the Unofficial Guide® to

the Best RV and Tent Campgrounds in the U.S.A.

Other Titles in the Series

California & the West
Mid-Atlantic States
Great Lakes States
Florida & the Southeast
Southwest & South Central Plains
Northeast
Northwest & Central Plains

Other Unofficial Guides

Beyond Disney: The Unofficial Guide to Universal, SeaWorld, and the Best of Central Florida

Inside Disney: The Incredible Story of Walt Disney World and the Man Behind the Mouse

Mini Las Vegas: The Pocket-Sized Unofficial Guide to Las Vegas

Mini-Mickey: The Pocket-Sized Unofficial Guide to Walt Disney World

The Unofficial Guides to Bed & Breakfasts and Country Inns:
California Great Lakes New England
Northwest Rockies Southeast Southwest

The Unofficial Guides to the Best RV and Tent Campgrounds:
California & the West Florida & the Southeast Great Lakes
Mid-Atlantic States Northeast Northwest Southwest U.S.A.

The Unofficial Guide to Branson, Missouri

The Unofficial Guide to Chicago

The Unofficial Guide to Cruises

The Unofficial Guide to Disneyland

The Unofficial Guide to Disneyland Paris

The Unofficial Guide to Florence, Rome, and the Heart of Italy

The Unofficial Guide to the Great Smoky and Blue Ridge Region

The Unofficial Guide to Golf Vacations in the Eastern U.S.

The Unofficial Guide to Hawaii

The Unofficial Guide to Las Vegas

The Unofficial Guide to London

The Unofficial Guide to New Orleans

The Unofficial Guide to New York City

The Unofficial Guide to Paris

The Unofficial Guide to San Francisco

The Unofficial Guide to South Florida, including Miami and the Keys

The Unofficial Guides to Traveling with Kids:
California Florida Mid-Atlantic New England and New York
Walt Disney World

The Unofficial Guide to Walt Disney World

The Unofficial Guide to Walt Disney World for Grown-Ups

The Unofficial Guide to Washington, D.C.

The Unofficial Guide to the World's Best Diving Vacations

the Unofficial Guide® to

the Best RV and Tent Campgrounds in the U.S.A.

1st Edition

Hungry Minds™

Best-Selling Books • Digital Downloads • e-Books • Answer Networks • e-Newsletters • Branded Web Sites • e-Learning

New York, NY • Indianapolis, IN • Cleveland, OH

Please note that prices fluctuate in the course of time, and travel information changes under the impact of many factors that influence the travel industry. We therefore suggest that you write or call ahead for confirmation when making your travel plans. Every effort has been made to ensure the accuracy of information throughout this book and the contents of this publication are believed correct at the time of printing. Nevertheless, the publishers cannot accept responsibility for errors or omissions or for changes in details given in this guide or for the consequences of any reliance on the information provided by the same. Assessments of attractions and so forth are based upon the author's own experience and therefore, descriptions given in this guide necessarily contain an element of subjective opinion, which may not reflect the publisher's opinion or dictate a reader's own experience on another occasion. Readers are invited to write to the publisher with ideas, comments, and suggestions for future editions.

Your safety is important to us, so we encourage you to stay alert and be aware of your surroundings. Keep a close eye on cameras, purses, and wallets, all favorite targets of thieves and pickpockets.

Published by Hungry Minds, Inc.
909 Third Avenue
New York, NY 10022

Produced by Menasha Ridge Press
COVER DESIGN BY MICHAEL J. FREELAND
INTERIOR DESIGN BY MICHELE LASEAU
CARTOGRAPHY BY JOHN DECAMILLIS, ROBERY STOCKWELL, AND NICHOLAS TROTTER

ISBN 0-7645-6587-7

ISSN 1536-9714

Manufactured in the United States of America

10 9 8 7 6 5 4 3 2 1

Contents

Part Three Supplemental Directory of Campgrounds 987

List of Maps

Introduction

Why Unofficial?

The material in this guide has not been edited or in any way reviewed by the campgrounds profiled. In this "unofficial" guide we represent and serve you, the consumer. By way of contrast with other campground directories, no ads were sold to campgrounds, and no campground paid to be included. Through our independence, we're able to offer you the sort of objective information necessary to select a campground efficiently and with confidence.

Why Another Guide to Campgrounds?

We developed *The Unofficial Guide to the Best RV and Tent Campgrounds in the United States* because we recognized that campers are as discriminating about their choice of campgrounds as most travelers are about their choice of hotels. As a camper, you don't want to stay in every campground along your route. Rather, you prefer to camp only in the best. A comprehensive directory with limited information on each campground listed does little to help you narrow your choices. What you need is a reference that tells you straight out which campgrounds are the best, and that supplies detailed information, collected by independent inspectors, that differentiates those campgrounds from all of the also-rans. This is exactly what *The Unofficial Guide to the Best RV and Tent Campgrounds* delivers.

The Choice Is All Yours

Life is short, and life is about choices. You can stay in a gravel lot, elbow to elbow with other campers, with tractor-trailers roaring by just beyond the fence, or with this guide, you can spend the night in a roomy, shaded site, overlooking a sparkling blue lake. The choice is yours.

The authors of this guide have combed the country inspecting and comparing hundreds of campgrounds. Their objective was to create a hit parade of the very best, so that no matter where you travel, you'll never have to spend another night in a dumpy, gravel lot.

The best campgrounds in each state are described in detail in individual profiles so you'll know exactly what to expect. In addition to the fully profiled campgrounds, we provide a Supplemental Directory of Campgrounds that lists over five thousand additional properties that are quite adequate, but that didn't make the cut for the top 2,450 in the guide. Thus, no matter where you are, you'll have plenty of campgrounds to choose from. None of the campgrounds appearing in this guide, whether fully profiled or in the supplemental list, paid to be included. Rather, each earned its place by offering a superior product. Period.

Letters, Comments, and Questions from Readers

Many who use the Unofficial Guides write to us with questions, comments, and reports of their camping experiences. We appreciate all such input, both positive and critical. Readers' comments are frequently incorporated into revised editions of the Unofficial Guides and have contributed immeasurably to their improvement. Please write to:

The Unofficial Guide to the Best RV and Tent Campgrounds
P.O. Box 43673
Birmingham, AL 35243
UnofficialGuides@menasharidge.com

For letters sent through the mail, please put your return address on both your letter and envelope; the two sometimes become separated. Also include your phone number and email address if you are available for a possible interview.

U.S.A Overview

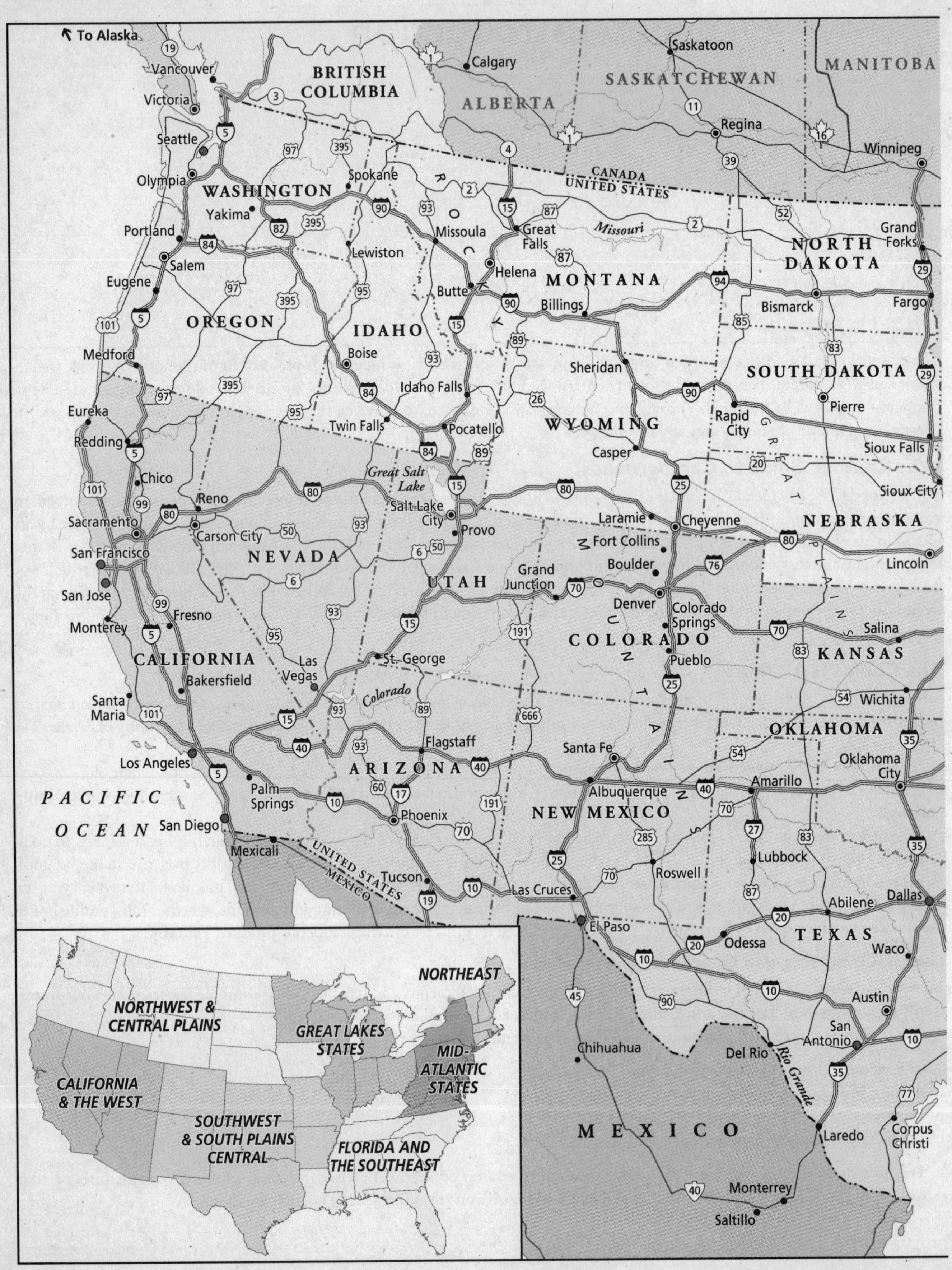

U.S.A. Overview

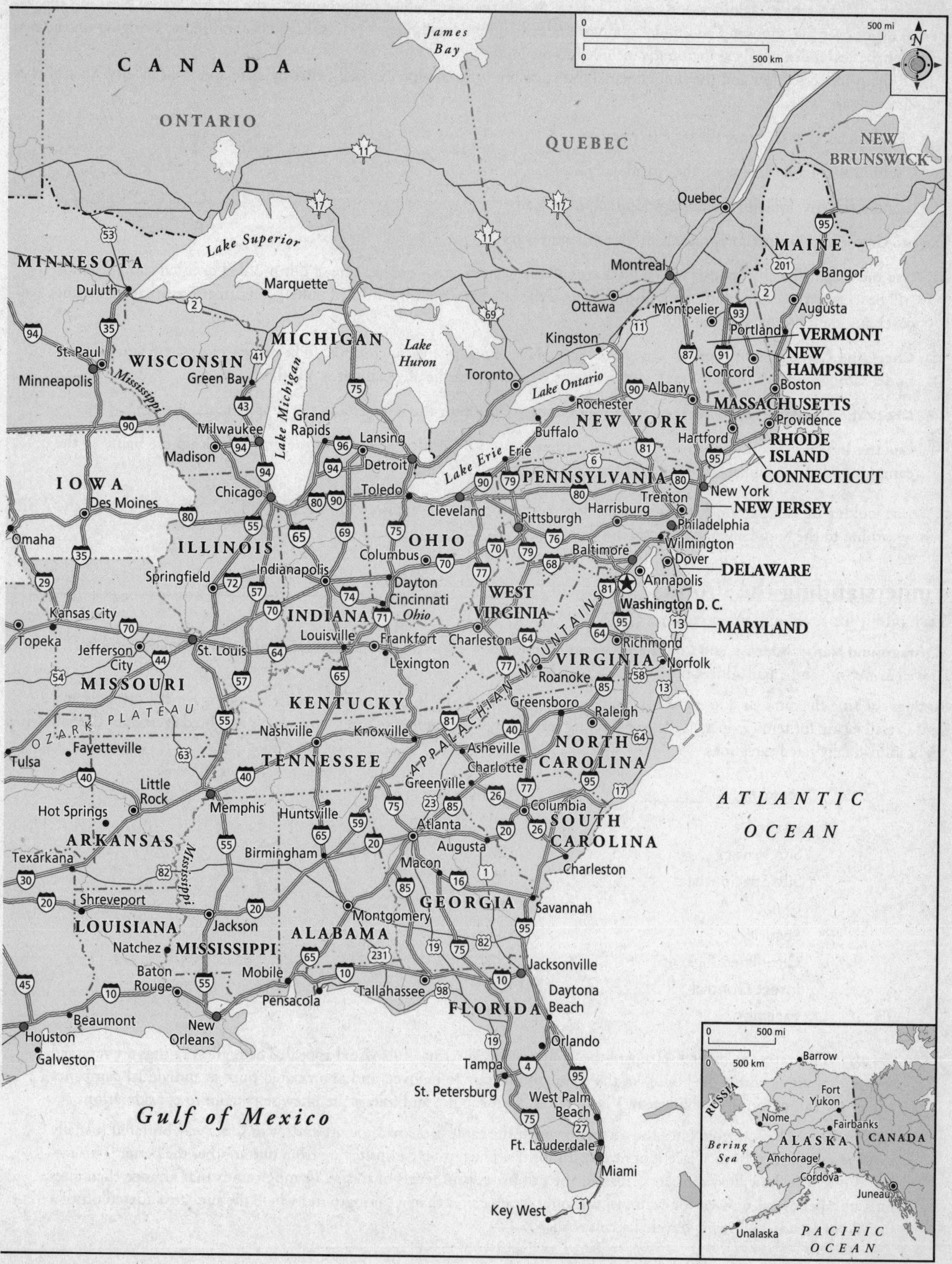

How to Use This Guide

Using this guide is quick and easy. We begin with this introduction followed by "Campground Awards," a list of the best campgrounds for RVers, tenters, families, and more. Then we profile the best 2,450 campgrounds in the United States. Next is a supplemental list of over five thousand additional campgrounds including details about prices, hookups, and more. Bringing up the rear is an alphabetical index of all campgrounds included in the guide.

Both the profiled section and the supplemental directory are ordered alphabetically, first by state and then by city. To see what campgrounds are available:

- Find the section covering the state in question.
- Within that section, look up the city alphabetically.
- Under the city, look up the campgrounds alphabetically.

You can choose and locate campgrounds in four different ways.

1. **Use the Map** If a city appears with a black, solid bullet on our map, at least one of our profiled or listed campgrounds will be located there. The converse is also the case: if the city has a hollow, outlined bullet, you can assume that we do not cover any campgrounds in that city.
2. **Check the Campground Profiles** In the section where we profile campgrounds, look up any city where you hope to find a campground. If the city isn't listed, it means we do not profile any campgrounds there.
3. **Check the Supplemental Directory of Campgrounds** Check for the same city in the supplemental listings.
4. **Use the Index** If you want to see if a specific campground is profiled or listed in the guide, look up the name of the campground in the alphabetical index at the back of the book.

When looking up campgrounds, remember that the best campgrounds are found in the profiled section; always check there first before turning to the Supplemental Directory of Campgrounds.

Understanding the Profiles

Each profile has seven important sections:

Campground Name, Address, and Contact Information In addition to the street address, we also provide phone and fax numbers as well as website and email addresses.

Ratings Using the familiar one- to five-star rating with five stars being best, we offer one overall rating for RV campers and a second overall rating for tent campers. The overall rating for each type of camper is based on a rough weighted average of the following eight individually rated categories:

Category	Weight
Beauty	15%
Site Privacy	10%
Site Spaciousness	10%
Quiet	15%
Security	13%
Cleanliness/upkeep	13%
Insect Control	10%
Facilities	14%

Beauty This rates the natural setting of the campground in terms of its visual appeal. The highest ratings are reserved for campgrounds where the beauty of the campground can be enjoyed and appreciated both at individual campsites and at the campground's public areas. Views, vistas, landscaping, and foliage are likewise taken into consideration.

Site Privacy This category rates the extent to which the campsites are set apart and/or in some way buffered (usually by trees and shrubs) from adjacent or nearby campsites. The farther campsites are from one another the better. This rating also reflects how busy the access road to the campsites is in terms of traffic. Campgrounds that arrange their sites on a number of cul-de-sacs, for example, will offer quieter sites than a campground where the sites are situated off of a busy loop or along a heavily traveled access road.

Site Spaciousness This rates the size of the campsite. Generally, the larger the better.

Quiet This rating indicates the relative quietness of the campground. There are three key considerations. The first is where the campground is located. Campgrounds situated along busy highways or in cities or towns are usually noisier, for example, than rural or wilderness campgrounds removed from major thoroughfares. The second consideration relates to how noise is managed at the campground. Does the campground forbid playing of radios or enforce a "quiet time" after a certain hour? Is there someone on site at night to respond to complaints about other campers being loud or unruly at a late hour? Finally, the rating considers the extent to which trees, shrubs, and the natural topography serve to muffle noise within the campground.

Security This rating reflects the extent (if any) to which management monitors the campground during the day and night. Physical security is also included in this rating: Is the campground fenced? Is the campground gated? If so, is the gate manned? Generally, a campground located in a city or along a busy road is more exposed to thieves or vandals than a more remote campground, and should more actively supervise access.

Cleanliness This rates the cleanliness, serviceability, and state of repair of the campground, including grounds, sites, and facilities.

Insect Control This rating addresses questions regarding insect and pest control. Does management spray or take other steps to control the presence of mosquitoes and other insect pests? Does the campground drain efficiently following a rain? Are garbage and sewage properly collected and disposed of?

Facilities This rates the overall variety and quality of facilities to include bath house/toilets, swimming pool, retail shops, docks, pavilions, playgrounds, etc. If the quality of respective facilities vary considerably within a given campground, inconsistencies are explained in the prose description of the campground.

Campground Description This is an informative, consumer-oriented description of the campground. It includes what makes the campground special or unique and what differentiates it from other area campgrounds. The description may additionally include the following:

- The general layout of the campground.
- Where the campground is located relative to an easily referenced city or highway.
- The general setting (wilderness, rural, or urban).
- Description of the campsites including most and least desirable sites.
- Prevailing weather considerations and best time to visit.
- Mention of any unusual, exceptional, or deficient facilities.
- Security considerations, if any (gates that are locked at night, accessibility of campground to non-campers, etc.).

Basics Key information about the campground including:

- *Operated By* Who owns and/or operates the campground.
- *Open* Dates or seasons the campground is open.
- *Site Assignment* How sites are most commonly obtained (first-come, first served; reservations accepted; reservations only; assigned on check-in, etc. Deposit and refund policy.
- *Registration* Where the camper registers on arrival. Information on how and where to register after normal business hours (late arrival).
- *Fee* Cost of a standard campsite for one night for RV sites and tent sites respectively. Forms of payment accepted. Uses the following abbreviations for credit cards: V = VISA, AE = American Express, MC = MasterCard, D = Discover, CB = Carte Blanche, and DC = Diner's Club International.
- *Parking* Usual entry will be "At campsite" or "On road," though some campgrounds have a central parking lot from which tent campers must carry their gear to their campsite.

Facilities This is a brief data presentation that provides information on the availability of specific facilities and services.

- *Number of RV Sites* Any site where RVs are permitted.
- *Number of Tent-Only Sites* Sites set aside specifically for tent camping, including pop-up tent trailers.
- *Hookups* Possible hookups include electric, water, sewer, cable TV, phone, and Internet connection. Electrical hookups vary from campground to campground. Where electrical hookups are available, the amperage available is stated parenthetically, for example: "Hookups: Electric (20 amps), water."

- *Each Site* List of equipment such as grill, picnic table, lantern pole, fire pit, water faucet, electrical outlet, etc., provided at each campsite. Are these items or services available on site? Dump station, laundry, pay phone, restrooms and showers, fuel, propane, RV service, general store, vending, playground, etc.
- *Internal Roads* Indicates the type of road (gravel, paved, dirt), and in what condition.
- *Market* Location and distance of closest supermarket or large grocery store.
- *Restaurant* Location and distance of closest restaurant.
- *Other* Boat ramp, dining pavilion, miniature golf, tennis court, lounge, etc.
- *Activities* Activities available at the campground or in the area.
- *Nearby Attractions* Can be natural or manmade.
- *Additional Information* The best sources to call for general information on area activities and attractions. Sources include local or area chambers of commerce, tourist bureaus, visitors and convention authorities, forest service, etc.

Restrictions Any restrictions that apply, including:

- *Pets* Conditions under which pets are allowed or not.
- *Fires* Campground rules for fires and fire safety.
- *Alcoholic Beverages* Campground rules regarding the consumption of alcoholic beverages.
- *Vehicle Maximum Length* Length in feet of the maximum size vehicle the campground can accommodate.
- *Other* Any other rules or restrictions, to include minimum and maximum stays; age or group size restrictions; areas off-limits to vehicular traffic; security constraints such as locking the main gate during the night; etc.

How to Get There Clear and specific directions, including mileage and landmarks, for finding the campground.

Supplemental Directory of Campgrounds

If you're looking for a campground within the territory covered in this guide and can't find a profiled campground that is close or convenient to your route, check the Supplemental Directory of Campgrounds. This directory of hundreds of additional campgrounds is organized alphabetically by state and city name. Each entry provides the campground's name, address, reservations phone, fax, website, number of sites, average fee per night, and hookups available.

Alabama

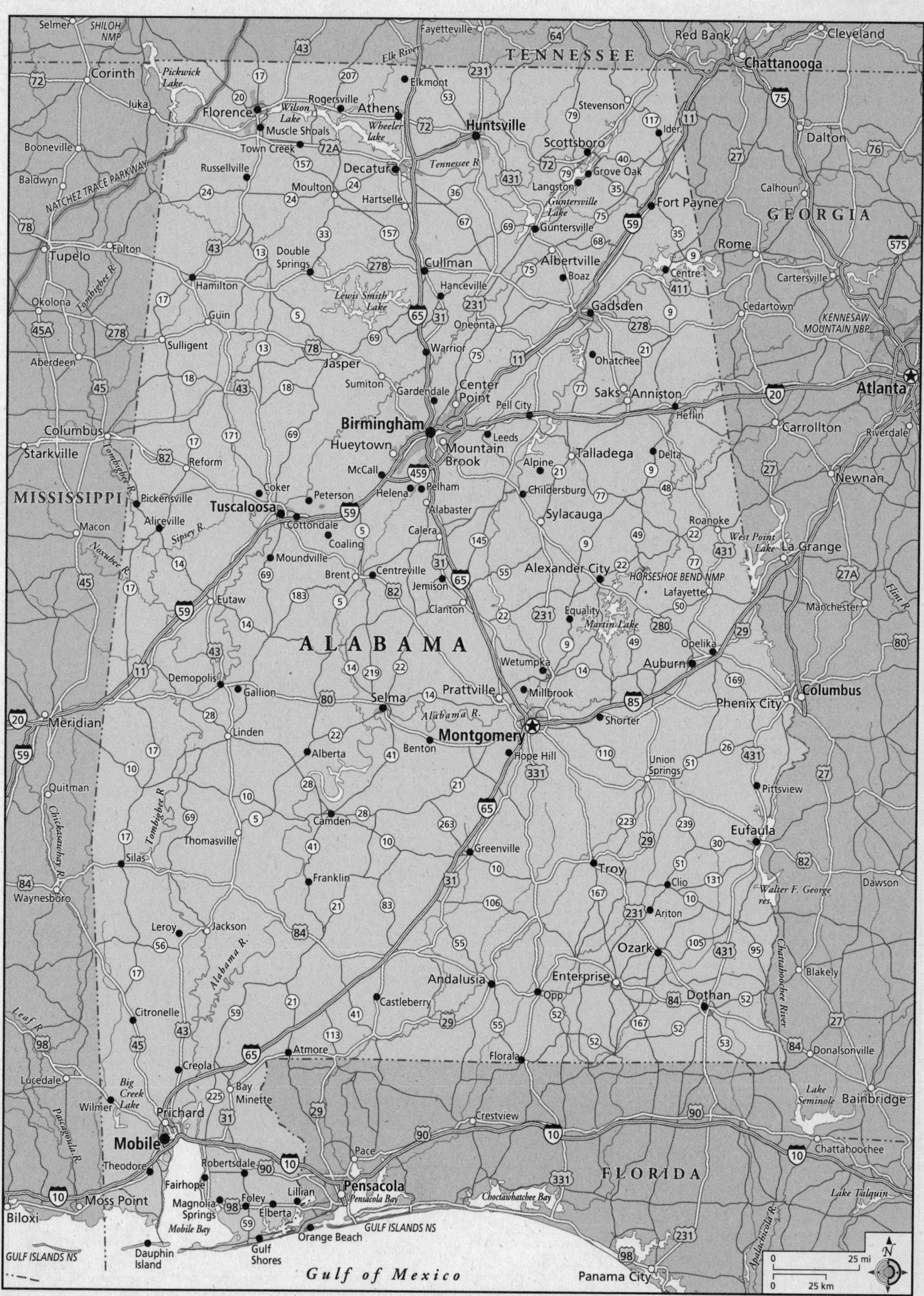

Selmer
SHILOH NMP
Fayetteville
TENNESSEE
Red Bank
Cleveland
Chattanooga
Elk River
Corinth
Pickwick Lake
Elkmont
Iuka
Florence
Rogersville
Athens
Wilson Lake
Muscle Shoals
Wheeler lake
Huntsville
Stevenson
Booneville
Town Creek
Scottsboro
Ider
Dalton
Russellville
Decatur
Tennessee R.
Grove Oak
Baldwyn
Moulton
Hartselle
Langston
Guntersville Lake
Calhoun
NATCHEZ TRACE PARKWAY
Fort Payne
GEORGIA
Guntersville
Tupelo
Fulton
Double Springs
Cullman
Albertville
Rome
Tombigbee R.
Hamilton
Centre
Boaz
Cartersville
Okolona
Hanceville
Lewis Smith Lake
Gadsden
Cedartown
Guin
Oneonta
KENNESAW MOUNTAIN NBP
Sulligent
Warrior
Ohatchee
Aberdeen
Jasper
Sumiton
Gardendale
Center Point
Saks
Anniston
Atlanta
Pell City
Heflin
Columbus
Birmingham
Carrollton
Hueytown
Mountain Brook
Leeds
Riverdale
Starkville
Reform
McCall
Talladega
Delta
Alpine
MISSISSIPPI
Pickensville
Coker
Peterson
Helena
Pelham
Childersburg
Newnan
Tuscaloosa
Alabaster
Aliceville
Cottondale
Sylacauga
Macon
Sipsey R.
Coaling
Calera
Roanoke
Noxubee R.
Moundville
West Point Lake
La Grange
Brent
Centreville
Alexander City
HORSESHOE BEND NMP
Jemison
Lafayette
Eutaw
Clanton
Manchester
Equality
Martin Lake
Flint R.
ALABAMA
Opelika
Wetumpka
Auburn
Demopolis
Gallion
Prattville
Millbrook
Columbus
Selma
Phenix City
Meridian
Alabama R.
Shorter
Linden
Montgomery
Benton
Hope Hill
Alberta
Union Springs
Quitman
Pittsview
Tombigbee R.
Camden
Thomasville
Eufaula
Chickasawhay R.
Greenville
Silas
Troy
Franklin
Clio
Walter F. George res.
Dawson
Waynesboro
Ariton
Leroy
Jackson
Ozark
Chattahoochee River
Alabama R.
Andalusia
Blakely
Enterprise
Castleberry
Opp
Dothan
Citronelle
Leaf R.
Florala
Atmore
Donalsonville
Lucedale
Creola
Big Creek Lake
Bay Minette
Lake Seminole
Bainbridge
Wilmer
Prichard
Crestview
Pascagoula R.
Mobile
Pace
Chattahoochee
Theodore
Robertsdale
FLORIDA
Fairhope
Lillian
Pensacola
Moss Point
Magnolia Springs
Foley
Pensacola Bay
Choctawhatchee Bay
Lake Talquin
Biloxi
Elberta
Mobile Bay
Orange Beach
GULF ISLANDS NS
Apalachicola R.
GULF ISLANDS NS
Dauphin Island
Gulf Shores
Gulf of Mexico
Panama City
0 25 mi
0 25 km
N

Alaska

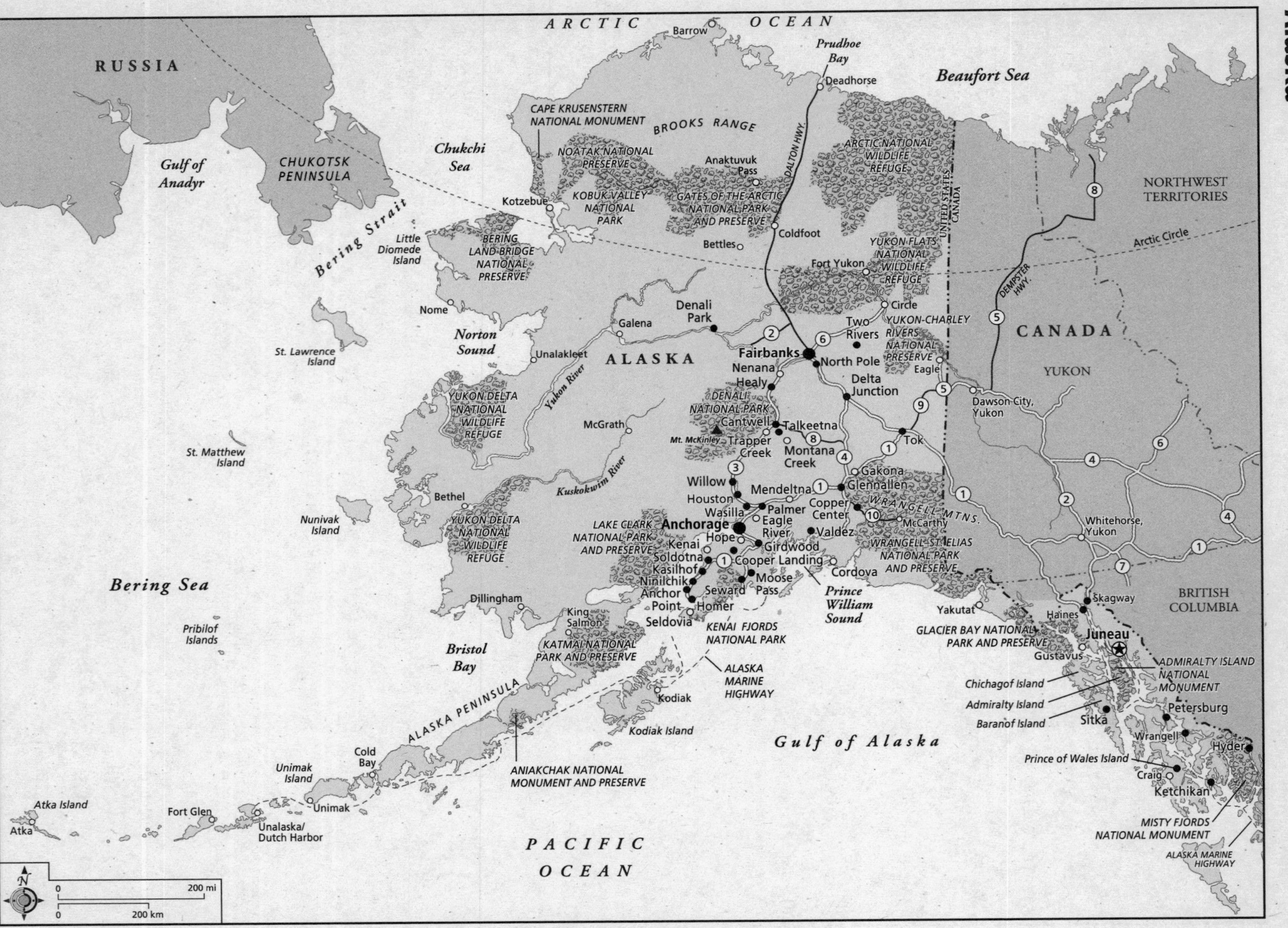

ARCTIC OCEAN
Beaufort Sea
Chukchi Sea
Bering Strait
Bering Sea
Gulf of Anadyr
Norton Sound
Bristol Bay
Gulf of Alaska
Prince William Sound
PACIFIC OCEAN
RUSSIA
CHUKOTSK PENINSULA
CANADA
NORTHWEST TERRITORIES
YUKON
BRITISH COLUMBIA
UNITED STATES
CANADA
ALASKA
Arctic Circle
BROOKS RANGE
ALASKA PENINSULA
WRANGELL MTNS.
DALTON HWY.
DEMPSTER HWY.
ALASKA MARINE HIGHWAY
Yukon River
Kuskokwim River
CAPE KRUSENSTERN NATIONAL MONUMENT
NOATAK NATIONAL PRESERVE
KOBUK VALLEY NATIONAL PARK
GATES OF THE ARCTIC NATIONAL PARK AND PRESERVE
ARCTIC NATIONAL WILDLIFE REFUGE
YUKON FLATS NATIONAL WILDLIFE REFUGE
YUKON-CHARLEY RIVERS NATIONAL PRESERVE
BERING LAND BRIDGE NATIONAL PRESERVE
YUKON DELTA NATIONAL WILDLIFE REFUGE
DENALI NATIONAL PARK
WRANGELL-ST. ELIAS NATIONAL PARK AND PRESERVE
GLACIER BAY NATIONAL PARK AND PRESERVE
KENAI FJORDS NATIONAL PARK
LAKE CLARK NATIONAL PARK AND PRESERVE
KATMAI NATIONAL PARK AND PRESERVE
ANIAKCHAK NATIONAL MONUMENT AND PRESERVE
ADMIRALTY ISLAND NATIONAL MONUMENT
MISTY FJORDS NATIONAL MONUMENT
Barrow
Prudhoe Bay
Deadhorse
Coldfoot
Anaktuvuk Pass
Bettles
Kotzebue
Nome
Little Diomede Island
St. Lawrence Island
Unalakleet
Galena
McGrath
Bethel
Nunivak Island
St. Matthew Island
Pribilof Islands
Dillingham
King Salmon
Cold Bay
Unimak
Unimak Island
Unalaska/Dutch Harbor
Fort Glen
Atka
Atka Island
Kodiak
Kodiak Island
Fort Yukon
Circle
Two Rivers
North Pole
Delta Junction
Eagle
Tok
Fairbanks
Nenana
Healy
Denali Park
Cantwell
Mt. McKinley
Talkeetna
Trapper Creek
Montana Creek
Willow
Houston
Wasilla
Palmer
Eagle River
Anchorage
Hope
Girdwood
Cooper Landing
Moose Pass
Seward
Kenai
Soldotna
Kasilhof
Ninilchik
Anchor Point
Homer
Seldovia
Mendeltna
Glennallen
Gakona
Copper Center
Valdez
Cordova
McCarthy
Yakutat
Dawson City, Yukon
Whitehorse, Yukon
Haines
Skagway
Gustavus
Juneau
Chichagof Island
Admiralty Island
Baranof Island
Sitka
Petersburg
Wrangell
Prince of Wales Island
Craig
Ketchikan
Hyder
0
200 mi
0
200 km
N

Arizona

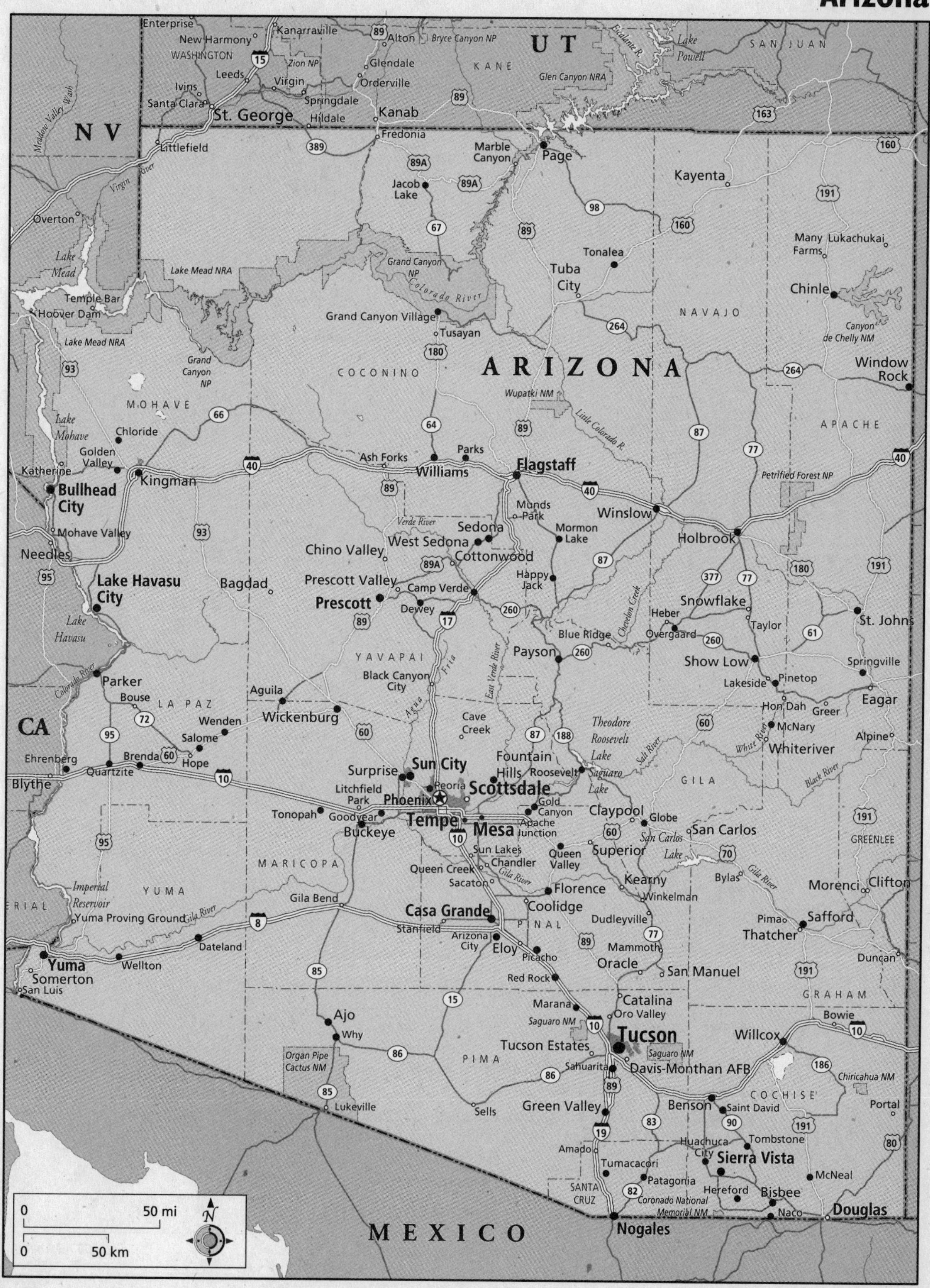
ARIZONA
NV
UT
CA
MEXICO
St. George
Kanab
Page
Kayenta
Tuba City
Chinle
Window Rock
Grand Canyon Village
Tusayan
Williams
Flagstaff
Winslow
Holbrook
Kingman
Bullhead City
Lake Havasu City
Sedona
Prescott
Payson
Show Low
Snowflake
St. Johns
Wickenburg
Sun City
Phoenix
Scottsdale
Tempe
Mesa
Casa Grande
Florence
Globe
Safford
Yuma
Ajo
Tucson
Sierra Vista
Bisbee
Douglas
Nogales
Willcox
Benson
Tombstone
Green Valley
COCONINO
MOHAVE
YAVAPAI
LA PAZ
MARICOPA
YUMA
PIMA
PINAL
GILA
NAVAJO
APACHE
GREENLEE
GRAHAM
COCHISE
SANTA CRUZ
0 50 mi
0 50 km
N

Arkansas

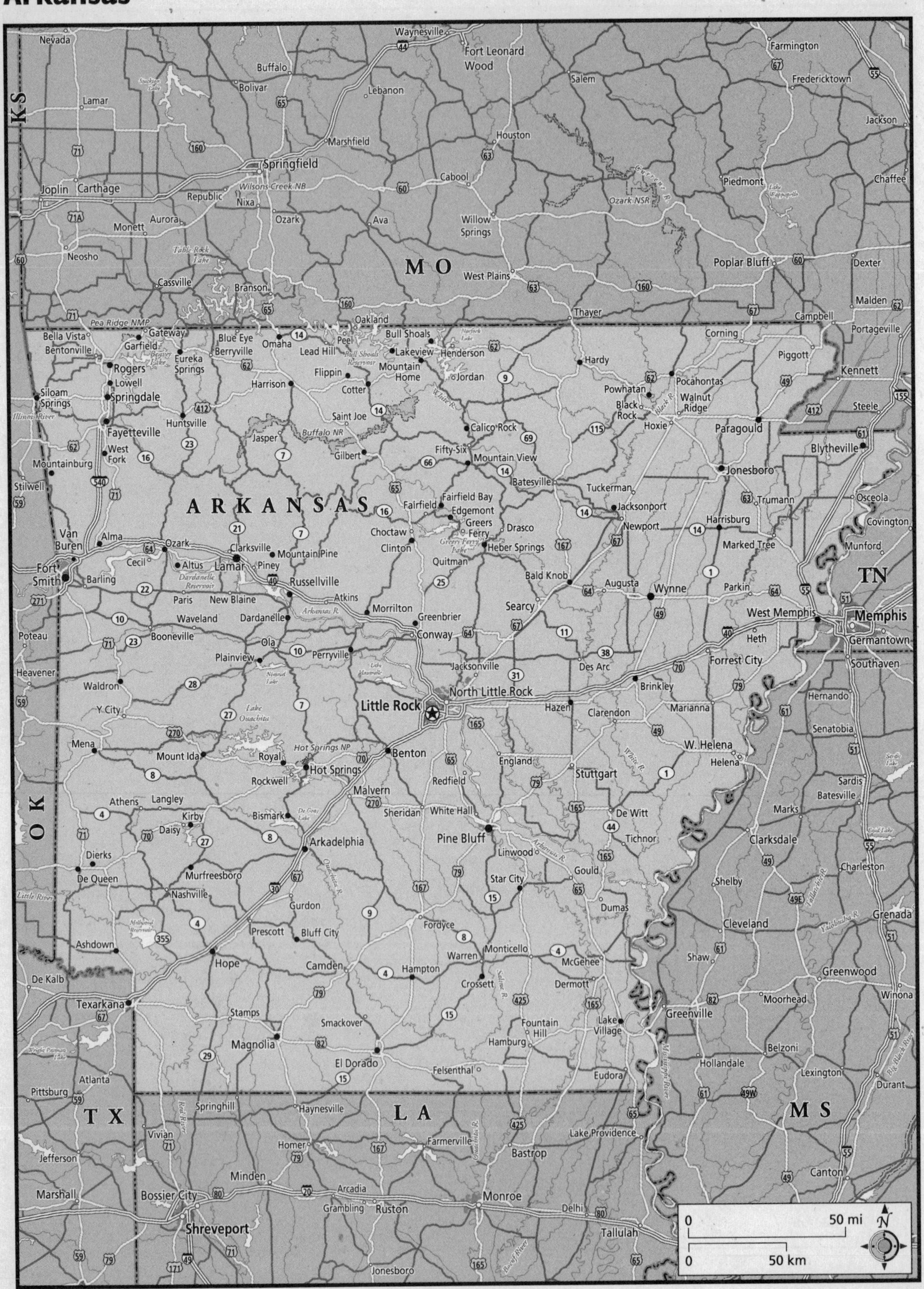

Nevada
Waynesville
Fort Leonard Wood
Farmington
Fredericktown
Buffalo
Bolivar
Lebanon
Salem
KS
Lamar
Jackson
Houston
Marshfield
Springfield
Wilsons Creek NB
Joplin
Carthage
Republic
Nixa
Cabool
Piedmont
Chaffee
Ozark NSR
Monett
Aurora
Ozark
Ava
Willow Springs
Neosho
Table Rock Lake
MO
West Plains
Poplar Bluff
Dexter
Cassville
Branson
Malden
Thayer
Oakland
Campbell
Portageville
Pea Ridge NMP
Bella Vista
Gateway
Garfield
Bentonville
Blue Eye
Berryville
Omaha
Peel
Lead Hill
Bull Shoals
Lakeview
Henderson
Corning
Hardy
Piggott
Kennett
Rogers
Lowell
Eureka Springs
Harrison
Flippin
Mountain Home
Jordan
Pocahontas
Powhatan
Black Rock
Walnut Ridge
Siloam Springs
Springdale
Cotter
Steele
Illinois River
Huntsville
Saint Joe
Calico Rock
Hoxie
Paragould
Fayetteville
Buffalo NR
Jasper
West Fork
Gilbert
Fifty-Six
Mountain View
Blytheville
Mountainburg
Batesville
Jonesboro
Stilwell
Tuckerman
ARKANSAS
Fairfield Bay
Fairfield
Edgemont
Greers Ferry
Jacksonport
Trumann
Osceola
Choctaw
Clinton
Drasco
Newport
Harrisburg
Covington
Van Buren
Alma
Ozark
Clarksville
Mountain Pine
Heber Springs
Marked Tree
Munford
Fort Smith
Cecil
Altus
Lamar
Piney
Quitman
TN
Barling
Dardanelle Reservoir
Russellville
Bald Knob
Augusta
Wynne
Parkin
Paris
New Blaine
Atkins
Arkansas R.
Morrilton
Searcy
West Memphis
Memphis
Waveland
Dardanelle
Greenbrier
Heth
Poteau
Booneville
Conway
Germantown
Ola
Perryville
Forrest City
Southaven
Plainview
Jacksonville
Des Arc
Heavener
Waldron
Brinkley
North Little Rock
Hernando
Little Rock
Hazen
Clarendon
Marianna
Y City
Lake Ouachita
Senatobia
Mena
Mount Ida
Royal
Hot Springs NP
Benton
W. Helena
Helena
Hot Springs
England
Stuttgart
Rockwell
Redfield
Sardis
Batesville
Athens
Langley
Malvern
Kirby
Bismark
Sheridan
White Hall
De Witt
Marks
OK
Daisy
Pine Bluff
Tichnor
Arkadelphia
Clarksdale
Dierks
Linwood
De Queen
Murfreesboro
Star City
Gould
Charleston
Nashville
Shelby
Gurdon
Dumas
Little River
Grenada
Prescott
Bluff City
Fordyce
Cleveland
Ashdown
Monticello
Hope
Camden
Warren
McGehee
Shaw
Hampton
De Kalb
Crossett
Dermott
Greenwood
Texarkana
Moorhead
Winona
Stamps
Lake Village
Greenville
Smackover
Fountain Hill
Magnolia
Hamburg
Belzoni
El Dorado
Hollandale
Felsenthal
Atlanta
Lexington
Eudora
Durant
Pittsburg
Springhill
Haynesville
TX
LA
MS
Vivian
Lake Providence
Homer
Farmerville
Bastrop
Jefferson
Canton
Minden
Arcadia
Marshall
Bossier City
Monroe
Grambling
Ruston
Delhi
Shreveport
Tallulah
Jonesboro
0
50 mi
0
50 km
N

Colorado

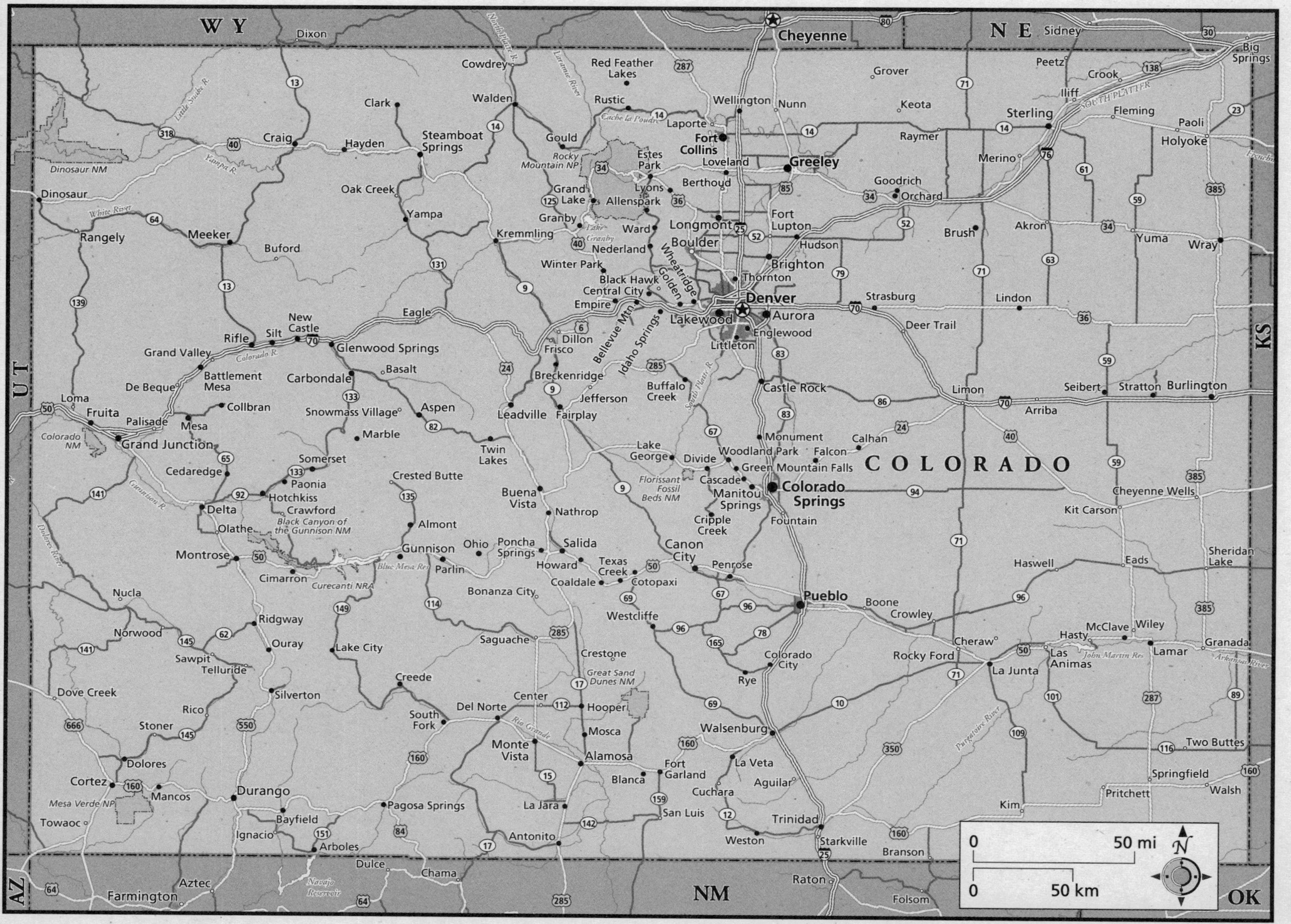

COLORADO
WY
NE
KS
OK
NM
AZ
UT
0
50 mi
0
50 km
N
Cheyenne
Sidney
Big Springs
Dixon
Cowdrey
Walden
Red Feather Lakes
Rustic
Wellington
Nunn
Grover
Keota
Peetz
Crook
Iliff
Sterling
Fleming
Paoli
Holyoke
Clark
Gould
Laporte
Fort Collins
Loveland
Greeley
Raymer
Merino
Craig
Hayden
Steamboat Springs
Rocky Mountain NP
Estes Park
Berthoud
Goodrich
Orchard
Dinosaur NM
Dinosaur
Oak Creek
Grand Lake
Lyons
Allenspark
Fort Lupton
Yampa
Granby
Ward
Longmont
Boulder
Brush
Akron
Yuma
Wray
Rangely
Meeker
Buford
Kremmling
Nederland
Hudson
Brighton
Winter Park
Black Hawk
Wheatridge
Golden
Thornton
Central City
Empire
Denver
Strasburg
Lindon
Aurora
Lakewood
Englewood
Deer Trail
Eagle
New Castle
Silt
Rifle
Glenwood Springs
Dillon
Frisco
Bellevue Mtn
Idaho Springs
Littleton
Grand Valley
Basalt
Carbondale
Battlement Mesa
Breckenridge
Buffalo Creek
Castle Rock
Limon
Seibert
Stratton
Burlington
De Beque
Jefferson
Loma
Fruita
Collbran
Snowmass Village
Aspen
Leadville
Fairplay
Arriba
Palisade
Mesa
Marble
Monument
Calhan
Colorado NM
Grand Junction
Twin Lakes
Lake George
Woodland Park
Falcon
Divide
Green Mountain Falls
Somerset
Crested Butte
Cedaredge
Paonia
Cascade
Colorado Springs
Florissant Fossil Beds NM
Manitou Springs
Cheyenne Wells
Hotchkiss
Buena Vista
Kit Carson
Delta
Crawford
Nathrop
Cripple Creek
Fountain
Black Canyon of the Gunnison NM
Olathe
Almont
Canon City
Gunnison
Ohio
Poncha Springs
Salida
Sheridan Lake
Haswell
Eads
Montrose
Howard
Texas Creek
Penrose
Parlin
Cimarron
Curecanti NRA
Coaldale
Cotopaxi
Nucla
Bonanza City
Pueblo
Boone
Crowley
Westcliffe
Ridgway
Norwood
McClave
Wiley
Hasty
Ouray
Saguache
Sawpit
Telluride
Lake City
Crestone
Cheraw
Granada
Colorado City
Rocky Ford
Las Animas
Lamar
Great Sand Dunes NM
La Junta
Rye
Creede
Dove Creek
Silverton
Center
Del Norte
Hooper
Rico
South Fork
Stoner
Walsenburg
Mosca
Two Buttes
Monte Vista
Dolores
Alamosa
Fort Garland
La Veta
Blanca
Aguilar
Springfield
Cortez
Pritchett
Walsh
Cuchara
Mesa Verde NP
Mancos
Durango
Pagosa Springs
La Jara
Kim
Towaoc
Bayfield
Trinidad
San Luis
Antonito
Weston
Starkville
Ignacio
Arboles
Branson
Dulce
Chama
Raton
Aztec
Farmington
Folsom

California

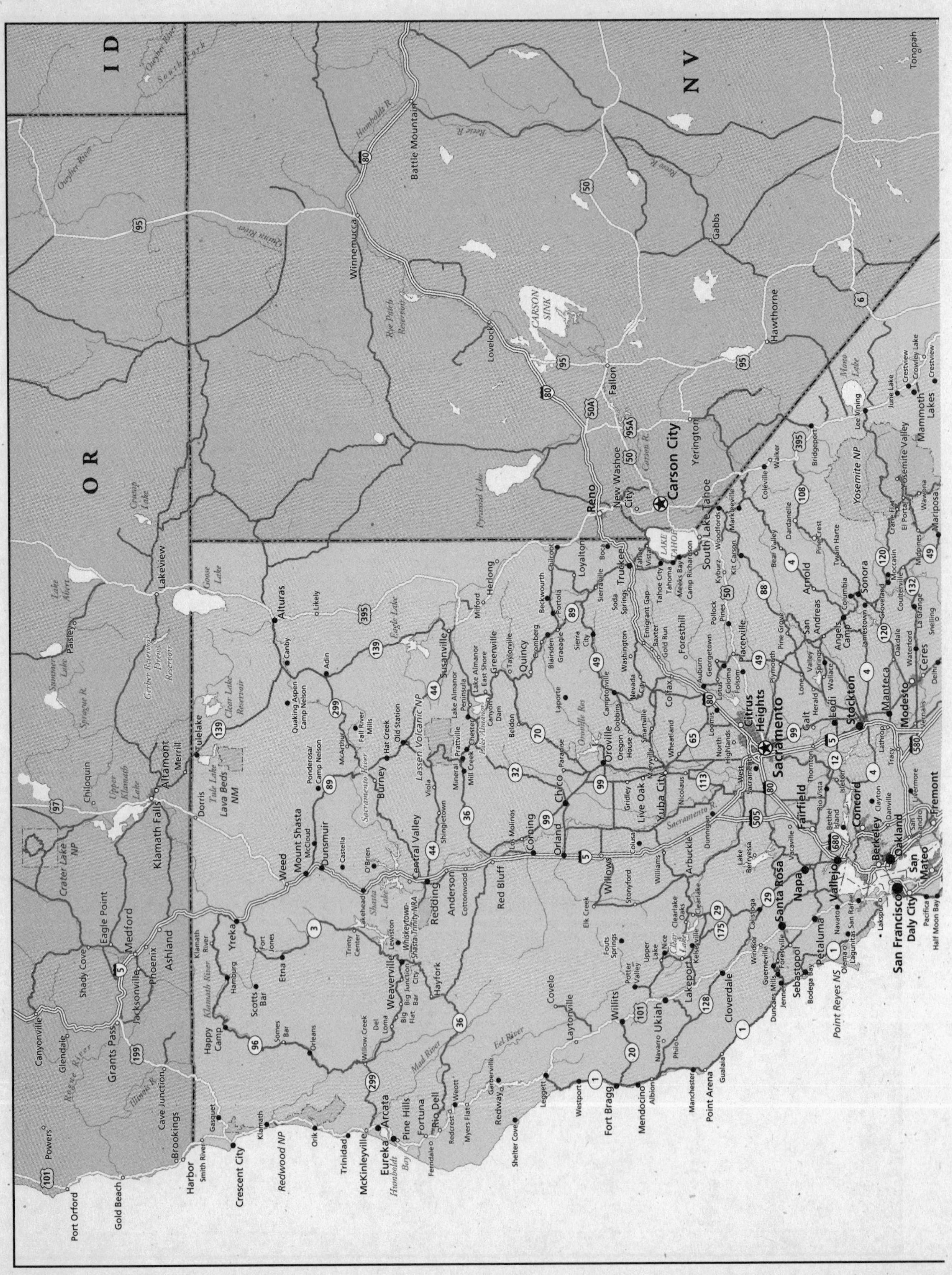

ID
OR
NV
Port Orford
Gold Beach
Brookings
Harbor
Crescent City
Redwood NP
Trinidad
McKinleyville
Arcata
Eureka
Fortuna
Rio Dell
Fort Bragg
Mendocino
Point Arena
Cloverdale
Ukiah
Willits
Lakeport
Santa Rosa
Petaluma
Napa
Vallejo
Fairfield
San Francisco
Daly City
Oakland
Berkeley
Concord
Fremont
San Mateo
Sacramento
Citrus Heights
Stockton
Lodi
Manteca
Modesto
Yuba City
Oroville
Chico
Red Bluff
Redding
Anderson
Weaverville
Mount Shasta
Weed
Yreka
Medford
Grants Pass
Ashland
Klamath Falls
Lakeview
Alturas
Susanville
Quincy
Truckee
Reno
Carson City
South Lake Tahoe
Placerville
Auburn
Sonora
Mariposa
Mammoth Lakes
Winnemucca
Lovelock
Fallon
Hawthorne
Yerington
Battle Mountain
Gabbs
Tonopah
Crater Lake NP
Lassen Volcanic NP
Lava Beds NM
Yosemite NP
Point Reyes NS
Lake Tahoe
Pyramid Lake
Goose Lake
Mono Lake
Carson Sink

California

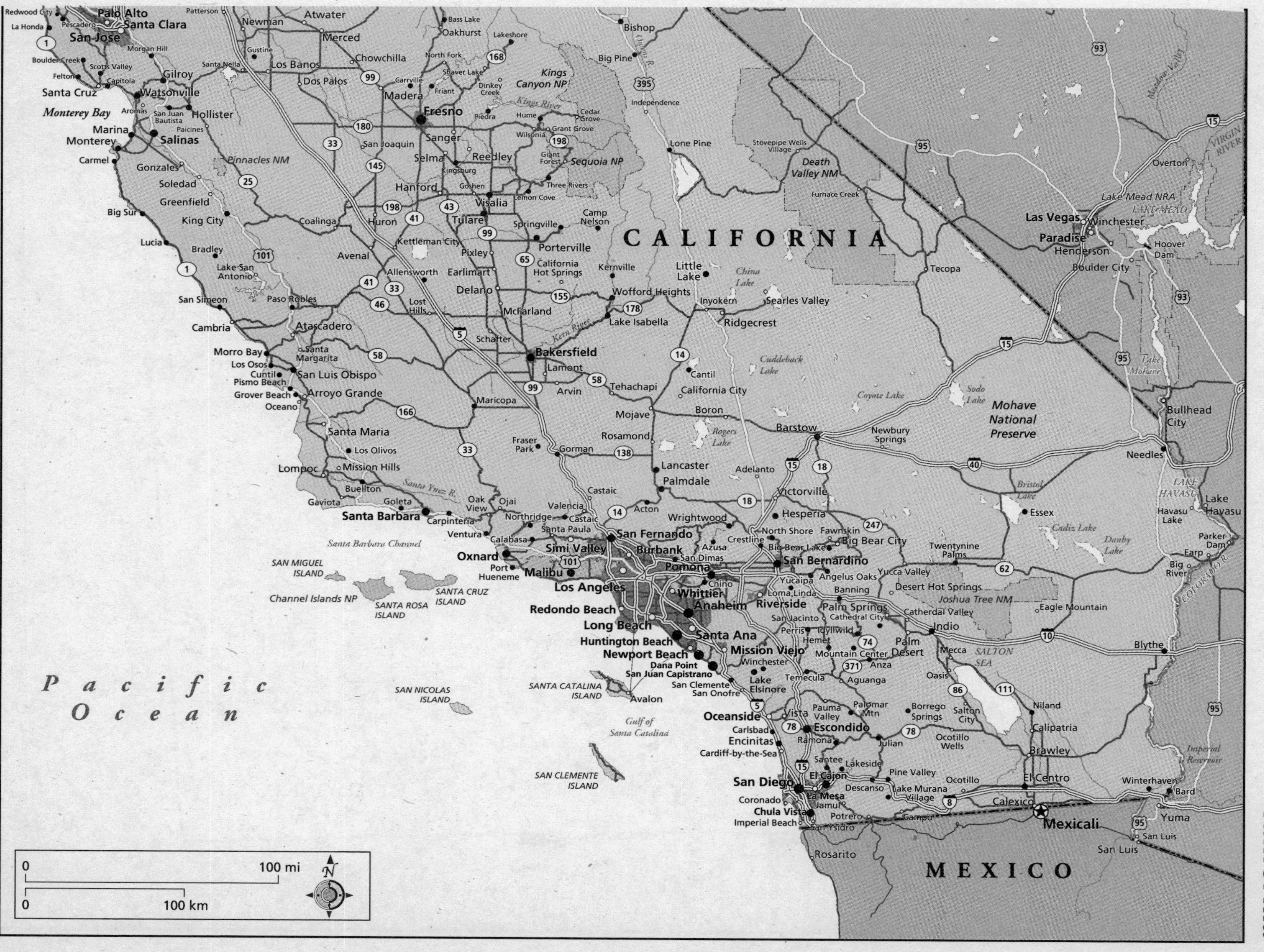

CALIFORNIA
MEXICO
Pacific Ocean
Las Vegas
Paradise
Henderson
Boulder City
Hoover Dam
Overton
Winchester
Lake Mead NRA
Bullhead City
Needles
Lake Havasu
Havasu Lake
Parker Dam
Earp
Big River
Blythe
Yuma
San Luis
Winterhaven
Bard
Mexicali
Calexico
El Centro
Brawley
Calipatria
Niland
Salton Sea
Salton City
Mohave National Preserve
Essex
Eagle Mountain
Joshua Tree NM
Twentynine Palms
Indio
Mecca
Oasis
Palm Desert
Palm Springs
Cathedral City
Desert Hot Springs
Yucca Valley
Banning
Borrego Springs
Ocotillo Wells
Ocotillo
Julian
Ramona
Escondido
Vista
Oceanside
Carlsbad
Encinitas
Cardiff-by-the-Sea
San Diego
La Mesa
El Cajon
Chula Vista
Coronado
Imperial Beach
Rosarito
Tecopa
Death Valley NM
Furnace Creek
Stovepipe Wells Village
Lone Pine
Independence
Big Pine
Bishop
Kings Canyon NP
Sequoia NP
Fresno
Madera
Merced
Atwater
Chowchilla
Los Banos
Dos Palos
Newman
Gustine
Patterson
Gilroy
Hollister
Morgan Hill
San Jose
Santa Clara
Palo Alto
Santa Cruz
Watsonville
Monterey Bay
Marina
Monterey
Salinas
Carmel
Big Sur
Gonzales
Soledad
Greenfield
King City
Pinnacles NM
Lucia
San Simeon
Cambria
Paso Robles
Atascadero
Morro Bay
San Luis Obispo
Pismo Beach
Arroyo Grande
Grover Beach
Oceano
Santa Maria
Lompoc
Buellton
Santa Barbara
Goleta
Carpinteria
Ventura
Oxnard
Port Hueneme
Malibu
Los Angeles
Simi Valley
San Fernando
Burbank
Pomona
Whittier
Anaheim
Santa Ana
Long Beach
Redondo Beach
Huntington Beach
Newport Beach
Mission Viejo
Dana Point
San Juan Capistrano
San Clemente
Riverside
San Bernardino
Hesperia
Victorville
Barstow
Lancaster
Palmdale
Mojave
Tehachapi
Bakersfield
Delano
Visalia
Tulare
Porterville
Hanford
Coalinga
Ridgecrest
Little Lake
Santa Barbara Channel
Channel Islands NP
SAN MIGUEL ISLAND
SANTA ROSA ISLAND
SANTA CRUZ ISLAND
SANTA CATALINA ISLAND
Avalon
SAN CLEMENTE ISLAND
SAN NICOLAS ISLAND
0
100 mi
100 km
N

Connecticut

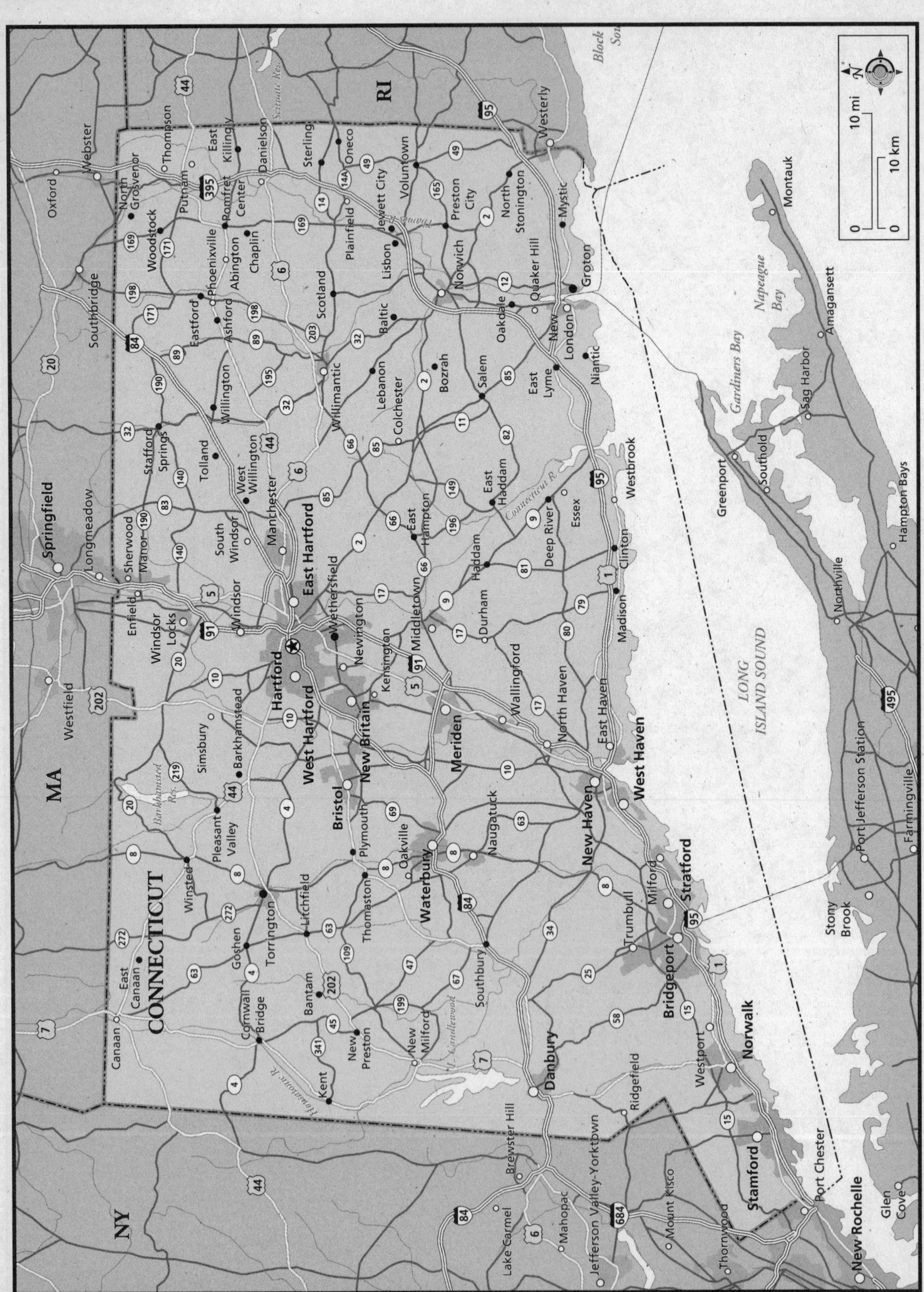

Delaware/Maryland

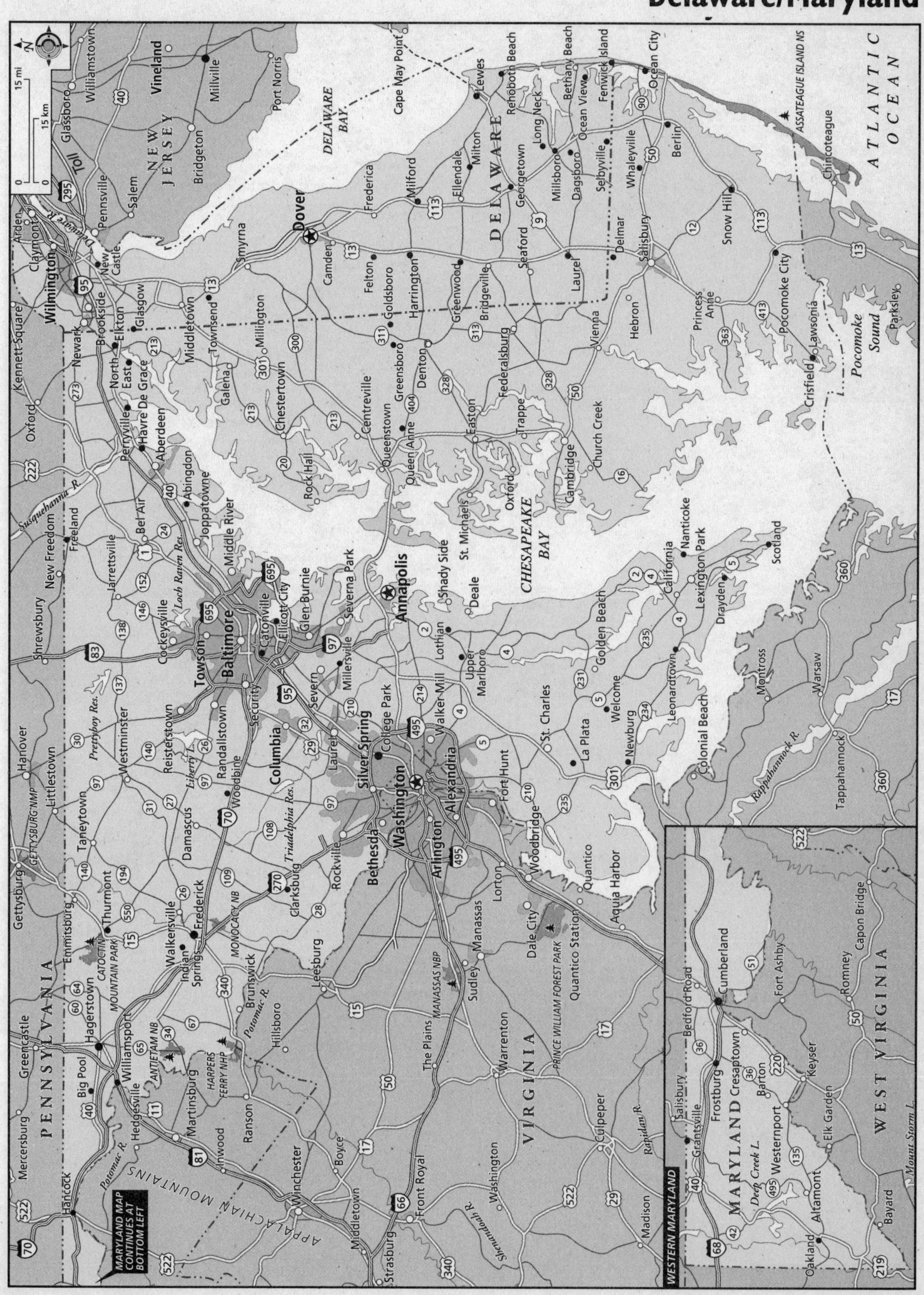

Florida

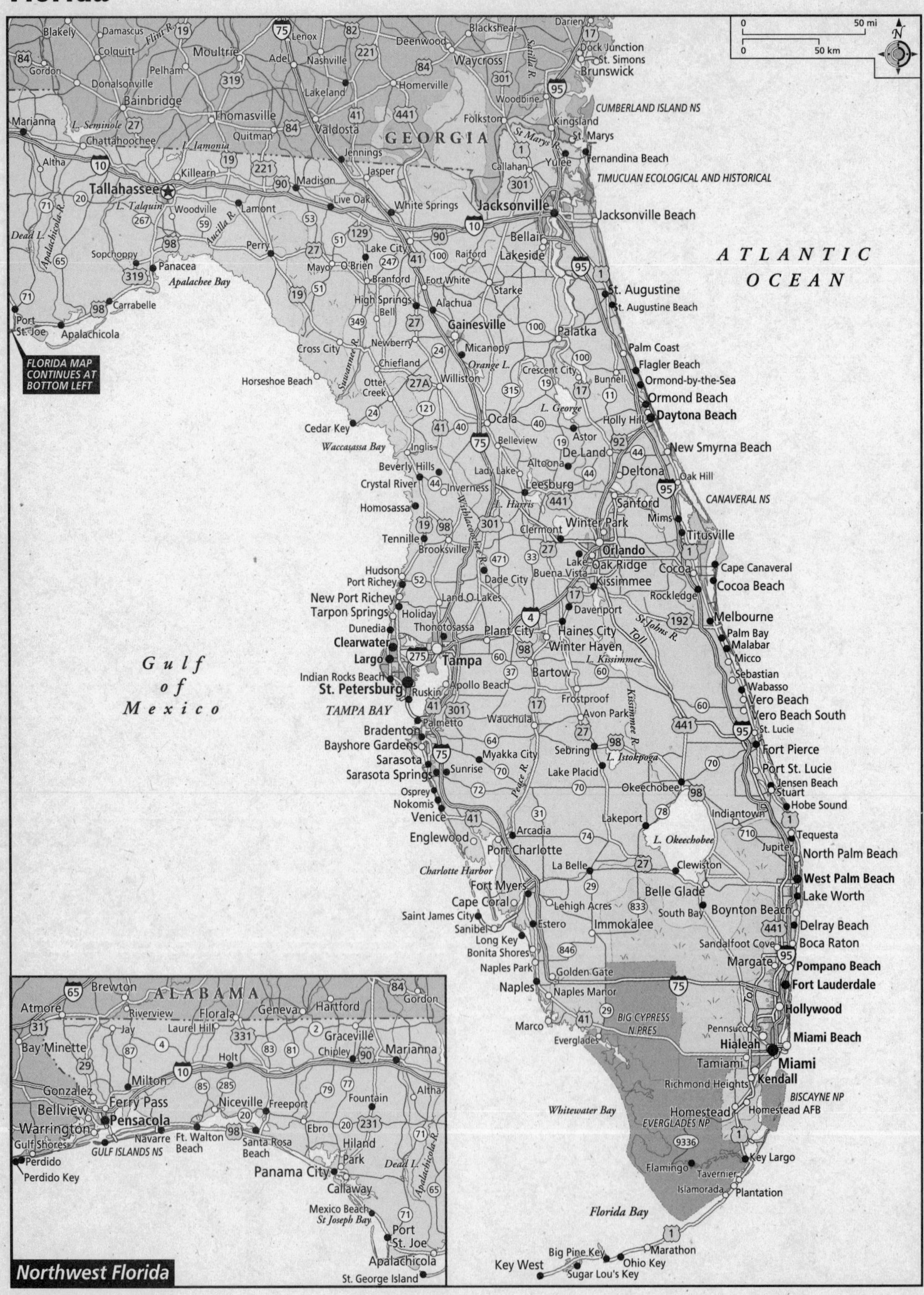

GEORGIA
ATLANTIC OCEAN
Gulf of Mexico
FLORIDA MAP CONTINUES AT BOTTOM LEFT
Blakely
Damascus
Colquitt
Moultrie
Adel
Lenox
Nashville
Deenwood
Waycross
Blackshear
Darien
Dock Junction
St. Simons
Brunswick
Gordon
Pelham
Donalsonville
Bainbridge
Lakeland
Homerville
Woodbine
CUMBERLAND ISLAND NS
Kingsland
St. Marys
Folkston
Marianna
L. Seminole
Chattahoochee
Thomasville
Quitman
Valdosta
L. Iamonia
Jennings
Callahan
Yulee
Fernandina Beach
TIMUCUAN ECOLOGICAL AND HISTORICAL
Altha
Killearn
Madison
Jasper
Tallahassee
Woodville
Lamont
Live Oak
White Springs
Jacksonville
Jacksonville Beach
L. Talquin
Dead L.
Bellair
Lakeside
Lake City
Raiford
O'Brien
Mayo
Perry
Sopchoppy
Panacea
Apalachee Bay
Branford
Fort White
Starke
St. Augustine
St. Augustine Beach
Carrabelle
Port St. Joe
Apalachicola
High Springs
Bell
Alachua
Gainesville
Palatka
Cross City
Newberry
Micanopy
Orange L.
Palm Coast
Flagler Beach
Chiefland
Crescent City
Bunnell
Ormond-by-the-Sea
Ormond Beach
Horseshoe Beach
Otter Creek
Williston
L. George
Daytona Beach
Holly Hill
Cedar Key
Ocala
Astor
Waccasassa Bay
Inglis
Belleview
De Land
New Smyrna Beach
Beverly Hills
Altoona
Deltona
Oak Hill
Crystal River
Inverness
Lady Lake
Leesburg
CANAVERAL NS
Homosassa
L. Harris
Sanford
Mims
Clermont
Winter Park
Titusville
Tennille
Brooksville
Orlando
Hudson
Port Richey
Dade City
Buena Vista
Lake
Oak Ridge
Cocoa
Cape Canaveral
Kissimmee
Cocoa Beach
New Port Richey
Tarpon Springs
Land O Lakes
Holiday
Davenport
Rockledge
Dunedia
Thonotosassa
Plant City
Haines City
Melbourne
Clearwater
Winter Haven
Palm Bay
Malabar
Largo
Tampa
L. Kissimmee
Micco
Indian Rocks Beach
St. Petersburg
Bartow
Sebastian
Ruskin
Apollo Beach
Wabasso
TAMPA BAY
Frostproof
Vero Beach
Palmetto
Wauchula
Avon Park
Vero Beach South
Bradenton
St. Lucie
Bayshore Gardens
Sebring
Fort Pierce
Sarasota
Myakka City
L. Istokpoga
Sarasota Springs
Sunrise
Lake Placid
Port St. Lucie
Osprey
Okeechobee
Jensen Beach
Nokomis
Stuart
Venice
Indiantown
Hobe Sound
Lakeport
Englewood
Arcadia
L. Okeechobee
Tequesta
Port Charlotte
Jupiter
North Palm Beach
Charlotte Harbor
La Belle
Clewiston
West Palm Beach
Fort Myers
Belle Glade
Lake Worth
Cape Coral
Lehigh Acres
South Bay
Boynton Beach
Saint James City
Immokalee
Delray Beach
Sanibel
Estero
Long Key
Sandalfoot Cove
Boca Raton
Bonita Shores
Margate
Pompano Beach
Naples Park
Golden Gate
Fort Lauderdale
Naples
Naples Manor
Hollywood
Marco
BIG CYPRESS N PRES
Pennsuco
Everglades
Hialeah
Miami Beach
Miami
Tamiami
Kendall
Richmond Heights
BISCAYNE NP
Whitewater Bay
Homestead
Homestead AFB
EVERGLADES NP
Key Largo
Flamingo
Tavernier
Islamorada
Plantation
Florida Bay
Marathon
Big Pine Key
Ohio Key
Key West
Sugar Lou's Key
Northwest Florida
ALABAMA
Brewton
Atmore
Riverview
Florala
Geneva
Hartford
Gordon
Jay
Laurel Hill
Graceville
Bay Minette
Chipley
Marianna
Holt
Milton
Gonzalez
Bellview
Ferry Pass
Niceville
Freeport
Fountain
Altha
Warrington
Pensacola
Ebro
Gulf Shores
Navarre
Ft. Walton Beach
Santa Rosa Beach
Hiland Park
GULF ISLANDS NS
Perdido
Perdido Key
Dead L.
Panama City
Callaway
Mexico Beach
St Joseph Bay
Port St. Joe
Apalachicola
St. George Island
50 mi
50 km
N

Georgia

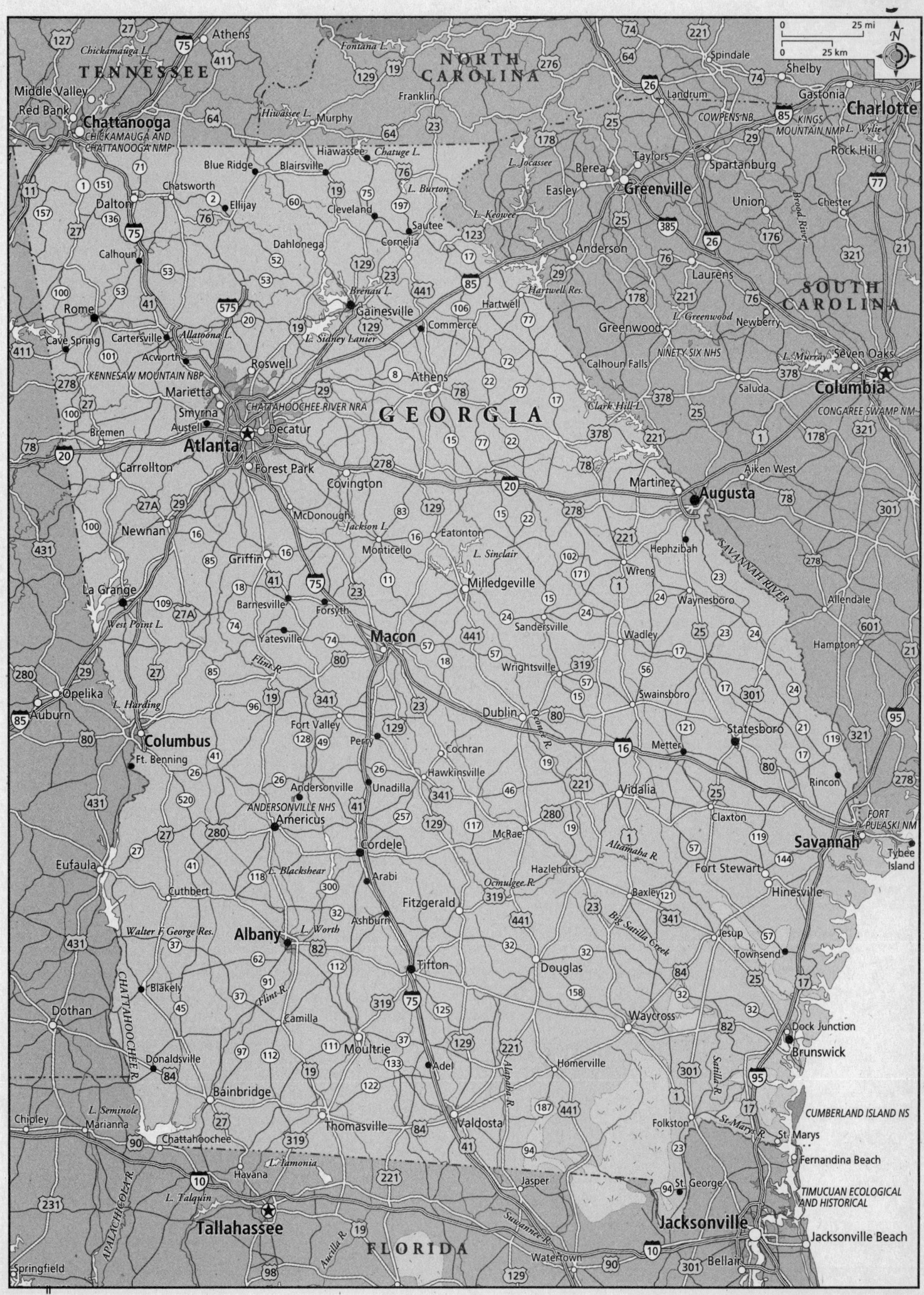

TENNESSEE
NORTH CAROLINA
SOUTH CAROLINA
GEORGIA
FLORIDA
Chattanooga
CHICKAMAUGA AND CHATTANOOGA NMP
Middle Valley
Red Bank
Athens
Chickamauga L.
Fontana L.
Hiwassee L.
Murphy
Franklin
Spindale
Shelby
Landrum
Gastonia
Charlotte
COWPENS NB
KINGS MOUNTAIN NMP
L. Wylie
Rock Hill
Blue Ridge
Blairsville
Hiawassee
Chatuge L.
L. Jocassee
Berea
Taylors
Spartanburg
Greenville
Easley
L. Burton
L. Keowee
Chatsworth
Dalton
Ellijay
Cleveland
Sautee
Cornelia
Dahlonega
Calhoun
Anderson
Union
Chester
Broad River
Laurens
Hartwell Res.
Hartwell
Rome
Cave Spring
Cartersville
Allatoona L.
Acworth
Gainesville
Brenau L.
L. Sidney Lanier
Commerce
Greenwood
L. Greenwood
Newberry
NINETY SIX NHS
Calhoun Falls
L. Murray
Seven Oaks
Columbia
Saluda
KENNESAW MOUNTAIN NBP
Roswell
Marietta
Athens
Smyrna
Austell
CHATTAHOOCHEE RIVER NRA
Clark Hill L.
CONGAREE SWAMP NM
Bremen
Atlanta
Decatur
Carrollton
Forest Park
Covington
Martinez
Augusta
Aiken West
Newnan
McDonough
Jackson L.
Eatonton
Monticello
L. Sinclair
Hephzibah
SAVANNAH RIVER
Griffin
Wrens
Milledgeville
La Grange
Barnesville
Forsyth
Waynesboro
Allendale
West Point L.
Sandersville
Yatesville
Macon
Wadley
Hampton
Flint R.
Wrightsville
Opelika
L. Harding
Auburn
Swainsboro
Dublin
Oconee R.
Columbus
Ft. Benning
Fort Valley
Perry
Cochran
Statesboro
Metter
Hawkinsville
Andersonville
Unadilla
Vidalia
Rincon
ANDERSONVILLE NHS
Americus
Claxton
FORT PULASKI NM
McRae
Savannah
Cordele
Altamaha R.
Tybee Island
Eufaula
L. Blackshear
Arabi
Hazlehurst
Fort Stewart
Cuthbert
Ocmulgee R.
Baxley
Hinesville
Fitzgerald
Ashburn
Big Satilla Creek
Walter F. George Res.
Albany
L. Worth
Jesup
Townsend
Tifton
Douglas
Blakely
CHATTAHOOCHEE R.
Dothan
Camilla
Waycross
Dock Junction
Brunswick
Moultrie
Adel
Donaldsville
Homerville
Alapaha R.
Satilla R.
Bainbridge
L. Seminole
Chipley
Marianna
Thomasville
Valdosta
CUMBERLAND ISLAND NS
Folkston
St. Marys R.
St. Marys
Chattahoochee
L. Iamonia
Fernandina Beach
Havana
Jasper
St. George
TIMUCUAN ECOLOGICAL AND HISTORICAL
APALACHICOLA R.
L. Talquin
Tallahassee
Suwannee R.
Jacksonville
Aucilla R.
Jacksonville Beach
Springfield
Watertown
Bellair
0 25 mi
0 25 km
N

Idaho

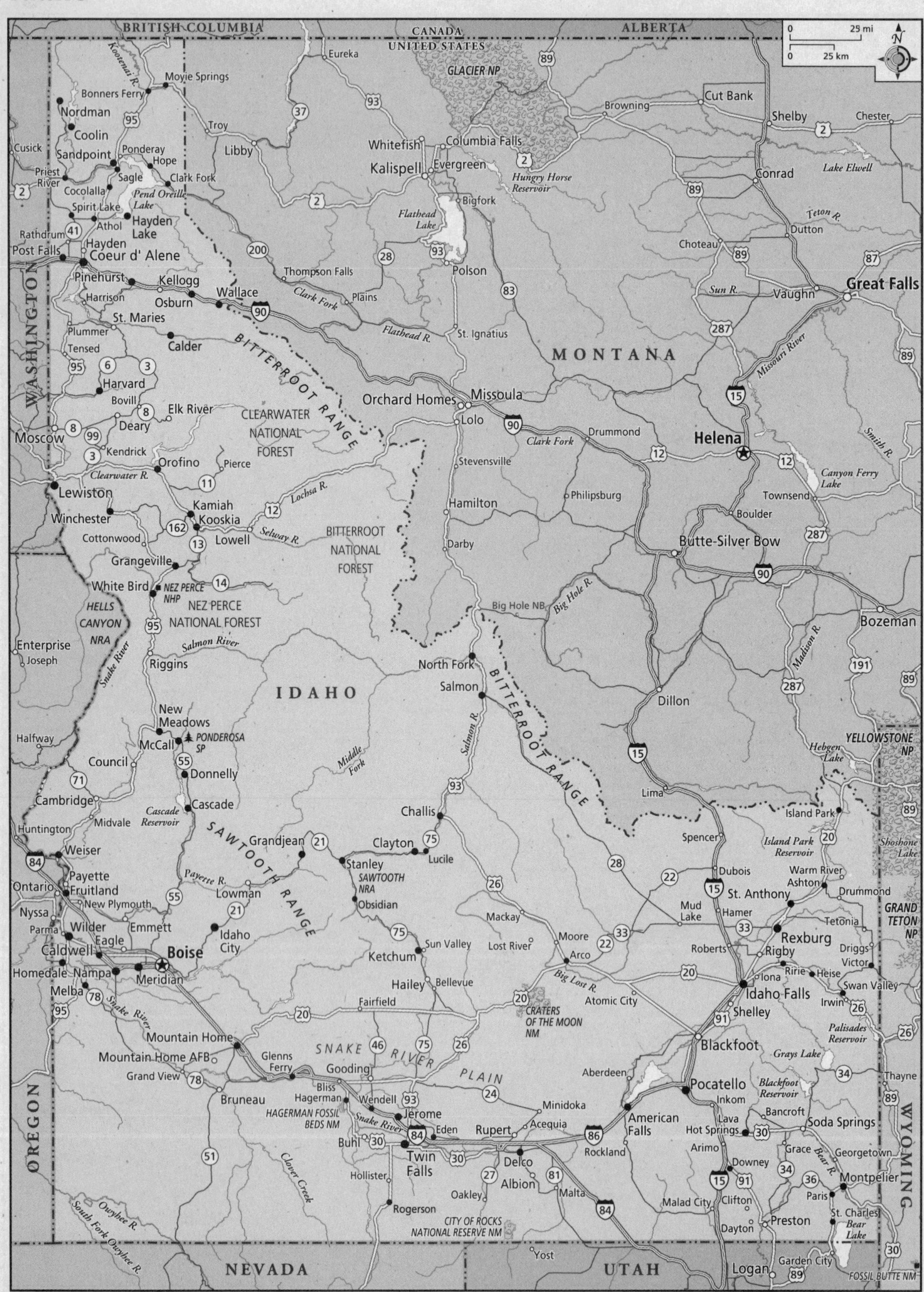

Illinois

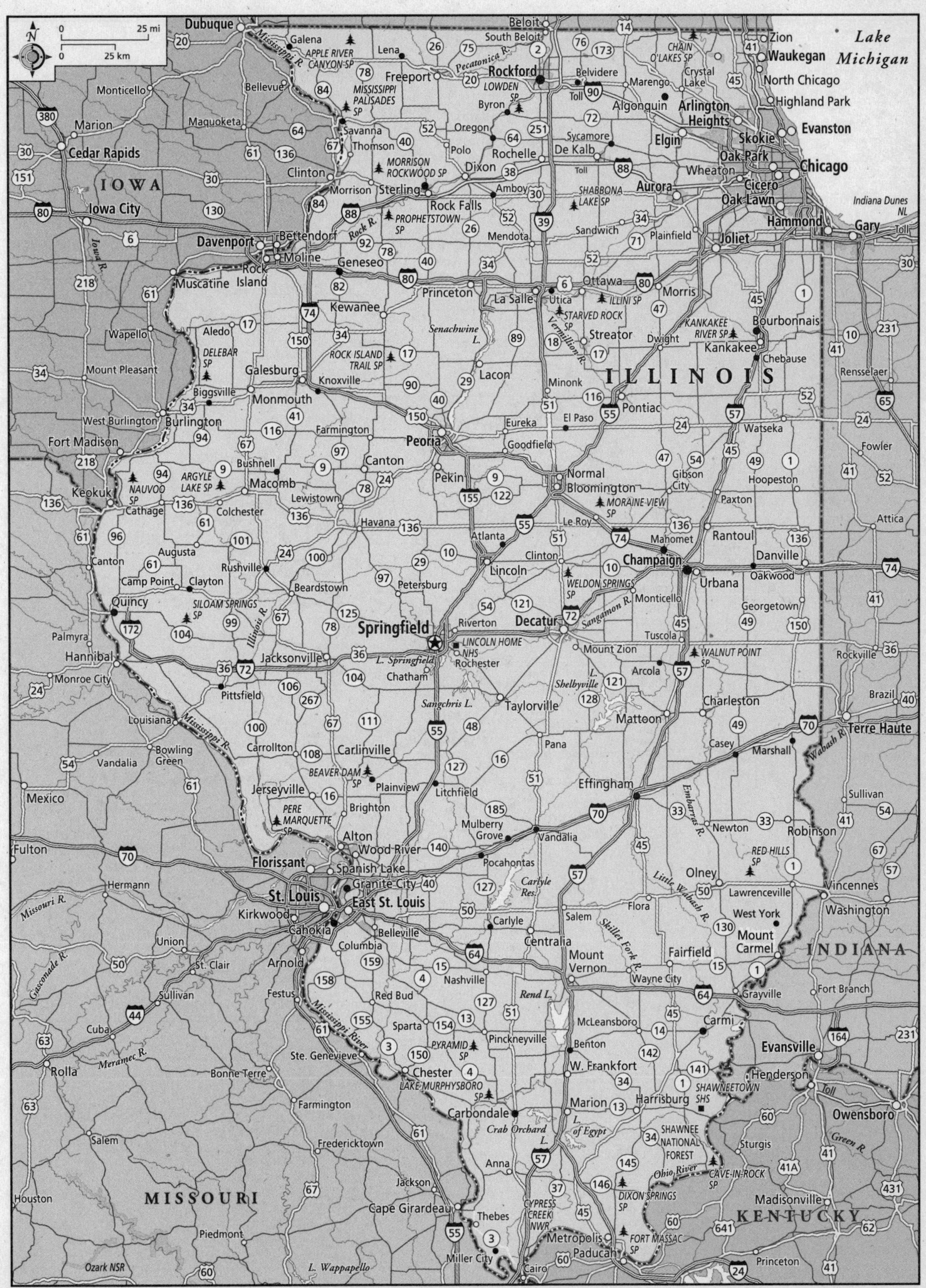

Indiana

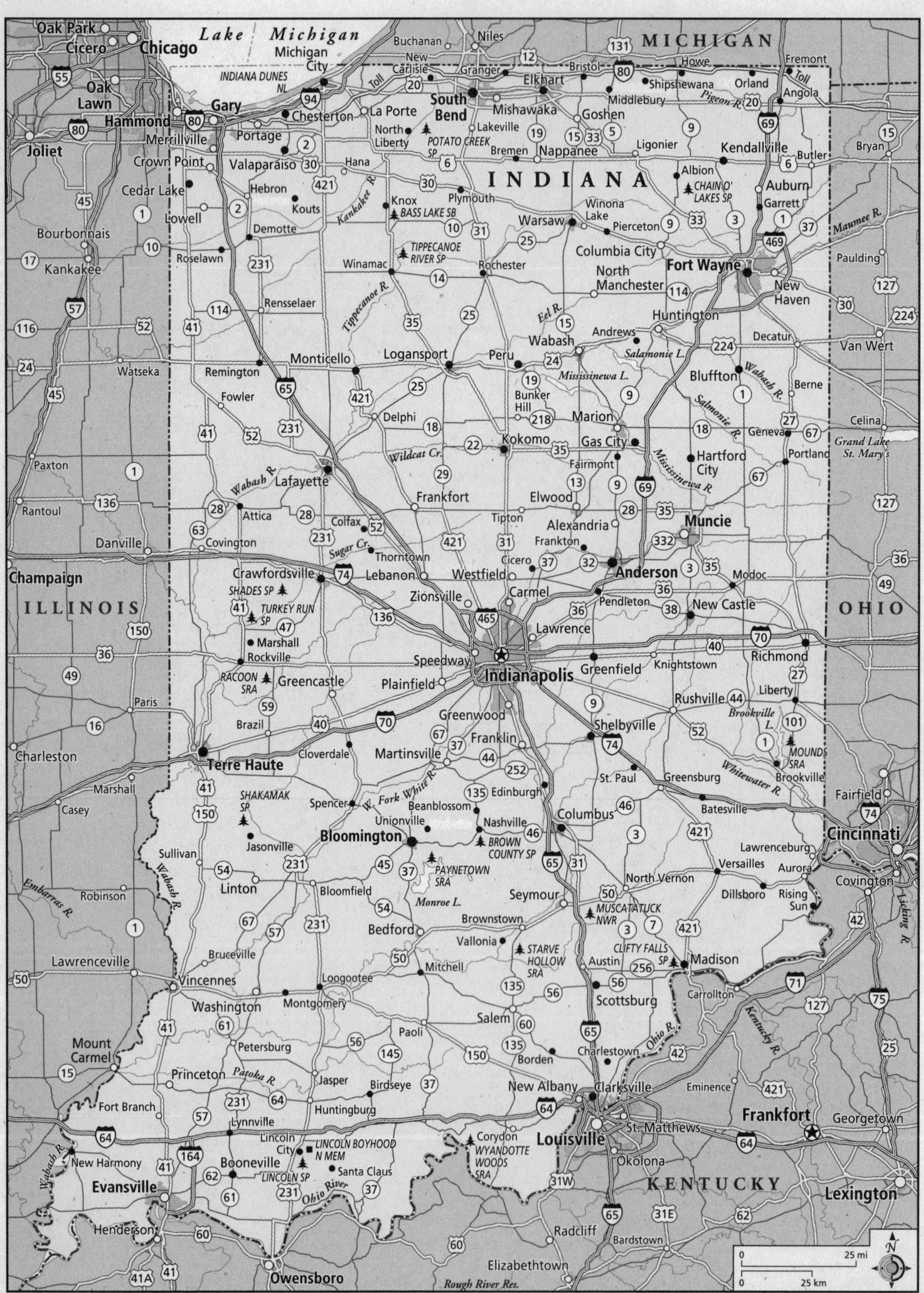
Lake Michigan
MICHIGAN
INDIANA
ILLINOIS
OHIO
KENTUCKY
Oak Park
Cicero
Chicago
Oak Lawn
Gary
Hammond
Joliet
Merrillville
Crown Point
Portage
Chesterton
Michigan City
INDIANA DUNES NL
La Porte
South Bend
Mishawaka
Elkhart
Goshen
Middlebury
Shipshewana
Orland
Angola
Fremont
Buchanan
Niles
New Carlisle
Granger
Bristol
Howe
Pigeon R.
Toll
Cedar Lake
Lowell
Valparaiso
Hebron
Kouts
Hana
North Liberty
POTATO CREEK SP
Lakeville
Bremen
Nappanee
Ligonier
Kendallville
Butler
Bryan
Albion
CHAIN O' LAKES SP
Auburn
Garrett
Kankakee R.
Knox
BASS LAKE SB
Plymouth
Warsaw
Winona Lake
Pierceton
Columbia City
Fort Wayne
New Haven
Maumee R.
Paulding
Bourbonnais
Kankakee
Demotte
Roselawn
TIPPECANOE RIVER SP
Winamac
Rochester
North Manchester
Huntington
Rensselaer
Tippecanoe R.
Eel R.
Wabash
Andrews
Salamonie L.
Decatur
Van Wert
Watseka
Remington
Monticello
Logansport
Peru
Mississinewa L.
Bluffton
Wabash R.
Berne
Fowler
Delphi
Bunker Hill
Marion
Salmonie R.
Geneva
Celina
Grand Lake St. Mary's
Kokomo
Gas City
Hartford City
Portland
Wildcat Cr.
Fairmont
Mississinewa R.
Paxton
Lafayette
Frankfort
Elwood
Rantoul
Attica
Tipton
Alexandria
Muncie
Colfax
Danville
Covington
Sugar Cr.
Thorntown
Frankton
Champaign
Crawfordsville
Lebanon
Westfield
Cicero
Anderson
Modoc
SHADES SP
TURKEY RUN SP
Zionsville
Carmel
Pendleton
New Castle
Lawrence
Marshall
Rockville
Speedway
Indianapolis
Greenfield
Knightstown
Richmond
RACOON SRA
Greencastle
Plainfield
Rushville
Liberty
Brookville L.
Paris
Brazil
Greenwood
Shelbyville
MOUNDS SRA
Charleston
Terre Haute
Cloverdale
Martinsville
Franklin
St. Paul
Greensburg
Whitewater R.
Brookville
Marshall
Casey
SHAKAMAK SP
Spencer
W. Fork White R.
Beanblossom
Edinburgh
Batesville
Fairfield
Unionville
Nashville
Columbus
BROWN COUNTY SP
Bloomington
Jasonville
Sullivan
Cincinnati
Lawrenceburg
Aurora
Covington
PAYNETOWN SRA
Linton
Bloomfield
Robinson
Embarras R.
Monroe L.
Seymour
North Vernon
Versailles
Dillsboro
Rising Sun
Licking R.
Brownstown
MUSCATATUCK NWR
Bedford
Vallonia
STARVE HOLLOW SRA
CLIFTY FALLS SP
Madison
Bruceville
Lawrenceville
Mitchell
Austin
Vincennes
Loogootee
Washington
Montgomery
Scottsburg
Carrollton
Kentucky R.
Salem
Paoli
Petersburg
Mount Carmel
Charlestown
Ohio R.
Borden
Princeton
Patoka R.
Jasper
Birdseye
New Albany
Clarksville
Eminence
Frankfort
Georgetown
Fort Branch
Huntingburg
Lynnville
St. Matthews
Louisville
Corydon
WYANDOTTE WOODS SRA
Lincoln City
LINCOLN BOYHOOD N MEM
New Harmony
Boonville
LINCOLN SP
Santa Claus
Ohio River
Okolona
Lexington
Evansville
Henderson
Radcliff
Bardstown
Elizabethtown
Owensboro
Rough River Res.
0
25 mi
0
25 km
N

Iowa

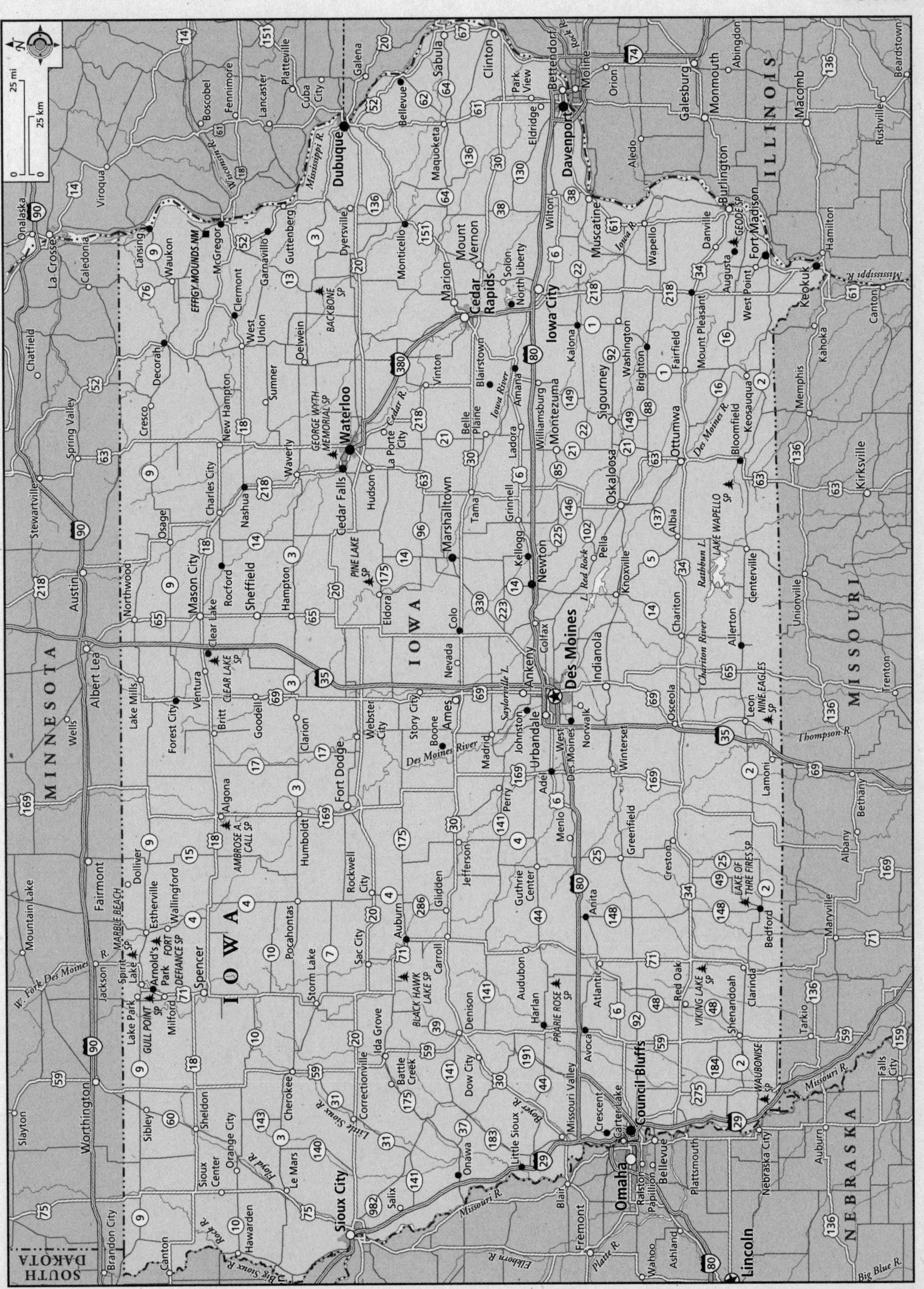

Kansas

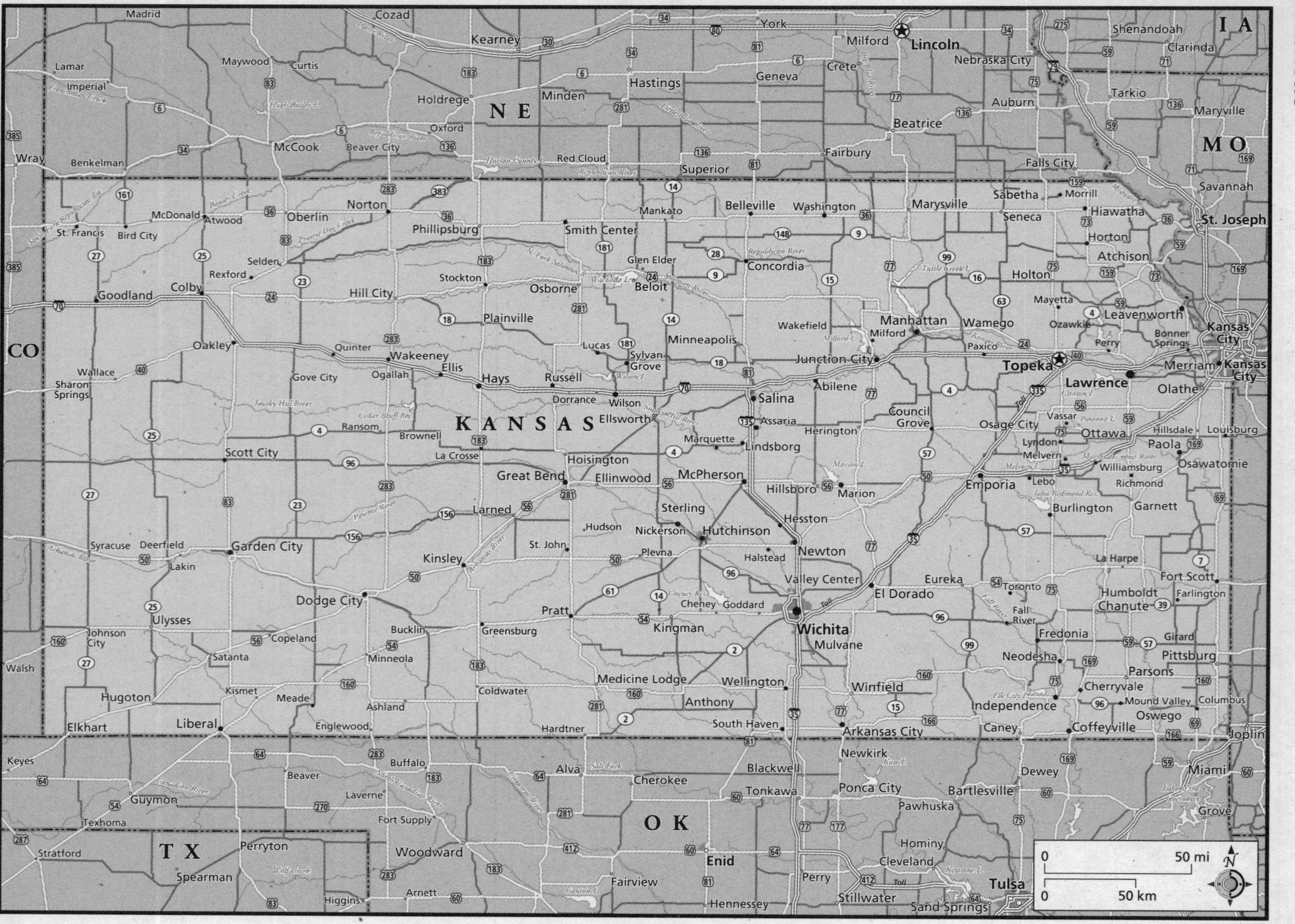
KANSAS
NE
MO
IA
OK
CO
TX
Topeka
Lawrence
Wichita
Kansas City
Salina
Manhattan
Hutchinson
Dodge City
Garden City
Lincoln
Tulsa
Enid
St. Joseph
50 mi
50 km

Kentucky

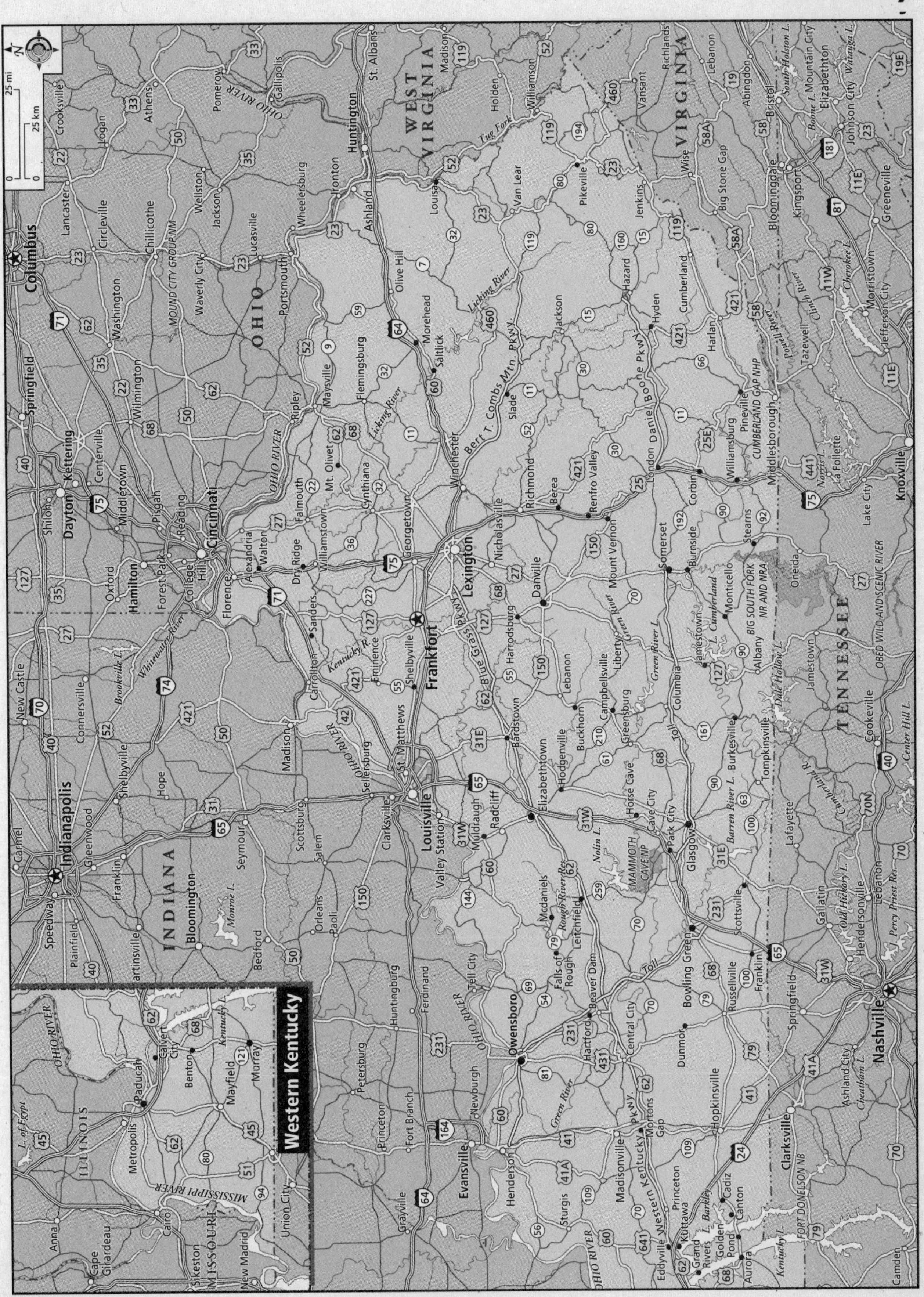

Western Kentucky
WEST VIRGINIA
VIRGINIA
OHIO
INDIANA
ILLINOIS
MISSOURI
TENNESSEE
Columbus
Springfield
Dayton
Kettering
Cincinnati
Hamilton
Indianapolis
Bloomington
Louisville
Frankfort
Lexington
Huntington
Ashland
Portsmouth
Maysville
Morehead
Winchester
Richmond
Berea
Danville
Harrodsburg
Bardstown
Elizabethtown
Owensboro
Evansville
Henderson
Bowling Green
Glasgow
Somerset
London
Corbin
Middlesborough
Pikeville
Hazard
Paducah
Murray
Mayfield
Clarksville
Nashville
Knoxville
Kingsport
Bristol
Johnson City
OHIO RIVER
MISSISSIPPI RIVER
Licking River
Green River
Kentucky R.
Bert T. Combs Mtn. Pkwy.
Daniel Boone Pkwy.
Blue Grass Pkwy.
Western Kentucky Pkwy.
MAMMOTH CAVE NP
BIG SOUTH FORK NR AND NRA
CUMBERLAND GAP NHP
L. Cumberland
Kentucky L.
L. Barkley
0
25 mi
25 km
N

Louisiana

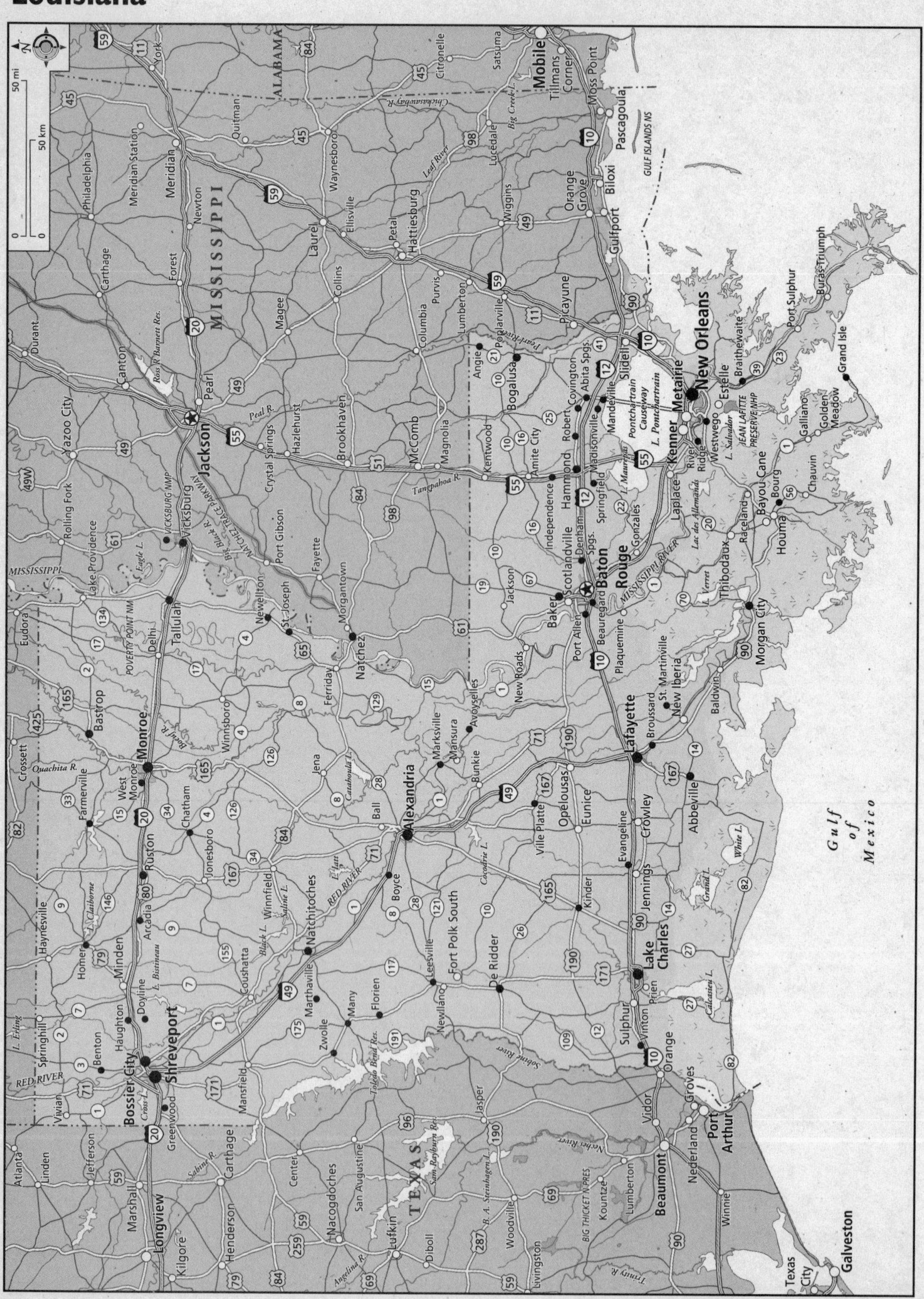

50 mi
50 km
N
MISSISSIPPI
ALABAMA
TEXAS
Gulf of Mexico
Mobile
Tillmans Corner
Moss Point
Pascagoula
GULF ISLANDS NS
Biloxi
Gulfport
Orange Grove
Wiggins
Lucedale
Citronelle
Satsuma
Quitman
Waynesboro
Meridian
Meridian Station
Philadelphia
Newton
Forest
Carthage
Laurel
Ellisville
Petal
Hattiesburg
Collins
Magee
Purvis
Lumberton
Poplarville
Picayune
Columbia
Durant
Canton
Pearl
Jackson
Yazoo City
Crystal Springs
Hazlehurst
Brookhaven
McComb
Magnolia
Rolling Fork
Vicksburg
VICKSBURG NMP
NATCHEZ TRACE PARKWAY
Port Gibson
Fayette
Morgantown
Natchez
Lake Providence
Tallulah
Newellton
St. Joseph
Ferriday
Eudora
Delhi
POVERTY POINT NM
Bastrop
Crossett
Monroe
West Monroe
Farmerville
Winnsboro
Jena
Chatham
Ruston
Jonesboro
Winnfield
Arcadia
Homer
Haynesville
Minden
Doyline
Haughton
Springhill
Benton
Bossier City
Shreveport
Vivian
Greenwood
Mansfield
Coushatta
Natchitoches
Marthaville
Many
Zwolle
Florien
Leesville
Newllano
Fort Polk South
De Ridder
Alexandria
Ball
Boyce
Marksville
Mansura
Avoyelles
Bunkie
Ville Platte
Opelousas
Eunice
Lafayette
Broussard
St. Martinville
New Iberia
Abbeville
Crowley
Evangeline
Jennings
Kinder
Lake Charles
Sulphur
Vinton
Prien
Orange
Vidor
Groves
Port Arthur
Beaumont
Nederland
Winnie
Galveston
Texas City
New Roads
Jackson
Baker
Scotlandville
Baton Rouge
Port Allen
Beauregard
Plaquemine
Denham Spgs.
Gonzales
Independence
Hammond
Amite City
Kentwood
Springfield
Madisonville
Mandeville
Covington
Abita Spgs.
Robert
Bogalusa
Angie
Slidell
Laplace
Kenner
Metairie
New Orleans
River Ridge
Westwego
Estelle
Braithewaite
JEAN LAFITTE PRESERVE NHP
Raceland
Thibodaux
Bayou Cane
Houma
Bourg
Chauvin
Morgan City
Baldwin
Galliano
Golden Meadow
Grand Isle
Port Sulphur
Buras-Triumph
L. Pontchartrain
Pontchartrain Causeway
L. Maurepas
L. Salvador
Lac des Allemands
MISSISSIPPI RIVER
RED RIVER
Sabine R.
Toledo Bend Res.
Sam Rayburn Res.
B. A. Steinhagen L.
Neches River
Sabine River
Calcasieu L.
Grand L.
White L.
Catahoula L.
Ouachita R.
Pearl R.
Leaf River
Big Black R.
Tangipahoa R.
Longview
Kilgore
Marshall
Henderson
Carthage
Linden
Atlanta
Jefferson
Center
Nacogdoches
San Augustine
Lufkin
Diboll
Jasper
Woodville
Livingston
Kountze
Lumberton
BIG THICKET N. PRES.
Angelina R.
Trinity R.

Maine

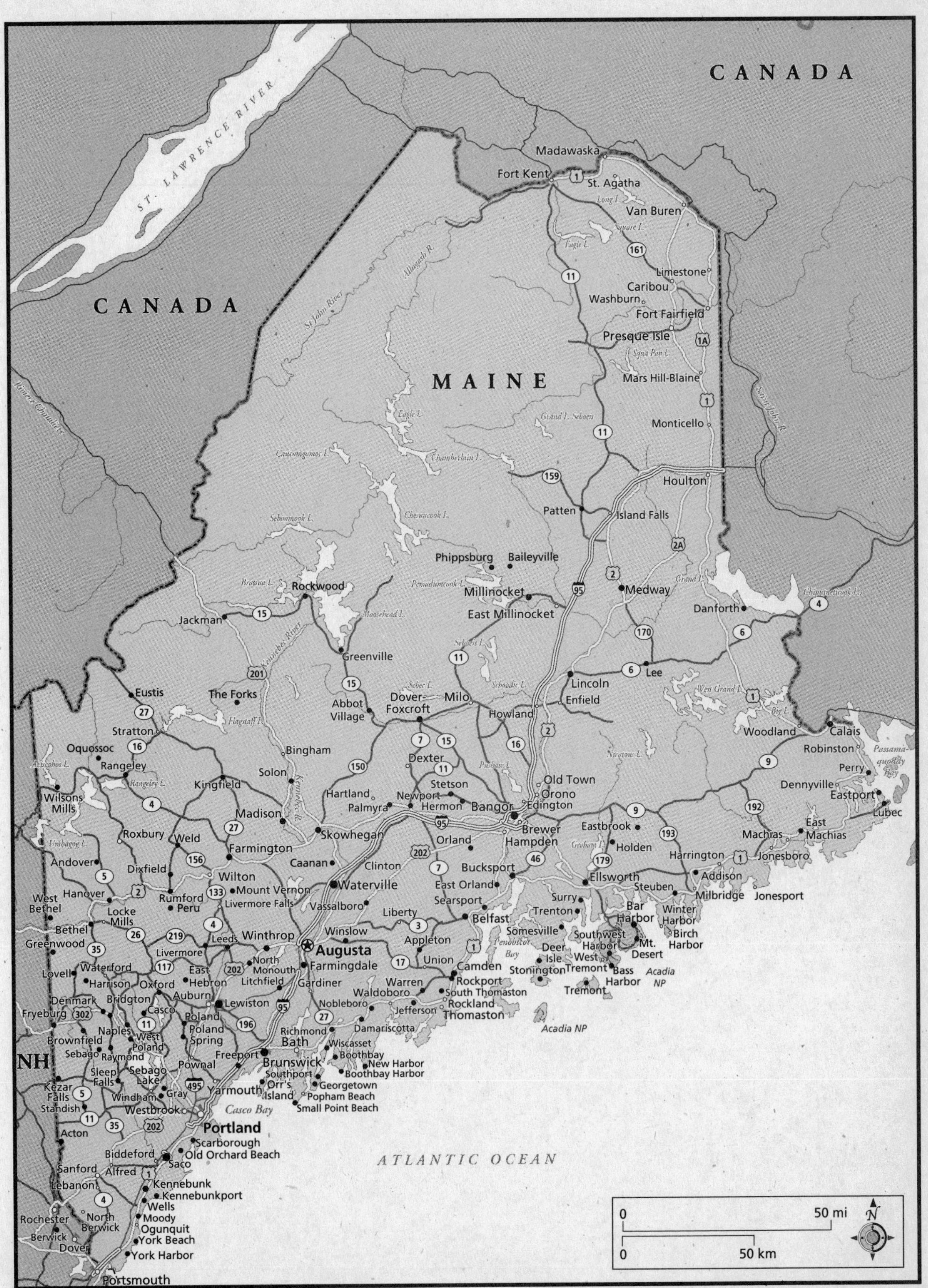
CANADA
CANADA
MAINE
ST. LAWRENCE RIVER
NH
ATLANTIC OCEAN
Madawaska
Fort Kent
St. Agatha
Van Buren
Limestone
Caribou
Washburn
Fort Fairfield
Presque Isle
Mars Hill-Blaine
Monticello
Houlton
Patten
Island Falls
Phippsburg
Baileyville
Millinocket
East Millinocket
Medway
Danforth
Rockwood
Jackman
Greenville
Lincoln
Enfield
Lee
Eustis
The Forks
Abbot Village
Dover-Foxcroft
Milo
Howland
Calais
Woodland
Robinston
Perry
Dennysville
Eastport
Lubec
Stratton
Oquossoc
Rangeley
Bingham
Solon
Kingfield
Dexter
Stetson
Old Town
Orono
Edington
Bangor
Brewer
Hampden
Hartland
Palmyra
Newport
Hermon
Wilsons Mills
Madison
Skowhegan
Orland
Eastbrook
Holden
Machias
East Machias
Jonesboro
Harrington
Roxbury
Weld
Farmington
Andover
Dixfield
Caanan
Clinton
Bucksport
Ellsworth
Addison
Milbridge
Jonesport
Steuben
Wilton
Mount Vernon
Livermore Falls
Waterville
East Orland
Searsport
West Bethel
Hanover
Rumford
Peru
Locke Mills
Vassalboro
Liberty
Belfast
Surry
Trenton
Bar Harbor
Winter Harbor
Birch Harbor
Bethel
Greenwood
Leeds
Winthrop
Winslow
Appleton
Somesville
Southwest Harbor
Mt. Desert
Livermore
Augusta
Union
Deer Isle
West Tremont
Bass Harbor
Lovell
Waterford
East Hebron
North Monouth
Farmingdale
Camden
Stonington
Tremont
Acadia NP
Harrison
Oxford
Litchfield
Gardiner
Warren
Rockport
Denmark
Bridgton
Auburn
Waldoboro
South Thomaston
Fryeburg
Casco
Lewiston
Nobleboro
Jefferson
Rockland
Thomaston
Naples
West Poland
Poland
Poland Spring
Damariscotta
Brownfield
Richmond
Bath
Sebago
Raymond
Freeport
Wiscasset
Boothbay
New Harbor
Boothbay Harbor
Sleep Falls
Sebago Lake
Pownal
Brunswick
Southport
Orr's Island
Georgetown
Popham Beach
Small Point Beach
Kezar Falls
Standish
Windham
Gray
Yarmouth
Westbrook
Casco Bay
Acton
Portland
Scarborough
Biddeford
Saco
Old Orchard Beach
Sanford
Alfred
Lebanon
Kennebunk
Kennebunkport
Wells
Moody
Ogunquit
York Beach
York Harbor
Rochester
North Berwick
Berwick
Dover
Portsmouth
0
50 mi
0
50 km
N

Massachusetts

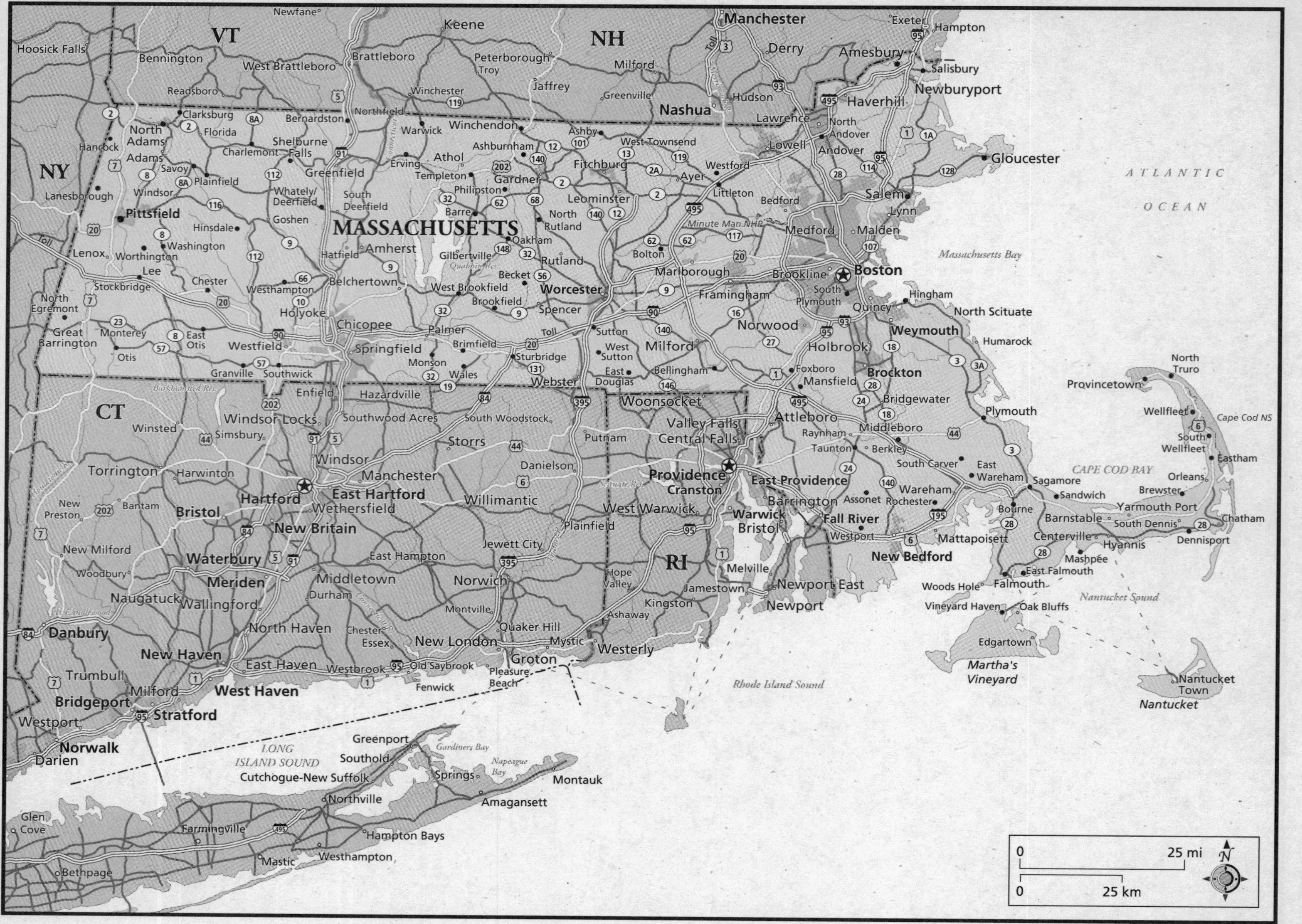

Michigan

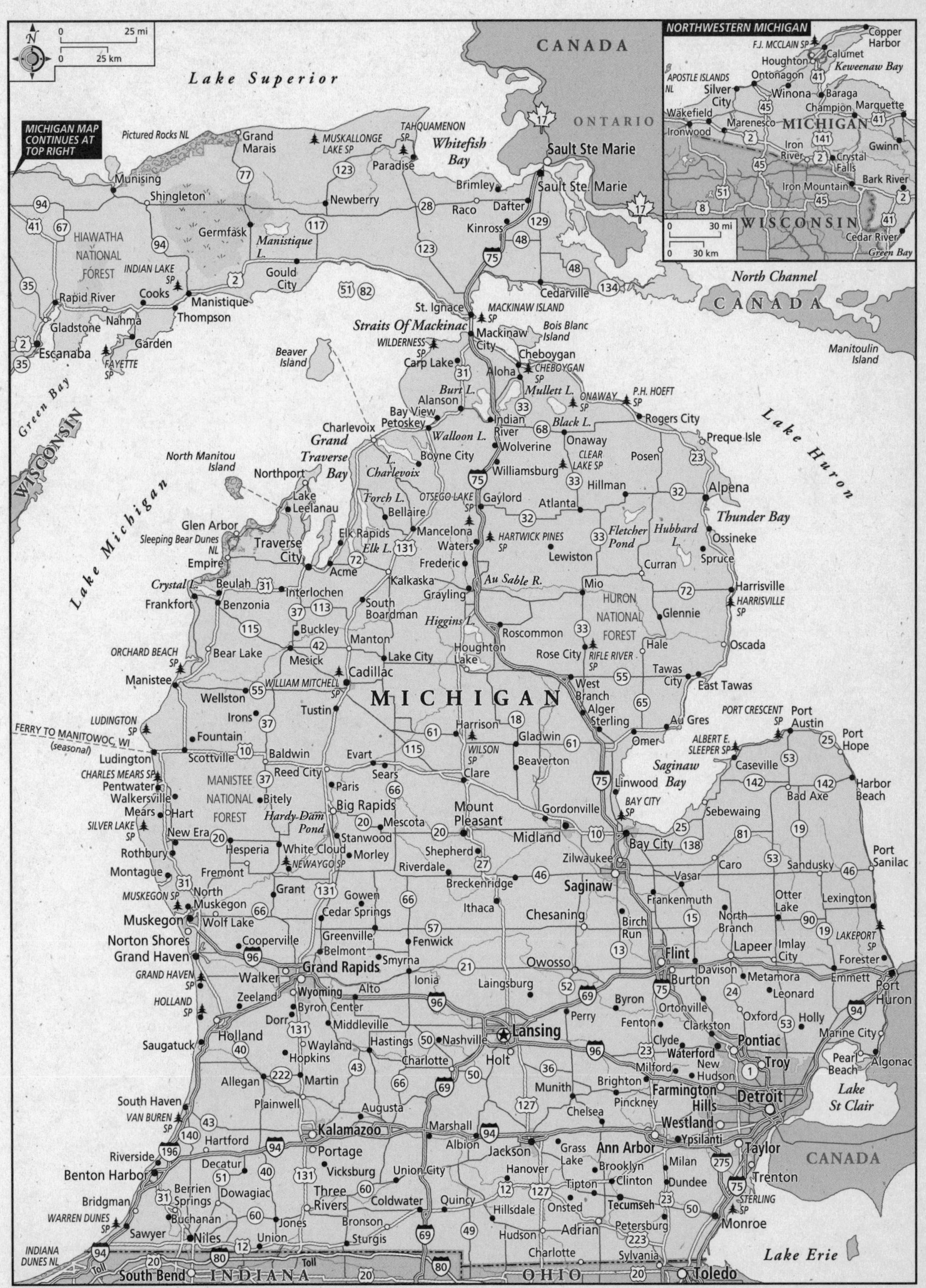

Minnesota

Winnipeg
Steinbach
MANITOBA
ONTARIO
Lake of the Woods
CANADA
UNITED STATES
Warroad
Roseau
Baudette
International Falls
South International Falls
Lake Bronson
Argyle
Warren
Thief River Falls
Grand Forks
Crookston
Erskine
Fosston
Bagley
Bemidji
Washkish
Upper Red L.
Lower Red L.
Kelliher
Tenstrike
Blackduck
Effie
Big Fork
Marcell
Orr
Buyck
Crane Lake
Tower
Ely
Babbitt
Isabella
Mountain Iron
Virginia
Hoyt Lakes
Gilbert
Chisholm
Hibbing
Deer River
Grand Rapids
Cass Lake
Walker
Bena
Federal Dam
Remer
Hill City
MINNESOTA
Two Harbors
Silver Bay
Knife River
Duluth
Superior
Cloquet
Esko
Lake Superior
Fargo
West Fargo
Moorhead
Glyndon
Mahnomen
Wauban
Lake Itasca
Ogema
Osage
Nevis
Akeley
Park Rapids
Ponsford
Detroit Lakes
Frazee
Perham
Pelican Rapids
Barnesville
Sebeka
Wadena
Hackensack
Fifty Lakes
Pine River
Backus
Breezy Point
Merrifield
Nisswa
Crosby
Aitken
Deerwood
Brainerd
Staples
Pillager
McGregor
Cromwell
Barnum
Moose Lake
Sturgeon Lake
Kerrick
Rutledge
Sandstone
Hinckley
Breckenridge
Fergus Falls
Battle Lake
Garfield
Ashby
Elbow Lake
Brandon
Alexandria
Carlos
Osakis
Burtrum
Long Prairie
Cushing
Little Falls
Garrison
Isle
Onamia
Mille Lacs L.
Mora
Ogilvie
Royalton
Milaca
Pine City
NORTH DAKOTA
WISCONSIN
Spooner
Sisseton
Morris
Starbuck
Glenwood
Sauk Centre
Melrose
St. Cloud
Princeton
North Branch
Taylor Falls
Center City
Lindstrom
Rice Lake
Barron
Ladysmith
Ortonville
Benson
Hawick
Richmond
South Haven
Clearwater
Big Lake
Elk River
Isanti
Ham Lake
Zimmerman
Marine on St. Croix
Forest Lake
Lino Lakes
Milbank
New London
Annandale
Andover
Willmar
Kandiyohi
Maple Plain
Cokato
Rogers
Plymouth
Maplewood
Dassel
Madison
Montevideo
Granite Falls
Olivia
Hutchinson
Glencoe
Minneapolis
St. Paul
Bloomington
Woodbury
Chippewa Falls
Eau Claire
Bloomer
Ellsworth
Watertown
Canby
Redwood Falls
Morton
Jordan
Savage
Belle Plaine
Apple Valley
Prior Lake
Red Wing
Durand
Mondovi
SOUTH DAKOTA
Marshall
Fairfax
Northfield
Cannon Falls
Lake City
Le Sueur
Nerstrand
Hastings
Wabasha
Brookings
Lake Benton
Tracy
New Ulm
Waterville
Faribault
Zumbrota
Mazeppa
Arcadia
Springfield
Mankato
Owatonna
Rochester
Altura
Winona
Madison
Pipestone
Currie
Madelia
Garden City
Waseca
Holmen
Dell Rapids
Jasper
Slayton
Windom
Stewartville
St. Charles
Lanesboro
Houston
La Crosse
Brandon City
Adrian
Lakefield
Welcome
Wells
Blooming Prairie
Austin
Preston
Sioux Falls
Luverne
Worthington
Jackson
Fairmont
Albert Lea
Le Roy
Caledonia
Estherville
Northwood
Cresco
Decorah
Sheldon
Milford
IOWA
Forest City
Osage
Waukon

Mississippi

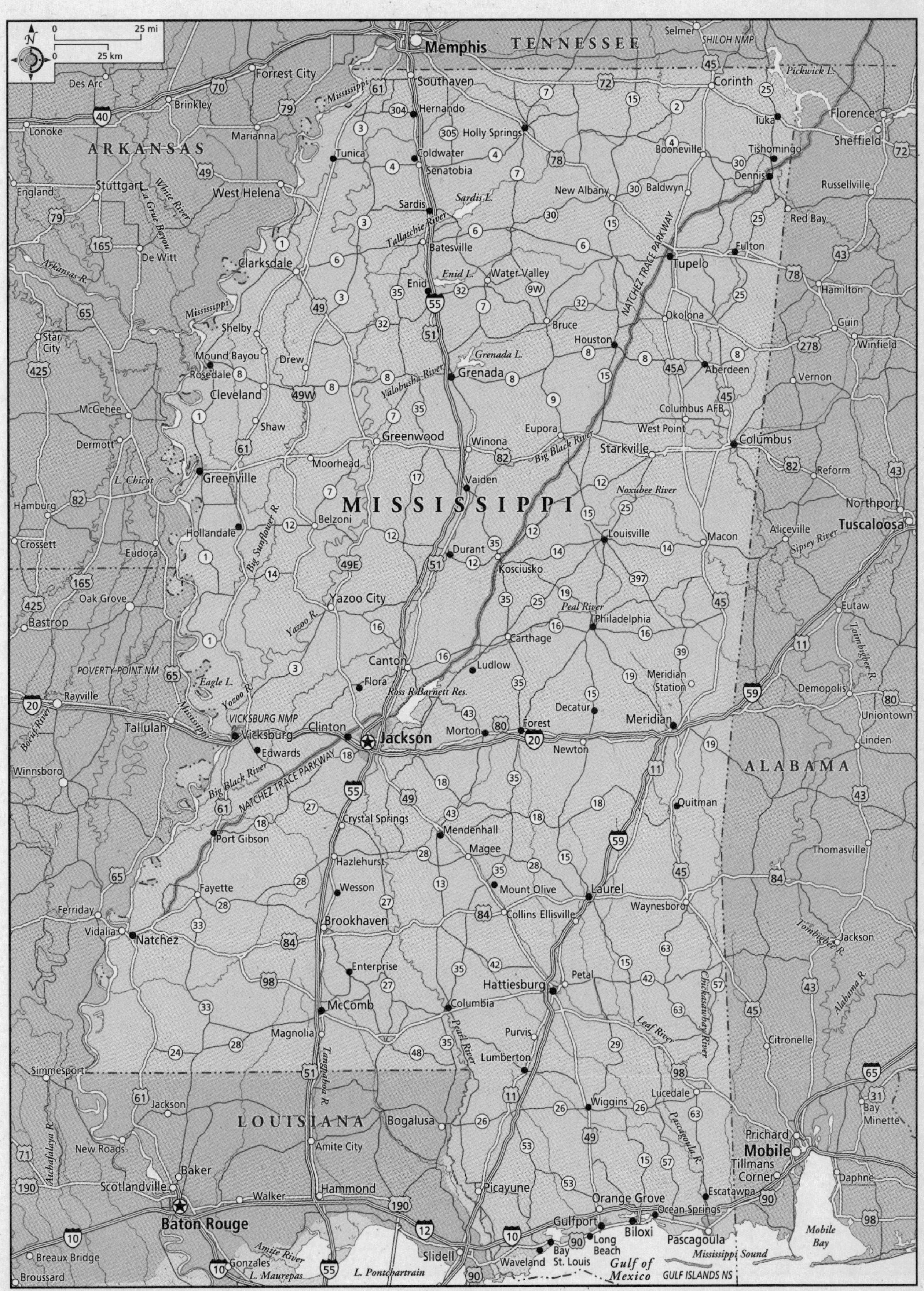

Missouri

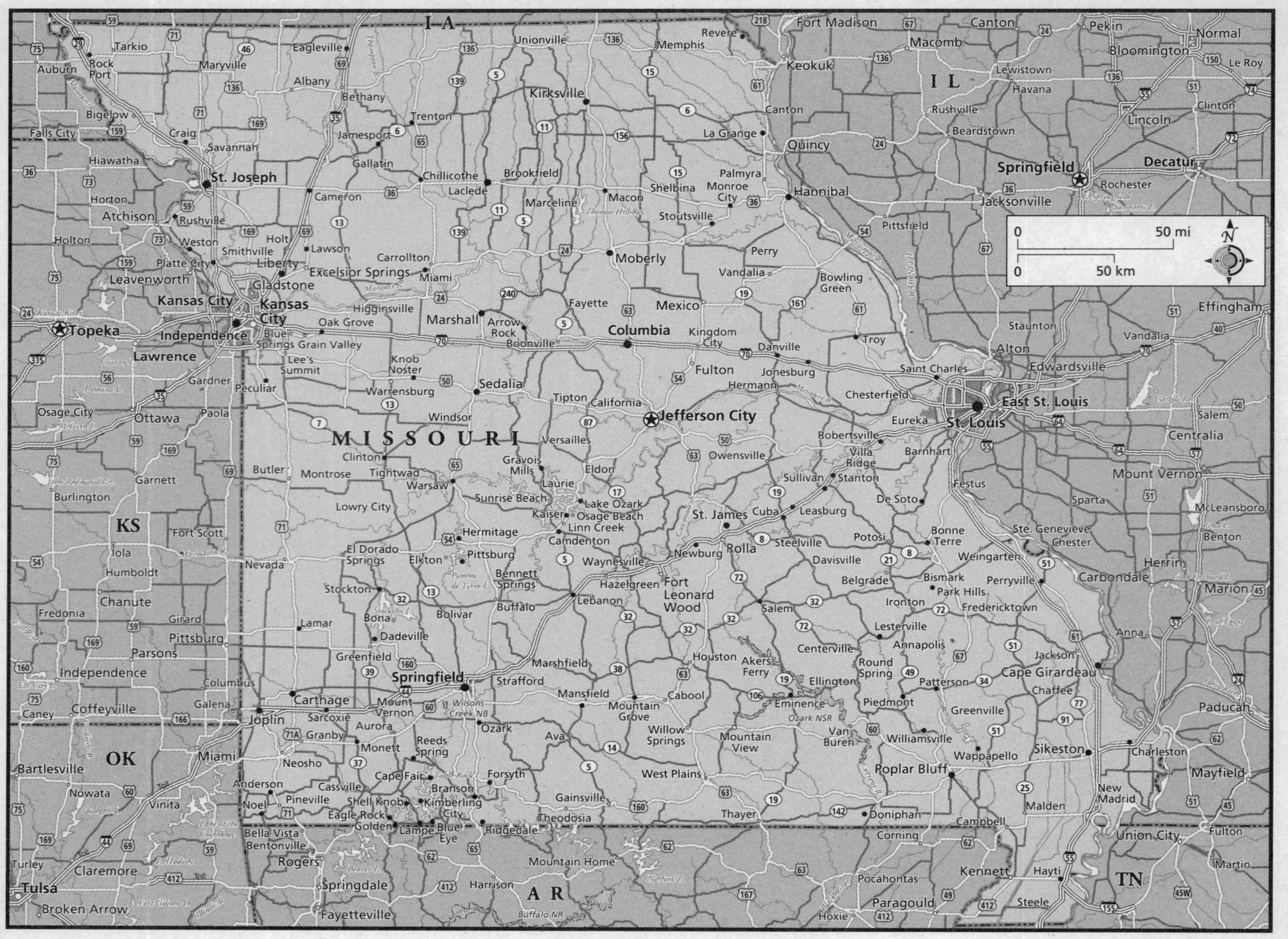

MISSOURI
IA
IL
KS
OK
AR
TN
0
50 mi
0
50 km
N
Tarkio
Rock Port
Auburn
Maryville
Eagleville
Albany
Bethany
Unionville
Memphis
Revere
Fort Madison
Macomb
Canton
Pekin
Bloomington
Normal
Le Roy
Keokuk
Lewistown
Havana
Kirksville
Trenton
Jamesport
Canton
La Grange
Quincy
Rushville
Beardstown
Lincoln
Clinton
Bigelow
Falls City
Craig
Savannah
Gallatin
Chillicothe
Laclede
Brookfield
Marceline
Macon
Shelbina
Palmyra
Monroe City
Hannibal
Stoutsville
Springfield
Decatur
Rochester
Jacksonville
Pittsfield
Hiawatha
St. Joseph
Cameron
Horton
Atchison
Rushville
Holton
Weston
Holt
Lawson
Smithville
Platte City
Liberty
Excelsior Springs
Leavenworth
Gladstone
Kansas City
Carrollton
Miami
Moberly
Perry
Vandalia
Bowling Green
Higginsville
Marshall
Arrow Rock
Fayette
Mexico
Topeka
Independence
Oak Grove
Blue Springs
Grain Valley
Lee's Summit
Lawrence
Columbia
Kingdom City
Boonville
Troy
Staunton
Alton
Edwardsville
Effingham
Vandalia
Danville
Jonesburg
Fulton
Hermann
Saint Charles
Chesterfield
Gardner
Peculiar
Knob Noster
Warrensburg
Sedalia
Tipton
California
Jefferson City
Eureka
St. Louis
East St. Louis
Salem
Centralia
Osage City
Ottawa
Paola
Windsor
Versailles
Owensville
Robertsville
Villa Ridge
Barnhart
Clinton
Tightwad
Warsaw
Gravois Mills
Laurie
Eldon
Sullivan
Stanton
Festus
Mount Vernon
Garnett
Butler
Montrose
Burlington
Lowry City
Sunrise Beach
Lake Ozark
Osage Beach
Kaiser
Linn Creek
St. James
Cuba
Leasburg
De Soto
Sparta
McLeansboro
Hermitage
Camdenton
Bonne Terre
Ste. Genevieve
Chester
Benton
Fort Scott
Iola
Humboldt
El Dorado Springs
Elkton
Pittsburg
Bennett Springs
Waynesville
Newburg
Rolla
Steelville
Potosi
Weingarten
Nevada
Davisville
Belgrade
Bismark
Park Hills
Perryville
Herrin
Carbondale
Marion
Stockton
Hazelgreen
Fort Leonard Wood
Lebanon
Buffalo
Bolivar
Salem
Ironton
Fredericktown
Chanute
Fredonia
Girard
Lamar
Bona
Dadeville
Lesterville
Annapolis
Centerville
Anna
Pittsburg
Parsons
Greenfield
Springfield
Marshfield
Strafford
Houston
Akers Ferry
Round Spring
Jackson
Independence
Columbus
Galena
Carthage
Mount Vernon
Wilsons Creek NB
Mansfield
Mountain Grove
Cabool
Ellington
Eminence
Piedmont
Patterson
Cape Girardeau
Chaffee
Paducah
Caney
Coffeyville
Joplin
Sarcoxie
Aurora
Ozark
Willow Springs
Ozark NSR
Greenville
Van Buren
Williamsville
Granby
Monett
Reeds Spring
Ava
Mountain View
Wappapello
Sikeston
Charleston
Bartlesville
Miami
Neosho
Cape Fair
Forsyth
West Plains
Poplar Bluff
Mayfield
Nowata
Anderson
Cassville
Branson
Kimberling City
Gainsville
Vinita
Noel
Pineville
Shell Knob
Eagle Rock
Golden
Lampe
Blue Eye
Ridgedale
Theodosia
Thayer
Doniphan
Campbell
Malden
New Madrid
Bella Vista
Bentonville
Corning
Union City
Fulton
Rogers
Mountain Home
Turley
Claremore
Tulsa
Springdale
Harrison
Pocahontas
Kennett
Hayti
Martin
Broken Arrow
Fayetteville
Buffalo NR
Hoxie
Paragould
Steele

Montana

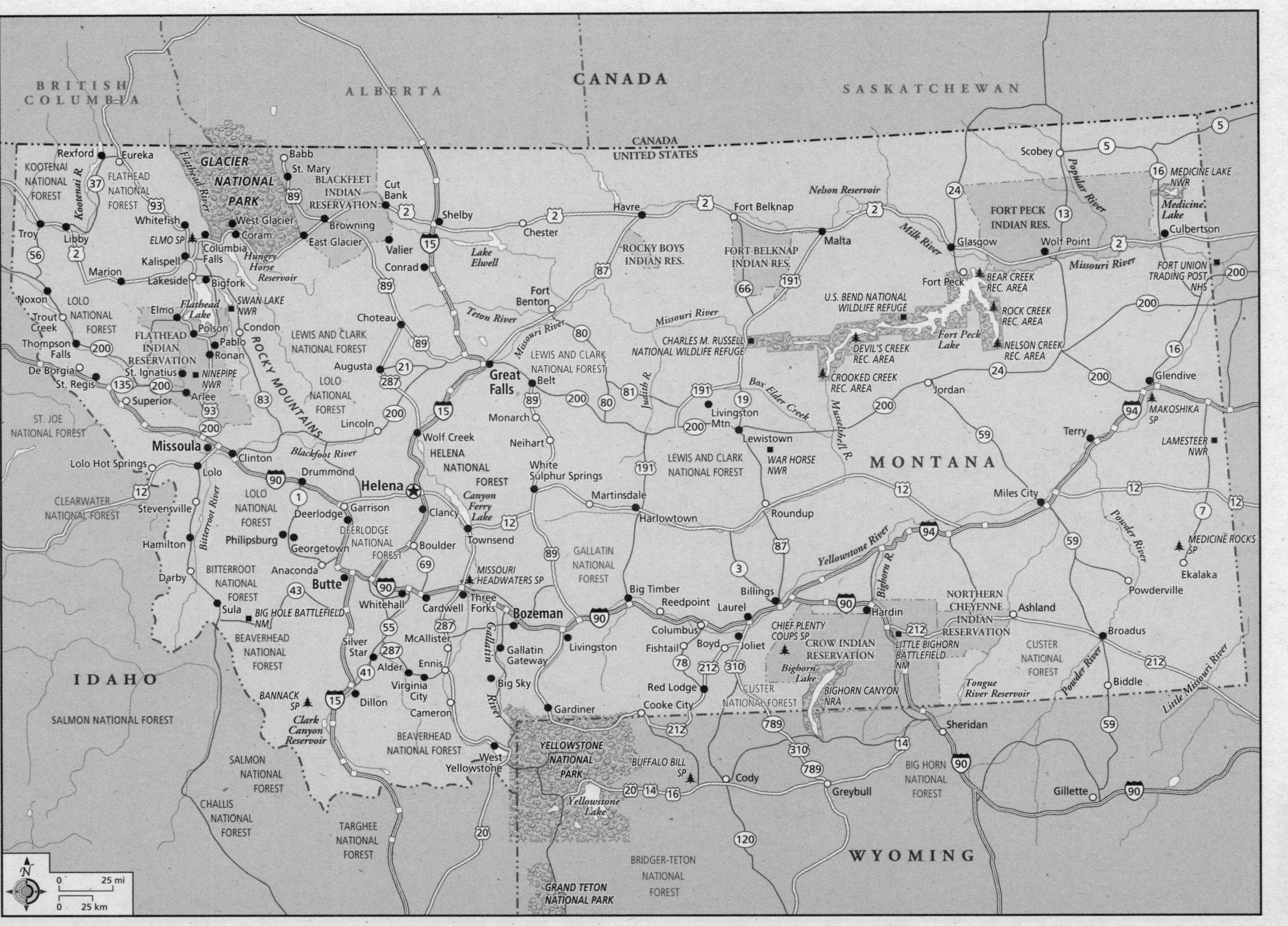
CANADA
UNITED STATES
ALBERTA
SASKATCHEWAN
BRITISH COLUMBIA
IDAHO
WYOMING
MONTANA
Helena
Great Falls
Missoula
Butte
Bozeman
Billings
Kalispell
Whitefish
Havre
Glasgow
Miles City
Lewistown
Glendive
Livingston
Dillon
Hamilton
Shelby
Cut Bank
Browning
Malta
Wolf Point
Scobey
Culbertson
Terry
Broadus
Ekalaka
Hardin
Roundup
Big Timber
Red Lodge
Cooke City
Gardiner
West Yellowstone
Ennis
Virginia City
Three Forks
Townsend
Deerlodge
Anaconda
Philipsburg
Drummond
Lincoln
Augusta
Choteau
Conrad
Chester
Fort Benton
Polson
Bigfork
Columbia Falls
West Glacier
Libby
Eureka
Troy
Superior
Thompson Falls
Lolo
Stevensville
Darby
Sula
Sheridan
Gillette
Cody
Greybull
GLACIER NATIONAL PARK
YELLOWSTONE NATIONAL PARK
GRAND TETON NATIONAL PARK
ROCKY MOUNTAINS
FORT PECK INDIAN RES.
FORT BELKNAP INDIAN RES.
ROCKY BOYS INDIAN RES.
BLACKFEET INDIAN RESERVATION
FLATHEAD INDIAN RESERVATION
NORTHERN CHEYENNE INDIAN RESERVATION
CROW INDIAN RESERVATION
CHARLES M. RUSSELL NATIONAL WILDLIFE REFUGE
LITTLE BIGHORN BATTLEFIELD NM
BIG HOLE BATTLEFIELD NM
Fort Peck Lake
Flathead Lake
Missouri River
Yellowstone River
Milk River
Powder River
Bighorn R.
Musselshell R.
Kootenai R.
Bitterroot River
Blackfoot River
Gallatin River
0 25 mi
0 25 km

Nebraska

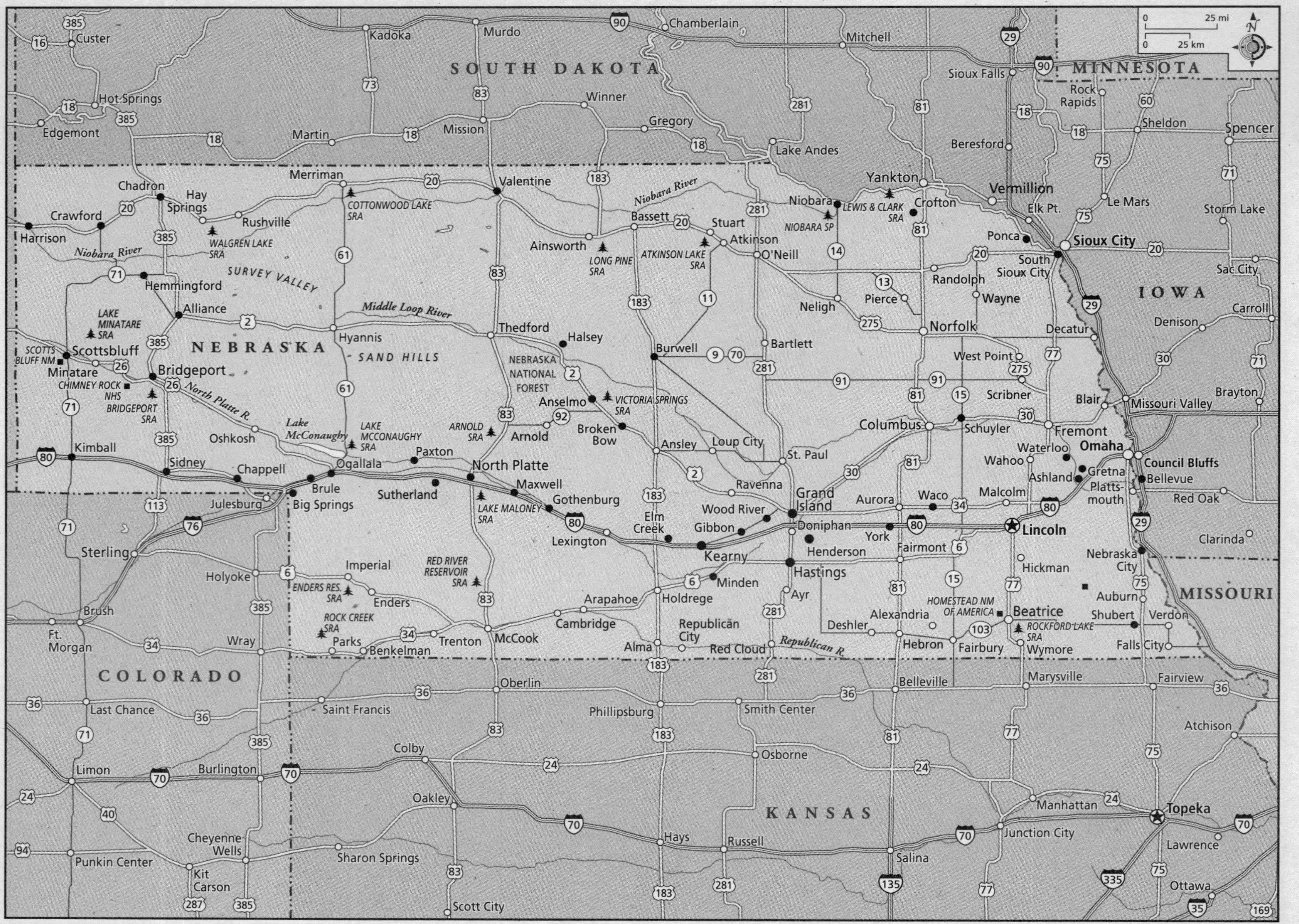

0 25 mi
0 25 km
N
MINNESOTA
IOWA
MISSOURI
SOUTH DAKOTA
NEBRASKA
KANSAS
COLORADO
Spencer
Storm Lake
Sac City
Carroll
Brayton
Clarinda
Sheldon
Le Mars
Sioux City
Denison
Missouri Valley
Council Bluffs
Bellevue
Red Oak
Rock Rapids
Sioux Falls
Beresford
Vermillion
Elk Pt.
South Sioux City
Ponca
Wayne
Randolph
Decatur
Blair
Omaha
Gretna
Platts-mouth
Nebraska City
Auburn
Verdon
Falls City
Shubert
Fremont
Waterloo
Ashland
Wahoo
Malcolm
Lincoln
Hickman
Beatrice
ROCKFORD LAKE SRA
Wymore
HOMESTEAD NM OF AMERICA
Fairbury
Scribner
West Point
Norfolk
Schuyler
Columbus
Waco
York
Fairmont
Hebron
Alexandria
Deshler
Aurora
Henderson
Hastings
Grand Island
Doniphan
Ayr
Republican R.
Yankton
Crofton
LEWIS & CLARK SRA
Pierce
Neligh
Niobara
NIOBARA SP
O'Neill
Atkinson
Stuart
Bartlett
St. Paul
Ravenna
Wood River
Gibbon
Kearny
Minden
Republican City
Red Cloud
Loup City
Burwell
Ansley
Elm Creek
Holdrege
Alma
Arapahoe
Cambridge
Bassett
ATKINSON LAKE SRA
Niobara River
VICTORIA SPRINGS SRA
Broken Bow
Anselmo
Halsey
Ainsworth
LONG PINE SRA
Thedford
NEBRASKA NATIONAL FOREST
Arnold
Gothenburg
Lexington
Maxwell
North Platte
LAKE MALONEY SRA
ARNOLD SRA
McCook
RED RIVER RESERVOIR SRA
Trenton
Valentine
Mission
Winner
Gregory
Lake Andes
Chamberlain
Mitchell
Murdo
Kadoka
Martin
Merriman
COTTONWOOD LAKE SRA
Middle Loop River
Hyannis
SAND HILLS
Paxton
Sutherland
Ogallala
LAKE McCONAUGHY SRA
Lake McConaughy
Brule
Big Springs
Imperial
Enders
ENDERS RES. SRA
ROCK CREEK SRA
Parks
Benkelman
SURVEY VALLEY
Rushville
WALGREN LAKE SRA
Alliance
Hemmingford
Hay Springs
Chadron
Bridgeport
North Platte R.
Oshkosh
Chappell
Julesburg
Sidney
Holyoke
Wray
BRIDGEPORT SRA
CHIMNEY ROCK NHS
LAKE MINATARE SRA
Scottsbluff
Minatare
SCOTTS BLUFF NM
Kimball
Crawford
Harrison
Niobara River
Sterling
Brush
Ft. Morgan
Last Chance
Limon
Burlington
Cheyenne Wells
Kit Carson
Punkin Center
Colby
Oakley
Sharon Springs
Saint Francis
Scott City
Hays
Russell
Osborne
Smith Center
Phillipsburg
Oberlin
Salina
Junction City
Manhattan
Marysville
Belleville
Topeka
Lawrence
Ottawa
Atchison
Fairview
Custer
Hot Springs
Edgemont

Nevada

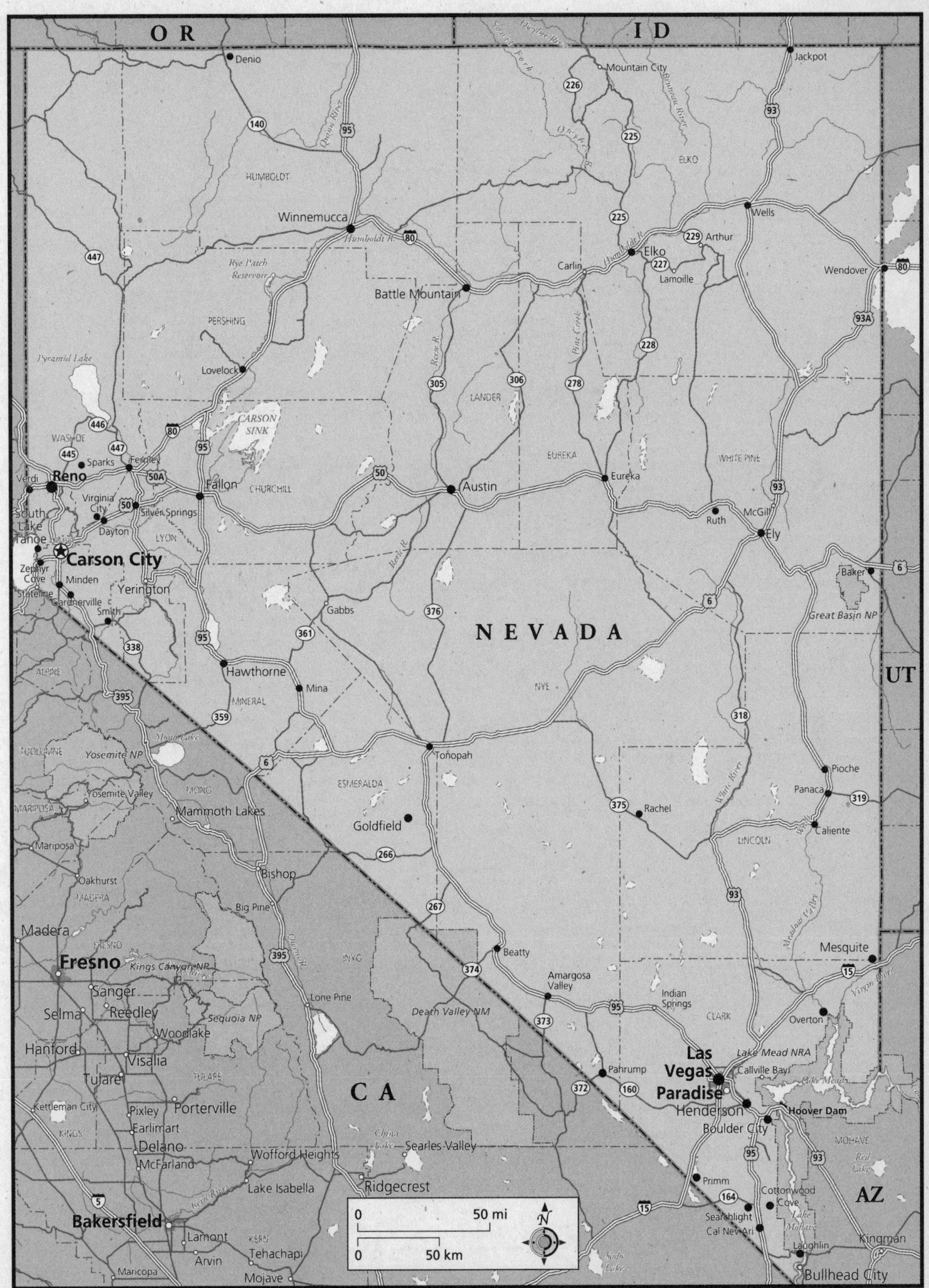
OR
ID
UT
AZ
CA
NEVADA
Denio
Jackpot
Mountain City
Winnemucca
Wells
Arthur
Elko
Carlin
Lamoille
Wendover
Battle Mountain
Lovelock
Pyramid Lake
Rye Patch Reservoir
CARSON SINK
HUMBOLDT
PERSHING
LANDER
EUREKA
WHITE PINE
ELKO
WASHOE
CHURCHILL
LYON
Sparks
Fernley
Reno
Verdi
Virginia City
Silver Springs
Fallon
Austin
Eureka
Ruth
McGill
Ely
South Lake Tahoe
Dayton
Carson City
Zephyr Cove
Minden
Stateline
Gardnerville
Yerington
Smith
Baker
Great Basin NP
Gabbs
Hawthorne
Mina
MINERAL
NYE
ALPINE
Mono Lake
Tonopah
TUOLUMNE
Yosemite NP
Yosemite Valley
MONO
MARIPOSA
Mariposa
Mammoth Lakes
ESMERALDA
Goldfield
Rachel
Pioche
Panaca
Caliente
LINCOLN
White River
Meadow Valley
Oakhurst
MADERA
Bishop
Big Pine
Madera
FRESNO
Fresno
Kings Canyon NP
Sanger
Selma
Reedley
Sequoia NP
Woodlake
Hanford
Visalia
Tulare
TULARE
INYO
Lone Pine
Death Valley NM
Beatty
Amargosa Valley
Indian Springs
CLARK
Mesquite
Overton
Lake Mead NRA
Callville Bay
Pahrump
Las Vegas
Paradise
Henderson
Boulder City
Hoover Dam
MOHAVE
Kettleman City
Pixley
Porterville
Earlimart
KINGS
Delano
McFarland
Wofford Heights
Searles Valley
China Lake
Ridgecrest
Lake Isabella
Bakersfield
Lamont
KERN
Tehachapi
Arvin
Maricopa
Mojave
Primm
Searchlight
Cal Nev Ari
Cottonwood Cove
Lake Mohave
Laughlin
Kingman
Bullhead City
Red Lake
0 50 mi
0 50 km
N
80
93
93A
95
50
50A
6
15
395
5
140
226
225
229
227
447
446
445
228
305
306
278
376
361
338
359
375
318
319
266
267
374
373
372
160
164

New Hampshire

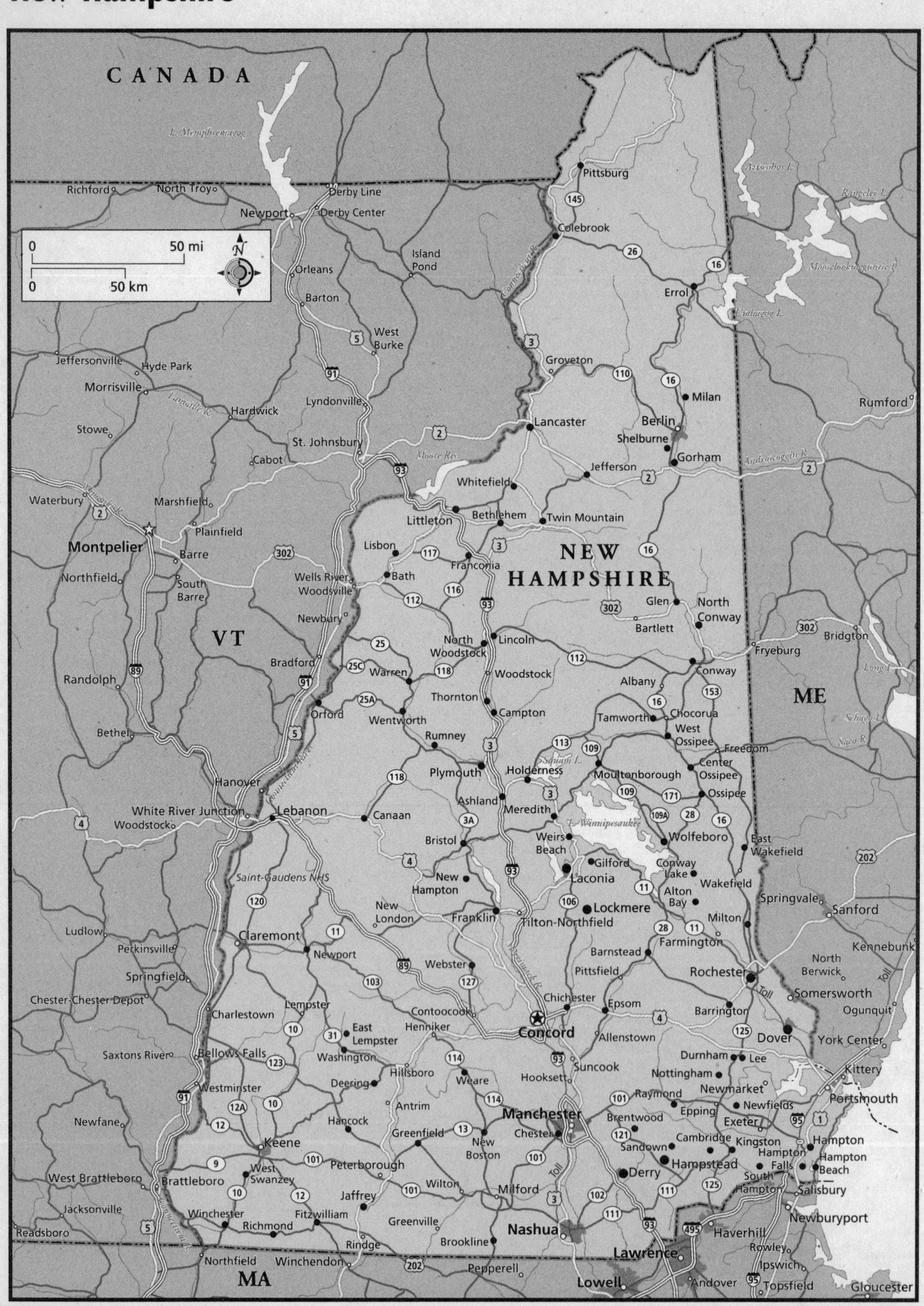

New Jersey

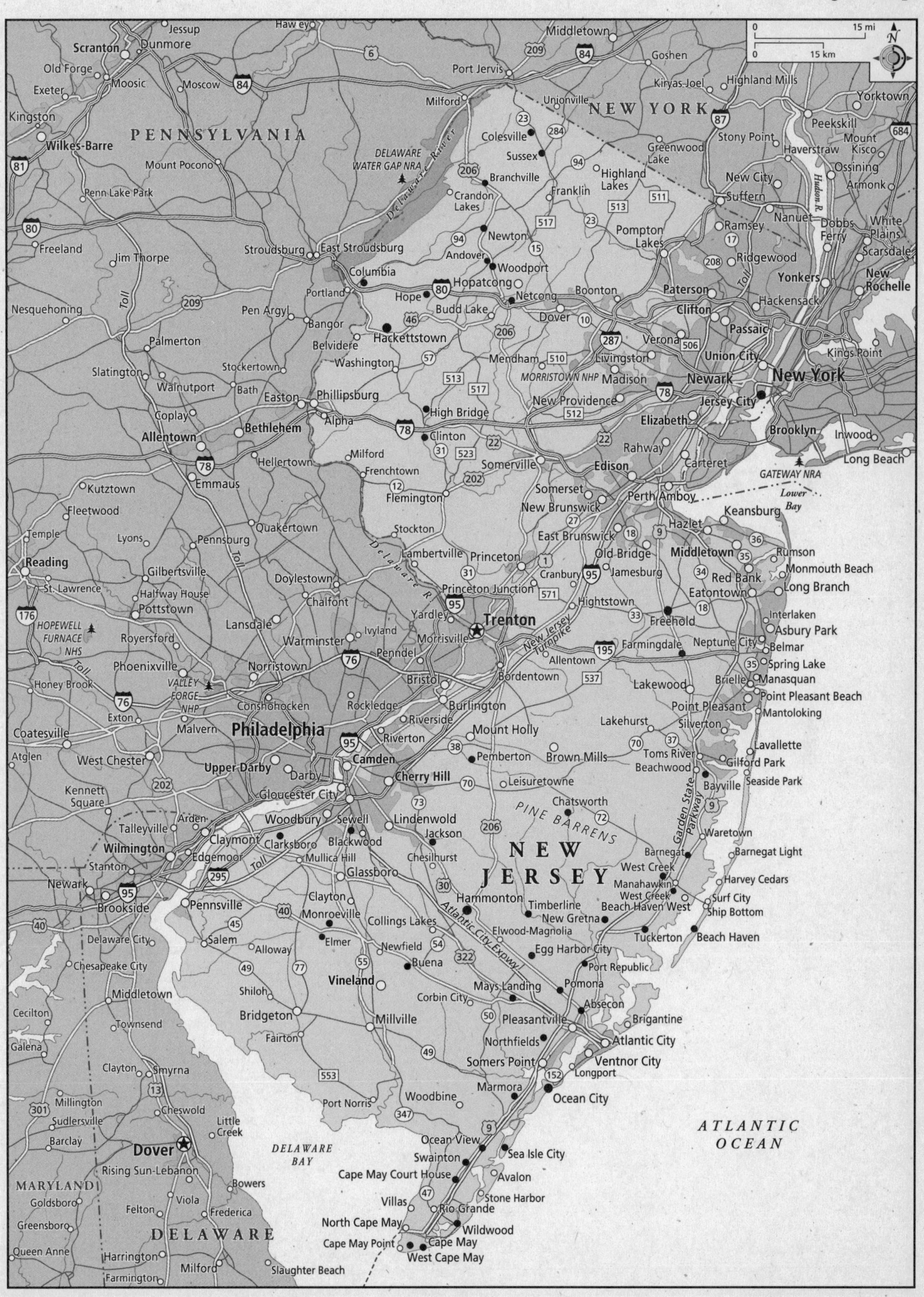
0 15 mi
0 15 km
N
NEW YORK
PENNSYLVANIA
NEW JERSEY
DELAWARE
MARYLAND
ATLANTIC OCEAN
DELAWARE BAY
DELAWARE WATER GAP NRA
Delaware River
Hudson R.
Lower Bay
GATEWAY NRA
MORRISTOWN NHP
HOPEWELL FURNACE NHS
VALLEY FORGE NHP
PINE BARRENS
Atlantic City Expwy
New Jersey Turnpike
Garden State Parkway
Toll
Scranton
Jessup
Dunmore
Old Forge
Moosic
Exeter
Kingston
Wilkes-Barre
Moscow
Hawley
Middletown
Goshen
Port Jervis
Milford
Kiryas Joel
Highland Mills
Unionville
Yorktown
Peekskill
Mount Kisco
Stony Point
Haverstraw
Ossining
Greenwood Lake
Colesville
Sussex
Branchville
Mount Pocono
Penn Lake Park
Crandon Lakes
Highland Lakes
Franklin
New City
Suffern
Armonk
Nanuet
Ramsey
Dobbs Ferry
White Plains
Scarsdale
Freeland
Jim Thorpe
Stroudsburg
East Stroudsburg
Newton
Andover
Woodport
Pompton Lakes
Ridgewood
Yonkers
New Rochelle
Columbia
Hopatcong
Portland
Hope
Netcong
Boonton
Paterson
Hackensack
Clifton
Passaic
Nesquehoning
Pen Argyl
Bangor
Budd Lake
Dover
Belvidere
Hackettstown
Verona
Palmerton
Washington
Mendham
Livingston
Union City
Kings Point
Stockertown
Slatington
Walnutport
Bath
Madison
Newark
New York
Easton
Phillipsburg
Alpha
High Bridge
New Providence
Jersey City
Coplay
Allentown
Bethlehem
Clinton
Elizabeth
Brooklyn
Inwood
Rahway
Long Beach
Milford
Hellertown
Somerville
Edison
Carteret
Emmaus
Frenchtown
Kutztown
Flemington
Somerset
Perth Amboy
New Brunswick
Keansburg
Fleetwood
Quakertown
Stockton
Hazlet
Temple
Lyons
Pennsburg
East Brunswick
Lambertville
Princeton
Old Bridge
Middletown
Rumson
Reading
Gilbertsville
Doylestown
Cranbury
Jamesburg
Red Bank
Monmouth Beach
St. Lawrence
Halfway House
Princeton Junction
Eatontown
Long Branch
Pottstown
Chalfont
Hightstown
Yardley
Interlaken
Lansdale
Ivyland
Trenton
Freehold
Asbury Park
Royersford
Warminster
Morrisville
Farmingdale
Neptune City
Belmar
Penndel
Allentown
Phoenixville
Norristown
Spring Lake
Bordentown
Brielle
Manasquan
Honey Brook
Bristol
Lakewood
Point Pleasant Beach
Conshohocken
Rockledge
Burlington
Point Pleasant
Mantoloking
Exton
Riverside
Lakehurst
Silverton
Coatesville
Malvern
Philadelphia
Mount Holly
Riverton
Lavallette
Atglen
West Chester
Upper Darby
Camden
Pemberton
Brown Mills
Toms River
Gilford Park
Beachwood
Darby
Cherry Hill
Leisuretowne
Seaside Park
Kennett Square
Gloucester City
Bayville
Chatsworth
Arden
Woodbury
Sewell
Lindenwold
Talleyville
Jackson
Claymont
Clarksboro
Blackwood
Waretown
Wilmington
Edgemoor
Mullica Hill
Chesilhurst
Barnegat
Barnegat Light
Stanton
Glassboro
West Creek
Newark
Manahawkin
Harvey Cedars
Hammonton
West Creek
Surf City
Brookside
Pennsville
Clayton
Timberline
Beach Haven West
Ship Bottom
Monroeville
New Gretna
Delaware City
Salem
Collings Lakes
Elwood-Magnolia
Tuckerton
Beach Haven
Elmer
Alloway
Newfield
Egg Harbor City
Chesapeake City
Buena
Port Republic
Vineland
Shiloh
Mays Landing
Pomona
Middletown
Corbin City
Absecon
Cecilton
Bridgeton
Millville
Pleasantville
Brigantine
Townsend
Fairton
Northfields
Atlantic City
Galena
Clayton
Smyrna
Somers Point
Ventnor City
Longport
Marmora
Ocean City
Millington
Port Norris
Woodbine
Sudlersville
Cheswold
Little Creek
Barclay
Dover
Ocean View
Sea Isle City
Swainton
Rising Sun-Lebanon
Cape May Court House
Avalon
Bowers
Goldsboro
Villas
Stone Harbor
Viola
Felton
Frederica
Rio Grande
Greensboro
North Cape May
Wildwood
Cape May
Queen Anne
Cape May Point
Harrington
West Cape May
Milford
Slaughter Beach
Farmington

New Mexico

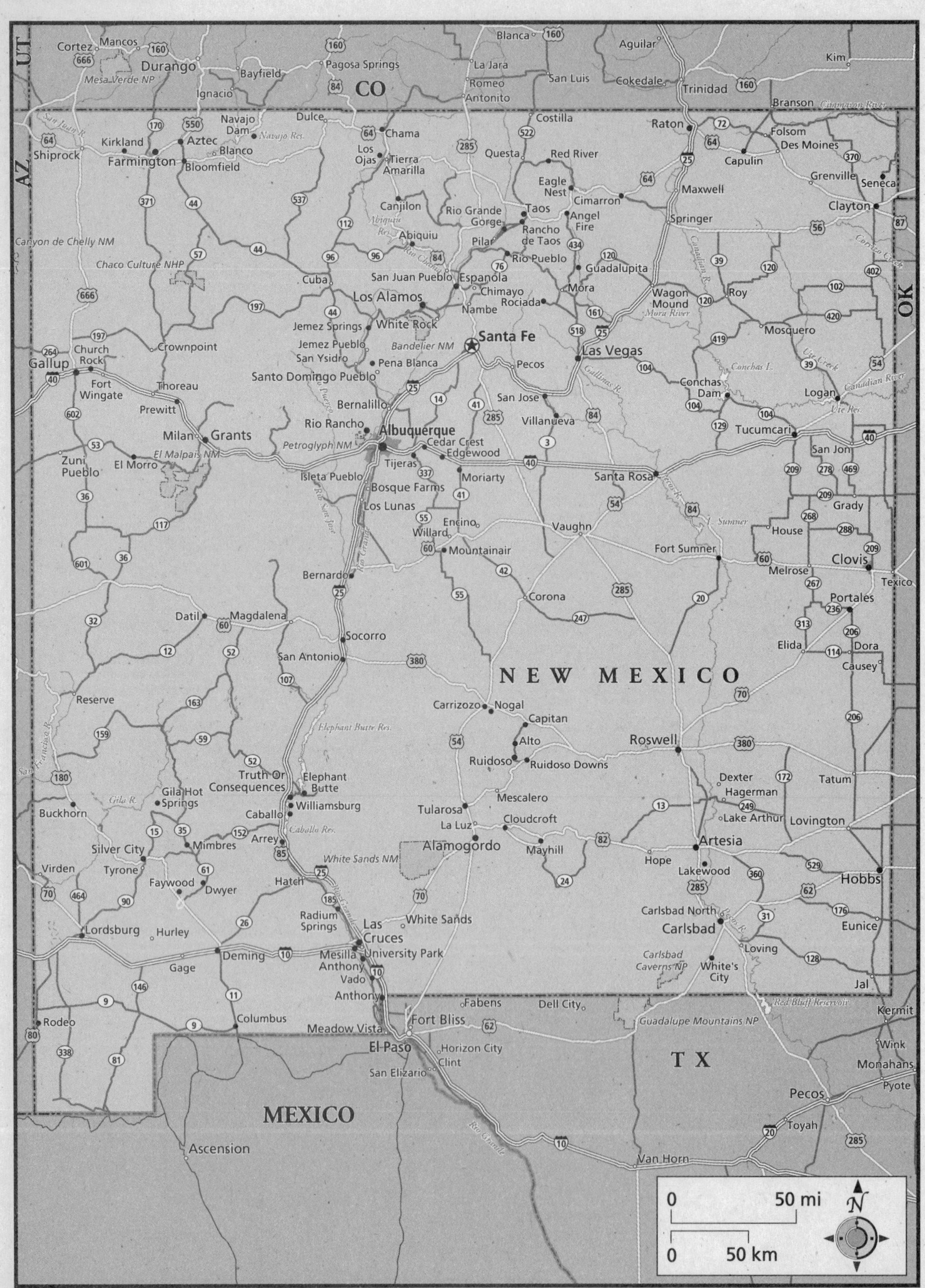

UT
CO
AZ
OK
TX
NEW MEXICO
MEXICO
Cortez
Mancos
Durango
Mesa Verde NP
Bayfield
Ignacio
Pagosa Springs
Blanca
La Jara
Romeo
Antonito
San Luis
Aguilar
Cokedale
Trinidad
Kim
Branson
Shiprock
Kirkland
Farmington
Aztec
Navajo Dam
Navajo Res.
Blanco
Bloomfield
Dulce
Chama
Los Ojas
Tierra Amarilla
Costilla
Questa
Red River
Raton
Folsom
Des Moines
Capulin
Grenville
Seneca
Maxwell
Clayton
Eagle Nest
Cimarron
Angel Fire
Taos
Rio Grande Gorge
Rancho de Taos
Pilar
Springer
Canjilon
Abiquiu
Rio Pueblo
Guadalupita
Mora
Canyon de Chelly NM
Chaco Culture NHP
Cuba
San Juan Pueblo
Espanola
Chimayo
Rociada
Nambe
Los Alamos
White Rock
Jemez Springs
Jemez Pueblo
Bandelier NM
San Ysidro
Santa Fe
Pena Blanca
Santo Domingo Pueblo
Pecos
Wagon Mound
Mora River
Roy
Mosquero
Las Vegas
Conchas L.
Conchas Dam
Logan
Canadian River
Ute Res.
Tucumcari
Crownpoint
Gallup
Church Rock
Fort Wingate
Thoreau
Prewitt
Milan
Grants
El Malpais NM
El Morro
Zuni Pueblo
Bernalillo
Rio Rancho
Albuquerque
Petroglyph NM
Cedar Crest
Edgewood
Tijeras
Moriarty
Isleta Pueblo
Bosque Farms
Los Lunas
San Jose
Villanueva
Santa Rosa
San Jon
Grady
House
Clovis
Texico
Melrose
Encino
Willard
Mountainair
Vaughn
Fort Sumner
Sumner
Bernardo
Corona
Portales
Elida
Dora
Causey
Datil
Magdalena
Socorro
San Antonio
Reserve
Carrizozo
Nogal
Capitan
Alto
Ruidoso
Ruidoso Downs
Roswell
Dexter
Hagerman
Lake Arthur
Tatum
Lovington
Elephant Butte Res.
Truth Or Consequences
Elephant Butte
Williamsburg
Caballo
Caballo Res.
Arrey
Gila Hot Springs
Buckhorn
Gila R.
Mimbres
Silver City
Tyrone
Virden
Faywood
Dwyer
Hatch
White Sands NM
Tularosa
Mescalero
La Luz
Cloudcroft
Alamogordo
Mayhill
Artesia
Hope
Lakewood
Hobbs
Eunice
Carlsbad North
Carlsbad
Carlsbad Caverns NP
White's City
Loving
Jal
Radium Springs
Las Cruces
White Sands
Lordsburg
Hurley
Deming
Gage
Mesilla
Anthony
University Park
Vado
Rodeo
Columbus
Fabens
Dell City
Red Bluff Reservoir
Kermit
Guadalupe Mountains NP
Meadow Vista
Fort Bliss
El Paso
Horizon City
Clint
San Elizario
Wink
Monahans
Pyote
Pecos
Toyah
Ascension
Van Horn
Rio Grande
0
50 mi
0
50 km
N

North Dakota

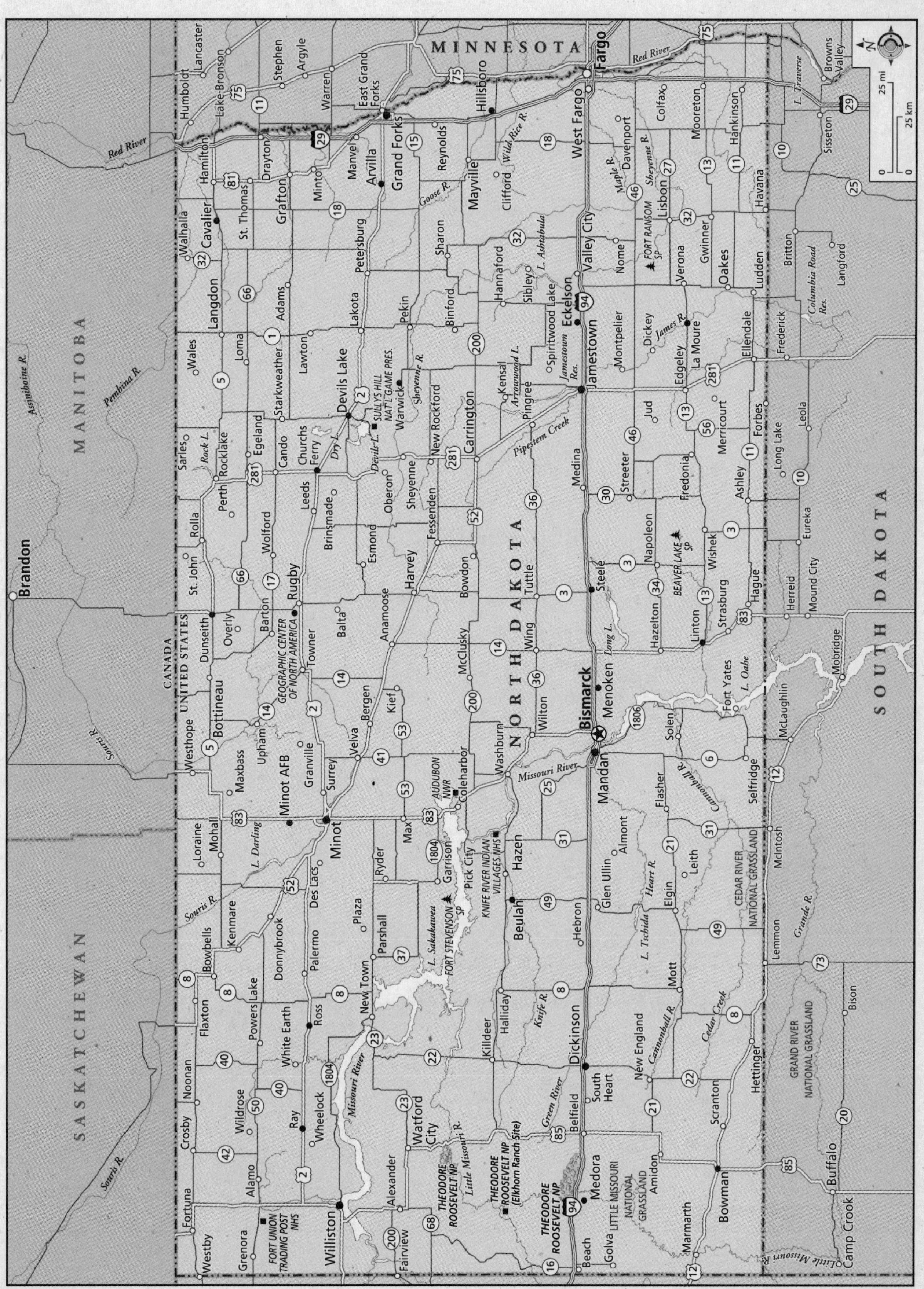

New York

0
25 mi
0
25 km
N
ONTARIO
Toronto
Kingston
Clayton
Cape Vincent
Dexter
Three Mile Bay
Sackets Harbor
Henderson Harbor
Woodville
Lake Ontario
Pulaski
Oswego
Mexico
Parish
Fair Haven
Red Creek
Sodus Point
Fulton
Baldwinsville
Wolcott
Alton
Youngstown
Newfane
Albion
Hamlin
Greece
Rochester
Lewiston
Gasport
Medina
Brockport
Niagara Falls
Lockport
Byron
Brighton
Newark
Weedsport
Liverpool
Fairmount
Tonawanda
Akron
Toll
Phelps
Montezuma
Syracuse
Buffalo
Cheektowaga
Batavia
Caledonia
LeRoy
Canandaigua
Waterloo
Darien Center
Lakeville
Auburn
La Fayette
West Seneca
Geneseo
Geneva
Seneca Falls
Moravia
Warsaw
Canandaigua L.
Finger Lakes
East Aurora
Bristol Center
Kendaia
Angola
Hamburg
Gainesville
Portageville
Mount Morris
Cohocton
Penn Yan
Ovid
Genoa
Lake Erie
Springwater
Prattsburgh
Cortland
North Java
Pike
Wayland
Keuka Park
Marathon
Willet
Dunkirk
Springville
Dansville
Lansing
Fredonia
Delevan
Caneadea
Himrod
Ithaca
Brocton
Houghton
Angelica
Hornell
Watkins Glen
Richford
Westfield
Dewittville
Ellicottville
Franklinville
Alfred
Bath
Odessa
Chautauqua L.
Chautauqua
Bemus Point
Stow
Randolph
Salamanca
Cold Spring
Campbell
Corning
Horseheads
Candor
Johnson City
Endicott
Findley Lake
Jamestown
Kennedy
ALLEGHENY SP
Olean
Wellsville
Gang Mills
Elmira
Addison
Bradford
Allegheny Res.
Athens
Union City
Port Allegany
Warren
Mansfield
Wellsboro
Towanda
Susquehanna R.
Genesee R.
PENNSYLVANIA
Tunkhannock
Jersey Shore
Williamsport
Montoursville
Nanticoke
Lock Haven
Berwick
Stamford
Bridgeport
Greenport
Norwalk
Montauk
Yonkers
Mattituck
New Rochelle
Riverhead
Sag Harbor
East Hampton
Smithtown
Huntington
Farmingville
Southampton
New York
Shirley
Hampton Bays
East Islip
Islip
Sayville
Mastic
LONG ISLAND
Long Beach
FIRE ISLAND NS
GATEWAY NRA

New York

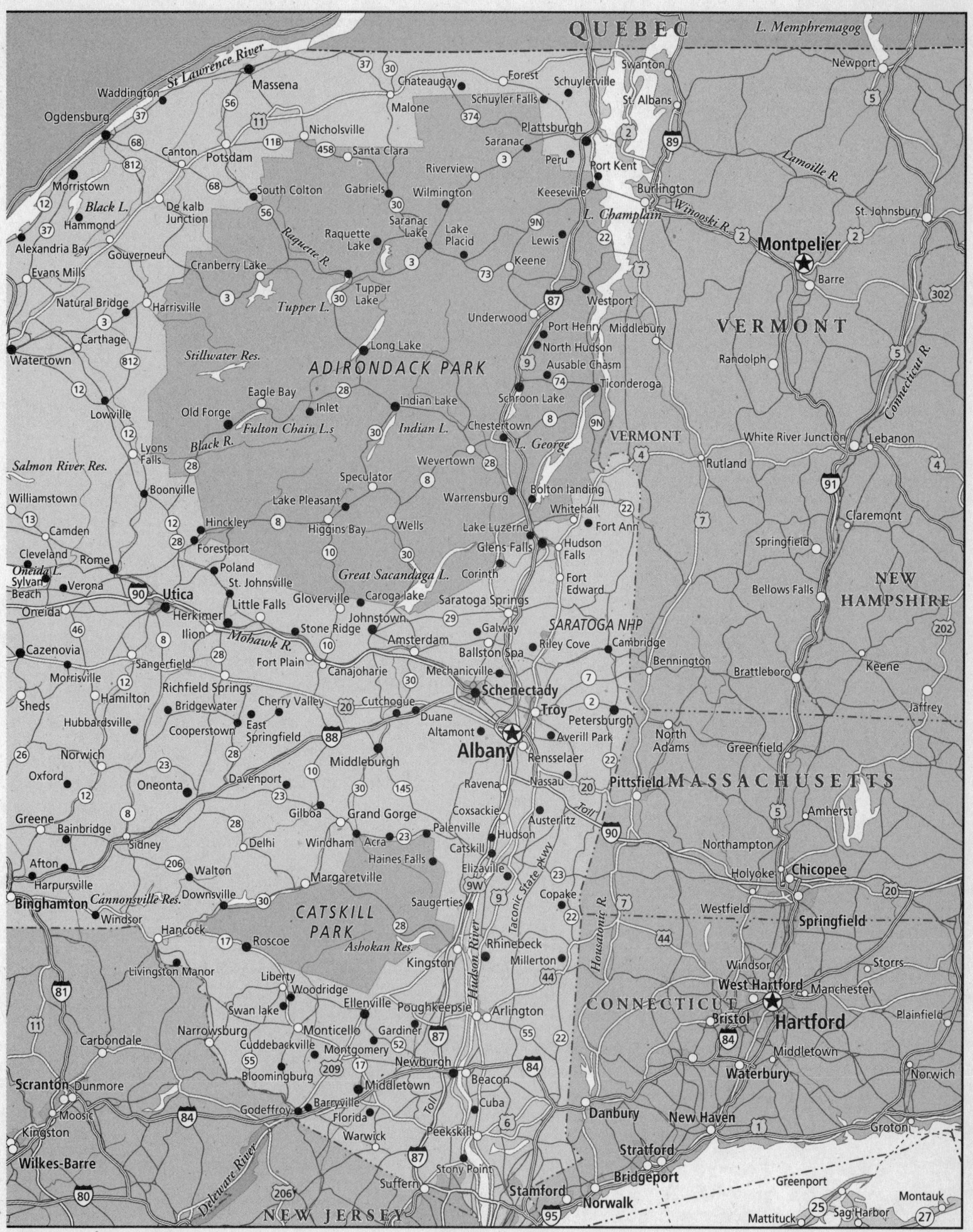

QUEBEC
L. Memphremagog
St Lawrence River
Waddington
Massena
Ogdensburg
Chateaugay
Forest
Schuylerville
Swanton
Newport
Malone
Schuyler Falls
St. Albans
Nicholsville
Plattsburgh
Canton
Potsdam
Santa Clara
Saranac
Peru
Riverview
Port Kent
Lamoille R.
Morristown
South Colton
Gabriels
Wilmington
Keeseville
Burlington
Black L.
De kalb Junction
Hammond
Winooski R.
L. Champlain
St. Johnsbury
Raquette Lake
Saranac Lake
Lake Placid
Lewis
Montpelier
Alexandria Bay
Gouverneur
Raquette R.
Barre
Evans Mills
Cranberry Lake
Keene
Tupper Lake
Westport
Natural Bridge
Harrisville
Tupper L.
Underwood
Carthage
Port Henry
Middlebury
VERMONT
Watertown
Long Lake
North Hudson
Randolph
Stillwater Res.
ADIRONDACK PARK
Ausable Chasm
Eagle Bay
Ticonderoga
Lowville
Old Forge
Inlet
Indian Lake
Schroon Lake
Connecticut R.
Fulton Chain L.s
Indian L.
Chestertown
Lyons Falls
Black R.
L. George
White River Junction
Lebanon
Salmon River Res.
Wevertown
Rutland
Speculator
Boonville
Bolton landing
Williamstown
Lake Pleasant
Warrensburg
Whitehall
Claremont
Camden
Hinckley
Higgins Bay
Wells
Lake Luzerne
Fort Ann
Springfield
Forestport
Glens Falls
Hudson Falls
Cleveland
Rome
Oneida L.
Poland
Great Sacandaga L.
Corinth
Fort Edward
NEW HAMPSHIRE
Sylvan Beach
Verona
St. Johnsville
Utica
Little Falls
Gloversville
Caroga lake
Saratoga Springs
Bellows Falls
Oneida
Herkimer
Johnstown
Ilion
Stone Ridge
Galway
SARATOGA NHP
Mohawk R.
Cazenovia
Amsterdam
Riley Cove
Cambridge
Ballston Spa
Bennington
Keene
Sangerfield
Fort Plain
Canajoharie
Mechanicville
Brattleboro
Morrisville
Schenectady
Hamilton
Richfield Springs
Jaffrey
Sheds
Bridgewater
Cherry Valley
Cutchogue
Troy
Hubbardsville
Duane
Petersburgh
East Springfield
Altamont
Cooperstown
North Adams
Greenfield
Albany
Averill Park
Norwich
Rensselaer
Middleburgh
Oxford
Davenport
Nassau
Pittsfield
MASSACHUSETTS
Oneonta
Ravena
Greene
Gilboa
Grand Gorge
Coxsackie
Austerlitz
Amherst
Bainbridge
Palenville
Toll
Sidney
Delhi
Windham
Acra
Hudson
Northampton
Catskill
Afton
Haines Falls
Walton
Elizaville
Chicopee
Holyoke
Harpursville
Margaretville
Binghamton
Cannonsville Res.
Downsville
Saugerties
Copake
Taconic State pkwy
Housatonic R.
Westfield
Windsor
CATSKILL PARK
Springfield
Hancock
Roscoe
Ashokan Res.
Rhinebeck
Hudson River
Millerton
Livingston Manor
Kingston
Storrs
Liberty
Windsor
Woodridge
West Hartford
Manchester
Ellenville
CONNECTICUT
Swan lake
Poughkeepsie
Arlington
Plainfield
Narrowsburg
Monticello
Gardiner
Bristol
Hartford
Carbondale
Cuddebackville
Montgomery
Middletown
Newburgh
Bloomingburg
Waterbury
Scranton
Dunmore
Middletown
Beacon
Norwich
Godeffroy
Barryville
Cuba
Danbury
Moosic
Florida
New Haven
Kingston
Warwick
Peekskill
Groton
Delaware River
Stratford
Wilkes-Barre
Stony Point
Bridgeport
Suffern
Greenport
Stamford
Montauk
Norwalk
NEW JERSEY
Mattituck
Sag Harbor

North Carolina

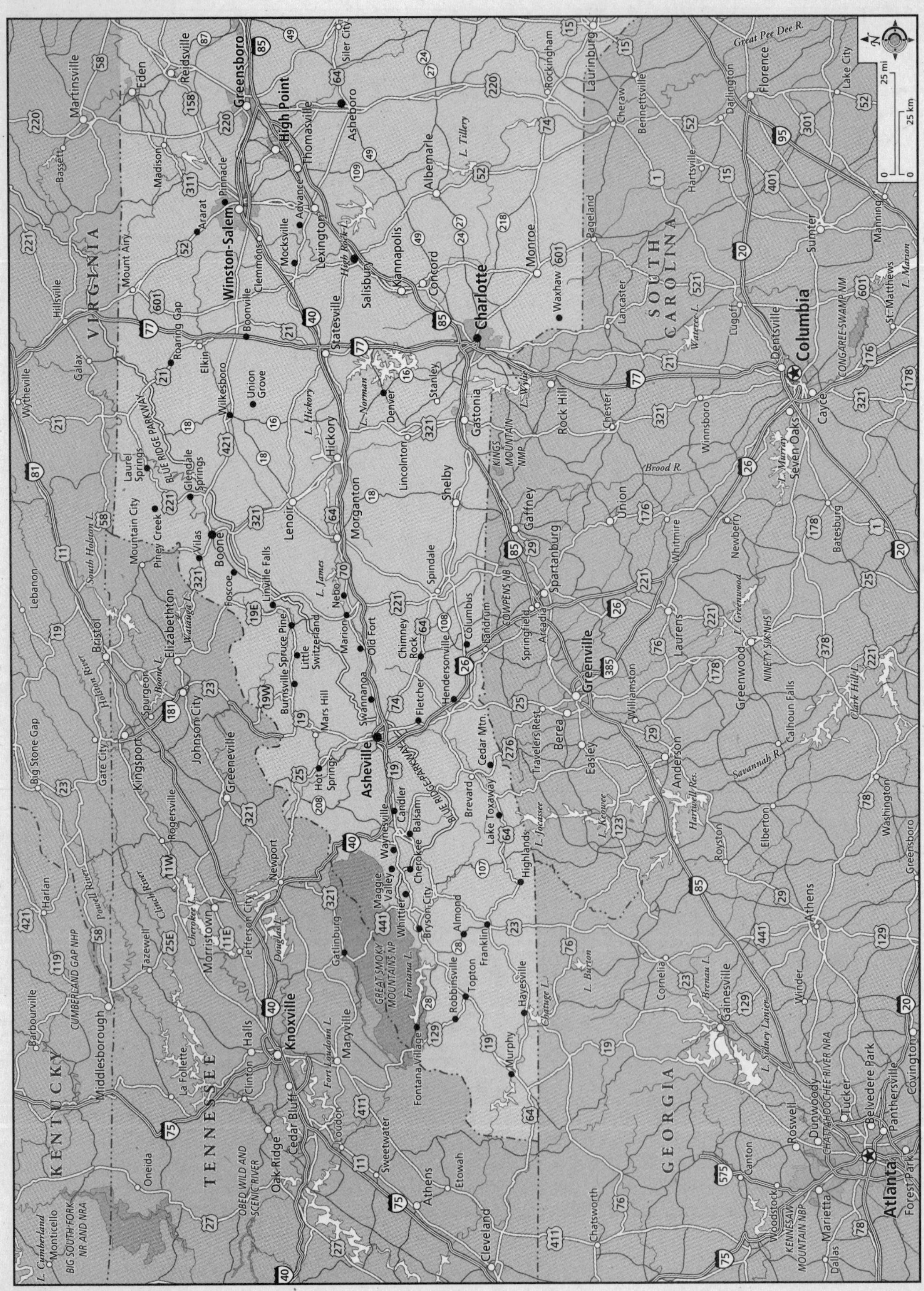

North Carolina

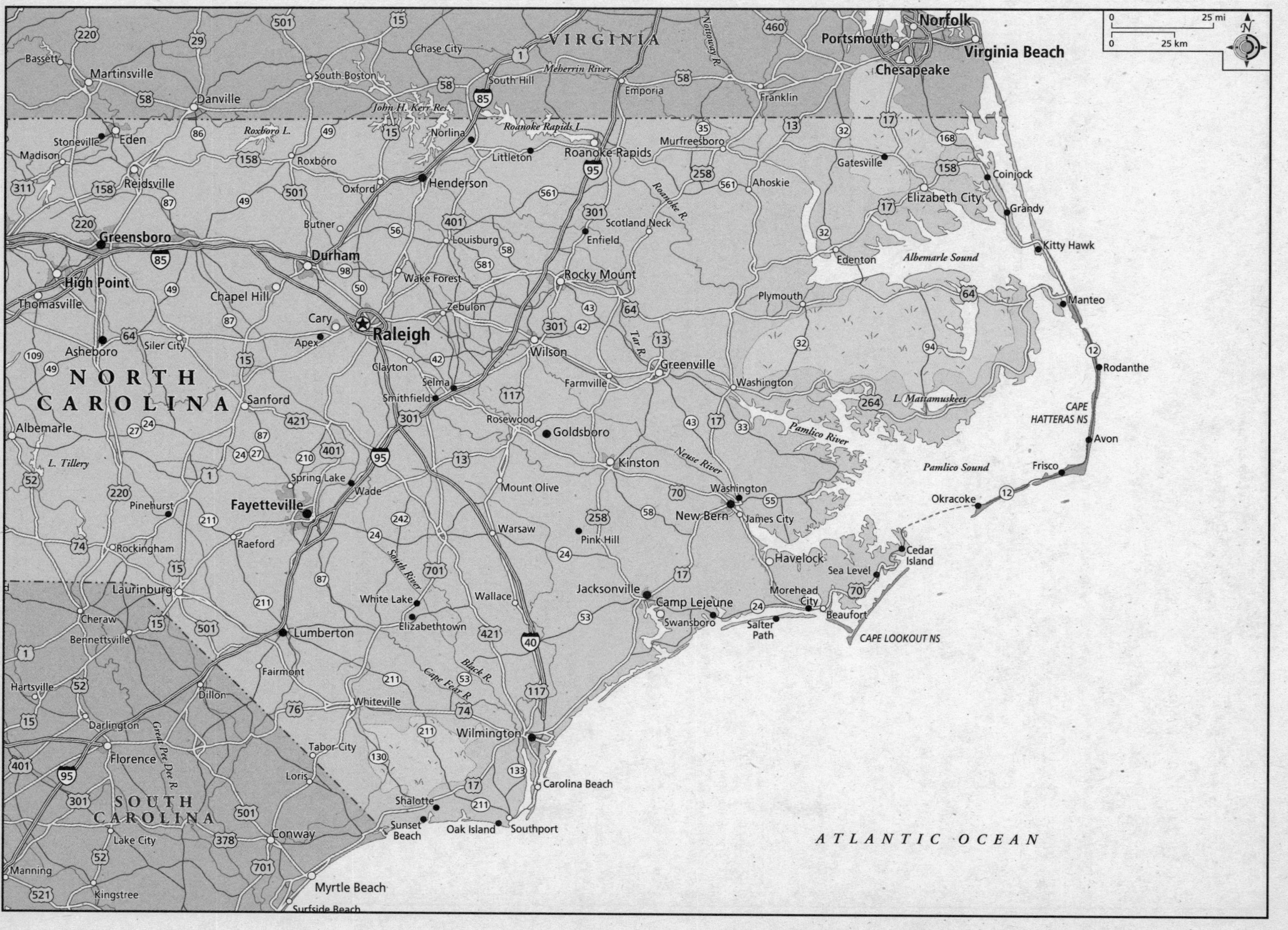

Ohio

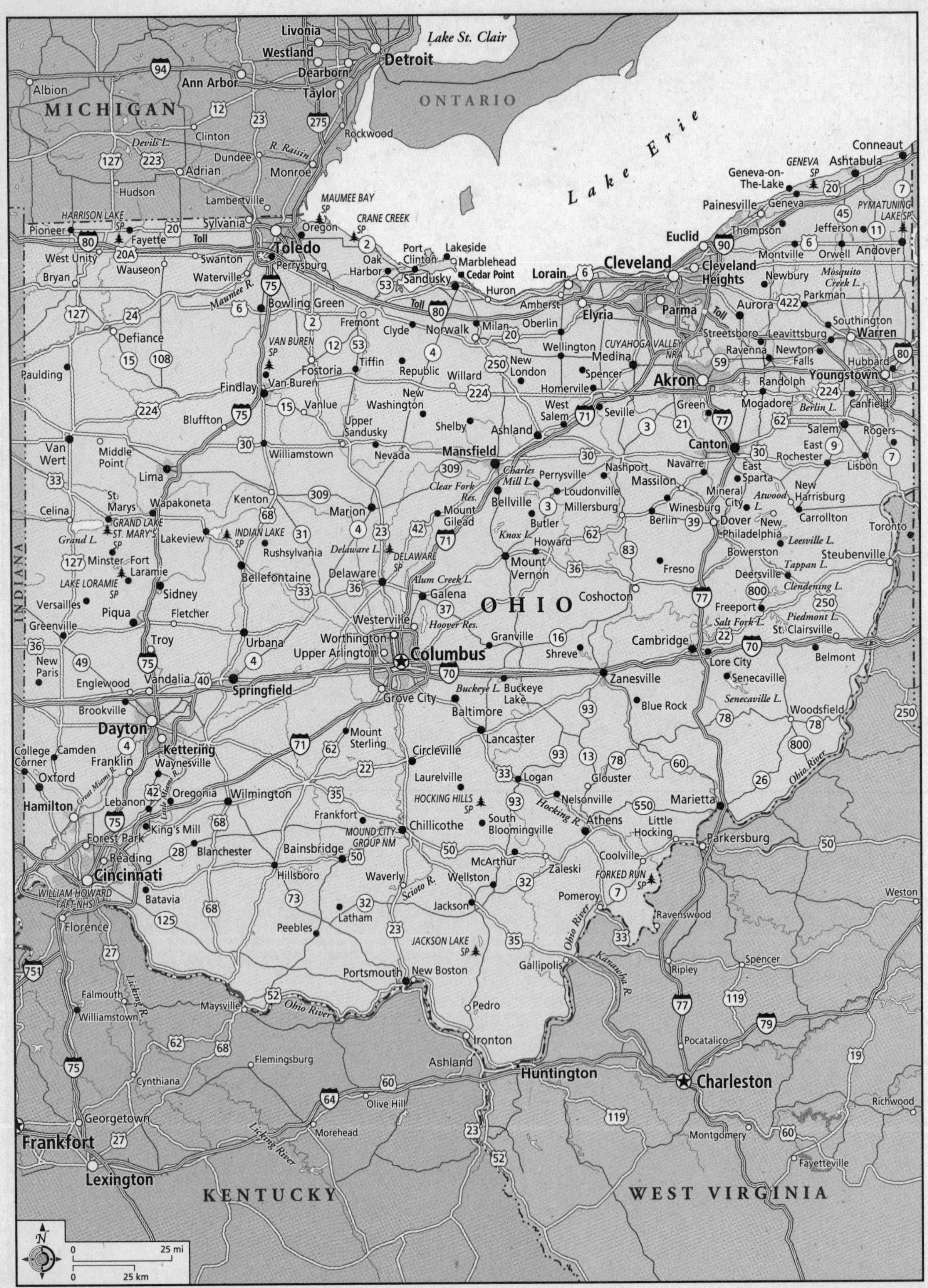

Livonia
Westland
Detroit
Lake St. Clair
Dearborn
Ann Arbor
Albion
Taylor
MICHIGAN
ONTARIO
Rockwood
Clinton
Devils L.
R. Raisin
Lake Erie
Dundee
Adrian
Monroe
Hudson
Lambertville
MAUMEE BAY SP
CRANE CREEK SP
HARRISON LAKE SP
Sylvania
Oregon
Pioneer
Fayette
Toll
Toledo
West Unity
Swanton
Wauseon
Perrysburg
Waterville
Bryan
Maumee R.
Bowling Green
Defiance
Paulding
Port Clinton
Lakeside
Marblehead
Cedar Point
Oak Harbor
Sandusky
Huron
Fremont
Clyde
Norwalk
Milan
VAN BUREN SP
Tiffin
Fostoria
Van Buren
Findlay
Vanlue
Republic
Willard
New London
New Washington
Upper Sandusky
Bluffton
Van Wert
Middle Point
Lima
Williamstown
Nevada
Shelby
Mansfield
Ashland
Kenton
Marion
Celina
St. Marys
Wapakoneta
GRAND LAKE ST. MARY'S SP
Grand L.
Lakeview
INDIAN LAKE SP
Rushsylvania
Minster
Fort Laramie
LAKE LORAMIE SP
Versailles
Sidney
Bellefontaine
Delaware
Delaware L.
DELAWARE SP
Alum Creek L.
Galena
Piqua
Fletcher
Greenville
Troy
Urbana
Westerville
Hoover Res.
Worthington
Upper Arlington
Columbus
New Paris
Englewood
Vandalia
Springfield
Grove City
Brookville
Dayton
Kettering
College Corner
Camden
Franklin
Waynesville
Oxford
Hamilton
Great Miami R.
Little Miami R.
Lebanon
Oregonia
Wilmington
King's Mill
Forest Park
Reading
Cincinnati
Blanchester
WILLIAM HOWARD TAFT NHS
Batavia
Florence
INDIANA
Lorain
Cleveland
Euclid
Cleveland Heights
Amherst
Elyria
Oberlin
Parma
Wellington
CUYAHOGA VALLEY NRA
Medina
Spencer
Homerville
Akron
West Salem
Seville
Green
Canton
Charles Mill L.
Perrysville
Clear Fork Res.
Mount Gilead
Bellville
Loudonville
Butler
Millersburg
Knox L.
Howard
Mount Vernon
OHIO
Coshocton
Granville
Shreve
Zanesville
Buckeye L.
Buckeye Lake
Baltimore
Lancaster
Mount Sterling
Circleville
Laurelville
Logan
HOCKING HILLS SP
Hocking R.
Nelsonville
Athens
South Bloomingville
Chillicothe
Frankfort
MOUND CITY GROUP NM
Bainsbridge
Hillsboro
Waverly
Scioto R.
McArthur
Zaleski
Wellston
Jackson
Latham
Peebles
JACKSON LAKE SP
Portsmouth
New Boston
Gallipolis
Pedro
Ironton
Conneaut
Ashtabula
GENEVA SP
Geneva-on-The-Lake
Geneva
Painesville
PYMATUNING LAKE SP
Thompson
Jefferson
Montville
Orwell
Andover
Newbury
Mosquito Creek L.
Parkman
Aurora
Southington
Streetsboro
Leavittsburg
Warren
Ravenna
Newton Falls
Hubbard
Youngstown
Randolph
Mogadore
Berlin L.
Canfield
Salem
Rogers
East Rochester
Lisbon
Navarre
Massilon
East Sparta
Nashport
Mineral City
Atwood L.
New Harrisburg
Winesburg
Berlin
Dover
New Philadelphia
Carrollton
Toronto
Leesville L.
Bowerston
Tappan L.
Steubenville
Fresno
Deersville
Clendening L.
Freeport
Salt Fork L.
Piedmont L.
St. Clairsville
Cambridge
Lore City
Belmont
Senecaville
Senecaville L.
Blue Rock
Woodsfield
Ohio River
Glouster
Marietta
Little Hocking
Parkersburg
Coolville
FORKED RUN SP
Pomeroy
Ravenswood
Weston
Kanawha R.
Ripley
Spencer
Pocatalico
Charleston
Huntington
Ashland
Falmouth
Licking R.
Williamstown
Maysville
Flemingsburg
Cynthiana
Olive Hill
Morehead
Licking River
Georgetown
Frankfort
Lexington
Richwood
Montgomery
Fayetteville
KENTUCKY
WEST VIRGINIA
N
0
25 mi
25 km

Oklahoma

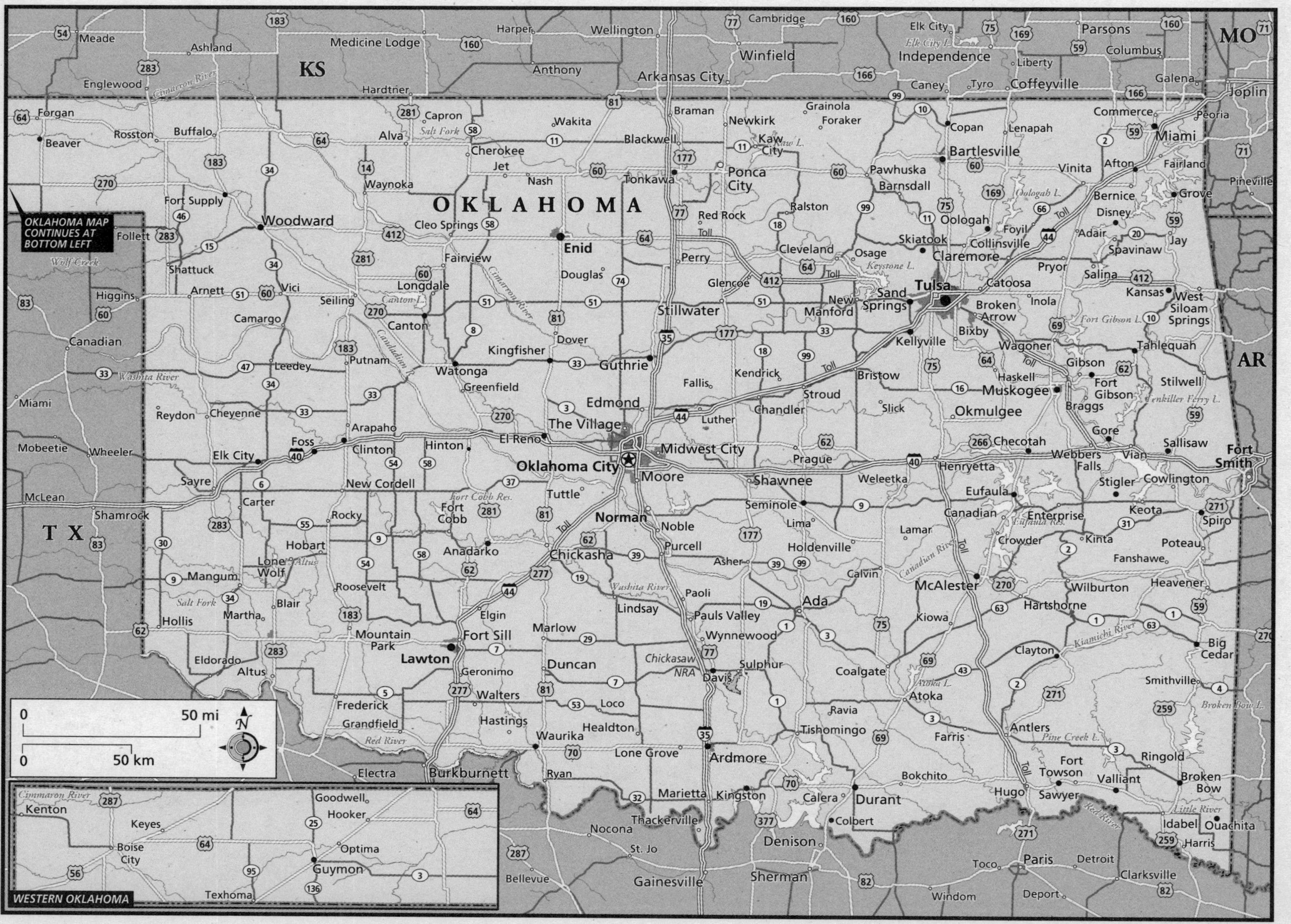

OKLAHOMA
KS
MO
AR
TX
OKLAHOMA MAP CONTINUES AT BOTTOM LEFT
WESTERN OKLAHOMA
0
50 mi
0
50 km
Oklahoma City
Tulsa
Norman
Lawton
Enid
Stillwater
Muskogee
Ardmore
McAlester
Shawnee
Ponca City
Bartlesville
Miami
Woodward
Guthrie
Edmond
The Village
Moore
Midwest City
El Reno
Chickasha
Duncan
Ada
Durant
Okmulgee
Tahlequah
Sallisaw
Fort Smith
Altus
Elk City
Clinton
Guymon
Boise City
Kenton
Keyes
Goodwell
Hooker
Optima
Texhoma
Alva
Kingfisher
Watonga
Anadarko
Fort Sill
Hugo
Idabel
Broken Bow
Poteau
Wilburton
Atoka
Sulphur
Pauls Valley
Purcell
Seminole
Weleetka
Holdenville
Henryetta
Sand Springs
Claremore
Pryor
Vinita
Grove
Wagoner
Broken Arrow
Perry
Blackwell
Pawhuska
Coffeyville
Independence
Arkansas City
Winfield
Sherman
Denison
Paris
Gainesville
Joplin
Medicine Lodge
Wellington
Burkburnett
Electra
Shamrock
McLean

Oregon

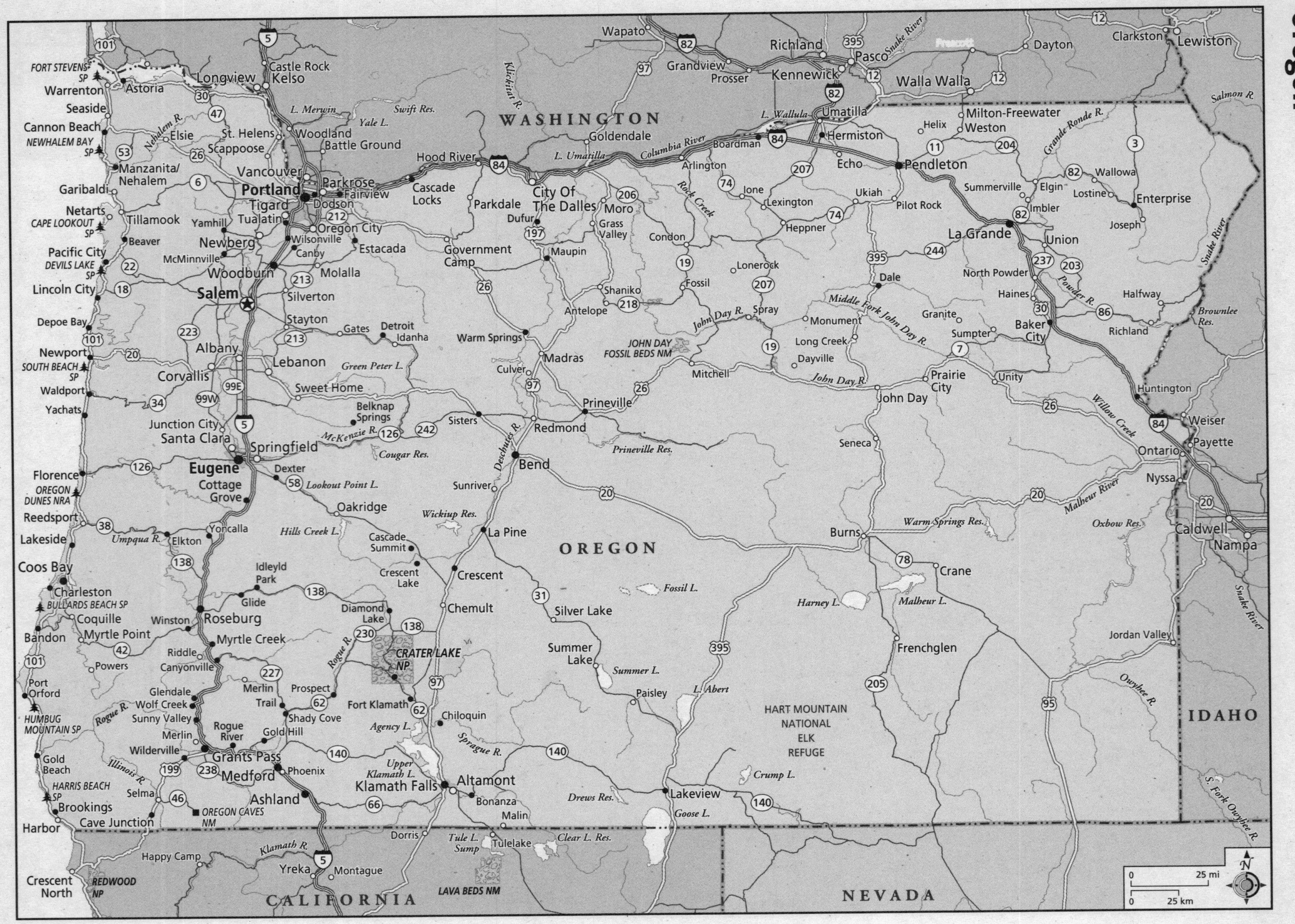
WASHINGTON
OREGON
IDAHO
NEVADA
CALIFORNIA
Portland
Salem
Eugene
Bend
Medford
Pendleton
La Grande
Baker City
Ontario
Burns
Lakeview
Klamath Falls
Roseburg
Coos Bay
Astoria
Newport
Corvallis
Albany
Springfield
Grants Pass
Ashland
Brookings
Florence
The Dalles
Hood River
Prineville
Redmond
John Day
Vancouver
Walla Walla
Kennewick
Pasco
Richland
Lewiston
Nampa
Caldwell
Yreka
Crescent North
Harbor
CRATER LAKE NP
HART MOUNTAIN NATIONAL ELK REFUGE
JOHN DAY FOSSIL BEDS NM
OREGON CAVES NM
LAVA BEDS NM
REDWOOD NP
OREGON DUNES NRA
Columbia River
Snake River
Malheur L.
Harney L.
Upper Klamath L.
Goose L.
25 mi
25 km

Rhode Island

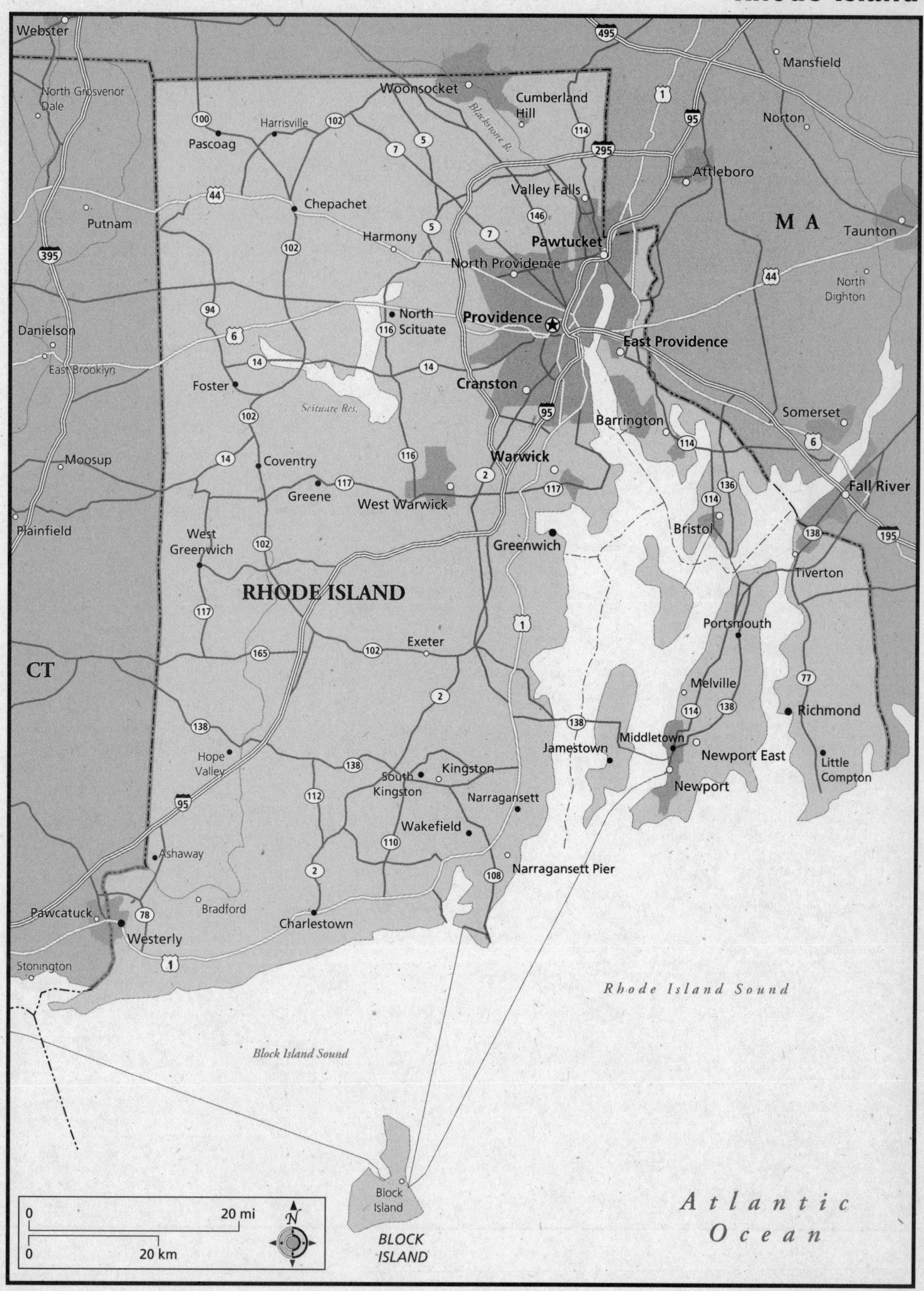

Pennsylvania

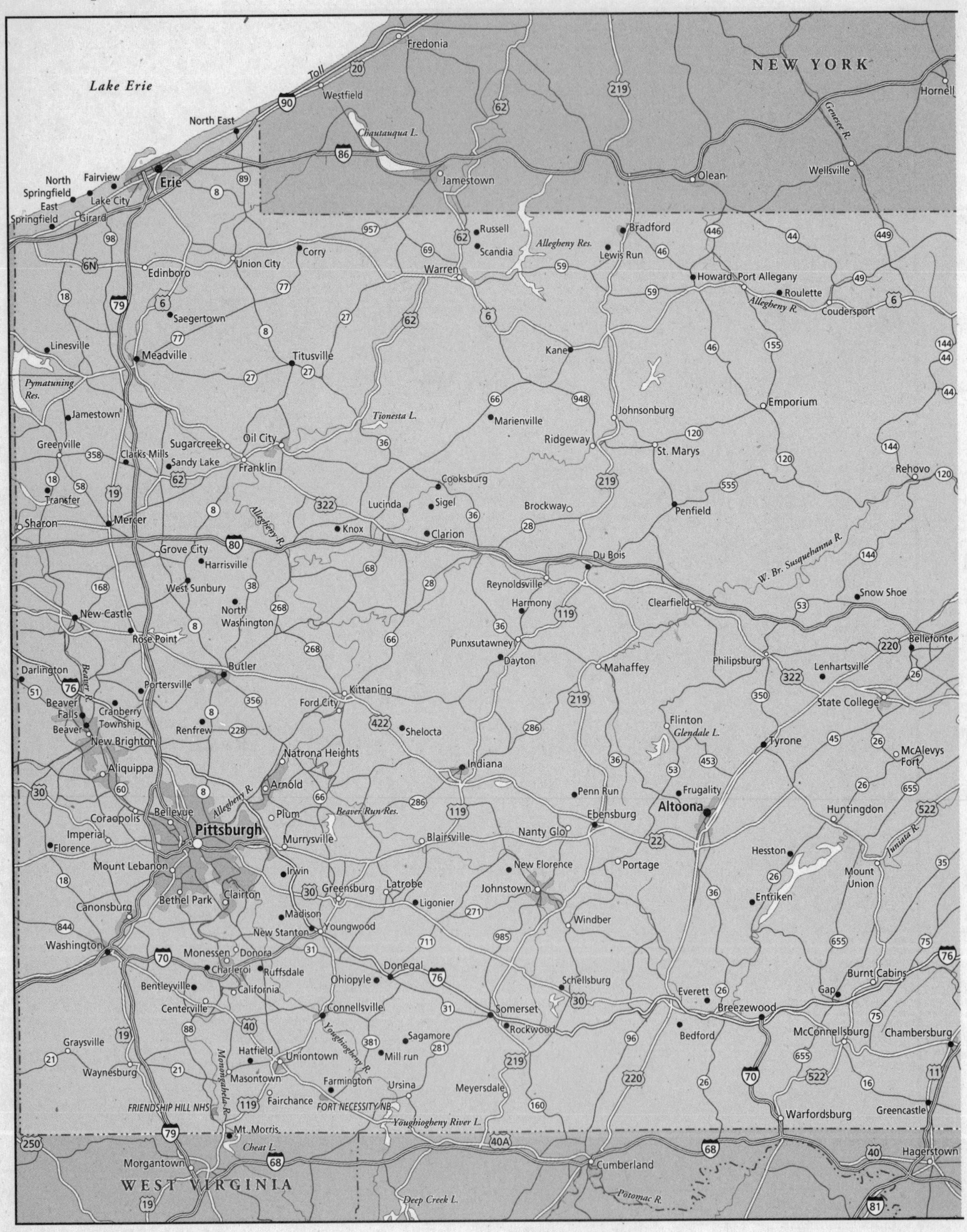

Pennsylvania

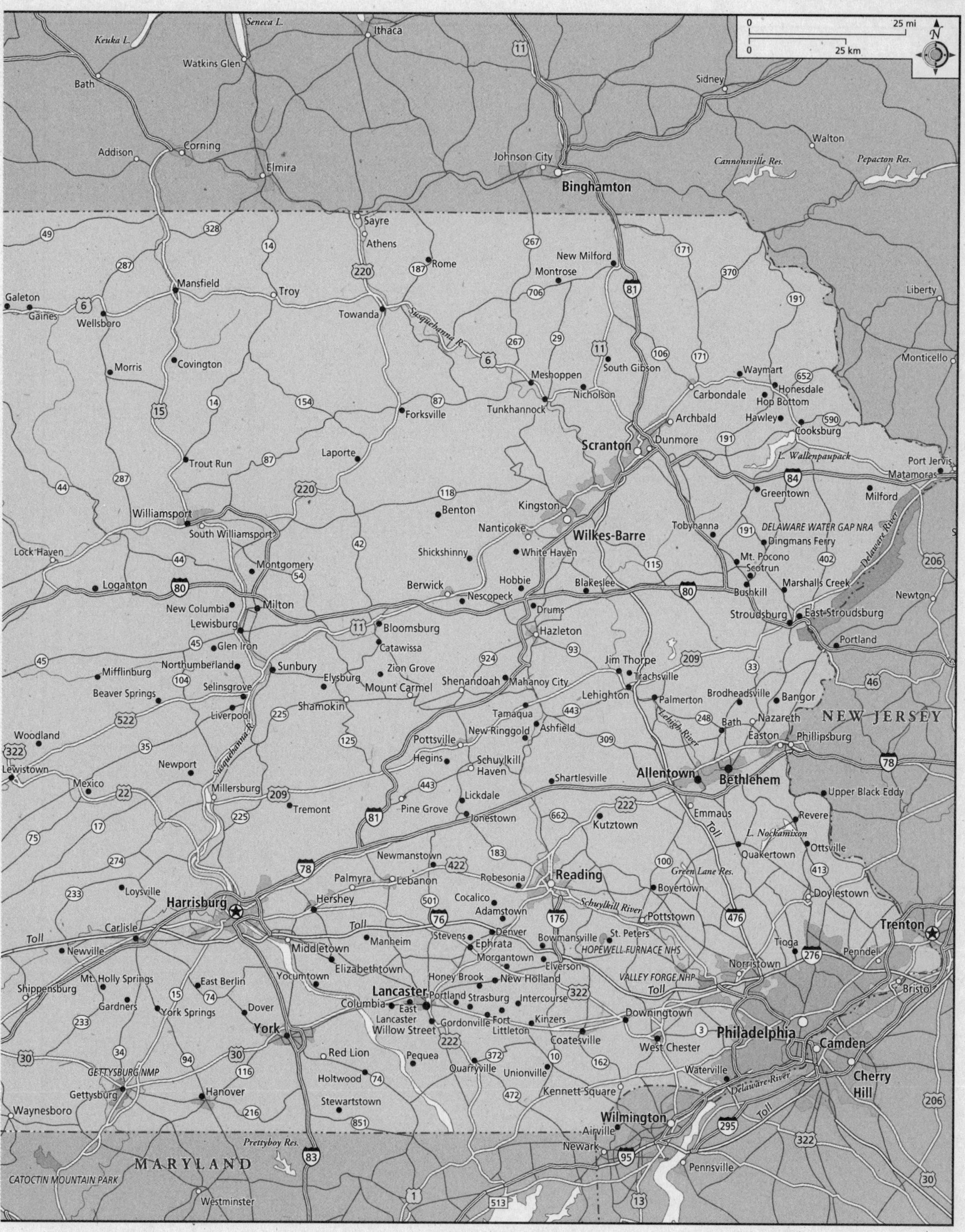

South Carolina

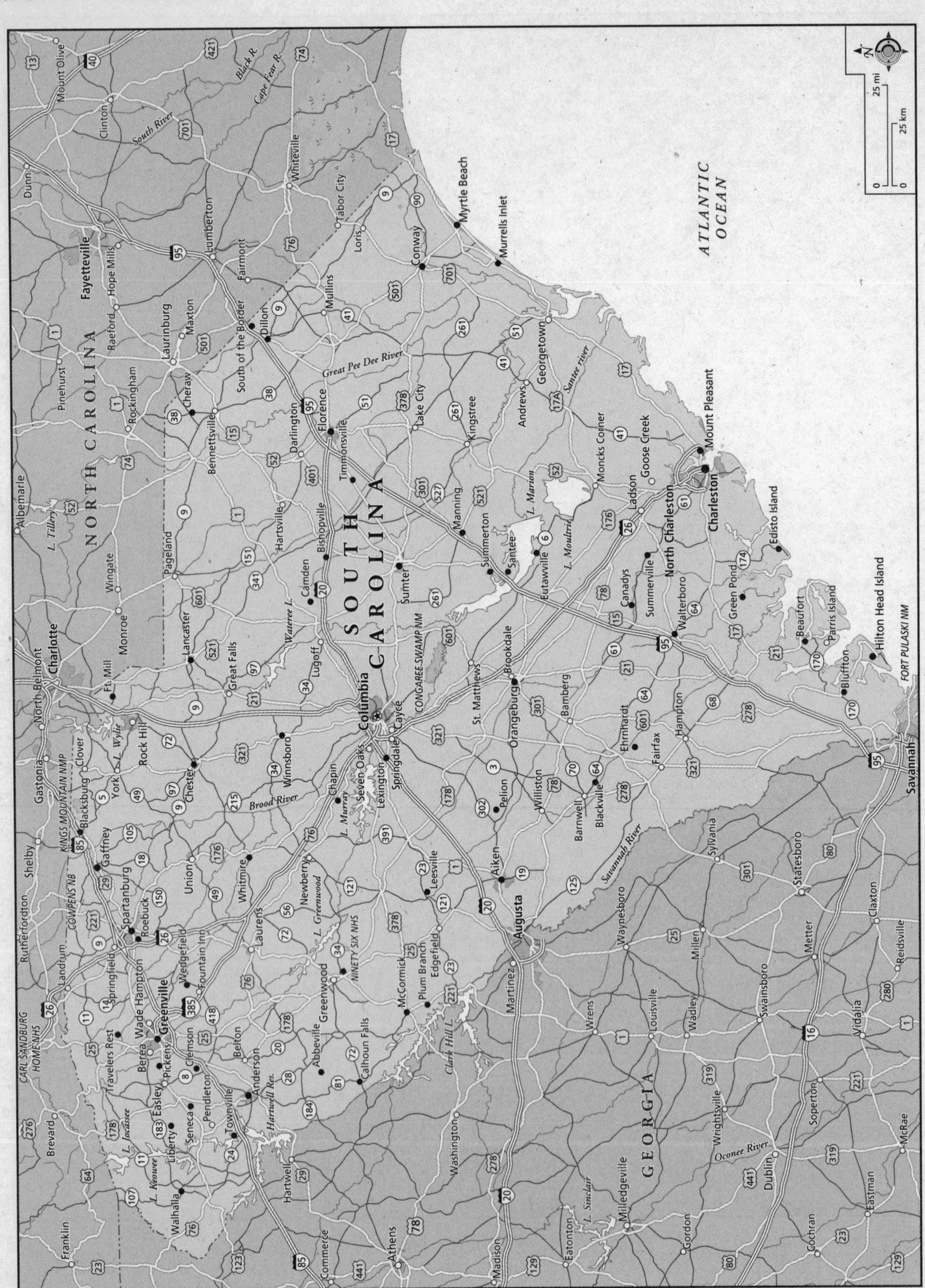

South Dakota

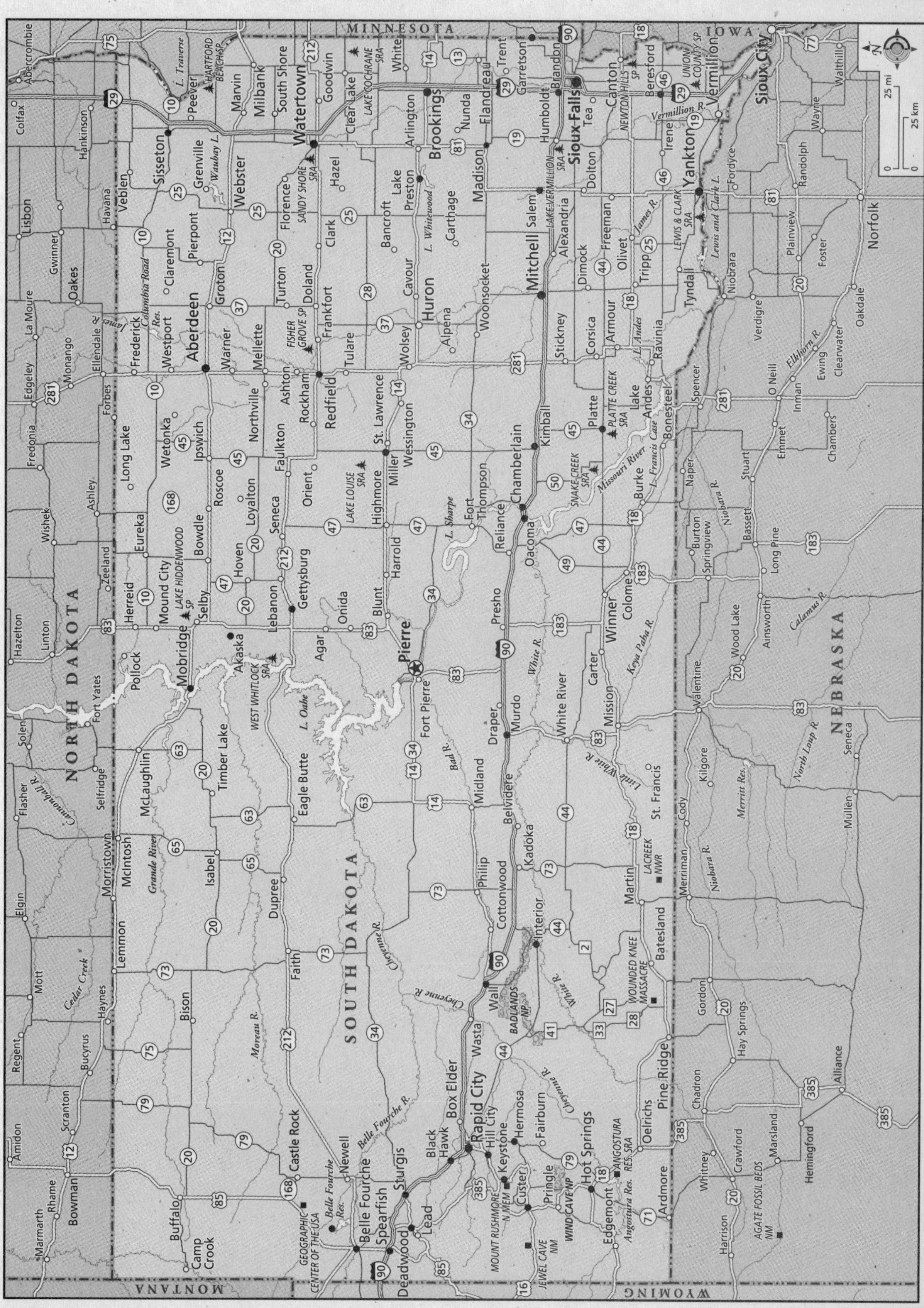

Tennessee

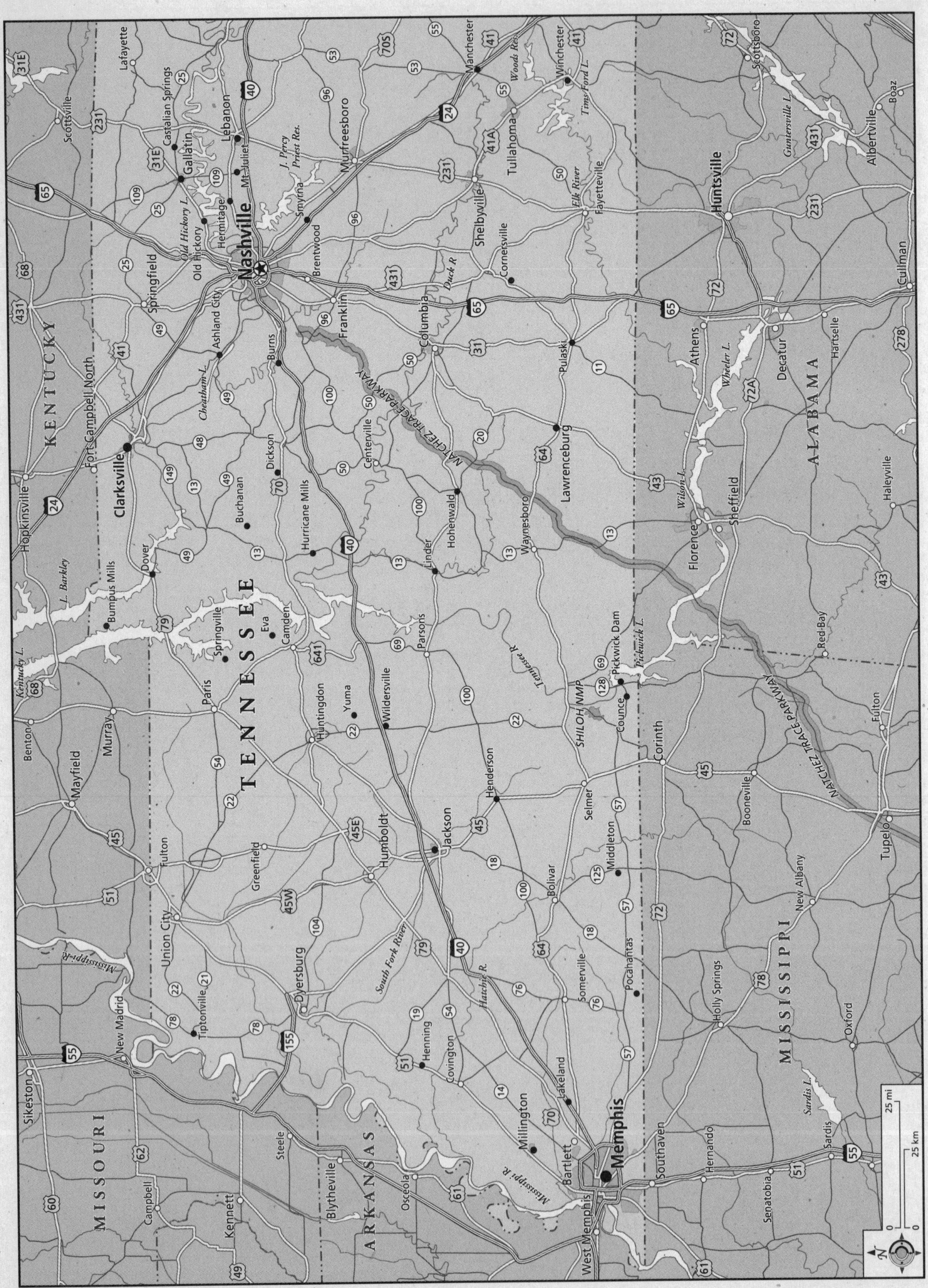

KENTUCKY
TENNESSEE
MISSOURI
ARKANSAS
MISSISSIPPI
ALABAMA
Nashville
Memphis
Huntsville
Clarksville
Jackson
Murfreesboro
Franklin
Columbia
Lebanon
Gallatin
Hendersonville
Hermitage
Old Hickory
Mt. Juliet
Smyrna
Brentwood
Springfield
Ashland City
Castalian Springs
Lafayette
Scottsville
Hopkinsville
Fort Campbell North
Dover
Bumpus Mills
Dickson
Burns
Centerville
Buchanan
Hurricane Mills
Camden
Eva
Springville
Paris
Murray
Mayfield
Benton
Fulton
Union City
Tiptonville
New Madrid
Sikeston
Dyersburg
Greenfield
Humboldt
Huntingdon
Yuma
Wildersville
Parsons
Linden
Hohenwald
Waynesboro
Lawrenceburg
Pulaski
Shelbyville
Cornersville
Tullahoma
Manchester
Winchester
Fayetteville
Henderson
Selmer
Bolivar
Middleton
Pocahontas
Somerville
Counce
Pickwick Dam
Corinth
Covington
Henning
Millington
Lakeland
Bartlett
West Memphis
Southaven
Hernando
Senatobia
Sardis
Holly Springs
Oxford
New Albany
Tupelo
Booneville
Fulton
Red Bay
Haleyville
Florence
Sheffield
Athens
Decatur
Hartselle
Cullman
Scottsboro
Albertville
Boaz
Steele
Blytheville
Osceola
Campbell
Kennett
SHILOH NMP
NATCHEZ TRACE PARKWAY
Kentucky L.
L. Barkley
Cheatham L.
Old Hickory L.
J. Percy Priest Res.
Woods Res.
Tims Ford L.
Elk River
Duck R.
Tennessee R.
Pickwick L.
Wilson L.
Wheeler L.
Guntersville L.
Sardis L.
Mississippi R.
South Fork River
Hatchie R.
25 mi
25 km
N

Tennessee

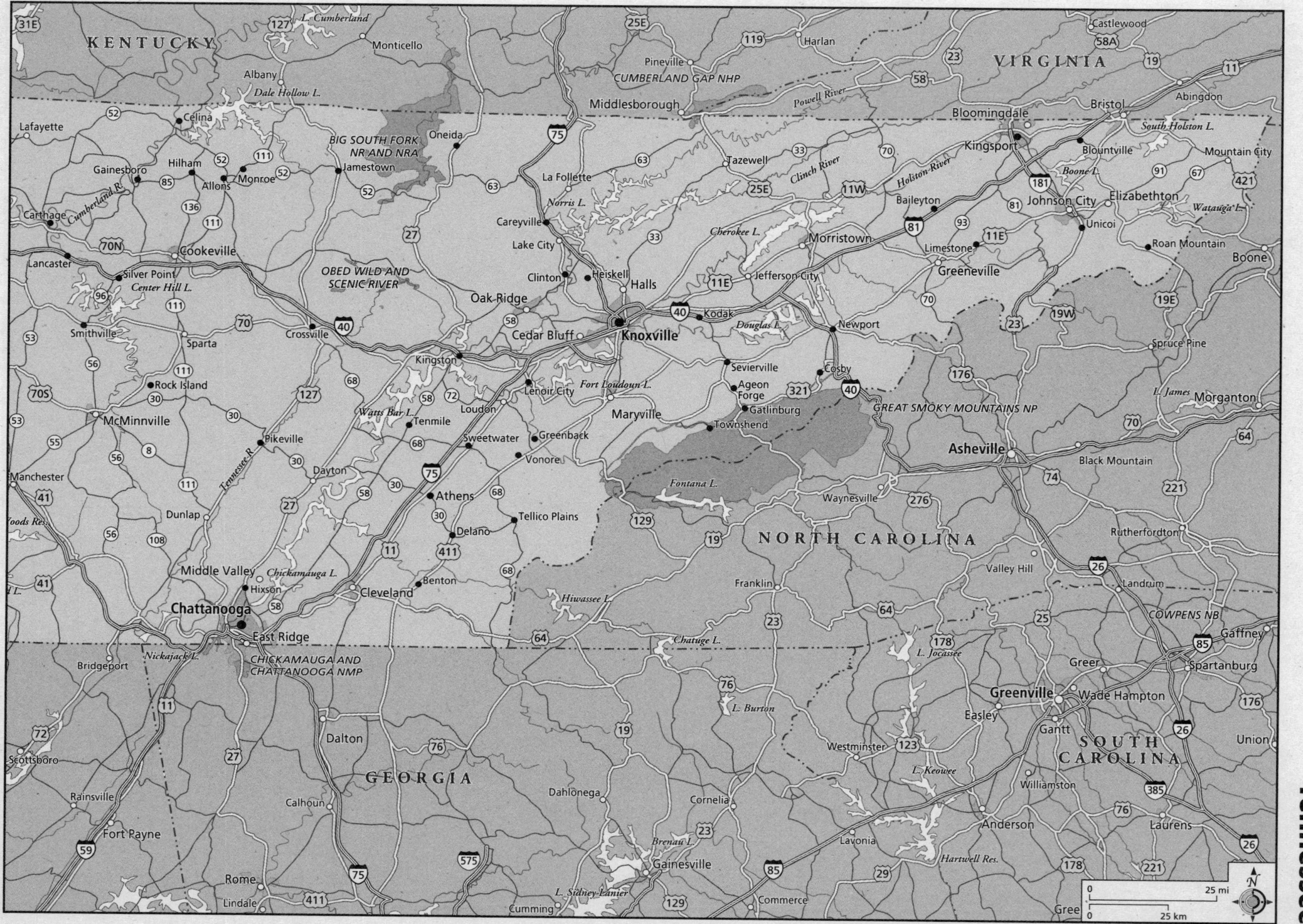

KENTUCKY
VIRGINIA
NORTH CAROLINA
SOUTH CAROLINA
GEORGIA
Knoxville
Chattanooga
Asheville
Greenville
Kingsport
Johnson City
Bristol
Morristown
Greeneville
Oak Ridge
Cookeville
Maryville
Gatlinburg
Ageon Forge
Sevierville
Cleveland
Athens
McMinnville
Crossville
GREAT SMOKY MOUNTAINS NP
CUMBERLAND GAP NHP
BIG SOUTH FORK NR AND NRA
OBED WILD AND SCENIC RIVER
CHICKAMAUGA AND CHATTANOOGA NMP
COWPENS NB
Fontana L.
Norris L.
Cherokee L.
Douglas L.
Tennessee R.
0
25 mi
25 km

Texas

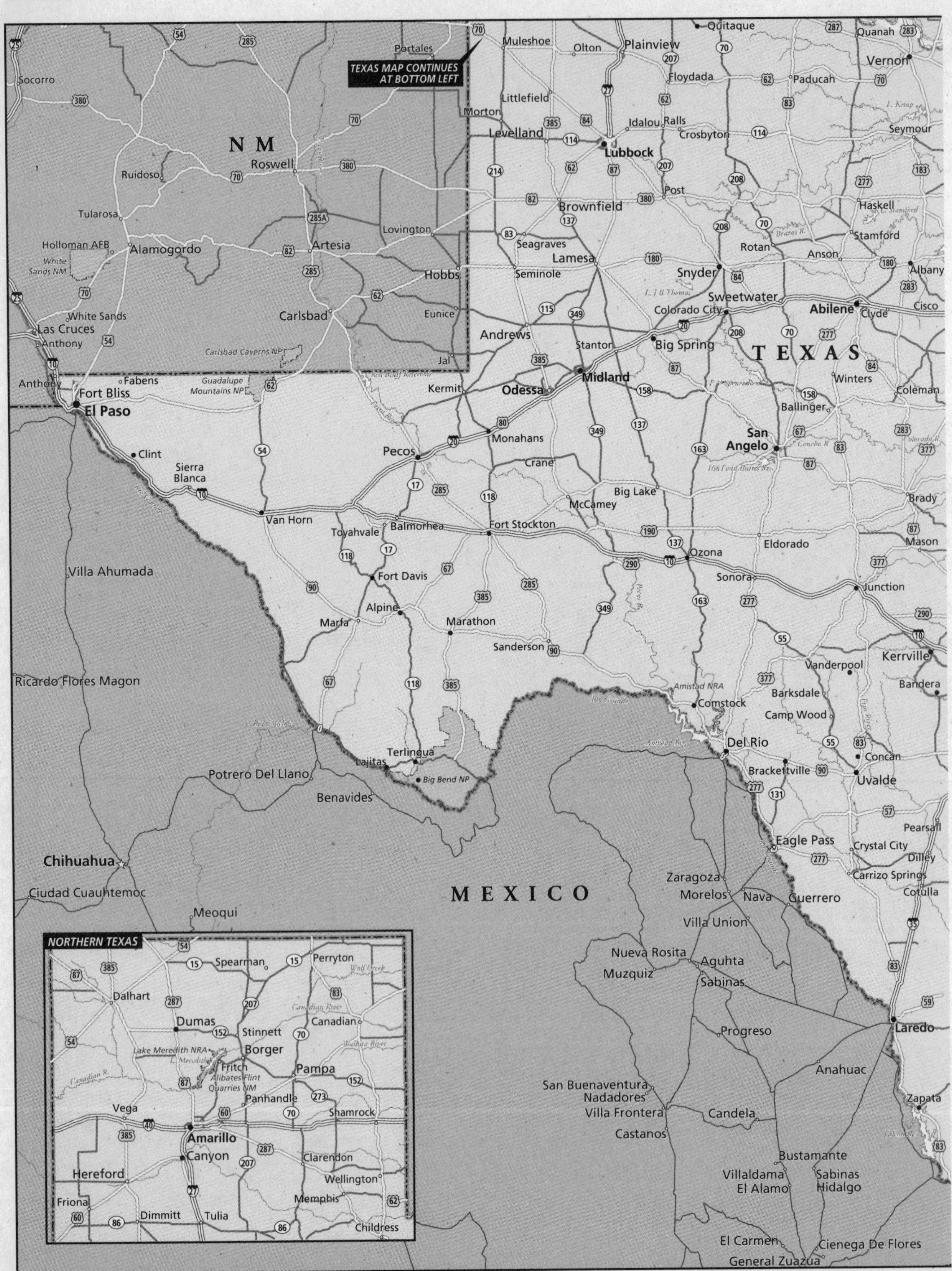

TEXAS MAP CONTINUES AT BOTTOM LEFT
NM
TEXAS
MEXICO
NORTHERN TEXAS
Socorro
Roswell
Ruidoso
Tularosa
Holloman AFB
Alamogordo
White Sands NM
White Sands
Las Cruces
Anthony
Artesia
Lovington
Hobbs
Carlsbad
Eunice
Carlsbad Caverns NP
Jal
Portales
Muleshoe
Olton
Plainview
Quitaque
Quanah
Vernon
Floydada
Paducah
Littlefield
Morton
Levelland
Idalou
Ralls
Crosbyton
Seymour
Lubbock
Post
Brownfield
Haskell
Stamford
Seagraves
Lamesa
Rotan
Anson
Seminole
Snyder
Albany
Sweetwater
Colorado City
Abilene
Clyde
Cisco
Andrews
Stanton
Big Spring
Winters
Coleman
Kermit
Odessa
Midland
Ballinger
Fabens
Fort Bliss
El Paso
Guadalupe Mountains NP
Anthony
Monahans
San Angelo
Clint
Sierra Blanca
Pecos
Crane
Big Lake
Brady
McCamey
Van Horn
Toyahvale
Balmorhea
Fort Stockton
Mason
Ozona
Eldorado
Sonora
Junction
Villa Ahumada
Fort Davis
Alpine
Marfa
Marathon
Sanderson
Kerrville
Vanderpool
Bandera
Ricardo Flores Magon
Amistad NRA
Comstock
Barksdale
Camp Wood
Del Rio
Concan
Terlingua
Lajitas
Big Bend NP
Brackettville
Uvalde
Potrero Del Llano
Benavides
Pearsall
Eagle Pass
Crystal City
Dilley
Carrizo Springs
Chihuahua
Zaragoza
Morelos
Nava
Guerrero
Cotulla
Ciudad Cuauhtemoc
Villa Union
Meoqui
Nueva Rosita
Aguhta
Muzquiz
Sabinas
Laredo
Progreso
Anahuac
San Buenaventura
Nadadores
Villa Frontera
Candela
Zapata
Castanos
Bustamante
Villaldama
El Alamo
Sabinas Hidalgo
El Carmen
Cienega De Flores
General Zuazua
Spearman
Perryton
Dalhart
Dumas
Stinnett
Canadian
Lake Meredith NRA
Fritch
Borger
Alibates Flint Quarries NM
Pampa
Panhandle
Vega
Shamrock
Amarillo
Canyon
Clarendon
Hereford
Wellington
Memphis
Friona
Dimmitt
Tulia
Childress

Texas

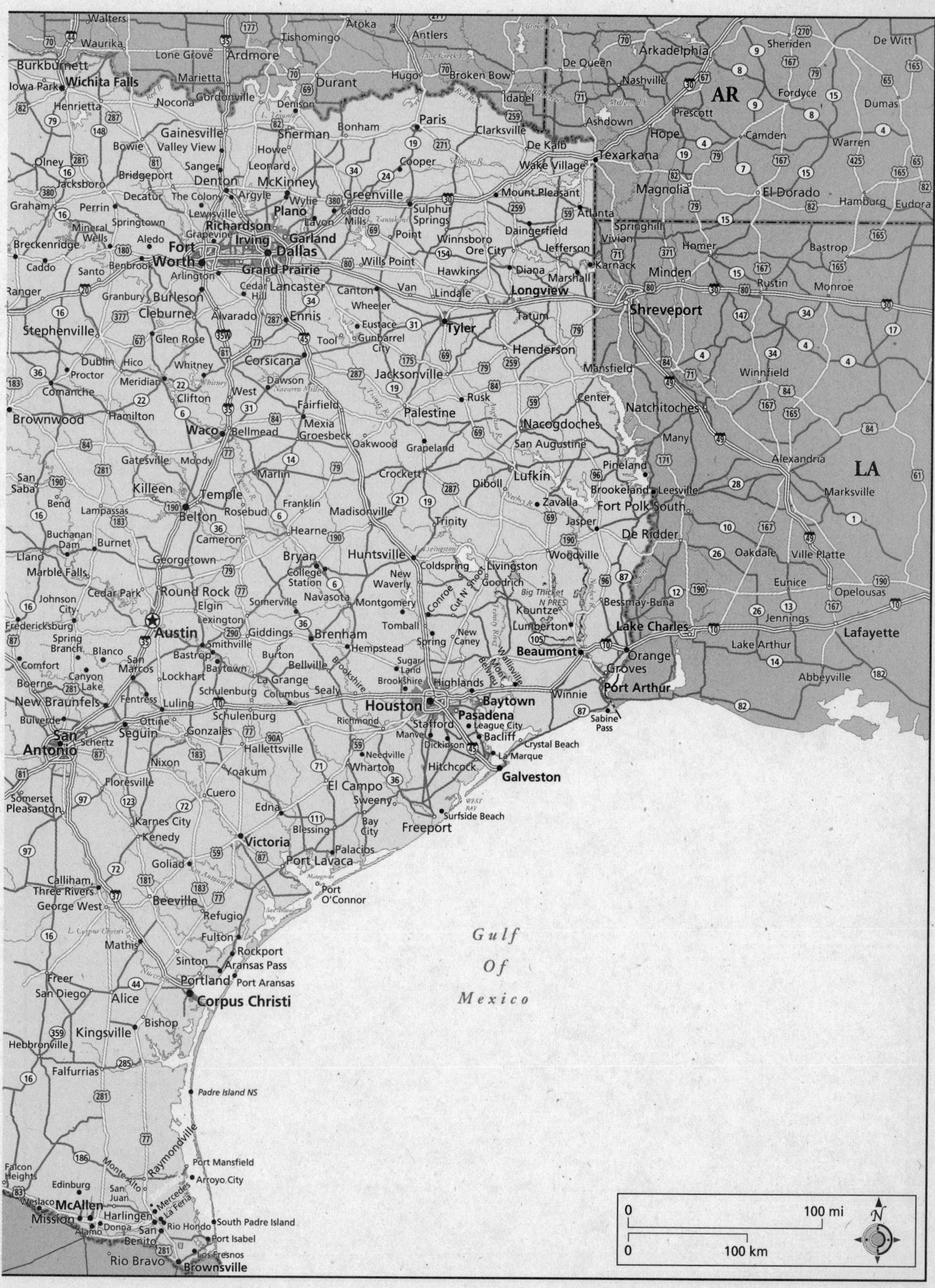

AR
LA
Gulf
Of
Mexico
Walters
Waurika
Atoka
Antlers
Tishomingo
Arkadelphia
Sheriden
De Witt
Burkburnett
Lone Grove
Ardmore
Iowa Park
Wichita Falls
Marietta
Durant
Hugo
Broken Bow
De Queen
Nashville
Fordyce
Dumas
Henrietta
Nocona
Gordonville
Denison
Idabel
Prescott
Ashdown
Hope
Camden
Warren
Gainesville
Valley View
Bonham
Sherman
Paris
Clarksville
De Kalb
Bowie
Howe
Olney
Sanger
Leonard
Cooper
Wake Village
Texarkana
Jacksboro
Bridgeport
Denton
McKinney
Magnolia
El Dorado
Hamburg
Eudora
Graham
Decatur
The Colony
Argyle
Wylie
Greenville
Mount Pleasant
Perrin
Lewisville
Plano
Lavon
Caddo Mills
Sulphur Springs
Atlanta
Springhill
Mineral Wells
Springtown
Richardson
Grapevine
Irving
Garland
Point
Daingerfield
Vivian
Homer
Bastrop
Breckenridge
Aledo
Fort Worth
Dallas
Winnsboro
Ore City
Jefferson
Benbrook
Grand Prairie
Wills Point
Diana
Karnack
Minden
Caddo
Santo
Arlington
Hawkins
Marshall
Rustin
Monroe
Ranger
Granbury
Burleson
Cedar Hill
Lancaster
Canton
Van
Lindale
Longview
Shreveport
Cleburne
Alvarado
Ennis
Wheeler
Tatum
Stephenville
Glen Rose
Eustace
Gunbarrel City
Tool
Tyler
Henderson
Dublin
Hico
Whitney
Corsicana
Jacksonville
Mansfield
Winnfield
Proctor
Meridian
Dawson
Comanche
Clifton
West
Rusk
Center
Natchitoches
Fairfield
Palestine
Brownwood
Hamilton
Mexia
Nacogdoches
Waco
Bellmead
Groesbeck
Oakwood
Grapeland
San Augustine
Many
Gatesville
Moody
Pineland
Alexandria
San Saba
Marlin
Crockett
Diboll
Lufkin
Killeen
Temple
Brookeland
Leesville
Marksville
Bend
Lampassas
Belton
Rosebud
Franklin
Madisonville
Zavalla
Fort Polk South
Trinity
Jasper
Buchanan Dam
Burnet
Cameron
Hearne
De Ridder
Llano
Georgetown
Bryan
Huntsville
Coldspring
Livingston
Woodville
Oakdale
Ville Platte
Marble Falls
College Station
New Waverly
Goodrich
Eunice
Johnson City
Cedar Park
Round Rock
Navasota
Somerville
Montgomery
Bessmay-Buna
Opelousas
Elgin
Conroe
Cut N' Shoot
Kountze
Jennings
Fredericksburg
Lexington
Austin
Tomball
Lumberton
Lake Charles
Lafayette
Spring Branch
Blanco
Giddings
Brenham
New Caney
Beaumont
Lake Arthur
San Marcos
Smithville
Hempstead
Spring
Orange
Comfort
Bastrop
Burton
Bellville
Sugar Land
Groves
Canyon Lake
Lockhart
Baytown
La Grange
Brookshire
Highlands
Mont Belvieu
Wallisville
Winnie
Port Arthur
Abbeyville
Boerne
Schulenburg
Columbus
Sealy
Baytown
New Braunfels
Fentress
Luling
Houston
Pasadena
Sabine Pass
Bulverde
Ottine
Schulenburg
Richmond
Stafford
League City
San Antonio
Schertz
Seguin
Gonzales
Hallettsville
Manvel
Bacliff
Dickinson
Crystal Beach
Needville
La Marque
Nixon
Wharton
Hitchcock
Galveston
Floresville
Yoakum
El Campo
Somerset
Pleasanton
Cuero
Sweeny
Edna
Karnes City
Blessing
Bay City
Freeport
Surfside Beach
Kenedy
Victoria
Palacios
Goliad
Port Lavaca
Port O'Connor
Calliham
Three Rivers
George West
Beeville
Refugio
Fulton
Mathis
Rockport
Sinton
Aransas Pass
Freer
Portland
Port Aransas
San Diego
Alice
Corpus Christi
Bishop
Kingsville
Hebbronville
Falfurrias
Padre Island NS
Raymondville
Monte Alto
Port Mansfield
Falcon Heights
Edinburg
San Juan
Arroyo City
Weslaco
McAllen
Mercedes
La Feria
Mission
Harlingen
Rio Hondo
South Padre Island
Alamo
Donna
San Benito
Port Isabel
Los Fresnos
Rio Bravo
Brownsville
0
100 mi
0
100 km
N

Utah

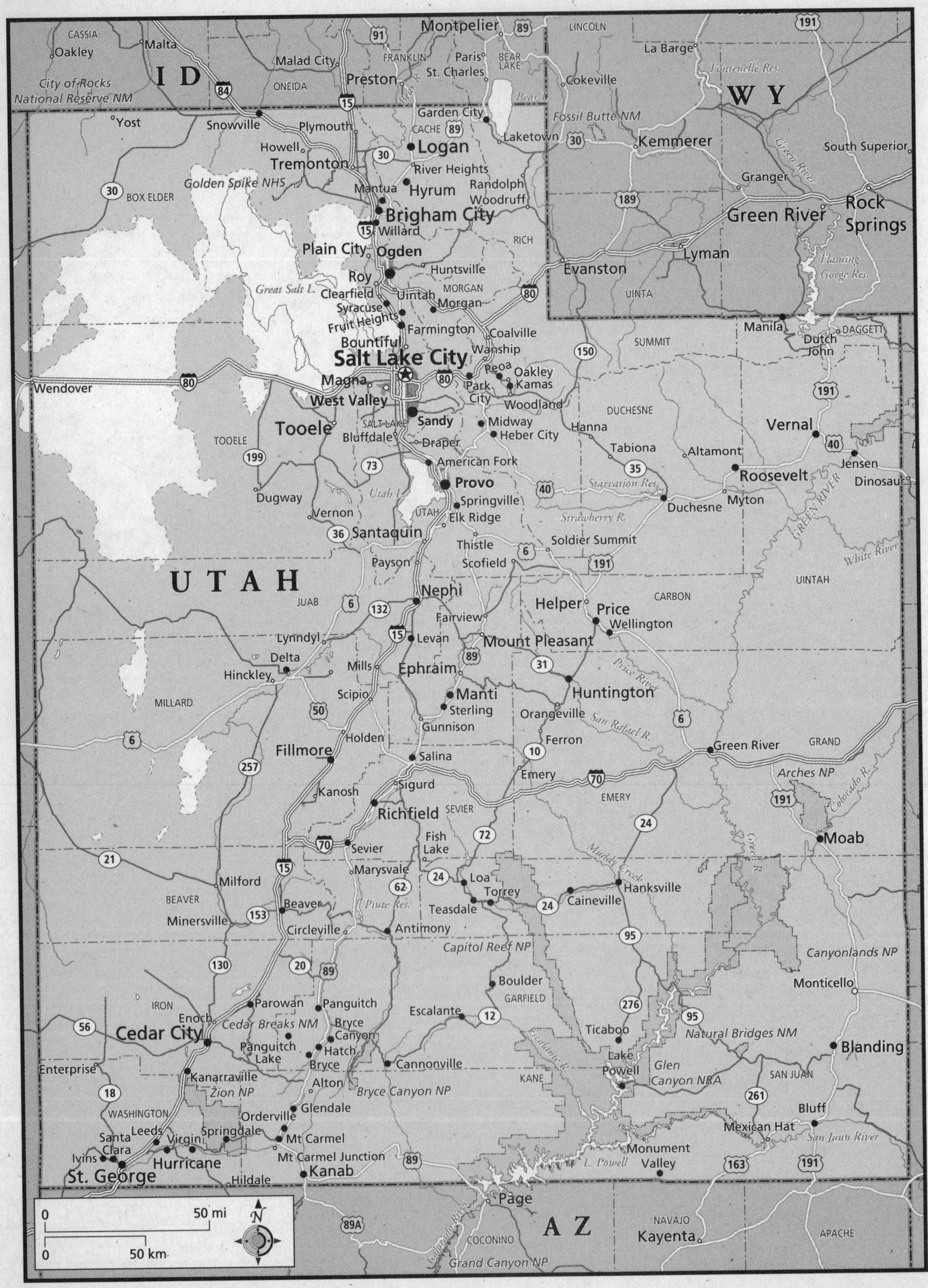

ID
WY
UTAH
AZ
CASSIA
Oakley
Malta
City of Rocks National Reserve NM
Malad City
ONEIDA
FRANKLIN
Preston
Montpelier
Paris
St. Charles
BEAR LAKE
Bear L.
LINCOLN
La Barge
Fontenelle Res.
Cokeville
Fossil Butte NM
Kemmerer
South Superior
Granger
Green River
Rock Springs
Flaming Gorge Res.
Lyman
Evanston
UINTA
Yost
Snowville
Plymouth
Howell
Tremonton
Golden Spike NHS
BOX ELDER
Garden City
CACHE
Logan
Laketown
River Heights
Hyrum
Mantua
Randolph
Woodruff
Brigham City
Willard
Plain City
Ogden
RICH
Roy
Huntsville
Great Salt L.
Clearfield
Uintah
MORGAN
Syracuse
Morgan
Fruit Heights
Farmington
Coalville
Bountiful
Wanship
Salt Lake City
Peoa
Oakley
Kamas
Park City
Woodland
Magna
West Valley
Wendover
Tooele
SALT LAKE
Sandy
Midway
Heber City
Bluffdale
Draper
TOOELE
American Fork
Provo
Utah L.
Springville
UTAH
Elk Ridge
Dugway
Vernon
Santaquin
Thistle
Scofield
Payson
Soldier Summit
SUMMIT
Manila
Dutch John
DAGGETT
DUCHESNE
Hanna
Tabiona
Altamont
Vernal
Jensen
Dinosaur
Roosevelt
Myton
Duchesne
Starvation Res.
Strawberry R.
GREEN RIVER
White River
UINTAH
JUAB
Nephi
Fairview
Helper
Price
Wellington
CARBON
Lynndyl
Levan
Mount Pleasant
Delta
Hinckley
Mills
Ephraim
Scipio
Manti
Sterling
Gunnison
Huntington
Orangeville
Price River
San Rafael R.
Ferron
MILLARD
Holden
Fillmore
Salina
Emery
Green River
GRAND
Arches NP
Colorado R.
Kanosh
Sigurd
Richfield
SEVIER
EMERY
Moab
Sevier
Fish Lake
Marysvale
Loa
Torrey
Teasdale
Caineville
Hanksville
Muddy Creek
Milford
BEAVER
Beaver
Minersville
Piute Res.
Circleville
Antimony
Capitol Reef NP
Canyonlands NP
Monticello
Boulder
GARFIELD
IRON
Parowan
Panguitch
Escalante
Enoch
Cedar City
Cedar Breaks NM
Bryce Canyon
Panguitch Lake
Hatch
Bryce
Ticaboo
Natural Bridges NM
Blanding
Enterprise
Kanarraville
Zion NP
Cannonville
Alton
Bryce Canyon NP
Escalante R.
KANE
Lake Powell
Glen Canyon NRA
SAN JUAN
WASHINGTON
Glendale
Orderville
Bluff
Mexican Hat
San Juan River
Santa Clara
Leeds
Virgin
Springdale
Mt Carmel
Mt Carmel Junction
Monument Valley
Ivins
Hurricane
St. George
Hildale
Kanab
L. Powell
Page
NAVAJO
Kayenta
APACHE
COCONINO
Grand Canyon NP
Colorado River
0
50 mi
0
50 km
N

Vermont

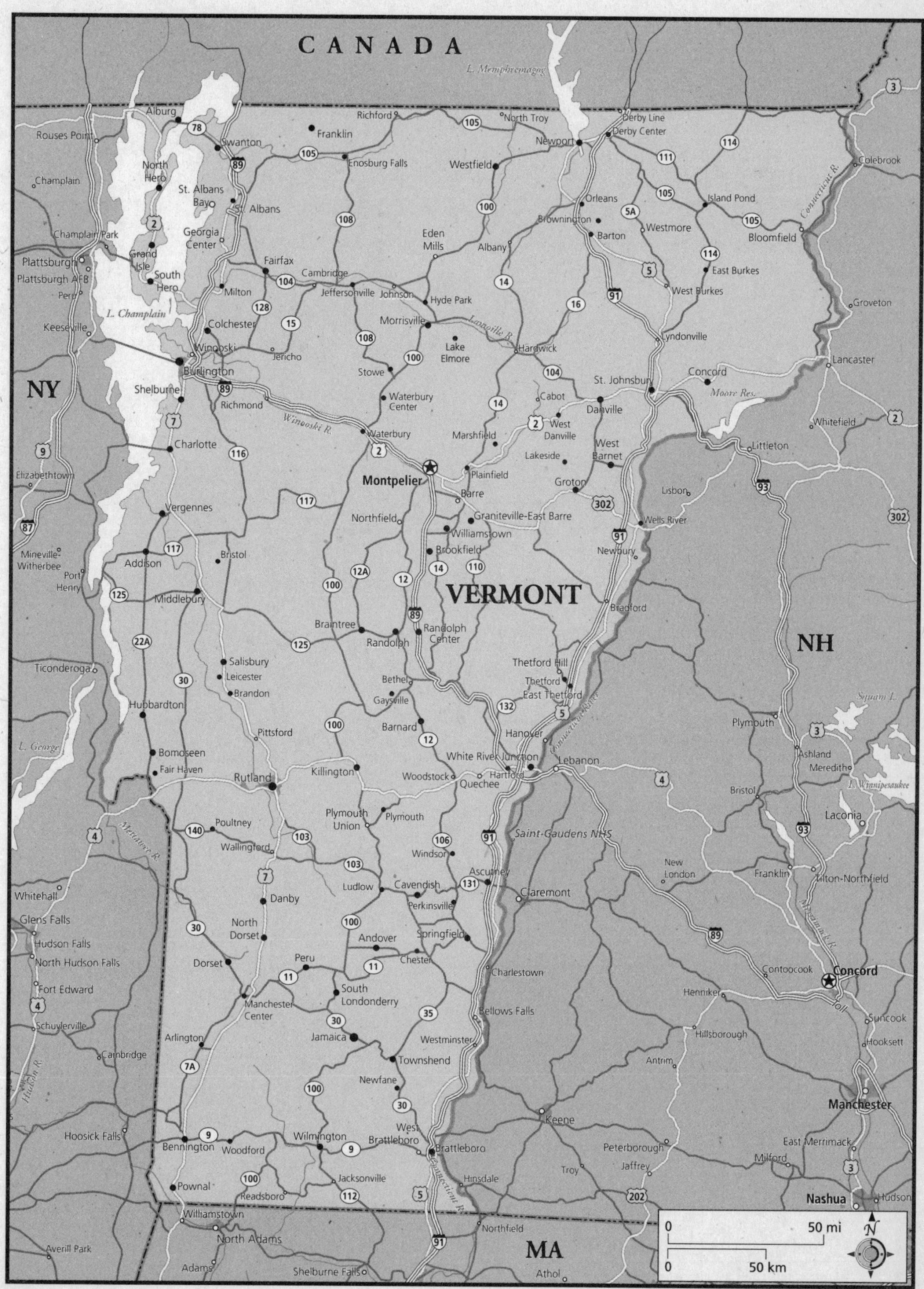
CANADA
L. Memphremagog
NY
NH
MA
VERMONT
Alburg
Rouses Point
Swanton
Franklin
Richford
North Troy
Derby Line
Derby Center
Newport
Enosburg Falls
Westfield
Champlain
North Hero
St. Albans Bay
St. Albans
Orleans
Brownington
Barton
Westmore
Island Pond
Bloomfield
Colebrook
Champlain Park
Grand Isle
Georgia Center
Eden Mills
Albany
East Burkes
West Burkes
Plattsburgh
Plattsburgh AFB
Peru
South Hero
Fairfax
Cambridge
Milton
Jeffersonville
Johnson
Hyde Park
L. Champlain
Keeseville
Colchester
Morrisville
Lamoille R.
Lake Elmore
Hardwick
Lyndonville
Groveton
Winooski
Jericho
Burlington
Stowe
Shelburne
Richmond
Waterbury Center
Cabot
St. Johnsbury
Concord
Moore Res.
Lancaster
Danville
West Danville
Whitefield
Winooski R.
Waterbury
Marshfield
Charlotte
Lakeside
West Barnet
Littleton
Elizabethtown
Montpelier
Plainfield
Barre
Groton
Lisbon
Vergennes
Northfield
Graniteville-East Barre
Williamstown
Wells River
Brookfield
Newbury
Mineville
Witherbee
Addison
Bristol
Port Henry
Middlebury
Bradford
Braintree
Randolph
Randolph Center
Salisbury
Leicester
Brandon
Ticonderoga
Thetford Hill
Thetford
East Thetford
Hubbardton
Bethel
Gaysville
Barnard
Hanover
Connecticut River
Squam L.
Plymouth
Pittsford
L. George
Bomoseen
Fair Haven
White River Junction
Lebanon
Ashland
Meredith
Rutland
Killington
Woodstock
Hartford
Quechee
L. Winnipesaukee
Bristol
Poultney
Plymouth Union
Plymouth
Laconia
Mettawee R.
Wallingford
Windsor
Saint-Gaudens NHS
New London
Franklin
Tilton-Northfield
Whitehall
Ludlow
Cavendish
Ascutney
Claremont
Danby
Perkinsville
Glens Falls
Hudson Falls
North Hudson Falls
North Dorset
Springfield
Andover
Dorset
Peru
Chester
Charlestown
Contoocook
Concord
Fort Edward
South Londonderry
Henniker
Manchester Center
Schuylerville
Bellows Falls
Suncook
Arlington
Jamaica
Westminster
Hillsborough
Hooksett
Cambridge
Townshend
Antrim
Hudson R.
Newfane
Manchester
Keene
Hoosick Falls
Bennington
Woodford
Wilmington
West Brattleboro
Brattleboro
Peterborough
East Merrimack
Milford
Troy
Jaffrey
Pownal
Readsboro
Jacksonville
Hinsdale
Nashua
Hudson
Williamstown
North Adams
Northfield
Averill Park
Adams
Shelburne Falls
Athol
0
50 mi
50 km
N

Virginia

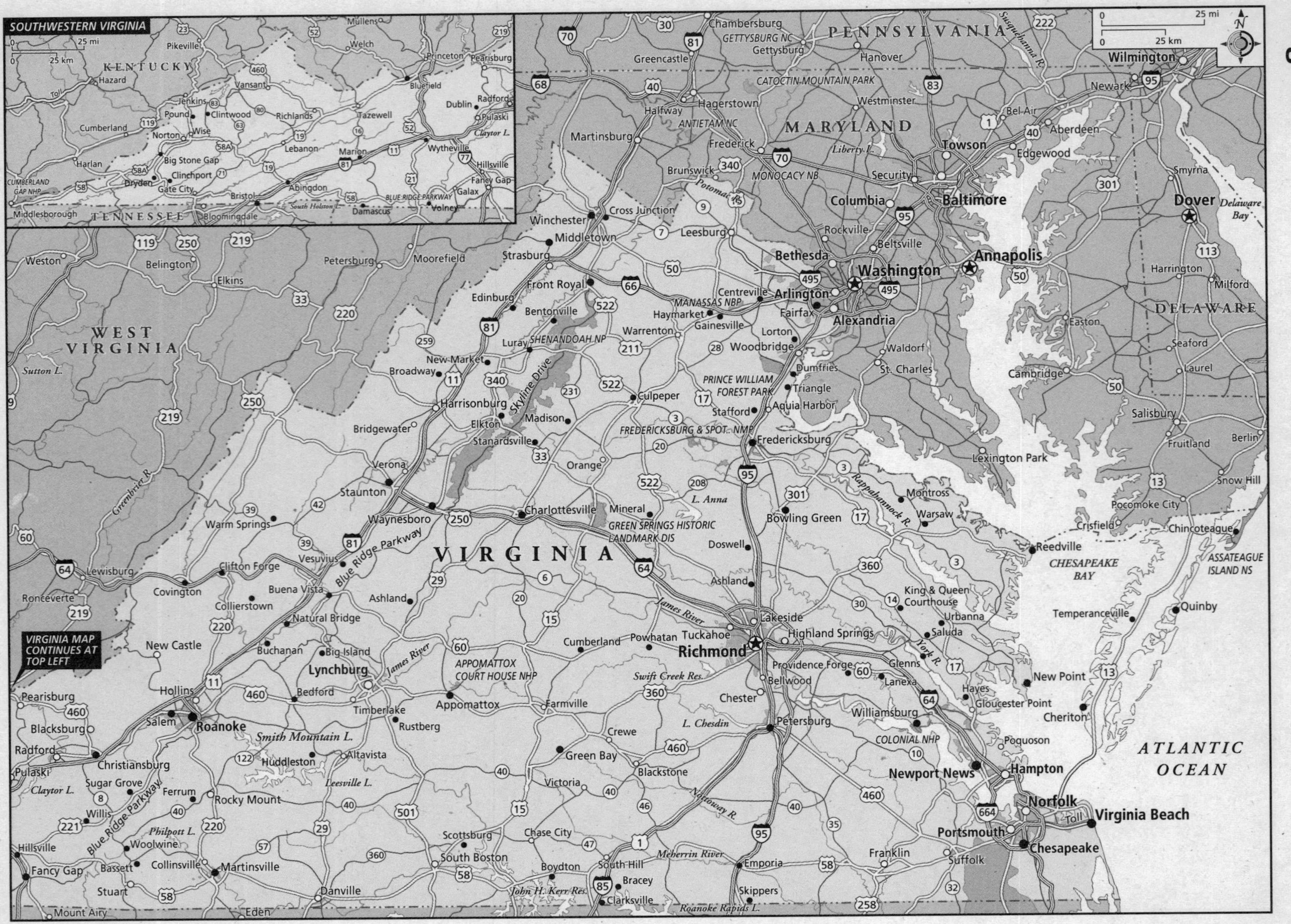

ATLANTIC OCEAN
PENNSYLVANIA
MARYLAND
DELAWARE
VIRGINIA
WEST VIRGINIA
KENTUCKY
TENNESSEE
SOUTHWESTERN VIRGINIA
VIRGINIA MAP CONTINUES AT TOP LEFT
CHESAPEAKE BAY
Delaware Bay
ASSATEAGUE ISLAND NS
GETTYSBURG NC
CATOCTIN MOUNTAIN PARK
ANTIETAM NC
MONOCACY NB
MANASSAS NBP
PRINCE WILLIAM FOREST PARK
FREDERICKSBURG & SPOT. NMP
GREEN SPRINGS HISTORIC LANDMARK DIS
SHENANDOAH NP
APPOMATTOX COURT HOUSE NHP
COLONIAL NHP
Skyline Drive
Blue Ridge Parkway
Washington
Richmond
Baltimore
Annapolis
Dover
Wilmington
Norfolk
Virginia Beach
Chesapeake
Portsmouth
Hampton
Newport News
Lynchburg
Roanoke
Alexandria
Arlington
Fredericksburg
Charlottesville
Williamsburg
Petersburg
Winchester
Harrisonburg
Staunton
Waynesboro
Danville
Martinsville
Blacksburg
Salem
25 mi
25 km

Washington

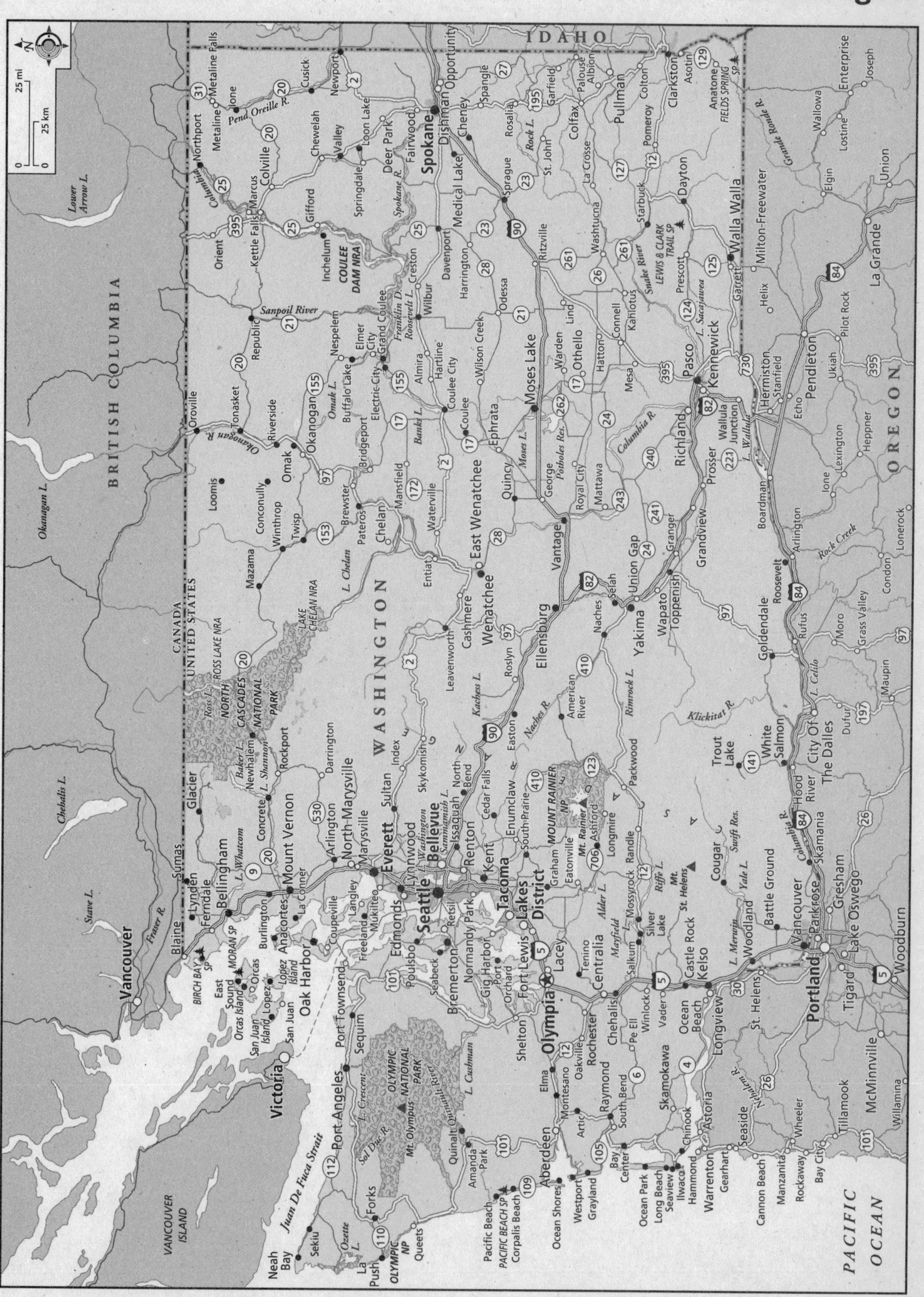

BRITISH COLUMBIA
CANADA
UNITED STATES
IDAHO
OREGON
WASHINGTON
PACIFIC OCEAN
VANCOUVER ISLAND
Juan De Fuca Strait
Vancouver
Victoria
Seattle
Bellevue
Tacoma
Spokane
Olympia
Everett
Bellingham
Yakima
Wenatchee
East Wenatchee
Ellensburg
Moses Lake
Richland
Kennewick
Pasco
Walla Walla
Pullman
Clarkston
Portland
Aberdeen
Port Angeles
Port Townsend
Oak Harbor
Anacortes
Mount Vernon
Centralia
Chehalis
Longview
Kelso
Vancouver
Bremerton
Renton
Kent
Lakes District
Fort Lewis
Lacey
Colville
Omak
Okanogan
Chelan
Leavenworth
Goldendale
White Salmon
Hood River
The Dalles
Pendleton
Hermiston
La Grande
Forks
Neah Bay
La Push
Sequim
Shelton
Raymond
Astoria
Seaside
OLYMPIC NATIONAL PARK
NORTH CASCADES NATIONAL PARK
MOUNT RAINIER NP
COULEE DAM NRA
LAKE CHELAN NRA
ROSS LAKE NRA
0 25 mi
0 25 km

West Virginia

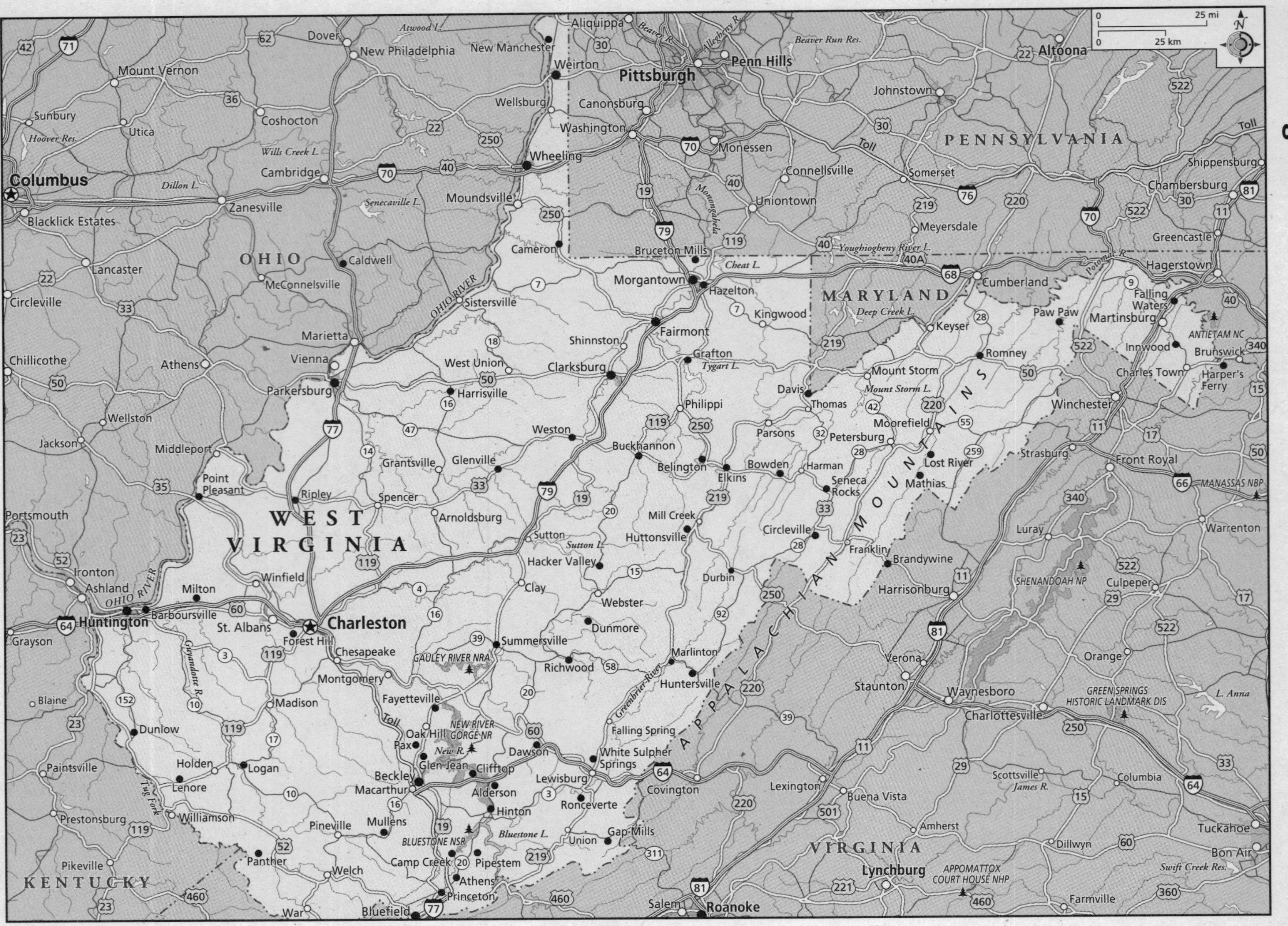

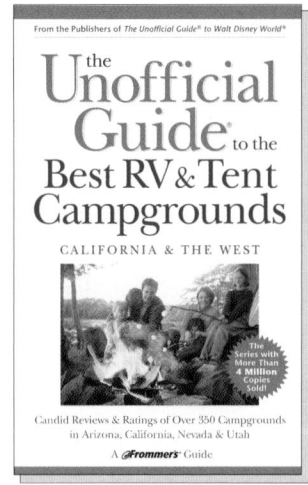

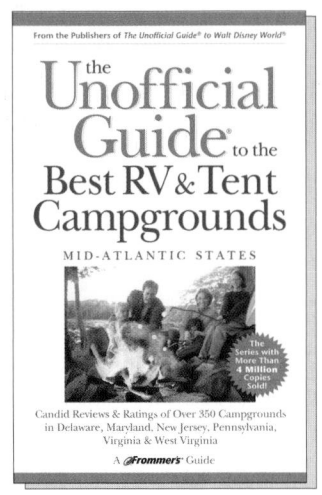

Wisconsin

ISLE ROYALE NP
0 25 mi
0 25 km
N
Grand Marais
Virginia
MINNESOTA
Lake Superior
Lake Superior
Meadowlands
APOSTLE ISLANDS NL
BIG BAY SP
Silver City
Ontonagon
Bayfield
Duluth
Superior
Cloquet
AMNICON FALLS SP
Washburn
La Pointe
Iron River
Ashland
Brule
WILDERNESS SP
Black River Harbor
LAKE GOGEBIC SP
L. Gogebic
L Anse
Marquette
Champion
OTTAWA NATIONAL FOREST
Bessemer
Wakefield
Barnum
Solon Springs
Mason
Drummond
Hurley
Mellen
MICHIGAN
Michigamme Res.
Gordon
Cable
CHEQUAMEGON NATIONAL FOREST
Mercer
Manitowish
Land O'Lakes
BEWABIC SP
Gwinn
Saint Croix NSR
Minong
Glidden
Lac Du Flambeau
Conover
Witch Lake
Channing
Crystal Falls
Escanaba R.
Hayward
L. Chippewa
Chippewa R.
Butternut
Arbor Vitae
NICOLET NATIONAL FOREST
Rapid River
St. Croix R.
Danbury
Trego
Webster
Spooner
Shell Lake
Grantsburg
Park Falls
Woodruff
Minocqua
Fifield
Eagle River
Florence
Iron Mountain
Escanaba
Exeland
Three Lakes
Hiles
Goodman
Merrimac
Luck
Cumberland
Flambeau R.
Phillips
Hazelhurst
Tripoli
Rhinelander
Pembine
St. Croix Falls
Balsam Lake
Rice Lake
Bruce
Ladysmith
Tomahawk
Crandon
Laona
Pelican Lake
Athelstane
ROCK ISLAND SP
Washington Island
Barron
Chetek
WISCONSIN
COUNCIL GROUNDS SP
Wabeno
Lakewood
Osceola
Holcombe
BRUNET ISLAND SP
Clear Lake
Cornell
Merrill
Antigo
Mountain
Crivitz
Ellison Bay
Sister Bay
Somerset
Medford
Menomonie
Fish Creek
Marinette
Baileys Harbor
Bloomer
Elton
Peshtigo
Hudson
Chippewa Falls
Dorchester
Wausau
Schofield
Spruce
Oconto
Egg Harbor
POTAWATOMI SP
Lower Saint Croix NSR
Eau Claire
Unity
Gresham
Tilleda
Sturgeon Bay
Spring Valley
Mosinee
Shawano
Green Bay
Augusta
Big Eau Pleine Res.
Marion
Suamico
Brussels
Red Wing
Marshfield
Stevens Point
Clintonville
Green Bay
Algoma
Osseo
Mondovi
Neillsville
Iola
Birchwood
Kewaunee
Alma Center
Merrillan
Wisconsin R.
Amherst Junction
Manawa
New London
De Pere
Wabasha
Blair
Hixton
Pittsville
Plover
Norman
Denmark
Zumbrota
Black River Falls
Nekoosa
Waupaca
Bancroft
Appleton
Maribel
Fountain City
Warrens
Petenwell L.
Coloma
L. Poygan
Wild Rose
Fremont
Kaukauna
Mississippi R.
Galesville
Big Flats
Hancock
L. Butte des Morts
Sherwood
Hilbert
Two Rivers
Rochester
Winona
Trempealeau
Tomah
Wyeville
Wisconsin Rapids
Wautoma
Redgranite
L. Winnebago
Manitowoc
FERRY TO LUDINGTON, MI
Sparta
Oakdale
Necedah
New Lisbon
Oshkosh
Elkhart Lake
MINNESOTA
Holmen
Wilton
Mauston
Oxford
Montello
Green Lake
Fond Du Lac
Greenbush
La Crosse
Ontario
Wonewoc
Lyndon Station
Marquette
Markesan
Eden
Sheboygan
Spring Valley
Babcock
Wisconsin Dells
Kingston
Cascade
KOHLER-ANDRAE SP
La Farge
Reedsburg
Lake Delton
Portage
Pardeeville
Waupun
Campbellsport
Viroqua
Viola
Baraboo
Dalton
Horicon
Kewaskum
HARRINGTON BEACH SP
De Soto
Richland Center
L. Wisconsin
DEVIL'S LAKE SP
Lodi
Beaver Dam
West Bend
Rio
Port Washington
Decorah
Columbus
IOWA
Effigy Mounds NM
Lynxville
Wisconsin R.
Blue River
Spring Green
Sun Prairie
Muscoda
Avoca
Madison
Wauwatosa
Milwaukee
TOWER HILL SP
Blue Mounds
Fort
Jefferson
West Allis
New Hampton
Prairie Du Chien
Atkinson
Eagle
Waukesha
Lake
West Union
Bagley
Dodgeville
Oregon
L. Koshkonong
Stoughton
Whitewater
Palmyra
Oak Creek
Lancaster
Guttenberg
Belmont
Mineral Point
Caledonia
Lake Michigan
Waverly
Cassville
Platteville
Evansville
Edgerton
Milton
Mukwonago
Racine
Blair
Janesville
Delevan
Burlington
Sturtevant
Monroe
Lake Geneva
Kenosha
Cedar Falls
Waterloo
Dubuque
Kieler
CADIZ SPRINGS SRA
Beloit
Bristol
Waukegan
ILLINOIS
North Chicago
Rockford
Highland Park

Wyoming

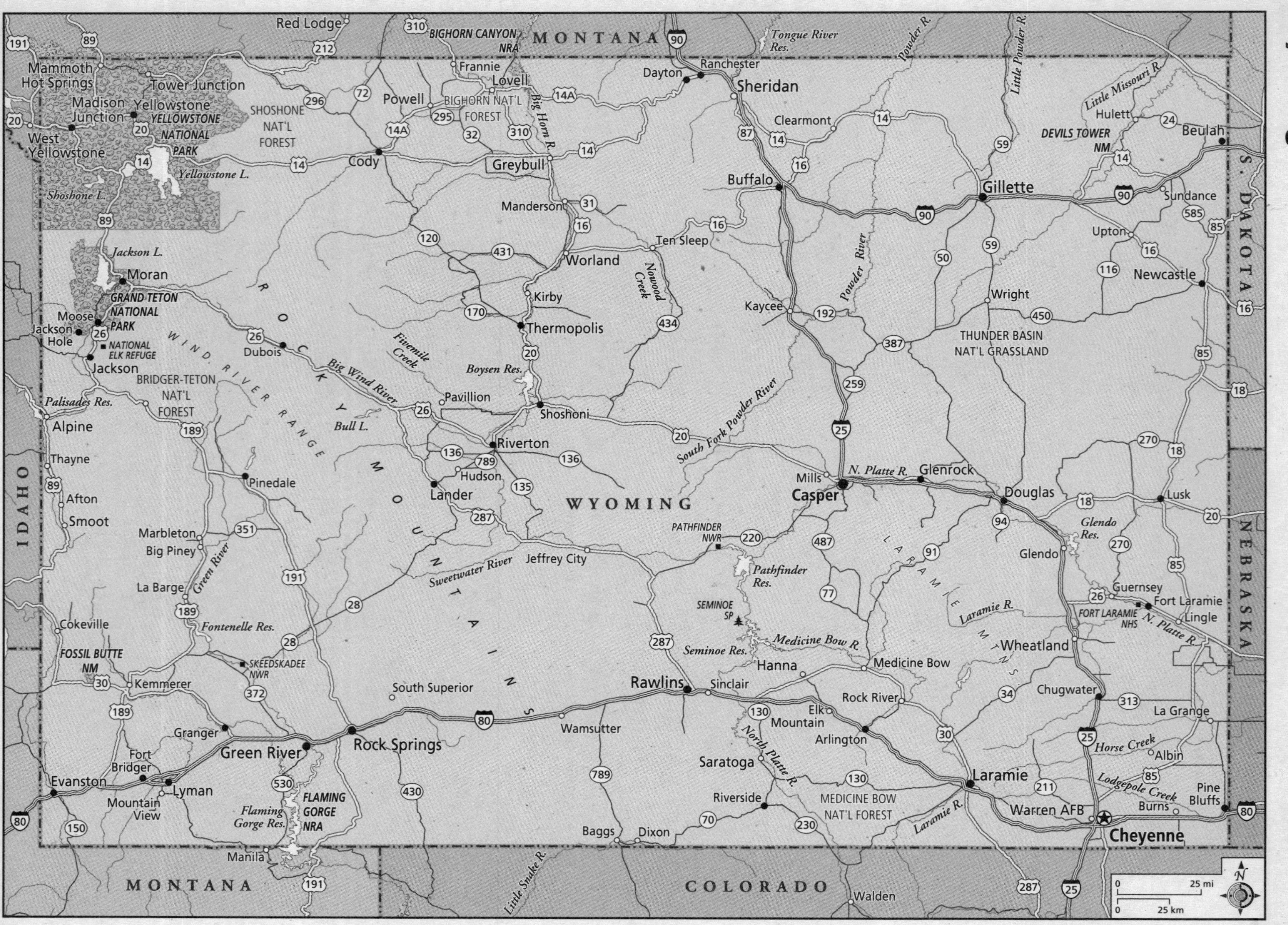

MONTANA
S. DAKOTA
NEBRASKA
COLORADO
IDAHO
WYOMING
ROCKY MOUNTAINS
LARAMIE MTNS
WIND RIVER RANGE
Red Lodge
BIGHORN CANYON NRA
Tongue River Res.
Powder R.
Little Powder R.
Little Missouri R.
Mammoth Hot Springs
Tower Junction
Madison Junction
Yellowstone
YELLOWSTONE NATIONAL PARK
West Yellowstone
Yellowstone L.
Shoshone L.
SHOSHONE NAT'L FOREST
Frannie
Lovell
Powell
BIGHORN NAT'L FOREST
Big Horn R.
Cody
Greybull
Dayton
Ranchester
Sheridan
Clearmont
Buffalo
Gillette
Hulett
DEVILS TOWER NM
Beulah
Sundance
Upton
Newcastle
Manderson
Ten Sleep
Worland
Nowood Creek
Powder River
Kaycee
Wright
THUNDER BASIN NAT'L GRASSLAND
Jackson L.
Moran
GRAND TETON NATIONAL PARK
Moose
Jackson Hole
NATIONAL ELK REFUGE
Jackson
Dubois
Kirby
Thermopolis
Fivemile Creek
Boysen Res.
Big Wind River
BRIDGER-TETON NAT'L FOREST
Palisades Res.
Alpine
Pavillion
Shoshoni
Bull L.
South Fork Powder River
Riverton
Hudson
Lander
Thayne
Afton
Smoot
Pinedale
Mills
N. Platte R.
Glenrock
Casper
Douglas
Lusk
Glendo Res.
Glendo
PATHFINDER NWR
Pathfinder Res.
Marbleton
Big Piney
Jeffrey City
Sweetwater River
La Barge
Green River
Guernsey
Fort Laramie
FORT LARAMIE NHS
Lingle
Laramie R.
Cokeville
Fontenelle Res.
SEMINOE SP
Medicine Bow R.
Seminoe Res.
Wheatland
FOSSIL BUTTE NM
SKEEDSKADEE NWR
Kemmerer
South Superior
Rawlins
Sinclair
Hanna
Medicine Bow
Rock River
Chugwater
La Grange
Elk Mountain
Arlington
Granger
Rock Springs
Wamsutter
Horse Creek
Albin
Fort Bridger
Green River
Saratoga
North Platte R.
Laramie
Lodgepole Creek
Pine Bluffs
Evanston
Lyman
Mountain View
Flaming Gorge Res.
FLAMING GORGE NRA
Riverside
MEDICINE BOW NAT'L FOREST
Warren AFB
Burns
Cheyenne
Baggs
Dixon
Manila
Little Snake R.
Walden
25 mi
25 km

British Columbia

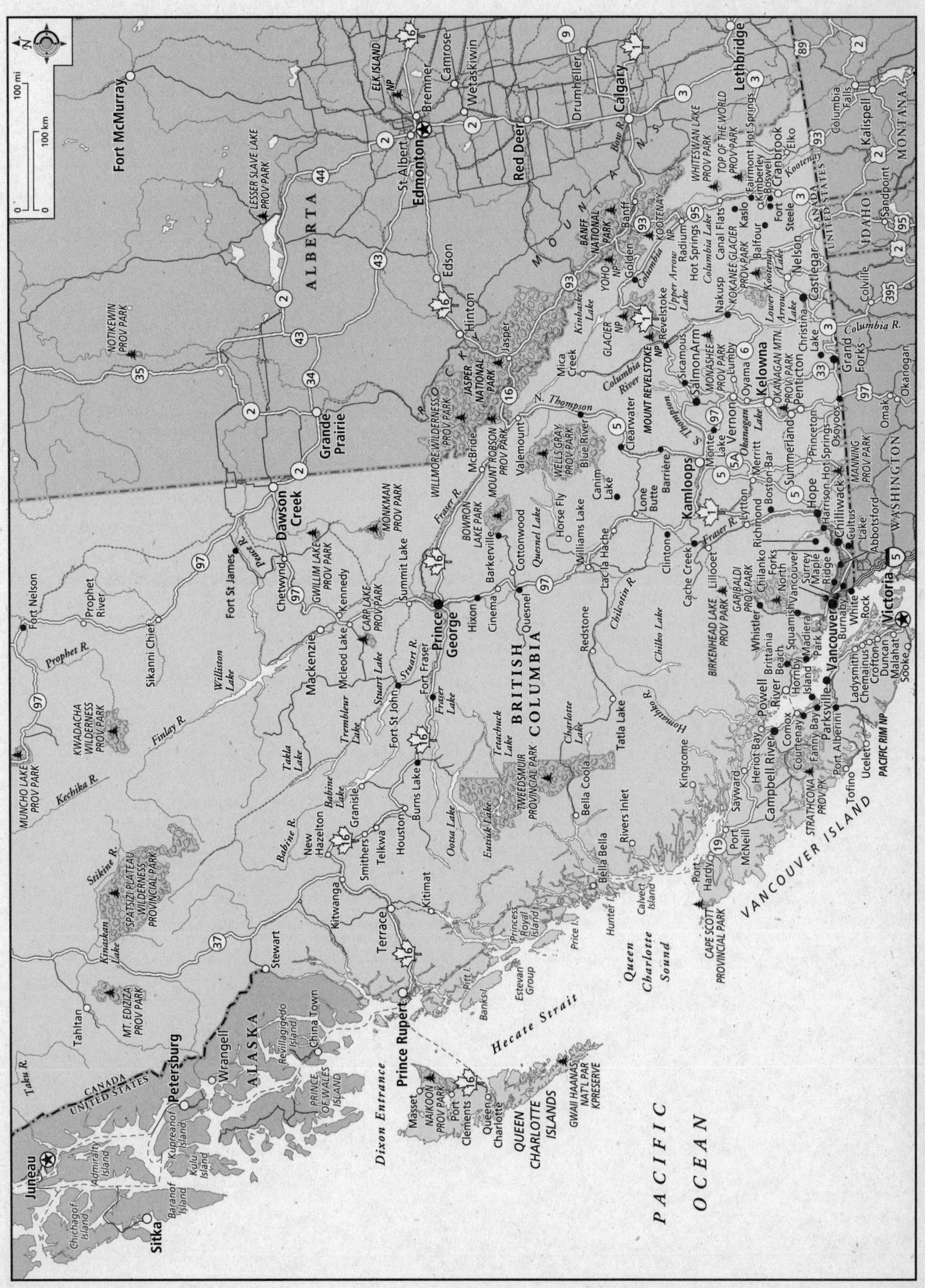

Campground Awards

ALABAMA

Best RV Camping
Clear Creek Recreation Area, Jasper
DeSoto State Park, Fort Payne
Joe Wheeler State Park, Rogersville
Sherling Lake, Greenville

Best Tent Camping
Buck's Pocket State Park, Grove Oak
Clear Creek Recreation Area, Jasper
De Soto State Park, Fort Payne
Joe Wheeler State Park, Rogersville

Most Beautiful Campgrounds
Buck's Pocket State Park, Grove Oak
Clear Creek Recreation Area, Jasper
De Soto State Park, Fort Payne
Joe Wheeler State Park, Rogersville
Sherling Lake, Greenville

Most Private Campsites
Clear Creek Recreation Area, Jasper

Most Spacious Campsites
Clear Creek Recreation Area, Jasper
De Soto State Park, Fort Payne

Quietest Campgrounds
Buck's Pocket State Park, Grove Oak
Clear Creek Recreation Area, Jasper
Sherling Lake, Greenville

Most Secure Campgrounds
Clear Creek Recreation Area, Jasper
Corinth Recreation Area, Double Springs
De Soto State Park, Fort Payne
Joe Wheeler State Park, Rogersville
Pickensville Recreation Area, Aliceville Lake, Pickensville
Sherling Lake, Greenville
Wind Creek State Park, Alexander City

Cleanest Campgrounds
Clear Creek Recreation Area, Jasper
Sherling Lake, Greenville

Best Campground Facilities
Gulf State Park, Gulf Shores
Joe Wheeler State Park, Rogersville
Lake Guntersville State Park, Guntersville
Lakepoint Resort State Park, Eufaula
Little Mountain Marina Resort, Guntersville/Langston
Noccalula Falls Park and Campground, Gadsden
Oak Mountain State Park, Birmingham/Pelham

Best Rural, Farm, or Ranch Settings
Noccalula Falls Park and Campground, Gadsden

Best Urban and Suburban Settings
Doc's RV Park, Gulf Shores
Gulf Breeze Resort, Gulf Shores
KOA Birmingham South, Birmingham/Pelham
McCalla/Tannehill KOA Kampground, McCalla
Perdido Bay KOA, Lillian

Best Mountain Settings
Buck's Pocket State Park, Grove Oak
De Soto State Park, Fort Payne
Monte Sano State Park, Huntsville
Oak Mountain State Park, Birmingham/Pelham

Best Waterfront Settings
Joe Wheeler State Park, Rogersville
Lake Guntersville State Park, Guntersville
Lake Lurleen State Park, Coker
Lakepoint Resort State Park, Eufaula
Little Mountain Marina Resort, Guntersville/Langston
Old Lock 16 Park, Holt Lake, Peterson
Pickensville Recreation Area, Aliceville Lake, Pickensville
Prairie Creek Campground, Woodruff Lake, Benton
Wind Creek State Park, Alexander City

Most Romantic Campgrounds
Clear Crek Recreation Area, Jasper
De Soto State Park, Fort Payne
Joe Wheeler State Park, Rogersville
Sherling Lake, Greenville

Best Family-Oriented Campgrounds
De Soto Caverns, Childersburg
Escatawpa Hollow Campground, Wilmer
Gulf State Park, Gulf Shores
Noccalula Falls Park and Campground, Gadsden

ALASKA

Best RV Camping
Anchorage RV Park, Anchorage
Denali Grizzly Bear Cabins & Campground, Denali Park
Riverside Camper Park, Houston

Best Tent Camping
Granite Creek Campground, Anchorage
Williwaw Campground, Anchorage

Most Beautiful Campgrounds
Bayside RV Park, Valdez
Denali View North Campground, Wasilla
Granite Creek Campground, Anchorage
Mountain View RV Park, Palmer
Oceanview RV Park, Homer
Scenic View RV Park, Ninilchik
Seaview RV Park, Hope
Waterfront Park, Seward
Williwaw Campground, Anchorage

Most Private Campsites
Centennial Park Municipal Campground, Soldotna
Granite Creek Campground, Anchorage

Most Spacious Campsites
Granite Creek Campground, Anchorage
Williwaw Campground, Anchorage

Quietest Campgrounds
Granite Creek Campground, Anchorage

Cleanest Campgrounds
Anchorage RV Park, Anchorage
Denali Grizzly Bear Cabins & Campground, Denali Park

ALASKA (continued)

***Cleanest Campgrounds** (continued)*
Montana Creek Campground, Anchorage
Oceanview RV Park, Homer
Williwaw Campground, Anchorage

Best Campground Facilities
Anchorage RV Park, Anchorage

Best Urban and Suburban Settings
Rainbow Denali RV Park, Denali Park
Ship Creek Landings RV Park, Anchorage

Best Mountain Settings
Bayside RV Park, Valdez
Bear Creek Campground, Seward
Denali Grizzly Bear Cabins and Campground, Denali Park
Denali View North Campground, Wasilla
Granite Creek Campground, Anchorage
Kenai Princess RV Park, Cooper Landing
Mountain View RV Park, Palmer
Oceanview RV Park, Homer
Rainbow Denali RV Park, Denali Park
Scenic View RV Park, Ninilchik
Seaview RV Park, Hope
Waterfront Park Campground, Seward
Williwaw Campground, Anchorage

Best Waterfront Settings
Bayside RV Park, Valdez
Oceanview RV Park, Homer
Scenic View RV Park, Ninilchick
Seaview RV Park, Hope
Waterfront Park Campground, Seward

Most Romantic Campgrounds
Denali View North Campground, Wasilla
Granite Creek Campground, Anchorage
Waterfront Park Campground, Seward
Williwaw Campground, Anchorage

Best Family-Oriented Campgrounds
Denali Grizzly Bear Cabins and Campground, Denali Park
Waterfront Park Campground, Seward

ARIZONA

Best RV Camping
Fool Hollow Lake Recreation Area, Show Low
Kartchner Caverns State Park, Benson
Rancho Sonora Inn & RV Park, Florence
Usery Mountain Recreation Area, Mesa

Best Tent Camping
Catalina State Park, Tucson
Cholla Recreation Site, Roosevelt
Fool Hollow Lake Recreation Area, Show Low
Kartchner Caverns State Park, Benson
Lake Havasu State Park (Windsor Beach), Lake Havasu City
Lost Dutchman State Park, Apache Junction
Picacho Peak State Park, Picacho Peak
Usery Mountain Recreation Area, Mesa

Most Beautiful Campgrounds
Cholla Recreation Site, Roosevelt
Hawley Lake Resort, Pinetop-Lakeside
Kartchner Caverns State Park, Benson
Lone Rock Beach, Page
Lost Dutchman State Park, Apache Junction
Organ Pipe Cactus National Monument, Lukeville
Picacho Peak State Park, Picacho Peak
Usery Mountain Recreation Area, Mesa

Most Private Campsites
Cholla Recreation Site, Roosevelt
Jacob Lake Campground, Jacob Lake
Kartchner Caverns State Park, Benson
Lake Havasu State Park (Windsor Beach), Lake Havasu City
Lost Dutchman State Park, Apache Junction
Organ Pipe Cactus National Monument, Lukeville
Painted Rock Petroglyph Site & Campground, Gila Bend
Picacho Peak State Park, Picacho Peak
Usery Mountain Recreation Area, Mesa

Most Spacious Campsites
Catalina State Park, Tucson
Cholla Recreation Site, Roosevelt
Gilbert Ray Campground, Tucson
Hawley Lake Resort, Pinetop-Lakeside
Jacob Lake Campground, Jacob Lake
Kartchner Caverns State Park, Benson
La Posa LTVA, Quartzsite
Lake Havasu State Park (Windsor Beach), Lake Havasu City
Lost Dutchman State Park, Apache Junction
McDowell Mountain Regional Park, Fountain Hills
Organ Pipe Cactus National Monument, Lukeville
Painted Rock Petroglyph Site & Campground, Gila Bend
Picacho Peak State Park, Picacho Peak
Rancho Sonora Inn & RV Park, Florence
Show Low Lake County Park, Show Low
Usery Mountain Recreation Area, Mesa
Voyager RV Resort, Tucson

Quietest Campgrounds
Cholla Recreation Site, Roosevelt
Fool Hollow Lake Recreation Area, Show Low
Hawley Lake Resort, Pinetop-Lakeside
Jacob Lake Campground, Jacob Lake
Kartchner Caverns State Park, Benson
Lake Havasu State Park (Windsor Beach), Lake Havasu City
Lost Dutchman State Park, Apache Junction
Lyman Lake State Park, St. Johns
Morenga Palms RV Park, Wenden
Painted Rock Petroglyph Site & Campground, Gila Bend

Quietest Campgrounds
Rancho Sonora Inn & RV Park, Florence
Usery Mountain Recreation Area, Mesa
Wheatfields Lake, Tsaile

Most Secure Campgrounds
Branson's Motel & RV Park, Parker
Fool Hollow Lake Recreation Area, Show Low
Havasu Springs Resort, Parker
Hawley Lake Resort, Pinetop-Lakeside
Hon-Dah RV Park, Pinetop-Lakeside
Islander RV Resort, Lake Havasu City
Laguna Beach Campground, Tortilla Flat
Lake Pleasant Regional Park, Peoria
Usery Mountain Recreation Area, Mesa

Cleanest Campgrounds
Black Rock RV Park & Cafe, Brenda
Cholla Recreation Site, Roosevelt
Fool Hollow Lake Recreation Area, Show Low
Havasu Springs Resort, Parker
Hawley Lake Resort, Pinetop-Lakeside
Holbrook/Petrified Forest KOA, Holbrook
Homolovi Ruins State Park, Winslow
Hon-Dah RV Park, Pinetop-Lakeside
Islander RV Resort, Lake Havasu City
Kartchner Caverns State Park, Benson
Kingman KOA, Kingman
LaPaz County Park, Parker
Lyman Lake State Park, St. Johns
Morenga Palms RV Park, Wenden
Organ Pipe Cactus National Monument, Lukeville
Picacho Peak RV Resort, Picacho Peak
Show Low Lake County Park, Show Low
Voyager RV Resort, Tucson

Best Campground Facilities
Black Rock RV Park & Cafe, Brenda
Havasu Springs Resort, Parker
Picacho Peak RV Resort, Picacho Peak
Sandpoint Marina and RV Park, Lake Havasu City
Voyager RV Resort, Tucson

Best Rural, Farm, or Ranch Settings
Black Rock RV Park & Cafe, Brenda
Circle "S" RV Park, Huachuca City
Hon-Dah RV Park, Pinetop-Lakeside
La Posa LTVA, Quartzsite
Morenga Palms RV Park, Wenden
Mountain View RV Ranch, Tumacacori
Picacho Campground, Picacho
Picacho Peak RV Resort, Picacho Peak
Rancho Sonora Inn & RV Park, Florence
De Anza Trails RV Resort, Tumacacori

Best Urban and Suburban Settings
Black Bart's RV Park, Flagstaff
Catalina State Park, Tucson
Cochise Terrace RV Resort, Benson
Covered Wagon RV Park, Phoenix
Crazy Horse Campground & RV Park, Tucson
Davis Camp, Bullhead City
Estrella Mountain Regional Park, Goodyear
Horspitality RV Park and Boarding Stable, Wickenburg
Islander RV Resort, Lake Havasu City
Kingman KOA, Kingman
Krazy K RV Park, Camp Verde
Lake Havasu State Park (Windsor Beach), Lake Havasu City
Manzanita, Sedona

ARIZONA (continued)

Mesa–Apache Junction KOA, Apache Junction
Ox Bow Estates RV Park, Payson
Queen Mine RV Park, Bisbee
Usery Mountain Recreation Area, Mesa
Voyager RV Resort, Tucson
Welcome Home RV Park, Phoenix
Wells Fargo RV Park, Tombstone

Best Mountain Settings

Buckskin Mountain State Park, Parker
Catalina State Park, Tucson
Gilbert Ray Campground, Tucson
Hawley Lake Resort, Pinetop-Lakeside
Jacob Lake Campground, Jacob Lake
Kaibab Camper Village, Jacob Lake
Laguna Beach Campground, Tortilla Flat
Lees Ferry Campground, Marble Canyon
Lost Dutchman State Park, Apache Junction
Lyman Lake State Park, St. Johns
Manzanita, Sedona
McDowell Mountain Regional Park, Fountain Hills
Ox Bow Estates RV Park, Payson
Picacho Peak State Park, Picacho Peak
Ponderosa Forest RV Park & Campground, Parks
Sandpoint Marina and RV Park, Lake Havasu City
Usery Mountain Recreation Area, Mesa
Virgin River Canyon Recreation Area, Littlefield
Wheatfields Lake, Tsaile

Best Waterfront Settings

Alamo Lake State Park, Wenden
Branson's Motel & RV Park, Parker
Buckskin Mountain State Park, Parker
Cholla Lake County Park, Holbrook
Cholla Recreation Site, Roosevelt
Davis Camp, Bullhead City
Fool Hollow Lake Recreation Area, Show Low
Havasu Springs Resort, Parker
Hawley Lake Resort, Pinetop-Lakeside
Islander RV Resort, Lake Havasu City
Kingman KOA, Kingman
Laguna Beach Campground, Tortilla Flat
Lake Havasu State Park (Windsor Beach), Lake Havasu City
LaPaz County Park, Parker
Lone Rock Beach, Page
Lyman Lake State Park, St. Johns
Patagonia Lake State Park, Patagonia
Red Rock Resort, Parker
Sandpoint Marina and RV Park, Lake Havasu City
Show Low Lake County Park, Show Low
Trailer Village, Grand Canyon
Wahweap Campground, Page
Wahweap RV Park, Page
Wheatfields Lake, Tsaile
Windy Hill Recreation Site, Roosevelt

Most Romantic Campgrounds

Catalina State Park, Tucson
Cottonwood Campground, Chinle
Fool Hollow Lake Recreation Area, Show Low
Havasu Springs Resort, Parker
Hawley Lake Resort, Pinetop-Lakeside
Kartchner Caverns State Park, Benson
Lake Havasu State Park (Windsor Beach), Lake Havasu City
Lost Dutchman State Park, Apache Junction
Lyman Lake State Park, St. Johns

Best Family-Oriented Campgrounds

Alamo Lake State Park, Wenden
Black Bart's RV Park, Flagstaff
Buckskin Mountain State Park, Parker
Cholla Lake County Park, Holbrook
Crazy Horse Campground & RV Park, Tucson
Davis Camp, Bullhead City
Estrella Mountain Regional Park, Goodyear
Fool Hollow Lake Recreation Area, Show Low
Holbrook/Petrified Forest KOA, Holbrook
Hon-Dah RV Park, Pinetop-Lakeside
Islander RV Resort, Lake Havasu City
Kartchner Caverns State Park, Benson
Kingman KOA, Kingman
Laguna Beach Campground, Tortilla Flat
Lake Havasu State Park (Windsor Beach), Lake Havasu City
LaPaz County Park, Parker
Lone Rock Beach, Page
Lyman Lake State Park, St. Johns
McDowell Mountain Regional Park, Fountain Hills
Mesa–Apache Junction KOA, Apache Junction
Patagonia Lake State Park, Patagonia
Picacho Campground, Picacho
Picacho Peak State Park, Picacho Peak
Sandpoint Marina and RV Park, Lake Havasu City

Best Family-Oriented Campgrounds

Show Low Lake County Park, Show Low
Usery Mountain Recreation Area, Mesa
Wahweap Campground, Page
Wahweap RV Park, Page

Best Swimming Pools

Covered Wagon RV Park, Phoenix
Crazy Horse Campground & RV Park, Tucson
Davis Camp, Bullhead City
De Anza Trails RV Resort, Tumacacori
Havasu Springs Resort, Parker
Holbrook/Petrified Forest KOA, Holbrook
Islander RV Resort, Lake Havasu City
Kingman KOA, Kingman
Mesa–Apache Junction KOA, Apache Junction
Mountain View RV Ranch, Tumacacori
Picacho Campground, Picacho
Picacho Peak RV Resort, Picacho Peak
Rancho Sonora Inn & RV Park, Florence
Voyager RV Resort, Tucson
Wahweap Campground, Page
Wahweap RV Park, Page
Welcome Home RV Park, Phoenix

ARKANSAS

Best RV Camping

Shadow Mountain, Mena

Best Tent Camping

Crowley's Ridge State Park, Paragould
Petit Jean State Park, Morrilton
Shadow Mountain, Mena
Jacksonport State Park, Jacksonport
Eureka Springs KOA, Eureka Springs
Cedar Ridge, Calico Rock

Most Beautiful Campgrounds

Petit Jean State Park, Morrilton
Jacksonport State Park, Jacksonport
Eureka Springs KOA, Eureka Springs
Blue Clouds RV & Cabin Resort, Edgemont
Cedar Ridge, Calico Rock

Most Private Campsites

Cedar Ridge, Calico Rock
Whispering Pines RV Park, Clinton
Moro Bay State Park, El Dorado
Hardy Camper Park, Hardy
Jacksonport State Park, Jacksonport
Pecan Grove RV Park, Lake Village
Petit Jean State Park, Morrilton
Wilderness Hills RV Park & Campground, Siloam Springs

Most Spacious Campsites

Whispering Pines RV Park, Clinton
Moro Bay State Park, El Dorado
Hardy Camper Park, Hardy
Parkers RV Park, Harrison
Jacksonport State Park, Jacksonport
Pecan Grove RV Park, Lake Village
Petit Jean State Park, Morrilton
Crowley's Ridge State Park, Paragould
Old Davidsonville State Park, Pocahontas
Wilderness Hills RV Park & Campground, Siloam Springs

Quietest Campgrounds

Cedar Ridge, Calico Rock
Moro Bay State Park, El Dorado
Jacksonport State Park, Jacksonport
Craighead Forest Park, Jonesboro
Petit Jean State Park, Morrilton
Crowley's Ridge State Park, Paragould
Saracen Trace RV Park, Pine Bluff
Old Davidsonville State Park, Pocahontas
Rogers/Pea Ridge KOA, Rogers
Wilderness Hills RV Park & Campground, Siloam Springs
Village Creek State Park, Wynne

Most Secure Campgrounds

Petit Jean State Park, Morrilton
Shadow Mountain, Mena
Pecan Grove RV Park, Lake Village
Craighead Forest Park, Jonesboro
Jacksonport State Park, Jacksonport
Young's Lakeshore RV Resort, Hot Springs
Fair Park RV Park, Hope
Hardy Camper Park, Hardy
Cedar Ridge, Calico Rock

Cleanest Campgrounds

Eureka Springs KOA, Eureka Springs
Parkers RV Park, Harrison
Jacksonport State Park, Jacksonport
Shadow Mountain, Mena

ARKANSAS (continued)

***Cleanest Campgrounds** (continued)*
Rogers/Pea Ridge KOA, Rogers
Trav-L-Park, West Memphis

Best Campground Facilities
Eureka Springs KOA, Eureka Springs
Fair Park RV Park, Hope
Little Rock North KOA, Little Rock
Trav-L-Park, West Memphis

Best Rural, Farm, or Ranch Settings
Pecan Grove RV Park, Lake Village

Best Urban and Suburban Settings
Hardy Camper Park, Hardy
Heritage Inn & RV Park, Brinkley

Best Waterfront Settings
Bull Shoals Recreationea, Bull Shoals
Moro Bay State Park, El Dorado

Most Romantic Campgrounds
Eureka Springs KOA, Eureka Springs

Best Family-Oriented Campgrounds
Petit Jean State Park, Morrliton

Best Swimming Pools
Arkadelphia KOA, Arkadelphia
Petit Jean State Park, Carrliton
Eureka Springs KOA, Eureka Springs
Trav-L-Park, West Memphis
Rogers KOA, Rogers

CALIFORNIA

Best RV Camping
Antlers RV Park and Campground, Redding
Casini Ranch Family Campground, Duncan Mills

Best Tent Camping
Figueroa, Buëllton
Grandview, Big Pine
Patrick's Point State Park, Trinidad

Most Beautiful Campgrounds
Big Basin Redwoods State Park, Santa Cruz
Ellery Lake, Lee Vining
Figueroa, Buëllton
Grover Hot Springs State Park, Markleeville
Henry W. Coe State Park, Headquarters Campground, Morgan Hill
Hidden Valley, Twentynine Palms
Red Rock Canyon State Park, Ricardo Campground, Mojave
Twin Lakes, Mammoth Lakes
Whitney Portal, Lone Pine

Most Private Campsites
Patrick's Point State Park, Trinidad

Most Spacious Campsites
Grandview, Big Pine
Tolkan, Shelter Cove

Quietest Campgrounds
Grandview, Big Pine

Best Campground Facilities
Beaver Creek RV Park & Campground, Middletown
Cachuma Lake Recreation Area, Santa Barbara
East Shore RV Park, Pomona
KOA Mount Shasta, Mount Shasta
Lake Skinner Recreation Area, Temecula
Malibu Beach RV Park, Malibu
Pacific Park RV Resort, San Francisco
Putah Creek Resort, Napa
Santee Lakes Regional Park & Campground, Santee

Best Rural, Farm, or Ranch Settings
Anthony Chabot Regional Park, Oakland
Austin Creek State Recreation Area and Armstrong Redwoods State Reserve, Bullfrog Pond Camp, Guerneville
Casini Ranch Family Campground, Duncan Mills
Del Valle Regional Park, Livermore
Henry W. Coe State Park, Headquarters Campground, Morgan Hill
KCL Campground, Carrizo Plain National Monument
Montaña de Oro State Park, Morro Bay
Prado Regional Park, Pomona
Selby Campground, Carrizo Plain National Monument
Woodson Bridge State Recreation Area, Corning

Best Urban and Suburban Settings
Anthony Chabot Regional Park, Oakland
Borrego Palm Canyon Campground, Anza-Borrego Desert State Park, Borrego Springs
Bothe–Napa Valley State Park, St. Helena
Camp Switzerland, San Bernardino
Candlestick RV Park, San Francisco
Carpinteria State Beach, Santa Barbara
Folsom Lake State Recreation Area, Beal's Point Campground, Sacramento
Pacific Park RV Resort, San Francisco
Pismo State Beach, North Beach Campground, Pismo Beach
Samuel P. Taylor State Park, San Rafael
San Onofre State Beach, San Mateo Campground, San Clemente
Santee Lakes Regional Park & Campground, Santee
South Carlsbad State Beach, Carlsbad
Spring Lake Regional Park, Santa Rosa
Yucaipa Regional Park, San Bernardino

Best Mountain Settings
Aspen Grove, Lee Vining
Azalea, Kings Canyon National Park
Big Pine Creek, Big Pine
Boulder Flat, Sonora
Butte Lake, Lassen Volcanic National Park
East Fork, Bishop
Ellery Lake, Lee Vining
Glass Creek, Mammoth Lakes
Goumaz, Susanville
Grandview, Big Pine
Grover Hot Springs State Park, Markleeville
Honeymoon Flat, Bridgeport
Ice House, Pollock Pines
Landslide, Hume
Leavitt Meadows, Dardanelle
Lundy Canyon Campground, Mono City
Mount San Jacinto State Park, Stone Creek Campground, Banning
Peppermint, Camp Nelson
Pine Cliff Resort, June Lake
Plumas-Eureka State Park, Upper Samson Creek Campground, Blairsden
Quaking Aspen, Quaking Aspen/Camp Nelson
Sonora Bridge, Coleville
Tuolumne Meadows, Yosemite National Park
Twin Lakes, Mammoth Lakes
Whitney Portal, Lone Pine

Best Waterfront Settings
Brannan Island State Recreation Area, Antioch
Buckhorn, Orland
Butte Lake, Lassen Volcanic National Park
Cachuma Lake Recreation Area, Santa Barbara
Carpinteria State Beach, Santa Barbara
Casini Ranch Family Campground, Duncan Mills
Clear Lake State Park, Lakeport
Cooper Gulch, Lewiston
D. L. Bliss State Park, South Lake Tahoe
Dixon Lake Recreation Area, Escondido
Doheny State Beach, Dana Point
El Capitan State Beach, Santa Barbara
Elam, Chester
Ellery Lake, Lee Vining
Fairview, Kernville
Fleming Meadows, La Grange
Folsom Lake State Recreation Area, Beal's Point Campground, Sacramento
Gaviota State Park, Santa Barbara
Grasshopper Flat, Portola
Holiday Harbor RV Park and Marina, Nice
Honeymoon Flat, Bridgeport
Ice House, Pollock Pines
Indian Creek, Markleeville
Kern River County Park, Kern River Campground, Bakersfield
Kirk Creek, Lucia
Ky-en, Ukiah
Lake Almanor Campground, Greenville
Lake Hemet, Banning
Lake Jennings Regional Park, El Cajon
Lake Kaweah Recreation Area, Horse Creek Campground, Visalia
Lake Morena County Park, South Shore Campground, San Diego

Best Waterfront Settings
Lake Oroville State Recreation Area, Bidwell Canyon Campground, Oroville
Lake Perris State Recreation Area, Luiseño Campground, Riverside
Lake Skinner Recreation Area, Temecula
Logger, Truckee
Malibu Beach RV Park, Malibu
Mayflower Park, Blythe
Meeks Bay, Tahoma

CALIFORNIA (continued)

Merrill, Susanville
Millerton Lake State Recreation Area, Madera
Moccasin Point, Groveland
Modesto Reservoir Regional Park, Modesto
Montaña de Oro State Park, Morro Bay
Needles Marina Park, Needles
Nelson Point, O'Brien
New Brighton State Beach, Capitola
New Hogan Lake, Acorn West and Acorn East Campgrounds, Stockton
North Pines, Yosemite National Park
Pacific Park RV Resort, San Francisco
Peninsula Recreation Area, Sunset Camp and Fashoda Camp, Pollock Pines
Pinecrest, Pinecrest
Pismo State Beach, North Beach Campground, Pismo Beach
Pit River, Fall River Mills
Pogie Point, Upper Lake
Putah Creek Resort, Napa
Salt Point State Park, Woodside and Gerstle Cove Campground, Jenner
Salton Sea State Recreation Area, Headquarters Campground, Mecca
San Clemente State Beach, San Clemente
San Luis Reservoir State Recreation Area, San Luis Creek Campground, Los Baños
Santee Lakes Regional Park & Campground, Santee
Sarah Totten, Hamburg
Shelter Cove RV Park & Campground, Garberville
Silverwood Lake State Recreation Area, Mesa Campground, San Bernardino
South Carlsbad State Beach, Carlsbad
Spring Creek, Portola
Spring Lake Regional Park, Santa Rosa
Sunset State Beach, Watsonville
Tannery Gulch, Weaverville
Tillie Creek, Wofford Heights
Tree of Heaven, Yreka
Tule Recreation Area, Porterville
Tuttletown Recreation Area, Manzanita Campground, Angels Camp
Twin Lakes, Mammoth Lakes
Wawona, Yosemite National Park
Whiskeytown National Recreation Area, Oak Bottom Campground, Whiskeytown
Wild Plum, Sierra City

Most Romantic Campgrounds

Aspen Grove, Lee Vining
Big Basin Redwoods State Park, Santa Cruz
Big Pine Creek, Big Pine
Boulder Flat, Sonora
Butano State Park, Palo Alto
Casini Ranch Family Campground, Duncan Mills
Culp Valley Primitive Camp, Anza-Borrego Desert State Park, Borrego Springs
East Fork, Bishop
Figueroa, Buëllton
Goumaz, Susanville
Grandview, Big Pine
Hidden Valley Campground, Willits
Honeymoon Flat, Bridgeport
Landslide, Hume
Lundy Canyon Campground, Mono City
Montaña de Oro State Park, Morro Bay
Owl Canyon, Barstow
Patrick's Point State Park, Trinidad
Prairie Creek Redwoods State Park, Elk Prairie Campground, Orick
Ronald W. Caspers Wilderness Park, San Juan Capistrano
Wawona, Yosemite National Park
Whitney Portal, Lone Pine
Wildrose, Death Valley
Wishon, Springville
Woodson Bridge State Recreation Area, Corning

Best Family-Oriented Campgrounds

Antlers RV Park and Campground, Redding
Azalea, Kings Canyon National Park
Beaver Creek RV Park & Campground, Middletown
Bothe–Napa Valley State Park, St. Helena
Buckhorn, Orland
Cachuma Lake Recreation Area, Santa Barbara
Carpinteria State Beach, Santa Barbara
Casini Ranch Family Campground, Duncan Mills
Cuyamaca Rancho State Park, Paso Picacho Campground, Julian
Del Valle Regional Park, Livermore
Dixon Lake Recreation Area, Escondido
Doheny State Beach, Dana Point
Dos Picos Regional Park, Escondido
East Shore RV Park, Pomona
El Capitan State Beach, Santa Barbara
Fleming Meadows, La Grange
Hume Lake, Hume
Kern River County Park, Kern River Campground, Bakersfield
KOA Mount Shasta, Mount Shasta
Ky-en, Ukiah
Lake Hemet, Banning
Lake Jennings Regional Park, El Cajon
Lake Kaweah Recreation Area, Horse Creek Campground, Visalia
Lake Oroville State Recreation Area, Bidwell Canyon Campground, Oroville
Lake Perris State Recreation Area, Luiseño Campground, Riverside
Lake Skinner Recreation Area, Temecula
Leo Carillo State Park, Malibu
Lupine-Cedar Bluff, Bass Lake
Malibu Beach RV Park, Malibu
Mayflower Park, Blythe
Merrill, Susanville
Millerton Lake State Recreation Area, Madera
Moccasin Point, Groveland
Modesto Reservoir Regional Park, Modesto
Needles Marina Park, Needles
New Hogan Lake, Acorn West and Acorn East Campgrounds, Stockton
North Pines, Yosemite National Park
Peninsula Recreation Area, Sunset Camp and Fashoda Camp, Pollock Pines
Pfeiffer Big Sur State Park, Big Sur
Pine Cliff Resort, June Lake
Pine Flat Lake Recreation Area, Fresno
Pinecrest, Pinecrest
Pismo State Beach, North Beach Campground, Pismo Beach
Prado Regional Park, Pomona
Saddle Mountain Recreation Park and RV & Campground, Carmel
Salton Sea State Recreation Area, Headquarters Campground, Mecca
Santee Lakes Regional Park & Campground, Santee
Silverwood Lake State Recreation Area, Mesa Campground, San Bernardino
Spring Creek, Portola
Tillie Creek, Wofford Heights
Tule Recreation Area, Porterville
Tuolumne Meadows, Yosemite National Park
Tuttletown Recreation Area, Manzanita Campground, Angels Camp
William Heise County Park, Julian

Best Swimming Pools

Aspen Grove, Lee Vining
Beaver Creek RV Park & Campground, Middletown
Bothe–Napa Valley State Park, St. Helena
Cachuma Lake Recreation Area, Santa Barbara
East Shore RV Park, Pomona
Furnace Creek, Death Valley National Park
Grover Hot Springs State Park, Markleeville
KOA Mount Shasta, Mount Shasta
Lake Skinner Recreation Area, Temecula
Needles Marina Park, Needles
North Pines, Yosemite National Park
Pacific Park RV Resort, San Francisco
Rio Bend RV Resort Ranch, El Centro
Santee Lakes Regional Park & Campground, Santee

COLORADO

Best RV Camping

Grape Creek RV Park, Westcliffe
Four Seasons RV Park, Salida
RV Ranch at Grand Junction, Grand Junction
North Park/Gould KOA, Gould
Lost Burro, Cripple Creek
Mt Views at River's Edge RV Resort, Creede
Pueblo South/Colorado City KOA, Colorado City
Gambler's Edge RV Park, Central City
Aspen Trails Campground and Resort, Cedaredge
Tiger Run RV Resort, Breckenridge

Best Tent Camping

Idlewild Campground, Winter Park
Camp Dick, Ward
North Park/Gould KOA, Gould
Horsetooth Campground (Stout Campground), Fort Collins
Pueblo South/Colorado City KOA, Colorado City
Steamboat Lake State Park, Clark
Aspen Trails Campground and Resort, Cedaredge
Arkansas River Rim Campground & RV Park, Buena Vista

COLORADO (continued)

Most Beautiful Campgrounds
Stillwater Campground, Yampa
Camp Dick, Ward
Parry Peak Campground, Twin Lakes
Rifle Falls/Rifle Gap, Rifle
Dowdy Lake Campground, Red Feather
Paonia State Park, Paonia
North Park/Gould KOA, Gould
Horsetooth Campground (Stout Campground), Fort Collins
Estes Park KOA, Estes Park
Lost Burro, Cripple Creek
Gambler's Edge RV Park, Central City
Bonny Lake State Park Campground, Burlington
Kelsey Campground, Buffalo Creek
Arkansas River Rim Campground & RV Park, Buena Vista
Tiger Run RV Resort, Breckenridge
Olive Ridge Campground, Allenspark

Most Private Campsites
Tiger Run RV Resort, Breckenridge
Castle Rock KOA, Castle Rock
Mt Views at River's Edge RV Resort, Creede
Lost Burro, Cripple Creek
Horsetooth Campground (Stout Campground), Fort Collins
North Park/Gould KOA, Gould
Four Seasons RV Park, Salida
Stillwater Campground, Yampa

Most Spacious Campsites
Tiger Run RV Resort, Breckenridge
Castle Rock KOA, Castle Rock
Mt Views at River's Edge RV Resort, Creede
Lost Burro, Cripple Creek
Horsetooth Campground (Stout Campground), Fort Collins
Stagecoach Campground, Meeker
Four Seasons RV Park, Salida
Stillwater Campground, Yampa

Quietest Campgrounds
Battlement Mesa RV Park, Battlement Mesa
Tiger Run RV Resort, Breckenridge
Bonny Lake State Park Campground, Burlington
Aspen Trails Campground and Resort, Cedaredge
Gambler's Edge RV Park, Central City
Steamboat Lake State Park, Clark
Mt Views at River's Edge RV Resort, Creede
Lost Burro, Cripple Creek
North Park/Gould KOA, Gould
Meadowlark Cafe, Motel & RV Park, Lindon
Montrose RV Resort (formerly KOA), Montrose
Ridgway State Park, Ridgway
Rifle Falls/Rifle Gap, Rifle
Glen Echo Resort, Rustic
Silver Summit, Silverton
Camp Dick, Ward
Grape Creek RV Park, Westcliffe
Stillwater Campground, Yampa

Most Secure Campgrounds
Prospect RV Park, Wheat Ridge
Denver North Campground & RV Park, Thornton
Yogi Bear Jellystone Camp Resort, Sterling
Pueblo KOA, Pueblo
Blue Mountain Village, Dinosaur
Pueblo South/Colorado City KOA, Colorado City
Gambler's Edge RV Park, Central City
Castle Rock KOA, Castle Rock
Tiger Run RV Resort, Breckenridge

Cleanest Campgrounds
Josey's Mogote Meadow, Antonito
Pinon Park Campground and RV Resort, Arboles
Aspen-Basalt Campground, Aspen
Battlement Mesa RV Park, Battlement Mesa
Tiger Run RV Resort, Breckenridge
Bonny Lake State Park Campground, Burlington
Castle Rock KOA, Castle Rock
Gambler's Edge RV Park, Central City
Cortez/Mesa Verde KOA, Cortez
Craig KOA Kampground, Craig
Mt Views at River's Edge RV Resort, Creede
Lost Burro, Cripple Creek
Durango East KOA, Durango
Estes Park KOA, Estes Park
Ami's Acres, Glenwood Springs
North Park/Gould KOA, Gould
RV Ranch at Grand Junction, Grand Junction
Elk Creek Campground, Grand Lake
Gunnison KOA, Gunnison
Red Mountain RV Park, Kremmling
Carter Valley Campground, Loveland
Montrose RV Resort (formerly KOA), Montrose
Cool Pines RV Park, Pagosa Springs
Pueblo KOA, Pueblo
Rifle Falls/Rifle Gap, Rifle
Glen Echo Resort, Rustic
Four Seasons RV Park, Salida
Silver Summit, Silverton
Denver North Campground & RV Park, Thornton
Fort Collins/Wellington KOA, Wellington
Grape Creek RV Park, Westcliffe
Prospect RV Park, Wheat Ridge

Best Campground Facilities
Aspen-Basalt Campground, Aspen
Tiger Run RV Resort, Breckenridge
Aspen Trails Campground and Resort, Cedaredge
Cortez/Mesa Verde KOA, Cortez
Craig KOA Kampground, Craig
Mt Views at River's Edge RV Resort, Creede
Durango East KOA, Durango
Estes Park KOA, Estes Park
North Park/Gould KOA, Gould
RV Ranch at Grand Junction, Grand Junction
Elk Creek Campground, Grand Lake
Gunnison KOA, Gunnison
Montrose RV Resort (formerly KOA), Montrose
Four Seasons RV Park, Salida
Steamboat Campground (formerly KOA), Steamboat Springs
Denver North Campground & RV Park, Thornton
Fort Collins/Wellington KOA, Wellington

Best Rural, Farm, or Ranch Settings
Meadowlark Cafe, Motel & RV Park, Lindon
Hitchin' Post RV Park, Wray

Best Urban and Suburban Settings
Deluxe RV Park, Denver
La Junta KOA, La Junta

Best Urban and Suburban Settings
La Junta KOA, La Junta
Memorial Park, Brush
Riverwood Inn, Delta

Best Mountain Settings
Battlement Mesa RV Park, Battlement Mesa
Tiger Run RV Resort, Breckenridge
Lost Burro, Cripple Creek
Mt Views at River's Edge RV Resort, Creede
Steamboat Lake State Park, Clark
Horsetooth Reservoir (Stout Campground), Fort Collins
Chief Hosa Campground, Golden
Gould KOA, Gould
North Park/Gould KOA, Gould
Paonia State Park, Paonia
Silver Summit, Silverton
Camp Dick, Ward
Stillwater Campground, Yampa

Best Waterfront Settings
Bonny Lake State Park, Burlington
Pinon Park Campground & RV Resort, Boles
Tiger Run RV Resort, Breckenridge
BRB Crystal River Resort, Carbondale
Cotopaxi KOA, Cotopaxi
Steamboat Lake State Park, Clark
Riverwood Inn, Delta
Horsetooth Reservoir (Stout Campground), Fort Collins
Jackson Lake State Park, Goodrich
Dowdy Lake Campground, Red Feather
Ridgway State Park, Ridgway
Rifle Falls/Rifle Gap Campgrounds, Rifle
Parry Peak Campground, Twin Lakes
Stillwater Campground, Yampa

Most Romantic Campgrounds
Aspen Trails Campground & Resort, Cedaredge
BRB Crystal River Resort, Carbondale
Cedar Ridge, Calico Rock
Lost Burro, Cripple Creek
Mt Views at River's Edge RV Resort, Creede
Estes Park KOA, Estes Park KOA
Gould KOA, Gould
Battlement Mesa RV Park, Battlement Mesa
Grape Creek RV Park, Westcliffe
Stillwater Campground, Yampa

Best Family-Oriented Campgrounds
Alamosa KOA, Alamosa
Bonny Lake State Park, Burlington
Tiger Run RV Resort, Breckenridge
Colorado City KOA, Colorado City
Cotopaxi KOA, Cotopaxi
Craig KOA, Craig
Mt Views at River's Edge RV Resort, Creede
Durango KOA, Durango
Estes Park KOA, Estes Park
Gould KOA, Gould
Gunnison KOA, Gunnison
RV Ranch at Grand Junction, Grand Junction
La Junta KOA, La Junta
La Junta KOA, La Junta
Lamar KOA, Lamar
Montrose RV Resort (formerly KOA), Montrose
Pueblo KOA, Pueblo
Steamboat Campground (formerly KOA), Steamboat Springs
Yogi Bear Jellystone Campground Resort, Sterling

COLORADO (continued)

Best Swimming Pools
Memorial Park, Brush
Castle Rock KOA, Castle Rock
Cortez KOA, Cortez
Cotopaxi KOA, Cotopaxi
Craig KOA, Craig
Durango KOA, Durango
Hudson KOA, Hudson
La Junta KOA, La Junta
Lamar KOA, Lamar
Hud's Campground, McClave
Montrose RV Resort (formerly KOA), Montrose
Pike's Peak RV Park & Campground, Manitou Springs
Pueblo KOA, Pueblo
Steamboat Campground (formerly KOA), Steamboat Springs
Yogi Bear Jellystone Campground Resort, Sterling
Wellington KOA, Wellington

CONNECTICUT

Most Beautiful Campgrounds
Highland Campground, Scotland
Island Campground & Cottages, East Lyme

Most Private Campsites
Beaver Pines Campground, Woodstock
Countryside Campground, Voluntown
Peppertree Camping, Oakdale

Most Spacious Campsites
Aces High RV Park, East Lyme
Lake Williams Campground, Lebanon
Seaport Campgrounds, Mystic

Quietest Campgrounds
Countryside Campground, Voluntown
Peppertree Camping, Oakdale

Most Secure Campgrounds
Highland Orchards Resort Park, North Stonington
Seaport Campgrounds, Mystic

Cleanest Campgrounds
Countryside Campground, Voluntown

Best Campground Facilities
Hemlock Hill Camp Resort, Litchfield
Seaport Campgrounds, Mystic

Best Rural, Farm, or Ranch Settings
Island Campground & Cottages, East Lyme

Best Waterfront Settings
Countryside Campground, Voluntown

Most Romantic Campgrounds
Countryside Campground, Voluntown
Island Campground & Cottages, East Lyme

Best Family-Oriented Campgrounds
Beaver Pines Campground, Woodstock
Brialee RV and Tent Park, Ashford
Deer Haven Campground, Lisbon
Hemlock Hill Camp Resort, Litchfield
Hidden Acres Family Campground, Preston
Seaport Campground, Mystic

Best Swimming Pools
Charlie Brown Campground, Eastford

DELAWARE

Best RV Camping
3 Seasons RV Resort, Rehoboth Beach

Most Beautiful Campground
Cape Henlopen State Park, Lewes

Most Private Campsites
3 Seasons RV Resort, Rehoboth Beach
Big Oaks Family Campground, Rehoboth Beach
Cape Henlopen State Park, Lewes
Lums Pond State Park, Glasgow
Trap Pond State Park , Laurel

Most Spacious Campsites
3 Seasons RV Resort, Rehoboth Beach
Big Oaks Family Campground, Rehoboth Beach
Cape Henlopen State Park, Lewes
Delaware Seashore State Park, Rehoboth Beach
Lums Pond State Park, Glasgow
Tall Pines, Lewes
Trap Pond State Park , Laurel

Quietest Campground
Cape Henlopen State Park, Lewes

Most Secure Campground
3 Seasons RV Resort, Rehoboth Beach

Cleanest Campground
3 Seasons RV Resort, Rehoboth Beach

Best Campground Facilities
3 Seasons RV Resort, Rehoboth Beach

Most Romantic Campground
Big Oaks Family Campground, Rehoboth Beach

Best Family-Oriented Campground
3 Seasons RV Resort, Rehoboth Beach

Best Swimming Pools
3 Seasons, Rehoboth Beach
Big Oaks Family Campground, Rehoboth Beach

FLORIDA

Best RV Camping
Camelot RV Park, Malabar
Emerald Coast RV Beach Resort, Panama City Beach
Florida Caverns State Park, Marianna
Lion Country Safari KOA, West Palm Beach
Nettles Island, Jensen Beach
Outdoor Resorts of Chokoluskee, Outdoor Resorts of Chokoluskee
Rock Crusher Canyon RV and Music Park, Crystal River
Top Sail Hill Preserve State Park: Gregory E. Moore RV Resort, Santa Rosa Beach
Travelers Campground, Alachua
Yogi Bear's Jellystone Park Camp Resorts, Madison

Best Tent Camping
Anastasia State Park, St. Augustine
Blackwater River State Park, Holt
Falling Waters State Recreation Area, Chipley
Florida Caverns State Park, Marianna
Grayton Beach State Recreation Area, Santa Rosa Beach
Highlands Hammock State Park, Sebring
Hillsborough River State Park, Thonotosassa (Tampa)
Jonathan Dickinson State Park, Hobe Sound
Ocala National Forest—Alexander Springs, Altoona
Paynes Prairie State Preserve, Micanopy
Spirit of the Suwannee Music Park, Live Oak

Most Beautiful Campgrounds
Anastasia State Park, St. Augustine
Blackwater River State Park, Holt
Dr. Julian G. Bruce St. George Island State Park, St. George Island

FLORIDA (continued)

Most Beautiful Campgrounds (continued)
Falling Waters State Recreation Area, Chipley
Florida Caverns State Park, Marianna
Fort Clinch State Park, Fernandina Beach, Amelia Island
Grayton Beach State Recreation Area, Santa Rosa Beach
Highlands Hammock State Park, Sebring
Hillsborough River State Park, Thonotosassa (Tampa)
Jonathan Dickinson State Park, Hobe Sound
Koreshan State Historic Site, Estero
Myaka River State Park, Sarasota
Ocala National Forest—Alexander Springs, Altoona
Paynes Prairie State Preserve, Micanopy
Spirit of the Suwannee Music Park, Live Oak

Most Private Campsites
Blackwater River State Park, Holt

Most Spacious Campsites
Craig's RV Park, Inc., Arcadia
Rock Crusher Canyon RV and Music Park, Crystal River
Spirit of the Suwannee Music Park, Live Oak

Quietest Campgrounds
Big Cypress State Preserve, Clewiston
Blackwater River State Park, Holt
Chokoluskee Island Park and Campground, Chokoluskee
Craig's RV Park, Inc., Arcadia
Dr. Julian G. Bruce St. George Island State Park, St. George Island
Falling Waters State Recreation Area, Chipley
Florida Caverns State Park, Marianna
Grayton Beach State Recreation Area, Santa Rosa Beach
Hillsborough River State Park, Thonotosassa (Tampa)
Jonathan Dickinson State Park, Hobe Sound
Myaka River State Park, Sarasota
Rock Crusher Canyon RV and Music Park, Crystal River
Steinhatchee RV Refuge, Tennille

Most Secure Campgrounds
Anastasia State Park, St. Augustine
Arrowhead RV Park, Marianna
Bayside Pensacola—Perdido Bay Kampground Resort, Lillian, AL (Pensacola, FL)
Camelot RV Park, Malabar
Craig's RV Park, Inc., Arcadia
Disney's Fort Wilderness Resort and Campground, Lake Buena Vista
Dr. Julian G. Bruce St. George Island State Park, St. George Island
Emerald Coast RV Beach Resort, Panama City Beach
Falling Waters State Recreation Area, Chipley
Florida Caverns State Park, Marianna
Fort Clinch State Park, Fernandina Beach, Amelia Island
Fort Myers Pine Island KOA, St. James City
Gamble Rogers Memorial State Recreation Area, Flagler Beach
Grayton Beach State Recreation Area, Santa Rosa Beach
High Springs Campground, High Springs
Highlands Hammock State Park, Sebring
Hillsborough River State Park, Thonotosassa (Tampa)
John Pennekamp Coral Reef State Park, Key Largo
Jonathan Dickinson State Park, Hobe Sound
Key Largo Kampground, Key Largo
Koreshan State Historic Site, Estero
Lazy K RV Park, Palm Bay
Lion Country Safari KOA, West Palm Beach
Miami/Everglades KOA Kampground, Miami
Myaka River State Park, Sarasota
Nettles Island, Jensen Beach
Ocala National Forest—Alexander Springs, Altoona
Paynes Prairie State Preserve, Micanopy
Rock Crusher Canyon RV and Music Park, Crystal River
San Carlos RV Park, Fort Myers Beach
Sebastian Inlet State Recreation Area, Melbourne Beach
Spirit of the Suwannee Music Park, Live Oak
Sunshine Key Fun Resort, Ohio Key
Tallahassee RV Park, Tallahassee
Top Sail Hill Preserve State Park: Gregory E. Moore RV Resort, Santa Rosa Beach
Zachary Taylor Camping Resort, Okeechobee

Cleanest Campgrounds
Bayside Pensacola—Perdido Bay Kampground Resort, Lillian, AL (Pensacola, FL)
Beverly Beach Camptown RV Resort, Flagler Beach/Beverly Beach
Blackwater River State Park, Holt
Camelot RV Park, Malabar
Cedar Key RV Park, Cedar Key
Craig's RV Park, Inc., Arcadia
Dr. Julian G. Bruce St. George Island State Park, St. George Island
Emerald Coast RV Beach Resort, Panama City Beach
Falling Waters State Recreation Area, Chipley
Florida Caverns State Park, Marianna
Fort Myers Pine Island KOA, St. James City
Gamble Rogers Memorial State Recreation Area, Flagler Beach
Grayton Beach State Recreation Area, Santa Rosa Beach
Highlands Hammock State Park, Sebring
John Pennekamp Coral Reef State Park, Key Largo
Koreshan State Historic Site, Estero
Lion Country Safari KOA, West Palm Beach
Markham Park, Sunrise
Miami/Everglades KOA Kampground, Miami
Nettles Island, Jensen Beach
Ocala National Forest—Alexander Springs, Altoona
Outdoor Resorts of Chokoluskee, Outdoor Resorts of Chokoluskee
Paradise Island Resort—formerly Buglewood RV Resort, Fort Lauderdale
Paynes Prairie State Preserve, Micanopy
Rock Crusher Canyon RV and Music Park, Crystal River
Sebastian Inlet State Recreation Area, Melbourne Beach
Sunshine Key Fun Resort, Ohio Key
Tallahassee RV Park, Tallahassee
Top Sail Hill Preserve State Park: Gregory E. Moore RV Resort, Santa Rosa Beach
Yogi Bear's Jellystone Park Camp Resorts, Madison
Zachary Taylor Camping Resort, Okeechobee

Best Campground Facilities
Anastasia State Park, St. Augustine
Bayside Pensacola—Perdido Bay Kampground Resort, Lillian, AL (Pensacola, FL)
Beverly Beach Camptown RV Resort, Flagler Beach/Beverly Beach
Camelot RV Park, Malabar
Craig's RV Park, Inc., Arcadia
Disney's Fort Wilderness Resort and Campground, Lake Buena Vista
Dr. Julian G. Bruce St. George Island State Park, St. George Island
Emerald Coast RV Beach Resort, Panama City Beach
Florida Caverns State Park, Marianna
Fort Clinch State Park, Fernandina Beach, Amelia Island
Fort Myers Pine Island KOA, St. James City
Grayton Beach State Recreation Area, Santa Rosa Beach
John Pennekamp Coral Reef State Park, Key Largo
Jonathan Dickinson State Park, Hobe Sound
Koreshan State Historic Site, Estero
Lion Country Safari KOA, West Palm Beach
Markham Park, Sunrise
Nettles Island, Jensen Beach
Ocala National Forest—Alexander Springs, Altoona
Paradise Island Resort—formerly Buglewood RV Resort, Fort Lauderdale
Sebastian Inlet State Recreation Area, Melbourne Beach
Spirit of the Suwannee Music Park, Live Oak
Sunshine Key Fun Resort, Ohio Key
Top Sail Hill Preserve State Park: Gregory E. Moore RV Resort, Santa Rosa Beach
Yogi Bear's Jellystone Park Camp Resorts, Madison
Zachary Taylor Camping Resort, Okeechobee

Most Romantic Campgrounds
Blackwater River State Park, Holt

Best Swimming Pools
Florida Caverns State Park, Marianna
Nettles Island, Jensen Beach
Ocala National Forest—Alexander Springs, Altoona
Outdoor Resorts of Chokoluskee, Outdoor Resorts of Chokoluskee
San Carlos RV Park, Fort Myers Beach

GEORGIA

Best RV Camping
Chestnut Ridge Campground, Flowery Branch
Doll Mountain Campground, Ellijay
Payne's Creek, Hartwell
Shoal Creek, Buford
Skidaway Island State Park, Savannah
Stephen Foster State Park, Fargo
Woodring Branch Campground, Chatsworth

Best Tent Camping
Chestnut Ridge Campground, Flowery Branch
Cloudland Canyon State Park, Rising Fawn
Doll Mountain Campground, Ellijay
Lake Blue Ridge Campground, Blue Ridge
Payne's Creek, Hartwell
Rabun Beach Campground, Clayton
Shoal Creek, Buford
Skidaway Island State Park, Savannah
Stephen Foster State Park, Fargo
Woodring Branch Campground, Chatsworth

Most Beautiful Campgrounds
Bald Ridge, Cumming
Blanton Creek Park, Fortson
Blythe Island Regional Park, Brunswick
Chestnut Ridge Campground, Flowery Branch
Cloudland Canyon State Park, Rising Fawn
Crooked River State Park, St. Mary's
Doll Mountain Campground, Ellijay
Fort McAllister State Historic Park, Richmond Hill
General Coffee State Park, Nicholls
Georgia Veterans Memorial State Park, Cordele
Hard Labor Creek State Park, Rutledge
Lake Blue Ridge Campground, Blue Ridge
Lake Lanier Islands, Lake Lanier Islands
Little Ocmulgee State Park, McRae
Mistletoe State Park, Appling
Payne's Creek, Hartwell
Rabun Beach Campground, Clayton
Shoal Creek, Buford
Skidaway Island State Park, Savannah
Stephen Foster State Park, Fargo
Unicoi State Park, Helen
Vogel State Park, Blairsville
Watsadler, Hartwell
Woodring Branch Campground, Chatsworth

Most Private Campsites
Chestnut Ridge Campground, Flowery Branch
Cloudland Canyon State Park, Rising Fawn
Doll Mountain Campground, Ellijay
Indian Springs State Park, Jackson
Lake Blue Ridge Campground, Blue Ridge
Payne's Creek, Hartwell
Rabun Beach Campground, Clayton
Shoal Creek, Buford
Skidaway Island State Park, Savannah
Stephen Foster State Park, Fargo
Woodring Branch Campground, Chatsworth

Most Spacious Campsites
Bald Ridge, Cumming
Blythe Island Regional Park, Brunswick
Chestnut Ridge Campground, Flowery Branch
Cloudland Canyon State Park, Rising Fawn
Crooked River State Park, St. Mary's
Doll Mountain Campground, Ellijay
Fort McAllister State Historic Park, Richmond Hill
General Coffee State Park, Nicholls
Georgia Veterans Memorial State Park, Cordele
Indian Springs State Park, Jackson
Lake Blue Ridge Campground, Blue Ridge
Payne's Creek, Hartwell
Rabun Beach Campground, Clayton
Shoal Creek, Buford
Skidaway Island State Park, Savannah
Stephen Foster State Park, Fargo
Woodring Branch Campground, Chatsworth

Quietest Campgrounds
Blanton Creek Park, Fortson
Blythe Island Regional Park, Brunswick
Chestnut Ridge Campground, Flowery Branch
Crooked River State Park, St. Mary's
Doll Mountain Campground, Ellijay
Eagles Roost Campground, Lake Park
Fort McAllister State Historic Park, Richmond Hill
General Coffee State Park, Nicholls
Lake Blue Ridge Campground, Blue Ridge
Rabun Beach Campground, Clayton
Shoal Creek, Buford
Skidaway Island State Park, Savannah
Stephen Foster State Park, Fargo
Woodring Branch Campground, Chatsworth

Most Secure Campgrounds
Bald Ridge, Cumming
Blanton Creek Park, Fortson
Bobby Brown State Park, Elberton
Chestnut Ridge Campground, Flowery Branch
Cloudland Canyon State Park, Rising Fawn
Elijah Creek State Park, Lincolnton
Lake Blue Ridge Campground, Blue Ridge
Lake Lanier Islands, Lake Lanier Islands
Mistletoe State Park, Appling
Old Salem, Greensboro
Parks Ferry, Greensboro
Payne's Creek, Hartwell
Red Top Mountain State Park, Cartersville
Shoal Creek, Buford
Stephen Foster State Park, Fargo
Tugaloo State Park, Lavonia
Woodring Branch Campground, Chatsworth

Cleanest Campgrounds
Bald Ridge, Cumming
Brookwood RV Resort Park, Marietta
Chestnut Ridge Campground, Flowery Branch
Eagles Roost Campground, Lake Park
Forsyth KOA Campground, Forsyth
Shoal Creek, Buford
Stephen Foster State Park, Fargo

Best Campground Facilities
F. D. Roosevelt State Park, Pine Mountain
General Coffee State Park, Nicholls
Georgia Veterans Memorial State Park, Cordele
Hard Labor Creek State Park, Rutledge
Lake Lanier Islands, Lake Lanier Islands
Little Ocmulgee State Park, McRae
Stone Mountain Family Campground, Stone Mountain
The Parks at Chehaw, Albany

Best Rural, Farm, or Ranch Settings
General Coffee State Park, Nicholls
The Parks at Chehaw, Albany

Best Urban and Suburban Settings
Atlanta South KOA RV Resort, McDonough
Brookwood RV Resort Park, Marietta
Fair Harbor RV Park & Campground, Perry
KOA Atlanta North, Kennesaw
KOA Chattanooga South, Ringgold
KOA Savannah South, Richmond Hill
Stone Mountain Family Campground, Stone Mountain
The Pottery Campgrounds, Commerce
Twin Oaks RV Park, Perry

Best Mountain Settings
Cloudland Canyon State Park, Rising Fawn
Doll Mountain Campground, Ellijay
Lake Blue Ridge Campground, Blue Ridge
Moccasin Creek State Park, Clarksville
Rabun Beach Campground, Clayton
Unicoi State Park, Helen
Vogel State Park, Blairsville

Best Waterfront Settings
Bald Ridge, Cumming
Blanton Creek Park, Fortson
Chestnut Ridge Campground, Flowery Branch
Crooked River State Park, St. Mary's
Doll Mountain Campground, Ellijay
Elijah Creek State Park, Lincolnton
Georgia Veterans Memorial State Park, Cordele
Hart State Park, Hartwell
Lake Blue Ridge Campground, Blue Ridge
Lake Lanier Islands, Lake Lanier Islands
Mistletoe State Park, Appling
Payne's Creek, Hartwell
Red Top Mountain State Park, Cartersville
Shoal Creek, Buford
Watsadler, Hartwell
Woodring Branch Campground, Chatsworth

Most Romantic Campgrounds
Bald Ridge, Cumming
Blythe Island Regional Park, Brunswick
Chestnut Ridge Campground, Flowery Branch
Cloudland Canyon State Park, Rising Fawn
Crooked River State Park, St. Mary's
Doll Mountain Campground, Ellijay
Fort McAllister State Historic Park, Richmond Hill
General Coffee State Park, Nicholls
Georgia Veterans Memorial State Park, Cordele
Lake Blue Ridge Campground, Blue Ridge
Payne's Creek, Hartwell
Rabun Beach Campground, Clayton
Shoal Creek, Buford
Skidaway Island State Park, Savannah
Stephen Foster State Park, Fargo
Woodring Branch Campground, Chatsworth

Best Family-Oriented Campgrounds
Elijah Creek State Park, Lincolnton
General Coffee State Park, Nicholls
Lake Lanier Islands, Lake Lanier Islands
Stone Mountain Family Campground, Stone Mountain
The Parks at Cheaha, Albany

IDAHO

Best RV Camping
Prospector's Gold RV Park and Campground, Lucile
Riverfront Gardens RV Park, Lucile
Rivers Inn and RV, North Fork
Water's Edge RV Resort, Cascade

Best Tent Camping
Chalis Hot Springs, Chalis
Riverfront Gardens RV Park, Lucile

Most Beautiful Campgrounds
Boise National Forest, Southwestern Idaho Region 3
Bruneau Dunes State Park, Mountain Home
Dworshak State Park, Orofino
Idaho Panhandle Natioanl Forest, Idaho Panhandle
Lake Cascade State Park, Cascade
Payette National Forest, Central Idaho
Ponderosa State Park, McCall
Priest Lake State Park, Coolin
Red Rock R.V. and Camping Park, Island Park
Riverfront Gardens RV Park, Lucile
Rivers Inn and RV, North Fork
Sawtooth National Recreation Area, Ketchum
Swiftwater RV Park & Store, White Bird
Winchester Lake State Park, Winchester

Most Private Campsites
Boise National Forest, Southwestern Idaho Region 3
Chalis Hot Springs, Chalis
Heyburn State Park, Plummer
Huckleberry Campground, Calder
Idaho Panhandle Natioanl Forest, Idaho Panhandle
Payette National Forest, Central Idaho
Prospector's Gold RV Park and Campground, Lucile
Riverfront Gardens RV Park, Lucile
Rivers Inn and RV, North Fork
Sawtooth National Recreation Area, Ketchum
Swiftwater RV Park & Store, White Bird

Most Spacious Campsites
Boise National Forest, Southwestern Idaho Region 3
Chalis Hot Springs, Chalis
Hells Gate State Park, Lewiston
Heyburn State Park, Plummer
High Adventure River Tours RV Park & Store , Hagerman
Idaho Panhandle Natioanl Forest, Idaho Panhandle
Payette National Forest, Central Idaho
Prospector's Gold RV Park and Campground, Lucile
Riverfront Gardens RV Park, Lucile
Rivers Inn and RV, North Fork
Sawtooth National Recreation Area, Ketchum

Quietest Campgrounds
Boise National Forest, Southwestern Idaho Region 3
Carmela Winery & Golf Course, Glenns Ferry
Heyburn State Park, Plummer
Huckleberry Campground, Calder
Idaho Panhandle Natioanl Forest, Idaho Panhandle
Payette National Forest, Central Idaho
Prospector's Gold RV Park and Campground, Lucile
Rivers Inn and RV, North Fork
Sawtooth National Recreation Area, Ketchum

Most Secure Campgrounds
Prospector's Gold RV Park and Campground, Lucile
Riverfront Gardens RV Park, Lucile
Rivers Inn and RV, North Fork
Water's Edge RV Resort, Cascade

Cleanest Campgrounds
Prospector's Gold RV Park and Campground, Lucile
Riverfront Gardens RV Park, Lucile
Rivers Inn and RV, North Fork
Swiftwater RV Park & Store, White Bird
Water's Edge RV Resort, Cascade

Best Campground Facilities
Prospector's Gold RV Park and Campground, Lucile
Riverfront Gardens RV Park, Lucile
Rivers Inn and RV, North Fork
Water's Edge RV Resort, Cascade

Best Rural, Farm, or Ranch Settings
Chalis Hot Springs, Chalis
Payette National Forest, Central Idaho

Best Urban and Suburban Settings
Anderson, Eden (Twin Falls)

Best Mountain Settings
Coeur d'Alene KOA RV, Tent & Kabin Resort, Couer d'Alene
Priest Lake State Park, Coolin
Red Rock R.V. and Camping Park, Island Park
Rivers Inn and RV, North Fork
Sawtooth Lodge, Grandjean
Sawtooth National Recreation Area, Ketchum

Best Waterfront Settings
Henry's Lake State Park, Island Park
Lake Cascade State Park, Cascade
Priest Lake State Park, Coolin
Water's Edge RV Resort, Cascade
Winchester Lake State Park, Winchester

Most Romantic Campgrounds
Boise National Forest, Southwestern Idaho Region 3
Idaho Panhandle Natioanl Forest, Idaho Panhandle
Payette National Forest, Central Idaho
Riverfront Gardens RV Park, Lucile
Rivers Inn and RV, North Fork
Sawtooth National Recreation Area, Ketchum

Best Family-Oriented Campgrounds
Idaho Falls KOA, Idaho Falls

Best Swimming Pools
Sawtooth Lodge, Grandjean
Three Island Crossing State Park, Glenn's Ferry

ILLINOIS

Best RV Camping
Casey KOA, Casey
O'Connell's Yogi Bear's Jellystone Park Camp Resort, Amboy

Best Tent Camping
Casey KOA, Casey
O'Connell's Yogi Bear's Jellystone Park Camp Resort, Amboy

Most Beautiful Campgrounds
Casey KOA, Casey
Green River Oaks Camping Resort, Amboy
Kickapoo State Park, Oakwood
Lincoln Trail State Park, Marshall
Mississippi Palisades, Savanna
Pine Lakes Camping and Fishing Resort, Pittsfield

Most Private Campsites
Casey KOA, Casey
O'Connell's Yogi Bear's Jellystone Park Camp Resort, Amboy

Most Spacious Campsites
Casey KOA, Casey
O'Connell's Yogi Bear's Jellystone Park Camp Resort, Amboy

Quietest Campgrounds
Casey KOA, Casey
O'Connell's Yogi Bear's Jellystone Park Camp Resort, Amboy

Most Secure Campgrounds
O'Connell's Yogi Bear's Jellystone Park Camp Resort, Amboy
Goodfield's Yogi Bear's Jellystone Park Camp Resort, Goodfield
Galesburg East Best Holiday, Knoxville
Lena KOA, Lena
Rainmaker Campground, Litchfield
Cedarbrook RV & Camper Park, Mulberry Grove
Tomahawk RV Park, Pocahontas
Rock Cut State Park, Rockford

Cleanest Campgrounds
Casey KOA, Casey
Lena KOA, Lena
Cedarbrook RV & Camper Park, Mulberry Grove
LaSalle-Peru KOA, Utica

Best Campground Facilities
Cedarbrook RV & Camper Park, Mulberry Grove
Casey KOA, Casey

Best Rural, Farm, or Ranch Settings
Casey KOA, Casey
Cedarbrook RV and Camper Park, Mulberry Grove

ILLINOIS (continued)

Green River Oaks Camping Resort, Amboy

Best Urban and Suburban Settings
Granite City KOA, Granite City
Tin Cup RV Park, Mahomet

Best Mountain Settings
Buckskin Mountain State Park, Parker

Best Waterfront Settings
Geneseo Campground, Geneseo
Green River Oaks Camping Resort, Amboy
Pine Lakes Camping and Fishing Resort, Pittsfield

Most Romantic Campgrounds
Casey KOA, Casey
Cedarbrook RV and Camper Park, Mulberry Grove
Green River Oaks Camping Resort, Amboy
Springfield Best Holiday Springfield

Best Family-Oriented Campgrounds
Goodfield's Yogi Bear's Jellystone Park Camp-Resort, Goodfield
O'Connell's Yogi Bear's Jellystone Park Camp-Resort, Amboy

Best Swimming Pools
Green River Oaks Camping Resort, Amboy
O'Connell's Yogi Bear's Jellystone Park Camp Resort, Amboy
Benton Best Holiday Trav-L Park, Benton
Casey KOA, Casey
Kankakee South KOA, Chebanse
Hickory Hills Campground, El Paso
Palace Campgrounds, Galena
Goodfield's Yogi Bear's Jellystone Park Camp Resort, Goodfield
Granite City KOA, Granite City
Galesburg East Best Holiday, Knoxville
Lena KOA, Lena
River Road Camping & Marina Inc., Oregon
Springfield Best Holiday, Springfield
Maple Aire Crow Valley Campground, Sterling
Ruffit Park, Sterling
LaSalle-Peru KOA, Utica
Okaw Valley Campground, Vandalia

INDIANA

Best RV Camping
South Bend East KOA Camping Resort, South Bend
Twin Mills Camping Resort, Howe
Yogi Bear's Jellystone Park Camp-Resort, Fremont
Woods-N-Waters , Columbus

Best Tent Camping
South Bend East KOA Camping Resort, South Bend
Twin Mills Camping Resort, Howe
Yogi Bear's Jellystone Park Camp-Resort, Fremont
Woods-N-Waters , Columbus

Most Beautiful Campgrounds
Twin Mills Camping Resort, Howe
Yogi Bear's Jellystone Park Camp-Resort, Fremont
Woods-N-Waters , Columbus

Most Private Campsites
South Bend East KOA Camping Resort, South Bend
Twin Mills Camping Resort, Howe
Yogi Bear's Jellystone Park Camp-Resort, Fremont
Woods-N-Waters , Columbus

Most Spacious Campsites
Woods-N-Waters , Columbus
Twin Mills Camping Resort, Howe
South Bend East KOA Camping Resort, South Bend
Yogi Bear's Jellystone Park Camp-Resort, Fremont

Quietest Campgrounds
South Bend East KOA Camping Resort, South Bend
Twin Mills Camping Resort, Howe
Yogi Bear's Jellystone Park Camp-Resort, Fremont
Woods-N-Waters , Columbus

Most Secure Campgrounds
Thousand Trails & NACO Indian Lakes, Batesville
Hidden Lake Campground, Fairmount
Yogi Bear's Jellystone Park Camp-Resort, Fremont
Twin Mills Camping Resort, Howe
Little Farm on the River RV Park Camping Resort, Rising Sun
South Bend East KOA Camping Resort, South Bend
Gordon's Camping, Kendallville

Cleanest Campgrounds
Thousand Trails & NACO Indian Lakes, Batesville
Woods-N-Waters , Columbus
Yogi Bear's Jellystone Park Camp-Resort, Fremont
Little Farm on the River RV Park Camping Resort, Rising Sun
South Bend East KOA Camping Resort, South Bend

Best Campground Facilities
Yogi Bear's Jellystone Park Camp-Resort, Fremont
Woods-N-Waters, Columbus
South Bend East KOA Camping Resort, South Bend

Best Rural, Farm, or Ranch Settings
Eby's Pines Campground, Bristol
Lake Monroe Village Recreation Resort, Bloomington
South Bend East KOA Camping Resort, South Bend
Woods-N-Waters, Columbus
Yogi Bear's Jellystone Park Camp-Resort at Barton, Lake Fremont

Best Urban and Suburban Settings
The Last Resort RV Park & Campground, Nashville

Best Waterfront Settings
Lakeview Campground, Rochester
Manapogo Park, Orland
Thousand Trails & NACO Indian Lakes, Batesville

Most Romantic Campgrounds
Crawfordsville KOA, Crawfordsville
Ely's Pines Campground, Bristol
Old Mill Run Park, Thorntown
Woods-N-Waters Columbus

Best Family-Oriented Campgrounds
Honey Bear Hollow Campground, Peru
Lake Rudolph Campground & RV Resort, Santa Claus
Manapogo Park, Orland
South Bend East KOA Camping Resort, South Bend
Twin Mills Camping Resort, Howe
Yogi Bear's Jellystone Park Camp-Resort at Barton Lake, Fremont
Yogi Bear's Jellystone Park Camp-Resort, Plymouth

Best Swimming Pools
Thousand Trails & NACO Indian Lake, Batesville
Eby's Pines Campground, Bristol
Broadview Lake Camping Resort, Colfax
Woods-N-Waters, Columbus
Lake Holiday Yogi Bear Jellystone Park Camp-Resort, DeMotte
Miami Camp, Frankton
Yogi Bear's Jellystone Park Camp-Resort, Fremont
Mar-brook Campground, Gas City
Sports Lake Camping Resort, Gas City
Twin Mills Camping Resort, Howe
Clifty Falls State Park, Madison
The Last Resort RV Park & Campground, Nashville
Honey Bear Hollow Campground, Peru
Lake Rudolph Campground & RV Resort, Santa Claus
South Bend East KOA Camping Resort, South Bend
Old Mill Run Park, Thorntown
Versailles State Park, Versailles
Lake Monroe Village Recreation Resort, Bloomington
Crawfordsville KOA, Crawfordsville
Gordon's Camping, Kendallville
Lafayette AOK Campground, Lafayette
Yogi Bear's Jellystone Park Camp-Resort, Plymouth

IOWA

Most Beautiful Campgrounds
Clearlake State Park, Clearlake
George Wyth State Park, Waterloo
Lewis and Clark State Park, Onawa
Saylorville Lake, Johnston
Springbrook State Park, Guthrie

Most Private Campsites
Onawa/Blue Lake KOA, Onawa
Saylorville Lake, Johnston
Springbrook State Park, Guthrie

Most Spacious Campsites
Onawa/Blue Lake KOA, Onawa
Saylorville Lake, Johnston
Springbrook State Park, Guthrie

Best Rural, Farm, or Ranch Settings
Onawa/Blue Lake KOA, Onawa

Best Urban and Suburban Settings
Cheyenne Koa, Cheyenne

Best Waterfront Settings
Clearlake State Park, Clearlake

Best Family-Oriented Campgrounds
Lewis and Clark State Park, Onawa
Skip-A-Way, Clermont
Timberland campground, West Des Moines

Best Swimming Pools
Clearlake State Park, Clearlake
George Wyth State Park, Waterloo
Springbrook State Park, Guthrie

KANSAS

Best RV Camping
Topeka KOA, Topeka
Tuttle Creek State Park, Manhatten
Fort Scott Campground, Fort Scott
Crawford State Park, Farlington
Council Grove Lake, Council Grove
Brome Ridge RV Park, Concordia
Covered Wagon RV Resort, Abilene

Best Tent Camping
Camp Lakeside, Scott City
Prairie Dog State Park, Norton
Tuttle Creek State Park, Manhatten
Elk City State Park, Independence
Crawford State Park, Farlington
Council Grove Lake, Council Grove
Covered Wagon RV Resort, Abilene

Most Beautiful Campgrounds
Elk City State Park, Independence
Crawford State Park, Farlington
Council Grove Lake, Council Grove
Evergreen Acres RV Park, Belleville

Most Private Campsites
Crawford State Park, Farlington
Tuttle Creek State Park, Manhatten

Most Spacious Campsites
Council Grove Lake, Council Grove
Crawford State Park, Farlington
Tuttle Creek State Park, Manhatten
Prairie Dog State Park, Norton

Quietest Campgrounds
Evergreen Acres RV Park, Belleville
Council Grove Lake, Council Grove
Crawford State Park, Farlington
Elk City State Park, Independence
Tuttle Creek State Park, Manhatten
Prairie Dog State Park, Norton
Webster State Park, Stockton

Most Secure Campgrounds
Garden City KOA Kampground, Garden City

Cleanest Campgrounds
Evergreen Acres RV Park, Belleville
Emporia RV Park, Emporia
Crawford State Park, Farlington
Fort Scott Campground, Fort Scott
Garden City KOA Kampground, Garden City
Country Squire Motel & RV Park, Hiawatha
Elk City State Park, Independence
Tuttle Creek State Park, Manhatten
Camp Lakeside, Scott City
Topeka KOA, Topeka
Wakeeney KOA Kampground, Wakeeney
USI RV Park, Wichita

Best Campground Facilities
Garden City KOA Kampground, Garden City
Goodland KOA, Goodland
Lawrence/Kansas City KOA, Lawrence
Topeka KOA, Topeka
Wakeeney KOA Kampground, Wakeeney
Wheatland RV Park, Wellington

Best Rural, Farm, or Ranch Settings
Evergreen Acres & RV Park, Belleville
Homewood RV Park, Ottawa-Williamsburg
Topeka KOA, Topeka

Best Urban and Suburban Settings
USI RV Park, Wichita

Best Waterfront Settings
Lake Atwood, Atwood
Evergreen Acres & RV Park, Belleville
Watersports Campground, Dodge City
Council Grove Lake, uncil Grove
Crawford State Park, Girard
Elk City State Park, Independence
Tuttle Creek State Park, Manhattan
Prairie Dog State Park, Norton
Camp Lakeside, Scott City
Webster State Park, Stockton
Topeka KOA, Topeka
Homewood RV Park, Ottawa-Williamsburg
Brome Ridge RV Park, Concordia

Most Romantic Campgrounds
Ft Scott Campground, Ft Scott

Best Family-Oriented Campgrounds
Watersports Campground, Dodge City
Ft Scott Campground, Fort Scott
Garden City KOA, Garden City
Goodland KOA, Goodland
Camp Lakeside, Scott City
Wakeeney KOA, Wakeeney

Best Swimming Pools
Covered Wagon RV Resort, Abilene
Ft Scott Campground, Fort Scott
Goodland KOA, Goodland
Lawrence KOA, Lawrence
Camp Inn & RV Park, Oakley
Wakeeney KOA, Wakeeney
Wheatland RV Park, Wellington

KENTUCKY

Best RV Camping
Cumberland Gap National Historical Park, Middlesboro
Mammoth Cave National Park, Mammoth Cave
Twin Knobs Recreation Area, Morehead

Best Tent Camping
Cumberland Gap National Historical Park, Middlesboro
Mammoth Cave National Park, Mammoth Cave
Twin Knobs Recreation Area, Morehead

Most Beautiful Campgrounds
Breaks Interstate Park, Elkhorn City
Carr Creek State Park, Sassafras
Cumberland Gap National Historical Park, Middlesboro
Dale Holow Lake SP, Bow
Lake Barkley State Resort Park, Cadiz
Mammoth Cave National Park, Mammoth Cave
Twin Knobs Recreation Area, Morehead

Most Private Campsites
Cumberland Gap National Historical Park, Middlesboro
Twin Knobs Recreation Area, Morehead

Most Spacious Campsites
Cumberland Gap National Historical Park, Middlesboro

KENTUCKY (continued)

Mammoth Cave National Park, Mammoth Cave
Twin Knobs Recreation Area, Morehead

Quietest Campgrounds

Cumberland Gap National Historical Park, Middlesboro
Pennyrile Forest SPR, Dawson Springs
Twin Knobs Recreation Area, Morehead

Most Secure Campgrounds

Barren River Lake State Park, Lucas
Big Bone Lick State Park, Union
Dale Holow Lake State Park, Bow
Mammoth Cave National Park, Mammoth Cave
Rough River Dam SRP, Falls of Rough
The Narrows, Barren River Lake, Scottsville
Twin Knobs Recreation Area, Morehead

Cleanest Campgrounds

Dale Holow Lake State Park, Bow
Mammoth Cave National Park, Mammoth Cave

Best Campground Facilities

Barren River Lake State Park, Lucas
Greenbo Lake State Resort Park, Greenup
Kenlake State Resort Park, Hardin
Kincaid Lake State Park, Falmouth
Lake Barkley State Resort Park, Cadiz
Lake Cumberland SRP, Jamestown
Pennyrile Forest SPR, Dawson Springs

Best Rural, Farm, or Ranch Settings

Kentucky Horse Park Campground, Lexington

Best Urban and Suburban Settings

Bowling Green, KY KOA Kampground, Bowling Green
Cincinnati South KOA, Cincinnati
John James Audubon State Park, Henderson
KOA Louisville South, Shepherdsville

Best Mountain Settings

Breaks Interstate Park, Elkhorn City
Carr Creek State Park, Sassafras
Cumberland Gap National Historical Park, Middlesboro

Best Waterfront Settings

General Butler SRP, Carrollton
Kenlake State Resort Park, Hardin
Lake Barkley State Resort Park, Cadiz
The Narrows, Barren River Lake, Scottsville
Twin Knobs Recreation Area, Morehead

Most Romantic Campgrounds

Cumberland Gap National Historical Park, Middlesboro
Mammoth Cave National Park, Mammoth Cave
Twin Knobs Recreation Area, Morehead

Best Family-Oriented Campgrounds

Kentucky Horse Park Campground, Lexington
Levi Jackson Wilderness Road State Park Campground, London
Yogi Bear's Jellystone Park, Cave City

Best Swimming Pools

Carr Creek State Park, Sassafras
Fort Boonesborough State Park, Richmond
KOA Louisville South, Shepherdsville
Levi Jackson Wilderness Road State Park Campground, London

LOUISIANA

Best RV Camping

Chicot State Park, Ville Platte
Kincaid Lake Recreation Area, Kisatchie National Forest, Gardner
North Toledo Bend State Park, Zwolle

Best Tent Camping

Chicot State Park, Ville Platte
Kincaid Lake Recreation Area, Kisatchie National Forest, Gardner
North Toledo Bend State Park, Zwolle

Most Beautiful Campgrounds

Caney Creek Lake State Park, Chatham
Caney Lakes Recreation Area, Kisatchie National Forest, Minden
Chicot State Park, Ville Platte
Kincaid Lake Recreation Area, Kisatchie National Forest, Gardner
Lake Bistineau State Park, Doyline
Lake Bruin State Park, St. Joseph
Lake Claiborne State Park, Homer
Lake D'Arbonne State Park, Farmerville
Lake Fausse Pointe State Park, St. Martinville
North Toledo Bend State Park, Zwolle
Tickfaw State Park, Springfield

Most Private Campsites

Caney Lakes Recreation Area, Kisatchie National Forest, Minden
Chicot State Park, Ville Platte
North Toledo Bend State Park, Zwolle

Most Spacious Campsites

Caney Creek Lake State Park, Chatham
Caney Lakes Recreation Area, Kisatchie National Forest, Minden
Chicot State Park, Ville Platte
Fontainebleau State Park, Mandeville
Kincaid Lake Recreation Area, Kisatchie National Forest, Gardner
Lake Bistineau State Park, Doyline
Lake Fausse Pointe State Park, St. Martinville
North Toledo Bend State Park, Zwolle
Tickfaw State Park, Springfield

Quietest Campgrounds

Caney Lakes Recreation Area, Kisatchie National Forest, Minden
Chicot State Park, Ville Platte
Kincaid Lake Recreation Area, Kisatchie National Forest, Gardner
Lake Bistineau State Park, Doyline
Lake Fausse Pointe State Park, St. Martinville
North Toledo Bend State Park, Zwolle
Tickfaw State Park, Springfield

Most Secure Campgrounds

Caney Creek Lake State Park, Chatham
Chicot State Park, Ville Platte
Grand Isle State Park, Grand Isle
Lake Claiborne State Park, Homer
Lake D'Arbonne State Park, Farmerville
Lake Fausse Pointe State Park, St. Martinville
Tickfaw State Park, Springfield

Cleanest Campgrounds

Caney Creek Lake State Park, Chatham
Grand Casino Coushatta Luxury RV Resort at Red Shoes Park, Kinder
Kincaid Lake Recreation Area, Kisatchie National Forest, Gardner
Lake D'Arbonne State Park, Farmerville
North Toledo Bend State Park, Zwolle

Best Urban and Suburban Settings

Bayou Segnette State Park, Westwego
KOA Kampground Lafayette, Lafayette
KOA Kampground Shreveport-Bossier, Shreveport
KOA Kampground, New Orleans West, River Ridge
Land-O-Pines, Covington
New Orleans/Hammond KOA Kampground, Hammond
Yogi Bear's Jellystone Park, Robert

Best Waterfront Settings

Caney Creek Lake State Park, Chatham
Caney Lakes Recreation Area, Kisatchie National Forest, Minden
Lake Bistineau State Park, Doyline
Lake Bruin State Park, St. Joseph
Lake Claiborne State Park, Homer
Lake D'Arbonne State Park, Farmerville
Lake Fausse Pointe State Park, St. Martinville

Most Romantic Campgrounds

Caney Creek Lake State Park, Chatham
Caney Lakes Recreation Area, Kisatchie National Forest, Minden
Chicot State Park, Ville Platte
Kincaid Lake Recreation Area, Kisatchie National Forest, Gardner
Lake Bistineau State Park, Doyline
Lake Claiborne State Park, Homer
Lake D'Arbonne State Park, Farmerville
Lake Fausse Pointe State Park, St. Martinville
North Toledo Bend State Park, Zwolle
Tickfaw State Park, Springfield

Best Family-Oriented Campgrounds

Yogi Bear's Jellystone Park, Robert

MAINE

Best RV Camping
Bar Harbor Campground, Bar Harbor
Barcadia Campground, Bar Harbor
Bayley's, Scarborough
Cathedral Pines, Eustis
Mount Desert Narrows, Bar Harbor
Narrows Too, Trenton
Palmyra Golf and RV Resort, Palmyra
Papoose Pond Resort & Campground, Waterford
Patten Pond Camping Resort, Ellsworth
Saco/Portland South KOA, Saco
Searsport Shores Camping Resort, Searsport
South Arm Campground, Andover

Best Tent Camping
Bar Harbor Campground, Bar Harbor
Camden Hills State Park, Camden
Cathedral Pines, Eustis
Katahdin Shadows, Medway
Mount Desert Narrows, Bar Harbor
Mt. Desert Campground, Somesville
Rangeley Lake State Park, Rangeley
Searsport Shores Camping Resort, Searsport
South Arm Campground, Andover

Most Beautiful Campgrounds
Bar Harbor Campground, Bar Harbor
Camden Hills State Park, Camden
Cathedral Pines Campground, Eustis
Chewonki Campgrounds, Wiscasset
Hermit Island Campground, Small Point
Horseneck Beach State Park, Westport
Katahdin Shadows, Medway
Lily Bay State Park, Greenville
Megunticook Campground by the Sea, Rockport
Mount Desert Narrows, Bar Harbor
Mt. Desert Campground, Somesville
Orr's Island Campground, Orr's Island
Searsport Shores Camping Resort, Searsport
Sebago Lake State Park, Casco
South Arm Campground, Andover
Barcadia, Bar Harbor
Lily Bay State Park, Greenville

Most Private Campsites
Blackwoods Campground, Acadia National Park
Cathedral Pines, Eustis
Lily Bay State Park, Greenville
Mt. Desert Campground, Somesville
Seawall Campground, Acadia National Park

Most Spacious Campsites
Blackwoods Campground, Acadia National Park
Cathedral Pines, Eustis
Lily Bay State Park, Greenville
Mt. Desert Campground, Somesville
Orr's Island Campground, Orr's Island
River Run, Brownfield
Seawall Campground, Acadia National Park
Woodland Acres Camp N Canoe, Brownfield

Quietest Campgrounds
Camden Rockport Camping, Rockport
Orr's Island Campground, Orr's Island
Seawall Campground, Acadia National Park
Whispering Pines, East Orland
Woodland Acres Camp N Canoe, Brownfield

Most Secure Campgrounds
Acres of Wildlife, Steep Falls
Bayley's, Scarborough
Beaver Brook Campground, North Monmouth
Blackwoods Campground, Acadia National Park
Camden Hills State Park, Camden
Family and Friends Campground, Standish
Four Seasons Family Camping, Naples
Hid 'n Pines, Old Orchard Beach
Honey Run Beach & Campground, Peru
Kezar Lake Camping Area, Lovell
Kokatosi Campground, Raymond
Lake Pemaquid Camping, Damariscotta
Little Ponderosa Campground, Boothbay
Old Orchard Beach Campground, Old Orchard Beach
Orr's Island Campground, Orr's Island
Point Sebago Golf and Beach Resort, Casco
Powder Horn Family Camping Resort, Old Orchard Beach
Rangeley Lake State Park, Rangeley
River Run, Brownfield
Saco/Portland South KOA, Saco
Sea-Vu Campground, Wells
Seawall Campground, Acadia National Park
Shady Oaks, Orland
Shore Hills Campground, Boothbay Harbor
Silver Springs, Saco
Thomas Point Beach , Brunswick

Cleanest Campgrounds
Camden Hills State Park, Camden
Camden Rockport Camping, Rockport
Honey Run Beach & Campground, Peru
Libby's Oceanside Camp, York Harbor
Meadowbrook Camping, Phippsburg
Megunticook Campground by the Sea, Rockport
Mount Desert Narrows, Bar Harbor
Mt. Desert Campground, Somesville
Narrows Too, Trenton
Palmyra Golf and RV Resort, Palmyra
Patten Pond Camping Resort, Ellsworth
Point Sebago Golf and Beach Resort, Casco
Poland Spring Campground, Poland Spring
Powder Horn Family Camping Resort, Old Orchard Beach
Saco/Portland South KOA, Saco
Saltwater Farm Campground, Thomaston
Searsport Shores Camping Resort, Searsport
Sennebec Lake Campground, Appleton
Skowhegan/Canaan KOA, Canaan
Thomas Point Beach, Brunswick

Best Campground Facilities
Bayley's, Scarborough
Megunticook Campground by the Sea, Rockport
Mount Desert Narrows, Bar Harbor
Narrows Too, Trenton
Palmyra Golf and RV Resort, Palmyra
Patten Pond Camping Resort, Ellsworth
Point Sebago Golf and Beach Resort, Casco
Powder Horn Family Camping Resort, Old Orchard Beach
Searsport Shores Camping Resort, Searsport
Thomas Point Beach, Brunswick

Best Rural, Farm, or Ranch Settings
Balsam Woods Campground, Abbott Village

Best Urban and Suburban Settings
Paul Bunyan Campground, Bangor
Pleasant Hill Campground, Hermon
Wassamki Springs, Scarborough

Best Mountain Settings
Katahdin Shadows, Medway
Lily Bay State Park, Greenville
Mount Blue State Park, Weld
Natanis Point Campground, Eustis

Most Romantic Campgrounds
Bar Harbor Campground, Bar Harbor
Lily Bay State Park, Greenville
Searsport Shores, Searsport
South Arm Campground, Andover

Best Family-Oriented Campgrounds
Acres of Wildlife, Steep Falls
Bayley's, Old Orchard Beach
Lake Pemaquid Camping, Damariscotta
Mount Desert Narrows, Bar Harbor
Narrow Too, Trenton
Papoose Pond Resort and Campground, Waterford
Point Sebago, Casco
Powder Horn, Old Orchard Beach
Wild Acres, Old Orchard Beach

Best Swimming Pools
Bar Harbor Campground, Bar Harbor
Megunticook Campground by the Sea, Rockport

MARYLAND

Best RV Camping
Morris Meadows Recreation Farm, Freeland

Best Tent Camping
Morris Meadows Recreation Farm, Freeland

Most Beautiful Campgrounds
Assateague Island National Seashore—Bayside Campground and Oceanside Campground, Berlin
Assateague State Park, Ocean City
Bar Harbor RV Park and Marina, Abingdon
Frontier Town Campground, Ocean City
Gambrill State Park, Frederick
Morris Meadows Recreation Farm, Freeland
Rocky Gap State Park, Cumberland
Assateague Island National Seashore—Bayside Campground and Oceanside Campground, Berlin

MARYLAND (continued)

Bar Harbor RV Park and Marina, Abingdon
Big Run State Park, Grantsville
Cherry Hill Park, College Park
Cunningham Falls State Park, Thurmont

Most Private Campsites
Holiday Park Campground, Greensboro
Janes Island State Park, Crisfield
Little Bennett Regional Park Campground, Clarksburg
Martinak State Park, Denton
Morris Meadows Recreation Farm, Freeland
Patapsco Valley State Park, Ellicott City
Rocky Gap State Park, Cumberland
Yogi Bear's Jellystone Park—Williamsport/Hagerstown, Hagerstown

Most Spacious Campsites
Assateague Island National Seashore—Bayside Campground and Oceanside Campground, Berlin
Bar Harbor RV Park and Marina, Abingdon
Big Run State Park, Grantsville
Cherry Hill Park, College Park
Cunningham Falls State Park, Thurmont
Gambrill State Park, Frederick
Greenbrier State Park, Hagerstown
Holiday Park Campground, Greensboro
Janes Island State Park, Crisfield
Little Bennett Regional Park Campground, Clarksburg
Martinak State Park, Denton
Morris Meadows Recreation Farm, Freeland
Patapsco Valley State Park, Ellicott City
Ramblin' Pines Family Campground, Woodbine
Rocky Gap State Park, Cumberland
Yogi Bear's Jellystone Park—Williamsport/Hagerstown, Hagerstown

Quietest Campgrounds
Assateague Island National Seashore—Bayside Campground and Oceanside Campground, Berlin
Rocky Gap State Park, Cumberland
Yogi Bear's Jellystone Park—Williamsport/Hagerstown, Hagerstown

Most Secure Campgrounds
Assateague Island National Seashore—Bayside Campground and Oceanside Campground, Berlin
Eagle's Nest Camping and Trailer Park, Ocean City
Frontier Town Campground, Ocean City
Holiday Park Campground, Greensboro
Janes Island State Park, Crisfield
KOA—Snug Harbor, Hagerstown
Martinak State Park, Denton
Morris Meadows Recreation Farm, Freeland
Patapsco Valley State Park, Ellicott City
Ramblin' Pines Family Campground, Woodbine
Rocky Gap State Park, Cumberland

Cleanest Campgrounds
Cherry Hill Park, College Park
Frontier Town Campground, Ocean City
Morris Meadows Recreation Farm, Freeland
Rocky Gap State Park, Cumberland
Yogi Bear's Jellystone Park—Williamsport/Hagerstown, Hagerstown

Best Campground Facilities
Cherry Hill Park, College Park
Frontier Town Campground, Ocean City
Morris Meadows Recreation Farm, Freeland
Rocky Gap State Park, Cumberland
Yogi Bear's Jellystone Park—Williamsport/Hagerstown, Hagerstown

Best Rural, Farm, or Ranch Settings
Morris Meadows, Freeland
Ramblin' Pines Family Campground and RV Park, Woodbine

Best Urban and Suburban Settings
Capitol KOA, Millersville
Cherry Hill Park, College Park

Best Waterfront Settings
Bar Harbor RV Park and Marina, Abingdon
Frontier Town Campground, Ocean City

Most Romantic Campgrounds
Frontier Town Campground, Ocean City

Best Family-Oriented Campgrounds
Frontier Town Campground, Ocean City
Morris Meadows, Freeland
Yogi Bear's Jellystone Park, Williamsport

Best Swimming Pools
Bar Harbor RV Park and Marina, Abingdon

MASSACHUSETTS

Best RV Camping
Normandy Farms Family Camping Resort, Foxboro
Pine Acres Family Camping Resort, Oakham
Pinewood Lodge, Plymouth
Salisbury Beach State Reservation, Salisbury

Best Tent Camping
Clarksburg State Park, Clarksburg
Pine Acres Family Camping Resort, Oakham
Pinewood Lodge, Plymouth
Shawme-Crowell State Forest, Sandwich
Wells State Park, Sturbridge

Most Beautiful Campgrounds
Boston Northwest/Minuteman KOA, Littleton
Cape Ann Camp Site, Gloucester
Clarksburg State Park, Clarksburg
Myles Standish State Forest, South Carver
Nickerson State Park, Brewster
Normandy Farms Family Camping Resort, Foxboro
Pine Acres Family Camping Resort, Oakham
Pittsfield State Forest, Pittsfield
Salisbury Beach State Reservation, Salisbury
Shawme-Crowell State Forest, Sandwich
Wells State Park, Sturbridge

Most Private Campsites
Shawme-Crowell State Forest, Sandwich
Wompatuck State Park, Hingham

Most Spacious Campsites
Peppermint Park Camping Resort, Plainfield
Shady Pines Campground, Savoy

Quietest Campgrounds
Harold Parker State Forest, North Andover
Lake Dennison State Recreation Area, Winchendon
Myles Standish State Forest, South Carver
Normandy Farms Family Camping Resort, Foxboro
Peppermint Park Camping Resort, Plainfield
Prospect Mountain Campground, Granville
Shady Acres Family Campground, South Carver
Shawme-Crowell State Forest, Sandwich
Wells State Park, Sturbridge

Most Secure Campgrounds
Boston South/Middleboro/Plymouth KOA, Middleboro
Campers Haven RV Resort, Dennisport
Canoe River Campgrounds, Mansfield
Cape Cod Campresort, East Falmouth
Circle CG Farm, Bellingham
Ellis Haven Camping Resort, Plymouth
Jellystone Park Sturbridge, Sturbridge
Outdoor World—Gateway to Cape Cod, Rochester
Peppermint Park Camping Resort, Plainfield
Peters Pond Park Family Camping, Sandwich
Pine Acres Family Camping Resort, Oakham
Rusnik Campground, Salisbury
Scusset Beach State Reservation Camping Area, Sagamore
Shady Pines Campground, Savoy
Shawme-Crowell State Forest, Sandwich
Sippewissett Campground and Cabins, Falmouth
Sodom Mountain Campground, Southwick
Sunsetview Farm Camping Area, Monson

Cleanest Campgrounds
Bay View Campgrounds, Bourne
Boston Northwest/Minuteman KOA, Littleton
Circle CG Farm, Bellingham
Ellis Haven Camping Resort, Plymouth
Maurice's Campground, Welfleet
Otter River State Forest, Templeton
Outdoor World Sturbridge Resort, Sturbridge
Pine Acres Family Camping Resort, Oakham
Pinewood Lodge, Plymouth

Best Campground Facilities
Bay View Campgrounds, Bourne
Jellystone Park Sturbridge, Sturbridge
Normandy Farms Family Camping Resort, Foxboro
Outdoor World Sturbridge Resort, Sturbridge
Outdoor World—Gateway to Cape Cod, Rochester
Pine Acres Family Camping Resort, Oakham

Best Rural, Farm, or Ranch Settings
Circle Campground Farm, Bellingham

MASSACHUSETTS (continued)

Best Urban and Suburban Settings
Boston Northwest KOA Minuteman Kampground, Littleton
Harold Parker State Forest, North Andover
Pinewood Lodge, Plymouth
Winter Island Park, Salem
Wompatuck State Park, Hingham

Best Family-Oriented Campgrounds
Pine Acres, Oakham
Pinewood Lodge, Plymouth
Sweetwater Forest, Brewster

Best Swimming Pools
Jellystone Park Sturbridge, Sturbridge
Normandy Farms Campground, Foxboro
Outdoor World Sturbridge Resort, Sturbridge

MICHIGAN

Best RV Camping
Petoskey KOA, Petoskey
Monroe County KOA Kampground, Petersburg
Poncho's Pond, Ludington
Indian River RV Resort & Campground, Indian River
Yogi Bear's Jellystone Park Camp-Resort, Indian River
Frankenmuth Jellystone Park, Frankenmuth
Vacation Trailer Park, Benzonia
Vacation Station RV Park, Ludington

Best Tent Camping
St. Ignace/Mackinac Island KOA, St. Ignace
Petoskey KOA, Petoskey
Monroe County KOA Kampground, Petersburg
Poncho's Pond, Ludington
Indian River RV Resort & Campground, Indian River
Yogi Bear's Jellystone Park Camp-Resort, Indian River
Frankenmuth Jellystone Park, Frankenmuth
Vacation Station RV Park, Ludington

Most Beautiful Campgrounds
Camp Cadillac, Cadillac
Castle Rock Mackinac Trail Campark, St. Ignace
Double R Ranch Camping Resort, Smyrna
Fort Trodd Family Campground Resort Inc., Port Huron
Holiday Park Campground, Traverse City
Indian River RV Resort & Campground, Indian River
Interstate State Park, Taylors Falls
Monroe County KOA Kampground, Petersburg
Oak Grove Resort Campgrounds, Holland
Petoskey KOA, Petoskey
Poncho's Pond, Ludington
St. Ignace/Mackinac Island KOA, St. Ignace
Vacation Station RV Park, Ludington
Yogi Bear's Jellystone Park Camp-Resort, Indian River
Vacation Station RV Park, Ludington

Most Private Campsites
St. Ignace/Mackinac Island KOA, St. Ignace
Fort Trodd Family Campground Resort Inc., Port Huron
Petoskey KOA, Petoskey
Monroe County KOA Kampground, Petersburg
Poncho's Pond, Ludington
Indian River RV Resort & Campground, Indian River
Yogi Bear's Jellystone Park Camp-Resort, Indian River
Oak Grove Resort Campgrounds, Holland
Frankenmuth Jellystone Park, Frankenmuth
Vacation Station RV Park, Ludington

Most Spacious Campsites
Fort Trodd Family Campground Resort Inc., Port Huron
Frankenmuth Jellystone Park, Frankenmuth
Indian River RV Resort & Campground, Indian River
Monroe County KOA Kampground, Petersburg
Oak Grove Resort Campgrounds, Holland
Petoskey KOA, Petoskey
Poncho's Pond, Ludington
St. Ignace/Mackinac Island KOA, St. Ignace
Yogi Bear's Jellystone Park Camp-Resort, Indian River
Vacation Station RV Park, Ludington

Quietest Campgrounds
St. Ignace/Mackinac Island KOA, St. Ignace
Fort Trodd Family Campground Resort Inc., Port Huron
Petoskey KOA, Petoskey
Monroe County KOA Kampground, Petersburg
Poncho's Pond, Ludington
Indian River RV Resort & Campground, Indian River
Yogi Bear's Jellystone Park Camp-Resort, Indian River
Oak Grove Resort Campgrounds, Holland
Frankenmuth Jellystone Park, Frankenmuth
Vacation Station RV Park, Ludington

Most Secure Campgrounds
Frankenmuth Jellystone Park, Frankenmuth
Yogi Bear's Jellystone Park Camp-Resort, Indian River
Poncho's Pond, Ludington
Harbortown RV Resort, Monroe
Petoskey KOA, Petoskey
Vacation Station RV Park, Ludington
Port Huron KOA, Port Huron

Cleanest Campgrounds
Frankenmuth Jellystone Park, Frankenmuth
Trails Campground, Frederic
Oak Grove Resort Campgrounds, Holland
Indian River RV Resort & Campground, Indian River
Poncho's Pond, Ludington
Harbortown RV Resort, Monroe
Monroe County KOA Kampground, Petersburg
Petoskey KOA, Petoskey
Fort Trodd Family Campground Resort Inc., Port Huron
St. Ignace/Mackinac Island KOA, St. Ignace
Driftwood Shores Resort & RV Park, Thompson
Headwaters Camping & Cabins, Waters
Vacation Station RV Park, Ludington

Best Campground Facilities
Poncho's Pond
Petoskey KOA, Petoskey
Monroe County KOA Kampground, Petersburg
Indian River RV Resort & Campground, Indian River
Harbortown RV Resort, Monroe
Frankenmuth Jellystone Park, Frankenmuth
Vacation Station RV Park, Ludington
Port Huron KOA, Port Huron

Best Rural, Farm, or Ranch Settings
Crystal Lake Best Holiday Trav-L Park, Ludington
Higgins Hills RV Park Roscommon,
Oak Shores Resort Campground, Vicksburg
Rockey's Campground, Albion
Yogi Bear's Jellystone Park Camp-Resort, Grayling

Best Urban and Suburban Settings
Dutch Treat Camping & Recreation, Zeeland
Frankenmuth Jellystone Park, Frankenmuth
Jerry's Campground, Montague
Lakeside Camp Park, Cedar Springs
Oak Grove Resort Campgrounds, Holland
Palace Campgrounds, Galena

Best Waterfront Settings
Mackinaw Mill Creek Camping, Mackinaw City
River Park Campground and Trout Pond, Grayling
River Pines RV Park & Campground, Ontonagon
Tee Pee Campground, Mackinaw City
Vacation Trailer Park, Benzonia

Most Romantic Campgrounds
Indian Lake Travel Resort, Manistique
Lake Leelanau RV Park, Lake Leelanau
Michigamme Shores Campground Resort, Champion
Poncho's Pond Ludington
Wandering Wheels Campground, Munising

Best Family-Oriented Campgrounds
Benton Harbor/St. Joseph KOA, Benton Harbor
Monroe County KOA Campground, Petersburg
River Ridge Campground, Midland
Spaulding Lake Campground, Niles
Yogi Bear's Jellystone Park of Holly, Holly

Best Swimming Pools
Campers Cove RV Park, Alpena
Benton Harbor/St. Joseph KOA, Benton Harbor
Vacation Trailer Park, Benzonia
Greenbriar Golf & Camping, Brooklyn
Camp Cadillac, Cadillac
Oak Shores Campground, Decatur
Hungry Horse Campground, Dorr
Snow Lake Kampground, Fenwick
Frankenmuth Jellystone Park, Frankenmuth

MICHIGAN (continued)

Gaylord Michaywe Wilderness Resort, Gaylord
Yogi Bear's Jellystone Park Camp-Resort, Grayling
Countryside Campground, Harrison
Whispering Waters Campground & Canoe Livery, Hastings
Oak Grove Resort Campgrounds, Holland
Yogi Bear's Jellystone Park Camp-Resort, Holly
Houghton Lake Travel Park, Houghton Lake
Sandyoak RV Park, Houghton Lake
Wooded Acres Family Campground, Houghton Lake
Indian River RV Resort & Campground, Indian River
Yogi Bear's Jellystone Park Camp-Resort, Indian River
Poncho's Pond, Ludington
Mackinaw Mill Creek Camping, Mackinaw City
Hide-A-Way Campground, Mears
Sandy Shores Campground & Resort, Mears
Silver Lake Yogi Bear's Jellystone Park Camp-Resort, Mears
River Ridge Campground, Midland
Valley Plaza RV Park, Midland
Harbortown RV Resort, Monroe
Shardi's Hide-Away, Mt. Pleasant
Wandering Wheels Campground, Munising
Petoskey KOA, Petoskey
Double R Ranch Camping Resort, Smyrna
St. Ignace/Mackinac Island KOA, St. Ignace
Timber Ridge Campground, Traverse City
Traverse City South KOA, Traverse City
Oak Shores Resort Campground, Vicksburg
Dutch Treat Camping & Recreation, Zeeland
Leisure Valley Campground, Decatur
Vacation Station RV Park, Ludington
Port Huron KOA, Port Huron

MINNESOTA

Best RV Camping
St. Cloud Campground and RV Park, St. Cloud
El Rancho Manana , Richmond
Lakeshore RV Park & Fruit Farm, Ortonville
Stony Point Resort Campground and RV Park, Cass Lake

Best Tent Camping
Interstate State Park, Taylors Falls
Timberline Campground, Sturgeon Lake
St. Cloud Campground and RV Park, St. Cloud
El Rancho Manana , Richmond
Lakeshore RV Park & Fruit Farm, Ortonville

Most Beautiful Campgrounds
Eagle Cliff Campground and Lodging Inc., Lanesboro
El Rancho Manana , Richmond
Interstate State Park, Taylors Falls
Itaska State Park Lake, Itaska
Lakeshore RV Park & Fruit Farm, Ortonville
Silver Rapids Lodge, Ely
St. Cloud Campground and RV Park, St. Cloud
St. Croix State Park, Hinckley
Sullivan's Resort and Campground, Brainerd
Timberline Campground, Sturgeon Lake

Most Private Campsites
Timberline Campground, Sturgeon Lake
St. Cloud Campground and RV Park, St. Cloud
El Rancho Manana , Richmond
Lakeshore RV Park & Fruit Farm, Ortonville

Most Spacious Campsites
El Rancho Manana , Richmond
Lakeshore RV Park & Fruit Farm, Ortonville
St. Cloud Campground and RV Park, St. Cloud
Timberline Campground, Sturgeon Lake
Vagabond Village, Park Rapids

Quietest Campgrounds
Timberline Campground, Sturgeon Lake
St. Cloud Campground and RV Park, St. Cloud
El Rancho Manana , Richmond
Lakeshore RV Park & Fruit Farm, Ortonville

Most Secure Campgrounds
Grand Casino Hinckley RV Resort, Hinckley
Fletcher Creek Campground, Little Falls
El Rancho Manana , Richmond
Silver Lake RV Park, Rochester
St. Cloud Campground and RV Park, St. Cloud

Cleanest Campgrounds
Grand Casino Hinckley RV Resort, Hinckley
Eagle Cliff Campground and Lodging Inc., Lanesboro
Lakeshore RV Park & Fruit Farm, Ortonville
Rochester KOA, Rochester
Silver Lake RV Park, Rochester
St. Cloud Campground and RV Park, St. Cloud
Timberline Campground, Sturgeon Lake

Best Campground Facilities
St. Cloud Campground and RV Park, St. Cloud
Lakeshore RV Park & Fruit Farm, Ortonville
Grand Casino Hinckley RV Resort, Hinckley

Best Rural, Farm, or Ranch Settings
El Rancho Manana, Richmond
Fritz's Resort and Campground, Nisswa
Lakeshore RV Park & Fruit Farm, Ortonville
Old Barn Resort Preston,
Silver Rapids Lodge, Ely
St. Cloud Campground and RV Park, St. Cloud
Whitewater State Park, Altura

Best Urban and Suburban Settings
Town & Country Campground, Savage

Best Waterfront Settings
Cokato Lake Campground, Cokato Lake
Don and Mayva's Crow Wing Lake Campground, Brainerd
Eagle Cliff Campground and Lodging Inc., Lanesboro
Gull Lake Campground, Bemidji
Shores of Leech Lake Campground & Marina, Walker
Stone Point Resort Campground and RV Park, Cass Lake
Two Rivers Park, Royalton

Most Romantic Campgrounds
Country Campground, Detroit Lakes
Old Barn Resort, Preston
St. Croix Haven Campground, Hinckley
Stony Point Campground and RV Park, Cass Lake
Sullivan's Resort and Campground, Brainerd
Timberline Campground, Sturgeon Lake

Best Family-Oriented Campgrounds
Bemidji KOA, Bemidji
El Rancho Manana, Richmond
Gull Lake Campground, Bemidji
Itaska State Park, Lake Itaska
Kiester's Campground, Waseca
Lakeshore RV Park and Fruit Farm, Ortonville
Vagabond Village Park, Rapids

Best Swimming Pools
Albert Lea-Austin KOA Kampground, Albert Lea
Hickory Hills Campground, Albert Lea
Sun Valley Resort and Campground, Alexandria
Beaver Trails Campgrounds, Austin
Bemidji KOA, Bemidji
Gull Lake Campground, Bemidji
Nodak Lodge , Bena
Don and Mayva's Crow Wing Lake Campground, Brainerd
Sullivan's Resort and Campground, Brainerd
Cloquet/Duluth KOA, Cloquet
Cokato Lake Campground, Cokato Lake
Camp Faribo, Faribault
Grand Casino Hinckley RV Resort, Hinckley
St. Croix Haven Campground, Hinckley
Money Creek Haven , Houston
South Isle Family Campground, Isle
Fletcher Creek Campground, Little Falls
Hilltop Family Campground, Ogilvie
Lakeshore RV Park & Fruit Farm, Ortonville
Vagabond Village, Park Rapids
Pokegama Lake RV Park and Golf Course, Pine City
Pipestone RV Campground, Pipestone
Old Barn Resort, Preston
Rochester KOA, Rochester
Town & Country Campground, Savage
Lazy D Campground, St. Charles
St. Cloud Campground and RV Park, St. Cloud
Timberline Campground, Sturgeon Lake
Wildwood RV Park and Campground, Taylors Falls
Pioneer Campsite, Wabasha
Moonlight Bay Resort and Campground on Leech Lake, Walker
Kiesler's Campground, Waseca
Winona KOA, Winona

MISSISSIPPI

Best RV Camping
Roosevelt State Park, Morton
South Abutment Campground, Arkabutla Lake, Hernando

Best Tent Camping
Roosevelt State Park, Morton
South Abutment Campground, Arkabutla Lake, Hernando

Most Beautiful Campgrounds
DeWayne Hayes Campground, Columbus
Piney Grove Campground, Dennis
Roosevelt State Park, Morton
South Abutment Campground, Arkabutla Lake, Hernando
Twitley Branch Camping Area, Okatibee Lake, Meridian
Whitten Park Campground (formerly called Fulton Campground), Fulton

Most Private Campsites
Roosevelt State Park, Morton
South Abutment Campground, Arkabutla Lake, Hernando

Most Spacious Campsites
DeWayne Hayes Campground, Columbus
Piney Grove Campground, Dennis
Roosevelt State Park, Morton
South Abutment Campground, Arkabutla Lake, Hernando
Town Creek Campground, Columbus

Quietest Campgrounds
Roosevelt State Park, Morton
South Abutment Campground, Arkabutla Lake, Hernando
Town Creek Campground, Columbus
Whitten Park Campground (formerly called Fulton Campground), Fulton

Most Secure Campgrounds
Blue Bluff, Aberdeen
DeWayne Hayes Campground, Columbus
Piney Grove Campground, Dennis
South Abutment Campground, Arkabutla Lake, Hernando
Twitley Branch Camping Area, Okatibee Lake, Meridian
Whitten Park Campground (formerly called Fulton Campground), Fulton

Cleanest Campgrounds
Piney Grove Campground, Dennis
South Abutment Campground, Arkabutla Lake, Hernando
Town Creek Campground, Columbus
Wallace Creek Campground Enid Lake, Enid
Whitten Park Campground (formerly called Fulton Campground), Fulton

Best Campground Facilities
LeFleur's Bluff State Park, Jackson
Percy Quinn State Park, McComb
Roosevelt State Park, Morton

Best Urban and Suburban Settings
Baywood Campground–RV Park, Gulfport
LeFleur's Bluff State Park, Jackson
Magnolia RV Park, Vicksburg
Mazalea Travel Park, Biloxi
Parker's Landing, Biloxi
Plantation Park, Natchez
Timberlake Campground and RV Park, Jackson

Best Waterfront Settings
Blue Bluff, Aberdeen
DeWayne Hayes Campground, Columbus
Paul B. Johnson State Park, Hattiesburg
Piney Grove Campground, Dennis
Roosevelt State Park, Morton
South Abutment Campground, Arkabutla Lake, Hernando
Town Creek Campground, Columbus
Twitley Branch Camping Area, Okatibee Lake, Meridian
Wallace Creek Campground, Enid Lake, Enid
Whitten Park Campground (formerly called Fulton Campground), Fulton

Most Romantic Campgrounds
Piney Grove Campground, Dennis
Roosevelt State Park, Morton
South Abutment Campground, Arkabutla Lake, Hernando
Whitten Park Campground (formerly called Fulton Campground), Fulton

Best Family-Oriented Campgrounds
Buccaneer State Park, Waveland

MISSOURI

Best RV Camping
Basswood Country Inn & RV Resort, Platte City
Perryville/Cape Girardeau KOA, Perryville
Peculiar Park Place, Peculiar
Kan-Do Kampground RV Park, Danville
Cottonwoods RV Park, Columbia

Best Tent Camping
Lake Wappapello State Park, Williamsville
Native Experience Adventure Campground, Sullivan
Perryville/Cape Girardeau KOA, Perryville
Long Branch Lake State Park, Macon
Gravois Creek Campground, Gravois Mills
Jacks Fork Campground, Eminence
Kan-Do Kampground RV Park, Danville
Trail of Tears State Park, Cape Girardeau
Down Under Camp Resort, Cameron

Most Beautiful Campgrounds
Lake Wappapello State Park, Williamsville
Pheasant Acres, St. James
Travelers Park Campground, Springfield
Elk River Floats Wayside Campground, Noel
Long Branch Lake State Park, Macon
Gravois Creek Campground, Gravois Mills
McCullough Park Campground, Chillicothe
Heavenly Days Resort & Campground, Camdenton

Most Private Campsites
Lamar KOA, Lamar
Pine Trails RV Ranch, Monett
Pheasant Acres, St. James
Lake Wappapello State Park, Williamsville

Most Spacious Campsites
McCullough Park Campground, Chillicothe
Jacks Fork Campground, Eminence
Lamar KOA, Lamar
Travelers Park Campground, Springfield
Lake Wappapello State Park, Williamsville

Quietest Campgrounds
Down Under Camp Resort, Cameron
Trail of Tears State Park, Cape Girardeau
McCullough Park Campground, Chillicothe
Parks Bluff Campground, Lesterville
Long Branch Lake State Park, Macon
Thompson Campground, Moberly
Pheasant Acres, St. James
Lake Wappapello State Park, Williamsville

Most Secure Campgrounds
Lake Wappapello State Park, Williamsville
Native Experience Adventure Campground, Sullivan
St. Louis RV Park, St. Louis
Pheasant Acres, St. James
Hinton Park, Sikeston
Basswood Country Inn & RV Resort, Platte City
Peculiar Park Place, Peculiar
Elk River Floats Wayside Campground, Noel
Pine Trails RV Ranch, Monett
Thompson Campground, Moberly
Long Branch Lake State Park, Macon
Parks Bluff Campground, Lesterville
Injun Joe Campground, Hannibal
Gravois Creek Campground, Gravois Mills
Rocky River Resort, Doniphan
Cottonwoods RV Park, Columbia
McCullough Park Campground, Chillicothe
Ballard's Campground, Carthage
Trail of Tears State Park, Cape Girardeau
Down Under Camp Resort, Cameron

Cleanest Campgrounds
Cottonwoods RV Park, Columbia
Kan-Do Kampground RV Park, Danville
Hayti-Portageville KOA, Hayti
Lamar KOA, Lamar
Lebanon KOA, Lebanon
Pine Trails RV Ranch, Monett
Peculiar Park Place, Peculiar
Perryville/Cape Girardeau KOA, Perryville
Basswood Country Inn & RV Resort, Platte City
Pheasant Acres, St. James
St. Louis RV Park, St. Louis
Native Experience Adventure Campground, Sullivan

MISSOURI (continued)

Best Campground Facilities
Cottonwoods RV Park, Columbia
Hayti-Portageville KOA, Hayti
Lamar KOA, Lamar
Lebanon KOA, Lebanon
Perryville/Cape Girardeau KOA, Perryville
Basswood Country Inn & RV Resort, Platte City
Native Experience Adventure Campground, Sullivan

Best Rural, Farm, or Ranch Settings
McCullough Park Campground, Chillicothe
Kan-Do Kampground & RV Park, Danville
Pheasant Acres Campground, St James

Best Urban and Suburban Settings
Ozark RV Park, Ozark
St Louis RV Park, St Louis

Best Waterfront Settings
Heavenly Days Resort & Campground, Camdenton
Trail of Tears State Park, Cape Girardeau
Truman Lake State Park (Sparrofoot Campground), Clinton
Gravois Creek Campground, Gravois Mills
Thousand Hills State Park, Kirksville
Parks Bluff Campground, Lesterville
Long Branch State Park, Macon
Elk River Floats Wayside Campground, Noel
Lake Wappapello State Park, Williamsville

Most Romantic Campgrounds
Heavenly Days Resort & Campground, Camdenton
Basswooduntry Inn & RV Resort, Platte City

Best Family-Oriented Campgrounds
Down Under Camp Resort, Cameron
Heavenly Days Resort & Campground, Camdenton
McCullough Park Campground, Chillicothe
Trail of Tears State Park, Cape Girardeau
Truman Lake State Park (Sparrofoot Campground), Clinton
Injun Joe Campground, Hannibal
Injun Joe Campground, Hannibal
KOA Hayti-Portageville, Hayti
Lamar KOA, Lamar
Lebanon KOA, Lebanon
Elk River Floats Wayside Campground, Noel
Oak Grove KOA, Oak Grove
Basswooduntry Inn & RV Resort, Platte City
Perryville KOA, Perryville
Native Experience Adventure Campground, Sullivan

Best Swimming Pools
Down Under Camp Resort, Cameron
Kan-Do Kampground & RV Park, Danville
Injun Joe Campground, Hannibal
KOA Hayti-Portageville, Hayti
Lamar KOA, Lamar
Lebanon KOA, Lebanon
Miller's Kampark, Liberty
Lazy Days Campground, Marshall
Missouri Park Campground, Mountain Grove
Thompson Campground, Moberly
Oak Grove KOA, Oak Grove
Basswooduntry Inn & RV Resort, Platte City
Perryville KOA, Perryville
AOK Overnite Kampground, St Joseph
Native Experience Adventure Campground, Sullivan
Pheasant Acres Campground, St James
St Louis RV Park, St Louis
Traveler's Park Campground, Springfield

MONTANA

Best RV Camping
Bismark KOA, Bismark
Madison River Cabins & RV, Cameron
Mountain Meadow Campground, Hungry Horse
Polson/Flathead Lake KOA, Polson
Timber Wolf Resort, Hungry Horse
Whitefish-Glacier KOA Kampground, Whitefish
Yellowstones Edge RV Park, Livingston

Best Tent Camping
Jefferson River Campground, Silver Star
Madison River Cabins & RV, Cameron
Mountain Meadow Campground, Hungry Horse
Polson/Flathead Lake KOA, Polson
Timber Wolf Resort, Hungry Horse
Whitefish-Glacier KOA Kampground, Whitefish
Yellowstones Edge RV Park, Livingston

Most Beautiful Campgrounds
Campground St. Regis, St. Regis
Flathead Lake State Park, Polson/Flathead Lake area
Glacier Campground, West Glacier
Glacier National Park, West Glacier
Lake Holter Recreation Area, Wolf Creek
Madison River and RV, Cameron
Mountain Meadow Campground, Hungry Horse
Paradise Valley KOA, Livingston
Pipestone Campground, Whitehall
Polson/Flathead Lake KOA, Polson
Timber Wolf Resort, Hungry Horse

Most Private Campsites
Campground St. Regis, St. Regis
Cardwell Store & RV Park, Cardwell
Glacier Campground, West Glacier
Mountain Meadow Campground, Hungry Horse
Yellowstone River RV Park & Campground, Billings
Yellowstones Edge RV Park, Livingston

Most Spacious Campsites
Campground St. Regis, St. Regis
Cardwell Store & RV Park, Cardwell
Glacier Campground, West Glacier
Helena Campground & RV Park, Helena
Mountain Meadow Campground, Hungry Horse
Yellowstone River RV Park & Campground, Billings
Yellowstones Edge RV Park, Livingston

Quietest Campgrounds
Mountain Meadow Campground, Hungry Horse
Shady Grove RV Park & Campground, Cut Bank
Timber Wolf Resort, Hungry Horse
Yellowstones Edge RV Park, Livingston

Most Secure Campgrounds
Illahe Campground, Gold Beach
Madison River Cabins & RV, Cameron

Most Secure Campgrounds
Mountain Meadow Campground, Hungry Horse
Polson/Flathead Lake KOA, Polson
Timber Wolf Resort, Hungry Horse
Whitefish-Glacier KOA Kampground, Whitefish
Yellowstones Edge RV Park, Livingston

Cleanest Campgrounds
Arrowhead Resort, Elmo
Campground St. Regis, St. Regis
Glacier Campground, West Glacier
Madison River and RV, Cameron
Madison River Cabins & RV, Cameron
Mountain Meadow Campground, Hungry Horse
Polson/Flathead Lake KOA, Polson
Yellowstones Edge RV Park, Livingston

Best Campground Facilities
Madison River Cabins & RV, Cameron
Mountain Meadow Campground, Hungry Horse
Polson/Flathead Lake KOA, Polson
Timber Wolf Resort, Hungry Horse
Whitefish-Glacier KOA Kampground, Whitefish
Yellowstones Edge RV Park, Livingston

Best Urban and Suburban Settings
Buffalo KOA Kampground, LLC, Buffalo

Best Mountain Settings
Glacier Campground, West Glacier
Glacier National Park, West Glacier
Mountain Meadow Campground, Hungry Horse
Whitefish-Glacier KOA Kampground, Whitefish

Best Waterfront Settings
Flathead Lake State Park, Polson/Flathead Lake area
Lake Holter Recreation Area, Wolf Creek

Most Romantic Campgrounds
Campground St. Regis, St. Regis
Glacier Campground, West Glacier
Mountain Meadow Campground, Hungry Horse

Best Family-Oriented Campgrounds
Whitefish-Glacier KOA Kampground, Whitefish

Best Swimming Pools
Arrowhead Resort, Elmo

NEBRASKA

Most Beautiful Campgrounds
Chadron State Park, Chadron
Fort Robinson State Park, Crawford
Lewis and Clark State Recreation Area, Crofton
Niobrara State Park, Niobrara

Best Rural, Farm, or Ranch Settings
Branched Oak State Recreation Area , Lincoln (Raymond)

Best Urban and Suburban Settings
Camp-A-Way, Lincoln

Best Family-Oriented Campgrounds
Double Nickel Campground, Waco
Eugene T Mahoney, Ashland

Best Swimming Pools
Lewis and Clark State Recreation Area, Crofton

NEVADA

Best Tent Camping
Cottonwood Cove, Cottonwood Cove
Echo Bay, Lake Mead National Recreation Area
Echo Canyon State Park, Pioche
Lower & Upper Lehman Creek Campgrounds, Great Basin National Park
Spring Valley State Park, Ursine
Valley of Fire State Park, Overton
Ward Mountain Campground, Ely

Most Beautiful Campgrounds
Boulder Beach, Boulder City
Cottonwood Cove, Cottonwood Cove
Echo Canyon State Park, Pioche
Hilltop Campground, Spring Mountain National Recreation Area
Lower & Upper Lehman Creek Campgrounds, Great Basin National Park
Sportsman's Beach Recreation Site, Walker Lake
Spring Valley State Park, Ursine
Valley of Fire State Park, Overton
Ward Mountain Campground, Ely

Most Private Campsites
Berlin Ichthyosaur State Park, Gabbs
Cottonwood Cove, Cottonwood Cove
Echo Canyon State Park, Pioche
Hilltop Campground, Spring Mountain National Recreation Area
Kyle Canyon & Fletcher View Campgrounds, Spring Mountain National Recreation Area
Lower & Upper Lehman Creek Campgrounds, Great Basin National Park
McWilliams & Dolomite Campgrounds, Lee Canyon Recreation Area
Spring Valley State Park, Ursine
Valley of Fire State Park, Overton
Ward Mountain Campground, Ely
Washoe Lake State Park, Carson City

Quietest Campgrounds
Berlin Ichthyosaur State Park, Gabbs
Boulder Beach, Boulder City
Cave Lake State Park, Ely
Cottonwood Cove, Cottonwood Cove
Hilltop Campground, Spring Mountain National Recreation Area
Lower & Upper Lehman Creek Campgrounds, Great Basin National Park
McWilliams & Dolomite Campgrounds, Lee Canyon Recreation Area
Spring Valley State Park, Ursine
Valley of Fire State Park, Overton

Most Secure Campgrounds
Cottonwood Cove, Cottonwood Cove
Silverton Hotel Casino RV Park, Las Vegas

Cleanest Campgrounds
Boulder Beach, Boulder City
Cottonwood Cove, Cottonwood Cove
Las Vegas Bay Campground, Henderson
Longstreet Inn, Casino, RV Park & Golf Club, Amargosa Valley
McWilliams & Dolomite Campgrounds, Lee Canyon Recreation Area

Best Campground Facilities
The Station House, Tonopah
Cottonwood Cove, Cottonwood Cove
Longstreet Inn, Casino, RV Park & Golf Club, Amargosa Valley
Silverton Hotel Casino RV Park, Las Vegas

Best Rural, Farm, or Ranch Settings
Davis Creek Regional Park, Carson City
Echo Canyon State Park, Pioche
Fort Churchill State Historic Park, Silver Springs
Quik-Pik Mini Mart & Campground, Rachel
Valley View RV Park, Elko

Best Urban and Suburban Settings
Hi-Desert RV Park, Winnemucca
Silverton Hotel Casino RV Park, Las Vegas
Young's RV Park, Caliente

Best Mountain Settings
Berlin Ichthyosaur State Park, Gabbs
Cathedral Gorge State Park, Panaca
Cave Lake State Park, Ely
Davis Creek Regional Park, Carson City
Hilltop Campground, Spring Mountain National Recreation Area
Lower & Upper Lehman Creek Campgrounds, Great Basin National Park
McWilliams & Dolomite Campgrounds, Lee Canyon Recreation Area
Spring Valley State Park, Ursine
13 Mile Campground, Red Rock Canyon National Conservation Area
Valley of Fire State Park, Overton
Ward Mountain Campground, Ely
Washoe Lake State Park, Carson City
Zephyr Cove RV Park & Campground, Lake Tahoe

Best Waterfront Settings
Boulder Beach, Boulder City
Cave Lake State Park, Ely
Echo Canyon State Park, Pioche
Lahontan State Recreation Area/Silver Springs Beach, Silver Springs
Las Vegas Bay Campground, Henderson
Overton Beach Marina, Overton
Sportsman's Beach Recreation Site, Walker Lake
Spring Valley State Park, Ursine

Most Romantic Campgrounds
Berlin Ichthyosaur State Park, Gabbs
Cathedral Gorge State Park, Panaca
Hilltop Campground, Spring Mountain National Recreation Area
Lahontan State Recreation Area/Silver Springs Beach, Silver Springs
Lower & Upper Lehman Creek Campgrounds, Great Basin National Park
Valley of Fire State Park, Overton

Best Family-Oriented Campgrounds
Davis Creek Regional Park, Carson City
Hi-Desert RV Park, Winnemucca
Katherine Campground, Boulder City
Lower & Upper Lehman Creek Campgrounds, Great Basin National Park

Best Swimming Pools
Davis Creek Regional Park, Carson City
Hi-Desert RV Park, Winnemucca
Lower & Upper Lehman Creek Campgrounds, Great Basin National Park
Riverside RV Park, Laughlin
Silverton Hotel Casino RV Park, Las Vegas

NEW HAMPSHIRE

Best RV Camping
Circle 9 Ranch, Epsom
Cold Springs Camp Resort, Weare
Friendly Beaver Campground, New Boston
Glen Ellis Family Campground, Glen
Mi-Te-Jo Campground, Milton
Moose Hillock Campground, Warren
Pine Acres, Raymond

Best Tent Camping
Beech Hill Campground, Twin Mountain
Glen Ellis Family Campground, Glen
Greenfield State Park Campground, Greenfield
Lafayette Campground, Franconia
Lost River Valley Campground, North Woodstock
Mi-Te-Jo Campground, Milton
Moose Hillock Campground, Warren
Pawtuckaway State Park, Nottingham
Swain Brook Campground, Wentworth
White Lake State Park, Tamworth

Most Beautiful Campgrounds
Glen Ellis Family Campground, Glen
Lost, River, North Woodstock
Mi-Te-Jo Campground, Milton
Swain Brook Campground, Wentworth
Umbagog Lake Campground, Cambridge
White Lake State Park, Tamworth
Swain Brook Campground, Wentworth

Most Private Campsites
Beech Hill Campground, Twin Mountain
Lost River Valley Campground, North Woodstock
Moose Hillock Campground, Warren
Passaconaway Campground, Bartlett

Most Spacious Campsites
Beech Hill Campground, Twin Mountain
Glen Ellis Family Campground, Glen
Lost River Valley Campground, North Woodstock
Moose Hillock Campground, Warren

Quietest Campgrounds
Living Water Campground, Twin Mountain

Most Secure Campgrounds
Ayers Lake Farm, Barrington
Barrington Shores, Barrington
Chocorua Camping Village, West Ossipee
Circle 9 Ranch, Epsom
Clearwater Campground, Meredith
Cold Springs Camp Resort, Weare
Ellacoya State Beach and RV Park, Gilford
Exeter Elms, Exeter
Glen Ellis Family Campground, Glen
Harbor Hill, Meredith
Hillcrest Campground, Chichester
Living Water Campground, Twin Mountain
Loon Lake, Newport
Lost River Valley Campground, North Woodstock
Meredith Woods, Meredith
Mi-Te-Jo Campground, Milton
Oxbow Campground, Deering
Roger's Family Camping Resort and Motel, Lancaster
Saco River Camping, North Conway
Tamworth Camping Area, Tamworth
Tidewater Campground, Hampton
Timberland, Gorham
Tuxbury Pond Camping Area, South Hampton
Twin Tamarack, New Hampton
Westward Shores, Ossipee
White Lake State Park, Tamworth

Cleanest Campgrounds
Circle 9 Ranch, Epsom
Cold Springs Camp Resort, Weare
Friendly Beaver Campground, New Boston
Glen Ellis Family Campground, Glen
Hillcrest Campground, Chichester
Lantern Motor Inn and Campground Resort, Jefferson
Littleton/Lisbon KOA, Lisbon
Living Water Campground, Twin Mountain
Lost River Valley Campground, North Woodstock
Mi-Te-Jo Campground, Milton
Twin Mountain KOA, Twin Mountain

Best Campground Facilities
Chocorua Camping Village, West Ossipee
Circle 9 Ranch, Epsom
Cold Springs Camp Resort, Weare
Friendly Beaver Campground, New Boston
Glen Ellis Family Campground, Glen
Gunstock Campground, Laconia
Hillcrest Campground, Chichester
Lantern Motor Inn and Campground Resort, Jefferson
Meredith Woods, Meredith
Mi-Te-Jo Campground, Milton
Moose Hillock Campground, Warren
Pine Acres, Raymond
Roger's Family Camping Resort and Motel, Lancaster
Tuxbury Pond Camping Area, South Hampton
Yogi Bear's Jellystone Park, Ashland

Best Rural, Farm, or Ranch Settings
3 Ponds, Raymond
Ames Brook, Ashland
Ayers Lake Farm, Barrington
Ferndale Acres, Lee

Best Urban and Suburban Settings
Circle 9 Campground, Epsom
Epsom Valley, Epsom
Hillcrest Campground, Chichester
Pine Acres, Raymond

Best Mountain Settings
Beech Hill, Twin Mountain
Cannon Mountain RV Park, Franconia Notch State Park
Crazy Horse, Littleton
Gunstock Campground, Laconia
Lafayette Campground, Franconia Notch State Park
Lantern Motor Inn and Campground Resort, Jefferson
Living Waters Campground, Twin Mountain
Rogers Family Camping Resort, Lancaster
Tarry Ho Campground, Twin Mountain
Timberland Campground, Gorham
Twin Mountain KOA, Twin Mountain
Twin Mountain Motor Court and RV Park, Twin Mountain
White Lake State Park, Tamworth

Most Romantic Campgrounds
Glen Ellis, Glen
Lost River, North Woodstock
Umbagog Lake Campground, Cambridge

Best Family-Oriented Campgrounds
Chocurua Camping Village, West Ossipee
Cold Springs, North Woodstock
Friendly Beaver, New Boston
Glen Ellis, Glen
Gunstock, Laconia
Lantern Motor Inn & Resort, Jefferson
Mi-Te-Jo, Milton
Moose Hillock, Warren
Pine Acres, Raymond
Tuxbury Pond Camping Area, South Hampton
Yogi Bear's Jellystone, Ashland

Best Swimming Pools
Cold Springs Camp Resort, Weare
Friendly Beaver, New Boston
Moose Hillock, Warren
Pine Acres, Raymond

NEW JERSEY

Best RV Camping
Beachcomber Camping Resort, Cape May
Pleasant Acres Farm Campground, Sussex

Best Tent Camping
Beachcomber Camping Resort, Cape May

Most Beautiful Campgrounds
Liberty Harbor RV Park, Jersey City
Outdoor World—Sea Pines Campground, Swainton
Pleasant Acres Farm Campground, Sussex

Most Private Campsites
Camp Taylor Campground, Columbia
Cape Island Campground, Cape May

Most Spacious Campsites
Camp Taylor Campground, Columbia
Pleasant Acres Farm Campground, Sussex
Sea Pirate Campground, West Creek
Timberline Lake Camping Resort, New Gretna
Triplebrook Family Camping Resort, Hope

Quietest Campgrounds
Camp Taylor Campground, Columbia
Triplebrook Family Camping Resort, Hope

Most Secure Campgrounds
Beachcomber Camping Resort, Cape May
Buena Vista Camping Park, Buena
Cape Island Campground, Cape May
Driftwood Camping Resort, Clermont
Green Valley Beach Family Campground, Newton
Holly Acres RV Park, Egg Harbor City
Indian Rock RV Resort and Campground, Jackson

NEW JERSEY (continued)

***Most Secure Campgrounds** (continued)*
North Wildwood Camping Resort, Cape May Court House
Ocean View Resort Campground, Ocean View
Pleasant Acres Farm Campground, Sussex
Sea Pirate Campground, West Creek
Thousand Trails–Chestnut Lake, Port Republic
Timberland Lake Campground, Jackson
Timberline Lake Camping Resort, New Gretna
Tip Tam Camping Resort, Jackson
Wading Pines Camping Resort, Chatsworth
Whippoorwill Campground, Marmora

Cleanest Campgrounds
Beachcomber Camping Resort, Cape May
Cape Island Campground, Cape May
Harmony Ridge Campground, Branchville

Best Campground Facilities
Beachcomber Camping Resort, Cape May
Ocean View Resort Campground, Ocean View
Outdoor World—Lake and Shore Campground, Sea Isle City
Outdoor World—Sea Pines Campground, Swainton
Pleasant Acres Farm Campground, Sussex
Yogi Bear's Jellystone Park at Tall Pines Resort, Elmer

Best Rural, Farm, or Ranch Settings
Outdoor World Sea Pines Campground, Swainton
Pleasant Acres Farm Campground, Sussex

Best Rural, Farm, or Ranch Settings
Triplebrook Family Camping Resort, Hope
Wading Pines Camping Resort, Chatsworth

Best Urban and Suburban Settings
Big Timber Lake Camping Resort, Cape May Court House
Liberty Harbor RV Park, Jersey City
Timberlane Campground, Clarksboro

Best Mountain Settings
Camp Taylor Campground, Columbia
Pleasant Acres Farm Campground, Sussex
Triplebrook Camping Resort, Hope

Best Waterfront Settings
Liberty Harbor RV Park, Jersey City
Winding River Campground, Mays Landing

Most Romantic Campgrounds
Cedar Creek Campground, Bayville
Liberty Harbor RV Park, Jersey City
Triplebrook Family Camping Resort, Hope
Wading Pines Campground, Chatsworth
Whippoorwill Campground, Marmora
Winding River Campground, Mays Landing

Best Family-Oriented Campgrounds
Beachcomber Camping Resort, Cape May
Buena Vista Camping Park, Buena
Camp Taylor Campground, Columbia
Holly Shores, Cape May
Pleasant Acres Farm Campground, Sussex
Triplebrook Family Camping Resort, Hope

Best Swimming Pools
Beachcomber Camping Resort, Cape May
Pleasant Acres Campground, Sussex
Timberline Lake Camping Resort, New Gretna

NEW MEXICO

Best RV Camping
Manzano's RV Park, Silver City
Santa Fe Skies RV Park, Santa Fe
Rio Penasco RV Camp, Mayhill
Best View RV Park, Las Cruces
Trail's End RV Park, Jemez Springs
Lakeside RV Park, Elephant Butte
Pancho Villa State Park, Columbus
Rio Chama RV Park, Chama
Alamogordo KOA, Alamogordo

Best Tent Camping
Pecos River Campground, San Jose
Bluewater Lake State Park, Prewitt
Trail's End RV Park, Jemez Springs
Faywood Hot Springs, Dwyer
Rio Chama RV Park, Chama
Riana Campground, Abiquiu

Most Beautiful Campgrounds
Monte Bello RV Park, Taos
Manzano's RV Park, Silver City
Santa Fe Skies RV Park, Santa Fe
Bluewater Lake State Park, Prewitt
Manzano Mountains State Park, Mountainair
Trail's End RV Park, Jemez Springs
Faywood Hot Springs, Dwyer
Pancho Villa State Park, Columbus
Rio Chama RV Park, Chama
Sierra Bonita Cabins & RV Park, Angel Fire
Riana Campground, Abiquiu

Most Private Campsites
Alamogordo KOA, Alamogordo
Artesia RV Park, Artesia
Kiva RV Park & Horse Motel, Bernardo
Rio Chama RV Park, Chama
Pancho Villa State Park, Columbus
Faywood Hot Springs, Dwyer
Lakeside RV Park, Elephant Butte
Trail's End RV Park, Jemez Springs
Ute Lake State Park, Logan
Lordsburg KOA, Lordsburg
Manzano Mountains State Park, Mountainair
Manzano's RV Park, Silver City

Most Spacious Campsites
Artesia RV Park, Artesia
Kiva RV Park & Horse Motel, Bernardo
Pancho Villa State Park, Columbus
Faywood Hot Springs, Dwyer
Lakeside RV Park, Elephant Butte
Trail's End RV Park, Jemez Springs
Ute Lake State Park, Logan
Lordsburg KOA, Lordsburg
Bluewater Lake State Park, Prewitt
Manzano's RV Park, Silver City
Monte Bello RV Park, Taos

Quietest Campgrounds
Riana Campground, Abiquiu
Faywood Hot Springs, Dwyer
Trail's End RV Park, Jemez Springs
Rio Penasco RV Camp, Mayhill
Manzano Mountains State Park, Mountainair
Bluewater Lake State Park, Prewitt
Bosque Birdwatcher's RV Park, San Antonio
Pecos River Campground, San Jose
Santa Fe Skies RV Park, Santa Fe
Manzano's RV Park, Silver City

Most Secure Campgrounds
Manzano's RV Park, Silver City
Pecos River Campground, San Jose
Bosque Birdwatcher's RV Park, San Antonio
Rodeo RV Park & Country Store, Rodeo
Best View RV Park, Las Cruces
Paramount RV Park, Kirtland
Trail's End RV Park, Jemez Springs
Gallup KOA, Gallup
Dad's RV Park, Farmington
Cottonwood RV Park, Espanola
Lakeside RV Park, Elephant Butte
Faywood Hot Springs, Dwyer
Ponil Campground, Cimarron
Rio Chama RV Park, Chama
Artesia RV Park, Artesia

Cleanest Campgrounds
Albuquerque Central KOA, Albuquerque
Sierra Bonita Cabins & RV Park, Angel Fire
Artesia RV Park, Artesia
Carlsbad RV Park & Campground, Carlsbad
Ponil Campground, Cimarron
Meadowlark KOA, Clayton
Faywood Hot Springs, Dwyer
West Lake RV Park, Eagle Nest
Lakeside RV Park, Elephant Butte
Gallup KOA, Gallup
Trail's End RV Park, Jemez Springs
Lordsburg KOA, Lordsburg
Rio Penasco RV Camp, Mayhill
Manzano Mountains State Park, Mountainair
Santa Fe Skies RV Park, Santa Fe
Manzano's RV Park, Silver City
Monte Bello RV Park, Taos

Best Campground Facilities
Alamogordo KOA, Alamogordo
Albuquerque Central KOA, Albuquerque
Carlsbad RV Park & Campground, Carlsbad
Gallup KOA, Gallup
Best View RV Park, Las Cruces
Lordsburg KOA, Lordsburg

Best Rural, Farm, or Ranch Settings
Kiva RV Park, Bernardo
Faywood Hot Springs, Dwyer
Cottonwood RV Park, Espanola
Bosque Birdwatcher's RV Park, San Antonio

Best Urban and Suburban Settings
Artesia RV Park, Artesia

NEW MEXICO (continued)

Dad's RV Park, Farmington
Sands RV Park & Motel, Carrizozo
Vegas RV Overnite Park, Las Vegas

Best Mountain Settings
Coyote Creek State Park, Angelfire
Riana Campground, Abiquiu
Trail's End RV Park, Jemez Springs
Manzano Mountains State Park, Mountainair

Best Waterfront Settings
Riana Campground, Abiquiu
Ute Lake State Park, Logan
Bluewater Lake State Park, Prewitt

Most Romantic Campgrounds
Coyote Creek State Park, Angelfire
Riana Campground, Abiquiu
Lakeside RV Park, Elephant Butte
Pancho Villa State Park, Columbus
Rio Chama RV Park, Chama
Faywood Hot Springs, Dwyer
Trail's End RV Park, Jemez Springs
Bosque Birdwatcher's RV Park, San Antonio
Manzano's RV Park, Silver City
Pecos River Campground, San Jose
Santa Fe Skies RV Park, Santa Fe

Best Family-Oriented Campgrounds
Alamogordo KOA, Alamogordo
Albuquerque KOA, Albuquerque
Riana Campground, Abiquiu
Carlsbad RV Park & Campground, Carlsbad
Clayton KOA, Clayton
Gallup KOA, Gallup
Lordsburg KOA, Lordsburg
Ute Lake State Park, Logan

Best Swimming Pools
Alamogordo KOA, Alamogordo
Albuquerque KOA, Albuquerque
Carlsbad RV Park & Campground, Carlsbad
Faywood Hot Springs, Dwyer
Redrow Campground, Edgewood
Gallup KOA, Gallup
Best View RV Park, Las Cruces
Lordsburg KOA, Lordsburg
Vado RV Park, Vado
AAA White's City RV Park, White's City

NEW YORK

Best RV Camping
Camp Chatauqua Camping Resort, Chautauqua
Cooperstown Shadow Brook Campground, Cooperstown
Deer Run Campground, Mechanicville
KOA—Newburgh/New York City North, Newburgh
Lake George Escape Resort, Lake George
Lake George RV Park, Lake George
Skyway Camping Resort, Ellenville
The Villages at Turning Stone RV Park, Verona
Yogi Bear's Jellystone Park at Birchwood Acres, Ellenville
Yogi Bear's Jellystone Park Camp Resort at Lazy River, Gardiner

Best Tent Camping
Camp Chatauqua Camping Resort, Chautauqua
Cooperstown Shadow Brook Campground, Cooperstown
KOA—Newburgh/New York City North, Newburgh
Lake George Escape Resort, Lake George
Skyway Camping Resort, Ellenville
Yogi Bear's Jellystone Park at Birchwood Acres, Ellenville
Yogi Bear's Jellystone Park Camp Resort at Lazy River, Gardiner

Most Beautiful Campgrounds
Camp Chatauqua Camping Resort, Chautauqua
Cooperstown Shadow Brook Campground, Cooperstown
KOA—Lake Placid/Whiteface Mountain, Wilmington
Lake George RV Park, Lake George
Lake George/Schroon Valley Resort, Warrensburg
North Pole Campground and Motor Inn, Wilmington
Skyway Camping Resort, Ellenville
Sugar Creek Glen Campground, Dansville
Yogi Bear's Jellystone Park at Birchwood Acres, Ellenville
Yogi Bear's Jellystone Park Camp Resort at Lazy River, Gardiner

Most Private Campsites
Ferenbaugh Campsites, Corning
Keewaydin State Park, Alexandria Bay
KOA—Lake Placid/Whiteface Mountain, Wilmington
Lake George Campsite, Lake George
Lakeside Beach State Park, Albion
Lei-Ti Campground, Batavia
Yogi Bear's Jellystone Park at Crystal Lake, Cooperstown

Most Spacious Campsites
Camp Bell Campground, Campbell
Keewaydin State Park, Alexandria Bay
KOA—Lake Placid/Whiteface Mountain, Wilmington
KOA—Newburgh/New York City North, Newburgh
Lakeside Beach State Park, Albion
Lei-Ti Campground, Batavia
Rip Van Winkle Campground, Saugerties

Quietest Campgrounds
KOA—Lake Placid/Whiteface Mountain, Wilmington
North Pole Campground and Motor Inn, Wilmington

Most Secure Campgrounds
Adirondack Camping Village, Lake George
Brennan Beach RV Park, Pulaski
Camp Chatauqua Camping Resort, Chautauqua
Chautauqua Heights Camping Resort, Dewittville
Deer River Campsite, Duane
Deer Run Campground, Mechanicville
Lake George Escape Resort, Lake George
Lake George RV Park, Lake George
Lake George/Schroon Valley Resort, Warrensburg
Ledgeview Village RV Park, Lake George
Massena International Kampground, Massena
Oleana Family Campground, Copake
Rip Van Winkle Campground, Saugerties
Skyline Camping Resort, Darien Center
Skyway Camping Resort, Ellenville
Trail's End Campground, Hinckley
Triple R Camping Resort, Franklinville
Yogi Bear's Jellystone Park Camp Resort at Lazy River, Gardiner
Yogi Bear's Jellystone Park Campground, Mexico

Cleanest Campgrounds
Cooperstown Shadow Brook Campground, Cooperstown
Deer Run Campground, Mechanicville
Hickory Hills Family Camping Resort, Bath
Lake George Escape Resort, Lake George
Lake George RV Park, Lake George
Lake George/Schroon Valley Resort, Warrensburg
Massena International Kampground, Massena
Skyway Camping Resort, Ellenville
The Villages at Turning Stone RV Park, Verona
Triple R Camping Resort, Franklinville
Yogi Bear's Jellystone Park at Birchwood Acres, Ellenville
Yogi Bear's Jellystone Park at Crystal Lake, Cooperstown
Yogi Bear's Jellystone Park Camp Resort at Lazy River, Gardiner

Best Campground Facilities
Alpine Lake Camping Resort, Corinth
Camp Chatauqua Camping Resort, Chautauqua
Deer River Campsite, Duane
Deer Run Campground, Mechanicville
Hickory Hills Family Camping Resort, Bath
KOA—Lake Placid/Whiteface Mountain, Wilmington
KOA—Newburgh/New York City North, Newburgh
Lake George Escape Resort, Lake George
Lake George RV Park, Lake George
Lake George/Schroon Valley Resort, Warrensburg
North Pole Campground and Motor Inn, Wilmington
Skyway Camping Resort, Ellenville
The Villages at Turning Stone RV Park, Verona
Yogi Bear's Jellystone Park at Birchwood Acres, Ellenville
Yogi Bear's Jellystone Park Camp Resort at Lazy River, Gardiner

NEW YORK (continued)

Best Rural, Farm, or Ranch Settings
Alps Family Campground, Averill Park
Camp at Mariposa Ponds, Houghton
Cheerful Valley Campground, Phelps
Hickory Hill Camping Resort, Bath
KOA—Herkimer Diamond Campground, Herkimer
KOA—Newburgh/NYC North, Newburgh
Paradise Pines Camping Resort, North Hudson
Shadow Brook Campground, Cooperstown
Triple R Camping Resort, Franklinville

Best Urban and Suburban Settings
Adirondack Camping Village, Lake George
Camp Bell Campground, Campbell
KOA—Newburgh/New York City, Plattekill
KOA—Niagara Falls, Grand Island
KOA—Old Forge, Old Forge
Lake George Campsite, Lake George
Massena International Kampground, Massena
Shadow Brook Campground, Cooperstown
Villages at Turning Stone RV Park, Verona

Best Mountain Settings
Alpine Lake Camping Resort, Corinth
Deer River Campsite, Duane
Deer Run Campground, Schaghticoke
Indian Ridge Campsites, Leeds
KOA—Lake Placid/Whiteface Mountain, Wilmington
Lake George Escape, Lake George
Lake George RV Park, Lake George
Lake George Schroon Valley Resort, Warrensburg
Ledgeview RV Park, Lake George
North Pole Campground and Motor Inn, Wilmington
Russell Brook Campsites, Roscoe
Skyway Camping Resort, Greenfield Park
Yogi Bear's Jellystone Park at Birchwood Acres, Woodridge

Best Waterfront Settings
Alpine Lake Camping Resort, Corinth
Brennan Beach RV Park, Pulaski
Camp Chautauqua Camping Resort, Stow
Deer River Campsite, Duane
KOA— Lake Placid/Whiteface Mountain, Wilmington
Lake George Escape, Lake George NY
Lake George Schroon Valley Resort, Warrensburg
North Pole Campground and Motor Inn, Wilmington
Russell Brook Campsite, Roscoe
Trail's End Campground, Hinkley
West Canada Creek Campsites, Poland
Yogi Bear's Jellystone Park at Lazy River, Gardiner
Yogi Bear's Jellystone Park at Paradise Pines, North Hudson

Most Romantic Campgrounds
Alpine Lake Camping Resort, Corinth
Camp Chautauqua Camping Resort, Stow
Deer River Campsite, Duane
Indian Ridge Campsites, Leeds
KOA—Herkimer Diamond Campground, Herkimer
KOA—Lake Placid/Whiteface Mountain, Wilmington
Lake George Escape, Lake George
North Pole Campground and Motor Inn, Wilmington
Yogi Bear's Jellystone Park at Birchwood Acres, Woodridge
Yogi Bear's Jellystone Park at Lazy River, Gardiner

Best Family-Oriented Campgrounds
Alpine Lake Camping Resort, Corinth
Brennan Beach Park, Pulaski
Camp Chautauqua Camping Resort, Stow
Hickory Hill Family Camping Resort, Bath
Lake George Escape, Lake George
Lake George RV Park, Lake George
Shadow Brook Campground, Cooperstown
Skyway Camping Resort, Greenfield Park
Yogi Bear's Jellystone Park at Birchwood Acres, Woodridge
Yogi Bear's Jellystone Park at Lazy River, Gardiner

Best Swimming Pools
Camp Chautauqua Camping Resort, Stow
KOA—Canandaigua/Rochester, Canandaigua
Lake George Escape, Lake George
Lake George RV Park, Lake George
Skyway Camping Resort, Greenfield Park

NORTH CAROLINA

Best RV Camping
Bear Den Campground, Spruce Pine
Hanging Rock State Park, Danbury
Hibernia, Henderson
Holly Point State Recreational Area, Wake Forest
Travel Resorts of America, Jackson Springs

Best Tent Camping
Bandits Roost Park, W. Kerr Scott Reservoir, Wilkesboro
Bear Den Campground, Spruce Pine
Hanging Rock State Park, Danbury
Hibernia, Henderson
Holly Point State Recreational Area, Wake Forest

Most Beautiful Campgrounds
Bandits Roost Park, W. Kerr Scott Reservoir, Wilkesboro
Bear Den Campground, Spruce Pine
Carolina Beach State Park, Carolina Beach
Hanging Rock State Park, Danbury
Hibernia, Henderson
High Rock Lake Marina and Campground, Southmont
Holly Point State Recreational Area, Wake Forest
Moonshine Creek Campground, Balsam
Morrow Mountain State Park, Albemarle
Ocracoke, Cape Hatteras
Oregon Inlet, Cape Hatteras
Standing Indian, Franklin
The Heritage, Whispering Pines

Most Private Campsites
Bear Den Campground, Spruce Pine
Carolina Beach State Park, Carolina Beach
Crosswinds Campground, Jordan Lake State Recreation Area, Apex
Hanging Rock State Park, Danbury
Hibernia, Henderson
Holly Point State Recreational Area, Wake Forest
Poplar Point Campground, Jordan Lake State Recreation Area, Apex

Most Spacious Campsites
Bandits Roost Park, W. Kerr Scott Reservoir, Wilkesboro
Carolina Beach State Park, Carolina Beach
Crosswinds Campground, Jordan Lake State Recreation Area, Apex
Hanging Rock State Park, Danbury
Hibernia, Henderson
Holly Point State Recreational Area, Wake Forest
Poplar Point Campground, Jordan Lake State Recreation Area, Apex
Standing Indian, Franklin

Quietest Campgrounds
Bandits Roost Park, W. Kerr Scott Reservoir, Wilkesboro
Bear Den Campground, Spruce Pine
Hanging Rock State Park, Danbury
Hibernia, Henderson
Holly Point State Recreational Area, Wake Forest
Ocracoke, Cape Hatteras
Travel Resorts of America, Jackson Springs

Most Secure Campgrounds
Bandits Roost Park, W. Kerr Scott Reservoir, Wilkesboro
Bear Den Campground, Spruce Pine
Cherokee KOA, Cherokee
Crosswinds Campground, Jordan Lake State Recreation Area, Apex
Hanging Rock State Park, Danbury
Hatteras Sands, Cape Hatteras
Holiday Trav-L-Park Resort, Emerald Isle
Linville Falls Campground, Linville Falls
Ocracoke, Cape Hatteras
Poplar Point Campground, Jordan Lake State Recreation Area, Apex
Stone Mountain State Park, Roaring Gap

Cleanest Campgrounds
Bandits Roost Park, W. Kerr Scott Reservoir, Wilkesboro
Bear Den Campground, Spruce Pine
Country Woods, Franklin
Doughton Campground, Asheville
Hanging Rock State Park, Danbury
Hibernia, Henderson
Holiday Trav-L-Park Resort, Emerald Isle

NORTH CAROLINA (continued)

Linville Falls Campground, Linville Falls
Morrow Mountain State Park, Albemarle
Stone Mountain State Park, Roaring Gap
Travel Resorts of America, Jackson Springs

Best Campground Facilities
Holiday Trav-L-Park Resort, Emerald Isle

Best Urban and Suburban Settings
Carolina Beach State Park, Carolina Beach
Carowinds, Charlotte
Holiday Trav-L-Park Resort, Emerald Isle
Water's Edge RV Park, Newport

Best Mountain Settings
Bear Den Campground, Spruce Pine
Country Woods, Franklin
Doughton Campground, Asheville
Great Smoky Mountains National Park Smokemont Campground, Cherokee
Hanging Dog, Murphy
Hanging Rock State Park, Danbury
Hidden Valley Campground and Waterpark, Marion
Moonshine Creek Campground, Balsam
Morrow Mountain State Park, Albemarle
Singing Waters Camping Resort, Tuckasegee
Standing Indian, Franklin
Steel Creek Park, Morganton
Stone Mountain State Park, Roaring Gap

Best Waterfront Settings
Bandits Roost Park, W. Kerr Scott Reservoir, Wilkesboro
Crosswinds Campground, Jordan Lake State Recreation Area, Apex
Hibernia Campground, Kerr Lake State Recreation Area, Henderson
High Rock Lake Marina and Campground, Southmont
Holly Point State Recreational Area, Falls Lake, Wake Forest
Morrow Mountain State Park, Albemarle
Poplar Point Campground, Jordan Lake State Recreation Area, Apex

Most Romantic Campgrounds
Bear Den Campground, Spruce Pine
Carolina Beach State Park, Carolina Beach
Hanging Rock State Park, Danbury
Hibernia Campground, Kerr Lake State Recreation Area, Henderson
Holly Point State Recreational Area, Falls Lake, Wake Forest
Standing Indian, Franklin

Best Family-Oriented Campgrounds
Bear Den Campground, Spruce Pine
Camp Hatteras, Waves
Cape Hatteras KOA Kampgound, Rodanthe
Holiday Trav-L-Park Resort, Emerald Isle
Steel Creek Park, Morganton
Yogi in the Smokies, Cherokee

NORTH DAKOTA

Best RV Camping
Crown Villa RV Park, Bend

Best Tent Camping
Bismark KOA, Bismark

Most Beautiful Campgrounds
Bismark KOA, Bismark
Fort Lincoln State Park, Mandan
Fort Stevenson State Park, Garrison
Graham's Island State Park, Cavalier
Icelandic State Park, Cavalier
Lake Metigoshe State Park, Bottineau
Lewis and Clark State Park, Epping
Turtle River State Park, Arvilla

Most Private Campsites
Bismark KOA, Bismark
Fort Stevenson State Park, Garrison
Graham's Island State Park, Cavalier
Jamestown KOA, Jamestown
Lake Metigoshe State Park, Bottineau
Larimore Dam Recreation Area and Campground, Larimore
Lewis and Clark State Park, Epping

Most Spacious Campsites
Bismark KOA, Bismark
Fort Stevenson State Park, Garrison
Graham's Island State Park, Cavalier
Jamestown KOA, Jamestown
Lake Metigoshe State Park, Bottineau
Larimore Dam Recreation Area and Campground, Larimore
Lewis and Clark State Park, Epping

Best Rural, Farm, or Ranch Settings
Icelandic State Park, Cavalier
Lewis and Clark State Park, Epping
Prairie Acres RV Park, Williston

Best Waterfront Settings
Lake Metigoshe State Park, Bottineau

Most Romantic Campgrounds
Bismark KOA, Bismark

Best Family-Oriented Campgrounds
Icelandic State Park, Cavalier
Turtle River State Park, Arvilla

OHIO

Best RV Camping
Indian Creek Camping Resort, Geneva-On-The Lake
Cross Creek Camping Resort, Delaware
Bear Creek Resort Ranch KOA, Canton
Dayton Tall Timbers KOA Resort, Brookville

Best Tent Camping
Indian Creek Camping Resort, Geneva-On-The Lake
Cross Creek Camping Resort, Delaware
Bear Creek Resort Ranch KOA, Canton

Most Beautiful Campgrounds
Alum Creek State Park Delaware
Bear Creek Resort Ranch KOA, Canton
Caesar Creek State Park Waynesville
Cross Creek Camping Resort, Delaware
Indian Creek Camping Resort, Geneva-On-The Lake
Rocky Fork State Park Hillsboro
Shawnee State Park Portsmouth

Most Private Campsites
Indian Creek Camping Resort, Geneva-On-The Lake
Cross Creek Camping Resort, Delaware
Bear Creek Resort Ranch KOA, Canton

Most Spacious Campsites
Bear Creek Resort Ranch KOA, Canton
Cross Creek Camping Resort, Delaware
Indian Creek Camping Resort, Geneva-On-The Lake

Quietest Campgrounds
Indian Creek Camping Resort, Geneva-On-The Lake
Cross Creek Camping Resort, Delaware
Bear Creek Resort Ranch KOA, Canton

Most Secure Campgrounds
Yogi Bear's Jellystone Park Camp-Resort, Aurora
Dayton Tall Timbers KOA Resort, Brookville
Indian Creek Camping Resort, Geneva-On-The Lake
Thousand Trails-Wilmington, Wilmington

Cleanest Campgrounds
Yogi Bear's Jellystone Park Camp-Resort, Aurora
Dayton Tall Timbers KOA Resort, Brookville
Bear Creek Resort Ranch KOA, Canton
Cross Creek Camping Resort, Delaware
Indian Creek Camping Resort, Geneva-On-The Lake
Thousand Trails-Wilmington, Wilmington

OHIO (continued)

Best Campground Facilities
Yogi Bear's Jellystone Park Camp-Resort, Aurora
Indian Creek Camping Resort, Geneva-On-The Lake
Dayton Tall Timbers KOA Resort, Brookville
Cross Creek Camping Resort, Delaware
Bear Creek Resort Ranch KOA, Canton

Best Rural, Farm, or Ranch Settings
Buckeye Lake KOA, Buckeye Lake
Camp Toodik Family Campground, Cabins, & Canoe Livery, Loudonville
Cross Creek Camping Resort, Delaware
Indian Creek Camping Resort, Geneva-On-The-Lake
Scenic Hills RV Park, Berlin
Spring Valley Campground, Cambridge

Best Waterfront Settings
Alum Creek State Park Campground, Delaware
Bear Creek Resort Ranch KOA, Canton
Camp Toodik Family Campground, Cabins, & Canoe Livery, Loudonville
Deerland Resort, Jackson
East Harbor State Park, Port Clinton

Most Romantic Campgrounds
Bear Creek Resort Ranch KOA, Canton
Carthage Gap Campground, Athens
Dayton Tall Timbers KOA Resort, Brookville
Deerland Resort, Jackson
Indian Creek Camping Resort, Geneva-On-The-Lake
Spring Valley Campground, Cambridge

Best Family-Oriented Campgrounds
Buckeye Lake KOA Buckeye, Lake
Cross Creek Camping Resort, Delaware
Pleasant View Recreation, Van Buren
Wapakoneta/Lima KOA, Wapakoneta
Yogi Bear's Jellystone Park Camp-Resort, Aurora

Best Swimming Pools
Yogi Bear's Jellystone Park Camp-Resort, Aurora
Dayton Tall Timbers KOA Resort, Brookville
Buckeye Lake KOA, Buckeye Lake
Butler Mohican KOA, Butler
Hillview Acres Campground, Cambridge
Spring Valley Campground, Cambridge
Bear Creek Resort Ranch KOA, Canton
Cross Creek Camping Resort, Delaware
Berkshire Lake Campground, Galena
Indian Creek Camping Resort, Geneva-On-The Lake
Yogi Bear's Jellystone Park Camp-Resort, Jackson
Camp Toodik Family Campground, Cabins & Canoe Livery, Loudonville
The Landings Family Campground, Marietta
Mt. Gilead Campground, Mt. Gilead
Maple Lakes Recreational Park, Seville
Whispering Hills Recreation Inc., Shreve
Pleasant View Recreation, Van Buren
Wapakoneta/Lima South KOA, Wapakoneta
Spring Valley Frontier Campground, Waynesville
Hidden Acres Campground, West Salem
Town & Country Camp Resort, West Salem
Thousand Trails-Wilmington, Wilmington

OKLAHOMA

Best RV Camping
Sawyer RV Park, Sawyer
Cedar Oaks RV Resort, Grove
High Point RV Park, Enid

Best Tent Camping
Red Rock Canyon State Park, Hinton
MarVal Family Resort, Gore
Cherokee State Park (Riverside Campground), Disney
Clayton Lake State Park, Clayton

Most Beautiful Campgrounds
Sawyer RV Park, Sawyer
Red Rock Canyon State Park, Hinton
Cedar Oaks RV Resort, Grove
Cherokee State Park (Riverside Campground), Disney

Most Private Campsites
High Point RV Park, Enid
Lakeside RV Park, Sallisaw

Most Spacious Campsites
Cherokee State Park (Riverside Campground), Disney
High Point RV Park, Enid
Lakeside RV Park, Sallisaw

Quietest Campgrounds
Indian City USA, Anadarko
Big Cedar RV Park, Big Cedar
Cherokee State Park (Riverside Campground), Disney
High Point RV Park, Enid
Cedar Oaks RV Resort, Grove
Red Rock Canyon State Park, Hinton
Sawyer RV Park, Sawyer
Diamondhead Resort, Talequah
Moneka Park, Waurika

Most Secure Campgrounds
Diamondhead Resort, Talequah
Sawyer RV Park, Sawyer
Cedar Oaks RV Resort, Grove
MarVal Family Resort, Gore
Bridgeport RV Park, Eufaula
High Point RV Park, Enid
Cherokee State Park (Riverside Campground), Disney
Big Cedar RV Park, Big Cedar

Cleanest Campgrounds
Ardmore/Marietta KOA, Ardmore
Big Cedar RV Park, Big Cedar
Wink's RV Park, Clinton
Best Western, El Reno
Bridgeport RV Park, Eufaula
Cedar Oaks RV Resort, Grove
Lakeside RV Park, Sallisaw
Sawyer RV Park, Sawyer
Tulsa NE KOA, Tulsa

Best Campground Facilities
Cedar Oaks RV Resort, Grove

Best Rural, Farm, or Ranch Settings
Ardmore/Marietta KOA, Ardmore
KOA Ardmore-Marietta, Ardmore
Oak Hill RV Park, Davis
Simmons RV Park, Durant
Southwind RV Park, Guymon
Sleepee Hollo, Kingfisher
Rockin' Horse RV Park, Spiro
Sawyer RV Park, Sawyer
Sawyer RV Park, Sawyer

Best Urban and Suburban Settings
Corky's Get & Go, Woodward

Best Waterfront Settings
Cherokee Riverside Campground, Disney
Cedar Oaks RV Park, Grove
MarVal Family Resort, Gore
Diamondhead Resort, Talequah

Best Family-Oriented Campgrounds
KOA Ardmore-Marietta, Ardmore
MarVal Family Resort, Gore
Diamondhead Resort, Talequah
Tulsa KOA, Tulsa

Best Swimming Pools
Indian City USA, Anadarko
Riverside RV Resort, Bartlesville
Sherrard RV KOA, Colbert
MarVal Family Resort, Gore
Red Rock Canyon State Park, Hinton
Sandstel, Oklahoma City
Lakeside RV Park, Sallisaw
Tulsa KOA, Tulsa

OREGON

Best RV Camping
Kah Nee Ta Resort, Warm Springs
Mt. Hood Village, Portland
Pacific Shores Motorcoach Resort, Newport
RV Resort At Cannon Beach, Cannon Beach
Stokes-Thomas Lake City Park, Watertown

Best Tent Camping
Jessie M. Honeyman Memorial State Park Campground, Florence
Manzama Campground, Crater Lake National Park

Most Beautiful Campgrounds
Bear Creek Campground, Maupin
Cape Blanco State Park, Port Orford
Cape Lookout State Park, Netarts
Cape Perpetua Scenic Area, Yachats
Crater Lake Resort Fort Creek Campground, Fort Klamath
Diamond Lake Campground, Diamond Lake
Eel Creek Campground, Winchester Bay
Elk Lake Campground, Detroit
Emmigrant Springs State Park, Meacham
Farewell Bend State Recreation Area, Huntington
Historic Arizona Beach RV Park, Port Orford
Jessie M. Honeyman Memorial State Park Campground, Florence
Lake Owyhee State Park, Ontario
Manzama Campground, Crater Lake National Park
Natural Bridge Campground, Prospect
Oxbow Park, Gresham
Princess Creek Campground, Cascade Summit
Rocky Point Resort, Klamath Falls
Saddle Mountain State Park, Cannon Beach
Shelter Cove Resort and Marina, Cascade Summit
Thielsen View Campground, Diamond Lake
Nehalem Bay State Park, Manzanita/Nehalem

Most Private Campsites
Cape Lookout State Park, Netarts
Eagle Creek Campground, Bonneville
Eel Creek Campground, Winchester Bay
Elk Lake Campground, Detroit
Illahe Campground, Gold Beach
Natural Bridge Campground, Prospect
Oxbow Park, Gresham
Thielsen View Campground, Diamond Lake

Most Spacious Campsites
Bear Creek Campground, Maupin
Cape Blanco State Park, Port Orford
Crown Villa RV Park, Bend
Eel Creek Campground, Winchester Bay
Elk Lake Campground, Detroit
Head of the River Campground, Chiloquin
Illahe Campground, Gold Beach
Oxbow Park, Gresham
Riverside Campground, Sisters
Thielsen View Campground, Diamond Lake

Quietest Campgrounds
Cinder Hill Campground, Bend
Eel Creek Campground, Winchester Bay
Elk Lake Campground, Detroit
Lake of the Woods Resort, Klamath Falls
Lake Owyhee State Park, Ontario
Paulina Lake Campground, Bend
Thielsen View Campground, Diamond Lake

Most Secure Campgrounds
Corps of Engineers Downstream, Pierre
Kah Nee Ta Resort, Warm Springs
Mt. Hood Village, Portland
Oxbow Park, Gresham
Pacific Shores Motorcoach Resort, Newport

Cleanest Campgrounds
Cape Blanco State Park, Port Orford
Cape Lookout State Park, Netarts
Crown Villa RV Park, Bend
Illahe Campground, Gold Beach
Kah Nee Ta Resort, Warm Springs
Lincoln City KOA Campground, Lincoln City
Natural Bridge Campground, Prospect
Pacific Shores Motorcoach Resort, Newport
Phoenix RV Park, Salem
Thielsen View Campground, Diamond Lake

Best Campground Facilities
Crown Villa RV Park, Bend
Kah Nee Ta Resort, Warm Springs
Mt. Hood Village, Portland
Pacific Shores Motorcoach Resort, Newport

Best Rural, Farm, or Ranch Settings
Richardson Park, Eugene

Best Mountain Settings
Mountain View RV Park, Pendelton
Saddle Mountain State Park, Cannon Beach

Best Waterfront Settings
Bastendorff Beach Campground, Coo's Bay
Diamond Lake Campground, Diamond Lake

Most Romantic Campgrounds
Cape Lookout State Park, Netarts
Eel Creek Campground, Winchester Bay
Elk Lake Campground, Detroit
Natural Bridge Campground, Prospect
Oxbow Park, Gresham
Thielsen View Campground, Diamond Lake

Best Family-Oriented Campgrounds
Astoria/Warrenton/Seaside KOA, Astoria
Bastendorff Beach Campground, Coo's Bay

PENNSYLVANIA

Best RV Camping
Drummer Boy Camping Resort, Gettysburg
Eagles Peak Family Camping Resort, Robesonia
Granite Hill Campground and Adventure Golf, Gettysburg
Keen Lake Camping and Cottage Resort, Waymart
Lake-In-Wood Camping Resort, Bowmansville
Sun Valley Campground, Bowmansville

Best Tent Camping
Lake-In-Wood Camping Resort, Bowmansville

Most Beautiful Campgrounds
Appalachian Campsites, Shartlesville
Bear Run Campground, Portersville
Brandywine Meadows Family Campground, Honey Brook
Drummer Boy Camping Resort, Gettysburg
Eagles Peak Family Camping Resort, Robesonia
Ferryboat Campsites, Liverpool
Foote Rest Campground, Kane
Gettysburg Campground, Gettysburg
Hickory Run Family Camping Resort, Denver
Locust Lake State Park, Mahanoy City
Nittany Mountain Campground, New Columbia
Otter Lake Camp Resort, Marshall's Creek
Pioneer Park Campground, Somerset
Pocono Vacation Park, East Stroudsburg
Promised Land State Park, Greentown
Robin Hill Camping Resort, Lenhartsville
Shangri-La on the Creek, Milton
Wolf's Camping Resort, Knox
Yogi Bear's Jellystone Park Camp Resort—Yogi-on-the-River, Northumberland

Most Private Campsites
Bald Eagle State Park (Russel P. Letterman Campground), Howard
Colonel Denning State Park, Newville
Kittatinny Campgrounds, Barryville
Locust Lake State Park, Mahanoy City
Mountain Vista Campground, East Stroudsburg
Ole Bull State Park, Galeton
World's End State Park, Laporte

Most Spacious Campsites
Bald Eagle State Park (Russel P. Letterman Campground), Howard
Brookdale Family Campground, Meadville
Bucktail Camping Resort, Mansfield
Colonel Denning State Park, Newville
French Creek State Park, Elverson
Hickory Run Family Camping Resort, Denver
Kittatinny Campgrounds, Barryville
Lake Raystown Resort and Lodge, Entriken
Lake-In-Wood Camping Resort, Bowmansville
Little Pine State Park, Waterville
Locust Lake State Park, Mahanoy City
Mount Pocono Campground and Resort, Mount Pocono
Mountain Vista Campground, East Stroudsburg
Ole Bull State Park, Galeton
Otter Lake Camp Resort, Marshall's Creek
Robin Hill Camping Resort, Lenhartsville
World's End State Park, Laporte

Quietest Campgrounds
Bucktail Camping Resort, Mansfield
Keen Lake Camping and Cottage Resort, Waymart
Otter Lake Camp Resort, Marshall's Creek
Pocono Vacation Park, East Stroudsburg
Warwick Woods Family Camping Resort, Morgantown
World's End State Park, Laporte

PENNSYLVANIA (continued)

Most Secure Campgrounds
Appalachian Campsites, Shartlesville
Artillery Ridge Camping Resort, Gettysburg
Brandywine Meadows Family Campground, Honey Brook
Brookdale Family Campground, Meadville
Driftstone on the Delaware, Portland
Eagles Peak Family Camping Resort, Robesonia
Hershey Highmeadow Campground, Hershey
Lake Raystown Resort and Lodge, Entriken
Oak Creek Campground, Bowmansville
Outdoor World—Circle M Campground, Lancaster
Rose Point Park Campground, Rose Point
Spring Gulch Resort Campground, New Holland
Thousands Trails—Hershey, Hershey
Wolf's Camping Resort, Knox

Cleanest Campgrounds
Brookdale Family Campground, Meadville
Eagles Peak Family Camping Resort, Robesonia
Friendship Village Campground, Bedford
Granite Hill Campground and Adventure Golf, Gettysburg
Hershey Highmeadow Campground, Hershey
Nittany Mountain Campground, New Columbia
Oak Creek Campground, Bowmansville
Outdoor World—Circle M Campground, Lancaster
Pioneer Park Campground, Somerset
Scottyland Camping Resort, Rockwood
Warwick Woods Family Camping Resort, Morgantown

Best Campground Facilities
Appalachian Campsites, Shartlesville
Bucktail Camping Resort, Mansfield
Colonial Woods Family Camping Resort, Upper Black Eddy
Drummer Boy Camping Resort, Gettysburg
Eagles Peak Family Camping Resort, Robesonia
Friendship Village Campground, Bedford
Gettysburg Campground, Gettysburg
Gettysburg Farm Campground/Outdoor World, Dover
Granite Hill Campground and Adventure Golf, Gettysburg
Hershey Highmeadow Campground, Hershey
Hidden Valley Camping Resort, Mifflinburg
Keen Lake Camping and Cottage Resort, Waymart
Lake Raystown Resort and Lodge, Entriken
Lake-In-Wood Camping Resort, Bowmansville
Mountain Springs Camping Resort, Shartlesville
Nittany Mountain Campground, New Columbia
Otter Lake Camp Resort, Marshall's Creek
Round Top Campground, Gettysburg
Scottyland Camping Resort, Rockwood
Spring Gulch Resort Campground, New Holland
Sun Valley Campground, Bowmansville
Thousands Trails—Hershey, Hershey
Wolf's Camping Resort, Knox

Best Rural, Farm, or Ranch Settings
Buttercup Campground, Butler
Deer Meadow Campground, Cooksburg
Foote Rest Campground, Kane
Hickory Run Family Camping Resort, Denver
Hidden Valley Camping Resort, Mifflinburg
Lake-in-Wood Resort, Narvon
Oak Creek Campground, Bowmansville
Outdoor World Gettysburg Farm Campground, Dover
Ridge Run Family Campground, Elizabethtown
Wolf's Camping Resort, Knox

Best Urban and Suburban Settings
Colonial Woods Family Camping Resort, Upper Black Eddy
Friendship Village RV Park and Campground, Bedford
Hershey Highmeadow Campground, Hershey
Western Village RV Park, Carlisle

Best Mountain Settings
Appalachian Campsites, Shartlesville
Eagles Peak Campground, Robesonia
Keen Lake Camping and Cottage Resort, Waymart
Mountain Creek Campground, Mt. Holly Springs
Mountain Springs Camping Resort, Shartlesville
Mountain Vista Campground, Stroudsburg
Mt. Pocono Campground Resort, Mt. Pocono
Nittany Mountain Campground, New Columbia
Otter Lake Camping Resort, Marshalls Creek
Pocono Vacation Park, Stroudsburg

Best Waterfront Settings
Driftstone on the Delaware, Portland
Ferryboat Campsites, Liverpool
Keen Lake Camping and Cottage Resort, Waymart
Otter Lake Camping Resort, Marshalls Creek
Pioneer Park Campground, Somerset
Yogi-on-the-River, Northumberland

Most Romantic Campgrounds
Keen Lake Camping Resort, Waymart
Lake-in-Wood Resort, Narvon
Mount Pocono Campground/Resort, Mount Pocono
Mountain Vista Campground, East Stroudsburg
Nittany Mountain Campground, New Columbia
Otter Lake Camping Resort, Marshalls Creek

Best Family-Oriented Campgrounds
Bucktail Camping Resort, Mansfield
Drummer Boy Camping Resort, Gettysburg
Eagles Peak Campground, Robesonia
Granite Hill Campground, Gettysburg
Spring Gulch Resort, New Holland

Best Swimming Pools
Drummer Boy Camping Resort, Gettysburg
Eagles Peak, Robesonia
Hershey Highmeadow Campground, Hershey
Keen Lake Camping and Cottage Resort, Waymart
Lake-in-Wood Resort, Narvon
Otter Lake Camp Resort, Marshalls Creek
Sun Valley Campground, Bowmansville
Warwick Woods Family Camping Resort, St. Peters

RHODE ISLAND

Best RV Camping
Card's Camps, Wakefield
Hickory Ridge Family Campground, Greene
Timber Creek RV Resort, Westerly

Best Tent Camping
George Washington Management Area, Chepachet

Most Beautiful Campgrounds
George Washington Management Area, Chepachet
Oak Embers Campground, West Greenwich
Peeper Pond Campground, Exeter
Whispering Pines Family Campground, Hope Valley

Most Private Campsites
Peeper Pond Campground, Exeter
Whippoorwill Hill Family Campground, Foster

Most Spacious Campsites
George Washington Management Area, Chepachet
Peeper Pond Campground, Exeter

Quietest Campgrounds
Legrand G. Reynolds Horsemen's Camping Area, Hope Valley

Cleanest Campgrounds
Legrand G. Reynolds Horsemen's Camping Area, Hope Valley

Best Campground Facilities
Timber Creek RV Resort, Westerly

Best Urban and Suburban Settings
Legrand G. Reynolds Horsemen's Camping Area, Hope Valley

Most Romantic Campgrounds
Legrand G. Reynolds Horsemen's Camping Area, Hope Valley

Best Family-Oriented Campgrounds
Card's Camp, Wakefield
Wawaloam Campground, Richmond
Timber Creek RV Resort, Westerly

Best Swimming Pools
Timber Creek RV Resort, Westerly
Wawaloam Campground, Richmond

SOUTH CAROLINA

Best RV Camping
- Calhoun Falls State Park, Calhoun Falls
- Modoc Campground, J. Strom Thurmond Lake, Modoc

Best Tent Camping
- Calhoun Falls State Park, Calhoun Falls
- Modoc Campground, J. Strom Thurmond Lake, Modoc

Most Beautiful Campgrounds
- Baker Creek State Park, McCormick
- Calhoun Falls State Park, Calhoun Falls
- Edisto Beach State Park, Edisto Island
- Hamilton Branch State Park, J. Strom Thurmond Reservoir, Plum Branch
- Hunting Island State Park, Hunting Island
- Lake Greenwood State Recreation Area, Ninety-Six
- Lake Hartwell State Park, Fair Play
- Lake Wateree State Recreation Area, Winnsboro
- Modoc Campground, J. Strom Thurmond Lake, Modoc
- Oconee State Park, Mountain Rest
- Santee State Park, Santee
- Springfield Campground, Hartwell Lake, Anderson

Most Private Campsites
- Calhoun Falls State Park, Calhoun Falls
- Lake Wateree State Recreation Area, Winnsboro
- Modoc Campground, J. Strom Thurmond Lake, Modoc

Most Spacious Campsites
- Calhoun Falls State Park, Calhoun Falls
- Hamilton Branch State Park, J. Strom Thurmond Reservoir, Plum Branch
- Lake Hartwell State Park, Fair Play
- Modoc Campground, J. Strom Thurmond Lake, Modoc
- Springfield Campground, Hartwell Lake, Anderson

Quietest Campgrounds
- Calhoun Falls State Park, Calhoun Falls
- Lake Wateree State Recreation Area, Winnsboro
- Modoc Campground, J. Strom Thurmond Lake, Modoc
- Oconee State Park, Mountain Rest
- Sesquicentennial State Park, Columbia

Most Secure Campgrounds
- Dreher Island State Park, Chapin
- Huntington Beach State Park, Murrells Inlet
- Kings Mountain State Park, Blacksburg
- Lake Greenwood State Recreation Area, Ninety-Six
- Lake Wateree State Recreation Area, Winnsboro
- Lakewood Camping Resort, Myrtle Beach
- Modoc Campground, J. Strom Thurmond Lake, Modoc
- Myrtle Beach State Park, Myrtle Beach
- Myrtle Beach Travel Park, Myrtle Beach
- Ocean Lakes Family Campground, Myrtle Beach
- Rocks Pond Campground and Marina, Eutawville
- Sesquicentennial State Park, Columbia
- Springfield Campground, Hartwell Lake, Anderson

Cleanest Campgrounds
- Calhoun Falls State Park, Calhoun Falls

Best Campground Facilities
- Kings Mountain State Park, Blacksburg
- Lakewood Camping Resort, Myrtle Beach
- Myrtle Beach Travel Park, Myrtle Beach
- Ocean Lakes Family Campground, Myrtle Beach

Best Rural, Farm, or Ranch Settings
- Kings Mountain State Park, Blacksburg

Best Urban and Suburban Settings
- Barefoot Camping Resort, Myrtle Beach
- Cunningham RV Park, Spartanburg
- Lakewood Camping Resort, Myrtle Beach
- Mt. Pleasant/Charleston KOA, Charleston/Mt. Pleasant
- Myrtle Beach State Park, Myrtle Beach
- Myrtle Beach Travel Park, Myrtle Beach
- Ocean Lakes Family Campground, Myrtle Beach
- Sesquicentennial State Park, Columbia

Best Mountain Settings
- Oconee State Park, Mountain Rest
- Table Rock State Park, Pickens

Best Waterfront Settings
- Baker Creek State Park, McCormick
- Calhoun Falls State Park, Calhoun Falls
- Dreher Island State Park, Chapin
- Lake Greenwood State Recreation Area, Ninety-Six
- Lake Hartwell State Park, Fair Play
- Lake Wateree State Recreation Area, Winnsboro
- Modoc Campground, J. Strom Thurmond Lake, Modoc
- Oconee State Park, Mountain Rest
- Santee State Park, Santee
- Springfield Campground, Hartwell Lake, Anderson

Most Romantic Campgrounds
- Calhoun Falls State Park, Calhoun Falls
- Hamilton Branch State Park, J. Strom Thurmond Reservoir, Plum Branch
- Lake Hartwell State Park, Fair Play
- Lake Wateree State Recreation Area, Winnsboro
- Modoc Campground, J. Strom Thurmond Lake, Modoc
- Oconee State Park, Mountain Rest
- Springfield Campground, Hartwell Lake, Anderson

Best Family-Oriented Campgrounds
- Hunting Island State Park, Hunting Island
- Kings Mountain State Park, Blacksburg
- Lakewood Camping Resort, Myrtle Beach
- Myrtle Beach State Park, Myrtle Beach
- Myrtle Beach Travel Park, Myrtle Beach
- Ocean Lakes Family Campground, Myrtle Beach

Best Swimming Pools
- River Plantation RV Park, Sevierville
- Standing Stone State Park, Hilham
- Twin Creek RV Resort, Gatlinburg
- Valley KOA Kampground, Pulaski

SOUTH DAKOTA

Best RV Camping
- Fort Worden State Park, Port Townsend

Best Tent Camping
- Corps of Engineers Downstream, Pierre
- Palisades State Park, Garretson
- Stokes-Thomas Lake City Park, Watertown

Most Beautiful Campgrounds
- Badlands National Park, Interior
- Custer Mountain Cabins and Campground, Custer
- Palisades State Park, Garretson
- Rafter J. Bar Ranch Campground, Hill

Most Private Campsites
- Corps of Engineers Downstream, Pierre
- Oakwood Lakes State Park, Brookings
- Palisades State Park, Garretson
- Stokes-Thomas Lake City Park, Watertown

Most Spacious Campsites
- Corps of Engineers Downstream, Pierre
- Oakwood Lakes State Park, Brookings
- Palisades State Park, Garretson
- Stokes-Thomas Lake City Park, Watertown

Quietest Campgrounds
- Custer Mountain Cabins and Campground, Custer

Most Secure Campgrounds
- Beckler River Campground, Skyhomish

Best Rural, Farm, or Ranch Settings
- Rafter J. Bar Ranch Campground, Hill

Best Urban and Suburban Settings
- Rushmore Shadows Resort, Rapid City

Best Mountain Settings
- Custer Mountain Cabins and Campground, Custer

Best Waterfront Settings
- Oakwood Lakes State Park, Brookings

Most Romantic Campgrounds
- Palisades State Park, Garretson

SOUTH DAKOTA (continued)

Best Family-Oriented Campgrounds
Horse Thief Campground and Resort, Hill City
Yogi Bear's Jellystone Park, Sioux Falls

Best Swimming Pools
Griffen Park, Pierre

TENNESSEE

Best RV Camping
Elkmont Campground, Great Smoky Mountains National Park, Gatlinburg
Fall Creek Falls State Park, Pikeville
Harrison Bay State Park, Chattanooga
Outdoor Resorts of America, Gatlinburg

Best Tent Camping
Chilhowee Campground, Cherokee National Forest, Benton
Cosby Campground, Great Smoky Mountains National Park, Cosby
Fall Creek Falls State Park, Pikeville
Harrison Bay State Park, Chattanooga
Indian Boundary Campground, Cherokee National Forest, Tellico Plains
Little Oak Campground, Cherokee National Forest, Unicoi

Most Beautiful Campgrounds
Cheatham Lake Lock A Campground, Ashland City
Chilhowee Campground, Cherokee National Forest, Benton
Cumberland Mountain State Park, Crossville
David Crockett State Park, Lawrenceburg
Indian Boundary Campground, Cherokee National Forest, Tellico Plains
Little Oak Campground, Cherokee National Forest, Unicoi
Outdoor Resorts of America, Gatlinburg
Piney Campground, Land Between the Lakes, Dover

Most Private Campsites
Fall Creek Falls State Park, Pikeville
Indian Boundary Campground, Cherokee National Forest, Tellico Plains
Little Oak Campground, Cherokee National Forest, Unicoi
Old Stone Fort State Archaeological Area, Manchester
Rock Island State Park, Rock Island

Most Spacious Campsites
Bandy Creek Campground, Big South Fork National River and Recreation Area, Oneida
Cheatham Lake Lock A Campground, Ashland City
Chilhowee Campground, Cherokee National Forest, Benton
Fall Creek Falls State Park, Pikeville
Harrison Bay State Park, Chattanooga
Indian Boundary Campground, Cherokee National Forest, Tellico Plains
Little Oak Campground, Cherokee National Forest, Unicoi
Old Stone Fort State Archaeological Area, Manchester

Quietest Campgrounds
Chilhowee Campground, Cherokee National Forest, Benton
Fall Creek Falls State Park, Pikeville
Little Oak Campground, Cherokee National Forest, Unicoi
Outdoor Resorts of America, Gatlinburg
Pickett State Park, Jamestown
Rock Island State Park, Rock Island
Standing Stone State Park, Hilham

Most Secure Campgrounds
Cheatham Lake Lock A Campground, Ashland City
Chilhowee Campground, Cherokee National Forest, Benton
Cumberland Mountain State Park, Crossville
David Crockett State Park, Lawrenceburg
Indian Boundary Campground, Cherokee National Forest, Tellico Plains
Little Oak Campground, Cherokee National Forest, Unicoi
Outdoor Resorts of America, Gatlinburg
Piney Campground, Land Between the Lakes, Dover

Cleanest Campgrounds
Cheatham Lake Lock A Campground, Ashland City
Little Oak Campground, Cherokee National Forest, Unicoi
Outdoor Resorts of America, Gatlinburg
Piney Campground, Land Between the Lakes, Dover
Reelfoot Lake State Park, South Campground, Tiptonville
Twin Creek RV Resort, Gatlinburg

Best Campground Facilities
Chickasaw State Park, Henderson
Cumberland Mountain State Park, Crossville
Fall Creek Falls State Park, Pikeville
Harrison Bay State Park, Chattanooga
Montgomery Bell State Park, Burns
Paris Landing State Resort Park, Buchanan
Pin Oak Campground, Natchez Trace State Resort Park, Wildersville
Piney Campground, Land Between the Lakes, Dover
Tims Ford State Park, Winchester
Warrior's Path State Park, Kingsport
Yogi Bear's Jellystone Park, Gatlinburg

Best Rural, Farm, or Ranch Settings
Loretta Lynn Dude Ranch, Hurricane Mills

Best Urban and Suburban Settings
Holiday Trav-L-Park of Chattanooga, Chattanooga
Manchester KOA, Manchester
Memphis-Graceland KOA, Memphis
Nashville KOA Kampground, Nashville
T.O. Fuller State Park, Memphis

Best Mountain Settings
Bandy Creek Campground, Big South Fork National River and Recreation Area, Oneida
Cades Cove Campground, Great Smoky Mountains National Park, Townesnd
Chilhowee Campground, Cherokee National Forest, Benton
Cosby Campground, Great Smoky Mountains National Park, Cosby
Elkmont Campground, Great Smoky Mountains National Park, Gatlinburg
Indian Boundary Campground, Cherokee National Forest, Tellico Plains
Little Oak Campground, Cherokee National Forest, Unicoi
Little River Village, Townsend
Outdoor Resorts of America, Gatlinburg
Tremont Hills Campground, Townsend
Twin Creek RV Resort, Gatlinburg
Yogi Bear's Jellystone Park, Gatlinburg

Best Waterfront Settings
Cheatham Lake Lock A Campground, Ashland City
Harrison Bay State Park, Chattanooga
Indian Boundary Campground, Cherokee National Forest, Tellico Plains
Little Oak Campground, Cherokee National Forest, Unicoi
Little River Village, Townsend
Pin Oak Campground, Natchez Trace State Resort Park, Wildersville
Piney Campground, Land Between the Lakes, Dover
Reelfoot Lake State Park, South Campground, Tiptonville
Tremont Hills Campground, Townsend
Warrior's Path State Park, Kingsport

Most Romantic Campgrounds
Chilhowee Campground, Cherokee National Forest, Benton
Fall Creek Falls State Park, Pikeville
Harrison Bay State Park, Chattanooga
Indian Boundary Campground, Cherokee National Forest, Tellico Plains
Little Oak Campground, Cherokee National Forest, Unicoi

Best Family-Oriented Campgrounds
Loretta Lynn Dude Ranch, Hurricane Mills
Yogi Bear's Jellystone Park, Gatlinburg

Best Swimming Pools
River Plantation RV Park, Sevierville
Standing Stone State Park, Hilham
Twin Creek RV Resort, Gatlinburg
Valley KOA Kampground, Pulaski

TEXAS

Best RV Camping
Angelina National Forest, Boykin Springs and Sandy Creek Recreation Areas, Zavalla
Guadalupe River State Park, Spring Branch
Lake Somerville State Park & Trailway, Somerville, Ledbetter
Buescher State Park, Smithville
Caprock Canyons State Park and Trailway, Quitaque
Lake Mineral Wells State Park and Trailway, Mineral Wells
Caddo Lake State Park, Karnack
Pedernales Falls State Park, Johnson City
Daingerfield State Park, Daingerfield
Seminole Canyon State Historical Park, Comstock
Cedar Hill State Park, Cedar Hill
Big Bend National Park Chisos Basin and Cottonwood Campgrounds, Big Bend National Park

Best Tent Camping
Cooper Lake State Park (South Sulpher Unit), Sulpher Springs
Guadalupe River State Park, Spring Branch
Lake Somerville State Park & Trailway, Somerville, Ledbetter
Buescher State Park, Smithville
Caprock Canyons State Park and Trailway, Quitaque
Mustang Island State Park, Port Aransas
Lake Mineral Wells State Park and Trailway, Mineral Wells
Meridian State Park, Meridian
Caddo Lake State Park, Karnack
Pedernales Falls State Park, Johnson City
Daingerfield State Park, Daingerfield
Cooper Lake State Park (Doctor's Creek Unit), Cooper
Garner State Park, Concan
Seminole Canyon State Historical Park, Comstock
Cedar Hill State Park, Cedar Hill
Big Bend National Park Chisos Basin and Cottonwood Campgrounds, Big Bend National Park
Atlanta State Park, Atlanta
Angelina National Forest, Boykin Springs and Sandy Creek Recreation Areas,

Most Beautiful Campgrounds
Angelina National Forest, Boykin Springs and Sandy Creek Recreation Areas, Zavalla
Lost Maples State Natural Area, Vanderpool
Guadalupe River State Park, Spring Branch
Lake Somerville State Park & Trailway, Somerville, Ledbetter
Buescher State Park, Smithville
Caprock Canyons State Park and Trailway, Quitaque
Bentson-Rio Grande Valley State Park, Mission
Lake Mineral Wells State Park and Trailway, Mineral Wells
Fort Parker State Park, Mexia
Meridian State Park, Meridian
Caddo Lake State Park, Karnack
Pedernales Falls State Park, Johnson City
Daingerfield State Park, Daingerfield
Garner State Park, Concan
Seminole Canyon State Historical Park, Comstock
Cedar Hill State Park, Cedar Hill
River Bend Resort, Brownsville
Big Bend National Park Chisos Basin and Cottonwood Campgrounds, Big Bend National Park
Bastrop State Park, Bastrop

Most Private Campsites
Daingerfield State Park, Daingerfield
Pedernales Falls State Park, Johnson City
Lake Mineral Wells State Park and Trailway, Mineral Wells
Buescher State Park, Smithville
Lake Somerville State Park & Trailway, Somerville, Ledbetter
Angelina National Forest, Boykin Springs and Sandy Creek Recreation Areas, Zavalla

Most Spacious Campsites
Daingerfield State Park, Daingerfield
Pedernales Falls State Park, Johnson City
Lake Mineral Wells State Park and Trailway, Mineral Wells
Caprock Canyons State Park and Trailway, Quitaque
Buescher State Park, Smithville
Lake Somerville State Park & Trailway, Somerville, Ledbetter
Guadalupe River State Park, Spring Branch
Angelina National Forest, Boykin Springs and Sandy Creek Recreation Areas, Zavalla

Quietest Campgrounds
Atlanta State Park, Atlanta
Big Bend National Park Chisos Basin and Cottonwood Campgrounds, Big Bend National Park
Cedar Hill State Park, Cedar Hill
Seminole Canyon State Historical Park, Comstock
Cooper Lake State Park (Doctor's Creek Unit), Cooper
Daingerfield State Park, Daingerfield
Eisenhower State Park, Denison
Pedernales Falls State Park, Johnson City
Caddo Lake State Park, Karnack
Village Creek State Park, Lumberton
Meridian State Park, Meridian
Fort Parker State Park, Mexia
Lake Mineral Wells State Park and Trailway, Mineral Wells
Caprock Canyons State Park and Trailway, Quitaque
Buescher State Park, Smithville
Lake Somerville State Park & Trailway, Somerville, Ledbetter
Guadalupe River State Park, Spring Branch
Cooper Lake State Park (South Sulpher Unit), Sulpher Springs
Ray Roberts State Park (Johnson Branch Unit), Valley View
Angelina National Forest, Boykin Springs and Sandy Creek Recreation Areas, Zavalla

Most Secure Campgrounds
Lost Maples State Natural Area, Vanderpool
Guadalupe River State Park, Spring Branch
Long Island Village, Port Isabel
Village Creek State Park, Lumberton
Mission RV Park, El Paso
Seminole Canyon State Historical Park, Comstock
Cedar Hill State Park, Cedar Hill
Palo Duro Canyon State Park, Canyon
Choke Canyon State Park, Calliham, Three Rivers
Possum Kingdom State Park, Caddo
Big Bend National Park Chisos Basin and Cottonwood Campgrounds, Big Bend National Park

Cleanest Campgrounds
Big Bend National Park Chisos Basin and Cottonwood Campgrounds, Big Bend National Park
River Bend Resort, Brownsville
Seminole Canyon State Historical Park, Comstock
Mission RV Park, El Paso
Pedernales Falls State Park, Johnson City
Long Island Village, Port Isabel
Caprock Canyons State Park and Trailway, Quitaque
Admiralty RV Resort, San Antonio
Lake Somerville State Park & Trailway, Somerville, Ledbetter
Ray Roberts State Park (Johnson Branch Unit), Valley View
Lost Maples State Natural Area, Vanderpool

Best Campground Facilities
Bastrop State Park, Bastrop
River Bend Resort, Brownsville
Choke Canyon State Park, Calliham, Three Rivers
Cedar Hill State Park, Cedar Hill
Garner State Park, Concan
Mission RV Park, El Paso
Long Island Village, Port Isabel
Buescher State Park, Smithville
Wagon Wheel Dude Ranch, Snyder

Best Rural, Farm, or Ranch Settings
Cedar Hill State Park, Cedar Hill
Wagon Wheel Dude Ranch, Snyder

Best Urban and Suburban Settings
Admiralty RV Resort, San Antonio
Austin Lone Star Resort, Austin
Bentson-Rio Grande Valley State Park, Mission
Chimney RV Park, Mission
Colonia del Rey RV Park, Corpus Christi
Fun 'n' Sun, San Benito
Galveston Island State Park, Galveston
Houston Leisure RV Resort, Houston
Long Island Village, Port Isabel
Pioneer RV Resort, Port Aransas
River Bend Resort, Brownsville
Trader's Village RV Park & Campground, Dallas/Fort Worth
Treetops RV Village, Arlington
United RV Resort, San Marcos
Victoria Palms, Donna

Best Mountain Settings
Big Bend National Park, Big Bend

Best Waterfront Settings
River Bend Resort, Brownsville
Cedar Hill State Park, Cedar Hill
Huntsville State Park, Huntsville
Guadalupe River RV Resort, Kerrville
Lake Corpus Christi State Park, Mathis
Fort Parker State Park, Mexia
Lake Mineral Wells State Park, Mineral Wells
Bentson-Rio Grande Valley State Park, Mission
Padre Island National Seashore, Padre Island
Pioneer RV Resort, Port Aransas
Long Island Village, Port Isabel

TEXAS (continued)

Best Waterfront Settings *(continued)*
Buescher State Park, Smithville
Lake Somerville State Park, Somerville
Angelina National Forest, Zavalla

Most Romantic Campgrounds
Big Bend National Park, Big Bend
Seminole Canyon State Historical Park, Comstock
Pedernales Falls State Park, Johnson City
Lake Miner al Wells State Park, Mineral Wells
Buescher State Park, Smithville
Lake Somerville State Park, Somerville
Angelina National Forest, Zavalla

Best Family-Oriented Campgrounds
Cedar Hill State Park, Cedar Hill
Guadalupe River RV Resort, Kerrville
Rusk/Palestine State Park, Rusk
Wagon Wheel Dude Ranch, Snyder

Best Swimming Pools
Alamo Palms, Alamo
Austin Lone Star RV Resort, Austin
Cowtown RV Park, Aledo
Treetops RV Village, Arlington
Alamo Fiesta RV Resort, Boerne
Bastrop State Park, Bastrop
River Bend Resort, Brownsville
Choke Canyon State Park, Calliham
Colonia del Rey RV Park, Corpus Christi
Trader's Village RV Park & Campground, Dallas-Fort Worth
Victoria Palms, Donna
Houston Leisure RV Resort, Houston
Guadalupe River RV Resort, Kerrville
Chimney RV Park, Mission
Las Aves RV Resort, Medina
Long Island Village, Port Isabel
Pioneer RV Resort, Port Aransas
Admiralty RV Resort, San Antonio
Fun 'n' Sun, San Benito
United RV Resort, San Marcos
Wagon Wheel Dude Ranch, Snyder

UTAH

Best RV Camping
Cannonville/Bryce Valley KOA, Cannonville
Rendezvous Beach, Bear Lake State Park
Ruby's RV Park & Campground, Bryce Canyon
Shady Acres RV Park & Campground, Green River
Wasatch Mountain State Park, Midway

Best Tent Camping
Calf Creek Campground, Escalante
Cannonville/Bryce Valley KOA, Cannonville
Devil's Canyon, Blanding
Devil's Garden Campground, Arches National Park
Escalante State Park, Escalante
Goblin Valley State Park, Hanksville
Green River State Park, Green River
Kodachrome Basin State Park, Cannonville
Minersville State Park, Beaver
Mitten View Campground, Monument Valley
Natural Bridges, Natural Bridges National Monument
North Campground, Bryce Canyon
Oasis Campground, Yuba State Park
Point Supreme Campground, Cedar Breaks National Monument
Red Canyon Campground, Bryce Canyon
Ruby's RV Park & Campground, Bryce Canyon
South & Watchman Campgrounds, Zion National Park
Squaw Flat Campground, Canyonlands National Park Needles District
Sunset Campground, Bryce Canyon
Wasatch Mountain State Park, Midway

Most Beautiful Campgrounds
Antelope Island State Park, Syracuse
Bullfrog Resort & Marina Campground/RV Park, Lake Powell
Calf Creek Campground, Escalante
Cedar Canyon Campground, Cedar City
Coral Pink Sand Dunes State Park, Kanab
Dead Horse Point State Park, Moab
Devil's Canyon, Blanding
Devil's Garden Campground, Arches National Park
Escalante State Park, Escalante
Fillmore KOA, Fillmore
Goblin Valley State Park, Hanksville
Goosenecks State Park, Mexican Hat
Kodachrome Basin State Park, Cannonville
Mitten View Campground, Monument Valley
Natural Bridges, Natural Bridges National Monument
Nephi KOA/Horseshoe Bar Ranch, Nephi
Oasis Campground, Yuba State Park
Point Supreme Campground, Cedar Breaks National Monument
Red Canyon Campground, Bryce Canyon
Red Cliffs Recreation Site, Leeds
Snow Canyon State Park, St. George
South & Watchman Campgrounds, Zion National Park
Squaw Flat Campground, Canyonlands National Park Needles District
Thousand Lakes RV Park, Torrey
Virgin River Canyon Recreation Area, Littlefield
Wasatch Mountain State Park, Midway
White Bridge Campground, Panguitch Lake
Willow Flat Campground, Canyonlands National Park Island in the Sky District

Most Private Campsites
Antelope Island State Park, Syracuse
Calf Creek Campground, Escalante
Cedar Canyon Campground, Cedar City
Coral Pink Sand Dunes State Park, Kanab
Devil's Canyon, Blanding
Devil's Garden Campground, Arches National Park
Escalante State Park, Escalante
Goblin Valley State Park, Hanksville
Green River State Park, Green River
Natural Bridges, Natural Bridges National Monument
Point Supreme Campground, Cedar Breaks National Monument
Red Canyon Campground, Bryce Canyon
Red Cliffs Recreation Site, Leeds
Squaw Flat Campground, Canyonlands National Park Needles District
Wasatch Mountain State Park, Midway
Willow Flat Campground, Canyonlands National Park Island in the Sky District

Most Spacious Campsites
Calf Creek Campground, Escalante
Coral Pink Sand Dunes State Park, Kanab
Dead Horse Point State Park, Moab
Goblin Valley State Park, Hanksville
Green River State Park, Green River
Oasis Campground, Yuba State Park
Red Canyon Campground, Bryce Canyon
Ruby's RV Park & Campground, Bryce Canyon
Shady Acres RV Park & Campground, Green River
Squaw Flat Campground, Canyonlands National Park Needles District
United Campground, Green River
Wasatch Mountain State Park, Midway

Quietest Campgrounds
Antelope Island State Park, Syracuse
Calf Creek Campground, Escalante
Goblin Valley State Park, Hanksville
Minersville State Park, Beaver
Natural Bridges, Natural Bridges National Monument
Nephi KOA/Horseshoe Bar Ranch, Nephi
Snow Canyon State Park, St. George
Squaw Flat Campground, Canyonlands National Park Needles District
White Bridge Campground, Panguitch Lake

Most Secure Campgrounds
Antelope Island State Park, Syracuse
Cadillac Ranch RV Park, Bluff
Canyonlands Campground, Moab
Coral Pink Sand Dunes State Park, Kanab
Dead Horse Point State Park, Moab

Most Secure Campgrounds
Goulding's Monument Valley Campground, Monument Valley
Green River State Park, Green River
Moab KOA, Moab
Panguitch Big Fish KOA, Panguitch
South & Watchman Campgrounds, Zion National Park
Squaw Flat Campground, Canyonlands National Park Needles District
United Campground, Green River

Cleanest Campgrounds
Cadillac Ranch RV Park, Bluff
Canyonlands Campground, Moab
Dead Horse Point State Park, Moab
Devil's Canyon, Blanding
Devil's Garden Campground, Arches National Park

UTAH (continued)

Fillmore KOA, Fillmore
Goosenecks State Park, Mexican Hat
Green River State Park, Green River
Hovenweep Campground, Hovenweep National Monument
Moab KOA, Moab
Moab Rim Campark, Moab
Natural Bridges, Natural Bridges National Monument
Nephi KOA/Horseshoe Bar Ranch, Nephi
Portal RV Park & Fishery, Moab
Squaw Flat Campground, Canyonlands National Park Needles District
Thousand Lakes RV Park, Torrey
United Campground, Green River
Willow Flat Campground, Canyonlands National Park Island in the Sky District
Wonderland RV Park, Torrey
Zion River Resort RV Park & Campground, Virgin

Best Campground Facilities

Bullfrog Resort & Marina Campground/RV Park, Lake Powell
Canyonlands Campground, Moab
Goulding's Monument Valley Campground, Monument Valley
Moab KOA, Moab
Ruby's RV Park & Campground, Bryce Canyon
Shady Acres RV Park & Campground, Green River
United Beaver Campground, Beaver

Best Rural, Farm, or Ranch Settings

Arch View Camp Park, Moab
Zion River Resort RV Park & Campground, Virgin
Brentwood RV Resort, Hurricane
Bryce/Zion KOA, Glendale
Cannonville/Bryce Valley KOA, Cannonville
Duck Creek Campground, Cedar City
Escalante State Park, Escalante

Best Rural, Farm, or Ranch Settings

Mitten View Campground, Monument Valley
Moab KOA, Moab
Moab Rim Campark, Moab
Nephi KOA/Horseshoe Bar Ranch, Nephi
Panguitch Big Fish KOA, Panguitch
Portal RV Park & Fishery, Moab
Red Rock Restaurant and Campground, Hanksville
Riverside Motel & RV Park, Hatch
Zion West RV Park, Leeds

Best Urban and Suburban Settings

Broken Bow RV Camp, Escalante
Butch Cassidy Campground, Salina
Cadillac Ranch RV Park, Bluff
Canyonlands Campground, Moab
Fillmore KOA, Fillmore
Green River KOA, Green River
Green River State Park, Green River
Shady Acres RV Park & Campground, Green River
United Beaver Campground, Beaver
United Campground, Green River
Zephyr Cove RV Park & Campground, Lake Tahoe

Best Mountain Settings

Bryce/Zion KOA, Glendale
Calf Creek Campground, Escalante
Cannonville/Bryce Valley KOA, Cannonville

Best Mountain Settings

Devil's Garden Campground, Arches National Park
Fruita Campground, Torrey
Goblin Valley State Park, Hanksville
Goulding's Monument Valley Campground, Monument Valley
Kodachrome Basin State Park, Cannonville
Mukuntuweep RV Park & Campground, Zion National Park
Nephi KOA/Horseshoe Bar Ranch, Nephi
North Campground, Bryce Canyon
Point Supreme Campground, Cedar Breaks National Monument
Red Cliffs Recreation Site, Leeds
Snow Canyon State Park, St. George
South & Watchman Campgrounds, Zion National Park
Squaw Flat Campground, Canyonlands National Park Needles District
Thousand Lakes RV Park, Torrey
White Bridge Campground, Panguitch Lake
Zion Canyon Campground, Springdale

Best Waterfront Settings

Antelope Island State Park, Syracuse
Bear Paw Lakeview Resort, Panguitch Lake
Escalante State Park, Escalante
Minersville State Park, Beaver
Oasis Campground, Yuba State Park
Palisade State Park, Manti
Quail Creek State Park, St. George
Willard Bay State Park, Willard

Most Romantic Campgrounds

Antelope Island State Park, Syracuse
Calf Creek Campground, Escalante
Devil's Garden Campground, Arches National Park
Fruita Campground, Torrey
Goblin Valley State Park, Hanksville
Hovenweep Campground, Hovenweep National Monument
Kodachrome Basin State Park, Cannonville
Mitten View Campground, Monument Valley
Nephi KOA/Horseshoe Bar Ranch, Nephi
Point Supreme Campground, Cedar Breaks National Monument
Red Canyon Campground, Bryce Canyon
Red Cliffs Recreation Site, Leeds
Rendezvous Beach, Bear Lake State Park
Snow Canyon State Park, St. George
Wasatch Mountain State Park, Midway

Best Family-Oriented Campgrounds

Arch View Camp Park, Moab
Bear Paw Lakeview Resort, Panguitch Lake
Brentwood RV Resort, Hurricane
Bryce/Zion KOA, Glendale
Butch Cassidy Campground, Salina
Cannonville/Bryce Valley KOA, Cannonville
Coral Pink Sand Dunes State Park, Kanab
Escalante State Park, Escalante
Fillmore KOA, Fillmore
Fruita Campground, Torrey
Goulding's Monument Valley Campground, Monument Valley
Green River KOA, Green River
Moab KOA, Moab
Nephi KOA/Horseshoe Bar Ranch, Nephi
Panguitch Big Fish KOA, Panguitch
Rendezvous Beach, Bear Lake State Park
Shady Acres RV Park & Campground, Green River
Snow Canyon State Park, St. George
United Beaver Campground, Beaver
United Campground, Green River
Wasatch Mountain State Park, Midway
Zion Canyon Campground, Springdale
Zion River Resort RV Park & Campground, Virgin

Best Swimming Pools

Arch View Camp Park, Moab
Bryce Canyon Pines, Bryce Canyon
Bryce/Zion KOA, Glendale
Butch Cassidy Campground, Salina
Cadillac Ranch RV Park, Bluff
Cannonville/Bryce Valley KOA, Cannonville
Canyonlands Campground, Moab
Fillmore KOA, Fillmore
Goulding's Monument Valley Campground, Monument Valley
Green River KOA, Green River
Moab KOA, Moab
Nephi KOA/Horseshoe Bar Ranch, Nephi
Panguitch Big Fish KOA, Panguitch
Ruby's RV Park & Campground, Bryce Canyon
Shady Acres RV Park & Campground, Green River
Thousand Lakes RV Park, Torrey
United Beaver Campground, Beaver
United Campground, Green River
Wonderland RV Park, Torrey
Zion Canyon Campground, Springdale
Zion River Resort RV Park & Campground, Virgin

VERMONT

Best Tent Camping
Gifford Woods State Park, Killington
Green Mountain National Forest Campgrounds, Rutland
Kettle Pond State Park, Marshfield
Knight Island State Park, St. Albans Bay
Mount Moosalamoo Campground, Middlebury

Most Beautiful Campgrounds
Belview Campground, Barton
Brighton State Park, Island Pond
Burton Island State Park, St. Albans Bay
Camp Skyland on Lake Champlain, South Hero
Elmore State Park, Lake Elmore
Gifford Woods State Park, Killington
Green Mountain National Forest Campgrounds, Rutland
Half Moon Pond State Park, Fair Haven
Kettle Pond State Park, Marshfield
Kings Bay Campground, North Hero
Knight Island State Park, St. Albans Bay
Mount Moosalamoo Campground, Middlebury
Mountain View Campground & Cabins, Morrisville
Sugar Ridge RV Village & Campground, Danville

Most Private Campsites
Half Moon Pond State Park, Fair Haven
Kettle Pond State Park, Marshfield
Knight Island State Park, St. Albans Bay
Mount Moosalamoo Campground, Middlebury

Most Spacious Campsites
Falls of Lana, Middlebury
Goose Point, Alburg
Green Mountain National Forest Campgrounds, Rutland
Kettle Pond State Park, Marshfield
Mount Moosalamoo Campground, Middlebury

Quietest Campgrounds
Burton Island State Park, St. Albans Bay
Champlain Adult Campground, Grand Isle
Falls of Lana, Middlebury
Green Mountain National Forest Campgrounds, Rutland
Kettle Pond State Park, Marshfield
Knight Island State Park, St. Albans Bay
Mount Moosalamoo Campground, Middlebury

Most Secure Campgrounds
Half Moon Pond State Park, Fair Haven

Cleanest Campgrounds
Brighton State Park, Island Pond
Covenant Hills Christian Camp, Marshfield
Half Moon Pond State Park, Fair Haven
Mount Moosalamoo Campground, Middlebury

Best Campground Facilities
Mountain View Campground & Cabins, Morrisville

Best Rural, Farm, or Ranch Settings
Brighton State Park, Island Pond
Kettle Pond State Park, Marshfield

Best Urban and Suburban Settings
Brewster River Campground, Jeffersonville
Burlington's North Beach Campground, Burlington
Fireside Campground, Derby
Lone Pine Campsites, Colchester

Best Mountain Settings
Camp Skyland on Lake Champlain, South Hero
Mountain View Campground & Cabins, Morrisville

Best Waterfront Settings
Alburg RV Resort, Alburg
Belview Campground, Barton
Gold Brook Campground, Stowe
Knight Island State Park, St. Albans Bay
Lakeside Camping, Island Pond
Mill Pond Campground, Franklin

Most Romantic Campgrounds
Burton Island State Park, St. Albans Bay
Camp Skyland on Lake Champlain, South Hero
Champlain Adult Campground, Grand Isle
Kettle Pond State Park, Marshfield

Best Family-Oriented Campgrounds
Apple Tree Bay Campground, South Hero
Hide-A-Way Cove Family Campground, East Killingly
Lone Pine Campsites, Colchester
Sugar Ridge RV Village & Campground, Danville

Best Swimming Pools
Sugar Ridge RV Village & Campground, Danville

VIRGINIA

Best RV Camping
Bethpage Camp-Resort, Urbanna
Cherrystone Family Camping and RV Resort, Cheriton

Best Tent Camping
Cherrystone Family Camping and RV Resort, Cheriton
Thousand Trails—Virginia Landing, Quinby

Most Beautiful Campgrounds
Candy Hill Campground, Winchester
KOA—Colonial Central, Williamsburg
Outdoor World—Williamsburg Campground, Williamsburg
Shenandoah Hills Campground, Madison
Thousand Trails—Chesapeake Bay, Glenns

Most Private Campsites
Battle of Cedar Creek Campground, Middletown
Big Meadows Campground, Luray
Cozy Acres Campground, Powhatan
Ed Allen's Campgrounds and Cottages—Chickahominy Recreational Park, Providence Forge
Hungry Mother State Park, Marion
Meadows of Dan Campground, Meadows of Dan
Thousand Trails—Virginia Landing, Quinby

Most Spacious Campsites
Big Meadows Campground, Luray
Shenandoah Hills Campground, Madison

Quietest Campground
Meadows of Dan Campground, Meadows of Dan

Most Secure Campgrounds
Americamps—Lake Gaston, Bracey
Christopher Run Campground, Mineral
Fairy Stone State Park, Bassett
Holiday Trav-L-Park, Virginia Beach
Meadows of Dan Campground, Meadows of Dan
Newport News Park Campground, Newport News
Outdoor Resorts—Virginia Beach, Virginia Beach
Riverside Campground, Abingdon
Thousand Trails—Virginia Landing, Quinby

Cleanest Campgrounds
Big Meadows Campground, Luray
Cherrystone Family Camping and RV Resort, Cheriton
Lewis Mountain Campground, Luray
Mathews Arm Campground, Luray

Best Campground Facilities
Bethpage Camp-Resort, Urbanna
Campground at Natural Bridge, Natural Bridge Station
Cherrystone Family Camping and RV Resort, Cheriton
Holiday Trav-L-Park, Virginia Beach
Outdoor World—Williamsburg Campground, Williamsburg
Thousand Trails—Chesapeake Bay, Glenns
Tom's Cove Park, Chincoteague
Yogi Bear's Jellystone Park Camp Resort, Luray

Best Rural, Farm, or Ranch Settings
A Wonderful Life Campground, Buchanan
Cozy Acres Campground, Powhatan
Greenville Farm Family Campground, Haymarket
Thousand Trails—Lynchburg, Rustburg

Best Urban and Suburban Settings
Aquia Pines Camp Resort, Stafford
Bull Run Regional Park, Centreville
Burke Lake Park, Fairfax Station
Candy Hill Campground, Winchester
Holiday Trav-L-Park, Virginia Beach
Jamestown Beach Campsites, Williamsburg
KOA—Fredericksburg/Washington, D.C., Fredericksburg
KOA—Williamsburg, Williamsburg
Lake Fairfax Park, Reston
Outdoor Resorts—Virginia Beach, Virginia Beach
Pohick Bay Regional Park, Lorton VA
Williamsburg Pottery Campground, Williamsburg

Best Mountain Settings
Campground at Natural Bridge, Natural Bridge Station
Candy Hill Campground, Winchester
Shenandoah Hills Campground, Madison
Yogi Bear's Jellystone Park, Luray

VIRGINIA (continued)

Best Waterfront Settings
Bethpage Camping Resort, Urbanna
Campground at Natural Bridge, Natural Bridge Station
Cherrystone Family Camping and RV Resort, Cheriton
Christopher Run Campground, Mineral
Tom's Cove Park, Chincoteague

Most Romantic Campgrounds
Campground at Natural Bridge, Natural Bridge Station
Cherrystone Family Camping and RV Resort, Cheriton
Christopher Run Campground, Mineral
Shenandoah Hills Campground, Madison
Tom's Cove Park, Chincoteague

Best Family-Oriented Campgrounds
Bethpage Camp-Resort, Urbanna
Cherrystone Family Camping and RV Resort, Cheriton

Best Swimming Pools
A Wonderful Life Campground, Buchanan
Bethpage Camp Resort, Urbanna
Cherrystone Family Camping and RV Resort, Cheriton
Ed Allen's Campgrounds and Cottages, Lanexa
Holiday Trav-L-Park, Virginia Beach
Lake Fairfax Park, Reston
Outdoor World—Williamsburg, Williamsburg
Shenandoah Hills Campground, Madison
Yogi Bear's Jellystone Park, Luray

WASHINGTON

Best RV Camping
Cheyenne KOA, Cheyenne
Hoh Rainforest Campground, Western Olympic National Park
Icicle River RV Resort, Leavenworth
Sunbanks Resort, Electric City
Trailer Inns RV Park, Seattle (Bellevue)
Trailer Inns RV Park, Yakima
Yakama Nation Resort RV Park, Yakima (Toppenish)
Yogi Bear's Camp Resort, Spokane

Best Tent Camping
Fort Flagler State Park, Port Townsend
Heart of the Hills Campground, Port Angeles (Olympic National Park)
Hoh Rainforest Campground, Western Olympic National Park

Most Beautiful Campgrounds
Altaire Campground, Port Angeles (Olympic National Park)
Beckler River Campground, Skyhomish
Birch Bay State Park, Birch Bay
Brooks Memorial State Park, Goldendale
Cougar Rock Campground, Longmire
Dash Point State Park, Federal Way (Tacoma)
Denny Creek Campground, North Bend
Dungeness Recreation Area, Sequim
Fields Spring State Park, Anatone
Fort Ebey State Park, Coupeville
Fort Flagler State Park, Port Townsend
Fort Worden State Park, Port Townsend
Hang Cove Campground, Kettle Falls
Harmony Lakeside RV Park, Silver Creek
Heart of the Hills Campground, Port Angeles (Olympic National Park)
Hoh Rainforest Campground, Western Olympic National Park
Icicle River RV Resort, Leavenworth
Illahee State Park, Bremerton
Lake Wenatchee State Park, Leavenworth
Larrabee State Park, Bellingham
Log Cabin Resort, Port Angeles
Lower Falls Recreation Area, Swift
Mora Campground, La Push
Ohanapecosh Campground (Mount Rainier National Park), Packwood
Panorama Point Campground, Baker Lake
Shadow Mountain Campground, Port Angeles
Sol Duc Resort, Port Angeles (Olympic National Park)
Spencer Spit State Park, Lopez
Steamboat Rock State Park Campground, Electric City
Sun Lakes State Park Campground, Coulee City
Takhlakh Campground, Randle

Most Private Campsites
American Heritage Campground, Olympia
Beacon Rock State Park, Skamania
Corral Pass Campground, Enumclaw
Dungeness Recreation Area, Sequim
Hang Cove Campground, Kettle Falls
Illahee State Park, Bremerton
Larrabee State Park, Bellingham
Lower Falls Recreation Area, Swift
Merrill Lake Campground, Cougar
Mora Campground, La Push
Panorama Point Campground, Baker Lake
Spencer Spit State Park, Lopez
The Cedars RV Resort, Ferndale

Most Spacious Campsites
Beacon Rock State Park, Skamania
Corral Pass Campground, Enumclaw
Dungeness Recreation Area, Sequim
Fields Spring State Park, Anatone
Fort Ebey State Park, Coupeville
Hang Cove Campground, Kettle Falls
Illahee State Park, Bremerton
Larrabee State Park, Bellingham
Lower Falls Recreation Area, Swift
Merrill Lake Campground, Cougar
Midway RV Park, Centralia
Mora Campground, La Push
Panorama Point Campground, Baker Lake
Spencer Spit State Park, Lopez

Quietest Campgrounds
Beacon Rock State Park, Skamania
Brooks Memorial State Park, Goldendale
Corral Pass Campground, Enumclaw
Hang Cove Campground, Kettle Falls
Hoh Rainforest Campground, Western Olympic National Park
Icicle River RV Resort, Leavenworth
Lower Falls Recreation Area, Swift
Merrill Lake Campground, Cougar
Mora Campground, La Push
Spencer Spit State Park, Lopez
Steamboat Rock State Park Campground, Electric City
Takhlakh Campground, Randle

Most Secure Campgrounds
Cheyenne KOA, Cheyenne
Evergreen Court Campground, Ocean Park
Fort Ebey State Park, Coupeville
Yogi Bear's Camp Resort, Spokane

Cleanest Campgrounds
Altaire Campground, Port Angeles (Olympic National Park)
Beacon Rock State Park, Skamania
Brooks Memorial State Park, Goldendale
Cougar Rock Campground, Longmire
Evergreen Court Campground, Ocean Park
Fields Spring State Park, Anatone
Illahee State Park, Bremerton
Larrabee State Park, Bellingham
Lower Falls Recreation Area, Swift
Panorama Point Campground, Baker Lake
Sandy Heights RV Park, Pasco
Trailer Inns RV Park, Seattle (Bellevue)
Trailer Inns RV Park, Yakima

Best Campground Facilities
Sunbanks Resort, Electric City
Trailer Inns RV Park, Seattle (Bellevue)
Trailer Inns RV Park, Yakima
Yakama Nation Resort RV Park, Yakima (Toppenish)
Yogi Bear's Camp Resort, Spokane

Best Rural, Farm, or Ranch Settings
Columbia Riverfront RV Resort, Vancouver
Snoqualmie River Campground and RV Park, Fall City

Best Mountain Settings
Shadow Mountain Campground, Port Angeles

Best Waterfront Settings
Birch Bay State Park, Birch Bay
Lake Pleasant RV Park, Seattle
Lake Wenatchee State Park, Leavenworth
Merrill Lake Campground, Cougar

Most Romantic Campgrounds
Dungeness Recreation Area, Sequim
Hang Cove Campground, Kettle Falls
Illahee State Park, Bremerton
Lower Falls Recreation Area, Swift
Mora Campground, La Push
Spencer Spit State Park, Lopez

Best Swimming Pools
Trailer Inns RV Park, Yakima

WEST VIRGINIA

Most Beautiful Campground
Audra State Park, Buckhannon

Most Private Campsites
Alpine Shores Campground, Elkins
Audra State Park, Buckhannon
KOA—Pipestem, Pipestem
Organ Cave Campground, Ronceverte
Twin Falls Resort State Park, Mullens

Quietest Campgrounds
Audra State Park, Buckhannon
Twin Falls Resort State Park, Mullens

Most Secure Campgrounds
Fox Fire Resort, Milton
Greenbrier River State Forest, Caldwell
Twin Falls Resort State Park, Mullens

Cleanest Campgrounds
Audra State Park, Buckhannon
Cedar Creek State Park, Glenville
Greenbrier River State Forest, Caldwell
Kanawha State Forest, Charleston
Moncove Lake State Park, Gap Mills

Best Campground Facilities
Fox Fire Resort, Milton
KOA—Harper's Ferry/Washington, D.C. Northwest, Harper's Ferry
Pipestem Resort State Park, Pipestem
Twin Falls Resort State Park, Mullens

Best Rural, Farm, or Ranch Settings
Foxfire Camping Resort, Milton

Best Mountain Settings
Revelle's Family Campground, Elkins

Best Waterfront Settings
KOA—Harper's Ferry/Washington, D.C. Northwest, Harper's Ferry
Revelle's Family Campground, Elkins

Best Swimming Pool
Foxfire Resort, Milton

WISCONSIN

Best RV Camping
Neshonoc Lakeside Campground, West Salem
Yogi Bear's Jellystone Park Camp-Resort, Warrens
Buffalo Lake Camping Resort, Montello
Kilby Lake Campground, Montello
Hidden Valley RV Resort and Campground, Milton
Wagon Trail Campground, Ellison Bay
Frontier Wilderness Campground, Egg Harbor
Vista Royalle Campground, Bancroft

Best Tent Camping
Neshonoc Lakeside Campground, West Salem
Yogi Bear's Jellystone Park Camp-Resort, Warrens
Kilby Lake Campground, Montello
Heaven's Up North Family Campground, Lakewood
Hixton-Alma Center KOA, Hixton
Wagon Trail Campground, Ellison Bay
Frontier Wilderness Campground, Egg Harbor
Hickory Hills Campground, Edgerton
Vista Royalle Campground, Bancroft

Most Beautiful Campgrounds
Frontier Wilderness Campground, Egg Harbor
Heaven's Up North Family Campground, Lakewood
Hixton-Alma Center KOA, Hixton
Kilby Lake Campground, Montello
Neshonoc Lakeside Campground, West Salem
Potawatomi State Park Daisy Field Campground Sturgeon Bay
Vista Royalle Campground, Bancroft
Wagon Trail Campground, Ellison Bay
Wyalusing State Park Bagley
Yogi Bear's Jellystone Park Camp-Resort, Warrens

Most Private Campsites
Neshonoc Lakeside Campground, West Salem
Yogi Bear's Jellystone Park Camp-Resort, Warrens
Kilby Lake Campground, Montello
Hidden Valley RV Resort and Campground, Milton
Heaven's Up North Family Campground, Lakewood
Hixton-Alma Center KOA, Hixton
Wagon Trail Campground, Ellison Bay
Frontier Wilderness Campground, Egg Harbor
Hickory Hills Campground, Edgerton
Vista Royalle Campground, Bancroft

Most Spacious Campsites
Frontier Wilderness Campground, Egg Harbor
Heaven's Up North Family Campground, Lakewood
Hickory Hills Campground, Edgerton
Hidden Valley RV Resort and Campground, Milton
Hixton-Alma Center KOA, Hixton
Kilby Lake Campground, Montello
Neshonoc Lakeside Campground, West Salem
Vista Royalle Campground, Bancroft
Wagon Trail Campground, Ellison Bay
Yogi Bear's Jellystone Park Camp-Resort, Warrens

Quietest Campgrounds
Neshonoc Lakeside Campground, West Salem
Yogi Bear's Jellystone Park Camp-Resort, Warrens
Kilby Lake Campground, Montello
Hidden Valley RV Resort and Campground, Milton
Heaven's Up North Family Campground, Lakewood
Hixton-Alma Center KOA, Hixton
Wagon Trail Campground, Ellison Bay
Frontier Wilderness Campground, Egg Harbor
Hickory Hills Campground, Edgerton
Vista Royalle Campground, Bancroft

Most Secure Campgrounds
Vista Royalle Campground, Bancroft
Hickory Hills Campground, Edgerton
Hidden Valley RV Resort and Campground, Milton
Kilby Lake Campground, Montello
Buffalo Lake Camping Resort, Montello
Yogi Bear's Jellystone Park Camp-Resort, Warrens
Neshonoc Lakeside Campground, West Salem

Cleanest Campgrounds
Vista Royalle Campground, Bancroft
Hickory Hills Campground, Edgerton
Frontier Wilderness Campground, Egg Harbor
Wagon Trail Campground, Ellison Bay
Hixton-Alma Center KOA, Hixton
Heaven's Up North Family Campground, Lakewood
Hidden Valley RV Resort and Campground, Milton
Kilby Lake Campground, Montello
Leon Valley Campground , Sparta
Yogi Bear's Jellystone Park Camp-Resort, Warrens
Neshonoc Lakeside Campground, West Salem

Best Campground Facilities
Yogi Bear's Jellystone Park Camp-Resort, Warrens
Wagon Trail Campground, Ellison Bay
Vista Royalle Campground, Bancroft
Neshonoc Lakeside Campground, West Salem
Kilby Lake Campground, Montello
Hidden Valley RV Resort and Campground, Milton
Hickory Hills Campground, Edgerton
Frontier Wilderness Campground, Egg Harbor

Best Rural, Farm, or Ranch Settings
Door County Camping Retreat, Egg Harbor
Heaven's Up North Family Campground, Lakewood
Rice Lake-Haugen KOA, Rice Lake
Tunnel Trail Campground, Wilton
Vista Royalle Campground, Bancroft

Best Urban and Suburban Settings
Buffalo Lake Camping Resort, Montello

Best Waterfront Settings
Kilby Lake Campground, Montello
Lake Chippewa Campground, Hayward
Lake Lenwood Beach and Campground, West Bend
O'Neil Creek Campground & RV Park, Chippewa Falls
Wilderness Campground, Montello

Most Romantic Campgrounds
Frontier Wilderness Campground, Egg Harbor
Hixton-Alma Center KOA, Alma Center
Pine Aire Resort & Campground, Eagle River
Wagon Wheel Campground, Ellison Bay
Wyalusing State Park, Bagley

WISCONSIN (continued)

Best Family-Oriented Campgrounds
Hickory Hills Campground, Edgerton
Hidden Valley RV Resort and Campground, Milton
Jellystone Park at Fort Atkinson, Fort Atkinson
Westward Ho Camp Resort, Fond de Lac
Yogi Bear's Jellystone Park Camp Resort, Warrens
Yogi Bear's Jellystone Park Camp-Resort, Fremont

Best Swimming Pools
Timber Trail Campground, Algoma
Yogi Bear's Jellystone Park Camp-Resort, Bagley
Baileys Grove Travel Park and Campground, Baileys Harbor
Turtle Creek Campsite, Beloit
Parkland Village Campground, Black River Falls
Happy Acres Kampground, Bristol
Quietwoods South Camping Resort, Brussels
Yogi Bear's Jellystone Park Camp-Resort, Caledonia
Chetek River Campground, Chetek
Coloma Camperland, Coloma
Hickory Hills Campground, Edgerton
Camp-Tel Family Campground, Egg Harbor
Door County Camping Retreat, Egg Harbor
Frontier Wilderness Campground, Egg Harbor
Westward Ho Camp Resort, Fond du Lac
Jellystone Park at Fort Atkinson, Fort Atkinson
Rivers Edge Campground & Resort, Galesville
Hixton-Alma Center KOA, Hixton
Cedar Valley Campground, Kewaunee
Kewaunee Village RV Park, Kewaunee
Heaven's Up North Family Campground, Lakewood
Maple Heights Campground, Lakewood
Edgewater Acres Campground, Menomonie
Hidden Valley RV Resort and Campground, Milton
Lakeland Camping Resort, Milton
Buffalo Lake Camping Resort, Montello
Kilby Lake Campground, Montello
Wilderness Campground, Montello
Oakdale KOA, Oakdale
Osseo Camping Resort, Osseo
Rice Lake-Haugen KOA, Rice Lake
Aqualand Camp Resort, Sister Bay
Leon Valley Campground , Sparta
Quietwoods North Camping Resort, Sturgeon Bay
Yogi Bear's Jellystone Park Camp-Resort, Sturgeon Bay
Turtle Lake RV Park, Turtle Lake
Yogi Bear's Jellystone Park Camp-Resort, Warrens
Timber Trail Campground, West Bend
Neshonoc Lakeside Campground, West Salem
Tunnel Trail Campground, Wilton
Yogi Bear's Jellystone Park Camp-Resort, Fremont
Rivers Edge Campground, Stevens Point

WYOMING

Best RV Camping
Country Campin' RV Park, Thermopolis

Most Beautiful Campgrounds
Grand Teton Park RV Resort, Moran
Grand Tetons, Moose
The Flagg Ranch Resort, Moran
Yellowstone National Park, Yellowstone National Park

Most Private Campsites
Buffalo KOA Kampground, LLC, Buffalo
Cheyenne KOA, Cheyenne
Country Campin' RV Park, Thermopolis
Lake DeSmet, Lake Stop Resort, Buffalo
Owl Creek, Riverton
Snake River Park KOA (Jackson/Hoback Junction KOA), Jackson Hole

Most Spacious Campsites
Buffalo KOA Kampground, LLC, Buffalo
Cheyenne KOA, Cheyenne
Country Campin' RV Park, Thermopolis
Lake DeSmet, Lake Stop Resort, Buffalo
Owl Creek, Riverton
Snake River Park KOA (Jackson/Hoback Junction KOA), Jackson Hole

Quietest Campgrounds
Country Campin' RV Park, Thermopolis

Most Secure Campgrounds
Country Campin' RV Park, Thermopolis

Cleanest Campgrounds
Cheyenne KOA, Cheyenne
Country Campin' RV Park, Thermopolis

Best Campground Facilities
Cheyenne KOA, Cheyenne

Best Rural, Farm, or Ranch Settings
Country Campin' RV Park, Thermopolis
Lyman KOA, Lyman
The Flagg Ranch Resort, Moran

Best Urban and Suburban Settings
Cheyenne KOA, Cheyenne

Best Mountain Settings
Grand Teton Park RV Resort, Moran
Grand Tetons, Moose

Best Family-Oriented Campgrounds
Cheyenne KOA, Cheyenne

Best Swimming Pools
Lyman KOA, Lyman
Rock Springs KOA, Rock Springs
Virginian Lodge and RV Resort , Jackson Hole

BRITISH COLUMBIA

Best RV Camping
Riverside RV Resort and Campground, Whistler

Best Tent Camping
Riverside RV Resort and Campground, Whistler

Most Beautiful Campgrounds
Alice Lake Provincial Park, Squamish
Brandywine Falls Provincial Park, Whistler/Squamish
Gold Creek Campground (Golden Ears Provincial Park), Maple Ridge
Nairn Falls Provincial Park, Pemberton
Porteau Cove Provincial Park, Britannia Beach
Sunnyside Family Campground, Cultus Lake

Most Private Campsites
Peace Arch RV Park, Vancouver (Surrey)

Cleanest Campgrounds
Riverside RV Resort and Campground, Whistler

Best Campground Facilities
Riverside RV Resort and Campground, Whistler

Best Rural, Farm, or Ranch Settings
Hazelmere RV Park and Campground, Vancouver (Surrey)

Best Waterfront Settings
Alice Lake Provincial Park, Squamish

Best Family-Oriented Campgrounds
Hope Valley Campground, Hope

Alabama

Called the "Cradle of the Confederacy," Alabama is steeped in Civil War history. Fascinating tours include Montgomery, the first capitol of the Confederacy. It was during the Battle of Mobile Bay that Admiral Farragut exclaimed "Damn the torpedoes! Full speed ahead!"

At the **USS Alabama Battleships Memorial Park** in Mobile, visitors can explore the park's namesake as well as over 20 other World War II–ships, aircraft, and weapons.

The Civil Rights movement thrust Alabama into the national media spotlight in the 1950s and 1960s. Defining events included the 1955 Montgomery Bus Boycott and the historic Selma to Montgomery March. Gain a deeper understanding of the movement at the **Birmingham Civil Rights Institute.** Across the street is the Sixteenth St. Baptist Church, site of the 1963 bombing that killed four little girls.

Natives call Alabama "The Beautiful," and we agree. Its northeast corner lies at the southernmost terminus of the **Appalachian Mountain range.** Quaint mountain towns such as Mentone offer rich fall foliage and excellent craft and antique shopping. **Little River Canyon** in Fort Payne is one of the deepest gorges east of the Mississippi. Four national forests and numerous lakes throughout the state provide enthusiasts with plenty of hunting and fishing.

Alabama's Gulf Coast region is home to moss-covered oak trees and white sand beaches. Orange Beach is known for top-notch saltwater fishing. The **Alabama Coastal Birding Trail** dots **Mobile Bay** with spots for viewing both wading and shore birds.

Golf is the feather in Alabama's outdoor cap. Anchoring Alabama's golf offerings are the eight facilities of the **Robert Trent Jones Golf Trail.** The trail lures golfers from all over the world with its championship courses and country club amenities. Other public, state park, and resort courses are open to visitors.

NASCAR racing fans are familiar with the **Talladega Superspeedway,** home of the Diehard 500 in April and the Winston 500 in October. Combination tickets for year-round track tours and admission to the **International Motorsports Hall of Fame** are available.

Other Alabama destinations include: The **U.S. Space and Rocket Center, VisionLand** theme park, **Mother Angelica's Eternal Word Television Network,** the **Alabama Jazz Hall of Fame, Birmingham Museum of Art, Sloss Furnaces National Historic Landmark, De Soto Caverns, Heart of Dixie Railroad Museum, Alabama Shakespeare Festival, Mercedes-Benz Visitor's Center, Hank Williams Sr. Boyhood Home and Museum, The Dauphin Island Sea Lab,** and numerous historic homes and plantations.

Campground Profiles

ALEXANDER CITY

Wind Creek State Park

4325 AL Hwy. 128, Alexander City 35010. T: (256) 329-0845; F: (256) 234-4870; www.dcnr.state.al.us/parks; windcreekstpk@mindspring.com.

RV: ★★★★ Tent: ★★★★

Beauty: ★★★★	Site Privacy: ★★
Spaciousness: ★★★	Quiet: ★★★
Security: ★★★★★	Cleanliness: ★★★★
Insect Control: ★★★	Facilities: ★★★★

On the shores of 40,000-acre Lake Martin in east central Alabama, Wind Creek State Park is an excellent choice for families. Children will enjoy the large playground and variety of natural and recreational programs. Campers with lakefront sites are allowed to swim and dock boats right at the sites. Fishermen will find catfish, crappie and bluegill as well as largemouth, salt water striped, white and hybrid bass. Wind Creek State Park is not the top choice for peace and quiet as it is full of children and boats. The park should be assiduously avoided on holiday weekends. Security is outstanding at this gated and extremely remote park. The campground at Wind Creek State Park is laid out in 5 main sections including a primitive overflow area. The large, flat, grid-like section B is nicely shaded by a stand of loblolly and longleaf pine. Section C includes sites on an open peninsula with unobscured views of Lake Martin. Sites C190, C191 and C192 are the prettiest in spite of their complete lack of privacy. Other attractive lakefront sites are found in Section D. Section E contains a few sites with lake views and a modicum of privacy (try E32, E33, E34, E36, E38, or E30). All the sites at Wind Creek State Park are small compared to other Alabama state parks. While some sites are extremely shady, the open sites tend to have better views of the lake. The back-in, paved parking spaces are in various states of repair and disrepair and may be peppered with pine straw, gravel or grass. However, the bathhouses here are in excellent condition—large and clean with no frills.

Basics

Operated By: Alabama State Parks. **Open:** All year. **Site Assignment:** First come, first served; Alabama State Park reservations system. **Registration:** Main entrance, open 24 hours in-season; night registration available in winter. **Fee:** $16 for RV camping, $14 for tent camping, $3 additional for sewer or waterfront sites, fee includes 4 people, $2 for each additional person, limit 8 people per site. **Parking:** Limit 2 cars per site, overflow parking available.

FACILITIES

Number of Multipurpose Sites: 642. **Hookups:** Water, electric (30, 50 amps), 235 sites w/ sewer. **Each Site:** Picnic table, grill. **Dump Station:** Yes. **Laundry:** Yes. **Pay Phone:** Yes. **Rest Rooms and Showers:** Yes. **Fuel:** No. **Propane:** No. **Internal Roads:** Paved. **RV Service:** 8 mi. northeast in Alexander City. **Market:** 8 mi. northeast in Alexander City. **Restaurant:** 8 mi. northeast in Alexander City. **General Store:** Camp store. **Vending:** Yes. **Swimming Pool:** No. **Playground:** Yes. **Other:** Marina, boat launches, 210-ft. fishing pier, picnic pavilions. **Activities:** Hiking trails, fishing, lake swimming, boating (limited boat rentals), waterskiing, organized summer activities, volleyball, horseshoes. **Nearby Attractions:** Lake Martin, Horseshoe Bend Military Park, Charles E. Bailey Sportsplex. **Additional Information:** Alexander City Chamber of Commerce, (256) 234-3461.

RESTRICTIONS

Pets: Leash only. **Fires:** Allowed. **Alcoholic Beverages:** At site only. **Vehicle Maximum Length:** 50 ft. **Other:** 2 week max. stay on the same site.

TO GET THERE

From Montgomery, take US Hwy. 231 north for 9 mi. At Wetumpka, turn right onto AL Hwy.170 and go east for 10 mi. At Eclectic follow signs to AL Hwy. 63 north. Follow Hwy. 63 for 18 mi. until you see park signs. Turn right onto AL Hwy.128 and travel east 5 mi. to the park. From Birmingham, take US Hwy. 280 east to Alexander City. Turn right onto AL Hwy. 63 and go south for 7 mi. Turn left onto Hwy. 128 and go east 5 mi.

ALPINE

Logan Landing RV Resort and Campground

1036 Paul Bear Bryant Blvd., Alpine 35014. T: (256) 268-0045; sites.netscape.net/sambo12h/loganlanding.

RV ★★★ Tent ★★★

Beauty: ★★★ Site Privacy: ★★★
Spaciousness: ★★★ Quiet: ★★★
Security: ★★★★ Cleanliness: ★★★
Insect Control: ★★★ Facilities: ★★★

Attractive and clean with friendly owners, Logan Landing is a good choice if you plan on spending a few days in the area. The campground offers boating and other activities and drive times are short to Logan Martin Lake, De Soto Caverns, and Talladega Superspeedway. Cheaha State Park can be reached in less than one hour. Because this is a popular recreation area, summer weekends are busy. By all means avoid the two biggest race weekends at Talladega Superspeedway—the Die Hard 500 in Apr. and the Winston 500 in Oct. If you want to stay here on a race weekend, make advance reservations. Two camping areas are situated next to a small private lake. Section A contains no lakefront sites and may be preferred by tent campers because the sites are wooded. We prefer section B for RVs because sites are generally larger and more level. Even-numbered sites 58–80 have lake-views but little shade. As you move away from the lake in Section B, sites become shadier. Each of the midsized sites in section B has gravel parking and a cement patio. Section C is unattractive. The variety of tree species in the campground includes some dogwood. Of the 145 campsites, only a few are pull-throughs. With its remote location in Alpine, Alabama and gated entrance, this campground has very good security.

BASICS

Operated By: Keith Bell. **Open:** All year. **Site Assignment:** First come, first served; reservations accepted for holiday weekends & Talladega Superspeedway race weekends. **Registration:** Guard house. **Fee:** $18 for sites w/ full hookup, $15 for sites w/ water & electric, $10 primitive, fee includes 2 adults, $5 per extra person. **Parking:** At sites.

FACILITIES

Number of RV Sites: 0. **Number of Tent-Only Sites:** 45. **Number of Multipurpose Sites:** 145. **Hookups:** Water, electric (30, 50, 80 amps), some sewer. **Each Site:** Picnic table, grill, fire ring, tent pads. **Dump Station:** Yes. **Laundry:** Yes. **Pay Phone:** Yes. **Rest Rooms and Showers:** Yes. **Fuel:** No. **Propane:** No. **Internal Roads:** Gravel. **RV Service:** 6 mi. north in Pell City. **Market:** 11 mi. north in Pell City. **Restaurant:** 6 mi. north in Pell City. **General Store:** 11 mi. north in Pell City. **Vending:** Beverages only. **Swimming Pool:** Yes. **Playground:** Yes. **Other:** Private lake, boat ramp, paddle boats, canoes, pontoons, pavilion, rental trailers. **Activities:** Fishing, croquet, horseshoes, Lake Logan Martin swimming beach, Bingo Fridays, live music, volleyball, hot dog cookout Saturdays. **Nearby Attractions:** Talladega Superspeedway (NASCAR), De Soto Caverns, Davey Allison Park, Kymulga Grist Mill & Covered Bridge, Cheaha State Park. **Additional Information:** Talladega Chamber of Commerce, (256) 362-9075.

RESTRICTIONS

Pets: Leash only. **Fires:** In fire ring, grill only. **Alcoholic Beverages:** At site only. **Vehicle Maximum Length:** 50 ft.

TO GET THERE

From I-20, take Exit 158 at Pell City. Go south on US Hwy. 231 for 9.5 mi.Turn left onto CR 54 and drive across Logan Martin Dam. Go straight through the first stop sign, cross the railroad tracks, and then turn left at the second stop sign onto CR 207. Go 1 mi. and turn left onto Paul Bear Bryant Blvd. The campground entrance is 1 mi. ahead on the right.

BENTON

Prairie Creek Campground, Woodruff Lake

8493 US Hwy. 80 West, Hayneville 36040. T: (334) 872-9554; F: (334) 875-1603; www.reserveusa.com.

RV ★★★★ Tent ★★★★

Beauty: ★★★★ Site Privacy: ★★★★
Spaciousness: ★★★★ Quiet: ★★★★
Security: ★★★★ Cleanliness: ★★★★
Insect Control: ★★★ Facilities: ★★★

Prairie Creek is typical of the top quality campgrounds managed by the Army Corps of Engineers. Sites are extremely spacious and most have uncluttered views of the Alabama River. Spanish moss-laden oak trees provide shade and privacy. Two of the three camping areas, Beaver Point and Eagles Roost, are newer and feature paved back-in parking. The older Whitetail Bluff camping area contains pull-throughs but is now used for overflow camping. At Beaver Point, sites 56–62 are reserved for tent campers. RV campers will not be disappointed with any of the waterfront sites, 27–51. Since so many sites are excellent, choose your site based on proximity to facilities. The campgrounds located on the Alabama River Lake system are all extremely remote. Prairie Creek makes a great summer destination as it only fills to capacity on the busiest holiday weekends. Gates lock at night making the park extremely safe. Prairie Creek is located six miles from Holy Ground Battlefield Park, site of 1813–1814 clashes between the Creek Indians and the U.S. Army, led by General Andrew Jackson. Today, Holy Ground Battlefield Park is a day-use only recreation area with swimming beach, boat launch, playground, bathhouse, picnic shelters, multi-purpose court, hiking trails and observation deck. Day-use fees are waived for Prairie Creek campground guests.

BASICS

Operated By: US Army Corps of Engineers. **Open:** All year. **Site Assignment:** First come, first served; 60% of sites are available for reservations, accepted through the National Recreation Reservation Service (NRRS) at (877) 444-6777 or www.reserveusa.com. Reservations can be made up to 240 days in advance, full payment required upon making reservation; credit card preferred (V, MC, D, AE), or pay by money order if at least 21 days in advance of arrival. $10 fee for cancellation or change of site or dates. Cancellation within three days of arrival charged first night, no-show charged $20 plus first night. **Registration:** Gatehouse or night access lane. **Fee:** $14 for waterfront multipurpose sites; $12 for other multipurpose sites, $10 for tent sites. **Parking:** At sites, overflow parking available.

FACILITIES

Number of RV Sites: 0. **Number of Tent-Only Sites:** 7. **Number of Multipurpose Sites:** 55. **Hookups:** Water, electric (50 amps). **Each Site:** Picnic tables, grills, fire rings, tent pad at tent sites. **Dump Station:** Yes. **Laundry:** Yes. **Pay Phone:** Yes. **Rest Rooms and Showers:** Yes. **Fuel:** No. **Propane:** No. **Internal Roads:** Paved. **RV Service:** 20 mi. west in Selma. **Market:** 20 mi. west in Selma. **Restaurant:** 10 mi. southeast in Lowndesboro. **General Store:** 20 mi. west in Selma. **Vending:** No. **Swimming**

Pool: No. **Playground:** Yes. **Other:** Courtesy docks, boat ramp, fish cleaning area, picnic shelters, sports court, scenic overlooks. **Activities:** Swimming, boating, waterskiing, hiking, hunting. **Nearby Attractions:** Brown Chapel A.M.E. Church & King Monument, Cahawba, National Voting Rights Museum & Institute, Old Depot Museum, Old Live Oak Cemetery Tour, Smitherman Historic Building. **Additional Information:** Selma/Dallas County Chamber of Commerce, (334) 875-7241.

Restrictions

Pets: Leash only. **Fires:** Fire rings only. **Alcoholic Beverages:** Allowed. **Vehicle Maximum Length:** 50 ft. **Other:** Limit 3 vehicles per site.

To Get There

From Montgomery, take US Hwy. 80 west for 25 mi. Turn right on CR 29 and follow the signs.

BIRMINGHAM

KOA Birmingham South

222 Hwy. 33, Pelham 35124. T: (205) 664-8832 or (800) KOA-4788 for reservations; F: (205) 620-1103.

RV ★★★★ Tent ★★

Beauty: ★★★	Site Privacy: ★★
Spaciousness: ★★★	Quiet: ★★★
Security: ★★★	Cleanliness: ★★★
Insect Control: ★★★★	Facilities: ★★★★

Though not as attractive as nearby Oak Mountain State Park, KOA Birmingham South is tidy and offers comfortably spaced sites. Campers sometimes prefer the aesthetically bland sites at KOA to the state park because sites are level and hookups include cable television. The KOA may also be quieter, as many of the campers here are retirees. Back-in sites numbered B-8 through B-30 are the shadiest, prettiest, and the most popular. If you prefer an open pull-through site, choose from sites numbered 1–36. All roads and RV parking spots are paved.

Basics

Operated By: KOA. **Open:** All year. **Site Assignment:** First come, first served; reservations accepted. **Registration:** Campground office. **Fee:** $25 water & electric, $20 tent, fee includes 2 people; extra charge for sewer, a/c, electric heat or 50 amp hookup. **Parking:** 2 vehicles per site, plus overflow lot.

Facilities

Number of RV Sites: 116. **Number of Tent-Only Sites:** 6. **Number of Multipurpose Sites:** None. **Hookups:** Water, electric (30, 50 amps), sewer. **Each Site:** Picnic table, paved area, grill on request. **Dump Station:** Yes. **Laundry:** Yes. **Pay Phone:** Yes. **Rest Rooms and Showers:** Yes. **Fuel:** No. **Propane:** Yes. **Internal Roads:** Some gravel, majority Paved. **RV Service:** 15 mi. **Market:** 1 mi. in Pelham. **Restaurant:** 0.5 mi. in Pelham. **General Store:** Camp store, Wal-Mart 2 mi. south in Pelham. **Vending:** Beverages only. **Swimming Pool:** Yes. **Playground:** Yes. **Other:** Gift shop, hot tub, covered pavilion. **Activities:** Game room, horseshoes, basketball, clubhouse w/ television. **Nearby Attractions:** Oak Mountain State Park (golf, fishing, horseback riding, boating, hiking), Birmingham Zoo & Botanical Gardens, Galleria Mall. **Additional Information:** Birmingham CVB, (800) 458-8085; Hoover Chamber of Commerce, (205) 988-5672.

Restrictions

Pets: Leash only. **Fires:** At tent sites only. **Alcoholic Beverages:** At site only. **Vehicle Maximum Length:** 50 ft.

To Get There

From I-65, take Exit 242, then Hwy. 152 west, then right on Hwy. 33, campground 1 block on the right.

BIRMINGHAM

Oak Mountain State Park

P.O. Box 278, Pelham 35124. T: (205) 620-2524; F: (205) 620-2531; www.dcnr.state.al.us/parks.

RV ★★★★ Tent ★★★★

Beauty: ★★★	Site Privacy: ★★★
Spaciousness: ★★★	Quiet: ★★★★
Security: ★★★	Cleanliness: ★★★
Insect Control: ★★★	Facilities: ★★★★★

While reasonably attractive, Oak Mountain State park doesn't boast the most gorgeous campground in the state. The camp sites are a little ghostly—we could tell that they used to be lovely. Sites are situated in two main areas, within which site shape, size and privacy vary immensely. Area A contains 71 sites, 24 of which have full hookups. Area A is prettier, shadier and more woodsy than B, which has 72 sites crammed into half the space of A. In fact, most of area B is downright unattractive, with the exception of tent sites B6, B8, B64, and B65. All RV parking is on untidy gravel and both areas have back-in and pull-through parking. Oak Mountain is exceptional for its proximity to Birmingham. It's a good place to stay while visiting Birmingham and it's also the favored outdoor playground for the city's natives. This means that hiking, mountain biking and other activities may not provide the solitude we would expect at other parks. Still, the park's broad offering of activities and its proximity to a number of restaurants and attractions make it a good choice for a visit. Security at Oak Mountain is fair. The back gate is never manned, but both gates are locked at night. Avoid Oak Mountain State Park like the plague on holiday weekends and during the hotter summer months.

Basics

Operated By: Alabama State Parks. **Open:** All year. **Site Assignment:** Reservations required for weekends & holidays, 2-night min. stay weekends, 3-night min. stay holiday weekends (Memorial Day, Labor Day, & 4th of July). **Registration:** Country store. **Fee:** $17 for sites w/ full hookups, $15 for sites w/ water & electric, $11 for tent sites, fee includes 3 people, $2.22 per extra person, senior discount over 65. **Parking:** Limit 2 cars per site.

Facilities

Number of RV Sites: 0. **Number of Tent-Only Sites:** 60. **Number of Multipurpose Sites:** 85. **Hookups:** Water, electric (30 amps), sewer. **Each Site:** Picnic table, grill, fire ring, lantern pole. **Dump Station:** Yes. **Laundry:** Yes. **Pay Phone:** Yes. **Rest Rooms and Showers:** Yes. **Fuel:** No. **Propane:** No. **Internal Roads:** Paved & gravel. **RV Service:** 2 mi. southwest. **Market:** 3 mi. southwest in Pelham. **Restaurant:** 3 mi. southwest in Pelham. **General Store:** Wal-Mart 6 mi. east in Inverness. **Vending:** Beverages only. **Swimming Pool:** No. **Playground:** Yes. **Other:** Boat ramp, lake beach, snack bar, petting zoo, information center, stables, marina, boat rental (no gasoline boats allowed on lake), tennis courts, BMX track, picnic area, Alabama Wildlife Rescue Center, 18-hole golf course, sports fields, picnic shelters & pavilions, conference center. **Activities:** Horseback riding, hiking, mountain biking, fishing. **Nearby Attractions:** VisionLand, Birmingham Zoo & Botanical Gardens, Birmingham Museum of Art, Alabama Jazz Hall of Fame, Birmingham Civil Rights Institute, Sloss Furnaces, Galleria Shopping Mall. **Additional Information:** Birmingham CVB, (205) 458-8001; Hoover Chamber of Commerce, (205) 988-5672.

Restrictions

Pets: Leash only. **Fires:** In grills, fire rings only. **Alcoholic Beverages:** At site only. **Vehicle Maximum Length:** 56 ft. **Other:** 14-day stay limit.

To Get There

From I-65, take Exit 246 and go west on US Hwy. 119. Take an immediate left onto State Park Rd. Drive for 3.5 mi. to a 4-way stop. Turn left onto Findlay Dr. The main park gate is ahead. Go 5.5 mi. past the gate to Campground Rd. and turn left.

CAMDEN

Roland Cooper State Park

285 Deer Run Dr., Camden 36726. T: (334) 682-4838; F: (334) 682-4050; www.dcnr.state.al.us/parks.

RV ★★★ Tent ★★★

Beauty: ★★★	Site Privacy: ★★★
Spaciousness: ★★★	Quiet: ★★★
Security: ★★★	Cleanliness: ★★★
Insect Control: ★★	Facilities: ★★★★

Golf and fishing are the primary draws at Roland Cooper State Park. Created by a dam on the Alabama River, 22,000-acre Dannelly Reservoir is home to numerous fish species, as well as beaver, waterfowl and American alligator. The nine-hole golf course is a bargain; greens fees are only $9 for 9 holes and $13 for eighteen holes. Here, the woodlands are dominated by pine. The majority of the campsites enjoy the shade of a mature stand of loblolly pine. A bit of privacy is provided by the trees, but none of the sites are entirely secluded. Most of the sites are situated on one loop and feature paved, back-in parking. Sites 22, 24 and 28 are pull-through sites, with views of the reservoir and gravel parking. In the primitive tent camping area, site number 10 has a nice view of the water. Site size is comfortable but not exceptional. Roland Cooper's rural location and gates that lock at night make it fairly secure. Avoid this park in July and Aug. when summer heat crescendos. Also avoid Memorial Day, 4th of July and Labor Day, when crowds are at a maximum.

Basics

Operated By: Alabama State Parks. **Open:** All year. **Site Assignment:** Reservations accepted; no credit cards accepted; cancellation w/ 24-hour notice; sites are first come, first served. **Registration:** Entrance office. **Fee:** $15. **Parking:** Limit 3 vehicles per site, overflow parking available.

Facilities

Number of RV Sites: 0. **Number of Tent-Only Sites:** 10. **Number of Multipurpose Sites:** 47. **Hookups:** 30 w/ electric & sewer, all w/ water. **Each Site:** Picnic table, grill, fire ring. **Dump Station:** Yes. **Laundry:** Yes. **Pay Phone:** Yes. **Rest Rooms and Showers:** Yes. **Fuel:** No. **Propane:** No. **Internal Roads:** Paved. **RV Service:** 75 mi. northeast in Montgomery. **Market:** Camp store. **Restaurant:** 5 mi. south in Camden. **General Store:** 5 mi. south in Camden. **Vending:** No. **Swimming Pool:** No. **Playground:** Yes. **Other:** Clubhouse, picnic pavilion, 9-hole golf course, driving range, boat ramps, fish cleaning area. **Activities:** Golf, fishing, boating, swimming, walking trails. **Nearby Attractions:** Bridgeport Beach, Dale Masonic Lodge, Wilcox Female Institute. **Additional Information:** Wilcox Development Council (334) 682-4929.

Restrictions

Pets: Leash only. **Fires:** In fire rings, grills only. **Alcoholic Beverages:** At site only. **Vehicle Maximum Length:** No limit.

To Get There

From I-65, take Exit 128. Drive west on Alabama Hwy. 10 for 40 mi. At Camden, turn right onto Alabama Hwy. 41 and drive north for 4 mi. The park is on the left.

CHILDERSBURG

De Soto Caverns

5181 De Soto Caverns Parkway, Childersburg 35044. T: (256) 378-7252; F: (256) 378-3678; www.desotocavernspark.com; awm3@mindspring.com.

RV ★★★ | Tent ★★★

Beauty: ★★★★	Site Privacy: ★★
Spaciousness: ★★	Quiet: ★★★
Security: ★★	Cleanliness: ★★★★
Insect Control: ★★★	Facilities: ★★★★

This small, privately owned campground is clean and attractive. Part of a complex that includes De Soto Caverns and a small amusement park, the campground is sandwiched into the front corner of the property. Because some sites are only a few feet from the amusement park, quiet afternoon naps may be out of the question when the park is busy. The triangular campground offers compact sites which are well shaded by pine trees. Parking is mainly back-in with a few pull-throughs, and patchy grass invading the gravel. Sites 2 and 3 are furthest away from 76 making them the quietest at night. Big rigs should avoid this tight, hilly campground altogether (opt for one of the sprawling campgrounds along Logan Martin Lake). Less than 60 miles from Birmingham, this kitschy-but-fun park will be appreciated by children especially. The Great-Onyx Cavern is the venue for a Laser Light Show and the amusement park includes a fishin' hole, gem panning and more. Keep in mind that there is no snack bar at the park. Count on driving about 5 miles to Childersburg if you're not cooking at your site. Security is poor here. There is no gate and the campground is visible from 76. Cave touring is a delightful summer time activity. Just steer clear of visits during holiday weekends and big event weekends at Talladega Superspeedway.

Basics

Operated By: The Mathis Family. **Open:** All year. **Site Assignment:** First come, first served; reservations accepted for holidays & Talladega Superspeedway race weekends only; full deposit required; one week cancellation policy. **Registration:** Gift shop or night registration. **Fee:** $20 for full hookups, $15 for tent camping, 4 person max., $2 per extra person. **Parking:** At site, overflow parking available.

Facilities

Number of RV Sites: 0. **Number of Tent-Only Sites:** 3. **Number of Multipurpose Sites:** 16. **Hookups:** Water, electric, sewer. **Each Site:** Picnic table, grill, some fire rings. **Dump Station:** Yes. **Laundry:** No. **Pay Phone:** Yes. **Rest Rooms and Showers:** Yes. **Fuel:** No. **Propane:** No. **Internal Roads:** Gravel. **RV Service:** 5 mi. southwest in Childersburg. **Market:** 5 mi. southwest in Childersburg. **Restaurant:** 5 mi. southwest in Childersburg. **General Store:** Camp Store, Wal-Mart 15 mi. south in Sylacauga. **Vending:** Yes. **Swimming Pool:** No. **Playground:** Yes. **Other:** Caverns, climbing wall, amusement park. **Activities:** Mazes, mini-golf, pedal boats, go-carts, gem stone panning, laser light show. **Nearby Attractions:** Talladega Superspeedway, Kymulga Grist Mill & Covered Bridge, Bryant's Vineyard, Blue Bell Creameries. **Additional Information:** Childersburg Chamber of Commerce, (256) 378-5482, Talladega Chamber of Commerce, (256) 362-9075.

Restrictions

Pets: Leash only. **Fires:** Allowed. **Alcoholic Beverages:** Not allowed. **Vehicle Maximum Length:** No limit.

To Get There

From US Hwy. 280 in Childersburg, drive northeast on AL Hwy. 76 (De Soto Caverns Parkway) for 5 mi. The entrance is on the left.

COKER

Lake Lurleen State Park

Rte. 1 Box 479, Coker 35452. T: (205) 339-1558; www.dcnr.state.al.us/parks.

RV ★★★★ | Tent ★★★★

Beauty: ★★★★	Site Privacy: ★★★
Spaciousness: ★★★★	Quiet: ★★★
Security: ★★★★	Cleanliness: ★★★
Insect Control: ★★	Facilities: ★★★

Named after Alabama's only woman governor, Lurleen Burns Wallace, this lake is popular with fishermen. The 250-acre lake is stocked with bream, catfish, crappie and largemouth and striped bass. Rather not fish? Swim, hike or canoe. Located 12 miles northwest of Tuscaloosa, this park stays busy all summer so we recommend weekday, spring, or fall visits. Four camping areas (A-D) offer nice sized sites. Most have paved back-in parking. A few sites have gravel parking. Section B is devoted to RV campers and contains 8 pull-through sites. Sites B33–B39 (odd numbers) feature wooden decks overlooking Lake Lurleen. In Section A, lakefront sites A2–A14 (even numbers) offer lovely views. While most sites have some shady trees, sites A15 and A16 are exceptionally shady and secluded. In spite of Lake Lurleen's proximity to Tuscaloosa, it feels remote. Gates lock at night making the park extremely secure.

Basics

Operated By: Alabama State Parks. **Open:** All year. **Site Assignment:** Reservations accepted w/ one night deposit; sites are first come, first served. **Registration:** Entrance station. **Fee:** $14 (MC, V, check, or cash). **Parking:** 2 vehicles per site.

Facilities

Number of Multipurpose Sites: 91. **Hookups:** Water, electric (30, 50 amps), 35 sites w/ sewer. **Each Site:** Picnic table, grill. **Dump Station:** Yes. **Laundry:** No. **Pay Phone:** Yes. **Rest Rooms and Showers:** Yes. **Fuel:** No. **Propane:** No. **Internal Roads:** Paved. **RV Service:** 15 mi. south in Tuscaloosa. **Market:** Camp store. **Restaurant:** 7 mi. east in Northport. **General Store:** 7 mi. east in Northport. **Vending:** Yes. **Swimming Pool:** No. **Playground:** Yes. **Other:** Boat ramps, fishing pier, marina, boat rentals, amphitheater, picnic area, group picnic shelters, swimming beach, beach snack stand, nature center, sports field. **Activities:** Fishing, boating, hiking, swimming. **Nearby Attractions:** Paul "Bear" Bryant Museum, Alabama Museum of Natural History, Moundville Indian Archeological Park, Mercedes Benz Visitor Center, Denny Chimes, Gorgas House, Children's Hands-On Museum, Kentuck Art Center, University of Alabama Arboretum. **Additional Information:** West Alabama Chamber of Commerce (205) 758-7588; Tuscaloosa CVB (800) 538-8696.

Restrictions

Pets: Leash only. **Fires:** In fire pits only. **Alcoholic Beverages:** Site only, Not allowed at beach. **Vehicle Maximum Length:** No limit. **Other:** No ATVs or horses allowed.

To Get There

From I-59, take Exit 71-B in Tuscaloosa. Go north on I-359 for 5 mi. Turn left onto US Hwy. 82 (McFarland Blvd.) and drive west for 5 mi. Turn right onto CR 21 and drive north for 4.5 mi. The park entrance is on the right.

DELTA

Cheaha State Park

Hwy. 281, 2141 Bunker Loop, Delta 36258. T: (256) 488-5111; F: (256) 488-5885; www.dcnr.state.al.us/parks; csparks@wrldnet.net.

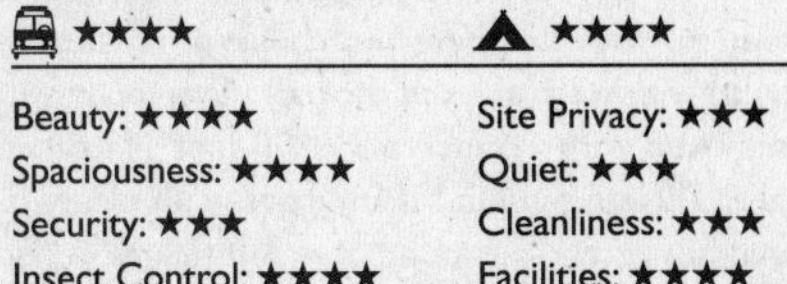

RV ★★★★ Tent ★★★★

Beauty: ★★★★ Site Privacy: ★★★
Spaciousness: ★★★★ Quiet: ★★★
Security: ★★★ Cleanliness: ★★★
Insect Control: ★★★★ Facilities: ★★★★

With an elevation of 2407 feet, Mt. Cheaha is the highest point in the state of Alabama. Park guests can enjoy the gorgeous mountain view from atop the observation tower. The campgrounds are also very attractive, with very spacious sites and a variety of shady hardwood species. Site privacy varies, with dense foliage buffering some sites from their neighbors. There are two campgrounds at Cheaha, Number 1, or "Upper", and Number 2, or "Lower". Campground Number 1 features mostly back-in parking, but there are a few spacious pull-throughs. Parking spots are an amalgamation of dirt and gravel. In campground Number 1, sites 4 and 5 are extremely private and wooded. Large pull-throughs include 30, 31, 34, 35, and 36. Of these, 34 is the shadiest. In campground Number 2, sites 56 and 57 have a gorgeous view. Most sites in Number 2 are pull-throughs. The popularity of Cheaha's campgrounds can sometimes detract from their beauty. The campgrounds are fairly well maintained, but the potties and trash bins sometimes need more attention than they get. Security is fair at this rural state park. We got the idea that gates may or may not go down at night. This Appalachian park stays cooler than most of Alabama during the summer. Nonetheless, we recommend avoiding Cheaha on summer weekends when the park's beauty and myriad activities attract the masses.

Basics

Operated By: Alabama State Parks. **Open:** All year. **Site Assignment:** First come, first served; reservations accepted w/ first night's fee in advance; no refunds allowed although date of stay can be changed. **Registration:** Country store. **Fee:** $17 multipurpose sites, $11 primitive sites, 15% discount for handicapped or 62 & over. **Parking:** Site, limit 2 vehicles per site.

Facilities

Number of RV Sites: 0. **Number of Tent-Only Sites:** Primitive tent area. **Number of Multipurpose Sites:** 73. **Hookups:** Water, electric (30 amps), sewer. **Each Site:** Picnic table, grill. **Dump Station:** No. **Laundry:** Yes. **Pay Phone:** Yes. **Rest Rooms and Showers:** Yes. **Fuel:** Yes. **Propane:** No. **Internal Roads:** Paved. **RV Service:** 25 mi. east in Oxford. **Market:** 25 mi. east in Oxford. **Restaurant:** In park. **General Store:** Wal-Mart 25 mi. east in Oxford. **Vending:** Beverages only. **Swimming Pool:** Yes. **Playground:** Yes. **Other:** Observation tower, CCC Museum, picnic & play area, sandy swimming beach. **Activities:** Fishing, pedal boat rental, hiking, mountain biking. **Nearby Attractions:** Anniston Museum of Natural History, Birmingham & Gadsden attractions. **Additional Information:** Inquire at campground.

Restrictions

Pets: Leash only. **Fires:** Allowed. **Alcoholic Beverages:** At site only. **Vehicle Maximum Length:** 40 ft. **Other:** 14-day stay limit.

To Get There

From I-20 take Exit 191. Go south on US Hwy. 431 for 5 mi. Turn right onto State Hwy. 281 and go south. This runs into the park.

DOUBLE SPRINGS

Corinth Recreation Area

P.O. Box 278, Double Springs 35553. T: (205) 489-5111; www.reserveusa.com.

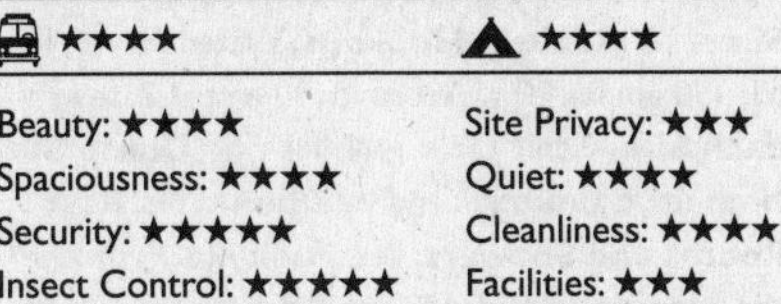

RV ★★★★ Tent ★★★★

Beauty: ★★★★ Site Privacy: ★★★
Spaciousness: ★★★★ Quiet: ★★★★
Security: ★★★★★ Cleanliness: ★★★★
Insect Control: ★★★★★ Facilities: ★★★

Located 28 miles from the hiking and equestrian trails at Sipsey Wilderness Area, Corinth Recreation Area offers 52 campsites with full hookups. Sites are attractive, spacious and heavily wooded. Dense brush between sites provides privacy. The campground is laid out in two main loops plus a group camp loop. The Yellow Hammer loop is much prettier than the Firefly loop. All parking is paved. While most of the parking is back-in style, there are five huge pull-through sites. Pull through sites 17 and 19 are lovely and very private. Although the bathhouses in Bankhead National Forest are small, they are some of the tidiest in the state. Security is excellent at Corinth; the campground is extremely remote and gated at all times. Day-use facilities at Corinth are minimal, so the atmosphere is usually incredibly laid back. This tranquil campground rarely fills up, so it's a good bet for a summer weekend (if you can stand the heat).

Basics

Operated By: Cradle of Forestry in America Interpretive Assoc. **Open:** Mar. 20–Oct. 31. **Site Assignment:** First come, first served; some loops reservable through National Recreation Reservation System (877) 444-6777. **Registration:** Gatehouse. **Fee:** $20 RV, $10 tent, fee includes 1 vehicle per site, $3 per extra vehicle. **Parking:** At site; wheels must be on pavement.

Facilities

Number of RV Sites: 0. **Number of Tent-Only Sites:** 8. **Number of Multipurpose Sites:** 50 (RV). **Hookups:** Water, electric (50 amps), sewer. **Each Site:** Picnic table, fire ring, grill, lantern post, tent pad. **Dump Station:** Yes. **Laundry:** No. **Pay Phone:** Yes. **Rest Rooms and Showers:** Yes. **Fuel:** No. **Propane:** No. **Internal Roads:** Paved. **RV Service:** 35 mi. east in Cullman. **Market:** 5 mi. northwest in Double Springs. **Restaurant:** 5 mi. northwest in Double Springs. **General Store:** 5 mi. northwest in Double Springs. **Vending:** No. **Swimming Pool:** No. **Playground:** No. **Other:** Boat launch, swimming beach, paddle boat rental, group picnic shelter. **Activities:** Fishing, swimming, hiking. **Nearby Attractions:** William B. Bankhead National Forest, Looney's Entertainment & Riverboat, Ave Maria Grotto in Cullman. **Additional Information:** Cullman Area Chamber of Commerce, (800) 313-5114.

Restrictions

Pets: Leash only. **Fires:** Fire rings only. **Alcoholic Beverages:** Not Allowed. **Vehicle Maximum Length:** 50 ft. **Other:** 14-day stay limit.

To Get There

From I-65, take Exit 308 at Cullman. Go west on US Hwy. 278 for approximately 30 mi. Turn left and drive south on CR 57 for 3 mi. to the park entrance.

EUFAULA

Lakepoint Resort State Park

P.O. Box 267, Eufaula 36072. T: (334) 687-8011 or (800) 544-5253; F: (334) 687-3273; www.dcnr.state.al.us/parks; lakepointstld@mindspring.com.

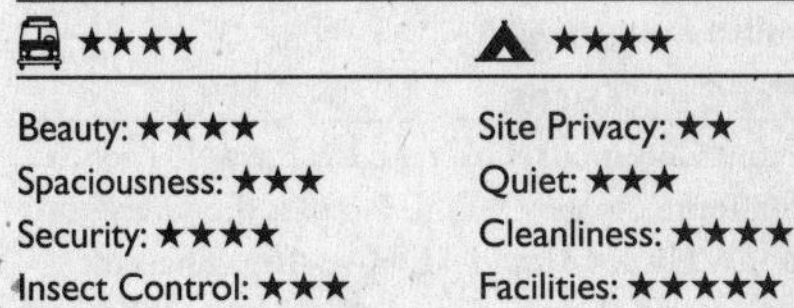

RV ★★★★ Tent ★★★★

Beauty: ★★★★ Site Privacy: ★★
Spaciousness: ★★★ Quiet: ★★★
Security: ★★★★ Cleanliness: ★★★★
Insect Control: ★★★ Facilities: ★★★★★

Hide your carrots. Lakepoint Resort Sate Park campgrounds are full of bunny rabbits. The flat campground is situated along Lake Eufaula, home to beaver and American alligator. Four camping areas provide over 500 sites. Of these areas, the Clark Loop, with sites along the lake, is the most attractive. Clark has only water and electric hookups, and is the best choice for tent campers. Even-numbered sites 20–42 have the prettiest views. RV campers should head for the Deer Court area, which has full hookups, and both back-in and pull-through sites. All parking is paved and ground cover consists of grass and pine straw. Site size varies, but sites are generally comfortable. Most sites are nicely wooded with a variety of tree species, some adorned with Spanish moss. None are very secluded. With excellent resort amenities, Lakepoint Resort State Park is a good choice for active families and couples, making its remote location worth the drive. Gated at all times, campground security is excellent. This park becomes chaotic on holiday weekends and should also be avoided in July and Aug. when it's bound to be unbearably hot and humid.

Basics

Operated By: Alabama State Parks Conservation Dept. **Open:** All year, except Thanksgiving & Christmas. **Site Assignment:** First come, first served; reservations accepted through Conservation Dept. or directly, one night deposit, 7-day cancellation notice; 3-night min. on holidays. **Registration:** Camp store, night registration available. **Fee:** $17 for sites w/ sewer, $15 for sites w/ water & electric, fees include 4 people, $1.10 per extra person. **Parking:** 2 cars per site, overflow parking available.

FACILITIES

Number of Multipurpose Sites: 190. **Hookups:** Water, electric (30 amps), 80 sites w/ sewer. **Each Site:** Picnic table, grill. **Dump Station:** Yes. **Laundry:** Yes. **Pay Phone:** Yes. **Rest Rooms and Showers:** Yes. **Fuel:** Boat fuel. **Propane:** Yes. **Internal Roads:** Paved. **RV Service:** 40 mi. north in Columbus, GA. **Market:** 6 mi. south in Eufaula. **Restaurant:** In park. **General Store:** Camp store. **Vending:** Yes. **Swimming Pool:** No. **Playground:** Yes. **Other:** Marina, Boat launches, swimming beach, picnic area, sports field, information/nature center, RV storage, tennis courts, volleyball courts, basketball courts, lodge, 18-hole golf course, lounge, resort motel, video arcade. **Activities:** Fishing, pontoon boat rental, hiking, tennis courts, lodge, 18-hole golf. **Nearby Attractions:** Downtown Eufaula, antebellum homes, walking & driving tours, antique shopping. **Additional Information:** Eufaula Chamber of Commerce, (334) 687-6664.

RESTRICTIONS

Pets: Leash. **Fires:** In grills, fire rings only. **Alcoholic Beverages:** At site only. **Vehicle Maximum Length:** 60 ft.

TO GET THERE

From Columbus, GA, take US Hwy. 431 south for approximately 50 mi. Go past the intersection of US Hwy. 431 and AL Hwy. 165. The park entrance is the next left.

FORT PAYNE

De Soto State Park

265 County Rd. 951, Fort Payne 35967. T: (800) 568-8840 State Park or (800) 760-4089 Camp Store; F: (256) 845-8286; www.dcnr.state.al.us/parks; desotostpk@mindspring.com.

RV ★★★★★ Tent ★★★★★

Beauty: ★★★★★	Site Privacy: ★★★★
Spaciousness: ★★★★★	Quiet: ★★★
Security: ★★★★★	Cleanliness: ★★★★
Insect Control: ★★★	Facilities: ★★★★

Situated about half way between De Soto Falls and Little River Canyon, De Soto State Park has a rugged ambience even though it's less than 10 miles northeast of Fort Payne. Sometimes referred to as "The Grand Canyon of the East," Little River Canyon has drops of up to 600 feet. Hardcore outdoorsfolk climb the canyon's sandstone bluffs and paddle the Little River's Class III-V White Water. The campground at De Soto State Park is laid out in two loops, each with its own playground and rest rooms. Sites are nicely spaced and the campground is heavily wooded with a variety of hardwoods and pines, making site size outstanding and site privacy excellent. RV parking spaces are gravel. Of the 78 campsites, 10 are pull-throughs. Since all of the sites are nice, choose your site based on proximity to (or distance from) playgrounds and rest rooms. RV campers may want to procure one of the 20 sites with full hookups. Gorgeous sites make this one of the most popular campgrounds in the state, so visit in the spring to avoid the masses. If you don't mind the constant crowds, visit for fall "leaf-peeping" in Sept. and Oct. Security at De Soto State Park is excellent; at night the gate must be opened with a "key card".

BASICS

Operated By: Alabama State Parks. **Open:** All year. **Site Assignment:** Reservations required. **Registration:** Country store. **Fee:** $17 water, electric, & sewer (4 people); $14 water & electric (4 people); $8 primitive (2 people); $3 per extra person; 8 people max.; children under 6 free. **Parking:** At site, limit 2 cars per site.

FACILITIES

Number of RV Sites: 78. **Number of Tent-Only Sites:** 50 acres open camp area (approximately 40 tents). **Number of Multipurpose Sites:** 78 (RV sites). **Hookups:** Water, 58 w/ electric (30 amps), 20 w/ electric (30 amps) & sewer. **Each Site:** Picnic table, grill, fire ring. **Dump Station:** Yes. **Laundry:** Yes. **Pay Phone:** Yes. **Rest Rooms and Showers:** Yes. **Fuel:** No. **Propane:** Yes. **Internal Roads:** Paved. **RV Service:** 35 mi. west in Rainsville. **Market:** Convenience 3 mi., grocery 7 mi. southwest in Fort Payne. **Restaurant:** In park. **General Store:** Convenience 3 mi., Wal-Mart 10 mi. southwest in Fort Payne. **Vending:** Yes. **Swimming Pool:** Yes. **Playground:** Yes. **Other:** Boat launch (7 mi.), nature trails, tennis courts, volleyball court, sports equipment, picnic & play area, lodge, country store. **Activities:** Whitewater paddling (class I-IV), rock climbing, hiking. **Nearby Attractions:** Little River Canyon National Preserve, Mentone crafts & antiques, Depot Museum, Cloudmont Ski & Golf Resort, various waterfalls. **Additional Information:** Fort Payne Chamber of Commerce, (256) 845-2741; Gadsden Chamber of Commerce, (256) 543-3472.

RESTRICTIONS

Pets: Leash only. **Fires:** Grills & fire rings only. **Alcoholic Beverages:** Not allowed. **Vehicle Maximum Length:** 50 ft. **Other:** 14-day stay limit.

TO GET THERE

From I-59, take Fort Payne Exit 218 and drive northeast on AL Hwy. 35. Drive 8 mi. to the top of Lookout Mountain. At the flashing caution light, turn left onto CR 89 and drive 5 mi. to the park entrance.

GADSDEN

Noccalula Falls Park and Campground

P.O. Box 267, Gadsden 35902. T: (256) 543-7412; www.rvcampground.com/al/noccalulafalls.

RV ★★★★ Tent ★★★★

Beauty: ★★★★	Site Privacy: ★★
Spaciousness: ★★★	Quiet: ★★★
Security: ★★★★	Cleanliness: ★★★
Insect Control: ★★★★	Facilities: ★★★★★

This city-owned park will be a big hit with the young'uns. The historic Pioneer Homestead consists of over 50 structures which have been preserved by the city of Gadsden. Buildings such as the blacksmith shop and the loom house contain tools typically used by early Appalachian pioneers. Children will also dig the passenger train, animal park, and mini-golf. Adults will appreciate the urban location, with shopping and choice of restaurants found within six miles of the park. Everybody will enjoy the park's center piece, 90-foot Noccalula Falls. The campground is attractive, with plenty of back-in sites and a handful of pull-throughs. A few sites have gravel parking, but most are paved. Here, site size varies greatly, with most sites being comfortably sized. The majority enjoy the shade of tall pine trees. But with little foliage between sites, privacy is poor. The prettiest sites (A19–A38) overlook the large bluff that leads down to Black Creek. Security is good at Noccalula Falls. Gates remain open throughout the night, but rangers patrol the park 24 hours a day. Avoid Gadsden in the hotter summer months. Avoid this park completely on holidays. School groups are more likely to visit the Pioneer Village on weekdays in Apr. and May. Call ahead if you would like to avoid them.

BASICS

Operated By: City of Gadsden. **Open:** All year. **Site Assignment:** First come, first served. **Registration:** Camp office. **Fee:** $23 for sites w/ full hookups, $17 for sites w/ water & electricity, seventh night is free, 10% senior discount. **Parking:** At site.

FACILITIES

Number of RV Sites: 83. **Number of Tent-Only Sites:** 47 (additional primitive tent area for large groups only). **Hookups:** 14 RV sites w/ water, electric (30, 50 amps), sewer & cable TV; 13 RV sites w/ water, electric (30, 50 amps), & sewer; 56 RV sites w/ water & electric (30, 50 amps); 47 tent sites w/ water & electric (30, 50 amps). **Each Site:** Picnic table, grill. **Dump Station:** Yes. **Laundry:** Yes. **Pay Phone:** Yes. **Rest Rooms and Showers:** Yes. **Fuel:** No. **Propane:** No. **Internal Roads:** Gravel. **RV Service:** 5 mi. east in Gadsden. **Market:** 1mi. south in Gadsden. **Restaurant:** In park. **General Store:** Country store in park; Wal-Mart, K-Mart & Lowe's 10 mi. south in Gadsden. **Vending:** No. **Swimming Pool:** Yes. **Playground:** Yes. **Other:** Botanical gardens, Noccalula Falls, Pioneer Village, animal park, passenger train, picnic pavilions, souvenir shop, concession stand, rec hall, information center. **Activities:** Hiking, carpet golf , swimming, nature & history study. **Nearby Attractions:** Inquire at campground. **Additional Information:** Inquire at campground.

RESTRICTIONS

Pets: Leash only. **Fires:** Allowed. **Alcoholic Beverages:** Not allowed. **Vehicle Maximum Length:** No limit.

TO GET THERE

From I-59 take Exit 188 onto AL Hwy. 211 (Noccalula Rd.). Go south 3.5 mi. to the first light and turn right. The park entrance is ahead.

GREENVILLE

Sherling Lake

P.O. Box 158, Greenville 36037. T: (800) 810-5253; F: (334) 382-7031; www.sherlinglake@alaweb.com; sherlinglake@alaweb.com.

RV ★★★★★ Tent ★★★★

Beauty: ★★★★★ Site Privacy: ★★★★
Spaciousness: ★★★★ Quiet: ★★★★★
Security: ★★★★★ Cleanliness: ★★★★★
Insect Control: ★★★★ Facilities: ★★★★

The city of Greenville operates this impeccably manicured campground. The tidy landscaping includes native azaleas and dogwoods with intermittent shade provided by tall pines. The park encompasses two fishing lakes, stocked with catfish, bluegill, brim, bass, and crappie. For golfers, 27-hole Cambrian Ridge (part of the Robert Trent Jones Golf Trail) is adjacent to Sherling Lake. Nearly deserted in the spring and fall, this campground is an excellent choice for golfers. For families, the playground is one of the nicest we've seen. The majority of the campsites are situated near the "Top Lake". All sites have ample paved parking and there are plenty of large pull-through sites. Folks with large campers should consider 1, 14, 18, and 25–41. Although all sites at Sherling Lake are spacious, back-in sites often feel a bit more secluded. Though most every site enjoys some shade, none are completely secluded by greenery. Sherling Lake is only three miles from Greenville, providing easy access to shopping and restaurants. The park fills to capacity on holidays and during coastal hurricane evacuations. The rest of the time it's an oasis of tranquility. Gates lock at night making security excellent.

BASICS

Operated By: City of Greenville. **Open:** All year. **Site Assignment:** First come, first served; reservations accepted, no deposit required. **Registration:** Office, late-comers register the next morning. **Fee:** $19 developed site for up to 4 people, $12 per tent in primitive area, Good Sam discount available. **Parking:** Limit 1 car per site, overflow parking available.

FACILITIES

Number of RV Sites: 0. **Number of Tent-Only Sites:** Primitive area holds up to 25 tent sites. **Number of Multipurpose Sites:** 41. **Hookups:** Water, electricity (30, 50 amps), sewer. **Each Site:** Picnic table, shelter, fire ring, grill; primitive area includes some tables, fire rings & grills. **Dump Station:** Yes. **Laundry:** No. **Pay Phone:** Yes. **Rest Rooms and Showers:** Yes. **Fuel:** No. **Propane:** No. **Internal Roads:** Paved. **RV Service:** 3.5 mi. south in Greenville. **Market:** 3.5 mi. south in Greenville. **Restaurant:** 3.5 mi. south in Greenville. **General Store:** Snack shop. **Vending:** Yes. **Swimming Pool:** No. **Playground:** Yes. **Other:** Boat launches, picnic pavilions, small meeting room. **Activities:** Fishing lakes, boat rentals, walking trail. **Nearby Attractions:** Adjacent to Cambrian Ridge Robert Trent Jones 18-hole golf course, Historic Greenville, Preesters Pecan Factory & Outlet. **Additional Information:** Greenville Chamber of Commerce, (334) 382-3251.

RESTRICTIONS

Pets: Leash. **Fires:** In grills, fire rings only. **Alcoholic Beverages:** At site only. **Vehicle Maximum Length:** 45 ft.

TO GET THERE

From I-65, take Exit 130 and head northwest on State Hwy. 185 for 1.5 mi. At State Hwy. 263, turn left and continue another 1.5 mi. The park entrance is on the left.

GROVE OAK

Buck's Pocket State Park

393 County Rd. 174, Grove Oak 35975. T: (256) 659-2000; F: (256) 659-2000; www.dcnr.state.al.us/parks.

RV ★★★★ Tent ★★★★★

Beauty: ★★★★★ Site Privacy: ★★★
Spaciousness: ★★★ Quiet: ★★★★★
Security: ★★★★ Cleanliness: ★★★★
Insect Control: ★★★★ Facilities: ★★★★

2,000-acre Buck's Pocket State park is exceedingly beautiful and not heavily visited. Built around the 400-foot deep Buck's Pocket Canyon and featuring five moderately difficult hiking trails, the park is appreciated by day hikers. Fishermen can access Lake Guntersville at Morgan Cove, seven miles from the park. We were very impressed with the quiet campground that lies in the flat valley of the canyon. Completely shaded by a stand of hardwood trees, the campground features sights adjacent to lovely boulder-lined Little South Sauty Creek. Campsites are not huge, but this campground rarely fills to capacity so you'll have plenty of elbow room. While internal roads are paved, sites offer back-in gravel parking. If you are looking for solitude, head for secluded site Number 17. At 900 feet above sea level, this little "pocket" of the southern Appalachians stays cooler than most of Alabama during the hot summer months. Visit Buck's Pocket comfortably during spring, summer, or fall. The park is very remote with poor signage. It is equipped with gates, but as one local said, "there ain't no need to lock 'em!"

BASICS

Operated By: Alabama State Parks. **Open:** All year. **Site Assignment:** First come, first served; reservations accepted for holiday weekends. **Registration:** Park office. **Fee:** $15 full hookups, $14 water & electric, fee includes 8 people, $1 per extra person. **Parking:** At sites.

FACILITIES

Number of RV Sites: 36. **Number of Tent-Only Sites:** 4. **Number of Multipurpose Sites:** 36 (RV sites). **Hookups:** 6 w/ water, electric (50 amps), & sewer; 30 w/ water & electric (50 amps). **Each Site:** Picnic table, grill, fire ring, tent pad at tent sites. **Dump Station:** Yes. **Laundry:** Yes. **Pay Phone:** Yes. **Rest Rooms and Showers:** Yes. **Fuel:** No. **Propane:** No. **Internal Roads:** Paved. **RV Service:** 12 mi. east in Rainsville. **Market:** Convenience store 3 mi. south, Grocery 10 mi. south in Geraldine. **Restaurant:** 10 mi. south in Geraldine. **General Store:** 10 mi. south in Geraldine. **Vending:** Yes. **Swimming Pool:** No. **Playground:** Yes. **Other:** Boat launch, observation overlook, picnic area. **Activities:** Hiking & walking trails, fishing, boating. **Nearby Attractions:** Cathedral Caverns, Huntsville Space Museum, Lake Guntersville State Park, TVA Guntersville Dam, Depot Museum. **Additional Information:** Guntersville Chamber of Commerce, (256) 582-3612.

RESTRICTIONS

Pets: Leash only. **Fires:** In fire rings & grills only. **Alcoholic Beverages:** Not allowed. **Vehicle Maximum Length:** No limit. **Other:** 14-day stay limit.

TO GET THERE

From I-59, take Exit 218 at Fort Payne. Go north on State Hwy. 35 for 7 mi. At Rainsville, turn left and drive south on State Hwy. 75 for 4 mi. At Fyffe, turn right on CR 50, and go 8 mi. Watch carefully for park signs. Turn right onto CR 19 and right again onto CR 556, then left onto CR 73. The park is on the right.

GULF SHORES

Doc's RV Park

17595 State 180/Fort Morgan Rd., Gulf Shores 36542. T: (334) 968-4511; F: (334) 968-1109; www.docsrvpark.com; docsrvpark@gulftel.com.

RV ★★★ Tent n/a

Beauty: ★★★ Site Privacy: ★★
Spaciousness: ★★★ Quiet: ★★★
Security: ★★★ Cleanliness: ★★★
Insect Control: ★★★★ Facilities: ★★★

When we visited Gulf Shores, Doc's RV Park was the quietest in town. Three miles from the beach and within easy distances to restaurants and shopping, Doc's isn't far from touristy hustle and bustle. Campsites at Doc's are built around an elliptical grassy park area. So even though sites are narrow, campers enjoy a view of the grass. Most sites have a little shade provided by trees on the periphery of the park. All sites have back-in, gravel parking which looks a little untidy in some places. The shadiest sites are numbers 46–30. If you want an open site, there are plenty to choose from. Doc's is popular with snowbirds in the winter and popular with families in the summer. For optimal peace and quiet, visit in Spring or Fall. Doc's is in a quiet Gulf Shores neighborhood, but there is no gate. Security is fair, so guard your valuables.

BASICS

Operated By: Roton & Bear. **Open:** All year. **Site Assignment:** Reservations recommended & accepted w/ deposit; 1-week cancellation notice required, 1 month in winter. **Registration:** Clubhouse, self-register at night. **Fee:** $24 in summertime, $21 in wintertime (good for 4 people); 2-day weekend min., 3-day holiday min.; Good Sam discount available. **Parking:** At site, limit 2 cars per site.

Facilities

Number of RV Sites: 75. **Number of Tent-Only Sites:** 0. **Number of Multipurpose Sites:** None. **Hookups:** Water, electric (30, 50 amps), cable, sewer. **Each Site:** Picnic table. **Dump Station:** Yes. **Laundry:** Yes. **Pay Phone:** Yes. **Rest Rooms and Showers:** Yes. **Fuel:** No. **Propane:** Yes. **Internal Roads:** Paved. RV Service: 10 mi. north in Foley. **Market:** 2 mi. in Gulf Shores. **Restaurant:** 2 mi. in Gulf Shores. **General Store:** 0.5 mi. in Gulf Shores, Wal-Mart 10 mi. north in Foley. **Vending:** Beverages only. **Swimming Pool:** Yes. **Playground:** Yes. **Other:** Clubhouse, fire grills in central location, RV storage. **Activities:** Volleyball, horseshoes, weekly campground gatherings in winter. **Nearby Attractions:** 3 mi. from the beach, outlet shopping, Bellingrath Gardens, boat tours, *USS Alabama* Battleship Memorial Park. **Additional Information:** Alabama Gulf Coast CVB, (800) 745-7263.

Restrictions

Pets: Welcome, on leash only. **Fires:** Grills only. **Alcoholic Beverages:** Allowed. **Vehicle Maximum Length:** No limit.

To Get There

From I-10, take Exit 44 onto Hwy. 59 south. Continue past the junction with Hwy. 98 another 9.5 mi. Turn west on State Hwy. 180/Fort Morgan Rd. and the park entrance will be 2 mi. down on the right. Web-site also has map and directions.

GULF SHORES
Gulf Breeze Resort

19800 Oak Rd. West, Gulf Shores 36542.
T: (251) 968-8884; F: (251) 968-8462;
www.ehodges.com;
wakefieldent@mindspring.com.

RV ★★★ | Tent n/a

Beauty: ★★★	Site Privacy: ★★
Spaciousness: ★★★	Quiet: ★★★
Security: ★★	Cleanliness: ★★★
Insect Control: ★★★★	Facilities: ★★★★

Gulf Breeze Resort offers extensive and well-maintained recreational facilities. It also boasts the nicest bathhouses in Gulf Shores and the tidiest landscaping. Even though the resort feels like it's off the beaten path, it's close to numerous restaurants and tourist attractions. The nearest beach is just four miles away. The campground is laid out in a giant grid and includes both back-in and pull-through spaces. Most of the spaces are paved although a few have gravel parking. Site size is average and very few sites have any shade. The nicest sites are 46–51, which are adjacent to the small fishing pond. Sites 164 and 171 overlook another small pond and are also attractive. This suburban resort is popular with snow-birds in the winter and popular with families in the summer, so it's almost always busy. Avoid visits during spring break, holiday weekends, and sweltering July and Aug. There is no gate at Gulf Breeze so protect your valuables.

Basics

Operated By: Wakefield Enterprises. **Open:** All year. **Site Assignment:** First come, first served; reservations accepted w/ one night deposit; 48-hour cancellation required, $2 cancellation fee if paid by credit card. **Registration:** Office, no late registration—check in next day by 10 a.m. **Fee:** $22 for 4 people, $2 per extra person up to 8. **Parking:** At site, limit 2 cars per site, overflow parking available.

Facilities

Number of RV Sites: 226. **Number of Tent-Only Sites:** 0. **Hookups:** Water, electric (30, 50 amps), sewer, cable TV, 6 overflow sites have water, electricity only. **Each Site:** Picnic table, concrete patios, some w/ concrete pads. **Dump Station:** No. **Laundry:** Yes. **Pay Phone:** Yes. **Rest Rooms and Showers:** Yes. **Fuel:** No. **Propane:** No. **Internal Roads:** Paved. **RV Service:** On call. **Market:** 3 mi. in Gulf Shores. **Restaurant:** 3 mi. in Gulf Shores. **General Store:** 0.25 mi., 5 mi. to Wal-Mart. **Vending:** Yes. **Swimming Pool:** Yes. **Playground:** Yes. **Other:** Pavilion, clubhouse for rent, indoor pool, outdoor pool, children's pool. **Activities:** Fishing lake, paddle boat rental, basketball, horseshoes, shuffleboard, 18-hole mini-golf, hot tub. **Nearby Attractions:** Gulf Shores beaches, Waterville USA, Bellingrath Gardens, Dauphin Island Sea Lab, Fort Conde Museum, USS Alabama Battleship Memorial Park, Mobile & Pensacola attractions. **Additional Information:** Alabama Gulf Coast CVB, (800) 745-7263.

Restrictions

Pets: Leash only, clean-up enforced. **Fires:** Not allowed. **Alcoholic Beverages:** At site only. **Vehicle Maximum Length:** No limit.

To Get There

From I-10, take Exit 44 (Loxley/Foley/Gulf Shores). Drive south on Hwy. 59 and go through Foley. Exit at CR 6 and turn right. The park is 1.5 blocks on the left.

GULF SHORES
Gulf State Park

22050 Campground Rd., Gulf Shores 36542. T: (334) 948-7275; F: (334) 948-4570;
www.dcnr.state.al.us/parks.

RV ★★★★ | Tent ★★★★

Beauty: ★★★★	Site Privacy: ★★★
Spaciousness: ★★★	Quiet: ★★★
Security: ★★★★	Cleanliness: ★★★★
Insect Control: ★★	Facilities: ★★★★★

Unfortunately, the large campground at Gulf State Park offers no campsites within walking distances of the beach. However, the campground is very attractive and perennially popular with families; don't expect any solitude here during the summer months. Site size is acceptable but the bustling atmosphere makes the campground feel crowded. 185 sites offer back-in parking and 25 offer pull-through parking. Parking areas may be paved, gravel or packed sand. Many of the sites are shady and a few offer views of small Middle Lake. Tent sites offer soft sand tent pads. Of those with lake views, sites 17–39 are the most picturesque. Unless you really want a pull-through, avoid the noisy, highly trafficked sites along the main road. Located just a few miles from the tourist town of Gulf Shores, campers have easy access to excellent dining and other tourist attractions. Amenities within the park are also outstanding, including the state's largest fishing pier (825 feet), an 18-hole golf course, and two-and-a-half miles of white sand beach. The gates at Gulf Shores State Park campground are locked at night and the entrance is manned all day, making security excellent.

Basics

Operated By: Alabama State Parks. **Open:** All year. **Site Assignment:** First come, first served; roughly half of the sites are available for reservation w/ a one-night, non-refundable deposit. **Registration:** Park entrance. **Fee:** $12–$16. **Parking:** At site, limit 2 vehicles per site.

Facilities

Number of Multipurpose Sites: 210. **Hookups:** Electric (15, 30 amps), water, sewer. **Each Site:** Picnic table, grill. **Dump Station:** Yes. **Laundry:** Yes. **Pay Phone:** Yes. **Rest Rooms and Showers:** Yes. **Fuel:** No. **Propane:** No. **Internal Roads:** Paved. **RV Service:** No. **Market:** 3 mi. in Gulf Shores. **Restaurant:** In park. **General Store:** 3 mi. in Gulf Shores. **Vending:** Beverages only. **Swimming Pool:** No. **Playground:** Yes. **Other:** Tennis courts, fishing pier, golf course, game room, bicycle rental, beach pavilion, boat ramp, nature center, resort hotel & conference center, picnic area. **Activities:** Swimming, hiking, fishing, golf. **Nearby Attractions:** Alabama Gulf Coast Zoo, Gulf Shores Beach, Dauphin Island Sea Lab, Adventure Island, Bellingrath Gardens & Home, Biophilia Nature Center & Native Nursery, Gulf Coast Museum of Science, Gulf Coast Amusement Park, Mobile Bay Ferry, Pirate Island Adventure Golf, *USS Alabama* Battleship Memorial Park, Wildland Expeditions, Waterville USA. **Additional Information:** Alabama Gulf Coast Visitor Information, (800) 745-7263.

Restrictions

Pets: On leash only. **Fires:** In grills & designated bonfire areas. **Alcoholic Beverages:** At site only. **Vehicle Maximum Length:** No limit.

To Get There

At the intersection of State Hwy. 59 and State Hwy. 182 (Beach Rd.), turn left. Drive east on State Hwy. 182 for 3.5 mi. Pass Gulf State Park Resort Hotel and take the next left onto CR 2. Campground is on the right.

GUNTERSVILLE
Lake Guntersville State Park

1155 Lodge Dr., Guntersville 35976-9126. T: (256) 571-5455; F: (256) 571-9043;
www.dcnr.state.al.us/parks.

Beauty: ★★★★ Site Privacy: ★★
Spaciousness: ★★★ Quiet: ★★
Security: ★★★ Cleanliness: ★★★
Insect Control: ★★★★ Facilities: ★★★★★

Lake Guntersville Sate Park is really lovely, but the campgrounds are often way too crowded for our tastes. Set in a beautiful stand of tall pines, the huge campground (with over 300 sites) stays full for much of the summer. If you don't mind spending your vacation with an entire village of new friends and neighbors, you may enjoy this park. Here you will find paved back-in sites with very little privacy. Sites are small compared to other Alabama State parks. The campground is laid out in eight grid-like areas (A–F). Tent campers should head for Area A, especially sites 16 and 17. RV campers should try to land a lakeside site in Area D or G. Sites G9, G11, G12, G13, G24, and G36 are among the most attractive. Area E should be avoided as it abuts the picnic pavilion and experiences heavy traffic. Families wishing to camp right next to the playground should head for C51–C59. Lake Guntersville State Park offers plenty of amenities and activities, but their pride and joy is the American bald eagles who winter there. The campground is gated and guarded, but security isn't fantastic because of the number of folks on the campground. We recommend visiting Lake Guntersville in spring or fall to avoid the crowds.

Basics

Operated By: Alabama State Parks. **Open:** All year. **Site Assignment:** First come, first served; about half of the sites can be reserved; 3 night min. weekends & holidays, one night deposit. **Registration:** Camp store, no late registration. **Fee:** $17 for up to 4 people. **Parking:** At site.

Facilities

Number of Multipurpose Sites: 320. **Hookups:** Water, electric (30 amps), sewer. **Each Site:** Picnic table, grill, fire ring. **Dump Station:** Yes. **Laundry:** Yes. **Pay Phone:** Yes. **Rest Rooms and Showers:** Yes. **Fuel:** No. **Propane:** No. **Internal Roads:** Paved. **RV Service:** Inquire at campground. **Market:** 7.5 mi. southwest in Guntersville. **Restaurant:** In park. **General Store:** Camp store, Wal-Mart 15 mi. southwest in Guntersville. **Vending:** Yes. **Swimming Pool:** No. **Playground:** Yes. **Other:** Beach, nature center, art gallery, 18-hole golf course, RV storage, activity building, fishing piers, picnic pavilion, 31 mi. of hiking trails. **Activities:** Swimming, fishing, boating, hiking, tennis. **Nearby Attractions:** American Bald Eagles Convention Center, Cathedral Caverns, Buck's Pocket State Park, Guntersville Museum & Cultural Center. **Additional Information:** Guntersville Chamber of Commerce, (256) 582-3612.

Restrictions

Pets: Leash only. **Fires:** Fire rings only. **Alcoholic Beverages:** At site only. **Vehicle Maximum Length:** No limit. **Other:** 14-day stay limit Apr.–Oct.

To Get There

From I-59, take the Gadsden exit and go north on US Hwy. 431 for approximately 38 mi. At Guntersville, turn right onto AL Hwy. 227 and go northeast for 7 mi. The park entrance is on the left.

GUNTERSVILLE/LANGSTON

Little Mountain Marina Resort

1001 Murphy Hill Rd., Langston 35755. T: (256) 582-8211; F: (256) 582-6344; www.ehodges.com; wakefieldent@mindspring.com.

RV ★★★★ Tent n/a

Beauty: ★★★ Site Privacy: ★★
Spaciousness: ★★★ Quiet: ★★
Security: ★★★★ Cleanliness: ★★★
Insect Control: ★★★★ Facilities: ★★★★★

Little Mountain Resort is noteworthy for its modern amenities rather than its natural beauty. Located on Guntersville Lake, the resort caters to active families and large groups. For fishing and boating enthusiasts, there's a boat launch, marina, fishing pier and two covered piers containing a total of 86 boat slips. Land amenities include a 500-seat great hall as well as multiple swimming pools and other activities. The gigantic campground is a no-frills affair with mid-sized sites. There are no barriers to provide privacy between sites. Back-in gravel parking is the rule and no tent camping is allowed. The prettiest sites are numbers 110–119 and 110A–119A, which are adjacent to the lake and have power and water only. The nicest sites with full hookups and views of the lake are 18–20, 27–29, 36, 37, 120, and 121. Avoid sites in the 200s and 300s, which have unattractive views of the boat and RV storage areas. Some sites are completely open while others provide plenty of shade. In spite of Little Mountain's extremely remote location, you may feel like you've arrived in Lower Manhattan once you're here. We recommend weekday visits in the summertime, or visits in spring or autumn. The guard house is staffed 24 hours a day, making security good.

Basics

Operated By: Earl & Elke Hodges. **Open:** All year. **Site Assignment:** First come, first served; 2-night min. for reservations; cancellation penalty is first night's fee on holidays. **Registration:** Guard house. **Fee:** $20, fee includes 4 people, $2 per extra person. **Parking:** Limit 2 vehicles per site.

Facilities

Number of RV Sites: 343. **Number of Tent-Only Sites:** 0. **Hookups:** 309 w/ sewer, water & electric (30, 50 amps); 34 w/ water & electric. **Each Site:** Picnic table, concrete patio, grill (at full hookup sites only). **Dump Station:** No. **Laundry:** Yes. **Pay Phone:** Yes. **Rest Rooms and Showers:** Yes. **Fuel:** No. **Propane:** Exchange only. **Internal Roads:** Gravel. **RV Service:** Mechanic On call. **Market:** 1 mi. **Restaurant:** 6 mi. south in Guntersville. **General Store:** Country store 0.5 mi., Wal-Mart 15 mi. south in Guntersville. **Vending:** Yes. **Swimming Pool:** Yes. **Playground:** Yes. **Other:** Marina, boat launch, 86-slip covered pier, fishing pier, indoor & outdoor pools, spa, sauna, game room, club house w/ great hall, exercise room, library, TV/card room, Florida room, dining room, chapel, activity pavilion. **Activities:** Tennis, shuffleboard, basketball, horseshoes, mini-golf, fishing, boating, swimming. **Nearby Attractions:** Cathedral Caverns, Huntsville Space Museum, Lake Guntersville State Park, TVA Guntersville Dam, Depot Museum. **Additional Information:** Guntersville Chamber of Commerce, (256) 582-3612.

Restrictions

Pets: Leash only. **Fires:** In grill only. **Alcoholic Beverages:** At site only. **Vehicle Maximum Length:** 40 ft.

To Get There

From I-59, take Exit 218 at Fort Payne. Go northwest on AL Hwy. 35 for 7 mi. to Rainsville. Turn left and drive south on AL Hwy. 75 for 18 mi. At AL Hwy. 227 turn right and drive north for 10 mi. Turn right onto Old Hwy. 227 and go 0.5 mi. Then, turn left onto Murphy Hill Rd. and go 0.5 mi.

HUNTSVILLE

Monte Sano State Park

5105 Nolen Ave., Huntsville 35801. T: (256) 534-3757; F: (256) 539-7069; www.dcnr.state.al.us/parks.

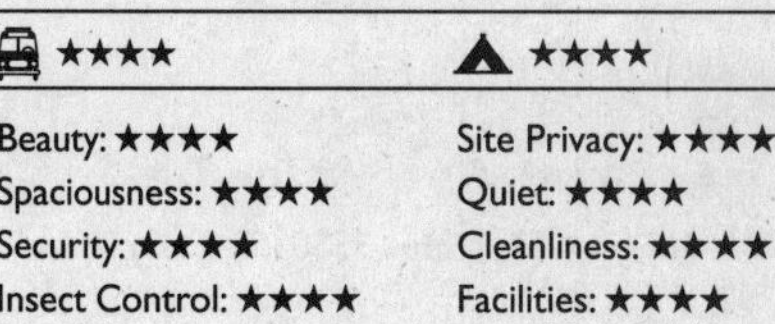

RV ★★★★ Tent ★★★★

Beauty: ★★★★ Site Privacy: ★★★★
Spaciousness: ★★★★ Quiet: ★★★★
Security: ★★★★ Cleanliness: ★★★★
Insect Control: ★★★★ Facilities: ★★★★

This flat campground on top of Monte Sano features lovely hardwoods with foliage between all campsites. In some instances, sites are very secluded by dense foliage. Site size is ample, and parking is mostly back-in. Four pull-throughs (numbers 14, 30, 62, and 82) are extremely large. Parking spaces are fine gravel. The prettiest sites are odd numbers 49–61 and only have water and electric hookups. Avoid sites 31–44, as they parallel a noisy road. The campground is laid out in two loops, each having its own bathhouse. With over 32 miles of trails, Monte Sano is a hiker's haven. This suburban park lies just outside of Huntsville city limits and is popular with the locals. Monte Sano Mountain has an elevation of approximately 1,500 feet, and stays about five degrees Fahrenheit cooler than Huntsville proper, making the park a fine summer destination. The park gates lock at night, but its suburban location necessitates caution with your valuables.

Basics

Operated By: Alabama State Parks. **Open:** All year. **Site Assignment:** First come, first served; no reservations taken. **Registration:** Camp store, night registration available. **Fee:** $16 for sites w/ full hookups, $15 for sites w/ water & electric, $10 for primitive tent sites. **Parking:** At site, overflow parking available.

Facilities

Number of RV Sites: 0. **Number of Tent-Only Sites:** 20. **Number of Multipurpose Sites:** 89. **Hookups:** Water, electric (30 amps), sewer. **Each Site:** Picnic table, fire ring, grill. **Dump Station:** Yes. **Laundry:** Yes. **Pay Phone:** Yes. **Rest Rooms and Showers:** Yes. **Fuel:** No. **Propane:** No. **Internal Roads:** Paved. **RV Service:** 8 mi. south in Huntsville. **Market:** 6 mi. south in Huntsville.

Restaurant: 6 mi. south in Huntsville. **General Store:** Inquire at campground. **Vending:** Yes. **Swimming Pool:** No. **Playground:** Yes. **Other:** Japanese Gardens, 32 mi. of hiking trials, planetarium, camp store, amphitheater w/ summertime film series. **Activities:** Hiking, walking. **Nearby Attractions:** Huntsville: U.S. Space & Rocket Center, Huntsville Museum of Art, Twickenham Historic District, Alabama Constitution Village, Cathedral Caverns, Children's Museum, Alabama State Black Archives Research Center & Museum. **Additional Information:** Huntsville CVB, (800) SPACE-4-U.

RESTRICTIONS

Pets: Leash only. **Fires:** Fire rings only. **Alcoholic Beverages:** Not allowed. **Vehicle Maximum Length:** No limit. **Other:** 14-night stay-limit.

TO GET THERE

From I-65, take Exit 340 and go east on I-565 to Huntsville. From I -565 take Exit 17 and go east on Governor's Dr. Go through Huntsville and turn left onto Monte Sano Blvd. At the top of the Mountain, turn right onto Nolen St. The park entrance is ahead.

JASPER

Clear Creek Recreation Area

8079 Fall City Rd., Jasper 35501. T: (205) 384-4792.

RV ★★★★★ Tent ★★★★★

Beauty: ★★★★★	Site Privacy: ★★★★★
Spaciousness: ★★★★★	Quiet: ★★★★★
Security: ★★★★★	Cleanliness: ★★★★★
Insect Control: ★★★★	Facilities: ★★★

In the heart of William B. Bankhead National Forest, Clear Creek offers incredibly spacious sites with majestic views of Lake Lewis Smith. The campground is incredibly remote and quiet, with a dense understory providing an additional noise barrier between campsites. Each site enjoys the cooling shade of mature trees. Parking is paved, and there are both back-in and pull-through spaces. Double sites are available for large families or small groups. Tent campers should head for picturesque lakefront sites 47, 49, and 51. For RV campers, we like a number of sites, including 5, 8, 17, 18, 51, 53, 55, 81, and 82. Site 53 is a pull-through with water view. Facilities here are nice, particularly the swimming beach. Bankhead National Forest and nearby Sipsey Wilderness (35 miles from campground) offer hiking galore. Security is excellent—the park is gated at all times. Visit in late spring, early summer, and fall. Avoid holiday weekends.

BASICS

Operated By: Cradle of Forestry in America Interpretive Assoc. **Open:** Mar. 20–Oct. 31. **Site Assignment:** First come, first served. **Registration:** Gatehouse 7 a.m.–9 p.m. Sunday–Thursday, 7 a.m.–10 p.m. Friday & Saturday; no late registration. **Fee:** $17.85–$18.90 single (up to 6 people, 2 vehicles plus RV or tent); $27.30–$31.50 double (up to 12 people, 4 vehicles plus RV or tent); Golden Age/Access discounts available. **Parking:** Limited space at sites, all wheels must be on pavement.

FACILITIES

Number of RV Sites: 102. **Number of Tent-Only Sites:** 2 group sites. **Number of Multipurpose Sites:** 102 (RV). **Hookups:** Water, electricity (30 amps). **Each Site:** Picnic table, grill, fire ring, lantern post, tent pad. **Dump Station:** Yes. **Laundry:** No. **Pay Phone:** Yes. **Rest Rooms and Showers:** Yes. **Fuel:** No. **Propane:** No. **Internal Roads:** Paved. **RV Service:** 15 mi. in Jasper. **Market:** 15 mi. in Jasper. **Restaurant:** 5 mi. west. **General Store:** 5 mi. south. **Vending:** No. **Swimming Pool:** No. **Playground:** Yes. **Other:** Boat launch. **Activities:** Lake beach, basketball, hiking, mountain biking, fishing, Interpretive programs, wildlife education. **Nearby Attractions:** Arrowhead & Twin Lakes golf, Walker County Lake, Rickwood Caverns State Park, William B. Bankhead National Forest, Smith Lake. **Additional Information:** Walker County Chamber of Commerce, (888) 384-4571.

RESTRICTIONS

Pets: Leash. **Fires:** Fire rings only. **Alcoholic Beverages:** Not allowed. **Vehicle Maximum Length:** Varies up to 50 ft. **Other:** 14-day max. stay.

TO GET THERE

From I-65, take Hwy. 78 west 41 mi. to Jasper, then Hwy. 195 north 8 mi. Turn right on CR 27, which dead ends at 5 mi. at the park entrance.

LILLIAN

Perdido Bay KOA

33951 Spinnaker Dr., Lillian 36549. T: (334) 961-1717; F: (334) 961-1717; www.koa.com; perdidokoa@gulftel.com.

RV ★★★ Tent ★★

Beauty: ★★★	Site Privacy: ★★
Spaciousness: ★★★	Quiet: ★★★
Security: ★★★	Cleanliness: ★★★
Insect Control: ★★★★	Facilities: ★★★

This KOA is situated on Perdido Bay, within 30 miles of Alabama's Gulf Coast. Though crabbing, fishing and dolphin watching are favored activities here, the campground is equipped with all the other amenities we expect from a KOA. The rectangular campground features rows of back-in and pull-through campsites. Parking areas are amoebic in shape and comprised of patchy sand, grass, and dirt. Sites are mid-sized and most afford no seclusion from neighbors. All sites are at least partially shaded by pine trees, with the shadiest sites on row F (F1–F14). Unfortunately, none of the RV sites are near the water. Tent campers should opt for a Kamping Kabin on the water's edge—the alternative is a noisy site adjacent to CR 99. Security is fair at this campground. There is no gate but the park is fairly remote. We recommend visiting Perdido Bay in the spring or fall, when the weather is mild.

BASICS

Operated By: Denise Valentyne. **Open:** All year. **Site Assignment:** Often assigned; reservations recommended; credit card deposit required for reservation; one day's notice required for full refund. **Registration:** Office & store. **Fee:** $19–$25 (cash, checks, V, MC, DISC). **Parking:** 1 vehicle per site, overflow parking available.

FACILITIES

Number of RV Sites: 100. **Number of Tent-Only Sites:** 6. **Number of Multipurpose Sites:** 100 (RV sites). **Hookups:** Water, electric (30, 50 amps), some sewer. **Each Site:** Picnic table. **Dump Station:** Yes. **Laundry:** Yes. **Pay Phone:** Yes. **Rest Rooms and Showers:** Yes. **Fuel:** No. **Propane:** Yes. **Internal Roads:** Paved & dirt. **RV Service:** Yes. **Market:** Camp store. **Restaurant:** 1.5 mi. north in Lillian. **General Store:** 8 mi. east in Myrtle Grove, FL. **Vending:** No. **Swimming Pool:** Yes. **Playground:** Yes. **Other:** Hot tub, fishing pier, boat launch, RV storage, fax service. **Activities:** Basketball, horseshoes, shuffleboard, fishing, crabbing, beaches. **Nearby Attractions:** Naval Air Museum, Bellingrath Gardens in Theodore, Gulf Shores beaches, Old Mobile. **Additional Information:** Mobile Convention & Visitor Corporation, (800) 5-MOBILE; Alabama Gulf Coast CVB, (800) 745-SAND.

RESTRICTIONS

Pets: Leash only. **Fires:** Allowed at tent sites w/ water hookups. **Alcoholic Beverages:** At site only. **Vehicle Maximum Length:** No limit.

TO GET THERE

From Pensacola, take Hwy. 98 West 15 mi. to Lillian, on the Alabama state line. From Mobile, take Hwy. 98 East 40 mi. to Lillian. At Lillian, turn south onto Spinnaker Dr. and go 2 mi. The campground entrance is on the left.

McCALLA

McCalla/Tannehill KOA Kampground

22191 Hwy. 216, McCalla 35111. T: (205) 477-4778.

RV ★★★ Tent ★★

Beauty: ★★★	Site Privacy: ★★
Spaciousness: ★★★	Quiet: ★★★
Security: ★★	Cleanliness: ★★★
Insect Control: ★★★	Facilities: ★★★

This suburban campground is a perfectly acceptable place to stay while visiting Birmingham and Tuscaloosa County. The park is located about halfway between downtown Birmingham and the Mercedes-Benz Plant and Visitor Center in Vance (approximately 12 miles to each). With all of the amenities folks expect at KOAs, this is a relaxing place to be after a day in the city. With the exception of untidy gravel and grass, this park is well kept and reasonably attractive. The campground is laid out in two sections divided by the pool, store, and other facilities. Site size is ample, especially when compared to sites at other KOA campgrounds. Sites numbering in the 60s and 70s are shaded by a variety of tree species. A few sites are completely open. Roads and parking spaces are gravel and almost all sites are pull-throughs. KOA McCalla is less than a quarter mile from I-59 and has no security gate, so protect your valuables. Avoid visits in July and Aug., when heat and humidity can be unbelievable in this part of Alabama.

Basics

Operated By: Andy Thompson & Judy Bogol. **Open:** All year. **Site Assignment:** First come, first served; reservations recommended; cancel w/ 24-hour notice or charge of 1st night. **Registration:** Camp office. **Fee:** $26 (50 amp), $23 full hookup (30 amp), $18 tent. **Parking:** 2 vehicles per site.

Facilities

Number of RV Sites: 42. **Number of Tent-Only Sites:** 8 (4 primitive, 4 w/ water & electricity). **Number of Multipurpose Sites:** None. **Hookups:** Water, electric (30, 50 amps), sewer, cable TV. **Each Site:** Picnic table, fire ring. **Dump Station:** Yes. **Laundry:** Yes. **Pay Phone:** Yes. **Rest Rooms and Showers:** Yes. **Fuel:** No. **Propane:** Yes. **Internal Roads:** Gravel. **RV Service:** 15 mi. **Market:** 8 mi. **Restaurant:** 0.75 mi. **General Store:** Camp store, 0.75 mi. **Vending:** No. **Swimming Pool:** Yes. **Playground:** Yes. **Other:** Lighted pavilion w/ kitchen, RV storage. **Activities:** Horseshoes, badminton, volleyball, basketball, game room. **Nearby Attractions:** VisionLand, Tannehill State Park, Mercedes Benz Plant & Visitor's Center, Birmingham Zoo & Botanical Gardens, Birmingham Museum of Art, McWane Center w/ IMAX theater. **Additional Information:** Tuscaloosa CVB, (800) 538-8696; Greater Birmingham CVB, (800) 458-8085.

Restrictions

Pets: Leash only. **Fires:** In grills, fire rings only. **Alcoholic Beverages:** At site only. **Vehicle Maximum Length:** No limit.

To Get There

From I-20/59, take Exit 100. Go 500 yards west on CR 20 to the park entrance.

MOBILE

Chickasabogue Park and Campground

760 Aldock Rd., Mobile 36613. T: (334) 574-2267; F: (334) 574-0541; www.mobilecounty.org-park; rjones@mobile-county.net.

RV ★★★★ Tent ★★★★

Beauty: ★★★★	Site Privacy: ★★★★
Spaciousness: ★★★★	Quiet: ★★★★
Security: ★★★	Cleanliness: ★★★
Insect Control: ★★	Facilities: ★★★

Operated by the Mobile County Commission, Chickasabogue Park campground includes 47 incredibly spacious sites. Most of the sites are pull-throughs, with plenty of shade and privacy provided by magnolia and post and live oak complete with Spanish moss. These surprisingly lovely sites have gravel parking. Tent campers should head for sites 40–47. RV campers should try sites 1–13, which are commodious, private and attractive pull-throughs. The campground includes a group camp and three other areas. The washhouses are nothing to write home about. Bring your own Lysol. This suburban park offers plenty of outdoor activities including an 18-hole disc golf course. Gates are not locked at night, but rangers patrol hourly, making security acceptable. The Mobile Bay should be avoided in July and Aug. when heat and humidity can be unbearable.

Basics

Operated By: Mobile County Commission. **Open:** All year. **Site Assignment:** First come, first served; reservations accepted w/ first night's fee deposit by check or credit card. **Registration:** Camp store, Security Guard after hours. **Fee:** $18 for sites w/ full hookups, $15 for sites w/ water & electric, $19 for tent sites; fee includes four people, $1 per extra person. **Parking:** At site.

Facilities

Number of RV Sites: 47. **Number of Tent-Only Sites:**. **Number of Multipurpose Sites:** 21. **Hookups:** Water, electric (50, 30 amps), 26 sites w/ sewer. **Each Site:** Picnic table, fire ring, grill. **Dump Station:** Yes. **Laundry:** Yes. **Pay Phone:** Yes. **Rest Rooms and Showers:** Yes. **Fuel:** No. **Propane:** No. **Internal Roads:** Paved. **RV Service:** 5 mi. north in Saraland. **Market:** 5 mi. north in Saraland. **Restaurant:** 5 mi. north in Saraland. **General Store:** Camp store in park, Wal-mart 5 mi. north in Saraland. **Vending:** Yes. **Swimming Pool:** No. **Playground:** Yes. **Other:** Canoe rentals, boat ramp, 18-hole disc golf course, picnic area, sports field, nature center. **Activities:** Boating, hiking, biking. **Nearby Attractions:** *USS Alabama,* Dauphin Island Sea Lab, Mobile attractions. **Additional Information:** Mobile Convention & Visitors Corporation, (800) 5-MOBILE.

Restrictions

Pets: Leash only. **Fires:** In grills & fire rings only. **Alcoholic Beverages:** At site only. **Vehicle Maximum Length:** No limit. **Other:** 2-week max. stay in summertime.

To Get There

From I-65 take Exit 13. If coming from the north, cross State Hwy. 158 (Industrial Rd.) and then turn left onto State Hwy. 213 South (Shelton beach Rd.). If coming from the south, turn left onto State Hwy. 158 (Industrial Rd.) and then left again onto State Hwy. 213 South. Go south on State hwy. 213 for 2 mi. At the first flashing light turn left onto Whistler St. Take the second left onto Aldock Rd. Go 1 mi. to the park entrance.

PELL CITY

Lakeside Landing

4600 Martin St. South, Cropwell 35054. T: (205) 525-5701; F: (205) 525-5423; www.loganmartin-guide.com.

RV ★★★ Tent ★★

Beauty: ★★	Site Privacy: ★★
Spaciousness: ★★	Quiet: ★★
Security: ★★	Cleanliness: ★★★
Insect Control: ★★	Facilities: ★★★

This park's location is its saving grace. On the banks of Logan Martin Lake, the park maintains boat launches, fishing piers, and a swimming area. Area attractions include the Talladega Superspeedway and De Soto Caverns. Campers hoping to enjoy the beauty of nature will have to leave Lakeside Landing. We suggest a drive to Pell City Lakeside Park where you'll find walking trails, picnic facilities, and boating and fishing facilities in a more natural setting. The huge campground at Lakeside Landing won't win any beauty contests, but it is clean and well equipped. There are back-in and pull-through sites that once featured paved parking. Now the parking areas are an untidy jumble of pavement, gravel and grass. The campground is almost completely tree-less and sites are on the small side. We hope you like your neighbors because you'll be able to hear them hiccup. Lakefront sites 174–193 are the most attractive. Some of these lakefront sites have a few shady trees. Avoid Lakeside Landing during summer holidays and major events at Talladega Superspeedway. If you want to camp here on a race weekend, make your reservations 6 to 12 months in advance. Security here is fair; the campground is located just outside Pell City and there are no gates, but the area is well patrolled at night.

Basics

Operated By: Mark & Cindy Bagley. **Open:** All year, except Christmas. **Site Assignment:** No reservations accepted, except race weekends (Apr. & Oct.). **Registration:** Camp store. **Fee:** $18, $16.20 w/ Good Sam discount. **Parking:** At site, overflow parking available.

Facilities

Number of Multipurpose Sites: 215. **Hookups:** Water, electric (50 amps), sewer. **Each Site:** Picnic table, grill. **Dump Station:** Yes. **Laundry:** Yes. **Pay Phone:** Yes. **Rest Rooms and Showers:** Yes. **Fuel:** Yes. **Propane:** Yes. **Internal Roads:** Paved. **RV Service:** 0.75 mi. **Market:** Camp store, supermarket 3 mi. north in Pell City. **Restaurant:** 0.75 mi. north in Pell City. **General Store:** Camp store, K-Mart 3 mi. north in Pell City. **Vending:** Beverages only. **Swimming Pool:** No. **Playground:** No. **Other:** Boat launch, fishing piers, RV storage, snack bar, picnic area, beach on Lake Logan Martin, meeting hall. **Activities:** Fishing, swimming. **Nearby Attractions:** Talladega Superspeedway (NASCAR), De Soto Caverns, Kymulga Grist Mill & Covered Bridge. **Additional Information:** Pell City Chamber of Commerce, (205) 338-3377; Greater Birmingham CVB, (800) 458-8085.

Restrictions

Pets: Leash only. **Fires:** Allowed. **Alcoholic Beverages:** Allowed. **Vehicle Maximum Length:** No limit. **Other:** No RV storage at sites.

To Get There

From I-20, take Exit 155B at Pell City/Asheville. Go 6 mi. south on Hwy. 231. The campground is on the left.

PETERSON

Old Lock 16 Park, Holt Lake

P.O. Box 295, Peterson 35478. T: (205) 553-9373; www.reserveusa.com.

RV ★★★★ Tent ★★★★

Beauty: ★★★★ Site Privacy: ★★★
Spaciousness: ★★★★ Quiet: ★★★★
Security: ★★★★ Cleanliness: ★★★★
Insect Control: ★★★ Facilities: ★★★

Old Lock 16 Park on Holt Lake will include 36 tranquil sites when construction is completed in 2002. When we visited, eight attractive sites had been completed. Every site is situated on the water and features paved back-in parking. Sites are larger than average and nicely spaced, making them quiet. There are a few shade trees, but not enough greenery to provide privacy between sites. At press time, we could not tell which sites would be the nicest.

BASICS

Operated By: US Army Corps of Engineers. **Open:** All year. **Site Assignment:** First come, first served; reservations accepted through the National Recreation Reservation Service (NRRS) at (877) 444-6777 or www.reserveusa.com. Reservations can be made up to 240 days in advance, full payment required upon making reservation; credit card preferred (V, MC, D, AE), or pay by money order if at least 21 days in advance of arrival. $10 fee for cancellation or change of site or dates. Cancellation within three days of arrival charged first night, no-show charged $20 plus first night. **Registration:** Gatehouse. **Fee:** $14. **Parking:** At site, limit 3 vehicles per site.

FACILITIES

Number of RV Sites: 0. **Number of Tent-Only Sites:** 2. **Number of Multipurpose Sites:** 36. **Hookups:** Water, electric (50 amps). **Each Site:** Picnic table, grill, fire ring, lantern post, some decks. **Dump Station:** Yes. **Laundry:** Yes. **Pay Phone:** Yes. **Rest Rooms and Showers:** Yes. **Fuel:** No. **Propane:** No. **Internal Roads:** Paved. **RV Service:** 35 mi. west in Tuscaloosa. **Market:** Country store 2.5 mi.; Grocery 25 mi. east in Hueytown. **Restaurant:** 10 mi. north in Oak Grove. **General Store:** 25 mi. east in Hueytown. **Vending:** Beverages only. **Swimming Pool:** No. **Playground:** Yes. **Other:** Boat ramp, swimming beach, picnic shelter. **Activities:** Fishing, boating, hiking in area. **Nearby Attractions:** VisionLand, Mercedes-Benz Visitor Center, Birmingham & Tuscaloosa attractions. **Additional Information:** Tuscaloosa CVB, (800) 538-8696; Greater Birmingham CVB, (800) 458-8085.

RESTRICTIONS

Pets: Leash only. **Fires:** In grills & fire rings only. **Alcoholic Beverages:** Not allowed. **Vehicle Maximum Length:** No limit. **Other:** 14-day stay limit.

TO GET THERE

From I-59, take the Brookwood exit onto CR 59 and go north approximately 5 mi. to AL Hwy. 216. Turn right and drive east for 2.5 mi. Then turn left back onto CR 59 and go north 18 mi. Turn left onto Lock 17 Rd. and go north. After 2 mi. (at Lock 17 Grocery) the road veers to the left. Continue 2.5 mi. north to the campground entrance.

PICKENSVILLE

Pickensville Recreation Area, Aliceville Lake

61 Camping Rd., Carrollton 35447. T: (205) 373-6328; F: (205) 373-8309; www.reserveusa.com; janalie.m.graham@sam.usace.army.mil.

RV ★★★★ Tent ★★★★

Beauty: ★★★★ Site Privacy: ★★★★
Spaciousness: ★★★★ Quiet: ★★★★
Security: ★★★★★ Cleanliness: ★★★★
Insect Control: ★★ Facilities: ★★★

The necessity of a waterway connecting the Tennessee River to Mobile Bay was noted as far back as 1770, when the Marquis de Montcalm made a report to King Louis XV. Since before Alabama attained statehood, governors have asked Congress to fund such a project. Finally completed in 1985, the Tennessee-Tombigbee Waterway currently flows [haha] south from the Tennessee River. Aliceville Lake is now one of many recreation destinations along the Tenn-Tom. Straddling the Alabama-Mississippi border, the lake provides fishing, swimming, and other activities. The Pickensville campground consists of 176 sites laid out in 3 loops and two spurs. Though mostly flat, the campground is very attractive. Sites are shaded by a variety of tree species and the water's edge is graced with lovely Cypress trees. All roads and parking spaces are paved. Most of the sites offer back-in parking and a good deal of privacy. Eight pull-through sites are gigantic, but lacking in privacy. Riverside sites, numbered 105–138, have the nicest views of the water. Built next to a cypress-lined creek, sites 49–61 are also very pretty. Security at Pickensville Campground is outstanding, with 24-hour gate attendance. We recommend avoiding this area in July and Aug. when insects, heat and humidity can be oppressive.

BASICS

Operated By: US Army Corps of Engineers. **Open:** All year. **Site Assignment:** First come, first served; reservations accepted through the National Recreation Reservation Service (NRRS) at (877) 444-6777 or www.reserveusa.com. Reservations can be made up to 240 days in advance, full payment required upon making reservation; credit card preferred (V, MC, D, AE), or pay by money order if at least 21 days in advance of arrival. $10 fee for cancellation or change of site or dates. Cancellation within three days of arrival charged first night, no-show charged $20 plus first night. **Registration:** Gatehouse. **Fee:** $14–$18 (cash, check, V, MC, D, AE). **Parking:** 2 large, 4 small vehicles per site, additional charge for more vehicles.

FACILITIES

Number of Multipurpose Sites: 176. **Hookups:** Water, electric (30, 50 amps), some sewer. **Each Site:** Picnic table, grill, fire ring, lantern post, concrete pads. **Dump Station:** Yes. **Laundry:** Yes. **Pay Phone:** Yes. **Rest Rooms and Showers:** Yes. **Fuel:** No. **Propane:** No. **Internal Roads:** Paved. **RV Service:** 25 mi. north in Columbus, MS. **Market:** 15 mi. southeast in Aliceville. **Restaurant:** 3 mi. east in Pickensville. **General Store:** 3 mi. east in Pickensville. **Vending:** Beverages only. **Swimming Pool:** No. **Playground:** Yes. **Other:** Boat launch, fish cleaning station, picnic shelters, group campfire ring, game courts, swimming beach, wildlife viewing area. **Activities:** Fishing, tennis, volleyball, basketball, boating, walking trails. **Nearby Attractions:** Antebellum Visitors Center in Pickensville, US Snag Boat Montgomery, Aliceville Museum & Cultural Arts Center w/ German POW Camp, attractions in Columbus, MS. **Additional Information:** Aliceville Chamber of Commerce, (205) 373-2820.

RESTRICTIONS

Pets: On leash only, not allowed on beach. **Fires:** Fire rings, grills only. **Alcoholic Beverages:** Not allowed. **Vehicle Maximum Length:** No limit. **Other:** Title 36 policies apply.

TO GET THERE

From Tuscaloosa, take US Hwy. 82 west 20 mi. to Alabama Hwy. 86. Go southwest 24 mi. to Pickensville. Continue 3 mi. west to the Recreation Area. From Columbus, MS take MS 69, which becomes AL 14, to Pickensville. Turn right onto Hwy. 86, and go 3 mi. west to the Recreation Area. The entrance is on the right.

ROGERSVILLE

Joe Wheeler State Park

201 McLean Dr., Rogersville 35652. T: (256) 247-1184; F: (256) 247-1449; www.dcnr.state.al.us/parks, joewheelerstpk.home.mindspring.com; joewheelerstpk@mindspring.com.

RV ★★★★★ Tent ★★★★★

Beauty: ★★★★★ Site Privacy: ★★★★
Spaciousness: ★★★★ Quiet: ★★★
Security: ★★★★★ Cleanliness: ★★★★
Insect Control: ★★★ Facilities: ★★★★★

Straddling Wheeler Lake, and connected by a bridge over Wheeler Dam, Joe Wheeler State Park is a favorite among fishermen. A variety of fish species is found in the lake. Two boat launches serve Wheeler Lake and a third provides access to adjoining Wilson Lake. A marina store augments the fishing experience with fuel and supplies. Joe Wheeler State Park provides a variety of activities on land as well as facilities for large groups. The campground is laid out in three loops with 116 improved sites, and one loop with primitive sites. Site size is ample but not outstanding. Parking is paved and most sites are back-in. The prettiest sites, 9, 10, 22, 24, and 26, have partial views of Lake Wheeler. The campground is surrounded by lovely thick woods, which provide shade at most sites but very little privacy between sites. The tent camping area consists of a nicely wooded loop of gravel road surrounded by trash cans and fire rings. Like many exceedingly attractive tent areas, there are no designated sites. This remote state park is gated and guarded, making security outstanding. Avoid late summer heat and humidity at Joe Wheeler State Park; plan a visit in spring, early summer, or fall.

Basics

Operated By: Alabama State Parks. **Open:** All year. **Site Assignment:** First come, first served. **Registration:** Campground office; Security will register late-comers. **Fee:** $16 for improved sites, $10 for primitive sites; fee includes 4 people; $2 each additional person, $5 for 2nd tent. **Parking:** At sites, limit 2 cars per site.

Facilities

Number of RV Sites: 0. **Number of Tent-Only Sites:** 50 (primitive). **Number of Multipurpose Sites:** 116. **Hookups:** Water, electric (20, 30 amps), sewer. **Each Site:** Picnic table, grill. **Dump Station:** Yes. **Laundry:** Yes. **Pay Phone:** Yes. **Rest Rooms and Showers:** Yes. **Fuel:** Boat fuel. **Propane:** No. **Internal Roads:** Paved. **RV Service:** 15 mi. west toward Florence. **Market:** 4 mi. east in Rogersville. **Restaurant:** In park. **General Store:** Camp store. **Vending:** Yes. **Swimming Pool:** No. **Playground:** Yes. **Other:** Marina, boat ramps, boat fuel, sandy beach, 18-hole golf course, group meeting room & lodge, resort lodge, picnic pavilions. **Activities:** Boating (rentals available), swimming, hiking trails, day-use tennis, basketball. **Nearby Attractions:** Athens, W.C. Handy birthplace Museum & Library in Florence, Civil War Walking Trail, Cook's Natural Science Museum, Oakville Indian Park & Museum. **Additional Information:** Decatur/Morgan County CVB, (256) 350-2028.

Restrictions

Pets: Leash only. **Fires:** In grills & fire rings only. **Alcoholic Beverages:** Not allowed. **Vehicle Maximum Length:** 50 ft. **Other:** 2-week stay limit.

To Get There

From I-65, take Hwy. 72 west for 22 mi. The Park entrance will be on the left 2 mi. west of Rogersville. The campground is 3 mi. inside the park.

WILMER

Escatawpa Hollow Campground

15551 Moffett Rd., Wilmer 36587. T: (334) 649-4233; F: (334) 649-1235; yerfdogjw@gateway.net.

RV: ★★★★ Tent: ★★★★

Beauty: ★★★★	Site Privacy: ★★★
Spaciousness: ★★★	Quiet: ★★★
Security: ★★★★	Cleanliness: ★★★
Insect Control: ★★★	Facilities: ★★★★

If your kids are the strong-swimming adventurous types, they will delight in the river and woods at Escatawpa Hollow. In the vernacular of youth, "this place is cool!" Because of its popularity with gregarious families, this campground is anything but quiet on summer weekends. The picturesque private campground is situated on the bank of the Escatawpa River near the Alabama-Mississippi border. An exceptionally clean blackwater river, here the Escatawpa is lined with white sand beach, creating a delightful swimming area. The bream, catfish, and bass in the river are purported to be the best-tasting in the state (if you can catch them). Paddlers enjoy the mellow flat water of the Escatawpa. Boat rental and shuttle arrangements are available at the campground.

Basics

Operated By: Larry & Janice Godfrey. **Open:** All year. **Site Assignment:** First come, first served; reservations accepted; deposit required on holidays; 2-day notice for refund. **Registration:** Office. **Fee:** $10–$15. **Parking:** 2 vehicles per site, overflow parking available.

Facilities

Number of RV Sites: 0. **Number of Tent-Only Sites:** 15. **Number of Multipurpose Sites:** 22. **Hookups:** Water, electric (20, 30 amps). **Each Site:** Picnic table, grill. **Dump Station:** Yes. **Laundry:** No. **Pay Phone:** No. **Rest Rooms and Showers:** Yes. **Fuel:** No. **Propane:** No. **Internal Roads:** Gravel & dirt. **RV Service:** 15 mi. southeast in Mobile. **Market:** 4 mi. east in Wilmer. **Restaurant:** 4 mi. east in Wilmer. **General Store:** 19 mi. southeast in Mobile. **Vending:** No. **Swimming Pool:** No. **Playground:** No. **Other:** Canoe & tube rentals, canoe trips including shuttle service (reservations required), walking trails, rope swings. **Activities:** River swimming, canoeing, kayaking, fishing. **Nearby Attractions:** Bellingrath Gardens in Theodore, Robert Trent Jones Golf Trail, *USS Alabama,* Mobile attractions. **Additional Information:** Mobile Convention & Visitors Corporation, (800) 5-MOBILE

Restrictions

Pets: In RV sites only, on leash only. **Fires:** At tent sites only. **Alcoholic Beverages:** Not allowed. **Vehicle Maximum Length:** 35 ft. **Other:** Tent sites max. 1-week stay, read all warnings concerning river swimming.

To Get There

From I-65, take exit 5B at Moffett Rd. and US Hwy. 98. Go 22 mi. west on US Hwy. 98 to the 0-mi. marker at the Mississippi state line. The park entrance is on the left.

Alaska

Alaska, seemingly the granddaddy of destinations for RVers and campers, lives up to its reputation as "the last frontier" in several ways. Glaciers, mountains, crystal-clear streams, and wildlife are certainly attractions that make you feel like you've entered another world. However, in Alaska you will also be entering another world of RV parks and campgrounds. After you cross the mountainous border, you notice the quality of both state and private campgrounds changes dramatically. Here, many private RV parks look like they were constructed hastily, without consideration for aesthetics and privacy. Bulldozed lots that sandwich vehicles together are more standard than not. State campgrounds and facilities aren't much better. Although generally more private, they tend to have bumpy roads, uneven campsites accommodating only the shortest of vehicles, few facilities, and no hookups.

Primitive though the campgrounds may be, they are nothing compared to the road system. If you look at a map of Alaska and see "highways," don't be fooled! Although most of the state's main roads are now paved (some just recently), what is a considered a highway in Alaska is a backcountry road to the rest of the nation. Except for **Anchorage** and **Fairbanks,** even modern thoroughfares are mostly narrow, single lanes without shoulders, curb banks, or passing areas. Factor in the many unexpected curves, a stargazing truck or trailer in front of you, slower speed limits, or the occasional moose blocking the way, and your travel time increases significantly. As a general rule, it would be very difficult to cover more than 300 miles in one day if you planned on making any pit stops. We recommend a three-week minimum stay to see Alaska, and many travel agencies and tour guides say that it takes at least two months to take in the primary attractions. Visitors are always surprised just how far it is from one civilized destination to another, and how slow the pace can be.

But we assure you that your trip will be worth every pothole, irregular campsite, and outhouse. The scenery in Alaska is unrivaled, and you will find yourself gasping and holding your breath countless times a day. In Alaska, just when you begin to think you've viewed **mountains** from every possible angle, suddenly you turn a corner to see a heart-stopping scene that makes you feel like you're glimpsing these giant rocky wonders for the first time. Add to this the massive hanging and piedmont **glaciers** that are visible right from the highway, the turquoise water of the lakes and streams, sprawling forests of spruce and birch, and seemingly endless fields of wildflowers, and you will feel certain that you have found heaven.

In addition, if viewing **wildlife** is your goal, there is nowhere like Alaska. Wake up early (we're talking between 4:30 and 7:00 am) to increase your chances of seeing moose by the roadside. Besides moose, there are caribou, Dall sheep, 300 varieties of migrating birds, whales, wolves, fox, coyotes, and bears are some of the animals you have a chance of glimpsing on your trip. But, of course, let's not forget the fish! Welcome, anglers, to the state where the fabled 98.5-pound King salmon and 395-pound halibut were caught. Fishing opportunities are as bountiful as mosquitoes in this state (and that means plenty bountiful).

The following facilities accept payment in checks or cash only:

Denali View North Campground, Wasilla
Granite Creek Campground, Anchorage
Montana Creek Campground, , Anchorage
Northern Nights RV Campground, Glennallen
Waterfront Park Campground, Seward

The following facility features 20 or fewer sites:

Granite Creek Campground, Anchorage

ANCHORAGE
Anchorage RV Park

1200 North Muldoon Rd., Anchorage 99506. T: (907) 338-7275 or (800) 400-7275; F: (907) 337-9007; www.anchrvpark.com.

RV ★★★★ Tent n/a

Beauty: ★★★	Site Privacy: ★★★
Spaciousness: ★★★	Quiet: ★★★★
Security: ★★★	Cleanliness: ★★★★★
Insect Control: ★★	Facilities: ★★★★★

Anchorage RV Park, located 15 minutes east of downtown, takes camping in Alaska to an entirely new level. This immaculate and well-maintained campground spoils RV travelers for all other parks. With 195 full-hookup sites, one might think that campers feel overcrowded here; however, plenty of birch and spruce trees, coupled with manicured flower gardens, make it easy to forget that you are at the largest campground in the state's largest city. And besides, one can always seek reprieve in the cedar-lined lounge area, where a fireplace, television, games, books, and coffee make guests feel like they are back home in their living rooms. For travelers who don't want to waste time shopping, Anchorage RV Park has a general store and gift shop right on the premises. And for those who can't quite get used to the cooler temperatures of the state, Anchorage RV Park offers bathrooms with heated floors to keep those toes toasty. Both back-in and pull-through sites are available, although the latter are a bit more expensive. We preferred the most wooded sites, numbers 101 through 115, but keep in mind these are quite far from the rest rooms and showers. Anchorage RV Park is located adjacent to Elmendorf Air Force Base, so if you hear a deep rumble, look up for F-16s flying daily maneuvers. Also keep your eyes peeled for the fox and moose that like this part of town.

BASICS

Operated By: CIRI Alaska Tourism. **Open:** May 15–Sept. 15 or later depending on the weather. **Site Assignment:** Reservations are strongly suggested in June & July. A credit card number is required to hold a spot & a $10 fee is charged for cancellations with 30-day notice. Cancellations within 30 days are nonrefundable. **Registration:** Office hours are from 6 a.m.–10 p.m. If you arrive after hours, a map w/ your site assignment will be posted on the door & payment can be settled by 8 a.m. the next morning. If you don't have a reservation, maps w/ highlighted available spots will be posted. Choose a spot & pay in the morning. **Fee:** $30–$35 per night. **Parking:** At site.

FACILITIES

Number of RV-Only Sites: 195. **Number of Tent-Only Sites:** 0. **Hookups:** Electric (20, 30, 50 amps), water, sewer, cable, telephone. **Each Site:** Picnic table. **Dump Station:** Yes. **Laundry:** Yes, coin operated washers & dryers cost $1.50. Laundry soap & change dispensers are available. **Pay Phone:** Yes, several w/ a terrace & chairs. **Rest Rooms and Showers:** Yes. Facilities are clean, modern & heated. **Fuel:** Available 3 mi. down the road at Muldoon Texaco. **Propane:** Available at Muldoon Texaco. **Internal Roads:** Gravel, pristine condition. **RV Service:** There are several service centers in Anchorage including mechanics that will come to you. Inquire in the office. **Market:** A Fred Meyers is located a few mi. south on Muldoon. **Restaurant:** Several to choose from in Anchorage. Ask for suggestions at the front office. **General Store:** Yes. **Vending:** Soda, candy & newspaper dispensers located by the rest rooms. **Swimming Pool:** No. **Playground:** No. **Other:** There is a covered picnic & grill area on the west side of the campground. **Activities:** Inquire at campground. **Nearby Attractions:** The Native Heritage Center is just across the street & downtown Anchorage is a 15 minute drive. There is also a paved bike trail nearby. Information on activities & a variety of brochures can be found at the front office. **Additional Information:** www.anchrvpark.com.

RESTRICTIONS

Pets: Must be leashed. Waste bags are available throughout to clean up after pets. **Fires:** No fires allowed. **Alcoholic Beverages:** Prohibited in communal areas. **Vehicle Maximum Length:** None. **Other:** A list of rules is distributed upon check-in.

TO GET THERE

Take the Glenn Hwy. to the Muldoon North Exit. Follow Muldoon north almost to the end of the road, where you will see the Elmendorf Air Force Base gates. Turn left just before these gates at the lighted Anchorage RV Park sign.

ANCHORAGE
Granite Creek Campground

Alaska Recreational Management, Inc., 800 East Diamond Blvd., Kenai Peninsula 99515. T: (907) 522-8368; F: (907) 522-8383; www.alaskacampground.com; arm@alaska.com.

RV ★★★★ Tent ★★★★★

Beauty: ★★★★★	Site Privacy: ★★★★★
Spaciousness: ★★★★★	Quiet: ★★★★★
Security: ★★★	Cleanliness: ★★★★
Insect Control: ★★	Facilities: ★★

If you are looking for a truly Alaskan camping experience, Granite Creek campground, tucked into a trio of Chugach mountain peaks, will not disappoint you. This campground is only a half-mile off the Seward Hwy.; but it can still be considered "off the beaten track," since Anchorage locals tend to occupy the campground on weekends, and out-of-state visitors rarely find their way here. You'll have to come prepared with plenty of food and fuel (as well as mosquito spray from mid-June to mid-July) because you will not find convenience stores or other amenities for at least 25 miles in any direction. However, the nature-lover will be entertained merely by listening to the rushing waters of Granite Creek, taking in the stunning views of the Chugach mountains, or identifying the lush variety of wildflowers that fill in the gaps between spruce trees. All sites are back-in, spacious, and private. However, the loop layout is a bit tight for extra-long vehicles, and it is not recommended for RVs 30 feet or longer. You'll find the most impressive views at sites 8, 11, 12, and 16, although a bad site does not exist at Granite Creek campground. Chances of spotting moose are high here, particularly if you are an early riser. Ask the campsite manager where to look.

BASICS

Operated By: Owned by USFS & managed by Alaska Recreational Management, Inc. A campground manager is on-site during operating months. **Open:** The campground may be utilized all year-round, but is only managed & maintained from Memorial Day weekend–Sept. 15. Sometimes snowy conditions prohibit opening until mid-June. **Site Assignment:** This campground is first come first served only. **Registration:** Occupy a site & return-the entrance sign within 30 minutes, fill out a fee envelope & settle payment. Tear the stub off the envelope & make sure it is visible through your car or RV windshield. **Fee:** All sites are $10 per night. Holders of a Golden Age Passport pay half price. Campground has a 14-day limit per camper. **Parking:** At site.

FACILITIES

Number of RV-Only Sites: 19. **Number of Tent-Only Sites:** 0. **Hookups:** 2 hand operated water pumps for entire campground. **Each Site:** Picnic table, fire grate. **Dump Station:** No. **Laundry:** No. **Pay Phone:** No. **Rest Rooms and Showers:** Two pit toilets both cleaned & well maintained by a campground manager. **Fuel:** Girdwood, 27 mi. north, or Seward, 63 mi. south. **Propane:** No. **Internal Roads:** Gravel, sometimes impassible up until mid-June due to high sNowfall in the area. **RV Service:** Girdwood, 27 mi. north, or Seward, 63 mi. south. **Market:** None in area. Go to Girdwood, 27 mi. north or Moose Pass, 34 mi. south. **Restaurant:** None in area. Go to Girdwood, 27 mi. north, Portage Lake Lodge near Portage Glacier, or Summit Lake Lodge 18 mi. south. **General Store:** None in area. Go to Girdwood, 27 mi. north, or Moose Pass, 34 mi. south. **Vending:** No. **Swimming Pool:** No. **Playground:** No. **Other:** The Johnson Pass hiking trailhead can be found on the highway 0.5 mi. north, & is a great family hike. There is also an 8-mi. paved biking trail that begins there. **Activities:** Go fishing for Dolly Vardens in Granite Creek, or take a walk & look for the many moose that reside in the area. **Nearby Attractions:** Portage Glacier & the access road to Whittier are only 30 minutes away & the gold mining town of Hope, although a 40-minute drive, would be worth an afternoon trip. **Additional Information:** www.alaskacampground.com.

RESTRICTIONS

Pets: All pets should be leashed & under owner supervision. **Fires:** Fires in fire grates only. **Alcoholic Beverages:** No restrictions. **Vehicle Maximum Length:** None, but RVs over 30 ft. may have difficulties. **Other:** No more than 8 people per site. Firearms & fireworks are not allowed. Food that is not properly stored or left unattended is subject to citation. Bear-proof food lockers are available free of charge from the campground manager.

TO GET THERE

Take the Seward Hwy. to mi. 63.5 and look for the large blue and white sign for Granite Creek Campground w/ an arrow directing you to Granite Creek Rd. Follow the road approximately 0.5 mi., and you will find a large entrance sign and fee box.

ANCHORAGE
Montana Creek Campground

816 Oceanview Dr., Montana Creek 99515. T: (907) 566-Camp or (907) 733-KAMP; montanacreekcampground@alaska.net

RV ★★★★ Tent ★★★★

Beauty: ★★★★	Site Privacy: ★★★
Spaciousness: ★★★	Quiet: ★★★★
Security: ★★★	Cleanliness: ★★★★★
Insect Control: ★★	Facilities: ★★

If you've been traveling awhile and feel that all campgrounds look alike, Montana Creek will offer a refreshing change of pace. Attention to detail is what makes this campground stand out from the rest. Sheila Lankford, the owner and operator of the campground, tends her perennial gardens and campsite grounds personally, and vibrant displays of wildflowers and berries are sure to delight those with or without a green thumb. Sheila was born and raised on a homestead in this area, and she can offer guests great stories and solid traveling advice. Look for her with her dog Cody. Montana Creek Campground has 18 back-in/pull-through sites with electric hookups available in a grassy area adjacent the creek. All-sized rigs can be easily accommodated here. These sites all have new fire pits and grills, as well as lanterns for the evening hours. For smaller RVs, more scenic, dry camping is available in the meandering campground loops tucked into birch and spruce woods. Campers will enjoy the private, heavily treed sites that have been uniquely named after regular guests. Our favorite spot was "Hilton's Hotel" located right next to the serene Montana Creek bed.

BASICS

Operated By: Owned & operated by Sheila Lankford. **Open:** May–Oct., exact days depend on snowmelt & weather conditions. **Site Assignment:** This campground is first come first served only. Space is usually available, but it is recommended that you arrive by Friday afternoon if you are planning to stay the weekend. **Registration:** A self-registration board & pay box are situated at the entrance of the campground. Find a site & return-the front-pay. **Fee:** Electric hookup costs $18, dry camping is $12. There is a $6 charge to park for the day & fish. **Parking:** At site.

FACILITIES

Number of RV-Only Sites: 74. **Number of Tent-Only Sites:** 0. **Hookups:** Electric (30, 50 amps), potable water is available near the tackle shop. **Each Site:** Picnic table, grill, lantern pole, fire pit, & some w/ electrical outlets. **Dump Station:** Available 3 mi. north at Sunshine One Stop or 5 mi. south at Mat-Su RV Park. **Laundry:** No. **Pay Phone:** No. **Rest Rooms and Showers:** No showers or flushable toilets. Only portables are available, but they are extremely well maintained & clean. **Fuel:** Available at Sunshine One Stop 3 mi. north or Ship Creek Lodge 8 mi. south. **Propane:** Available at Sunshine One Stop 3 mi. north or Mat-Su RV Park 5 mi. south. **Internal Roads:** Gravel, well-maintained. **RV Service:** Talkeetna Auto Care is located 3 mi. north of the campground. **Market:** The Store is located one mi. north & has basic, albeit pricey, food & supplies. Sunshine One Stop is 3 mi. north & also stocks basic amenities. **Restaurant:** His & Hers Lounge & Restaurant located 3 mi. north. Also several restaurants to choose from in Talkeetna. The Store just north of the campground also has a small baker w/ soups & sandwiches. **General Store:** The Store one mi. north. **Vending:** No. **Swimming Pool:** No. **Playground:** No. **Other:** A paved walkway & pedestrian bridge allows guests views of Montana Creek & several access points to the creek offer excellent fishing opportunities for silvers, kings, pink (even numbered years), grayling, & trout. A tackle shop on site offers fishing gear for sale or for rent. **Activities:** Live music is available on the campground July 4th. Feature artists vary every year. The Talkeetna Bluegrass Festival takes place the first week of Aug. just five mi. north of the campground. **Nearby Attractions:** This campground is a hop, skip & a jump from the endearing town of Talkeetna (the town which the show *Northern Exposure* was designed after). In addition, information is available at the campground on dog sledding, flight seeing, fishing, & boating opportunities in the area.

RESTRICTIONS

Pets: Should be leashed at all times. **Fires:** Allowed in campground fire pits & grills. Sometimes high forest fire conditions trigger temporary fire restrictions. **Alcoholic Beverages:** No restrictions. **Vehicle Maximum Length:** None. **Other:** There are several resident bald eagles in this area. Ask about recent sightings.

TO GET THERE

Take the Parks Hwy. to mi. 96.5 and look to the east. The large sign and a picnic table w/ a statue of two bear cubs sitting on it make this campground easy to find.

ANCHORAGE
Ship Creek Landings RV Park

150 North Ingra St., Anchorage 99520. T: (907) 277-0877 or reservations: (888) 778-7700; www.alaskarv.com; alaskarv@aol.com.

RV ★★ Tent ★★

Beauty: ★	Site Privacy: ★
Spaciousness: ★★	Quiet: ★★
Security: ★★★	Cleanliness: ★★★
Insect Control: ★★	Facilities: ★★★

Only blocks away from downtown, Ship Creek Landings offers guests a resting spot that is within minutes of the highlights of Alaska's largest city. However, this campground is not one to choose for its scenery or quality. Located in Anchorage's warehouse district, dilapidated buildings surround the area, and the Alaska railroad passes directly by. Looming power lines cut through the center of the campground, and even though the city's hub is so close, a steep hill and industrial traffic do not make walking ideal. All of this said, Ship Creek does offer full hookup camping, clean bathrooms and showers, and a convenient location. It is also within the vicinity of Anchorage's prime fishing creek—you guessed it, Ship Creek. This loop-shaped campground consists of mostly back-in sites, but four pull-throughs are also available for larger rigs. A separate area at the back of the campground offers respite for tenters only. Besides a steep birch-lined hill bordering one side of the campground, there is little plant life here. About five feet of grass separates individual spaces. We found no one site to be better than another. It is simply a choice between being next to a power line or a fence.

BASICS

Operated By: Best of Alaska RV Parks, Alaska Travel Adventures. **Open:** May 1–Sept. 30. **Site Assignment:** Reservations are strongly suggested as the campground fills up quickly. The toll-free reservation number is for all of Alaska Travel Adventures' campgrounds, so have the name of the one you want in mind. **Registration:** Office hours are from 8 a.m.–8 p.m. If you arrive after hours, choose a spot that doesn't have a name card posted on the electrical outlet & pay by 9 a.m. the next morning. **Fee:** RVs $14–$32, tents $13. **Parking:** At site.

FACILITIES

Number of RV-Only Sites: 153. **Number of Tent-Only Sites:** 20. **Hookups:** Electric (30, 50 amps), water, sewer. **Each Site:** Picnic table. **Dump Station:** Yes. **Laundry:** Yes, coin operated washers for $1 & dryers for $1.25. Laundry soap can be purchased at the office. **Pay Phone:** Yes. **Rest Rooms and Showers:** Yes, flushable toilets & unlimited showers. **Fuel:** Available at Tesoro on 5th & Gambell. **Propane:** Available at Tesoro on 5th & Gambell. **Internal Roads:** Gravel, some potholes. **RV Service:** Several service stations available in Anchorage. **Market:** A Carrs/Safeway is located on 13th & Gambell. **Restaurant:** Several to choose from in Anchorage. Ask for suggestions & menus at the front office. We enjoyed the Glacier Brewhouse on 5th Ave. **General Store:** Basic items & snacks are for sale in the office. **Vending:** Soda & newspaper dispensers located by the office. **Swimming Pool:** No. **Playground:** No. **Other:** Inquire at campground. **Activities:** Inquire at campground. **Nearby Attractions:** Downtown Anchorage has many attractions. Visit the 4th Ave. Visitor Center for maps & brochures. Some tours can be booked at the campground. **Additional Information:** www.alaskarv.com.

RESTRICTIONS

Pets: Must be leashed & attended. **Fires:** No fires allowed. **Alcoholic Beverages:** No restrictions. **Vehicle Maximum Length:** None. **Other:** A list of rules is distributed upon check-in.

TO GET THERE

Coming from the north, take the Glenn Hwy. to Anchorage and turn right on Ingra St. (Coming from the south, take the New Seward Hwy. to Anchorage. The highway will become a one-way street named Ingra.) Go the end of Ingra, down a steep hill, and turn left on 1st St. You will see the Ship Creek Landings sign on your left. If you cross the railroad tracks, you have gone too far.

ANCHORAGE

Williwaw Campground

USFS, 800 East Diamond Blvd., Portage 99515. T: (877) 444-NRRS; www.reserveusa.com.

RV ★★★★ Tent ★★★★★

Beauty: ★★★★★ Site Privacy: ★★★★★
Spaciousness: ★★★★★ Quiet: ★★★★
Security: ★★★ Cleanliness: ★★★★★
Insect Control: ★★ Facilities: ★★

Relatively new to the RV scene, this immaculate and newly paved campground is a stone's throw away from Portage and Whittier, as well as an ideal overnight stopover for travelers heading to Seward or Homer. Williwaw is a USFS campground, and therefore without hookups or other amenities—but waking up to the dynamic blue of the hanging Middle Glacier that is the campground backdrop is an experience sure to delight young and old alike. Campsites are spacious and private here and can easily accommodate the largest of RVs. With both pull-through and back-in spaces available, it is worth planning ahead and making reservations for a campsite with a view of the Glacier. We recommend sites 2–6 or 34–36.

BASICS

Operated By: USFS. **Open:** Apr. 15–Sept. 30. **Site Assignment:** By reservation or on a space available basis. **Registration:** Occupy a site & return the entrance sign within 30 minutes—fill out a fee envelope & settle payment. Tear the stub off the envelope & make sure it is visible through your RV windshield or on the front of your tent. **Fee:** $12 per single site & $18 for a double. **Parking:** At site.

FACILITIES

Number of RV-Only Sites: 60. **Number of Tent-Only Sites:** Several. **Hookups:** None. **Each Site:** Picnic table, fire pit. **Dump Station:** No. **Laundry:** No. **Pay Phone:** No, go to Portage Glacier Lodge 1.5 mi. down the road. **Rest Rooms and Showers:** Several brand new pit toilets. No showers or wash facilities available. **Fuel:** None in area, fuel up in Anchorage or Girdwood before arriving. The next gas station will not be available until Seward. **Propane:** No. **Internal Roads:** Newly paved & in excellent condition. **RV Service:** No. **Market:** No. The closest market is 10 mi. north in Girdwood. **Restaurant:** Tidewater Cafe is at the Seward Hwy. & Portage Rd. junction. They are open from 8 a.m.–8 p.m. Portage Glacier Lodge is 1.5 mi. beyond the campground. This cafeteria-style restaurant has great soups & sells assorted varieties of homemade fudge. Hours are 9 a.m.–7 p.m. **General Store:** The closest general store is in Girdwood, 10 mi. north. **Vending:** No, but there is a soda & candy machine at Portage Glacier Lodge. **Swimming Pool:** No. **Playground:** No. **Other:** Check out the salmon spawning viewing area adjacent the campground, or take the pleasant Williwaw Nature trail to get a better look at the glacier. **Activities:** Inquire at campground. **Nearby Attractions:** Portage Lake & the Begich Boggs Visitor Center are just 1 1/2 mi. down the road. It is worth catching the movie Voices from the Ice at the visitor center (shown 20 minutes after every hour). Boat tours to the face of the Glacier are also available. Portage road then continues to Whittier but there is a fee to drive through the tunnel. Many people catch glacier boat tours out of Whittier. **Additional Information:** www.reserveusa.com.

RESTRICTIONS

Pets: All pets should be on leashed & under owner supervision. **Fires:** Fires in fire grates only. **Alcoholic Beverages:** Inquire at campground. **Vehicle Maximum Length:** None.

TO GET THERE

Take the Seward Hwy. to mi. 78. Although your map may say Portage, the town was destroyed in the 1964 earthquake and only a few dilapidated remnants remain. Turn north on Portage Rd. and go 5 mi. to the Williwaw Campground sign (not to be confused w/ the Williwaw Viewing Area sign that you'll see 0.25 mi. before the campground). Turn right at the sign, and you will find the entrance board and campsite manager just down the road.

COOPER LANDING

Kenai Princess RV Park

P.O.Box 676, Cooper Landing 99572. T: (907) 595-1425; www.princessalaskalodges.com.

RV ★★★ Tent n/a

Beauty: ★★★ Site Privacy: ★
Spaciousness: ★★ Quiet: ★★★
Security: ★★★ Cleanliness: ★★★★
Insect Control: ★★ Facilities: ★★★★

When you begin to feel the need to pamper yourself after long days on the highway, spend a night at the Kenai Princess RV Park for a bit of luxury. The park itself is nothing extraordinary; however, it's adjacent to the beautiful Kenai Princess Lodge, where RV guests are welcome to dine in the restaurant, enjoy an evening cocktail outside at the bar, use the facility exercise equipment, or dip into the indoor and outdoor Jacuzzis located on the grounds. During your time at this facility, you will feel like coach passenger who just got bumped to first class. A small campground tucked well away from the main roads, Kenai Princess RV Park is quiet and without traffic. The peak of Cecil Rhode Mountain makes for a stunning backdrop, and the glacial waters of the Kenai River are a just short walk away. The campground has a pleasant border of Sitka spruce, but the individual sites are without trees, and only about 10 feet separates campers. All sites are back-ins—the longest being 55 feet—so extra-large rigs might find the campground to be a tight squeeze. No sites stand out as superior or inferior, but we do recommend a spot that is away from the dump station since the tour busses going to and from the lodge utilize the area throughout the day and can be somewhat distracting.

BASICS

Operated By: Princess Cruise Lines. **Open:** May 15–Sept. 15. **Site Assignment:** In June & July reservations are necessary. Spots are held w/ a credit card number & cancellations must be made at least 24 hours beforehand. Reservations are recommended for all months, but occasionally there are spaces available in the early & late days of the season. **Registration:** Office hours are from 8 a.m.–10 p.m. Call if you're going-be late & a map w/ your site assignment will be posted on the door. **Fee:** $22–$27 per night. Good Sam discounts available. **Parking:** At site.

FACILITIES

Number of RV-Only Sites: 28. **Number of Tent-Only Sites:** 0. **Hookups:** Electric (20, 30 amps), water, sewer. **Each Site:** Picnic table. **Dump Station:** Yes. **Laundry:** Yes, $2 per machine. **Pay Phone:** Yes. **Rest Rooms and Showers:** Yes, flushable toilets & coin-operated showers. $1.25 buys about 15 minutes. **Fuel:** Available in Cooper Landing 2.5 mi. away. **Propane:** Available in Cooper Landing. **Internal Roads:** Gravel, well-maintained. **RV Service:** No. **Market:** The Shrew's Nest in Cooper Landing has sundries, including unique Alaskan gifts. Larger supermarkets are available in Soldotna. **Restaurant:** The Kenai Princess lodge offers fine dining, or eat at the bar for a simpler venue. Gwin's Restaurant in Cooper Landing also comes recommended. **General Store:** Yes, at the campground. **Vending:** A soda machine is by the office. **Swimming Pool:** No. **Playground:** No. **Other:** A gift shop is located across from the lodge. **Activities:** Tours & charters can be booked from the lodge. Many include transportation. **Nearby Attractions:** Most visitors are in this region are passionate anglers as the Kenai River is one of the most famous salmon fishing rivers in the state. There are also several local hikes for all skill ranges, including a nature hike on the Kenai Princess Lodge grounds. There are lots of moose in this area—wake up early to find them along Bean Creek Rd. **Additional Information:** www.princessalaskalodges.com.

RESTRICTIONS

Pets: Must be leashed & supervised. **Fires:** No fires allowed. **Alcoholic Beverages:** No restrictions. **Vehicle Maximum Length:** Sites are 55 ft. in length & back-in. **Other:** All prices include use of lodge facilities.

TO GET THERE

Take the Sterling Hwy. to mi. 47.7 just before the bridge crossing the Kenai River. You will see a sign for the Kenai Princess Wilderness Lodge and RV Park, followed by the Bean Creek Rd. turnoff to the right. Follow Bean Creek Rd. for 2 mi. and turn left at the lodge sign. Another sign directs you to the campground tucked just down the hill from the lodge.

DENALI PARK

Denali Grizzly Bear Cabins & Campground

P.O.Box 7, Denali Park 99755. T: (907) 683-2696; www.alaskaone.com/dengrzly.

RV ★★★★ Tent ★★★★

Beauty: ★★★★ Site Privacy: ★★★
Spaciousness: ★★★ Quiet: ★★★★
Security: ★★★ Cleanliness: ★★★★★
Insect Control: ★★ Facilities: ★★★★

If you're looking to capture some of the hearty Alaskan spirit from the days of yore, Denali Grizzly Bear Campground will make you feel like you're back in the pioneer times. One of the highlights of this campground is chatting with the workers here. Most of them are part of the Reisland clan, descendents of the family that homesteaded this land decades ago. Siblings and cousins now run the campground in the summer, and they have gone to great lengths to preserve some of the flavor of yesteryear. Take a few moments to admire the unique Alaska paraphernalia that decorates the general store and office. Almost everything you see has a story behind it. With several thickly wooded back-in sites (and two pull-through sites) available, all-sized rigs can be accommodated, but longer vehicles may have some difficulty maneuvering if they wander beyond their designated area. This campground has many loops and turns, making campers feel like they're much further away from the park highway than they really are. The rushing Nenana River that borders the campground, coupled with the snow-capped mountains in the background, complete the effect of being away from it all. Ask for a riverside site if possible.

Basics

Operated By: Owned & operated by the Reisland's. **Open:** May 15–Sept. 12, exact days depend on snowmelt & weather conditions. **Site Assignment:** Reservations are recommended, particularly in June & July. A one-night deposit is required to secure a campsite, & a 15% service fee is charged for cancellations. No refunds are given w/ 48 hours of the reserved date. Walk-ins are also welcome, just check into the office before settling into a site. **Registration:** Payments should be made at the front office prior-going-your site. Check-in is from 3-10 p.m. If you are not going-be able-make it during office hours (8 a.m.-10 p.m.) call ahead. A map will w/ your site assignment will be waiting for you on a pegboard outside the office. **Fee:** Each campsite (up to four people) is $17.50. Extra people are $3 each. An extra vehicle or tent is $1. Electric hookup is $5 per vehicle & water is $1 per vehicle. All major credit cards or cash accepted. **Parking:** At site for most spots. Some tent sites are walk-in only w/ designated parking in a separate area.

Facilities

Number of RV-Only Sites: 89. **Number of Tent-Only Sites:** Several. **Hookups:** Electric (30 amps), water, sewer. **Each Site:** Picnic table, electrical outlet, water faucet. **Dump Station:** Yes, two on campground property. **Laundry:** Yes, tokens available for purchase at campground office. Laundry soap is sold in the general store. **Pay Phone:** Yes, three. **Rest Rooms and Showers:** Three buildings w/ flushable toilets & pay showers are available to park guests. Shower is coin operated; five minutes cost 75 cents. Facilities are clean & accessible. **Fuel:** A Tesoro station is located in Denali Village 7 mi. north. **Propane:** Yes. **Internal Roads:** Dirt, curvy but well maintained. **RV Service:** A service garage is available just a mi. away. Ask the front desk to call & schedule a time for you. **Market:** Basic food items are available at the campground general store. The Park Mart in Denali Village is also fairly well stocked, but costly. **Restaurant:** Two restaurants available just across the highway at McKinley Village Resort. Several more restaurants to choose from in Denali Village. **General Store:** A well-stocked general store is located adjacent the office & includes coffee & rolls, ice cream, snacks & groceries, ice, liquor, & Alaskan gifts. Hours are 8 a.m–10 p.m. **Vending:** No. **Swimming Pool:** No. **Playground:** No. **Other:** There are 7 covered pavilions for picnics & barbeques. **Activities:** Inquire at campground. **Nearby Attractions:** The Denali National Park entrance is located 6 mi. north of the RV Park. In addition, a wide array of local tours can be booked in the front office. **Additional Information:** www.alaskaone.com/dengrzly.

Restrictions

Pets: Should not be left unattended. **Fires:** Restricted to pit areas only. **Alcoholic Beverages:** No restrictions. Liquor is sold in the campground general store. **Vehicle Maximum Length:** No restrictions, but only 2 pull-through sites available. **Other:** A list of sensible campground rules is distributed to all campers.

To Get There

Take the Parks Hwy. to mi. 231. When you near this mi., slow down—the large Denali Grizzly Bear Cabins & Campground sign on the west side of the road sneaks up on you suddenly.

DENALI PARK

Rainbow Denali RV Park

P.O.Box 777, Denali Park 99755. T: (907) 683-7777; F: (907) 683-7275; www.denalirainbowrvpark.com.

RV ★★ Tent ★★

Beauty: ★★★	Site Privacy: ★
Spaciousness: ★★	Quiet: ★★
Security: ★★	Cleanliness: ★★★
Insect Control: ★★★	Facilities: ★★★

Located at the apex of Denali Village, the development of hotels, restaurants, and gift shops that has sprouted just outside the entrance of Denali National Park, Rainbow Denali RV Park puts you where the action is. Use this RV Park during your allotted time in Denali, and you will be able to grab a bagel and morning cup of coffee, catch a shuttle to the Park, book various tours around the area, go shopping, and find evening entertainment all within walking distance of your tent or RV. Rainbow Denali RV Park is simply a barren gravel lot set behind a boardwalk of tourist shops and attractions, but the facilities are clean, and there are plenty of back-in and pull-through sites that can accommodate all vehicles. There are no superior or inferior individual sites at this campground, as all share the same sweeping views of the Alaska Range and all are equidistant from the hubbub of Denali Village.

Basics

Operated By: Owned & operated by the amicable Ed Regan. **Open:** May 20–Sept. 20, exact days depend on snowmelt & weather conditions. **Site Assignment:** Either just show up or make reservations in advance. Sites can be held w/ a credit card, but must be canceled at least 24 hours beforehand if you can't make it. June & July are the busiest months. **Registration:** Check in at the front office before settling on a site. Office hours are 9 a.m.–9 p.m. If you arrive after hours, find a site & place your payment in the box located on the front of the office building. **Fee:** Full hookups cost $28, electric only is $25, & dry camping costs $18. Tents are $14. These prices include tax. After two nights, a 25% discount is given for subsequent nights. All major credit cards accepted. **Parking:** At site.

Facilities

Number of RV-Only Sites: 77. **Number of Tent-Only Sites:** 10. **Hookups:** Electric (20, 50 amps), water, sewer. **Each Site:** Picnic table, electrical outlet, water faucet. **Dump Station:** Yes. **Laundry:** Yes. **Pay Phone:** Yes. **Rest Rooms and Showers:** Flushable toilets & pay showers available to park guests. Shower is coin operated & costs $2. **Fuel:** The Park Mart Tesoro station is directly adjacent to the campground. **Propane:** Available at the Park Mart Tesoro station. **Internal Roads:** Gravel, flat & well maintained. **RV Service:** Available 11 mi. north in Healy. **Market:** The Tesoro station has convenience items available (at inconvenient prices!). **Restaurant:** Black Bear Cafe is next to the campground office. This Internet cafe is Notable for its soups & sandwiches. The carrot cake also comes recommended. **General Store:** Again, the Tesoro station is your best bet for basic items, but it is preferable to stock up on supplies before arriving in Denali. **Vending:** Soda machines are located on the boardwalk. **Swimming Pool:** No. **Playground:** No. **Other:** The boardwalk offers a jewelry shop, several gift stores, a one-hour photo gallery, & offices where rafting, horseback riding, flight seeing, & golfing tours can be booked. **Activities:** Inquire at campground. **Nearby Attractions:** The Denali National Park entrance is located just south of the RV Park. **Additional Information:** www.denalirainbowrvpark.com.

Restrictions

Pets: No restrictions. **Fires:** Restricted to pit areas only. **Alcoholic Beverages:** No restrictions. Ed only asks that you "behave.". **Vehicle Maximum Length:** None.

To Get There

Take the Parks Hwy. to mi. 238. This mi., known unofficially as Denali Village, is a strip of hotels, restaurants, and gift shops for guests to the National Park. Rainbow Denali is smack in the center of this area. On the east side of the highway, look for a boardwalk of cabin-style shops and a large green sign that says Rainbow Denali (just to the left of the Tesoro Station).

FAIRBANKS

River's Edge RV Park & Campground

4140 Boat St., Fairbanks 99709. T: (907) 474-0286 or (800) 770-3343; F: (907) 474-3695; www.riversedge.net; reresort@alaska.net.

RV ★★★ Tent ★★★

Beauty: ★★★	Site Privacy: ★
Spaciousness: ★★	Quiet: ★★★
Security: ★★★	Cleanliness: ★★★★
Insect Control: ★★★	Facilities: ★★★★

River's Edge RV Park offers the style of camping guests are accustomed to finding in the lower 48 states. Clean, pristine, and modern, this campground allows guests easy access to downtown Fairbanks and nearby tourist attractions, while at the same time providing a tranquil setting on the Chena River. Rest rooms and showers are well maintained here, and the friendly atmosphere, coupled with the knowledge of campground staff regarding the general area, will impress guests. This vast horseshoe-shaped campground has several treed sites on the eastside with more open, grassy spots on the west. Back-ins and pull-through sites are available, with approximately 20 feet between sites. Larger vehicles are easily accommodated. Sites located near the office seemed heavily trafficked and a bit noisy. We preferred the riverside sites, especially sites B-9, D-17, and E-16.

Basics

Operated By: Owned & operated by husband & wife team Steve Frank & Linda Anderson. **Open:** Memorial Day weekend–Sept. 15. **Site Assignment:** General reservations can be made, but specific sites are not assigned until arrival. Reservations require advance payment in full. Drop-in guests are welcome & usually accommodated. **Registration:** Check-in is required at the office before obtaining a site. If you will be arriving after hours (7 a.m.–10 p.m.) call ahead. A map & instructions will be hung on a bulletin board for you-pick up when you arrive. **Fee:** Full hookups are $26.95 & partial hookups cost $23.95. Dry camping available for $15.95. Good Sam discounts available. **Parking:** At site.

Facilities

Number of RV-Only Sites: 179. **Number of Tent-Only Sites:** 10. **Hookups:** Electric (30 amps), water, sewer, modem access. **Each Site:** Picnic table. **Dump Station:** Yes. **Laundry:** Coin operated machines available. Purchase soap & get change in the front office. **Pay Phone:** Yes. **Rest Rooms and Showers:** Flushable toilets & clean showers available free of charge to all guests. **Fuel:** Available on Airport Way (0.25 mi. away) in several places. Fred Meyer is kNown to have the lowest prices. **Propane:** Available on Airport Way (0.25 mi. away) at several gas stations. **Internal Roads:** Gravel, well-maintained. **RV Service:** Several service stations available in Fairbanks. The front office will assist you in making calls. **Market:** Fred Meyer & Safeway are both located on Airport Way. Safeway is open 24 hours. **Restaurant:** The front office lists the daily specials for the nearby Chena's Restaurant & staff will happily make reservations for you. Sample menus for other Fairbanks restaurants are also available. **General Store:** A gift shop & some general items are located on site. Other shopping is abundant throughout Fairbanks. **Vending:** Soda machines & newspaper dispensers on site. **Swimming Pool:** No. **Playground:** No. **Other:** Walk to the banks of the Chena River & try your hand at catch-and-release if you're inclined. There is also a sunny deck area adjacent the office where you can relax & read the newspaper. **Activities:** Reservations for fishing & rafting tours, historical city tours, gold mine tours, & Riverboat Discovery tours can all be booked at the front office. Transportation is provided for most tours. **Nearby Attractions:** The Fairbanks CVB has a toll free number: (800) 327-5774 for information. They can also be visited at 550 First Ave. Lots of website information is also available at www.explorefairbanks.com. **Additional Information:** www.riversedge.net.

Restrictions

Pets: No restrictions. **Fires:** Because campground is in city limits, no fires are allowed. **Alcoholic Beverages:** No restrictions. **Vehicle Maximum Length:** None. **Other:** There is a 1-week max. stay unless otherwise arranged by the campground manager.

To Get There

From the Parks Hwy. take the East Fairbanks Exit. Take a left on Sportsmans Way and another left on Boat St. From the Richardson Hwy. take a left on Airport Way, cross University Ave., and turn right on Sportsmans Way. Take an immediate left onto Boat St. Blue camping signs will point you in the right direction.

GLENNALLEN

K.R.O.A. Kamping Resorts of Alaska

HC1 Box 2560, Glennallen 99588. T: (907) 822-3346; F: (907) 835-3346.

RV ★★★ Tent ★★★

Beauty: ★★★	Site Privacy: ★★★
Spaciousness: ★★★	Quiet: ★★★
Security: ★★★	Cleanliness: ★★★
Insect Control: ★★	Facilities: ★★★

This campground, the halfway point between Tok and Anchorage, is not a destination in itself, but rather a place to layover before journeying to your next checkpoint. However, the highway-weary traveler will find a surprisingly unique experience at K.R.O.A. Set in the gnarly black spruce forest with the sinuous Mendeltna Creek flowing by, the campground has a bit of a rustic, wild feel to it. Jerry and Carol, the hardy Alaskan owners who have been here for over 30 years, do not believe in the creature comforts of the rest of the world. Ask them about computers or highway improvements and they will grunt and remind you that, "This is Alaska!" However, Carol is happy to serve you a hot sourdough pancake breakfast in the charming log cabin lodge, and Jerry can be found working at the bar in the evening offering you a shot of whiskey. This campground has treed sites with plenty of back-ins and pull-throughs. The several loops and slightly bumpy road make some parts of the campground difficult for larger rigs, but ultimately all can be accommodated. The sites are not numbered and seem slightly scattered about. We preferred the creekside sites, but they are the furthest away from the showers and bathrooms. Overall, the campground is clean and on par with Alaska's other RV sites—it simply has a very "seasoned" feel to it.

Basics

Operated By: Jerry Snow & Carol Adkins. **Open:** Year round. **Site Assignment:** Reservations are recommended for holiday weekends & July 4th. Deposits are required during busy times. Otherwise, there is usually room for RVers who just show up. The only exception might be if the campground is accommodating a caravan. **Registration:** Stop in the restaurant/office & pay before you park. If you arrive after hours, find a spot & settle payment in the morning. **Fee:** Full hookup is $17, dry camping is $10, & tents are $6. Cabins range from $35–$55 per night. Good Sam discounts available. Cash or CC accepted, no checks. **Parking:** At site.

Facilities

Number of RV-Only Sites: 60. **Number of Tent-Only Sites:** Several. **Hookups:** Electric (20 amps), water, sewer, phone access. **Each Site:** Picnic table. **Dump Station:** Yes. **Laundry:** Yes, coin operated. **Pay Phone:** No, but calling cards may be used in the office. Phone cards available for purchase in the restaurant. **Rest Rooms and Showers:** Family style bathrooms available in the restaurant & on the campground. Showers cost $1. **Fuel:** Yes, on site. **Propane:** No. **Internal Roads:** Gravel, a bit bumpy. **RV Service:** Closest is available in Glenallen. **Market:** Closest is in Glenallen. **Restaurant:** A restaurant & bar are on site & are open from 7 a.m. to 10 p.m. Carol makes the dough for the pizzas, & the cinnamon rolls come recommended. Sandwiches & simple meals are also available at relatively reasonable prices. **General Store:** Some basic items available for purchase in the restaurant. **Vending:** No. **Swimming Pool:** No. **Playground:** No. **Other:** Cozy cabins are available for rent if you want a night out of your camper/tent. **Activities:** Inquire at campground. **Nearby Attractions:** The Drunken Forest museum is on site. This is a fenced in collection of unusually shaped wood pieces & artifacts that have been found in the local area.

Restrictions

Pets: Jerry says make sure your pets don't eat his!. **Fires:** No restrictions. **Alcoholic Beverages:** No restrictions, alcohol available at the bar. **Vehicle Maximum Length:** None.

To Get There

Take the Glenn Hwy. to mi. 153. You'll see the log lodge and the wooden K.R.O.A. sign on the south side of the highway.

GLENNALLEN

Northern Nights RV Campground

P.O.Box 528, Glennallen 99588. T: (907) 822-3199; F: (907) 822-3199; www.alaska-rv-campground-glennallen-northernnights.net; nnites@yahoo.com.

RV ★★★ Tent ★★★★

Beauty: ★★★★	Site Privacy: ★★
Spaciousness: ★★	Quiet: ★★★
Security: ★★★	Cleanliness: ★★★★
Insect Control: ★★	Facilities: ★★★

Set just where the Glenn Hwy. T-bones the Richardson Hwy., Northern Nights is a convenient stopover for those en route to Tok, Fairbanks, Valdez, or Anchorage. This spruce-lined campground is tucked away from the roar of the trucks and cars on the highways and has a quaint, cozy atmosphere. It is a good place to refuel, get a hot meal in town, and make preparations for the following day's travel. As an added bonus, if you stay at Northern Nights on a Monday or Wednesday, you can join in on their free bonfire and dessert nights—an attraction worth timing your visit for. Northern Nights is a small campground with a parking lot layout. There are plenty of pull-through sites for larger vehicles, and tenters are able to enjoy a comfortable night's sleep at a padded tent spot. Sites are only about 10 feet apart, but a few young trees between each camping space provide a little more privacy. We recommend sites 13–18, simply because they are farthest away from the office and the incoming and outgoing RVs.

Basics

Operated By: Richard & Tomi Hawes. **Open:** Apr. 10–Sept. 29. **Site Assignment:** Reservations are strongly recommended for June & July. No deposit is required but please call by 4 p.m. if you have to cancel. Visitors without reservations will be accommodated on a space available basis. **Registration:** Register at the front office before settling in. If you are going-arrive after hours, call ahead, & a map w/ your assignment will be left on the front door. For those without reservations, find a spot & settle payment before 9 a.m. the next morning. **Fee:** RVs are $19–$22, tents are $12. No credit cards accepted. **Parking:** At site.

Facilities

Number of RV-Only Sites: 18. **Number of Tent-Only Sites:** 5. **Hookups:** Electric (30 amps), water, phone access. **Each Site:** Picnic table, fire pit. **Dump Station:** Yes. **Laundry:** In the process of being constructed at the time of publication. **Pay Phone:** No, but calling cards can be used in the front office. **Rest Rooms and Showers:** In the process of being constructed at the time of publication. **Fuel:** A gas station is directly across the street. **Propane:** Available at the gas station. **Internal Roads:** Gravel, pot-holed in some areas. **RV Service:** The Glennallen Chevron has complete mechanical service. **Market:** Park's Place is 0.5 mi. down the road. **Restaurant:** Check out the Hitchin' Post one mi. west for $2.99 breakfasts & large burgers. The Great Alaskan Freeze & The Caribou Restaurant are other close dining options. **General Store:** Spark's general store is across the road, & the Hub of Alaska is just east of the campground. **Vending:** No. **Swimming Pool:** No. **Playground:** No. **Other:** Inquire at campground. **Activities:** Glennallen has a large 4th of July celebration complete w/ a parade, raft races, & a salmon bake. **Nearby Attractions:** The Glennallen Visitor Center, mi. 189 on the Glenn Hwy., can help you find hiking, hunting, & fishing opportunities. Hours are 8 a.m. to 7 p.m. in the summer, (907) 822-5555. **Additional Information:** www.alaska-rv-campground-glennallen-northernnights.net.

Restrictions

Pets: Must be leashed. Pet sitting is available for a small fee. **Fires:** Restricted to fire pits. Firewood is free!. **Alcoholic Beverages:** Glennallen is a dry city. One cannot purchase alcohol here, but if you have your own you may imbibe at your site. **Vehicle Maximum Length:** None. **Other:** Quiet hours are from 10 p.m.–6 a.m. No generators or radios during these times. Vehicle washing is also not allowed on site.

To Get There

Take the Glenn Hwy. to mi. 188.7. The campground is right at the Glenn/Richardson junction in the town of Glennallen on the north side.

HOMER

Oceanview RV Park

Geri Barling, Homer 99603. T: (907) 235-3951; F: (907) 235-1065; www.oceanview-rv.com; camp4fun@xyz.net.

RV ★★★ | Tent ★★★

Beauty: ★★★★★	Site Privacy: ★★
Spaciousness: ★★	Quiet: ★★★
Security: ★★★	Cleanliness: ★★★★★
Insect Control: ★★★	Facilities: ★★★★

This full-hookup campground offers a magnificent panoramic view of Katchemak Bay and is conveniently located next to downtown Homer, the very last town on the Alaska highway system. Probably the cleanest and most modern facility on the Kenai Peninsula, Oceanview is an ideal place to get a hot shower, browse a well-stocked gift shop, and get a free cup of coffee in the morning. With both back-in and pull-through sites, Oceanview is a parking lot–style facility with few trees and little privacy between sites. However, the friendly atmosphere and numerous amenities make Oceanview an ideal resting spot. Reserve a waterside site if you can. Sites 26, 43, 64, 83, and 86 are recommended. For shade-lovers, ask for 17B.

Basics

Operated By: Geri Barling. **Open:** Apr. 1–Oct. 1. **Site Assignment:** By reservation or on a space available basis. Sometimes the entire park is booked by caravans, so a phone call is recommended. **Registration:** Do not occupy a site until you have registered at the front office. If you are going-be arriving after hours (8 a.m.–9 p.m. Monday through Saturday, 9 a.m.–8 p.m. Sunday) call ahead & the campground manager will make arrangements w/ you. **Fee:** Full **Hookups:** $26.95, electricity $19.95, & dry camping $14.95. Showers are included for all campers. There are no discounts or coupons, but seniors do receive a 10% discount at the gift shop. **Parking:** At site.

Facilities

Number of RV-Only Sites: 100. **Number of Tent-Only Sites:** 11. **Hookups:** Electric (30, 50 amps), water, cable, phone. **Each Site:** Trash can. **Dump Station:** Not on site. City dump is located just down the road. **Laundry:** Yes, coin-operated washers & dryers are available for $2. Change is available in the gift shop. **Pay Phone:** Yes. **Rest Rooms and Showers:** Flush toilets & hot showers available free of charge to all campers. Facilities are clean & well-maintained. **Fuel:** Available just a few blocks away at Tesoro. **Propane:** Available at Homer Tesoro. **Internal Roads:** Gravel roads in good condition. **RV Service:** Available in Homer. **Market:** Located eight blocks away & open 24/7. **Restaurant:** None on site, but several to choose from in downtown Homer. We recommend Sal's for sourdough french toast or Cups for lunch & dinner. **General Store:** No, but there is a gift shop w/ some basic food & camping items. **Vending:** Ice, soda, & newspaper machines are all available outside the front office. **Swimming Pool:** No. **Playground:** No. **Other:** There is a covered picnic area for large groups or grill parties. Guests can also take a walk down the hill to the beach for an up close look at the shimmering waters of Katchemak Bay. **Activities:** A fish-fry is hosted for campground guests every Fourth of July. **Nearby Attractions:** Find information at the Chamber of Commerce located on the Sterling Hwy. between Bartlett & Main St. Their number is (907) 235-7740. **Additional Information:** www.oceanview-rv.com.

Restrictions

Pets: All pets should be leashed & under owner supervision. More than two animals requires manager approval. **Fires:** No fires in the RV Park. **Alcoholic Beverages:** No restrictions. **Vehicle Maximum Length:** None. **Other:** RV Park guests can arrange for several boating & fishing charters at a 10% discount.

To Get There

Take the Sterling Hwy. to mi. 172.7. Just before you reach downtown Homer, you will see the RV park's large sign off to the right.

HOPE

Seaview RV Park

P.O. Box 110, Hope 99605. T: (907) 782-3300; F: (907) 782-3344; www.home.gci.net/~hopeak; hopeak@gci.net.

RV ★★ | Tent ★★

Beauty: ★★★	Site Privacy: ★
Spaciousness: ★★	Quiet: ★★
Security: ★★★	Cleanliness: ★★★
Insect Control: ★★★	Facilities: ★★★

The town of Hope is a tiny speck on the Alaska map that is often overlooked by tourists. However, the traveler who ventures off the Seward Hwy. and down the curvy 18-mile road to this vintage gold-mining community will not regret the detour. Seaview RV Park lies on the edge of Hope and is host to the downtown area's only bar and dinner restaurant. Sweeping views of the Turnagain Arm, coupled with a convenient placement, allow one to ignore the fact that the RV Park itself is a barren, crowded lot with back-in and pull-through sites to accommodate all vehicles. Since there is little to no privacy between sites (and because there is a bar next door) this is not a campground for a person who sleeps lightly. However, for the more sociable, Seaview RV Park is an ideal place to meet local Alaskans, fish for salmon in Resurrection Creek, and explore a few well-preserved remnants of the gold rush.

Basics

Operated By: Owned & operated by a friendly Australian, Greg Stanley-Harris. Sometimes you'll find him running the bar. **Open:** May 1–Sept. 20. **Site Assignment:** First come, first served or by reservation. There is usually plenty of space at the beginning & end of the season, but reservations are recommended from mid-July until the end of Aug. **Registration:** Occupy a site & find someone in the bar or restaurant for payment. If you arrive after hours simply pay the next day. This campground operates on the honor system. **Fee:** $10 per RV site, $15 w/ electric. Tents are $5. **Parking:** At site or on road.

Facilities

Number of RV-Only Sites: 28. **Number of Tent-Only Sites:** As many as can be squeezed in. **Hookups:** Electric (20, 30 amps), one water hose available on the side of the bar. **Each Site:** Electrical outlet, fire pit. **Dump Station:** No, but can go to Henry's One Stop 1 mi. down the road. **Laundry:** No, Henry's One Stop is available. **Pay Phone:** No, but calling cards can be used in the bar or restaurant. **Rest Rooms and Showers:** Several portables of dubious cleanliness are available. Showers can be taken at Henry's One Stop for a miniscule fee. **Fuel:** Hope has a gas station, but the availability of fuel is hit or miss & there are No set hours of operation. Fuel-up beforehand in Anchorage (when coming from the north) or Seward (when leaving the south). **Propane:** Available at Henry's One Stop. **Internal Roads:** Gravel, average condition. **RV Service:** None. **Market:** No. Hope has a small gift shop w/ the basics, but it is expensive here. **Restaurant:** The Seaview Restaurant is famed for its seafood chowder & homemade pasta sauces. Also featured at various times are exotic meats such as ostrich, caribou, musk ox, kangaroo, & rattlesnake. Discovery Cafe, the town's other restaurant, is just down the road &, unlike the Seaview Restaurant, is open for breakfast. **General Store:** Again, you'll find the basics at the local gift shop, but be prepared to pay a hefty price. **Vending:** No. **Swimming Pool:** No. **Playground:** No. **Other:** Inquire at campground. **Activities:** Ask in the restaurant or bar for Gold Rush Peck. This eccentric Alaskan will give you a two-hour gold panning lesson for $5. Fish for salmon in Resurrection Creek from mid-July through the end of the summer. From Aug. through mid Sep., pick raspberries along the Turnagain Arm or follow Hope Junction to the end of the road & hike the scenic Gull Rock Trail. **Nearby Attractions:** There are several nearby hiking trails that cater to all levels. Rafting trips & guided fishing tours are also available in the area. Inquire in the restaurant or bar. **Additional Information:** www.home.gci.net/~hopeak.

Restrictions

Pets: No restrictions. **Fires:** In fire pits only. Firewood is available for sale. **Alcoholic Beverages:** No restrictions. **Vehicle Maximum Length:** None. **Other:** Inquire at campground.

To Get There

Take the Seward Hwy. to mi. 56 just over the Canyon Creek Bridge and turn north at Hope junction. There is a large sign pointing the way. Follow the Hope Hwy. 16.9 mi. and turn right on Old Hope Rd. A short stretch on Old Hope brings you to Main St. Turn left and follow this road to its end.

HOUSTON

Riverside Camper Park

P.O.Box 87, Houston 99694. T: (907) 892-9020; F: (907) 892-9020; aksalmon@mtaonline.net.

RV ★★★★ Tent ★★★

Beauty: ★★★	Site Privacy: ★★★
Spaciousness: ★★★	Quiet: ★★★
Security: ★★★	Cleanliness: ★★★★
Insect Control: ★★	Facilities: ★★★★

Riverside Camper Park is a clean, tranquil park that offers the perfect break before going to the big city of Anchorage just an hour's drive away. This loop-shaped campground is just off the park highway and is conveniently located within walking distance of a restaurant, post office, grocery store, and service station. It can also be commended for its clean bathrooms and home-style showers. For fishing fans, bank fishing on the Little Susitna River is available all summer, and boat charters can be arranged at the campground. There are plenty of spacious back-in and pull-through sites available. Spruce and birch line Riverside Camper Park, but no trees or flowers separate the grassy campsites. Request the spots furthest from the highwa;. sites 27 and 28 are next to the water.

Basics

Operated By: Owned & operated by Kenny & Sheila Mortensen. **Open:** May–Sept., exact days depend on snowmelt & weather conditions. **Site Assignment:** Either just show up or make reservations in advance. Sites can be held w/ a credit card, but must be cancelled at least 24 hours beforehand if you can't make it. **Registration:** Check in at the front office before settling on a site. Office hours are 9 a.m.–9 p.m. If you arrive after hours, instructions are on the front gate for check-in. **Fee:** Full hookups cost $20. Good Sam & Military discounts given. All major credit cards accepted. **Parking:** At site.

Facilities

Number of RV-Only Sites: 56. **Number of Tent-Only Sites:** 2. **Hookups:** Electric (30 amps), water, sewer, modem access available in the front office. **Each Site:** Picnic table, electrical outlet, water faucet. **Dump Station:** Yes. **Laundry:** Yes, $1.50 to wash & $1.50 to dry. An iron & ironing board are available free of charge. **Pay Phone:** Yes, phone cards can also be purchase here. **Rest Rooms and Showers:** Clean & modern bathroom facilities are available free of charge to all guests. **Fuel:** There is a service station adjacent to the campground. **Propane:** Yes. **Internal Roads:** Gravel, well-maintained. **RV Service:** Available in Wasilla 15 mi. away. **Market:** Miller's Place is located next to the campground within easy walking distance. Items are cheaper in Anchorage, but immediate needs can be met here & fishing licenses are also available. Ice cream fans will find the largest soft-serve cones in Alaska at this market!. **Restaurant:** Hamburgers are available at Miller's Place. For more variety, The Houston Lounge is located just down the road. **General Store:** Miller's Place stocks a variety of basic supplies. **Vending:** Soda & candy machines, newspapers, & phone cards are all vendable items in the Riverside front office. One can also buy or trade from a large variety of used books here. **Swimming Pool:** No. **Playground:** No. **Other:** There is a boat ramp & bank access to the Little Susitna River, & horseshoe pits on site. **Activities:** The 3rd Saturday of Aug. is Houston's Annual Founder's Day. This is a community BBQ w/ games, activities, & the best fireworks display you've ever witnessed!. **Nearby Attractions:** This area of the state is famed for lake & river fishing. Houston is also renown for its fireworks stores.

Restrictions

Pets: No restrictions. **Fires:** Restricted to pit areas only. **Alcoholic Beverages:** No restrictions. **Vehicle Maximum Length:** None. **Other:** Barcley, the office pooch, is not much of a watch dog, but he is fun to pet & play with!.

To Get There

Take the Parks Hwy. to mi. 57.7. You cannot miss the tiny strip of convenience shops and the large, dark brown building w/ Riverside Camper Park displayed above the front door.

NINILCHIK

Scenic View RV Park

P.O.Box 39253, Ninilchik 99639. T: (907) 567-3909; www.scenicviewrv.com; scenicrv@yahoo.com.

RV ★★★ Tent ★★★

Beauty: ★★★★	Site Privacy: ★★
Spaciousness: ★★	Quiet: ★★★
Security: ★★★	Cleanliness: ★★★
Insect Control: ★★★	Facilities: ★★★

This campground is justly named. On a clear day, the view of the famous mountain trio I.R.S. (Iliamna, Redoubt, and Spur) will remind you why you came to Alaska. Although just off of the Sterling Hwy., Scenic View feels more remote than other RV Parks on the Kenai Peninsula, with very little development in the surrounding area. Scenic View would make a wonderful stopover on the way to Homer, as well as offer a great rest stop for adventurers who want to try their hand at digging up razor clams at the nearby Clam Gulch. Scenic View Campground is located on a gently sloping hill reaching downward toward the Cook Inlet. All sites here are back-in, but larger vehicles can be accommodated. There is about 5–10 feet between camping spots, and grass or shrub-covered strips separate sites. Request a site next to the ocean and away from the highway. Wherever you end up, you'll have an amazing view.

Basics

Operated By: Ann Musarra. **Open:** May 15–Sept. 1. **Site Assignment:** Reservations are strongly suggested. A credit card number is required to hold a spot & one night's charge will be applied to the card if cancellations are made within 24 hours. **Registration:** Office hours are from 7 a.m.–10 p.m. If you arrive after hours, occupy a spot & find Ann in the morning-settle payment. **Fee:** $12–$19 per night. **Parking:** At site.

Facilities

Number of RV-Only Sites: 27. **Number of**

Tent-Only Sites: As many as can be squeezed in. **Hookups:** Electric (20, 30 amps), water, sewer, phone access. **Each Site:** None. **Dump Station:** Yes. **Laundry:** Yes, coin operated washers & dryers for $1.75. **Pay Phone:** No, calling cards may be used in the office. **Rest Rooms and Showers:** Yes. Showers are clean but cost $3. **Fuel:** Available 6 mi. west in Ninilchik. **Propane:** Available 6 mi. west in Ninilchik. **Internal Roads:** Gravel & in good condition. **RV Service:** Available in Ninilchik. **Market:** Available in Ninilchik. **Restaurant:** Available in Ninilchik, ask at the front desk for recommendations. **General Store:** No. **Vending:** No. **Swimming Pool:** No. **Playground:** No. **Other:** There is a shared picnic & BBQ area at the center of the campground. **Activities:** Fishing charters can be arranged at the front office. **Nearby Attractions:** Fishing, hunting, & clamming are the main activities that draw travelers to this area. The quaint Russian Orthodox town of Ninilchik is just a 15 minute drive away, & Homer, the famous "end-of-the-road" Alaskan town is another hour beyond that. **Additional Information:** www.scenicviewrv.com.

Restrictions

Pets: No restrictions. **Fires:** No restrictions. **Alcoholic Beverages:** No restrictions. **Vehicle Maximum Length:** None.

To Get There

Simply take the Sterling Hwy. to mi. 127 and turn right at the large Scenic View sign.

PALMER

Mountain View RV Park

P.O.Box 2521, Palmer 99645. T: (907) 745-5747 or (800) 264-4582; F: (907) 745-1700; str@matnet.com.

RV ★★★ Tent ★★

Beauty: ★★★★	Site Privacy: ★
Spaciousness: ★★	Quiet: ★★★★
Security: ★★★	Cleanliness: ★★★
Insect Control: ★★★	Facilities: ★★★

We chose to feature this park because it is a bit off the beaten path, and during busy times when other RV parks are bursting at the seams, Mountain View RV Park will likely be able to accommodate you even at the last minute. This pleasant campground is located three miles off the Glenn Hwy. in Palmer and offers close and personal views of Marsh, Byers, and Lazy Mountains. With spacious, grassy sites and farms on either side, Mountain View RV Park feels more like a stay in the country than a wilderness getaway. Of course, one does have to overlook the many trucks, cars, and engine parts stored behind the campground office. Come here on the Fourth of July, when the owners throw their BBQ bash for the whole town, and you can join the festivities for free. Mountain View RV Park consists of mostly pull-through sites that easily accommodate all rigs. There are no trees on the campground, as the owners say this keeps away insects. Anywhere from 5 to 10 feet separates the sites. We found that sites 1–5 and 22–25 offered the best view of the mountains and were conveniently located.

Basics

Operated By: Red & Dee Starr. **Open:** May 1–Oct. 1. **Site Assignment:** When possible it is best to make reservations. No deposit is required, but please phone if you can't make it. Usually, there is also space for last minute arrivals who haven't called in advance. **Registration:** Office hours are from 8 a.m.-10 p.m. If you arrive after hours, a map w/ your site assignment will be posted on the door & payment can be settled the next morning. If you don't have a reservation, choose a spot & pay in the morning. **Fee:** Spaces are $20–$22 per night. This includes showers. Senior & Good Sam discounts available. **Parking:** At site.

Facilities

Number of RV-Only Sites: 119. **Number of Tent-Only Sites:** 0. **Hookups:** Electric (30 amps), water, sewer, phone access. **Each Site:** Picnic table. **Dump Station:** No. **Laundry:** Yes, coin operated washers are $2 & dryers cost $1.25. Laundry soap & change available in the front office. **Pay Phone:** Yes. **Rest Rooms and Showers:** Yes, 8 separate bathrooms & showers. **Fuel:** Available at Tesoro 3 mi. away. **Propane:** Available at Tesoro. **Internal Roads:** Gravel, good condition. **RV Service:** RV Service is available 10 mi. away in Wasilla. **Market:** A Carrs/Safeway is located 4 mi. away on the Glenn Hwy. The farm adjacent the campground (Arctic Organics) sells freshly picked produce every Friday from 5 p.m.–7 p.m. **Restaurant:** Several to choose from in Palmer. Ask for suggestions at the front office. **General Store:** No. **Vending:** Newspaper dispensers located by the office. **Swimming Pool:** No. **Playground:** No. **Other:** There is a covered picnic & grill area in the center of the campground. **Activities:** A 4th of July grill party is hosted on the grounds. It is free to guests. **Nearby Attractions:** The campground owner operates a boat tour to the Knik Glacier that is reputed to be the best new attraction in South Central Alaska. The Palmer reindeer farm is also very near. If you arrive on Labor Day weekend, the Alaska State Fairgrounds are only a few mi. away. Brochures of other local charters & tours can be found at the front office..

Restrictions

Pets: Must be supervised. **Fires:** No fires allowed except in the grill area. **Alcoholic Beverages:** No restrictions. **Vehicle Maximum Length:** None.

To Get There

Take the Glenn Hwy. to Palmer and turn east at the Old Glenn Hwy. stoplight (also called Arctic St.). There is a Tesoro station on the corner to use for a landmark. Go 2.8 mi. on the Old Glenn Hwy., over the Matanuska River, and look for the Mt. View RV Park Sign. Turn left at the sign (Smith St.) and follow this road around a sharp right turn. You will see the campground off to the left. For travelers coming from Anchorage, be sure not to take the first Old Glenn Hwy. Exit you see. Go all the way to Palmer, through the Parks Hwy. intersection, and the next light will be the Old Glenn Hwy. access point you're looking for.

SEWARD

Bear Creek Campground

P.O.Box 2209, Seward 99664. T: (907) 224-5725; F: (907) 224-2283; www.bearcreekrv.com; bearcreekrvpk@symbolseward.net.

RV ★★ Tent ★★

Beauty: ★★★	Site Privacy: ★
Spaciousness: ★★	Quiet: ★★★
Security: ★★★	Cleanliness: ★★★
Insect Control: ★★	Facilities: ★★

Just off the Seward Hwy., six-and-a-half miles before you arrive in the town of Seward, Bear Creek Campground offers the only full-hookup camping on the south side of the Kenai Peninsula. The campground itself is not much more than an expansive gravel lot carved out of spruce forest, but the Kenai Mountains are in view, and pristine Bear Lake is within walking distance. This campground is a less crowded alternative for travelers who want to avoid the throngs of RVs and tourists in Seward, particularly during the fishing months of June, July, and Aug. However, despite the campground's generally tranquil location, be forewarned of the early morning train that whistles when passing Bear Creek Rd.

Basics

Operated By: Owned & operated by Lynn Hettick. **Open:** All year. **Site Assignment:** Reservations accepted or just show up. No deposit is required to hold a spot, however, reservations cannot be made for July 4th. This day is first come first served only. **Registration:** Office is well marked & is open from 8 a.m.–9 p.m. If you arrive after hours, simply choose a site & settle payment the following day. **Fee:** Full hookups cost $28. Parking & facility use without hookup costs $20. Tent sites are $20. MC & D accepted. Good Sam, AAA, AARP, & military receive 10% discount. **Parking:** At site.

Facilities

Number of RV-Only Sites: 60. **Number of Tent-Only Sites:** Space available basis. **Hookups:** Electric (30 amps), water, sewer, cable, phone. **Each Site:** Picnic table, electrical outlet, water faucet, cable hookup (some have fire pits, but campground is currently in a "no fire" zone). **Dump Station:** Yes. **Laundry:** Yes. **Pay Phone:** Yes. **Rest Rooms and Showers:** Yes, campers are provided w/ a punch code to use facilities. **Fuel:** a gas station is located 0.5 mi. away from the campground. **Propane:** Yes. **Internal Roads:** gravel, sometimes in poor condition, particularly in the spring. **RV Service:** in Seward, 6.5 mi. **Market:** Eagle/Safeway in Seward; open 24 hours. **Restaurant:** several to choose from in Seward; ask for sample menus in the office. **General Store:** Convenience shop & liquor store on site. **Vending:** No. **Swimming Pool:** No, but if you're brave & like cold water you can jump into Bear Lake. **Playground:** No. **Other:** Inquire at campground. **Activities:** Jet-ski rentals available at the gas station. **Nearby Attractions:** Explore the nearby fishing weir & watch the spawning red salmon in Aug. **Additional Information:** www.bearcreekrv.com.

Restrictions

Pets: no restrictions. **Fires:** no fires currently allowed due to state regulations. **Alcoholic Beverages:** no restrictions. **Vehicle Maximum Length:** None. **Other:** Management is on site 24/7.

To Get There

Take the Seward Hwy. to mi. 6.5 (mileposts mark the entire highway) and begin looking for the large blue-and-white sign showing Bear Creek Campground w/ an arrow directing you to Bear Creek Rd. Follow Bear Creek Rd. 0.5 mi. over the railroad tracks, past Gary's Gas, and around the bend. The campground is clearly marked on the right side of the road.

SEWARD
Waterfront Park

Camp Management, P.O. Box 167, Seward 99664. T: (907) 224-4055; F: (907) 224-4088; www.sprd.org; campsprd@seward.net.

RV ★★★ Tent ★★★★

Beauty: ★★★★★	Site Privacy: ★
Spaciousness: ★★	Quiet: ★★
Security: ★★	Cleanliness: ★★
Insect Control: ★★★	Facilities: ★★★

This sprawling campground spans almost the entire Seward waterfront, and it's probably one of the most popular RV destinations on the Kenai Peninsula. Visitors will understand why when they arrive; the panoramic views of the Kenai Mountains and Resurrection Bay are breathtaking, and the variety of activities within walking distance from this campground will make you want to schedule more than one night here. Waterfront Park is always active with the hustle and bustle of tourists, and there is very little distance or privacy between RVs. However, you will be too busy sighting bald eagles, looking for whale spouts, and enjoying the ever-changing sunlight in the mountains to notice the crowds. Make reservations for a waterside campsite (sites 12–82 are best), and then bring your walking shoes and take the scenic paved trail either to the Small Boat Harbor, where you can watch the fisherman bring in their daily cache, or to downtown, where shopping and dining are bountiful.

Basics

Operated By: The City of Seward. **Open:** Apr. 15–Sept. 30. **Site Assignment:** Reservations can be made for caravans of 10 or more vehicles only. Everyone else is first come first served. Spaces fill up quickly on the 4th of July & for the Silver Salmon Derby the second week of Aug. **Registration:** Occupy a site & return-an entrance within 15 minutes-fill out a fee envelope & settle payment. Tear the stub off the envelope & make sure it is visible through your RV windshield or on the front of your tent. **Fee:** $15 for hookups, $10 for dry camping, $6 for tents. **Parking:** At site or extra parking on road.

Facilities

Number of RV-Only Sites: 400. **Number of Tent-Only Sites:** 50. **Hookups:** Electric (20, 30 amps), water (23 sites). **Each Site:** Picnic table, fire pit. **Dump Station:** Yes. **Laundry:** No, but there is a laundromat on C & Ballaine. **Pay Phone:** Yes, in the shower house, at the Harbor Master's Office or at City Hall. **Rest Rooms and Showers:** There are flush toilets in three locations & a shower house in the center of the campground (make sure & have $2 worth of quarters, as there are No change machines). Showers are also available at the Harbor Master's Office on the north end of the campground. **Fuel:** Tesoro is located on the Seward Hwy. when arriving in Seward. **Propane:** Available at Bay City Motors on 3rd Ave. or at the Seward Hwy. Tesoro station. **Internal Roads:** Gravel roads that become somewhat pitted during the rainy months of July & Aug. **RV Service:** Available at Bay City Motors on 3rd Ave. **Market:** Eagle Grocery is a 24-hour market just off the highway when you arrive in Seward. **Restaurant:** There are several to choose from. Try Ray's in the Small Boat Harbor for dinner or check out the baked goods at the Ranting Raving on 4th Ave. for breakfast. **General Store:** Fourth Ave. has all varieties of gift & supply shops. **Vending:** No. **Swimming Pool:** No. **Playground:** Yes. **Other:** There are two large picnic pavilions, a baseball diamond, a sand volleyball court, a scenic gazebo, & a paved walkway lined w/ placards showcasing Seward's history & geography. The public boat ramp is adjacent to the campground. **Activities:** Inquire at campground. **Nearby Attractions:** There is a lot to do in Seward including fishing, glacier boat cruises, hiking, shopping, sled dog rides, etc. Information booths are available downtown, at the Small Boat Harbor, or at the Chamber of Commerce Visitors Center just off the Seward Hwy. before you get to town. Call (907) 224-8051. **Additional Information:** www.sprd.org.

Restrictions

Pets: All pets should be on leashes 6 ft. or less. **Fires:** Fires in fire pits only. **Alcoholic Beverages:** No alcoholic beverages allowed. **Vehicle Maximum Length:** No restrictions, back-in sites only. **Other:** Quiet hours between 11p.m. & 7 a.m.

To Get There

Take the Seward Hwy. to the town of Seward. When the speed limit drops to 20 mph, the Seward Hwy. becomes 3rd Ave. Take 3rd Ave. to D St. and turn left. D St. turns into Ballaine, and this street parallels the entire campground. There are several well-marked entrances on Ballaine St.

SOLDOTNA
Centennial Park Municipal Campground

City of Soldotna Parks & Recreation, 538 Arena Dr., Soldotna 99669. T: (907) 262-3151; F: (907) 262-3152; www.ci.soldotna.ak.us.

RV ★★ Tent ★★★

Beauty: ★★	Site Privacy: ★★★★
Spaciousness: ★★★	Quiet: ★★
Security: ★★★	Cleanliness: ★★
Insect Control: ★★	Facilities: ★★

If you are going to Alaska to fish, you might as well head straight for Centennial Park Municipal Campground in Soldotna. Located directly on the Kenai River, this campground includes a popular fishwalk where guests can cast for dolly vardens, red salmon, and king salmon within walking distance from their campsite. Be careful not to tell too many friends about this coveted fishing hole, since it is a favored area for locals and annually returning guests. Evenings at this campground are lively as fisherman fry up their daily catch and talk about "the one that got away". Centennial Park consists of a series of winding loops and is snugly tucked into a forest of spruce and birch. Vehicles of all sizes can be accommodated, but some of the curves will be a bit tight for larger RVs, and all sites are back-ins. Riverside sites are far superior to the inland ones. Campsites on the water include sites 6, 7, 9, 21, 23, 24, 25, 27–31, 84, 86, 88, 91, 93, 95, 97, 98, 100, and 102.

Basics

Operated By: City of Soldotna Parks & Recreation. **Open:** May 1–Oct. 1. If there is snow before Oct., the campground closes early. **Site Assignment:** Reservations are not accepted at this campground. Come early in the day to obtain a site. **Registration:** Choose a site from a map available at the registration area upon arrival, & pay before setting up camp. The registration booth is usually manned 24/7 during the high tourist season, but hours of operation are not set at the beginning & end of the camping season. **Fee:** RVs & tents are $9 a night. There is a $5 fee for day-use & a $7 charge for the boat launch. **Parking:** Cars can be kept at the site. Boat trailers are parked in a designated parking area.

Facilities

Number of RV-Only Sites: 180. **Number of Tent-Only Sites:** 14. **Hookups:** Potable water available at two campsground well houses. **Each Site:** Picnic table, fire grate. **Dump Station:** Two available on site, but the fee is $10. However, dumping is free of charge w/ a fuel purchase at the Soldotna Tesoro or Chevron. **Laundry:** No. **Pay Phone:** Yes. **Rest Rooms and Showers:** Several pit toilets. **Fuel:** Available in Soldotna. **Propane:** Available in Soldotna at any Chevron, Tesoro, or Thompson's Center Gas Station. **Internal Roads:** Gravel, average condition. **RV Service:** Available in Soldotna. **Market:** Fred Meyers & Safeway are two large & well-stocked grocery stores in Soldotna. Stock up on food items here as prices will be higher everywhere else on the Kenai Peninsula. **Restaurant:** All varieties to choose from in Soldotna. **General Store:** No. **Vending:** Soda machines available at the covered picnic area. Ice & newspapers can be purchased at the entrance. **Swimming Pool:** No. **Playground:** No. **Other:** A covered picnic area can accommodate large groups. **Activities:** There is a public boat launch & angler walk at the end of the campground. A small hut in the parking lot contains several brochures highlighting local charters & tours. Coffee can be purchased here for $1. **Nearby Attractions:** Fishing is definitely the highlight here, but non-anglers can inquire about other attractions at the Kenai Peninsula Visitor Center located on the Sterling Hwy. Their number is (907) 262-1337. **Additional Information:** www.ci.soldotna.ak.us.

Restrictions

Pets: Required to be on a leash at all times. **Fires:** In the designated fire grates only. Firewood is for sale at the entrance. **Alcoholic Beverages:** No restrictions. **Vehicle Maximum Length:** None.

To Get There

Take the Sterling Hwy. through Soldotna to mi. 96. Here you will see the junction for Kalifornsky

Beach Rd. Take this road west 0.1 mi. (just follow the vehicles pulling boats). You won't miss that campground sign on the right side of the road.

VALDEZ

Bayside RV Park

P.O.Box 466, Valdez 99686. T: (907) 835-4425 or (888) -835-4425; F: (907) 835-4425; www.alaska.net/~bayside1; bayside1@alaska.net.

RV ★★★ Tent ★★

Beauty: ★★★★★	Site Privacy: ★
Spaciousness: ★★	Quiet: ★★★
Security: ★★★	Cleanliness: ★★★★
Insect Control: ★★★	Facilities: ★★★★

Bayside RV Park is set amongst several other RV parks in Valdez, but this campground stands out for its cleanliness, friendly atmosphere, and waterfront campsites. Chuck Dennis, a retired Alaskan who does a lot of RVing himself, started this business as a way to meet people from around the world. If you're looking for information about the surrounding area, or are just in the mood to chat with someone, Chuck is the man to talk to. Bayside RV Park is basically an open gravel lot, but it's set on the edge of tranquil Prince William Sound with 360° views of the Chugach mountains. The campground is within walking distance from all the major attractions, and local tours can be booked directly through Chuck. There are no trees at this campground, so privacy is minimal, but this is the case at most RV parks in Valdez. At Bayside, the availability of full-hookup sites (plus cable) coupled with unlimited hot showers make this campground a welcome sight after driving the somewhat grueling Richardson Hwy. We preferred the waterside sites, odd numbers 1–41. Sites 45–66 are closer to the highway and tend to be a bit noisier. Both back-ins and pull-throughs campsites are available, and all size rigs can be accommodated.

Basics

Operated By: Charles C. Dennis. **Open:** May 1–Oct. 10, later if weather allows. **Site Assignment:** Reservations are recommended, particularly in June, July & Aug. However, visitors are also welcomed to just show up. If a campsite w/ hookups is not available, Chuck will still find space for you. **Registration:** Payments should be made at the front office prior-going-your site. If you are not going-be able-make it during office hours (8 a.m.–10 p.m.), find an open space & pay in the morning. **Fee:** RVs are $15–$24, Tents cost $12. Showers are included w/ all prices. **Parking:** At site.

Facilities

Number of RV-Only Sites: 89. **Number of Tent-Only Sites:** Several. **Hookups:** Electric (20, 30, 50 amps), water, sewer, cable, Internet access. **Each Site:** Picnic table. **Dump Station:** Yes. **Laundry:** Yes, $1.50 for washers & dryers. Change is available at campground office. **Pay Phone:** Yes, two. **Rest Rooms and Showers:** Home-style bathrooms have recently been installed & offer handicap accessible showers that are included w/ the camping price. Chuck suggests limiting showers to 20 minutes, but if it's been awhile since your last one, he doesn't mind if you take your time. **Fuel:** A Tesoro station is located just across the street. **Propane:** Yes. **Internal Roads:** Crushed rock. **RV Service:** A service garage is available in Valdez. Sometimes Chuck's brother is on-site & available to help w/ mechanical problems. **Market:** Eagle Grocery is a block away & is open from 5 a.m. to midnight. **Restaurant:** The Totem Restaurant is just across the street & is reputed to have the best breakfast in Valdez. **General Store:** No. **Vending:** Both soda & newspaper dispensers are located on the site. A microwave & coffee maker can be found in the office. **Swimming Pool:** No. **Playground:** No. **Other:** The public boat ramp is 0.25 mi. away. **Activities:** Not officially, but Chuck will gladly introduce you to his tamed squirrel, Squeaky. Put a peanut in your mouth, & Squeaky will climb on your shoulder to fetch it!. **Nearby Attractions:** Visit the Valdez Visitor Center for an impressive array of handouts & brochures regarding the surrounding area. They lay out a walking tour of Valdez as well as offer flyers that outline the general history of the area, the pipeline, & other interesting tidbits. **Additional Information:** www.alaska.net/~bayside1.

Restrictions

Pets: No restrictions. **Fires:** No restrictions. **Alcoholic Beverages:** No restrictions. **Vehicle Maximum Length:** None.

To Get There

Take the Richardson Hwy. to Valdez. Just when you are in view of the town look to the left. You will see a light blue sign w/ Bayside RV Park in dark letters. It is the first RV Park you'll see.

WASILLA

Denali View North Campground

AK State Parks, Mat-su/CB Area, HC 32 Box 6706, Denali State Park 99654. T: (907) 745-3975; F: (907) 745-0938; www.dnr.state.ak.us/parks/units/denali1.htm.

RV ★★★ Tent n/a

Beauty: ★★★★★	Site Privacy: ★
Spaciousness: ★	Quiet: ★★★
Security: ★★	Cleanliness: ★★★★
Insect Control: ★★	Facilities: ★★

For many, one of the primary goals of visiting Alaska is to see the longest rock face in the world, Mt. McKinley (more commonly referred to as Denali by Alaskans). Unfortunately, 75% of the tourists who visit this area do not even get a glimpse of this elusive monolith, since it is usually cloaked in a thick layer of clouds. However, if you are willing to take a chance that during your visit the weather will break, then the Denali View North Campground is the place you'll want to be when the sun finally does shine. Views of Mt. McKinley are the sole reason this campground was constructed, as there are no other attractions or guided activities for 30 miles in any direction. However, if the mountain does reveal itself, seeing it from this campground will be the highlight of your trip. A newly paved lot with extra-long pull-through sites makes this campground easily accessible to even the longest of vehicles. There are no hookups here, but a campground water pump is available, as well as regularly maintained outhouses. Some picnic tables and grill areas line the campground. There are also informational placards, a spotting scope, and benches to rest and enjoy the view. The campground is designed so that all RVs face the mountain. However, this really is a parking lot–style campground, and there is little to no space between sites.

Basics

Operated By: Denali State Park. **Open:** From snowmelt till the first snowfall (Approximately mid May–mid Sep.). **Site Assignment:** First come, first served. **Registration:** There is a self registration box located at the entrance. Park your vehicle & fill out a fee envelope shortly thereafter. Display the receipt in a visible area of your vehicle. **Fee:** $10 per night. **Parking:** At site.

Facilities

Number of RV-Only Sites: 23. **Number of Tent-Only Sites:** 0. **Hookups:** None. **Each Site:** None. **Dump Station:** No. **Laundry:** No. **Pay Phone:** No. **Rest Rooms and Showers:** Outhouses are available that are relatively clean. **Fuel:** The nearest fuel station is either north in Cantwell or south at Trapper Creek. **Propane:** No. **Internal Roads:** Newly paved & in excellent condition. **RV Service:** No. **Market:** No. **Restaurant:** Mary's McKinley View Lodge is located at mi. 134.5. **General Store:** No. **Vending:** No. **Swimming Pool:** No. **Playground:** No. **Other:** A short loop trail allows weary travels to walk & stretch their legs. **Activities:** Inquire at campground. **Nearby Attractions:** The entrance to the Denali State Park (not to be confused w/ Denali National Park) is located at mi. 132.2 & offers several hiking trails for all levels. Flightseeing, horsebackriding, & other area tours can be booked at Mt. McKinley Princess Lodge just up Mt. McKinley Princess Dr. at mi. 132.9. **Additional Information:** www.dnr.state.ak.us/parks/units/denali1.htm.

Restrictions

Pets: Must be leashed. **Fires:** Restricted to grill areas at the back of the campground. **Alcoholic Beverages:** No restrictions. **Vehicle Maximum Length:** None. **Other:** Campground rules & regulations are posted next to the fee box.

To Get There

Take the Parks Hwy. to mi. 162.7 and turn west at the Denali View sign. Since there are no landmarks before or after the campground, it can be difficult to find if you're not paying attention. A short paved road leads straight to the camp parking lot.

Arkansas

Rice paddies. Catfish filets. Only country-and-western radio stations. A polite "Sir" or "Madam" in every sentence. Life in Arkansas draws on the Deep South in ways outsiders may consider out of sync with modern America. With county bans on alcohol sales reminiscent of Prohibition, one native went so far as to call the state "backwards," but that depends on your perception. Residents possess an intimate knowledge and palpable love of the land they inhabit, and visitors are welcomed warmly in the best tradition of Southern hospitality.

Arkansas calls itself "The Natural State," and this moniker is reinforced by its inhabitants—even businessmen don safety orange for a weekend hunting trip. Nearly everyone you meet has a fishing pole, knows where to catch a trophy bass (or maybe just dinner), or has photos in his pocket from his last fishing trip. Perhaps the best way to get to know this state is to camp at some of the many state parks—they give you a feel for the breadth of the state's natural diversity and the depth of its history.

Aside from the hunting, the fishing, the boating, and the hot springs, even just driving Arkansas is a pleasure. Lush vegetation wraps around small roads like snug clothing. Wildlife abounds, including armadillos and even alligators. Go for a drive through the **Ozark National Forest** or along the **Mississippi River,** and you'll never think of Arkansas the same way again. Arkansas is such a verdent state you can't help but revel in its greenery. **Bull Shoals** and the **Ouachita Mountains** are as representative of Arkansas as **Little Rock** and **Texarkana.**

The question to ask yourself isn't "Why should I go to *Arkansas*?" but "Why haven't I gone there before?"

The following facilities accept payment in checks or cash only:

- Craighead Forest Park, Jonesboro
- Crossett Harbor RV Park, Crossett
- Fair Park RV Park, Hope
- Freppon's RV Park, Bald Knob
- Hardy Camper Park, Hardy
- Pecan Grove RV Park, Lake Village
- Whispering Pines RV Park, Clinton
- Wilderness Hills RV Park & Campground, Siloam Springs
- Young's Lakeshore RV Resort, Hot Springs

The following facilities feature 20 sites or fewer:

- Bull Shoals Recreation Area, Bull Shoals
- Cedar Ridge, Calico Rock
- Jacksonport State Park, Jacksonport
- Wiederkehr Wine Cellars RV Park, Altus

Campground Profiles

ALTUS
Wiederkehr Wine Cellars RV Park

3324 Swiss Family Dr., Altus 72821. T: (800) 622-WINE or (501) 468-WINE; F: (501) 468-4791; winear62@ar-digit.net.

RV ★★★	Tent ★★★
Beauty: ★★★★	Site Privacy: ★★★
Spaciousness: ★★★	Quiet: ★★★★
Security: ★★★★	Cleanliness: ★★★★
Insect Control: ★★★★	Facilities: ★★

This campground is west of a restaurant, gift shop, and office complex, and north of Arkansas River Valley vineyards. The park itself is little more than a large open parking lot of a gravel, grass, and dirt. Sites 1–10 back up to woods, while 11–20 back up to a pretty agricultural setting. Site 1 is partly in long prairie-type grass, but is close to a shade tree. Sites 7 and 8 are shaded, as is 20. This latter site is probably in the nicest location, as it is furthest from the restaurant complex and next to a large tree. Sites 9–12 are closest to the visitor parking lot. While there is no real maximum length to the vehicles this park can accommodate during off-season, it is unrealistic to haul more than 50 feet during the wine fest—the best time to come to this park (at least, if you don't mind crowds). Tents can cover the entire field to the west during the September wine fest, making it difficult to find a spot. There are few trees anyway, so most tenters will be in the same boat—camping on a hill with no shower facility. Of course, the atmosphere of the festival can override other concerns, but tenters (and RVers without indoor showers) must remember that they will have to spend a day or so without showering. There is one modern unisex rest room that must surely be packed during the festival. This campground is a somewhat dull park without many facilities, although the atmosphere of the restaurant and the wine fest help make up for these shortcomings.

Basics

Operated By: Don Neumeier. **Open:** All year. **Site Assignment:** First come, first served (reservations only for wine fest) **Registration:** In office, shop, or restaurant. (Late arrivals select an available site & pay in the morning.) **Fee:** RV $10 (water, electric), tent $10 (checks, MC, AE, D, CB, DC). **Parking:** At site.

Facilities

Number of RV Sites: 20. **Number of Tent-Only Sites:** Undesignated sites. **Hookups:** Water, electric (30 amps). **Dump Station:** No. **Laundry:** No. **Pay Phone:** Yes. **Rest Rooms and Showers:** Rest rooms; no shower. **Fuel:** No. **Propane:** No. **Internal Roads:** Gravel. **RV Service:** No. **Market:** 2 mi. to Altus. **Restaurant:** On site. **General Store:** No. **Vending:** No. **Swimming:** No. **Playground:** No. **Other:** Gift shop, vineyards **Activities:** Picnics in vineyards, shopping, wine tasting. **Nearby Attractions:** Wineries, antique shops. **Additional Information:** Altus Chamber of Commerce, (501) 468-4684.

Restrictions

Pets: On leash, cleaned up after. **Fires:** In grills only; subject to seasonal bans. **Alcoholic Beverages:** At sites. **Vehicle Maximum Length:** None.

To Get There

From I-40 (Exit 41), turn south onto Hwy. 186 and go 4.6 mi. Turn right at the sign into the entrance.

ARKADELPHIA

Arkadelphia KOA

221 Frost Rd., Arkadelphia 71923. T: (800) KOA-4207 or (870) 246-4922; F: (870) 246-4922; www.koa.com.

RV ★★★★ | Tent ★★★

Beauty: ★★★★	Site Privacy: ★★★
Spaciousness: ★★★	Quiet: ★★★
Security: ★★★★	Cleanliness: ★★★★
Insect Control: ★★★★	Facilities: ★★★★

Most of the sites in this campground are well-shaded, which is good news to summer campers in this part of the state. Laid out in an arc with internal sites, the main camping area has 12 sites around the perimeter that can be used for tents or for small RVs. Site 1 is very close to the road that leads to the northern camping area, and all other sites (except 7 and 8) require either pitching a tent on a serious slope or right on the internal road. RVers may find this normal, but tenters will not like the space. Sites 7 and 8 are the exceptions, with larger spaces and nice trees. Site 24 is an enormous (100-feet-long) pull-through, while the sites next to it (20–23) are half the size and only pull-throughs if the adjacent site is unoccupied. These sites are all next to the forest, under a canopy of trees. Nice 50-foot back-ins that are likewise shaded include 50, 52, 59, and 62. These sites are in the north area of the campground, off the main camping area. Pull-throughs include 51, 55, 58, 60, and 62, which can accommodate a rig of any size. Less pleasant are sites 30 and 31, which are very open, and site 27, which is close to the entrance, Frost Rd., and the propane vending area. The laundry room is clean and spacious, and has a television to help while away the time while your clothes are being cleaned. The rest room is very clean but looks a little outdated. The campground is undergoing remodeling, and hopefully the rest rooms are slated for modernization. Overall, this is a nice campground, although RVers will enjoy it a little more than tenters.

Basics

Operated By: The Cristoffersons. **Open:** All year. **Site Assignment:** Assigned upon registration (Credit card required for reservations, recommended during holidays. Cancellation by 4 p.m. the day before arrival) **Registration:** In office. (Late arrivals use drop box.) **Fee:** RV $20 (full), $18 (water, electric), tent $14. **Parking:** At site.

Facilities

Number of RV Sites: 44. **Number of Tent-Only Sites:** 12. **Hookups:** Water, sewer, electric (30, 50 amps), cable. **Each Site:** Picnic table. **Dump Station:** Yes. **Laundry:** Yes. **Pay Phone:** Yes. **Rest Rooms and Showers:** Yes. **Fuel:** No. **Propane:** Yes. **Internal Roads:** Gravel. **RV Service:** No. **Market:** 7 mi. (Exit 73). **Restaurant:** 1 mi. **General Store:** Yes. **Vending:** No. **Swimming:** Pool. **Playground:** Yes. **Other:** Pet walk area, cabins, fishing pond, cottage (w/kitchen). **Activities:** Fishing, horseshoes, tetherball, hopscotch, hiking, biking. **Nearby Attractions:** Lake DeGray, Lake Hamilton, Lake Catherine, Lake Ouachita, Hot Springs, Crater of Diamonds. **Additional Information:** Arkadelphia Area Chamber of Commerce (870) 246-5542.

Restrictions

Pets: On leash, cleaned up after. **Fires:** In grills; subject to seasonal bans. **Alcoholic Beverages:** At sites, not by pool, subject to dry county regulations. **Vehicle Maximum Length:** None.

To Get There

From I-30, take Exit 78 and turn north onto Hwy. 7. Go 0.25 mi. and turn right onto Frost Rd. Go 1.5 mi. and turn left at the sign into the entrance.

BALD KNOB

Freppon's RV Park

Hwy. 167 North, Bald Knob 72010. T: (501) 724-6476.

RV ★★★ | Tent n/a

Beauty: ★★	Site Privacy: ★★★
Spaciousness: ★★★	Quiet: ★★★
Security: ★★★★	Cleanliness: ★★★
Insect Control: ★★★	Facilities: ★★

This campground has RV sites and mobile homes. RV sites are situated on the outside of a looped internal road around a large open grassy area. Sites 1–7 are 70-foot back-ins set in a row along the east side, close to the manager's house and the entrance. Sites 10–16, 45-foot back-ins along the north edge, back up to a forested area. Of these, sites 15 and 16 are less desirable, as they are so close to a storage unit that navigating a large rig into one of these sites may be problematic (especially 16). Back-ins 17–26 are located along the southern edge of the park. Of these 17 is the nicest, as it has a tree and more space than the others. There are five pull-throughs (also numbered 1–5) to the west of the manager's house. These are 75-foot sites, with grassy patches. The campground unfortunately does not offer rest rooms or showers, so self-contained units are the only RVs that should stop here. Campers who require outside rest room facilities may wish to press on.

Basics

Operated By: David Freppon. **Open:** All year. **Site Assignment:** Flexible when sites are available; verbal reservations OK. **Registration:** In mgr.'s house. (Late arrivals use drop box or settle in morning.) **Fee:** $15. **Parking:** At site.

Facilities

Number of RV Sites: 27. **Number of Tent-Only Sites:** 0. **Hookups:** Water, sewer, electric (30, 50 amps). **Dump Station:** Yes. **Laundry:** No. **Pay Phone:** No. **Rest Rooms and Showers:** No. **Fuel:** No. **Propane:** No. **Internal Roads:** Gravel. **RV Service:** No. **Market:** 3 mi. south. **Restaurant:** Less than 1 mi. south. **General Store:** No. **Vending:** No. **Swimming:** No. **Playground:** No. **Other:** Fishing pond. **Activities:** Fishing. **Nearby Attractions:** Bald Knob National Wildlife Reserve, Big Creek Natural Area. **Additional Information:** Bald Knob Chamber of Commerce, (501) 724-3140.

Restrictions

Pets: On leash, cleaned up after. **Fires:** In grills. **Alcoholic Beverages:** At sites subject to dry county regulations. **Vehicle Maximum Length:** None.

To Get There

From the junction of Hwy. 64, 67, and 167, go 0.5 mi. north on Hwy. 167. Turn right at the sign into the campground.

BRINKLEY

Heritage Inn and RV Park

1507 North Hwy. 17, Brinkley 72021. T: (870) 734-2121; F: (870) 734-3538.

RV ★★★ | Tent n/a

Beauty: ★★	Site Privacy: ★★★
Spaciousness: ★★★	Quiet: ★★★
Security: ★★★★	Cleanliness: ★★★
Insect Control: ★★★	Facilities: ★★★

Run in conjunction with a motel, this RV park is located in a commercial complex next to a gas station with convenience store, and it is within a block of Wal-Mart and several fast-food restaurants. Sites face either the motel or Wal-Mart. Sites are 75-foot pull-throughs with mostly gravel and some grass. Shade trees grow in even numbers 2–10 and odd numbers 11–21. End sites 1 and 22 seem short-changed for space, and 9 is encroached upon by a storage shed. The campground offers the convenience of a commercial location, and the recreation possibilities of a pool.

Basics

Operated By: Pam & Sam. **Open:** All year. **Site**

Assignment: First come, first served Credit card required for reservations. 24 hour cancellation policy. **Registration:** In motel office. **Fee:** $17.22. **Parking:** At site.

Facilities

Number of RV Sites: 24. **Number of Tent Sites:** 0. **Hookups:** Water, sewer, electric (30, 50 amps). **Dump Station:** No (sewer at all sites). **Laundry:** No. **Pay Phone:** No. **Rest Rooms and Showers:** Yes. **Fuel:** No. **Propane:** No. **Internal Roads:** Gravel. **RV Service:** No. **Market:** Less than 0.25 mi. south. **Restaurant:** Less than 0.25 mi. south. **General Store:** No. **Vending:** Yes. **Swimming:** Pool. **Playground:** No. **Activities:** Swimming, hiking, wildlife watching. **Nearby Attractions:** White River Natural Wildlife Reserve. **Additional Information:** Chamber of Commerce, (870) 734-2262.

Restrictions

Pets: On leash, cleaned up after. **Fires:** In grills. **Alcoholic Beverages:** At sites. **Vehicle Maximum Length:** None.

To Get There

From I-40, take Exit 216. Turn south onto Hwy. 49 and take the first right into the motel complex. Register in the motel office.

BULL SHOALS

Bull Shoals Recreation Area

P.O. Box 748, Bull Shoals 72619. T: (870) 445-4424 or (870) 445-4166; F: (870) 445-8354; www.bullshoals.com/boatdock; boatdock@bullshoals.net.

RV: ★★★ Tent: ★★★

Beauty: ★★★★ Site Privacy: ★★
Spaciousness: ★★★ Quiet: ★★★
Security: ★★★★ Cleanliness: ★★★
Insect Control: ★★★ Facilities: ★★★

Sites in this park are situated on a hill that overlooks the marina and the lake. All sites are 30-foot long and 40-foot wide paved back-ins, with the exception of 10, which is 40 feet Sites 1 and 2 have a partial view of the marina—for what it's worth. Sites 3 and 4, set further back into the woods, are combined, making them best for groups who arrive together—and a possible nuisance if incompatible groups are forced to share these sites. Sites 6–8 are forested sites located along the entrance in the northeast corner, but have the least impressive views. The remaining sites (9–12) are situated just above the marina parking lot, and are closest to the action. This can, however, be both good and bad: they have a great view, but are subjected to the most amount of traffic and noise from a loudspeaker. The pit toilet can get quite messy, and those who depend on it will likely not enjoy their stay as much as fully self-contained units. (Likewise, there are no showers.) This is definitely a place to come to enjoy your boat, and not a place to stay otherwise.

Basics

Operated By: US Army Corps of Engineers. **Open:** All year. **Site Assignment:** First come, first served no reservations. **Registration:** Pick a site, then register in the office. **Fee:** $7.50 (water, electric), $15 (includes boat stall). **Parking:** At site.

Facilities

Number of RV Sites: 12. **Number of Tent-Only Sites:** 0. **Hookups:** Water, electric (30 amps). **Each Site:** Picnic table, grill, cement prep table. **Dump Station:** No. **Laundry:** No. **Pay Phone:** Yes. **Rest Rooms and Showers:** Rest rooms; no shower. **Fuel:** No. **Propane:** Yes. **Internal Roads:** Paved. **RV Service:** No. **Market:** 0.25 mi. north. **Restaurant:** 0.25 mi. north. **General Store:** Yes. **Vending:** No. **Swimming:** No. **Playground:** No. **Other:** Boat stall. **Activities:** Fishing, boating. **Nearby Attractions:** Mountain Village, Bull Shoals Caverns, Top O' The Ozarks. **Additional Information:** Bull Shoals Lake–White River Chamber of Commerce, (800) 447-1290, (870) 445-4443.

Restrictions

Pets: On leash, cleaned up after. **Fires:** In grills. **Alcoholic Beverages:** At sites; subject to dry county regulations. **Vehicle Maximum Length:** 30 ft.

To Get There

From the town's westernmost name sign, go 2.1 mi. west on Hwy. 178. Turn left onto Shorecrest Dr., then take the first left onto Boat Dock Rd., which leads to the marina.

CALICO ROCK

Cedar Ridge

P.O. Box 236, Calico Rock 72519. T: (870) 297-4282.

RV: ★★★★★ Tent: ★★★★★

Beauty: ★★★★★ Site Privacy: ★★★★★
Spaciousness: ★★★★ Quiet: ★★★★★
Security: ★★★★★ Cleanliness: ★★★★
Insect Control: ★★★★ Facilities: ★★

This campground is wild, undeveloped, natural, and quiet. It is subtlely but attractively landscaped with rock, cacti, and juniper. Sites 1–3 are 42-foot back-ins that back up to the (rather quiet) road. Site 4 is an unshaded site that also abuts the road, but backs to thick vegetation. Sites 5–7 are pull-throughs that average 55 feet in length; 5 and 7 are shaded, 6 is not. Two unnumbered sites in the northeast corner are in an open field, and can accommodate a rig of any size, as can a third site slightly below these two. (This third site, being sheltered somewhat by a juniper, is more welcoming than the two open sites next to it.) The largest sites are 9–11, which average 70 feet in length. The rest room and shower are contained in a single unit, which is modern and decently clean. There is an absolutely wonderful scenic view of the river down a gravel road at the southernmost edge of the campground, which campers should make a point of seeing. In fact, the campground itself is an extremely attractive natural setting that will please campers of all kinds—definitely a destination campground to return to.

Basics

Operated By: Gene & Reva Lockie. **Open:** Mar 1–Oct. 30. **Site Assignment:** First come, first served; verbal reservations OK. **Registration:** In office. (Late arrivals sign register; "Gene will see you later".) **Fee:** RV $12 (full), $10 (water, electric), tent $7. **Parking:** At site.

Facilities

Number of RV Sites: 17. **Number of Tent-Only Sites:** 3. **Hookups:** Water, sewer, electric (20, 30 amps). **Each Site:** Picnic table, grill. **Dump Station:** Yes. **Laundry:** No. **Pay Phone:** No. **Rest Rooms and Showers:** Yes. **Fuel:** No. **Propane:** No. **Internal Roads:** Gravel. **RV Service:** No. **Market:** 3 mi. into town. **Restaurant:** 1 mi. into town. **General Store:** No. **Vending:** No. **Swimming:** No. **Playground:** Yes. **Other:** Firewood. **Activities:** Fishing, hunting. **Nearby Attractions:** Blanchard Springs Caverns, White River. **Additional Information:** Mountain Home, Chamber of Commerce, (870) 425-5111.

Restrictions

Pets: On leash, cleaned up after. **Fires:** In grills. **Alcoholic Beverages:** At sites. **Vehicle Maximum Length:** None.

To Get There

From the junction of Hwy. 56 and Hwy. 5, go 1 block south on Hwy. 5 (Main St.) to Calico St. Turn right and go 0.7 mi. Turn left at the sign into the campground.

CLINTON

Whispering Pines RV Park

8575 Hwy. 65 North, Clinton 72031. T: (888) 745-4291 or (501) 745-4291.

RV: ★★★★ Tent: ★★★★

Beauty: ★★★★ Site Privacy: ★★★★★
Spaciousness: ★★★★★ Quiet: ★★★★
Security: ★★★★ Cleanliness: ★★★★
Insect Control: ★★★★ Facilities: ★★★

Located in a residential area, this property is a quiet, campground, with a large forested area at the back. Sites are extremely large (85 × 50 feet), with a mixture of pull-throughs and back-ins. Sites 1–14 are divided up into three rows, with 1–5 off to the west of the others. Site 11 is a particularly nice pull-through located next to the pavilion. Sites 15–24 are back-ins along the eastern edge of the property. These sites back up to a strip of trees, beyond which lies the highway. (This proximity to the road and the requirement that drivers back in make these sites a little less desirable.) Tenting is possible in a huge open field to the west, beyond which lie acres of forest. (The owner tells of a bear that has been seen in these woods, so hiding food and toiletries in your vehicle couldn't hurt.) Two other sites are located in front of the office, right off the highway, but you'd have to be crazy to camp there: they are literally a dozen steps from the road. The laundry facility is exceptionally clean and cozy, as are the rest rooms. The showers, while clean, are beginning to show their age and could use an overhaul. This is a cute campground with fruit trees, pines, and country kitsch decorating the grounds. RVers and tenters alike will be comfortable staying here.

BASICS

Operated By: Vilene Borgman & Donna Adkins. **Open:** Mar.–Nov. **Site Assignment:** Flexible, according to availbility; verbal reservations OK. **Registration:** In office. (Late arrivals pay in morning). **Fee:** RV $17 (full), tent $10. (checks, but no credit cards). **Parking:** At site.

FACILITIES

Number of RV Sites: 23. **Number of Tent-Only Sites:** Undesignated sites. **Hookups:** Water, sewer, electric (20, 30, 50 amps). **Each Site:** Picnic table, grill. **Dump Station:** No (sewer hookup at all sites). **Laundry:** Yes. **Pay Phone:** Yes. **Rest Rooms and Showers:** Yes. **Fuel:** No. **Propane:** No. **Internal Roads:** Gravel. **RV Service:** No. **Market:** 7.5 mi. south. **Restaurant:** 0.5 mi. north. **General Store:** Yes. **Vending:** No. **Swimming:** No. **Playground:** No. **Other:** Pavilion, dog run, rec room. **Activities:** Boating, swimming, fishing, darts, horseshoes. **Nearby Attractions:** Branson, Greers Ferry Lake. **Additional Information:** Clinton Chamber of Commerce, (501) 745-6500.

RESTRICTIONS

Pets: On leash, cleaned up after. **Fires:** In grills. **Alcoholic Beverages:** At sites. **Vehicle Maximum Length:** None.

TO GET THERE

From the junction of Hwy. 16 and Hwy. 65, turn north onto Hwy. 65 (towards Marshall), and go 7.3 mi. Turn left into the campground at the sign.

CROSSETT

Crossett Harbor RV Park

P.O. Box 338, Crossett 71635. T: (501) 364-6136.

RV ★★★★ Tent ★★★★

Beauty: ★★★★ Site Privacy: ★★★★
Spaciousness: ★★★★ Quiet: ★★★★
Security: ★★★★ Cleanliness: ★★
Insect Control: ★★★ Facilities: ★★★

This campground is divided into a south loop and an east loop. The south loop is further divided into an inner and outer loop. The most desirable sites are in general on the outer loop 9 especially even 102–106, 109, and odd 113–117), as they have more space and back up to forest, not other campsites. Site 85 is set back away from the other sites, and therefore has more privacy. Site 67 (and 69, to a lesser extent) is adjacent to a pond. Sites 86–91 are doubles. Some sites (especially 86, 87, 95, 97, and 98) seem prone to flooding after a rain. Sites on the outside of the east loop back to seemingly endless forest, and the loop feels more "lost" (in a good way) because of this. However, there is also a lot of stuff strewn about this part of the campground: an old bed frame, wood, and even the charred remains of a burnt vehicle! Sites 1–3 are smack dab on the intersection of two roads, and certainly must receive more passing traffic due to their location. Sites 31, 33, 35, 48, and 50 seem prone to flooding. The rest rooms in both areas look well used, and the floors are in a desperate need of a paint job. Despite the bizarre junk found in a few sites, the east loop seems the nicer of the two areas, and campers will certainly enjoy a stay here.

BASICS

Operated By: US Army Corps of Engineers. **Open:** All year. **Site Assignment:** First come, first served; no reservations. **Registration:** In office (late arrivals check manager's trailer to left of registration kiosk) **Fee:** $12, $9 for seniors (no credit cards.) **Parking:** At site.

FACILITIES

Number of RV Sites: 119. **Number of Tent-Only Sites:** 0. **Hookups:** Water, electric (30, 50 amps). **Each Site:** Picnic table, grill, fire ring, 50-ft. camping pad, 18x12 tent pad, lantern pole. **Dump Station:** Yes. **Laundry:** No. **Pay Phone:** Yes. **Rest Rooms and Showers:** Yes. **Fuel:** No. **Propane:** No. **Internal Roads:** Paved. **RV Service:** No. **Market:** 9 mi. east. **Restaurant:** 8.5 mi. east. **General Store:** Yes. **Vending:** Yes. **Swimming:** No. **Playground:** Yes. **Other:** Boat ramp, picnic shelter. **Activities:** Hiking, boating, fishing. **Nearby Attractions:** Felsenthal Wildlife Refuge. **Additional Information:** Crossett Area Chamber of Commerce, (870) 364-6591, (870) 364-8648.

RESTRICTIONS

Pets: On leash, cleaned up after. **Fires:** In grills; subject to bans. **Alcoholic Beverages:** None. **Vehicle Maximum Length:** None.

TO GET THERE

From the junction of Hwy. 133 and Hwy. 82 in town, turn west onto Hwy. 82 and go 8.1 mi. Turn left at the sign into the entrance.

EDGEMONT

Blue Clouds RV and Cabin Resort

10645 Edgemont Rd., Edgemont 72044. T: (501) 723-4999; www.greersferry.com/blueclouds.htm; bcrvcabins@aol.com.

RV ★★★★ Tent ★★★★

Beauty: ★★★★★ Site Privacy: ★★★★
Spaciousness: ★★★★ Quiet: ★★★★
Security: ★★★★ Cleanliness: ★★★★
Insect Control: ★★★★ Facilities: ★★★

This campground is built at the bottom of a hill, upon which are the office and the cafe. As a result there is a very nice forested view from many of the sites, which are all naturally landscaped. (While this has some appeal, the dirt road may be tricky for some rigs. Sites 1 and 9 are 90-foot pull-throughs, and 14 is a 120-foot pull-through, making it the longest site in the campground. Sites 2–6 are 40-foot back-ins, and 17–25 are 60-foot back-ins. Sites 40–48 back to woods on the south side, making them very attractive sites. All of the sites in this campground, however, are forested and therefore well-shaded. This is a very nice, natural campground for those who enjoy a woodsy feel without being 25 miles from the nearest conveniences. RVers and tenters alike will enjoy a stay here, although the forested setting and dirt road may make for challenging driving for long rigs—especially those with tows.

BASICS

Operated By: Janice. **Open:** All year. **Site Assignment:** Assigned upon registration (Credit card required or telephone number for reservation. 24 hours cancellation policy.) **Registration:** In office. (Late arrivals select an available site & pay in the morning.) **Fee:** RV $15 (checks, V, MC, D). **Parking:** At site.

FACILITIES

Number of RV Sites: 25. **Number of Tent-Only Sites:** 0. **Hookups:** Water, sewer, electric (30, 50 amps). **Dump Station:** No. **Laundry:** Yes. **Pay Phone:** No. **Rest Rooms and Showers:** Yes. **Fuel:** No. **Propane:** Yes. **Internal Roads:** Dirt. **RV Service:** No. **Market:** 3 mi. east. **Restaurant:** 3 mi. east. **General Store:** No. **Vending:** Yes. **Swimming:** No. **Playground:** No. **Other:** Cabins. **Activities:** Fishing, boating, swimming, golfing, folk music. **Nearby Attractions:** Greers Ferry Lake. **Additional Information:** Heber Springs Chamber of Commerce, (501) 362-2444.

RESTRICTIONS

Pets: On leash, cleaned up after. **Fires:** In grills. **Alcoholic Beverages:** At sites. **Vehicle Maximum Length:** None.

TO GET THERE

From the westernmost town name sign on Hwy. 16, go west on Hwy. 16 for 0.4 mi. Turn left at the sign into the entrance.

EL DORADO

Moro Bay State Park

6071 Hwy. 15 South, Jersey 71651. T: (870) 463-8555; www.arkansasstateparks.com.

RV ★★★★ Tent ★★★

Beauty: ★★★★ Site Privacy: ★★★★★
Spaciousness: ★★★★★ Quiet: ★★★★★
Security: ★★★★ Cleanliness: ★★★
Insect Control: ★★★ Facilities: ★★★

Sites 1–9 are built along the edge of a hill, and some of the space is unusable due to an extreme slope. However, there is a large fenced-in area that contains the picnic table and a large concrete slab for camping. Sites are 42-feet-long back-ins, with two pull-throughs (4 and 9), of 42 feet and 75 feet in length, respectively. Site 1 backs to a large open field, and can allow for recreation right off the site. The rest room is across from site 8, and noise from a large fan in the men's room may be bothersome at this site. The rest rooms are relatively clean and modern, but up on our visit the shower needed a good cleaning. Site 10 is located at the crossroads of two internal roads, and may receive more traffice because of this fact. The rest of the sites are along this other road, and are all 42-foot back-ins. Of the sites on this strip, 16 and 17 have a more secluded location at the end of the roundabout. The other sites are pretty much indistinguishable. Tenters will enjoy the wooded sites, but may wish for grassy ground cover instead of a more developed site. Campers of any stripe will enjoy this campground—however, especially those with boats.

Basics

Operated By: Arkansas State Parks. **Open:** All year. **Site Assignment:** First come, first served. Reservations require cash, credit card, or postal money order deposit; in case of cancellation, one night's fee is not refunded. **Registration:** In office. (Late arrivals occupy an available site & register at 8 the next morning.) **Fee:** $14. **Parking:** At site.

Facilities

Number of RV Sites: 20. **Number of Tent-Only Sites:** 0. **Hookups:** Water, electric (20, 30 amps). **Each Site:** Picnic table, grill, fire pit. **Dump Station:** Yes. **Laundry:** No. **Pay Phone:** Yes. **Rest Rooms and Showers:** Yes. **Fuel:** No. **Propane:** No. **Internal Roads:** Paved. **RV Service:** No. **Market:** 15 mi. to Strong or Hermitage. **Restaurant:** 15 mi. to Strong, Hermitage, or Union. **General Store:** Yes. **Vending:** Yes. **Swimming:** No. **Playground:** Yes. **Other:** Picnic area, hunting & fishing licenses. **Activities:** Boating, fishing, basketball, soccer, volleyball. **Nearby Attractions:** Ouachita River, South Arkansas Arbortoreum. **Additional Information:** El Dorado Chamber of Commerce, (870) 863-6113.

Restrictions

Pets: On leash, cleaned up after. **Fires:** In grills. **Alcoholic Beverages:** At sites. **Vehicle Maximum Length:** None.

To Get There

From the junction of Hwy. 167 and Hwy. 15, go 20 mi. northeast on Hwy. 15. Turn left at the sign and continue on to the park entrance.

EUREKA SPRINGS

Eureka Springs KOA

15020 Hwy. 187 South, Eureka Springs 72632. T: (501) 253-8036; F: (501) 253-2249; www.eureka-net.com/koa; koa4fun@ipa.net.

RV: ★★★★ Tent: ★★★★★

Beauty: ★★★★★	Site Privacy: ★★★
Spaciousness: ★★★	Quiet: ★★★
Security: ★★★★	Cleanliness: ★★★★★
Insect Control: ★★★★	Facilities: ★★★★★

There are loads of neat ornaments, plants, logs, rocks, and garden spots in this campground, giving it a somewhat artsy wilderness feel. All of the sites in this campground are forested, undeveloped gravel sites. Sites 1–19 ranging from 30 to 45-feet long on either side of an internal road, Of these, 1–12 back to a hedge, beyond which lies the highway. Sites 11 and 12 are fenced off, giving them added privacy. Site 32 is an exceptionally large (120 feet) pull-through, and 58–69 are only slightly shorter at 115 feet. Sites 41–44 are 60-foot back-ins by the Garden of Meditation, but are slightly sloped. Better sites by the garden are 49–51, which are also 60-foot back-ins, but more level. Tents sites are to the north, away from the RV sites. An exceptional feature of these tent pads is that they contain sawdust instead of crushed gravel, giving tenters a much more comfy bed to sleep on. These dirt sites are located under a canopy of trees, ensuring that all sites are shaded. Many of these sites are along the highway, which is normally quite quiet, but does, of course, carry the occasional vehicle. Sites M and N are the most remote, and R and S are also quite secluded. The rest rooms and showers are all very clean and spacious. Showers are all tile, which makes them seem as comfy as home. One really neat detail is the wooden number plates at each site, which each have a unique hand-carved cartoon. The Garden of Meditation, also a unique detail, comprises stone, twisted wood, plants, and sculptures, and is an extremely peaceful place to rest for a moment.

Basics

Operated By: Jane Shonka. **Open:** All year. **Site Assignment:** Assigned upon registration. Credit card required for reservation; 48 hours cancellation policy. **Registration:** In office. (Late arrivals select an available site & pay in the morning.) **Fee:** RV $24.00 (full), $22.00 (water, electric), tent $15.50. **Parking:** At site.

Facilities

Number of RV Sites: 65. **Number of Tent-Only Sites:** 24. **Hookups:** Water, sewer, electric (30, 50 amps). **Each Site:** Picnic table, fire pit. **Dump Station:** Yes. **Laundry:** Yes. **Pay Phone:** Yes. **Rest Rooms and Showers:** Yes. **Fuel:** No. **Propane:** Yes. **Internal Roads:** Paved. **RV Service:** No. **Market:** 5 mi. to Eureka Springs. **Restaurant:** 0.75 mi. towards Eureka. **General Store:** Yes. **Vending:** Yes. **Swimming:** Pool. **Playground:** Yes. **Other:** Mini golf, game room, dataport, picnic pavilion, Garden of Meditation. **Activities:** Fishing, boating, swimming. **Nearby Attractions:** White River, Beaver Lake, passion play, hoedowns, downtown (on National Registry of Historic Places), Onyx Cave Park. **Additional Information:** Eureka Springs Chamber of Commerce, (800) 638-7352 or (501) 253-8737.

Restrictions

Pets: On leash, cleaned up after. **Fires:** In grills. **Alcoholic Beverages:** At sites. **Vehicle Maximum Length:** None. **Other:** Consult handout when registering.

To Get There

From the junction of Hwy. 62 and Hwy. 187, turn south onto Hwy. 187 and go 1.1 mi. Turn left at the sign into the entrance.

FAYETTEVILLE

Fayetteville RV Park

2310 South School Ave., Fayetteville 72701. T: (501) 443-5864.

RV: ★★★ Tent: n/a

Beauty: ★★★	Site Privacy: ★★★
Spaciousness: ★★★	Quiet: ★★★
Security: ★★★★	Cleanliness: ★★★
Insect Control: ★★★★	Facilities: ★★

This park has gravel sites that average 45 × 27 feet Sites 1–7 are back-ins on the south side of the park, and 8–10 are open-ended back-ins on the north end. These latter sites may be able to accommodate slightly longer rigs. Sites 11–14 are 45-foot pull-throughs in the middle of the park. The best sites in the park, and the only ones with shade, are 3, 4, and 14. Much less desirable is site 1, which is crammed up against the house. This is a small park that is fine as a short stay for RVers. Tenters will have to move on, however.

Basics

Operated By: Private Operator. **Open:** All year. **Site Assignment:** First come, first served; verbal reservations OK. **Registration:** Park & pay when someone is around. (Late arrivals select an available site & pay in the morning.) **Fee:** RV $18 (checks, V, MC). **Parking:** At site, plus guest parking.

Facilities

Number of RV Sites: 13. **Number of Tent-Only Sites:** 0. **Hookups:** Water, sewer, electric (30, 50 amps), cable. **Dump Station:** No. **Laundry:** Yes. **Pay Phone:** No. **Rest Rooms and Showers:** Yes. **Fuel:** No. **Propane:** No. **Internal Roads:** Gravel. **RV Service:** No. **Market:** 5 mi. west. **Restaurant:** 3 mi. west. **General Store:** No. **Vending:** No. **Swimming:** No. **Playground:** No. **Activities:** Visiting museums. **Nearby Attractions:** Arkansas Air Museum, Fine Arts Center, University Museum. **Additional Information:** Fayetteville Chamber of Commerce, (800) 766-4626 or (501) 521-1710.

Restrictions

Pets: On leash, cleaned up after. **Fires:** In grills. **Alcoholic Beverages:** At sites. **Vehicle Maximum Length:** 45 ft.

To Get There

From I-540 (Exit 61), exit onto Hwy. 71 and go 1.3 mi. east. Get into the left-hand lane and turn left onto Hwy. 71B (School Ave.). Go 0.8 mi., then turn right at the sign into the entrance.

HARDY

Hardy Camper Park

P.O. Box 150 South Springs St., Hardy 72542. T: (870) 856-2356.

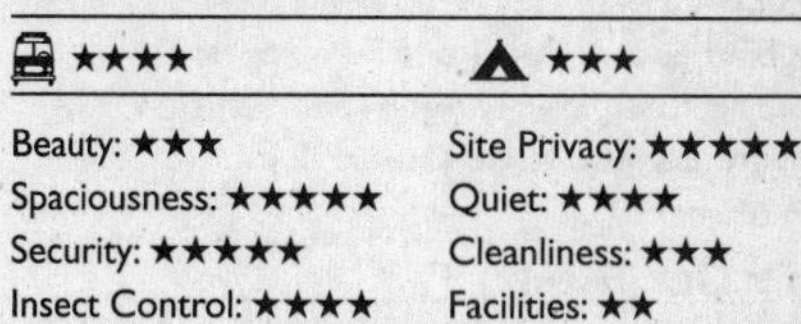

RV: ★★★★ Tent: ★★★

Beauty: ★★★	Site Privacy: ★★★★★
Spaciousness: ★★★★★	Quiet: ★★★★
Security: ★★★★★	Cleanliness: ★★★
Insect Control: ★★★★	Facilities: ★★

While the north and east sides of this campground face an industrial complex, the south has gorgeous rock cliffs over the river, and the west faces lush vegetation. Just 2 blocks from Main Street, this campground is convenient for visiting Old Hardy Town on foot, and has a comfortable, city park–like feel. RV sites are mostly open-ended, and can take a vehicle of any size. River sites (42-foot back-ins) have truly wonderful views, and are worth the slightly higher price. While you can't go wrong with any of these sites, 20–23 are definitely the best of the bunch: they are well-shaded and furthest from the entrance. Sites 10 and 11 are also well-shaded, and close to the bath house, while shaded sites 1–5 are closest to the entrance/exit. For a cheaper site (not on the river) or a pull-through, 58–63 are better than average. They are well-shaded, full-length (120-

feet) pull-throughs. (The other pull-throughs have two sites in an area the same size.) The tenting area is a nice, unmarked grassy area behind the office. There is some shade, but no protection in the event of rain. The bathhouse is a disappointment. The inside is old cement with untreated cement floors. In stark contract with the attractiveness of the rest of the park, this is an obviously old facility in desperate need of renovation. (It might spur the city to action if enough campers contact the town of Hardy to let them know of this situation.) One further surprise arrives with every train—loud whistles and rumblings. While infrequent, this may be enough to put off some campers, which is a shame given the camp's enjoyable environment.

Basics

Operated By: City of Hardy. **Open:** All year. **Site Assignment:** Flexible, depending on availability. Reservations require deposit if made more than 3 weeks in advance; cancellation requires 24-hours notice. **Registration:** In office. (Late arrivals either use drop box or pay in the morning.) **Fee:** Riverside, 17.50, other, $15.30, tent, $13.10. **Parking:** At site.

Facilities

Number of RV Sites: 76. **Number of Tent-Only Sites:** Undesignated sites. **Hookups:** Water, electric (15, 30, 50 amps). **Each Site:** Picnic table. **Dump Station:** Yes. **Laundry:** Yes. **Pay Phone:** Yes. **Rest Rooms and Showers:** Yes. **Fuel:** No. **Propane:** No. **Internal Roads:** Gravel/dirt. **RV Service:** No. **Market:** 2 blocks (on Main). **Restaurant:** 2 blocks (on Main). **General Store:** No. **Vending:** Yes. **Swimming:** River. **Playground:** No. **Activities:** Swimming, canoeing, fishing. **Nearby Attractions:** Veterans Military Museum, Old Hardy Town, antique stores. **Additional Information:** Spring River Area Chamber of Commerce, (870) 856-3210.

Restrictions

Pets: On leash, cleaned up after. **Fires:** In grills; subject to bans. **Alcoholic Beverages:** At sites, subject to dry county regulations. **Vehicle Maximum Length:** None. **Other:** Key for rest rooms in office.

To Get There

From the junction of Hwy. 62/412 and Hwy. 63, go 0.25 mi. on Hwy. 62/412 (Main St.) to Spring St. Turn south onto Spring St. (at a building with a large mural). Go 0.2 mi. (just south of the train depot) and turn right at the sign into the campground.

HARRISON

Parkers RV Park

3629 Hwy. 65 North, Harrison 72601. T: (888) 590-2267 or (870) 743-2267; F: (870) 743-0011; www.parkersrvinc.com; parkersrv@critter.net.

RV ★★★★ Tent ★★★

Beauty: ★★★★	Site Privacy: ★★★★
Spaciousness: ★★★★★	Quiet: ★★★
Security: ★★★★	Cleanliness: ★★★★★
Insect Control: ★★★★	Facilities: ★★★

This campground has very cute landscaping (including shrubs and a bridge), and very tidy gravel and grass sites. sites 1–3 are 75 × 44-foot pull-throughs on the north side of the park, near the highway. These are some of the largest sites. (Site 4, for example, is only 52 feet long.) The only sites that are larger are 10 (a 90-foot pull-through) and 24, which can be a 105-foot pull-through if site 23 is unoccupied. A strip in the middle of the park contains sites 12–17, which are 66 × 44-foot back-ins. On the north side of the "island" in the middle, sites 18–22 are slightly smaller (60-feet) back-ins. For more shade, try sites 25–39, which back to woods on the south side of the campground. There is a covered pavilion between sites 29 and 30, which increases traffic near these two sites. Tenting is restricted to small parties of responsible adults. Tenting groups are discouraged. The rest room facility is one of the nicest you'll find. It is modern, very clean, and extremely comfortable. This park is a very nice stop for RVers, but tenters with children or groups of more than two or three should look elsewhere.

Basics

Operated By: Gregg Parker. **Open:** All year. **Site Assignment:** Assigned upon registration. Credit card required for reservation; 24 hours cancellation policy. **Registration:** In office. (Late arrivals park, "someone will be out to see you".) **Fee:** RV $16.95, tent $. (checks, V, MC, AE, D). **Parking:** At site.

Facilities

Number of RV Sites: 42. **Number of Tent-Only Sites:** 0. **Hookups:** Water, sewer, electric (50 amps), cable. **Each Site:** Picnic table. **Dump Station:** Yes. **Laundry:** Yes. **Pay Phone:** Yes. **Rest Rooms and Showers:** Yes. **Fuel:** No. **Propane:** Yes. **Internal Roads:** Gravel. **RV Service:** No. **Market:** 1 mi. south. **Restaurant:** 1 mi. south. **General Store:** Yes. **Vending:** Yes. **Swimming:** No. **Playground:** No. **Other:** RV supplies, rec room, pool table, fooseball, dataport. **Activities:** Fishing, boating, swimming. **Nearby Attractions:** Buffalo River National Park, Hot Springs National Park. **Additional Information:** Harrison Chamber of Commerce, (870) 741-2659.

Restrictions

Pets: On leash, cleaned up after. **Fires:** In grills. **Alcoholic Beverages:** At sites. **Vehicle Maximum Length:** None. **Other:** No fireworks.

To Get There

From the junction of Hwy. 62 and Hwy. 165/412, turn east onto Hwy. 62/65/412 and go 1.3 mi. Turn right at the sign into the entrance.

HAZEN

T. Ricks RV Park

3001 North Hwy. 11, Hazen 72064. T: (870) 255-4914.

RV ★★★ Tent ★★

Beauty: ★★★	Site Privacy: ★★★★
Spaciousness: ★★★★	Quiet: ★★
Security: ★★★★	Cleanliness: ★★★★
Insect Control: ★★★★	Facilities: ★★★

This campground is run by the convenience store adjacent to it. Sites are laid out in two strips of 65-foot pull-throughs (1–14 and 20–26) running from east (closest to the highway) to west (towards the forest). There is agricultural land to the south, which enhances the aesthetics of the campground. A strip of unfinished sites lies at the northwest end. The best sites are towards the western edge (9–14 and 20–22), as these sites have shade trees and are located furtehst from the convenience store and the highway. Less desirable sites are closer to the traffic: 1–3 and 26. There are swing chairs located between sites 10 and 11, 21 and 22, and 23 and 24. They say that tenting is possible on the RV sites, but a much better bet is a grassy area under one of the many trees around the perimter—especially towards the north side. This park provides visitors decent overnight stay. It does offer the convenience of a store and gas station, but the drawbacks include no showers, plenty of traffic noise, and not much to do or to look at.

Basics

Operated By: Rick Adams & Rick Kent. **Open:** All year. **Site Assignment:** First come, first served; verbal reservations OK. **Registration:** In convenience store (Open 24 hrs.) **Fee:** RV $18 (30 amps), $20 (50 amps), tent $5. **Parking:** At site.

Facilities

Number of RV Sites: 21. **Number of Tent-Only Sites:** 0. **Hookups:** Water, sewer, electric (30, 50 amps). **Each Site:** Picnic table. **Dump Station:** Yes. **Laundry:** No. **Pay Phone:** Yes (in store). **Rest Rooms and Showers:** Yes; no shower. **Fuel:** Yes. **Propane:** Yes. **Internal Roads:** Gravel. **RV Service:** No. **Market:** 3 mi. south. **Restaurant:** Across street. **General Store:** Yes. **Vending:** No. **Swimming:** No. **Playground:** No. **Activities:** Fishing, boating, swimming, hiking. **Nearby Attractions:** Peckerwood Lake. **Additional Information:** Stuttgart Chamber of Commerce, (870) 673-1602.

Restrictions

Pets: On leash, cleaned up after. **Fires:** In grills. **Alcoholic Beverages:** At sites. **Vehicle Maximum Length:** None.

To Get There

From I-40, take Exit 193. Turn south onto Hwy. 63 and take first the right. Go straight into the entrance and register in the convenience store.

HOPE

Fair Park RV Park

P.O. Box 596, Hope 71802. T: (870) 777-7500.

RV ★★★ Tent ★★★

Beauty: ★★★	Site Privacy: ★★★★
Spaciousness: ★★★★	Quiet: ★★★★
Security: ★★★★★	Cleanliness: ★★★
Insect Control: ★★★	Facilities: ★★★★★

This campground is in a large city park, and there are hundreds of RV sites available, divided up into sections. Section A is open and grassy, to the north of the ballfield and the collesium, with open-ended pull-through sites. There are a few trees, but most sites are not shaded. A2 is between the barns and the collesium, and consists of open, grassy sites. Section B is to the south of A, and is likewise an open grassy field with no real shade. C is similar, but consists of open-ended back-ins around the baseball field. Section D backs to the woods on the perimeter of the park. Sites to the southeast are better shaded, and are some of the better sites in the park for this reason. Sections E and F are on either side of the office, closest to the rest rooms. This is where tenters are encouraged to stay. There is a decent grass covering, and a tree at the far end of the fence to the north of the office complex. The most outstanding area of the park, however, is Section G. This area is shaded, has full hookups, and backs to the woods. sites are open-ended pull-throughs, which means that any rig could fit in pretty much any site. RVers are advised to check out Section G, and tenters can pitch tents in a number of pleasant spots at no cost.

Basics

Operated By: Paul G. Henley. **Open:** All year. **Site Assignment:** First come, first served; no reservations. **Registration:** In office. (Late arrivals use drop box.) **Fee:** RV $10, tent free (checks, no credit cards). **Parking:** At site.

Facilities

Number of RV Sites: 400. **Number of Tent-Only Sites:** Undesignated sites. **Hookups:** Water, sewer, electric (30 amps). **Dump Station:** Yes. **Laundry:** Yes. **Pay Phone:** Yes. **Rest Rooms and Showers:** Yes. **Fuel:** No. **Propane:** No (6 blocks away). **Internal Roads:** Paved. **RV Service:** No. **Market:** 6 blocks west. **Restaurant:** less than 1 mi. west. **General Store:** No. **Vending:** Yes. **Swimming:** Pool. **Playground:** Yes. **Other:** Arena, colliseum, wrestling matches, rodeo. **Activities:** Basketball, swimming, baseball/softball, tennis. **Nearby Attractions:** Watermelon festival. **Additional Information:** Hope Hempstead County Chamber of Commerce, (800) 777-3640.

Restrictions

Pets: On leash, cleaned up after. **Fires:** In grills. **Alcoholic Beverages:** At sites. **Vehicle Maximum Length:** None.

To Get There

From I-30, take Exit 30 and go 1.35 mi. south on Hwy. 4. Turn right onto Hwy. 67 and go 0.25 mi. west. Turn left onto Hwy. 174 and go 0.3 mi. south. Turn right onto Park Dr. and go 0.5 mi. through the park to the T intersection. Turn right and go 0.5 block to the office (green building) on the left.

HOT SPRINGS

Young's Lakeshore RV Resort

1601 Lakeshore Dr., Hot Springs 71913. T: (501) 767-7946; F: (501) 767-0084; www.hsnp.com/yougsrv; rvresort@hsnp.com.

RV ★★★★ Tent n/a

Beauty: ★★★★ Site Privacy: ★★★
Spaciousness: ★★★ Quiet: ★★★
Security: ★★★★★ Cleanliness: ★★★★
Insect Control: ★★★★ Facilities: ★★★

A campground whose motto is "in the city, on the lake", this RV park has nearly lakeside sites towards the back (37 is the closest). Most back-ins around the perimter are open-ended, with no maximum vehicle size. These sites back to a row of trees that provide some shade, but sites elsewhere in the park are open to the sun. Sites 1–6 are 42-feet back-ins in a strip on the north side of the park. Of these, 6 is the nicest, as it is closest to the trees and furthest from the entrance. Sites 7–20 are in two rows along the entrance road. These are 60-foot pull-throughs with grassy strips. Site 24 is next to both the propane and the entrance, making it less desirable. The lower numbered sites (1; 12, 13) are closer to the entrance, while the higher numbers (6; 7, 20) are further away. The laundry is slightly unkempt but clean and well-lit. The rest rooms are small with an open toilet, so guests may only want to use them one at a time (which is slightly inconvenient). Children must be accompanied and kept under supervision at all times, so families may want to reconsider this as a destination. Other campers who do not wish to camp with children will be happiest here.

Basics

Operated By: Jimmy & Ev Young. **Open:** All year. **Site Assignment:** Assigned upon registration; verbal reservations OK. **Registration:** In office. (Late arrivals use mailbox next to the door.) **Fee:** $21 (50 amps), $19 (30 amps). **Parking:** At site.

Facilities

Number of RV Sites: 40. **Number of Tent-Only Sites:** 0. **Hookups:** Water, sewer, electric (30, 50 amps), cable. **Each Site:** Picnic table. **Dump Station:** Yes. **Laundry:** Yes. **Pay Phone:** Yes. **Rest Rooms and Showers:** Yes. **Fuel:** No. **Propane:** Yes. **Internal Roads:** Gravel. **RV Service:** No. **Market:** 1.5 mi. east on Hwy. 7. **Restaurant:** 1.5 mi. west or east. **General Store:** No. **Vending:** Yes. **Swimming:** No. **Swimming:** No. **Playground:** No. **Other:** Dataport, boat ramp, lake beach, rec room, picnic area by lake. **Activities:** Fishing, boating, hot spring baths, canoeing, hiking. **Nearby Attractions:** Hot Springs National Park, Josephine Tussaud Wax Museum, Arkansas Alligator Farm & Petting Zoo. **Additional Information:** Hot Springs CVB: (800) 772-2489, (501) 321-2277.

Restrictions

Pets: On leash, cleaned up after. **Fires:** None. **Alcoholic Beverages:** At sites. **Vehicle Maximum Length:** None. **Other:** Adults preferred (children must be accompanied at all times).

To Get There

From Hwy. 270 (south of town), take Exit 3 and go west onto McLeod St. Go 0.25 mi. straight into the entrance of the park.

JACKSONPORT

Jacksonport State Park

Jacksonport State Park P.O. Box 8, Jacksonport 72075. T: (870) 523-2143; www.arkansas.com; jacksonport@arkansas.com.

 ★★★★ Tent ★★★★★

Beauty: ★★★★★ Site Privacy: ★★★★★
Spaciousness: ★★★★★ Quiet: ★★★★★
Security: ★★★★★ Cleanliness: ★★★★★
Insect Control: ★★★★ Facilities: ★★★

This park is located in a wilderness setting about 5 miles out of town. There is a boat ramp, swimming beach, picnic area, and museum that explains the history of the area. All of the sites in this park are grassy 50-foot back-ins on either side of a looped road. Sites are extremely spacious, and most contain several shade trees. (All sites but 1, 10, and 11 are well-shaded.) Site 1 has a parking pad for an extra vehicle. Even numbered sites 4–10 and 9, 13, and 16 back to the river, while 2, 5, 7, 11, 12, 15, and 19 back to a large, open recreation field on the interior of the looped drive. Site 7 and 9 are closest to the rest rooms. The rest rooms and showers are very clean and modern, and quite comfortable.

Basics

Operated By: Arkansas Dept. of Parks & Tourism. **Open:** All year. **Site Assignment:** First come, first served; first night's reservation must be paid 5 days in advance of arrival date; no refunds. **Registration:** In Visitor Center or self-pay station. (Late arrivals use self-pay station.) **Fee:** $14.28 (checks, V, MC, AE, D) **Parking:** At site.

Facilities

Number of RV Sites: 20. **Number of Tent-Only Sites:** 0. **Hookups:** Water, electric (30 amps). **Each Site:** Picnic table, grill, fire pit, lantern pole. **Dump Station:** Yes. **Laundry:** No. **Pay Phone:** Yes. **Rest Rooms and Showers:** Yes. **Fuel:** No. **Propane:** No. **Internal Roads:** Paved. **RV Service:** No. **Market:** 3 mi. to Newport. **Restaurant:** 3 mi. to Newport. **General Store:** Yes. **Vending:** Yes. **Swimming:** River. **Playground:** Yes. **Other:** Hunting & fishing licenses, picnic area, gift shop, boat ramp, nature trail. **Activities:** Fishing, swimming, boating, interprative programs. **Nearby Attractions:** White River, Old Jacksonport Courthouse Museum. **Additional Information:** Newport Area Chamber of Commerce, (870) 523-3618.

Restrictions

Pets: On leash, cleaned up after. **Fires:** In grills or pits. **Alcoholic Beverages:** None. **Vehicle Maximum Length:** None. **Other:** No metal detectors, no glass near river.

To Get There

From the junction of Hwy. 367 and Hwy. 69, go 2.9 mi. north. Turn left onto Hwy. 69 Spur (South), and go 0.8 mi. Take a tricky left turn at the sign into the campground entrance.

JONESBORO

Craighead Forest Park

P.O. Box 1845, Jonesboro 72403. T: (870) 933-4604.

Beauty: ★★★★ Site Privacy: ★★★★
Spaciousness: ★★★★ Quiet: ★★★★★

Security: ★★★★★ Cleanliness: ★★★
Insect Control: ★★★ Facilities: ★★★

Situated in the easternmost edge of the park, this small campground has forested sites on either side of a single road. All sites back to the forest. Sites on the northwest side slope down towards the lake, while those on the southeast side back to flat land, making these sites a little longer than the 50-foot paved parking spaces. All campsites are extremely well-spaced: there is loads of room between you and your neighbor and plenty of space for extra vehicles. Sites 12–15 are closest to the fishing dock (but there is no swimming access). Sites 14 and 15 are the nicest, as they are adjacent to a grassy field that can be used for recreation and has picnic tables. The rest rooms are a little unkempt, but not any more than those who often camp in public forests might come to expect. This is a small and comfortable campground, well away from even the recreation areas within the park, offering a night of tranquility.

Basics

Operated By: City of Jonesboro. **Open:** All year. **Site Assignment:** First come, first served; no reservations, no refunds. **Registration:** Campsite attendant (across from site 8). **Fee:** $15 (water, electric), tent $7 (checks, but no credits cards.) **Parking:** At site.

Facilities

Number of RV Sites: 26. **Number of Tent-Only Sites:** 0. **Hookups:** Water, electric (30 amps). **Each Site:** Picnic table, grill, trash. **Dump Station:** Yes. **Laundry:** No. **Pay Phone:** Yes. **Rest Rooms and Showers:** Yes. **Fuel:** No. **Propane:** No. **Internal Roads:** Paved. **RV Service:** No. **Market:** 4 mi. to Hwy. 63. **Restaurant:** 4 mi. to Hwy. 63. **General Store:** No. **Vending:** Yes. **Swimming:** Lake. **Playground:** Yes. **Other:** Picnic pavilions, ballfields, basketball court, paddle boat rentals, ATV trails. **Activities:** Boating, swimming, fishing, hiking, outdoor sports. **Nearby Attractions:** Craighead Forest Lake, Arkansas State University Museum. **Additional Information:** Chamber of Commerce, (870) 932-6691.

Restrictions

Pets: On leash, cleaned up after. **Fires:** In grills. **Alcoholic Beverages:** None. **Vehicle Maximum Length:** 50 ft. **Other:** No ATVs in campground, no fireworks.

To Get There

From the junction of Hwy. 63 and Hwy. 1B, turn south onto Hwy. 1B and take the first right onto the service road (Parker Rd.). Follow this road 0.9 mi., then turn left onto Hwy. 141 (Culberhouse St.), and go 1.9 mi. Turn left onto Forest Park Dr. and go 1.25 mi. to the east end of Forest Park Loop, past pavilion 1, to the campground.

LAKE VILLAGE

Pecan Grove RV Park

3768 Hwy. 82 & 65 South, Lake Village 71653. T: (877) RV-4-FUNN or (870) 265-3005; F: (870) 265-2200; deebill@cei.net.

 ★★★★  ★★★★

Beauty: ★★★★ Site Privacy: ★★★★★
Spaciousness: ★★★★★ Quiet: ★★★
Security: ★★★★★ Cleanliness: ★★★
Insect Control: ★★★★ Facilities: ★★★★

An old pecan orchard, this campground has a small-farm feel to it. There is very cute landscaping around the grounds (flowers around trees and light-poles), and remnants of the farm it once was (barn, farmhouse). Towering pecan trees grow at almost every site. There is also, however, an air of oldness that could be swept away: cobwebs in the corners, dirt from many hands opening doors, etc. The laundry is small, and while the rest rooms are clean, the building itself looks old. Further more, the cement walls are speckled with reddish paint. But don't let that scare you. The campground is very nice, and nearly every site is an excellent choice. Numbered sites in the first five rows are reserved for overnighters—the rest are for monthly renters. All sites are 80-foot pull-throughs on grassy patches. Sites at the far end of the highway (10, 27, and 35 especially) are the best, as they receive less traffic noise and not much passing traffic. (18, also an end site, is directly across from the bathhouse.) Those at the highway end are a little noisier (9, 17, 26, 34, 42). The tent area is to the northwest of the bathhouse. There is an excellent grass cover. Several large trees lend shade, but may be too high to provide much protection from rain. While the campground needs a nice spring cleaning and a little less traffic noise to earn a full rating, it is very nice, and a destination that many campers will be sure to return to.

Basics

Operated By: Bill & Dee Bunker. **Open:** All year. **Site Assignment:** Flexible, according to availability; verbal reservations OK. **Registration:** In office. (Late arrivals use drop box.) **Fee:** RV $16.67 (full), tent $12.50 (add $1 for cable or 50 amps.) **Parking:** At site.

Facilities

Number of RV Sites: 116. **Number of Tent-Only Sites:** 4. **Hookups:** Water, sewer, electric (30, 50 amps), cable. **Each Site:** Picnic table. **Dump Station:** No (sewer at all sites). **Laundry:** Yes. **Pay Phone:** Yes. **Rest Rooms and Showers:** Yes. **Fuel:** Next door. **Propane:** 1 mi. **Internal Roads:** Gravel. **RV Service:** On-call. **Market:** 1.5 mi. north. **Restaurant:** 1 mile north. **General Store:** Yes. **Vending:** Yes. **Swimming:** Lake. **Playground:** Yes. **Other:** Cabins, recreation hall, Lake Chicot, boat ramp, pavilion, dataport, dock, fish cleaning area. **Activities:** fishing, swimming, boating, volleyball, horseshoes. **Nearby Attractions:** Lake Chicot, Mississippi River. **Additional Information:** Chamber of Commerce, (870) 265-5997.

Restrictions

Pets: On leash, cleaned up after. **Fires:** In fire ring. **Alcoholic Beverages:** At sites. **Vehicle Maximum Length:** None.

To Get There

From the junction of Hwy. 65 South, 82 East, and 278 East, go 2.8 mi. on Hwy. 65/82. Turn right at the sign into the entrance. The office is the white house on the left.

LITTLE ROCK

Little Rock North KOA

7820 Crystal Hill Rd., North Little Rock 72118. T: (800) KOA-4598 or (501) 758-4598; www.koa.com; nlrkoa@aol.com.

★★★★ ★★★★

Beauty: ★★★★ Site Privacy: ★★★
Spaciousness: ★★★ Quiet: ★★
Security: ★★★★ Cleanliness: ★★★★
Insect Control: ★★★★ Facilities: ★★★★★

Campers in large rigs will be happy with the numerous pull-throughs in this campground, which include all sites except those around the perimter. Rows G19–24 and R8–14 are closest to the road, and include 40-foot back-ins. (G sites 15–24 are all in a forested corner of the campground, with gravel sites.) Sites R1–7 are well-shaded 56-foot pull-throughs, while G11– 14 are even longer (75 feet). Row B has 75-foot pull-throughs, of which 1–3 face a residence. B15–20 is along the northwest side of the grounds, and has 40-foot grassy back-ins. (19 is located directly next to the dog walk area.) Row Y, along the northern perimeter, has the least developed sites, but the many pine trees in this area give it a nice, natural feel. Sites Y1–13 are 75 pull-throughs amidst the trees, while Y14–28 back into the forest. Tent site T1 is off in the woods above RV site G24, and T2–3 are even more remote, in the northeast corner. All sites have a finely crushed gravel bed for a tent and plenty of trees. The rest room is very clean, and campers will be delighted to know that it has airconditioning. The toilet stalls are a little narrow, but everything is clean as a whistle. This is a fine campground to make your home base while exploring the Little Rock area. It has a nice woodsy feel and is close enough to the attractions to allow for plenty of day trips.

Basics

Operated By: The Clay Family. **Open:** All year. **Site Assignment:** Assigned upon registration. Reservations require credit card; cancellation requires 24 hours notice. **Registration:** In office. (Late arrivals use drop box.) **Fee:** RV $23–31, tent $20–23 (checks V, MC, AE, & D). **Parking:** At site.

Facilities

Number of RV Sites: 100. **Number of Tent-Only Sites:** 10. **Hookups:** Water, sewer, electric (20, 30, 50 amps), cable. **Each Site:** Picnic table, grill. **Dump Station:** Yes. **Laundry:** Yes. **Pay Phone:** Yes. **Rest Rooms and Showers:** Yes. **Fuel:** No. **Propane:** Yes. **Internal Roads:** Paved. **RV Service:** No. **Market:** 4 mi. west. **Restaurant:** Across street. **General Store:** Yes. **Vending:** Yes. **Swimming:** Pool. **Playground:** Yes. **Other:** Dataport, sauna, hot tub, exercise equipment, snack bar, pool table, dog walk. **Activities:** Basketball, volleyball, horseshoes, swimming, golf, shopping. **Nearby Attractions:** Burns Park, Wild River Country, Little Rock, Aerospace Education Center, State Capitol, Museum of Dy. **Additional Information:** North Little Rock Advertising & Promotion Commission, (800) 643-4690, (501) 758-1424.

Restrictions

Pets: On leash, cleaned up after; do not leave unattended. **Fires:** In grills only. **Alcoholic Beverages:** At sites. **Vehicle Maximum Length:** None.

To Get There

(If coming north from Little Rock on I-30, take I-40 West to I-40.) From I-40, take Exit 148. Turn west onto Crystal Hill Rd. and go 1.2 mi. Turn right at the sign into the entrance.

MENA

Shadow Mountain

3708 Hwy. 71 South, Mena 71953. T: (501) 394-6299; F: (501) 394-7378.

RV ★★★★★ Tent ★★★★★

Beauty: ★★★★	Site Privacy: ★★★★
Spaciousness: ★★★★	Quiet: ★★★★
Security: ★★★★★	Cleanliness: ★★★★★
Insect Control: ★★★★	Facilities: ★★★★

Touted by the proprietor as the "only full-service campground within 50 miles", this campground has full hookups, a pool, and modern facilities in a forested, rural setting. Sites in this campground are not overly developed, adding to the natural charm of the grounds. All RV sites are 65-foot pull-throughs. Sites at the ends of the rows on the east side (2, 7, 13, 14, 28) are generally the best, as they face the forest and are slightly away from the other sites in the rows. Sites 41–51 are right off the highway, making them less desirable than other sites. Unnumbered tent sites are situated down the slope of the RV park and to the south, towards the highway. Sites are grassy, with ample tree coverage, but due to some amount of passing traffic noise is inevitable. The rest rooms are very clean and fairly modern. Showers are very spacious. The laundry room is spacious and contains enough machines for a campground of this size. This is a nice little getaway with an off-the-beaten-path feel but the convenience of a highway location.

Basics

Operated By: Bonnie & Aaron Trawiek. **Open:** All year. **Site Assignment:** Assigned upon registration; reservations require credit card. **Registration:** In office. (Late arrivals use drop box.) **Fee:** RV $18 (full), $17 (water, electric), $13 (electric), tent $10. **Parking:** At site.

Facilities

Number of RV Sites: 51. **Number of Tent-Only Sites:** Undesignated sites. **Hookups:** Water, sewer, electric (30 amps). **Each Site:** Picnic table. **Dump Station:** Yes. **Laundry:** Yes. **Pay Phone:** Yes. **Rest Rooms and Showers:** Yes. **Fuel:** No. **Propane:** No. **Internal Roads:** Paved. **RV Service:** No. **Market:** 5 mi. to Mena. **Restaurant:** 5 mi. to Mena. **General Store:** Yes. **Vending:** Yes. **Swimming:** Pool. **Playground:** Yes. **Other:** Lake, antique soda fountain, firewood. **Activities:** Basketball, swimming. **Nearby Attractions:** Talimena scenic Drive, Ouachita National Forest, Janssen Park, Queen Wilhelmina State Park. **Additional Information:** Mean/Polk County Chamber of Commerce, (501) 394-2912.

Restrictions

Pets: On leash, cleaned up after. **Fires:** In rings. **Alcoholic Beverages:** At sites; subject to dry county regulations. **Vehicle Maximum Length:** None.

To Get There

From the junction of Hwy. 8 and Hwy. 59/71, in Mena, go 4.5 mi. south on Hwy. 59/71. Turn right at the sign into the entrance. The office is on the left; park to the right.

MORRILTON

Petit Jean State Park

1285 Petit Jean Mountain Rd., Morrilton 72110. T: (501) 727-5441; www.arkansasstateparks.com; petitjean@arkansas.com.

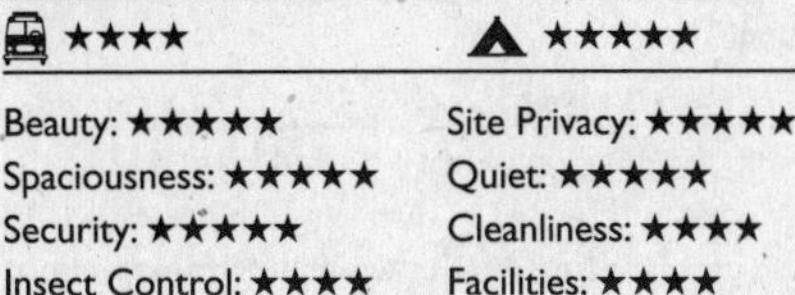

RV ★★★★ Tent ★★★★★

Beauty: ★★★★★	Site Privacy: ★★★★★
Spaciousness: ★★★★★	Quiet: ★★★★★
Security: ★★★★★	Cleanliness: ★★★★
Insect Control: ★★★★	Facilities: ★★★★

Sites in this state park, Arkansas' first, are divided into 4 areas, A–D. Area A is east of the Visitors Center, and contains sites 1–35, all 80-foot pull-throughs (except 32, which is 105 feet). Many of these sites are along (or near) the lake, and therefore are preferred or premium sites, costing more than the others. Premium sites closest to the lake are 19, 26, and 27. Preferred sites near the lake are 8, 9, 29, and 30. The end sites 1 and 35 are closest to the entrance, and may not be as desirable. Area B contains the reservable sites. Of these, 44–48 are the nicest, as they back to thick woods and are quieter than other sites. Sites 36–42 back to a road, and suffer from more noise as a result. Area C contains 45–50-foot back-ins. Sites 74–76, 89, and 91 back to thick woods, making them quite nice. Site 71 is across from the bathhouse, making access quite convenient. Site 77 is right by the entrance. Area D is for overflow camping. The rest rooms and showers in all of these areas are clean and spacious. This is a wonderful park with loads to do. It makes a great destination for families and anyone in a tent. RVers will enjoy their stay, but do not have the benefit of full hookups.

Basics

Operated By: Arkansas State Parks. **Open:** All year. **Site Assignment:** Assigned upon registration during the day; first come, first served at night. Reservations require deposit of one's night's stay, made 5 days in advance; cancellation requires 5-days notice; first night's deposit non-refundable. **Registration:** In visitor's center. (Late arrivals select an available site & pay in the morning.) **Fee:** $17.50 (premium site), $16 (preferred site), $14.50 (water, electric). **Parking:** At site.

Facilities

Number of RV Sites: 127. **Number of Tent-Only Sites:** 0. **Hookups:** Water, electric (20, 30 amps). **Each Site:** Picnic table, grill, lantern pole. **Dump Station:** Yes. **Laundry:** No. **Pay Phone:** Yes. **Rest Rooms and Showers:** Yes. **Fuel:** No. **Propane:** No. **Internal Roads:** Paved. **RV Service:** No. **Market:** 20 mi. to Morrilton. **Restaurant:** On site; 20 mi. to Morrilton. **General Store:** Yes. **Vending:** Yes. **Swimming:** Pool. **Playground:** Yes. **Other:** Tennis courts, picnic pavilion, snack bar, boat rentals, amphitheater, Mather Lodge Restaurant, horse facilities. **Activities:** Fishing, boating, swimming, horseback riding, hiking, tennis. **Nearby Attractions:** Waterfall, Museum of Automobiles. **Additional Information:** Morrilton Chamber of Commerce, (501) 354-2393.

Restrictions

Pets: On leash, cleaned up after. **Fires:** In grills. **Alcoholic Beverages:** At sites. **Vehicle Maximum Length:** None.

To Get There

From the junction of Hwy. 9 and Hwy. 154, turn west onto Hwy. 154 and go 11.3 mi. into the park.

MURFREESBORO

Miner's Camping and Rock Shop

2235 Hwy. 301 South, Murfreesboro 71958. T: (870) 285-2722; jgoodin776@aol.com.

RV ★★★★ Tent ★★★★

Beauty: ★★★★	Site Privacy: ★★★
Spaciousness: ★★★	Quiet: ★★★
Security: ★★★★	Cleanliness: ★★★
Insect Control: ★★★	Facilities: ★★★

This campground is divided into two sections on either side of the highway, the north and south sections. In the north section, sites are arranged on the outside of an internal loop. All sites are back-ins: 5–11 back to the forest, 12–17 to a dirt road. Sites are open-ended, meaning that a rig of any size can fit in most sites. Site 17 is somewhat less desirable due to its proximity to the highway. The main rest rooms are in this section, and are small, modern, and cozy. The shower is extremely spacious, but shares one drawback with the rest room—a cement floor. Sites on the south side of the park all back to the woods. Sites H–K are the best sites, as they are furthest from the highway. Site A is closest to the highway, and therefore less desirable. There are two non-flush toilets here, which are as clean as can be expected. (Take the time to cross the highway and use the full rest room!) Tenting is allowed in an open field on the south side, to the east of the RV sites. There is a good grass cover, but no trees for shade or protection from the elements. Rockhounds—and others—will enjoy this campground just south of Murfreesboro and a couple hundred feet from the Crater of Diamonds State Park. The services are decent, and the campground is cute and woodsy.

Basics

Operated By: J. Goodin. **Open:** All year. **Site Assignment:** Assigned upon registration. Verbal reservations OK; call to cancel.) **Registration:** In gift shop. (Late arrivals select an available site & settle in the morning.) **Fee:** RV $15 (full), $12 (water, electric), tent $10. **Parking:** At site.

Facilities

Number of RV Sites: 33. **Number of Tent-Only Sites:** 10. **Hookups:** Water, sewer, electric (30, 50 amps). **Each Site:** Picnic table, trash can.

Dump Station: Yes. **Laundry:** No. **Pay Phone:** Yes. **Rest Rooms and Showers:** Yes. **Fuel:** No. **Propane:** No. **Internal Roads:** Dirt. **RV Service:** No. **Market:** 2 mi. north. **Restaurant:** 2 mi. north. **General Store:** No. **Vending:** Yes. **Swimming:** No. **Playground:** Yes. **Other:** Gift shop, 3 cabins, firewood, fishing pond, pavilion. **Activities:** Hiking, rock collecting. **Nearby Attractions:** Crater of Diamonds State Park, Ka-Do-Ha Indian Village, Hot Springs, Quartz Mines, Washington State Park. **Additional Information:** Murfreesboro Chamber of Commerce, (870) 425-5111.

Restrictions

Pets: On leash, cleaned up after. **Fires:** In pits. **Alcoholic Beverages:** Subject to dry county regulations. **Vehicle Maximum Length:** None. **Other:** No washing of vehicles.

To Get There

From the junction of Hwy. 26/27 and Hwy. 301, go 2.3 mi. east on Hwy. 301. Turn left at the sign into the entrance.

PARAGOULD

Crowley's Ridge State Park

2092 Hwy. 168 North, Paragould 72450. T: (800) 264-2405 or (870) 573-6751; F: (870) 573-6758; www.arkansasstateparks.com; crowleys@arkansas.com.

RV ★★★★ Tent ★★★★★

Beauty: ★★★★ Site Privacy: ★★★★
Spaciousness: ★★★★★ Quiet: ★★★★★
Security: ★★★★ Cleanliness: ★★★
Insect Control: ★★★ Facilities: ★★★

Campsites in the park are situated along a single internal road. Sites on the north side have a sudden slope at the rear, while those on the south side have a more gradual slope. (All parking strips are level.) Tent sites (19–26) are mostly 30 feet off the main road, although sites 22–24 are set back further. These are extremely spacious (45-feet-wide) dirt campsites set, as all campsites in the park are, back in the forest. Of the RV sites (so designated solely by their electric hookups), 1 is a gigantic (120-feet) pull-through, while the others are mostly 45–50-foot back-ins. (Site 7 is an exception, being only 30 feet long and set very close to the road.) Site 9 offers the most privacy, being set well back from the road; while 8 has much less privacy due to its proximity to a hiking trail head. The rest rooms and showers are astonishingly clean, modern, and spacious (but do lack air conditioning). This is an intimate state park with extraordinarily clean facilities that both tenters and RVers will definitely enjoy.

Basics

Operated By: Arkansas Dept. of Parks & Tourism. **Open:** All year. **Site Assignment:** First come, first served. Reservations require deposit of one's night's stay, made 5 days in advance; cancellation requires 5-days notice; first night's deposit non-refundable. **Registration:** In Visitors Center. (Late arrivals select available site & register next morning after 8.) **Fee:** $14 (water, electric), tent $8 (checks, V, MC, AE, & D). **Parking:** At site.

Facilities

Number of RV Sites: 18. **Number of Tent-Only Sites:** 8. **Hookups:** Water, electric (30 amps). **Each Site:** Picnic table, grill, lantern pole. **Dump Station:** Yes. **Laundry:** No. **Pay Phone:** Yes. **Rest Rooms and Showers:** Yes. **Fuel:** No. **Propane:** No. **Internal Roads:** Paved. **RV Service:** No. **Market:** 9 mi. to Paragould. **Restaurant:** 9 mi. to Paragould. **General Store:** No. **Vending:** Yes. **Swimming:** Lake. **Playground:** Yes. **Other:** Gift shop. **Activities:** Boating, canoeing, hiking, swimming, paddleboating. **Nearby Attractions:** Lake Ponder, Walcott Lake. **Additional Information:** Paragould-Greene County Chamber of Commerce, (870) 236-7684.

Restrictions

Pets: On leash, cleaned up after. **Fires:** In pits. **Alcoholic Beverages:** At sites (preferably in non-descript containers). **Vehicle Maximum Length:** None.

To Get There

From the junction of Hwy. 49 and Hwy. 412, go 9 mi. west on Hwy. 412. Turn left onto Hwy. 168 and go 2 mi. Turn left at the sign into campground.

PINE BLUFF

Saracen Trace RV Park

P.O. Box 7676, Pine Bluff 71611. T: (870) 536-0920; parks@seark.net.

RV ★★★★ Tent n/a

Beauty: ★★★★ Site Privacy: ★★★★
Spaciousness: ★★★★ Quiet: ★★★★★
Security: ★★★★ Cleanliness: ★★★★
Insect Control: ★★ Facilities: ★★★

Located within a large city park, this campground has open, grassy sites situated along a looped internal road. All sites are 60-foot back-ins, and most (if not all) are very well shaded. Sites on the eastern side of the campground (7–17) back to the lake, and seem to be sought after for this reason. Sites 21–24 back to a golf course adjacent to the campground. Site 43 is desirable for the large amount of open space (large enough for another RV site) adjacent to it. Sites 29 and 30, on the other hand, are less desirable, as they are very close to the entrance and receive more passing traffic than other sites. There is a disabled-access fishing pier between sites 12 and 13, which may also account for increased traffic past these two sites. This campground is on the whole a very pleasant, extremely quiet campground. Sites are grassy and shaded, and campers seeking a relaxing atmosphere should find them extremely comfortable.

Basics

Operated By: Pine Bluff Parks Commission. **Open:** All year. **Site Assignment:** First come, first served; no reservations. **Registration:** Registration kiosk. **Fee:** $10. **Parking:** At site.

Facilities

Number of RV Sites: 54. **Number of Tent-Only Sites:** 0. **Hookups:** Water, sewer, electric (20, 30 amps). **Each Site:** Picnic table, grill, trees. **Dump Station:** Yes. **Laundry:** Yes. **Pay Phone:** Yes. **Rest Rooms and Showers:** No. **Fuel:** No. **Propane:** No. **Internal Roads:** Paved. **RV Service:** No. **Market:** 6 mi. to town. **Restaurant:** 6 mi. to town. **General Store:** No. **Vending:** Yes. **Swimming:** Lake. **Playground:** Yes. **Activities:** Swimming, fishing, baseball, soccer, horseshoes, hiking, golf. **Nearby Attractions:** Lake Langhofer, The Band Museum, Southeast Arkansas Arts & Science Center. **Additional Information:** Greater Pine Bluff Area Chamber of Commerce, (870) 535-0110.

Restrictions

Pets: On leash, cleaned up after. **Fires:** In grills. **Alcoholic Beverages:** At sites. **Vehicle Maximum Length:** None.

To Get There

From the junction of Hwy. 79B and Hwy. 65B, go 1.2 mi. east on Hwy. 65B. Turn left at the light onto Convention Center Drive and follow this road into the park. The campground is at the extreme north end of the park.

POCAHONTAS

Old Davidsonville State Park

7953 Hwy. 166 South, Pocahontas 72455. T: (870) 892-4708 or (870) 892-7650; www.arkansasstateparks.com; olddavidson@arkansas.com.

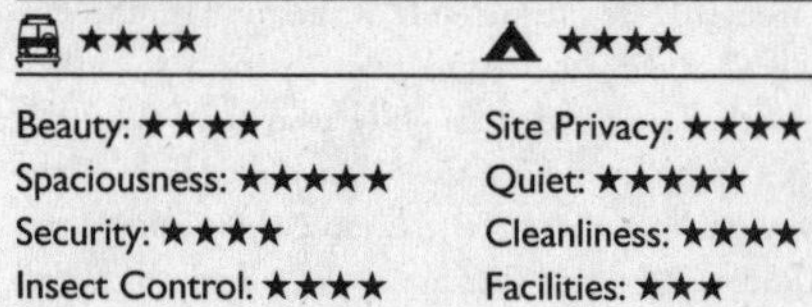

RV ★★★★ Tent ★★★★

Beauty: ★★★★ Site Privacy: ★★★★
Spaciousness: ★★★★★ Quiet: ★★★★★
Security: ★★★★ Cleanliness: ★★★★
Insect Control: ★★★★ Facilities: ★★★

RV sites in this park are located on either side of a single internal looped road. Tent sites are walk-ins from a common parking area in the southeast corner. All campsites are spacious, forested spaces with a (mostly) dirt floor. Of the RV sites, 4, 8, 16, and 20 are 120-foot pull-throughs, while the rest of the sites run from 45 feet (1) or 75 feet (3) in length. Sites 10 and 11 are a double, suitable for a group camping. Sites 18, 19, and 24 are slightly less desirable sites: 18 is set right on the road, with little privacy; 19 is extremely close to several tent sites; and 24 is located right on the path that leads to the bath house, ensuring loads of passing foot traffic. All other sites are very nice, and even these three are only slightly worse-off. The tenting area consists of a very spacious walk-in area behind site 19. One (unnumbered) site in the northeast corner of this area is situated well away from the others, and therefore offers more privacy. The rest rooms and showers are extremely clean, modern, and spacious. The campground is very comfortable for both tenters and RVers, and offers a glimpse into frontier life in Arkansas from the early 1800s.

Basics

Operated By: Arkansas Dept. of Parks & Tourism. **Open:** All year (limited services Dec.–Feb.). **Site Assignment:** First come, first served; reservations require deposit of one's night's stay, made 5 days in advance; cancellation requires 5-days notice; first night's deposit non-refundable. **Registration:** In Visitor Center. (Late arrivals select available site & register next morning after 8.) **Fee:** $14.28 (water, electric), tent $8.16 (checks, V, MC, AE, & D). **Parking:** At site.

Facilities

Number of RV Sites: 24. **Number of Tent-Only Sites:** 15. **Hookups:** Water, electric (20 amps). **Each Site:** Picnic table, grill, fire pit, trees. **Dump Station:** Yes. **Laundry:** No. **Pay Phone:** Yes. **Rest Rooms and Showers:** Yes. **Fuel:** No. **Propane:** No. **Internal Roads:** Paved. **RV Service:** No. **Market:** 10 mi. to Pocahontas. **Restaurant:** 9 mi. to Pocahontas. **General Store:** No. **Vending:** Yes. **Swimming:** No. **Playground:** Yes. **Other:** Pavilion, boat ramp, historical exhibits, canoe rentals, gift shop, campfire ring. **Activities:** Boating, hiking, fishing, volleyball. **Nearby Attractions:** Black River, Old Davidsonville. **Additional Information:** Randolph County Chamber of Commerce, (870) 892-3956.

Restrictions

Pets: On leash, cleaned up after. **Fires:** In grills. **Alcoholic Beverages:** At sites (preferably in nondescript containers). **Vehicle Maximum Length:** None. **Other:** No fireworks, no firearms, no metal detectors, no excavating.

To Get There

From the junction of Hwy. 62 and Hwy. 166, turn south onto Hwy. 166 and go 8.5 mi. (Be sure to follow Hwy. 166 as it turns to the left after 8 mi.) Follow the road straight into the park.

ROGERS

Rogers/Pea Ridge KOA

P.O. Box 456, Rogers 72757. T: (800) 562-6572 or (501) 451-8566; www.koa.com.

RV: ★★★★ Tent: ★★★★

Beauty: ★★★★	Site Privacy: ★★★
Spaciousness: ★★★	Quiet: ★★★★★
Security: ★★★★	Cleanliness: ★★★★★
Insect Control: ★★★★	Facilities: ★★★★

Sites in this campground are mostly undeveloped, being grassy or, at most, gravel. However, this lends a natural feel to the entire campground that many campers will enjoy. Sites 1–15 are 75-foot pull-throughs, of which 1–8 are mostly without shade. (Sites 10–15 are forested.) Sites 22–26 are smaller (42–54-feet) back-ins, and a little crunched for space. 23 is a 60-foot pull-through at the tip of the island inside the looped road. Sites 44 and 45 are 75-foot back-ins that back to the forest, and are the most secluded sites in the park. The tent spaces, 32–40, are in fact one large open space fit for tents. This area has lots of trees but a rather thin grass cover. Tent sites 48 and 50, by the entrance, have crushed gravel pads and loads of shade. The laundry facility is small but very clean. The rest rooms are likewise clean and very bright. This campground is a very comfortable stay for both RVers and tenters.

Basics

Operated By: Leslie Thomas & Jack Maertens. **Open:** All year. **Site Assignment:** Assigned upon registration; V or MC required for reservation, 24-hours cancellation policy. **Registration:** In office. (Late arrivals use drop box.) **Fee:** RV $22 (full), $20 (water, electric), tent $13.50 (checks, V, MC). **Parking:** At site.

Facilities

Number of RV Sites: 41. **Number of Tent-Only Sites:** Undesignated sites. **Hookups:** Water, sewer, electric (20, 30, 50 amps). **Each Site:** Picnic table, grill. **Dump Station:** Yes. **Laundry:** Yes. **Pay Phone:** Yes. **Rest Rooms and Showers:** Yes. **Fuel:** No. **Propane:** No. **Internal Roads:** Gravel. **RV Service:** No. **Market:** 2 mi. on Hwy. 62. **Restaurant:** 6 mi. west. **General Store:** Yes. **Vending:** No. **Swimming:** Pool. **Playground:** Yes. **Other:** Game room, within 15 minutes of fishing areas, cabins, pet walk. **Activities:** Fishing, boating, swimming. **Nearby Attractions:** Pea Ridge Military Park, War Eagle Cavern. **Additional Information:** Rogers Chamber of Commerce, (501) 636-1240.

Restrictions

Pets: On leash, cleaned up after. **Fires:** In grills. **Alcoholic Beverages:** At sites. **Vehicle Maximum Length:** None. **Other:** Extended-stay campers have a 3 dog limit.

To Get There

From I-340 (Exit 82), exit onto Hwy. 62 and go 10.6 mi. Turn left at the sign into the entrance.

RUSSELLVILLE

Outdoor Living Center RV Park

10 Outdoor Ct., Russellville 72802. T: (501) 968-7705; olcrv@mail.cswnet.com.

RV: ★★★ Tent: n/a

Beauty: ★★	Site Privacy: ★★★
Spaciousness: ★★★	Quiet: ★★★
Security: ★★★★	Cleanliness: ★★★★
Insect Control: ★★★★	Facilities: ★★★

Although this campground is bordered to the northwest by woods, unsightly storage units to the south detract significantly from the beauty of this park. Sites are laid out in two central rows of 65-foot pull-throughs, with 60-foot back-ins around the perimiter. The nicest of the back-ins (17–25) are along the northern edge, just in front of the woods. Sites 1–16 also back to trees, but the trees don't shade the sites. The pull-throughs are grassy and level, but open to the sun. Site 25 is next to the rec room, and may receive more than the normal amount of passing foot traffic. Likewise, 46, closest to the rest rooms, may be a high-traffic site. The rest rooms are clean and comfortable, and kept locked for added security. This park is a decent overnight stay, but not a destination for most travelers. One word of note: during our visit, the managers were involved in multi-level marketing, and tended to push their product on visitors—to the extent of including a product brochure with each site map!

Basics

Operated By: Richard Shilling. **Open:** All year. **Site Assignment:** Flexible, depending on availability; reservations require credit card if arriving after 4 p.m.; cancellation requires 24-hours' notice. **Registration:** In office. (Late arrivals pay in morning.) **Fee:** RV $ 16.32 (50 amps), $ 15.30 (30 amps) (check, V, MC, & D). **Parking:** At site.

Facilities

Number of RV Sites: 50. **Number of Tent-Only Sites:** 0. **Hookups:** Water, sewer, electric (30, 50 amps), cable. **Dump Station:** Yes. **Laundry:** Yes. **Pay Phone:** Yes. **Rest Rooms and Showers:** Yes. **Fuel:** No. **Propane:** No. **Internal Roads:** Gravel/paved. **RV Service:** No. **Market:** 2 mi. south. **Restaurant:** 0.25 mi. south. **General Store:** Yes. **Vending:** Yes. **Swimming:** No. **Playground:** No. **Other:** Dataport, rec hall, RV supplies. **Activities:** Hot springs bathing, tours, hiking. **Nearby Attractions:** Lake Dardanelle State Park, Hot Springs National Park. **Additional Information:** Chamber of Commerce, (501) 968-2530.

Restrictions

Pets: On leash, cleaned up after; long-term residents may only have a "few" dogs. **Fires:** In grills; subject to bans. **Alcoholic Beverages:** At sites; subject to dry county regulations. **Vehicle Maximum Length:** 65 ft.

To Get There

From I-40 Exit 81, turn west onto Hwy. 7 and go 0.3 mi. north to campground entrance.

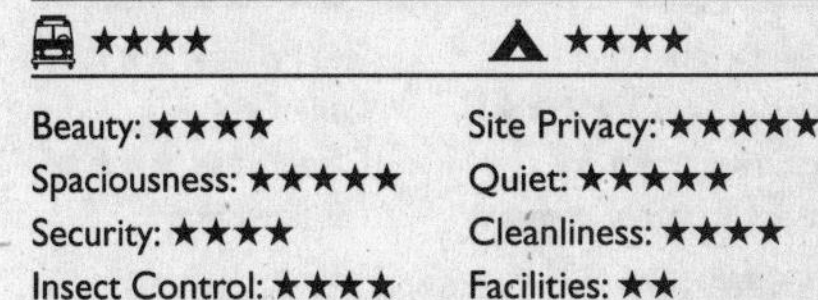

SILOAM SPRINGS

Wilderness Hills RV Park and Campground

13776 Taylor Orchard Rd., Gentry 72734. T: (501) 524-4955; F: (501) 524-4414; whcg@coxinternet. com.

RV: ★★★★ Tent: ★★★★

Beauty: ★★★★	Site Privacy: ★★★★★
Spaciousness: ★★★★★	Quiet: ★★★★★
Security: ★★★★	Cleanliness: ★★★★
Insect Control: ★★★★	Facilities: ★★

Located in a wilderness setting and surrounded by forest, this campground is shady and quiet. RV sites are huge pull-throughs (75–95-feet) laid out in two strips, and all are well-shaded. Sites 1–10 are furthest from the office, but closest to the entrance. (Sites 1–5 are the furthest from everything—but not by much.) Sites 3 and 4,as well as 5 and 6, are angled into each other, which makes them slightly less private. The longest sites in the campground are 11–15, which are an impressive 95 feet in length. Tenting space is located in the southeast corner. Like the RV sites, this area is well-shaded, and it is closest to the undeveloped forest. While there is but thin grass cover, the dirt is soft and will easily take tent spikes. Tenters will especially enjoy the "lost" atmosphere of this park, although anyone in search of a quiet night in the woods will appreciate it.

Basics

Operated By: Robert Hammersla. **Open:** All year. **Site Assignment:** Assigned upon registration; verbal reservations OK. **Registration:** In office. (Late arrivals use drop box.) **Fee:** RV $15 (full), $12 (water, electric), tent $10 (checks, no credit cards.) **Parking:** At site.

Facilities

Number of RV Sites: 25. **Number of Tent-Only Sites:** Undesignated sites. **Hookups:** Water, sewer, electric (30, 50 amps). **Each Site:** Picnic table, grill. **Dump Station:** No (sewer at all sites). **Laundry:** No. **Pay Phone:** Yes. **Rest Rooms and Showers:** Yes. **Fuel:** No. **Propane:** No. **Internal Roads:** Gravel. **RV Service:** No. **Market:** 3 mi. southwest. **Restaurant:** 3 mi. southwest. **General Store:** No. **Vending:** Yes. **Swimming:** No. **Playground:** No. **Other:** Dataport, lake, stream, golf course, cabins. **Activities:** Fishing, golf, antique, flea markets. **Nearby Attractions:** Ozark National Forest, Beaver Lake. **Additional Information:** Chamber of Commerce, (501) 524-6466.

Restrictions

Pets: On leash, cleaned up after, quiet. **Fires:** In grills. **Alcoholic Beverages:** At sites. **Vehicle Maximum Length:** None.

To Get There

From the junction of Hwy. 595 and Hwy. 412 East in town (just west of the Arkansas state line), go east on Hwy. 412 for 1.5 mi. Turn left onto Mt. Olive St. and go 1.9 mi. Turn right onto Dawn Hill Rd. and go 1.85 mi. Turn left onto Taylor Orchard Rd. and go 1.3 mi. Turn right at the sign into the campground.

TEXARKANA

Texarkana RV Park

8225 Camper Ln., Texarkana 71854. T: (870) 772-0751; rbparksr@msn.com.

RV: ★★★ Tent: n/a

Beauty: ★★★	Site Privacy: ★★★
Spaciousness: ★★★★	Quiet: ★★
Security: ★★★★	Cleanliness: ★★★★
Insect Control: ★★★★	Facilities: ★★★

Divided into three sections (A, B, and C), this campground has only RV sites, and does not accommodate tenting. Sites are all level, grassy pull-throughs. Row A has 65-foot sites that are all very open. Site 8 has the largest tree (across the internal road, by the grill), making it the best of this row. Site 12 is closest to the highway, making it the least desirbale. Row B has 45-foot sites that are mostly open—sites 8, 11, 12, and 14 have shade trees. Row C has 60-foot sites, with the best sites in the higher numbers. Sites 11–14 face a nice field to the north, and have trees across the internal road that provide some shade, but 14 is close to the highway. The campground in general is not highly developed, which lends a natural feel to the sites but also provides for a sometimes choppy road. RVers should take the internal road at a slow speed. The restooms are clean and very modern. However, the showers could benefit from a tile scrubbing, and some of the lights were not working when the campground was inspected. The laundry is spacious and clean. This is a very reasonable campground to spend several days in, and depending on which site you get, it may prove to be worthy of a longer stay.

Basics

Operated By: Janet Park. **Open:** All year. **Site Assignment:** Assigned upon registration. Reservations require credit card in busy season; 24-hours cancellation policy. **Registration:** In office. (Late arrivals use drop box.) **Fee:** RV $20–23 depending on 30 or 50 amps (V, MC, AE, & D.) **Parking:** At site.

Facilities

Number of RV Sites: 41. **Number of Tent-Only Sites:** 0. **Hookups:** Water, sewer, electric (20, 30, 50 amps), cable. **Each Site:** Picnic table, grill, trash can. **Dump Station:** Yes. **Laundry:** Yes. **Pay Phone:** Yes. **Rest Rooms and Showers:** Yes. **Fuel:** No. **Propane:** Yes. **Internal Roads:** Dirt. **RV Service:** No. **Market:** 5 mi. to Texarkana. **Restaurant:** 5 mi. to Texarkana. **General Store:** Yes. **Vending:** No. **Swimming:** Pool. **Playground:** Yes. **Other:** Small TV lounge, game room. **Activities:** Games, visiting museums, swimming. **Nearby Attractions:** Crater of Diamonds State Park, Dy Place Children's Museum. **Additional Information:** Texarkana Chamber of Commerce, (903) 792-7191.

Restrictions

Pets: On leash, cleaned up after, do not leave tied up. **Fires:** In grills. **Alcoholic Beverages:** At sites. **Vehicle Maximum Length:** None.

To Get There

From I-30, take Exit 7 to Mandeville. Go 0.2 mi. north on Hwy. 108 West, then take the first right onto the north service road and go 0.4 mi. straight into the campground.

VAN BUREN

Overland RV Park

1716 Fayetteville Hwy., Van Buren 72956. T: (501) 471-5474; olcrv@mail.cswnet.com.

RV: ★★★ Tent: n/a

Beauty: ★	Site Privacy: ★★★
Spaciousness: ★★	Quiet: ★★★
Security: ★★★	Cleanliness: ★★★★
Insect Control: ★★★★	Facilities: ★★★

This RV park is part of an RV-oriented complex in a commercial area off a main road. The park is located next to a sales and service center, while a fence running around the park hides a supermarket, restaurants, and shops. Sites are laid out in three rows. The south row (even 2–32 and 33) contains back-ins of 40 × 22 feet and offers phone hookups. The north row (34–49) offers 50 amps service. pull-throughs are located in the north and middle rows. These sites are 65 feet in length, with a mixture of gravel and grass. 33 is slightly less desirable, as fencing on two sides seems to hem it in. The most desirable sites are in the north row, since they have the greatest amount of open space behind them, while the easternmost sites are furthest from the entrance. The shower facility is cleaner than the rest rooms, which are acceptable but not spectacular. At the time of our visit, the floors were utterly exhausted, and needed to be replaced. This campground is a reasonable overnight stay—and an extremely convenient one for those in need of RV servicing—but shouldn't make anyone's destination list.

Basics

Operated By: Richard Shilling. **Open:** All year. **Site Assignment:** First come, first served Credit card required for reservation; 24-hours cancellation policy. **Registration:** In RV at entrance, on right. If unattended, use mail slot. **Fee:** RV $17 (50 amps), $16 (30 amps) (checks, V, MC, & D). **Parking:** At site.

Facilities

Number of RV Sites: 49. **Number of Tent-Only Sites:** 0. **Hookups:** Water, sewer, electric (30, 50 amps), phone. **Dump Station:** Yes. **Laundry:** Yes. **Pay Phone:** Yes. **Rest Rooms and Showers:** Yes. **Fuel:** No. **Propane:** Yes. **Internal Roads:** Gravel. **RV Service:** Yes. **Market:** 1 block. **Restaurant:** 2 blocks. **General Store:** No. **Vending:** No. **Swimming:** No. **Playground:** No. **Other:** Pet walk area, pavilion. **Activities:** Railroad rides. **Nearby Attractions:** Arkansas & Missouri Railroad. **Additional Information:** Van Buren Visitors Center, (800) 332-5889.

Restrictions

Pets: On leash, cleaned up after. **Fires:** In grills. **Alcoholic Beverages:** At sites. **Vehicle Maximum Length:** None.

To Get There

From I-40 Exit 5, turn south onto Hwy. 59. On the south side of the highway crossover, go 0.1 mi. to the first left turn. Drive straight into the entrance.

WALDRON

Big Pine RV Park

1085 North Main St., Waldron 72958. T: (501) 420-5732 or (903) 665-8648; bjem@ipa.net.

RV: ★★★ Tent: ★★★

Beauty: ★★	Site Privacy: ★★
Spaciousness: ★★★★	Quiet: ★★★
Security: ★★★	Cleanliness: ★★★
Insect Control: ★★★★	Facilities: ★★

This overnight park is located in a residential area, with little to enhance its beauty. Sites are grassy and open, and situated rather close to the road. (Sites 12–16 are especially close. Mainly unshaded, they are as open to the sun as they are to passer-by.) While sites are open-ended, anything larger than 60 feet or so seems unfeasible, especially if a number of sites are occupied. Sites 10 and 11 are perhaps the nicest, with a couple of trees around them to reduce the amount of direct sunlight that reaches them. Site 16 also has a tree, making it slightly better than the other roadside sites. Of the remaining sites, 1–8, are the better sites, being furthest from the highway. Perhaps a telling detail: a warning sign that reads "Not Responsible For Accidents" is displayed prominently in the campground, suggesting that entering and exiting the premises is somewhat difficult in traffic. But then, unless you are running late you probably won't want to bother to find out.

Basics

Operated By: Billy & Esther Murphy. **Open:** All year. **Site Assignment:** First come, first served; verbal reservations OK. **Registration:** "Pick a spot & park." Register when someone is around. **Fee:** RV $12. **Parking:** At site.

Facilities

Number of RV Sites: 16. **Number of Tent-Only Sites:** Undesignated sites. **Hookups:** Water, sewer, electric (30, 50 amps). **Dump Station:** Yes. **Laundry:** Yes. **Pay Phone:** Yes. **Rest Rooms and Showers:** Yes. **Fuel:** No. **Propane:** No. **Internal Roads:** Gravel. **RV Service:** No. **Market:** 1 mi. south. **Restaurant:** 1 mile south. **General Store:** No. **Vending:** No. **Swimming:** No. **Playground:** No. **Activities:** Fishing, boating, swimming, hiking. **Nearby Attractions:** Ouachita National Forest, Blue Mountain Lake. **Additional Information:** Chamber of Commerce, (501) 637-2775.

Restrictions

Pets: On leash, cleaned up after. **Fires:** In grills. **Alcoholic Beverages:** At sites. **Vehicle Maximum Length:** 60 ft.

To Get There

From the junction of Hwy. 71 and Hwy. 71 B north of town, turn south onto Hwy. 71B South, and go 0.7 mi. Turn left at the sign into the park.

WEST MEMPHIS

Trav-L-Park

7037 I-55, Marion 72364. T: (888) 857-4890 or (870) 739-4801; F: (870) 739-4801; www.tldirectory. com; tennpop@aol.com.

RV ★★★★ Tent ★★★★

Beauty: ★★★★	Site Privacy: ★★★★
Spaciousness: ★★★	Quiet: ★★★
Security: ★★★★	Cleanliness: ★★★★★
Insect Control: ★★★	Facilities: ★★★★★

West of the highway, with a cornfield to the north and an agricultural field to the south, this campground has attractive landscaping (using bushes at the ends of rows) and towering shade trees. Nearly all sites in the park are very well shaded, with a grass floor. Sites 1, 2, 4, and 9 are enormous (100-feet) pull-throughs, while 3 and 5–8 are 75-foot back-ins. End sites 16, 24, 32, 40, 48, and H have enormous leftover space at the ends of the rows. Sites 50–54 are 60-foot back-ins in a strip across from the office. Adjacent to these sites are sites 55–62, arranged in a semi-circle in the grass. These are undeveloped sites in a wooded area, with a very natural, almost wild, feel. (These sites can accommodate any size of rig, and can be pull-throughs if the adjacent area is clear.) Sites A–H face a residential area, and A and B are the least best sites in the campground, lacking shade trees. However, there is nary a truly bad site in the park. The rest rooms and showers are immaculate, well-lit, and tastefully decorated. The laundry is contained in its own cute little cabin, and is open 24 hrs. Located 15 miles to most attractions, and 22 miiles to Graceland, this park boasts very friendly management and is worth the drive out, especially given the state of other local campgrounds.

Basics

Operated By: Joyce & Ramon Mitchell. **Open:** All year. **Site Assignment:** Assigned upon registration. Reservations require credit card or cell phone number, & are recommended; cancellation must be made 4 days before arrival. **Registration:** In office. (Late arrivals use drop box.) **Fee:** RV $22 (full), $18 (water, electric), tent $13. Winter RV rates are $18 & $16. **Parking:** At site, w/ plenty of visitor parking.

Facilities

Number of RV Sites: 125. **Number of Tent-Only Sites:** 3. **Hookups:** Water, sewer, electric (30, 50 amps). **Each Site:** Picnic table, grill. **Dump Station:** Yes. **Laundry:** Yes. **Pay Phone:** Yes. **Rest Rooms and Showers:** Yes. **Fuel:** No. **Propane:** Yes. **Internal Roads:** Gravel. **RV Service:** No. **Market:** 4 mi. south (Exit 10). **Restaurant:** 4 mi. south (Exit 10). **General Store:** Yes. **Vending:** No. **Swimming:** Pool. **Playground:** Yes. **Other:** Dataport, rec room, pet walk area, horseshoes. **Activities:** Swimming, visiting museums, city tours, shopping. **Nearby Attractions:** Graceland, Sun Studio, Beale St., Pink Palace Museum, Rock 'n' Soul Museum, IMAX Theater. **Additional Information:** Visitor information Desk, (901) 543-5333.

Restrictions

Pets: On leash, cleaned up after. **Fires:** In grills. **Alcoholic Beverages:** At sites, no bottles. **Vehicle Maximum Length:** None. **Other:** No semis, operators prefer no large animals that must be kept outside of RVs.

To Get There

From I-55, take Exit 14. Take the first right (following the sign for Memphis). Follow the road around and take the right turn so that you are driving parallel to the interstate on the west service road. Go 0.2 mi. and turn right at the sign into the campground.

WYNNE

Village Creek State Park

201 CR 754, Wynne 72396. T: (870) 238-9406; F: (870) 238-9415; www.arkansasstateparks.com; villagecrk@arkansas.com.

RV ★★★★ Tent ★★★★

Beauty: ★★★★	Site Privacy: ★★★★
Spaciousness: ★★★★	Quiet: ★★★★★
Security: ★★★★	Cleanliness: ★★★
Insect Control: ★★★	Facilities: ★★★★

This is a large campground divided up into three camping areas: South (1–41), West (42–73), and North (74–104), in order from the entrance. All sites are forested, and have a paved parking area for an RV or other vehicle. Most sites open to a grassy field that campers can use for recreation. The South Area consists of two loops in a figure 8, the more northernly of the two loops containing reservable sites. Sites 1 and 8 are set very close to the road, which makes them less desirable; while 7 is set back further than most, making it rather more private. Sites 23 and 24 are on either side of a hiking trail head, and may experience more foot traffic for this reason. Sites 25 and 26 together form a double. The West Area is close to Lake Dunn; sites 46–50 are the closest campsites to the swimming beach. Sites 53–57 back to the lake (with a strip of forest behind them), while 59 is close to the rest room facility. Sites 48 and 49 make a double, and 72 and 73 are very close to one another. 60–67 are located on a side street, making them slightly more private. Of these sites, 61 and 62 are the most remote. The North Area contains the most number of doubles, which will interest groups of campers. These include sites 75 and 76, 93 and 94, and 101 and 102. Site 74 is right at the entrance, but 85 and 86 are tucked away in a corner. This is a pleasant wilderness campground that will appeal to many campers for its quiet and natural setting.

Basics

Operated By: Arkansas Dept. of Parks & Tourism. **Open:** All year. **Site Assignment:** First come, first served. Reservations require deposit of one's night's stay, made 5 days in advance; cancellation requires 5-days notice; first night's deposit non-refundable. **Registration:** In Visitors Center. (Late arrivals select available site & register next morning after 8.) **Fee:** $14 (checks, V, MC, AE, & D). **Parking:** At site.

Facilities

Number of RV Sites: 104. **Number of Tent-Only Sites:** 0. **Hookups:** Water, electric (20, 30, 50 amps). **Each Site:** Picnic table, fire pit, tent pad. **Dump Station:** Yes. **Laundry:** No. **Pay Phone:** Yes. **Rest Rooms and Showers:** Yes. **Fuel:** No. **Propane:** No. **Internal Roads:** Paved. **RV Service:** No. **Market:** 7 mi. to Wynne. **Restaurant:** 7 mi. to Wynne. **General Store:** Yes. **Vending:** Yes. **Swimming:** Lake. **Playground:** Yes. **Other:** Cabins, auditorium. **Activities:** Golf, tennis, hiking. **Nearby Attractions:** Village Creek State Park, Parkin Arch State Park. **Additional Information:** Chamber of Commerce, (870) 238-2601.

Restrictions

Pets: On leash, cleaned up after, not in cabins. **Fires:** In grills. **Alcoholic Beverages:** At sites (preferably in a nondescript containers). **Vehicle Maximum Length:** None.

To Get There

From the junction of Hwy. 1 and Hwy. 64B/284, turn east onto Hwy. 64B/284, and go 1.9 mi., making sure to take the two turns within the first 0.7 mi. to stay on this highway. At the junction of Hwy. 64B and Hwy. 284, go 4.9 mi. south on Hwy. 284. Turn left at the sign into the park entrance.

Arizona

Arizona blends a rich Native American past and present with a Wild West legacy of cowboys, cattle, and mining. Snowbirds annually flock to Arizona's deserts for the mild winter temperatures, golf and Major League Baseball's spring training Cactus League. Hundreds of RV parks with every imaginable amenity come to life to handle the winter influx, and most book full well in advance of the annual RV migration.

The desert has its own kind of beauty, and the hardiest heat lovers will brave summer temperatures soaring past 110 degrees in **Phoenix** at **Organ Pipe Cactus National Monument.** But most opt for the cooler months from fall through the spring wildflower season. **Tucson** summer temperatures are about 10 degrees cooler than those in Phoenix, though still in the 100s, and summer monsoons bring flash floods. By August, birdwatchers invade the **Upper San Pedro River Valley** southeast of Tucson, an area about 15 degrees cooler than Phoenix. History abounds in **Bisbee,** an old copper mining town with an RV Park overlooking an open pit mine. Few ghost towns rival **Tombstone's** ambiance, and **Kartchner Caverns** satisfies cravings for geological oddities.

Arizona is also a land of mountains, which means winter sports and summer campgrounds that are a refuge from the desert heat. Both deserts and mountains abound with lakes and reservoirs, and fishing and boating are a popular part of the cooling summer mix. The **Colorado River** along Arizona's western border is a water playground with a mix of private RV parks, marinas, and state and county campgrounds between Parker and Lake Havasu, home of the old **London Bridge.** Nearby **Quartzsite** becomes a giant winter flea market and gem show, attracting over a million visitors who park their RVs on Bureau of Land Management (BLM) land all over the desert.

The **Grand Canyon,** to the north, is an international attraction and gateway to the Navajo Nation. **Canyon de Chelley,** just east of the Hopi Indian mesas, is also on most international itineraries. There is no camping inside the **Painted Desert** or **Petrified Forest National Park,** but choices outside the parks, between **Winslow** and **Holbrook,** range from archaeological sites and powerplant cooling reservoirs to commercial campgrounds. South of the Petrified Forest is high mountain country, with a number of forest, lake, and reservoir campgrounds, and even a White Mountain Apache casino RV park for those wanting some Nevada style action.

The following facilities accept payment in checks or cash only:

Alamo Lake State Park, Wenden
Betatakin, Betatakin (Navajo National Monument)
Buckskin Mountain State Park, Parker
Burro Creek Recreation Site, Wikieup
Catalina State Park, Tucson
Cholla Lake County Park, Holbrook
Fool Hollow Lake Recreation Area, Show Low
Gilbert Ray Campground, Tucson
Homolovi Ruins State Park, Winslow
Horspitality RV Park and Boarding Stable, Wickenburg
Jacob Lake Campground, Jacob Lake
Kaibab Camper Village, Jacob Lake
Krazy K RV Park, Camp Verde
La Posa LTVA, Quartzsite
Lake Havasu State Park (Windsor Beach), Lake Havasu City
Lake Pleasant Regional Park, Peoria
LaPaz County Park, Parker
Lees Ferry Campground, Marble Canyon
Lone Rock Beach, Page
Lost Dutchman State Park, Apache Junction
Lyman Lake State Park, St. Johns
Manzanita, Sedona
Mather Campground, Grand Canyon
McDowell Mountain Regional Park, Fountain Hills
Organ Pipe Cactus National Monument, Lukeville
Painted Rock Petroglyph Site & Campground, Gila Bend
Patagonia Lake State Park, Patagonia
Picacho Peak State Park, Picacho Peak
Queen Mine RV Park, Bisbee
Shady Dell RV Park, Bisbee
Temple Bar, Temple Bar
Wheatfields Lake, Tsaile

The following facility features 50 sites or fewer:

Shady Dell RV Park, Bisbee

APACHE JUNCTION

Lost Dutchman State Park

6109 N. Apache Tr., Apache Junction 85219. T: (602) 982-4485; www.pr.state.az.us.

 ★★★★ ★★★★★

Beauty: ★★★★★ Site Privacy: ★★★★★
Spaciousness: ★★★★★ Quiet: ★★★★★
Security: ★★★ Cleanliness: ★★★★
Insect Control: ★★★ Facilities: ★★

The big news at Lost Dutchman State Park is the addition of showers, though being without hookups this was never the sort of place people came for RV amenities. The major attractions here are the great views of the spire-like Praying Hand rock formation backed by the tall Flatiron formation, plus many nature trails for hiking and horseback riding. The area's intriguing eroded rock formations are fronted with saguaros, palo verde cholla, and other desert vegetation tall enough to screen the campsites and add privacy. The campground's 35 sites are divided into three small loops within a larger loop, so the natural environment predominates over camping neighbors. It is these natural environment qualities, not the presence or absence of standard amenities, that causes this campground to fill up fast. The group-camping area sometimes doubles as overflow.

BASICS

Operated By: Arizona State Parks. **Open:** All year. **Site Assignment:** First come, first served. **Registration:** Office or self-pay fee station. **Fee:** $10 (cash or check only). **Parking:** At site.

FACILITIES

Number of RV Sites: 35. **Number of Tent-Only Sites:** 0. **Hookups:** None. **Each Site:** Table, grill. **Dump Station:** Yes. **Laundry:** No. **Pay Phone:** Yes. **Rest Rooms and Showers:** Yes. **Fuel:** No. **Propane:** No. **Internal Roads:** Paved & gravel, good condition. **RV Service:** No. **Market:** Apache Junction, 5 mi. **Restaurant:** Apache Junction, 3 mi. **General Store:** No. **Vending:** Yes. **Swimming:** No. **Playground:** No. **Other:** Group pavilion, amphitheater, native-plant trail near ranger station. **Activities:** Horseback riding. **Nearby Attractions:** Tortilla Flat, Phoenix. **Additional Information:** Pinal County Visitor Center, (520) 868-9433.

RESTRICTIONS

Pets: On leash. **Fires:** In grills only; ground fires strictly prohibited; no wood gathering). **Alcoholic Beverages:** Allowed. **Vehicle Maximum Length:** None. **Other:** 15-day stay limit.

TO GET THERE

From junction of US Hwy. 60 & AZ Hwy. 88 go 6 mi. northeast on Hwy. 88.

APACHE JUNCTION

Mesa-Apache Junction KOA

1520 South Tomahawk Rd., Apache Junction 85219. T: (800) KOA-3404, (480) 982-4015; www.koa.com

 ★★★★  ★★★

Beauty: ★★★ Site Privacy: ★★
Spaciousness: ★★★★ Quiet: ★★★★
Security: ★★★★ Cleanliness: ★★★★★
Insect Control: ★★★ Facilities: ★★★★

Without the age restriction of many of the mega-lots in the Apache Junction/Mesa area, this campground is a great family destination. The combination of decent-sized lots (50 × 25 feet on average), attractive landscaping, views of the Superstition Mountains, and full services makes this a campground worth your while to visit. Tent sites are well tucked away, but would be improved with grass instead of gravel. RV sites 116 and 177 sport a fine mature shade tree, making them the best for the money. Sites to avoid are 65, 113, 113A, 114, and 114A, as they have no tree to speak of and are located next to the rec room and an intersection in the campground road. Tent sites H–L are located next to shrubs along the border of the property, which adds to their charm. Tent sites E and F are situated closest to the playground, and worse, E has no tree whatsoever.

BASICS

Operated By: Mike & Rosemary Mortensen. **Open:** All year. **Site Assignment:** Assigned on registration. **Registration:** At office. (Late arrivals: select site from map of open sites, use drop slot in door.). **Fee:** $20–$27. **Parking:** At site.

FACILITIES

Number of RV Sites: 140. **Number of Tent-Only Sites:** 8. **Hookups:** Water, sewer, electric (30, 50 amps). **Each Site:** Picnic table, some shade trees, some trash receptacles. **Dump Station:** Yes. **Laundry:** Yes. **Pay Phone:** Yes. **Rest Rooms and Showers:** Yes. **Fuel:** No. **Propane:** Yes. **Internal Roads:** Hard-packed dirt, gravel, & pavement mix; in very drivable condition. **RV Service:** No. **Market:** On site. **Restaurant:** Next door. **General Store:** Yes. **Vending:** Yes. **Swimming:** Yes. **Playground:** Yes. **Other:** Rec building, "dog relief pen." **Activities:** Shuffleboard, river tubing, TV, some fitness equipment, ping pong, basketball, horseshoes, desert Jeep tours, horseback tours, helicopter tours. **Nearby Attractions:** Mesa Southwest Museum, Champlin Fighter Museum, Superstition Springs Center, Casa Grande Ruins, Roosevelt Dam, Tonto National Monument. **Additional Information:** Apache Junction Chamber of Commerce, (602) 982-3141.

RESTRICTIONS

Pets: On leash, clean up after. **Fires:** Yes (only charcoal in grills). **Alcoholic Beverages:** At sites only. **Vehicle Maximum Length:** None. **Other:** No clotheslines, no generators, no For Sale signs.

TO GET THERE

From Hwy. 60, take Exit 197 onto Tomahawk Rd., turn north and drive for 1 mi. The entrance is on the left.

BENSON

Cochise Terrace RV Resort

1030 South Barrel Cactus Ridge, Benson 85602. T: (520) 586-0600 or (800) 495-9005; F: (520) 586-3200; www.cochise-terrace.com; rvresort@theriver.com.

 ★★★★ ★

Beauty: ★★★★ Site Privacy: ★★★★
Spaciousness: ★★★★ Quiet: ★★★★
Security: ★★★★ Cleanliness: ★★★★
Insect Control: ★★★★ Facilities: ★★★★

Far enough from the main highways so that the only external sound is the wind blowing, Cochise Terrace is like a little city with street lights. Streets have bird names like Raven Road and Quail Run, and an 80-foot-tall American flag near the front entrance office doubles as a navigation landmark. Barrel cactus, ocotillo, mesquite, and a wash are reminders that there is a desert surrounding this little oasis of paved streets. There are almost 100 annual residents of Cochise Terrace, and the 200-plus remaining RV sites are particularly popular with snowbirds. So, if the largest 42-foot site is needed for a winter visit, call ahead and reserve it. As far as locations go, this is about as central a base for touring southeast Arizona as there is, being an easy drive to almost all the sights from Tucson and Tumacacori to Tombstone and Bisbee.

BASICS

Operated By: Art & Pat Bale. **Open:** All year. **Site Assignment:** First come, first served; winter reservations recommended. **Registration:** Office. **Fee:** $20–$23 (V, MC, AE, D). **Parking:** At site.

FACILITIES

Number of RV Sites: 223. **Number of Tent-Only Sites:** 0. **Hookups:** Electric (20, 30, 50 amp), water, sewer, cable TV, phone. **Each Site:** Table. **Dump Station:** Yes. **Laundry:** Yes. **Pay Phone:** Yes. **Rest Rooms and Showers:** Yes. **Fuel:** No. **Propane:** Yes. **Internal Roads:** Paved, excellent. **RV Service:** No. **Market:** Benson, 2 mi. **Restaurant:** Benson, 2 mi. **General Store:** No. **Vending:** Yes. **Swimming:** Pool. **Playground:** No. **Other:** Clubhouse, whirlpool, kitchen, BBQ, picnic area, basketball court, pet walk, mail service. **Activities:** Golf, horseshoes, square dancing. **Nearby Attractions:** Kartchner Caverns, Fort Huachuca, Tombstone, Bisbee, Dragoon Mountains, Cochise Stronghold, San Pedro Riparian National Conservation Area, Tucson. **Additional Information:** Benson Chamber of Commerce, (520) 586-2842, www.bensonchamberaz.com.

RESTRICTIONS

Pets: On leash and never left unattended. **Fires:** No. **Alcoholic Beverages:** Allowed. **Vehicle Maximum Length:** 42 ft. **Other:** No firearms.

TO GET THERE

From I-10 Exit 302 go south on AZ Hwy. 90 and west on S. Barrel Cactus Ridge.

BENSON

Kartchner Caverns State Park

P.O. Box 1849, Benson 85602. T: (520) 586-4100; www.pr.state.az.us.

 ★★★★★ ★★★★★

Beauty: ★★★★★ Site Privacy: ★★★★★
Spaciousness: ★★★★★ Quiet: ★★★★★
Security: ★★★★ Cleanliness: ★★★★★
Insect Control: ★★★★ Facilities: ★★★

The Caverns, which require separate admission tickets (520) 586-CAVE for cavern tour reservations), are limestone caves with pooling shelfstones, spar crystals, cave pearls, dripping stalactites, stalagmites, coral pipes, columns, and drapery. Discovered 49 miles southeast of Tucson by two cave explorers in 1974, the caverns were kept secret until purchased as a state park in 1988. The Discovery Center has an explanatory video, plus a hummingbird garden. The campsites are very large, and include 16 50-amp pull-through sites. Thick mesquite barriers between sites provide privacy, and agave, ocotillo, and prickly pear make this campground one of the most beautiful in the desert. However, the attractive sites fill up early almost every day of the year. Since there are no campground reservations, be prepared to make this a day trip and find alternative campsites in Benson, Huachuca City, and other nearby areas.

Basics

Operated By: Arizona State Parks. **Open:** All year. **Site Assignment:** First come, first served. **Registration:** Entrance kiosk (after hours self-pay station). **Fee:** $20 (V, MC; cash only after hours). **Parking:** At site.

Facilities

Number of RV Sites: 64. **Number of Tent-Only Sites:** 0. **Hookups:** Electric (30, 50 amp), water. **Each Site:** Table. **Dump Station:** Yes. **Laundry:** No. **Pay Phone:** Yes. **Rest Rooms and Showers:** Yes. **Fuel:** No. **Propane:** No. **Internal Roads:** Paved, good. **RV Service:** No. **Market:** Benson, 10 mi. **Restaurant:** Benson, 10 mi. **General Store:** No. **Vending:** Yes. **Swimming:** No. **Playground:** No. **Other:** Some grills, Discovery Center. **Activities:** Cave tours. **Nearby Attractions:** Ramsey Canyon Preserve, Patagonia Lake, Sonoita, Fort Huachuca, Tombstone. **Additional Information:** Sierra Vista Vistor Center, (800) 288-3861, www.visitsierravista.com; Sierra Vista Ranger District, (520) 378-0311.

Restrictions

Pets: On leash under owner's control. **Fires:** Yes (gas stoves only, no wood or charcoal fires). **Alcoholic Beverages:** Allowed. **Vehicle Maximum Length:** 74 ft. **Other:** 14-day stay limit.

To Get There

From I-10, 1 mi. west of Benson, take Exit 302 and go 9 mi. south on AZ Hwy. 90.

BETATAKIN (NAVAJO NATIONAL MONUMENT)

Betatakin

National Park Service, Navajo National Monument, HC-71 Box 3, Tonalea 86044. T: (520) 672-2700; www.nps.gov/nava.

RV: ★★ Tent: ★★★★★

Beauty: ★★★★★	Site Privacy: ★★★★
Spaciousness: ★★★	Quiet: ★★★★★
Security: ★	Cleanliness: ★★★★
Insect Control: ★★★	Facilities: ★

Roughly 10 miles from the nearest highway and 30 miles to the nearest town of any size, Betatakin campsite is rustic and isolated in the extreme. Hidden amidst pinyon, juniper, sage, and a smattering of yucca, sites are far enough away from the visitor center to avoid light pollution. On a clear night, the sky comes alive with stars, and the only sounds to be heard are the chirping, fluttering, or howling of nocturnal animals. This campsite is so natural that there are even black bear warnings issued, and campers would be wise to keep their sites free of trash or food that might attract a bear. The visitor center contains a small display of artifacts, and shows informative videos upon request. Guided tours to the ruins can be reserved up to two months before your trip, but are only offered between Memorial Day and Labor Day. The canyon is still used by Navajo Indians, who herd sheep and gather herbs that can only be found in this canyon. Hopi Indians also still make a yearly pilgrimage to a sacred spot for a Sun Clan ritual.

Basics

Operated By: National Parks Service. **Open:** All year. **Site Assignment:** First come, first served. **Registration:** None. **Fee:** None. **Parking:** At site.

Facilities

Number of RV Sites: 31. **Number of Tent-Only Sites:** 0. **Hookups:** None. **Each Site:** Picnic table. **Dump Station:** No. **Laundry:** No. **Pay Phone:** Yes. **Rest Rooms and Showers:** Toilets; no showers. **Fuel:** No. **Propane:** No. **Internal Roads:** Paved. **RV Service:** No. **Market:** 15 mi. in Black Mesa. **Restaurant:** 15 mi. in Black Mesa. **General Store:** No. **Vending:** Yes. **Swimming:** No. **Playground:** No. **Activities:** Hiking, seasonal tours to Betatakin & Keet Seel ruins, evening presentations at the Fire Circle. **Nearby Attractions:** Aspen Forest Overlook nature trail.

Restrictions

Pets: On leash. **Fires:** No. **Alcoholic Beverages:** None permitted on tribal land. **Vehicle Maximum Length:** 25 ft. **Other:** Hiking off trails onto tribal land is prohibited, no gathering of artifacts or natural objects.

To Get There

From Kayenta, go 19 mi. west on Hwy. 160 and turn right at the sign for the Navajo National Monument at Black Mesa. Go 9.5 mi. to the visitor center. Follow the road around the center and straight into the campground.

BISBEE

Queen Mine RV Park

P.O. Box 488, Bisbee 85603. T: (520) 432-5006.

RV: ★★★★ Tent: ★

Beauty: ★★★★	Site Privacy: ★★★★
Spaciousness: ★★★★	Quiet: ★★★★
Security: ★★★★	Cleanliness: ★★★★
Insect Control: ★★★★	Facilities: ★★★

Perched on a circular hilltop just opposite and above the Queen Mine Tour, with RVs circled around the perimeter like a wagon train, the Queen Mine RV Park looks out on orange, ochre, and gray hillside layers exposed by a deep pit copper mine known as the Lavender Pit. Some may call the pit mine a scar on the face of the Earth, but it has its beauty, particularly after a rain when the hillside colors become deeply saturated. For at least a brief moment it is possible to fantasize that a mighty river, rather than copper miners, carved out this three-quarter-mile wide, 950-foot-deep chasm filled with water at the bottom. In any event, it is just a block downhill from this clean, well-run, breezy hillside RV park to the start of Bisbee's historic old Main St. and all the shops, restaurants, hotels, galleries, theaters, and saloons.

Basics

Operated By: Stan Dupuy. **Open:** All year. **Site Assignment:** First come, first served. **Registration:** Office. **Fee:** $19 (cash or check). **Parking:** At site.

Facilities

Number of RV Sites: 25. **Number of Tent-Only Sites:** 0. **Hookups:** Electric (20, 30 amp), water, sewer, cable TV. **Each Site:** Rock planter w/ small tree. **Dump Station:** Yes. **Laundry:** Yes. **Pay Phone:** Yes. **Rest Rooms and Showers:** Yes. **Fuel:** No. **Propane:** No. **Internal Roads:** Gravel, good. **RV Service:** No. **Market:** Bisbee, 2 mi. **Restaurant:** Bisbee, 2 blocks. **General Store:** No. **Vending:** No. **Swimming:** No. **Playground:** No. **Activities:** Golf, bird-watching. **Nearby Attractions:** Mine tour, museums, Tombstone, San Pedro Riparian National Conservation Area. **Additional Information:** Bisbee Chamber of Commerce, (520) 432-5421, www.bisbeearizona.com.

Restrictions

Pets: On leash under owner's control. **Fires:** Yes. **Alcoholic Beverages:** Allowed. **Vehicle Maximum Length:** None.

To Get There

From AZ Hwy. 80, take downtown Bisbee Exit and follow road to Queen Mine Tour.

BISBEE

Shady Dell RV Park

1 Douglas Rd., Bisbee 85603. T: (520) 432-3567.

RV: ★★★★ Tent: ★★

Beauty: ★★★★	Site Privacy: ★★★★
Spaciousness: ★★★★	Quiet: ★★★
Security: ★★★★	Cleanliness: ★★★★
Insect Control: ★★★★	Facilities: ★★★★

Located off a roundabout southeast of the Lavender Pit mine, Shady Dell got its start in 1927 when copper mining was going strong and Bisbee was better known than Phoenix. Getting a campsite here is tough, and late afternoon arrivals are usually of out of luck, as most of the campground is rented out to year-round campers. Even more coveted than the camping sites are the furnished aluminum travel trailer rentals, an homage to American road travel that includes a 1949 Airstream, 1950 Spartanette, 1951 Royal Mansion, and 1954 Crown, all furnished in near original blonde woods and polished aluminum with vintage radios, black-and-white TVs, phonographs, and vinyl records of early rhythm and blues and big bands. Dot's Diner, a ten-stool 1957 art deco Valentine model, makes Shady Dell a good early breakfast stop even if not camping.

Basics

Operated By: Ed Smith & Rita Personette. **Open:** All year. **Site Assignment:** First come, first served. **Registration:** Office. **Fee:** $10–$15 (cash or check only). **Parking:** At site.

Facilities

Number of RV Sites: 10. **Number of Tent-Only Sites:** 2. **Hookups:** Electric (30 amp), water, sewer, cable TV. **Each Site:** Grass & gravel. **Dump Station:** Yes. **Laundry:** Yes. **Pay Phone:** Yes. **Rest Rooms and Showers:** Yes. **Fuel:** Yes. **Propane:** Yes. **Internal Roads:** Gravel, good. **RV Service:** No. **Market:** Bisbee, 2 mi. **Restaurant:** Yes. **General Store:** No. **Vending:** No. **Swimming:** No. **Playground:** No. **Other:** Vintage travel trailer rentals. **Activities:** Golf, bird-watching, rock hunting. **Nearby Attractions:** Mine tour, museums, Tombstone, San Pedro Riparian National Conservation Area. **Additional Information:** Bisbee Chamber of Commerce, (520) 432-5421, www.bisbeearizona.com.

Restrictions

Pets: On leash. **Fires:** Yes. **Alcoholic Beverages:** Allowed. **Vehicle Maximum Length:** 24 ft.

To Get There

From AZ Hwy. 80, 1.5 mi. southeast of Bisbee, follow the roundabout at the Chevron station to Douglas Rd.

BRENDA

Black Rock RV Park & Cafe

46751 East Hwy. 60, Salome 85348. T: (520) 927-4206; F: (520) 927-4210; www.blackrockrv-park.com.

RV ★★★★ Tent n/a

Beauty: ★★★★	Site Privacy: ★★★
Spaciousness: ★★★★	Quiet: ★★★★
Security: ★★★★	Cleanliness: ★★★★★
Insect Control: ★★★★	Facilities: ★★★★★

A small, friendly village with a great little bakery guaranteed to defeat efforts to keep off the pounds, Black Rock is a welcome refuge from the Jan. and Feb. crowds jamming nearby Quartzsite. A few trees and cacti line gravel streets with names like Which Way, What Street, Wash Way, Fun Gully, and Easy Street. Desert amenities abound for snowbirds, and people here enjoy walking alongside the road. Winter activities include Sunday afternoon ice cream socials, bean bag baseball, line dancing, cribbage, crafts, painting classes, exercise programs, bingo, darts, pinochle, and jam sessions. The rec hall attracts entertainers like Terry Raff, the singing mountain man. The area to the north is BLM land with ATV and hiking trails, as well as 18 holes of golf and a remote control airfield for flying model planes. For some this is enough to rent a post office box and take up residence.

Basics

Operated By: Black Rock RV Park. **Open:** All year. **Site Assignment:** First come, first served. **Registration:** Office inside cafe. **Fee:** $21 (V, MC). **Parking:** At site.

Facilities

Number of RV Sites: 350. **Number of Tent-Only Sites:** 0. **Hookups:** Electric (30, 50 amp), water, sewer, phone (modem), satellite TV. **Each Site:** Table. **Dump Station:** Yes. **Laundry:** Yes. **Pay Phone:** Yes. **Rest Rooms and Showers:** Yes. **Fuel:** No. **Propane:** Yes. **Internal Roads:** Gravel, good. **RV Service:** No. **Market:** Brenda, 0.5 mi. **Restaurant:** Yes. **General Store:** Yes. **Vending:** Yes. **Swimming:** No. **Playground:** No. **Other:** Soft water car/RV wash, barber, beauty shop, bakery, jeweler, post office, motel, 9-hole golf, R/C model flying field, rec hall, reverse osmosis water, oil change area. **Activities:** Golf, horseshoes. **Nearby Attractions:** Colorado River. **Additional Information:** McMullen Valley Chamber of Commerce, (520) 859-3846, www.azoutback.com.

Restrictions

Pets: On leash (quantity, size, & breed may be limited by management). **Fires:** Yes. **Alcoholic Beverages:** Allowed. **Vehicle Maximum Length:** 100 ft. **Other:** No subletting sites.

To Get There

From Quartzsite go 11 mi. east on I-10 and take Exit 31 to US Hwy. 60; stay on US Hwy. 60 heading east for 4 mi.

BULLHEAD CITY

Davis Camp

P.O. Box 2078, Bullhead City 86430. T: (520) 754-4606 or (877) 757-0915 (toll free); www.daviscamp.com.

RV ★★★★ Tent ★★

Beauty: ★★★★	Site Privacy: ★★★
Spaciousness: ★★★	Quiet: ★★★
Security: ★★★★	Cleanliness: ★★★★
Insect Control: ★★★★	Facilities: ★★★★

On the northern outskirts of Bullhead City, along Hwy. 68, between Davis Dam and the Laughlin Bridge, there are three clusters of camping sites with palms and eucalyptus along the banks of the Colorado River. This former federal housing area for Davis Dam workers, now a regional county park, looks across the river a mile to Laughlin, Nevada's glimmering casinos, and is the area's best combination of outdoor activities and casino proximity. Hardy outdoor types can swim, boat, jet ski, fish for world record striped bass (59 lbs., 12 oz. caught just below Davis Dam), and walk to Laughlin for food, gaming, and outlet shopping. Children have a safe, shallow swimming cove and spacious play areas with swings, slides, and basketball hoops. Dogs are commonplace, and the roar of the nearby highway and river traffic add to the noise. The most coveted sites, particularly for tents, are the 50 beachfront ramadas with tables and grills near the north beach fishing pier.

Basics

Operated By: Mohave County Parks Dept. **Open:** All year. **Site Assignment:** First come, first served; reservations required for group area. **Registration:** At entrance kiosk. **Fee:** $10–$16 (V, MC). **Parking:** At site.

Facilities

Number of RV Sites: 171. **Number of Tent-Only Sites:** 0. **Hookups:** Electric (up to 50 amps), water, sewer. **Each Site:** Wide pull through. **Dump Station:** Yes. **Laundry:** Yes. **Pay Phone:** Yes. **Rest Rooms and Showers:** Yes. **Fuel:** In Bullhead City & Laughlin. **Propane:** In Bullhead City & Laughlin. **Internal Roads:** Paved, in good condition. **RV Service:** In Bullhead City & Laughlin. **Market:** In Bullhead City & Laughlin. **Restaurant:** Many in nearby Laughlin, Bullhead City. **General Store:** In Bullhead City & Laughlin. **Vending:** Yes. **Swimming:** Children's wading pool. **Playground:** Yes. **Other:** Boat ramp, dock. **Activities:** River fishing, swimming, boating. **Nearby Attractions:** Laughlin casinos & outlet shopping; Colorado River Museum, Lake Mead National Recreation Area. **Additional Information:** Bullhead Area Chamber of Commerce, (520) 754-4121.

Restrictions

Pets: Must be under handlers' control; leash laws strictly enforced. **Fires:** Grills only. **Alcoholic Beverages:** Arizona law enforced by park rangers. **Vehicle Maximum Length:** 40 ft. **Other:** No loaded firearms, 14-day stay limit for beach sites.

To Get There

At junction of Bullhead Pkwy. (Laughlin Casino Bridge) and Hwy. 68.

CAMP VERDE

Krazy K RV Park

2075 Arena Del Loma, Camp Verde 86322. T: (520) 567-0565.

RV ★★★ Tent ★★

Beauty: ★★	Site Privacy: ★★★
Spaciousness: ★★★	Quiet: ★★★
Security: ★★★	Cleanliness: ★★★★
Insect Control: ★★★	Facilities: ★★

Overlooked by a scrub-covered hill with exclusive houses at the crest, this campground is pretty, with well-tended landscaping. The campground is laid out in rows, half located by the entrance, and the other half or so on a terrace at the foot of the hill at the west end of the grounds. Sites are a spacious (30-feet wide), with both pull-throughs and back-ins. This campground is definitely geared more to the RVer than to tenters: tent sites are not clearly defined, and crammed in by the restrooms. The top terrace and the strip closest to the office are reserved for monthly visitors. Although the campground is close to the highway, traffic noise is not noticeable, but the proximity offers a convenient quick jaunt into town. Overall, the campground presents a very pretty face, with tasteful decorations inside the bathrooms and laundry, and landscaping using volcanic rock and local plants. Its proximity to area attractions or to destinations such as scenic Sedona are an added bonus to a charming campground.

Basics

Operated By: Steve & Marlys Parks. **Open:** All year. **Site Assignment:** Assigned upon registration (especially when getting full). **Registration:** At office. Late arrivals go to lot #5 (Sun.–Tues.) or lot #14 (Wed.–Sat.). **Fee:** RV $18, tent $12 (no credit cards). **Parking:** At site.

Facilities

Number of RV Sites: 36. **Number of Tent-Only Sites:** Undesignated sites. **Hookups:** Water, sewer, electric (30, 50 amps). **Each Site:** Tree, most have tables. **Dump Station:** Yes. **Laundry:** Yes. **Pay Phone:** Yes. **Rest Rooms and Showers:** Yes. **Fuel:** No. **Propane:** Delivered. **Internal Roads:** Gravel. **RV Service:** No. **Market:** 1 mi. into town. **Restaurant:** 1 mi. into town. **General Store:** No. **Vending:** Yes. **Swimming:** Spa. **Playground:** No. **Other:** Dog walk, planned rec room w/ Internet access. **Activities:** Sightseeing, cycling, relaxing in nearby hot springs. **Nearby Attractions:** Montezuma Castle National Monument, Tuzigoot National Monument, Childs hot springs. **Additional Information:** Chamber of Commerce Visitor Center, (520) 567-9294.

Restrictions

Pets: 1 animal limit, on leash. **Fires:** No. **Alcoholic Beverages:** At sites only. **Vehicle Maximum Length:** 50 ft. **Other:** Rule sheet given upon registration.

To Get There

From the intersection of Hwy. 260 and I-17, go north on I-17 for 2.5 mi., then turn right onto Middle Verde Rd. (Exit 289). Turn right and follow the road east for 1 mi. Turn right again onto Arena Del Loma, and after 1 mi., make a right turn into the gravel entrance at the sign.

CHINLE

Cottonwood Campground

P.O. Box 588, Chinle 86503. T: (520) 674-5501 or (520) 674-5510; www.nps.gov/cach.

RV ★★★★ Tent ★★★★

Beauty: ★★★★	Site Privacy: ★★★★
Spaciousness: ★★★	Quiet: ★★★★
Security: ★★★★	Cleanliness: ★★★★
Insect Control: ★★★	Facilities: ★★★★

Ancient Puebloans occupied 83,000-acre Canyon de Chelly National Monument at least as long ago as 350 AD, and sites like the White House Ruins, Canyon del Muerto, and Spider Rock attract visitors from around the world. At least 20 Navajo families still seasonally graze their sheep and plant corn crops here, and four-wheel-drive and all-terrain vehicle guided tours into Canyon de Chelly are a tourist staple. Overlook views and the White House Ruins trail are free, as amazingly enough is the campground. When Cottonwood's free sites are gone, private Spider Rock RV Park (P.O. Box 2509, Chinle, AZ 86503; (520) 674-8261; no hookups) 10 miles southeast on South Rim Drive is happy to have the business. But with tall cottonwood trees providing plenty of shade and the Thunderbird Lodge Cafeteria next door staying open odd hours, this is the place to camp.

Basics

Operated By: National Park Service. **Open:** All year. **Site Assignment:** First come, first served; group site reservations (Apr. 1–Oct. 31). **Registration:** Office. **Fee:** None. **Parking:** At site.

Facilities

Number of RV Sites: 96. **Number of Tent-Only Sites:** 0. **Hookups:** None. **Each Site:** Table, grill. **Dump Station:** Yes. **Laundry:** No. **Pay Phone:** Yes. **Rest Rooms and Showers:** No showers. **Fuel:** No. **Propane:** No. **Internal Roads:** Paved, good condition. **RV Service:** No. **Market:** Chinle, 1 mi. **Restaurant:** Thunderbird Lodge, adjacent. **General Store:** No. **Vending:** No. **Swimming:** No. **Playground:** No. **Other:** Museum, Visitor Center. **Activities:** Horseback riding, Canyon de Chelly guided tours, summer campfire programs & hogan talks. **Nearby Attractions:** Hubbell Trading Post, Navajo National Monument, Kayenta Burger King Navajo Code Breakers exhibit. **Additional Information:** Canyon de Chelly National Monument, (520) 674-5500, www.nps.gov/cach.

Restrictions

Pets: On leash (do not feed stray dogs, which are being live trapped). **Fires:** Yes (in grill, ground fires & wood collection prohibited). **Alcoholic Beverages:** Prohibited on Navajo reservation. **Vehicle Maximum Length:** 35 ft. **Other:** 5-day stay limit.

To Get There

From junction of US Hwy. 91 and Indian Hwy. 7 in Chinle, go 4 mi. east on Hwy. 7 and then 0.25 mi. south on South Rim Dr.

FLAGSTAFF

Black Bart's RV Park

2760 East Butler Ave., Flagstaff 86004. T: (520) 774-1912.

RV ★★★ Tent ★

Beauty: ★★★★	Site Privacy: ★★★
Spaciousness: ★★★	Quiet: ★★
Security: ★★	Cleanliness: ★★★
Insect Control: ★★★	Facilities: ★★★

Although the campground is sandwiched between two busy roads, one side borders woods, and there are enough trees in the park itself (most sites have several) that the camp feels more rural than its urban location should warrant. Noise is a bit of a problem, given the proximity of Hwy. 40 and the 75 trains that run daily through town. Further, since tent sites are simply RV sites that "for one reason or another" are unusable for RVs, tenters would be advised to push on to the Ponderosa Forest campground in Parks. However, RV campers don't have it nearly so bad, and there are some impressive views of Arizona's highest mountain (Humphreys Peak) from inside the park. One RVer who had stayed several nights rated the park an 8 out of 10, and the park is a reasonable, family-oriented destination.

Basics

Operated By: Helen Kelley. **Open:** All year. **Site Assignment:** Assigned at regsitration. **Registration:** At antique store; after hours, enclose fee in envelope & slip into slot in door. **Fee:** $15–$20. **Parking:** At site.

Facilities

Number of RV Sites: 174. **Number of Tent-Only Sites:** 15. **Hookups:** Water, sewer, electric (50 amps; will provide converter for 30 amp vehicles). **Each Site:** Picnic table, trees. **Dump Station:** Yes. **Laundry:** Yes. **Pay Phone:** Yes. **Rest Rooms and Showers:** Yes. **Fuel:** No. **Propane:** No. **Internal Roads:** Paved but potholed. **RV Service:** No. **Market:** Yes. **Restaurant:** Yes. **General Store:** Yes. **Vending:** Yes. **Swimming:** No. **Playground:** No. **Other:** Nightly musical revue (singing waiters/waitresses) from 5:30 to close, antique store. **Activities:** Skiing, biking, hiking. **Nearby Attractions:** Coconino National Forest, Lowell Observatory, Arizona Snowbowl, volcanic crater hikes, Humphreys Peak, several museums in town. **Additional Information:** Flagstaff Visitors Bureau, (800) 842-7293.

Restrictions

Pets: On leash. **Fires:** No open fires, in summer, "prefer" no open grills due to fire hazard. **Alcoholic Beverages:** At sites only. **Vehicle Maximum Length:** None. **Other:** "Cattle rustling is punishable by hanging."

To Get There

On Hwy. 40, take Exit 198 and take a quick left into the park entrance.

FLORENCE

Rancho Sonora Inn & RV Park

9160 Hwy. 79, Florence 85232. T: (520) 868-8000 or (800) 205-6817; F: (520) 868-8000; www.c2i2.com/~rancho/index.htm; rancho@c2i2.com.

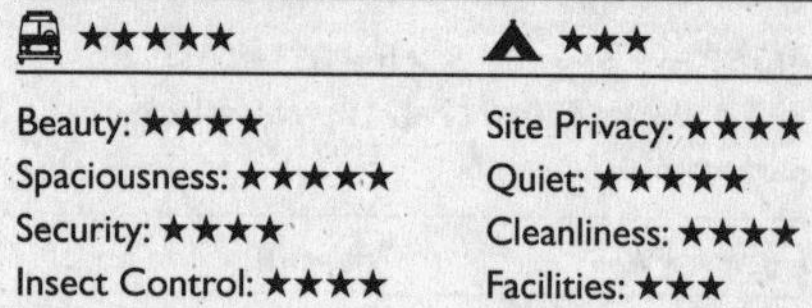

RV ★★★★★ Tent ★★★

Beauty: ★★★★	Site Privacy: ★★★★
Spaciousness: ★★★★★	Quiet: ★★★★★
Security: ★★★★	Cleanliness: ★★★★
Insect Control: ★★★★	Facilities: ★★★

An extremely attractive campground studded with saguaro cacti, Rancho Sonora fills with snowbirds every winter. Halfway between Tucson and Phoenix (60 miles), this extremely well-run family operation has an attractive pool area with relaxing desert views that attract visitors from as far away as Alaska. The surprising beauty found here makes it a welcome haven and escape for those visiting the neighboring state facility, as well as for those using Rancho Sonora as a tourism base to explore surrounding areas. Florence has a good Mexican restaurant and old street façades that show up in Hollywood movies and TV shows. Nearby Coolidge has major chain stores for stocking up on sundries. The extended host family is very welcoming, and does its best to help guests enjoy their stay to the maximum.

Basics

Operated By: Brent & Linda Freeman. **Open:** All year. **Site Assignment:** Reservations needed mid-Oct. to end of Mar. (45-day cancellation, or 1 month's charge applicable to following year's space rental; $35 cancellation fee). **Registration:** Office. **Fee:** $18 tent, $22 RV (V, MC, AE). **Parking:** At site.

Facilities

Number of RV Sites: 62. **Number of Tent-Only Sites:** 4. **Hookups:** Electric (20, 30, 50 amp), water, sewer, phone (modem). **Each Site:** Table, cement pad. **Dump Station:** Yes. **Laundry:** Yes. **Pay

Phone: Yes. **Rest Rooms and Showers:** Yes. **Fuel:** No. **Propane:** Yes. **Internal Roads:** Gravel, excellent. **RV Service:** No. **Market:** Florence, 5 mi. **Restaurant:** Florence, 5 mi. **General Store:** No. **Vending:** Yes. **Swimming:** Pool. **Playground:** No. **Other:** Putting green, whirlpool, horseshoes, BBQ, kitchen, clubhouse, pet walk, fax service, Friday night bonfire. **Activities:** Golf. **Nearby Attractions:** Casa Grande Ruins, McFarland Historical State Park, museums. **Additional Information:** Pinal County Visitor Center, (520) 868-9433.

Restrictions

Pets: On leash (not allowed in clubhouse). **Fires:** No (clubhouse fire pit only). **Alcoholic Beverages:** "Drink all you want." **Vehicle Maximum Length:** None (40 ft. width). **Other:** Children must be supervised at all times.

To Get There

Go 5 mi. south of Florence on AZ Hwy. 79.

FOUNTAIN HILLS

McDowell Mountain Regional Park

P.O. Box 18415, Fountain Hills 85269. T: (602) 506-2930; F: (602) 506-4692; www.maricopa.gov/recsev; McDowellMountainPark@mail.maricopa.gov.

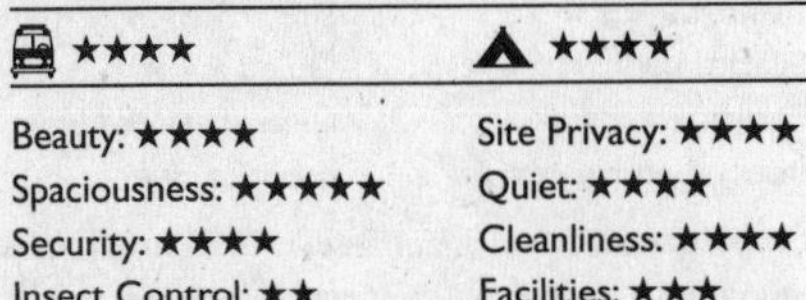

Beauty: ★★★★ Site Privacy: ★★★★
Spaciousness: ★★★★★ Quiet: ★★★★
Security: ★★★★ Cleanliness: ★★★★
Insect Control: ★★ Facilities: ★★★

One of the excellent Maricopa County Parks ringing the Phoenix area, McDowell Mountain attracts many groups, individuals using the Mayo Clinic in Fountain Hills, and mountain bikers coming to race on the competitive track. With over 100 picnic tables and grills, this is also a popular day-use park, featuring 50 miles of mountain biking and horsback riding trails traversing several ecosystems with six different rattlesnake species. Even though surrounded by the Superstition, McDowell, and Four Peaks Mountains, the park is conveniently located near urban areas. An Native American casino is nearby, downtown Phoenix is just 20 miles away, and Scottsdale is within six miles for those wanting to shop and enjoy the urban amenities. The campsites at McDowell's E. I. Rowland Campground are very large and far apart. Barriers of tall desert plants like saguaro, ocotillo, and palo verde between the campsites make the privacy even more absolute.

Basics

Operated By: Maricopa County Parks & Recreation. **Open:** All year. **Site Assignment:** First come, first served; group reservations. **Registration:** Self-pay fee station. **Fee:** $15. **Parking:** At site.

Facilities

Number of RV Sites: 80. **Number of Tent-Only Sites:** 0. **Hookups:** Electric (20, 30 amp), water. **Each Site:** Table, grill, fire ring. **Dump Station:** Yes. **Laundry:** No. **Pay Phone:** Yes. **Rest Rooms and Showers:** Yes. **Fuel:** No. **Propane:** No. **Internal Roads:** Gravel, good. **RV Service:** No. **Market:** Fountain Hills, 5 mi. **Restaurant:** Fountain Hills, 5 mi. **General Store:** No. **Vending:** Yes. **Swimming:** No. **Playground:** Yes. **Other:** Competitive bike track. **Activities:** Horseback riding, biking. **Nearby Attractions:** Phoenix, Scottsdale, Rio Verde. **Additional Information:** McDowell Park Assoc., (602) 837-3026; Fountain Hills Chamber of Commerce, (480) 837-1654, www.fhchamberofcommerce.org.

Restrictions

Pets: On leash under owner's control. **Fires:** Yes. **Alcoholic Beverages:** Allowed. **Vehicle Maximum Length:** None. **Other:** No glass bottles.

To Get There

From Fountain Hills go 4 mi. north on Fountain Hills Blvd. to N. McDowell Mountain Rd.

GILA BEND

Painted Rock Petroglyph Site & Campground

2015 West Deer Valley Rd., Phoenix 85027. T: (602) 580-5500 or (602) 780-8090; F: (602) 581-9535.

RV ★★ Tent ★★★★

Beauty: ★★★★ Site Privacy: ★★★★★
Spaciousness: ★★★★★ Quiet: ★★★★★
Security: ★★★★ Cleanliness: ★★★★
Insect Control: ★★★ Facilities: ★

Near Painted Rocks Dam and Reservoir, Painted Rock Petroglyph Site & Campground is a place for self-sufficient campers carrying their own water and firewood. It also makes a good picnic lunch stop when approaching or leaving Organ Pipe Cactus National Monument via I-8. The drive to the campground has lots of dips and flood warning signs as sculpted hills and grain and alfalfa fields teeming with birds give way to desert scrub. The one-acre rock outcropping behind the covered tables chained to the ground in the eating area is densely covered with petroglyphs depicting spirals and animals as varied as deer, lizards, snakes, coyotes, and birds. During the hot summer months of May to Oct., the campground is rarely used, and there is no fee. The only noise most nights is that of howling coyotes, though there are three huge group areas that have the potential to cause noise disturbance.

Basics

Operated By: Bureau of Land Management. **Open:** All year. **Site Assignment:** First come, first served. **Registration:** Self-pay fee station. **Fee:** $4 (no fee May 1–Sept. 30; cash or check only). **Parking:** At site.

Facilities

Number of RV Sites: 40. **Number of Tent-Only Sites:** 0. **Hookups:** None. **Each Site:** Metal table, grill. **Dump Station:** No. **Laundry:** No. **Pay Phone:** No. **Rest Rooms and Showers:** No showers. **Fuel:** No. **Propane:** No. **Internal Roads:** Gravel, good. **RV Service:** No. **Market:** Gila Bend, 30 mi. **Restaurant:** Gila Bend, 30 mi. **General Store:** No. **Vending:** No. **Swimming:** No. **Playground:** No. **Other:** Picnic & group area. **Activities:** Looking at petroglyphs. **Nearby Attractions:** Organ Pipe Cactus National Monument. **Additional Information:** Gila Bend Tourist Information Center, (520) 683-7395.

Restrictions

Pets: On leash under owner's control (not allowed on petroglyph rocks). **Fires:** Yes. **Alcoholic Beverages:** Allowed. **Vehicle Maximum Length:** None. **Other:** No climbing, walking on, rubbing, or defacing petroglyph rocks.

To Get There

From Gila Bend go 16 mi. west on I-8 to Exit 102, then go 15 mi. north on Painted Rocks Dam Rd. to intersection w/ Rocky Point Rd.

GOODYEAR

Estrella Mountain Regional Park

14805 West Vineyard Ave., Goodyear 85338. T: (623) 932-3811; F: (623) 932-7718; www.maricopa.gov/recsev.

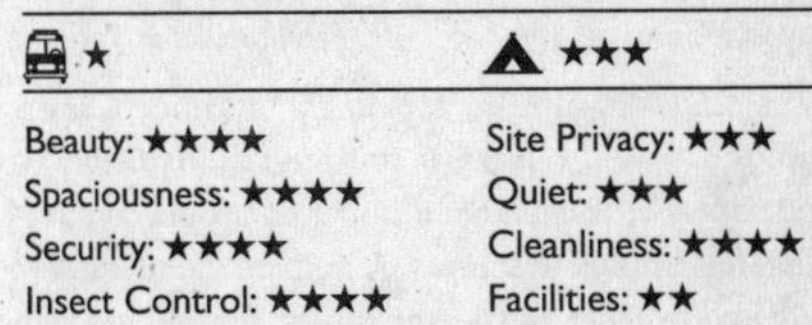

Beauty: ★★★★ Site Privacy: ★★★
Spaciousness: ★★★★ Quiet: ★★★
Security: ★★★★ Cleanliness: ★★★★
Insect Control: ★★★★ Facilities: ★★

One of the Phoenix area's six little-known Maricopa County parks, Estrella is scenically situated 18 miles southwest of Phoenix in 19,200 acres of mountainous terrain with horse and hiking trails. Weekends during the school year, Estrella is crowded with scout and school groups, many camping in the deep mesquite shade of the Navy Area and using the park's many playgrounds. Weekdays and school vacations, with the exception of special events like dog shows and medieval pageants, Estrella is relatively empty. The six sites with RV hookups are near the amphitheater and stable area. Tent campers can camp almost anywhere on acres of flat grass, in the open or among shady mesquite groves. The mesquite tree shade can cool the area underneath by ten degrees, enough to make summer camping bearable.

Basics

Operated By: Maricopa County Parks & Recreation Dept. **Open:** All year. **Site Assignment:** First come, first served; reservations required for group area. **Registration:** Entrance kiosk. **Fee:** $8–$15 (V, MC). **Parking:** At site.

Facilities

Number of RV Sites: 6. **Number of Tent-Only Sites:** 100. **Hookups:** Electric (30 amp), water, sewer. **Each Site:** Table, grill. **Dump Station:** No. **Laundry:** No. **Pay Phone:** Yes. **Rest Rooms and Showers:** No showers. **Fuel:** No. **Propane:** No. **Internal Roads:** Paved, in good condition. **RV Service:** No. **Market:** Litchfield Park, 6 mi. **Restaurant:** Litchfield Park, 6 mi. **General Store:** No. **Vending:** Yes. **Swimming:** No. **Playground:** Yes. **Other:** Amphitheater, horse, rodeo, & picnic areas, softball field, sheltered tables. **Activities:** Golf, horseback riding, archery. **Nearby Attractions:** Phoenix International Raceway, museums. **Additional Information:** Maricopa County Parks, (602) 506-2930.

RESTRICTIONS

Pets: On leash under owner's control (leash laws strictly enforced). **Fires:** Yes (grills only). **Alcoholic Beverages:** Beer in cans or kegs; no glass bottles or hard liquor. **Vehicle Maximum Length:** 20 ft.

TO GET THERE

From I-10 east of Phoenix, go south on Estrella Pkwy. (Exit 126) 5 mi. to W. Vineyard Rd.

GRAND CANYON

Mather Campground

P.O. Box 129, Grand Canyon 86023. T: Reservations, (800) 365-CAMP or Ranger, (520) 638-7953.

RV ★★★★ Tent ★★★★

Beauty: ★★★★ Site Privacy: ★★★
Spaciousness: ★★★★ Quiet: ★★
Security: ★★ Cleanliness: ★★★★
Insect Control: ★★ Facilities: ★★

One can imagine by looking at Mather Campground how the Anasazi slowly ground their way out of existence: a large number of people competing for limited resources. Campers are definitely advised to arrive early—the earlier, the better. Large numbers of people want to camp within the Grand Canyon's boundaries, and with hikers taking advantage of the maximum stay of seven nights, numerous campsites will already be taken when you arrive. By 4 p.m., it is a scramble to pick up any spot, which, naturally, leaves the slimmest picking for the late arrivals. Sites to avoid (if possible) are those closest to the restrooms, as the lights remain on all night and the doors slam with a thud that can raise the dead. In addition, try to avoid sites close to the busy roads (such as sites 53 and 54 on the Aspen Loop or 318 and 319 on the Pine Loop), with foot and car traffic that will annoy all but the soundest sleepers. Having said that, this is the Grand Canyon after all, and perhaps the greatest natural wonder of the world is only a few minutes' drive away. Further, the campground offers an extremely rugged and wild flavor. If you can abide the few annoyances inherent in a campground of this size, it is definitely worth the stay.

BASICS

Operated By: Spherics. **Open:** All year. **Site Assignment:** Reservations recommended (Apr. 1–Nov. 30); first come, first served (Dec. 1–Mar. 31). **Registration:** At kiosk at entrance. **Fee:** $15 (Apr. 1–Nov. 30); $10 (Dec. 1–Mar. 31); half price for Golden Age/Access cardholders. Cash only. **Parking:** At site.

FACILITIES

Number of RV Sites: 312. **Number of Tent-Only Sites:** 0. **Hookups:** None. **Each Site:** Picnic table, grill. **Dump Station:** Yes. **Laundry:** Yes. **Pay Phone:** Yes. **Rest Rooms and Showers:** Yes. **Fuel:** 0.5 mi. away in Market Plaza. **Propane:** No. **Internal Roads:** Paved. **RV Service:** No. **Market:** 0.5 mi. away in Market Plaza. **Restaurant:** 0.5 mi. away in Market Plaza. **General Store:** No. **Vending:** No. **Swimming:** No. **Playground:** No. **Activities:** Hiking, helicopter, plane & horseback rides through the Grand Canyon. **Nearby Attractions:** Grand Canyon National Park. **Additional Information:** North Rim park info: (520) 638-7864, South Rim park info: (520) 638-7888 or (520) 638-7770.

RESTRICTIONS

Pets: On leash, in campground only. **Fires:** Charcoal or wood in grills only. **Alcoholic Beverages:** At sites only. **Vehicle Maximum Length:** 50 ft. **Other:** 7-day stay limit; max. of 6 people or 1 family per site.

TO GET THERE

From the Grand Canyon South Entrance, take Hwy. 64 North for 2.6 mi., then turn left at the traffic light. Continue for.4 mi. and turn right onto Market Plaza Rd. Drive.9 mi., then turn right into the entrance at the sign for the campground.

GRAND CANYON

Trailer Village

1 Main St., P.O. Box 699, Grand Canyon 86023. T: (303) 29-PARKS; F: (303) 297-3175; www.amfac.com; reservations@amfac.com.

RV ★★★ Tent ★

Beauty: ★★ Site Privacy: ★★★
Spaciousness: ★★ Quiet: ★★★
Security: ★★ Cleanliness: ★★★★★
Insect Control: ★★★ Facilities: ★★★★

Imagine a department store parking lot during a Christmas tree liquidation sale. That pretty much sums up the asthetics of Trailer Village. Most lots are divided by low shrubs, and the lucky few contain trees, while some have no vegetation at all. However, as nearby Mather Campground does not offer RV hookups, those who want fuller service should consider Trailer Village—especially as there are no other full-service RV parks on the South Rim. (Some services, such as showers and laundry are shared between Mather and Trailer Village.) Arranged as a grid, the campground offers 50-foot pull-through sites spaced a scant 20 feet apart. Although tents are permitted, the mere thought of camping here in a tent seems ridiculous—unless the campgrounds are all full and you've got to stay in the Grand Canyon. Not nearly as sylvan as Mather Campground, Trailer Village is recommended to travelers who desire a less primitive experience than the campground, and don't mind taking in the sight of equal parts RV and forest while at home base.

BASICS

Operated By: AmFac Parks & Resorts. **Open:** All year. **Site Assignment:** Assigned at registration. **Registration:** At kiosk. **Fee:** $20 for 2 adults, $1.75 extra per additional adult (no Golden Access discount). **Parking:** At site & parking lot.

FACILITIES

Number of RV Sites: 84. **Number of Tent-Only Sites:** 0. **Hookups:** Water, sewer, electric (30 amps). **Each Site:** Picnic table, grill. **Dump Station:** Yes. **Laundry:** Yes (at Mather Campground). **Pay Phone:** Yes. **Rest Rooms and Showers:** Rest room on-site, showers at Mather Campground. **Fuel:** No. **Propane:** No. **Internal Roads:** Paved. **RV Service:** No. **Market:** 0.5 mi. away in Market Plaza. **Restaurant:** 0.5 mi. away in Market Plaza. **General Store:** No. **Vending:** Yes. **Swimming:** No. **Playground:** No. **Other:** Kennel for pets. **Activities:** Hiking, helicopter, plane, & horseback rides through the Grand Canyon. **Nearby Attractions:** Grand Canyon National Park. **Additional Information:** www.amfac.com.

RESTRICTIONS

Pets: On leash. **Fires:** Charcoal only in grills. **Alcoholic Beverages:** At sites only. **Vehicle Maximum Length:** 50 ft.

TO GET THERE

From the Grand Canyon South Entrance, take Hwy. 64 north for 2.6 mi., then turn left at the traffic light. Continue for 0.4 mi. and turn right onto Market Plaza Rd. Drive 1 mi., turn right at the sign for Trailer Village, and follow the road 0.2 mi. to the entrance.

HOLBROOK

Cholla Lake County Park

Navajo County Parks & Recreation Dept., Holbrook 86025. T: (520) 524-4251 or (520) 288-3717; www.parksrec@navajo.az.us; parksrec@navajo.az.us.

RV ★★★ Tent ★★★

Beauty: ★★★★ Site Privacy: ★★★★
Spaciousness: ★★★★ Quiet: ★★★★
Security: ★★★★ Cleanliness: ★★★★
Insect Control: ★★★ Facilities: ★★

Situated around a manmade cattail-ringed lake whose waters cool and generate electricity at the four adjacent coal-burning Cholla Power Plant units, rustic Cholla Lake County Park provides travelers on I-40 between Flagstaff and Gallup, New Mexico, with a convenient overnight stop or a base for exploring the Petrified Forest, Painted Desert, Mogollon Rim, and nearby Hopi and Navajo Indian Reservations. The lake, one of the largest in northeastern Arizona, can be used for boating and water sports or fished for large mouth bass, sunfish, and catfish. For some campers, the power pylons, tall cement smokestacks, and piles of coal waiting to be pulverized will seem a visual blight. Others may enjoy the educational displays explaining how scrubbers remove sulfur dioxides and particulates.

BASICS

Operated By: Navajo County Parks & Recreation Dept. **Open:** All year. **Site Assignment:** First come, first served; reservations available by email. **Registration:** Self-pay fee station. **Fee:** $8–$14 (cash or check only). **Parking:** At site.

FACILITIES

Number of RV Sites: 25. **Number of Tent-Only Sites:** 0. **Hookups:** Electric (30 amp), water. **Each Site:** Table, grill. **Dump Station:** Yes. **Laundry:** No. **Pay Phone:** Yes. **Rest Rooms and Showers:** Yes. **Fuel:** No. **Propane:** No. **Internal Roads:** Gravel, good condition. **RV Service:** No. **Market:** Holbrook, 8 mi. **Restaurant:** Holbrook, 8 mi. **General Store:** No. **Vending:** No. **Swimming:** Lake. **Playground:** Yes. **Other:** Group pavilion, water ski course, jet ski landing, fishing dock, horseshoe pits, sand volleyball court. **Activi-**

ties: Fishing, boating, bird-watching. **Nearby Attractions:** Navajo Indian Reservation, Petrified Forest, Painted Desert, Homolovi Ruins, Mongollon Rim, White Mountains. **Additional Information:** Holbrook Chamber of Commerce, (800) 524-2459.

RESTRICTIONS

Pets: On leash, crated or caged (not allowed on swimming beach or in structures). **Fires:** Yes (in grills only). **Alcoholic Beverages:** Allowed. **Vehicle Maximum Length:** 35 ft. **Other:** No glass bottles, boaters must observe no wake zone.

TO GET THERE

From Holbrook go 8 mi. west on I-40 to Exit 277 (Joseph City), then south onto park access road for 2 mi.

HOLBROOK

Holbrook/Petrified Forest KOA

102 Hermosa Dr., Holbrook 86025. T: (520) 524-6689 or (800) 562-3389; www.koa.com.

RV ★★★ Tent ★★

Beauty: ★★★ Site Privacy: ★★
Spaciousness: ★★ Quiet: ★★★★
Security: ★★★★ Cleanliness: ★★★★★
Insect Control: ★★★★★ Facilities: ★★★

Flanked at the entrance by a 200-million-year-old petrified log, the Holbrook/Petrified Forest KOA has more than enough amenities for families and is an excellent location for exploring the area's geologic (Petrified Forest, Painted Desert), kitsch (teepee motel, Rte. 66), and Native American (Hopi and Navajo Indian Reservations) sights. Trees line the perimeter and a small cafe serves up pancake breakfasts and cowboy-style barbecue dinners during the peak tourist season. Fortunately, the campground is far enough from the interstate highway that truck noise is not a major problem. Though RVs are sometimes parked seemingly close enough to touch, the campground is usually relatively quiet. Pull-through sites 1–20 have cable TV ($2 extra), and sites 10, 20, 40, 50, 92, and 102 are 50 amp. Tent campers have grass sites, and pet owners are warned to keep their animals off the grass and on the pet walks.

BASICS

Operated By: KOA. **Open:** All year. **Site Assignment:** First come, first served. **Registration:** Office. **Fee:** $18–$28 (V, MC, D). **Parking:** At site.

FACILITIES

Number of RV Sites: 109. **Number of Tent-Only Sites:** 20. **Hookups:** Electric (20, 30, 50 amp), water, sewer, cable TV, phone (modem). **Each Site:** Table, grill. **Dump Station:** Yes. **Laundry:** Yes. **Pay Phone:** Yes. **Rest Rooms and Showers:** Yes. **Fuel:** No. **Propane:** Yes. **Internal Roads:** Gravel, good. **RV Service:** No. **Market:** Holbrook, 1 mi. **Restaurant:** Holbrook, 1 mi. (small cafe on premises). **General Store:** Yes. **Vending:** Yes. **Swimming:** Pool. **Playground:** Yes. **Other:** Game room, mini-golf, pet walk, mail pickup, seasonal cowboy barbecues, cabins. **Activities:** Volleyball, basketball, tetherball, horseshoes. **Nearby Attractions:** Petrified Forest, Painted Desert, Canyon de Chelly, Second Mesa. **Additional Information:** Holbrook Chamber of Commerce, (800) 524-2459; Petrified Forest National Park, (520) 524-6228, www.nps.gov/pefo.

RESTRICTIONS

Pets: On leash & under owner's control. **Fires:** In grills only; no open fires). **Alcoholic Beverages:** Allowed. **Vehicle Maximum Length:** 50 ft. **Other:** No fireworks; tents must be removed from grass during day for watering & mowing; children & teenagers must be under parental supervision at night.

TO GET THERE

From I-40 Exit 289 to 1.5 mi. south on Navajo Blvd.

HUACHUCA CITY

Circle "S" RV Park

2224 Graham Cir., Huachuca City 85616. T: (520) 456-9801; F: (520) 456-9847; jerryrv@C212.com.

RV ★★★★ Tent ★★★★

Beauty: ★★★★ Site Privacy: ★★★★
Spaciousness: ★★★★ Quiet: ★★★★
Security: ★★★★ Cleanliness: ★★★★
Insect Control: ★★★★ Facilities: ★★★★

A hardworking couple formerly in the lodging business in Florida have taken over what was formerly a combination mobile home and RV park. Jerry and Glenna Scott have been adding tent and RV sites to Circle "S," along with putting in new power, sewer, and water lines. Not to be outdone in amenities, they are also bringing in natural gas, cable TV, and phones. In contrast to the parking lot lights so common to RV parks, new light poles balancing five round bulb fixtures attractively light this campground. Large old shade trees add an attractive rural ambiance. Except for military retirees in Sierra Vista taking advantage of Fort Huachuca and bird watchers passing through to catch the Upper San Pedro River Valley migrations, few know this area. But this is a good base for exploring southeast Arizona.

BASICS

Operated By: Jerry & Glenna Scott. **Open:** All year. **Site Assignment:** First come, first served. **Registration:** Self-pay entrance fee station. **Fee:** $5 tents, $15–$18 RV. **Parking:** At site.

FACILITIES

Number of RV Sites: 25. **Number of Tent-Only Sites:** 7. **Hookups:** Electric (20, 30, 50 amp), water, sewer, cable TV, phone, natural gas. **Each Site:** Table, fireplace, cement patio. **Dump Station:** Yes. **Laundry:** Yes. **Pay Phone:** No. **Rest Rooms and Showers:** Yes. **Fuel:** No. **Propane:** No. **Internal Roads:** Gravel, good. **RV Service:** No. **Market:** Sierra Vista, 10 mi. **Restaurant:** Sierra Vista, 10 mi. **General Store:** Yes. **Vending:** No. **Swimming:** No. **Playground:** No. **Other:** Free fax & email. **Activities:** Horseback riding, bird-watching. **Nearby Attractions:** Fort Huachuca, Tombstone, Bisbee, Kartchner Caverns, San Pedro Riparian National Conservation Area. **Additional Information:** Sierra Vista Vistor Center, (800) 288-3861, www.visitsierravista.com.

RESTRICTIONS

Pets: Yes ("everybody has pets"). **Fires:** Yes. **Alcoholic Beverages:** Allowed. **Vehicle Maximum Length:** 70 ft.

TO GET THERE

1 mi. east of junction of AZ Hwys. 90 & 82.

JACOB LAKE

Jacob Lake Campground

Jacob Lake Inn, Jacob Lake 86022. T: (520) 643-7395; (520) 203-4334 (group reservations).

RV ★★★★ Tent ★★★★

Beauty: ★★★★ Site Privacy: ★★★★★
Spaciousness: ★★★★★ Quiet: ★★★★★
Security: ★★★★ Cleanliness: ★★★★
Insect Control: ★★★ Facilities: ★★★★

It's camping at its best along five secluded loops in the pine forest at 7,900 feet, just an hour's drive (40 miles south via a slow, windy road) from the forested North Rim of the Grand Canyon. Widely dispersed pull-through sites provide plenty of forested privacy, yet Jacob Lake Campground is within one-quarter mile of a 24-hour gas station, general store, counter cafe, restaurant, ranger-staffed Visitor Center and motel. However, water is scarce and available only by the bucketful. In contrast to the North Rim Campground (see Appendix), which books up over a month in advance with reservations, the key to getting a spot here is a very early afternoon arrival, as Jacob Lake Campground fills up just after 4 p.m. most June, July, and Aug. afternoons. Campers wanting hookups should head to nearby Kaibab Camper Village. For a more primitive experience at a smaller campground (23 sites; 30 foot maximum) run by the same concessionaire, head south on US Hwy. 89A towards the North Rim another 23 miles to De Motte Campground (see Appendix).

BASICS

Operated By: US Forest Service/Resource Recreation Management (concessionaire). **Open:** May 15–Nov. 1. **Site Assignment:** First come, first served; group site reservations. **Registration:** Select a site, hosts collect fee later. **Fee:** $12 (cash). **Parking:** Paved loop in front of site.

FACILITIES

Number of RV Sites: 54. **Number of Tent-Only Sites:** 0. **Hookups:** None. **Each Site:** Table, fire ring. **Dump Station:** Yes. **Laundry:** No. **Pay Phone:** Yes. **Rest Rooms and Showers:** Yes. **Fuel:** No. **Propane:** No. **Internal Roads:** Paved, bumpy in spots. **RV Service:** No. **Market:** 0.3 mi. south, near Visitor Center. **Restaurant:** 0.3 mi. south, near Visitor Center. **General Store:** No. **Vending:** No. **Swimming:** No. **Playground:** No. **Activities:** Evening ranger programs, mule deer watching. **Nearby Attractions:** North Rim of Grand Canyon, Pipe Springs National Monument, Kanab, Lees Ferry. **Additional Information:** Kaibab Plateau Visitor Center, (520) 643-7298; North Kaibab Ranger District, (520) 643-7395.

RESTRICTIONS

Pets: On 6 ft leash under owner's control. **Fires:** Yes (firewood sold). **Alcoholic Beverages:**

Allowed. **Vehicle Maximum Length:** 30 ft. **Other:** 14-day stay limit; wheelchair accessible site; no fireworks.

To Get There

From junction of US 89A and AZ 67, drive 0.3 mi. north on US 89A.

JACOB LAKE

Kaibab Camper Village

P.O. Box 3331, Flagstaff 86003. T: (520) 643-7804 (May 15–Oct. 15) or (800) 525-0924 (Oct. 15–May 15, outside AZ) or (520) 526-0924 (Oct. 15–May 15, inside AZ); F: (520) 527-9398; www.canyoneers.com; answers@canyoneers.com.

RV ★★★★ Tent ★★★★

Beauty: ★★★★ Site Privacy: ★★★★
Spaciousness: ★★★★ Quiet: ★★★★
Security: ★★★★ Cleanliness: ★★★★
Insect Control: ★★★ Facilities: ★★★

Tall pines, grassy meadows with picnic tables, the closest hookups to the Grand Canyon's North Rim, and wide pull-through sites make Kaibab Camper Village a top choice for quiet relaxation and North Rim excursions. Management goes to great lengths to keep the campground quiet, even banning electrical generators. Tent campers will appreciate the grassy sites separate from the RV loop. Although it feels isolated in a tall pine forest surrounded by horse pastures and tall mountain backdrops, the campground is only one mile (half via a dusty but extra wide gravel road) from a 24-hour gas station anchoring the US Forest Service's helpful Kaibab Plateau Visitor Center, a motel, an old-fashioned counter cafe, a sit-down restaurant decorated with Native American rugs, and a general store loaded with curios. All in all, it is hard to go wrong with this combination of wilderness and comforts.

Basics

Operated By: Canyoneers (Flagstaff, AZ). **Open:** May 15–Oct. 15. **Site Assignment:** First come, first served; reservations accepted (nonrefundable prepayment of first night). **Registration:** Entrance station office. **Fee:** $12 (tents, dry sites); $22 (hookups); cash, traveler's checks, personal checks w/ 2 valid IDs. **Parking:** At site.

Facilities

Number of RV Sites: 67. **Number of Tent-Only Sites:** 50. **Hookups:** Electric (20, 30 amp), water, sewer. **Each Site:** Table, fire ring. **Dump Station:** Yes. **Laundry:** No. **Pay Phone:** Yes. **Rest Rooms and Showers:** Yes. **Fuel:** No. **Propane:** No. **Internal Roads:** Gravel, good but dusty. **RV Service:** No. **Market:** 1 mi., near Visitor Center. **Restaurant:** 1 mi., near Visitor Center. **General Store:** No. **Vending:** No. **Swimming:** No. **Playground:** No. **Other:** Modem hookup at office; 30-ft.-wide pull-throughs; noon check-out. **Activities:** Horseback riding. **Nearby Attractions:** Grand Canyon North Rim (40 mi.), Bryce (115 mi.). **Additional Information:** Kaibab Plateau Visitor Center, (520) 643-7298; North Kaibab Ranger District, (520) 643-7395.

Restrictions

Pets: On 10 ft. leash & kept quiet at all times; designated dog walking area. **Fires:** Yes (only in metal firepits, firewood sold). **Alcoholic Beverages:** Allowed. **Vehicle Maximum Length:** 60 ft. **Other:** Electrical generator use not allowed, no gathering of firewood, water is scarce, & cannot be used for washing people, pets, vehicles, or clothes.

To Get There

From junction of US Hwy. 89A and AZ Hwy. 67, go 0.3 mi. south on Hwy. 67 and then 0.5 mi. west on gravel road.

KINGMAN

Kingman KOA

3820 North Roosevelt, Kingman 86401. T: (520) 757-4397 or (800) 562-3991; www.koa.com; kingkoa@citylink.net.

RV ★★★ Tent ★★★

Beauty: ★★★ Site Privacy: ★★★
Spaciousness: ★★★ Quiet: ★★★★
Security: ★★★★ Cleanliness: ★★★★★
Insect Control: ★★★★ Facilities: ★★★★

Kingman, a stop en route to the Grand Canyon from Las Vegas, had its heyday when local boy Andy Devine was playing Jingles in cowboy movies and Rte. 66 was still the place for getting your "kicks" when driving cross country from Chicago to Los Angeles. Downtown Kingman is just now coming out of a deep boarded-up funk, and the KOA is just about the only campground away from the noise of I-40 with a little space for campers to spread out, short of heading out of town into the Hualapai Mountains. The KOA is a little oasis with oleanders and trees between the campsites, a pleasant ambiance, free morning coffee, 50 TV channels, and newspaper machines. Tent campers have their own area, and a policy of not running generators ensures quiet.

Basics

Operated By: KOA. **Open:** All year. **Site Assignment:** First come, first served; reservations accepted. **Registration:** Office. **Fee:** $17–$24 (V, MC, AE, D). **Parking:** At site.

Facilities

Number of RV Sites: 78. **Number of Tent-Only Sites:** 12. **Hookups:** Electric (30, 50 amp), water, sewer, cable TV, phone (modem). **Each Site:** Table, grill. **Dump Station:** Yes. **Laundry:** Yes. **Pay Phone:** Yes. **Rest Rooms and Showers:** Yes. **Fuel:** No. **Propane:** Yes. **Internal Roads:** Paved, good. **RV Service:** No. **Market:** Kingman, 1 mi. **Restaurant:** Kingman, 1 mi. **General Store:** Yes. **Vending:** Yes. **Swimming:** Pool. **Playground:** Yes. **Other:** Rec hall w/ kitchen & TV, video game room, mini-golf, cabins. **Activities:** Golf. **Nearby Attractions:** Rte. 66, Laughlin casinos, Colorado River recreation. **Additional Information:** Kingman Chamber of Commerce, (520) 753-6106, www.kingmanchamber.org; Powerhouse Visitor Center, www.arizonaguide.com/visitkingman.

Restrictions

Pets: On leash & under owner's control. **Fires:** Yes (only in approved grills). **Alcoholic Beverages:** Allowed. **Vehicle Maximum Length:** None. **Other:** No running of generators.

To Get There

From I-40 Exits 51 & 53 take Stockton Hill Rd. or Andy Devine to intersection of Airway and Roosevelt.

LAKE HAVASU CITY

Islander RV Resort

751 Beachcomber Blvd., Lake Havasu City 86403. T: (520) 680-2000; F: (520) 855-1261; www.islanderrv.com.

RV ★★★★ Tent n/a

Beauty: ★★★★ Site Privacy: ★★★
Spaciousness: ★★★★ Quiet: ★★★★
Security: ★★★★★ Cleanliness: ★★★★★
Insect Control: ★★★★ Facilities: ★★★

On the shores of Lake Havasu, Islander boasts ample amenities, including two swimming pools, boat docks, fish cleaning stations, and winter activities for snowbirds. Premium and waterfront sites have the best lake views, but inland sites have tall eucalyptus trees and some decent mountain views. Unlike Beachcomber Resort (see Appendix) down the road, which rents empty mobile home spots to RVs, Islander terminates the rental agreement of anyone showing signs of residency like enrolling kids in local schools or taking a job in town. The typical 36-foot wide space has a patio pad and enough space for parking a tow vehicle and boat. Those who like it quiet will appreciate that the park is far from noisy highways, though only a short jaunt from the London Bridge, whose 10,276 granite stones were reassembled in this planned desert city by developer Robert McCulloch.

Basics

Operated By: Islander RV Resort. **Open:** All year. **Site Assignment:** First come, first served; reservations do not guarantee specific sites. **Registration:** Office. **Fee:** $30–$42 (waterfront sites most expensive; V, MC). **Parking:** At site.

Facilities

Number of RV Sites: 500. **Number of Tent-Only Sites:** 0. **Hookups:** Electric (30, 50 amp), water, sewer. **Each Site:** Patio pad, table, fire ring. **Dump Station:** Yes. **Laundry:** Yes. **Pay Phone:** Yes. **Rest Rooms and Showers:** Yes. **Fuel:** No. **Propane:** Yes. **Internal Roads:** Paved, excellent. **RV Service:** No. **Market:** Lake Havasu City, 1 mi. **Restaurant:** Lake Havasu City, 1 mi. **General Store:** Yes. **Vending:** Yes. **Swimming:** Lake, 2 pools. **Playground:** Yes. **Other:** Rec hall, billiards, shuffleboard & horseshoe areas, boat docks & launch ramp, fish cleaning station. **Activities:** Biking, golf, fishing, boating, volleyball. **Nearby Attractions:** London Bridge, Havasu National Wildlife Refuge. **Additional Information:** Lake Havasu Tourism Bureau, (520) 453-3444, (800) 242-8278.

Restrictions

Pets: Allowed (subject to separate signed agreement; aggressive breeds like pit bulls not allowed). **Fires:** In fire ring. **Alcoholic Beverages:** Excessive use prohibited. **Vehicle Maximum Length:** 50 ft. **Other:** RVIA approved self-contained RVs only; no clotheslines, firearms, or fireworks.

To Get There

Get off AZ Hwy. 95 at Mesquite Ave. and go east on Lake Havasu Blvd., south to McCullough Blvd., and west across the London Bridge.

LAKE HAVASU CITY

Lake Havasu State Park (Windsor Beach)

1801 Hwy. 95, Lake Havasu City 86406. T: (520) 855-2784; F: (520) 855-9394; www.pr.state.az.us.

RV ★★★★ Tent ★★★★★

Beauty: ★★★★	Site Privacy: ★★★★★
Spaciousness: ★★★★★	Quiet: ★★★★★
Security: ★★★★	Cleanliness: ★★★★
Insect Control: ★★★	Facilities: ★★

Formed when the Colorado River was dammed near Parker to end the area's annual spring floods and provide water for Arizona and southern California, 45-mile-long Lake Havasu's boating, fishing, and bird-watching recreational possibilities can be accessed at Lake Havasu State Park's Windsor Beach Campground. The large gravel campsites at Windsor Beach combine camping in the desert scrub with a lakeside location. Plus the palo verde, mesquite, and other desert plants are lush enough here to provide each campsite with a barrier of privacy. For those desiring even more of an escape, Lake Havasu State Park also has 55 campsites accessible only by boat. For those wanting to stay closer to urban amenities, Windsor Beach has the added advantage of being only three miles from the London Bridge and Lake Havasu City's restaurants, three microbreweries, movie theaters, nightclubs, and shops.

Basics

Operated By: Arizona State Parks. **Open:** All year. **Site Assignment:** First come, first served. **Registration:** Entrance kiosk. **Fee:** $8–$13 (cash or check only). **Parking:** At site.

Facilities

Number of RV Sites: 73. **Number of Tent-Only Sites:** 55. **Hookups:** None. **Each Site:** Table, grill, fire ring. **Dump Station:** Yes. **Laundry:** No. **Pay Phone:** Yes. **Rest Rooms and Showers:** Yes. **Fuel:** No. **Propane:** No. **Internal Roads:** Paved, good. **RV Service:** No. **Market:** Lake Havasu City, 3 mi. **Restaurant:** Lake Havasu City, 2 mi. **General Store:** No. **Vending:** No. **Swimming:** Lake. **Playground:** Yes. **Other:** Botanical garden, group pavilion. **Activities:** Boating, fishing, water sports, bird-watching, golf. **Nearby Attractions:** London Bridge, Havasu National Wildlife Refuge. **Additional Information:** Lake Havasu Tourism Bureau, (520) 453-3444, (800) 242-8278.

Restrictions

Pets: On leash; water & shade must be provided. **Fires:** Yes (no fires when high winds). **Alcoholic Beverages:** Allowed (state liquor laws strictly enforced). **Vehicle Maximum Length:** None. **Other:** No glass containers on beaches or in day-use areas.

To Get There

From the junction of London Bridge Rd. & AZ Hwy. 95, go 2.5 mi. west on London Bridge Rd.

LAKE HAVASU CITY

Sandpoint Marina and RV Park

P.O. Box 1469, Lake Havasu City 86405. T: (520) 855-0549; F: (520) 855-3008; www.lakehavasucity.com/sandpoint.

RV ★★★ Tent ★★★

Beauty: ★★★	Site Privacy: ★★
Spaciousness: ★★★	Quiet: ★★★★
Security: ★★★★	Cleanliness: ★★★★
Insect Control: ★★★	Facilities: ★★★★★

A swimming beach, a marina with 104 boat slips, and rentals of everything from pontoons and sea doos to fishing boats and houseboats makes Sandpoint Marina a worthwhile destination on the shores of Lake Havasu. Sandpoint Marina is actually within Cattail Cove State Park, and is reached via a fork in the road at the entrance to Cattail Cove Campground (see Appendix), which makes a good alternative for large vehicles and has 40 campsites accessible only by boat. Besides the water action and karaoke in the marina cafe, the London Bridge and Lake Havasu City's three microbreweries are only a short journey away. During the winter, Sandpoint has its own newsletter and a variety of snowbird get-togethers. Monthly fishing tournaments reward the boat catching the largest stripers, catfish, carp, and bass with a trophy and up to $50 in prize money.

Basics

Operated By: Arizona State Parks concession. **Open:** All year. **Site Assignment:** First come, first served. **Registration:** Office. **Fee:** $20–$35 (more for waterfront sites; V, MC). **Parking:** At site.

Facilities

Number of RV Sites: 173. **Number of Tent-Only Sites:** 0. **Hookups:** Electric (30 amp), water, sewer, satellite TV. **Each Site:** Sheltered table, grill. **Dump Station:** Yes. **Laundry:** Yes. **Pay Phone:** Yes. **Rest Rooms and Showers:** Yes. **Fuel:** Yes. **Propane:** Yes. **Internal Roads:** Paved & gravel, good. **RV Service:** No. **Market:** Lake Havasu City, 7 mi. **Restaurant:** On premises. **General Store:** Yes. **Vending:** Yes. **Swimming:** River. **Playground:** Yes. **Other:** Marina, boat rentals, dry storage, horseshoe pits, shuffleboard, rec room. **Activities:** Boating, fishing, water sports. **Nearby Attractions:** London Bridge, Buckskin Mountain State Park, Havasu National Wildlife Refuge. **Additional Information:** Lake Havasu Tourism Bureau, (520) 453-3444, (800) 242-8278.

Restrictions

Pets: On leash at all times (subject to fees; not allowed on swimming beach). **Fires:** In grills only. **Alcoholic Beverages:** Allowed (excessive or underage consumption is grounds for eviction). **Vehicle Maximum Length:** 37 ft. **Other:** No fireworks; no watercraft refueling from portable containers.

To Get There

From Lake Havasu City go 12 mi. south on AZ Hwy. 95 to Cattail Cove State Park.

LUKEVILLE

Organ Pipe Cactus National Monument

Rte. 1 Box 100, Ajo 85321. T: (520) 387-6849; www.nps.gov/orpi.

RV ★★★ Tent ★★★★

Beauty: ★★★★★	Site Privacy: ★★★★★
Spaciousness: ★★★★★	Quiet: ★★★
Security: ★★★★	Cleanliness: ★★★★★
Insect Control: ★★★	Facilities: ★★

Designated an International Biosphere Reserve by the United Nations in 1976, Organ Pipe Cactus National Monument showcases Sonoran Desert plants (28 cactus species) and animals adapted to extremes like summer air temperatures of 118 degrees and ground temperatures of 175 degrees. The Monument's namesake organ pipe cactus copes in part by only opening its lavender-white flowers at night. Campers cope best by coming from Oct. to Apr., when daytime temperatures are in the 60s and 70s. The campground stays open through the torrid summer, when the organ pipe and other cacti colorfully bloom and storms suddenly appear out of nowhere, triggering flash floods. Hardy tent campers can head to more primitive campgrounds, some in cooler mountains with juniper, oak, rosewood, agave, and jojoba. Lukeville has Mexican food, and plenty of hookups are available in Why and Ajo, 22 and 36 miles north, respectively.

Basics

Operated By: National Park Service. **Open:** All year. **Site Assignment:** First come, first served. **Registration:** Visitor Center. **Fee:** $10 ($5 w/ Gold Access; cash only). **Parking:** At site.

Facilities

Number of RV Sites: 208. **Number of Tent-Only Sites:** 0. **Hookups:** None. **Each Site:** Table, grill, cement pad. **Dump Station:** Yes. **Laundry:** No. **Pay Phone:** Yes. **Rest Rooms and Showers:** No showers. **Fuel:** No. **Propane:** No. **Internal Roads:** Gravel, good. **RV Service:** No. **Market:** Lukeville, 5 mi. **Restaurant:** Lukeville, 5 mi. **General Store:** No. **Vending:** Yes. **Swimming:** No. **Playground:** No. **Other:** Amphitheater. **Activities:** Bird-watching. **Nearby Attractions:** Mexico, Ajo, Tohono O'odham Indian Reservation. **Additional Information:** Ajo Chamber of Commerce, (520) 387-7742.

Restrictions

Pets: On leash under owner's control. **Fires:** In grills only. **Alcoholic Beverages:** Allowed. **Vehicle Maximum Length:** 35 ft. **Other:** No wood gathering.

To Get There

From Gila Bend, go 80 mi. south on AZ Hwy. 85.

MARBLE CANYON

Lees Ferry Campground

P.O. Box 1507, Page 86040. T: (520) 355-2234 or (520) 645-2471.

RV ★★★ Tent ★★★★

Beauty: ★★★★ Site Privacy: ★★★★
Spaciousness: ★★★★ Quiet: ★★★★
Security: ★★★★ Cleanliness: ★★★★
Insect Control: ★★★ Facilities: ★★

The surrounding mountains have red, orange, chocolate brown, white, and green bands of sandstone that give the area its name, Marble Canyon. In the 1920s, this was an important area for crossing the Colorado River by ferry, as well as the site of Jerry Johnson's polygamous Mormon colony at Lonely Dell Ranch. Ferry service ended after a deadly accident in 1928, when the historic Navajo Bridge opened. The boat launch near Lees Ferry Campground is still one of the best places to enter the Colorado River where it flows smooth and green beneath both the old and new Navajo Bridges. The National Park Service has an interpretative center at Navajo Bridge, near where the river splits into its upper and lower basins. Only a few camp sites have trees or manmade structures for shade. Noises echo at the campground, but when the neighbors are quiet this is a peaceful spot. Few places are better for river recreation, and it's away from the hubbub of Lake Powell and Page.

BASICS

Operated By: National Park Service. **Open:** All year. **Site Assignment:** First come, first served. **Registration:** Self-pay fee station at entrance. **Fee:** $10 ($5 w/ Golden Age or Golden Access Passport; cash only). **Parking:** At site.

FACILITIES

Number of RV Sites: 50. **Number of Tent-Only Sites:** 0. **Hookups:** None. **Each Site:** Table, fire ring. **Dump Station:** Yes. **Laundry:** No. **Pay Phone:** Yes. **Rest Rooms and Showers:** No showers. **Fuel:** No. **Propane:** No. **Internal Roads:** Paved, good condition. **RV Service:** No. **Market:** 6 mi. southwest at Marble Canyon Lodge. **Restaurant:** 6 mi. southwest at Marble Canyon Lodge. **General Store:** No. **Vending:** No. **Swimming:** No. **Playground:** No. **Other:** Boat launch ramp, fish cleaning station. **Activities:** Colorado River fishing, canoeing. **Nearby Attractions:** Navajo Bridge, Lake Powell, Jacob Lake, Grand Canyon North Rim. **Additional Information:** US National Park Service, Southern AZ Group, (602) 640-5250; Marble Canyon Lodge, (520) 355-2225; Glen Canyon National Recreation Area, (520) 608-6404.

RESTRICTIONS

Pets: On 6 ft. leash under owner's control. **Fires:** In fire receptacles only, no ground fires. **Alcoholic Beverages:** Allowed. **Vehicle Maximum Length:** 20 ft. **Other:** 14 consecutive days limit, 30 days per year max., noon checkout.

TO GET THERE

From US Hwy. 89A, go 5.7 mi. north at Marble Canyon.

MESA

Usery Mountain Recreation Area

3939 North Usery Pass Rd., Mesa 85207. T: (480) 984-0032; F: (480) 357-1542; www.maricopa.gov/recsvc/usery.

RV ★★★★★ Tent ★★★★★

Beauty: ★★★★★ Site Privacy: ★★★★★
Spaciousness: ★★★★★ Quiet: ★★★★★
Security: ★★★★★ Cleanliness: ★★★★
Insect Control: ★★★ Facilities: ★★★

Conveniently close to Mesa's urban amenities, Usery Mountain Recreation Area's Buckhorn Family Campground combines lower Sonoran Desert foreground scenery with the majestic backdrop of the Usery, Goldfield, McDowell, and Superstition Mountains. Campsites at this excellent Maricopa County campground named for King Usery, a cattle rancher who robbed stagecoaches to make ends meet, are very private thanks to intervening patches of mesquite, ocotillo, palo verde, cholla, and saguaro. During spring and fall, Mexican and Basque shepherds can be spotted with their dogs moving sheep across Usery Pass between the high country and the Salt River Valley, an area of ancient Native American village and canal ruins. Seven miles north is Saguaro Lake and Salt River tubing near Stewart Mountain Dam. Campers can also ride their horses or mountain bike park trails. During hot summer months, four covered sites are available ($110 a week in advance; 2-week limit).

BASICS

Operated By: Maricopa County Parks & Recreation Dept. **Open:** All year. **Site Assignment:** First come, first served; group reservations required. **Registration:** Host site near entrance. **Fee:** $8–$15 (V, MC). **Parking:** At site.

FACILITIES

Number of RV Sites: 73. **Number of Tent-Only Sites:** 0. **Hookups:** Electric (30, 50 amp), water. **Each Site:** Table, grill. **Dump Station:** Yes. **Laundry:** No. **Pay Phone:** Yes. **Rest Rooms and Showers:** Yes. **Fuel:** No. **Propane:** No. **Internal Roads:** Paved, good. **RV Service:** No. **Market:** Mesa, 4 mi. **Restaurant:** Mesa, 4 mi. **General Store:** No. **Vending:** Yes. **Swimming:** No. **Playground:** Yes. **Other:** Horse staging area, archery range, gun range, model airplane field, flood lights for group area. **Activities:** Horseback riding, mountain biking, river tubing, golf. **Nearby Attractions:** Phoenix, colleges, museums, botanic gardens. **Additional Information:** Mesa CVB, (602) 969-1307.

RESTRICTIONS

Pets: On leash under owner's control (horses OK). **Fires:** In grills only. **Alcoholic Beverages:** Allowed (glass bottles prohibited). **Vehicle Maximum Length:** None. **Other:** 2-week stay limit; no horses in picnic areas.

TO GET THERE

From Mesa go 7.5 mi. north on US Hwy. 60 (Ellsworth/Usery Pass Rd.) to Usery Park Rd.

PAGE

Lone Rock Beach

P.O. Box 1507, Page 86040. T: (520) 608-6404; www.nps.gov/glca.

RV ★★ Tent ★★

Beauty: ★★★★★ Site Privacy: ★★★
Spaciousness: ★★★★ Quiet: ★★★★
Security: ★★★★ Cleanliness: ★★★★
Insect Control: ★★ Facilities: ★★

National Park Service rangers patrol Lone Rock Beach, making this two miles of Lake Powell's 1,960 miles of shoreline among the more secure stretches of beach for camping. A large lone monolithic sandstone rock sticking out of the lake and straddling the Arizona/Utah border gives the beach its name. It seems like southern California, complete with beach bums, albeit sans surfboards and backed by the incomparable beauty of Glen Canyon sandstone. Motor homes share the hard beach sand with tents and people sleeping in the open. Off-road vehicle enthusiasts flock here for the sand dunes, and boaters sail in from Wahweap Marina for beach camping. Though a primitive beach camping experience, don't expect much privacy in July and Aug., when summer traffic jams Page and crowds flock to the beach to beat the heat. Indeed, escaping the summer crowds requires taking a boat (even houseboats are for rent) to the more remote, roadless parts of this 186-mile-long lake.

BASICS

Operated By: National Park Service. **Open:** All year. **Site Assignment:** First come, first served. **Registration:** Entrance kiosk. **Fee:** $6. **Parking:** On beach.

FACILITIES

Number of RV Sites: Unlimited (not designated sites). **Number of Tent-Only Sites:** 0. **Hookups:** None. **Each Site:** Beach sand. **Dump Station:** Yes. **Laundry:** No. **Pay Phone:** Yes. **Rest Rooms and Showers:** Yes. **Fuel:** No. **Propane:** No. **Internal Roads:** Pavement ends in hard sand. **RV Service:** No. **Market:** 9 mi. south at Wahweap. **Restaurant:** 9 mi. south at Wahweap. **General Store:** No. **Vending:** No. **Swimming:** In Lake Powell. **Playground:** No. **Other:** Boat launch. **Activities:** Beach sports, fishing, off-road vehicles on sand dunes. **Nearby Attractions:** Wahweap Marina, Glen Canyon Dam, Page, Antelope Canyon, Rainbow Bridge National Monument, Escalante Staircase National Monument. **Additional Information:** Glen Canyon National Recreation Area, (520) 608-6404.

RESTRICTIONS

Pets: On 6 ft. leash under owner's control. **Fires:** Yes. **Alcoholic Beverages:** Allowed. **Vehicle Maximum Length:** None. **Other:** Portable toilets are mandatory when camping away from restrooms; heavy fines for sewage pollution.

TO GET THERE

Go 6 mi. north from Page on US Hwy. 89, crossing AZ border into UT, then 2 mi. west down road to Lone Rock Beach.

PAGE

Wahweap Campground

P.O. Box 1597, Page 86040. T: (800) 528-6154 or (928) 645-2313; www.visitlakepowell.com.

RV ★★★ Tent ★★★★

Beauty: ★★★★
Site Privacy: ★★★★
Spaciousness: ★★★★
Quiet: ★★★★
Security: ★★★★
Cleanliness: ★★★★
Insect Control: ★★★
Facilities: ★★★★

Wahweap Campground is more spacious and private in feel than Wahweap RV Park, and the Lake Powell views are surpassed only by camping at Lone Rock Beach. However, RV campers may prefer downtown Page and the more amenity-laden Page–Lake Powell Campground (see appendix) over Wahweap Campground when Wahweap RV Park's hookups are full. Indeed, the spacious campsites and small loops are tailored to tents and small trailers, with plenty of shade trees and desert scrub separating sites from each other along smallish loops. It is slightly over a mile to the showers ($2) and Wahweap Marina amenities like pizza, a restaurant, groceries, and the Wahweap Lodge pool (open to campers). Overall, Wahweap Campground is a good tent and trailer choice, combining the feel of camping out with Lake Powell's nearby amenities.

BASICS

Operated By: Aramark. **Open:** Mar. 15–Oct. 31. **Site Assignment:** First come, first served; group reservations. **Registration:** At office/store. **Fee:** $15 (V, MC, AE, D, DC). **Parking:** At site.

FACILITIES

Number of RV Sites: 112. **Number of Tent-Only Sites:** 0. **Hookups:** None. **Each Site:** Table, grill. **Dump Station:** Yes. **Laundry:** Yes. **Pay Phone:** Yes. **Rest Rooms and Showers:** Yes. **Fuel:** No. **Propane:** No. **Internal Roads:** Paved, good condition. **RV Service:** No. **Market:** Limited groceries at office store; more at RV park. **Restaurant:** At Wahweap Marina. **General Store:** Yes. **Vending:** Yes. **Swimming:** At lodge pool; in lake. **Playground:** No. **Other:** Fine dining at Wahweap Lodge. **Activities:** Boat tours & rentals; float trips on river. **Nearby Attractions:** Rainbow Bridge, Page, Glen Canyon Dam, Antelope Canyon, Lees Ferry, Escalante Staircase National Monument. **Additional Information:** Glen Canyon National Recreation Area, (520) 608-6404; Page–Lake Powell Chamber of Commerce, 644 North Navajo Dr., Dam Plaza, P.O. Box 727, Page, AZ 86040; (888) 261-7243; www.PageLakePowellChamber.org; info@pagelakepowellchamber.org.

RESTRICTIONS

Pets: On leash under owner's control (including barking). **Fires:** In grills only. **Alcoholic Beverages:** Allowed. **Vehicle Maximum Length:** 35 ft. **Other:** 14 consecutive days, 30 days per year camping limit; no loaded firearms, fireworks or water balloon launchers.

TO GET THERE

Take US Hwy. 198 north from Glen Canyon Dam for 4 mi., turn on Lake Shore Dr. and go to corner of Wahweap Blvd.

PAGE

Wahweap RV Park

P.O. Box 1597, Page 86040. T: (800) 528-6154 or (928) 645-2313; www.visitlakepowell.com.

RV ★★★★ Tent n/a

Beauty: ★★★
Site Privacy: ★★★
Spaciousness: ★★★
Quiet: ★★★★
Security: ★★★★
Cleanliness: ★★★★
Insect Control: ★★★
Facilities: ★★★★

Wahweap RV Park offers plenty of boat parking for nearby Wahweap Marina. An attractive grassy area with trees separates the RV Park from the road, but once inside it is more like a huge parking lot full of boats and vehicles. If hookups and amenities are of more interest than boats and the lake, downtown Page and the Page–Lake Powell Campground (see Appendix) are an attractive alternative. For a more primitive beach camping experience, head to Lone Rock Beach. The views are nothing to write home about, but the whole idea here seems to be get out on the water and play until dark. Despite the tightly-packed nature of the RV park, it stays fairly quiet. Tables on cement and shade are among the nice touches. If boating on Lake Powell plus RV amenities equal a good time, then this is the best place to be.

BASICS

Operated By: Aramark. **Open:** All year. **Site Assignment:** First come, first served; reservations (first night deposit). **Registration:** Self-pay entrance fee station. **Fee:** $17–$27 (V, MC, AE, D, DC). **Parking:** At site.

FACILITIES

Number of RV Sites: 123. **Number of Tent-Only Sites:** 0. **Hookups:** Electric (20, 30, 50 amp). **Each Site:** Table, grill. **Dump Station:** Yes. **Laundry:** Yes. **Pay Phone:** Yes. **Rest Rooms and Showers:** Yes. **Fuel:** Yes. **Propane:** Yes. **Internal Roads:** Gravel, good condition. **RV Service:** No. **Market:** Yes. **Restaurant:** At Wahweap Marina. **General Store:** Yes. **Vending:** Yes. **Swimming:** In lodge pool or lake. **Playground:** Yes. **Other:** Boat ramp & boat rentals. **Activities:** Fishing, boating, summer ranger programs, free use of lodge facilities. **Nearby Attractions:** Antelope Canyon, Glen Canyon Dam, Lees Ferry, Rainbow Bridge, Escalante Staircase National Monument. **Additional Information:** Glen Canyon National Recreation Area, (520) 608-6404; Page–Lake Powell Chamber of Commerce, 644 North Navajo Dr., Dam Plaza, P.O. Box 727, Page, AZ 86040; (888) 261-7243; www.PageLakePowellChamber.org; info@pagelakepowellchamber.org.

RESTRICTIONS

Pets: On leash under owner's control. **Fires:** Yes. **Alcoholic Beverages:** Allowed. **Vehicle Maximum Length:** 45 ft. **Other:** No tents.

TO GET THERE

From Glen Canyon Dam go 4 mi. north on US Hwy. 89, then take Lake Shore Dr. to 100 Stateline Dr.

PARKER

Branson's Motel & RV Park

7804 Riverside Dr., Parker 85344. T: (520) 667-3346; F: (520) 667-2085.

RV ★★★ Tent n/a

Beauty: ★★★
Site Privacy: ★★
Spaciousness: ★★
Quiet: ★★★★
Security: ★★★★★
Cleanliness: ★★★★
Insect Control: ★★
Facilities: ★★★★

With card games, ice cream socials, and potlucks in the rec hall, Branson's caters to snowbirds in winter with its tightly packed concrete pads and grass strip RV sites. German tourists are among those flocking in summer to this hybrid mixture of marina, mobile homes, RV park, and motel units with kitchens. The motel and front row of mobile homes get the river views. But RV patrons can relax on breezy beachfront lawns under palm frond umbrellas and gaze across the lapping waters of the Colorado River to California or use the ample boat facilities for water sports. A public golf course, the top-rated Emerald Canyon, is just across the street. LaPaz County Park's abundant day-use areas and occasional swap meets are next door. After a visit to the nearby solar saloon, younger party animals will want to leave this little community to the elders and head further north on the road to Lake Havasu.

BASICS

Operated By: Branson's Resort. **Open:** All year. **Site Assignment:** First come, first served; reservations needed in winter. **Registration:** Self-pay entrance fee station. **Fee:** $21 & up (V, MC). **Parking:** At site.

FACILITIES

Number of RV Sites: 70. **Number of Tent-Only Sites:** 0. **Hookups:** Electric (30 amp), water, sewer, cable TV. **Each Site:** Table, grill. **Dump Station:** Yes. **Laundry:** Yes. **Pay Phone:** Yes. **Rest Rooms and Showers:** Yes. **Fuel:** No. **Propane:** No. **Internal Roads:** Paved, good. **RV Service:** No. **Market:** Parker, 8 mi. **Restaurant:** Parker, 2 mi. **General Store:** Yes. **Vending:** Yes. **Swimming:** River. **Playground:** No. **Other:** Boat ramps, slips & storage, horseshoe pits, volleyball court, exercise room, pool table. **Activities:** Fishing, boating, water sports, golf. **Nearby Attractions:** Nellie E. Saloon, Blythe Intaglios (CA), Quartzsite, Lake Havasu. **Additional Information:** Parker Chamber of Commerce, (520) 669-2174, www.riverinfo.com/parker.

RESTRICTIONS

Pets: Not allowed. **Fires:** Yes (when wind is not blowing). **Alcoholic Beverages:** Allowed. **Vehicle Maximum Length:** None.

TO GET THERE

From Parker go 7.5 mi. north on Riverside Dr.

PARKER
Buckskin Mountain State Park

5476 Hwy. 95, Parker 85344. T: (520) 667-3231; www.pr.state.az.us.

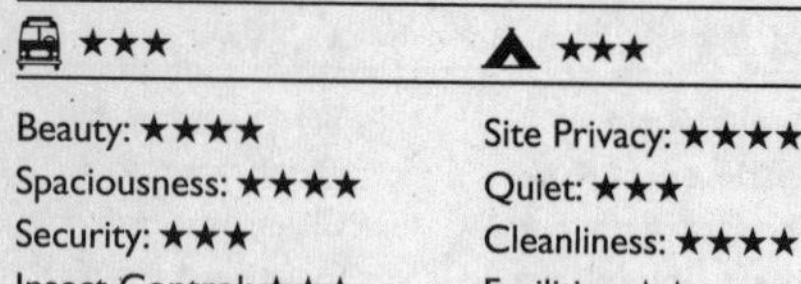

★★★ ★★★

Beauty: ★★★★ Site Privacy: ★★★★
Spaciousness: ★★★★ Quiet: ★★★
Security: ★★★ Cleanliness: ★★★★
Insect Control: ★★★ Facilities: ★★

If relaxation and plenty of play space for the children are more important than partying, then Buckskin Mountain's paved sites separated by dirt and trees are a better choice than Fox's Pierpoint Landing and Tony's Road Runner. A group-use area with sheltered tables is one mile north at Buckskin Mountain State Park's River Island Unit, which has another 22 campsites and large grass play areas but no hookups on 420 acres with a boat ramp and a Colorado River swimming beach. Island Unit is closer to the highway and further from the water, but is quieter when not overrun with weekend groups. During the cooler winter months, hiking the short steep trails into the surrounding mountains for spectacular overviews of the area is a worthwhile alternative to water play. Some trails go by abandoned mines and have interpretative stops to get to better know the local ecosystems and vegetation.

BASICS

Operated By: Arizona State Parks. **Open:** All year. **Site Assignment:** First come, first served. **Registration:** Self-pay entrance fee station. **Fee:** $12–$20 (cash or check only). **Parking:** At site.

FACILITIES

Number of RV Sites: 83. **Number of Tent-Only Sites:** 0. **Hookups:** Electric (30 amp), water, sewer. **Each Site:** Table, grill. **Dump Station:** Yes. **Laundry:** No. **Pay Phone:** Yes. **Rest Rooms and Showers:** Yes. **Fuel:** No (boat fuel only). **Propane:** No. **Internal Roads:** Paved, good. **RV Service:** No. **Market:** Buckskin Market, in park. **Restaurant:** In park. **General Store:** Yes. **Vending:** Yes. **Swimming:** River. **Playground:** Yes. **Other:** Cactus garden, interpretative center, boutique, boat ramp, basketball court, volleyball, horseshoe pit. **Activities:** Boating, fishing, water sports, golf. **Nearby Attractions:** Lake Havasu. **Additional Information:** Parker Chamber of Commerce, (520) 669-2174, www.riverinfo.com/parker.

RESTRICTIONS

Pets: On leash. **Fires:** In fire grill **Alcoholic Beverages:** Allowed. **Vehicle Maximum Length:** None. **Other:** No loud nuisance noises; 15-day stay limit.

TO GET THERE

From Parker go 11 mi. north on AZ Hwy. 95.

PARKER
Havasu Springs Resort

2581 Hwy. 95, Parker 85344. T: (520) 667-3361; F: (520) 667-1098; www.havasusprings.com; havasusprings@hotmail.com.

★★★★ n/a

Beauty: ★★★ Site Privacy: ★★★
Spaciousness: ★★★ Quiet: ★★★★
Security: ★★★★★ Cleanliness: ★★★★★
Insect Control: ★★★ Facilities: ★★★★★

A true destination resort with plenty of amenities, including an Olympic-sized pool, and enough winter activities to keep snowbirds happy, Havasu Springs Resort has over 250 boat slips, three motels, a restaurant with a bar and lounge, and everything from par 3 golf to houseboat and fishing boat rentals. In contrast to the Colorado River and Havasu partying areas, even teenagers must be under tight adult reign here. Motorcycles are also banned, which helps keep the park quiet. Gate security is also relatively tight, and visitors must obtain passes. Though the cement pads here are good, it will be a few years before the trees are large enough to provide some shade to the RV sites. But if protection from noisy Harleys and rowdy party animals is part of the Colorado River recreation game plan, then reservations here may fit the bill.

BASICS

Operated By: Havasu Springs Resort L.L.C. **Open:** All year. **Site Assignment:** First come, first served; reservations a necessity. **Registration:** Office. **Fee:** $26–$30 (V, MC, AE, D). **Parking:** At site.

FACILITIES

Number of RV Sites: 150. **Number of Tent-Only Sites:** 0. **Hookups:** Electric (30, 50 amp), water, sewer, phone, cable TV. **Each Site:** Table, grill. **Dump Station:** Yes. **Laundry:** Yes. **Pay Phone:** Yes. **Rest Rooms and Showers:** Yes. **Fuel:** Yes (boat fuel also available). **Propane:** Yes. **Internal Roads:** Paved, good. **RV Service:** No. **Market:** On premises. **Restaurant:** On premises. **General Store:** Yes. **Vending:** Yes. **Swimming:** Pool. **Playground:** No. **Other:** Marina, houseboat & fishing boat rentals, fish-cleaning stations, lighted tennis courts, 9-hole golf course, 3 motels, sporting goods store, pool tables, video games. **Activities:** Boating, fishing, golf, tennis, hunting. **Nearby Attractions:** Parker Dam, Lake Havasu. **Additional Information:** Parker Chamber of Commerce, (520) 669-2174, www.riverinfo.com/parker.

RESTRICTIONS

Pets: On leash at all times (subject to management discretion). **Fires:** Yes. **Alcoholic Beverages:** Allowed. **Vehicle Maximum Length:** None. **Other:** Only RVIA approved units w/ hard sides allowed; teenagers must be accompanied by parents; no motorcycles or go-carts.

TO GET THERE

From Parker go 17 mi. north on AZ Hwy. 95.

PARKER
LaPaz County Park

7350 Riverside Dr., Parker 85344. T: (520) 667-2069; F: (520) 667-2757; j.bennett@co.la-paz.az.us.

★★★★ ★★★★

Beauty: ★★★★ Site Privacy: ★★★★
Spaciousness: ★★★★ Quiet: ★★★★
Security: ★★★★ Cleanliness: ★★★★★
Insect Control: ★★★ Facilities: ★★★

Though lacking ice cream socials and some of the snowbird amenities of Branson's Resort next door, LaPaz offers lots of open space and green grass. Golfers can practice on the putting green and cross the street to use the driving range or play 18 holes, and there is a baseball field, tennis court, and plenty else to do besides boating, fishing, and swimming in the Colorado River. During the winter, tent campers have a prime dirt beachfront area along the river, and designated sites are kept open for RVs. But RV sites are open to tent camping during the summer months when the snowbird migration has reversed. Tents can also be placed under trees near the group area when it does not conflict with irrigation schedules. The two-mile-long park has some big pines surrounding the inland RV sites, but beachfront RV sites 5–47 and 84–113 have the best river views.

BASICS

Operated By: LaPaz County Parks. **Open:** All year. **Site Assignment:** First come, first served. **Registration:** Self-pay entrance fee station. **Fee:** $10–$15 (cash or check only). **Parking:** At site.

FACILITIES

Number of RV Sites: 114. **Number of Tent-Only Sites:** 35. **Hookups:** Electric (30 amp), water, cable TV, phone. **Each Site:** Table, grill. **Dump Station:** Yes. **Laundry:** No. **Pay Phone:** Yes. **Rest Rooms and Showers:** Yes. **Fuel:** No. **Propane:** No. **Internal Roads:** Gravel, good. **RV Service:** No. **Market:** Parker, 8 mi. **Restaurant:** Parker, 2 mi. **General Store:** No. **Vending:** Yes. **Swimming:** River. **Playground:** Yes. **Other:** Boat ramps, putting green, tennis court, softball field, volleyball court, rec hall, horseshoe pits, some sites w/ sheltered tables. **Activities:** Boating, fishing, golf, horseshoes, volleyball, tennis. **Nearby Attractions:** Nellie E. Saloon, Blythe Intaglios (CA), Quartzsite, Lake Havasu. **Additional Information:** Parker Chamber of Commerce, (520) 669-2174, www.riverinfo.com/parker.

RESTRICTIONS

Pets: On leash at all times (barking dogs not tolerated; no dogs on beachfront walkways). **Fires:** Yes. **Alcoholic Beverages:** Allowed. **Vehicle Maximum Length:** None. **Other:** No bands allowed; no firearms.

TO GET THERE

From Parker go 8 mi. north on US Hwy. 95.

PARKER
Red Rock Resort

6400 Riverside Dr., Parker 85344. T: (520) 667-3116; F: (520) 667-3116; www.redrockresort.com; redrock4@gte.net.

★★★ ★★★

Beauty: ★★★★ Site Privacy: ★★★
Spaciousness: ★★★ Quiet: ★★★★
Security: ★★★★ Cleanliness: ★★★★
Insect Control: ★★★ Facilities: ★★

Boating, fishing, and water sports are the chief attraction at Red Rock Resort, which is notable for its waterfront cabana campsites. The large pull-through sites (41–56) and sites 64–71 near the winter overflow and RV and trailer storage areas are furthest from the Colorado River. However, site 41, a large lawn corner pull-through is closer to the water and worth the small rental premium. The best sites are right on the Colorado River, and are open only to smaller vehicles and tent camping. These waterfront cabanas, which offer the opportunity to barbecue on the banks of the Colorado River and sit in the shade, are numbered 1–40 and are difficult to score, as they are often rented for four months solid during the peak winter season. Good boat facilities, including repair, salvage, and storage, as well as RV and trailer storage, also help make this small waterfront resort with its own bar and cafe a popular destination.

BASICS

Operated By: Red Rock Resort. **Open:** All year. **Site Assignment:** First come, first served; reservations advised for peak season, holidays, weekends. **Registration:** Front desk. **Fee:** $20–$25 (V, MC). **Parking:** At site.

FACILITIES

Number of RV Sites: 90. **Number of Tent-Only Sites:** 0. **Hookups:** Electric (30, 50 amp), water, sewer, cable TV, phone. **Each Site:** Table, grill. **Dump Station:** Yes. **Laundry:** Yes. **Pay Phone:** Yes. **Rest Rooms and Showers:** Yes. **Fuel:** No. **Propane:** Yes. **Internal Roads:** Paved, good. **RV Service:** No. **Market:** Parker, 9 mi. **Restaurant:** On premises. **General Store:** Yes. **Vending:** Yes. **Swimming:** River. **Playground:** No. **Other:** Boat ramp, RV & boat storage, boat repair, game room, cafe, bar. **Activities:** Fishing, boating, water sports. **Nearby Attractions:** Parker Dam, Lake Havasu. **Additional Information:** Parker Chamber of Commerce, (520) 669-2174, www.riverinfo.com/parker.

RESTRICTIONS

Pets: On leash. **Fires:** Yes. **Alcoholic Beverages:** Allowed. **Vehicle Maximum Length:** None.

TO GET THERE

From Parker go 9 mi. north on AZ Hwy. 95.

PARKS

Ponderosa Forest RV Park & RVCampground

P.O. Box 50640, Parks 86018. T: (888) 635-0456, (520) 635-045; F: (520) 635-0659.

RV ★★★★★ Tent ★★★★

Beauty: ★★★★★	Site Privacy: ★★★★
Spaciousness: ★★★★	Quiet: ★★★★★
Security: ★★★★	Cleanliness: ★★★★★
Insect Control: ★★★	Facilities: ★★★★

It is hard to imagine a more beautiful campground. Sites are spacious (average 25 feet wide) and nearly all are set into the forest. (There is a treeless strip of gravel for seven larger rigs in the middle of the park that strikes one as slightly out of place.) A gorgeous ponderosa forest surrounds the park for at least ten acres, giving this campground both a rustic feel and the clean fresh air of a mountain forest. Accommodating both pull-throughs and back-ins, Ponderosa Forest offers full amenities while giving the impression of being lost in the woods. While the tent sites could stand a little more room, the overall experience is superior to any of the campgrounds in Williams or Flagstaff. Owner Jane is extremely friendly and full of stories. Whether your destination is the Grand Canyon or Flagstaff, this campground makes a wonderful jumping-off point, and should not be missed!

BASICS

Operated By: Jane & Guren Stinson. **Open:** All year. **Site Assignment:** Assigned at registration. **Registration:** At office; late arrivals go to manager's office at back of park. **Fee:** RV $19, tent $13. **Parking:** At sites; will help park vehicles of any size.

FACILITIES

Number of RV Sites: 29. **Number of Tent-Only Sites:** 16. **Hookups:** Water, sewer, electric (30, 50). **Each Site:** Picnic table, fire ring, trash can, most have several trees. **Dump Station:** Yes. **Laundry:** Yes. **Pay Phone:** Yes. **Rest Rooms and Showers:** Yes. **Fuel:** No. **Propane:** Yes. **Internal Roads:** Packed dirt & gravel, mostly good condition. **RV Service:** No. **Market:** 0.5 mi. to Parks. **Restaurant:** 0.5 mi. **General Store:** Yes. **Vending:** Yes. **Swimming:** No. **Playground:** No. **Other:** Gift shop on premises; post office, fax, copies, hair salon, massage parlor in front of RV park. **Activities:** Hiking, fishing, hunting, 4th of July & Labor Day BBQ & potluck. **Nearby Attractions:** Kendrik Peak, historic Rte. 66. **Additional Information:** Williams–Grand Canyon Chamber of Commerce, (520) 635-4061.

RESTRICTIONS

Pets: On leash; some dog breed restrictions; do not leave unattended; no barking. **Fires:** In fire ring. **Alcoholic Beverages:** At sites. **Vehicle Maximum Length:** None. **Other:** Motorcycles & ATVs in/out use only; no generators; no clotheslines; no wood gathering.

TO GET THERE

From Hwy. 40, take Exit 178, turn north, then take immediate left and follow the road behind the shops.

PATAGONIA

Patagonia Lake State Park

P.O. Box 274, Patagonia 85624. T: (520) 287-6965; F: (520) 287-5618; www.pr.state.az.us.

RV ★★★★ Tent ★★★★

Beauty: ★★★★	Site Privacy: ★★★★
Spaciousness: ★★★★	Quiet: ★★★★
Security: ★★★★	Cleanliness: ★★★★
Insect Control: ★★★	Facilities: ★★★★

Situated between Patagonia and Nogales on the Mexican border, Patagonia Lake is reached from AZ Hwy. 82 via a curving paved road through housing developments and a hillside forest of mesquite and ocotillo. The campground is nestled in low rolling foothills amongs shady mesquite trees, yucca, and cacti. The best campsites for views of the 265-acre manmade lake are numbered 1–37, and are also nearest the swimming beach. Boaters may wish to opt for the other loops, nearer the launch ramps. There are a dozen tent-only areas scattered around the lake, but they are only accessible by boat. Besides being stocked with trout every three weeks between Nov. and late Feb., the lake offers fishing for crappie, bluegill, bass, and catfish and birding tours. Almost every Friday the campground fills early for the weekend, and peak season park closures are common.

BASICS

Operated By: Arizona State Parks. **Open:** All year. **Site Assignment:** First come, first served. **Registration:** Self-pay fee station. **Fee:** $10–$15. **Parking:** At site (except for tent areas only accessible by boat).

FACILITIES

Number of RV Sites: 106. **Number of Tent-Only Sites:** 12. **Hookups:** Water, electric (20, 30 amp). **Each Site:** Table, grill. **Dump Station:** Yes. **Laundry:** No. **Pay Phone:** Yes. **Rest Rooms and Showers:** Yes. **Fuel:** No. **Propane:** No. **Internal Roads:** Paved, good. **RV Service:** No. **Market:** Patagonia, 12 mi. **Restaurant:** Patagonia, 12 mi. **General Store:** Yes. **Vending:** Yes. **Swimming:** Lake. **Playground:** No. **Other:** Marina, boat rentals, disabled-access fishing dock, picnic area. **Activities:** Boating, fishing, bird-watching. **Nearby Attractions:** Tubac Presidio, Tumacacori National Monument, Patagonia-Sonoita Creek Preserve. **Additional Information:** Mariposa Books/Patagonia Visitors Center, (520) 394-9186; Nogales Santa Cruz County Chamber of Commerce, (520) 287-3685.

RESTRICTIONS

Pets: On 6 ft. leash under owner's control. **Fires:** In grills provided; no wood gathering. **Alcoholic Beverages:** Allowed. **Vehicle Maximum Length:** 30 ft. **Other:** 2 weeks per month max. stay; 12 people & 2 vehicles per site- no water or jet skiing or recreational device towing May 1–Oct. 1; park gate closes 10 p.m.–4 a.m.

TO GET THERE

From AZ Hwy. 82, go 4 mi. north on park access road.

PAYSON

Ox Bow Estates RV Park

HC6 Box 1050 D, Payson 85541. T: (800) 520-5239; F: (520) 474-4538.

RV ★★★★ Tent ★★

Beauty: ★★★	Site Privacy: ★★★
Spaciousness: ★★★★	Quiet: ★★★★
Security: ★★★	Cleanliness: ★★★★★
Insect Control: ★★★★	Facilities: ★★★

With its log cabin–style office and wooded lots and stream, this campground has a very woodsy atmosphere. And well it should, since it abuts Tonto National Forest on one side. (From an aerial photo in the office, you can see just how lost in the woods this campground really is.) The rest of the surrounding area is quiet residential property. Sites are laid out in a grid, with one section divided from the rest by a small creek. Most sites are shaded, including the tent sites, and average a spacious 40 × 50 feet. The campground is peaceful, laid-back, and quiet. Besides Tonto National Forest, which you can be lost in within five minutes of leaving the park, the other local attractions are a quick drive away, making this campground a relaxing yet convenient stop. Proprietors Fred and Mimi are friendly, helpful, and full of information about the region.

Basics

Operated By: Fred & Mimi Hendrix. **Open:** All year. **Site Assignment:** Assigned at registration. **Registration:** At office; if no one is available, use courtesy phone & call number listed; late arrivals: pick a spot & use drop slot in door. **Fee:** RV $21–23, tent $19. **Parking:** At site.

Facilities

Number of RV Sites: 50. **Number of Tent-Only Sites:** 0. **Hookups:** Water, sewer, electric (30, 50), TV. **Each Site:** Picnic table, fire pit, charcoal grill, tree. **Dump Station:** Yes. **Laundry:** Yes. **Pay Phone:** Yes. **Rest Rooms and Showers:** Yes. **Fuel:** No. **Propane:** Yes. **Internal Roads:** Gravel, in very good condition. **RV Service:** No. **Market:** 2 miles to casino. **Restaurant:** 2 mi. to casino. **General Store:** Yes. **Vending:** Yes. **Swimming:** No. **Playground:** No. **Other:** Creek. **Activities:** Hiking, biking, fishing, summer potlucks. **Nearby Attractions:** Tonto National Forest, Tonto National Bridge Park, Tonto Cliff Dwellings. **Additional Information:** Payson Chamber of Commerce, (520) 474-4515.

Restrictions

Pets: On leash. **Fires:** In pit or grill. **Alcoholic Beverages:** Not in buildings. **Vehicle Maximum Length:** 45 ft. **Other:** No clotheslines.

To Get There

From the intersection of Hwy. 260 and Hwy. 87 in Payson, go south on 87 (towards Rye) for 4.2 mi., then turn right at the sign for the campground (there is no street sign). Drive 0.8 mi. through a residential area and turn into the entrance on the right.

PEORIA

Lake Pleasant Regional Park

41835 North Castle Hot Springs Rd., Peoria 85382. T: (520) 501-0107; F: (520) 501-1704; www.maricopa.gov/recsev.

RV ★★★★ Tent ★★★★

Beauty: ★★★★	Site Privacy: ★★★★
Spaciousness: ★★★★	Quiet: ★★★★
Security: ★★★★★	Cleanliness: ★★★★
Insect Control: ★★★	Facilities: ★★★

One of six excellent Phoenix area county parks, Lake Pleasant Regional Park contains both the Desert Tortoise and Roadrunner Campgrounds. Roadrunner's hillside sites 7–24 fill up first because of their excellent views. Desert Tortoise's tent-only and improved pull-through sites along Den and Bajada Loop Roads have coveted lake views that are also snapped up fast. On long holiday weekends it seems like all Phoenix is headed here with boats. Since there are no reservations, an early Thursday arrival is advised to ensure snagging a holiday weekend campsite. Most sites easily accommodate vehicles in the mid-30 to mid-45-foot range, though the sites tend to be narrow (e.g. the 80-foot-long site is only 13 foot wide). The native desert hillside saguaro, octotillo, and brittlebush landscape blooms with yellow, purple, and blue wildflowers after Apr. showers. Park animals include bald eagles, wild burros, javelina, and desert tortoises.

Basics

Operated By: Maricopa County Parks & Recreation Dept. **Open:** All year. **Site Assignment:** First come, first served. **Registration:** Entrance kiosk (or camp host). **Fee:** $8–$15 (cash or check only). **Parking:** At site.

Facilities

Number of RV Sites: 146. **Number of Tent-Only Sites:** 4. **Hookups:** Electric (20, 30, 50 amp), water. **Each Site:** Sheltered table, grill. **Dump Station:** No. **Laundry:** No. **Pay Phone:** Yes. **Rest Rooms and Showers:** Yes. **Fuel:** No. **Propane:** No. **Internal Roads:** Paved, good. **RV Service:** No. **Market:** Peoria, 8 mi. **Restaurant:** Peoria, 8 mi. **General Store:** No. **Vending:** Yes. **Swimming:** Lake. **Playground:** Yes. **Other:** Boat ramp, dam visitor center. **Activities:** Boating, fishing, shooting range, golf. **Nearby Attractions:** Factory shops, museums, Cave Creek, Carefree. **Additional Information:** Carefree–Cave Creek Chamber of Commerce, (602) 488-3381.

Restrictions

Pets: On leash under owner's control. **Fires:** In grills only; no ground fires. **Alcoholic Beverages:** Allowed. **Vehicle Maximum Length:** 80 ft. **Other:** No wood gathering.

To Get There

From I-17 north of Phoenix take Exit 223, go west on AZ Hwy. 74 (Carefree Hwy.).

PHOENIX

Covered Wagon RV Park

6540 North Black Canyon Hwy., Phoenix 85017. T: (602) 242-2500.

RV ★★★ Tent ★★

Beauty: ★★★	Site Privacy: ★★★
Spaciousness: ★★★★	Quiet: ★★
Security: ★★★★	Cleanliness: ★★★★
Insect Control: ★★★★	Facilities: ★★★

This campground is slightly less pretty than Welcome Home, due to a cement retaining wall that runs along the edge of the property from sites 34–44. In addition, while the park seems equally well insulated from highway traffic sounds, noise from a ballpark located across the street invades the entire park when games are on. Still, this is not a bad place to park your RV while you explore the humongous city of Phoenix—and it is certainly much more convenient than the several campgrounds located 30 miles out of town. There are some wonderful flowering trees, giving the grounds a city park–like feel: you know you're in the city, but removed a bit from the action. Definitely not for the tenter looking for a wilderness experience. The Covered Wagon makes a reasonable base of operations for exploring Phoenix, but one more exit on I-17 will bring you to a slightly quieter park.

Basics

Operated By: Ted Heiser. **Open:** All year. **Site Assignment:** Assigned at registration. **Registration:** Ring bell at office. **Fee:** RV $21–$32, depending on size, tent $18. **Parking:** At site.

Facilities

Number of RV Sites: 47. **Number of Tent-Only Sites:** 0. **Hookups:** Water, sewer, electric (20, 30, 50 amps). **Each Site:** Mature shade trees. **Dump Station:** Yes. **Laundry:** Yes. **Pay Phone:** Yes. **Rest Rooms and Showers:** Yes. **Fuel:** No. **Propane:** No. **Internal Roads:** Paved. **RV Service:** No. **Market:** 4 blocks. **Restaurant:** 4 blocks. **General Store:** No. **Vending:** Yes. **Swimming:** Yes. **Playground:** No. **Activities:** Swimming, shopping, hiking, sightseeing. **Nearby Attractions:** Mesa Southwest Museum, Champlin Fighter Museum, Superstition Springs Center, Casa Grande Ruins, Roosevelt Dam, Tonto National Monument. **Additional Information:** Phoenix Visitors Center, (602) 254-6500.

Restrictions

Pets: On leash, clean up after. **Fires:** Only charcoal in grills. **Alcoholic Beverages:** At sites only. **Vehicle Maximum Length:** None. **Other:** No clotheslines.

To Get There

From the junction of I-17 and Glendale Rd. (Exit 205), merge into the far right-hand lane. Take the frontage road 0.5 mi., turn right, then take the second right (not the immediate right) into the entrance, follow the driveway to the end and turn right. The office is the white building on the left.

PHOENIX

Welcome Home RV Park

2501 Missouri Ave., Phoenix 85017. T: (602) 249-9852.

RV ★★★ Tent n/a

Beauty: ★★★	Site Privacy: ★★★★
Spaciousness: ★★★★	Quiet: ★★★★
Security: ★★★	Cleanliness: ★★★★★
Insect Control: ★★★★	Facilities: ★★

Certainly one of the closest campgrounds to downtown Phoenix, this park is being converted to accept only RVs. (It currently does not accept tents, but has a few remaining mobile homes.) The grounds are laid out on a loop, with well-shaded, comfortable lots on either side. Lots are 30 feet wide, making them spacious enough for evening outdoor activities. Although situated right next to the highway, there is very little traffic noise spillover. Located on a quiet residential street, the park presents a great little urban getaway without an overly urban feel. Downtown Phoenix is a 20-minute drive away, while the quick access to I-17 provides a convenien way to depart for further destinations.

Basics

Operated By: Ed Little. **Open:** All year. **Site Assignment:** Assigned at registration. **Registration:** At office; if closed, go to house next door. **Fee:** $21–$24; cash preferred, no credit cards. **Parking:** At site.

Facilities

Number of RV Sites: 52. **Number of Tent-Only Sites:** 0. **Hookups:** Water, sewer, electric (30, 50). **Each Site:** Trees & grass, some flowering bushes. **Dump Station:** No (sewer available at all sites). **Laundry:** Yes. **Pay Phone:** No (1 block). **Rest Rooms and Showers:** No shower. **Fuel:** No (1 block). **Propane:** No. **Internal Roads:** Paved. **RV Service:** No. **Market:** 1 mi. **Restaurant:** 2 mi. **General Store:** No (1 block). **Vending:** No. **Swimming:** Yes. **Playground:** No. **Activities:** Shuffleboard, clubhouse, Christmas dinner. **Nearby Attractions:** Mesa Southwest Museum, Champlin Fighter Museum, Superstition Springs Center, Casa Grande Ruins, Roosevelt Dam, Tonto National Monument. **Additional Information:** Phoenix Visitors Center, (602) 254-6500.

Restrictions

Pets: On leash, clean up after. **Fires:** Yes (only charcoal in grills). **Alcoholic Beverages:** At sites only. **Vehicle Maximum Length:** None. **Other:** 30 ft. min. length, must be 1991 or newer RV.

To Get There

From the junction of I-17 and Bethany Rd. (Exit 204), merge into the far right-hand lane heading south. Follow the frontage road 0.5 mi. to the entrance on the right.

PICACHO

Picacho Campground

P.O. Box 368, Picacho 85241. T: (520) 466-7401 or (888) 562-7453; www.pichachocampground.com.

RV ★★★★ Tent ★★★★

Beauty: ★★★★	Site Privacy: ★★★
Spaciousness: ★★★★	Quiet: ★★★
Security: ★★★★	Cleanliness: ★★★★
Insect Control: ★★★★	Facilities: ★★★★

Just off I-10, 75 miles south of Phoenix and 42 miles north of Tucson, Picacho Campground is popular with horse owners because it provides corrals ($10). Children are also welcome here, though parents must keep them in sight and under control at all times, particularly around the pool. Visitors here are mostly snowbirds and overnighters. Many put out their TV antennas to pull in Phoenix and Tucson stations, which means two NBC and two CBS channels, one each from PBS and ABC and two independents. An attractive oleander perimeter mutes much of the highway truck noise, though not all of it. Cacti, eucalyptus, and an abundance of other trees shade these extra long and extra wide sites, which easily accommodate sliders. The store and office stay open from 8 a.m. to 8 p.m., adding convenience at this well-run family operation.

Basics

Operated By: Jerry & Frankie Cross. **Open:** All year. **Site Assignment:** First come, first served; winter reservations advised. **Registration:** Office. **Fee:** $17 tent, $22–$24 RV (V, MC, D). **Parking:** At site.

Facilities

Number of RV Sites: 70. **Number of Tent-Only Sites:** 8. **Hookups:** Electric (30, 50 amp), water, sewer. **Each Site:** Table. **Dump Station:** Yes. **Laundry:** Yes. **Pay Phone:** Yes. **Rest Rooms and Showers:** Yes. **Fuel:** Yes. **Propane:** Yes. **Internal Roads:** Gravel, good. **RV Service:** No. **Market:** Eloy, 4 mi. **Restaurant:** Steakhouse on premises (Dec.–Mar.). **General Store:** Yes. **Vending:** Yes. **Swimming:** Pool. **Playground:** Yes. **Other:** Hot tub, shuffleboard, dog walk, cabin. **Activities:** Horseback riding, golf. **Nearby Attractions:** Picacho Peak State Park, Casa Grande Ruins, Sasco ghost town. **Additional Information:** Sunland Visitor Center, (520) 466-3007.

Restrictions

Pets: On leash under owner's control (horses welcome). **Fires:** In fire pits in tent & picnic areas only. **Alcoholic Beverages:** Allowed. **Vehicle Maximum Length:** None. **Other:** No vehicle washing or repairs.

To Get There

From I-10 Picacho Exit (211A from Phoenix; 212 from Tucson), go 0.5–1 mi. on frontage road.

PICACHO PEAK

Picacho Peak RV Resort

P.O. Box 1100, Red Rock 85245. T: (520) 466-7841.

RV ★★★★ Tent n/a

Beauty: ★★★	Site Privacy: ★★★
Spaciousness: ★★★★	Quiet: ★★★
Security: ★★★★	Cleanliness: ★★★★★
Insect Control: ★★★★	Facilities: ★★★★★

Often confused with Picacho Campground seven miles to the north, Picacho Peak RV Resort exudes a very different atmosphere. Though the sites are attractively landscaped with medium-sized ocotillo, cacti, and trees, Picacho Peak RV Resort feels like an upscale RV parking annex for the mobile home park sharing the rear of the property. The benefit of mixing mobile homes and RVs is sharing the clean, well-maintained mobile home amenities. The RVs are closer to the interstate highway than the mobile homes, and the sandstone-colored perimeter wall and trees do not keep out all the truck noises and nightly train sounds. Also, there is not a convenience store here with the long hours found at Picacho Campground. However, the Resort is affiliated with Adventure Outdoor Resorts, Coast to Coast Network, and Resort Parks International, and members of those groups are promised good deals here.

Basics

Operated By: Picacho Peak Resort. **Open:** Oct.–May. **Site Assignment:** First come, first served; winter reservations advised. **Registration:** Office (hosts will come by site to collect money after hours). **Fee:** $23 (V, MC). **Parking:** At site.

Facilities

Number of RV Sites: 159. **Number of Tent-Only Sites:** 0. **Hookups:** Electric (30, 50 amp), water, sewer, phone (modem). **Each Site:** Table. **Dump Station:** Yes. **Laundry:** Yes. **Pay Phone:** Yes. **Rest Rooms and Showers:** Yes. **Fuel:** No. **Propane:** Yes. **Internal Roads:** Paved, excellent. **RV Service:** No. **Market:** Picacho Peak, 1 mi. **Restaurant:** Picacho Peak, 1 mi. **General Store:** No. **Vending:** Yes. **Swimming:** Pool. **Playground:** No. **Other:** Rec room, whirlpool, shuffleboard & volleyball courts, horseshoes, planned activities. **Activities:** Golf, horseback riding. **Nearby Attractions:** Picacho Peak SP, Casa Grande Ruins. **Additional Information:** Sunland Visitor Center, (520) 466-3007, Picacho SP, (520) 466-3183.

Restrictions

Pets: On leash under owner's control. **Fires:** Yes (where designated). **Alcoholic Beverages:** Allowed. **Vehicle Maximum Length:** 32 ft.

To Get There

From I-10, get off at Exit 219 and go south 0.5 mi. on frontage road.

PICACHO PEAK

Picacho Peak State Park

P.O. Box 275, Picacho 85241. T: (520) 466-3183; www.pr.state.az.us.

RV ★★★★ Tent ★★★★★

Beauty: ★★★★★	Site Privacy: ★★★★★
Spaciousness: ★★★★★	Quiet: ★★★★
Security: ★★★★	Cleanliness: ★★★★
Insect Control: ★★	Facilities: ★★

Picacho Peak, an ancient Hohokam Indian site, is a colorful mixture of 22-million-year-old lava flows and sedimentary rock strata rich in saguaro, cacti, grasses, and cottontail rabbits. Though it doesn't have the swimming pools and amenities of the nearby private campgrounds, Picacho Peak State Park is the best place to experience the raw nature of this historic area. The three loops are far enough back from the interstate highway that noise is not a problem. The 14-site hookup loop closest to the peak and park entrance is literally just a paved parking lot, albeit with a spectacular view and natural surroundings. Indeed, those who end up here as Catalina State Park overflow casualties are pleasantly surprised by the historic peak that served as a landmark for Father Kino, the Butterfield Overland Stage, and the forty-niners headed to the California gold fields.

Basics

Operated By: Arizona State Parks. **Open:** All year. **Site Assignment:** First come, first served; group area requires reservations. **Registration:** Self-pay station. **Fee:** $10–$15 (cash or check only). **Parking:** At site.

FACILITIES

Number of RV Sites: 109. **Number of Tent-Only Sites:** 0. **Hookups:** Electric (30 amp), water. **Each Site:** Table, grill. **Dump Station:** Yes. **Laundry:** No. **Pay Phone:** Yes. **Rest Rooms and Showers:** Yes. **Fuel:** No. **Propane:** No. **Internal Roads:** Paved, good. **RV Service:** No. **Market:** Picacho Peak, 1 mi. **Restaurant:** Picacho Peak, 1 mi. **General Store:** No. **Vending:** No. **Swimming:** No. **Playground:** Yes. **Other:** Small visitor center, some sheltered tables. **Activities:** Horseback riding, golf, bird & wildlife watching. **Nearby Attractions:** Casa Grande Ruins, Catalina State Park, Saguaro National Park West. **Additional Information:** Sunland Visitor Center, (520) 466-3007.

RESTRICTIONS

Pets: On leash under owner's control. **Fires:** Yes (except summer, when fire danger). **Alcoholic Beverages:** Allowed. **Vehicle Maximum Length:** None. **Other:** No fireworks.

TO GET THERE

From I-10, take Exit 219, Picacho Peak Rd.

PINETOP-LAKESIDE

Hawley Lake Resort

P.O. Box 448, McNary 85930. T: (520) 335-7511; F: (520) 335-7434.

RV: ★★★★ Tent: n/a

Beauty: ★★★★★ Site Privacy: ★★★★
Spaciousness: ★★★★★ Quiet: ★★★★★
Security: ★★★★★ Cleanliness: ★★★★★
Insect Control: ★★★ Facilities: ★★★★

Created in the 1950s by impounding Trout Creek, 300-acre Hawley Lake offers rustic waterfront camping on the lands of the White Mountain Apache. Tall ponderosa pine trees, boulder-strewn meadows, small waterfalls, roadside fishing (requires daily White Mountain Apache permit), and good lake views from many hillside campsites are among the attractions. Rainbow trout thrive in the lake, though Apache, brown, cutthroat, and brook trout are also caught summer and winter (ice fishing). Many prefer fall fishing when the browns come up in the shallows. Wild turkey, deer, elk, and black bear make for good wildlife viewing and attract hunters. Be prepared for cold weather here, as at 8,200 feet elevation, summer temperatures can drop below freezing at night. The last two miles into the lake are on a gravel road, and big vehicles should call ahead to make sure they can be accommodated.

BASICS

Operated By: White Mountain Apache Tribe. **Open:** All year. **Site Assignment:** First come, first served; reservations up to 1 year in advance. **Registration:** Office in store. **Fee:** $8 regular site, $25 hookups (V, MC, debit cards). **Parking:** At site.

FACILITIES

Number of RV Sites: 100. **Number of Tent-Only Sites:** 0. **Hookups:** Electric (30 amp), water, sewer. **Each Site:** Table, grill. **Dump Station:** Yes. **Laundry:** Yes. **Pay Phone:** Yes. **Rest Rooms and Showers:** Yes. **Fuel:** Yes. **Propane:** Yes. **Internal Roads:** Gravel, good (chains or 4x4 required in winter). **RV Service:** No. **Market:** Pinetop-Lakeside, 24 mi. **Restaurant:** Cafe on premises. **General Store:** Yes (summer only). **Vending:** No. **Swimming:** No. **Playground:** No. **Other:** Marina, boat rentals, lodge, cabins, summer home rentals. **Activities:** Boating, fishing, hunting, horseback riding, biking, backpacking, archery. **Nearby Attractions:** Lakes, forest, casino. **Additional Information:** White Mountain Apache Tribe Office of Tourism, (520) 338-1230, www.wmat.nsn.us.

RESTRICTIONS

Pets: On leash under owner's control. **Fires:** Yes. **Alcoholic Beverages:** Allowed (drunk driving laws strictly enforced). **Vehicle Maximum Length:** No stated limit (but check w/ tribe before bringing in big vehicles). **Other:** No tents, fireworks, ATVs, cattle rustling, or fence cutting.

TO GET THERE

From Pinetop-Lakeside, go 16 mi. southeast on AZ Hwy. 260 and 8 mi. south on AZ Hwy. 473.

PINETOP–LAKESIDE

Hon-Dah RV Park

One Hwy. 73, Pinetop 85935. T: (520) 369-7400 or (800) 929-8744+1+7400# (reservations).

RV: ★★★★ Tent: n/a

Beauty: ★★★★ Site Privacy: ★★★
Spaciousness: ★★★★ Quiet: ★★★
Security: ★★★★★ Cleanliness: ★★★★★
Insect Control: ★★★★ Facilities: ★★★★

A popular destination requiring advance reservations, Hon-Dah RV Park is across the street from Hon-Dah Casino's 500 slot machines and offers ample amenities to those visiting the area for boating, fishing, or winter skiing at nearby (20 miles) Sunrise Park Resort. The RV Park is in a wetlands area bisected by Corduroy Creek. There are 140 RV campsites south of the creek, and 58 reached by crossing a bridge and going uphill to the north side of the creek. Though the RV Park is near enough the highway to hear the hum of passing traffic, tall pines and gravel roads make the campground feel rustic, almost like camping in the wilderness. For those who want their forests and lake country with gambling and nighttime entertainment, this is a friendly place to put down after a day of fishing or boating.

BASICS

Operated By: White Mountain Apache Tribe. **Open:** All year. **Site Assignment:** First come, first served; reservations necessary. **Registration:** Office. **Fee:** $21 (V, MC). **Parking:** At site.

FACILITIES

Number of RV Sites: 198. **Number of Tent-Only Sites:** 0. **Hookups:** Electric (20, 30, 50 amp), water, sewer, satellite TV, phone. **Each Site:** Table, grill. **Dump Station:** Yes. **Laundry:** Yes. **Pay Phone:** Yes. **Rest Rooms and Showers:** Yes. **Fuel:** Yes. **Propane:** Yes. **Internal Roads:** Gravel, well-maintained. **RV Service:** No. **Market:** Pinetop-Lakeside, 5 mi. **Restaurant:** Casino, across street. **General Store:** Yes. **Vending:** Yes. **Swimming:** No. **Playground:** Yes. **Other:** Rec hall, casino, conference center. **Activities:** Shuffleboard, horseshoes, gambling, fishing, hunting, boating, winter sports. **Nearby Attractions:** Lakes, forests. **Additional Information:** White Mountain Apache Tribe Office of Tourism, (520) 338-1230, www.wmat.nsn.us; Sunrise Park Resort, (520) 735-7600, www.sunriseskipark.com.

RESTRICTIONS

Pets: On leash (requires prior approval; loud barking not tolerated). **Fires:** Yes. **Alcoholic Beverages:** At site only. **Vehicle Maximum Length:** None. **Other:** Pets must be walked along fence outside park perimeter; no smoking in buildings; pedestrians should carry flashlight at night; units over 10 years old must pass visual inspection (refund if turned away).

TO GET THERE

From Pinetop-Lakeside go 5 mi. east on AZ Hwy. 260 to junction w/ AZ Hwy. 73.

QUARTZSITE

La Posa LTVA

2555 Gila Ridge Rd., Yuma 85365. T: (520) 726-6300 or (520) 317-3200; www.az.blm.gov.

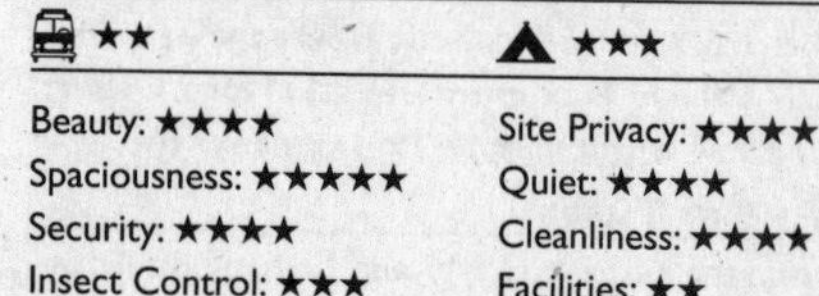

RV: ★★ Tent: ★★★

Beauty: ★★★★ Site Privacy: ★★★★
Spaciousness: ★★★★★ Quiet: ★★★★
Security: ★★★★ Cleanliness: ★★★★
Insect Control: ★★★ Facilities: ★★

Every winter Quartzsite's few thousand permanent residents are joined by 200,000 in RVs, and during the giant Gemboree (gem show/flea market) the population surges into the millions before its annual contraction back to almost nothing during the scorching summer months. Hundreds of unofficial RV parks spring up to join the official ones. Literally any patch of desert along the roadsides becomes RV habitat, though there is more security in Long-Term Visitor Areas (LTVA) like La Posa, operated by the US Department of Interior's Bureau of Land Management (BLM). Besides La Posa, BLM operates five smaller no-fee, 14-day limit camping areas (Plomosa Rd., Hi Jolly/MM112, Dome Rock Mountain, Scaddan Wash, Road Runner/MM99) around Quartzsite. Though La Posa lacks RV park amenities, it has the beauty of literally camping out in the desert wherever you choose, provided it is not too near another campsite (to reduce the danger of a fire spreading).

BASICS

Operated By: Bureau of Land Management. **Open:** All year. **Site Assignment:** First come, first served. **Registration:** Brown brick entrance contact stations. **Fee:** $20 (7-day permit; cash or check only). **Parking:** At site.

FACILITIES

Number of RV Sites: 2,000. **Number of Tent-Only Sites:** 0. **Hookups:** None. **Each Site:** At least 15 ft. distance from neighbors. **Dump Sta-**

tion: Yes. **Laundry:** No. **Pay Phone:** Yes. **Rest Rooms and Showers:** No showers. **Fuel:** No. **Propane:** No. **Internal Roads:** Gravel, adequate. **RV Service:** No. **Market:** Quartzsite, 1 mi. **Restaurant:** Quartzsite, 1 mi. **General Store:** No. **Vending:** No. **Swimming:** No. **Playground:** No. **Activities:** Winter ranger presentations, gem show. **Nearby Attractions:** Colorado River. **Additional Information:** Quartzsite Chamber of Commerce, (520) 927-5600, www.quartzsitechamber.com.

Restrictions

Pets: On leash under owner's control. **Fires:** Yes (subject to posted rules). **Alcoholic Beverages:** Allowed. **Vehicle Maximum Length:** None. **Other:** No camping in desert washes.

To Get There

From junction of I-10 and AZ Hwy. 95 in Quartzsite, go south 1 mi. on AZ Hwy. 95.

ROOSEVELT

Cholla Recreation Site

Tonto Basin Ranger District, HC02 Box 4800, Roosevelt 85545. T: (520) 467-3200; F: (520) 467-3239; www.fs.fed.us/r3/tonto.

RV: ★★★ Tent: ★★★★★

Beauty: ★★★★★	Site Privacy: ★★★★★
Spaciousness: ★★★★★	Quiet: ★★★★★
Security: ★★★★	Cleanliness: ★★★★★
Insect Control: ★★★	Facilities: ★★

The largest completely solar-powered campground in the United States, Cholla Campground and Boating Site is located on the shores of central Arizona's largest lake, Theodore Roosevelt Lake. Blue shelters make the campground look like a blue-roofed village with solar panels amidst the tall saguaro, mesquite, and palo verde providing the campsites a privacy barrier. The 13 tent-only sites furthest from the boat ramp on the steep slopes at the end of Christmas Cholla Loop and the five tent-only sites at Cane Cholla Loop on the slopes closer to the campground entrance have the best waterfront views. The gravel and sand campsites are flat, and many double sites are available for those with multiple vehicles and big boats. For those wanting a more primitive experience, head to Indian Point on the northeast side of the lake or checkout the sometimes crowded beach camping nearby at Bachelor Cove or Cholla Cove.

Basics

Operated By: US Forest Service. **Open:** All year. **Site Assignment:** First come, first served. **Registration:** Kiosk or self-pay station. **Fee:** $11–$17 (highest for double sites; half price for Golden Age pass holders; V, MC). **Parking:** At site; separate walk-in tent site parking near restrooms.

Facilities

Number of RV Sites: 188. **Number of Tent-Only Sites:** 18. **Hookups:** None. **Each Site:** Sheltered table, grill, fire pit. **Dump Station:** Yes. **Laundry:** No. **Pay Phone:** No. **Rest Rooms and Showers:** Yes. **Fuel:** No. **Propane:** No. **Internal Roads:** Paved, good. **RV Service:** No. **Market:** Globe, 36 mi. **Restaurant:** Roosevelt, 5 mi. **General Store:** No. **Vending:** No. **Swimming:** Lake. **Playground:** Yes. **Other:** Boat ramp, campfire circle, fish cleaning station, barrier-free wheelchair accessibility. **Activities:** Boating, fishing. **Nearby Attractions:** Tonto National Monument, Roosevelt Dam, Globe, Payson. **Additional Information:** Salt River Project (for water level information), (602) 236-3929, www.srpnet.com; Roosevelt Lake Marina, (520) 467-2245.

Restrictions

Pets: On leash under owner's control. **Fires:** Yes. **Alcoholic Beverages:** Allowed. **Vehicle Maximum Length:** None. **Other:** No ATVs or firearms.

To Get There

From Globe take AZ Hwy. 88/188 west for 36 mi.

ROOSEVELT

Windy Hill Recreation Site

HC02 Box 4800, Roosevelt 85545. T: (520) 467-3200; F: (520) 467-3239; www.fs.fed.us/r3/tonto.

RV: ★★★ Tent: ★★★★

Beauty: ★★★★	Site Privacy: ★★★★
Spaciousness: ★★★★	Quiet: ★★★
Security: ★★★★	Cleanliness: ★★★★
Insect Control: ★★★★	Facilities: ★★

Often packed full with local boaters on summer weekends, Windy Hill feels isolated because it is two miles from the main highway and the campsites are widely dispersed among ten loops. Each loop has its own trailheads and is named after a different animal that might be seen in the area, such as javelina, desert bighorn, gray fox, and coati. However, it is the rattlesnake (which does not have a loop named after it) which has to be watched out for here and in most other Arizona campgrounds. Double sites are big enough for a small beach party, packing in up to four cars, two boats, and 20 people. The level ground is good for tenting, and abundant desert plants like palo verde, ocotillo, and mesquite between the campsites add to the feeling of isolation and privacy.

Basics

Operated By: US Forest Service. **Open:** All year. **Site Assignment:** First come, first served; group reservations. **Registration:** Self-pay fee machines. **Fee:** $10–$11 single & tent sites, $16–$17 double sites (V, MC; no checks). **Parking:** At site.

Facilities

Number of RV Sites: 320. **Number of Tent-Only Sites:** 27. **Hookups:** None. **Each Site:** Sheltered table, grill. **Dump Station:** Yes (5 mi. east). **Laundry:** No. **Pay Phone:** No. **Rest Rooms and Showers:** Yes. **Fuel:** No. **Propane:** No. **Internal Roads:** Gravel, good. **RV Service:** No. **Market:** Globe, 27 mi. **Restaurant:** Roosevelt, 6 mi. **General Store:** No. **Vending:** No. **Swimming:** Lake. **Playground:** Yes. **Other:** Amphitheater, fish cleaning station, high- & low-water boat ramps, day-use picnic sites, wheelchair accessible sites. **Activities:** Boating, fishing. **Nearby Attractions:** Tonto National Monument, Roosevelt Dam, Globe. **Additional Information:** Salt River Project (for water level information), (602) 236-3929, www.srpnet.com; Roosevelt Lake Marina, (520) 467-2245.

Restrictions

Pets: On leash. **Fires:** Yes (fires prohibited when high winds). **Alcoholic Beverages:** Allowed. **Vehicle Maximum Length:** 30 ft. **Other:** No glass containers.

To Get There

From Globe take AZ Hwy. 88/188 west for 25 mi., then go east for 2 mi. on Frontage Rd. 82 at Windy Hill Recreation Site entrance sign.

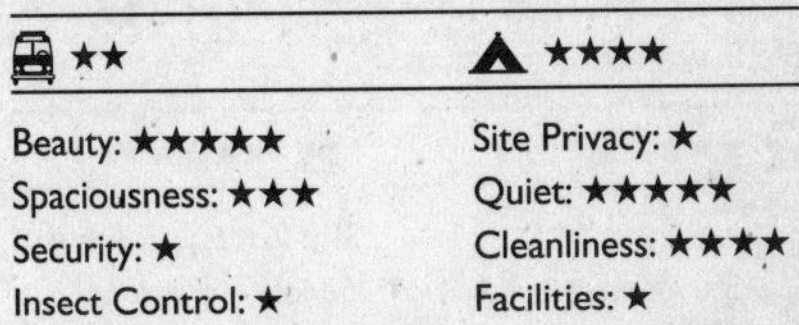

SEDONA

Manzanita

2323 East Greenlaw Ln., Flagstaff 86004. T: (520) 527-3600.

RV: ★★ Tent: ★★★★

Beauty: ★★★★★	Site Privacy: ★
Spaciousness: ★★★	Quiet: ★★★★★
Security: ★	Cleanliness: ★★★★
Insect Control: ★	Facilities: ★

Charming, gorgeous, breathtaking, revitalizing—pick any superlative, they all fit. But so does "filled quickly." This campsite is a favorite in the well-traveled Oak Creek Canyon—and for good reason. Striking red rock bursts out of the forested hills above the creek, while rocky crags jut overhead. The entire canyon is beautiful and, as one local resident put it, "plum fulla history." The campsites mostly string out along the creek, and these sites (along with 10 and 19 on the ends) are the most highly-prized. The sites to avoid are 6 and 7 situated by the outhouse and up against the road. Admittedly, this campsite is not for everyone, and the lack of services or the hairpin turn in the road that prohibits larger rigs may put off more than one. (Those who do want full hookups or don't want to negotiate that curve could press on down Hwy. 89A to the lovely Rio Verde in Cottonwood.) However, campers looking for a great base for outdoor activities or a really romantic nook should definitely try their luck at scoring one of these spots.

Basics

Operated By: National Forest Service. **Open:** All year. **Site Assignment:** First come, first served. **Registration:** Pick a site, register w/ camp host. **Fee:** $15. **Parking:** At sites.

Facilities

Number of RV Sites: 18. **Number of Tent-Only Sites:** 0. **Hookups:** None. **Each Site:** Picnic table, concrete fire pit, trees. **Dump Station:** No. **Laundry:** No. **Pay Phone:** No. **Rest Rooms and Showers:** Pit toilets, no showers. **Fuel:** No. **Propane:** No. **Internal Roads:** Paved. **RV Service:** No. **Market:** 2 mi. south on Hwy. 89A. **Restaurant:** 1 mi. south on Hwy. 89A. **General Store:** No. **Vending:** No. **Swimming:** In creek. **Playground:** No. **Other:** Well water, murmur of Oak Creek. **Activities:** Hiking, fishing, swimming, mountain biking; boating & other water sports at nearby Mormon Lake. **Nearby Attractions:** Oak

Creek Canyon, Mormon Lake (seasonally the largest lake in Arizona). **Additional Information:** Sedona-Oak Creek Chamber of Commerce, (800) 228-7336.

RESTRICTIONS

Pets: On leash. **Fires:** In pit or grill. **Alcoholic Beverages:** At sites only. **Vehicle Maximum Length:** Larger than 24 ft. is unfeasible, due to a hairpin bend in the road. **Other:** 7-day stay limit.

TO GET THERE

Five mi. north of "Midgely Bridgely" at the northernmost edge of town on Hwy. 89A.

SHOW LOW

Fool Hollow Lake Recreation Area

P.O. Box 288, Show Low 85901. T: (520) 537-3680; www.pr.state.az.us.

RV ★★★★★ Tent ★★★★★

Beauty: ★★★★	Site Privacy: ★★★★
Spaciousness: ★★★★	Quiet: ★★★★★
Security: ★★★★★	Cleanliness: ★★★★★
Insect Control: ★★★	Facilities: ★★★

Established in 1991 as a partnership between the city of Show Low, the US Forest Service, Arizona State Parks, and Arizona Game and Fish, Fool Hollow provides RV campers with large cement pads and hookups in four separate loops (Red Head, Mallard, Ruddy Duck, and Cinnamon Teal). Tent campers have good lake views from their three separate loops (Northern Harrier, Osprey, Bald Eagle). Pines, tall junipers, volcanic boulders, and jack rabbits contribute to the rustic feel. Show Low Creek feeds Fool Hollow Lake, which is stocked with rainbow trout by Arizona Game and Fish. There is also a good chance of catching brown trout, large and small mouth bass, black crappie, and green sunfish. Away from the water are 103 miles of hiking trails within 15 miles and golf links in the rapidly suburbanizing surrounding area.

BASICS

Operated By: Arizona State Parks. **Open:** All year. **Site Assignment:** First come, first served. **Registration:** Self-pay station. **Fee:** $10 tent, $15 RV. **Parking:** At site.

FACILITIES

Number of RV Sites: 92. **Number of Tent-Only Sites:** 31. **Hookups:** Electric (30, 50 amp), water. **Each Site:** Table, grill. **Dump Station:** Yes. **Laundry:** No. **Pay Phone:** Yes. **Rest Rooms and Showers:** Yes. **Fuel:** No. **Propane:** No. **Internal Roads:** Paved, excellent. **RV Service:** No. **Market:** Show Low, 4 mi. **Restaurant:** Show Low, 4 mi. **General Store:** No. **Vending:** No. **Swimming:** Lake. **Playground:** Yes. **Other:** Boat ramps, fish cleaning station, fishing docks, covered picnic tables w/ grills, wildlife island. **Activities:** Boating, fishing, golf. **Nearby Attractions:** Lakes, forests, Mogollon Rim, Petrified Forest. **Additional Information:** Show Low Chamber of Commerce, (520) 537-2326.

RESTRICTIONS

Pets: On leash (not allowed on beaches or in buildings). **Fires:** In grills only; firewood sold. **Alcoholic Beverages:** Allowed. **Vehicle Maximum Length:** None. **Other:** Entrance gate closed 10 p.m. to 5 a.m.; no fireworks; food must be secured from bears; 8 horsepower limit on boat motors.

TO GET THERE

From junction of US Hwy. 60 and AZ Hwy. 260, go 2 mi. west on Hwy. 260 and 1.5 mi. east on Old Linden Rd. to Fool Hollow Rd.

SHOW LOW

Show Low Lake County Park

Navajo County Parks & Recreation Dept., Holbrook 86025. T: (520) 537-4126 or (520) 524-4251; www.parksrec@navajo.az.us.

RV ★★★ Tent ★★★★

Beauty: ★★★★	Site Privacy: ★★★★
Spaciousness: ★★★★★	Quiet: ★★★★
Security: ★★★★	Cleanliness: ★★★★★
Insect Control: ★★★	Facilities: ★★★★

Show Low Lake was formed when the Phelps Dodge Corporation built Show Low Dam as part of a water exchange agreement with the Salt River Project to supply water to its mining and metallurgical operations elsewhere in the state. Indeed, the park land is leased from Phelps Dodge. Navajo County recently issued a private vendor a special permit to run the park and take campsite reservations. At 7,000 feet elevation in the White Mountains, the area makes a relatively cool summer retreat for Phoenix and the hot desert valleys. Show Low Lake is also a popular fishing spot for trout, walleyes, bluegills, large mouth bass, and catfish. The large crushed brown volcanic gravel campsites are shaded by very tall pine trees. For electric hookups request sites 25, 26, 28, 31, 32, 33, or 35. When the need for manmade necessities strikes, the local Walmart is only a mile away.

BASICS

Operated By: Recreation Resource Management of America. **Open:** All year. **Site Assignment:** First come, first served; reservations available. **Registration:** Store (adjacent host trailer when store is closed). **Fee:** $8–$16. **Parking:** At site.

FACILITIES

Number of RV Sites: 73. **Number of Tent-Only Sites:** 0. **Hookups:** Electric (30 amp), water. **Each Site:** Table, fire pit. **Dump Station:** Yes. **Laundry:** No. **Pay Phone:** Yes. **Rest Rooms and Showers:** Yes. **Fuel:** No. **Propane:** No. **Internal Roads:** Gravel, good. **RV Service:** No. **Market:** Show Low, 1 mi. **Restaurant:** Show Low, 1 mi. **General Store:** Yes. **Vending:** Yes. **Swimming:** Lake. **Playground:** Yes. **Other:** Boat ramp, boat rental, visitor center. **Activities:** Boating, fishing. **Nearby Attractions:** Lakes, forests, Mogollon Rim, Petrified Forest. **Additional Information:** Show Low Chamber of Commerce, (520) 537-2326.

RESTRICTIONS

Pets: On leash. **Fires:** Yes (firewood sold). **Alcoholic Beverages:** Allowed. **Vehicle Maximum Length:** None. **Other:** Boats limited to one 8 horsepower motor; no firearms or woodcutting; secure food from bears.

TO GET THERE

From Show Low go 6 mi. south on AZ Hwy. 260.

ST. JOHNS

Lyman Lake State Park

P.O. Box 1428, St. Johns 85936. T: (520) 337-4441; F: (520) 337-4649; www.pr.state.az.us.

RV ★★★★ Tent ★★★★

Beauty: ★★★★	Site Privacy: ★★★★
Spaciousness: ★★★★	Quiet: ★★★★★
Security: ★★★★	Cleanliness: ★★★★★
Insect Control: ★★★★	Facilities: ★★★★

A favorite of local windsurfers and waterskiiers because of the lake's smooth surface, boaters like 6,000-foot-elevation Lyman Lake because it doesn't have boat size and motor horsepower restrictions (though there is a no-wake area near the fishing dock). There is a self-guided petroglyph trail on Peninsula Point, as well as a ranger-guided weekend boat trip to another petroglyph trail on the opposite side of the lake. Rangers also lead a summer tour to fourteenth-century Rattlesnake Pueblo for those curious about the ancient Mogollon and Pueblo cultures formerly inhabiting this high plains area. RV campers have 38 electrical and water hookup sites attractively separated by grass and aspen and juniper trees. Tent campers can opt out of the designated sites altogether for more of a wilderness experience and camp along the shoreline beaches of this 1,500-acre reservoir.

BASICS

Operated By: Arizona State Parks. **Open:** All year. **Site Assignment:** First come, first served; group reservations. **Registration:** Office. **Fee:** $10–$15 (cash or check only). **Parking:** At site.

FACILITIES

Number of RV Sites: 61. **Number of Tent-Only Sites:** Undesignated sites. **Hookups:** Electric (30 amp), water. **Each Site:** Table, fire pit. **Dump Station:** Yes. **Laundry:** No. **Pay Phone:** Yes. **Rest Rooms and Showers:** Yes. **Fuel:** No. **Propane:** No. **Internal Roads:** Paved, good. **RV Service:** No. **Market:** St. Johns, 10 mi. **Restaurant:** St. Johns, 10 mi. **General Store:** Yes. **Vending:** Yes. **Swimming:** Lake. **Playground:** No. **Other:** Boat ramp, boat rentals, fish-cleaning station, sheltered picnic tables, tournamen-grade water ski slalom course, petroglyph trails. **Activities:** Fishing, boating, water sports, volleyball, horseshoes. **Nearby Attractions:** Sunrise Ski Area, White Mountains, Petrified Forest, Navajo Reservation. **Additional Information:** St. Johns Regional Chamber of Commerce, (520) 337-2000.

RESTRICTIONS

Pets: On leash. **Fires:** In fire pits or grills only; no wood gathering. **Alcoholic Beverages:** Allowed (provided quiet hours observed). **Vehicle Maximum Length:** 45 ft. **Other:** No harassing or removing birds.

To Get There

From St. Johns go 11 mi. south on the combined US Hwy. 191/180.

TEMPLE BAR

Temple Bar

601 Nevada Hwy., Boulder City 89005. T: (702) 293-8907; F: (702) 293-8936; www.nps.gov/lame.

RV ★★★ Tent ★★★★

Beauty: ★★★★ Site Privacy: ★★★★
Spaciousness: ★★★★ Quiet: ★★★★
Security: ★★★★ Cleanliness: ★★★★★
Insect Control: ★★★ Facilities: ★★★

On the Arizona side of Lake Mead, across yucca-studded desert that yields to creosote bush interspersed with brown and black chunks of lava and white hills, Temple Bar is one of the most remote designated campgrounds on Lake Mead. The Temple, a huge monolithic chunk of sandstone that glows brilliant orange at sunset, was an early landmark for Mormon settlers and the site of placer mining operations in the 1800s. The campground is a tightly packed cluster of sites beautifully landscaped with palms, oleander. and eucalyptus that provide privacy. Gravel pads make for good tent camping, and lake and mountain views are common. The campground's remoteness and isolation are part of its beauty, and like the rest of Lake Mead, the activities center around the water. There are 64 boat slips.

Basics

Operated By: National Park Service. **Open:** All year. **Site Assignment:** First come, first served. **Registration:** Self-pay entrance fee station. **Fee:** $10. **Parking:** At site.

Facilities

Number of RV Sites: 166. **Number of Tent-Only Sites:** 0. **Hookups:** None. **Each Site:** Table, grill. **Dump Station:** Yes. **Laundry:** Yes. **Pay Phone:** Yes. **Rest Rooms and Showers:** Yes. **Fuel:** Yes. **Propane:** Yes. **Internal Roads:** Paved, good. **RV Service:** No. **Market:** Boulder City, 60 mi. **Restaurant:** At Temple Bar Resort. **General Store:** Yes. **Vending:** Yes. **Swimming:** In lake at own risk. **Playground:** No. **Other:** Wheelchair accessible sites, boat ramp, row boat rentals, motel, landing strip. **Activities:** Boating, fishing. **Nearby Attractions:** Lake Mead, Hoover Dam, Las Vegas. **Additional Information:** Temple Bar Resort (Seven Crowns), (800) 752-9669, (520) 767-3211.

Restrictions

Pets: On leash under owner's control. **Fires:** Yes. **Alcoholic Beverages:** Allowed. **Vehicle Maximum Length:** None. **Other:** 30-night stay limit.

To Get There

From Hoover Dam go 19 mi. southeast on US Hwy. 93 and turn northeast on Temple Bar Rd. for 28 mi.

TOMBSTONE

Wells Fargo RV Park

Box 1076, Tombstone 85638. T: (520) 457-3966 or (800) 269-8266; F: (520) 457-2307; si-systems.com/wellsfargorv; wellsfargorv@si-systems.com.

RV ★★★ Tent ★★★

Beauty: ★★★ Site Privacy: ★★★★
Spaciousness: ★★★ Quiet: ★★★★
Security: ★★★ Cleanliness: ★★★★
Insect Control: ★★★★ Facilities: ★★★★

Though at the edge of Tombstone's historic boardwalk, Wells Fargo RV Park becomes almost as quiet as a tomb at night, as this once brawling, saloon and brothel-filled frontier mining town now shuts down at sundown. Some claim to hear ghosts at night, but usually the only commotion at this tree-lined campground is dogs in a howling frenzy as deer and javelina strolling through like they own the place. Wells Fargo's year-round residents are mostly a friendly group, and many work at local establishments like Big Nose Kate's Saloon. Next door is what locals call the best breakfast place in town, the O.K. Cafe, which also charbroils emu, ostrich, and buffalo burgers. It's "just a biscuit sling from the OK Corral," where Doc Holliday joined Wyatt and the Earp brothers for the famous shootout with the Clanton and McLaury families.

Basics

Operated By: Joe & Buff Huntsman. **Open:** All year. **Site Assignment:** First come, first served; reservations advised Dec. 26–Memorial Day. **Registration:** Office. **Fee:** $21.50. **Parking:** At site.

Facilities

Number of RV Sites: 71. **Number of Tent-Only Sites:** 0. **Hookups:** Electric (20, 30 amp), water, sewer, cable TV. **Each Site:** Table, cement pad. **Dump Station:** Yes. **Laundry:** Yes. **Pay Phone:** Yes. **Rest Rooms and Showers:** Yes. **Fuel:** No. **Propane:** No. **Internal Roads:** Gravel, good. **RV Service:** No. **Market:** Bisbee, 19 mi. **Restaurant:** Tombstone, next door. **General Store:** No. **Vending:** Yes. **Swimming:** No. **Playground:** No. **Activities:** 2 p.m. daily OK Corral shootout. **Nearby Attractions:** OK Corral, Tombstone Courthouse State Park, Bird Cage Theatre, Bisbee. **Additional Information:** Tombstone Chamber of Commerce, (520) 457-9317 or (888) 457-3929, www.tombstone.org.

Restrictions

Pets: On leash under owner's control. **Fires:** No. **Alcoholic Beverages:** Allowed. **Vehicle Maximum Length:** 30 ft.

To Get There

From junction of US Hwy. 80 & AZ Hwy. 82, go 3 mi. south on US Hwy. 80.

TORTILLA FLAT

Laguna Beach Campground

P.O. Box 4978, Apache Junction 85278. T: (602) 944-6504 (voice option #1); F: (480) 380-9301; www.canyonlakemarinaaz.com; customer.service@canyonlakemarinaaz.com.

RV ★★★ Tent ★★

Beauty: ★★★★ Site Privacy: ★★
Spaciousness: ★★★ Quiet: ★★★
Security: ★★★★★ Cleanliness: ★★★★
Insect Control: ★★★ Facilities: ★★★★

At Canyon Lake, 17 miles north of Apache Junction, a gated kiosk and steel fence encloses Laguna Beach Campground, a lakeside stretch of parking lot and grassy campsites (ten hookups) within Canyon Lake Marina. The Marina prides itself on round-the-clock security and being "a gated community with the lake as one border and steel fencing preventing land access." Campers must adhere to strict rules, like no fishing around the boat dock or restaurant without a Marina member. Jet skies, mini-bikes, boats, and trailers are among the items banned from the campground, though they can be left in the parking lot on the other side of the steel fence or stored for a fee. Getting to this maximum security campground is a scenic ordeal via a slow twisting mountain road with one-lane bridges for added adventure. If this sounds like too much of an ordeal, there is always Roosevelt Lake.

Basics

Operated By: Canyon Lake Marina. **Open:** All year. **Site Assignment:** First come, first served; reservations recommended (no refund on cancellation of reservation made 60 days in advance or for a Friday). **Registration:** Gated entrance kiosk. **Fee:** $12–$15 tent; $15–$30 RV (V, MC, AE, DC). **Parking:** At site.

Facilities

Number of RV Sites: 27. **Number of Tent-Only Sites:** 19. **Hookups:** Electric (30 amp), water. **Each Site:** Table, fire ring. **Dump Station:** No. **Laundry:** No. **Pay Phone:** Yes. **Rest Rooms and Showers:** Yes. **Fuel:** No (boat fuel only). **Propane:** No. **Internal Roads:** Paved, good. **RV Service:** No. **Market:** Apache Junction, 17 mi. **Restaurant:** Marina, adjacent. **General Store:** No. **Vending:** No. **Swimming:** Lake. **Playground:** No. **Other:** Storage, boat & slip rentals. **Activities:** Boating, fishing, steamboat ride. **Nearby Attractions:** Roosevelt Lake, Tonto National Monument, parks. **Additional Information:** Apache Junction Chamber of Commerce, (800) 252-3141 or (602) 982-3141.

Restrictions

Pets: On leash. **Fires:** In fire rings only. **Alcoholic Beverages:** Allowed (glass containers prohibited; $50 bottle fine). **Vehicle Maximum Length:** 40 ft. **Other:** No gas containers; no weapons; gate closed sunset to sundown.

To Get There

From Apache Junction, go northeast 17 mi. on AZ Hwy. 88 (Apache Trail).

TSAILE

Wheatfields Lake

P.O. Box 9000, Window Rock 86515. T: (520) 871-6645 or (520) 871-7307.

 ★★ ▲ ★★★★

Beauty: ★★★★ Site Privacy: ★★★★
Spaciousness: ★★★★ Quiet: ★★★★★
Security: ★★★ Cleanliness: ★★
Insect Control: ★★★ Facilities: ★

Just east of Canyon de Chelly at 7,200 feet elevation, Wheatfields Lake is a relatively uncrowded place to catch cutthroat and rainbow trout, though a fishing permit first needs to be obtained from Navajo Fish & Wildlife (call (520) 871-6451) in Window Rock. Unlike Camp Asaayi Campground at Asaayi Lake where the terrain mitigates against RVs, smaller vehicles can squeeze into Wheatfields Lake when the weather is favorable. If the beer cans left behind by those not observing the tribal prohibition on alcohol are too much of an eyesore while shoreline fishing near the roadside, the other side of the lake can be reached by vehicle, and a boat can be launched from the base of the Chuska Mountains. The campground gets plenty of shade from tall ponderosa pines, though with port-a-potties this is a primitive spot in a rural area where careful driving is advised to avoid hitting horses grazing too close to the road.

BASICS

Operated By: Navajo Nation. **Open:** All year. **Site Assignment:** First come, first served. **Registration:** Self-pay fee station. **Fee:** $5. **Parking:** At site.

FACILITIES

Number of RV Sites: 25. **Number of Tent-Only Sites:** 0. **Hookups:** None. **Each Site:** Table, grill. **Dump Station:** No. **Laundry:** No. **Pay Phone:** Yes. **Rest Rooms and Showers:** No showers. **Fuel:** No. **Propane:** No. **Internal Roads:** Dirt, bumpy. **RV Service:** No. **Market:** Window Rock, 43 mi. **Restaurant:** Tsaile, 12 mi. **General Store:** Yes (sporadically open). **Vending:** No. **Swimming:** Lake. **Playground:** No. **Activities:** Fishing, boating. **Nearby Attractions:** Canyon de Chelly, Window Rock. **Additional Information:** Navajo Nation Visitor Center, (520) 871-6436.

RESTRICTIONS

Pets: On leash under owner's control. **Fires:** Yes. **Alcoholic Beverages:** Prohibited on Navajo Reservation. **Vehicle Maximum Length:** 20 ft.

TO GET THERE

From Window Rock, go 43 mi. north on Indian Hwy. 12.

TUCSON

Catalina State Park

P.O. Box 36986, Tucson 85740. T: (520) 628-5798; www.pr.state.az.us.

 ★★★★ ▲ ★★★★★

Beauty: ★★★★ Site Privacy: ★★★★
Spaciousness: ★★★★★ Quiet: ★★★★
Security: ★★★★ Cleanliness: ★★★★
Insect Control: ★★★ Facilities: ★★

Big patches of mesquite ensure privacy at Catalina State Park, where the smallest campsite length is 55 feet and half the sites have hookups. Ten years ago this Santa Catalina Mountains desert foothill cattle ranching area was considered remote. Now Tangerine Rd. between I-10 and the park and the whole Oro Valley is filling up with subdivisions for retirees and aerospace engineers commuting to Tucson. Park roads run through a floodplain with flat ridges that provided the ancient Hohokams a home with water. When Sutherland Wash, the key floodplain drainage, becomes impossible to cross, access to hiking trails and Romero Ruins is blocked, though the campground is still reachable. From Jan. through Apr., Tucson's peak season, morning arrivals snag all the campsites by noon. Afternoon arrivals (overflow) are typically sent to either Gilbert Ray Campground or Picacho Peak State Park. Plans call for alleviating winter-use pressures by adding 75 campsites with electric hookups.

BASICS

Operated By: Arizona State Parks. **Open:** All year. **Site Assignment:** First come, first served; group reservations required. **Registration:** Self-pay station. **Fee:** $10–$15 (cash or check only). **Parking:** At site.

FACILITIES

Number of RV Sites: 48. **Number of Tent-Only Sites:** 0. **Hookups:** Electric (20, 30, 50 amp), water. **Each Site:** Table, grill. **Dump Station:** Yes. **Laundry:** No. **Pay Phone:** Yes. **Rest Rooms and Showers:** Yes. **Fuel:** No. **Propane:** No. **Internal Roads:** Paved, good condition. **RV Service:** No. **Market:** Oro Valley, 2 mi. **Restaurant:** Oro Valley, 2 mi. **General Store:** No. **Vending:** Yes. **Swimming:** Seasonal pools along hiking trails. **Playground:** No. **Other:** Romero Ruin Hohokam Indian archaeological site. **Activities:** Horseback riding, bird-watching, golf. **Nearby Attractions:** Santa Catalina Mountains, Coronado National Forest, Biosphere 2. **Additional Information:** Santa Catalina Ranger District, (520) 749-8700.

RESTRICTIONS

Pets: On leash under owner's control. **Fires:** Yes (charcoal only; no wood fires, except 1 campfire pit in group area). **Alcoholic Beverages:** Allowed. **Vehicle Maximum Length:** 136 ft. **Other:** 14-day stay limit.

TO GET THERE

Go 9 mi. north of Tucson on AZ Hwy. 77 (Oracle Rd.) to mi. marker 81.

TUCSON

Crazy Horse Campground & RV Park

6660 South Craycroft Rd., Tucson 85706. T: (520) 574-0157 or (800) 279-6279.

★★★★ ▲ ★★★

Beauty: ★★★ Site Privacy: ★★★★
Spaciousness: ★★★★ Quiet: ★★★★
Security: ★★★★ Cleanliness: ★★★★
Insect Control: ★★★★ Facilities: ★★★★

Far enough back from I-10 to be quiet and near enough a truck stop to have a gas station, mini-mart, and restaurant next door, Crazy Horse is especially attractive to families with children. Thomas Jay Littletown Park, a quiet Pima County–run park two blocks north, is popular with kids and an easy walk from Crazy Horse. Most sites are pull-through, mostly 24-feet wide and accommodating vehicles up to 45 feet in length (one site accommodates a 60-foot vehicle). The attractive oleander, mesquite and agave landscaping is concentrated around the front of the campground. For more amenities and the feel of a small luxury city, the adult-oriented Voyager RV Resort a few miles down the road is a good alternative. Cochise Terrace in Benson should also be considered if the objective is establishing a base camp near Tucson for exploring places like Tombstone and Bisbee.

BASICS

Operated By: Frank & Billie Anne Weingart. **Open:** All year. **Site Assignment:** First come, first served; reservations accepted seasonally (nonrefundable fee for confirmation by mail). **Registration:** Office. **Fee:** $19–$21 (V, MC). **Parking:** At site.

FACILITIES

Number of RV Sites: 154. **Number of Tent-Only Sites:** 0. **Hookups:** Electric (20, 30, 50 amp), water, sewer, cable TV, phone. **Each Site:** Table. **Dump Station:** Yes. **Laundry:** Yes. **Pay Phone:** Yes. **Rest Rooms and Showers:** Yes. **Fuel:** Yes. **Propane:** Yes. **Internal Roads:** Paved, good. **RV Service:** No. **Market:** Tucson, 3 mi. **Restaurant:** Tucson, 1 block. **General Store:** Yes. **Vending:** Yes. **Swimming:** Pool. **Playground:** Yes. **Other:** Dog walk, rec hall. **Activities:** Golf, horseback riding. **Nearby Attractions:** Pima Air & Space Museum, Saguaro National Park East, Colossal Cave, Kartchner Caverns, museums. **Additional Information:** Tucson CVB, (800) 638-8350, www.visitTucson.org.

RESTRICTIONS

Pets: On leash under owner's control. **Fires:** In approved containers & hibachis; no open fires. **Alcoholic Beverages:** Allowed. **Vehicle Maximum Length:** 60 ft.

TO GET THERE

Take Exit 268 from I-10 and go north on S. Craycroft Rd.

TUCSON

Gilbert Ray Campground

1204 West Silverlake Rd., Tucson 85713. T: (520) 740-2690 or (520) 883-4200.

 ★★★★  ★★★★

Beauty: ★★★★ Site Privacy: ★★★★
Spaciousness: ★★★★★ Quiet: ★★★★
Security: ★★★ Cleanliness: ★★★★
Insect Control: ★★★ Facilities: ★

A favorite of many for its low cost and location west of Tucson near Saguaro National Park West and the Desert Museum, Gilbert Ray's river gravel sites are a particularly convenient stopping place when driving from Ajo or Organ Pipe Cactus National Monument through the Tohono O'odham Indian Reservation en route to Tucson on Arizona Hwy. 86 (Ajo Hwy.). This large, looping Pima County campground in Tucson Mountain Park is as close as camping gets to Saguaro National Park West without backpacking. Though there are hookups, the campground has few other amenities besides newspaper machines and a large recycling area. Campers here are mostly self-sufficient types whose idea of amenities is an undeveloped landscape with saguaro-studded mountains. Kinney, Gates Pass, and McCain Loop Rds. have roller coaster–like ups and downs near Gilbert Ray, and numerous roadside pullouts double as trailheads for traversing saguaro-rich Tucson Mountain Park.

Basics

Operated By: Pima County Parks & Recreation. **Open:** All year. **Site Assignment:** First come, first served. **Registration:** Self-pay station. **Fee:** $7 tent; $12 RV (cash or check only). **Parking:** At site.

Facilities

Number of RV Sites: 136. **Number of Tent-Only Sites:** 5. **Hookups:** Electric (30 amp), water, sewer. **Each Site:** Table, grill. **Dump Station:** Yes. **Laundry:** No. **Pay Phone:** No. **Rest Rooms and Showers:** No showers. **Fuel:** No. **Propane:** No. **Internal Roads:** Paved, excellent. **RV Service:** No. **Market:** Tucson Estates, 5 mi. **Restaurant:** Tucson Estates, 5 mi. **General Store:** No. **Vending:** No. **Swimming:** No. **Playground:** No. **Other:** Some sheltered tables, recycling station. **Activities:** Rifle range, archery, horseback riding, biking. **Nearby Attractions:** Old Tucson Studios, Arizona-Sonora Desert Museum, Saguaro National Park West. **Additional Information:** Friends of Saguaro National Park, (520) 622-1080, www.friendsofsaguaro.org.

Restrictions

Pets: On leash under owner's control. **Fires:** Charcoal only in grills only; no wood fires. **Alcoholic Beverages:** Allowed. **Vehicle Maximum Length:** 30 ft. **Other:** 7-day stay limit; $160 automatic noncompliance citation if site not paid for within 15 min. of occupancy.

To Get There

From intersection of W. Gates Pass & Kinney Rds., go northwest to McCain Loop Rd.

TUCSON

Voyager RV Resort

8701 South Kolb Rd., Tucson 85706. T: (520) 574-5000 or (800) 424-9191; F: (520) 574-5037; www.VoyagerRV.com; info@VoyagerRV.com.

RV ★★★★★ Tent n/a

Beauty: ★★★ Site Privacy: ★★★
Spaciousness: ★★★★★ Quiet: ★★★★
Security: ★★★★★ Cleanliness: ★★★★★
Insect Control: ★★★★★ Facilities: ★★★★★

Tucson's largest RV resort opened in 1984 with 37,000 square feet of enclosed recreational space, including special crafts rooms for stained glass, lapidary, ceramics, and silver. With its own bank branch, restaurant, travel desk, store, and other facilities, Voyager has the feel of a small self-contained city. Streets are numbered 1st through 18th, and then skip by tens from 20th through 50th for the pull-through area surrounding the recreational facilities. Though daily RV rentals are welcome, the orientation is adult, like many southern Arizona RV parks catering to snowbird retirees. Except during summer, when kids are welcome, families with children will do better at the more child- and family-oriented Crazy Horse Campground. Since the fees are higher here, commensurate with the myriad of recreation options, Voyager is best thought of as a destination resort. But Voyager also works well as a luxury tourism base for exploring Tucson and southeastern Arizona.

Basics

Operated By: Ike & Blanche Issacson. **Open:** All year. **Site Assignment:** First come, first served. **Registration:** Self-pay entrance fee station. **Fee:** $24–$27 (V, MC, D). **Parking:** At site.

Facilities

Number of RV Sites: 1,576. **Number of Tent-Only Sites:** 0. **Hookups:** Electric (20, 30, 50 amp), water, sewer, cable TV, phone. **Each Site:** Paved, table. **Dump Station:** Yes. **Laundry:** Yes. **Pay Phone:** Yes. **Rest Rooms and Showers:** Yes. **Fuel:** Yes. **Propane:** Yes. **Internal Roads:** Paved, excellent. **RV Service:** No. **Market:** Tucson, 2 mi. **Restaurant:** On premises. **General Store:** Yes. **Vending:** Yes. **Swimming:** Pool. **Playground:** No. **Other:** Bocce, tennis, basketball & volleyball courts, mini-golf & 9-hole courses, exercise, poker, computer, & crafts rooms, ballroom, library, beautician, whirlpool, pet walk, pet grooming. **Activities:** Golf, shuffleboard, billiards. **Nearby Attractions:** Pima Air & Space Museum, Saguaro National Park East, Colossal Cave, Kartchner Caverns, museums. **Additional Information:** Tucson CVB, (800) 638-8350, www.visitTucson.org.

Restrictions

Pets: On leash under owner's control. **Fires:** Yes. **Alcoholic Beverages:** Allowed. **Vehicle Maximum Length:** 100 ft. **Other:** Children welcome May 1–day after Labor Day.

To Get There

From I-10 Exit 270 go 0.5 mi. south on Kolb Rd.

TUMACACORI

De Anza Trails RV Resort

HC 65 Box 381, Tumacacori 85640. T: (520) 398-8628 or (866) 332-6022; F: 520-398-2314; www.deanzatrailsrvresort.com; DeAnzaTrailsRVResort@msn.com.

RV ★★★ Tent n/a

Beauty: ★★★ Site Privacy: ★★★
Spaciousness: ★★★ Quiet: ★★★★
Security: ★★★ Cleanliness: ★★★★
Insect Control: ★★★★ Facilities: ★★★★

A collection of mundane RV parking spaces packaged with an impressive array of amenities, including an indoor pool and weight room, De Anza Trails offers 50 amp electric power, unlike Mountain View next door. However, De Anza falls short in parking convenience, as its spaces are all back-ins and require a security guard to supervise placement, in contrast to Mountain View's pull-through sites. Higher prices than the RV park next door have not helped, and on a recent summer day (admittedly the slow season this far south), De Anza had one customer while the funkier Mountain View was packed with RVs. Tents are prohibited, as are noisy trucks, cars, and motorcycles. Noise from trucks traversing the adjacent highway linking Tucson and Mexico might bother some people, but inside the clubhouse, library, and other facilities it should not be a problem.

Basics

Operated By: De Anza Trails. **Open:** All year. **Site Assignment:** First come, first served; reservations accepted (payment in full; 30-days notice for 90% refund, otherwise "No refunds!! No exceptions!!"). **Registration:** Self-pay entrance fee station. **Fee:** $23–$28 (V, MC). **Parking:** At site.

Facilities

Number of RV Sites: 82. **Number of Tent-Only Sites:** 0. **Hookups:** Electric (20, 30, 50 amp), water, sewer, cable TV, phone. **Each Site:** Pole lights. **Dump Station:** Yes. **Laundry:** Yes. **Pay Phone:** Yes. **Rest Rooms and Showers:** Yes. **Fuel:** No. **Propane:** No. **Internal Roads:** Paved, excellent. **RV Service:** No. **Market:** Green Valley, 15 mi. **Restaurant:** Tumacacori, seasonal coffeeshop on premises. **General Store:** Yes. **Vending:** Yes. **Swimming:** Indoor pool. **Playground:** No. **Other:** Pet walk, jacuzzi, rec center, library, exercise/weight room, modem access. **Activities:** Cards, billiards, golf, boating, fishing. **Nearby Attractions:** Missions, Tubac Presidio, Madera Canyon, Buenos Aires Wildlife Refuge, museums, copper mine tour. **Additional Information:** Green Valley Chamber of Commerce, (520) 625-7575, (800) 858-5872, sraney@concentric.net.

Restrictions

Pets: On leash under owner's control. **Fires:** Yes (limited). **Alcoholic Beverages:** Allowed. **Vehicle Maximum Length:** 50 ft. **Other:** 1 RV & vehicle per site; no street parking; shirts & shoes required in clubhouse; swim attire permitted in swim area only; 11 a.m. checkout.

To Get There

From I-19 south of Green Valley, take Exit 48 (Arivaca Junction) and go south 2 mi. on frontage road.

TUMACACORI

Mountain View RV Ranch

HRC 65 Box 380, Tumacacori 85640. T: (520) 398-9401; www.woodalls.com; desertpark@aol.com.

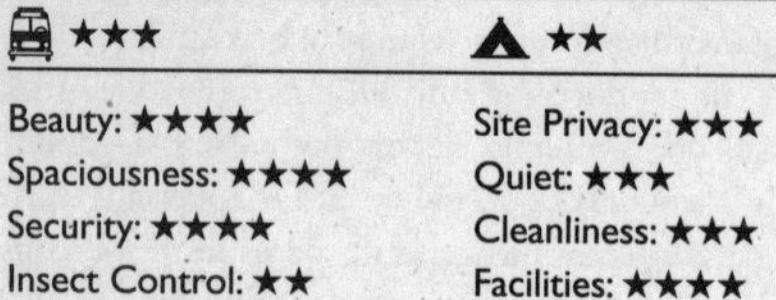

RV ★★★ Tent ★★

Beauty: ★★★★ Site Privacy: ★★★
Spaciousness: ★★★★ Quiet: ★★★
Security: ★★★★ Cleanliness: ★★★
Insect Control: ★★ Facilities: ★★★★

Along the highway linking Tucson with Nogales, Mexico, a brick wall separates Mountain View RV Ranch from the newer De Anza Trails RV Resort next door. A loyal coterie of supporters keeps Mountain View humming year-round, even during the summer slow season when many other nearby RV parks look like deserted ghost towns. The virtually unlimited vehicle length and 49 40-ft. wide pull-through spaces accommodating slide-outs is one reason for Mountain View's popularity. Tent campers can choose their spot anywhere along a grass strip extending from the small rear mobile home park to near the front of the park for pool, laundry, and snack bar convenience. Sunday mornings the snack bar serves up free coffee with breakfast, and home-made soups and sandwiches top off the lunch menu. The action here includes Monday night football on a big screen TV, pot lucks, card games, Friday night bingo, and darts.

Basics

Operated By: Esther Geisman. **Open:** All year. **Site Assignment:** First come, first served; winter reservations advised. **Registration:** In office. **Fee:** $15 tent, $17–$21 RV (V, MC, AE, D). **Parking:** At site.

Facilities

Number of RV Sites: 72. **Number of Tent-Only Sites:** Undesignated sites. **Hookups:** Electric (20, 30 amp), water, sewer, cable TV, phone. **Each Site:** Table. **Dump Station:** Yes. **Laundry:** Yes. **Pay Phone:** Yes. **Rest Rooms and Showers:** Yes. **Fuel:** No. **Propane:** Yes. **Internal Roads:** Gravel, good condition. **RV Service:** No. **Market:** Green Valley, 15 mi. **Restaurant:** Tumacacori, snack bar on premises. **General Store:** Yes. **Vending:** Yes. **Swimming:** Pool. **Playground:** No. **Other:** Dog walk, rental cabins. **Activities:** Shuffleboard, golf, boating, fishing. **Nearby Attractions:** Tubac Presidio, Tumacacori National Monument, Madera Canyon, Buenos Aires Wildlife Refuge, Native American casinos, museums, copper mine tour. **Additional Information:** Green Valley Chamber of Commerce, (520) 625-7575, (800) 858-5872, sraney@concentric.net.

Restrictions

Pets: On leash. **Fires:** In designated area only. **Alcoholic Beverages:** Allowed. **Vehicle Maximum Length:** None.

To Get There

From I-19 south of Green Valley, take Amado Exit 48 South or 42 North.

WENDEN

Alamo Lake State Park

P.O. Box 38, Wenden 85357. T: (520) 669-2088; www.pr.state.az.us.

RV ★★★★ Tent ★★★★

Beauty: ★★★★ Site Privacy: ★★★
Spaciousness: ★★★ Quiet: ★★★★
Security: ★★★★ Cleanliness: ★★★★
Insect Control: ★★★ Facilities: ★★★★

Nestled amongst saguaros and ocotillos where wild burros roam and golden and bald eagles soar in the Bill Williams River Valley, bass-filled Alamo Lake has a collection of eight developed and primitive camping areas on widely separated loops. The section of camping area A nearest the general store, sheltered picnic tables, and ranger station has 19 coveted sites with electric and water hookups. Camping areas A and B have sites with paved pads topped with a pebble layer, and are popular for both RVs and tents. Camping area C off Cholla Rd. also has hookups, though those willing to trade hookups for maximum privacy and beauty should continue down Cholla Rd. towards the lakeshore and camping areas D and E. Though furthest from the showers, store, and other amenities, camping area E, which has portable restrooms and picnic tables because it is sometimes underwater, is best situated to enjoy beautiful lake views.

Basics

Operated By: Arizona State Parks. **Open:** All year. **Site Assignment:** First come, first served. **Registration:** Self-pay entrance fee station. **Fee:** $8–$15 (cash or check only). **Parking:** At site.

Facilities

Number of RV Sites: 250. **Number of Tent-Only Sites:** 0. **Hookups:** Electric (30 amp), water. **Each Site:** Table, grill, fire ring. **Dump Station:** Yes. **Laundry:** No. **Pay Phone:** No. **Rest Rooms and Showers:** Yes. **Fuel:** No. **Propane:** No. **Internal Roads:** Paved or pebbly, good condition. **RV Service:** No. **Market:** Quartzite, 79 mi. **Restaurant:** Wenden, 38 mi. **General Store:** Yes. **Vending:** Yes. **Swimming:** Lake. **Playground:** No. **Other:** Boat ramps, fish cleaning & battery recharge station. **Activities:** Mountain biking, fishing, boating. **Nearby Attractions:** None. **Additional Information:** Alamo Lake Store (boat rental), (520) 925-0133.

Restrictions

Pets: On leash. **Fires:** In fire rings only. **Alcoholic Beverages:** Allowed. **Vehicle Maximum Length:** 30 ft. **Other:** OHV's must be street legal to operate in park.

To Get There

From US Hwy. 60 in Wenden, go 38 mi. north on Alamo Dam Access Rd.

WENDEN

Morenga Palms RV Park

P.O. Box 68, Wenden 85357. T: (520) 859-3722.

RV ★★★★ Tent ★★

Beauty: ★★★★ Site Privacy: ★★★
Spaciousness: ★★★★ Quiet: ★★★★★
Security: ★★★★ Cleanliness: ★★★★★
Insect Control: ★★★ Facilities: ★★

During the five-month winter season, this small RV park is filled by regulars from around the country and Canada, some of whom have been coming here for over a decade to form part of a small community that gathers for evening cocktails while watching the sunset from the clubhouse porch before evening games commence. During the hot summer, when there is space for tent campers to plug into the electric hookups left behind by migrating snowbirds, the surrounding fields are growing cotton, cantaloupes, watermelons, and a variety of fruit and vegetables for the Delmonte cannery. Parker and the Colorado River recreation is 64 miles to the north, but Alamo Lake State Park is within about 30 miles. Wickenburg's bowling alley and many restaurants are 46 miles to the west. All in all, a small isolated gem of a stopping place for those venturing into the Arizona outback.

Basics

Operated By: Dorothy & Bruce O'Hara. **Open:** All year. **Site Assignment:** First come, first served; winter reservations advised. **Registration:** Office. **Fee:** $16. **Parking:** At site.

Facilities

Number of RV Sites: 52. **Number of Tent-Only Sites:** 0. **Hookups:** Electric (30 amp), water, sewer, phone. **Each Site:** Table, bench, fire ring. **Dump Station:** Yes. **Laundry:** Yes. **Pay Phone:** Yes. **Rest Rooms and Showers:** Yes. **Fuel:** No. **Propane:** No. **Internal Roads:** Gravel, good. **RV Service:** No. **Market:** Wenden, 3 mi. **Restaurant:** Wenden, 3 mi. **General Store:** No. **Vending:** Yes. **Swimming:** No. **Playground:** No. **Other:** Clubhouse, exercise room, picnic area w/ fire ring. **Activities:** ATVs, golf, fishing, boating. **Nearby Attractions:** Alamo Lake State Park, Quartzsite. **Additional Information:** McMullen Valley Chamber of Commerce, (520) 859-3846, www.azoutback.com.

Restrictions

Pets: On leash under owner's control. **Fires:** Yes. **Alcoholic Beverages:** Allowed. **Vehicle Maximum Length:** 40 ft. **Other:** Need own satellite dish for TV.

To Get There

From Wenden go 3 mi. east on US Hwy. 60.

WICKENBURG

Horspitality RV Park and Boarding Stable

51802 Hwy. 60, Wickenburg 85390. T: (520) 684-2519.

RV ★★★ Tent n/a

Beauty: ★★★ Site Privacy: ★★
Spaciousness: ★★★ Quiet: ★★★★

Security: ★★★★ Cleanliness: ★★★★
Insect Control: ★★★★ Facilities: ★★★

Founded by German immigrant Henry Wickenburg after the discovery of gold at the Vulture Mine in 1863, Wickenburg sprang into existence 60 miles northwest of Phoenix with the motto "Horses have the right of way on all Wickenburg streets." Though horses no longer wander the streets of this crossroads town of motels and restaurants, Horspitality RV Park continues the tradition of catering to horses with a boarding stable with 65 horse pens. Horspitality also borders BLM land with miles of trails for horses, hikers, and ATVs. There is no general store, but major chain stores and markets are within a mile of the RV park. Palms and deciduous trees add to the country ambiance, and some residents settle in for the winter by spreading Astroturf on their concrete porch pads. All in all, a friendly stop for those who don't want to leave their horses at home.

Basics

Operated By: Craig & Pam Dyer. **Open:** All year. **Site Assignment:** First come, first served; reservations advised for special events. **Registration:** Office. **Fee:** $17–$20 (cash or check only). **Parking:** At site.

Facilities

Number of RV Sites: 109. **Number of Tent-Only Sites:** 0. **Hookups:** Electric (15, 30 amp), water, sewer. **Each Site:** Table, grill. **Dump Station:** Yes. **Laundry:** Yes. **Pay Phone:** Yes. **Rest Rooms and Showers:** Yes. **Fuel:** No. **Propane:** No. **Internal Roads:** Gravel, good. **RV Service:** No. **Market:** Wickenburg, 1 mi. **Restaurant:** Wickenburg, 1 mi. **General Store:** No. **Vending:** Yes. **Swimming:** No. **Playground:** No. **Other:** Open pens for horses, dog walk, horseshoes, adjacent BLM trails. **Activities:** Horseback riding, golf. **Nearby Attractions:** Museums, Phoenix, Prescott. **Additional Information:** Wickenburg Chamber of Commerce, (520) 684-5479.

Restrictions

Pets: On leash (horses welcome). **Fires:** Yes. **Alcoholic Beverages:** Allowed. **Vehicle Maximum Length:** None.

To Get There

From junction of US Hwys. 60 & 89/93 in Wickenburg, go east 2 mi. on US Hwy. 60 to milepost 112.5.

WIKIEUP

Burro Creek Recreation Site

2475 Beverly Ave., Kingman 86401. T: (520) 692-4400.

 ★★★★ ▲ ★★★★

Beauty: ★★★★ Site Privacy: ★★★★
Spaciousness: ★★★★ Quiet: ★★★★
Security: ★★★★ Cleanliness: ★★★★
Insect Control: ★★★ Facilities: ★★

Nine miles north of the town of Nothing and near old copper mining towns like Bagdad, Burro Creek Recreation Site is seemingly in the middle of nowhere, though it is just off US Hwy. 93, the main artery linking Phoenix and Las Vegas, Nevada. Many regulars come back here every year because it is such a good place to just sit and relax, with little else to do besides hiking along the tree-lined creek and looking for the blue and purple agates and Apache tears that endear the area to rock hounds. Day use of the park is free, including the solar-lighted restrooms and the ample picnic area surrounded by saguaros and mesquite. The small cactus garden is a good introduction to desert botany and nesting desert pack rats. Fishing in the year-round water pools is taboo, as the Sonoran suckers and roundtail chubb are endangered. Bird watchers can spot great blue herons and bald eagles.

Basics

Operated By: Bureau of Land Management. **Open:** All year. **Site Assignment:** First come, first served; group site reservations. **Registration:** Self-pay fee station. **Fee:** $10 (cash or check only). **Parking:** At site.

Facilities

Number of RV Sites: 30. **Number of Tent-Only Sites:** 0. **Hookups:** None. **Each Site:** Table, fire ring. **Dump Station:** Yes. **Laundry:** No. **Pay Phone:** No. **Rest Rooms and Showers:** No showers. **Fuel:** No. **Propane:** No. **Internal Roads:** Gravel, good. **RV Service:** No. **Market:** Wickenburg, 60 mi. **Restaurant:** Wickenburg, 60 mi. **General Store:** No. **Vending:** No. **Swimming:** No. **Playground:** No. **Other:** Some sheltered tables; 1 wheelchair-accessible site; cactus botanical garden. **Activities:** Rock collecting, bird-watching. **Nearby Attractions:** Hualapai Indian Reservation, Alamo Lake State Park. **Additional Information:** BLM Kingman Field Office, (520) 692-4400.

Restrictions

Pets: On leash under owner's control. **Fires:** Yes. **Alcoholic Beverages:** Allowed. **Vehicle Maximum Length:** None.

To Get There

From Kingman go 17 mi. east on I-40, then 53 mi. south on US Hwy. 93 to signed turnoff 1 mi. south of Burro Creek Bridge and follow gravel road 1.5 mi. to campground.

WINSLOW

Homolovi Ruins State Park

HCR 63 Box 5, Winslow 86047. T: (520) 289-4106; F: (520) 289-2021; www.pr.state.az.us; homolovi@pr.state.az.us.

★★★★ ▲ ★★★

Beauty: ★★★★ Site Privacy: ★★★★
Spaciousness: ★★★★ Quiet: ★★★★
Security: ★★★★ Cleanliness: ★★★★★
Insect Control: ★★★ Facilities: ★★★

Mostly used as an overnight stop by travelers on I-40, Homolovi Ruins is further from the highway and not near a power plant or lake like the nearby and more rustic Cholla Lake County Park. The paved sites have small trees that should eventually grow up to provide some shade. Raised dirt pads make for comfortable tenting, though it is advisable to shake your boots for scorpions before putting them on in the morning. The name Homolovi means little hills in the Hopi language, and the area was a sacred gathering place of the clans and is still visited as a sacred place by the Hopi. The park opened in 1993, but archaeological excavations date to 1896. The over 1,000-room pueblo is the most accessible site in this park, which has good wildlife viewing areas along the Little Colorado River.

Basics

Operated By: Arizona State Parks. **Open:** All year. **Site Assignment:** First come, first served. **Registration:** Entrance kiosk (use self-pay slot when closed). **Fee:** $10–$15 (cash or check only). **Parking:** At site.

Facilities

Number of RV Sites: 53. **Number of Tent-Only Sites:** 0. **Hookups:** Electric (30 amp), water. **Each Site:** Table, grill. **Dump Station:** Yes. **Laundry:** No. **Pay Phone:** Yes. **Rest Rooms and Showers:** Yes (showers May–Oct. only). **Fuel:** No. **Propane:** No. **Internal Roads:** Paved, excellent. **RV Service:** No. **Market:** Winslow, 3 mi. **Restaurant:** Winslow, 3 mi. **General Store:** No. **Vending:** Yes. **Swimming:** No. **Playground:** No. **Other:** Visitor center, museum, covered picnic tables, wildlife viewing turnouts, archaelogical sites. **Activities:** Archaeological dig tours (June, July). **Nearby Attractions:** Little Painted Desert, Second Mesa, Mogollon Rim, Meteor Crater, Walnut Canyon, Flagstaff, Petrified Forest. **Additional Information:** Winslow Chamber of Commerce Visitor Center, (520) 289-2434, www.winslowarizona.org.

Restrictions

Pets: On leash (not allowed in buildings). **Fires:** In designated areas only. **Alcoholic Beverages:** Allowed. **Vehicle Maximum Length:** None. **Other:** Gates closed from 7 p.m. to 6 a.m.

To Get There

From Winslow go east 2 mi. on I-40 to Exit 257 and then north 1.5 mi. on AZ Hwy. 87.

California

California's motto, eureka, means "I have found it!" That sentiment is just as applicable to campers today as it was when it was first adopted a century and a half ago by the '49ers of the Gold Rush era. Indeed, the camping prospects are richer by far than what remains of the Golden State's mineral resources. From its 840 miles of shoreline, millions of acres of federal land, and 264 state parks (with scores more on the county level), California's scenery is a glittering reflection of all that is rare and wonderful in the natural beauty of the United States. And with its relatively mild climate, many campgrounds remain open year-round.

As one might expect in a state California's size, it is a land packed with extremes and superlatives: from **Mt. Whitney,** the highest peak in the lower 48 states, to **Badwater,** in **Death Valley,** the lowest point in the western hemisphere. Its coast redwoods are the tallest trees in the world, while the bristlecone pines of the **Inyo National Forest** are the planet's oldest living things. To the south are sun-parched deserts awash in cacti and colorfully eroded landscapes that explode with wildflowers in the spring. Up north are the **Cascade Mountains,** iced with snow, scarred by lava, laced with trout streams, alpine lakes, and thousands of miles of hiking trails. In between are snow-crusted glaciers in the **Sierra Nevada Mountains,** one crashing waterfall after another, especially in **Yosemite Valley,** more national parks and monuments than any other state in the country, and a number of historical sites honoring Native American, Spanish and Mexican explorers, and African and Chinese pioneers, among others.

Beyond its silky smooth beaches and tide pools, where passing whales and nesting seals can be observed, in addition to the superb fishing and boating in pristine lakes, rivers, and reservoirs, California's abundance of wildlife is icing on the camper's cake. Grizzly bears are long gone, but you will find Tule elk, Roosevelt elk, and fallow deer among the animals gracing the coastal preserves, big horn sheep, kangaroo rats, and desert tortoises in the arid areas, while black bears, coyotes, and black-tail deer seem to roam throughout. And one needn't be a sharp-eyed birder to enjoy the sight of condors, Canada geese, bald and golden eagles, acorn woodpeckers, hummingbirds, valley quails, and herons of various types warbling among the oaks or winging across the marshlands.

Under the Clinton presidency the Golden State gained the newly-created **Mojave National Preserve** and two national monuments, **Carrizo Plain** and **Giant Sequoia,** while the domains of **Pinnacles National Monument, Death Valley,** and **Joshua Tree National Parks** were substantially expanded. In 2000, when the state enjoyed a substantial budget surplus, it lowered its day-use and camping fees, making access to state parks one of the better deals around. Hundreds of properties within California's national forests have been revamped and are now run by concessionaires intent on keeping them clean, secure, and profitable. Dispersed camping on lands administered by the National Forest Service and Bureau of Land Management offers serious solitude-seekers and the budget-minded a less structured approach to camping.

Whatever your interests, however you like to camp, California has so much beauty and space that on pulling into a campground you may well feel like imitating the '49ers by exclaiming with exuberance, "Eureka!"

The following facilities accept payment in checks or cash only:

Afton Canyon, Barstow
Aspen Grove, Lee Vining
Azalea, Kings Canyon National Park
Bogard, Susanville
Boulder Flat, Sonora
Bow Willow Campground, Anza-Borrego Desert State Park, Borrego Springs
Butte Lake, Lassen Volcanic National Park
Coldbrook, Azusa
Cooper Gulch, Lewiston
Cottonwood, Twentynine Palms
Culp Valley Primitive Camp, Anza-Borrego Desert State Park, Borrego Springs
El Cariso North Campground, Lake Elsinore
Elam, Chester
Ellery Lake, Lee Vining
Fossil Falls, Ridgecrest
Fowlers Campground, McCloud
Gaviota State Park, Santa Barbara
Goumaz, Susanville
Hole-in-the-Ground, Mill Creek
Hole-in-the-Wall, Mojave National Preserve
Howards Gulch, Alturas
Indian Creek, Markleeville

The following facilities accept payment in checks or cash only (continued):

Indian Well, Lava Beds National Monument
Kern River County Park, Kern River Campground, Bakersfield
Lake Almanor Campground, Greenville
Leavitt Meadows, Dardanelle
Lundy Canyon Campground, Mono City
Mesquite Spring, Death Valley
Monte Cristo, Pasadena
Owl Canyon, Barstow
Pine Cliff Resort, June Lake
Pine Flat Lake Recreation Area, Fresno
Pit River, Fall River Mills
Plumas-Eureka State Park, Upper Samson Creek Campground, Blairsden
Pogie Point, Upper Lake
Ponderosa, Lucia
Potwisha, Sequoia National Park
Red Rock Canyon State Park, Ricardo Campground, Mojave
Sarah Totten, Hamburg
Sonora Bridge, Coleville
The Pines, Groveland
Tolkan, Shelter Cove
Tuttletown Recreation Area; Manzanita Campground, Angels Camp
Twin Lakes, Mammoth Lakes
Upper Rush Creek, Adin
Wild Plum, Sierra City

The following facilities feature 50 sites or fewer:

Bogard, Susanville
Bow Willow Campground, Anza-Borrego Desert State Park, Borrego Springs
Cooper Gulch, Lewiston
Culp Valley Primitive Camp, Anza-Borrego Desert State Park, Borrego Springs
Elam, Chester
Ellery Lake, Lee Vining
Goumaz, Susanville
Hole-in-the-Ground, Mill Creek
Howards Gulch, Alturas
KCL, Carrizo Plain National Monument
Landslide, Hume
Leavitt Meadows, Dardanelle
Monte Cristo, Pasadena
Nelson Point, O'Brien
Pit River, Fall River Mills
Sarah Totten, Hamburg
Selby, Carrizo Plain National Monument
The Pines, Groveland
Tolkan, Shelter Cove
Upper Rush Creek, Adin

Campground Profiles

ADIN

Upper Rush Creek

CR 198A, Adin 96006. T: (530) 299-3215; F: (530) 299-8409; www.r5.fs.fed.us/modoc.

RV ★★★ Tent ★★★★

Beauty: ★★★★ Site Privacy: ★★★
Spaciousness: ★★★ Quiet: ★★★★
Security: ★★ Cleanliness: ★★★
Insect Control: ★★★ Facilities: ★

You will have to pass Lower Rush Creek to reach this campground and may very well feel inclined to stop there for the night. No problem, the two are comparably pleasant, and Lower Rush has several walk-in sites, hidden away beyond a small wooden bridge, that are perfect for reclusive tenters. Upper Rush, though, is the more densely forested, tranquil of the two and offers a better array of sites. Conifers tower over the hilly dominion, providing shade and—through their fallen needles—soft padding for tents. To the north of camp is a volcanic outcropping, while the narrow, trickling Rush Creek sluices along its southern boundary. Some of the real estate here is not very level, but sites overall are very roomy and scattered well apart. Units 3–5, nestled above the creek, are the most picturesque. This facility is in the Modoc National Forest, 35 miles southwest of Alturas, off of Hwy. 299. It is nearly a mile high in altitude, making for cold nights early and late in the season. In winter, spigots are capped and no potable water is available.

BASICS

Operated By: Modoc National Forest, Big Valley Ranger District. **Open:** May–Oct. **Site Assignment:** First come, first served. **Registration:** At entrance kiosk. **Fee:** $6, cash or check; no fee in winter when water spigots are capped. **Parking:** At site.

FACILITIES

Number of RV Sites: 13. **Number of Tent-Only Sites:** 0. **Hookups:** None. **Each Site:** Picnic table, fire grate, barbecue grill. **Dump Station:** No. **Laundry:** No. **Pay Phone:** No. **Rest Rooms and Showers:** Vault toilets, no showers. **Fuel:** No. **Propane:** No. **Internal Roads:** Dirt, good condition. **RV Service:** No. **Market:** 10 mi. south in Adin. **Restaurant:** 10 mi. south in Adin. **General Store:** No. **Vending:** No. **Swimming:** No. **Playground:** No. **Activities:** Hiking, fishing. **Nearby Attractions:** Lava Beds National Monument; Modoc National Wildlife Refuge & Modoc County Historical Museum in Alturas. **Additional Information:** Alturas Chamber of Commerce, (530) 233-4434.

RESTRICTIONS

Pets: On leash. **Fires:** In fire grates only. **Alcoholic Beverages:** Allowed. **Vehicle Maximum Length:** 22 ft. **Other:** 14-day stay limit.

BANNING

Lake Hemet

56570 Hwy. 74, #4, Mountain Center 92561. T: (909) 659-2680; F: (909) 659-8509.

RV ★★★★ Tent ★★★

Beauty: ★★★ Site Privacy: ★★
Spaciousness: ★★ Quiet: ★★★★
Security: ★★★★★ Cleanliness: ★★★
Insect Control: ★★ Facilities: ★★★★

To paraphrase Dickens, Lake Hemet offers the best of campgrounds and the worst of campgrounds. It has a fine sandy beach but doesn't allow swimming in its namesake lake (wading is allowed in Hurkey Creek by the playground). The rugged, natural atmosphere radiating from the surrounding San Jacinto and Thomas mountain ranges is partly diminished by the cluttered cluster of the long-term residences. Several stands of mature ponderosa pines are scattered around the property but sites of dirt, sand, and a smattering of grass are largely exposed to the sun. And unless you like plenty of company, forget about a waterside location, especially among the RV hookups; the outlying areas without electricity are your best bet for space and seclusion. Security is one feature this facility is unequivocal about, with an entrance gate, regular patrols, and a county sheriff's office on the edge of the grounds.

Basics

Operated By: Lake Hemet Municipal Water District. **Open:** All year. **Site Assignment:** First come, first served. **Registration:** At entrance office. **Fee:** $13, cash, V, MC. **Parking:** At site.

Facilities

Number of RV Sites: 275. **Number of Tent-Only Sites:** Undesignated sites. **Hookups:** Water, electric (20, 30 amps), sewer. **Each Site:** Picnic table, fire ring, some with a barbecue grill. **Dump Station:** Yes. **Laundry:** Yes. **Pay Phone:** Yes. **Rest Rooms and Showers:** Yes. **Fuel:** No. **Propane:** Yes. **Internal Roads:** Mostly paved, some dirt roads. **RV Service:** No. **Market:** 9 mi. north in Idyllwild. **Restaurant:** 9 mi. north in Idyllwild. **General Store:** Yes. **Vending:** Yes. **Swimming:** In creek. **Playground:** Yes. **Other:** Wheelchair-accessible facilities, boat launch. **Activities:** Fishing, hiking, volleyball, basketball, horseshoe pit, boat rentals. **Nearby Attractions:** Pacific Crest Trail, Gilman Historic Ranch & Wagon Museum in Banning, San Jacinto Valley Museum. **Additional Information:** Banning Chamber of Commerce, (909) 849-4695.

Restrictions

Pets: On leash no longer than 15 ft., $1 fee. **Fires:** In fire rings only. **Alcoholic Beverages:** Allowed. **Vehicle Maximum Length:** 40 ft. **Other:** 14-day stay limit for tents, no shooting.

To Get There

From Banning head south on Hwy. 243, off I-10, and drive 31 mi. Turn left on route 74 and continue for 5 mi. to the campground on the right.

BANNING

Mount San Jacinto State Park, Stone Creek Campground

25905 Hwy. 243, P.O. Box 308, Idyllwild 92549. T: (909) 659-2607 or reservations (800) 444-7275; F: (909) 659-4769; www.sanjac.statepark.org.

RV: ★★★★ Tent: ★★★

Beauty: ★★★★	Site Privacy: ★★★
Spaciousness: ★★★	Quiet: ★★★
Security: ★★★	Cleanliness: ★★★★
Insect Control: ★	Facilities: ★★

The scenic mountain drive along Hwy. 243 to Stone Creek is a good warm-up for your arrival at this gorgeous highland park. Set in a hilly, boulder-strewn forest of oak and incense cedar, manzanita, and ponderosa pine, the camp lies at 5,900 feet of elevation, so plan for cool evenings throughout the year. Regrettably, the somewhat wild, natural look of the place is balanced by sites that tend to be grouped a bit close together, with several lacking level tenting space. Best choices for RVers from the series of loops are sites 45, with a large pull-through slot, and 50, for privacy. Site 26 is the most secluded among the tent options. Birders will enjoy the lively community of acorn woodpeckers nesting in the vicinity and hikers should aim their boots in the direction of trails that lead into the neighboring San Jacinto Wilderness.

Basics

Operated By: California Dept. of Parks & Recreation. **Open:** All year. **Site Assignment:** Reservations accepted w/ V, MC, D. **Registration:** At entrance kiosk. **Fee:** $7, cash or CA check. **Parking:** At site.

Facilities

Number of RV Sites: 23. **Number of Tent-Only Sites:** 27. **Hookups:** None. **Each Site:** Picnic table, fire grate, food storage box. **Dump Station:** No. **Laundry:** No. **Pay Phone:** Yes. **Rest Rooms and Showers:** Vault toilets, no showers. **Fuel:** No. **Propane:** No. **Internal Roads:** Paved. **RV Service:** No. **Market:** 2 mi. south in Pine Cove. **Restaurant:** 6 mi. south in Idyllwild. **General Store:** No. **Vending:** No. **Swimming:** No. **Playground:** No. **Other:** Some wheelchair-accessible facilities. **Activities:** Hiking, birding, nature programs in summer. **Nearby Attractions:** Palm Springs Aerial Tramway, Palm Springs Desert Museum, Oasis Water Park in Palm Springs, Gilman Historic Ranch & Wagon Museum in Banning. **Additional Information:** Idyllwild Chamber of Commerce, (909) 659-3259.

Restrictions

Pets: On 6 ft. leash. **Fires:** In fire grates only. **Alcoholic Beverages:** Allowed at site. **Vehicle Maximum Length:** 24 ft. **Other:** 14-day stay limit; no firearms; no wood gathering.

To Get There

From I-10 in Banning exit south on Hwy. 243. Drive 20 mi. and turn left at the campground sign.

BARSTOW

Afton Canyon

Afton Canyon Rd., Barstow 92311. T: (760) 252-6000; F: (760) 252-6099; www.ca.blm.gov/caso/information.html.

RV: ★★★ Tent: ★★★★

Beauty: ★★★★	Site Privacy: ★★★
Spaciousness: ★★★★	Quiet: ★★★
Security: ★★	Cleanliness: ★★
Insect Control: ★★★★	Facilities: ★

Your first impression of Afton Canyon may well be that it is a dusty God-forsaken over-sized sandbox where even the lowly creosote bush has difficulty putting down roots. And your second impression might echo your first, especially if a freight train should chance to rattle down the nearby tracks while you are there. But give your eyes—and your other senses—an opportunity to take in the surroundings and you may just find the low-key beauty of the place growing on you. Some of the level, sandy sites are screened by mesquite bushes, and most are spaced well apart, while desert dunes and the russet colored namesake canyon lend texture to the setting. (So, too, does a disturbing amount of litter, but that's another story.) There's a chance you'll see the elusive desert tortoise here, though rosy boas and kangaroo rats are more likely visitors. Bring plenty of water—the source here is unreliable—and note that while the campground is less than four miles south of I-15, a hairpin curve on the dirt and gravel washboard of an access road is all but impassable for vehicles over 22 feet in length.

Basics

Operated By: Bureau of Land Management. **Open:** All year. **Site Assignment:** First come, first served. **Registration:** At entrance kiosk. **Fee:** $6, cash or check. **Parking:** At site.

Facilities

Number of RV Sites: 22. **Number of Tent-Only Sites:** 0. **Hookups:** None. **Each Site:** Picnic table, fire ring; most sites have ramada & barbecue grill. **Dump Station:** No. **Laundry:** No. **Pay Phone:** No. **Rest Rooms and Showers:** Vaulted toilets, no showers. **Fuel:** No. **Propane:** No. **Internal Roads:** Packed, rocky dirt but manageable. **RV Service:** No. **Market:** 35 mi. west in Barstow. **Restaurant:** 35 mi. west in Barstow. **General Store:** No. **Vending:** No. **Swimming:** No. **Playground:** No. **Other:** Some wheelchair-accessible facilities. **Activities:** Hiking, birding, rock & mineral collecting, horseback riding, 4WD exploring. **Nearby Attractions:** Mojave National Preserve, Early Man Site, Death Valley National Park. **Additional Information:** Bureau of Land Management, Barstow Field Office, (760) 252-6091; Baker Area Chamber of Commerce, (760) 733-4469.

Restrictions

Pets: Allowed. **Fires:** In fire rings. **Alcoholic Beverages:** Allowed. **Vehicle Maximum Length:** 22 ft. **Other:** 14-day stay limit; no shooting.

To Get There

From Barstow drive 40 mi. east on I-15. Exit on Afton Rd. and drive 3.5 mi south on a dirt and gravel accordion road that leads to the campground on the left.

BARSTOW

Owl Canyon

Fossil Bed Rd., Barstow 92311. T: (760) 252-6000; F: (760) 252-6099; www.ca.blm.gov/caso/information.html.

RV: ★★★ Tent: ★★★★

Beauty: ★★★★	Site Privacy: ★★★
Spaciousness: ★★★★	Quiet: ★★★★
Security: ★★	Cleanliness: ★★★★
Insect Control: ★★★★	Facilities: ★

Rock hounds like this area for its abundance of fossils, but they're overlooking the obvious: Owl Canyon is a diamond-in-the-rough. Conveniently located next to Rainbow Basin National Natural Landmark, just 11 miles north of Barstow, this campground is dramatically set against a colorful, eroded canyon of bentonite and limestone. Roomy, level sites are well spaced along a tri-pronged loop, with numbers 12–23 among the more private. Tableside ramadas are an essential campsite accouterment in an otherwise primitive locale that consists of just desert scrub and a few sparse Joshua trees for vegetation. Owl Canyon lies at an elevation of 2,600 feet and can be scorching hot from mid-spring through early autumn. Whenever you visit pack plenty of water, as none is available at the campground. And drive carefully, as the last time we traveled through we encountered a large, shy desert tortoise crossing the camp's dirt access road.

Basics

Operated By: Bureau of Land Management. **Open:** All year. **Site Assignment:** First come, first served. **Registration:** At entrance kiosk. **Fee:** $6, cash or check. **Parking:** At site.

Facilities

Number of RV Sites: 31. **Number of Tent-Only Sites:** 0. **Hookups:** None. **Each Site:** Picnic table, fire ring, barbecue grill, ramada. **Dump Station:** No. **Laundry:** No. **Pay Phone:** No. **Rest Rooms and Showers:** Vaulted toilets, no showers. **Fuel:** No. **Propane:** No. **Internal Roads:** Gravel, decent condition. **RV Service:** No. **Market:** 10 mi. south in Barstow. **Restaurant:** 10 mi. south in Barstow. **General Store:** No. **Vending:** No. **Swimming:** No. **Playground:** No. **Other:** Some wheelchair-accessible facilities. **Activities:** Hiking, horseback riding, scenic loop drive through canyon, birding, rock & mineral collecting. **Nearby Attractions:** Rainbow Basin National Natural Landmark, Mojave National Preserve, Afton Canyon. **Additional Information:** Bureau of Land Management, Barstow Field Office, (760) 252-6091; Barstow Area Chamber of Commerce, (760) 256-8617.

Restrictions

Pets: On leash. **Fires:** In fire rings only. **Alcoholic Beverages:** Allowed. **Vehicle Maximum Length:** None. **Other:** 14-day stay limit; no firearms; no wood gathering.

To Get There

In Barstow follow the I-15 Business Loop and head north on 1st St. After 0.8 mi. turn left on Irwin Rd. and drive 6 mi., then turn left on Fossil Bed Rd. Proceed for 3 mi. and turn right. The campground is located 1.6 mi. down the road. The last 4.6 mi. are dirt w/ washboard stretches.

BASS LAKE

Lupine-Cedar Bluff

CR 222, Bass Lake 93604. T: (559) 877-2218 or reservations (877) 444-6777; F: (559) 877-3108; www.r5.fs.fed.us/sierra or www.reserveusa.com.

RV ★★★★ Tent ★★

Beauty: ★★★★ Site Privacy: ★★
Spaciousness: ★★ Quiet: ★★★
Security: ★★★ Cleanliness: ★★★
Insect Control: ★★ Facilities: ★★★

A question to ask before heading out to this campground is, how much time will you be spending at the site? Bass Lake, a pretty green mountain reservoir, is right across the street, an attractive venue for fishing, boating, and waterskiing. The surrounding national forest land and Yosemite National Park, 25 miles away, beckon to hikers. If you plan to put in most of your time soaking up the natural splendor of the environment, go ahead and book a spot at Lupine-Cedar Bluff. On second thought, make that a double. For while its hilltop setting, among an array of manzanita, oak, cedar, and pines, is superb, the exposed, grassy sites are disappointingly small and crammed right up against each other. In many cases the dimensions are so tight you won't be able to set up a tent and safely light a fire. The dozen walk-ins are a sop to tenters, as this is more of a camp for motor homes, with paved parking slips and the vast majority of its spots set aside as multiple units. There are a handful of fine single sites, but the concession that runs this property—and dares to charge $16 a night—does not permit reservations by number, only by type (single, double, on up to quadruple).

Basics

Operated By: California Land Management, concessionaire. **Open:** All year. **Site Assignment:** Reservations recommended w/ V, MC, D. **Registration:** At Forest Service office 2.7 mi. west of campground. **Fee:** $16, cash or check; up to $64 for quadruple site. **Parking:** At site or designated area for walk-ins.

Facilities

Number of RV Sites: 62. **Number of Tent-Only Sites:** 12. **Hookups:** None. **Each Site:** Picnic table, fire grate. **Dump Station:** No. **Laundry:** No. **Pay Phone:** No. **Rest Rooms and Showers:** Flush toilets, no showers. **Fuel:** No. **Propane:** No. **Internal Roads:** Paved. **RV Service:** No. **Market:** 10 mi. west in Oakhurst. **Restaurant:** Several options on Bass Lake. **General Store:** No. **Vending:** No. **Swimming:** In Bass Lake. **Playground:** No. **Other:** Some wheelchair-accessible facilities. **Activities:** Fishing, hiking, waterskiing, boating, eavesdropping on your neighbors. **Nearby Attractions:** Yosemite National Park; Fresno Flats Historical Site in Oakhurst; Yosemite Mountain Sugar Pine Railroad in Fish Camp. **Additional Information:** Bass Lake Chamber of Commerce, (559) 642-3676.

Restrictions

Pets: On leash. **Fires:** In fire grates only. **Alcoholic Beverages:** Allowed. **Vehicle Maximum Length:** 40 ft. **Other:** 14-day stay limit.

To Get There

From Oakhurst drive 3 mi. north on Hwy. 41. Turn right on CR 222 and continue for 7 mi., bearing right at 2 consecutive forks, to the campground on the right.

BIG PINE

Big Pine Creek

Glacier Lodge Rd., Big Pine 93513. T: (760) 873-2500 or reservations (877) 444-6777; F: (760) 873-2563; www.r5.fs.fed.us/inyo or www.reserveusa.com.

RV ★★★★ Tent ★★★★

Beauty: ★★★★ Site Privacy: ★★★
Spaciousness: ★★ Quiet: ★★★
Security: ★★★ Cleanliness: ★★★
Insect Control: ★★★ Facilities: ★★

Of the several campgrounds along Glacier Lodge Rd., Big Pine Creek, at an elevation of 7,700 feet, is preferable for its green grassy look and close proximity to the rocky jaw-line of the overhanging mountains. It is a gorgeous, natural setting, shot-through with Sierra granite, a creek running by, and an abundance of Jeffrey pines complementing its flush of aspens. There is only one blemish to all this beauty, the presence of a handful of private cabins at the center of the property. As is typical of mountain camps, many sites run toward the miniature, and seem to offer less privacy than you'd enjoy at a nudist colony. The exceptions, though, make this a winner, with the spots by the creek providing the best space and seclusion. The pick of the park are numbers 9, appealingly set in an old stone foundation, and 21–23, which are roomy and private. Showers, a snack bar, bait and tackle, and other basic supplies are available at the lodge.

Basics

Operated By: American Land & Leisure, concessionaire. **Open:** May to mid-Oct., weather permitting. **Site Assignment:** Reservations accepted with V, MC, D. **Registration:** At entrance kiosk. **Fee:** $13, cash or check. **Parking:** At site.

Facilities

Number of RV Sites: 25. **Number of Tent-Only Sites:** 5. **Hookups:** None. **Each Site:** Picnic table, fire grate. **Dump Station:** No. **Laundry:** No. **Pay Phone:** No. **Rest Rooms and Showers:** Vault toilets, no showers. **Fuel:** No. **Propane:** No. **Internal Roads:** Paved, narrow & bumpy. **RV Service:** No. **Market:** 9.5 mi. east in Big Pine. **Restaurant:** 9.5 mi. east in Big Pine. **General Store:** Yes. **Vending:** No. **Swimming:** No. **Playground:** No. **Other:** Some wheelchair-accessible facilities. **Activities:** Hiking, fishing, horseback riding, photography. **Nearby Attractions:** Inyo National Forest; Ancient Bristlecone Pine Forest & Laws Railroad Museum & Historic Site in Bishop; Death Valley National Park; John Muir Wilderness. **Additional Information:** Bishop Area Chamber of Commerce & Visitors Bureau, (760) 873-8405.

Restrictions

Pets: On leash. **Fires:** In fire grates only. **Alcoholic Beverages:** Allowed. **Vehicle Maximum Length:** 35 ft. **Other:** 14-day stay limit.

To Get There

From Big Pine on US 395 head west on Crocker St. (which becomes Glacier Lodge Rd.). Drive 9.5 mi. to the campground entrance on the left.

BIG PINE

Grandview

White Mountain Rd., Big Pine 93513. T: (760) 873-2500; F: (760) 873-2563; www.r5.fs.fed.us/inyo.

Beauty: ★★★★ Site Privacy: ★★★★
Spaciousness: ★★★★★ Quiet: ★★★★★
Security: ★ Cleanliness: ★★★★
Insect Control: ★★★★ Facilities: ★

Your first question on arriving at this notably primitive place will probably be, "Where's the view?" Don't despair. While none of the remarkably spacious, well-separated sites offer vistas of anything much beyond the sage-covered meadow at the center of the large loop, walk a few minutes in almost any direction and you will find rewarding panoramas of the outlying valleys and mountain ranges. The best of this national forest land, though, lies five miles farther up the road, at the Ancient Bristlecone Pine Forest, with trails leading past some of the oldest trees on the planet. (The relatively new visitor center there keeps irregular hours.) Pull-through parking slots are available at a number of sites, and most of the latter benefit at least partly from the shade cast by mature junipers, piñons, and other conifers. Weather can be scorching in late spring and early autumn, but at 8,600 feet of elevation, expect nights to be cool and quite breezy. There is no water available, and trash must be packed out.

Basics

Operated By: Inyo National Forest, White Mountain Ranger District. **Open:** May through Oct., weather permitting. **Site Assignment:** First come, first served. **Registration:** None. **Fee:** None. **Parking:** At site.

Facilities

Number of RV Sites: 26. **Number of Tent-Only Sites:** 0. **Hookups:** None. **Each Site:** Picnic table, fire grate. **Dump Station:** No. **Laundry:** No. **Pay Phone:** No. **Rest Rooms and Showers:** Vault toilets, no showers. **Fuel:** No. **Propane:** No. **Internal Roads:** Packed dirt, good condition. **RV Service:** No. **Market:** 13 mi. south in Big Pine. **Restaurant:** 13 mi. south in Big Pine. **General Store:** No. **Vending:** No. **Swimming:** No. **Playground:** No. **Activities:** Hiking, photography, star-gazing. **Nearby Attractions:** Inyo National Forest; Ancient Bristlecone Pine Forest & Laws Railroad Museum & Historic Site in Bishop; Death Valley National Park. **Additional Information:** Bishop Area Chamber of Commerce & Visitors Bureau, (760) 873-8405.

Restrictions

Pets: On leash. **Fires:** In fire grates only. **Alcoholic Beverages:** Allowed. **Vehicle Maximum Length:** 34 ft. **Other:** 14-day stay limit.

To Get There

From Big Pine on US 395 drive 13 mi. east on Hwy. 168. Turn left on White Mountain Rd. and continue 5.5 mi. to the campground entrance on the left.

BIG SUR

Pfeiffer Big Sur State Park

47225 Hwy. 1, Big Sur 93920. T: (831) 667-2315 or reservations (800) 444-7275; F: (831) 667-2886; www.cal-parks.ca.gov or www.reserveamerica.com.

 ★★★ 

Beauty: ★★★★ Site Privacy: ★★
Spaciousness: ★★ Quiet: ★★★
Security: ★★★★ Cleanliness: ★★★
Insect Control: ★ Facilities: ★★★

The redwood trees of Pfeiffer Big Sur are neither the largest nor oldest along the California coast. In fact, there is a more impressive grove just two miles south, at the privately-operated Ventana Campground. The trees are so numerous there and grow so close together that the property, with small sites priced around $40 a night, seems perpetually moist and dark. The trees at Pfeiffer, on the other hand, are big without blocking the sunlight. They compose only one part of three distinct habitats represented over the five dispersed loops, with an oak woodland and grassy meadows making up the balance. The Big Sur River parallels the campground, which consists of level sites of dirt and leaves. Those in the first two loops are a bit more spacious than elsewhere. There are some excellent hiking trails in this ever-popular park, with Buzzards Roost in particular delivering superb views of the surrounding hills. Poison oak is abundant around the campground and beggar squirrels can strip your table of food before you're even aware they've invaded.

Basics

Operated By: California Dept. of Parks & Recreation. **Open:** All year. **Site Assignment:** Reservations recommended; V, MC, D. **Registration:** At entrance booth. **Fee:** $12, cash or CA check. **Parking:** At site.

Facilities

Number of RV Sites: 214. **Number of Tent-Only Sites:** 0. **Hookups:** None. **Each Site:** Picnic table, fire grate, barbecue grill. **Dump Station:** Yes. **Laundry:** Yes. **Pay Phone:** Yes. **Rest Rooms and Showers:** Yes. **Fuel:** No. **Propane:** No. **Internal Roads:** Paved. **RV Service:** No. **Market:** 1 mi. north in Big Sur. **Restaurant:** In Big Sur Lodge, within the park. **General Store:** Yes. **Vending:** Yes. **Swimming:** In Big Sur Lodge pool. **Playground:** No. **Other:** Some wheelchair-accessible facilities, Big Sur Lodge. **Activities:** Hiking, beaching, winter whale-watching, redwoods exploring, photography. **Nearby Attractions:** Several state parks in the vicinity: Julia Pfeiffer Burns, Andrew Molera, Garrapata, Limekiln State Park in Lucia, Big Sur coastal vistas. **Additional Information:** Big Sur Chamber, (831) 667-2100.

Restrictions

Pets: On 6 ft. leash. **Fires:** In fire grates only. **Alcoholic Beverages:** Allowed at site. **Vehicle Maximum Length:** 32 ft. **Other:** 14-day stay limit; no firearms; no wood gathering.

To Get There

From the Big Sur Post Office on Hwy. 1, drive 1.5 mi. north and turn right into the campground.

BISHOP

East Fork

Rock Creek Rd., Toms Place 93514. T: (760) 873-2500 or reservations (877) 444-6777; F: (760) 873-2563; www.r5.fs.fed.us/inyo or www.reserveamerica.com.

★★★★ ★★★

Beauty: ★★★★ Site Privacy: ★★★
Spaciousness: ★★ Quiet: ★★★
Security: ★★★ Cleanliness: ★★★
Insect Control: ★★★ Facilities: ★

East Fork is nestled in a rocky canyon with snow-capped Sierra peaks looming above, a thrilling setting very near the gorgeous Rock Creek Lake. The creek itself gurgles through the property, which consists of a hodge-podge of sites, some shaded by lodgepole pines and junipers, others screened by aspen trees, and many exposed to the sun. While most are respectably scattered apart, sites are on the small side, with some so snug there's not enough room to set up anything but a bivvy tent. Still, we find this Inyo National Forest facility infinitely preferable to that at the lake, which is basically a campers' corral in a parking lot. Creek-side site 86 is especially recessed and private, 108 is quite large, and 110–112 and 114 are very good runners-up. At 9,000 feet elevation, this high altitude camp can get hit by snow at almost any time of year, so plan your trip accordingly.

Basics

Operated By: American Land & Leisure. **Open:** Mid-May through Oct., weather permitting. **Site Assignment:** Reservations accepted w/ MC, V, D. **Registration:** At entrance kiosk. **Fee:** $13 , cash or check. **Parking:** At site.

Facilities

Number of RV Sites: 80. **Number of Tent-Only Sites:** 53. **Hookups:** None. **Each Site:** Picnic table, fire grate, barbecue grill. **Dump Station:** No. **Laundry:** No. **Pay Phone:** No. **Rest Rooms and Showers:** Flush toilets, no showers. **Fuel:** No. **Propane:** No. **Internal Roads:** Paved. **RV Service:** No. **Market:** 21 mi. north in Mammoth Lakes. **Restaurant:** 3 mi. northeast in Toms Place. **General Store:** No. **Vending:** No. **Swimming:** No. **Playground:** No. **Activities:** Hiking, fishing, bicycling. **Nearby Attractions:** Devil's Postpile National Monument, outlet shopping in Mammoth Lakes, museums in Bishop, Ancient Bristlecone Pine Forest in the Inyo National Forest. **Additional Information:** Bishop Area Chamber of Commerce & Visitors Bureau, (760) 873-8405.

Restrictions

Pets: On leash. **Fires:** In fire grates only. **Alcoholic Beverages:** Allowed. **Vehicle Maximum Length:** 45 ft. **Other:** 14-day stay limit.

To Get There

From Bishop head north on US 395 for 24 mi. Turn west (left) on Rock Creek Rd.; continue for 6 mi. and turn left to the campground access road.

BLAIRSDEN

Plumas-Eureka State Park, Upper Samson Creek Campground

310 Johnsville Rd., Blairsden 96103. T: (530) 836-2380; F: (530) 836-0498; www.cal-parks.ca.gov or www.ceres.ca.gov/sierradsp/plumas.html.

★★★★ ★★★★

Beauty: ★★★★ Site Privacy: ★★★
Spaciousness: ★★★ Quiet: ★★★★
Security: ★★★ Cleanliness: ★★★
Insect Control: ★★ Facilities: ★★★

"Stunning," "drop-dead gorgeous," and "breathtaking," all describe the spectacular beauty of this high altitude campground that is encircled by a series of jagged, snow-patched Sierra Nevada peaks. The rugged landscape is enhanced by its position next to Jamison Creek and the great variety of conifers, as well as willows, alders, and cottonwoods, that provide it with shade. Flourishing though the forest is, a fair degree of sunlight manages to warm the property. Most sites are roomy and set pretty well apart along a small series of loops. Eureka Peak was once known as Gold Mountain, a testimony to the extensive mining activity that went on in the Jamison area from the gold rush days through the end of the first world war. A mining history museum within the park preserves buildings and equipment from that era. Once a month, in summer, docents in period dress attempt to recreate a sense of what camp life was like in the 1890s.

Basics

Operated By: California Dept. of Parks & Recreation. **Open:** May 15–Oct. 15, weather permitting. **Site Assignment:** First come, first served. **Registration:** At park office. **Fee:** $12, cash or CA check. **Parking:** At site.

Facilities

Number of RV Sites: 59. **Number of Tent-Only Sites:** 8. **Hookups:** None. **Each Site:** Picnic table, fire grate, bearproof box. **Dump Station:** Yes. **Laundry:** No. **Pay Phone:** Yes. **Rest Rooms and Showers:** Yes. **Fuel:** No. **Propane:** No. **Internal Roads:** Paved. **RV Service:** No. **Market:** 6 mi. east in Graegle. **Restaurant:** 6 mi. east in Graegle. **General Store:** No. **Vending:** No. **Swimming:** No. **Playground:** No. **Other:** Some wheelchair-accessible facilities, visitor center & museum. **Activities:** Hiking, bicycling, fishing. **Nearby Attractions:** Portola Railroad Museum; Lakes Basin Recreation Area in Graegle; Plumas County Museum in Quincy; Plumas National Forest. **Additional Information:** Plumas County Visitors Bureau, (530) 283-6345 or (800) 326-2247.

Restrictions

Pets: On 6 ft. leash. **Fires:** In fire grates only. **Alcoholic Beverages:** Allowed at site. **Vehicle Maximum Length:** 30 ft. **Other:** 14-day stay limit; no firearms; no wood gathering.

To Get There

From Portola drive 10 mi. west on Hwy. 70. 1 mi. beyond Blairsden after the junction w/ Hwy. 89, turn left towards Johnsville and continue for 0.6 mi. At the stop sign turn right on the Graegle-Johnsville Rd./A14. The park entrance is 4.5 mi. ahead.

BLYTHE

Mayflower Park

4980 Colorado River Rd., Blythe 92225. T: (760) 922-4665; www.riversidecountyparks.org/parks/mayflower.htm.

★★★★ ★★★

Beauty: ★★★ Site Privacy: ★★
Spaciousness: ★★ Quiet: ★★★
Security: ★★★★ Cleanliness: ★★★★
Insect Control: ★★★ Facilities: ★★★★

In the dusty desert landscape common to this part of the state, Mayflower is a welcome oasis and, situated just seven miles north of I-10, a convenient one to pilgrims sailing along the highway. Well manicured, grassy sites are partially shaded by mesquite trees, eucalyptus and cottonwoods, with the tent area—separated from two other RV loops—especially appealing. The view of the Plomosa Mountains across the state line in Arizona is superb, but it is the border itself, marked here by the Colorado River (which flows just below the campground and is accessible via an in-camp boat ramp and swimming lagoon) that is the real attraction for most visitors. Peace-and-quiet seekers take note: boating on this stretch of river during summer months—weekends especially—is more popular than a high school prom queen, so be prepared to hear the constant whine of two-stroke engines being pushed to their limits. That activity largely fades away in the off-season, but winter brings hordes of a different sort of camper, snowbirds by the RV-load.

Basics

Operated By: Riverside County. **Open:** All Year. **Site Assignment:** First come, first served. **Registration:** At entrance office. **Fee:** $15–$16, cash, CA check or V, MC, D. **Parking:** At site.

Facilities

Number of RV Sites: 145. **Number of Tent-Only Sites:** 19. **Hookups:** Water, electric (30, 50 amps). **Each Site:** Picnic table, fire grate. **Dump Station:** Yes. **Laundry:** No. **Pay Phone:** Yes. **Rest Rooms and Showers:** Yes. **Fuel:** No. **Propane:** No. **Internal Roads:** Mostly paved. **RV Service:** No. **Market:** 7 mi. southwest in Blythe. **Restaurant:** 7 mi. southwest in Blythe. **General Store:** No. **Vending:** Yes. **Swimming:** In mudwallow lagoon & Colorado River. **Playground:** No. **Other:** Some wheelchair-accessible facilities, boat ramp. **Activities:** Fishing, horseshoe pits, bowling lawn, shuffleboard. **Nearby Attractions:** Colorado River, Mojave National Preserve, Cibola & Imperial National Wildlife Refuges, in Arizona. **Additional Information:** Riverside County, Regional Park & Open Space District, (909) 955-4397.

Restrictions

Pets: On leash, $2 fee. **Fires:** In fire grates only. **Alcoholic Beverages:** Allowed. **Vehicle Maximum Length:** None. **Other:** 14-day stay limit from Apr. 1–Sept. 30; no ORVs; no generators; no loaded firearms.

To Get There

From I-10/US 95 drive 3.7 mi. north on Inlake Blvd. Turn right on 6th Ave. and drive 3.2 mi. into the campground.

BODEGA BAY

Sonoma Coast State Beach, Bodega Dunes Campground

Hwy. 1, Bodega Bay 94923. T: (707) 875-3483 or reservations (800) 444-7275; www.cal-parks.ca.gov or www.reserveamerica.com.

★★★★ ★★★★

Beauty: ★★★★ Site Privacy: ★★★★
Spaciousness: ★★★ Quiet: ★★★★
Security: ★★★ Cleanliness: ★★★
Insect Control: ★★★ Facilities: ★★

This good-looking, spacious campground is right off of Hwy. 1, just a short trail's walk from the ocean. Three separate loops undulate across sandy dunes in a semi-forested environment colored by ferns, dune grass, Monterey pines, and eucalyptus. Sites of grass and sand are decently roomy and planted well apart, with a number of pull-through parking slips on hand. Of the latter, numbers 3 and 4 are very private and shaded by conifers. Similarly isolated are 24, 32, 36, 69, 86, and 88, and their nestled-in-the-dunes position is a welcome buffer against road noise and brisk coastal breezes. The steady drone of a distant foghorn is less a disturbing influence than a contributor to the pleasant seaside atmosphere. In spite of its beauty, this facility is often wonderfully under-populated. With whales routinely passing in winter months and a seal rookery located by the egress of the Russian River, you will want to pack binoculars.

Basics

Operated By: California Dept. of Parks & Recreation. **Open:** All year. **Site Assignment:** Reservations accepted w/ V, MC, D. **Registration:** At entrance booth. **Fee:** $12, cash or CA check. **Parking:** At site.

Facilities

Number of RV Sites: 98. **Number of Tent-Only Sites:** 0. **Hookups:** None. **Each Site:** Picnic table, fire grate, food storage box. **Dump Station:** Yes. **Laundry:** No. **Pay Phone:** Yes. **Rest Rooms and Showers:** Yes. **Fuel:** No. **Propane:** No. **Internal Roads:** Paved. **RV Service:** No. **Market:** 2 mi. south in Bodega Bay. **Restaurant:** 2 mi. south in Bodega Bay. **General Store:** No. **Vending:** No. **Swimming:** No. **Playground:** No. **Other:** Some wheelchair-accessible facilities. **Activities:** Fishing, sunning, surfing, tidepooling, beachcombing, horseback riding, bicycling, winter whale-watching at Bodega Head. **Nearby Attractions:** Santa Rosa museums & Luther Burbank Home & Memorial Gardens; Fort Ross, Kruse Rhododendron State Reserve & Salt Point State Park in Jenner. **Additional Information:** Bodega Bay Area Chamber of Commerce, (707) 875-3422.

Restrictions

Pets: On 6 ft. leash. **Fires:** In fire grates only. **Alcoholic Beverages:** Allowed at site. **Vehicle Maximum Length:** 31 ft. **Other:** 10-day stay limit from Apr. 1–Nov. 30; no firearms; no wood gathering.

To Get There

From Bodega Bay drive 2 mi. north on Hwy. 1. Turn left into the park.

BORREGO SPRINGS

Borrego Palm Canyon Campground, Anza-Borrego Desert State Park

200 Palm Canyon Dr., Borrego Springs 92004. T: (760) 767-5311; F: (760) 767-3427; www.calparks.ca.gov, www.reserveamerica.com.

RV ★★★ Tent ★★★

Beauty: ★★★ Site Privacy: ★★★
Spaciousness: ★★★ Quiet: ★★★
Security: ★★★ Cleanliness: ★★★
Insect Control: ★★★★ Facilities: ★★★

This campground is situated in the mouth of the expansive Borrego Palm Canyon near the heart of Anza-Borrego Desert State Park. That central location insures a level of use and popularity well beyond most of the many other camps in this, the largest of state parks in the lower 48 states. A good range of facilities adds to its appeal, with drinking water, showers, full hookups, and even a few partially enclosed stone shelters (complete with fireplaces) available. Though shade is scarce, ramadas over tables provide some relief from a sun that is scorching much of the year. Tent pads are of a coarse gravel, but the overall landscape is hardly lunar, with fan palms lining one stretch of the camp road and ironwood, ocotillo, staghorn cholla, and creosote bushes sprinkled throughout. Largely comparable sites are fairly well fanned apart, with a good number equipped with pull-through parking slots.

BASICS

Operated By: California Dept. of Parks & Recreation. **Open:** All year. **Site Assignment:** Reservations accepted w/ V, MC. **Registration:** At entrance booth. **Fee:** $10–$16, cash, CA checks or V, MC. **Parking:** At site.

FACILITIES

Number of RV Sites: 117. **Number of Tent-Only Sites:** 0. **Hookups:** Water, electric (30 amps), sewer. **Each Site:** Picnic table, fire grate, ramada (tent loop only). **Dump Station:** Yes. **Laundry:** No. **Pay Phone:** Yes. **Rest Rooms and Showers:** Yes. **Fuel:** No. **Propane:** No. **Internal Roads:** Paved. **RV Service:** No. **Market:** 2 mi. east in Borrego Springs. **Restaurant:** 2 mi. east in Borrego Springs. **General Store:** No. **Vending:** No. **Swimming:** No. **Playground:** No. **Other:** Some wheelchair-accessible facilities. **Activities:** Hiking, bicycling, seasonal nature programs. **Nearby Attractions:** Anza-Borrego Desert State Park, San Diego Wild Animal Park in Escondido. **Additional Information:** Borrego Springs Chamber of Commerce, (760) 767-5976.

RESTRICTIONS

Pets: On 6 ft. leash. **Fires:** In fire grates only. **Alcoholic Beverages:** Allowed at site. **Vehicle Maximum Length:** 35 ft. **Other:** 14-day stay limit; no firearms; no wood gathering.

TO GET THERE

From Borrego Springs drive 1 mi. west on CR S22. At the bend in the road continue straight on Palm Canyon Dr. for 0.2 mi. The campground access road is 1 mi. ahead to the right.

BORREGO SPRINGS

Bow Willow Campground, Anza-Borrego Desert State Park

CR S2, Borrego Springs 92004. T: (760) 767-5311; F: (760) 767- 3427; www.anzaborrego.statepark.org.

RV ★★★ Tent ★★★★

Beauty: ★★★★ Site Privacy: ★★★
Spaciousness: ★★★ Quiet: ★★★★
Security: ★ Cleanliness: ★★★
Insect Control: ★★★★ Facilities: ★

As the largest state park in the lower 48 states, Anza-Borrego has many attractions: a varied desert landscape, beautiful wildflowers in the spring, a mastodon site, and no shortage of fine camping options. Of these latter, Bow Willow is one of the standouts, with a pair of loops meandering along the lower contours of a rocky canyon. Sandy sites are marginally screened from each other by ocotillo, mesquite, salt bush, and cholla cacti, with numbers 1 and 16 at the periphery the most private. An easy one-and-a-half-mile trail out of camp leads to several shady groves of California fan palms, where we spotted a black hooded oriole and a fluorescent green hummingbird our last time through. No-fee overflow camping is available one mile up the road at the primitive Mountain Palm Springs.

BASICS

Operated By: California Dept. of Parks & Recreation. **Open:** All year. **Site Assignment:** First come, first served. **Registration:** At entrance kiosk. **Fee:** $7, cash or CA check. **Parking:** At site.

FACILITIES

Number of RV Sites: 16. **Number of Tent-Only Sites:** 0. **Hookups:** None. **Each Site:** Picnic table, fire grate, ramada. **Dump Station:** No. **Laundry:** No. **Pay Phone:** No. **Rest Rooms and Showers:** Pit toilets, no showers. **Fuel:** No. **Propane:** No. **Internal Roads:** Sandy washboard, decent condition. **RV Service:** No. **Market:** 44 mi. northwest in Julian. **Restaurant:** 44 mi. northwest in Julian. **General Store:** 10.5 mi. north in Agua Caliente Hot Springs. **Vending:** No. **Swimming:** No. **Playground:** No. **Activities:** Hiking, rock scrambling, birding. **Nearby Attractions:** Palm Springs Desert Museum, Agua Caliente Cultural Museum. **Additional Information:** Borrego Springs Chamber of Commerce, (800) 559-5524.

RESTRICTIONS

Pets: On 6 ft. leash. **Fires:** In fire grates only. **Alcoholic Beverages:** Allowed at site. **Vehicle Maximum Length:** None. **Other:** 14-day stay limit; no firearms; no wood gathering.

TO GET THERE

Turn off I-8 at the Ocotillo Exit. Follow CR S2 north through Ocotillo, and turn left into campground after 18 mi.

BORREGO SPRINGS

Culp Valley Primitive Camp, Anza-Borrego Desert State Park

CR S22, Borrego Springs 92004. T: (760) 767-5311; F: (760) 767-3427.

RV ★★★★ Tent ★★★★

Beauty: ★★★★ Site Privacy: ★★★★
Spaciousness: ★★★★ Quiet: ★★★★
Security: ★ Cleanliness: ★★★★
Insect Control: ★★★★ Facilities: ★

To those who appreciate the low key beauty of the desert and enjoy roughing it, Culp Valley, nine miles west of Borrego Springs, is a hidden gem. Large granite boulders litter a chaparral landscape punctuated by buckwheat, cat's claw, staghorn cholla, and dwarf oak. Most sites are extraordinarily spacious, and several are shielded from view by high hedges of sugar bush, which makes for a more peaceful experience than what is possible in the more popular—and populated—developed campgrounds elsewhere in Anza-Borrego. The trade-off is that creature comforts are limited to surprisingly clean vaulted toilets; no water is available and you will have to pack out your trash. A greater nuisance though is the biting wind that tends to whistle through camp from late fall through early spring. That and an altitude of 3,400 feet will make you glad you packed a heavy sweater, should you visit in the off-season. If you come in summer, well, you'll very likely find yourself alone in the whole blazing park.

BASICS

Operated By: California Dept. of Parks & Recreation. **Open:** All year. **Site Assignment:** First come, first served. **Registration:** At entrance kiosk. **Fee:** $5, cash or CA check; no fee in winter. **Parking:** At site.

FACILITIES

Number of RV Sites: 15. **Number of Tent-Only Sites:** 0. **Hookups:** None. **Each Site:** Space & privacy. **Dump Station:** No. **Laundry:** No. **Pay Phone:** No. **Rest Rooms and Showers:** Vault toilets, no showers. **Fuel:** No. **Propane:** No. **Internal Roads:** Hard sand, some rock, some washboard, negotiable. **RV Service:** No. **Market:** 9 mi. west in Borrego Springs. **Restaurant:** 9 mi. west in Borrego Springs. **General Store:** No. **Vending:** No. **Swimming:** No. **Playground:** No. **Activities:** Hiking, photography, stargazing, rock scrambling. **Nearby Attractions:** Anza-Borrego Desert State Park, San Diego Wild Animal Park in Escondido, historic Julian, scenic views. **Additional Information:** Borrego Springs Chamber of Commerce, (760) 767-5976.

RESTRICTIONS

Pets: On 6 ft. leash. **Fires:** No. **Alcoholic Beverages:** Allowed. **Vehicle Maximum Length:** None, but think twice if over 22 ft. **Other:** 14-day stay limit; no shooting.

TO GET THERE

From Borrego Springs drive 9 mi. east on CR S22. Check for a sign between mi. markers 9 and 10 on the right (north) side of the road.

BRIDGEPORT

Honeymoon Flat

Twin Lakes Rd., Bridgeport 93517. T: (760) 932-7070 or reservations (877) 444-6777; F: (760)

932-1299; www.r5.fs.fed.us/htnf/honecamp.htm or www.reserveusa.com.

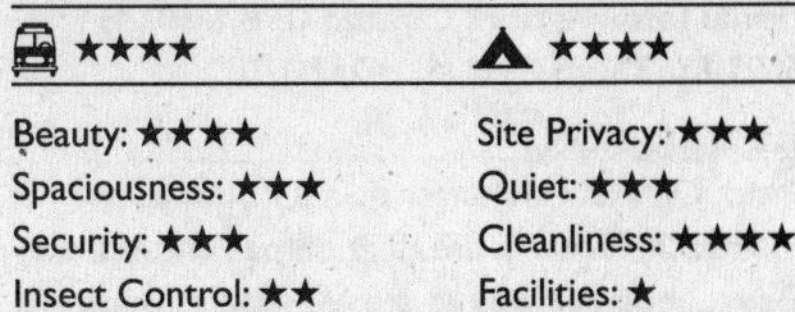

RV ★★★★ Tent ★★★★

Beauty: ★★★★ Site Privacy: ★★★
Spaciousness: ★★★ Quiet: ★★★
Security: ★★★ Cleanliness: ★★★★
Insect Control: ★★ Facilities: ★

A campground sporting the name Honeymoon Flat had better be the sort of cozily romantic place you'd want to take your sweetheart. Well, go right ahead, as this idyllic spot lives up to that promise, and then some. Twin Lakes Rd. divides it into two sections, with both hugging Robinson Creek. Many of the grassy sites along the camp's series of sandy loops abut the water, allowing you to fish for trout from tent-side, or simply dandle your toes in the rippling water. Though sites are a shade small, privacy is well above average, with screening provided by a mix of pines and, especially, the luminescent leaves of quaking aspen. Site 3, very recessed and with water flowing by on three sides, might well be the envy of Diana. Number 5 is similarly romantic. There are half a dozen other campgrounds in the neighborhood, but this is the only one that hasn't been smothered by an excess of asphalt. When you are at 7,000 feet, surrounded by the high Sierras, a campground shouldn't look like a parking lot. The pit toilets are reportedly going to be replaced with new restrooms; we expect the concessionaire will raise the rates as a consequence.

Basics

Operated By: American Land & Leisure, concessionaire. **Open:** Mid-Apr. through Oct., weather permitting. **Site Assignment:** Reservations accepted w/ V, MC, D. **Registration:** At entrance kiosk. **Fee:** $10, cash or check. **Parking:** At site.

Facilities

Number of RV Sites: 31. **Number of Tent-Only Sites:** 4. **Hookups:** None. **Each Site:** Picnic table, fire grate. **Dump Station:** No. **Laundry:** No. **Pay Phone:** No. **Rest Rooms and Showers:** Pit toilets, no showers. **Fuel:** No. **Propane:** No. **Internal Roads:** Sandy & somewhat bumpy. **RV Service:** No. **Market:** 8.5 mi. north in Bridgeport. **Restaurant:** 8.5 mi. north in Bridgeport. **General Store:** No. **Vending:** No. **Swimming:** No. **Playground:** No. **Activities:** Hiking, fishing, whispering sweet nothings into your sweetheart's ear. **Nearby Attractions:** Bodie State Historic Park in Bridgeport; Lower Twin Lake, Mono Lake Tufa State Reserve in Lee Vining. **Additional Information:** Eastern Sierra Interagency Visitor Center, (760) 876-6222; Bridgeport Chamber of Commerce, (760) 932-7500.

Restrictions

Pets: On leash. **Fires:** In fire grates only. **Alcoholic Beverages:** Allowed. **Vehicle Maximum Length:** 45 ft. **Other:** 14-day stay limit.

To Get There

From US 395 on Bridgeport's west side, turn south onto Twin Lakes Rd. Drive 8.2 mi. to the campground entrance on both sides of the road.

BUËLLTON

Figueroa

Figueroa Mountain Rd., Los Olivos 93441.
T: (805) 925-9538; F: (805) 681-2781; www.r5.fs.fed.us/lospadres.

RV ★★★ Tent ★★★★★

Beauty: ★★★★★ Site Privacy: ★★★★
Spaciousness: ★★★★ Quiet: ★★★★
Security: ★★ Cleanliness: ★★★★
Insect Control: ★★★★ Facilities: ★

As far as rustic campgrounds go, this one, set at 4,000 feet among alpine meadows and mixed tree communities high in the rugged mountains of the Los Padres National Forest, is almost perfect. It is so far out—the nearest town is more than 15 miles away—that the only sounds likely to disturb you will come from Stellar's jays, acorn woodpeckers, owls, or coyotes. Unless you happen to have particularly obnoxious neighbors. Even so, most of the dirt and pebbly sites along the double loop are regally spacious and far apart, screened by manzanita, live oak, and Coulter pines, with an accent here and there of shiny, putty colored rock outcroppings. Shade is abundant, though several units are open and sunny, and a few offer superb vistas of sunsets and the valley far below. In spring the hills are a velvety green that is a delight to behold, but be alert to changing weather as the pockmarked road leading here can be very tricky when wet. Figueroa is a pack-in, pack-out facility with an unreliable water supply.

Basics

Operated By: Los Padres National Forest, Santa Lucia Ranger District. **Open:** All year. **Site Assignment:** First come, first served. **Registration:** No. **Fee:** No fee, but National Forest Adventure Pass ($5 per day, $30 annual pass) required. **Parking:** At site.

Facilities

Number of RV Sites: 33. **Number of Tent-Only Sites:** 0. **Hookups:** None. **Each Site:** Picnic table, fire grate, barbecue grill. **Dump Station:** No. **Laundry:** No. **Pay Phone:** No. **Rest Rooms and Showers:** Vault toilets, no showers. **Fuel:** No. **Propane:** No. **Internal Roads:** Paved. **RV Service:** No. **Market:** 23 mi. southwest in Buëllton. **Restaurant:** 23 mi. southwest in Buëllton. **General Store:** No. **Vending:** No. **Swimming:** No. **Playground:** No. **Other:** Some wheelchair-accessible facilities. **Activities:** Hiking, birding, stargazing. **Nearby Attractions:** Mission Santa Inés & museums in Solvang, La Purísima Mission State Historic Park in Lompoc, Lake Cachuma. **Additional Information:** Buëllton Visitors Bureau, (805) 688-7829.

Restrictions

Pets: On leash. **Fires:** In fire grates only. **Alcoholic Beverages:** Allowed. **Vehicle Maximum Length:** 22 ft. **Other:** 14-day stay limit.

To Get There

In Los Olivos on Hwy. 154 head north on Figueroa Mountain Rd. Watch out for potholes on this narrow, windy road. Drive 13.8 mi. and turn right into the campground.

CAMP NELSON

Peppermint

FR 21S07A, Ponderosa/Camp Nelson 93208.
T: (559) 539-2607; www.r5.fs.fed.us/sequoia.

RV ★★★★ Tent ★★★★

Beauty: ★★★★ Site Privacy: ★★★★
Spaciousness: ★★★★ Quiet: ★★★
Security: ★ Cleanliness: ★★
Insect Control: ★★★ Facilities: ★

The last time we stopped by this primitive camp we were surprised to find half a dozen motor homes in residence. Not that the dirt access road off of Western Divide Hwy. is bad—it isn't (though the internal lane verges on abominable in places). It's just that for ages Peppermint has been a refuge for budget-minded tenters. Word of its rustic appeal must have spread. There are about a dozen tables scattered around this rocky, forested mountain knoll, mostly downhill by Peppermint Creek. There is also a dilapidated outhouse, of a similar vintage to the one at Quaking Aspen, just up the road. If you want more in creature comforts, you best bring 'em with you or go elsewhere. Undesignated sites are well hidden among lodgepole, ponderosa and Jeffrey pines, alders and aspens, cedars and dirt. Those with tables are snapped up first, but there are many more across the hill with simply a crude ring of stones as an amenity. Bring your own drinking water, pack out trash, and, since you'll be camping at an altitude of 7,100 feet, dress warmly. Telephone, gasoline, propane, and a general store are available 1.5 miles north at Ponderosa Lodge.

Basics

Operated By: Sequoia National Forest, Tule River Ranger District. **Open:** May through Oct., weather permitting. **Site Assignment:** First come, first served. **Registration:** None. **Fee:** None. **Parking:** No restriction.

Facilities

Number of RV Sites: Unspecified, dispersed camping. **Number of Tent-Only Sites:** 0. **Hookups:** None. **Each Site:** 12 scattered picnic tables, many makeshift fire rings. **Dump Station:** No. **Laundry:** No. **Pay Phone:** No. **Rest Rooms and Showers:** Vault toilets, no showers. **Fuel:** No. **Propane:** No. **Internal Roads:** Rocky forest floor. **RV Service:** No. **Market:** 45 mi. west in Porterville. **Restaurant:** 30 mi. west in Springville. **General Store:** No. **Vending:** No. **Swimming:** No. **Playground:** No. **Activities:** Hiking, fishing, whittling. **Nearby Attractions:** Sequoia National Forest; Porterville Historical Museum & Zauld House & Gardens; California Hot Springs. **Additional Information:** Springville Chamber of Commerce, (559) 539-2312; Porterville Chamber of Commerce, (559) 784-7503.

Restrictions

Pets: On leash. **Fires:** By permit, issued at the Tule River Ranger District in Springville; use fire ring. **Alcoholic Beverages:** Allowed. **Vehicle Maximum Length:** 22 ft. **Other:** 14-day stay limit.

To Get There
From Porterville drive 44 mi. east on Hwy. 190 (which becomes the Western Divide Hwy.). Turn left on FR 21S07B and after 0.5 mi. turn left again on 21S07A. The campground lies straight ahead.

CAPITOLA
New Brighton State Beach
1500 Park Ave., Hwy. 1, Capitola 95010. T: (831) 464-6330 or reservations (800) 444-7275; www.cal-parks.ca.gov or www.reserveamerica.com.

RV ★★★★ Tent ★★★★

Beauty: ★★★★ Site Privacy: ★★★
Spaciousness: ★★★★ Quiet: ★★★
Security: ★★★ Cleanliness: ★★★★
Insect Control: ★★ Facilities: ★★

Tired of sweeping buckets of sand out of your tent or RV after every trip to the beach? Then you owe it to yourself to check out this splendid campground, located just five miles east of Santa Cruz off of Hwy. 1. The bluff-top real estate is lush and grassy, graced with a comforting balance of shade and sun that filters through a high canopy of pines and eucalyptus trees. Many of the refreshingly spacious spots enjoy great vistas of the crashing surf. And of those that do not, a hefty share have the edge in privacy, being buffered by dense hedges of coastal chaparral. Sites 25 and 94 are the most isolated, while 36 is the best screened of the view options. And if sand in your shelter isn't a problem, you can always bring a bucketful back from the idyllic beach, reachable via a short trail next to site 50. Poison oak thrives around the edges of this park.

Basics
Operated By: California Dept. of Parks & Recreation. **Open:** All year. **Site Assignment:** Reservations recommended; V, MC, D. **Registration:** At entrance booth. **Fee:** $12, cash or CA check. **Parking:** At site.

Facilities
Number of RV Sites: 112. **Number of Tent-Only Sites:** 0. **Hookups:** None. **Each Site:** Picnic table, fire grate, food storage box. **Dump Station:** Yes. **Laundry:** No. **Pay Phone:** Yes. **Rest Rooms and Showers:** Yes. **Fuel:** No. **Propane:** No. **Internal Roads:** Paved. **RV Service:** No. **Market:** 5 mi. west in Santa Cruz. **Restaurant:** 5 mi. west in Santa Cruz. **General Store:** No. **Vending:** No. **Swimming:** In Pacific Ocean. **Playground:** No. **Other:** Some wheelchair-accessible facilities. **Activities:** Surf fishing, sunning, hiking, ranger-led programs in summer. **Nearby Attractions:** Santa Cruz Beach Boardwalk, mission, museums, Seymour Marine Discovery Center, Arboretum & Natural Bridges State Beach; Roaring Camp Railroads in Felton. **Additional Information:** Capitola Chamber of Commerce, (831) 475-6522; Santa Cruz County Conference & Visitors Council, (831) 425-1234 or (800) 833-3494.

Restrictions
Pets: On 6 ft. leash. **Fires:** In fire grates only. **Alcoholic Beverages:** Allowed at site. **Vehicle Maximum Length:** 36 ft. **Other:** 7-day stay limit from Apr. 1–Oct. 31; no firearms; no wood gathering.

To Get There
From Santa Cruz drive 5 mi. south on Hwy. 1 and take the New Brighton Beach Exit. Drive 1 block west to the stop sign. Turn left on McGregor Dr. After 0.2 mi. turn right into the park.

CARLSBAD
South Carlsbad State Beach
Carlsbad Blvd./Pacific Coast Hwy. 101, Carlsbad 92008. T: (760) 438-3143; www.cal-parks.ca.gov or www.reserveamerica.com.

RV ★★★★ Tent ★★

Beauty: ★★★ Site Privacy: ★★
Spaciousness: ★★★ Quiet: ★
Security: ★★★ Cleanliness: ★★
Insect Control: ★★ Facilities: ★★★★

There is much to like about South Carlsbad State Beach. Such as the pretty beach, and its convenient location just off I-5, 25 miles north of San Diego. Sites are positioned side-by-side high above the sea on a sandy bluff, and are both spacious and buffered with thick hedges that provide a certain degree of privacy. The straight-in linear layout of the camp road endows half the property with fine views of the Pacific Ocean. Of course, the narrowness of the bluff means that you are likely to have neighbors on three of your spot's four sides when the camp is busy, which is most of the year, given its near-constant use by hordes of college-age campers. At those times the flow of traffic can seem never-ending, a problem compounded by the busy external road that parallels the park's entire length. True, that constant hum of vehicles helps drown out the boisterousness of other campers and the squealing whistles of Amtrak trains that tend to pass the property on an hourly basis, but that may be of small consolation to light sleepers. At least the ocean-side sites benefit from the sonorous sound of the surf. Overall, South Carlsbad is quieter than San Elijo State Beach to the south, where the deafening roar of railroad and highway vehicles seems to be bearing down on one's tent. San Elijo does, however, offer some sites with hookups.

Basics
Operated By: California Dept. of Parks & Recreation. **Open:** All year. **Site Assignment:** Reservations recommended; V, MC, D. **Registration:** At entrance booth. **Fee:** $12, cash, CA check or V, MC, D. **Parking:** At site.

Facilities
Number of RV Sites: 222. **Number of Tent-Only Sites:** 0. **Hookups:** None. **Each Site:** Picnic table, fire ring. **Dump Station:** Yes. **Laundry:** Yes. **Pay Phone:** Yes. **Rest Rooms and Showers:** Yes. **Fuel:** No. **Propane:** Yes. **Internal Roads:** Paved. **RV Service:** No. **Market:** 4 mi. north in Carlsbad. **Restaurant:** 4 mi. north in Carlsbad. **General Store:** Yes. **Vending:** Yes. **Swimming:** In Pacific Ocean. **Playground:** No. **Other:** Some wheelchair-accessible facilities. **Activities:** Sunning, surfing, rock & shell hounding, surfboard & boogie board rentals. **Nearby Attractions:** Coastal air tours, outlet shopping, Museum of Making Music, Legoland. **Additional Information:** Carlsbad CVB, (760) 434-6093; San Diego CVB, (619) 232-3101.

Restrictions
Pets: On leash no longer than 6 ft.; not allowed on the beach. **Fires:** In fire rings only. **Alcoholic Beverages:** Allowed at site. **Vehicle Maximum Length:** 35 ft. **Other:** 14-day stay limit; no firearms.

To Get There
From Carlsbad drive 4.5 miles south on Hwy. 101. Bear to the right into the campground, which is easy to overshoot since signs are lacking.

CARMEL
Saddle Mountain Recreation Park and RV & Campground
27625 Schulte Rd., Carmel 93923. T: (831) 624-1617; F: (831) 624-4470.

RV ★★★ Tent ★★

Beauty: ★★★ Site Privacy: ★★
Spaciousness: ★★ Quiet: ★★★★
Security: ★★★ Cleanliness: ★★
Insect Control: ★★ Facilities: ★★★

Planning to be in the Monterey vicinity? If you are hauling a trailer or driving an RV you will find that Saddle Mountain has a lot going for it. Like full hookups, including cable television, a heated swimming pool (Memorial Day through Labor Day), basketball, volleyball, horseshoes, hiking, and even fishing in the nearby Carmel River. Its suburban location is a plus, too, just five miles from Carmel in the hills of Potrero Canyon, with great vistas of the surrounding mountains. Terraced clusters of sites are rather close together but shady and well-screened by cypress trees, Monterey pines, and flowering oleanders, with a pretty rock garden adding to the attractive landscaping. Tent sites, sequestered up the hill from RVs, are similarly shaded and slightly more spacious. A latticed picnic area and deck overlook the pool. Although the moderate climate makes it possible for this privately-operated campground to remain open throughout the year, maintenance slackens somewhat in the off-season.

Basics
Operated By: Saddle Mountain Recreation Park & RV & Campground. **Open:** All year. **Site Assignment:** Reservations accepted w/ V, MC. **Registration:** At office. **Fee:** $25–$40, cash or V, MC. **Parking:** At site.

Facilities
Number of RV Sites: 25. **Number of Tent-Only Sites:** 25. **Hookups:** Water, electric (20, 30 amps), sewer, cable TV. **Each Site:** Picnic table, barbecue grill. **Dump Station:** Yes. **Laundry:** No. **Pay Phone:** Yes. **Rest Rooms and Showers:** Yes. **Fuel:** No. **Propane:** No. **Internal Roads:** Paved, dirt in the tent area. **RV Service:** No. **Market:** 5 mi. west in Carmel. **Restaurant:** 5 mi. west in Carmel. **General Store:** No. **Vending:** Yes. **Swimming:** In heated pool seasonally. **Playground:** Yes.

Other: Limited wheelchair-accessible facilities, game room. **Activities:** Hiking, volleyball, horseshoe pit, golf. **Nearby Attractions:** Mission San Carlos Borromeo del Rio Carmelo & outlet shopping in Carmel; Monterey peninsula w/ its museums & aquarium. **Additional Information:** Carmel Valley Chamber of Commerce, (831) 659-4000.

RESTRICTIONS

Pets: On leash no longer than 6 ft.; not allowed in the tent area. **Fires:** In grills only. **Alcoholic Beverages:** Allowed at site. **Vehicle Maximum Length:** 40 ft. **Other:** 14-day stay limit.

TO GET THERE

From Carmel on Hwy. 1 follow the Carmel Valley Rd. inland for 4.7 miles. Turn right on Schulte Rd. The park is one mile ahead on the windy road.

CARRIZO PLAIN NATIONAL MONUMENT

KCL Campground

Soda Lake Rd., Maricopa 93252. T: (805) 475-2131 or (661) 391-6000; www.ca.blm.gov.

RV ★★★ Tent ★★★★

Beauty: ★★★★	Site Privacy: ★★★
Spaciousness: ★★★	Quiet: ★★★★
Security: ★	Cleanliness: ★★★
Insect Control: ★★★★	Facilities: ★

Formerly the ranch of Kern County Land Company, KCL is now one of two camps in Carrizo Plain National Monument, a park established near the end of president Clinton's term in office. The monument's staff suggests upgraded facilities are coming, but for now this campground offers nil beyond a portable toilet. No water, no trash pickup, no host, just a pretty setting alongside a photogenic barn and corral. The large sites are shaded by ancient eucalyptus trees, backed up against the base of the Caliente Mountains and with a view across the grasslands to the San Andreas fault and the Temblor Range. Ten miles to the east is Painted Rock, a pictograph-covered relic from when Native Americans still roamed the plains. Near that is Soda Lake, a glistening salt-crusted body of water that attracts migrating birds, most notably the sandhill crane, throughout the winter. The tall grass of the plains, where pronghorn antelope and black-tailed deer frequently graze, is streaked yellow with wildflowers in the spring before the scorching heat of summer turns everything brown. Note that the deeply rutted dirt camp road is impassable when wet, and the nearest telephone is at the intersection of Soda Lake Rd. and Hwy. 166, 20 miles southeast of KCL.

BASICS

Operated By: Bureau of Land Management, Bakersfield Field Office. **Open:** All year. **Site Assignment:** First come, first served. **Registration:** No. **Fee:** No fee, donations accepted. **Parking:** At site.

FACILITIES

Number of RV Sites: 8. **Number of Tent-Only Sites:** 0. **Hookups:** None. **Each Site:** Picnic table, fire ring. **Dump Station:** No. **Laundry:** No. **Pay Phone:** No. **Rest Rooms and Showers:** Pit toilet, no showers. **Fuel:** No. **Propane:** No. **Internal Roads:** Dirt, can be slick when wet. **RV Service:** No. **Market:** 35 mi. east in Taft. **Restaurant:** 35 mi. east in Taft. **General Store:** No. **Vending:** No. **Swimming:** No. **Playground:** No. **Other:** Limited wheelchair-accessible facilities. **Activities:** Hiking, birding, wildflower walks, photography, pictographs & old farm structures to explore. **Nearby Attractions:** Tule Elk State Reserve in Buttonwillow; Kern Oil Museum in Taft. **Additional Information:** Taft District Chamber of Commerce, (661) 765-2165.

RESTRICTIONS

Pets: Allowed. **Fires:** In fire rings only. **Alcoholic Beverages:** Allowed. **Vehicle Maximum Length:** None. **Other:** 14-day stay limit; no loaded firearms; no wood gathering.

TO GET THERE

From San Luis Obispo drive 8.8 mi. north on US 101. Exit on Hwy. 58 and head east for 47 mi., through Santa Margarita and California Valley. Turn right on Soda Lake Rd. and drive 26 mi. to the campground entrance on the right.

CARRIZO PLAIN NATIONAL MONUMENT

Selby Campground

Soda Lake Rd., Maricopa 93252. T: (805) 475-2131 or (661) 391-6000; www.ca.blm.gov.

RV ★★★ Tent ★★★

Beauty: ★★★★	Site Privacy: ★★★
Spaciousness: ★★★	Quiet: ★★★★
Security: ★	Cleanliness: ★★
Insect Control: ★★★★	Facilities: ★

This campground is in a park that is way the heck off the beaten track, with just a portable toilet and non-potable water for amenities. Most of the year wind howls through camp, and when it finally ceases the heat of summer feels like a blast furnace. So why bother to visit Carrizo Plain, one of the newest monuments in the national park system? For several reasons, actually, such as to see sandhill cranes—and many other water fowl—nesting during the winter by the salt-glistening shores of Soda Lake. And for ranger-led tours of Painted Rock, a 55-foot high rock decorated with Native American pictographs, with some estimated to be as old as 2,000 years. There is also a trail to the San Andreas fault that showcases the awesome power of earthquakes. Spring wildflower displays, too, are sensational. Trails into a Wilderness Study Area, part of the Caliente Mountains, start at Selby and pass through hills dotted with juniper, sage and salt bush. Selby, set at the base of a slanting escarpment, features five oversize, unshaded sites with plenty of parking for even the largest of RVs. The nearest telephone is 14.5 miles away in California Valley.

BASICS

Operated By: Bureau of Land Management, Bakersfield Field Office. **Open:** All year. **Site Assignment:** First come, first served. **Registration:** No. **Fee:** No fee, donations accepted. **Parking:** At site.

FACILITIES

Number of RV Sites: 5. **Number of Tent-Only Sites:** 0. **Hookups:** None. **Each Site:** Picnic table, fire ring. **Dump Station:** No. **Laundry:** No. **Pay Phone:** No. **Rest Rooms and Showers:** Portable toilet, no showers. **Fuel:** No. **Propane:** No. **Internal Roads:** Dirt, can be slick when wet. **RV Service:** No. **Market:** 45 mi. east in Taft. **Restaurant:** 45 mi. east in Taft. **General Store:** No. **Vending:** No. **Swimming:** No. **Playground:** No. **Other:** Limited wheelchair-accessible facilities. **Activities:** Hiking, birding, wildflower walks, photography, pictographs & old farm structures to explore. **Nearby Attractions:** Tule Elk State Reserve in Buttonwillow; Kern Oil Museum in Taft. **Additional Information:** Taft District Chamber of Commerce, (661) 765-2165.

RESTRICTIONS

Pets: Allowed. **Fires:** In fire rings only. **Alcoholic Beverages:** Allowed. **Vehicle Maximum Length:** None. **Other:** 14-day stay limit; no loaded firearms; no wood gathering.

TO GET THERE

From San Luis Obispo drive 8.8 mi. north on US 101. Exit on Hwy. 58 and continue east for 47 mi., through Santa Margarita and California Valley. Turn right on Soda Lake Rd. and drive 16.5 mi. to the campground entrance on the right. Follow the windy access road for 4.7 mi. into camp.

CHESTER

Elam

Hwy. 32, Chester 96020. T: (530) 258-2141; F: (530) 258-5194; www.r5.fs.fed.us/lassen.

RV ★★★ Tent ★★

Beauty: ★★★	Site Privacy: ★★
Spaciousness: ★★	Quiet: ★★★
Security: ★★	Cleanliness: ★★★
Insect Control: ★★	Facilities: ★

Elam is a small, primitive national forest facility that is about 15 miles west of Chester, to the south of Lassen Volcanic National Park. It would be quite an appealing camp if it were not overcrowded so much of the time. A bubbling creek flows by one side of its short access lane, a steep embankment parallels the other, and granite rocks and boulders litter the narrow grounds. Why is Elam so popular? The answer, in a word, is trout. The creek is regularly stocked, and unlike other bodies of water in the area, fishermen are allowed to keep what they catch. You can spend the day trying to lure the fish onto your hook, then while away the evenings swapping stories with newly-made fishing buddies about the huge ones that got away. Level, dirt-surfaced sites are small and exposed—not just to each other but also to the picnic area directly across the creek—major shortcomings in such a highly trafficked property. Number 15, at the end of the lane, is the most private site, followed by 14, at the water's edge, and 11, also creekside. The altitude of 4,400 feet justifies packing a sweater, even in summer.

Basics

Operated By: CSU Chico Research Foundation, concessionaire, & Lassen National Forest, Almanor Ranger District. **Open:** May through Oct., weather permitting. **Site Assignment:** First come, first served. **Registration:** At entrance kiosk. **Fee:** $12, cash or check. **Parking:** At site.

Facilities

Number of RV Sites: 15. **Number of Tent-Only Sites:** 0. **Hookups:** None. **Each Site:** Picnic table, fire grate. **Dump Station:** No. **Laundry:** No. **Pay Phone:** No. **Rest Rooms and Showers:** Vault toilets, no showers. **Fuel:** No. **Propane:** No. **Internal Roads:** Paved. **RV Service:** No. **Market:** 16 mi. east in Chester. **Restaurant:** 16 mi. east in Chester. **General Store:** No. **Vending:** No. **Swimming:** No. **Playground:** No. **Activities:** Fishing, hiking, bicycling, bragging about the fish that got away. **Nearby Attractions:** Westwood Museum & Paul Bunyan & Babe the Blue Ox Statues; Lassen National Scenic Byway (Hwys. 89-44-36); Lassen Volcanic National Park; Lake Almanor. **Additional Information:** Chester–Lake Almanor Chamber of Commerce, (530) 258-2426 or (800) 350-4838.

Restrictions

Pets: On leash. **Fires:** In fire grates only. **Alcoholic Beverages:** Allowed. **Vehicle Maximum Length:** 22 ft. **Other:** 14-day stay limit from Memorial Day through Labor Day, 21-day stay limit for the rest of the year.

To Get There

From Chester on Hwy. 36 drive 13 mi. west to the junction w/ Hwy. 32. Turn left on Hwy. 32 and continue for 3.6 mi. The campground is to the right.

COLEVILLE

Sonora Bridge

Hwy. 108, Coleville 96107. T: (760) 932-7070; F: (760) 932-1299; www.r5.fs.fed.us/htnf/soncamp.htm.

RV ★★★★ Tent ★★★★

Beauty: ★★★★	Site Privacy: ★★★
Spaciousness: ★★★	Quiet: ★★★★
Security: ★★★	Cleanliness: ★★★★
Insect Control: ★★★★	Facilities: ★

There is a rough-surfaced russet knob of granite on one flank of this expansive camp, a steep rocky slope on another, and all around are fabulous views of the mountains. Thick-trunked Jeffrey pines are the dominant trees in these parts, though the campground is also accented by juniper and such chaparral as salt bush and sage. Unlike Leavitt Meadows, just up the road, there's no river flowing by this turf, but sites here are clearly superior, and many offer pull-through parking. Most are roomier and largely more private, owing partly to a thick undergrowth of mountain mahogany, and partly to their wider distribution along a series of four loops. Additionally, the breathtaking views of the Sierras simply cannot be beat. Unless, that is, you strap a pack to your back and hoof it higher into the mountains, or head out to the Walker River to fish for rainbow trout. Elevation at Sonora Bridge, which is 20 miles west of Bridgeport, is 6,800 feet; icy winds whistle through camp early and late in the year, so bring along some warm clothing.

Basics

Operated By: American Land & Leisure, concessionaire. **Open:** Mid-May through mid-Oct., weather permitting. **Site Assignment:** First come, first served. **Registration:** At entrance kiosk. **Fee:** $10, cash or check. **Parking:** At site.

Facilities

Number of RV Sites: 23. **Number of Tent-Only Sites:** 0. **Hookups:** None. **Each Site:** Picnic table, fire grate. **Dump Station:** No. **Laundry:** No. **Pay Phone:** No. **Rest Rooms and Showers:** Vault toilets, no showers. **Fuel:** No. **Propane:** No. **Internal Roads:** Dirt but smooth. **RV Service:** No. **Market:** 19 mi. east in Bridgeport. **Restaurant:** 19 mi. east in Bridgeport. **General Store:** No. **Vending:** No. **Swimming:** No. **Playground:** No. **Activities:** Hiking, fishing, star-gazing. **Nearby Attractions:** Bodie State Historic Park in Bridgeport; Sonora Pass. **Additional Information:** Eastern Sierra Interagency Visitor Center, (760) 876-6222; Bridgeport Chamber of Commerce, (760) 932-7500.

Restrictions

Pets: On leash. **Fires:** In fire grates only. **Alcoholic Beverages:** Allowed. **Vehicle Maximum Length:** 30 ft. **Other:** 14-day stay limit.

To Get There

From Bridgeport drive 17 mi. north on US 395. Turn west (left) onto Hwy. 108 and drive 1.5 mi. to the campground entrance on the left.

CORNING

Woodson Bridge State Recreation Area

South Ave., Corning 96021. T: (530) 839-2112 or reservations (800) 444-7275; www.cal-parks.ca.gov or www.norcal.parks.ca.us or www.reserveamerica.com.

RV ★★★★ Tent ★★★★

Beauty: ★★★★	Site Privacy: ★★★
Spaciousness: ★★★	Quiet: ★★★
Security: ★★★★	Cleanliness: ★★★★
Insect Control: ★	Facilities: ★★

The marked increase in visitation to this sweet gem of a park proves The Secret is out. No wonder, with its grounds, which overlap the Sacramento River, so fertile and grassy, and its recessed, scattered campsites framed by massive, aged valley oaks. Unbelievably, this sylvan glade is not concealed in some forested outback, but instead is located a scant six miles east of Corning and I-5, three miles west of Hwy. 99 and Vina. If fishing is your game, prepare to mark your datebook: king salmon runs are optimum from Oct. through May, the peak for shad is in July and Aug., striped bass in early fall, steelhead in Oct. and Nov., and catfish may be caught just about any time of year. If that is not enough to lure you to this appealing recreation area, perhaps its extraordinary birding will, with yellow-billed cuckoos, hummingbirds, pheasants, hawks, falcons, and many other species commonly seen. So are swarms of mosquitoes, from spring through mid-summer—plan to bring repellant. Older guidebooks list Woodson Bridge as having a dump station but fallen trees now make that inaccessible. There are no plans yet to restore it.

Basics

Operated By: California Dept. of Parks & Recreation. **Open:** All year. **Site Assignment:** Reservations accepted w/ V, MC, D. **Registration:** At entrance booth. **Fee:** $14 from May 15–Sept. 15, $10 the rest of the year; cash or CA check. **Parking:** At site.

Facilities

Number of RV Sites: 37. **Number of Tent-Only Sites:** 0. **Hookups:** None. **Each Site:** Picnic table, fire grate. **Dump Station:** No, inaccessible because of fallen trees. **Laundry:** No. **Pay Phone:** Yes. **Rest Rooms and Showers:** Yes. **Fuel:** No. **Propane:** No. **Internal Roads:** Paved. **RV Service:** No. **Market:** 6 mi. west in Corning. **Restaurant:** 6 mi. west in Corning. **General Store:** No. **Vending:** No. **Swimming:** In Sacramento River. **Playground:** No. **Other:** Some wheelchair-accessible facilities. **Activities:** Fishing, hiking, birding, boating. **Nearby Attractions:** Tejama County Park in Corning; Chico museums & Bidwell Mansion State Historic Park; outlet shopping in Anderson; William B. Ide Adobe State Historic Park near Red Bluff. **Additional Information:** Corning District Chamber of Commerce, (530) 824-5550; Chico Chamber of Commerce & Visitor Bureau, (530) 891-5556 or (800) 852-8570.

Restrictions

Pets: On 6 ft. leash. **Fires:** In fire grates only. **Alcoholic Beverages:** Allowed at site. **Vehicle Maximum Length:** 31 ft. **Other:** 14-day stay limit from June through Sept., 30-day stay limit from Oct. through May; no firearms; no wood gathering.

To Get There

In Corning on I-5 take the South Ave. Exit. Head east for 6.3 mi. and turn left into the campground.

CRESCENT CITY

Del Norte Coast Redwoods State Park, Mill Creek Campground

US 101 South, Crescent City 95532. T: (707) 464-6101, ext. 5102 or reservations (800) 444-7275; www.cal-parks.ca.gov or www.reserveamerica.com.

RV ★★★★ Tent ★★★★

Beauty: ★★★★	Site Privacy: ★★★★
Spaciousness: ★★★	Quiet: ★★★
Security: ★★★	Cleanliness: ★★★★
Insect Control: ★★★	Facilities: ★★

This campground is set in the heart of Mill Creek Canyon among a concentration of red alders and second-growth redwoods. It is a moist, antediluvian environment, with winter rainfall, which averages 100 inches, contributing to a fertile, mossy, jungle-like luminescence. Rhododendrons, azaleas, maples, and ferns thrive here, along with pale yellow slugs as thick as a thumb and a good deal longer. A sextet of loops features level grass and dirt sites that are smallish and rather crowded together, but fairly well-screened by the flourishing foliage and equipped with capacious car slips. One of the larger spots is 38, by the creek, and of the many walk-up units, 4, 5, and 6 offer the best privacy. A pristine stretch of beach is accessible via the challenging Damnation Creek Trail, an old Native American path that loses 1,000 feet as it descends through a grove of old-growth redwoods. Mill Creek is closed to fishing from Oct. through Apr. to protect spawning salmon.

Basics

Operated By: California Dept. of Parks & Recreation. **Open:** Apr. through Sept. **Site Assignment:** Reservations accepted w/ V, MC, D. **Registration:** At entrance booth. **Fee:** $12, cash or CA check. **Parking:** At site.

Facilities

Number of RV Sites: 145. **Number of Tent-Only Sites:** 0. **Hookups:** None. **Each Site:** Picnic table, fire grate, food storage box. **Dump Station:** Yes. **Laundry:** No. **Pay Phone:** No. **Rest Rooms and Showers:** Yes. **Fuel:** No. **Propane:** No. **Internal Roads:** Paved, w/ bumps & potholes. **RV Service:** No. **Market:** 6 mi. north in Crescent City. **Restaurant:** 6 mi. north in Crescent City. **General Store:** No. **Vending:** No. **Swimming:** In Smith River. **Playground:** No. **Other:** Some wheelchair-accessible facilities. **Activities:** Hiking, bicycling, fishing. **Nearby Attractions:** Redwood National & State Parks; Battery Point Lighthouse, Ocean World & Del Norte County Historical Museum in Crescent City. **Additional Information:** Crescent City–Del Norte County Chamber of Commerce, (707) 464-3174 or (800) 343-8300.

Restrictions

Pets: On 6 ft. leash. **Fires:** In fire grates only. **Alcoholic Beverages:** Allowed at site. **Vehicle Maximum Length:** 31 ft. **Other:** 14-day stay limit from May 1–Sept. 30; no firearms; no wood gathering; no mushroom-plucking.

To Get There

From Crescent City head 6 mi. south on US 101 to the marked access road for the State Park. Turn left; the park entrance is 1.5 mi. ahead.

CRESCENT CITY

Jedediah Smith Redwoods State Park

US 199 South, Crescent City 95532. T: (707) 464-6101, ext. 5112 or reservations (800) 444-7275; www.cal-parks.ca.gov or www.reserveamerica.com.

★★★★ ★★★★

Beauty: ★★★★ Site Privacy: ★★★
Spaciousness: ★★★★ Quiet: ★★★
Security: ★★★ Cleanliness: ★★★★
Insect Control: ★★★ Facilities: ★★★

Heading south from Oregon along Hwy. 199, Jedediah Smith Redwoods State Park is the northernmost of several redwoods-focused state parks. Named for the first white man known to cross the Coast Range of mountains, Jed Smith is a striking introduction to Sequoia sempervirens. These giant redwood trees are the tallest living things in the world, with several old-growth groves towering over the 10,000-acre preserve. The campground is less than ten miles northeast of Crescent City, set beside the emerald-green Smith River. Tan oaks, maples, and rhododendrons thrive among the red barked atavars, with moss and hanging lichen contributing to the cool, shady, rainforest atmosphere. The roomy and well-screened sites are spread decently apart over a series of loops, the most private being 68 (with a river view), 70 (a spacious end spot), and 77. 60 has pull-through parking. Years ago local American Indians gathered the green, stringy lichen that hangs from the trees and dried it to use as soft bedding material. It—and all other vegetation within the park—is now protected by the state.

Basics

Operated By: California Dept. of Parks & Recreation. **Open:** All year. **Site Assignment:** Reservations recommended; V, MC, D. **Registration:** At entrance booth. **Fee:** $12, cash or CA check. **Parking:** At site.

Facilities

Number of RV Sites: 106. **Number of Tent-Only Sites:** 5. **Hookups:** None. **Each Site:** Picnic table, fire grate, food storage box. **Dump Station:** Yes. **Laundry:** No. **Pay Phone:** Yes. **Rest Rooms and Showers:** Yes. **Fuel:** No. **Propane:** No. **Internal Roads:** Paved. **RV Service:** No. **Market:** 9 mi. west in Crescent City. **Restaurant:** 9 mi. west in Crescent City. **General Store:** No. **Vending:** No. **Swimming:** No. **Playground:** No. **Other:** Some wheelchair-accessible facilities. **Activities:** Hiking, fishing, bicycling, horseback riding, canoeing, rafting. **Nearby Attractions:** Redwood National & State Parks; Battery Point Lighthouse, Ocean World & Del Norte County Historical Museum in Crescent City. **Additional Information:** Crescent City–Del Norte County Chamber of Commerce, (707) 464-3174 or (800) 343-8300.

Restrictions

Pets: On 6 ft. leash. **Fires:** In fire grates only. **Alcoholic Beverages:** Allowed at site. **Vehicle Maximum Length:** 36 ft. **Other:** 14-day stay limit from May 1–Sept. 30; no firearms; no wood gathering.

To Get There

From Crescent City drive 3.5 mi. north on US 101. Exit on US 199 and head east towards Grants Pass. Continue for 5 mi. to the park entrance on the right.

DANA POINT

Doheny State Beach

25300 Dana Point Harbor Dr., Dana Point 92629. T: (949) 496-6171; www.cal-parks.ca.gov or www.reserveamerica.com.

Beauty: ★★★★ Site Privacy: ★★★
Spaciousness: ★★ Quiet: ★★
Security: ★★★ Cleanliness: ★★★★
Insect Control: ★ Facilities: ★★

This state park provides sun and surf lovers access to more than a mile of beautiful beach, with the good news for campers being that a healthy number of sites are set right on the sand. Stroll from your tent to the shore in one fluid motion, or bask in a sunset radiating over the water from the comfort of your picnic table. If it is high tide, this must be "surfin' USA"! And if the water is low, grab your children and go check out the tide pools. All of these somewhat tightly packed sites benefit from the fresh breeze of the salty sea, but the ones to the rear of camp are annoyingly close to railroad tracks, and also have the dubious distinction of facing a large housing development across the interstate. Best by far are those on the beach, such as 38–43, and odd numbers from 45–59. Though swimming is ideal from late June through early autumn, solitude-seekers will enjoy camping here in winter, when daytime temperatures are still comfortable.

Basics

Operated By: California Dept. of Parks & Recreation. **Open:** All year. **Site Assignment:** Reservations recommended; w/ V, MC, D. **Registration:** At entrance booth. **Fee:** $12, cash or CA check. **Parking:** At site.

Facilities

Number of RV Sites: 120. **Number of Tent-Only Sites:** 0. **Hookups:** None. **Each Site:** Picnic table, fire grate. **Dump Station:** Yes. **Laundry:** No. **Pay Phone:** Yes. **Rest Rooms and Showers:** Yes (cold beach showers). **Fuel:** No. **Propane:** No. **Internal Roads:** Paved. **RV Service:** No. **Market:** 1 mi. east in Dana Point. **Restaurant:** 1 mi. east in Dana Point. **General Store:** No. **Vending:** No. **Swimming:** In Pacific Ocean. **Playground:** No. **Other:** Some wheelchair-accessible facilities. **Activities:** Surfing, swimming, fishing, people-watching, tide pool exploring, volleyball, whale-watching. **Nearby Attractions:** San Clemente, Dana Point, Mission San Juan Capistrano. **Additional Information:** Dana Point Chamber of Commerce, Tourism & Visitors Center, (949) 496-1555.

Restrictions

Pets: On 6 ft. leash. **Fires:** In fire grates only. **Alcoholic Beverages:** Not allowed. **Vehicle Maximum Length:** 35 ft. **Other:** 7-day stay limit from June 1–Sept. 30, 14-day stay limit for the rest of the year; no firearms; no wood gathering.

To Get There

From San Juan Capistrano head 3 mi. south on I-5 to the Beach Cities/Pacific Coast Hwy. Exit. Turn left onto Dana Point Harbor Dr., then left again onto Park Lantern into the park.

DARDANELLE

Leavitt Meadows

Hwy. 108, Dardanelle 95314. T: (760) 932-7070; F: (760) 932-1299; www.r5.fs.fed.us/htnf/bpcamp.htm.

Beauty: ★★★★ Site Privacy: ★★★
Spaciousness: ★★ Quiet: ★★
Security: ★★★ Cleanliness: ★★★
Insect Control: ★★ Facilities: ★

If you are looking for a taste of the high Sierras without having to venture too far off the road, Leavitt Meadows, at 7,000 feet elevation and 25 miles west of Bridgeport, should be a good fit. This roadside camp, ensconced in a bend in the West Walker River, is close enough to the water that the raging current drowns out much of the noise of passing traffic. Rising across the river is a flinty outcropping, and a granite-streaked ridge looms above camp. Juniper, aspen, sage, and various conifers set the stage around the single loop, where diminutive, dirt sites are well spread apart. The handful of spots nearest the water are the most exposed, and tenters may find the water-ward tilt challenging. An exception is number 9, which is well-screened and has pull-through parking. Away from the river, 15, while a touch small, is under a large pine and shielded by aspens. Drinking water is shut off early and late in the year, due to the higher risk of freezing weather. That is, nonetheless, our preferred time to visit this part of the Sierra Nevadas, when visitation is at its lightest.

Basics

Operated By: American Land & Leisure, concessionaire. **Open:** Late Apr. to mid-Oct., weather permitting. **Site Assignment:** First come, first served. **Registration:** At entrance kiosk. **Fee:** $10, cash or check; $5 in winter when no water. **Parking:** At site.

Facilities

Number of RV Sites: 16. **Number of Tent-Only Sites:** 0. **Hookups:** None. **Each Site:** Picnic table, fire grate. **Dump Station:** No. **Laundry:** No. **Pay Phone:** No. **Rest Rooms and Showers:** Vault toilets, no showers. **Fuel:** No. **Propane:** No. **Internal Roads:** Dirt, somewhat bumpy. **RV Service:** No. **Market:** 25 mi. east in Bridgeport. **Restaurant:** 25 mi. east in Bridgeport. **General Store:** No. **Vending:** No. **Swimming:** No. **Playground:** No. **Activities:** Fishing, hiking, horseback riding, star-gazing. **Nearby Attractions:** Bodie State Historic Park in Bridgeport; Pinecrest Lake, Sonora Pass. **Additional Information:** Eastern Sierra Interagency Visitor Center, (760) 876-6222; Bridgeport Chamber of Commerce, (760) 932-7500.

Restrictions

Pets: On leash. **Fires:** In fire grates only. **Alcoholic Beverages:** Allowed. **Vehicle Maximum Length:** 22 ft. **Other:** 14-day stay limit.

To Get There

From Bridgeport drive 17 mi. north on US 395. Turn west (left) onto Hwy. 108 and drive 7.5 mi. to the campground entrance on the left.

DEATH VALLEY
Mesquite Spring

Grapevine Rd., Death Valley 92328. T: (760) 786-23317; F: (760) 786-3283; www.nps.gov/deva.

RV ★★★ Tent ★★★

Beauty: ★★★★ Site Privacy: ★★★
Spaciousness: ★★★ Quiet: ★★★
Security: ★★★★ Cleanliness: ★★★
Insect Control: ★★★★ Facilities: ★★

The vast tract of land that is Death Valley National Park is far more than a barren, stagnant desert. Give it a chance and your appreciation for the parched beauty of the scenery will likely grow as you explore the park: from the volcanic craters in the north to the salt water basins to its south, from its shifting sand dunes to the multicolored mountains that range like twin spines up its entire length. You'll be in good position at Mesquite Spring to check out Ubehebe Crater and Scotty's Castle, a lavish 1920s vacation home built in Spanish mission style. This campground is more exposed than Furnace Creek, but it benefits, after the sun goes down, from being 2,000 feet higher. It is set against a mud-colored canyon wall and a dry creek, with two low mountain ridges paralleling its double loop. Dusty, pebbly sites are on the spacious side, and they are grouped farther apart than at Furnace Creek, allowing for a greater degree of privacy. A couple of cottonwoods mark where the spring is. The nearest pay phone is at the Grapevine Ranger Station, 2.5 miles north; fuel is available at Scotty's Castle; a general store is in Stovepipe Wells, 41 miles south.

Basics

Operated By: National Park Service. **Open:** All year. **Site Assignment:** First come, first served. **Registration:** At entrance kiosk. **Fee:** $10–$16, cash or check (in addition to the park entrance fee). **Parking:** At site.

Facilities

Number of RV Sites: 30. **Number of Tent-Only Sites:** 0. **Hookups:** None. **Each Site:** Picnic table, fire grate. **Dump Station:** Yes. **Laundry:** No. **Pay Phone:** No. **Rest Rooms and Showers:** Flush toilets, no showers. **Fuel:** No. **Propane:** No. **Internal Roads:** Paved. **RV Service:** No. **Market:** 53 mi. east in Beatty. **Restaurant:** 41 mi. south in Stovepipe Wells. **General Store:** No. **Vending:** No. **Swimming:** No. **Playground:** No. **Other:** Some wheelchair-accessible facilities. **Activities:** Hiking, driving tours, stargazing, photography. **Nearby Attractions:** Badwater, Scotty's Castle, Dantes View, Stovepipe Wells Village, mountains, mines & more in Death Valley National Park. **Additional Information:** Death Valley Chamber of Commerce, (760) 852-4524.

Restrictions

Pets: On leash no longer than 6 ft., not allowed on trails. **Fires:** In fire grates only. **Alcoholic Beverages:** Allowed at site. **Vehicle Maximum Length:** 50 ft. **Other:** 30-day stay limit; no loaded firearms; no wood gathering.

To Get There

From Furnace Creek head north on Hwy. 190 and drive 19 mi. to Sand Dune Junction. Turn right, direction Scotty's Castle, and continue for 32 mi. Turn left onto the campground access road. Proceed for another 2 mi. into the campground.

DEATH VALLEY
Wildrose

Wildrose Canyon Rd., Death Valley National Park 92328. T: (760) 786-2331; F: (760) 786-3283; www.nps.gov/deva.

RV ★★★★ Tent ★★★★

Beauty: ★★★★ Site Privacy: ★★★
Spaciousness: ★★★★ Quiet: ★★★★
Security: ★★ Cleanliness: ★★★★
Insect Control: ★★★★ Facilities: ★

The wonderful, oleander-shaded picnic area in the dramatically eroded Wildrose Canyon is misleading. You will find nothing so pleasant in the way of plantings at the similarly-named campground. Still, there is a Spartan beauty to this arid, primitive camp. Very Spartan. It is located in a side gully of the canyon, with rumpled hills on either side. There are no shade trees to shelter the dusty, pebbly ground, only such scrub as creosote and salt bushes. The same, of course, might also be said of most of Death Valley's other campgrounds; at least Wildrose has potable water (from late spring through early autumn). Because the campground, which is 30 miles south of Stovepipe Wells Village, is at 4,100 feet of elevation, evenings are blessedly cooler here than elsewhere in the park. Comparable spots are roomy but exposed, and dispersed in two sections (the upper one being reserved for tents). Even when Furnace Creek and Stovepipe Wells are brimming with campers, you are likely to find plenty of space and tranquility at this remote place. Use it as a base for exploring such Death Valley attractions as the beehive-shaped charcoal kilns, Skidoo, a ghost town, and the Eureka mine.

Basics

Operated By: National Park Service. **Open:** All year. **Site Assignment:** First come, first served. **Registration:** None. **Fee:** None (but there is a park entrance fee). **Parking:** At site.

Facilities

Number of RV Sites: 11. **Number of Tent-Only Sites:** 11. **Hookups:** None. **Each Site:** Picnic table, fire grate and/or barbecue grill. **Dump Station:** No. **Laundry:** No. **Pay Phone:** No. **Rest Rooms and Showers:** Vault toilets, no showers. **Fuel:** No. **Propane:** No. **Internal Roads:** Gravel, good condition. **RV Service:** No. **Market:** 65 mi. south in Ridgecrest. **Restaurant:** 30 mi. north in Stovepipe Wells. **General Store:** No. **Vending:** No. **Swimming:** No. **Playground:** No. **Activities:** Hiking, solitudinous meditation, stargazing. **Nearby Attractions:** Ballarat Ghost Town; Trona Pinnacles. **Additional Information:** Death Valley Chamber of Commerce, (760) 852-4524.

Restrictions

Pets: On leash no longer than 6 ft., not allowed on trails. **Fires:** In fire grates only. **Alcoholic Beverages:** Allowed at site. **Vehicle Maximum Length:** 25 ft. **Other:** 30-day stay limit; no loaded firearms; no wood gathering.

To Get There

From Ridgecrest drive 13 mi. east on Hwy. 178. Turn left on Trona Rd. and continue for 42 mi. to

Wildrose Canyon Rd. Turn right and proceed for 9 mi. Bear right at the fork in the road; the campground is 0.25 mi. ahead on the left.

DEATH VALLEY NATIONAL PARK

Furnace Creek

Hwy. 190, Death Valley 92328. T: (760) 786-2331 or reservations (800) 365-2267; F: (760) 786-3283; www.nps.gov/deva or reservations.nps.gov.

RV ★★★★ | Tent ★★★

Beauty: ★★★★	Site Privacy: ★★
Spaciousness: ★★	Quiet: ★★★
Security: ★★★★	Cleanliness: ★★★
Insect Control: ★★★★	Facilities: ★★

Visit this campground between May and Sept. and you'll have a good idea of what Hades is all about; you are also likely to have most of the domain to yourself. Certainly the "furnace" half of its name seems apt, with an oppressive blanket of heat clinging to the dry terrain in much the manner that bark hugs the trunk of a tree. As to the "creek," just be thankful for water spigots. Level sites of hard clay are closely grouped around a series of loops, with a bit of shade provided by mesquite, creosote bushes, a few palms, and tamarisk trees. (These latter are non-native, and the park service intends to uproot them.) The blistering heat seems magnified by the camp's position at 196 feet below sea level, but we prefer it to Stovepipe Wells, which is little more than a pebbly parking lot without a twig of shade. The park visitor center is next to the campground, and a number of excellent hikes and drives are in the vicinity. Laundry machines, showers, swimming pool, general store, and gasoline are available at Furnace Creek Ranch.

BASICS

Operated By: National Park Service. **Open:** All year. **Site Assignment:** Reservations recommended; V, MC, D. **Registration:** At entrance booth. **Fee:** $10–$16, cash or check (in addition to the park entrance fee). **Parking:** At site.

FACILITIES

Number of RV Sites: 101. **Number of Tent-Only Sites:** 35. **Hookups:** None. **Each Site:** Picnic table, fire grate, barbecue grill. **Dump Station:** Yes. **Laundry:** No. **Pay Phone:** Yes. **Rest Rooms and Showers:** Flush toilets, no showers. **Fuel:** No. **Propane:** No. **Internal Roads:** Paved. **RV Service:** No. **Market:** 47 mi. north in Beatty. **Restaurant:** At Furnace Creek Ranch. **General Store:** No. **Vending:** No. **Swimming:** No. **Playground:** No. **Other:** Some wheelchair-accessible facilities, visitor center, museum. **Activities:** Hiking, driving tours, ranger-led activities, photography, frying eggs on the sidewalk. **Nearby Attractions:** Badwater, Scotty's Castle, Dantes View, Stovepipe Wells Village, mountains, mines, & more in Death Valley National Park. **Additional Information:** Death Valley Chamber of Commerce, (760) 852-4524.

RESTRICTIONS

Pets: On 6 ft. leash; not allowed on trails. **Fires:** In fire grates only. **Alcoholic Beverages:** Allowed at site. **Vehicle Maximum Length:** 50 ft. **Other:** 7-day stay limit from Oct. 15 to Apr. 15, 14-day stay limit for the rest of the year; no loaded firearms; no wood gathering.

TO GET THERE

From the Furnace Creek Visitor Center drive 0.5 mi. north on Hwy. 190 to the campground entrance on the left.

DUNCAN MILLS

Casini Ranch Family Campground

22855 Moscow Rd., Duncan Mills 95430. T: (707) 865-2255 Ext. 13 or reservations (800) 451-8400; www.caohwy.com/c/casinirf.htm.

RV ★★★★★ | Tent ★★★★

Beauty: ★★★★	Site Privacy: ★★★★
Spaciousness: ★★★★	Quiet: ★★★★
Security: ★★★★	Cleanliness: ★★★
Insect Control: ★★★	Facilities: ★★★★

Not too many years ago this family-operated campground was a dairy farm and many of the rustic buildings from that era remain, along with miscellaneous farm implements that have been decoratively strewn about the property. It is hard to imagine, though, that the scene was any prettier when cows lowed through the grassy meadows and varied woodland than it is today, even when brimming with campers. The level property sits in an oxbow bend of the Russian River, a perfect position that blesses it not only with a number of waterview sites but also a greater amount of serenity than the bucolic camp's road-side counterparks. True, the full hookup area next to a row of pollarded trees at Casini's core is typically congested. If you don't require pull-through parking and can get by without a sewer connection, such pleasantly secluded spots as 88–90, 92–94, and 96–98 are infinitely more appealing. Similarly, 36–40 are the pick of the primitive options, where grassy sites are so spacious and well buttressed by vegetation as to satisfy even the most finicky of tent campers.

BASICS

Operated By: Casini family. **Open:** All year. **Site Assignment:** Reservations accepted w/ V, MC, D, AE. **Registration:** At entrance booth or office. **Fee:** $20–$27 plus 9% local tax, cash or V, MC, AE, D. **Parking:** At site.

FACILITIES

Number of RV Sites: 225. **Number of Tent-Only Sites:** 0. **Hookups:** Water, electric (30 amps), sewer, cable TV. **Each Site:** Picnic table, fire grate. **Dump Station:** Yes. **Laundry:** Yes. **Pay Phone:** Yes. **Rest Rooms and Showers:** Yes. **Fuel:** No. **Propane:** Yes. **Internal Roads:** Packed gravel & dirt, good condition. **RV Service:** No. **Market:** 0.75 mi. away in Duncans Mills. **Restaurant:** 0.75 mi. away in Duncans Mills. **General Store:** Yes. **Vending:** Yes. **Swimming:** In Russian River. **Playground:** Yes. **Other:** Some wheelchair-accessible facilities, rec hall, boat ramp. **Activities:** Fishing, kayak & canoe rentals. **Nearby Attractions:** Fort Ross State Historic Park, Kruse Rhododendron State Reserve & Salt Point State Park in Jenner; Austin Creek State Recreation Area & Armstrong Redwoods State Reserve in Guerneville; winery tours. **Additional Information:** Russian River Chamber of Commerce & Visitors Center, (707) 869-9212 or (877) 644-9001.

RESTRICTIONS

Pets: On leash. **Fires:** In fire grates only. **Alcoholic Beverages:** Allowed. **Vehicle Maximum Length:** None. **Other:** 30-day stay limit; no firearms; no wood gathering.

TO GET THERE

From Guerneville head west on Hwy. 116 and drive 8.4 mi. to Duncans Mills. Turn left on Moscow Rd. and continue for 0.75 mi. to the well-signed campground entrance.

DUNSMUIR

Castle Crags State Park

Castle Creek Rd., Castella 96017. T: (530) 235-2684 or reservations (800) 444-7275; www.calparks.ca.gov or www.norcal.parks.state.ca.us or www.reserveamerica.com.

RV ★★★ | Tent ★★★

Beauty: ★★★★	Site Privacy: ★★
Spaciousness: ★★	Quiet: ★★
Security: ★★★	Cleanliness: ★★★
Insect Control: ★★★	Facilities: ★★

The stark, saw-toothed spires that give this small park its name rise some 4,000 feet from the Sacramento River to the tips of their granite peaks. If the challenging, highly strenuous hike up there from the campground doesn't take your breath away, the spectacular views will. The domain straddles I-5, with the larger part of it, including the crags, lying west of the highway. To the east, just beyond the railroad tracks and right alongside the river, are 12 grassy sites that are ideal for anglers. The main campground, though, is across the road, higher up toward the summit. Its three ascending loops snake through an attractively wooded hillside of oaks, cedars, and pines, with mediocre screening between closely-set, shallow sites. The most private is 11, though its rear faces a chain-link fence. Similarly recessed are 14 and 15, and both 26 and 37 have pull-through parking. The stone masonry of the fire pits dates from when the Civilian Conservation Corps was active here more than 60 years ago. The continuous roar of traffic emanating from the interstate is a jarring note to an otherwise splendid setting.

BASICS

Operated By: California Dept. of Parks & Recreation. **Open:** All year. **Site Assignment:** Reservations accepted w/ V, MC, D. **Registration:** At entrance booth. **Fee:** $12, cash or CA check. **Parking:** At site.

FACILITIES

Number of RV Sites: 76. **Number of Tent-Only Sites:** 6. **Hookups:** None. **Each Site:** Picnic table, fire grate, food storage box. **Dump Station:** No. **Laundry:** No. **Pay Phone:** Yes. **Rest Rooms and Showers:** Yes. **Fuel:** No. **Propane:** No. **Internal Roads:** Paved. **RV Service:** No. **Market:** 7 mi. north in Dunsmuir. **Restaurant:** 7 mi. north in Dunsmuir. **General Store:** No. **Vending:** No. **Swimming:** In Sacramento River. **Playground:** No. **Other:** Some wheelchair-accessible facilities. **Activities:** Hiking, fishing, canoeing, rafting, bicycling. **Nearby Attractions:** Lake Siskiyou; Mount Shasta Ski Park, Mount Shasta Hatchery & Sisson Museum; downtown Dunsmuir. **Additional Information:** Mount Shasta Chamber of Commerce & Visitors Bureau, (530) 926-4865 or (800) 926-4865; Dunsmuir Chamber of Commerce, (530) 235-2177.

Restrictions

Pets: On 6 ft. leash. **Fires:** In fire grates only. **Alcoholic Beverages:** Allowed at site. **Vehicle Maximum Length:** 27 ft. **Other:** 14-day stay limit from May 1–Sept. 30, 30-day limit the rest of the year; no firearms; no wood gathering.

To Get There

From Dunsmuir on I-5 drive 6.5 mi. south to the Castella Exit. Turn west (right) and continue for 0.3 mi. Turn right into the well-signed park. The campground is 0.7 mi. beyond the entrance station.

EL CAJON

Lake Jennings Regional Park

10108 Bass Rd., Lakeside 92046. T: (858) 69403049 or reservations (858) 565-3600; www.co.san-diego.ca.us/parks.

RV ★★★★ Tent ★★★

Beauty: ★★★★	Site Privacy: ★★★★
Spaciousness: ★★★	Quiet: ★★★
Security: ★★★★	Cleanliness: ★★★
Insect Control: ★★★	Facilities: ★★★

People familiar with Lake Jennings from previous years may be excused if they fail to recognize it in its current state. The most obvious change is the spruced up landscaping, with geraniums and other annuals lending a welcome splash of color to a ridge-top setting marked by holly, acacia, prickly pear cacti, eucalyptus, pepper trees, and a variety of conifers. That's not all, as structural renovations have encompassed the restrooms and showers, as well as upgraded electrical hookups. Unaffected by these alterations, alas, are the gravel sites themselves, which are shoe-horned close together, several resting on ground so tilted that hammocks might seem preferable to tents. Thankfully, abundant vegetation yields some privacy and many units along the park's spiraling loop road enjoy excellent vistas. Numbers 20, 22, 24, 43, and 45 are among the standout tenting options, with 89–91 tops for RVs. The lake is stocked with trout in the winter and catfish summertime, but boating is only allowed on weekends.

Basics

Operated By: County of San Diego, Dept. of Parks & Recreation. **Open:** All year. **Site Assignment:** Reservations accepted w/ V, MC, D. **Registration:** At entrance booth. **Fee:** $12–$16, cash or V, MC, D. **Parking:** At site.

Facilities

Number of RV Sites: 90. **Number of Tent-Only Sites:** 6. **Hookups:** Water, electric (20, 30 amps), sewer. **Each Site:** Picnic table, fire grate, barbecue grill. **Dump Station:** Yes. **Laundry:** No. **Pay Phone:** Yes. **Rest Rooms and Showers:** Yes. **Fuel:** No. **Propane:** No. **Internal Roads:** Paved. **RV Service:** No. **Market:** 2 mi west in Lakeside. **Restaurant:** 2 mi. west in Lakeside. **General Store:** No. **Vending:** Yes. **Swimming:** No. **Playground:** Yes. **Other:** Some wheelchair-accessible facilities. **Activities:** Fishing, hiking, horseshoe pit. **Nearby Attractions:** San Diego & its waterfront, museums, zoo, historic district. **Additional Information:** Lakeside Chamber of Commerce, (619) 561-1031; City of El Cajon, (619) 441-1776.

Restrictions

Pets: On 6 ft. leash; $1 fee. **Fires:** In fire grates only. **Alcoholic Beverages:** Allowed at site, not exceeding 40 proof. **Vehicle Maximum Length:** 35 ft. **Other:** 14-day stay limit; no firearms.

To Get There

From I-8 in El Cajon take Hwy. 67 north and drive 4.5 mi. Turn right onto Maple View St. and drive 2.2 mi. The road changes into Lake Jennings Park Rd. The campground entrance is on the left.

EL CENTRO

Rio Bend RV Resort Ranch

1589 Drew Rd., El Centro 92243. T: (760) 352-7061; F: (760) 352-0055; www.riobendrv.com.

RV ★★★★ Tent ★

Beauty: ★★	Site Privacy: ★★
Spaciousness: ★★	Quiet: ★★★
Security: ★★★	Cleanliness: ★★★★
Insect Control: ★	Facilities: ★★★★

In many ways Rio Bend is a community unto itself. RVs are parked side by side along dirt lanes attractively lined with palms, eucalyptus, and citrus trees; the central plaza is colorfully accented with flowering oleanders, a couple of Conestoga wagons, and some bales of hay; there are even a post office, swimming pool, nine-hole golf course, and two stocked fishing ponds on the premises. No wonder then that the resort is also well stocked each winter with snowbirds looking to ride out the cooler months at 50 feet below sea level. True, shade trees are scarce in the short term camping area and tents, relegated to the thick grass outside the office, are given short shrift. But with so many amenities, these small hardships are a little easier to wink at.

Basics

Operated By: Wayne & Shirlee Miller, managers. **Open:** All year. **Site Assignment:** Reservations accepted w/ V, MC. **Registration:** In office at the end of the driveway. **Fee:** $13–$26, cash or V, MC. **Parking:** At site.

Facilities

Number of RV Sites: 270. **Number of Tent-Only Sites:** Undesignated sites. **Hookups:** Water, electric (50 amps), cable TV, Internet. **Each Site:** Full hookups. **Dump Station:** Yes. **Laundry:** Yes. **Pay Phone:** Yes. **Rest Rooms and Showers:** Yes. **Fuel:** No. **Propane:** No. **Internal Roads:** Paved & packed dirt. **RV Service:** No. **Market:** 8.5 mi. east in El Centro. **Restaurant:** 8.5 mi. east in El Centro. **General Store:** Yes. **Vending:** No. **Swimming:** In heated pool. **Playground:** No. **Other:** Some wheelchair-accessible facilities, post office, 2 fishing ponds. **Activities:** 9-hole golf course, pool, spa, fishing, shuffleboard, horseshoe pit. **Nearby Attractions:** Shopping in Mexicali across the Mexican border, Anza-Borrego Desert State Park, Salton Sea National Wildlife Refuge, Imperial (Algodones) Sand Dunes (east of El Centro). **Additional Information:** El Centro Chamber of Commerce & Visitors Bureau, (760) 352-3681.

Restrictions

Pets: On leash. **Fires:** No. **Alcoholic Beverages:** Allowed. **Vehicle Maximum Length:** None. **Other:** No stay limit.

To Get There

From El Centro head west on I-8 for 8 mi. Take the Drew Rd. Exit and turn left (south). Drive 0.5 mi. to the resort on the right.

ESCONDIDO

Dixon Lake Recreation Area

1700 North La Honda Dr., Escondido 92027. T: (760) 741-3328 or reservations (760) 839-4680; www.dixonlake.com.

RV ★★★ Tent ★★★★

Beauty: ★★★★	Site Privacy: ★★★★
Spaciousness: ★★★	Quiet: ★★★★
Security: ★★★	Cleanliness: ★★★
Insect Control: ★★	Facilities: ★★★

Dixon Lake is almost too good to be true: the camp's hilltop location lies at just over 1,000 feet elevation, with a dramatic panorama of greater Escondido on one side and the small lake on the other. This latter is actually a stocked reservoir with great fishing for trout in the fall and catfish and bass year-round. Like the fish you'll throw back, some sites may be a tad small, but they are spaced fairly well apart amid a field of granite boulders that just beg to be scrambled over, and amply shaded by an appealing potpourri of trees, including the ubiquitous eucalyptus, live oak, a variety of pines, toyon, and ceanothus, as well as a healthy accent of agave. Aside from the handful of spots near the park road, it is hard to go wrong, with numbers 8, 11, 12, and 37 particularly private and 26 and 29 yielding great city views. And when you tire of boating, fishing, and hiking, the San Diego Wild Animal Park is just a 15 minutes' drive away.

Basics

Operated By: City of Escondido. **Open:** All year. **Site Assignment:** Reservations accepted w/ V, MC. **Registration:** At ranger office. **Fee:** $12–$16, cash or V, MC. **Parking:** At site.

Facilities

Number of RV Sites: 44. **Number of Tent-Only Sites:** 0. **Hookups:** Water, electric (20, 30 amps), sewer. **Each Site:** Picnic table, fire grate, trash bin. **Dump Station:** Yes. **Laundry:** No. **Pay Phone:** Yes. **Rest Rooms and Showers:** Yes. **Fuel:** No. **Propane:** No. **Internal Roads:** Paved.

RV Service: No. **Market:** 3 mi. south in Escondido. **Restaurant:** 3 mi. south in Escondido. **General Store:** Yes. **Vending:** No. **Swimming:** No. **Playground:** Yes. **Other:** Some wheelchair-accessible facilities, snackbar, boat launch. **Activities:** Fishing, bicycling, hiking, horseshoe pit, boat rentals. **Nearby Attractions:** Heritage Walk & Museum, San Pascal Battlefield State Historic Park, Deer Park Auto Museum, San Diego Wild Animal Park. **Additional Information:** Escondido Chamber of Commerce, (760) 745-2125.

RESTRICTIONS

Pets: Not allowed. **Fires:** No. **Alcoholic Beverages:** Allowed at site, not exceeding 28 proof. **Vehicle Maximum Length:** 50 ft. **Other:** 14-day stay limit; no firearms.

TO GET THERE

From I-15 in Escondido take the El Norte Pkwy. Exit and drive 3.3 mi. north. Turn left on La Honda Dr. and continue 1.2 mi. straight into the rec area.

ESCONDIDO

Dos Picos Regional Park

17953 Dos Picos Park Rd., Ramona 92065.
T: (858) 694-3049 or reservations (858) 565-3600; www.co.san-diego.ca.us/parks.

RV ★★★★ Tent ★★★

Beauty: ★★★★ Site Privacy: ★★
Spaciousness: ★★★ Quiet: ★★★
Security: ★★ Cleanliness: ★★
Insect Control: ★ Facilities: ★★★

In the "location is everything" department, Dos Picos comes up a winner. It lies in a hillside riparian forest just a half hour drive from downtown San Diego, and a little less than that from the San Diego Wild Animal Park in Escondido. The dirt and grass surfaced sites, spread out over several loops, are amply shaded by eucalyptus and live oak, with several enormous 300-year-olds among the latter. Of the many amenities here, highlights include a jogging track, soccer field, hiking trails, and a kids-only fishing pond. The park loses points, though, for its rundown lavatories, in which three of four toilets in one men's room were out of commission on a recent weekend visit, and such noise problems as many low-flying aircrafts and neighborhood dogs barking throughout the night. Drivers of long RVs should plan to reserve site 56, one of the few with pull-through parking, while 9 and 12 are the more private, roomier tent options.

BASICS

Operated By: County of San Diego, Dept. of Parks & Recreation. **Open:** All year. **Site Assignment:** Reservations accepted w/ V, MC. **Registration:** At entrance booth. **Fee:** $10–$14, cash or V, MC. **Parking:** At site.

FACILITIES

Number of RV Sites: 60. **Number of Tent-Only Sites:** 0. **Hookups:** Water, electric (20 amps). **Each Site:** Picnic table, fire grate, barbecue grill. **Dump Station:** Yes. **Laundry:** No. **Pay Phone:** Yes. **Rest Rooms and Showers:** Yes. **Fuel:** No. **Propane:** No. **Internal Roads:** Paved. **RV Service:** No. **Market:** 5.5 mi. northeast in Ramona. **Restaurant:** 5.5 mi. northeast in Ramona. **General Store:** No. **Vending:** Yes. **Swimming:** No. **Playground:** Yes. **Other:** Limited wheelchair-accessible facilities. **Activities:** Hiking, children's fishing, horseshoe pit, jogging track, soccer field. **Nearby Attractions:** San Diego Wild Animal Park, San Pasqual Battlefield. **Additional Information:** Ramona Chamber of Commerce, (760) 789-1311.

RESTRICTIONS

Pets: On leash, $1 fee. **Fires:** In fire grates only. **Alcoholic Beverages:** Allowed at site, not exceeding 40 proof. **Vehicle Maximum Length:** 35 ft. **Other:** 14-day stay limit; no firearms.

TO GET THERE

In Escondido drive 20 mi. east on Hwy. 78 to Ramona. Turn south on Hwy. 67 and drive 3.5 mi., then turn left on Mussey Grade Rd. and drive 1.1 mi. Turn right on Dos Picos Park Rd. The entrance is less than 1 mi. ahead.

ESCONDIDO

Palomar Mountain State Park

19952 State Park Rd., Palomar Mountain 92060.
T: (760) 765-0755; www.palomar.statepark.org.

RV ★★★ Tent ★★★★

Beauty: ★★★★ Site Privacy: ★★★
Spaciousness: ★★★ Quiet: ★★★
Security: ★★★ Cleanliness: ★★★
Insect Control: ★★★★ Facilities: ★★

Palomar Mountain State Park is located very near an observatory that houses one of America's largest ground-based telescopes, a testimony to the clarity of the night sky in these parts. That facility is off-limits to the public, but barring an overcast sky you should be able to see plenty of stars from the privacy of your campsite. Most are pretty spacious and hug the contours of the hilly mountainside, which compensates for an overall lack of screening. Which is not to suggest that the terraced loops meander over a denuded knob (though there is a fair share of gray granite and mossy rocks scattered about the domain). On the contrary, this charming campground is well forested with cedars, live oak, Douglas firs, and Coulter pines. The restrooms and a couple of sites are wheelchair accessible, but most of the rest involve negotiating a few stone stairs, solid relics from when the Civilian Conservation Corps was working in the area 60 years ago. The best seasons to camp here are spring and fall, though at an elevation of 4,700 feet the risk of snowfall exists from Nov. through early Apr. Plan accordingly.

BASICS

Operated By: California Dept. of Parks & Recreation. **Open:** All year. **Site Assignment:** Reservations accepted w/ V, MC, D. **Registration:** At entrance kiosk. **Fee:** $12, cash or CA check. **Parking:** At site.

FACILITIES

Number of RV Sites: 12. **Number of Tent-Only Sites:** 19. **Hookups:** None. **Each Site:** Picnic table, fire grate, barbecue grill, food storage box. **Dump Station:** No. **Laundry:** No. **Pay Phone:** Yes. **Rest Rooms and Showers:** Yes. **Fuel:** No. **Propane:** No. **Internal Roads:** Paved. **RV Service:** No. **Market:** 47 mi. northwest in Temecula. **Restaurant:** 47 mi. northwest in Temecula. **General Store:** No. **Vending:** No. **Swimming:** No. **Playground:** No. **Other:** Some wheelchair-accessible facilities. **Activities:** Hiking, fishing, ranger-led activities in summer. **Nearby Attractions:** Palomar Mountain Observatory, San Diego Wild Animal Park, Mission San Antonio de Pala. **Additional Information:** Escondido Chamber of Commerce, (760) 745-2125.

RESTRICTIONS

Pets: On 6 ft. leash. **Fires:** In fire grates only. **Alcoholic Beverages:** Allowed at site. **Vehicle Maximum Length:** 27 ft. **Other:** 7-day stay limit; no firearms; no wood gathering.

TO GET THERE

From Escondido on I-15 drive 15 mi. north. Turn east on Hwy. 76 and continue for 21 mi. Turn left on CR S6 direction Palomar Mountain. Follow S6/South Grade Rd. for 7 mi., then turn left on East Grade/State Park Rd. The park entrance is 3.5 mi. ahead.

EUREKA

Humboldt Redwoods State Park, Burlington Campground

Ave. of the Giants, Weott 95571. T: (707) 946-2409 or (707) 946-2015 or reservations (800) 444-7275; F: (707) 946-2326; www.cal-parks.ca.gov or www.reserveamerica.com; hrsp@humboldtredwoods.org.

RV ★★★ Tent ★★★

Beauty: ★★★★ Site Privacy: ★★
Spaciousness: ★★★ Quiet: ★★
Security: ★★★ Cleanliness: ★★★
Insect Control: ★★★ Facilities: ★★

Unlike many of the other state-run campgrounds situated in redwood forests, this one is easy to get to on a smooth piece of road just five miles off US 101, 40 miles south of Eureka. The highly scenic Ave. of the Giants flows through the park, threading for 32 miles past several impressive groves, including the must-see Rockefeller Forest. Of the three campgrounds here, only Burlington is open year-round. Its sites are grouped fairly closely together across a convoluted double loop, with 29 one of the more spacious and 37 a roomy corner spot. There are some impressive specimens of Sequoia sempervirens within Burlington, sturdy red pillars that allow only filtered streaks of sunlight through to the dirt and pine needle-layered forest floor. There are also a handful of decaying logs and a shocking number of redwood stumps. These latter serve as sober reminders of what might well have befallen the remaining giants had it not been for the efforts of conservationists.

BASICS

Operated By: California Dept. of Parks & Recreation. **Open:** All year. **Site Assignment:** Reservations recommended; V, MC, D. **Registration:** At entrance booth. **Fee:** $12, cash or CA check. **Parking:** At site.

Facilities

Number of RV Sites: 57. **Number of Tent-Only Sites:** 0. **Hookups:** None. **Each Site:** Picnic table, fire grate, food storage box. **Dump Station:** No. **Laundry:** No. **Pay Phone:** Yes. **Rest Rooms and Showers:** Yes. **Fuel:** No. **Propane:** No. **Internal Roads:** Paved. **RV Service:** No. **Market:** 4 mi. south in Meyers Flat. **Restaurant:** 4 mi. south in Meyers Flat. **General Store:** No. **Vending:** No. **Swimming:** In Eel River. **Playground:** No. **Other:** Some wheelchair-accessible facilities, visitor center. **Activities:** Hiking, bicycling, horseback riding, fishing. **Nearby Attractions:** Ave. of the Giants; Richardson Grove State Park in Garberville; Pacific Lumber Company Logging Museum in Scotia, Ferndale museums. **Additional Information:** Garberville-Redway Area Chamber of Commerce, (707) 923-2613; Ferndale Chamber of Commerce, (707) 786-4477.

Restrictions

Pets: On 6 ft. leash. **Fires:** In fire grates only. **Alcoholic Beverages:** Allowed at site. **Vehicle Maximum Length:** 33 ft. **Other:** 14-day stay limit; no firearms; no wood gathering.

To Get There

Exit US 101 at Meyers Flat, turning west on Ave. of the Giants. Drive 4.5 mi. to the campground entrance on the right, immediately behind the visitor center.

FALL RIVER MILLS

Pit River

Pit No. 1 Powerhouse Rd., Fall River Mills 96028. T: (530) 233-4666; F: (530) 233-5696; www.ca.blm.gov/alturas.

RV ★★ | Tent ★★★★

Beauty: ★★★★	Site Privacy: ★★★
Spaciousness: ★★★	Quiet: ★★★★
Security: ★★★	Cleanliness: ★★
Insect Control: ★★	Facilities: ★

This inauspiciously-named campground, also known as Pit No. 1, is actually in a very pretty—if somewhat overgrown—forested setting abutting the Pit River. You may find it totally vacant, which is ideal since the best site, which is right on the water looking across to a tiny island, is also the most popular. Or the twin loops might be choked with vehicles, especially on weekends from late spring through summer. Most of the level, leaf-strewn sites lie in the shadow of oaks and a few pines, next to a scruffy meadow. The handful of spots by the water are crammed closely together; otherwise there is space and privacy galore. Pit lies at 3,000 feet of elevation, which is quite comfortable for this region of the Cascade Mountain range. Though not exactly an Eden, Pit River has had its share of serpents, in the form of litterers, despite the presence of plenty of trash bins. No potable water is available, nor does the Bureau of Land Management seem to supervise the land. Local police, though, occasionally patrol. The nearest telephone is in Fall River Mills.

Basics

Operated By: Bureau of Land Management, Alturas Field Office. **Open:** All year, weather permitting. **Site Assignment:** First come, first served. **Registration:** No. **Fee:** None. **Parking:** No designated slips.

Facilities

Number of RV Sites: 10. **Number of Tent-Only Sites:** 0. **Hookups:** None. **Each Site:** Picnic table, fire ring. **Dump Station:** No. **Laundry:** No. **Pay Phone:** No. **Rest Rooms and Showers:** Pit toilets, no showers. **Fuel:** No. **Propane:** No. **Internal Roads:** Dirt, bumpy. **RV Service:** No. **Market:** 6 mi. east in Fall River Mills. **Restaurant:** 6 mi. east in Fall River Mills. **General Store:** No. **Vending:** No. **Swimming:** No. **Playground:** No. **Other:** Natural small boat launch. **Activities:** Fishing, hiking, canoeing, birding. **Nearby Attractions:** Lassen Volcanic National Park; Fort Crook Museum in Fall River Mills; McArthur-Burney Falls Memorial State Park in Burney; Ahjumawi Lava Springs State Park in McArthur; Hat Creek Recreation Area in Old Station. **Additional Information:** Fall River Valley Chamber of Commerce, (530) 336-5840; Burney Chamber of Commerce, (530) 335-2111.

Restrictions

Pets: Allowed. **Fires:** In fire rings only. **Alcoholic Beverages:** Allowed. **Vehicle Maximum Length:** 22 ft. is an absolute max. **Other:** 14-day stay limit.

To Get There

From Fall River Mills drive 4.5 mi. west on Hwy. 299. Turn left on Pit No. 1 Powerhouse Rd. and continue 1.1 mi. to the campground, bearing right at the entrance to Pit River Lodge. The road turns to dirt here and becomes impassable when wet.

FELTON

Henry Cowell Redwoods State Park

101 North Big Trees Park Rd., Felton 95018. T: (831) 438-2396 or reservations (800) 444-7275; www.cal-parks.ca.gov or www.reserveamerica.com.

RV ★★★ | Tent ★★★

Beauty: ★★★★	Site Privacy: ★★★
Spaciousness: ★★★	Quiet: ★★
Security: ★★	Cleanliness: ★★★
Insect Control: ★★★	Facilities: ★★

The first thing you may notice on pulling into the pair of double loops that comprise this campground is that despite the park's name there are precious few burly-looking redwoods in evidence. The natural forested atmosphere derives from an abundance of knob cone pines, madrone trees, and moss-covered oaks. The Cowell grove of redwoods is a 40-minute hike (or 5-minute drive) away. Such minor misrepresentations aside, this is a fine park with roomy leaf- and dirt-based sites ranging from sun-dappled to shady, from exposed to well-shielded. Unfortunately, noise carries here and can be a big problem on weekends when Bay Area residents descend in droves. The presence of a summer-time host augments an otherwise lax enforcement of quiet time. Trash tossed into fire grates is another nuisance. Be alert to poison oak and if you plan to visit in the spring pack along insect repellant.

Basics

Operated By: California Dept. of Parks & Recreation. **Open:** Feb. 15–Nov. 30. **Site Assignment:** Reservations accepted w/ V, MC. **Registration:** At entrance booth. **Fee:** $12, cash or CA check. **Parking:** At site.

Facilities

Number of RV Sites: 112. **Number of Tent-Only Sites:** 0. **Hookups:** None. **Each Site:** Picnic table, fire grate, food storage box. **Dump Station:** No. **Laundry:** No. **Pay Phone:** Yes. **Rest Rooms and Showers:** Yes. **Fuel:** No. **Propane:** No. **Internal Roads:** Paved. **RV Service:** No. **Market:** 2 mi. west in Felton. **Restaurant:** 2 mi. west in Felton. **General Store:** No. **Vending:** No. **Swimming:** No. **Playground:** No. **Other:** Some wheelchair-accessible facilities. **Activities:** Hiking, bicycling, horseback riding, horseshoe pit. **Nearby Attractions:** Santa Cruz Beach Boardwalk, mission, museums, Seymour Marine Discovery Center, Arboretum & Natural Bridges State Beach; Roaring Camp Railroads in Felton. **Additional Information:** Santa Cruz County Conference & Visitors Council, (831) 425-1234 or (800) 833-3494.

Restrictions

Pets: On 6 ft. leash. **Fires:** In fire grates only. **Alcoholic Beverages:** Allowed at site. **Vehicle Maximum Length:** 35 ft. **Other:** 7-day stay limit from Apr. 1–Oct. 31; no firearms; no wood gathering.

To Get There

From Santa Cruz on Hwy. 1 take Hwy. 9 north. Drive 6.5 mi. to the stop light; bear right on Graham Hill Rd. The campground is 2.7 mi. ahead on the right.

FRESNO

Pine Flat Lake Recreation Area

Pine Flat Rd., Piedra 93649. T: (559) 488-3004; F: (559) 488-1988.

RV ★★★★ | Tent ★★★

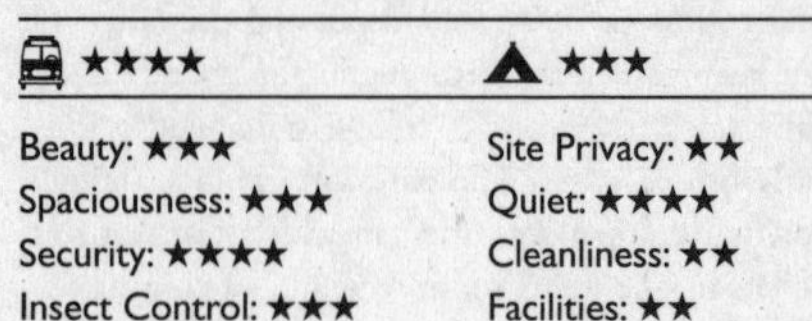

Beauty: ★★★	Site Privacy: ★★
Spaciousness: ★★★	Quiet: ★★★★
Security: ★★★★	Cleanliness: ★★
Insect Control: ★★★	Facilities: ★★

One of the more pleasant aspects of this county park is that it does not get over-run by hordes of campers, unlike other lakeside camps in the area. Boaters are not in dry-dock country, though; there is good fishing in the Kings River, which flows from the Pine Flat Dam past one side of camp, and boat-ramp access to the reservoir is nearby. The level, grassy turf is attractively punctuated here and there by a great range of such shade trees as oak, sycamore, and black walnut, and encompassed by undulating hills of golden grass and traces of granite. There is a uniformity to the double-loop layout, with open sites so comparable that one is as good as another. This is an invaluable oasis during the summer, which runs in these parts from May through Sept. The grounds are raked and well maintained, though some restrooms lack taps and have a neglected air to them. There is a general store and fuel station in Piedra, three miles to the west.

BASICS

Operated By: Fresno County Parks Dept. **Open:** All year. **Site Assignment:** First come, first served. **Registration:** At entrance booth. **Fee:** $11, cash or CA check. **Parking:** At site.

FACILITIES

Number of RV Sites: 55. **Number of Tent-Only Sites:** 0. **Hookups:** None. **Each Site:** Picnic table, barbecue grill. **Dump Station:** Yes. **Laundry:** No. **Pay Phone:** Yes. **Rest Rooms and Showers:** Flush toilets, no showers. **Fuel:** No. **Propane:** No. **Internal Roads:** Paved. **RV Service:** No. **Market:** 20 mi. southwest in Sanger. **Restaurant:** 20 mi. southwest in Sanger. **General Store:** No. **Vending:** No. **Swimming:** In Kings River. **Playground:** No. **Other:** Some wheelchair-accessible facilities. **Activities:** Fishing, hiking. **Nearby Attractions:** Museums, Forestiere Underground Gardens, Chaffee Zoological Gardens, Rotary Storyland & Playland in Fresno; Sanger Depot Museum. **Additional Information:** Sanger District Chamber of Commerce, (559) 875-4575; Fresno City & County CVB, (800) 788-0836.

RESTRICTIONS

Pets: On 6 ft. leash. **Fires:** In fire grills only. **Alcoholic Beverages:** Allowed. **Vehicle Maximum Length:** None. **Other:** 14-day stay limit.

TO GET THERE

From Fresno drive 15 mi. east on Hwy. 180/Kings Canyon Rd. to Centerville. Bear left on Trimmer Springs Rd. Continue for 10 mi., past the small town of Piedra, then turn right on Pine Flat Rd. Proceed for 2.5 mi., over the bridge, to the campground entrance on the right.

GARBERVILLE

Shelter Cove RV Park & Campground

492 Machi Rd., Shelter Cove 95589. T: (707) 986-7474; F: (707) 986-7101; www.sojourner2000.com.

RV ★★★ Tent ★★

Beauty: ★★★★	Site Privacy: ★★
Spaciousness: ★★	Quiet: ★★
Security: ★★	Cleanliness: ★★
Insect Control: ★★★	Facilities: ★★★★

Shelter Cove RV Park is for the Bohemian at heart, for people who love the ocean, enjoy fishing for salmon, and don't mind stray dogs wandering through their campsite. It is also for people who live to socialize and don't require much sleep, because in peak season the entire patch of gently tilting grassland that makes up this domain can seem like one continuous block party. On summer weekends there is live music on the patio and sizzling barbecues are centered around the giant crab cooker. Sites are small and shoe-horned together, but enjoy unobstructed views of the ocean, which is a few yards off the lot. Rugged highlands loom over the inland side of Shelter Cove. A small public park—complete with a diminutive lighthouse—lies immediately to its south, and at the opposite end is a county airport. Unfortunately, the occasional plane that approaches the airstrip comes in so low you might think it's trying to land on top of your RV. Of the single lavatory located at the deli/snack bar, we've seen cleaner facilities at the end of a four-day beer festival. Your best bet is to use the toilets in the public park. This campground lies 25 tortuous miles west of Garberville across the King Range National Conservation Area, a drive that requires your vehicle's brakes to be in good working order.

BASICS

Operated By: Shelter Cove Enterprises. **Open:** All year. **Site Assignment:** Reservations recommended; V, MC, D. **Registration:** At store. **Fee:** $16–$27, cash, check or V, MC, D. **Parking:** At site.

FACILITIES

Number of RV Sites: 103. **Number of Tent-Only Sites:** 0. **Hookups:** Water, electric (30 amps), sewer, Internet. **Each Site:** Picnic table, fire grate. **Dump Station:** Yes. **Laundry:** Yes. **Pay Phone:** Yes. **Rest Rooms and Showers:** Yes. **Fuel:** No. **Propane:** Yes. **Internal Roads:** Gravel, good condition. **RV Service:** No. **Market:** 22 mi. east in Redway. **Restaurant:** 1 mi. away in Shelter Cove. **General Store:** Yes, w/ deli. **Vending:** No. **Swimming:** No. **Playground:** No. **Other:** Limited wheelchair-accessible facilities, 6-lane boat launch. **Activities:** Fishing, beachcombing, clamming, hiking, whale-watching. **Nearby Attractions:** Richardson Grove State Park in Garberville; Smithe Redwoods State Reserve & Standish Hickey State Recreation Area in Leggett; Ave. of the Giants north of Garberville; Humboldt Redwoods State Park in Weott. **Additional Information:** Shelter Cove Information Bureau, (707) 923-1830; Garberville-Redway Area Chamber of Commerce, (707) 923-2613.

RESTRICTIONS

Pets: On leash, $1 fee. **Fires:** In fire grates only. **Alcoholic Beverages:** Allowed. **Vehicle Maximum Length:** 40 ft. **Other:** No stay limit.

TO GET THERE

Exit US 101 at Garberville and drive through the downtown, turning left on Redwood Rd. at the sign for the King Range National Conservation Area. After 2.6 mi. turn left on Briceland Rd. which becomes the meandering and steep Shelter Cove Rd. Drive 22.2 mi., turn south on Upper Pacific Rd. and continue for 0.5 mi. to the campground on the right.

GASQUET

Smith River National Recreation Area, Panther Flat Campground

10600 US 199 South, Gasquet 95543. T: (707) 457-3131 or reservations (877) 444-6777; F: (707) 457-3794; www.r5.fs.fed.us/sixrivers or www.reserveusa.com.

RV ★★★★ Tent ★★★★

Beauty: ★★★★	Site Privacy: ★★★
Spaciousness: ★★★★	Quiet: ★★★
Security: ★★★	Cleanliness: ★★★★
Insect Control: ★★★	Facilities: ★★

This tidy, well-maintained campground is perched just above the Middle Fork of the Smith River, about 20 miles northeast of Crescent City along Hwy. 199. Though a rather average facility, it is a worthy alternative to Jedediah Smith Redwood State Park, just down the road, if the latter is full, or if the wild, moldering atmosphere of a moss-encrusted old-growth forest leaves you shivering. Its central location within the Smith River National Recreation Area also makes Panther Flat a suitable base camp for day hikes and fishing the several rivers in the locale. There are only a few redwoods here, of the spindly second-growth variety, and they are overshadowed by tan oaks and madrones. Level gravel sites, well-groomed and equipped with large back-in parking slips, are moderately spacious and evenly distributed around a small grassy meadow at the heart of the elongated double-oval camp lane. The nearest telephone is in Gasquet, three miles west.

BASICS

Operated By: Six Rivers National Forest, Smith River National Recreation Area. **Open:** All year. **Site Assignment:** Reservations accepted w/ V, MC. **Registration:** At entrance kiosk. **Fee:** $15, cash or check. **Parking:** At site.

FACILITIES

Number of RV Sites: 39. **Number of Tent-Only Sites:** 0. **Hookups:** None. **Each Site:** Picnic table, fire grate. **Dump Station:** No. **Laundry:** No. **Pay Phone:** No. **Rest Rooms and Showers:** Yes. **Fuel:** No. **Propane:** No. **Internal Roads:** Paved. **RV Service:** No. **Market:** 2 mi. south in Gasquet. **Restaurant:** 2 mi. south in Gasquet. **General Store:** No. **Vending:** No. **Swimming:** In Smith River. **Playground:** No. **Other:** Some wheelchair-accessible facilities. **Activities:** Fishing, hiking, kayaking. **Nearby Attractions:** Redwood National & State Parks; Battery Point Lighthouse, Ocean World, & Del Norte County Historical Museum in Crescent City; Rowdy Creek Fish Hatchery in Smith River. **Additional Information:** Crescent City–Del Norte County Chamber of Commerce, (707) 464-3174 or (800) 343-8300.

RESTRICTIONS

Pets: On leash. **Fires:** In fire grates only. **Alcoholic Beverages:** Allowed. **Vehicle Maximum Length:** 40 ft. **Other:** 14-day stay limit.

TO GET THERE

From Crescent City drive 3.5 mi. north on US 101. Exit on US 199 and head east towards Grants Pass. Continue for 17 mi. to the well-marked campground entrance on the left.

GILROY

Mount Madonna County Park

Pole Line Rd., Gilroy 95020. T: (408) 358-3741 or group reservations (408) 358-3751; www.parkhere.org/prkpages/madonna.htm.

RV ★★★★ Tent ★★★★

Beauty: ★★★★	Site Privacy: ★★★
Spaciousness: ★★★	Quiet: ★★★★
Security: ★★★	Cleanliness: ★★★
Insect Control: ★★★	Facilities: ★★★

Redwood trees are what this park is all about, with some groves so dense you may find yourself wondering whether the sun has gone into eclipse. Madrone trees and tan oaks round out a very natural, attractive hilltop forest habitat that is laced with 20 miles of hiking trails. Sites of matted leaves and grass are above average in size and distributed over four separate loops, with those in Tan Oak both more private and open to diffused sunlight. There is also a generous amount of gravel-surfaced pull-through parking slips available throughout the campground. The Civilian Conservation Corps was based here in the early 1930s; fieldstone fire pits in some sites are solid reminders of their efforts. Around the same time, William Hearst donated a pair of white fallow deer to the park. Their descendants are still present, housed in a pen near the visitor center. Black tailed deer, coyotes, foxes, and bobcats also call this part of the Santa Cruz Mountain range home.

Basics

Operated By: County of Santa Clara, Parks & Recreation Dept. **Open:** All year. **Site Assignment:** First come, first served. **Registration:** At entrance booth. **Fee:** $15–$25, cash, CA check, V, MC. **Parking:** At site.

Facilities

Number of RV Sites: 117. **Number of Tent-Only Sites:** 0. **Hookups:** Water, electric (20, 30 amps). **Each Site:** Picnic table, fire grate, food storage box. **Dump Station:** Yes. **Laundry:** No. **Pay Phone:** Yes. **Rest Rooms and Showers:** Yes. **Fuel:** No. **Propane:** No. **Internal Roads:** Paved. **RV Service:** No. **Market:** 8 mi. west in Watsonville. **Restaurant:** 8 mi. west in Watsonville. **General Store:** No. **Vending:** No. **Swimming:** No. **Playground:** No. **Other:** Some wheelchair-accessible facilities, visitor center. **Activities:** Hiking, horseback riding, archery, fishing for children. **Nearby Attractions:** Mission San Juan Bautista; John Steinbeck House & Library in Salinas; outlet shopping in Gilroy; Monterey peninsula. **Additional Information:** Gilroy Visitors Bureau & Information Center, (408) 842-6436.

Restrictions

Pets: On 6 ft. leash. **Fires:** In fire grates only. **Alcoholic Beverages:** Allowed at site & picnic area. **Vehicle Maximum Length:** 35 ft. **Other:** 14-day stay limit; no firearms; no wood gathering.

To Get There

From Gilroy on US 101 take the Hwy. 152 Exit and drive west for 10.5 mi. Turn right on Pole Line Rd., which leads to the park.

GRASS VALLEY

Schoolhouse

Marysville Rd., Camptonville 95922. T: (530) 288-3231 or reservations & marina (530) 692-3200; F: (530) 288-0727; www.r5.fs.fed.us/tahoe.

★★★★ ★★★

Beauty: ★★★★ Site Privacy: ★★★
Spaciousness: ★★★ Quiet: ★★★★
Security: ★★★ Cleanliness: ★★★
Insect Control: ★★★ Facilities: ★★

Dark Day Campground, a tent-only, walk-in facility just up the road from Schoolhouse, is blessed from its bluff-top aerie with a heavenly vista of Bullards Bar Reservoir. Sites at Schoolhouse, on the other hand, enjoy no water views. Even so, it is a peaceful, engaging camp, located above the lake on a hill that is thick with conifers, madrone, toyon, and dogwood. The triple loop winds its way across an undulating terrain, where roomy sites are granted a fair degree of privacy. There is plenty of pull-through parking available, and many of the back-ins are large enough for vehicles hauling boats. The most secluded spots are 24, 37, and 40, while 26, a pull-through, is very deep. From mid-Oct. through early spring only sites 1–14 are kept open and no potable water is available. Bullards Bar Dam, constructed in 1969, is California's largest, and ranks fourth in size in the United States.

Basics

Operated By: Tahoe National Forest, North Yuba/ Downieville Ranger District & Yuba City Water Agency. **Open:** All year. **Site Assignment:** Reservations accepted w/ V, MC. **Registration:** At Emerald Cove Marina at the dam; permit required. **Fee:** $14 from Apr. 15–Oct. 15, cash, check or V, MC; no fee in winter when water spigots are capped. **Parking:** At site.

Facilities

Number of RV Sites: 56. **Number of Tent-Only Sites:** 0. **Hookups:** None. **Each Site:** Picnic table, fire grate. **Dump Station:** No. **Laundry:** No. **Pay Phone:** Yes. **Rest Rooms and Showers:** Flush & vault toilets, no showers. **Fuel:** No. **Propane:** No. **Internal Roads:** Paved, more potholes than pavement. **RV Service:** No. **Market:** 26 mi. east in Downieville. **Restaurant:** 26 mi. east in Downieville. **General Store:** Yes, at marina. **Vending:** No. **Swimming:** In Bullards Bar Reservoir. **Playground:** No. **Other:** Boat ramp, marina. **Activities:** Fishing, hiking, horseback riding, mountain biking, boating. **Nearby Attractions:** Empire Mine State Historic Park in Grass Valley; Malakoff Diggins State Historic Park in Nevada City; Downieville Foundry/Museum, Gallows & County Museum. **Additional Information:** Grass Valley–Nevada County Chamber of Commerce, (530) 273-4667; Sierra County Chamber of Commerce, (530) 862-0308 or (800) 200-4949.

Restrictions

Pets: On leash. **Fires:** In fire grates only. **Alcoholic Beverages:** Allowed. **Vehicle Maximum Length:** 35 ft. **Other:** 14-day stay limit.

To Get There

Exit Hwy. 70 at Marysville and drive twelve mi. east on Hwy. 20. Turn left on Marysville Rd./E21, at the sign for Bullards Bar Reservoir, and continue for 11 mi. Head right on Old Marysville Rd. and drive 17 mi., across the dam, to the campground on the left.

GREENVILLE

Lake Almanor Campground

15778 Hwy. 89, Pratville 95923. T: (916) 386-5164; www.r5.fs.fed.us/lassen.

★★★★ ★★★★

Beauty: ★★★★ Site Privacy: ★★★
Spaciousness: ★★★ Quiet: ★★★
Security: ★★★ Cleanliness: ★★★★
Insect Control: ★★★ Facilities: ★★

Of the many level, rather spacious sites here, there is a healthy balance between those that are open and exposed and others that are flanked by incense cedars, manzanita, Douglas firs, and ponderosa pines. Shade or sun, boating and fishing versus hiking or swimming, one thing that everybody can agree on is that the sightlines are magnificent from camp to glimmering Lake Almanor and the rumpled mountains looming above. Access to the lake is easy, too, with only a gentle tilt to the ground near the water—instead of the steep embankments of many other reservoir lakes—and loops that hug the meandering contours of the shore. Arguably, the very finest site is 40, isolated on a finger of land projecting into the lake; its neighbor, 41, is a very good runner-up. Similarly situated is 50, a double site that's ideal for large groups or oversize RVs. Tent campers should angle for 12, a cedar-shaded walk-in near the shore. A "camp library" of paperbacks is located in a cabinet across from the "supervisor," an on-site employee of American Land & Leisure, which operates the property for Pacific Gas & Electric.

Basics

Operated By: American Land & Leisure, concessionaire. **Open:** May through Oct. **Site Assignment:** First come, first served. **Registration:** At entrance kiosk. **Fee:** $15, cash or check. **Parking:** At site.

Facilities

Number of RV Sites: 125. **Number of Tent-Only Sites:** 6. **Hookups:** None. **Each Site:** Picnic table, fire grate, food storage box. **Dump Station:** Yes. **Laundry:** No. **Pay Phone:** Yes. **Rest Rooms and Showers:** Vault toilets, no showers. **Fuel:** No. **Propane:** No. **Internal Roads:** Paved. **RV Service:** No. **Market:** 12 mi. south in Greenville. **Restaurant:** 12 mi. south in Greenville. **General Store:** No. **Vending:** No. **Swimming:** In Lake Almanor. **Playground:** No. **Other:** Some wheelchair-accessible facilities, boat ramp. **Activities:** Fishing, boating, waterskiing, hiking, birding. **Nearby Attractions:** Westwood Museum & Paul Bunyan & Babe the Blue Ox Statues; Lassen National Scenic Byway (Hwys. 89-44-36); Lassen Volcanic National Park. **Additional Information:** Chester–Lake Almanor Chamber of Commerce, (530) 258-2426 or (800) 350-4838.

Restrictions

Pets: On leash, $1 fee. **Fires:** In fire grates only. **Alcoholic Beverages:** Allowed. **Vehicle Maximum Length:** 40 ft. **Other:** 14-day stay limit.

To Get There

From Greenville drive 12 mi. north on Hwy. 89. The campground entrance is on the right.

GROVELAND

Moccasin Point

Jacksonville Rd., Moccasin 95347. T: (209) 852-2396 or marina (209) 989-2206; F: (209) 857-2780; www.donpedrolake.com.

★★★★ ★★★

Beauty: ★★★★ Site Privacy: ★★★
Spaciousness: ★★★ Quiet: ★★★
Security: ★★★★ Cleanliness: ★★★
Insect Control: ★★★ Facilities: ★★★★

Given a choice between camping at Moccasin Point or Fleming Meadows, just down the road, the first wins hands down. For one thing, sites at Moccasin are not wedged together quite as tightly, and they benefit from a greater concentration of such shade and privacy providers as oaks, various conifers, and manzanita. Another point in its favor is the picturesque landscape, which ranges from chaparral-covered Sierra foothills to rolling fields of wildflower-dotted golden grass. The layout consists of a figure-8 loop and a triple circuit, both of which descend toward the jade-green water over a series of tiers. The most private sites are B 6, 10, 17, C 7, 8, 15, and 16. One drawback of this fine campground is the dearth of lake views. Oddly, the best water access is available via its primitive D and E overflow loops, the latter being graced with its own lagoon. Site distribution is more concentrated there, but shade is abundant.

Basics

Operated By: Don Pedro Recreation Agency. **Open:** All year. **Site Assignment:** Reservations accepted w/ V, MC or check. **Registration:** At entrance booth. **Fee:** $12–$22, cash or V, MC. **Parking:** At site.

Facilities

Number of RV Sites: 91. **Number of Tent-Only Sites:** 0. **Hookups:** Water, electric (20, 30 amps), sewer. **Each Site:** Picnic table, barbecue grill, food storage box. **Dump Station:** Yes. **Laundry:** No. **Pay Phone:** Yes. **Rest Rooms and Showers:** Yes. **Fuel:** No. **Propane:** Yes. **Internal Roads:** Paved. **RV Service:** No. **Market:** 8 mi. east in Groveland. **Restaurant:** 8 mi. east in Groveland. **General Store:** Yes. **Vending:** Yes. **Swimming:** In Don Pedro Lake. **Playground:** No. **Other:** Some wheelchair-accessible facilities, boat ramp, marina. **Activities:** Fishing, waterskiing, motorboat & houseboat rentals, sailing. **Nearby Attractions:** Northern Mariposa County History Center in Coulterville; Tuolumne County Museum & History Center in Sonora; Yosemite National Park. **Additional Information:** Coulterville Visitors Center, (209) 878-3074; Tuolumne County Visitors Bureau, (209) 533-4420 or (800) 446-1333.

Restrictions

Pets: Not allowed. **Fires:** Groundfires not allowed. **Alcoholic Beverages:** Allowed. **Vehicle Maximum Length:** None. **Other:** 14-day stay limit; no fireworks.

To Get There

From Groveland on Hwy. 120 head 7 mi. west to the junction w/ Hwy. 49. Turn north (right) on Hwy. 49 and continue for 2 mi. Turn right on Jacksonville Rd., followed by another right into the campground.

GROVELAND

The Pines

Hwy. 120, Groveland 95321. T: (209) 962-7825; F: (209) 962-6406; www.r5.fs.fed.us/stanislaus.

Beauty: ★★★ Site Privacy: ★★
Spaciousness: ★★★ Quiet: ★★★★
Security: ★★★ Cleanliness: ★★★
Insect Control: ★★★ Facilities: ★

No one cares to stay at The Pines very long, seldom more than one night. That is no reflection on this peaceful haven just off of Hwy. 120, nine miles east of Groveland. It's just that with the entrance to Yosemite National Park 15 miles farther on, this serves more as a brief lay-over camp than a destination in its own right. The clean, attractive campground, located behind a forest ranger station, features level, grassy sites scattered over an L-shaped access road. There are plenty of oak trees, manzanita, and cedars sprinkled in among the mature pines, yielding abundant shade to this lush sward. Even so, sites, while somewhat roomy, are rather exposed. Best of the group are a pair of walk-ins, 6 and 7, which are well-recessed amid a clutch of stumps and a small marsh. Elevation is 3,200 feet, auguring for cool-but-pleasant nights most of the year.

Basics

Operated By: American Land & Leisure, concessionaire. **Open:** All year. **Site Assignment:** First come, first served. **Registration:** At entrance kiosk. **Fee:** $10, cash or check. **Parking:** At site.

Facilities

Number of RV Sites: 7. **Number of Tent-Only Sites:** 5. **Hookups:** None. **Each Site:** Picnic table, fire grate. **Dump Station:** No. **Laundry:** No. **Pay Phone:** No. **Rest Rooms and Showers:** Vault toilets, no showers. **Fuel:** No. **Propane:** No. **Internal Roads:** Paved. **RV Service:** No. **Market:** 9 mi. west in Groveland. **Restaurant:** 9 mi. west in Groveland. **General Store:** No. **Vending:** No. **Swimming:** No. **Playground:** No. **Activities:** Hiking, rafting on the Tuolumne River. **Nearby Attractions:** Yosemite National Park; Don Pedro Lake; Northern Mariposa County History Center in Coulterville. **Additional Information:** Tuolumne County Visitors Bureau, (209) 533-4420 or (800) 446-1333; Yosemite Area Traveler Information, (209) 723-3153.

Restrictions

Pets: On leash. **Fires:** In fire grates only. **Alcoholic Beverages:** Allowed. **Vehicle Maximum Length:** 22 ft. **Other:** 14-day stay limit.

To Get There

From Groveland drive 8.5 mi. east on Hwy. 120. Turn right at the sign for the Groveland Ranger District Office and follow the signs to the campground, 0.6 mi. ahead.

GUERNEVILLE

Austin Creek State Recreation Area, Bullfrog Pond Campground

17000 Armstrong Woods Rd., Guerneville 95446. T: (707) 869-2015; F: (707) 869-5629; www.cal-parks.ca.gov.

Beauty: ★★★★ Site Privacy: ★★★
Spaciousness: ★★★ Quiet: ★★★★
Security: ★★★ Cleanliness: ★★★★
Insect Control: ★★ Facilities: ★★

Shortly after the end of World War II, renowned ceramist Marguerite Wildenhain of the Bauhaus school came to settle in this area. She found inspiration in the sublime beauty of her surroundings, a feeling that countless campers have shared since then. If you are able to get your vehicle up the steep, narrow, meandering access road—and that's a big if—you will find stunning mountain views and an enchanting forested atmosphere. Feral pigs, wild turkeys, bobcats, and the elusive spotted owl make their homes in these redwood- and tan oak–covered hills. You are more likely, though, to see frogs by the pond, where the camp lane ends. Fern-freckled sites are distributed fairly well apart and though they are a tad small and some are planted on slanting ground, such minor discomforts seem an acceptable tradeoff for camping in so attractive a place. The park closes when the fire risk is extreme, so be sure to call ahead in summer.

Basics

Operated By: California Dept. of Parks & Recreation. **Open:** All year, weather & fire danger permitting. **Site Assignment:** First come, first served. **Registration:** At kiosk, 3.2 mi. beyond entrance booth. **Fee:** $12, cash or CA check. **Parking:** At site.

Facilities

Number of RV Sites: 23. **Number of Tent-Only Sites:** 0. **Hookups:** None. **Each Site:** Picnic table, fire grate, food storage box. **Dump Station:** No. **Laundry:** No. **Pay Phone:** Yes. **Rest Rooms and Showers:** Flush toilets, no showers. **Fuel:** No. **Propane:** No. **Internal Roads:** Paved, narrow & bumpy. **RV Service:** No. **Market:** 5.5 mi. south in Guerneville. **Restaurant:** 5.5 mi. south in Guerneville. **General Store:** No. **Vending:** No. **Swimming:** No. **Playground:** No. **Other:** Some wheelchair-accessible facilities. **Activities:** Hiking, fishing, horseback riding, birding, canoeing (in the Russian River). **Nearby Attractions:** Healdsburg Museum & Sonoma County Wine Library; Fort Ross State Historic Park, Kruse Rhododendron State Reserve & Salt Point State Park in Jenner; winery tours. **Additional Information:** Healdsburg Chamber of Commerce & Visitors Center, (707) 823-3032 or (877) 828-4748; Russian River Chamber of Commerce & Visitors Center, (707) 869-9212 or (877) 644-9001.

Restrictions

Pets: On 6 ft. leash; not allowed on trails. **Fires:** In fire grates only; not allowed when fire danger is extreme. **Alcoholic Beverages:** Allowed at site. **Vehicle Maximum Length:** 20 ft.; no trailers allowed. **Other:** 14-day stay limit; no firearms; no wood gathering.

To Get There

From downtown Guerneville on Hwy. 116, turn north on Armstrong Woods Rd. The park entrance is 2.3 mi. ahead, w/ the campground entrance is 3.2 mi. beyond that.

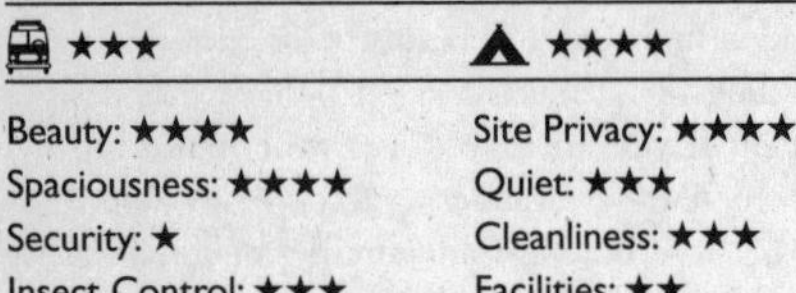

HAMBURG

Sarah Totten

Hwy. 96, Hamburg 96086. T: (530) 493-2243 or reservations (877) 444-6777; F: (530) 493-1796; www.r5.fs.fed.us/klamath; wrwilliams@fs.fed.us.

★★★ ★★★★

Beauty: ★★★★ Site Privacy: ★★★★
Spaciousness: ★★★★ Quiet: ★★★
Security: ★ Cleanliness: ★★★
Insect Control: ★★★ Facilities: ★★

A popular rafting stretch of the Klamath River flows right by this pretty little campground, with easy put-in access to the water. Like Fort Goff to the west, this is a roadside facility, with a key difference being that Sarah Totten is recessed from Hwy. 96 and thus approaching autos do not seem to be bearing down on one's tent. In fact, road noise in most sites is pretty effectively muffled by the melodious churning of the Klamath. Of the two neighboring loops, the left-hand one contains five walk-in sites, with the oak-shaded number 3 the most spacious. Oak, pines, and horsetail grass also thrive in the second circuit, where peculiar mounds of river stones near the entrance are relics from the Gold Rush era, circa 1850, when extensive mining of the river occurred. Sites 6 and 7, with paved back-in parking, are tailor-made for RVs. The most private spot is 9, hidden behind an overgrown thicket of vines and weeds; it also has a water view. This is a splendid property, 40 miles east of Happy Camp, albeit somewhat neglected and overgrown.

Basics

Operated By: Klamath National Forest. **Open:** May to Nov. **Site Assignment:** First come, first served; reservations required for group site. **Registration:** At entrance kiosk. **Fee:** $10, cash or check; no fee when in winter when spigots are capped. **Parking:** At site.

Facilities

Number of RV Sites: 5. **Number of Tent-Only Sites:** 12. **Hookups:** None. **Each Site:** Picnic table, barbecue grill, fire ring. **Dump Station:** No. **Laundry:** No. **Pay Phone:** No, emergency phone only. **Rest Rooms and Showers:** Vault toilets, no showers. **Fuel:** No. **Propane:** No. **Internal Roads:** Mostly paved, also dirt & rocks. **RV Service:** No. **Market:** 10 mi. east in Seiad Valley. **Restaurant:** 10 mi. east in Seiad Valley. **General Store:** No. **Vending:** No. **Swimming:** In Klamath River. **Playground:** No. **Other:** Limited wheelchair-accessible facilities. **Activities:** Fishing, hiking, rafting, kayaking, birding. **Nearby Attractions:** Klamath National Forest; Yreka National Historic District, Western Railroad, Siskiyou County Courthouse & Museum in Yreka. **Additional Information:** Siskiyou County Visitors Bureau, (530) 926-3850; Yreka Chamber of Commerce, (530) 842-1649.

Restrictions

Pets: On 6 ft. leash. **Fires:** In fire rings only. **Alcoholic Beverages:** Allowed. **Vehicle Maximum Length:** 22 ft. **Other:** 14-day stay limit.

To Get There

From Happy Camp drive 30 mi. east on Hwy. 96. The campground entrance is on the left side of the road.

HAPPY CAMP

Elk Creek Camp & RV Park

921 Elk Creek Rd., Happy Camp 96039. T: (530) 493-2208; www.elkcreekcampground.com; eddiedav@sisqtel.net.

★★★ ★★

Beauty: ★★★ Site Privacy: ★★
Spaciousness: ★★ Quiet: ★★★
Security: ★★★★ Cleanliness: ★★★★
Insect Control: ★★★ Facilities: ★★★★

Elk Creek is a privately operated campground with a rocky creek running through it, offering good fishing and swimming opportunities within easy walking distance of sites. The rustic feeling of the locale stems in part from its being thinly forested with maple, oak, madrone, and several types of pine, but also from its chaotic criss-crossing layout of lanes. Sites are level and surfaced either with grass, gravel, or dirt; the ones just above the creek are the roomiest and most secluded. While the setting is generally quite attractive, the appeal of Elk Creek is diminished by the presence of several unsightly long-term trailers, some of which sport license tags that haven't been renewed in years. A recent change in management, though, bodes well, with a rec room, equipped with ping pong and pool tables, recently installed and the genial new owners determined to turn this place around. Miniature show horses are bred on the premises.

Basics

Operated By: Eddie & Jean Davenport, owners. **Open:** All year. **Site Assignment:** Reservations accepted w/ V, MC, D, AE. **Registration:** At the office. **Fee:** $10–$20, cash, check or V, MC, C, AE. **Parking:** At site.

Facilities

Number of RV Sites: 78. **Number of Tent-Only Sites:** Undesignated sites. **Hookups:** Water, electric (30, 50 amps), sewer, cable TV, Internet. **Each Site:** Picnic table, fire grate. **Dump Station:** Yes. **Laundry:** Yes. **Pay Phone:** Yes. **Rest Rooms and Showers:** Yes. **Fuel:** No. **Propane:** Yes. **Internal Roads:** Dirt & gravel, negotiable. **RV Service:** No. **Market:** 1 mi. northeast in Happy Camp. **Restaurant:** 1 mi. northeast in Happy Camp. **General Store:** No. **Vending:** Yes. **Swimming:** In Elk Creek & Klamath River. **Playground:** No. **Other:** Some wheelchair-accessible facilities, rec room. **Activities:** Hiking, fishing, kayaking, rafting. **Nearby Attractions:** Oregon Caves National Monument; Yreka National Historic District; Klamath National Forest. **Additional Information:** Siskiyou County Visitors Bureau, (530) 926-3850.

Restrictions

Pets: On leash. **Fires:** In fire grates only. **Alcoholic Beverages:** Allowed. **Vehicle Maximum Length:** None. **Other:** No stay limit; no wood gathering.

To Get There

From Happy Camp drive 0.5 mi. south on Hwy. 96 to Elk Creek Rd. Turn left and drive 1 mi. to the campground entrance on the right. The unpaved access road descends steeply.

HUME

Hume Lake

Hume Lake Rd., Hume 93628. T: (599) 338-2251 or reservations (877) 444-6777; F: (559) 338-2131; www.r5.fs.fed.us/sequoia or www.reserveusa.com.

★★★ ★★★

Beauty: ★★★★ Site Privacy: ★★★
Spaciousness: ★★★ Quiet: ★★★
Security: ★★★★ Cleanliness: ★★★
Insect Control: ★★ Facilities: ★★

Hume Lake lies just below this good-looking woodland campground. Fishing and boating are popular pastimes here, so much so that you'll need reservations on summer weekends. It is well situated as a base camp for exploring the newly-minted Giant Sequoia National Monument, of which it is a part, and launching into the neighboring Kings Canyon National Park. Manzanita, Jeffrey and ponderosa pines, oak, and cedar thrive across this hilly domain, where dirt- and pine needle–surfaced sites are spread decently apart over a convoluted series of six loops. That's the good news. The bad news is that few spots are blessed with lake vistas, and those that are, such as 63 and 64, are not specifically reservable. The concession that manages Hume Lake for the national forest service restricts reservations to "type," not site number. Thus, car campers with a tent might reserve a "type one" spot, while a motor home would require a "type two" or "type three," at a higher fee. Unfortunately, many in the first category have parking slips that are so tight you may wish you rolled in on two wheels instead of four. Gasoline and a general store are available at the Christian camp in Hume, two miles south.

Basics

Operated By: California Land Management, concessionaire. **Open:** May through Sept., weather permitting. **Site Assignment:** Reservations accepted w/ V, MC, D. **Registration:** At entrance booth. **Fee:** $16, cash or check; $32 for a double site; add $2 per night for holiday weekends. **Parking:** At site.

Facilities

Number of RV Sites: 74. **Number of Tent-Only Sites:** 0. **Hookups:** None. **Each Site:** Picnic table, fire grate, some sites have bearproof box. **Dump Station:** No. **Laundry:** No. **Pay Phone:** No. **Rest Rooms and Showers:** Flush toilets, no showers. **Fuel:** No. **Propane:** No. **Internal Roads:** Paved. **RV Service:** No. **Market:** 41 mi. west in Sanger. **Restaurant:** 10 mi. southwest in Grant Grove Village. **General Store:** Yes. **Vending:** No. **Swimming:** In Hume Lake. **Playground:** No. **Other:** Boat ramp. **Activities:** Fishing, boat rentals, hiking. **Nearby Attractions:** Giant Sequoia National Monument; Kings Canyon & Sequoia National Parks; Reedley Opera House, Museum & Mennonite Quilting Center. **Additional Information:** Fresno City & County CVB, (800) 788-0836; Reedley District Chamber of Commerce & Visitors Bureau, (559) 638-3548.

RESTRICTIONS

Pets: On leash. **Fires:** In fire grates only. **Alcoholic Beverages:** Allowed. **Vehicle Maximum Length:** 30 ft. **Other:** 14-day stay limit.

TO GET THERE

From Grant Grove on Hwy. 180 in Kings Canyon National Park drive 6.2 mi. north, direction Cedar Grove. At the sign for Hume Lake make a right onto Hume Rd. and continue for 3.2 mi. to the Hume Lake campground turnoff. Make a left and proceed for 0.4 mi. to the campground straight ahead.

HUME

Landslide

Ten Mile Creek Rd., Hume 93628. T: (559) 338-2251 or reservations (877) 444-6777; F: (559) 338-2131; www.r5.fs.fed.us/sequoia or www.reserveusa.com.

RV ★★★ Tent ★★★★

Beauty: ★★★★	Site Privacy: ★★★
Spaciousness: ★★★★	Quiet: ★★★
Security: ★★★	Cleanliness: ★★★
Insect Control: ★★	Facilities: ★

Located just down the road from Hume Lake (and 15 miles from Grant Grove Village in Kings Canyon National Park), this thickly-forested campground is a worthy alternative to that oft-overrun facility. It's small, and picks up traffic noise from the forest road, but the setting reflects an authentic Sierra Nevada flavor, with granite boulders highlighting the rolling turf, and several meandering streams trickling through. Sizable sites of dirt and grass are positioned well apart along the curvilinear camp lane, with abundant shade provided by incense cedars and Jeffrey pines—but no sequoias. Late spring, when neon-red snow plants push up through the ground, is a good time to visit, but at an altitude of 5,800 feet, evenings then can be downright chilly. Formerly, Landslide was a no-fee national forest camp, but now that it is part of the newly-minted Giant Sequoia National Monument, the concession that operates it has imposed a $10 fee. Gasoline and a general store are located at the Christian camp in Hume, three miles north.

BASICS

Operated By: California Land Management, concessionaire. **Open:** May 25 through Oct., weather permitting. **Site Assignment:** Reservations accepted for some sites; V, MC, D. **Registration:** At entrance kiosk. **Fee:** $10, cash or check. **Parking:** At site.

FACILITIES

Number of RV Sites: 7. **Number of Tent-Only Sites:** 2. **Hookups:** None. **Each Site:** Picnic table, fire grate. **Dump Station:** No. **Laundry:** No. **Pay Phone:** No. **Rest Rooms and Showers:** Vault toilets, no showers. **Fuel:** No. **Propane:** No. **Internal Roads:** Mostly dirt, but smooth. **RV Service:** No. **Market:** 44 mi. west in Sanger. **Restaurant:** 13 mi. southwest in Grant Grove Village. **General Store:** Yes. **Vending:** No. **Swimming:** No. **Playground:** No. **Other:** Limited wheelchair-accessible facilities. **Activities:** Fishing, boat rentals, hiking. **Nearby Attractions:** Giant Sequoia National Monument; Kings Canyon & Sequoia National Parks; Reedley Opera House, Museum & Mennonite Quilting Center. **Additional Information:** Fresno City & County CVB, (800) 788-0836; Reedley District Chamber of Commerce & Visitors Bureau, (559) 638-3548.

RESTRICTIONS

Pets: On leash. **Fires:** In fire grates only. **Alcoholic Beverages:** Allowed. **Vehicle Maximum Length:** 30 ft. **Other:** 14-day stay limit.

TO GET THERE

From Grant Grove on Hwy. 180 in Kings Canyon National Park drive 6.2 mi. north, direction Cedar Grove. At the sign for Hume Lake make a right onto Hume Rd. (which becomes Ten Mile Creek Rd.) and continue for 7.5 mi. to the campground on the right.

JENNER

Salt Point State Park, Woodside and Gerstle Cove Campground

Hwy. 1, Jenner 95450. T: (707) 865-2391 or (707) 847-3221 or reservations (800) 444-7275; F: (707) 865-2046; www.cal-parks.ca.gov or www.reserveamerica.com.

RV ★★★ Tent ★★★

Beauty: ★★★	Site Privacy: ★★★
Spaciousness: ★★★★	Quiet: ★★★
Security: ★★★	Cleanliness: ★★★
Insect Control: ★★★	Facilities: ★

Hwy. 1 is a sleepy, sparsely-traveled stretch of pavement in this part of the state, which is a good thing as it cuts directly through Salt Point State Park. The campground's two loops lie on either side of the road and that quirk of geography could not result in more contrasting realms. The west-facing Gerstle Cove consists of 30 roomy sites spaced well apart around a small grassy meadow. Most of the pines at the perimeter died years ago, victims of a forest fire. As a result, their skeletal limbs have an eerie appearance, especially when veiled in the fog that frequently cloaks this section of the park. When the air is clear the camp commands a great view of the sandy cove below, one of a series of small bays and inlets in the vicinity. Inland is Woodside, where the dense concentration of mixed conifers, madrones, and ferns emerged unscathed from the fire. Sites here are no less roomy than across the road, but the forest environment contributes to better screening and thus superior privacy. Amateur mycologists will be delighted to find that king boletes and chanterelles thrive in these woods. Divers will want to explore the protected underwater reserve just off shore.

BASICS

Operated By: California Dept. of Parks & Recreation. **Open:** All year. **Site Assignment:** Reservations accepted w/ V, MC, D. **Registration:** At entrance booth. **Fee:** $12, cash or CA check. **Parking:** At site.

FACILITIES

Number of RV Sites: 109. **Number of Tent-Only Sites:** 30. **Hookups:** None. **Each Site:** Picnic table, fire grate, food storage box. **Dump Station:** No. **Laundry:** No. **Pay Phone:** Yes. **Rest Rooms and Showers:** Flush toilets, no showers. **Fuel:** No. **Propane:** No. **Internal Roads:** Paved. **RV Service:** No. **Market:** 1 mi. south on Hwy. 1. **Restaurant:** 1 mi. south on Hwy. 1. **General Store:** No. **Vending:** No. **Swimming:** No. **Playground:** No. **Other:** Some wheelchair-accessible facilities, underwater park. **Activities:** Hiking, fishing, bicycling, horseback riding, mushroom collecting, abalone diving, tidepooling. **Nearby Attractions:** Fort Ross State Historic Park & Kruse Rhododendron State Reserve in Jenner; Armstrong Redwoods State Reserve & Austin Creek State Recreation Area in Guerneville; Sonoma County Wine Library in Healdsburg. **Additional Information:** Sebastopol Area Chamber of Commerce & Visitors Center, (707) 823-3032 or (877) 828-4748.

RESTRICTIONS

Pets: On leash no longer than 6 ft., not allowed on trails. **Fires:** In fire grates only. **Alcoholic Beverages:** Allowed at site. **Vehicle Maximum Length:** 31 ft. **Other:** 10-day stay limit; no firearms; no wood gathering.

TO GET THERE

From Guerneville drive 12.3 mi. west on Hwy. 116 to Jenner. Turn right (north) onto Hwy. 1 and continue for 20 mi. Woodside is to the right, Gerstle Cove is 2 mi. farther on Hwy. 1, to the left.

JULIAN

Cuyamaca Rancho State Park, Paso Picacho Campground

12551 Hwy. 79, Descanso 92016. T: (760) 765-0755; www.cuyamaca.statepark.org.

RV ★★★ Tent ★★★★

Beauty: ★★★★	Site Privacy: ★★★
Spaciousness: ★★★	Quiet: ★★★
Security: ★★★★	Cleanliness: ★★★
Insect Control: ★★★	Facilities: ★★

Paso Picacho is open all year but if you come in the winter plan to dress warmly and don't be surprised if there is snow on the ground. That's because at an elevation of nearly 5,000 feet this is one of the higher camps in southern California, and thus one of the more pleasant—and hugely popular—in summer. Of course its rough-hewn mountainous setting has something to do with that appeal, with roomy sites shaded by oak, manzanita, and pines, and dispersed through a series of loops that snake across the hilly contours of the park. As with many mountain camps, finding a level site can be a challenge: Best in that department (as well as for privacy and space) are numbers 3–12. Rangers report that area mountain lions have become bold, with a number of sightings, two attacks and one fatality over the last 14 years.

BASICS

Operated By: California Dept. of Parks & Recreation. **Open:** All year. **Site Assignment:** Reservations recommended; V, MC, AE. **Registration:** At entrance booth. **Fee:** $12, cash or CA check. **Parking:** At site.

Facilities

Number of RV Sites: 85. **Number of Tent-Only Sites:** 0. **Hookups:** None. **Each Site:** Picnic table, fire grate. **Dump Station:** Yes. **Laundry:** No. **Pay Phone:** Yes. **Rest Rooms and Showers:** Yes. **Fuel:** No. **Propane:** No. **Internal Roads:** Paved. **RV Service:** No. **Market:** 11 mi. north in Julian. **Restaurant:** 11 mi. north in Julian. **General Store:** No. **Vending:** No. **Swimming:** No. **Playground:** No. **Other:** Some wheelchair-accessible facilities. **Activities:** Hiking, horseback riding, boating & fishing in Lake Cuyamaca less than 2 mi. away, ranger-led activities in summer. **Nearby Attractions:** San Diego Wild Animal Park in Escondido, historic Julian. **Additional Information:** Julian Chamber of Commerce, (760) 765-1857.

Restrictions

Pets: On 6 ft. leash. **Fires:** In fire grates only. **Alcoholic Beverages:** Allowed at site. **Vehicle Maximum Length:** 27 ft. **Other:** 30-day stay limit; no firearms; no wood gathering.

To Get There

From San Diego head east on I-8 for 43 mi. Exit on Rte. 79 north and drive 12.2 mi. The campground entrance is on the left.

JULIAN

William Heise County Park

4945 Heise Park Rd., Julian 92036. T: (858) 694-3049; www.co.san-diego.ca.us/parks.

RV: ★★★ Tent: ★★★

Beauty: ★★★★	Site Privacy: ★★★
Spaciousness: ★★★	Quiet: ★★★
Security: ★★★	Cleanliness: ★★★
Insect Control: ★	Facilities: ★★★

This agreeable campground mixes grassy meadows with a forest environment and comes up with a series of loops laid out in a terracing of such shade trees as live oaks, Coulter pines, and incense cedars. The largely comparable sites have coarse sand and dirt for tent pads, with 73 and 84 giving tenters the most space and 36 optimum for RVers. You're likely to hear acorn woodpeckers clowning around up in the leafy canopy, and last time we camped here a number of wild turkeys gobbled through our site. There are seven miles of hiking trails in the park, with the scenic overlook on Desert View Trail especially rewarding. Looking for more? How about heated restrooms, a nicely civilized touch of comfort. The park is just six miles from the scenic mountain town of Julian, making it a great base when the latter holds its Apple Days festival throughout Oct.

Basics

Operated By: County of San Diego, Dept. of Parks & Recreation. **Open:** All year. **Site Assignment:** Reservations accepted w/ V, MC, D. **Registration:** At entrance booth & park office. **Fee:** $12–$14, cash or V, MC, D. **Parking:** At site.

Facilities

Number of RV Sites: 61. **Number of Tent-Only Sites:** 43. **Hookups:** None. **Each Site:** Picnic table, fire ring, some w/ a barbecue grill. **Dump Station:** Yes. **Laundry:** Yes. **Pay Phone:** Yes. **Rest Rooms and Showers:** Yes. **Fuel:** No. **Propane:** No. **Internal Roads:** Paved. **RV Service:** No. **Market:** 5.5 mi. north in Julian. **Restaurant:** 5.5 mi. north in Julian. **General Store:** No. **Vending:** Yes. **Swimming:** No. **Playground:** Yes. **Other:** Some wheelchair-accessible facilities. **Activities:** Hiking, bicycling, horseback riding, horseshoe pit. **Nearby Attractions:** Anza-Borrego Desert State Park, historic Julian, Lake Cuyamaca. **Additional Information:** Julian Chamber of Commerce, (760) 765-1857.

Restrictions

Pets: On 6 ft. leash; $1 fee. **Fires:** In fire rings only. **Alcoholic Beverages:** Allowed at site, not exceeding 40 proof. **Vehicle Maximum Length:** 40 ft. **Other:** 14-day stay limit; no firearms.

To Get There

From Julian head west on Hwy. 78 for 1 mi. Turn left on Pine Hills Rd. and drive 2.3 mi. Turn left again on Frisius Rd. and continue for 2.2 mi. to the park.

JUNE LAKE

Pine Cliff Resort

Pine Cliff Rd., June Lake 93529. T: (760) 648-7558; F: (760) 648-7428.

RV: ★★★★ Tent: ★★★

Beauty: ★★★★	Site Privacy: ★★
Spaciousness: ★★	Quiet: ★★★★
Security: ★★★★	Cleanliness: ★★★★
Insect Control: ★★★	Facilities: ★★★★

June Lake is a lovely body of water, encircled by wavy, golden grasslands, with the choppy, rocky eastern Sierra range looming above. Pine Cliff Resort capitalizes on this rugged setting by positioning many of its sandy, mostly level sites among large gray boulders, while others rub up against high desert chaparral. Jeffrey pines thrive throughout the tilting, mountainous domain, providing shade and highlighting its natural beauty. Despite the trees, there is little screening here, and sites, which are on the small side, are too often crowded together. For the most privacy, try to reserve such perimeter slots as 133, 135, and 136; or any of 66–72, for their dramatic location amid a rift of Sierra uplift. Management deserves credit for the competitive pricing of its fuel and basic supplies, though for "people skills," campers give it mixed reviews. Pine Cliff Resort lies at 7,600 feet altitude, less than 15 miles south of Lee Vining. The sandy access road to the beach and boat ramp is very bumpy.

Basics

Operated By: Pine Cliff Resort. **Open:** All year. **Site Assignment:** Reservations recommended; checks only. **Registration:** At entrance booth. **Fee:** $10–$18, cash only. **Parking:** At site.

Facilities

Number of RV Sites: 190. **Number of Tent-Only Sites:** 60. **Hookups:** Water, electric (20, 30 amps), sewer. **Each Site:** Half-size picnic table, fire grate. **Dump Station:** No. **Laundry:** Yes. **Pay Phone:** Yes. **Rest Rooms and Showers:** Yes. **Fuel:** Yes. **Propane:** Yes. **Internal Roads:** Sandy & smooth. **RV Service:** No. **Market:** 13 mi. north in Lee Vining. **Restaurant:** 13 mi. north in Lee Vining. **General Store:** Yes. **Vending:** No. **Swimming:** In June Lake. **Playground:** Yes. **Other:** Some wheelchair-accessible facilities, boat launch, beach. **Activities:** Fishing, hiking, volleyball, basketball, horseshoe pit, boat & tackle rentals. **Nearby Attractions:** Mono Lake Tufa State Reserve in Lee Vining; Devils Postpile National Monument, Mammoth Mountain Bike Park, Mammoth Museum & outlet shopping in Mammoth Lakes. **Additional Information:** Mono County Tourism Commission, (760) 924-3699; Mammoth Lakes Visitors Bureau, (888) GO-MAMMOTH

Restrictions

Pets: On leash. **Fires:** In fire grates only & out by 10:30 p.m. **Alcoholic Beverages:** Allowed. **Vehicle Maximum Length:** None. **Other:** No stay limit.

To Get There

From Lee Vining drive 11 mi. south on US 395, ignoring the 1st turnoff for Hwy. 158 north. Turn right on the 2nd turnoff, Hwy. 158 south for the June Lake Loop. Drive 1 mi. to North Shore Dr. and turn right on it. Continue for 0.6 mi., then turn left on Pine Cliff Rd. The campground entrance is 0.4 mi. ahead on the right, well-signed.

KERNVILLE

Fairview

Sierra Way, Fairview/Kernville 93238. T: (760) 376-3781 or reservations (877) 444-6777; F: (760) 376-3795; www.r5.fs.fed.us/sequoia or www.reserveusa.com.

RV: ★★★★ Tent: ★★★

Beauty: ★★★★	Site Privacy: ★★★
Spaciousness: ★★	Quiet: ★★★
Security: ★★★	Cleanliness: ★★★
Insect Control: ★★★	Facilities: ★★

The turbulent Kern River is a rafters' delight, and Fairview puts campers where the action is, right alongside that purling cascade of water. The saw-toothed Sierra range circles this rocky, mountainous setting, which is at an altitude of 3,500 feet. Very small, level sites, with equally tight parking slips, are crowded together over rocky, sandy ground. The host's spot has the best shade; elsewhere over the three loops it is sparsely provided by a few pines and cottonwoods, with Mormon tea and other chaparral making up the ground cover. Spring, when snow melt adds to the Kern's power, is the best time to visit, but bear in mind that the concession operating this national forest property charges the same fee whether you picnic, day-use, or camp. There are many maverick camps along the Kern that budget-minded campers may want to investigate. Many are sizable enough to handle small RVs and if they don't have facilities, at least they offer more seclusion and fairer river access than this and the many other developed camps in the area.

Basics

Operated By: California Land Management, concessionaire. **Open:** Apr. through Nov. **Site Assign-**

ment: Reservations recommended; V, MC, D. **Registration:** With campground host. **Fee:** $12, cash or check; $24 for double site; add $2 per night for holiday weekends. **Parking:** At site.

FACILITIES

Number of RV Sites: 55. **Number of Tent-Only Sites:** 0. **Hookups:** None. **Each Site:** Picnic table, fire grate, coffee can ashtray. **Dump Station:** No. **Laundry:** No. **Pay Phone:** Yes. **Rest Rooms and Showers:** Vault toilets, no showers. **Fuel:** No. **Propane:** No. **Internal Roads:** Paved & meandering. **RV Service:** No. **Market:** 17 mi. south in Kernville. **Restaurant:** 17 mi. south in Kernville. **General Store:** Yes. **Vending:** No. **Swimming:** No. **Playground:** No. **Other:** Some wheelchair-accessible facilities. **Activities:** Rafting, fishing, hiking, bicycling. **Nearby Attractions:** Sequoia National Forest; Isabella Lake; California Hot Springs; Porterville Historical Museum & Zauld House & Gardens. **Additional Information:** Porterville Chamber of Commerce, (559) 784-7503.

RESTRICTIONS

Pets: On leash. **Fires:** In fire grates only. **Alcoholic Beverages:** Allowed. **Vehicle Maximum Length:** 40 ft. **Other:** 14-day stay limit.

TO GET THERE

From Kernville drive 17 mi. north on Sierra Way. The campground entrance is on the left.

KINGS CANYON NATIONAL PARK

Azalea

Hwy. 180, Grant Grove Village, Kings Canyon National Park 93633. T: (559) 565-3341; www.nps.gov/seki.

RV ★★★★ Tent ★★★

Beauty: ★★★★	Site Privacy: ★★
Spaciousness: ★★★	Quiet: ★★★
Security: ★★★	Cleanliness: ★★★
Insect Control: ★★★	Facilities: ★★

One of the more appealing aspects of this campground is its central location, within easy walking distance of the General Grant Grove of massive redwood trees and the Grant Grove Visitor Center. The first thing you may notice, though, on driving in is that many sites are considerably less than mediocre—tiny, unshaded, and exposed, as if carved out of the pine needle–packed ground as an afterthought. Indeed, for a rugged, hilly setting that is rich in redwoods, cedar, manzanita, madrone, and various pines, the overall absence of privacy throughout the many loops is hugely disappointing. Still, spacing between sites is not that bad, and if you persevere you'll notice a few that take advantage of protruding boulders for a little extra cover, with 89 and 113 in this better category. There are also several tent-only spots, though many are grouped closely together. If you have the time, be sure to drive the awe-inspiring Kings Canyon Scenic Byway (closed in winter). Sentinel, near the road's end, is a beautiful, wooded campground laid out around a small meadow.

BASICS

Operated By: National Park Service. **Open:** All year. **Site Assignment:** First come, first served. **Registration:** At entrance kiosk. **Fee:** $14, cash or check (in addition to the park entrance fee). **Parking:** At site.

FACILITIES

Number of RV Sites: 93. **Number of Tent-Only Sites:** 17. **Hookups:** None. **Each Site:** Picnic table, fire grate, some sites have bearproof box. **Dump Station:** No. **Laundry:** No. **Pay Phone:** Yes. **Rest Rooms and Showers:** Yes. **Fuel:** No. **Propane:** No. **Internal Roads:** Paved. **RV Service:** No. **Market:** 31 mi. west in Sanger. **Restaurant:** In Grant Grove Village. **General Store:** Yes. **Vending:** Yes. **Swimming:** No. **Playground:** No. **Other:** Some wheelchair-accessible facilities. **Activities:** Hiking, horseback riding, ranger-led activities. **Nearby Attractions:** Giant Sequoia National Monument; Sequoia National Park; Reedley Opera House, Museum & Mennonite Quilting Center. **Additional Information:** Fresno City & County CVB, (800) 788-0836; Reedley District Chamber of Commerce & Visitors Bureau, (559) 638-3548.

RESTRICTIONS

Pets: On 6 ft. leash; not allowed on trails. **Fires:** In fire grates only. **Alcoholic Beverages:** Allowed at site. **Vehicle Maximum Length:** 32 ft. **Other:** 14-day stay limit; no firearms; no food in vehicles (bear habitat).

TO GET THERE

From Grant Grove Village drive 0.2 mi. north on Hwy. 180. Turn left at the sign for Azalea and a quick left again into the campground.

LA GRANGE

Fleming Meadows

81 Bonds Flat Rd., La Grange 95329. T: (209) 852-2396 or marina (209) 852-2369; www.donpedrolake.com.

RV ★★★★ Tent ★★★

Beauty: ★★★★	Site Privacy: ★★
Spaciousness: ★★★	Quiet: ★★★
Security: ★★★★	Cleanliness: ★★★
Insect Control: ★★★	Facilities: ★★★★

In an area where summers are long and hot, Don Pedro Lake, 35 miles east of Modesto, is a marvelous sight. The rolling hills around its multi-pronged arms are speckled green with oaks and awash in golden grass. The reservoir features 160 miles of shoreline, endowing Fleming Meadows campground with no end of water vistas. There is a trade-off for those splendid views; many of the dirt-surfaced sites lack privacy and space. Of the four loops, sites in the A group are better shaded and seem a little more spacious. The optimum are A 24 and 25, which overlook the lake and are framed by a large oak; A 34, a comfortable unit with pull-through parking; and A 58, 59, 61, 62, and 64. Boaters may also indulge in primitive camping along the opposite shoreline. Not that a boat is necessary to enjoy this huge recreation area. Facilities include a sandy swimming lagoon that is six feet deep and two acres across, a softball field, horseshoe pits, volleyball, and no end of fishing opportunities. Boat service, fuel, a snack bar, and store are available at the marina.

BASICS

Operated By: Don Pedro Recreation Agency. **Open:** All year. **Site Assignment:** Reservations accepted w/ V, MC or check. **Registration:** At entrance booth. **Fee:** $12–$22, cash or V, MC. **Parking:** At site or designated area for walk-ins.

FACILITIES

Number of RV Sites: 231. **Number of Tent-Only Sites:** 36. **Hookups:** Water, electric (20, 30 amps), sewer. **Each Site:** Picnic table, fire grate, food storage box, some sites have a ramada. **Dump Station:** Yes. **Laundry:** Yes. **Pay Phone:** Yes. **Rest Rooms and Showers:** Yes. **Fuel:** No. **Propane:** Yes. **Internal Roads:** Paved. **RV Service:** No. **Market:** 8.5 mi south in La Grange. **Restaurant:** 8.5 mi. south in La Grange. **General Store:** Yes. **Vending:** Yes. **Swimming:** In lagoon. **Playground:** No. **Other:** Some wheelchair-accessible facilities, boat ramp, marina, beach. **Activities:** Fishing, waterskiing, motorboat & houseboat rentals, sailing, horseshoe pit, volleyball, softball. **Nearby Attractions:** Northern Mariposa County History Center in Coulterville; Turlock Lake State Recreation Area; Yosemite National Park. **Additional Information:** Coulterville Visitors Center, (209) 878-3074; Tuolumne County Visitors Bureau, (209) 533-4420 or (800) 446-1333.

RESTRICTIONS

Pets: Not allowed. **Fires:** In fire grates only. **Alcoholic Beverages:** Allowed. **Vehicle Maximum Length:** 50 ft. **Other:** 14-day stay limit; no fireworks.

TO GET THERE

From La Grange on Hwy. 132 drive 5 mi. north on La Grange Rd./J59. Turn right on Bonds Flat Rd. and proceed for another 3.3 mi. to the park entrance on the left.

LA HONDA

Portola Redwoods State Park

9000 Portola State Park Rd. Box F, La Honda 94020. T: (650) 948-9098 or reservations (800) 444-7275; F: (650) 948-0137; www.cal-parks.ca.gov or www.reserveamerica.com.

RV ★★★ Tent ★★★★

Beauty: ★★★★	Site Privacy: ★★★
Spaciousness: ★★★	Quiet: ★★★★
Security: ★★	Cleanliness: ★★★
Insect Control: ★★★	Facilities: ★★

As you make your way along the access road to Portola Redwoods State Park you'll enjoy some breathtaking valley views. Some may feel that is small reward for the clutch-grinding, white-knuckle drive from one hairpin curve to another. But on finally arriving at the park you may have the entire campground to yourself, especially if visiting midweek or out of season. The three small loops are deftly arranged across a hilly canyon to maximize the usable space. That is a good thing, as aside from the fallen giants that border some of the fern-dappled sites, screening is minimal. Still, this is a handsomely forested camp, with ancient moss-covered sentinels surrounded by their smaller, second-growth descendants, as well as oaks and azaleas. Site 28 overlooks a creek and is, with neighboring 29, among the better ones for privacy. Numbers 37 and 39 are attractive, too, though on the small side. Pull-through slots are available but drivers of long rigs should think twice about trying to navigate the goat-path of a road up to Portola.

Basics

Operated By: California Dept. of Parks & Recreation. **Open:** Mar.–Nov. **Site Assignment:** Reservations accepted w/V, MC, D. **Registration:** At entrance booth or visitor center. **Fee:** $12, cash or CA check. **Parking:** At site.

Facilities

Number of RV Sites: 46. **Number of Tent-Only Sites:** 14. **Hookups:** None. **Each Site:** Picnic table, fire grate, food storage box. **Dump Station:** No. **Laundry:** No. **Pay Phone:** Yes. **Rest Rooms and Showers:** Yes. **Fuel:** No. **Propane:** No. **Internal Roads:** Paved. **RV Service:** No. **Market:** 25 mi. east in Palo Alto. **Restaurant:** 25 mi. east in Palo Alto. **General Store:** No. **Vending:** No. **Swimming:** No. **Playground:** No. **Activities:** Hiking, ranger-led activities in summer, exploring redwood forests. **Nearby Attractions:** Palo Alto museums; state beaches along the coast; Mission Santa Clara de Asis & various museums in Santa Clara; San Jose museums, architecture & zoo. **Additional Information:** Palo Alto Chamber of Commerce, (650) 324-3121; Santa Clara CVB, (408) 224-9660 or (800) 272-6822; San Jose CVB, (888) SAN-JOSE.

Restrictions

Pets: On 6 ft. leash; not allowed on trails or in creeks. **Fires:** In fire grates only. **Alcoholic Beverages:** Allowed at site. **Vehicle Maximum Length:** 24 ft. **Other:** 14-day stay limit from Apr. 1–Oct. 31; no loaded firearms; no wood gathering; no bicycling; no horseback riding; no fishing.

To Get There

From Palo Alto drive south on I-280 and take the Page Mill Rd. Exit. Turn right (south) and drive 8.8 mi., straight through the stop sign, to Alpine Rd. Follow this road for 3.5 mi., then turn left on Portola State Park Rd. The park entrance is 3.1 mi. ahead.

LAKE ELSINORE

El Cariso North Campground

Hwy. 74/Ortega Hwy., Lake Elsinore 92530. T: (909) 736-1811; F: (909) 736-3002; www.r5.fs.fed.us/cleveland; mailroomr5cleveland@fs.fed.us.

RV ★★★ Tent ★★★

Beauty: ★★★	Site Privacy: ★★
Spaciousness: ★★★	Quiet: ★
Security: ★★★	Cleanliness: ★★★
Insect Control: ★★	Facilities: ★

This is a small roadside campground in the Cleveland National Forest, conveniently located along Hwy. 74, just ten miles west of I-15. It is a primitive facility with a single loop passing through a grove of aged oak trees and a sprinkling of pines. Sites are well shaded and deep, largely level, and equipped with dirt tent pads. Because Hwy. 74 connects to I-5 on the coast there tends to be a good deal of traffic flowing past El Cariso, making spots 10, 14, 19, 21, and 24, positioned toward the rear of the campground, the most desirable. The meandering creek (dry most of the year) that bisects the camp has been found to be the habitat of the endangered Southwestern Arroyo Toad. To protect it during its breeding cycle El Cariso North is closed from Apr. 1 through Sept. 30. A public telephone is available just across the street at the national forest fire station.

Basics

Operated By: Cleveland National Forest, Trabuco Ranger District. **Open:** From Oct. 1–Mar. 31. **Site Assignment:** First come, first served. **Registration:** At entrance kiosk. **Fee:** $15, cash or CA check. **Parking:** At site.

Facilities

Number of RV Sites: 24. **Number of Tent-Only Sites:** 0. **Hookups:** None. **Each Site:** Picnic table, fire grate, barbecue grill. **Dump Station:** No. **Laundry:** No. **Pay Phone:** No. **Rest Rooms and Showers:** Pit toilets, no showers. **Fuel:** No. **Propane:** No. **Internal Roads:** Paved. **RV Service:** No. **Market:** 1 mi. west in El Cariso Village. **Restaurant:** 10 mi. east in Lake Elsinore. **General Store:** No. **Vending:** No. **Swimming:** No. **Playground:** No. **Activities:** Hiking, boating, fishing. **Nearby Attractions:** Lake Elsinore, Orange Empire Railway Museum in Perris, Ortega Falls. **Additional Information:** Lake Elsinore Valley Chamber of Commerce, (909) 245-8848.

Restrictions

Pets: On 6 ft. leash. **Fires:** In fire grates only. **Alcoholic Beverages:** Allowed. **Vehicle Maximum Length:** 35 ft. **Other:** 14-day stay limit.

To Get There

From I-15 in Lake Elsinore drive 10 mi. west on Hwy. 74. The campground is on the right.

LAKEPORT

Clear Lake State Park

5300 Soda Bay Rd., Kelseyville 95451. T: (707) 279-4293 or reservations (800) 444-7275; www.cal-parks.ca.gov or www.reserveamerica.com.

RV ★★★★ Tent ★★★★

Beauty: ★★★★	Site Privacy: ★★★
Spaciousness: ★★★	Quiet: ★★★
Security: ★★★★	Cleanliness: ★★★
Insect Control: ★★	Facilities: ★★★

Clear Lake is one of the largest freshwater lakes in California. The angling in its shimmering blue-green waters is so good, particularly for bass, bluegill, and catfish, that you just might forget for a moment the other liquids for which this wine-producing region is renowned. There is an appealingly wild, untamed air to the forested hills around the lake, and the park takes full advantage of that by dispersing its campground into four zones ranging from lake and creekside on up into the higher woodland. The prime water sites are 58–60 in the Kelsey Creek loop, where plant life is highlighted by manzanita, willow, cottonwood, and black walnut. The opposite side of that loop overlooks a creek (very buggy in spring) and numbers 29, 31, 32, 38, 39, 41, 42, 44, and 45 are gratifyingly spacious and private. Pines, oak, and sycamore are the dominant tree species at the two Bayview circuits up the road, with 110–112, shady and overlooking the lake, ideal for small RVs. Cole Creek, close and parallel to the access road near the park entrance, is the least attractive of the camping areas.

Basics

Operated By: California Dept. of Parks & Recreation. **Open:** All year. **Site Assignment:** Reservations accepted w/V, MC, D. **Registration:** At entrance booth. **Fee:** $12, cash or CA check. **Parking:** At site.

Facilities

Number of RV Sites: 145. **Number of Tent-Only Sites:** 2. **Hookups:** None. **Each Site:** Picnic table, fire grate. **Dump Station:** Yes. **Laundry:** No. **Pay Phone:** Yes. **Rest Rooms and Showers:** Yes. **Fuel:** No. **Propane:** No. **Internal Roads:** Paved. **RV Service:** No. **Market:** 4 mi. south in Kelseyville. **Restaurant:** 4 mi. south in Kelseyville. **General Store:** No. **Vending:** No. **Swimming:** In Clear Lake. **Playground:** No. **Other:** Some wheelchair-accessible facilities, boat ramp, visitor center. **Activities:** Fishing, hiking, waterskiing, birding, kayak rentals. **Nearby Attractions:** Lakeport County Museum in Lakeport; Clear Lake Queen, Outrageous Waters Water Park & Fun Center & Anderson Marsh State Historic Park in Clearlake. **Additional Information:** Lakeport Chamber of Commerce, (707) 263-5092; Clearlake Chamber of Commerce, (707) 994-3600.

Restrictions

Pets: On 6 ft. leash. **Fires:** In fire grates only. **Alcoholic Beverages:** Allowed at site. **Vehicle Maximum Length:** 35 ft. **Other:** 14-day stay limit from Apr. 1–Oct. 1; no firearms; no wood gathering.

To Get There

From Lakeport head 8 mi. south on Hwy. 29 to Kelseyville. Turn left on Merritt Rd. which leads into Gaddy Ln. Drive 3.5 mi., then turn right on Soda Bay and continue for 1 mi. to the park entrance on the left.

LASSEN VOLCANIC NATIONAL PARK

Butte Lake

Butte Lake Rd., Mineral 96063. T: (530) 595-4444; F: (530) 595-3262; www.nps.gov/lavo.

RV ★★★★ Tent ★★★★

Beauty: ★★★★	Site Privacy: ★★★
Spaciousness: ★★★	Quiet: ★★★
Security: ★★★★	Cleanliness: ★★★
Insect Control: ★★★	Facilities: ★

The remote location of Butte Lake campground provides a tranquil respite from the crowds of sightseers thronging to Manzanita Lake, Summit Lakes, and such main attractions of Lassen Volcanic National Park as Bumpass Hell and the Sulfur Works. While only one site, B-1, actually enjoys a view of the stunning Butte Lake, the campground's proximity to the water, to a cinder peak, and to several fine hikes, makes it a winner. Roomy sites, evenly positioned across a slightly undulating hillside, are partially shaded by lodgepole pines and a smattering of ponderosas. As is typical in national park venues, few of them offer much privacy. Of the A and B circuits, the second area has the larger sites and more pull-through parking: best bets, in addition to B-1, are B-3, which overlooks the lava flow field, and the partly screened B-55. A pay phone, gasoline, and a general store are available at Old Station, 17 miles west on Hwy. 44. Butte Creek, a national forest camp on the dirt and gravel access road to Butte Lake, is a passable alternative when the latter is full or closed.

Basics

Operated By: National Park Service. **Open:** June 16 to Sept. 25, weather permitting. **Site Assignment:** First come, first served. **Registration:** At entrance kiosk. **Fee:** $10, cash or check (in addition to the park entrance fee). **Parking:** At site.

Facilities

Number of RV Sites: 42. **Number of Tent-Only Sites:** 0. **Hookups:** None. **Each Site:** Picnic table, fire grate, bearproof box. **Dump Station:** No. **Laundry:** No. **Pay Phone:** No. **Rest Rooms and Showers:** Vault toilets, no showers. **Fuel:** No. **Propane:** No. **Internal Roads:** Gravel, good condition. **RV Service:** No. **Market:** 48 mi. east in Susanville. **Restaurant:** 48 mi. east in Susanville. **General Store:** No. **Vending:** No. **Swimming:** In Butte Lake. **Playground:** No. **Other:** Some wheelchair-accessible facilities, boat launch. **Activities:** Hiking, fishing, boating (no motors), birding. **Nearby Attractions:** Hat Creek Recreation Area in Old Station; Lassen Historical Museum & Railroad Depot in Susanville. **Additional Information:** Burney Chamber of Commerce, (530) 335-2111.

Restrictions

Pets: On 6 ft. leash; not allowed on trails. **Fires:** In fire grates only. **Alcoholic Beverages:** Allowed at site. **Vehicle Maximum Length:** 35 ft. **Other:** 14-day stay limit; no loaded firearms; no wood gathering.

To Get There

From Old Station at the junction of Hwys. 44 and 89 drive 11 mi. east on Hwy. 44. Turn south (right) on Butte Lake Rd. and follow this dirt road for 6.5 mi. to the campground entrance on the right.

LASSEN VOLCANIC NATIONAL PARK

Manzanita Lake

Lassen Park Rd., Mineral 96063. T: (530) 595-4444; F: (530) 595-3262; www.nps.gov/lavo.

 ★★★  ★★★

Beauty: ★★★★ | Site Privacy: ★★★
Spaciousness: ★★★ | Quiet: ★★
Security: ★★★ | Cleanliness: ★★★
Insect Control: ★★★ | Facilities: ★★★

Lassen Volcanic National Park was established as a monument in 1907, and upgraded to national park status nine years later. An astoundingly beautiful chunk of the Cascade Mountain range, the park has hundreds of miles of hiking trails, several geothermal attractions, an abundance of wildlife, and a handful of excellent campgrounds. Of those, Manzanita Lake is one of the best, with its namesake body of glimmering water abutting it and snow-capped Mt. Lassen hovering above. Just five miles from Lassen's north entrance, the camp enjoys an illusion of privacy that stems in part from its thick concentration of various conifers, as well as from the pull-through and back-in sites being well-dispersed through a series of many loops. The shade provided by those evergreens keeps things cool and on the dark side, but tenters will find comfort in the spongy layer of pine needles that has accumulated on the forest floor. Best time to visit is Sept. to mid-Oct., when the park sees fewer visitors. Just remember, at an altitude of 5,890 feet, Manzanita Lake can be chilly most anytime of year: Extra layers of clothing and rain gear are advised. And use the bearproof boxes to protect your vehicle from a furry intruder. Many sites are wheelchair accessible.

Basics

Operated By: National Park Service. **Open:** May 25 to Sept. 25 w/ water, then without water until snow requires closure. **Site Assignment:** First come, first served. **Registration:** Self-registration at entrance kiosk. **Fee:** $14, cash or check (in addition to the park entrance fee). **Parking:** At site.

Facilities

Number of RV Sites: 179. **Number of Tent-Only Sites:** 0. **Hookups:** None. **Each Site:** Picnic table, fire ring, barbecue grill, bearproof box. **Dump Station:** Yes. **Laundry:** Yes. **Pay Phone:** Yes. **Rest Rooms and Showers:** Yes. **Fuel:** No. **Propane:** Yes. **Internal Roads:** Paved. **RV Service:** No. **Market:** 50 mi. west in Redding. **Restaurant:** 19 mi. west in Shingletown. **General Store:** Yes. **Vending:** Yes. **Swimming:** In Manzanita Lake. **Playground:** No. **Other:** Some wheelchair-accessible facilities, boat launch, Loomis Museum. **Activities:** Hiking, fishing, boating (no motors), bike rentals, ranger-led programs. **Nearby Attractions:** Westwood Museum & Paul Bunyan & Babe the Blue Ox Statues; Lassen National Scenic Byway (Hwys. 89-44-36); Lake Almanor; Hat Creek Recreation Area in Old Station. **Additional Information:** Burney Chamber of Commerce, (530) 335-2111.

Restrictions

Pets: On 6 ft. leash; not allowed on trails. **Fires:** In fire rings only. **Alcoholic Beverages:** Allowed at site. **Vehicle Maximum Length:** 35 ft. **Other:** 14-day stay limit; no firearms; no fireworks.

To Get There

From Redding drive 48 mi. east on Hwy. 44 to the junction w/ Hwy. 89. Drive 1 mi. south on Hwy. 89 (which becomes Lassen Park Rd. once you pass the park entrance station). Turn right onto the campground access road and continue for 0.5 mi. to the campground.

LAVA BEDS NATIONAL MONUMENT

Indian Well

Lava Beds National Monument Rd., Tulelake 96134. T: (530) 667-2282, ext. 230; F: (530) 667-2737; www.nps.gov/labe.

★★★ ★★★

Beauty: ★★★★ | Site Privacy: ★★★
Spaciousness: ★★★ | Quiet: ★★★
Security: ★★★ | Cleanliness: ★★★★
Insect Control: ★★★★ | Facilities: ★★

At just over 46,000 acres, Lava Beds National Monument may not seem a very large preserve. It manages, though, to pack a great deal within the confines of its boundaries. Located 55 miles south of Klamath Falls, Oregon, this high desert terrain has been dramatically painted by lava runoff from the Medicine Lake volcano, and a large swath of its rugged, rocky tufa–terrain saw the final curtain drawn on the Modoc war. Most dramatically, there are over 380 lava tube caves in the park, with two dozen developed for easy—and often thrilling—exploration. Most of those are a short drive from the campground, which is divided into a pair of loops. Cinder and spatter cones mark the approach to camp, and such desert scrub as sage brush, rabbit brush, bitter brush, and mountain mahogany contribute a hint of green to the bituminous landscape. Aged, gnarly junipers scattered over the undulating lava meadow shed shade on a few fortunate sites, such as the roomy, recessed B 25 and both A 5 and A 6, the latter two also being graced with expansive valley views. At 4,770 feet of elevation, nights at Indian Well can be quite windy and cold from late Oct. through early Apr. Keep an eye out for kangaroo rats after dark.

Basics

Operated By: National Park Service. **Open:** All year. **Site Assignment:** First come, first served. **Registration:** At entrance kiosk. **Fee:** $10, cash or check. **Parking:** At site.

Facilities

Number of RV Sites: 43. **Number of Tent-Only Sites:** 0. **Hookups:** None. **Each Site:** Picnic table, fire ring, barbecue grill. **Dump Station:** No. **Laundry:** No. **Pay Phone:** Yes. **Rest Rooms and Showers:** Seasonal flush toilets, vault toilets, no showers. **Fuel:** No. **Propane:** No. **Internal Roads:** Paved. **RV Service:** No. **Market:** 14 mi. south in Tionesta (basic supplies). **Restaurant:** 30 mi. north in Tulelake. **General Store:** No. **Vending:** Yes. **Swimming:** No. **Playground:** No. **Other:** Some wheelchair-accessible facilities, visitor center. **Activities:** Hiking, lava tube dwelling, birding. **Nearby Attractions:** Tule Lake & Klamath National Wildlife Refuges; Medicine Lake Recreation Area; Petroglyph Section at the northeast entrance of Lava Beds National Monument. **Additional Information:** Tulelake Chamber of Commerce, (530) 667-5312.

Restrictions

Pets: On 6 ft. leash; not allowed on trails. **Fires:** In fire rings only. **Alcoholic Beverages:** Allowed at site. **Vehicle Maximum Length:** 30 ft. **Other:** 14-day stay limit; no loaded firearms; wood gathering only in designated areas.

To Get There

From Tulelake drive 26 mi. south on Hwy. 139. Turn right (west) on Tionesta Rd. and continue for 2.7 mi. Turn right again on Lava Beds National Monument Rd. and proceed for 14 mi. The campground entrance is to the right, directly across the visitor center.

LEE VINING

Aspen Grove

Hwy. 120, Lee Vining 93541. T: (760) 932-5451; F: (760) 932-5458.

RV ★★★ Tent ★★★

Beauty: ★★★★ Site Privacy: ★★★
Spaciousness: ★★★ Quiet: ★★★
Security: ★★ Cleanliness: ★★★
Insect Control: ★★★ Facilities: ★

There is an enchanting quality to the raw, mountainous beauty of Aspen Grove, particularly in spring, just after its many aspens have leafed out into a fluttering luminescence. Jeffrey pines, sage, and other high desert scrub compose the complement of vegetation at this creekside, county-operated camp, which is just five miles west of Lee Vining along the Tioga Rd. At 7,500 feet elevation, you'll find breathtaking views of the snow-laced Sierra Nevada peaks all around, with Mono Dome, at 10,622 feet, dominating the scene. Some of the dirt-packed, somewhat rocky sites are on uneven ground, others (most notably, those by the creek) are squeezed for space. The lion's share, though, are delightfully large and very recessed. Among the better choices for RVs are 22, 23, and 25, facing the creek. Great tenting spots include 54, also by the creek; 18, hidden among pines and horsetail grass; and, away from the water, 37 and 39, both being very private. Similarly rustic sites are available at Big Bend campground, half a mile east.

Basics

Operated By: Mono County Building & Parks Dept. **Open:** May through Oct., weather permitting. **Site Assignment:** First come, first served. **Registration:** At entrance kiosk. **Fee:** $7, cash only. **Parking:** At site.

Facilities

Number of RV Sites: 58. **Number of Tent-Only Sites:** 0. **Hookups:** None. **Each Site:** Picnic table, makeshift fire ring. **Dump Station:** No. **Laundry:** No. **Pay Phone:** No. **Rest Rooms and Showers:** Pit & portable toilets, no showers. **Fuel:** No. **Propane:** No. **Internal Roads:** Dirt, rocky & bumpy. **RV Service:** No. **Market:** 6 mi. northeast in Lee Vining. **Restaurant:** 6 mi. northeast in Lee Vining. **General Store:** No. **Vending:** No. **Swimming:** No. **Playground:** No. **Activities:** Fishing, hiking, photography. **Nearby Attractions:** Yosemite National Park; Mono Lake Tufa State Reserve in Lee Vining; Bodie State Historic Park in Bridgeport. **Additional Information:** Lee Vining Chamber of Commerce, (760) 647-6629; Yosemite Area Traveler Information, (209) 723-3153.

Restrictions

Pets: On 10 ft. leash. **Fires:** In fire rings only. **Alcoholic Beverages:** Allowed. **Vehicle Maximum Length:** 40 ft. **Other:** No stay limit.

To Get There

Just south of Lee Vining on US 395 head west on Hwy. 120. Drive 3.2 mi. and turn left onto Poole Power Plant Rd. Make a quick right onto the campground access road and continue for 1.5 mi. to the entrance on the left.

LEE VINING

Ellery Lake

Hwy. 120, Lee Vining 93541. T: (760) 873-2400 or (760) 647-3044; F: (760) 647-3046; www.r5.fs.fed.us/inyo.

RV ★★★★ Tent ★★★

Beauty: ★★★★★ Site Privacy: ★★
Spaciousness: ★★ Quiet: ★★
Security: ★★★★ Cleanliness: ★★★
Insect Control: ★ Facilities: ★

There is only one site here with a view of the camp's namesake Ellery Lake, lucky 13, a walk-in. Don't let that, or the overall lack of privacy and elbowroom, nettle you, though. This is an exquisite environment, surrounded by the jagged, snow-iced mountain peaks of Lee Vining Canyon, with a small creek gurgling by. The ground is level, parking slips paved, and a smattering of lodgepole pines and low-lying willows vie with boulders and campers for ground space. You can fish for trout in the creek or, better still, the nearby lake. The campground, which is at an altitude of 9,500 feet, is also a fine base for day trips into Yosemite National Park's high country, its east entrance being a scant three miles away. Nearly half the sites are walk-ins for tenters, with access to them cutting directly through other sites, an unfortunate sacrifice in privacy. The better spots are 9–14, shielded from Hwy. 120 in a nook behind talus rock. A general store is 0.5 miles to the west.

Basics

Operated By: Sierra Recreation, concessionaire. **Open:** June through Oct., weather permitting. **Site Assignment:** First come, first served. **Registration:** At entrance kiosk. **Fee:** $11, cash or check. **Parking:** At site.

Facilities

Number of RV Sites: 6. **Number of Tent-Only Sites:** 6. **Hookups:** None. **Each Site:** Picnic table, fire grate. **Dump Station:** No. **Laundry:** No. **Pay Phone:** No. **Rest Rooms and Showers:** Vault toilets, no showers. **Fuel:** No. **Propane:** No. **Internal Roads:** Paved. **RV Service:** No. **Market:** 11 mi. east in Lee Vining. **Restaurant:** 11 mi. east in Lee Vining. **General Store:** No. **Vending:** No. **Swimming:** No. **Playground:** No. **Other:** Some wheelchair-accessible facilities. **Activities:** Fishing, hiking, photography. **Nearby Attractions:** Yosemite National Park; Mono Lake Tufa State Reserve in Lee Vining; Bodie State Historic Park in Bridgeport. **Additional Information:** Lee Vining Chamber of Commerce, (760) 647-6629; Yosemite Area Traveler Information, (209) 723-3153.

Restrictions

Pets: On leash. **Fires:** In fire grates only. **Alcoholic Beverages:** Allowed. **Vehicle Maximum Length:** 30 ft. **Other:** 14-day stay limit.

To Get There

Just south of Lee Vining on US 395, head west on Hwy. 120. Drive 10 mi. and turn left into the campground.

LEWISTON

Cooper Gulch

Trinity Dam Blvd., Lewiston 96052. T: (530) 623-2121; F: (530) 623-6010; www.r5.fs.fed.us/shasta-trinity.

RV ★★★★ Tent ★★★

Beauty: ★★★★ Site Privacy: ★★
Spaciousness: ★★ Quiet: ★★★
Security: ★★★★ Cleanliness: ★★★★
Insect Control: ★★★ Facilities: ★

The first thing you may notice about Cooper Gulch is the high tension wires that run directly over the campground. That impression won't linger. Not when you see how close the five level sites are to the edge of Lewiston Lake. That they are also close to each other and lack privacy is not really a problem, either, since almost everybody devotes their attention to the rippling water just a few steps away. Bring your hammock and anchor it to a couple of the pines and incense cedars that shade this charming spot. And don't forget your canoe or kayak, which can be launched from the small dirt ramp right in camp. It is hard to go wrong with any of these medium-small, pine needle–carpeted sites, but 4 is closest to the lake and 5, sheltered by oaks, is the most private. Amazingly, a host occupies one of the five coveted slots in summer.

Basics

Operated By: Hodge Management, concessionaire. **Open:** Apr. through Nov. **Site Assignment:** First come, first served. **Registration:** At entrance kiosk. **Fee:** $11; cash or check. **Parking:** At site.

Facilities

Number of RV Sites: 5. **Number of Tent-Only Sites:** 0. **Hookups:** None. **Each Site:** Picnic table, fire grate. **Dump Station:** No. **Laundry:** No. **Pay Phone:** No. **Rest Rooms and Showers:** Vault toilets, no showers. **Fuel:** No. **Propane:** No. **Internal Roads:** Paved. **RV Service:** No. **Market:** 4 mi. south in Lewiston. **Restaurant:** 4 mi. south in Lewiston. **General Store:** No. **Vending:** No. **Swimming:** No. **Playground:** No. **Other:** Some wheelchair-accessible facilities, small boat launch. **Activities:** Fishing, boating, hiking, birding. **Nearby Attractions:** Weaverville museums, National Historic District & Joss House State Historic Park; Historic Trinity River Bridge in Lewiston. **Additional Information:** Weaverville Chamber of Commerce, (530) 623-3840; Trinity County Chamber of Commerce, (530) 623-6101 or (800) 487-4648.

RESTRICTIONS

Pets: On 6 ft. leash. **Fires:** In fire grates only. **Alcoholic Beverages:** Allowed. **Vehicle Maximum Length:** 16 ft. **Other:** 14-day stay limit.

TO GET THERE

From Redding drive 26 mi. west on Hwy. 299 to Trinity Dam Blvd./Lewiston Exit. Turn right and continue for 8.6 mi. to the campground entrance on the right.

LIVERMORE

Del Valle Regional Park

7000 Del Valle Rd., Livermore 94550. T: (510) 636-1684 or reservations (510) 562-2267; www.ebparks.org.

RV: ★★★★ Tent: ★★★★

Beauty: ★★★★	Site Privacy: ★★★
Spaciousness: ★★★	Quiet: ★★★
Security: ★★★★	Cleanliness: ★★
Insect Control: ★★★	Facilities: ★★★

Del Valle Regional Park is a quiet, unassuming place that just happens to be one of the more beautiful of the many parklands in the immediate Bay Area. A part of the Diablo Range, this rugged canyon setting consists of grassy hills, meadows punctuated by thick concentrations of oak, eucalyptus, knob cone pine, and sycamore, and at its heart a narrow reservoir lake that stretches five miles from end to end. Windsurfers and sailing enthusiasts take to the water like a child to chocolate, with motorboats restricted to a maximum speed of ten miles per hour. Fishing conditions are only average, despite regular plantings of rainbow trout. There are no views of the lake from the campground, but roomy, grass-covered sites are spaced well apart over a double loop, helping to compensate for that handicap. Birders will find pleasure in the many species that make this territory their home, including several wild turkeys and a pair of peacocks. The park loses points, though, for haphazard maintenance: during a recent tour we found sites littered with above average amounts of plastic, paper, bottle caps, and cigarette butts. The open-air restrooms are also in urgent need of an overhaul.

BASICS

Operated By: East Bay Regional Park District. **Open:** All year. **Site Assignment:** Reservations accepted w/ V, MC. **Registration:** At entrance booth. **Fee:** $15–$18, cash or V, MC. **Parking:** At site.

FACILITIES

Number of RV Sites: 150. **Number of Tent-Only Sites:** 0. **Hookups:** Water, sewer. **Each Site:** Picnic table, fire grate. **Dump Station:** Yes. **Laundry:** No. **Pay Phone:** Yes. **Rest Rooms and Showers:** Yes. **Fuel:** No. **Propane:** No. **Internal Roads:** Paved. **RV Service:** No. **Market:** 9.5 mi. north in Livermore. **Restaurant:** 9.5 mi. north in Livermore. **General Store:** Yes, in summer. **Vending:** No. **Swimming:** In designated areas of Lake Del Valle. **Playground:** No. **Other:** Some wheelchair-accessible facilities, marina, boat launch. **Activities:** Hiking, fishing, horseback riding, bicycling, boat & sailboard rentals, windsurfing, sailing, nature programs. **Nearby Attractions:** Mission San Jose & Ardenwood Historic Farm in Fremont; winery tours. **Additional Information:** Livermore Chamber of Commerce, (925) 447-1606.

RESTRICTIONS

Pets: On leash, $1 fee. **Fires:** In fire grates only. **Alcoholic Beverages:** Allowed at site & picnic areas. **Vehicle Maximum Length:** 35 ft. **Other:** 14-day stay limit; no firearms.

TO GET THERE

From Livermore and Hwy. 84 head south on South Livermore Ave., which changes into Tesla Rd. After 2.4 mi. turn right on Mines Rd. Continue for 3.6 mi. and bear right on Del Valle Park Rd. The park entrance is 3.2 mi. ahead.

LONE PINE

Whitney Portal

Whitney Portal Rd., Lone Pine 93545. T: (760) 876-6200 or reservations (877) 444-6777; F: (760) 876-6202; www.r5.fs.fed.us/inyo or www.reserveusa.com.

RV: ★★★★ Tent: ★★★★

Beauty: ★★★★★	Site Privacy: ★★★
Spaciousness: ★★★	Quiet: ★★★
Security: ★★★	Cleanliness: ★★★
Insect Control: ★★★	Facilities: ★★

Even if you don't plan to hike Mt. Whitney, which, at 14,495 feet, is the highest peak in the lower 48 states, this campground is a worthwhile, breathtaking retreat. From its rocky, pine-shrouded sites, up to the aspen-fringed trailhead, from the many streams noisily cascading down the mountain to the saw-toothed, jaw-like peaks that hover menacingly above, this is one spectacular, picture-perfect scene. As you lounge by your tent at 8,000 feet elevation, low-floating clouds seem close enough to reach out and grab. Boulders provide respectable privacy between closely-grouped sites, and shade is derived from Jeffrey and ponderosa pines, as well as mountain mahogany. The most secluded sites are 8 and 9, flanked by large slabs of granite. Avoid the spots just below Whitney Portal Rd., which pick up more traffic noise than the others, and try to visit on a weekday, when there are fewer mountain climbers in camp. The trailhead picnic area is an Arcadian delight.

BASICS

Operated By: American Land & Leisure, concessionaire. **Open:** Mid-May through mid-Oct., weather permitting. **Site Assignment:** Reservations accepted w/ V, MC, D. **Registration:** At entrance kiosk. **Fee:** $14, cash or check. **Parking:** At site.

FACILITIES

Number of RV Sites: 43. **Number of Tent-Only Sites:** 0. **Hookups:** None. **Each Site:** Picnic table, fire grate or barbecue grill, some sites have bearproof box. **Dump Station:** No. **Laundry:** No. **Pay Phone:** No. **Rest Rooms and Showers:** Chemical toilets, no showers. **Fuel:** No. **Propane:** No. **Internal Roads:** Paved, windy. **RV Service:** No. **Market:** 12 mi. east in Lone Pine. **Restaurant:** 12 mi. east in Lone Pine. **General Store:** Yes. **Vending:** No. **Swimming:** No. **Playground:** No. **Other:** Some wheelchair-accessible facilities, snack bar. **Activities:** Hiking, fishing, photography. **Nearby Attractions:** Manzanar National Historic Site & Eastern California Museum in Independence; Diaz Lake Recreation Area in Lone Pine; Mount Whitney. **Additional Information:** Lone Pine Chamber of Commerce, (760) 876-4444; Independence Chamber of Commerce, (760) 878-0084.

RESTRICTIONS

Pets: On leash. **Fires:** In fire grates only. **Alcoholic Beverages:** Allowed. **Vehicle Maximum Length:** 32 ft. **Other:** 7-day stay limit.

TO GET THERE

From Lone Pine on US 395 drive 12 mi. west on Whitney Portal Rd. to the campground on the left.

LOS BAÑOS

San Luis Reservoir State Recreation Area, San Luis Creek Campground

31426 Gonzaga Rd., Gustine 95322. T: (209) 826-1196 or reservations (800) 444-7275; F: (209) 826-0284; www.cal-parks.ca.gov or www.reserveamerica.com.

RV: ★★★★ Tent: ★★★

Beauty: ★★★★	Site Privacy: ★★
Spaciousness: ★★★	Quiet: ★★★★
Security: ★★★★	Cleanliness: ★★★★
Insect Control: ★★★	Facilities: ★★★

San Luis Reservoir lies in the heart of California's valley region, just off of I-5, about 40 miles south of Modesto. Summer starts early in these parts, with the sun scorching the neighboring hills brown by Apr. Water sports are therefore the logical activity of choice and fortunately there is usually enough H_2O in the reservoir to satisfy boaters and swimmers throughout the hot season. Of the three campgrounds in the park, only San Luis Creek on the O'Neill Forebay has hookups. It is a grassy, peaceful camp with many of its fairly exposed, roomy sites set close to the shore. Adding a splash of color to the setting are eucalyptus trees, pines, and sycamores. The latter are still too small to cast much shade but they are just large enough to attract larks and other song birds. The only off-key note is the presence of power lines looming above a few of the sites. Showers are available across the street at Basalt Campground.

BASICS

Operated By: California Dept. of Parks & Recreation. **Open:** All year. **Site Assignment:** Reservations accepted w/ V, MC, D. **Registration:** At entrance booth. **Fee:** $14, cash or CA check. **Parking:** At site.

FACILITIES

Number of RV Sites: 53. **Number of Tent-Only Sites:** 0. **Hookups:** Water, electric (30 amps). **Each Site:** Picnic table, fire grate. **Dump Station:** Yes. **Laundry:** No. **Pay Phone:** Yes. **Rest Rooms and Showers:** Pit toilets, no showers. **Fuel:** No. **Propane:** No. **Internal Roads:** Paved. **RV Service:** No. **Market:** 15 mi. east in Los Baños. **Restaurant:** 15 mi. east in Los Baños. **General Store:** No. **Vending:** No. **Swimming:** In the reservoir. **Playground:** No. **Other:** Some wheelchair-accessible facilities. **Activities:** Fishing, boating, birding, hiking. **Nearby Attractions:** Modesto museums; Mission San Juan Bautista; Los Baños Great Valley Grasslands State Park & Wildlife Area. **Additional Information:** Santa Nella Chamber of Commerce, (209) 826-8282; Los Baños Chamber of Commerce, (209) 826-2495.

Restrictions

Pets: On 6 ft. leash. **Fires:** In fire grates only. **Alcoholic Beverages:** Allowed at site. **Vehicle Maximum Length:** 30 ft. **Other:** 14-day stay limit from May 1– Sept. 30; no firearms; no wood gathering.

To Get There

From Gilroy on US 101 follow Hwy. 152 east for 36 mi. Turn left into the park. The campground entrance is 1 mi. ahead to the left.

LUCIA
Kirk Creek

Hwy. 1, Lucia 93921. T: (831) 385-5434; F: (831) 385-0628; www.r5.fs.fed.us/lospadres.

RV ★★★ Tent ★★★★

Beauty: ★★★★ Site Privacy: ★★★
Spaciousness: ★★ Quiet: ★★★
Security: ★★★ Cleanliness: ★★★
Insect Control: ★★ Facilities: ★

This is a rough-cut, wild-looking campground with a grassy, unmanicured feel to its sites. One might even say "bucolic," a quality that is entirely appropriate given its location, just off Hwy. 1 along the unspoiled Big Sur coast. Coastal chaparral and shrubs provide excellent screening for sites that are mostly small, unshaded and tend to tilt toward the ocean. That the handsome national forest land slopes steeply water-ward has an upside in the auditorium effect of projecting the roar of the surf into camp—thus drowning out the din of passing traffic—and endowing most slots with commanding views of the Pacific. Best for privacy along the figure-8 loop are 8, 9, 21, 22, and 11, with the latter located next to the beach. Be sure to avoid tiny number 1, which picks up too much road noise. The only abrasive chord is struck by the nightly fee of $16, a hefty sum given the Spartan facilities. Golden poppies color the hillside in spring.

Basics

Operated By: Parks Management, concessionaire. **Open:** All year. **Site Assignment:** First come, first served. **Registration:** At entrance kiosk. **Fee:** $16, cash or check. **Parking:** At site.

Facilities

Number of RV Sites: 32. **Number of Tent-Only Sites:** 3. **Hookups:** None. **Each Site:** Picnic table, fire ring, barbecue grill. **Dump Station:** No. **Laundry:** No. **Pay Phone:** No. **Rest Rooms and Showers:** Flush toilets, no showers. **Fuel:** No. **Propane:** No. **Internal Roads:** Paved. **RV Service:** No. **Market:** 4 mi. north in Lucia. **Restaurant:** 4 mi. north in Lucia. **General Store:** No. **Vending:** No. **Swimming:** No. **Playground:** No. **Activities:** Hiking, fishing. **Nearby Attractions:** Hearst Castle & National Geographic Theater in San Simeon; Mission San Antonio de Padua in Jolon; Limekiln State Park; Big Sur coast. **Additional Information:** Big Sur Chamber, (831) 667-2100.

Restrictions

Pets: On leash. **Fires:** In fire rings only. **Alcoholic Beverages:** Allowed. **Vehicle Maximum Length:** 30 ft. **Other:** 14-day stay limit; no firearms; no wood gathering.

To Get There

From Lucia on Hwy. 1 drive 4 mi. south and turn right into the campground.

LUCIA
Ponderosa

Nacimiento Fergusson Rd., Lucia 93921. T: (831) 385-5434; F: (831) 385-0628; www.r5.fs.fed.us/lospadres.

RV ★★★ Tent ★★★★

Beauty: ★★★★ Site Privacy: ★★★★
Spaciousness: ★★★★ Quiet: ★★★★
Security: ★ Cleanliness: ★★★
Insect Control: ★ Facilities: ★

This isolated camp is located within the tree-choked Los Padres National Forest, 15 miles and an hour's drive from the coast along the windy, occasionally broken up, mountainous Nacimiento Rd. On pulling into Ponderos,a don't expect that Hoss and Little Joe will be there to greet you. In fact, there may not be anyone present at all, which is one of the virtues of this pretty property, in contrast to its overflowing counterparts along the Big Sur coast. Roomy sites of dirt and grass are well separated along the serpentine loop, with a babbling creek running by several and a handful of walk-ins especially secluded. This hilly campground lies at 1,650 feet of elevation near the crest of the Santa Lucia Mountain range and is shaded more by live oaks, oddly, than its namesake pines. We prefer this facility to Nacimiento, two miles to the west, the latter featuring exposed, shallow sites that are very close to the road.

Basics

Operated By: Parks Management Company, concessionaire. **Open:** All year, weather permitting. **Site Assignment:** First come, first served. **Registration:** At entrance kiosk. **Fee:** $12, cash or check. **Parking:** At site.

Facilities

Number of RV Sites: 18. **Number of Tent-Only Sites:** 5. **Hookups:** None. **Each Site:** Picnic table, fire ring, barbecue grill. **Dump Station:** No. **Laundry:** No. **Pay Phone:** No. **Rest Rooms and Showers:** Vault toilets, no showers. **Fuel:** No. **Propane:** No. **Internal Roads:** Paved. **RV Service:** No. **Market:** 20 mi. northwest in Lucia. **Restaurant:** 20 mi. northwest in Lucia. **General Store:** No. **Vending:** No. **Swimming:** In Pacific Ocean, if you dare. **Playground:** No. **Other:** Some wheelchair-accessible facilities. **Activities:** Hiking, fishing. **Nearby Attractions:** Hearst Castle & National Geographic Theater in San Simeon; Mission San Antonio de Padua in Jolon; Limekiln State Park; Big Sur coast; Pinnacles National Monument. **Additional Information:** Big Sur Chamber, (831) 667-2100.

Restrictions

Pets: On leash. **Fires:** In fire rings only. **Alcoholic Beverages:** Allowed. **Vehicle Maximum Length:** 35 ft. **Other:** 14-day stay limit.

To Get There

From Lucia on Hwy. 1 drive 4 mi. south. Turn inland (left) on Nacimiento Fergusson Rd. and follow this windy, ascending road for 14 mi. The campground entrance is to the right.

MADERA
Millerton Lake State Recreation Area

5290 Millerton Rd., Friant 93626. T: (559) 822-2332 or reservations (800) 444-7275; F: (559) 822-2319; www.cal-parks.ca.gov or www.reserveamerica.com.

RV ★★★★ Tent ★★★★

Beauty: ★★★★ Site Privacy: ★★★★
Spaciousness: ★★★ Quiet: ★★★
Security: ★★★ Cleanliness: ★★★
Insect Control: ★★ Facilities: ★★★

State officials estimate that on holiday weekends as many as 25,000 people descend on Millerton Lake, an indication of its popularity, as well as when to avoid visiting. Beyond the charming setting, amid a series of wrinkly, dimpled hills, with long, golden grass and monzo-granite gleaming in the sun, the attraction is obvious, given the scorching temperatures here during summer months. But while the lake is the main show, the campground is no ugly stepchild. Its level sites of grass and dirt are very well scattered over an extended series of loops, endowing many with privacy and prime vantages of the water. Several kinds of oak grace the domain, as well as sycamores, willow, eucalyptus, and various conifers, providing a balance of shade and filtered sun. The best of many fine sites is 59, on a point of land jutting out into the lake; 6–8 are on the small side but secluded. There are also 25 boat-in spots, and a marina with a snackbar and vending machines. Be sure to visit the Millerton Courthouse, circa 1867, preserved within the park.

Basics

Operated By: California Dept. of Parks & Recreation. **Open:** All year. **Site Assignment:** Reservations accepted w/ V, MC, D. **Registration:** At entrance booth. **Fee:** $12–$18, cash or CA check. **Parking:** At site.

Facilities

Number of RV Sites: 138. **Number of Tent-Only Sites:** 0. **Hookups:** Water, electric (20, 30, 50 amps), sewer. **Each Site:** Picnic table, fire grate, some sites have food storage box and/or ramada. **Dump Station:** Yes. **Laundry:** No. **Pay Phone:** Yes. **Rest Rooms and Showers:** Yes. **Fuel:** No. **Propane:** No. **Internal Roads:** Paved. **RV Service:** No. **Market:** 23 mi. west in Madera.

Restaurant: 23 mi. west in Madera. **General Store:** No. **Vending:** No. **Swimming:** In Millerton Lake. **Playground:** No. **Other:** Some wheelchair-accessible facilities, marina, boat launch, beach when water level drops. **Activities:** Fishing, boat rentals, horseback riding, hiking, waterskiing, windsurfing. **Nearby Attractions:** Museums, Forestiere Underground Gardens, Chaffee Zoological Gardens, Rotary Storyland & Playland in Fresno; Madera County Historical Museum & Quady Winery. **Additional Information:** Fresno City & County CVB, (800) 788-0836; Madera Chamber of Commerce, (559) 673-3563.

Restrictions

Pets: On 6 ft. leash. **Fires:** In fire grates only. **Alcoholic Beverages:** Allowed at site. **Vehicle Maximum Length:** 36 ft. **Other:** 14-day stay limit from May 1–Sept. 15, 30 for the rest of the year; no firearms; no wood gathering.

To Get There

From Madera drive 16 mi. east on Hwy. 145. Proceed through the intersection w/ Hwy. 41 (where Hwy. 145 becomes Millerton Rd.). Continue 3.5 mi., then bear left. After 1.3 mi. turn right. The campground is 2.2 mi. ahead.

MALIBU
Leo Carillo State Park

Pacific Coast Hwy., Malibu 90265. T: (805) 488-5223; www.cal-parks.ca.gov or www.reserveamerica.com.

RV: ★★★★ Tent: ★★★★

Beauty: ★★★★	Site Privacy: ★★★
Spaciousness: ★★★★	Quiet: ★★★
Security: ★★★★	Cleanliness: ★★★
Insect Control: ★★	Facilities: ★★★

The campground at Leo Carillo State Park is located directly across the Pacific Coast Hwy. from a wide sandy beach. While this detached position may at first appear to be a drawback, it is in fact the best of two worlds, with easy access to the ocean via a walkway under the road and a campground free of coastal winds due to its dramatic nest by the base of the steep Santa Monica Mountains. Gnarly sycamore trees overhang grassy sites along a double loop, with most being fairly spacious and decently screened by such riparian chaparral as bay willow, buckwheat, coastal sage and black walnut. The largest and most private sites, 54, 57, 59, 61, 63, and 66, are on the west side of camp along the creek. On weekends, restrooms can be in an atrocious state, but overall the campground is surprisingly clean, given the high traffic it receives from large family groups. Reservations are highly recommended from Easter through mid-Sept. Rangers routinely patrol the grounds.

Basics

Operated By: California Dept. of Parks & Recreation. **Open:** All year. **Site Assignment:** Reservations recommended; V, MC, D. **Registration:** At entrance booth. **Fee:** $12, cash or CA check. **Parking:** At site.

Facilities

Number of RV Sites: 139. **Number of Tent-Only Sites:** 1. **Hookups:** None. **Each Site:** Picnic table, fire ring. **Dump Station:** Yes. **Laundry:** No. **Pay Phone:** Yes. **Rest Rooms and Showers:** Yes. **Fuel:** No. **Propane:** No. **Internal Roads:** Paved. **RV Service:** No. **Market:** 5.5 mi. east in Malibu. **Restaurant:** 5.5 mi. east in Malibu. **General Store:** No. **Vending:** No. **Swimming:** In Pacific Ocean. **Playground:** No. **Other:** Some wheelchair-accessible facilities. **Activities:** Surfing, fishing, beachcombing, tide pools, cave & reef exploring. **Nearby Attractions:** Hollywood's theme parks, J. P. Getty Museum, La Brea Tar Pits, Will Rogers State Historic Park, Disneyland, historic Ventura. **Additional Information:** Santa Monica Mountains District, (810) 706-1310.

Restrictions

Pets: On 6 ft. leash. **Fires:** In fire rings only. **Alcoholic Beverages:** Allowed at site. **Vehicle Maximum Length:** 36 ft. **Other:** 7-day stay limit in summer, 14-day stay limit for the rest of the year; no firearms; no wood gathering.

To Get There

At the intersection of Trancas Canyon and Broad Beach in Malibu, drive 5.5 mi. west on the Pacific Coast Hwy. The park entrance is on the right (north) side of the road.

MALIBU
Malibu Beach RV Park

25801 Pacific Coast Hwy., Malibu 90265. T: (800) 622-6052 or (310) 456-6052; F: (310) 456-2532; www.malibubeachrv.com; info@maliburv.com.

RV: ★★★★ Tent: ★★★

Beauty: ★★★★	Site Privacy: ★★
Spaciousness: ★★	Quiet: ★★★
Security: ★★★	Cleanliness: ★★★★
Insect Control: ★★★	Facilities: ★★★★★

On the surface Malibu Beach looks like just another run-of-the-mill RV facility. Caravans are wedged one next to another, with a tenting area attached to the end of the serpentine camp lane seemingly as an afterthought. Probe a bit, though, and you will find this a superior property, just six miles west of Malibu on the Pacific Coast Hwy. on the inland side of the road. Shrewd terracing stretches sites up a bluff, thus maximizing vistas of the ocean. Yes, site privacy is nearly nil, but with that ocean panorama and the beautiful sunsets, who cares! Eucalyptus, palms, pines, and sycamores decorate the landscape and while they do little to provide shade, at least they don't obstruct the view. Though they will probably be taken already, try to get any of numbers 6–33 or V1–V13. Even the dirt walk-in tenting area atop the bluff is attractive, with small sycamores providing shade. Double-wide sites and pull-throughs are available, as well as a hot tub, game room, and Internet connection.

Basics

Operated By: Malibu Beach RV Park. **Open:** All year. **Site Assignment:** Reservations recommended; V, MC, D, AE, DC. **Registration:** At entrance office. **Fee:** $22–$48 in summer (May 1–Sept. 30); $18–$40 in winter (Oct. 1–Apr. 30). **Parking:** At site.

Facilities

Number of RV Sites: 115. **Number of Tent-Only Sites:** 50. **Hookups:** Water, electric (30, 50 amps), sewer, cable TV, Internet. **Each Site:** Picnic table, barbecue grill. **Dump Station:** Yes. **Laundry:** Yes. **Pay Phone:** Yes. **Rest Rooms and Showers:** Yes. **Fuel:** No. **Propane:** Yes. **Internal Roads:** Paved. **RV Service:** No. **Market:** 3 mi. east in Malibu. **Restaurant:** 3 mi. east in Malibu. **General Store:** Yes. **Vending:** Yes. **Swimming:** In Pacific Ocean. **Playground:** Yes. **Other:** Some wheelchair-accessible facilities, game room. **Activities:** Surfing, fishing, hiking, dolphin & whale-watching. **Nearby Attractions:** Hollywood's theme parks, J. P. Getty Museum, La Brea Tar Pits, Will Rogers State Historic Park, Venice Beach Boardwalk, Santa Monica Pier & museums. **Additional Information:** Malibu Chamber of Commerce, (310) 456-9025.

Restrictions

Pets: Well behaved pets in RV sites only; no rotweilers, pit bulls, German sheperds, Doberman pinschers. **Fires:** No wood fires allowed. **Alcoholic Beverages:** Allowed. **Vehicle Maximum Length:** 45 ft. **Other:** 7-month stay limit in winter.

To Get There

From the Pacific Coast Hwy. in Malibu turn inland just 3 mi. west of Coral Canyon Rd. The campground is well signposted.

MALIBU
Malibu Creek State Park

1925 Las Virgenes Rd., Calabasas 91302. T: (818) 880-0367; www.cal-parks.ca.gov or www.reserveamerica.com.

RV: ★★★ Tent: ★★★★

Beauty: ★★★★	Site Privacy: ★★★
Spaciousness: ★★★	Quiet: ★★★
Security: ★★★★	Cleanliness: ★★★
Insect Control: ★★★	Facilities: ★★

If you managed to get a site here without a reservation it may be time to buy a lottery ticket, that's how good your luck is. "Popular" doesn't begin to describe this park, which lies just six miles north of Malibu, on the sloping side of a grassy hill in the shadow of the Santa Monica Mountains. Though a forest of live oak borders the camp, there is scant shade to be found within its single loop. A recent round of plantings holds the promise of many shade trees to come, albeit years from now. And while the tilt of the terrain and small parking slips make RV camping a challenge, most sites are large enough for tenters to scratch out a satisfactory patch of turf. Heavy visitation means that restrooms tend toward the messy, especially on weekends. Overall, though, this is a remarkably well-maintained place. There are some Hollywood sets in the park, leftover from when it was owned by Universal Studios, but most people come for the great hiking, mountain biking, and horseback riding. Try to get here in spring, while the long flowing grass is still green and wildflowers are in bloom.

Basics

Operated By: California Dept. of Parks & Recreation. **Open:** All year. **Site Assignment:** Reservations highly recommended; V, MC, D.

Registration: At entrance booth. **Fee:** $12, cash or CA check. **Parking:** At site.

Facilities

Number of RV Sites: 63. **Number of Tent-Only Sites:** 0. **Hookups:** None. **Each Site:** Picnic table, fire grate. **Dump Station:** Yes. **Laundry:** No. **Pay Phone:** Yes. **Rest Rooms and Showers:** Yes. **Fuel:** No. **Propane:** No. **Internal Roads:** Paved. **RV Service:** No. **Market:** 6 mi. south in Malibu. **Restaurant:** 6 mi. south in Malibu. **General Store:** No. **Vending:** No. **Swimming:** No. **Playground:** No. **Other:** Some wheelchair-accessible facilities. **Activities:** Hiking, mountain biking, horseback riding, birding. **Nearby Attractions:** Santa Monica Pier & museums, Venice Beach Boardwalk, Hollywood's theme parks, La Brea Tar Pits. **Additional Information:** Malibu Chamber of Commerce, (310) 456-9025.

Restrictions

Pets: On 6 ft. leash. **Fires:** In fire grates only, not allowed after the grass turns brown late spring/early summer. **Alcoholic Beverages:** Allowed at site. **Vehicle Maximum Length:** 30 ft. **Other:** 7-day stay limit June 1–Sept. 30, 14-day stay limit Oct. 1–May 31; no firearms; no wood gathering.

To Get There

From the Pacific Coast Hwy. in Malibu head north on CR N1/Malibu Canyon Rd. Drive 6 mi. to the campground entrance on the left.

MAMMOTH LAKES

Glass Creek

Glass Creek Rd., Crestview 93546. T: (760) 647-3044; F: (760) 647-3046; www.r5.fs.fed.us/inyo.

RV: ★★★★ Tent: ★★★★

Beauty: ★★★	Site Privacy: ★★★
Spaciousness: ★★★★	Quiet: ★★★
Security: ★	Cleanliness: ★★★
Insect Control: ★★★★	Facilities: ★

It may be true that there is no such thing as a free lunch, but fortunately for budget-minded campers there are still a few no-fee campgrounds left. Glass Creek is one of those, a primitive national forest camp with no potable water, no trash pick-up, and rickety-looking vaulted toilets. It is also a quietly attractive piece of land that straddles its namesake creek (where the fishing for trout is pretty good), with generously large, dispersed sites on either side of the smooth, dirt access road. The slightly rolling terrain is partly shaded by very mature Jeffrey and ponderosa pines, and aspens that grow alongside the creek. Its great location, just 12 miles north of Mammoth Lakes, makes Glass Creek a popular base camp for the RV set. While ranger patrols are few and far between, the presence of vacation homes at the perimeter of the property is a reassuring sign of civilization. The nearest pay phone is at the intersection with US 395, directly across the road.

Basics

Operated By: Inyo National Forest, Mono Lake Ranger District. **Open:** Mid-May through Oct., weather permitting. **Site Assignment:** First come, first served. **Registration:** None. **Fee:** None. **Parking:** At site.

Facilities

Number of RV Sites: 50. **Number of Tent-Only Sites:** 0. **Hookups:** None. **Each Site:** Picnic table, fire grate or pit. **Dump Station:** No. **Laundry:** No. **Pay Phone:** No. **Rest Rooms and Showers:** Vault toilets, no showers. **Fuel:** No. **Propane:** No. **Internal Roads:** Dirt, sand, & rocks, but negotiable. **RV Service:** No. **Market:** 12 mi. south in Mammoth Lakes. **Restaurant:** 12 mi. south in Mammoth Lakes. **General Store:** No. **Vending:** No. **Swimming:** No. **Playground:** No. **Activities:** Fishing, hiking, photography. **Nearby Attractions:** Mono Lake Tufa State Reserve in Lee Vining; Devils Postpile National Monument, Mammoth Mountain Bike Park, Mammoth Museum & outlet shopping in Mammoth Lakes. **Additional Information:** Mono County Tourism Commission, (760) 924-3699; Mammoth Lakes Visitors Bureau, (888) GO-MAMMOTH.

Restrictions

Pets: On leash. **Fires:** In fire grates or pits only. **Alcoholic Beverages:** Allowed. **Vehicle Maximum Length:** 40 ft. **Other:** 42-day stay limit.

To Get There

From Mammoth Junction drive 10 mi. north on US 395, past the Caltrans Crestview Maintenance Station. Make a U-turn and head 0.5 mi. south on US 395. Turn right on Glass Creek Rd., a forest service road, and continue for 0.3 mi. to the campground access road on the right.

MAMMOTH LAKES

Twin Lakes

Twin Lakes Loop Rd., Mammoth Lakes 93546. T: (760) 924-5500; F: (760) 924-5537; www.r5.fs.fed.us/inyo.

RV: ★★★★ Tent: ★★★★

Beauty: ★★★★★	Site Privacy: ★★
Spaciousness: ★★★	Quiet: ★★★
Security: ★★★	Cleanliness: ★★★
Insect Control: ★★	Facilities: ★★★

To describe this camp as dramatic and pretty, peaceful and exhilarating, is to fall frustratingly short of its true splendor. The pair of lakes that inspired its name rest smack in the middle of a high Sierra canyon, jagged granite spires soaring well above the tops of the highest lodgepole pines. In spring, snow melt courses into Twin Falls, making for a spectacular cascade, visible from the campground. The very best site, with a prime panorama of the lakes, has been taken by the host. But there are many other agreeable options among the three zones that make up this park-like setting. Forget about the area by the entrance; those sites are too exposed to passing traffic. Better by far are the spots just across the bridge that divides the two lakes: 23, 25, 26, and 28 are small but enjoy their own private lakefront; 31, 33, 36, and 39, at the base of a steep hill, are fairly roomy, and detached from their neighbors; 62 and 70 are tucked into a thicket and blessed with a stunning view of the craggy canyon. The upper loop, in a more mountainous setting away from the lakes, is the roomiest; even the interior sites seem well separated. Given the elevation of 8,600 feet, you'll want to pack, along with a fishing rod, some heavy-weight fleece as a precaution against windy evenings.

Basics

Operated By: Rocky Mountain Recreation Company, concessionaire. **Open:** June through Oct., weather permitting. **Site Assignment:** First come, first served. **Registration:** At entrance kiosk. **Fee:** $14, cash or check. **Parking:** At site.

Facilities

Number of RV Sites: 95. **Number of Tent-Only Sites:** 0. **Hookups:** None. **Each Site:** Picnic table, fire grate, barbecue grill. **Dump Station:** Yes. **Laundry:** No. **Pay Phone:** Yes. **Rest Rooms and Showers:** Yes. **Fuel:** No. **Propane:** No. **Internal Roads:** Paved. **RV Service:** No. **Market:** 4 mi. northeast in Mammoth Lakes. **Restaurant:** 4 mi. northeast in Mammoth Lakes. **General Store:** Yes. **Vending:** No. **Swimming:** No. **Playground:** No. **Other:** Some wheelchair-accessible facilities, boat launch. **Activities:** Fishing, horseback riding, hiking, boat rentals. **Nearby Attractions:** Mono Lake Tufa State Reserve in Lee Vining; Devils Postpile National Monument, Mammoth Mountain Bike Park, Mammoth Museum & outlet shopping in Mammoth Lakes. **Additional Information:** Mono County Tourism Commission, (760) 924-3699; Mammoth Lakes Visitors Bureau, (888) GO-MAMMOTH.

Restrictions

Pets: On leash. **Fires:** In fire grates only. **Alcoholic Beverages:** Allowed. **Vehicle Maximum Length:** 46 ft. **Other:** 7-day stay limit.

To Get There

From Mammoth Junction on US 395 head west on Hwy. 203, leading into Mammoth Lakes' Main St., and continue 4 mi. to where Main St. becomes Lake Mary Rd. Proceed straight ahead for 2.3 mi., then turn right onto Twin Lakes Loop Rd. The campground is 0.5 mi. ahead.

MARKLEEVILLE

Grover Hot Springs State Park

Hot Springs Rd., Markleeville 96120. T: (530) 694-2248 or reservations (800) 444-7275; F: (530) 694-2502; www.cal-parks.ca.gov or www.grover@gbis.com or www.reserveamerica.com.

RV: ★★★★ Tent: ★★★★

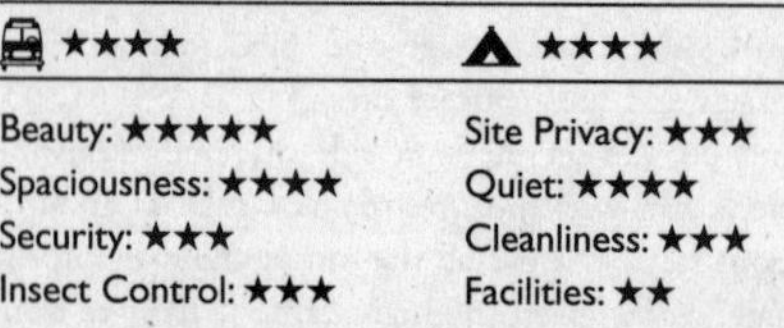

Beauty: ★★★★★	Site Privacy: ★★★
Spaciousness: ★★★★	Quiet: ★★★★
Security: ★★★	Cleanliness: ★★★
Insect Control: ★★★	Facilities: ★★

The mineral springs of Grover Hot Springs remain a constant 102° year-round, making its hot and cool pools a major therapeutic attraction. There is more to this state park, though, than the chance to bathe oneself in simmering water. Like miles of hiking and riding trails, as well as cross-country skiing in winter. First and foremost, though, is its strikingly beautiful campground, set at 5,900 feet of altitude, with a series of corrugated Sierra peaks contributing an Arcadian quality to its forested, creekside location. The undefiled, natural look of this gorgeous preserve is furthered by its undulating terrain being well-salted with granite boulders, juniper, incense cedar and Jeffrey and lodgepole pines. Sites, covered with grass and pine needles, are generally shady, generously large and fairly well separated, though several lie on uneven turf. The most private are 11, tucked behind boulders, and 22, by a row of Jeffrey pines and a grassy meadow; 58, 66–68, and 73–75 are also worth shooting for. The pools close for maintenance the last two weeks of Sept., and shut down during thunderstorms, which occur regularly throughout July and Aug.

Basics

Operated By: California Dept. of Parks & Recreation. **Open:** All year. **Site Assignment:** Reservations recommended; V, MC, D. **Registration:** At entrance booth. **Fee:** $12, cash or CA check. **Parking:** At site.

Facilities

Number of RV Sites: 76. **Number of Tent-Only Sites:** 0. **Hookups:** None. **Each Site:** Picnic table, fire grate, bearproof box. **Dump Station:** No. **Laundry:** In tubs. **Pay Phone:** Yes. **Rest Rooms and Showers:** Yes. **Fuel:** No. **Propane:** No. **Internal Roads:** Paved. **RV Service:** No. **Market:** 3.6 mi. east in Markleeville. **Restaurant:** 3.6 mi. east in Markleeville. **General Store:** No. **Vending:** No. **Swimming:** In hot springs pool. **Playground:** No. **Other:** Some wheelchair-accessible facilities. **Activities:** Hiking, fishing, bicycling, taking the "cure." **Nearby Attractions:** Alpine County Museum in Markleeville; Lake Tahoe & Lake Tahoe Historical Museum in South Lake Tahoe. **Additional Information:** Alpine County Chamber of Commerce, (530) 694-2475.

Restrictions

Pets: On 6 ft. leash. **Fires:** In fire grates only. **Alcoholic Beverages:** Allowed at site. **Vehicle Maximum Length:** 27 ft. **Other:** 14-day stay limit from May 15 to the first week in Sept., 30-day stay limit for the rest of the year; no firearms; no wood gathering.

To Get There

From Markleeville on Hwy. 89 turn west on Hot Springs Rd. and drive 3.6 mi. The well-signed state park entrance is on the right.

MARKLEEVILLE

Indian Creek

Airport Rd., Markleeville 96120. T: (775) 885-6000; www.nv.blm.gov/carson/information.html.

RV ★★★★ Tent ★★★★

Beauty: ★★★★ Site Privacy: ★★★
Spaciousness: ★★★ Quiet: ★★★★
Security: ★★★ Cleanliness: ★★★★
Insect Control: ★★★ Facilities: ★★

Indian Creek is easily reached along a well-signed, smoothly paved roadway, a rare double-treat for a Bureau of Land Management property. Then, when you pull into camp—the trifecta!—as this is as sweet as it gets for BLM land. It's a beautiful lakeside campground, backed up against the Sierra range, with its two loops enhanced by mature stands of piñon, ponderosa, and Jeffrey pines, as well as a few boulders and such high desert shrubs as salt bush and brittle bush. The first loop, which features walk-in sites for tents, offers the better vantage over Indian Creek Reservoir, where white pelicans were noisily cavorting our last time through. Birding is no less rewarding at the second circuit, which faces the lake on one side and a grassy marsh on another. The optimum sites there are 44, 48, and 49. The ground slopes gently toward the water, but most units are level, distributed well apart and surprisingly clean; even the sandy tent pads are raked by a conscientious host. Situated on the west side of the reservoir, Indian Creek is pleasantly illuminated by morning light, when it is almost too pretty for words.

Basics

Operated By: Bureau of Land Management, Carson City Field Office. **Open:** First weekend in May through last weekend in Sept. **Site Assignment:** First come, first served. **Registration:** At entrance kiosk. **Fee:** $8–$10, cash or check. **Parking:** At site or in parking lot for walk-ins.

Facilities

Number of RV Sites: 19. **Number of Tent-Only Sites:** 10. **Hookups:** None. **Each Site:** Picnic table, makeshift fire ring, barbecue grill, bear-proof box. **Dump Station:** Yes. **Laundry:** No. **Pay Phone:** No. **Rest Rooms and Showers:** Yes. **Fuel:** No. **Propane:** No. **Internal Roads:** Paved. **RV Service:** No. **Market:** 6.5 mi. south in Markleeville. **Restaurant:** 6.5 mi. south in Markleeville. **General Store:** No. **Vending:** No. **Swimming:** No. **Playground:** No. **Other:** Boat ramp. **Activities:** Fishing, hiking, birding, horseback riding, sailing, mountain biking. **Nearby Attractions:** Alpine County Museum in Markleeville; Lake Tahoe & Lake Tahoe Historical Museum in South Lake Tahoe. **Additional Information:** Alpine County Chamber of Commerce, (530) 694-2475.

Restrictions

Pets: On leash. **Fires:** In fire rings only. **Alcoholic Beverages:** Allowed. **Vehicle Maximum Length:** 30 ft. **Other:** 14-day stay limit.

To Get There

From Markleeville drive 2.5 mi. north on Hwy. 89. Turn right onto Airport Rd. and continue for 4 mi., then make a left into the campground.

McCLOUD

Fowlers Campground

FR 39N28, McCloud 96057. T: (530) 964-2184; F: (530) 964-2938; www.r5.fs.fed.us/shastatrinity.

RV ★★★ Tent ★★★★

Beauty: ★★★★ Site Privacy: ★★★
Spaciousness: ★★★ Quiet: ★★★★
Security: ★★★ Cleanliness: ★★★
Insect Control: ★★★ Facilities: ★★

You are barreling along on Hwy. 89 bound toward McCloud, with a fishing rod in the back of your vehicle and a kayak strapped to its roof. Where do you pull over for some R&R? Fowlers Campground is one of the better options in the area. The McCloud River flows right behind this clean, well-maintained national forest–operated property. Brown trout inhabit the river and rainbow trout are regularly stocked from this point clear down to Lake McCloud. A small put-in for kayaks and canoes is just past the photogenic series of cascades by the day-use picnic area, 0.5 miles beyond camp along the dirt road. The campground's double loop threads by level sites that are situated reasonably well apart and decently shielded by a densely forested mix of incense cedar, manzanita, and various conifers. The tree-to-tree carpet of pine needles is speckled with pumice rocks, which enhances the natural beauty of this wheelchair-accessible camp.

Basics

Operated By: Shasta-Trinity National Forest, McCloud Ranger District. **Open:** May 1–Oct. 31. **Site Assignment:** First come, first served. **Registration:** At entrance kiosk. **Fee:** $12, cash or check. **Parking:** At site.

Facilities

Number of RV Sites: 38. **Number of Tent-Only Sites:** 0. **Hookups:** None. **Each Site:** Picnic table, fire grate. **Dump Station:** No. **Laundry:** No. **Pay Phone:** No. **Rest Rooms and Showers:** Vault toilets, no showers. **Fuel:** No. **Propane:** No. **Internal Roads:** Paved, narrow. **RV Service:** No. **Market:** 6 mi. west in McCloud. **Restaurant:** 6 mi. west in McCloud. **General Store:** No. **Vending:** No. **Swimming:** At the base of Middle & Lower Falls. **Playground:** No. **Other:** Some wheelchair-accessible facilities, small boat launch. **Activities:** Fishing, hiking, kayaking. **Nearby Attractions:** McCloud River Falls & Shasta Sunset Dinner Train; Mount Shasta Ski Park, Mount Shasta Hatchery, & Sisson Museum in Mount Shasta; Lake Siskiyou. **Additional Information:** Mount Shasta Chamber of Commerce & Visitors Bureau, (530) 926-4865 or (800) 926-4865; McCloud Chamber of Commerce, (530) 964-3113.

Restrictions

Pets: On leash. **Fires:** In fire grates only. **Alcoholic Beverages:** Allowed. **Vehicle Maximum Length:** 30 ft. **Other:** 14-day stay limit.

To Get There

From Mount Shasta drive 2 mi. south on I-5. Head east on Hwy. 89 and drive 16 mi., past the town of McCloud, and turn right at the campground sign. Continue for 0.6 mi. and bear left at the fork. The campground is straight ahead.

MECCA

Salton Sea State Recreation Area, Headquarters Campground

100–225 State Park Rd., North Shore 92254. T: (760) 393-3052; F: (760) 393-2466; www.saltonsea.statepark.org.

RV ★★★ Tent ★★★

Beauty: ★★★ Site Privacy: ★★★
Spaciousness: ★★★ Quiet: ★★★
Security: ★★★ Cleanliness: ★★★
Insect Control: ★★ Facilities: ★★★

The attraction here is the Salton Sea, a vast lake that lies 227 feet below sea level and is 25 percent saltier than the Pacific Ocean. The palm-fringed body of water is a Mecca of sorts to boaters and fishermen, as well as birders drawn by hopes of sighting some of the great range of migratory fowl that wing through between late fall and early spring. The mildest weather is from Jan. through Mar., a time that coincides with free ranger-led kayak tours of the lake (call ahead to make reservations). Of the state-run campgrounds in the area, Mecca Beach gives tenters the best beach access, but only has six spots with hookups. Headquarters, on the other hand, has the better fishing. It consists of two loops; one with 15 full-hookup sites facing the water across a paved, level parking area, the other with more space and privacy among desert ironwood trees, brittle bush, and desert scrub. A visitor center, located between the loops, has a short film strip on the lake and some interesting exhibits. This would be a delightfully peaceful bivouac if not for the occasional rattling of trains along the tracks by the park road. When the winds blow from the west side of the lake, that sweet briny air that is so reminiscent of the seaside can change in the twitch of a nose to such a strong stench of sulphur you may think you're camping next to a match factory.

Basics

Operated By: California Dept. of Parks & Recreation. **Open:** All year. **Site Assignment:** Reservations accepted w/ V, MC, D, but not for primitive sites. **Registration:** At entrance booth. **Fee:** $10–$14, cash or CA check. **Parking:** At site.

Facilities

Number of RV Sites: 50. **Number of Tent-Only Sites:** 0. **Hookups:** Water, electric (30 amps). **Each Site:** Picnic table, barbecue grill, some w/ a ramada. **Dump Station:** Yes. **Laundry:** No. **Pay Phone:** Yes. **Rest Rooms and Showers:** Yes. **Fuel:** No. **Propane:** No. **Internal Roads:** Paved. **RV Service:** No. **Market:** 11 mi. north in Mecca. **Restaurant:** 11 mi. north in Mecca. **General Store:** No. **Vending:** No. **Swimming:** In Salton Sea. **Playground:** Yes. **Other:** Some wheelchair-accessible facilities. **Activities:** Fishing, boating, hiking, birding, horseshoe pit. **Nearby Attractions:** Joshua Tree National Park, San Andreas Trail, Wister Mud Pots. **Additional Information:** Coachella Chamber of Commerce, (760) 398-8089.

Restrictions

Pets: On 6 ft. leash. **Fires:** No ground fires. **Alcoholic Beverages:** Allowed at site. **Vehicle Maximum Length:** 32 ft. **Other:** 30-day stay limit; no firearms; no wood gathering.

To Get There

Take Hwy. 111 south from Mecca, drive 12 mi. and turn right into the state recreation area.

MIDDLETOWN

Beaver Creek RV Park & Campground

14417 Bottle Rock Rd., Cobb Mountain 95426. T: (707) 928-4322 or reservations (800) 307-CAMP; F: (707) 928-5341; www.campbeavercreek.com.

RV: ★★★★ Tent: ★★

Beauty: ★★★ Site Privacy: ★★
Spaciousness: ★★ Quiet: ★★★
Security: ★★★★ Cleanliness: ★★★
Insect Control: ★★★ Facilities: ★★★★★

This is not a campground where you are likely to feel comfortable sitting in an easy chair watching the clouds drift by. Not in the summer, anyway, when a smorgasbord of activities and distractions keeps the place humming. The family-oriented entertainment ranges from such stalwarts as fishing, kayaking, softball, and basketball, to crafts and games, campfire programs, karaoke, and bingo. Bring the "bug juice" and you will have the complete summer camp experience. The flat grassy camping meadow, tucked below an attractive array of hills, is open, rather crowded, and lacking in shade. The most desirable site is 11, set back under a large oak and pine, right by the creek. There are also clean cabins for rent by the small boat pond. Beaver Creek recently changed its name from Yogi Bear's Jellystone Park Camp Resort, a sure indicator of the declining fortune of the cartoon character and his pal, Booboo. Although open year-round, upkeep tends to slide in the off-season.

Basics

Operated By: Beaver Creek RV Park & Campground. **Open:** All year. **Site Assignment:** Reservations accepted w/ V, MC, D, AE. **Registration:** At office. **Fee:** $19–$24, cash or V, MC, AE, D. **Parking:** At site.

Facilities

Number of RV Sites: 97. **Number of Tent-Only Sites:** 14. **Hookups:** Water, electric (30, 50 amps), sewer. **Each Site:** Picnic table, fire grate. **Dump Station:** Yes. **Laundry:** Yes. **Pay Phone:** Yes. **Rest Rooms and Showers:** Yes. **Fuel:** No. **Propane:** Yes. **Internal Roads:** Dirt & gravel, good condition. **RV Service:** No. **Market:** 12 mi. south in Middletown. **Restaurant:** 12 mi. south in Middletown. **General Store:** Yes. **Vending:** Yes. **Swimming:** In small pool. **Playground:** Yes. **Other:** Some wheelchair-accessible facilities, rec hall, trout creek. **Activities:** Fishing, hiking, birding, shuffleboard, soccer, softball, kayak & paddleboat rentals. **Nearby Attractions:** Clear Lake Queen, Outrageous Waters Water Park & Fun Center, & Anderson Marsh State Historic Park in Clearlake. **Additional Information:** Lake County Marketing Program/Visitor Information Center, (707) 263-9544 or (800) 525-3743; Clearlake Chamber of Commerce, (707) 994-3600.

Restrictions

Pets: On leash. **Fires:** In fire grates only. **Alcoholic Beverages:** Allowed. **Vehicle Maximum Length:** None. **Other:** 180-day stay limit; no wood gathering.

To Get There

From Middletown on Hwy. 29 take Hwy. 175 north for 8.7 mi. Turn left on Bottle Rock Rd. and drive 3.4 mi. to the park entrance on the left.

MILL CREEK

Hole-in-the-Ground

FR 28NO6, Mill Creek 96061. T: (530) 258-2141; F: (530) 258-5194; www.r5.fs.fed.us/lassen.

RV: ★★★ Tent: ★★★★

Beauty: ★★★★ Site Privacy: ★★★
Spaciousness: ★★★ Quiet: ★★★★
Security: ★ Cleanliness: ★★★
Insect Control: ★★★ Facilities: ★

In spite of its name, this camp is far more than just a "hole-in-the-ground." In fact, the contrast to Elam, a few miles to the southeast, couldn't be more striking. While both consist of sites sprinkled along short camp lanes that are flanked by gurgling streams, the ones here are roomy, well-separated, and thickly populated with ponderosa pines and Douglas firs. Privacy is further enhanced by the remoteness of the setting, some three miles down a gravel washboard off of Hwy. 172, about 14 miles from the south entrance to Lassen Volcanic National Park. Amazingly, while Elam is often packed to the gills with rod-slinging campers, you may find Hole-in-the-Ground occupied by only a small handful of visitors, if at all. The reason for that is fishing here in Mill Creek is limited to catch-and-release, with barbless hooks. With an elevation of 4,300 feet, snowfall can block access to this park-like campground from mid-Oct. through May. The rusty, old-fashioned water pump is a good incentive to bring plenty of drinking water.

Basics

Operated By: CSU Chico Research Foundation, concessionaire, & Lassen National Forest, Almanor Ranger District. **Open:** May through Oct., weather permitting. **Site Assignment:** First come, first served. **Registration:** At entrance kiosk. **Fee:** $11, cash or check. **Parking:** At site.

Facilities

Number of RV Sites: 13. **Number of Tent-Only Sites:** 0. **Hookups:** None. **Each Site:** Picnic table, fire grate or makeshift stone ring, some old-fashioned camp stoves. **Dump Station:** No. **Laundry:** No. **Pay Phone:** No. **Rest Rooms and Showers:** Vault toilets, no showers. **Fuel:** No. **Propane:** No. **Internal Roads:** Packed dirt & coarse gravel. **RV Service:** No. **Market:** 4 mi. north in Mineral. **Restaurant:** 4 mi. north in Mineral. **General Store:** No. **Vending:** No. **Swimming:** No. **Playground:** No. **Activities:** Fishing, kayaking, hiking. **Nearby Attractions:** Westwood Museum & Paul Bunyan & Babe the Blue Ox Statues; Lassen National Scenic Byway (Hwys. 89-44-36); Lassen Volcanic National Park; Lake Almanor. **Additional Information:** Chester–Lake Almanor Chamber of Commerce, (530) 258-2426 or (800) 350-4838.

Restrictions

Pets: On leash. **Fires:** In fire grates or rings only. **Alcoholic Beverages:** Allowed. **Vehicle Maximum Length:** 25 ft., trailers not recommended. **Other:** 14-day stay limit.

To Get There

From Chester on Hwy. 36 drive 23 mi. west to the junction w/ Hwy. 172. Turn left and continue for

3.6 mi., then turn left onto FR 28N06 (campground is signposted). After 2.8 mi. take another left onto the access road. The campground is 0.6 mi. ahead. A few sudden rises in the road surface may cause problems for trailers and oversize RVs.

MODESTO

Modesto Reservoir Regional Park

Reservoir Rd. 18143, Waterford 95386. T: (209) 874-9540; F: (209) 874-4513; www.co.stanislaus.ca.us.

RV ★★★★ Tent ★★

Beauty: ★★★★	Site Privacy: ★★
Spaciousness: ★★	Quiet: ★★★
Security: ★★★	Cleanliness: ★★★
Insect Control: ★★	Facilities: ★★★★

Summer seems to last for six or seven months in this steamy stretch of California's Central Valley. That's a major reason why Modesto Reservoir is so popular for much of the year; its cool, shimmering water brings relief from temperatures that frequently top 100°. Even on busy weekends, you are apt to find spots available in the sparsely shaded, full-hookup parking meadow. Far better are the smaller slots that are lined up one against another following the amoeba-like contours of the reservoir's wandering shoreline. What those lack in privacy they more than gain in shade from eucalyptus, plane trees, pines, and juniper. Their tent-side access to the lake is an added bonus. The many small islands that dot the surface of the water not only bless it with pleasing aesthetics, but also serve as safe havens for a variety of bird life, including pelicans, Canada geese, blue herons, bald eagles, red tail hawks, pheasants, and burrowing owls. An undeveloped section on the opposite side of the lake allows for more privacy, but lacks tables, fire rings, and potable water.

Basics

Operated By: Stanislaus County Parks Dept. **Open:** All year. **Site Assignment:** First come, first served. **Registration:** At entrance kiosk. **Fee:** $12–$16, cash, CA check or V, MC; $2 per night extra for 3-day holiday weekends. **Parking:** At site.

Facilities

Number of RV Sites: 186. **Number of Tent-Only Sites:** Undesignated sites. **Hookups:** Water, electric (20, 30 amps), sewer. **Each Site:** Picnic table, fire grate, barbecue grill. **Dump Station:** Yes. **Laundry:** No. **Pay Phone:** Yes. **Rest Rooms and Showers:** Yes. **Fuel:** No. **Propane:** No. **Internal Roads:** Paved. **RV Service:** No. **Market:** 7 mi. west in Waterford. **Restaurant:** 7 mi. west in Waterford. **General Store:** Yes. **Vending:** No. **Swimming:** In Modesto Reservoir. **Playground:** No. **Other:** Some wheelchair-accessible facilities, boat ramp, marina, beach, archery range. **Activities:** Fishing, boat rentals, waterskiing,. **Nearby Attractions:** McHenry Mansion & museums in Modesto; Turlock Lake State Recreation Area in La Grange. **Additional Information:** Modesto CVB, (209) 571-6480 or (800) 266-4282.

Restrictions

Pets: Not allowed. **Fires:** In fire grates only. **Alcoholic Beverages:** Allowed at site. **Vehicle Maximum Length:** None. **Other:** 14-day stay limit; MBTE-free fuel only; no fuel containers; no firearms; no wood gathering.

To Get There

From Modesto drive 13 mi. east on Hwy. 132/Yosemite Blvd. Turn left on Reservoir Rd. and continue 0.5 mi. to the park entrance.

MOJAVE

Red Rock Canyon State Park, Ricardo Campground

Hwy. 14, Cantil 93519. T: (661) 942-0662; F: (661) 940-7327; www.cal-parks.ca.gov.

RV ★★★★ Tent ★★★★

Beauty: ★★★★★	Site Privacy: ★★★
Spaciousness: ★★★★	Quiet: ★★★
Security: ★★★	Cleanliness: ★★★★
Insect Control: ★★★★	Facilities: ★

White House Cliffs is a fabulous fairyland canyon of melting sandstone and fluted folds, where cliff swallows nest and great horned owls occasionally perch during their nocturnal vigils. This feast for the eyes, a part of the El Paso Mountain range, serves as host to Ricardo Campground, right at its base, and has been a featured backdrop in more than 130 movies. Coarse sand-surfaced sites are backed up against the eroded nooks and alcoves of the canyon, gaining, in addition to a touch of privacy from their neighbors, a solid shield from the afternoon sun. From this primitive setting one can look across the valley floor, an arid landscape that is enlivened by creosote bushes, Joshua trees, and rabbit brush, to the headlights of distant autos humming along on Hwy. 14, while still enjoying a brilliantly starry sky. Indeed, the star-gazing here is so exceptional that star charts have been posted by the latrines and kiosk. A visitor center and the remains of an 1890s mining operation are in the vicinity. The nearest pay phone is 14 miles south by the Cantil post office.

Basics

Operated By: California Dept. of Parks & Recreation. **Open:** All year. **Site Assignment:** First come, first served. **Registration:** At entrance booth. **Fee:** $8, cash or CA check. **Parking:** At site.

Facilities

Number of RV Sites: 50. **Number of Tent-Only Sites:** 0. **Hookups:** None. **Each Site:** Picnic table, fire grate. **Dump Station:** Yes. **Laundry:** No. **Pay Phone:** No. **Rest Rooms and Showers:** Pit toilets, no showers. **Fuel:** No. **Propane:** No. **Internal Roads:** Gravel, good condition. **RV Service:** No. **Market:** 35 mi. northeast in Ridgecrest. **Restaurant:** 25 mi. southwest in Mojave. **General Store:** No. **Vending:** No. **Swimming:** No. **Playground:** No. **Other:** Some wheelchair-accessible facilities, visitor center. **Activities:** Hiking, driving tour, photography, birding, stargazing, ranger-led activities. **Nearby Attractions:** Trona Pinnacles; Fossil Falls; Last Chance Canyon & Maturango Museum in Ridgecrest; Desert Tortoise Natural Area in California City. **Additional Information:** Mojave Chamber of Commerce, (661) 824-2481; Ridgecrest Area CVB, (760) 375-8202 or (800) 847-4830.

Restrictions

Pets: On 6 ft. leash. **Fires:** In fire grates only. **Alcoholic Beverages:** Allowed at site. **Vehicle Maximum Length:** 30 ft. **Other:** 14-day stay limit; no firearms.

To Get There

From Mojave on Hwy. 14 drive 24 mi. northeast to the park entrance on the left. The campground is 1 mi. ahead.

MOJAVE NATIONAL PRESERVE

Hole-in-the-Wall

Black Canyon Rd., Mojave National Preserve 92311. T: (760) 255-8801; www.nps.gov/moja.

RV ★★★ Tent ★★★★

Beauty: ★★★★	Site Privacy: ★★★
Spaciousness: ★★★	Quiet: ★★★★
Security: ★★★	Cleanliness: ★★★★
Insect Control: ★★★★	Facilities: ★★★

If you chanced to visit this campground when the Mojave National Preserve was first created in 1994, there was a very good likelihood that you had the entire grounds to yourself. Times have changed as word has spread about the subtle beauty of this area, and now you will probably have neighbors. Unless, of course, you make the mistake of visiting this piece of desert in summer when it becomes a sweltering inferno without a single shade tree to be found in the camp's single loop. But at an elevation of 4,400 feet, Hole-in-the-Wall can be pretty comfortable in both autumn and spring, even if late afternoon winds often require the donning of jackets and hats for warmth. And while the yucca plants and pencil chollas don't provide much in the way of screening, sites, with both pull-through and back-in parking, are roomy, well spaced apart, and attractively positioned just below a rough looking canyon. The sunset view of the surrounding mountains is an added plus, as is the Rings Trail hike, with its trailhead half a mile to the south.

Basics

Operated By: National Park Service. **Open:** All year. **Site Assignment:** First come, first served. **Registration:** At entrance kiosk. **Fee:** $12, cash or check. **Parking:** At site.

Facilities

Number of RV Sites: 35. **Number of Tent-Only Sites:** 2. **Hookups:** None. **Each Site:** Picnic table, fire ring. **Dump Station:** Yes. **Laundry:** No. **Pay Phone:** Yes, at Hole-in-the Wall Visitor Center, 0.5 mi south. **Rest Rooms and Showers:** Vaulted toilets, no showers. **Fuel:** No. **Propane:** No. **Internal Roads:** Dirt, in good condition. **RV Service:** No. **Market:** 60 mi. west in Baker. **Restaurant:** 60 mi. west in Baker. **General Store:** No. **Vending:** No. **Swimming:** No. **Playground:** No. **Other:** Some wheelchair accessible sites. **Activities:** Hiking, bicycling, horseback riding. **Nearby Attractions:** Mitchell Caverns, Desert Museum, Kelso Dunes, Teutonia Peak. **Additional Information:** Mojave Desert Information Center, (760) 733-4040.

RESTRICTIONS

Pets: On 6 ft. leash; not allowed on trails. **Fires:** In fire rings only. **Alcoholic Beverages:** Allowed at site. **Vehicle Maximum Length:** None. **Other:** 14-day stay limit; no loaded firearms.

TO GET THERE

Exit I-40 at Essex Rd., drive 10 mi. north and turn right on Black Canyon Rd. Drive 10.3 mi. and turn left into campground. Or: Exit I-15 at Cima Rd. and drive south for 22 mi. Turn left on Cedar Canyon Rd. and after 6 mi. turn right on Black Canyon Rd. Proceed for 9.5 mi. to the campground on the right.

MONO CITY

Lundy Canyon Campground

Lundy Lake Rd., Mono City 93541. T: (760) 932-5252 or (760) 932-5231; F: (760) 932-5458.

RV ★★★★ Tent ★★★★

Beauty: ★★★★ Site Privacy: ★★★★
Spaciousness: ★★★★ Quiet: ★★
Security: ★★ Cleanliness: ★★
Insect Control: ★★★ Facilities: ★

Lundy Canyon, a county park, is one of the better bargains around, especially with the explosion of price hikes at the concession-run national forest options. There is a subtle, understated beauty to this scruffy glen, where Lundy Creek discreetly trickles through and the Sierras tower above. Level, largely grassy sites, which range in size from shoeboxes to palatial, are spread out over several access points along Lundy Lake Rd. Skip the first 15 or so, as many later choices are endowed with superior privacy and a more generous amount of space. Excellent screening between spots is derived from thickets of aspen, as well as juniper and high desert chaparral. This diamond-in-the-rough, at 7,800 feet elevation, lacks potable water, but the county has recently installed new tables and fire grates in several sites; new vaulted toilets are reportedly on the way. A boat ramp, boat rental,s and groceries are available at Lundy Lake Resort, just up the road.

BASICS

Operated By: Mono County Building & Parks Dept. **Open:** May through Oct., weather permitting. **Site Assignment:** First come, first served. **Registration:** At entrance kiosk, pay at site 37. **Fee:** $7, cash or CA check. **Parking:** At site.

FACILITIES

Number of RV Sites: 54. **Number of Tent-Only Sites:** 0. **Hookups:** None. **Each Site:** Picnic table, fire grate. **Dump Station:** No. **Laundry:** No. **Pay Phone:** No. **Rest Rooms and Showers:** Pit & vault toilets, no showers. **Fuel:** No. **Propane:** No. **Internal Roads:** Gravel & dirt, decent condition. **RV Service:** No. **Market:** 10 mi. southeast in Lee Vining. **Restaurant:** 10 mi. southeast in Lee Vining. **General Store:** No. **Vending:** No. **Swimming:** No. **Playground:** No. **Other:** Some wheelchair-accessible facilities. **Activities:** Fishing, hiking, boating. **Nearby Attractions:** Mono Lake Tufa State Reserve in Lee Vining; Lundy Lake; Bodie State Historic Park in Bridgeport. **Additional Information:** Mono County Tourism Commission, (760) 924-3699; Lee Vining Chamber of Commerce, (760) 647-6629.

RESTRICTIONS

Pets: On 10 ft. leash. **Fires:** In fire grates only. **Alcoholic Beverages:** Allowed at site. **Vehicle Maximum Length:** 24 ft. **Other:** No stay limit.

TO GET THERE

From Lee Vining drive 7 mi. north on US 395. Turn left on Lundy Lake Rd. and continue for 2.5 mi. to the campground entrance on the left. Lundy Lake Rd. offers several access points.

MORGAN HILL

Henry W. Coe State Park, Headquarters Campground

East Dunne Ave., Morgan Hill 95038. T: (408) 779-2728 or reservations (800) 444-7275; www.coepark.parks.ca.gov or www.cal-parks.ca.gov or www.reserveamerica.com.

RV ★★★ Tent ★★★★

Beauty: ★★★★★ Site Privacy: ★★
Spaciousness: ★★ Quiet: ★★★★
Security: ★★★ Cleanliness: ★★
Insect Control: ★★★ Facilities: ★★

Much of the 135 square miles that compose Henry Coe State Park are devoted to hiking trails, making the largest state park in northern California one of the better places for backpacking. You won't need to strap a 50-pound sack to your back to appreciate the beauty of this area, though, an RV or a tent will do nicely, too. Headquarters Campground, at 2,600 feet elevation, is located on the edge of a steep hillside, a few dozen yards from the well-maintained ranch buildings that date from when the Coe family resided here half a century ago (one of those structures now houses a visitor center). This sloping terrain limits both sites (several of which are on unlevel turf) and parking slips to very confined space. Even the old-style outhouses—which look as if they, too, date from the Coe era—seem smaller than a telephone booth. Happily, the extraordinary views across the hills toward distant mountains are more than expansive enough to compensate. In springtime the hilltop meadows erupt in an array of wildflowers.

BASICS

Operated By: California Dept. of Parks & Recreation. **Open:** All year. **Site Assignment:** Reservations accepted w/ V, MC, D. **Registration:** At visitor center. **Fee:** $7, cash or CA check. **Parking:** At site.

FACILITIES

Number of RV Sites: 20. **Number of Tent-Only Sites:** 0. **Hookups:** None. **Each Site:** Picnic table, fire ring, ramada or shade tree. **Dump Station:** No. **Laundry:** No. **Pay Phone:** Yes. **Rest Rooms and Showers:** Vault toilets, no showers. **Fuel:** No. **Propane:** No. **Internal Roads:** Paved. **RV Service:** No. **Market:** 13 mi. west in Morgan Hill. **Restaurant:** 13 mi. west in Morgan Hill. **General Store:** No. **Vending:** No. **Swimming:** No. **Playground:** No. **Other:** Old farmhouse buildings, nature center. **Activities:** Hiking, mountain biking, fishing, stargazing, horseback riding. **Nearby Attractions:** Mission San Juan Bautista, San Jose museums, zoo, & parks. **Additional Information:** Morgan Hill Chamber of Commerce, (408) 779-9444.

RESTRICTIONS

Pets: On 6 ft. leash. **Fires:** In fire rings only. **Alcoholic Beverages:** Allowed at site. **Vehicle Maximum Length:** 22 ft. **Other:** 14-day stay limit; no firearms; no wood gathering.

TO GET THERE

In Morgan Hill on US 101 take the East Dunne Ave. Exit. Drive for 13 mi. along the windy, narrow, ascending road straight to the park entrance. Use a pull-out along the way to absorb the magnificent valley views.

MORRO BAY

Montaña de Oro State Park

Pecho Valley Rd., Los Osos 93402. T: (805) 528-0513; www.cal-parks.ca.gov or www.reserveamerica.com.

RV ★★★ Tent ★★★★

Beauty: ★★★★ Site Privacy: ★★
Spaciousness: ★★★ Quiet: ★★★★
Security: ★★★ Cleanliness: ★★★★
Insect Control: ★★★ Facilities: ★

In many respects this is a very ordinary campground, with adequate elbow room in the grass and dirt sites but little privacy. Facilities are minimal, and even the camp's immediate setting, with a few Bishop pines punctuating the green confines of the narrow canyon, is just a notch or two above average in pulchritude. Give the park a chance, though—all 8,000 acres of it—and what you will find is a spectacular coastal wilderness that rivals the Big Sur area in its unspoiled beauty. The drive into Montaña de Oro threads past dense groves of aromatic eucalyptus, with eye-popping views of the dune-draped shore and Morro Rock out in the bay. Tall stands of cottonwood, oak, maple, willow, and box elder thrive elsewhere. Add to that miles of pristine beaches, highland bluffs and miscellaneous meadows, and you have a nature-lover's nirvana. For sun bathers there is Spooner's Cove, a romantic patch of sand and tide pools, just below the campground off the road. The vast array of wildflowers scattered over the hills in late spring is a heaven-scent sight.

BASICS

Operated By: California Dept. of Parks & Recreation. **Open:** All year. **Site Assignment:** Reservations accepted w/ V, MC, D. **Registration:** At entrance kiosk. **Fee:** $12, cash or CA check. **Parking:** At site.

FACILITIES

Number of RV Sites: 50. **Number of Tent-Only Sites:** 4. **Hookups:** None. **Each Site:** Picnic table, fire grate, food storage box. **Dump Station:** No. **Laundry:** No. **Pay Phone:** Yes. **Rest Rooms**

and Showers: Vault toilets, no showers. **Fuel:** No. **Propane:** No. **Internal Roads:** Paved. **RV Service:** No. **Market:** 5 mi. northeast in Los Osos. **Restaurant:** 5 mi. northeast in Los Osos. **General Store:** No. **Vending:** No. **Swimming:** In Pacific Ocean. **Playground:** No. **Activities:** Hiking, birding, bicycling, horseback riding, tidepooling, fishing, nature programs. **Nearby Attractions:** Mission San Luis Obispo; Morro Bay State Beach & Museum of Natural History. **Additional Information:** Los Osos/Baywood Park Chamber of Commerce, (805) 528-4884.

RESTRICTIONS

Pets: On 6 ft. leash. **Fires:** In fire grates only. **Alcoholic Beverages:** Allowed at site. **Vehicle Maximum Length:** 27 ft. **Other:** 14-day stay limit; no firearms; no wood gathering.

TO GET THERE

From San Luis Obispo head 3 mi. south on US 101 and exit at Los Osos Valley Rd. Drive 11.7 mi. west, then bear left on Pecho Valley Rd. The park entrance is 1 mi. ahead and the campground is to the left after that.

MOUNT SHASTA

KOA Mount Shasta

900 North Mount Shasta Blvd., Mount Shasta 96067. T: (530) 926-4029 or reservations (800) 562-3617; www.koa.com.

★★★★ ★★

Beauty: ★★★	Site Privacy: ★★
Spaciousness: ★★	Quiet: ★★★
Security: ★★★★	Cleanliness: ★★★★
Insect Control: ★★★	Facilities: ★★★★★

Admit it, you've always wondered what it was like to camp at a KOA. Well, stop your wondering and get your butane-burner over to this campground. As you might expect, the facilities are top-notch, ranging from a small pool (summer season) and cabin rentals to a game room, volleyball, basketball, and even a horse corral. With snow-capped Mt. Shasta towering over the downtown property, you can imagine that you are roughing it while flipping burgers by the barbecue grill. Sites are crowded into two environments, open meadow and sparsely forested. The latter is composed mostly of pines, with support from cottonwoods, cedars, maples, and manzanita. The resulting shade and screening make that area preferable, especially for tent campers, but the narrow, meandering lanes are not recommended for big rigs. The meadow, on the other hand, while exposed to both sun and neighbors, has the virtue of pull-through parking.

BASICS

Operated By: KOA Kampgrounds. **Open:** All year. **Site Assignment:** Reservations accepted w/ V, MC, D. **Registration:** At entrance office. **Fee:** $19–$26, cash or V, MC, D. **Parking:** At site.

FACILITIES

Number of RV Sites: 40. **Number of Tent-Only Sites:** 68. **Hookups:** Water, electric (30, 50 amps), sewer, Internet. **Each Site:** Half-size picnic table, fire grate, some sites have a barbecue grill. **Dump Station:** Yes. **Laundry:** Yes. **Pay Phone:** Yes. **Rest Rooms and Showers:** Yes. **Fuel:** No. **Propane:** Yes. **Internal Roads:** Paved & forest floor. **RV Service:** Yes, mobile. **Market:** 1 mi. south in Mount Shasta. **Restaurant:** 1 mi. south in Mount Shasta. **General Store:** Yes. **Vending:** Yes. **Swimming:** In small pool seasonally. **Playground:** Yes. **Other:** Some wheelchair-accessible facilities, game room, movie rentals. **Activities:** Horseshoe pit, volleyball, basketball, shuffleboard, nearby hiking, rafting, & fishing. **Nearby Attractions:** Lake Siskiyou; Mount Shasta Ski Park, Mount Shasta Hatchery & Sisson Museum; downtown Dunsmuir; Castle Crags State Park in Castella. **Additional Information:** Mount Shasta Chamber of Commerce & Visitors Bureau, (530) 926-4865 or (800) 926-4865; Dunsmuir Chamber of Commerce, (530) 235-2177.

RESTRICTIONS

Pets: On leash. **Fires:** In fire grates only; no wood fires allowed. **Alcoholic Beverages:** Allowed. **Vehicle Maximum Length:** 85 ft. **Other:** No fireworks.

TO GET THERE

On I-5 take the central Mount Shasta Exit and drive 0.5 mi. into town on West Lake St. At the stoplight turn left on North Mount Shasta Blvd. and proceed for 0.6 mi. Turn right on East Hinkley Blvd. and drive 1 block to the campground entrance on the left.

NAPA

Putah Creek Resort

7600 Knoxville Rd., Napa 94558. T: (707) 966-2116 or (707) 966-2368; F: (707) 966-0593; www.napavalleyonline.com/directory/wsparks.html.

★★★★ ★★

Beauty: ★★★	Site Privacy: ★★
Spaciousness: ★★	Quiet: ★★★
Security: ★★★★	Cleanliness: ★★★
Insect Control: ★★★	Facilities: ★★★★★

Like every story, there are two sides to Putah Creek Resort. As in lakeside and creekside. The main compound overlooks lovely Lake Berryessa, a glimmering body of water that was created by the Bureau of Land Reclamation back in the 1950s. Yuccas and palms, knob cone pines and oaks, oleanders and pollarded hibiscus lend an appealing dash of beauty to a camp so developed it even has motel rooms and a restaurant-bar. Partial hookups are available near the boat launch, painfully close to the bar's open-air patio and within easy earshot of the motorboats and jet skis that often zip by. Across the road is the creek camp, in a greener, more serene setting. It is also endowed with a boat launch, and though many sites are too close to each other for camping comfort, a healthy majority overlook the water. Of the latter, 21–28 offer RVers a fine lateral view of the creek, while 3–8t put tent campers at the shore's edge. One negative to the creek area is that upkeep of restrooms is sometimes neglected. Both zones are fenced and protected by gate house entrance booths.

BASICS

Operated By: Putah Creek Resort. **Open:** All year. **Site Assignment:** Reservations accepted w/ V, MC, AE. **Registration:** At entrance gate or in store. **Fee:** $21–$26, cash or V, MC, AE. **Parking:** At site.

FACILITIES

Number of RV Sites: 255. **Number of Tent-Only Sites:** 0. **Hookups:** Water, electric (30, 50 amps), sewer. **Each Site:** Picnic table, barbecue grill. **Dump Station:** Yes. **Laundry:** Yes. **Pay Phone:** Yes. **Rest Rooms and Showers:** Yes. **Fuel:** Yes. **Propane:** Yes. **Internal Roads:** Paved. **RV Service:** No. **Market:** 27 mi. east in St. Helena. **Restaurant:** 27 mi. east in St. Helena. **General Store:** Yes, also deli & snack bar. **Vending:** Yes. **Swimming:** In Lake Berryessa. **Playground:** No. **Other:** Boat ramp, motel, restaurant. **Activities:** Fishing, boat rentals. **Nearby Attractions:** Bale Gristmill State Historic Park & Bothe–Napa Valley State Park in St. Helena; winery tours. **Additional Information:** Winters District Chamber of Commerce, (530) 795-2329; Napa-Sonoma Wine Country Visitor Center, (707) 624-0686 or (800) 723-0575.

RESTRICTIONS

Pets: On leash, $2. **Fires:** No. **Alcoholic Beverages:** Allowed. **Vehicle Maximum Length:** 50 ft. **Other:** 14-day stay limit from May 15–Oct. 15, 3-month stay limit in winter.

TO GET THERE

From Napa head 16 mi. north on Hwy. 121/Monticello Rd. Turn left on Hwy. 128 and drive 5 mi. Turn right on Berryessa Knoxville Rd. and continue for 13 mi. The resort entrance is on the right, just after the Pope Canyon Rd. turnoff.

NEEDLES

Needles Marina Park

100 Marina Dr., Needles 92363. T: (760) 326-2197; F: (760) 326-4125; www.needlesmarina.com.

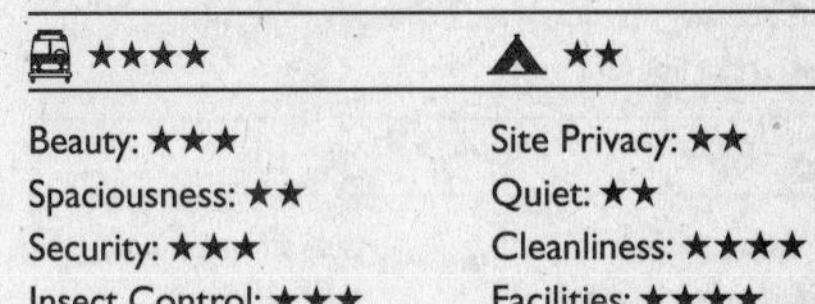

Of the many campgrounds located along the Colorado River, few are quite as visually appealing as Needles Marina Park, where palm trees blend seamlessly with eucalyptus, mulberry with mesquite, and flowering oleanders lend a splash of color to the desert scene. Add to that a swimming pool and lagoon, a small sandy beach by the river, a boat ramp and marina, a hot tub, cabin rentals, and even a rec room equipped with billiard tables and dart boards, and you've got the recipe for one fine vacation spot. All of which is not exactly a well kept secret, as is easily observed in winter when the campground seems more crowded than the Santa Monica Freeway at rush hour. Even though loops are dispersed in clusters and many sites feature pull-through parking, space is definitely on the small side, and the hard-packed pebbly dirt is inhospitable to comfortable tenting. Sites 162–166, overlooking the lagoon, are the best screened for privacy.

Basics

Operated By: Needles Marina Park. **Open:** All year. **Site Assignment:** Reservations accepted w/ V, MC. **Registration:** At office in store. **Fee:** $26–$28, cash or V, MC. **Parking:** At sites.

Facilities

Number of RV Sites: 194. **Number of Tent-Only Sites:** 0. **Hookups:** Water, electric (30, 50 amps), sewer, Internet. **Each Site:** Picnic table, barbecue grill. **Dump Station:** Yes. **Laundry:** Yes. **Pay Phone:** Yes. **Rest Rooms and Showers:** Yes. **Fuel:** No. **Propane:** No. **Internal Roads:** Paved. **RV Service:** No. **Market:** 1 mi. south in Needles. **Restaurant:** 1 mi. south in Needles. **General Store:** Yes. **Vending:** Yes. **Swimming:** In pool & lagoon. **Playground:** Yes. **Other:** Boat ramp & boat slips, marina, rec room, spa. **Activities:** Fishing, pool tables, dart board, waterskiing, Needles Municipal Golf Course. **Nearby Attractions:** London Bridge, Mitchell Caverns, Lake Havasu, Providence Mountains State Recreation Area. **Additional Information:** Needles Area Chamber of Commerce, (760) 326-2050.

Restrictions

Pets: On leash. **Fires:** In barbecue grills only. **Alcoholic Beverages:** Allowed. **Vehicle Maximum Length:** None. **Other:** No washing of vehicles; no motorcycle riding; no ATVs.

To Get There

From Needles drive 0.8 mi. north on Needles Hwy. Bear right as it turns into River Rd. Take a left on Marina Dr. and continue 0.1 mi. to the park entrance on the left side.

NICE
Holiday Harbor RV Park and Marina

3605 Lakeshore Blvd., Nice 95464. T: (707) 274-1136; www.sojourner2000.com/clc/hh; jsbartz@pacific.net.

RV ★★★ | Tent n/a

Beauty: ★★★	Site Privacy: ★★
Spaciousness: ★★	Quiet: ★★
Security: ★★★	Cleanliness: ★★★
Insect Control: ★★★	Facilities: ★★★★

Holiday Harbor is at the northern end of Clear Lake, California's second largest freshwater lake and one of the top places for bass fishing in the entire country, according to reputable angling organizations. This is more of a marina than a campground, with comparable gravel-surfaced sites encircling the boat slips at the center of the property. There are a few sycamores and junipers on the lot, and though situated in a residential neighborhood, within easy walking distance of the commercial district of Nice, a wooden fence at the perimeter lends a degree of protective privacy to the lot. A county-owned stretch of beach abuts Holiday Harbor and sunsets viewed from its pier are heart-stoppers. This is one of the few places in which you can sleep within eyeshot of your boat, but if you are not hauling one there really is not much point in staying here. Tent camping is not permitted.

Basics

Operated By: Holiday Harbor RV Park & Marina. **Open:** All year. **Site Assignment:** Reservations accepted w/ V, MC. **Registration:** At office. **Fee:** $18–$20 plus 9% local tax, cash, CA check or V, MC. **Parking:** At site.

Facilities

Number of RV Sites: 34. **Number of Tent-Only Sites:** 0. **Hookups:** Water, electric (20, 30 amps), sewer, Internet. **Each Site:** Half-size picnic table, garden lantern. **Dump Station:** Yes. **Laundry:** Yes. **Pay Phone:** Yes. **Rest Rooms and Showers:** Yes. **Fuel:** No. **Propane:** No. **Internal Roads:** Gravel, good condition. **RV Service:** No. **Market:** Within 0.5 mi. in Nice. **Restaurant:** Within 0.5 mi. in Nice. **General Store:** No. **Vending:** Yes. **Swimming:** At swim beach on Clear Lake. **Playground:** No. **Other:** Marina, boat ramp. **Activities:** Fishing, boating, waterskiing, hiking, bicycling, birding. **Nearby Attractions:** Lake County Museum in Lakeport; Clear Lake State Park in Kelseyville. **Additional Information:** Lakeport Chamber of Commerce, (707) 263-5092; Lake County Marketing Program/Visitor Information Center, (707) 263-9544 or (800) 525-3743.

Restrictions

Pets: On 6 ft. leash. **Fires:** No. **Alcoholic Beverages:** Allowed. **Vehicle Maximum Length:** None. **Other:** No stay limit; no tents.

To Get There

From the town of Nice on Hwy. 20 at the north end of Clear Lake, turn left on Howard St. Drive 1 block, then turn left again onto Lakeshore Blvd. The campground entrance is 1 block away on the right.

O'BRIEN
Nelson Point

Conflict Point Rd., O'Brien 96070. T: (530) 275-1587 or reservations (800) 444-6777; www.r5.fs.fed.us/shastatrinity or www.reserveusa.com.

RV ★★★ | Tent ★★★★

Beauty: ★★★★	Site Privacy: ★★★★
Spaciousness: ★★	Quiet: ★★
Security: ★	Cleanliness: ★★
Insect Control: ★	Facilities: ★

Nelson Point is a cozy property that rests on a grassy hill just above one rippling arm of Shasta Lake, a little more than 20 miles north of Redding. It is a convenient hop just off I-5, and that is also its major drawback: you may wake up in the middle of the night to the sound of traffic and think for a moment you're in a highway rest area. Oaks and pines hover over the dirt-surfaced sites, which are also spaced well apart along the meandering camp lane. While most spots enjoy water views, number 5, a walk-in of some 20 steps, is tops in spaciousness and occupies a small promontory that is blessed with a 180-degree panorama of the lake. More private is 7, though it lies close to the road, and 6, too, is tucked away from its neighbors. The apalling amount of broken glass, food debris, bottle caps, and even bullet shells littering the ground indicates that the concessionaire operating this diamond-in-the-rough for the forest service must do more to maintain the property than simply emptying the cash box. An elevation of just 1,000 feet makes for very comfortable evenings early and late in the year.

Basics

Operated By: Shasta Recreation Company, concessionnaire. **Open:** Apr. through Sept. **Site Assignment:** Reservations accepted w/ V, MC, D for groups & limited number of sites. **Registration:** At entrance kiosk. **Fee:** $8, cash or check. **Parking:** At site.

Facilities

Number of RV Sites: 8. **Number of Tent-Only Sites:** 0. **Hookups:** None. **Each Site:** Picnic table, fire grate, some sites have stone fire ring. **Dump Station:** No. **Laundry:** No. **Pay Phone:** No. **Rest Rooms and Showers:** Vault toilets, no showers. **Fuel:** No. **Propane:** No. **Internal Roads:** Paved. **RV Service:** No. **Market:** 4 mi. north in Lakehead. **Restaurant:** 14 mi. south in Shasta Lake. **General Store:** No. **Vending:** No. **Swimming:** In Shasta Lake inlet. **Playground:** No. **Activities:** Fishing, boating, waterskiing. **Nearby Attractions:** Carter House Natural Science Museum, Turtle Bay Museums & Arboretum, Waterworks Park in Redding; Shasta Lake, Caverns, & Dam; Shasta State Historic Park; Whiskeytown National Recreation Area. **Additional Information:** Redding CVB, (530) 225-4100.

Restrictions

Pets: On 6 ft. leash. **Fires:** In fire grates only. **Alcoholic Beverages:** Allowed. **Vehicle Maximum Length:** 16 ft. **Other:** 14-day stay limit.

To Get There

From Redding drive 22 mi. north on I-5 and exit at Salt Creek Rd./Gilman Rd. Turn left and drive 1 block, then veer right onto Salt Creek Rd. After 0.3 mi. hang a left onto Conflict Point Rd. (opposite the highway underpass). The campground is 0.3 mi. ahead on the left.

OAKLAND
Anthony Chabot Regional Park

9999 Redwood Rd., Oakland 94619. T: (510) 562-2267; www.ebparks.org.

RV ★★★★ | Tent ★★★

Beauty: ★★★★	Site Privacy: ★★
Spaciousness: ★★★	Quiet: ★★★★
Security: ★★★	Cleanliness: ★★★
Insect Control: ★★	Facilities: ★★★

This wooded, pastoral setting is an oasis of calm and beauty only a few minutes drive from the urban bustle of Oakland and Berkeley. Five small loops are spread over a hilltop that is abundantly populated with fragrant eucalyptus trees—though contrary to what may be implied by the name of the access lane, Redwood Rd.—and a few sycamores. Some of the slim, exposed sites enjoy vistas of Lake Chabot, while others overlook a fertile pasture where goats often graze. Best of the latter are 10–12 in the hookup area. The most private of the drive-to sites is number 69 but ardent tenters should consider the even more secluded walk-ins in the direction of the water. In addition to several hiking trails there is a 12-mile bicycling path that is very popular with the thin tire set. The lake, which covers 315 acres, is stocked with fish on a regular basis. Security is good, with ranger patrols and a gate that is locked nightly at 10 p.m.

BASICS

Operated By: East Bay Regional Park District. **Open:** All year. **Site Assignment:** Reservations recommended; V, MC, D. **Registration:** At entrance booth. **Fee:** $15–$20, cash or V, MC, D. **Parking:** At site.

FACILITIES

Number of RV Sites: 65. **Number of Tent-Only Sites:** 10. **Hookups:** Water, electric (30 amps), sewer. **Each Site:** Picnic table, fire grate. **Dump Station:** Yes. **Laundry:** No. **Pay Phone:** Yes. **Rest Rooms and Showers:** Yes. **Fuel:** No. **Propane:** No. **Internal Roads:** Paved. **RV Service:** No. **Market:** 17 mi. west in Oakland. **Restaurant:** 17 mi. west in Oakland. **General Store:** No. **Vending:** No. **Swimming:** No. **Playground:** No. **Other:** Some wheelchair-accessible facilities, boat launch, marina, shooting range. **Activities:** Hiking, fishing, bicycling, horseback riding, kayaking, canoeing. **Nearby Attractions:** Berkeley Botanical Garden & museums; Oakland museums, zoo, Dunsmuir House & Gardens Historic Estate, Chabot Space & Science Center, Jack London Square & more. **Additional Information:** Oakland CVB, (510) 839-5924.

RESTRICTIONS

Pets: On 6 ft. leash; $1 fee. **Fires:** In fire grates only. **Alcoholic Beverages:** Allowed at site, beer & wine only. **Vehicle Maximum Length:** 39 ft. **Other:** 15-day stay limit; no loaded firearms; no wood gathering.

TO GET THERE

From Oakland on I-580 drive 5.5 mi. east. Exit on Hwy. 13 north and after 1 mi. turn right onto Redwood Rd. Continue for 7.8 mi. to the park entrance on the right. The campground is 2 mi. ahead.

ORICK

Prairie Creek Redwoods State Park, Elk Prairie Campground

Newton B. Drury Scenic Pkwy., Orick 95555. T: (707) 464-6101 ext. 5301 or 5064 or reservations (800) 444-7275; www.cal-parks.ca.gov or www.reserveamerica.com.

RV ★★★★	Tent ★★★★
Beauty: ★★★★	Site Privacy: ★★★★
Spaciousness: ★★★★	Quiet: ★★★★
Security: ★★★	Cleanliness: ★★★★
Insect Control: ★★★	Facilities: ★★

Tall as they are, it is easy to overlook the redwood trees when you visit this delightful park. That is largely due to the presence of a good-sized herd of photogenic Roosevelt elk, which can usually be observed grazing in the open grassland near the park's entrance along US 101, as well as down by the shore close to the primitive Gold Bluff Beach campground. The latter is in a beautiful location, between the ocean and 100-foot-high bluffs, but to reach it you will have to navigate six miles along a dirt minefield of potholes, a stress test for your nerves as well as your vehicle's axles. Prairie Creek's other campground, Elk Prairie, is inland from the bluffs and far easier to reach. Its single meadow loop—favored by RVs—is prime elk-viewing territory, and its wooded double loop allows for shade, space, and privacy. Curiously, there are few redwoods present, but an abundance of other conifers as well as maples and moss-encrusted alders contribute to a lush, rain forest atmosphere. The largest, most private sites are those nearest to the creek, where the gently gurgling water will serenade you to sleep at night.

BASICS

Operated By: California Dept. of Parks & Recreation. **Open:** All year. **Site Assignment:** Reservations recommended; V, MC, D. **Registration:** At entrance booth. **Fee:** $12, cash or CA check. **Parking:** At site.

FACILITIES

Number of RV Sites: 75. **Number of Tent-Only Sites:** 0. **Hookups:** None. **Each Site:** Picnic table, fire grate, food storage box. **Dump Station:** Yes. **Laundry:** No. **Pay Phone:** Yes. **Rest Rooms and Showers:** Yes. **Fuel:** No. **Propane:** No. **Internal Roads:** Paved, narrow, & winding. **RV Service:** No. **Market:** 4 mi. south in Orick. **Restaurant:** 4 mi. south in Orick. **General Store:** No. **Vending:** No. **Swimming:** No. **Playground:** No. **Other:** Some wheelchair-accessible facilities, visitor center. **Activities:** Hiking, bicycling, wildlife viewing, photography, beachcombing. **Nearby Attractions:** Humboldt Lagoons State Park & Redwood National & State Parks in Orick; Trees of Mystery in Klamath. **Additional Information:** Orick Chamber of Commerce, (707) 488-2885; Klamath Chamber of Commerce, (707) 482-7165.

RESTRICTIONS

Pets: On 6 ft. leash. **Fires:** In fire grates only. **Alcoholic Beverages:** Allowed at site. **Vehicle Maximum Length:** 27 ft. **Other:** 14-day stay limit from May 1–Sept. 30; no firearms; no wood gathering; no mushroom-plucking.

TO GET THERE

From Crescent City drive 37 mi. south on US 101. Exit and turn right on the Newton B. Drury Scenic Pkwy. Continue for 1.2 mi. to the park entrance on the left.

ORLAND

Buckhorn

Buckhorn Rd., Orland 95963. T: (530) 865-4781 or reservations (877) 444-6777 or marina (530) 865-2665; F: (530) 865-5283; www.spk.usace.army.mil/cespk-co/lakes/blackbutte.html or www.reserveusa.com; blackbutte-info@spk.usace.army.mil.

RV ★★★★	Tent ★★★★
Beauty: ★★★★	Site Privacy: ★★
Spaciousness: ★★★	Quiet: ★★★
Security: ★★★★	Cleanliness: ★★★
Insect Control: ★★★	Facilities: ★★★★

Black Butte Lake may seem like a mirage at first glance, its blue-green surface shimmering in the middle of sun-baked brown hills, with black-mauve volcanic rocks crowning the scene. Go ahead and pinch yourself, it's really there. It is also, as one of the largest lakes in the region, a hugely popular summertime recreation area that attracts anyone with a boat for miles around. Buckhorn is one of two campgrounds on this US Army Corps of Engineers domain, 12 miles west of Orland and I-5. Several loops cling to the undulating contours of the hillside abutting the lake, which results in a high percentage of lake-view sites. A sprinkling of oaks shed adequate shade, and screening and space are average. While all types of watercrafts are permitted, the stiff breezes that often sweep across the lake make sailing especially rewarding. Black Butte Lake is one of the better locations for crappie fishing in northern California.

BASICS

Operated By: US Army Corps of Engineers. **Open:** All year. **Site Assignment:** Reservations accepted w/ MC, V, D. **Registration:** At entrance booth. **Fee:** $14 from Mar. 1–Sept. 30, $10 the rest of the year; cash or check. **Parking:** At site.

FACILITIES

Number of RV Sites: 87. **Number of Tent-Only Sites:** 5. **Hookups:** None. **Each Site:** Picnic table, fire grate, barbecue grill. **Dump Station:** Yes. **Laundry:** No. **Pay Phone:** Yes. **Rest Rooms and Showers:** Flush & portable toilets, no showers. **Fuel:** No. **Propane:** Yes. **Internal Roads:** Paved. **RV Service:** No. **Market:** 12 mi. east in Orland. **Restaurant:** 12 mi. east in Orland. **General Store:** Yes, at marina. **Vending:** No. **Swimming:** In Black Butte Lake. **Playground:** Yes. **Other:** Some wheelchair-accessible facilities, boat launch, marina. **Activities:** Fishing, hiking, sailing, windsurfing, boat rentals. **Nearby Attractions:** Tejama County Park in Corning; Chico museums & Bidwell Mansion State Historic Park; outlet shopping in Anderson; William B. Ide Adobe State Historic Park near Red Bluff. **Additional Information:** Corning District Chamber of Commerce, (530) 824-5550; Chico Chamber of Commerce & Visitor Bureau, (530) 891-5556 or (800) 852-8570.

RESTRICTIONS

Pets: On leash. **Fires:** In fire grates only. **Alcoholic Beverages:** Allowed. **Vehicle Maximum Length:** 35 ft. **Other:** 14-day stay limit.

TO GET THERE

In Orland on I-5 take the Black Butte Lake Exit. Head west on Rd. 200/Newville Rd. for 12 mi. Turn left on Buckhorn Rd. and continue straight to the campground.

OROVILLE

Lake Oroville State Recreation Area, Bidwell Canyon Campground

Arroyo Dr., Oroville 95966. T: (530) 538-2219 or (530) 538-2200 or reservations (800) 444-7275; www.cal-parks.ca.gov or www.norcal.parks.state.ca.us or www.reserveamerica.com.

RV ★★★★ Tent ★★

Beauty: ★★★ Site Privacy: ★★
Spaciousness: ★★ Quiet: ★★★
Security: ★★★ Cleanliness: ★★★
Insect Control: ★★★ Facilities: ★★★★

When Lake Oroville is full it is a beautiful sight. Unfortunately, its level depends both on winter snow melt and how much it has been drawn down during the summer. Management tries to keep the water near capacity at least through the fourth of July holiday, when the recreation area overflows with campers, but Mother Nature does not always cooperate. Not that campsites are affected either way, since few are endowed with water views. Of the two double circuits, Loop I (numbers 1–39) is the grassier, with limited space between pine- and live oak–shaded sites. The crowding is no better in Loop II (40–75), where the live oaks are complemented by madrone and manzanita. Two of the better sites for privacy are 31 and 44, but overall the constricted layout of this facility makes it more suitable for RV campers than tenters. The exceptions are the remote boat-in sites, assuming there is water available to provide access.

Basics

Operated By: California Dept. of Parks & Recreation. **Open:** All year. **Site Assignment:** Reservations accepted w/ V, MC, D. **Registration:** At entrance booth. **Fee:** $16, cash or CA check. **Parking:** At site.

Facilities

Number of RV Sites: 75. **Number of Tent-Only Sites:** 0. **Hookups:** Water, electric (20, 30 amps), sewer. **Each Site:** Picnic table, fire grate. **Dump Station:** No. **Laundry:** No. **Pay Phone:** Yes. **Rest Rooms and Showers:** Yes. **Fuel:** No. **Propane:** Yes. **Internal Roads:** Paved. **RV Service:** No. **Market:** 10 mi. west in Oroville. **Restaurant:** 10 mi. west in Oroville. **General Store:** Yes, w/ snack bar at marina. **Vending:** No. **Swimming:** In Lake Oroville. **Playground:** No. **Other:** Some wheelchair-accessible facilities, 7-lane boat ramp, marina. **Activities:** Fishing, waterskiing, hiking, windsurfing, horseback riding, boat rentals. **Nearby Attractions:** Oroville Dam, Chinese Temple & Garden, Pioneer Museum, Freeman Bicycle Trail; Gold Nuggett Museum in Paradise. **Additional Information:** Oroville Area Chamber of Commerce, (530) 538-2542 or (800) 655-GOLD.

Restrictions

Pets: On 6 ft. leash. **Fires:** In fire grates only. **Alcoholic Beverages:** Allowed at site. **Vehicle Maximum Length:** 40 ft. **Other:** 30-day stay limit; no firearms; no wood gathering.

To Get There

From Oroville drive 7 mi. east on Hwy. 162. Turn left on Kelly Ridge Rd. and continue for 1.6 mi. to Arroyo Dr. Turn right and proceed to the park entrance 0.5 mi. ahead.

PALO ALTO

Butano State Park

1500 Cloverdale Rd., Pescadero 94060. T: (650) 879-2040 or reservations (800) 444-7275; www.cal-parks.ca.gov or www.reserveamerica.com.

RV ★★★ Tent ★★★★

Beauty: ★★★★ Site Privacy: ★★★★
Spaciousness: ★★★★ Quiet: ★★★
Security: ★★★★ Cleanliness: ★★★★
Insect Control: ★★★ Facilities: ★★

You've heard the expression "good things come in small packages"? That is certainly true of this beautiful park, another in the fine constellation of coast redwood preserves that are located above Santa Cruz and to the east of San Jose. The drive to Butano is easier than the others, along a marginally wider road without quite as many mountainous turns. Sites, too, are roomier and scattered farther apart than those at Portola Redwoods State Park a few miles away. Direct sunlight onto the double loop is largely blocked by the magnificent stands of Sequoia sempervirens, which are so dominant that only a few tan oaks have been able to lay down roots. Tenters will enjoy the privacy of the many recessed walk-in sites, and of the drive-to options, 6 is level and very roomy, and 9, tucked behind a fallen giant, is quite private. We encountered quails, rabbits ,and a doe and its tiny fawn on our last visit; they were attracted to the grounds by a small creek that runs through camp.

Basics

Operated By: California Dept. of Parks & Recreation. **Open:** All year. **Site Assignment:** Reservations accepted w/ V, MC, D. **Registration:** At entrance booth. **Fee:** $12, cash or CA check. **Parking:** At site.

Facilities

Number of RV Sites: 21. **Number of Tent-Only Sites:** 17. **Hookups:** None. **Each Site:** Picnic table, fire grate, food storage box. **Dump Station:** No. **Laundry:** No. **Pay Phone:** Yes. **Rest Rooms and Showers:** Flush & pit toilets, no showers. **Fuel:** No. **Propane:** No. **Internal Roads:** Paved. **RV Service:** No. **Market:** 24 mi. north in Half Moon Bay. **Restaurant:** 24 mi. north in Half Moon Bay. **General Store:** No. **Vending:** No. **Swimming:** No. **Playground:** No. **Other:** Some wheelchair-accessible facilities, visitor center. **Activities:** Hiking, birding, exploring redwood forests. **Nearby Attractions:** Pigeon Point Lighthouse & downtown Half Moon Bay; Montara & Gray Whale Cove State Beaches; several redwood forests. **Additional Information:** Half Moon Bay Coastside Chamber of Commerce & Visitors Bureau, (650) 726-8380.

Restrictions

Pets: On 6 ft. leash. **Fires:** In fire grates only. **Alcoholic Beverages:** Allowed at site. **Vehicle Maximum Length:** 27 ft. **Other:** 14-day stay limit; no firearms; no wood gathering.

To Get There

From the junction of Hwy. 1 and Hwy. 92 in Half Moon Bay, drive 17 mi. south on Hwy. 1. Turn left on Pescadero Rd., drive 2.7 mi. and turn right on Cloverdale Rd. The park entrance is 4.5 mi. ahead on the left.

PASADENA

Monte Cristo

12371 North Little Tujunga Canyon Rd., San Fernando 91342. T: (818) 899-1900; F: (818) 896-6727; www.r5.fs.fed.us/angeles.

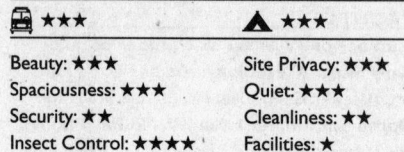

RV ★★★ Tent ★★★

Beauty: ★★★ Site Privacy: ★★★
Spaciousness: ★★★ Quiet: ★★★
Security: ★★ Cleanliness: ★★
Insect Control: ★★★★ Facilities: ★

To reach Monte Cristo you will have to drive 20 miles north of La Cañada along steep, windy roads, with the stretch on CR N3 showcasing highly dramatic craggy peaks. There is no let down at the campground, either, which is tucked under sycamores and oaks in a mountain knoll (3,600 feet elevation) deep in the Angeles National Forest. Agaves and pines round out a setting that is often overrun with family groups, especially on weekends. And no wonder, given that deep sites, surfaced with a mix of grass and dirt, are planted well apart along the camp's figure-8 loop, which is bisected by a small creek. Those spots are largely comparable, though we prefer the ones at the far end of the camp's entrance because that area picks up less road noise. As is typical of many national forest properties, security and maintenance are lax, with the result that litter is often to be found in the fire grates.

Basics

Operated By: Angeles National Forest, Los Angeles River Ranger District. **Open:** All year, weather permitting. **Site Assignment:** First come, first served. **Registration:** At entrance kiosk. **Fee:** $8, cash or check. **Parking:** At site.

Facilities

Number of RV Sites: 19. **Number of Tent-Only Sites:** 0. **Hookups:** None. **Each Site:** Picnic table, fire grate. **Dump Station:** No. **Laundry:** No. **Pay Phone:** No. **Rest Rooms and Showers:** Vault toilets, no showers. **Fuel:** No. **Propane:** No. **Internal Roads:** Paved. **RV Service:** No. **Market:** 20 mi. south in La Cañada. **Restaurant:** 20 mi. south in La Cañada. **General Store:** No. **Vending:** No. **Swimming:** No. **Playground:** No. **Other:** Some wheelchair-accessible facilities. **Activities:** Hiking, wading in creek. **Nearby Attractions:** Six Flags Magic Mountain, downtown Pasadena, Hollywood's theme parks. **Additional Information:** La Cañada Flintridge Chamber of Commerce, (818) 790-4289.

Restrictions

Pets: On leash. **Fires:** In fire grates only. **Alcoholic Beverages:** Allowed. **Vehicle Maximum Length:** 30 ft. **Other:** 14-day stay limit.

To Get There

From I-210 in La Cañada/Flintridge head north on Hwy. 2. After 9 mi. turn left onto CR N3, direction Palmdale. Drive 10 mi. and turn right into the campground.

PINECREST

Pinecrest

Pinecrest Lake Rd., Pinecrest 95364. T: (209) 965-3434 or reservations (877) 444-6777; F: (209) 965-3372; www.r5.fs.fed.us/stanislaus or www.reserveusa.com.

RV ★★★★	Tent ★★★
Beauty: ★★★★	Site Privacy: ★★★
Spaciousness: ★★★	Quiet: ★★
Security: ★★	Cleanliness: ★★
Insect Control: ★★★	Facilities: ★★★

There is more than merely the aura of a resort town to Pinecrest, it actually delivers the goods. Activities range from hiking and bicycling to fishing, swimming, and boating; amenities include an expansive picnic area near the water, a marina, and, across the street, a post office, restaurant and general store stocked with everything from fresh produce to liquor to hardware. The huge campground, which is 30 miles east of Sonora, is handsomely framed by its high altitude (5,600 feet) Sierra Nevada locale, rubbing up against the clear blue Pinecrest Lake, with pine and granite studded hills all around. Even Shrangi-la had its downside, however, and Pinecrest is no different. Sites of grass and pine needles pinch a bit as space is at a premium over the camp's multiple series of loops. That constricted feeling is accentuated by the presence of private vacation cabins off to one side of the property, which also detract from the rustic atmosphere. Nonetheless, privacy is not bad, as thick groves of cedars, ponderosa, and lodgepole pines, as well as a widespread debris field of glacial erratics, contribute a degree of screening. The grungy, pitted restrooms are in urgent need of renovation.

Basics

Operated By: Dodge Ridge Corp., concessionaire. **Open:** May through Oct., weather permitting. **Site Assignment:** Reservations required from May 15 to Sept. 5; V, MC, D, AE. **Registration:** At entrance booth. **Fee:** $16, cash or check. **Parking:** At site.

Facilities

Number of RV Sites: 200. **Number of Tent-Only Sites:** 0. **Hookups:** None. **Each Site:** Picnic table, fire grate. **Dump Station:** No. **Laundry:** No. **Pay Phone:** Yes. **Rest Rooms and Showers:** Yes. **Fuel:** No. **Propane:** No. **Internal Roads:** Paved. **RV Service:** No. **Market:** Across the street is a large, well-stocked general store. **Restaurant:** Across the street. **General Store:** Yes. **Vending:** No. **Swimming:** In Pinecrest Lake. **Playground:** No. **Other:** Limited wheelchair-accessible facilities, boat ramp, marina. **Activities:** Hiking, fishing, boat rentals, bicycling. **Nearby Attractions:** Tuolumne County Museum & History Center in Sonora; Yosemite National Park; Ahwahnee Whitewater Rafting in Columbia. **Additional Information:** Yosemite Area Traveler Information, (209) 723-3153; Tuolumne County Visitors Bureau, (209) 533-4420 or (800) 446-1333.

Restrictions

Pets: On leash. **Fires:** In fire grates only. **Alcoholic Beverages:** Allowed. **Vehicle Maximum Length:** 22 ft. **Other:** 14-day stay limit.

To Get There

From Sonora drive 28 mi. east on Hwy. 108. Turn right at the sign for Pinecrest Lake and continue for 0.7 mi. to the campground entrance on the right.

PISMO BEACH

Pismo State Beach, North Beach Campground

Hwy. 1, Pismo Beach 93445. T: (805) 489-2684; www.cal-parks.ca.gov or www.reserveamerica.com.

RV ★★★	Tent ★★★★
Beauty: ★★★★	Site Privacy: ★★★
Spaciousness: ★★★	Quiet: ★★★
Security: ★★★	Cleanliness: ★★★
Insect Control: ★★	Facilities: ★★

Sand and surf, in a nutshell, are two attributes that make this a central coast standout, one of the prettier stretches of beach in the area. Add to that the wintertime presence of tens of thousands of monarch butterflies, drawn to the park by its towering eucalyptus trees, and it's clear why swarms of tourists descend on the camp like ants to a picnic throughout the summer and most weekends the rest of the year. Located just off of Hwy. 1, one mile south of town, North Beach is separated from the water by a high series of dunes. These obstruct views of the ocean, but also buffer the campground from its blustery breezes. Grassy sites are level and of average size, with Monterey pines and flowering bottle brush enhancing the modest screening provided by the fragrant eucalyptus. Unlike Oceano, two miles to the south, North Beach does not allow day use, meaning that campers enjoy their piece of shore without the added crush of daytrippers. This is also the prettier of the two camps, but its lack of hookups means that if you need electricity Oceano is the place to be.

Basics

Operated By: California Dept. of Parks & Recreation. **Open:** All year. **Site Assignment:** Reservations accepted w/ V, MC, D. **Registration:** At entrance booth. **Fee:** $12, cash or CA check. **Parking:** At site.

Facilities

Number of RV Sites: 103. **Number of Tent-Only Sites:** 0. **Hookups:** None. **Each Site:** Picnic table, fire grate, food storage box. **Dump Station:** Yes. **Laundry:** No. **Pay Phone:** Yes. **Rest Rooms and Showers:** Yes. **Fuel:** No. **Propane:** No. **Internal Roads:** Paved. **RV Service:** No. **Market:** 1 mi. north in Pismo Beach. **Restaurant:** 1 mi. north in Pismo Beach. **General Store:** No. **Vending:** Yes. **Swimming:** In Pacific Ocean, if you can tolerate it. **Playground:** No. **Other:** Some wheelchair-accessible facilities. **Activities:** Fishing, surfing, clamming, horseback riding, hiking, golf. **Nearby Attractions:** Wineries; San Luis Obispo mission & musems; Oceano Dunes State Vehicular Recreation Area. **Additional Information:** Pismo Beach Chamber of Commerce, (805) 773-4382; San Luis Obispo County Visitors & Conference Bureau, (800) 634-1414 or (805) 541-8000.

Restrictions

Pets: On 6 ft. leash. **Fires:** In fire grates only. **Alcoholic Beverages:** Allowed at site. **Vehicle Maximum Length:** 36 ft. **Other:** 7-day stay limit from Apr. 1–Oct. 29; no firearms; no wood gathering.

To Get There

In Pismo Beach on US 101 take the Pismo Beach State Park Exit. Drive 2.8 mi. west (toward the ocean) on East Grand Ave. and turn right on Hwy. 1. After 0.8 mi. turn left into the campground.

POLLOCK PINES

Ice House

FR 32, Pollock Pines 95726. T: (530) 644-2349 or reservations (877) 444-6777; F: (530) 647-5405; www.r5.fs.fed.us/eldorado or www.reserveusa.com.

RV ★★★★	Tent ★★★★
Beauty: ★★★★	Site Privacy: ★★★
Spaciousness: ★★★	Quiet: ★★★★
Security: ★★★	Cleanliness: ★★★
Insect Control: ★★★	Facilities: ★★

The concession that operates Ice House delivers primitive camping conditions for its nightly fee of $15, which seems appalling at first blush. Don't let price-gouging deter you, though, from coming to this beautiful, rough-cut campground. Its wild, unspoiled appearance is an idiosyncratic reminder of the relative youth and vitality of the Sierra Nevada range, and a bit reminiscent of Grover Hot Springs State Park, at Markleeville. Ice House reflects two sorts of environments, from the reservoir below its two undulating loops to the lofty, snow-dusted mountain peaks high above. Sites of dirt and pine needles are grouped closely together, but are well-buffered by an abundance of enormous boulders and concentrations of ponderosa and Jeffrey pines, incense cedar, and manzanita. The latter appears in especially thick concentrations in the second circuit, which also holds more of the quirkily engaging sites. With an elevation of 5,436 feet, roads in this area can be snow-covered from late Oct. until mid-May.

Basics

Operated By: American Land & Leisure, concessionaire. **Open:** Mid-May to mid-Oct., weather permitting. **Site Assignment:** Reservations accepted w/ V, MC, D. **Registration:** At entrance kiosk. **Fee:** $15, cash or check; $30 for double site. **Parking:** At site.

Facilities

Number of RV Sites: 66. **Number of Tent-Only Sites:** 17. **Hookups:** None. **Each Site:** Picnic table, fire grate, barbecue grill. **Dump Station:** Yes. **Laundry:** No. **Pay Phone:** No. **Rest Rooms and Showers:** Vault toilets, no showers. **Fuel:** No. **Propane:** No. **Internal Roads:** Paved but bumpy, windy & narrow. **RV Service:** No. **Market:** 21 mi. southwest in Pollock Pines. **Restaurant:** 21 mi. southwest in Pollock Pines. **General Store:** No. **Vending:** No. **Swimming:** In Ice House Reservoir. **Playground:** No. **Other:** Some wheelchair-accessible facilities, boat ramp. **Activities:** Fishing, hiking, boating, bicycling, boulder scrambling. **Nearby Attractions:** Fountain-Tallman Museum in Placerville; El Dorado National Forest in Camino; Sly Park Recreation Area in Pollock Pines. **Additional Information:** El Dorado County Visitors Authority, (530) 642-8029 or (887) 588-4FUN; Pollock Pines–Camino Chamber of Commerce, (530) 644-3970 or (530) 644-2498.

Restrictions

Pets: On leash. **Fires:** In fire grates only. **Alcoholic Beverages:** Allowed. **Vehicle Maximum Length:** 22 ft. **Other:** 14-day stay limit.

To Get There

From Placerville drive 20 mi. east on US 50. Turn north (left) on Ice House Rd. and continue for 11 mi. to FR 32. Hang a right, direction Ice House Reservoir, and proceed for 1.2 mi. to the campground entrance.

POLLOCK PINES

Peninsula Recreation Area, Sunset Camp and Fashoda Camp

Ice House Rd., Pollock Pines 95726. T: (530) 644-2349 or reservations (877) 444-6777; F: (530) 647-5405; www.r5.fs.fed.us/eldorado or www.reserveusa.com.

RV: ★★★ Tent: ★★★

Beauty: ★★★★	Site Privacy: ★★★
Spaciousness: ★★★	Quiet: ★★★★
Security: ★★★	Cleanliness: ★★★
Insect Control: ★★★	Facilities: ★★

When we first saw the overnight fee for this Eldorado National Forest camp our eyes bugged out from sticker shock. Fifteen dollars seems pretty pricy for a primitive place that doesn't have showers, flush toilets, or even cold-water sinks. The charm of this handsome lakeside forest, though, can easily put one in a forgiving mood. For one thing, the campground, which is divided into Sunset and Fashoda units, occupies a densely treed peninsula that juts out into and rises above Union Valley Reservoir. The woodsy and watery setting is majestically framed by a surrounding series of jagged Sierra peaks. An odor of vanilla often permeates the air, emanating from the many stands of Jeffrey pine. Fair-sized sites are mostly level; the walk-ins at Fashoda are shady and fairly private, while Sunset's slots are screened by fallen trees and large stumps. The lake is best for boating and fishing from spring through early summer, before it gets drawn down too much. Mushroom-picking is a popular pastime in these woods.

Basics

Operated By: American Land & Leisure, concessionaire. **Open:** Late May through Sept., weather permitting. **Site Assignment:** Reservations accepted w/ V, MC, D. **Registration:** Every loop has a kiosk for payment. **Fee:** $15, cash or check; $30 for double site. **Parking:** At site or designated lot for walk-ins.

Facilities

Number of RV Sites: 131. **Number of Tent-Only Sites:** 30. **Hookups:** None. **Each Site:** Picnic table, fire grate, barbecue grill. **Dump Station:** Yes. **Laundry:** No. **Pay Phone:** No. **Rest Rooms and Showers:** Vault toilets, no showers. **Fuel:** No. **Propane:** No. **Internal Roads:** Paved but narrow, bumpy, & windy. **RV Service:** No. **Market:** 25 mi. southwest in Pollock Pines. **Restaurant:** 25 mi. southwest in Pollock Pines. **General Store:** No. **Vending:** No. **Swimming:** In Union Valley Reservoir. **Playground:** No. **Other:** Some wheelchair-accessible facilities, boat ramp, beach. **Activities:** Fishing, hiking, boating, mushroom-plucking. **Nearby Attractions:** Fountain-Tallman Museum in Placerville; El Dorado National Forest in Camino; Sly Park Recreation Area in Pollock Pines. **Additional Information:** El Dorado County Visitors Authority, (530) 642-8029 or (887) 588-4FUN; Pollock Pines–Camino Chamber of Commerce, (530) 644-3970 or (530) 644-2498.

Restrictions

Pets: On leash. **Fires:** In fire grates only. **Alcoholic Beverages:** Allowed. **Vehicle Maximum Length:** 22 ft. **Other:** 14-day stay limit.

To Get There

From Placerville drive 20 mi. east on US 50. Turn north (left) on Ice House Rd. and continue for 15.2 mi. to the Peninsula Creek Recreation Area turnoff. Turn left and proceed for another mi. to the campground entrance.

POMONA

East Shore RV Park

Puddingstone Lake, 1440 Camperview Rd., San Dimas 91773. T: (909) 599-8355; F: (909) 592-7481; www.holidayguide.com/camp-usa/california/eastshorervpark; esrv@pacbell.net.

RV: ★★★★ Tent: ★★

Beauty: ★★	Site Privacy: ★★
Spaciousness: ★★★	Quiet: ★★★
Security: ★★★★	Cleanliness: ★★★
Insect Control: ★★★	Facilities: ★★★★★

When you arrive at East Shore RV Park you will be handed map of the property, which is a good thing as without it you can forget about navigating your way through its maze of loops. Located just 30 miles east of downtown Los Angeles, above the shores of Puddingstone Lake and within the Frank Bonelli Regional Park, not only is this place attractively landscaped, with undulating meadows accented by such trees as alder, eucalyptus, sycamore, magnolia, and a range of conifers, but it is well endowed with a whole host of facilities. You want boating or fishing? You've got it. Looking to play some golf? No problem. Need to hook up to the Internet? That's a "can-do," too. And security is tighter than a martinet's collar, with both an entrance booth check point and regular ranger patrols. That sites tend to be wedged rather snugly together only really impacts tenters. And for them East Shore has set aside a "wilderness area" meadow, a dubious amenity with undesignated sites on ground so curvaceous as to be unusable by RVs. Two small knocks on this outfit are the occasional buzz of airplanes using the neighboring county airport and restrooms that should be equipped with real mirrors instead of the shatterproof stainless steel more commonly seen in cut-rate national forest properties.

Basics

Operated By: East Shore RV Park, Phyllis Cook. **Open:** All year. **Site Assignment:** Reservations accepted w/ MC, V, D. **Registration:** At office. **Fee:** $24–$29. **Parking:** At site.

Facilities

Number of RV Sites: 518. **Number of Tent-Only Sites:** 25. **Hookups:** Water, electric (20, 30, 50 amps), sewer, cable TV, Internet. **Each Site:** Picnic table, fire grate. **Dump Station:** Yes. **Laundry:** Yes. **Pay Phone:** Yes. **Rest Rooms and Showers:** Yes. **Fuel:** No. **Propane:** Yes. **Internal Roads:** Paved. **RV Service:** No. **Market:** 3 mi. north in San Dimas. **Restaurant:** 3 mi. north in San Dimas. **General Store:** Yes. **Vending:** Yes. **Swimming:** 2 pools. **Playground:** Yes. **Other:** Some wheelchair-accessible facilities. **Activities:** Fishing, boating, waterskiing, hiking, bicycling, volleyball, horseshoe pit, horseback riding rentals, golf. **Nearby Attractions:** Disneyland, Six Flags Magic Mountain, Riverside & its museums, gardens, & historic buildings. **Additional Information:** Pomona Chamber of Commerce, (909) 622-1256.

Restrictions

Pets: On leash, $2 fee. **Fires:** In fire grates only. **Alcoholic Beverages:** Allowed. **Vehicle Maximum Length:** 45 ft. **Other:** 7-day stay limit for tents, no stay limit for RVs.

To Get There

From I-10 at Pomona, take Exit 44A/Fairplex Dr. Proceed north for 0.7 mi. and turn left on Via Verde. After 0.5 mi., at the stop sign, turn right on Campers View. The park is straight ahead.

POMONA

Prado Regional Park

16700 Euclid Ave., Chino 91710. T: (909) 597-4260; F: (909) 393-8428; www.co.san-bernardino.ca.us/parks/prado.htm.

RV: ★★★★ Tent: ★★★

Beauty: ★★★★	Site Privacy: ★★★
Spaciousness: ★★★★	Quiet: ★★★★
Security: ★★★★	Cleanliness: ★★★
Insect Control: ★★	Facilities: ★★★★

This attractive park is just 35 miles east of downtown Los Angeles, and yet to look at its verdant grounds you might think you were in the middle of farm country. That impression is accentuated by the presence of a neighboring ranch that pens cattle up near one of Prado's two loops. The pitiful sight of so many beasts herded together in a small parcel of muddy, denuded soil is outdone only by the powerful reek of ammonia emanating from their direction, a one-two sensory punch that could convert the most committed of meat eaters to vegetarianism. You won't have much to beef about though if you bring your fishing rod to

Prado, as the lake is well stocked w/ trout in winter and catfish in summer. Grassy sites are exposed but roomy, set under young sycamores, eucalyptus, and pines. Aim for any of 7–75, as they are not only among the shadier, but also out of view of the bovine stalag. Of the great number of amenities here, one of the more unusual is an area set aside on the lake for radio-controlled model boats.

BASICS

Operated By: San Bernardino County, Regional Parks Dept. **Open:** All year. **Site Assignment:** Reservations accepted w/ V, MC, D. **Registration:** At entrance booth. **Fee:** $15, cash, check or V, MC, D. **Parking:** At site.

FACILITIES

Number of RV Sites: 75. **Number of Tent-Only Sites:** 0. **Hookups:** Water, electric (50 amps), sewer. **Each Site:** Picnic table, fire ring. **Dump Station:** Yes. **Laundry:** Yes. **Pay Phone:** Yes. **Rest Rooms and Showers:** Yes. **Fuel:** No. **Propane:** No. **Internal Roads:** Paved. **RV Service:** No. **Market:** 8 mi. south in Corona. **Restaurant:** 8 mi. south in Corona. **General Store:** No. **Vending:** No. **Swimming:** No. **Playground:** Yes. **Other:** Some wheelchair-accessible facilities, boat ramp. **Activities:** Fishing, horseback riding rentals, soccer field, boat rentals, golf. **Nearby Attractions:** Disneyland, Six Flags Magic Mountain, Riverside & its museums, gardens, & historic buildings. **Additional Information:** San Bernardino County, Regional Parks Dept., (909) 38-PARKS.

RESTRICTIONS

Pets: On leash no longer than 6 ft., $1 fee. **Fires:** In fire rings only. **Alcoholic Beverages:** Allowed at site. **Vehicle Maximum Length:** 60 ft. **Other:** 14-day stay limit; no loaded firearms; no wood gathering.

TO GET THERE

In Pomona exit Hwy. 60 on Euclid Ave./Hwy. 83 and head south for 0.6 mi. Turn left at the sign for the regional park.

PORTERVILLE

Tule Recreation Area

Hwy. 190, Porterville 93258. T: (559) 784-0215 or reservations (877) 444-6777; F: (559) 784-5469; www.spk.usace.army.mil/cespk-co/lakes/success.html or www.reserveusa.com.

RV ★★★★ Tent ★★★

Beauty: ★★★	Site Privacy: ★★
Spaciousness: ★★★★	Quiet: ★★★
Security: ★★★★	Cleanliness: ★★★
Insect Control: ★★★	Facilities: ★★★

Sun-scorched buttes rise above the multi-pronged lake that serves as a focal point to this recreation area. How people cooled off here before the US Army Corps of Engineers created Lake Success in 1961 is anybody's guess. With plenty of iced-down beer, perhaps, and that might still be considered an essential ingredient to any summertime visit. There is a scattered presence of such trees as oak, eucalyptus, buttonwood, oleander, juniper, and various conifers throughout the double-looped campground, but shade remains scarcer than candy in a dentist's office. In a facility that appears to put function ahead of aesthetics, ramadas would be a welcome addition to the sites. But hey!, the extra exposure to the blazing sun is just one more excuse to jump in the water. Not convinced? Then try to land 26, 29, 30, or 41, some of the few, the proud, the shaded. Located just off Hwy. 190, nine miles east of Porterville, the campground is subject to traffic noise. Unfortunately, an above average amount of bottles, 'butts, and plastic pollute the grounds.

BASICS

Operated By: US Army Corps of Engineers. **Open:** All year. **Site Assignment:** Reservations recommended; V, MC, D. **Registration:** At office at the end of the driveway. **Fee:** $16–$21, cash or check. **Parking:** At site.

FACILITIES

Number of RV Sites: 104. **Number of Tent-Only Sites:** 0. **Hookups:** Water, electric (30 amps). **Each Site:** Picnic table, fire grate, barbecue grill, lantern pole. **Dump Station:** Yes. **Laundry:** No. **Pay Phone:** Yes. **Rest Rooms and Showers:** Yes. **Fuel:** No. **Propane:** No. **Internal Roads:** Paved. **RV Service:** No. **Market:** 9 mi. west in Porterville. **Restaurant:** 9 mi. west in Porterville. **General Store:** Yes. **Vending:** Yes. **Swimming:** In Lake Success. **Playground:** Yes. **Other:** Some wheelchair-accessible facilities, two boat ramps, marina. **Activities:** Fishing, boat rentals, sailing, waterskiing, hiking, horseback riding. **Nearby Attractions:** Porterville Historical Museum & Zauld House & Gardens; Kaweah Oaks Preserve in Exeter; California Hot Springs. **Additional Information:** Porterville Chamber of Commerce, (559) 784-7503.

RESTRICTIONS

Pets: On leash. **Fires:** In fire grates only. **Alcoholic Beverages:** Allowed. **Vehicle Maximum Length:** 30 ft. **Other:** 14-day stay limit.

TO GET THERE

From Porterville drive 9 mi. east on Hwy. 190 to Lake Success. The campground entrance is on the left.

PORTOLA

Grasshopper Flat

Beckwourth-Taylorsville Rd., Beckwourth 96129. T: (530) 836-2575 or reservations (877) 444-6777; F: (530) 836-0493; www.r5.fs.fed.us/plumas or www.reserveamerica.com.

RV ★★★★ Tent ★★★★

Beauty: ★★★★	Site Privacy: ★★★
Spaciousness: ★★★	Quiet: ★★★
Security: ★★★	Cleanliness: ★★★★
Insect Control: ★★★	Facilities: ★★

If you are not towing a boat to this delightful lakeside facility you will probably be in the minority. A simple fishing rod will do, though pole-less nature lovers should find the natural beauty of the setting gratifying enough. No sites verge on Lake Davis, but many of them offer excellent pine-filtered vistas of the water and short trails make access to the shore as easy as putting a night crawler on a hook. The tidy campground's three loops wind through medium-size Jeffrey and ponderosa pines. As a result, this facility, at 5,785 feet of altitude, is carpeted with pine needles and cones. There is a respectable amount of space between most sites, and the presence of both double units and pull-through parking simplifies the maneuvering of larger vehicles and trailers. A dump station is located on the opposite side of the street, two-tenths of a mile south of camp, and the Grizzly store, two miles south across the dam, has basic supplies and pay showers.

BASICS

Operated By: UST Wilderness Management Corp, concessionaire. **Open:** May through Oct. **Site Assignment:** Reservations accepted w/ V, MC, D for a limited number of sites. **Registration:** At entrance kiosk. **Fee:** $13, cash or check. **Parking:** At site.

FACILITIES

Number of RV Sites: 70. **Number of Tent-Only Sites:** 0. **Hookups:** None. **Each Site:** Picnic table, fire grate. **Dump Station:** No. **Laundry:** No. **Pay Phone:** Yes. **Rest Rooms and Showers:** Flush toilets, no showers. **Fuel:** No. **Propane:** No. **Internal Roads:** Paved. **RV Service:** No. **Market:** 8 mi. south in Portola. **Restaurant:** 8 mi. south in Portola. **General Store:** No. **Vending:** No. **Swimming:** In Frenchman Lake. **Playground:** No. **Other:** Boat launch 1 mi. north. **Activities:** Fishing, boating, hiking. **Nearby Attractions:** Portola Railroad Museum; Lakes Basin Recreation Area & Plumas-Eureka State Park in Graegle; Plumas County Museum in Quincy; Plumas National Forest. **Additional Information:** Plumas County Visitors Bureau, (530) 283-6345 or (800) 326-2247.

RESTRICTIONS

Pets: On leash. **Fires:** In fire grates only. **Alcoholic Beverages:** Allowed. **Vehicle Maximum Length:** 32 ft. **Other:** 14-day stay limit.

TO GET THERE

From downtown Portola head north on West St. and follow the sign for Lake Davis Recreation Area. West St. becomes Lake Davis Rd. Drive 7.7 mi. to the stop sign across the dam and turn left onto Beckwourth-Taylorsville Rd. The campground is 0.5 mi. ahead on the left.

PORTOLA

Spring Creek

Frenchman Lake Rd., Chilcoot 96105. T: (530) 836-2575 or reservations (877) 444-6777; F: (530) 836-0493; www.r5.fs.fed.us/plumas or www.reserveusa.com.

RV ★★★★ Tent ★★★★

Beauty: ★★★★	Site Privacy: ★★★
Spaciousness: ★★★★	Quiet: ★★★
Security: ★★★	Cleanliness: ★★★★
Insect Control: ★★★	Facilities: ★★

Spring Creek is a splendid oasis of pines and saltbush, and a smattering of aspen, standing in contrast to the refreshing blue-green waters of Frenchman Lake, just below the campground. This arid, mountain-fringed, high desert domain sits on a hillside that is handsomely studded with volcanic rocks and tufa outcroppings. There is little screening between the level, pine needle–carpeted sites, but they are decently spaced apart, with many—even those on the upper tier of the double loop—enjoying great pine-filtered views of the lake. While sites on average are rather spacious, the central positioning of fire rings and tables may pose problems for campers with large tents. Despite the rock-rimmed shore, access to the lake for boating and fishing is as easy as capsizing a canoe, with a boat ramp located at Frenchman Campground, just up the road. Of the reservable spots, the best for space, privacy and water view are 30, 32, and 35. The concession that operates this Plumas National Forest facility offers double-size sites for twice the price of singles, and small bundles of firewood for $6, indications that inflation is making a comeback.

Basics

Operated By: UST Wilderness Management Corp., concessionaire. **Open:** May through Oct., weather permitting. **Site Assignment:** Reservations accepted w/ V, MC, D. **Registration:** At entrance kiosk. **Fee:** $13, cash or check, $26 for double site. **Parking:** At site.

Facilities

Number of RV Sites: 35. **Number of Tent-Only Sites:** 0. **Hookups:** None. **Each Site:** Picnic table, fire grate. **Dump Station:** No. **Laundry:** No. **Pay Phone:** No. **Rest Rooms and Showers:** Vault toilets, no showers. **Fuel:** No. **Propane:** No. **Internal Roads:** Paved. **RV Service:** No. **Market:** 10 mi. south in Chilcoot. **Restaurant:** 10 mi. south in Chilcoot. **General Store:** No. **Vending:** No. **Swimming:** In Lake Davis. **Playground:** No. **Other:** Some wheelchair-accessible facilities. **Activities:** Fishing, boating, birding, hiking. **Nearby Attractions:** Frenchman Lake; Portola Railroad Museum; Lakes Basin Recreation Area in Graegle; Plumas National Forest; Plumas-Eureka State Park near Graegle. **Additional Information:** Plumas County Visitors Bureau, (530) 283-6345 or (800) 326-2247.

Restrictions

Pets: On leash. **Fires:** In fire grates only. **Alcoholic Beverages:** Allowed. **Vehicle Maximum Length:** 55 ft. **Other:** 14-day stay limit; no wood gathering.

To Get There

From Portola on Hwy. 70 drive 17 mi. to Chilcoot and turn left on Frenchman Lake Rd. Continue for 8.6 mi., bear right and cross the dam. Proceed for 1.2 mi. and turn left into the campground.

QUAKING ASPEN/ CAMP NELSON

Quaking Aspen

Western Divide Hwy., Quaking Aspen/Camp Nelson 93208. T: (559) 539-2607 or reservations (877) 444-6777; www.r5.fs.fed.us/sequoia or www.reserveusa.com.

 ★★★  ★★★

Beauty: ★★★★ Site Privacy: ★★★
Spaciousness: ★★★ Quiet: ★★★★
Security: ★★★ Cleanliness: ★★★
Insect Control: ★★★ Facilities: ★

In most respects Quaking Aspen is a very average, unextraordinary campground. Yet its position, at 7,000 feet elevation in the heart of Giant Sequoia National Monument's southern unit, makes it an ideal base for day hikes into the area's redwood groves. There is a grassy meadow on one side of this pretty, peaceful, hillside camp, and Freeman Creek flows nearby. Fair-sized sites of dirt and pine needles are set reasonably far apart around the double loop, and shaded by an abundance of lodgepole pines—but curiously few aspens. Units 12, 19, 21, and 29 are among the more recessed and shady, and 23 and 24 the more private ones in the meadow area. Tenters may want to consider Belknap (no trailers or RVs allowed), nine miles west on Hwy. 190, where they can strike camp under the protective aura of redwood trees. Telephone, gasoline, propane, and a general store are available two miles south at Ponderosa Lodge.

Basics

Operated By: California Land Management, concessionaire. **Open:** Mid-Apr. to mid-Nov., weather permitting. **Site Assignment:** Reservations accepted w/ V, MC, D. **Registration:** At entrance kiosk. **Fee:** $14, cash or check. **Parking:** At site or in designated area.

Facilities

Number of RV Sites: 32. **Number of Tent-Only Sites:** 0. **Hookups:** None. **Each Site:** Picnic table, fire grate. **Dump Station:** No. **Laundry:** No. **Pay Phone:** No. **Rest Rooms and Showers:** Vault toilets, no showers. **Fuel:** No. **Propane:** No. **Internal Roads:** Paved. **RV Service:** No. **Market:** 40 mi. west in Porterville. **Restaurant:** 25 mi. west in Springville. **General Store:** No. **Vending:** No. **Swimming:** No. **Playground:** No. **Other:** Some wheelchair-accessible facilities. **Activities:** Hiking, fishing, horseback riding. **Nearby Attractions:** Sequoia National Forest; Porterville Historical Museum & Zauld House & Gardens; California Hot Springs. **Additional Information:** Springville Chamber of Commerce, (559) 539-2312; Porterville Chamber of Commerce, (559) 784-7503.

Restrictions

Pets: On leash. **Fires:** In fire grates only. **Alcoholic Beverages:** Allowed. **Vehicle Maximum Length:** 24 ft. **Other:** 14-day stay limit.

To Get There

From Porterville drive 40 mi. east on Hwy. 190 (which becomes the Western Divide Hwy.). The campground entrance is on the right.

REDDING

Antlers RV Park and Campground

20682 Antler Rd., Lakehead 96051. T: (530) 238-2322 or reservations (800) 642-6849; www.antlersrv.com.

★★★★★ ★★★★

Beauty: ★★★★ Site Privacy: ★★★★
Spaciousness: ★★★★ Quiet: ★★★
Security: ★★★ Cleanliness: ★★★★
Insect Control: ★★★ Facilities: ★★★★

During a recent winter, snow and rain combined with gale-force winds to topple dozens of trees in Antlers RV Park. A lesser property would have been left scarred for years to come by such decimation. Not Antlers. The trunks and limbs were carved up and hauled away, and the campground continues to be a standout beauty. Its lovely perch above the iridescent Shasta Lake offers campers a balance of sun and shade among an abundance of such trees as oak, pine, cedar, and manzanita. Most sites are level, grassy, and surprisingly spacious for an RV-oriented campground. Even those with full hookups have plenty of elbow-room, with 108 one of the best in that class. In the ever-popular lake-view area, A 38 and A 39, decked with ramadas as well as shade trees, are the prime slots. Tent campers, too, will find more than enough space to spread their canvas, with the forested loops, where mossy boulders accentuate the natural look, providing the most privacy. Although Antlers is a mere two miles from I-5, surprisingly little road noise reaches it.

Basics

Operated By: Antlers RV Park & Campground. **Open:** All year. **Site Assignment:** Reservations accepted w/ V, MC. **Registration:** At office. **Fee:** $12–$27.50, cash or V, MC. **Parking:** At site.

Facilities

Number of RV Sites: 70. **Number of Tent-Only Sites:** 37. **Hookups:** Water, electric (30, 50 amps), sewer, Internet. **Each Site:** Picnic table, fire grate, food storage box. **Dump Station:** No. **Laundry:** Yes. **Pay Phone:** Yes. **Rest Rooms and Showers:** Yes. **Fuel:** No. **Propane:** Yes. **Internal Roads:** Paved & gravel. **RV Service:** No. **Market:** 2 mi. north in Lakehead. **Restaurant:** 18 mi. south in Shasta Lake. **General Store:** Yes, open from Memorial Day to Labor Day, w/ snack bar. **Vending:** No. **Swimming:** Pool. **Playground:** Yes. **Other:** Some wheelchair-accessible facilities, marina, game room, video rentals. **Activities:** Fishing, boat rentals, waterskiing, hiking, horseshoe pit, ping pong, volleyball, basketball. **Nearby Attractions:** Carter House Natural Science Museum, Turtle Bay Museums & Arboretum, Waterworks Park in Redding; Shasta Lake, Caverns & Dam; Shasta State Historic Park; Whiskeytown National Recreation Area. **Additional Information:** Redding CVB, (530) 225-4100.

Restrictions

Pets: On leash, $3 fee. **Fires:** In fire grates only. **Alcoholic Beverages:** Allowed. **Vehicle Maximum Length:** 40 ft. **Other:** 14-day stay limit in summer; no wood gathering.

To Get There

From Redding drive 26 mi. north on I-5 and exit at Lakeshore/Antlers Rd. Turn right and drive 1 block, then turn right again on Antlers Rd. Continue for 1.5 mi. to the campground entrance straight ahead.

RIDGECREST

Fossil Falls

Cinder Rd., Little Lake 93542. T: (760) 384-5400; www.ca.blm.gov/caso/index.html.

RV ★★★★ Tent ★★★★

Beauty: ★★★★ Site Privacy: ★★★★
Spaciousness: ★★★★ Quiet: ★★★
Security: ★ Cleanliness: ★★★★
Insect Control: ★★★★ Facilities: ★

Heading north toward Lone Pine along US 395, a sign points the way to Fossil Falls, a geological site and campground. The falls in question are not fossilized, but rather a fantastic flow of hardened basaltic lava, spewed out of the eastern Coso Mountain range during a massive eruption 440,000 years ago. This little-known campground lies in a volcanic debris field in the arid Rose Valley, between the green-dappled Sierra Nevadas to the west, China Lake naval base to the east, and a red cinder peak marking its north side. The sublime beauty of this desolate place is not universally appreciated, especially as the grounds are exposed to an unyielding sun and periodic high winds. There are no shade trees here, just low-lying desert scrub across the mildly undulating terrain. Level cinder-based sites, spread well apart over three loops, are among the largest we've come across, and they take advantage of volcanic tufts, spires and mounds as privacy screening. Though this Bureau of Land Management facility lacks potable water and trash pick-up, the absence of ramadas is the most sorely-felt omission. Gasoline and a pay phone are available three miles south at Little Lake.

BASICS

Operated By: Bureau of Land Management, Ridgecrest Field Office. **Open:** All year. **Site Assignment:** First come, first served. **Registration:** At entrance kiosk. **Fee:** $6, cash or check. **Parking:** At site.

FACILITIES

Number of RV Sites: 5. **Number of Tent-Only Sites:** 6. **Hookups:** None. **Each Site:** Picnic table, fire grate. **Dump Station:** No. **Laundry:** No. **Pay Phone:** No. **Rest Rooms and Showers:** Vault toilets, no showers. **Fuel:** No. **Propane:** No. **Internal Roads:** Cinder gravel, wide, & bumpy. **RV Service:** No. **Market:** 31 mi. south in Ridgecrest. **Restaurant:** 21 mi. south in Inyokern. **General Store:** No. **Vending:** No. **Swimming:** No. **Playground:** No. **Other:** Limited wheelchair-accessible facilities, Fossil Falls geological site. **Activities:** Hiking, birding, stargazing, rock scrambling, philosophical ruminating. **Nearby Attractions:** Trona Pinnacles; Last Chance Canyon & Maturango Museum/Death Valley Tourist Center in Ridgecrest; Death Valley National Park. **Additional Information:** Ridgecrest Area CVB, (760) 375-8202 or (800) 847-4830.

RESTRICTIONS

Pets: On leash. **Fires:** In fire grates only. **Alcoholic Beverages:** Allowed. **Vehicle Maximum Length:** 30 ft. **Other:** 14-day stay limit.

TO GET THERE

From Ridgecrest drive 14 mi. west on Hwy. 178. Turn right on Hwy. 14/US 395. Continue 15 mi. and turn right at the sign for Fossil Falls. Proceed for 0.5 mi. and turn right again. The campground is 0.5 mi. ahead on the left.

RIVERSIDE

Lake Perris State Recreation Area, Luiseño Campground

17801 Lake Perris Dr., Perris 92571. T: (909) 940-5603; www.cal-parks.ca.gov or www.reserveamerica.com.

RV ★★★★ Tent ★★★★

Beauty: ★★★★ Site Privacy: ★★★★
Spaciousness: ★★★★ Quiet: ★★★
Security: ★★★★ Cleanliness: ★★★
Insect Control: ★★ Facilities: ★★★★

If time weighs heavily on your hands during your stay at Lake Perris you will only have yourself to blame. That's because this recreation area has a little bit of something for everyone, from fishing and boating (rentals available at the marina), hiking, biking and horseback riding trails, and an Native American museum (open Wednesdays and weekends), to a pair of swimming beaches and a waterslide (summer season only). It is a pretty park, too, with lush grassy turf sloping gently toward the water and rocky hills coloring the horizon. Sites are open but spacious, many shaded by conifers, eucalyptus and pepper trees. That shade is essential, as summer temperatures typically hit 110 degrees, scorching the grass brown and sending everyone with a swimsuit into the water. The weather is milder in the spring, when a fabulous explosion of wildflowers makes this place a must-see. Boating to Alessandro Island for a romantic picnic is considered by many to be a Lake Perris rite-of-passage.

BASICS

Operated By: California Dept. of Parks & Recreation. **Open:** All year. **Site Assignment:** Reservations accepted w/ V, MC, D. **Registration:** At entrance booth. **Fee:** $8–$14, cash or CA check. **Parking:** At site.

FACILITIES

Number of RV Sites: 254. **Number of Tent-Only Sites:** 177. **Hookups:** Water, electric (30, 50 amps). **Each Site:** Picnic table, fire grate. **Dump Station:** Yes. **Laundry:** No. **Pay Phone:** Yes. **Rest Rooms and Showers:** Yes. **Fuel:** No. **Propane:** No. **Internal Roads:** Paved. **RV Service:** No. **Market:** 5 mi. south in Perris. **Restaurant:** 5 mi. south in Perris. **General Store:** Yes. **Vending:** No. **Swimming:** In Lake Perris. **Playground:** Yes. **Other:** Some wheelchair-accessible facilities, boat ramp, coffee shop. **Activities:** Fishing, bicycling, hiking, horseback riding, horseshoe pit, surfing, boat rentals, golf. **Nearby Attractions:** Perris Valley Historical Museum & Orange Empire Railway Museum; Riverside & its museums, gardens & historic buildings. **Additional Information:** Perris Valley Chamber of Commerce, (909) 657-3555.

RESTRICTIONS

Pets: On 6 ft. leash. **Fires:** In fire grates only. **Alcoholic Beverages:** Allowed at site. **Vehicle Maximum Length:** 34 ft. **Other:** 14-day stay limit from June 1–Sept. 30, 30-day stay limit for the rest of the year; no firearms; no wood gathering.

TO GET THERE

From Riverside follow I-215/Hwy. 60 east. When the 2 roads split remain on Hwy. 60 for another 4.6 mi. Exit on Moreno Beach Dr. and continue south for 3.5 mi. Turn left on Via del Lago. The park entrance is just 1 mi. ahead.

SACRAMENTO

Folsom Lake State Recreation Area, Beal's Point Campground

7806 Folsom-Auburn Rd., Folsom 95630. T: (916) 988-0205 or reservations (800) 444-7275 or marina (916) 933-1300; F: (916) 988-9062; www.cal-parks.ca.gov or www.reserveamerica.com.

RV ★★★★ Tent ★★★★

Beauty: ★★★★ Site Privacy: ★★★
Spaciousness: ★★★★ Quiet: ★★★
Security: ★★★★ Cleanliness: ★★★
Insect Control: ★★★ Facilities: ★★★

Beal's Point is just 20 miles from Sacramento, a convenient proximity that explains why camping reservations are essential between May and mid-Sept. Once you get over the shock of so many people—and the absence of lake vistas from the campground—you'll be in for a treat. That's because this is a splendid woodland habitat that offers a little bit of something for everyone. At the top of that list are grassy campsites that are roomy, recessed, and shaded by conifers, blue and live oaks, and buttonwood trees. The many walk-ins make tenting here especially pleasant, though RVers do well with any of 16–38, which are level and shady. The lake features 75 miles of shoreline when it is full, and there are hiking, riding, and biking trails in the surrounding foothills. The marina offers both wet and dry slips (the latter when the water drops below 435 feet), as well as a snack bar, marine supplies and fuel. Full hookups are coming in 2002—er, make that 2003. Or maybe 2004. . . .

BASICS

Operated By: California Dept. of Parks & Recreation. **Open:** All year. **Site Assignment:** Reservations recommended; V, MC, D. **Registration:** At entrance booth. **Fee:** $12, cash or CA check. **Parking:** At site.

FACILITIES

Number of RV Sites: 31. **Number of Tent-Only Sites:** 18. **Hookups:** None. **Each Site:** Picnic table, fire grate. **Dump Station:** Yes. **Laundry:** No. **Pay Phone:** Yes. **Rest Rooms and Showers:** Yes. **Fuel:** No. **Propane:** No. **Internal Roads:** Paved. **RV Service:** No. **Market:** 3 mi. south in Folsom. **Restaurant:** 3 mi. south in Folsom. **General Store:** No. **Vending:** No. **Swimming:** In Folsom Lake. **Playground:** No. **Other:** Some wheelchair-accessible facilities, 4-lane boat ramp, marina, beach, snackbar in summer. **Activities:** Fishing, boat rentals, horseback riding, hiking, bicycling. **Nearby Attractions:** Folsom City Zoo, Dam, Powerhouse, museums, historic downtown, &

outlet shopping; Sacramento Zoo, museums, Esquire Imax Theatre, & state parks. **Additional Information:** Folsom Chamber of Commerce & Visitors Center, (916) 985-2698; Sacramento CVB, (916) 264-7777 or (800) 292-2334.

Restrictions

Pets: On 6 ft. leash. **Fires:** In fire grates only. **Alcoholic Beverages:** Allowed at site. **Vehicle Maximum Length:** 31 ft. **Other:** 7-day stay limit from May 18 to Sept. 30, 30-day stay limit for the rest of the year; no firearms; no wood gathering.

To Get There

From Sacramento drive 15 mi. east on US 50 and take Folsom Blvd. Exit. Head north on Folsom Blvd. (which becomes Folsom-Auburn Rd.). After 6.3 mi. turn right into the park.

SAN BERNARDINO
Camp Switzerland

24558 Lake Dr., Crestline 92325. T: (909) 338-2731.

RV ★★★ Tent ★★

Beauty: ★★★ Site Privacy: ★★
Spaciousness: ★★ Quiet: ★★★
Security: ★★★★★ Cleanliness: ★★★
Insect Control: ★★ Facilities: ★★

If you have ever wondered what campgrounds were like in the old days, wonder no longer: Camp Switzerland may be just what you are looking for. Established in 1939, this forested facility looks like something of a relic, but it is also a classic, with boulders and pines, cedars and locust trees in harmony with sites that are packed tightly along a steeply descending lane. The most private of those are at the lowest tier, but if your rig is longer than 22 feet forget about trying to maneuver it down there. The campground lies at 4,500 feet altitude at the north end of Lake Gregory in the San Bernardino Mountains, where it is not uncommon to find snow on the ground well into Apr. Though the property lacks a view of the water, the attractive lakeside town of Crestline is within modest yodeling distance a few minutes walk away.

Basics

Operated By: Camp Switzerland, Earl & Bernie Silva, managers. **Open:** All year. **Site Assignment:** Reservations accepted w/ V, MC, D. **Registration:** At entrance office. **Fee:** $19–$23, cash, check or V, MC, D. **Parking:** At site.

Facilities

Number of RV Sites: 30. **Number of Tent-Only Sites:** 10. **Hookups:** Water, electric (15, 30 amps), sewer. **Each Site:** Picnic table in most sites. **Dump Station:** Yes. **Laundry:** No. **Pay Phone:** No. **Rest Rooms and Showers:** Yes. **Fuel:** No. **Propane:** Yes. **Internal Roads:** Paved. **RV Service:** No. **Market:** 1 mi. west in Crestline. **Restaurant:** 1 mi. west in Crestline. **General Store:** No. **Vending:** No. **Swimming:** In Lake Gregory. **Playground:** No. **Activities:** Fishing & boating on Lake Gregory, hiking. **Nearby Attractions:** Lake Gregory, Silverwood Lake, Lake Arrowhead, Big Bear Lake. **Additional Information:** Crestline Chamber of Commerce, (909) 338-2706.

Restrictions

Pets: On leash, $3. **Fires:** No ground fires. **Alcoholic Beverages:** Allowed. **Vehicle Maximum Length:** 25 ft. **Other:** 29-day stay limit.

To Get There

From San Bernardino drive twelve mi. north on Hwy. 18. Exit left on Hwy. 138. Drive 1 mi. north, then turn right onto Lake Dr.; Camp Switzerland is 3 mi. ahead on the left.

SAN BERNARDINO
Silverwood Lake State Recreation Area, Mesa Campground

14651 Cedar Cir., Hesperia 92345. T: (760) 389-2303 or (800) 444-7275; www.cal-parks.ca.gov or www.reserveamerica.com.

RV ★★★ Tent ★★★

Beauty: ★★★★ Site Privacy: ★★★★
Spaciousness: ★★★ Quiet: ★★
Security: ★★ Cleanliness: ★★★
Insect Control: ★★ Facilities: ★★★

Mesa Campground offers something for everyone, from private, well-screened sites situated among thick stands of manzanita, oak, and ponderosa pines, to a network of bike paths and hiking trails. And don't overlook Silverwood Lake, below the campground, which serves triple duty among swimmers, boaters and fishermen. No wonder then that reservations are advisable, especially for weekends, from late spring through Sept. At a distance of less than 30 miles from San Bernardino, Mesa is close enough to Los Angeles to be hugely popular as a getaway destination and yet far enough out that it occasionally has problems with black bears raiding its dumpsters. You are more likely to hear, though, distant sounds of planes, trains, and automobiles, and, alas, your neighbors, as enforcement of quiet hours tends to be lax. Fortunately, sites are well dispersed through a series of eight loops, with numbers 101–106 appealingly shady and both 76 and 86 a little more secluded than the rest. The only site with a water view is 16, but gusty evening breezes make that a mixed blessing.

Basics

Operated By: California Dept. of Parks & Recreation. **Open:** All year. **Site Assignment:** Reservations recommended; V, MC, D. **Registration:** At entrance booth. **Fee:** $8, cash or CA check. **Parking:** At site.

Facilities

Number of RV Sites: 136. **Number of Tent-Only Sites:** 7. **Hookups:** None. **Each Site:** Picnic table, fire grate, barbecue grill. **Dump Station:** Yes. **Laundry:** No. **Pay Phone:** Yes. **Rest Rooms and Showers:** Yes. **Fuel:** No. **Propane:** No. **Internal Roads:** Paved. **RV Service:** No. **Market:** 9 mi. south in Crestline. **Restaurant:** 9 mi. south in Crestline. **General Store:** Yes, at the marina. **Vending:** No. **Swimming:** In Silverwood Lake. **Playground:** No. **Other:** Some wheelchair-accessible facilities, boat launch, marina. **Activities:** Hiking, fishing, bicycling, boat rentals, horseshoe pit, birding. **Nearby Attractions:** Pacific Crest Trail, California Theater of Performing Arts in San Bernardino. **Additional Information:** San Bernardino CVB, (909) 889-3980 or (800) 867-8366.

Restrictions

Pets: On 6 ft. leash. **Fires:** In fire grates only. **Alcoholic Beverages:** Allowed at site. **Vehicle Maximum Length:** None. **Other:** 14-day stay limit in summer, 30-day stay limit in winter; no firearms; no wood gathering.

To Get There

From San Bernardino drive 17 mi. north on I-215/I-15. Take the Silverwood Lake Exit onto Rte. 138 and drive 11 mi. Turn left into the campground.

SAN BERNARDINO
Yucaipa Regional Park

33900 Oak Glen Rd., Yucaipa 92399. T: (909) 790-3127; F: (909) 790-3121; www.co.san-bernardino.ca.us/parks.

RV ★★★★ Tent ★★★★

Beauty: ★★★★ Site Privacy: ★★
Spaciousness: ★★★★ Quiet: ★★★
Security: ★★★★★ Cleanliness: ★★★★
Insect Control: ★★ Facilities: ★★★

There is quite a lot to like about Yucaipa Regional Park, from its easy-to-find suburban location just five miles off of I-10, to the lushly manicured grounds that include three ponds stocked with trout and catfish and a one acre swimming lagoon. Add to this a sandy beach and a pair of 350-foot waterslides, pull-through parking large enough to handle most of the larger RVs, and a separate area for tents complete with soft, sandy pads, and you have the makings for good family fun. Security is tight, with a gate that typically closes at 9 p.m., and there are five hosts in residence throughout the year. Critics may carp that the handsome mix of trees does not do much to shade sites, but at least they don't obscure the fine view of the San Bernardino Mountains, either. One thing to watch: a city park development going up at the campground's periphery threatens to become an eyesore.

Basics

Operated By: San Bernardino County Regional Parks Dept. **Open:** All year. **Site Assignment:** Reservations accepted w/ V, MC, D. **Registration:** At entrance booth. **Fee:** $11–$18, cash, check or V, MC, D. **Parking:** At site.

Facilities

Number of RV Sites: 26. **Number of Tent-Only Sites:** 8. **Hookups:** Water, electric (30 amps). **Each Site:** Picnic table, barbecue grill. **Dump Station:** Yes. **Laundry:** No. **Pay Phone:** Yes. **Rest Rooms and Showers:** Yes. **Fuel:** No. **Propane:** No. **Internal Roads:** Paved. **RV Service:** No. **Market:** 5 mi. south in Yucaipa. **Restaurant:** 5 mi. south in Yucaipa. **General Store:** Yes. **Vending:** Yes. **Swimming:** In lake. **Playground:** Yes. **Other:** Wheelchair-accessible facilities, snack-bar. **Activities:** Fishing, horseshoe pit, pedal boat rentals. **Nearby Attractions:** Asistencia Misión de San Gabriel, Historical Glass Museum, both in Redlands. **Additional Information:** San Bernardino County Regional Parks, (909) 38-PARKS.

RESTRICTIONS

Pets: On 10 ft. leash. **Fires:** Yes (In grills only). **Alcoholic Beverages:** Allowed at site. **Vehicle Maximum Length:** None. **Other:** 14-day stay limit; no firearms.

TO GET THERE

From San Bernardino follow I-10 east for 15 mi. to the Yucaipa Exit. Drive 2.8 mi. east on Yucaipa Blvd., turn left on Oak Glen Rd. and proceed for 2 mi. to the campground on the left.

SAN CLEMENTE

San Clemente State Beach

3030 Avenida del Presidente, San Clemente 92672. T: (949) 492-3156 or (949) 492-0802; www.cal-parks.ca.gov or www.reserveamerica.com.

RV ★★★★ Tent ★★★

Beauty: ★★★	Site Privacy: ★★★
Spaciousness: ★★★	Quiet: ★★
Security: ★★★★	Cleanliness: ★★★★
Insect Control: ★★★★	Facilities: ★★★

San Clemente seems to be in a constant state of renewal. A few years ago a tent loop was renovated, about a year later it was the picnic area's turn for a face lift, and recently the electrical hookups were upgraded. Now if only some vegetation could be planted in the RV hookup loop to provide buffers between its crowded slots. Until that happens, your best bet is to steer toward the two loops that lack hookups; marginally more spacious and with a bit of screening, sites there are also positioned on grass instead of the dirt surface of the RV lot. Especially roomy are 83 and 85, both of which overlook the beach and cliffs. Monterey pines, eucalyptus, and flowering ceanothus are scattered throughout the park, lending an attractive look to the domain. Less appealing is the occasional use of prison labor for landscaping.

BASICS

Operated By: California Dept. of Parks & Recreation. **Open:** All year. **Site Assignment:** Reservations recommended; V, MC, D. **Registration:** At entrance booth. **Fee:** $12–$18, cash or CA check. **Parking:** At site.

FACILITIES

Number of RV Sites: 160. **Number of Tent-Only Sites:** 0. **Hookups:** Water, electric (30 amps), sewer. **Each Site:** Picnic table, fire grate; non-hookup sites have ramada, barbecue grill, spigot. **Dump Station:** Yes. **Laundry:** No. **Pay Phone:** Yes. **Rest Rooms and Showers:** Yes. **Fuel:** No. **Propane:** No. **Internal Roads:** Paved. **RV Service:** No. **Market:** 2 mi. north in San Clemente. **Restaurant:** 2 mi. north in San Clemente. **General Store:** No. **Vending:** No. **Swimming:** In Pacific Ocean, less than 0.5 mi. **Playground:** No. **Other:** Some wheelchair-accessible facilities. **Activities:** Surfing, swimming, bicycling, 2 mi. of hiking trails. **Nearby Attractions:** San Clemente, Dana Point, Mission San Juan Capistrano. **Additional Information:** San Clemente Chamber of Commerce, (949) 492-1131.

RESTRICTIONS

Pets: On 6 ft. leash. **Fires:** In fire grates only. **Alcoholic Beverages:** Allowed at site. **Vehicle Maximum Length:** 30 ft. **Other:** 7-day stay limit; no firearms; no wood gathering.

TO GET THERE

In San Clemente exit I-5 on Avenida Calafia and proceed for 0.2 mi. Turn left (west) into the park.

SAN CLEMENTE

San Onofre State Beach, San Mateo Campground

830 Cristianitos Rd., San Clemente 92672. T: (949) 361-2531; www.cal-parks.ca.gov or www.reserveamerica.com.

RV ★★★★ Tent ★★★

Beauty: ★★★	Site Privacy: ★★★
Spaciousness: ★★★	Quiet: ★★★
Security: ★★★	Cleanliness: ★★★
Insect Control: ★★★	Facilities: ★★★

San Onofre State Beach is composed of two campgrounds, the Bluff Area by the beach and San Mateo, one mile inland off of I-5. Forget about privacy at the Bluff Area, where sites are lined up one after another on a tiny stretch of turf alongside the parking area. Tranquility is another lost cause: trains hurtle along tracks just 100 feet from camp, basically paralleling its linear layout, and a few yards beyond an interstate highway reverberates to the continuous roar of traffic. Then there is the multitude of college-age campers that descends on the park from mid-spring through early Sept., filling it with the off-key melodies of their raucous partying and straining facilities beyond the capacity of the maintenance staff. Sites at San Mateo, by contrast, while not large, are at least scattered over three loops and enjoy decent privacy. The atmosphere is calmer—dare we say more sedate?—and setting more lush, though fine views of the coastal hills are somewhat offset by opposing vistas of power lines and produce fields. Both camps suffer from occasional helicopter overflights from neighboring Camp Pendleton. The best time to visit is from early spring through mid-summer, while the grass in the sites is still soft and green. Your San Mateo receipt covers the day-use fee at the Bluff Area beach.

BASICS

Operated By: California Dept. of Parks & Recreation. **Open:** All year. **Site Assignment:** Reservations recommended; V, MC, D. **Registration:** At entrance booth. **Fee:** $12–$18, cash or CA check, good for day use at San Onofre State Beach Bluffs Area. **Parking:** At site.

FACILITIES

Number of RV Sites: 157. **Number of Tent-Only Sites:** 0. **Hookups:** Water, electric (30 amps). **Each Site:** Picnic table, fire grate. **Dump Station:** Yes. **Laundry:** No. **Pay Phone:** Yes. **Rest Rooms and Showers:** Yes. **Fuel:** No. **Propane:** No. **Internal Roads:** Paved. **RV Service:** No. **Market:** 2 mi. north in San Clemente. **Restaurant:** 2 mi. north in San Clemente. **General Store:** No. **Vending:** No. **Swimming:** In Pacific Ocean, 1.1 mi. **Playground:** No. **Other:** Some wheelchair-accessible facilities. **Activities:** Surfing, bicycling, nature trails, skate boarding, helicopter spotting. **Nearby Attractions:** San Clemente, Dana Point, Mission San Juan Capistrano. **Additional Information:** San Clemente Chamber of Commerce, (949) 492-1131.

RESTRICTIONS

Pets: On 6 ft. leash. **Fires:** In fire grates only. **Alcoholic Beverages:** Allowed at site. **Vehicle Maximum Length:** 36 ft. **Other:** 14-day stay limit from Memorial Day through Labor Day.

TO GET THERE

From I-5 in San Clemente take the Cristianitos Rd. Exit and proceed inland for 1 mi. Turn right into the campground, which lacks adequate signposting.

SAN DIEGO

Lake Morena County Park, South Shore Campground

2550 Lake Morena Dr., Lake Morena Village 91906. T: (619) 565-3600; www.co.san-diego.ca.us/parks.

RV ★★★★ Tent ★★★

Beauty: ★★★★	Site Privacy: ★★★
Spaciousness: ★★★	Quiet: ★★★★
Security: ★★★	Cleanliness: ★★★
Insect Control: ★★	Facilities: ★★★

Lake Morena Reservoir is home to some of the better bass and trout fishing in the area, with the record for the former weighing in at a whopping 19 pounds, 3 ounces. But even when the water has been drawn down to the size of a pond, typically by late July or early Aug., there is still plenty to do here, from biking and hiking the nature trails to hooking up to the Pacific Crest Trail, which cuts through the park. Granite-spiked hills surround the domain, with the campground's grassy, fairly tightly concentrated sites well shaded by thick-limbed live oaks, incense cedars, and Jeffrey and Coulter pines. Best for spaciousness and lake view—at least when water levels are high—are sites 81 and 85, with 6–14 good fall-back options. And though restrooms are a bit shabby looking, they are kept reasonably clean. Dogs are supposed to be kept on leashes, but enforcement is lax. Tent campers looking for more space and privacy may want to stake out a spot at the North Shore primitive area.

BASICS

Operated By: County of San Diego, Dept. of Parks & Recreation. **Open:** All year. **Site Assignment:** Reservations accepted w/ V, MC, D. **Registration:** At entrance booth or ranger office. **Fee:** $12–$16, cash or V, MC, D. **Parking:** At site.

FACILITIES

Number of RV Sites: 86. **Number of Tent-Only Sites:** 0. **Hookups:** Water, electric (20, 30 amps). **Each Site:** Picnic table, fire grate. **Dump Station:** Yes. **Laundry:** No. **Pay Phone:** Yes. **Rest Rooms and Showers:** Yes. **Fuel:** No.

Propane: No. **Internal Roads:** Mostly paved. **RV Service:** No. **Market:** 1 mi. south in Lake Morena Village. **Restaurant:** 1 mi. south in Lake Morena Village. **General Store:** No. **Vending:** Yes. **Swimming:** No. **Playground:** No. **Other:** Some wheelchair-accessible facilities, boat launch. **Activities:** Fishing, bicycling, hiking, campfire programs, boat rentals. **Nearby Attractions:** Coral Canyon OHV Area, Pacific Crest Trail, only 8 mi. from the Mexican border, historic Campo. **Additional Information:** County of San Diego, Dept. of Parks & Recreation, (858) 694-3049.

RESTRICTIONS

Pets: On 6 ft. leash. **Fires:** In fire grates only. **Alcoholic Beverages:** Allowed at site, not exceeding 40 proof. **Vehicle Maximum Length:** 45 ft. **Other:** 14-day stay limit; no firearms; no wood gathering.

TO GET THERE

From San Diego head east on I-8 for 54 mi. Exit on Buckman Springs Rd. and continue south for 5.5 mi. Turn right on Oak Dr. and proceed for 1.5 mi. Turn right again on Lake Morena Dr. The park is 0.5 mi. ahead.

SAN FRANCISCO

Candlestick RV Park

650 Gilman Ave., San Francisco 94124. T: (415) 822-2299 or (800) 888-CAMP; F: (415) 822-7638; www.gocampingamerica.com/candlestick; candlestickrv@msn.com.

RV: ★★★★ Tent: ★

Beauty: ★★★ Site Privacy: ★
Spaciousness: ★ Quiet: ★★
Security: ★★★★ Cleanliness: ★★★★
Insect Control: ★★★★ Facilities: ★★★★

Short of setting up camp in Golden Gate Park, it is hard to imagine bivouacking much closer to San Francisco than in Candlestick RV Park. This facility is located directly across the street from 3Com Stadium, nee Candlestick Park, just five miles south of downtown. While its parking lot layout and the chain link security fence that encompasses the compound are not very appealing, management has done an admirable job of sewing a variety of exotic plants and trees around the perimeter. As usual for this sort of property, parking slots seem crowded together on the asphalt with no screening and negligible shade. A narrow strip of grass has been set aside for tenters but it seems to get more traffic from dogs, despite a rule that mandates dog-walking outside the fence. The washrooms, on the other hand, tend to be immaculate. Just down the street is Candlestick Point State Recreation Area, with a bike trail, picnic area, and Bay access via a boat ramp. Also nearby, alas, is the airport, with loud flyovers common enough to make you wish your RV had double-pane glass. A shuttle service is available to ferry campers to downtown San Francisco.

BASICS

Operated By: Candlestick RV Park. **Open:** All year. **Site Assignment:** Reservations recommended; V, MC, AE. **Registration:** At entrance office. **Fee:** $46–$49, cash or V, MC, AE. **Parking:** At site.

FACILITIES

Number of RV Sites: 165. **Number of Tent-Only Sites:** 12. **Hookups:** Water, electric (30, 50 amps), sewer, Internet. **Each Site:** Picnic table in some sites. **Dump Station:** No. **Laundry:** Yes. **Pay Phone:** Yes. **Rest Rooms and Showers:** Yes. **Fuel:** No. **Propane:** Yes. **Internal Roads:** Paved. **RV Service:** No. **Market:** 5 mi. north in San Francisco. **Restaurant:** 5 mi. north in San Francisco. **General Store:** Yes. **Vending:** Yes. **Swimming:** No. **Playground:** No. **Other:** Some wheelchair-accessible facilities, game room, free video tapes. **Activities:** Touring San Francisco, hiking the Bay shoreline, surfing. **Nearby Attractions:** Candlestick Point State Recreation Area; museums, Ghirardelli Square, Fisherman's Wharf, zoo, aquarium, Golden Gate Park, & much more in San Francisco. **Additional Information:** San Francisco CVB, (415) 391-2000.

RESTRICTIONS

Pets: On leash, must be under 20 pounds. **Fires:** No. **Alcoholic Beverages:** Allowed. **Vehicle Maximum Length:** 45 ft. **Other:** 29-day stay limit; no generators.

TO GET THERE

From San Francisco drive south on US 101 to the 3Com Stadium Exit. Drive around the stadium, about 1 mi., to gate 4. The park entrance is directly opposite to that, to the right.

SAN FRANCISCO

Pacific Park RV Resort

700 Palmetto Ave., Pacifica 94044. T: (800) 992-0554 or (650) 355-7093; F: (650) 355-7102; www.sanfranciscorv.com; frontdesk@sanfranciscorv.com.

RV: ★★★★ Tent: n/a

Beauty: ★★★ Site Privacy: ★
Spaciousness: ★ Quiet: ★★
Security: ★★★★ Cleanliness: ★★★★
Insect Control: ★★★★ Facilities: ★★★★★

Pacific Park RV Resort is conveniently located just ten miles south of San Francisco, right off of Hwy. 1 in Pacifica. It is loaded with amenities, from cable television and Internet connections to a small swimming pool and Jacuzzi, from a horseshoe pit to a video game room. The Pacific Ocean abuts the lot, filling the air with a pleasant brininess, and a very short trail leads down to the sandy beach. The view across the busy road is not bad, either, highlighted by a wavy series of grass-covered hills. The bad news is the parking slots are wedged one against another, and there are no shade trees, no privacy, and no tents allowed. The best bet is to set up as far to the western edge of the grounds as possible, where an unobstructed view of the sun setting into the water is a killer, and the crashing surf is almost loud enough to drown out the noise of incessant air and auto traffic. A shuttle service is available to ferry campers to downtown San Francisco.

BASICS

Operated By: Pacific Park RV Resort; Carol Motl, manager. **Open:** All year. **Site Assignment:** Reservations recommended; V, MC. **Registration:** At entrance office. **Fee:** $38–$69 plus 10% local tax, cash or V, MC. **Parking:** At site.

FACILITIES

Number of RV Sites: 250. **Number of Tent-Only Sites:** 0. **Hookups:** Water, electric (30, 50 amps), sewer, cable TV, Internet. **Each Site:** Communal picnic table. **Dump Station:** Yes. **Laundry:** Yes. **Pay Phone:** Yes. **Rest Rooms and Showers:** Yes. **Fuel:** No. **Propane:** Yes. **Internal Roads:** Paved. **RV Service:** No. **Market:** 1 mi. away in Pacifica. **Restaurant:** 1 mi. away in Pacifica. **General Store:** Yes. **Vending:** Yes. **Swimming:** In small heated pool. **Playground:** No. **Other:** Some wheelchair-accessible facilities, spa, game room. **Activities:** Sunning, surfing, beachcombing, horseshoe pit, touring San Francisco. **Nearby Attractions:** Candlestick Point State Recreation Area; museums, Ghirardelli Square, Fisherman's Wharf, zoo, aquarium, Golden Gate Park, & much more in San Francisco; Montara & Gray Whale Cove State Beaches. **Additional Information:** San Francisco CVB, (415) 391-2000.

RESTRICTIONS

Pets: On leash, must be under 20 pounds. **Fires:** No. **Alcoholic Beverages:** Allowed. **Vehicle Maximum Length:** 60 ft. **Other:** No stay limit; no generators.

TO GET THERE

From San Francisco drive 8 mi. south on Hwy. 1 to Pacifica. Exit on Manor Dr. and continue straight through the stop sign. Manor Dr. becomes Palmetto Ave. The resort entrance is 0.5 mi. ahead on the right.

SAN JUAN CAPISTRANO

Ronald W. Caspers Wilderness Park

Ortega Hwy. 33401, San Juan Capistrano 92675. T: (949) 728-0235; F: (949) 728-0346; www.coparks.com/caspers.

RV: ★★★ Tent: ★★★

Beauty: ★★★★ Site Privacy: ★★★
Spaciousness: ★★★ Quiet: ★★★
Security: ★★★★ Cleanliness: ★★
Insect Control: ★★ Facilities: ★★★

Caspers Wilderness Park does not allow pets on the property for the same reason that minors must be accompanied by an adult: concern about mountain lions following a fatal attack 18 years ago. These restrictions have a positive side-effect, endowing the property with a greater degree of quietude than similar establishments elsewhere. Just eight miles inland from San Juan Capistrano and I-5, among the ranch lands and the rolling foothills of the Cleveland National Forest, Caspers occupies a transitional zone, with vegetation ranging from open grassy meadows fringed with prickly pear cacti and agaves, to sycamores and live oak. Most of the sites are rather close to each other, with about half in open grassland and the remainder appealingly sheltered under the high canopy of aged oaks. In spring there is just enough water flowing through the campside creek to generate a tremendous insect population. So either bring plenty of repellant or aim to bivouac from mid-summer on, when biting bugs should no longer be a problem. There are some fine hiking and riding trails in Caspers, as well as a separate horse camp.

BASICS

Operated By: City of Orange Public Facilities. **Open:** All year. **Site Assignment:** First come, first served. **Registration:** At entrance booth. **Fee:** $12, cash or CA check. **Parking:** At site.

FACILITIES

Number of RV Sites: 52. **Number of Tent-Only Sites:** 0. **Hookups:** None. **Each Site:** Picnic table, fire grate, barbecue grill. **Dump Station:** Yes. **Laundry:** No. **Pay Phone:** Yes. **Rest Rooms and Showers:** Yes. **Fuel:** No. **Propane:** No. **Internal Roads:** Paved & gravel. **RV Service:** No. **Market:** 8 mi. southwest in San Juan Capistrano. **Restaurant:** 8 mi. southwest in San Juan Capistrano. **General Store:** No. **Vending:** No. **Swimming:** No. **Playground:** No. **Other:** Some wheelchair-accessible facilities. **Activities:** 35 mi. of hiking trails, horseback riding, mountain biking, stargazing. **Nearby Attractions:** Mission San Juan Capistrano, Dana Point. **Additional Information:** San Juan Capistrano Chamber of Commerce, (949) 493-4700.

RESTRICTIONS

Pets: Not allowed. **Fires:** In fire grates only. **Alcoholic Beverages:** Not allowed. **Vehicle Maximum Length:** 44 ft. **Other:** 14-day stay limit; no firearms.

TO GET THERE

From I-5 in San Juan Capistrano take Hwy. 74/Ortega Hwy. east and drive 8 mi. Turn left into the park.

SAN RAFAEL

Samuel P. Taylor State Park

Sir Francis Drake Blvd., Lagunitas 94938. T: (415) 488-9897 or reservations (800) 444-7275; F: (415) 488-4315; www.cal-parks.ca.gov or www.reserveamerica.com.

RV ★★★ | Tent ★★★

Beauty: ★★★★ | Site Privacy: ★★★
Spaciousness: ★★★ | Quiet: ★★★
Security: ★★★ | Cleanliness: ★★★★
Insect Control: ★★ | Facilities: ★★

In 1854 Samuel Taylor stumbled into a redwood grove here and was so enchanted by the sight that he promptly purchased 100 acres of land and set up a paper mill. Present-day visitors to this dark, densely forested park may wish that he had exercised less discretion in his timber harvesting to allow more sunshine to penetrate. No matter, it remains an appealing woodland of intermingled second-growth redwoods, tan oaks, madrones, laurels, and Douglas firs. The compact campground is tightly woven through two loops, with small dirt-surfaced sites rather crowded together. Although the preserve is open to RVs and even has six pull-through spots, narrow cornering and limited parking space make it more practical for tenting. Yet even the nylon roof set may find most sites a bit shy of elbow room. Of the two circuits, there is slightly more space and privacy in Orchard Hill (numbers 25–60). If you plan on coming between May and Oct., you will need to reserve far ahead.

BASICS

Operated By: California Dept. of Parks & Recreation. **Open:** All year. **Site Assignment:** Reservations accepted w/ V, MC, D. **Registration:** At entrance booth. **Fee:** $12, cash or CA check. **Parking:** At site or adjacent to it.

FACILITIES

Number of RV Sites: 50. **Number of Tent-Only Sites:** 11. **Hookups:** None. **Each Site:** Picnic table, fire grates, food storage box. **Dump Station:** No. **Laundry:** No. **Pay Phone:** Yes. **Rest Rooms and Showers:** Yes. **Fuel:** No. **Propane:** No. **Internal Roads:** Paved, narrow, & windy. **RV Service:** No. **Market:** 2 mi. southeast in Lagunitas. **Restaurant:** 2 mi. southeast in Lagunitas. **General Store:** No. **Vending:** No. **Swimming:** No. **Playground:** No. **Other:** Some wheelchair-accessible facilities. **Activities:** Hiking, mountain biking, horseback riding. **Nearby Attractions:** Mission San Rafael Archangel, Marin County Frank Lloyd Wright Civic Center & China Camp State Park in San Rafael; Muir Woods National Monument & Mount Tamalpais State Park in Mill Valley. **Additional Information:** San Rafael Chamber of Commerce, (415) 454-4163; Mill Valley Chamber of Commerce, (415) 388-9700.

RESTRICTIONS

Pets: On leash no longer than 6 ft., not allowed on trails. **Fires:** In fire grates only. **Alcoholic Beverages:** Allowed at site. **Vehicle Maximum Length:** 28 ft. **Other:** 7-day stay limit from Apr. 1–Oct. 31; no firearms; no wood gathering.

TO GET THERE

From San Rafael take I-580 south to the Sir Francis Drake Blvd. Exit. Head west for 17 mi. The park entrance is on the left.

SAN SIMEON

San Simeon State Park, San Simeon Creek Campground

San Simeon Creek Rd., San Simeon 93452. T: (805) 927-2035 or (805) 927-2020 or reservations (800) 444-7275; www.cal-parks.ca.gov or www.reserveamerica.com.

RV ★★★ | Tent ★★★

Beauty: ★★★ | Site Privacy: ★★★
Spaciousness: ★★★ | Quiet: ★★
Security: ★★★ | Cleanliness: ★★★★
Insect Control: ★★★ | Facilities: ★★★

The two campgrounds in this state preserve are very average in nearly every respect. San Simeon Creek is the more developed, with lavatories equipped with showers, water fill-up and dump stations for RVs, and good size Monterey pines sprinkled along its five paved loops. One of those circuits, adjacent to a noisy highway overpass, is reserved for tents. That awkward position makes the more primitive Washburn, up the hill along the park road, a more peaceful option for sleeping in nylon shelters. The cinder surface to Washburn's twin loops is smooth and the vaulted toilets well-maintained. In both camps sites are level and grassy, but in need of more shade trees. The high use this rather ordinary park receives throughout the year has little to do with the neighboring beach (which, like the campgrounds themselves, is often cloaked in fog). Rather, it is the location of the magnificent Hearst Castle just five miles north on Hwy. 1 that makes this the ideal overnight spot either before or after visits to the mansion. Just remember to book your tours at (800) 444-4445 well in advance.

BASICS

Operated By: California Dept. of Parks & Recreation. **Open:** All year. **Site Assignment:** Reservations accepted w/ V, MC, D. **Registration:** At entrance booth. **Fee:** $12, cash or CA check. **Parking:** At site.

FACILITIES

Number of RV Sites: 115. **Number of Tent-Only Sites:** 19. **Hookups:** None. **Each Site:** Picnic table, fire grate. **Dump Station:** Yes. **Laundry:** No. **Pay Phone:** Yes. **Rest Rooms and Showers:** Yes. **Fuel:** No. **Propane:** No. **Internal Roads:** Paved. **RV Service:** No. **Market:** 2 mi. south in Cambria. **Restaurant:** 1 mi. north in San Simeon Acres. **General Store:** No. **Vending:** No. **Swimming:** In Pacific Ocean. **Playground:** No. **Other:** Some wheelchair-accessible facilities. **Activities:** Hiking, fishing, birding, horseshoe pit, campfire programs. **Nearby Attractions:** Hearst Castle & National Geographic Theater, wineries around Paso Robles. **Additional Information:** San Simeon Chamber of Commerce, (805) 927-3500.

RESTRICTIONS

Pets: On 6 ft. leash; not allowed on trails. **Fires:** In fire grates only, not allowed on the beach. **Alcoholic Beverages:** Allowed at site. **Vehicle Maximum Length:** 40 ft. **Other:** 10-day stay limit from Memorial Day through Labor Day; no firearms; no wood gathering.

TO GET THERE

From San Simeon on Hwy. 1 take the Hearst Castle' Exit and drive 4.7 mi. south. Turn left on San Simeon Creek Rd., then right into the well signposted park.

SANTA BARBARA

Cachuma Lake Recreation Area

HC 58, Hwy. 154, Santa Barbara 93105. T: (805) 686-5054; F: (805) 686-5075; www.cachuma.com or www.sbparks.org.

RV ★★★★ | Tent ★★★

Beauty: ★★★★ | Site Privacy: ★★★
Spaciousness: ★★★ | Quiet: ★★★
Security: ★★★★ | Cleanliness: ★★★★
Insect Control: ★★ | Facilities: ★★★★★

Confusion is an understandable state of mind for first-time visitors to Cachuma Lake. For one thing, this is a huge campground, with more than 500 mostly level, grassy sites dispersed through an intricate maze of loops. For another, though the recreation area is less than 20 miles from Santa Barbara, the large shimmering body of water is surrounded by the relatively undeveloped Santa Ynez and San Rafael Mountains, giving the impression that you are much farther out than you really are. There will be no roughing it here, though, because Cachuma has just about every possible amenity necessary to comfortable camping (and a good deal that probably aren't), including a snack bar and on-site gas station, and rentals of various size boats, bikes, golf clubs, and even yurts. The large domain is semi-forested with mature sycamores, oaks, manzanita, and holly, and if most sites lack privacy, at least a good percentage overlook the water. At an elevation of only 800 feet, weather at this park is pleasant throughout the year. Be sure to check out the excellent nature center (open weekends) for its Native American exhibits and to make reservations for naturalist-led wildlife cruises.

Basics

Operated By: Santa Barbara County Parks. **Open:** All year. **Site Assignment:** Reservations accepted w/V, MC, D. **Registration:** At entrance booth. **Fee:** $16–$22, cash or CA check. **Parking:** At site.

Facilities

Number of RV Sites: 573. **Number of Tent-Only Sites:** 0. **Hookups:** Water, electric (20, 30 amps), sewer. **Each Site:** Picnic table, fire ring (not in full hookup sites). **Dump Station:** Yes. **Laundry:** Yes. **Pay Phone:** Yes. **Rest Rooms and Showers:** Yes. **Fuel:** Yes. **Propane:** Yes. **Internal Roads:** Paved. **RV Service:** No. **Market:** 10 mi. west in Santa Ynez. **Restaurant:** In campground or 10 mi. west in Santa Ynez. **General Store:** Yes. **Vending:** No. **Swimming:** Pool, $1 per hour. **Playground:** Yes. **Other:** Some wheelchair-accessible facilities, marina, boat launch, family fun center, nature center. **Activities:** Fishing, hiking, horseshoe pit, boat & bicycle rentals, mini-golf, volleyball, horseback riding, wildlife cruises. **Nearby Attractions:** Solvang & its mission & museums; Chumash Painted Cave State Historic Park; Santa Barbara & its mission, museums, historic buildings, zoo, Stearns Wharf, & Botanic Garden. **Additional Information:** Santa Barbara Region Chamber of Commerce, (805) 965-3023.

Restrictions

Pets: On 6 ft. leash; proof of rabies vaccination required; $2 fee. **Fires:** In fire rings only. **Alcoholic Beverages:** Allowed at site. **Vehicle Maximum Length:** None. **Other:** 14-day stay limit from Apr. 1–Sept. 14, 90-day limit the rest of the year.

To Get There

In Santa Barbara exit US 101 on Hwy. 154 and drive 18 mi. north to the park entrance on the right.

SANTA BARBARA

Carpinteria State Beach

5361 6th St., Carpinteria 93013. T: (805) 684-2811 or reservations (805) 968-3294; www.cal-parks.ca.gov or www.reserveamerica.com.

RV ★★★ Tent ★★

Beauty: ★★★ Site Privacy: ★★
Spaciousness: ★★ Quiet: ★★
Security: ★★★ Cleanliness: ★★★
Insect Control: ★★★ Facilities: ★★★

The bad news about this state-run property is that many sites border the park road and some industrial buildings, and if you happen to occupy one of those near the railroad tracks you may confuse a passing freight train with an earthquake. The good news? Never mind the distant off-shore oil platforms, a fair number of sites enjoy stunning views of the ocean, and the crashing surf nearby will drown out most of the noise emanating from your neighbors. The campground, which features an attractive balance of palm trees, eucalyptus, conifers, and sycamores, is broken into four separate sections, with Santa Cruz, Santa Rosa, and San Miguel providing beach access, while the shady Anacapa is situated away from the water. Not so coincidentally, the latter is the quietest, least crowded area in which to camp, while the former three loops feature sandy sites that are packed together like sardines in a can. The beach at Carpinteria, which is just one mile from Hwy. 101, 12 miles south of Santa Barbara, is also open to day-use and picnicking, and a large grassy meadow near it is excellent for kites and frisbee.

Basics

Operated By: California Dept. of Parks & Recreation. **Open:** All year. **Site Assignment:** Reservations recommended; V, MC, D. **Registration:** At entrance booth. **Fee:** $12–$18, cash, CA check or V, MC, D. **Parking:** At site.

Facilities

Number of RV Sites: 261. **Number of Tent-Only Sites:** 1. **Hookups:** Water, electric (30 amps), sewer. **Each Site:** Picnic table, fire grate. **Dump Station:** Yes. **Laundry:** No. **Pay Phone:** Yes. **Rest Rooms and Showers:** Yes. **Fuel:** No. **Propane:** No. **Internal Roads:** Paved. **RV Service:** No. **Market:** 1 mi. north in Carpinteria. **Restaurant:** 1 mi. north in Carpinteria. **General Store:** No. **Vending:** No. **Swimming:** In Pacific Ocean. **Playground:** Yes. **Other:** Some wheelchair-accessible facilities. **Activities:** Surfing, tide pool exploring, seal watching, volleyball. **Nearby Attractions:** Mission San Buenaventura, historic Ventura, Mission Santa Barbara, Santa Barbara & its museums, historic buildings, zoo, Stearns Wharf, Botanic Garden, historic Ventura. **Additional Information:** Santa Barbara Region Chamber of Commerce, (805) 965-3023.

Restrictions

Pets: On 6 ft. leash. **Fires:** In fire grates only, not on the beach. **Alcoholic Beverages:** Allowed at site. **Vehicle Maximum Length:** 35 ft. **Other:** 7-day stay limit from June 1–Oct. 15; no firearms; no wood gathering.

To Get There

From Santa Barbara drive 12 mi. southeast on US 101 and exit on Casitas Pass. Follow Casitas Pass Rd. to the right for 0.2 mi., then turn right on Carpinteria Ave. After 1 block turn left onto Palm St. Continue for 0.4 mi. straight into the campground.

SANTA BARBARA

El Capitan State Beach

10 Refugio Beach Rd., Goleta 93117. T: (805) 968-1033; www.cal-parks.ca.gov or www.reserveamerica.com.

RV ★★★★ Tent ★★★★

Beauty: ★★★★ Site Privacy: ★★★
Spaciousness: ★★★ Quiet: ★★★
Security: ★★★ Cleanliness: ★★★★
Insect Control: ★★★ Facilities: ★★★

El Capitan is not your typical beach campground. Though its four loops are set amidst a series of coastal bluffs, there is more of grass and dirt than sand in the surprisingly roomy, agreeably private sites. And aside from the time you spend on the beach, you won't need a parasol: much of the domain, which is just off Hwy. 101, 17 miles northwest of Santa Barbara, lies within a lush forest of live oak, with a few eucalyptus, sycamores, and pines tossed in for good measure. Tent campers looking for a water view should try for sites 75, 76, 78, and 80 in the third loop; RVers desiring the same will do well with 110, 111, 114, and 116 in the fourth and highest loop. The first circuit (sites 1–31), on the other hand, is one to avoid, lying nearest the railroad tracks and with no view of the ocean. This is one of the prettier beach campgrounds we've seen, with the terrain particularly green and delightful in spring.

Basics

Operated By: California Dept. of Parks & Recreation. **Open:** All year. **Site Assignment:** Reservations recommended; V, MC, D. **Registration:** At entrance booth. **Fee:** $12, cash or CA check. **Parking:** At site.

Facilities

Number of RV Sites: 142. **Number of Tent-Only Sites:** 0. **Hookups:** None. **Each Site:** Picnic table, fire ring. **Dump Station:** Yes. **Laundry:** No. **Pay Phone:** Yes. **Rest Rooms and Showers:** Yes. **Fuel:** No. **Propane:** Yes. **Internal Roads:** Paved. **RV Service:** No. **Market:** 13 mi. east in Goleta. **Restaurant:** 13 mi. east in Goleta. **General Store:** Yes. **Vending:** No. **Swimming:** In Pacific Ocean. **Playground:** No. **Other:** Some wheelchair-accessible facilities. **Activities:** Fishing, hiking, bicycling, boogie board rentals. **Nearby Attractions:** Santa Barbara & its museums, historic buildings, zoo, Stearns Wharf, Botanic Garden, Mission Santa Barbara, Goleta South Coast Railroad Museum. **Additional Information:** Goleta Valley Chamber of Commerce, (805) 967-4618.

Restrictions

Pets: On 6 ft. leash. **Fires:** In fire rings only. **Alcoholic Beverages:** Allowed at site. **Vehicle Maximum Length:** 30 ft. **Other:** 14-day stay limit from June 1–Sept. 30; no firearms; no wood gathering.

To Get There

From Santa Barbara drive 17 mi. west on US 101 and exit on El Capitan State Beach. Turn left (west) and proceed for 0.3 mi., under the railroad trestle, straight into the campground.

SANTA BARBARA

Gaviota State Park

Hwy. 101, Goleta 93117. T: (805) 968-1033; www.cal-parks.ca.gov.

RV ★★★ Tent ★★★

Beauty: ★★★★ Site Privacy: ★★
Spaciousness: ★★ Quiet: ★★
Security: ★★★ Cleanliness: ★★★
Insect Control: ★★★ Facilities: ★★

Gaviota was completely renovated recently after flooding buried one loop in mud and stripped out the sod in the other. Aside from the mature eucalyptus trees at the edge of the dusty, drab-looking campground, the few saplings here have only recently been planted; it will be ten or more years before they mature into shade trees—if they survive. Yet this park, which lies just off Hwy. 101, 30 miles northwest of Santa Barbara, is thrillingly set between a steep series of scenic bluffs and an unspoiled beach. To reach the shore you must walk beneath a century-old railroad trestle (more of a curiosity than noise nuisance) elevated some 75 feet off the ground. The pier by the water is fine for fishing and is equipped with a hoist for launching boats. A hot spring is located in the hills above Gaviota. The strong coastal breezes funneling through camp most afternoons and evenings make the packing of a jacket or sweater advisable.

BASICS

Operated By: California Dept. of Parks & Recreation. **Open:** All year. **Site Assignment:** First come, first served. **Registration:** At entrance booth. **Fee:** $10, cash or CA check. **Parking:** At site.

FACILITIES

Number of RV Sites: 52. **Number of Tent-Only Sites:** 0. **Hookups:** None. **Each Site:** Picnic table, fire grate. **Dump Station:** No. **Laundry:** No. **Pay Phone:** Yes. **Rest Rooms and Showers:** Yes. **Fuel:** No. **Propane:** No. **Internal Roads:** Paved. **RV Service:** No. **Market:** 11 mi. north in Buëllton. **Restaurant:** 11 mi. north in Buëllton. **General Store:** Yes (summer only). **Vending:** No. **Swimming:** In Pacific Ocean. **Playground:** No. **Other:** Some wheelchair-accessible facilities. **Activities:** Fishing, hiking, surfing, horseback riding. **Nearby Attractions:** Mission Santa Inés & museums in Solvang, La Purísima Mission State Historic Park in Lompoc, Santa Barbara & its museums, historic buildings, zoo, Stearns Wharf, Botanic Garden. **Additional Information:** Goleta Valley Chamber of Commerce, (805) 967-4618.

RESTRICTIONS

Pets: On 6 ft. leash. **Fires:** In fire grates only. **Alcoholic Beverages:** Allowed at site. **Vehicle Maximum Length:** 27 ft. **Other:** 14-day stay limit; no firearms; no wood gathering.

TO GET THERE

From Santa Barbara drive 30 mi. west on US 101 and take the Gaviota State Beach Exit to the left. Continue straight for 5 mi. to the park entrance.

SANTA CRUZ

Big Basin Redwoods State Park

21600 Big Basin Way, Boulder Creek 95006. T: (831) 338-8860 or reservations (800) 444-7275; F: (831) 338- 8863; www.bigbasin.org or www.cal-parks.ca.gov or www.reserveamerica.com.

RV ★★★★ Tent ★★★★

Beauty: ★★★★★ Site Privacy: ★★★
Spaciousness: ★★★ Quiet: ★★
Security: ★★★ Cleanliness: ★★★★
Insect Control: ★★★ Facilities: ★★★

Unlike the nearby Henry Cowell Redwoods State Park, Big Basin puts campers right in the center of a dramatic redwood forest. A fair amount of sunlight filters through the dense cluster of giants—which dwarf the tan oaks and hemlocks among them—and an abundance of mossy rocks and fallen trees decorate the thick blanket of pine needles layered on the ground. Average-size sites offer minimal privacy but their distribution over three separate campgrounds helps to reduce incidental noise. The more spacious and private spots are in the hilly Huckleberry loop, which also has tent cabins. Big Basin was established 100 years ago as California's first state park. Of its more than 80 miles of trails, the Berry Creek Falls hike (9.5 miles round trip), which threads past a superb series of redwoods to a pretty waterfall, should be atop your to-do list. Although just 24 miles northwest of Santa Cruz, the road into the park, Hwy. 236, is very slow and windy.

BASICS

Operated By: California Dept. of Parks & Recreation. **Open:** All year. **Site Assignment:** Reservations recommended; V, MC, D. **Registration:** At park headquarters. **Fee:** $12, cash or CA check. **Parking:** At site.

FACILITIES

Number of RV Sites: 39. **Number of Tent-Only Sites:** 108. **Hookups:** None. **Each Site:** Picnic table, fire grate, food storage box. **Dump Station:** Yes. **Laundry:** Yes. **Pay Phone:** Yes. **Rest Rooms and Showers:** Yes. **Fuel:** No. **Propane:** Yes. **Internal Roads:** Paved, some potholes. **RV Service:** No. **Market:** 9.5 mi. southeast in Boulder Creek. **Restaurant:** 9.5 mi. southeast in Boulder Creek. **General Store:** Yes. **Vending:** No. **Swimming:** No. **Playground:** No. **Other:** Some wheelchair-accessible facilities. **Activities:** Hiking, photography, exploring redwood forests. **Nearby Attractions:** Mission Santa Clara de Asis & various museums in Santa Clara; Hakone Japanese Gardens & Saso Herb Gardens in Saratoga; state beaches along the coast. **Additional Information:** Santa Clara CVB, (408) 224-9660 or (800) 272-6822; Saratoga Chamber of Commerce, (408) 867-0753.

RESTRICTIONS

Pets: On 6 ft. leash. **Fires:** In fire grates only. **Alcoholic Beverages:** Allowed at site. **Vehicle Maximum Length:** 27 ft. **Other:** 30-day stay limit; no firearms; no wood gathering.

TO GET THERE

From Santa Cruz drive 13.3 mi. north on Hwy. 9 to Boulder Creek. Turn left (west) on Hwy. 236 and continue for 8 mi. to the park entrance. The park headquarters are 1 mi. down the road.

SANTA ROSA

Spring Lake Regional Park

5585 Newanga Ave., Santa Rosa 95403. T: (707) 539-8092 or reservations (707) 565-2267; F: (707) 538-8038; www.sonoma-county.org/parks.

RV ★★★ Tent ★★★

Beauty: ★★★★ Site Privacy: ★★★
Spaciousness: ★★★ Quiet: ★★★
Security: ★★★ Cleanliness: ★★★
Insect Control: ★★★ Facilities: ★★★

Spring Lake is a small body of water encircled by rolling hills of mature oaks, pines, and bay trees. It is a calm retreat just a few minutes from the heart of suburban Santa Rosa. As such, it is hardly a well-kept secret and you are liable to have company here at almost any time of year. No problem, the grass-covered sites are large enough for you to comfortably spread out your gear, and decently spaced apart around a tree-dotted meadow. Lichen-speckled rocks are scattered across the turf, adding to the natural feel of this agreeable camp. Some sites are impacted by a gentle slope toward the water, and none are graced with a view of the lake. Still, there is a good amount of fine slots, with 28 and 30, at the loop's periphery, ideal for RVers desiring privacy. Five, 26, and 27 are equipped with pull-through parking. Tent campers who don't mind being some distance from their cars should grab 12 or 14, which are secluded and give access to the lake. Note that from Oct. first through Apr. the campground is only open on weekends and holidays.

BASICS

Operated By: County of Sonoma, Regional Parks Dept. **Open:** Every day from May 1–Sept. 30; weekends & holidays only from Oct. 1–Apr. 30. **Site Assignment:** Reservations accepted w/ V, MC. **Registration:** At entrance office. **Fee:** $16, cash or CA check. **Parking:** At site.

FACILITIES

Number of RV Sites: 27. **Number of Tent-Only Sites:** 4. **Hookups:** None. **Each Site:** Picnic table, fire grate, food storage box. **Dump Station:** Yes. **Laundry:** No. **Pay Phone:** Yes. **Rest Rooms and Showers:** Yes. **Fuel:** No. **Propane:** No. **Internal Roads:** Paved. **RV Service:** No. **Market:** 2 mi. west in Santa Rosa. **Restaurant:** 2 mi. west in Santa Rosa. **General Store:** No. **Vending:** No. **Swimming:** In swimming lagoon. **Playground:** No. **Other:** Some wheelchair-accessible facilities, boat ramp, fishing pier, visitor center. **Activities:** Hiking, bicycling, horseback riding, windsurfing, canoe & paddle boat rentals. **Nearby Attractions:** Santa Rosa museums & Luther Burbank Home & Gardens; San Francisco Solano Mission & winery tours in Sonoma. **Additional Information:** Santa Rosa

CVB, (800) 404-ROSE; Sonoma County Tourism Program, (800) 5-SONOMA or (707) 565-5383.

RESTRICTIONS

Pets: On 6 ft. leash; rabies certificate required; $1 fee. **Fires:** In fire grates only. **Alcoholic Beverages:** Allowed at site. **Vehicle Maximum Length:** 40 ft. **Other:** 10-day stay limit; no firearms; no wood gathering.

TO GET THERE

From Santa Rosa on US 101 take Hwy. 12 east. After 1.25 mi. exit onto Hoen Frontage Rd. which will turn into Hoen Ave. After 1.5 mi. turn left on Newanga Ave., which veers sharply to the right. The park entrance is 0.6 mi. ahead.

SANTEE

Santee Lakes Regional Park & Campground

9040 Carlton Oaks Dr., Santee 92071. T: (619) 596-3141; F: (619) 449-4694; www.padredam.org/santee.html.

RV ★★★★ Tent ★★

Beauty: ★★★ Site Privacy: ★★★
Spaciousness: ★★★ Quiet: ★★★
Security: ★★★★★ Cleanliness: ★★★★
Insect Control: ★★ Facilities: ★★★★★

For comfort in camping, Santee Lakes merits an enthusiastic "thumbs up." From tight security to remarkably clean restrooms, from a heated pool to modem hookup in the office, RV camping does not get much better than this. California sycamores, eucalyptus, and palm trees hover over the lush, grassy grounds, which also encompass a series of seven lakes—ponds, really. One of those is dotted with tiny islands and has been set aside for canoeing and pedal boats. Two others are stocked with fish, and the great number of waterfront sites means that fishermen can camp where the action is. Still, despite respectable screening and level terrain, tent camping purists are likely to find the slots a bit too close together. Their best option—short of decamping altogether—is the remote and barren-looking Cottonwood loop (only open weekends), where an absence of such amenities as shade, screening, and barbecue grills guarantees a high level of solitude. An added plus for this park is its close proximity to a San Diego trolley stop.

BASICS

Operated By: Padre Dam Municipal Water District. **Open:** All year. **Site Assignment:** Reservations accepted w/ V, MC, D. **Registration:** At entrance booth. **Fee:** $18–$35, cash or V, MC, D. **Parking:** At site.

FACILITIES

Number of RV Sites: 224. **Number of Tent-Only Sites:** 0. **Hookups:** Water, electric (20, 30, 50 amps), sewer, Internet. **Each Site:** Picnic table, barbecue grill. **Dump Station:** Yes. **Laundry:** Yes. **Pay Phone:** Yes. **Rest Rooms and Showers:** Yes. **Fuel:** No. **Propane:** Yes. **Internal Roads:** Paved. **RV Service:** No. **Market:** 3 mi. east in Santee. **Restaurant:** 3 mi. east in Santee. **General Store:** Yes. **Vending:** Yes. **Swimming:** In heated pool. **Playground:** Yes. **Other:** Some wheelchair-accessible facilities. **Activities:** Fishing, bicycling, horseshoe pit, volleyball, canoe & pedal boat rentals. **Nearby Attractions:** San Diego & its waterfront, museums, zoo, historic district. **Additional Information:** San Diego CVB, (619) 232-3101.

RESTRICTIONS

Pets: On leash; not allowed in day-use area; $1 fee. **Fires:** No. **Alcoholic Beverages:** Allowed. **Vehicle Maximum Length:** 45 ft. **Other:** 14-day stay limit.

TO GET THERE

From Hwy. 67 in Santee exit at Woodside/Santee. Woodside changes into Mission Gorge. Drive 2 mi. on Mission Gorge, turn right onto Carlton Hills Blvd. and after 0.5 mi. turn left onto Carlton Oaks. The campground is 0.4 mi. ahead on the right.

SEQUOIA NATIONAL PARK

Potwisha

Generals Hwy., Sequoia National Park 93262. T: (559) 565-3341; www.nps.gov/seki.

RV ★★★★ Tent ★★★

Beauty: ★★★★ Site Privacy: ★★★
Spaciousness: ★★★ Quiet: ★★★
Security: ★★★ Cleanliness: ★★★★
Insect Control: ★★ Facilities: ★★

Potwisha is named for the Native Americans who once roamed these parts. It is four miles north of Sequoia National Park's south entrance station, 12 miles from the Giant Forest grove of impossibly large redwood trees. Situated at 2,100 feet elevation, Potwisha enjoys an understated beauty, especially in spring when buttercups and other wildflowers decorate its tall green grass, the buckeye trees are ablaze with white blossoms, and the steeply sloping hills are ripe with flowering yucca. There is an authentically natural flavor to this campground, in contrast to the mega-sized Lodgepole, a camper-corral in the heart of the park. Several sites are equipped with pull-through parking, and those along the lower loop, nearer the river, are the more private. Number 18 is all by itself next to a large boulder; 21, 22, and 24, above the river, are roomy and shaded by oaks. Regular bear sightings make using the metal storage lockers a necessity. A highly scenic trail along the Marble Fork leads out of camp by site 17. The road from Potwisha to the Giant Forest and Lodgepole, an uphill, serpentine, white-knuckle drive, ascends 4,500 feet and is not recommended for vehicles over 22 feet in length.

BASICS

Operated By: National Park Service. **Open:** All year. **Site Assignment:** First come, first served. **Registration:** At entrance kiosk. **Fee:** $14, cash or check (in addition to the park entrance fee). **Parking:** At site.

FACILITIES

Number of RV Sites: 42. **Number of Tent-Only Sites:** 0. **Hookups:** None. **Each Site:** Picnic table, fire grate, bearproof box. **Dump Station:** Yes. **Laundry:** No. **Pay Phone:** Yes. **Rest Rooms and Showers:** Flush toilets, no showers. **Fuel:** No. **Propane:** No. **Internal Roads:** Paved. **RV Service:** No. **Market:** 10 mi. southwest in Three Rivers. **Restaurant:** 10 mi. southwest in Three Rivers. **General Store:** No. **Vending:** No. **Swimming:** No. **Playground:** No. **Other:** Some wheelchair-accessible facilities. **Activities:** Hiking, wildlife viewing, white-water rafting on Kaweah River. **Nearby Attractions:** Kings Canyon National Park; Tulare County Museum in Visalia; Kaweah Oaks Preserve in Exeter; Kaweah Lake. **Additional Information:** Visalia Chamber of Commerce & Visitors Bureau, (559) 734-5876; Three Rivers–Lemoncove Business Assoc., (550) 561-0410.

RESTRICTIONS

Pets: On 6 ft. leash; not allowed on trails. **Fires:** In fire grates only. **Alcoholic Beverages:** Allowed at site. **Vehicle Maximum Length:** 32 ft. **Other:** 14-day stay limit; no loaded firearms; no food in vehicles.

TO GET THERE

From Visalia drive 37 mi. east on Hwy. 198 to the park's Ash Mountain entrance station. Continue 4 mi. north on Generals Hwy. The well-signed campground entrance is on the left.

SHELTER COVE

Tolkan

Kings Peak Rd., Shelter Cove 95589. T: (707) 986-7731 or (707) 825-2300; F: (707) 825-2301; www.ca.blm.gov/arcata/campground.html.

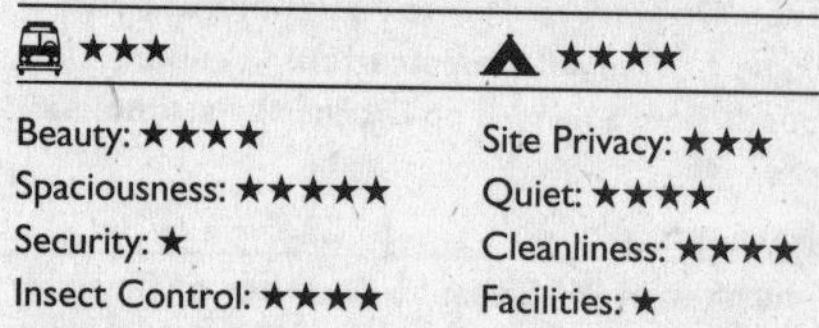

RV ★★★ Tent ★★★★

Beauty: ★★★★ Site Privacy: ★★★
Spaciousness: ★★★★★ Quiet: ★★★★
Security: ★ Cleanliness: ★★★★
Insect Control: ★★★★ Facilities: ★

The Bureau of Land Management has begun an ambitious campaign to revamp many of its long-neglected properties. Nowhere is that more apparent than at this hidden gem, cloaked within the overgrown heart of the rugged King Range National Conservation Area high above the Lost Coast, about ten miles inland from Shelter Cove (the last three are a dirt washboard). After the recent refurbishing, Tolkan now features royally spacious, gravel and dirt sites equipped with new tables, fire grates, and back-in parking slots large enough to handle the most colossal of motor homes. The units have been distributed so far apart that it is hard to go wrong with any, but the most isolated, and largest, is number seven, handsomely ensconced under a massive pine tree. An old-fashioned water tower rests on four stilts in the center of the single loop, partially screened by the varied conifers, manzanita, tan oak, madrone, and ceanothus that grow so abundantly throughout this mountainous ridge.

BASICS

Operated By: Bureau of Land Management, Arcata Field Office. **Open:** All year. **Site Assignment:** First come, first served. **Registration:** At entrance kiosk. **Fee:** $8, cash or check. **Parking:** At site.

FACILITIES

Number of RV Sites: 9. **Number of Tent-Only Sites:** 0. **Hookups:** None. **Each Site:** Picnic table, fire grate. **Dump Station:** No. **Laundry:** No. **Pay Phone:** No. **Rest Rooms and Showers:** Vault toilets, no showers. **Fuel:** No. **Propane:** No. **Internal Roads:** Gravel & dirt, decent condition. **RV Service:** No. **Market:** 18.3 mi. east in Redway. **Restaurant:** 3.7 mi. west in Shelter Cove. **General Store:** No. **Vending:** No. **Swimming:** No. **Playground:** No. **Other:** Some wheelchair-accessible facilities. **Activities:** Hiking, mushroom-plucking (permit required). **Nearby Attractions:** Richardson Grove State Park in Garberville; Smithe Redwoods State Reserve & Standish Hickey State Recreation Area in Leggett; Ave. of the Giants north of Garberville; Humboldt Redwoods State Park in Weott. **Additional Information:** Shelter Cove Information Bureau, (707) 923-1830; Garberville-Redway Area Chamber of Commerce, (707) 923-2613.

RESTRICTIONS

Pets: On leash. **Fires:** In fire grates only. **Alcoholic Beverages:** Allowed. **Vehicle Maximum Length:** 22 ft. **Other:** 14-day stay limit.

TO GET THERE

Exit US 101 at Garberville and drive through the downtown, turning left on Redwood Rd. at the sign for the King Range National Conservation Area. After 2.6 mi. turn left on Briceland Rd. which becomes the meandering and steep Shelter Cove Rd. Drive 18.3 mi. and turn right on Kings Peak Rd. Continue for 3.8 mi. to the well-marked campground on the right.

SIERRA CITY

Wild Plum

Wild Plum Rd., Sierra City 96125. T: (530) 288-3231 or (530) 993-1410; F: (530) 288-0727; www.r5.fs.fed.us/tahoe.

RV ★★★ Tent ★★★★

Beauty: ★★★★	Site Privacy: ★★★
Spaciousness: ★★★	Quiet: ★★★★
Security: ★★★★	Cleanliness: ★★★
Insect Control: ★★★	Facilities: ★

Gadzooks! What has this book steered me to, a construction zone? may be the first words you voice when, after maneuvering down the bad camp road, you arrive at an expansive mound of river stones. Persevere; the campground, right alongside the musical, rollicking Haypress Creek (which flows into the Yuba River), is a delight and well worth your initial discomfort. Of the three separate loops to this mountainous pine forest, the middle one climbs uphill to the best sites for views of the water as well as neighboring ridge-tops. The most spacious is 32, but 33–36 also overlook the creek. On the lower tracks, 7 is set well back in a corner location and 19 is tucked behind an embankment. While the ground throughout the property is rather rocky, most dirt- and pine needle–surfaced sites have enough smooth, level ground for the staking of a tent. Parking, too, is ample for medium-size RVs and trailers. Wild Plum, which rests at 4,400 feet elevation, is often over-run by youthful kayakers, especially on summer weekends. If you find it full, there is also a fair amount of secluded sites at the less-popular Loganville Campground, 1.5 miles west of Sierra City.

BASICS

Operated By: High Sierra Campground Management, concessionaire. **Open:** May through Oct. **Site Assignment:** First come, first served. **Registration:** At entrance kiosk. **Fee:** $13, cash or check. **Parking:** At site.

FACILITIES

Number of RV Sites: 47. **Number of Tent-Only Sites:** 0. **Hookups:** None. **Each Site:** Picnic table, fire grate, some equipped w/ bearproof box. **Dump Station:** No. **Laundry:** No. **Pay Phone:** No. **Rest Rooms and Showers:** Vault toilets, no showers. **Fuel:** No. **Propane:** No. **Internal Roads:** Paved, bumpy. **RV Service:** No. **Market:** 2 mi. west in Sierra City. **Restaurant:** 2 mi. west in Sierra City. **General Store:** No. **Vending:** No. **Swimming:** No. **Playground:** No. **Activities:** Hiking, kayaking, fishing, gold panning. **Nearby Attractions:** Kentucky Mine, Stampmill & Museum in Sierra City; Empire Mine State Historic Park in Grass Valley; Malakoff Diggins State Historic Park in Nevada City; Downieville Foundry/Museum, Gallows, & County Museum; Tahoe National Forest. **Additional Information:** Grass Valley–Nevada County Chamber of Commerce, (530) 273-4667; Sierra County Chamber of Commerce, (530) 862-0308 or (800) 200-4949.

RESTRICTIONS

Pets: On leash. **Fires:** In fire grates only. **Alcoholic Beverages:** Allowed. **Vehicle Maximum Length:** 22 ft. **Other:** 14-day stay limit.

TO GET THERE

From Grass Valley drive about 55 mi. north on Hwy. 49 to Sierra City. Continue for 0.5 mi. and turn right on Wild Plum Rd. Cross a narrow bridge and follow the gravel road for 1.5 mi. over another bridge into the campground.

SONORA

Boulder Flat

Hwy. 108, Dardanelle 95314. T: (209) 965-3434; F: (209) 965-3372; www.r5.fs.fed.us/stanislaus.

RV ★★★★ Tent ★★★

Beauty: ★★★★	Site Privacy: ★★★
Spaciousness: ★★★	Quiet: ★★★
Security: ★★★	Cleanliness: ★★
Insect Control: ★★★★	Facilities: ★★

Of the great number of national forest campgrounds along Hwy. 108, Boulder Flat is perhaps the most appropriately-named, given its granite-strewn appearance. It is also arguably one of the prettier facilities, reflecting something of a wild, high Sierra Nevada ambiance. A spiny alpine ridge flanks one side of camp, the Stanislaus River purls by another, while a series of pointy peaks hover over the scene. Grass and dirt sites, punctuated by several stands of enormous red-bark cedars, are larger and more dispersed than at nearby Brighton Flat, and less barren-looking and exposed than those at Eureka Valley (though the latter also features an impressive array of boulders, and has the river sluicing past on two sides). It is true that Boulder Flat picks up auto noise from the Sonora Pass, but the same might be said of all the other campgrounds along this stretch of road. The town of Sonora is 50 miles west, and Dardanelle, where you will find a telephone and general store, two miles east.

BASICS

Operated By: Dodge Ridge Corp., concessionaire. **Open:** May through Sept., weather permitting. **Site Assignment:** First come, first served. **Registration:** At entrance kiosk. **Fee:** $13, cash or check. **Parking:** At site.

FACILITIES

Number of RV Sites: 20. **Number of Tent-Only Sites:** 0. **Hookups:** None. **Each Site:** Picnic table, fire grate. **Dump Station:** No. **Laundry:** No. **Pay Phone:** No. **Rest Rooms and Showers:** Vault toilets, no showers. **Fuel:** No. **Propane:** No. **Internal Roads:** Paved. **RV Service:** No. **Market:** 36 mi. southwest in Twain Harte. **Restaurant:** 36 mi. southwest in Twain Harte. **General Store:** No. **Vending:** No. **Swimming:** No. **Playground:** No. **Activities:** Fishing, hiking. **Nearby Attractions:** Tuolumne County Museum & History Center in Sonora; Pinecrest Lake; Sonora Pass. **Additional Information:** Tuolumne County Visitors Bureau, (209) 533-4420 or (800) 446-1333.

RESTRICTIONS

Pets: On leash. **Fires:** In fire grates only. **Alcoholic Beverages:** Allowed. **Vehicle Maximum Length:** 22 ft. **Other:** 14-day stay limit.

TO GET THERE

From Sonora drive 49 mi. east on Hwy. 108. The campground entrance is on the left, just beyond Clark Fork Rd.

SOUTH LAKE TAHOE

D. L. Bliss State Park

Hwy. 89, West Shore Lake Tahoe, Tahoma 96142. T: (530) 525-7277 or (530) 525-7232 or reservations (800) 444-7275; www.cal-parks.ca.gov or www.reserveamerica.com.

RV ★★★ Tent ★★★

Beauty: ★★★★	Site Privacy: ★★
Spaciousness: ★★★	Quiet: ★★★
Security: ★★★	Cleanliness: ★★★
Insect Control: ★★★	Facilities: ★★

D. L. Bliss was a pioneering lumberman, banker, and railroad owner whose family donated 744 acres of this land to the state park system in 1929. More than 70 years later, the campground retains an appealingly rustic look. That it lacks the "Hooverville" feel of so many other facilities its size may be chalked up to its pleasingly chaotic Sierra Nevada setting. Huge granite boulders vie for space with incense cedars, lodgepole, and Jeffrey pines across a steep hillside that ends at a sandy beach and picnic area on the shore of Lake Tahoe. Roomy sites are tightly clustered over a series of loops, but they don't seem crowded, due to a degree of buffering provided by the boulders. For the most space and best views of the indigo water, try for the loop with sites 141–168, which also has a number of pull-through parking slots. Make time for hiking the Rubicon trail (four-and-a-half miles, one way), which offers stellar views of the lake and a chance to see osprey nesting in the tall trees. It ends at Vikingsholm Mansion (worth a visit), at scenic Emerald Bay. The shorter Balancing Rock nature trail (half a mile long) winds through the forest to a precariously positioned granite boulder.

Basics

Operated By: California Dept. of Parks & Recreation. **Open:** Late May to mid-Sept., weather permitting. **Site Assignment:** Reservations recommended;V, MC, D. **Registration:** At entrance booth. **Fee:** $12, cash or CA check. **Parking:** At site.

Facilities

Number of RV Sites: 168. **Number of Tent-Only Sites:** 0. **Hookups:** None. **Each Site:** Picnic table, fire grate, bearproof box, some sites have barbecue grill. **Dump Station:** Yes. **Laundry:** No. **Pay Phone:** Yes. **Rest Rooms and Showers:** Yes. **Fuel:** No. **Propane:** No. **Internal Roads:** Paved. **RV Service:** No. **Market:** 11 mi. south in South Lake Tahoe. **Restaurant:** 11 mi. south in South Lake Tahoe. **General Store:** No. **Vending:** No. **Swimming:** In Lake Tahoe. **Playground:** No. **Other:** Beach. **Activities:** Hiking, fishing, birding. **Nearby Attractions:** Emerald Bay State Park & Vikingsholm Mansion in Tahoma; Lake Tahoe Historical Museum in South Lake Tahoe. **Additional Information:** South Lake Tahoe Chamber of Commerce, (530) 541-5255.

Restrictions

Pets: On 6 ft. leash. **Fires:** In fire grates only. **Alcoholic Beverages:** Allowed at site. **Vehicle Maximum Length:** 18 ft. **Other:** 14-day stay limit; no firearms; no wood gathering.

To Get There

From South Lake Tahoe, at the junction of US 50 and Hwy. 89, follow Hwy. 89 north for 11.4 mi. to the entrance of the state park on the right. After making that turn, the campground is straight ahead.

SPRINGVILLE

Wishon

Camp Wishon Rd./CR 208, Springville 93265. T: (559) 539-2607 or reservations (877) 444-6777; www.r5.fs.fed.us/sequoia or www.reserveusa.com.

RV ★★★ Tent ★★★★

Beauty: ★★★★	Site Privacy: ★★★
Spaciousness: ★★★	Quiet: ★★★★
Security: ★★★★	Cleanliness: ★★★
Insect Control: ★★	Facilities: ★★

Wishon, at 4,000 feet elevation, is not for the tidy at heart. It's a sprawling campground that overlaps a congested tangle of trees and rocks. The boulder-larded landscape adds convincingly to the mountainous feel here, and to the difficulty in walking through the domain after dark. The unspoiled allure of this primitive, peaceful setting is accentuated by craggy Sierra ridges that seem to brush the sky overhead. Middle Fork of the North Tule River cuts the camp in half, with the more appealing sites across the small bridge, where aged, spidery-limbed oaks bestow the gift of shade. Additional shelter and screening are provided by ponderosa pines, madrone, manzanita, and cedar. Sites 20, 21, and 28, tucked behind boulders, are the most private. This national forest campground is in the southern unit of the new Giant Sequoia National Monument, making it a great base for exploring trails in the area. The host's residence is adjacent to the property.

Basics

Operated By: California Land Management, concessionaire. **Open:** All year, weather permitting. **Site Assignment:** Reservations accepted w/ V, MC, D. **Registration:** At entrance kiosk. **Fee:** $14, cash or check; $28 for double site. **Parking:** At site.

Facilities

Number of RV Sites: 35. **Number of Tent-Only Sites:** 0. **Hookups:** None. **Each Site:** Picnic table, fire grate, barbecue grill. **Dump Station:** No. **Laundry:** No. **Pay Phone:** Yes. **Rest Rooms and Showers:** Vault toilets, no showers. **Fuel:** No. **Propane:** No. **Internal Roads:** Paved. **RV Service:** No. **Market:** 28 mi. west in Porterville. **Restaurant:** 13 mi. west in Springville. **General Store:** No. **Vending:** No. **Swimming:** No. **Playground:** No. **Activities:** Hiking, fishing. **Nearby Attractions:** Sequoia National Forest; Porterville Historical Museum & Zauld House & Gardens; California Hot Springs. **Additional Information:** Springville Chamber of Commerce, (559) 539-2312; Porterville Chamber of Commerce, (559) 784-7503.

Restrictions

Pets: On leash. **Fires:** In fire grates only. **Alcoholic Beverages:** Allowed. **Vehicle Maximum Length:** 24 ft. **Other:** 14-day stay limit.

To Get There

From Porterville drive 24 mi. east on Hwy. 190 to Camp Wishon Rd. Turn left and proceed 4 mi. to the campground entrance on the right.

ST. HELENA

Bothe-Napa Valley State Park

3801 St. Helena Hwy. (Hwy. 29), Calistoga 94515. T: (707) 942-4574 or reservations (800) 444-7275; www.cal-parks.ca.gov or www.reserveamerica.com.

RV ★★★ Tent ★★★★

Beauty: ★★★★	Site Privacy: ★★★★
Spaciousness: ★★★	Quiet: ★★★
Security: ★★★	Cleanliness: ★★★
Insect Control: ★	Facilities: ★★

The Wappo Indians used to call this part of the valley home until being displaced by white settlers in the middle of the nineteenth century. In honor of its first inhabitants the park maintains a small "Native American garden" of herbs and vegetables the Wappos are believed to have cultivated. Indigenous plants are featured in a more natural setting around the campground, its lollipop loop being abundantly furnished with a variety of conifers and oaks, toyon, bay, madrone, manzanita, and poison oak. Most campers gravitate to the top of the cul-de-sac near the latrines. The more private sites, though, are 1–9 at the front end of the drive, and their gravel parking slips are long enough to accommodate almost any size RV. One of the better trails in Bothe-Napa leads to volcanic ash cliffs atop Upper Ritchey Canyon. And for unusual amenities in a state park, how about the swimming pool, open from Memorial Day through Labor Day? That sure beats wading in the stream that trickles by one side of camp, spawning hordes of mosquitoes in the spring.

Basics

Operated By: California Dept. of Parks & Recreation. **Open:** All year. **Site Assignment:** Reservations accepted w/ V, MC, D. **Registration:** At kiosk opposite site 11. **Fee:** $12, cash or CA check. **Parking:** At site.

Facilities

Number of RV Sites: 40. **Number of Tent-Only Sites:** 9. **Hookups:** None. **Each Site:** Picnic table, fire grate, food storage box. **Dump Station:** No. **Laundry:** No. **Pay Phone:** Yes. **Rest Rooms and Showers:** Yes. **Fuel:** No. **Propane:** No. **Internal Roads:** Paved. **RV Service:** No. **Market:** 3 mi. north in Calistoga. **Restaurant:** 3 mi. north in Calistoga. **General Store:** No. **Vending:** No. **Swimming:** In pool seasonally. **Playground:** No. **Other:** Some wheelchair-accessible facilities, visitor center. **Activities:** Hiking, bicycling, horseback riding, birding, interpretive programs, horseshoe pit. **Nearby Attractions:** Luther Burbank Home & Gardens, Annadel State Park & museums in Santa Rosa; winery tours. **Additional Information:** Santa Rosa CVB, (800) 404-ROSE; Napa-Sonoma Wine Country Visitor Center, (707) 642-0686 or (800) 723-0575.

Restrictions

Pets: On 6 ft. leash. **Fires:** In fire grates only. **Alcoholic Beverages:** Allowed at site. **Vehicle Maximum Length:** 31 ft. **Other:** 14-day stay limit; no firearms; no wood gathering.

To Get There

From St. Helena follow Hwy. 29 north for 4.5 mi. The well-marked park entrance is on the left, beyond Bale Grist Mill State Park.

STOCKTON

New Hogan Lake, Acorn West and Acorn East Campgrounds

2713 Hogan Dam Rd., Valley Springs 95252. T: (209) 772-1343 or reservations (877) 444-6777 or marina (209) 772-1462; F: (209) 772-9352; www.spk.usace.army.mil/cespk-co/lakes/newhogan.html or www.reserveusa.com; newhogan-info@spk.usace.army.mil.

RV ★★★★ Tent ★★★

Beauty: ★★★★	Site Privacy: ★★
Spaciousness: ★★★	Quiet: ★★
Security: ★★★★	Cleanliness: ★★
Insect Control: ★★★	Facilities: ★★★★

The US Army Corps of Engineers created this reservoir in 1964 and continues to manage it. Which is not to suggest that you'll be rousted out of your sleeping bag by reveille at 0500 hours. It's more likely that the roar of motorboats will get you up, as this is a popular—though seldom full—boating and fishing spot. The only overt reminders that this is army land is the presence of uniformed volunteers at the entrance booths. In a sense that's a shame, since the oak-fringed, grassy meadows of the three camp loops, which slope water-ward, could tolerate more thorough litter control. On weekend nights, too, excessive noise, including barking, wandering dogs, can be severe enough to make you want to call in the MPs. Yet sites are well dispersed, if somewhat open, and many are shaded by toyon, pines, and oaks. There are also 30 boat-in spots available (first come, first served) from May through Sept. Oak Knoll, the primitive overflow area, costs $6 less per night and offers a few decently private, lake view sites.

Basics

Operated By: US Army Corps of Engineers. **Open:** All year. **Site Assignment:** Reservations for 70% of the sites accepted w/ V, MC, D. **Registration:** At entrance booth. **Fee:** $16, cash or check. **Parking:** At site.

Facilities

Number of RV Sites: 127. **Number of Tent-Only Sites:** 0. **Hookups:** None. **Each Site:** Picnic table, fire grate, lantern pole. **Dump Station:** Yes. **Laundry:** No. **Pay Phone:** Yes. **Rest Rooms and Showers:** Yes. **Fuel:** No. **Propane:** No. **Internal Roads:** Paved. **RV Service:** No. **Market:** 3 mi. northwest in Valley Springs. **Restaurant:** 3 mi. northwest in Valley Springs. **General Store:** No. **Vending:** No. **Swimming:** In New Hogan Lake. **Playground:** No. **Other:** Some wheelchair-accessible facilities, boat ramp, marina. **Activities:** Fishing, boat rentals, hiking, birding, horseback riding, mountain biking, cussing out your noisy neighbors. **Nearby Attractions:** Calaveras County Historical Society & Museum Complex in San Andreas; Amador County Museum in Jackson; planetarium & museums in Stockton. **Additional Information:** Calaveras County Visitors Bureau, (209) 736-0049.

Restrictions

Pets: On leash. **Fires:** In fire grates only. **Alcoholic Beverages:** Allowed. **Vehicle Maximum Length:** None. **Other:** 14-day stay limit.

To Get There

From Stockton on Hwy. 99 drive 30 mi. east to Hogan Dam Rd. Turn right and continue for 1 mi. to the well-signed campground access road on the left. The campground entrance is 0.8 mi. from there.

SUSANVILLE

Bogard

FR 31N21, Susanville 96130. T: (530) 257-4188; F: (530) 257-4150; www.r5.fs.fed.us/lassen.

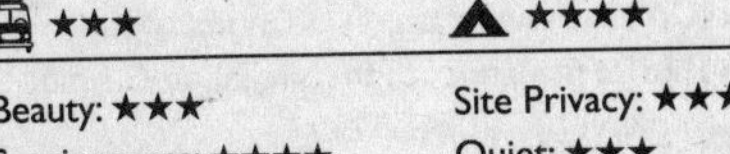

Beauty: ★★★ | Site Privacy: ★★★
Spaciousness: ★★★★ | Quiet: ★★★
Security: ★★ | Cleanliness: ★★★
Insect Control: ★★★ | Facilities: ★

Searching for a peaceful camp where you are more likely to hear birds chirping and the tapping of woodpeckers than another camper's voice? Then Bogard is just the place. Its single loop winds through a mountainous—though level—pine and alder forest, with rocks, pine needle, and grass coloring the floor of sites. That there are so few of the latter is refreshing, considering how easily another dozen could be shoe-horned into such a sizable piece of turf. Of the many good spots, the very best for privacy are 4, 6, 7, 10, and 11. We prefer Bogard as a base camp to Butte Creek, also a Lassen National Forest campground, even though the second is closer to the Butte Lake section of Lassen National Park. Bogard is used less often by hunters and has thus suffered less wear and tear during the off-season. There is no trash pick-up, and the rustic pump delivers rusty water, so plan to pack-in drinking water and pack-out your rubbish. Surprisingly, the back-in parking slots are paved.

Basics

Operated By: CSU Chico Research Foundation, concessionaire. **Open:** May through Oct., weather permitting. **Site Assignment:** First come, first served. **Registration:** At entrance kiosk. **Fee:** $10, cash or check. **Parking:** At site.

Facilities

Number of RV Sites: 13. **Number of Tent-Only Sites:** 0. **Hookups:** None. **Each Site:** Picnic table, fire grate. **Dump Station:** No. **Laundry:** No. **Pay Phone:** No. **Rest Rooms and Showers:** Vault toilets, no showers. **Fuel:** No. **Propane:** No. **Internal Roads:** Paved. **RV Service:** No. **Market:** 28 mi. east in Susanville. **Restaurant:** 28 mi. east in Susanville. **General Store:** No. **Vending:** No. **Swimming:** No. **Playground:** No. **Activities:** Hiking, fishing, wildlife viewing. **Nearby Attractions:** Bizz Johnson National Recreation Trail; Railroad Depot & Lassen Historical Museum in Susanville; Lassen Volcanic National Park; Eagle Lake Recreation Area. **Additional Information:** Lassen County Chamber of Commerce, (530) 257-4323.

Restrictions

Pets: On leash. **Fires:** In fire grates only. **Alcoholic Beverages:** Allowed. **Vehicle Maximum Length:** 28 ft. **Other:** 14-day stay limit.

To Get There

From Susanville drive 6 mi. west on Hwy. 36. Bear right on Hwy. 44 and continue for 20 mi., then turn left on FR 31N26 (a dirt washboard immediately after the rest area sign). Proceed for 1.6 mi. and take a right on FR 31N21. The campground is 0.5 mi. ahead.

SUSANVILLE

Goumaz

FR 30N03, Susanville 96130. T: (530) 257-4188; F: (530) 252-5803; www.r5.fs.fed.us/lassen.

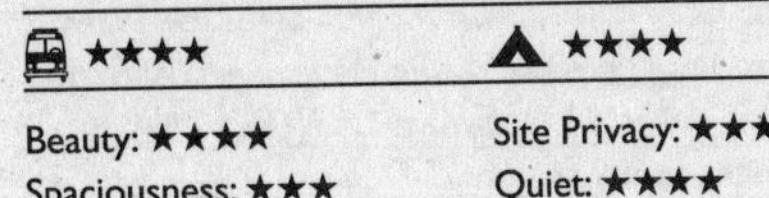

Beauty: ★★★★ | Site Privacy: ★★★
Spaciousness: ★★★ | Quiet: ★★★★
Security: ★ | Cleanliness: ★★★
Insect Control: ★ | Facilities: ★

Aside from a new-ish vaulted toilet, which is shared with hikers doing the Bizz Johnson "rails to trails" path that runs by the camp, this place has nada for facilities. If you can do without the other comforts, though, you'll have it made in the glade. Goumaz, at 5,200 feet elevation, is a thinly-forested, delightfully pretty, alpine campground in a level, sunny spot right alongside the Susan River. There is plenty of elbow room between the five sites, and four of those abut the water. Thus, it is hard to go wrong with any of these units, though number 2 enjoys a commanding view of a bend in the river and 4, which has pull-through parking (as does 1), is just 15 feet from a melodic cascade. Pine trees and grassy meadows contribute to a peaceful atmosphere that is marred only occasionally by the buzzing of a passing military jet. Biting flies can be a nuisance from mid-spring through early summer, so bring repellant. Susanville lies less than 20 miles to the east.

Basics

Operated By: CSU Chico Research Foundation, concessionaire, & Lassen National Forest, Eagle Lake Ranger District. **Open:** May through Oct., weather permitting. **Site Assignment:** First come, first served. **Registration:** At entrance kiosk. **Fee:** $8, cash or check. **Parking:** At site.

Facilities

Number of RV Sites: 5. **Number of Tent-Only Sites:** 0. **Hookups:** None. **Each Site:** Picnic table, fire grate. **Dump Station:** No. **Laundry:** No. **Pay Phone:** No. **Rest Rooms and Showers:** Vault toilets, no showers. **Fuel:** No. **Propane:** No. **Internal Roads:** Packed dirt & volcanic cinder, decent condition. **RV Service:** No. **Market:** 16 mi. east in Susanville. **Restaurant:** 16 mi. east in Susanville. **General Store:** No. **Vending:** No. **Swimming:** No. **Playground:** No. **Activities:** Hiking, bicycling, horseback riding, birding. **Nearby Attractions:** Lassen National Scenic Byway (Highways 89/44/36); Lassen Volcanic National Park; Bizz Johnson National Recreation Trail & Lassen Historical Museum in Susanville; Lake Almanor. **Additional Information:** Lassen County Chamber of Commerce, (530) 257-4323.

Restrictions

Pets: On leash. **Fires:** In fire grates only. **Alcoholic Beverages:** Allowed. **Vehicle Maximum Length:** 30 ft. **Other:** 14-day stay limit.

To Get There

From Susanville drive 6 mi. west on Hwy. 36. Turn right on Hwy. 44 and continue for 7.1 mi. Turn left on FR 30N03/Goumaz Rd. The campground is 3.4 mi. ahead on the right.

SUSANVILLE

Merrill

Eagle Lake Rd., Susanville 96130. T: (530) 257-4188 or reservations (877) 444-6777; F: (530) 252-5803; www.r5.fs.fed.us/lassen or www.reserveusa.com.

Beauty: ★★★★ Site Privacy: ★★★
Spaciousness: ★★★ Quiet: ★★★
Security: ★★★★ Cleanliness: ★★★
Insect Control: ★★★ Facilities: ★★

The deep blue Eagle Lake is California's second largest natural body of water, a magnificent mountain lake that is ringed by ponderosa, Jeffrey and white pines, with low-slung peaks nuzzling the horizon. The beauty of the scene more than compensates for the shocking impression made by the clear-cutting of national forest land along the drive to Eagle Summit, a process that appears to be turning large patches of forest into mountain heath. Sites at Merrill are evenly distributed over six loops and are either grassy or covered in pine needles, and partially shaded by pines. Many of those lie just 100 feet from the water, with 164 and 180 the most isolated. Also worth reserving are 167, 169, 171, 172, 174, 176, and 178. Security is above average for a national forest camp, with two separate hosts patrolling the domain. Also vigilant in summer are omnipresent game wardens, something to remember if you intend to fish. Showers, pay phones, fuel, groceries, and laundry machines are available at the marina, three miles away.

Basics

Operated By: CSU Chico Research Foundation, concessionaire, & Lassen National Forest, Eagle Lake Ranger District. **Open:** May through Oct., weather permitting. **Site Assignment:** Reservations accepted w/ V, MC, D for Aspen & Pine loops. **Registration:** At entrance kiosk. **Fee:** $14–$16, cash or check. **Parking:** At site.

Facilities

Number of RV Sites: 180. **Number of Tent-Only Sites:** 0. **Hookups:** None, but planned. **Each Site:** Picnic table, fire grate. **Dump Station:** Yes. **Laundry:** No. **Pay Phone:** No. **Rest Rooms and Showers:** Flush toilets, no showers. **Fuel:** No. **Propane:** No. **Internal Roads:** Paved. **RV Service:** No. **Market:** 14 mi. north in Spaulding. **Restaurant:** 14 mi. north in Spaulding. **General Store:** No. **Vending:** No. **Swimming:** In Eagle Lake. **Playground:** No. **Other:** Some wheelchair-accessible facilities, boat ramp, marina. **Activities:** Fishing, waterskiing, canoeing, bicycling. **Nearby Attractions:** Bizz Johnson National Recreation Trail; Railroad Depot & Lassen Historical Museum in Susanville; Lassen Volcanic National Park. **Additional Information:** Lassen County Chamber of Commerce, (530) 257-4323.

Restrictions

Pets: On leash. **Fires:** In fire grates only. **Alcoholic Beverages:** Allowed. **Vehicle Maximum Length:** 45 ft. **Other:** 14-day stay limitexcept in one loop w/ a 30-day stay limit.

To Get There

From Susanville drive 4 mi. west on Hwy. 36. Turn right on Eagle Lake Rd./CR A1 and continue for 13.7 mi. to Gallatin Rd. Take a right and proceed for 1 mi. to the campground entrance on the right. The marina is 1 mi. farther.

TAHOMA
Meeks Bay

Hwy. 89, West Shore Lake Tahoe, Meeks Bay 96142. T: (530) 573-2674 or (530) 583-3642; F: (530) 573-2693; www.r5.fs.fed.us/ltbmu or www.reserveusa.com.

RV: ★★★ Tent: ★★

Beauty: ★★★★ Site Privacy: ★★
Spaciousness: ★★★ Quiet: ★★
Security: ★★★ Cleanliness: ★★★
Insect Control: ★★★ Facilities: ★★

If your idea of a restful vacation spot is a quiet place to pitch your tent or park your camper, don't even think about stopping at Meeks Bay. Just 11 miles south of Tahoe City, this national forest camp is hunkered up against a bend in Hwy. 89 as it follows the contours of Lake Tahoe, subjecting it to the roar of an ongoing stream of traffic. If, on the other hand, beach time is what makes you tick, drive on in and sink your toes into the soft sandy stretch of shore here at the heart of the scenically gorgeous Meeks Bay. Soak up the rays and enjoy the hazy view of Nevada and its mountains across the lake. Or get out on the water via the boat ramp at the resort next door. As for the attractive campground, at 6,300 feet elevation, its level, sandy, and grassy sites are dispersed around a convoluted series of loops. Though they are rather exposed, many are shaded by mature Jeffrey pines, with smaller conifers, some manzanita, and young incense cedars adding to the beauty of the scene. The Meeks Bay trailhead leads into the Desolation Wilderness, across the road.

Basics

Operated By: California Land Management, concessionaire. **Open:** Mid-May to end Sept. **Site Assignment:** Reservations recommended; V, MC, D. **Registration:** At entrance kiosk. **Fee:** $14, cash or check. **Parking:** At site.

Facilities

Number of RV Sites: 40. **Number of Tent-Only Sites:** 0. **Hookups:** None. **Each Site:** Picnic table, fire ring, barbecue grill. **Dump Station:** No. **Laundry:** No. **Pay Phone:** Yes. **Rest Rooms and Showers:** Flush toilets, no showers. **Fuel:** No. **Propane:** No. **Internal Roads:** Paved. **RV Service:** No. **Market:** 4 mi. north in Homewood. **Restaurant:** 2 mi. north in Tahoma. **General Store:** Yes. **Vending:** No. **Swimming:** In Lake Tahoe. **Playground:** No. **Other:** Beach. **Activities:** Fishing, boating, bicycle rentals, counting the passing cars. **Nearby Attractions:** Gatekeeper's Museum/Marion Steinbach Indian Basket Museum & Watson Cabin Museum in Tahoe City; Emerald Bay State Park & Vikingsholm Mansion in Tahoma. **Additional Information:** South Lake Tahoe Chamber of Commerce, (530) 541-5255.

Restrictions

Pets: On 6 ft. leash; not allowed on beach. **Fires:** In fire rings only. **Alcoholic Beverages:** Allowed at site. **Vehicle Maximum Length:** 20 ft. **Other:** 14-day stay limit.

To Get There

From Tahoe City drive 11.2 mi. south on Hwy. 89. The campground entrance is on the left, right after Meeks Bay RV Resort & Marina.

TAHOMA
Sugar Pine Point State Park, General Creek Campground

Hwy. 89, West Shore Lake Tahoe 7360, Tahoma 96142. T: (530) 525-7982 or (530) 525-7232 or reservations (800) 444-7275; www.cal-parks.ca.gov or www.reserveamerica.com.

RV: ★★★ Tent: ★★★

Beauty: ★★★★ Site Privacy: ★★★
Spaciousness: ★★★ Quiet: ★★★
Security: ★★★ Cleanliness: ★★★
Insect Control: ★★★ Facilities: ★★★

So close to Lake Tahoe, and yet so far. That, in a phrase, sums up one of the more frustrating aspects of this otherwise fine state park. General Creek Campground, at an altitude of 6,250 feet, consists of several loops that wind through a level pine forest that is uphill and across the street from the lake, but offers no views of the water. There is decent screening between sites, which is fortunate, given how closely they are clustered. The circuit with units 126–175 features the most dispersed spots, while that containing 76–125 runs a close second. This is the only state park in the area to stay open all year, a boon to cross-country skiers and hardy, hot-blooded campers. Spring, though, is one of the better times to come, before the roads are clogged by tourists, and while the snow plants and manzanita are in bloom. The Hellman-Ehrman Mansion, an opulent, pine-paneled summer home built a century ago, is open for tours from July through Labor Day.

Basics

Operated By: California Dept. of Parks & Recreation. **Open:** All year. **Site Assignment:** Reservations recommended; V, MC, D. **Registration:** At entrance booth. **Fee:** $12, cash or CA check. **Parking:** At site.

Facilities

Number of RV Sites: 175. **Number of Tent-Only Sites:** 0. **Hookups:** None. **Each Site:** Picnic table, fire ring, bearproof box, most sites have barbecue grill. **Dump Station:** Yes. **Laundry:** No. **Pay Phone:** Yes. **Rest Rooms and Showers:** Yes, showers closed in winter. **Fuel:** No. **Propane:** No. **Internal Roads:** Paved. **RV Service:** No. **Market:** 3 mi. north in Homewood. **Restaurant:** 1 mi. north in Tahoma. **General Store:** No. **Vending:** No. **Swimming:** In Lake Tahoe. **Playground:** No. **Other:** Lighthouse, beach, Nature Center, Hellman-Ehrman Mansion. **Activities:** Hiking, fishing, bicycle rentals, birding, cross-country skiing. **Nearby Attractions:** Gatekeeper's Museum/Marion Steinbach Indian Basket Museum & Watson Cabin Museum in Tahoe City; Emerald Bay State Park & Vikingsholm Mansion in Tahoma. **Additional Information:** South Lake Tahoe Chamber of Commerce, (530) 541-5255.

RESTRICTIONS

Pets: On 6 ft. leash. **Fires:** In fire rings only. **Alcoholic Beverages:** Allowed at site. **Vehicle Maximum Length:** 32 ft. **Other:** 14-day stay limit from June 15 to Sept. 30, 30-day stay limit for the rest of the year; no firearms; no wood gathering.

TO GET THERE

From Tahoe City drive 9.7 mi. south on Hwy. 89, past Tahoma. The campground entrance is on the right.

TEMECULA

Lake Skinner Recreation Area

37701 Warren Rd., Winchester 92596. T: (909) 926-1541 or reservations (800) 234-7275; www.riversidecountyparks.org.

RV ★★★★ Tent ★★

Beauty: ★★★ Site Privacy: ★★
Spaciousness: ★★★ Quiet: ★★★★
Security: ★★★★ Cleanliness: ★★
Insect Control: ★★★ Facilities: ★★★★★

Forget the hiking and equestrian trails at Lake Skinner and its proximity to nearly a dozen wineries. There is really only one reason to visit this huge campground, and that reason is spelled f-i-s-h-i-n-g. The lake is stocked weekly from Nov. through May, making it one of the better fishing spots in southern California for trout, bass, bluegill, catfish, and crappie. Serious anglers will appreciate the lake-wide speed limit of ten miles per hour and may want to plan their trips around the derbies held for catfish in Aug. and trout in Nov., when cash prizes are awarded. Keep in mind, though, that boats must be at least ten feet long and canoes and kayaks are not permitted on the water. Of the campground itself, there are three large loops spread over grassy meadows, with few of the average-looking sites endowed with a lake view. Shade, too, is scarce, despite the scattered presence of sycamores and pepper trees. B and C loops offer sites that appear marginally less crowded together than those in loop A.

BASICS

Operated By: Riverside County Regional Park. **Open:** All year. **Site Assignment:** Reservations accepted w/ V, MC, D. **Registration:** At entrance booth. **Fee:** $15–$18, cash or CA check. **Parking:** At site.

FACILITIES

Number of RV Sites: 300. **Number of Tent-Only Sites:** 0. **Hookups:** Water, electric (30, 50 amps), sewer. **Each Site:** Picnic table, fire grate. **Dump Station:** Yes. **Laundry:** Yes. **Pay Phone:** Yes. **Rest Rooms and Showers:** Yes. **Fuel:** Yes, for boats. **Propane:** Yes. **Internal Roads:** Paved. **RV Service:** No. **Market:** 8 mi. southwest in Temecula. **Restaurant:** 8 mi. southwest in Temecula. **General Store:** Yes. **Vending:** Yes. **Swimming:** In pool seasonally. **Playground:** Yes. **Other:** Some wheelchair-accessible facilities, two boat ramps. **Activities:** Fishing, hiking, horseback riding, horseshoe pit, volleyball, boat rentals. **Nearby Attractions:** Numerous wineries, Palomar Mountain Observatory. **Additional Information:** Temecula Valley Chamber of Commerce (909) 676-5090.

RESTRICTIONS

Pets: On 6 ft. leash; $2. **Fires:** In fire grates only. **Alcoholic Beverages:** Allowed at site. **Vehicle Maximum Length:** 45 ft. **Other:** 14-day stay limit; no firearms.

TO GET THERE

From I-15 in Temecula take Rancho California Rd. Exit and head east for 9.5 mi. Turn right on Warren Rd. Campground entrance is straight ahead.

TRINIDAD

Patrick's Point State Park

4150 Patrick's Point Dr., Trinidad 95570. T: (707) 677-3570 or reservations (800) 444-7275; www.cal-parks.ca.gov or www.reserveamerica.com; ncrdppsp@humboldt1.com.

RV ★★★★ Tent ★★★★★

Beauty: ★★★★ Site Privacy: ★★★★★
Spaciousness: ★★★★ Quiet: ★★★★
Security: ★★★ Cleanliness: ★★★
Insect Control: ★★★ Facilities: ★★

Visitors to this breathtakingly beautiful state park are in for a special treat. We're not referring to Sumeg, its reconstructed Yurok Indian village. Nor to the thriving tide pools and pretty beach. Beyond the chance of seeing passing whales from towering, pine-shrouded bluffs, Patrick's Point has an ace up its figurative sleeve: its campground is one of the finest in the entire state park system. There is a wild, untamed atmosphere to the domain, with the rock-studded undergrowth thick with ferns and moss. Three detached loop areas feature sites that are uncommonly spacious and well-screened, a generous allowance of space that grants campers a refreshing dignity of privacy. Those in the shady Abalone circuit (from 16–85) are the roomiest, while Agate's (86 –97) enjoy more sun exposure and have stunning views of the surf. The RV section, admittedly, is typically tight, but its ocean vistas are a balancing amelioration. Cabin and yurt rentals are also available.

BASICS

Operated By: California Dept. of Parks & Recreation. **Open:** All year. **Site Assignment:** Reservations recommended; V, MC, D. **Registration:** At entrance booth. **Fee:** $12, cash or CA check. **Parking:** At site.

FACILITIES

Number of RV Sites: 124. **Number of Tent-Only Sites:** 0. **Hookups:** None. **Each Site:** Picnic table, fire grate, food storage box. **Dump Station:** No. **Laundry:** No. **Pay Phone:** Yes. **Rest Rooms and Showers:** Yes. **Fuel:** No. **Propane:** No. **Internal Roads:** Paved. **RV Service:** No. **Market:** 6.5 mi. south in Trinidad. **Restaurant:** 6.5 mi. south in Trinidad. **General Store:** No. **Vending:** No. **Swimming:** No. **Playground:** No. **Other:** Some wheelchair-accessible facilities. **Activities:** Hiking, fishing, whale-watching, agate hunting, tidepooling. **Nearby Attractions:** Trinidad State Beach, museums, Memorial Lighthouse & Aquarium in Trinidad; Sumeg Village; Fort Humboldt State Historic Park, Humboldt Bay Harbor Cruise & Maritime Museum, Romano Gabriel Wooden Sculpture Garden, Carson Mansion, Main St., zoo, & more in Eureka. **Additional Information:** Trinidad Chamber of Commerce, (707) 677-1610; Greater Eureka Chamber of Commerce, (707) 442-3738.

RESTRICTIONS

Pets: On 6 ft. leash. **Fires:** In fire grates only. **Alcoholic Beverages:** Allowed at site. **Vehicle Maximum Length:** 31 ft. **Other:** 14-day stay limit from May 1–Sept. 30; no firearms; no wood gathering.

TO GET THERE

From Eureka drive 28 mi. north on US 101 and take the Patrick's Point State Park Exit. Drive 0.4 mi. west on Patrick's Point Dr. to the park entrance on the right.

TRUCKEE

Logger

Stampede Valley Rd., Boca 96161. T: (530) 587-3558 or (530) 544-0426 or reservations (877) 444-6777; F: (530) 587-6914; www.r5.fs.fed.us/tahoe or www.reserveusa.com.

RV ★★★★ Tent ★★★

Beauty: ★★★★ Site Privacy: ★★
Spaciousness: ★★★ Quiet: ★★★
Security: ★★★ Cleanliness: ★★★
Insect Control: ★★★ Facilities: ★★

Campers who make a practice of shying away from oversize properties with numerous loops may want to make an exception for Logger, which is so vast it has west and east entrances. In spite of its inauspicious name, there is an abundance of ponderosa pines across its hillside perch, above the south shore of the deep blue Stampede Reservoir. Sage-colored salt bush and other low-lying shrubs don't add much to the minimal screening between dirt- and pine needle–surfaced sites, but in general space and shade are above average for such a crowded campground. One of the more private sites is 22, and 39 is well-shaded, with a water view; two of the larger pull-through slots are 32, also with a lake view, and 37. Other fine options include 25, 79, 83, and 84. Logger, which is less than 20 miles from Truckee, is at an elevation of 5,949 feet, making a coat or sweater essential apparel, even in summer. Stampede Reservoir is a popular fishing spot for Kokanee salmon, so don't forget your rod. Seasonal drawdowns, however, can leave the lake disappointingly low by late summer.

BASICS

Operated By: California Land Management, concessionaire. **Open:** May 15 to Sept. 30, weather permitting. **Site Assignment:** Reservations accepted w/ V, MC, D. **Registration:** At entrance booth. **Fee:** $13, cash or check. **Parking:** At site.

FACILITIES

Number of RV Sites: 252. **Number of Tent-Only Sites:** 0. **Hookups:** None. **Each Site:** Picnic table, fire grate, barbecue grill. **Dump Station:** Yes. **Laundry:** No. **Pay Phone:** No. **Rest Rooms and Showers:** Vault toilets, no showers. **Fuel:**

No. **Propane:** No. **Internal Roads:** Paved. **RV Service:** No. **Market:** 11 mi. south in Boca. **Restaurant:** 18 mi. south in Truckee. **General Store:** No. **Vending:** No. **Swimming:** In Stampede Reservoir. **Playground:** No. **Other:** Some wheelchair-accessible facilities, boat ramp. **Activities:** Fishing, boating, waterskiing, hiking, meeting your neighbors. **Nearby Attractions:** Boreal Mountain Ski Resort, Donner Memorial State Park, Western Skisport Museum, & historic downtown in Truckee; Lake Tahoe. **Additional Information:** Truckee Donner Chamber of Commerce & Visitors Center, (530) 587-2757.

RESTRICTIONS

Pets: On leash. **Fires:** In fire grates only. **Alcoholic Beverages:** Allowed. **Vehicle Maximum Length:** 32 ft. **Other:** 14-day stay limit.

TO GET THERE

From Truckee drive 7 mi. east on I-80. Take the Boca/Stampede-Hirschdale Rd. Exit and proceed north for 8.7 mi., past the Boca Reservoir. Turn left onto CR S261 and drive 2 mi. to the campground entrance on the right.

TWENTYNINE PALMS
Cottonwood

74485 National Park Dr., Twentynine Palms 92277. T: (760) 367-5525; F: (760) 367-5583; www.nps.gov/jotr.

★★★ ▲ ★★★

Beauty: ★★★ Site Privacy: ★★
Spaciousness: ★★ Quiet: ★★
Security: ★★★ Cleanliness: ★★★★
Insect Control: ★★★★ Facilities: ★★

This is a neat looking camp located near the southern entrance to Joshua Tree National Park, just seven miles north of I-10. It is a long drive from here to the park's concentration of granite boulders, which are looked upon almost as totemic objects by amateur climbers, and the celebrated stands of Joshua trees that thrive at higher altitudes. Thus, this facility is usually the last to fill, even on weekends. It is popular nonetheless among RVers, partly because this is one of the few campgrounds in Joshua Tree to provide potable water, and pull-up parking is the norm throughout the two loops. Despite the sites being rather small and closely situated, most are pretty well screened by a mix of mesquite, jojoba, cholla cacti, and other desert scrub. The trail to Mastodon Peak starts in the campground, and that to Lost Palms Oasis is nearby. The nearest telephone is 12 miles east on I-10 at Chiriaco Summit.

BASICS

Operated By: National Park Service. **Open:** All year. **Site Assignment:** First come, first served. **Registration:** At entrance kiosk. **Fee:** $10, cash only. **Parking:** At site.

FACILITIES

Number of RV Sites: 62. **Number of Tent-Only Sites:** 0. **Hookups:** None. **Each Site:** Picnic table, fire grate. **Dump Station:** Yes. **Laundry:** No. **Pay Phone:** No. **Rest Rooms and Showers:** Flush toilets, no showers. **Fuel:** No. **Propane:** No. **Internal Roads:** Paved. **RV Service:** No. **Market:** 12 mi. east in Chiriaco Summit. **Restaurant:** 12 mi. east in Chiriaco Summit. **General Store:** No. **Vending:** No. **Swimming:** No. **Playground:** No. **Other:** Very limited wheelchair-accessible facilities. **Activities:** Hiking, mountain climbing, bicycling, horseback riding, ranger-led programs. **Nearby Attractions:** Salton Sea National Wildlife Refuge. **Additional Information:** Twentynine Palms Chamber of Commerce & Visitors Bureau, (760) 367-3445.

RESTRICTIONS

Pets: On 6 ft. leash; not allowed on trails. **Fires:** In fire rings only. **Alcoholic Beverages:** Allowed at site. **Vehicle Maximum Length:** 27 ft. **Other:** 14-day stay limit from Oct. through May; no firearms; no wood gathering.

TO GET THERE

From the I-10 Exit for Joshua Tree National Park drive 7 mi. north. Turn right at the sign and proceed 0.7 mi. to the campground on the left.

TWENTYNINE PALMS
Hidden Valley

Park Blvd., Twentynine Palms 92277. T: (760) 367-5525; F: (760) 367-5583; www.nps.gov/jotr.

★★ ▲ ★★★★

Beauty: ★★★★★ Site Privacy: ★★★★
Spaciousness: ★★★ Quiet: ★★★
Security: ★★ Cleanliness: ★★★★
Insect Control: ★★★★ Facilities: ★

Hidden Valley is fairly typical of the decidedly primitive campgrounds in Joshua Tree National Park. There is no telephone, no water, and the only shade comes from the oversize boulders that decorate much of the park. It is those boulders, composed of tan-colored monzo-granite, that lend Joshua Tree much of its visual appeal. Unfortunately, because monzo-granite is enticingly easy to scale, campground boulders attract amateur climbers at all hours of the day (and occasionally night), something privacy-seekers should keep in mind when selecting their site. The sandy sites here are fairly spacious and decently far apart, with creosote bushes, Joshua trees, and rabbit brush complementing the rocky terrain. Spring, when wildflowers pop up all over the desert, is our preferred time to visit this area, with autumn and the milder temperatures it brings running a close second. Daytime temperatures are mild from late Oct. through Mar., but nights can be downright icy. Outside of summer months, when the desert heat is blistering, campgrounds fill up most weekends. Beware of beggar coyotes prowling the grounds.

BASICS

Operated By: National Park Service. **Open:** All year. **Site Assignment:** First come, first served. **Registration:** At entrance kiosk. **Fee:** None. **Parking:** At site.

FACILITIES

Number of RV Sites: 39. **Number of Tent-Only Sites:** 0. **Hookups:** None. **Each Site:** Picnic table, fire ring. **Dump Station:** No. **Laundry:** No. **Pay Phone:** No, only an emergency phone. **Rest Rooms and Showers:** Vault toilets, no showers. **Fuel:** No. **Propane:** No. **Internal Roads:** Paved, but 1 loop is a sandy washboard. **RV Service:** No. **Market:** 15 mi. north in Joshua Tree. **Restaurant:** 15 mi. north in Joshua Tree. **General Store:** No. **Vending:** No. **Swimming:** No. **Playground:** No. **Other:** Very limited wheelchair-accessible facilities. **Activities:** Hiking, rock climbing, bicycling, horseback riding, ranger-led programs. **Nearby Attractions:** Old Shoolhouse Museum in Twentynine Palms, Hi-Desert Nature Museum in Yucca Valley. **Additional Information:** Twentynine Palms Chamber of Commerce & Visitors Bureau, (760) 367-3445.

RESTRICTIONS

Pets: On 6 ft. leash; not allowed on trails. **Fires:** In fire rings only. **Alcoholic Beverages:** Allowed at site. **Vehicle Maximum Length:** 27 ft. **Other:** 14-day stay limit from Oct. through May; no firearms; no wood gathering.

TO GET THERE

From the town of Joshua Tree on Hwy. 62 turn south on Park Blvd. After 14 mi. turn left into the campground.

UKIAH
Ky-en

1160 Lake Mendocino Dr., Ukiah 95482. T: (707) 462-7581 or reservations (877) 444-6777; F: (707) 462-3372; www.spn.usace.army.mil/mendocino.html or www.reserveusa.com.

★★★ ▲ ★★★

Beauty: ★★★★ Site Privacy: ★★★
Spaciousness: ★★ Quiet: ★★★
Security: ★★★★ Cleanliness: ★★
Insect Control: ★★★ Facilities: ★★★

You do not need to have a fishing rod or boat to enjoy Lake Mendocino, but it will certainly add to your pleasure. This green gleaming body of water receives quite a lot of use, with most of that falling between Memorial Day and Labor Day. Ky-en (also rendered Kyen) is typical of the three campgrounds here (a fourth, Miti, is a boat-in camp), nestled against a sloping hillside between Hwy. 20 and the lake. The most popular sites abut the shore, with 75, 82, and 103 the most private. The screening and shade are far better, though, up the hill where the loops snake through such varied vegetation as juniper, pine trees, oak, toyon, manzanita, and flowering ceanothus. Best of that section are 18 and 22 (both with pull-through parking), and 15, 16, 26, and 42. Security is good, with regular ranger patrols and entrance gates that are locked between 10:30 p.m. and 7:30 a.m. Rest rooms, though, could use a face-lift, and the grounds are disturbingly littered with bottles and cans.

BASICS

Operated By: US Army Corps of Engineers. **Open:** All year. **Site Assignment:** Reservations accepted w/ V, MC, D, AE. **Registration:** At entrance booth. **Fee:** $16–$18, cash or check. **Parking:** At site.

FACILITIES

Number of RV Sites: 103. **Number of Tent-

Only Sites: 0. **Hookups:** None. **Each Site:** Picnic table, fire grate, lantern holder. **Dump Station:** Yes. **Laundry:** No. **Pay Phone:** Yes. **Rest Rooms and Showers:** Yes. **Fuel:** No. **Propane:** No. **Internal Roads:** Paved & narrow. **RV Service:** No. **Market:** 1 mi. east in Calpella. **Restaurant:** 1 mi. east in Calpella. **General Store:** Yes, in summer. **Vending:** No. **Swimming:** In Lake Mendocino. **Playground:** Yes. **Other:** Some wheelchair-accessible facilities, 6-lane boat ramp, visitor center. **Activities:** Fishing, waterskiing, sailing, boat rentals, hiking, disc golf. **Nearby Attractions:** Ukiah museums & Cow Mountain Recreation Area; Mendocino County Museum & Roots of Motive Power/Antique Steam Logging Equipment in Willits; Skunk Train from Willits to Fort Bragg. **Additional Information:** Greater Ukiah Chamber of Commerce, (707) 462-4705.

RESTRICTIONS

Pets: On 6 ft. leash. **Fires:** In fire grates only. **Alcoholic Beverages:** Allowed. **Vehicle Maximum Length:** 35 ft. **Other:** 14-day stay limit.

TO GET THERE

Drive 6 mi. north of Ukiah on US 101. Turn east on Hwy. 20 and after 2.3 mi. turn right on Marina Drive Rd. The campground is 0.3 mi. ahead.

UPPER LAKE

Pogie Point

Hull Mountain Rd., Potter Valley 95469. T: (916) 386-5164; www.r5.fs.fed.us/mendocino.

RV ★★★ Tent ★★★

Beauty: ★★★★ Site Privacy: ★★★
Spaciousness: ★★ Quiet: ★★★
Security: ★★★ Cleanliness: ★★★
Insect Control: ★★ Facilities: ★★

Forget the jokes about "doughboy" campers and "poppin' fresh" fish: Lake Pillsbury is one pretty haven for boating, fishing, hiking, or just lazing around. There are four campgrounds in this region of the Mendocino National Forest, with Oak Flat, two miles up the road, offering better lake access than Pogie Point. The former, though, is a primitive facility and there is some truth to the waggish suggestion that this status owes more to the people it attracts than its limited amenities. Pogie Point is marginally better in the creature comforts department (though its latrines could use more regular maintenance), but leagues ahead in aesthetics. It rests above a tiny cove that is ideal for launching canoes and kayaks. The grounds are thinly forested with tan oak, moss-covered pines, madrone trees, and oversize manzanita. Sites along its double loop range from uncomfortably small and exposed to reasonably roomy and recessed. Elk, black-tailed deer, and wild turkey frequent these parts.

BASICS

Operated By: Pacific Gas & Electric. **Open:** All year, weather permitting. **Site Assignment:** First come, first served. **Registration:** At entrance kiosk. **Fee:** $12, cash or check. **Parking:** At site.

FACILITIES

Number of RV Sites: 45. **Number of Tent-Only Sites:** 0. **Hookups:** None. **Each Site:** Picnic table, fire grate. **Dump Station:** No. **Laundry:** No. **Pay Phone:** No. **Rest Rooms and Showers:** Vault toilets, no showers. **Fuel:** No. **Propane:** No. **Internal Roads:** Paved. **RV Service:** No. **Market:** 19 mi. west in Potter Valley. **Restaurant:** 19 mi. west in Potter Valley. **General Store:** No. **Vending:** No. **Swimming:** In Lake Pillsbury. **Playground:** No. **Other:** Some wheelchair-accessible facilities, small boat launch. **Activities:** Fishing, hiking, horseback riding, mountain biking, windsurfing, boating. **Nearby Attractions:** Lakeport County Museum & Clear Lake in Lakeport. **Additional Information:** Lake County Marketing Program/Visitor Information Center, (707) 263-9544 or (800) 525-3743; Mendocino National Forest, Upper Lake Ranger District, (707) 275-2361.

RESTRICTIONS

Pets: On leash, $1 fee. **Fires:** In fire grates only. **Alcoholic Beverages:** Allowed. **Vehicle Maximum Length:** 40 ft. **Other:** 14-day stay limit.

TO GET THERE

From Hwy. 20 in Upper Lake head north on Mendenhall Ave., which becomes Elk Mountain Rd./FR M1. After 17 mi. the scenic road turns to graded dirt, then pavement again after another 9 mi. From that point, the campground access is 5.5 mi. ahead on the right.

VISALIA

Lake Kaweah Recreation Area, Horse Creek Campground

Hwy. 198, Lemoncove 93244. T: (550) 597-2301 or reservations (877) 444-6777 or marina (559) 597-2526; F: (559) 597-2468; www.spk.usace.army.mil/cespk-co/lakes/kaweah.html or www.reserveusa.com.

RV ★★★★ Tent ★★★

Beauty: ★★★★ Site Privacy: ★★
Spaciousness: ★★★ Quiet: ★★★
Security: ★★★★ Cleanliness: ★★★
Insect Control: ★★ Facilities: ★★★

Lake Kaweah is a refreshing body of water that provides welcome relief in a part of the state where summer starts early and runs late. Its level was so high last spring that several of Horse Creek's sites were underwater. Nonetheless it remains a popular weekend retreat for area families, and for good reason: you can soak yourself in Kaweah's cool waters while the campgrounds in Sequoia and Kings Canyon National Parks are still under snow. Nestled in the Sierra foothills at an elevation of 694 feet, Horse Creek's environment is framed by the boulder-streaked, grassy ridges that hover over it. Nearer at hand, sites are plentifully shaded by oak, sycamore, buckeye, and cottonwood trees. An elongated loop, with three spur circuits, puts a great number of grass and dirt sites right at the edge of the lake. Privacy-seekers, though, should look toward higher ground, where numbers 4 and 5 are roomy, set back from the camp lane and enjoy a premium vantage of the water. The marina at Lemon Hill has propane and basic supplies.

BASICS

Operated By: US Army Corps of Engineers. **Open:** All year. **Site Assignment:** Reservations recommended; V, MC, D, AE. **Registration:** At entrance booth. **Fee:** $16, cash or check. **Parking:** At site.

FACILITIES

Number of RV Sites: 80. **Number of Tent-Only Sites:** 0. **Hookups:** None. **Each Site:** Picnic table, fire grate, lantern pole. **Dump Station:** Yes. **Laundry:** No. **Pay Phone:** Yes. **Rest Rooms and Showers:** Yes. **Fuel:** No. **Propane:** No. **Internal Roads:** Paved & occasionally flooded. **RV Service:** No. **Market:** 8 mi. east in Three Rivers. **Restaurant:** 8 mi. east in Three Rivers. **General Store:** No. **Vending:** No. **Swimming:** In Lake Kaweah. **Playground:** Yes. **Other:** Some wheelchair-accessible facilities, boat ramp. **Activities:** Fishing, boat rentals, waterskiing, hiking, whitewater rafting on the Kaweah River, bailing out your tent. **Nearby Attractions:** Sequoia & Kings Canyon National Parks; Tulare County Museum in Visalia; Kaweah Oaks Preserve in Exeter. **Additional Information:** Visalia Chamber of Commerce & Visitors Bureau, (559) 734-5876; Three Rivers–Lemoncove Business Assoc., (550) 561-0410.

RESTRICTIONS

Pets: On leash. **Fires:** In fire grates only. **Alcoholic Beverages:** Allowed. **Vehicle Maximum Length:** 45 ft. **Other:** 14-day stay limit.

TO GET THERE

From Visalia drive 24 mi. east on Hwy. 198 to Lake Kaweah's south shore. The well-signed campground entrance is on the left.

WALNUT CREEK

Mount Diablo State Park

96 Mitchell Canyon Rd., Clayton 94517. T: (925) 837-2525 or reservations (800) 444-7275; www.mdia.org or www.cal-parks.ca.gov or www.reserveamerica.com.

RV ★★ Tent ★★★★

Beauty: ★★★★ Site Privacy: ★★★
Spaciousness: ★★ Quiet: ★★★★
Security: ★★★ Cleanliness: ★★★
Insect Control: ★★★ Facilities: ★★

The rolling grass-covered hills that make up this highly scenic park are dappled with live oak, knob cone pines, and juniper. If the extraordinary valley views don't take your breath away, you had better check your pulse! Or come back in spring, when an explosion of wildflowers should stimulate even the most colorblind of campers. There are three campgrounds here set at different altitudes, with the no-reservations Junction the least appealing. We prefer the Juniper loop (3,000 feet elevation) because, in a park where sites run toward petite, its are the larger and better screened. Additionally, many are blessed with outstanding westward vistas. Prime among many fine choices is number 20, detached from its neighbors and nursed by a superannuated, overhanging tree. In summer months when the heat intensifies, the cool, shady Live Oak loop (1,450 feet elevation) is the sounder choice. As the risk of wildfires escalates in summer, the park may close. Plan to call ahead, therefore, from June through Sept.

BASICS

Operated By: California Dept. of Parks & Recreation. **Open:** All year, but may close in summer due to extreme fire danger—call ahead. **Site Assignment:** Reservations recommended; V, MC, D. **Registration:** At entrance kiosk. **Fee:** $12, cash or CA check. **Parking:** At site.

FACILITIES

Number of RV Sites: 64. **Number of Tent-Only Sites:** 0. **Hookups:** None. **Each Site:** Picnic table, fire grate, food storage box in some sites. **Dump Station:** No. **Laundry:** No. **Pay Phone:** Yes. **Rest Rooms and Showers:** Yes. **Fuel:** No. **Propane:** No. **Internal Roads:** Paved & windy. **RV Service:** No. **Market:** 10 mi. north in Livermore. **Restaurant:** 10 mi. north in Livermore. **General Store:** No. **Vending:** No. **Swimming:** No. **Playground:** No. **Other:** Some wheelchair-accessible facilities, visitor center, observation deck, Summit Museum. **Activities:** Hiking, horseback riding, star gazing, mountain biking, rock climbing. **Nearby Attractions:** Berkeley Botanical Garden & museums; Dunsmuir House & Gardens Historic Estate, Chabot Space & Science Center, Jack London Square, museums, zoo, & more in Oakland. **Additional Information:** Walnut Creek Chamber of Commerce, (925) 934-2007.

RESTRICTIONS

Pets: On 6 ft. leash. **Fires:** In fire grates only; restrictions are in effect when wildfire risk is extreme. **Alcoholic Beverages:** Not allowed. **Vehicle Maximum Length:** 20 ft. **Other:** 30-day stay limit; no firearms; no wood gathering.

TO GET THERE

From I-680 at Walnut Creek take the North Main St. Exit. Head east (toward downtown) to Ygnacio Valley Rd. Follow that for 2.1 mi. to the traffic light and turn right on Walnut Ave., which turns into North Gate Rd. Proceed to park entrance booth; Junction campground is 6.7 mi. beyond that.

WATSONVILLE

Sunset State Beach

201 Sunset Beach Rd., Watsonville 95076. T: (831) 763-7062 or reservations (800) 444-7275; www.cal-parks.ca.gov or www.reserveamerica.com.

RV ★★★★ Tent ★★★★

Beauty: ★★★★ Site Privacy: ★★★
Spaciousness: ★★★ Quiet: ★★★★
Security: ★★★ Cleanliness: ★★★★
Insect Control: ★★★ Facilities: ★★

Too often beach-side campgrounds are a compromise in comfort, especially in the southern part of the state. Sites are compact, they are laid out in a parking lot, there's no view of the water, trains thunder by at regular intervals. Sunset State Beach, located just 15 miles south of Santa Cruz, avoids most of those pitfalls, presenting campers with a stellar setting in the process. Plenty of shade is provided by the Monterey pines and eucalyptus trees that thrive throughout the property's three loops, yet sun-worshippers will appreciate that there is also an abundance of open space. Level sites are grassy, surprisingly roomy, and buffered from ocean breezes by a series of high sand dunes. Arguably, the most appealing loop is South Camp, with 26 particularly private and 25 offering a decent ocean view. The sandy beach is stunningly gorgeous, though slightly marred by the presence of a cookie-cutter housing development at its south end. Surf fishing here is reportedly very good. If you value tranquility don't even think about arriving on weekends from Easter through Labor Day.

BASICS

Operated By: California Dept. of Parks & Recreation. **Open:** All year. **Site Assignment:** Reservations recommended; V, MC, D. **Registration:** At entrance booth. **Fee:** $12, cash or CA check. **Parking:** At site.

FACILITIES

Number of RV Sites: 90. **Number of Tent-Only Sites:** 0. **Hookups:** None. **Each Site:** Picnic table, fire grate, food storage box. **Dump Station:** No. **Laundry:** No. **Pay Phone:** Yes. **Rest Rooms and Showers:** Yes. **Fuel:** No. **Propane:** No. **Internal Roads:** Paved. **RV Service:** No. **Market:** 3 mi. northeast in Watsonville. **Restaurant:** 3 mi. northeast in Watsonville. **General Store:** No. **Vending:** No. **Swimming:** In Pacific Ocean. **Playground:** No. **Other:** Some wheelchair-accessible facilities. **Activities:** Fishing, surfing, beachcombing, hiking, hang gliding. **Nearby Attractions:** Mission San Juan Bautista; John Steinbeck House & Library in Salinas; outlet shopping in Gilroy; Monterey peninsula. **Additional Information:** Castroville Chamber of Commerce, (831) 633-6545.

RESTRICTIONS

Pets: On 6 ft. leash. **Fires:** In fire grates only. **Alcoholic Beverages:** Allowed at site, not on the beach. **Vehicle Maximum Length:** 31 ft. **Other:** 7-day stay limit from Apr. 1–Oct. 31; no wood gathering.

TO GET THERE

From Hwy. 1 near Watsonville take the Riverside Dr. Exit and head toward the ocean. Turn right after 1 block onto Lee Rd., then a quick left onto West Beach St. Proceed for 1.5 mi. to San Andreas Rd., where you should hang a right. In 2.1 mi. steer left onto Sunset Beach Rd. and follow it into the park.

WEAVERVILLE

Tannery Gulch

CR 172, Weaverville 96093. T: (530) 623-2121 or reservations (877) 444-6777; F: (530) 623-6010; www.r5.fs.fed.us/shastatrinity or www.reserveusa.com.

RV ★★★★ Tent ★★★

Beauty: ★★★★ Site Privacy: ★★
Spaciousness: ★★★ Quiet: ★★★★
Security: ★★★ Cleanliness: ★★★★
Insect Control: ★★★ Facilities: ★★

Gold was discovered in the Trinity River in 1848. The rush that followed left its mark on this entire region, from hillsides washed away with hydraulic pumps to the colorful names attached to various locales. Tannery Gulch is an example of the second, and fortunately in its beautiful pine-forested perch above the jade-green Trinity Lake there is little evidence of the first. A few oaks and dogwoods are sprinkled among the tall conifers, and while the forest is fairly dense, a good deal of sunlight radiates through the canopy. As in any hilly area, some sites lack level ground. Most, though, are fine, being above average in spaciousness and distributed reasonably far apart over the property's five loops. Among the better choices for space and their partial views of the lake are 33, 34, 35, 40, 41, and 42. Most people come here for the water sports, but hikers (and horse riding enthusiasts) won't have to sit idly by watching the moss grow: there are many outstanding trails immediately to the north in the Trinity Alps Wilderness. Weaverville is 12 miles south along Hwy. 3.

BASICS

Operated By: Hodge Management, concessionaire. **Open:** May through Sept. **Site Assignment:** Reservations accepted w/ V, MC, D for most sites; First come, first served for sites 50 through 62. **Registration:** At entrance kiosk. **Fee:** $12–$18, cash or check. **Parking:** At site.

FACILITIES

Number of RV Sites: 83. **Number of Tent-Only Sites:** 0. **Hookups:** None. **Each Site:** Picnic table, fire grate. **Dump Station:** No. **Laundry:** No. **Pay Phone:** No. **Rest Rooms and Showers:** Flush & vault toilets, no showers. **Fuel:** No. **Propane:** No. **Internal Roads:** Paved. **RV Service:** No. **Market:** 13 mi. south in Weaverville. **Restaurant:** 13 mi. south in Weaverville. **General Store:** No. **Vending:** No. **Swimming:** In Trinity Lake. **Playground:** No. **Other:** Limited wheelchair-accessible facilities, seasonal boat ramp. **Activities:** Fishing, hiking, boating, waterskiing. **Nearby Attractions:** Weaverville museums, National Historic District, & Joss House State Historic Park; Historic Trinity River Bridge in Lewiston. **Additional Information:** Weaverville Chamber of Commerce, (530) 623-3840; Trinity County Chamber of Commerce, (530) 623-6101 or (800) 487-4648.

RESTRICTIONS

Pets: On leash. **Fires:** In fire grates only. **Alcoholic Beverages:** Allowed. **Vehicle Maximum Length:** 40 ft. **Other:** 14-day stay limit.

TO GET THERE

Exit Hwy. 299 in Weaverville onto Hwy. 3, northward direction. After 12 mi. turn right on CR 172. The campground entrance is 1.25 mi. ahead.

WHISKEYTOWN

Whiskeytown National Recreation Area, Oak Bottom Campground

Hwy. 299, Whiskeytown 96095. T: (530) 359-2027 or (530) 242-3400 or reservations (800) 365-CAMP; F: (530) 246-5154; www.nps.gov/whis.

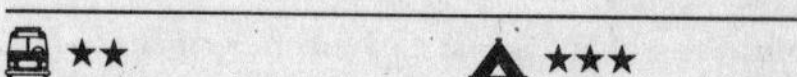

RV ★★ Tent ★★★

Beauty: ★★★★ Site Privacy: ★★
Spaciousness: ★★ Quiet: ★★★
Security: ★★★ Cleanliness: ★★★
Insect Control: ★★★ Facilities: ★★★★

Some jokingly refer to this campground as "Rock Bottom," but you will probably not be laughing if you roll in hauling a motor home. That is because the area designated for RVs, right by the boat launch, is a paved parking lot with no shade trees or privacy. At least it is near the water, a good thing since you'll want to spend most of your time swimming or boating in summer, when it is so hot in these parts you could fry a trout on the blistering pavement. Tent campers fare far better with grassy walk-in sites situated on an oak and pine-shaded knoll overlooking Whiskeytown Lake. A number of those are just a few steps from the park loop, but there is less litter and more privacy as you walk farther toward the lake. On average, the walk-ins are surprisingly level, and though many are wedged closely together, they are decently buffered by manzanita, madrone, and ceanothus. The concession that operates this National Park Service property, which is located 13 miles west of Redding along Hwy. 299, needs to devote more attention to the dilapidated restrooms and neglected grounds. Note that from Apr. 20, 2002, personal watercrafts (e.g. jet skis) will no longer be permitted on Whiskeytown Lake.

Basics

Operated By: Ken Smith, concessionaire. **Open:** All year. **Site Assignment:** Reservations recommended; V, MC, D. **Registration:** At campground store. **Fee:** $7–$18, cash, check or V, MC, D. **Parking:** At site or designated area for walk-ins.

Facilities

Number of RV Sites: 22. **Number of Tent-Only Sites:** 102. **Hookups:** None. **Each Site:** Picnic table, fire grate, bearproof box. **Dump Station:** Yes. **Laundry:** No. **Pay Phone:** Yes. **Rest Rooms and Showers:** Yes. **Fuel:** No. **Propane:** No. **Internal Roads:** Paved. **RV Service:** No. **Market:** 13 mi. east in Redding. **Restaurant:** 13 mi. east in Redding. **General Store:** Yes, in summer; also snack bar. **Vending:** Yes. **Swimming:** In Whiskeytown Lake at swim beach. **Playground:** No. **Other:** Some wheelchair-accessible facilities, boat ramp, marina. **Activities:** Hiking, bicycling, boat rentals, sailing, windsurfing, fishing. **Nearby Attractions:** Carter House Natural Science Museum, Turtle Bay Museums & Arboretum, Waterworks Park in Redding; Shasta Lake & Dam, Shasta State Historic Park. **Additional Information:** Redding CVB, (530) 225-4100.

Restrictions

Pets: On 6 ft. leash. **Fires:** In fire grates only. **Alcoholic Beverages:** Allowed at site. **Vehicle Maximum Length:** 35 ft. **Other:** 14-day stay limit from May 15–Sept. 14, 30-day limit the rest of the year.

To Get There

From Redding drive 13 mi. west on Hwy. 299. Turn left at the sign for the campground.

WILLITS

Hidden Valley Campground

29801 North U.South 101, Willits 95490. T: (707) 459-2521; F: (707) 459-3396; www.rvdestinations.com/hiddenvalley; hvcgd@jps.net.

RV ★★★ Tent ★★

Beauty: ★★★ Site Privacy: ★★
Spaciousness: ★★ Quiet: ★★
Security: ★★★ Cleanliness: ★★★
Insect Control: ★★ Facilities: ★★★

There are campgrounds worth building a vacation around, little islands of paradise one would willingly drive hours to reach. Places where the passing of time is happily marked in days, even weeks, and when the moment finally arrives—all too soon, alas—to decamp, sighs of resignation involuntarily rise up from one's chest. Then there are the in-transit campgrounds, those we use while on our way to someplace else. Hidden Valley falls into the second category. It is a pleasant, average-looking camp, conveniently located just off of US 101 about midway between Eureka and San Francisco, six miles north of Willits. Its single lane leads gently uphill from the entrance and several long-term RVs, past pines, oaks, locusts, and bay trees. The most private and quiet of the somewhat closely grouped sites are 42 and 43, ensconced at the far end of the acreage. Other grass- and dirt-based sites worth reserving include 23, 25, 26, and 28. The security gate is closed between 8:30 p.m. and 6:30 a.m.

Basics

Operated By: Hidden Valley Campground, Ed & Carol Rotramel, owners. **Open:** All year. **Site Assignment:** Reservations accepted w/ V, MC. **Registration:** At entrance office. **Fee:** $17–$21, cash or V, MC. **Parking:** At site.

Facilities

Number of RV Sites: 50. **Number of Tent-Only Sites:** 0. **Hookups:** Water, electric (30 amps), sewer, cable TV, Internet. **Each Site:** Half-size picnic table, fire grate. **Dump Station:** Yes. **Laundry:** Yes. **Pay Phone:** Yes. **Rest Rooms and Showers:** Yes. **Fuel:** No. **Propane:** No. **Internal Roads:** Paved & gravel, good condition. **RV Service:** No. **Market:** 6.5 mi. south in Willits. **Restaurant:** 6.5 mi. south in Willits. **General Store:** No. **Vending:** Yes. **Swimming:** No. **Playground:** No. **Other:** Some wheelchair-accessible facilities. **Activities:** Hiking, horseshoe pit, ping pong, basketball. **Nearby Attractions:** Skunk Train from Willits to Fort Bragg; Ukiah museums & Cow Mountain Recreation Area; Mendocino County Museum & Roots of Motive Power/Antique Steam Logging Equipment in Willits. **Additional Information:** Willits Chamber of Commerce, (707) 459-7910.

Restrictions

Pets: On leash; rabies certificate required. **Fires:** In fire grates only. **Alcoholic Beverages:** Allowed. **Vehicle Maximum Length:** 40 ft. **Other:** No stay limit; no wood gathering.

To Get There

From Willits on US 101 drive 6.5 mi. north. The well-marked campground entrance is on the right side of the road.

WOFFORD HEIGHTS

Tillie Creek

Hwy. 155, Wofford Heights 93285. T: (760) 379-5646 or reservations (877) 444-6777; F: (760) 379-8597; www.r5.fs.fed.us/sequoia or www.reserveusa.com.

RV ★★★★ Tent ★★★

Beauty: ★★★★ Site Privacy: ★★★
Spaciousness: ★★ Quiet: ★★★
Security: ★★★ Cleanliness: ★★★
Insect Control: ★★★ Facilities: ★★★

Isabella Lake is a Mecca of sorts for windsurfing, waterskiing, and year-round fishing. Cottonwoods skirt its meandering shoreline, whereas oak trees and pines populate the higher ground, especially around Tillie Creek, on the lake's western rim. The rocky locale, in the foothills of the Sierra Nevadas, is attractively wild, in a sun-baked area of wavy brown hills. There is plenty of shade throughout most of the multiple loops, with the exception of sites nearest the water, which are uncomfortably exposed. Across the domain, units are so shallow and small that tent campers will find it challenging to use the fire ring without singing their nylon. There are some larger-size spots available in the type three and four categories, but none may be reserved by specific number. Thus, you have no guarantee of getting a shady site, or even a lake view. A distressing amount of broken glass litters an otherwise tidy camp. Basic supplies and laundry machines are available in Wofford Heights.

Basics

Operated By: California Land Management, concessionaire. **Open:** All year. **Site Assignment:** Reservations accepted w/ V, MC, D. **Registration:** With campground host. **Fee:** $14, cash or check. **Parking:** At site.

Facilities

Number of RV Sites: 155. **Number of Tent-Only Sites:** 0. **Hookups:** None. **Each Site:** Picnic table, fire grate, barbecue grill. **Dump Station:** Yes. **Laundry:** No. **Pay Phone:** Yes. **Rest Rooms and Showers:** Yes. **Fuel:** No. **Propane:** No. **Internal Roads:** Paved. **RV Service:** No. **Market:** 6.5 mi. south in Lake Isabella. **Restaurant:** 6.5 mi. south in Lake Isabella. **General Store:** No. **Vending:** No. **Swimming:** In Lake Isabella. **Playground:** Yes. **Other:** Some wheelchair-accessible facilities. **Activities:** Fishing, hiking, boating, waterskiing. **Nearby Attractions:** Sequoia National Forest; California Hot Springs; Greenhorn Mountain Park in Alta Sierra. **Additional Information:** Kern County Board of Trade, (661) 861-2367 or (800) 500-KERN.

Restrictions

Pets: On leash. **Fires:** In fire grates only. **Alcoholic Beverages:** Allowed. **Vehicle Maximum Length:** 45 ft. **Other:** 14-day stay limit.

To Get There

From Wofford Heights drive 1 mi. south on Hwy. 155. Turn left at the campground sign; the entrance is just ahead.

YOSEMITE NATIONAL PARK
North Pines

Southside Dr., Yosemite Valley, Yosemite National Park 95389. T: (209) 372-0265 or reservations (800) 436-7275; F: (209) 372-0371; www.nps.gov/yose or www.reservations.nps.gov.

RV ★★★★ Tent ★★★

Beauty: ★★★★ Site Privacy: ★★
Spaciousness: ★★★ Quiet: ★★
Security: ★★★★ Cleanliness: ★★★
Insect Control: ★★ Facilities: ★★★

Given a choice, it is best to see Yosemite Valley in late spring, when its many waterfalls are at their peak and the dogwoods are in bloom. You'll be joining thousands of others then, so make your campground reservations well in advance. There are three campgrounds situated near each other, and which you end up at may come down to the one with available space. If possible, aim for North Pines, which is superior for its views of the granite environs and its thrilling position at the confluence of the Merced River and Tenaya Creek. Like the neighboring camps, this is a family-friendly atmosphere that makes a great launching point for a number of excellent hikes. Level sites are, alas, packed rather closely together, and the many stands of lodgepole pine and oak provide only minimal screening. Best for privacy and access to the river are 136, 502, 503, 504, and 506. Do pay attention to the bear warnings, use the metal food lockers, and keep a whistle—or other noise maker—handy after dark. The nearest gas station is at Crane Flat, just outside the valley.

BASICS

Operated By: National Park Service. **Open:** Apr. through Sept., weather permitting. **Site Assignment:** Reservations required; V, MC. **Registration:** At reservation office. **Fee:** $18, cash, check or V, MC (in addition to the park entrance fee). **Parking:** At site.

FACILITIES

Number of RV Sites: 81. **Number of Tent-Only Sites:** 0. **Hookups:** None. **Each Site:** Picnic table, fire ring, barbecue grill, bearproof box. **Dump Station:** Yes. **Laundry:** Yes. **Pay Phone:** Yes. **Rest Rooms and Showers:** Yes. **Fuel:** No. **Propane:** No. **Internal Roads:** Paved. **RV Service:** No. **Market:** In Yosemite Valley. **Restaurant:** In Yosemite Valley. **General Store:** Yes. **Vending:** No. **Swimming:** At Ahwahnee Lodge & Curry Village. **Playground:** No. **Other:** Visitor center, several stores, post office. **Activities:** Hiking, fishing, horse & bicycle rentals, mountaineering classes, free art classes, rafting, ranger-led activities, bear-spotting. **Nearby Attractions:** El Capitan, waterfalls, LeConte Memorial Lodge, sightseeing tours, museum & gallery in Yosemite Valley. **Additional Information:** Yosemite Public Information Office, (209) 372-0200.

RESTRICTIONS

Pets: On 6 ft. leash; not allowed on trails. **Fires:** In fire rings only, from May 1 to Oct. 15, 5–10 p.m. only. **Alcoholic Beverages:** Allowed at site. **Vehicle Maximum Length:** 40 ft. **Other:** 14-day stay limit; no firearms; no fireworks; no metal detectors; no food in vehicles (bear habitat); no wood gathering.

TO GET THERE

On entering the park from the west via Hwy. 120, follow the signs first to Yosemite Valley, then to Curry Village. Proceed straight ahead, past Lower and Upper Pines, drive over Clarks Bridge and turn left into the campground.

YOSEMITE NATIONAL PARK
Tuolumne Meadows

Tioga Rd./Hwy. 120, Yosemite National Park 95389. T: (209) 372-0265 or reservations (800) 436-7275; F: (209) 372-0371; www.nps.gov/yose or www.reservations.nps.gov.

RV ★★★★ Tent ★★★★

Beauty: ★★★★ Site Privacy: ★★
Spaciousness: ★★★ Quiet: ★★
Security: ★★★★ Cleanliness: ★★★★
Insect Control: ★ Facilities: ★★★

Summer doesn't last long in Yosemite National Park's high country, which translates to a short season for Tuolumne Meadows Campground, elevation 8,600 feet. Perhaps it's that scarcity of available time that lends an extra frisson to the delights of being in this glacier-wracked wilderness camp, which is only 20 miles west of Lee Vining. It is surprisingly attractive, given its enormous dimensions. Young lodgepole pines rise up off ubiquitous slanting slabs of granite and poke past giant boulders, while the fresh, clear Tuolumne River twists and bends, churning noisily by the campground. In late spring, and after heavy rainfalls, the river brims to the very edge of sites, verging on overflowing the campground. Of this camp's two sections, the A loops run closer to the river and offers vistas of Lembert Dome. Best for views, river access or privacy are A 50, 51, 52, 55, 63, 65, 66, 67, 71, 74, and 89. Sites in the B area are in a more forested setting, recessed from the road and a touch roomier. We find the $18 fee outrageous, given the austere facilities, but if you don't take the site, some one else will. The Tioga Rd. closes in winter, depending on snowfall; call ahead if traveling in late fall or early spring.

BASICS

Operated By: National Park Service. **Open:** July through Sept., weather permitting. **Site Assignment:** Half by advanced reservations, half by same-day reservations; V, MC. **Registration:** At entrance kiosk. **Fee:** $18, cash, check or V, MC (in addition to the park entrance fee). **Parking:** At site.

FACILITIES

Number of RV Sites: 304. **Number of Tent-Only Sites:** 25. **Hookups:** None. **Each Site:** Picnic table, fire ring, barbecue grill, bearproof box. **Dump Station:** Yes. **Laundry:** No. **Pay Phone:** Yes. **Rest Rooms and Showers:** Yes. **Fuel:** Yes. **Propane:** Yes. **Internal Roads:** Partly paved, partly dirt, but decent. **RV Service:** No. **Market:** 20 mi. east in Lee Vining. **Restaurant:** In Tuolumne Meadows. **General Store:** Yes. **Vending:** No. **Swimming:** No. **Playground:** No. **Other:** Visitor center, bookstore, sport shop, post office. **Activities:** Hiking, fishing, horse rentals, mountaineering classes, ranger-led activities. **Nearby Attractions:** Mono Lake Tufa State Reserve in Lee Vining; Bodie State Historic Park in Bridgeport. **Additional Information:** Yosemite Public Information Office, (209) 372-0200.

RESTRICTIONS

Pets: On 6 ft. leash; not allowed on trails. **Fires:** In fire rings only. **Alcoholic Beverages:** Allowed at site. **Vehicle Maximum Length:** 35 ft. **Other:** 14-day stay limit; no firearms; no fireworks; no food in vehicles (bear habitat).

TO GET THERE

Just south of Lee Vining on US 395 head west on Hwy. 120. Drive 20 mi., past the Yosemite National Park entrance, to the campground on the left.

YOSEMITE NATIONAL PARK
Wawona

Wawona Rd./Hwy. 41, Yosemite National Park 95389. T: (209) 372-0265 or reservations (800) 436-7275; F: (209) 372-0371; www.nps.gov/yose or www.reservations.nps.gov.

RV ★★★★ Tent ★★★

Beauty: ★★★★ Site Privacy: ★★
Spaciousness: ★★★ Quiet: ★★★
Security: ★★★★ Cleanliness: ★★★
Insect Control: ★★ Facilities: ★★★

Sitting in a camp chair, gazing over the South Fork Merced River as the afternoon sun radiates through the oaks, cedars, and cinnamon-barked ponderosa pines onto the enormous boulders protruding from the hilly domain, you may well feel a part of Eden. Go ahead and look for snakes, though bears are more likely nighttime visitors. Wawona, 21 miles north of Oakhurst, near Yosemite's southern entrance, is one of the national park's prettier, more sedate campgrounds. It is also one of the more spacious, as its series of loops are elongated alongside the Merced, rather than being concentrated one against another. As a result of that thoughtful layout, dirt- and grass-covered sites seem less jammed together, and a high number are favored with waterfront locations. Highly recommended are 34 and 37, and to a lesser extent, 51–53; while tent campers should consider such prime river sites as walk-ins 1–4. Away from the water, 42 and 44 are among the more private. The nearby Mariposa Grove trail leads into a forest of numerous spectacular sequoia trees, as well as many other impressive conifers.

BASICS

Operated By: National Park Service. **Open:** All Year. **Site Assignment:** Reservations required May–Sept.; V, MC; first come, first served Oct.–Apr. **Registration:** At entrance kiosk. **Fee:** $18, cash, check or V, MC (in addition to the park entrance fee). **Parking:** At site.

FACILITIES

Number of RV Sites: 89. **Number of Tent-Only Sites:** 4. **Hookups:** None. **Each Site:** Picnic table, fire ring, barbecue grill, bearproof box. **Dump Station:** Yes. **Laundry:** No. **Pay Phone:** No. **Rest Rooms and Showers:** Flush toilets, no showers. **Fuel:** No. **Propane:** No. **Internal Roads:** Paved, many potholes. **RV Service:** No. **Market:** 20 mi. east in Lee Vining. **Restaurant:** 1.25 mi. south in the Wawona Hotel. **General Store:** Yes. **Vending:** No. **Swimming:** In South Fork Merced River. **Playground:** No. **Other:** Some wheelchair-accessible facilities, hotel, golf course, bookstore. **Activities:** Hiking, fishing, horse rentals. **Nearby Attractions:** Mariposa Grove of giant redwoods; Yosemite Mountain Sugarpine Railroad in Fish Camp; Yosemite Valley & its attractions. **Additional Information:** Yosemite Sierra Visitors Bureau, (559) 683-5697.

Restrictions

Pets: On 6 ft. leash; not allowed on trails. **Fires:** In fire rings only. **Alcoholic Beverages:** Allowed at site. **Vehicle Maximum Length:** 35 ft. **Other:** 7-day stay limit; no firearms; no fireworks; no food in vehicles (bear habitat).

To Get There

From Oakhurst drive 15 mi. north on Hwy. 41 to the Yosemite National Park entrance station. Continue for 6 mi. to the campground on the left.

YREKA

Tree of Heaven

Hwy. 96, Yreka 96097. T: (530) 468-5351; F: (530) 468-1290; www.r5.fs.fed.us/klamath.

RV: ★★★★ Tent: ★★★

Beauty: ★★★★	Site Privacy: ★★
Spaciousness: ★★★	Quiet: ★★★
Security: ★★	Cleanliness: ★★★
Insect Control: ★★★	Facilities: ★★

Tree of Heaven is the common name for *Ailantus altissima,* a non-native tree that grows in this small campground, which lies just eight miles west of I-5. The forest service has thoughtfully installed a sign informing visitors that *Ailantus altissima* were "planted by early settlers for soil conservation and resistance to air pollution." That they were a fast-growing source of shade is a more likely reason miners settled on them, something campers can be glad of, too. Pines, junipers, and maples round out the shady mix of trees here, with grassy, level sites evenly spaced out along a single loop. The grounds and limited facilities show none of the neglect so ubiquitous to forest service campgrounds elsewhere. On the contrary, scrupulous manicuring may leave some campers feeling that the "wilderness" has been snipped right out of the domain. The frothy waters of the Klamath River, which is popular for its rafting opportunities, churn right alongside the property. A fish-cleaning station is located next to the river.

Basics

Operated By: Klamath National Forest, Scott River Ranger District. **Open:** All year; no water in winter. **Site Assignment:** Reservations accepted w/ V, MC. **Registration:** At central kiosk. **Fee:** $10, cash or check. **Parking:** At site.

Facilities

Number of RV Sites: 21. **Number of Tent-Only Sites:** 0. **Hookups:** None. **Each Site:** Picnic table, fire grate, barbecue grill. **Dump Station:** Yes. **Laundry:** No. **Pay Phone:** No. **Rest Rooms and Showers:** Vault toilets, no showers. **Fuel:** No. **Propane:** No. **Internal Roads:** Paved. **RV Service:** No. **Market:** 12 mi. east in Yreka. **Restaurant:** 12 mi. east in Yreka. **General Store:** No. **Vending:** No. **Swimming:** In Klamath River. **Playground:** No. **Other:** Some wheelchair-accessible facilities, small boat ramp. **Activities:** Fishing, hiking, rafting, kayaking, canoeing. **Nearby Attractions:** Klamath National Forest; Yreka National Historic District, Western Railroad, Siskiyou County Courthouse & Museum in Yreka. **Additional Information:** Siskiyou County Visitors Bureau, (530) 926-3850; Yreka Chamber of Commerce, (530) 842-1649.

Restrictions

Pets: On leash. **Fires:** In fire grates only. **Alcoholic Beverages:** Allowed. **Vehicle Maximum Length:** 34 ft. **Other:** 14-day stay limit.

To Get There

From Yreka drive 8 mi. north on Hwy. 263. Turn west (left) on Hwy. 96 and continue for 4 mi. to the campground entrance on the left.

Colorado

Colorado boasts what must be some of the best camping in the entire world. Mountains, rivers, forests, lakes, cliffs, wildlife, fishing, hiking, canoeing—Colorado has it all. Ranging from forested mountains to nearly desert plains, the geography and climate vary wildly from region to region and month to month. (Some would even say minute to minute.) It can be 80° in Denver with blizzard conditions in the mountains less than two hours away. For this reason, campers in the mountains should bring much warmer clothing than they would need in the city. Weather in the mountains changes quickly, and even summer nights can be downright cold.

Interstate 25 slices the state neatly into two vastly differing regions: the almost featureless grasslands of the east and the mountainous west, where the lion's share of exciting camping opportunities exist. **Bonny State Park** is an excellent welcome to visitors in search of outdoor recreation entering the state from Kansas. To the west, **Dinosaur National Monument** and the **Grand Mesa** area likewise show the state at its best. In fact, entering Colorado on nearly any road from the surrounding states quickly puts you in prime camping territory. And once you've made it to the center, opportunities for outdoor recreation abound.

With large tracts of national forest, plenty of state parks, and numerous private campgrounds, the mountains of Colorado provide endless possibilities for those who like to stretch their legs and breathe in clean mountain air. But let's not forget skiing! In some people's dictionaries, the entry for *snow skiing* says "see Colorado." **Vail, Aspen, Breckenridge, Steamboat Springs**—these are ski towns with nearly mythical status. All of these areas accommodate campers, whether they come in the largest RVs available or hike in with a tent. And every level of amenity is available, from the most basic primitive campgrounds with no running water to full-service resorts with a hot tub, Internet connection, and ice cream socials.

In-state attractions are nearly too numerous to mention, but **Mesa Verde National Park, Rocky Mountain National Park,** the **Great Sand Dunes National Monument, Telluride,** the **Durango and Silverton Narrow Gauge Railroad, Royal Gorge, Garden of the Gods, Denver, Boulder, Leadville, Cache La Poudre wilderness,** and **Central City** all deserve a mention—as well as a visit. Colorado is a camper's state, and boasts opportunities for any outdoor activity you can possibly imagine.

The following facilities accept payment in checks or cash only:

Cadillac Jack's Campground, Calhan
Camp Dick, Ward
Dakota Campground, Walsenburg
Horsetooth Reservoir (Stout Campground), Fort Collins
Hud's Campground, McClave
Kelly-Dahl Campground, Nederland
Lake Fork Campground & RV Resort, Lake City
Paonia State Park, Paonia
Parry Peak Campground, Twin Lakes
Ridgway State Park, Ridgway
Rifle Falls/Rifle Gap Campgrounds, Rifle
Stillwater Campground, Yampa

The following facilities feature 20 sites or fewer:

Hud's Campground, McClave
Paonia State Park, Paonia
Meadowlark Cafe, Motel & RV Park, Lindon
Mobile Manor RV Park, Monte Vista

ALAMOSA

Alamosa KOA

6900 Juniper Ln., Alamosa 81101. T: (800) 562-9157 or (719) 589-9757; www.koa.com.

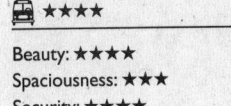

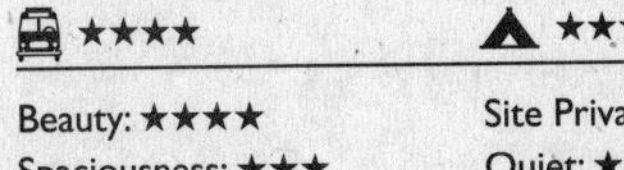

RV ★★★★ Tent ★★★

Beauty: ★★★★ Site Privacy: ★★★
Spaciousness: ★★★ Quiet: ★★★★
Security: ★★★★ Cleanliness: ★★★★
Insect Control: ★★★★ Facilities: ★★★★

This campground, offering spectacular views of mountains to the east, has pull-through sites that average 60 × 22 feet in size—large enough to camp comfortably in almost any vehicle. End sites 16, 24, 32, and 42 have superb views, making them more attractive. Sites 41 and 42 are even longer (80-foot) pull-throughs, also with excellent views, although 42 shares space with a light standard. The last row of RV sites on Rd. 6 (sites 33–42) are arguably the nicest, as they are away from the office and closest to the grassy tent sites. (Of course, this row is also furthest from the rest rooms, so some campers may prefer not to take a site.) Tent sites on the north side of the campground have nice grass and great views, but no shade. (Tent sites at the northwest side have more trees, and are therefore a better bet for tenters.) The rest room and shower facilities are clean and spacious, although the showers share a cement floor, which is slightly less comfortable and clean-looking than tile. The laundry is clean, with loads of room.

Basics

Operated By: Private operator. **Open:** May 1–Oct. 25. **Site Assignment:** Assigned upon registration. Credit card required for reservation; 24-hour cancellation policy. $5 cancellation fee). **Registration:** In office. (Late arrivals use drop box.) **Fee:** RV $25 (full), $22 (water, electric), tent $19. **Parking:** At site.

Facilities

Number of RV Sites: 42. **Number of Tent-Only Sites:** 15. **Hookups:** Water, sewer, electric (30 amps). **Each Site:** Picnic table, grill. **Dump Station:** Yes. **Laundry:** Yes. **Pay Phone:** Yes. **Rest Rooms and Showers:** Yes. **Fuel:** No. **Propane:** No. **Internal Roads:** Gravel. **RV Service:** No. **Market:** 5 mi. west. **Restaurant:** 1 west. **General Store:** Yes. **Vending:** No. **Swimming:** No. **Playground:** Yes. **Other:** Pool table, video games, cabins, dog walk area. **Activities:** Hiking, viewing wildlife, volleyball, horseshoes. **Nearby Attractions:** Great Sand Dunes, Alamosa National Wildlife Refuge, San Luis Valley Alligator Farm. **Additional Information:** Alamosa County Chamber of Commerce, (800) 258-7597 or (719) 589-3681.

Restrictions

Pets: 1 per camper; on leash, cleaned up after. **Fires:** In community fire pit. **Alcoholic Beverages:** At sites. **Vehicle Maximum Length:** 40 ft.

To Get There

From the junction of Hwy. 17 and Hwy. 160, go 3.2 mi. east on Hwy. 160. Turn north onto Juniper Ln., then take the first right into the campground. The office is on the left.

ALLENSPARK

Olive Ridge Campground

Boulder Ranger Office, 2140 Yarmouth Ave., Boulder 80301. T: (877) 444-6777 or (303) 444-6600 or (303) 747-2647; F: (303) 747-2647; www.reserveusa.com or www.fs.fed.us/arns.

RV ★★★★ Tent ★★★★

Beauty: ★★★★★ Site Privacy: ★★★★
Spaciousness: ★★★★ Quiet: ★★★★
Security: ★★★★ Cleanliness: ★★★★
Insect Control: ★★★★ Facilities: ★

Almost in the shadow of Long's Peak, this campground has very natural campsites scattered in a ponderosa pine forest. Sites average 40 feet, and all but 50 are back-ins. (Site 50 is a 45-foot "parallel-parking" site similar to a pull-through.) Sites 26 and 40 are oversized sites, roughly twice as large as a regular site. Sites 10, 42, 45, and 46 are reserved for campground hosts and administration. There is a hiking trail that starts by site 35, perhaps increasing foot traffic past this site. Water pumps are located near sites 2, 8, 16, 20, 30, 34, 36, and 49. Several sites have huge boulders that may either be seen as an encroachment on site space or as a source of shade and beauty. This is a slice of nature developed with a minimal impact, allowing campers to experience the beauty of nature. Facilities are limited to pit toilets, but the photos on the walls are an attempt to make the campground as comfortable as possible, considering its basic facilities. Tenters in particular may prefer this campground, but there is no reason why RVers willing to forego hookups for a night shouldn't enjoy it equally well.

Basics

Operated By: Thousand Trails Management. **Open:** May–Oct. (dates may vary). **Site Assignment:** First come, first served. Credit card required for reservation; 3-days cancellation policy. less $10.00 service fee; refunds must be requested within 30 days. **Registration:** At pay kiosk. (Camp Host will verify that campers have paid.) **Fee:** $12, $15 for oversized sites (checks, but no credit cards). **Parking:** At site.

Facilities

Number of RV Sites: 54. **Number of Tent-Only Sites:** 0. **Hookups:** None. **Each Site:** Picnic table, grill, fire pit. **Dump Station:** No. **Laundry:** No. **Pay Phone:** No. **Rest Rooms and Showers:** Rest rooms; no shower. **Fuel:** No. **Propane:** No. **Internal Roads:** Gravel/dirt. **RV Service:** No. **Market:** 12 mi. to Estes Park. **Restaurant:** 2 mi. to Allenspark. **General Store:** No. **Vending:** No. **Swimming:** No. **Playground:** Yes. **Other:** Amphitheater, 1 free picnic site. **Activities:** Fishing, hiking, mountain climbing, cross-country skiing. **Nearby Attractions:** Rocky Mountain National Park, Blackhawk, Central City Casinos. **Additional Information:** Thousand Trails Management, (303) 258-3610.

Restrictions

Pets: On leash, cleaned up after. **Fires:** In fire pits. **Alcoholic Beverages:** At sites. **Vehicle Maximum Length:** None.

To Get There

From the junction of Hwy. 72 and Hwy. 7, turn north onto Hwy. 7 and go 5.6 mi. Turn left at the sign into the entrance, then take the immediate left to go to the fee station.

ANTONITO

Josey's Mogote Meadow

34127 Hwy. 17, Antonito 81120. T: (719) 376-5774.

RV ★★★★ Tent ★★★★

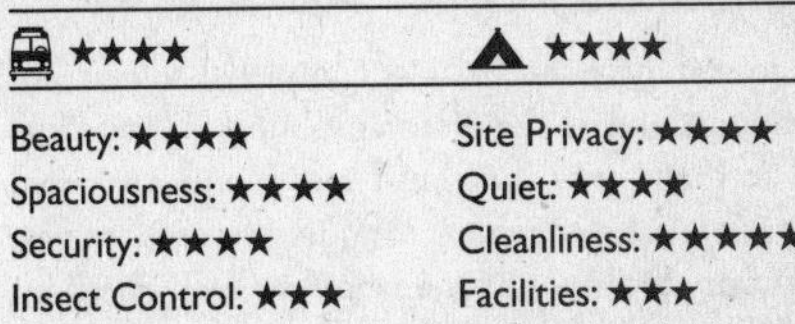

Beauty: ★★★★ Site Privacy: ★★★★
Spaciousness: ★★★★ Quiet: ★★★★
Security: ★★★★ Cleanliness: ★★★★★
Insect Control: ★★★ Facilities: ★★★

This park consists of a large field that can take any-sized rig (except for sites 8–16, which are restricted to 55 feet in length). 40-feet wide sites are in a rural location with trees on all sides. (Some houses to the north belie the proximity to human habitation, but do not damage the scenery overly.) End site 27 is set slightly apart from the others, and has a large open space to the west. Sites 1–7 are situated along the entrance, and therefore receive more traffic than other sites. The laundry facility is slightly cramped and hot (it shares the building with a furnace and has no windows). The men's and women's rest rooms are separated—the men's being out in the middle of the park and the women's being in the same building as the laundry facility. These facilities are quite clean and comfortable. This is a fine campground in a great location.

Basics

Operated By: Bob & Anne Josey. **Open:** May 1–Oct. 20. **Site Assignment:** Flexible depending on fullness; no reservations. **Registration:** In office. (Late arrivals select an available site & pay in the morning.) **Fee:** $16, tax (no credit cards, but checks). **Parking:** At site.

Facilities

Number of RV Sites: 45. **Number of Tent-Only Sites:** 0. **Hookups:** Water, sewer, electric (30, 50 amps). **Each Site:** Most have cement slab & large cottonwood. **Dump Station:** No (sewer at all sites). **Laundry:** Yes. **Pay Phone:** Yes. **Rest Rooms and Showers:** Yes. **Fuel:** No. **Propane:** Yes. **Internal Roads:** Gravel. **RV Service:** No. **Market:** 5 mi. to Antonito. **Restaurant:** 5 mi. to Antonito. **General Store:** Yes. **Vending:** No. **Swimming:** No. **Playground:** Yes. **Other:** Cabins, meeting hall. **Activities:** Fishing, volleyball, horseshoes, ping pong. **Nearby Attractions:** Scenic Byway, Cumbres & Toltect Scenic Railroad. **Additional Information:** Antonito Tourist Information Center & Chamber of Commerce, (719) 376-5441.

Restrictions

Pets: On leash, cleaned up after. **Fires:** No fires. **Alcoholic Beverages:** At sites. **Vehicle Maximum Length:** None.

To Get There

From the junction of Hwy. 285 and Hwy. 17, go 4.8 mi. southwest on Hwy. 17. Turn right at the sign into the entrance. The office is immediately on the left.

ARBOLES

Pinon Park Campground and RV Resort

19 Lazy Ln., Arboles 81121. T: (970) 883-3636.

★★★★ ★★★★

Beauty: ★★★★ Site Privacy: ★★★★
Spaciousness: ★★★ Quiet: ★★★★
Security: ★★★★ Cleanliness: ★★★★★
Insect Control: ★★★ Facilities: ★★★★

This campground has just completed some renovations, and is therefore absolutely immaculate. The brand-new individual rest rooms are clean, spacious, and extremely comfortable, as is the new laundry facility. Anyone who frets over questionable rest rooms may want to stay an extra few days to luxuriate in the clean and comfortable facilities. The park itself is in a wilderness setting, not too far (0.5 miles) from Navajo State Park, which offers lake recreation. Both back-ins and pull-throughs are grassy but open sites 14–26 offer no shade at all, making them slightly less attractive. (There is not a lot of shade to begin with.) Tenters, on the other hand, will delight in the trees offered for the tenting area. All tent sites have water and a grill, and the sites are a mix of grass and dirt. Campers of either stripe (RV or tent) will be happy to stay in this park, which offers great views of the reservoir to the east. The RV experience would, however, be improved with the addition of more shade trees.

Basics

Operated By: Nannette Colaizzy. **Open:** Apr.–Nov. **Site Assignment:** Assigned upon registration; flexible, depending on site availability. Credit card required for reservation; cancellation fees are $5 w/ 14-days notice & 50% of deposit within less than 14 days notice. **Registration:** In office. (Late arrivals use drop box.) **Fee:** RV $18.50 (full hookups), $14.50 (water, electric), tent $12 (V, MC, D). **Parking:** At site.

Facilities

Number of RV Sites: 35. **Number of Tent-Only Sites:** 30. **Hookups:** Water, sewer, electric (30, 50 amps). **Each Site:** Picnic table, grill. **Dump Station:** Yes. **Laundry:** Yes. **Pay Phone:** Yes. **Rest Rooms and Showers:** Yes. **Fuel:** No. **Propane:** No. **Internal Roads:** Primitive. **RV Service:** No. **Market:** 0.25 mi. to Arboles. **Restaurant:** 0.25 mi. to Arboles. **General Store:** Yes. **Vending:** Yes. **Swimming:** Reservoir. **Playground:** Yes. **Other:** RV rentals, pavillion, dog walk area, storage. **Activities:** 6 organized parties in summer. **Nearby Attractions:** San Juan National Forest, Vallecito Reservoir, Florida River, Mesa Verde National Park. **Additional Information:** Durango Chamber of Commerce, (800) 525-8855.

Restrictions

Pets: On leash, cleaned up after. **Fires:** Community fire pit only. **Alcoholic Beverages:** At sites. **Vehicle Maximum Length:** 40 ft.

To Get There

From Hwy. 151 in town, go 0.2 mi. north of Navajo State Park—look for the sign on the east side. Turn east into the driveway, then, at the T intersection, take the 2nd left into the campground. The office is the brown building ahead and to the right.

ASPEN

Aspen-Basalt Campground

Box 880 Aspen Hwy. 82, Aspen-Basalt Campground 81621. T: (800) KMP-ASPEN or (970) 927-3405; abc@soperis.net.

★★★★ n/a

Beauty: ★★★★ Site Privacy: ★★★★
Spaciousness: ★★★★ Quiet: ★★★
Security: ★★★★ Cleanliness: ★★★★★
Insect Control: ★★★★ Facilities: ★★★★★

With red hills to the southwest, forested hills to the east, south, and west, and loads of trees in and around the park, this campground is a comfortable location for an overnight or extended stay. Each site has at least one shade tree and a section of fence for increased privacy. Sites 1–6 are small (30-foot) back-ins and have no hookups. Sites 54–61, right next to these sites, are even smaller (25 feet in length), but have larger fences and are located in a beautiful, shaded corner. These are by far the most attractive sites, but very small. Sites 8–27 and 37–53 are 60-foot pull-throughs laid out in two rows. There are mobile homes located to the east of the row containing sites 8–27. Sites 28–36 to the south and 64–90 to the north (by the entrance) are reserved for monthly guests. These are 45-foot back-ins that back to trees and the road (in both areas). The rest rooms and showers are very clean, and the laundry is big and clean. This is an extremely pleasant destination located in a wonderful area.

Basics

Operated By: Rich & Bonnie Nichols. **Open:** All year. **Site Assignment:** Assigned upon registration. Credit card required for reservation; 24-hours cancellation policy. **Registration:** In office. (Late arrivals use drop box.) **Fee:** $30 (full), $26 (water, electric, cable), $23 (no hookups) (checks, V, MC). **Parking:** At site.

Facilities

Number of RV Sites: 75. **Number of Tent-Only Sites:** 0. **Hookups:** Water, sewer, electric (20, 30, 50 amps), cable. **Each Site:** Picnic table. **Dump Station:** Yes. **Laundry:** Yes. **Pay Phone:** Yes. **Rest Rooms and Showers:** Yes. **Fuel:** No. **Propane:** Yes. **Internal Roads:** Gravel. **RV Service:** On-call. **Market:** 1 mi. north. **Restaurant:** 1 mi. north. **General Store:** Yes. **Vending:** Yes. **Swimming:** Pool & hot tub. **Playground:** Yes. **Other:** Dataport, game room. **Activities:** Movies, skiing, ATV riding, fishing, golfing, hunting, mountain biking, rafting, horseback riding, swimming, hiking. **Nearby Attractions:** Roaring Fork River, Aspen, golf courses. **Additional Information:** Aspen Chamber of Commerce, (970) 925-1940.

Restrictions

Pets: On leash, cleaned up after; no more than 2 pets. **Fires:** In grills. **Alcoholic Beverages:** At sites. **Vehicle Maximum Length:** None. **Other:** No smoking in buildings.

To Get There

From the junction of Hwy. 133 and Hwy. 82, turn southeast onto Hwy. 82 and go 8.8 mi. Turn right, then take the immediate left and go straight into the campground.

BATTLEMENT MESA

Battlement Mesa RV Park

0095 Eldora Dr., P.O. Box 6000, Battlement Mesa 81635. T: (888) 828-0681 or (970) 285-7023 or (970) 285-9740; F: (970) 285-9721.

★★★★ ★★

Beauty: ★★★★ Site Privacy: ★★★
Spaciousness: ★★★ Quiet: ★★★★★
Security: ★★★★ Cleanliness: ★★★★★
Insect Control: ★★★★ Facilities: ★★★

This campground offers wonderous views of Battlement Mesa and other volcano-like peaks from any site. The location is very rural, and sites are level, grassy, and large. Super-long (70-foot) forked pull-throughs share a common entrance, but angle so that privacy is maximized given the site arrangment. Site 106 is next to a residence, and 139 and 144 are adjacent to electrical hardware, making these the least desirable sites. Sites 133, 145 have superior grass, bushes, and views, making these two highly desirable. Other coveted sites include odd numbers 101–109, which back to a dried river bed and forested hills and therefore receive less traffic and noise. The rest rooms and showers are very clean and modern, and Mr. Gibson is extremely affable, making the RV experience quite pleasant. However, tenters are at the mercy of the high winds or the occasional rainstorm, as there is absolutely no coverage to protect a tent. RVers should definitely check out this park, but tenters should consider moving on to Rifel, if possible.

Basics

Operated By: Charles Gibson. **Open:** All year. **Site Assignment:** Assigned upon registration; verbal reservations OK. **Registration:** In office. (Late arrivals go to 86 Partachute Way.) **Fee:** RV $22, tent $9.36 (checks, V, MC, AE, D, CB, DC). **Parking:** At site.

Facilities

Number of RV Sites: 135. **Number of Tent-Only Sites:** 12. **Hookups:** Water, sewer, electric (30, 50 amps), cable. **Each Site:** Picnic table. **Dump Station:** Yes. **Laundry:** Yes. **Pay Phone:** Yes. **Rest Rooms and Showers:** Yes. **Fuel:** No. **Propane:** Yes. **Internal Roads:** Paved. **RV Service:** No. **Market:** 2.5 mi. into Battlement Mesa. **Restaurant:** 2.5 mi. into Battlement Mesa. **General Store:** No. **Vending:** No. **Swimming:** No. **Playground:** No. **Other:** Dataport, dog walk, rec center (2.5 mi. away; free w/ park receipt). **Activities:** Skiing, fishing, swimming, golf, biking, horseshoes, tennis. **Nearby Attractions:** Aspen, Powederhorn, Vail, Grand Mesa, natural hot springs. **Additional Information:** Rifle Visitor Information Center, (970) 625-2085.

Restrictions

Pets: On 6-ft. leash, cleaned up after. **Fires:** Charcoal in grills. **Alcoholic Beverages:** At sites. **Vehi-**

cle **Maximum Length:** None. **Other:** Call if late, no motorcycles or ATVs.

To Get There

From Hwy. I-70, take Exit 75, turn south, and go 0.75 mi. Turn right onto West Battlement Parkway, drive 1.5 mi., then turn right onto Stone Quarry Rd. Drive 2 mi., then turn right onto Thunderberg Trail. Take the 2nd left and keep straight to get to the office.

BRECKENRIDGE

Tiger Run RV Resort

85 Tiger Run Rd., Breckenridge 80424. T: (970) 453-9690; F: (970) 453-6782; www.tigerrunresort.com.

RV: ★★★★★ Tent: n/a

Beauty: ★★★★★ Site Privacy: ★★★★★
Spaciousness: ★★★★★ Quiet: ★★★★★
Security: ★★★★★ Cleanliness: ★★★★★
Insect Control: ★★★★★ Facilities: ★★★★★

The manager here calls this resort "its own little town," and this is not an exaggeration. With roughly 400 sites (70% of which are available to overnighters), tennis courts, indoor swimming pools, a recreation building with TV rooms and pool tables, laundry facilities, double-wide parking spaces, and chalet-style cabins on nearly each RV site, as well as incredible landscaping (lawns, trees, and brick walks), this resort feels more like a quiet suburban neighborhood than an overnight RV park. RVers who wish to use this resort as a travel park (as opposed to buying property) should speak to the manager about which sites are available, as some are privately owned or up for sale. Sites 122–129 and 147–151 are closest to the lake, while 1–7, 129–147, 204–243, and 345–367 are riverside sites. For those who like proximity to the facilities, sites 16–39 and 275–291 are closest to the recreation building. This is a top-notch RV park that deserves the title resort.

Basics

Operated By: The Whitt family. **Open:** All year. **Site Assignment:** Assigned upon registration Credit card required for reservation; 48-hours cancellation policy. **Registration:** In office 24 hours (Dial *9). **Fee:** RV $29–39 (checks, V, MC, AE, D, DC, CB; 10% cash discount). **Parking:** At site.

Facilities

Number of RV Sites: 358. **Number of Tent-Only Sites:** 0. **Hookups:** Water, sewer, electric (30, 50 amps), cable. **Each Site:** Picnic table, full-service cabin. **Dump Station:** No (sewer at all sites). **Laundry:** Yes. **Pay Phone:** Yes. **Rest Rooms and Showers:** Yes. **Fuel:** No. **Propane:** Yes. **Internal Roads:** Paved. **RV Service:** No. **Market:** 3.5 mi. to Breckenridge. **Restaurant:** 3.5 mi. to Breckenridge. **General Store:** Yes. **Vending:** Yes. **Swimming:** Pool & hot tub. **Playground:** Yes. **Other:** Cabins, dataport, TV room, pool table, free bus service, lake. **Activities:** Rafting, fishing, ping pong, biking, Wed. night free wine & cheese, Fri. night smores, live entertainment on weekends, tennis, rock climbing, GPS orienteering, teambuilding activities. **Nearby Attractions:** 14,000-ft.-plus mountains, Summit County. **Additional Information:** Breckenridge Resort Chamber, (970) 453-5579.

Restrictions

Pets: On leash, cleaned up after. **Fires:** In grills. **Alcoholic Beverages:** At sites. **Vehicle Maximum Length:** None. **Other:** No pop-ups or tents.

To Get There

From Hwy. I-70 Exit 203, turn south onto Hwy. 9 and go 6.3 mi. Turn left at the sign onto the entrance (past MM 91) and turn left into the office complex.

BRUSH

Memorial Park

Mayor of Brush, P.O. Box 363, Brush 80723. T: (970) 842-5001; F: (970) 842-5909; www.brushcolo.com.

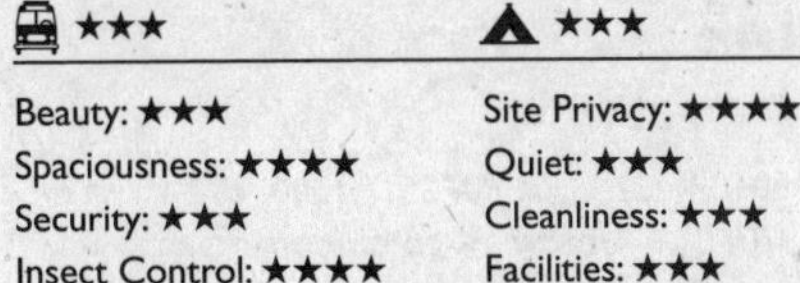

RV: ★★★ Tent: ★★★

Beauty: ★★★ Site Privacy: ★★★★
Spaciousness: ★★★★ Quiet: ★★★
Security: ★★★ Cleanliness: ★★★
Insect Control: ★★★★ Facilities: ★★★

A city park set in an urban environment with industrial and commercial lots around the perimeter, this park tries its best to present a comfortable stay to Brush visitors. Grassy areas and a cute schoolhouse definitely add to the attractiveness of the park, and visitors here should feel rather comfortable. (Especially knowing that their first night is free!) The sites are somewhat undistinguished, and can number more than the electrical boxes that dot the parking area, depending on how people park. There are rows of seemingly just 3–6 sites each, but the city employees who tend to the RV park insist that there are 50 possible sites. The south side of the park is conducive to pull-alongside sites, while the north is better suited to back-ins. The south side is slightly more industrial, and therefore less visibly attractive. All sites are located on the gravel interior road and do not have a picnic area in their immediate vicinity. Tenters can camp on the lush grass or the crushed gravel tent pads located at the entrance to the RV park. The facilities are city park–clean, and the shower is enormous. They are all open, lacking curtains or dividers of any kind. Overall, this is a rather comfortable city park

Basics

Operated By: City of Brush. **Open:** All year. **Site Assignment:** First come, first served; no reservations. **Registration:** At pay station. **Fee:** first night free; $10, night thereafter (checks). **Parking:** At site.

Facilities

Number of RV Sites: 50. **Number of Tent-Only Sites:** Undesignated sites. **Hookups:** Electric (20, 30, 50 amps). **Each Site:** Picnic table, grill (tent pads at tent sites). **Dump Station:** Yes. **Laundry:** No. **Pay Phone:** Yes. **Rest Rooms and Showers:** Yes. **Fuel:** No. **Propane:** No. **Internal Roads:** Gravel. **RV Service:** No. **Market:** 0.5 mi. northwest. **Restaurant:** 0.5 mi. north. **General Store:** No. **Vending:** No. **Swimming:** Pool. **Playground:** Yes. **Other:** Covered picnic area, schoolhouse museum. **Activities:** Basketball, volleyball, baseball, swimming. **Nearby Attractions:** Brush Rodeo (July 1–4), buildings on National Historic Registry. **Additional Information:** Brush Chamber of Commerce, (970) 842-2666.

Restrictions

Pets: On leash, cleaned up after. **Fires:** In grills. **Alcoholic Beverages:** Beer only. **Vehicle Maximum Length:** None.

To Get There

From Hwy. I-76 (Exit 90A), turn south onto Hwy. 1 and go 0.75 mi. Turn right onto Hwy. 34, then take the first left onto Clayton. Go 0.4 mi. Turn right at the sign into the entrance.

BUENA VISTA

Arkansas River Rim Campground and RV Park

33198 Hwy. 24 North, Buena Vista 81211. T: (719) 395-8883; www.coloradodirectory.com/arkansas river rimcamp; www.arkriverrim@chaffee.net.

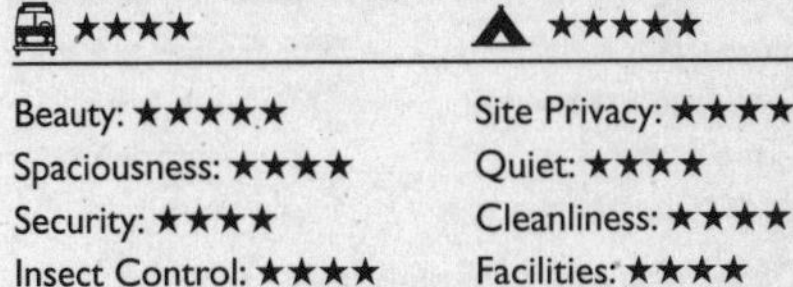

RV: ★★★★ Tent: ★★★★★

Beauty: ★★★★★ Site Privacy: ★★★★
Spaciousness: ★★★★ Quiet: ★★★★
Security: ★★★★ Cleanliness: ★★★★
Insect Control: ★★★★ Facilities: ★★★★

Located in a beautiful valley next to the Arkansas River, this campground offers comfortable sites with beautiful mountain views to the northeast. Sites 1–15 are 75-foot pull-throughs, and 16–24 are 40-foot back-ins located in the north part of the campground. Behind these sites are woods, and beyond those, distant mountains. Sites 25–31 are smaller back-ins (30-foot), while 28–32 are slightly larger (40-foot). Sites 30–32 back to a residence. Sites 33–36 are 60-foot pull-throughs, and 37 and 38, in the same row, are 42-foot pull-throughs. All sites are mostly open, although there is some shade throughout the park. Tent sites are located at the top of the embankment above the Arkansas River. These sites are wooded and very attractive in their natural state. The rest rooms and showers are located in a mobile home. The facilities aren't elaborate, but are comfortably clean. This is a very attractive campground in a stunning part of state—a worthwhile stop in a highly recommended area.

Basics

Operated By: Dale & Debbie Jantz. **Open:** All year. **Site Assignment:** Flexible, depending on site availability; reservations highly recommended in summer. Credit card required for reservation; call to cancel. **Registration:** In office. (Late arrivals select an available site & pay in the morning.) **Fee:** RV $20 (full), tent $15 (checks, V, MC, & D). **Parking:** At site.

Facilities

Number of RV Sites: 36. **Number of Tent-Only Sites:** 8. **Hookups:** Water, sewer, electric (30, 50 amps). **Each Site:** Picnic table. **Dump Station:** Yes. **Laundry:** Yes. **Pay Phone:** Yes. **Rest Rooms and Showers:** Yes. **Fuel:** No. **Propane:** No. **Internal Roads:** Gravel. **RV Service:** No. **Market:** 4.5 mi. south. **Restaurant:** 4 mi. south. **General**

Store: Yes. **Vending:** No. **Swimming:** No. **Playground:** No. **Other:** Ice, fishing licenses. **Activities:** Fishing, gold panning, hiking, mountain climbing. **Nearby Attractions:** Classic auto show (July), ghost towns. **Additional Information:** Buena Vista Chamber of Commerce, (719) 395-6612.

Restrictions

Pets: On leash, cleaned up after. **Fires:** In grills. **Alcoholic Beverages:** At sites. **Vehicle Maximum Length:** None. **Other:** Children and groups discouraged.

To Get There

From the junction of Hwy. 285 and Hwy. 24, turn north onto Hwy. 24 and go 7 mi. Turn right at the sign into the entrance. The office is to the right.

BUFFALO CREEK

Kelsey Campground

P.O. Box 636, Woodland Park 80866. T: (800) 416-6992 or (877) 444-6777; www.fs.fed.us/r2/psicc/spl.

RV ★★★ | Tent ★★★★

Beauty: ★★★★★ | Site Privacy: ★★★★
Spaciousness: ★★★★ | Quiet: ★★★★
Security: ★★★★ | Cleanliness: ★★★★
Insect Control: ★★★★ | Facilities: ★

Of the many campgrounds in the area, this is perhaps the best for RVers, as the sites are paved. Having said that, of course, there are no hookups, and some of the sites are quite severely sloped. A refined statement might read: this is the area's best campground for adventurous RVers in small rigs. Some of the sites (of which all are back-ins) are truly small: 1 is the smallest at 35 feet, 5 is 40 feet, and most of the rest range from 51 to 60 feet. Site 13 is by far the largest at 66 feet. Sites 8 and 9 are quite a bit less shaded than the rest of the sites. Sites 10, 11, and 13 are also somewhat unshaded, and are quite noticeably sloped. The best bets for RVers are 13 (for its size), 12 (level and close to the rest room), or one of the smaller sites 1–5. Tenters need not worry as much about the slope, as there is plenty of level ground to pitch a tent. In fact, this campground is practically a tenter's paradise, and the scenery is absolutely unbeatable. More adventurous RVers can also enjoy a foray into the wild at this campground.

Basics

Operated By: US Forest Service. **Open:** May 24–Sept. 1 (or later). **Site Assignment:** First come, first served. Credit card required for reservation; reservations can be made 4–240 days in advance. $8.65 reservation fee, $10 cancellation fee; cancellations within 3 days pay first night, no-shows pay $20 fee. (2-nights min. stay on weekends, 3-nights on holidays.) **Registration:** At pay station. **Fee:** $13. (checks). **Parking:** At site.

Facilities

Number of RV Sites: 17. **Number of Tent-Only Sites:** 0. **Hookups:** None. **Each Site:** Picnic table, grill. **Dump Station:** No. **Laundry:** No. **Pay Phone:** No. **Rest Rooms and Showers:** Pit toilets; no shower. **Fuel:** No. **Propane:** No. **Internal Roads:** Gravel. **RV Service:** No. **Market:** 18 mi. to Conifer. **Restaurant:** 9 mi. to Pine. **General Store:** No. **Vending:** No. **Swimming:** No. **Playground:** No. **Activities:** Hiking, mountain biking, fishing. **Nearby Attractions:** Arapaho National Forest. **Additional Information:** South Platte Peak Ranger District: (303) 275-5610.

Restrictions

Pets: On leash, cleaned up after. **Fires:** In grills. **Alcoholic Beverages:** At sites. **Vehicle Maximum Length:** None. **Other:** $4 per day park pass;$5 dollar 2nd vehicle fee. (2-nights min. stay on weekends, 3-nights on holidays.)

To Get There

From the junction of Hwy. 285 and Hwy. 126, turn southeast onto Hwy. 126 and go 19.9 mi. (7.2 mi. from National Forest Service Buffalo Creek Work Center). Turn right at the sign into the entrance.

BURLINGTON

Bonny Lake State Park Campground

30010 Rd. 3, Idalia 80735. T: (800) 678-CAMP or (970) 354-7306; www.coloradoparks.org; bonny@plains.net.

RV ★★★★ | Tent ★★★★

Beauty: ★★★★★ | Site Privacy: ★★★★
Spaciousness: ★★★★ | Quiet: ★★★★★
Security: ★★★ | Cleanliness: ★★★★★
Insect Control: ★★★ | Facilities: ★★★★

The best time to go to this campground, strung out along the perimeter of Lake Bonny, is in later spring or summer, when full facilities are provided and it's warm enough to tempt you into the water. Variety is the name of the game here: laid out in a series of loops, the campground offers sites both lakeside and further up the banks in the forest. (All sites are within a quarter mile of the lake.) There are both pull-throughs (average length 50 feet) and back-ins (average length 35 feet), all of which are grassy and mostly level. Tents or RVs can occupy any sites, although you may see primitive sites (without hookups) referred to as "tent sites". This forested campground has a secluded, wilderness feel to it, and is a fun destination for families who enjoy lake recreation. Campers should remember to bring along enough provisions for their stay, however, as the campground is a fair hike (25 miles) from the nearest full services. The marina inside the campground can, however, provide limited groceries, propane, and gasoline in proper containers.

Basics

Operated By: Colorado State Parks. **Open:** All year (limitied services Oct.–mid-Apr.). **Site Assignment:** First come, first served. Reservations recommended in summer; credit card required. Cancellation fees are $12 w/ 14-days notice & $7 plus one night w/ less than 14 days notice. **Registration:** Check information board for reserved sites, select available campsite, then return to self-pay station to pay fee (in drop slot). **Fee:** Electric: $14, primitive: $10, plus $4 day pass (cash only for pay station). **Parking:** At site, some parking in lots.

Facilities

Number of RV Sites: 100. **Number of Tent-Only Sites:** 90. **Hookups:** Electric (30, 50 amps). **Each Site:** Picnic table, grill. **Dump Station:** Yes. **Laundry:** No. **Pay Phone:** Yes. **Rest Rooms and Showers:** Pit toilets; no shower. **Fuel:** Yes (marina). **Propane:** Yes (marina). **Internal Roads:** Paved/dirt. **RV Service:** No. **Market:** 25 mi. to Burlington. **Restaurant:** 25 mi. to Burlington. **General Store:** Marina. **Vending:** Yes. **Swimming:** Lake. **Playground:** No. **Other:** Boat ramp, amphitheater. **Activities:** Swimming, boating, fishing, ranger presentations. **Nearby Attractions:** Bonny Lake, wildlife viewing areas. **Additional Information:** Burlington Chamber of Commerce, (719) 346-8070.

Restrictions

Pets: On 6-ft. leash, cleaned up after. **Fires:** In fire pits. **Alcoholic Beverages:** Beer only. **Vehicle Maximum Length:** None. **Other:** Vehicle pass required.

To Get There

From I-70, take Exit 437, then turn north onto Hwy. 385 and go 22 mi. Turn right at the sign (0.7 mi. after mile marker 209) onto CR-2, and follow the road 3.7 mi. to the park entrance. (You can also take CR-3, 1 mi. further north on Hwy. 385, to go directly to the north side of the lake.)

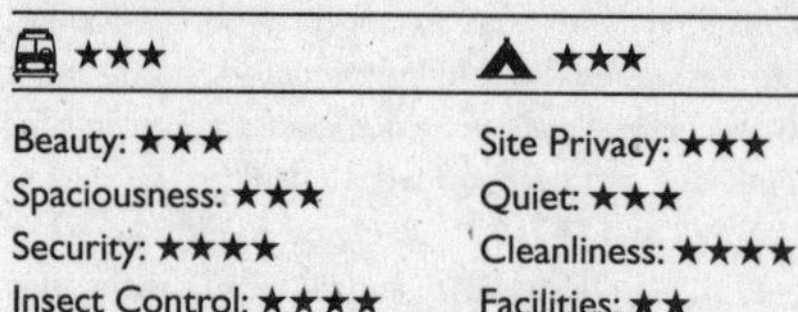

CALHAN

Cadillac Jack's Campground

1001 5th St., Calhan 80808. T: (719) 347-2000; F: (719) 347-2760.

RV ★★★ | Tent ★★★

Beauty: ★★★ | Site Privacy: ★★★
Spaciousness: ★★★ | Quiet: ★★★
Security: ★★★★ | Cleanliness: ★★★★
Insect Control: ★★★★ | Facilities: ★★

Like most of eastern side of Colorado, this campground is largely barren and unshaded. It is, however, a comfortable place to camp, that offers several pull-throughs (1–6) able to accommodate a rig of any size, including a tow. Sites 7–16 (mostly unnumbered) are 30-foot back-ins that back to a row of large shrubs. These are the most shaded sites in the campground, but quite small. Larger sites (but not as large as 1–6) are laid out in a row along the northern edge of the campground. These sites are 33-foot (17–25) and 42-foot (26–37) pull-throughs that offer full hookups. Sites 15 and 16 deserve warning, as they are quite close to the highway that passes by the campground. The tent area is an open grassy space near the storage units in the southern part of the campground. Tenters will not enjoy this campground as much as self-contained RVs with shower and toilet, as there are no facilities for campers to use.

Basics

Operated By: Tom Covington. **Open:** All year. **Site Assignment:** First come, first served; no reservations. **Registration:** In A-frame kiosk in campground. **Fee:** RV $22 (full), $20 (water, electric), tent $10 (checks). **Parking:** At site, extra parking for tows.

Facilities

Number of RV Sites: 42. **Number of Tent-Only

Sites: 5. **Hookups:** Water, sewer, electric (30, 50 amps). **Dump Station:** No. **Laundry:** 1 block away. **Pay Phone:** Yes. **Rest Rooms and Showers:** No. **Fuel:** Next door. **Propane:** Across street. **Internal Roads:** Gravel. **RV Service:** No. **Market:** 20 mi. west. **Restaurant:** Across street. **General Store:** Next door. **Vending:** No. **Swimming:** No. **Playground:** No. **Other:** Covered pavilion, antique store, barber shop, bowling alley. **Activities:** Bowling, antique shopping. **Nearby Attractions:** Paint Mines, El Paso County Fair (late July), Colorado Springs. **Additional Information:** Colorado Springs Chamber of Commerce, (719) 635-1551.

Restrictions

Pets: On leash, cleaned up after. **Fires:** In grills. **Alcoholic Beverages:** At sites. **Vehicle Maximum Length:** None.

To Get There

From Hwy. 24, 0.75 mi. west of the town center on the north side of the street. (Look for the antique shop.)

CANON CITY

RV Campground

3120 East Main, Canon City 81212. T: (719) 275-4576.

RV ★★★ Tent ★★

Beauty: ★★★	Site Privacy: ★★★
Spaciousness: ★★★	Quiet: ★★
Security: ★★★★	Cleanliness: ★★★
Insect Control: ★★★★	Facilities: ★★

This is one of the few RV campgrounds in the area that is *not* a tacky theme park exploiting the Royal Gorge. Hwy. 50 is immediately to the north of this campground, and sites 1–10 are less desirable due to their proximity to this road. The sites to the south and east (11–16, 28–31, 36, and 40–48) have grass instead of gravel, and are therefore better picks. Best of these are 40–48, which are well away from the highway, grassy, and back to an open field to the south. Tent sites, along the interior road, are not very long (12-foot) but wide (45-foot). All tent sites but 50 have a tree, and all are right up against the fence along the border of the park. They are grassy but with bare patches. The rest rooms are clean but oldish, and the showers are not built-in but rather add-on units. All in all, this park is a decent stop for RVers, and not as cheesy as a lot of area parks.

Basics

Operated By: John & Conney Palmer. **Open:** All year. **Site Assignment:** Assigned upon registration. Check required for reservation; 24-hours cancellation policy. **Registration:** In office. (Late arrivals select an available site & pay in the morning.) **Fee:** RV $18.25 (full), tent $15 (checks, no credits cards). **Parking:** At site.

Facilities

Number of RV Sites: 47. **Number of Tent-Only Sites:** 9. **Hookups:** Water, sewer, electric (20, 30 amps). **Dump Station:** Yes. **Laundry:** No. **Pay Phone:** Yes. **Rest Rooms and Showers:** Yes. **Fuel:** No. **Propane:** No. **Internal Roads:** Dirt. **RV Service:** No. **Market:** Across street. **Restaurant:** Across street. **General Store:** No. **Vending:** Yes. **Swimming:** No. **Playground:** No. **Other:** Close to shopping. **Activities:** Rafting. **Nearby Attractions:** Rodeos in town, Royal Gorge, Museum of Colorado Prisons. **Additional Information:** Greater Canon City Chamber of Commerce, (800) 876-7922, (719) 275-2331.

Restrictions

Pets: On leash, cleaned up after. **Fires:** No fires. **Alcoholic Beverages:** At sites. **Vehicle Maximum Length:** 40 ft.

To Get There

From the junction of Hwy. 115 and Hwy. 50, go 2.3 mi. east on Hwy. 50 (Royal Gorge Blvd. in town). Turn right at the Dozier St. light, and take the immediate left. Turn right at the sign and a then quick left into the campground.

CARBONDALE

BRB Crystal River Resort

7202 Hwy. 133, Carbondale 81623. T: (800) 963-2341 or (970) 963-2341; www.cabinscolorado.com; brbresort@cs.com.

RV ★★★★ Tent ★★★★

Beauty: ★★★★	Site Privacy: ★★★★
Spaciousness: ★★★	Quiet: ★★★★
Security: ★★★★	Cleanliness: ★★★★
Insect Control: ★★★	Facilities: ★★

This campground bills itself as the "ultimate resort," which isn't far from the truth. It is surrounded on three sides by towering hills and a mountain, and offers a relaxing rustic experience and wonderful views from any site. Sites K–O and 24–31, on the river's edge, are smaller (21-foot) back-ins for pop-ups. Site 25 looks a little cramped, but 26 and N have nice trees and grass. Sites A and B have tall trees, nice grass, and easy access. Tent sites are inside a loop, with excellent trees and wild grass (7–9, right off the highway, are less desirable). Sites E-J and V (all back-ins; there are no pull-throughs in the park) are a little too open and lacking in shade, are situated by the highway, and have more gravel than grass. The rest room and shower facility is a wooden structure that is rustic but cozy—probably chilly on a cold fall day but great in summer. A sign warns campers to keep the doors closed "due to bears". There is rather intimate space between the showers, but on the whole, the facility—as well as the park itself—is quite comfortable.

Basics

Operated By: Omar Sultan. **Open:** Memorial Day–Oct. 31. **Site Assignment:** Flexible depending on availability. Credit card or check required for reservation; 24-hours cancellation policy. **Registration:** In office. (Late arrivals select an available site & pay in the morning.) **Fee:** RV $23, tent $15 (V, MC, D). **Parking:** At site.

Facilities

Number of RV Sites: 24. **Number of Tent-Only Sites:** 24. **Hookups:** Water, electric (30 amps). **Each Site:** Picnic table. **Dump Station:** Yes. **Laundry:** No. **Pay Phone:** Yes. **Rest Rooms and Showers:** Yes. **Fuel:** No. **Propane:** No. **Internal Roads:** Gravel. **RV Service:** No. **Market:** 5 mi. in Carbondale. **Restaurant:** 5 mi. in Carbondale. **General Store:** Yes. **Vending:** No. **Swimming:** Pool. **Playground:** Yes. **Other:** River, cabins. **Activities:** Volleyball, basketball, horseshoes, skiing, fishing, hunting. **Nearby Attractions:** McClure Pass, Hanging Lake. **Additional Information:** Glenwood Springs Chamber Resort Assoc.: (970) 945-6589.

Restrictions

Pets: On leash, cleaned up after. **Fires:** In fire pits. **Alcoholic Beverages:** At sites. **Vehicle Maximum Length:** None.

To Get There

From the junction of Hwy. 82 and Hwy. 133, go 7 mi. south on Hwy. 133. The entrance is on the left, and the office to the right.

CASTLE ROCK

Castle Rock KOA

6527 South I-25, Castle Rock 80104. T: (800) KOA-3102 or (303) 681-3169; F: (303) 681-2592; www.koa.com.

RV ★★★★ Tent ★★★★

Beauty: ★★★★	Site Privacy: ★★★★★
Spaciousness: ★★★★★	Quiet: ★★★★
Security: ★★★★★	Cleanliness: ★★★★★
Insect Control: ★★★★	Facilities: ★★★★

A large campground with sites scattered over the side of a hill, this KOA offers extremely private sites separated from each other by large swaths of vegetation. Sites 1 and 2 are 75-foot pull-throughs right by the entrance. Sites 12, 14, 15, 17, and 19 are "pull-alongsides" that can accommodate 70 feet. Site 72 is an extra-long (100-foot) pull-through. Back-in sites in this area average 54 × 24 feet. Even sites 74–78 and 127 and 129 command a view to the northeast from the top of the hill, making these quite attarctive sites. Sites 85–89 are unshaded pull-throughs in the eastern section of the campground. Sites 174 and 175 have views of the volcano cones to the east. Sites 160–169 have approximately 45 feet of usable space (the rest has too much slope). Even 140–148 have views to the east, but are completely unshaded and are closest to the railroad tracks. Tent sites are mostly open and unshaded. These include walk-in sites T9–11 and sites T3–8, which are located on the side of the hill. This is quite an attractive campground with lots of vegetation. It is a very nice destination for both tenters and RVers.

Basics

Operated By: Private operator. **Open:** All year. **Site Assignment:** Assigned upon registration Credit card required for reservation; 24-hours cancellation policy. **Registration:** In office. (Late arrivals use drop box.) **Fee:** RV $29.64 (full, 50 amps), $26.62 (full, 30 amps), $24.44 (water, electric), $22.36 (electric), tent $19.24 (checks, V, MC, D). **Parking:** At site.

Facilities

Number of RV Sites: 179. **Number of Tent-Only Sites:** 24. **Hookups:** Water, sewer, electric (30, 50 amps). **Each Site:** Picnic table, grill. **Dump Station:** Yes. **Laundry:** Yes. **Pay Phone:** Yes. **Rest**

Rooms and Showers: Yes. **Fuel:** No. **Propane:** Yes. **Internal Roads:** Dirt. **RV Service:** No. **Market:** 8 mi. north. **Restaurant:** 8 mi. north. **General Store:** Yes. **Vending:** Yes. **Swimming:** Pool. **Playground:** Yes. **Other:** Snack bar, cabins, movie caboose, video games, dog walk. **Activities:** Shopping, swimming. **Nearby Attractions:** Castlewood Canyon State Park, outlet stores, Denver, Colorado Springs, Roxborough State Park. **Additional Information:** Castle Rock Chamber of Commerce, (303) 688-4597.

Restrictions

Pets: On leash, cleaned up after. **Fires:** In grills. **Alcoholic Beverages:** At sites. **Vehicle Maximum Length:** None. **Other:** No ATVs or motorcycles.

To Get There

From Hwy. I-25 (Exit 174), turn west onto Tomah Rd. and go across the railroad tacks. Take the first left into the campground parking lot.

CEDAREDGE

Aspen Trails Campground and Resort

1997 Hwy. 65, Cedaredge 81413. T: (888) 856-1101 or (970) 856-6321.

RV ★★★★★ Tent ★★★★★

Beauty: ★★★★ Site Privacy: ★★★★
Spaciousness: ★★★★ Quiet: ★★★★★
Security: ★★★★ Cleanliness: ★★★★
Insect Control: ★★★★ Facilities: ★★★★★

This campground is beautifully landscaped with grass, trees lining the perimeter and dotting the park, and rocks demarking RV sites. (Sites 1–12 are clearly marked, but 13–22 as yet do not have numbers.) All pull-throughs are 72 × 28 feet. The RV site possibly numbered 13 (at any rate, the site southeast of 1) is closest to the road, although a fence does add some extra security. While there is no shade in the RV park, angling your vehicle can reduce direct sunlight dramatically—especially in conjunction with the use of an awning. The large tenting area to the west of the RV sites is wild and good: with lots of grass and tons of trees. Children should be careful of large rocks in the grass around the playground area near the tenting sites. The rest rooms have finely finished wood interiors with a Western theme. Showers share a partition and a drain, and the toilet stall doors are only 5 feet high—but otherwise, the facilities are quite comfortable. Located on a scenic byway, this campground is worth the drive up.

Basics

Operated By: Dolly, Pat, & Tony Mercep. **Open:** Memorial Day–Nov 15. **Site Assignment:** Flexible depending on availability. Credit card required for reservation; 7-days cancellation policy, less one night's fee. **Registration:** In office. **Fee:** RV $19.50, tent $14 (V, MC, AE, D, checks). **Parking:** At site.

Facilities

Number of RV Sites: 22. **Number of Tent-Only Sites:** Undesignated sites. **Hookups:** Water, sewer, electric (30, 50 amps). **Each Site:** Picnic table, grill. **Dump Station:** Yes. **Laundry:** No. **Pay Phone:** Yes. **Rest Rooms and Showers:** Yes. **Fuel:** No. **Propane:** No. **Internal Roads:** Dirt/gravel. **RV Service:** No. **Market:** 2 mi. to Cedaredge. **Restaurant:** 2 mi. to Cedaredge. **General Store:** Yes. **Vending:** No. **Swimming:** No. **Playground:** Yes. **Other:** Ice cream & soda fountain, deli, cabins, pavillion, pet exercise area, groups welcome. **Activities:** Skiing, biking, hiking, fishing. **Nearby Attractions:** Grand Mesa, motorcycle rally (early Aug.). **Additional Information:** Delta Area Chamber of Commerce, (970) 874-8616.

Restrictions

Pets: On leash, cleaned up after; not allowed to chase deer. **Fires:** Depends on seasonal bans. **Alcoholic Beverages:** At sites. **Vehicle Maximum Length:** None.

To Get There

From the Cedaredge town name signpost, go 2 mi. north. Turn west at the signs into the entrance.

CENTRAL CITY

Gambler's Edge RV Park

605 Lake Gulch Rd., Central City 80427. T: (877) 660-3465 or (303) 582-9345.

RV ★★★★★ Tent n/a

Beauty: ★★★★★ Site Privacy: ★★★★
Spaciousness: ★★★★ Quiet: ★★★★★
Security: ★★★★★ Cleanliness: ★★★★★
Insect Control: ★★★★ Facilities: ★★★★

Still under construction, this campground did not offer all of the planned services at the time of review, but is already a very nice destination. Sites are uniform gravel back-ins 55 × 30 feet with exceptional landscaping. In addition to an attractive interior, this park benefits from stunning views to the east and northwest. Sites 1–10 back to a stone retaining wall and a beautiful view of Central City and the hills beyond. Sites 11–25 are laid out in two rows on the "island" inside the road that loops around the park. These are nice, but do not offer the views that most other sites enjoy. Sites 33–42 back to an open view to the east and are among the best sites in the park. While there are 80 sites planned for this park, work is still being done on about half. However, from the looks of the existing sites and facilities, this park promises to be a top-notch resort that is well worth a return trip.

Basics

Operated By: Barb & Bob. **Open:** All year. **Site Assignment:** First come, first served; reservations recommended & preferred. Credit card required for reservation; 24-hours cancellation policy. **Registration:** In office. (Late arrivals come to office or use drop box). **Fee:** RV $28–30 (V, MC, D, checks). **Parking:** At site, next to huge parking lot.

Facilities

Number of RV Sites: 45. **Number of Tent-Only Sites:** 0. **Hookups:** Water, sewer, electric (30, 50 amps), telephone, dataport. **Dump Station:** No (sewer at all sites). **Laundry:** Yes. **Pay Phone:** Yes. **Rest Rooms and Showers:** Yes. **Fuel:** No. **Propane:** Yes. **Internal Roads:** Gravel. **RV Service:** No. **Market:** 8 mi. to Idaho Springs. **Restaurant:** 1 mi. to Central City. **General Store:** Yes. **Vending:** No. **Swimming:** No (hot tub). **Playground:** No. **Other:** Clubhouse. **Activities:** Rafting, hiking, mountain biking, skiing. **Nearby Attractions:** Ghost towns, Coors Brewery. **Additional Information:** Gilpin County Chamber of Commerce, (303) 582-5077.

Restrictions

Pets: On leash, cleaned up after. **Fires:** In grills. **Alcoholic Beverages:** At sites. **Vehicle Maximum Length:** None. **Other:** 1 vehicle only.

To Get There

From I-70 (Exit 244), turn east onto Hwy. 6 and go 2.85 mi. Turn north onto Hwy. 119 and go 7.3 mi. Turn left onto Gregory St. and go 1 mi. Turn left onto Spring St. (turns into Hooper) and go 2 mi. Turn right onto Lake Gulch Rd. and go 0.15 mi. Turn left at the sign into the entrance.

CLARK

Steamboat Lake State Park

Box 750, Clark 80428. T: (800) 678-CAMP or (970) 879-7019 or (970) 879-3922; www.colorado parks.org; steamboat.lake@state.co.us.

RV ★★★★ Tent ★★★★★

Beauty: ★★★★ Site Privacy: ★★★★
Spaciousness: ★★★★ Quiet: ★★★★★
Security: ★★★★ Cleanliness: ★★★★
Insect Control: ★★★★ Facilities: ★★★

This campground has forested campsites that include 60-foot back-ins and some 90-foot pull-throughs. (pull-throughs include 116, 118, 120, 121, 123, and 127.) Sites with electric hookups are limited to 116–165. All sites are laid out in loops, with the Baker Loop being slightly closer to the boat ramps and the swimming beach. Sites 131, 146, and 160 are all located at the end of roundabouts, and they are therefore more secluded than most others. Bridge Island is a separate section of the campground connected by the interior road. It contains sites 166–200, of which about half (181–200) are walk-in tent sites. The rest rooms and showers are large, clean, and comfortable. The showers cost 50 cents for three minutes. There are change machines in the rest rooms.

Basics

Operated By: Colorado State Parks. **Open:** All year. **Site Assignment:** First come, first served. Credit card required for reservation; 3-days cancellation policy. **Registration:** At pay station. **Fee:** RV $14 (electric), tent $10 (checks, no credits cards). **Parking:** At site.

Facilities

Number of RV Sites: 50. **Number of Tent-Only Sites:** 148. **Hookups:** Electric (20, 30, 50 amps). **Each Site:** Picnic table, grill, fire pit, tent pad. **Dump Station:** Yes (at Dutch Hill). **Laundry:** Yes (at Dutch Hill). **Pay Phone:** Yes (at Visitor Center). **Rest Rooms and Showers:** Yes (at Dutch Hill). **Fuel:** No. **Propane:** No. **Internal Roads:** Gravel. **RV Service:** No. **Market:** 26 mi. south. **Restaurant:** 26 mi. south. **General Store:** Marina. **Vending:** Yes. **Swimming:** Lake. **Playground:** No.

Other: Boat ramp, fire wood, amphitheater, cabins, boat rentals, indoor picnic area. **Activities:** Fishing, boating, swimming, hiking. **Nearby Attractions:** Steamboat Springs. **Additional Information:** Steamboat Springs Chamber Resort Assoc., (970) 879-0880.

Restrictions

Pets: On leash, cleaned up after. **Fires:** In grills. **Alcoholic Beverages:** At sites. **Vehicle Maximum Length:** None. **Other:** $4 per vehicle for day-use fee.

To Get There

From the junction of Hwy. 40 and CR-129, turn north onto CR-129 and go 25 mi. to Visitor Center. Continue 0.9 mi. to first campground on the left.

COLORADO CITY

Pueblo South/Colorado City KOA

9040 I-25 South, Colorado City 81004. T: (800) 562-8646 or (719) 676-3376; www.koa.com; cocitykoa@juno.com.

RV ★★★★★ Tent ★★★★★

Beauty: ★★★★ Site Privacy: ★★★★
Spaciousness: ★★★★ Quiet: ★★★
Security: ★★★★★ Cleanliness: ★★★★
Insect Control: ★★★★ Facilities: ★★★★

This desert campground uses attractive indiginous plants and rocks in its landscaping, including at least one huge flowering cactus. RV sites are laid out in three rows, with tent sites occupying another distinct row. Row A, along the north side of the campground, has 60-foot back-ins that are mostly quite shady. (Sites 13 and 14 do not have shade trees.) Site A2 is next to the hot tub, which is convenient, but may attract more foot traffic. Site A9 has an extra large grassy site (27-foot wide), which makes it more desirable. Site A14, on the other hand, has "views" of a gas station and residences and backs to a mobile home, making it the least desirable site in the campground. Row B has grassy pull-throughs 60 × 18 feet. Sites B7–10 are especially shaded. Site B1 has a giant overhanging tree, and is closest to the rest rooms. Sites in Row C have views of an open field to the east, which is more attractive than, for example, A14's view. These sites are all grassy, and C7–10 are especially shaded. Site C16 has an electric pole and wires that encroach on its space. Tent sites are located along the south side of the campground. These sites have beautiful grass and loads of trees. There are also some very nice views of hills to the southwest. (Unfortunately, there is RV storage to the southeast.) Each of these spacious sites is separated by shrubs. The rest rooms are very nicely decorated, but had soap residue on the shower floors. Otherwise, the rest rooms were spotless. This is a very attractive campground that will appeal to most RV campers, and has excellent facilities for tenters.

Basics

Operated By: Tim & Elena Johnson. **Open:** All year. **Site Assignment:** Assigned upon registration Credit card required for reservation; 24-hours cancellation policy. **Registration:** In office. (Late arrivals use drop box.) **Fee:** RV $26, tent $18 (V, MC, D, checks). **Parking:** At site.

Facilities

Number of RV Sites: 67. **Number of Tent-Only Sites:** 16. **Hookups:** Water, sewer, electric (30, 50 amps). **Each Site:** Picnic table. **Dump Station:** Yes. **Laundry:** Yes. **Pay Phone:** Yes. **Rest Rooms and Showers:** Yes. **Fuel:** No. **Propane:** Yes. **Internal Roads:** Gravel. **RV Service:** No. **Market:** 2 mi. west. **Restaurant:** 0.25 mi. west. **General Store:** Yes. **Vending:** Yes. **Swimming:** No. **Playground:** Yes. **Other:** Mini golf, pavilion, pet walk, cabins. **Activities:** Basketball, fishing, offroad riding, swimming, boating. **Nearby Attractions:** Hollydot Golf Course, Bishop's Castle, Lake Beckweth, Lake Isabel. **Additional Information:** Visitor Information Center, (719) 543-1742.

Restrictions

Pets: On leash, cleaned up after. **Fires:** In fire pits. **Alcoholic Beverages:** At sites. **Vehicle Maximum Length:** 42 ft.

To Get There

From I-25 (Exit 74): from the south side of the exit, take the first right after the highway and go 0.25 mi. Turn left at the sign into the entrance.

COLORADO SPRINGS

Garden of the Gods Campground

3704 West Colorado Ave., Colorado Springs 80904. T: (800) 248-9451 or (719) 475-9450; www.coloradocampgrounds.com.

RV ★★★★ Tent ★★★★

Beauty: ★★★★ Site Privacy: ★★★
Spaciousness: ★★★ Quiet: ★★★
Security: ★★★★ Cleanliness: ★★★★
Insect Control: ★★★★ Facilities: ★★★★

This is a vast campground that offers a large selection of back-ins and pull-throughs, with some creekside spaces. Most sites are very well-shaded (the M, N, and O sites being one notable exception). Back-in sites range from 30 feet (A, B, and P sections), 45 feet (D, E, K, and S sections), to 60 feet (C section) long. pull-throughs are located in the F, G, M, N, and O sections. F and G sites are extra-long, 80-feet, sites used as end-to-end doubles, making each site roughly 40 feet. Longer single sites are located in sections M, N, and O, which are 60 feet in length. Creekside sites (indicated on the campground map by "CS") are located in the southwest corner. The tenting area is found on the west side of the campground, but there are also creekside tenting sites, marked on the map as "CRT." These are nice, shaded sites with some grass cover. Although they are closer to the road that passes by the campground, tenters may prefer these sites for their natural feel and the sound of the creek at night. The pool, the laundry, the rest rooms, and all other facilties are well-maintained, clean, and comfortable. This is a great campground to stay at while visiting the Garden of the Gods or any of the other numerous attractions in the area.

Basics

Operated By: Chuck Murphy. **Open:** All year. **Site Assignment:** Assigned upon registration Credit card required for reservation; 24-hours cancellation policy, less $5 fee. **Registration:** In office. (Late arrivals use drop box.) **Fee:** RV $37 (full, deluxe), $40 (full, creekside), $35 (full, standard), $32 (water, electric), tent $27 (checks, V, MC, D). **Parking:** At site.

Facilities

Number of RV Sites: 300. **Number of Tent-Only Sites:** 30. **Hookups:** Water, sewer, electric (30, 50 amps), phone. **Each Site:** Picnic table, grill. **Dump Station:** Yes. **Laundry:** Yes. **Pay Phone:** Yes. **Rest Rooms and Showers:** Yes. **Fuel:** No. **Propane:** No. **Internal Roads:** Paved. **RV Service:** No. **Market:** 0.5 mi. east. **Restaurant:** 1 block east. **General Store:** Yes. **Vending:** Yes. **Swimming:** Pool. **Playground:** Yes. **Other:** Clubhouse, jukebox, gift shop, coffee & donuts, pancake breakfasts, watermelon feasts, ice cream socials, fajitas, bus stop in front, cabins. **Activities:** Bus tours. **Nearby Attractions:** Garden of the Gods, Florissant Fossil Beds National Monument, Cripple Creek & Victor Narrow Guage Railroad, Air Force Base Visitor Center, Mining Museum. **Additional Information:** Colorado Springs Chamber of Commerce, (719) 635-1551.

Restrictions

Pets: On leash, cleaned up after. **Fires:** In grills. **Alcoholic Beverages:** At sites. **Vehicle Maximum Length:** None.

To Get There

From I-25 (Exit 141), turn west onto Hwy. 24 and go 2.6 mi. Turn north onto 31st St. and go 1 block. Turn left onto Colorado Ave. and go 0.8 mi. Turn right at the sign into the entrance.

CORTEZ

Cortez/Mesa Verde KOA

27432 East Hwy. 160, Cortez 81321. T: (800) 562-3901 or (970) 565-9301; F: (970) 565-2107; www.koa.com; cortezkoa@fone.net.

RV ★★★★ Tent ★★★★

Beauty: ★★★★ Site Privacy: ★★★★
Spaciousness: ★★★★ Quiet: ★★★
Security: ★★★★ Cleanliness: ★★★★★
Insect Control: ★★★★ Facilities: ★★★★★

This beautiful campground is surrounded on three sides by mountains, and has an excellent view of Sleeping Ute Mountain to the north. To the south are scrub-covered hills, and over everything looms big, open sky. RV sites are almost exclusively 70-foot pull-throughs, with a handful of 45-foot back-ins mostly used by long-term guests. Tent sites have both water and electric hookups. The tenting area is grassy, shaded, and very comfortable. The rest rooms and showers are spacious, comfortable, and absolutely spotless. The laundry room is bright and roomy, and all other facilities (pool, game room) are clean and tidy. This campground is centrally located for trips to Mesa Verde, Four Corners, and even further reaches such as Canyonlands or Monument Valley. Campers in tents or RVs will be pleased by this campground, which is worth making a destination on their itinerary.

BASICS

Operated By: Billy Sanders. **Open:** Apr 1–Oct. 15. **Site Assignment:** Assigned upon registration. **Registration:** In office. (Late arrivals use drop box.) **Fee:** RV $28 (full), $26 (water, electric), tent $20 (V, MC, D). **Parking:** At site.

FACILITIES

Number of RV Sites: 78. **Number of Tent-Only Sites:** 26. **Hookups:** Water, sewer, electric (30, 50 amps). **Each Site:** Picnic table, grill. **Dump Station:** Yes. **Laundry:** Yes. **Pay Phone:** Yes. **Rest Rooms and Showers:** Yes. **Fuel:** No. **Propane:** No. **Internal Roads:** Gravel. **RV Service:** No. **Market:** 1 mi. west. **Restaurant:** 0.25 mile west. **General Store:** Yes. **Vending:** Yes. **Swimming:** Pool. **Playground:** Yes. **Other:** Dataport, hot tub/sauna, firewood, game room, cabins, pet walk, teepees. **Activities:** Fishing, boating, swimming, golf, horseback riding, visiting ruins, volleyball, basketball. **Nearby Attractions:** Mesa Verde, Four Corners, Lake McPhee, Monument Valley, Canyonlands, Hovenweep National Monument. **Additional Information:** Cortez Area Chamber of Commerce, (800) 346-6526 or (970) 565-3414.

RESTRICTIONS

Pets: On leash, cleaned up after. **Fires:** In fire pits. **Alcoholic Beverages:** At sites. **Vehicle Maximum Length:** None.

TO GET THERE

From the junction of Hwy. 145 and Hwy. 160, turn east onto Hwy. 160 and go 0.4 mi. Turn right at the sign into the entrance.

COTOPAXI

Arkansas River KOA

21435 US Hwy. 50, Cotopaxi 81223. T: (800) 562-2686 or (719) 275-9308; F: (719) 275-2249; www.koa.com.

RV ★★★★ Tent ★★★★

Beauty: ★★★★	Site Privacy: ★★★
Spaciousness: ★★★★	Quiet: ★★★
Security: ★★★★	Cleanliness: ★★★★
Insect Control: ★★★★	Facilities: ★★★★

This riverside campground has three strips of pull-throughs (1–13, 14–29, and 30–49) between the highway and the river. These pull-through sites range from 60 feet to 80 feet in length. Sites with nice shade trees include 14, and 17–23. These sites also have beautiful vistas of the rocky hills across the river to the west. End site 30 is a slightly shorter (50-foot) pull-through, but has extra space around it. This site might be a tough spot to park in for a larger rig, due to its proximity to a cabin. Tent sites are back-ins, 35 × 18 feet, along the riverfront. These sandy sites (51–80) have trees and vegetation, and they face the river and the woods on the far shore. These are excellent sites that tenters will be happy to occupy for a stay of any length. The rest rooms are clean, though slightly run-down, and appear to have been decorated in the 1970s. (There are additional porta-potties along the river for tenters' use.) Likewise, the laundry is dark and a little musty, but spacious and relatively clean. This is a pleasant campground in a beautiful setting that will appeal slightly more to tenters, but is still an excellent stay for RVers.

BASICS

Operated By: Jim & Amy Burnham. **Open:** Apr. 15–Oct. 30. **Site Assignment:** Flexible, depending on site availability. Credit card required for reservation; cancellation by 4 p.m. same day. **Registration:** In office. (Late arrivals go to night registration at building to left of entrance.) **Fee:** RV $26 (full), $24 (water, electric), tent $20 (V, MC, D). **Parking:** At site.

FACILITIES

Number of RV Sites: 49. **Number of Tent-Only Sites:** 30. **Hookups:** Water, sewer, electric (30, 50 amps). **Each Site:** Picnic table, fire pit. **Dump Station:** Yes. **Laundry:** Yes. **Pay Phone:** Yes. **Rest Rooms and Showers:** Yes. **Fuel:** No. **Propane:** Yes. **Internal Roads:** Dirt. **RV Service:** No. **Market:** 25 mi. to Salida or Canon City. **Restaurant:** 25 mi. to Salida or Canon City. **General Store:** Yes. **Vending:** Yes. **Swimming:** Pool. **Playground:** Yes. **Other:** Pool table. **Activities:** Basketball, fishing, rafting, horseshoes, nightly hay ride, nightly kids movies, mini golf, tetherball, shuffleboard. **Nearby Attractions:** Royal Gorge. **Additional Information:** Canon City Chamber of Commerce, (719) 275-2331.

RESTRICTIONS

Pets: On leash, cleaned up after, $5 per pet. **Fires:** In fire pits. **Alcoholic Beverages:** At sites. **Vehicle Maximum Length:** None. **Other:** Protect trees, do not tie anything to trees.

TO GET THERE

From the easternmost town name sign, go 1.3 mi. east on Hwy. 50 (just south of mi. marker 247). Turn left at the sign into the entrance. The office is on the right; night registration is to the left.

CRAIG

Craig KOA Kampground

2800 East US 40, Craig 81625. T: (970) 824-5105; www.koa.com.

RV ★★★ Tent ★★

Beauty: ★★★	Site Privacy: ★★★
Spaciousness: ★★★	Quiet: ★★★
Security: ★★★★	Cleanliness: ★★★★★
Insect Control: ★★★★	Facilities: ★★★★★

Just at the east end of town, and 2 miles from downtown Craig, this campground has grassy fields and plenty of trees to the south and west. Its super-long (90-foot) double pull-throughs (sites 28–44) can be used by one long rig if the campground is not too full. Sites are level and grassy, averaging 27 feet wide. Sites 6–10 are wide open in the middle of the interior road with only two decent trees, thus they are the least desirable sites. Tent sites are located along the south fence, which presents one significant drawback: trains roll right past the park boundary by the fence. The rest room and shower facilities are spotless and well-lit. The laundry is spacious and clean, with a pleasant waiting area. Overall, the park is a decent place to stay, but tenters might have better luck elsewhere.

BASICS

Operated By: Rocky Mt RV Park. **Open:** All year (monthly tenants only Dec 1–Apr 15). **Site Assignment:** Reservations recommended Apr. 1–Nov. 30; first come, first served Dec. 1–Mar. 31st. **Registration:** In store. (Late arrivals use drop box.) **Fee:** RV $27, tent $20 (V, MC, AE, D). **Parking:** At site only.

FACILITIES

Number of RV Sites: 83. **Number of Tent-Only Sites:** 20. **Hookups:** Water, sewer, electric (30, 50 amps). **Each Site:** Picnic table, tree. **Dump Station:** Yes. **Laundry:** Yes. **Pay Phone:** Yes. **Rest Rooms and Showers:** Yes. **Fuel:** No. **Propane:** Yes. **Internal Roads:** Gravel. **RV Service:** No. **Market:** 2 mi. west. **Restaurant:** 2 mi. west. **General Store:** Yes. **Vending:** Yes. **Swimming:** Pool. **Playground:** Yes. **Other:** 4 cabins, RV parts, dataport, pet walk area, hot tub, rec room, soccer field. **Activities:** Soccer, swimming, horseshoes, hiking. **Nearby Attractions:** Sandrocks Nature Trail & Petroglyphs, Museum of Northwest Colorado, Dinosaur National Monument. **Additional Information:** Craig Chamber of Commerce, (800) 864-4405, (970) 824-5689.

RESTRICTIONS

Pets: On leash, cleaned up after. **Fires:** In fire pits; subject to seasonal bans. **Alcoholic Beverages:** At sites only. **Vehicle Maximum Length:** None.

TO GET THERE

On Hwy. 40, go 0.5 mi. west of the easternmost Craig town name signpost. Turn south into the entrance. The office is straight ahead.

CREEDE

Mt. Views at River's Edge RV Resort

539 Airport Rd., Box 680, Creede 81130. T: (719) 658-2710; F: (719) 658-2711.

RV ★★★★★ Tent n/a

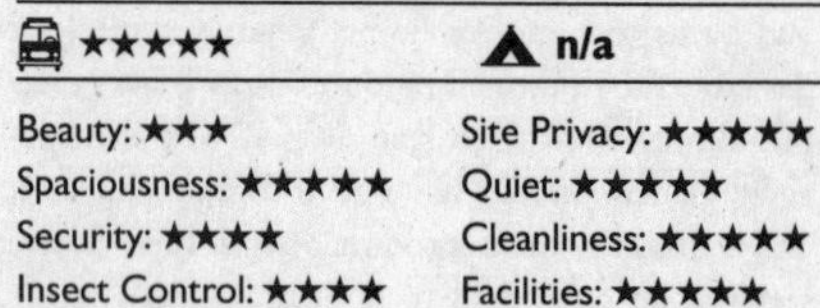

Beauty: ★★★	Site Privacy: ★★★★★
Spaciousness: ★★★★★	Quiet: ★★★★★
Security: ★★★★	Cleanliness: ★★★★★
Insect Control: ★★★★	Facilities: ★★★★★

This beautiful park is surrounded on all four sides by mountains and features all brand-new facilities. The laundry is spacious, clean, well-lit, and has lots of machines. The rest rooms are similarly brand-new and immaculate. (Management says that other new, unnamed, services will be added this year, making this park all the more luxurious.) There is truly a space for any rig of any size in this park: back-ins are 60 feet long, while pull-throughs are a lengthy 70 feet; both types are 40 feet wide, with a designated space for extra vehicles to the side of the main parking area. The best sites in this park (which is a difficult thing to judge!) are probably 107–110 on the north side, as they face nice pasture land, hills, and an attractive wooden fence, they are as long as anyone would need, and they are close to the rest rooms without being right next to them. Although shade trees—and perhaps a paved road—would improve this park, the location is so nice, the spaces so big, and the facilities so new and clean that it deserves top honors. This is a top-notch resort; make sure to get reservations, or you may not get in.

Basics

Operated By: Roland & Helen Zimmerman. **Open:** May–Oct. **Site Assignment:** Assigned upon registration. Reservations require deposit; $20 cancellation fee. **Registration:** In office. (Late arrivals use map on bulletin board to find available site, pay in the morning.) **Fee:** $21 (no credit cards). **Parking:** At site.

Facilities

Number of RV Sites: 100. **Number of Tent-Only Sites:** 0. **Hookups:** Water, sewer, electric (30, 50 amps). **Each Site:** Picnic table, sectioned-off picnic area. **Dump Station:** No (sewer at all sites). **Laundry:** Yes. **Pay Phone:** Yes. **Rest Rooms and Showers:** Yes. **Fuel:** No. **Propane:** Yes. **Internal Roads:** Gravel. **RV Service:** No. **Market:** 1.4 mi. west. **Restaurant:** 1.2 mi. west. **General Store:** Yes. **Vending:** No. **Swimming:** No. **Playground:** No. **Other:** Enclosed phone/dataport pavillion (5 units), group picnic/BBQ area, extremely large rec room, pool table, sofa, TV. **Activities:** Potlucks, Mexican-themed dinners, shared meat from hunting. **Nearby Attractions:** Creede Repertory Theater, Creede Underground Mining Museum. **Additional Information:** Creede-Mineral Chamber of Commerce, (800) 327-2102, or (719) 658-2374.

Restrictions

Pets: On leash, cleaned up after, no barking. **Fires:** In pavillion. **Alcoholic Beverages:** At sites. **Vehicle Maximum Length:** None.

To Get There

From the south edge of Creede, take Hwy. 149 0.75 mi. southwest. Turn south onto Airport Rd. (unmarked—look for blue trailer sign). Drive 0.5 mi. and take the first left into the gravel driveway. Continue straight ahead to get to the office.

CRIPPLE CREEK

Lost Burro

P.O. Box 614, Cripple Creek 80813. T: (719) 689-2345; www.lostburro.com; burrocamp@aol.com.

RV ★★★★★ Tent ★★★★

Beauty: ★★★★★	Site Privacy: ★★★★★
Spaciousness: ★★★★★	Quiet: ★★★★★
Security: ★★★★	Cleanliness: ★★★★★
Insect Control: ★★★★	Facilities: ★★★

Get lost in the pines! If you'd like to, you certainly can at the Lost Burro. Located in a small valley with wooded and rocky hills on all four sides, imposing cliffs to the north, and dense forest to the south, this campground feels truly "lost". Campsites are located in tiers up the hillside and down near the stream. Sites are well-spaced, and include some enormous pull-throughs (16 measures 100-feet), as well as long (60-foot) back-ins (8, 12, 13, 14, 15). RV site 11 is a long pull-through like the others, but only about 48 feet are level—the rest drop off quite quickly. Tents sites (by the stream) are mostly open, although sites 15 and 16 (up in the forest away from the stream) are wooded and separated from the rest, making them the best tent sites. The campground is wild and not overly built-up: sites are not much more than bulldozed strips in the woods, making them quite natural and beautiful. For some, the primitive sites, along with the lack of full hookups at every site, may represent too much of a step away from civilization. However, those savvy enough to realize that water spouts and a dump station make full hookups unnecessary will love this campground. Make sure you have reservations—once others "discover" the Lost Burro, it may be harder to get lost than you'd like.

Basics

Operated By: Kent Goza & Mary Eddleman. **Open:** All year. **Site Assignment:** Assigned upon registration. Credit card or check required for reservation; 24-hours cancellation policy. **Registration:** In office. (Late arrivals select an available site & pay in the morning.) **Fee:** RV $18, tent $14 (checks, V, MC, D). **Parking:** At site.

Facilities

Number of RV Sites: 13. **Number of Tent-Only Sites:** 23. **Hookups:** Electric (30, 50 amps). **Each Site:** Picnic table, fire pit. **Dump Station:** Yes. **Laundry:** No. **Pay Phone:** Yes. **Rest Rooms and Showers:** Yes. **Fuel:** No. **Propane:** No. **Internal Roads:** Dirt. **RV Service:** No. **Market:** 20 mi. to Woodland/Divide. **Restaurant:** 4 mi. to Cripple Creek. **General Store:** Yes. **Vending:** Yes. **Swimming:** No. **Playground:** No. **Other:** Stream, burgers. **Activities:** Hiking. **Nearby Attractions:** Casinos, Cripple Creek, Royal Gorge, Florissant Fossil Beds National Monument, Pike's Peak, Cripple Creek & Victor Narrow Gauge Railroad. **Additional Information:** Cripple Creek Chamber of Commerce, (719) 689-2169.

Restrictions

Pets: On leash, cleaned up after. **Fires:** In fire pits. **Alcoholic Beverages:** At sites. **Vehicle Maximum Length:** None. **Other:** Quiet at 9 p.m., no ATVs or motorcycles, no wood cutting or gathering.

To Get There

From the northwestern sign for the town of Cripple Creek on Carr Ave. (CR-Teller 1), go 3.2 mi. north. Turn left at the signs into the entrance. (Those coming from Canon City on CR-Teller 1 will find the campground on their right, just at the Open Air Chapel dome.) Follow the dirt drive down to the office on the right.

DELTA

Riverwood Inn

677 Hwy. 50 North, Delta 81416. T: (970) 874-5787; F: (970) 874-4872; www.riverwoodn.com; info@ riverwoodn.com.

RV ★★★ Tent ★★★

Beauty: ★★★	Site Privacy: ★★★★
Spaciousness: ★★★	Quiet: ★★★
Security: ★★★	Cleanliness: ★★★
Insect Control: ★★★	Facilities: ★★★

This park, on the Gunnison River, has large back-ins (56–70-foot), and absolutely enormous pull-throughs (90–100-foot). Further more, there are loads of trees throughout the park, making shade a given for any site. Arguably the best sites are 5–7 in the northeast corner near the tenting area, with fine towering trees at the back, nice grass, and enough distance from the mobile homes to the west (behind 8–13) to allow increased privacy. The least desirable sites are 14 and 15, right along Hwy. 50 (with no fence at the perimiter), and sites 16 and 17, which back to the park entrance (again without a fence). The laundry facility is a little small (1 of each machine) and dingy. The tent sites are located on an "island" to the northeast of the RV sites. These are unmarked, virtually unlimited, and unkempt. While the wild grass and other vegetation, including lots of trees, is appealing to tenters, there was old wood and some cast away furniture littering the area during our inspection. Additionally, the only rest room on the "island" is a porta-potty. Disregarding this slight slap in the face to tenters, the actual tenting area is quite nice. Campers of all stripes will find it a reasonable stop, as it is easily accessed from Hwy. 50 or 92, and is quite close to town.

Basics

Operated By: Loren & Merced Pogue. **Open:** All year. **Site Assignment:** Assigned upon registration. Credit card required for reservation; 24-hours cancellation policy. **Registration:** In office. (Late arrivals select an available site & pay in the morning.) **Fee:** Pull-through: $21.50, back-in: $19.50, tent $11 (V, MC, D, DC, CB, check). **Parking:** At site.

Facilities

Number of RV Sites: 28. **Number of Tent-Only Sites:** Undesignated sites. **Hookups:** Water, sewer, electric (30, 50 amps). **Each Site:** Picnic table, grill; most have several trees & shrubs. **Dump Station:** No (sewer at all sites). **Laundry:** Yes. **Pay Phone:** Yes. **Rest Rooms and Showers:** Yes. **Fuel:** No. **Propane:** No. **Internal Roads:** Gravel. **RV Service:** No. **Market:** 0.5 mi. **Restaurant:** On site. **General Store:** No. **Vending:** No. **Swimming:** No. **Playground:** No. **Other:** River, 11-room hotel. **Activities:** Fishing, hiking, biking. **Nearby Attractions:** Grand Mesa, Fort Uncompahgre, Delta County Museum. **Additional Information:** Delta Area Chamber of Commerce, (970) 874-8616.

Restrictions

Pets: On leash, cleaned up after. **Fires:** In fire pits. **Alcoholic Beverages:** At sites. **Vehicle Maximum Length:** None.

To Get There

From the junction of Hwy. 92 and Hwy. 50, turn north onto Hwy. 50, go 0.5 mi., and turn right into the entrance.

DENVER

Delux RV Park

5520 North Federal Blvd., Denver 80221. T: (303) 433-0452.

RV ★★★ Tent n/a

Beauty: ★★	Site Privacy: ★★★
Spaciousness: ★★★	Quiet: ★★★
Security: ★★★	Cleanliness: ★★★
Insect Control: ★★★★	Facilities: ★★★

Laid out in a horseshoe around the office and manager's residence, this campground features back-ins roughly 40 feet long, with a 30-foot cement slab at most sites. The campground is located in an urban residential area, and some of the sites lie next to houses and a lounge (18–22). Some of the sites are unnumbered, and the numbering scheme appears somewhat haphazard. Probably the nicest sites are 12–17, located on the inside of the internal road loop. Site 27 is less desirable, as it lies adjacent to the office parking lot. Sites 32–34 are even worse, as they lie right off of (busy) Federal Blvd. A number of the sites appear to be given over to long-term residents, especially those in the lower number (2–11) on the north side of the loop. The RV park, during our visit, was slightly run-down, but not uncomfortable. Being the only RV park in Denver proper, it is a convenient place to stay while checking out the sights in Denver.

Basics

Operated By: Tony Clemons. **Open:** All year. **Site Assignment:** Assigned upon registration. Credit card required for reservation; 24-hours cancellation policy. **Registration:** In office. (Late arrivals select an available site & pay in the morning.) **Fee:** RV $30 (V, MC, D). **Parking:** At site.

Facilities

Number of RV Sites: 31. **Number of Tent-Only Sites:** 0. **Hookups:** Water, sewer, electric (30, 50 amps), cable, phone. **Each Site:** Picnic table. **Dump Station:** Yes. **Laundry:** Yes. **Pay Phone:** Yes. **Rest Rooms and Showers:** Yes. **Fuel:** No. **Propane:** No. **Internal Roads:** Gravel. **RV Service:** No. **Market:** 2 mi. north. **Restaurant:** 1 mi. south. **General Store:** No. **Vending:** Yes. **Swimming:** No. **Playground:** No. **Other:** Dataport, 10 minutes to downtown Denver, Mile High Stadium, Civic Center, Elitch Gardens; 20 minutes to Denver Zoo, dataport. **Activities:** Visiting museums, sightseeing, amusement park. **Nearby Attractions:** Denver, Mile High Stadium, Civic Center, Elitch Gardens amusement park. **Additional Information:** Denver Chamber of Commerce, (303) 458-0220.

Restrictions

Pets: On leash, cleaned up after. **Fires:** In grills. **Alcoholic Beverages:** At sites. **Vehicle Maximum Length:** 39 ft.

To Get There

From the junction of Hwy. I-25 and Hwy. I-70, turn west onto Hwy. I-70 and go 2 mi. Turn north onto Federal Blvd and go 0.8 mi. Turn right at the sign into the entrance.

DINOSAUR

Blue Mountain Village

P.O. Box 7, Dinosaur 81610. T: (970) 374-2747; dinoma@nwco.quik.com.

RV ★★ Tent ★

Beauty: ★★ Site Privacy: ★★★
Spaciousness: ★★ Quiet: ★★★★
Security: ★★★★★ Cleanliness: ★★★
Insect Control: ★★★ Facilities: ★★

This fenced-in park has some views of mountains to the north, but is otherwise not much to look at, with few trees to speak of, gravel (not grassy) sites, and mobile homes at the front area of the RV park. However, that being said, this park is a middling palce to stay. The pull-throughs are long (85 feet), but narrow (16 feet). The pull-throughs in the southwest corner (70–80) are probably the nicest of the lot: they are well away from the road and have decent views to the south, west, and east. The laundry facility is clean and well-lit, but the showers are a little cramped. The rest rooms are otherwise reasonably clean and modern. Tent sites are located on a strip of grass along the fence at the south edge of the park. This strip is ratyher narrow, and provides no protection from the elements. Tenters would be advised to give the park a pass, while RVers could reasonably stay a couple of days—but not make a destination out of the park.

Basics

Operated By: Jeanne & Jim. **Open:** Apr. 1–Nov. 1. **Site Assignment:** Assigned upon registration. Credit card required for reservation; 24-hours cancellation policy. **Registration:** In office. (Late arrivals ring doorbell.) **Fee:** RV $17.50, tent $11 (V, MC, many discounts honored). **Parking:** At site.

Facilities

Number of RV Sites: 88. **Number of Tent-Only Sites:** 12. **Hookups:** Water, sewer, electric (30, 50 amps). **Dump Station:** No (sewer at all sites). **Laundry:** Yes. **Pay Phone:** Yes. **Rest Rooms and Showers:** Yes. **Fuel:** No. **Propane:** No. **Internal Roads:** Gravel. **RV Service:** No. **Market:** 3 mi. to Vernal (mini market 0.5 mi.). **Restaurant:** 1 mi. **General Store:** No. **Vending:** No. **Swimming:** No. **Playground:** Yes. **Other:** Covered picnic shelter. **Activities:** Viewing dinosaur fossils, rafting. **Nearby Attractions:** Dinosaur National Monument. **Additional Information:** Dinosaur National Monument, (970) 374-3000.

Restrictions

Pets: On leash, cleaned up after. **Fires:** In fire pits. **Alcoholic Beverages:** At sites. **Vehicle Maximum Length:** None.

To Get There

From the junction of Hwy. 40 and Hwy. 64, turn south onto Hwy. 64 (going east). Drive 0.5 mi. to 7th St. (go right at the fork in the road). Turn right onto Blue Mountain Village, then take the first left onto Morrison Ave. The office is at the end of the drive.

DURANGO

Durango East KOA

30090 US Hwy. 160, Durango 81303. T: (800) KOA-0793 or (970) 247-0783; F: (970) 247-3655; www.koa; 104117.3442@compuserve.com.

RV ★★★★ Tent ★★★★

Beauty: ★★★★ Site Privacy: ★★★★
Spaciousness: ★★★★ Quiet: ★★★★
Security: ★★★★ Cleanliness: ★★★★★
Insect Control: ★★★★ Facilities: ★★★★★

This campground, on the northeast side of town, has mostly back-ins, but of such large proportions (40–60 feet) that campers should not be put off by the prospect of not finding a pull-through. Indeed, the pull-throughs on the east side of the campground are less desirable than most back-ins due to the absence of any shade trees, and their "views" of nearby houses. Site 43 is a gigantic pull-through that will accommodate any rig, while 66 is a pull-through with a great view. Most sites have a row of trees and shrubs between them for an added sense of privacy. With the exception of the more open sites to the east, many spots have a lost-in-the-woods feel. The least desirable sites (1 and 2), however, are quite open and close to the propane storage, a separate storage unit, and the registration office; hopefully they are only used as overflow sites. This campground's ruggedness will appeal especially to tenters, who have lots of protection in a wilderness atmosphere. The rest rooms are clean, modern, and spacious, as is the laundry. This is a great campground in a wonderful location, and will suit both tenters and RVers.

Basics

Operated By: Jay & Carol Coates. **Open:** May 1–Oct. 15. **Site Assignment:** Assigned upon registration. Reservations require deposit; 24-hours cancellation policy. **Registration:** In office. (Late arrivals use drop box.) **Fee:** RV $29 (full), $27 (water, electric), tent $22 (V, MC, checks). **Parking:** At site.

Facilities

Number of RV Sites: 60. **Number of Tent-Only Sites:** 24. **Hookups:** Water, sewer, electric (30, 50 amps), cable. **Each Site:** Picnic table, grill, trees. **Dump Station:** Yes. **Laundry:** Yes. **Pay Phone:** Yes. **Rest Rooms and Showers:** Yes. **Fuel:** No. **Propane:** Yes. **Internal Roads:** Gravel. **RV Service:** No. **Market:** 4 mi. southwest. **Restaurant:** 5 mi. southwest. **General Store:** Yes. **Vending:** No. **Swimming:** Pool. **Playground:** Yes. **Other:** Cabins, cottage, game room, TV lounge, group site, dataport, pool table, river. **Activities:** Mini golf, volleyball, fishing, ice cream socials, pancake breakfast, nightly movie. **Nearby Attractions:** Durango/ Silverton Railroad, Mesa Verde. **Additional Information:** Durango Chamber of Commerce, (800) 525-8855.

Restrictions

Pets: On leash, cleaned up after; do not leave unattended. **Fires:** Subject to seasonal bans. **Alcoholic Beverages:** At sites. **Vehicle Maximum Length:** None.

To Get There

From the northwest junction of Hwy. 550 and Hwy. 160/550 (at the western edge of town), go 2.7 mi. northeast on Hwy. 550. Turn right at the sign into the entrance. The office is straight ahead.

ESTES PARK

Estes Park KOA

2051 Big Thompson Ave., Estes Park 80517. T: (800) KOA-1887 or (970) 586-2888; F: (970) 577-0518; www.koa.com; estesparkkoa @compuserve.com.

RV ★★★★ Tent ★★★

Beauty: ★★★★★ Site Privacy: ★★★
Spaciousness: ★★★ Quiet: ★★★★

Security: ★★★★ Cleanliness: ★★★★★
Insect Control: ★★★★★ Facilities: ★★★★★

The fourth KOA campground ever built, this tiered campground is admittedly not for big rigs. Sites are somewhat cramped by today's standards (although the odd large 5th wheel can still be found, tucked in sideways), and space between sites is negligible. And yet the campground is still worth a visit—after all, you can't beat the gorgeous mountain views from all sides or the cooler weather in summer, and even the natural landscaping is very attractive. Sites 1–7 in the southwest corner along the highway are rather small back-ins (30 × 22 feet). Sites 8–29 are larger (40-foot) back-ins, as are 37–48 (40–42-feet). Sites 30–36 and 49–54 are longer (40–45-feet) "parallel parking" sites that resemble pull-throughs, and may be more convenient than a straight back-in. There are stairs between the tiered levels at sites 24,26, and 44, increasing the likelihood of foot traffic past these sites. Tent sites are located in the southeast corner (accessed on the road by cabins 9 and 12). Each tent site has at least one (two maximum) sides fenced in by a solid fence, with a wooden barricade on one other side, lending more privacy to these sites. There is one gravel pad and one astroturf pad per tent site. At 21 × 33 feet, the sites are medium-sized, but they are packed in one atop the other with little space between them. Despite the confined spaces, this is a beautiful campground and well worth a visit.

Basics

Operated By: Wendy. **Open:** May 1–Oct. 20. **Site Assignment:** Assigned upon registration. Credit card required for reservation; 24-hours cancellation policy. **Registration:** In office. (Late arrivals use drop box.) **Fee:** RV $20 (full), $18 (water, electric), tent $10 (V, MC). **Parking:** At site.

Facilities

Number of RV Sites: 46. **Number of Tent-Only Sites:** 19. **Hookups:** Water, sewer, electric (30, 50 amps), cable. **Each Site:** Picnic table on wooden platform, grill. **Dump Station:** Yes. **Laundry:** Yes. **Pay Phone:** Yes. **Rest Rooms and Showers:** Yes. **Fuel:** No. **Propane:** Yes. **Internal Roads:** Dirt. **RV Service:** No. **Market:** 1.5 mi. west. **Restaurant:** 1.5 mi. west. **General Store:** Yes. **Vending:** No. **Swimming:** No. **Playground:** Yes. **Other:** 16 cabins, 7 cottages, teepees, gift shop, lounge, game room, across from lake. **Activities:** Fishing, boating, swimming, hiking, skiing, mountain climbing. **Nearby Attractions:** Rocky Mountain National Park, elk bugling, aspens turning. **Additional Information:** Estes Park Chamber of Commerce, (800) 443-7837 or (970) 586-4431.

Restrictions

Pets: On leash, cleaned up after. **Fires:** In fire pits. **Alcoholic Beverages:** At sites. **Vehicle Maximum Length:** 40 ft.

To Get There

From the junction of Hwy. 36 and Hwy. 34, turn east onto Hwy. 34 and go 1.8 mi. Turn left at the sign into the entrance.

FAIRPLAY

Western Inn and RV Park

490 Hwy. 285 P.O. Box 187, Fairplay 80440. T: (877) 306-3037 or (719) 836-2026; F: (719) 836-0758; westerninn@chaffeee.net.

RV ★★★ Tent ★★★

Beauty: ★★ Site Privacy: ★★★★
Spaciousness: ★★★★ Quiet: ★★★
Security: ★★★★ Cleanliness: ★★★★
Insect Control: ★★★★ Facilities: ★★★

This is a small RV park operated in conjunction with a motel. The complex is located in a rural area with some industrial development especially towards the southeast. The RV sites are located on a gravel interior road. Each site contains a tree that is more decorative than shading. Sites 1–3 and 7–11 are open-ended pull-throughs that can easily accommodate 90 feet. Sites 4–6 are back-ins that can take approximately 55 feet. Tenters can pitch a tent to the southeast of the RV sites, pretty much wherever they can find room. The tenting area has sparse grass, and, like the RV section of the park, offers no shade. This campground is conveniently located clsoe to the town of Fairplay, and is a decent stop on the highway, but is not a destination in itself.

Basics

Operated By: Jack & Linda Sanderson. **Open:** All year. **Site Assignment:** Flexible, depending on site availability. Credit card required for reservation; 24-hours cancellation policy. **Registration:** In office. (Late arrivals can call manager 24 hrs.) **Fee:** RV $20 (full), tent $10 (checks, V, MC, AE, D, DC). **Parking:** At site.

Facilities

Number of RV Sites: 11. **Number of Tent-Only Sites:** Undesignated sites. **Hookups:** Water, sewer, electric (30, 50 amps). **Each Site:** Picnic table. **Dump Station:** No (sewer at all sites). **Laundry:** 4 blocks. **Pay Phone:** Yes. **Rest Rooms and Showers:** Yes. **Fuel:** No. **Propane:** No. **Internal Roads:** Gravel. **RV Service:** No. **Market:** 6 blocks on Hwy. 9. **Restaurant:** Next door. **General Store:** No. **Vending:** Yes. **Swimming:** No (hot tub). **Playground:** Yes (in park 2 blocks away). **Other:** Some frozen foods in office. **Activities:** Hiking, hunting, skiing, fishing. **Nearby Attractions:** South Park city, 14,000-ft. mountains. **Additional Information:** Fairplay Chamber of Commerce, (719) 836-3410.

Restrictions

Pets: On leash, cleaned up after. **Fires:** In grills. **Alcoholic Beverages:** At sites. **Vehicle Maximum Length:** None.

To Get There

From the junction of Hwy. 285 and Hwy. 9, turn north onto Hwy. 285 and go 0.2 mi. Turn left at the sign into the entrance.

FORT COLLINS

Horsetooth Campground (Stout Campground)

1800 South CR 31, Loveland 80537. T: (970) 679-4554; www.abouthorsetooth.com; info@abouthorsetooth.com.

RV ★★★★ Tent ★★★★★

Beauty: ★★★★★ Site Privacy: ★★★★★
Spaciousness: ★★★★★ Quiet: ★★★★
Security: ★★★★ Cleanliness: ★★★★
Insect Control: ★★★★ Facilities: ★★

Beautiful views of rocks, hills, and trees surround this park to the northeast and northwest. In addition to its beauty, the lake offers many recreational opportunities, including swimming, boating, and scuba diving. There are lots of trees throughout the park, and most sites are at least partially shaded. Site 1 is close to the entrance and the rest rooms. Site 8 is a 90-foot pull-through, and 14 and 15 are even longer (105-foot) pull-throughs. Sites 21, 26, 27, 29, and 30 are among the handful of back-ins in the park. Sites 32–42 are on a separate loop to the southeast of the main campground area. Site 37 has a water pump. Tent sites are walk-ins, with a central parking area for all sites. (There are a large number of tenting sites around the reservoir.) This campground is a decent stop for outdoor enthusiasts, and although it does not offer full services, many campers will enjoy a stay here.

Basics

Operated By: Larimer County. **Open:** All year. **Site Assignment:** First come, first served; no reservations. **Registration:** Ranger or Camp Host will collect fees. **Fee:** $10 (electric), tent $7. (checks). **Parking:** At site.

Facilities

Number of RV Sites: 42. **Number of Tent-Only Sites:** 0. **Hookups:** Electric (20, 30, 50 amps). **Each Site:** Picnic table, grill, tent pad. **Dump Station:** Yes. **Laundry:** No. **Pay Phone:** No. **Rest Rooms and Showers:** Pit toilets; no shower. **Fuel:** No. **Propane:** No. **Internal Roads:** Gravel. **RV Service:** No. **Market:** 6.5 mi. east. **Restaurant:** 6.5 mi. east. **General Store:** Yes. **Vending:** No. **Swimming:** Reservoir. **Playground:** No. **Other:** Boat ramp, covered picnic area. **Activities:** Fishing, boating, swimming, hiking, rock climbing, scuba diving, horseback riding. **Nearby Attractions:** Lory State Park, Horsetooth Mountain Park. **Additional Information:** Larimer City Parks & Open Lands Dept., (970) 679-4570.

Restrictions

Pets: On leash, cleaned up after. **Fires:** In grills. **Alcoholic Beverages:** Beer only. **Vehicle Maximum Length:** None. **Other:** Counter-clockwise boating only; $6 day pass for all vehicles.

To Get There

From I-25 (Exit 265), turn west onto Harmony Rd. and go 10.8 mi. Turn right at the sign into the entrance.

FRUITA

Monument RV Park

607 Hwy. 340, Fruita 81521. T: (888) 977-6777 or (970) 858-3155; F: (970) 858-4777.

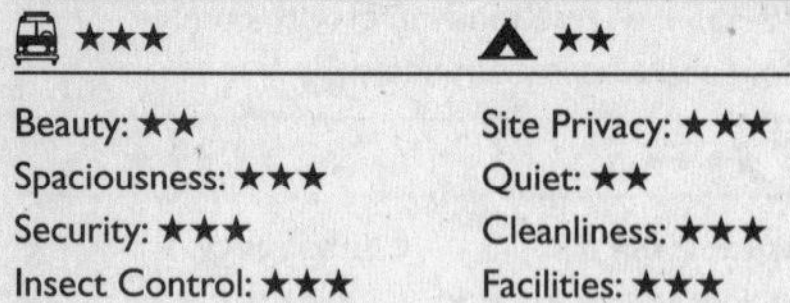

RV ★★★ Tent ★★

Beauty: ★★ Site Privacy: ★★★
Spaciousness: ★★★ Quiet: ★★
Security: ★★★ Cleanliness: ★★★
Insect Control: ★★★ Facilities: ★★★

This is a functional jumping-off point to explore the Colorado National Monument, Devil's Canyon, and other destinations in Colorado or Utah. Despite the proximity of several gas stations and fast-food restaurants, the campground retains a semi-rural feel, with a horse pasture abutting the southeast corner. However, this rectangular campground is situated close to both the highway and the train tracks that run through town, and light-sleepers would be well-advised to bring earplugs. Likewise, the security floodlights are kept on all night, and (tent) campers may want to consider sleeping blinders. (No tent sites can escape the floodlights.) Travelers who do not wish to turn off of I-70 for lodging will find a reasonable place to spend the night here, but those who seek the wilder side would be advised to take the short drive up to Saddlehorn Campground at the Colorado National Monument.

Basics

Operated By: Lonnie & Angie. **Open:** All year. **Site Assignment:** First-come, first served. **Registration:** At office (Late arrivals select an available site & pay in the morning.) **Fee:** $24 (full), $21 (water, electric), $18 (tent). **Parking:** At site only.

Facilities

Number of RV Sites: 80. **Number of Tent-Only Sites:** 33. **Hookups:** Full. **Each Site:** Picnic table, some grills. **Dump Station:** Yes. **Laundry:** Yes. **Pay Phone:** Yes. **Rest Rooms and Showers:** Yes. **Fuel:** Yes. **Propane:** Yes. **Internal Roads:** Gravel, in good condition. **RV Service:** No (on-call mobile service). **Market:** 1.5 mi. **Restaurant:** No. **General Store:** Yes. **Vending:** Yes. **Swimming:** No. **Playground:** No. **Other:** Dog run, communal area. **Activities:** Fishing, hiking, boating. **Nearby Attractions:** Devil's Canyon, Colorado National Monument, Country Jam in nearby Mack (3rd weekend in June). **Additional Information:** Fruita Chamber of Commerce, (970) 858-3894.

Restrictions

Pets: On leash, cleaned up after. **Fires:** At sites only. **Alcoholic Beverages:** At sites. **Vehicle Maximum Length:** None.

To Get There

From I-70, take the Fruita exit (Exit 19), turn left onto Hwy. 340, and then left into the park.

GLENWOOD SPRINGS

Ami's Acres

50235 Hwy. 6 & 24, Glenwood Springs 81602. T: (970) 945-5340; F: (970) 947-9169; amisacres@yahoo.com.

RV ★★★★ Tent ★★★★

Beauty: ★★★★ Site Privacy: ★★★
Spaciousness: ★★ Quiet: ★★
Security: ★★★★ Cleanliness: ★★★★★
Insect Control: ★★★★ Facilities: ★★★

This terraced RV park on the slope of a hill facing gorgeous rock cliffs across the highway has long (90-foot) but narrow (15-foot) pull-throughs. Sites 51–56 are smaller back-ins for pop-ups, but back to a beautiful grassy hill, and are quite attractive sites. Tent sites are located up the slope from the RV sites, a nice distance from park traffic. These are nice, natural sites with plenty of tree coverage and soft dirt floor. The rest room and shower facilities are quite clean and modern, although the building they are housed in looks a little run-down. The laundry is small but clean. The landscaping is rather attractive, with plenty of trees and shrubs making a nice, natural setting. Another nice touch are the picnic tables, which are painted a variety of different colors. One downside is that the park is plagued by both train and traffic noise. However, if you can get past the minor inconvenience, this park is a nice stay.

Basics

Operated By: John & Roxanne Christner. **Open:** Mar 15– Nov. 1. **Site Assignment:** Assigned upon registration. Credit card required for reservation; 48-hours cancellation policy. **Registration:** In office. (Late arrivals use drop box.) **Fee:** RV $23, tent $16 (V, MC). **Parking:** At site.

Facilities

Number of RV Sites: 62. **Number of Tent-Only Sites:** 18. **Hookups:** Water, sewer, electric (30, 50 amps). **Each Site:** Picnic table, tree. **Dump Station:** No (sewer at all site). **Laundry:** Yes. **Pay Phone:** Yes. **Rest Rooms and Showers:** Yes. **Fuel:** No. **Propane:** No. **Internal Roads:** Gravel. **RV Service:** No. **Market:** 1 mi. east. **Restaurant:** 1 mi. east. **General Store:** No. **Vending:** No. **Swimming:** No. **Playground:** Yes. **Other:** Easy access from I-70. **Activities:** Rafting, hiking, biking, hunting, fishing, golf. **Nearby Attractions:** Glenwood Hot Springs Pool, Hanging Lake, Frontier Historical Museum, Yampa Spa & Vapour Cave. **Additional Information:** Glenwood Springs Chamber Resort Assoc., (970) 945-6589.

Restrictions

Pets: On leash, cleaned up after; no pets in tent sites. **Fires:** No wood fires. **Alcoholic Beverages:** At sites. **Vehicle Maximum Length:** None. **Other:** No ATVs or motorcycles.

To Get There

From I-70, take Exit 114, go 1 mi. west on the frontage road to the north of the highway. The entrance is on the right.

GOLDEN

Chief Hosa Campground

27661 Genesee Dr., Golden 80401. T: (303) 526-0242; F: (303) 526-2685; www.chiefhosa.com; info@chiefhosa.com.

RV ★★★ Tent ★★★★

Beauty: ★★★★ Site Privacy: ★★★★
Spaciousness: ★★★★ Quiet: ★★★★
Security: ★★★★ Cleanliness: ★★★★
Insect Control: ★★★★ Facilities: ★★

This is a giant campground that occupies both sides of the highway. (The western side of the campground closes on Sept. 1.) All of the sites in this campground are back-ins, averaging 40 feet in length. Sites 1–13 are 40-foot sites in a row along the northeast side. Sites 14–19 are located in the southeast, and 20–42 are in the central "island" of the park. Sites 43–48 are clustered around the bathhouse. There are numerous tent sites in this campground. The heavily forested sites are rough and natural. The road leading up to the hill on which sites 26–40 are located is very poorly maintained, and difficult to negotiate. Other tent sites are scattered around the park, and not quite as challenging to get to. The rest rooms and showers are located in a mobile home parked in the southwest corner. The facilities are quite clean, although the showers are slightly less so than the rest rooms. This is an enjoyable place to take the family for a camping outing, or just to get away for a weekend alone.

Basics

Operated By: City & County of Denver. **Open:** All year (limited services Labor Day–Memorial Day). **Site Assignment:** Assigned upon registration. Credit card required for reservation; 24-hours cancellation policy. **Registration:** In office or use drop box. **Fee:** RV $20 (water, electric), tent $15 (V, MC, AE, D). **Parking:** At site.

Facilities

Number of RV Sites: 50. **Number of Tent-Only Sites:** 38. **Hookups:** Water, electric (30, 50 amps). **Each Site:** Picnic table. **Dump Station:** Yes. **Laundry:** No. **Pay Phone:** Yes. **Rest Rooms and Showers:** Yes. **Fuel:** No. **Propane:** No. **Internal Roads:** Gravel. **RV Service:** No. **Market:** 3.2 mi. west. **Restaurant:** 1 mi. east or west. **General Store:** No. **Vending:** No. **Swimming:** No. **Playground:** Yes. **Other:** Communal fire pit, dog walk. **Activities:** Volleyball, basketball, horseshoes. **Nearby Attractions:** Buffalo Bill's Grave, Buffalo Herd Overlook. **Additional Information:** Golden Chamber of Commerce, (303) 279-3113.

Restrictions

Pets: On leash, cleaned up after. **Fires:** In grills. **Alcoholic Beverages:** At sites. **Vehicle Maximum Length:** None.

To Get There

From I-70 (Exit 253), on the southeast side of the highway, go straight on Genesee Rd. to campground entrance on right.

GOODRICH

Jackson Lake State Park Cove Campground

26363 Rd. 3, Orchard 80649. T: (877) 444-6777 or (970) 645-2551; F: (970) 645-1535; www.parks. state.co.us; jackson.lake@state.co.us.

 ★★★ ▲ ★★★★

Beauty: ★★★★	Site Privacy: ★★★
Spaciousness: ★★★★	Quiet: ★★★★
Security: ★★★★	Cleanliness: ★★★★
Insect Control: ★★★★	Facilities: ★★★

Seemingly its own little world, this state park offers water-oriented recreation in a wilderness setting. The sparse grass and low vegetation gives it a typical southwestern feel, and it is beautiful in its own way. There are several campgrounds with several hundred sites; those reviewed here are the Cove and Pelican Campgrounds, containing roughly 20 sites combined. Sites 1–4 in Cove Campground are unshaded 40-foot back-ins that do not provide much in the way of privacy. Sites 5 and 6 are 63-foot pull-throughs located near the amphitheater. Site 5 has much better shade than 1–4 or 6. There is an unnumbered, 60-foot "pull-alongside" near the swimming beach, and several possible campsites along the parking lot for the swim beach. (If the parking lot is full, there is no parking for these sites.) Sites 7–10 and 13–14 are 40-foot back-ins that back to woods. These sites have the best shade in the park. (Sites 15 and 16 are also well-shaded.) Sites 11 and 12 are much more open 45-foot back-ins. In the Pelican Campground, sites 5–10 are 60-foot pull-throughs that overlook the beach. There are also some tenting sites that are even closer to the edge of the beach. These are undoubtedly among the best tenting sites. The low shade trees and sandy cover make tent camping quite comfortable. This is a fun park for the entire family, whether in tents or an RV.

Basics

Operated By: Colorado State Parks. **Open:** All year. **Site Assignment:** First come, first served. Credit card required for reservation; 3-days cancellation policy, less $10 service fee. **Registration:** At pay station. **Fee:** $14 (electric), tent $10. (checks). **Parking:** At site.

Facilities

Number of RV Sites: 250. **Number of Tent-Only Sites:** 0. **Hookups:** Electric (20, 30, 50 amps). **Each Site:** Covered picnic table, grill, fire pit. **Dump Station:** Yes. **Laundry:** No. **Pay Phone:** Yes. **Rest Rooms and Showers:** Yes. **Fuel:** No. **Propane:** No. **Internal Roads:** Paved/dirt. **RV Service:** No. **Market:** 18 mi. south in Wiggins. **Restaurant:** 18 mi. south in Wiggins. **General Store:** Marina. **Vending:** No. **Swimming:** Lake. **Playground:** No. **Other:** Boat ramp, ampitheater, hunting blinds, nature trails. **Activities:** Fishing, boating, swimming, hiking, ice skating, interpretive programs, hunting. **Nearby Attractions:** Riverside Reservoir, Pawnee National Grasslands. **Additional Information:** Fort Morgan Chamber of Commerce, (970) 867-6702.

Restrictions

Pets: On 6-ft. leash, cleaned up after. **Fires:** In grills. **Alcoholic Beverages:** Beer only. **Vehicle Maximum Length:** None. **Other:** $4 per day park pass; no cutting of firewood.

To Get There

From the junction of I-76 and Hwy. 39, turn north onto Hwy. 39 and go 7.65 mi. Turn west onto CR Y5 and go 2.4 mi. Turn right to go to the south end or continue straight to the north end and the office.

GOULD

North Park/Gould KOA

53337 Hwy. 14, Walden 80480. T: (800) 562-3596 or (970) 723-4310; www.koa.com.

RV ★★★★★ ▲ ★★★★★

Beauty: ★★★★★	Site Privacy: ★★★★★
Spaciousness: ★★★★	Quiet: ★★★★★
Security: ★★★★	Cleanliness: ★★★★★
Insect Control: ★★★★	Facilities: ★★★★★

Ahhh . . . This is what camping is all about! Smack-dab in the middle of the forest in North Park, this campground is wooded, quiet, and clean. Now, campers should keep in mind the fact that North Park is 8,900 feet above sea level, and nights get pretty chilly here—even well into spring, when there can still be snow on the ground. Bring your long johns (especially tent campers) for cold nights and possible use during the day. Tenters should count on bringing more "winter woolies" and bed layers when camping at lower elevations. That said, this is a gorgeous campground that RVers and tenters alike will love. Back-in sites are quite long (50-foot), while pull-throughs are an incredible 90-foot—there's something for every rig here! Sites could be wider (they are just 22 feet), but should suffice for all but the widest RVs with slide-outs. Sites are well-spaced and private, located along a single giant loop. The only site that may present any incovneience is 30, which is located on the tip of the inner "island" of the loop, and may thus get a little more passing traffic than the others. All other sites are a camper's delight. The playground includes a neat wooden fort, and all of the facilities are spotless. There are a number of state, national, and private campgrounds in the area, but this campground is unequalled in services. If you are considering a trip to this region, by all means, plan to stop for a night at this KOA.

Basics

Operated By: The Vlasmans. **Open:** May 26–Nov 15. **Site Assignment:** Assigned upon registration. **Registration:** In office. (Late arrivals use drop box.) **Fee:** RV $25 (full), $22 (water, electric), tent $20. **Parking:** At site.

Facilities

Number of RV Sites: 30. **Number of Tent-Only Sites:** 7. **Hookups:** Water, sewer, electric (30 amps). **Each Site:** Picnic table. **Dump Station:** Yes. **Laundry:** Yes. **Pay Phone:** Yes. **Rest Rooms and Showers:** Yes. **Fuel:** Yes. **Propane:** Yes. **Internal Roads:** Gravel. **RV Service:** No. **Market:** 3 mi. to Gould. **Restaurant:** 3 mi. to Gould. **General Store:** Yes. **Vending:** No. **Swimming:** Lake. **Playground:** Yes. **Other:** Game room. **Activities:** Fishing, hiking, mountain biking, hunting, horseshoes, basketball. **Nearby Attractions:** North Park, North sandhills Recreation Area, Arapahoe National Wildlife Refuge. **Additional Information:** North Park Tourism Information Center, (970) 723-4344.

Restrictions

Pets: On leash, cleaned up after. **Fires:** In fire pits. **Alcoholic Beverages:** At sites. **Vehicle Maximum Length:** None.

To Get There

From the westernmost Gould town name signpost, drive 2.7 mi. west on Hwy. 14. Turn north at the sign into the campground entrance. The office is straight ahead.

GRANBY

Stillwater Campground

8590 US Hwy. 39, Granby 80446. T: (877) 444-6777 or (970) 887-0056; www.reserveusa.com.

RV ★★★★ ▲ ★★★★

Beauty: ★★★★	Site Privacy: ★★★★
Spaciousness: ★★★	Quiet: ★★★★
Security: ★★★★	Cleanliness: ★★★★
Insect Control: ★★★★	Facilities: ★★★

Overlooking Lake Granby, this campground has a myriad of sites offering a combination of camping possibilities: great views, electrical hookups, facilities. One combination that does not seem possible, however, is an electric site with a superb view, as all of the electric sites are on the north side of the hill and the lake is further south. However, most sites are at least partially forested, and all seem very comfortable. Sites 1–4 accommodate tents only, as there is separate parking away from these sites. Electric sites include 12–14, 16–18, 20–23, and about half of the sites numbered in the 30s, 40s, and 50s. These sites range from 25-foot back-ins (12) to 42-foot back-ins (14). The only electric sites that have somewhat of a view are 12 and 23. Sites 61–92 offer spectacular views of the lake and the marina, but are entirely unshaded. Moreover, a number of these sites (76–83) do not permit tent camping. Loop C offers some great views—especially amongst the higher numbers—but is mostly unshaded. Tent sites include 24–28 and 32–35, which are walk-in sites overlooking the lake. The rest room is small and the showers made of crude cement, but they are otherwise modern and comfortable. This is a large and attractive campground that will appeal mostly to those interested in water recreational.

Basics

Operated By: Thousand Trails Management. **Open:** Memorial Day–early Sept. **Site Assignment:** First come, first served. Credit card required for reservation; 3-days cancellation policy, less $10 service fee. **Registration:** At pay station. **Fee:** $20 (water, electric), no hookups, $15. (checks). **Parking:** At site.

Facilities

Number of RV Sites: 20. **Number of Tent-Only Sites:** 128. **Hookups:** Water, electric (10, 20, 30, 50 amps). **Each Site:** Picnic table, fire pit. **Dump Station:** Yes. **Laundry:** No. **Pay Phone:** Yes. **Rest Rooms and Showers:** Yes. **Fuel:** No. **Propane:** No. **Internal Roads:** Gravel. **RV Service:** No. **Market:** 9 mi. south. **Restaurant:** 9 mi. south. **General Store:** No. **Vending:** No. **Swimming:** Lake. **Playground:** No. **Other:** Boat ramp, ampitheater. **Activities:** Fishing, boating, swimming, hiking, skiing. **Nearby Attractions:** Lake Granby. **Additional Information:** Forestry Office, (970) 887-4100.

Restrictions

Pets: On leash, cleaned up after. **Fires:** In grills. **Alcoholic Beverages:** At sites. **Vehicle Maximum Length:** None. **Other:** Max. 5 people per site.

To Get There

From the junction of Hwy. 40 and Hwy. 34, turn north onto Hwy. 34 and go 8.5 mi. Turn right at the sign into the entrance.

GRAND JUNCTION

RV Ranch at Grand Junction

3238 East I-70 Business Loop, Grand Junction 81520. T: (800) 793-0041 or (970) 434-6644; F: (970) 434-5681; www.rvranches.com; rvranch@gj.net.

RV ★★★★★ Tent ★★

Beauty: ★★★★	Site Privacy: ★★
Spaciousness: ★★★	Quiet: ★★★★
Security: ★★★★	Cleanliness: ★★★★★
Insect Control: ★★★★	Facilities: ★★★★★

This perfectly manicured, wonderfully clean park has loads of trees offering shade, nice landscaping, and long (75-foot) pull-throughs. The one downside is that sites are slightly narrow: the RVs with slide-outs on some of the 30-foot-wide spaces were practically touching on my visit. Besides this, however, it is hard to find a less-than-wonderful site in this park. (Although, 53 seems slightly chinsed on space and doesn't have a tree, and 54 is a little close to the basketball court.) Pull-throughs 44–52 and back-ins 23–35 are personal favorites due to their semi-isolated feeling and good trees. The rest rooms are immaculate and beautiful, with nice tiling and decorations. Showers have inner and outer doors for added privacy, and are spacious enough for anyone. A sign in the rest rooms asks guests to report any problems to management, and you can tell that these folks are on top of things. Tenters, unfortunately, don't fare quite as well, and the concrete slabs that pass for tent sites (ouch!) might as well be converted to RV sites for all they're worth. Tent campers should skip this park. However, anyone with an RV who is passing through Colorado should make a point to check out this park—it is what an RV park is supposed to be!

Basics

Operated By: RV Resorts Co. **Open:** All year. **Site Assignment:** Assigned upon registration. Credit card required for reservation; 24-hours cancellation policy. **Registration:** In office. (Late arrivals use drop box.) **Fee:** RV $26–33, tent $28 (V, MC, AE, D). **Parking:** At site.

Facilities

Number of RV Sites: 139. **Number of Tent-Only Sites:** 0. **Hookups:** Water, sewer, electric (20, 30, 50 amps). **Each Site:** Picnic table, grill. **Dump Station:** Yes. **Laundry:** Yes. **Pay Phone:** Yes. **Rest Rooms and Showers:** Yes. **Fuel:** No. **Propane:** Yes. **Internal Roads:** Perfect paved. **RV Service:** Can call. **Market:** 0.5 mi. east. **Restaurant:** 0.5 mi. east (cafe on-site). **General Store:** Yes. **Vending:** Yes. **Swimming:** Pool. **Playground:** Yes. **Other:** Dog walk area, TV room, e-mail booth, exercise room, kitchen, nightly movies in summer, RV supplies. **Activities:** Hiking, wine-tasting, swimming, volleyball, horseshoes, pancake breakfasts, ice cream socials, fishing, golf, crafts. **Nearby Attractions:** Colorado National Monument, Dionosaur National Monument, Dinosaur Trail, Grand Mesa, wineries. **Additional Information:** Grand Junction Visitor & Convention Bureau, (800) 962-2547 or (970) 244-1480.

Restrictions

Pets: On leash, cleaned up after. **Fires:** In fire pits. **Alcoholic Beverages:** At sites. **Vehicle Maximum Length:** None. **Other:** No generators, no kennels, no clotheslines, no vehicle washing.

To Get There

From I-70, take Exit 30 onto the I-70 Business Loop. Go-0.75 mi. southwest, then turn right at the light onto F Rd. and take the first (sharp) right turn behind the Park-Ride. Drive 0.1 mi. and take the first left into the entrance.

GRAND LAKE

Elk Creek Campground

143 CR 48 (Golf Course Rd.) P.O. Box 549, Grand Lake 80447. T: (800) ELK-CREEK or (970) 627-8502; F: (970) 627-5456; www.coloradodirectory.com; elkcreek@rkymtnhi.com.

RV ★★★★ Tent ★★★★

Beauty: ★★★★	Site Privacy: ★★★★
Spaciousness: ★★★★	Quiet: ★★★★
Security: ★★★★	Cleanliness: ★★★★★
Insect Control: ★★★★	Facilities: ★★★★★

Located in a very rural area just outside of town, this campground has campsites laid out in a loop that extends almost into the forest. As a result, most sites are well-shaded. (Sites 1–3 and 27–33 are on the edge of a clearing and are therefore less shaded.) All sites are back-ins, averaging 45 feet in length, with little variation. Sites 20 and even numbers 34–40 are located at the foot of a forested hill, which makes these sites somewhat more attractive. Site 42 is by far the most secluded site, set well into the forest at the far end of the internal road loop. Tent sites are located across the Elk River opposite the playground. The management is planning to build more cabins, however, and these sites may no longer be available. The rec room is extremely cozy, and contains comfortable sofas as well as cable TV. The rest rooms are spic-and-span. The showers are individual unisex units just outside the rest rooms. While clean, they are extremely narrow, a little dark, and almost intimidating. Otherwise, this campground is a wonderful destination for any camper, along or with a family.

Basics

Operated By: Linda Stanley. **Open:** All year. **Site Assignment:** Assigned upon registration; reservations recommended. Credit card required for reservation; cancellation required by noon the day before a scheduled stay. **Registration:** In office. (Late arrivals select an available site & pay in the morning.) **Fee:** RV $25 (full), $23 (water, electric), tent $20 (checks, V, MC, D, AE). **Parking:** At site.

Facilities

Number of RV Sites: 50. **Number of Tent-Only Sites:** Undesignated sites. **Hookups:** Water, sewer, electric (30, 50 amps). **Each Site:** Picnic table, grill, fire pit. **Dump Station:** Yes. **Laundry:** Yes. **Pay Phone:** Yes. **Rest Rooms and Showers:** Yes. **Fuel:** No. **Propane:** Yes. **Internal Roads:** Gravel. **RV Service:** No. **Market:** 0.5 mi. toward Grand Lake. **Restaurant:** 0.75 mi. toward Grand Lake. **General Store:** Yes. **Vending:** No. **Swimming:** No. **Playground:** Yes. **Other:** 14 cabins, game room, rec room (w/ cable TV & pool table), dataport, RV supplies, fishing pond. **Activities:** Fishing, boating, swimming, hiking, golfing, horseback riding, hunting, snowmobiling, tennis, horseshoes, volleyball. **Nearby Attractions:** Rocky Mountain National Park. **Additional Information:** Grand Lake Chamber of Commerce, (970) 627-3402.

Restrictions

Pets: On leash, cleaned up after. **Fires:** In grills. **Alcoholic Beverages:** At sites. **Vehicle Maximum Length:** None. **Other:** No pets or food in game room or rec room.

To Get There

From the junction of Hwy. 278 and Hwy. 34, turn north onto Hwy. 34 and go 0.25 mi. Turn west onto CR 48 (Golf Course Rd.) and go 0.2 mi. Turn right at the sign into the entrance.

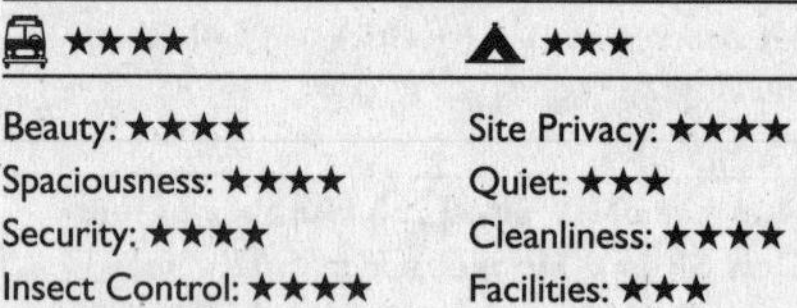

GREELEY

Greeley Campground and RV Park

501 East 27 St., Greeley 80631. T: (970) 353-6476; www.greeleyrvpark.com.

RV ★★★★ Tent ★★★

Beauty: ★★★★	Site Privacy: ★★★★
Spaciousness: ★★★★	Quiet: ★★★
Security: ★★★★	Cleanliness: ★★★★
Insect Control: ★★★★	Facilities: ★★★

Made up of uniform 65-foot pull-throughs, this campground offers many shaded sites and a comfortable environment. The western side of the campground is more shaded than the east. Many sites have a cement pad for picnicking, although some (especially towards the southwest) do not. Sites 2–12 along the north side face a row of vegetation, offering a very pleasant view. This row, and perhaps the row immediately to the south (60–71), is the nicest area in the park due to the large amount of shade and the view. There is a storage unit by sites 2 and 71 that makes these sites less desirable. Site 15, on the other hand, has exceptionally attractive landscaping (including flowers and a section of fence) that makes it the prettiest site in the park. The row containing sites 39–52 is closest to the highway, and therefore a less desirable place to camp. The tenting area is lcoated to the east of the office, and consists of a large grassy area with two huge shade trees. This area is even closer to the highway than the closest row of RV sites. The rest rooms and showers are aging slightly, but are very clean. This campground provides a pretty location for campers who wish to explore the Greeley area, and is very convenient for longer rigs.

Basics

Operated By: Marlin & Shirley Ness. **Open:** All year. **Site Assignment:** Assigned upon registration Credit card required for reservation; 24-hours cancellation policy. **Registration:** In office. (Late arrivals use drop box.) **Fee:** RV $23.50 (full, 50 amps), $21.50 (full, 30 amps), tent $13 (checks, V, MC). **Parking:** At site, plenty of extra parking.

Facilities

Number of RV Sites: 95. **Number of Tent-Only Sites:** 10. **Hookups:** Water, sewer, electric (30, 50 amps). **Each Site:** Picnic table. **Dump Station:** No (sewer at all sites). **Laundry:** Yes. **Pay Phone:** Yes. **Rest Rooms and Showers:** Yes. **Fuel:** No. **Propane:** Yes. **Internal Roads:** Paved. **RV Service:** No. **Market:** 1 mi. west. **Restaurant:** 1 mi. west. **General Store:** Yes. **Vending:** Yes. **Swimming:** No. **Playground:** No. **Other:** RV parts, dataport, woodworking shop, dog walk area, cabins. **Activities:** Hiking, woodworking. **Nearby Attractions:** Pawnee Grasslands, Centennial Village, Greeley Independence Stampede (July 4th). **Additional Information:** Greeley/Weld Chamber of Commerce, (970) 352-3566.

Restrictions

Pets: On leash, cleaned up after, small pets only. **Fires:** In grills. **Alcoholic Beverages:** At sites. **Vehicle Maximum Length:** None. **Other:** Adult-oriented.

To Get There

From the junction of Hwy. 85 and Hwy. 34 (Fort Morgan Exit), turn east onto Hwy. 34 and go 0.6 mi. Turn north at the blue trailer sign onto an unmarked road. Turn right at the sign into the entrance.

GUNNISON

Gunnison KOA

105 CR 50, Gunnison 81230. T: (800) 562-1248 or (970) 641-1358; F: (970) 641-5329; www.koa.com.

RV ★★★★ Tent ★★★

Beauty: ★★★★ Site Privacy: ★★★★
Spaciousness: ★★★ Quiet: ★★★★
Security: ★★★★ Cleanliness: ★★★★★
Insect Control: ★★★★ Facilities: ★★★★★

This campground on the southwest side of town features level, grassy sites laid out on two loops. The rural location and the attractive decor make for a pleasant camping experience. There is a farm to the southwest, and cars are greeted by curious geese upon entry. The interior spaces of the loops are large enough that vehicles of any size can park on the sites (which average 75 feet long). Except for the lack of shade, most sites are extremely nice. RV sites E-H are very close to the playground, which some campers may wish to avoid. Tent areas are grassy, with some large trees to the northeast. While the RV experience would be improved with more trees, this campground is pleasant enough to warrant a return visit. Tenters will likewise be pleased.

Basics

Operated By: Norman & Karen. **Open:** Apr. 15–Nov. 1. **Site Assignment:** Assigned upon registration. Credit card required for reservation; 24-hours cancellation policy. **Registration:** In office. (Late arrivals use drop box.) **Fee:** RV $21–27, tent $18 (V, MC, AE, D). **Parking:** At site.

Facilities

Number of RV Sites: 126. **Number of Tent-Only Sites:** 0. **Hookups:** Water, sewer, electric (30, 50 amps). **Each Site:** Picnic table, grill. **Dump Station:** Yes. **Laundry:** Yes. **Pay Phone:** Yes. **Rest Rooms and Showers:** Yes. **Fuel:** No. **Propane:** Yes. **Internal Roads:** Gravel. **RV Service:** Can call. **Market:** 1.5 mi. **Restaurant:** 1 mi. **General Store:** Yes. **Vending:** Yes. **Swimming:** No. **Playground:** Yes. **Other:** Trout pond, covered picnic area, pet walk area, cabins. **Activities:** Fishing, golf, hunting, ATV riding. **Nearby Attractions:** Aspen trees at Kebler Pass, Curecanti National Recreation Area. **Additional Information:** Gunnison Chamber of Commerce, (800) 274-7580 or (970) 641-1501.

Restrictions

Pets: On leash, cleaned up after. **Fires:** In fire pits. **Alcoholic Beverages:** At sites. **Vehicle Maximum Length:** None. **Other:** No clotheslines, no vehicle washing/maintenance.

To Get There

From the junction of Hwy. 135 and US 50, go 1.6 mi. west on Hwy. 50. Turn south onto CR 38 (just east of the bridge across the street). Go 0.5 mi., then turn right after the sign. Take the first right into the entrance. The office is on the right.

HOTCHKISS

Mountain Valley Meadows RV Park

1083 Hwy. 133 P.O. Box 893, Hotchkiss 81419. T: (800) 782-4037 or (970) 872-2351; F: (970) 872-4961; www.mountainvalleymeadows.com; mrvpark@aol.com.

RV ★★★ Tent ★★

Beauty: ★★★ Site Privacy: ★★★
Spaciousness: ★★★★ Quiet: ★★★★
Security: ★★★★ Cleanliness: ★★★
Insect Control: ★★★★ Facilities: ★★

This campground offers 54-foot grassy back-ins in a loop, with a 40-foot space at each site for an extra vehicle. Sites 15–17 at the end of the loop back to woods to the west and a fence to the rear. They feel slightly apart from the other sites, and have an incomparable view of the mountains to the east (as do 28–30). Sites 21 and 24 are at the corner of two internal roads, and may receive more traffic due to this location. Long-term residents occupy several of the RV sites. Tent sites are to the southeast of the RV sites in a strip, on either side of the internal road. While these sites have gorgeous grass, there is no shade to protect from the sun or rain. Site T2 is less desirable due to a dumpster that encroaches on it. The rest rooms have composting, non-flush toilets and curtained-off showers that are extremely clean. This is a worthwhile campground for either tenters or RVers, although RVers may find it slightly more comfortable.

Basics

Operated By: Private operator. **Open:** All year. **Site Assignment:** First come, first served. **Registration:** In office. (Late arrivals use drop box.) **Fee:** RV $18.90 (full), $15.75 (water, electric), tent $10.50 (V, MC, D). **Parking:** At site.

Facilities

Number of RV Sites: 30. **Number of Tent-Only Sites:** 5. **Hookups:** Water, sewer, electric (30, 50 amps). **Each Site:** Picnic table, fire ring. **Dump Station:** Yes. **Laundry:** Yes. **Pay Phone:** Yes. **Rest Rooms and Showers:** Yes. **Fuel:** No. **Propane:** No. **Internal Roads:** Gravel/dirt. **RV Service:** No. **Market:** No. **Restaurant:** No. **General Store:** No. **Vending:** No. **Swimming:** No. **Playground:** Yes. **Other:** Well water. **Activities:** Hiking, fishing, hunting, boating, swimming. **Nearby Attractions:** Gunnison National Forest, Crawford State Park, Gunnison Gorge National Conservation Area. **Additional Information:** Delta Chamber of Commerce, (970) 874-8616.

Restrictions

Pets: On leash, cleaned up after. **Fires:** In fire pits. **Alcoholic Beverages:** At sites. **Vehicle Maximum Length:** None.

To Get There

From the junction of Hwy. 92 and Hwy. 133, turn east onto Hwy. 133 and go 1 mi. Turn left at the sign into the entrance. The office is the first building on the left.

HUDSON

Pepper Pod KOA

P.O. Box 445, Hudson 80642. T: (303) 536-4763 or (303) 536-9554; www.koa.com; koahudson@qwest.net.

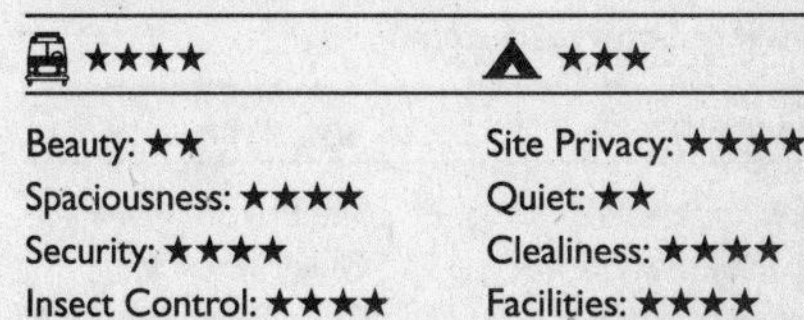

RV ★★★★ Tent ★★★

Beauty: ★★ Site Privacy: ★★★★
Spaciousness: ★★★★ Quiet: ★★
Security: ★★★★ Clealiness: ★★★★
Insect Control: ★★★★ Facilities: ★★★★

Laid out as a square with rows on the inside and sites ringing the perimter, this campground is adjacent to some industrial and commercial areas, and it has a definite urban feel. There is a railroad that passes to the east of the campground. Sites to the northwest (especially 19 and 29) have the most industrial views, and are less attractive as a result. Sites 2–10 are 30-foot back-ins on thick grass that is even better than the grass in the tenting area. Site 2 is directly next to the trash dumpster and the RV dump, and is the least desirable site. The row containing 32–39 is perhaps the nicest section, as it is furthest from the highway and the residences around the park. Sites 42 and 52 are adjacent to the manager's residence, and sites 52–59 border an external residential area. The tenting area occupies the entire western side of the campground. There is sparse vegetation covering the ground, and little shade except in the northwest corner. The camper kitchen did not have running water at the time of this review. This is an acceptable overnight campground, but neither the area nor the campground itself present any reason to make a special trip out.

Basics

Operated By: Neal Pontius. **Open:** All year. **Site Assignment:** Assigned upon registration Credit card required for reservation; 24-hours cancellation policy. **Registration:** In office. (Late arrivals use drop box.) **Fee:** RV $27 (full), $23 (water, electric), tent $18 (checks, V, MC, D). **Parking:** At site.

Facilities

Number of RV Sites: 65. **Number of Tent-Only Sites:** 10. **Hookups:** Water, sewer, electric (20, 30, 50 amps). **Each Site:** Picnic table, grill. **Dump Station:** Yes. **Laundry:** Yes. **Pay Phone:** Yes. **Rest Rooms and Showers:** Yes. **Fuel:** No. **Propane:** Yes. **Internal Roads:** Gravel. **RV Service:** No. **Market:** 18 mi. to Brighton. **Restaurant:** 1 block. **General Store:** Yes. **Vending:** No. **Swimming:** Pool. **Playground:** Yes. **Other:** 2 cabins, game room, pet walk, dataport, community building. **Activities:** Swimming, meetings, volleyball, touring Denver. **Nearby Attractions:** Denver. **Additional Information:** Fort Lupton Chamber of Commerce, (303) 857-4474.

Restrictions

Pets: On leash, cleaned up after. **Fires:** In grills. **Alcoholic Beverages:** At sites. **Vehicle Maximum Length:** 65 ft.

To Get There

From I-76 (Exit 33), turn east onto Hwy. 52 and go 0.1 mi., then turn right and go 0.2 mi. Turn left at the sign into the entrance. The office is on the right.

KREMMLING

Red Mountain RV Park

P.O. Box 1267, Kremmling 80459. T: (970) 724-9593 or (877) 375-9593; www.redmtnrvpark.com.

RV ★★★ Tent ★★★

Beauty: ★★★	Site Privacy: ★★★
Spaciousness: ★★★	Quiet: ★★★★
Security: ★★★★	Cleanliness: ★★★★★
Insect Control: ★★★★	Facilities: ★★★★

The presence or abscence of trees in this park will make or break your stay—at least in summer. Sites 1–10 are shaded 54-foot gravel pull-throughs laid out horizontally to the highway. The dump station is right at site 10, making this site less desirable. The rest of the sites, however, are entirely unshaded. In effect, this park consists of hookups set around a large, open gravel space. To the north are long-term residents and RV storage. There is a baseball field to the east and a large antenna to the west. The sites that have grass (mostly towards the north) are in large part overgrown. The tent area is a cordoned-off section of thick grass that has two covered picnic tables. This area is nice, but only large enough to comfortably fit about 6 tents. The rest rooms and showers are very clean and roomy enough. They are often used by hunters who only pass through for a shower. For campers who wish to stay and explore the area, this park is a pleasant stay.

Basics

Operated By: Jeff & Sara Miller. **Open:** All year. **Site Assignment:** Flexible, depending on site availability. Credit card required for reservation; 24-hours cancellation policy. **Registration:** In office. (Late arrivals select an available site & pay in the morning.) **Fee:** RV $19 (full), tent $12 (checks, V, MC, & D). **Parking:** At site.

Facilities

Number of RV Sites: 45. **Number of Tent-Only Sites:** Undesignated sites. **Hookups:** Water, sewer, electric (30, 50 amps). **Each Site:** Picnic table. **Dump Station:** Yes. **Laundry:** Yes. **Pay Phone:** Yes. **Rest Rooms and Showers:** Yes. **Fuel:** No. **Propane:** Yes. **Internal Roads:** Gravel. **RV Service:** No. **Market:** 1 mi. west. **Restaurant:** 1 mi. west. **General Store:** Yes. **Vending:** Yes. **Swimming:** No. **Playground:** Yes. **Other:** Dataport, lounge, RV storage. **Activities:** Hunting, fishing, hiking. **Nearby Attractions:** Rocky Mountain National Park, Steamboat Springs. **Additional Information:** Kremmling Area Chamber of Commerce, (970) 724-3472.

Restrictions

Pets: On leash, cleaned up after. **Fires:** In grills. **Alcoholic Beverages:** At sites. **Vehicle Maximum Length:** None.

To Get There

From the junction of Hwy. 9 and Hwy. 40, turn east onto Hwy. 40 and go 1 mi. Turn north onto CR 22 and go 1 block. Turn right at the sign into the entrance.

LA JUNTA

La Junta KOA

26680 West Hwy. 50, La Junta 81050. T: (800) 562-9501 or (719) 384-9580; F: (719) 384-5221; www.koa.com.

RV ★★★★ Tent ★★★

Beauty: ★★	Site Privacy: ★★★
Spaciousness: ★★★★	Quiet: ★★★
Security: ★★★★	Cleanliness: ★★★★
Insect Control: ★★★★	Facilities: ★★★★

Pull-throughs in this campground range from 30 feet to 60 feet in length, and all are very level, grassy, and open. End sites 31, 41, and 49 are at the small end of this scale, making them slightly less desirable. The best RV site is 25, as it contains large shade trees on both sides. This is an important consideration, as most sites (and most campgrounds in the area) have very little shade. Site 49 comes in second thanks to a single towering shade tree. Tenters have it a little nicer with regards to shade. The strip of tent sites at the north end of the campground (just off the highway, unfortunately) and to the west of the pool have a line of overarching trees that protect tenters from the sun's rays. The earth is quite hard here, however, and the sites receive a fair amount of traffic noise. The group tenting area at the extreme south end of the campground does not have shade trees like the strip at the north end, and is therefore not quite as nice. The rest room facility is a little small but quite clean. The shower curtains and floors look dated, but the facility is otherwise comfortable. The laundry room is clean and roomy, and open 24 hours. RVers will enjoy this campground, but tenters may want to push on.

Basics

Operated By: Hank & Margy Rogers. **Open:** All year. **Site Assignment:** Assigned upon registration Credit card required for reservation; 24-hours cancellation policy. **Registration:** In office. (Late arrivals). **Fee:** RV $24.50 (full, 30 amps), $26.50 (full, 50 amps), $23.50 (water, electric), tent $18 (V, MC, D). **Parking:** At site; additional lots.

Facilities

Number of RV Sites: 52. **Number of Tent-Only Sites:** 5. **Hookups:** Water, sewer, electric (30, 50 amps), cable. **Each Site:** Picnic table, tree or shrub. **Dump Station:** Yes. **Laundry:** Yes. **Pay Phone:** Yes. **Rest Rooms and Showers:** Yes. **Fuel:** No. **Propane:** Yes. **Internal Roads:** Gravel. **RV Service:** No. **Market:** 0.2 mi. west (limited on site). **Restaurant:** 0.2 mi. west. **General Store:** Yes. **Vending:** Yes. **Swimming:** Pool. **Playground:** Yes. **Other:** Meeting room, dog walk area, pool table, covered patio, dataport. **Activities:** Fishing, golf, boating, horseshoes, video games. **Nearby Attractions:** Bent's Fort. **Additional Information:** La Junta Chamber of Commerce, (719) 384-7411.

Restrictions

Pets: On leash, cleaned up after, max. of 2 (small) dogs. **Fires:** In grills only. **Alcoholic Beverages:** At sites. **Vehicle Maximum Length:** None.

To Get There

From the junction of Hwy. 10 and Hwy. 50, go 1.5 mi. west on Hwy. 50. Turn left at the sign into the entrance. Keep straight to enter the campground. The office is on the left.

LA VETA

Circle the Wagons RV Park and Motel

124 North Main St., P.O. Box 122, La Veta 81055. T: (719) 742-3233.

RV ★★ Tent ★

Beauty: ★★	Site Privacy: ★★★
Spaciousness: ★★★	Quiet: ★★
Security: ★★★★	Cleanliness: ★★★
Insect Control: ★★★	Facilities: ★★★

This campground is divided into two parks, with a much different experience depending on which campground you stay at. The main campground (where the office is located) has much more of an urban feel to it. The pull-throughs near the office are 75 feet long, while the internal road is so wide that any rig can manoeuvre within it, and even stick out from any site. End sites 63 and 56 have trees and grass in a strip that effectively adds 10–15 feet to their site width. (Most other sites have neither grass nor trees.) Back-ins 49–53 back to undeveloped land with hills in the distance, making them more scenic, while 42–48 back to a residential area, which lessens their appeal. 55, by the bathhouse, is a pull-through that could take a rig of any size and has grass and extra width. The facilities are clean but unremarkable. Now for the park's better half. The west campground is much prettier and even cleaner than the east campground. All sites are grassy, the campground is surrounded by trees, and there are views of hills and distant peaks. The best of these 60-foot back-ins are probably 10 and 12, which are near the pond, with decent trees, and even 1, which is by the entrance but has great trees and perhaps a little more space. The rest rooms and laundry facilities are much nicer, and there is even a small sitting area with books in the same building. Unless a pull-through is absolutely necessary, be sure to get a space in the western campground. The road leading in is on the rough side (drive slowly!), but once you're in, you'll be happier than in the east side park.

BASICS

Operated By: Lonnie Hawkins. **Open:** All year. **Site Assignment:** First come, first served; verbal reservations OK. **Registration:** In office; inform management if staying multiple nights. (Late arrivals ring bell.) **Fee:** Pull-through: $20, tent $12 (V, MC, AE, D, DC, CB). **Parking:** At site.

FACILITIES

Number of RV Sites: 63. **Number of Tent-Only Sites:** 0. **Hookups:** Water, sewer, electric (30, 50 amps), cable. **Each Site:** Picnic table. **Dump Station:** No (sewer at all sites). **Laundry:** Yes. **Pay Phone:** Yes. **Rest Rooms and Showers:** Yes. **Fuel:** No. **Propane:** No. **Internal Roads:** Gravel. **RV Service:** Small repairs possible. **Market:** Next door. **Restaurant:** On site. **General Store:** No. **Vending:** Yes. **Swimming:** No. **Playground:** No. **Other:** Dance hall, children's fishing pond, gift shop, clubhouse, special events room. **Activities:** Scenic drives, horseracing, horseshoes. **Nearby Attractions:** La Mesa horse track, Royal Gorge, Highway of Legends Scenic Byway, Great Sand Dunes National Monument. **Additional Information:** La Veta/Cuchara Chamber of Commerce, (719) 742-3676.

RESTRICTIONS

Pets: On leash, cleaned up after. **Fires:** In fire rings. **Alcoholic Beverages:** At sites. **Vehicle Maximum Length:** None.

TO GET THERE

From the junction of Hwy. 160 and Hwy. 12, go 4.3 mi. south on Hwy. 12, turn right at the sign into the entrance. (The entrance to the second part of the campground is on the left side of Main St., south of 1st St.)

LAKE CITY

Lake Fork Campground and RV Resort

P.O. Box 1086, Lake City 81235. T: (970) 944-9519 or (970) 944-2217.

RV ★★★ Tent ★★★

Beauty: ★★★★	Site Privacy: ★★★★
Spaciousness: ★★★	Quiet: ★★★★
Security: ★★★★	Cleanliness: ★★★
Insect Control: ★★★	Facilities: ★★★

Beautiful views of mounatins to the southwest, a river to the east, and plenty of trees around and inside the park make this campground a serene rural escape. The proximity to downtown makes it a convenient stop for motorists who wish to relax in town for a day or an evening. While sites are a little on the narrow side (20 feet wide), some are doubles that can pass as super-long (90-foot) pull-throughs if the opposite site is unoccupied. The rest rooms are clean, spacious, and still comfortable, though old. Showers have a curtained off changing area that adds to the privacy, although accessing the second shower stall requires walking through the first. The best RV sites are 21–24 on the east side, facing trees, a garden, and wooded hills. These sites also have lots of trees and are close to the rest room facilities. Tent sites would be better if they were grassy, not gravel. Please note that this campground has recently come under new management, and some policies (such as reservations and cancellations) had not been established before we went to press.

BASICS

Operated By: Charles Sansing, Cecil Bergerson. **Open:** June–Sept. 6. **Site Assignment:** Flexible, depending on availability. Check required for reservation. **Registration:** In office. (Late arrivals settle in morning.) **Fee:** RV $22, tent $17.50 (checks, no credit cards). **Parking:** At site.

FACILITIES

Number of RV Sites: 23. **Number of Tent-Only Sites:** 3. **Hookups:** Water, sewer, electric (30 amps). **Each Site:** Overturned cable spool for table, fencing, tree. **Dump Station:** No (sewer at all sites). **Laundry:** Yes. **Pay Phone:** Yes. **Rest Rooms and Showers:** Yes. **Fuel:** No. **Propane:** No. **Internal Roads:** Gravel. **RV Service:** No. **Market:** 2 block (limited). **Restaurant:** 1 block. **General Store:** No. **Vending:** Yes. **Swimming:** No. **Playground:** No. **Activities:** Fishing, mountain climbing, hiking, cross-country skiing. **Nearby Attractions:** Uncompahgre Peak, Lake San Cristobal, Lake Fork. **Additional Information:** Lake City Chamber of Commerce, (800) 569-1874 or (970) 944-2527.

RESTRICTIONS

Pets: On leash, cleaned up after. **Fires:** In fire pits. **Alcoholic Beverages:** At sites. **Vehicle Maximum Length:** 40 ft.

TO GET THERE

From Hensen Creek Bridge at the south edge of town, go 1 block north on Hwy. 149. Turn right at the sign for the museum onto 2nd St. Take the first right onto Hensen St., and follow the signs to the office at the south end of the park.

LAKEWOOD

Bear Creek Lake Campground

15600 West Morrison Rd., Morrison 80465. T: (303) 697-6159.

RV ★★★★ Tent ★★★★

Beauty: ★★★★	Site Privacy: ★★★★
Spaciousness: ★★★★	Quiet: ★★★★
Security: ★★★★	Cleanliness: ★★★★
Insect Control: ★★★	Facilities: ★★★★

Almost appearing out of place, this campground is in a desert-like field with few trees and low, sparse vegetation. Sites are mostly dirt, with some vegetation cover. The campground is at the far southeast end of the park. The electric sites (more suitable for RVs) are on a hill overlooking the primitive sites. Sites are laid out in rows of roughly five units. Sites 13–16 are closest to the railroad that passes by the park, and are therefore less desirable. Of the primitive sites, 45–49 are extremely long (100–105-foot) pull-throughs. Others are quite long (65–70-foot) back-ins. Sites 65–70 are located just off the internal raod, making them more susceptible to passing vehicular traffic. Walk-in tent sites are found to the northeast of the RV sites. These are surrounded by both fences and trees. This is a nice, wild campground located surprisingly close to the highway to Denver. It is a welcome relief from the busy city, that most campers should enjoy.

BASICS

Operated By: Lakewood Community Resources. **Open:** Apr. 1–Oct. 31. **Site Assignment:** First come, first served; no reservations. **Registration:** At pay station. **Fee:** Electric: $10, primitive: $7 (checks). **Parking:** At site.

FACILITIES

Number of RV Sites: 52. **Number of Tent-Only Sites:** 0. **Hookups:** Electric (20, 30, 50 amps). **Each Site:** Picnic table, grill, fire pit. **Dump Station:** No. **Laundry:** No. **Pay Phone:** Yes. **Rest Rooms and Showers:** Yes. **Fuel:** No. **Propane:** No. **Internal Roads:** Paved/gravel. **RV Service:** No. **Market:** 3 mi. east. **Restaurant:** 0.5 mi. into Morrison. **General Store:** Marina. **Vending:** No. **Swimming:** Lake. **Playground:** Yes. **Other:** Amphitheater, swim beach, picnic areas, horse rentals, archery range, boat rentals, boat ramp, yurt. **Activities:** Fishing, boating, swimming, hiking, volleyball. **Nearby Attractions:** Denver. **Additional Information:** Denver Chamber of Commerce, (303) 458-0220.

RESTRICTIONS

Pets: On 6-ft. leash, cleaned up after. **Fires:** In grills. **Alcoholic Beverages:** At sites. **Vehicle Maximum Length:** None. **Other:** $3/vehicle/day.

TO GET THERE

From the junction of Hwy. 470 (Bear Creek Lake Exit), turn east onto Hwy. 8. Go 1 mi. Turn right at the sign into the entrance.

LAMAR

Lamar KOA

5385 Hwy. 50, Lamar 81052. T: (800) KOA-7626 or (719) 336-7625; www.koa.com.

RV ★★★★ Tent ★★★

Beauty: ★★★	Site Privacy: ★★★
Spaciousness: ★★★	Quiet: ★★★
Security: ★★★★	Cleanliness: ★★★★
Insect Control: ★★★★	Facilities: ★★★★

This campground has all pull-throughs laid out in rows, with level grassy sites. Like other campgrounds in the area, the sites are open with little shade. There is, however, a row of dense trees to the north that blocks off views of a residential area, and provides some shade to campers in those sites. Otherwise, there are very few trees or bushes in the campground itself. Sites average 24 feet wide and

60–70 feet in length. The best sites for RVers are the end sites 10, 16, and 21. These sites are significantly wider than the others, are closest to the row of trees, and furthest from the highway. (End sites 31 and 43 are also wide, but not as close to the trees.) Tent sites are located in Row A and the southwest section of Row F. Row A is wide open, with no shade at all. These are less desirable sites than those in Row F. Sites in Row F (33–37) have a decent grass covering and, even more important, a half-covering over the picnic tables, which affords campers at these sites more shade than nearly any other sites. The rest rooms and showers are very clean, well-lit, and modern, as is the laundry facility. This is probably the nicest campground in the area, and campers should make a note to head here when in southeast Colorado.

Basics

Operated By: Bill Rich. **Open:** All year (limited facilities in winter). **Site Assignment:** Flexible, depending on availability. Credit card required for reservation; same-day cancellation policy. **Registration:** In office. (Late arrivals use drop box.) **Fee:** RV $25 (full), $23 (water, electric), tent $18. **Parking:** At site.

Facilities

Number of RV Sites: 28. **Number of Tent-Only Sites:** 15. **Hookups:** Water, sewer, electric (20, 30 amps). **Each Site:** Picnic table (half are covered), grill. **Dump Station:** Yes. **Laundry:** Yes. **Pay Phone:** Yes. **Rest Rooms and Showers:** Yes. **Fuel:** No. **Propane:** Yes. **Internal Roads:** Gravel. **RV Service:** No. **Market:** 5 mi. southeast. **Restaurant:** 1 mi. southeast. **General Store:** Yes. **Vending:** No. **Swimming:** Pool. **Playground:** Yes. **Other:** Mini golf, dog walk area, cabin, outdoor patio. **Activities:** Hunting, fishing, golf, video games. **Nearby Attractions:** Big Timbers Museum, Madonna of the Trail, Arkansas River, Bent's Old Fort. **Additional Information:** Lamar Chamber of Commerce, (719) 336-4379.

Restrictions

Pets: On leash, cleaned up after. **Fires:** In grills only. **Alcoholic Beverages:** At sites. **Vehicle Maximum Length:** None. **Other:** Children under 7 must be accompanied by an adult in the swimming pool.

To Get There

From the junction of Hwy. 50 and Hwy. 287 (Olive and Main Sts. in town), go 4.3 mi. northwest on Hwy. 50/287. Turn right at the sign into the entrance. The office is on the left.

LEADVILLE

Leadville RV Corral

135 West 2nd St., Leadville 80461. T: (719) 486-3111.

RV ★★★ Tent ★★★

Beauty: ★★	Site Privacy: ★★★
Spaciousness: ★★★	Quiet: ★★★
Security: ★★★★	Cleanliness: ★★★★
Insect Control: ★★★★	Facilities: ★★★

Within walking distance to downtown, this campground offers a convenient place to stay the night while visiting the Leadville area. However, spacious and beautifully landscaped it is not. This is a rather urban overnighter, with uniform 45-foot spaces laid out in a ring around the perimeter, surrounded by residences and semi-industrial lots surrounding it. All sites are gravel, but most have a grassy strip for picnicking located next to the drive. (Sites 1 and 2 do not.) Sites 1–8 are back-ins; all the rest of the sites are pull-throughs. Sites 17 and 33 are located along an external road, and are less deisrable for this fact. Sites 1 and 2 double as the entrance and exit, which raises the question of how to get in or out when they are occupied. A tenting area is located next to the office. This is an open, grassy, but rather small area. Three tents could reasonably stay there, and five could probably squeeze in, especially if they were together. The facilities are clean, and the management quite friendly, making this an acceptable location for a stay of a night or two.

Basics

Operated By: Rudy Klucik, Steve Anerson. **Open:** All year. **Site Assignment:** Flexible, depending on site availability. Credit card required for reservation; 24-hours cancellation policy. **Registration:** In office. (Late arrivals use drop box.) **Fee:** RV $23.94 (full), tent $16.32 (checks, V, MC). **Parking:** At site.

Facilities

Number of RV Sites: 33. **Number of Tent-Only Sites:** 5. **Hookups:** Water, sewer, electric (30, 50 amps), cable. **Each Site:** Picnic table, grill. **Dump Station:** Yes. **Laundry:** Yes. **Pay Phone:** Yes. **Rest Rooms and Showers:** Yes. **Fuel:** No. **Propane:** No. **Internal Roads:** Gravel. **RV Service:** No. **Market:** 2 mi. north. **Restaurant:** 2 mi. north. **General Store:** Planned. **Vending:** Yes. **Swimming:** No. **Playground:** No. **Other:** Walking distance to downtown. **Activities:** Fishing, hunting, hiking. **Nearby Attractions:** Boom Days (first weekend in Aug.), 100-mile footrace. **Additional Information:** Leadville Chamber of Commerce, (719) 486-3900.

Restrictions

Pets: No dogs outside. **Fires:** In grills. **Alcoholic Beverages:** At sites. **Vehicle Maximum Length:** 45 ft.

To Get There

From the junction of Hwy. 24 (Harrison) and West 2nd St., turn west onto West 2nd St. and take 2nd parking lot entrance.

LIMON

Limon KOA

575 Colorado Ave., Limon 80828. T: (719) 775-2151; www.koa.com.

RV ★★★ Tent ★★

Beauty: ★★	Site Privacy: ★★★
Spaciousness: ★★★	Quiet: ★★★
Security: ★★★★	Cleanliness: ★★★★
Insect Control: ★★★★	Facilities: ★★★★

Hunkered down in the middle of nowhere, this campground serves mainly overnighters and is not close to any specific attractions for tourists. The land it is located on is likewise mainly devoid of trees and grass, and sites in the campground mostly lack shade. There are residences to the southwest of the campground and storage units to the west, making the area surrounding the campground less than attractive. The row of sites to the north consists of 33-foot back-ins (43–46) and 75-foot pull-throughs (47–59). The row of pull-throughs to the south (1–26) consists of 70-foot sites that face out to the residences and storage facility. Tenting sites in the west end of the park are entirely unshaded, although two sites have shaded picnic tables.

Basics

Operated By: Private operator. **Open:** All year (services are weather-dependent). **Site Assignment:** Assigned upon registration. Credit card required for reservation; 24-hours cancellation policy, less $5 fee. **Registration:** In office. (Late arrivals use drop box.) **Fee:** RV $24.95 (full), $22.95 (water, electric), tent $18.95 (checks, V, MC). **Parking:** At site.

Facilities

Number of RV Sites: 50. **Number of Tent-Only Sites:** 10. **Hookups:** Water, sewer, electric (30, 50 amps), cable. **Each Site:** Picnic tables, grills. **Dump Station:** Yes. **Laundry:** Yes. **Pay Phone:** Yes. **Rest Rooms and Showers:** Yes. **Fuel:** No. **Propane:** No. **Internal Roads:** Dirt. **RV Service:** No. **Market:** Small market 1 mi. east. **Restaurant:** 0.25 mi. towards I-40. **General Store:** Yes. **Vending:** No. **Swimming:** Pool. **Playground:** Yes. **Other:** Cabins, RV supplies, dataport, dog walk. **Activities:** Swimming, fishing (at Bonny State Park), volleyball, basketball. **Nearby Attractions:** Denver, Colorado Springs, Burlington. **Additional Information:** Limon Chamber of Commerce, P.O. Box 101, Limon, Colorado, 80828.

Restrictions

Pets: On leash, cleaned up after; no horses. **Fires:** In fire pits. **Alcoholic Beverages:** At sites. **Vehicle Maximum Length:** None.

To Get There

From I-70 (Exit 361), on the south side of the highway, turn west onto Main St. and go 0.2 mi. Turn right onto Hwy. 24/40/287 and go 0.2 mi. Turn left at the sign into the entrance.

LINDON

Meadowlark Cafe, Motel and RV Park

12120 CR South, Lindon 80740. T: (970) 383-2298.

RV ★★★ Tent ★★

Beauty: ★★	Site Privacy: ★★★
Spaciousness: ★★★★	Quiet: ★★★★★
Security: ★★★★	Cleanliness: ★★★★
Insect Control: ★★★★	Facilities: ★★

This part of Colorado does not, unfortunately, lend itself to tourism in general, and camping specifically. There are no attractions in the immediate area, and this campground (if it can be called that) offers little more than a place to park an RV for the night. (Bonny State Park, the nearest area for recreation, is a good 50 miles distant.) The park consists of one row of hookups in a large, open grassy field, with two other sites located to the east of this row. None of the sites offers shade, but on the positive side, all of these sites can accommodate a rig of any size. There are open fields to the north, west, and east, and a motel and a row of bushes to the south and east. The grain silos to the immediate north are at least something to look at, but many campers here may want to catch up on their reading or television-watching. Outside of such activities, there is, alas, little else to do in this campground.

Basics

Operated By: Doug or Dwayne Bowers. **Open:** All year. **Site Assignment:** Assigned upon registration; verbal reservations OK. **Registration:** In office. (Late arrivals register at night office.) **Fee:** RV $15 (full), tent $8 (checks, V, MC, AE, D). **Parking:** At site.

Facilities

Number of RV Sites: 12. **Number of Tent-Only Sites:** Undesignated sites. **Hookups:** Water, sewer, electric (20, 50 amps). **Dump Station:** Yes. **Laundry:** Yes. **Pay Phone:** Yes. **Rest Rooms and Showers:** Yes. **Fuel:** No. **Propane:** No. **Internal Roads:** Gravel. **RV Service:** No. **Market:** 6 mi. northeast/northwest. **Restaurant:** On site. **General Store:** No. **Vending:** No. **Swimming:** No. **Playground:** No. **Other:** Cafe, motel rooms, pet walk. **Activities:** Swimming, fishing, boating, hunting. **Nearby Attractions:** Bonny State Park. **Additional Information:** Limon Chamber of Commerce, P.O. Box 101, Limon, Colorado, 80828.

Restrictions

Pets: On leash, cleaned up after. **Fires:** In fire pits. **Alcoholic Beverages:** At sites. **Vehicle Maximum Length:** None.

To Get There

From the easternmost town sign on Hwy. 36, go 0.1 mi. west, and take first right onto the dirt road. Follow the road 0.15 mi. to the entrance on the right.

LONGMONT

Barbour Ponds State Park

4995 Weld CR 24 1/2, Longmont 80504.
T: (303) 678-9402; www.coloradoparks.org.

RV: ★★★ Tent: ★★★

Beauty: ★★★ Site Privacy: ★★★★
Spaciousness: ★★★★ Quiet: ★★★
Security: ★★★★ Cleanliness: ★★★
Insect Control: ★★★★ Facilities: ★★★

Divided into the North, West, and East campgrounds, this park offers rather undeveloped sites with both back-ins and pull-throughs. The North Campground is located quite close to I-25, and cannot be recommended due to the amount of traffic noise it receives. Sites in this campground include 40-foot (57–60) to 66-foot back-ins (48–50, 52–54), and 70-foot pull-throughs (46, 47, 51). Many of these sites are well-shaded. The West Campground has 45–54-foot back-ins that lie closest to the water. Some of these sites are right on the banks of the ponds. Furthest west, the unattractive view of mines to the south opens up. The views to the north, however, are much nicer. The East Campground has several tent sites in a stand of trees right at the entrance (site 28). Other sites are 45-foot back-ins, and many of these are unshaded. Facilities are limited to pit toilets (no showers). This is a pleasant but rather small state park that attracts mostly fishermen and does not offer much in terms of facilities or activities.

Basics

Operated By: Colorado State Parks. **Open:** All year. **Site Assignment:** First come, first served; reservations available Memorial Day–Labor Day. Credit card required for reservation; 3 days cancellation policy. **Registration:** At pay kiosk. **Fee:** $10 (checks, no credits cards). **Parking:** At site, lots of extra parking.

Facilities

Number of RV Sites: 60. **Number of Tent-Only Sites:** 0. **Hookups:** None. **Each Site:** Picnic table, grill, fire pit, tent pad. **Dump Station:** No. **Laundry:** No. **Pay Phone:** No. **Rest Rooms and Showers:** Rest rooms; no shower. **Fuel:** No. **Propane:** Rest rooms, but no showers. **Internal Roads:** Dirt. **RV Service:** No. **Market:** less than 10 mi. to 17th & Pace Sts. **Restaurant:** 3 mi. to I-25. **General Store:** No. **Vending:** No. **Swimming:** No. **Playground:** Yes. **Other:** Firewood, nature trails, wildlife, views of Rocky Mountains, covered picnic areas. **Activities:** Non-motorized boating, fishing. **Nearby Attractions:** Denver, Boulder, Rocky Mountain National Park. **Additional Information:** Boulder CVB, (303) 442-2911.

Restrictions

Pets: On 6-ft. leash, cleaned up after. **Fires:** In fire pits. **Alcoholic Beverages:** At sites. **Vehicle Maximum Length:** None. **Other:** Pack out trash, $4 entrance fee, no swimming, no bills larger than $20.

To Get There

From the junction of Hwy. I-25 (Exit 240), turn west onto Hwy. 179 and go 1.1 mi. Turn right onto Rd. 7 and go 1.3 mi. to the entrance.

LOVELAND

Carter Valley Campground

1326 North Carter Lake Rd., Loveland 80537.
T: (970) 663-3131.

RV: ★★★★ Tent: ★★★

Beauty: ★★★★ Site Privacy: ★★★
Spaciousness: ★★★ Quiet: ★★★★
Security: ★★★★ Cleanliness: ★★★★★
Insect Control: ★★★★ Facilities: ★★★

Sites in this campground are laid out in rows on three tiers up a hillside. The campground is surrounded by farms, and there are forests and mountains to the northwest. Sites around the office are open-ended back-ins that can accommodate a vehicle of about 40 feet Sites 15–25 on the second tier are 40-foot angled back-ins with parking in front of the sites. Sites 53–62 measure 25 × 35 feet and are laid out by the highway. These sites are somewhat cramped and (although well-shaded) rather undesirable. The top tier, adjacent to a large grassy hill, contains long-term residents. This is probably the nicest section of the park. Sites 37–40 are located along the south edge, perpendicular to the rows on the three tiers. There is RV storage to the west of site 37, making this area less attractive. Tent sites are located on the second tier, above the office. These are grassy but unshaded sites. This campground is in an attractive area and close to a number of recreation opportunities. It is a pleasant stay for RVers or tenters.

Basics

Operated By: Tammy Johnson. **Open:** All year. **Site Assignment:** Assigned upon registration; verbal reservations OK. **Registration:** In office. (Late arrivals ring bell.) **Fee:** RV $20 (full), $18 (water, electric), tent $10 (checks, V, MC, D). **Parking:** At site.

Facilities

Number of RV Sites: 58. **Number of Tent-Only Sites:** 6. **Hookups:** Water, sewer, electric (30, 50 amps). **Each Site:** Picnic table. **Dump Station:** Yes. **Laundry:** Yes. **Pay Phone:** Yes. **Rest Rooms and Showers:** Yes. **Fuel:** No. **Propane:** No. **Internal Roads:** Gravel. **RV Service:** No. **Market:** 4 mi. east. **Restaurant:** 2.5 mi. east. **General Store:** Yes. **Vending:** Yes. **Playground:** Yes. **Other:** Potlucks every 2 weeks, rec room w/ pool table & TV. **Activities:** Skiing, hiking, rock climbing, fishing, boating, swimming, bicycling, mountain climbing. **Nearby Attractions:** Golf courses, Rocky Mountain National Park, flea markets, antique malls. **Additional Information:** Loveland Visitor Center: (970) 667-5728.

Restrictions

Pets: On leash, cleaned up after. **Fires:** In grills. **Alcoholic Beverages:** At sites. **Vehicle Maximum Length:** 42 ft.

To Get There

From the junction of Hwy. 287 and Hwy. 34, turn west onto Hwy. 34 and go 7.25 mi. Turn left onto Carter Lake Rd. and go 0.45 mi. Turn left at the sign into the entrance.

MANITOU SPRINGS

Pike's Peak RV Park and Campground

320 Manitou Dr., Manitou Springs 80829.
T: (719) 685-9459.

RV: ★★★★ Tent: ★★★

Beauty: ★★★★ Site Privacy: ★★★
Spaciousness: ★★ Quiet: ★★★
Security: ★★★★ Cleanliness: ★★★★
Insect Control: ★★★★ Facilities: ★★★

Laid out in a giant loop that rings the entire campground, RV sites are a tight 19 feet wide and a maximum of 40 feet in length. Sites 1–19 back to woods along the northern edge of the campground. Besides 24–27, which are quite near the basketball court and may find games there disruptive, these are among the best sites due to the natural scenery. Sites 26–47 back to the creek, which would make these the nicest sites, except the highway lies just beyond, bringing traffic noise to these sites. Sites 48–58 are in the middle of the park. Sites 58 and 59 are close by a private residence, but definitely the most spacious sites. Tent sites are on a crushed gravel drive. Sites 70 and 71 are wide open to the sun, but 72–74 are very well-shaded. All of these sites are just off the highway.

BASICS

Operated By: Allen & Jackie Branine. **Open:** Apr. 1–Oct. 31. **Site Assignment:** Assigned upon registration. Credit card required for reservation; 24-hours cancellation policy. **Registration:** In office. (Late arrivals select an available site & pay in the morning.) **Fee:** RV $26 (full), $26 (water, electric), tent $20 (checks, V, MC). **Parking:** At site.

FACILITIES

Number of RV Sites: 60. **Number of Tent-Only Sites:** 6. **Hookups:** Water, sewer, electric (30, 50 amps). **Each Site:** Picnic table. **Dump Station:** No. **Laundry:** Yes. **Pay Phone:** Yes. **Rest Rooms and Showers:** Yes. **Fuel:** No. **Propane:** No. **Internal Roads:** Gravel. **RV Service:** On-call. **Market:** less than 0.25 mi. **Restaurant:** Across street. **General Store:** Yes. **Vending:** Yes. **Swimming:** Pool. **Playground:** No. **Other:** Dataport, next door to city park & pool, central location, fishing in creek. **Activities:** Swimming, fishing, sightseeing, mountain climbing, hiking, tours. **Nearby Attractions:** Garden of the Gods, Pike's Peak. **Additional Information:** Manitou Springs Chamber of Commerce, (719) 685-5089.

RESTRICTIONS

Pets: On leash, cleaned up after. **Fires:** In grills. **Alcoholic Beverages:** At sites. **Vehicle Maximum Length:** 40 ft.

TO GET THERE

From the junction of Hwy. 24 and Hwy. Business 24 (Manitou Ave.), turn west onto Manitou Ave. and go 0.25 mi. Turn right at the sign into the entrance.

McCLAVE

Hud's Campground

29995 Hwy. 50, McClave 81057. T: (719) 829-4344.

RV ★★★ Tent ★★★

Beauty: ★★★	Site Privacy: ★★★★
Spaciousness: ★★★★	Quiet: ★★★
Security: ★★★★	Cleanliness: ★★★
Insect Control: ★★★★	Facilities: ★★★★

This rural campground consists of a large open field. There is a mobile home to the west of the park, which is slightly unattractive, and the highway is just off the east edge. A big plus in this campground is that sites are defined by width, but not by length. Therefore, pull-throughs measure 30 × 60 feet or longer. Rigs of any size can easily park here. Sites are open, grassy spaces situated in rows. The campground contains only sparse bushes, and, as a result, not much shade. The best sites, at the northern edge of the campground, are slightly larger but situated right on the internal road. Tenting sites, to the south of the pool, are also quite open, but the grass is rather thick, making for a decent ground covering. The shower and rest room facility is a large concrete building, reminiscent of a public swimming pool changing room. The floor needed painting during our inspection, and the showers, while certainly adequate, were due for a good scrubbing.

BASICS

Operated By: Bob & Patty Boyer. **Open:** All year (limited facilities in winter). **Site Assignment:** First come, first served; verbal reservations OK. **Registration:** In store. (Late arrivals select an available site & settle in the morning.) **Fee:** RV $14, tent $11. **Parking:** At site.

FACILITIES

Number of RV Sites: 20. **Number of Tent-Only Sites:** 5. **Hookups:** Water, sewer, electric (30 amps). **Each Site:** Some picnic tables. **Dump Station:** No (sewer at all sites). **Laundry:** Yes. **Pay Phone:** Yes. **Rest Rooms and Showers:** Yes. **Fuel:** No. **Propane:** No. **Internal Roads:** Gravel. **RV Service:** No. **Market:** 15 mi. into Lamar. **Restaurant:** 15 mi. into Lamar. **General Store:** Yes. **Vending:** No. **Swimming:** Pool. **Playground:** Yes. **Other:** RV parts, horseshoes, lake (7 mi. away). **Activities:** Swimming, fishing. **Nearby Attractions:** John Martin Lake. **Additional Information:** Lamar Chamber of Commerce, (719) 336-4379.

RESTRICTIONS

Pets: On leash, cleaned up after. **Fires:** In fire pits. **Alcoholic Beverages:** At sites. **Vehicle Maximum Length:** None. **Other:** No BB guns.

TO GET THERE

At the junction of Hwy. 50 and Hwy. 196, on the southwest side.

MEEKER

Stagecoach Campground

39084 Hwy. 13, Meeker 81641. T: (970) 878-4334.

RV ★★★★ Tent ★★★

Beauty: ★★★★	Site Privacy: ★★★★
Spaciousness: ★★★★★	Quiet: ★★★★
Security: ★★★★	Cleanliness: ★★★
Insect Control: ★★★	Facilities: ★★

This is a beautiful campground with lush grass and giant cottonwoods surrounded by natural scenery on all sides: grassy hills to the south and west, a rocky hill to the north, and wetlands to the east. Sites 30–34 are long enough (120 feet) to be used as doubles, but, surprisingly, are not. Sites are a generous 45 feet wide, grassy, and forested. Sites 11–18C may require some manoeuvering to park in, but are still excellent places to camp. RV sites 1–10 are shorter (36-foot) back-ins, much more cramped than the humongous pull-throughs. Tent sites are on a strip of thick grass to the west of the RV sites, but there is only one fire pit, under a cottonwood by the river. Whoever can grab that one spot has quite possibly the best tenting space for 20 miles around! The laundry is small, and the rest rooms are small and darkish, with sealant flaking off the cement floors. Showers are spacious, but one light didn't work when inspected. These facilities are rough, but not uncomfortable. Don't let the less-than-perfect toilet facilities put you off: this is a park to return to again and again!

BASICS

Operated By: Gerry Meislohn. **Open:** May 1–Nov. 15. **Site Assignment:** Flexible, depending on fullness; verbal reservations OK. **Registration:** In office. (Late arrivals knock on door or use drop box). **Fee:** RV $20 (full), $18 (water, electric), tent $5 per person (max. $10), (V, MC). **Parking:** At site.

FACILITIES

Number of RV Sites: 31. **Number of Tent-Only Sites:** Undesignated sites. **Hookups:** Water, sewer, electric (20, 30, 50 amps). **Each Site:** Picnic table, fire ring. **Dump Station:** Yes. **Laundry:** Yes. **Pay Phone:** Yes. **Rest Rooms and Showers:** Yes. **Fuel:** No. **Propane:** No. **Internal Roads:** Gravel. **RV Service:** No. **Market:** 2 mi. into town. **Restaurant:** 2 mi. into town. **General Store:** No. **Vending:** No. **Playground:** No. **Other:** River, meat-hanging area for hunters, cottonwoods, wildlife. **Activities:** Fishing, hunting, skiing, backpacking, snowmobiling. **Nearby Attractions:** White River Museum, White River National Forest, Meeker Classic Sheepdog Trials (Sep.). **Additional Information:** Meeker Chamber of Commerce, (970) 878-5510.

RESTRICTIONS

Pets: On leash, cleaned up after. **Fires:** In fire rings/pits. **Alcoholic Beverages:** At sites. **Vehicle Maximum Length:** None.

TO GET THERE

On the south side at the junction of Hwy. 13 and Hwy. 64 (2 mi. out of town). The office is on the left of the driveway.

MONTE VISTA

Mobile Manor RV Park

2830 US Hwy. 160 West, Monte Vista 81144. T: (719) 852-5921; F: (719) 852-0122.

RV ★★ Tent n/a

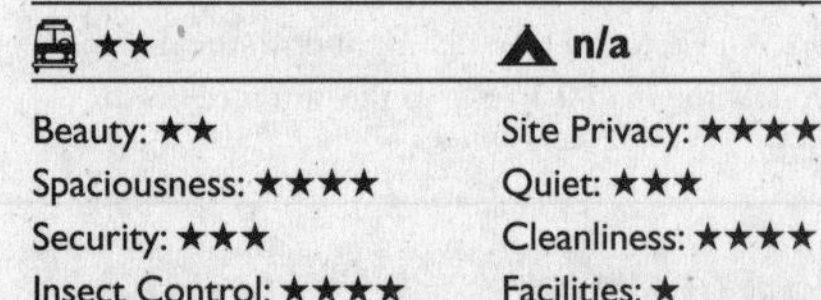

Beauty: ★★	Site Privacy: ★★★★
Spaciousness: ★★★★	Quiet: ★★★
Security: ★★★	Cleanliness: ★★★★
Insect Control: ★★★★	Facilities: ★

This RV park is a wide-open gravel parking area with two rows of six RV sites. As a result, a rig of any size could park in any of the sites, but the park itself is not very appealing. While it is true that there are nice views on three sides (woods and mountains), the park lacks any kind of landscaping or trees. Furthermore, the adjacent motel occupies the view to the southeast, and a drive-in movie screen picks up where the motel leaves off. The higher-numbered sites in both rows are progressively further away from the motel and drive-in, and it is recommended that campers who stay the night here use one of these sites. Tents need not apply.

BASICS

Operated By: George Kelloff. **Open:** All year. **Site Assignment:** First come, first served. **Registration:** In motel office. **Fee:** RV $18 (full; by reservation only), $15 (water, electric), $12 (electric) (checks, V, MC, D). **Parking:** At site.

FACILITIES

Number of RV Sites: 12. **Number of Tent-Only Sites:** 0. **Hookups:** Water, sewer, electric (30, 50 amps). **Each Site:** Picnic table. **Dump Station:** No. **Laundry:** No. **Pay Phone:** Yes. **Rest Rooms**

and Showers: Yes. **Fuel:** No. **Propane:** No. **Internal Roads:** Gravel. **RV Service:** No. **Market:** 2 mi. east. **Restaurant:** On site. **General Store:** No. **Vending:** No. **Swimming:** No. **Playground:** No. **Other:** Drive-in movies. **Activities:** Hiking, watching wildlife. **Nearby Attractions:** Monte Vista National Wildlife Reserve. **Additional Information:** Alamosa County Chamber of Commerce, (800) BLU-SKYS or (719) 589-3681.

Restrictions

Pets: On leash, cleaned up after. **Fires:** In fire pits. **Alcoholic Beverages:** At sites. **Vehicle Maximum Length:** None. **Other:** Full hookups by reservation only.

To Get There

From the junction of Hwy. 285 and Hwy. 160, turn west onto Hwy. 160 and go 2.9 mi. Turn left at the sign into the entrance (next to the drive-in movies).

MONTROSE

Montrose RV Resort (formerly KOA)

200 North Cedar Ave., Montrose 81401. T: (888) 249-9554 or (970) 249-9177.

RV ★★★★ Tent ★★★

Beauty: ★★★ Site Privacy: ★★★★
Spaciousness: ★★★★ Quiet: ★★★★★
Security: ★★★★ Cleanliness: ★★★★★
Insect Control: ★★★★ Facilities: ★★★★★

All sites are level and grassy here and the landscaping makes this an attractive park. (Storage units to the south detract a little from the beauty.) Sites 1–7 are 36-foot back-ins; although 4 does not have a shade tree, making it less desirable. Sites 8–13 and 18–23 are 56-foot pull-throughs with a shared covered picnic area separated by a wooden divider. 24–31 are slightly larger (66 × 24 feet). Tent sites are in a fenced-off area to the north of the RV sites and west of the cabins. Beyond this, there is an open grassy field with trees at the far end and views of distant hills to the north and west. (43 has the only shade tree among the tent sites.) The rest rooms and showers are spotless, modern, and spacious. There is a bench running along one side for towels and toiletries as well as a clothes rack. Note that the door locks are is a little complicated to use. The laundry is spacious and clean. All in all, this is quite a nice park—especially for RVers.

Basics

Operated By: Ray & Angeline Wells. **Open:** All year. **Site Assignment:** Flexible, depending on availability. Credit card required for reservation; 24-hours cancellation policy. **Registration:** In office. (Late arrivals use drop box.) **Fee:** RV $23.95 (full), $21.95 (water, electric), tent $18.50 (V, MC, AE, D). **Parking:** At site.

Facilities

Number of RV Sites: 26. **Number of Tent-Only Sites:** 17. **Hookups:** Water, sewer, electric (30, 50 amps). **Each Site:** Picnic table, grill. **Dump Station:** Yes. **Laundry:** Yes. **Pay Phone:** Yes. **Rest Rooms and Showers:** Yes. **Fuel:** No. **Propane:** Yes. **Internal Roads:** Nice gravel. **RV Service:** No. **Market:** 1 mi. into town. **Restaurant:** 1 mi. into town. **General Store:** Yes. **Vending:** No. **Swimming:** Pool. **Playground:** Yes. **Other:** Dog walk area, nightly movies on large screen TV, covered pavillion, cabins. **Activities:** Basketball, movies, swimming, hunting, hiking, biking, rafting, boating. **Nearby Attractions:** Montrose County Historical Museum, Ute Indian Museum & Ouray Memorial Park. **Additional Information:** Montrose Chamber of Commerce, (800) 923-5515 or (970) 249-5000, (970) 249-5515.

Restrictions

Pets: On leash, cleaned up after. **Fires:** In grills. **Alcoholic Beverages:** At sites. **Vehicle Maximum Length:** None.

To Get There

From the junction of Hwy. 50 and Hwy. 550, go 0.8 mi. east on Hwy. 50 (Main St. in town), then 0.2 mi. north on Cedar Ave. Turn right at the sign into the entrance.

NEDERLAND

Kelly-Dahl Campground

Boulder Ranger Office, 2140 Yarmouth Ave., Boulder 80301. T: (877) 444-6777, (800) 280-2267, or (303) 444-6600; www.reserveusa.com or www.fs.fed.us/arns; pmdelong@yahoo.com.

RV ★★★★ Tent ★★★★

Beauty: ★★★★ Site Privacy: ★★★★
Spaciousness: ★★★★ Quiet: ★★★★
Security: ★★★★ Cleanliness: ★★★
Insect Control: ★★★★ Facilities: ★

The campgrounds in this area of the Roosevelt National Forest unfortunately do not include hookups. RVers wishing to camp here therefore has to make a bit of a sacrifice. However, this sacrifice may well be worth it, as the forest and the surrounding area is beautiful and wonderfully peaceful. This campground is laid out in three loops, with site driveways ranging from 20 feet (site 39) to 45 feet (site 30) in length. Average length is between 35 feet and 40 feet Site 11 is a 72-foot quasi pull-through (that actually requires parallel parking). The rest of the sites are straightforward back-ins. Sites 16, 18, and 20 have a hill that provides a view when climbed. Both the Aspen Loop and the Pine Loop are quite forested. The Fir Loop is more open. Reservable sites are located in the Fir and Pine Loops. Site 30 (in the Pine Loop) is located extremely close to the playground, which may make it less desirable to some campers. The toilets are typical pit toilets, with no running water or showers. This campground offers the chance to get close to nature, which, of course, entails giving up some modern conveniences.

Basics

Operated By: Thousand Trails Management. **Open:** May–Oct. (dates may vary). **Site Assignment:** First come, first served. Credit card required for reservation; 3-days cancellation policy, less $10 fee. **Registration:** At pay kiosk. (Camp Host will verify that campers have paid.) **Fee:** $12. (checks, no credit cards). **Parking:** At site.

Facilities

Number of RV Sites: 46. **Number of Tent-Only Sites:** 0. **Hookups:** None. **Each Site:** Picnic table, grill, fire pit. **Dump Station:** No. **Laundry:** No. **Pay Phone:** No (in Rollingsville). **Rest Rooms and Showers:** Rest rooms; no shower (showers in downtown Nederland mall). **Fuel:** No. **Propane:** No. **Internal Roads:** Gravel/dirt. **RV Service:** No. **Market:** 3.5 mi. to Nederland. **Restaurant:** 3.5 mi. to Nederland. **General Store:** No. **Vending:** No. **Swimming:** No. **Playground:** Yes. **Other:** Firewood for sale. **Activities:** Hiking, gambling, horseback riding, mountain biking. **Nearby Attractions:** Rocky Mountain National Park, Blackhawk, Central City. **Additional Information:** Thousand Trails Management, (303) 258-3610.

Restrictions

Pets: On leash, cleaned up after. **Fires:** In fire pits. **Alcoholic Beverages:** At sites. **Vehicle Maximum Length:** None.

To Get There

From the junction of Hwy. 72 and Hwy. 119, turn south onto Hwy. 119/72 and go 3 mi. Turn left at the sign into the entrance and follow the dirt road to the pay kiosk.

OURAY

4J+1+1 Trailer Park

P.O. Box F, Ouray 81427. T: (970) 325-4418.

RV ★★★★ Tent ★★★★

Beauty: ★★★★ Site Privacy: ★★★★
Spaciousness: ★★★★ Quiet: ★★★★
Security: ★★★★ Cleanliness: ★★★★
Insect Control: ★★★★ Facilities: ★★★★

Located in an outstandingly beautiful part of Colorado, this campground offers spectacular scenes from any site. This rural park has level gravel sites close to the river as well as further back. "R" sites are back-ins by the river. 1–6 are quite small (24 feet long), but 7–13 get progressively longer: 27 feet to 45 feet. The pull-throughs in the middle of the park (14–19) are 55–60 feet long and contain shade trees, making them the best pull-through sites. Tent sites are along the western edge of the park right at the base of the mountain. (No worry about rockfall, though, as the mountain side is all trees.) The least appealing spot is 15, which is located next to a concrete slab as well as a telephone pole and dumpster. The rest of the tent sites are quite nice, however, and 6–10 are all the nicer for the overhanging trees they contain. Tent sites 1–4 have attractive wooden fencing for added privacy, and it appears as though all tent sites will soon have this added feature. The rest rooms are clean but rather cramped—so much so, in fact, that only 1 of 4 stalls has a door, and only 1 of 3 showers has a curtain—which may make for an awkward bathroom experience. The playground is located across a road, and, while it is fenced in, it would be wise to keep an eye on children playing there. The RV experience here would be improved with more trees, and tenters would enjoy more grass, but either experience is quite satisfactory in this campground.

Basics

Operated By: Jack & Jackie Clark & Family. **Open:** May 15–Oct. 15 (fully self-contained units may come before & after these dates). **Site Assignment:** Flexible, depending on site availability. Credit card required for reservation; 24-hours cancellation policy, 72-hours for 4th of July.) **Registration:** In office. (Late arrivals park & register in the morning.) **Fee:** RV $26 (Full), tent $18 (V, MC). **Parking:** At site.

Facilities

Number of RV Sites: 55. **Number of Tent-Only Sites:** 10. **Hookups:** Water, sewer, electric (30, 50 amps). **Each Site:** Picnic table, grill. **Dump Station:** Yes. **Laundry:** Across street. **Pay Phone:** Yes. **Rest Rooms and Showers:** Yes. **Fuel:** No. **Propane:** No. **Internal Roads:** Paved. **RV Service:** No. **Market:** 3 blocks. **Restaurant:** 1 block. **General Store:** No. **Vending:** Yes. **Swimming:** No. **Playground:** Yes. **Other:** River, conveniently located near downtown & hot springs. **Activities:** Jeep tours, hiking, mountain biking, skiing (Telluride). **Nearby Attractions:** Hot springs, historic district. **Additional Information:** Ouray Chamber Resort Assoc.: (800) 228-1876 or (970) 325-4746.

Restrictions

Pets: On leash, cleaned up after. **Fires:** In fire pits. **Alcoholic Beverages:** At sites. **Vehicle Maximum Length:** None.

To Get There

From Hwy. 550 in town, turn west onto 7th Ave. Drive 2 blocks to the end (just past the river), then turn right at the end of 7th Ave. onto Oak St. Take the first right into the entrance. The office is on the left.

PAGOSA SPRINGS

Cool Pines RV Park

1501 West Hwy. 160, Pagosa Springs 81147. T: (970) 264-9130; coolpinesrv@frontier.net.

RV: ★★★★ Tent: ★★★

Beauty: ★★★★ Site Privacy: ★★★★
Spaciousness: ★★★ Quiet: ★★★★
Security: ★★★★ Cleanliness: ★★★★★
Insect Control: ★★★ Facilities: ★★★★

This attractive park is surrounded by "cool pines," and offers some mountain views from within. Terraced sites are situated on a loop with a grassy patch between each site. Pull-throughs are 60 feet long, while back-ins are only slightly smaller (50–55 feet long). There is one unmarked RV site directly by the office, which may get more traffic, but also has a better view of the mountains. Tent sites are unmarked on a grassy patch behind the shops to the north, which could comfortably fit five or so tents. (There are only 3 trees to provide coverage, however, and one fire ring.) The rest rooms are individual units, which can be locked when in use. They are all very clean and spacious. The rec room, which houses the rest rooms, is likewise very clean and comfortable. RVers should definitely make a point to come to Cool Pines. Tenters will also be comfortable, but would benefit from more coverage, and more fire rings or pits and some tables. This is a peaceful, wilderness location with convenient proximity both to the highway and to town.

Basics

Operated By: The Robinsons. **Open:** Mid-Apr.–mid-Nov. **Site Assignment:** Flexible depending on fullness. Credit card required for reservation; 3-days cancellation policy. **Registration:** In office. (Late arrivals come to office.) **Fee:** RV $24, tent $16 (V, MC). **Parking:** At site.

Facilities

Number of RV Sites: 22. **Number of Tent-Only Sites:** Undesignated sites. **Hookups:** Water, sewer, electric (30, 50 amps), cable. **Each Site:** Picnic table, several trees. **Dump Station:** Yes. **Laundry:** Yes. **Pay Phone:** Yes. **Rest Rooms and Showers:** Yes. **Fuel:** No. **Propane:** No. **Internal Roads:** Gravel. **RV Service:** No. **Market:** 1 mi. **Restaurant:** 1 mi. **General Store:** No. **Vending:** No. **Swimming:** No (hot tub). **Playground:** Yes. **Other:** Handicap accessible. **Activities:** Hiking, mountain biking, river rafting, fishing. **Nearby Attractions:** Chimney Rock. **Additional Information:** Pagosa Springs Area Chamber of Commerce, (800) 252-2204, (970) 264-2360.

Restrictions

Pets: On leash, cleaned up after. **Fires:** In grills. **Alcoholic Beverages:** At sites. **Vehicle Maximum Length:** 42 ft.

To Get There

From the junction of Hwy. 84 and Hwy. 160, go 2.5 mi. west on Hwy. 160. Turn right at the sign, and drive down behind the store fronts to get to the RV park.

PAONIA

Paonia State Park

Paonia State Park, P.O. Box 147, Crawford 81415. T: (800) 678-2267 or (303) 470-1144; www.parks.state.co.us.

RV: ★★★ Tent: ★★★★

Beauty: ★★★★★ Site Privacy: ★★★★
Spaciousness: ★★★★ Quiet: ★★★★
Security: ★★★★ Cleanliness: ★★★★
Insect Control: ★★★★ Facilities: ★

Of the two campgrounds in this state park, Hawsapple Campground is the closest to the reservoir boat and swimming access areas. Sites 1–3 are scrunched together at the end of the roundabout, near a pit toilet. These are 27 feet long, but have ample parking space, as they are 25 feet wide. Site 0 is a "pull-alongside" that can accommodate 42–45 feet If you turn left at the entrance, you continue on to sites 4–7. Of these, 4–6 are large pull-throughs, measuring 84–90 feet each. Site 7 is a 54-foot shaded back-in. The reservoir access area is a mile further up this road. Spruce Campground is located just off Hwy. 133, and contains sites 8–15. Sites 8–12 are located together by the entrance, and sites 8 and 10 seem to be sharing parking spaces as do 11 and 12. Site 13 is a smallish back-in (36 feet long), but extremely well-shaded. Site 15 is a 60-foot "pull-alongside" with an open picnic area down by the edge of the river. The two campgrounds in this state park offer a variety of recreational opportunities related to the reservoir, and campers of all stripes will enjoy an adventurous stay here.

Basics

Operated By: Colorado State Parks. **Open:** Apr. 1–Sept. 30. **Site Assignment:** First come, first served. Credit card or check required for reservation; 24-hours cancellation policy. **Registration:** At pay station. **Fee:** $6, plus $4 day use fee (checks). **Parking:** At site.

Facilities

Number of RV Sites: 15. **Number of Tent-Only Sites:** 0. **Hookups:** None. **Each Site:** Picnic table, grill. **Dump Station:** No. **Laundry:** No. **Pay Phone:** No. **Rest Rooms and Showers:** Pit toilets; no shower. **Fuel:** No. **Propane:** No. **Internal Roads:** Gravel. **RV Service:** No. **Market:** 16 mi. to Paonia. **Restaurant:** At bottom of reservoir. **General Store:** No. **Vending:** No. **Swimming:** Reservoir. **Playground:** No. **Other:** Boat ramp, picnic area. **Activities:** Fishing, boating, swimming, hiking. **Nearby Attractions:** Gunnison National Forest. **Additional Information:** Gunnison National Forest (970) 921-5721.

Restrictions

Pets: On 6-ft. leash, cleaned up after. **Fires:** In grills. **Alcoholic Beverages:** At sites. **Vehicle Maximum Length:** None.

To Get There

From the junction of Hwy. 133 and CR2 (at the sign for Paonia State Park), turn left and cross the bridge. (A 2nd campground is 0.1 mi. south on Hwy. 133, on the left.) Take the first right and go 0.5 mi. Turn right into the campground.

PONCHA SPRINGS

Monarch Spur RV Park and Campground

18989 West Hwy. 50, P.O. Box 457, Poncha Springs 81242. T: (888) 814-3001 or (719) 530-0341; www.monarchspurrvpark.com; jerry@monarch spurRVPark.com.

RV: ★★★★ Tent: ★★★★

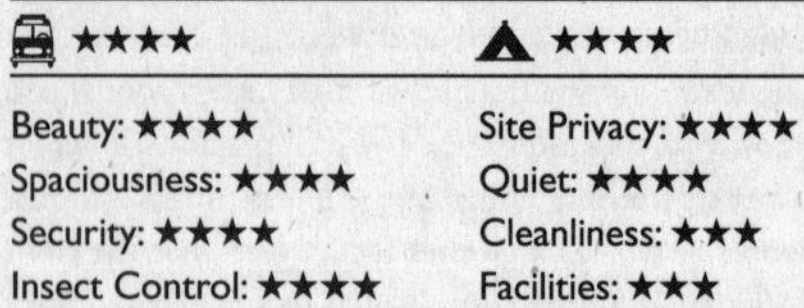

Beauty: ★★★★ Site Privacy: ★★★★
Spaciousness: ★★★★ Quiet: ★★★★
Security: ★★★★ Cleanliness: ★★★
Insect Control: ★★★★ Facilities: ★★★

Billing itself as a "big rig park", this campground makes good on its promise with decent 60-foot sites. This park uses its natural setting to its best advantage, employing rows of large rocks to designate site boundaries, and setting tent sites (and some RV sites) in the thick forest and on the grassy hills that encompass the park. RV sites are arranged in two rows of sites sixe 60 × 30 feet. All pull-throughs are level with a grass and gravel mix. Unmarked tent sites are scattered along the river on grassy patches. These are fairly wild sites with good grass, lots of trees, and the constant sound of the river (which helps drown out traffic noise). The owner is apparently building many new sites in the forest, which should be ready by summer 2002. Of the current sites, 22–31 are scattered up in the forest, making them slightly more isolated and definitely more shaded. However, accessing these sites requires navigating a very primitive road that leads up a slight hill; sites 1–21 are definitely easier to pull into. The laundry room is clean and spacious, as are the rest rooms. The showers are, however, slightly dingy. Tucked away on Hwy. 50, this campground can be a little difficult to locate. However, if you call, the staff will help you locate the park and even come out and get you.

BASICS

Operated By: Jerry Gunkel. **Open:** All year. **Site Assignment:** Flexible, depending on site availability. Credit card required for reservation; 48-hours cancellation policy, less $5 fee. **Registration:** In office. (Late arrivals select an available site & pay in the morning.) **Fee:** RV $22, tent $17. **Parking:** At site.

FACILITIES

Number of RV Sites: 30. **Number of Tent-Only Sites:** 20. **Hookups:** Water, sewer, electric (20, 30, 50 amps). **Each Site:** Picnic table, grass strip. **Dump Station:** No (sewer at all sites). **Laundry:** Yes. **Pay Phone:** Yes. **Rest Rooms and Showers:** Yes. **Fuel:** No. **Propane:** Yes. **Internal Roads:** Gravel/dirt. **RV Service:** No. **Market:** 10 mi. to Salida. **Restaurant:** 7 mi. to Poncha Springs. **General Store:** Yes. **Vending:** Yes. **Swimming:** No. **Playground:** No. **Other:** ATV rentals, picnic deck. **Activities:** Hiking, ATV trails, horseshoes, swimming, hunting. **Nearby Attractions:** San Isabel National Forest, San Juan National Forest. **Additional Information:** Heart of the Rockies Chamber of Commerce, (877) 772-5432 or (719) 539-2068.

RESTRICTIONS

Pets: On leash, cleaned up after. **Fires:** In fire pits; subject to seasonal bans. **Alcoholic Beverages:** At sites. **Vehicle Maximum Length:** 60 ft. **Other:** Read policy sheet.

TO GET THERE

From the junction of Hwy. 285 and Hwy. 50 in Salida, go 8.2 mi. west on Hwy. 50. Turn south at the sign onto a dirt road and follow it to the office.

PUEBLO

Pueblo KOA

4131 I-25 North, Pueblo 81008. T: (800) 562-7453 or (719) 542-2273; www.koa.com; pueblokoa@juno.com.

RV ★★★★ Tent ★★★

Beauty: ★★★★ Site Privacy: ★★★
Spaciousness: ★★★★ Quiet: ★★★
Security: ★★★★★ Cleanliness: ★★★★★
Insect Control: ★★★★ Facilities: ★★★★

This campground in a desert setting has scattered rows of sites, each designated by a letter. Row A has pull throughs measuring 60 × 18 feet that are separated from each other by a row of bushes. Sites A5 and A6 share a large shade tree. Towards the south are Rows N and P. Row N has pull-throughs of 45 × 30 feet, and is separated from Row P by a hedge. All sites are well-shaded. Row P, at the southern edge of the campground, has 40-foot back-ins. Sites P1 and P2 are separated from each other by a wooden fence, which offers these sites more privacy than practically any others. They back to the hedge and open to the pool and a dirt road. There is a private residence next to P6. On the other side of P6 is a hedge that separates it from P5, making this latter site very private. In the middle and northern side of the campground, Rows B, C, D, and E have unshaded pull-throughs that average 60 feet in length. (Row C has some slightly shorter pull-throughs, 42–57 feet long) Rows F, G, and H are primitive sites good for tenting and possibly a pop-up. These sites are nicer, in fact, than the designated tent area between Rows C and D, which has completely open sites on sparse grass set amongst a number of RV sites. The rest rooms are pristine; the showers are a little worn but still acceptable. This is a beautiful campground for those who appreciate the austere beauty of the desert.

BASICS

Operated By: Mark & Alexis Whitworth. **Open:** All year. **Site Assignment:** Assigned upon registration. Credit card required for reservation; 24-hours cancellation policy. **Registration:** In office. (Late arrivals use drop box.) **Fee:** RV $26 (full), $24 (water, electric), tent $18 (Colorado checks, V, MC, AE, D). **Parking:** At site.

FACILITIES

Number of RV Sites: 60. **Number of Tent-Only Sites:** 25. **Hookups:** Water, sewer, electric (50 amps). **Each Site:** Picnic table. **Dump Station:** Yes. **Laundry:** Yes. **Pay Phone:** Yes. **Rest Rooms and Showers:** Yes. **Fuel:** No. **Propane:** Yes. **Internal Roads:** Gravel. **RV Service:** No. **Market:** 8 mi. south to Hwy. 50. **Restaurant:** 2 mi. north. **General Store:** Yes. **Vending:** Yes. **Swimming:** Pool. **Playground:** Yes. **Other:** Rec room (pool table, video games), dataport, dog walk, nature trail. **Activities:** Swimming, hiking, mountain climbing, boating, swimming, caving. **Nearby Attractions:** Lake Pueblo State Park, Royal Gorge Bridge, Pikes Peak, Seven Falls, Cave of the Winds, Garden of the Gods, Manitou Cliff Dwellings. **Additional Information:** Visitor Information Center: (719) 543-1742.

RESTRICTIONS

Pets: On leash, cleaned up after; or must stay inside at night. **Fires:** Charcoal only. **Alcoholic Beverages:** At sites. **Vehicle Maximum Length:** None.

TO GET THERE

From I-25 (Exit 108): on the west side of the highway, take the first right and go 0.6 mi. straight into the campground. (From northbound I-25, there is a single lane underpass 13 ft. 6 in. high to negotiate. The owner assures there has never been a rig that can't pass through.)

RED FEATHER

Dowdy Lake Campground

Red Feather Lakes, Bellevue 80512. T: (877) 444-6777; www.reserveusa.com/nrrs/co/dowd.

RV ★★ Tent ★★★★

Beauty: ★★★★★ Site Privacy: ★★★
Spaciousness: ★★★ Quiet: ★★★★
Security: ★★★★ Cleanliness: ★★★★
Insect Control: ★★★ Facilities: ★

This National Forest campground is divided up into Loops A–E, each containing a varying number of campsites. The average size of a site is 24 × 18 feet, which, of course, limits the number of RVs that can camp here. As there are no RV hookups, the campground is more geared towards tenters. However, RVers who don't mind roughing it for a night or two will also enjoy the natural beauty and the quiet this campground has to offer. Sites 1–3 in Loop A are spacious and quite close to the lake (3 is closest) and some neat rock formations. These are quite possibly the best sites in the campground, as they boast terrific views of the lake, are close to the camp hosts, and aren't bothered by too much passing traffic. Sites right on the water include 27, 28, 30–32, 35, and 37. Sites 33 and 34 are very close together, and they may be best for a group that is camping together. Group sites that require a double fee include 44–46, 50, 53, and 54. These are aimed at groups of 10 people or more. Sites 52 and 57 are outside the woods that most of the other sites are located in. The rest rooms are pit toilets, and, unfortunately, there are no showers. Some RVers may hesitate to camp in a park without hookups, but those hardy enough to do so will join adventurous tenters in an excellent wilderness of woods, grass, wildflowers, rock outcroppings, and gorgeous lake views.

BASICS

Operated By: Thousand Trails. **Open:** May 15–Sept. **Site Assignment:** First come, first served; reservations can be made 5–240 days in advance. Credit card required for reservation; 24-hours cancellation policy. **Registration:** Self-pay station. **Fee:** $11 (checks, no credits cards). **Parking:** At site, Loop C parking lot.

FACILITIES

Number of RV Sites: 48. **Number of Tent-Only Sites:** 14. **Hookups:** None. **Each Site:** Picnic table, grill, flat tent space. **Dump Station:** No. **Laundry:** No. **Pay Phone:** No. **Rest Rooms and Showers:** Toilets; no shower. **Fuel:** No. **Propane:** No. **Internal Roads:** Dirt. **RV Service:** No. **Market:** 35 mi. west to Wellington. **Restaurant:** 3 mi. west. **General Store:** No. **Vending:** No. **Swimming:** No. **Playground:** No. **Other:** Boat ramp, no fee day use. **Activities:** Fishing, boating, hiking, cycling. **Nearby Attractions:** Dowdy Lake, North Park. **Additional Information:** Red Feather Lakes Tourist Council, (800) 462-5870.

RESTRICTIONS

Pets: On leash, cleaned up after. **Fires:** In fire pits. **Alcoholic Beverages:** At sites. **Vehicle Maximum Length:** 40 ft. **Other:** Wakeless boating, no swimming, do not fill water reserves, no ATVs.

TO GET THERE

From the junction of Prairie Divide Rd. and Red Feather Lakes Rd. (74 East), go 1 mi. east on 74 East. Turn north onto Dowdy Lake Rd. and go 1 mi. (keep right on Dowdy Rd.) to pay station.

RIDGWAY

Ridgway State Park

28555 Hwy. 50, Ridgway 81432. T: (800) 678-2267/(303) 470-1144 or (970) 626-5822; www.coloradoparks.org/ridgway.

RV ★★★★ Tent ★★★★

Beauty: ★★★★ Site Privacy: ★★★★
Spaciousness: ★★★ Quiet: ★★★★★
Security: ★★★★ Cleanliness: ★★★★
Insect Control: ★★★ Facilities: ★★

This state park includes three separate campgrounds (Elk Ridge, Dakota Terraces, and Pa-Co-Chu-Puk), each offering a slightly different experience. All campgrounds are organized in loops, offering back-ins that range from 25-foot backins for pop-ups to 65-foot pull-throughs for longer RVs. The first campground on the way in from the entrance and the Visitor Center, Dakota Terraces is also closest to the swimming beach at the reservoir (especially sites 56–79 in Loop C). Elevated wooden tent decks are offered at sites 10 and 50, while shade shelters can be found at 4, 6, 8–10, 79, and others (indicated on the state park map). This campground has many trees, and is the best bet for those who want to take advantage of the reservoir. Elk Ridge Campground is located on top of a hill overlooking the reservoir. It is thus a little further from the water than Dakota Terraces, as well as more open. The most remote, and thus most private, sites are odd numbers 139–149 in Loop E, as well as 184–187. Wooden tent decks are provided at sites 99–103 (and others), while improved tent sites include 80, 83, 87, 123, 124, 165, 170 and others. Most difficult to pronounce, Pa-Co-Chu-Pak (also known as "Cow Creek") offers full hookups (sites 200–280) and walk-in tent sites (281–295). This campground is the most remote, and possibly the best for tenters—as long as they don't mind parking first and trekking in with their stuff. This campground offers two fishing ponds and almost exclusively pull-throughs. The most private sites include 200–208 in Loop F and 251, 254, and 257 in Loop G. This is a rare example of a state park offering full hookups, and those campers who enjoy getting out into the wild a little should definitely take advantage of these campgrounds.

Basics

Operated By: Colorado State Parks. **Open:** All year (closed during bad weather; limited facilities in winter). **Site Assignment:** First come, first served; reservations can be made 3–90 days in advance. Credit card required for reservation. **Registration:** At self-pay kiosk. **Fee:** $14–16 ($10 for tent walk-in sites), $4 park pass (checks, no credit card). **Parking:** At site.

Facilities

Number of RV Sites: 267. **Number of Tent-Only Sites:** 15. **Hookups:** Water, sewer, electric (50 amps). **Each Site:** Picnic table, grill. **Dump Station:** Yes. **Laundry:** Yes. **Pay Phone:** Yes. **Rest Rooms and Showers:** Yes. **Fuel:** No. **Propane:** No. **Internal Roads:** Paved. **RV Service:** No. **Market:** 6 mi. in Ridgway. **Restaurant:** 6 mi. in Ridgway. **General Store:** Yes. **Vending:** Yes. **Swimming:** Lake. **Playground:** Yes. **Other:** Marina. **Activities:** Hiking, swimming, biking, hunting, fishing. **Nearby Attractions:** Ridgway Reservoir. **Additional Information:** Ridgway Visitor Center, (970) 626-5868.

Restrictions

Pets: On 6-ft. leash, cleaned up after. **Fires:** In fire pits/grills. **Alcoholic Beverages:** Beer only. **Vehicle Maximum Length:** 65 ft. **Other:** No gathering firewood.

To Get There

From the junction of Hwy. 62 and Hwy. 550, go 4.6 mi. north on Hwy. 550. Turn northwest at "Dutch Charlie" sign into the entrance. Go 0.4 mi. to the pay station or to the park HQ.

RIFLE

Rifle Falls/Rifle Gap

0050 CR 219, Rifle 81650. T: (800) 678-2267 or (303) 470-1144 or (970) 625-1607; F: (970) 625-4327; www.coloradoparks.org; rifle.gap.park@ state.co.us.

RV ★★★★ Tent ★★★★

Beauty: ★★★★★ Site Privacy: ★★★★
Spaciousness: ★★★★ Quiet: ★★★★★
Security: ★★★ Cleanliness: ★★★★★
Insect Control: ★★★ Facilities: ★★★★

The Rifle Falls/Rifle Gap State Park Camping area consists of five small campgrounds—four in Rifle Gap, one in rifle Falls—each of which is described below. The Cottonwood Campground in Rifle Gap has absolutely huge pull-throughs that can accommodate a rig of any size. These sites, which average 100 × 100 feet, are scattered around the lake edge—some right up to the water, which would allow for an easy morning dip or an afternoon cast. This is the first campground one would approach from the main entrance, and well worth occupying for the night. Next in line is Cedar Campground, which contains mostly back-ins (average 48 feet in length), and one single pull-through. Also close to the water, this campground is better for smaller RVs, such as pop-ups or vans. Sage Campground, as the name implies, is "dry"—that is, has no direct water access. There are, however, 100-foot pull-throughs in a loop along the road, each with a large covered picnic area—ideal for landlubbers who only want to dip once or twice in the lake. Pinion Campground is perhaps the prettiest, crowded as it is with pinions and juniper. Like Cedar Campground, sites are smaller, and best suited for small vehicles or tents. (Tenters won't be thrilled by the gravel bed in each site, however.) Rifle Falls Campground, which offers easy access to the falls and caves that accompany them, has back-ins and pull-throughs that range in length from 28 feet to 120 feet. Tent sites are walk-ins to the south of the RV sites. The more remote sites, while offering better privacy, also require lugging equipment several hundred feet. Campers in tents or RVs will enjoy the beautiful sites—and sights—of Rifle Falls, and should definitely consider making a stop here.

Basics

Operated By: Colorado State Parks. **Open:** All year. **Site Assignment:** First come, first served. **Registration:** At pay kiosk. **Fee:** $10, $4 park pass (checks). **Parking:** At site.

Facilities

Number of RV Sites: 60. **Number of Tent-Only Sites:** 7. **Hookups:** Electric (30, 50 amps). **Each Site:** Picnic table, grill. **Dump Station:** Yes. **Laundry:** No. **Pay Phone:** No (at golf course). **Rest Rooms and Showers:** Pit toilets; no shower. **Fuel:** No. **Propane:** No. **Internal Roads:** Gravel. **RV Service:** No. **Market:** 10 mi. to Rifle. **Restaurant:** 10 mi. to Rifle. **General Store:** No. **Vending:** No. **Swimming:** Lake. **Playground:** No. **Other:** Creek, lake, falls. **Activities:** Boating, swimming, fishing, water skiing, scuba diving, ice skating, golf, caving, hiking, windsurfing. **Nearby Attractions:** Rifle Falls, Rifle Gap Reservoir. **Additional Information:** Rifle Visitor Information Center/Chamber of Commerce, (970) 625-2085.

Restrictions

Pets: On 6-ft. leash, cleaned up after. **Fires:** In fire pits. **Alcoholic Beverages:** Beer only. **Vehicle Maximum Length:** None. **Other:** No removing of plants or artifacts; cell phones may not work.

To Get There

From the junction of Hwy. 13 and Hwy. 325, go 6 mi. northeast on Hwy. 325. At the fork, stay on the paved road to reach the campground. (You can take the dirt road to the park office.) Turn left at the sign into the Rifle Gap Reservation, or continue for another 4 mi. to get to Rifle Falls.

RUSTIC

Glen Echo Resort

31503 Poudre Canyon Dr./Hwy. 14, Rustic 80512. T: (800) 348-2208 or (970) 881-2208; F: (970) 881-2066.

RV ★★★★ Tent ★★★

Beauty: ★★★★ Site Privacy: ★★★
Spaciousness: ★★ Quiet: ★★★★★
Security: ★★★★ Cleanliness: ★★★★★
Insect Control: ★★★ Facilities: ★★★

Situated on scenic Hwy. 14, this campground delivers on the beauty promised by the scenic drive to get there. Hills surround the campground on all four sides, and a river runs at the back, behind the cabins. The air is fresh, birds sing constantly, and there is green everywhere you look. Even the wood and stone buildings blend in well with the natural surroundings. Now, for the sites themselves. The best sites by far are those in the south portion of the park, which is divided by a retaining wall running east-west down the middle. Unfortunately, nearly half of the sites in the park (including, you guessed it, the choicest south sites) are occupied by long-term residents. There are still some very nice sites available (pull-throughs 64–68 are 80 feet long and have good tree coverage), but chances are good that you will end up on the north side, in a back-in facing to the highway. Not that that's a bad place to be. Sites are level, grassy, and for the most part, shaded by numerous trees. (Sites 14–21 one row in from the highway have no shade to speak of and are therefore less desirable.) The rest room and shower facilities (both in the main living and laundry complex and the secondary building to the south) are immaculate and brand-spanking new. The laundry is likewise clean and comfortable, with a sofa and bookshelf stocked with loaners. Note that the "playground" consists of one merry-go-round, but since most of the residents are retirees, there probably isn't call for much more than that. There is a fine group picnic shelter that even has electric outlets. Living up to the name of the town, this campground is "rustic," and makes a scenic as well as comfortable destination. Make a special trip to come out!

Basics

Operated By: Lloyd & Gaile Rowe. **Open:** All year. **Site Assignment:** First come, first served. **Registration:** In store until 7 p.m. (Late arrivals not allowed.) **Fee:** RV $25, tent $16 (V, MC). **Parking:** At site.

Facilities

Number of RV Sites: 77. **Number of Tent-Only Sites:** 2. **Hookups:** Water, sewer, electric (30, 50 amps). **Each Site:** Picnic table, trees. **Dump Station:** No (sewer at all sites). **Laundry:** Yes. **Pay Phone:** Yes. **Rest Rooms and Showers:** Yes. **Fuel:** Yes, including diesel. **Propane:** Yes. **Internal Roads:** Dirt, in good condition. **RV Service:** No. **Market:** Limited on-site (full, 40 mi. east to La Porte). **Restaurant:** Yes. **General Store:** Yes. **Vending:** No. **Swimming:** No. **Playground:** Yes. **Other:** 9 cabins, 2 duplex cabins, group picnic shelter. **Activities:** Special dinner on Mother's Day, hiking, driving. **Nearby Attractions:** Roosevelt National Forest, Cache La Poudre Scenic Byway. **Additional Information:** North Park Chamber of Commerce, (970) 723-4600.

Restrictions

Pets: On leash. **Fires:** In grills. **Alcoholic Beverages:** No alcohol permitted. **Vehicle Maximum Length:** None.

To Get There

On Hwy. 14, just west of the Rustic town name sign and mile marker 91.

SALIDA

Four Seasons RV Park

4305 East US Hwy. 50, Salida 81201. T: (888) 444-3626 or (719) 539-3084; fourseasons@amigo.net.

RV ★★★★★ Tent n/a

Beauty: ★★★★	Site Privacy: ★★★★★
Spaciousness: ★★★★★	Quiet: ★★★★
Security: ★★★★	Cleanliness: ★★★★★
Insect Control: ★★★★	Facilities: ★★★★★

This two-tiered campground offers sites just off the highway as well as sites down by the river. All of the long back-ins in the B row are gorgeous, and most river sites are equally nice. (R15 has exceptionally great shade.) The D row, one in from the river, is also quite pleasant, with lush grass, two pull-throughs (in addition to the lengthy back-ins), and fencing between sites. Most sites in the park have one side to either the river or to an embankment, adding privacy and security, and a shade tree of considerable size. The exceptions to this are 11–13 by the river, which lack grass as well as shade and are undoubtedly the least desirable sites. The rest rooms are immaculate and spacious, as is the laundry. There is also a community room with microwave, fridge, books, and nine tables. Although big rigs will have to unhook, you really can't go wrong with any site in the D or R rows. Ask for a site on the lower tier by the river, and you will be pleased with virtually any site you get.

Basics

Operated By: Paul & Candy Draper. **Open:** May–Oct. 1. **Site Assignment:** Assigned upon registration. Credit card required for reservation. 72-hours to 1-week cancellation policy, depending on legth of stay. **Registration:** In office. (Late arrivals use drop box.) **Fee:** Full: $23, water, electric: $18.50 (V, MC, D). **Parking:** At site.

Facilities

Number of RV Sites: 67. **Number of Tent-Only Sites:** 0. **Hookups:** Water, sewer, electric (30, 50 amps). **Each Site:** Picnic table. **Dump Station:** No (sewer at all sites). **Laundry:** Yes. **Pay Phone:** Yes. **Rest Rooms and Showers:** Yes. **Fuel:** No. **Propane:** Yes. **Internal Roads:** Dirt. **RV Service:** No. **Market:** 2 mi. west to Salida. **Restaurant:** 2 mi. west to Salida. **General Store:** No. **Vending:** Yes. **Swimming:** No. **Playground:** Yes. **Other:** Meeting room, storage. **Activities:** Rafting, horseshoes, shuffleboard, fishing, Jeep tours, hiking, mountain biking, skiing, golf, hunting, rockhounding. **Nearby Attractions:** Hot springs pools, ghost towns, kayaking competition. **Additional Information:** Heart of the Rockies Chamber of Commerce, (877) 772-5432 or (719) 539-2068.

Restrictions

Pets: On leash, cleaned up after. **Fires:** No open fires. **Alcoholic Beverages:** At sites. **Vehicle Maximum Length:** None.

To Get There

From the junction of Hwy. 291 and Hwy. 50, go 1.4 mi. east on Hwy. 50. Turn north at the sign into the entrance. The office is on the right.

SEIBERT

Shadey Grove Campground

306 Colorado St., Seibert 80834. T: (970) 664-2218; F: (970) 664-2222.

RV ★★★★ Tent ★★★★

Beauty: ★★★★	Site Privacy: ★★★★
Spaciousness: ★★★★	Quiet: ★★★★
Security: ★★★★	Cleanliness: ★★★★
Insect Control: ★★★★	Facilities: ★★★

This campground is split up into three separate areas. The two main camping areas are on either side of the office. On the north side, there are 12 50-foot pull-throughs with cable TV hookups. These sites are mainly open, with some trees. The 2nd main area is on the south side of the office. There are 11 60-foot pull-throughs in this area (without cable). This area is more heavily forested, and most every site is shaded. The third area, for overflow, consists of an open grassy field with six 70-foot back-ins. These sites are completely unshaded and do not offer any facilities (other than electric hookups). The town and surrounding area are devoid of attractions.

Basics

Operated By: Linda & Jerry Starks. **Open:** Apr–Oct. **Site Assignment:** Assigned upon registration; verbal reservations OK. **Registration:** In office. (Late arrivals use drop box.) **Fee:** RV $20 (full), tent $11 (checks, no credits cards). **Parking:** At site.

Facilities

Number of RV Sites: 29. **Number of Tent-Only Sites:** Undesignated sites. **Hookups:** Water, sewer, electric (20, 30, 50 amps), cable. **Dump Station:** No (sewer at all sites). **Laundry:** Yes. **Pay Phone:** Yes. **Rest Rooms and Showers:** Yes. **Fuel:** No. **Propane:** No. **Internal Roads:** Gravel. **RV Service:** No. **Market:** Less than 0.25 mi. north. **Restaurant:** Less than 1 mi. south. **General Store:** No. **Vending:** No. **Swimming:** No. **Playground:** No. **Activities:** Fishing, boating, swimming, hiking. **Nearby Attractions:** Bonny State Park. **Additional Information:** Burlington Chamber of Commerce, (719) 346-8070.

Restrictions

Pets: On leash, cleaned up after. **Fires:** In grills. **Alcoholic Beverages:** At sites. **Vehicle Maximum Length:** None.

To Get There

From I-70 (Exit 405), turn north onto Hwy. 59 and go 0.2 mi. Turn right onto 4th St. and go 0.2 mi. Turn right onto Colorado and go 1 block to the office on the right.

SILVERTON

Silver Summit

640 Mineral St., P.O. Box 656, Silverton 81433. T: (800) 352-1637 or (970) 387-0240; F: (970) 387-5495; www.silverton.org/silversummit; slvrsmmt@ frontier.net.

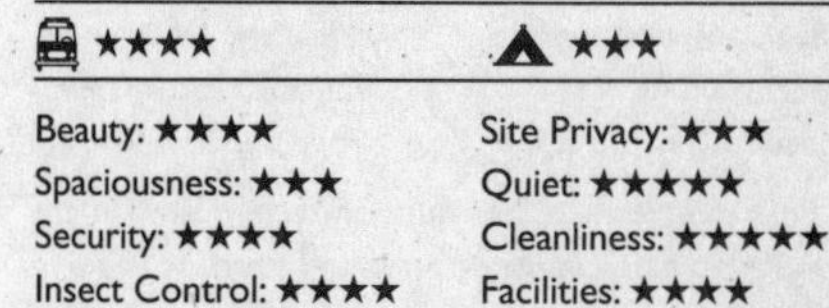

RV ★★★★ Tent ★★★

Beauty: ★★★★	Site Privacy: ★★★
Spaciousness: ★★★	Quiet: ★★★★★
Security: ★★★★	Cleanliness: ★★★★★
Insect Control: ★★★★	Facilities: ★★★★

At the southern edge of town, this campground is surrounded on all four sides by mountains (including Kendell Mountain to the east). There are beautiful vistas from anywhere inside this campground, making it a wonderful place to stop and relax. While there are no shade trees around the park, summers do not get overly hot and the park remains quite comfortable. End site 23 is an open pull-through that could accommodate a rig of any size. All other sites (pull-throughs and back-ins) range from 50 feet to 55 feet. Tents are allowed on any of the RV spaces, which are all level, grassy, and open, making them a fine place to set up a tent. The rest rooms are fantastically clean, and there is plenty of space in the showers. The laundry room is also quite clean and spacious. This is a very pretty campground with unbeatable vistas that both tenters and RVers will enjoy.

Basics

Operated By: Denny & Sigrun Martin. **Open:** May 15–Oct. 15. **Site Assignment:** Assigned upon registration. Credit card required for reservation; 48-hours cancellation policy. **Registration:** In office. (Late arrivals select an available site & pay in the morning.) **Fee:** RV $22, tent $17 (V, MC, AE, D). **Parking:** At site.

Facilities

Number of RV Sites: 39. **Number of Tent-Only Sites:** 0. **Hookups:** Water, sewer, electric (30, 50 amps). **Each Site:** Picnic table, grill. **Dump Station:** Yes. **Laundry:** Yes. **Pay Phone:** Yes. **Rest Rooms and Showers:** Yes. **Fuel:** No. **Propane:** No. **Internal Roads:** Gravel. **RV Service:** No. **Market:** 1 block. **Restaurant:** 6 blocks. **General Store:** Yes. **Vending:** No. **Swimming:** No (hot tub). **Playground:** No. **Other:** Jeep rentals. **Activities:** Jeeping, hiking, fishing, horseback riding, guided tours, gold mining tours. **Nearby Attractions:** Ghost towns, railroad, scenic byway, national historic district, wild flowers, native crafts, museum. **Additional Information:** Silverton Chamber of Commerce, (800) 752-4494 or (970) 387-5654.

Restrictions

Pets: On leash, cleaned up after. **Fires:** In fire pits. **Alcoholic Beverages:** At sites. **Vehicle Maximum Length:** 42 ft.

To Get There

From the junction of Hwy. 550 and Hwy. 110, go 0.2 mi. north on Hwy. 110. Turn east onto East 7th St. Turn right onto Mineral St. The office is on the left.

SOUTH FORK

Grandview Cabins and RV

P.O. Box 189, South Fork 81154. T: (719) 873-5541.

RV ★★★★ Tent n/a

Beauty: ★★★	Site Privacy: ★★★
Spaciousness: ★★★	Quiet: ★★★★
Security: ★★★★	Cleanliness: ★★★★
Insect Control: ★★★	Facilities: ★★★★

This campground has quite attractive sites in the southern part, but more open and unshaded sites to the north. There are level grassy pull-throughs as well as back-ins, which average 35 × 25 feet. Back-ins in the southwest (16–24) back to a wall of trees that makes these sites quite attractive. Sites 25–34 are larger (40 × 27 feet), but do not have as many trees. Sites 51–54 are very nice back-ins with shade trees and nice landscaping that back to an attractive fence. Site 48, next to the cabins, is also quite a nice spot, with several trees in the corner. The laundry, which shares a room with a furnace and water tanks, is a little hot and cramped and in need of a paint job, but has quite a few machines. The rest rooms are housed individually, and are very clean and comfortable.

Basics

Operated By: Gary & Maria Hodges. **Open:** All year. **Site Assignment:** Assigned upon registration. Credit card required for reservation; 1-week cancellation policy. **Registration:** In office. (Late arrivals park by the river & settle in the morning). **Fee:** $16–18 (V, MC, D). **Parking:** At site.

Facilities

Number of RV Sites: 92. **Number of Tent-Only Sites:** 0. **Hookups:** Water, sewer, electric (30 amps). **Each Site:** Picnic table. **Dump Station:** Yes. **Laundry:** Yes. **Pay Phone:** Yes. **Rest Rooms and Showers:** Yes. **Fuel:** No. **Propane:** No. **Internal Roads:** Gravel. **RV Service:** No. **Market:** 0.5 mi. to South Fork. **Restaurant:** 0.5 mi. to South Fork. **General Store:** No. **Vending:** No. **Swimming:** No (hot tub). **Playground:** No. **Other:** Fish cleaning station, cabins, meeting room, free RV storage, kitchenette. **Activities:** Hunting, fishing, Jeep tours, evening camp fires, skiing, snow mobiling, rafting, hiking, country & western dancing, potlucks, ice cream socials. **Nearby Attractions:** Great Sand Dunes, Creede, Silver Thread Scenic Byway, Mesa Verde, Rio Grande River, Durango-Silverton RR, Royal Gorge Bridge. **Additional Information:** Durango Chamber of Commerce, (800) 525-8855.

Restrictions

Pets: Only in north RV sites; on leash, cleaned up after. **Fires:** In fire rings. **Alcoholic Beverages:** At sites. **Vehicle Maximum Length:** None.

To Get There

From the junction of Hwy. 148 and Hwy. 160, go 0.6 mi. northwest on Hwy. 149. Turn left at the sign onto a dirt road. Keep straight and follow the signs to the office.

STEAMBOAT SPRINGS

Steamboat Campground

3603 Lincoln Ave., Steamboat Springs 80487. T: (800) 562-7549; skitownkoa@springsips.com.

RV ★★★★ Tent ★★★★

Beauty: ★★★★	Site Privacy: ★★★
Spaciousness: ★★★	Quiet: ★★★
Security: ★★★★	Cleanliness: ★★★★
Insect Control: ★★★★	Facilities: ★★★★★

At the very western tip of town, this campground is split in half by the Yampa River: RVs on the north side, tents on the south. There are stunning mountain views from practically anywhere in the campground. However, Hwy. 40 is just a stone's throw away, and noise can be heard as far away as in the tent sites. The grounds are clean, with immaculately manicured, lush grass. The rest room facilities are clean and modern, as is the laundry, although the latter is a little cramped. Some of the best sites (36–39, 41, 42) are back-ins, that may exclude some larger rigs, but they sport nice trees along the southwest fence. Another drawback to this area are the mobile homes parked along this strip—some of which look quite run-down. Other RV sites are laid out in a grid, with decent-sized pull throughs among them (73 × 28 feet). (Back-in spaces run 42 feet in length and a comparable width.) The RV section of the park is mostly open, and all sites are level and grassy. The tent area is a whole different ballgame, left nicely wild with loads of trees and grass. Some tent sites (99A–106) are right on the river's edge, while the rest have a more forested feel. In all, this park offers a very nice stay in a location that can't be beat.

Basics

Operated By: the Sabia family. **Open:** All year. **Site Assignment:** Assigned upon registration. **Registration:** In office. (Late arrivals use drop box.) **Fee:** RV $30 (full), $25 (water, electric), tent $20 (V, MC, D). **Parking:** At site.

Facilities

Number of RV Sites: 104. **Number of Tent-Only Sites:** 36. **Hookups:** Water, sewer, electric (30, 50 amps). **Each Site:** Picnic table, grill. **Dump Station:** Yes. **Laundry:** Yes. **Pay Phone:** Yes. **Rest Rooms and Showers:** Yes. **Fuel:** No. **Propane:** Yes. **Internal Roads:** Paved, gravel to tent area. **RV Service:** No. **Market:** 2 mi. into town. **Restaurant:** 2 mi. into town. **General Store:** Yes. **Vending:** Yes. **Swimming:** Pool. **Playground:** Yes. **Other:** TV room w/ pool table, RV parts, mini golf, free local bus service, cabins, river, dataport, hot tub, breakfast patio, snack bar, pet walk area. **Activities:** Volleyball, horseshoes, fishing, hiking, skiing. **Nearby Attractions:** Steamboat Springs ski area, Routt National Forest, Fish Creek Falls, Haymaker Golf Course, Flat Tops Wilderness Area, Tread of Pioneers Museum. **Additional Information:** Steamboat Springs Chamber Resort Assoc., (970) 879-0880.

Restrictions

Pets: On leash, cleaned up after use pet walk area. **Fires:** In fire ring only. **Alcoholic Beverages:** At sites. **Vehicle Maximum Length:** None. **Other:** In winter, only open to monthly rentals.

To Get There

0.1 mi. from the western town name signpost on Hwy. 40. Entrance is on the south side.

STERLING

Yogi Bear's Jellystone Camp Resort

22018 Hwy. 6, Sterling 80751. T: (970) 522-2233 or (970) 522-6701; www.gocampingamerica.com/yogisterling/index.html; ranger@campjellystonepark.com.

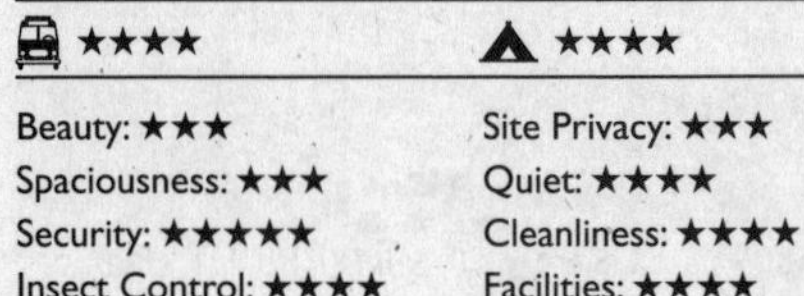

RV ★★★★ Tent ★★★★

Beauty: ★★★	Site Privacy: ★★★
Spaciousness: ★★★	Quiet: ★★★★
Security: ★★★★★	Cleanliness: ★★★★
Insect Control: ★★★★	Facilities: ★★★★

This family-oriented campground offers lots of activities within the park itself, with facilities from a swimming pool to volleyball nets to meeting rooms. There are two separate RV areas, offering very different experiences. Sites E1–E14 are laid out in two wings along a central row, and are entirely unshaded. These are, of course, electric sites only, and lack of other hookups and shade trees makes them less desirable than sites in the main camping area. The main camping area contains both RV sites (laid out in a large loop) and tenting sites (occupying the middle of the loop). These 47 RV sites are uniformly forested, and all of them are pull-throughs. Sites average 75 feet in length—easily large enough for any vehicle, even with a tow. About half of these sites are large enough for double slide-outs, but all sites are certainly roomy enough for pleasant family camping. Sites with the highest numbers (40–47) are closest to the pool and the office, while those in the 20s and 30s are furthest away from the action. The tenting area is likewise well-shaded, and very comfortable. The rest rooms and showers are exceptionally clean and comfrotable. This is a family-oriented campground that offers enough in the way of recreation opportunities to be a destination in itself.

Basics

Operated By: "Ranger" Bill. **Open:** All year. **Site Assignment:** Assigned upon registration. **Regis-**

tration: In office. (Late arrivals use drop box.) **Fee:** RV $27.74 (full), $25.57 (water, electric), tent $21.22 (checks, V, MC). **Parking:** At site.

Facilities

Number of RV Sites: 61. **Number of Tent-Only Sites:** Undesignated sites. **Hookups:** Water, sewer, electric (20, 30 amps). **Each Site:** Picnic table, grill. **Dump Station:** Yes. **Laundry:** Yes. **Pay Phone:** Yes. **Rest Rooms and Showers:** Yes. **Fuel:** No. **Propane:** Yes. **Internal Roads:** Gravel. **RV Service:** No. **Market:** 5 mi. to Sterling. **Restaurant:** 0.5 mi. to I-76. **General Store:** Yes. **Vending:** Yes. **Swimming:** Pool. **Playground:** Yes. **Other:** Mini golf, game room, meeting room, pet walk. **Activities:** Volleyball, swimming, planned activities, horseshoes, basketball, fishing, boating. **Nearby Attractions:** North Sterling State Park, North Sterling Reservoir. **Additional Information:** Logan County Chamber of Commerce, (800) 544-8609 or (970) 522-5070.

Restrictions

Pets: On leash, cleaned up after. **Fires:** In fire pits. **Alcoholic Beverages:** At sites. **Vehicle Maximum Length:** None.

To Get There

From Hwy. I-76 (Exit 125), turn east onto Hwy. 6 and go 0.5 mi. Turn right at the sign into the entrance.

THORNTON

Denver North Campground and RV Park

16700 North Washington St., Broomfield 80020. T: (800) 851-6521 or (303) 452-4120; F: (303) 452-4156; campdenver@aol.com.

RV ★★★★ Tent ★★★★

Beauty: ★★★★	Site Privacy: ★★★★
Spaciousness: ★★★★	Quiet: ★★★★
Security: ★★★★★	Cleanliness: ★★★★★
Insect Control: ★★★★	Facilities: ★★★★★

Just off the highway and offering easy on and off access, this campground has plenty of long pull-throughs for larger rigs with tows. Laid out in 5 rows, sites 1–60 are pull-throughs in the middle of the campground. Sites 1–24 are 54 feet in length, while 25–60 are 40 feet. To the east, sites in the 100s and 200s are more open (with fewer shade trees) and closer to the highway. However, these sites include the longest (75-foot) pull-throughs. Close to the entrance are 45-foot back-ins reserved for long-term residents. This area also contains the tenting sites, which offer wooden partitions for increased privacy and sand tent pads for increased comfort. However, these sites are just off the road and may suffer from passing traffic noise. The rest rooms are small but clean. They are housed in a mobile home that seems to be showing its age slightly. The showers are individual units, and very clean. This is a quite decent stop for tenters or RVers who wish to stay in the area for several days.

Basics

Operated By: Steve & Chris Hennings. **Open:** All year. **Site Assignment:** Assigned upon registration Credit card required for reservation; cancellation requires same-day notice by 10 a.m. **Registration:** In office. (Late arrivals use drop box.) **Fee:** RV $29.50 (full, 50 amps), $27.90 (full, 30 amps), $26.50 (water, electric), tent $21 (checks, V, MC, D). **Parking:** At site.

Facilities

Number of RV Sites: 140. **Number of Tent-Only Sites:** 15. **Hookups:** Water, sewer, electric (30, 50 amps). **Each Site:** Picnic table, grill. **Dump Station:** Yes. **Laundry:** Yes. **Pay Phone:** Yes. **Rest Rooms and Showers:** Yes. **Fuel:** No. **Propane:** Yes. **Internal Roads:** Paved/dirt. **RV Service:** No. **Market:** 5 mi. south. **Restaurant:** 5 mi. south. **General Store:** Yes. **Vending:** Yes. **Swimming:** Pool. **Playground:** Yes. **Other:** 2 cabins, dataport, meeting room, game room, dog walk. **Activities:** Pancake corral (Memorial Day–Labor Day), swimming. **Nearby Attractions:** Denver, Boulder, Rocky Mountain National Park. **Additional Information:** Denver Chamber of Commerce, (303) 458-0220.

Restrictions

Pets: On leash, cleaned up after. **Fires:** In grills. **Alcoholic Beverages:** At sites. **Vehicle Maximum Length:** None.

To Get There

From I-25 (Exit 229), on the east side of the highway, take the first right turn and go 0.2 mi. Turn left at the sign into the entrance.

TRINIDAD

Summit Inn Motel and RV Park

9800 Santa Fe Trail, Trinidad 81082. T: (719) 846-2251; F: (719) 846-2251.

RV ★★★ Tent n/a

Beauty: ★★	Site Privacy: ★★★
Spaciousness: ★★★★	Quiet: ★★★
Security: ★★★★	Cleanliness: ★★★★
Insect Control: ★★★★	Facilities: ★★★

RV sites are located behind this motel. To the east and south are woods-covered hills, giving rise to the motel's claim of "great views". There are two rows of RV sites, with back-ins on the north side and pull-throughs on the south side. Each site has a gravel strip and cement pad. pull-throughs are 75 × 33 feet, back-ins are 70 × 33 feet. The best sites are to the east, as these have the best views, and are furthest away from the entrance and the highway. Sites 9–12 are closest to the motel and slightly apart from the others. Site 10 is just off the parking lot, while 9 is actually on the parking lot behind the motel. This motel/RV park is an acceptable overnighter for RVers, and close enough to Trinidad State Park to make day recreation at the lake possible. Tenters, however, will have to move on, either to Walsenburg or on into New Mexico.

Basics

Operated By: JoAnn Tortorelli. **Open:** All year. **Site Assignment:** First come, first served; verbal reservations OK. **Registration:** In office. **Fee:** RV $23 (full), $19 (water, electric) (checks, V, MC, D). **Parking:** At site.

Facilities

Number of RV Sites: 32. **Number of Tent-Only Sites:** 0. **Hookups:** Water, sewer, electric (20, 30, 50 amps). **Each Site:** Table. **Dump Station:** Yes. **Laundry:** Yes. **Pay Phone:** Yes. **Rest Rooms and Showers:** Yes. **Fuel:** No. **Propane:** No. **Internal Roads:** Gravel, paved. **RV Service:** No. **Market:** At Exit 11. **Restaurant:** At Exit 11. **General Store:** No. **Vending:** No. **Swimming:** Pool & indoor spa. **Playground:** No. **Other:** Free continental breakfast. **Activities:** Soaking in spa, boating, fishing, hiking, wildlife watching. **Nearby Attractions:** Trinidad State Park. **Additional Information:** Trinidad Chamber of Commerce, (719) 846-9285.

Restrictions

Pets: On leash, cleaned up after. **Fires:** In fire pits. **Alcoholic Beverages:** At sites. **Vehicle Maximum Length:** None.

To Get There

From I-25 Exit 11, take the first right on the east side of the highway (Santa Fe Trail) and go 0.25 mi. Turn left at the sign into the motel entrance.

TWIN LAKES

Parry Peak Campground

2015 North Poplar, Leadville 80461. T: (800) 416-6992; F: (719) 395-9022.

RV ★★★★ Tent ★★★★

Beauty: ★★★★★	Site Privacy: ★★★★
Spaciousness: ★★★★	Quiet: ★★★★
Security: ★★★★	Cleanliness: ★★★★
Insect Control: ★★★★	Facilities: ★

At the foot of a large mountain and by a river, this campground offers a very natural escape from the world. Unfortunately, that world drives past quite close to the campground, and no site is immune to passing traffic noise. Sites 1, 3–5, 7, and 9 back to the highway and receive the worst traffic noise. Most of the sites are 50–54-foot back-ins, although there are large pull-throughs, including 6 (78-foot) and 8 (70-foot), as well as an oversized back-in (site 26 measures 30 × 36 feet) and at least one smaller site (5 is a 30-foot back-in). While most sites in this forested campground are well-shaded, 12 is an exception, and many campers may wish to avoid this site for that reason. Sites 16–26, located across a small bridge from the main campground area, also offer tent pads at each site. Some of these sites (17–21 especially) are among the quietest sites, as they are furthest from the highway. Although there are no hookups in this campground, drinking water is found at several sites, including 10 and between 17 and 18. Besides the RV sites and the sites with tent pads, tenters can also choose from several extremely attractive walk-in sites. These are just off the road (no fear of dragging your gear for hundreds of yards), and three are located just off the river. While lacking hookups, this campground offers a great escape for those willing to give up luxury for a night or two.

Basics

Operated By: National Forest Service. **Open:** Memorial Day–after Labor Day. **Site Assignment:** First come, first served; reservations can be made 4–240 days in advance. Credit card required for reservation; $8.65 reservation fee, $10 cancellation fee; cancellations within 3 days pay first night, no-shows pay $20 fee. 2-nights min. stay on weekends,

3-nights on holidays. **Registration:** At pay station. **Fee:** $10 (checks). **Parking:** At site.

FACILITIES

Number of RV Sites: 26. **Number of Tent-Only Sites:** 4. **Hookups:** None. **Each Site:** Picnic table, grill. **Dump Station:** No. **Laundry:** No. **Pay Phone:** No. **Rest Rooms and Showers:** Pit toilets; no shower. **Fuel:** No. **Propane:** No. **Internal Roads:** Gravel. **RV Service:** No. **Market:** 22 mi. to Leadville. **Restaurant:** 2.8 mi. to Twin Lakes. **General Store:** No. **Vending:** No. **Swimming:** Lake. **Playground:** No. **Other:** Firewood. **Activities:** Fishing, boating, swimming, hiking. **Nearby Attractions:** Leadville, Rocky Mountains, San Isabel National Forest. **Additional Information:** Leadville Chamber of Commerce, (719) 486-3900.

RESTRICTIONS

Pets: On leash, cleaned up after. **Fires:** In grills. **Alcoholic Beverages:** At sites. **Vehicle Maximum Length:** None. **Other:** $3 day use fee.

TO GET THERE

From the junction of Hwy. 24 and Hwy. 82, turn west onto Hwy. 82 and go 9 mi. Turn left at the sign into the entrance.

WALDEN

Roundup Motel

365 Main, Walden 80480. T: (970) 723-4680; F: (970) 723-4959; www.roundupmotel.com; bobbie@roundupmotel.com.

RV: ★★★ Tent: n/a

Beauty: ★★★	Site Privacy: ★★★
Spaciousness: ★★★	Quiet: ★★★★
Security: ★★★★	Cleanliness: ★★★★
Insect Control: ★★★★	Facilities: ★★★

Recently opened as an RV park, the Roundup Motel has only a few spaces available, but these are the only full hookups within several miles of town. (There are two other pull-through sites with full hookups at the North Park Motel, also on Main.) The "park" consists of five back-ins, 25 feet wide and virtually as long as you want. On the opposite side of the fence that runs around the park are mobile homes, and the surrounding area has a destinct small town feel. The sites are a mix of gravel and grass. The middle sites are slightly more desirbale, as they do not abut a residence. The advantage of this park over the National Forest campgrounds in the surrounding area is twofold: full hookups (as opposed to electrical or none) and proximity to town. Everything in town is within walking distance of this park. Tenters can pitch a tent in the town park or continue on to one of the National Forest parks. This RV park is extremely small but convenient.

BASICS

Operated By: Mark & Bobbie Scott. **Open:** All year. **Site Assignment:** First come, first served. Credit card required for reservation; 24-hours cancellation policy. **Registration:** In office. (Late arrivals ring manager's number on phone.) **Fee:** RV $20 (checks, V, MC, D, AE). **Parking:** At site.

FACILITIES

Number of RV Sites: 5. **Number of Tent-Only Sites:** 0. **Hookups:** Water, sewer, electric (20, 30 amps), cable. **Dump Station:** No (sewer at all sites). **Laundry:** No (in town). **Pay Phone:** Yes. **Rest Rooms and Showers:** Yes. **Fuel:** No. **Propane:** No. **Internal Roads:** Gravel. **RV Service:** No. **Market:** Less than 1 mi. north. **Restaurant:** 1 block south. **General Store:** Across street. **Vending:** Across street. **Swimming:** No. **Playground:** No. **Other:** Motel rooms. **Activities:** Fishing, boating, swimming, hiking, cross-country skiing, hunting. **Nearby Attractions:** Steamboat Springs, Laramie, wildlife, natural sand dunes, Big Creek Lakes, North Platte River, Routt National Forest. **Additional Information:** North Park Chamber of Commerce, (970) 723-4600.

RESTRICTIONS

Pets: On leash, cleaned up after. **Fires:** In grills. **Alcoholic Beverages:** At sites. **Vehicle Maximum Length:** None.

TO GET THERE

From the junction of Hwy. 14 and Hwy. 125, Turn right at the sign into the entrance.

WALSENBURG

Dakota Campground

P.O. Box 206, Walsenburg 81089. T: (719) 738-9912.

RV: ★★★ Tent: ★★

Beauty: ★★	Site Privacy: ★★★
Spaciousness: ★★★	Quiet: ★★★
Security: ★★★★	Cleanliness: ★★★
Insect Control: ★★★★	Facilities: ★★★

Next to an RV service shop, dry storage, and mobile homes, this campground is surrounded by commercial/industrial space, and only the trees along the west liven it up slightly. Sites are grassy and unshaded 90-foot and 100-foot pull-throughs. Sites 1–22 are mobile homes along the south. RV sites 23–34, located behind the office, measure 90 × 16 feet. Rigs with slide-outs will feel the squeeze in these sites, especially if situated next to one another. Sites 35–46 are longer (100 feet), and include the best sites: 35–37 and 44–46, which are away from the office and playground, have views of the trees to the west. Sites 47–68 are 100-foot sites close to a commercial area and the highway, making them less desirable. The tenting area is located ot the north, adjacent to a shed. Grass and a few tables make this area acceptable, but it is far from a haven for tenters. The rest rooms are reasonably clean, but showing their age. This campground is a reasonable stop—especially for RVs—but won't likely make anyone's destination list.

BASICS

Operated By: George & Mikell Birrer. **Open:** All year. **Site Assignment:** Assigned upon registration; verbal reservations OK. **Registration:** In office. (Late arrivals go to house.) **Fee:** RV $20 (full), tent $10 (no checks, no credit cards). **Parking:** At site.

FACILITIES

Number of RV Sites: 72. **Number of Tent-Only Sites:** 10. **Hookups:** Water, sewer, electric (30, 50 amps). **Each Site:** Picnic table. **Dump Station:** Yes. **Laundry:** Yes. **Pay Phone:** Yes. **Rest Rooms and Showers:** Yes. **Fuel:** No. **Propane:** Yes. **Internal Roads:** Gravel. **RV Service:** Yes. **Market:** 1 mi. north. **Restaurant:** 0.5 mi. north. **General Store:** Yes. **Vending:** No. **Swimming:** No. **Playground:** Yes. **Activities:** Boating, fishing, golf. **Nearby Attractions:** Lathrop State Park. **Additional Information:** Huerfano County Chamber of Commerce, (719) 738-1065.

RESTRICTIONS

Pets: On leash, cleaned up after. **Fires:** In fire pits. **Alcoholic Beverages:** At sites. **Vehicle Maximum Length:** None.

TO GET THERE

From I-25 Exit 52, turn south onto Business Loop I-25 and go 0.3 mi. from the south side of the highway. Turn right at the sign into the entrance.

WARD

Camp Dick

Boulder Ranger Office, 2140 Yarmouth Ave., Boulder 80301. T: (877) 444-6777 or (303) 444-6600; www.reserveusa.com or www.fs.fed.us/arns.

RV: ★★★ Tent: ★★★★★

Beauty: ★★★★★	Site Privacy: ★★★★
Spaciousness: ★★★★	Quiet: ★★★★★
Security: ★★★★	Cleanliness: ★★★
Insect Control: ★★★★	Facilities: ★

Nature lovers will enjoy this campground, but those who rely on campground facilities may have mixed feelings. The beauty of this location is undeniable: the entire campground is surrounded by forested hills and most of the sites are at least partially forested. On the downside, of course, is the lack of RV hookups and narrow road in—hopefully, two giant 5th wheels will never meet on this road. Most of the sites are 40-foot back-ins, but there are exceptions to this. Site 16 is a large (75-foot) pull-through, and sites 7 and 21 are oversized sites—large enough for two vehicles and much wider than ordinary sites. Sites to the north (10, 12, and 13–16) back to a lovely stream, making these more desirable sites. Sites 26 and 28, on the other hand, are totally unshaded, making them less desirable. Site 35 offers more privacy, located as it is at the end of a roundabout. Sites 30–38 offer somewhat more seclusion, as they are located on a separate road from the other sites. The facilities include pit toilets but no showers or running water. Hardier campers will enjoy the chance to be close to nature, but those who prefer to be pampered will want to look elsewhere.

BASICS

Operated By: Thousand Trails Management. **Open:** May–Oct. (dates may vary). **Site Assignment:** First come, first served. Credit card required for reservation; 3-days cancellation policy, less $10.00 service fee. **Registration:** At pay kiosk. (Camp host will verify that campers have paid.) **Fee:** $12, $15 for oversized sites (checks, no credit cards). **Parking:** At site.

FACILITIES

Number of RV Sites: 41. **Number of Tent-Only Sites:** 0. **Hookups:** None. **Dump Station:** No. **Laundry:** No. **Pay Phone:** No. **Rest Rooms and Showers:** Rest rooms; no shower. **Fuel:** No.

Propane: No. **Internal Roads:** Paved. **RV Service:** No. **Market:** 12 mi. (in Nederland). **Restaurant:** 5 mi. north (in town). **General Store:** No. **Vending:** No. **Swimming:** No. **Playground:** No. **Activities:** Fishing, hiking, mountain climbing, cross-country skiing, gambling. **Nearby Attractions:** Rocky Mountain National Park, Blackhawk, Central City. **Additional Information:** Thousand Trails Management, (303) 258-3610.

Restrictions

Pets: On leash, cleaned up after. **Fires:** In fire pits. **Alcoholic Beverages:** At sites. **Vehicle Maximum Length:** None.

To Get There

From the junction of Hwy. 7 and Hwy. 72, turn south onto Hwy. 72 and go 4.1 mi. Turn right at the sign into the entrance. Pass through Peaceful Valley Campground to get to Camp Dick.

WELLINGTON

Fort Collins/Wellington KOA

P.O. Box 130, Wellington 80549. T: (800) KOA-8142 or (970) 568-7486; www.koa.com.

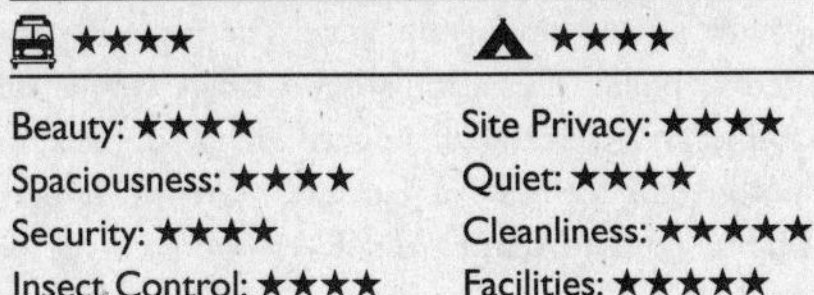

RV ★★★★ Tent ★★★★

Beauty: ★★★★	Site Privacy: ★★★★
Spaciousness: ★★★★	Quiet: ★★★★
Security: ★★★★	Cleanliness: ★★★★★
Insect Control: ★★★★	Facilities: ★★★★★

With the exception of a small row of back-ins for long-term guests, this campground offers all pull-throughs. Sites average 70 feet (60 feet in Row Cougar). The sites consist of gravel and sparse grass, and have only limited amounts of shade from small trees. The views to the west are best enjoyed from sites A12, B14, C10, and D10. These end sites are also the furthest from the entrance (especially in rows Antelope, Buffalo, and Cougar) and the office. The 50-amp sites are in the southeast corner of the RV sites (A 1–5 and B 1–5). There are 19 tent sites on a semi-circle to the southeast. These sites are also sparsely shaded at best. The rest rooms and showers are very clean and spacious. There are four individual units inside the office complex that are open during business hours. These are equally spotless. This campground is a pleasant place to stay, whether visiting the Ft. Collins area or continuing on to the Poudre valley.

Basics

Operated By: Guenter Kippschull, Helmut Roy. **Open:** All year. **Site Assignment:** Credit card required for reservation; 24-hours cancellation policy, less $4 fee. **Registration:** In office. (Late arrivals use drop box.) **Fee:** RV $25 (full), $23 (water, electric), tent $19 (checks, V, MC, AE). **Parking:** At site.

Facilities

Number of RV Sites: 75. **Number of Tent-Only Sites:** 19. **Hookups:** Water, sewer, electric (30, 50 amps). **Each Site:** Picnic table. **Dump Station:** Yes. **Laundry:** Yes. **Pay Phone:** Yes. **Rest Rooms and Showers:** Yes. **Fuel:** No. **Propane:** Yes. **Internal Roads:** Gravel. **RV Service:** No. **Market:** 12 mi. south to Fort Collins. **Restaurant:** 12 mi. south to Fort Collins. **General Store:** Yes. **Vending:** No. **Swimming:** Pool. **Playground:** Yes. **Other:** Pavilion, rec room (w/ TV), dog walk, storage, patio, bicycle rentals. **Activities:** Rafting, fishing, swimming. **Nearby Attractions:** Cache La Poudre, Fort Collins, Budweiser Brewery, Cheyenne Days Rodeo (July). **Additional Information:** Fort Collins CVB, (970) 491-3388.

Restrictions

Pets: On leash, cleaned up after; monthly guests must pay deposit. **Fires:** In grills. **Alcoholic Beverages:** At sites. **Vehicle Maximum Length:** None. **Other:** No speeding (5 mph limit).

To Get There

From I-25 (Exit 281), turn east onto CR 70 and go 0.3 mi. Turn into 2nd driveway (to the east) and continue to the office.

WESTCLIFFE

Grape Creek RV Park

56491 Hwy. 69, Westcliffe 81252. T: (888) 783-CAMP or (719) 783-2588; grapecreekrv@rmi.net.

RV ★★★★★ Tent ★★★

Beauty: ★★★★	Site Privacy: ★★★★
Spaciousness: ★★★★	Quiet: ★★★★★
Security: ★★★★	Cleanliness: ★★★★★
Insect Control: ★★★★	Facilities: ★★★★

A destination for peace, quiet, and, in the words of Mr. Latham, "some of the most beautiful sunsets you've ever seen," this campground has beautiful sites with lush grass and gorgeous views of snow-capped peaks to the west. Pretty much all sites are wonderful, although 25–32 are closest to the offices and may get a little more passing traffic than other sites. Sites 1–12 and end site 24 have the best views of the mountains and the valley, and are therefore more desirable. All RV sites are grassy pull-throughs averaging 50 × 30 feet. The rest rooms and showers are immaculate, spacious, and modern, as is the laundry room. Tenting is possible to the west of the RV sites or below the park by the river. Either location has beautiful grass but no cover. In fact, pretty much the only conceivable complaint anyone could have here is the lack of shade. But why complain when you're in such a beautiful site? Sit back, relax, and enjoy the quiet and scenery!

Basics

Operated By: Zane & Diana Latham. **Open:** May 10–Oct. 1. **Site Assignment:** Assigned upon registration. Credit card required for reservation; 30-days cancellation policy. **Registration:** In office. (Late arrivals come to office.) **Fee:** RV $24 (full), water, electric: $20, tent $14. **Parking:** At site.

Facilities

Number of RV Sites: 34. **Number of Tent-Only Sites:** 10. **Hookups:** Water, sewer, electric (30, 50 amps). **Each Site:** Bushes between sites, space for extra vehicle. **Dump Station:** Yes. **Laundry:** Yes. **Pay Phone:** Yes. **Rest Rooms and Showers:** Yes. **Fuel:** No. **Propane:** No. **Internal Roads:** Gravel. **RV Service:** No. **Market:** 2 mi. to Westcliffe. **Restaurant:** 2 mi. to Westcliffe. **General Store:** No. **Vending:** No. **Swimming:** No. **Playground:** No. **Other:** Cabins. **Activities:** Fishing, mountain climbing, mountain biking, hunting. **Nearby Attractions:** Bishop Castle, Kit Carson Mountain, Carson Mountain, Crestone Peak, Crestone Needle, Humboldt Peak, Grape Creek. **Additional Information:** Custer County Chamber, (719) 783-9163.

Restrictions

Pets: On leash, cleaned up after. **Fires:** In rings (not at sites). **Alcoholic Beverages:** At sites. **Vehicle Maximum Length:** 45 ft.

To Get There

From the junction of Hwy. 96 and Hwy. 69, go 2 mi. south on Hwy. 69. Turn right at the sign onto a dirt lane and follow it into the campground.

WHEAT RIDGE

Prospect RV Park

11600 West 44th Ave., Wheat Ridge 80033. T: (800) 344-5702 or (303) 424-4414.

RV ★★★★ Tent n/a

Beauty: ★★★★	Site Privacy: ★★★
Spaciousness: ★★★	Quiet: ★★★★
Security: ★★★★★	Cleanliness: ★★★★★
Insect Control: ★★★★	Facilities: ★★★★

Although this campground is located in an urban residential area, it abuts a park and a lake, so it feels much more like a hideaway. The red barn and horses in the southwest corner only add to this feeling. Sites consist of shaded gravel spaces a uniform 24 feet wide. pull-throughs average 50 feet in length, and back-ins average 35 feet. Sites 5–10 have a very nice view of the neighboring lake. Sites 21–35 and 42–47 are quite attractive back-ins that back to a hedge that runs along the perimeter of the manager's residence. Sites 49–71 are laid out in three rows. These pull-throughs are somewhat smaller than the others in the park (30–42 feet). Sites 41 and 55 have the nicest views of the farmland to the southwest, but 64 has the least desirable view (a storage shed). The rest rooms are bright, modern, and absolutely immaculate. This campground offers urban convenience, but the surprise it holds up its sleeve is the quiet, pretty retreat it creates in the middle of the city.

Basics

Operated By: Nancy Laird. **Open:** All year. **Site Assignment:** Assigned upon registration. Credit card required for reservation; call to cancel. **Registration:** In office. (Late arrivals select an available site & pay in the morning.) **Fee:** RV $28 (full), $24 (water, electric) (checks, V, MC). **Parking:** At site.

Facilities

Number of RV Sites: 71. **Number of Tent-Only Sites:** 0. **Hookups:** Water, sewer, electric (30, 50 amps). **Each Site:** Picnic table on concrete slab. **Dump Station:** Yes. **Laundry:** Yes. **Pay Phone:** Yes. **Rest Rooms and Showers:** Yes. **Fuel:** No. **Propane:** No. **Internal Roads:** Gravel. **RV Service:** On-call. **Market:** 6 blocks west. **Restaurant:** 3 blocks west. **General Store:** No. **Vending:** Yes. **Swimming:** No. **Playground:** Yes (next door). **Other:** Pet walk, dataport. **Activities:** Fishing, biking, hiking. **Nearby Attractions:** Prospect Park, Prospect Lake. **Additional Information:** Denver Chamber of Commerce, (303) 458-0220.

Restrictions

Pets: On leash, cleaned up after, some problem

breeds not allowed. **Fires:** In grills. **Alcoholic Beverages:** At sites. **Vehicle Maximum Length:** None.

To Get There

From the junction of I-25 and I-70, take Exit 214A and turn west onto I-70. Go 8.1 mi. to Exit 266, then turn south onto Ward Rd. and go 1 block south. Turn east onto 44th Ave. and go 0.6 mi. (past the RV service center). Turn right at the sign into the entrance. The office is on the right.

WINTER PARK

Idlewild Campground

9 Ten Mile Rd., Granby 80446. T: (970) 887-4100 www.fs.fed.us/recreation; hmcolburn@fs.fed.us.

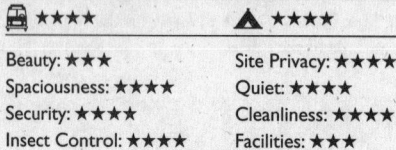

RV ★★★ Tent ★★★★★

Beauty: ★★★★	Site Privacy: ★★★★
Spaciousness: ★★★★	Quiet: ★★★★
Security: ★★★★	Cleanliness: ★★★★
Insect Control: ★★★★	Facilities: ★

Laid out in two levels, the majority of sites here are located on the upper level. The lower level is mainly given over to a cycling path, and the right turn immediately at the bottom of the (steep) road between levels leads to a dead end where only bicycles can continue. All sites in this campground are well shaded, but there is not much grass growing below the pines. On the lower level, site 3 is dedicated to the camp host. Several sites (including 4 and 16) can accommodate two vehicles. Site 18 is a 70-foot pull-through located close to the rest rooms. On the upper level, site 5 is a 90-foot pull-through and 8 is a 60-foot "parallel parking" site to the side of the road. Sites 9–11 are located by the rest room in a small, secluded area. Of these sites, 11 backs to the internal road, making it much less private than 9 or 10. Near the exit, site 13 is an extremely sloped 30-foot back-in. This campground is as natural and wild as they come. It will appeal to tenters and RVers who have both a sense of adventure and a toilet and shower facility.

Basics

Operated By: Fraser Valley Lion's Club. **Open:** May to Sept. 15. **Site Assignment:** First come, first served; no reservations. **Registration:** At pay station. **Fee:** $10 (checks). **Parking:** At site.

Facilities

Number of RV Sites: 26. **Number of Tent-Only Sites:** 0. **Hookups:** None. **Each Site:** Picnic table, grill. **Dump Station:** No. **Laundry:** No. **Pay Phone:** No. **Rest Rooms and Showers:** Pit toilets; no shower. **Fuel:** No. **Propane:** No. **Internal Roads:** Gravel. **RV Service:** No. **Market:** 1.5 mi. north. **Restaurant:** 1.5 mi. north. **General Store:** No. **Vending:** No. **Swimming:** No. **Playground:** No. **Other:** Firewood for sale. **Activities:** Hiking, biking, hunting, skiing. **Nearby Attractions:** Arapaho Nat'l Forest, Berthoud Pass. **Additional Information:** Sulpher Ranger District: (970) 887-4100.

Restrictions

Pets: On leash, cleaned up after. **Fires:** In grills. **Alcoholic Beverages:** At sites. **Vehicle Maximum Length:** None. **Other:** No fireworks.

To Get There

From the junction of Hwy. 40 and Vasquez Rd. (the southernmost traffic light in town), turn south onto Hwy. 40 and go 1.2 mi. Turn left at the sign into the entrance.

WRAY

Hitchin' Post RV Park

34172 Hwy. 385, Wray 80758. T: (970) 332-3128; www.plains.net//hitchinpost; hitchinpost@plains.net.

RV ★★★★ Tent ★★★★

Beauty: ★★★	Site Privacy: ★★★★
Spaciousness: ★★★★	Quiet: ★★★★
Security: ★★★★	Cleanliness: ★★★★
Insect Control: ★★★★	Facilities: ★★★

This campground consists solely of two rows of pull-throughs. These unshaded gravel sites can accommodate RVs of any size. There is a third row of back-ins/tent sites to the south of the RV sites. These back-ins, (which can also be used by tents), are located on a lush grassy field. Sites are 40 feet in length. While the sites themselves do not offer any facilities, the campground has attractive landscaping that uses flowers, trees, and white fencing. The rest rooms are perfectly clean, and the showers only slightly less so. This is a pleasant campground that will appeal equally well to tenters and to RVers.

Basics

Operated By: Noble & Virgene Burns. **Open:** All year. **Site Assignment:** Assigned upon registration; verbal reservations OK. **Registration:** In office. (Late arrivals select an available site & pay in the morning.) **Fee:** RV $20 (full), tent $10 (checks, no credits cards). **Parking:** At site.

Facilities

Number of RV Sites: 19. **Number of Tent-Only Sites:** Undesignated sites. **Hookups:** Water, sewer, electric (15, 30, 50 amps). **Each Site:** Hitchin' Post RV Park. **Dump Station:** Yes. **Laundry:** Yes. **Pay Phone:** Yes. **Rest Rooms and Showers:** Yes. **Fuel:** No. **Propane:** Yes. **Internal Roads:** Gravel. **RV Service:** No. **Market:** 1 mi. north. **Restaurant:** 1 mi. north. **General Store:** No. **Vending:** No. **Swimming:** No. **Playground:** No. **Other:** Dog pen. **Activities:** Fishing, boating, swimming. **Nearby Attractions:** Bonny State Park. **Additional Information:** Chamber of Commerce, (970) 332-4609.

Restrictions

Pets: On leash, cleaned up after. **Fires:** In grills. **Alcoholic Beverages:** At sites. **Vehicle Maximum Length:** None. **Other:** See rule sheet.

To Get There

From the junction of Hwy. 34 and Hwy. 385, turn south onto Hwy. 385 and go 1.1 mi. Turn left at the sign into the entrance, then right towards the office.

YAMPA

Stillwater Campground

P.O. Box 7, 300 Roselawn Ave., Yampa 80483. T: (970) 879-1722.

RV ★★★★ Tent ★★★★

Beauty: ★★★★★	Site Privacy: ★★★★★
Spaciousness: ★★★★★	Quiet: ★★★★★
Security: ★★★★	Cleanliness: ★★★
Insect Control: ★★★★	Facilities: ★

The long but beautiful drive in to this campground is worth the effort once you are there, as this campground offers spectacular views of lakes and the mountains that rise above them. The recreational opportunities for outdoor enthusiasts are also limitless. The campground itself is very small (7 sites), but there are a number of campsites along the road in. Some of these (including 28, just across from the campground, and 33, a pull-through overlooking Bear Lake) are at the tops of hills, allowing a view overlooking the entire area. Site 1 in the campground is right by the entrance, and may be less desirable for this location. Sites 2–4 are 45–50-foot back-ins; of these, 3 has the best views to the southeast. Site 5 is an 80-foot back-in, and 6 and 7 are 75-foot pull-throughs. All of these sites are at least partially forested and some (2 and 4) are completely lost in trees. Come to this campground in Sept., when the aspens are turning. You will see a startle of yellow aspens among the stately deep-green ponderosa pines. This campground offers wonderful scenic and recreational opportunities but next to nothing in the way of facilities. As such, it may appeal most to tenters and RVers with a sense of adventure.

Basics

Operated By: US Forest Service. **Open:** All year. **Site Assignment:** First come, first served; no reservations. **Registration:** At pay station. **Fee:** Site in campground: $10, developed campsites along road: $3 (checks). **Parking:** At site.

Facilities

Number of RV Sites: 29. **Number of Tent-Only Sites:** 0. **Hookups:** None. **Each Site:** Picnic table, fire pit. **Dump Station:** No. **Laundry:** No. **Pay Phone:** No. **Rest Rooms and Showers:** Toilets; showers in town. **Fuel:** No. **Propane:** No. **Internal Roads:** Dirt. **RV Service:** No. **Market:** 16 mi. northeast. **Restaurant:** 16 mi. northeast. **General Store:** No. **Vending:** No. **Swimming:** Reservoir. **Playground:** No. **Activities:** Fishing, boating, swimming, hiking, hunting, horseback riding. **Nearby Attractions:** Stillwater Reservoir, Yamcolo Reservoir, Bear Lake, Devil's Causeway, Stagecoach State Park. **Additional Information:** Yampa Ranger District, (970) 638-4516.

Restrictions

Pets: On leash, cleaned up after. **Fires:** In grills. **Alcoholic Beverages:** At sites. **Vehicle Maximum Length:** None. **Other:** $3 per vehicle day use pass, no cutting firewood.

To Get There

From the junction of Hwy. 131 and Moffat Ave. (by gas station complex at southeastern edge of town), turn southwest onto Moffat Ave. and go 0.4 mi. to Main St. Cross over Main and continue on CR 7 (which becomes unpaved FR 900) for 13.3 mi. to Bear Lake Campground. The campground is on the left.

Connecticut

A small state with a surprising variety of terrain, Connecticut offers an impressive array of camping options. Though even the most remote parts of the state aren't far from civilization (or a mall), campgrounds range from isolated to right in the middle of a town. There's almost no type of camping that you can't find here, and if you're looking for variety, you could easily spend one day at a rural site, another near the ocean, and the next one by a small mountain.

Since it takes at most three hours to drive across Connecticut, you're never that far from anything. Of course, the big attraction for most people are the **Foxwoods** and **Mohegan Sun** casinos. These gigantic Native American–run facilities are accessible from nearly anywhere in the state and are close to numerous campgrounds.

The other big attraction in Connecticut is the town of **Mystic** with its aquarium, seaport, and numerous quaint attractions. There's also an uncountable number of towns with lively downtowns full of little shops, restaurants, and attractions. Much of the state is traditional New England, where the center of town is still the center of activity.

In addition to the varying terrain of the state's campgrounds, its cities and towns tend to vary quite a bit within a small distance. Take the capital of **Hartford** as an example—you have a city with most of the amenities of its bigger counterparts that's also a five-minute ride from open space. And if you go in different directions you get a wide choice of towns that cater to different needs. Some offer gourmet dining and theater while others have great pizza places, movie theaters, and bowling alleys.

For campers, the main appeal of Connecticut has to be that it's easy to do anything from anywhere in this state, but there's enough to do to keep you busy for a while. In general, if you're looking for rustic, you'll want to stay away from the southern parts of the state, and there might be less to do outside your campground in the west. But, with the small size and many highways, you're never more than half-hour ride from pretty much anything.

Campground Profiles

ASHFORD

Brialee RV and Tent Park

174 Laurel Ln., P.O. Box 125, Ashford 06278.
T: (800) 303-CAMP; F: (860) 429-5930; www.brialee.net;brialee@gocampingamerica.com.

RV: ★★★★ Tent: ★★

Beauty: ★★★★	Site Privacy: ★★★★
Spaciousness: ★★★★	Quiet: ★★★★
Security: ★★★★	Cleanliness: ★★★★
Insect Control: ★★★	Facilities: ★★★★

A very active seasonal community, Brialee focuses most of its energy on pleasing seasonal guests and their RVs. Tent campers can still find a good site here, but they are definitely in the minority. With state forests all around and large, private sites, the scenery is definitely pleasant. There are also stone walls around the campground, a sparklingly clean lake, and a water fountain.

Basics

Operated By: Brian, Addie, & Ed Specyalski. **Open:** Apr. 1–Dec. 1. **Site Assignment:** Reservations recommended. **Registration:** At office. **Fee:** $55 for 2 nights; 1-week min. stay in season, 2 nights otherwise. **Parking:** At site.

Facilities

Number of RV Sites: 180. **Number of Tent-Only Sites:** 0. **Hookups:** Electric (30 amps), sewer, cable TV. **Each Site:** Fire pit, picnic table. **Dump Station:** Yes. **Laundry:** Yes. **Pay Phone:** Yes. **Rest Rooms and Showers:** Yes. **Fuel:** No. **Propane:** Yes. **Internal Roads:** Paved. **RV Service:** No. **Market:** Bubba T's **General Store:** 259 Ference Rd., Ashford, CT (4.4 mi.). Take a left onto Rte. 89 & follow for 4.4 mi. **Restaurant:** Snack bar, Midway Restaurant & Pizza, 174 Ashford Center Rd., Ashford, CT (4.1 mi.). Take a right onto Rte. 89 followed by a left onto Rte. 44. **General Store:** Yes. **Vending:** Yes. **Swimming Pool:** Yes, heated. **Playground:** Yes. **Other:** Beach, pond, stocked fishing, arcade, walking trails. **Activities:** Band or DJ on Saturday nights, bingo. **Nearby Attractions:** Great Natchaug Forest, Sturbridge Village. **Additional Information:** Northeast Connecticut Visitors District, (860) 779-6383 or (888) 628-1228, www.ctquietcorner.org.

Restrictions

Pets: On leash only. **Fires:** Allowed. **Alcoholic Beverages:** Allowed. **Vehicle Maximum Length:** 40 ft. **Other:** No smoking.

To Get There

Take 84 east to Exit 69 and follow Rte. 74 east for 6 mi. to Rte. 44. Take a left onto Rte. 44 east and follow for 1 mi. At the junction of Rtes. 89 and 44 take a left onto Rte. 89 north, then take the first left onto Perry Hill Rd. and the second right onto Laurel Ln., which leads to Briarlee.

BARKHAMSTEAD

White Pines Campsites

232 Old North Rd., Barkhamstead 06063.
T: (800) 622-6614; www.whitepinescamp.com; campwp@whitepinescamp.com.

RV: ★★★★ Tent: ★★★

Beauty: ★★	Site Privacy: ★★
Spaciousness: ★★★	Quiet: ★★
Security: ★★★★	Cleanliness: ★★★
Insect Control: ★★★	Facilities: ★★★★

With tons of activities and planned events, this is not the campground for quiet contemplation or for people who want to keep to themselves. A visit to White Pines is definitely for those who want an active vacation but don't want to do much themselves. However, despite the summer-camp feel, you'll find fishing and other outdoor activities, which makes White Pines a nice compromise between the resort campgrounds and those that offer a decidedly rustic experience.

Basics

Operated By: Owners Peter Lawrence & Pete Finkel. **Open:** Mid-Apr.–mid-Oct. **Site Assignment:** Reservations. **Registration:** At office. **Fee:** $25–$32. **Parking:** At site.

Facilities

Number of RV Sites: 200. **Number of Tent-Only Sites:** 9. **Hookups:** Electric (30 amps), cable TV. **Each Site:** Water, electric. **Dump Station:** Yes. **Laundry:** No. **Pay Phone:** Yes. **Rest Rooms and Showers:** Yes. **Fuel:** No. **Propane:** Yes. **Internal Roads:** Stone. **RV Service:** No, but on-site handyman can do some repairs. **Market:** Pleasant Valley. **General Store:** Take a right on CT-101 & follow for 0.4 mi. **Restaurant:** Sophie's Pizza Restaurant, 200 New Hartford, Rd., Winsted, CT. Take a right on CT-181 & follow until it becomes CT-318. Stay straight on CT-318 until CT-44. Take a right on CT-44 & follow for 1.4 mi. **General Store:** Yes. **Vending:** Yes. **Swimming Pool:** Yes. **Playground:** Yes. **Other:** Paddle boat rentals. **Activities:** Every weekend has a theme & special activities, such as the mid-Aug. Las Vegas weekend & the early Sep. Mexican fiesta. **Nearby Attractions:** Fishing & tubing. **Additional Information:** Litchfield Hills Visitors Bureau, (860) 567-4506, www.litchfieldhills.com.

Restrictions

Pets: Yes. **Fires:** Allowed. **Alcoholic Beverages:** Allowed. **Vehicle Maximum Length:** None. **Other:** No bicycles after dark, keep only two fish per day.

To Get There

Take US 44 Old North Rd.

BOZRAH

Acorn Acres

135 Lake Rd., Bozrah 06334. T: (860) 859-1020; F: (609) 886-8228; www.acorncampground.com.

RV ★★★★ Tent ★★

Beauty: ★★★★	Site Privacy: ★★★★
Spaciousness: ★★★★	Quiet: ★★★★
Security: ★★★★	Cleanliness: ★★★★
Insect Control: ★★★	Facilities: ★★★★

Tucked into a hill, this campground offers large sites. Though its literature claims it's a quiet spot, the sometimes large number of kids means that's not the case during the day. At night things settle down, but Acorn Acres is definitely more of a family place than a secluded spot for grown-ups. The campground caters to RVs, although the sites along the river make a nice place to pitch your tent.

Basics

Operated By: Private operator. **Open:** May 1–Columbus Day. **Site Assignment:** Reservations required. **Registration:** Office. **Fee:** $27–$33. **Parking:** At site.

Facilities

Number of RV Sites: 200. **Number of Tent-Only Sites:** 0. **Hookups:** Water, electric (50 amps), phone, cable TV. **Each Site:** Picnic table, stone fireplace. **Dump Station:** Yes. **Laundry:** Yes. **Pay Phone:** Yes. **Rest Rooms and Showers:** Yes. **Fuel:** No. **Propane:** Yes. **Internal Roads:** Paved. **RV Service:** No. **Market:** Main's Country Store Inc., 318 Fitchville Rd., Bozrah, CT (5.5 mi.). Turn left onto Lake Rd., followed by a left onto Rte. 136, then a left onto Haughton Rd. & a left onto Fitchville Rd. **Restaurant:** Exit 23 Restaurant, 318 Fitchville Rd., Bozrah, CT (5.5 mi.). Follow above directions. **General Store:** Yes. **Vending:** No. **Swimming Pool:** Yes. **Playground:** No. **Other:** Swimming & fishing pond, trout stream, rec hall. **Activities:** Organized sports. **Nearby Attractions:** Gardner Lake. **Additional Information:** Southeastern Connecticut Tourism District, (860) 444-2206 or (800) TO-ENJOY, www.mysticmore.com.

Restrictions

Pets: Yes. **Fires:** Allowed. **Alcoholic Beverages:** Allowed. **Vehicle Maximum Length:** 40 ft. **Other:** No cutting live trees.

To Get There

Take Rte. 2 east to Exit 22 and make a right at the end of the ramp. Go 2 mi. and make a left at the "T", take the next right and go down the second hill on your left to the campground.

CLINTON

Nickerson Park

Rte. 198, Chaplin 06235. T: (860) 455-0007; www.nickersonpark.com.

RV ★★★ Tent ★★★

Beauty: ★★	Site Privacy: ★★
Spaciousness: ★★	Quiet: ★★
Security: ★★★	Cleanliness: ★★★★
Insect Control: ★★★	Facilities: ★★

Though the campground is nothing special, it makes an excellent home base for hunting in the Nautchag State Forest (in season, of course). The forest also offers great cross-country skiing trails for winter visitors. Since the campground is open year-round, those who don't hunt may want to try an off-season visit. Campsites are wooded and fairly private but aren't very big and could be farther apart. Note: When making a reservation here, be sure not to confuse it with a similarly named campground in Massachusetts.

Basics

Operated By: The Nickerson family. **Open:** All year. **Site Assignment:** Reservations recommended; required during holiday weekends. **Registration:** At office. **Fee:** $45–$50; 3-day min. stay. **Parking:** At site.

Facilities

Number of RV Sites: 80. **Number of Tent-Only Sites:** 32. **Hookups:** Water, electric, sewer, cable TV, phone. **Each Site:** Fire ring, picnic table. **Dump Station:** Yes. **Laundry:** Yes. **Pay Phone:** Yes. **Rest Rooms and Showers:** Yes. **Fuel:** No. **Propane:** Yes. **Internal Roads:** Paved. **RV Service:** Yes. **Market:** Ted's Mini Market, 315 Boston Post Rd., North Windham, CT (5.5 mi.). Go south on Rte. 198 towards Pumpkin Hill Rd. by turning right, then take a slight right onto Rte. 6. Rte. 6 becomes N. Windham Rd. & then becomes Boston Post Rd. **Restaurant:** Chaplin Pizza, 52 Willimantic Rd. Chaplin, CT. Follow above directions to Willimantic Rd. **General Store:** No. **Vending:** Yes. **Swimming Pool:** No. **Playground:** No. **Other:** Rec hall. **Activities:** Trout fishing, swimming, river tubing, hiking, mountain biking, wildlife, scheduled events during peak season, hunting in season. **Nearby Attractions:** Natchaug State Forest. **Additional Information:** Connecticut River Valley & Shoreline Visitors Council, (860) 347-0028 or (800) 486-3346, www.visitctrivershore.org.

Restrictions

Pets: Yes. **Fires:** Allowed. **Alcoholic Beverages:** Allowed. **Vehicle Maximum Length:** Sites vary, check ahead. **Other:** Check w/ park regarding firearms.

To Get There

Take 84 to Exit 59. Follow Rte. 384 onto Rte. 6 toward Providence and Willimantic. Take Rte. 6 east to the junction of Rte. 198 and take 198 north for 4.5 mi.

EAST CANAAN

Lone Oak Campsites

360 Norfolk Rd., East Canaan 06024. T: (800) 422-2267; F: (860) 422-2267; www.loneoak-campsites .com; loneoakinc@aol.com.

RV ★★★★ Tent ★★

Beauty: ★	Site Privacy: ★★
Spaciousness: ★★	Quiet: ★★
Security: ★★★	Cleanliness: ★★
Insect Control: ★★	Facilities: ★★★★

More of a summer resort that happens to have camping and RV facilities, Lone Oak targets families looking for a camping experience without too much "roughing it." Like a summer camp for families, the campground has a daily schedule of activities that inlcude arts and crafts, ping-pong, various sports, and more conducted by the staff. For adults, there's the Hayloft Lounge, which has a full bar and a dance floor. All of these amenities make Lone Oak a good place for a family vacation but not the place for a real outdoors experience. For those who don't even want to brave the elements, Lone Oak also rents cabins and trailers.

Basics

Operated By: The Brown family. **Open:** Apr. 15–Oct. 15. **Site Assignment:** Reservations accepted; otherwise first come, first served. **Registration:** At office. **Fee:** $19–$35; V, MC, D; 2-night min. stay June, July, & Aug.; 3-night min. stay Columbus Day weekend. **Parking:** At site.

Facilities

Number of RV Sites: 70. **Number of Tent-Only Sites:** 430. **Hookups:** Water, electric (30 amps), sewer, cable TV. **Each Site:** Picnic table, fire ring. **Dump Station:** Yes. **Laundry:** Yes. **Pay Phone:** Yes. **Rest Rooms and Showers:** Yes. **Fuel:** No. **Propane:** Yes. **Internal Roads:** Gravel. **RV Service:** No. **Market:** Stop & Shop Supermarket, Rte. 44 & East Main St. , Canaan, 1.3 mi. away. **Restaurant:** The Chipmunk Deli is located on the premises. The Collins Diner is found at Rte. 7 & 44,

Canaan, 1.3 mi. away. **General Store:** Yes. **Vending:** No. **Swimming Pool:** Yes. **Playground:** Yes. **Other:** Volleyball court, softball field, rec hall w/ planned activities (bingo, movies, card games). **Activities:** Fishing in the state stocked Blackberry River, which runs through the property, special events (like 50s/60s Weekend & the Country Music Double Header) nearly every weekend during the summer. **Nearby Attractions:** Appalachian Trail, Lime Rock Race Park, Norman Rockwel Museum, golf courses, Tanglewood canoe & tube rentals. **Additional Information:** Litchfield Hills Visitors Bureau, (860) 567-4506, www.litchfieldhills.com.

Restrictions

Pets: Yes. **Fires:** Allowed in specified area. **Alcoholic Beverages:** At site, sold in recreation areas. **Vehicle Maximum Length:** None. **Other:** Partial handicap access.

To Get There

Lone Oak is off of Rt. 44 and is clearly visible from the road. From Hartford the trip takes approximately 1 hour. From Springfield and Boston take the Mass Pike to Exit 2 (Lee). Follow Rt. 102 to Stockbridge. Take Rt. 7 South (at the Red Lion Inn). Follow Rt. 7 to the center of Canaan. At the junction of Rt. 7 and Rt. 44 take a left (heading east on 44). Lone Oak is 4 mi. on the right.

EAST HADDAM

Wolf's Den Family Campground

256 Town St., East Haddam 06423. T: (860) 873-9681; F: (860) 873-1248; wolfsdencampground.com; information@wolfsdencampground.com.

RV: ★★★★ Tent: ★★★

Beauty: ★★★ Site Privacy: ★★★
Spaciousness: ★★ Quiet: ★★★
Security: ★★★★ Cleanliness: ★★★★
Insect Control: ★★★★ Facilities: ★★★★

A popular campground due to its many on-site family acitivities, Wolf's Den never has a dull moment, which makes it a good place for kids. Because it's located in an area with plenty to do, Wolf's Den is an excellent place to park your RV and enjoy the surrounding sights. Since the campground tends to be booked solid throughout the entire tourist season, reservations are absolutely required for weekends and are a good idea even during the week.

Basics

Operated By: Judt Kulisch (manager), Glen Gustine (owner). **Open:** First weekend in May–last weekend in Oct. **Site Assignment:** Reservations. **Registration:** At office. **Fee:** $27 (includes electricity & water). **Parking:** At site.

Facilities

Number of RV Sites: 209. **Number of Tent-Only Sites:** 0. **Hookups:** Water, electric (30, 50 amps), phone, cable TV. **Each Site:** Picnic table, fireplace. **Dump Station:** Yes. **Laundry:** Yes. **Pay Phone:** Yes. **Rest Rooms and Showers:** Yes. **Fuel:** No. **Propane:** Yes. **RV Service:** No. **Market:** Adams Super Food, 5.6 mi. away. Go southeast on Town St. towards River Ed. by turning left, turn right onto River Rd., River becomes Geer Hill Rd., which becomes CT-148. Follow until Middlesex Turnpike & take a left. Follow until Turnpike becomes Main, & make a left onto Essex. **Restaurant:** Hale 'N Heart Restaurant, 381 Town St. (take a right on town & follow for 1.2 mi.). **General Store:** Yes. **Vending:** Yes. **Swimming Pool:** Yes, olympic-sized. **Playground:** Yes. **Other:** Game room, rental cabin, tennis courts, basketball, mini-golf, group & club areas. **Activities:** Each weekend has a theme, such as mid-September's "toga party" & late August's "Christmas in August". **Nearby Attractions:** Essex Steam Train (1 Railroad Ave., Essex). **Additional Information:** Middlesex County Chamber of Commerce, (860) 347-1043, www.middlesexchamber.com.

Restrictions

Pets: Yes. **Fires:** At site only. **Alcoholic Beverages:** Allowed. **Vehicle Maximum Length:** None. **Other:** Ask on arrival.

To Get There

From New York (north) or Rhode Island (south) take 95 to Rte. 9 North. Rte. 9 North to Exit 7, east on Rte. 82, then go 4 mi. From Massachusetts take 91 South to Rte. 9 South to Exit 7, then go east on Rte. 82 for 4 mi.

EAST KILLINGLY

Hide-A-Way Cove Family Campground

North Rd., P.O. Box 129, East Killingly 06243. T: (860) 774-1128; hide-awaycove@webtv.net.

RV: ★★★ Tent: ★

Beauty: ★★ Site Privacy: ★★
Spaciousness: ★ Quiet: ★★
Security: ★★★ Cleanliness: ★★★
Insect Control: ★★★ Facilities: ★★★

On the positive side, the campground is located on Hide-a-Way lake, an otherwise undeveloped body of water that's fairly nice to look at. The lake allows for boating (motors up to seven horsepowers) and has some pretty good fishing. On the other hand, the campground is not much to look at. The sites are packed tightly and some of them are just plain ugly. Many of the best, lakefront sites are snapped up by seasonal customers, so you'll want to move quickly or else you'll end up with a crowded site looking at another RV. There's not much for tent campers here.

Basics

Operated By: Edward & Jacquelyn Benoit. **Open:** May 1–Oct. 15. **Site Assignment:** Reservations required in season; best sites often reserved seasons in advance. **Registration:** Store. **Fee:** $18. **Parking:** At site.

Facilities

Number of RV Sites: 300. **Number of Tent-Only Sites:** 0. **Hookups:** Water, electric (20 amps). **Each Site:** Picnic table, fire ring. **Dump Station:** Yes. **Laundry:** Yes. **Pay Phone:** Yes. **Rest Rooms and Showers:** Yes. **Fuel:** No. **Propane:** Yes. **RV Service:** No. **Market:** A&P Food Stores 1058 N. Main St., Dayville, CT (3.8 Miles). Turn right onto Rte. 101 & follow for 3.7 mi., before making a sharp left onto Rte. 12. **Restaurant:** Pizza King, 430 Ledge Rd., Dayville, CT. Go east on Rte. 101 by turning left, then turn right onto East Killingly Rd. & then right onto Shippee Schoolhouse Rd., which runs into Ledge Rd. **General Store:** Yes. **Vending:** Yes. **Swimming Pool:** Yes. **Playground:** No. **Other:** Volleyball courts, horseshoe pits, lake, rec hall. **Activities:** Lots of organized activities, including bingo & arts & crafts. **Nearby Attractions:** Inquire at campground. **Additional Information:** Northeast Connecticut Visitors District, (860) 779-6383 or (888) 628-1228, www.ctquietcorner.org.

Restrictions

Pets: On leash only. **Fires:** At site only. **Alcoholic Beverages:** Allowed. **Vehicle Maximum Length:** 35 ft. **Other:** Ask on arrival.

To Get There

395 to Exit 83 onto Rte. 101 east. Go 3.5 mi. to North Rd. (Turn left onto North Rd. just prior to the blinking light). Follow North Rd. a short distance to campground on right.

EAST LYME

Aces High RV Park

301 Chesterfield Rd., East Lyme 06333. T: (860) 739-8858; www.aceshighrvpark.com; sales@aceshighpark.com.

RV: ★★★★ Tent: n/a

Beauty: ★★★★ Site Privacy: ★★★
Spaciousness: ★★★★★ Quiet: ★★★★
Security: ★★★ Cleanliness: ★★★
Insect Control: ★★★ Facilities: ★★★

An RV-only park, Aces High manages to remain attractive despite the fact it's basically a grass field surrounding a pond and bordered by forest. Sites are large but fairly close together for such a large park. There are plenty of family activities, including movies and some things for adults only.

Basics

Operated By: Private operator. **Open:** Apr. 1–Oct. 31. **Site Assignment:** Reservations recommended. **Registration:** At office. **Fee:** $34 for pop-ups, $37 for all others. **Parking:** At site.

Facilities

Number of RV Sites: 43. **Number of Tent-Only Sites:** 0. **Hookups:** Water, electric (50 amps), sewer, cable TV. **Dump Station:** Yes. **Laundry:** Yes. **Pay Phone:** Yes. **Rest Rooms and Showers:** No. **Fuel:** Yes. **Propane:** Yes. **RV Service:** Yes. **Market:** Oakdale Market, 430 Chapel Hill Rd., Oakdale, CT (5.5 mi.). Take a right onto Rte. 161, then a slight left onto Rte.85, followed by a right onto Chesterfield Rd. & a left onto Chapel Hill Rd. **Restaurant:** Flanders Fish Market, 22 Chesterfield Rd., East Lyme (2.7 mi.). Follow above directions through Chesterfield Rd. **General Store:** No. **Vending:** No. **Swimming Pool:** No. **Playground:** Yes. **Other:** Game room, stocked trout pond, volleyball court. **Activities:** Paddle boats, surf bikes. **Nearby Attractions:** Inquire at campground. **Additional Information:** Southeastern Connecticut Tourism District, (860) 444-2206 or (800) TO-ENJOY, www.mysticmore.com.

RESTRICTIONS

Pets: Yes. **Fires:** Allowed. **Alcoholic Beverages:** Allowed. **Vehicle Maximum Length:** 45 ft. **Other:** No tents.

TO GET THERE

Take 95 to Exit 74 and go north on Rte. 161 for 3 mi. Campground will be on your right.

EAST LYME

Island Campground & Cottages

P.O. Box 2, Islanda Court, East Lyme 06333. T: (860) 739-8316.

RV ★★★ Tent ★★★★

Beauty: ★★★★★ Site Privacy: ★★★★
Spaciousness: ★★★ Quiet: ★★★★
Security: ★★★★ Cleanliness: ★★★★
Insect Control: ★★★ Facilities: ★★

This isolated campground that's basically an island on Lake Pattagansett doesn't offer much to do, but it's perfect for grown-ups looking to get away from it all. Most of the shaded sites overlook the lake and are perfect for quiet contemplation. You can fish and swim in the lake, but most of the activity here is of the hat-tipped-over-your-eyes variety. All sites allow tents and RVs, but you might be better off leaving the RV at home and just pitching a tent and enjoying the simple life.

BASICS

Operated By: Private operator. **Open:** May 1–Oct. 30. **Site Assignment:** Reservations absolutely necessary; campground is small & fills up fast. **Registration:** At office. **Fee:** $18 & up. **Parking:** At site.

FACILITIES

Number of RV Sites: 35. **Number of Tent-Only Sites:** 0. **Hookups:** Water, electric. **Each Site:** Table. **Dump Station:** Yes. **Laundry:** No. **Pay Phone:** Yes. **Rest Rooms and Showers:** Yes. **Fuel:** No. **Propane:** Yes. **RV Service:** No. **Market:** Adam's Super Food Stores, 58 Pennsylvania Ave., Niantic, CT (4.4 mi.). Go south on Islanda Ct. towards Pattangnasett Dr., making a left onto Rte. 1, then a right onto Rte. 161, followed by a slight left onto Pennsylvania Ave. **Restaurant:** Bee Bee Dairy Restaurant, 324 Flanders Rd., East Lyme, CT (1.4 mi.). Go south on Islanda Ct. towards Pattangnasett Dr., making a left onto Rte. 1, followed by a slight right onto Flanders Rd./Rte. 161. **General Store:** No. **Vending:** No. **Swimming Pool:** No. **Playground:** Yes. **Other:** Private beach. **Activities:** Swimming, fishing. **Nearby Attractions:** Mystic is pretty remote but relatively accessible. **Additional Information:** Southeastern Connecticut Tourism District, (860) 444-2206 or (800) TO ENJOY, www.mysticmore.com.

RESTRICTIONS

Pets: On leash only. **Fires:** Ask on arrival. **Alcoholic Beverages:** Allowed. **Vehicle Maximum Length:** None. **Other:** Ask on arrival.

TO GET THERE

95 to Exit 74. Turn left onto Rte. 161 to junction of Rte. 1 and Rte. 161 and turn left. Go for 1 mi. until you see Islanda Court Rd. on your right. Follow to campground.

EASTFORD

Charlie Brown Campground

Rte. 198, 98 Chaplin Rd., Eastford 06242. T: (860) 974-0142.

RV ★★★★ Tent ★★★

Beauty: ★★★★ Site Privacy: ★★★★
Spaciousness: ★★★★ Quiet: ★★★★
Security: ★★★ Cleanliness: ★★★★
Insect Control: ★★★ Facilities: ★★★★

The campground uses fences to separate sites in some areas, while other areas have bushes or open grassy spaces to protect privacy. The swimming hole is better than your average Olympic-size pool and is almost as clean—without the chlorine. Sites are mostly flat and nearly all are shaded.

BASICS

Operated By: Steve & Gary St. John. **Open:** Apr. 15–Oct. 15. **Site Assignment:** Reservations recommended. **Registration:** Store. **Fee:** $20 & up. **Parking:** At site.

FACILITIES

Number of RV Sites: 100. **Number of Tent-Only Sites:** 25. **Hookups:** Water, electric, sewer. **Each Site:** Picnic table, fire barrel. **Dump Station:** Yes. **Laundry:** Yes. **Pay Phone:** Yes. **Rest Rooms and Showers:** Yes. **Fuel:** No. **Propane:** Yes. **RV Service:** Supply shop. **Market:** Eastford Village Store, 192 Eastford Rd., Eastford, CT (6.5 Miles). Take Rte. 198 until it becomes Rte. 171 & look for store in 0.2 mi. **Restaurant:** Midway Restaurant & Pizza, 174 Ashford Center Rd., Ashford, CT (4.5 mi.). Take a left onto Rte. 198 & follow it until Rte. 44. Take a left onto Rte. 44 & follow for 2 mi. **General Store:** Yes. **Vending:** Yes. **Swimming Pool:** No. **Playground:** No. **Other:** Picnic area, rec hall, basketball courts, fields. **Activities:** Band performances, planned activities, mountain biking. **Nearby Attractions:** Natchaug State Forest. **Additional Information:** Northeast Connecticut Visitors District, (860) 779-6383 or (888) 628-1228, www.ctquietcorner.org.

RESTRICTIONS

Pets: On leash only. **Fires:** Allowed. **Alcoholic Beverages:** Allowed. **Vehicle Maximum Length:** None. **Other:** Ask on arrival.

TO GET THERE

Take 84 to Exit 69 and follow 74 east to Rte. 44, east to 198 south.

JEWITT CITY

Campers World of Connecticut

P.O. Box 337, Jewitt City 06351. T: (860) 376-2340.

RV ★★★ Tent n/a

Beauty: ★★ Site Privacy: ★
Spaciousness: ★ Quiet: ★
Security: ★★ Cleanliness: ★★
Insect Control: ★★★ Facilities: ★★★★

Given the adults-only policy, one wonders why this crowded campground set on a tiny beach has a playground. Seasonal campers make up most of the clientele here, so maybe the joy of this fairly bleak, RV-packed setting is the camaraderie. Some sites do have their own boat docks, and many are shaded.

BASICS

Operated By: George Barr. **Open:** May 1–Oct. 7. **Site Assignment:** Reservations recommended. **Registration:** At office. **Fee:** $16. **Parking:** At site.

FACILITIES

Number of RV Sites: 92. **Number of Tent-Only Sites:** 0. **Hookups:** Water, electric (30, 50 amps), sewer, phone. **Dump Station:** No. **Laundry:** No. **Pay Phone:** No. **Rest Rooms and Showers:** Yes. **Fuel:** No. **Propane:** No. **RV Service:** No. **Market:** Plainfield Food Mart, 518 Norwich Rd., Plainfield, CT (4.8 mi.). **Restaurant:** Altone's Italian American, 47 Main St., No. A, Jewett City, CT (1.4 mi.). Take a right onto Carely Ave., followed by a right onto Ashland St. & a left onto Rte. 12. **General Store:** No. **Vending:** No. **Swimming Pool:** No. **Playground:** Yes. **Other:** Beach, pond, boat docks. **Activities:** Fishing, swimming. **Nearby Attractions:** Inquire at campground. **Additional Information:** Northeast Connecticut Visitors District, (860) 779-6383 or (888) 628-1228, www.ctquietcorner.org.

RESTRICTIONS

Pets: Yes. **Fires:** Ask on arrival. **Alcoholic Beverages:** Allowed. **Vehicle Maximum Length:** None. **Other:** No children.

TO GET THERE

Take 395 to Exit 86 and go east on Rte. 201 for 0.5 of a mi. Take a right onto First Rd. and look for campground on the left.

LEBANON

Lake Williams Campground

1742 Exeter Rd. (Rte. 207), Lebanon 06249. T: (860) 642-7761; F: (860) 642-4602; www.lakewilliamscampground.com; lakewilliamscampgd@snet.com.

RV ★★★ Tent ★★

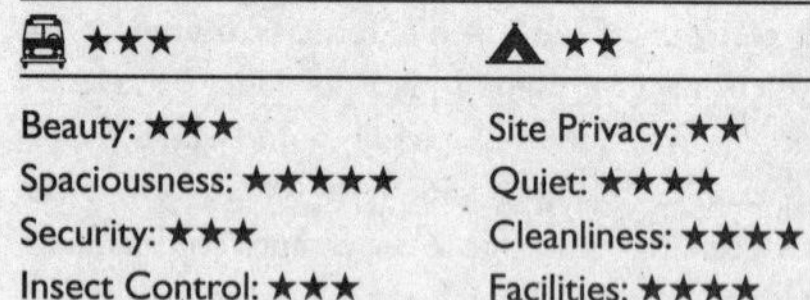

Beauty: ★★★ Site Privacy: ★★
Spaciousness: ★★★★★ Quiet: ★★★★
Security: ★★★ Cleanliness: ★★★★
Insect Control: ★★★ Facilities: ★★★★

Despite being on an enormous plot of land, the sites at Lake Williams are crowded. However, this does allow the campground's staff to better serve its visitors. In some ways, Lake Williams feels more like a hotel than a campground, as you see the employees more than you do at most places—which is generally a good thing. The entire area feels a bit too industrial to be described as "pretty" or to seem like you're taking an outdoors vacation. Still, the lake offers plenty of recreation, including fishing and boating.

BASICS

Operated By: Lee & Sandra Rider. **Open:** Apr. 15–Oct. 15. **Site Assignment:** Reservations in season. **Registration:** At office. **Fee:** $32.95 (in season), $19.95 (off-season). **Parking:** At site.

FACILITIES

Number of RV Sites: 87. **Number of Tent-Only

Sites: 0. **Hookups:** Water, electric (30, 50 amps), cable TV. **Each Site:** Picnic table, fire ring. **Dump Station:** Yes. **Laundry:** Yes. **Pay Phone:** Yes. **Rest Rooms and Showers:** Yes. **Fuel:** No. **Propane:** Yes. **Internal Roads:** Paved. **RV Service:** No. **Market:** Ted's Food Center, 127 Main St., Hebron, CT (4.5 mi.). Go northwest on Exeter Rd./CT-207 towards Levita Rd. by turning right. Turn right onto Rte. 85, then right onto Main St. **Restaurant:** Gina Marie's Family Restaurant, 71 Main St., Hebron, CT (4.8 mi.). Follow same directions as above. **General Store:** Yes. **Vending:** Yes. **Swimming Pool:** No. **Playground:** Yes. **Other:** Rec. hall, horseshoe pits, pool room, swimming beach. **Activities:** Bass fishing, waterskiing, boat rentals. **Nearby Attractions:** Dr. William Beaumont House (West Town St., Lebanon). **Additional Information:** Northeast Connecticut Visitors District, (860) 779-6383 or (888) 628-1228, www.ctquietcorner.org.

Restrictions

Pets: Yes. **Fires:** Allowed. **Alcoholic Beverages:** Allowed. **Vehicle Maximum Length:** 40 ft. **Other:** Ask on arrival.

To Get There

From 95, take 85 north through Colchester. About 3.5 mi. north of Colchester take a right onto Rte. 207 East. Go about 2.4 mi. and the campground will be on the left.

LISBON

Deer Haven Campground

15 Kenyon Rd., Lisbon 06351. T: (860) 376-1081; F: (860) 376-3240; deerhaven@gocamping america.com.

RV: ★★★★ Tent: ★★★

Beauty: ★★★ Site Privacy: ★★★
Spaciousness: ★★★ Quiet: ★★★
Security: ★★★★ Cleanliness: ★★★★
Insect Control: ★★★ Facilities: ★★★★

With both open and wooded sites as well as a separate area for tent camping, Deer Haven has a bit of everything. There's a nice mix of adult and family activities here, so this might be a good place to bring older kids who can occupy themselves at night while you head off to the adult lounge.

Basics

Operated By: Jane & Randy Pawlikowski. **Open:** May 1–Oct. 18. **Site Assignment:** Reservations recommended. **Registration:** Store. **Fee:** $17–$28. **Parking:** At site.

Facilities

Number of RV Sites: 50. **Number of Tent-Only Sites:** 30. **Hookups:** Water, electric (30 amps), sewer. **Each Site:** Picnic table, fire ring. **Dump Station:** Yes. **Laundry:** Yes. **Pay Phone:** Yes. **Rest Rooms and Showers:** Yes. **Fuel:** No. **Propane:** Yes. **RV Service:** No. **Market:** Russ's Market, 754 North Main St., Norwich, CT (4.5 mi.). Turn right onto Kenyon Rd., which becomes Strand Rd., which becomes Kendall Rd. Ext. Take a sharp right onto Rte. 169, followed by a left onto Rte. 97, then a slight right onto Rte. 12. Follow Rte. 12 until it becomes Main St. **Restaurant:** Corner Restaurant, 337 Old Canterbury Turnpike, Norwich, CT (3.1 mi.). Turn right onto Kenyon Rd., which becomes Strand Rd., which becomes Kendall Rd. Ext. Take a sharp right onto Rte. 169, followed by the I-395 south ramp. Get off 395 at Exit 83, turning left onto Rte. 97. Turn left onto Rte. 97 & go straight onto the Old Canterbury Turnpike. **General Store:** Yes. **Vending:** Yes. **Swimming Pool:** No. **Playground:** Yes. **Other:** Rec hall, arcade, pool tables, swimming pond. **Activities:** Planned activities, basketball, horseshoes. **Nearby Attractions:** Public golf course, casinos, Norwich Navigators baseball. **Additional Information:** Southeastern Connecticut Tourism District, (860) 444-2206 or (800) TO-ENJOY, www.mysticmore.com.

Restrictions

Pets: Yes. **Fires:** Allowed. **Alcoholic Beverages:** Allowed. **Vehicle Maximum Length:** None. **Other:** Ask on arrival.

To Get There

Take 395 north to Exit 83A (Exit 83 from 395 south), then take a left onto Rte. 169. Follow for approximately 0.5 mi. to the Kendall Rd. Exit and bear left onto Strand, following signs to campground.

LITCHFIELD

Hemlock Hill Camp Resort

P.O. Box 828 Hemlock Hill Rd., Litchfield 06759. T: (860) 567-2267.

RV: ★★★ Tent: ★★★

Beauty: ★★★ Site Privacy: ★★★★
Spaciousness: ★★★ Quiet: ★★★★
Security: ★★★ Cleanliness: ★★★
Insect Control: ★★★ Facilities: ★★★★★

Sites are set on a hillside (don't worry, the sites themselves are flat) shaded by large hemlock trees. Fairly spacious but not enormous, some overlook the brook that runs through the campground. Canoes can be used on the brook, but the real attraction at Hemlock Hills are its planned activities. There's a lot going on during weekends, making this a good choice for families. People can own sites here, so many RV campers stay the entire summer or split ownership of a site. Since many of the guests here already know each other, Hemlock Hills is a very friendly place. Tent campers are welcome but find themselves in a heavy minority.

Basics

Operated By: Jerry & Mary Hughes. **Open:** Apr. 29–Oct. 23. **Site Assignment:** Reservations w/ deposit suggested; sites can be purchased. **Registration:** At office. **Fee:** $20–$29. **Parking:** At site.

Facilities

Number of RV Sites: 125. **Number of Tent-Only Sites:** 10. **Hookups:** Electric (20, 30 amps). **Each Site:** Fire pit, picnic table. **Dump Station:** Yes. **Laundry:** Yes. **Pay Phone:** Yes. **Rest Rooms and Showers:** Yes. **Fuel:** No. **Propane:** Yes. **RV Service:** No. **Market:** Stop & Shop Supermarket, 331 West St., Litchfield, CT (4.5 mi.). Take a left onto Maple St., followed by a left onto Milton Rd. Make a left onto Rte. 202, which becomes West St. **Restaurant:** Snack bar, Ming's Chinese Restaurant, Rte. 202, Litchfield, CT (3.4 mi. Follow directions above. **General Store:** No. **Vending:** Yes. **Swimming Pool:** Yes. **Playground:** Yes. **Other:** Bocce, whirlpool, sports area, fishing pond, hot tub. **Activities:** Every weekend has a heavy schedule of planned family activities. **Nearby Attractions:** Town of Litchfield has shopping & other activities. **Additional Information:** Litchfield Hills Visitors Bureau, (860) 567-4506, www.litchfieldhills.com.

Restrictions

Pets: On leash only. **Fires:** Allowed. **Alcoholic Beverages:** Allowed. **Vehicle Maximum Length:** 40 ft. **Other:** Ask on arrival.

To Get There

Take 84 east to Exit 7. Follow Rte. 7 north to Rte. 202 east for 19 mi. to Maple St. Follow Maple St. for 4 mi. to Hemlock Hill Rd.

MYSTIC

Seaport Campgrounds

P.O. Box 104, Hwy. 184, Mystic 06372. T: (860) 536-4044; F: (860) 536-4461; www.seaport-campground.com; seaport@gocampingamerica.com.

RV: ★★★★ Tent: ★★

Beauty: ★★ Site Privacy: ★★★
Spaciousness: ★★★★★ Quiet: ★★★
Security: ★★★★★ Cleanliness: ★★★★
Insect Control: ★★★ Facilities: ★★★★★

A wide-open campground with nicely sized sites but not much in the way of shade, Seaport is a well-run facility with many activities and impressive facilities. But the biggest attraction might be the easy accessibility to Mystic and its multitude of activities. There are more RVs than tenters here, but the layout makes it a pleasant place for both.

Basics

Operated By: Private operator. **Open:** Varies, call ahead. **Site Assignment:** Reservations generally required Memorial Day–Labor Day. **Registration:** Store. **Fee:** $28. **Parking:** At site.

Facilities

Number of RV Sites: 130. **Number of Tent-Only Sites:** Undesignated sites. **Hookups:** Water, electric (30, 50 amps). **Each Site:** Picnic table, fire pit. **Dump Station:** Yes. **Laundry:** Yes. **Pay Phone:** Yes. **Rest Rooms and Showers:** Yes. **Fuel:** No. **Propane:** Yes. **RV Service:** No. **Market:** Central Market, 118 Fort Hill Rd., Groton, CT (3.7 mi.). Take a right onto High St., followed by a right onto Rte. 1. Follow Rte. for about 3 mi. until it becomes Fort Hill Rd. **Restaurant:** 41 Degrees North Restaurant, 21 W. Main St., Mystic, CT (0.6 mi.). Take a right onto High St. followed by a slight left onto Rte. 1. **General Store:** Yes. **Vending:** Yes. **Swimming Pool:** Yes. **Playground:** No. **Other:** Mini-golf, rec room, fishing pond. **Activities:** Live music on weekends. **Nearby Attractions:** Town of Mystic. **Additional Information:** Southeastern Connecticut Tourism District, (860) 444-2206 or (800) TO-ENJOY, www.mysticmore.com.

Restrictions

Pets: On leash only. **Fires:** Allowed. **Alcoholic Beverages:** Allowed. **Vehicle Max. Length:** 55 ft.

To Get There

Take 95 to Exit 90 and go 1.25 mi. to Rte. 72, then take a right and go 0.5 mi. east on Rte. 184. The campground is on the left.

NIANTIC

Camp Niantic by the Atlantic

271 Main St. (Rte. 156), Niantic 06357. T: (800) 739-9308; www.campniantic.com; campniantic@aol.com.

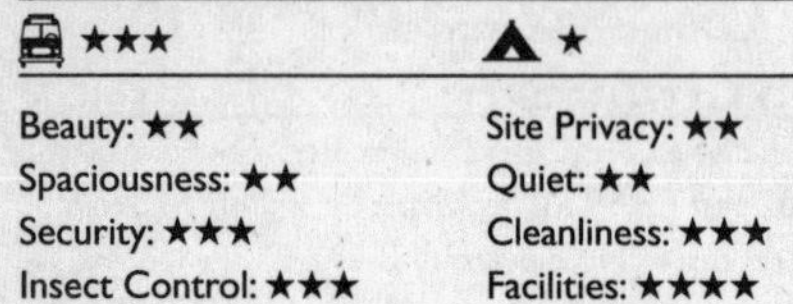

RV ★★★ Tent ★

Beauty: ★★ Site Privacy: ★★
Spaciousness: ★★ Quiet: ★★
Security: ★★★ Cleanliness: ★★★
Insect Control: ★★★ Facilities: ★★★★

Though tent camping is allowed here, we can't see why anyone would choose to pitch their tent at Camp Niantic. RVs absolutely fill the entire place and a tent would get lost among them. Despite all the RVs, the campground manages to remain attractive, as most of its hillside is wooded. Free passes are offered to McCook Point Beach, located a short drive away.

Basics

Operated By: Terell & Carole Rice. **Open:** May 1–Oct. 15. **Site Assignment:** Reservations recommended. **Registration:** At office. **Fee:** $23–$27. **Parking:** At site.

Facilities

Number of RV Sites: 100. **Number of Tent-Only Sites:** 0. **Hookups:** Water, electric, sewer. **Each Site:** Fireplace, picnic table. **Dump Station:** No. **Laundry:** Yes. **Pay Phone:** Yes. **Rest Rooms and Showers:** Yes. **Fuel:** No. **Propane:** Yes. **RV Service:** No. **Market:** Colonial Market, 243 Main St., Niantic, CT (0.1 mi.). Take a left onto Main St. **Restaurant:** Constantine's, 252 Main St., Niantic, CT (0.1 mi.). Take a left onto Main St. **General Store:** No. **Vending:** No. **Swimming Pool:** No. **Playground:** No. **Other:** Free access to town beach, game room, basketball courts. **Activities:** Planned weekend activities, sports tournaments. **Nearby Attractions:** Rocky Neck State Park & McCook Point Beach. **Additional Information:** Southeastern Connecticut Tourism District, (860) 444-2206 or (800) TO-ENJOY, www.mysticmore.com.

Restrictions

Pets: On leash only. **Fires:** Allowed. **Alcoholic Beverages:** Allowed. **Vehicle Maximum Length:** None. **Other:** Ask on arrival.

To Get There

95 to Exit 72. Turn right onto Rte. 156 south and follow to campsite.

NIANTIC

Rocky Neck State Park

244 W. Main St., Niantic 06357. T: (860) 739-1339; www.reserveamerica.com.

RV ★★★ Tent ★★★

Beauty: ★★★ Site Privacy: ★★★
Spaciousness: ★★★★ Quiet: ★★★★
Security: ★★ Cleanliness: ★★★
Insect Control: ★★★ Facilities: ★★★

Rocky Neck State Park is a big place. Yet despite its 700 acres, it seems fairly quiet and cozy. Its proximity to Long Island Sound, the salt marsh, and the forest make it a prime choice for birdwatching; there's a nature center on the grounds, and you'll want to take time on your way down the walking/biking trail to the beach to enjoy the salt marsh you'll pass. You may even want to do some fishing or try netting some blue crabs. The park's big, open grassy areas are great for playing Frisbee or tossing a football; lots of people are just walking about, biking, or in-line skating. (Consequently, drivers should be cautious!) There's a community fire ring, so you may make some new friends there. Tent campers will be hard pressed to find a softer surface on which to pitch their sleeping bags.

Basics

Operated By: CT Dept. of Environmental Protection. **Open:** Memorial Day–Labor Day. **Site Assignment:** Reservations or first come, first served. **Registration:** Reserve America. **Fee:** $15. **Parking:** At site.

Facilities

Number of RV Sites: 120. **Number of Tent-Only Sites:** 48. **Hookups:** None. **Dump Station:** Yes. **Laundry:** No. **Pay Phone:** Yes. **Rest Rooms and Showers:** Yes. **Fuel:** No. **Propane:** No. **Internal Roads:** Paved. **RV Service:** No. **Market:** No. **Restaurant:** No. **General Store:** Concessions. **Vending:** Yes. **Swimming Pool:** No. **Playground:** No. **Activities:** Hiking, picnicking, shellfishing, swimming, scuba diving, saltwater fishing, field sports. **Nearby Attractions:** McCook Point Beach, casinos. **Additional Information:** Southeastern Connecticut Tourism District (860) 444-2206 or (800) TO-ENJOY, www.mysticmore.com.

Restrictions

Pets: No. **Fires:** In fire ring. **Alcoholic Beverages:** No. **Vehicle Maximum Length:** None. **Other:** Ask on arrival.

To Get There

From Rte. 95, take Exit 72 and follow the signs to the park.

NORTH STONINGTON

Highland Orchards Resort Park

P.O. Box 222, North Stonington 06359. T: (800) 624-0829; F: (860) 599-8944; www.highlandorchards.com; camp@highlandorchards.com.

RV ★★★★ Tent ★★★

Beauty: ★★★ Site Privacy: ★★★★
Spaciousness: ★★★★ Quiet: ★★★
Security: ★★★★★ Cleanliness: ★★★★
Insect Control: ★★★ Facilities: ★★★

Mostly grassy rolling meadows with trees here and there, Highland Orchards does have a few wooded areas that are dedicated to the tent sites. A combination destination park and travel park, Highland Orchards is a good home base for excursions to the local beaches, Mystic, and, of course, the Connecticut casinos. It's quieter than many RV-dominated campgrounds because the staff zealously enforces its quiet policy. There aren't as many planned activities here as at some places, but there's always something scheduled for Saturday evenings in season. Make weekend reservations well in advance during summer, but you'll usually find a space during the week.

Basics

Operated By: Bob, Elaine, & Joe Boissevain. **Open:** All year. **Site Assignment:** Reservations. **Registration:** At office. **Fee:** $30–$41.50. **Parking:** 1 car at site; other cars in lot.

Facilities

Number of RV Sites: 250. **Number of Tent-Only Sites:** 20. **Hookups:** Water, electric (30, 50 amps), sewer, cable TV. **Each Site:** Picnic table, fire ring, some w/ phone. **Dump Station:** Yes. **Laundry:** Yes. **Pay Phone:** Yes. **Rest Rooms and Showers:** Yes. **Fuel:** No. **Propane:** Yes. **Internal Roads:** Paved, some gravel. **RV Service:** Yes. **Market:** A&P Super Food Market, 179 Stonington Rd., Stonington, CT. **Restaurant:** Ashby Restaurant, Rte. 27 Stonington, CT. **General Store:** Yes. **Vending:** Yes. **Swimming Pool:** Yes. **Playground:** Yes. **Other:** Fishing ponds, mini-golf, basketball court, shuffleboard, rec room, fireplace lounge. **Activities:** Free shuttle to Foxwoods casino, special events every weekend during the summer. **Nearby Attractions:** Mystic seaport, Mystic aquarium. **Additional Information:** Southeastern Connecticut Tourism District, (860) 444-2206 or (800) TO-ENJOY, www.mysticmore.com.

Restrictions

Pets: Yes. **Fires:** Allowed. **Alcoholic Beverages:** Quietly at site. **Vehicle Maximum Length:** None. **Other:** Quiet hours begin at 10:30 p.m.

To Get There

95 to Exit 92. Take a left onto Rte. 2, passing under 95, and turn right onto the service road for Rte. 49. Turn left onto Rte. 49 and enter the first driveway on the right.

OAKDALE

Peppertree Camping

Rte. 198, Chaplin 06235. T: (860) 974-1439; www.campconn.com/peppertree.

RV ★★★★ Tent ★★★

Beauty: ★★★ Site Privacy: ★★★★★
Spaciousness: ★★★★ Quiet: ★★★★★
Security: ★★★★ Cleanliness: ★★★★
Insect Control: ★★★ Facilities: ★★★

Nicer than neighboring Nickerson Campground, Peppertree Camping also borders the Natchaug State Forest but features more attractive sites that offer a little more privacy. There are no tent-specific sites here and any site should work fine for both tents and RVs. Quite a few planned activities are offered, but your best bet might be to just spend time walking the numerous forest trails.

Basics

Operated By: Dan & Camille Wilson. **Open:** Apr. 15–Oct. 15. **Site Assignment:** Reservations recommended. **Registration:** Store. **Fee:** $22–$23.50. **Parking:** At site.

Facilities

Number of RV Sites: 55. **Number of Tent-Only**

Sites: 0. **Hookups:** Water, electric, sewer. **Each Site:** Picnic table, fireplace. **Dump Station:** Yes. **Laundry:** Yes. **Pay Phone:** Yes. **Rest Rooms and Showers:** Yes. **Fuel:** No. **Propane:** Yes. **RV Service:** No. **Market:** Ted's Mini Market, 315 Boston Post Rd., North Windham, CT (5.5 mi.). Go south on Rte. 198 towards Pumpkin Hill Rd. by turning right, then take a slight right onto Rte. 6. Rte. 6 becomes N. Windham Rd. & then becomes Boston Post Rd. **Restaurant:** Chaplin Pizza, 52 Willimantic Rd. Chaplin, CT. Follow above directions to Willimantic Rd. **General Store:** Yes. **Vending:** Yes. **Swimming Pool:** No. **Playground:** Yes. **Other:** Baseball field, horseshoe pits, basketball court. **Activities:** Swimming, rafting, river tubing, hiking, biking, bingo, pot-luck suppers. **Nearby Attractions:** Natchaug State Forest. **Additional Information:** Northeast Connecticut Visitors District, (860) 779-6383 or (888) 628-1228, www.ctquietcorner.org.

Restrictions

Pets: On leash only. **Fires:** Allowed. **Alcoholic Beverages:** Allowed. **Vehicle Maximum Length:** None. **Other:** Ask on arrival.

To Get There

84 to Exit 69. Right onto Rte. 74 east to Rte. 44 east. Take 44 east to Rte. 198 south. Campground is on the left.

PLYMOUTH

Gentiles Campground

Rte. 262, Mt. Tobe Rd., Plymouth 06782. T: (860) 283-8437; F: (203) 755-3582.

RV: ★★★ Tent: ★★

Beauty: ★ Site Privacy: ★
Spaciousness: ★★ Quiet: ★★
Security: ★★★ Cleanliness: ★★★★
Insect Control: ★★★ Facilities: ★★★

If you're looking for nature, the actual campground here might not be the place to find it. Sites are packed close together, and it seems like most of the RVs parked here plan to remain for the season, so your view is likely to be of the side of someone's RV. However, you don't have to go far to find nature, because Gentiles borders Mattatuck State Forest, which offers stocked fishing, trails, and a chance to commune with nature. Gentiles has a lot to offer—especially if you plan to get away from your campsite a bit.

Basics

Operated By: Irene & Ray Gentile. **Open:** May 1–Oct. 15. **Site Assignment:** Reservations required. **Registration:** Store. **Fee:** Rates available by request only. **Parking:** At site.

Facilities

Number of RV Sites: 110. **Number of Tent-Only Sites:** 0. **Hookups:** Water, electric (30 amps), sewer. **Each Site:** Picnic table, fire ring. **Dump Station:** Yes. **Laundry:** No. **Pay Phone:** Yes. **Rest Rooms and Showers:** Yes. **Fuel:** No. **Propane:** Yes. **RV Service:** No. **Market:** Village Mart, 1815 Thomaston Ave., Waterbury, CT (2.4 Miles). Left onto Rte. 262 & then a left onto Thomaston Ave. **Restaurant:** Giovanni's Restaurante, 1622 Thomaston Ave., Waterbury, CT (2.6 mi.). Follow directions above. **General Store:** Yes. **Vending:** Yes. **Swimming Pool:** Yes. **Playground:** No. **Other:** Picnic area, tennis courts, bocce, mini-golf, volleyball courts, basketball court, petting zoo, 2 rec halls. **Activities:** Tennis, swimming, hiking. **Nearby Attractions:** City of Waterbury (3 mi. south). **Additional Information:** Litchfield Hills Visitors Bureau, (860) 567-4506, www.litchfieldhills.com.

Restrictions

Pets: Yes. **Fires:** Allowed. **Alcoholic Beverages:** Allowed. **Vehicle Maximum Length:** None. **Other:** Ask on arrival.

To Get There

Take 84 to Rte. 8 north to Exit 39. Go east on Rte. 6 for 2 mi., take a right at the light onto Rte. 262, and follow for 3 mi. until you see the campground on the left.

PRESTON

Hidden Acres Family Campground

47 River Rd., Preston 06365. T: (860) 887-9633; F: (860) 887-6359; hacampgd@aol.com.

RV: ★★★★ Tent: ★★

Beauty: ★★ Site Privacy: ★★★
Spaciousness: ★★ Quiet: ★★
Security: ★★★★ Cleanliness: ★★★
Insect Control: ★★ Facilities: ★★★★

Not the place to go if you're camping with a tent, this loud campground is dedicated to RVs. Despite bordering the Quinebaug River, the scenery here is nothing special, though most sites at least have fairly large trees on them. This is also not the place to go for a quiet weekend away, but it might be a good place to take the kids, as there are many children around and numerous planned activities.

Basics

Operated By: The Migliaccio Family. **Open:** May 1–Columbus Day. **Site Assignment:** Reservations. **Registration:** At office. **Fee:** $20–$26. **Parking:** At site.

Facilities

Number of RV Sites: 180. **Number of Tent-Only Sites:** 0. **Hookups:** Water, electric (20, 30, 50 amps). **Each Site:** Picnic table, fire ring. **Dump Station:** Yes. **Laundry:** Yes. **Pay Phone:** Yes. **Rest Rooms and Showers:** Yes. **Fuel:** No. **Propane:** Yes. **RV Service:** No. **Market:** Russ's Market, 754 N. Main St., Norwich, CT (2.8 mi.). **Restaurant:** Snack bar on site. Eli's Pizza Place, 500 Norwich Ave., Taftville, CT (2 mi.). **General Store:** Yes. **Vending:** Yes. **Swimming Pool:** No. **Playground:** No. **Other:** Stocked fishing pond, animal-visiting area, horseshoe pits, basketball & volleyball courts, craft shop w/ ceramics, rec hall, game room. **Activities:** Hayrides, weekend entertainment, bingo. **Nearby Attractions:** Quinebaug River (offers tubing & fishing). **Additional Information:** Southeastern Connecticut Tourism District, (860) 444-2206 or (800) TO-ENJOY, www.mysticmore.com.

Restrictions

Pets: On leash only. **Fires:** At site only. **Alcoholic Beverages:** At site. **Vehicle Maximum Length:** None. **Other:** Ask on arrival.

To Get There

Rte. 395 to Exit 85. Go south 1 mi. on Rte. 164 and turn right on George Palmer Rd. Continue 3 mi. to campground, bearing right the whole way.

SALEM

Indianfield Campground

Gardner Lake, Rte. 354, 306 Old Colchester Rd., Salem 06420. T: (860) 859-1320; F: (860) 859-1320.

RV: ★★★ Tent: n/a

Beauty: ★★★ Site Privacy: ★★★
Spaciousness: ★★★ Quiet: ★★★
Security: ★★★ Cleanliness: ★★★
Insect Control: ★★★ Facilities: ★★★

A large RV-based campground located on Gardner Lake, Indianfield makes for an excellent family camping destination. The entire clientele seems to be families in enormous RVs who come for extended vacations, and the campsite caters to that. There are many planned activities as well as spontaneous ones that pop up due to the sheer volume of people here. The campground itself is actually quite large and the lakefront offers a large beach. There's also boat docks and every other kind of waterfront activity imaginable.

Basics

Operated By: Larry & Marlene Harrington. **Open:** May 1–Oct. 30. **Site Assignment:** At time of Registration. **Registration:** Store. **Fee:** $12–$28. **Parking:** At site.

Facilities

Number of RV Sites: 228. **Number of Tent-Only Sites:** 0. **Hookups:** Water, electric (30 amps), phone. **Dump Station:** Yes. **Laundry:** Yes. **Pay Phone:** Yes. **Rest Rooms and Showers:** Yes. **Fuel:** No. **Propane:** Yes. **RV Service:** No. **Market:** Oakdale Market, 430 Chapel Hill Rd., Oakdale, CT (3.9 mi.). Turn left onto Rte. 354, then take a right onto Rte. 82, followed by an immediate left onto OldColchester Rd. Follow until Forsyth Rd. & make a right, followed by a left on Chapel Hill Rd. **Restaurant:** Grumpy Joe's Restaurant & Bar, 627 Rte. 82, Oakdale, CT (2.1 mi.). Go left onto Rte. 354 & then left onto Rte. 82. **General Store:** Yes. **Vending:** Yes. **Swimming Pool:** No. **Playground:** Yes. **Other:** Rec hall, open pavilion, dock slips. **Activities:** Planned events on weekends. **Nearby Attractions:** Inquire at campground. **Additional Information:** Southeastern Connecticut Tourism District, (860) 444-2206 or (800) TO-ENJOY, www.mysticmore.com.

Restrictions

Pets: Must be leashed, quiet, & cleaned up after. **Fires:** Ask on arrival. **Alcoholic Beverages:** Allowed. **Vehicle Maximum Length:** 40 ft. **Other:** Ask on arrival.

To Get There

395 to Exit 80. Go west on Rte. 82 for 8 mi. to Rte. 354. Turn right and go 1 mi. looking for campground sign on the right.

SCOTLAND

Highland Campground

Toleration Rd., P.O. Box 305, Scotland 06264. T: (860) 423-5684; F: (860) 456-2697; www.highlandcampground.com; info@highlandcampground.com.

RV ★★★★ Tent ★★★

Beauty: ★★★★ Site Privacy: ★★★★
Spaciousness: ★★★★ Quiet: ★★★★
Security: ★★★★ Cleanliness: ★★★★
Insect Control: ★★★ Facilities: ★★★★

A beautiful campground, Highland is set back well off the road. Each site has ample space, and most sites are well hidden by the forest. Unlike many campgrounds that cater to RVs, this one is also a friendly place for tent campers, as the privacy of the sites means you won't be pitching your tent too close to an RV. A well-situated campground, Highland is near a lot of recreation, both within walking distance (hiking and fishing) and within a short drive.

BASICS

Operated By: The Davis family. **Open:** All year, but limited in winter. **Site Assignment:** Reservations necessary in season, though sites are sometimes available. **Registration:** Store. **Fee:** $24 & up. **Parking:** At site.

FACILITIES

Number of RV Sites: 160. **Number of Tent-Only Sites:** 0. **Hookups:** Electric (20, 30 amps). **Each Site:** Fireplace, picnic table. **Dump Station:** Yes. **Laundry:** Yes. **Pay Phone:** Yes. **Rest Rooms and Showers:** Yes. **Fuel:** No. **Propane:** Yes. **RV Service:** No. **Market:** Yadiras Grocery Store, 157 Valley St., Windham, CT. **Restaurant:** Snack bar, Liberty's Restaurant, 451 Main Windham, CT. **General Store:** Yes. **Vending:** Yes. **Swimming Pool:** Yes. **Playground:** Yes. **Other:** Stocked fishing pond, mini-golf, rec hall, adult lounge, bocce court. **Activities:** Catch & release fishing, hiking, potluck suppers, volleyball, bingo, dancing. **Nearby Attractions:** Foxwoods, USS Nautilus, Plainfield Greyhound Park. **Additional Information:** Northeast Connecticut Visitors District, (860) 779-6383 or (888) 628-1228, www.ctquietcorner.org.

RESTRICTIONS

Pets: On leash only. **Fires:** Allowed. **Alcoholic Beverages:** Allowed. **Vehicle Maximum Length:** 40 ft. **Other:** Ask on arrival.

TO GET THERE

395 to Exit 83. Follow Rte. 97 north for 7.5 mi. to Toleration Rd. and take a right onto Toleration Rd.

THOMASTON

Branch Brook Campground

435 Watertown Rd., Thomaston 06787. T: (860) 283-8144.

RV ★★★ Tent ★★

Beauty: ★★ Site Privacy: ★★★
Spaciousness: ★★★ Quiet: ★★★
Security: ★★★★ Cleanliness: ★★
Insect Control: ★★★ Facilities: ★★★

Filled mostly with seasonal campers, Branch Brook has a "lived in" feel. Though the campground has a pretty brook and some other nice scenery, it's hard to get past the feeling that you're staying in a trailer park. However, you're near Mattatuck State Forest, so walking trails and less-spoiled nature are only a little way down the road.

BASICS

Operated By: Kip & Denise Brammer. **Open:** Apr. 1–Nov. 1. **Site Assignment:** Reservations recommended. **Registration:** At office. **Fee:** Around $20 & up; 3-day min. stay required for holiday weekends. **Parking:** At site.

FACILITIES

Number of RV Sites: 63. **Number of Tent-Only Sites:** 0. **Hookups:** Water, electric (20, 30, 50 amps), sewer. **Each Site:** Picnic table, fire ring. **Dump Station:** Yes. **Laundry:** Yes. **Pay Phone:** Yes. **Rest Rooms and Showers:** Yes. **Fuel:** No. **Propane:** Yes. **RV Service:** Yes. **Market:** New Daily Mart, 9 N. Main St., Thomaston, CT (2 mi.). Go northeast on Rte. 6, following it untul it becomes Waterbury Rd., then turn back to Rte. 6 & finally N. Main St. **Restaurant:** Goose & The Gander Inc., 370 Watertown Rd., Thomaston, CT (0.1 mi.). Take a right onto Watertown Rd. **General Store:** No. **Vending:** Yes. **Swimming Pool:** Yes. **Playground:** No. **Other:** Rec hall. **Activities:** Fishing. **Nearby Attractions:** Black Rock State Park. **Additional Information:** Waterbury Region CVB, (203) 597-9527, www.waterburyregion.com.

RESTRICTIONS

Pets: On leash only. **Fires:** Allowed. **Alcoholic Beverages:** Allowed. **Vehicle Maximum Length:** None. **Other:** Ask on arrival.

TO GET THERE

From Rte. 8 take Exit 38 and go 1 mi. west on Rte. 6. Campground is across from Black Rock State Park.

TOLLAND

Del Aire

Shepsit Lake Rd., Tolland 06084. T: (860) 875-8325.

RV ★★★ Tent ★★★★

Beauty: ★★★★ Site Privacy: ★★★
Spaciousness: ★★ Quiet: ★★★
Security: ★★★ Cleanliness: ★★★★
Insect Control: ★★★ Facilities: ★★★

Del Aire caters to seasonal campers, and you can generally get a reservation. RV sites are somewhat close together, but they're flat and dotted with a reasonable number of trees offering shade. Tent sites are a little more remote, which makes them seem bigger. Two brooks run through the grounds, adding to the scenery, and the neighboring lake offers boating, fishing, and swimming. There's also an easily accessible trail up Soapstone Mountain that offers access to a lookout tower and some spectacular views.

BASICS

Operated By: Albert & Germaine Ouelette. **Open:** May 1–Oct. 15. **Site Assignment:** Reservations recommended July–Labor Day. **Registration:** Store. **Fee:** $14–$18. **Parking:** At site.

FACILITIES

Number of RV Sites: 100. **Number of Tent-Only Sites:** 25. **Hookups:** Water, electric (15, 20 amps). **Each Site:** Picnic table, stone fireplace. **Dump Station:** Yes. **Laundry:** No. **Pay Phone:** Yes. **Rest Rooms and Showers:** Yes. **Fuel:** No. **Propane:** Yes. **RV Service:** No. **Market:** Tolland IGA, 200 Merrow Rd. 208, Tolland, CT (1.3 mi.). Go right on Rte. 74 & make a sharp left onto Rte. 195. **Restaurant:** Lee's Garden, 200 Merrow Rd., Tolland, CT (1.3 mi.). Follow directions above. **General Store:** Yes (limited). **Vending:** Yes. **Swimming Pool:** No. **Playground:** Yes. **Other:** Rec hall, sports field. **Activities:** Fishing, swimming. **Nearby Attractions:** Shenipsit Lake. **Additional Information:** Greater Hartford Tourism District, (860) 244-8181 or (800) 793-4480, www.enjoyhartford.com.

RESTRICTIONS

Pets: On leash only. **Fires:** Allowed. **Alcoholic Beverages:** Allowed. **Vehicle Maximum Length:** None. **Other:** Ask on arrival.

TO GET THERE

Take 84 to Exit 67. Go north on Rte. 31 for 0.25 mi. to Rte. 30. Take a right at the light and go 4 mi. to Brown Bridge Rd. Follow signs to campground.

VOLUNTOWN

Circle "C" Campground

RFD 1, P.O. Box 23A Bailey Rd., Voluntown 06384. T: (860) 564-4534; F: (860) 564-4339; www.campcirclec.com; circleccampground@prodigy.net.

RV ★★★★ Tent ★★★

Beauty: ★★★ Site Privacy: ★★★
Spaciousness: ★★★ Quiet: ★★★
Security: ★★★ Cleanliness: ★★★★
Insect Control: ★★★ Facilities: ★★★★

Whether you prefer wooded sites or wide-open ones, Circle "C" has the site for you. The open sites are grassy, and some overlook Bailey Pond, which is located on the premises. You can powerboat on Bailey (up to 10 mph) and swim and fish in the other two ponds at the campground. There's a decent mix of tent and RV campers who stay here, and a handful of sites are definitely best suited for tents.

BASICS

Operated By: John & Jeanette Richard. **Open:** Apr. 19–Oct. 16. **Site Assignment:** Reservations recommended. **Registration:** Store. **Fee:** $22 tent, $25 hookups. **Parking:** At site.

FACILITIES

Number of RV Sites: 100. **Number of Tent-Only Sites:** 0. **Hookups:** Water, electric (30, 50 amps), sewer. **Each Site:** Picnic table, fire pit. **Dump Station:** Yes. **Laundry:** Yes. **Pay Phone:** Yes. **Rest Rooms and Showers:** Yes. **Fuel:** No. **Propane:** No. **RV Service:** No. **Market:** Better Val-U Supermarket, 104 Beach Pond Rd., Voluntown, CT 06384 (10.7 mi.). Turn left onto Bailey Pond Rd., followed by a right onto Hazard Rd., which becomes Escoheag Hill Rd. Turn right onto Rte. 165, which becomes Beach Pond Rd. **Restaurant:** Town Pizza & Restaurant, 104 Beach Pond Rd., Voluntown, CT (10.7 mi.). Follow above directions. **General Store:** Yes (mini-store). **Vending:** Yes. **Swimming Pool:** No. **Playground:** Yes. **Other:** Rec hall, arcade, basketball court, badminton court, mini-golf, horseshoe pits. **Activities:** Boat rentals, fishing, lots of planned activities, including "Murder Mystery" weekend. **Nearby Attractions:** Plainfield Greyhound Park. **Additional Information:** Southeastern Connecticut Tourism District, (860) 444-2206 or (800) TO-ENJOY, www.mysticmore.com.

RESTRICTIONS

Pets: Yes. **Fires:** Allowed. **Alcoholic Beverages:** Allowed. **Vehicle Maximum Length:** 40 ft. **Other:** Ask on arrival.

TO GET THERE

Take 95 to Exit 5A and make a right onto Rte. 3, followed by a right into Rte. 165. Follow until Rte. 40 north. Go 2.6 mi. and take a right onto Brown Rd. Follow to end and make a right onto Gallup Homestead Rd. Follow to end and make a right onto Bailey Pond Rd.

VOLUNTOWN

Countryside Campground

75 Cook Hill Rd., Voluntown 06384. T: (860) 376-0029; F: (860) 376-3120; countryside-camp@email.com.

 ★★★★ ▲ ★★★★

Beauty: ★★★★ Site Privacy: ★★★★★
Spaciousness: ★★★★ Quiet: ★★★★★
Security: ★★★★ Cleanliness: ★★★★★
Insect Control: ★★★ Facilities: ★★★

Quiet is the operative word here—the goal is to keep the noise level to a mimimum. Trees shield the sites from each other (and add to the beauty of the place). The spring-fed swimming pond is at the center of the camp, and occassional whoops of joy while taking a dip are acceptable during the day. The private sites are ideal for tent campers who don't want to feel like they're penned in by RVs.

BASICS

Operated By: Linda Mackin. **Open:** May 1–Oct. 15. **Site Assignment:** Reservations w/ nonrefundable deposit recommended. **Registration:** At office. **Fee:** $18 tent, $20 hookups. **Parking:** At site.

FACILITIES

Number of RV Sites: 59. **Number of Tent-Only Sites:** 9. **Hookups:** Water, electric (30, 50 amps). **Each Site:** Picnic table, stone fireplace. **Dump Station:** Yes. **Laundry:** No. **Pay Phone:** Yes. **Rest Rooms and Showers:** Yes. **Fuel:** No. **Propane:** No. **RV Service:** No. **Market:** Sunny Supermarket, 129 Main St., Voluntown, CT (1.1 mi.). Turn left onto Cook Hill Rd., followed by a slight left onto Sheldon Rd. & a right onto Rte. 138, which becomes Main St. **Restaurant:** Town Pizza & Restaurant, 104 Beach Pond Rd., Voluntown, CT (1.7 mi.). Follow above directions, staying on Main St. until it becomes Beach Pond Rd. **General Store:** No. **Vending:** No. **Swimming Pool:** No. **Playground:** No. **Other:** Swimming pond, fishing pond. **Activities:** Swimming, fishing. **Nearby Attractions:** Next to Pachaug State Forest. **Additional Information:** Southeastern Connecticut Tourism District, (860) 444-2206 or (800) TO-ENJOY, www.mysticmore.com.

RESTRICTIONS

Pets: On leash only. **Fires:** Allowed. **Alcoholic Beverages:** Allowed. **Vehicle Maximum Length:** 36 ft. **Other:** Ask on arrival.

TO GET THERE

Take 395 to Exit 85. Go east on Rte. 138 for 4 mi., then take a right onto Rte. 201 south. Follow for 1 mi. to Cook Hill Rd. on the left. Campground will be 0.5 mi. down on the right.

WOODSTOCK

Beaver Pines Campground

1728 Rte. 198, Woodstock 06281. T: (860) 974-0110; www.beaverpinescampground.com; e-mail form on website.

 ★★★ ▲ ★★★★

Beauty: ★★★★ Site Privacy: ★★★★★
Spaciousness: ★★★★ Quiet: ★★★★
Security: ★★★★ Cleanliness: ★★★★
Insect Control: ★★★ Facilities: ★★★★

A tent camper's paradise, Beaver Pines offers enormous sites in an attractive wooded setting. Though the regular sites are reasonably private, anyone wanting complete seclusion can reserve a remote site set away from the rest of the campground. The RV facilities are relatively limited in number, and the entire campground is somewhat small, which gives it a family feel—that's mostly what you find here.

BASICS

Operated By: Private operator. **Open:** Apr. 15–Oct. 15. **Site Assignment:** Reservations recommended, required for secluded sites. **Registration:** Store. **Fee:** $22–$25. **Parking:** At site.

FACILITIES

Number of RV Sites: 8. **Number of Tent-Only Sites:** 14. **Hookups:** Water, electric, cable TV. **Each Site:** Picnic table, fire ring. **Dump Station:** Yes. **Laundry:** No. **Pay Phone:** Yes. **Rest Rooms and Showers:** Yes. **Fuel:** No. **Propane:** No. **RV Service:** No. **Market:** La Bonne's Epicure Market, 544 Straits Turnpike, Watertown, CT. **Restaurant:** Anthony's, 308 Main St., Watertown, CT. **General Store:** Yes. **Vending:** No. **Swimming Pool:** No. **Playground:** Yes. **Other:** Sports field, pond, game room. **Activities:** Fishing, kayaking, hiking, mountain biking. **Nearby Attractions:** Bigelow Hollow State Park. **Additional Information:** Northeast Connecticut Visitors District, (860) 779-6383 or (888) 628-1228, www.ctquietcorner.org.

RESTRICTIONS

Pets: Yes. **Fires:** Allowed. **Alcoholic Beverages:** Allowed. **Vehicle Maximum Length:** Large vehicles must make reservations. **Other:** Ask on arrival.

TO GET THERE

Take 84 to Exit 73 and follow Rte. 190 for 2 mi. Turn left onto Rte. 197 and follow for 2 mi., then make a left onto Rte. 198. The campground is 1.5 mi. on the left.

WOODSTOCK

Chamberlain Lake Campground

1397 Rte. 197, Woodstock 06281. T: (860) 974-0567; www.gocampingamerica/chamberlain; chamberlainlakecampground@yahoo.com.

★★★★ ▲ ★★★

Beauty: ★★★ Site Privacy: ★★★★
Spaciousness: ★★★ Quiet: ★★★★
Security: ★★★★ Cleanliness: ★★★★
Insect Control: ★★★ Facilities: ★★★★

While the wooded sites here aren't particularly large (around 25–35 feet), they're fairly private, with trees and other growth shielding you from your neighbors. Sites on the lakefront cost a bit more, but the others are almost as nice. Tent campers should enjoy the relative seclusion and quiet of this campground, and nature lovers will appreciate that all fishing done at the campground's lake is catch and release.

BASICS

Operated By: Private operator. **Open:** May 1–Oct. 15. **Site Assignment:** Reservations recommended. **Registration:** Store. **Fee:** $26–$28; 3-night min. stay required in season. **Parking:** At site.

FACILITIES

Number of RV Sites: 120. **Number of Tent-Only Sites:** 30. **Hookups:** Water, electric (30, 40 amps), phone. **Each Site:** Fireplace, picnic table. **Dump Station:** Yes. **Laundry:** Yes. **Pay Phone:** Yes. **Rest Rooms and Showers:** Yes. **Fuel:** No. **Propane:** Yes. **RV Service:** No. **Market:** Xtra Mart, 251 West Main St., Dudley, MA (4.5 mi.). Turn left onto Rte. 197 & follow for 4.5 mi. **Restaurant:** No. **General Store:** Yes. **Vending:** Yes. **Swimming Pool:** Bogey's Restaurant, 80 Airport Rd., Dudley, MA (5.2 mi.). Turn left onto Rte. 197 & follow until Dudley Hill Rd. Make a left onto Dudley Hill Rd. & follow for 1.7 mi. **Playground:** No. **Other:** Rec hall, basketball court, volleyall courts, lake. **Activities:** Boat & canoe rentals, fishing. **Nearby Attractions:** Brimfield flea markets, Old Sturbridge Village. **Additional Information:** Northeast Connecticut Visitors District, (860) 779-6383 or (888) 628-1228, www.ctquietcorner.org.

RESTRICTIONS

Pets: On leash only. **Fires:** Allowed. **Alcoholic Beverages:** Allowed. **Vehicle Maximum Length:** 40 ft. **Other:** Ask on arrival.

TO GET THERE

Take 84 to Exit 73 and go east on Rte. 190. Take a right onto Rte. 171 and follow for 2.2 mi., then take a left onto Rte. 197 and follow for 3.5 mi. until you see the campground on the left.

Delaware

From the cobblestone streets of New Castle to the 18th-century cupola-topped state house in Dover, or from the rolling hills and sprawling meadows of Brandywine Valley to the picturesque beach towns on the Atlantic Coast, Delaware is a compact but diverse place. America's second-smallest state after Rhode Island, Delaware is rich with early American history, natural splendor, and small-town charm. The state capital of Dover was laid out by William Penn around a beautiful green. A contrasting landscape, Delaware features forested hills in the north, stretches of sand dunes in the south, and miles of marshland along the coast.

In northern Delaware, historic **New Castle** is a well-preserved colonial town and the state's first capital. The state's largest city is **Wilmington,** settled in the Brandywine Valley by Swedes in the 17th century and regarded as the chemical capital of the world. Minutes from Wilmington's skyline are numerous lavish country estates, including the 300-acre **Nemours Mansion and Gardens,** once the home of Alfred I. du Pont. Options for outdoor jaunts include the 1,000-acre day-use **Brandywine Creek State Park,** which offers nature trails, fishing holes, and a nature center; and **Fort Delaware State Park,** with its Civil War-era stockade.

Set in the heart of Delaware, the state capital of **Dover** is known for its tranquil beauty. The **Delaware State Museums Complex** includes the **Delaware Archaeology Museum,** the **Johnson Victrola Museum,** and the **Museum of Small Town Life. Killens Pond State Park** and the **Delaware Agricultural Museum and Village** are also located in the Dover area.

The coastal side of southern Delaware is renowned for its mammoth sandy beaches. **Bethany Beach** and **Dewey Beach** are popular oceanside towns. **Rehoboth Beach** is one of the Atlantic Coast's busiest resort areas. Away from the bustle of the resort area, **Delaware Seashore State Park** is a seven-mile strip of land separating Rehoboth and Indian River Bays from the Atlantic Ocean. **Lewes,** originally called Zwaanendael when it was the first Dutch settlement in Delaware, is a quaint town perched on Delaware Bay. Outdoor recreation is plentiful at **Cape Henlopen State Park**. Daytrippers can board the **Lewes–Cape May Ferry** and visit **Cape May, NJ,** the immaculately preserved town that boasts more Victorian homes than any community in the United States.

The following facilities accept payment in checks or cash only:

Treasure Beach RV Park and Campground, Fenwick Island

Campground Profiles

FELTON

Killens Pond State Park

5025 Killens Pond Rd., Felton 19943. T: (302) 284-4526 or (877) 987-2757; www.destateparks.com; parkinfo@dnrec.state.de.us.

RV: ★★★★ Tent: ★★★★

Beauty: ★★★★	Site Privacy: ★★★
Spaciousness: ★★★	Quiet: ★★★★
Security: ★★★★	Cleanliness: ★★★★
Insect Control: ★★★★	Facilities: ★★★★

Located in the heart of Kent County about 15 miles south of Dover, Killens Pond State Park is within a 1.5-hour drive from the northern and southern borders of Delaware, making the campground an ideal base to explore the state. The wooded sites for both RVs and tents are arranged around six loops, all a short walk from the southeastern end of Killens Pond. A secluded primitive tenting area is separated from the other sites. The park office and water park complex are located on the north side of the pond, a short drive from the campground. Killens Pond is stocked with largemouth bass, catfish, carp, perch, crappie, bluegill and pickerel. Canoes, rowboats, surfbikes, kayaks, and pedal boats are available for rent during the summer. The water park has a concession stand and swim shop. An 18-hole disc golf course and a network of wooded hiking trails offer additional recreation.

BASICS

Operated By: State of Delaware. **Open:** All year. **Site Assignment:** Reservations accepted (pay in advance to confirm site; $10 fee for canceling reservation with notice of 30 days or more, 1-night charge for canceling reservation with notice of less than 30 days), walk-ins accepted. **Registration:** At campground office. **Fee:** $18–$24 (VISA, MC). **Parking:** At site.

FACILITIES

Number of RV Sites: 59. **Number of Tent-Only Sites:** 17. **Hookups:** Electric (20 amps), water. **Each Site:** Fire ring, picnic table. **Dump Station:** Yes. **Laundry:** No. **Pay Phone:** Yes. **Rest Rooms and Showers:** Yes. **Fuel:** No. **Propane:** No. **Internal Roads:** Paved and dirt, in fair condition. **RV Service:** No. **Market:** Within 2 mi. **Restaurant:** Within 2 mi. **General Store:** No. **Vending:** Yes. **Playground:** Yes. **Other:** Cabin rentals, Killens Pond Water Park. **Activities:** Swimming, boating, canoeing, boat rentals, pond fishing, shuffleboard, sports field, volleyball, hiking trails, horseshoes, badminton, disc golf. **Nearby Attractions:** Delaware Archaeology Museum, Museum of Small Town Life, Johnson Victrola Museum, Delaware State Visitor Center, Dover Heritage Trail, John Dickinson Plantation, Old State House, Delaware State Fair. **Additional Information:** Kent County Convention and Visitors Bureau, (800) 233-KENT, www.visitdover.com.

RESTRICTIONS

Pets: On leash. **Fires:** At site. **Alcoholic Beverages:** At site. **Vehicle Maximum Length:** 30 ft. **Other:** Max. 14-day stay during 21-day period from Memorial Day to Labor Day.

TO GET THERE

From Felton, go 1 mi. south on US 13 and 1.5 mi. east on Paradise Alley Rd. Follow signs to campground.

FENWICK ISLAND

Treasure Beach RV Park and Campground

Route 54 Box 150A, Selbyville 19975. T: (302) 436-8001; F: (302) 436-9515; www.bayvillede.com; camping@bayvillede.com.

RV ★★★★ Tent ★★★★

Beauty: ★★★★ Site Privacy: ★★★
Spaciousness: ★★★ Quiet: ★★★★
Security: ★★★★ Cleanliness: ★★★★
Insect Control: ★★★★ Facilities: ★★★★

Watching the sun set over the Atlantic Ocean is a spectacular sight from Treasure Island RV Park and Campground, located along the ocean and Little Assawoman Bay one mile west of Fenwick Island at the southeastern tip of Delaware. Rehoboth Beach is a 20-minute drive to the north, and Ocean City (MD) is a 20-minute jaunt to the south. With 1,000 sites in a relatively small area, campers have little privacy, but the campground has many amenities, such as a crabbing pier, two swimming pools, and a recreation center. The campground is close to the Bayville Marina and the well-kept Bayville Shopping Center. Sailboats are rented here. For an added adventure, campers can drive to Lewes, less than 10 miles north of Rehoboth Beach, and board the Lewes–Cape May (NJ) Ferry. The 16-mile, 70-minute journey ends at historic Cape May, where a tour of the town's historic Victorian district is a must for history enthusiasts.

BASICS

Operated By: Private operator. **Open:** May 1–Oct. 15. **Site Assignment:** Reservations accepted (3-day min. stay on weekends in July and Aug., and on holiday weekends), walk-ins accepted. **Registration:** At campground office. **Fee:** $25–$40. **Parking:** At site.

FACILITIES

Number of RV Sites: 900. **Number of Tent-Only Sites:** 100. **Hookups:** Electric (30, 50 amps), cable TV, 30 full hookups. **Each Site:** Fireplace, picnic table. **Dump Station:** Yes. **Laundry:** Yes. **Pay Phone:** Yes. **Rest Rooms and Showers:** Yes. **Fuel:** No. **Propane:** Yes. **Internal Roads:** Gravel and paved, in good condition. **RV Service:** No. **Market:** Within 2 mi. **Restaurant:** Within 2 mi. **General Store:** Yes. **Vending:** Yes. **Playground:** Yes. **Other:** Little Assawoman Bay. **Activities:** Saltwater fishing, boating, shuffleboard, planned activities, rec hall, game room. **Nearby Attractions:** Fenwick Island Lighthouse, DiscoverSea Shipwreck Museum, Thunder Lagoon, Fenwick Island State Park, Bethany Beach, Rehoboth Beach, Ocean City (MD). Additional Information: Bethany-Fenwick Area Chamber of Commerce, (800) 962-7873, www.bethany-fenwick.org.

RESTRICTIONS

Pets: On leash. **Fires:** In fireplace. **Alcoholic Beverages:** At site only. **Vehicle Maximum Length:** 40 ft. **Other:** Two cars and one RV per campsite.

TO GET THERE

From SR 1, go 2 mi. west on SR 54. Follow sign to campground.

GLASGOW

Lums Pond State Park

1068 Howell School Rd., Bear 19701. T: (877) 987-2757 or (302) 368-6989; www.destateparks.com; parkinfo@dnrec.state.de.us.

RV ★★★ Tent ★★★★

Beauty: ★★★★ Site Privacy: ★★★★
Spaciousness: ★★★★ Quiet: ★★★★
Security: ★★★★ Cleanliness: ★★★★
Insect Control: ★★★★ Facilities: ★★★★

Built around the largest freshwater pond in Delaware, Lums Pond State Park is located on the north side of the Chesapeake and Delaware Canal south of Newark and southwest of culture-rich Wilmington. Covering 200 acres, Lums Pond itself has a sandy swimming beach and a place where rowboats, sailboats, canoes, and pedal boats are rented. For campers who bring their own boats, a launching ramp and two piers allow easy access to the water. The campground is located off Rte. 71 south of the widest section of the pond, not far from the boat ramp. Sites are spacious and wooded, and six have electric hookups. The shower facilities here are modern and clean. The swimming area, boat rental station, sports complex, nature center, and park office are located on the opposite end of the pond. These sites are accessible through the main entrance off Howell School Rd.

BASICS

Operated By: State of Delaware. **Open:** Apr. 1–Oct. 31. **Site Assignment:** Reservations accepted (pay in advance to confirm site; $10 fee for canceling reservation with notice of 30 days or more, 1-night charge for canceling reservation with notice of less than 30 days), walk-ins accepted. **Registration:** At campground office. **Fee:** $20–$23 (VISA, MC). **Parking:** At site.

FACILITIES

Number of RV Sites: 68. **Number of Tent-Only Sites:** None. **Hookups:** Electric (20 amps). **Each Site:** Grill, picnic table. **Dump Station:** Yes. **Laundry:** No. **Pay Phone:** Yes. **Rest Rooms and Showers:** Yes. **Fuel:** No. **Propane:** No. **Internal Roads:** Paved, in good condition. **RV Service:** No. **Market:** Within 5 mi. **Restaurant:** Within 5 mi. **General Store:** No. **Vending:** Yes. **Playground:** No. **Other:** Yurt (tent) rentals, nature center, gift shop in park office. **Activities:** Disc golf, pond swimming and fishing, boating, boat rentals, tennis, badminton, sports field, hiking trails, volleyball, horseshoes. **Nearby Attractions:** Wilmington, Fort Delaware State Park, Brandywine Zoo and Park, Brandywine Springs Park, Delaware Art Museum, Fort Christina Monument, Delaware Museum of Natural History, Rockwood Museum, Nemours Mansion and Gardens, New Castle, Amstel House Museum, Old New Castle Court House, University of Delaware. **Additional Information:** Greater Wilmington CVB, (800) 489-6664.

RESTRICTIONS

Pets: On leash. **Fires:** At site. **Alcoholic Beverages:** No alcohol permitted. **Vehicle Maximum Length:** 40 ft. **Other:** 14-day max. stay limit within 21-day period between Mem. Day and Labor Day.

TO GET THERE

From Glasgow, go 3 mi. south on Hwy. 896 and east on Howell School Rd. Follow signs to campground.

LAUREL

Trap Pond State Park

RD 2 Box 331, Laurel 19956. T: (877) 987-2757 or (302) 875-2392; www.destateparks.com; parkinfo@dnrec.state.de.us.

RV ★★★ Tent ★★★★

Beauty: ★★★★ Site Privacy: ★★★★
Spaciousness: ★★★★ Quiet: ★★★★
Security: ★★★★ Cleanliness: ★★★★
Insect Control: ★★★★ Facilities: ★★★

Trap Pond State Park retains the picturesque mystique of the freshwater wetlands of southwestern Delaware. In fact, Trap Pond contains the northernmost stand of baldcypress trees in the nation. Hiking trails surround the pond, and observant hikers may spot a great blue heron, hummingbird, warbler, bald eagle, or pileated woodpecker. Our favorite activity at Trap Pond is boating amid the baldcypress. Guided pontoon boat tours hosted by a park interpreter are conducted on weekends and holidays. One of the streams that flows into Trap Pond has been marked as a wilderness canoe trail, which leads further into the swamp's interior. The campground is located at the northwest end of the pond, and sites are arranged in five loops beneath tall pines. Overall, 130 sites are equipped with water and electric hookups. Two primitive camping areas are also available for youth groups by reservation .

BASICS

Operated By: State of Delaware. **Open:** Apr. 1–Oct. 31. **Site Assignment:** Reservations accepted (pay in advance to confirm site; $10 fee for cancelling reservation with notice of 30 days or more, 1-night charge for cancelling reservation with notice of less than 30 days), walk-ins accepted. **Registration:** At campground office. **Fee:** $18–$23 (VISA, MC). **Parking:** At site.

FACILITIES

Number of RV Sites: 130. **Number of Tent-Only Sites:** 12. **Hookups:** Electric (20 amps), water. **Each Site:** Fire ring, picnic table. **Dump Station:** Yes. **Laundry:** Yes. **Pay Phone:** Yes. **Rest Rooms and Showers:** Yes. **Fuel:** No. **Propane:** No. **Internal Roads:** Dirt, in fair condition. **RV Service:** No. **Market:** Within 5 mi. **Restaurant:** Within 5 mi. **General Store:** No. **Vending:** No. **Playground:** Yes. **Other:** Trap Pond, Baldcypress Nature Center. **Activities:** Pond swimming, fishing, boating, canoeing, boat rentals, hiking trails, volleyball, horseshoes. **Nearby Attractions:** Barnes Woods Nature Preserve, Old Christ Church, Nutter D. Marvel Carriage Museum, Fenwick Island, Nanticoke River, Delaware Seashore State Park, Rehoboth Beach. **Additional Information:** Laurel Chamber, (302) 875-9319, www.laurelchamber.com.

RESTRICTIONS

Pets: On leash, under control. **Fires:** At site. **Alcoholic Beverages:** No alcohol permitted. **Vehicle Maximum Length:** 40 ft. **Other:** Max. 14-day stay within 21-day period from Mem. Day to Labor Day.

To Get There

From US 13, go 4 mi. east on Hwy. 24 and 1 mi. south on CR 449. Follow signs to campground.

LEWES
Cape Henlopen State Park

42 Cape Henlopen Drive, Lewes 19958. T: (877) 987-2757 or (302) 645-2103; www.destateparks.com; parkinfo@dnrec.state.de.us.

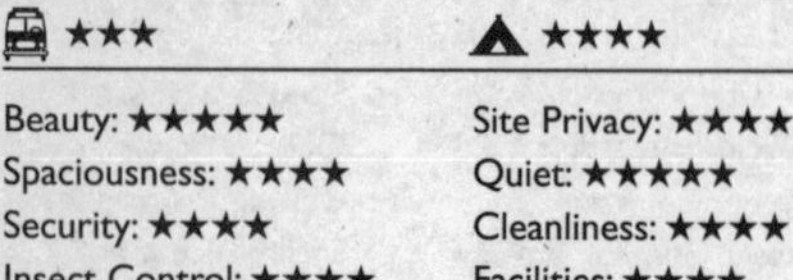

RV ★★★ Tent ★★★★

Beauty: ★★★★★ Site Privacy: ★★★★
Spaciousness: ★★★★ Quiet: ★★★★★
Security: ★★★★ Cleanliness: ★★★★
Insect Control: ★★★★ Facilities: ★★★★

The beaches attract most visitors to Cape Henlopen State Park, located on the Atlantic Ocean at the mouth of Delaware Bay. Yet this park on Delaware's southeastern shore is not just about basking in the sun and swimming in the ocean. Gordon's Pond Wildlife Area has a unique saltwater impoundment. Along the coast, the Great Dune rises 80 feet above sea level. Further inland, the famous "walking dunes" stretch across the pine forests. A broad salt marsh meanders along the park's western boundary. Fittingly, the campground is nestled amid pine-covered dunes and has 159 sites, most of which have water hookups. For anglers, a quarter-mile-long pier offers access to Delaware Bay. The pier's bait and tackle shop also sells snacks and beverages. Two designated swimming beaches are monitored by lifeguards, and the northern swimming area has a modern bath house with showers, changing rooms, and a concession stand.

Basics

Operated By: State of Maryland. **Open:** Apr. 1–Oct. 31. **Site Assignment:** Reservations accepted (pay in advance to confirm site; $10 fee for cancelling reservation with notice of 30 days or more, 1-night charge for cancelling reservation with notice of less than 30 days), walk-ins accepted. **Registration:** At campground office. **Fee:** $25–$27 (VISA, MC). **Parking:** At site.

Facilities

Number of RV Sites: 142. **Number of Tent-Only Sites:** 17. **Hookups:** Water. **Each Site:** Grill, picnic table. **Dump Station:** Yes. **Laundry:** Yes. **Pay Phone:** Yes. **Rest Rooms and Showers:** Yes. **Fuel:** No. **Propane:** No. **Internal Roads:** Paved, in good condition. **RV Service:** No. **Market:** Within 4 mi. **Restaurant:** Within 4 mi. **General Store:** No. **Vending:** No. **Playground:** No. **Other:** Seaside Nature Center. **Activities:** Saltwater fishing and swimming, basketball, disc golf, tennis, hiking trails, sports field, rec hall. **Nearby Attractions:** Lewes–Cape May (NJ) Ferry, Beach Plum Island Nature Preserve, Lewes Historical Society Complex (including Cannon Ball House and Marine Museum, Thompson Country Store, Doctor's Office, log cabins and farmhouse), Zwaanendael Museum, Rehoboth Beach. **Additional Information:** Lewes Chamber of Commerce and Visitors Bureau, (302) 645-8073, www.leweschamber.com.

Restrictions

Pets: On leash, must be kept attended. **Fires:** At site. **Alcoholic Beverages:** No alcohol permitted. **Vehicle Maximum Length:** 35 ft. **Other:** Max. of 14-day stay limit within 21-day period from Memorial Day to Labor Day.

To Get There

From Hwy. 1, go 4 mi. northeast on US 9. Follow signs to the campground.

LEWES
Tall Pines

RD 1 Box 221, Lewes 19958. T: (302) 684-0300; F: (302) 684-1045; www.tallpines-del.com; tpinfo@ezol.com.

RV ★★★★ Tent ★★★★

Beauty: ★★★★ Site Privacy: ★★★
Spaciousness: ★★★★ Quiet: ★★★★
Security: ★★★★ Cleanliness: ★★★★
Insect Control: ★★★★ Facilities: ★★★★

As the name suggests, Tall Pines is a camping resort snuggled beneath a forest of loblolly pines. Located in Lewes near Delaware's southeastern shore, the campground is only a few minutes from the Atlantic Ocean and the mouth of Delaware Bay, where campers can frolic on beaches and explore the rolling sand dunes at Cape Henlopen State Park. The bulk of the RV sites are situated in the center and north end of Tall Pines. Seasonal sites are concentrated from the center to the north, while transient sites are located from the center to the south. Though Tall Pines is shaded by pines and is well-maintained, campers should know that the eastern side of the campground is bordered by railroad tracks. Tent sites are located on the southwestern end of the campground along the stream.

Basics

Operated By: Private operator. **Open:** All year. **Site Assignment:** Reservations accepted (2-night deposit required, 3 nights on holiday weekends), walk-ins accepted. **Registration:** At campground office. **Fee:** $30–$33 (VISA, MC). **Parking:** At site.

Facilities

Number of RV Sites: 430. **Number of Tent-Only Sites:** 26. **Hookups:** Electric (20, 30 amps), water, 400 full hookups. **Each Site:** Fire ring, picnic table. **Dump Station:** Yes. **Laundry:** Yes. **Pay Phone:** Yes. **Rest Rooms and Showers:** Yes. **Fuel:** No. **Propane:** Yes. **Internal Roads:** Paved, in fair condition. **RV Service:** No. **Market:** Within 4 mi. **Restaurant:** Within 4 mi. **General Store:** Yes. **Vending:** Yes. **Playground:** Yes. **Other:** Pavilion. **Activities:** Basketball, rec hall, Olympic-size pool, game room, badminton, shuffleboard, volleyball, horseshoes. **Nearby Attractions:** Lewes–Cape May (NJ) Ferry; Cape Henlopen State Park, Lewes Historical Society Complex (including Cannon Ball House and Marine Museum, Thompson Country Store, Doctor's Office, log cabins and farmhouse), Zwaanendael Museum, Rehoboth Beach. **Additional Information:** Lewes Chamber of Commerce and Visitors Bureau, (302) 645-8073, www.leweschamber.com.

Restrictions

Pets: On leash, at site; no pets permitted in recreation areas. **Fires:** At site. **Alcoholic Beverages:** At site. **Vehicle Maximum Length:** None. **Other:** Quiet hours are 11 p.m.–9 a.m.; rates are based on a family of four people. Additional campers may stay at a rate of $2 per person per day.

To Get There

From Hwy. 1, go 3 mi. southwest on US 9 and 0.75 mi. southwest on service road. Entrance is on the right.

NEW CASTLE
Delaware Motel and RV Park

235 S. Dupont Hwy., New Castle 19720. T: (302) 328-3114.

RV ★★★ Tent n/a

Beauty: ★ Site Privacy: ★
Spaciousness: ★ Quiet: ★★
Security: ★★★ Cleanliness: ★★★★
Insect Control: ★★★★ Facilities: ★★★

As far as campgrounds go, Delaware Motel and RV Park offers few amenities. There are rest rooms and showers. No tents are allowed. Scenery is non-existent; the park features 28 sites behind a motel. There is no playground, sports courts, or fishing ponds. In fact, there is no on-site recreation, period. Simply put, the park is best used as a base for sight-seeing in New Castle, Fort Delaware State Park, Wilmington, and even Philadelphia. Located in historic New Castle, this property is near many interesting towns and attractions in northern Delaware. Delaware's first capital and located on the Delaware River, New Castle is a haven for history buffs who love colonial architecture. The town's buildings date back to the 17th century, and many of them surround The Green, a public square. The Old Court House, built in 1732, is the oldest surviving court house in Delaware.

Basics

Operated By: Private operator. **Open:** All year. **Site Assignment:** Reservations and walk-ins accepted. **Registration:** At motel. **Fee:** $20 (VISA, MC, AE, D). **Parking:** At site.

Facilities

Number of RV Sites: 28. **Number of Tent-Only Sites:** None. **Hookups:** Electric (30 amps), phone, all sites have full hookups. **Each Site:** Full hookups. **Dump Station:** No. **Laundry:** Yes. **Pay Phone:** Yes. **Rest Rooms and Showers:** No. **Fuel:** No. **Propane:** No. **Internal Roads:** Paved, in good condition. **RV Service:** No. **Market:** Within 2 mi. **Restaurant:** Within 0.5 mi. **General Store:** No. **Vending:** No. **Playground:** No. **Other:** Motel. **Activities:** None. **Nearby Attractions:** Colonial New Castle, Amstel House Museum, The Green, George Read II House, Old Library Museum, Old Dutch House, Old New Castle Court House, Wilmington, Delaware History Museum, Hagley Museum, Brandywine Zoo and Park, Brandywine Creek State Park, Nemours Mansion and Gardens, Rockwood Museum Fort Delaware State Park, Philadelphia. **Additional Information:** Historic New Castle Visitors Bureau, (800) 758-1550, www.hsd.org.

Restrictions

Pets: On leash, at campsite. **Fires:** At site. **Alcoholic Beverages:** At site. **Vehicle Maximum Length:** 35 ft. **Other:** No tents or camping motorcyclists allowed.

To Get There

Located at the junction of US 13 and Hwy. 40 in New Castle.

OCEAN VIEW

Sandy Cove Campground

RD 1 Box 256, Ocean View 19970.
T: (302) 539-6245; F: (302) 539-2344;
www.sandycovede.com;
scc@sandycovede.com.

RV ★★★ Tent ★★★

Beauty: ★★★ Site Privacy: ★★★
Spaciousness: ★★★ Quiet: ★★★
Security: ★★★★ Cleanliness: ★★★★
Insect Control: ★★★★ Facilities: ★★★

We like sunsets over the water, and the sunset from Sandy Cove Campground's location on Indian River Bay did not disappoint us. Sandy Cove is based in Ocean View, a few miles west of the Atlantic Ocean, where the waters of Indian River Bay flow. Sandy Cove is central to Rehoboth Beach (about 12 miles north) and Fenwick Island (about eight miles south). Campers have their choice of open and wooded sites, all of which have water and electric hookups. Sandy Cove does not have a swimming pool, but it does have a private beach. The marina rents rowboats and canoes, and the campground has a crabbing pier that lures the youngsters, who also flock to the game room and playground. If you want to enjoy the ocean and the beach without the crowds that often gather at Ocean City and Rehoboth Beach, try Bethany Beach, which is just south of Ocean View.

Basics

Operated By: Private operator. **Open:** Apr. 1–Nov. 1. **Site Assignment:** Reservations accepted (3-night min. stay June 15–Aug. 15), walk-ins accepted. **Registration:** At campground office. **Fee:** $25–$27.50 (VISA, MC). **Parking:** At site.

Facilities

Number of RV Sites: 180. **Number of Tent-Only Sites:** None. **Hookups:** Electric (20, 30 amps), water. **Each Site:** Fire ring, picnic table. **Dump Station:** Yes. **Laundry:** No. **Pay Phone:** Yes. **Rest Rooms and Showers:** Yes. **Fuel:** No. **Propane:** Yes. **Internal Roads:** Gravel, in good condition. **RV Service:** Yes. **Market:** Within 2 mi. **Restaurant:** Within 2 mi. **General Store:** Yes. **Vending:** Yes. **Playground:** Yes. **Other:** Boat ramp and dock. **Activities:** Boating, canoeing, boat rentals, saltwater fishing, volleyball, horseshoes. **Nearby Attractions:** Indian River Bay, Fenwick Island, DiscoverSea Shipwreck Museum, Fenwick Island Lighthouse, Bethany Beach, Fenwick Island State Park, Delaware Seashore State Park, Rehoboth Beach, Lewes–Cape May Ferry, Ocean City (MD). **Additional Information:** Bethany-Fenwick Area Chamber of Commerce, (800) 962-7873, www.bethany-fenwick.org.

Restrictions

Pets: On leash. **Fires:** At site. **Alcoholic Beverages:** At site. **Vehicle Maximum Length:** 35 ft. **Other:** Pets and fires may not be left unattended.

To Get There

From Hwy. 1, go 2 mi. west on Hwy. 26, 2.5 mi. north on Central Ave., and 0.5 mi. west on CR 358. Entrance is on the left.

REHOBOTH BEACH

3 Seasons RV Resort

727 Country Club Rd., Rehoboth Beach 19971.
T: (302) 227-2564 or (800) 635-4996; F: (302) 227-9418; www.3seasons.com;
threesns@dmv.com.

RV ★★★★★ Tent n/a

Beauty: ★★★★ Site Privacy: ★★★★
Spaciousness: ★★★★ Quiet: ★★★★
Security: ★★★★★ Cleanliness: ★★★★★
Insect Control: ★★★★ Facilities: ★★★★★

Located about 2.5 miles from Rehoboth Beach, 3 Seasons RV Resort is hands-down the nicest RV campground to stay at in Delaware (no tents allowed though). The park has a shuttle that takes passengers to the Rehoboth Beach boardwalk. Campers have their choice of open and wooded sites, each of which has full hookups and is comfortably spaced. Amenities here are so abundant that you do not have to leave the park to stay entertained or relaxed—unless you want to bask on the beach or stroll along the boardwalk. Captain Wag's Cruises will arrange fishing trips, dolphin watch excursions, and sunset cruises. Campers can rent bikes and scooters, and they can even embark on guided bike tours. The Cottage Day Spa provides massages and waxing among other services. Most of the activity centers are located near the entrance, including the swimming pool, playground, basketball court, registration center, and beach shuttle stop.

Basics

Operated By: Private operator. **Open:** Mar. 17–Dec. 17; fully operational between Memorial Day and Labor Day. **Site Assignment:** Reservations recommended (2-night deposit required), walk-ins accepted. **Registration:** At campground office. **Fee:** $30–$46 (VISA, MC, AE, D). **Parking:** At site.

Facilities

Number of RV Sites: 304. **Number of Tent-Only Sites:** None. **Hookups:** Electric (20, 30, 50 amps), cable TV, phone, all sites have full hookups. **Each Site:** Fire ring, picnic table. **Dump Station:** Yes. **Laundry:** Yes. **Pay Phone:** Yes. **Rest Rooms and Showers:** Yes. **Fuel:** No. **Propane:** Yes. **Internal Roads:** Paved, in good condition. **RV Service:** No. **Market:** Within 2 mi. **Restaurant:** Within 2 mi. **General Store:** Yes. **Vending:** Yes. **Playground:** Yes. **Other:** Equipped pavilion. **Activities:** Basketball, mini-golf, game room, kiddie pool in addition to swimming pool, shuffleboard, movies, planned activities, volleyball, horseshoes, sports field, badminton, lounge with fireplace. **Nearby Attractions:** Rehoboth Beach boardwalk attractions and beach, Cape Henlopen State Park, Delaware Seashore State Park, Lewes–Cape May Ferry. **Additional Information:** Rehoboth Beach-Dewey Beach Chamber of Commerce, (800) 441-1329, www.beach-fun.com.

Restrictions

Pets: On leash. **Fires:** At site. **Alcoholic Beverages:** At site. **Vehicle Maximum Length:** None. **Other:** No tents are allowed.

To Get There

From Hwy. 1, go 1.5 mi. west on CR 273. Entrance is on the right.

REHOBOTH BEACH

Big Oaks Family Campground

Box 53 Route 1, Rehoboth Beach 19971.
T: (302) 645-6838; F: (302) 644-4644;
www.bigoakscamping.com;
campbigoaks@aol.com.

RV ★★★★ Tent ★★★★

Beauty: ★★★★ Site Privacy: ★★★★
Spaciousness: ★★★★ Quiet: ★★★★
Security: ★★★★ Cleanliness: ★★★★
Insect Control: ★★★★ Facilities: ★★★★

Located three miles north of Rehoboth Beach and three miles south of the Lewes–Cape May Ferry, Big Oaks Family Campground caters to campers interested in the boardwalk amusements and beach frolicking. Big Oaks operates a free shuttle service to and from Rehoboth Beach. Campers can choose from level open and wooded sites, 125 of which have full hookups. Yes, the wooded sites are snuggled under mighty oak trees. The campground has a new swimming pool, as well as a clubhouse, game room, and snack bar. The restrooms and shower facilities at Big Oaks are well-maintained. During the summer, Big Oaks stirs with special activities like dances, hayrides, art contests, and bingo games, as well as tournaments for basketball, horseshoes, shuffleboard, and billiards. For those without RVs or tents, Big Oaks has two-room cabins, RVs, and mobile homes for rent. Big Oaks also sells tickets to Atlantic City casinos, a short drive north of Lewes.

Basics

Operated By: Private operator. **Open:** May 1–Oct. 1. **Site Assignment:** Reservations accepted (2-night min. stay in July and Aug.), walk-ins accepted. **Registration:** At campground office. **Fee:** $30–$35 (VISA, MC). **Parking:** At site.

Facilities

Number of RV Sites: 150. **Number of Tent-Only Sites:** 25. **Hookups:** Electric (20, 30, 50 amps), water, cable TV, phone, 125 full hookups. **Each Site:** Fire ring, picnic table. **Dump Station:** Yes. **Laundry:** Yes. **Pay Phone:** Yes. **Rest Rooms and Showers:** Yes. **Fuel:** No. **Propane:** No. **Internal Roads:** Gravel and paved, in good condition. **RV Service:** No. **Market:** Within 1 mi. **Restaurant:** Within 1 mi. **General Store:** Yes. **Vending:** Yes. **Playground:** Yes. **Other:** RV rentals, beach shuttle. **Activities:** Basketball, game room, rec hall, shuffleboard, movies, planned activities on weekends, horseshoes. **Nearby Attractions:** Rehoboth Beach boardwalk attractions and beach, Cape Henlopen State Park, Delaware Seashore State Park, Lewes–Cape May (NJ) Ferry. **Additional Information:** Rehoboth Beach-Dewey Beach Chamber of Commerce, (800) 441-1329, www.beach-fun.com.

Restrictions

Pets: On leash. **Fires:** At site. **Alcoholic Beverages:** At site. **Vehicle Maximum Length:** 40 ft. **Other:** One camping unit for site; pets may not be left unattended.

To Get There

At Hwy. 1 and Hwy. 24, go 0.5 mi. east on CR 270. Entrance is on the left.

REHOBOTH BEACH
Delaware Seashore State Park

Inlet 850, Rehoboth Beach 19971. T: (877) 987-2757 or (302) 539-7202; www.destateparks.com; parkinfo@dnrec.state.de.us.

RV ★★★★ Tent ★★★★

Beauty: ★★★★ Site Privacy: ★★★
Spaciousness: ★★★★ Quiet: ★★★★
Security: ★★★★ Cleanliness: ★★★★
Insect Control: ★★★★ Facilities: ★★★★

Bounded on the east by the Atlantic Ocean and on the west by Rehoboth Bay and Indian River Bay, the 2,799-acre Delaware Seashore State Park covers six miles of ocean and bay shoreline. Surf fishing is big here, and several charter boats offer deep-sea excursions. Also, fishing boats operate from the Indian River Marina, located on the bay side north of the inlet. A special access pier at the inlet allows people with disabilities to more easily fish. Umbrellas, chairs, and rafts can be rented on the beach. The park office and the Indian River Marina are located north of Indian River Inlet, while the campground is situated on the water south of the inlet. Of the 278 sites, 145 have full hookups. The new Thompson Island Preserve, located on Rehoboth Bay northwest of the inlet, is a prime example of the salt marsh habitat that once thrived around inland bays.

Basics

Operated By: State of Maryland. **Open:** All year; fully operational mid-Mar.–mid-Nov. **Site Assignment:** Reservations accepted (pay in advance to confirm site; $10 fee for canceling reservation with notice of 30 days or more, 1-night charge for canceling reservation with notice of less than 30 days), walk-ins accepted. **Registration:** At campground office. **Fee:** $25–$33 (VISA, MC). **Parking:** At site.

Facilities

Number of RV Sites: 145. **Number of Tent-Only Sites:** 133. **Hookups:** Electric (20, 50 amps), 145 full hookups. **Each Site:** Picnic table. **Dump Station:** Yes. **Laundry:** Yes. **Pay Phone:** Yes. **Rest Rooms and Showers:** Yes. **Fuel:** No. **Propane:** No. **Internal Roads:** Paved and dirt, in good condition. **RV Service:** No. **Market:** Within 3 mi. **Restaurant:** Within 3 mi. **General Store:** No. **Vending:** No. **Playground:** No. **Other:** Indian River Bay. **Activities:** Saltwater fishing and swimming, boating, hiking trails. **Nearby Attractions:** Rehoboth Beach boardwalk attractions and beach, Fenwick Island, Lewes–Cape May Ferry, Cape Henlopen State Park. **Additional Information:** Rehoboth Beach-Dewey Beach Chamber of Commerce, (800) 441-1329, www.beach-fun.com.

Restrictions

Pets: On leash. **Fires:** At site. **Alcoholic Beverages:** No alcohol permitted. **Vehicle Maximum Length:** 40 ft. **Other:** 14-day max. stay in 21-day period from Memorial Day to Labor Day.

To Get There

From Rehoboth Beach, go 2 mi. south on Hwy. 1. Follow signs to campground.

REHOBOTH BEACH
Holly Lake Campsites

RD 6 Box 141, Millsboro 19966. T: (302) 945-3410 or (800) 227-7170; F: (302) 945-3411; www.hollylakecampsites.com; camping@dmv.com.

RV ★★★ Tent ★★★

Beauty: ★★★ Site Privacy: ★★★
Spaciousness: ★★★ Quiet: ★★★★
Security: ★★★★ Cleanliness: ★★★
Insect Control: ★★★★ Facilities: ★★★

A kidney-shaped 4,000-square-foot swimming pool, two miles of hiking trails through dense woodlands, a wildlife area with two observation platforms, and a petting zoo where barnyard animals roam are among the attractions that lure campers to Holly Lake Campsites, located outside of Rehoboth Beach. The campground also has Old Holly River, Deep Branch Creek, and Ivy Branch Creek within its boundaries. The camp store serves breakfast, lunch, and dinner as well as ice cream, camping supplies, snacks, beverages, and ice. With 600 sites, including 500 with full hookups, Holly Lake is a large campground with 11 bathhouses scattered about. Sites are arranged in four large areas. Many sites are nestled between Deep Branch Creek and Old Holly Lake. A mass of sites is also located east of Deep Branch. Though the campground is adorned with lush woods around the bodies of water, and some sites are wooded, many sites have little privacy.

Basics

Operated By: Private operator. **Open:** All year, fully operational May 1–Sept. 30. **Site Assignment:** Reservations accepted (2-night min. stay on weekends, 3-nights stay on holiday weekends), walk-ins accepted. **Registration:** At campground office. **Fee:** $35 (VISA, MC). **Parking:** At site.

Facilities

Number of RV Sites: 500. **Number of Tent-Only Sites:** 100. **Hookups:** Electric (20, 30 amps), water, 500 full hookups. **Each Site:** Fire ring, picnic table. **Dump Station:** Yes. **Laundry:** Yes. **Pay Phone:** Yes. **Rest Rooms and Showers:** Yes. **Fuel:** Yes. **Propane:** Yes. **Internal Roads:** Dirt, in fair condition. **RV Service:** No. **Market:** Within 6 mi. **Restaurant:** Within 4 mi. **General Store:** Yes. **Vending:** Yes. **Playground:** No. **Other:** Petting zoo. **Activities:** Hiking trails, game room, volleyball, horseshoes, rec hall, planned activities on weekends. **Nearby Attractions:** Rehoboth Beach boardwalk attractions and beach, Cape Henlopen State Park, Delaware Seashore State Park, Lewes–Cape May Ferry. **Additional Information:** Rehoboth Beach-Dewey Beach Chamber of Commerce, (800) 441-1329, www.beach-fun.com.

Restrictions

Pets: On leash, do not leave unattended. **Fires:** At site. **Alcoholic Beverages:** No alcohol permitted. **Vehicle Maximum Length:** 45 ft. **Other:** No motorcycles or mini-bikes; no outside refrigerators.

To Get There

From Hwy. 1, go 6 mi. southwest on Hwy. 24. Entrance is on the right.

REHOBOTH BEACH
Sea Air Village

Hwy. 1 and Sea Air Ave., Rehoboth Beach 19971. T: (302) 227-8118.

RV ★★★★ Tent n/a

Beauty: ★★ Site Privacy: ★★
Spaciousness: ★★★ Quiet: ★★★
Security: ★★★★ Cleanliness: ★★★★
Insect Control: ★★★★ Facilities: ★★★★

Convenient to boardwalk attractions, outlet malls, and the eponymous beach in Rehoboth Beach, Sea Air Village is an RV and manufactured home community and park where no tents are allowed. In fact, Sea Air Village only accepts full hookup units. The park has two swimming pools, a large playground, a softball diamond, and a volleyball court. There is also a rec room and a pavilion for special events. Sea Air Village is ideal for campers who want clean facilities while enjoying Rehoboth Beach's attractions, of which there are many. Funland, a family-operated amusement center along the boardwalk, has 18 rides, 12 midway games, and a video arcade. Even closer to Sea Air Village, in the Midway Shopping Center, is Midway Speedway and Water Park. Many Sea Air Village campers wander over to Rehoboth Outlets, where 140 stores line a two-mile stretch of Rte. 1.

Basics

Operated By: Private operator. **Open:** All year. **Site Assignment:** Reservations and walk-ins accepted. **Registration:** At campground office. **Fee:** $40 per family (VISA, MC). **Parking:** At site.

Facilities

Number of RV Sites: 157. **Number of Tent-Only Sites:** None. **Hookups:** Electric (20, 30, 50 amps), cable TV, phone, all sites have full hookups. **Each Site:** Fire ring, picnic table. **Dump Station:** No. **Laundry:** No. **Pay Phone:** Yes. **Rest Rooms and Showers:** Yes. **Fuel:** No. **Propane:** No. **Internal Roads:** Paved, in good condition. **RV Service:** No. **Market:** Within 2 mi. **Restaurant:** Within 2 mi. **General Store:** No. **Vending:** No. **Playground:** Yes. **Other:** Pavilion. **Activities:** Badminton, sports field, rec hall, volleyball. **Nearby Attractions:** Rehoboth Beach boardwalk attractions and beach, Cape Henlopen State Park, Delaware Seashore State Park, Lewes–Cape May Ferry. **Additional Information:** Rehoboth Beach-Dewey Beach Chamber of Commerce, (800) 441-1329, www.beach-fun.com.

Restrictions

Pets: On leash. **Fires:** At site. **Alcoholic Beverages:** At site. **Vehicle Maximum Length:** None. **Other:** No tents allowed.

To Get There

From Hwy. 274, go 1.5 mi. south on Hwy. 1 and 2 blocks west on Sea Air Ave. Entrance is on the right.

Florida

You may think of Florida as the home of Mickey Mouse, roller coasters, and long, long lines. Or maybe the Sunshine State inspires dreams of endless surf and all-night parties on glittery South Beach. You'd be right, but you'd also be missing out on about 54,000 other unique square miles. Although much of Florida's 1,197 miles of coastline is obscured by high-rise condos, there is still a wealth of undiscovered beauty and charm behind the glamorous façade, along the back roads and quiet coastal towns. Perhaps you've visited the Space Coast, the Treasure Coast, and the Gold Coast, but next time you come to Florida, take time to explore with us the Undiscovered Coast, the Forgotten Coast, the Nature Coast, the Emerald Coast, the First Coast, and the Interior.

Join us for a tour of US 19/98 along the **Gulf Coast** through **Pasco County** and north to the **Nature Coast,** a beautiful, wonderful old road through the countryside where road signs warn of bear habitats and others offer such Florida cracker staples as churches, guns and palm readers, boiled peanuts, fresh scallops, and oysters. We'll take I-10 antiquing across the top to the **First Coast,** and stop by **Amelia Island** for succulent copper shrimp. We'll canoe the rivers that course through the central part of the state, and kayak the east and west shorelines, scuba-dive and snorkel the coral reef in the south. We'll take an airboat ride into the depths of the **Everglades** and sample gator tail, frog legs, and swamp cabbage along with a little Indian fry bread. Let's amble around the 700 square miles of **Lake Okeechobee**, buying juicy mangoes and crisp okra from local farmers who've been here all their lives. When we're done with all that, we'll hit the beach. We'll dig for shark's teeth and tales of pirates, and we'll be on the lookout for giant sea turtles, dolphins, and manatees. Come along, we'll have a great time.

Campers need to remember that summertime is swelter time in our fair state, when temperatures can soar into the 90s and higher. Afternoon rains help to cool the air, but the heat can be brutal for those who haven't acclimated to it. Bugs are worse in summertime, especially at night. Mosquitoes and No-See-Ums, too small to see and tiny enough to pass through window screens, are the most annoying. Bug sprays and citronella candles will help, but there will be times when the only solution is to seek shelter. Some folks prefer Florida in the wintertime, when bugs and temperatures are more moderate; but expect to encounter more crowds then, too. No need to let a little nature scare you off—be prepared and you can count on an adventure you'll never forget.

Cinderella's Castle is truly a sight to behold, but just wait until you've had the chance to see the untouched wonders of nature still waiting here in Florida for you to discover. Come explore our treasure.

The following facilities accept payment in checks or cash only:

Cedar Key RV Park, Cedar Key
High Springs Campground, High Springs

Campground Profiles

ALACHUA

Travelers Campground

17701 April Blvd., Alachua 32615. T: (386) 462-2505; GreenCamper1@juno.com.

RV ★★★★★ Tent ★★

Beauty: ★★★ Site Privacy: ★★
Spaciousness: ★★ Quiet: ★★★★
Security: ★★★ Cleanliness: ★★★★
Insect Control: ★★★★ Facilities: ★★★★

Designed for travelers as its name implies, this campground is super convenient to the highway, clean and quick to get in and out of. Although some larger sites occupy a friendly hill graced with tall trees, most overnighters are placed in the back lot, six rows of seven drive-through sites. Privacy is not an option. The new shower house is impeccably clean, and further renovations are underway to provide phone hookups and updated electricity. New roads are slated to follow. The perimeter of the campground houses the owners menagerie, which includes a single horse, donkeys, an emu, a pink pig, chickens and chicks, albino peacocks, goats, and an aviary with macaws and other exotic birds. A quiet rec hall hosts occasional dinners, and guests can check e-mail while doing laundry—there is an Internet connection in the laundry room for lap-top hookups.

BASICS

Operated By: Owners Harold & Linda. **Open:** All year. **Site Assignment:** First come, first served; also reservations. **Registration:** Office. **Fee:** $22; cash or checks only. **Parking:** Yes.

FACILITIES

Number of RV Sites: 100. **Number of Tent-Only Sites:** 50. **Hookups:** Water, electric (20, 30, 50 amps), sewer, cable TV. **Each Site:** Picnic table on request. **Dump Station:** Yes. **Laundry:** Yes. **Pay Phone:** Yes. **Rest Rooms and Showers:** Yes. **Fuel:** No. **Propane:** Yes. **Internal Roads:** Some paved, some smooth dirt and limerock, all in good condition. **RV Service:** Referral. **Market:** 1.5 mi. east on US 441. **Restaurant:** 2 mi. east on US 441. **General Store:** Yes. **Vending:** No. **Swimming Pool:** Yes. **Playground:** Yes. **Other:** Rec hall, horseshoes, shuffleboard, field for golf and ballgames. **Activities:** Monthly pot-luck dinner. **Nearby Attractions:** Freshwater springs offer tubing and canoeing; Antique mall in Micanopy, University of Florida in Gainesville.

Additional Information: Alachua County CVB, (352) 374-5260.

Restrictions

Pets: On leash only. **Fires:** Grills only. **Alcoholic Beverages:** Yes, but not openly displayed. **Vehicle Maximum Length:** None.

To Get There

I-75 Exit 78 at US 441 east 200 ft. to April Blvd. (on north side of road next to Waffle House), north 1 mi. to campground on right.

ALTOONA

Ocala National Forest—Alexander Springs

49525 CR 445, Altoona 32702. T: (352) 669-3522; F: (353) 669-0600; www.camprrm.com; rrmfl@atlantic.net.

RV ★★★ Tent ★★★★★

Beauty: ★★★★★ Site Privacy: ★★★
Spaciousness: ★★★ Quiet: ★★★
Security: ★★★★★ Cleanliness: ★★★★★
Insect Control: ★★★ Facilities: ★★★★★

If you're in the mood to take a break from luxury camping for a dip into the wild side, the Ocala National Forest is a great place for the adventure. Rangers report finding bear droppings and paw prints on the beaches in the mornings, and say that a mama bear and her cubs have been known to reside nearby. Sightings are frequent along CR 445 leading to the Alexander Springs Recreation Area—you may want to cruise a bit more slowly than the 55 mph speed limit allows. Other creatures include alligators in the springs (yes, the place is crowded with swimmers), wild hogs, and deer. Osprey and American bald eagles can be seen above. Camping is confined to four loops, each site shielded by a rim of brush and trees offering a little privacy, but paths cross through the back of some sites to the bath houses (some brand new), so you might get to know your neighbors. The nights are so quiet, you'll probably get to hear the giggles of other scouts and campers even if you don't get to meet them—even generators must be silenced during the night. But if you get a little sweaty at night, you'll be instantly refreshed if you take a dip in the perpetually 70° water that replenishes itself at the rate of 70 million gallons a day.

Basics

Operated By: Recreation Resource Management for the US Government. **Open:** All year. **Site Assignment:** First come, first served. **Registration:** Park office. **Fee:** $15; MC,V for bills of $20 or more. **Parking:** Yes.

Facilities

Number of RV Sites: 67. **Number of Tent-Only Sites:** 0. **Hookups:** None. **Each Site:** Picnic table, grill, lantern pole. **Dump Station:** Yes. **Laundry:** No. **Pay Phone:** Yes. **Rest Rooms and Showers:** Yes. **Fuel:** No. **Propane:** No. **Internal Roads:** Paved in good condition. **RV Service:** Referral. **Market:** 3 mi. south on Hwy. 445 to convenience market, 6 mi. north on Hwy. 445 to supermarket in Astor. **Restaurant:** 6 mi. north on Hwy. 445 to Astor. **General Store:** Yes. **Vending:** Yes. **Swimming Pool:** Freshwater-spring swimming area w/ beach. **Playground:** No. **Other:** Hiking and biking trails, canoe launch. **Activities:** Hiking, biking, swimming, fishing, canoeing. **Nearby Attractions:** National Forest surrounds recreation area. **Additional Information:** Ocala National Forest Visitors Center, (352) 669-7495.

Restrictions

Pets: On leash only, designated areas. **Fires:** Grill only. **Alcoholic Beverages:** Not allowed. **Vehicle Maximum Length:** 35 ft. **Other:** Gate closes at 8 p.m.; quiet time 10 p.m.–6 a.m.

To Get There

From US 441, 6 mi. north on Hwy. 19 to CR 445, 6 mi. north to entrance on left.

ARCADIA

Craig's RV Park, Inc.

7895 NE Hwy. 17, Arcadia 34266. T: (863) 494-1820 or (877) 750-5129; F: (863) 494-1079; www.craigsrv.com; craigsrv@desoto.net.

RV ★★★★ Tent ★★★

Beauty: ★★★ Site Privacy: ★★★★
Spaciousness: ★★★★★ Quiet: ★★★★★
Security: ★★★★★ Cleanliness: ★★★★★
Insect Control: ★★★★★ Facilities: ★★★★★

Tucked into Florida's beautiful countryside, Arcadia is a rural town surrounded by a long-standing agricultural community. The scenic Peace River meanders through the cattle ranches, forests, and swamps without a trace of commercial interference for miles on end. The river is very popular for canoeists who pack a few-days-worth of supplies and camp along its banks. The practice is allowed by the ranch owners, but you're at your own risk—the territory is rich with alligators and other wildlife. Craig's RV Park is conveniently situated, with river access just three miles away, and it provides a peaceful place for those seeking the country atmosphere but who still love country fun, such as the bluegrass festivals and informal music nights. Laid out like a suburban neighborhood, sites are tightly packed though spacious, with more trees on the north side of the park than on the south, and a few dozen pull-through sites as well. One great feature is the private bathrooms and showers, but campers must pay 25 cents for 6 minutes of water, thanks to some vandals who once left the taps running and drained the water supply. The camp is run very professionally and kept immaculate by its family owners.

Basics

Operated By: Owners Vicky & Allen Wickey & Sara & Victor Craig. **Open:** All year. **Site Assignment:** Reservations accepted, $20 deposit required, refundable up to 24 hours in advance w/ 10% service charge. **Registration:** Office. **Fee:** $20; M,V, D. **Parking:** Yes.

Facilities

Number of RV Sites: 356. **Number of Tent-Only Sites:** 0. **Hookups:** Water, electric (20, 30, 50 amps), sewer. **Each Site:** Concrete pad. **Dump Station:** Yes. **Laundry:** Yes. **Pay Phone:** Yes. **Rest Rooms and Showers:** Yes. **Fuel:** No. **Propane:** Yes. **Internal Roads:** Paved in good condition. **RV Service:** Referral. **Market:** 9 mi. south to Arcadia, convenience mart 2 mi. south. **Restaurant:** 9 mi. south to Arcadia. **General Store:** Yes. **Vending:** Yes. **Swimming Pool:** Yes. **Playground:** No. **Other:** Shuffleboard, bocci court, horseshoes, game room w/ pool tables, golf driving range. **Activities:** Monthly calendar of events Nov.–Apr. includes bingo, live music, bluegrass festivals in Nov. & Mar., shuffleboard, bocci & horseshoe tournaments. **Nearby Attractions:** Peace River canoe ramp 3 mi. south, antique shops in Arcadia. **Additional Information:** DeSoto County Chamber of Commerce, (863) 494-4033.

Restrictions

Pets: On leash & in designated areas only, proof of insurance policy for dogs over 30 lbs. required. **Fires:** In grill or designated campfire areas only. **Alcoholic Beverages:** On individual sites only. **Vehicle Maximum Length:** 45 ft., call ahead for availability.

To Get There

I-75 Exit 29/Hwy. 17 north 32 mi. to campground

ARCADIA

Peace River Campground

2998 NW Hwy. 70, Arcadia 34266. T: (863) 494-9693 or (800) 559-4011; F: (863) 494-9110; www.peacerivercampground.com; ceorge@peacerivercampground.com.

RV ★★★★ Tent ★★★★

Beauty: ★★★★ Site Privacy: ★★★
Spaciousness: ★★★★ Quiet: ★★★★
Security: ★★★★ Cleanliness: ★★★★
Insect Control: ★★ Facilities: ★★★★

This wonderfully rustic and wooded campground might let you forget you're in a campground at all—almost. The shady camp overlooks the Peace River, and the campground has become home to a fossil museum, thanks to the excavation of the bones of three mammoths from the riverbed. Sharks teeth continue to be a popular find for those who like to wade in the scenic river waters and sift through the sands along the bottom and shorelines. The laid-back, peaceful campground hosts an interesting group each year—The Ruckus Society gathers here in the spring to train peaceful demonstrators in the techniques of getting attention without getting in trouble. Lots of wildlife live in the surrounding environs, including alligators, bobcats, deer, grey foxes, even the occasional panther passes through. There are a few pull-through sites among the trees, and although there is plenty of room and plenty of trees, there are not specific site buffers in many cases.

Basics

Operated By: Owners George & Johnny Lempenau. **Open:** All year. **Site Assignment:** Reservations accepted, $50 deposit plus 3-night min. stay required for holidays. **Registration:** Office. **Fee:** $25 May–Sept., $32 Oct.–Apr. **Parking:** Yes.

Facilities

Number of RV Sites: 182. **Number of Tent-

Only Sites: 0. **Hookups:** Water, electric (20, 30, 50 amps), sewer. **Each Site:** Picnic table. **Dump Station:** Yes. **Laundry:** Yes. **Pay Phone:** Yes. **Rest Rooms and Showers:** Yes. **Fuel:** No. **Propane:** Yes. **Internal Roads:** Crushed shell in good condition. **RV Service:** Referral. **Market:** 4 mi. east to Arcadia. **Restaurant:** 4 mi. east to Arcadia. **General Store:** Yes. **Vending:** Yes. **Swimming Pool:** Yes. **Playground:** Yes. **Other:** Boat ramp, video room w/ pool tables, shuffleboard, horseshoes, fishing pond, miniature animal farm, snowbird dance hall, computers. **Activities:** Canoeing, fishing, fossil hunting. **Nearby Attractions:** Peace River, antique shops in Arcadia. **Additional Information:** DeSoto County Chamber of Commerce, (863) 494-4033.

Restrictions

Pets: Leash only. **Fires:** Yes. **Alcoholic Beverages:** Allowed. **Vehicle Maximum Length:** None.

To Get There

I-75 Exit 29/Hwy. 17, 22 mi. east to Hwy. 70, north/left 4 mi. to campground.

CEDAR KEY

Cedar Key RV Park

P.O. Box 268, Cedar Key 32625. T: (352) 543-5150.

RV ★★★★ Tent ★★★

Beauty: ★★★ Site Privacy: ★
Spaciousness: ★★ Quiet: ★★★
Security: ★★★★ Cleanliness: ★★★★★
Insect Control: ★★ Facilities: ★★★

A rustic trailer park on an out-of-the-way island that seems to be just beginning to commercialize—find it quickly before this waterfront property has been consumed by the ubiquitous oceanfront condominiums, which have gone up on both sides already. This low-key park may not offer a wide range of amenities or frills—no rec room, modem, or laundry, but the rest room is immaculate and refreshingly private. Although the park itself is unspectacular, the location is unbeatable, with a few prime sites overlooking the shore on a slight bluff with steps leading down to a long dock for fishing and boating. Price listed reflect choice waterfront location—the other sites are packed unceremoniously together without buffers or the slightest charm—incomparable to the pleasure of an unobstructed view of the Gulf of Mexico. Don't miss it.

Basics

Operated By: Shirley Gulley, manager. **Open:** All year. **Site Assignment:** By phone, deposits accepted by mail. **Registration:** Park office. **Fee:** $22; cash or checks only. **Parking:** Yes.

Facilities

Number of RV Sites: 30. **Number of Tent-Only Sites:** 4 (beachfront, not divided into sites). **Hookups:** Electric (30 amps), water, sewer, cable TV. **Each Site:** Picnic table. **Dump Station:** No. **Laundry:** No. **Pay Phone:** Yes. **Rest Rooms and Showers:** Yes. **Fuel:** No. **Propane:** No. **Internal Roads:** Gravel in good condition. **RV Service:** No. **Market:** 3 blocks south, 3 blocks east to down town Cedar Key. **Restaurant:** 3 blocks south. **General Store:** No. **Vending:** No. **Swimming Pool:** No. **Playground:** No. **Other:** Fishing pier. **Activities:** Fishing, crabbing, clamming, bird-watching. **Nearby Attractions:** State Museum & County Museum. **Additional Information:** Cedar Key Chamber of Commerce, (352) 543-5600, www.cedarkey.org.

Restrictions

Pets: On leash only. **Fires:** In grill only. **Alcoholic Beverages:** Allowed. **Vehicle Maximum Length:** 35 ft. **Other:** Office closes at 8 p.m.

To Get There

From I-75 in Gainesville Exit Hwy. 24, 70 mi. west to Cedar Key, (24 mi. west on Hwy. 24 past US 19/98), right on 6th St. to G St., right to campground at 7th St.

CHIPLEY

Falling Waters State Recreation Area

1130 State Park Rd., Chipley 32428. T: (850) 638-6130; www.myflorida.com.

RV ★★★ Tent ★★★★★

Beauty: ★★★★★ Site Privacy: ★★★★
Spaciousness: ★★★★ Quiet: ★★★★★
Security: ★★★★★ Cleanliness: ★★★★★
Insect Control: ★★★★★ Facilities: ★★★★

Falling Waters State Recreation Area boasts an unusually high elevation for Florida—and that's a great advantage during mosquito season when larvae thrive in puddles and lakes. The campground itself is particularly high within the park, which adds to the interest of the area. Once a camper has made the slow climb to the top of the hill, campsites form a single small circle around central rest rooms and a playground for kids. The quiet, wooded setting is peaceful and friendly. Seven of the 24 sites are pull-through half circles.

Basics

Operated By: Florida Dept. of Environmental Protection, Division of Recreation & Parks. **Open:** All year. **Site Assignment:** First come, first served; reservations accepted w/ 1-night deposit, refundable w/ up to 24 hours advance notice. **Registration:** Office. **Fee:** $8 Nov.–Feb., $10 Mar.–Oct.; MC,V.

Parking: Yes.

Facilities

Number of RV Sites: 24. **Number of Tent-Only Sites:** 0. **Hookups:** Water, electric. **Each Site:** Picnic table, grill. **Dump Station:** Yes. **Laundry:** No. **Pay Phone:** Yes. **Rest Rooms and Showers:** Yes. **Fuel:** No. **Propane:** No. **Internal Roads:** Paved in good condition. **RV Service:** Referral. **Market:** 3 mi. north on 77A to supermarket. **Restaurant:** 3 mi. north on 77A. **General Store:** No. **Vending:** Yes. **Swimming Pool:** No (Lake). **Playground:** Yes. **Other:** Lake, hiking trails, sinkholes, waterfall, amphitheater. **Activities:** Hiking, swimming, fishing. **Nearby Attractions:** Florida Caverns State Park. **Additional Information:** Washington County Chamber of Commerce, (850) 638-4157, www.washcomall.com.

Restrictions

Pets: On leash only, proof of vaccinations required. **Fires:** In grill only. **Alcoholic Beverages:** Not allowed. **Vehicle Maximum Length:** 45 ft. **Other:** No firearms, no fireworks, quiet time 11 p.m.

To Get There

Exit I-10 or Hwy. 90 at Chipley, 3 mi. south of town on Hwy. 77A.

CHOKOLUSKEE

Chokoluskee Island Park and Campground

P.O. Box 430, Chokoluskee 34138. T: (941) 695-2414; F: (941) 695-3033; chokislpark@aol.com.

RV ★★★ Tent ★★

Beauty: ★★ Site Privacy: ★★
Spaciousness: ★★ Quiet: ★★★★★
Security: ★★★★ Cleanliness: ★★★★
Insect Control: ★★ Facilities: ★★★

Rustic like the entire community of Chokoluskee, this park has the advantage of a boat dock right on the Ten Thousand Islands, which form a sort of barrier between coastline and the Florida Bay. The anglers—and that's who most like to come to this town—love the easy access. This town is best known as the home of stone crabs, because this is where the practice of harvesting the crabs claws, then tossing them back to sea to grow a new claw for next year's harvest. Fresh stone crabs, boiled in garlic or raw, are available all over town during the season Oct. 15 to May 15. The park is really a fish camp, home to some live-ins and rental trailers, but also offers sites to travelers. Although there are some nice, tall mature palms and trees throughout the park, the sites are crowded quite close together. Not what most of us might consider a vacation paradise, but quite possibly the most beautiful place in Florida to watch the sunset, especially if you love to fish.

Basics

Operated By: Managers Ray & Sheilah Strobel. **Open:** All year. **Site Assignment:** Reservations accepted, deposit of 1-night stay. **Registration:** Office. **Fee:** $18 June–Oct., $26 Nov.–May; M,V,AE. **Parking:** Yes.

Facilities

Number of RV Sites: 20. **Number of Tent-Only Sites:** 0. **Hookups:** Water, electric (30 amps), sewer. **Each Site:** Picnic Table. **Dump Station:** Yes. **Laundry:** Yes. **Pay Phone:** Yes. **Rest Rooms and Showers:** Yes. **Fuel:** No. **Propane:** Yes. **Internal Roads:** Paved in good condition. **RV Service:** Referral. **Market:** 1 block east. **Restaurant:** 1 block east. **General Store:** Yes. **Vending:** Yes. **Swimming Pool:** No. **Playground:** No. **Other:** Boat ramp, shuffleboard, horseshoes, marina. **Activities:** Fishing trips. **Nearby Attractions:** Florida Bay (for fishing & exploring), Ten Thousand Islands (for canoeing), Ted Smallwood's Historic Store, Everglades National Park. **Additional Information:** Everglades Area Chamber of Commerce, (800) 914-6355, www.florida-everglades.com.

Restrictions

Pets: Leash only. **Fires:** Grill only. **Alcoholic Beverages: Allowed. **Vehicle Maximum Length:** 28 ft. **Other:** Quiet time 10 p.m.–8 a.m.

To Get There

US 41 east approximately 22 mi. from Naples (approximately 75 mi. west from Miami) to US 29, south 8 mi. to DeMere St., right past the Church of God, then left to the park on right.

CLERMONT

Clerbrook Golf and RV Resort

20005 US Hwy. 27, Clermont 34711. T: (352) 394-6165; F: (352) 394-8251; www.n1florida-camping.lu; ClerbrookResort@aol.com.

RV: ★★★ Tent: n/a

Beauty: ★★★ Site Privacy: ★
Spaciousness: ★ Quiet: ★★
Security: ★★★★ Cleanliness: ★★★★
Insect Control: ★★★★ Facilities: ★★★★

This large mobile-home community is a golfer's paradise in Florida's heartland. The three residential sections offer rental and permanent RVs, cabins and family tents, with those on the perimeter more spacious and scenic than those in the interior of each section. Trees and a wildlife conservation area surround Clerbrook, and the golf course provides a lovely rolling landscape in the center of the community, restful to the eyes and mind. Three large clubhouses, ball fields, stocked fishing ponds, whirlpool spas, and three swimming pools promise fun for those less interested in golf, which is clearly the main activity in this locale. Overnight travelers are bunked into a large, grassy parking area with pull-throughs. that lack trees and privacy but have hookups and picnic tables. The community is accessed through a manned security gate closing at 11 p.m.

Basics

Operated By: Florida Mobile Home Camping. **Open:** All year. **Site Assignment:** Reservations accepted, deposit required. **Registration:** Office. **Fee:** $18, MC, V, D. **Parking:** Yes.

Facilities

Number of RV Sites: 1250. **Number of Tent-Only Sites:** 0. **Hookups:** Electric (30, 50 amps), water, sewer, phone, modem, cable TV. **Each Site:** Picnic table. **Dump Station:** Yes. **Laundry:** Yes. **Pay Phone:** Yes. **Rest Rooms and Showers:** Yes. **Fuel:** No. **Propane:** Yes. **Internal Roads:** Paved in good condition. **RV Service:** No. **Market:** 6 mi. southwest in Clermont. **Restaurant:** 6 mi. southwest in Clermont. **General Store:** Yes. **Vending:** Yes. **Swimming Pool:** Yes. **Playground:** Yes. **Other:** 18-hole golf course, rec room, softball field, whirlpool. **Activities:** Golf, horseshoes, shuffleboard, fishing, winter recreation program. **Nearby Attractions:** Disney World & Orlando 45 min. east on Florida Turnpike. **Additional Information:** Lake County CVB, (352) 429-3673, (800) 798-1071.

Restrictions

Pets: On leash only. **Fires:** Grill only. **Alcoholic Beverages:** Allowed. **Vehicle Max. Length:** None.

To Get There

Florida Turnpike Exit 285, south on US 27 1.5 mi. to Clerbrook on right.

CLEWISTON

Big Cypress State Preserve

HC Box 54A, Clewiston 33440. T: (863) 983-1330 or (800) 437-4102; F: (863) 983-3122; www.semiletribe.com/campground.

RV: ★★★ Tent: ★★★

Beauty: ★★★ Site Privacy: ★★★
Spaciousness: ★★★★ Quiet: ★★★★★
Security: ★★★★ Cleanliness: ★★★
Insect Control: ★★ Facilities: ★★★

If you're looking for wilderness in the Everglades, you've found it here in the Big Cypress National Preserve and the Big Cypress Seminole Indian Reservation. And if you think the glades are just a big swamp, you'll be pleasantly surprised to find that there is plenty of high ground, thickly forested with flora, including water oak trees, sabal palms, and shrubbery. The large park also has abundant hibiscus flowers and a pretty pond and garden area.

Basics

Operated By: Seminole Indian Reservation. **Open:** All year. **Site Assignment:** Reservations accepted, $50 credit card deposit, at least 30-day cancellation. **Registration:** Park office. **Fee:** $22. **Parking:** Yes.

Facilities

Number of RV Sites: 110. **Number of Tent-Only Sites:** Primitive camping area. **Hookups:** Water, electric (20, 50 amps), sewer, phone. **Each Site:** Picnic table, grill. **Dump Station:** Yes. **Laundry:** Yes. **Pay Phone:** Yes. **Rest Rooms and Showers:** Yes. **Fuel:** No. **Propane:** Yes. **Internal Roads:** Paved & gravel in good condition. **RV Service:** Referral. **Market:** 2 mi. southeast on CR 833. **Restaurant:** 3 mi. west on Safari Rd. **General Store:** Yes. **Vending:** Yes. **Swimming Pool:** Yes. **Playground:** Yes. **Other:** Rec hall, mini-golf, shuffleboard, basketball, horseshoes. **Activities:** Fishing, swimming, boating, safari air boat & swamp buggy rides. **Nearby Attractions:** Boat ramp, Lake Okeechobee, Billie Swamp Safari Wildlife Park, Seminole Indian park featuring airboat rides, eco-tours, restaurant w/ authentic Indian food plus animals including the Florida panther; Ah-Tah-Thi-Ki Museum w/ exhibits depicting the history of the Seminole Indians in Florida. **Additional Information:** Big Cypress National Preserve, (941) 695-2000.

Restrictions

Pets: On leash only, max. 2 pets per rig. **Fires:** In grill or designated area only. **Alcoholic Beverages:** Not allowed. **Vehicle Maximum Length:** 36 ft. **Other:** No firearms or fireworks.

To Get There

I-75 (Alligator Alley between Fort Lauderdale and Naples) Exit 14 at mile marker 49 onto Snake Rd., north 19 mi. to park.

CRYSTAL RIVER

Rock Crusher Canyon RV and Music Park

275 South Rock Crusher Rd., Crystal River 34429. T: (352) 795-3870; www.rccrvpark.com; information@rccrvpark.com.

RV: ★★★★★ Tent: ★★★

Beauty: ★★★★ Site Privacy: ★★★
Spaciousness: ★★★★★ Quiet: ★★★★★
Security: ★★★★★ Cleanliness: ★★★★★
Insect Control: ★★★ Facilities: ★★★

This hidden new RV paradise of rolling green hills with shaded, level, grassy sites is like an oasis on Florida's west central coast. Once you've found it, though, you're not likely to forget it for future travels, especially if you're a music lover. The park offers regular concerts with famous vintage and country headliners like Glen Campbell, the Tommy Dorsey Orchestra, and The Ink Spots. The top-rated park features individual rest room/showers, wide sites with plenty of bushes and trees providing privacy, and the unusual bonus of several elevations. The park also offers a fitness center, country store, pool, country store, and clubhouse. It's easy to see how this park has received top ratings from industry experts.

Basics

Operated By: Private operator. **Open:** All year. **Site Assignment:** Reservations accepted, 1-night deposit required except for special events, which require multi-night stays & non-refundable tickets. **Registration:** Park office. **Fee:** $35. **Parking:** Yes.

Facilities

Number of RV Sites: 398. **Number of Tent-Only Sites:** 0. **Hookups:** Water, electric (50 amps), sewer, cable TV, phone. **Each Site:** Picnic table. **Dump Station:** Yes. **Laundry:** Yes. **Pay Phone:** Yes. **Rest Rooms and Showers:** Yes. **Fuel:** No. **Propane:** Yes. **Internal Roads:** Paved in good condition. **RV Service:** Referral. **Market:** 2.5 mi. west to Crystal River/Hwy. 19. **Restaurant:** 2.5 mi. west to Crystal River/Hwy. 19. **General Store:** Yes. **Vending:** Yes. **Swimming Pool:** Yes. **Playground:** Yes. **Other:** Amphitheater, lakes, shuffleboard, horseshoes, fitness center. **Activities:** Country music & bluegrass concerts & festivals, fishing. **Nearby Attractions:** Crystal River Springs, Homosassa Springs (home to manatees), Weeki Wachee Springs, mermaid amusement park. **Additional Information:** Nature Coast Tourism Development, Inc. & Welcome Center, (352) 564-9197, www.crystalriver-ecotours.com.

Restrictions

Pets: On leash only. **Fires:** Designated areas only. **Alcoholic Beverages:** Allowed. **Vehicle Maximum Length:** None. **Other:** Quiet hours 11 p.m.–7:30 a.m.

To Get There

From Hwy. 19/Crystal River, turn east on Venable Rd. (by the Home Depot store), 2.3 mi. to Rock Crusher Rd., right/south to entrance on the left.

ESTERO

Koreshan State Historic Site

P.O. Box 7, Estero 33928. T: (941) 992-0311; F: (941) 992-1607; www.myflorida.com.

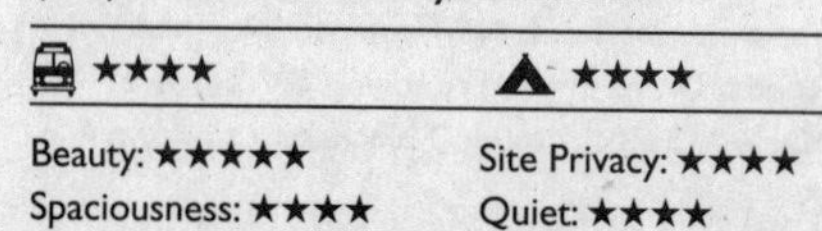

RV: ★★★★ Tent: ★★★★

Beauty: ★★★★★ Site Privacy: ★★★★
Spaciousness: ★★★★ Quiet: ★★★★

Security: ★★★★★ Cleanliness: ★★★★★
Insect Control: ★★★ Facilities: ★★★★★

This small, unassuming park with the somewhat daunting name (the 'e' in Koreshan is pronounced as a short vowel like 'eh') offers a fascinating glimpse into a tiny but powerful piece of history. The site is the preserved settlement of a religious sect founded in 1894 by New York doctor Cyrus Teed, who called himself by the Biblical name Koresh. Teed believed in immortality, therefore the sect practiced celibacy. Teed died in 1908, but not before establishing the settlement of a few hundred followers which included a group kitchen, machine shop, and cultural arts hall, where several paintings are still displayed. One depicts Teed's vision of the world, an inverted Earth with Heaven in its center. The buildings and their well-preserved contents make it clear that the group was well educated, musical, and artistic. The gardens they created of bamboo, monkey trees, pineapple, citrus, and mangoes still stand, although the last of the sect members expired in the early 1960s, leaving the settlement to the state for preservation. Campers will enjoy the long loops of very private sites surrounded by an abundance of trees, in close proximity to the Estero River, a prime site for canoeing (rentals available); swimming is prohibited, perhaps because of alligators.

Basics

Operated By: Florida Dept. of Environmental Protection, Division of Recreation & Park. **Open:** All year. **Site Assignment:** Reservations accepted up to 11 months in advance, 1-night deposit, refundable up to 24 hours in advance. **Registration:** Office. **Fee:** $14.11 May–Nov., $20.70 Dec.–Apr. **Parking:** Yes.

Facilities

Number of RV Sites: 50. **Number of Tent-Only Sites:** 10. **Hookups:** Water, electric (30 amps). **Each Site:** Picnic table, fire ring. **Dump Station:** Yes. **Laundry:** Yes. **Pay Phone:** Yes. **Rest Rooms and Showers:** Yes. **Fuel:** No. **Propane:** No. **Internal Roads:** Paved & crushed shell in good condition. **RV Service:** Referral. **Market:** 0.25 mi. across US Hwy. 41. **Restaurant:** 0.25 mi. across US Hwy. 41. **General Store:** No, but in future plans. **Vending:** Yes. **Swimming Pool:** No. **Playground:** Yes. **Other:** Beach, volleyball court, boat launch, historic settlement. **Activities:** Fishing, canoeing (rentals available). **Nearby Attractions:** Corkscrew Swamp Sanctuary, an Audubon Society nature preserve; Everglades Wonder Gardens in Bonita Springs; Dog Racing Track in Bonita Springs; beach; Mound Key Archaeological State Park, an adjacent island; Edison Ford estate in Fort Myers. **Additional Information:** Lee Island Coast CVB, (800) 237-6444, www.leeislandcoast.com.

Restrictions

Pets: On leash only, proof of vaccinations required, not allowed in buildings or canoes. **Fires:** In grill or fire ring only. **Alcoholic Beverages:** After hours only. **Vehicle Maximum Length:** 45 ft. **Other:** No firearms or fireworks.

To Get There

I-75 Exit 19, Estero onto Corkscrew Rd., 2 mi. west to Koreshan State Historic Site just 0.3 mi. west of US 41.

FERNANDINA BEACH, AMELIA ISLAND

Fort Clinch State Park

2601 Atlantic Ave., Fernandina Beach 32034.T: (904) 277-7274; F: (904) 277-7225; www.myflorida.com.

RV ★★★★ Tent ★★★★

Beauty: ★★★★★ Site Privacy: ★★★
Spaciousness: ★★★★ Quiet: ★★★★
Security: ★★★★★ Cleanliness: ★★★★
Insect Control: ★★★ Facilities: ★★★★★

How does watching the sunset from the riverfront or the beach sound? It's not unlikely that you might see dolphins jumping in the surf, and even possible you might catch sight of the elusive right whales that come to calve in the offshore waters. Train your binoculars on Cumberland Island across the channel and you just might see the wild horses that still live there, left over from the island's days of glory as home to Carnegies and Rockefellers. The campgrounds at Fort Clinch State Park provide shoreside benches to enjoy the view. Campsites are all back-in, but fairly spacious, with a path through the woods behind sites at the river campground leading to the beach—watch out for huge wolf spiders that weave webs among the trees! Take time for a tour of historic Fort Clinch itself, built for the Civil War but never used in battle; the place is fully equipped as a living-history exhibit, with touchable replicas so kids—and adults—can really feel what military life in the late 1800s must have been like. While you're on the island, be sure to sample the delicious local copper shrimp that makes the region famous.

Basics

Operated By: Florida Dept. of Environmental Protection, Division of Recreation & Parks. **Open:** All year. **Site Assignment:** First come, first served, reservations accepted w/ 1-day deposit, refundable up to 24 hours in advance. **Registration:** Ranger Station. **Fee:** $19; MC, V, D. **Parking:** Yes.

Facilities

Number of RV Sites: 54. **Number of Tent-Only Sites:** 6. **Hookups:** Water, electric. **Each Site:** Picnic table, fire ring. **Dump Station:** Yes. **Laundry:** Yes. **Pay Phone:** Yes. **Rest Rooms and Showers:** Yes. **Fuel:** No. **Propane:** No. **Internal Roads:** Paved in good condition. **RV Service:** Referral. **Market:** 1.4 mi. south from main gate on Atlantic Blvd. (A1A). **Restaurant:** 0.25 mi. south on Atlantic Blvd., continuing 1.5 mi. **General Store:** Yes, firewood & souvenirs. **Vending:** Yes. **Swimming Pool:** No. **Playground:** Yes. **Other:** Civil War era Fort Clinch, beach, pier, river, forest. **Activities:** Tours of historic fort, Civil War reenactments (first weekend of each month), Civil War encampment (first weekend in May), guided nature hikes (9 a.m. Saturdays), kids fishing clinic (June), Memorial & Veterans Day observations. **Nearby Attractions:** Historic town of Fernandina Beach. **Additional Information:** Amelia Island Tourist Development Council, (800) 2-AMELIA, www.ameliaisland.org.

Restrictions

Pets: On leash and in designated areas only, proof of vaccinations required; no pets on beach, in buildings, or on boardwalks. **Fires:** In grill only. **Alcoholic Beverages:** Not allowed. **Vehicle Maximum Length:** 50 ft. or more. **Other:** No firearms or fireworks; do not damage or disturb dunes, nature, or wildlife, digging prohibited; quiet time 11 p.m.–7 a.m.

To Get There

Exit I-95 north of Jacksonville onto A1A, east 14 mi. to Fernandina Beach, right on Atlantic Ave. 3 mi. to park.

FLAGLER BEACH

Gamble Rogers Memorial State Recreation Area

3100 South A1A, Flagler Beach 32136.T: (386) 517-2086; F: (386) 517-2088; www.myflorida.com.

RV ★★★★ Tent ★★★★

Beauty: ★★★★ Site Privacy: ★★
Spaciousness: ★★ Quiet: ★★★★
Security: ★★★★★ Cleanliness: ★★★★★
Insect Control: ★★★ Facilities: ★★★★

This park was named for troubadour Gamble Rogers, a Floridian who drowned off Flagler Beach while saving another man from drowning in the mid-1980s. The campground, on the beach-side, or east of A1A, is a small, gated facility with closely packed sandy sites shielded from the ocean by a bushy barrier of sea oats. Boardwalk paths lead to the beach, but there is no ocean view for campers. Sites have slight bushy buffers, but no trees to break the ocean breezes. The rest of the park is on the west side of A1A—a thin strip of native land bordered by the highway and the Intracoastal Waterway. The park office displays an interesting but sad collection of roadkill collected from the highway—a skunk, ruby-throated hummingbird, luna moth, rattlesnake, and a dozen or so other snakes. All victims of progress, reminding visitors to drive carefully.

Basics

Operated By: Florida Dept. of Environmental Protection, Division of Recreation & Parks. **Open:** All year. **Site Assignment:** Reservations accepted up to 11 months in advance, 1-night deposit refundable up to 24 hours in advance. **Registration:** Park office (across Hwy. A1A from the beach campground). **Fee:** $19; M, V, D. **Parking:** Yes.

Facilities

Number of RV Sites: 24. **Number of Tent-Only Sites:** 8. **Hookups:** Water, electric (30 amps). **Each Site:** Picnic table, ground grill. **Dump Station:** Yes. **Laundry:** No. **Pay Phone:** Yes. **Rest Rooms and Showers:** Yes. **Fuel:** No. **Propane:** No. **Internal Roads:** Sand roads in good condition. **RV Service:** Referral. **Market:** 3 mi. north on A1A. **Restaurant:** 3 mi. north on A1A. **General Store:** No. **Vending:** No. **Swimming Pool:** No (beach). **Playground:** No. **Other:** Sand box, boat ramp, nature trails. **Activities:** Swimming, fish, boating, hiking.

Restrictions

Pets: Leash only, not in buildings or on beach. **Fires:** Grill/fire ring only. **Alcoholic Beverages:**

Not allowed. **Vehicle Maximum Length:** 46 ft.—call ahead to ensure availability.

To Get There

Exit I-95 at SR 100, 6 mi. east to Hwy. A1A, 3 mi. south to park.

FLAGLER BEACH/ BEVERLY BEACH

Beverly Beach Camptown RV Resort

P.O. Box 1048, Flagler Beach 32136. T: (904) 439-3111 or (800) 255-2706; F: (904) 439-6555

RV ★★★★ Tent ★★★

Beauty: ★★★★	Site Privacy: ★
Spaciousness: ★	Quiet: ★★
Security: ★★★★	Cleanliness: ★★★★★
Insect Control: ★★★★	Facilities: ★★★★★

We're generally not impressed with campgrounds that look like parking lots, but this one's directly on the beach—campers pull right up to the seawall, so they can literally wake up and watch the sun rise over the ocean without leaving their beds. That's pretty hard to beat, even without trees and wall-to-wall neighbors. The campground also offers a few tent sites right on the beach. Beverly Beach Camptown has a well-stocked store, too, with everything from souvenirs to beer and wine, plus a small restaurant in case you're tired of cooking. But the best bonus here—at least for those who like to travel with their pets—is that leashed dogs are allowed on the beach, an unusual treat for our furry friends.

Basics

Operated By: Manager Karen Siefken. **Open:** All year. **Site Assignment:** Reservations accepted w/ credit card guarantee—recommended on holidays and during Daytona special events. **Registration:** Office. **Fee:** $37 Oct.–Jan., $41 Feb.–Sept.; M, V, D. **Parking:** Yes.

Facilities

Number of RV Sites: 127. **Number of Tent-Only Sites:** 5. **Hookups:** Water, electric (30, 50 amps), sewer, cable TV. **Each Site:** Picnic table. **Dump Station:** Yes. **Laundry:** Yes. **Pay Phone:** Yes. **Rest Rooms and Showers:** Yes. **Fuel:** No. **Propane:** No. **Internal Roads:** Paved, in good condition. **RV Service:** Referral. **Market:** On site or 4 mi. south on A1A. **Restaurant:** On site for breakfast & lunch or 4 mi. south on A1A. **General Store:** Yes. **Vending:** No. **Swimming Pool:** No (beach). **Playground:** No. **Other:** Beach, meeting room & café. **Activities:** Swimming, fishing, boogie board surfing. **Nearby Attractions:** Daytona Beach 20 mi. south. **Additional Information:** Flagler Beach Chamber of Commerce, (800) 298-0995 www.flaglercounty.com/fbcc.

Restrictions

Pets: On leash only. **Fires:** Allowed on beach when weather permitting. **Alcoholic Beverages:** Allowed. **Vehicle Maximum Length:** 40 ft.

To Get There

I-95 Exit 91, 3.5 mi. east on SR 100 to A1A, 3 mi. north to campground.

FORT LAUDERDALE

Paradise Island Resort (Formerly Buglewood Resort)

2121 NW 29th Ct., Fort Lauderdale 33311-2175. T: (954) 485-1150; (800) 487-7395; buglewood.com; buglewood@aol.com.

RV ★★★ Tent n/a

Beauty: ★★	Site Privacy: ★★
Spaciousness: ★★	Quiet: ★★★★
Security: ★★★★	Cleanliness: ★★★★★
Insect Control: ★★★	Facilities: ★★★★★

Paradise Island Resort is a quaint, peaceful oasis smack in the middle of downtown Fort Lauderdale, just a few minutes from beaches, restaurants, and the historic arts and science district. Popular with snowbirds who visit during the winter months from the northern states and Canada for 24 years, Paradise Island has a strong sense of community demonstrated by the heavily attended petanque (a Canadian game similar to bocci) tournaments during the winter and several dog-walkers out in the early evenings. Shade trees provide a cool breeze. Named a Good Sam Club, Paradise Island Resort is a pleasant park for RVers just passing through and for those looking to stay for awhile. There are 19 pull-through sites and most are 20 feet long, with some as long as 55 feet. Although less-savory areas abut the community, Paradise Island is surrounded by a six-foot hedge and maintains a security system with a night attendant who reports minimal disturbances. It is well-lit, gated park with regular police patrols.

Basics

Operated By: Managers Bill & Karen Price. **Open:** All year. **Site Assignment:** Reservations required in winter, $10 deposit for 1 night. **Registration:** Office. **Registration:** Office. **Fee:** $36 Nov.–May; $29 May–Nov.; MC, V, D, AE. **Parking:** Yes.

Facilities

Number of RV Sites: 232. **Number of Tent-Only Sites:** 0. **Hookups:** Electric (30, 50 amps), water, sewer, phone. **Each Site:** Full hookups,. **Dump Station:** No. **Laundry:** Yes. **Pay Phone:** Yes. **Rest Rooms and Showers:** Yes. **Fuel:** No. **Propane:** No. **Internal Roads:** Paved, in good condition. **RV Service:** Mechanic on call. **Market:** Groceries 3 mi. east on Oakland Park Blvd., pharmacy next door to campground to the north. **Restaurant:** Several within walking distance. **General Store:** Yes. **Vending:** Yes, plus free ice at pool area. **Swimming Pool:** Yes. **Playground:** No. **Other:** Clubhouse w/ full kitchen & 2 rec halls. **Activities:** Horseshoes, shuffleboard, petanque tournaments, billiards; planned activities during the winter include monthly dinners w/ music, holiday parties, live entertainment. **Nearby Attractions:** Fort Lauderdale beach 6 mi. east on Oakland Park Blvd., the Swap Shop flea market about 5 mi. west on Sunrise Blvd., an Indian Casino & Bingo hall north approximately 5 mi. in Coconut Creek. Car rentals available through the office. **Additional Information:** Greater Fort Lauderdale CVB, (800) 231-SUNNY, www.sunny.org.

Restrictions

Pets: On leash only, small pets preferred. **Fires:** In grill only, portable grills available at pool area. **Alcoholic Beverages:** Allowed. **Vehicle Maximum Length:** 45 ft.

To Get There

Exit I-95 in Fort Lauderdale at Oakland Park Blvd, Exit 31, Oakland Park west about a mile to NW 21st. Ave., turn south to campground entrance on right.

FORT MYERS BEACH

San Carlos RV Park

18701 San Carlos Blvd., Fort Myers Beach 33931. T: (941) 466-3133; F: (941) 466-3133; www.gocampingamerica.com/sancarlos; sancarrv@aol.com.

RV ★★★ Tent ★

Beauty: ★★★	Site Privacy: ★★
Spaciousness: ★★	Quiet: ★★★
Security: ★★★★★	Cleanliness: ★★★★
Insect Control: ★★★	Facilities: ★★★★

Although a bit crowded, this RV park has been family owned for 20 years and is clearly a favorite among its guests—and likely has been for years. The owners live on-site, and 19 of the park's mobile-home units are available as efficiency rentals. A small plot of land jutting out into the back bay waters of Hurricane Bay off the Gulf of Mexico, the park provides a quiet, unassuming means of being a tourist without feeling trapped by a circus of attractions. Fishers can appreciate the boat docks and marina, and tenters will appreciate the waterfront sites. Swimming in the bay is discouraged, however, because of the sharp barnacles clinging to the rocks covering the ocean floor. Luckily, Fort Myers Beach is just a mile away.

Basics

Operated By: Owner Vernon Underwood & family. **Open:** All year. **Site Assignment:** Reservations accepted, 1-night deposit required, refundable up to 24 hours in advance. **Registration:** Office. **Fee:** $25 May–Oct., $26 Nov.–Dec. 14, $32.50 Dec. 15–Apr. **Parking:** Yes.

Facilities

Number of RV Sites: 145. **Number of Tent-Only Sites:** 0. **Hookups:** Water, electric (20, 30 amps), sewer. **Each Site:** Picnic table, concrete pad. **Dump Station:** Yes. **Laundry:** Yes. **Pay Phone:** Yes. **Rest Rooms and Showers:** Yes. **Fuel:** No. **Propane:** No. **Internal Roads:** Paved in good condition. **RV Service:** Referral. **Market:** 1.5 mi. north, convenience mart 2 blocks south. **Restaurant:** 2–4 blocks north & south. **General Store:** Yes. **Vending:** Yes. **Swimming Pool:** Yes (w/ Jacuzzi). **Playground:** No. **Other:** Rec hall, shuffleboard, horseshoes, boat dock & marina, kayak & paddleboat rentals. **Activities:** Shuffleboard & horseshoe tournaments, potluck dinners, holiday parties, arts & crafts, all during winter season. **Nearby Attractions:** Beach, Sanibel & Captiva islands, dog race track in Bonita Springs, Edison & Ford homes in Fort Myers. **Additional Information:** Lee Island Coast CVB, (800) 237-6444, www.leeislandcoast.com.

RESTRICTIONS

Pets: No pit bulls or rottweilers, max. 2 pets per site, kept on 4-ft. leash. **Fires:** In grill only. **Alcoholic Beverages:** Allowed. **Vehicle Maximum Length:** 40 ft., call ahead for availability. **Other:** No firearms, no feeding wildlife, quiet hours 10 p.m.–8 a.m., pool closes at dusk.

TO GET THERE

I-75 Exit 21/Daniels Pkwy., west 5.5 mi. to Summerlin Rd., left/west 5.5 mi. to San Carlos Blvd., left/south 1.5 mi. to park on left.

HIGH SPRINGS

High Springs Campground

24004 NW Old Bellamy Rd., High Springs 32643. T: (386) 454-1688; HSCamping@aol.com.

RV ★★★ Tent ★★

Beauty: ★★★ Site Privacy: ★★
Spaciousness: ★★ Quiet: ★★★
Security: ★★★★★ Cleanliness: ★★★★
Insect Control: ★★★★ Facilities: ★★★★

There's a pleasant country atmosphere at this small, quiet, older campground that's right off the highway. The camping and playground areas are shaded with tall trees, although the sites themselves are not particularly wooded nor private. With some pull-through sites and grass underfoot, this makes a pleasant place to stop for a night or for a few days. Rustic and far from fancy, High Springs offers a laid-back feeling for those anxious to escape the city bustle. But real life is only a few clicks away, since Internet access is available in the laundry room. Even Fido can relax here—well-mannered dogs are welcome to go without leashes so long as they remain on best behavior and under their master's control. A popular spot for campers in town to canoe, tube, or swim the area springs as well as those planning to attend the annual Gator National Drag races in Gainesville the third weekend of Mar.

BASICS

Operated By: Jason Outler, manager; Linda McDonald, owner. **Open:** All year. **Site Assignment:** Reservations accepted, 50% deposit for holidays or special events, refundable w/ 7-day notice. **Registration:** Campground office. **Fee:** $18; cash or check only. **Parking:** Yes.

FACILITIES

Number of RV Sites: 48. **Number of Tent-Only Sites:** 5. **Hookups:** Water, electric (30 amps.), sewer. **Each Site:** Picnic table, fire rings. **Dump Station:** Yes. **Laundry:** Yes. **Pay Phone:** Free. **Rest Rooms and Showers:** Yes. **Fuel:** No. **Propane:** No. **Internal Roads:** Paved, in good condition. **RV Service:** Referral. **Market:** South 4 mi. on Hwy. 236 to US 441, right 1 mi. to supermarket on right. **Restaurant:** South 4 mi. on Hwy. 236 to High Springs. **General Store:** Ice only. **Vending:** Yes. **Swimming Pool:** Yes. **Playground:** Yes. **Activities:** Inquire at campground. **Nearby Attractions:** Fresh water springs nearby (driving distance) at Ichnetucknee Springs & Santa Fe River. **Additional Information:** Alachua County CVB, (352) 374-5260.

RESTRICTIONS

Pets: On leash if necessary. **Fires:** In fire rings unless restriction in effect. **Alcoholic Beverages:** Allowed. **Vehicle Maximum Length:** None.

TO GET THERE

I-75 Exit 79 at Hwy. 236 (just north of Gainesville), west to entrance at Old Bellamy Rd., north 1,000 ft. to campground.

HOBE SOUND

Jonathan Dickinson State Park

16450 SE Federal Hwy., Hobe Sound 33455. T: (561)546-2771; www.myflorida.com.

RV ★★★★ Tent ★★★★★

Beauty: ★★★★★ Site Privacy: ★★★★
Spaciousness: ★★★★ Quiet: ★★★★★
Security: ★★★★★ Cleanliness: ★★★★
Insect Control: ★★★ Facilities: ★★★★★

Frequently cited as one of the best camping opportunities in South Florida, Jonathan Dickinson State Park offers a range of ecosystems to study and enjoy, from the Loxahatchee River, Florida's first federally designated Wild and Scenic River (which protects the river from future development and restructuring), to the pine scrub, cypress swamp, and pine flatwoods laced with hiking, biking, and nature trails. Try to visit Trapper Nelson's place on the Loxahatchee—the restored homesite of a Florida pioneer trapper who died in 1968 under mysterious circumstances. Boat tours are offered Wednesday–Sunday. The park offers two campgrounds for RVers plus primitive trail camping areas for backpackers. The Pine Grove campground near the park entrance just off US 1 is the largest and provides both small and large sites. Most offer bushy buffers and shade cover from the many tall pine trees throughout the campground. Groups may appreciate the conference building and campfire circle at Pine Grove. The river campground, named for its proximity to the Loxahatchee River that runs along the western border of the park, has less tall trees but more native bushy vegetation, which provides greater privacy at each site but little shade. There are no pull-through sites at either campground.

BASICS

Operated By: Florida Dept. of Environmental Protection, Division of Recreation & Parks. **Open:** All year. **Site Assignment:** Reservations accepted, deposit required (call for amount). **Registration:** Park office. **Fee:** $14–$20; M, V, D, AE. **Parking:** Yes.

FACILITIES

Number of RV Sites: 120. **Number of Tent-Only Sites:** 10. **Hookups:** Water, electric (30 amps). **Each Site:** Picnic table, grill. **Dump Station:** Yes. **Laundry:** No. **Pay Phone:** Yes. **Rest Rooms and Showers:** Yes. **Fuel:** No. **Propane:** No. **Internal Roads:** Paved, in good condition. **RV Service:** Referral. **Market:** 3–5 mi. north or south on US 1. **Restaurant:** 3–5 mi. north or south on US 1. **General Store:** Yes. **Vending:** Yes. **Swimming Pool:** No. **Playground:** Yes. **Other:** Boat dock, hiking trails, observation tower, paved & off-road bike trails, nature trails. **Activities:** Hiking, boating (rentals available include motorboats, canoes, & kayaks), fishing, biking, bird & nature study, boat tours. **Nearby Attractions:** Beaches. **Additional Information:** Hobe Sound Chamber of Commerce, (561) 546-4724.

RESTRICTIONS

Pets: On leash & in designated areas only, proof of rabies vaccination required. **Fires:** In grill only. **Alcoholic Beverages:** After hours only. **Vehicle Maximum Length:** 35 ft. **Other:** No firearms or fireworks.

TO GET THERE

Exit I-95 at SR 708 (Hobe Sound Exit), east to US 1, south to park.

HOLT

Blackwater River State Park

7720 Deaton Bridge Rd., Holt 32564. T: (850) 983-5363; www.myflorida.com.

RV ★★★★ Tent ★★★★★

Beauty: ★★★★★ Site Privacy: ★★★★★
Spaciousness: ★★★★ Quiet: ★★★★★
Security: ★★★ Cleanliness: ★★★★★
Insect Control: ★★ Facilities: ★★★★

Amazingly remote, this campground entrance was unmanned when we arrived, with self-sign in instructions based on the honor system. Campers were advised to revisit the camp office between 5 and 7 p.m. to register and pay for the campsite. Sites around the two circles were all back-in or pull-in sites, but quite large, with generous buffers. Although peaceful and quiet, the campground was nearly full, and even more visitors were found at the rivers edge—Blackwater River is said to be one of the cleanest, most pristine rivers in the world. Happy groups of canoeists, swimmers, kayakers, and tubing enthusiasts frolicked in the cold, fresh, dark water as it wound its way through the park, dotted with wide, white-sand shores. Bobcats and deer are said to be common in this section of state forest. This one is clearly a Florida treasure. Pack the cooler and plan to stay a few days to enjoy the wilderness.

BASICS

Operated By: Florida Dept. of Environmental Protection, Division of Recreation & Parks. **Open:** All year. **Site Assignment:** First come, first served self-select. **Registration:** Office. **Fee:** $10; M, V, D. **Parking:** Yes.

FACILITIES

Number of RV Sites: 30. **Number of Tent-Only Sites:** 0. **Hookups:** Water, electric. **Each Site:** Picnic table, fire ring, clothesline poles. **Dump Station:** Yes. **Laundry:** No. **Pay Phone:** Yes. **Rest Rooms and Showers:** Yes. **Fuel:** No. **Propane:** No. **Internal Roads:** Paved, in good condition. **RV Service:** No. **Market:** 2 mi. south on Deaton Bridge Rd. **Restaurant:** 3 mi. south to Hwy. 90. **General Store:** No. **Vending:** No. **Swimming Pool:** No (River). **Playground:** No. **Other:** Picnic pavilions, hiking trails & boardwalks, river. **Activities:** Fishing, hiking, swimming, canoeing & kayaking. **Nearby Attractions:** Blackwater Canoe Outpost—rents canoes & tubes. **Additional Informa-**

tion: Main Street Milton, (850) 623-2339, www.src-chamber.com; Pensacola Convention & Visitor Center, (800) 87401234, www.visitpensacola.com.

Restrictions

Pets: On leash only, not allowed at riverside pavilions, beaches, or in river. **Fires:** In grill only. **Alcoholic Beverages:** Not allowed. **Vehicle Maximum Length:** 45 ft. **Other:** No firearms or intoxicants.

To Get There

Exit Hwy. 90 at Harold onto Deaton Bridge Rd., north 3 mi. to park.

JENSEN BEACH

Nettles Island

9803 S. Ocean Dr., Jensen Beach 34957. T: (561) (229) 1300; F: (561) 229-1304; www.vnirealty.com; Bev@vnirealty.com.

RV ★★★★★ Tent n/a

Beauty: ★★ Site Privacy: ★
Spaciousness: ★ Quiet: ★★★
Security: ★★★★★ Cleanliness: ★★★★★
Insect Control: ★★★★★ Facilities: ★★★★★

Quite different from most of the RV parks we've visited, Nettle's Island is very popular with retirees who want Florida's great lifestyle at a high value. Nettle's Island is wall-to-wall, privately owned sites, some available as rentals, others available for travelers and snow birds. It is a complete village unto itself, with streets and nicely landscaped grassy lawns on the perimeter sites. Nettle's Island includes a recreational section of property across the road, directly on the beach, with pool and cabana club. Fisher's delight.

Basics

Operated By: VNI Realty. **Open:** All year. **Site Assignment:** Reservations necessary Jan.–Mar., full payment due 30 days before arrival. **Registration:** Office. **Fee:** $39–$44 (waterfront) Dec.–Apr., $30–$35 May–Nov. **Parking:** Yes.

Facilities

Number of RV Sites: 1589. **Number of Tent-Only Sites:** 0. **Hookups:** Water, electric (50 amps), cable TV, phone. **Each Site:** Varies—some tables, grills. **Dump Station:** No. **Laundry:** Yes. **Pay Phone:** Yes. **Rest Rooms and Showers:** Yes. **Fuel:** Yes. **Propane:** Yes. **Internal Roads:** Paved, in good condition. **RV Service:** Referral. **Market:** On site. **Restaurant:** On site. **General Store:** Yes. **Vending:** Yes. **Swimming Pool:** Yes (2). **Playground:** Yes. **Other:** Mini-golf, volleyball & tennis courts, jacuzzi, sauna, gas station, bank, hair salon, marina, clothing store. **Activities:** Fishing off sites, off bridges, in the ocean. **Nearby Attractions:** Ocean. **Additional Information:** Jensen Beach Chamber of Commerce, (561) 334-3444, www.jensenchamber.com.

Restrictions

Pets: On leash only. **Fires:** In grill only (not provided). **Alcoholic Beverages:** Allowed. **Vehicle Maximum Length:** None. **Other:** No tents or pop-ups–full hookups only.

To Get There

Exit I-95 66 at Fort Pierce (Orange Ave.), east to US 1, north 0.5 mi. to A1A, east across Indian River (Fort Pierce Bridge to Hutchinson Island) then continue south on A1A about 14 mi. to Nettles Island.

KEY LARGO

John Pennekamp Coral Reef State Park

P.O. Box 1560, Key Largo 33037. T: (305) 451-1202; F: (305) 853-3555; www.myflorida.com.

RV ★★★★ Tent ★★★★

Beauty: ★★★★ Site Privacy: ★★
Spaciousness: ★★★ Quiet: ★★★★
Security: ★★★★★ Cleanliness: ★★★★★
Insect Control: ★★★ Facilities: ★★★★★

Boasting numerous awards as one of the best parks and campgrounds in the state, John Pennekamp Coral Reef State Park offers several unique treats thanks to its location in the Florida Keys, just minutes from Miami. The first undersea park in the nation, 178 square miles of this park extend into the Atlantic Ocean, including a portion of the only coral reef in the country. Park management takes advantage of the prime location to offer boat tours for snorkelers, scuba divers, and scenic viewers—glass-bottom boat rides are also offered daily. Equipment and instruction are available. All RV campsites are back-in only, and many are waterfront but don't afford a view because the camping area is surrounded by protected mangrove trees, revered around the world for their erosion protection and their root system (which can get a little smelly at times) which provides nutrients for the tiniest sea creatures forming the foundation of the food chain.

Basics

Operated By: Florida Dept. of Environmental Protection, Division of Recreation & Parks. **Open:** All year. **Site Assignment:** Reservations recommended, accepted up to 11 months in advance, 1-night deposit required, refundable up to 24 hours in advance. **Registration:** Park office. **Fee:** $29. **Parking:** Yes.

Facilities

Number of RV Sites: 41. **Number of Tent-Only Sites:** 6. **Hookups:** Water, electric. **Each Site:** Picnic table, grill. **Dump Station:** Yes. **Laundry:** No. **Pay Phone:** Yes. **Rest Rooms and Showers:** Yes. **Fuel:** No. **Propane:** No. **Internal Roads:** Paved & gravel, in good condition. **RV Service:** Referral. **Market:** 1 mi. south or north of the campground entrance. **Restaurant:** 1 mi. north or south of the campground entrance. **General Store:** Yes. **Vending:** Yes. **Swimming Pool:** No. **Playground:** Yes. **Other:** Coral reef, nature trails, canoe trails, scuba & snorkel boat tours. **Activities:** Swimming, fishing, boating, scuba, snorkeling. **Nearby Attractions:** Florida Keys Wild Bird Center, Tavernier; Key West (100 mi. south). **Additional Information:** Key Largo Chamber of Commerce, (800) 822-1088, www.keylargo.org.

Restrictions

Pets: No. **Fires:** In grill only. **Alcoholic Beverages:** Used discreetly after park hours only. **Vehicle Maximum Length:** 40 ft. **Other:** No firearms or fireworks.

To Get There

US 1 south from Miami to mile marker 102.5

KEY LARGO

Key Largo Kampground

101551 Overseas Hwy., Key Largo 33037. T: (305) 451-1431; F: (305) 451-8083; www.Key-Largo.org/accommodations.

RV ★★★★ Tent ★★

Beauty: ★★★ Site Privacy: ★★
Spaciousness: ★★★ Quiet: ★★★★
Security: ★★★★★ Cleanliness: ★★★★
Insect Control: ★★★ Facilities: ★★★★

This campground is occupied partly by those who own the sites; rentals are not uncommon but are made available on an individual basis through the office. Travelers can overnight in the tent area—a grassy, shaded park near the entrance. The atmosphere is made even more peaceful with coconut palm trees, mahogany, gumbo limbo, and mangroves lining the park, providing habitat to tiny crabs and raccoons. Manatees sometimes venture into the marina from the surrounding bone flats—shallow waterways dotted with protected mangrove islands. Owner's sites reveal an interesting crowd, with fragrant flower and tropical-fruit gardens, wind chimes, and colorful flags. The campground employs interpreters during the winter season to accommodate guests from German, French, and Spanish-speaking countries.

Basics

Operated By: Key Largo Kampground, Inc. **Open:** All year. **Site Assignment:** Reservations requested, 1-night non-refundable deposit. **Registration:** Office. **Fee:** $24.50–$52.50 (waterfront); M,V. **Parking:** Yes.

Facilities

Number of RV Sites: 171. **Number of Tent-Only Sites:** 38. **Hookups:** Water, electric (20, 30 50 amps), sewer, cable TV. **Each Site:** Some tables & grills. **Dump Station:** Yes. **Laundry:** Yes. **Pay Phone:** Yes. **Rest Rooms and Showers:** Yes. **Fuel:** No. **Propane:** No. **Internal Roads:** Paved, in good condition. **RV Service:** Referral. **Market:** 2 blocks south. **Restaurant:** 2 blocks south. **General Store:** Yes. **Vending:** Yes. **Swimming Pool:** Yes. **Playground:** Yes. **Other:** Marina, boat dock, beach, volleyball, horseshoe & shuffleboard courts. **Activities:** Bingo, game nights, pot-luck dinners, BBQ nights. **Nearby Attractions:** Coral reef, scuba, snorkeling, deep-sea fishing. **Additional Information:** Key Largo Chamber of Commerce, (800) 822-1088, www.keylargo.org.

Restrictions

Pets: On leash only. **Fires:** In grill only. **Alcoholic Beverages:** On site only, no offensive behavior. **Vehicle Maximum Length:** 35 ft. **Other:** No firearms or fireworks.

To Get There

US 1 south from Miami to Key Largo (first Key), left on Samson Rd. at mile marker 101.5, 2 blocks to campground.

LAKE BUENA VISTA

Disney's Fort Wilderness Resort and Campground

4510 North Fort Wilderness Trail, Lake Buena Vista 32830. T: (407) 824-2900; F: (407) 824-3508; www.disneyworld.com.

RV ★★★★ Tent ★★★

Beauty: ★★★★ Site Privacy: ★★★
Spaciousness: ★★★★ Quiet: ★★★★
Security: ★★★★★ Cleanliness: ★★★★★
Insect Control: ★★★★★ Facilities: ★★★★★

There's something very different at Disney's Campground. Just as the Magic Kingdom is like no other country and its Main Street like no other town, Disney's Fort Wilderness is a far cry from any other campground we've seen in Florida. For example, you'll be hard-pressed to find a mosquito here, even though the little blood-sucking bugs are a veritable plague throughout most of the rest of the state and beyond. Just as in the Magic Kingdom, the campgrounds are perfectly landscaped and maintained, and plenty of trees and shrubs create a nice sense of seclusion from neighboring campsites. Fort Wilderness offers 20 loops of campsites, plus another 8 for cabins, all spread comfortably across the more than 700-acre campground. Entertainment is also true Disney style, with two video arcades, nightly musical shows around the campfire, two swimming pools, a beach, fitness walks, bike, boat, and ski rentals available. Horseback trails, pony rides and hay rides, canoeing and kayaking add to the fun. But perhaps the best thing about Fort Wilderness is its convenient location close to all of Disney's parks—and early daily admission and free transportation to them all is allowed for campers. Enjoy!

BASICS

Operated By: Walt Disney World. **Open:** All year. **Site Assignment:** Reservations accepted through www.disneyworld.com or (407) 934-7639; 1-night stay deposit, refundable up to 72 hours in advance. **Registration:** Park office. **Fee:** $39; M,V, D,AE, DC, CB. **Parking:** Yes.

FACILITIES

Number of RV Sites: 784. **Number of Tent-Only Sites:** 83. **Hookups:** Water, electric (20, 30, 50 amps), sewer, cable TV. **Each Site:** Picnic table, grill. **Dump Station:** No. **Laundry:** Yes. **Pay Phone:** Yes. **Rest Rooms and Showers:** Yes. **Fuel:** No. **Propane:** Yes. **Internal Roads:** Paved, in good condition. **RV Service:** Referral. **Market:** Yes. **Restaurant:** Yes. **General Store:** Yes. **Vending:** Yes. **Swimming Pool:** Yes. **Playground:** Yes. **Other:** Tennis, basketball & volleyball courts, beach, bike paths, fitness trail, marina, shuffleboard, horseshoes, horse stables, petting farm. **Activities:** Fishing, musical campfire shows, boating, biking, horseback riding, sports. **Nearby Attractions:** Disneyworld Magic Kingdom & MGM, Epcot Center & Animal Kingdom theme parks. **Additional Information:** Orlando Official Visitor Center, (407) 363-5872, www.orlandoinfo.com.

RESTRICTIONS

Pets: On leash only, proof of rabies, please mention pets when booking reservation. **Fires:** In grill only. **Alcoholic Beverages:** Allowed. **Vehicle Maximum Length:** None. **Other:** No fireworks, firearms must be stored at front desk.

TO GET THERE

Exit I-4 at and follow signs to the Magic Kingdom.

LIVE OAK

Spirit of the Suwannee Music Park

3076 95th Dr., Live Oak 32060. T: (904) 364-1683 or (800) 224-5656; F: (386) 364-2998; www.musicliveshere.com; spirit@musicliveshere.com.

RV ★★★★ Tent ★★★★★

Beauty: ★★★★★ Site Privacy: ★★★
Spaciousness: ★★★★★ Quiet: ★★★★
Security: ★★★★★ Cleanliness: ★★★★
Insect Control: ★★★★ Facilities: ★★★★★

Music is a mainstay of the local activities—bring your own and join in or come for the frequent concerts, which include nationally known musicians of a variety of genres, from bluegrass and country to Christian and rock. Campers can choose from full-hookup RV sites to rentable trailers called cabins to a tree house overlooking the outdoor amphitheater.

BASICS

Operated By: The Cornett family. **Open:** All year. **Site Assignment:** Reservations accepted, deposit 20%, refundable up to 15 days in advance. **Registration:** Park office. **Fee:** $25; M,V, D. **Parking:** Yes.

FACILITIES

Number of RV Sites: 1100. **Number of Tent-Only Sites:** 600 acres of primitive camping. **Hookups:** Water, electric (20, 30, 50 amps), sewer, cable. **Each Site:** Picnic table. **Dump Station:** Yes. **Laundry:** Yes. **Pay Phone:** Yes. **Rest Rooms and Showers:** Yes. **Fuel:** No. **Propane:** No. **Internal Roads:** Paved & gravel in good condition. **RV Service:** Referral. **Market:** 4.5 mi. south on Hwy. 129 to I-10. **Restaurant:** 4.5 mi. north on Hwy. 129 to I-75. **General Store:** Yes. **Vending:** Yes. **Swimming Pool:** Yes. **Playground:** Yes. **Other:** Paddle-boat & canoe rentals, amphitheater, restaurant, pickin' shed, horse stables, 15 mi. of trails, 3 stages, gamefield for up to 20,000 people. **Activities:** Playing and/or listening to music, canoeing, fishing, hiking, horseback riding. **Nearby Attractions:** Inquire at campground. **Additional Information:** Suwannee County Tourist Development Council, (386) 362-3071, www.suwanneechamber.com.

RESTRICTIONS

Pets: On leash only. **Fires:** Must be attended. **Alcoholic Beverages:** Allowed. **Vehicle Maximum Length:** None. **Other:** No firearms.

TO GET THERE

4.5 mi. south of I-75 at Hwy. 129/Live Oak; 4.5 mi. north of I-10 at Hwy. 129/Live Oak.

MADISON

Yogi Bear's Jellystone Park Camp Resort

Rte. 1 Box 3199J, Ragans Lake Rd., Madison 32340. T: (850) 97308269; F: (850) 973-4114; www.madisonfl.com/jellystone; yogibear@madisonfl.com.

RV ★★★★★ Tent ★★★★

Beauty: ★★★ Site Privacy: ★★★
Spaciousness: ★★★★ Quiet: ★★★★
Security: ★★★★ Cleanliness: ★★★★★
Insect Control: ★★★★ Facilities: ★★★★★

Although this campground is conveniently situated right off the highway in north-central Florida, it's much more than a parking lot for overnight travelers. This campground offers plenty of opportunities for play—it is quickly becoming a destination in itself. It is the only Yogi Bear Jellystone campground in Florida, and Yogi himself often visits to cheer the children in a wide variety of activities, from mini-golf to a water slide. Regular tram rides take visitors to the back lot to see the frontier village, often the site of paint-ball showdowns. Some of the largest and most scenic sites are located on the lakeshore. Others are opposite a small pine forest, giving the campground a very spacious and comfortable feel with grass underfoot. Rest rooms are private, individual shower/toilet rooms. About half the sites are pull-throughs, but most people want to stay awhile to relax and enjoy the activities. Kids are entertained throughout the days, and karaoke and even an "opry" hall features occasional performances for older travelers.

BASICS

Operated By: Jim & Latrelle Ragans. **Open:** All year. **Site Assignment:** Reservations accepted w/ credit card, deposit $25, refundable if cancelled 48 hours in advance. **Registration:** Park office. **Fee:** $25; MC,V, D,AE. **Parking:** Yes.

FACILITIES

Number of RV Sites: 92. **Number of Tent-Only Sites:** 8. **Hookups:** Water, electric (20, 30, 50 amps), sewer. **Each Site:** Picnic table, grill, fire ring, lantern. **Dump Station:** Yes. **Laundry:** Yes. **Pay Phone:** Yes. **Rest Rooms and Showers:** Yes. **Fuel:** No. **Propane:** No. **Internal Roads:** Gravel, in good condition. **RV Service:** Referral. **Market:** 4 mi. north on Hwy. 53. **Restaurant:** 2 mi. north on Hwy. 53. **General Store:** Yes. **Vending:** Yes. **Swimming Pool:** Yes. **Playground:** Yes. **Other:** Lake, waterslide, frontier town, tram tours, mini-golf, rec hall, movie room. **Activities:** Holiday parties, volleyball tournaments (June), kids weekends (July), bingo, paintball. **Nearby Attractions:** Capitol city, Tallahassee. **Additional Information:** Madison County Tourism Development Council, (850) 973-2788, www.madisonfl.org.

RESTRICTIONS

Pets: On leash only, in designated areas. **Fires:** In grill & fire rings only. **Alcoholic Beverages:** At site only. **Vehicle Maximum Length:** None. **Other:** Don't feed the alligators.

TO GET THERE

Exit I-10 east of Tallahassee at Madison, Exit 37, take Hwy. 53 south to Ragans Lake Rd. (first road to right), turn right and follow 0.75 mi. to campground.

MALABAR

Camelot RV Park

1600 US Hwy. 1, Malabar 32950. T: (321) 724-5396; F: (321) 724-9022; www.camelotrvpark.com; Camelot@camelotrvpark.com.

RV ★★★★★ Tent n/a

Beauty: ★★★ Site Privacy: ★★★
Spaciousness: ★★★ Quiet: ★★★
Security: ★★★★★ Cleanliness: ★★★★★
Insect Control: ★★★★★ Facilities: ★★★★★

More like a small village than a typical RV park, this 15-acre complex seems a comfortable location for travelers with time to stay awhile in this quiet and peaceful section of Florida's central east coast. Owners help visitors get to know their neighbors by organizing frequent leisure events such as pitch-in dinners and dances. If the office happens to be closed when you arrive, you may self-select from among many large, grassy sites dotted with oak and palm trees, then register at your convenience. The campground offers a nice view of the Intracoastal Waterway/Indian River across the road, where a private fishing dock is available for guests. Dolphins and manatees can often be spotted passing by in the river. Snowbirds will appreciate that this park offers RV storage, too.

BASICS

Operated By: Owners Bob Sr., Bobby, Liz & John Ritter. **Open:** All year. **Site Assignment:** Reservations accepted, deposit recommended. **Registration:** Office. **Fee:** $23 May–Nov., $27 Nov.–May; M, V. **Parking:** Yes.

FACILITIES

Number of RV Sites: 130. **Number of Tent-Only Sites:** 0. **Hookups:** Water, electric (30, 50 amps), sewer, cable TV, phone, modem. **Each Site:** Picnic table, grill, patio. **Dump Station:** Yes. **Laundry:** Yes. **Pay Phone:** Yes. **Rest Rooms and Showers:** Yes. **Fuel:** No. **Propane:** Yes. **Internal Roads:** Paved, in good condition. **RV Service:** Referral. **Market:** 2 mi. south on US 1. **Restaurant:** Walking distance south. **General Store:** No. **Vending:** Yes. **Swimming Pool:** No. **Playground:** No. **Other:** Basketball, shuffleboard, & bocci courts, rec hall, fishing dock. **Activities:** Bingo, musical performances & dances, BBQ dinners, craft groups, boating, fishing. **Nearby Attractions:** Intracoastal Waterway (Indian River), Beach. **Additional Information:** Melbourne/Palm Bay Area Chamber of Commerce, (800) 771-9922, www.melpb-chamber.org.

RESTRICTIONS

Pets: On leash only. **Fires:** In grill only. **Alcoholic Beverages:** Allowed. **Vehicle Maximum Length:** Big rigs welcome. **Other:** Quiet time 10 p.m.–8 a.m.

TO GET THERE

I-95 Exit 70 east on Hwy. 514, 4.5 mi. to US 1, south 2 blocks to park.

MARIANNA

Arrowhead RV Park

4820 US Hwy. 90 East, Marianna 32446. T: (850) 482-5583 or (800) 643-9166; www.arrowheadcamp.com.

RV ★★★★ Tent ★★★

Beauty: ★★★ Site Privacy: ★★
Spaciousness: ★★ Quiet: ★★★★
Security: ★★★★★ Cleanliness: ★★★★
Insect Control: ★★★★ Facilities: ★★★★

This large, friendly campground offers a comfortable place to stay for those visiting the Marianna area not far from Tallahassee. Although it. is on the main highway of the small town, the adjacent lake and plenty of tall trees give the camp a rural atmosphere. The half of the campground north of the pool and pavilion and running along the water's edge is more desirable, with curving roads and more wooded sites, although even the less private sites are still pleasant, with grass underfoot and a few trees. There's plenty to do here, too, with boat rentals and fishing docks on Merritt's Mill Pond, a spring-fed lake that boasts the world-record red-eye fish (called a shell cracker in these parts) ever caught. Kids like the mini-golf and game room, and families appreciate the security of the gated entrance adjacent to the office.

BASICS

Operated By: Bill Reddoch. **Open:** All year. **Site Assignment:** Reservations. **Registration:** Park office. **Fee:** $16; MC, V, D, AE. **Parking:** Yes.

FACILITIES

Number of RV Sites: 200. **Number of Tent-Only Sites:** 45. **Hookups:** Water, electric (20, 30 amps), sewer, cable TV. **Each Site:** Picnic table, trash can. **Dump Station:** Yes. **Laundry:** Yes. **Pay Phone:** Yes. **Rest Rooms and Showers:** Yes. **Fuel:** Yes. **Propane:** Yes. **Internal Roads:** Hard-packed dirt, in good condition. **RV Service:** Referral. **Market:** 0.5 mi. **Restaurant:** 0.5 mi. west on US 90. **General Store:** Yes. **Vending:** Yes. **Swimming Pool:** Yes. **Playground:** Yes. **Other:** Lake, boat launch, fishing docks, recreation pavilion, game room. **Activities:** Swimming, fishing, boating. **Nearby Attractions:** Florida Caverns State Park, Falling Waters State Park, 3 golf courses. **Additional Information:** Jackson County Tourist Development Council, (850) 482-8061.

RESTRICTIONS

Pets: On leash only. **Fires:** In fire rings only. **Alcoholic Beverages:** Allowed. **Vehicle Maximum Length:** None.

TO GET THERE

1.5 mi. from I-10 Exit 21 (Marianna), 1 mi. north on Hwy. 71 to US 90, 0.5 mi. west to campground.

MARIANNA

Florida Caverns State Park

3345 Caverns Rd. (SR 166), Marianna 32446. T: (850) 482-1228; www.dep.state.fl.us/parks.

RV ★★★★★ Tent ★★★★★

Beauty: ★★★★★ Site Privacy: ★★★★
Spaciousness: ★★★★ Quiet: ★★★★★
Security: ★★★★★ Cleanliness: ★★★★★
Insect Control: ★★★★ Facilities: ★★★★★

Who knew there were caves in Florida? Sure enough when the land rises just a bit above sea level, caverns are revealed beneath the surface of the earth. Left behind by the retreating sea millions of years ago, a dozen caves have been discovered in this state park (but only one is open for public exploration). The park also features a beautiful blue swimming hole. This is one of the nicest parks we've visited in Florida.

BASICS

Operated By: Florida Dept. of Environmental Protection, Division of Recreation & Parks. **Open:** All year. **Site Assignment:** Reservations accepted. **Registration:** Park office. **Fee:** $14; MC, V. **Parking:** Yes.

FACILITIES

Number of RV Sites: 32. **Number of Tent-Only Sites:** 0. **Hookups:** Water, electric. **Each Site:** Picnic table, fire ring, clothes poles. **Dump Station:** Yes. **Laundry:** No. **Pay Phone:** Yes. **Rest Rooms and Showers:** Yes. **Fuel:** No. **Propane:** No. **Internal Roads:** Paved, in good condition & somewhat bumpy dirt roads. **RV Service:** No. **Market:** 3 mi. south on SR 166 to US 90, 2 mi. east to town. **Restaurant:** 3 mi. south on SR 166 to US 90, 2 mi. east to town. **General Store:** Yes. **Vending:** Yes. **Swimming Pool:** Blue Hole spring-fed pond & beach. **Playground:** No. **Other:** Cave, visitors center features geologic & historic exhibits, golf course, boat launch. **Activities:** Guided cave tours, swimming, canoeing, hiking, fishing, golf. **Additional Information:** Jackson County Chamber of Commerce, (850) 482-8061.

RESTRICTIONS

Pets: On leash only. **Fires:** Fire ring only. **Alcoholic Beverages:** Not allowed. **Vehicle Maximum Length:** 30 ft. **Other:** No firearms, no fireworks.

TO GET THERE

On SR 166 (Caverns Rd), 3 mi. north of US 90.

MELBOURNE BEACH

Sebastian Inlet State Recreation Area

9700 S. A1A, Melbourne Beach 32951. T: (407) 984-4852 or (561) 589-9659 or (321) 984-4852; www.myflorida.com.

RV ★★★★ Tent ★★★★

Beauty: ★★★★ Site Privacy: ★★
Spaciousness: ★★★ Quiet: ★★★★
Security: ★★★★★ Cleanliness: ★★★★★
Insect Control: ★★★★ Facilities: ★★★★★

Although there aren't a lot of trees to shade the campsites at Sebastian Inlet State Recreation Area, neither are there many obstructions to the view. This is one of the few campgrounds we found that allows campers overnight positions on the waterfront. In this case, sites 1–14 look across the road and directly over Sebastian Inlet, and sites 35–50 on the other side of the campground sit on a tidal lagoon, although the view may be somewhat obscured by brush and sea grape trees, a few strangler figs, sabal palm, and gumbo limbo trees. Wood storks and mocking birds can be seen foraging along the shoreline and among the plants. This state park also offers an unusual bonus, the waterfront restaurant that serves lunch and breakfast. Finally, this beach is known as one of the best surfing areas in the world and hosts several international surfing competitions.

BASICS

Operated By: Florida Dept. of Environmental Protection, Division of Recreation & Parks. **Open:** All year. **Site Assignment:** Reservations accepted up to 11 months in advance, 1-night stay refundable up to 24 hours in advance. **Registration:** Ranger's office or park entrance gate. **Fee:** $15 May–Nov., $19 Dec.–Apr.; M,V, D,AE. **Parking:** Yes.

FACILITIES

Number of RV Sites: 51. **Number of Tent-Only Sites:** 0. **Hookups:** Water, electric (30 amps). **Each Site:** Picnic table, fire ring. **Dump Station:** Yes. **Laundry:** Yes. **Pay Phone:** Yes. **Rest Rooms and Showers:** Yes. **Fuel:** No. **Propane:** No. **Internal Roads:** Paved, in good condition. **RV Service:** Referral. **Market:** About 6 mi. north on Hwy. A1A in Melbourne Beach. **Restaurant:** Park offers ocean-side café serving breakfast & lunch, or 6 mi. north on A1A. **General Store:** Yes. **Vending:** Yes. **Swimming Pool:** No (Indian River & Ocean). **Playground:** No. **Other:** Boat dock, ramp & marina w/ boat, canoe, kayak, & pontoon rentals; Fishing museum & Treasure museum. **Activities:** Fishing, boating, swimming, surfing. **Nearby Attractions:** Pelican Island National Wildlife Refuge, immediately south of Sebastian Inlet State Recreation Area on A1A. **Additional Information:** Melbourne/Palm Bay Area Chamber of Commerce, (800) 771-9922, www.melpb-chamber.org.

RESTRICTIONS

Pets: On leash only. **Fires:** In grill or fire ring only. **Alcoholic Beverages:** Not allowed. **Vehicle Maximum Length:** None. **Other:** Quiet time 11 p.m.–8 a.m., no firearms or fireworks.

TO GET THERE

US 1 to Wabasso, CR 510 east 5 mi. through "Town of Orchid" to A1A, north 7 mi. to Sebastian State Recreation Area.

MEXICO BEACH/PANAMA CITY

Rustic Sands RV Resort

800 N 15th St., Mexico Beach 32456. T: (850) 648-5229; F: (850) 648-4349; rentacabin@aol.com.

RV ★★★	Tent ★★
Beauty: ★★	Site Privacy: ★★
Spaciousness: ★★	Quiet: ★★
Security: ★★★	Cleanliness: ★★★★
Insect Control: ★★★	Facilities: ★★★

This campground is near, but not on, the busy strip near Panama City Beach. It's less than a mile away from the ocean and has a boat ramp and all the joys that come with both. The campground itself offers a small fishing pond for those content with the more restful atmosphere under tall pine trees. Bird houses have been erected to provide habitat for the feathered snow birds known to pass through on annual treks. A pool was under construction so should be available by time of publication, and kids will enjoy the playground and basketball courts. Pleasantly grassy campsites are 20 feet wide and laid out in circles. Some have bushy buffers, but they're not very private. Some have pull-through capability. Tiny cabins and mobile-home sites are available for rental, but traveling RVers and tenters are welcome.

BASICS

Operated By: Manager. **Open:** All year. **Site Assignment:** First come, first served. **Registration:** Office. **Fee:** $18; MC, D,V. **Parking:** Yes.

FACILITIES

Number of RV Sites: 32. **Number of Tent-Only Sites:** 16. **Hookups:** Water, electric (30 amps.), sewer, cable TV, phone. **Each Site:** Picnic table. **Dump Station:** Yes. **Laundry:** Yes. **Pay Phone:** Yes. **Rest Rooms and Showers:** Yes. **Fuel:** No. **Propane:** Yes. **Internal Roads:** Crushed shell in good condition. **RV Service:** Referral. **Market:** 0.75 mi. to US 98. **Restaurant:** 0.75 mi. to US 98. **General Store:** Yes. **Vending:** Yes. **Swimming Pool:** Yes. **Playground:** Yes. **Other:** Fishing pond, rec hall. **Activities:** Fishing, swimming, boating. **Nearby Attractions:** Beach, marina w/ boat ramp & boat charters. **Additional Information:** Panama City Beaches Chamber of Commerce, (850) 235-1159, www.pcbeach.org.

RESTRICTIONS

Pets: On leash only. **Fires:** Yes. **Alcoholic Beverages:** Allowed. **Vehicle Maximum Length:** None.

TO GET THERE

US 98 to N. 15th St., 0.75 mi. north to entrance on left.

MIAMI

Miami/Everglades KOA Kampground

20675 SW 162nd Ave., Miami 33187. T: (305) 233-5300 or (800) 562-7732; www.miami-camp.com; admin@koamiami.com.

RV ★★★	Tent ★
Beauty: ★★	Site Privacy: ★★
Spaciousness: ★★	Quiet: ★★★★
Security: ★★★★★	Cleanliness: ★★★★★
Insect Control: ★★★	Facilities: ★★★★

Miami/Everglades KOA Kampground provides the standards ensured by KOA, so while crowds can be expected, travelers can also rely on cleanliness and comfort. Set amid Miami-Dade County farms—which feed the nation during the winter months—this quiet and peaceful yet somewhat lonely campground was once a grove and still boasts mature avocado and mango trees throughout the grounds and even on several sites. Fruit is free for those who wish to pluck it from the branches. Coconut trees and cascading fuchsia bouganvillea complete the subtropical atmosphere. The park is 25 miles south of Miami and 6 miles east of Everglades National Park, providing easy access to the best attractions South Florida has to offer. Sites are side-by-side, most are pull-through, almost giving the less-than-pleasant effect of a parking lot. The best sites are on the outer edges, the west side of the campground offers more shade trees. Tent sites offer no privacy and no ambience. A fine place to park while visiting the area, but not a destination in itself.

BASICS

Operated By: Managers Jim & Julia Champion. **Open:** All year. **Site Assignment:** Reservations recommended, $25 deposit, refunds up to 4 p.m. day prior. **Registration:** Camp office. **Fee:** $34; MC,V, D,AE. **Parking:** Yes.

FACILITIES

Number of RV Sites: 257. **Number of Tent-Only Sites:** 13. **Hookups:** Water, electric (30, 50 amps), sewer. **Each Site:** Picnic table, tree. **Dump Station:** Yes. **Laundry:** Yes. **Pay Phone:** Yes. **Rest Rooms and Showers:** Yes. **Fuel:** No. **Propane:** Yes. **Internal Roads:** Paved, in good condition. **RV Service:** Mobile RV service available. **Market:** Farmers markets open Dec.–May, 1.5 mi. west on Krome Ave., or go about 5 mi. south on Krome to find a grocery in Homestead. **Restaurant:** 5 mi. east on Quail Roost to Miami or 5 mi. southwest in Homestead. **General Store:** Yes. **Vending:** Yes. **Swimming Pool:** Yes. **Playground:** Yes. **Other:** Soccer field. **Activities:** Soccer, shuffleboard, volleyball. **Nearby Attractions:** Monkey Jungle, Everglades National Park, city of Miami, Florida Keys, Indian Casino. **Additional Information:** Greater Miami CVB, (888) 76-MIAMI, www.tropicoolmiami.com.

RESTRICTIONS

Pets: On leash only. **Fires:** In grills only. **Alcoholic Beverages:** Allowed. **Vehicle Maximum Length:** None.

TO GET THERE

Exit Florida Turnpike 13, Eureka Dr. (SW 184 St.), west to SW 117 Ave., south 1 mi. to Quail Roost Dr., west 5 mi. to campground.

MICANOPY

Paynes Prairie State Preserve

100 Savannah Blvd., Micanopy 32667. T: (352) 466-3397; F: (352) 466-4297; www.AFN.org/`prairie; Prairie@AFN.org.

RV ★★★★	Tent ★★★★★
Beauty: ★★★★★	Site Privacy: ★★★★
Spaciousness: ★★★★	Quiet: ★★★★
Security: ★★★★★	Cleanliness: ★★★★★
Insect Control: ★★★	Facilities: ★★★★

This 21,000-acre wildlife preserve is quite unique, as it provides a safe home for free roaming wild horses, herds of bison, and "cracker" cattle brought to the state by Spanish pioneers. Visitors are quite likely to encounter deer and perhaps even these more unusual animals during a camp stay. An observation tower provides a panoramic view of the prairie—take binoculars so you'll be sure to capture images when you see the buffalo roam across the prairie. The two small campground loops of the Puc Puggy Campground (named for the nickname of the prairie's founder, William Bartram) provide a quiet hideaway, with wooded terrain and sand and dirt underfoot. None of the sites are pull-through, but there is some vegetation separating each from the next. The camping area is a short hike from the lake.

Basics

Operated By: Florida Dept. of Environmental Protection, Division of Recreation & Parks. **Open:** All year. **Site Assignment:** First come, first served, reservations accepted up to 11 months in advance by credit card, cancellations refundable up to 24 hours in advance. **Registration:** Park office. **Fee:** $13; MC, V. **Parking:** Yes.

Facilities

Number of RV Sites: 35. **Number of Tent-Only Sites:** 15. **Hookups:** Electric, water. **Each Site:** Picnic table, grill. **Dump Station:** Yes. **Laundry:** No. **Pay Phone:** Yes. **Rest Rooms and Showers:** Yes. **Fuel:** No. **Propane:** No. **Internal Roads:** Paved, in good condition. **RV Service:** No. **Market:** US 441 south 1 mi. to small grocery store. **Restaurant:** US 441 north 8 mi. to Gainesville. **General Store:** No. **Vending:** No. **Swimming Pool:** No. **Playground:** Yes. **Other:** Wildlife preserve, hiking, biking, horse trails, observation tower, visitors center. **Activities:** Fishing, boating, hiking, horseback riding, educational programs, guided trail hikes. **Nearby Attractions:** Antique stores in historic Old Micanopy, Historic home of Marjorie Kinnan Rawlings in nearby Cross Creek. **Additional Information:** Alachua County CVB, (352) 374-5260.

Restrictions

Pets: On leash & on paved roads only, not allowed in campground. **Fires:** In grills unless restrictions in effect. **Alcoholic Beverages:** Not allowed. **Vehicle Maximum Length:** None. **Other:** No firearms, no fireworks, no feeding wildlife, no collecting firewood, stay on established trails.

To Get There

I-75 to Exit 75/Micanopy, 2 mi. east to US 441 north 1 mi. to park entrance on right.

OHIO KEY

Sunshine Key Fun Resort

38801 Overseas Hwy., Big Pine Key 33043. T: (305) 872-2217; F: (305) 872-3801; www.RVONTHEGO.com; NHCFLSK@Terranova.net.

RV ★★★ Tent ★★★

Beauty: ★★	Site Privacy: ★
Spaciousness: ★	Quiet: ★★
Security: ★★★★★	Cleanliness: ★★★★★
Insect Control: ★★★★	Facilities: ★★★★★

A great campground for RVers who love to boat and fish—this Encore property offers a boat dock as well as a few waterfront sites under the perpetual sunshine of the Florida Keys. Book early, especially for winter visits. Gravel and white sand underfoot and scattered small trees and bushes give a stark appearance. There are virtually no buffers between sites: this location is here for recreation, not the wilderness experience, although registered campers can visit a bird sanctuary across the highway. Tennis and basketball courts at the campground add to the fun, and a pool-side snack bar provides refreshment.

Basics

Operated By: National Homes Community/ Encore. **Open:** All year. **Site Assignment:** By request on site or by phone in advance, 1-night rental deposit by credit card, refundable up to 7 days prior. **Registration:** Office. **Fee:** $25; MC, V, D, AE. **Parking:** Yes.

Facilities

Number of RV Sites: 397. **Number of Tent-Only Sites:** 0. **Hookups:** Electric (30, 50 amps), water, sewer, cable TV. **Each Site:** Tables. **Dump Station:** Yes. **Laundry:** Yes. **Pay Phone:** Yes. **Rest Rooms and Showers:** Yes. **Fuel:** Yes. **Propane:** Yes. **Internal Roads:** Paved & gravel, in good condition. **RV Service:** Referral. **Market:** 8 mi. south to Big Pine Key. **Restaurant:** 8 mi. south to Big Pine Key (plus pool side café for breakfast & lunch). **General Store:** Yes. **Vending:** Yes. **Swimming Pool:** Yes. **Playground:** No. **Other:** Game room, basketball, volleyball, horseshoes, tennis court, shuffleboard, boat marina. **Activities:** Boating, fishing, kayaking, scuba, snorkeling (rentals available), winter recreation program includes bingo, shows, & dinners. **Nearby Attractions:** Beach, Key West is 61 mi. away. **Additional Information:** Florida Keys & Key West Tourist Council, (800) 648-5510, www.fla-keys.com.

Restrictions

Pets: On leash only. **Fires:** In grill only (not provided). **Alcoholic Beverages:** Allowed. **Vehicle Maximum Length:** 45 ft. **Other:** Max. 6 campers per site.

To Get There

US 1 south from Miami 61 mi. to mile marker 39, campground on west (Gulfside).

OKEECHOBEE

Zachary Taylor Camping Resort

2995 Hwy. 441 S.E., Okeechobee 34974. T: (863) 763-3377 or (reservations only): 888-282-6523; www.campfloridarv.com; ZTResort@ictransnet.com.

RV ★★★★ Tent ★★★

Beauty: ★★★★	Site Privacy: ★★
Spaciousness: ★★★	Quiet: ★★★★
Security: ★★★★★	Cleanliness: ★★★★★
Insect Control: ★★★★	Facilities: ★★★★★

This rural campground has been run by Chuck Freed for a quarter century. A haven for fisherpeople, the most scenic campsites abut Taylor creek, which flows into Lake Okeechobee, the state's largest lake and well known for its premium bass fishing. In times of drought the connection to the lake is blocked by manmade dike. Nonetheless, proximity to the lake makes this campground a favorite for those who love to fish. Supplies are only a short distance away in the town of Okeechobee, too. Tall moss-draped cypress trees shade many sites and lean out over the river, narrow wooden docks lead out from the waterfront sites for boaters access, and alligators, turtles, and herons share the river while gray squirrels scamper along the banks. Bird calls and the whistling of a nearby train provide a nighttime lullaby. Paved circular roads shared by about 100 permanent renters and 150 sites for travelers (each with concrete pads surrounded by grass and trees) wind through the camp. Cabins, a rec hall, and screened pool are provided as well as small separate toilet and shower stalls—be sure to ask for the key to the always-locked facilities reserved for overnight guests. Late arrivals can call ahead, and instructions will be posted at the entrance gate or on-site security guard will greet and guide you after hours.

Basics

Operated By: Owners Chuck & Fran Freed. **Open:** All year. **Site Assignment:** Reservations welcome, non-refundable deposit required. **Registration:** Office. **Fee:** $29; MC, V. **Parking:** Yes.

Facilities

Number of RV Sites: 250. **Number of Tent-Only Sites:** 0. **Hookups:** Electric (30 amps), water, sewage. **Each Site:** Picnic table, fire rings on waterfront sites. **Dump Station:** Yes. **Laundry:** Yes. **Pay Phone:** Yes. **Rest Rooms and Showers:** Yes ($2 key deposit). **Fuel:** No. **Propane:** No. **Internal Roads:** Paved, in good condition. **RV Service:** Referral. **Market:** 3 mi. north on US 441 in Okeechobee. **Restaurant:** 3 mi. north on US 441 in Okeechobee. **General Store:** Yes. **Vending:** Yes. **Swimming Pool:** Yes. **Playground:** No. **Other:** Boat Ramp, open grassy field for play. **Activities:** Fishing, boating (rental available), shuffleboard, horseshoes, group crafts in winter, holiday parties, fishing tournaments. **Nearby Attractions:** Lake Okeechobee, Brighton Indian gaming casino. **Additional Information:** Okeechobee County Tourist Development Council, (863) 763-3959, (800) 871-4403.

Restrictions

Pets: On leash only. **Fires:** In grill or fire ring only. **Alcoholic Beverages:** Allowed. **Vehicle Maximum Length:** 40 ft.—call for availability. **Other:** 1 car per site, 1 family per site.

To Get There

From US 441 south from Okeechobee 2 mi. to US 441 east 1 mi. to SE 30th Terrace, left (north) to campground entrance.

OUTDOOR RESORTS OF CHOKOLUSKEE

Outdoor Resorts of Chokoluskee

P.O. Box 39, Chokoluskee 34138. F: (941) 695-3338; www.outdoor-resorts.com.

RV ★★★★★ Tent ★★★★

Beauty: ★★★	Site Privacy: ★★★
Spaciousness: ★★★	Quiet: ★★★
Security: ★★★★	Cleanliness: ★★★★★
Insect Control: ★★★	Facilities: ★★★★

This owner-occupied park offers rental units as well as sites for travelers. Sites are large, with concrete pads and grass, some on the waterfront. On the Turner River, which runs from the Everglades and out to the Gulf of Mexico after passing through the Ten Thousand Islands, the park offers a marina and boat, canoe and kayak rentals as well as fishing gear. But with many other amenities, such as three swimming pools and tennis courts, there's plenty to do for those who aren't interested in fishing.

BASICS

Operated By: Manager Kenny Brown. **Open:** All year. **Site Assignment:** Reservations accepted, 1-night deposit required, refunded w/ at least 7-day notice cancellation. **Registration:** Office. **Fee:** $40. **Parking:** Yes.

FACILITIES

Number of RV Sites: 283. **Number of Tent-Only Sites:** 0. **Hookups:** Water, electric (30, 50 amps), sewer, cable TV, phone. **Each Site:** None. **Dump Station:** Yes. **Laundry:** Yes. **Pay Phone:** No. **Rest Rooms and Showers:** Yes. **Fuel:** Yes. **Propane:** No. **Internal Roads:** Paved, in good condition. **RV Service:** Referral. **Market:** 2 mi. north in Everglades City. **Restaurant:** 2 mi. north in Everglades City. **General Store:** Yes. **Vending:** No. **Swimming Pool:** Yes (3 pools). **Play-ground:** No. **Other:** Tennis courts, shuffleboard, rec hall, weight room, marina. **Activities:** Winter activities include dinners, bingo, ice cream socials, craft exhibits, etc. **Nearby Attractions:** Ten Thousand Islands, Everglades National Park. **Additional Information:** Everglades Chamber of Commerce.

RESTRICTIONS

Pets: Yes. **Fires:** In grill only. **Alcoholic Beverages:** Yes, in moderation. **Vehicle Maximum Length:** 45 ft. plus.

TO GET THERE

US 41 from Miami (60 mi.) or Naples (40 mi.) to CR 29, south through Everglades City across 3 mi. causeway to Chokoluskee, to campground on left.

PALM BAY

Lazy K RV Park

5150 Dixie Hwy., N.E., Palm Bay 32905. T: (321) 724-1639.

RV ★★★ Tent n/a

Beauty: ★★ Site Privacy: ★
Spaciousness: ★ Quiet: ★★★
Security: ★★★★★ Cleanliness: ★★★★
Insect Control: ★★★ Facilities: ★★

This small, private RV park is one of only a few along this central eastern segment of Florida's coastline. Clean and well maintained by owners, who live on the premises, sites are large and grassy, with a concrete pad, with a few trees and bushes scattered among them, and a backdrop of trees surrounding the U-shaped park. A dog walk runs along the adjacent railroad track, but one of the nicest features at this small mom-and-pop park is the view. Across the street from the park is the Intracoastal Waterway (known here as the Indian River), providing a lovely scene.

BASICS

Operated By: Owners Terry & Pat. **Open:** All year. **Site Assignment:** First come, first served. **Registration:** Park office. **Fee:** $18; M,V. **Parking:** Limited.

FACILITIES

Number of RV Sites: 63. **Number of Tent-Only Sites:** 0. **Hookups:** Water, electric (30, 50 amps), sewer, cable TV, phone. **Each Site:** Picnic table. **Dump Station:** Yes. **Laundry:** Yes. **Pay Phone:** Yes. **Rest Rooms and Showers:** Yes. **Fuel:** No. **Propane:** No. **Internal Roads:** Paved, in good condition. **RV Service:** Referral. **Market:** 3 mi. north to Palm Bay Rd., 2 mi. west. **Restaurant:** 3 mi. north to Palm Bay Rd., 2 mi. west. **General Store:** No. **Vending:** No. **Swimming Pool:** No. **Playground:** No. **Other:** Intracoastal Waterway across the street. **Activities:** Fishing, swimming, boating. **Nearby Attractions:** Beach. **Additional Information:** Palm Bay Area Chamber of Commerce, (800) 276-9130, www.palmbaychamber.com.

RESTRICTIONS

Pets: On leash only. **Fires:** In grill only. **Alcoholic Beverages:** Allowed. **Vehicle Maximum Length:** Big rigs welcome. **Other:** No tents.

TO GET THERE

I-95 Exit 70, east on Hwy. 514 4 mi. to US 1, north 0.5 mi.

PANAMA CITY BEACH

Emerald Coast RV Beach Resort

1957 Allison Ave., Panama City Beach 32407. T: (850)235-0924 or (800) BEACH-RV; F: (850) 235-9609; www.RVResort.com; ECRVBR@aol.com.

RV ★★★★★ Tent ★★

Beauty: ★★★ Site Privacy: ★★
Spaciousness: ★★★ Quiet: ★★★
Security: ★★★★★ Cleanliness: ★★★★★
Insect Control: ★★★★★ Facilities: ★★★★★

Given top designations by industry campground rating services, the Emerald Coast RV Beach Resort bills itself as "the highest-rated resort in North America." The four-year-old resort has earned the compliment by creating a clean, well-manicured park with comfortable clubhouse and amenities—including big-screen TV—all kept in top condition. Premium cable channels are available on-site as well. For those who find concrete roads, pads, and patios plus two trees too ascetic, a pair of stocked fishing lakes and recreational area abut the camper lots, providing a taste of nature. Colorful lilies and oleander bloom throughout the park, lending the tropical flair of Florida to the easy living provided at Emerald Coast. Even mosquitoes aren't too bad, thanks to an underground drainage system that eliminates bug-breeding grounds. Daily trash pickup at each site is another big plus that helps keep the park spotless and vermin-free. Many sites are pull-through, and "super sites" can accommodate the largest vehicles with triple slideouts.

BASICS

Operated By: Owners Mr. & Mrs. Hartka. **Open:** All year. **Site Assignment:** Reservations accepted by phone w/ 1-day deposit, $50 for week, or $100 for month; cancellations w/ 14-day notice, less $10 administrative fee. **Registration:** Office. **Fee:** $32; MC,V. **Parking:** Yes.

FACILITIES

Number of RV Sites: 143. **Number of Tent-Only Sites:** No tents or pop-ups allowed. **Hookups:** Water, electric (30, 50 amps), sewer, cable TV, phone. **Each Site:** Table. **Dump Station:** Yes. **Laundry:** Yes. **Pay Phone:** Yes. **Rest Rooms and Showers:** Yes. **Fuel:** No. **Propane:** Yes. **Internal Roads:** Paved, in good condition. **RV Service:** Referral. **Market:** 0.75 mi. west on US 98 to supermarket. **Restaurant:** 0.75 mi. west on US 98. **General Store:** Yes. **Vending:** Yes. **Swimming Pool:** Yes. **Playground:** Yes. **Other:** Rec room w/ computer & free e-mail, free coffee, putting green, shuffleboard, sand volleyball, fishing lake, bike rentals, horseshoes, sandbox. **Activities:** Free shuttle to the beach, family cookouts, breakfasts, bingo, card games, movies, organized outings to area restaurants & attractions. **Nearby Attractions:** Zoo next door, beach, pier & boat charters, outlet shopping mall, 18-hole golf course, amusement park. **Additional Information:** Panama City Beach CVB, (800) PC-BEACH, www.800pcbeach.com.

RESTRICTIONS

Pets: Gentle breeds only, leash required. **Fires:** In grill only. **Alcoholic Beverages:** Allowed. **Vehicle Maximum Length:** None. **Other:** No tents or pop-ups.

TO GET THERE

Park is on Allison Ave. between US 98 and Alt. 98, 1.5 mi. west of Hathaway Bridge (SR 231).

PENSACOLA

Bayside Pensacola—Perdido Bay Kampground Resort

33951 Spinnaker Dr., Lillian 36549. T: (334) 961-1717 or (800) 562-3471; F: (334) 961-1717; www.koa.com/where/fl/01102.htm; perdidokoa@gulftel.com.

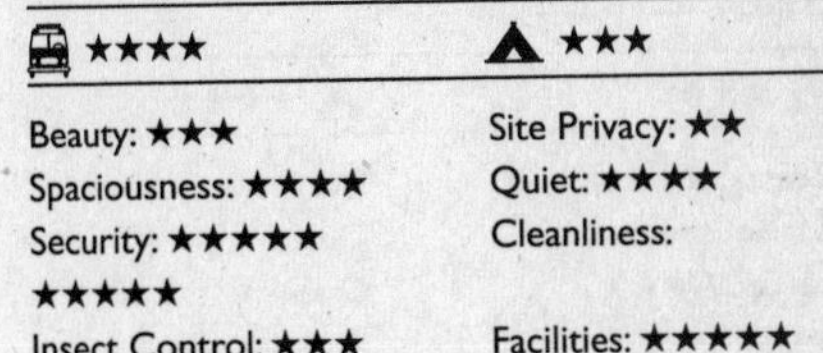

RV ★★★★ Tent ★★★

Beauty: ★★★ Site Privacy: ★★
Spaciousness: ★★★★ Quiet: ★★★★
Security: ★★★★★ Cleanliness: ★★★★★
Insect Control: ★★★ Facilities: ★★★★★

We planned to end our day on Perdido Key outside Pensacola so we could spend the evening at the legendary rock/country pub and club, the Florabama on the state line. Alas, each campground we found on the island appeared to be nothing more than a beach-side or near-beach parking lot, wall-to-wall with metal traveling vehicles. We kept on going, right across the Florida line into Alabama, where suddenly rolling green hills and a herd of frolicking deer in the twilight convinced us that we had found the best place around. We settled in at the KOA on Perdido Bay. With 80 pull-through sites and a dock that runs down to the bay, this campground looked like paradise.

BASICS

Operated By: Owner Denise Valentyne. **Open:** All year. **Site Assignment:** Reservations accepted,

1-night deposit, refundable 24 hours. **Registration:** Park office. **Fee:** $23. **Parking:** Yes.

Facilities

Number of RV Sites: 100. **Number of Tent-Only Sites:** 10. **Hookups:** Water, electric (30, 50 amps), sewer, cable TV. **Each Site:** Picnic table. **Dump Station:** Yes. **Laundry:** Yes. **Pay Phone:** Yes. **Rest Rooms and Showers:** Yes. **Fuel:** No. **Propane:** No. **Internal Roads:** Paved, in good condition. **RV Service:** Referral. **Market:** 4 mi. east. **Restaurant:** 3 mi. east or west. **General Store:** Yes. **Vending:** Yes. **Swimming Pool:** Yes. **Playground:** Yes. **Other:** Basketball court, boat ramp & pier, rec room, shuffleboard, horseshoes, RV wash station. **Activities:** Saturday wagon rides & ice-cream socials. **Nearby Attractions:** Gulf Shores National Seashore. **Additional Information:** Pensacola Convention & Visitor Center, (800) 874-1234, www.visitpensacola.com; Perdido Key Area Chamber of Commerce, (800) 328-0107, www.perdidochamber.com.

Restrictions

Pets: On leash only. **Fires:** In grills & designated areas only. **Alcoholic Beverages:** Allowed. **Vehicle Maximum Length:** None. **Other:** No fireworks, no generators, no clotheslines, quiet hours 10 p.m.–8 a.m.

To Get There

From I-10 or Alt 90 in Pensacola, west to Hwy. 297 south to Blue Angel Rd., south to Bauer Rd./US 98, 3 mi. west across Perdido Bay into Alabama, first left after bridge is Hwy. 99, south to campground.

PORT ST. JOE (APALACHICOLA, PANAMA CITY)

Indian Pass Campground

2817 Indian Pass Rd., Port St. Joe 32456. T: (850) 227-7203; www.indianpasscharters.com/campground; daniel2@gtcom.net.

RV: ★★★ Tent: ★★★★

Beauty: ★★★★	Site Privacy: ★★★
Spaciousness: ★★★	Quiet: ★★★★
Security: ★★★	Cleanliness: ★★★
Insect Control: ★★	Facilities: ★★★★

Bugs! A pod of dolphin has been seen playing in adjacent Indian Pass Sound, alligators live there and swim past the campground occasionally, a 12-foot shark sighted recently, swimming the off-shore waters. St. Vincent Island, visible from the campground, is a national wildlife refuge and home to a red wolf–breeding and reintroduction program as well as to 500–600 pound sambar deer, exotic animals from southeast Asia, introduced by the island's previous private owners in the early 1900s along with other non-native game for hunters. The campground itself is beautiful and scenic, with honeysuckle-scented air, although just as rustic as you might guess for a fisherman's hideout.

Basics

Operated By: Owners, the Captains of Indian Pass Charters. **Open:** All year. **Site Assignment:** First come, first served; reservations accepted, no deposit required. **Registration:** Office. **Fee:** Call ahead for details. **Parking:** Yes.

Facilities

Number of RV Sites: 38. **Number of Tent-Only Sites:** 0. **Hookups:** Water, electric (30, 50 amps.). **Each Site:** Picnic table. **Dump Station:** Yes. **Laundry:** Yes. **Pay Phone:** Yes. **Rest Rooms and Showers:** Yes. **Fuel:** Yes. **Propane:** No. **Internal Roads:** Gravel. **RV Service:** Referral. **Market:** 3.5 mi. west to Indian Pass. **Restaurant:** 3.5 mi. west to Indian Pass. **General Store:** Yes. **Vending:** Yes. **Swimming Pool:** Yes. **Playground:** No. **Other:** Boat ramp. **Activities:** Fishing, charters available. **Nearby Attractions:** National Wildlife Habitat. **Additional Information:** Apalachicola Bay Chamber of Commerce, (850) 653-9419, www.baynavigator.com.

Restrictions

Pets: Welcome, leashed if necessary. **Fires:** Fire rings only. **Alcoholic Beverages:** Allowed. **Vehicle Maximum Length:** 45 ft.

To Get There

From Apalachicola, travel west on Hwy. 98 approximately 6 mi., follow left fork on C30, 9 mi. west/left, to C30B/Indian Pass Rd. south/left 3.5 mi.

SANTA ROSA BEACH

Grayton Beach State Recreation Area

357 Main Park Rd., Santa Rosa Beach 32549. T: (850) 231-4210; www.myflorida.com.

RV: ★★★★ Tent: ★★★★★

Beauty: ★★★★★	Site Privacy: ★★★★
Spaciousness: ★★★	Quiet: ★★★★★
Security: ★★★★★	Cleanliness: ★★★★★
Insect Control: ★★★	Facilities: ★★★★★

Sandwiched between the tourist meccas of Seaside—an urban demonstration project touted as an ecologically-sound pedestrian community but looking more like a lot of tightly packed tourist dwellings—and Sandestin, a resort hotel community that similarly packs in huge numbers of vacationers, Grayton Beach State Recreation Area offers a glimpse of the world's best beaches without being marred by rows of rooftops or other burdens of civilization. Here is a place where citizens can really appreciate the preservation of land via government park systems. The broad, white-sand beaches and turquoise waters clearly deserve the recurring annual recognitions they receive, and thousands upon thousands of people (and birds) flock to this haven of American beauty. Park rangers distribute a guide to area birds visitors might watch for, from grosbeaks to grebes, herons to hawks, with a cuckoo or two, loons, and starlings. Though small, Grayton Beach provides a perfect, quiet respite from the booming cities surrounding it, perhaps one of the last bastions of safety for passing birds and snowbirds alike.

Basics

Operated By: Florida Dept. of Environmental Protection, Division of Recreation & Parks. **Open:** All year. **Site Assignment:** Reservations accepted up to 11 months in advance, 1-night deposit required. **Registration:** Office. **Fee:** $10 Oct.–Feb., $16 Mar.–Sept.; AE, MC, V, D. **Parking:** Yes.

Facilities

Number of RV Sites: 37. **Number of Tent-Only Sites:** 0. **Hookups:** Water, electric. **Each Site:** Picnic table, fire ring, clothesline poles. **Dump Station:** Yes. **Laundry:** No. **Pay Phone:** Yes. **Rest Rooms and Showers:** Yes. **Fuel:** No. **Propane:** No. **Internal Roads:** Paved & shell, in good condition. **RV Service:** Referral. **Market:** 12 mi. west on Hwy. 98. **Restaurant:** 12 mi. west on Hwy. 98. **General Store:** No. **Vending:** Yes. **Swimming Pool:** No. **Playground:** No. **Other:** One of the best beaches in the nation, hiking trails, boat ramp. **Activities:** Swimming, fishing, boating, hiking, birding. **Nearby Attractions:** Eglin Air Force Base. **Additional Information:** South Walton Tourist Development Council, (800) 822-6877, www.beachesofsouthwalton.com.

Restrictions

Pets: Not allowed in campground. **Fires:** In grill only. **Alcoholic Beverages:** Not allowed. **Vehicle Maximum Length:** None.

To Get There

US 98 west from Panama City Beach to CR 30A—scenic coastal route—to park, just west of Seaside.

SANTA ROSA BEACH

Top Sail Hill Preserve State Park: Gregory E. Moore RV Resort

7525 W. County Hwy. 30A, Santa Rosa Beach 32459. T: (850) 267-0299; (877) BEACH-RV; F: (850) 267-9014; www.topsailhill.com; topsailhill@gnt.net.

RV: ★★★★★ Tent: n/a

Beauty: ★★★	Site Privacy: ★★★★
Spaciousness: ★★★★	Quiet: ★★★★
Security: ★★★★★	Cleanliness: ★★★★★
Insect Control: ★★★★★	Facilities: ★★★★★

Proud recipient of top ratings from two RV industry watchdogs, the Gregory E. Moore RV Resort at Topsail Hill Preserve State Park is the crown of camper habitats. Well-manicured and trimmed, the RV parking areas offer bushy buffers amid scattered tall pines lining concrete drives, pads, and patios. Twenty pull-through sites are available for the largest rigs around.

Basics

Operated By: Florida Dept. of Environmental Protection, Division of Recreation & Parks. **Open:** All year. **Site Assignment:** First come, first served or reservations accepted w/ deposit, refundable up to 24 hours in advance. **Registration:** Office. **Fee:** $32; MC, V, D. **Parking:** Yes.

Facilities

Number of RV Sites: 156. **Number of Tent-Only Sites:** 0. **Hookups:** Water, electric (30, 50 amps), sewer, cable TV. **Each Site:** Picnic table, grills at pull-through sites. **Dump Station:** No. **Laundry:** Yes. **Pay Phone:** Yes. **Rest Rooms and Showers:** Yes. **Fuel:** No. **Propane:** Yes. **Internal**

Roads: Paved. **RV Service:** Referral. **Market:** 2 mi. east on Hwy. 98. **Restaurant:** 0.25 mi. south on Hwy. 30A. **General Store:** Yes. **Vending:** Yes. **Swimming Pool:** Yes. **Playground:** No. **Other:** 1,650-acre preserve w/ hiking trails & bike path, tennis courts, shuffleboard, basketball, 3 lakes, clubhouse w/ library. **Activities:** Fishing, biking, hiking,. **Nearby Attractions:** 1 mi. walking trail to top-rated beach. **Additional Information:** South Walton Tourist Development Council, (800) 822-6877, www.beachesofsouthwalton.com.

Restrictions

Pets: On leash only, proof of vaccinations required. **Fires:** In grill only. **Alcoholic Beverages:** After hours only. **Vehicle Maximum Length:** None. **Other:** No tents (pop-ups okay), quiet hours 11 p.m.–7 a.m.

To Get There

From US 98 and Hwy. 30A near Sandestin, south 0.25 mi. on 30A to park entrance.

SARASOTA

Myaka River State Park

13207 SR 72, Sarasota 34241. T: (941) 361-6511; F: (941) 361-6501; www.myaka.sarasota.fl.us.

RV ★★★ Tent ★★★★

Beauty: ★★★★★	Site Privacy: ★★★
Spaciousness: ★★★	Quiet: ★★★★★
Security: ★★★★★	Cleanliness: ★★★★
Insect Control: ★★★	Facilities: ★★★★

Scenic and swampy, this alligator habitat is well known as home to a number of incredible birds, including bald eagles, great blue herons, great horned owls, sandhill cranes, wild turkeys, and ruby-throated hummingbirds, and as rest stop for passers-by, such as the roseate spoonbill, loons, Canadian geese, mallards, and peregrine falcons. Local volunteers even built a bridge that lifts observers seven flights of stairs into the tree tops to gain perspective on life among their feathered friends. Other creatures include fox, bobcat, deer, wild hogs, and the occasional black bear. Campers can enjoy the campgrounds, which can get a bit swampy during rainy season, usually Aug. and Sept., when the mosquitoes are out in full force. Many visitors bring their boats along to explore the lakes and the wild and scenic Myaka River, so named as part of a government preservation program that will protect it from scientific "engineering," a common practice designed to improve conditions but which ultimately is often discovered to bring negative results for tampering with nature. Myaka was one of Florida's first state parks, so it has been well preserved. Cabins here are very nice, built by the Civilian Conservation Corps in the 1930s and still sturdy—much larger and nicer than modern campground 'cabins'.

Basics

Operated By: Florida Dept. of Environmental Protection, Division of Recreation & Parks. **Open:** All year. **Site Assignment:** Reservations accepted up to 11 months in advance, 1-night deposit, refundable if cancelled by 5 p.m. the day before. **Registration:** Office. **Fee:** $15 May–Nov., $18 Dec.–Apr.; M,V, D, AE. **Parking:** Yes.

Facilities

Number of RV Sites: 48. **Number of Tent-Only Sites:** 28. **Hookups:** Water, electric (20, 30 amps). **Each Site:** Picnic table, grill or fire ring. **Dump Station:** Yes. **Laundry:** No. **Pay Phone:** Yes. **Rest Rooms and Showers:** Yes. **Fuel:** No. **Propane:** No. **Internal Roads:** Paved & dirt, in good condition. **RV Service:** Referral. **Market:** A little less than 10 mi. west to Sarasota. **Restaurant:** A little less than 10 mi. west to Sarasota. **General Store:** Yes. **Vending:** Yes. **Swimming Pool:** No. **Playground:** Yes. **Other:** Canopy walkway for tree-top-level bird-watching, boat ramp, tram & airboat rides, nature trails. **Activities:** Fishing, birding (a favorite Audubon Society bird habitat), hiking, horseback riding, biking. **Nearby Attractions:** Selby Botanical Gardens & Ringling Museum in Sarasota. **Additional Information:** Sarasota CVB, (800) 522-9799, www.sarasotafl.org.

Restrictions

Pets: Not allowed in camping areas because of alligators. **Fires:** Contained only, provided there is no burn ban. **Alcoholic Beverages:** Not allowed. **Vehicle Maximum Length:** 34 ft. **Other:** No firearms or fireworks.

To Get There

I-75 Exit 37/ SR 72, east 9 mi. to park on left.

SEBRING

Highlands Hammock State Park

5931 Hammock Rd., Sebring 33872. T: (863) 386-6094; www.myflorida.com.

RV ★★★★ Tent ★★★★★

Beauty: ★★★★★	Site Privacy: ★★★
Spaciousness: ★★★	Quiet: ★★★★
Security: ★★★★★	Cleanliness: ★★★★★
Insect Control: ★★★★	Facilities: ★★★★

This beautiful central Florida state park boasts a pristine hardwood hammock featuring tall pines and oak trees alongside cypress and native palms. Nature trails wind through samples of ancient hardwoods as well as swampy marshlands. A wide variety of native fauna has been found in the decades-old protected area, including the rare Florida panthers, black bears, river otters, raccoons, and foxes. Dual camping rings offer quiet sites under cover of the trees with easy access to shower and laundry facilities. Back-in only, dirt-ground sites are about 20 ξ 30 to 50 feet, with slight wooded buffer between each. A community campfire circle is available for evening activities. Although Florida summers are known for their heat, humidity, and mosquitoes, this forested atmosphere in the central state offers the promise of cooler, less humid nights than some. Park gates are locked at night, with security lock codes distributed to campers for access.

Basics

Operated By: State Dept. of Environmental Protection. **Open:** All year. **Site Assignment:** Reservations up to 11 months in advance, no deposit but credit card number to guarantee, cancel by 5 p.m. day before. **Registration:** Park Ranger office. **Fee:** $8 May–Oct., $13 Nov.–Apr.; MC, V. **Parking:** Yes.

Facilities

Number of RV Sites: 138. **Number of Tent-Only Sites:** 24. **Hookups:** Electric, water. **Each Site:** Picnic tables. **Dump Station:** Yes. **Laundry:** Yes. **Pay Phone:** Yes. **Rest Rooms and Showers:** Yes. **Fuel:** No. **Propane:** No. **Internal Roads:** Paved & smooth dirt roads, good condition. **RV Service:** Referral. **Market:** 6 mi. south on US 27. **Restaurant:** Yes. **General Store:** Yes. **Vending:** Yes. **Swimming Pool:** No. **Playground:** Yes. **Other:** Horseshoes, shuffleboard, checkers. **Activities:** Horse trails (bring your own horse), nature trails, bike trails, guided ranger walks & tram tours. **Nearby Attractions:** Prestigious annual auto race & year-round activities at nearby Sebring Raceway. **Additional Information:** Highlands County CVB, (863) 385-1316, (800) 255-1711.

Restrictions

Pets: On leash only. **Fires:** In grill only. **Alcoholic Beverages:** Not allowed. **Vehicle Maximum Length:** 45 ft. **Other:** No firearms, no fireworks, no intoxicants.

To Get There

Four mi. west of Sebring on SR 634

ST. AUGUSTINE

Anastasia State Park

1340A A1A South, St. Augustine 32080. T: (904) 461-2033; F: (904) 461-2006; www.myflorida.com.

RV ★★★★ Tent ★★★★★

Beauty: ★★★★★	Site Privacy: ★★★
Spaciousness: ★★	Quiet: ★★★
Security: ★★★★★	Cleanliness: ★★★★
Insect Control: ★★★	Facilities: ★★★★★

Crowded and very popular, this ocean-side park provides a beautiful example of Florida's coastal dunes undisturbed by development. Although all sites are back-in in the seven U-shaped camping areas, some are more crowded than others, and none are actually on the water. The Sea Bean circle seemed to offer the most privacy, and the Coquina circle, where we stayed, was most crowded. Nonetheless, the park was quiet by 11 p.m., and the dense trees and bush buffer provided a sense of seclusion. In addition to preserved and protected sand dunes and sea oats, endangered sea turtles are common to the shoreline here during nesting season, May to Sept. If you should happen to be lucky enough to spot a turtle laying eggs, or her hatchlings making their way from nest back to the ocean, be careful not to interfere with the process with sound or lights.

Basics

Operated By: Florida Dept. of Environmental Protection, Division of Recreation & Parks. **Open:** All year. **Site Assignment:** Reservations accepted up to 11 months in advance, 1-night deposit, refundable up to 24 hours in advance. **Registration:** Park office. **Fee:** $18; M,V, D. **Parking:** Yes.

Facilities

Number of RV Sites: 104. **Number of Tent-Only Sites:** 35. **Hookups:** Water, electric. **Each Site:** Picnic table, fire ring. **Dump Station:** Yes.

Laundry: Yes. **Pay Phone:** Yes. **Rest Rooms and Showers:** Yes. **Fuel:** No. **Propane:** No. **Internal Roads:** Paved & dirt, in good condition. **RV Service:** Referral. **Market:** 3 mi. south from park entrance. **Restaurant:** 1 mi. north or south from park entrance. **General Store:** Yes. **Vending:** Yes. **Swimming Pool:** No (beach). **Playground:** Yes. **Other:** Windsurf, kayak & canoe rentals; beach, fishing pier, hiking trails. **Activities:** Summer evening programs at the campfire circle, surfing, kayaking, canoeing, sailing, swimming, fishing, hiking. **Nearby Attractions:** Historic Fort Castillo de San Marcos; Lighthouse Museum; historic St. Augustine, Florida's oldest city; farmer's market (south from park on A1A about 3 mi. at public fishing pier & information center), dog-friendly beach 3 mi. south of the city fishing pier. **Additional Information:** St. Augustine, Ponte Vedra & the Beaches CVB, (800) OLD-CITY, www.visitoldcity.com.

RESTRICTIONS

Pets: In designated areas (not on beach), on leash only, proof of vaccination. **Fires:** In grills & designated areas only. **Alcoholic Beverages:** Not during park hours. **Vehicle Maximum Length:** 35 ft.—call ahead for up to 40 ft. **Other:** No driving on beach, do not damage or disturb dunes, nature, or wildlife.

TO GET THERE

Exit I-95 at Rte. 207, north approximately 5 mi. to SR 312, east 3 mi. to Anastasia Island, left on A1A 1.5 mi. north to park on right.

ST. GEORGE ISLAND

Dr. Julian G. Bruce St. George Island State Park

1900 E. Gulf Beach Dr., St. George Island 32328. T: (850) 927-2111; www.myflorida.com.

RV ★★★★ Tent ★★★★

Beauty: ★★★★★ Site Privacy: ★★★★
Spaciousness: ★★★★ Quiet: ★★★★★
Security: ★★★★★ Cleanliness: ★★★★★
Insect Control: ★★★★ Facilities: ★★★★★

St. George Island Park is a beautifully preserved example of Florida's famous Emerald Coast beaches—the park has nine miles of pristine beach front, half accessible only by boat or foot. The rather stark park is largely made up of drifts of snow-white sands covered with small, wind-bent pines and sea oats, pink and purple flower vines crawling across them. The smooth, soft slopes may call upon your instincts to climb, but you must resist the urge—this weather-shaped landscape is fragile, and the island depends on the dunes to protect against erosion. A number of interesting creatures make their home in the park and on the island. There were eight eagles nests when we visited, and we saw several eagles, standing proudly atop pine trees, light poles, and cellular towers, living comfortably amid civilization. Strangely, a coyote has been detected on the island, and there are alligators, nesting sea turtles, cardinals, pelicans, and osprey. Campers will appreciate the nicely wooded camping areas, with nice bushy buffers around the rather smallish sites. The full-facility campground offers 60 back-in sites, but no pull-throughs. A primitive camping area is available for tenters willing to hike two-and-a-half miles.

BASICS

Operated By: Florida Dept. of Environmental Protection, Division of Recreation & Parks. **Open:** All year. **Site Assignment:** Reservations accepted up to 11 months in advance, 1-night deposit, refundable up to 24 hours in advance. **Registration:** Park office. **Fee:** $10 Sept.–Jan., $16 Feb.–Aug. **Parking:** Yes.

FACILITIES

Number of RV Sites: 60. **Number of Tent-Only Sites:** Primitive camping area. **Hookups:** Water, electric. **Each Site:** Picnic table, fire ring. **Dump Station:** Yes. **Laundry:** No. **Pay Phone:** Yes. **Rest Rooms and Showers:** Yes. **Fuel:** No. **Propane:** No. **Internal Roads:** Paved & crushed shell, in good condition. **RV Service:** Referral. **Market:** Approx. 4 mi. west on Gulf Beach Dr. to St. George. **Restaurant:** Approx. 4 mi. west on Gulf Beach Dr. to St. George. **General Store:** No. **Vending:** Yes. **Swimming Pool:** No (beach). **Playground:** Yes. **Other:** Boat ramp, nature trails. **Activities:** Swimming, fishing, hiking. **Nearby Attractions: Nearby Attractions:. Additional Information:** Apalachicola Bay Chamber of Commerce, (850) 653-9419, www.baynavigator.com.

RESTRICTIONS

Pets: On leash only, not allowed on beaches, boardwalks, or dunes. **Fires:** In grill only. **Alcoholic Beverages:** Not during park hours. **Vehicle Maximum Length:** 35 ft. **Other:** No firearms or fireworks, no vehicles off roadways, do not walk over dunes or vegetation, do not feed wildlife, quiet hours starting 11 p.m.

TO GET THERE

From US 98 at Eastpoint (just east of Apalachicola), cross Eastpoint Bridge/Hwy. 300 to St. George Island, then turn left on Gulf Beach Blvd. (still Hwy. 300) to park, about 5 mi.

ST. JAMES CITY

Fort Myers Pine Island KOA

5120 Stringfellow, St. James City 33956. T: (941) 283-2415 or (800) KOA-8505; F: (941) 283-2415; www.pineislandkoa.com; pineislkoa@aol.com.

RV ★★★★ Tent ★★

Beauty: ★★ Site Privacy: ★★
Spaciousness: ★★★★ Quiet: ★★★★
Security: ★★★★★ Cleanliness: ★★★★★
Insect Control: ★★ Facilities: ★★★★★

To say that this RV park is out of the way would be a great understatement—and that is exactly why so many campers love it. Pine Island is one of the last remaining rural outposts on Florida's southwest coast, offering a down-home feeling, farmers markets, and fishing villages. Although there are no pull-through sites, most are very large. The campground is on the waterfront, but views are completely obscured by mangrove trees. Most sites have a palm tree, and there is a nice expanse of green grass, but little shade. If you plan to visit in July, be sure to ask about MangoMania, an island festival that celebrates the many varieties of mangoes and avocados that grow on the island, and features live music and entertainment plus foods from area restaurants.

BASICS

Operated By: Manager John Streeter. **Open:** All year. **Site Assignment:** Reservations accepted, $20 deposit required, refundable up to 24 hours in advance. **Registration:** Office. **Fee:** $27 May–Nov., $45 Dec.–Apr. **Parking:** Yes.

FACILITIES

Number of RV Sites: 368. **Number of Tent-Only Sites:** 0. **Hookups:** Water, electric (30 amps), sewer, cable TV. **Each Site:** Picnic table. **Dump Station:** Yes. **Laundry:** Yes. **Pay Phone:** No. **Rest Rooms and Showers:** Yes. **Fuel:** No. **Propane:** Yes. **Internal Roads:** Paved, in good condition. **RV Service:** Maintenance on-site & referral. **Market:** 5 mi. north or convenience mart 2 mi. south. **Restaurant:** 2–4 mi. south. **General Store:** Yes. **Vending:** Yes. **Swimming Pool:** Yes. **Playground:** Yes. **Other:** Clubhouse, exercise room, hot tub, game room w/ computers & Internet access, library, big-screen TV. **Activities:** Shuttle to beach, cultural activities, flea market, etc. **Nearby Attractions:** Island is surrounded by the Gulf of Mexico. **Additional Information:** Greater Pine Island Chamber, (941) 283-0888, www.pineislandchamber.org.

RESTRICTIONS

Pets: On leash only, max. 2 pets. **Fires:** In grill only. **Alcoholic Beverages:** Allowed. **Vehicle Maximum Length:** None. **Other:** Quiet time 10 p.m., no swimming in lakes.

TO GET THERE

I-75 Exit 26 at Hwy. 78/Bayshore Rd. (becomes Pine Island Rd.) west 21 mi. to Stringfellow, south 6 mi. to KOA.

SUGARLOAF KEY

Sunburst RV Park

P.O. Box 440179, Sugarloaf Key 33044. T: (305) 745-1079 or (800) 354-5524; F: (305) 745-1680; www.RVONTHEGO.com; NHCFLLL@Terra-nova.net.

RV ★★★ Tent ★★★

Beauty: ★★★ Site Privacy: ★★
Spaciousness: ★★★ Quiet: ★★★★
Security: ★★★★ Cleanliness: ★★★★
Insect Control: ★★★ Facilities: ★★★★

Several campers have discovered that Lazy Lake—now called Sunburst since being bought by National Homes Communities in 1999—can provide an affordable stay in the Florida Keys, an increasingly rare circumstance. This small campground recalls the truly rustic atmosphere that made the Keys famous but which is quickly being replaced by all things shiny and new, big and corporate. Permanent guests have added on sun rooms and wooden decks, large potted palms and hanging parrot lights. Built around a manmade lake and surrounded by mud flats, Lazy Lake offers several waterfront sites plus free kayaks and paddle boats for exploring the turquoise waters. Mangrove trees lines the edges of the campground, a plus for their erosion prevention benefits, but they can get a little smelly, as their roots are in constant state of decay from standing in water. Mangroves are protected thanks to their role as foundation for ecosystems around the world, so they are revered and there is no getting rid of them without special compensation. There's nothing fancy about Sunburst, but some will find that the rural atmosphere is a welcome reprieve from busy city life as well as from the heavily commercialized atmosphere found in Key West and increasingly throughout the Keys. For those who prefer a more modern, standardized environment, there are plenty of campgrounds nearby that will fit the bill.

Basics

Operated By: National Home Communities. **Open:** All year. **Site Assignment:** Length of stay. **Registration:** Office. **Fee:** $35; MC,V, D,AE. **Parking:** Yes.

Facilities

Number of RV Sites: 94. **Number of Tent-Only Sites:** 6. **Hookups:** Electric (30, 50 amps), water, sewage, cable TV. **Each Site:** Picnic table, some w/ grill. **Dump Station:** Yes. **Laundry:** Yes. **Pay Phone:** Yes. **Rest Rooms and Showers:** Yes. **Fuel:** No. **Propane:** No. **Internal Roads:** Paved, in good condition. **RV Service:** Referral. **Market:** Convenience mart 1.5 mi. west to US 1 (Overseas Hwy.), supermarket 8 mi. north on US 1. **Restaurant:** 1.5 mi. west to US 1. **General Store:** Yes. **Vending:** Yes. **Swimming Pool:** Yes. **Playground:** No. **Other:** Paddleboat & kayak rentals, rec room. **Activities:** Boating, fishing, winter recreation activities include bingo & group dinners. **Nearby Attractions:** Beach, Key West. **Additional Information:** Florida Keys & Key West Tourist Council, (800) 648-5510, www.fla-keys.com.

Restrictions

Pets: On leash only. **Fires:** In grill only. **Alcoholic Beverages:** Allowed. **Vehicle Maximum Length:** 42 ft.—call ahead.

To Get There

US 1 south from Miami 81 mi. to mile marker 19, less than a mile further south to Johnson Rd., left 1 mile to campground on right, sign says Lazy Lake.

SUNRISE

Markham Park

16001 W. SR 84, Sunrise 33326. T: (954) 389-2000; www.broward.org/parks.

RV: ★★★ Tent: ★★★★

Beauty: ★★★	Site Privacy: ★★★
Spaciousness: ★★★	Quiet: ★★★★
Security: ★★★★	Cleanliness: ★★★★★
Insect Control: ★★★	Facilities: ★★★★★

Markham Park may be smaller than other nearby RV campgrounds like C.B. Smith Park, but its proximity to the Everglades gives this park an edge than can't be matched in the area. An abundance of alligators fill the waterways, canals, and lakes of the park, so keep dogs leashed and away from water. Other fauna include raccoons, foxes, and deer, and there have even been sightings of Florida's endangered panther on the outskirts of the park. Hike through the woods in the southwest corner of the park to a land bridge over the canal and to the dike, which provides a rare hilltop hike along the edge of the Everglades. It's a great place to enjoy the sunset—but don't stay too late, the walk back through darkened woodlands can be eerie! Ample trees give a wilderness feel that is largely missing in most of South Florida. Cul-de-sacs provided for camping create small, private enclaves for small groups.

Basics

Operated By: Broward County. **Open:** All year. **Site Assignment:** First come, first served; weekends fill up fast so reservations suggested, deposit full amount or arrangement by agreement. **Registration:** At park office. **Fee:** $19 plus $4 for non-Florida residents Dec. 1–Mar. 31; MC,V, D. **Parking:** Yes.

Facilities

Number of RV Sites: 88. **Number of Tent-Only Sites:** 10. **Hookups:** Water, electric (20, 50 amps), sewer. **Each Site:** Grills or fire ring, picnic table. **Dump Station:** Yes. **Laundry:** No. **Pay Phone:** Yes. **Rest Rooms and Showers:** Yes. **Fuel:** No. **Propane:** No. **Internal Roads:** Paved, in good condition. **RV Service:** No. **Market:** Grocery & pharmacy across the street from entrance to the park. **Restaurant:** Snack bar at pool Feb.–Labor Day, restaurants across the street from the park entrance. **General Store:** No. **Vending:** No. **Swimming Pool:** Yes. **Playground:** Yes. **Other:** Boat ramp. **Activities:** Bike rentals, bike & jogging paths, canoe, paddleboat & johnboat rentals, fishing permitted, model airplane field, tennis, racquetball & target range. **Nearby Attractions:** Sawgrass Mills Mall (the world's largest outlet mall) is 5 mi. northwest, beaches are 15 mi. east in Fort Lauderdale & Hollywood. **Additional Information:** Greater Fort Lauderdale CVB, (800) 231-SUNNY, www.sunny.org.

Restrictions

Pets: On leash only. **Fires:** Ground fires in fire pits w/ park ranger permission only. **Alcoholic Beverages:** In designated areas only, no glass containers. **Vehicle Maximum Length:** None.

To Get There

I-595 west from Fort Lauderdale, about 15 mi. to Exit at SW 136th Ave., continue west on SR 84 about 1 mi. to park entrance on right.

TALLAHASSEE

Tallahassee RV Park

6504 Mahan Dr., Tallahassee 32308. T: (850) 878-7641; F: (850) 878-7082.

RV: ★★★ Tent: ★★

Beauty: ★	Site Privacy: ★
Spaciousness: ★★	Quiet: ★★★
Security: ★★★★★	Cleanliness: ★★★★★
Insect Control: ★★★	Facilities: ★★★

Made for you if you're just passing through, the Tallahassee RV Park is the long, grassy backyard of the Schlinger family home. Surrounded by pine trees, pretty oleanders, crepe myrtle, and honeysuckle, the park provides a clean, quiet, and restful spot for relaxing the road-weary. A bird house provides a similar way-station for feathered friends. Grassy, mostly pull-through sites are neat with a little extra greenery—each has a bush and a tree—if not as private as longer-term visitors might prefer. A central modem connection is provided in the office, along with basic supplies. A few extra sites are available in front when needed, which should keep the back lot from getting too crowded. This is a nice, rural residential location in spite of its easy access to the adjacent intersection of I-10 and US 90.

Basics

Operated By: Don Schlinger. **Open:** All year. **Site Assignment:** Reservations accepted w/ credit card number, refunds w/ 24 hour cancellation. **Registration:** Office, late registrants self-register. **Fee:** $22.75; MC,V, D. **Parking:** Yes.

Facilities

Number of RV Sites: 66. **Number of Tent-Only Sites:** 0. **Hookups:** Water, electric (20, 30, 50 amps) Sewer. **Each Site:** Picnic table, pine tree, & a bush. **Dump Station:** No. **Laundry:** No. **Pay Phone:** No. **Rest Rooms and Showers:** Yes. **Fuel:** No. **Propane:** No. **Internal Roads:** Paved, in good condition. **RV Service:** Referral. **Market:** 3 mi. west on US 90 to Publix. **Restaurant:** 2 mi. west on US 90. **General Store:** Yes. **Vending:** No. **Swimming Pool:** No. **Playground:** No. **Activities:** Inquire at campground. **Nearby Attractions:** Capitol city of Tallahassee, Florida State University. **Additional Information:** Tallahassee Area CVB, (800) 628-2866.

Restrictions

Pets: On leash only. **Fires:** In grill only. **Alcoholic Beverages:** Allowed. **Vehicle Maximum Length:** None.

To Get There

I-10 Exit 31A at US 90, west 0.5 mi. to campground on right.

TENNILLE

Steinhatchee RV Refuge

P.O. Box 48, Perry 32348. T: (352) 498-5192 or (800) 589-1541; www.steinhatcheeoutpost.com; steinhatchee@perry.gulfnet.com.

RV: ★★★ Tent: ★★

Beauty: ★★	Site Privacy: ★★
Spaciousness: ★★★	Quiet: ★★★★★
Security: ★★★	Cleanliness: ★★★
Insect Control: ★★	Facilities: ★★★★

Lonely but not forgotten, this hunters' haven is one of the last vestiges of natural Florida. How long it will last, sandwiched between high-tourist traffic areas of the Gulf Coast and Panama Beach, isn't likely to be long. Not to mention the fact that ammunition is offered for sale at area convenient stores—perhaps wildlife is as at risk now as it will be in the near future when development comes to town. RVers may enjoy the extreme quiet and laid-back atmosphere of the park, especially if they're here to enjoy the adjacent nature opportunities along Steinhatchee River and the Gulf of Mexico. Wide, grassy sites provide an easy backdrop and parking spot, but don't expect the polished shine of some other RV resorts. This rustic piece of Old Florida is for hearty Florida crackers (our slang for natives).

Basics

Operated By: Private operator. **Open:** All year. **Site Assignment:** Reservations available. **Registration:** Camp store. **Fee:** $18. **Parking:** Yes.

Facilities

Number of RV Sites: 100. **Number of Tent-Only Sites:** 0. **Hookups:** Water, electric, sewer. **Each Site:** Picnic table, grill, some w/ patio. **Dump Station:** Yes. **Laundry:** Yes. **Pay Phone:** Yes. **Rest Rooms and Showers:** Yes. **Fuel:** Yes. **Propane:** Yes. **Internal Roads:** Grass. **RV Service:** Referral. **Market:** On site. **Restaurant:** If livers, gizzards, & okra work for you, restaurant on site at the camp store. **General Store:** Yes. **Vending:** Yes. **Swimming Pool:** No. **Playground:** Yes. **Other:** Volleyball, basketball courts. **Activities:** Fishing, volleyball, basketball, boating. **Nearby Attractions:** Beaver Spring Creek, Cooper Spring Creek, Steinhatchee Falls.

Restrictions

Pets: On leash only. **Fires:** In grill only. **Alcoholic Beverages:** Allowed. **Vehicle Maximum Length:** None.

To Get There

US 19 to Tennille at Hwy. 51, camp to the left/southwest.

THONOTOSASSA (TAMPA)

Hillsborough River State Park

15402 US 301 North, Thonotosassa 33592. T: (813) 987-6771; www.myFlorida.com.

RV ★★★★ Tent ★★★★★

Beauty: ★★★★★ Site Privacy: ★★★
Spaciousness: ★★★★ Quiet: ★★★★★
Security: ★★★★★ Cleanliness: ★★★
Insect Control: ★★★ Facilities: ★★★★

Designated a park in 1936, this 2,994-acre plot of land boasts oak, hickory, magnolia, and native sabal palm trees, with an undergrowth of palms that ensures you'll remember you're in Florida. Wild deer, bobcat, foxes, alligators, raccoons, grey squirrels, armadillos, and snakes take cover in the brush and along the scenic Hillsborough River, which runs through the park and features a unique set of rapids for canoeists and kayakers. A suspension bridge carries hikers across the river to hike a section of the Florida Trail.

Basics

Operated By: Florida Dept. of Environmental Protection, Division of Recreation & Parks. **Open:** All year. **Site Assignment:** First come, first served; reservations accepted by phone w/ credit card up to 11 months in advance, full refund if cancelled by 5 p.m. the day prior. **Registration:** Park office. **Fee:** $16.70; MC, V. **Parking:** Yes.

Facilities

Number of RV Sites: 64. **Number of Tent-Only Sites:** 30. **Hookups:** Water, electric (30 amps). **Each Site:** Picnic table, fire ring. **Dump Station:** Yes. **Laundry:** Yes. **Pay Phone:** Yes. **Rest Rooms and Showers:** Yes. **Fuel:** No. **Propane:** No. **Internal Roads:** Paved & crushed shell, in good condition. **RV Service:** No. **Market:** 9 mi. south to Tampa. **Restaurant:** 9 mi. south to Tampa. **General Store:** Yes. **Vending:** Yes. **Swimming Pool:** Yes. **Playground:** Yes. **Other:** Boat ramp, hiking trails, bridges over river, Historic Fort Foster. **Activities:** Hiking, canoeing, kayaking, fishing, guided tours of fort on weekends, special events. **Nearby Attractions:** Busch Gardens, Adventure Island Water Park, Museum of Science & Industry. **Additional Information:** Tampa Bay CVB, (800) 44-TAMPA, www.visittampabay.com.

Restrictions

Pets: On leash only and in designated areas only, proof of rabies vaccination. **Fires:** In grills or fire rings only. **Alcoholic Beverages:** Not allowed. **Vehicle Maximum Length:** None. **Other:** No firearms, no fireworks, no collecting of firewood or any other flora or fauna, no feeding of wildlife.

To Get There

I-75 Exit at Fowler Ave., east 5 mi. to US 301, north 9 mi. to park on left.

WEST PALM BEACH

Lion Country Safari KOA

2000 Lion Country Safari Rd., Loxahatchee 33470. T: (561) 793-9797 or (800) 562-9115; F: (561) 793-9603; www.lioncountrysafari.com; koa@lioncountrysafari.com.

RV ★★★★★ Tent ★★★★

Beauty: ★★★ Site Privacy: ★★
Spaciousness: ★★★ Quiet: ★★★
Security: ★★★★★ Cleanliness: ★★★★★
Insect Control: ★★★★ Facilities: ★★★★★

Through the village of Royal Palm Beach and past the interesting city of Wellington where many residents are aviators and share runways for driveways, finally you'll find a very unique attraction—Lion Country Safari, home to hundreds of African animals for more than 30 years.

Basics

Operated By: Managers. **Open:** All year. **Site Assignment:** Reservations accepted, 1-night deposit required, refundable up to 48 hours in advance, less a $4 administrative fee. **Registration:** Park office. **Fee:** $27.50; M, V, D, AE. **Parking:** Yes.

Facilities

Number of RV Sites: 203. **Number of Tent-Only Sites:** 22. **Hookups:** Water, electric (30, 50 amps), sewer. **Each Site:** Picnic table, concrete pad. **Dump Station:** Yes. **Laundry:** Yes. **Pay Phone:** Yes. **Rest Rooms and Showers:** Yes. **Fuel:** No. **Propane:** Yes. **Internal Roads:** Paved, in good condition. **RV Service:** Referral. **Market:** Approx. 10 mi. east on Southern Blvd. **Restaurant:** Approx. 4 mi. east on Southern Blvd. **General Store:** Yes. **Vending:** Yes. **Swimming Pool:** Yes. **Playground:** Yes. **Other:** Horseshoes, shuffleboard, volleyball, basketball & petanque (similar to bocci) courts. **Activities:** Swimming, horseshoes, shuffleboard, basketball, petanque, visiting the adjacent Lion Country Safari. **Nearby Attractions:** Lion Country Safari, a 500-acre wildlife preserve park where African animals such as rhinoceroses, elephants, lions, tigers are among the more than 1,000 animals who roam free throughout the preserve. Visitors may observe the animals from the safety of enclosed vehicles as they drive through the preserve. An amusement park offers rides, mini-golf, paddle boats, petting zoo. **Additional Information:** Palm Beach County CVB, (800) 554-PALM, www.palmbeachfl.com.

Restrictions

Pets: On leash only. **Fires:** In grill only. **Alcoholic Beverages:** Allowed. **Vehicle Maximum Length:** Big rigs welcome. **Other:** Quiet hours 10 p.m.–8 a.m., no bike riding after dusk, children must wear helmets when riding.

To Get There

Exit I-95 at Southern Blvd., west 20 mi. to campground.

Georgia

It is with her high Appalachian views; her rich history memorialized in stately mansions and great plantations; her primordial swamps crawling with creatures and draped in moss; her golden coast graced with wide beaches and magical islands; and with her great winding rivers feeding the land and imagination that Georgia beckons. Likely, after you journey through the state and experience firsthand her richness, the memory of your stay will be slow to fade. Begin your camping expedition in north Georgia's mountainous region. The days are cool, even when summer swelters below, and thundering waterfalls, miles of hiking trails, and lazy floats down the **Chattahoochee River** occupy visitors. Just around the corner, you might be surprised by **Helen,** a Bavarian town seemingly transplanted from the Alps to America's Deep South.

Move on to the **Atlanta** metro region. While it may seem strange to choose a campsite near this bustling metropolis, the number of recreational opportunities in this area will surprise you. The Chattahoochee River meanders through Atlanta, where river recreation opportunities await. Be sure to visit **Stone Mountain,** a monolith of granite displaying one of the world's largest relief sculptures. Venture on foot up the side of the mountain or take a sky lift to the top to enjoy a breathtaking view. Below, visit the **Antebellum Plantation,** where you can wander through both an 1800's mansion and slave quarters. After exploring, brush yourself off and visit some of Atlanta's cultural treasures including the **Civil War Museum, High Museum of Art,** and the **Margaret Mitchell House,** where the author penned *Gone With the Wind.*

As you travel southward, you can't help but be mesmerized by the scenic expanse of 90 miles of Georgian coastline. Feel the warm salt air hug you as you adventure to one of the state's many islands. **Cumberland Island** admits only 300 visitors each day to enjoy and explore its untamed wilderness, but camping is allowed. Enjoy the **Okefenokee National Wildlife Refuge** from a boat, or dare yourself to paddle a canoe through the blackwater swamp as you watch the surface bubble with the teeming life below. Visit sweet **Savannah,** whose curious inhabitants and beautiful scenery were recently popularized by the book and film *Midnight in the Garden of Good and Evil.* You'll soon learn that Savannah didn't need Hollywood's endorsement; she is a star of her own making. Savannah makes a nice transition to Georgia's Historic South, where campers can hike the trails of **Oconee National Forest** or fish on **Oconee Lake.** Canoeing and camping along the **Altamaha River,** lined by swamps and sandbars, provides campers and nature lovers a grand adventure. With so much to do, Georgia and her charm will likely entice you to a second visit.

Campground Profiles

ALBANY

The Parks at Chehaw

Philema Rd. (Hwy. 91N), Albany 31701. T: (229) 430-5275; www.parsatchehaw.org.

★★★★ ★★★★

Beauty: ★★★★
Site Privacy: ★★
Spaciousness: ★★★★
Quiet: ★★★★
Security: ★★★★
Cleanliness: ★★★★
Insect Control: ★★★
Facilities: ★★★★★

Located just outside of Albany, this 800-acre park is a great destination for families. Fairly suburban in nature, the park has 52 RV sites that are moderately spaced but offer little privacy. Each site has water and electrical hookups and all back-in parking. The camping is not remarkable, but the activities nearby are. Within short walking distance is an amazing contemporary playground with slides, rungs, and other fun activities. Fishing, cycling, mountain biking, and hiking are all recreation possibilities, and those wishing to see cheetahs, beers, bison or elk in the Georgia piney woods only need walk a short distance to the Wild Animal Park.

BASICS

Operated By: John Fowler. **Open:** All year. **Site Assignment:** First come, first served. **Registration:** At ticket booth prior to set up. **Fee:** $14 RV, $8 tent. **Parking:** 2 vehicles per site.

FACILITIES

Number of Multipurpose Sites: 52. **Hookups:** Water, electric (30 amps). **Each Site:** Water, electricity. **Dump Station:** Yes. **Laundry:** Yes. **Pay Phone:** No. **Rest Rooms and Showers:** Yes. **Fuel:** 5 min. on Philema Rd. **Propane:** No. **Internal Roads:** Dirt. **RV Service:** No. **Market:** 5 min. on Philema Rd. **Restaurant:** Savanna Café. **General Store:** Gift shop. **Vending:** Yes. **Swimming Pool:** No. **Playground:** Yes. **Other:** Covered picnic shelters by reservation. **Activities:** BMX riding, hiking, fishing, mountain biking, train rides, playground. **Nearby Attractions:** Public boat ramp (1 mi.), Wild Animal Park, Mt. Zion Albany Civil Rights Movement Museum, Albany Museum of Art.

RESTRICTIONS

Pets: On leash only. **Fires:** Allowed. **Alcoholic Beverages:** Not allowed. **Vehicle Maximum Length:** None. **Other:** 14-day max. stay limit.

TO GET THERE

From Atlanta, take I-75S to Exit 32 (Hwy. 300). Go south on Hwy. 300, then turn right on Hwy. 32. Follow Hwy. 32 and turn left on Hwy. 91 (Philema Rd.); go 9 mi. to the park, which is on the right.

APPLING

Mistletoe State Park

Rte. 1 Box 335, Appling 30802. T: (706) 541-0321; www.gastateparks.org.

Beauty: ★★★★★	Site Privacy: ★★★★
Spaciousness: ★★★★	Quiet: ★★★
Security: ★★★★★	Cleanliness: ★★★★
Insect Control: ★★★★	Facilities: ★★★

Located immediately northwest of Augusta, Mistletoe State Park is known as one of the best bass fishing destinations in the United States. Camping is relegated to the northern part of the 1,900 acre park, but comes with great views of the lake. Primitive camping is limited to four walk-in sites. For RVs, back-in sites dominate, but there are a few pull-throughs. Site size and privacy vary quite a bit; look around, and try to get sites 20 or 79—these are the cream of the crop. Shuffleboard, volleyball, and hiking are available, if you didn't come to fish. Two trails leave from the campground to connect with the rest of the park.

Basics

Operated By: Georgia Dept. of Natural Resources. **Open:** All year. **Site Assignment:** Reservations or first come, first served. **Registration:** At camp office. **Fee:** $13–$15. **Parking:** Yes.

Facilities

Number of Multipurpose Sites: 92. **Hookups:** Water, electric (30 amps). **Each Site:** Grill, fire ring, picnic table, lantern pole. **Dump Station:** Yes. **Laundry:** Yes. **Pay Phone:** Yes. **Rest Rooms and Showers:** Yes. **Fuel:** No. **Propane:** No. **Internal Roads:** Gravel. **RV Service:** 15 mi. in Thompson. **Market:** In Thompson. **Restaurant:** In Thompson. **General Store:** No. **Vending:** Yes. **Swimming Pool:** No. **Playground:** Yes. **Activities:** Shuffleboard, volleyball, canoe rental, hiking, biking. **Nearby Attractions:** Augusta, Fun City, Golf Museum, Riverwalk.

Restrictions

Pets: On leash only. **Fires:** Allowed. **Alcoholic Beverages:** Not allowed. **Vehicle Maximum Length:** 50 ft. **Other:** 14-day max. stay limit.

To Get There

From I-20, take Exit 175 (Hwy. 150). Go north 7.9 mi. to the park.

BISHOP

Pine Lake RV Campground

5540 High Shoals Rd., Hwy. 186, Bishop 30621. T: (706) 769-5486; F: (706) 769-6553; members.aol.com/pinelakerv/index.html; pinelakerv@aol.com.

RV ★★★★ Tent ★★★

Beauty: ★★★★	Site Privacy: ★★★★
Spaciousness: ★★	Quiet: ★★★★
Security: ★★★	Cleanliness: ★★★★
Insect Control: ★★★	Facilities: ★★★

If you can get past the kitschy "Happy Campers are Our Business" slogan, this is a surprisingly nice, nature-oriented private campground. The pretty setting and the people (a mostly older crowd when we visited) together make this a pleasant place to be, picturesque and heavily wooded. It is a rural spot in north-central Georgia, with good security in part due to its remoteness. There are both back-in and pull-through sites, and although they are smallish, they have foliage between them for better privacy than is offered at a lot of commercial campgrounds. Also, despite the lovely hilly surroundings, the campsites themselves are flat, with gravel ground cover. We recommend sites 3, 15, and 16 in particular. The ponds here are stocked with catfish, bass, and bluegill, but they do have a bit of an algae problem. For its privacy, beauty, friendliness, and character, this campground is a delight.

Basics

Operated By: Britt, Linda, & John Chandler. **Open:** All year. **Site Assignment:** Revervations preferred. **Registration:** At camp office. **Fee:** $21. **Parking:** On site.

Facilities

Number of RV Sites: 23. **Number of Tent-Only Sites:** 7. **Hookups:** Water, electric (30 amps), sewer. **Each Site:** Gravel site. **Dump Station:** Yes. **Laundry:** Yes. **Pay Phone:** Yes. **Rest Rooms and Showers:** Yes. **Fuel:** No. **Propane:** No. **Internal Roads:** Gravel. **RV Service:** In Athens. **Market:** In Athens or Watkinsville. **Restaurant:** In Athens or Watkinsville. **General Store:** Yes. **Vending:** Yes. **Swimming Pool:** No. **Playground:** Yes. **Activities:** Bird-watching, nature trails. **Nearby Attractions:** State Botanical Gardens, antebellum homes, University of Georgia.

Restrictions

Pets: On leash only. **Fires:** Not allowed. **Alcoholic Beverages:** Not allowed. **Vehicle Maximum Length:** None.

To Get There

From I-20, go north on Hwy. 441-129 to Bishop. Turn west on Hwy. 186 and go 1.4 mi. to entrance.

BLAIRSVILLE

Vogel State Park

7485 Vogel State Park Rd., Blairsville 30512. T: (706) 745-2628; www.gastateparks.org.

RV ★★★★ Tent ★★★★

Beauty: ★★★★★	Site Privacy: ★★★★
Spaciousness: ★★★★	Quiet: ★★★
Security: ★★★★	Cleanliness: ★★★★
Insect Control: ★★★★	Facilities: ★★★

Many of today's state parks wouldn't exist, at least not as we reocognize them, if not for the work of the Civilian Conservation Corps—Vogel State Park is one such park. The CCC's handiwork is easily seen here, and a small museum honors their work. When the heat of the summer hits the rest of the state, Vogel is a great place to visit. The 85 sites have electric and water hookups (there are 18 walk-in sites without these amenities). The sites are all large, but some of them are practically on top of one another. This place is very woody, hence quite shady, but the ground cover is minimal, reducing privacy in some areas. Recommended sites are toward the back of the campground. In addition to hiking, visitors can take a boat out on beautiful Lake Trahlyta.

Basics

Operated By: Georgia Dept. of Natural Resources. **Open:** All year. **Site Assignment:** Reservations or first come, first served. **Registration:** At Visitors Center. **Fee:** $10–$25. **Parking:** Yes.

Facilities

Number of RV Sites: 84. **Number of Tent-Only Sites:** 18. **Hookups:** Water, electric (50 amps). **Each Site:** Grassy, gravel pads. **Dump Station:** Yes. **Laundry:** Yes. **Pay Phone:** Yes. **Rest Rooms and Showers:** Yes. **Fuel:** No. **Propane:** No. **Internal Roads:** Paved. **RV Service:** No. **Market:** In Blairsville. **Restaurant:** In Owltown or Hiawasee. **General Store:** Yes. **Vending:** Yes. **Swimming Pool:** No. **Playground:** Yes. **Activities:** Swimming, fishing, hiking, paddle boating, mini golf. **Nearby Attractions:** CCC Museum, Appalachian Trail, Walasi-Yi Center, Dahlonega Gold Museum, numerous waterfalls.

Restrictions

Pets: Yes. **Fires:** In fire rings only. **Alcoholic Beverages:** Restricted. **Vehicle Max. Length:** 50 ft.

To Get There

11 mi. south of Blairsville via US Hwy. 19-129.

BLUE RIDGE

Lake Blue Ridge Campground

6050 Appalachian Hwy, Blue Ridge 30513. T: (706) 632-3031.

RV ★★★★ Tent ★★★★★

Beauty: ★★★★★	Site Privacy: ★★★★★
Spaciousness: ★★★★★	Quiet: ★★★★★
Security: ★★★★★	Cleanliness: ★★★
Insect Control: ★★★★★	Facilities: ★★★

Pretty much everything is secondary to the lake at Lake Blue Ridge, including campsite amenities. The surrounding North Georgia mountains and Chattahoochee National Forest lend the place a pristine air. This is not a great place for RVers though, as there are no hookups and no pull-throughs and few of the sites are level. However, if you're a camper who doesn't mind roughing it a bit (including a long walk to the outhouse), this is otherwise a really beautiful place to camp. Campsites are palatial in size and completely wooded, and the sites located in the lake loop (sites 49–56) are absolutely gorgeous. The lake offers the typical roster of water sports, and anglers can fish for bass, bream, catfish, perch, and crappie. A six-tenths-mile loop trail follows the lakeshore, providing good views of the water.

Basics

Operated By: USDA Forest Service. **Open:** Apr. 1–Oct. 31. **Site Assignment:** Inquire at campground. **Registration:** At campsite or w/ host. **Fee:** $8–$10. **Parking:** On site.

Facilities

Number of RV Sites: 0. **Number of Tent-Only Sites:** 58. **Hookups:** None. **Each Site:** Picnic table, grill, tent pads. **Dump Station:** No. **Laundry:** No. **Pay Phone:** No. **Rest Rooms and Showers:** Yes. **Fuel:** No. **Propane:** No. **Internal Roads:** Paved. **RV Service:** No. **Market:** In Blue Ridge. **Restaurant:** In Blue Ridge. **General Store:** Nearby on Old US 76. **Vending:** No. **Swimming Pool:** No. **Playground:** No. **Activities:** Hiking, boating, fishing, water skiing, swimming. **Nearby Attractions:** Blue Ridge Lake, scenic railway, fish hatchery, Chattahoochee National Forest. **Addi-**

tional Information: Fannin County Chamber, (800) 899-6867 or www.blueridgemountains.com.

RESTRICTIONS

Pets: On leash only. **Fires:** In fire rings only. **Alcoholic Beverages:** Allowed. **Vehicle Maximum Length:** None. **Other:** 14-day max. stay limit.

TO GET THERE

Take Old US 76 east for 1.5 mi. to Dry Branch Road. Turn right and go 3 mi. to entrance sign.

BRUNSWICK

Blythe Island Regional Park

6616 Blythe Island Hwy., Brunswick 31523.
T: (800) 343-7855 or (912) 261-3805.

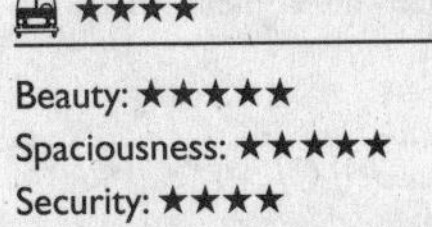

RV ★★★★ Tent ★★★★

Beauty: ★★★★★ Site Privacy: ★★★★
Spaciousness: ★★★★★ Quiet: ★★★★★
Security: ★★★★ Cleanliness: ★★★★
Insect Control: ★★★ Facilities: ★★★

This campground is a great place to use as a base for touring the Jekyll Island area and nearby beaches. Pretty and well-maintained, Blythe Island's sites are surprisingly large. Lovely shade trees and a variety of native scrub brush provide some privacy between sites. Sites 54, 56, 57, 60, 61, 63, 65, and 67 are the largest, most secluded, and most attractive in the campground. The small lake is stocked with fish for anglers, and a nice swimming beach serves one section. None of the sites are actually lakeside, though none are very far from the water; the closest sites to the swimming beach are 1–13. The wide variety of on-site activities include hiking and biking trails, boat and kayak rentals, tournament horseshoes, and a field archery range. Campers can also make use of the nearby Blythe Island Marina to arrange for fishing or touring excursions or to dock their own boats.

BASICS

Operated By: County Glynn. **Open:** All year. **Site Assignment:** Reservations or first come, first served. **Registration:** At camp office. **Fee:** $20–$23. **Parking:** Yes.

FACILITIES

Number of RV Sites: 97. **Number of Tent-Only Sites:** 26. **Hookups:** Water, electric (30 amps), sewer. **Each Site:** Shell covering. **Dump Station:** Yes. **Laundry:** Yes. **Pay Phone:** Yes. **Rest Rooms and Showers:** Yes. **Fuel:** No. **Propane:** Yes. **Internal Roads:** Gravel. **RV Service:** In Brunswick. **Market:** In Brunswick or Dock Junction. **Restaurant:** In Fancy Bluff or Brunswick. **General Store:** No. **Vending:** Yes. **Swimming Pool:** No. **Playground:** Yes. **Activities:** Swimming, fishing, boating, horseshoes, archery. **Nearby Attractions:** Saint Simons, Sea Island, & Jekyll Islands, Cumberland Island.

RESTRICTIONS

Pets: On leash only. **Fires:** Allowed. **Alcoholic Beverages:** Not allowed. **Vehicle Maximum Length:** 40 ft.

TO GET THERE

From I-95, take Exit 29 (US 17 S.). Go 1 mi. to GA 303 N., then 3 mi. to campground.

BUFORD

Shoal Creek

6300 Shadburn Ferry Rd., Buford 30518.
T: (877) 444-6777.

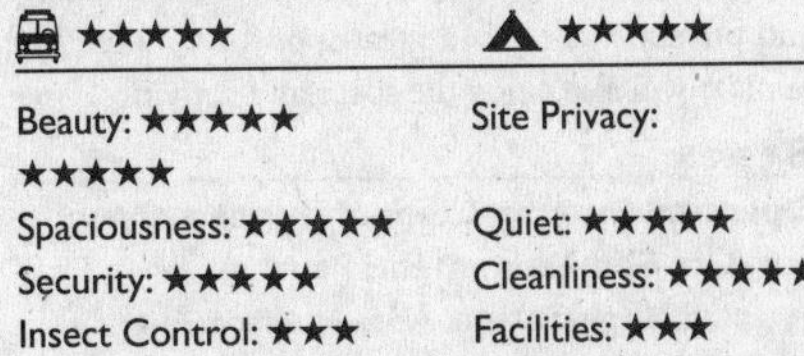

RV ★★★★★ Tent ★★★★★

Beauty: ★★★★★ Site Privacy: ★★★★★
Spaciousness: ★★★★★ Quiet: ★★★★★
Security: ★★★★★ Cleanliness: ★★★★★
Insect Control: ★★★ Facilities: ★★★

This pretty, well-run campground is one of the finest in Georgia. Set on the shores of Lake Lanier in a ritzy, suburban neighborhood and overseen by the U.S. Army Corps of Engineers, Shoal Creek is a popular place that can get packed with campers. In addition, the lakeside setting means that boat noise is a fact of life for visitors; ask attendants for recommendations on quieter campsites. All sites here are quite large, with lovely shade trees above and screening foliage in between. Sites 55–57 are particularly shady and private; nearby, sites 36–39 and 51–54 are also particularly sizable and secluded, site 40 even more so. The half-loop that makes up sites 31–35 has breathtaking lake views. Lake Lanier features ten other campgrounds (see profiles for Lake Lanier Islands and Chestnut Ridge in Flowery Branch), 43 day-use parks, ten marinas, and nine state, county, and city parks.

BASICS

Operated By: Army Corps of Engineers. **Open:** Mar. 30–Sept. 23. **Site Assignment:** Reservations accepted. **Registration:** Entrance station. **Fee:** $12–$22, plus day use fees. **Parking:** limited.

FACILITIES

Number of Multipurpose Sites: 107. **Hookups:** Some water, some electric (30 amps). **Each Site:** Table, grill, lantern posts, fire pit. **Dump Station:** Yes. **Laundry:** Yes. **Pay Phone:** Yes. **Rest Rooms and Showers:** Yes. **Fuel:** No. **Propane:** No. **Internal Roads:** Paved. **RV Service:** No. **Market:** In Buford. **Restaurant:** In Buford. **General Store:** Less than 10 mi. **Vending:** Drinks only. **Swimming Pool:** No. **Playground:** Yes. **Other:** Swim area, boat ramp. **Activities:** Baseball, horseshoes. **Nearby Attractions:** Lake Lanier Island water park & golf course, concerts. **Additional Information:** Visitor Center, (770) 945-9531.

RESTRICTIONS

Pets: On leash only. **Fires:** In fire rings only. **Alcoholic Beverages:** Not allowed. **Vehicle Maximum Length:** None. **Other:** 14-day max. stay limit.

TO GET THERE

From Atlanta, take I-85N to I-985 take Exit 8 and turn left onto Hwy. 347. Turn left onto McEver Rd. then right on Shadburn Ferry Rd., which ends at the campground.

CARTERSVILLE

Allatoona Landing Campground

24 Allatoona Landing Rd., Cartersville 30121.
T: (770) 974-6068.

RV ★★★ Tent ★★★

Beauty: ★★★★ Site Privacy: ★★★
Spaciousness: ★★ Quiet: ★★★
Security: ★★★★ Cleanliness: ★★★★
Insect Control: ★★★★ Facilities: ★★★

This large campground is very popular, which means it's often crowded. Combine that with small- to mid-size campsites, and you lose a little when it comes to spaciousness and privacy. The owners of Allatoona Landing do run a tight ship, so the property is well-maintained and reasonably clean. Be aware that railroad tracks pass very near the campground, so some train noise is inevitable (especially for those sites nearest the campground office). Allatoona Lake offers plenty of options for water sports enthusiasts, including elaborate boating facilities, and an extensive swimming beach. Sites 85, 86, 93, 95–101, and 103 are shaded and pretty, while 87 and 89–92 are the nicest waterfront sites. Sites 60–73 and 75, 77, 79, 81, 83, and 88 are closest to the swimming beach.

BASICS

Operated By: Private operator. **Open:** All year. **Site Assignment:** By reservation. **Registration:** At camp office. **Fee:** $20–$25. **Parking:** 2 vehicles per site.

FACILITIES

Number of RV Sites: 120. **Number of Tent-Only Sites:** 20. **Hookups:** Water, electric (30, 50 amps), sewer. **Each Site:** Picnic table. **Dump Station:** Yes. **Laundry:** Yes. **Pay Phone:** Yes. **Rest Rooms and Showers:** Yes. **Fuel:** Yes. **Propane:** Yes. **Internal Roads:** Paved. **RV Service:** Yes. **Market:** In Bartow or Acworth. **Restaurant:** In Cartersville or Acworth. **General Store:** Yes. **Vending:** Yes. **Swimming Pool:** Yes. **Playground:** Yes. **Activities:** Fishing, boating. **Nearby Attractions:** Barnsly Gardens, Coopers Iron Works, Dellinger Park Complex, Etowah Arts Gallery, Etowah Indian Mounds, Lake Allatoona, Red Top State Park, Royal Oaks Golf Course. **Additional Information:** Cartersville-Barton County Welcome Center, (770) 387-1357.

RESTRICTIONS

Pets: On leash, some restrictions. **Fires:** In designated areas only. **Alcoholic Beverages:** Allowed. **Vehicle Maximum Length:** 25 ft.

TO GET THERE

From I-75, take Exit 283. Go 2 mi. to campground entrance (in front of 2nd set of RR tracks).

CARTERSVILLE

Red Top Mountain State Park

50 Lodge Rd., Cartersville 30120. T: (770) 975-4226; www.gastateparks.org.

RV ★★★★ Tent ★★★★

Beauty: ★★★★ Site Privacy: ★★★
Spaciousness: ★★★ Quiet: ★★★★
Security: ★★★★★ Cleanliness: ★★★★
Insect Control: ★★★★ Facilities: ★★★

Red Top Mountain was once an important mining area for iron—the red-colored soil gives this away.

Located a short distance from I-75 and near the town of Acworth, this park offers great camping opportunities on Allatoona Lake. Tent campers have a section all to themselves (sites 37–60), but water and power hookups are only available in the 63 other sites. Sites 1–12 are pull-throughs; the rest are back-ins. The area is nicely wooded, offering shade to small but picturesque sites. Every Saturday from May until early September, the park has a bluegrass and storytelling program. In addition to tennis, mini golf, and boating, the park has 11.5 miles of trails to explore.

BASICS

Operated By: Georgia Dept. of Natural Resources. **Open:** All year. **Site Assignment:** Reservations or first come, first served. **Registration:** At visitor center or lodge. **Fee:** $12–$18. **Parking:** 2 vehicles per site.

FACILITIES

Number of RV Sites: 63. **Number of Tent-Only Sites:** 29. **Hookups:** Water, electric (50 amps). **Each Site:** Wooded w/ tent pad, grill, fire ring. **Dump Station:** Yes. **Laundry:** No. **Pay Phone:** Yes. **Rest Rooms and Showers:** Yes. **Fuel:** No. **Propane:** No. **Internal Roads:** Paved. **RV Service:** In Acworth. **Market:** In Acworth. **Restaurant:** In Cartersville or Acworth. **General Store:** In visitor center. **Vending:** Yes. **Swimming Pool:** Yes. **Playground:** Yes. **Other:** Gated park. **Activities:** Tennis, mini golf, hiking, boating, swimming, game room. **Nearby Attractions:** Etowah Indian Mounds State Historic Site, Kennesaw Mountain National Battlefield Park, Weinman Mineral Museum. **Additional Information:** Cartersville-Barton County Welcome Center, (770) 387-1357.

RESTRICTIONS

Pets: On leash only. **Fires:** In fire rings only. **Alcoholic Beverages:** At sites only. **Vehicle Maximum Length:** 40 ft. **Other:** No bicycles allowed on trails.

TO GET THERE

From Atlanta, go north on I-75 to Exit 285. Go right on Red Top Mountain Rd. across Lake Allatoona to the state park.

CHATSWORTH

Woodring Branch Campground

5026 Woodring Branch Rd., Oakman 30732. T: (706) 334-2248; www.reserveusa.com or www.sam.usace.army.mil/op/rec/carters.

RV ★★★★★ Tent ★★★★★

Beauty: ★★★★★	Site Privacy: ★★★★★
Spaciousness: ★★★★★	Quiet: ★★★★★
Security: ★★★★★	Cleanliness: ★★★★
Insect Control: ★★★★	Facilities: ★★★

This Corps of Engineers Campground is exceptionally beautiful and quiet, with most sites very close to the shores of Carters Lake. A very rural spot in the northwest corner of the state, this campground boasts huge wooded sites, with some foliage in between. All of the sites are back-ins, with paved RV and car spaces, fine (pea-sized) gravel pads for tents, picnic tables, and so on. Almost every site has a gorgeous lake view, and the most amazing is from site 35. Site 31 is especially secluded, although its view is not as stunning, and 17 is the most impressively huge. Don't let the spacious, peaceful atmosphere fool you, however. There is plenty of recreation to choose from, including water sports. The beauty and privacy make this a great spot for couples, but families will also enjoy the space and activities.

BASICS

Operated By: Army Corps of Engineers. **Open:** Apr.–Oct. **Site Assignment:** Reservations accepted. **Registration:** At camp office. **Fee:** $8–$18. **Parking:** Yes.

FACILITIES

Number of RV Sites: 31. **Number of Tent-Only Sites:** 11. **Hookups:** Water, electric (20, 30 amps). **Each Site:** Tent pad, picnic table. **Dump Station:** Yes. **Laundry:** Yes. **Pay Phone:** Yes. **Rest Rooms and Showers:** Yes. **Fuel:** No. **Propane:** No. **Internal Roads:** Paved. **RV Service:** No. **Market:** In Chatsworth. **Restaurant:** In Chatsworth. **General Store:** No. **Vending:** Soft drinks. **Swimming Pool:** Yes. **Playground:** Yes. **Activities:** Boating, hiking trails, water skiing. **Nearby Attractions:** Antique shopping, outlet mall, Cherokee Indian Museum, Fort Mountain State Park.

RESTRICTIONS

Pets: On leash only. **Fires:** In designated areas. **Alcoholic Beverages:** At sites only. **Vehicle Maximum Length:** None.

TO GET THERE

From Ellijay, travel west on Hwy. 282. Follow signs approximately 4 mi. to the campground

CLARKESVILLE

Moccasin Creek State Park

3655 Hwy. 197, Clarkesville 30523. T: (706) 947-3194.

RV ★★★★ Tent ★★★★

Beauty: ★★★★	Site Privacy: ★★★★
Spaciousness: ★★★★	Quiet: ★★★★
Security: ★★★★	Cleanliness: ★★★★
Insect Control: ★★★★	Facilities: ★★★

High in the Blue Ridge Mountains and surrounded on three sides by the enormous Lake Burton, Moccasin Creek State Park offers a unique opportunity for campers with disabilities. The majority of the property is wheelchair-accessible, including a fishing pier reserved exclusively for handicapped visitors, seniors, and children. Despite its mountainous location, the campground is relatively flat. This makes it easy to maneuver around in large RVs, bicycles, and wheelchairs. Canoeing on the lake is a treat, though the high elevation and terrain mean that sudden winds can blow up (some strong enough to tip canoes over in the lake's center). Several trails wind through the mountains around the lake, including an easy walk to Hemlock Falls and a more rugged trek to Moccasin Creek Falls. The fall colors are especially beautiful here, making it very difficult to score a vacancy during Oct.

BASICS

Operated By: Georgia Dept. of Natural Resources. **Open:** All year. **Site Assignment:** First come, first served. **Registration:** Office. **Fee:** $18–$22. **Parking:** On site.

FACILITIES

Number of RV Sites: 54. **Number of Tent-Only Sites:**. **Hookups:** Water, electric. **Dump Station:** Yes. **Laundry:** Yes. **Pay Phone:** Yes. **Rest Rooms and Showers:** Yes. **Fuel:** No. **Propane:** No. **Internal Roads:** Yes. **RV Service:** No. **Market:** In Clarkesville. **Restaurant:** In Clarkesville. **General Store:** On Hwy. 197. **Vending:** Yes. **Swimming Pool:** No. **Playground:** Yes. **Other:** Observation tower. **Activities:** Hiking, fishing, canoeing (seasonal). **Nearby Attractions:** Appalachian Trail, Chattahoochee National Forest.

RESTRICTIONS

Pets: On leash only. **Fires:** In fire rings only. **Alcoholic Beverages:** Not allowed. **Vehicle Maximum Length:** 40 ft.

TO GET THERE

20 mi. north of Clarkesville on GA 197 or 15 mi. west of Clayton on GA 76 & GA 197.

CLAYTON

Rabun Beach Campground

5100 Lake Rabun Rd., Lakemont 30552. T: (706) 782-3320; F: (706) 782-3320.

RV ★★★★ Tent ★★★★★

Beauty: ★★★★★	Site Privacy: ★★★★★
Spaciousness: ★★★★★	Quiet: ★★★★★
Security: ★★★★	Cleanliness: ★★★★
Insect Control: ★★★★★	Facilities: ★★

Those wanting a beautiful and secluded camping experience in rural Georgia will do well to visit Rabun Beach. A gravel road leads campers to 80 sites (5 of which are tent-only). Most of the RV-friendly sites, with water and electric hookups, are back-ins, but a few are pull-throughs. Though the entire area is attractive, sites 49 and 53 are truly gorgeous. No sites are situated directly on Lake Rabun, but all are within easy walking distance. Visitors have their pick of sites during the week, but even on busy weekends visitors will have little problem finding one of the many spacious and well-shaded sites unoccupied. Not far from this extraordinary campground is Tallulah Gorge State Park, sometimes referred to as the Grand Canyon of the southeast, and a 1.3 mile trail leads to 50-foot Angel Falls.

BASICS

Operated By: US Forest Service. **Open:** May–Nov. **Site Assignment:** First come, first served. **Registration:** At camp office; no reservations; cash or check only. **Fee:** $10–$18. **Parking:** In campground.

FACILITIES

Number of RV Sites: 75. **Number of Tent-Only Sites:** 5. **Hookups:** Water, electric (20 amps). **Each Site:** Grill, picnic table, tent pad. **Dump Station:** Yes. **Laundry:** No. **Pay Phone:** Yes. **Rest Rooms and Showers:** Yes. **Fuel:** No. **Propane:** No. **Internal Roads:** Gravel. **RV Service:** No. **Market:** 6 mi. **Restaurant:** 2 mi. **General Store:** No. **Vending:** No. **Swimming Pool:** No. **Playground:** No.

Other: Lake on site. **Activities:** Hiking, swimming, boating, fishing. **Nearby Attractions:** Angel Falls, Tallulah Gorge overlook. **Additional Information:** Rabun County Civic Center, (706) 212-2149.

RESTRICTIONS

Pets: On leash only. **Fires:** In fire rings only. **Alcoholic Beverages:** Allowed. **Vehicle Maximum Length:** 35 ft.

TO GET THERE

From Hwy. 441 in Clayton, go 2 mi. and turn right on the Wiley Connector. Go 0.1 mi. and turn left on Old Hwy. 441. Go 2 mi. and turn right on Lake Rabun Rd. The campground is 4 mi. ahead on the right.

COMMERCE

The Pottery Campgrounds

Exit 53, I-85, Commerce 30529. T: (800) 223-0667; www.cravenpottery.com.

RV ★★★ Tent n/a

Beauty: ★★★ Site Privacy: ★★★
Spaciousness: ★★★ Quiet: ★★★
Security: ★★★★ Cleanliness: ★★★
Insect Control: ★★★ Facilities: ★

A relatively new campground associated with The Pottery home and garden outlet store, The Pottery Plant greenhouse and gardens, and Stringers Fish Camp and Oyster Bar, the Pottery Campground is a no-frills way station for campers visiting area attractions. There are no activities or facilities of note—just hookups and a bathhouse. That said, the sites are of good size and mostly shady. Campsite 13 is long and shady, while site 48 is new and nicely set into the hillside; both are pull-throughs. If pottery-related shopping doesn't thrill you, both Lake Hartwell and Lake Lanier are nearby, along with a plethora of recreational options.

BASICS

Operated By: Craven, Inc. **Open:** All year. **Site Assignment:** First come, first served, 24-hours cancellation policy. **Registration:** At back house office, w/ security guard, or by envelope. **Fee:** $20. **Parking:** On site.

FACILITIES

Number of RV Sites: 52. **Number of Tent-Only Sites:** 0. **Hookups:** Water, electric (30 amps), sewer. **Each Site:** Brick oven, picnic table. **Dump Station:** Yes. **Laundry:** No. **Pay Phone:** Yes. **Rest Rooms and Showers:** Yes. **Fuel:** No. **Propane:** No. **Internal Roads:** Paved. **RV Service:** 10 mi. **Market:** 0.5 mi. **Restaurant:** Stringer's Fish Camp, 0.5 mi. **General Store:** 0.5 mi. **Vending:** Yes. **Swimming Pool:** No. **Playground:** No. **Activities:** Outlet shopping, watersports at nearby lakes. **Nearby Attractions:** Tanger outlet stores, The Pottery store, Pottery Plant greenhouse/gardens.

RESTRICTIONS

Pets: On leash only. **Fires:** In grills only. **Alcoholic Beverages:** Not allowed. **Vehicle Maximum Length:** None.

TO GET THERE

From I-85 N., take exit 149. Turn right onto Hwy. 441. The campground is on the right behind The Pottery store.

CORDELE

Georgia Veterans Memorial State Park

2459-A US Hwy 280 West, Cordele 31015. T: (229) 276-2371.

RV ★★★★ Tent ★★★★

Beauty: ★★★★★ Site Privacy: ★★★★
Spaciousness: ★★★★★ Quiet: ★★★★
Security: ★★★★ Cleanliness: ★★★★
Insect Control: ★★★ Facilities: ★★★★★

This popular campground, only a few miles from Cordele, has ample sites with moderate hardwood shade. The generally flat landscape is very picturesque and tranquil. RV Camping Areas 1 and 2 (sites 1–53) are arranged by Lake Blackshear, with campsites 1–27 set on the lakefront itself. These are the best sites in the campground, especially sites 25–27 (all are pretty, but site 27 is especially huge and gorgeous). Sites 52 and 53 are particularly large pull-throughs. Camping Area 3 (sites 54–76) is a separate loop set back in the woods; its sites are not as nice as the others. Across the lake are the park's main facilities (the visitor center, a museum, military exhibits, nature trails, etc.); that's also where you'll find tent camping areas and cottages. This campground has plenty of options for groups, from a fully equipped conference center to a separately-reserved, secluded area for group primitive camping.

BASICS

Operated By: Georgia Dept. of Natural Resources. **Open:** All year. **Site Assignment:** Can reserve waterfront or non-waterfront. **Registration:** At visitor center. **Fee:** RV $10.35–$20, tent $9.15–$18, cottages $75–$90. **Parking:** At site or in park.

FACILITIES

Number of RV Sites: 77. **Number of Tent-Only Sites:**. **Hookups:** Water, electric (30, 50 amps), cable. **Each Site:** Grills. **Dump Station:** Yes. **Laundry:** Yes. **Pay Phone:** Yes. **Rest Rooms and Showers:** Yes. **Fuel:** Nearby. **Propane:** Nearby. **Internal Roads:** Paved. **RV Service:** No. **Market:** In Codele. **Restaurant:** In Cordele. **General Store:** Yes. **Vending:** Yes. **Swimming Pool:** Yes. **Playground:** Yes. **Other:** 10 Cottages. **Activities:** Nature trail, golf, boating, water skiing, fishing model airplane flying. **Nearby Attractions:** Warner Robins Air Museum, Chehaw Wild Animal Park. **Additional Information:** Cordele Chamber of Commerce, (229) 273-1668 or www.cordele-crisp-chamber.com.

RESTRICTIONS

Pets: On leash only. **Fires:** In fire rings only. **Alcoholic Beverages:** At sites only. **Vehicle Maximum Length:** 50 ft.

TO GET THERE

The park is 9 mi. west of I-75 (Exit 101) near Cordele on US Hwy 280.

CUMMING

Bald Ridge

4100 Bald Ridge Rd., Cumming 30040. T: (770) 889-1591.

RV ★★★★ Tent ★★★★

Beauty: ★★★★★ Site Privacy: ★★★★
Spaciousness: ★★★★★ Quiet: ★★★★
Security: ★★★★★ Cleanliness: ★★★★★
Insect Control: ★★★ Facilities: ★★★

This extraordinarily well-manicured campground is situated in a nice suburban to rural area about 30 miles northeast of Atlanta. The sites vary from shady to open, with gorgeous views, though not a great deal of privacy, at lakefront sites 39–53. We also recommend lakefront sites 70–72, which offer lovely views and are also fairly secluded. Avoid sites 81 and 82 if possible, as they are adjacent to the sewer, and keep in mind noisy boats when choosing a site near the water. Lake Sidney Lanier is host to several Corps of Engineers campgrounds, and Bald Ridge is the flagship, with facilities to accommodate RVs and tents quite well (although the rest rooms are nicer at a couple of the other campgrounds). Some back-ins and some pull-throughs, the extremely large, paved sites also include a sizeable gravel picnic and tent area. Between the gates and general seclusion, security here is excellent, and it's a wonderful spot for families.

BASICS

Operated By: Army Corps of Engineers. **Open:** Feb. 22–Nov. 19. **Site Assignment:** Reservations accepted. **Registration:** Park entry station. **Fee:** $12–$22. **Parking:** On site.

FACILITIES

Number of RV Sites: 82. **Number of Tent-Only Sites:** 0. **Hookups:** Water, electric (30, 50 amps),sewer. **Each Site:** Picnic table, grill, fire pits. **Dump Station:** Yes. **Laundry:** Yes. **Pay Phone:** No. **Rest Rooms and Showers:** Yes. **Fuel:** Nearby. **Propane:** Nearby. **Internal Roads:** Paved. **RV Service:** No. **Market:** In Cumming. **Restaurant:** In Cumming. **General Store:** Nearby. **Vending:** Yes. **Swimming Pool:** No. **Playground:** Yes. **Activities:** Boating, fishing, swimming. **Nearby Attractions:** Lake Lanier Island water park & golf course. **Additional Information:** Cumming-Forsyth County Chamber of Commerce, (770) 887-6461 or www.forsythchamber.org,.

RESTRICTIONS

Pets: On leash only. **Fires:** In fire rings only. **Alcoholic Beverages:** Not allowed. **Vehicle Maximum Length:** None. **Other:** 14-day stay limit.

TO GET THERE

400N to Exit 16. Turn right on Pilgrim Mill Rd., then turn right on Sinclair Shores Rd. Turn left on Bald Rich Rd, which ends at the campground.

DARIEN

Inland Harbor RV Park

Hwy. 251 E, Darien 31305. T: (912) 437-6172.

RV ★★ Tent n/a

Beauty: ★★★ Site Privacy: ★★
Spaciousness: ★★★ Quiet: ★★
Security: ★★ Cleanliness: ★★★
Insect Control: ★★★ Facilities: ★

The sites, all pull-throughs, at Inland Harbor RV Park are of medium size overall, though they're still large for a private campground. Strictly a stopover on the way up or down the coast on I-95, this campground caters to big rigs and through-travelers. Sites are relatively well shaded, but there is not much screening between you and your neighbor. You probably wouldn't stick around the property to do anything but relax between road trips. That said, the campground is perfectly fine as a practical base for exploring coastal attractions. The proximity of the highway creates significant road noise, so ask for quieter sites away from the road.

Basics

Operated By: Lois Truhlar. **Open:** All year. **Site Assignment:** First come, first served. **Registration:** At office. **Fee:** $17. **Parking:** In campground.

Facilities

Number of RV Sites: 60. **Number of Tent-Only Sites:** 0. **Hookups:** Water, electric (50 amps), sewer, phone, cable. **Each Site:** Picnic table, grill. **Dump Station:** Yes. **Laundry:** Yes. **Pay Phone:** Yes. **Rest Rooms and Showers:** Yes. **Fuel:** No. **Propane:** No. **Internal Roads:** Paved. **RV Service:** No. **Market:** 1 mi. **Restaurant:** Less than 1 mi. **General Store:** No. **Vending:** No. **Swimming Pool:** No. **Playground:** No. **Activities:** Visiting the coast. **Nearby Attractions:** Rice Plantation, Sapalo Island.

Restrictions

Pets: Yes. **Fires:** In grills only. **Alcoholic Beverages:** Allowed. **Vehicle Maximum Length:** 70 ft.

To Get There

From I-95, go 2.5 mi. east on Hwy. 251 to the campground.

ELBERTON

Bobby Brown State Park

2509 Bobby Brown State Park Rd., Elberton 30635. T: (706) 213-2046; www.gastateparks.org.

RV: ★★★★ Tent: ★★★

Beauty: ★★★★ Site Privacy: ★★
Spaciousness: ★★★ Quiet: ★★★★
Security: ★★★★★ Cleanliness: ★★★★
Insect Control: ★★★★ Facilities: ★★★

One of several camping areas located on the Georgia–South Carolina border, Bobby Brown State Park is situated on what was once the historic boomtown of Petersburg, established in 1798. Now campers come to the 665-acre park to relax and take part in the many activities available here, including fishing, boating, swimming, and hiking. Water and electric hookups are available at the park's 61 sites, which are a mix of pull-throughs and back-ins. When compared to other state parks, these sites are a bit small, but they still are larger than many private campgrounds. If you want premium access to the Broad River, pay $1 more and stay at sites 3–13, but look to see if site 60 is open—it's arguably one of the best in the park. Visitors who get the itch to explore will want to check out Pioneer Nancy Hart's Cabin or the Granite Museum.

Basics

Operated By: Georgia Dept. of Natural Resources. **Open:** All year. **Site Assignment:** Reservations or first come, first served. **Registration:** At main office. **Fee:** $13–$16. **Parking:** 2 vehicles per site.

Facilities

Number of RV Sites: 61. **Number of Tent-Only Sites:** 2 primitive areas. **Hookups:** Water, electric (30, 50 amps). **Each Site:** Picnic table, grill, fire ring, lantern pole. **Dump Station:** Yes. **Laundry:** Yes. **Pay Phone:** Yes. **Rest Rooms and Showers:** Yes. **Fuel:** No. **Propane:** No. **Internal Roads:** Paved. **RV Service:** 22 mi. **Market:** 22 mi. **Restaurant:** 10 mi. **General Store:** No. **Vending:** Soft drinks. **Swimming Pool:** Yes. **Playground:** Yes. **Activities:** Hiking trails, boat launch, 72,000-acre lake, fishing pier, canoes, pedal boats. **Nearby Attractions:** Pioneer Nancy Hart's Cabin, Granite Museum.

Restrictions

Pets: On leash (6 ft. or less) only. **Fires:** In fire rings only. **Alcoholic Beverages:** At sites only. **Vehicle Max. Length:** 40 ft. **Other:** 14-day stay limit.

To Get There

From I-85, exit at Hwy. 175 and go to Elberton. Then take Hwy. 72 east for 15 mi. Turn right on Bobby Brown State Park Rd. Go 7 mi. to the park entrance.

ELLIJAY

Doll Mountain Campground

P.O. Box 96, Oakman 30732. T: (706) 276-4413; www.carterslake.com or www.reserveusa.com.

RV: ★★★★★ Tent: ★★★★★

Beauty: ★★★★★ Site Privacy: ★★★★★
Spaciousness: ★★★★★ Quiet: ★★★★★
Security: ★★★★ Cleanliness: ★★★★
Insect Control: ★★★★★ Facilities: ★★★

Doll Mountain Campground is an excellent property located on the shores of Carter Lake, itself an outdoor activity paradise. There are several camping and recreation areas to choose from on the lake, and Doll Mountain is among the nicest. Most campsites are very spacious, and all are heavily wooded. However, because the sites are strung out along a thin spit of land projecting into the lake, almost all sites have beautiful lake views. Sites 1, 2, 4, 6, and 7 are small, pretty pull-throughs, but they are not as secluded as the other sites. Sites 15, 15A, and 16 are somewhat cramped and distastefully close to the dump station. The best location by far is the loop containing sites 39–46; site 45 is particularly gorgeous. Doll Mountain's sites also vary a bit in terms of overall privacy; some don't have much, but others are some of the most secluded we've seen.

Basics

Operated By: Army Corps of Engineers. **Open:** Apr.–Oct. **Site Assignment:** Reservations preferred. **Registration:** At camp office. **Fee:** $12–$18. **Parking:** On site.

Facilities

Number of RV Sites: 39. **Number of Tent-Only Sites:** 25. **Hookups:** Water, electric (30 amps). **Each Site:** Picnic table, fire pit. **Dump Station:** Yes. **Laundry:** Yes. **Pay Phone:** Yes. **Rest Rooms and Showers:** Yes. **Fuel:** Nearby. **Propane:** No. **Internal Roads:** Paved. **RV Service:** Yes. **Market:** In Ellijay. **Restaurant:** In Ellijay. **General Store:** No. **Vending:** Soft drinks. **Swimming Pool:** Yes. **Playground:** Yes. **Activities:** Basketball, boating, ampitheather, hiking, swimming. **Nearby Attractions:** Battle ground, Lake Chattahoochee.

Restrictions

Pets: On leash only. **Fires:** In designated areas only. **Alcoholic Beverages:** At sites only. **Vehicle Maximum Length:** 35 ft. **Other:** 2-day min. on weekends.

To Get There

From Ellijay, travel 11 mi. southwest on Hwy. 382. Follow signs to campground.

EULONIA

Lake Harmony RV Park

Rte. 3 Box 3128, Townsend 31331. T: (888) 767-7864; www.lakeharmonypark.com.

RV: ★★★ Tent: ★★

Beauty: ★★★ Site Privacy: ★★
Spaciousness: ★★ Quiet: ★★★★
Security: ★★★★ Cleanliness: ★★★★
Insect Control: ★★★ Facilities: ★★★

Located south of Savanah and just north of Brunswick, Lake Harmony provides visitors with a place to rest within easy reach of Georgia's coastal attractions. Access to I-95 is convenient, yet the park is quiet and has rural feel. The 50 sites are a mixture of pull-throughs and back ins, with 25 additional sites designated as tent-only. The sites are small, with sand and pine straw ground cover, which is sufficient but could use a little work. With a few exceptions, the sites are shady. Fishing, boating, and swimming are available, but those campers wanting to explore may venture onto nearby Saint Simons for hiking, kayaking, or shopping. Others may wish to visit Cumberland Island National Seashore, which is accessed by ferry only.

Basics

Operated By: Larry Kosior. **Open:** All year. **Site Assignment:** Reservations preferred. **Registration:** At camp office. **Fee:** $18–$20. **Parking:** In campground.

Facilities

Number of RV Sites: 50. **Number of Tent-Only Sites:** 25. **Hookups:** Water, electric (30 amps), sewer, cable. **Each Site:** Picnic tale, grill. **Dump Station:** No. **Laundry:** Yes. **Pay Phone:** Yes. **Rest Rooms and Showers:** Yes. **Fuel:** No. **Propane:** Yes. **Internal Roads:** Packed sand. **RV Service:** No. **Market:** 5 mi. **Restaurant:** 0.5 mi. **General Store:** Limited groceries. **Vending:** No. **Swimming Pool:** No. **Playground:** No. **Other:** Lake w/ swimming beach on site. **Activities:** Fishing, boating, swimming, bird-watching, game room, shuffleboard. **Nearby Attractions:** St. Simons Island, Brunswick, Cumberland Island, Okefenokee Swamp.

Restrictions
Pets: On leash only. **Fires:** In designated areas only. **Alcoholic Beverages:** Restricted. **Vehicle Maximum Length:** 65 ft.

To Get There
Take I-95 Exit 58 in Townsend. Park is 0.6 mi. from exit.

FARGO
Stephen Foster State Park

Route 1 Box 131, Fargo 31631. T: (912) 637-5274.

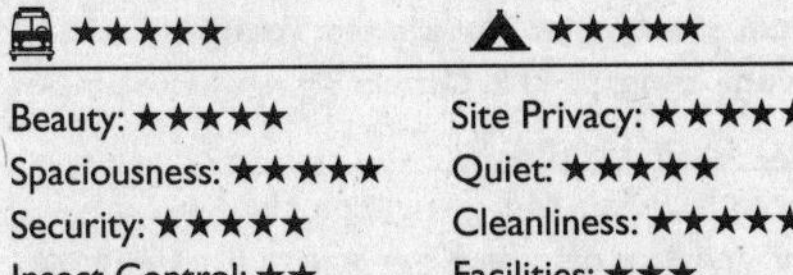

The extremely remote location of Stephen C. Foster State Park means that its campground is extraordinarily peaceful and serene. The park is the main Georgia entrance to the Okefenokee Swamp and related Okefenokee National Wild-life Refuge. Campsites are huge, densely shaded, and wooded for offering plenty of privacy. The natural scenery and wildlife are the obvious attractions here, and all that prevents this campground from getting five stars in beauty are the occasional intrusions of telephone lines and unsightly utility buildings. Even so, the quiet blackwater of the swamp, the stately cypress groves, and the hanging curtains of Spanish moss still make this one of the prettiest campgrounds in the region. Families often walk the grounds at night to watch the droves of wild deer that wander placidly by. Be sure to bring insect repellant and mosquito netting, since the swampy conditions are heaven for all manner of bloodsuckers.

Basics
Operated By: Georgia Dept. of Natural Resources. **Open:** All year. **Site Assignment:** First come, first served except during peak season when sites are assigned. **Registration:** Office. **Fee:** $18–$20. **Parking:** On site.

Facilities
Number of RV Sites: 49. **Number of Tent-Only Sites:** 17. **Hookups:** Water, electric (20, 30 amps). **Each Site:** Picnic table, grill. **Dump Station:** Yes. **Laundry:** Yes. **Pay Phone:** Yes. **Rest Rooms and Showers:** Yes. **Fuel:** No. **Propane:** No. **Internal Roads:** Paved. **RV Service:** No. **Market:** In Ernest. **Restaurant:** In Ernest. **General Store:** Yes. **Vending:** Yes. **Swimming Pool:** No. **Playground:** Yes. **Activities:** Fishing, boating, canoeing. **Nearby Attractions:** Okefenokee Swamp, Suwanee Canal Recreational Area, Laura S. Walker State Park.

Restrictions
Pets: Leash only. **Fires:** Allowed. **Alcoholic Beverages:** Sites only. **Vehicle Max. Length:** 50 ft.

To Get There
Take US 441 to Fargo. Go 18 mi. on Hwy 177N to the state park.

FLOWERY BRANCH
Chestnut Ridge Campground

6515 Chestnut Ridge Rd., Flowery Branch 30542. T: (770) 967-6710.

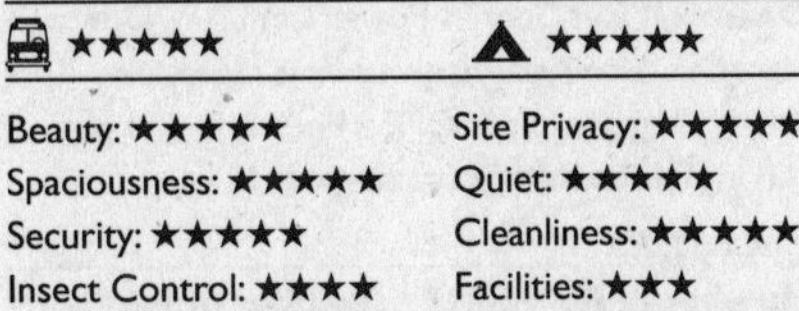

Another gorgeous campground in the Lake Lanier resort area (see profiles for Shoal Creek in Buford and Lake Lanier Islands), Chestnut Ridge sits on a small peninsula in an upscale residential neighborhood. Campsites are large, shaded, and many have screening foliage between them. Most sites are fairly close together; campsites 1–13 have the most elbow room, while sites 23–29 are the most secluded. As with other properties in this Army Corps of Engineers–managed area, boat noise is often the only downside; ask attendants for recommendations about the quietest sites. Chestnut Ridge is most often full on weekends. This campground offers little more than nice accommodations, as most visitors come for lake activities and water sports. However, there's plenty to do in the area, since Lake Lanier has 43 day-use parks, ten marinas, and nine state, county, and city parks.

Basics
Operated By: Army Corps of Engineers. **Open:** Mar. 29–Sept. 8. **Site Assignment:** 60% reservable, 40% first come, first served. **Registration:** Park entry station. **Fee:** $12–$22 plus day use fees. **Parking:** On site.

Facilities
Number of RV Sites: 85. **Number of Tent-Only Sites:**. **Hookups:** Water, electric (30,50 amps), sewer. **Each Site:** Grills, fire pits, picnic table. **Dump Station:** Yes. **Laundry:** Yes. **Pay Phone:** No. **Rest Rooms and Showers:** Yes. **Fuel:** No. **Propane:** Nearby. **Internal Roads:** Paved. **RV Service:** No. **Market:** In Flowery Branch. **Restaurant:** In Flowery Branch. **General Store:** Nearby. **Vending:** Drink only. **Swimming Pool:** No. **Playground:** Yes. **Activities:** Boating, lake swimming, fishing. **Nearby Attractions:** Lake Lanier Island water park & golf course. **Additional Information:** City of Flowery Branch, (770) 967-6371 or www.cityofflowerybranch.org.

Restrictions
Pets: On leash only. **Fires:** In fire rings only. **Alcoholic Beverages:** Not allowed. **Vehicle Maximum Length:** None. **Other:** 14-day max. stay limit.

To Get There
From Atlanta, take I-85N to I-985. Take Exit 8 and turn left onto Hwy. 347, turn right onto McEver Rd., and turn left on Gaines Ferry Rd. Then turn right onto Chestnut Ridge Rd., which ends at the campground.

FORSYTH
Forsyth KOA Campground

414 South Frontage Rd., Forsyth 31029. T: (478) 994-2019; www.koa.com.

★★★ ★★

Beauty: ★★★★ Site Privacy: ★★
Spaciousness: ★★★ Quiet: ★★★
Security: ★★★ Cleanliness: ★★★★★
Insect Control: ★★★★ Facilities: ★★★

In some ways a typical private campground, this KOA is recommended on the basis of friendly owners, cleanliness, and the general sweetness of kids feeding ducks and geese at the fishing pond. Privacy and site size are average for a private campground, and the main detractor is certainly the parks proximity to I-75. Forsyth is a lovely small town, but the noise of the interstate warrants seeking out sites as far from the traffic as possible. Most of the sites are pull-throughs, with gravel, gras,s or pine straw ground cover. The plentiful pine trees help make this an attractive campground, but be mindful of limited security. There is no gate, and again—it is very close to the interstate. The combination of activities in Forsyth and several possible day-trips do add up to a good family camping spot. Located in the center of the state, we recommend this as an ideal midway stop for midwesterners en route to Florida.

Basics
Operated By: KOA Kampgrounds. **Open:** All year. **Site Assignment:** Reservations accepted. **Registration:** At camp office. **Fee:** $17–$23. **Parking:** 2 vehicles per site.

Facilities
Number of RV Sites: 130. **Number of Tent-Only Sites:** 10. **Hookups:** Water, electric (30 amps), sewer. **Each Site:** Picnic table, grill. **Dump Station:** Yes. **Laundry:** Yes. **Pay Phone:** Yes. **Rest Rooms and Showers:** Yes. **Fuel:** 1 mi. **Propane:** Yes. **Internal Roads:** Gravel. **RV Service:** Yes. **Market:** In Forsyth. **Restaurant:** In Forsyth. **General Store:** No. **Vending:** No. **Swimming Pool:** Yes. **Playground:** Yes. **Activities:** Volleyball, badminton, fishing, basketball, boating. **Nearby Attractions:** Historic Juliette, Six Flags.

Restrictions
Pets: On leash only. **Fires:** In designated areas. **Alcoholic Beverages:** At sites only. **Vehicle Maximum Length:** None.

To Get There
Exit I-75 at Exit 186 and follow the signs.

FORTSON
Blanton Creek Park

1516 Bartletts Ferry Rd., Fortson 31808. T: (706) 643-7737.

★★★★ ★★★

Beauty: ★★★★★ Site Privacy: ★★★★
Spaciousness: ★★★★ Quiet: ★★★★★
Security: ★★★★★ Cleanliness: ★★★
Insect Control: ★★★ Facilities: ★★★

Blanton Creek Park is one of numerous Georgia Power–owned campgrounds scattered across the state. This lakeside property has an unusual layout. The hilly terrain rolls down to the shores of Lake Harding, and the roads and campsites form terraces on the hillside. The overall effect is quite lovely, and the only real aesthetic downside to the campground are the less-than-clean facilities (the bathrooms were particularly gross on our visit). Assuming that gets taken care of, there's little to fault in the large campsites set under gorgeous woods. If you're looking for a good pull-through, there aren't many to choose from; however, site 7 is a nice one, and site 12 is even better. Sites 44–47 have fantastic lake views. The tent area here has a nice views too, but it's really too crowded to recommend.

Basics

Operated By: Georgia Power Company. **Open:** Apr.–Labor Day. **Site Assignment:** Reservations accepted. **Registration:** Office. **Fee:** $14 per vehicle. **Parking:** In campground.

Facilities

Number of RV Sites: 43. **Number of Tent-Only Sites:** 8. **Hookups:** Electric. **Each Site:** Picnic tables, grills. **Dump Station:** Yes. **Laundry:** Yes. **Pay Phone:** Yes. **Rest Rooms and Showers:** Yes. **Fuel:** No. **Propane:** No. **Internal Roads:** Paved & gravel. **RV Service:** In Columbus. **Market:** In Columbus. **Restaurant:** In Columbus. **General Store:** No. **Vending:** Yes. **Swimming Pool:** Yes. **Playground:** Yes. **Other:** Group wilderness camping. **Activities:** Boating, fishing, hiking. **Nearby Attractions:** Calloway Gardens, Pine Mountain, Franklin D. Roosevelt State Park. **Additional Information:** Georgia Power, (888) GPC-LAKE.

Restrictions

Pets: On leash only; 2 pet max. **Fires:** In grills only. **Alcoholic Beverages:** Not allowed. **Vehicle Maximum Length:** Call ahead for details. **Other:** big rigs welcome.

To Get There

From I-185, take Exit 21 and go 0.25 mi. west on Hwy. 116, then 3.5 mi. west on Hwy. 103, then 1 mi. south on Lick Skillet Rd.

GREENSBORO

Old Salem

1530 Old Salem Rd., Greensboro 30642. T: (706) 467-2850.

RV: ★★★ Tent: ★★★

Beauty: ★★★ Site Privacy: ★★★
Spaciousness: ★★★ Quiet: ★★★
Security: ★★★★★ Cleanliness: ★★★★
Insect Control: ★★★★ Facilities: ★★★

The most elaborate of Georgia Power's campgrounds on Lake Oconee (see the following profile for Parks Ferry), Old Salem focuses mostly on lake activities and water sports. This campground is quite popular, and the large number of children and vehicles can make it less than tranquil. Campsites vary in size, but most are acceptably large; all are nicely wooded. The best campsites by far are 85, 87, 89, and 91, with 91 leading the pack. All of these are extremely choice and hard to get due to their lakeside setting and close proximity to the campers-only boat dock. Families might prefer sites 78–80, which are adjacent to the beach house and playground.

Basics

Operated By: Georgia Power Company. **Open:** Mar.–Oct. **Site Assignment:** First come, first served. **Registration:** Office. **Fee:** $12–$14 plus parking fee. **Parking:** In campground.

Facilities

Number of RV Sites: 67. **Number of Tent-Only Sites:** 25. **Hookups:** Water, electric (20, 30 amps). **Each Site:** Picnic areas. **Dump Station:** Yes. **Laundry:** Yes. **Pay Phone:** Yes. **Rest Rooms and Showers:** Yes. **Fuel:**. **Propane:** Yes. **Internal Roads:** Paved. **RV Service:** Yes. **Market:** Nearby. **Restaurant:** Nearby. **General Store:** Inquire at campground. **Vending:** Inquire at campground. **Swimming Pool:** No. **Playground:** Yes. **Activities:** Swimming areas, fishing, boating, volleyball. **Nearby Attractions:** Iron Horse, museum, Green County Courthouse. **Additional Information:** Chamber of Commerce, (800) 886-5253 www.greeneccoc.org.

Restrictions

Pets: Yes. **Fires:** Allowed. **Alcoholic Beverages:** Inquire at campground. **Vehicle Maximum Length:** Call ahead for details. **Other:** Big rigs welcome.

To Get There

From Jct. I-20 Exit 130 and Hwy. 44: Go 7 mi. SW on Hwy. 44, then 0.75 mi. SE on Linger Longer Rd. then 1 mi. SW on paved road. Follow signs.

GREENSBORO

Parks Ferry

125 Wallace Dam Rd., Eatonton 31024. T: (706) 453-4308.

RV: ★★★★ Tent: ★★★

Beauty: ★★★★ Site Privacy: ★★
Spaciousness: ★★★ Quiet: ★★★★
Security: ★★★★★ Cleanliness: ★★★★
Insect Control: ★★★★ Facilities: ★★★

One of several Georgia Power campgrounds on Lake Oconee (see the preceeding profile of Old Salem), Parks Ferry is a tight triple loop of campsites set next to the lake and a tiny "wildlife habitat." This property is not as nice as nearby Old Salem, and its long sites are a bit sandwiched together. However, it's also not as crowded as its Oconee sibling, which translates to a bit more quiet and overall privacy. A forest of hardwoods on the grounds also makes the place more attractive than it might otherwise be. A small beach and boat facilities make Parks Ferry a viable alternative when other Lake Oconee campgrounds are overwhelmed with visitors.

Basics

Operated By: Georgia Power Company. **Open:** Apr. 13–Sept. 4. **Site Assignment:** First come, first served, reservations. **Registration:** Gatehouse. **Fee:** $12–$14. **Parking:** On site.

Facilities

Number of RV Sites: 85. **Number of Tent-Only Sites:** 40. **Hookups:** Water, electric. **Each Site:** Grill, picnic, fire pit. **Dump Station:** Yes. **Laundry:** Yes. **Pay Phone:** Yes. **Rest Rooms and Showers:** Yes. **Fuel:** No. **Propane:** No. **Internal Roads:** Paved. **RV Service:** 10 mi. **Market:** 5 mi. **Restaurant:** 10 mi. **General Store:** 10 mi. **Vending:** Drink only. **Swimming Pool:** No. **Playground:** Yes. **Activities:** Beachfront, boat ramp, volleyball. **Nearby Attractions:** Iron Horse, museum, Green County Courthouse. **Additional Information:** Green County Chamber of Commerce, (800) 886-5253 or www.greeneccoc.org.

Restrictions

Pets: On leash only. **Fires:** In fire rings only. **Alcoholic Beverages:** Not allowed. **Vehicle Maximum Length:** 40 ft. **Other:** Big rigs welcome.

To Get There

From I-20 Exit 130, go right on Hwy. 44 for 5.5 mi. and turn right on Kerry Station Rd. Continue for 3.5 mi, turn left on Parkshill Rd., and continue for1 mi. to the park on your right

HARTWELL

Hart State Park

330 Hart State Park Rd., Hartwell 30643. T: (706) 376-8756; www.gastateparks.org.

RV: ★★★★ Tent: ★★★★

Beauty: ★★★★ Site Privacy: ★★★★
Spaciousness: ★★★★ Quiet: ★★★
Security: ★★★★ Cleanliness: ★★★★
Insect Control: ★★★ Facilities: ★★★★

The 55,590-acre Hartwell Reservoir is the main attraction at Hart State Park Campground. Anglers can fish for largemouth and hybrid bass, striper, black crappie, bream, rainbow trout, and walleyed pike in the reservoir's waters, and the campground's boat ramp and six docks make water access easy. Both the size and overall privacy of these campsites vary immensely. Sites 28–37 are a bit more spacious than most, and they have decent shade and good lake views. Two big pull-throughs can be found at sites 59 and 60. The adjacent sites 56–58 are not level enough to suit most RVers. A few nature trails lace the edge of the property, and a multi-use trail for hiking and biking offers a good jaunt south of the campground. No visit to the area could possibly be complete with a pilgrimage to nearby Elberton, the "Granite Capital of the World."

Basics

Operated By: Georgia Dept. of Natural Resources. **Open:** All year. **Site Assignment:** First come, first served. **Registration:** Park entry station. **Fee:** Call ahead for details. **Parking:** On site.

Facilities

Number of RV Sites: 76. **Number of Tent-Only Sites:** 25. **Hookups:** Water, electric (20, 30 amps), sewer. **Each Site:** Picnic, fire ring, grill, lantern pole. **Dump Station:** Yes. **Laundry:** Yes. **Pay Phone:** Yes. **Rest Rooms and Showers:** Yes. **Fuel:** No. **Propane:** No. **Internal Roads:** Paved. **RV Service:** 30 mi. **Market:** 5 mi. **Restaurant:** 5 mi. **General Store:** 5 mi. **Vending:** Yes. **Swimming Pool:** No. **Playground:** Yes. **Activities:** Hiking, fishing, biking, swimming beach, picnic shelters, Cricket

Theater, boat ramps, canoes, pedal boats. **Nearby Attractions:** Hartwell Golf Club, Tugaloo State Park, Granite Capital of World, Hartwell Lake & Dam. **Additional Information:** Hart County Chamber of Commerce, (706) 376-8590 or www.hart-chamber.org.

Restrictions

Pets: On leash only. **Fires:** Fire rings only. **Alcoholic Beverages:** At sites only. **Vehicle Max. Length:** 35 ft. **Other:** No entry after 11 p.m.

To Get There

From Hartwell, drive north on Hwy. 29. Turn left on Ridge Rd. and go 2 mi. to the park.

HARTWELL

Payne's Creek

P.O. Box 248, Hartwell 30645-0298. T: (877) 444-6777; www.reserveusa.com.

 ★★★★★ ★★★★★

Beauty: ★★★★★ Site Privacy: ★★★★★
Spaciousness: ★★★★★ Quiet: ★★★★
Security: ★★★★★ Cleanliness: ★★★★
Insect Control: ★★★★ Facilities: ★★★

Situated on the Georgia–South Carolina border, this lakeside campground is in easy striking distance from I-85, yet remains fairly remote. Incredibly large sites lie throughout the grounds. Heavy vegetation between sites offers great privacy, and all but a few are on the water. The best of these sites—20, 21, 23, 27–29, 34, and 35—offer wide, beautiful views of the lake. Both back-ins and pull-throughs are available, though the preferred areas have large, circular pull-throughs. No developed sites are designated tents-only, though there is a nearby primitive area. A boat-ramp provides great opportunity to access the nearly 56,000-acre Hartwell Lake, and those wishing to see a working power plant can visit the Hartwell Power plant a few miles away.

Basics

Operated By: Army Corps of Engineers. **Open:** May–Sept. **Site Assignment:** Reservation only. **Registration:** By phone or at the website, at least 2 days in advance. **Fee:** 12. **Parking:** At site or designated areas.

Facilities

Number of RV Sites: 0. **Number of Tent-Only Sites:** Unnumbered primitive. **Number of Multipurpose Sites:** 52. **Hookups:** Water, electric (20, 30, 50 amps), sewer. **Each Site:** Water, electricity. **Dump Station:** Yes. **Laundry:** No. **Pay Phone:** Yes. **Rest Rooms and Showers:** Yes. **Fuel:** No. **Propane:** No. **Internal Roads:** Paved. **RV Service:** In Hartwell. **Market:** In Hartwell. **Restaurant:** In Hartwell. **General Store:** No. **Vending:** No. **Swimming Pool:** No. **Playground:** Yes. **Activities:** Boating, swimming. **Nearby Attractions:** Marinas, boat slips, rentals.

Restrictions

Pets: On leash (6 ft. or less) only. **Fires:** In fire rings or grills; burn only fallen or purchased wood. **Alcoholic Beverages:** Not allowed. **Vehicle Maximum Length:** 60 ft. **Other:** 14-day stay limit; no guns or fireworks.

To Get There

From I-85, take Exit 177. Proceed south on Hwy. 77 for 5 mi. Follow directional signs the last 10 mi. to the campground.

HARTWELL

Watsadler

P.O. Box 278, Hartwell 30643. T: (888) 893-0678; www.reserveusa.com.

★★★★ ★★★★

Beauty: ★★★★★ Site Privacy: ★★★★
Spaciousness: ★★★ Quiet: ★★★★
Security: ★★★★ Cleanliness: ★★★★
Insect Control: ★★★ Facilities: ★★★

Another U.S. Army Corps of Engineers property, Watsadler is one of several campgrounds resting on the shores of Hartwell Lake (but this is the only one open year-round). You'd expect this remote property to be dead quiet, but the large number of vehicles in the park tends to create a lot of background noise. Site size varies from fair to huge, with shade ranging from slight to heavy. A few campsites are extremely private, but most are not. Lakeside sites 9 and 10 are among the exceptions, boasting not only a good amount of screening foliage, but also a lot of room and fantastic lake views. Site 5 is also quite picturesque. The July Fourth fireworks here are said to be particularly impressive.

Basics

Operated By: Army Corps of Engineers. **Open:** Mar. 1–Nov. 30. **Site Assignment:** Reservations accepted. **Registration:** Office. **Fee:** $16–40. **Parking:** On site.

Facilities

Number of Multipurpose Sites: 51. **Hookups:** Water, electric (50 amps), sewer. **Each Site:** Fire pit. **Dump Station:** Yes. **Laundry:** No. **Pay Phone:** Yes. **Rest Rooms and Showers:** Yes. **Fuel:** No. **Propane:** No. **Internal Roads:** Paved. **RV Service:** In Hartwell. **Market:** In Hartwell. **Restaurant:** In Hartwell. **General Store:** No. **Vending:** No. **Swimming Pool:** No. **Playground:** Yes. **Other:** Boat ramp, courtesy dock. **Activities:** Inquire at campground. **Nearby Attractions:** Clemson University, Hartwell Dam, July 4th fireworks. **Additional Information:** Hart County Chamber of Commerce, (706) 376-8590 or www.hart-chamber.org.

Restrictions

Pets: On leash only. **Fires:** In fire rings only. **Alcoholic Beverages:** Not allowed. **Vehicle Maximum Length:** Call ahead for details. **Other:** 14-day max. stay limit.

To Get There

From I-85, take Exit 177 onto Hwy. 77 towards Hartwell. In Hartwell, take Hwy. 29N towards Anderson, South Carolina. The campground is 4 mi. outside of Hartwell.

HELEN

Cherokee Campground

45 Bethel Rd., Sautee 30571. T: (706) 878-2267.

★★★ ★★

Beauty: ★★★ Site Privacy: ★★★
Spaciousness: ★★★ Quiet: ★★★
Security: ★★★★ Cleanliness: ★★★★
Insect Control: ★★★★ Facilities: ★★

The 48 sites of this private campground are small but sufficient, with some shade provided by young trees. The absence of underbrush allows easy walking between sites but does little for privacy. Tenters will enjoy soft-mulch tent pads, and all visitors can listen to live music performed on weekends during peak season. This private campground may not have astounding views, but it's proximity to the area's cultural and outdoor activities definitely recommends it. Unicoi State Park, the Appalachian Trail, Anna Ruby Falls, and Brasstown Bald provide some of the outdoor fun. Those wanting an Old World experience can drive to nearby Helen, where German crafts and food are readily available in this Alpine-theme town. Reserve far in advance if you intend to camp during the annual Oktoberfest (mid-Sept. through the beginning of Nov.).

Basics

Operated By: Ed & Julie Digiorgion. **Open:** All year. **Site Assignment:** First come, first served. **Registration:** At camp office. **Fee:** Full hookups $20, no hookups $18, for cable add $2. **Parking:** In campground.

Facilities

Number of RV Sites: 48. **Number of Tent-Only Sites:** Tent area. **Hookups:** Water, electric (20, 30 amps), sewer, phone, cable. **Each Site:** Picnic table. **Dump Station:** Yes. **Laundry:** Yes. **Pay Phone:** Yes. **Rest Rooms and Showers:** Yes. **Fuel:** No. **Propane:** No. **Internal Roads:** Half paved, half gravel. **RV Service:** 15 mi. **Market:** 5 mi. **Restaurant:** 1 mi. **General Store:** Yes. **Vending:** No. **Swimming Pool:** No. **Playground:** No. **Other:** Pavilion available. **Activities:** Hiking, trout fishing, horseback riding. **Nearby Attractions:** Anna Ruby Falls, Appalachian Trail, whitewater rafting.

Restrictions

Pets: On leash only. **Fires:** Allowed. **Alcoholic Beverages:** Allowed. **Vehicle Max. Length:** 45 ft.

To Get There

Take I-85N to I-985N, which becomes Hwy. 365. At the second light, turn left onto Hwy. 384. When the road ends, turn right onto Hwy. 75. 1 mi. north of Helen, take a left onto Hwy. 356 at mi. marker 5.

HELEN

Unicoi State Park

1788 Hwy. 356, Helen 60543. T: (706) 878-3982; www.gastateparks.org.

★★★★ ★★★★

Beauty: ★★★★★ Site Privacy: ★★★★
Spaciousness: ★★★★ Quiet: ★★★★
Security: ★★★★ Cleanliness: ★★★★
Insect Control: ★★★★ Facilities: ★★★★

Platform camping and walk-in tent sites are only some of the camping possibilities found in this

1023-acre state park. RVers will find comfort in the 52 back-in sites with water, electric, and sewer hookups. Gorgeous hardwoods and pines tower over most of the sites, and though the camping areas are beautiful throughout, the most notable areas are those near Big Brook Spur. Weekend visitors should plan ahead, as the park often fills up. Even weekday camping here is not be a solitary experience. Though the alpine village of Helen and the Dahlonega Gold Museum lie within easy driving distance, visitors will want to remain in the park and take advantage of its offerings as well. Activities include hiking, biking, fishing, and canoeing, and the on-site restaurant and conference center provide resources for groups of all sizes.

Basics

Operated By: Georgia Dept. of Natural Resources. **Open:** All year. **Site Assignment:** First come, first served. **Registration:** At camp office. **Fee:** Full hookup $20, RV w/ electric & water hookups $18, tent w/ electric & water hookups $16, walk-in tent $14. **Parking:** On site.

Facilities

Number of RV Sites: 52. **Number of Tent-Only Sites:** 48. **Hookups:** Water, electric (30 amps), sewer. **Each Site:** Grill, picnic table, tent pad. **Dump Station:** Yes. **Laundry:** Yes. **Pay Phone:** Yes. **Rest Rooms and Showers:** Yes. **Fuel:** No. **Propane:** No. **Internal Roads:** Paved. **RV Service:** On site. **Market:** 3 mi. **Restaurant:** On site. **General Store:** Yes. **Vending:** Yes. **Swimming Pool:** No. **Playground:** Yes. **Other:** Programs, tours, lake on site, conference center on site. **Activities:** Hiking, mountain biking, fishing, swimming, boating. **Nearby Attractions:** Anna Ruby Falls, Dahlonega Gold Museum, Appalachian Trail.

Restrictions

Pets: On leash (6 ft. or less) only. **Fires:** Allowed. **Alcoholic Beverages:** Allowed. **Vehicle Maximum Length:** 40 ft. **Other:** 14-day max. stay limit.

To Get There

Take I-85N to I-195 N., which becomes Hwy. 365. At the second light, turn left onto Hwy. 384. At end of the road, turn right onto Hwy. 75. 1 mi. north of Helen, take a right onto Hwy. 356 and follow signs to the campground.

HIAWASSEE
Bald Mountain Park

3540 Fodder Creek Rd., Hiawassee 30546. T: (706) 896-8896; www.baldmountainpark.com.

RV ★★★ Tent ★★★

Beauty: ★★★★ Site Privacy: ★★
Spaciousness: ★★ Quiet: ★★★
Security: ★★★★ Cleanliness: ★★★
Insect Control: ★★★★ Facilities: ★★★★

In the far north of the state, this extremely rural private resort campground lies in a flat valley with pretty views of the surrounding mountains. Sites with good views are 2–18 on Lakeside Ln., and more open, with even better views, are sites 1–54 between Doe Lane Dr. and Lakeside Ln. For nicely wooded sites with pine straw ground cover, go for 64, 66, 68, 70,73, 75 and 77. All of the sites are back-in, some open, others beautifully wooded. Most of the sites are grass-covered, though some have gravel or pine straw. The campground is fairly secure in terms of its rural setting, but it is also very crowded, so privacy is not generally the best here. The resort hosts rodeo events and fairs during the summer, so check the schedule. Despite the cigarette butts that cover some areas, the recreational opportunities and the vicinity to the Appalachian Trail and other attractions, make this a family-friendly campground.

Basics

Operated By: Family owned. **Open:** Apr. 1–Oct. 31. **Site Assignment:** First come, first served. **Registration:** Office or night box. **Fee:** $17–$21. **Parking:** On site.

Facilities

Number of RV Sites: 300. **Number of Tent-Only Sites:**. **Hookups:** Electric (20, 30 amps), water sewer. **Each Site:** Picnic table, fire pit. **Dump Station:** Yes. **Laundry:** Yes. **Pay Phone:** Yes. **Rest Rooms and Showers:** Yes. **Fuel:** No. **Propane:** No. **Internal Roads:** Gravel. **RV Service:** Yes. **Market:** In Hiawasee. **Restaurant:** In Hiawasee. **General Store:** Yes. **Vending:** Yes. **Swimming Pool:** Yes. **Playground:** Yes. **Activities:** Fishing, golf, volleyball, boating, gameroom. **Nearby Attractions:** Brasstown Valley Resort, Lake Chatuge, Appalachian Trail, Helen (Bavarian village). **Additional Information:** Towns County Chamber of Commerce, (800) 981-1543 or www.towns-county-chamber.org.

Restrictions

Pets: Yes. **Fires:** Designated areas only. **Alcoholic Beverages:** At sites only. **Vehicle Maximum Length:** 35 ft. **Other:** Firearms prohibited.

To Get There

From Rt. 288, turn onto Fodder Creek Rd. The entrance is 4 mi. south on the left.

JACKSON
High Falls State Park

76 High Falls Park Dr., Jackson 30233. T: (478) 993-3053; www.gastateparks.org.

RV ★★★★ Tent ★★★★

Beauty: ★★★★ Site Privacy: ★★★
Spaciousness: ★★★★ Quiet: ★★
Security: ★★★ Cleanliness: ★★★★
Insect Control: ★★★ Facilities: ★★★★

In spite of its proximity to I-75, this park has a real rural feel to it. RVers and tent-campers share all 112 sites, which have full hookups available. Moderately wooded with tall hardwoods, most sites have ample shade, though the limited underbrush reduces privacy. Those wishing to fall asleep to the sound of rushing water should camp in Area 2, situated next to the Towaliga River. Rigs needing lots of space should head for Loop B (sites 82–90). It's more open here, but the new bathhouse is nice. For a more secluded experience, look to Area 1 (sites 109–122). The curious will find trails that wind past ruins in this former industrial town. Canoes and paddleboats are available to explore High Falls Lake. But, if it has been rainy, you may want to just stare at the water rushing over the park's namesake.

Basics

Operated By: Georgia Dept. of Natural Resources. **Open:** All year. **Site Assignment:** Reservations available. **Registration:** At camp office. **Fee:** $18–$20. **Parking:** In campground.

Facilities

Number of RV Sites: 112. **Number of Tent-Only Sites:** 0. **Hookups:** Water, electric (50 amps). **Each Site:** Water, electricity, grill, picnic table. **Dump Station:** Yes. **Laundry:** Yes. **Pay Phone:** Yes. **Rest Rooms and Showers:** Yes. **Fuel:** No. **Propane:** No. **Internal Roads:** Paved. **RV Service:** No. **Market:** Across the street from park. **Restaurant:** Across the street from park. **General Store:** Across the street from park. **Vending:** Soft drinks. **Swimming Pool:** Yes. **Playground:** Yes. **Activities:** Hiking, fishing, paddle boating, boat rental, mini golf. **Nearby Attractions:** Jarrell Plantation State Historic Site, Indian Springs State Park, Piedmont National Wildlife Refuge, Oconee National Forest.

Restrictions

Pets: On leash only. **Fires:** Allowed. **Alcoholic Beverages:** Not allowed. **Vehicle Maximum Length:** None. **Other:** 2 tents max. per site.

To Get There

The park is 1.8 mi. east of I-75, Exit 198, at High Falls Rd.

JACKSON
Indian Springs State Park

678 Lake Clark Rd., Flovilla 30216. T: (770) 504-2277; www.gastateparks.org.

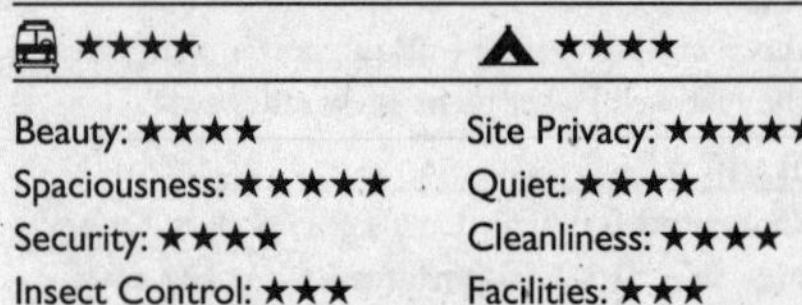

RV ★★★★ Tent ★★★★

Beauty: ★★★★ Site Privacy: ★★★★★
Spaciousness: ★★★★★ Quiet: ★★★★
Security: ★★★★ Cleanliness: ★★★★
Insect Control: ★★★ Facilities: ★★★

Campers with a penchant for history will want to visit Indian Springs State Park, believed to be the oldest park in the nation The park has 88 sites for RVs, trailers and tents, as well as 30 more primitive sites for tents only. All the sites are pull-throughs, and include electrical, water, and cable hookups. The area is nicely shaded, with pines and the occasional hardwood. Each sight has ample space in which to relax, but the phone lines running through the park and the well-used outhouses detract from the overall beauty. Those wishing to explore can find a spring house built by the Civilian Conservation Corps. The Creek Native Americans used this spring to heal the ill and impart vigor to the healthy. Today, visitors can participate in a number of activities, including swimming, fishing, and boating. Nearby points of interest include the Jarrell Plantation State Historic Site and the Historic Indian Springs Hotel.

Basics

Operated By: Georgia Dept. of Natural Resources. **Open:** All year. **Site Assignment:** Sites assigned based on vehicle size. **Registration:** At camp office. **Fee:** $15–$18. **Parking:** In campground.

Facilities

Number of RV Sites: 88. **Number of Tent-Only Sites:** 0. **Hookups:** Water, electric (30 amps), cable. **Each Site:** Picnic table, fire pit. **Dump Station:** Yes. **Laundry:** Yes. **Pay Phone:** Yes. **Rest Rooms and Showers:** Yes. **Fuel:** No. **Propane:** No. **Internal Roads:** Paved. **RV Service:** 30 mi. **Market:** 5 mi. in Jackson. **Restaurant:** 5 mi. in Jackson. **General Store:** Outside park. **Vending:** Soft drinks. **Swimming Pool:** No. **Playground:** No. **Activities:** Pedal boats, fishing, swimming, golf. **Nearby Attractions:** Jarrell Plantation State Historic Site, High Falls State Park, Piedmont National Wildlife Refuge, Historic Indian Springs Hotel.

Restrictions

Pets: On leash only. **Fires:** Allowed but subject to seasonal bans. **Alcoholic Beverages:** Not allowed. **Vehicle Maximum Length:** None.

To Get There

From I-75 S., take Exit 205 to Jackson. Proceed south on Hwy. 42 to the park. From I-75 N., take Exit 188 and proceed north on Hwy. 42. The park is approximately 15 mi. from the interstate.

JEKYLL ISLAND

Jekyll Island Campground

1197 Riverview Dr., Jekyll Island 31527. T: (912) 635-3021; www.jekyllisland.com; campground@jekyllisland.com.

RV ★★★★ Tent ★★★★

Beauty: ★★★★ Site Privacy: ★★★
Spaciousness: ★★★★ Quiet: ★★★★
Security: ★★★★ Cleanliness: ★★★★
Insect Control: ★★★ Facilities: ★★★

Located in a historic resort community, Jekyll Island Campground offers spectacular views of the ocean and shoreline. Covered with gorgeous live oak and pine trees, the area has a wonderfully serene and laid back vibe. Since the sites vary greatly in size, we recommend sites J7, J11, H15, and H16, as they are the most spacious and secluded. The back tent areas of the campground are generally much nicer. The facilities on the campground are satisfactory but basic. Georgia's mild winters make the campground a perfect winter destination. The campground is more crowded in the spring and summer, and therefore we recommend that you call in advance for availability during these times. Security at Jekyll Island is mediocre, but the campground does have the advantage of being secluded.

Basics

Operated By: Private operator. **Open:** All year. **Site Assignment:** Reservations accepted. **Registration:** Office. **Fee:** $12–$20. **Parking:** On site.

Facilities

Number of RV Sites: 158. **Number of Tent-Only Sites:** 41. **Hookups:** Water, electric, sewer. **Each Site:** Picnic table. **Dump Station:** Yes. **Laundry:** Yes. **Pay Phone:** No. **Rest Rooms and Showers:** Yes. **Fuel:** No. **Propane:** Yes. **Internal Roads:** Paved. **RV Service:** No. **Market:** In Brunswick. **Restaurant:** In Brunswick. **General Store:** Yes. **Vending:** Yes. **Swimming Pool:** Yes. **Playground:** No. **Activities:** Biking, golfing, fishing, tennis. **Nearby Attractions:** Sea turtle walks, nature center, carriage tours, historic district. **Additional Information:** Jekyll Island CVB, www.jekylisland.com or (877) 453-5955.

Restrictions

Pets: On leash only. **Fires:** Allowed. **Alcoholic Beverages:** At sites only. **Vehicle Maximum Length:** None. **Other:** $3 daily parking fee.

To Get There

Take I-95 to Exit 29. Follow the signs on US 17 for 10 mi. and turn right onto Drowning Musgrove Causeway (GA 520). The Jekyll Island Welcome Center is 4 mi. on the left.

KENNESAW

KOA–Atlanta North

2000 Old US 41, Kennesaw 30152. T: (770) 427-2406; F: (770) 429-1014; www.koa.com.

RV ★★★ Tent ★★

Beauty: ★★★ Site Privacy: ★★
Spaciousness: ★★★ Quiet: ★★★
Security: ★★★ Cleanliness: ★★★★
Insect Control: ★★★★ Facilities: ★★★

Situated 20 miles northwest of Atlanta, this KOA campground provides easy access to the city. Located just off a busy, suburban road, the campground has a pretty fish pond with large koi and a waterfall at the entrance. Though the atmosphere is relaxing, the experience is more residential than rural. Numbered "streets" help orient people in this large facility, creating a sense of home away from home. Both pull-throughs and back-ins are available, all paved, and those who tent camp have a designated area located right at the entrance. The campground is mostly shady, though a few areas have more sunlight than others, and sites 165–170 and 65–67 have more than their share of tree shade. Besides the many attractions found in Atlanta, nearby Kennesaw Mountain offers over 16 miles of trails, and the Big Shanty Museum retells the history of The General, a famous Civil War Locomotive.

Basics

Operated By: People, Inc. **Open:** All year. **Site Assignment:** First come, first served. **Registration:** At camp office. **Fee:** 30 amp hookups $28, 50 amp hookups $30, 10% AAA, AARP, or KOA discount. **Parking:** 2 vehicles per site.

Facilities

Number of RV Sites: 231. **Number of Tent-Only Sites:** 17. **Hookups:** Water, electric (20, 30, 50 amps), sewer. **Each Site:** Picnic table, tent pad. **Dump Station:** Yes. **Laundry:** Yes. **Pay Phone:** Yes. **Rest Rooms and Showers:** Yes. **Fuel:** No. **Propane:** Yes. **Internal Roads:** Paved. **RV Service:** 2 mi. **Market:** 0.5 mi. **Restaurant:** 1 mi. **General Store:** 0.5 mi. **Vending:** Yes. **Swimming Pool:** Yes. **Playground:** Yes. **Activities:** Basketball, TV room, game room. **Nearby Attractions:** Whitewater rafting, Kennesaw Battlefield Park, American Adventures, Six Flags.

Restrictions

Pets: On leash only. **Fires:** In fire rings only. **Alcoholic Beverages:** At sites only. **Vehicle Maximum Length:** None. **Other:** 14-day stay limit.

To Get There

Take I-75N to Exit 269. Turn left and go 3 mi. At Old US 41, turn right. After 0.5 mi., the campground is on the right.

KINGSLAND

Country Oaks Campground

6 Carlton Cemetary Rd., Kingsland 31548. T: (912) 729-6212.

RV ★★★ Tent n/a

Beauty: ★★★ Site Privacy: ★★
Spaciousness: ★★★ Quiet: ★★★★
Security: ★★★★ Cleanliness: ★★★★
Insect Control: ★★★ Facilities: ★

A middling campground with few frills, Country Oaks does enjoy the benefits of very courteous and helpful owner/managers. Campsites vary significantly in size, and some are quite small (the pull-through sites are largest). All are shaded, with a scattering of nice oaks, but there is not much privacy. The campsites are laid out in three rows, with sites 19–28 being the most secluded (they're also near a small creek). Sites 12–18 and 29–44 are nearest the general store and bathhouse; sites 1–11 are just off the access road and I-95, and these sites may experience significant road noise. Toilet cleanliness leftsomething to be desired on our visit. The owners encourage guests to pet the friendly horses, and buggy rides are available. The mostly older clientele seems to relish the relaxed pace here, often enjoying an afternoon in swinging chairs and rockers on the general store's wraparound porch

Basics

Operated By: Lonnie & Karen Gay. **Open:** All year. **Site Assignment:** First come, first served. **Registration:** Office. **Fee:** $20–$22. **Parking:** On site.

Facilities

Number of RV Sites: 44. **Number of Tent-Only Sites:** 0. **Hookups:** Water, electric (30, 50 amps), sewer. **Each Site:** Picnic table. **Dump Station:** No. **Laundry:** Yes. **Pay Phone:** Yes. **Rest Rooms and Showers:** Yes. **Fuel:** No. **Propane:** Yes. **Internal Roads:** Paved. **RV Service:** 2.5 mi. **Market:** 2.5 mi. **Restaurant:** 2.5 mi. **General Store:** Yes. **Vending:** Yes. **Swimming Pool:** No. **Playground:** No. **Activities:** Boating, fishing, horseshoe. **Nearby Attractions:** Jacksonville Flea Market, Fernandina, Daytona Jacksonville Beaches, Okefenokee Wetlands, Summer Wars. **Additional Information:** Kingsland CVB, (800) 433-0225 or www.visitkingsland.com.

Restrictions

Pets: On leash only. **Fires:** In fire rings only. **Alcoholic Beverages:** Allowed. **Vehicle Maximum Length:** None.

To Get There

Take I-95 to Exit 1 in Georgia and go 0.2 mi.

LAKE LANIER ISLANDS

Lake Lanier Islands

6950 Holiday Rd., Lake Lanier Islands 30518.
T: (770) 932-7270; www.lakelanierislands.com; wbeavers@llimail.com.

★★★★ ★★★★

Beauty: ★★★★★ Site Privacy: ★★★
Spaciousness: ★★★★ Quiet: ★★★★
Security: ★★★★★ Cleanliness: ★★★★
Insect Control: ★★★★ Facilities: ★★★★★

This huge property is a complete vacation destination. Lake Lanier Islands is spread over the eponymous clumps of land in Lake Lanier, a U.S. Army Corps of Engineers project which has many recreational options of its own. Like the other ten campgrounds on the lake (see profiles of Shoal Creekin Buford and Chestnut Ridge in Flowery Branch), boat noise is always a factor for campers; ask attendants for recommendations on quieter campsites. Most sites are well shaded, and some have screening foliage; size varies greatly. In contrast to some nearby campgrounds that are entirely lake-focused, Lake Lanier Islands has several other choices for campers—two golf clubs, an equestrian center, mountain bike rentals, a water park, and more. If you want to explore the surrounding area, the region offers 43 day-use parks, ten marinas, and nine state, county, and city parks.

BASICS

Operated By: Winston Beaver-Manager. **Open:** May–Sept. **Site Assignment:** First come, first served, also reservations. **Registration:** Campground office. **Fee:** $20–$30. **Parking:** On site.

FACILITIES

Number of RV Sites: 271. **Number of Tent-Only Sites:** 31. **Hookups:** Water, electric, some sewer. **Each Site:** Picnic areas. **Dump Station:** Yes. **Laundry:** Yes. **Pay Phone:** Yes. **Rest Rooms and Showers:** Yes. **Fuel:** No. **Propane:** Yes. **Internal Roads:** Paved. **RV Service:** 4 mi. **Market:** 7 mi. **Restaurant:** Less than 7 mi. **General Store:** Yes. **Vending:** No. **Swimming Pool:** No. **Playground:** Yes. **Other:** Full golf course. **Activities:** Boating, beach, waterpark, wave pool, equistrian center, mountain biking. **Nearby Attractions:** Lake Lanier Islands Resort.

RESTRICTIONS

Pets: On leash only. **Fires:** In fire rings only. **Alcoholic Beverages:** Not allowed. **Vehicle Maximum Length:** None. **Other:** 2 vehicles per family.

TO GET THERE

From Atlanta, take I-85N to I-985N (Exit 113). Take Exit 8 (Friendship Rd.), and turn left. Continue 4 mi. to the campground.

LAKE PARK

Eagles Roost Campground

5465 Mill Store Rd., Lake Park 31636. T: (229) 559-0141; www.eaglesroostcampground.com; camp@eaglesroostcampground.com.

Beauty: ★★★★ Site Privacy: ★★★
Spaciousness: ★★★ Quiet: ★★★★★
Security: ★★★★ Cleanliness: ★★★★★
Insect Control: ★★★★ Facilities: ★★★

Located right off I-75, just a few miles from the Florida state line, this park offers convenience as well as all the amenities of a top notch vacation spot. Surrounded by gorgeous hardwoods draped in Spanish moss, the Eagle's Roost offers its guests the tranquility of a rural setting, along with a myriad of activities both inside and outside the park. There is a swimming pool, playground and a rec room for the kids inside the campground itself, while nearby, guests can enjoy Georgia's Wild Adventures , Okefenokee Swamp, or Reed Bingham State Park. Section A, or the Club Deluxe area, is our pick for the best spots at the Eagle's Roost, as the internal roads here are paved and each site is equipped with a concrete pad. Of the 42 available spots in this section, we would have to say that sites 34 through 42 are the most beautiful, surrounded by plenty of those moss-covered hardwoods. For families with children, however, our pick for the best spots would have to be sites 5, 6, and 7, as they are the closest to the pool, playground, and store. The sites in the B and C sections aren't up to par with those in the A section, being closer together, and the roads here are packed sand instead of asphalt. Overall, this is an attractive, well run facility. However, our advice to anyone planning to travel in this area is to do so in the early to mid-spring, as this part of Georgia is nearly unbearable when summer is in full swing.

BASICS

Operated By: Terry Herndon. **Open:** All year. **Site Assignment:** First come, first served. **Registration:** Office. **Fee:** $19–$25. **Parking:** On site.

FACILITIES

Number of RV Sites: 160. **Number of Tent-Only Sites:**. **Hookups:** Water, electric (50 amps). **Each Site:** Picnic table. **Dump Station:** Yes. **Laundry:** Yes. **Pay Phone:** Yes. **Rest Rooms and Showers:** Yes. **Fuel:** No. **Propane:** Yes. **Internal Roads:** Gravel. **RV Service:** Yes. **Market:** Yes. **Restaurant:** Nearby. **General Store:** Yes. **Vending:** No. **Swimming Pool:** Yes. **Playground:** Yes. **Activities:** Okeefenokee Swamp Park, Wild Adventures, Reed Bingham State Park, Stephen C. Foster Park. **Nearby Attractions:** Inquire at campground.

RESTRICTIONS

Pets: On leash only. **Fires:** None. **Alcoholic Beverages:** Allowed. **Vehicle Max. Length:** None.

TO GET THERE

From I-75 Exit 5, go northbound and take a right at the first light. The campground is 1 mi. on left.

LAVONIA

Tugaloo State Park

1763 Tugaloo State Park Rd., Lavonia 30553.
T: (706) 356-4362; www.gastateparks.org.

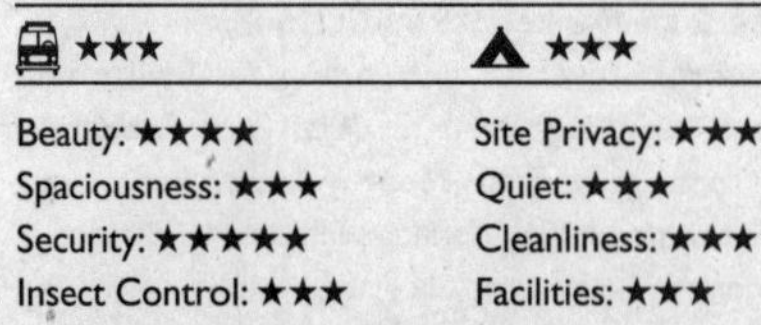

★★★ ★★★

Beauty: ★★★★ Site Privacy: ★★★
Spaciousness: ★★★ Quiet: ★★★
Security: ★★★★★ Cleanliness: ★★★
Insect Control: ★★★ Facilities: ★★★

Between the lovely Pine stand and the views of Hartwell Lake, beauty is the major draw of this State Park campground. Located in the northeast corner of the state, the campground feels quite rural despite its proximity to I-85. And it is well-guarded, making this is one of the region's more secure spots for camping. Unfortunately the restrooms are lousy, and the facilities are lacking in general. But the nearby recreation opportunities and the natural setting help make this an attractive spot nonetheless. With roughly equal numbers of back-in and pull-through sites, the campground sits on a peninsula, and the sites closest to the water are recommended, naturally. The sites, all gravel, vary greatly in size, but are all pretty and wooded. Fishing—especially for large-mouth bass—and water sports make this a fun, if noisy, campground that is excellent for families. Keeping in mind the larger crowds in warmer weather, due to the allure of the water, this park offers a pleasant stay in a tent or RV.

BASICS

Operated By: Georgia Dept. of Natural Resources. **Open:** All year. **Site Assignment:** Reservations accepted. **Registration:** At camp office. **Fee:** $16. **Parking:** In campground.

FACILITIES

Number of Multipurpose Sites: 117. **Hookups:** Water, electric (30 amps), sewer. **Each Site:** Picnic shelter. **Dump Station:** Yes. **Laundry:** Yes. **Pay Phone:** Yes. **Rest Rooms and Showers:** Yes. **Fuel:** No. **Propane:** Yes. **Internal Roads:** Paved. **RV Service:** Yes. **Market:** No. **Restaurant:** No. **General Store:** Yes. **Vending:** Yes. **Swimming Pool:** Yes. **Playground:** Yes. **Activities:** Fishing, boating, hiking, volleyball, horseshoes, mini golf. **Nearby Attractions:** Ty Cobb Museum, Victoria Bryant State Park & Golf Course, Tallulah Gorge State Park, Hartwell Dam.

RESTRICTIONS

Pets: On leash only. **Fires:** In fire rings only. **Alcoholic Beverages:** At sites. **Vehicle Maximum Length:** 35 ft.

TO GET THERE

Take I-85 to Exit 173. Follow the signs to Gerrard Rd. Turn right and go 1.5 mi. to Hwy. 328. Turn left and proceed 3.3 mi. to the park.

LINCOLNTON

Elijah Creek State Park

2959 McCormick Hwy., Lincolnton 30817.
T: (706) 359-3458 or (800) 864-7275; www.gastateparks.org.

★★★★ ★★★★

Beauty: ★★★★ Site Privacy: ★★★
Spaciousness: ★★★ Quiet: ★★★
Security: ★★★★★ Cleanliness: ★★★★
Insect Control: ★★★ Facilities: ★★★★

Named after the frontiersman and Revolutionary War hero Elijah Clark, this is one of the more popular state parks in the area. Expect lots of running kids, buzzing boats, and other noises associated with large camps. RVers and tent campers have a choice of 165 sites. Most of the sites have some shade but with very little undergrowth. In Campground 1, sites 38 and 53 are gorgeous, 56 is quite secluded, and 23–31 have lovely open views (though all are a bit crowded). Campground 2 has sites that are quite shady (108–115) and some with nice views (116–118). Be sure to avoid all sites near boat ramps, especially during summer weekends. The park offers hiking, swimming and fishing thanks to Clarks Hill Lake, as well as a museum depicting colonial life. Several annual events, including an arts and crafts festival and a bluegrass festival, mean potential visitors should call well in advance.

Basics

Operated By: Georgia Dept. of Natural Resources. **Open:** All year. **Site Assignment:** Reservations or first come, first served. **Registration:** At camp office. **Fee:** $18–$20. **Parking:** 2 vehicles per site.

Facilities

Number of RV Sites: 165. **Number of Tent-Only Sites:** 0. **Hookups:** Water, electric (50 amps), cable. **Each Site:** Picnic table, fire pit. **Dump Station:** Yes. **Laundry:** Yes. **Pay Phone:** Yes. **Rest Rooms and Showers:** Yes. **Fuel:** 2 mi. **Propane:** 2 mi. **Internal Roads:** Paved & gravel. **RV Service:** Housecalls available. **Market:** In Martins Crossroads. **Restaurant:** 7 mi. **General Store:** No. **Vending:** Soft drinks. **Swimming Pool:** No. **Playground:** Yes. **Other:** 3rd weekend in October—Oldtimer's Festival. **Activities:** Boating, water skiing, fishing, museum tours, hiking, miniatue golf, swimming, volleyball. **Nearby Attractions:** Mistletoe State Park, Bobby Brown State Park, historic Washington, Clarks Hill Dam.

Restrictions

Pets: On leash only. **Fires:** In fire rings only. **Alcoholic Beverages:** Not allowed. **Vehicle Maximum Length:** 40 ft.

To Get There

7 mi. northeast of Lincolnton on US Hwy. 378.

MARIETTA

Brookwood RV Resort Park

1031 Wylie Rd., Marietta 30067. T: (877) 727-5787; F: (770) 427-8410; www.brookwoodrvresortparks.com; info@brookwoodrvresortparks.com.

RV ★★★ Tent n/a

Beauty: ★★★	Site Privacy: ★★
Spaciousness: ★★	Quiet: ★★
Security: ★★	Cleanliness: ★★★★★
Insect Control: ★★★★	Facilities: ★★★

For those desiring a camping experience convenient to exploring Atlanta, Brookwood Resort Park is the place. Just 13 miles from downtown, the campground provides a refreshing oasis amidst the bustle of the metroplitan area. Visitors won't mistake this for a more secluded, mountain experience (a car dealership lies next door), but setting up beneath the tall pine trees beats a musty hotel room. Full hookups along with cable and phones are complemented by a concierge service that will deliver rental cars as needed. Most of the sites are spacious (a few are not), with either gravel, grass or a mixture of the two on the ground.

Basics

Operated By: The Sullivan family. **Open:** All year. **Site Assignment:** Reservations preferred. **Registration:** At camp office. **Fee:** $37. **Parking:** In campground.

Facilities

Number of RV Sites: 70. **Number of Tent-Only Sites:** 0. **Hookups:** Water, electric (20, 30, 50 amps), sewer, phone, cable. **Each Site:** Level, paved, full hookups. **Dump Station:** Yes. **Laundry:** Yes. **Pay Phone:** Yes. **Rest Rooms and Showers:** Yes. **Fuel:** No. **Propane:** Yes. **Internal Roads:** Paved. **RV Service:** Concierge service. **Market:** In Marietta. **Restaurant:** In Marietta. **General Store:** No. **Vending:** Soft drinks. **Swimming Pool:** Yes. **Playground:** No. **Activities:** Inquire at campground. **Nearby Attractions:** White Water Park, Kennesaw Civil War Museum, Underground Atlanta.

Restrictions

Pets: Yes. **Fires:** No. **Alcoholic Beverages:** At sites only. **Vehicle Maximum Length:** 45 ft.

To Get There

From downtown Atlanta, go 13 mi. on I-75N to exit 261 and drive west.

McDONOUGH

Atlanta South KOA RV Resort

281 Mt. Olive Rd., McDonough 30253. T: (800) 562-6073; www.koa.com.

RV ★★★ Tent ★

Beauty: ★★★★	Site Privacy: ★★★
Spaciousness: ★★★	Quiet: ★★★
Security: ★★★	Cleanliness: ★★★★
Insect Control: ★★★	Facilities: ★★★

Campers come to Atlanta South KOA for convenience rather than escape, as the area is suburban in nature. Located 30 minutes south of Atlanta, this campground is 15 miles from the Atlanta Speedway, so potential visitors should check far in advance to insure a spot during speedway weekends. Most of the sites are pull-throughs, though back-ins are found along the campground's perimeter. Water, sewer, and electric hookups are available. There is a beautiful tent-only area, but it isn't very level. Each site is mix of pine straw and gravel, and though there are sufficient trees to provide shade, mostly pine and maple, the understory does little to provide privacy.

Basics

Operated By: Don Goetz. **Open:** All year. **Site Assignment:** Reservations or first come, first served. **Registration:** At camp office. **Fee:** $26–$28. **Parking:** In campground.

Facilities

Number of RV Sites: 144. **Number of Tent-Only Sites:** 10. **Hookups:** Water, electric (30, 50 amps), sewer. **Each Site:** Picnic table, grill. **Dump Station:** Yes. **Laundry:** Yes. **Pay Phone:** Yes. **Rest Rooms and Showers:** Yes. **Fuel:** No. **Propane:** Yes. **Internal Roads:** Gravel. **RV Service:** Washing $5. **Market:** In McDonough. **Restaurant:** In McDonough. **General Store:** No. **Vending:** No. **Swimming Pool:** Yes. **Playground:** Yes. **Other:** Cabins available, $36. **Activities:** Swimming, pond fishing, nature trails. **Nearby Attractions:** Atlanta Motor Speedway.

Restrictions

Pets: On leash w /restrictions. **Fires:** In fire rings only. **Alcoholic Beverages:** Allowed. **Vehicle Maximum Length:** 70 ft.

To Get There

From I-75 N., take Exit 222 (or Exit 72 from I-75 S.). Go west on Jodeco Rd. Mt. Olive Rd. and the campground are on the left.

McRAE

Little Ocmulgee State Park

P.O. Drawer 149, McRae 31055. T: (229) 868-7474; www.gastateparks.org.

RV ★★★★ Tent ★★★★

Beauty: ★★★★★	Site Privacy: ★★★
Spaciousness: ★★★★	Quiet: ★★★★
Security: ★★★★	Cleanliness: ★★★★
Insect Control: ★★★	Facilities: ★★★★★

A small park created by private land donations and the work of the Civilian Conservation Corps, Little Ocmulgee State Park offers a pleasant retreat from the more popular (and populated) campgrounds in the area. The lodge is the center of activity here, and only lodge and cottage guests can use its swimming pool (though its restaurant is open to everyone, of course). However, you don't need the pool when you can just take a dip in the lake, which has its own pleasant little beach. A fairly low-key place, most campers seem to visit here to stroll along the nature trail or to tee off on the 18-hole golf course. Be sure to keep moving on the trail, though—the path passes near a buzzard rookery, and stationary campers might draw some interested, circling birds above.

Basics

Operated By: Georgia Dept. of Natural Resources. **Open:** All year. **Site Assignment:** First come, first served. **Registration:** At lodge prior to set up. **Fee:** $15–$19. **Parking:** On site.

Facilities

Number of RV Sites: 55. **Number of Tent-Only Sites:** 0. **Hookups:** Water, electric (50 amps), cable. **Each Site:** Fire pit. **Dump Station:** Yes. **Laundry:** Yes. **Pay Phone:** Yes. **Rest Rooms and Showers:** Yes. **Fuel:** No. **Propane:** No. **Internal Roads:** Paved. **RV Service:** No. **Market:** 2 mi. in McRae. **Restaurant:** At lodge. **General Store:** No. **Vending:** Yes. **Swimming Pool:** No. **Playground:** No. **Activities:** Fishing, boating, beach area, tennis, nature trails, mini golf. **Nearby Attractions:** Georgia Veterans State Park & Golf Course, General Coffee State Park & Heritage Farm, Jefferson Davis Memorial State Historic Site.

Restrictions

Pets: On leash (6 ft. or less) only. **Fires:** In fire rings only. **Alcoholic Beverages:** Allowed, cups only at the beach. **Vehicle Max. Length:** 40 ft.

To Get There

The park is 2 mi. north of McRae via US Hwys. 319 and 441.

NICHOLLS

General Coffee State Park

46 John Coffee Rd., Nicholls 31554. T: (912) 384-7082.

RV ★★★★ Tent ★★★★

Beauty: ★★★★★ Site Privacy: ★★★★
Spaciousness: ★★★★★ Quiet: ★★★★★
Security: ★★★★ Cleanliness: ★★★★
Insect Control: ★★★ Facilities: ★★★★★

Approximately six miles from Douglas, this rural park includes Seventeen Mile River, which creates six small lakes as it winds through a Cypress swamp. The variety of foliage includes pines and hardwoods draped with Spanish moss. The park was donated to the state by a group of Coffee County citizens in 1970 and was named after General John Coffee, a planter, US Congressman and military leader. In addition to camping, it offers several exhibits at Heritage Farm, including a tobacco barn, a cane mill, and, yes, barnyard animals as well. With comfortable, gravel pull-through sites, the campground has a relatively serene, spacious feel. Both multipurpose camping Areas 1 and 2 are loops, and Area 1 includes a grassy field and playground, although the playground at the picnic area is much nicer. There are separate tent areas, but the facilities overall make both tent and RV camping quite pleasant here. This is a secure spot, largely due to the rural setting and sparse crowds, good for families and privacy.

BASICS

Operated By: Georgia Dept. of Natural Resources. **Open:** All year. **Site Assignment:** First come, first served. **Registration:** Inside main gate. **Fee:** $13–$15. **Parking:** On site.

FACILITIES

Number of Multipurpose Sites: 50. **Hookups:** Electric (30 amps), water, sewer. **Each Site:** Picnic shelters. **Dump Station:** Yes. **Laundry:** Yes. **Pay Phone:** Yes. **Rest Rooms and Showers:** Yes. **Fuel:** No. **Propane:** No. **Internal Roads:** Gravel. **RV Service:** Yes. **Market:** No. **Restaurant:** No. **General Store:** No. **Vending:** Yes. **Swimming Pool:** Yes. **Playground:** Yes. **Other:** Amphitheater. **Activities:** Hiking, nature programs, fishing, boating. **Nearby Attractions:** Historical farm w/ live animals. **Additional Information:** (800) 864-PARK.

RESTRICTIONS

Pets: No. **Fires:** Allowed. **Alcoholic Beverages:** Allowed. **Vehicle Maximum Length:** Must park in 120-ft. pull-through. **Other:** $2 parking pass.

TO GET THERE

From Rt. 221, exit at Rt 32, and turn right at the Keystone Dr. Entrance after the train tracks.

OCHLOCKNEE

Sugar Mill Plantation RV Park

4857 McMillan Rd., Ochlocknee 31773. T: (229) 227-1451 or (888) 375-3246; sugarmillrv@yahoo.com.

RV ★★★ Tent ★★★

Beauty: ★★★ Site Privacy: ★★
Spaciousness: ★★★ Quiet: ★★★★
Security: ★★★ Cleanliness: ★★★★
Insect Control: ★★★ Facilities: ★★★

This is a lovely private campground in a rural area near the Florida panhandle a few miles from the small town of Thomasville. We found very nice folks here and a positive atmosphere all around, with a generally older crowd. The sites are medium in size, both back-ins and pull-throughs, and the quiet is one of the park's more attractive features. The campground is fairly wooded, with about half the sites in some shade, and ground cover is of grass or pine straw. Especially quiet and wooded are sites 15–18. The landscaping includes palmetto bushes and pampas grass. There is a goose pond, and the fishing ponds are stocked with bass and catfish. This is not the most private or spacious campground, but it is quite pleasant, more so than many commercial campgrounds. And, as the name implies, there are plantations and sites of historic interest to be enjoyed nearby.

BASICS

Operated By: Private operator. **Open:** All year. **Site Assignment:** Reservations accepted. **Registration:** At camp office. **Fee:** $19. **Parking:** In campground.

FACILITIES

Number of RV Sites: 120. **Number of Tent-Only Sites:** 0. **Hookups:** Water, electric (20, 30, 50 amps), sewer. **Each Site:** Picnic table. **Dump Station:** Yes. **Laundry:** Yes. **Pay Phone:** Yes. **Rest Rooms and Showers:** Yes. **Fuel:** No. **Propane:** Yes. **Internal Roads:** Paved & gravel. **RV Service:** Yes. **Market:** In Ochlocknee. **Restaurant:** In Ochlocknee. **General Store:** Yes. **Vending:** No. **Swimming Pool:** No. **Playground:** No. **Activities:** Fishing, basketball, potluck dinners, game nights, shuffleboard. **Nearby Attractions:** Thomas County Historical Museum, historic plantation tours, antique shops.

RESTRICTIONS

Pets: On leash only. **Fires:** In designated areas. **Alcoholic Beverages:** At sites only. **Vehicle Maximum Length:** None.

TO GET THERE

The campground is located 8 mi. north of Thomasville on Hwy. 19.

PERRY

Fair Harbor RV Park & Campground

515 Marshallville Rd., Perry 31069. T: (877) 988-8844; www.fairharborrvpark.com.

RV ★★★★ Tent n/a

Beauty: ★★★★ Site Privacy: ★★
Spaciousness: ★★ Quiet: ★★★★
Security: ★★★ Cleanliness: ★★★★
Insect Control: ★★★★ Facilities: ★★★

Not far from the Georgia National Fairgrounds, Fair Harbor provides a nice, under-developed camping experience just two-tenths of a mile from I-75. The 100-acre park has 150 RV sites, mostly pull-throughs. The 30, densely wooded, tent-only sites are well removed from the rest of the area and have water and electric hookups. Though less shady, the RV sites are quite large, which provides a bit of privacy. For a quieter experience, campers should choose sites closer to the tent-only area. Breakfast is served Tuesday through Saturday. Campers may want to visit during the Georgia National Livestock Show and Rodeo in February as well as the Georgia State Fair in August, but plan ahead as the park fills quickly.

BASICS

Operated By: Tim McCord & Kirk Morris. **Open:** All year. **Site Assignment:** Reservations or first come, first served. **Registration:** At camp office. **Fee:** $11–$22. **Parking:** In campground.

FACILITIES

Number of RV Sites: 150. **Number of Tent-Only Sites:** 30. **Hookups:** Water, electric (20, 30, 50 amps), sewer, cable. **Each Site:** Picnic table, grill. **Dump Station:** Yes. **Laundry:** Yes. **Pay Phone:** Yes. **Rest Rooms and Showers:** Yes. **Fuel:** No. **Propane:** Yes. **Internal Roads:** Paved, sites gravel. **RV Service:** 15 min. **Market:** In. Perry. **Restaurant:** Less than 1 mi. **General Store:** Limited. **Vending:** No. **Swimming Pool:** No. **Playground:** No. **Other:** Breakfast Tue.–Sat.; RV storage available. **Activities:** Pond fishing, horseshoes. **Nearby Attractions:** Georgia Music Hall of Famr, the Hay House, Andersonville National Cemetery, Massee Lane Gardens, Museum of Aviation, Georgia Agricenter, fairgrounds.

RESTRICTIONS

Pets: On leash only. **Fires:** Allowed. **Alcoholic Beverages:** Allowed. **Vehicle Maximum Length:** None.

TO GET THERE

Take I-75 Exit 135. Go 0.1 mi. to campground.

PERRY

Twin Oaks RV Park

Hwy. 26, Perry 31069. T: (478) 987-9361.

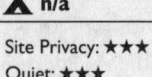

RV ★★★ Tent n/a

Beauty: ★★★★ Site Privacy: ★★★
Spaciousness: ★★★ Quiet: ★★★
Security: ★★★ Cleanliness: ★★★★
Insect Control: ★★★★ Facilities: ★★

In the center of the state, this private campground has a rural feel despite its proximity to I-75. The RV park itself boasts huge sites and welcomes big rigs, but not tents. Among its pluses are spanking new restrooms and showers, shade at almost all sites, and RV-friendly facilities. There are both back-in and pull-through sites, with gravel and a nice grassy spot at each site. The whole place is landscaped, pretty, and pleasant, and there is even a little green between some of the sites. Security may be a concern due to the nearby interstate traffic and the lack of a gate, however. Recreation at the RV park is available, and there is plenty in Perry to keep the whole family entertained. With the possible exception of the highway noise, we agree with the park's advertisement: this is a "quiet country" vacation spot, good for families and all ages.

BASICS

Operated By: Harvey Youngblood. **Open:** All year. **Site Assignment:** First come, first served. **Regis-**

tration: At camp office. **Fee:** $17. **Parking:** In campground.

Facilities

Number of RV Sites: 72. **Number of Tent-Only Sites:** 0. **Hookups:** Water, electric (50 amps), sewer. **Each Site:** Gravel w/ concrete patio, picnic table. **Dump Station:** Yes. **Laundry:** Yes. **Pay Phone:** Yes. **Rest Rooms and Showers:** Yes. **Fuel:** No. **Propane:** Yes. **Internal Roads:** Gravel. **RV Service:** No. **Market:** In Perry. **Restaurant:** 1 mi. **General Store:** Across from park. **Vending:** No. **Swimming Pool:** No. **Playground:** No. **Activities:** Horseshoes, volleyball. **Nearby Attractions:** Andersonville, fairground, Civil War Museum..

Restrictions

Pets: On leash only. **Fires:** Some sites. **Alcoholic Beverages:** At sites only. **Vehicle Maximum Length:** None.

To Get There

Take I-75S from Atlanta to Exit 127. The campground is just below Perry on Hwy. 26.

PINE MOUNTAIN
F. D. Roosevelt State Park

2970 Hwy. 190, Pine Mountain 31822. T: (706) 663-4858; www.gastateparks.org.

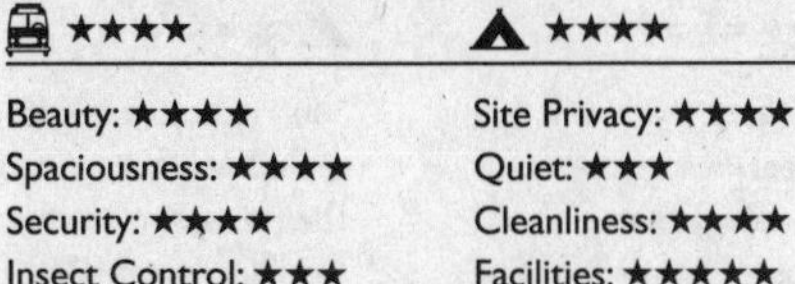

Beauty: ★★★★ Site Privacy: ★★★★
Spaciousness: ★★★★ Quiet: ★★★
Security: ★★★★ Cleanliness: ★★★★
Insect Control: ★★★ Facilities: ★★★★★

In west-central Georgia, this state park is—you guessed it—all about Franklin D. Roosevelt. Actually, they also have the nature thing going for them, in the form of hiking and horseback riding amongst hardwoods and pines and fishing on the lovely Lake Delanor. Despite its secluded, rural setting, the campground stays busy on holidays and weekends, and we suggest going during the off-season if you seek quiet. There are both back-in and pull-through sites, mostly gravel. Although most sites are plenty shady, there is little if any foliage between them. We recommend Campground 5 for its privacy and huge pull-throughs, and the great lake views are in Campground 1 at sites 3 and 4. In Campground 2, sites 33–41 are nicely wooded, and the best tent camping is in Campground 3, as it is more wooded and private (although it is not paved). For the natural beauty of the setting and the historical interest of the attractions in the area, this is a well-rounded spot for families and all generations.

Basics

Operated By: Georgia Dept. of Natural Resources. **Open:** All year. **Site Assignment:** Reservations accepted. **Registration:** At camp office. **Fee:** $15–$17. **Parking:** In campground.

Facilities

Number of Multipurpose Sites: 140. **Hookups:** Water, electric (50 amps). **Each Site:** Picnic area. **Dump Station:** Yes. **Laundry:** Yes (on weekends). **Pay Phone:** Yes. **Rest Rooms and Showers:** Yes. **Fuel:** No. **Propane:** No. **Internal Roads:** Paved. **RV Service:** No. **Market:** No. **Restaurant:** No. **General Store:** No. **Vending:** No. **Swimming Pool:** Yes. **Playground:** Yes. **Activities:** Hiking, biking, fishing, boating, horseback riding. **Nearby Attractions:** Little White House State Park, Sprewell Bluff State Park, West Point Lake.

Restrictions

Pets: Yes. **Fires:** In designated areas. **Alcoholic Beverages:** At sites only. **Vehicle Maximum Length:** 40 ft.

To Get There

The park is located just off I-185 near Callaway Gardens, west of Warm Springs on Hwy. 190, and south of Pine Mountain off US Hwy. 27.

PINE MOUNTAIN
Pine Mountain Campground

8804 Hamilton Rd. (Hwy. 27), Pine Mountain 31822. T: (706) 663-4329; F: (706) 663-9837; www.gocampingamerica.com/pinemountain; jenningspmcg@aol.com.

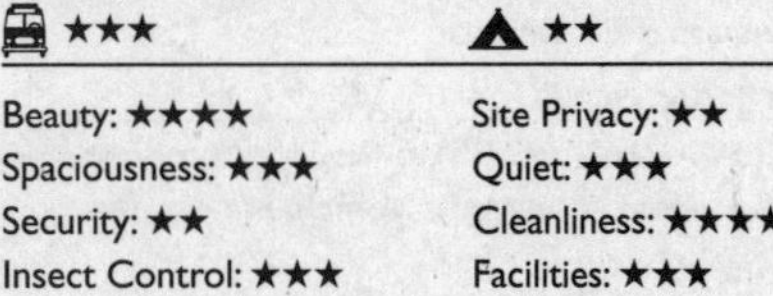

Beauty: ★★★★ Site Privacy: ★★
Spaciousness: ★★★ Quiet: ★★★
Security: ★★ Cleanliness: ★★★★
Insect Control: ★★★ Facilities: ★★★

Located in the foothills of the Appalachian Mountains, this private campground is a rural spot in the vicinity of small town charm and historic tourist attractions such as Callaway Gardens and FDR's Little White House. This is a pretty campground with private, relatively large sites and lots of pine trees. Between kids and highway noise, this is not a terribly quiet campground, but there are extensive facilities and they are well maintained. The pull-through sites in the back are more spacious and are further from the highway noise, but beware the large chunky gravel (the sites in the front have smaller gravel). There are no gates, and the campground is quite visible from the highway, so security is not great. Ideal for families, the campground also offers some adult amenities, including a spa. Bring the kids (or not) and enjoy the trees!

Basics

Operated By: Private operator. **Open:** Apr.–Oct. **Site Assignment:** Reservations accepted. **Registration:** At camp office. **Fee:** $18–$26. **Parking:** In campground.

Facilities

Number of RV Sites: 154. **Number of Tent-Only Sites:** 0, tenters use RV sites. **Hookups:** Water, electric (20, 30, 50 amps), sewer. **Each Site:** Picnic area. **Dump Station:** Yes. **Laundry:** Yes. **Pay Phone:** Yes. **Rest Rooms and Showers:** Yes. **Fuel:** Yes. **Propane:** Yes. **Internal Roads:** Paved & gravel. **RV Service:** No. **Market:** No. **Restaurant:** No. **General Store:** No. **Vending:** No. **Swimming Pool:** Yes. **Playground:** Yes. **Activities:** Miniature golf, swimming, boating. **Nearby Attractions:** Callaway Gardens, FDR's Little White House, Warm Springs, Wild Animal Safari Park. **Additional Information:** Inquire at campground

Restrictions

Pets: Yes. **Fires:** Allowed. **Alcoholic Beverages:** Inquire at campground. **Vehicle Maximum Length:** 40 ft. **Other:** No fireworks.

To Get There

Take I-85S to I-185. Take Exit 42, Hwy. 27. Turn left and go 8 mi. to the campground.

RICHMOND HILL
Fort McAllister State Historic Park

3984 Ft. McAllister Rd., Richmond Hill 31324. T: (912) 727-2339; www.ftmcallister.org or www.gastateparks.org; ftmcallr@coastalnow.net.

RV ★★★★ Tent ★★★★

Beauty: ★★★★★ Site Privacy: ★★★★
Spaciousness: ★★★★★ Quiet: ★★★★★
Security: ★★★★ Cleanliness: ★★★★
Insect Control: ★★★ Facilities: ★★★★

Not far from the Georgia coast on the banks of the Great Ogeechee River, campers at Fort McAllister will find a place to rest their heads among civil war history. The 57 RV sites and 12 tent-only sites lie beneath the giant live oaks that grow in this former battlefield. Water and electric hookups are available in this first come, fist served campground. A Civil War Museum and tours of the fort are possible, just call for reservations.

Basics

Operated By: Georgia Dept. of Natural Resources. **Open:** All year. **Site Assignment:** First come, first served. **Registration:** Museum office. **Fee:** RV $17, tent $5–$15. **Parking:** On site.

Facilities

Number of RV Sites: 53. **Number of Tent-Only Sites:** 12. **Hookups:** Water, electric (30 amps). **Each Site:** Grill, picnic table. **Dump Station:** Yes. **Laundry:** Yes. **Pay Phone:** Yes. **Rest Rooms and Showers:** Yes. **Fuel:** Nearby. **Propane:** Nearby. **Internal Roads:** Paved; sites grass & gravel. **RV Service:** In Richmond Hill. **Market:** 10 mi. **Restaurant:** Nearby. **General Store:** 4 mi. **Vending:** Soft drinks. **Swimming Pool:** No. **Playground:** Yes. **Activities:** Hiking, picknicking, salt water fishing, canoeing, kayaking. **Nearby Attractions:** Civil War museum, fort tours (call for reservations). **Additional Information:** Richmond Hill CVB, (912) 756-2676 or www.richmondhillcvb.org.

Restrictions

Pets: On leash & attended. **Fires:** In fire rings only. **Alcoholic Beverages:** At sites only. **Vehicle Maximum Length:** 50 ft.

To Get There

Take I-95 Exit 90. Go 10 mi. east to Georgia Spur 144. Turn left, then go until the road dead-ends at the park (4.4 mi.).

RICHMOND HILL
KOA–Savannah South

P.O. Box 309, Richmond Hill 31324. T: (912) 756-3396.

Beauty: ★★★★ Site Privacy: ★★★
Spaciousness: ★★★ Quiet: ★★★★

Security: ★★★ Cleanliness: ★★★★
Insect Control: ★★★ Facilities: ★★★

Located in a suburban setting, this campground contains sites that are small but attractive. The area is mostly shady with a few open sites scattered throughout the site. For the nature lover, the campground has a 35-acre fishing lake that also contains hundreds of ducks, geese, swans, and egrets. The sites closest to the lakefront are by far the prettiest. However, the sites do not offer much privacy. We recommend visiting Savanna South in the fall or the spring when the weather is most pleasant. Reservations are preferred for this KOA campground. However, the campground's security measures are lacking, so be mindful.

Basics

Operated By: Private operator. **Open:** All year. **Site Assignment:** First come, first served. **Registration:** Office. **Fee:** $27–$36. **Parking:** On site.

Facilities

Number of RV Sites: 130. **Number of Tent-Only Sites:** 15. **Hookups:** Electric (50 amps), water. **Each Site:** Picnic table, fire pit. **Dump Station:** Yes. **Laundry:** Yes. **Pay Phone:** Yes. **Rest Rooms and Showers:** Yes. **Fuel:** No. **Propane:** Yes. **Internal Roads:** Paved. **RV Service:** No. **Market:** In Richmond Hill. **Restaurant:** In Richmond Hill. **General Store:** Yes. **Vending:** Yes. **Swimming Pool:** Yes. **Playground:** Yes. **Activities:** Fishing, boating, bird-watching, basketball, shuffleboard, game room. **Nearby Attractions:** Savannah, Fort Stewart, Fort McAllister State Historic Park. **Additional Information:** Richmond Hill CVB (912) 756-2676 or www.richmondhillcvb.org.

Restrictions

Pets: Yes. **Fires:** Designated areas only. **Alcoholic Beverages:** Not allowed. **Vehicle Maximum Length:** None.

To Get There

From I-95 take Exit 87 and turn left onto US 17 South. The campground is 0.5 mi. on left.

RINGGOLD

KOA–Chattanooga South

199 KOA Blvd., Ringgold 30736. T: (706) 937-4166; www.koa.com; koakamp@catt.com.

RV ★★★ Tent ★★

Beauty: ★★★★ Site Privacy: ★★★
Spaciousness: ★★★ Quiet: ★★★★
Security: ★★★ Cleanliness: ★★★
Insect Control: ★★★★ Facilities: ★★★

Whether civil war enthusiasts or just families on vacation, campers will find this KOA park offers a relaxing camp experience within easy reach of Chattanooga. A mix of gravel and paved roads provides access to the sites, some of which have tent pads. The prettiest and shadiest sites are located on the east side, near the pet kennel. A minimal understory limits privacy, but campers have some room to move about, as sites are medium to large in size. Those wishing to remain in the campground will find an outdoor theater, volleyball court, basketball court, and horseshoe pits. Campers venturing beyond the park can visit to civil war battlefields (Chickamauga and Chattanooga National Military Park) or the Tennessee Aquarium, Ruby Falls, or the Tennessee Valley Railroad.

Basics

Operated By: KOA Kampgrounds. **Open:** All year. **Site Assignment:** Reservations accepted. **Registration:** At camp office. **Fee:** $25. **Parking:** In campground.

Facilities

Number of RV Sites: 65. **Number of Tent-Only Sites:** 21. **Hookups:** Water, electric (30, 50 amps). **Each Site:** Picnic table, fire pit. **Dump Station:** Yes. **Laundry:** Yes. **Pay Phone:** Yes. **Rest Rooms and Showers:** Yes. **Fuel:** Yes. **Propane:** Yes. **Internal Roads:** Paved & gravel. **RV Service:** Yes. **Market:** In Chattanooga. **Restaurant:** In Chattanooga. **General Store:** Yes. **Vending:** No. **Swimming Pool:** Yes. **Playground:** Yes. **Activities:** Outdoor theater, volleyball, basketball, horseshoes. **Nearby Attractions:** Tennessee Aquarium, Ruby Falls, outlet malls, Rock City, Lost Sea, area flea markets, Southern Belle riverboat.

Restrictions

Pets: On leash only. **Fires:** Allowed. **Alcoholic Beverages:** At sites only. **Vehicle Maximum Length:** None.

To Get There

From I-75, take the Battlefield Pkwy./Fort Oglethorpe exit and proceed west on Hwy. 2 for 300 yards to the camp entrance.

RISING FAWN

Cloudland Canyon State Park

122 Cloudland Canyon Park Rd., Rising Fawn 30738. T: (706) 657-4050; www.gastateparks.org.

RV ★★★★ Tent ★★★★★

Beauty: ★★★★★ Site Privacy: ★★★★★
Spaciousness: ★★★★★ Quiet: ★★★★
Security: ★★★★★ Cleanliness: ★★★★
Insect Control: ★★★★ Facilities: ★★★★

Cloudland is one of the most scenic parks in Georgia. The 2,200-acre park has 75 sites with an additional 30 primitive tent sites. All of the back-in sites are huge, while the size of the pull-throughs varies greatly. Still, the entire area is gorgeous and heavily wooded, providing great privacy between sites, some of which are quite large and secluded. The nearby town of Trenton provides supplies to the forgetful camper. Tennis and swimming are available, but the hiking trails take visitors to the park's centerpiece—the canyon, which varies in depth between 800 and nearly 2000 feet. Those who come to relax at Cloudland may still hear the call of Rock City, a private attraction located close by. Visitors may even want to zip up to Chattanooga, where a myriad of activities, including the Tennessee Aquarium, and the Chattanooga Choo Choo, await

Basics

Operated By: Georgia Dept. of Natural Resources. **Open:** All year. **Site Assignment:** Reservations preferred. **Registration:** At camp office. **Fee:** $10–$19. **Parking:** 2 vehicles per site.

Facilities

Number of RV Sites: 75. **Number of Tent-Only Sites:** 30. **Hookups:** Water, electric (30 amps). **Each Site:** Picnic table, fire pit. **Dump Station:** Yes. **Laundry:** Yes. **Pay Phone:** Yes. **Rest Rooms and Showers:** Yes. **Fuel:** No. **Propane:** No. **Internal Roads:** Paved. **RV Service:** No. **Market:** In Trenton. **Restaurant:** In Trenton. **General Store:** No. **Vending:** Soft drinks. **Swimming Pool:** Yes. **Playground:** Yes. **Other:** Waterfall trails. **Activities:** Hiking, backpacking, tennis, swimming. **Nearby Attractions:** Chief Van House State Historic Site, Ruby Falls, Incline Railroad, Lookout Mountain, Tennessee Aquarium.

Restrictions

Pets: On leash only. **Fires:** Allowed. **Alcoholic Beverages:** Yes, in a cup. **Vehicle Maximum Length:** None.

To Get There

The campground is located 5 mi. east of Trenton or 18 mi. northwest of Lafayette via GA 136.

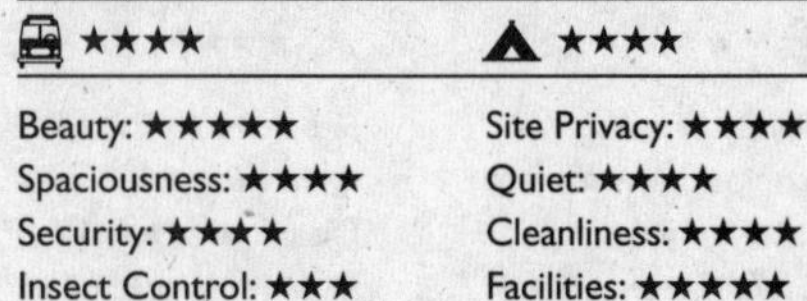

RUTLEDGE

Hard Labor Creek State Park

P.O. Box 247, Rutledge 30663. T: (706) 557-3001; www.gastateparks.org.

RV ★★★★ Tent ★★★★

Beauty: ★★★★★ Site Privacy: ★★★★
Spaciousness: ★★★★ Quiet: ★★★★
Security: ★★★★ Cleanliness: ★★★★
Insect Control: ★★★ Facilities: ★★★★★

Named either by slaves working in nearby fields or by Indians who thought the creek was difficult to ford, Hard Labor Creek State Park conjures up very different associations these days. The park's golf course is known as a good value, offering a pro shop, driving range, and unlimited weekday play packages. Campsite sizes vary, but most are spacious and nicely wooded. The campground abuts a swimming beach on the small but pleasant Lake Brantley. Lakeside sites 50 and 51 have nice water views, and sites 22 and 27 are pleasantly secluded; site 42 is a particularly nice pull-through. Nearby, campers can visit Stone Mountain or the Oconee National Forest. There's also a large on-site horse stable with special campsites for equestrians, as well as access to multi-use trails open to both horses and hikers.

Basics

Operated By: Georgia Dept. of Natural Resources. **Open:** All year. **Site Assignment:** Reservations only. **Registration:** At camp office. **Fee:** $15–$17. **Parking:** 2 vehicles per site.

Facilities

Number of RV Sites: 47. **Number of Tent-Only Sites:** 4. **Hookups:** Water, electric (30 amps). **Each Site:** Picnic table, grill, fire ring. **Dump Station:** Yes. **Laundry:** Yes. **Pay Phone:** Yes. **Rest Rooms and Showers:** Yes. **Fuel:** No. **Propane:** No. **Internal Roads:** Paved. **RV Service:** 20 mi. **Market:** 5 mi. **Restaurant:** 5 mi. **General Store:** 15 mi. **Vending:** Yes. **Swimming Pool:** No. **Playground:** Yes. **Activities:** Beach area, golf, hiking trails, horse stable. **Nearby Attractions:** Stone Mountain,

Oconee National Forest, Athens, Panola Mountain & State Conservation Park.

Restrictions

Pets: On leash only. **Fires:** In fire rings only. **Alcoholic Beverages:** Allowed. **Vehicle Maximum Length:** None. **Other:** 14-day max. stay limit.

To Get There

Take exit 105 on I-20E. Proceed 3 mi. on Fairplay Rd.

SAVANNAH

Skidaway Island State Park

52 Diamond Causeway, Savannah 31411-1102. T: (912) 598-2300; www.gastateparks.org.

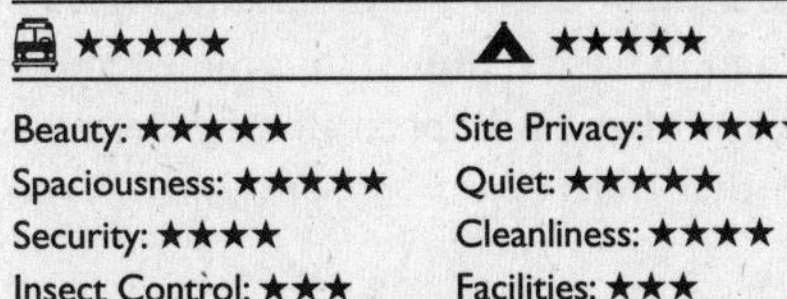

RV ★★★★★ Tent ★★★★★

Beauty: ★★★★★ Site Privacy: ★★★★★
Spaciousness: ★★★★★ Quiet: ★★★★★
Security: ★★★★ Cleanliness: ★★★★
Insect Control: ★★★ Facilities: ★★★

Historic Savannah is the cultural anchor of this state park, and the rich, diverse physical environment makes it a stunner for nature lovers as well. It is a glorious, beautiful place offerig both fresh and salt water, oodles of wildlife viewing, and plenty of natural variety in the forest portions of the park. It is an urban to suburban setting, so we do not recommend sites near the main road, but the sites themselves are indeed quite large and attractive, with spanish moss dripping from the trees above. All of the sites are pull-throughs, and they have pine straw and packed dirt ground cover. Especially huge are sites 1–10, and exceptionally gorgeous are 55, 57, and 59. The only turn-off here are the yucky facilities, but if you can tolerate that, the beauty and privacy more than make up for it. Savannah is a large enough town to provide entertainment for all travelers, and the campground itself is good for families and all ages. For history and/or nature nuts, this is a supreme vacation spot.

Basics

Operated By: Georgia Dept. of Natural Resources. **Open:** All year. **Site Assignment:** Reservations accepted. **Registration:** At camp office. **Fee:** $16–$18. **Parking:** 2 vehicles per site.

Facilities

Number of Multipurpose Sites: 88. **Hookups:** Water, electric (30 amps), cable. **Each Site:** Picnic table. **Dump Station:** Yes. **Laundry:** Yes. **Pay Phone:** Yes. **Rest Rooms and Showers:** Yes. **Fuel:** Nearby. **Propane:** No. **Internal Roads:** Paved. **RV Service:** No. **Market:** In Savannah. **Restaurant:** In Savannah. **General Store:** No. **Vending:** Yes. **Swimming Pool:** Yes. **Playground:** Yes. **Activities:** Hiking, nature trail, bird-watching, swimming, museum & interpretative center. **Nearby Attractions:** Wormsloe State Historic Site, Fort McAllister State Historic Park, Fort Morris State Historic Site, Skidaway Marine Institute, historic Savannah, Tybee Island beaches.

Restrictions

Pets: On 6-ft leash. **Fires:** Allowed. **Alcoholic Beverages:** Not allowed. **Vehicle Maximum Length:** None.

To Get There

From I-16 in Savannah, exit at I-518 (Exit 164A), which merges with DeReene Ave. Turn right on Waters Ave. and go straight ahead to Diamond Causeway.

ST. MARY'S

Crooked River State Park

6222 Charlie Smith Sr. Hwy., St. Mary's 31558. T: (912) 882-5256; www.gastateparks.org.

RV ★★★★ Tent ★★★★

Beauty: ★★★★★ Site Privacy: ★★★★
Spaciousness: ★★★★★ Quiet: ★★★★★
Security: ★★★★ Cleanliness: ★★★★
Insect Control: ★★ Facilities: ★★★

Situated in a gorgeous pine stand, this State Park campground also boasts Spanish moss-draped oaks at most campsites. This is a serene campground near the small coastal town of St. Mary's in the southernmost part of the state. Most of the sites are pull-throughs, and they tend to be spacious (some are huge) with pine straw and packed dirt for ground cover. The best views of the intercoastal marshland can be found at sites 10, 11, and 39. Some other sites offer more privacy, such as 44, which is a giant pull-through that would be great for big-rigs. This is a wonderful place for families who want privacy, with plenty of outdoor recreation and water sports available to campers. In addition, the historical intrigue of the nearby McIntosh Sugar Works and the wild horses and mansion ruins at Cumberland Island National Seashore make this a lovely place for a vacation.

Basics

Operated By: Georgia Dept. of Natural Resources. **Open:** All year. **Site Assignment:** Reservations or first come, first served. **Registration:** At camp office. **Fee:** $18. **Parking:** In campground.

Facilities

Number of RV Sites: 62. **Number of Tent-Only Sites:** 0. **Hookups:** Water, electric (30, 50 amps), cable. **Each Site:** Picnic shelter. **Dump Station:** Yes. **Laundry:** Yes. **Pay Phone:** Yes. **Rest Rooms and Showers:** Yes. **Fuel:** In St. Mary's. **Propane:** In St. Mary's. **Internal Roads:** Paved. **RV Service:** In Brunswick or Jacksonville. **Market:** 10 min. **Restaurant:** In St. Mary's. **General Store:** 3 mi. **Vending:** Soft drinks. **Swimming Pool:** Yes. **Playground:** Inquire at campground. **Activities:** Saltwater fishing, boating, kayaking, hiking, mini golf. **Nearby Attractions:** Cumberland Island National Seashore, Jekyll Island, Okefenokee National Wildlife Refuge, Fernandina Beach.

Restrictions

Pets: On leash (6 ft. or less) only. **Fires:** In fire ring or grill. **Alcoholic Beverages:** Yes, in a cup. **Vehicle Maximum Length:** None.

To Get There

The campground is located 7 mi. north of St. Mary's on GA Spur 40 or 12 mi. east of Kingsland off US Hwy. 17 (8 mi. off I-95).

STONE MOUNTAIN

Stone Mountain Family Campground

Hwy. 78 East, Stone Mountain 30086. T: (800) 385-9807 or (770) 498-5710; F: (770) 413-5082; www.stonemountain.com.

RV ★★★ Tent ★★★

Beauty: ★★★★ Site Privacy: ★★
Spaciousness: ★★★ Quiet: ★★
Security: ★★★ Cleanliness: ★★★★
Insect Control: ★★★★ Facilities: ★★★★★

In spite of touting 441 wooded campsites (43 of these primitive tent sites), Stone Mountain is quite a friendly and relaxing place. Campers expecting a remote experience won't find it, but visitors ready to take advantage of the many activities available at Stone Mountain will have a field day. Nearby activities include a swimming beach with a water slide, Stone Mountain Museum, a train ride, and a hike to the top of Stone Mountain. The famous laser light show occurs on Saturdays in season (everyday between mid-May and mid-August). Keep in mind that camping costs are in addition to the entrance fee. Most sites have water, electric, and sewer hookups in addition to a grill, picnic table and tent pad. Not all sites are on the water, but all are within easy walking distance.

Basics

Operated By: Silver Dollar City, Inc. **Open:** All year. **Site Assignment:** First come, first served. **Registration:** At camp office. **Fee:** $37 lakeside full, $32 lakeside partial, $28 lakeside tent, $22 primitive tent. **Parking:** 2 vehicles per site.

Facilities

Number of RV Sites: 398. **Number of Tent-Only Sites:** 43. **Hookups:** Water, electric (20, 30, 50 amps), sewer. **Each Site:** Grill, picnic table, tent pad, fire ring. **Dump Station:** Yes. **Laundry:** Yes. **Pay Phone:** Yes. **Rest Rooms and Showers:** Yes. **Fuel:** No. **Propane:** Yes. **Internal Roads:** Paved. **RV Service:** 6 mi. **Market:** 2 mi. **Restaurant:** In park. **General Store:** 1 mi. **Vending:** Yes. **Swimming Pool:** Yes. **Playground:** Yes. **Other:** Laser show, sky lift. **Activities:** Tennis, golf, fishing, hiking, volleyball, lake, horseshoes, riverboat cruise, antebellum plantation, petting zoo. **Nearby Attractions:** Beach & waterslide complex, Stone Mountain Museum, Children's Barn, Cross Roads attraction.

Restrictions

Pets: On leash only. **Fires:** In fire rings only. **Alcoholic Beverages:** Not allowed. **Vehicle Maximum Length:** 50 ft. **Other:** 14-day max. stay limit.

To Get There

From Atlanta, take I-285E to Exit 39B, Hwy. 78E Go 7.5 mi. to the park. After entering the park, take first left and go 2 mi. to campground.

Idaho

A visit to Idaho is a journey in time, with much of the country looking exactly as it did for Lewis and Clark and early Native American tribes. Still, proud pines spiral into the cerulean blue, and bald eagles, prouder still, dare the limits of the mountain tops. As you wander into the backcountry wilderness, it's not hard to imagine that you're the first human to have ventured into these remote places. The number of Idaho parks, both state and private, and the diversity of Idaho's landscape offer a full spectrum of experience for all outdoor enthusiasts. From campsites accessible only by foot (where you're reminded that toilets are a modern amenity) to comfortable RV campgrounds, it's nearly impossible to escape the feeling of wilderness.

As you journey to your camping destinations, take the opportunity to enjoy the views provided by the Gem State. In the north, you might visit **Lake Coeur d'Alene** or **Lake Pend Oreille,** the largest lake in Idaho or you could motor along the **Lake Coeur d'Alene Scenic Byway**, making sure to stop at a scenic lookout to glimpse an eagle on the prowl. Take the **Northwest Passage Scenic Byway** and recapture moments of Lewis and Clark along 191 miles of their trail, and venture into **Hell's Canyon** where you can experience the sheer cliffs from water's edge. RV campers will enjoy a stop in **Kamiah** where the RV community is strong. In Central Idaho make a stop in the **Clear Lake Region** where you can stay at one of many Lewis and Clark Expedition campsites. Explore the area alone, take a guided tour, or horseback ride, or mountain bike through the remote territories. Drive the **Salmon River Scenic Byway,** with its awesome views of the **Sawtooth Mountains** and **Grand Tetons.**

Venturing east and southward, watch as the Idaho landscape transforms itself, as subtle desert colors begin to emerge and contrast with the deep evergreen. Ride the **Mesa Falls Scenic Byway** through the **Targhee National Forest** where glimpses of rushing waterfalls will beg for your attention. The **Bear Lake-Caribou Byway** takes you south past **Bear Lake, Minnetonka Caves,** and to the **Lava Hot Springs** established by the Bannock and Shoshone Tribes. Move farther south along the **Thousand Springs Scenic Byway** where you can visit the **City of Rocks.** Here, 60-foot granite pillars reach skyward like stalagmites from a cave floor. Nearby, the **Albion Mountain Range** provides a number of hiking, climbing, and wildlife-viewing experiences. Drive to the west along **Hells Canyon Scenic Byway** (it's short but steep) and visit southwest Idaho's **Bruneau Sand Dunes,** with sand peaks reaching 400 feet in height, the tallest dunes in North America. Choose a campsite in the **Payette National Forest** and enjoy the extensive hiking, biking, and fishing opportunities there. Wherever you travel, Idaho is sure to satisfy your spirit for adventure and quest for beauty if you seek more than the average camping experience.

The following facilities accept payment in checks or cash only:

Bruneau Dunes State Park, Mountain Home
Dent Acres Recreation Area, Orofino
Elk Mountain RV Resort, Stanley
Hells Gate State Park, Lewiston
Lake Cascade State Park, Cascade

Campground Profiles

ATHOL

Farragut State Park

13400 East Ranger Rd., Athol 83801. T: (208) 638-2425; F: (208) 683-7416; www.idahoparks.org; FAR@idpr.state.id.us.

RV ★★★ Tent ★★★★

Beauty: ★★★★
Spaciousness: ★★★
Security: ★★★★
Insect Control: ★★★★
Site Privacy: ★★★
Quiet: ★★★★
Cleanliness: ★★★
Facilities: ★★★

Farragut State Park once served as a vital stop along the Pony Express route and was later purchased by the US Navy, which transformed it into the second-largest navel-training center in the world. Located only 14 miles north of Coeur d'Alene, this 4,000-acre state park is a perfect retreat, set in a forest of lodgepole pine, douglas fir, white pine, and western red cedar. Farragut State Park has five camping areas with 219 sites altogether. Its Snowberry Campground offers 44 hookup sites, with over 18 pull-throughs situated in a forest atmosphere. The eastern portion of the park is positioned on Idaho's largest lake, Lake Pend Oreille, with depths of 1,150 feet. The surrounding forest and mountain peaks are home to white-tail deer, black bear, coyote, and bald eagle. The elevation is 2,054 feet, offering crisp mornings and comfortable days. Each camping area has a camp host and day-use areas, and the marina gates are locked at 10 p.m.

BASICS

Operated By: Idaho Dept. of Parks & Recreation. **Open:** All year. **Site Assignment:** Reservations are recommended in the summer; $6 non-refundable reservation fee, which must be paid 5 days prior to arrival. **Registration:** In the visitors center. **Fee:** $12 no hookups, $16 w/ hookups. **Parking:** At site.

FACILITIES

Number of RV-Only Sites: 44. **Number of Tent-Only Sites:** 0. **Number of Multipurpose Sites:** 175. **Hookups:** Electric (30 amps), water. **Each Site:** Picnic table, fire pit. **Dump Station:** Yes. **Laundry:** No. **Pay Phone:** Yes. **Rest Rooms and Showers:** Yes. **Fuel:** No. **Propane:** No. **Internal Roads:** Mostly paved, some gravel. **RV Service:** 11 mi. south in Coeur d'Alene. **Market:** In Athol. **Restaurant:** In Athol. **General Store:** No. **Vending:** Yes. **Swimming Pool:** No, but there is lakefront swimming. **Playground:** Yes. **Other:** Visitor Center Park Museum, picnic areas, swimming area, model-airplane/glider flying field, boat launch & dock, amphitheater, Boy Scout monument, view points w/ coin-op. binoculars. **Activities:** Swimming, fishing (rainbow trout, bull trout, kokanee, machinaw, perch, blue gill, bass), boating, whitewater rafting, hiking, biking, hard path trails, volleyball, horseshoe pits, horseback riding, 18-hole golf course, shooting range, guided nature walks, interpretive programs, cross-country skiing. **Nearby Attractions:** Silverwood Theme Park, Lake Coeur d'Alene Cruises, Museum of North Idaho, Wild Water (water park). **Additional Information:** Coeur d'Alene Chamber of Commerce, (208) 664-3194 or (877) 782-9232 or www.coeurdalene.org.

RESTRICTIONS

Pets: On 6-ft. leash only or confined, not tied to trees or vegetation, always attended. **Fires:** In fire pits only (fires may be prohibited due to weather, ask park official before starting any fire). **Alcoholic Beverages:** Yes. **Vehicle Maximum Length:** 60 ft. **Other:** Max. 8 people per site, 14-day limit, group camps available, check-out 1 p.m; tents must be pitched on tent pads; extra-vehicle fee of $5 per night.

TO GET THERE

15 mi. north of Coeur d'Alene or 17 mi. south of sandpoint off of Hwy. 95, turn west on Hwy. 54, park is directly off of Hwy. 54.

ATHOL

Silverwood RV Park

North 26225 Hwy. 95, Athol 83801. T: (208) 683-3400 ext. 139; F: (208) 683-2268; www.silverwood4fun.com; info@silverwood4fun.com.

RV ★★★ Tent ★★★

Beauty: ★★★	Site Privacy: ★★★
Spaciousness: ★★★	Quiet: ★★★
Security: ★★★	Cleanliness: ★★★
Insect Control: ★★★	Facilities: ★★★

If you are looking for a great time and enjoy the thrill of a roller coaster or a water flume, this is the park for you. Silverwood RV Park is operated in conjunction with Silverwood Theme Park, one of the Northwest's largest amusement parks, just north of Coeur d'Alene. The RV park is located adjacent to the theme parks main parking lot and offers discount admissions for its patrons. The campground consists of six wagon-wheel loops of 10–12 sites per loop, plus one larger main loop also with sites. The park offers both back-in and pull-through grass sites with paved trailer pads. The campground is clean and functional, with laundry and a convenience store. Silverwood campground's main function is to provide comfortable alternative lodging for the theme park customers. Security is handled through the main theme park, and the campground operates near full capacity all summer.

BASICS

Operated By: Silverwood Theme Park. **Open:** May–Oct. **Site Assignment:** By reservation. **Registration:** In RV office/general store. **Fee:** $21.42 first night, $19.35 the second, $18.28 per night for 3 or more nights. **Parking:** At site.

FACILITIES

Number of Multipurpose Sites: 126. **Hookups:** Electric (30 amps), water, sewer. **Each Site:** Picnic table. **Dump Station:** No. **Laundry:** Yes. **Pay Phone:** Yes. **Rest Rooms and Showers:** Yes. **Fuel:** No. **Propane:** No. **Internal Roads:** Gravel. **RV Service:** In Coeur D'Alene. **Market:** In Athol. **Restaurant:** In Athol. **General Store:** Yes. **Vending:** Yes. **Swimming Pool:** No. **Playground:** No. **Other:** Owned in junction to Silverwood Theme Park. **Activities:** Fishing, hiking, rafting, volleyball, horseshoe pits. **Nearby Attractions:** Silverwood Theme Park, Museum of North Idaho, Wild Waters, Farragut State Park. **Additional Information:** Silverwood Theme Park tickets sold at a discount, (208) 683-3400, www.silverwood4fun.com. Coeur d'Alene area Chamber of Commerce & Visitor's Center, (208) 664-3194, (877) 782-9232, www.coeurdalene.org.

RESTRICTIONS

Pets: On leash only, may not be left in RVs or tied (Kickaboo Dog & Cat Boarding available in town, (208) 683-3210). **Fires:** No open fires allowed. **Alcoholic Beverages:** In moderation. **Vehicle Maximum Length:** None. **Other:** Discounted admission tickets to Silverwood Theme Park.

TO GET THERE

15 mi. North of Coeur d'Alene, on Hwy. 95.

BOISE

Boise National Forest

1249 South Vinnell Way, Suite 200, Boise 83709. T: (208) 373-4100; F: (208) 373-4111; www.fs.fed.us/r4/boise; r4boiseinfo@fs.fed.us.

RV ★★★ Tent ★★★★

Beauty: ★★★★★	Site Privacy: ★★★★
Spaciousness: ★★★★	Quiet: ★★★★★
Security: ★★★	Cleanliness: ★★★
Insect Control: n/a	Facilities: ★★

If you enjoy outdoor activity, then Boise National Forest is the place to go. Surrounded by gorgeous scenery, there are breath-taking views in just about every direction. The sites are spacious, and quiet, as well as providing adequate privacy for the guests. All of the sites are equipped with on-site parking (most of them paved), fire pits, and picnic tables. There are any number of activities available, such as hiking, skiing, horseback riding, and backpacking, and even a ghost town nearby. The only thing to remember is that Boise National Forest is quite large and somewhat remote in spots, so be sure you keep an eye on your fuel levels.

BASICS

Operated By: US Forest Service. **Open:** Most are May–Sept. **Site Assignment:** Several are by reservation (877) 444-6777 or www.reserveusa.com, you may reserve 240 days in advance or self serve. **Registration:** Registration kiosk or camp hosts trailer. **Fee:** Sites vary in price from $5–$20 per night/ 6 max-a site. **Parking:** At site.

FACILITIES

Number of Multipurpose Sites: There are 70 campgrounds in the Boise National Forest, 6 to 200 sites each. (on average 12). **Hookups:** Potable water. **Each Site:** Level parking spurs (most are paved), picnic table, grated fire pit. **Dump Station:** Dumps are located in several locations through out the forest. **Laundry:** There are laundry facilities in the small communities scattered through out the forest, but Not at the individual campgrounds. **Pay Phone:** No. **Rest Rooms and Showers:** All the campgrounds have rest rooms, mostly w/ vaulted toilets. **Fuel:** The Boise National Forest is very large area & there are very few areas to fuel, & even less places w/ diesel. Please be careful. **Propane:** Can be found most anyplace that sales fuel. **Internal Roads:** Most are paved. **RV Service:** Boise. **Market:** There are groceries in most every small community within the forest. **Restaurant:** There are very few restaurants, please pack dinner, especially if you don't eat hamburgers & fries. **General Store:** No. **Vending:** No. **Swimming Pool:** No, but there are many areas on the rivers & lakes open to public for swimming. There are also many natural hot springs in the area. Please use caution, many of the hot springs are too hot for swimming & will cause second- & third-degree burns. **Playground:** No. **Other:** Horse camps (there is 1 commercial horse camp in Idaho City), Boise River, Payette River. **Activities:** Hiking, mountain biking, fishing, skiing, horseback riding, backpacking, mountaineering, visiting ghost towns, cross-country skiing. **Nearby Attractions:** Arrowrock Reservoir, Anderson Ranch Reservoir, Idaho Historical Museum, Boise Zoo. **Additional Information:** www.fs.fed.us/r4/boise.

RESTRICTIONS

Pets: On leash. **Fires:** In fire rings only (the forest may prohibit open fires due to weather conditions, always check w/ a ranger or camp host before starting any fires). **Alcoholic Beverages:** Allowed. **Vehicle Maximum Length:** Sites vary in size, the campgrounds on the national reservation service are better equipped to handle larger RVs. **Other:** Golden Access & Golden Age Passes are honored & can be purchased at any ranger station; 14-day limit.

TO GET THERE

Hwy. 21, mile post 38.5.

BOISE

United Campground

7373 Federal Way, Boise 83716. T: (208) 343-4379

RV ★★ | Tent n/a

Beauty: ★★ | Site Privacy: ★★★
Spaciousness: ★★ | Quiet: ★★
Security: ★★ | Cleanliness: ★★
Insect Control: ★★★ | Facilities: ★★

United Campground is located directly off I-84 in Boise. The campground is open to self-contained hard-shelled campers. There is no tent camping allowed. United Campground is a large facility with a full-service convenient store, fuel, and supplies. It is mostly gravel with sprouts of grass and a few trees. The sites are close together and moderate in size. This campground seems to cater to a lot of transient workers. Boise is a large metropolitan city as well as Idaho's state capital and offers a large variety of activities, festivals, and events. It is home to Boise State University, numerous museums, motor speedway, parks, and theater. There are tours available of the downtown area, as well as the state capital building and surrounding grounds. United Campground makes for a nice base camp while patrons enjoy all Boise has to offer.

BASICS

Operated By: Western Construction. **Open:** All year. **Site Assignment:** By reservation, no deposit required. **Registration:** In convenience store. **Fee:** $15. **Parking:** At site.

FACILITIES

Number of RV-Only Sites: 106. **Number of Tent-Only Sites:** 0. **Hookups:** Electric (20, 30, 50 amps), water, sewer. **Each Site:** Some sites have picnic tables. **Dump Station:** Yes. **Laundry:** Yes. **Pay Phone:** Yes. **Rest Rooms and Showers:** Yes. **Fuel:** Yes. **Propane:** Yes. **Internal Roads:** Gravel, in good condition. **RV Service:** In Boise. **Market:** In Boise. **Restaurant:** In Boise. **General Store:** Yes. **Vending:** Yes. **Swimming Pool:** No. **Playground:** Yes. **Other:** Convenient store & fuel on site. **Activities:** Horseshoes, playground. **Nearby Attractions:** Basque Museum & Cultural Center, Discovery Center of Idaho, Idaho Botanical Garden, Morrison-Knudsen Nature Center, Boise National Forest, zoo, shopping, dinning. **Additional Information:** Boise CVB, (800) 635-5240.

RESTRICTIONS

Pets: Not permitted. **Fires:** No open fires. **Alcoholic Beverages:** Allowed. **Vehicle Maximum Length:** 40 ft.

TO GET THERE

From I-84 Exit 57, go east on Godwin Rd. and within 0.25 mi. turn right on Federal Way.

CALDER

Huckleberry Campground

1808 North Third St., Coeur d'Alene 83814. T: (208) 769-5030; F: (208) 769-5050; www.id.blm.gov/recreation/sites/huckle.htm.

RV ★★★ | Tent ★★★★

Beauty: ★★★★ | Site Privacy: ★★★★
Spaciousness: ★★★ | Quiet: ★★★★★
Security: ★★ | Cleanliness: ★★★
Insect Control: ★★★ | Facilities: ★★

Located in the Idaho Panhandle National Forest along the St. Joe River, this BLM campground is a hidden treasure to campers looking for a beautiful spot to relax, fish, or bike. The scenery is spectacular and the area is full of history. Huckleberry Campground is just one of many BLM campgrounds in the area offers electrical and water hookups, paved trailer pads, and gravel tent pads. The campsites are private and very well maintained. The security of the campground is overseen by the local ranger, but a camp host is there during the summer season to assist with any needs that may arise. (Please note this is bear country). The air is crisp in the spring and fall, and days are warm in the summer. The St. Joe area is popular for its fly-fishing and elk hunting.

BASICS

Operated By: Bureau of Land Management. **Open:** May–Oct. **Site Assignment:** Self serve. **Registration:** Self register at the cash box. **Fee:** $12 w/ hookups, $9 no hookups, $3 RV dump fee. **Parking:** At site.

FACILITIES

Number of Multipurpose Sites: 33. **Hookups:** Electric (30 amps), water. **Each Site:** Picnic table, fire pit. **Dump Station:** Yes. **Laundry:** No. **Pay Phone:** No. **Rest Rooms and Showers:** Vaulted toilets, no showers. **Fuel:** No. **Propane:** No. **Internal Roads:** Gravel. **RV Service:** Avery. **Market:** 35 mi. west in St. Maries. **Restaurant:** St. Joe in Marble Creek about 7 mi. east. **General Store:** No. **Vending:** No. **Swimming Pool:** No, but you may swim in the river. **Playground:** No. **Activities:** Fishing (horseshoe fly fishing), hiking, backpacking, non-motorized boating, hunting. **Nearby Attractions:** St. Joe Discovery Tour, Hobo Cedar Grove Botanical Area, Splash Dam, Marble Creek Interpretive Site, Big Creek National Recreation Trail. **Additional Information:** St. Maries Chamber of Commerce, (208) 245-3562.

RESTRICTIONS

Pets: On leash. **Fires:** In fire pits only (open fires may be restricted due to dry weather, check w/ the local forest ranger, (208) 245-2531). **Alcoholic Beverages:** Contained on site only. **Vehicle Maximum Length:** None. **Other:** 50% discount w/ Golden Age or Golden Access passport.

TO GET THERE

Take Hwy. 3 north from St. Maries for not quite a mile, then right on St. Joe River Rd. (FH-50) to between mile markers 29 and 30.

CALDER (MARBLE SPRINGS)

St. Joes Lodge and Resort

RR 3 Box 350, Calder 83808. T: (208) 245-3462; F: (208) 245-3367.

RV ★★★ | Tent ★★★

Beauty: ★★★★ | Site Privacy: ★★
Spaciousness: ★★ | Quiet: ★★★★
Security: ★★★ | Cleanliness: ★★★
Insect Control: ★★★ | Facilities: ★★★

Hidden away in the Idaho Panhandle National Forest along the St. Joe River is St. Joes Lodge and Resort. This small resort offers cabins, a six-room motel, 24 camping sites, and a warm, cozy rustic lodge with the best home-cooked food around. The campground sits on the riverbank surrounded by a diverse evergreen forest. The sites are hard-packed dirt and gravel with some grass, that indicative of a forest floor. Most RV sites are back-ins, with a few pull-throughs. Tent sites are fairly open along the river. The campground has a tubing outfitter and some fishing supplies. The area is home to many wildlife species, such as deer, elk, and bear and offers great hunting or photography. The area is also along the St. Joe Discovery Tour and the Marble Creek Interpretive Site. There are several national recreation-hiking trails and mountain-biking trails. Temperatures are cool during the evening, with comfortable summer days.

BASICS

Operated By: Richard & Sharie Larson. **Open:** All year. **Site Assignment:** Reservations recommended. **Registration:** In the lodge. **Fee:** Tent $8, RV $18. **Parking:** At site.

FACILITIES

Number of RV-Only Sites: 24. **Number of Tent-Only Sites:** Open tent area. **Hookups:** Electric (30, 50 amps), water, sewer. **Each Site:** Picnic table, fire pit. **Dump Station:** No. **Laundry:** No. **Pay Phone:** Yes. **Rest Rooms and Showers:** Yes. **Fuel:** Yes. **Propane:** Yes. **Internal Roads:** Gravel. **RV Service:** 20 mi. east in Avery. **Market:** 20 mi. east in Avery. **Restaurant:** St. Joes Lodge. **General Store:** No. **Vending:** Yes. **Swimming Pool:** No, but you may swim in the river. **Playground:** No. **Other:** Riverfront beach area, tube rental, 6-room motel, & a cabin. **Activities:** Fly-fishing (cut throat & rainbow trout), tubing, hunting, mountain biking, whitewater rafting, horseback riding, hiking. **Nearby Attractions:** There are many outfitters in the area & a lot of scenic drives. **Additional Information:** North Idaho Visitors Information Center, (888) 333-3737; St. Maries Chamber of Commerce, (208) 245-3563, www.stmarieschamber.org.

RESTRICTIONS

Pets: On leash only. **Fires:** In fire pits only (fires may be prohibited due to weather, ask management before starting any fire). **Alcoholic Beverages:** Yes. **Vehicle Maximum Length:** 40 ft.

TO GET THERE

33.5 mi. from St. Maries down FH-50 (St. Joe River Rd.).

CASCADE

Arrowhead Mountain Village

P.O. Box 387, Cascade 83611. T: (208) 382-4534

RV ★★★★ | Tent ★★★

Beauty: ★★★★ | Site Privacy: ★★★
Spaciousness: ★★ | Quiet: ★★★★
Security: ★★★★ | Cleanliness: ★★★★
Insect Control: ★★★★ | Facilities: ★★★★

Located just within the Cascade city limits, this 115-site RV park is like a home to many returning seasonal visitors. Arrowhead Mountain Village is a pristine community catering to its guests. It offers full amenities, craft classes, totem-pole carving, and many other scheduled activities. Sites are comfortably spaced and most are shaded. The majority of the sites are pull-through, with a few back-ins along the Payette River. The river runs along the southern portion of the property, offering great fishing and non-motorized boating. The park provides a fish cleaning area and boat ramp. There is a central fire pit on the riverbank, available for campfires. The Cascade Reservoir is only a few miles north, attracting water-skiers, jet-skiers, and serious fishermen. Perch, coho salmon, and rainbow trout are only a few of the many fish found in the reservoir. A constant breeze comes from the adjacent mountains, making summer days very pleasant.

Basics

Operated By: Gerald & Bobbie Patterson. **Open:** May–Oct. 15. **Site Assignment:** Reservations recommended & held w/ credit card. **Registration:** In camp office. **Fee:** Tent $15, RV $20 per 2 people, extra people $2, children under age 6 free. **Parking:** At site.

Facilities

Number of RV-Only Sites: 110. **Number of Tent-Only Sites:** 5. **Hookups:** Electric (30, 50 amps), water, sewer, satellite TV. **Each Site:** Picnic tables. **Dump Station:** Yes. **Laundry:** Yes. **Pay Phone:** Yes. **Rest Rooms and Showers:** Yes. **Fuel:** Across the street. **Propane:** Yes. **Internal Roads:** Gravel. **RV Service:** 12 mi. North in Lake Fork. **Market:** In Cascade. **Restaurant:** In Cascade. **General Store:** Yes. **Vending:** Yes. **Swimming Pool:** No. **Playground:** Yes. **Other:** 2 yurts (circular, Mongolian-style tent), pet area, boat launch & parking, cabins, flower garden, butterfly garden, rec hall, pavilion, fish-cleaning house, secure storage yard. **Activities:** Archery, horseshoes, craft classes, carving classes, ice-cream socials, many scheduled activities, fishing (perch, rainbow trout, coho salmon), hiking, boating, waterskiing, snowmobiling, golf, basketball, skeet shooting, horseback trips, fly-fishing trips, wagon rides. **Nearby Attractions:** Nature trails, Idaho Historical Railroads. **Additional Information:** Cascade Chamber of Commerce, (208) 382-3833, www.cascadeid.com.

Restrictions

Pets: On leash only. **Fires:** No open fires allowed, 1 central fire pit. **Alcoholic Beverages:** Allowed. **Vehicle Maximum Length:** None.

To Get There

Located directly off of Hwy. 55, within the city limits of Cascade.

CASCADE
Lake Cascade State Park

P.O. Box 709, Cascade 83611.T: (208) 382-6544; F: (208) 382-4071; www.idahoparks.org; cas@idpr.state.id.us.

RV ★★★ Tent ★★★

Beauty: ★★★★	Site Privacy: ★★
Spaciousness: ★★	Quiet: ★★★
Security: ★★★	Cleanliness: ★★★
Insect Control: ★★★★	Facilities: ★★

Lake Cascade State Park is composed of five camping areas surrounding the Cascade Reservoir. The Cascade Reservoir stretches over 20 miles bordered by grass plains and framed with timbered mountains. The reservoir is known for its constant mountain breeze and attracts water-skiers, jet-skiers, windsurfers, and sailors. It is stocked with trophy coho salmon, rainbow trout, and perch. Each campground is located along the banks of the reservoir. Campground areas range in size from 5 to15 acres, each offering a picnic table, fire pit, potable water, and toilet facilities. Lake Cascade State Park does not offer full hookups; however, it does offer 300 campsites accommodating trailers up to 55 feet. Each campsite has a registration box and charges a fee. Lake Cascade State Park has five boat launches, boat parking, and a marine dump. Stop at the Lake Cascade visitors center for a map of campsite locations. All day-use areas of the park are closed at 10 p.m.

Basics

Operated By: Idaho Dept. of Parks & Recreation, Rick Brown Manager. **Open:** All year. **Site Assignment:** First come, first served; no reservations except groups. **Registration:** Self-serve at the entrance of each camping area (except for groups). **Fee:** $7–$9 (cash or check). **Parking:** At site.

Facilities

Number of Multipurpose Sites: 300 within 5 campground areas. **Hookups:** Water. **Each Site:** Picnic table, fire pit. **Dump Station:** 2 dump locations. **Laundry:** No. **Pay Phone:** On the west side of the lake. **Rest Rooms and Showers:** Vaulted toilets, no showers. **Fuel:** In Cascade. **Propane:** In Cascade. **Internal Roads:** Paved & packed dirt/gravel. **RV Service:** 12 mi. north in Lake Fork. **Market:** In Cascade. **Restaurant:** In Cascade. **General Store:** No. **Vending:** No. **Swimming Pool:** No pool, but there is swimming in the lake. **Playground:** Yes. **Other:** 3 yurts (circular, Mongolian-style domed tents for groups), lakefront beach, group picnic shelters, dump station, 5 boat launches. **Activities:** Fishing (rainbow trout, coho salmon), fly-fishing trips, windsurfing, sailing, boating, waterskiing, jet-skiing, swimming, whitewater rafting, horseback trips, horseshoes, skeet shooting, golf. **Nearby Attractions:** Boating, fishing, & hunting outfitters, snowmobile trails, cross-country nordic trails, flea market, biking trails. **Additional Information:** Cascade Chamber of Commerce, (208) 382-3833, www.cascadeid.com; Idaho Dept. of Parks & Recreation, (208) 334-4199.

Restrictions

Pets: On 6-ft. leash only. **Fires:** In fire pits only (fires may be prohibited due to weather, check w/ park officials before starting any fires). **Alcoholic Beverages:** Allowed. **Vehicle Maximum Length:** 55 ft. **Other:** Lake Cascade State Park circles all of Lake Cascade but not all the land is Cascade State Park—much of it is private, US Forestry, or US Bureau of Reclamation; read all posted signs for directions & instructions; max. 8 people per site, 14-day stay limit.

To Get There

The main entrance is located off Hwy. 55, approx. 4 mi. north of Cascade.

CASCADE
Pinewood Lodge Motel, RV Park and Storage

900 South Main, Cascade 83611.T: (208) 382-4948; F: (208) 382-5521; www.thepinewood-lodge.com; pinewood@micron.net.

RV ★★★ Tent ★★

Beauty: ★★★	Site Privacy: ★★
Spaciousness: ★★	Quiet: ★★★
Security: ★★★	Cleanliness: ★★★★
Insect Control: ★★★★	Facilities: ★★★★

Located within the city limits of Cascade, the Pinewood Lodge Motel, RV Park, and Storage offers a pleasant and comfortable atmosphere. The campground sits behind a charming motel and offers wooded sites, both pull-throughs and back-ins. Tent camping is available, but the sites are small and backed up to the fence line. The Pinewood Lodge is convenient to the Cascade Reservoir and Lake Cascade State Park. The Cascade area is renown for attracting water-skiers, boaters, and fishermen. The breeze on the reservoir is perfect for windsurfing and sailing. In the winter the area is popular for its nordic trails, cross-country snow skiing, and snowmobiling. The Pinewood Lodge offers a canoe shuttle, fish-cleaning facilities, and a large screened-in pavilion with a kitchen area and two gas grills. Staff is on duty around the clock.

Basics

Operated By: Paul & Audrey Parton. **Open:** All year. **Site Assignment:** Reservations recommended & held w/ a credit card. **Registration:** Lodge office. **Fee:** Tent $15, RV $21 per 2 people, extra person $3, children under age 2 free; cash, credit cards, checks; 10% senior discount. **Parking:** At site.

Facilities

Number of RV-Only Sites: 36. **Number of Tent-Only Sites:** 9. **Hookups:** Electric (20, 30, 50 amps), water, sewer, cable. **Each Site:** Picnic table, some fire pit. **Dump Station:** Yes. **Laundry:** Yes. **Pay Phone:** Yes. **Rest Rooms and Showers:** Yes. **Fuel:** Across the street. **Propane:** Across the street. **Internal Roads:** Paved. **RV Service:** 12 mi. north in Lake Fork. **Market:** In Cascade. **Restaurant:** In Cascade, 2 within 300 yards. **General Store:** No. **Vending:** Yes. **Swimming Pool:** Yes. **Playground:** Yes. **Other:** Large screened pavilion w/ 2 gas grills, kitchen area, & fire place, fish-cleaning facilities, group fire ring, canoe shuttle. **Activities:** Basketball, horseshoes, boating, whitewater rafting, skeet trap shooting, hiking, fishing, fly-fishing trips, trail rides, wagon rides, sleigh rides. **Nearby Attractions:** Lake Cascade, Lake Cascade State Park, Gem State Rock Hunting, summer flee markets. **Additional Information:** Cascade Chamber of Commerce, (208) 382-3833, www.cascadeid.com; Big Creek Wilderness Outfitters, (208) 382-4872; Snowbank Outfitters, (208) 382-4872; snowmobile rentals, (208) 382-3465.

Restrictions

Pets: On leash only. **Fires:** In fire pits. **Alcoholic Beverages:** Allowed. **Vehicle Maximum Length:** Call ahead for details.

To Get There

Hwy. 55 on the south side of Cascade within the city limits.

CASCADE

Water's Edge RV Resort

P.O. Box 1018, Cascade 83611. T: (208)382-0120 or (800) 574-2038; F: (208) 382-3035; www.watersedgervpark.com; we2are1@cyberhighway.net.

RV ★★★★ Tent ★★★

Beauty: ★★★★ Site Privacy: ★★★
Spaciousness: ★★★ Quiet: ★★★★
Security: ★★★★ Cleanliness: ★★★★★
Insect Control: ★★★★ Facilities: ★★★★★

Located on the beautiful Payette River and only a few short miles from the Cascade Reservoir, Water's Edge RV Resort is the ideal location for water-sport enthusiasts. Water's Edge offers free canoeing and kayaking from its own riverfront beach. There are 92 lakes and 169 streams in a 50-mile radius with trophy sockeye, chinook, and rainbow trout. The campground itself offers level gravel sites, with all the amenities, beautifully landscaped common areas, and a brand-new covered picnic pavilion. Water's Edge is famous for its evening campfires on the beach and the hot, fresh cinnamon rolls on summer weekend mornings. And Cascade is known for its cool mountain breeze, which makes summer days pleasant and evenings cool. In winter, the Cascade area offers miles of cross-country skiing and snowmobile trails.

Basics

Operated By: Ashley & Katrin Thompson. **Open:** May–Oct. **Site Assignment:** Reservations recommended & held w/ a credit card number. **Registration:** In camp office. **Fee:** Tent 19, RV $22–$29 per 2 people. Extra person $2. **Parking:** At site.

Facilities

Number of RV-Only Sites: 100. **Number of Tent-Only Sites:** 10. **Hookups:** Electric (30, 50 amps), water, sewer, cable, phone, Internet. **Each Site:** Picnic table. **Dump Station:** Yes. **Laundry:** Yes. **Pay Phone:** Yes. **Rest Rooms and Showers:** Yes. **Fuel:** No. **Propane:** Yes. **Internal Roads:** Gravel, in excellent condition. **RV Service:** 12 mi. north in Lake Fork. **Market:** In Cascade. **Restaurant:** In Cascade. **General Store:** Yes. **Vending:** Yes. **Swimming Pool:** No, but there is riverfront swimming. **Playground:** No. **Other:** 2 pavilions w/ grills, 2 riverfront fire pits, private riverfront beach (Payette River), cabins, covered picnic area, rec hall w/ kitchen area, free canoes & kayaks, fax & copier service, cinnamon rolls on Saturday morning in the summer. **Activities:** Canoeing, kayaking, beach volleyball, horseshoes, paddleboats, evening campfires, bird-watching, fishing (rainbow trout, perch, coho salmon), river nature walks, sailing, biking, hiking, windsurfing, whitewater rafting, skeet trap shoots, wilderness fly-fishing trips, horseback trips, wagon rides, golf. **Nearby Attractions:** Lake Cascade State Park. **Additional Information:** Cascade Chamber of Commerce, (208) 382-3833, www.cascadeid.com; Snowbank Outfitter, (208) 382-4872; Big Creek Wilderness Outfitter, (208) 382-4872.

Restrictions

Pets: On leash only. **Fires:** In central fire pits only. **Alcoholic Beverages:** Allowed. **Vehicle Maximum Length:** 40 plus.

To Get There

Directly off Hwy. 55 on the north side of Cascade.

CHALLIS

Challis Hot Springs

HC 63 Box 1779, Challis 83226. T: (208) 879-4442; www.scenicriver.com; fish@scenicriver.com.

RV ★★★★ Tent ★★★★★

Beauty: ★★★★ Site Privacy: ★★★★
Spaciousness: ★★★★ Quiet: ★★★★
Security: ★★★★ Cleanliness: ★★★★
Insect Control: ★★★★ Facilities: ★★★★

Nestled between the Lost River Range and Salmon River Mountains, this rustic campground is the perfect place to get away from the hubbub of city life. The 27 RV and 12 tent-only sites make a great base camp from which to explore a number of Idaho's spectacular resources, including the Frank Church River of No Return Wilderness, the Salmon River, and the Rocky Mountains. Wildlife frequently pass through the campgrounds, and the Salmon River, which is in easy walking distance, provides a great place to wet some lines. Though the campground is remote, campers can find most amenities in the town of Challis, including food, auto parts, and banking. Challis, the country seat of Custer County, is still the area's economic center of mines, ranches, and farms. This area is still known as one of the richest mineral belts in North America.

Basics

Operated By: Tom & Sandi Coates. **Open:** All year. **Site Assignment:** By reservation, 50% deposit required. **Registration:** In camp office. **Fee:** Tent $15.50, RV $21.50 per 2 people, extra person $6. **Parking:** At site.

Facilities

Number of RV-Only Sites: 27. **Number of Tent-Only Sites:** 12. **Number of Multipurpose Sites:** 4. **Hookups:** Electric (30 amps), water, sewer. **Each Site:** Picnic table, fire pit. **Dump Station:** Yes. **Laundry:** No. **Pay Phone:** Yes. **Rest Rooms and Showers:** Yes. **Fuel:** 3 mi. in Challis. **Propane:** 3 mi. in Challis. **Internal Roads:** Gravel, in good condition. **RV Service:** 3 mi. in Challis. **Market:** 3 mi. in Challis. **Restaurant:** Gourmet meals served once a week on site, & some Dutch-oven cooking, otherwise 3 mi. in Challis. **General Store:** Yes. **Vending:** No. **Swimming Pool:** Yes. **Playground:** Yes. **Other:** Natural hot water swimming pool open year-round, hot mineral pool, driving range, Dutch-oven cooking, beautiful bed-&-breakfast, nice pavilion, rafting outfitters, horseback outfitters, fly-fishing school. **Activities:** Swimming, fly fishing, rafting, golf, cross-country skiing, snowmobile trails. **Nearby Attractions:** Scenic drives, many recreational outfitters. **Additional Information:** Challis Chamber, (208) 879-2771.

Restrictions

Pets: On leash only. **Fires:** In fire pits only (fires may be restricted due to dry weather, always ask management before starting any open fire). **Alcoholic Beverages:** Allowed. **Vehicle Maximum Length:** None.

To Get There

Challis is at the junction of Hwy. 75 and Hwy. 93. From there go 3 mi. east on Hwy. 93 and turn left on Challis Hot Springs Rd.; this road will dead-end into the property. (There are excellent signs directing you into this property.)

COOLIN

Priest Lake State Park

314 Indian Creek Park Rd., Coolin 83821-9076. T: (208) 443-6710; www.idahoparks.org/parks/priest.html; PRI@idpr.state.id.us.

RV ★★★ Tent ★★★

Beauty: ★★★★ Site Privacy: ★★★
Spaciousness: ★★★ Quiet: ★★★
Security: ★★★★ Cleanliness: ★★★
Insect Control: ★★★★ Facilities: ★★★

If you are looking for abundance, spectacular scenery, and cool summer days, then Priest Lake State Park is the vacation spot for you. Priest Lake State Park offers two fully equipped campgrounds situated on a 19-mile lake of crystal-clear water. The campgrounds are under canopies of mature cedars and hemlocks that open to the panoramic view of Priest Lake and the Selkirk Mountain Range. Each site is comfortable in size and offers a sense of privacy. There are both pull-through and back-in sites available, as well as packed-sand trailer pads. Some sites are more level than others, and rain does seem to cause minor flooding. The area is home to diverse wildlife inhabitants (i.e. bears and moose), and it is wise to leave all food packed in a safe and secure place outside of your sleeping area. The campground is open year-round, with utilities functioning from spring until late fall. Activities differ with each season—from waterskiing in the summer to snowmobiling and cross-country skiing in winter. The park is fully staffed with park officials on duty around the clock.

Basics

Operated By: Idaho State Parks. **Open:** All year. **Site Assignment:** First come, first served. **Registration:** Entrance gate. **Fee:** $12 no hookups, $16 w/ hookups. **Parking:** $ 4 extra-vehicle fee.

Facilities

Number of Multipurpose Sites: 151. **Hookups:** Electric (30 amps), water at both campgrounds. **Each Site:** Picnic table, fire pit. **Dump Station:** Yes. **Laundry:** Yes. **Pay Phone:** Yes. **Rest Rooms and Showers:** Yes. **Fuel:** Yes (also boat fuel). **Propane:** Yes. **Internal Roads:** Combination of sand & dirt (watch for water after hard rain). **RV Service:** No. **Market:** No. **Restaurant:** In Coolin. **General Store:** Yes. **Vending:** General store only. **Swimming Pool:** No, but you may swim in the lake. **Playground:** Yes. **Other:** Amphitheater, marina, picnic area, cabins, picnic shelters, day-use area. **Activities:** Fishing, swimming, boating, volleyball, horseshoes, guided walks, picking huckleberries, evening summer programs; skiing, ice-fishing, & snowmobiling in winter. **Nearby Attractions:** Lionhead. **Additional Information:** Idaho State Parks & Recreation, (208) 334-4199.

RESTRICTIONS

Pets: On 6-ft. leash only. **Fires:** In fire pits only (fires may be prohibited due to dry weather, check w/ park officials before starting any fire). **Alcoholic Beverages:** Allowed, if used w/ good judgement & in moderation. **Vehicle Maximum Length:** 50 ft. **Other:** 14-day limit.

TO GET THERE

From N US-95 to N US-2 to SH-57, then follow signs into the park.

COUER D'ALENE

Coeur d'Alene KOA RV, Tent, and Kabin Resort

East 10588 Wolf Lodge Bay Rd., Coeur d'Alene 83814. T: (208) 664-4471 or (800) 562-2609; F: (208) 765-4109; www.koa.com.

RV: ★★★ Tent: ★★★

Beauty: ★★★★	Site Privacy: ★★★
Spaciousness: ★★★	Quiet: ★★★★
Security: ★★★	Cleanliness: ★★★
Insect Control: ★★★★	Facilities: ★★★★

Positioned on the side of Coeur d'Alene Mountain and adjacent to Lake Coeur d'Alene, KOA RV, Tent, & Kabin Resort is ideal for recreation. The park is located directly off I-90, only nine miles east of Coeur d'Alene. The campground offers 89 RV sites and19 cabins terraced up the side of Coeur d'Alene Mountain, with 79 tent sites and 2 tepees in the valley. The grounds are nicely landscaped and the view is spectacular. Sites, however, are relatively close together, with pull-through sites offering little shade. All sites are gravel climbing the hill, and many are difficult to maneuver. A bird and wildlife sanctuary is found in the basin of the valley. The weather can change with a snap of a finger; evenings are cool. This KOA offers two adult-only hot tubs, and kayaking from a boat dock. The campground is patrolled on a regular basis.

BASICS

Operated By: David & Karen Striker. **Open:** Apr. 1–Oct. 15. **Site Assignment:** Reservations recommended w/ 50% deposit. **Registration:** In camp store. **Fee:** Tent $19, RV $21–$29 per 2 people, $2.75 per extra person; cash, credit cards, checks. **Parking:** At site, very little extra.

FACILITIES

Number of RV-Only Sites: 86. **Number of Tent-Only Sites:** 79. **Hookups:** Electric (30 amps), water, sewer. **Each Site:** Picnic table, grill, fire pit. **Dump Station:** Yes. **Laundry:** Yes. **Pay Phone:** Yes. **Rest Rooms and Showers:** Yes. **Fuel:** No. **Propane:** Yes. **Internal Roads:** Gravel, in good condition. **RV Service:** 9 mi. west in Coeur d'Alene. **Market:** 9 mi. west in Coeur d'Alene. **Restaurant:** Steak house on the north frontage road about 0.5 mi., or in Coeur d'Alene. **General Store:** Yes, w/ snacks & homemade pizza. **Vending:** In general store only. **Swimming Pool:** Heated pool & 2 hot tubs. **Playground:** Yes. **Other:** Amphitheater, camp kitchen, tepees, cabins, non-motorized boat launch, kayak rentals. **Activities:** Outside movies, paddleboat, canoeing, kayaking, fishing, mini-golf, horseshoes, horseback riding, hiking, bike trails. **Nearby Attractions:** Silverwood Theme Park, Wild Water Slides, Silver Mountain Gondola ride, shopping, seaplane & helicopter rides, museums, parasailing, casinos. **Additional Information:** Coeur d'Alene Chamber of Commerce, (208) 664-3194, (877) 782-9232, www.coeurdalene.org.

RESTRICTIONS

Pets: On 6-ft. leash only, cleaned up after, always attended or a fee will be imposed; not allowed in any building or the pool area; pet walk provided. **Fires:** In fire pits only (fires may be prohibited during dry weather). **Alcoholic Beverages:** Allowed. **Vehicle Maximum Length:** None. **Other:** Free modem access.

TO GET THERE

Exit 22 off I-90, go south on SR 97 for 0.5 mi. and turn left onto Wolf Lodge Bay Rd.

COEUR D'ALENE

Idaho Panhandle National Forest

3815 Schreiber Way, Coeur d'Alene 83815-8363. T: (208) 765-7223; F: (208) 765-7307; www.fs.fed.us/outernet/ipnf.

RV: ★★★ Tent: ★★★★

Beauty: ★★★★★	Site Privacy: ★★★★
Spaciousness: ★★★★	Quiet: ★★★★★
Security: ★★★	Cleanliness: ★★★
Insect Control: n/a	Facilities: ★★

Camping in the Panhandle Idaho National Forest is for all outdoor enthusiasts, especially those who seek breathtaking views and pristine lakes and rivers. Most of the sites are accessible by cars and RVs (some even by boat), but this camping experience is relatively rustic for the most part. Whether you want to do some serious outdoor recreation or just to hang out under the pines (fir, spruce, cedar and hemlock, to name a few) and breathe the delicious northwest air, the beauty of this national forest will not disappoint. For the most part, you will find level parking spots at the campsites, but be prepared to do some research to choose the most practical site for your style of camping. These rural, quiet campgrounds will provide you with a private, gorgeous wonderland. Rock-climbing, hiking, hunting, fishing, and other such diversions will keep you busy.

BASICS

Operated By: US Forest Service. **Open:** Most are May–Sept. **Site Assignment:** Several reservable, (877) 444-6777 or www.reserveusa.com, 240 days in advance or self-serve. **Registration:** Registration kiosk or camp hosts trailer. **Fee:** $5–$20 per night; max. 6 per site. **Parking:** At site.

FACILITIES

Number of Multipurpose Sites: 60 campgrounds in the Idaho Panhandle National Forest, 6–35 sites each. **Hookups:** Potable water. **Each Site:** Level parking spurs (most are paved), picnic table, grated fire pit. **Dump Station:** In several locations throughout the forest. **Laundry:** In the small communities scattered throughout the forest, but not at the individual campgrounds. **Pay Phone:** No. **Rest Rooms and Showers:** Rest rooms, mostly w/ vaulted toilets; no showers. **Fuel:** Many places to fuel throughout the forest. **Propane:** Inquire at campground. **Internal Roads:** Most are paved. **RV Service:** Couer d'Alene. **Market:** Groceries in most every small community within the forest. **Restaurant:** Plenty of restaurants & a nice variety of dining. **General Store:** No. **Vending:** No. **Swimming Pool:** No, but many areas on the rivers & lakes open to public for swimming; many natural hot springs. (Use caution: many of the hot springs are too hot for swimming & will cause second- & third-degree burns.) **Playground:** No. **Other:** Many sites on lakes & rivers, excellent boating & blue-ribbon fishing. **Activities:** Hiking, mountain biking, fishing (Priest Lake, Lake Pend Oreille, St. Joe River), boating, waterskiing,swimming, lakefront beaches,backpacking, mountaineering, motorized bike trailheads, cross-country skiing, hunting. **Nearby Attractions:** Museum of North Idaho, Silverwood Theme Park, Stateline & Speedway, Fort Sherman Museum, Hells Canyon. **Additional Information:** North Idaho Visitors Center, (888) 333-3737.

RESTRICTIONS

Pets: On leash only. **Fires:** In fire rings only (the forest may prohibit open fires due to weather conditions, always check w/ a ranger or camp host before starting any fires). **Alcoholic Beverages:** Allowed. **Vehicle Maximum Length:** Sites vary in size, the campgrounds on the national reservation service are better equipped to handle larger RVs. **Other:** Golden Access & Golden Age Passes are honored & can be purchased at any ranger station; 14-day stay limit.

TO GET THERE

I-90 passes right through the middle of the Idaho Panhandle National Forest. Coeur d'Alene is on I-90, acting as a hub for forest access.

DELCO

Village of the Trees

Exit 216, I-84, Delco 83323. T: (208) 654-2133; www.travelstop216.com; facility@travelstop216.com.

RV: ★★★ Tent: ★★★

Beauty: ★★	Site Privacy: ★★
Spaciousness: ★★★	Quiet: ★★★★
Security: ★★★	Cleanliness: ★★★★
Insect Control: ★★★	Facilities: ★★★★

Not quite an hour east of Twin Falls, off I-84 is Delco's, Village of the Trees. This is a moderately-sized, comfortable, and clean RV park. The sites are configured in rows with level, gravel parking spurs. The majority are pull-throughs, with a small lawn between sites. There are several, although not a lot, nice shade trees and a large, open tenting area separate from the RVs, with green grass and adequate shade. The tent area, however, is in plain view of the interstate and not the quietest spot. A large common area with playground is found by the pool; the camp store and restaurant are entrance to the park. There are not a lot of activities in Delco, but several state parks and the Sawtooth Nation Forest are only a short drive away.

Basics

Operated By: John & Gerry Temperley. **Open:** All year. **Site Assignment:** By reservations with credit card. **Registration:** In camp store. **Fee:** Tent $18, RV $25 per 4 people. **Parking:** At site.

Facilities

Number of RV-Only Sites: 120. **Number of Tent-Only Sites:** 30. **Hookups:** Electric (30, 50 amps), water, sewer. **Each Site:** Picnic table, grill. **Dump Station:** Yes. **Laundry:** Yes. **Pay Phone:** Yes. **Rest Rooms and Showers:** Yes. **Fuel:** Yes. **Propane:** Yes. **Internal Roads:** Gravel, in good condition. **RV Service:** 15 mi. in Burley. **Market:** In Burley. **Restaurant:** On site or in town. **General Store:** Yes. **Vending:** Yes. **Swimming Pool:** Yes, w/ hot tub. **Playground:** Yes. **Other:** Arcade, large recreation center, trout pond. **Activities:** Fishing, games, biking, nature walks. **Nearby Attractions:** City of Rocks, Lake Walcott State Park. **Additional Information:** Mini-Cassia of Commerce, (208) 679-4793.

Restrictions

Pets: On leash only. **Fires:** In grills only, 1 central fire ring. **Alcoholic Beverages:** Allowed. **Vehicle Maximum Length:** None.

To Get There

I-84 Exit 216, directly off the ramp.

EDEN (TWIN FALLS)

Anderson Camp & RV Sales and Service

1188 East 99 US, Eden 83325. T: (208) 825-9800 or (888) 480-9400; F: (208) 825-9715; www.andersoncamp.cjb.net; andercmp@pmt.org.

RV ★★★★ Tent ★★★

Beauty: ★★★	Site Privacy: ★★★
Spaciousness: ★★★	Quiet: ★★★
Security: ★★★	Cleanliness: ★★★
Insect Control: ★★★★	Facilities: ★★★

This facility is more aptly described as a resort for campers rather than just a basic campground. Excellently maintained, the RV sites are spacious, with full hookups provided. For those who like to "rough it," a beautiful, open tent area is provided, with convenient access to laundry and shower facilities. Even though this campground is larger than most we've seen, it still manages to provide adequate privacy to the guests, as well as lots of peace and quiet. But the most attractive characteristic of this vacation spot is the huge list of activities. There is a water slide, mini-golf, and a game room, to name just a few. This park is a very popular spot, so be sure to make a reservation.

Basics

Operated By: Gerry & Carleen Miller. **Open:** All year. **Site Assignment:** By reservation. **Registration:** In camp office. **Fee:** Tent $17.50, RV $21.50 per 2 people, extra person $2. **Parking:** At site.

Facilities

Number of RV-Only Sites: 87. **Number of Tent-Only Sites:** Open tent area. **Hookups:** Electric (30, 50 amps), water, sewer. **Each Site:** Picnic table. **Dump Station:** Yes. **Laundry:** Yes. **Pay Phone:** Yes. **Rest Rooms and Showers:** Yes. **Fuel:** Yes. **Propane:** Yes. **Internal Roads:** Gravel, in good condition. **RV Service:** Next door. **Market:** In Twin Falls. **Restaurant:** On site, or in Twin Falls. **General Store:** Yes. **Vending:** Yes. **Swimming Pool:** Yes, w/ waterslide. **Playground:** Yes. **Other:** Natural hot water swimming pool, gas station, game room, large hall, fruit trees in season, homemade pizza. **Activities:** Waterslide, swimming, 18 bankshot basketball, mini-golf, square dancing, skiing, hiking, horseback riding. **Nearby Attractions:** Trout farms, Herrett Center, shopping. **Additional Information:** Twin Falls Chamber of Commerce, (208) 733-3974.

Restrictions

Pets: On leash only. **Fires:** No open fires, there is 1 central fire ring & a few grills. **Alcoholic Beverages:** Allowed. **Vehicle Maximum Length:** None.

To Get There

Located at mile post 204 on US Hwy. 95.

GLENNS FERRY

Carmela Winery & Golf Course

795 West Madison, P.O. Box 790, Glenns Ferry 83623. T: (208) 366-7531; F: (208) 366-2458; www.carmelawinery.com; info@carmelawinery.com.

RV ★★★ Tent ★★

Beauty: ★★★	Site Privacy: ★★★
Spaciousness: ★★★	Quiet: ★★★★★
Security: ★★★	Cleanliness: ★★★
Insect Control: ★★★	Facilities: ★★★

This tiny RV campground set between the Carmela Winery and Three Island Crossing State Park is little more than a cluster of hookup sites and a dump station. It's patronized almost exclusively by campers visiting the winery grounds, which, in addition to the fermented-grape-juice concern, also sports a golf course, gift shop, bar, and an excellent restaurant. There are no rest rooms at the campground itself, but you can use those at the winery's stone château across the street; showers are available at the nearby state park for $2. This is definitely just a stop-over while visiting the winery or passing through.

Basics

Operated By: Roger & Nancy Jones. **Open:** All year. **Site Assignment:** By reservation or walk-in. **Registration:** The Stone Château (the main building at the winery). **Fee:** $12. **Parking:** At site.

Facilities

Number of Multipurpose Sites: 15. **Hookups:** Electric (30 amps), water. **Each Site:** Some picnic tables. **Dump Station:** Yes. **Laundry:** No. **Pay Phone:** Yes. **Rest Rooms and Showers:** None in the campground area; rest rooms across the street at the Stone Château (winery), showers for $2 at the state park next door. **Fuel:** No. **Propane:** No. **Internal Roads:** Gravel, in good condition. **RV Service:** Limited local service. **Market:** In town. **Restaurant:** On-site; excellent restaurant at the Stone Château. **General Store:** Gift shop only. **Vending:** No. **Swimming Pool:** No. **Playground:** No, but large recreation area & playground at the state park next door. **Other:** Winery, restaurant, bar, banquet & conference rooms, gift shop, golf course. **Activities:** Wine-tasting, golf. **Nearby Attractions:** Three Island Crossing State Park, Oregon Trail History & Education Center. **Additional Information:** Glenns Ferry Chamber of Commerce, (208) 366-7345.

Restrictions

Pets: On leash only. **Fires:** No open fires. **Alcoholic Beverages:** Allowed. **Vehicle Maximum Length:** 45 ft.

To Get There

I-84 to Glenns Ferry Exit; follow signs, winery is next door to Three Island State Park.

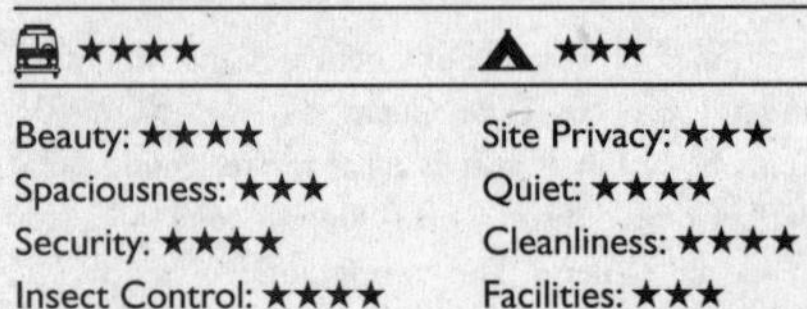

GLENNS FERRY

Three Island Crossing State Park

P.O.Box 609, Glenns Ferry 83623. T: (208) 366-2394; F: (208) 366-2060; www.idahoparks.org/parks/threeisland/html; thr@idpr.state.id.us.

RV ★★★★ Tent ★★★

Beauty: ★★★★	Site Privacy: ★★★
Spaciousness: ★★★	Quiet: ★★★★
Security: ★★★★	Cleanliness: ★★★★
Insect Control: ★★★★	Facilities: ★★★

Three Island Crossing State Park is situated on the Oregon Trail where travelers moving west would cross the Snake River. You can see remnants of trail ruts and artifacts along the riverbank. Located only a few miles from I-84 in Glenns Ferry, this 513-acre park represents a piece of early American history. The park also is home to the Oregon Trail Three Island Crossing History and Education Center, where annually they reenact the crossing. The campground offers large shaded sites in two loops with large common areas of green grass. The park also offers a more primitive area with tepees. There is a day-use area with a riverfront swimming beach, picnic area, and grills. Sites are paved and level back-ins or pull-throughs. This park is located in high desert, so the days are warm and the nights are cool. Park officials and rangers are on duty 24 hours a day and are there to assist.

Basics

Operated By: Idaho Dept. of Parks & Recreation. **Open:** All year. **Site Assignment:** First come, first served. **Registration:** At visitor center. **Fee:** $12 no hookups, $16 hookups, double camp sites $22, $5 extra-vehicle fee. **Parking:** At site.

Facilities

Number of Multipurpose Sites: 101. **Hookups:** Electric (20, 30 amps), water. **Each Site:** Picnic table, grated fire pit, grill. **Dump Station:** Yes. **Laundry:** No. **Pay Phone:** Yes. **Rest Rooms and

Showers: Yes. **Fuel:** No. **Propane:** No. **Internal Roads:** Paved. **RV Service:** No. **Market:** In Glenns Ferry. **Restaurant:** In Glenns Ferry or next door at the Carmela Vineyard. **General Store:** No. **Vending:** No. **Swimming Pool:** No. **Playground:** Yes. **Other:** 3 tepees, amphitheater, Oregon Trail Three Island Crossing History & Education Center, picnic shelters, grills, riverfront beach (Snake River), group picnic shelter. **Activities:** Fishing, hiking, weekend campfire program, swimming, guided nature walks. **Nearby Attractions:** Glenn's Ferry Historical Museum, Carmela Winery & Golf Club. **Additional Information:** Idaho Dept. of Parks & Recreation, (208) 334-4199; Glenns Ferry Chamber of Commerce, (208) 366-7345, www.cyberhighway.net/~gfcity; the second weekend in August Oregon Trail river-crossing reenactment takes place.

RESTRICTIONS

Pets: On leash only. **Fires:** In fire pits only. **Alcoholic Beverages:** Allowed. **Vehicle Maximum Length:** None. **Other:** Max. 8 people per site, 14-day stay limit.

TO GET THERE

I-84 to Exit 120, take a left, then take a left on First Ave., right on Commercial St., right on Madison Avenue, left into park.

GRANDJEAN

Sawtooth Lodge

130 North Haines, Boise 83712. T: (208) 259-3331 May–Oct. or (208) 344-2437 Oct. 15–May 15; www.sawtoothlodge.com.

RV ★★★	Tent ★★★★
Beauty: ★★★★	Site Privacy: ★★★
Spaciousness: ★★★	Quiet: ★★★★
Security: ★★★	Cleanliness: ★★★
Insect Control: ★★★	Facilities: ★★★

Situated in the Sawtooth National Forest, Sawtooth Lodge is a favorite destination amongst outdoor enthusiasts. Opened in 1927, Sawtooth Lodge offers a great place to relax and enjoy the serene beauty of the surrounding wilderness. Pines and spruce give background to a lovely meadow available for tent camping. The RV campground is a simple row of grass pull-through sites, shaded by towering mature pines. Well-maintained trails and majestic mountains envelope the property. The swimming-pool water is from a natural hot spring. The south fork of the Payette River and Trail Creek make for great fly fishing. Mornings are crisp with cool mountain air warming as the day progresses. Nights are chilly after sunset. Fresh home-style meals are served daily in the lodge, with ice-cream potatoes as a favorite desert. Cabins are available, and a there is a barn to board your horse.

BASICS

Operated By: Rodney & Linda Lockett. **Open:** Memorial Day weekend–Oct. 15. **Site Assignment:** Reservations highly recommended, 2-night min. on the weekend, 3-night min. over holidays. **Registration:** In camp lodge. **Fee:** Tent $6, RV $15 (pool is extra). **Parking:** At site.

FACILITIES

Number of RV-Only Sites: 22. **Number of Tent-Only Sites:** Open tent area. **Hookups:** Electric (20 amps, but for lights only), water, sewer. **Each Site:** Picnic tables. **Dump Station:** Yes. **Laundry:** No. **Pay Phone:** Yes. **Rest Rooms and Showers:** Yes. **Fuel:** 15 mi. south at the Sourdough Lodge. **Propane:** Yes. **Internal Roads:** Dirt & gravel. **RV Service:** Boise. **Market:** 40 mi. east in Stanley. **Restaurant:** In lodge, but with dinner reservations. **General Store:** Yes. **Vending:** General store only. **Swimming Pool:** Yes, natural hot spring water. **Playground:** No. **Other:** Lodge w/ cafe, barn, cabins, lovely open meadow. **Activities:** Fishing (trout & cutthroat), whitewater rafting, hiking, horseback riding, backpacking, mountain biking. **Nearby Attractions:** Natural hot springs, Sawtooth National Recreation Area. **Additional Information:** Stanley-Sawtooth Chamber of Commerce, (208) 744-3411 or (800) 878-7950, www.stanleycc.org.

RESTRICTIONS

Pets: On leash only (you may bring your horse, call about use of barn & fees). **Fires:** In grills only, there is a central fire pit (fire may be prohibited due to weather conditions, ask management before starting any fire). **Alcoholic Beverages:** Allowed. **Vehicle Maximum Length:** None.

TO GET THERE

Hwy. 21 between Lowman and Stanley in Grandjean. There is a sign right at the cross guards where they close parts of Hwy. 21 in the winter. Grandjean is 6 mi. back a narrow dirt road. Feel free to get a map of the Sawtooth Recreational area from either the Lowman or Stanley ranger station.

HAGERMAN

High Adventure River Tours RV Park & Store

1211 East 2350 South, Hagerman 83332. T: (800) 286-4123 or (208) 837-9005; www.inidaho.com.

RV ★★★	Tent ★★★
Beauty: ★★★	Site Privacy: ★★★
Spaciousness: ★★★★	Quiet: ★★★
Security: ★★★★	Cleanliness: ★★★★
Insect Control: ★★★	Facilities: ★★★★

High Adventure River Tours RV Park & Store is conveniently located off I-84 in Hagerman. It specializes in rafting trips and river tours of the Snake River and Snake River Canyon Area. The campground is located behind a small store/outfitter on level ground, with nice green grass. The campground is configured into rows, with the first row being an open lawn for tent camping. There are no trees on the tent lawn, and spaces are not divided out. The RV sites are all pull-throughs with level gravel parking spurs, divided by nice-size lawns and the occasional shade tree. Hagerman is half way between Twin Falls and Boise. There are some wonderful geological finds in the area and excellent fishing. The staff at High Adventure River Tours RV Park & Store is friendly and inviting.

BASICS

Operated By: Private operator. **Open:** Mar.–Dec. **Site Assignment:** By reservations or first available. **Registration:** In camp store. **Fee:** Tent $4 per person, RV $20 per 2 people, extra person $1. **Parking:** At site.

FACILITIES

Number of RV-Only Sites: 26. **Number of Tent-Only Sites:** Open tent area. **Hookups:** Electric (20, 30, 50 amps), water, sewer. **Each Site:** Picnic table. **Dump Station:** Yes. **Laundry:** Yes. **Pay Phone:** Yes. **Rest Rooms and Showers:** Yes. **Fuel:** No. **Propane:** Yes. **Internal Roads:** Gravel, in good condition. **RV Service:** In Wendall. **Market:** In Wendall. **Restaurant:** Small, limited food service on site. **General Store:** Yes. **Vending:** Yes. **Swimming Pool:** No. **Playground:** Yes. **Other:** River tour outfitter. **Activities:** Rafting, river tours (Snake River), fishing, boating, hiking, horseshoes. **Nearby Attractions:** Hagerman Fossil Beds National Monument, Snake River Canyon, Blue Heart Springs, Box Canyon Springs, the Heron Rookery. **Additional Information:** Hagerman Valley Chamber of Commerce, (208) 837-9131.

RESTRICTIONS

Pets: On leash only. **Fires:** In grills only. **Alcoholic Beverages:** Yes. **Vehicle Maximum Length:** Call ahead for details.

TO GET THERE

I-84 Exit 141.

IDAHO CITY

Warm Springs Resort

P.O. Box 28, Idaho City 83631. T: (208) 392-4437

RV ★★★	Tent ★★
Beauty: ★★★	Site Privacy: ★★★
Spaciousness: ★★★	Quiet: ★★★★
Security: ★★★	Cleanliness: ★★★
Insect Control: ★★★★	Facilities: ★★★

Deep inside the Boise National Forest, about five miles south of Idaho City along the Payette River is Warm Spring Resort. This unique campground offers cabins, gravel RV sites, and an open tenting area. The highlight of the campground is a natural pebble-lined hot spring mineral pool. The pool stays a constant 98° and is open year-round. The RV sites are fairly close together and require leveling in most cases. The tenting area is a large, open grass field with a small stream. The area is rich in history and natural wonders, the forest is full of wildlife, flowers, and streams. This is a nice base camp for those wishing to fish, hunt, or bike. The days are very comfortable during the summer, but the evenings get very cool through the end of June. Security is overseen by the local forestry.

BASICS

Operated By: Private Operator. **Open:** May 1–Labor Day Weekend, pool open year-round. **Site Assignment:** Reservations recommended. **Registration:** At pool desk. **Fee:** Tent $7.50 per 4 people, pool not included, RV $18 per 2 people & 2 swims per day, extra person $2; cash, credit, or in-state checks. **Parking:** At site.

FACILITIES

Number of RV-Only Sites: 22. **Number of Tent-Only Sites:** 38. **Hookups:** Electric (50 amps), water, sewer. **Each Site:** Some picnic table, some fire pit. **Dump Station:** Yes. **Laundry:** No. **Pay Phone:** Yes. **Rest Rooms and Showers:** Yes. **Fuel:** No. **Propane:** No. **Internal Roads:** Gravel, w/ some pot holes. **RV Service:** 23 mi. south in Boise. **Market:** In Idaho City. **Restaurant:** Small cafe w/ grill in the resort, or in Idaho City. **General Store:** No. **Vending:** No. **Swimming Pool:** Yes, natural hot-spring pool open year-round, stays a constant 98°. **Playground:** No. **Other:** Meeting rooms, cooking units, waterfront access, 2 cabins. **Activities:** Fishing, hiking, horseshoes, volleyball, cross-country skiing, rafting, boating, snowmobiling. **Nearby Attractions:** Boise Basin Historical Museum. **Additional Information:** Idaho City Chamber of Commerce, (208) 392-4148, www.idahocitychamber.com.

RESTRICTIONS

Pets: On leash only, not allowed in any buildings, cabins, or pool area. **Fires:** In fire pits or grills only. **Alcoholic Beverages:** Not permitted. **Vehicle Maximum Length:** None.

TO GET THERE

Located off Hwy. 21 about 4 mi. south of Idaho City (mile marker 37).

IDAHO FALLS

Idaho Falls KOA

1440 Lindsay Blvd., Idaho Falls 83402. T: (800) 562-7644 or (208) 523-3362; www.koa.com.

RV ★★★ Tent ★★★

Beauty: ★★★ Site Privacy: ★★★
Spaciousness: ★★★ Quiet: ★★★★
Security: ★★★★ Cleanliness: ★★★★
Insect Control: ★★★ Facilities: ★★★

This KOA campground, located in Idaho Falls, is one of the cleanest parks we've seen. The roads are gravel, but in excellent condition, and the facilities are well maintained. We preferred the RV sites over the tent sites in terms of beauty, but, both were spacious, private, and quiet. The park offers all the amenities for our convenience, including a laundry on the premises. The range of activities is adequate to entertain the whole family, with the usual fishing, playground, and horseshoes, but the thing we liked best was the hot tub and sauna. For the sports fans, Idaho Falls is home to a minor league baseball team, and there are several area golf courses.

BASICS

Operated By: Private Operator. **Open:** All year. **Site Assignment:** By reservations or first available. **Registration:** In camp store. **Fee:** Tent $19–$22 per person, RV $24–$28 per 2 people, extra people $2. **Parking:** At site.

FACILITIES

Number of RV-Only Sites:. **Number of Tent-Only Sites:** 0. **Hookups:** Electric (20, 30, 50 amps), water, sewer. **Each Site:** Picnic table. **Dump Station:** Yes. **Laundry:** Yes. **Pay Phone:** Yes. **Rest Rooms and Showers:** Yes. **Fuel:** No. **Propane:** Yes. **Internal Roads:** Gravel, in good condition. **RV Service:** In town. **Market:** In town. **Restaurant:** There are many restaurants in town including several national chains. **General Store:** Yes. **Vending:** Store only. **Swimming Pool:** Yes, w/ hot tub & sauna. **Playground:** Yes. **Other:** Cabins, hot tub, sauna, snack bar. **Activities:** Game room, playground, fishing, mini-gold, horseshoes, volleyball, basketball. **Nearby Attractions:** Golf, professional baseball team. **Additional Information:** Idaho Falls Chamber of Commerce, (208) 523-1010.

RESTRICTIONS

Pets: On leash only. **Fires:** In grills only. **Alcoholic Beverages:** Allowed. **Vehicle Maximum Length:** Call ahead for details.

TO GET THERE

I-15 Exit 119 E 0.2 mi. to Lindsay.

ISLAND PARK

Henry's Lake State Park

HC 66 Box 20, Island Park 83429. T: (208) 558-7532

RV ★★★ Tent ★★★

Beauty: ★★★ Site Privacy: ★★★
Spaciousness: ★★★ Quiet: ★★★
Security: ★★★★ Cleanliness: ★★★
Insect Control: ★★★ Facilities: ★★

This beautiful park is surrounded on three sides by the Continental Divide in the rugged Targhee National Forest. The larger Island Park area offers most any kind of outdoor recreation imaginable, in any season, including hiking, snowmobiling, cross-country skiing, ATV-riding, snowshoeing, hunting, biking, and more. And if you want still more options, Yellowstone National Park is just 15 miles to the east. The Henry's Lake campground itself is nice but unremarkable, although that doesn't really matter—you'll spend most of your time marveling at the scenery. Trout-fishing is the main draw here; angling choices include Henry's Lake and the nearby Henry's Fork, Madison River, and Gallatin River. A boat ramp and docks are available for campers' use, but boaters should be careful of choppy water on the lake caused by occasionally unpredictable high winds. A three-mile hiking trail originates from the campground as well.

BASICS

Operated By: Private operator. **Open:** Call ahead for details. **Site Assignment:** First come, first served. **Registration:** In camp office. **Fee:** $22 w/ hookup, $18 no hookup. **Parking:** At site.

FACILITIES

Number of RV-Only Sites: 25. **Number of Tent-Only Sites:** 0. **Number of Multipurpose Sites:** 17. **Hookups:** Electric (20, 30 amps), water, sewer. **Each Site:** Picnic table, grated fire pit. **Dump Station:** Yes. **Laundry:** Yes. **Pay Phone:** Yes. **Rest Rooms and Showers:** Yes. **Fuel:** No. **Propane:** No. **Internal Roads:** Paved. **RV Service:** Mobile RV service. **Market:** In town. **Restaurant:** In town. **General Store:** No. **Vending:** No. **Swimming Pool:** No. **Playground:** Yes. **Activities:** Fishing (rainbow trout, cutthroat, brook), hiking, golf. **Nearby Attractions:** Yellowstone National Park 16 miles east, Red Rock Lakes National Wildlife Refuge, Mesa Falls Scenic Byway. **Additional Information:** Idaho Dept. of Parks & Recreation (208) 334-4199.

RESTRICTIONS

Pets: On leash only. **Fires:** Inquire at campground. **Alcoholic Beverages:** Inquire at campground. **Vehicle Maximum Length:** Call ahead for details.

TO GET THERE

From Hwy. 20 out of Idaho Falls go north approx. 80 mi. until you see park signs; go 2.5 mi. west to the entrance.

ISLAND PARK

Red Rock RV and Camping Park

HC 66 P.O. Box 7, Island Park 83429. T: (800) 473-3762 or (208) 558-7442; www.8004redrock.com.

RV ★★★★ Tent ★★★★

Beauty: ★★★★★ Site Privacy: ★★★
Spaciousness: ★★★ Quiet: ★★★★
Security: ★★★★ Cleanliness: ★★★★
Insect Control: ★★★ Facilities: ★★★

Only 20 miles from the western gateway to Yellowstone Park, Red Rock is situated in a pristine valley that offers panoramic views of the many 8,000–10,000-foot mountains in the area. Adjacent to Targhee National Forest and Henry's Lake State Park, Red Rock is a great base camp for every outdoor activity imaginable. For cycling enthusiasts, the Great Western Bike Trail borders the park. A working dude ranch with weekly rodeos is close by, and there's plenty of scenic driving for those who don't want to cozy to the many amenities available at Red Rock. Further afield, history buffs can visit Montana's Virginia City and Nevada City. Visitors wishing for a more "civilized" day-trip can travel south to Island Park.

BASICS

Operated By: Gordon Glenn. **Open:** May 15–Sept. 20. **Site Assignment:** By reservation. **Registration:** In the general store. **Fee:** Tent $14, RV $16 per 2 people. **Parking:** At site.

FACILITIES

Number of RV-Only Sites: 44. **Number of Tent-Only Sites:** 6. **Hookups:** Electric (30 amps), water, sewer. **Each Site:** Picnic table, fire pit. **Dump Station:** Yes. **Laundry:** Yes. **Pay Phone:** Yes. **Rest Rooms and Showers:** Yes. **Fuel:** No. **Propane:** No. **Internal Roads:** Gravel, in good condition. **RV Service:** Mobile RV service. **Market:** 3 mi. in Island Park. **Restaurant:** The Model Ranch next door, or Island Park. **General Store:** Limited general store. **Vending:** No. **Swimming Pool:** No. **Playground:** Yes. **Other:** Fish photo gallery, Internet dataport in the office for checking e-mail only. **Activities:** Blue-ribbon trout fishing, boating, hiking, biking, bird- & wildlife-watching. **Nearby Attractions:** Meadow Vue Ranch, Lake Henry, Yellowstone National Park, Red Rock Lakes National Wildlife Refuge, The Great Western Bike Trail, Mesa Falls Scenic Byway. **Additional Information:** www.8004redrock.com.

RESTRICTIONS

Pets: On leash only. **Fires:** In grills or fire pits only. **Alcoholic Beverages:** Allowed. **Vehicle Maximum Length:** None. **Other:** Good Sam discount.

To Get There

From Hwy. 20 in Island Park turn west at mile post 398, follow signs on Red Rock Rd., approx. 5 mi.

JEROME

Twin Falls-Jerome KOA

5431 US 93, Jerome 83338. T: (800) 562-4169 or (208) 324-4169; F: (208) 324-7064; www.koa.com; twinkoa@filertel.com.

RV ★★★ Tent ★★★

Beauty: ★★★ Site Privacy: ★★★
Spaciousness: ★★★ Quiet: ★★★
Security: ★★★ Cleanliness: ★★★
Insect Control: ★★★ Facilities: ★★★

This KOA isn't as nice as some we have visited, but it is clean and well maintained. The RV and tent sites are medium sized, but still have some privacy and the park itself is quiet. Some of the RV sites offer full hookups, and all sites come equipped with a picnic table and grill. What this campground lacks in beauty, it makes up for in amenities. Over and above the normal activities usually found in parks, this KOA offers a hot tub, sauna, camp kitchen, and a snack bar. Nearby, guests can also try several more adventurous pastimes, like fishing on the Snake River, rafting, mountain biking, or waterskiing. If you'd like to visit, be sure to call ahead: this KOA is a "reservation-only" campground.

Basics

Operated By: Robert Tanner. **Open:** Mar. 20–Oct. 30. **Site Assignment:** By reservations with a credit card. **Registration:** In camp store. **Fee:** Tent $19, RV $25–$30 per 2 people, extra person $2.50. **Parking:** No extra parking.

Facilities

Number of RV-Only Sites: 69. **Number of Tent-Only Sites:** 21. **Hookups:** Electric (20, 30, 50 amps), water, sewer. **Each Site:** Picnic table, grill. **Dump Station:** Yes. **Laundry:** Yes. **Pay Phone:** Yes. **Rest Rooms and Showers:** Yes. **Fuel:** No, in town. **Propane:** Yes. **Internal Roads:** Gravel, in good condition. **RV Service:** 5 mi. west in Twin Falls. **Market:** In Twin Falls. **Restaurant:** On site or in town. **General Store:** Yes. **Vending:** No. **Swimming Pool:** Yes, w/ hot tub. **Playground:** Yes. **Other:** 6 cabins, sauna, hot tub, camp kitchen, snack bar. **Activities:** Mini-golf, horseshoes, games, fishing, rafting, hiking, mountain biking, waterskiing, boating. **Nearby Attractions:** Snake River, many outfitters, gold. **Additional Information:** Twin Falls Chamber of Commerce, (208) 733-3974.

Restrictions

Pets: On leash only. **Fires:** In grills only. **Alcoholic Beverages:** Allowed. **Vehicle Maximum Length:** 92 ft. w/ tow.

To Get There

From I-84 Exit 173, go 1 mi. north on US 93.

KETCHUM

Sawtooth National Recreation Area

HC 64 Box 8291, Ketchum 83340. T: (208) 727-5000 or (800) 260-5970; F: (208) 727-5029; www.fs.fed.us/r4/sawtooth/camplist.html or www.fs.fed.us/r4/sawtooth/; cgalvez@ff.fed.us.

RV ★★★ Tent ★★★★

Beauty: ★★★★★ Site Privacy: ★★★★
Spaciousness: ★★★★ Quiet: ★★★★★
Security: ★★★ Cleanliness: ★★★
Insect Control: n/a Facilities: ★★

This campground is located in the heart of Sawtooth National Forest, which stretches for over two million acres, covering four mountain ranges that provide a scenic landscape in any direction, with more than 40 peaks over 10,000 feet in elevation. With over 300 mountain lakes and several major rivers, there are endless opportunities for fishing, bird-watching, and viewing wildlife. While the RV sites are quite peaceful and spacious, the campground's facilities are not very good. The campground's location is clearly its best-selling point. Prospective campers should note that this recreation area is very large, with very few gas stations. The campgrounds are open from May to September, and we recommend that you make reservations in advance.

Basics

Operated By: US Forest Service. **Open:** Mostly May–Sept. **Site Assignment:** Several are by reservation, (877) 444-6777, or self-serve. **Registration:** Registration kiosk or camp hosts trailer. **Fee:** Sites vary in price from $5–$20 per night/ max. 6 per site. **Parking:** At site.

Facilities

Number of Multipurpose Sites: 32 campgrounds suitable for RVs, 6–65 sites each. **Hookups:** Potable water. **Each Site:** Level parking spurs (most are paved), picnic table, grated fire pit. **Dump Station:** Dumps in several locations throughout the forest. **Laundry:** Laundry facilities in the towns of Hailey, Ketchum, Lowman, Sawtooth City, Stanley, Sunbeam, Redfish, Challis, Salmon, & Mackay. **Pay Phone:** No. **Rest Rooms and Showers:** Rest rooms, mostly w/ vaulted toilets. **Fuel:** The Sawtooth National Recreation Area is very large, with very few areas to fuel, even fewer places w/ diesel. **Propane:** Inquire at campground. **Internal Roads:** Most are paved. **RV Service:** Ketchum-Sun Valley. **Market:** Groceries in most every small community within the forest. **Restaurant:** Restaurants through the area, excellent dinning in the Ketchum-Sun Valley. **General Store:** No. **Vending:** No. **Swimming Pool:** No, but many areas on the rivers & lakes open to public for swimming; natural hot springs. (Use caution: many hot springs are too hot for swimming & will cause second- & third-degree burns.) **Playground:** No. **Other:** Horse camps. **Activities:** Hiking, mountain biking, fishing, skiing, horseback riding, backpacking, mountaineering, visiting ghost towns, cross-country skiing. **Nearby Attractions:** Trail Creek Canyon, Sun Valley, Sawtooth Fish. **Additional Information:** Central Idaho Rockies Assoc.

Restrictions

Pets: On leash only. **Fires:** In fire rings only (the forest may prohibit open fires due to weather conditions, always check w/ a ranger or camp host before starting any fires). **Alcoholic Beverages:** Allowed. **Vehicle Maximum Length:** Sites vary in size, the campgrounds on the national reservation service are better equipped to handle larger RVs. **Other:** Golden Access & Golden Age Passes are honored & can be purchased at any ranger station; 14-day stay limit.

To Get There

The main roads in the recreation area are Hwy. 21 and Hwy. 75

LEWISTON

Aht Wy Plaza RV Park

17818 Nez Perce, Lewiston 83501. T: (208) 750-0231

RV ★★★ Tent ★★

Beauty: ★★★ Site Privacy: ★★★
Spaciousness: ★★ Quiet: ★★★
Security: ★★★ Cleanliness: ★★★
Insect Control: ★★★★ Facilities: ★★★

Aht Wy Plaza RV Park offers visitors to the Lewiston area a comfortable place to rest. This simple yet well-maintained RV park is conveniently located off Hwy. 95 on the Nez Perce Reservation, only five miles southeast of Lewiston. The campground offers level gravel and grass sites with varying degrees of shade. The tent area has just been expanded, so the foliage is young and there is little shade. The Clearwater River runs parallel to the property just across the highway. The Aht Wy Plaza offers Clearwater River Casino (next door) and free shuttle service to the Casino, as well as to Lapwai, Lewiston, and Clarkston. There are many nearby attractions, including the Nez Perce Historical Society Museum. Summers are warm during the day and cool in the evening; first snow is normally sometime in October. The park has a camp host in residence.

Basics

Operated By: Nez Perce Tribal Enterprises. **Open:** All year. **Site Assignment:** Either by reservation or first available. **Registration:** In camp office. **Fee:** Tent $10, RV $15 per 4 people; cash, credit cards, checks. **Parking:** At site.

Facilities

Number of RV-Only Sites: 33. **Number of Tent-Only Sites:** 15. **Number of Multipurpose Sites:** 8. **Hookups:** Electric (20, 30, 50 amps), water, sewer, some phone. **Each Site:** Picnic table, grill. **Dump Station:** No. **Laundry:** Yes. **Pay Phone:** Yes. **Rest Rooms and Showers:** Yes. **Fuel:** No. **Propane:** No. **Internal Roads:** Gravel. **RV Service:** In Lewiston. **Market:** In Lewiston. **Restaurant:** In Lewiston. **General Store:** No. **Vending:** Yes. **Swimming Pool:** Yes. **Playground:** No. **Activities:** Fishing, hiking, swimming, whitewater rafting, hunting, skiing. **Nearby Attractions:**

Hells Canyon, The Nez Perce National Historical Park & Museum, Clearwater River Casino. **Additional Information:** Lewiston Chamber of Commerce, (208) 734-3531 or (800) 473-3543, www.lewistonchamber.org.

Restrictions

Pets: Allowed. **Fires:** In fire pits only. **Alcoholic Beverages:** Allowed. **Vehicle Maximum Length:** None.

To Get There

5 mi. south of Lewiston on Hwy. 95.

LEWISTON

Hells Gate State Park

3620A Snake River Ave., Lewiston 83501. T: (208) 799-5015 (office) or (208) 799-5016 (marina); F: (208) 799-5187; www.idahoparks.org; helgate@lewiston.com.

RV ★★★★ Tent ★★★

Beauty: ★★★	Site Privacy: ★★★
Spaciousness: ★★★★	Quiet: ★★★
Security: ★★★★	Cleanliness: ★★★★
Insect Control: ★★★★	Facilities: ★★★

Hells Gate State Park is a 960-acre facility located in the city limits of Lewiston. Hells Gate offers 96 campsites, in 3 circular loops. The sites are spacious and well shaded, both pull-throughs and back-ins available. The Snake River runs along the west side of the property, also serving as a boundary line between Idaho and Washington. Many of the campsites are in viewing distance of the river. The campground area is not as quiet as most due to Washington Hwy. 129 running directly across the river. Hells Gate offers a full-service marina with boat fuel and marine dump. Hells Gate is the opening to the Hells Canyon National Recreation Area. (At 9,393 feet, Hells Canyon is the deepest gorge in North America, surpassing the Grand Canyon.) Jet-boat tours of the canyon leave from the parks marina. Hells Gate is known for its moderate weather and has an elevation of only 733 feet. Camp rangers and camp host are available 24 hours a day, with day-use areas closing at 10 p.m. Quiet hours are strictly enforced.

Basics

Operated By: Idaho State Parks. **Open:** All year. **Site Assignment:** By reservation. **Registration:** Reservation can be made for a $6 non-refundable reservation fee. **Fee:** No hookups $12, w/ hookups $16, $5 extra-vehicle fee. Cash or check. **Parking:** At site.

Facilities

Number of RV-Only Sites: 64. **Number of Tent-Only Sites:** 0. **Number of Multipurpose Sites:** 28. **Hookups:** Electric (20, 30, 50 amps), water. **Each Site:** Picnic table, grated fire pit. **Dump Station:** Yes. **Laundry:** Yes. **Pay Phone:** Yes. **Rest Rooms and Showers:** Yes. **Fuel:** Boat Fuel Only. **Propane:** No. **Internal Roads:** Paved. **RV Service:** In Lewiston. **Market:** In Lewiston. **Restaurant:** In Lewiston. **General Store:** Yes. **Vending:** Yes. **Swimming Pool:** No. **Playground:** Yes. **Other:** 2 amphitheaters, counsel ring, covered pavilions, Riverside conference room, marina. **Activities:** Hells Canyon jet-boat tours, fishing, boating, picnicking, interpretive programs. **Nearby Attractions:** Nez Perce National Historical Park. **Additional Information:** www.idahoparks.org.

Restrictions

Pets: On leash only. **Fires:** In fire pits only (fires may be prohibited due to weather, ask park officials before starting any fire). **Alcoholic Beverages:** Allowed, but no kegs. **Vehicle Maximum Length:** None. **Other:** Max. 15 days in a 30-day period.

To Get There

From Hwy. 95 take Hwy. 12 towards Walla Walla, WA. Just before the bridge going into Washington make a left on Snake River Ave. (Hwy. 505); the park is 2.5 mi. on the right.

LUCILE

Prospector's Gold RV Park and Campground

P.O.Box 313, Lucile 83542. T: (208) 628-3773

RV ★★★★ Tent ★★★

Beauty: ★★★★	Site Privacy: ★★★★
Spaciousness: ★★★★	Quiet: ★★★★★
Security: ★★★★	Cleanliness: ★★★★★
Insect Control: ★★★★	Facilities: ★★★★★

Prospector's Gold is small in comparison to some other campgrounds we've visited, but none of the others can compete with the service here. The scenery is breath-taking and the facilities are exceptionally well kept. All of the sites are medium to large, quiet, and with ample privacy. The facilities available on-site are clean and more than adequate for anyone's needs. Activities center around outdoor activities, such as fishing, hunting (elk and deer), and panning for gold. There is a riverfront beach and a nearby outfitter for those who want to try whitewater rafting. Just remember that reservations are required.

Basics

Operated By: Tucker & Gay Lindsey. **Open:** All year. **Site Assignment:** By reservation. **Registration:** In camp office. **Fee:** $15–$16 per 2. **Parking:** At site.

Facilities

Number of RV-Only Sites: 24. **Number of Tent-Only Sites:** 10. **Hookups:** Electric (30, 50 amps), water, sewer. **Each Site:** Picnic table. **Dump Station:** Yes. **Laundry:** Yes. **Pay Phone:** Yes. **Rest Rooms and Showers:** Yes. **Fuel:** 9 mi. south in Riggins. **Propane:** In Riggins. **Internal Roads:** Gravel, in good condition. **RV Service:** Limited service in Riggins. **Market:** In Riggins. **Restaurant:** In the area & in Riggins. **General Store:** Yes. **Vending:** Yes. **Swimming Pool:** No, but there a riverfront beach. **Playground:** Yes. **Other:** Northwest Voyageurs rafting outfitters, contacts for jet-boat trip, video rental. **Activities:** Gold panning, fishing (salmon), hunting (deer & elk), horseshoes, volleyball, rafting, boating. **Nearby Attractions:** Scenic drives, Hells Canyon, Riggins, many outfitters. **Additional Information:** Riggins Chamber of Commerce, (208) 628-3778.

Restrictions

Pets: On leash only. **Fires:** No open fires. **Alcoholic Beverages:** Allowed. **Vehicle Maximum Length:** None. **Other:** Good Sam discount, group rates.

To Get There

Located at mile post 204 on US Hwy. 95.

LUCILE

Riverfront Gardens RV Park

HCO 1 Box 15, Lucile 83542. T: (208) 628-3777; F: (208) 628-3221; snmoore@cyberhighway.net.

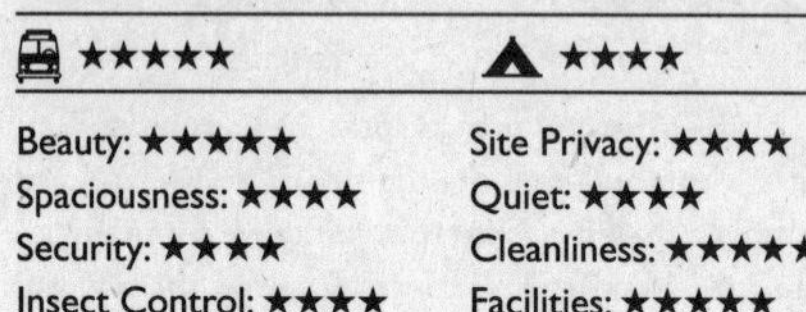

RV ★★★★★ Tent ★★★★

Beauty: ★★★★★	Site Privacy: ★★★★
Spaciousness: ★★★★	Quiet: ★★★★
Security: ★★★★	Cleanliness: ★★★★★
Insect Control: ★★★★	Facilities: ★★★★★

Riverfront Gardens RV Park is an incredible work of art. Home of Stan and Norma Moore, this spectacular property could grace the cover of *Home and Garden Magazine.* The owners and horticulture students from the university in Boise have formally landscaped the entire campground. If fact, the grounds are so elegant you might want to bring along your best linen and china for dinner on the beach. All the sites are grass, with large shade trees strategically placed for optimal shade and growth. There is a riverfront beach area with a gazebo, fully equipped with a grill. The surrounding area is high desert, with very dry summers and cool winters. The Little Salmon River is famous for it chinook salmon. There are many fishing and rafting outfitters in the Riggins area, and great hunting in the fall.

Basics

Operated By: Stan & Norma Moore. **Open:** All year. **Site Assignment:** First come, first served. **Registration:** Self-serve envelopes at the entrance. **Fee:** Tents $15, RV $18 (cash). **Parking:** Very limited.

Facilities

Number of RV-Only Sites: 24. **Number of Tent-Only Sites:** Open tent area. **Hookups:** Electric (30 amps), water, sewer. **Each Site:** Some picnic tables. **Dump Station:** No. **Laundry:** No. **Pay Phone:** No. **Rest Rooms and Showers:** Yes. **Fuel:** No. **Propane:** No. **Internal Roads:** Gravel, in excellent condition. **RV Service:** 11 mi. south in Riggins. **Market:** 11 mi. south in Riggins. **Restaurant:** South to Riggins or North White Bird, there a snack shop/cafe in Lucile. **General Store:** No. **Vending:** No. **Swimming Pool:** No, but there is a riverfront beach w/ swimming. **Playground:** No. **Other:** Formal flower gardens, gazebo, riverfront beach, fax/copier service, handicapped equipped. **Activities:** Fishing (steelhead fishing Sept.–Mar., bass, sturgeon, & trout year-round), hunting (elk, deer, black bear, cougar, turkey, pheasant, chukar), whitewater rafting, jet-skiing. **Nearby Attractions:** Boat launch 0.25 mile, Hells Canyon National Recreation Area, Salmon River. **Additional Information:** Salmon River Chamber of Commerce, (208) 628-3778, www.rigginsidaho.com; cfriend@ctcweb.net.

RESTRICTIONS

Pets: On leash only. **Fires:** In fire pits only. **Alcoholic Beverages:** Allowed. **Vehicle Maximum Length:** None.

TO GET THERE

Directly off Hwy. 95 at milepost 210.5, 11 mi. north of Riggins.

McCALL

Payette National Forest

800 West Lakeside Ave., McCall 83638. T: (208) 634-0700; F: (208) 634-0744; www.fs.fed.us/r4/payette; rbidiman@fs.fed.us.

RV ★★★ Tent ★★★★

Beauty: ★★★★★ Site Privacy: ★★★★
Spaciousness: ★★★★ Quiet: ★★★★★
Security: ★★★ Cleanliness: ★★★
Insect Control: n/a Facilities: ★★

Rustic camping, clean air, stunning photo opportunities, and many ways to enjoy the dramatic terrain will serve to make campers at Payette brag to their friends. Many of the campsites accommodate RVs, all of them are tent-friendly. Most sites have a paved parking spot, but facilities are primitive to basic (and we mean basic). Surrounded by two deep river canyons, this remote area varies in altitude changes and climate, ranging from hot desert grasslands to conifer forests to snow-capped peaks. You can enjoy cross-country skiing, hiking, rock-climbing, hunting, fishing, and lots of outdoor recreation. Plan ahead, bring a good camera, and expect to find privacy, quiet, and legendary beauty.

BASICS

Operated By: US Forest Service. **Open:** Most are May–Sept. **Site Assignment:** Several are by reservation, (877) 444-6777 or www.reserveusa.com, reservable 240 days in advance or self-serve. **Registration:** Registration kiosk or camp hosts trailer. **Fee:** $5–$20 per night; max. 6 per site. **Parking:** At site.

FACILITIES

Number of Multipurpose Sites: There are 22 campgrounds in the Payette National Forest, 6–35 sites each. **Hookups:** Potable water. **Each Site:** Level parking spurs (most are paved), picnic table, grated fire pit. **Dump Station:** Dumps are located in several locations through-out the forest. **Laundry:** In the small communities scattered throughout the forest, but not at the individual campgrounds. **Pay Phone:** No. **Rest Rooms and Showers:** Rest rooms mostly w/ vaulted toilets; no showers. **Fuel:** The Payette National Forest is a very large area with very few places to fuel, even fewer w/ diesel. **Propane:** Inquire at campground. **Internal Roads:** Most are paved. **RV Service:** McCall. **Market:** Groceries in most every small community within the forest. **Restaurant:** Very few, mostly café/grills & pizza. **General Store:** No. **Vending:** No. **Swimming Pool:** No, but many areas on the rivers & lakes open to public for swimming; natural hot springs. (Use caution: many hot springs are too hot for swimming & will cause second- & third-degree burns.) **Playground:** No. **Other:** Horse camps (1 commercial horse camp in Idaho City), Boise River, Payette River. **Activities:** Hiking, mountain biking w/ 6 trailheads, fishing, skiing, horseback riding w/ over 27 trailheads, backpacking, mountaineering, motorized bike trailheads, cross-country skiing. **Nearby Attractions:** Arrowrock Reservoir, Anderson Ranch Reser-voir, Idaho Historical Museum, Boise Zoo, Ponderosa State Park. **Additional Information:** McCall Recreation Report, (208) 634-0409; Idaho Fish & Game, (208) 634-8137; McCall Area Chamber of Commerce, (208) 634-7631; Weiser Area Chamber, (208) 549-0452.

RESTRICTIONS

Pets: On leash only. **Fires:** In fire rings only (the forest may prohibit open fires due to weather conditions, always check w/ a ranger or camp host before starting any fires). **Alcoholic Beverages:** Allowed. **Vehicle Maximum Length:** Sites vary in size, the campgrounds on the national reservation service are better equipped to handle larger RVs. **Other:** Golden Access & Golden Age Passes are honored & can be purchased at any ranger station; 14-day stay limit.

TO GET THERE

From McCall, east and west off US 95, follow signs.

McCALL

Ponderosa State Park

P.O. Box 84, McCall 83638. T: (208) 634-2164; F: (208) 634-5370; www.idahoparks.org; PON@idpr.state.id.us.

RV ★★★ Tent ★★★

Beauty: ★★★ Site Privacy: ★★★
Spaciousness: ★★ Quiet: ★★★
Security: ★★★★ Cleanliness: ★★★
Insect Control: ★★★ Facilities: ★★★

Ponderosa State Park, named for the 150-foot tall ponderosa pines that inhabit the diverse 1,400-acre area, is known as one of Idaho's favorite recreational spots. It is a sanctuary for the wildlife and a nesting ground for the osprey and the bald eagle. The park is on a large peninsula in the Payette Lake, with a public beach on its north end. The campground is the center of activity, with sites both primitive and developed. It is shaded by evergreens, and the ground is level. Sites are fairly close together, and the park reaches full capacity during the summer months. Most sites are located in one of three loops, are paved, and provide electricity. The park offers a large variety of activities for patrons of all ages, including paved walking paths, scheduled activities, and an education center. The weather is cool in the spring and fall, with dry, warm summers. The park is fully staffed around clock and camp host and rangers are always there to assist.

BASICS

Operated By: Idaho Dept. of Parks & Recreation. **Open:** State park is open all year, the campgrounds are open Memorial Day weekend–the first snow (after Labor Day). **Site Assignment:** Reservations recommended, $6 non-refundable reservation fee to be paid 5 days prior to arrival. **Registration:** In visitors center. **Fee:** $12 water only, $16 electric & water, plus reservation fee. **Parking:** At site.

FACILITIES

Number of Multipurpose Sites: 137. **Hookups:** Electric (20, 30 amps), water. **Each Site:** Picnic table, grated fire pit. **Dump Station:** Yes. **Laundry:** No. **Pay Phone:** Yes. **Rest Rooms and Showers:** Yes. **Fuel:** No. **Propane:** No. **Internal Roads:** Paved. **RV Service:** In McCall. **Market:** In McCall. **Restaurant:** In McCall. **General Store:** No. **Vending:** Yes. **Swimming Pool:** No, but you may swim in the lake. **Playground:** Yes. **Other:** 2 yurts (a circular, Mongolian-style domed tent 20 ft. in diameter w/ a plywood floor, insulated & heated in the winter, sleeps 4–6 people), group picnic shelters, boat ramp, lakefront swimming. **Activities:** Fishing, hiking, biking, boating, horseshoes, volleyball, cross-country skiing, golf, interpretive programs, guided nature walks, hard path trail, youth programs for children 6–12. **Nearby Attractions:** Culture Center Museum, Meadow Creek natural hot springs, Brundage Mountain Ski Resort, scenic chair lifts, outdoor concerts, Cascade Reservoir, Payette lake. **Additional Information:** McCall Chamber & Visitor Bureau, (208) 634-7631 or (800) 260-5130, www.mccall-idchamber.org.

RESTRICTIONS

Pets: On 6-ft. leash only. **Fires:** In fire pits only (fires may be prohibited due to weather, ask park officials before starting any fire). **Alcoholic Beverages:** Allowed. **Vehicle Maximum Length:** Some spaces are up to 80 ft. **Other:** Max. 8 people per site, 14-day limit; group camps are available.

TO GET THERE

Located 108 mi. north of Boise on Hwy. 55, you will need to follow signs once in McCall.

MOUNTAIN HOME

Bruneau Dunes State Park

HC 85 Box 41, Mountain Home 83647. T: (208) 366-7919; F: (208) 366-2844; www.idahoparks.org; BRU@idpr.state.id.us.

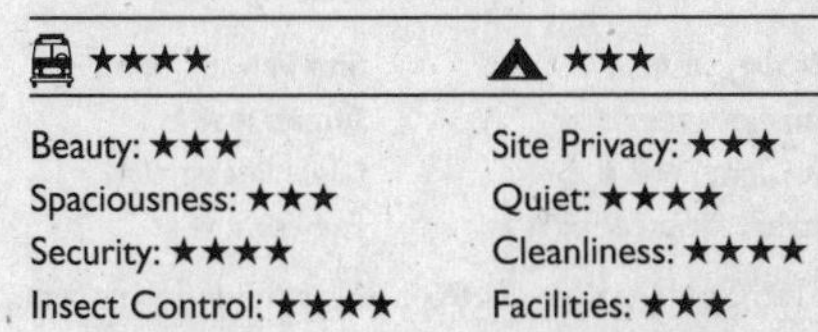

RV ★★★★ Tent ★★★

Beauty: ★★★ Site Privacy: ★★★
Spaciousness: ★★★ Quiet: ★★★★
Security: ★★★★ Cleanliness: ★★★★
Insect Control: ★★★★ Facilities: ★★★

Bruneau Dunes State Park is home to the largest single sand dune in North America, with a peak 470 feet above the lake surface. Situated in the high desert, Bruneau Dunes receives less than 10 inches of rain a year, with temperatures over a 100° in the summer to well below 0° in the winter. The park offers a unique feature, an observatory, as well as fascinating geological formations. There are two camping areas with electricity and water, both circular. The older campsite offers better shade and some covered picnic tables, while the new area offers larger pull-through sites and 50-amp hookups. However, the trees have not had time to mature. The park also has primitive camping near its horse coral for those campers wishing to take advantage of the equestrian trails. There are day-use areas in the park as well as great bluegill and large-mouth bass fishing in the lakes. The Natural Science Center and Observatory offers interpretive programs available with reservations.

BASICS

Operated By: Idaho State Parks. **Open:** All year. **Site Assignment:** Yes. **Registration:** at visitor center. **Fee:** No hookups $12, hookups $16, equestrian camping $7; cash, checks. **Parking:** At site.

FACILITIES

Number of RV-Only Sites: 57. **Number of Tent-Only Sites:** 16. **Number of Multipurpose Sites:** 5. **Hookups:** Electric (30, 50 amps), water. **Each Site:** Picnic table, grill or grated fire pit. **Dump Station:** Yes. **Laundry:** No. **Pay Phone:** Yes. **Rest Rooms and Showers:** Yes. **Fuel:** No. **Propane:** No. **Internal Roads:** Paved. **RV Service:** In Mountain Home. **Market:** In Mountain Home. **Restaurant:** In Mountain Home. **General Store:** Yes. **Vending:** No. **Swimming Pool:** No. **Playground:** Yes. **Other:** Horse corral, picnic area, Bruneau Dunes State Park Astronomical Complex & Natural Science Center, Interpretive Services, non-motorized boat dock. **Activities:** Hiking, fishing, equestrian trails, picnicking. **Nearby Attractions:** 1 hour from Boise. **Additional Information:** Idaho State Parks & Recreation, Boise, (208) 334-4199.

RESTRICTIONS

Pets: On leash only. **Fires:** In fire pits only. **Alcoholic Beverages:** Yes. **Vehicle Maximum Length:** None. **Other:** 14-day limit.

TO GET THERE

From I-84 take Exit 90, bear right onto US 30 (Sunset Strip), south on SR 51, left (east) on SR 78, go about 3.4 mi. and turn right into park.

MOUNTAIN HOME

Golden Rule KOA

220 East 10th N, Mountain Home 83647. T: (800) 562-8695 or (208) 587-5111; www.koa.com.

RV ★★★ Tent ★★

Beauty: ★★ Site Privacy: ★★
Spaciousness: ★★ Quiet: ★★★
Security: ★★★ Cleanliness: ★★
Insect Control: ★★★ Facilities: ★★

The Golden Rule KOA is located in downtown Mountain Home. It is one of the smaller and older KOAs in the system and seems to cater more to longterm guest. It is centrally located within walking distance to the Mountain Home public park and pool as well as to restaurants. The campground has both pull-through and back-in sites, but due to the age of the park there is limited space for the new, larger RVs. The rest rooms are clean, kept locked at all times, and are available only to guests. There is a small store on premises, but not the normally large KOA-type gift shop. There is very limited space for children to play and there are several mobile homes within view. The staff is friendly and helpful; the weather is dry and windy; and Mountain Home is a delightful small community with an inviting atmosphere.

BASICS

Operated By: Private Operator. **Open:** Mar.–Nov. **Site Assignment:** By reservations or first available. **Registration:** In camp store. **Fee:** Tent $18–$19 per person, RV $26–$28 per 2 people, extra person $2.70. **Parking:** At site.

FACILITIES

Number of RV-Only Sites: 50. **Number of Tent-Only Sites:** 5. **Hookups:** Electric (20, 30, 50 amps), water, sewer, cable. **Each Site:** Picnic table, grill. **Dump Station:** Yes. **Laundry:** Yes. **Pay Phone:** Yes. **Rest Rooms and Showers:** Yes. **Fuel:** No. **Propane:** Yes. **Internal Roads:** Gravel, in good condition. **RV Service:** Terry RV on Hwy. 30. **Market:** Alberson, 1 block. **Restaurant:** Serval in walking distance. **General Store:** Yes. **Vending:** Store only. **Swimming Pool:** No, but the public city pool is 1 block away. **Playground:** Yes. **Other:** Game room. **Activities:** Fishing, golf. **Nearby Attractions:** City park within walking distance w/ pool, tennis, & recreation area. **Additional Information:** Mountain Home Valley Chamber of Commerce, (208) 837-9131.

RESTRICTIONS

Pets: On leash only. **Fires:** In grills only. **Alcoholic Beverages:** Allowed. **Vehicle Maximum Length:** Call ahead for details.

TO GET THERE

I-84 Exit 95 go towards Mountain Home on Hwy. 51 to third stop light, turn right on 2nd E St. to Chevron Station, right 2 blocks.

NORTH FORK

Rivers Inn and RV

P.O Box 68, North Fork 83466. T: (208) 865-2301; www.riversforkinn.com.

RV ★★★★★ Tent n/a

Beauty: ★★★★★ Site Privacy: ★★★★
Spaciousness: ★★★★ Quiet: ★★★★★
Security: ★★★★ Cleanliness: ★★★★★
Insect Control: ★★★ Facilities: ★★★★★

Twenty five miles south of the Montana, Idaho line off Hwy. 93, in the Salmon National Forest is the small Rivers Fork Inn and RV Park. This quaint eight-site campground is hands down the most naturally beautiful full hookup campground in the state. Its eight sites are all in a row, lined up only yards from the bank of the Salmon River. The veranda from the log lodge permit guests to view the merging of the North Fork River and Salmon River while gazing up into mountains of the Salmon National Forest. Both rivers are famous for their steelhead fishing, and the Joseph Pass Ski resort is only a few miles north. There are several fishing, hunting, and rafting outfitters in the area, and the snow skiing is wonderful in the winter. There is also a small hotel on the property of resort quality and the owners meticulously maintain the property. In addition, the owners are quite affable people and live full time on the property.

BASICS

Operated By: Noel & Betty Stone. **Open:** All year. **Site Assignment:** By reservation or walk-in. **Registration:** In the lodge. **Fee:** $18. **Parking:** At site.

FACILITIES

Number of RV-Only Sites: 8. **Number of Tent-Only Sites:** 0. **Hookups:** Electric (30, 50 amps), water, sewer. **Each Site:** A few tables. **Dump Station:** No. **Laundry:** No. **Pay Phone:** Yes. **Rest Rooms and Showers:** No, campground was build for self contained RVs, there are rest rooms in the lodge. **Fuel:** No, in North Fork about 3 mi. **Propane:** No, in North Fork about 3 mi. **Internal Roads:** Gravel, in good condition. **RV Service:** Limited local service. **Market:** In town. **Restaurant:** In North Fork. **General Store:** No. **Vending:** Yes. **Swimming Pool:** No. **Playground:** No. **Other:** Large lodge, 8-room motel, all sites sit on the river. **Activities:** Mountain biking, hiking, fishing (property is on the Salmon River) & backs up to the Salmon National Forest. **Nearby Attractions:** Whitewater rafting, fishing tours, float trips, skiing both cross-country & downhill (10 miles for the ski resorts). There are several outfitters in the area. **Additional Information:** Salmon Valley Chamber of Commerce, (208) 756-2100.

RESTRICTIONS

Pets: On leash only. **Fires:** No open fires. **Alcoholic Beverages:** Allowed. **Vehicle Maximum Length:** 45 ft.

TO GET THERE

From I-90 in Missoula, MT, the campground is 180 mi. south on Hwy. 93, 25 mi. south of the MT/ID border.

OROFINO

Dent Acres Recreation Area

P.O. Box 48, Ahsahka 83520. T: (208) 476-1261; F: (208) 476-1262; www.nww.usace.army.mil; eric.s.peterson@nww.usace.army.mil (project manager).

RV ★★★ Tent ★★★★

Beauty: ★★★★ Site Privacy: ★★★
Spaciousness: ★★★ Quiet: ★★★★
Security: ★★★★ Cleanliness: ★★★
Insect Control: ★★★ Facilities: ★★★

Dent Acres Recreation Area sits on the east side of the Dworshak Reservoir, 19 miles northeast of Orofino. The Dworshak Dam is the largest straight-axis dam in North America and its reservoir has 54 miles of tree-lined shore. This 500 area recreation area offers 50 full-hookup campsites situated in an open meadow. The campgrounds consist of an "S," configuration offering both shaded and open sites. The elevation of the park is 1,600 feet, offering warm summer days and cool nights. Most sites are spacious and private, both pull-throughs and back-ins. Dent Acres Recreation Area offers trophy fishing (kokanee salmon, small mouth bass, and rainbow trout), 18 miles of hiking trials, and an additional 100 primitive campsites accessible only by boat. The park also has a full marina with boat dump. Park rangers and camp attendant are on duty 24 hours a day to provide you with any assistance.

BASICS

Operated By: US Army Corp of Engineers (Walla Walla District). **Open:** Recreation area year-round, the campground Apr.–Nov. **Site Assignment:** Dent Acres Recreation Area uses the National Recreation Reservation Service (877) 444-6777, 60% of the campsites are reservable, www.reserveusa.com. **Registration:** See camp attendant. **Fee:** $16 (cash or check, unless using the reservation service). **Parking:** At site.

Facilities

Number of Multipurpose Sites: 50. **Hookups:** Electric (20, 30 amps), water, sewer. **Each Site:** Picnic table, fire pit. **Dump Station:** Yes. **Laundry:** No. **Pay Phone:** Yes. **Rest Rooms and Showers:** Yes. **Fuel:** 20 mi. in Orofino (except by boat & then Big Eddy Marina approx. 5 mi. down the res. **Propane:** 20 mi. in Orofino. **Internal Roads:** Paved. **RV Service:** 20 mi. south in Orofino. **Market:** 20 mi. south in Orofino. **Restaurant:** 20 mi. south in Orofino. **General Store:** No. **Vending:** Inquire at campground. **Swimming Pool:** No, you make swim in the reservoir. **Playground:** Yes. **Other:** Boat launch, floating marine dump, group shelters, weather station, camp attendant, boat parking. **Activities:** Fishing (kakanee salmon, small mouth bass, rainbow trout), hunting (elk, deer, black bear, cougar), boating, waterskiing, cross-country skiing, 18 miles of hiking trails, backpacking, mountain biking. **Nearby Attractions:** Dworshak State Park, Dworshak National Steelhead Fish Hatchery, Clearwater County Museum, Lewis & Clark National Historic Trail. **Additional Information:** There are 100 primitive sites surrounding the Dworshak Reservoir, accessible only by boat, featuring picnic tables, fire pits, & vaulted toilets. Orofino Chamber of Commerce, (208) 476-4335, www.orofino.com.

Restrictions

Pets: On 6-ft. leash only. **Fires:** In fire pits only (fires may be prohibited due to weather, ask park official before starting any fire). **Alcoholic Beverages:** Yes. **Vehicle Maximum Length:** Some sites up to 50 ft. **Other:** Max. 8 people per site, 14-day limit.

To Get There

Hwy. 12 to Orofino, in Orofino there are signs to the Dworshak Reservoir Visitor Center. Please stop and obtain a map of the reservoir and recreation area. They will direct you into the area. The roads leading in to recreation area are narrow and curvy. It is 19 mi. from the visitors center into the recreation area. Please note the visitor center closes most days at 4 p.m.

OROFINO

Dworshak State Park

P.O. Box 2028, Orofino 83544. T: (208) 476-5994; www.idahoparks.org; DWO@idpr.state.id.us.

RV ★★★ Tent ★★★★

Beauty: ★★★★	Site Privacy: ★★★
Spaciousness: ★★★	Quiet: ★★★★
Security: ★★★	Cleanliness: ★★★
Insect Control: ★★★	Facilities: ★★

Located on the west side of the Dworshak Reservoir, Dworshak State Parks offers a spectacular secluded setting of pine forest and open meadows. This 105-campsite park is seated along side the Dworshak Reservoir with many walk-in tent sites right on the bank. The Dworshak Dam is the largest straight-axis dam in North America and its reservoir has 54 miles of tree-lined shore. The campground consists of three circular loops offering both shaded and open sites. The elevation of the park is 1,600 feet, translating into warm summer days and cool nights. Most sites are spacious and private, providing both pull-through and back-in sites. Dworshak State Park offers trophy fishing, miles of hiking trials, and a full service group camp. The park also offers weekend interpretive programs throughout the spring and summer in a large outdoor amphitheater. Park rangers and camp host are on duty 24 hours a day to provide you with any assistance.

Basics

Operated By: Idaho Dept. of Parks & Recreation. **Open:** All year (electric & water are only on Apr.–Oct.). **Site Assignment:** Some sites are reservable, there is a $6 non-refundable reservation fee. **Registration:** At entrance gate or see camp hosts. **Fee:** $12 no hookups, $16 w/ electric & water. **Parking:** At site.

Facilities

Number of RV-Only Sites: 45. **Number of Tent-Only Sites:** 20. **Number of Multipurpose Sites:** 40. **Hookups:** Electric (20, 30 amps), water. **Each Site:** Picnic table, fire pit. **Dump Station:** Yes. **Laundry:** No. **Pay Phone:** Yes. **Rest Rooms and Showers:** Yes. **Fuel:** No. **Propane:** No. **Internal Roads:** The main roads are paved, some of the campground loops are gravel. **RV Service:** 25 mi. south in Orofino. **Market:** 25 mi. south in Orofino. **Restaurant:** 25 mi. south in Orofino. **General Store:** No. **Vending:** No. **Swimming Pool:** No, but you may swim in the reservoir. **Playground:** Yes. **Other:** Marina, boat launch, boat parking, floating boat dump (shared w/ the corp of engineers), group picnic shelter, dry storage, Three Meadows Group Area w/ cabins, lodge, & kitchen facilities. **Activities:** Fishing (kakanee salmon, smallmouth bass, rainbow trout), weekend interpretive programs, hiking, swimming, boating, waterskiing, jet skiing. **Nearby Attractions:** Hunting (no hunting on state park property), Dent Acres Recreational Area, Dworshak National Steelhead Fish Hatchery, Clearwater County Museum, Lewis & Clark National Historic Trail. **Additional Information:** Idaho Dept. of Parks & Recreation, (208) 334-4199; Orofino Chamber of Commerce, (208) 476-4335, www.orofino.com.

Restrictions

Pets: On 6-ft. leash only. **Fires:** In fire pits only (fires may be prohibited due to weather, ask park official before starting any fire). **Alcoholic Beverages:** Allowed. **Vehicle Maximum Length:** 50 ft. **Other:** Max. 8 people per site; 14-day limit; group camps available; $4 extra-vehicle fee per night.

To Get There

Take Hwy. 12, 40 mi. east of Lewiston into Orofino. Stop at the visitor center or ranger station in Orofino, they will give you a map of the Dworshak reservoir and direct you to the park. The park is 26 mi. north of Orofino on the west side of the reservoir, the road is paved but narrow and curves.

OSBURN

Blue Anchor Trailer and RV Park

P.O.Box 645, Osburn 83849. T: (208) 752-3443 or (877) 590-7275; www.blueanchorrv.homestead.com; reservations@blueanchor-rv.com or manager@blueanchor-rv.com.

RV ★★★ Tent ★★★

Beauty: ★★★	Site Privacy: ★★★
Spaciousness: ★★★	Quiet: ★★★
Security: ★★★	Cleanliness: ★★★
Insect Control: ★★★	Facilities: ★★★

Tucked into the hills of Northern Idaho, Blue Anchor Trailer and RV Park is great for a cozy hideaway. The campground is abundant in evergreens providing shade and gorgeous scenery. The spring and summer months are the best time to visit because of the stunning foliage and warmer temperatures. The 24 pull-through RV sites are grassy and average in size compared to others in the area. Off Exit 57 on I-90 this campground is easily accessible. Surprisingly, in the nearby small town of Osburn there are attractions appealing to all age groups.

Basics

Operated By: Jim. **Open:** All year. **Site Assignment:** Reservations recommended. **Registration:** In general store. **Fee:** Tent $14, RV $17–$19. **Parking:** At site.

Facilities

Number of RV-Only Sites: 24. **Number of Tent-Only Sites:** Open tent area. **Hookups:** Electric (30, 50 amps), water, sewer. **Each Site:** Picnic tables, fire pit. **Dump Station:** Yes. **Laundry:** Yes. **Pay Phone:** Yes. **Rest Rooms and Showers:** Yes. **Fuel:** 1 mi. by I-90. **Propane:** 1 mi. by I-90. **Internal Roads:** Gravel. **RV Service:** Limited service in town. **Market:** In town. **Restaurant:** There are a few in town. **General Store:** Yes. **Vending:** No. **Swimming Pool:** No. **Playground:** Yes. **Other:** Dataport, river access. **Activities:** Volleyball, skiing, hiking nature trails, fishing, basketball, recreation area. **Nearby Attractions:** Wallace Melodrama, mining town tours & museums, Silver Mt. Ski Resort, many outfitters. **Additional Information:** Montana Visitors Information, (406) 649-2290.

Restrictions

Pets: On leash only. **Fires:** In fire pits only. **Alcoholic Beverages:** Allowed. **Vehicle Maximum Length:** None. **Other:** Good Sam Member.

To Get There

Exit 57 off I-90, follow signs.

PINEHURST

Kellogg/Silver Valley

801 North Division, Pinehurst 83850. T: (208) 682-3612; www.koa.com.

RV ★★★★ Tent ★★★

Beauty: ★★★	Site Privacy: ★★★
Spaciousness: ★★★	Quiet: ★★★★
Security: ★★★	Cleanliness: ★★★★
Insect Control: ★★★	Facilities: ★★★★

Only a few short mile away from the historic Silver Valley, directly off I-90 is the Kellogg/Silver Valley KOA. This well manicured campground offers a full array of services from cable TV and internet access to fishing and miniature-golf. There is a small stocked stream that runs through the campground adding ambiance. The campground is a completely gated community and patrons must have a code to enter the camping area. Campsites are moderate in size with gravel parking spurs. The further back you go into the campground, the smaller and closer together the sites get. There are both pull-through and back-in sites, with limited room for extra large big rigs. The area around the campground is full of silver mining history, several museums, and wonderful fishing and hiking. Summer days are warm and almost always windy.

BASICS

Operated By: Mike & Kim Jones. **Open:** Apr. 15–Oct. 15. **Site Assignment:** By reservations held on a credit card number. **Registration:** In camp store. **Fee:** Tent $22–$24, RV $27–$34 per 2 people, extra people $2.50, children under 5 stay free. **Parking:** At site.

FACILITIES

Number of RV-Only Sites: 56. **Number of Tent-Only Sites:** 16. **Hookups:** Electric (30, 50 amps), water, sewer, cable, phone. **Each Site:** Picnic table, grated fire pit. **Dump Station:** Yes. **Laundry:** Yes. **Pay Phone:** Yes. **Rest Rooms and Showers:** Yes. **Fuel:** Next door. **Propane:** Next door. **Internal Roads:** Gravel, in good condition. **RV Service:** Inquire at campground. **Market:** In Pinehurst. **Restaurant:** In town. **General Store:** Yes. **Vending:** Yes. **Swimming Pool:** Yes, w/ hot tub. **Playground:** Yes. **Other:** 6 cabins, 1 pond front cottage, pedal boat dock, day-use area. **Activities:** Fishing, games, bikes, nature walks, fun cycles, pedal boats, croquet, golf. **Nearby Attractions:** Coeur d'Alene National Forest, Wallace, Idaho–Silver Capital of the World, Silverwood Theme Park, Idaho Panhandles, mtn. bike trails, Silver Mountain. **Additional Information:** Kellogg Chamber of Commerce, (208) 784-0821.

RESTRICTIONS

Pets: On leash only. **Fires:** In fire pits only. **Alcoholic Beverages:** Allowed. **Vehicle Maximum Length:** 75 ft. w/ tow. **Other:** Special holiday rates, KOA discount.

TO GET THERE

I-90 Exit 45.

PLUMMER

Heyburn State Park

1291 Chatcolet, Plummer 83851. T: (208) 686-1308; F: (208) 686-3003; www.idahoparks.org/parks/heyburn.html; hey@idpr.state.id.us.

RV: ★★★★	Tent: ★★★
Beauty: ★★★★	Site Privacy: ★★★★
Spaciousness: ★★★★	Quiet: ★★★★★
Security: ★★★★	Cleanliness: ★★★★
Insect Control: n/a	Facilities: ★★★

Heyburn State Park was created from the Coeur d'Alene Indian Reservation by an act of Congress on April 28, 1908. It is the oldest State Park in the Pacific Northwest. The lakes provide an abundance of fish, the marsh areas are filled with waterfowl, and the heavily timbered slopes and open meadows are ideal for deer, bears and upland birds. Birdwatching is terrific at Heyburn, with osprey and blue heron as common as sparrows elsewhere. Trails for hikers or horseback riders are shaded by 400-year-old ponderosa pines. Heyburn has three campgrounds with sites that range from full hookup to primitive camping. The sites provide the ultimate get away, as they are quiet, spacious and clean. The campgrounds are open year-round and sites are available on a first come first serve basis.

BASICS

Operated By: Idaho Dept. of Parks & Recreation. **Open:** All year. **Site Assignment:** First come, first served. **Registration:** Registration kiosk or entrance gate. **Fee:** $7–$22 depending on site & amenities. **Parking:** At site.

FACILITIES

Number of RV-Only Sites: 57. **Number of Tent-Only Sites:** 34. **Number of Multipurpose Sites:** 40. **Hookups:** Electric (30 amps), water, sewer. **Each Site:** Level parking spurs, picnic table, grated fire pit. **Dump Station:** Yes. **Laundry:** No. **Pay Phone:** Yes. **Rest Rooms and Showers:** Yes. **Fuel:** In the Rocky Point Day-Use Area. **Propane:** No, in town. **Internal Roads:** Most are paved. **RV Service:** St. Maries. **Market:** 5 mi. east in Plummer. **Restaurant:** Plummer or St. Maries. **General Store:** In the Rocky Point Day-Use Area. **Vending:** No. **Swimming Pool:** No, but there is a lakefront beach w/ swimming. **Playground:** Yes. **Other:** Boat launch, boat rentals, interpretive center, public docks, amphitheater, boat moorage, boat sewage station, cabins, group shelters. **Activities:** Hiking, boating, fishing, swimming, interpretive programming, audio scenic drives (pick tapes up at local ranger station). **Nearby Attractions:** Garnet digging, St. Joe's river, rafting & fishing outfitters. **Additional Information:** St. Maries Chamber of Commerce, (208) 245-3563.

RESTRICTIONS

Pets: On leash, not allowed on waterfront. **Fires:** In fire rings only (the forest service may prohibit open fires due to weather conditions, check w/ a ranger or camp host before starting any fires). **Alcoholic Beverages:** Allowed. **Vehicle Max. Length:** 40 ft.

TO GET THERE

Between Plummer & St. Maries, ID (SH 5, off US 95).

STANLEY

Elk Mountain RV Resort

Box 115, Stanley 83278. T: (208) 774-2202

RV: ★★★	Tent: ★★
Beauty: ★★★	Site Privacy: ★★
Spaciousness: ★★	Quiet: ★★★★
Security: ★★★	Cleanliness: ★★★
Insect Control: ★★★	Facilities: ★★★

Elk Mountain RV resort is a small private campground on the outskirts of the Sawtooth National Recreation Area. If offers a wooded ambiance amongst giant aged pine trees. The property is on a small slope; therefore sites are laid out in a non-uniformed manor. Tent sites are very close together and do not allow for very much privacy. Stanley and Redfish Lakes are in close proximity for trophy sockeye, chinook, and rainbow trout fishing. The Sawtooth recreation area offers miles of hiking trails, and mountain biking. There are several outfitters in the Stanley Area offering a vast assortment of activities from whitewater rafting trips, to guided fly-fishing expeditions. The campground offers a friendly and hospitable atmosphere, making this a great location to set up base camp or just relax and enjoy the summer. Days are warm with a nice mountain breeze, but bring a jacket for the evening.

BASICS

Operated By: Kenneth & Patti Butts. **Open:** Memorial Day–Labor Day. **Site Assignment:** Reservations recommended. **Registration:** In general store. **Fee:** Tents $15, RV $21.40 per 2 people, Cash & checks. **Parking:** At site.

FACILITIES

Number of RV-Only Sites: 20. **Number of Tent-Only Sites:** 5. **Hookups:** Electric (30 amps), water, sewer, phone. **Each Site:** Picnic table. **Dump Station:** No. **Laundry:** Yes. **Pay Phone:** No. **Rest Rooms and Showers:** Yes. **Fuel:** No. **Propane:** No. **Internal Roads:** Gravel. **RV Service:** None. **Market:** Stanley, ID. **Restaurant:** Stanley, ID. **General Store:** Yes. **Vending:** General store only. **Swimming Pool:** No. **Playground:** No. **Other:** Central fire pit. **Activities:** Hiking, rafting, fishing, hiking. **Additional Information:** Stanley-Sawtooth Chamber of Commerce, (208) 744-3411, (800) 878-7950, www.stanleycc.org.

RESTRICTIONS

Pets: Allowed. **Fires:** In fire pits only. **Alcoholic Beverages:** Not allowed. **Vehicle Maximum Length:** None.

TO GET THERE

Hwy. 21, about 5 mi. southwest of Stanley.

WHITE BIRD

Swiftwater RV Park & Store

HC 01 Box 24, White Bird 83554. T: (208) 839-2700 or (888) 291-5065; www.swiftwaterrv-park.com; jamie46@ctc.net.

RV: ★★★★	Tent: ★★★
Beauty: ★★★★★	Site Privacy: ★★★★
Spaciousness: ★★★	Quiet: ★★★★
Security: ★★★★	Cleanliness: ★★★★★
Insect Control: ★★★★	Facilities: ★★★★

Swiftwater RV Park & Store is located in the Salmon River Valley, eight miles south of Grangeville. This quiet park has beautifully landscaped level sites, both pull-through and back-in. Situated in an open meadow on the banks of the Salmon River an attractive gazebo with fire pit and grill that overlooks the riverfront beach. White Bird is also located on the Lewis and Clark trail, with

Meriweather Lewis being the first white man to visit the Salmon River Valley in 1805. Swiftwater is surrounded by recreational activities, and interesting historic areas. The area is home to many species of wildlife and offers trophy fishing and hunting. The weather is dry and the area is high desert, summer days can be very warm, with cool evenings. The owners live on the property and are there to assist in anyway.

Basics

Operated By: Mark & Jamie Mortenson. **Open:** All year. **Site Assignment:** Reservations recommended. **Registration:** In the general store, located on the second floor. **Fee:** Tent $14, RV $18, per 2 people. Weekly & monthly rates available. $2.50 charge for extra people. **Parking:** At site.

Facilities

Number of RV-Only Sites: 27. **Number of Tent-Only Sites:** Open tent area. **Hookups:** Electric (30, 50 amps), water, sewer, satellite, phone. **Each Site:** Some picnic tables. **Dump Station:** Yes. **Laundry:** Yes. **Pay Phone:** Yes. **Rest Rooms and Showers:** Yes. **Fuel:** No. **Propane:** Yes. **Internal Roads:** Gravel. **RV Service:** 8 mi. north in Grangeville. **Market:** No. **Restaurant:** 1 mi. North. **General Store:** Yes. **Vending:** No. **Swimming Pool:** No, but you may swim in the river. **Playground:** No. **Other:** TV room, gazebo w/ gas grill, central fire pit, river front beach. **Activities:** Fishing (chinook salmon, sockeye, rainbow trout,& perch), hiking, hunting, backpacking. **Nearby Attractions:** Rafting, skiing, snowmobiling, Hell's Canyon, Jet boating, kayaking, canoeing, guided hunting & fishing expeditions. **Additional Information:** www.swiftwaterrvpark.com.

Restrictions

Pets: Allowed. **Fires:** In central fire pit only. **Alcoholic Beverages:** Allowed. **Vehicle Maximum Length:** None.

To Get There

From mile post 222 on Hwy. 95 at White Bird take a Hammer Creek turn off; campground is 0.5 mi. on the left.

WINCHESTER

Winchester Lake State Park

P.O.Box 186, Winchester 83555. T: (208) 924-7563; F: (208) 924-5941; www.idahoparks.org/parks/winchester.html; WIN@idpr.state.id.us.

RV ★★★★ Tent ★★★

Beauty: ★★★★	Site Privacy: ★★★
Spaciousness: ★★★	Quiet: ★★★
Security: ★★★★	Cleanliness: ★★★★
Insect Control: ★★★★	Facilities: ★★★★

Located in the Nez Perce Indian Reservation, Winchester Lake State Park is a beautiful 418- acre park on a 103-acre lake at the foot of the Craig Mountains. The park offers modern camping facilities and yurt rentals. The campground is configured in three loops on the west side of the lake. Campsites are both back-in and pull-through, with sites in loop A on the lake shaded by Douglas firs and ponderosa pines. The park offers boating, fishing (rainbow trout,) hiking trials, and biking trails in the summer; cross-country skiing, ice stating and ice fishing in the winter. In addition the park conducts educational programs and guided walks. Many different types of wildlife inhabit the park. The park staff is there to assist with any needs that may arise, along with volunteer host during the summer.

Basics

Operated By: Idaho State Parks & Recreation. **Open:** All year. **Site Assignment:** First come, first served. **Registration:** Park office or self registration box at entrance gate. **Fee:** $12 no-hookups & $16 w/ hookups. **Parking:** Yes, but there is an extra vehicle fee of $3.

Facilities

Number of RV-Only Sites: 50. **Number of Tent-Only Sites:** 23. **Hookups:** Electric & water. **Each Site:** Picnic table, grated fire pit. **Dump Station:** 0.5 mi. in town. **Laundry:** No. **Pay Phone:** Yes. **Rest Rooms and Showers:** Yes. **Fuel:** No. **Propane:** No. **Internal Roads:** Paved. **RV Service:** No. **Market:** In Winchester. **Restaurant:** In Winchester. **General Store:** No. **Vending:** No. **Swimming Pool:** No. **Playground:** Yes. **Other:** Three yurts, lake side picnic area, non-motorized boat ramp, amphitheater. **Activities:** Fishing, picnicking, boating, hiking, wildlife viewing. **Nearby Attractions:** Inquire at campground. **Additional Information:** Idaho State Parks & Recreation, (208) 334-4199.

Restrictions

Pets: On leash only, dogs are not allowed on waterfront or day-use area of the park. **Fires:** In fire pits or grills only. **Alcoholic Beverages:** At sites only. **Vehicle Maximum Length:** 60 ft. **Other:** 15-day limit in a 30-day period.

To Get There

From US 95 take right on US 95 business, then right on Camas St. and follow signs to park.

Illinois

The "Land of Lincoln" has a welcome blend of history and outdoor activities, along with much more to keep anyone happy. Bordered on almost all sides by water, Illinois is awash with water sports. It's also home to the grasslands that inspired poet Carl Sandburg and the mighty "Windy City" of Chicago. Sandburg's ashes are scattered under **Remembrance Rock** in his hometown of **Galesburg,** just as he requested.

Historic stops across Illinois trace the political career of Abraham Lincoln on the **Lincoln Heritage Trail.** In **Springfield, Lincoln's Tomb State Historic Site** contains the tomb of Lincoln, his wife, and three of their four children. Near Chicago, **Oak Park** showcases the **Frank Lloyd Wright Home and Studio** where the architect's love for the prairie is evident in his creations. Superman may not really exist, but his legendary home of **Metropolis** honors the man of steel with monuments to the super hero.

In **Chicago,** the **Field Museum** is home to Sue, the largest and most complete T. Rex ever found. Once the largest Mississippi River port north of St. Louis, **Galena** has a vibrant downtown and some of the finest period architecture in the Midwest. John Deere settled in the village of **Grand Detour** and developed his famed steel plow. See Deere's restored homestead and other farming memorabilia at the **John Deere Historic Site.** A huge manmade pile of earth, Monk's Mound is the remnant of a prehistoric civilization at **Cahokia Mounds State Historic Site** in **Collinsville.**

At **Starved Rock State Park** in **La Salle,** Mother Nature presents an unusual show—in the spring, water cascades from the park's many canyons; in the winter, the falls become crystal icefalls. A 55-mile trail that begins in **Elmhurst,** the **Illinois Prairie Path** is a bicyclist's dream. Near **Mount Vernon,** the 19,000-acre **Rend Lake** draws campers, swimmers, boaters, and anglers, as does the **Shawnee National Forest** that covers most of the southern tip of Illinois. **Horseshoe Lake** and **Union County Wildlife Refuge** near **Cairo** attract one of the nation's largest gatherings of geese each winter.

The twin cities of **Champaign/Urbana** are separated by a single street but united in a wealth of attractions, such as the **University of Illinois** and the **John Philip Sousa Library and Museum.** The Amish brought their way of life to **Arcola** and **Arthur** where quilts are still made by hand and baked goods tempt with homemade goodness.

The following facilities accept payment in checks or cash only:

- Benton Best Holiday Trav-L Park, Benton
- Hickory Hills Campground, El Paso
- Hickory Holler Campground, West York
- Kickapoo State Park, Oakwood
- Lake Le-Aqua-Na State Park, Lena
- Lincoln Trail State Park, Marshall
- Mississippi Palisades State Park, Savanna
- Palace Campgrounds, Galena
- Rainmaker Campground, Litchfield
- River Road Camping & Marina Inc., Oregon
- Rock Cut State Park, Rockford
- Ruffit Park, Sterling
- Schuy-Rush Lake & Campground, Rushville
- Sycamore RV Resort, Sycamore
- Tomahawk RV Park, Pocahontas
- Valley View Campground, Quincy

AMBOY
Green River Oaks Camping Resort

P.O. Box 131, Amboy 61310. T: (815) 857-2815

RV ★★★★ Tent ★★★★

Beauty: ★★★★ Site Privacy: ★★★★
Spaciousness: ★★★★ Quiet: ★★★★
Security: ★★★★ Cleanliness: ★★★★
Insect Control: None Facilities: ★★★★

A river runs through Green River Oaks, located three miles southwest of Amboy. Two creeks also meander through the campground, and giant oaks and pines help account for its beauty and its name. Two heated pools are an unusual plus, but swimming is not allowed in Arrow Lake. A schedule of events is always posted so campers can know what's going on. Arranged in a series of loops, the campground offers mostly grassy sites with an average site width of 35 feet. All sites are back-in and most are shady. More than half the sites are occupied by seasonal residents. Seasonals sites are clumped together in sections—one sizable group by each pool. The remaining RV sites are in rows by themselves. Tent sites are in a separate area with privacy and more grassy and shady surroundings.

BASICS
Operated by: Mike Ciaccio. **Open:** May 1–Oct. 15. **Site Assignment:** Reservations are required w/ 1-night deposit; refunds w/ 7-day notice, plus $5 service charge. **Registration:** At campground office. **Fee:** $30 (cash, check, credit cards). **Parking:** At site.

FACILITIES
Number of RV Sites: 225. **Number of Tent-Only Sites:** 10. **Hookups:** Electric (30 amps), water, sewer. **Each Site:** Picnic table. **Dump Station:** Yes. **Laundry:** Yes. **Pay Phone:** Yes. **Rest Rooms and Showers:** Yes. **Fuel:** No. **Propane:** Yes. **Internal Roads:** Paved, in good condition. **RV Service:** No. **Market:** 3 mi. northeast in Amboy. **Restaurant:** 3 mi. northeast in Amboy. **General Store:** Yes. **Vending:** Yes. **Swimming Pool:** Two. **Playground:** Yes. **Other:** Sports court, tennis courts, 18-hole mini-golf, softball field, shuffleboard, horseshoes, fishing lake, family center. **Activities:** Swimming, fishing, lumberjack breakfasts on weekends (Memorial Day through Labor Day), planned weekend activities. **Nearby Attractions:** Flea markets, Amboy Depot Museum, wood carvings at Amboy City Park East, scenic drive, bike trail. **Additional Information:** Blackhawk Waterways CVB, (800) 678-2108.

RESTRICTIONS
Pets: Leash only. **Fires:** Fire pits only. **Alcoholic Beverages:** Permitted. **Vehicle Maximum Length:** 40 ft. **Other:** 2-night min. on weekends, 3-night min. on holidays, w/ all 3 nights paid at least a month in advance.

TO GET THERE
From I-88 take the Sugar Grove Rte. 30 West Exit. Go to Rte. 52, turn south to Main St. in downtown Amboy. Turn west and go to the west end of town. Take Rockyford Rd. to the left and go 3 mi. to Sleepy Hollow Rd. and turn right into Green River Oaks. Sleepy Hollow Rd. has poor shoulders.

AMBOY
O'Connell's Yogi Bear's Jellystone Park Camp Resort

970 Green Wing Rd., Amboy 61310. T: (800) FOR-YOGI; F: (815) 857-2916; www.jellystoneamboy.com; reservations@mail.jellystoneamboy.com.

RV ★★★★ Tent ★★★★

Beauty: ★★★★ Site Privacy: ★★★★
Spaciousness: ★★★★ Quiet: ★★★★
Security: ★★★★★ Cleanliness: ★★★★
Insect Control: None Facilities: ★★★★

O'Connell's Yogi Bear's Yellowstone Park Camp Resort is a destination. Folks come to visit because they know they can count on a clean, secure campground with enough recreation and programs to wear anyone out. Campers are escorted to their sites when they arrive or can opt for express check-in on Fridays for reservations paid in full in advance. A rolling, grassy campground with shaded and open sites, O'Connell's is a rural facility, five miles east of Amboy, laid out in a series of loops. The typical site width for the 275 pull-throughs is 40 feet. Tent sites are away from RVs and offer more shade and privacy. Because the campground is so large, it features multiple facilities, such as three outdoor pools, three spas, three kiddie pools, three laundromats, and five large rest room/shower combinations. Laundromats and showers are open 24 hours a day. Security is tops owing to a locked entrance gate with gate codes and regular patrols of the area. To ensure safety and quiet, the enforced speed limit is 7 mph, quiet hours are from 11 p.m. to 7 a.m., no bicycle riding is permitted after dusk, and visitor checkout time is 11 p.m.

BASICS
Operated by: Jane & Daniel O'Connell. **Open:** Apr. 7–Oct. 25. **Site Assignment:** Reservations w/ 1-night deposit; refund (minus $10) or a certificate of credit for full amount of deposit w/ 14-day notice. Holiday weekends require pre-pay, 1 month in advance, & a 3-night min. stay; there is a 2-night min. for weekend camping. **Registration:** At campground office. **Fee:** $40 (cash, check, credit cards). **Parking:** At site.

FACILITIES
Number of RV Sites: 635. **Number of Tent-Only Sites:** 250. **Hookups:** Electric (30, 50 amps), water, sewer. **Each Site:** Picnic table. **Dump Station:** Yes. **Laundry:** Yes. **Pay Phone:** Yes. **Rest Rooms and Showers:** Yes. **Fuel:** No. **Propane:** Yes. **Internal Roads:** Paved, in good condition. **RV Service:** Yes. **Market:** 5 mi. west in Amboy. **Restaurant:** 5 mi. west in Amboy. **General Store:** Yes. **Vending:** Yes. **Swimming Pool:** Yes. **Playground:** Yes. **Other:** Two lakes, spas, kiddie pools, mini-golf, soccer & softball fields, snack bar, ranger station, game room, pavilion, banquet center, swimming beach, horseshoes, movies, Green River, hiking trails, RV sales. **Activities:** Swimming, fishing, hiking, haywagon rides, boating (rental kayak & paddleboats available), planned daily activities, Sunday church services. **Nearby Attractions:** Flea markets, festivals, Ambody Depot Museum, wood carvings at Amboy City Park East, scenic drive, bike trail. **Additional Information:** Blackhawk Waterways CVB, (800) 678-2108.

RESTRICTIONS
Pets: Leash only. **Fires:** Fire pits only. **Alcoholic Beverages:** Permitted. **Vehicle Maximum Length:** None. **Other:** Spa for 18 years & older.

TO GET THERE
From junction Hwy. 52 and Main St., drive 1.5 mi. east on Main St., then 2.5 mi. southeast on Shaw Rd., then 1 mi. north on Green Wing Rd. Roads are wide and well maintained with good shoulders.

BENTON
Benton Best Holiday Trav-L Park

Rte. 1, Whittington 62897. T: (618) 439-4860

RV ★★★★ Tent ★★★

Beauty: ★★★ Site Privacy: ★★★
Spaciousness: ★★★ Quiet: ★★★★
Security: ★★★★ Cleanliness: ★★★★
Insect Control: None Facilities: ★★★★

Tall oak trees shade Benton Best Holiday Trav-L-Park, located five miles north of Benton. Level campsites with a typical width of 25 feet and easy access from the interstate make this a popular stop for travelers. With 20 pull-throughs, the sites are mostly shaded and grassy with gravel pads for RVs. A big pavilion is a draw for camping clubs. Primitive tent camping is provided on the perimeters of the campground, where tenters have more privacy away from RVs. Quiet time from 11 p.m. to 7 a.m. is enforced, as is a 5 mph speed limit. Laid out in a series of loops, the campground has security provided by owners who live on the site and offer regular patrols. It also has 20 seasonal campers. Many campers come for the 1,900-acre Rend Lake Recreation Area nearby for fishing, boating, and swimming. Although it is open year-round, the campground offers limited facilities from Nov. through Apr. 1.

BASICS
Operated by: Phil & Mary Poninski. **Open:** All year. **Site Assignment:** Reservations w/ no deposit for non-holidays; for holidays, 1-night deposit required; refund w/ 7-day notice. **Registration:** At campground office. **Fee:** $21 (cash, check). **Parking:** At site.

FACILITIES
Number of RV Sites: 97. **Number of Tent-Only Sites:** 23. **Hookups:** Electric (30, 50 amps), water, sewer. **Each Site:** Picnic table, fire ring. **Dump Station:** Yes. **Laundry:** Yes. **Pay Phone:** Yes. **Rest Rooms and Showers:** Yes. **Fuel:** No. **Propane:** No. **Internal Roads:** Gravel, in good condition. **RV Service:** No. **Market:** 5 mi. south in Benton. **Restaurant:** 5 mi. south in Benton. **General Store:** Yes. **Vending:** Yes. **Swimming Pool:** Yes. **Playground:** Yes. **Other:** Game room, pavilion, basketball, horseshoes, shuffleboard, video games,

sports field. **Activities:** Swimming, bingo, & hayrides on holiday weekends. **Nearby Attractions:** Rend Lake Recreation Area, tennis, golf, Benton Civic Center, marina, winery, antiques, Old Franklin County Jail, Franklin County Garage 1910s Museum. **Additional Information:** Southern Tourism Development Office, (618) 998-9397.

Restrictions

Pets: Leash only. **Fires:** Fire ring only. **Alcoholic Beverages:** Permitted. **Vehicle Maximum Length:** None..

To Get There

From junction of I-57 and Hwy. 154, take Exit 77, drive 0.25 mi. east on Hwy. 154, then 0.5 mi. south on Hwy. 37. Roads are wide and well maintained with good shoulders.

CASEY

Casey KOA

P.O. Box 56, Casey 62420. T: (800) 554-9206; www.koa.com.

RV ★★★★ Tent ★★★★

Beauty: ★★★★ Site Privacy: ★★★★
Spaciousness: ★★★★ Quiet: ★★★★
Security: ★★★★ Cleanliness: ★★★★★
Insect Control: None Facilities: ★★★★

The owners of the Casey KOA wax the campground's rest room floors. That's an indication of the attention to detail shown at the campground. Arranged in a series of loops, the campground offers an average site width of 30 feet, along with 45 pull-throughs. Each site is level, has a tree, and offers a good combination of gravel for an RV and grass for the picnic table. A major plus is the short distance and easy access from the interstate. Travelling campers will find this a good place for an overnight stay—it is a popular stopping-off point for people going to Branson, which is one day away. Located three miles north of Casey, the campground also is a good place to come as a destination, because of its recreation facilities and planned activities. Owners sell RVs and offer on-site service. The best RV site is 11, because it is close to the pool, rec room, and other activities. The most popular site for tent campers is 53, because it is more private and tenters can walk to the lake.

Basics

Operated by: Gene & Patti Shanks. **Open:** Mar. 1–Oct. 31. **Site Assignment:** Reservations accepted w/ 1-night deposit, refunded for cancellations w/ 24-hour notice, or 72-hour notice for holidays. **Registration:** At campground office. **Fee:** $23 (cash, check, credit cards). **Parking:** At site.

Facilities

Number of RV Sites: 79. **Number of Tent-Only Sites:** 2. **Hookups:** Electric (20, 30, 50 amps), water, sewer. **Each Site:** Picnic table, fire ring. **Dump Station:** Yes. **Laundry:** Yes. **Pay Phone:** Yes. **Rest Rooms and Showers:** Yes. **Fuel:** No. **Propane:** Yes. **Internal Roads:** Gravel, in good condition. **RV Service:** Yes. **Market:** 3 mi. south in Casey. **Restaurant:** 3 mi. south in Casey. **General Store:** Yes. **Vending:** Yes. **Swimming Pool:** Yes. **Playground:** Yes. **Other:** Game room, stocked fishing lake, horseshoes, basketball, volleyball. **Activities:** Fishing, boating (rental rowboats & paddle-boats available), Sunday pancake breakfast, weekly planned activities. **Nearby Attractions:** Amish country, Lincoln log cabin, antique malls, golf course, outlet shopping. **Additional Information:** Arthur Information Center, (800) 722-6474.

Restrictions

Pets: Leash only. **Fires:** Fire ring only. **Alcoholic Beverages:** Permitted. **Vehicle Maximum Length:** None.

To Get There

From I-70 and Hwy. 49 junction, take Exit 129, drive 0.25 mi. north on Hwy. 49, then 0.25 mi. west on CO 1250 N. Roads are wide and well maintained; all except the county road have broad shoulders.

CHEBANSE

Kankakee South KOA

425 East 6000 South Rd., Chebanse 60922. T: (815) 939-4603; www.koa.com.

RV ★★★ Tent ★★★

Beauty: ★★★ Site Privacy: ★★★
Spaciousness: ★★★ Quiet: ★★★★
Security: ★★★ Cleanliness: ★★★
Insect Control: None Facilities: ★★★

KOA Kankakee South offers the best of both worlds—ease of access to the interstate, yet a quiet location off the main highway. Six miles south of Kankakee, the campground is shielded from road noise by a row of oak trees and bushes. Farm fields ring the campground. Quiet hours are enforced from 11 p.m. to 7 a.m. The speed limit is a strict 4 mph. Laid out in a series of loops, the campground has gravel, shaded RV sites. The typical site width is 30 feet and 90 percent of the sites offer pull-through access. Only an hour from Chicago, the campground attracts many Chicagoans looking for some country peace. The best RV sites are in row 40, because these offer concrete pads and sewer hookups. Tent sites are located in a back area, where they have more privacy, greenery, and quiet. Security is good, with an owner who lives on the site and offers regular campground patrols.

Basics

Operated by: Sam Kwak. **Open:** Apr. 1–Oct. 31. **Site Assignment:** Reservations w/ 1-night deposit; refund w/ 24-hour notice. **Registration:** At campground office. **Fee:** $15 (cash, credit cards). **Parking:** At site.

Facilities

Number of RV Sites: 59. **Number of Tent-Only Sites:** 22. **Hookups:** Electric (30 amps), water, sewer. **Each Site:** Picnic table, fire ring. **Dump Station:** Yes. **Laundry:** Yes. **Pay Phone:** Yes. **Rest Rooms and Showers:** Yes. **Fuel:** No. **Propane:** Yes. **Internal Roads:** Gravel, in good condition. **RV Service:** No. **Market:** 6 mi. north in Kankakee. **Restaurant:** 6 mi. north in Kankakee. **General Store:** Yes. **Vending:** No. **Swimming Pool:** Yes. **Playground:** Yes. **Other:** Pool table, basketball court, volleyball, sports field, video games, picnic shelter. **Activities:** Swimming. **Nearby Attractions:** Golf, canoe trips, Friday night stockcar races, scenic drive, antique mall, skydiving, Model Railroad Museum. **Additional Information:** Kankakee County CVB, (900) 74-RIVER.

Restrictions

Pets: Leash only. **Fires:** Fire ring only. **Alcoholic Beverages:** At sites only. **Vehicle Maximum Length:** 40 ft.

To Get There

Take Exit 308 off I-57 onto US 45/32. Drive 3 mi. south on US 45/52, then 0.5 mi. east on Rd. 6000 to Kankakee South KOA. Roads wide and well maintained with decent shoulders.

EFFINGHAM

Camp Lakewood

1217 West Rickelman Ave., Effingham 62401. T: (217) 342-6233

RV ★★★ Tent ★★★

Beauty: ★★★ Site Privacy: ★★★★
Spaciousness: ★★★★ Quiet: ★★★★
Security: ★★★★ Cleanliness: ★★★★
Insect Control: None Facilities: ★★★

Camp Lakewood has many good things going for it, but it doesn't offer swimming. For campers who expect that as a normal part of their camping recreation, it may be hard to do without. Located on the north shores of Lake Pauline, one mile north of Effingham, the campground has 45 pull-throughs and the typical site width is 25 feet. Sites are generally gravel and shady. Camp Lakewood is conveniently located near the interstate and city restaurants, shopping, and movies. Security is good, with owners who live on the grounds, providing regular patrols, and city police nearby who keep an eye on the property. Campers are given a good first impression when escorted to their sites instead of just being handed a map with a red line indicating where to go. Tent sites are set off in a more primitive area. The price also is right; very economical for such a clean campground in a good location. But for some campers all the positive aspects might not balance out that one missing element—swimming.

Basics

Operated by: Deb & Gary Gregory. **Open:** All year. **Site Assignment:** Reservations w/ no deposit. **Registration:** At campground office. **Fee:** $18.50 (cash, check, credit cards). **Parking:** At site.

Facilities

Number of RV Sites: 65. **Number of Tent-Only Sites:** 10. **Hookups:** Electric (30, 50 amps), water, sewer, cable TV. **Each Site:** Picnic table, fire ring. **Dump Station:** Yes. **Laundry:** Yes. **Pay Phone:** Yes. **Rest Rooms and Showers:** Yes. **Fuel:** No. **Propane:** No. **Internal Roads:** Gravel, in good condition. **RV Service:** No. **Market:** 1 mi. south in Effingham. **Restaurant:** 1 mi. south in Effingham. **General Store:** Yes. **Vending:** No. **Swimming Pool:** No. **Playground:** Yes. **Other:** Boat ramp, game room, fishing dock, horseshoes. **Activities:** Fishing, boating (rental rowboats available). **Nearby Attractions:** Golf, mini-golf, movie theater, outlet mall, marina, art galleries, restaurants. **Additional Information:** Effingham CVB, (800) 772-0750.

Restrictions
Pets: Leash only. **Fires:** Fire ring only. **Alcoholic Beverages:** At sites only. **Vehicle Maximum Length:** None.

To Get There
From I-57 and I-70, take Effingham Exit 160. Turn north on Rte. 33/32. Go about 0.25 mi. to Ford Ave. and turn right. Follow signs 1 mi. to Camp Lakewood Campground. Roads are wide and well maintained, with broad shoulders.

EL PASO
Hickory Hills Campground
RR 1 Box 157, Secor 61771. T: (888) 801-4469; F: (309) 744-2407; www.hickoryh@elpaso.net.

RV ★★★ Tent ★★★

Beauty: ★★★ Site Privacy: ★★★
Spaciousness: ★★★ Quiet: ★★★★
Security: ★★★★ Cleanliness: ★★★★
Insect Control: None Facilities: ★★★

Hickory Hills Campground is what it sounds like—a grassy rural facility with a lot of trees. The typical site width is 25 feet and the campground has ten pull-throughs. About half of the sites are occupied by seasonal campers. Located four miles west of El Paso, the campground is level with a mix of grassy and gravel sites, along with shady or open ones. Many campers are repeats who come for the family atmosphere and recreation. Safety measures are enforced, including a 5 mph speed limit. Anyone driving a golf cart must be licensed and all golf carts must be insured if they are driven on the road. Quiet time is 10 p.m. to 8 a.m. on weekdays and midnight to 8 a.m. on weekends. The campground has one entrance road and owners who live on site providing a regular patrol of the campgrounds.

Basics
Operated by: Bryan & Ficki Outinen. **Open:** Apr. 1–Nov. 1. **Site Assignment:** Reservations w/ no deposit; holiday weekends require 1-night deposit. **Registration:** At campground office. **Fee:** $22 (cash, check). **Parking:** At site.

Facilities
Number of RV Sites: 179. **Number of Tent-Only Sites:** 110. **Hookups:** Electric (20, 30 amps), water, sewer. **Each Site:** Picnic table, fire ring. **Dump Station:** Yes. **Laundry:** Yes. **Pay Phone:** Yes. **Rest Rooms and Showers:** Yes. **Fuel:** No. **Propane:** Yes. **Internal Roads:** Gravel, in good condition. **RV Service:** No. **Market:** 4 mi. east in El Paso. **Restaurant:** 4 mi. east in El Paso. **General Store:** Yes. **Vending:** Yes. **Swimming Pool:** Yes. **Playground:** Yes. **Other:** Mini-golf, rec hall, video games, horseshoes, volleyball, basketball, fishing stream, hiking trails, sports field. **Activities:** Swimming, fishing, hiking, planned weekend activities. **Nearby Attractions:** Nature center, zoo, museum, casino, antique shops, art galleries, botanical garden, golf. **Additional Information:** Peoria Area CVB, (800) 747-0302.

Restrictions
Pets: Leash only. **Fires:** Fire ring only. **Alcoholic Beverages:** Permitted. **Vehicle Maximum Length:** None.

To Get There
From junction of I-39 and US 24, take Exit 14, drive 4 mi. west on US 24, then 0.25 mi. south on a county road. Roads are wide and well maintained with adequate shoulders.

GALENA
Palace Campgrounds
11357 Rte. 20 West, Galena 61036. T: (815) 777-2466; F: (815) 777-3739; www.palacecampground.com; palace@galenalink.net.

RV ★★★★ Tent ★★★★

Beauty: ★★★★ Site Privacy: ★★★★
Spaciousness: ★★★★ Quiet: ★★★
Security: ★★★★ Cleanliness: ★★★★
Insect Control: None Facilities: ★★★★

Palace Campgrounds is a rural campground that is rapidly becoming an urban campground as the city of Galena, grows out to meet it. That means the campground is surrounded by city amenities such as restaurants and gas stations. A restaurant and hotel/motel is located next door. Bordered by farm fields in the back, the campground features rolling hills, woods, and a tree-lined road. The typical site width is 28 feet with eight pull-throughs. Laid out in a series of loops, the campground has gravel sites for RVs and grassy ones for tents. Some RV sites are open, others shady. Free fishing is available at the four-acre pond. Tent sites are off by themselves, away from RVs in a more secluded, natural area. The campground is fenced with one major entrance/exit road. and speed bumps on interior roads help keep traffic speeds down.

Basics
Operated by: Teenie McCarthy. **Open:** Apr. 1–Oct. 31. **Site Assignment:** Reservations w/ $10 deposit, 1-night deposit required on holidays; refund w/ 10-day notice. **Registration:** At campground office. **Fee:** $23 (cash, check). **Parking:** At site.

Facilities
Number of RV Sites: 133. **Number of Tent-Only Sites:** 100. **Hookups:** Electric (30, 50 amps), water, sewer. **Each Site:** Picnic table, fire ring. **Dump Station:** Yes. **Laundry:** Yes. **Pay Phone:** Yes. **Rest Rooms and Showers:** Yes. **Fuel:** No. **Propane:** No. **Internal Roads:** Gravel, in good condition. **RV Service:** No. **Market:** 1 mi. east in Galena. **Restaurant:** Next door. **General Store:** No. **Vending:** Yes. **Swimming Pool:** Yes. **Playground:** Yes. **Other:** Basketball, snack bar, arcade, mini-golf, rec hall, pool table, outdoor movies, wading pool, fishing pond, sports field, horseshoes. **Activities:** Swimming, fishing, Saturday night hayrides, planned weekend activities. **Nearby Attractions:** Historic Galena, go-cart track, golf, riverboat casino, antique shops, fishing, flea markets, trail rides, cave tours, mountain resort, Alpine slide & chair lift rides. **Additional Information:** Galena/Jo Davies County CVB, (800) 747-9377.

Restrictions
Pets: Leash only. **Fires:** Fire ring only. **Alcoholic Beverages:** Permitted. **Vehicle Maximum Length:** 40 ft. **Other:** Must be at least 21 to reserve a site.

To Get There
From the west edge of Galena, drive 1 mi. west on US 20. US 20 has no shoulders and a steep hill coming out of Galena.

GENESEO
Geneseo Campground
22978 Illinois Hwy. 82, Geneseo 61254. T: (309) 944-6465; F: (309) 944-8879; www.fulltiming-america.com/geneseo; w6465@geneseo.net.

RV ★★★★ Tent ★★★

Beauty: ★★★★ Site Privacy: ★★★
Spaciousness: ★★★ Quiet: ★★★★
Security: ★★★★ Cleanliness: ★★★★
Insect Control: None Facilities: ★★★★

A rural campground adjacent to the historic Hennepin Canal, Geneseo Campground offers grassy, mostly shaded sites. The campground has 25 pull-through sites and a typical site width of 24 feet. Rustic cabins with air conditioning are a popular plus. Along with being a quiet spot, the biggest thing Geneseo Campground has going for it is its location adjacent to the Hennepin Canal. Listed in the National Register of Historic Places, the canal joins the Mississippi and Illinois Rivers. There are 32 of the original 33 locks still visible on the canal. Located within walking distance of the campground is one of the five locks restored to working condition and one of the six remaining aqueducts that carry the Hennepin across larger rivers and streams. You can rent a canoe or kayak for a Hennepin Canal trip that begins and ends at the campground. Fully watered, the canal also is a good fishing spot.

Basics
Operated by: Craig & Shari Weber. **Open:** Apr. 1–Oct. 31. **Site Assignment:** Reservations w/ 1-night deposit; refund w/ 7-day notice. **Registration:** At campground office. **Fee:** $16 (cash, check, credit cards). **Parking:** At site.

Facilities
Number of RV Sites: 63. **Number of Tent-Only Sites:** 0. **Hookups:** Electric (20, 30, 50 amps), water, sewer, phone. **Each Site:** Picnic table, fire ring. **Dump Station:** Yes. **Laundry:** Yes. **Pay Phone:** Yes. **Rest Rooms and Showers:** Yes. **Fuel:** No. **Propane:** Yes. **Internal Roads:** Gravel, in good condition. **RV Service:** No. **Market:** 2 mi. south in Geneseo. **Restaurant:** 2 mi. south in Geneseo. **General Store:** Yes, limited. **Vending:** No. **Swimming Pool:** No. **Playground:** Yes. **Other:** Sports field, horseshoes, rental cabins, rec room, fishing stream, badminton, hiking trails, volleyball. **Activities:** Fishing, canoeing & kayaking (rental canoes & kayaks available), hiking. **Nearby Attractions:** Victorian architecture, antiques, arts & crafts, golf, Grand Illinois Trail, Hennepin Canal, Bishop Hill, John Deere Museum, Rock Island Arsenal, riverboat cruises, casinos, Niabi Zoo, Wacky Waters, Geneseo Historical Museum, community swimming pool. **Additional Information:** Henry County Tourism Council, (309) 937-1255.

Restrictions
Pets: Leash only. **Fires:** In fire ring. **Alcoholic Beverages:** Permitted. **Vehicle Max. Length:** None.

To Get There

From junction of I-80 and Hwy. 82, take Exit 19 and drive 1.25 mi. north on Hwy. 82. Follow blue camping signs through town, pick up Hwy. 82 again and drive 2 mi. north. Roads are wide and well maintained with some narrow shoulders.

GOODFIELD

Goodfield's Yogi Bear's Jellystone Park Camp Resort

P.O. Box 92, Goodfield 61742. T: (800) 558-2954, ext. 116; F: (309) 965-2156; www.campjellystone.com.

RV ★★★★ Tent ★★★★

Beauty: ★★★	Site Privacy: ★★★★
Spaciousness: ★★★★	Quiet: ★★★★
Security: ★★★★★	Cleanliness: ★★★★
Insect Control: Yes	Facilities: ★★★★

Located 20 miles northwest of Bloomington, Goodfield's Yogi Bear's Jellystone Park Resort offers open and shaded grassy sites on a rolling terrain. Arranged in a series of loops, the rural campground has a typical site width of 30 feet with 20 pull-throughs. The campground offers separate sections for about 100 seasonal campers. Primitive areas for tent campers are scattered around the perimeter of the campground offering more privacy and natural beauty. Most popular tent sites are by the lake and by the ravine. Best RV sites are 113–122 because they are pull-throughs with small trees for shade. Safety measures include a speed limit of 5 mph, no bike riding after dark, and some restrictions for children. Quiet hours are between 10:30 p.m. and 8 a.m., visitors must leave by 10 p.m., and no generators are allowed in the campground. The owners live on site and a guard helps control access and makes regular patrols of the campgrounds.

Basics

Operated by: Bruce & Kathy Watkins. **Open:** All year. **Site Assignment:** Reservations w/ 1-night deposit; refunds (minus $5) w/ 7-day notice. **Registration:** At campground office. **Fee:** $26 (cash, check, credit cards). **Parking:** At site.

Facilities

Number of RV Sites: 387. **Number of Tent-Only Sites:** 200. **Hookups:** Electric (30, 50 amps), water, sewer. **Each Site:** Some picnic tables, fire sites. **Dump Station:** Yes. **Laundry:** Yes. **Pay Phone:** Yes. **Rest Rooms and Showers:** Yes. **Fuel:** No. **Propane:** Yes. **Internal Roads:** Gravel, in fair condition. **RV Service:** No. **Market:** 7 mi. north in Eureka. **Restaurant:** 3 mi. south in Goodfield. **General Store:** Yes. **Vending:** Yes. **Swimming Pool:** Yes. **Playground:** Yes. **Other:** Stocked fishing lake, mini-golf, bocci ball court, volleyball, horseshoes, softball, rec hall, chapel, clubhouse, hiking trails, boat dock. **Activities:** Swimming, fishing, hiking, boating (rental paddleboats, rowboats available) planned weekend activities. **Nearby Attractions:** Horse racing track, historic sites, museums, art galleries, antique shops, zoo, casino, golf, Prairie Aviation Museum, dinner theater, Factory Outlet Mall. **Additional Information:** Bloomington-Normal Area CVB, (800) 433-8226.

Restrictions

Pets: Leash only. **Fires:** Fire pits only. **Alcoholic Beverages:** At sites only. **Vehicle Maximum Length:** 65 ft. **Other:** 3-day min. stay on holidays.

To Get There

From junction of I-74 and Hwy. 117, take Exit 112 and drive 1 mi. north on Hwy. 117, then 0.75 mi. east on Timberline Rd. Roads are wide and well maintained with broad shoulders.

GRANITE CITY

Granite City KOA

3157 West Chain of Rocks Rd., Granite City 62040. T: (618) 931-5160; www.koa.com.

RV ★★★★ Tent ★★★

Beauty: ★★★	Site Privacy: ★★★
Spaciousness: ★★★	Quiet: ★★★★
Security: ★★★★	Cleanliness: ★★★★
Insect Control: None	Facilities: ★★★★

It's sort of a trade-off. At Granite City KOA, you are 11 miles north of downtown St. Louis on historic Rte. 66. It's an easy place to use as a base for all the wonderful St. Louis area attractions. But, since it is in the city limits, you cannot have a campfire at Granite City KOA. You can use a grill for cooking but no open fires are permitted in the city limits. Granite City KOA does have a lot of other amenities going for it, though. A rural/urban campground laid out in a series of loops, Granite City KOA offers mostly wooded, grassy, or gravel, level sites. There are few open sites available. The typical site width is 35 feet and there are 70 pull-throughs. A secluded area set aside for tents is shaded with big elm and maple trees, offering privacy. There are no scheduled activities. With all St. Louis has to offer, most campers don't seem to mind.

Basics

Operated by: Cuvar Family. **Open:** Mar. 15–Nov. 1. **Site Assignment:** Reservations accepted w/ 1-night deposit of $10 on credit card by mail; refund w/ 24-hour notice. **Registration:** At campg office. **Fee:** $23 (cash, credit cards). **Parking:** At site.

Facilities

Number of RV Sites: 80. **Number of Tent-Only Sites:** 50. **Hookups:** Electric (20, 30, 50 amps), water, sewer. **Each Site:** Picnic table. **Dump Station:** Yes. **Laundry:** Yes. **Pay Phone:** Yes. **Rest Rooms and Showers:** Yes. **Fuel:** No. **Propane:** Yes. **Internal Roads:** Paved/gravel, in good condition. **RV Service:** No. **Market:** 3 mi. south in Granite City. **Restaurant:** 3 mi. south in Granite City. **General Store:** Yes. **Vending:** No. **Swimming Pool:** Yes. **Playground:** Yes. **Other:** Basketball, horseshoes, game room, rental cabins, recreation field, pavilion, badminton. **Activities:** Swimming. **Nearby Attractions:** St. Louis Arch, raceway, bike trails, historic sites, museums, zoo, riverboat gambling, Six Flags, Busch Stadium, Laclede's Landing. **Additional Information:** St. Louis Convention & Visitors Commission, (800) 916-0040.

Restrictions

Pets: Leash only. **Fires:** None. **Alcoholic Beverages:** Permitted. **Vehicle Max. Length:** None.

To Get There

From junction I-270 and Hwy. 3, take Exit 3A, drive 0.25 mi. south on Hwy. 3, then 0.5 mi. east on Chain of Rocks Rd. Roads are wide and well maintained with broad shoulders.

KNOXVILLE

Galesburg East Best Holiday

1081 US Hwy. 150 East, Knoxville 61448. T: (309) 289-CAMP; F: (309) 289-0079; .

RV ★★★★ Tent ★★★

Beauty: ★★★	Site Privacy: ★★★
Spaciousness: ★★★	Quiet: ★★★★
Security: ★★★★★	Cleanliness: ★★★★
Insect Control: None	Facilities: ★★★★

Located in a secluded country setting with farm fields around it, Galesburg East Best Holiday Trav-L-Park offers a quiet, secure facility. With easy access from the Hwy., the campground has level, shady spots with an average width of 25 feet and 55 pull-throughs. Tent sites are somewhat separated from RVs and offer more shade and grass. Campers often stay at Galesburg East to do geneaology work in the area and enjoy the local festivals. A welcome touch in the hot summer is the air-conditioned laundry and store. Security is tops thanks to lights on buildings, security cameras, owners who live on the property, and regular patrols of the campground, which is seven miles east of Galesburg.

Basics

Operated by: Stan & Judy Herrick. **Open:** Apr. 1–Nov. 1. **Site Assignment:** Reservations w/ 1-night deposit; refund w/ 24-hour notice. **Registration:** At campground headquarters. **Fee:** $20 (cash, credit cards). **Parking:** At site.

Facilities

Number of RV Sites: 58. **Number of Tent-Only Sites:** 10. **Hookups:** Electric (30, 50 amps,) water, sewer. **Each Site:** Picnic table, fire ring. **Dump Station:** Yes. **Laundry:** Yes. **Pay Phone:** Yes. **Rest Rooms and Showers:** Yes. **Fuel:** No. **Propane:** Yes. **Internal Roads:** Gravel, in fair condition. **RV Service:** Next door. **Market:** 7 mi. west in Galesburg. **Restaurant:** 3 mi. west in Knoxville. **General Store:** Yes. **Vending:** No. **Swimming Pool:** Yes. **Playground:** Yes. **Other:** Fishing pond, lounge w/ TV, enclosed shelter, heated swimming pool. **Activities:** Fishing. **Nearby Attractions:** Carl Sandburg's Birthplace, Bishop Hill Swedish colony, scenic drive, golf, railroad museum, Wolf Covered Bridge spanning Spoon River. **Additional Information:** Galesburg Area CVB, (309) 343-1194.

Restrictions

Pets: Leash only. **Fires:** Fire ring only. **Alcoholic Beverages:** At sites only. **Vehicle Maximum Length:** 40 ft.

To Get There

From Exit 54 on US 150, drive 1 mi. east to the campground. Roads are wide and well maintained with broad shoulders.

LENA

Lake Le-Aqua-Na State Park

8542 North Lake Rd., Lena 61048. T: (815) 369-4282; www.dnr.state.il.us.

RV ★★ Tent ★★★★

Beauty: ★★★★ Site Privacy: ★★★
Spaciousness: ★★★ Quiet: ★★★★
Security: ★★★★ Cleanliness: ★★★★
Insect Control: None Facilities: ★★

Six miles south of the Illinois-Wisconsin state line, Lake Le-Aqua-Na State Park was dedicated as a state park in 1958. The unusual name is the result of a contest to name the park; it's a combination of the town name of Lena and the Latin word for water, aqua. Oak, hickory, walnut, and other hardwood trees grow in abundance here, along with large tracts of pines. Campsites are grouped into three designated areas. Class A facilities include gravel pads, conveniently located water hydrants, a dumping station, and a shower building with flush toilets. Class B facilities offer vehicular access and the use of the shower building. Big Buck Campground is separate from the other areas and is maintained for equestrians. It is accessed from the county roads bordering the park. Alcohol is prohibited in the campgrounds. The average site width is 20 feet and there are three pull-throughs. The campground offers a mix of shady and open sites. The best RV sites are 42 and 43, because they are the biggest. The best tent sites are Hickory Hill sites 1–7 and 150–153 because they are more wooded and offer more privacy. Internal roads in the park are often twisty with no shoulders. Some of the hilly terrain makes it difficult for RVs to maneuver, but the views are worth it.

Basics

Operated by: State of Illinois. **Open:** All year. **Site Assignment:** 28 sites available for reservations; 1-night deposit required, plus $5 reservation fee; refund w/ 7-day notice. **Registration:** At camp office. **Fee:** $11 (cash, check). **Parking:** At site.

Facilities

Number of RV Sites: 141. **Number of Tent-Only Sites:** 30. **Hookups:** Electric (30, 50 amps). **Each Site:** Picnic table, fire ring. **Dump Station:** Yes. **Laundry:** No. **Pay Phone:** Yes. **Rest Rooms and Showers:** Yes. **Fuel:** No. **Propane:** No. **Internal Roads:** Paved, in good condition. **RV Service:** No. **Market:** 3 mi. south in Lena. **Restaurant:** 3 mi. south in Lena. **General Store:** Yes. **Vending:** Yes. **Swimming Pool:** No. **Playground:** Yes. **Other:** Lake w/ beach, hiking trails, boat ramp, boat dock, equestrian trail. **Activities:** Swimming, fishing, boating (rental rowboats & paddleboats available), hiking. **Nearby Attractions:** Lena Area Historical Museum, Stagecoach Trail, Stephenson–Black Hawk Trail, *Field of Dreams* movie site, cheese companies, golf, casino. **Additional Information:** Northern Illinois Tourism Development Office, (815) 547-3740.

Restrictions

Pets: Leash only. **Fires:** Fire ring only. **Alcoholic Beverages:** Not permitted. **Vehicle Maximum Length:** None. **Other:** 2-week stay limit.

To Get There

From junction US 20 and Hwy. 73, drive 5 mi. north on Hwy. 73 and Lake Park Rd. US 20 is well maintained but narrow with no shoulders.

LENA

Lena KOA

10982 West Hwy. 20, Lena 61048. T: (815) 369-2612; F: (815) 369-5338; www.koa.com; reservations@lenakoa.com.

RV ★★★ Tent ★★★

Beauty: ★★★ Site Privacy: ★★★
Spaciousness: ★★★ Quiet: ★★★★
Security: ★★★★★ Cleanliness: ★★★★★
Insect Control: None Facilities: ★★★

Surrounded by cornfields and woods, Lena KOA is a quiet, family campground one mile north of Lena. The typical site width is 27 feet and the campground has 25 pull-throughs. There is a mixture of wooded and open sites. A Kamping Kitchen, with three cooking stations with sinks and electric stoves, plus six picnic tables, provides cooking and eating facilities for campers to use. Tent sites are grassy with wooden platforms for tents. RV sites are grassy with gravel pads for RVs. The best RV sites are M6–11, because they are long sites offering easy in and out; L1–5, because they are away from the road and closer to the woods; and I1–5, because they are long, level, have 50 amps electricity and a variety of trees. Tent sites are spacious and level, with a short walk to rest rooms and showers. Campers are escorted to their sites when they check in. Security is good thanks to an owner who lives on the grounds, a staffed office from 8 a.m. to 9 p.m., enforced quiet time from 10 p.m. to 7 a.m., and regular patrols of the campground.

Basics

Operated by: Denny Drake & Bonnie Phillips. **Open:** May 1–Nov. 1. **Site Assignment:** Reservations w/ $20 deposit; refund (minus $5 service fee) w/ 3-day notice. **Registration:** At campground office. **Fee:** $26 (cash, check, credit cards). **Parking:** At site.

Facilities

Number of RV Sites: 83. **Number of Tent-Only Sites:** 5. **Hookups:** Electric (30, 50 amps), water, sewer, phone, Internet. **Each Site:** Picnic table, fire ring. **Dump Station:** Yes. **Laundry:** Yes. **Pay Phone:** Yes. **Rest Rooms and Showers:** Yes. **Fuel:** No. **Propane:** Yes. **Internal Roads:** Gravel, in good condition. **RV Service:** No. **Market:** 1 mi. north in Lena. **Restaurant:** 1 mi. north in Lena. **General Store:** Yes. **Vending:** Yes. **Swimming Pool:** Yes. **Playground:** Yes. **Other:** Video arcade, rec room, volleyball, horseshoes, basketball, sports field, pavilion, Kamping Kitchen. **Activities:** Swimming, biking (rental low-rider bikes available), planned activities on weekends. **Nearby Attractions:** Lena Area Historical Museum, Stagecoach Trail, *Field of Dreams* movie site, Stephenson–Black Hawk Trail, cheese companies, golf, casino. **Additional Information:** Northern Illinois Tourism Development Office, (815) 547-3740.

Restrictions

Pets: Leash only. **Fires:** Fire ring only. **Alcoholic Beverages:** At sites only. **Vehicle Maximum Length:** 45 ft.

To Get There

From junction of Hwy. 73 and US 20, drive 0.25 mi. east on US 20. US 20 has no shoulders so be careful turning into the campground.

LITCHFIELD

Rainmaker Campground

865 Rainmaker Tr., Litchfield 62056. T: (217) 532-6370

RV ★★★ Tent ★★

Beauty: ★★★ Site Privacy: ★★★
Spaciousness: ★★★ Quiet: ★★★★
Security: ★★★★★ Cleanliness: ★★★★
Insect Control: None Facilities: ★★★

The fourth generation of campers are now visiting Rainmaker Campground, six miles east of Litchfield. And the same owners are there who started it almost four decades ago. Prices must not have changed much over those years because the campground is a real bargain—$10 for an RV or tent site. Seasonals campers have taken up 140 of the sites and seem to spend considerable time fixing up their second homes with flowers, shrubs, and decorations. The owners don't charge storage if RVs are left year-round on the site. The campground is a destination. Very few RVs would drive those country roads just for an overnight place to stay. The drive is pretty but the winding, narrow roads can get tiresome. RV sites are gravel with a choice of open or shaded. Typical site width is 25 feet and there are five pull-throughs in front of the shower facility. Those are the most popular RV sites. Tent campers can use any of the RV sites which puts them at a bit of a disadvantage if they want privacy. The family campground has solid security measures—owners who live on the grounds, regular patrols, a security camera, and an access gate that is locked from 11 p.m. to 6 a.m.

Basics

Operated by: Rex & June Brawley. **Open:** Apr. 1–Oct. 31. **Site Assignment:** Reservations w/ no deposit. **Registration:** At campground office. **Fee:** $10 (cash, check). **Parking:** At site.

Facilities

Number of RV Sites: 220. **Number of Tent-Only Sites:** 0. **Hookups:** Electric (20, 30 amps), water, sewer. **Each Site:** Picnic table, fire ring. **Dump Station:** Yes. **Laundry:** No. **Pay Phone:** Yes. **Rest Rooms and Showers:** Yes. **Fuel:** No. **Propane:** Yes. **Internal Roads:** Paved/gravel, in good condition. **RV Service:** Yes. **Market:** 6 mi. west in Litchfield. **Restaurant:** 6 mi. west in Litchfield. **General Store:** Yes. **Vending:** No. **Swimming Pool:** No. **Playground:** Yes. **Other:** Fishing pond, Lake Yeager, nature trails, horseshoes, volleyball, tetherball, basketball, bait, boat ramp, boat dock, rec hall, pavilion, adults room, recreation field. **Activities:** Swimming, fishing, boating, hiking, Sunday church services, planned weekend activities.

Nearby Attractions: Golf, drive-in theater, nature conservation area, Sportsman's Family Fun Park, nature trails, water sports, swimming. **Additional Information:** Central Illinois Tourism Development Office, (217) 525-7980.

Restrictions

Pets: Leash only. **Fires:** Fire ring only. **Alcoholic Beverages:** Permitted. **Vehicle Maximum Length:** None.

To Get There

From junction of I-55 and Hwy. 16, take Exit 52, drive 5.5 mi. east on Hwy. 16, then 4 mi. northwest on Parsons. The country roads are very winding and narrow at times.

MAHOMET

Tin Cup RV Park

1715 East Tincup Rd., Mahomet 61853. T: (217) 586-3011

RV ★★★ Tent ★★★

Beauty: ★★★	Site Privacy: ★★★
Spaciousness: ★★★	Quiet: ★★★★
Security: ★★★★	Cleanliness: ★★★★
Insect Control: Yes	Facilities: ★★★

At first glance, Tin Cup RV Park looks like a golf course. The slopes of the grassy campground are so well maintained they could be a golf green. Located in the small town of Mahomet, eight miles west of Champaign, the campground offers a country setting just down the road from the Champaign Country Forest Preserve. A favorite with golfers, the campground also has an updated golf driving range with a ball dispenser. Most sites offer shade with mature trees. Typical site width is 30 feet and the campground has 18 pull-throughs. Laid out in a series of loops, the campground has mostly gravel pads on grassy sites for RVs. Best RV sites are 33–40 because they are spacious and well shaded and offer easy access. Primitive sites are set aside in three acres of woods where RVs aren't allowed to camp. The tent sites are promoted as being unlimited but could probably accommodate an estimated 700 tent campers. However, the tent area is never filled up so tent campers have a bit more privacy and rustic surroundings. Security is good with a co-owner who lives on the premises and provides regular patrols of the area. Set back from the road, the campground is quiet. Many campers probably spend their days at the nearby 18-hole golf course.

Basics

Operated by: Stephen Robinson. **Open:** All year. **Site Assignment:** Reservations w/ no deposit. **Registration:** At campground office. **Fee:** $22 (cash, check, credit cards). **Parking:** At site.

Facilities

Number of RV Sites: 65. **Number of Tent-Only Sites:** 700. **Hookups:** Electric (30 amps), water, sewer. **Each Site:** Picnic table, fire ring. **Dump Station:** Yes. **Laundry:** No. **Pay Phone:** Yes. **Rest Rooms and Showers:** Yes. **Fuel:** No. **Propane:** No. **Internal Roads:** Paved/gravel, in good condition. **RV Service:** No. **Market:** 0.5 mi. west on Mahomet. **Restaurant:** 0.5 mi. west on Mahomet. **General Store:** No. **Vending:** Yes. **Swimming Pool:** No. **Playground:** Yes. **Other:** Golf driving range w/ ball dispenser, sports field. **Activities:** None on-site. **Nearby Attractions:** Golf course, fishing lakes, swimming area, Early American Museum, University of Illinois, hiking trails, paved bike trails. **Additional Information:** Mahomet Chamber of Commerce, (217) 586-3165.

Restrictions

Pets: Leash only. **Fires:** Fire ring only. **Alcoholic Beverages:** At sites only. **Vehicle Maximum Length:** 40 ft.

To Get There

From junction of I-57 and I-74, take Exit 174 and drive 5 mi. northwest on I-74, then 0.5 mi. north on Prairie View Rd., then 0.5 mi. west on Tincup Rd. Roads are wide and well maintained with broad shoulders.

MARSHALL

Lincoln Trail State Park

RR 1 Box 117, Marshall 62441. T: (217) 826-2222; www.dnr.state.il.us.

RV ★★★ Tent ★★★★

Beauty: ★★★★	Site Privacy: ★★★★
Spaciousness: ★★★★	Quiet: ★★★★
Security: ★★★★	Cleanliness: ★★★★
Insect Control: None	Facilities: ★★★

Officially dedicated in 1958, Lincoln Trail State Park was named after the trail Abraham Lincoln's family followed en route from Indiana to Illinois in 1831. With 3,000 markers showing the way, the trail winds through Kentucky, Indiana, and Illinois. Located five miles south of Marshall, the 1,023-acre park centers around the 146-acre Lincoln Trail Lake. Two campgrounds, Plainview and Lakeside, offer amenities, including mostly gravel, open sites with 23 pull-throughs. For those who wish to be atuned to nature without the distractions of modern conveniences, Lakeside Campground also includes a camping area for tents. Tent sites offer more privacy, grass, and shade. A full-service concession stand near the boat docks offers a wide variety of refreshments and supplies, as well as boat and dock rentals. The Beech Tree Trail is just a half mile long, extending from the boat dock parking lot and concession stand, past the large picnic shelter, and on to the campground. The trail includes a series of stairways and foot bridges, which provide an excellent view of the beech maple forest contained within the nature preserve. Now, if only Lincoln Trail State Park had someplace nice to swim.

Basics

Operated by: State of Illinois. **Open:** All year. **Site Assignment:** First come, first served. **Registration:** At campground office. **Fee:** $11 (cash, check). **Parking:** At site.

Facilities

Number of RV Sites: 208. **Number of Tent-Only Sites:** 24. **Hookups:** Electric (20, 30, 50 amps). **Each Site:** Picnic table, fire ring. **Dump Station:** Yes. **Laundry:** No. **Pay Phone:** Yes. **Rest Rooms and Showers:** Yes. **Fuel:** No. **Propane:** No. **Internal Roads:** Paved, in good condition. **RV Service:** No. **Market:** 5 mi. north in Marshall. **Restaurant:** On site. **General Store:** No. **Vending:** Yes. **Swimming Pool:** No. **Playground:** Yes. **Other:** Lincoln Trail Lake, boat ramp, boat dock, hiking trails. **Activities:** Fishing, hiking, boating (rental motorboats, canoes, paddleboats, & rowboats available). **Nearby Attractions:** The Archer House former stagecoach stop, Clark County Museum, Stone Arch Bridges, hunting, Amish country, antique shops, golf. **Additional Information:** Central Illinois Tourism Development Office, (217) 525-7980.

Restrictions

Pets: Leash only. **Fires:** Fire ring only. **Alcoholic Beverages:** Permitted. **Vehicle Maximum Length:** 60 ft. **Other:** 2-week stay limit.

To Get There

From junction US 40 and Hwy. 1, drive 5 mi. south on Hwy. 1, then 1 mi. west on blacktop road. Roads are wide and well maintained with good shoulders.

MULBERRY GROVE

Cedarbrook RV & Camper Park

1109 Mulberry Grove Rd., Mulberry Grove 62262. T: (618) 326-8865

RV ★★★★ Tent ★★★★

Beauty: ★★★★	Site Privacy: ★★★★
Spaciousness: ★★★	Quiet: ★★★★
Security: ★★★★★	Cleanliness: ★★★★★
Insect Control: None	Facilities: ★★★★

Not only are the rest rooms at Cedarbrook RV and Camper Park very clean, they are also decorated: scatter rugs lay on the floor, a fan supplies cooling breezes, and a fancy bottle of liquid soap adorns the sink. The owners obviously care. The secluded wilderness setting eight miles west of Vandalia, features nine pull-through sites—the most popular with RVs—and an average site width of 25 feet. A wooded ravine and a small lake for fishing and swimming add to the amenities, but there are no scheduled activities. RV sites are generally gravel with a mixture of sunny and shady places. Tent sites are more primitive and grassy. The campground has a gate for security, owners who live on the grounds, and regular patrols of the area.

Basics

Operated by: Howard & Donna Kunder. **Open:** Apr. 1–Nov. 1. **Site Assignment:** Reservations w/ 1-night deposit; refund w/ 24-hour notice. **Registration:** At campground office. **Fee:** $18 (cash, credit cards). **Parking:** At site.

Facilities

Number of RV Sites: 57. **Number of Tent-Only Sites:** 15. **Hookups:** Electric (20, 30, 50 amps), water, sewer. **Each Site:** Picnic table, fire ring. **Dump Station:** Yes. **Laundry:** Yes. **Pay Phone:** Yes. **Rest Rooms and Showers:** Yes. **Fuel:** No. **Propane:** Yes. **Internal Roads:** Gravel, in good condition. **RV Service:** No. **Market:** 8 mi. east in Vandalia. **Restaurant:** 1 mi. north in Mulberry Grove. **General Store:** Yes. **Vending:** Yes. **Swimming Pool:** No. **Playground:** Yes. **Other:** Small lake, clubhouse w/ complete kitchen, horseshoes, ping-pong, volleyball, TV, pool table. **Activities:**

Swimming in lake, fishing. **Nearby Attractions:** Carlyle Lake, biggest man-made lake in Illinois; Vandalia, first capitol of Illinois; scenic drives. **Additional Information:** Crawford County Tourism Council, (800) 445-7006.

RESTRICTIONS

Pets: Leash only. **Fires:** Fire ring only. **Alcoholic Beverages:** Permitted. **Vehicle Maximum Length:** None.

TO GET THERE

From I-70, take Exit 52, drive 1 mi. south. Roads are wide and well maintained with broad shoulders.

OAKWOOD

Kickapoo State Park

10906 Kickapoo Park Rd., Oakwood 61858. T: (217) 442-4915; www.dnr.state.il.us.

RV ★★★ Tent ★★★★

Beauty: ★★★★	Site Privacy: ★★★
Spaciousness: ★★★	Quiet: ★★★★
Security: ★★★★	Cleanliness: ★★★
Insect Control: None	Facilities: ★★★

Easily reached by I-74, Kickapoo State Park has a wealth of natural beauty and outdoor activities. Oddly, that is not how it all started. Once a scarred wasteland ravaged by strip-mine operations, Kickapoo State Park's 2,842 acres now provide an outdoor playground with something to appeal to every member of the family. For campers, Kickapoo has two major campgrounds for tent and RV camping. Campers occupying electrical sites are required to pay for the availability of electricity even if the service is not used. A limited number of walk-in sites are available for primitive campers. Sites are mostly shaded and level. The park is said to be the first in the nation built on strip-mined land and one of the first to be subsidized through public contributions. The spoil piles and mine pits left behind after nearly a century (1850–1940) of mining were the base from which nature had to recover to transform Kickapoo State Park into the outdoor playground it is today. The park has 22 deep-water ponds providing a total of 221 acres of water for boaters, canoeists, and anglers.

BASICS

Operated by: State of Illinois. **Open:** All year. **Site Assignment:** Some sites available for reservations; 1-night deposit, plus $5 for reservation; refund w/ 7-day notice. **Registration:** At campground office. **Fee:** $11 (cash, check). **Parking:** At site.

FacilitiesNumber of RV Sites: 108. **Number of Tent-Only Sites:** 75. **Hookups:** Electric (20, 50 amps). **Each Site:** Picnic table, fire ring. **Dump Station:** Yes. **Laundry:** No. **Pay Phone:** Yes. **Rest Rooms and Showers:** Yes. **Fuel:** No. **Propane:** No. **Internal Roads:** Paved, in good condition. **RV Service:** No. **Market:** 1 mi. south in Oakwood. **Restaurant:** 1 mi. south in Oakwood. **General Store:** No. **Vending:** No. **Swimming Pool:** No. **Playground:** Yes. **Other:** Vermilion River, lakes, ponds, horseshoes, boat ramp, shelters, hiking trails, mountain bike trails. **Activities:** Fishing, boating (rental boats available), canoeing, hiking, hunting, scuba diving. **Nearby Attractions:** Danville Stadium, Vermilion County Museum, Middle Fork National Scenic River, Vermilion County War Museum Society, antique & arts & crafts stores. **Additional Information:** Danville Area CVB, (800) 383-4386.

RESTRICTIONS

Pets: Leash only. **Fires:** Fire ring only. **Alcoholic Beverages:** Not permitted. **Vehicle Maximum Length:** None. **Other:** 2-week stay limit.

TO GET THERE

From Oakwood, drive 1 mi. north on New Town Rd. Roads are wide and well maintained with mostly broad shoulders.

OREGON

Lake LaDonna Family Campground

1302 Harmony Rd., Oregon 61061. T: (815) 732-6804

RV ★★★ Tent ★★★

Beauty: ★★★	Site Privacy: ★★★
Spaciousness: ★★★	Quiet: ★★★
Security: ★★★★	Cleanliness: ★★★
Insect Control: None	Facilities: ★★★

Campers often stop and ask if they have to be veterans to stay at Lake LaDonna Family Campground. They don't, of course. But the campground is dedicated to veterans and has the nation's first Vietnam Memorial Wall. The 80-foot wall was built in 1982 by the owner, himself a Vietnam vet whose limp attests to his war injuries. Flags fly everywhere, POW and MIA signs are prominently displayed, and military branch symbols are affixed to RVs and campers. Special memorial services also are held several times a year to honor veterans. Laid out in a series of loops, the campground has well-shaded grassy and gravel sites. The average site width is 28 feet, with 50 pull-throughs. The campground has 135 seasonal campers. The campground's white sand beach and spring-fed lake are its biggest draws. The lake has a 16-foot waterfall, a boardwalk with huge thatched huts for shade, a diving board, and a life guard on duty.

BASICS

Operated by: Lamont Gaston. **Open:** Apr. 15–Oct. 15. **Site Assignment:** Reservation required, w/ 1-night deposit; full refund w/ 1-week notice; cancellations w/ 24-hour notice receive half the deposit amount. **Registration:** At campground office. **Fee:** $25 (cash, check, credit cards). **Parking:** At site.

FACILITIES

Number of RV Sites: 351. **Number of Tent-Only Sites:** 6. **Hookups:** Electric (20, 30, 50 amps), water. **Each Site:** Picnic table. **Dump Station:** Yes. **Laundry:** No. **Pay Phone:** Yes. **Rest Rooms and Showers:** Yes. **Fuel:** No. **Propane:** Yes. **Internal Roads:** Paved, in good condition. **RV Service:** No. **Market:** 5 mi. north in Oregon. **Restaurant:** 5 mi. north in Oregon. **General Store:** Yes. **Vending:** Yes. **Swimming Pool:** No. **Playground:** Yes. **Other:** Manmade lake, beach, rope swing dock, boardwalk, basketball court, lodge, video game arcade, pool tables, pinball, juke box, fast-food restaurant, amphitheater. **Activities:** Swimming, planned activities. **Nearby Attractions:** Go-karts, mini-golf, bumper boats, ultralight flying lessons, shooting gallery, 4 state parks, paddlewheel boat, 48-ft. tall Black Hawk statue overlooking Rock River. **Additional Information:** Northern Illinois Tourism Development Office, (815) 547-3740.

RESTRICTIONS

Pets: Leash only. **Fires:** Fire pits only. **Alcoholic Beverages:** Permitted. **Vehicle Maximum Length:** 40 ft. **Other:** 2-night min. for weekends, 3-night min. on holiday weekends.

TO GET THERE

From Rte. 64 west, turn left at the 3rd stoplight (Rte. 2) in Oregon. Continue south to edge of town. Follow signs to White Pines State Park by turning right onto Pines Rd. Continue on Pines Rd., following signs to White Pines State Park. Two miles before the state park, turn right off Pines Rd. onto Harmony Rd. Lake LaDonna is 0.5 mile on right on Harmony Rd., marked by a large, lighted sign. Road is well maintained with sufficient shoulders.

OREGON

River Road Camping & Marina

3922 River Rd., Oregon 61061. T: (815) 234-5383; F: (815) 234-5386; www.gocampingamerica.com/riverroadcpmar/index.html.

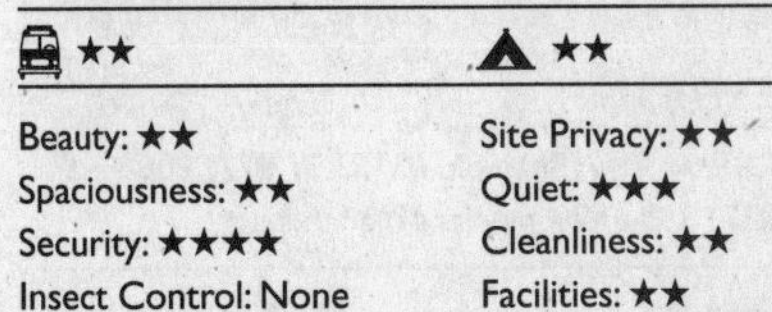

RV ★★ Tent ★★

Beauty: ★★	Site Privacy: ★★
Spaciousness: ★★	Quiet: ★★★
Security: ★★★★	Cleanliness: ★★
Insect Control: None	Facilities: ★★

The Rock River is the centerpiece of River Road Camping and Marina, five miles north of Oregon. Most people come for water recreation and the most popular sites are right by the river, especially sites 36–41 that are around a big oak tree and near the boat launch. Sites on the river also get a cooling breeze which can be a welcome relief in a Midwest summer. The campground tends to get crowded, so reservations are recommended. Laid out in a series of loops, the rural campground has a typical site width of 26 feet and offers 30 pull-throughs. RV sites are level with a mix of grass and gravel with shaded or open areas. A primitive area is set aside for tent campers, offering more privacy, shade, and grass. A creek runs through the campground, winding through some of the sites. Security measures are good with owners living in the campground, a regular patrol of the area, and entrance gates that are locked from 10 p.m. to 8 a.m. on weekdays and 11 p.m. to 8 a.m. on weekends.

BASICS

Operated by: Al & Ada Overton. **Open:** Apr. 15–Oct. 30. **Site Assignment:** Reservations w/ 1-night deposit; 2-night min.; 3-night min. on holidays, paid in advance. No refunds. **Registration:** At campground office. **Fee:** $26 (cash, check). **Parking:** At site.

FACILITIES

Number of RV Sites: 150. **Number of Tent-Only Sites:** 200. **Hookups:** Electric (30 amps), water. **Each Site:** Picnic table, fire ring. **Dump Station:** Yes. **Laundry:** Yes. **Pay Phone:** Yes. **Rest Rooms and Showers:** Yes. **Fuel:** Yes. **Propane:** Yes. **Internal Roads:** Paved, in good condition. **RV Service:** No. **Market:** 5 mi. south in Oregon. **Restaurant:** 5 mi. south in Oregon. **General Store:** Yes. **Vending:** Yes. **Swimming Pool:** Yes. **Playground:** Yes. **Other:** Rock River, Spring Creek, game room, boat dock, boat launch, horseshoes, basketball, pavilion, badminton, sports field, volleyball. **Activities:** Swimming, waterskiing, fishing, boating (rental pontoons, rowboats, & canoes available), planned weekend activities. **Nearby Attractions:** Go-karts, mini-golf, bumper boats, ultralight flying lessons, shooting gallery, 4 state parks, paddlewheel boat, 48-ft. tall Black Hawk statue overlooking Rock River. **Additional Information:** Northern Illinois Tourism Development Office, (815) 547-3740.

RESTRICTIONS

Pets: Leash only. **Fires:** Fire ring only. **Alcoholic Beverages:** Permitted. **Vehicle Maximum Length:** 40 ft.

TO GET THERE

From junction of Hwy. 2 and Hwy. 64, drive 0.5 mi. east on Hwy. 64, then 4 mi. north on River Rd. Roads are wide and well maintained with broad shoulders.

PITTSFIELD

Pine Lakes Camping & Fishing Resort

RR 3, Box 3077, Pittsfield 62363. T: (877) 808-PINE; F: (217) 285-1439; pinelake@adams.net.

RV ★★★★ | Tent ★★★★

Beauty: ★★★★	Site Privacy: ★★★★
Spaciousness: ★★★★	Quiet: ★★★★
Security: ★★★★	Cleanliness: ★★★★
Insect Control: None	Facilities: ★★★★

Pine Lakes Camping and Fishing Resort in Pittsfield, has natural beauty—to begin with, 45-acre Pine Lake with a pretty shoreline, a ravine, and sandy swimming beach. The campground also has little touches to add to its scenic attractions—flower gardens, flower boxes, large wooden carvings, and a totem pole. Laid out in a series of loops, the campground's typical site width is 35 feet and it has 16 pull-throughs. RV sites are a mixture of grass and gravel. Many RV sites have concrete pads and picnic tables covered with wooden canopies. RVs have a choice of shady or open sites. A primitive site for tents offers more privacy, trees, and grass. The best RV sites are in the 400 section along the lake, and the heavily-shaded 100 section. The speed limit is 7.5 mph, no bicycles or golf carts are allowed after dark (bike helmets are encouraged), and each vehicle must exhibit a camper or visitor pass. Security and noise regulations are enforced. Bug zappers are not permitted and quiet hours are 11 p.m. to 8 a.m. Children must be on their site during quiet hours unless accompanied by an adult. A security gate guards the entrance to the campground and the area is patrolled.

BASICS

Operated by: Jim & Marsha. **Open:** All year, limited winter facilities. **Site Assignment:** Reservations w/ 1-night deposit; refunds (minus $7 service charge) w/ 14-day notice; cancellations within 3–14 days will be issued credit for current season; 2-night min. reservation, 3-night min. for holiday weekends. **Registration:** At campground office. **Fee:** $21 (cash, check, credit cards). **Parking:** At site.

FACILITIES

Number of RV Sites: 130. **Number of Tent-Only Sites:** 50. **Hookups:** Electric (20, 30, 50 amps), water, sewer, cable TV. **Each Site:** Picnic table, fire ring. **Dump Station:** Yes. **Laundry:** Yes. **Pay Phone:** Yes. **Rest Rooms and Showers:** Yes. **Fuel:** No. **Propane:** Yes. **Internal Roads:** Paved/gravel, in good condition. **RV Service:** No. **Market:** 0.5 mi. south in Pittsfield. **Restaurant:** 0.5 mi. south in Pittsfield. **General Store:** Yes. **Vending:** Yes. **Swimming Pool:** No. **Playground:** Yes. **Other:** Pine Lake, sandy swimming beach, arcade, fish-cleaning building, tetherball, horseshoes, volleyball, basketball, hiking trail, outdoor movies, bait shop. **Activities:** Swimming, fishing (no license required), boating (rental rowboats, canoes, & paddleboats), rental golf carts, hiking, planned activities. **Nearby Attractions:** Hunting, horseback riding, golf, antique shops, craft shops, ostrich farm, geneaology resources, apple orchard. **Additional Information:** Western Illinois Tourism Development Office, (309) 837-7460.

RESTRICTIONS

Pets: Leash only. **Fires:** Fire ring only. **Alcoholic Beverages:** At sites only. **Vehicle Maximum Length:** None. **Other:** Pole fishing only, limit 4 catfish & 4 bass a day; no private boats or motors allowed; no boats on water before dawn or after dusk; swimming beach open 10 a.m. to dusk.

TO GET THERE

From junction of I-72/US 36 and Pittsfield/New Salem Rd., take Exit 31 and drive 4.5 mi. south on Pittsfield/New Salem Rd. Roads are wide and well maintained with broad shoulders.

POCAHONTAS

Tomahawk RV Park

119 Tomahawk Dr., Pocahontas 62275. T: (618) 669-2781

RV ★★★ | Tent ★

Beauty: ★★★	Site Privacy: ★★★★
Spaciousness: ★★★★	Quiet: ★★★★
Security: ★★★★★	Cleanliness: ★★★★
Insect Control: Yes	Facilities: ★★★

Small camping clubs love Tomahawk RV Park because of its large rec hall with kitchen facilities for get togethers. Other nice touches are concrete patios and wooden canopies over picnic tables at some RV sites. But the campground, ten miles. east of Highland, has a high percentage of seasonal campers. About 100 of the sites are taken by seasonals. The campground also doesn't have a special section for tent campers. Tents are allowed on RV sites but those don't allow for the type of private setting most tent campers are seeking. Typical site width is 28 feet and the campground has 15 pull-throughs. RV sites are primarily gravel and open. Best RV sites are 5-8 because they are the most level. Other sites have a slight slope to them. Security and quiet measures are strictly enforced, including a 5 mph speed limit. Quiet hours are 11 p.m. to 7 a.m., the swimming beach is open noon to 7:30 p.m. on weekdays and 10:30 a.m. to 7:30 p.m. on weekends. The campground has security gates, security lights, an owner who lives on the premises, regular patrols, motion sensor lights, and a driveway warning bell for approaching vehicles.

BASICS

Operated by: Ron Griffith. **Open:** All year. **Site Assignment:** Reservations w/ no deposit. **Registration:** At campground office. **Fee:** $16 (cash, check). **Parking:** At site.

FACILITIES

Number of RV Sites: 135. **Number of Tent-Only Sites:** 0. **Hookups:** Electric (20, 30 amps), water. **Each Site:** Picnic table, fire ring. **Dump Station:** Yes. **Laundry:** Yes. **Pay Phone:** Yes. **Rest Rooms and Showers:** Yes. **Fuel:** No. **Propane:** Yes. **Internal Roads:** Gravel, in good condition. **RV Service:** Limited. **Market:** 10 mi. west in Highland. **Restaurant:** 10 mi. west in Highland. **General Store:** Yes. **Vending:** No. **Swimming Pool:** No. **Playground:** Yes. **Other:** 2 lakes, swimming beach, horseshoes, bait & tackle shop, rec hall, pavilion, coin games, basketball, sports field, volleyball. **Activities:** Swimming, fishing, planned activities. **Nearby Attractions:** Carlyle Lake, antique shops, boating, scenic drives, Louis Latzer Homestead. **Additional Information:** Illinois Bureau of Tourism, (800) 226-6632.

RESTRICTIONS

Pets: Leash only. **Fires:** Fire ring only. **Alcoholic Beverages:** Permitted. **Vehicle Maximum Length:** None. **Other:** No mini-bikes or motorcycles are to be ridden inside camp area; no fishing license required but fee of $3 per pole to fish in either lake.

TO GET THERE

From junction of I-70 and Hwy. 143, take Exit 30 and drive 6 mi. east on Hwy. 143, then 1 mi. south on Jamestown Rd. Roads are wide and well maintained with adequate shoulders. Entry road to campground is narrow.

QUINCY

Valley View Campground

2300 Bonansinga Dr., Quincy 62301. T: (217) 222-7229

RV ★★ | Tent ★★

Beauty: ★★	Site Privacy: ★★★
Spaciousness: ★★★	Quiet: ★★★
Security: ★★	Cleanliness: ★★
Insect Control: Yes	Facilities: ★★

Valley View Campground, two miles west of Quincy, has great potential, but needs some work. A closed swimming pool is an eyesore and the whole campground could use a general spiffing up. Arranged in a series of loops, the hilly campground offers grassy sites—some shaded, some open—in a rural setting. The campground has a typical site width of 30 feet and offers no pull-through sites.

Boat launching ramps to the Mississippi River and the many lakes and streams surrounding Quincy are accessible across from the campground. Most popular RV sites are 18–24 because they are more level and easier to back into. Most popular tent sites are by the shelter house. Many campers come from the area or are construction workers in the area for the summer. Some campers are also overnighters passing through. A manager lives on the site and city police regularly patrol the campground.

BASICS

Operated by: Bob Mays. **Open:** All year. **Site Assignment:** Reservations w/ no deposit. **Registration:** At campground office. **Fee:** $20 (cash, check). **Parking:** At site.

FACILITIES

Number of RV Sites: 36. **Number of Tent-Only Sites:** 100. **Hookups:** Electric (30, 50 amps), water, sewer. **Each Site:** Picnic table, fire ring. **Dump Station:** Yes. **Laundry:** Yes. **Pay Phone:** Yes. **Rest Rooms and Showers:** Yes. **Fuel:** No. **Propane:** No. **Internal Roads:** Paved/gravel, in fair condition. **RV Service:** No. **Market:** 2 mi. east in Quincy. **Restaurant:** 2 mi east in Quincy. **General Store:** No. **Vending:** Yes. **Swimming Pool:** No. **Playground:** Yes. **Other:** Pavilion, sports field, television lounge. **Activities:** None on-site. **Nearby Attractions:** Historic district, 7 museums, Mississippi River, Quinsippi Island, public marina, boating, fishing, swimming, hunting. **Additional Information:** Quincy CVB, (800) 978-4748.

RESTRICTIONS

Pets: Leash only. **Fires:** Fire ring only. **Alcoholic Beverages:** At sites only. **Vehicle Maximum Length:** 40 ft.

TO GET THERE

From junction of I-172 and US 24W, take Exit 19 and drive 3 mi. west and 4 mi. south on US 24. Entrance to campground is through a mobile home park with rough roads, speed bumps, and a steep hill going down to the campground.

ROCKFORD

Rock Cut State Park

7318 Harlem Rd., Loves Park 61111.T: (815) 885-3311; dnr.state.il.us.

RV ★★★ Tent ★★★★

Beauty: ★★★★ Site Privacy: ★★★
Spaciousness: ★★★ Quiet: ★★★
Security: ★★★★★ Cleanliness: ★★★★
Insect Control: None Facilities: ★★★

Chiseled out of the state's far northern region, Rock Cut State Park got its name from the blasting operations that railroad crews conducted during the 1859 construction of the Kenosha-Rockford Rail Line. It's an area of rollling plains and two lakes. Pierce Lake, with 162 acres, is a retreat for people wanting to fish, ice fish, or ice skate. The 50-acre Olson Lake is especially for swimmers. Laid out in a series of one-way loops, the wilderness campground, two miles north of Loves Park, offers grassy sites for tent campers and gravel pads for RVs with hookups. Sitting on a point overlooking Pierce Lake, site 20 is the most popular for tents. Reservations are not accepted for the site so campers often start arriving around noon, looking to see if the site will be vacated at the 3 p.m. check-out time. For RVs, the 400 loop of sites on the even side are the most popular because of the trees and privacy. The campground has a mix of shady and open sites for RVs but offers no pull-throughs. Security is excellent with a gate that is locked at 10 p.m. and regular patrols of the grounds. A big sign at the entrance warns visitors "Don't get locked in" because the park closes at 10 p.m. Rock Cut has speed bumps as well as speed checked by radar. The campground is very serious about its one-way entrance and exit—nails will chew up the tires of any vehicle that tries to go "in" the "out" or vice versa.

BASICS

Operated by: State of Illinois. **Open:** All year. **Site Assignment:** Reservations w/ 1-night deposit plus $5; refund (minus $5) w/ 3-day notice. **Registration:** At campground office. **Fee:** $11 (cash, check). **Parking:** At site.

FACILITIES

Number of RV Sites: 220. **Number of Tent-Only Sites:** 60. **Hookups:** Electric (30, 50 amps). **Each Site:** Picnic table, grill. **Dump Station:** Yes. **Laundry:** No. **Pay Phone:** Yes. **Rest Rooms and Showers:** Yes. **Fuel:** No. **Propane:** No. **Internal Roads:** Paved, in good condition. **RV Service:** No. **Market:** 2 mi. south in Loves Park. **Restaurant:** On site. **General Store:** Yes. **Vending:** Yes. **Swimming Pool:** No. **Playground:** Yes. **Other:** Pierce Lake, Olson Lake, swimming beach, hiking trails, boat launch, equestrian trails, fishing pier, concession stand, bait shop. **Activities:** Fishing, swimming, hiking, boating (rental rowboats & paddleboats). **Nearby Attractions:** Museums, BMX track, bowling, golf, nature preserve, tennis, Magic Waters, horseback riding, theater, speedway, antique & art shops. **Additional Information:** Rockford Area CVB, (800) 521-0849.

RESTRICTIONS

Pets: Leash only. **Fires:** In grills only; ground fires prohibited. **Alcoholic Beverages:** Not permitted. **Vehicle Maximum Length:** 40 ft. **Other:** 2-week stay limit.

TO GET THERE

From junction of US 51 and Hwy. 173, drive 3 mi. west on Hwy. 173. Roads are wide and well maintained with good shoulders.

RUSHVILLE

Schuy-Rush Lake & Campground

RR 3, Rushville 62681.T: (217) 322-6628; www.rushville.org.

RV ★★ Tent ★★★

Beauty: ★★★ Site Privacy: ★★★
Spaciousness: ★★★ Quiet: ★★★★
Security: ★★★★ Cleanliness: ★★★
Insect Control: None Facilities: ★★

The centerpiece of Schuy-Rush is a 225-acre lake which has been stocked with bass, channel cat, walleye, blue gill, and crappie fish. Laid out in a series of loops, the rural campground three miles south of Rushville, offers a mix of grassy and gravel sites with 12 pull-throughs. Tent sites are set away from RVs in a woodsy area for more privacy and shade. The campground does a great deal of repeat business and is especially busy around holidays and the annual gas engine show in June. Best RV sites are 1–20 near the showers and rest rooms. Favorite tent sites are in the primitive area in the woods. The road leading to the back RV sites is narrow and winding on a steep hill. Security measures are good with a manager who lives on site, gates that are locked from 10 p.m. to 6 a.m., security patrols, plus regular drive-throughs by city police.

BASICS

Operated by: City of Rushville. **Open:** Apr. 1–Nov. 1. **Site Assignment:** Reservations w/ 1-night deposit; no refund. **Registration:** At campground office. **Fee:** $10 (cash, check). **Parking:** At site.

FACILITIES

Number of RV Sites: 81. **Number of Tent-Only Sites:** 100. **Hookups:** Electric (20, 30 amps), water. **Each Site:** Picnic table, fire ring. **Dump Station:** Yes. **Laundry:** No. **Pay Phone:** No. **Rest Rooms and Showers:** Yes. **Fuel:** No. **Propane:** No. **Internal Roads:** Paved, in good condition. **RV Service:** No. **Market:** 3 mi. north in Rushville. **Restaurant:** 3 mi. north in Rushville. **General Store:** No. **Vending:** Yes. **Swimming Pool:** No. **Playground:** Yes. **Other:** Schuy-Rush Lake, hiking trails, boat ramp, baseball. **Activities:** Fishing, boating, hiking, planned activities. **Nearby Attractions:** Community theater, genealogical center, hunting, antique shops, golf, Schuyler County Jail Museum, art galleries, nature preserve, tennis. **Additional Information:** Rushville Area Chamber of Commerce, (217) 322-3689.

RESTRICTIONS

Pets: Leash only. **Fires:** Fire ring only. **Alcoholic Beverages:** At sites only. **Vehicle Maximum Length:** None.

TO GET THERE

Take US 67 out of Rushville and drive 3 mi. south. Entrance road to campground is sloping and has narrow shoulders.

SAVANNA

Mississippi Palisades State Park

16327 A IL Rte. 84, Savanna 61074.T: (815) 273-2731; www.dnr.state.il.us.

RV ★★★ Tent ★★★★

Beauty: ★★★★ Site Privacy: ★★★★
Spaciousness: ★★★★ Quiet: ★★★★
Security: ★★★★ Cleanliness: ★★★★
Insect Control: None Facilities: ★★

Palisades is the word used to describe a line of lofty, steep cliffs usually seen along a river. Mississippi Palisades, three miles north of Savanna, handsomely lives up to its name. Caves are evident, as are dangerous sink holes—limestone caves that go straight down. Atop the bluffs, erosion has carved intriguing rock formations, such as Indian Head and Twin Sisters—which bears keen resemblance to a pair of human figures. With sites in both shaded and open areas, the campground is in demand. Because of its popularity, reservations are not accepted. RV sites have gravel pads and are generally open; 12 are pull-throughs. The best RV site is 64, on the corner of a one-way road and away from tent campers. The best tent site is 25, private and grassy and located over the edge of a hill so no headlights hit it. Three primitive walk-in sites are also tucked into Mississippi Palisades. By hiking about a half mile, you'll be able to enjoy rustic camping along the park's serene northern trails. Natural beauty abounds, but Mississippi Palisades sure could use a good swimming spot.

BASICS

Operated by: State of Illinois. **Open:** All year. **Site Assignment:** First come, first served. **Registration:** At campground office. **Fee:** $11 (cash, check). **Parking:** At site.

FACILITIES

Number of RV Sites: 110. **Number of Tent-Only Sites:** 121. **Hookups:** Electric (20, 30, 50 amps). **Each Site:** Picnic table, fire ring. **Dump Station:** Yes. **Laundry:** No. **Pay Phone:** Yes. **Rest Rooms and Showers:** Yes. **Fuel:** No. **Propane:** No. **Internal Roads:** Paved, in good condition. **RV Service:** No. **Market:** 3 mi. south in Savanna. **Restaurant:** 3 mi. south in Savanna. **General Store:** Yes. **Vending:** Yes. **Swimming Pool:** No. **Playground:** Yes. **Other:** Mississippi River, boat ramp, boat dock, hiking trails. **Activities:** Fishing, boating, hiking, hunting, nature programs, slide shows. **Nearby Attractions:** Antique mall, marinas, Savanna-Sabula Bridge, playhouse, scenic drives, golf. **Additional Information:** Northern Illinois Tourism Development Office, (815) 547-3740.

RESTRICTIONS

Pets: Leash only. **Fires:** Fire ring only. **Alcoholic Beverages:** Not permitted. **Vehicle Maximum Length:** None. **Other:** 2-week stay limit.

TO GET THERE

From junction of US 52 and SR 84, drive 2 mi. north on SR 84. The state road is narrow and winding with limited shoulders.

SPRINGFIELD

Mr. Lincoln's Campground

3045 Stanton St., Springfield 62703. T: (800) 657-1414; F: (217) 529-6725.

RV ★★★ Tent ★★★

Beauty: ★★★	Site Privacy: ★★★
Spaciousness: ★★★	Quiet: ★★★
Security: ★★★★	Cleanliness: ★★★★
Insect Control: None	Facilities: ★★★

Location is everything, and Mr. Lincoln's Campground sure has it. The urban campground in Springfield, is in the midst of more historical sites and recreational opportunities than most other facilities dream of. First and foremost, the area is filled with Abraham Lincoln attractions. The campground also is on the bus line to downtown and the White Oaks Mall. In addition to being the only campground in Lincoln's hometown, the facility also offers the area's largest RV center with parts and service. The campground is laid out in a series of loops, with 30 feet the typical site width. All RV sites have gravel pads, some are shady, and others open. There are 15 pull-throughs. The tent area is separated from RVs and offers more shade and privacy. Because it has a large yard, 51 is the best RV site. All tent sites are similar—secluded, quiet, and tree-lined. The campground has good security measures including a manager staying on the premises, regular staff patrols, one entrance/exit, and patrols by city police. The campground also is completely fenced.

BASICS

Operated by: Sue Johnson. **Open:** All year. **Site Assignment:** Reservations w/ 1-night deposit; refund w/ 24-hour notice. **Registration:** At campground office. **Fee:** $21 (cash, check, credit cards). **Parking:** At site.

FACILITIES

Number of RV Sites: 42. **Number of Tent-Only Sites:** 108. **Hookups:** Electric (30, 50 amps), water, sewer, cable TV. **Each Site:** Picnic table, fire ring. **Dump Station:** Yes. **Laundry:** Yes. **Pay Phone:** Yes. **Rest Rooms and Showers:** Yes. **Fuel:** No. **Propane:** Yes. **Internal Roads:** Gravel, in fair condition. **RV Service:** Yes. **Market:** Across street. **Restaurant:** 0.5 mi. in either direction. **General Store:** Yes. **Vending:** Yes. **Swimming Pool:** No. **Playground:** No. **Other:** Horseshoes, volleyball, softball, sauna, sports field, rec room, coin games, badminton, movies, RV parts & accessory store. **Activities:** Local tours. **Nearby Attractions:** Lincoln historical sites, golf, theaters, shopping center, antique malls, lake, universities, walking tours, Old State Capitol, Museum of Funeral Customs, zoo, botanical gardens, wildlife sanctuary. **Additional Information:** Springfield CVB, (800) 545-7300.

RESTRICTIONS

Pets: Leash only. **Fires:** Fire ring only. **Alcoholic Beverages:** Permitted. **Vehicle Maximum Length:** 45 ft.

TO GET THERE

From junction of I-55 and Stevenson Dr., take Exit 94 and drive 1 mi. west on Stevenson Dr., then 1 block north on Stanton St. Roads are wide and well maintained with broad shoulders.

SPRINGFIELD

Springfield Best Holiday

P.O. Box 11231, Springfield 62629. T: (217) 483-9998

RV ★★★★ Tent ★★★★

Beauty: ★★★	Site Privacy: ★★★★
Spaciousness: ★★★	Quiet: ★★★★
Security: ★★★★	Cleanliness: ★★★★
Insect Control: No	Facilities: ★★★★

Located 15 minutes from downtown Springfield, the campground is a popular spot for folks enjoying the area's historical attractions. The campground also gets many repeat campers who come mainly for the facilities and activities. Arranged in a series of loops, the campground offers a rural setting with mostly pull-through sites. Typical site width is 30 feet and sites are a mixture of gravel and grass. Most sites are wooded and shady but some are open. RVs favor the sites in the 90s section because they are pull-throughs and offer 50 amps electricity. Tent sites are fairly isolated from the general campground, offering more privacy, grass, and trees. Security is good, with owners who live on the grounds, regular patrols, and the presence of state police from headquarters two miles away.

BASICS

Operated by: N. J. & Joyce Bucklin. **Open:** Apr. 1–Nov. 1. **Site Assignment:** Reservations w/ 1 night deposit. No refunds. **Registration:** At campground office. **Fee:** $21 (cash, check, credit cards). **Parking:** At site.

FACILITIES

Number of RV Sites: 105. **Number of Tent-Only Sites:** 20. **Hookups:** Electric (30, 50 amps), water, sewer. **Each Site:** Picnic table, grill. **Dump Station:** Yes. **Laundry:** Yes. **Pay Phone:** Yes. **Rest Rooms and Showers:** Yes. **Fuel:** No. **Propane:** No. **Internal Roads:** Gravel, in good condition. **RV Service:** Yes. **Market:** 5 mi. west in Chatham. **Restaurant:** 5 mi. west in Chatham. **General Store:** Yes. **Vending:** Yes. **Swimming Pool:** Yes. **Playground:** Yes. **Other:** Mini-golf, tennis, rec room, baseball, basketball. **Activities:** Swimming, planned weekend activities. **Nearby Attractions:** Lincoln-related historical sites, Illinois State Museum, Children's Zoo, Frank Lloyd Wright Home, scenic drive, bike trail, golf. **Additional Information:** Springfield CVB, (800) 545-7300.

RESTRICTIONS

Pets: Leash only. **Fires:** Fire pits only. **Alcoholic Beverages:** Permitted. **Vehicle Maximum Length:** None.

TO GET THERE

On I-55 Frontage Rd., 1 mi. south of Springfield, between Exits 88 and 83. Roads are wide and well maintained with broad shoulders.

STERLING

Maple Aire Crow Valley Campground

23807 Moline Rd., Sterling 61081. T: (815) 626-5376

RV ★★ Tent ★

Beauty: ★★	Site Privacy: ★★
Spaciousness: ★★	Quiet: ★★
Security: ★★	Cleanliness: ★★
Insect Control: None	Facilities: ★★

Maple Aire Crow Valley Campground is a work in progress. In fact, even the name is changing. The Maple Aire part was just added and the original Crow Valley may eventually be dropped. The new owner hopes to implement a bunch of improvements—a laundry, gate house, electric pedestals, more sites, better hookups. The rural campground offers open, grassy RV sites with concrete pads to park on, an average site width of 28 feet, and seven pull-throughs. At press time, roads in the area are under construction and may be considerably improved. The Rock River is the centerpiece of the campground and activities. The most popular sites are by the river, and many local people like to come for the fishing and boating. The campground is conveniently located off I-88, five miles west of Rock Falls. However, the campground is so close to the interstate that the noise of cars and trucks whizzing by can be heard in the campground.

Basics

Operated by: Mike & Beth Johnson. **Open:** Apr. 15–Oct. 15. **Site Assignment:** Reservations w/ 1-night deposit; refunds w/ 7-day notice. **Registration:** At campground office. **Fee:** $20 (cash, credit cards). **Parking:** At site.

Facilities

Number of RV Sites: 100. **Number of Tent-Only Sites:** 0. **Hookups:** Electric (30 amp), water. **Each Site:** Picnic table, fire ring. **Dump Station:** Yes. **Laundry:** No. **Pay Phone:** No. **Rest Rooms and Showers:** Yes. **Fuel:** No. **Propane:** No. **Internal Roads:** Gravel, in poor condition. **RV Service:** No. **Market:** 5 mi. east in Rock Falls. **Restaurant:** 5 mi. east in Rock Falls. **General Store:** No. **Vending:** No. **Swimming Pool:** Yes. **Playground:** Yes. **Other:** Rock River, boat ramp, basketball, volleyball, badminton, horseshoes, shuffleboard, sports field. **Activities:** Fishing, swimming. **Nearby Attractions:** Bison ranch, Dillon Home Museum, bike trails, Behren's Country Village. **Additional Information:** Northern Illinois Tourism Development Office, (815) 547-3740.

Restrictions

Pets: Leash only. **Fires:** Fire ring only. **Alcoholic Beverages:** At sites only. **Vehicle Maximum Length:** None.

To Get There

From junction of I-88 and Hwy. 2/30, take Exit 36, drive 1 mi. west on Moline Rd. The road is in fair condition with adequate shoulders.

STERLING

Ruffit Park

24832 Rock Falls Rd., Sterling 61081. T: (815) 626-0221

RV ★★★ Tent ★★

Beauty: ★★ Site Privacy: ★★★
Spaciousness: ★★★ Quiet: ★★★
Security: ★★★★ Cleanliness: ★★★
Insect Control: None Facilities: ★★★

Ruffit Park Camping Resort offers easy access from the interstate and good parking with about 50 pull-through sites. The grassy campground five miles west of Sterling, offers shaded or open sites with a typical site width of 28 feet. Laid out in a series of loops, the campground has 34 seasonal campers. The fast-flowing Elkhorn Creek runs through the park and is filled with game fish. Favorite campsites are by the river. Quiet hours from 11 p.m. to 7 a.m. are enforced, as is a 5 mph speed limit. In the Gaumer family for over three decades, the campground is bordered by a small cemetery. For security measures, the owners live on site, offer regular patrols, and have a gate that is shut at night.

Basics

Operated by: Gaumer Family. **Open:** May 1–Oct. 1. **Site Assignment:** Reservations w/ 1-night deposit; refund w/ 7-day notice. **Registration:** At campground office. **Fee:** $16 (cash, check). **Parking:** At site.

Facilities

Number of RV Sites: 100. **Number of Tent-Only Sites:** 25. **Hookups:** Electric (30, 50 amps), water. **Each Site:** Picnic table, fire ring. **Dump Station:** Yes. **Laundry:** Yes. **Pay Phone:** Yes. **Rest Rooms and Showers:** Yes. **Fuel:** No. **Propane:** No. **Internal Roads:** Paved/gravel, in fair condition. **RV Service:** No. **Market:** 5 mi. east in Sterling. **Restaurant:** 5 mi. east in Sterling. **General Store:** Yes. **Vending:** Yes. **Swimming Pool:** Yes. **Playground:** Yes. **Other:** Basketball, hiking trails, horseshoes, game room, wading pool, fishing stream, basketball, badminton, sports field, volleyball. **Activities:** Swimming, fishing, hiking. **Nearby Attractions:** Bison ranch, Dillon Home Museum, bike trails, Behren's Country Village, golf, John Deere Museum, casino. **Additional Information:** Northern Illinois Tourism Development Office, (815) 547-3740.

Restrictions

Pets: Leash only. **Fires:** Fire ring only. **Alcoholic Beverages:** Not permitted. **Vehicle Maximum Length:** None.

To Get There

From junction of I-88 and Hwy. 2/30, take Exit 36 and drive 0.25 mi. east on Hwy. 2/30. Roads are wide and well maintained with broad shoulders.

SYCAMORE

Sycamore RV Resort

375 East North Ave., Sycamore 60178. T: (815) 895-5590; F: (815) 895-5729; www.sycamorervresort.com.

RV ★★★ Tent n/a

Beauty: ★★★ Site Privacy: ★★★
Spaciousness: ★★★ Quiet: ★★★★
Security: ★★★ Cleanliness: ★★★★
Insect Control: None Facilities: ★★★

Sycamore RV Resort is surprisingly quiet, especially since it is located right in the town of Sycamore. Surrounded on three sides by water and woods, the campground has a natural buffer to keep out urban noises. The owners also enforce rules to keep the peace. Beach hours are 11 a.m. to 6 p.m. and no scheduled activities are planned. The campground also does not allow motorcycle campers or tent campers. All fishing in the two lakes is catch-and-release only and stops at dusk. Laid out in a series of loops, the campground has a typical site width of 30 feet and 15 pull-throughs. RVs park in a level gravel site with a choice of trees or open. Most popular RV sites are 22–46 because they are located along the lake. The campground tends to be crowded and reservations are recommended. Sycamore's annual pumpkin festival in Oct. and other town activities and attractions are located within walking distance.

Basics

Operated by: Dale & Anita Cappel. **Open:** Apr. 1–Nov. 1. **Site Assignment:** Reservations w/ no deposit. **Registration:** At campground office. **Fee:** $22 (cash, check). **Parking:** At site.

Facilities

Number of RV Sites: 56. **Number of Tent-Only Sites:** 0. **Hookups:** Electric (30, 50 amps), water, sewer, phone, Internet. **Each Site:** Picnic table, fire ring. **Dump Station:** Yes. **Laundry:** Yes. **Pay Phone:** Yes. **Rest Rooms and Showers:** Yes. **Fuel:** No. **Propane:** Yes. **Internal Roads:** Gravel, in good condition. **RV Service:** No. **Market:** 3 blocks in Sycamore. **Restaurant:** 2 blocks in Sycamore. **General Store:** Yes. **Vending:** Yes. **Swimming Pool:** No. **Playground:** Yes. **Other:** 2 spring-fed lakes, swimming beach, boat launch, badminton, sports field, volleyball. **Activities:** Swimming, fishing, boating (rental paddleboats & rowboats). **Nearby Attractions:** Golf, speedway, nature trail, Northern Illinois University, historic district walking tour. **Additional Information:** Northern Illinois Tourism Development Office, (815) 547-3740.

Restrictions

Pets: Leash only. **Fires:** Fire ring only. **Alcoholic Beverages:** At sites only. **Vehicle Maximum Length:** 40 ft. **Other:** No tent camping; no camping motorcyclists.

To Get There

From junction of Hwy. 64 and Hwy. 23, drive 0.5 mi. north on Hwy. 23, then 200 yards east on East North Ave. Roads are wide and well maintained with adequate shoulders.

UTICA

LaSalle-Peru KOA

756 North 3150th Rd., Rte. 2, Utica 61373. T: (800) KOA-9498; www.koa.com.

RV ★★★★ Tent ★★★★

Beauty: ★★★★ Site Privacy: ★★★
Spaciousness: ★★★ Quiet: ★★★★
Security: ★★★★ Cleanliness: ★★★★★
Insect Control: None Facilities: ★★★

LaSalle-Peru KOA is a clean, quiet campground out in the country. No highway noise or passing trains disturb the setting. Located one-and-a-half hours from Chicago, the campground is a popular getaway for city dwellers wanting some peace and quiet, along with good recreation facilities. Quiet hours are enforced between 10 p.m. and 7 a.m. Bicycle riding is not allowed after dark and generators are not permitted at any time. Another rule enforcing the quiet time requires that pets be confined in an enclosed vehicle or tent at night. If campers leave the campground, they must take their pets with them. Sites are mostly grassy and shady, with a common width of 30 feet. Laid out in a series of loops, the campground has 40 pull-through sites. The laundry uses soft water and the camp store offers rental videos. TV reception varies between excellent and poor. Prime time reception is usually better. Tent sites offer some privacy from RVs, grass, and shade from tall oak trees.

Basics

Operated by: Denny & Ginny Lazar. **Open:** Apr. 1–Oct. 15. **Site Assignment:** Reservations w/ no deposit. **Registration:** At campground office. **Fee:** $29 (cash, credit cards). **Parking:** At site.

Facilities

Number of RV Sites: 65. **Number of Tent-Only Sites:** 40. **Hookups:** Electric (20, 30 amps), water, sewer. **Each Site:** Picnic table, fire ring. **Dump Station:** Yes. **Laundry:** Yes. **Pay Phone:** Yes. **Rest Rooms and Showers:** Yes. **Fuel:** No. **Propane:** No. **Internal Roads:** Gravel, in good condition. **RV Service:** Yes. **Market:** 4 mi. south in Utica. **Restaurant:** 2 mi. south in Utica. **General Store:** Yes. **Vending:** Yes. **Swimming Pool:** Yes. **Playground:** Yes. **Other:** Small fishing creek, game room, horseshoes, recreation field, badminton, volleyball. **Activities:** Swimming, fishing, planned weekend activities. **Nearby Attractions:** Antique shops, golf, stock car races, horseback riding, I & M Canal State Trail, LaSalle County Historical Society, Matthiessen State Park, Starved Rock State Park. **Additional Information:** Heritage Corridor Visitors Bureau, (800) 746-0550.

Restrictions

Pets: Leash only. **Fires:** Fire ring only. **Alcoholic Beverages:** Permitted. **Vehicle Maximum Length:** None. **Other:** No visitors, everyone must be a registered guest; if friends or family are visiting, they must register on a separate campsite.

To Get There

From junction of I-80 and SR 178, take Exit 81, drive north 1.5 mi. on SR 178 to North 3150th Rd., drive west 0.5 mi. Roads are wide and well maintained with broad shoulders.

VANDALIA

Okaw Valley Campground

RR 2 Box 55A, Brownstown 62418. T: (888) 470-3968

RV: ★★★ Tent: ★★★

Beauty: ★★★★	Site Privacy: ★★★★
Spaciousness: ★★★★	Quiet: ★★★
Security: ★★★	Cleanliness: ★★★★
Insect Control: None	Facilities: ★★★

A partially shaded campground on rolling terrain five miles east of Vandalia, Okaw Valley Campground is a popular overnight destination with travelers passing through on I-70. The campground is located 330 miles, or about a day's drive, from Branson. The typical site width is 30 feet and the campground has 25 pull-throughs. Arranged in a series of loops, the rural campground offers both shady and open sites, with mostly gravel spots for RVs. There is a section for tent sites away from RVs, as well as a primitive tent site featuring more grass, trees, and privacy. A five-acre lake allows boating and fishing but no swimming. No license is required to fish in the lake; the catch is mostly bass, catfish, and bluegill. The TV lounge and laundromat are open 24 hours a day. A service sink on the north wall outside the washrooms is provided for washing pots, pans, and dishes. A 5 mph speed limit is enforced, as is a 10 p.m. to 7 a.m. quiet time.

Basics

Operated by: Dennis & Vikki Ramsey. **Open:** Apr. 1–Nov. 1. **Site Assignment:** Reservations w/ 1-night deposit; refunds w/ 24-hour notice. **Registration:** At campground office. **Fee:** $22 (cash, check, credit cards). **Parking:** At site.

Facilities

Number of RV Sites: 51. **Number of Tent-Only Sites:** 40. **Hookups:** Electric (20, 30 amps), water, sewer. **Each Site:** Picnic table, fire ring. **Dump Station:** Yes. **Laundry:** Yes. **Pay Phone:** Yes. **Rest Rooms and Showers:** Yes. **Fuel:** No. **Propane:** Yes. **Internal Roads:** Gravel, in good condition. **RV Service:** No. **Market:** 3 mi. east in Brownstown. **Restaurant:** 5 mi. west in Vandalia. **General Store:** Yes. **Vending:** No. **Swimming Pool:** Yes. **Playground:** Yes. **Other:** Lake, volleyball, basketball, TV lounge, game room, horseshoes, boat dock, adults room, rec room, sports field, pavilion. **Activities:** Swimming, fishing, boating (rental paddleboats & rowboats), biking (rental bikes), planned activities. **Nearby Attractions:** Vandalia State House, Fayette County Museum, Steam Engine Museum, golf, rollerskating, stock car races, Alwerdt's Gardens. **Additional Information:** Vandalia Chamber of Commerce, (618) 283-2728.

Restrictions

Pets: Leash only. **Fires:** Fire ring only. **Alcoholic Beverages:** Permitted. **Vehicle Maximum Length:** None.

To Get There

From junction of I-70 and US 40, take Exit 68 and drive 1,000 feet north on US 40, then 0.25 mi. west on frontage road. Roads are wide and well maintained with broad shoulders.

WEST YORK

Hickory Holler Campground

9876 East 2000th Ave., West York 62478. T: (618) 563-4779

RV: ★★★ Tent: ★★★

Beauty: ★★★	Site Privacy: ★★★★
Spaciousness: ★★★★	Quiet: ★★★★
Security: ★★★★	Cleanliness: ★★★★
Insect Control: Yes	Facilities: ★★★

A quiet, rural campground (eight miles north of West Union) with an emphasis on Christian activities, Hickory Holler Campground offers spacious, peaceful surroundings. The typical site width is 40 feet with grassy sites and a good mixture of shaded and open areas. As the name implies, Hickory Holler is blessed with mature hickory trees. Gospel sing-alongs are held in an old remodeled cattle barn and nightly campfires offer community get-togethers. Despite the absence of a swimming pool, the campground offers a lot of varied activities and clean surroundings for a low fee (the $13 rate is about half what other area campgrounds charge). Primitive sites for tent campers feature trees and privacy from RV campers. Security lights, an owner who lives on the grounds, and regular patrols add to campground security.

Basics

Operated by: Leola Guyer. **Open:** All year. **Site Assignment:** Reservations w/ 1-night deposit, refunds w/ 24-hour notice. **Registration:** At campground office. **Fee:** $13 (cash, check). **Parking:** At site.

Facilities

Number of RV Sites: 100. **Number of Tent-Only Sites:** 15. **Hookups:** Electric (20, 30, 50 amps), water, sewer. **Each Site:** Picnic table, fire ring. **Dump Station:** Yes. **Laundry:** Yes. **Pay Phone:** No. **Rest Rooms and Showers:** Yes. **Fuel:** No. **Propane:** No. **Internal Roads:** Gravel, in good condition. **RV Service:** No. **Market:** 12 mi. south in Robinson. **Restaurant:** 7 mi. north in West Union. **General Store:** Yes. **Vending:** Yes. **Swimming Pool:** No. **Playground:** Yes. **Other:** Mini-golf, rec hall, video games, pool table, 2 lakes. **Activities:** Fishing, boating (rental paddleboats available), nightly community campfires, monthly gospel sing-alongs, talent night. **Nearby Attractions:** Crawford County Historical Museum, military museum, Lincoln Trail College, parks. **Additional Information:** Springfield CVB, (800) 545-7300.

Restrictions

Pets: Leash only. **Fires:** Fire ring only. **Alcoholic Beverages:** Not permitted. **Vehicle Maximum Length:** 40 ft.

To Get There

From Marshall, drive 18 mi. south on Rte. 1 to Annapolis Rd. Drive 4 mi. west of Rte. 1 on Rte. 33 to Hickory Holler Campground. Roads are wide and well maintained with broad shoulders.

Indiana

Home of icons like James Dean and the Indy 500, the Hoosier State offers unique treats from its "crossroads of America." For starters, the May speedway extravaganza in Indianapolis boasts some of the fastest speeds, smoothest racecars, and most skilled drivers in the racing world. Indianapolis also is home to 113 city parks, including the 250-acre White River State Park right in the heart of the city.

The short life of James Dean is celebrated in his hometown of **Fairmount** where the *Rebel Without a Cause* star is buried. A continuously changing artwork is seen at the **Indiana Dunes** where winds swirl the sand into surreal landscapes. Howl with the wolves at **Wolf Park** in **Lafayette** or hike through the scenic hills of 195,000-acre **Hoosier National Forest.** See the many species of coral and prehistoric ocean life in the fossil bed at **Falls of the Ohio State Park** in **Clarksville** or enjoy the unusual limestone formations and waterfalls at **McCormick's Creek State Park,** east of **Spencer.**

Spelunking is special in Indiana where an electric boat takes visitors through **Bluespring Caverns** in **Bedford.** Hear the story of how **Marengo Cave** was discovered by two youngsters or see the cave where Daniel Boone's brother, Squire, is buried in **Corydon.** An underground mountain and huge helicties mark the passages of Wyandotte caves.

Rent a pontoon boat and cruise **Bloomington's Lake Monroe** to catch a glimpse of a nesting bald eagle, or head to **Madison** to experience the timeless treasure of this beautifully preserved river town. **Auburn's** history as a luxury car manufacturer is recalled at the **Auburn Cord Duesenberg Museum** while **Columbus** has architectural landmarks designed by the master, including I. M. Pei.

French Lick and next door neighbor, **West Baden, were** early resorts and health centers because of the abundant artisan springs. Take a ride on the historic 1920s railroad and visit the amazing **West Baden Springs Hotel,** whose domed atrium was once considered the Eighth Wonder of the World. In **Nashville,** the area's beauty led to the establishment of an artists colony that still thrives today, along with the **Little Nashville Opry** which showcases top country music stars. Remnants of a Utopian community draws visitors to **New Harmony,** and the nation's first theme park thrills families at **Holiday World and Splashin' Safari** in **Santa Claus.** Home to one of the world's largest Amish communities, **Shipshewana** also has what is said to be the biggest flea market in America.

The following facilities accept payment in checks or cash only:

Bixler Lake Campground, Kendallville
Broadview Lake Camping Resort, Colfax
Gordon's Camping, Kendallville
Mar-brook Campground, Gas City
Miami Camp, Frankton
Oak Lake Family Campground, Roselawn
Sports Lake Camping Resort, Gas City

Campground Profiles

BATESVILLE
Thousand Trails & NACO Indian Lakes

7234 East Hwy. 46, Batesville 47006. T: (800) 427-3392; www.1000trails.com.

RV ★★★★ | Tent ★★

Beauty: ★★★★
Spaciousness: ★★★★
Security: ★★★★★
Insect Control: None
Site Privacy: ★★★★
Quiet: ★★★★
Cleanliness: ★★★★★
Facilities: ★★★★

Thousand Trails NACO-Indian Lakes is part of a nationwide network of 57 campground resorts for members of a private camping club. Membership options with annual dues allow members to camp at every preserve in the system or choose only a favorite region. Nonmembers are allowed a get-acquainted visit and will be invited, but not required, to attend a presentation regarding membership offerings. Located eight miles east of Batesville, the campground is on a preserve of wooded land, open spaces. and several lakes. The typical site width is 35 feet and the campground has 100 pull-throughs. Sites are mostly shaded from mature oak, maple, and ash trees. Members have access to a wide array of recreational opportunities, including indoor and outdoor swimming pools and a wading pool, as well as a boat ramp and dock. Quiet time is enforced from 11 p.m. to 8 a.m. when outside patio and decorative lights must be turned off. Golf carts also are prohibited during quiet hours. Speed limit is 15 mph on the main road and five mph in the camping areas. Security measures are great with a gate that requires a code to get in, a manager on site and regular patrols.

Basics

Operated by: Thousand Trails Inc. **Open:** May 1–Nov. 1. **Site Assignment:** Reservations w/ 1-

night deposit; refund w/ 24-hour notice. **Registration:** At campground office. **Fee:** $25 (cash, check, credit cards). **Parking:** At site.

Facilities

Number of RV Sites: 1,200. **Number of Tent-Only Sites:** 0. **Hookups:** Electric (30 amps), water. **Each Site:** Picnic table, fire ring. **Dump Station:** Yes. **Laundry:** Yes. **Pay Phone:** Yes. **Rest Rooms and Showers:** Yes. **Fuel:** Yes. **Propane:** Yes. **Internal Roads:** Paved, in great condition. **RV Service:** No. **Market:** 8 mi. west in Batesville. **Restaurant:** 8 mi. west in Batesville. **General Store:** Yes. **Vending:** Yes. **Swimming Pool:** Yes. **Playground:** Yes. **Other:** Indian Lake, adult lounge, ballfield, rental cabins, gazebos, golf course, horseshoes, basketball, shuffleboard, tennis, lodges, mini golf, nature trail, volleyball, amphitheater, game room, boat ramp, boat dock, coin games, trading post. **Activities:** Swimming, boating, hiking, scheduled activities. **Nearby Attractions:** Metamora antique village, covered bridge, riverboat casinos, museums, historic homes, Cincinnati Zoo. **Additional Information:** Batesville Chamber of Commerce, (812) 934-3101.

Restrictions

Pets: Leash only. **Fires:** Fire ring only. **Alcoholic Beverages:** At sites only. **Vehicle Maximum Length:** None. **Other:** 14-day stay limit.

To Get There

From junction I-74 and Hwy. 46, take Exit 156 and drive 3.5 mi. west on Hwy. 46. Roads are wide and well maintained with broad shoulders.

BEANBLOSSOM

Bill Monroe Memorial Music Park & Campground

5163 IN 135N, Bean Blossom 46160. T: (800) 414-4677; www.beanblossom.com.

RV ★★★ Tent ★★★

Beauty: ★★★ Site Privacy: ★★
Spaciousness: ★★★ Quiet: ★★
Security: ★★★★ Cleanliness: ★★★★
Insect Control: None Facilities: ★★★

This countryside campground is the home of Bill Monroe's famous "Bean Blossom Bluegrass Festival," the longest running annual bluegrass festival in the world. Its wooded amphitheater, with a seating capacity of 5,000, also features other music festivals when camping sites are at a premum. A Pickin' Parlor is a popular site for impromptu music sessions by campers and performers, as are campsites and the parking lot. For music lovers, it's the place to be when events are going on. For folks who want to sleep, it might be a bit noisy during festivals. An on-site museum tells the story of bluegrass and displays some of Monroe's memorabilia, along with the Bluegrass Hall of Fame room. Hillside vistas and natural ambience like cows grazing in nearby fields add a country touch. Air-conditioned showers and restrooms are a welcome respite during hot, humid Hoosier summers. The best sites for tenters are on Miller Hill and Rude Dog where the spots are bigger and shaded. Best places for RVs are sites 43–115 in the woods. The typical site width is 35 feet and the campground offers eight pull-throughs. Located five miles north of Nashville, the campground provides good security with one entry road and regular patrols.

Basics

Operated by: Dwight Dillman. **Open:** All year. **Site Assignment:** Reservations accepted w/ full payment; no refund. **Registration:** At campground office. **Fee:** $16 (cash, check, credit cards). **Parking:** At site.

Facilities

Number of RV Sites: 237. **Number of Tent-Only Sites:** 300. **Hookups:** Electric (30, 50 amps), water. **Each Site:** Grill, picnic table, fire ring. **Dump Station:** Yes. **Laundry:** No. **Pay Phone:** Yes. **Rest Rooms and Showers:** Yes. **Fuel:** No. **Propane:** No. **Internal Roads:** Gravel, in good condition. **RV Service:** No. **Market:** Walking distance. **Restaurant:** Food concessions during festivals. **General Store:** No. **Vending:** Yes. **Swimming Pool:** No. **Playground:** Yes. **Other:** Small fishing lake, fitness trail, cabins, gift shop. **Activities:** Fishing, biking. **Nearby Attractions:** Brown County State Park, Nashville artist colony w/ more than 350 specialty shops, scenic drives, winter skiing, Little Nashville Opry, golf, Indiana University. **Additional Information:** Brown County CVB, (800) 753-3255.

Restrictions

Pets: Leash only. **Fires:** Fire rings, campfires. **Alcoholic Beverages:** At sites only. **Vehicle Maximum Length:** 40 ft.

To Get There

Take I-65 to Exit 68 in Columbus, Indiana. Take Hwy. 46 west 15 mi. to Nashville, Indiana. Bean Blossom is 5 mi. north of Nashville on IN 135. Roads are wide and well maintained with adequate shoulders, but the area is known for its winding roads and steep hills.

BLOOMINGTON

Lake Monroe Village Recreation Resort

8107 South Fairfax Rd., Bloomington 47401. T: (812) 824-CAMP; www.lakemonroevillage.com.

RV ★★★★ Tent ★★★★

Beauty: ★★★★ Site Privacy: ★★★★
Spaciousness: ★★★★ Quiet: ★★★★
Security: ★★★★ Cleanliness: ★★★★
Insect Control: None Facilities: ★★★★

Arriving at Lake Monroe Village Recreation Resort, visitors are greeted with a smile and escorted on a tour of the facilities. Campers have a choice of any available sites and are allowed to see them before choosing. Located eight miles southeast of Bloomington, the campground has 30 seasonal campers, 25 pull-through sites, and a typical site width of 24 feet. Laid out in a series of loops, the rural campground offers open and shaded sites. The chlorine-free pool uses electronic purification. Other water recreation choices are an adults-only hot tub and a baby pool. Security measures include surveillance cameras and gates at the entrance and exit. Speed limit is five mph and quiet times are from 11 p.m. to 8 a.m. Little touches such as stone walls used as terraces between some sites add to the beauty and quietness of the campground.

Basics

Operated by: Sandy & Nelson Cicchitto. **Open:** All year. **Site Assignment:** Reservations w/ 1-night deposit; refund w/ 7-day notice. **Registration:** At campground office. **Fee:** $30 (cash, check, credit cards). **Parking:** At site.

Facilities

Number of RV Sites: 125. **Number of Tent-Only Sites:** 50. **Hookups:** Electric (20, 30, 50 amps), water, sewer. **Each Site:** Picnic table, fire ring. **Dump Station:** Yes. **Laundry:** Yes. **Pay Phone:** Yes. **Rest Rooms and Showers:** Yes. **Fuel:** No. **Propane:** Yes. **Internal Roads:** Gravel, in good condition. **RV Service:** No. **Market:** 6 mi. north in Bloomington. **Restaurant:** 1.5 mi. north in Fairfax. **General Store:** Yes. **Vending:** Yes. **Swimming Pool:** Yes. **Playground:** Yes. **Other:** Pavilion, baseball, hot tub, volleyball, basketball, horseshoes, rec hall, rental cabins, badminton, sports field. **Activities:** Swimming. **Nearby Attractions:** Lake Monroe, Indiana University, golf, antiques, arts & crafts, boating, fishing, museums, historic homes, bike park, speedway, horseback riding, wineries. **Additional Information:** Bloomington/Monroe County CVB, (800) 800-0037.

Restrictions

Pets: Leash only. **Fires:** Fire ring only. **Alcoholic Beverages:** At sites only. **Vehicle Maximum Length:** None.

To Get There

From junction of Hwy. 45 and Hwy. 31, drive 6 mi. south on Hwy. 37, then 1.8 mi. east on Smithville Rd., then 1.25 mi. south on Fairfax Rd. Roads are wide and well maintained with broad shoulders.

BRISTOL

Eby's Pines Campground

14583 SR 120, Bristol 46507. T: (574) 848-4583; F: (574) 848-7291; www.Ebyspines.com; Ebyspinescamp@juno.com.

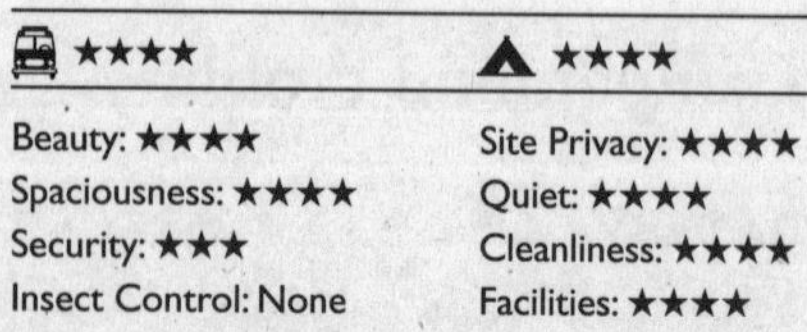

RV ★★★★ Tent ★★★★

Beauty: ★★★★ Site Privacy: ★★★★
Spaciousness: ★★★★ Quiet: ★★★★
Security: ★★★ Cleanliness: ★★★★
Insect Control: None Facilities: ★★★★

Harry Eby was a conservationist with a particular fondness for trees. Campers can now enjoy his legacy at Eby's Pines Campground, located three miles east of Bristol. Most of the trees, of course, are pines—white pine, scotch pine and red pine. Laid out in a series of loops, the campground sites are level, mostly shaded and grassy with gravel parking spots. The typical site width is 40 feet; there are 96 seasonal campers and 69 pull-through sites. Best RV spots are 71–76 because they are located by the fishing pond, shower facilities, and swimming pools. The best tent sites are in the Poplars section because they are surrounded by poplar trees and have privacy from RVs. For being so close to the interstate, the campground is surprisingly quiet and peaceful with the pines, the ponds, and the Little Elkhart River providing a natural buffer. At one time a tree farm, the campground has a nicely equipped new camp store and Amish hand-built, rustic log camping cabins that can be rented. A large 2,400-square-foot heated pool has a double tube slide, water umbella, and—most importantly—a certified lifeguard on duty.

Basics

Operated by: Barry Lang. **Open:** Apr. 1–Oct. 31. **Site Assignment:** Reservations w/ 1-night deposit; refunds (minus $6) w/ 48-hour notice. **Registration:** At campground office. **Fee:** $28 (cash, credit cards). **Parking:** At site.

Facilities

Number of RV Sites: 330. **Number of Tent-Only Sites:** 13. **Hookups:** Electric (30 amps), water, sewer. **Each Site:** Picnic table, fire ring. **Dump Station:** Yes. **Laundry:** Yes. **Pay Phone:** Yes. **Rest Rooms and Showers:** Yes. **Fuel:** No. **Propane:** Yes. **Internal Roads:** Paved/gravel, in good condition. **RV Service:** No. **Market:** 3 mi. west in Bristol. **Restaurant:** 3 mi. west in Bristol. **General Store:** Yes. **Vending:** Yes. **Swimming Pool:** Yes. **Playground:** Yes. **Other:** Basketball, tennis, volleyball, roller skating, horseshoes, rec room, video games, rental cabins, fishing pond, hiking trail, spa pool, pavilion, sports field. **Activities:** Swimming, fishing, hiking, scheduled weekend activities. **Nearby Attractions:** Amish country, Shipshewana Flea Market, golf, RV History Museum, antique shops, arts & crafts shops, museums, historic homes, Notre Dame University. **Additional Information:** Amish Country/Elkhart County Visitors Center, (800) 860-5949.

Restrictions

Pets: Leash only. **Fires:** Fire ring only. **Alcoholic Beverages:** At sites only. **Vehicle Maximum Length:** 40 ft.

To Get There

From junction of I-80/90 (Indiana Turnpike) and Hwy. 13, take Exit 101 and drive 1 mi. south on Hwy. 13, then 3 mi. west on Hwy. 120. Roads are wide and well maintained with broad shoulders.

CLOVERDALE

Cloverdale RV Park

2789 East CR 800S, Cloverdale 46120. T: (888) 298-0035; cdalervp@ccrtc.com.

RV ★★★ Tent ★★★

Beauty: ★★★	Site Privacy: ★★★
Spaciousness: ★★★	Quiet: ★★★★
Security: ★★★★	Cleanliness: ★★★★
Insect Control: None	Facilities: ★★★

Cloverdale RV Park is a nice, quiet, comfortable place to stay and hosts many return campers. That's why reservations are strongly recommended. Laid out in a series of loops, the campground has 50 pull-throughs and a typical site width of 35 feet. The rural campground two miles north of Cloverdale, has a fishing pond but doesn't allow swimming or boating. Regulations to keep the campground quiet and safe are strictly enforced. Quiet times are between 9 p.m. and 8 a.m. and children must be accompanied by an adult in public areas at all time. The campground has a eight mph speed limit which might be better set at five mph. Children camping are more concerned about play than about watching for cars. Security measures include one entrance; an exit is closed at night so vehicles have to drive by the office to enter. Owners live on site and provide regular patrols.

Basics

Operated by: Dan & Cher Nickerson. **Open:** All year. **Site Assignment:** Reservations accepted w/ 1-night deposit; refund w/ 48-hour notice. **Registration:** At campground office. **Fee:** $22 (cash, check, credit card). **Parking:** At site.

Facilities

Number of RV Sites: 52. **Number of Tent-Only Sites:** 20. **Hookups:** Electric (30 amps), water, sewer, telephone. **Each Site:** Picnic table, fire ring. **Dump Station:** Yes. **Laundry:** Yes. **Pay Phone:** Yes. **Rest Rooms and Showers:** Yes. **Fuel:** No. **Propane:** No. **Internal Roads:** Gravel, in good condition. **RV Service:** No. **Market:** 2 mi. south in Cloverdale. **Restaurant:** 2 mi. south in Cloverdale. **General Store:** Yes. **Vending:** Yes. **Swimming Pool:** No. **Playground:** Yes. **Other:** Rec room, fax & copy service, fishing pond, horseshoes, basketball, nature trail, coin games, sports field. **Activities:** Fishing, hiking. **Nearby Attractions:** Covered bridges, raceway, antiques, Victory Field, zoo, Cataract Falls. **Additional Information:** Putnam County CVB, (800) 829-4639.

Restrictions

Pets: Leash only. **Fires:** Fire ring only. **Alcoholic Beverages:** At sites only. **Vehicle Maximum Length:** None. **Other:** No clotheslines permitted.

To Get There

From junction of I-70 and US 231, take Exit 41, drive 0.8 mi. north on US 231 to CR 800S, drive east 0.5 mi. Roads are wide and well maintained with broad shoulders.

COLFAX

Broadview Lake Camping Resort

4850 South Broadview Rd., Colfax 46035. T: (765) 324-2622

RV ★★ Tent ★★

Beauty: ★★	Site Privacy: ★★
Spaciousness: ★★	Quiet: ★★★
Security: ★★★	Cleanliness: ★★
Insect Control: None	Facilities: ★★

Located two miles north of Colfax, Broadview Lake Camping Resort is set back from major roads and surrounded by cornfields. Almost every site has a tree including quite a few tall maples. A primitive camping area is bordered on two sides by a creek. The typical site width is 30 feet; there are four pull-throughs and 70 seasonal campers. Most sites are grassy and a few have gravel pads for RVs. Speed limit is five mph. Campers and visitors over the age of ten must buy a fishing pass at $5 a day for campers and $6 for visitors. No swimming or wading is allowed in the lake or creeks.

Basics

Operated by: Fred & Karen Culross. **Open:** Apr. 1–Oct. 15. **Site Assignment:** Reservations w/ no deposit. **Registration:** At campground office. **Fee:** $15 (cash). **Parking:** At site.

Facilities

Number of RV Sites: 100. **Number of Tent-Only Sites:** 30. **Hookups:** Electric (30 amps), water, sewer. **Each Site:** Picnic table, fire ring. **Dump Station:** Yes. **Laundry:** No. **Pay Phone:** Yes. **Rest Rooms and Showers:** Yes. **Fuel:** No. **Propane:** No. **Internal Roads:** Paved/gravel, in fair condition. **RV Service:** No. **Market:** 13 mi. north in Frankfort. **Restaurant:** 2 mi. south in Colfax. **General Store:** Yes. **Vending:** Yes. **Swimming Pool:** Yes. **Playground:** Yes. **Other:** Stocked fishing lake, game room, rec hall, badminton, horseshoes, volleyball, sports field. **Activities:** Swimming, fishing, scheduled weekend activities. **Nearby Attractions:** Golf, Purdue University, antiques, Tippecanoe Battlefield, Wolf Park, Fort Quiatenon, museums, historic homes. **Additional Information:** Greater Lafayette CVB, (800) 872-6648.

Restrictions

Pets: Leash only. **Fires:** Fire ring only. **Alcoholic Beverages:** Permitted. **Vehicle Maximum Length:** 38 ft. **Other:** Tents may not remain in one spot for longer than 5 days; limit of 6 catfish per day per person; limit of 2 poles per person.

To Get There

From junction of I-65 and Hwy. 28, take Exit 158 and drive 2.5 mi. west on Hwy. 28, then 3 mi. south on US 52, then 0.25 mi. west on Broadview Rd./CR 800W. Roads are wide and well maintained with broad shoulders, with one bad curve on Broadview Rd.

COLUMBUS

Woods–Waters

8855 South 300 West, Columbus 47201. T: (800) 799-3928

RV ★★★★ Tent ★★★★

Beauty: ★★★★	Site Privacy: ★★★★
Spaciousness: ★★★★	Quiet: ★★★★
Security: ★★★★	Cleanliness: ★★★★★
Insect Control: None	Facilities: ★★★★

Woods–Waters offers a quiet country setting close to the interstate and other attractions. Located five miles south of Columbus, the rural campground has level gravel sites with a typical site width of 35 feet. The campground has 15 seasonal campers and 15 pull-throughs. Situated in a forest, the campground is well maintained and decorated with flowers, as well as a wishing well and a wooden swing. The bathrooms are not only extremely clean, but brightened with wallpaper, artificial flowers, framed paintings, and plenty of mirrors over the sink, along with a full-length mirror on the wall. A well-stocked campstore with friendly folks makes it an even more pleasant place. Security and safety measures are good with a five mph speed limit, quiet hours from eight p.m. to 7 a.m., a year-round resident manager, and three deputy sheriffs who are seasonal campers at the campground.

Basics

Operated by: Larry & Betty York. **Open:** All year. **Site Assignment:** Reservations w/ 1-night deposit; refund w/ 7-day notice. **Registration:** At campground office. **Fee:** $22 (cash, check, credit cards). **Parking:** At site.

Facilities

Number of RV Sites: 100. **Number of Tent-Only Sites:** 10. **Hookups:** Electric (30, 50 amps), water, sewer. **Each Site:** Picnic table, fire ring. **Dump Station:** Yes. **Laundry:** Yes. **Pay Phone:** Yes. **Rest Rooms and Showers:** Yes. **Fuel:** No. **Propane:** Yes. **Internal Roads:** Gravel, in good condition. **RV Service:** No. **Market:** 5 mi. north in Columbus. **Restaurant:** 5 mi. north in Columbus. **General Store:** Yes. **Vending:** No. **Swimming Pool:** Yes. **Playground:** Yes. **Other:** Game room, movies clubhouse, lounge, coin games, pavilion, nature trail, fishing lake, basketball, badminton, sports field, volleyball, horseshoes. **Activities:** Swimming, fishing, hiking, scheduled weekend activities. **Nearby Attractions:** Columbus architecture tour, museums, historic homes, golf, Brown County & Nashville, crafts shops, antiques, Indianapolis Zoo, Indy 500. **Additional Information:** Columbus Area Visitor Center, (800) 468-6564.

Restrictions

Pets: Leash only. **Fires:** Fire ring only. **Alcoholic Beverages:** At sites only. **Vehicle Maximum Length:** None.

To Get There

From junction of I-65 and Hwy. 58 (Ogilville), take Exit 64, drive 0.5 mi. west on Hwy. 58, then 1 mi. south on CR 300W. Roads are wide and well maintained with broad shoulders, except for CR 300W which has narrow shoulders.

CRAWFORDSVILLE

Crawfordsville KOA

1600 Lafayette Rd., Crawfordsville 47933. T: (317) 362-4190; www.koa.com; cvillkoa@tetc.com.

RV: ★★★★ Tent: ★★★★

Beauty: ★★★★ Site Privacy: ★★★★
Spaciousness: ★★★★ Quiet: ★★★
Security: ★★★★ Cleanliness: ★★★★
Insect Control: No Facilities: ★★★★

Crawfordsville KOA is conveniently located, clean, and secure. It also offers spacious spots, almost all of which are pull-throughs, with a typical site width of 48 feet. Laid out in a series of loops, the rural campground offers a choice of shady or open, grassy or gravel sites. Large patches of iris and peonies brighten the campgrounds, as do shrubs and other landscaping. Located two miles north of Crawfordsville, the campground is convenient to several popular local festivals—Feast of the Hunters Moon, Strawberry Festival, Covered Bridge Festival, to name a few—so be sure there is an open space if you know when you want to stay there. Easy access and good roads pull a lot of travelers from the interstate looking for a night's rest. Security is good with one entrance road and owners who live on site.

Basics

Operated by: Richard Nelson. **Open:** Mar. 15–Nov. 25. **Site Assignment:** Reservations accepted w/ no deposit. **Registration:** At campground office. **Fee:** $23 (cash, check, credit cards). **Parking:** At site.

Facilities

Number of RV Sites: 60. **Number of Tent-Only Sites:** 7. **Hookups:** Electric (30, 50 amps), water, sewer, cable TV. **Each Site:** Picnic table, fire ring. **Dump Station:** Yes. **Laundry:** Yes. **Pay Phone:** Yes. **Rest Rooms and Showers:** Yes. **Fuel:** No. **Propane:** Yes. **Internal Roads:** Paved/gravel, in good condition. **RV Service:** Yes. **Market:** 2 mi. south in Crawfordsville. **Restaurant:** 2 mi. south in Crawfordsville. **General Store:** Yes. **Vending:** Yes. **Swimming Pool:** Yes. **Playground:** Yes. **Other:** RV supply store, rec room, horseshoes, pavilion, volleyball, coin games, sports field, rental cabins. **Activities:** Swimming. **Nearby Attractions:** Ben Hur Museum, antiques, Old Jail Museum, 42 covered bridges, golf, canoe trips. **Additional Information:** Crawfordsville CVB, (800) 866-3973.

Restrictions

Pets: Leash only. **Fires:** Fire ring only. **Alcoholic Beverages:** Permitted. **Vehicle Maximum Length:** 38 ft.

To Get There

From junction of I-74 and US 231, take Exit 34, then drive 1 mi. south on US 231. Roads are wide and well maintained with good shoulders.

DEMOTTE

Lake Holiday Yogi Bear Jellystone Park Camp-Resort

11780 West SR 10, DeMotte 46310. T: (219) 345-3132; F: (219) 345-4422; www.jellystonedemotte.com.

RV: ★★★ Tent: ★★

Beauty: ★★★ Site Privacy: ★★★
Spaciousness: ★★★ Quiet: ★★★
Security: ★★★★ Cleanliness: ★★★★
Insect Control: None Facilities: ★★★

Located right off I-65 in DeMotte, this campground offers convenience and easy access with the feel of a country setting in a city location. Sites are level and mostly shaded with a typical site width of 40 feet. Laid out in a series of loops, Lake Holiday has five pull-through sites and 115 seasonal campers. As with most Yogi Bear resorts, the campground has many activities and recreation facilities. Speed limit is five mph, but at the time of our visit, golf carts were zipping around much faster As a family campground, Lake Holiday requires that shirts and shoes be worn in the ranger station and restaurant, that alcoholic beverages be kept in a covered container or at campsites and that children under seven are not to be in restrooms unless accompanied by an adult. Security measures include an on-site manager, regular ranger patrols, and a security gate that requires a card to open. The gate is manned 24 hours a day.

Basics

Operated by: Jim Rose. **Open:** Apr. 1–Oct. 31. **Site Assignment:** Reservations paid in full; refund (minus $5) w/ 5-day notice. **Registration:** At campground office. **Fee:** $29 (cash, check, credit cards). **Parking:** At site.

Facilities

Number of RV Sites: 674. **Number of Tent-Only Sites:** 20. **Hookups:** Electric (30 amps), water, sewer. **Each Site:** Picnic table, fire ring. **Dump Station:** Yes. **Laundry:** Yes. **Pay Phone:** Yes. **Rest Rooms and Showers:** Yes. **Fuel:** No. **Propane:** Yes. **Internal Roads:** Paved/gravel, in good condition. **RV Service:** No. **Market:** 1 block in DeMotte. **Restaurant:** On site. **General Store:** Yes. **Vending:** Yes. **Swimming Pool:** Yes. **Playground:** Yes. **Other:** Lake Holiday, swimming beach, sports area, rec hall, waterslide, splash boats, mini-golf, rental golf carts, horseshoes, tennis, basketball, volleyball, shuffleboard, pool tables, video games. **Activities:** Swimming, fishing, canoeing, scheduled activities. **Nearby Attractions:** Golf, dragstrip, Amish Acres, antiques, historic sites, museums, Indiana Beach. **Additional Information:** DeMotte Chamber of Commerce, (219) 987-5800.

Restrictions

Pets: Leash only. **Fires:** Fire ring only. **Alcoholic Beverages:** Permitted. **Vehicle Maximum Length:** 40 ft.

To Get There

From junction of I-65 and Hwy. 10, take Exit 230 (DeMotte-Roselawn Exit), drive 1 block west on Hwy. 10. Roads are wide and well maintained with broad shoulders.

FAIRMOUNT

Hidden Lake Campground

11460 SR 37, Fairmount 46928. T: (765) 948-4862; hiddnlake@aol.com.

RV: ★★ Tent: ★★

Beauty: ★★ Site Privacy: ★★
Spaciousness: ★★★ Quiet: ★★★
Security: ★★★★★ Cleanliness: ★
Insect Control: Yes Facilities: ★★

A '57 Chevy rests at the bottom of a lake at Hidden Lake Campground. It seems a fitting memento for a campground outside actor James Dean's hometown. The sunken auto is used for scuba diving and lessons. A cabin cruiser also is sunk there to further interest scuba divers in the 100-foot-deep lake. The best things about the campground are its proximity to Fairmount (about eight miles), its spring-fed lake, and its security system. Video cameras are placed in several locations and the owner lives on site to help monitor quiet and safety. The campground has one entrance and exit. An air-conditioned gameroom is a welcome spot on humid Hoosier summers. The typical site width is 35 feet and the campground offers ten pull-throughs. Unfortunately, the campground is not as well maintained as others we've seen. At the time of our visit, it was long overdue for an intensive cleaning. Junk cars need to be towed off, buildings need painting, and trash and brush need to be removed. After all, this is the area where the "King of Cool" once roamed. With some work, this could be a cool campground.

Basics

Operated by: Colin Johnstone. **Open:** Apr. 1–Oct. 15. **Site Assignment:** Reservations accepted, no deposit. **Registration:** At campground office. **Fee:** $22.50 (cash, check, credit cards). **Parking:** At site.

Facilities

Number of RV Sites: 125. **Number of Tent-Only Sites:** 36. **Hookups:** Electric (20, 30 amps), water. **Each Site:** Fire ring. **Dump Station:** Yes. **Laundry:** No. **Pay Phone:** Yes. **Rest Rooms and Showers:** Yes. **Fuel:** No. **Propane:** No. **Internal Roads:** Gravel, in fair condition. **RV Service:** No. **Market:** 8 mi. south in Elwood. **Restaurant:** 8 mi. south in Elwood. **General Store:** No. **Vending:** Yes. **Swimming Pool:** No. **Playground:** Yes. **Other:** Spring-fed lake, sandy beach, rec hall, video games, horseshoes, volleyball, badminton. **Activities:** Swimming, fishing, scuba diving, rental kayak & paddleboats available. **Nearby Attractions:** Fairmount (home of actor James Dean), museums, boating, James Dean's final resting place. **Additional Information:** Grant County CVB, (800) 662-9474.

Restrictions

Pets: Leash only. **Fires:** Fire ring only. **Alcoholic Beverages:** At sites only. **Vehicle Maximum Length:** None.

To Get There

From junction of I-69 and Hwy. 26, take Exit 55, drive 9 mi. west on Hwy. 26, then 3 mi. south on Hwy. 37. Roads are wide and well maintained with adequate shoulders.

FRANKTON

Miami Camp

8851 West 400N, Frankton 46044. T: (765) 734-1365; www.campgrounds.com/icoa; miamicamp@worldnet.att.net.

RV ★★ Tent ★★

Beauty: ★★	Site Privacy: ★★
Spaciousness: ★★	Quiet: ★★★★
Security: ★★★	Cleanliness: ★★
Insect Control: Yes	Facilities: ★★

Miami Camp got its name from its location, the site of an old Miami Indian encampment in a grove of huge sycamore trees along a half mile of Pipe Creek. All the sites are wooded with abundant shade and a mix of grassy and gravel sites. The local health department sprays for mosquitos when necessary. Laid out in a series of loops, the campground offers a large, shady, primitive area where tenters have more natural surroundings and privacy away from RVs. Miami Camp has two pull-through sites and access to pizza delivery from seven miles away. The larger city of Anderson, is 11 miles south. Living on site, the owner enforces quiet and safety rules. Pets must be in the units at night.

Basics

Operated by: Millie Burkhart. **Open:** Apr. 15–Oct. 15. **Site Assignment:** Reservations accepted w/ no deposit. **Registration:** At campground office. **Fee:** $19 (cash, check). **Parking:** At site.

Facilities

Number of RV Sites: 50. **Number of Tent-Only Sites:** 50. **Hookups:** Electric (20, 30, 50 amps), water, sewer. **Each Site:** Picnic table, fire ring. **Dump Station:** Yes. **Laundry:** No. **Pay Phone:** Yes. **Rest Rooms and Showers:** Yes. **Fuel:** No. **Propane:** No. **Internal Roads:** Gravel, in fair condition. **RV Service:** No. **Market:** 7 mi. north in Elwood. **Restaurant:** 7 mi. north in Elwood. **General Store:** No. **Vending:** Yes. **Swimming Pool:** Yes. **Playground:** Yes. **Other:** Hiking trails, horseshoes, volleyball, badminton, bocce ball, fishing creek. **Activities:** Swimming, fishing, hiking. **Nearby Attractions:** Antiques, fine arts center, Historic Military Armor Museum, horse race track. **Additional Information:** Madison County CVB, (800) 533-6569.

Restrictions

Pets: Leash only. **Fires:** Fire ring only. **Alcoholic Beverages:** At sites only. **Vehicle Maximum Length:** None.

To Get There

From south junction of Hwy. 13, Hwy. 37 and CR 400N, drive 1.25 mi. east on CR 400N. Roads are wide and well maintained with adequate shoulders.

FREMONT

Yogi Bear's Jellystone Park Camp-Resort

140 Lane 201, Fremont 46737. T: (219) 833-1114; www.jellystonesbest.com.

RV ★★★★ Tent ★★★★

Beauty: ★★★★	Site Privacy: ★★★★
Spaciousness: ★★★★	Quiet: ★★★★
Security: ★★★★★	Cleanliness: ★★★★★
Insect Control: Yes	Facilities: ★★★★★

The campground's name indicates that it is a resort, and that is a good way to describe Yogi Bear's Jellystone Park Camp-Resort at Barton Lake. Located seven miles west of Fremont, the campground offers enough activities to keep families happily busy for days. With its snack bar and well-stocked campstore, it is possible for campers to come, park their vehicles, and not leave the campground for little errands. Campers have a choice of open or shady spots with 35 feet being the typical site width. Sites are generally grassy with concrete patios. The facility has 216 seasonal campers and 50 pull-through sites. Swimmers have a choice of a sandy beach at Barton Lake, a heated outdoor pool or an indoor solarium pool. Tent campers can choose a rustic area with more greenery and privacy from RVs or tents may be put on any of the RV sites. Security is tops with a locked card-coded gate, surveillence cameras, regular patrols, and owners who live on site.

Basics

Operated by: The Barry & Corcimiglia families. **Open:** Apr. 15–Nov. 1. **Site Assignment:** Reservations w/ 1-night deposit; refund w/ 7-day notice. **Registration:** At campground office. **Fee:** $38 (cash, check, credit cards). **Parking:** At site.

Facilities

Number of RV Sites: 460. **Number of Tent-Only Sites:** 25. **Hookups:** Electric (30, 50 amps), water, sewer. **Each Site:** Picnic table, fire ring. **Dump Station:** Yes. **Laundry:** Yes. **Pay Phone:** Yes. **Rest Rooms and Showers:** Yes. **Fuel:** No. **Propane:** Yes. **Internal Roads:** Paved, in excellent condition. **RV Service:** Yes. **Market:** 7 mi. east in Fremont. **Restaurant:** 7 mi. east in Fremont. **General Store:** Yes. **Vending:** Yes. **Swimming Pool:** Yes. **Playground:** Yes. **Other:** Fishing lake, rental cabins, spa, snack bar, volleyball, basketball, arcade building, horseshoes, mini-golf, boat launch, rec hall, pavilion, sandy beach. **Activities:** Swimming, fishing, boating (rental rowboats, paddleboats available), movies, scheduled activities. **Nearby Attractions:** Outlet shopping malls, water slide, Amish area, flea market, amusement park, car musuem, lakes, golf, antiques, arts & crafts shops. **Additional Information:** Amish County/Elkhart County Visitors Center, (800) 860-5949.

Restrictions

Pets: Leash only. **Fires:** Fire ring only. **Alcoholic Beverages:** At sites only. **Vehicle Maximum Length:** None. **Other:** Campfires must be extinguished by midnight.

To Get There

From I-80/90 (Indiana Turnpike), take Exit 144 to Hwy. 120, drive 3.25 mi. west on Hwy. 120, then 0.5 mi. north on CR 300W. Roads are wide and well maintained with broad shoulders.

GARRETT

Indian Springs Campground

981 CR 64, Garrett 46738. T: (219) 357-5194; F: (219) 357-5194; indiansprings@ctlnet.com.

RV ★★ Tent ★★

Beauty: ★★	Site Privacy: ★★
Spaciousness: ★★★	Quiet: ★★★★
Security: ★★★★	Cleanliness: ★★
Insect Control: Yes	Facilities: ★★

Indian Springs Campground is blessed with three lakes—two for fishing, one for fishing and swimming—and an abundance of mature oak and hickory trees. Laid out in a series of loops, the campground offers 15 pull-throughs and an average site width of 35 feet. Most sites are grassy and shaded. A separate section is set aside for tent campers, away from RVs. Security is good with a traffic control gate requiring a pass. Owners live on site and the campground is patrolled regularly. A game room is a good addition but needs to be spiffed up in our opinion. If you go, be careful entering and exiting the campground because of a hill that makes it difficult to see oncoming traffic. Also be cautious of a narrow bridge crossing at the campground entrance.

Basics

Operated by: Karen & Kenneth Steele; Kathy, Deborah, Dale, & Don Moore. **Open:** All year. **Site Assignment:** Reservations accepted w/ 1-night deposit; refund (minus $5 fee) w/ 48-hour notice. **Registration:** At campground office. **Fee:** $23 (cash, check, credit cards). **Parking:** At site.

Facilities

Number of RV Sites: 400. **Number of Tent-Only Sites:** 17. **Hookups:** Electric (20, 30, 50 amps), water, sewer. **Each Site:** Picnic table, fire ring. **Dump Station:** No. **Laundry:** Yes. **Pay Phone:** Yes. **Rest Rooms and Showers:** Yes. **Fuel:** No. **Propane:** Yes. **Internal Roads:** Gravel, in fair condition. **RV Service:** No. **Market:** 4 mi. north in Garrett. **Restaurant:** 4 mi. north in Garrett. **General Store:** Yes. **Vending:** Yes. **Swimming Pool:** No. **Playground:** Yes. **Other:** 3 small lakes, hiking trails, basketball, volleyball, horseshoes, game room. **Activities:** Swimming, fishing, boating (rental pontoon, rowboats, canoes, paddleboats available), church services, hiking, scheduled weekend activities. **Nearby Attractions:** Amish communities, nation's 2nd largest genealogy library, Lincoln Museum, zoo, Auburn Cord Duesenberg Museum. **Additional Information:** Fort Wayne/Allen County CVB, (800) 767-7752.

Restrictions

Pets: Leash only. **Fires:** Fire ring only. **Alcoholic Beverages:** At sites only. **Vehicle Maximum Length:** None. **Other:** Pet owners must show proper vaccination records.

To Get There

From junction of I-69 and Hwy. 8, take Exit 129, drive 3 mi. west on Hwy. 8, then 5 mi. south on Hwy. 327, then 0.5 mi. west on CR 64. Roads are in good condition with adequate shoulders.

GAS CITY

Mar-brook Campground

6690 East 600 South, Marion 46953. T: (765) 674-4383

RV ★★★ Tent ★★★

Beauty: ★★★ Site Privacy: ★★★
Spaciousness: ★★★ Quiet: ★★
Security: ★★★★ Cleanliness: ★★★
Insect Control: Yes Facilities: ★★★

Mar-brook Campground is so close to I-69 that you can almost read the license plates on vehicles speeding by. The convenience of such easy access comes with a price, though. Highway noise is very loud, particularly during rush hours. The noise is less noticeable on the back side of the campground. The typical site width is 22 feet, with 15 pull-throughs. Laid out in a loop, the riverside park offers mostly shady spots. Security measures are good with one entrance road, owners who live on site, and regular patrols. Safety also is emphasized in the family campground, located four miles west of Gas City. No motor bike riding is allowed, bicycles must be put up when the dusk to dawn lights come on, and bikes are not allowed at any time on the hill in front of the recreation building. Children under 13 are not allowed in the pool unsupervised and small children are not to go to the restrooms alone. To make sure the rules are understood, campers must read and sign a copy of the regulations.

Basics

Operated by: Paul & Joyce Martin. **Open:** Apr. 15–Oct. 15. **Site Assignment:** Reservations w/ 1-night deposit; refund w/ 4-day notice. **Registration:** At campground office. **Fee:** $17 (cash, check). **Parking:** At site.

Facilities

Number of RV Sites: 160. **Number of Tent-Only Sites:** 30. **Hookups:** Electric (20, 30 amps), water, sewer. **Each Site:** Picnic table, fire ring. **Dump Station:** Yes. **Laundry:** Yes. **Pay Phone:** Yes. **Rest Rooms and Showers:** Yes. **Fuel:** No. **Propane:** Yes. **Internal Roads:** Paved/gravel, in fair condition. **RV Service:** No. **Market:** 4 mi. east in Gas City. **Restaurant:** 4 mi. east in Gas City. **General Store:** Yes. **Vending:** Yes. **Swimming Pool:** Yes. **Playground:** Yes. **Other:** Mississinewa River, hiking trails, horseshoes, basketball court, recreation field, volleyball, arcade, mini-golf. **Activities:** Swimming, fishing, hiking, scheduled weekend activities. **Nearby Attractions:** James Dean hometown, museums, golf, antiques, Mississinewa Battlefield. **Additional Information:** Grant County CVB, (800) 662-9474.

Restrictions

Pets: Leash only. **Fires:** Fire ring only. **Alcoholic Beverages:** At sites only. **Vehicle Maximum Length:** None. **Other:** No cotton garments, suntan oil, or lotion allowed in pool.

To Get There

From junction of I-69 and Hwy. 22, take Exit 59, drive 0.25 mi. east on Hwy. 22, then 1 mi. south on CR 700E, then 1 mi. southwest on CR 600S. The county road is narrow and rough in spots.

GAS CITY

Sports Lake Camping Resort

7230 East 400 South, Marion 46953. T: (765) 998-2558; F: (765) 674-9229.

RV ★★★ Tent ★★★

Beauty: ★★★ Site Privacy: ★★★
Spaciousness: ★★★ Quiet: ★★★★
Security: ★★★★ Cleanliness: ★★★
Insect Control: None Facilities: ★★★

With two golf courses nearby, Sports Lake Camping Resort is a popular campground for golfers and other sports enthusiasts. Located two miles east of Gas City, the campground also offers many recreational opportunities on site. Not surprisingly, about half the sites are occupied by seasonal campers and only two full hookups spots remain. A heavily wooded lakeside campground in a secluded rural area, Sports Lake offers a common site width of 30 feet with ten pull-throughs. A five mph speed limit is strictly enforced and motorists who try to enter the exit will find their tires in trouble from a one-way apparatus. Security features include an electric gate that is closed from 10 p.m. to 8 a.m. The owner lives nearby and helper campers also assist in keeping an eye on the campground. About the only noise is what drifts over from the Friday night races nearby. Best spots for RVs are 1A–10A because they are larger pull-throughs. Favorite sites for tent campers are in the woods.

Basics

Operated by: Randy & Peggy Richards. **Open:** Apr. 15–Oct. 15. **Site Assignment:** Reservations accepted w/ 1-night deposit; no refunds. **Registration:** At campground office. **Fee:** $25 (cash, check). **Parking:** At site.

Facilities

Number of RV Sites: 150. **Number of Tent-Only Sites:** 25. **Hookups:** Electric (20, 30 amps), water, sewer. **Each Site:** Picnic table, fire ring. **Dump Station:** Yes. **Laundry:** No. **Pay Phone:** No. **Rest Rooms and Showers:** Yes. **Fuel:** No. **Propane:** No. **Internal Roads:** Gravel, in fair condition. **RV Service:** No. **Market:** 2 mi. west in Gas City. **Restaurant:** 2 mi. west in Gas City. **General Store:** Yes. **Vending:** Yes. **Swimming Pool:** Yes. **Playground:** Yes. **Other:** Rec hall, pavilion, fishing lake, mini-golf, shuffleboard, badminton, sports field, horseshoes, volleyball. **Activities:** Swimming, fishing, boating (rental rowboats, paddleboats available), scheduled weekend activities. **Nearby Attractions:** James Dean's hometown, golf, antiques, museums, Mississinewa Battlefield. **Additional Information:** Grant County CVB, (800) 662-9474.

Restrictions

Pets: Leash only. **Fires:** Fire ring only. **Alcoholic Beverages:** At sites only. **Vehicle Maximum Length:** None. **Other:** Visitors must park in the lot outside & pay $2 each to visit; no swimming in the lake.

To Get There

From junction of I-69 and Hwy. 22, take Exit 59, drive 0.5 mi. east on Hwy. 22, then 1 mi. north on CR 700E, then 0.25 mi. east on CR 400S. Roads are wide and well maintained with narrow shoulders in spots.

HOWE

Twin Mills Camping Resort

1675 West SR 120, Howe 46746. T: (219) 562-3212; www.twinmillscamping.com.

RV ★★★★ Tent ★★★★

Beauty: ★★★★ Site Privacy: ★★★★
Spaciousness: ★★★★ Quiet: ★★★★
Security: ★★★★★ Cleanliness: ★★★★
Insect Control: Yes Facilities: ★★★★

Twin Mills Camping Resort has the beauty and paved roads of a state park, along with the facilities of a private resort. The result is a winning combination for campers. Located two miles east of Howe, the campground has wooded and open sites with a typical site width of 35 feet. Each site is plainly marked with a white pole and red number sign. Mature pine trees and other greenery add to the privacy, quiet, and attractiveness. Laid out in a series of loops, the campground has 280 seasonals and 20 pull-through sites. Most popular sites are in Campers Cove which is close to the activities. A full-time recreation director keeps the activities going. A five mph speed limit and one-way roads help with safety. Security measures are tops with a key-card gate, one entrance/exit road, owners who live on site, surveillance cameras, and regular patrols of the campground.

Basics

Operated by: Dave & Vicki Cagley. **Open:** Apr. 15–Oct. 15. **Site Assignment:** Reservations w/ 1-night deposit; refund (less $5) w/ 48-hour notice. **Registration:** At campground office. **Fee:** $32 (cash, check, credit cards). **Parking:** At site.

Facilities

Number of RV Sites: 559. **Number of Tent-Only Sites:** 10. **Hookups:** Electric (30 amps), water, sewer. **Each Site:** Picnic table, fire ring. **Dump Station:** Yes. **Laundry:** Yes. **Pay Phone:** Yes. **Rest Rooms and Showers:** Yes. **Fuel:** Yes. **Propane:** Yes. **Internal Roads:** Paved, in good condition. **RV Service:** Yes. **Market:** 2 mi. east in Howe. **Restaurant:** 2 mi. east in Howe. **General Store:** Yes. **Vending:** Yes. **Swimming Pool:** No. **Playground:** Yes. **Other:** Lake beach, mini-golf, biking & hiking trails, shuffleboard, basketball, horseshoes, volleyball, game room, coin games, rec hall, rental cabins, pavilion, nature lookout, boat dock, badminton. **Activities:** Swimming, hiking, fishing, boating (rental rowboats, canoes available), scheduled weekend activities. **Nearby Attractions:** Amish community, flea market, antique mall, auto museum, golf, arts & crafts, Borkholder Dutch Village. **Additional Information:** LaGrange County CVB, (800) 254-8090.

Restrictions

Pets: Leash only. **Fires:** Fire ring only. **Alcoholic Beverages:** At sites only. **Vehicle Maximum Length:** None.

To Get There

From junction of I-80/90 and Hwy. 9, take Exit 121, drive 2.5 mi. south on Hwy. 9, then 1.75 mi. west on Hwy. 120. Roads are wide and well maintained with broad shoulders.

KENDALLVILLE

Bixler Lake Campground

211 Iddings St., Kendallville 46755. T: (219) 347-1064

RV ★★★ Tent ★★★

Beauty: ★★★	Site Privacy: ★★★
Spaciousness: ★★★	Quiet: ★★★
Security: ★★★	Cleanliness: ★★★
Insect Control: None	Facilities: ★★★

Located in the woods and wilds, yet close to town and separated by a 120-acre lake, Bixler Lake Campground is a popular spot with local campers and with groups that can be in adjoining sites. Despite the lengthy directions, Bixler Lake Campground is easy to find with signs to point the way. But much of the access travel must be done on residential streets which can be narrow with inadequate shoulders. The campground offers a choice of grassy or gravel sites, shady or open, 20 pull-throughs. Rates are surprisingly low and discounts are given to groups with ten units or more. The campground offers wheelchair-accessible rest rooms and showers. Security is good with a check-in point, as well as regular patrols by local officers.

Basics

Operated by: Kendallville Parks & Recreation Dept. **Open:** May 15–Oct. 15. **Site Assignment:** Reservations accepted w/ no deposit. **Registration:** At campground office. **Fee:** $14 (cash, check). **Parking:** At site.

Facilities

Number of RV Sites: 80. **Number of Tent-Only Sites:** 20. **Hookups:** Electric (20, 30, 50 amps), water. **Each Site:** Picnic table, fire ring. **Dump Station:** Yes. **Laundry:** No. **Pay Phone:** Yes. **Rest Rooms and Showers:** Yes. **Fuel:** No. **Propane:** No. **Internal Roads:** Paved/gravel, in good condition. **RV Service:** No. **Market:** 2 mi. west in Kendallville. **Restaurant:** 2 mi. west in Kendallville. **General Store:** No. **Vending:** Yes. **Swimming Pool:** No. **Playground:** Yes. **Other:** Fishing lake, swimming beach, boat launch, fishing piers, volleyball, duck pond, nature trails, observation platforms, herb garden, butterfly plots, bee-keeping display, recreation field, tennis court. **Activities:** Fishing, swimming, boating (rental paddleboats available), scheduled weekend activities. **Nearby Attractions:** Windmill museum, golf, nation's 2nd largest genealogy library, Lincoln Museum, zoo, Auburn Cord Duesenberg Museum. **Additional Information:** Fort Wayne/Allen County CVB, (800) 767-7752.

Restrictions

Pets: Leash only. **Fires:** Fire ring only. **Alcoholic Beverages:** Not permitted. **Vehicle Maximum Length:** None. **Other:** 14-day stay limit.

To Get There

From junction of US 6 and US 3, drive 1.3 mi. east on US 6 to Fair St., then 0.4 mi. south to Wayne St., 500 feet east to Park Ave., and finally 0.4 mi. south to Lake Park Dr. Roads are well maintained, residential streets, some narrow with poor shoulders.

KENDALLVILLE

Gordon's Camping

9500 South 600E, Wolcottville 46755. T: (219) 351-3383; www.gordonscamping.com; info@gordonscamping.com.

RV ★★★ Tent ★★★

Beauty: ★★★	Site Privacy: ★★★
Spaciousness: ★★★	Quiet: ★★★
Security: ★★★★★	Cleanliness: ★★★★
Insect Control: None	Facilities: ★★★

Calling itself "the cure for summertime blues," Gordon's Camping has enough recreation and activities to keep most anyone happy. Located 35 miles north of Kendallville, the campground also is convenient to many attractions. So, not surprisingly, Gordon's is popular. Offering wooded sites on rolling terrain, Gordon's has 150 pull-throughs and some sites as large as 50 feet wide. Sites are mostly shady and grassy. The best sites for tents are along the pond in the Black Willow section where it is quieter and more natural. The best sites for RVs are in the Black Walnut and Tulip Tree sections because the sites offer 50 amp electricity, are pull-throughs, and feature more shade. Security is tops with a traffic-control gate requiring a pass, owners who live on site, and regular patrols of the campground.

Basics

Operated by: Jerry & Sandi Bubb. **Open:** May 13–Oct. 15. **Site Assignment:** First come; first served. **Registration:** At campground office. **Fee:** $25 (cash, check). **Parking:** At site.

Facilities

Number of RV Sites: 300. **Number of Tent-Only Sites:** 0. **Hookups:** Electric (20, 30, 50 amps), water. **Each Site:** Picnic table, fire ring. **Dump Station:** Yes. **Laundry:** Yes. **Pay Phone:** Yes. **Rest Rooms and Showers:** Yes. **Fuel:** No. **Propane:** Yes. **Internal Roads:** Paved/gravel, in good condition. **RV Service:** No. **Market:** 8 mi. south in Kendallville. **Restaurant:** 8 mi. south in Kendallville. **General Store:** Yes. **Vending:** Yes. **Swimming Pool:** Yes. **Playground:** Yes. **Other:** Mini-golf, hiking trails, pavilion, video rental, basketball, volleyball, horseshoes, kids' fishing pond, coin games, wading pool, sports field. **Activities:** Swimming, boating (rental rowboats available), biking (rental bikes available), church services, scheduled activities, rental cabins. **Nearby Attractions:** Golf, Auburn Cord Duesenberg Museum, zoo, nation's 2nd largest geneaology library, windmill museum. **Additional Information:** Fort Wayne/Allen County CVB, (800) 767-7752.

Restrictions

Pets: Leash only. **Fires:** Fire ring only. **Alcoholic Beverages:** Permitted. **Vehicle Maximum Length:** None.

To Get There

From junction of US 20 and Hwy. 3, drive 7 mi. south on Hwy. 3, then 1.25 mi. east on CR 600S. Roads are well maintained but narrow with adequate shoulders.

LAFAYETTE

Lafayette AOK Campground

225 East 300 South, Lafayette 47909. T: (765) 474-5030

RV ★★★★ Tent ★★★★

Beauty: ★★★	Site Privacy: ★★★
Spaciousness: ★★★	Quiet: ★★★
Security: ★★★★	Cleanliness: ★★★★
Insect Control: None	Facilities: ★★★★

It is no typo and your eyes aren't playing tricks. This is the Lafayette AOK Campground, not a KOA, but that is a common misconception. Campers often think they are pulling into a KOA. Laid out in a series of loops, the Lafayette AOK offers a choice of shaded or open sites in a rolling terrain. The typical site width is 30 feet and the campground has mostly pull-through sites and 50 seasonals. The best RV sites are in the first row in the campground which offers easier access and more trees. The best tent sites are in a corner of the grounds with more woods, shade, and privacy. A five mph speed limit is enforced as are quiet times from 10 p.m. to 8 a.m. No outside clotheslines are permitted but laundry facilities are open 24 hours a day. Security includes one entrance/exit road, a manager living on site, and seasonal campers who keep an eye on their area.

Basics

Operated by: Ted Riehle. **Open:** All year. **Site Assignment:** Reservations w/ 1-night deposit; refund w/ 24-hour notice. **Registration:** At campground office. **Fee:** $24 (cash, check, credit card). **Parking:** At site.

Facilities

Number of RV Sites: 76. **Number of Tent-Only Sites:** 150. **Hookups:** Electric (30, 50 amps), water, sewer, cable TV, phone. **Each Site:** Picnic table. **Dump Station:** Yes. **Laundry:** Yes. **Pay Phone:** Yes. **Rest Rooms and Showers:** Yes. **Fuel:** No. **Propane:** Yes. **Internal Roads:** Paved/gravel, in good condition. **RV Service:** No. **Market:** 0.25 mi. north in Lafayette. **Restaurant:** 0.25 mi. east in Lafayette. **General Store:** Yes. **Vending:** Yes. **Swimming Pool:** Yes. **Playground:** Yes. **Other:** Coin games, pool table, exercise machines, horseshoes, recreation field, rec hall, game room, hiking trails, creek. **Activities:** Swimming, hiking. **Nearby Attractions:** Tippecanoe Battlefield, Wolf Park, Fort Quiatenon, golf, Purdue University, museums, historic homes, antiques, Indiana Beach amusement park. **Additional Information:** Greater Lafayette CVB, (800) 872-6648.

Restrictions

Pets: Leash only. **Fires:** Fire ring only. **Alcoholic Beverages:** Permitted. **Vehicle Maximum Length:** None.

To Get There

From junction of I-65 and Hwy. 38, take Exit 168, drive 1.25 mi. west on Hwy. 38, then 4 mi. west on CR 475E and CR 350S, then 0.5 mi. north on CR 100E, then 0.9 mi. west on CR 300S. Roads are wide and well maintained with broad shoulders.

MADISON

Clifty Falls State Park

1501 Green Rd., Madison 47250. T: (812) 273-8885; F: (812) 265-6662; www.state.in.us/dnr.

RV ★★★ Tent ★★★★

Beauty: ★★★★ Site Privacy: ★★★
Spaciousness: ★★★ Quiet: ★★★★
Security: ★★★★ Cleanliness: ★★★★
Insect Control: None Facilities: ★★★

It's easy to see where Clifty Falls State Park got its name. With four plunging waterfalls, 70-foot gorges, sheer cliffs, and a narrow valley, Clifty Falls shows the awesome forces of nature at work. The park is popular with campers who like to hike in the area. Winter and spring hiking show the falls at their best. July through Nov. offer meager falls and the easiest hiking in Clifty Creek's wonderful stone bed. A muddy, rock- strewn, 600-foot tunnel piercing the hillside beneath Oak Grove is the most prominent remnant of the Madison and Indianapolis Railroad, begun in 1852 and abandoned in bankruptcy. It is passable on foot with flashlight. Security is good, with passes needed to enter the campground and a ranger on patrol. Despite the lack of water hookups and laundry, Clifty Falls has a dedicated following of campers, both RV and tents. The natural beauty, the programs, and the security are the main draws.

Basics

Operated by: Indiana Dept. of Natural Resources. **Open:** All year. **Site Assignment:** Written reservations w/ 1-night deposit; no refunds. **Registration:** At campground office. **Fee:** $12 (check, credit cards). **Parking:** At site.

Facilities

Number of RV Sites: 140. **Number of Tent-Only Sites:** 60. **Hookups:** Electric (30 amps). **Each Site:** Picnic table, fire ring. **Dump Station:** Yes. **Laundry:** No. **Pay Phone:** Yes. **Rest Rooms and Showers:** Yes. **Fuel:** No. **Propane:** No. **Internal Roads:** Paved, in good condition. **RV Service:** No. **Market:** 1 mi. east in Madison. **Restaurant:** Yes. **General Store:** Yes. **Vending:** Yes. **Swimming Pool:** Yes. **Playground:** Yes. **Other:** Nature center, inn w/ indoor swimming pool, picnic shelters, tennis court. **Activities:** Swimming, hiking, guided nature walks, summer weekday programs & evening activities offered by naturalist. **Nearby Attractions:** Scenic drives, golf, historic Madison, Ohio River, Lanier State Historic Site, vineyards, marina. **Additional Information:** Madison Area CVB, (800) 559-2956.

Restrictions

Pets: Leash only. **Fires:** Fire rings & grills only. **Alcoholic Beverages:** At sites only. **Vehicle Maximum Length:** 35 ft. **Other:** 14-day stay limit.

To Get There

From Madison, drive 1 mi. west on IN 56/62. Roads are generally wide and well maintained. Shoulders are often poor. The area is popular for its scenic, hilly, winding roads but they can be difficult to maneuver.

NASHVILLE

The Last Resort RV Park & Campground

2248 East SR 46, Nashville 47448. T: (812) 988-4675

RV ★★★★ Tent ★★★★

Beauty: ★★★★ Site Privacy: ★★★★
Spaciousness: ★★★★ Quiet: ★★★★
Security: ★★★★ Cleanliness: ★★★★
Insect Control: None Facilities: ★★★★

Location is everything. And The Last Resort RV Park & Campground has a prime spot to be a campground. The Last Resort is in the midst of beautiful Brown County, two-and-a-half miles east of Nashville, Indiana, but it offers the peacefulness and beauty of a woodland setting. Situated atop a hill, and surrounded by ravines, the campground has both open and shaded sites that are level and grassy with gravel parking spots. Laid out in a loop, the campground has 16 seasonals, 18 pull-through sites and a typical site width of 35 feet. Nice touches include private shower stalls, each with a door and a curtain. Speed limit is five mph and quiet hours are 10 p.m. to 8 a.m.; generators are not permitted at any time. Sites 114–117 are popular because they back up into the woods and are away from the main activity. Security includes one entrance/exit road and an on-site manager. The campground is particularly lovely when autumn foliage is showing peak colors.

Basics

Operated by: Frank & Dot Moser. **Open:** Apr. 1–Nov. 1. **Site Assignment:** Reservations w/ 1-night deposit; refund w/ 7-day notice. **Registration:** At campground office. **Fee:** $25 (cash, check, credit cards). **Parking:** At site.

Facilities

Number of RV Sites: 80. **Number of Tent-Only Sites:** 36. **Hookups:** Electric (30, 50 amps), water, sewer, cable TV. **Each Site:** Picnic table, fire ring. **Dump Station:** Yes. **Laundry:** Yes. **Pay Phone:** Yes. **Rest Rooms and Showers:** Yes. **Fuel:** No. **Propane:** Yes. **Internal Roads:** Paved/gravel, in good condition. **RV Service:** No. **Market:** 2.5 mi. west in Nashville. **Restaurant:** 2.5 mi. west in Nashville. **General Store:** Yes. **Vending:** Yes. **Swimming Pool:** Yes. **Playground:** Yes. **Other:** Rec room, horseshoes, recreation field, pavilion, coin games, basketball, hiking trails. **Activities:** Swimming, hiking, scheduled weekend activities. **Nearby Attractions:** Brown County State Park, Nashville artist colony w/ more than 350 specialty shops, scenic drives, winter skiing, Little Nashville Opry, golf, Indiana University. **Additional Information:** Brown County CVB, (800) 753-3255.

Restrictions

Pets: On leash. **Fires:** In fire ring. **Alcoholic Beverages:** At sites. **Vehicle Max. Length:** None.

To Get There

From junction of I-65 and Hwy. 46, take Exit 68, drive 14 mi. west on Hwy. 46. Roads are wide and well maintained with broad shoulders.

ORLAND

Manapogo Park

5495 W 760N, Orland 46776. T: (260) 833-3902; www.manapogo.com.

RV ★★★★ Tent ★★★★

Beauty: ★★★ Site Privacy: ★★★★
Spaciousness: ★★★★ Quiet: ★★★★

Security: ★★★★ Cleanliness: ★★★★
Insect Control: Yes Facilities: ★★★★

A wooded, grassy campground, Manapogo Park centers around 425-acre Lake Pleasant. Located four miles east of Orland, Indiana, the campground has a typical site width of 50 feet. The campground has 247 seasonal campers and no pull-through sites. A five mph speed limit is enforced for vehicles and bicycles. Bicycles may not be ridden after sundown and motorcycles may be used only for entering or leaving the campground, when idle speed is required. A separate section for tent campers allows more greenery and privacy from RVs. Overnight sites are generally placed together instead of being scattered throughout the park's seasonals. Security measures include entrance gates that require a $5 deposit fee for cards, refundable upon return of the card. The campground owner lives on site and provides regular patrols.

Basics

Operated by: John West. **Open:** 3rd week in Apr.–1st week in Oct. **Site Assignment:** Reservations w/ 1-night deposit; refund (minus $5) w/ 5-day notice. **Registration:** At campground office. **Fee:** $32. **Parking:** At site.

Facilities

Number of RV Sites: 304. **Number of Tent-Only Sites:** 15. **Hookups:** Electric (30 amps), water, sewer. **Each Site:** Picnic table, fire ring. **Dump Station:** Yes. **Laundry:** Yes. **Pay Phone:** Yes. **Rest Rooms and Showers:** Yes. **Fuel:** Yes. **Propane:** Yes. **Internal Roads:** Paved/gravel, in good condition. **RV Service:** No. **Market:** 4 mi. west in Orland. **Restaurant:** 4 mi. west in Orland. **General Store:** Yes. **Vending:** Yes. **Swimming Pool:** No. **Playground:** Yes. **Other:** Lake Pleasant, swimming beach, pavilion, boat piers, boat ramp, basketball, volleyball, shuffleboard, horseshoes, rental cabins, fish-cleaning station, rec room, coin games, mini-golf, fishing pond. **Activities:** Swimming, fishing, boating (rental fishing boats, paddleboats, canoes & water bikes available), scheduled weekend activities. **Nearby Attractions:** Golf, Shipshewana flea market, factory outlet stores, amusement park, car museum, go-cart raceway, antiques, arts & crafts shops. **Additional Information:** Amish County/Elkhart County Visitors Center, (800) 860-5949.

Restrictions

Pets: Leash only; walking of pets in park is not allowed; pets must be carried or transported in vehicle to the designated walking area near the dump station. **Fires:** Fire ring only. **Alcoholic Beverages:** Permitted but must be kept in covered container if taken off campsite. **Vehicle Maximum Length:** None. **Other:** No golf carts or mopeds permitted, except for park staff.

To Get There

From junction of Hwy. 327 and Hwy. 120, drive 3.25 mi. east on Hwy. 120, then 0.75 mi. north on CR 650W, then 1 mi. east on CR 760N. Roads are wide and well maintained with broad shoulders, except for a narrow section and steep curve on CR 760N.

PERU

Honey Bear Hollow Campground

4252 West 200 N, Peru 46970. T: (765) 473-4342; F: (765) 473-5366; jelly@netusal.net.

RV ★★★★ Tent ★★★★

Beauty: ★★★ Site Privacy: ★★★★
Spaciousness: ★★★★ Quiet: ★★★★
Security: ★★★★ Cleanliness: ★★★★
Insect Control: Yes Facilities: ★★★★

The entryway to Honey Bear Hollow Campground lets guests know that the owners care about the facility. A small pond and water display along with flowers and other greenery add a nice welcoming touch. Well-tended flower barrels also decorate bathroom entrances. Laid out in a series of loops, the campground has a typical site width of 30 feet with 50 seasonal campers and pull-through sites for all overnight campers. Locted four miles north of Peru, Indiana, the campground has a well-stocked camp store and is surrounded by woods. Sites are mostly shady and grassy with gravel pads to park on. Quiet time is 11 p.m. to 8 a.m. and there is a curfew for children under age 18. Security measures include an alarm system, one entrance/exit and owners who live on site.

Basics

Operated by: Dawn Thomas & her parents, Bob & Toni Billetz. **Open:** All year. **Site Assignment:** Reservations w/ 1-night deposit; refund (minus $5) w/ 7-day notice; no refunds on holiday weekends. **Registration:** At campground office. **Fee:** $23 (cash, check, credit cards). **Parking:** At site.

Facilities

Number of RV Sites: 105. **Number of Tent-Only Sites:** 5. **Hookups:** Electric (30, 50 amps), water. **Each Site:** Picnic table, fire ring. **Dump Station:** Yes. **Laundry:** Yes. **Pay Phone:** Yes. **Rest Rooms and Showers:** Yes. **Fuel:** No. **Propane:** Yes. **Internal Roads:** Gravel, in good condition. **RV Service:** No. **Market:** 4 mi. south in Peru. **Restaurant:** 4 mi. south in Peru. **General Store:** Yes. **Vending:** Yes. **Swimming Pool:** Yes. **Playground:** Yes. **Other:** Rec hall, pavilion, fishing pond, mini-golf, horseshoes, volleyball, game room, disc golf course, cartoons & video games. **Activities:** Swimming, fishing, scheduled weekend activities. **Nearby Attractions:** Grissom Air Museum, historic homes, golf, Big Top Circus & Hall of Fame Museum, antiques, arts & crafts shops. **Additional Information:** Howard County CVB, (800) 837-0971.

Restrictions

Pets: Leash only. **Fires:** Fire ring only. **Alcoholic Beverages:** At sites only. **Vehicle Maximum Length:** None. **Other:** No fireworks of any kind, including sparklers, are permitted.

To Get There

From junction of US 31 and Bypass US 24, go 1 mi. north on US 31, then 1.25 mi. west on CR 200N. Roads are wide and well maintained with broad shoulders, except for CR 200N which is narrow with small shoulders.

PLYMOUTH

Yogi Bear's Jellystone Park Camp-Resort

7719 Redwood Rd., Plymouth 46563. T: (219) 936-7851

RV ★★★★ Tent ★★

Beauty: ★★★ Site Privacy: ★★★★
Spaciousness: ★★★★ Quiet: ★★★★
Security: ★★★★ Cleanliness: ★★★★
Insect Control: None Facilities: ★★★★

Yogi Bear's Jellystone Park Camp-Resort is owned by the people who live there, the Marshall County Membership Corp. That helps keep the campground well maintained and attractive. People take pride in what they own. For example, lights in the main bathroom are triggered to come on when somone comes in; the water faucet in the sink releases a certain amount of water when a person's hands are under it. Those measures are both convenient and energy saving. The facilities also are very clean and nicely decorated. A 5.5 mph speed limit is enforced and campers are warned if they "exceed the speed limit at Yogi Bear, you'll find yourself walking." Laid out in a series of loops, the campground has 946 owner/campers, leaving 150 sites for visitors and 32 spots in the primitive tent area which is used only on Labor Day weekend. Located four miles west of Plymouth, Indiana, the campground has ten pull-through sites and a typical site width of 40 feet. Security measures are excellent with a controlled gate entry system and 24-hour security on the premises.

Basics

Operated by: Marshall County Membership Corp. **Open:** May 1–Oct. 1. **Site Assignment:** Reservations w/ 1-night deposit; refund (minus 10 percent) w/ 10-day notice. **Registration:** At campground office. **Fee:** $32 (cash, check, credit cards). **Parking:** At site.

Facilities

Number of RV Sites: 1,096. **Number of Tent-Only Sites:** 32. **Hookups:** Electric (30 amps), water, sewer. **Each Site:** Picnic table, fire ring. **Dump Station:** Yes. **Laundry:** Yes. **Pay Phone:** Yes. **Rest Rooms and Showers:** Yes. **Fuel:** No. **Propane:** Yes. **Internal Roads:** Paved/gravel, in good condition. **RV Service:** No. **Market:** 3 mi. east in Plymouth. **Restaurant:** 3 mi. east in Plymouth. **General Store:** Yes. **Vending:** Yes. **Swimming Pool:** Yes. **Playground:** Yes. **Other:** Snack bar, gameroom, fishing pond, pavilion, rec hall, rental cabins, tennis, basketball, mini-golf, horseshoes, adults room, recreation field, coin games, wading pool, boat dock. **Activities:** Swimming, fishing, boating (rental kayaks & paddleboats available), scheduled activities. **Nearby Attractions:** Golf, Amish Acres, Culver Military Academy, University of Notre Dame, Studebaker Museum, College Football Hall of Fame, Trail of Courage, antiques, arts & crafts, historic homes. **Additional Information:** Marshall County CVB, (800) 626-5353.

Restrictions

Pets: Leash only. **Fires:** Fire ring only. **Alcoholic Beverages:** At sites only. **Vehicle Maximum Length:** None. **Other:** Roller skates, skateboards, & roller blades are not allowed.

To Get There

From junction of Hwy. 17 and US 30, drive 4 mi. west on US 30. Roads are wide and well maintained with broad shoulders.

REMINGTON

Caboose Lake Campground

3657 West US 24, Remington 47977. T: (800) 726-6982; www.cabooselake.com; cabooselake@yahoo.com.

RV ★★ Tent ★★

Beauty: ★★ Site Privacy: ★★
Spaciousness: ★★ Quiet: ★★
Security: ★★★★ Cleanliness: ★★★
Insect Control: None Facilities: ★★

Caboose Lake Campground, located two miles east of Remington, Indiana, is a work in progress. Already, the campground has a great location—a stone's throw off I-65, right on the travel route for snowbirds and other folks heading north or south. Starting with a nice little lake, the owners (a father/daughter team) have some great plans, including the addition of a brand new comfort station, go-kart track, mini-golf, and rental cabooses and cabins. As a new facility, Caboose Lake has planted lots of small trees that don't offer much shade yet. Sites are level and grassy with a typical site width of 40 feet and six pull-throughs. Favorite RV and tent sites are ones facing the lake. Security measures include a five mph speed limit, regular patrols, and an owner who lives on site. Open all year, Caboose Lake is an easy stopping-off point for travelers. However, you can't be this close to an interstate without hearing the rumbling noise of trucks and autos.

Basics

Operated by: Douglas McGill & Christiane Palladino. **Open:** All year. **Site Assignment:** Reservations w/ 1-night deposit; refund w/ 1-week notice. **Registration:** At campground office. **Fee:** $20 (cash, check, credit card). **Parking:** At site.

Facilities

Number of RV Sites: 38. **Number of Tent-Only Sites:** 10. **Hookups:** Electric (20, 30, 50 amps), water, sewer. **Each Site:** Picnic table, fire ring. **Dump Station:** Yes. **Laundry:** No. **Pay Phone:** Yes. **Rest Rooms and Showers:** Yes. **Fuel:** No. **Propane:** Yes. **Internal Roads:** Gravel, in good condition. **RV Service:** No. **Market:** 2 mi. west in Remington. **Restaurant:** 0.5 mi. west in Remington. **General Store:** No. **Vending:** Yes. **Swimming Pool:** No. **Playground:** Yes. **Other:** Caboose Lake, pavilion, swimming beach, volleyball, horseshoes. **Activities:** Swimming, fishing, boating (rental paddleboats, sailboats & fishing boats available), scheduled activities. **Nearby Attractions:** Purdue University, Wolf Park, Lake Shafer, Indiana Beach amusement park, Tippecanoe Battlefield & Museum. **Additional Information:** Greater Lafayette CVB, (800) 872-6569.

Restrictions

Pets: Leash only. **Fires:** Fire ring only. **Alcoholic Beverages:** At sites only. **Vehicle Maximum Length:** None.

To Get There

From junction of I-65 and US 24E, take Exit 201, drive 500 feet east on US 24. Roads are wide and well maintained with broad shoulders.

RISING SUN

Little Farm on the River RV Park Camping Resort

1343 East Bellview Ln., Rising Sun 47040. T: (812) 438-4500; F: (812) 438-9135; www.littlefarmrvresort.com; littlefarmrv@hotmail.com.

RV ★★★ Tent ★★★

Beauty: ★★★ Site Privacy: ★★
Spaciousness: ★★★ Quiet: ★★★
Security: ★★★★★ Cleanliness: ★★★★★
Insect Control: None Facilities: ★★★★

The good thing about Little Farm on the River RV Park Camping Resort is that it's new. Sparkling clean facilities still have the fresh smell of construction and the owner is energetic and enthusiastic. The bad thing about Little Farm on the River is that it's new. More than 300 trees have been planted and still have some growing to do for adequate shade in the upper camp sites. At press time, facilities are still being constructed and activities are being added. Located a mile east of Rising Sun, Indiana, the country campground is situated on the Ohio River with a natural sand bank and towering trees alongside the river bank—the prime camping spots. Autumn and spring would be best times for a stay—the flowering dogwood and pear trees and 3,000 newly planted flower bulbs put on quite a spring show. A series of three loops offers spacious grassy or gravel sites, pull-through or back-in spots. Open all year, the campground has underground water hookups so water is available even in freezing temperatures. Security is tops with an on-site manager, as well as both county and town police patrolling every hour all night and the Dept. of Natural Resources keeping a watch from the river. Some campers will enjoy the campground's close proximity to three riverboat gambling casinos.

Basics

Operated by: Little Farm on the River LLC. **Open:** All year. **Site Assignment:** Reservations w/ 1-night deposit; full refund w/ 7-day notice. **Registration:** At campground headquarters. **Fee:** $21.50 (check, credit cards, cash). **Parking:** At sites & headquarters.

Facilities

Number of RV Sites: 142. **Number of Tent-Only Sites:** 41. **Hookups:** Electric (20, 30, 50 amps), water, sewer. **Each Site:** Fire ring, picnic table. **Dump Station:** Yes. **Laundry:** Yes. **Pay Phone:** Yes. **Rest Rooms and Showers:** Yes. **Fuel:** No. **Propane:** Yes. **Internal Roads:** Gravel, in good condition. **RV Service:** Yes. **Market:** 1 mi. west in Rising Sun. **Restaurant:** 1 mi. west in Rising Sun. **General Store:** Yes. **Vending:** Yes. **Swimming Pool:** No. **Playground:** Yes. **Other:** Stocked fishing pond, rec room, pool table, card table, free Internet access, pavilion, TV, basketball court, RV storage & cleaning, baby animal petting zoo, Native American artifact display, shuffleboard court, tetherball, horseshoes, badminton, volleyball, free shuttle to Grand Victoria Casino & historic district of Rising Sun. **Activities:** Fishing, bike riding (rental bikes available), horseback riding (rental horses available), bingo, poker, crafts, fishing tournament. **Nearby Attractions:** Scenic river drive, golf, historic Rising Sun, Ohio River, marina, 3 riverboat casinos. **Additional Information:** Rising Sun/Ohio County Convention & Tourism Bureau (888) RSNGSUN.

Restrictions

Pets: Leash only. **Fires:** Fire rings & grills only. **Alcoholic Beverages:** Permitted. **Vehicle Maximum Length:** None.

To Get There

From US 50 in Aurora, drive east 7 mi. to East Bellview Ln. The state highway is wide and well maintained; Bellview Ln. was recenly paved by the county.

ROCHESTER

Lakeview Campground

7781 East 300 North, Rochester 46975. T: (219) 353-8114; F: (219) 353-8114; www.perfectmatrix.com/lakeview; lakeview@medt.com.

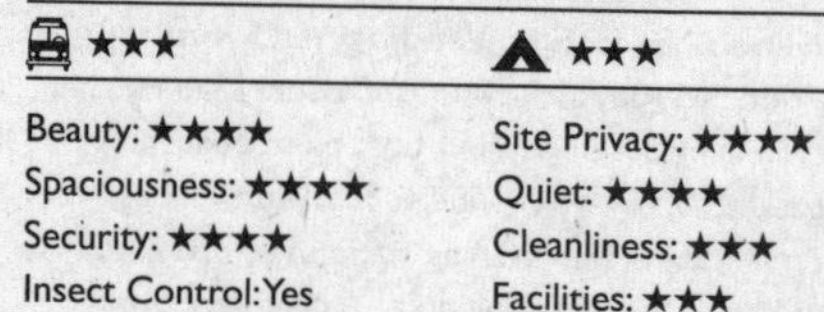

Campers don't have to worry about getting a lakefront site at Lakeview Campground. Each site is on Barr Lake. Located seven miles northeast of Rochester, Indiana, the campground has a surprising amount of shade for lakefront sites. Laid out in a half loop, the campground has a typical site width of 30 feet with 45 seasonals and eight pull-through sites. Lakeview is well maintained with freshly painted buildings, a mowed bank that goes down to a small creek, and a colorful mini-golf setup with a little teepee, windmill, log cabin, bridge, and other gizmos to offer challenge. Tents have a separate area with more greenery and privacy from RVs. Security includes one entrance/exit road, surveillance cameras and owners who live on site. Quiet hours are 11 p.m. to 8 a.m.

Basics

Operated by: Jim, Roberta, & Jeff Bever. **Open:** Apr. 15–Oct. 15. **Site Assignment:** Reservations w/ 1-night deposit; refund w/ 48-hour notice. **Registration:** At campground office. **Fee:** $25 (cash, check, credit cards). **Parking:** At site.

Facilities

Number of RV Sites: 105. **Number of Tent-Only Sites:** 25. **Hookups:** Electric (30 amps), water, sewer. **Each Site:** Picnic table, fire ring.

Dump Station: Yes. **Laundry:** No. **Pay Phone:** Yes. **Rest Rooms and Showers:** Yes. **Fuel:** No. **Propane:** No. **Internal Roads:** Gravel, in good condition. **RV Service:** No. **Market:** 7 mi. southwest in Rochester. **Restaurant:** 7 mi. southwest in Rochester. **General Store:** Yes, limited. **Vending:** No. **Swimming Pool:** No. **Playground:** Yes. **Other:** Barr Lake, swimming beach, mini-golf, pavilion, volleyball, basketball, hiking trails, rec hall, badminton, sports field, fish-cleaning house. **Activities:** Swimming, fishing, boating (rental rowboats, canoes, paddleboats available), hiking, scheduled weekend activities. **Nearby Attractions:** Golf, outlet stores, Rounds Barn Museum, Fulton County Museum, antiques, Living History Village. **Additional Information:** Fulton County Historical Society, (219) 223-4436.

Restrictions

Pets: Leash only. **Fires:** Fire ring only. **Alcoholic Beverages:** Permitted. **Vehicle Maximum Length:** None.

To Get There

From junction of Hwy. 31 and Hwy. 14, drive 6.5 mi. east on Hwy. 14 to Athens, then 3 mi. north on CR 650E, then 1 mi. east on CR 300N. Roads are wide and well maintained with broad shoulders.

ROSELAWN

Oak Lake Family Campground

5310 East 900 North, Fair Oaks 47943. T: (219) 345-3153

RV ★★★ Tent n/a

Beauty: ★★	Site Privacy: ★★
Spaciousness: ★★	Quiet: ★★★
Security: ★★★★	Cleanliness: ★★★
Insect Control: Yes	Facilities: ★★★

Located on the outskirts of Roselawn, Indiana, Oak Lake Family Campground is an RV park only. Sites are mostly grassy and shady with a typical site width of 35 feet. The campground has 40 pull-throughs and 175 seasonal campers. The camp area is heavily wooded with oaks trees; wild roses, berries, and mushrooms decorate the grounds. For RV clubs, Oak Lake has two clusters of sites set around a central bonfire pit. A small lake offers fishing, a sandy beach for swimming, and a fun island with a footbridge. Limited supplies are available at the camp store which also offers a small gift shop and lending library. Fast-food items include hot sandwiches and pizza and, in season, fresh farm vegetables. Security measures include a locked laundry room (key is available at office), owners who live on site and provide regular patrols, and a security gate which is locked at night. Campers need a plastic entry card to enter the security gate.

Basics

Operated by: Paul & Allegra McCurtain. **Open:** Apr. 15–Oct. 15. **Site Assignment:** Reservations w/ 1-night deposit; refund w/ 7-day notice. **Registration:** At campground office. **Fee:** $24 (cash, check). **Parking:** At site.

Facilities

Number of RV Sites: 250. **Number of Tent-Only Sites:** 0. **Hookups:** Electric (30, 50 amps), water, sewer. **Each Site:** Picnic table, fire ring. **Dump Station:** Yes. **Laundry:** Yes. **Pay Phone:** Yes. **Rest Rooms and Showers:** Yes. **Fuel:** No. **Propane:** No. **Internal Roads:** Paved/gravel, in good condition. **RV Service:** Yes. **Market:** 1.5 mi. north in Roselawn. **Restaurant:** 1.5 mi. north in Roselawn. **General Store:** Yes, limited. **Vending:** Yes. **Swimming Pool:** No. **Playground:** Yes. **Other:** Oak Lake, swimming beach, hiking trails, island, footbridge, duck pond, baby animal pen, recreation building, rental cabins, badminton, volleyball, picnic shelter, pavilion, coin games. **Activities:** Swimming, fishing, hiking, scheduled weekend activities. **Nearby Attractions:** Indiana Beach, museums, historic sites, antiques, golf, arts & crafts shops. **Additional Information:** North Newton Chamber of Commerce, (219) 345-2525.

Restrictions

Pets: Leash only. **Fires:** Fire ring only. **Alcoholic Beverages:** At sites only. **Vehicle Maximum Length:** 40 ft.

To Get There

From junction of I-65 and Hwy. 10, take Exit 230 (Roselawn) exit, drive 0.25 mi. west on CR 900N. Roads are wide and well maintained with broad shoulders.

SANTA CLAUS

Lake Rudolph Campground & RV Resort

78 North Holiday Blvd., Santa Claus 47579. T: (877) 478-3657; F: (812) 937-4470; www.lakerudolph.com.

RV ★★★★ Tent ★★★★

Beauty: ★★★	Site Privacy: ★★★
Spaciousness: ★★★	Quiet: ★★★
Security: ★★★★	Cleanliness: ★★★★
Insect Control: None	Facilities: ★★★★

A touch of Christmas lives year-round at Lake Rudolph Campground & RV Resort. Located in the small Indiana town of Santa Claus, Lake Rudolph got its name from, of course, the famed red-nosed reindeer. Sections of the two big loops are named Dasher, Kringer, and Prancer. Next door to Holiday World Theme Park & Splashin' Safari Water Park, the campground is a summertime favorite with folks who like to be a free shuttle ride or a ten-minute walk from their campsite and the amusement park. The spacious, forested campground with its southern Indiana hills features beautiful fall foliage and a quieter refuge when the theme park starts closing down after Labor Day. The best sites for RVs are 2, 11, 17, 35, 37, 39, and 92 in the Dasher section because they are easier to back in (no pull-through sites are available). Sites have gravel pads with a grassy area; no two lots are the same. Tenters favor sites 125–130 in the Dasher section for the huge pine, maple and oak trees. Though open all year, the freezing temperatures, snow, and lack of on-site water make Lake Rudolph a good-weather option for all but the most hardy—or those who want to experience Santa Claus in his true element.

Basics

Operated by: Koch Development Corp. **Open:** All year. **Site Assignment:** Reservations w/ 1-night deposit; refunds w/ 48-hour notice, 10-day notice on RV & cabin rentals. **Registration:** At campground headquarters. **Fee:** $20 (credit cards, cash), $75 for cabin, $59 for RV rental. **Parking:** At sites or at headquarters parking lot.

Facilities

Number of RV Sites: 200. **Number of Tent-Only Sites:** 50. **Hookups:** Electric (30, 50 amps), water, sewer. **Each Site:** Fire ring, picnic table. **Dump Station:** Yes. **Laundry:** Yes. **Pay Phone:** Yes. **Rest Rooms and Showers:** Yes. **Fuel:** No. **Propane:** Yes. **Internal Roads:** Paved, in good condition. **RV Service:** No. **Market:** 0.25 mi. west in Santa Claus. **Restaurant:** 0.25 mi. west in Santa Claus. **General Store:** Yes. **Vending:** Yes. **Swimming Pool:** Yes. **Playground:** Yes. **Other:** Game room, billiard room, basketball, horseshoes, volleyball, nature trail, fishing lake, mini-golf, free shuttle to Holiday World Theme Park & Splashin' Safari Water Park, cabin rentals, RV rentals. **Activities:** Fishing, bingo, occasional cookouts, special Halloween weekends w/ hayrides & other activities. **Nearby Attractions:** Holiday World Theme Park & Splashin' Safari Water Park, golf, Santa Claus post office, Lincoln Boyhood National Memorial, caves, Lincoln State Park, Young Abe Lincoln Outdoor Drama. **Additional Information:** Santa Claus–Lincoln City Area Visitors Bureau, (800) GO-SANTA.

Restrictions

Pets: Leash only (not in rentals). **Fires:** Fire rings & grills only. **Alcoholic Beverages:** At sites only. **Vehicle Maximum Length:** 40 ft. **Other:** Rentals 2-night min. stay, holiday weekends 3-day min. stay.

To Get There

Take Exit 63 off I-64, travel 7 mi. south on SR 162, turn right at Holiday World parking lot, then go 200 yards and turn right into campgrounds. Roads are wide and well maintained.

SOUTH BEND

South Bend East KOA Camping Resort

50707 Princess Way, Granger 46530. T: (219) 277-1335; www.southbendeastkoa.com; marshkoa@aol.com.

RV ★★★★ Tent ★★★★

Beauty: ★★★★	Site Privacy: ★★★★
Spaciousness: ★★★★	Quiet: ★★★★
Security: ★★★★★	Cleanliness: ★★★★★
Insect Control: None	Facilities: ★★★★

Little touches add up to some pleasing results at the South Bend KOA Camping Resort in the town of Granger, Indiana. Pink rose bushes are planted to help conceal a propane tank, framed pictures and artificial flowers brighten the restrooms, and clean, private shower rooms have lights that turn on when the door is closed. An urban campground with level shaded sites, the facility has no seasonal campers, 40 pull-throughs and a typical site width of 24 feet. The rec room is modem friendly for computer users. A five mph speed limit is enforced for safety and to prevent vehicles from kicking up dust. Security measures include owners who live on site, a traffic control gate, and surveillance cameras. A list of campground guidelines is nicely worded with more than a list of the usual "no's." Instead, the campground requests that "we don't want any of our trees or guests strangled, so please no clotheslines." If campers are not satisfied within one hour of check in, registration fees are refunded.

Basics

Operated by: Terry & Beverlee Marsh. **Open:** Mar. 15–Nov. 15. **Site Assignment:** Reservations w/ 1-night deposit; refund w/ 7-day notice. **Registration:** At campground office. **Fee:** $30 (cash, check, credit cards). **Parking:** At site.

Facilities

Number of RV Sites: 88. **Number of Tent-Only Sites:** 12. **Hookups:** Electric (30, 50 amps), water, sewer, cable TV. **Each Site:** Picnic table, fire ring. **Dump Station:** Yes. **Laundry:** Yes. **Pay Phone:** Yes. **Rest Rooms and Showers:** Yes. **Fuel:** No. **Propane:** Yes. **Internal Roads:** Paved/gravel, in good condition. **RV Service:** No. **Market:** Two blocks in Granger. **Restaurant:** Two blocks in Granger. **General Store:** Yes. **Vending:** Yes. **Swimming Pool:** Yes. **Playground:** Yes. **Other:** Game room, basketball, volleyball, horseshoes, mini-golf, nature trail, rental cabins, pavilion w/ kitchen, coin games, badminton, sports field, adults room. **Activities:** Swimming, hiking, scheduled weekend activities. **Nearby Attractions:** College Football Hall of Fame, golf, Studebaker National Museum, Notre Dame University, zoo, Amish acres, RV museum, Shipshewana Flea Market, antiques, St. Mary's College, historic homes. **Additional Information:** South Bend/Mishawaka CVB, (800) 282-2330.

Restrictions

Pets: Leash only. **Fires:** Fire ring only. **Alcoholic Beverages:** Permitted. **Vehicle Maximum Length:** None.

To Get There

From junction of I-80/90 (Indiana Turnpike), take Exit 83 and drive 0.5 mi. to Hwy. 23, then 2 mi. north on Hwy. 23, then 0.3 mi. north on Princess Way. Roads are wide and well maintained with broad shoulders.

THORNTOWN

Old Mill Run Park

8544 West 690 North, Thorntown 46071. T: (765) 436-7190; www.frontiernet.net/~oldmill; oldmill@frontiernet.net.

RV ★★★★ Tent ★★★★

Beauty: ★★★★	Site Privacy: ★★★★
Spaciousness: ★★★★	Quiet: ★★★★
Security: ★★★★	Cleanliness: ★★★★
Insect Control: Yes	Facilities: ★★★★

Little touches like coordinated wallpaper in the bathrooms, an entrance way decorated with day lilies, and a mill water fountain make this campground stand out. Mature trees and newly planted ones are mingled to ensure future shade. Campers have a choice of open or shaded areas and mostly pull-through sites. Laid out in a series of loops, Old Mill Run Camp has 197 seasonal campers and a separate section for tents. The average site width is 35 feet and sites are mostly grassy with patios. As a family campground located one mile west of Thorntown, Old Mill doesn't allow alcohol at any activities or facilities, including walking around the park with it. Quiet hours are 11 p.m. to 7 a.m. Clotheslines are not permitted in the park, nor are mopeds, four-wheelers, or motorized bikes. Electric golf carts are permitted for seasonal campers age 21 and up. The best RV sites are 216–248 because they are bigger, offer cable TV, and cement pads. The best tent sites are P13–P24 because they are behind the pond and provide more greenspace and privacy. A security patrol, an owner who lives on site, and one entrance/exit to the campground help assure campers' safety.

Basics

Operated by: Ralph & Sandy Christman. **Open:** Apr. 1–Oct. 15. **Site Assignment:** Reservations w/ no deposit. **Registration:** At campground office. **Fee:** $24 (cash, check, credit card). **Parking:** At site.

Facilities

Number of RV Sites: 347. **Number of Tent-Only Sites:** 25. **Hookups:** Electric (30 amps), water, sewer, cable TV, phone. **Each Site:** Picnic table, fire ring. **Dump Station:** Yes. **Laundry:** Yes. **Pay Phone:** Yes. **Rest Rooms and Showers:** Yes. **Fuel:** No. **Propane:** Yes. **Internal Roads:** Gravel/paved, in good condition. **RV Service:** No. **Market:** 9 mi. east in Lebanon. **Restaurant:** 1 mi. east in Thorntown. **General Store:** Yes. **Vending:** No. **Swimming Pool:** Yes. **Playground:** Yes. **Other:** Mini-golf, horseshoes, rental cabin, rally area, shelter house, 2 fishing ponds, hot tub, 5-hole golf course, basketball, volleyball, shuffleboard, Sugar Creek, coin games, sports field, badminton. **Activities:** Swimming, fishing, scheduled activities, Sunday church services. **Nearby Attractions:** Indianapolis Zoo, Children's Museum, Indianapolis Motor Speedway, antiques, museums, historic sites. **Additional Information:** Boone County Chamber of Commerce, (765) 482-1320.

Restrictions

Pets: Leash only. **Fires:** Fire ring only. **Alcoholic Beverages:** At sites only. **Vehicle Maximum Length:** None. **Other:** Limit of 6 fish per day.

To Get There

From I-65W, take Exit 146, drive 6.5 mi. west on Hwy. 47, then 1 mi. north on CR 825W. Roads are wide and well maintained with broad shoulders.

VERSAILLES

Versailles State Park

Box 205, US 50, Versailles 47042. T: (812) 689-6424; www.state.in.us/dnr.

RV ★★★ Tent ★★★

Beauty: ★★★★	Site Privacy: ★★★
Spaciousness: ★★★	Quiet: ★★★
Security: ★★★★	Cleanliness: ★★★★
Insect Control: None	Facilities: ★★★

At 5,905 acres, Versailles State Park is the second largest state park in Indiana. It also has the second busiest state park swimming pool, a 25-meter pool with a 100-foot waterslide. In peak summer time, the park, campgrounds, and pool are overrun with visitors. Hillsides with limestone outcroppings, ravines, upland wooded areas, fields, and a 230-acre lake help make this one of the state's prettiest parks. Oct. is a peak time for fall foliage, as well as the annual Bluegrass Festival. At the entrance to the park, you can drive over Busching Bridge, one of the two remaining covered bridges in Ripley County. Located two miles east of Versailles, Indiana, the park is one of the few state parks to offer horseback riding. The horseback trails are open year-round but the saddle barn is open only Apr. through Oct. The park also has more than six miles of scenic hiking trails marked for skilled and beginning hikers. All camping sites will accommodate both RVs and tents. Security measures are strict with passes needed to enter the campground; the area is patrolled by rangers.

Basics

Operated by: Indiana Dept. of Natural Resources. **Open:** All year. **Site Assignment:** Written reservations w/ 1-night deposit, no refunds. **Registration:** At campground office. **Fee:** $12 (check, credit cards). **Parking:** At site.

Facilities

Number of RV Sites: 226. **Number of Tent-Only Sites:** 0. **Hookups:** Electric (30 amps). **Each Site:** Picnic table, fire ring. **Dump Station:** Yes. **Laundry:** No. **Pay Phone:** Yes. **Rest Rooms and Showers:** Yes. **Fuel:** No. **Propane:** No. **Internal Roads:** Paved, in good condition. **RV Service:** No. **Market:** 2 mi. west in Vincennes. **Restaurant:** 2 mi. west in Vincennes. **General Store:** Yes. **Vending:** Yes. **Swimming Pool:** Yes. **Playground:** Yes. **Other:** Boat ramp (only electric trolling motors permitted), nature center, picnic shelters. **Activities:** Hiking, fishing, boating (rental rowboats, paddleboats, & canoes available), summer weekday programs, nature walks & evening activities offered by naturalist. **Nearby Attractions:** Scenic drives, 27-mi. Hoosier Hills Bicycle Route, golf, Ripley County Historical Society. **Additional Information:** Ripley County Tourism Bureau, (888) 747-3827.

Restrictions

Pets: Leash only. **Fires:** Fire rings & grills only. **Alcoholic Beverages:** At sites only. **Vehicle Maximum Length:** 35 ft. **Other:** 14-day stay limit.

To Get There

From junction of US 421 and US 50, drive 1 mi. east on US 50. Roads are wide and well maintained with adequate shoulders.

Iowa

If the state of Iowa registers at all to non-residents, it comes across as an endless field of corn where little, other than farming, ever happens. And yet, to view the Hawkeye state solely in this light is to ignore the many cultural and historical contributions Iowa has made to the nation. The 31st president of the United States (Herbert Hoover) was born here, as was famous TV personality Johnny Carson. Other notable Iowans include Grant Wood, Glenn Miller, and Ann Landers.

Before Europeans settled in Iowa, a number of Native American tribes livend in the area, including the Sauk, Mesquakie, Sioux, Potawatomi, Otoe, and Missouri, and before them, pre-historic ancestors roamed along the banks of the Mississippi. In 1673, the French explorers Louis Joliet and Father Jacques Marquette were the first Europeans to set foot in Iowa. As in other parts of the United States, pioneers soon came flooding into the state, displacing its native populations. Despite the lack of trees, pioneers remained to discover a land with exceedingly rich soil.

As settlement proceeded, Iowa became a melting pot of cultures. Between 1860 and 1870, the population nearly doubled due to an influx of immigrants. Germans were the largest group of immigrants and could be found in every county in the state. Iowa also became home for many other nationalities, including Swedes, Norwegians, Danes, Dutch, Czechs, Italians, and Croatians. Most of these people came to farm, but, interestingly, a thriving coal industry also emerged, once making Iowa the major coal producer for the U.S.

The state has had its share of hard times. The coal industry collapsed in the early 1900s, leaving many towns deserted, and the stock market crash of 1929 led to many farmers losing their land. In spite of these setbacks, the citizens and the economy of Iowa ultimately prospered: the state is today the number one producer of corn and pork in the country.

Visitors to Iowa will find much to enjoy, including historic frontier forts, authentic American farms, and culturally rich cities.

In the southeast corner of the state, near **Cedar Rapids** (the second largest city), campers can visit the **Amana Colonies,** founded 150 years ago by Germans seeking religious freedom. Other sites include **Ushers Ferry Historic Village,** the **National Czech and Slovak Museum,** and the **Indian Creek Nature Center,** which has more than 11 miles of trails. About 50 miles away in **Davenport,** visitors can see the **Davenport Museum of Art's Grant Wood** collection as well as the **Adler Theater,** once part of the RKO theater chain. Outdoor enthusiasts will admire the many opportunities offered by the **Upper Mississippi River National Wildlife and Fish Refuge,** which runs along the state's eastern border.

The northeast section of Iowa stands in sharp contrast to the rest of the state. Instead of rolling hills and farmlands, this region, often referred to as **"Little Switzerland,"** has large forested swaths of land amidst its rugged geography. Outdoor enthusiasts will find much to do here, including paddling opportunities on the **Turkey, Upper Iowa,** and **Volga Rivers.** The access to the Mississippi also made this a valuable location for prehistoric Native Americans, as visitors will discover at the **Effigy Mounds National Monument.** For travellers seeking more cosmopolitan fare, **Cedar Falls/Waterloo** hosts many festivals, including the **Cedar Basin Jazz Festival** and **College Hill Arts Festival.**

Though lacking in major metropolitan areas, northwest Iowa has plenty to offer. There are numerous state parks and recreation areas within the Natural Lakes region, which was shaped by glacial activity thousands of years ago. **Gull Point State Park** and the **Lost Island Prairie Wetland Nature Center** are two recommended sites. Most winter outdoor activities center around cross-country skiing or snowmobile riding, but during the summer, visitors should seek out the **Inkpaduta Canoe Trail,** which follows the meandering **Little Sioux River.**

One of the richest regions in the state, the **Loess Hills,** is located in the southwest section of the state. Those wanting to see what the Iowa landscape looked like before European settlement should visit **Neal Smith National Wildlife Reserve,** where tall-grass prairie is being reintroduced along with natural herds of buffalo and other critters. The capital also offers numerous options for fun and recreation, including the **Des Moines Art Center** and the **Historic Jordan House.**

ADEL

Des Moines West KOA

3418 L Ave., Adel 50003. T: (515) 834-2729 or (800) KOA-2181; www.koa.com.

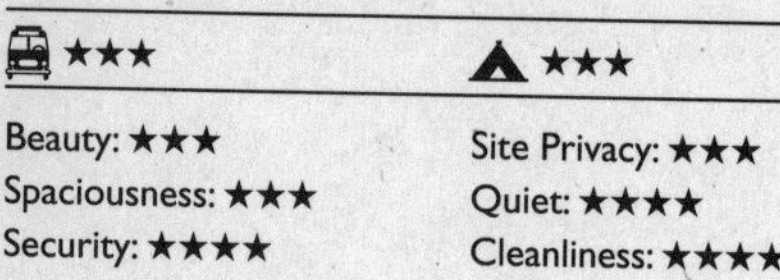

★★★ ▲★★★

Beauty: ★★★ Site Privacy: ★★★
Spaciousness: ★★★ Quiet: ★★★★
Security: ★★★★ Cleanliness: ★★★★
Insect Control: ★★★ Facilities: ★★★

Seventeen miles outside Des Moines and conveniently located directly off I-80 is the West Des Moines KOA. This KOA offers its patrons full amenities, a separate tent area, and all pull-through sites. Each site is has a level parking area and a small grass lawn. The campground is nicely landscaped and offers some shade. Hot coffee is served daily, just in time for an early morning dip in the pool. The area is rich in history, with numerous places to visit such as the Blank Park Zoo, the botanical center, and the now-famous bridges of Madison County. The staff is friendly and helpful, and the park offers excellent security. The park is open year round, but remember to pack according to the season; Iowa is bitterly cold and windy in the winter.

Basics

Operated By: Howard & Katie Hudson. **Open:** Year round. **Site Assignment:** By reservation w/ credit card. **Registration:** In camp store. **Fee:** Tent $16, RV $18–$26; fee covers 2 people, $2. per additional guest, children under 5 free. **Parking:** At site.

Facilities

Number of RV-Only Sites: 110. **Number of Tent-Only Sites:** 70. **Hookups:** Electric (20, 30, 50 amps), water, sewer. **Each Site:** Picnic table. **Dump Station:** Yes. **Laundry:** Yes. **Pay Phone:** Yes. **Rest Rooms and Showers:** Yes. **Fuel:** No, in Adel or West Des Moines. **Propane:** No. **Internal Roads:** Paved, in good condition. **RV Service:** In West Des Moines. **Market:** 10 mi. in Castana, IA. **Restaurant:** In West Des Moines. **General Store:** Yes. **Vending:** No. **Swimming Pool:** Yes. **Playground:** Yes. **Other:** Cabins, fishing pond. **Activities:** Fishing, swimming, horseshoes. **Nearby Attractions:** Living History Farms, State Capitol, John Wayne birthplace, Blank Park Zoo, botanical center, art & science center. Valley West Mall. **Additional Information:** West Des Moines Chamber of Commerce, (515) 225-6009.

Restrictions

Pets: On leash. **Fires:** No open fires. **Alcoholic Beverages:** Allowed. **Vehicle Maximum Length:** None. **Other:** $2 extra to run heat or a/c.

To Get There

From I-80 Exit 106, go north 1 mi. on paved CR P-58.

CEDAR FALLS

Black Hawk Park

2410 West Lone Tree Rd., Cedar Falls 50613. T: (319) 266-6813 or 266-0328; F: (319) 277-1536; www.co.black-hawk.ia.us/depts/conservation.html; conservation@co.black-hawk.ia.us.

★★★★ ▲★★★★

Beauty: ★★★★ Site Privacy: ★★★
Spaciousness: ★★★ Quiet: ★★★★
Security: ★★★★ Cleanliness: ★★★
Insect Control: ★★★ Facilities: ★★

Named after Chief Black Hawk of the Sauk Indian Tribe, Black Hawk Park is one of the largest county parks in the state. The park is part of a conservation area over 1,300 acres in size with a 142-site modern campground, complete with rest room facilities and showers. The sites are comfortable and well shaded by mature oak and other hardwoods. The park roads are paved and there are large sites, both pull-throughs and back-ins. Activities here include archery, a rifle range, and public hunting and fishing. There are even boat ramps. A full-time residential staff person and a host family are available to assist campers. The natural setting is a combination of woodland and prairie with a constant breeze.

Basics

Operated By: Black Hawk County Conservation Board. **Open:** All year, weather permitting. **Site Assignment:** First come, first served & a small number of sites by reservation. **Registration:** Registration kiosk. **Fee:** $10–$13. **Parking:** At site.

Facilities

Number of Multipurpose Sites: 142. **Hookups:** Electric (20, 30, 50 amps), water. **Each Site:** Picnic table, fire pit. **Dump Station:** Yes. **Laundry:** No. **Pay Phone:** Yes. **Rest Rooms and Showers:** Yes. **Fuel:** No, in Cedar Falls. **Propane:** No, in Cedar Falls. **Internal Roads:** Paved, in good condition. **RV Service:** In Cedar Falls. **Market:** In Cedar Falls. **Restaurant:** In Cedar Falls. **General Store:** No. **Vending:** No. **Swimming Pool:** No. **Playground:** Yes. **Other:** 2 cabins, primitive camping, picnic shelters. **Activities:** Recreation trails, boating, rifle & pistol range, archery range, hunting, fishing, water activities, winter activities, ice fishing. **Nearby Attractions:** Sturgis Falls Celebrations, University of Northern Iowa Museum, the Grout Museums, Cedar Valley Nature Trail. **Additional Information:** Cedar Falls Chamber, (319) 266-3593.

Restrictions

Pets: On leash. **Fires:** Fire pits only. **Alcoholic Beverages:** Allowed. **Vehicle Max. Length:** 45 ft.

To Get There

From Cedar Falls where US 218 and SR 58 meet, go north a little more than 1.7 mi. Turn left on East Lone Tree Rd and continue about 2.5 mi. to the campground.

CLEAR LAKE

Clear Lake State Park

2730 South Lakeview Dr., Clear Lake 50428. T: (515) 357-4212; F: (515) 357-4242; www.state.ia.us/parks; clear_lake@dnr.state.ia.us.

★★★ ▲★★★

Beauty: ★★★ Site Privacy: ★★
Spaciousness: ★★ Quiet: ★★★
Security: ★★★★ Cleanliness: ★★★
Insect Control: ★★★ Facilities: ★★

Located on the southeast shores of Clear Lake, this state park offers a verity of outdoor activities and is considered one of Northern Iowa's premiere recreation areas. The campground has over 215 sites in a series of loops surrounded by mature oaks and smaller vegetation. The park offers both pull-throughs and back-ins with level trailer pads, as well as modern rest rooms and showers. Clear Lake State Park offers a sandy beach perfect for swimming and tanning, along with many other water activities, all only a short walk for the main campground area. A large variety of fish can be caught in the lake, including walleye, catfish, and northern pike. Iowa's four distinct seasons include hot, dry summers, but it is never a bad idea to pack a rain jacket; sun screen and bug spray are imperitive. There is an entrance fee and camping permits are granted through self registration.

Basics

Operated By: Iowa Department of Natural Resources. **Open:** All year. **Site Assignment:** First come, first served. **Registration:** Self-registration at entrance gate. **Fee:** $16 w/ hookups, $11 no hookups. **Parking:** At site.

Facilities

Number of Multipurpose Sites: 215. **Hookups:** Electric (20, 30 amps). **Each Site:** Picnic table, grated fire pits. **Dump Station:** Yes. **Laundry:** No. **Pay Phone:** Yes. **Rest Rooms and Showers:** Yes. **Fuel:** At marina. **Propane:** At marina. **Internal Roads:** Paved, in good condition. **RV Service:** 10 mi. east in Mason City. **Market:** In Clear Lake or Mason City. **Restaurant:** In Clear Lake or Mason City. **General Store:** No, at nearby private marina. **Vending:** No, at nearby private marina. **Swimming Pool:** No. **Playground:** Yes. **Other:** Lodge w/ kitchen & rustic fireplace, enclosed picnic shelters, 900-ft. sandy beach. **Activities:** Fishing, boating, jetskiing, waterskiing, wind surfing, swimming, hiking, biking, cross-country skiing, snowmobiling, & ice sailing. **Nearby Attractions:** Iowa Trolley Park, shopping. **Additional Information:** Mason City Chamber of Commerce, (641) 423-5724.

Restrictions

Pets: Dogs on leash only, see web site for rules on horses & mules. **Fires:** In fire rings only. **Alcoholic Beverages:** At sites, beer & wine only. **Vehicle Maximum Length:** None. **Other:** No metal detectors in campground, max. 6 people per site.

To Get There

From I-35 Exit 193, take SR 106 (4th Ave. S.) west, turn left on S. Shore Dr., right onto 26th Ave. S., and left onto S. Lakeview Dr.

CLEAR LAKE

Oakwood RV Park

541 240th St., Clear Lake 50428. T: (641) 357-4019

★★★ ▲ n/a

Beauty: ★★★ Site Privacy: ★★
Spaciousness: ★★ Quiet: ★★★★
Security: ★★★★ Cleanliness: ★★★
Insect Control: ★★★ Facilities: ★★

Only a short drive from Clear Lake, Oakwood RV Park is ideal for visitors with large and long RVs. Campsites each have a gravel parking pad, a small lawn (some much larger than others), and many have a concrete patio with a picnic table. The campground offers full hookups with lockable rest room and shower facilities. As a result of an expansion, the two camping areas sit side by side, and the entire park backs up to a large corn field. There is a delightful small white church next door. However, this campground does have some strange regulations, and only accepts campers on reservations. There is no tent camping allowed, with or without an RV. The weather is warm in the summer and the grounds offer little shade. Campers are permitted one tow, and Clear Lake is a wonderful vacation spot to fish and boat.

Basics

Operated By: Bob & Lee Speakar. **Open:** All year. **Site Assignment:** By reservation, all charges are payable in advance. **Registration:** Camp office. **Fee:** $15 per two people, a $2 daily charge for extra people. **Parking:** At site.

Facilities

Number of RV-Only Sites: 68. **Number of Tent-Only Sites:** 0. **Hookups:** Electric (30, 50 amps), water, sewer, phone. **Each Site:** Picnic table, some fire pits. **Dump Station:** Yes. **Laundry:** Yes. **Pay Phone:** Yes. **Rest Rooms and Showers:** Yes. **Fuel:** No. **Propane:** Yes, but delivered on Friday's only. **Internal Roads:** Gravel, in fair condition. **RV Service:** 10.5 mi. in Mason City. **Market:** In Clear Lake. **Restaurant:** In Clear Lake. **General Store:** No. **Vending:** Yes. **Swimming Pool:** No. **Playground:** Yes. **Other:** Some concrete patios, rally room, game room, firewood sold. **Activities:** Games, hiking. **Nearby Attractions:** Fire museum, trolley tours, fishing, boating, golf. **Additional Information:** Clear Lake Chamber, (641) 357-2159.

Restrictions

Pets: On leash only, no pets over 30 lbs. **Fires:** In fire pits only. **Alcoholic Beverages:** Allowed. **Vehicle Maximum Length:** Will accommodate very large RVs. **Other:** All RVs must be a 1987 model or newer & are subject to managers approval; firearms & firecrackers prohibited; no tent camping.

To Get There

From I-35 take Exit 193 south, merge onto SR 106 (4th Ave. S), go a little more than 1 mi. and turn left onto S. Shore Dr. Veer right, go another 0.5 mi. and turn left on 240th St. Look for campground.

CLERMONT

Skip-A-Way

3825 Harding Rd., Clermont 52135. T: (800) 728-1167; F: (563) 423-5239; www.gocamping.com/skipaway.

★★★★ ★★★

Beauty: ★★	Site Privacy: ★★
Spaciousness: ★★	Quiet: ★★★
Security: ★★★	Cleanliness: ★★★
Insect Control: ★★★	Facilities: ★★★★

With a little imagination and some foresight, Skip and Bev Baker have created a camper's playground at Skip-A-Way Resort. The hosts' aim, to make your stay comfortable and fun, is accomplished by providing a full range of amenities and a number of family and community activities. Enjoy a round of miniature golf, a game of Norwegian horseshoes, or a leisurely float down the Turkey River after an afternoon of fishing on Quarry Lake. Saturday evenings can be spent in the lodge watching a movie with other campers or bouncing through the campground on a wagon ride. Other scheduled events change each year and may include anything from square dancing to eating contests. For a truly unusual experience, spend a night in the rustic 1800s log cabin that is available for rent. With an eye for improvement, the owners continue to upgrade their campground with new landscaping, fresh paint, and added sites, making it increasingly popular. While walk-ins are welcome, it is best to reserve a site early, especially on holiday weekends. Certainly, the highlight of a stay here is the hosts eagerness to help guests have fun.

Basics

Operated By: Skip & Bev Baker. **Open:** May 1–Oct. 15. **Site Assignment:** Reservations taken. **Registration:** Call for reservations, otherwise at lodge. **Fee:** $14–$21. **Parking:** At site.

Facilities

Number of RV-Only Sites: 77. **Number of Tent-Only Sites:** 6. **Hookups:** Electric (20, 30, 50 amps), water, sewer. **Each Site:** None. **Dump Station:** Yes. **Laundry:** Yes. **Pay Phone:** Yes. **Rest Rooms and Showers:** Yes. **Fuel:** No. **Propane:** No. **Internal Roads:** Gravel. **RV Service:** Yes. **Market:** No. **Restaurant:** Yes. **General Store:** Yes. **Vending:** No. **Swimming Pool:** Yes. **Playground:** Yes. **Other:** Lake and river access. **Activities:** Mini golf, fishing (need license on river, but not for lake), swimming, boating, weekend movies. **Nearby Attractions:** 1800s log cabin for rent, Echo Valley Speedway.

Restrictions

Pets: On leash. **Fires:** In fire rings only. **Alcoholic Beverages:** Allowed. **Vehicle Maximum Length:** Call for limits.

To Get There

From Hwy. 18, take Exit 3825.The campground is visible from the road.

DAVENPORT

Interstate RV Park

8448 North Fairmont, Davenport 52806. T: (563) 386-7292 or (888) 387-6573; F: (563) 386-7299; www.gocampingamerica.com/interstatervia/; interstatervia@gocampingamerica.com.

★★★ ★★

Beauty: ★★★	Site Privacy: ★★
Spaciousness: ★★	Quiet: ★★★★
Security: ★★★	Cleanliness: ★★★★
Insect Control: ★★★	Facilities: ★★★

Interstate RV Park is conveniently located for anyone wishing to visit the Davenport Metropolitan area. Wthin the city limits, this campground offers a full range of amenities. There are close to 100 sites, 15 of which are considered super sites, with extra parking space and 50-amp service (sites 80–97). The campground offers several activities, a large pool, and a gift shop. Interstate RV Park is next door to restaurants, fuel, and a large water park. Campsite's each have a gravel parking pad and light post, but some are tightly arranged, with little grass or shade. However, the grounds are well maintained. This campground is ideal for visitors wishing to see area attractions. The weather can be very warm in Davenport during the summer, and windy, so skin protection is a good idea. The office is staffed daily to assist campers.

Basics

Operated By: Private operator. **Open:** All year. **Site Assignment:** By reservation, credit card required for deposit. **Registration:** In office or drop box. **Fee:** $20–$25 for 2 people, additional adults are $3 each, children $2. **Parking:** At site.

Facilities

Number of RV-Only Sites: 98. **Number of Tent-Only Sites:** 0. **Hookups:** Electric (20, 30, 50 amps), water, sewer. **Each Site:** Picnic table, light posts. **Dump Station:** Yes. **Laundry:** Yes. **Pay Phone:** Yes. **Rest Rooms and Showers:** Yes. **Fuel:** No, next door. **Propane:** Yes. **Internal Roads:** Gravel, in good condition. **RV Service:** In Davenport. **Market:** In Davenport. **Restaurant:** In walking distance or in Davenport. **General Store:** Yes. **Vending:** Yes. **Swimming Pool:** Yes, open June–Aug. **Playground:** Yes. **Other:** Enclosed group pavilion, dataport. **Activities:** Horseshoes, swimming. **Nearby Attractions:** Quad City Botanical Center, District Rock Island, several malls, President Casino, golf, Family Museum of Art. **Additional Information:** Davenport Chamber of Commerce, (563) 322-1706.

Restrictions

Pets: On leash. **Fires:** In fire pits only. **Alcoholic Beverages:** Allowed. **Vehicle Maximum Length:** None. **Other:** Good Sam honored.

To Get There

I-80 Exit 292, bear right on Northwest Blvd, then turn right onto the ramp and left onto N. Pine Street. Go 1.1 mi., turn right onto W. 49th St., then right on to N. Fairmount.

GUTHRIE

Springbrook State Park

2437 160th Rd., Guthrie Center 50115. T: (641) 747-3591; F: (641)747-3957; www.state.ia.us/parks/springbr.htm; springbrook@dnr.state.ia.us.

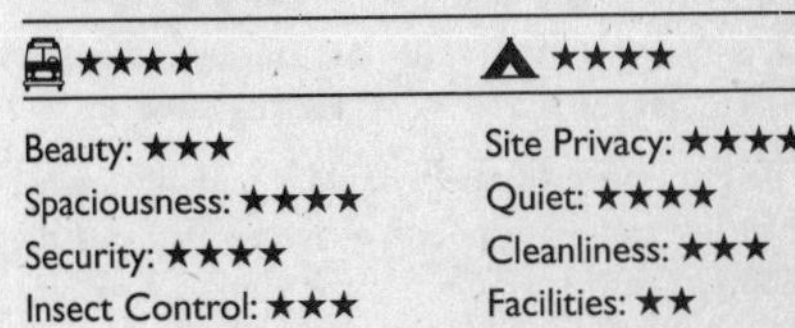

★★★★ ★★★★

Beauty: ★★★	Site Privacy: ★★★★
Spaciousness: ★★★★	Quiet: ★★★★
Security: ★★★★	Cleanliness: ★★★
Insect Control: ★★★	Facilities: ★★

If you're a serious outdoorsman, this park will suit your needs well. Operated by the Iowa Department of Natural Resources, it is open all year and is well maintained. The sites for both RVs and tents are very nice, being spacious, private, and quiet. Some of the RV sites have electric and water hookups, and all of the sites are equipped with a picnic table and grated fire pit. Activities within the park include fishing, boating, and hiking. There is also swimming, biking, water skiing and wind surfing in the summer. Nearby, visitors will find a golf course and river fishing. Reservations are not required.

Basics

Operated By: Iowa Department of Natural Resources. **Open:** All year. **Site Assignment:** First come, first served. **Registration:** Self-registration at entrance gate. **Fee:** $9-19 depending on site & hookups. **Parking:** At site.

Facilities

Number of RV-Only Sites: 81. **Number of Tent-Only Sites:** 0. **Number of Multipurpose Sites:** 40. **Hookups:** Electric (20, 30 amps), water. **Each Site:** Picnic table, grated fire pits. **Dump Station:** Yes. **Laundry:** No. **Pay Phone:** Yes. **Rest Rooms and Showers:** Yes. **Fuel:** In town. **Propane:** In town. **Internal Roads:** Paved, in good condition. **RV Service:** In Des Moines. **Market:** In Guthrie. **Restaurant:** There are several in the area. **General Store:** No. **Vending:** No. **Swimming Pool:** No, but there is a lake front beach. **Playground:** Yes. **Other:** 6 cabins, enclosed picnic shelters, boat ramps, boat rentals, beach, fishing dock, large group camp w/ kitchen, dinning hall, & meeting rooms. **Activities:** Fishing (walleye, muskie, yellow bass), boating, jet skiing, water skiing, wind surfing, swimming,miles of trails, in-line skating, hiking, biking in the summer. Part of The Central Iowa State Park Bike Route. **Nearby Attractions:** River fishing, golf. **Additional Information:** Panora Chamber of Commerce, (641) 755-3300.

Restrictions

Pets: Dogs on leash. **Fires:** In fire rings only. **Alcoholic Beverages:** Beer & wine only in sites. **Vehicle Maximum Length:** None. **Other:** No metal detectors in campground; max of 6 people to a site.

To Get There

From I-80 Exit 86 go north on SR 25 for about 20 mi.(you will go through Guthrie Center) and east on SR 384 about 3 mi. into park.

IOWA CITY

Colony Country Campground

1275 Forever green Rd., Iowa City 52240. T: (319) 626-2221; www.gocampingamerica.com/colonycountry.

RV ★★★★ Tent ★★★

Beauty: ★★★★	Site Privacy: ★★★
Spaciousness: ★★★	Quiet: ★★★★
Security: ★★★	Cleanliness: ★★★★
Insect Control: ★★★	Facilities: ★★

This family owned campground is centrally located to many east Iowa points of interest such as the Hoover Historical Site and the Amana Colonies. The staff is friendly and more than willing to provide helpful tips on which attractions are worth visiting. The grounds are well kept, with meticulously groomed gravel roads and flowered grassy plots throughout. Most sites are tight and may be difficult to maneuver for oversized rigs. Many sites provide both privacy and shade. With plenty of activities on site such as basketball, volleyball, and horseshoes, leisure time at Colony Country is relaxing and plentiful.

Basics

Operated By: Private Operator. **Open:** Apr.–Nov 30. **Site Assignment:** By reservations or first available. **Registration:** In camp store. **Fee:** Tent $15, RV $22 per 4 people. **Parking:** At site.

Facilities

Number of RV-Only Sites: 29. **Number of Tent-Only Sites:** 20. **Hookups:** Electric (20, 30, 50 amps), water, sewer. **Each Site:** Picnic table. **Dump Station:** Yes. **Laundry:** Yes. **Pay Phone:** Yes. **Rest Rooms and Showers:** Yes. **Fuel:** No. **Propane:** No. **Internal Roads:** Gravel, in good condition. **RV Service:** In town. **Market:** In town. **Restaurant:** There are many restaurants in town. **General Store:** Yes. **Vending:** Store only. **Swimming Pool:** Yes, w/ hot tub & sauna. **Playground:** Yes. **Other:** Cabins, hot tub, sauna, snack bar, central Internet data port. **Activities:** Basketball, volleyball, playground. **Nearby Attractions:** Hoover Historic Site, Amana Colonies, Kalona & Iowa City/Coralville area. **Additional Information:** Iowa City Chamber of Commerce, (319) 337-9637.

Restrictions

Pets: On leash. **Fires:** Grills only. **Alcoholic Beverages:** Allowed. **Vehicle Maximum Length:** Big rigs welcome.

To Get There

I-15 Exit 119 E. Go 0.1 mi. to Lindsay.

JOHNSTON

Saylorville Lake

5600 NorthWest 78th Ave., Johnston 50131. T: (515) 276-4656 or (515) 964-0672 or Daily Lake Info (515) 276-0433; www.mvr.usace.army.mil/saylor/index.htm; jerry.l.demarce@usace.army.mil (project manager).

RV ★★★★ Tent ★★★★

Beauty: ★★★★	Site Privacy: ★★★★
Spaciousness: ★★★★	Quiet: ★★★★
Security: ★★★	Cleanliness: ★★★
Insect Control: ★★★	Facilities: ★★★

Approximately, ten miles north of Des Moines is the US Army Corp of Engineers Saylorville Lake Project. This 5950 acre area is a wonderful recreation haven for outdoor enthusiast. It features five campgrounds with over 500 camping sites. Camping sites have level paved parking pads and there is a variety of amenities including full hook ups on some sites. Modern rest rooms and showers can be found in all the camping areas. There are over 25 miles of biking trails, in addition to hiking and cross country ski trails. Boating and fishing are amongst the favorite activities with the project offering a full service marina, repair, and fuel. There is a year round visitor center and camping reservations are recommended. The area is a combination of woodland and prairie, and all the campsites are well groomed. There is a registration gate at the entrance to each camping area staffed by seasonal volunteers or corp employees.

Basics

Operated By: US Army Corps of Engineers. **Open:** The park is open year round, the campgrounds are open May–Sept. **Site Assignment:** The park is 60% reservable, the remainder are first come first served. Call the National Recreation reservation service toll free (877) 444-6777. **Registration:** At the entrance gate, or the registration kiosk. **Fee:** $12–$24 based on day of the week & amenities. **Parking:** At site.

Facilities

Number of Multipurpose Sites: over 100 in each campground, 558 total. **Hookups:** Electric (20, 30, 50 amps), water, sewer. **Each Site:** Picnic table, paved trailer pad, fire pit. **Dump Station:** Yes. **Laundry:** No. **Pay Phone:** Yes. **Rest Rooms and Showers:** Yes. **Fuel:** No. **Propane:** No. **Internal Roads:** Paved, in good condition. **RV Service:** In Des Moines. **Market:** In Des Moines. **Restaurant:** In Des Moines. **General Store:** Yes. **Vending:** Yes. **Swimming Pool:** No, but there are two beaches. **Playground:** Yes. **Other:** Two beaches, three boat ramps, picnic shelters, scheduled activities. **Activities:** Softball, bike trails, hiking trails, fishing, volleyball, horseshoes, swimming, boating, waterskiing, jet skiing, playground, horse trails, golf, winter recreation, scheduled activities, & nature program. **Nearby Attractions:** state capital, Historical Museum, botanical center, Des Moines zoo, Des Moines Science Center. **Additional Information:** West Des Moines Chamber, (515) 225-6009.

Restrictions

Pets: On leash only (6 ft. maximum). **Fires:** In approved places only. **Alcoholic Beverages:** Yes, w/ discretion. **Vehicle Maximum Length:** 45 ft. **Other:** 50% discount w/ Golden Age or Golden Access passport.

To Get There

From I-35 Exit 96 go west on NE 126th Ave. for 7.2 mi., then turn left on NW Sheldahl Dr. Go 0.5 mi. and continue south on N. 3rd St.; 1 mi. later turn right on SR 415; go about 5 mi. and follow the signs to the park or visitors center.

KELLOGG

Kellogg RV Park

1570 Hwy. 224 South, P.O. Box 380, Kellogg 50135. T: (641) 526-8535; F: (641)526-8060.

RV ★★★ Tent n/a

Beauty: ★★★	Site Privacy: ★★★
Spaciousness: ★★★	Quiet: ★★★
Security: ★★★	Cleanliness: ★★★
Insect Control: ★★★	Facilities: ★★★

Directly off I-80 halfway between Grinnell and Newtown, is the Kellogg Campground. Set in the backdrop of a small service station and adjacent to a large crop of corn, this small campground gives you the feeling of home. The campsites are arranged in a loop with a few in the center. All the campsites are large, level, and have gravel parking pads. Shaded by large, mature maple trees, most of the sites are pull-throughs and come with a barbeque grill. The lawn is plush and well kept, and the area is clean. The rest rooms and showers are located in the mini-mart (the Kellduff 5 and 10), and all campground patrons receive a $.10 per gallon discount on fuel. The campground is simple, warm, and a nice place to relax from a long day's drive. There is a small cafe in the mini-mart as well as basic supplies. The weather varies from season to season, but sun and bug protection are always a good idea.

Basics

Operated By: Richard Wenndt. **Open:** All year. **Site Assignment:** First come, first served. **Registration:** In mini-mart. **Fee:** $11. **Parking:** At site.

Facilities

Number of RV-Only Sites: 23. **Number of Tent-Only Sites:** 0. **Hookups:** Electric (20, 30, 50 amps), water. **Each Site:** Picnic table, grill, light post. **Dump Station:** Yes. **Laundry:** No. **Pay Phone:** Yes. **Rest Rooms and Showers:** Yes. **Fuel:** Yes. **Propane:** Yes. **Internal Roads:** Gravel, in good condition. **RV Service:** 21 mi. in Marshalltown. **Market:** 8 mi. in either Grinnell or Newtown. **Restaurant:** On site or in Grinnell or Newton. **General Store:** Yes. **Vending:** At the mini-mart on property. **Swimming Pool:** No. **Playground:** Yes. **Activities:** Playground, walking, bicycling. **Nearby Attractions:** Inquire at campground. **Additional Information:** Grinnel Chamber, (641) 236-6555, or Marshaltown Chamber, (641) 792-5545.

Restrictions

Pets: On leash. **Fires:** Grills only. **Alcoholic Beverages:** Allowed. **Vehicle Max. Length:** None.

To Get There

From I-80, take Exit 173 and go north on SR 224 about 0.2 mi. to the Kellduff 5 and 10.

ONAWA

Lewis and Clark State Park

21914 Park Loop, Onawa 51040. T: (712) 423-2829; F: 712-423-2829; www.state.ia.us/parks/lewisclk.htm; lewis_&_clark@dnr.state.ia.us.

RV ★★★ Tent ★★★

Beauty: ★★★	Site Privacy: ★★★
Spaciousness: ★★★	Quiet: ★★★
Security: ★★★	Cleanliness: ★★★
Insect Control: ★★★	Facilities: ★★★

Located in an "ox bow" on the Blue Lake, Lewis and Clark State Park is a delightful place to relax and enjoy a small piece of American history. In August of 1804, Lewis and Clark explored this area, making note of its natural beauty. The park features 81 camping sites, all with electrical hookups, along the lakeshore. Most sites have level parking pads and are back-ins, though there are some pull-throughs. The foliage is splendid in the spring, and the wind off the lake is crisp. The park, officially part of the Lewis and Clark National Trail, celebrates the Lewis and Clark festival around the second weekend in June, so call in advance for details and schedules. There are numerous activities available, including self-guided nature trails and a large lodge that's great for family gatherings. The park is well staffed and maintained. Winds in the area can be strong.

Basics

Operated By: Iowa Dept. of Natural Resources. **Open:** All year. **Site Assignment:** First come, first served. **Registration:** Self registration at kiosks. **Fee:** $12–$16. **Parking:** At site.

Facilities

Number of Multipurpose Sites: 81. **Hookups:** Electric (20, 30 amps), water. **Each Site:** Picnic table, fire pit, trailer pad. **Dump Station:** Yes. **Laundry:** No. **Pay Phone:** Yes. **Rest Rooms and Showers:** Yes. **Fuel:** No. **Propane:** No. **Internal Roads:** Paved, in good condition. **RV Service:** 33 mi. northwest in South Sioux City. **Market:** In Onawa. **Restaurant:** In Onawa. **General Store:** No. **Vending:** Yes. **Swimming Pool:** No. **Playground:** Yes. **Other:** Beach, boat ramp, covered picnic tables, historic site. **Activities:** Fishing, hiking, biking, horseshoes, swimming, water activities, hunting. **Nearby Attractions:** The Kiwanis Railroad Depot Museum Complex, The Monona County Historical Museum, Lewis & Clark Festival. **Additional Information:** Onawa Chamber, (712) 423-1801.

Restrictions

Pets: On leash. **Fires:** Yes in fire pits only. **Alcoholic Beverages:** Allowed. **Vehicle Maximum Length:** 45 ft.

To Get There

From I-29, take Exit 112 and go west on SR 175. Turn right on SR 324 and continue to the park.

ONAWA

Onawa/Blue Lake KOA

21788 Dogwood Ave., Onawa 51040. T: (712) 423-1633; F: 712-423-2494; www.koa.com; kampkoa@willinet.net.

RV ★★★★ Tent ★★★★

Beauty: ★★★★	Site Privacy: ★★★★
Spaciousness: ★★★★	Quiet: ★★★★
Security: ★★★★	Cleanliness: ★★★★
Insect Control: ★★★★	Facilities: ★★★★

Set in a rural area in the heart of the Loess Hills in western Iowa is the Onawa/Blue Lake KOA. This campground is situated on a 250-acre lake with excellent bass fishing and water-skiing. The campground offers large pull-through sites under a canopy of large oaks and other mature deciduous trees. It provides a full array of amenities and activities such as boating and swimming. The campground takes part in Lewis and Clark Festival activities in June, and there are fireworks over the lake on the 4th of July. The KOA is conveniently located near a public golf course, a Museum complex, and one of the most beautiful scenic byways in the country. The campground is well kept, and the service is friendly and helpful. It can be very windy, so don't forget your skin protection.

Basics

Operated By: Brian & Cherry Dye. **Open:** Apr.–Oct. 15. **Site Assignment:** By reservation, credit card required. **Registration:** In camp store. **Fee:** Tent $17, RV $21–$25 for 2 people, $2 per additional guest, children under 5 free. **Parking:** At site.

Facilities

Number of RV-Only Sites: 54. **Number of Tent-Only Sites:** 11. **Hookups:** Electric (20, 30, 50 amps), water, sewer. **Each Site:** Picnic table, grated fire pits. **Dump Station:** Yes. **Laundry:** Yes. **Pay Phone:** Yes. **Rest Rooms and Showers:** Yes. **Fuel:** No. **Propane:** Yes. **Internal Roads:** Gravel. **RV Service:** 32 mi. in Sioux City. **Market:** In Onawa. **Restaurant:** In Onawa. **General Store:** Yes. **Vending:** No. **Swimming Pool:** Yes. **Playground:** Yes. **Other:** Cabins, fishing docks, boat rentals. **Activities:** Fishing, swimming, horseshoes, rowboating, paddleboating, basketball, volleyball. **Nearby Attractions:** Onawa Aquatic Center Monona County Historical Complex/Depot Museum, Monona County Arboretum, Loess Hills. **Additional Information:** Onawa Chamber, (712) 423-1801.

Restrictions

Pets: On leash. **Fires:** In fire pits only. **Alcoholic Beverages:** Allowed. **Vehicle Maximum Length:** None. **Other:** 30-day limit.

To Get There

From I-29 Exit 112, merge west onto SR 175 and go about 1 mi. Turn left on to Dogwood Ave. and continue 1 mi.

ROCKFORD

George Wyatt Park

1st. Northwest, Rockford 50468. T: (641) 756-3618; www.netins.net/ricweb/community/rockford/rockford.htm.

RV ★★★ Tent ★★★

Beauty: ★★★	Site Privacy: ★★★
Spaciousness: ★★★	Quiet: ★★★★
Security: ★★★	Cleanliness: ★★★
Insect Control: ★★	Facilities: ★★★

George Wyatt Park, not to be confused with George Wyatt State Park, is a delightful small city park in the town of Rockford. This charming little park is located on the Shell Rock River at the edge of town. The campground is simple, with grass sites and mature trees, and overlooks the river. The park offers a small boat ramp for non-motorized boats and a lovely picnic area. There are also clean rest room facilities and warm showers. The price is great, and the town is full of charm and history. The area is known for its fossil beds, and there is a public pool and golf course in town. This is a wonderful hide away and a great value. The Rockford Fire Department is right next door, and although the city maintains the park, you could not ask for better security or nicer people.

Basics

Operated By: City of Rockford, Denny Ginther Manager. **Open:** Year round, weather permitting. **Site Assignment:** First come, first served. **Registration:** Self registration. **Fee:** $7. no hookups, $8 electric. **Parking:** At site.

Facilities

Number of RV-Only Sites: 8. **Number of Tent-Only Sites:** 0. **Number of Multipurpose Sites:** 16. **Hookups:** Electric (20, 30, 50 amps), water. **Each Site:** Some picnic tables. **Dump Station:** Yes. **Laundry:** No. **Pay Phone:** No. **Rest Rooms and Showers:** Yes. **Fuel:** No. **Propane:** No. **Internal Roads:** Paved & gravel. **RV Service:** 26 mi. away in Hanlontown. **Market:** In Rockford.

Restaurant: In Rockford. **General Store:** No. **Vending:** No. **Swimming Pool:** No, but there is a public pool in town. **Playground:** Yes. **Other:** Small boat ramp, picnic area, river access. **Activities:** Fishing, hiking, biking. **Nearby Attractions:** The Rockford Fossil Beds, Rockfort Public Pool, golf, Iowa Trolley Park, Aladdin's Castle. **Additional Information:** Charles City Chamber, (641) 228-4234.

RESTRICTIONS

Pets: On leash. **Fires:** In approved areas. **Alcoholic Beverages:** Allowed. **Vehicle Max. Length:** None.

TO GET THERE

From Madison City on US 65, go east 9 mi. to US 18, then south on CR-S70 for another 5 mi. Follow the signs to the city park.

SPIRIT LAKE

Cenla RV Park

3400 US Hwy. 71, Spirit Lake 51360. T: (712) 336-2925; www.smithsrv.com.

RV ★★★ Tent ★★★

Beauty: ★★★ Site Privacy: ★★
Spaciousness: ★★ Quiet: ★★★
Security: ★★★ Cleanliness: ★★★
Insect Control: ★★★ Facilities: ★★★

Situated in the center of Iowa's lake region, Cenla RV Park is perfect for lake enthusiasts. The campground itself backs up to Center Lake, and there are five other lakes in very close proximity. Cenla RV Park has more than 100 RV sites with excellent amenities, activities, and a separate tenting cul-de-sac. The campground is laid out in a series of rows with both back-in and pull-through sites. Each site has a gravel parking pad, and several of the sites offer cable television from May through September. The campground features both shaded and open areas, as well as the lakeshore and two fishing docks. The Spirit Lake area is home to several lake beaches, fishing outfitters, boat rentals, and golf courses.

BASICS

Operated By: Private operator. **Open:** Apr.–Oct. **Site Assignment:** By reservation, $25 deposits. **Registration:** In camp office. **Fee:** Tent $17.50, RV $21.50–$24.50. **Parking:** At site.

FACILITIES

Number of RV-Only Sites: 120. **Number of Tent-Only Sites:** 5. **Hookups:** Electric (30, 50 amps), water, sewer, cable. **Each Site:** Picnic tables, w/ some fire pits. **Dump Station:** Yes. **Laundry:** Yes. **Pay Phone:** Yes. **Rest Rooms and Showers:** Yes. **Fuel:** No. **Propane:** No. **Internal Roads:** Gravel & dirt. **RV Service:** 28 mi. in Worthington, MN. **Market:** In Spirit Lake. **Restaurant:** In Spirit Lake. **General Store:** Yes. **Vending:** Yes. **Swimming Pool:** Yes. **Playground:** Yes. **Other:** Game room, fish cleaning station. **Activities:** Volleyball, swimming, games. **Nearby Attractions:** Spirit Lake Fish Hatchery, The Ranch Amusement Park, Marble Beach State Park. **Additional Information:** Spirit Lake Chamber of Commerce, (712) 336-4978.

RESTRICTIONS

Pets: On leash. **Fires:** In fire pits only. **Alcoholic Beverages:** Allowed. **Vehicle Maximum Length:** None. **Other:** Good Sam honored.

TO GET THERE

From I-90 Exit 73 in Jackson, Minnesota, go south on US Hwy. 71. The campground will be about 25 mi. directly off US Hwy. 71 in Spirit Lake, Iowa.

WATERLOO

George Wyth State Park

3659 Wyth Rd., Waterloo 50703. T: (319) 232-5505; F: (319) 232-1508; www.state.ia.us/parks; george_wyth@dnr.state.ia.us.

RV ★★★ Tent ★★★

Beauty: ★★★ Site Privacy: ★★
Spaciousness: ★★ Quiet: ★★★
Security: ★★★★ Cleanliness: ★★★
Insect Control: ★★★ Facilities: ★★

If you love water, biking, or fishing, then George Wyth State Park is a perfect spot to camp. The park is unique, because it offers extraordinary water access. The campground is surrounded by the Cedar River to the south and George Wyth Lake to the northeast. There are wonderful sites right on the waters edge offering level trailer pads. Most sites are back-in, but there are a limited number of pull-throughs. There is a wonderful public beach area with concessions and boat rentals. The park offers a variety of multipurpose trails, which includes part of a lake-to-lake bike route that covers over 50 miles and links to Pine Lake. The campground offers self registration, and fees can be paid at the site. However, the park is staffed around the clock and someone is always there to assist. The park offers a broad spectrum of activities from swimming in the summer to cross-country skiing in the winter.

BASICS

Operated By: Iowa Dept. of Natural Resources. **Open:** All year. **Site Assignment:** First come, first served. **Registration:** Self-registration. **Fee:** $16 hookups, $11 no hookups. **Parking:** At site.

FACILITIES

Number of Multipurpose Sites: 58. **Hookups:** Electric (20, 30 amps), water. **Each Site:** Picnic table, grated fire pits. **Dump Station:** Yes. **Laundry:** No. **Pay Phone:** Yes. **Rest Rooms and Showers:** Yes. **Fuel:** At Marina. **Propane:** At Marina. **Internal Roads:** Paved, in good condition. **RV Service:** In Waterloo. **Market:** In Waterloo. **Restaurant:** In Waterloo. **General Store:** Concession stand at the beach. **Vending:** No. **Swimming Pool:** No. **Playground:** Yes. **Other:** Lodge w/ kitchen & rustic fireplace, enclosed picnic shelters, boat ramps, boat rentals, beach, fish pier, 4 lakes & the Cedar River, 5.5 mi. of paved muti-purpose trails linked to a 45 mi. trail network. **Activities:** Fishing, boating, jet skiing, waterskiing, wind surfing, swimming, hiking, biking, cross-country skiing, snowmobiling, ice sailing. **Nearby Attractions:** Lake-to-Lake State Park Bike Route (bike rentals), Grout Museum of History & Science, Ice House Museum, John Deere Tours. **Additional Information:** Waterloo Chamber, (319) 233-8431.

RESTRICTIONS

Pets: Dogs on leash only, see web site for rules on horses & mules. **Fires:** In fire rings only. **Alcoholic Beverages:** At sites, beer & wine only. **Vehicle Maximum Length:** None. **Other:** No metal detectors in campground, max. 6 people to a site.

TO GET THERE

From Waterloo, go west on US 218 (W. Washington St.), take the Broadway St. Exit, turn left onto Broadway St., and go 0.3 mi. to the park entrance.

WEST DES MOINES

Timberland Campground

3165 Ashworth Rd., Waukee 50263. T: (515) 987-1714; F: (515) 987-3455; www.timberlineiowa.com; timberr@aol.com.

RV ★★★ Tent ★★★

Beauty: ★★★ Site Privacy: ★★★
Spaciousness: ★★★ Quiet: ★★★
Security: ★★★ Cleanliness: ★★★
Insect Control: ★★★ Facilities: ★★★

Timberline Campground is a comfortable and relaxing getaway, conveniently located on the outskirts of Des Moines, less than two miles from I-80. It offers over 40 acres of scenic woodland, with mature shade trees and nature trails full of different wildlife. The campground provides a large selection of amenities, including a RV wash barn and an ice cream shop. There is a large pool, a full playground, and a rec room with games. The campsites are a nice size, most being level pull-throughs. The campground has many nearby attractions, such as the botanical center, the Blank Park Zoo, and the bridges of Madison County. The weather can be windy, and you will likely need sunscreen. The staff is kind, and there is a family-friendly atmosphere. All visitors must register in the office, and security is tight.

BASICS

Operated By: Dick & Deborah Christensen. **Open:** Apr.–Nov. **Site Assignment:** By reservation, credit card & first night deposit required. **Registration:** In general store. **Fee:** Tent $16.80, RV $21–$24. **Parking:** At site.

FACILITIES

Number of RV-Only Sites: 100. **Number of Tent-Only Sites:** 16. **Hookups:** Electric (20, 30, 50 amps), water, sewer, phone. **Each Site:** Picnic table. **Dump Station:** Yes. **Laundry:** Yes. **Pay Phone:** No. **Rest Rooms and Showers:** Yes. **Fuel:** No. **Propane:** Yes. **Internal Roads:** Gravel, in good condition. **RV Service:** In Des Moines. **Market:** In Des Moines. **Restaurant:** In Des Moines. **General Store:** Yes. **Vending:** Yes. **Swimming Pool:** Yes. **Playground:** Yes. **Other:** 3 camping cabins, pavilion, RV wash, game room. **Activities:** Swimming, playground, horseshoes, basketball. **Nearby Attractions:** State capitol & historical museum, botanical center, art center, zoo, Sugar Creek golf course. **Additional Information:** West Des Moines Chamber, (515) 225-6009.

RESTRICTIONS

Pets: On leash (no large, aggressive breeds). **Fires:** Fire pits only. **Alcoholic Beverages:** Allowed. **Vehicle Maximum Length:** 45 ft.

TO GET THERE

from I-80 Exit 117, go 1 mi. north and 0.5 mi. east; there are signs to follow.

Kansas

Kansas isn't what you might think: cornfield and tornado country with nothing to see. While there are cornfields and twisters, there's also much more available to visitors than you might guess by looking over the guardrail as you speed down I-70. If you turn off the main routes, you'll find an honest vision of America struggling in the face of same-as-everywhere megamarts and fast-food chains.

Kansas is a small-town state. But that is good news for campers, as this makes for a lot of quiet rural camping. While Kansas has its share of overnighters, many campgrounds are in rural areas where you're as likely to encounter a horse as a human being. For outdoor enthusiasts, nearly every county has a state fishing lake open to anglers and campers alike.

For a look at what Kansas was like in the nineteenth century, go to **Dodge City** or **Meade** or **Coffeyville.** The museums that remain offer tourists a chance to relive history. You will see why lawmakers in Clint Eastwood movies shook in their boots when they heard talk of dreaded Kansas.

To see Kansas as it faces the future, visit the large cities of **Wichita, Kansas City,** and **Topeka.** These make convenient destinations (or even just stopping points) on a cross-Kansas trip. Spend a few days in these urban centers to soak up some culture, then venture forth into the special small places Kansas has to offer—such as the Amish community of **Yoder,** the weird rock formations at **Monument Rocks National Landmark,** or "the living ghost town" of **Elk Falls.** One highway slogan sums it up: "Drive through Kansas and you'll miss it."

The following facilities accept payment in checks or cash only:

Bourquin's RV Park, Colby
Circle-O, Meade
Crawford State Park, Girard
Elk City State Park, Independence
Homewood RV Park, Ottawa-Williamsburg
Prairie Dog State Park, Norton
Tarrant Overnight Camping, El Dorado
Tuttle Creek State Park, Manhattan

The following facilities feature 20 sites or fewer:

Evergreen Inn & RV Park, Pratt
Country Squire Motel & RV Park, Hiawatha
Payne Oil CO, Newton
Pleasant View Motel & Overnight RV Park, Greensburg

Campground Profiles

ABILENE
Covered Wagon RV Resort

803 South Buckeye, Abilene 67410. T: (800) 864-4053 or (785) 263-2343.

RV ★★★★★ Tent ★★★★★

Beauty: ★★★★
Site Privacy: ★★★★
Spaciousness: ★★★★
Quiet: ★★★★
Security: ★★★
Cleanliness: ★★★★
Insect Control: ★★★★
Facilities: ★★★★

Two dramatically different experiences await RVers at this park, depending on which portion of the park you find yourself parked in. Those parked close to the house will find a forested campsite with level, grassy sites and plenty of (deciduous) tree coverage. Sites 26–31 at the edge of the park are treed-off from the rest of the sites and face a grassy field under a canopy of trees. Site 7 would make a particularly nice tent site due to the protection of trees. However, sites 52–57 sit on an open gravel/grassy strip at the edge of the property with no coverage whatsoever. Adding insult to injury, a row of storage units faces this landing strip, degrading the visual aesthetic even further. For an enjoyable stay, insist on a site closer to the house.

BASICS

Operated By: Richard & Cathy Osborn. **Open:** All year. **Site Assignment:** Upon registration, reservations OK, credit card to hold, must cancel within 24 hours. **Registration:** In house, late arrivals use drop box. **Fee:** $15–$21; V, MC, D, $1 discount for cash or check. **Parking:** At site.

FACILITIES

Number of RV Sites: 40. **Number of Tent-Only Sites:** 0. **Hookups:** Water, sewer, electric (30, 50 amp), phone. **Each Site:** Picnic table, tree. **Dump Station:** Yes. **Laundry:** Yes. **Pay Phone:** Yes. **Rest Rooms and Showers:** Yes. **Fuel:** No. **Propane:** No. **Internal Roads:** Yes. **RV Service:** No. **Market:** 1 mi. **Restaurant:** 0.25 mi. **General Store:** Yes. **Vending:** No. **Swimming:** Pool. **Playground:** Yes. **Other:** Accepts horses, makes reservations for lunch/dinner in town or for tours, horseshoes. **Activities:** Swimming, basketball, tennis, volleyball at nearby Eisenhower Park. **Nearby Attractions:** Dwight D. Eisenhower Presidential Center, Greyhound Hall of Fame, antique doll museum. **Additional Information:** Abilene Chamber of Commerce, (913) 263-1770.

Restrictions

Pets: On leash only. **Fires:** In grills. **Alcoholic Beverages:** At sites. **Vehicle Maximum Length:** None.

To Get There

From I-70, take Exit 275. Turn south onto Hwy. 15, then drive 2.3 mi. The entrance is on the right. Park behind the house to go to the office.

ATWOOD

Linis Park at Lake Atwood

4th St. & Lake Rd., Atwood 67730. T: (785) 626-3020 or (785) 626-9503.

RV ★★★ Tent ★★

Beauty: ★★★ Site Privacy: ★★★
Spaciousness: ★★★ Quiet: ★★★★
Security: ★★★ Cleanliness: ★★★★
Insect Control: ★★★★ Facilities: ★★★

Campsites are located in a strip a few hundred feet away from the edge of the lake. With the lake to the northwest, a cute pavillion, and a romantic lit walkway around the circumference of the lake, the campground is pretty, with a quiet, small-town park atmosphere. Sites 1–4 are situated on the paved parking lot (with grass behind), while 5–9 are all grass. All sites are open back-ins with full hookups. Tent sites are located between the RV sites and the lake, in a large, open grassy field with virtually unlimited sites. Be forewarned of the hot-rod rally that occurs May 18–20, as sites fill up quickly. Site 1, being an end site, has much more space than all the others except 9, the other end site. (There is a 10th water hookup and space for another vehicle next to site 9 that isn't rented out, but it seems hard to believe someone might not take advantage of it in the busy season.) While the restroom and showers are in the park, other all services (such as phone and vending) are located at the Vista mart.

Basics

Operated By: Lion's Club. **Open:** All year. **Site Assignment:** First come, first served. **Registration:** In Vista mart 6 a.m.–midnight. **Fee:** RV $15, $5 refundable key deposit, tents free. **Parking:** At site.

Facilities

Number of RV Sites: 9. **Number of Tent-Only Sites:** Undesignated sites. **Hookups:** Water, sewer, electric (20, 30, 50 amp). **Each Site:** Grill, picnic table, tree. **Dump Station:** No (sewer at all sites). **Laundry:** No. **Pay Phone:** Yes. **Rest Rooms and Showers:** Yes. **Fuel:** Yes. **Propane:** No. **Internal Roads:** Paved. **RV Service:** No. **Market:** 6 blocks. **Restaurant:** 2 blocks. **General Store:** Yes. **Vending:** Yes. **Swimming:** No. **Playground:** Yes. **Other:** Fishing lake, lit walkway around lake. **Activities:** Fishing, 9-hole golf, softball, basketball, volleyball, boating. **Nearby Attractions:** Lake Atwood 10 mi. race, Hayden Nature Trail, Atwood Country Club & Golf Course. **Additional Information:** Atwood Chamber of Commerce, (785) 626-9630.

Restrictions

Pets: On leash. **Fires:** In grills. **Alcoholic Beverages:** At sites. **Vehicle Maximum Length:** None.

To Get There

From Hwy. 36 and 4th St. in town, turn north onto 4th St. At the end of the block, turn left onto Lake Rd., then take the immediate right into the park. Select a spot, then walk to the Coastal/Vista gas station on the south side of Hwy. 36 and 4th St. to register.

BELLEVILLE

Evergreen Acres RV Park

1880 Elm Rd., Belleville 66935. T: (785) 987-5544.

RV ★★★★ Tent ★★★★

Beauty: ★★★★★ Site Privacy: ★★★
Spaciousness: ★★★ Quiet: ★★★★★
Security: ★★★★ Cleanliness: ★★★★★
Insect Control: ★★★★ Facilities: ★★★★

This isolated campground offers an authentic farm experience in a beautiful pastoral setting. Traffic noise is supplanted by the croaking of frogs, the calling of birds, and the sighing of the wind. Large mature evergreens shield the campground from the road and add to the verdant beauty. The campground is divided into two sections: one near the house, one barely a quarter mile away by the lake. (To get to the second section, continue on the road just past the authentic, functional barn with the authentic, functional cows, take the first left turn, then again the immediate left turn onto the white gravel driveway.) The lake is located at the second section, but in fact, the better sites are closer to the house. Sites near the lake (1–10) are a little more tightly crammed together and are lined up in a single row. Sites at the house are more scattered (offering more privacy) and contain more trees. All sites are grassy and level pull-throughs, however, and the least desirable site is located in the campground you have to go to when all the spaces at Evergreen Acres are full.

Basics

Operated By: Henry & Mildred Blecha. **Open:** All year (lake area may close for winter). **Site Assignment:** Upon registration. **Registration:** In office. **Fee:** RV $10, tent $6; checks OK, no credit cards. **Parking:** At site.

Facilities

Number of RV Sites: 15. **Number of Tent-Only Sites:** Undesignated sites. **Hookups:** Water, sewer, electric (30 amp). **Each Site:** Picnic table. **Dump Station:** No (sewer at all sites). **Laundry:** No. **Pay Phone:** Yes. **Rest Rooms and Showers:** Yes. **Fuel:** No. **Propane:** No. **Internal Roads:** Gravel. **RV Service:** No. **Market:** 4 mi. north to Chester, Nebraska. **Restaurant:** 4 mi. North to Chester, Nebraska. **General Store:** No. **Vending:** No. **Swimming:** No. **Playground:** Yes. **Other:** Lake. **Activities:** Fishing. **Nearby Attractions:** Pawnee Indian museum. **Additional Information:** Belleville Chamber of Commerce, (913) 527-5519.

Restrictions

Pets: On leash, cleaned up after. **Fires:** Stoves only. **Alcoholic Beverages:** At sites. **Vehicle Maximum Length:** None.

To Get There

From the junction of Hwy. 36 and Hwy. 81, travel North on Hwy. 81 for 9.5 mi., then turn East onto a gravel road. Follow this road 0.8 mi., then turn left at the sign into the entrance. Keep left to go to the office.

COLBY

Bourquin's RV Park

155 East Willow, I-70 Frontage Rd., Colby 67701. T: (785) 462-3300; www.colby.ixks.com; shirleyb@colby.ixks.com.

RV ★★★ Tent ★★

Beauty: ★★★ Site Privacy: ★★
Spaciousness: ★★ Quiet: ★★★★
Security: ★★★ Cleanliness: ★★★
Insect Control: ★★★ Facilities: ★★

Conveniently close (half a mile) to town, this campground is still far enough removed to avoid most of the lights and noise. Most sites are back-in, with the possibility of pull-throughs in the inner circle of the loop (requiring pulling out over a strip of grass that looks like it can take it—and has.) Sites are not well shaded, so the summer sun could prove a little overwhelming—as could a strong spring rain or windstorm. The Prairie Art Museum to the north offers a cute view of a miniaturized church, barn, and windmill. Unmarked tent sites are off in the northwest corner, next to a charming red one-room schoolhouse with several large shrubs, but are equally unprotected and sit next to a road. Tenters might optimally give this campground a miss and continue on to Oakley or Goodland. The best RV sites are 19–36, which lie on the outside of the loop away from town-side, and next to open land and a pond to the east. The least desirable sites are 37–48, which are a little squashed together and share tables and grills.

Basics

Operated By: Shirley Bourquin. **Open:** Apr. 15–Sept. 30. **Site Assignment:** First come, first served. **Registration:** In office, late arrivals use drop box; verbal reservations OK. **Fee:** RV $18, coach $20, van/pop-up $16, tent $12. **Parking:** At site.

Facilities

Number of RV Sites: 50. **Number of Tent-Only Sites:** Undesignated sites. **Hookups:** Water, sewer, electric (20, 30, 50 amp). **Each Site:** Some tables, grills, trees. **Dump Station:** Yes. **Laundry:** No. **Pay Phone:** Yes. **Rest Rooms and Showers:** Yes. **Fuel:** No. **Propane:** No. **Internal Roads:** Gravel, good condition. **RV Service:** No. **Market:** 0.5 mi. to Colby. **Restaurant:** On site. **General Store:** Yes. **Vending:** No. **Swimming:** No. **Playground:** No. **Other:** Homemade organic foods. **Activities:** Bluegrass festival in July. **Nearby Attractions:** Prairie Art Museum. **Additional Information:** Prairie Museum of Art & History, Northwest Research Extension Center.

Restrictions

Pets: On leash, cleaned up after. **Fires:** In grills. **Alcoholic Beverages:** At sites. **Vehicle Maximum Length:** None.

To Get There

From I-70, take Exit 53 and turn north. Take the first right onto the frontage road along I-70. Follow the road 0.5 mi. to the entrance.

CONCORDIA

Brome Ridge RV Park

RR1 Box 149, Concordia 66901. T: (785) 243-4539.

RV ★★★★★ Tent ★★★★

Beauty: ★★★★ Site Privacy: ★★★
Spaciousness: ★★★ Quiet: ★★★
Security: ★★★★ Cleanliness: ★★★★
Insect Control: ★★★★ Facilities: ★★★★

This campground is charming and pictoresque. Along the drive into the campground are several items of country kitsch ("Coyote Crossing" sign, animal statuettes) that are—surprisingly—tastefully done. Trees line the drive half of the way down, while the rest of the grounds open up to reveal scenes of rural Kansas: rolling hills, farms, cows, and a large pond. Indeed, the entire park feels like it's on a farm. All RV sites are level and grassy pull-throughs situated on a giant loop. While it is hard to think of a "least desirable site" in the campground, site 1 does sit right at the tip of the loop, and may therefore receive more internal traffic than a camper would care for. But it's still not bad! Sites 18–20 are slightly nicer than others due to their size and proximity to a large open field. Please note that the hot and cold water knobs were inverted—there really is hot water, you just have to turn it to maximum blue (cold) instead of red (hot).

Basics

Operated By: Stan & Maxine Van Meter. **Open:** All year. **Site Assignment:** First come, first served. **Registration:** At self-pay station. **Fee:** RV $14 full, $8 dry; tent $5. **Parking:** At site.

Facilities

Number of RV Sites: 21. **Number of Tent-Only Sites:** Undesignated sites. **Hookups:** Water, sewer, electric (30, 50 amp). **Each Site:** Picnic table, deciduous shrub. **Dump Station:** No (sewer at all sites). **Laundry:** Yes. **Pay Phone:** No. **Rest Rooms and Showers:** Yes. **Fuel:** No. **Propane:** No. **Internal Roads:** Gravel, in good condition. **RV Service:** No. **Market:** 7 mi. to Concordia. **Restaurant:** 7 mi. to Concordia. **General Store:** No. **Vending:** Yes. **Swimming:** No. **Playground:** Yes. **Other:** Storm shelter, cabins, pond, catering, club house w/ kitchenette. **Activities:** Hunting, fishing. **Nearby Attractions:** Brown Grand Theatre, Cloud County Historical Museum, Republican River. **Additional Information:** Concordia Chamber, (785) 243-4290.

Restrictions

Pets: On leash, cleaned up after. **Fires:** In grills. **Alcoholic Beverages:** At sites. **Vehicle Maximum Length:** None.

To Get There

From Hwy. 81, drive 7 mi. south of Concordai. Between mile markers 195 and 196, turn west at the sign into the entrance. Follow the drive to the self-pay station.

COUNCIL GROVE

Council Grove Lake

RT2 Box 110, Council Grove 66846. T: (877) 444-6777 or (316) 767-5195; F: (620) 767-6919; www.reserveusa.com.

RV ★★★★★ Tent ★★★★★

Beauty: ★★★★★ Site Privacy: ★★★★
Spaciousness: ★★★★★ Quiet: ★★★★★
Security: ★★★★ Cleanliness: ★★★★
Insect Control: ★★ Facilities: ★★★

Eight different campgrounds surround the lake, with sites ranging from lakeside higher ground. All sites are spacious, level, and grassy, with some as big as 100 × 100 feet. Although there are too many campsites to enumerate, several distinguish themselves as particularly nice. Sites 21–26 on the peninsula in Ritchie Cove and 1–13 on a strip by the waterfront, for example, have spectacular views of the sunset. All campgrounds have a wilderness feel, and if you come on a weekday in spring, you may get the whole place to yourself! A wonderful destination for a fun-filled stay of any length.

Basics

Operated By: U.S. Army Corps of Engineers. **Open:** All year. **Site Assignment:** First come, first served; reservations OK, need credit card to hold, $10 cancellation fee, first-night's-use fee if not cancelled within 3 days of arrival date. **Registration:** Self-pay station. **Fee:** RV $14, tent $10. **Parking:** At site, additional parking available.

Facilities

Number of RV Sites: 180. **Number of Tent-Only Sites:** 0. **Hookups:** Water, sewer, electric (30, 50 amp). **Each Site:** Covered picnic table, fire pit/grill, trees. **Dump Station:** Yes. **Laundry:** No. **Pay Phone:** No. **Rest Rooms and Showers:** Yes. **Fuel:** No. **Propane:** No. **Internal Roads:** Paved. **RV Service:** No. **Market:** 2 mi. to Council Grove. **Restaurant:** 2 mi. to Council Grove. **General Store:** Yes. **Vending:** Yes. **Swimming:** Yes (lake). **Playground:** Yes. **Activities:** Fishing, swimming, boating, waterskiing, hunting. **Nearby Attractions:** July 4th fireworks in town, Kay Mission State Historic Site. **Additional Information:** Council Grove Chamber of Commerce, (316) 767-5413.

Restrictions

Pets: On leash. **Fires:** In fire rings only. **Alcoholic Beverages:** At sites. **Vehicle Maximum Length:** None. **Other:** No fireworks.

To Get There

From the junction of Hwy. 56 & Hwy. 57/177 in town, take Hwy. 57/177 2 mi. north, then turn left at the sign for Council Grove Lake. Follow the road 1.3 mi. across the lake, then cross the intersection to arrive at the office. (You may also go to any campsite & then to a self-pay station.)

DODGE CITY

Watersports Campground

500 East Cherry St., Dodge City 67801. T: (316) 225-8044 or (316) 225-9003; F: (316) 225-4407; www.gocampingamerica.com.

RV ★★★★ Tent ★★★

Beauty: ★★★ Site Privacy: ★★★
Spaciousness: ★★★ Quiet: ★★★★
Security: ★★★★ Cleanliness: ★★★★
Insect Control: ★★★ Facilities: ★★★★

This popular RV park sits just west of the lake from which its name derives. (The RV park on the east side of the lake is for members only.) Sites 31–52 have an attractive view of the lake, but 51 and 52 are very close to the playground. Full hookup pull-throughs 1–10 face open grassy land with an attractive row of trees at the far end. Site 31 has extra space to the north side, while site 38 is known among visitors as "the best site," presumably for its commanding view of the lake. Sites may be a little cramped for larger rigs (45–50 feet long), and spare vehicles may have to be parked crosswise in a space. Tents can be pitched on the well-manicured lawn that extends between the RV park and the lake.

Basics

Operated By: Deana Vogel. **Open:** All year. **Site Assignment:** At registration, verbal reservations OK except for holidays. **Registration:** In office, late arrivals use slot in door. **Fee:** $15, $1 utility (water free); no credit cards. **Parking:** At site.

Facilities

Number of RV Sites: 56. **Number of Tent-Only Sites:** Undesignated sites. **Hookups:** Water, sewer, electric (30, 50 amp). **Each Site:** Tree. **Dump Station:** Yes. **Laundry:** Yes. **Pay Phone:** Yes. **Rest Rooms and Showers:** Yes. **Fuel:** No. **Propane:** Yes. **Internal Roads:** Dirt/gravel. **RV Service:** No. **Market:** 4 blocks. **Restaurant:** 10 blocks. **General Store:** Yes. **Vending:** Yes. **Swimming:** Yes (lake). **Playground:** Yes. **Other:** Courtesy van to Boot Hill, lifeguard, walking path. **Activities:** Swimming, fishing, pool table, video games, self-guiding tours. **Nearby Attractions:** Boot Hill, Fort Dodge, Home of Stone. **Additional Information:** Dodge City Chamber of Commerce, (316) 227-3119.

Restrictions

Pets: "We do not like rotweilers, dobermans, or pit bulls." **Fires:** In fire pits only. **Alcoholic Beverages:** At sites. **Vehicle Maximum Length:** 45 ft.

To Get There

From the junction of Hwy. 50 and 2nd Ave. in town, turn south at the light onto 2nd Ave., then drive 0.5 mi. and turn left onto Cherry St. Take Cherry St. 0.4 mi. to the end, and follow the dirt road to the right to go to the office.

EL DORADO

Tarrant Overnight Camping

RR2 Box 272, El Dorado 67042. T: (316) 321-6272.

RV ★★★ Tent n/a

Beauty: ★★★ Site Privacy: ★★★
Spaciousness: ★★ Quiet: ★★★
Security: ★★★ Cleanliness: ★★
Insect Control: ★★★ Facilities: ★★★

Vehicle length is not a problem in this campground, but even according to management, width can pose problems. Sites are laid out in two rows of 18 sites, 1–18 being doubled-up pull-throughs parked back-to-back, 19–36 being back-ins. Sites 32–26 look quite cramped, while 20 has a telephone pole that encroaches, and 19 (next to the rest rooms) has a patch of tulips that enlivens the site but also clips a corner. The best sites are 13–18, closest to the forested southeast corner, with the convenience of a pull-through. The rest-room facilities are less than thrilling: the shower stalls share a curtain divider and floor, and the toilet is not enclosed, making for inconvenient use of the toilet while someone else is showering. This campground is the only one in the immediate area this is open during the winter season, making it a convenient—or perhaps necessary—stop, but not a haven to plan around.

Basics

Operated By: Doug & Sharon Varner. **Open:** All year. **Site Assignment:** Assigned when getting full, verbal reservations OK. **Registration:** In office, late arrivals use drop box. **Fee:** Under 35 ft. $15, 35 ft. or longer $17. **Parking:** At site.

Facilities

Number of RV Sites: 36. **Number of Tent-Only Sites:** 0. **Hookups:** Water, sewer, electric (30, 50 amp). **Each Site:** Picnic table, mature shade tree. **Dump Station:** No. **Laundry:** No. **Pay Phone:** No. **Rest Rooms and Showers:** Yes. **Fuel:** No. **Propane:** No. **Internal Roads:** Gravel. **RV Service:** Across street. **Market:** 4 mi. to El Dorado. **Restaurant:** 2.5 mi. to El Dorado. **General Store:** No. **Vending:** No. **Swimming:** No. **Playground:** No. **Other:** Storm shelter, notary public. **Activities:** Swimming, fishing, shopping, visiting museums. **Nearby Attractions:** State lake (4 mi.), Wichita, art museum, historical museum, antique stores. **Additional Information:** El Dorado Chamber of Commerce, (316) 321-3150.

Restrictions

Pets: On leash, cleaned up after. **Fires:** In grill or stove. **Alcoholic Beverages:** At sites. **Vehicle Maximum Length:** None. **Other:** No vehicle washing.

To Get There

From the junction of Hwy. 35 and Hwy. 254, take Exit 71 onto Hwy. 254 and go east (after 0.3 mi., Hwy. 254 becomes Hwy. 54). Stay on Hwy. 54 going east for 3 mi., then turn right into the entrance, half block west of the El Dorado State Lake Park entrance. Follow the drive to the back of the park and to the office straight ahead.

EMPORIA

Emporia RV Park

4601 West Hwy. 50, Emporia 66801. T: (316) 343-3422; F: (316) 341-0105; www.gocampingamerica.com/emporia; emprv@valu-line.com.

RV ★★★ Tent ★★★

Beauty: ★★	Site Privacy: ★★★
Spaciousness: ★★★	Quiet: ★★★
Security: ★★★★	Cleanliness: ★★★★★
Insect Control: ★★★★	Facilities: ★★★

The proximity to the highway to the north and east detracts slightly from the ambiance, but adds greatly to the convenience of the campsite. A forested area to the east/southeast and to the west helps create a rural feel in the campground, as does the fish pond to the northwest. Each site has at least one tree, but some are too small to afford any real shade. Sites are pull-throughs laid out in two strips. Sites 20 and 39 on the ends are slightly shortchanged for space, and odd numbers 21–39 face the highway. The better sites are odd numbers 1–19, which face the woods on the western border of the property. Average site size is 75 × 27 feet, large enough for a big rig with slide-outs.

Basics

Operated By: Paul & Charlotte Pinick. **Open:** All year. **Site Assignment:** Upon registration, reservations OK, credit card to hold, must cancel within 24 hours. **Registration:** In office, late arrivals use drop box. **Fee:** RV $20, tent $18. **Parking:** At site.

Facilities

Number of RV Sites: 39. **Number of Tent-Only Sites:** Undesignated sites. **Hookups:** Water, sewer, electric (20, 30, 50 amp), cable. **Each Site:** Picnic table, tree. **Dump Station:** Yes. **Laundry:** Yes. **Pay Phone:** Yes. **Rest Rooms and Showers:** Yes. **Fuel:** No. **Propane:** Yes. **Internal Roads:** Gravel. **RV Service:** No. **Market:** 0.5 mi. to Emporia. **Restaurant:** 0.5 mi. to Emporia. **General Store:** Yes. **Vending:** No. **Swimming:** No. **Playground:** Yes. **Other:** Fishing pond, rec room, dog walk area, skate ramp. **Activities:** Fishing, skating, boating, swimming in nearby reservoirs. **Nearby Attractions:** Tallgrass Prairie National Preserve, farmer's market. **Additional Information:** Emporia Chamber of Commerce, (316) 342-1600.

Restrictions

Pets: On leash, not tied up. **Fires:** None. **Alcoholic Beverages:** On sites only. **Vehicle Maximum Length:** 70 ft.

To Get There

From the junction of I-35 (Exit 127C) and Hwy. 50, turn west onto Hwy. 50 and begin to merge left as soon as possible. The entrance is on the left, barely 0.5 mi. from the junction.

FARLINGTON

Crawford State Park

1 Lake Rd., Farlington 66734. T: (620) 362-3671.

RV ★★★★★ Tent ★★★★★

Beauty: ★★★★★	Site Privacy: ★★★★★
Spaciousness: ★★★★★	Quiet: ★★★★★
Security: ★★★	Cleanliness: ★★★★★
Insect Control: ★★★	Facilities: ★★★

Campsites around this lake are enormous (some 100 × 100 feet) and vary from waterfront to higher up and set into woods. There are four separate camping areas, several nature trails, a mountain biking/hiking trail, as well as scads of picnic and water-use areas. Some of these areas (evening Breeze Point, Osage Bluff, Cherokee Landing, Lonesome point) offer primitive camping (and toilets) only. All RV sites are back-in only, but spacious and private enough to make up for this small inconvenience. Washrooms are surprisingly clean but sparse—possibly a drive away from some campsites. This campground is a great destination to bring the kids.

Basics

Operated By: Kansas Dept. of Wildlife & Parks. **Open:** All year. **Site Assignment:** First come, first served. **Registration:** At office or self-pay station. **Fee:** $7–$18, $5/day vehicle permit. **Parking:** At site.

Facilities

Number of RV Sites: 72. **Number of Tent-Only Sites:** 35. **Hookups:** Water, electric (30 amp); no water Oct. 15–Apr. 1. **Each Site:** Picnic table, fire pit/grill, trees. **Dump Station:** Yes. **Laundry:** Yes. **Pay Phone:** Yes. **Rest Rooms and Showers:** Yes. **Fuel:** No. **Propane:** No. **Internal Roads:** Paved. **RV Service:** No. **Market:** 10 mi. to Farlington. **Restaurant:** 10 mi. to Farlington. **General Store:** Yes. **Vending:** Yes. **Swimming:** Yes (lake). **Playground:** Yes. **Other:** Boat ramp, ampitheater. **Activities:** Boating, swimming, fishing, hiking. **Nearby Attractions:** Fort Scott. **Additional Information:** Girard Chamber of Commerce, (620) 724-4715.

Restrictions

Pets: On leash. **Fires:** In fire pits; subject to seasonal bans. **Alcoholic Beverages:** Beer only. **Vehicle Maximum Length:** None. **Other:** 1 vehicle/site, boat registration.

To Get There

From the junction of Hwy. 57 and Hwy. 7, turn north onto Hwy. 7 and drive 8.7 mi. Turn right at the sign onto 710 Ave. and continue 1 mi. to the entrance.

FORT SCOTT

Fort Scott Campground

2162 Native Rd., Fort Scott 66701. T: (800) 538-0216 or (620) 223-3440; F: (620) 223-4950.

RV ★★★★★ Tent ★★★★

Beauty: ★★★★	Site Privacy: ★★★
Spaciousness: ★★★	Quiet: ★★★★
Security: ★★★	Cleanliness: ★★★★★
Insect Control: ★★★	Facilities: ★★★

A very cute, tidy campground with 40 pull-throughs and 10 back-ins. An average site measures 24 × 70 feet, leaving a potentially restricted area around some bigger rigs. However, the ambiance is virtually unbeatable, more than making up for possible space shortages. This is the kind of campground you want to take a walk around as soon as you arrive, just to take in the natural beauty. Sites are very clearly labeled with attractive wooden signs. Many sites have two or more trees, increasing the impression of privacy. Site 33 is slightly encroached upon by signs, and 34 (which may not be assigned) appears to be part of a through-road. Any other sites really can't be beat. As an added bonus, end site 42 seems to have inherited some extra space, and 16 (closest to the fishing pond and cow pasture) has a wide-open east side. One glaring exception to this pristine idyll is the swingsets, which are rusted and unstable looking. A safer bet for kids are the other swings, teeter-totter, and merry-go-round. The tent site to the north of the office offers thick grass, mature shade trees, and almost unlimited number of spaces. A sure bet for campers of any stripe!

Basics

Operated By: Jack & Ruth Jaro. **Open:** All year (limited services Nov. 16–Feb. 28). **Site Assignment:** Fist come, first served or assigned upon registration, verbal reservations OK, cancel within 48 hours. **Registration:** In office, late arrivals use drop box. **Fee:** RV $19 full, $17 water/ electric, $12 winter; checks, V, MC, AE. **Parking:** At site.

Facilities

Number of RV Sites: 50. **Number of Tent-Only Sites:** 15. **Hookups:** Water, sewer, electric (30, 50 amp). **Each Site:** Picnic table, trees. **Dump Station:** Yes. **Laundry:** Yes. **Pay Phone:** No. **Rest Rooms and Showers:** Yes. **Fuel:** No. **Propane:** No. **Internal Roads:** Gravel. **RV Service:** No. **Market:** 4 mi. in Fort Scott. **Restaurant:** 0.25 mi. **General Store:** Yes. **Vending:** No. **Swimming:** Pool. **Playground:** Yes. **Other:** Stocked fishing pond, free firewood, 1 cabin, central fire ring, pet walk area, video games. **Activities:** Fishing, volleyball, horseshoes, pool. **Nearby Attractions:** Fort Scott. **Additional Information:** Fort Scott Chamber of Commerce, (316) 223-3566.

Restrictions

Pets: On leash, always attended, cleaned up after. **Fires:** In fire ring or grill. **Alcoholic Beverages:** Prefer cans (due to pool). **Vehicle Maximum Length:** 70 ft. **Other:** Some pool restrictions.

To Get There

From the junction of Hwy. 69 and Hwy. 54, take Hwy. 64 west for 0.5 mi., turn north immediately at the sign. Follow the road 0.4 mi., then turn right into the entrance and take the second right to the office.

GARDEN CITY

Garden City KOA Kampground

4100 East Hwy. 50, Garden City 67846. T: (800) KOA-8613 or (620) 276-9741; F: (620) 276-1987.

RV: ★★★★ Tent: ★★

Beauty: ★★★	Site Privacy: ★★★
Spaciousness: ★★★	Quiet: ★★★
Security: ★★★★★	Cleanliness: ★★★★★
Insect Control: ★★★★	Facilities: ★★★★★

This is a clean, respectable campground packed with facilities. All RV sites are pull-throughs arranged in a grid, and can accommodate a 60-foot rig. All sites are grassy, level, 25-feet wide, and most have 50 amp electrical. There are lots of shade trees except where they are most sorely needed: in the tening area. (The tent area benefits from a fence to the back, but no other real protection.) RV sites 68, 70, 72, and 76 and tent site 5 are extremely close to the playground. Site 87 is carved into part of the internal road. A mobile-home park to the north and one to the east are potential sources of loud music, but otherwise, most sites are pleasant and quiet. Shower and toilet facilities are clean, modern, and well lit. The tenting experience would improve with more and larger trees, as well as more distance from the campground road. Security is not an issue, as there are frequent sheriff patrols.

Basics

Operated By: Paul Foster. **Open:** All year. **Site Assignment:** Assigned until 9 p.m, verbal reservations OK. **Registration:** In office, late arrivals use drop box. **Fee:** RV $20–$22, tent $15. **Parking:** At site.

Facilities

Number of RV Sites: 60. **Number of Tent-Only Sites:** 20. **Hookups:** Water, sewer, electric (30, 50 amp), cable. **Each Site:** Picnic table, grill, tree. **Dump Station:** Yes. **Laundry:** Yes. **Pay Phone:** Yes. **Rest Rooms and Showers:** Yes. **Fuel:** Yes. **Propane:** Yes. **Internal Roads:** Paved/dirt. **RV Service:** Yes. **Market:** 2.5 mi. in Garden City. **Restaurant:** 2.5 mi. in Garden City. **General Store:** Yes. **Vending:** Yes. **Swimming:** Pool. **Playground:** Yes. **Other:** Cabins, dog walk area. **Activities:** Shuffleboard, horseshoes, basketball. **Nearby Attractions:** Finnup Park & Lee Richardson Zoo, Finney Game Refuge. **Additional Information:** Garden City Chamber of Commerce, (316) 276-3264.

Restrictions

Pets: On leash, cleaned up after. **Fires:** In grills. **Alcoholic Beverages:** At sites. **Vehicle Maximum Length:** 60 ft. **Other:** Quiet after 9 p.m.

To Get There

From the junction of Hwy. 83 (*not* the business loop of Hwy. 83) and Hwy. 50 (Fulton St. in town), go 1 mi. east on Hwy. 50. Turn right into the entrance.

GOODLAND

Goodland KOA

1114 East Hwy. 24, Goodland 67735. T: (800) 562-5704 or (785) 899-5701; www.koa.com; goodl&koa@nwkansas.com.

RV: ★★★★ Tent: ★★★

Beauty: ★★	Site Privacy: ★★★
Spaciousness: ★★★	Quiet: ★★★
Security: ★★★	Cleanliness: ★★★★
Insect Control: ★★★★	Facilities: ★★★★★

Located just off the highway, this campground is an easy-on, easy-off stop. Most campsites have at least two trees, with other trees scattered around the campground, lending a back-to-nature feel. Back-in sites 66–71 have a more than normal number of trees, which gives them woodsy feel. The east side of the campground is partitioned off from neighboring land by dense vegetation, and an open grassy field lies to the north. In addition, cute landscaping using shrubs, flower beds, and several tree trunk carvings liven up the grounds. On the downside, there is unattractive commercial development to the west, but not enough to detract terribly from the environment. Laundry and restroom/shower facilities are large, well lit, and immaculate. Some sites in the 28–42 area are not clearly marked, making their location a minor hassle. Overall, however, this is a convenient and enjoyable stay.

Basics

Operated By: Dale & Wally Neill. **Open:** Mar. 15–Nov. 1. **Site Assignment:** Upon registration, reservations with credit card or check to hold, must cancel within 24 hours for refund. **Registration:** At office, late arrivals use drop box. **Fee:** RV $21–$26, tent $15. **Parking:** At site only.

Facilities

Number of RV Sites: 51. **Number of Tent-Only Sites:** 17. **Hookups:** Water, sewer, electric (30, 50 amp), cable. **Each Site:** Picnic table, some fire grills. **Dump Station:** Yes. **Laundry:** Yes. **Pay Phone:** Yes. **Rest Rooms and Showers:** Yes. **Fuel:** No. **Propane:** No. **Internal Roads:** Gravel/dirt. **RV Service:** No. **Market:** 1.5 mi. (into Goodland). **Restaurant:** 0.25 mi. (into Goodland). **General Store:** Yes. **Vending:** No. **Swimming:** Pool. **Playground:** Yes. **Other:** 4 cabins, dog walk area. **Activities:** Mini golf, horseshoes, basketball. **Nearby Attractions:** 18-hole golf course, Goodland High Plains Museum. **Additional Information:** Goodland Chamber of Commerce, (913) 899-7130.

Restrictions

Pets: On leash only. **Fires:** Grills only. **Alcoholic Beverages:** At sites. **Vehicle Maximum Length:** None.

To Get There

From I-70, take exit 19, turn North onto Hwy. 24 and follow it for 0.8 mi. The entrance is on the right.

GREENSBURG

Pleasant View Motel and Overnight RV Park

800 West Kansas Ave., Greensburg 67054. T: (316) 723-2105.

RV: ★★ Tent: ★

Beauty: ★	Site Privacy: ★★★
Spaciousness: ★★★	Quiet: ★★★
Security: ★★★	Cleanliness: ★★★
Insect Control: ★★★	Facilities: ★★★

The name says it all for this campground—it is certainly an overnight stop devoid of attractions to warrant a longer stay. The campground is a large, open dirt parking lot in an urban setting. All sites (nine back-ins, six pull-throughs) are in extremely level rows. Tenting is possible on grassy spots to both the east and the west of the RV park. This is a reasonable stop on the way to Dodge City, Wichita, or Oklahoma. The proprietors are, however, quite friendly, making this stop a little nicer.

Basics

Operated By: Lila. **Open:** All year. **Site Assignment:** Upon registration, reservations OK, credit card to hold if spaces filling up. **Registration:** In motel office, late arrivals ring bell. **Fee:** Varies; V, MC, AE, D. **Parking:** At site.

Facilities

Number of RV Sites: 15. **Number of Tent-Only Sites:** Undesignated sites. **Hookups:** Water, sewer, electric (30, 50 amp). **Dump Station:** No (sewer at all sites). **Laundry:** No. **Pay Phone:** Yes. **Rest Rooms and Showers:** Yes. **Fuel:** No. **Propane:** No. **Internal Roads:** Dirt. **RV Service:** No. **Market:** 0.5 mi. **Restaurant:** Next door. **General Store:** No. **Vending:** No. **Swimming:** No. **Playground:** No. **Other:** Storage room, 24 hour gas station within 100 yards. **Activities:** Fishing, swimming, wildlife-viewing (at nearby Kiowa State Fishing Lake). **Nearby Attractions:** Big Well, Pallasite Meteorite. **Additional Information:** Greensburg Chamber of Commerce, (316) 723-2261.

Restrictions

Pets: On leash only. **Fires:** In (own) grill. **Alcoholic Beverages:** At sites. **Vehicle Maximum Length:** None.

To Get There

From the junction of Hwy. 183 and Hwy. 54, go 1 mi. east on Hwy. 54. Going west on Hwy. 54, drive to the west end of town, 0.5 mi. west of Main St. Turn at the motel sign (across the street from the John Deere dealership).

HAYS

Sunflower Creek RV Park and Campground

6th & Vine, Hays 67601. T: (785) 623-4769 or (785) 625-7518; www.kansasrvroads.com; jshaver@comlinkusa.net.

RV ★★★ Tent ★

Beauty: ★★ Site Privacy: ★★★★
Spaciousness: ★★★★ Quiet: ★★★
Security: ★★★★ Cleanliness: ★★★
Insect Control: ★★★ Facilities: ★★★★

This park was converted from a mobile-home park, so sites are ultra-wide, situated on one island and one row. The tent area is sectioned off by a chain-link fence on a grassy, but slightly uneven, area. One large shade tree provides protection from the sun for several tents, but there is no protection in the case of rain. Further, the area to the north is wide open to passing pedestrians and motorists, although set back about 100 feet from the sidewalk. (There is no fence around the perimeter of the property.) RV sites 7 and 8 abut a neighboring mobile-home park. Better sites are 1–5, which are located away from both the mobile homes and the road. This park offers the convenience of many services within walking distance, and owners John and Nancy promise many changes in their second year of operation.

Basics

Operated By: John & Nancy Shaver. **Open:** All year. **Site Assignment:** Upon registration. **Registration:** In office, late arrivals use drop box. **Fee:** RV $16–$18, tent or no hookups $15. **Parking:** At site.

Facilities

Number of RV Sites: 28. **Number of Tent-Only Sites:** 25. **Hookups:** Water, sewer, electric (30, 50 amp). **Each Site:** Some picnic tables, some trees. **Dump Station:** Yes. **Laundry:** Yes. **Pay Phone:** No. **Rest Rooms and Showers:** Yes. **Fuel:** No. **Propane:** No. **Internal Roads:** Gravel. **RV Service:** No. **Market:** 2 mi. into Hays. **Restaurant:** 1 block. **General Store:** No. **Vending:** Yes. **Swimming:** No. **Playground:** No. **Other:** Produce stand. **Activities:** Old Fort Hays Days. **Nearby Attractions:** Fort Hays, Sternberg Museum of Natural History, Aqua park. **Additional Information:** Hays Chamber of Commerce, (913) 628-8201.

Restrictions

Pets: On leash, cleaned up after. **Fires:** In grills. **Alcoholic Beverages:** At sites. **Vehicle Maximum Length:** None.

To Get There

From the junction of I-70 and Hwy. 183, turn south onto Hwy. 183 (which becomes Vine St.) and go 2.5 mi. through town to 6th St. Turn right onto 6th Ave. then take the immediate left at the sign.

HIAWATHA

Country Squire Motel and RV Park

2000 West Oregon St., Hiawatha 66434. T: (785) 742-2877.

RV ★★★ Tent ★★

Beauty: ★★★ Site Privacy: ★★★
Spaciousness: ★★★ Quiet: ★★★
Security: ★★★★ Cleanliness: ★★★★★
Insect Control: ★★★★ Facilities: ★★★★

Despite its proximity to urban amenities, this campground has a definite rural feel. Trees line the east and west perimeters and block off most of the road to the south. In addition, a visually appealing chunk of pine forest blocks view of the office from the RV park. To the west is a large, open grassy field. The north is slightly less attractive, with a ball park that can become noisy during games. Campsites are situated on a loop, with back-in sites around the perimiter. All sites are grassy and level, with trees close to the edges. Two exceptions to this are sites 15 and 16, which are not close to any trees and consequently have an open, almost vulnerable feel. The most favorable is site 1 (which is surrounded on two sides by trees), followed by odd-number sites 3–11 (which are away from both the road and the ball park and face a grassy field with trees at the opposite end). Tucked behind the motel buildings, the campground is well away from motel traffic. Tenting sites occupy the tip of the island, with enough space to comfortbaly fit 10–12 tents. Five large trees (four deciduous) provide enough shelter for a comfortable tent stay.

Basics

Operated By: Leland & Carla Oplinger. **Open:** All year. **Site Assignment:** Depends on availability. **Registration:** In office, late arrivals ring bell. **Fee:** RV $10 no hookups, $2 hookup, $1 cable; tent $5–$7. **Parking:** At site.

Facilities

Number of RV Sites: 16. **Number of Tent-Only Sites:** 10. **Hookups:** Water, sewer, electric (30, 50 amp), cable. **Each Site:** Picnic table. **Dump Station:** Yes. **Laundry:** No. **Pay Phone:** Yes. **Rest Rooms and Showers:** Yes. **Fuel:** No. **Propane:** No. **Internal Roads:** Gravel. **RV Service:** No. **Market:** 1 mi. **Restaurant:** 1 mi. **General Store:** No. **Vending:** Yes. **Swimming:** No. **Playground:** No. **Other:** Free coffee, golf course. **Activities:** Mini golf. **Nearby Attractions:** Old town clock, Davis Memorial, flea markets, casinos. **Additional Information:** Hiawatha Chamber of Commerce, (785) 742-7136.

Restrictions

Pets: On leash. **Fires:** Stove or grill only. **Alcoholic Beverages:** At sites. **Vehicle Maximum Length:** None.

To Get There

From Hwy. 36, turn north onto Oregon St. (West Exit). Continue 0.3 mi. on Oregon St.—the entrance is on the right-hand side, slightly east (and across the road) from the water tower.

HUTCHINSON

Melody Acres Campground

1009 East Blanchard, Hutchinson 67501. T: (316) 665-5048; F: (316) 663-4134.

RV ★★★★ Tent ★★★★

Beauty: ★★★★ Site Privacy: ★★★★
Spaciousness: ★★★★ Quiet: ★★★
Security: ★★★ Cleanliness: ★★★
Insect Control: ★★★ Facilities: ★★★

This cute campground is lined by cedars on the east, is forested to the west, and has a line of mature shade trees to the north, which gives it a real forested feel. Most camping sites have at least one tree, although some too small to provide any real shade. Tent sites, by contrast, are right in the middle of the treed area providing lots of overhead protection and an honest middle-of-the-forest ambiance. While the campgrounds themselves are clean, the rest room/shower facility is a little dingey. The unfinished cement floors and peeling paint make the facilities feel more like a storage area than a comfortble washroom. The most convenient sites are the pull-throughs (1–10 and others in the bizarrely-numbered scheme) in the middle of the loop, while the prettiest are the back-ins (8–19 and A–G) that abut the forested area. All sites are level and grassy, with pull-throughs an enormous 45 × 100 feet. (The back-ins are equally wide but not as long.) Sites C and D have a particularly pleasing mulberry tree overhanging them.

Basics

Operated By: Judy Mitchell. **Open:** All year. **Site Assignment:** First come, first served; verbal reservations OK. **Registration:** In office, late arrivals pay in morning. **Fee:** RV $18, tent $10; no credit cards. **Parking:** At site.

Facilities

Number of RV Sites: 32. **Number of Tent-Only Sites:** Undesignated sites. **Hookups:** Water, sewer, electric (30, 50 amp). **Dump Station:** Yes. **Laundry:** Yes. **Pay Phone:** No. **Rest Rooms and Showers:** Yes. **Fuel:** No. **Propane:** No. **Internal Roads:** Dirt. **RV Service:** No. **Market:** 1 mi. to Hutchinson. **Restaurant:** 1 mi. to Hutchinson.

General Store: No. **Vending:** No. **Swimming:** No. **Playground:** No. **Other:** Storm shelter. **Activities:** Viewing IMAX films, visiting museums. **Nearby Attractions:** Kansas Cosmosphere & Space Center, Reno County Museum. **Additional Information:** Hutchinson Chamber of Commerce, (316) 662-3391.

RESTRICTIONS

Pets: No dogs over 20 lbs in park. **Fires:** Subject to seasonal bans. **Alcoholic Beverages:** At sites. **Vehicle Maximum Length:** 70 ft.

TO GET THERE

From the junction of Hwy. 61 and Hwy. 50, go 0.25 mi. west on Hwy. 50. Take the first right turn into the entrance and drive through the campground to the office.

INDEPENDENCE

Elk City State Park

P.O. Box 945, Independence 67301. T: (316) 331-6295.

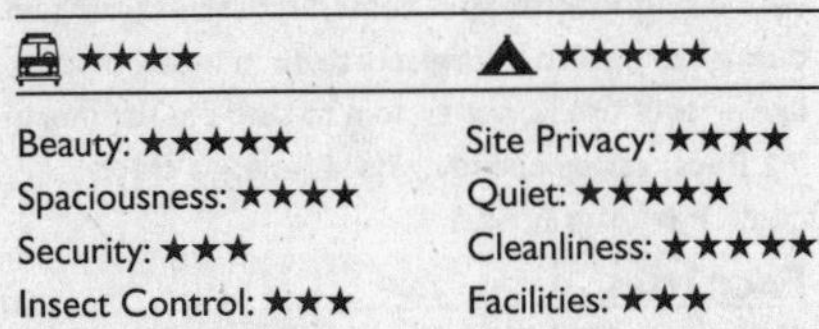

RV ★★★★ Tent ★★★★★

Beauty: ★★★★★ Site Privacy: ★★★★
Spaciousness: ★★★★ Quiet: ★★★★★
Security: ★★★ Cleanliness: ★★★★★
Insect Control: ★★★ Facilities: ★★★

This campground is another of the many attractive state parks in Kansas. Sites are well-groomed, located close to the water's edge, as well as further away. Those further away tend to be more open, with more trees closer to the edge of the lake. (For this reason, tenters may want to consider a site close to the water for the increased shelter.) Most sites are back-ins, with a limited number of pull-throughs. Sites fill up quickly for major holidays (Memorial Day, July 4th, Labor Day), so get there early in the day to ensure a spot for yourself.

BASICS

Operated By: Kansas Dept. of Wildlife & Parks. **Open:** All year. **Site Assignment:** First come, first served. **Registration:** In office. **Fee:** $7–$18, $5/day vehicle permit; no credit cards. **Parking:** At site, plenty of additional parking.

FACILITIES

Number of RV Sites: 150. **Number of Tent-Only Sites:** 56. **Hookups:** Water, sewer, electric (30, 50 amp). **Each Site:** Picnic table, fire pit/grill, trees. **Dump Station:** Yes. **Laundry:** No. **Pay Phone:** Yes. **Rest Rooms and Showers:** Yes. **Fuel:** No. **Propane:** No. **Internal Roads:** Paved. **RV Service:** No. **Market:** 5 mi. to Independence. **Restaurant:** 5 mi. to Independence. **General Store:** No. **Vending:** Yes. **Swimming:** Yes (lake). **Playground:** Yes. **Other:** Wildlife. **Activities:** Fishing, swimming, boating, waterskiing, hiking, hunting. **Nearby Attractions:** Little House on the Prairie, Riverside Park. **Additional Information:** Independence Chamber of Commerce, (316) 331-1890.

RESTRICTIONS

Pets: On leash only. **Fires:** In fire ring. **Alcoholic Beverages:** At sites. **Vehicle Maximum Length:** None.

TO GET THERE

From the junction of Hwy. 75 and Hwy. 160 (Main St. and 10th St. in town), go west on Hwy. 160 for 1.7 mi. Turn right onto Peter Pan Rd. Go 1 mi. north on this road (which turns into CR 3525), then turn left onto CR 4800. Continue west to the office or to a pay station.

KINSLEY

Four Aces RV Campground and Mobile Home

104 South Massechusettes Ave., Kinsley 67547. T: (620) 659-2060.

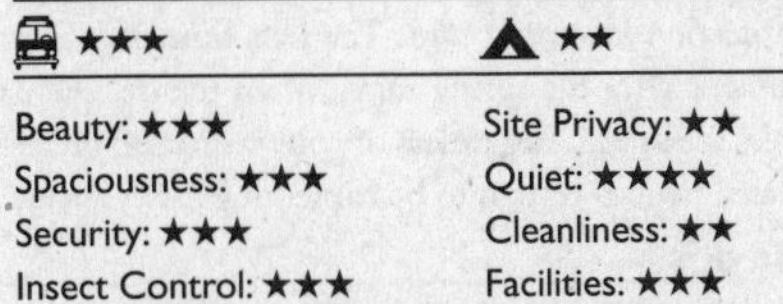

RV ★★★ Tent ★★

Beauty: ★★★ Site Privacy: ★★
Spaciousness: ★★★ Quiet: ★★★★
Security: ★★★ Cleanliness: ★★
Insect Control: ★★★ Facilities: ★★★

This campground lies in an open rural setting with woods to the south and east and agricultural land to the west. Detracting a little are houses to the north and several white buildings and tanks to the west that stand out sharply. Sites are level pull-throughs with large concrete slabs and a dirt/grass mixture beteen spaces. The ground is relatively barren, and there are no shade trees within the park. While the campground itself is clean enough with somewhat pretty surroundings, it could benefit from renovated rest rooms. The rest room and shower facilities are shared men/women, and toilets are separated by wooden sides that do not enclose each stall from floor to ceiling. Despite somewhat off-putting toilet facilities, this campground is an agreeable stay.

BASICS

Operated By: Private operator. **Open:** All year. **Site Assignment:** First come, first served. **Registration:** In office, late arrivals use drop box. **Fee:** $16. **Parking:** At site.

FACILITIES

Number of RV Sites: 20. **Number of Tent-Only Sites:** Undesignated sites. **Hookups:** Water, sewer, electric (20, 30, 50 amp). **Dump Station:** Yes. **Laundry:** Yes. **Pay Phone:** No. **Rest Rooms and Showers:** Yes. **Fuel:** No. **Propane:** No. **Internal Roads:** Dirt. **RV Service:** No. **Market:** 1 mi. into Kinsley. **Restaurant:** 1 mi. into Kinsley. **General Store:** No. **Vending:** Yes. **Swimming:** No. **Playground:** No. **Activities:** None on site. **Nearby Attractions:** Edwards County Historical Museum. **Additional Information:** Kinsley Chamber of Commerce, (316) 659-3642.

RESTRICTIONS

Pets: On leash only, cleaned up after. **Fires:** In grills. **Alcoholic Beverages:** At sites. **Vehicle Maximum Length:** None.

TO GET THERE

From the junction of Hwy. 183 and Hwy. 50, go 3 blocks west on Hwy. 50, turn left onto Massachusettes Ave., and follow the dirt road into the entrance.

LAWRENCE

Lawrence/Kansas City KOA

1473 Hwy. 40, Lawrence 66044. T: (800) 562-3708 or (785) 842-3877; F: (785) 312-9186; www.lawrencekoa.com.

RV ★★★★ Tent ★★★★

Beauty: ★★★ Site Privacy: ★★★★
Spaciousness: ★★★★ Quiet: ★★★
Security: ★★★★ Cleanliness: ★★★
Insect Control: ★★★★ Facilities: ★★★★★

A little messy due to renovations (scheduled for completion in 2002) but otherwise attractive, this campground is surrounded by seven acres of undeveloped land to the north and a sod farm with lush green grass to the east. Flowering trees and flowers planted in surprising nooks add color and charm to the grounds. All sites are grassy, level pull-throughs located on loops that are separated by rows of trees. Already packed with features, this campground promises exciting additional services when the renovations are completed. The best time to come is when the flowers and trees are in bloom. Keep in mind, however, the NASCAR schedule and be sure to cancel well in advance, if necessary, to avoid losing your deposit during these busy times.

BASICS

Operated By: Ralph & Kim Newell. **Open:** All year. **Site Assignment:** Upon registration, credit card for reservation; must cancel 24 hours in advance, except for race weekends, when cancellation must be made 1 week in advance for refund. **Registration:** In store, late arrivals select site from map & use drop box. **Fee:** RV $26, tent $20. **Parking:** At site, additional parking available.

FACILITIES

Number of RV Sites: 69. **Number of Tent-Only Sites:** 26. **Hookups:** Water, sewer, electric (30, 50 amp). **Each Site:** Picnic table, fire pit, trees. **Dump Station:** Yes. **Laundry:** Yes. **Pay Phone:** Yes. **Rest Rooms and Showers:** Yes. **Fuel:** No. **Propane:** Yes. **Internal Roads:** Paved/dirt. **RV Service:** Yes. **Market:** 2 mi. into Lawrence. **Restaurant:** 0.5 mi. into Lawrence. **General Store:** Yes. **Vending:** Yes. **Swimming:** Pool. **Playground:** Yes. **Other:** Game room, cabins, group meeting room, dog walk area, cycling/running trail. **Activities:** Volleyball, basketball, badminton, canoe trips, tetherball. **Nearby Attractions:** NASCAR track, golf course, Kansas City. **Additional Information:** Lawrence Chamber of Commerce, (913) 865-4411.

RESTRICTIONS

Pets: On leash, not left outside, cleaned up after. **Fires:** Fire pits only. **Alcoholic Beverages:** At sites. **Vehicle Maximum Length:** None. **Other:** Pay attention to speed limits, no parking on grass; no clotheslines.

TO GET THERE

From the junction of I-70 and Hwy. 59, drive 0.5 mi. north on 59, veer right (east) onto Hwy. 24, and follow Hwy. 24 for 0.2 mi. Take the first right at the KOA sign into the entrance. Follow the driveway to the end to register at the store.

LIBERAL

B&B Overnite RV Camp

Rte. 1 Box 66, Liberal 67901. T: (620) 624-5581; bbonc@midusa.net.

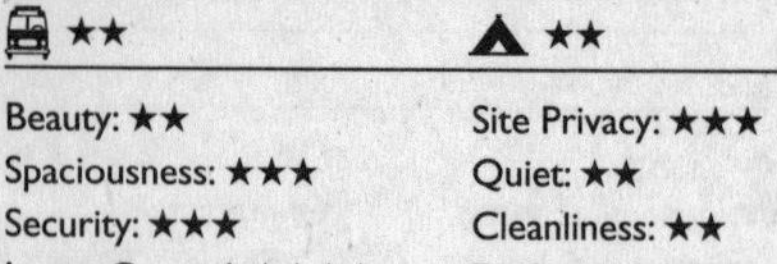

RV ★★ Tent ★★

Beauty: ★★	Site Privacy: ★★★
Spaciousness: ★★★	Quiet: ★★
Security: ★★★	Cleanliness: ★★
Insect Control: ★★★★	Facilities: ★★★★

Just on the outskirts of town, this campground has the potential to be quite attractive, but requires some renovations and beautification to achieve this goal. Sites are of a decent size (average 24 × 55 feet), with some quite lengthy pull-throughs (over 100 feet). Sites 23–25 offer good shade, while sites 28–30 in the southeast corner (the best sites) have good tree shade and abut the vegetation along the perimeter of the property. The east side of the property boasts a row of trees, and behind that, undeveloped land. However, there are some unsightly vehicles parked on the neighboring land in the southwest corner. One shower stall was quite clean, but the remaining two were less so. Additionally, dog waste was a problem in several campsites. Overall, this campground is a reasonable stopover, but not yet a destination in itself.

Basics

Operated By: Betty Booth. **Open:** All year. **Site Assignment:** First come, first served; verbal reservations OK. **Registration:** In office, late arrivals use drop box. **Fee:** RV $21, tent $16. **Parking:** At site.

Facilities

Number of RV Sites: 30. **Number of Tent-Only Sites:** 8. **Hookups:** Water, sewer, electric (30, 50 amp), cable. **Each Site:** Tree; most have picnic tables. **Dump Station:** Yes. **Laundry:** Yes. **Pay Phone:** Yes. **Rest Rooms and Showers:** Yes. **Fuel:** No. **Propane:** No. **Internal Roads:** Gravel. **RV Service:** No. **Market:** 5 mi. (into Liberal). **Restaurant:** Less than 0.25 mi. **General Store:** Yes. **Vending:** Yes. **Swimming:** No. **Playground:** Yes. **Other:** RV parts. **Activities:** Visit museums. **Nearby Attractions:** Mid-America Air Museum, Dorothy's House/Coronado Museum. **Additional Information:** Liberal Chamber, (316) 624-3855.

Restrictions

Pets: On leash, not tied up, cleaned up after. **Fires:** In grills only. **Alcoholic Beverages:** At sites. **Vehicle Maximum Length:** None. **Other:** No generators.

To Get There

From the junction of Hwy. 54 and Western Ave. in town (last light on western edge of town), go 2.5 mi. west on Hwy. 54. Turn left at the sign into the entrance.

MANHATTEN

Tuttle Creek State Park

5800A River Pond Rd., Manhatten 66502. T: (785) 539-7941; www.wp.state.ks.us; tuttlecreeksp@wp.state.ks.us.

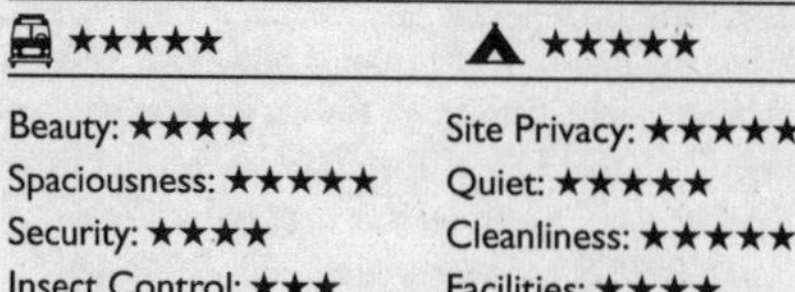

RV ★★★★★ Tent ★★★★★

Beauty: ★★★★	Site Privacy: ★★★★★
Spaciousness: ★★★★★	Quiet: ★★★★★
Security: ★★★★	Cleanliness: ★★★★★
Insect Control: ★★★	Facilities: ★★★★

Located to the northwest of Manhatten, this humungous state park (1,100-plus acres) offers four camping areas with grassy sites on large loops. Like other state parks, this campground offers a variety of sites, from waterfront to woodsy. The River Pond campground, for example, offers some spacious, well-groomed pull-throughs, although the back-ins (sites 71–104) are a little more pressed together. Tenters should be aware that some sites offer no protection in case of rain. The best time of year to come is after the spring rains, when the deciduous trees are in leaf. Regardless of your tastes and preferences, there is certain to be something for everyone.

Basics

Operated By: Kansas Dept. of Wildlife & Parks. **Open:** All year. **Site Assignment:** First come, first served; 10 reservable sites, must have credit card to hold, no refunds. **Registration:** At office or self-pay station. **Fee:** Varies, $5/day vehicle permit, add $2 for prime sites indicated by red. **Parking:** At site.

Facilities

Number of RV Sites: 116. **Number of Tent-Only Sites:** 500. **Hookups:** Water, electric (30, 50 amp). **Each Site:** Picnic table, fire pit, trees. **Dump Station:** Yes. **Laundry:** No. **Pay Phone:** Yes. **Rest Rooms and Showers:** Yes. **Fuel:** No. **Propane:** No. **Internal Roads:** Paved. **RV Service:** No. **Market:** 3 mi. to Manhatten. **Restaurant:** 3 mi. to Manhatten. **General Store:** Yes. **Vending:** Yes. **Swimming:** Yes (lake). **Playground:** Yes. **Other:** Boat ramp, group picnic shelters, fish cleaning station, canoe rentals. **Activities:** Swimming, boating, waterskiing, windsurfing, cycling, hiking, softball, hunting. **Nearby Attractions:** Flint Hills, Riley County Historical Museum, Wonder Workshop. **Additional Information:** Manhatten CVB, (800) 759-0134.

Restrictions

Pets: On 10-ft. leash. **Fires:** In rings or grills. **Alcoholic Beverages:** Beer only. **Vehicle Maximum Length:** None. **Other:** $5 per day vehicle permit.

To Get There

From the junction of Hwy. 24 and Hwy. 13, turn east onto Hwy. 13 and drive 1.8 mi. Take the tricky right turn at the sign (this may be problematic for larger rigs) and follow the road 1 mi. to the office or self-pay station. Alternately, take Hwy. 24 0.5 mi. east from the junction with Hwy. 13, and turn left at the sign. This takes you away from the office, but avoids the hair-brained/hair-pin turn.

MEADE

Circle-O Motel and RV Park

P.O. Box 203, Meade 67864. T: (620) 873-2405 or (620) 873-2543.

RV ★★ Tent ★

Beauty: ★★	Site Privacy: ★★★
Spaciousness: ★★★	Quiet: ★★★
Security: ★★	Cleanliness: ★★★
Insect Control: ★★★	Facilities: ★★

This campground has an urban feel, with motor homes occupying the northwest corner, a residential area to the north, a commercial area to the south, and a total paucity of shade trees throughout the campground. A residential back alley runs through the campground, and sites 25 and 31 occupy a portion of it. The average site is 25-feet wide, but there are some absolutely humungous pull-throughs (sites 35 and 36). Shower facilities are slightly cramped but reasonably clean. The least desirable sites are 15–17, which are just off the back alley and next to the dump station. Better sites are 26, 32, and 33, close to the grassy tent area. (The tent area is a well-mowed lawn, but lacking the protection of trees.) Circle-O Motel is a reasonable place to spend a night, and if you are lucky, you can hit on a choice spot. Beware the lack of shade in the summer, however. Tenters: move on!

Basics

Operated By: Mick & Pat Ohnick. **Open:** All year. **Site Assignment:** First come, first served; assigned during busy season. **Registration:** In motel office, late arrivals use honor system to settle in the morning. **Fee:** Varies depending on vehicle; no credit cards. **Parking:** At site.

Facilities

Number of RV Sites: 24. **Number of Tent-Only Sites:** Undesignated sites. **Hookups:** Water, sewer, electric (30, 50 amp). **Dump Station:** Yes. **Laundry:** No. **Pay Phone:** Yes. **Rest Rooms and Showers:** Yes. **Fuel:** Next door. **Propane:** No. **Internal Roads:** Gravel/dirt. **RV Service:** No. **Market:** 7 blocks. **Restaurant:** 6 blocks. **General Store:** Across the street. **Vending:** No. **Swimming:** No. **Playground:** Yes. **Other:** Pet area. **Activities:** Visiting museums. **Nearby Attractions:** Dalton Gang Hideout, Meade County Historical Society Museum. **Additional Information:** Meade Economic Development, (316) 873-8795.

Restrictions

Pets: On leash only. **Fires:** In grills. **Alcoholic Beverages:** At sites. **Vehicle Maximum Length:** None. **Other:** No vehicle washing.

To Get There

From the junction of Hwy. 23 and Hwy. 54/160, turn east onto Hwy. 54/160 and go 0.4 mi. Turn north onto State St., then turn right into the second driveway at the motel.

NEWTON

Payne Oil Co. RV Park

Rte. 2, Junction I-135 & K-15, Exit 34, Newton 67114. T: (316) 283-5530.

RV ★★★ Tent ★

Beauty: ★★	Site Privacy: ★★★
Spaciousness: ★★★	Quiet: ★★
Security: ★★	Cleanliness: ★★★★
Insect Control: ★★★	Facilities: ★★★★

This small RV park located next to the highway is a convenient stop for those requiring RV parts or servicing or too tired to push on. Part gas station, part RV service, part campground, Payne Oil Co. makes up in services what it lacks in beauty. (Note that the rest room and shower facilities are located within the office and are unavailable outside office hours. The park does supply a porta-potty for campers' use.) Laid out as spokes radiating from a central road, sites are open and grassy, with 15 pull-thrus and 5 back-ins. The average site size is 30 × 100 feet. The most advantageous sites (10, 20) are located on the end closest to the golf course, where the park abuts a large grassy field. The gas station to the northwest and storage units and the highway to the west conspire to make the scenery rather unattractive, although a sparse number of small trees do their best to liven up the grounds. Seemingly any number of tents can be pitched on the grassy area to the south of the RV sites. This is a great service stop, but not a destination in itself.

Basics

Operated By: Rick & Maura Payne. **Open:** All year. **Site Assignment:** First come, first served. **Registration:** At gas station, late arrivals use drop box under picnic shelter. **Fee:** RV $15, tent $5; V, MC, AE, D. **Parking:** At site.

Facilities

Number of RV Sites: 20. **Number of Tent-Only Sites:** Undesignated sites. **Hookups:** Water, sewer, electric (30, 50 amp). **Dump Station:** Yes. **Laundry:** Yes. **Pay Phone:** No. **Rest Rooms and Showers:** Yes. **Fuel:** Yes. **Propane:** Yes. **Internal Roads:** Dirt. **RV Service:** Yes. **Market:** 2 mi. in Newton. **Restaurant:** 2 mi. in Newton. **General Store:** No. **Vending:** No. **Swimming:** No. **Playground:** No. **Other:** 9-hole golf course. **Activities:** Jogging, cycling, golf. **Nearby Attractions:** Kauffman Museum. **Additional Information:** Newton Chamber of Commerce, (316) 283-2560.

Restrictions

Pets: On leash only. **Fires:** In grills. **Alcoholic Beverages:** At sites. **Vehicle Maximum Length:** None.

To Get There

From I-135, take Exit 34 and turn east onto Hwy. 15. Drive 0.1 mi. on Hwy. 15 and turn right into the gas-station entrance.

NORTON

Prairie Dog State Park

RR 431, Norton 67654. T: (785) 877-2953.

RV ★★★★ | Tent ★★★★★

Beauty: ★★★★	Site Privacy: ★★★★
Spaciousness: ★★★★★	Quiet: ★★★★★
Security: ★★★★	Cleanliness: ★★★★
Insect Control: ★★★	Facilities: ★★★

Named for the prairie dog town at the entrance, this park is renowned for the excellent fishing it provides in the Sebelius Reservoir. Best in the spring or fall, the park is extremely crowded during the summer, and especially so for the holidays. Sites are grassy and open, averaging 60-feet long and up to 65-feet wide, with both back-ins and pull-throughs. Despite the number of new trees planted, sites do not benefit from their shade. Branded Cedar sites W1–W6 have a commanding view of the lake and proximity to the showers, while Medowlark campsites have fire pits and are situated right on the lake. Tenting areas are separated from the RV sites and also offer fire pits. This park is a beautiful alternative to the overnight RV spots in town, with only slightly fewer facilities.

Basics

Operated By: Camp Hosts Ray & Leta Koel. **Open:** All year. **Site Assignment:** First come, first served; 8 reservable sites. **Registration:** At office or self-pay stations. **Fee:** $7–$18, $5/day vehicle permit; no credit cards. **Parking:** At site.

Facilities

Number of RV Sites: 58. **Number of Tent-Only Sites:** 139. **Hookups:** Water, electric (30, 50 amp). **Each Site:** Picnic table, tree, some lantern poles. **Dump Station:** Yes. **Laundry:** No. **Pay Phone:** Yes. **Rest Rooms and Showers:** Yes. **Fuel:** Yes. **Propane:** Yes. **Internal Roads:** Paved/gravel. **RV Service:** No. **Market:** 6 mi. to Norton. **Restaurant:** 6 mi. to Norton. **General Store:** Yes. **Vending:** No. **Swimming:** Yes (lake). **Playground:** Yes. **Other:** Boat ramp, renovated adobe home, one-room schoolhouse, marina concessions, picnic shelters, some free firewood. **Activities:** Fishing, boating, swimming, waterskiing, archery, wildlife-watching, fireworks over lake on July 4th w/ free watermelon. **Nearby Attractions:** Gallery of Also Rans (First State Bank building). **Additional Information:** Norton Chamber of Commerce, (785) 877-2501.

Restrictions

Pets: On leash only. **Fires:** In grills. **Alcoholic Beverages:** None (kegs w/ a permit). **Vehicle Maximum Length:** None. **Other:** No washing of vehicles or boats.

To Get There

From the junction of Hwy. 283 and Hwy. 36, turn west onto Hwy. 36 and drive 4.3 mi. through the town of Norton. Turn right at the sign for the park onto Hwy. 261 and drive 1 mi. to the office or to a self-pay station.

OAKLEY

Camp Inn RV Park

462 US 83, Oakley 67748. T: (785) 672-4440.

RV ★★★★ | Tent ★★★★

Beauty: ★★★★	Site Privacy: ★★★
Spaciousness: ★★★	Quiet: ★★★★
Security: ★★★	Cleanliness: ★★★★
Insect Control: ★★★★	Facilities: ★★★

Despite its proximity to the commercial area of Oakley (half a mile), this campground retains a secluded feel. Laid out on loops, sites are spacious, open, and grassy, with both back-ins and pull-throughs. Average sites are 30-feet wide, although several (M1, M10, M11, D12) seem short-changed for space. Sites M1–M10 feel slightly as if they were in a fishbowl for all to look at, but M12–M20 are more removed and private. The best sites are D13–17 and E13–17, which are more secluded but have a convenient proximity to facilities. The tent area is fenced-off from the RV sites, next to a large open field. Although the unmarked sites lack overhead protection, this campground is a better bet for tenters than the campground in nearby Colby.

Basics

Operated By: Marvin Huelsmann. **Open:** All year. **Site Assignment:** First come, first served (unless close to full). **Registration:** In office, late arrivals use drop box. **Fee:** Summer (Apr. 15–Oct. 15) $20, winter $15. **Parking:** At site.

Facilities

Number of RV Sites: 86. **Number of Tent-Only Sites:** Undesignated sites. **Hookups:** Water, sewer, electric (30, 50 amp). **Each Site:** Picnic table, shade tree. **Dump Station:** No (sewer at all sites). **Laundry:** Yes. **Pay Phone:** Yes. **Rest Rooms and Showers:** Yes. **Fuel:** Yes. **Propane:** No. **Internal Roads:** Gravel. **RV Service:** No. **Market:** 1 mi. in Oakley. **Restaurant:** Next door. **General Store:** Yes. **Vending:** No. **Swimming:** Pool (Memorial Day–Labor Day). **Playground:** Yes. **Other:** Mini-golf, ATM, discount at Conoco gas station w/ valid RV park receipt. **Activities:** Golf, horseshoes, volleyball, video games. **Nearby Attractions:** Monument Rocks, Fick Fossil & History Museum, Prairie Dog Town. **Additional Information:** Oakley Chamber of Commerce, (913) 672-4862.

Restrictions

Pets: On leash only. **Fires:** In grills. **Alcoholic Beverages:** At sites. **Vehicle Maximum Length:** None.

To Get There

From I-70, take Exit 70, then turn south onto Hwy. 83. Drive 0.2 mi. on Hwy. 83 and take the first right after the I-70 junction. Go straight into the entrance.

PRATT

Evergreen Inn and RV Park

20001 West US 54, Pratt 67124. T: (800) 456-6424 or (620) 672-6431.

RV ★★★ | Tent ★★★

Beauty: ★★★	Site Privacy: ★
Spaciousness: ★	Quiet: ★★★
Security: ★★★	Cleanliness: ★★★★
Insect Control: ★★★	Facilities: ★★★

This is a fairly attractive park with decent services, but a little cramped. The south side is bordered by an open grassy field with dogwood, fir, and deciduous trees at the far end, while the building complex is somewhat shielded by large shade trees. Spaces, however, are a meager 15-feet wide, posing potential difficulties for larger rigs with slide-outs. Sites 13 and 14 are situated well away from the rest of the sites and from each other and can accommodate a larger-sized vehicle. Site 13 is particularly nice, tucked away under mature shade trees and sided by an open grassy field and a wooden fence. Sites 1 and 12 also benefit from an extra bit of grassy space. There is plenty of extra space at the head of the sites to park an extra vehicle. The shower and rest room facilities are quite clean, but can accommodate only one person at a time. Tent space is located between the RV park and the motel on a grassy area with a fair number of shade trees.

Basics

Operated By: Mike. **Open:** All year. **Site Assignment:** First come, first served; reservations only after 4 p.m. & with credit card, cancel before 4 p.m. same day for refund. **Registration:** In motel office, late arrivals ring doorbell. **Fee:** RV $16, tent $10;V, MC,AE, D. **Parking:** At site.

Facilities

Number of RV Sites: 14. **Number of Tent-Only Sites:** Undesignated sites. **Hookups:** Water, sewer, electric (30 amp). **Dump Station:** Yes. **Laundry:** Yes. **Pay Phone:** No. **Rest Rooms and Showers:** Yes. **Fuel:** No. **Propane:** No. **Internal Roads:** Gravel. **RV Service:** No. **Market:** 2 mi. to Pratt. **Restaurant:** Next door. **General Store:** No. **Vending:** Yes. **Swimming:** Pool. **Playground:** Yes. **Other:** Trampoline. **Activities:** Basketball. **Nearby Attractions:** Kansas State Fish Hatchery. **Additional Information:** Pratt Chamber of Commerce, (316) 672-5501.

Restrictions

Pets: On leash only. **Fires:** No. **Alcoholic Beverages:** Not in pool. **Vehicle Maximum Length:** 60 ft.

To Get There

From the junction of Hwy. 281 and Hwy. 54, go 2 mi. west on Hwy. 54, then turn left at the sign into the entrance.

RUSSELL

Triple J Campground

187 Edwards, Russell 67665. T: (785) 483-4826; F: (785) 483-4826.

RV ★★★★ Tent ★★★

Beauty: ★★★ Site Privacy: ★★★★
Spaciousness: ★★★★ Quiet: ★★★
Security: ★★★ Cleanliness: ★★★★
Insect Control: ★★★★ Facilities: ★★★★

This campground has pull-throughs that could accommodate all but the largest monster rig on the road without unhooking. Average site size is 40 ¥ 60 feet. The grounds are spacious and open, with a rural feel; an open field and horses in the west corner add to the ambiance. Unmarked tent sites are on a grassy strip that is set away from the RV sites. Trees provide a natural barricade to the neighboring land to the north, and the best sites (even numbers 34–38 and odd numbers 39–47) face this direction. The least favorable sites—still nowhere near a bad spot to end up—are on the east side, facing the distant shopping complex. (The campground is quite removed from this complex, and these sites are offset from the entrance, which gives them extra space and privacy.) RVers will be happy with any available spot; tenters, however, fare a little worse, being closer to the highway and its attendant noise.

Basics

Operated By: Lana Zorn. **Open:** All year. **Site Assignment:** First come, first served. **Registration:** In office. **Fee:** RV $18, tent $12; no credit cards. **Parking:** At site.

Facilities

Number of RV Sites: 52. **Number of Tent-Only Sites:** Undesignated sites. **Hookups:** Water, sewer, electric (30, 50 amp). **Each Site:** Picnic table; grill & tree at most sites. **Dump Station:** No (sewer at all sites). **Laundry:** Yes. **Pay Phone:** Yes. **Rest Rooms and Showers:** Yes. **Fuel:** No. **Propane:** No. **Internal Roads:** Paved/gravel. **RV Service:** No (within 1 block). **Market:** 1 block. **Restaurant:** 1 block. **General Store:** Yes. **Vending:** Yes. **Swimming:** No. **Playground:** Yes. **Other:** Storm shelter, dataport hookups. **Activities:** Mini-golf, horseshoes, video games. **Nearby Attractions:** Sternberg Museum, Cathedral of the Plains, Garden of Eden sculptures. **Additional Information:** Russell CVB, (800) 658-4686.

Restrictions

Pets: On leash only, cleaned up after. **Fires:** In grills only. **Alcoholic Beverages:** At sites. **Vehicle Maximum Length:** None.

To Get There

From I-70, turn north onto Hwy. 281 and follow it for 1 block. The entrance is on the left. Follow the driveway around to the right; the office is across from the mini-golf.

SCOTT CITY

Camp Lakeside

520 West Scott Lake Dr., Scott City 67871. T: (620) 872-2061; scottsp@wp.state.ks.us.

RV ★★★★ Tent ★★★★★

Beauty: ★★★★ Site Privacy: ★★★★
Spaciousness: ★★★★ Quiet: ★★★★
Security: ★★★ Cleanliness: ★★★★★
Insect Control: ★★★ Facilities: ★★★

The Scott Lake campgrounds are divided into several campgrounds around the lake, with sites close to the water (Lakeside campground) as well as further up the embankment, with a more woodsy feel (Elm Grove). Sites are laid out on a series of loops, with both pull-throughs and back-ins. All sites are spacious and level, and the lake offers a variety of activities for a day, a week, or even just an afternoon. Rocky outcrops around part of the lake add to the natural beauty, but the lack of water facilities in winter may make this campground too natural for some campers. Those who don't mind roughing it a little (in winter only) should definitely make a point to stop here—and bring the kids.

Basics

Operated By: Kansas Dept. of Wildlife & Parks. **Open:** All year. **Site Assignment:** First come, first served. **Registration:** At office or self-pay stations. **Fee:** $7–$18, $5/day vehicle permit. **Parking:** At site.

Facilities

Number of RV Sites: 60. **Number of Tent-Only Sites:** 170. **Hookups:** Electric, water (no water Oct.–Apr.). **Each Site:** Grill. **Dump Station:** Yes. **Laundry:** No. **Pay Phone:** Yes. **Rest Rooms and Showers:** Yes. **Fuel:** No. **Propane:** No. **Internal Roads:** Paved/gravel. **RV Service:** No. **Market:** 14 mi. to Scott City (limited market on site). **Restaurant:** 14 mi. to Scott City. **General Store:** Yes. **Vending:** Yes. **Swimming:** Yes (lake). **Playground:** Yes. **Other:** Boat ramp, canoe/boat rentals. **Activities:** Boating, fishing, cycling, hiking, horseback riding, hunting. **Nearby Attractions:** El Cuartelego pueblo ruins. **Additional Information:** Scott City Chamber of Commerce, (316) 872-3525.

Restrictions

Pets: On leash only. **Fires:** In grills only. **Alcoholic Beverages:** Beer only. **Vehicle Maximum Length:** None.

To Get There

From the junction of Hwy. 83 and Hwy. 95, turn north onto Hwy. 95. To go to the office (or a pay station), follow Hwy. 95 to West Scott Lake Drive, and turn left into the office park-ing lot. To get to other pay stations and campsites, turn right onto East Scott Lake Drive and drive 2.5 mi.

STOCKTON

Webster State Park

1210 Nine Rd., Stockton 67669. T: (785) 425-6775; F: (785) 425-6180; webstersp@wp.state.ks.us.

RV ★★★★ Tent ★★★

Beauty: ★★★★ Site Privacy: ★★★★
Spaciousness: ★★★★ Quiet: ★★★★★
Security: ★★★ Cleanliness: ★★★★
Insect Control: ★★★ Facilities: ★★★

Sites in this campground vary from water's edge to further up the embankment. Thus the camper can experience woods, beach, and park all in one. All sites are level and grassy, averaging 50 × 60 feet in size (some pull-throughs are even longer), situated on a series of large loops and some grid sites. The reservoir itself is surrounded by reeds (at the water's edge) and fields with short pines. Sites close to the water generally have more trees, while those away from the water are more open. While parking is available at each of the sites, there is enough additional parking (for day use) to accommodate extra vehicles. Facilities are clean but a hike away from some campsites. Overall, this is a fun, family-oriented destination with plenty of activities for kids and grandparents alike.

Basics

Operated By: Kansas department of Wildlife & Parks. **Open:** All year. **Site Assignment:** First come, first served; 18 reservable sites, can be reserved 2 weeks in advance by check or credit card or 1 week in advance in person, no refunds. **Registration:** At station or self-pay sites (Apr. 1–Sept. 30 self-pay only). **Fee:** Campsite $7, 1 utility $17, 2 utilities $18, 3 utilities $20, add $2 for prime sites marked red. **Parking:** At site.

Facilities

Number of RV Sites: 72. **Number of Tent-Only Sites:** 100. **Hookups:** Water, electric (20, 30, 50 amp). **Each Site:** Picnic table, fire pit, trees; some lantern poles, some free firewood. **Dump Station:** Yes. **Laundry:** No. **Pay Phone:** Yes. **Rest Rooms and Showers:** Yes. **Fuel:** No. **Propane:** No. **Internal Roads:** Paved. **RV Service:** No. **Market:** 9 mi. to Stockton. **Restaurant:** 9 mi. to

Stockton. **General Store:** Yes. **Vending:** Yes. **Swimming:** Yes (lake). **Playground:** Yes. **Other:** Picnic shelters, fishing dock, fish cleaning station, wildlife. **Activities:** Swimming, fishing, baseball, boating, hiking, volleyball, horseshoes. **Nearby Attractions:** Webster Reservation Wildlife Area. **Additional Information:** Stockton Chamber of Commerce & Economic Development: (785) 425-6162.

Restrictions

Pets: On leash only. **Fires:** In grills or pits. **Alcoholic Beverages:** Beer only. **Vehicle Maximum Length:** 60 ft.

To Get There

From the junction of Hwy. 183 and Hwy. 24, turn north onto Hwy. 24 and drive 9 mi. The entrance is on the left (past the overpass). Follow the road to the office or to a self-pay station. (The turn-off for Webster Reservoir onto Hwy. 283 leads to the Goose Flats camping area.)

TOPEKA

Topeka KOA

3366 KOA Rd., Topeka 66429. T: (800) 562-8717 or (785) 246-3419; www.koa.com.

RV ★★★★★ Tent ★★★

Beauty: ★★★★ Site Privacy: ★★★
Spaciousness: ★★★ Quiet: ★★★★
Security: ★★★★ Cleanliness: ★★★★★
Insect Control: ★★★★ Facilities: ★★★★★

This campground has the feeling of being lost in the woods. The land in front of the office is undeveloped, and Area A (in back) is surrounded on three sides by undeveloped land. There is, accordingly, no highway noise; however, trains pass close enough to be heard from all over the campground. Sites are grassy, with level pull-throughs in Area B. Area A, has some slope—all sites but end site 26 seemed to require jacks. However, this is the nicer area of the campground if you can tolerate some slope. Area B has longer but narrower sites: 25 feet vs. 30 feet in Area A. Area B is also open to office, road, and pool traffic. The best sites are 25 and 26 in Area A, as they are level and in the prettiest part of the park. Sites 1 and 2 are the least desirable, being close to the office, to the parking lot, and to a garbage dumpster. The tent area is a long strip of grass at the front of the property. Sites are separated by a small length of wooden fencing providing better privacy. Although located a fair distance outisde of the metroplois of Topeka, this campground is worth the trip and offers a relaxing, quiet stay in the middle of the woods.

Basics

Operated By: Private operator. **Open:** Apr. 1–Nov. 15 (otherwise limited services). **Site Assignment:** Upon registration; credit card to reserve site, cancel before 4 p.m. the day before arrival for refund. **Registration:** In office, late arrivals use drop box. **Fee:** RV $20 full, $19 water/electric, tent $16. **Parking:** At site.

Facilities

Number of RV Sites: 36. **Number of Tent-Only Sites:** 11. **Hookups:** Water, sewer, electric (20, 30, 50 amp). **Each Site:** Picnic table, grill or fire pit, tree. **Dump Station:** Yes. **Laundry:** Yes. **Pay Phone:** No. **Rest Rooms and Showers:** Yes. **Fuel:** No. **Propane:** No. **Internal Roads:** Gravel. **RV Service:** No. **Market:** 2 mi. to Topeka. **Restaurant:** 2 mi. to Topeka. **General Store:** Yes. **Vending:** Yes. **Swimming:** Pool. **Playground:** Yes. **Other:** Pond, cabins, rec room, antique shop. **Activities:** Golf, shopping, visiting museums, sightseeing, swimming. **Nearby Attractions:** Combat Air Museum, Gage Park, Kansas Center for Historical Research, State Capitol, Ward-Meade Park, golf course, antique malls, casinos. **Additional Information:** Topeka CVB, (800) 235-1030.

Restrictions

Pets: On leash only, cleaned up after. **Fires:** In fire ring. **Alcoholic Beverages:** At sites. **Vehicle Maximum Length:** None.

To Get There

From the junction of I-70 and Hwy. 75, take Exit 358 and drive 9 mi. to Hwy. 24. Take the Hwy. 24 east Exit, then turn left at the KOA sign (at mile marker 374) onto KOA Rd. Follow the gravel drive 1.3 mi. through a residential area and over the bridge. The entrance is on the right, north of 31st St.

WAKEENEY

Wakeeney KOA Kampground

P.O. Box 235, Wakeeney 67672. T: (800) 562-2761 or (785) 743-5612.

RV ★★★★ Tent ★★★

Beauty: ★★★ Site Privacy: ★★★★
Spaciousness: ★★★★ Quiet: ★★★
Security: ★★★★ Cleanliness: ★★★★★
Insect Control: ★★★ Facilities: ★★★★★

This campground features modern, clean, and tastefully decorated facilities. All sites are level and grassy, the majority (all except those in C area) being pull-throughs. Sites and rows are clearly marked, and site sizes average 30 × 62 feet (up to 80 feet). The playground and pool facilities are well away from camping sites. Tent sites are likewise separated from the RV sites by the internal road and from each other by a half-length of wood fencing. The back-ins in the C area face a screen of trees, but are closest to the highway. Site 75 in the southeast corner faces two unattractive sheds and a slightly crumbling fence. Besides this minor insult to the senses, you really can't go wrong with any site, nor can the facilities be beat. There is definitely a site to fit all preferences: large shade tree, proximity to the restroom facilities, to the pool, etc.

Basics

Operated By: Fred & Sue Wallace. **Open:** Mar. 15–Nov. 15. **Site Assignment:** Upon registration, reservations w/ credit card, cancel same day. **Registration:** In office, late arrivals use drop box. **Fee:** RV $20–$22, tent $16. **Parking:** At site.

Facilities

Number of RV Sites: 79. **Number of Tent-Only Sites:** 13. **Hookups:** Water, sewer, electric (30, 50 amp). **Each Site:** Picnic table, tree. **Dump Station:** Yes. **Laundry:** Yes. **Pay Phone:** Yes. **Rest Rooms and Showers:** Yes. **Fuel:** No. **Propane:** Yes. **Internal Roads:** Dirt/gravel. **RV Service:** No. **Market:** 1 mi. to Wakeeney. **Restaurant:** 2 blocks. **General Store:** No. **Vending:** Yes. **Swimming:** Pool. **Playground:** Yes. **Other:** 3 cabins. **Activities:** Volleyball. **Nearby Attractions:** Cedar Bluff State Park, Castle rock. **Additional Information:** Wakeeney Chamber of Commerce, (913) 743-2077.

Restrictions

Pets: On leash. **Fires:** In grills. **Alcoholic Beverages:** At sites. **Vehicle Maximum Length:** None.

To Get There

From I-70, take Exit 127 and turn south onto Hwy. 283. Go 100 yards on Hwy. 283 onto the frontage road, which dead-ends at the KOA entrance.

WELLINGTON

Wheatland RV Park

R.R. 1 Box 227, Wellington 67152. T: (877) 914-6114 or (620) 326-6114.

RV ★★★ Tent ★★★

Beauty: ★★★ Site Privacy: ★★★
Spaciousness: ★★★ Quiet: ★★★★
Security: ★★★ Cleanliness: ★★
Insect Control: ★★★ Facilities: ★★★★★

A little unkempt and ragged around the edges, this campground suffers from a few shortcomings that could easily be set right to turn the park around. Bordered on the south and east by wooded land and to the west by a grassy field, it offers quite a good deal of shade. Trees and shrubs around the office and driveway give a secluded feeling. Tent sites are in a row among the shrubs around the periphery of the campsite. From here, however, the campground slides downhill: a mobile-home park abuts the south western side, longer rigs (55 feet) will stick out from both ends, there seems to be lax enforcement of the leash law, and the curve in the road near sites 38–43 and 25–27 seems prone to flooding after a rain. (The dirt road had dried into a choppy, difficult mess after a recent rain, with no obvious attempts to smooth it out.) Sites include both back-ins and pull-throughs, all of which are both level and grassy. End site 27 seems to have been invaded by the road. Other less desriable sites include 15–20 (trees severely cut back) and 25–26 (trees too young for shade). The best sites are 21–24, followed closely by odd numbers 51–55—these are pull-throughs that face the shrubbery to the east and rest under a canopy of shade trees.

Basics

Operated By: Richard D. McCue. **Open:** All year. **Site Assignment:** Upon registration or first come, first served; verbal reservations OK. **Registration:** In office, late arrivals use drop box. **Fee:** RV $22, tent $16; V, MC, AE, D; 10% discount for KOA, Good Sam, or AARP membership or cash. **Parking:** At site.

Facilities

Number of RV Sites: 72. **Number of Tent-Only Sites:** 15. **Hookups:** Water, sewer, electric (30, 50 amp). **Each Site:** Picnic table, grill, tree; every other tent site has a fire pit. **Dump Station:** Yes. **Laundry:** Yes. **Pay Phone:** Yes. **Rest Rooms and Showers:** Yes. **Fuel:** No. **Propane:** Yes. **Internal Roads:** Dirt. **RV Service:** No. **Market:** 5 mi. into Wellington. **Restaurant:** 0.5 mi. into Wellington. **General Store:** Yes. **Vending:** No. **Swimming:** Pool. **Playground:** Yes. **Other:** 1 cabin, hot tub, video games, dog walk. **Activities:** Swimming, visiting museums. **Nearby Attractions:** Chisholm Trail Museum. **Additional Information:** Wellington Chamber of Commerce, (316) 326-7466.

Restrictions

Pets: On leash only. **Fires:** In fire ring or grill. **Alcoholic Beverages:** At sites. **Vehicle Maximum Length:** None.

To Get There

From the junction of I-35 and Hwy. 160, go west on 160 for 1.5 mi. Turn left into the entrance at the sign.

WICHITA

USI RV Park

2920 East 33rd North, Wichita 67219. T: (800) 782-1531 or (316) 838-8699 or (316) 838-0435; F: (316) 838-1193.

RV: ★★★★ Tent: n/a

Beauty: ★★	Site Privacy: ★★
Spaciousness: ★★★	Quiet: ★★★
Security: ★★★★	Cleanliness: ★★★★★
Insect Control: ★★★★	Facilities: ★★★★

This popular park consists of gravel and grassy sites laid out in strips 25-feet wide and long enough to accommodate almost any rig. Most sites are pull-throughs with very little grass—there is slightly more grass at the sites around the perimeter. The most favorable sites are in the A area, which boasts trees (sites 6–8 are especially nice), more grass, and proximity to the rest rooms. Sites 13–14 are jammed between the office and a garage and seem to have been added as an afterthought. All facilities are fantastically clean, and there are separate phone and dataport rooms, which give excellent privacy. While the wooden fence around the west side does a fine job of blocking out the view of neighboring land, there is a storage area to the southeast and a large radio antenna due north that detract from the setting.

Basics

Operated By: Sheila Wagner. **Open:** All year. **Site Assignment:** Upon registration, reservations strongly recommended, credit card to hold site; for shorter stay, cancel within 24 hours; for longer stay, within 5 days. **Registration:** In office, late arrivals use drop box. **Fee:** $21–$23. **Parking:** At site.

Facilities

Number of RV Sites: 75. **Number of Tent-Only Sites:** 0. **Hookups:** Water, sewer, electric (30, 50 amp). **Each Site:** Picnic table, tree. **Dump Station:** Yes. **Laundry:** Yes. **Pay Phone:** Yes. **Rest Rooms and Showers:** Yes. **Fuel:** No. **Propane:** Yes. **Internal Roads:** Gravel. **RV Service:** No. **Market:** 3 mi. east. **Restaurant:** 3 mi. east. **General Store:** Yes. **Vending:** Yes. **Swimming:** No. **Playground:** No. **Other:** Dataports, rec room, storm shelter. **Activities:** Sightseeing, shopping. **Nearby Attractions:** Wichita Grdens, Sedgwick County Zoo, Indian Center Museum, Wichita Art Museum, Wichita Center for the Arts, Omnisphere & Science Center, Wichita Greyhound Park. **Additional Information:** Wichita Chamber of Commerce, (316) 265-7771, Wichita CVB, (800) 288-9424.

Restrictions

Pets: 2 pets per vehicle; must sign pet agreement. **Fires:** None. **Alcoholic Beverages:** No kegs. **Vehicle Maximum Length:** None. **Other:** 10-year age limit of vehicle.

To Get There

From Hwy. 135 (southbound Exit 10, northbound Exit 10A), turn east onto Hwy. 96 and go 1 mi. Take the Hillside Exit and turn left onto Hillside Rd., then make an immediate left after the overpass onto 33rd St. Drive 1 block and turn right at the sign.

WILLIAMSBURG

Homewood RV Park

2161 Idaho Rd., Williamsburg 66095. T: (785) 242-5601.

RV: ★★★★ Tent: ★★★

Beauty: ★★★★	Site Privacy: ★★★
Spaciousness: ★★★	Quiet: ★★★
Security: ★★★	Cleanliness: ★★★★
Insect Control: ★★★	Facilities: ★★★★

This campground, one corner of a 55-acre farm, is a very pretty and convenient stopover from the highway, and proprietor Betty is friendly and full of life. (If interested, ask to see historical family photos.) The park is ringed on all sides by trees, some of them flowering. There is a small picnic area in a stand of woods bordering the farmland, and an unused (and somewhat unattractive) pond to the north. The audible traffic noise is quickly forgotten in the natural surroundings. Sites 1–3, 10–13, and 17 have particularly nice rustic views, while sites 16, 16b (unmarked), and 17 are off the main loop and back into woods, beyond which lies only farmland. Slightly less desirable sites are 1 (a little too close to the rest rooms) and 15 (tip of an island in the loop, and slightly cut off). Tent sites are unmarked, but adequate both in number and in overhead protection.

Basics

Operated By: Larry & Betty Shaffer. **Open:** All year. **Site Assignment:** Upon registration. **Registration:** In office, verbal reservations OK. **Fee:** Pull-through $16, back-in $15, tent $12. **Parking:** At site.

Facilities

Number of RV Sites: 24. **Number of Tent-Only Sites:** Undesignated sites. **Hookups:** Water, sewer, electric (30, 50 amp), some phone. **Each Site:** Trees, some picnic tables. **Dump Station:** Yes. **Laundry:** Yes. **Pay Phone:** Yes. **Rest Rooms and Showers:** Yes. **Fuel:** No. **Propane:** No. **Internal Roads:** Gravel. **RV Service:** No. **Market:** 8 mi. to Ottawa. **Restaurant:** 8 mi. to Ottawa. **General Store:** No. **Vending:** No. **Swimming:** No. **Playground:** No. **Other:** Walking trail, library, dogwalk area, country & western singer. **Activities:** Impromptu dinners. **Nearby Attractions:** Rail Trail, architecture, antique stores in Ottawa. **Additional Information:** Ottawa Chamber of Commerce, (913) 242-1000.

Restrictions

Pets: No rottweilers or pit bulls. **Fires:** In grills or fire ring. **Alcoholic Beverages:** At sites. **Vehicle Maximum Length:** 70 ft. **Other:** No hunting, no swimming in pond, no children near pond, children must be accompanied by an adult at all times.

To Get There

From I-35, take Exit 176, then turn north and go 1 block to the entrance on the right. Keep left to go to the office.

Kentucky

The state of Kentucky has a rich historical heritage going back to colonial times and before. Thousands of years before Europeans came to America, regions in western Kentucky along the Ohio and Mississippi rivers were inhabited by bands of ancient mound-building Indians. Later, tribes of Shawnee, Iroquois, Delaware, and Chickasaw lived in the area as well. Many of these fought or were allied with American pioneers during skirmishes and wars before and during the American Revolution. Many frontiersmen established settlements in eastern and central Kentucky. One of these was Boonesborough, on the Kentucky River about 45 miles east of present-day Harrodstown, founded by the famous Daniel Boone.

Following the Revolutionary War, Kentucky became the 15th state of the Union. Native American claims to Kentucky were erased in 1818, when the last Chickasaw lands in the western part of the state were acquired by the US government. In the years leading up the Civil War, large portions of Kentucky were cleared for farming, especially tobacco. As the agricultural industry kicked into high gear and steamboats appeared, the city of Louisville (located on the Ohio River) became the state's principal trade center.

Kentucky was sharply divided at the outbreak of the Civil War, having strong pro-slavery and pro-Union factions. Though Kentucky's government declared itself neutral in the fighting and refused calls for volunteers from both the Union and Confederacy, neither side really respected the state's neutrality. Both moved armies through Kentucky at various times, and several large battles were fought there early in the war. Eventually, both the Confederacy and Union claimed Kentucky as an ally (there was a star for the state on both governments' flags). After suffering repeated Confederate invasion, the state government finally sided with the Union, which spared Kentucky from the Union's harsh Reconstruction policies.

The post-Civil War era saw many outbreaks of local strife and discord (including the infamous Hatfield-McCoy feud on the West Virginia border). However, the state as a whole began to prosper economically. Through the twentieth century, Kentucky has become known for its thriving urban centers **(Louisville, Lexington, Bowling Green),** its rich natural beauty **(Land Between the Lakes, Mammoth Cave National Park, Big South Fork National River & Recreation Area, Daniel Boone National Forest, Cumberland Gap National Historic Park),** fine Kentucky bourbon (**Maker's Mark Distillery** near Loretto), horse racing (the **Kentucky Derby** at Louisville's Churchill Downs), and the Bluegrass region (the Shaker village of Pleasant Hill, Stephen Foster balladry in Bardstown, the historic state capital of **Frankfort**).

In addition to hundreds of private campgrounds of every size and type, Kentucky has a great deal of parkland with its own share of camping choices. Five nationally designated outdoor recreation areas cover close to a million acres of Kentucky soil. In addition there are many more state resort parks, wildlife refuges, and private campgrounds to enjoy nature at its most pristine. Throughout the state, you can find miles of trails, acres of lakes, and uncountable rivers, streams, mountains, and forests that make great places to park an RV or pitch a tent.

Campground Profiles

BARDSTOWN

My Old Kentucky Home State Park

P.O. Box 323, Bardstown 40004-0323. T: (502) 348-3502.

RV ★★★★ Tent ★★★★

Beauty: ★★★★	Site Privacy: ★★★
Spaciousness: ★★★	Quiet: ★★
Security: ★★★	Cleanliness: ★★★★
Insect Control: ★★★★	Facilities: ★★★★

Though it's proper name is Federal Hill Mansion, this parks centerpiece was immortalized in Stephen Foster's ballad "My Old Kentucky Home." Visiting My Old Kentucky Home is a religious pilgrimage for many Kentuckians. For others, it's a fascinating way to learn about lifestyles of the aristocracy in antebellum Kentucky. The campground is just around the corner from the mansion. It's fairly attractive, with ample-sized sites. All sites are paved, with back-in parking. Though the campground would be a lot nicer without the telephone lines, sites are shaded by gorgeous mature trees. Our favorite sites, 19 and 21, enjoy views of the state park golf course. The campground is locatedin the heart of Bardstown and has no gates, making security fair. For less crowded touring, avoid My Old Kentucky Home on summer and holiday weekends.

BASICS

Operated By: State of Kentucky. **Open:** Apr.–Oct. **Site Assignment:** First come, first served. **Registration:** Office. **Fee:** $16; 10% senior discount. **Parking:** On site.

FACILITIES

Number of RV Sites: 39. **Number of Tent-Only Sites:**. **Hookups:** Water, electric. **Each Site:** None. **Dump Station:** Yes. **Laundry:** Nearby. **Pay Phone:** Yes. **Rest Rooms and Showers:** Yes. **Fuel:** No. **Propane:** No. **Internal Roads:** Paved. **RV Service:** No. **Market:** Nearby. **Restaurant:** Nearby. **General Store:** Nearby. **Vending:** Yes. **Swimming Pool:** No. **Playground:** Yes. **Activities:** picnicking, golfing, tennis. **Nearby Attractions:** Amphitheater, house museum.

RESTRICTIONS

Pets: On leash. **Fires:** Fire ring. **Alcoholic Beverages:** Not allowed. **Vehicle Maximum Length:** No limit. **Other:** Check out at 2 p.m.

TO GET THERE

Located in Bardstown on US Hwy. 150.

BENTON

Sportsman's Anchor Resort & Marina

12800 US Hwy. 68 East, Benton 42025. T: (270) 354-6568 or (800) 326-3625; www.kentucky-lake.com/anchor; anchor@vci.net.

RV ★★★ Tent ★★★

Beauty: ★★★★ Site Privacy: ★★★
Spaciousness: ★★ Quiet: ★★★
Security: ★★★ Cleanliness: ★★★★
Insect Control: ★★★ Facilities: ★★★

Sportsman's Anchor is located in a remote though touristy area on Ruff Creek, a branch of Kentucky Lake. The RV sites are a bit small and on top of each other (no understory adds to lack of privacy), but those with boats will appreciate the adjacent full-service marina. The 15 tent-only primitive sites have more elbow room, and they are very attractive, especially for a private campground. The entire campground is shaded by pines and hardwood trees. However, there are no waterside sites, though the creek can be seen through the trees. There are not a lot of activities on the grounds—a pool and playground are located at the entrance—but Land Between the Lakes Recreation Area is only a five-minute car drive away. There, visitors can hike, boat, ride horses, bike, or hunt.

BASICS

Operated By: Raymond & Lynn Meyers. **Open:** Seasonal. **Site Assignment:** Assigned at registration. **Registration:** Office. **Fee:** $16–$23. **Parking:** On site.

FACILITIES

Number of RV Sites: 49. **Number of Tent-Only Sites:**. **Hookups:** Water, electric, sewer, cable TV. **Each Site:** Tent pad, picnic table. **Dump Station:** Yes. **Laundry:** Yes. **Pay Phone:** Emergency use only. **Rest Rooms and Showers:** Yes. **Fuel:** No (Gas dock in progress). **Propane:** Gas dock in progress. **Internal Roads:** Gravel. RV Service: 15 mi. north. **Market:** Yes. **Restaurant:** 1 mi. **General Store:** Yes. **Vending:** No. **Swimming Pool:** Yes (seasonal). **Playground:** Yes. **Other:** Gift shop, country store. **Activities:** game room, shuffleboard, fishing, boat rentals. **Nearby Attractions:** Kentucky Dam Village SRP, Land Between the Lakes. **Additional Information:** Park Manager.

RESTRICTIONS

Pets: On leash/not in rental units. **Fires:** Small on site (no fire rings). **Alcoholic Beverages:** In covered container only. **Vehicle Max. Length:** 40 ft.

TO GET THERE

I-24 Exit 25 A east on Purchase Parkway, turn east on Hwy. 68, 14 mi. on right (large blue/white sign).

BOW

Dale Hollow Lake SP

6371 State Park Rd., Bow 42717-9728. T: (270) 433-7431.

RV ★★★★ Tent ★★★★

Beauty: ★★★★★ Site Privacy: ★★
Spaciousness: ★★★ Quiet: ★★★★
Security: ★★★★★ Cleanliness: ★★★★★
Insect Control: ★★★ Facilities: ★★★★

Known for its clear, clean waters, Dale Hollow Lake attracts scuba divers, water skiers, and anglers. With a former world record for smallmouth bass, the lake is hailed as one of the best fishing spots in the Southeast. Other catches include crappie, bream, muskie, walleye, and four more bass species. The campground is laid out on 18 cul-de-sacs containing 8 sites each. Though sites are small, the campground feels open due to its layout and lack of understory. A few areas enjoy shade, but most lack trees. Parking pads are paved, back-in style. The equestrian camping area is the prettiest. If you left your horse at home, try areas L and N, which offer shady trees. Lucky for campers, there's a swimming pool at the campground. Remote and gated, this campground is very safe. Avoid Dale Hollow Lake on busy holiday weekends.

BASICS

Operated By: State of Kentucky. **Open:** year-round. **Site Assignment:** First come, first served. **Registration:** At camp office. **Fee:** 12. **Parking:** On site.

FACILITIES

Number of RV Sites: 144. **Number of Tent-Only Sites:**. **Number of Multipurpose Sites:** Combined. **Hookups:** Electric, water. **Each Site:** Picnic Shelter. **Dump Station:** Yes. **Laundry:** Yes. **Pay Phone:** Yes. **Rest Rooms and Showers:** Yes. **Fuel:** 9 mi. away. **Propane:** 9 mi. **Internal Roads:** Paved & gravel. RV Service: No. **Market:** No. **Restaurant:** Dining, 3 meals. **General Store:** No. **Vending:** Drink only. **Swimming Pool:** Yes. **Playground:** Yes. **Other:** Public swimming lake. **Activities:** Skiing, fishing, boating hiking, scuba diving, biking, amphitheater. **Nearby Attractions:** Nature trails, Tomkind Field, Cordell Hall, Alvin York's Birth place. **Additional Information:** Check out 2 p.m.

RESTRICTIONS

Pets: On leash. **Fires:** Fire ring. **Alcoholic Beverages:** Not allowed. **Vehicle Maximum Length:** No limit.

TO GET THERE

From I-65, exit at Cumberland parkway (Exit No. 43) & take KY 90 east at Glasgow.

BOWLING GREEN

Bowling Green, KY KOA Kampground

1960 Three Springs Rd., Bowling Green 42104. T: (270) 843-1919; www.bgkoa.com.

 ★★★  ★★

Beauty: ★★★★ Site Privacy: ★★
Spaciousness: ★★★ Quiet: ★★★★
Security: ★★ Cleanliness: ★★★★
Insect Control: ★★★★ Facilities: ★★★

Convenient to I-65, the Bowling Green KOA offers attractive sites laid out in five rows of pull-through sites with back-in sites along the back of the park. Sites, which tend to be long and narrow, are average sized. Almost every site enjoys the shade of mature trees. Parking pads are gravel. Our favorite site, shady number 60, is an excellent place for a tent or pop-up. RV campers should head for a more spacious pull-through site in the 40s or 76–78. The campground is located in the bustling town of Bowling Green, and has no gates, making security poor. Bowling Green is home to the National Corvette Museum, which displays over 50 rare Corvettes. Plan ahead for a memorable day trip to Mammoth Cave National Park—with so many cave tours offered, you may have trouble choosing. Avoid the area on summer holidays.

BASICS

Operated By: Koa Kampgrounds, Dan & Yvonne Goad. **Open:** Year-round. **Site Assignment:** First come, first served. **Registration:** Office. **Fee:** $20–$30. **Parking:** On site.

FACILITIES

Number of RV Sites: 124. **Number of Tent-Only Sites:** 6. **Hookups:** Water, electric (20, 30, 50 amps), sewer. **Each Site:** Fire ring. **Dump Station:** Yes. **Laundry:** Yes. **Pay Phone:** Yes. **Rest Rooms and Showers:** Yes. **Fuel:** No. **Propane:** Yes. **Internal Roads:** Paved. **RV Service:** No. **Market:** No. **Restaurant:** No. **General Store:** Yes. **Vending:** Yes. **Swimming Pool:** Yes. **Playground:** Yes. **Other:** Lake & duck pond. **Activities:** Fishing, tennis, golf. **Nearby Attractions:** Mammoth Cave National Park, skating rink, Corvette assembly plant tours, Shaker Museum. **Additional Information:** check out at noon.

RESTRICTIONS

Pets: On leash. **Fires:** Only in designated areas. **Alcoholic Beverages:** At site only. **Vehicle Maximum Length:** No limit.

TO GET THERE

From I-65 take Exit 22, then turn north on US 231. Turn left on KY 884 (Three Springs Rd.) and campground is app. 1.5 mi.

BURNSIDE

General Burnside State Park

P.O. Box 488, Burnside 36119-0488. T: (606) (561) 4104.

RV ★★★★ Tent ★★★★

Beauty: ★★★★ Site Privacy: ★★★★
Spaciousness: ★★★★ Quiet: ★★★★
Security: ★★★★ Cleanliness: ★★★★
Insect Control: ★★★ Facilities: ★★★★

General Burnside Island's campground rests on gentle, verdant hills and offers uncommonly tidy sites. Though site size varies, most are larger than average. About a dozen sites are totally open, but the rest are shaded by lovely mature trees. Many enjoy a measure of privacy. Sites offer paved, back-in style parking. Families should head for sites 1–4, right next to the playground. Other RV campers should try sites 30, 31, or 88, which are secluded. Very shady sites include 74 and 76. General Burnside Island is accessible by a bridge across 50, 000-acre Lake Cumberland, and boasts excellent amenities. A well-appointed marina aids fishermen in their quest for crappie and largemouth, smallmouth, and striped bass. The park is incredibly isolated, making security good. Visit any time except summer holidays—there's plenty of elbow room on the island.

Basics

Operated By: State of Kentucky. **Open:** Apr. 1–Oct. 31. **Site Assignment:** Reservations not accepted, first come, first serve. **Registration:** Control station. **Fee:** $14. **Parking:** Site plus overflow parking.

Facilities

Number of RV Sites: 110. **Number of Tent-Only Sites:** Tent area. **Hookups:** Water, elec-tric. **Each Site:** Picnic shelter. **Dump Station:** Yes. **Laundry:** Yes. **Pay Phone:** Yes. **Rest Rooms and Showers:** Yes. **Fuel:** No (8 mi., Somerset). **Propane:** Yes (8 mi., Somerset). **Internal Roads:** Paved. **RV Service:** No. **Market:** No. **Restaurant:** No. **General Store:** No. **Vending:** Yes. **Swimming Pool:** Yes. **Playground:** Yes. **Activities:** Boating, fishing, golf. **Nearby Attractions:** Cumberland State Resort Park. **Additional Information:** Somerset CVB, (800) 642-6287.

Restrictions

Pets: On leash, no tying to trees or bushes, clean up after. **Fires:** Fire ring only. **Alcoholic Beverages:** Not allowed. **Vehicle Maximum Length:** No limit. **Other:** Firearms & fireworks.

To Get There

From US 27 south in Somerset go 8 mi.

CADIZ

Lake Barkley State Resort Park

Box 790, Cadiz 42211-0790. T: (270) 924-1131.

RV ★★★★ Tent ★★★★

Beauty: ★★★★★ Site Privacy: ★★★★
Spaciousness: ★★★★ Quiet: ★★★★
Security: ★★★ Cleanliness: ★★★★
Insect Control: ★★★ Facilities: ★★★★★

There are an abundance of campgrounds to choose from in western Kentucky. Campers wishing to pamper themselves should visit Lake Barkley. Located close to the Land Between the Lakes Recreation Area, Lake Barkley has 78 RV sites with water and electric hookups. The sites are larger than average, and a gorgeous forest surrounds the campground. What's intriguing is the number of activities available, both on site and off. The heart of the resort is the Fitness Center, where Nautilus machines and fitness cycles await, preceding an inviting sauna and massage. There is also an indoor heated pool for the winter months. Those desiring more outdoors-oriented activities can fish, swim, or water-ski on Lake Barkley, practice their aim at the local trap-shoot range, or enjoy over nine miles of hiking trails. This is a popular place; the lodge and cottages book nearly a year in advance—RVs have a distinct advantage as there are no advance reservations.

Basics

Operated By: State of Kentucky. **Open:** Year round. **Site Assignment:** First come, first served. **Registration:** Office. **Fee:** $10–$14. **Parking:** On site.

Facilities

Number of RV Sites: 78. **Number of Tent-Only Sites:**. **Hookups:** Water, electric (15 amps). **Each Site:** None. **Dump Station:** Yes. **Laundry:** Yes. **Pay Phone:** Yes. **Rest Rooms and Showers:** Yes. **Fuel:** No. **Propane:** No. **Internal Roads:** Paved. **RV Service:** No. **Market:** Nearby. **Restaurant:** Nearby. **General Store:** No. **Vending:** Yes. **Swimming Pool:** No. **Playground:** Yes. **Other:** Fitness center. **Activities:** Fishing, boating, lake swimming, golf, tennis, hiking. **Nearby Attractions:** Jefferson Davis Monument State Historic Site.

Restrictions

Pets: On leash. **Fires:** Fire pits. **Alcoholic Beverages:** Not allowed. **Vehicle Max. Length:** 45 ft.

To Get There

29 mi. west of Hopkinsville. Take US 68 west to KY 1489.

CARROLLTON

General Butler SRP

P.O. Box 325, Carrollton 41008-0325. T: (502) 732-4384.

RV ★★★★ Tent ★★★

Beauty: ★★★★ Site Privacy: ★★★
Spaciousness: ★★★ Quiet: ★★★
Security: ★★★ Cleanliness: ★★★★
Insect Control: ★★★★★ Facilities:

Named for William Orlando Butler, a Carrollton veteran of the War of 1812 and the US-Mexican War, General Butler State Resort Park has a pretty campground just outside of Carrollton. Set in a pleasant stretch of river valley at the confluence of the Kentucky and Ohio Rivers (and on the shores of the 30-acre Butler Lake), the park is well forested with oaks and a variety of other trees. Campsites vary in size, and the parking areas are somewhat small, but the space between sites is usually acceptable. Lakeside campsites 55–59 and 86 are the most secluded and attractive. However, though Butler Lake has a swimming beach accessible to campers, swimming is contingent upon lifeguard availability. Also, the lake was noticeably overgrown with algae when we visited. Regardless, the variety of on-site activities make this campground a popular choice for families.

Basics

Operated By: Kentucky State Parks. **Open:** Apr. 1–Oct. 31. **Site Assignment:** First come, first served. **Registration:** Camp gate or front desk, no reservations. **Fee:** $18, over 2 adults $1 extra. **Parking:** On site.

Facilities

Number of RV Sites: 0. **Number of Tent-Only Sites:** 0. **Number of Multipurpose Sites:** 111. **Hookups:** Electric, water. **Each Site:** Table, grill. **Dump Station:** Yes. **Laundry:** Yes. **Pay Phone:** Yes. **Rest Rooms and Showers:** Yes. **Fuel:** No. **Propane:** No. **Internal Roads:** Paved. **RV Service:** No. **Market:** No. **Restaurant:** Yes. **General Store:** No. **Vending:** Drinks only. **Swimming Pool:** No. **Playground:** Yes. **Activities:** Nature trail, boat dock, golf course for fee. **Nearby Attractions:** Historic Carrollton, Outlet Shopping. **Additional Information:** www.carrolltonky.com.

Restrictions

Pets: On leash. **Fires:** Fire ring. **Alcoholic Beverages:** Not allowed. **Vehicle Maximum Length:** No limit.

To Get There

44 mi. northeast of Louisville. Take I-71 to Carrollton.

CAVE CITY

Yogi Bear's Jellystone Park

1002 Mammoth Cave Rd., Cave City 42127. T: (270) 773-3840.

RV ★★★ Tent ★★★

Beauty: ★★★★ Site Privacy: ★★
Spaciousness: ★★★ Quiet: ★★★
Security: ★★★ Cleanliness: ★★★★
Insect Control: ★★★★ Facilities: ★★★★

Located three miles from the Entrance to Mammoth Cave National Park, Yogi's is a good choice for families with small children. The marvelous national park includes the world's largest surveyed cave plus vast acres of rolling hills above it. The cave was used by people as early as 2000 BC, when prehistoric Americans mined for minerals. This isn't the most attractive Jellystone Park we've seen, but it has the kind of family-friendly amenities folks expect from Yogi, including a duck pond. Sites tend to be long and narrow and larger than average. Most sites offer pull-through, gravel parking. Choose from sites in Area A, which is more level, or Area B, which contains more spacious sites. Avoid this touristy area on summer and holiday weekends. And watch your valuables, as there are no gates at this bustling campground.

Basics

Operated By: Joe & Pat Baffuto. **Open:** Year round. **Site Assignment:** First come, first served except weekends & holidays. **Registration:** ranger station. **Fee:** $25–$30. **Parking:** On site.

Facilities

Number of RV Sites: 150. **Number of Tent-Only Sites:** 60. **Hookups:** Water, electric (30 amps); sewer extra. **Each Site:** Picnic table, fire ring. **Dump Station:** Yes. **Laundry:** Yes. **Pay Phone:** Yes. **Rest Rooms and Showers:** Yes. **Fuel:** No. **Propane:** Yes. **Internal Roads:** Paved & gravel. **RV Service:** Yes. **Market:** No. **Restaurant:** Yes. **General Store:** Yes. **Vending:** Yes. **Swimming Pool:** Yes. **Playground:** Yes. **Other:** Water slide, cabins. **Activities:** Planned events, nature hikes, mini-golf. **Nearby Attractions:** Mammoth Cave National Park, wax museum, antique shops, Alpine Slide Fun Park. **Additional Information:** Checks are only accepted 2 weeks or more prior to arrival.

RESTRICTIONS

Pets: On leash. **Fires:** Fire ring. **Alcoholic Beverages:** At site only. **Vehicle Maximum Length:** No limit.

TO GET THERE

Take Cave City Exit No. 53 off I-65 and go 0.5 mi. west on Hwy. 70 to the park.

CORBIN

Cumberland Falls State Resort/Park

7351 Hwy. 90, Corbin 40701-8857. T: (606) 528-4121 or (800) 325-0063; www.kystateparks.com.

RV ★★★ Tent ★★★

Beauty: ★★★★ Site Privacy: ★★★
Spaciousness: ★★★ Quiet: ★★★
Security: ★★★★ Cleanliness: ★★★
Insect Control: ★★★ Facilities: ★★★★

The campgrounds at Cumberland Falls aren't the tidiest we've ever seen, but they're reasonably attractive. Though site size varies, most are adequate. In the main campground, parking is paved. The nicest sites, 126–137, surround the cul-de-sac at the rear of the campground and offer back-in style parking. Sites 111–155 are downright plain. The smaller campground near the swimming pool is less developed and more attractive. Here, 13 sites with gravel parking line a shady mountain ridge. Known as the "Niagara of the South, " Cumberland Falls measures 125 feet in width and plunges 60 feet into the Cumberland River. Folks flock to the waterfall on full moons, when its mist creates a spectacular moon-bow. Park offerings, including numerous planned activities, are outstanding. To see the sights without hordes of people around you, try to plan a mid-week, full moon visit. Security is good at this remote park.

BASICS

Operated By: Kentucky State Parks. **Open:** Apr.–Oct. **Site Assignment:** First come, first served; no reservations. **Registration:** Camp store, after hours register next morning. **Fee:** $14 RV, $10.50 tent; prices for 2 people, $1 per additional person; 16 & under free; senior discount available (cash, personal check, V, MC, D, AE). **Parking:** At site (2 cars), in parking lot.

FACILITIES

Number of RV Sites: 35. **Number of Tent-Only Sites:** 15. **Number of Multipurpose Sites:** None. **Hookups:** Water, electric (20, 30, 50 amps). **Each Site:** Picnic table, fire ring w/ grill. **Dump Station:** Yes. **Laundry:** Yes. **Pay Phone:** Yes. **Rest Rooms and Showers:** Yes. **Fuel:** No. **Propane:** No. **Internal Roads:** Paved. **RV Service:** 15 mi. in Corbin. **Market:** 15 mi. in Corbin. **Restaurant:** Park restaurant. **General Store:** Camp store, Wal-Mart 15 mi. in Corbin. **Vending:** Yes. **Swimming Pool:** Yes. **Playground:** Yes. **Other:** Lodge, meeting room, Bob Blair Museum, stables, picnic areas & pavilion. **Activities:** Fishing, boating, canoeing, rafting, nature trails, tennis, horseshoes, shuffleboard, bird-watching, guided equestrian trails, naturalist & recreation programs in summer, square dancing. **Nearby Attractions:** Cumberland, Eagle, Yahoo & Dog Slaughter Falls, Daniel Boone National Forest, Berea Crafts Center, White Hall State Historic Site, Fort Boonesborough State Park, Colonel Harland Sanders Café & Museum. **Additional Information:** Corbin Chamber of Commerce, (606) 528-6390.

RESTRICTIONS

Pets: On leash only. **Fires:** Allowed, in fire ring only. **Alcoholic Beverages:** Not allowed. **Vehicle Maximum Length:** 36 ft. (sites vary). **Other:** 14-day stay limit, quiet hours enforced.

TO GET THERE

From I-75, take Exit 15 (from the south) or 25 (from the north) and head west on US Hwy. 25. Drive 7 mi. until merging w/ Hwy. 90. Drive another 7–8 mi. to the park, and the campground is on the left.

CRITTENDON

Cincinnati South KOA

P.O. Box 339, Crittendon 41030. T: (859) 428-2000.

RV ★★★ Tent ★★★

Beauty: ★★★★ Site Privacy: ★★★
Spaciousness: ★★ Quiet: ★★
Security: ★★ Cleanliness: ★★★★
Insect Control: ★★★★★ Facilities: ★★★

With friendly new owners, this nice-looking KOA is inviting. The campground is laid out on a gently sloping hillside with a pond at the bottom. Sites are average sized, with plenty of grass and shady trees. Parking is on gravel, and most sites are pull-through style. Unfortunately, this KOA is sandwiched between two noisy roads. For quiet, we recommend sites in the 30s and 40s, in the campground's interior. Sites 85 and 86 are the prettiest, offering views of the small fishing pond. Tent campers should also ask for pond-side sites. The campground is 27 miles south of Cincinnati, making it convenient to Paramount's King's Island theme park and river-boat casinos on the mighty Ohio. Security is passable—there are no gates, but the surrounding suburban neighborhood is very nice.

BASICS

Operated By: Doug Mullins. **Open:** All year. **Site Assignment:** First come, first served also reservations. **Registration:** Office, self-register after hours. **Fee:** $30 full hookup w/ 50 amps, $25 full hookup, $23 water & electric, $20 primitive; prices for 2 people, $4 per additional adult, $3 child; KOA discounts available (cash, V, MC, D). **Parking:** At sites.

FACILITIES

Number of RV Sites: 86. **Number of Tent-Only Sites:** 8 primitive. **Number of Multi-purpose Sites:** 10. **Hookups:** Water, electric (15, 30, 50 amps), sewer at 25 sites. **Each Site:** Picnic table, most sites w/ fire ring and/or grill. **Dump Station:** Yes. **Laundry:** Yes. **Pay Phone:** Courtesy. **Rest Rooms and Showers:** Yes. **Fuel:** No. **Propane:** Yes. **Internal Roads:** Paved. **RV Service:** 6 mi. in Walton. **Market:** 6 mi. in Dry Ridge. **Restaurant:** 5 mi. in Dry Ridge. **General Store:** Convenience store on-site, 6 mi. in Dry Ridge. **Vending:** Yes. **Swimming Pool:** Yes. **Playground:** Yes. **Other:** Rec. lodge, dock, game room, picnic areas. **Activities:** Fishing lake, paddle boats, basketball. **Nearby Attractions:** Cincinnati Zoo & Botanical Gardens, casino cruises, Taft Museum of Art, American Classical Music Hall of Fame, Krohn Conservatory, National Underground Railroad Freedom Center. **Additional Information:** Greater Cincinnati CVB, (513) 621-2142.

RESTRICTIONS

Pets: On leash only. **Fires:** Allowed, fire rings only. **Alcoholic Beverages:** Not allowed (dry county). **Vehicle Maximum Length:** 85 ft.

TO GET THERE

From I-75 take Exit 166 (5 mi. south of the junction w/ I-71) and head east to US 25. Drive south 2.5 mi. on Hwy. 25 and the campground is on the right.

DAWSON SPRINGS

Pennyrile Forest State Park Resort

20781 Pennyrile Lodge Rd., Dawson Springs 42408-9212. T: (270) 797-3421.

RV ★★★★ Tent ★★★★

Beauty: ★★★★ Site Privacy: ★★★
Spaciousness: ★★★ Quiet: ★★★★★
Security: ★★★★ Cleanliness: ★★★★
Insect Control: ★★★★ Facilities: ★★★★★

This campground is set in one of the most lush and beautiful forests in western Kentucky. Despite its relative closeness to the highway, the property has a remote and rural feel. Campsites are of moderate size, and all have at least partial shade. With a huge range of on-site activities, Pennyrile Forest is a big hit with families; expect large crowds of children. There's plenty for everyone to do, including good fishing on Pennyrile Lake for bluegill, channel catfish, crappie, and largemouth bass. If you're done with water sports, seven hiking trails weave their way through the forested hills around the lake, ranging from easy, level rambles to more rugged hikes. Both a nine-hole regulation golf course and a quirky mini-golf course are available for campers' use.

BASICS

Operated By: Kentucky State Parks. **Open:** Mar.–Oct. **Site Assignment:** First come, first served. **Registration:** Office. **Fee:** $14 for adults, $1 additional adults. **Parking:** On site.

FACILITIES

Number of RV Sites: 0. **Number of Tent-Only Sites:** 0. **Number of Multipurpose Sites:** 68. **Hookups:** Electric, water during season. **Each Site:** Table, grill. **Dump Station:** Yes. **Laundry:** Yes. **Pay Phone:** Yes. **Rest Rooms and Showers:** Yes. **Fuel:** No. **Propane:** No. **Internal Roads:** Paved. **RV Service:** No. **Market:** 3 mi. on hwy 109. **Restaurant:** Yes. **General Store:** Yes. **Vending:** Yes. **Swimming Pool:** No. **Playground:** Yes. **Other:** Public beach, nature trails. **Activities:** Golf course for fee, mini-golf for fee, boat dock, fishing. **Nearby Attractions:** Trail of Tears.

RESTRICTIONS

Pets: On leash. **Fires:** Fire ring. **Alcoholic Beverages:** Not allowed. **Vehicle Maximum Length:** No limit.

TO GET THERE

20 mi. northeast of Hopkinsville on KY 109 North from western Kentucky Parkway, exit at Dawson Springs and take KY 103 south.

EDDYVILLE

Indian Point

1136 Indian Hills Trail, Eddyville 42038. T: (270) 388-2730.

RV ★★★ Tent ★

Beauty: ★★★ Site Privacy: ★★
Spaciousness: ★★ Quiet: ★★★
Security: ★★★★ Cleanliness: ★★
Insect Control: ★★★ Facilities: ★★★

This campground on Lake Barkley is not nearly as attractive as nearby Lake Barkley State Resort Park or the beautiful campgrounds at Land Between the Lakes National Recreation Area. It's laid out in three areas with small sites. Sites have back-in, gravel parking. There are shady trees at most sites. Without greenery between sites, there is no privacy. The prettiest sites, 226–237, are situated on a cul-de-sac near the lake and are generally leased seasonally. If you can't get one of these, choose a site based on location in the campground. Incidentally, on our visit this campground's bathrooms left much to be desired in terms of cleanliness. There are no gates, but the campground is a rural location, making security fine. Avoid this place like the plague on holiday weekends.

BASICS

Operated By: Robert & Kathy Murphy. **Open:** Apr. 1–Nov. 1. **Site Assignment:** First come, first served. **Registration:** Office. **Fee:** $19–$22. **Parking:** Yes.

FACILITIES

Number of RV Sites: 200. **Number of Tent-Only Sites:** Available. **Hookups:** sewer, electric.water. **Each Site:** None. **Dump Station:** Yes. **Laundry:** Yes. **Pay Phone:** Yes. **Rest Rooms and Showers:** Yes. **Fuel:** No. **Propane:** Yes. **Internal Roads:** Paved. **RV Service:** Yes. **Market:** Nearby. **Restaurant:** Nearby. **General Store:** Yes. **Swimming Pool:** Yes. **Playground:** Yes. **Other:** Boat dock & ramp, tennis courts, volleyball courts. **Nearby Attractions:** Inquire at campground.

RESTRICTIONS

Pets: On leash. **Fires:** Fire ring. **Alcoholic Beverages:** On Campsites only. **Vehicle Maximum Length:** Call ahead for details.

TO GET THERE

Exit 45 off I-24. Take Hwy. 293 south. Follow signs.

ELKHORN CITY

Breaks Interstate Park

P.O. Box 100, Breaks 24607. T: (540) 865-4413; www.breakspark.com.

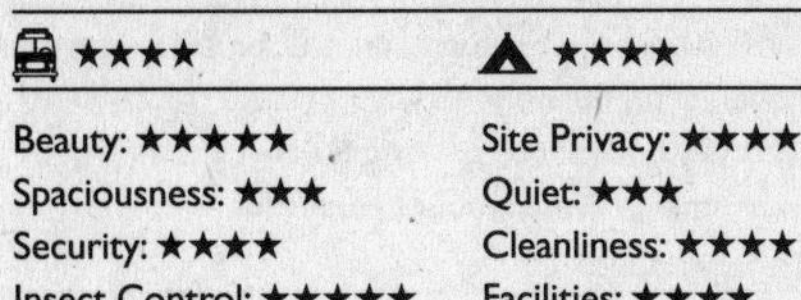

RV ★★★★ Tent ★★★★

Beauty: ★★★★★ Site Privacy: ★★★★
Spaciousness: ★★★ Quiet: ★★★
Security: ★★★★ Cleanliness: ★★★★
Insect Control: ★★★★★ Facilities: ★★★★

Administered jointly by the states of Kentucky and Virginia, Breaks Interstate contains the largest canyon east of the Mississippi. The canyon was formed by the Russell Fork River over a period of 250 million years. Today, the Russell Fork is frequented by whitewater rafters and stocked with trout. Anglers can also head for 12-acre Laurel Lake, which is stocked with bass and bluegill. Equestrian trails meander through the wooded uplands. Twelve miles of hiking trails include a demanding path to the river. The lovely campground features small, but picturesque sites situated on a heavily wooded mountainside. Parking is on gravel, and there are both back-in and pull-through sites, with a little bit of greenery between them. Loop B offers more spacious, yet less private sites than Loop A. Our favorite sites in Loop A are 56, 60, and 61. On Loop B, we like site 34. Section C is our absolute favorite, containing some large pull-through sites on top of the mountain. Security is fine at this remote park. Treat yourself—visit in June when the rhododendrons are in bloom.

BASICS

Operated By: VA & KY state parks. **Open:** Apr.–Oct. **Site Assignment:** First come, first served. **Registration:** Office. **Fee:** $7–$10. **Parking:** On site.

FACILITIES

Number of RV Sites: 122. **Number of Tent-Only Sites:** 0. **Hookups:** Water, electric (50 amps), sewer. **Each Site:** Picnic tables, grill. **Dump Station:** Yes. **Laundry:** Yes. **Pay Phone:** Yes. **Rest Rooms and Showers:** Yes. **Fuel:** No. **Propane:** No. **Internal Roads:** Paved. **RV Service:** Yes. **Market:** Yes. **Restaurant:** Yes. **General Store:** Yes. **Vending:** Yes. **Swimming Pool:** Yes. **Playground:** Yes. **Other:** Horseback riding stable. **Activities:** Boating, fishing, mountain biking, hiking. **Nearby Attractions:** Red River Gorge. **Additional Information:** (800) 982-5122.

RESTRICTIONS

Pets: On leash. **Fires:** Only in designated areas. **Alcoholic Beverages:** Not allowed. **Vehicle Maximum Length:** 40 ft.

TO GET THERE

I-64 East to Exit 98 onto Bert T. Combs Mtn. Pkwy. East. Turn right onto US 460. Stay straight onto KY 114. Take US 23 South to US 199 South. Take the US 460/KY 80 ramp. Stay straight to go onto US 460. Turn right onto KY 80 East that goes by the park.

FALLS OF ROUGH

North Fork Park, Rough River Lake

14500 Falls Of Rough Rd., Fall of Rough 95313. T: (270) 257-8139.

 ★★★  ★★★

Beauty: ★★★★ Site Privacy: ★★★
Spaciousness: ★★★ Quiet: ★★★
Security: ★★★★ Cleanliness: ★★★★
Insect Control: ★★★ Facilities: ★★★

North Fork Park lies in the northern area of the Pennyroyal Region of Kentucky, a place where ancient sandstone, shale, and limestone cliffs abound. This is also the land of caves, and Mammoth Cave lies about 40 miles to the south. North Fork Park is rural in the extreme; if you aren't content to enjoy the peepers and birds while camping here, you'll feel quite isolated. You'll have plenty to do if you enjoy hiking, boating and swimming. Be sure to provision yourself well—it is a long drive to pick-up anything forgotten. There are only a few pull-through sites in this 107-site park, with electric and water hookups available at most sites. The best views can be had from sites 6–11, though 86–88 have nice views too.

BASICS

Operated By: Corps of Engineers. **Open:** Apr. 19–Sept. 14. **Site Assignment:** Reservation 2 day advance, (888) 444-6777. **Registration:** Tollhouse. **Fee:** $14–$22 night. **Parking:** In designated areas.

FACILITIES

Number of RV Sites: 107. **Number of Tent-Only Sites:**. **Number of Multipurpose Sites:** Combined. **Hookups:** Electric (some), water. **Each Site:** Picnic Shelters. **Dump Station:** Yes. **Laundry:** No. **Pay Phone:** Yes. **Rest Rooms and Showers:** Yes. **Fuel:** No. **Propane:** No. **Internal Roads:** Paved. **RV Service:** No. **Market:** No. **Restaurant:** No. **General Store:** No. **Vending:** No. **Swimming Pool:** No. **Playground:** Yes. **Activities:** Boating, hiking. **Nearby Attractions:** Mammoth Caves, Limestone Cliffs. **Additional Information:** (270) 257-8139.

RESTRICTIONS

Pets: On leash. **Fires:** Only in designated areas. **Alcoholic Beverages:** Not allowed. **Vehicle Maximum Length:** 64 ft.

TO GET THERE

The Campground is 70 mi. southwest of Louisville, KY. Take US 60., go 10 mi. to Harred, KY. Go 9 mi. west on Hwy. 79 to the campground entrance.

FALLS OF ROUGH

Rough River Dam State Resort Park

450 Lodge Rd., Falls of Rough 40119-9701. T: (270) 257-2311.

RV ★★★ Tent ★★★

Beauty: ★★★★ Site Privacy: ★★★
Spaciousness: ★★★ Quiet: ★★★★
Security: ★★★★★ Cleanliness: ★★★★
Insect Control: ★★★★ Facilities: ★★★★

Situated on 4, 860-acre Rough River Lake, this state resort park runs a marina with 150 rental slips. Fishermen head back to shore with Kentucky bass, bluegill, channel catfish, crappie, and rough fish. Unique park facilities include a 3,200-foot airstrip, air camp, and shuttle service to the lodge. Though the attractive campground lines the Rough River, sites don't enjoy water views. There are both back-in and pull-through sites, with patchy gravel parking. Most sites are well shaded, but there is little undergrowth to provide privacy between sites. Sites are larger than average. RV campers should head for one of the pull-through sites, 32–66. Tent campers should head fot site 4 or 5, at the end of a pretty little spur. This park rarely fills to capacity, so it's an excellent destination for all but the busiest holiday weekends. Visit in spring in order to enjoy dogwood and redbud blooms. Security is excellent at this isolated park.

Basics

Operated By: Kentucky State Parks. **Open:** Apr. 1–Oct. 31. **Site Assignment:** First come, first served. **Registration:** Office. **Fee:** $8.50–$16. **Parking:** Camp Site & Main Lodge.

Facilities

Number of RV Sites: 66. **Number of Tent-Only Sites:**. **Hookups:** Electric, water on some. **Each Site:** Fire ring. **Dump Station:** Yes. **Laundry:** Yes. **Pay Phone:** Yes. **Rest Rooms and Showers:** Yes. **Fuel:** No. **Propane:** No. **Internal Roads:** Paved & gravel. **RV Service:** No. **Market:** No. **Restaurant:** Yes. **General Store:** Nearby. **Vending:** Yes. **Swimming Pool:** No. **Playground:** Yes. **Other:** Public beach. **Activities:** Marina fishing, nature trail, golf, mini-golf, recreation courts. **Nearby Attractions:** Manmade Falls antique shops, outdoor theatre. **Additional Information:** (270) 257-2311.

Restrictions

Pets: On leash. **Fires:** Fire ring. **Alcoholic Beverages:** Not allowed. **Vehicle Maximum Length:** Call ahead for details. **Other:** 14 day max.

To Get There

Located on KY 79. From Western Kentucky Parkway, Exit KY 79 north from Caneyville or exit on KY 259 north at Leithfield and travel to park via KY 54 from Leithfield. Driving south form Hardinsburg and US 60.

FALMOUTH

Kincaid Lake State Park

565 Kincaid Park Rd., Falmouth 41040. T: (859) 654-3531; www.kystateparks.com.

RV ★★★ Tent ★★★

Beauty: ★★★ Site Privacy: ★★
Spaciousness: ★★★ Quiet: ★★★
Security: ★★★★ Cleanliness: ★★★★
Insect Control: ★★★ Facilities: ★★★★★

Located near the historic town of Falmouth, Kincaid Lake is a quaint state park tucked far from any major development and noise. Tent-only sites, which outnumber RV sites, are mainly primitive. The RV sites are fairly close together, but some of them are pretty deep. Phone lines running throughout the campground detract from it's beauty. The shadiest and most tranquil area of the campground can be found at sites 42–52. All of these sites are back-in, and have electric and water hookups during the season. Activities include boating on Kincaid Lake (rentals available), hiking along the parks nature trail, as well as swimming and mini-golf. Those who brig a fishing rod will be pleased with the large population of keeper- and trophy-sized largemouth bass. The Licking River is also nearby; a livery rents boats for interested parties.

Basics

Operated By: Kentucky State Parks. **Open:** Year round. **Site Assignment:** No reservations, first come first serve. **Registration:** At camp office. **Fee:** $8.50–$16. **Parking:** Inquire at registration.

Facilities

Number of RV Sites: 84. **Number of Tent-Only Sites:** 125. **Hookups:** Water, electric (seasonal). **Each Site:** Table. **Dump Station:** Yes. **Laundry:** Yes. **Pay Phone:** Yes. **Rest Rooms and Showers:** Yes. **Fuel:** Yes. **Propane:** Yes. **Internal Roads:** Paved. **RV Service:** No. **Market:** Yes. **Restaurant:** No. **General Store:** Yes. **Vending:** Yes. **Swimming Pool:** Yes (fee). **Playground:** Yes. **Other:** Amphitheater. **Activities:** Boat rental, fishing, mini-golf (fee), hiking, tennis, athletic multi-courses. **Nearby Attractions:** Historic Falmouth, Kincaid regional Theatre. **Additional Information:** Park Manager (Jeff P. Auchter).

Restrictions

Pets: On leash. **Fires:** Fire rings only. **Alcoholic Beverages:** Not allowed. **Vehicle Maximum Length:** No limit. **Other:** 14-day max. stay.

To Get There

48 mi. southeast of Covington. Take I-275 East to US 27 South to Falmouth and KY 159 to the park.

FRANKLIN

Franklin KOA Kampground

2889 Scottsville Rd., Franklin 32135. T: (270) 586-5622; F: (270) 586-9123; www.KOA.com/whereKY; camping@KOA.net.

RV ★★★ Tent ★★

Beauty: ★★★ Site Privacy: ★★
Spaciousness: ★★ Quiet: ★★
Security: ★★★ Cleanliness: ★★★★
Insect Control: ★★★ Facilities: ★★★

Located just east of the historic town of Franklin, this KOA campground is easily accessible from the interstate. However, this means the grounds can be a bit noisy. Those wishing a quieter experience should look for sites toward the back of the campground (sites 34–68), while campers with children may want to choose sites 26–30 because of their proximity to the playground and pool. History buffs will be interested to know that due to a surveyor's error, people with disputes were able to duel here legally until about 1920. Two famous duelists included Sam Houston, the Governor of Tennessee, and Andrew Jackson, the winning general at the Battle of New Orleans and the seventh president of the United States.

Basics

Operated By: Clyde Dittbenner. **Open:** Year round. **Site Assignment:** Reservations accepted, site assigned a time of registration. **Registration:** Office. **Fee:** Tent $18–$23, Cabins $37–$49, accepted MC, V, D, $2.50 for add'l person. **Parking:** Designated area assigned/no parking on the grass.

Facilities

Number of RV Sites: 82. **Number of Tent-Only Sites:** 22. **Hookups:** Water, electric (30, 50 amps), sewer. **Each Site:** Table, fire rings. **Dump Station:** Yes. **Laundry:** Yes. **Pay Phone:** Yes. **Rest Rooms and Showers:** Yes. **Fuel:** Yes. **Propane:** Yes. **Internal Roads:** Paved. **RV Service:** No, storage & supplies. **Market:** Nearby. **Restaurant:** No. **General Store:** Yes. **Vending:** Yes. **Swimming Pool:** Yes. **Playground:** Yes. **Activities:** Game room, horseshoe, volleyball. **Nearby Attractions:** Opryland, Mammoth Caves, Dueling Grounds, Kentucky Downs. **Additional Information:** Franklin KOA, (800) 562-5631.

Restrictions

Pets: On leash. **Fires:** Fire ring only. **Alcoholic Beverages:** Allowed. **Vehicle Maximum Length:** No limit. **Other:** Check out is noon.

To Get There

From I-65 take Exit 6 onto Hwy. 100, go 100 yards west on Hwy. 100, entrance on the left.

GREENUP

Greenbo Lake State Resort Park

HC 60 Box 52, Greenup 41144-9517. T: (606) 473-7324; F: (606) 473-7741; www.kystateparks.com; bobby.bowe@mail.state.ky.us.

RV ★★★ Tent ★★★

Beauty: ★★★★ Site Privacy: ★★
Spaciousness: ★★★ Quiet: ★★★
Security: ★★★★ Cleanliness: ★★★★
Insect Control: ★★★ Facilities: ★★★★★

The attractive campground at Greenbo Lake is laid out in three spurs and a loop adjacent to Claylick Creek. There are average sized sites with paved, back-in parking. With woods flanking the campground, some sites enjoy cool shade, while others are totally open. Privacy is minimal. For families we recommend sites 29 and 30 near the wash house and playground. For tent campers, we recommend 16 and 17, tucked into the back of the primitive area. Security is passable; there are no gates, but the park is remote. Visit during the week in the summertime. This park's myriad recreation draws massive crowds. Children love the corkscrew water slide at the swimming pool. The state park is also a hiking haven, with 25 miles of easy to challenging hiking. With two largemouth bass records, fishing in the 225-acre Greenbo Lake is excellent.

Basics

Operated By: Kentucky State Parks. **Open:** Apr.–Oct. (lodge etc. open all year). **Site Assignment:** First come, first served; no reservations. **Registration:** Check in station. **Fee:** $16 full hookup, $10 primitive; price for 2 people, $1 per additional adult, 16 & under free; senior & disabled discounts available, Kentucky POWs free (cash, personal checks, AE, V, MC, D). **Parking:** At site (2 cars), in parking lot.

Facilities

Number of RV Sites: 0. **Number of Tent-Only Sites:** 31 primitive. **Number of Multipurpose Sites:** 63. **Hookups:** Water, electric (30 amps). **Each Site:** Picnic table, grill, fire ring, asphalt pad.

Dump Station: Yes. **Laundry:** Yes. **Pay Phone:** Yes. **Rest Rooms and Showers:** Yes. **Fuel:** No. **Propane:** Yes. **Internal Roads:** Paved. **RV Service:** 10 mi. in Greenup. **Market:** 5–10 mi. in Greenup. **Restaurant:** Park restaurant. **General Store:** Camp store, 10 mi. in Greenup. **Vending:** Yes. **Swimming Pool:** Yes (Memorial Day–Labor Day). **Playground:** Yes. **Other:** Lodge, marina, picnic area & shelters. **Activities:** Water sports (no jet-ski), canoe, pontoon, paddle boat, rowboat & motorboat rentals, fishing, hiking trails, mini-golf, tennis, basketball, bicycle rentals, summer organized activities. **Nearby Attractions:** Golf course, Jesse Stuart Birthplace, Kentucky Highlands Museum & Discovery Center, Paramount Arts Center, McConnell House, Carter Caves & Grayson Lake state Parks. **Additional Information:** Boyd/ Greenup Counties Chamber of Commerce, (606) 324-5111.

Restrictions

Pets: On leash only. **Fires:** Allowed in sites, fire rings, only. **Alcoholic Beverages:** Not allowed. **Vehicle Maximum Length:** 45 ft. (sites vary). **Other:** 14-day stay limit, no ATVs.

To Get There

From I-64, take Exit 172 and drive 18 mi. north on KY 1. Turn left onto KY 1711/State Park Rd. and the campground is 3 mi. on the left.

HARDIN

Kenlake State Resort Park

542 Kenlake Rd., Hardin 42048-937. T: (270) 474-2211 or (800) 325-0143; www.state.ky.us.

RV ★★★★ Tent ★★★★

Beauty: ★★★★	Site Privacy: ★★★★
Spaciousness: ★★★★	Quiet: ★★★★
Security: ★★★★	Cleanliness: ★★★★
Insect Control: ★★★	Facilities: ★★★★★

Located minutes from the 170,000-acre Land Between the Lakes National Recreation Area, the campground at Kenlake State Resort Park rests on the western shore of Kentucky Lake. You don't have to be a boat enthusiast to visit, but water activities are a significant reason people come here. The 90 back-in sites (each with water and electric hookups) have small parking areas, but the space in between sites is more than adequate. There are only a few waterfront sites (62–69 and 24–29); they are pretty but the ground is not level. The campground is separated from the rest of the resort by Hwy. 68, so while the resort offers tennis, golfing and some hiking, you might as well visit Land Between the Lakes since you have to get in your car anyway. The resort is host to several festivals throughout the year, including the Hot August Blues Festival and the Aurora County Festival.

Basics

Operated By: State of Kentucky. **Open:** All year. **Site Assignment:** Reservations not accepted, first come, first served. **Registration:** Contact station. **Fee:** $14. **Parking:** In designated areas assigned, must have car pass/visitor pass visible.

Facilities

Number of RV Sites: 90. **Number of Tent-Only Sites:** Tent area. **Hookups:** Water, electric (30, 50 amps), sewer. **Each Site:** Picnic shelters, fire ring. **Dump Station:** Yes. **Laundry:** Yes. **Pay Phone:** Yes. **Rest Rooms and Showers:** Yes. **Fuel:** 2–3 mi. away. **Propane:** 2.5 mi. **Internal Roads:** Paved. **RV Service:** No. **Market:** No, 0.5 mi. away. **Restaurant:** Yes. **General Store:** No. **Vending:** No. **Swimming Pool:** Yes. **Playground:** Yes. **Other:** Meeting rooms. **Activities:** Fishing, boating, golf, tennis, nature trails. **Nearby Attractions:** Kentucky Dam Village SRP, Hardin Southern Railway, The Homeplace 1850, North-South Trail. **Additional Information:** State of Kentucky, (859) 384-3522.

Restrictions

Pets: On leash. **Fires:** Fire ring. **Alcoholic Beverages:** Not allowed. **Vehicle Maximum Length:** No limit. **Other:** No firearms or fireworks.

To Get There

40 mi. southeast of Paducah. Going east on I-24 exit to the Purchase Parkway, then exit on US 68 east, going west on I-24, take the Cadiz exit to US 68/KY 80 West.

HENDERSON

John James Audubon State Park

P.O. Box 576, Henderson 42419-0576. T: (270) 826-2247; F: (270) 826-2286; www.kystateparks.com; maryd.miller@mail.state.ky.us.

RV ★★★ Tent ★★★

Beauty: ★★★★	Site Privacy: ★★★
Spaciousness: ★★★	Quiet: ★★
Security: ★★	Cleanliness: ★★★★
Insect Control: ★★★★	Facilities: ★★★★

Audubon State Park, a little green oasis in the city of Henderson, maintains nice sports facilities including a nine-hole golf course and fishing on the park's small lake. Anglers are rewarded with largemouth bass, bluegill, and catfish. Henderson residents are proud to know that John James Audubon lived here. Today, over 20 species of warblers visit the state park every spring. The campground is laid out in one large loop with three partitions. RV sites 1–28 and tent sites 8T–17T abut the highway and are not recommended. Quieter sites include RV sites 40–63 and tent sites 1T–7T. Site size and distance between sites vary, but most are adequate. Parking is paved, back-in style. Almost all sites are well shaded by sycamore, cottonwood and other species. There are no gates at this urban campground, making security iffy. Visit during the week to avoid summer crowds.

Basics

Operated By: Kentucky State Parks. **Open:** Year round. **Site Assignment:** First come, first served; no reservations; honor system in winter. **Registration:** Entrance kiosk, self-register after hours. **Fee:** $18 RV; $10 winter flat rate; prices for 2 people, $1 per additional person; 16 & under free (cash, personal check, V, MC, D, AE). **Parking:** At site (2 cars), in parking lot.

Facilities

Number of RV Sites: 0. **Number of Tent-Only Sites:** 10 primitive. **Number of Multipurpose Sites:** 69. **Hookups:** Water, electric (50 amps). **Each Site:** Picnic table, grill, fire ring. **Dump Station:** Yes. **Laundry:** Yes. **Pay Phone:** Yes. **Rest Rooms and Showers:** Yes. **Fuel:** No. **Propane:** No. **Internal Roads:** Paved. **RV Service:** 8 mi. in Evansville, Indiana. **Market:** 0.25 mi. **Restaurant:** Within 1 mi. in Henderson. **General Store:** 0.5 mi. in Henderson. **Vending:** Yes. **Swimming Pool:** No. **Playground:** Yes. **Other:** John James Audubon Museum & Nature Center, meeting rooms, picnic area & shelters, boat dock (trolling motors only). **Activities:** 9-hole golf course, pro shop, club & cart rentals, fishing, paddle boat, canoe & hydrobike rentals (seasonal), hiking trails, tennis (seasonal), ropes challenge course (w/ facilitator only), interpretive & recreation programs year-round. **Nearby Attractions:** Ellis Park Race Course, Aztar Casino Riverboat, Audubon Mill Park, Wesselman Woods Nature Preserve, Angel Mounds Prehistoric Native American Site. **Additional Information:** Henderson Tourism Commission (270) 826-3128, Evansville CVB (800) 433-3025 www.evansvillecvb.org.

Restrictions

Pets: On leash only. **Fires:** Allowed, in fire ring only. **Alcoholic Beverages:** Not allowed. **Vehicle Maximum Length:** 45 ft. (sites vary). **Other:** 14-day stay limit, no pets on trails except designated pet trail.

To Get There

From the Pennyrile Parkway, drive north until it merges w/ US 41. The park is 1.5 mi. north on the right.

JAMESTOWN

Lake Cumberland State Resort Park

5465 State Park Rd., Jamestown 42629. T: (270) 343-3111.

RV ★★★★ Tent ★★★★

Beauty: ★★★★	Site Privacy: ★★★★
Spaciousness: ★★★★	Quiet: ★★★
Security: ★★★	Cleanliness: ★★★★
Insect Control: ★★★	Facilities: ★★★★★

Set on a large peninsula protruding into the 50, 250-acre Lake Cumberland, this extremely popular state resort park has plenty to do and an upscale feel. Unfortunately, the large crowds make for a hectic atmosphere, and they also somewhat overwhelm the staff's efforts to keep the campground clean. Many families means many children, as well as lots of cars, trucks, and other vehicles. Though campsite size varies, most are large, and some are quite close together. Some sites have both a nice forest canopy as well as screening ground foliage for privacy. The prettiest campsites are sites 19–21, 38, and 72–75. An unsightly telephone wire runs right through the loop of sites 49–52. Generally, the most visually attractive sites are not as level as others. The large lake means that all varieties of boating and water sports take up most campers' time here, but there's also various sports activities and a four-mile loop nature trail.

Basics

Operated By: State of Kentucky. **Open:** Apr.–Nov. **Site Assignment:** First come, first served. **Regis-**

tration: Entrance Gate. **Fee:** $8.50 Tent, $10 RV. **Parking:** On site.

Facilities

Number of RV Sites: 113. **Number of Tent-Only Sites:** 34. **Hookups:** Water, electric (20 amps). **Each Site:** Picnic Tables. **Dump Station:** Yes. **Laundry:** Yes. **Pay Phone:** Yes. **Rest Rooms and Showers:** Yes. **Fuel:** 5 mi. **Propane:** 5 mi. **Internal Roads:** Paved. **RV Service:** No. **Market:** No. **Restaurant:** Yes. **General Store:** Yes. **Vending:** Yes. **Swimming Pool:** Yes. **Playground:** Yes. **Activities:** Golf, game room, mini-golf, stables, hiking, fishing. **Nearby Attractions:** Wolf Greek Dam & Fish Hatchery.

Restrictions

Pets: On leash. **Fires:** Fire ring. **Alcoholic Beverages:** Not allowed. **Vehicle Maximum Length:** No limit.

To Get There

Located 45 min. West of Somerset. Take Cumberland Parkway to US 127.

LEXINGTON

Kentucky Horse Park Campground

4089 Iron Works Parkway, Lexington 40511. T: (859) 259-4257 or (800) 370-6416; F: (859) 255-2690; www.kyhorsepark.com; campground@kyhorsepark.com.

★★★ ★★★

Beauty: ★★★★	Site Privacy: ★★
Spaciousness: ★★★	Quiet: ★★★
Security: ★★	Cleanliness: ★★★★
Insect Control: ★★★★	Facilities: ★★★★

Beautiful Kentucky Horse Park rests on 1, 200 acres of verdant rolling horse pasture enclosed and subdivided by 30 miles of pristine white fence. The park's mission is multi-fold. It's a working horse farm, educational facility (with two superb museums and two theaters), competition venue, and tasteful theme park. Children can pet ponies and enjoy a number of exhibitions and shows. The flat campground is passably attractive, with spruce fir and pine shading the sites. It's laid out in two concentric figure eights, with sites in the rear (160–171 and 29–41) enjoying views of the polo fields. Medium-sized sites feature paved, back-in style parking, with short parking pads. The campground is convenient to restaurants in Lexington and outlet mall shopping in Georgetown. Security is marginal at this giant campground with no gates. Visit during the week for less crowded touring, but avoid weekdays in late spring when armies of school children invade.

Basics

Operated By: Kentucky Tourism Development Cabinet. **Open:** Year round. **Site Assignment:** First come, first served. **Registration:** Trading post, host makes rounds after hours. **Fee:** $23 developed, $20 seniors, $15 primitive; prices for 6 people, $2 per additional person (cash, checks, V, MC, D, AE). **Parking:** At site (2 cars), in parking lot.

Facilities

Number of RV Sites: 0. **Number of Tent-Only Sites:** Primitive, undesignated. **Number of Multipurpose Sites:** 260. **Hookups:** Water, electric (20, 30, 50 amps). **Each Site:** Picnic table, fire ring, paved pad. **Dump Station:** Yes. **Laundry:** Yes. **Pay Phone:** Yes. **Rest Rooms and Showers:** Yes. **Fuel:** No. **Propane:** No. **Internal Roads:** Paved. **RV Service:** 5 mi. in Lexington. **Market:** 10 mi. in Georgetown. **Restaurant:** Park Restaurant, within 4 mi. **General Store:** Camp store, 10 mi. in Georgetown (Wal-Mart). **Vending:** Yes. **Swimming Pool:** Yes. **Playground:** Yes. **Other:** Pavilion, museum, gallery, gift shop. **Activities:** Horse drawn tours, riding shows, events, square dancing (occasional), tennis, croquet, volleyball, basketball, horseshoes. **Nearby Attractions:** Aviation Museum of Kentucky, Keeneland Race Course, Lexington Center/ Rupp Arena, Mary Todd Lincoln House, Thoroughbred Center, University of Kentucky. **Additional Information:** Lexington CVB, (800) 845-3959, www.visitlex.com.

Restrictions

Pets: On leash only. **Fires:** Allowed, fire rings only. **Alcoholic Beverages:** Not allowed. **Vehicle Max. Length:** 45 ft. **Other:** 14-day stay limit.

To Get There

From I-75 (2 mi. north of the junction w/ I-64), take Exit 120. The Park is immediately on the east and the campground is on the east side of the park.

LONDON

Levi Jackson Wilderness Road State Park Campground

998 Levi Jackson Mill Rd., London 40744-8944. T: (606) 878-8000; F: (606) 864-3825; www.kystateparks.com; william.meadors@mail.state.ky.us.

★★★★ ★★★★

Beauty: ★★★★	Site Privacy: ★★★
Spaciousness: ★★★	Quiet: ★★★★
Security: ★★★★	Cleanliness: ★★★★
Insect Control: ★★★	Facilities: ★★★★

Levi Jackson Wilderness Road offers diverse family recreation, including a large swimming pool with a water slide and an 18-hole mini-golf course. Traversing the park, the Wilderness Road is believed by many historians to be the most significant trail in the westward flow of English colonists. Lucky hikers can retrace the steps of Daniel Boone. The pretty campground is laid out in many small areas containing both back-in and pull-through sites. Sites have paved parking and are larger than average. Most sites are shady, while a few are open. Many sites are lovely, especially the larger pull-throughs. We particularly fancy sites in Area D, which enjoy a dense tree canopy. Parents, keep your children away from the vexing, ugly, old, and rusty barbed wire fence that runs the length of the campground. Security is passable—there are no gates at this small town campground. Avoid this park on summer weekends and holidays.

Basics

Operated By: Kentucky State Parks. **Open:** Year round. **Site Assignment:** First come, first served; no reservations; honor system in winter. **Registration:** Camp store, after hours register next day (honor system in winter). **Fee:** $18 developed, $14 tent, pop-up, designated areas; prices for 2 people, $2 per additional person; 16 & under free; $10 winter flat rate; Seniors & KY disabled discounts available (cash, personal check, V, MC, D, AE). **Parking:** At site (2 cars), in parking lot.

Facilities

Number of Multipurpose Sites: 146. **Hookups:** Water, electric (20, 30, 50 amps). **Each Site:** Picnic table, fire ring. **Dump Station:** Yes. **Laundry:** Yes. **Pay Phone:** Yes. **Rest Rooms and Showers:** Yes. **Fuel:** No. **Propane:** No. **Internal Roads:** Paved. **RV Service:** 12 mi. in Corbin. **Market:** Within 5 mi. in London. **Restaurant:** Within 5 mi. in London. **General Store:** camp store, Wal-Mart 5 mi. in London. **Vending:** Beverages only. **Swimming Pool:** Yes (& wading pool & waterslides). **Playground:** Yes. **Other:** Rec. room, Mountain Life Museum, McHargue's Grist Mill (operational summertime), picnic areas, gazebo, amphitheater, bird sanctuary. **Activities:** Mini-golf, hiking trails, horseshoes, basketball, summer organized activities. **Nearby Attractions:** Daniel Boone Motocross Park, Renfro Valley Entertainment Center, Berea Crafts Center, White Hall State Historic Site, Fort Boonesborough State Park, Colonel Harland Sanders Café & Museum. **Additional Information:** London Chamber of Commerce, (606) 864-4789.

Restrictions

Pets: On leash only. **Fires:** Allowed, fire ring only. **Alcoholic Beverages:** Not allowed. **Vehicle Maximum Length:** 60 ft. (sites vary). **Other:** 14-day stay limit.

To Get There

From I-75, take Exit 38 and drive 3 mi. east on Hwy. 192. Turn south on US Hwy. 25 and drive 2 mi. to the first traffic light. Turn left onto State Rte. 1006. Drive 1.5 mi. into the park.

LUCAS

Barren River Lake State Park

1149 State Park Rd., Lucas 42156-9709. T: (270) 646-2151.

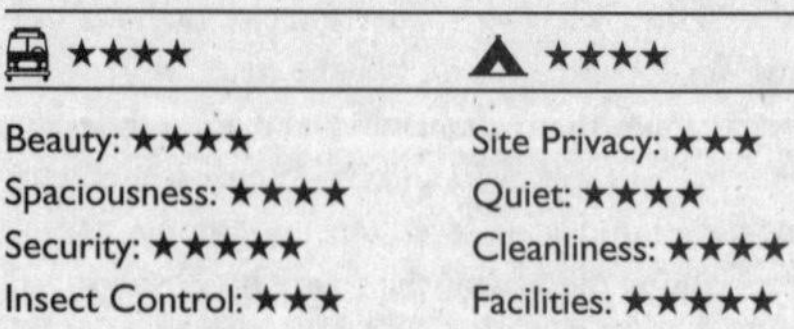

★★★★ ★★★★

Beauty: ★★★★	Site Privacy: ★★★
Spaciousness: ★★★★	Quiet: ★★★★
Security: ★★★★★	Cleanliness: ★★★★
Insect Control: ★★★	Facilities: ★★★★★

The campground at Barren River Lake lies in graceful rolling hills surrounded by woods. The pretty campground contains back-in and pull-through sites with paved parking. Pull-through sites are often huge and open. Some, like 79A and 79B, enjoy view s of a green hillside. Back-in sites tend to be average sized and shadier. Our favorite back-in sites numbered in the 80s and 90s. Security is very good, with gates at the campground entrance. Barren River Lake offers outstanding recreational facilities, including a marina with rental slips (100 open and 40 covered). The lake supports bluegill, channel catfish, crappie, rough fish, and largemouth, white, and hybrid striped bass. The park's many planned events climax with the annual Glasgow Highland Games in June. Approximately 35 miles north of the park, Mammoth Cave National Park makes an excellent day trip. Avoid this popular state park on summer holidays and weekends.

Basics

Operated By: State of Kentucky. **Open:** Apr. 1–Oct. 31. **Site Assignment:** First come, first served. **Registration:** Office. **Fee:** $14. **Parking:** On site.

Facilities

Number of RV Sites: 99. **Number of Tent-Only Sites:** Tent area. **Hookups:** Water, electric. **Each Site:** Picnic table. **Dump Station:** Yes. **Laundry:** Yes. **Pay Phone:** Yes. **Rest Rooms and Showers:** Yes. **Fuel:** 3.5 mi. **Propane:** 3.5 mi. **Internal Roads:** Paved. **RV Service:** No. **Market:** No. **Restaurant:** Dining room. **General Store:** Yes. **Vending:** Yes. **Swimming Pool:** Yes (beach). **Playground:** Yes. **Activities:** Basketball, golf, nature trails, horseback riding, boating. **Nearby Attractions:** Dale Hollow Lake, Old Mulkey historic site. **Additional Information:** Corps of Engineers, (606) 642-3308.

Restrictions

Pets: On leash. **Fires:** Fire rings only. **Alcoholic Beverages:** No. **Vehicle Max. Length:** No limit.

To Get There

From Bowling Green, take I-65 south to the Cumberland Parkway and drive east, then go south on US 31 East to the park.

MAMMOTH CAVE

Mammoth Cave National Park

P.O. Box 7, Mammoth Cave 42259. T: (270) 758-2328.

RV ★★★★★ Tent ★★★★★

Beauty: ★★★★★ Site Privacy: ★★★★
Spaciousness: ★★★★★ Quiet: ★★★★
Security: ★★★★★ Cleanliness: ★★★★★
Insect Control: ★★★ Facilities: ★★★★

Fascinating Mammoth Cave has seen plenty of adventure during its 4000-year relationship with humans. Tour guides are full of anecdotes about the characters who've contributed to the cave's colorful history—of course many of these folks were just trying to make a buck. With over 345 miles of mapped passages, it's the longest cave in the world. Above ground, the rolling woodlands within the park contain 70 miles of multi-use trails. The beautiful Headquarters Campground is laid out in three loops, with paved back-in and pull-through sites. Site size is ample, with pull-through sites tending to be larger than back-in sites. Most sites enjoy a fair amount of seclusion. Sites 65–83, on the second loop are pretty and quiet. Sites 26–34 are also quite nice-looking, but maybe noisy. Situated near a noisy road, sites 1–10 and 11–21 should be avoided. The campground is remote and gated, making it ultra-safe. Visit during the week in the summer.

Basics

Operated By: National Park Service. **Open:** Mar.–Oct. **Site Assignment:** First come, first served. **Registration:** Entrance kiosk. **Fee:** $14. **Parking:** In designated areas.

Facilities

Number of RV Sites: 106. **Number of Tent-Only Sites:** 0. **Hookups:** None. **Each Site:** Picnic table, fire grate. **Dump Station:** Yes. **Laundry:** Yes. **Pay Phone:** Yes. **Rest Rooms and Showers:** Yes. **Fuel:** Yes. **Propane:** Yes. **Internal Roads:** Paved. **RV Service:** No. **Market:** No. **Restaurant:** No. **General Store:** Yes. **Vending:** No. **Swimming Pool:** No. **Playground:** No. **Activities:** Hiking, horseback riding, fishing. **Nearby Attractions:** Mammoth Cave, water slides, golfing. **Additional Information:** Check out at 11 a.m.

Restrictions

Pets: On leash. **Fires:** Only in designated areas. **Alcoholic Beverages:** Not allowed. **Vehicle Maximum Length:** 32 ft. **Other:** Mopeds & motorcycles only on improved roads.

To Get There

Exit 53 off I-60.

MIDDLESBORO

Cumberland Gap National Historical Park

US 25 E South, Middlesboro 40965. T: (606) 248-2817.

RV ★★★★★ Tent ★★★★★

Beauty: ★★★★★ Site Privacy: ★★★★★
Spaciousness: ★★★★★ Quiet: ★★★★★
Security: ★★★★ Cleanliness: ★★★★
Insect Control: ★★★★ Facilities: ★★★★

Millions of years of wind and water carved this natural gap in the Appalachian Mountains. It was first used by migrating animals, then by Native Americans, and more recently by frontiers-people headed to settle the American West, Historians estimate that 12,000 settlers passed through Cumberland Gap by the end of the American Revolution. Learn about these folks, including Daniel Boone, who shaped the gap's history at the Visitor's Center in Kentucky. The national historic park straddles the Kentucky-Virginia border and dips into Tennessee at its southern tip. The beautiful Wilderness Road campground is actually in Virginia. Sites are commodious. With plenty of space and foliage between them, sites are also secluded. Campsites feature gravel, back-in parking under a canopy of oak, poplar, and hickory. Our favorite sites, E1, E2, E4, and F9, are extremely private. The campground at Cumberland Gap is fairly remote, making it safe. Visit the park during the week for less crowded touring.

Basics

Operated By: State of Kentucky. **Open:** Year round. **Site Assignment:** First come, first served. **Registration:** Ranger station. **Fee:** $10–$15. **Parking:** On site.

Facilities

Number of RV Sites: 41. **Number of Tent-Only Sites:** 119. **Hookups:** Electric (30 amps), sewer. **Each Site:** Picnic shelters. **Dump Station:** Yes. **Laundry:** No. **Pay Phone:** Yes. **Rest Rooms and Showers:** Yes. **Fuel:** Nearby. **Propane:** Nearby. **Internal Roads:** Gravel. **RV Service:** Nearby. **Market:** Nearby. **Restaurant:** Nearby. **General Store:** Nearby. **Vending:** No. **Swimming Pool:** No. **Playground:** No. **Activities:** Hiking, horseback riding. **Nearby Attractions:** Abraham Lincoln Museum, Pine Mountain State Park, Museum of Appalachia, antique shops.

Restrictions

Pets: On leash. **Fires:** Fire ring. **Alcoholic Beverages:** At site only. **Vehicle Max. Length:** No limit.

To Get There

From I-75, take Exit 25E on Corbin.

MOREHEAD

Twin Knobs Recreation Area

5195 KY Hwy. 801 South, Morehead 40351. T: (606) 784-8816.

RV ★★★★★ Tent ★★★★★

Beauty: ★★★★★ Site Privacy: ★★★★★
Spaciousness: ★★★★★ Quiet: ★★★★★
Security: ★★★★★ Cleanliness: ★★★★
Insect Control: ★★★ Facilities: ★★★

Gorgeous Twin Knobs Recreation Area includes quite a few sites with gorgeous views of 8, 270-acre Cave Run Lake. Anglers know the lake for its muskie, but it also supports largemouth bass, bluegill, crappie, and catfish. The lake lies within the northern tip of giant Daniel Boone National Forest, which maintains 115 miles of multi-use trails in this district alone. The campground at Twin Knobs offers incredibly spacious with dense undergrowth providing a lush barrier between sites. Most sites are shaded by various hardwoods. Some parking is on pavement, while other parking is on fine gravel. All sites offer back-in parking. Large groups looking for double sites should head for J9 and J10. Gorgeous lakefront sites include D9, D11, and D13, F22–F28, and I7–I9. Elegant loop B is tucked into the woods and offers the most secluded sites. Security is excellent—the campground is remote and gated. Avoid Twin Knobs on busy summer holidays.

Basics

Operated By: Recreation Resource Management. **Open:** Mar. 30–Oct. 29. **Site Assignment:** Most sites first come, first served; $8.35 reservation fee for few select sites. **Registration:** Entrance station. **Fee:** $12–$25. **Parking:** On site.

Facilities

Number of RV Sites: 216. **Number of Tent-Only Sites:**. **Hookups:** Water, electric (50 amps), sewer. **Each Site:** Picnic table, grill. **Dump Station:** Yes. **Laundry:** No. **Pay Phone:** Yes. **Rest Rooms and Showers:** Yes. **Fuel:** No. **Propane:** No. **Internal Roads:** Paved. **RV Service:** No. **Market:** No. **Restaurant:** No. **General Store:** Yes. **Vending:** No. **Swimming Pool:** No. **Playground:** No. **Other:** Large sandy beach w/ summer concessions. **Activities:** Hiking, volleyball, lake swimming, boating, fishing, weekly amphitheater programs. **Nearby Attractions:** Cave Run Lake, Minor E. Clark Fish Hatchery, Clear Creek Furnace. **Additional Information:** (606) 784-6428.

Restrictions

Pets: On leash. **Fires:** In grills only. **Alcoholic Beverages:** Not allowed. **Vehicle Maximum Length:** No limit.

To Get There

From I-64 take Exit 133 and go south on KY 801. Campground is 9 mi. on right.

OLIVE HILL

Grayson Lake State Park

314 Grayson Lake Park Rd., Olive Hill 41164-9213.T: (606) 474-9727.

RV ★★★	Tent ★★★
Beauty: ★★★★	Site Privacy: ★★★
Spaciousness: ★★★	Quiet: ★★★
Security: ★★★★	Cleanliness: ★★★★
Insect Control: ★★★★	Facilities: ★★★

Grayson Lake's geology, terrain, and scenery make this a particularly striking place to camp, even though the property is fairly mediocre overall. A walled canyon of sandstone bluffs looms over the lake's waters. Historically, Shawnee and Cherokee Indians camped in the area while hunting, and European frontiersman used the cliffs as a source of flint and saltpeter (an ingredient of gunpowder). A short nature trail allows one to view the distinctive flora and rock formations of the area. Most of the campsites are open, with a few well shaded; all are medium-sized. Sites 13, 14, and 27 are pretty and shaded, while sites 29–32 are completely open. Site 57 is a nice, big pull-through. Lots of children were in evidence when we visited, and it looks like the campground might serve as a sort of local teen hangout.

Basics

Operated By: Kentucky State Parks. **Open:** Apr. 1–Oct. 31. **Site Assignment:** First come, first served. **Registration:** Check in station. **Fee:** $16. **Parking:** On site.

Facilities

Number of RV Sites: 71. **Number of Tent-Only Sites:** 0. **Hookups:** Electric, water. **Each Site:** Table, fire ring. **Dump Station:** Yes. **Laundry:** Yes. **Pay Phone:** Yes. **Rest Rooms and Showers:** Yes. **Fuel:** No. **Propane:** No. **Internal Roads:** Paved. **RV Service:** Ashland, 45 minutes. **Market:** Soft Drinks, ice, fire wood. **Restaurant:** Grayson, 12 mi. **General Store:** No. **Vending:** No. **Swimming Pool:** No. **Playground:** Yes. **Other:** Marina, beach available Memorial Day & Labor Day. **Activities:** Boating, hiking, golf course available summer 2002. **Nearby Attractions:** Carter Caves State Resort Park, Greenbo Lake.

Restrictions

Pets: On leash. **Fires:** Fire ring. **Alcoholic Beverages:** Not allowed. **Vehicle Maximum Length:** No limit. **Other:** 14 day max.

To Get There

Take I-64 to the Grayson exit, go south on KY 7 through the town of Grayson. Park is 12 mi. from I-64.

PRESTONBURG

Jenny Wiley State Resort Park

75 Theatre Ct., Prestonberg 41653-9799. T: (606) 886-2711 or (800) 325-0142; www.state.ky.us.

RV ★★★	Tent ★★★
Beauty: ★★★★	Site Privacy: ★★
Spaciousness: ★★★	Quiet: ★★★
Security: ★★★★	Cleanliness: ★★★
Insect Control: ★★	Facilities: ★★★★

Jenny Wiley State Resort Park offers excellent recreational facilities in the hills of eastern Kentucky. The park roads follow the shoreline of Dewey Lake, which supports largemouth and hybrid striped bass, bluegill, catfish, and crappie. There are 10 miles of hiking trails in the park, with 60 more miles in the surrounding countryside. It's a shame the campground isn't as pretty as the rest of the park. Sites are laid out on four spurs. Sites are frighteningly similar. Each square, mid-sized site features paved, back-in parking. Sites are totally open to each other, with woods behind them providing partial shade. Since the sites are all the same, choose your site based on location. Jenny Wiley State Park stages musicals and hosts festivals all summer long, keeping the campground busy. It's best to plan a mid-week trip to avoid the crowds Security is excellent—the park is gated and rural.

Basics

Operated By: US Army Corps of Engineers. **Open:** Apr. 1–Oct.31. **Site Assignment:** First come, first served. **Registration:** Office lodge. **Fee:** $14. **Parking:** in designated areas.

Facilities

Number of RV Sites: 111. **Number of Tent-Only Sites:** 30. **Hookups:** Water, electric. **Each Site:** Picnic shelter. **Dump Station:** Yes. **Laundry:** Yes. **Pay Phone:** Yes. **Rest Rooms and Showers:** Yes. **Fuel:** 5 mi. **Propane:** 5 mi. **Internal Roads:** Paved. **RV Service:** No. **Market:** Yes. **Restaurant:** No. **General Store:** Yes. **Vending:** Yes. **Swimming Pool:** Yes. **Playground:** Yes. **Other:** Hiking, nature, mt. Bike trails, fishing, boating, golfing. **Activities:** Inquire at campground. **Nearby Attractions:** Breaks Interstate Park, Grave of Jenny Wiley, Pioneer Village, Tunder Ridge, The Samuel May House. **Additional Information:** Corps of Engineers, (606) 642-3308.

Restrictions

Pets: On leash. **Fires:** Fire ring. **Alcoholic Beverages:** Not allowed. **Vehicle Maximum Length:** No limit.

To Get There

From I-64 West take the Mtn. Pkwy. Exit. From I-64 East take the US 23 South Exit. From I-75 take the Daniel Boone Pkwy. Exit. From I-75 south, take the I-64 East Exit.

RENFRO VALLEY

Renfro Valley KOA Kampground

P.O. Box 54 Red Foley Rd., Renfro Valley 40473.T: (606) 256-2474 or (800) KOA-2475; F: (606) 256-2474; www.renfrovalley.com.

RV ★★★	Tent ★★
Beauty: ★★★	Site Privacy: ★★
Spaciousness: ★★★	Quiet: ★★★★
Security: ★★★	Cleanliness: ★★★★
Insect Control: ★★★★	Facilities: ★★★

This passably attractive KOA is convenient if you're headed to Renfro Valley Village for a concert or festival. Renfro Valley is Kentucky's country music capitol and home to the Kentucky Country Music Hall of Fame. There's also oodles of outdoor recreation in this area, which lies at the western edge of massive Daniel Boone National Forest. The campground offers long, narrow, average-sized sites. Many enjoy partial shade, but most are totally open. Most parking is on paved pull-through pads, but internal roads are gravel—oh well. If you're looking for full shade, head to one of the handful of back-in sites. Otherwise, choose your site based on location and rig size. There are no gates, but Renfro Valley is a nice little town. In order to score a site, make advance reservations for special events weekends.

Basics

Operated By: Don & Pat Miller. **Open:** Year round. **Site Assignment:** First come, first served; reservations accepted w/ first night deposit; 24-hour cancellation notice for full refund. **Registration:** Store, after hours self-register. **Fee:** $28 full (cable), $23 water & electric, $19 tent; prices for 2 adults or family of four, $1.50 per additional adult; KOA discount (cash, V, MC, D, AE). **Parking:** 1 car at site.

Facilities

Number of RV Sites: 0. **Number of Tent-Only Sites:** 40. **Number of Multipurpose Sites:** 100. **Hookups:** Water, electric (20, 30, 50 amps), some sewer, some cable. **Each Site:** Picnic table, fire ring, grill. **Dump Station:** Yes. **Laundry:** Yes. **Pay Phone:** Yes. **Rest Rooms and Showers:** Yes. **Fuel:** No. **Propane:** Yes. **Internal Roads:** Paved. **RV Service:** 25 mi. in Somerset. **Market:** On site, plus RV supplies. **Restaurant:** 0.25 mi. **General Store:** 14 mi. in Berea. **Vending:** Yes. **Swimming Pool:** Yes. **Playground:** Yes. **Other:** Game room, pavilion, outdoor kitchen. **Activities:** Basketball, volleyball, shuffleboard, horseshoes. **Nearby Attractions:** Renfro Valley Country Music Center, Great Saltpeter Cave, Daniel Boone National Forest, 14 mi. to Berea College & crafts, 50 mi. to Lexington. **Additional Information:** Renfro Valley information (800) 765-7464 or www.renfrovalley.com, Berea Chamber, (859) 986-9760.

Restrictions

Pets: On leash only. **Fires:** Allowed. **Alcoholic Beverages:** Not allowed (dry county). **Vehicle Maximum Length:** No limit.

To Get There

From I-75, take Exit 62 and drive north 1 mi. on US 25. The campground is on the right.

RICHMOND

Fort Boonesborough State Park

4375 Boonesboro Rd., Richmond 40475.T: (859) 527-3131; www.kystateparks.com.

RV ★★★	Tent ★★★
Beauty: ★★★★	Site Privacy: ★★
Spaciousness: ★★★	Quiet: ★★
Security: ★★★	Cleanliness: ★★★★
Insect Control: ★★★	Facilities: ★★★

Here's a rhetorical question: Why build a campground next to a sewage treatment plant? Suffice to say that the campground at Fort Boonesborough would be much more desirable without the aforementioned eyesore. The campground is situated on a gentle hill partially shaded by mature hardwoods. Mid-sized sites offer paved, back-in parking (there is one pull-through), and the campground feels claustrophobic due to its popularity. The shadiest sites, in the back of the campground, include 61–74 and 137–139. Security is okay—there are no gates, but the park is in a rural location. Park facilities are excellent. Fort Boonesborough is a reconstruction based on the fort built here by Daniel Boone and Richard Henderson in the 1770s. Costumed guides and artisans perform demonstrations. Fishing on the Kentucky River is also available. Catches include bluegill, bass, and catfish. Avoid Fort Boonesborough on summer holidays and weekends.

Basics

Operated By: Kentucky State Parks. **Open:** Year round. **Site Assignment:** First come, first served; no reservations. **Registration:** Entrance booth, night arrival register next morning. **Fee:** $18 RV, $10 primitive; price for 2 people, $1 per additional adult, 16 & under free; senior & disabled discounts available, Kentucky POWs free (cash, local checks, AE, V, MC, D). **Parking:** At site, in parking lot.

Facilities

Number of RV Sites: 0. **Number of Tent-Only Sites:** Primitive, undesignated. **Number of Multipurpose Sites:** 167. **Hookups:** Water, electric (20, 30, 50 amps). **Each Site:** Picnic table, grill, fire rings in primitive area. **Dump Station:** Yes. **Laundry:** Yes. **Pay Phone:** Yes. **Rest Rooms and Showers:** Yes. **Fuel:** No. **Propane:** No. **Internal Roads:** Paved. **RV Service:** 25 mi. in Lexington. **Market:** 8 mi. in Winchester. **Restaurant:** 0.25 mi. **General Store:** Camp store, 8 mi. in Winchester. **Vending:** Yes. **Swimming Pool:** Yes (seasonal, w/ waterslide). **Playground:** Yes. **Other:** Rec building, gift shop, meeting room, picnic shelters, boat ramp. **Activities:** Fishing, mini-golf, nature trails, seasonal organized activities. **Nearby Attractions:** Boone Station State Historic Site, Natural Bridge State Resort Park, Daniel Boone National Forest, 15 mi. to Lexington. **Additional Information:** Lexington CVB (800) 845-3959, www.visitlex.com.

Restrictions

Pets: On leash only. **Fires:** Allowed, fire ring only. **Alcoholic Beverages:** Not allowed. **Vehicle Maximum Length:** No limit. **Other:** 14-day stay limit.

To Get There

From I-75, take Exit 95 and drive 5.5 mi. northeast on State Rte. 627. Turn right on KY Hwy. 388 and the campground is on the left. From I-64, take Exit 94/Winchester and drive 10 mi. southwest on Rte. 627. Turn left on Hwy. 388.

SASSAFRAS

Carr Creek State Park

P.O. Box 249, Sassafras 41759. T: (606) 642-4050.

Beauty: ★★★★★ Site Privacy: ★★
Spaciousness: ★★★★ Quiet: ★★★★
Security: ★★★★ Cleanliness: ★★★★
Insect Control: ★★★★ Facilities: ★★★

The flat, pretty campground at Carr Creek State Park rests in an Appalachian Mountain valley. It offers large sites with paved, back-in parking. Each site also has either a gravel or paved picnic area. Most sites are open to each other, with pleasant woods surrounding the campground. The campground is laid out in two loops, with the nicest sites in the back. Sites 14, 16, 18, 20, 22, and 23, are partially shady, with views of the mountains. The state park offers a full-service marina and fishing on a 750-acre lake. Common catches include bass, crappie and walleye. Carr Creek is so isolated, we thought we would never arrive. But it's definitely worth the drive. Though there is no gate, security is fine. Avoid the park on holiday weekends. Otherwise, these cool mountain highlands are a good summer destination.

Basics

Operated By: Corps of Engineers. **Open:** Apr. 1–Oct. 31. **Site Assignment:** First come, first served. **Registration:** Office. **Fee:** $16. **Parking:** Designated areas.

Facilities

Number of RV Sites: 39. **Number of Tent-Only Sites:**. **Hookups:** Water, electric. **Each Site:** Picnic shelter. **Dump Station:** Yes. **Laundry:** Yes. **Pay Phone:** Yes. **Rest Rooms and Showers:** Yes. **Fuel:** 1 mi. **Propane:** 1 mi. **Internal Roads:** Paved. **RV Service:** No. **Market:** No. **Restaurant:** No. **General Store:** No. **Vending:** Yes. **Swimming Pool:** Beach area. **Playground:** Yes. **Activities:** Fishing, boating, hiking, pontoons, theatre. **Nearby Attractions:** Inquire at campground. **Additional Information:** US Army Corps of Engineers, (606) 642-3308.

Restrictions

Pets: On leash. **Fires:** Fire ring. **Alcoholic Beverages:** Not allowed. **Vehicle Maximum Length:** No limit.

To Get There

From Hazard on KY 15, Carr Creek is located 15 mi.

SCOTTSVILLE

Tailwater Recreation Area

11088 Finney Rd., Glasgow 42141-9642. T: (270) 646-2055.

RV ★★★★ Tent ★★★

Beauty: ★★★★ Site Privacy: ★★★
Spaciousness: ★★★★ Quiet: ★★★★
Security: ★★★★ Cleanliness: ★★★★
Insect Control: ★★★ Facilities: ★★★

The campground at the Tailwater Recreation Area was designed with the avid angler in mind. Most of the 49 sites are right on the water, and those that aren't lie nearby. Most of these sites are long and narrow, and while the trees provide ample shade throughout, the minimal ground cover reduces the privacy between sites. If campers can snag it, site 5 is one of the best in the area; it has one of the only pull-throughs, and the huge site has a gorgeous view. Though the campground can get quite crowded on summer weekends, it seldom fills up. At the time of our visit, the showers were under construction, though they should be completed for the 2002 season. Besides fishing, in-camp activities include horseshoes and hiking.

Basics

Operated By: US Army Corps of Engineers. **Open:** Apr.–Oct. **Site Assignment:** First come, first served. **Registration:** fee station. **Fee:** $14–$50. **Parking:** On site.

Facilities

Number of RV Sites: 49. **Number of Tent-Only Sites:**. **Hookups:** Water, electric (30, 50 amps). **Each Site:** Picnic shelter. **Dump Station:** Yes. **Laundry:** Yes. **Pay Phone:** No. **Rest Rooms and Showers:** Yes. **Fuel:** No. **Propane:** Nearby. **Internal Roads:** Paved. **RV Service:** No. **Market:** Nearby. **Restaurant:** No. **General Store:** Nearby. **Vending:** Yes. **Swimming Pool:** No. **Playground:** Yes. **Activities:** Fishing, boating, horseshoes, hiking. **Nearby Attractions:** Buckhorn Lake State Resort.

Restrictions

Pets: On leash. **Fires:** Only in designated areas. **Alcoholic Beverages:** Not allowed. **Vehicle Maximum Length:** 45 ft.

To Get There

From Glasgow, take Hwy. 31E south for 4 mi.; turn right on 252. Go 8 mi. & cross the dam. The Tailwater entrance road is at the south end of the dam.

SCOTTSVILLE

The Narrows, Barren River Lake

11088 Finney Rd., Glasgow 42141-9642. T: (502) 646-3094.

RV ★★★★ Tent ★★★★

Beauty: ★★★★ Site Privacy: ★★★
Spaciousness: ★★★★ Quiet: ★★★★
Security: ★★★★★ Cleanliness: ★★★
Insect Control: ★★★ Facilities: ★★★

This campground is a bit disappointing compared to other superb US Army Corps of Engineers Campgrounds in the Southeast. Though attractive, parts of the campground need maintenance work. There are weeds popping up through the gravel parking pads. Campsites are larger than average, with back-in parking. Some are well shaded, while others are more open. If you have a big rig, your site choices may be limited, as pad length varies. Our favorites are in Area B. Sites 31 and 32 boast lake views and ample shade. For tent campers, sites 1, 2, 43, 45, 47, 49, and 50 have no hookups, but nestle into the woods and offer seclusion. Remote and gated, security is outstanding here. Fishing in Barren River Lake affords shots at bluegill, channel catfish, crappie, rough fish, and largemouth, white, and hybrid striped bass. In the area, many commercial marinas and bait shops cater to fishermen. Avoid Barren River Lake on busy summer holidays and weekends.

Basics

Operated By: US Army Corps of Engineers. **Open:** Apr.–Sept. **Site Assignment:** First come, first served. **Registration:** fee station. **Fee:** $16–$19. **Parking:** On site.

Facilities

Number of RV Sites: 97. **Number of Tent-Only Sites:**. **Hookups:** Water, electric (50 amps). **Each Site:** Picnic table. **Dump Station:** Yes. **Laundry:** Yes. **Pay Phone:** No. **Rest Rooms and Showers:** Yes. **Fuel:** No. **Propane:** No. **Internal Roads:** Paved. **RV Service:** No. **Market:** Nearby. **Restaurant:** Nearby. **General Store:** Nearby. **Vending:** Yes. **Swimming Pool:** No. **Playground:** Yes. **Activities:** Fishing, boating, swimming in lake. **Nearby Attractions:** Buckhorn Dam Overlook.

Restrictions

Pets: On leash. **Fires:** Only in designated areas. **Alcoholic Beverages:** Not allowed. **Vehicle Maximum Length:** 45 ft. **Other:** Max 6 person, 2 vehicles per site.

To Get There

From Glasgow, take Hwy. 31 east for 10 mi.; turn right on 1318. Follow the signs.

SHEPHERDSVILLE

KOA–Louisville South

2433 Hwy. 44 East, Shepherdsville 40165. T: (502) 543-2041.

RV ★★★ Tent ★★★

Beauty: ★★★★	Site Privacy: ★★★
Spaciousness: ★★★★	Quiet: ★★★
Security: ★★	Cleanliness: ★★★★
Insect Control: ★★★	Facilities: ★★★

This attractive KOA offers both back-in and pull-through sites laid out in numerous areas. Some sites are wide and as long as 70 feet, while others are pretty dinky. Most sites are shady, though a few are totally open. Parking is on gravel. In the back of the park, the prettiest sites (75–89, 126–130, and 181–191) overlook a cliff leading to the Salt River. The swimming pool and other facilities are in tip-top shape. Security is so-so. The area is densely populated and the campground has no gates. Suburban Shepherdsville is about 20 miles from downtown Louisville. There are plenty of restaurants and shops near the campground. For a pleasant day trip, visit My Old Kentucky Home in Bardstown. Unless you have tickets to an event, avoid the Louisville area on Kentucky Derby weekend (first Saturday in May) as well as summer holidays.

Basics

Operated By: Roy J. Tanner & Carol Hylton. **Open:** Year round. **Site Assignment:** First come, first served. **Registration:** Office. **Fee:** $21–$29. **Parking:** On site.

Facilities

Number of RV Sites: 108. **Number of Tent-Only Sites:** 37. **Hookups:** Water, electric (50 amps), some sewer, Internet ports. **Each Site:** Fire ring. **Dump Station:** Yes. **Laundry:** Yes. **Pay Phone:** Yes. **Rest Rooms and Showers:** Yes. **Fuel:** No. **Propane:** Yes. **Internal Roads:** Gravel. **RV Service:** No. **Market:** No. **Restaurant:** No. **General Store:** Yes. **Vending:** Yes. **Swimming Pool:** Yes, heated. **Playground:** Yes. **Other:** hot tub. **Activities:** Horse shoes, boating, hiking mini-golf. **Nearby Attractions:** Derby Museum, General Patton Museum, Jim Beam. **Additional Information:** (800) KOA-1880.

Restrictions

Pets: On leash. **Fires:** Fire ring. **Alcoholic Beverages:** Allowed. **Vehicle Maximum Length:** 100 ft. **Other:** 21 or older in hot tub.

To Get There

I-65 to Exit 117. Go 2 mi. east on Rte. 44.

SLADE

Natural Bridge State Park

2135 Natural Bridge Rd., Slade 40376. T: (606) 663-2214.

RV ★★★ Tent ★★★

Beauty: ★★★★	Site Privacy: ★★
Spaciousness: ★★★	Quiet: ★★★
Security: ★★★★	Cleanliness: ★★★★
Insect Control: ★★★★★	Facilities: ★★★★

It's a shame that the campgrounds at Natural Bridge are so mediocre, given the natural beauty of the land in this part of the Daniel Boone National Forest. With the campgrounds squeezed into tight mountain hollers, sites are on the small side of average. What's more, this park is extremely popular and the campgrounds stay full all summer. Sites offer gravel, back-in parking. Shadiness varies. We recommend shady RV sites in the back of the Whittleton Campground, particularly A33–A35. For tent campers, we like sites in the primitive area, numbered C4–C10. The state park's namesake is a giant sandstone arch. Nearby, the Red River Gorge contains a plethora of rock climbing routes catering to novices and experts. The Red River is known for gorgeous canoeing as well as Class II–III whitewater. Security is passable at this isolated state park. Visit in spring or fall if you value solitude.

Basics

Operated By: State of Kentucky. **Open:** Apr.–Oct. **Site Assignment:** First come, first served. **Registration:** Booth at campground entry. **Fee:** $10–$20. **Parking:** In designated areas.

Facilities

Number of RV Sites: 86. **Number of Tent-Only Sites:**. **Hookups:** Water, electric (20, 30 amps). **Each Site:** Picnic shelters. **Dump Station:** Yes. **Laundry:** Yes. **Pay Phone:** Yes. **Rest Rooms and Showers:** Yes. **Fuel:** Nearby. **Propane:** Nearby. **Internal Roads:** Paved. **RV Service:** No. **Market:** No. **Restaurant:** Yes. **General Store:** No. **Vending:** Yes. **Swimming Pool:** Yes. **Playground:** Yes. **Other:** Nature center. **Activities:** Fishing, mini-golf, hiking. **Nearby Attractions:** Buckhorn Lake State Resort Park. **Additional Information:** Check out at 2 p.m.

Restrictions

Pets: On leash. **Fires:** Fire ring. **Alcoholic Beverages:** Not allowed. **Vehicle Max. Length:** None.

To Get There

I-64 E to Exit 98 onto Bert T. Combs Mtn. Pkwy East. Take KY 11 Exit No. 33 towards Slade/Beattyville. Keep right at the fork in the ramp. Merge onto KY 11. Park is 0.33 mi.

UNION

Big Bone Lick State Park

3380 Beaver Rd., Union 41091-9627. T: (859) 384-3522; www.state.ky.us.

RV ★★★★ Tent ★★★★

Beauty: ★★★★	Site Privacy: ★★
Spaciousness: ★★★	Quiet: ★★★
Security: ★★★★★	Cleanliness: ★★★★
Insect Control: ★★★	Facilities: ★★★★

The institutional-looking campground at Big Bone Lick is not gorgeous, but it's pleasant. Set on a large, gentle hill, the campground features average-sized sites with minimal privacy. Some sites are shady, but the campground is open enough that you can easily see one end from the other. Sites offer paved, back-in parking. Many of the parking pads are short. Our favorite sites, 25–29, are on a cul-de-sac at the end of the campground. Fascinating Big Bone Lick State Park, the birthplace of American vertebrate paleontology, was a swamp at the end of the Ice Age. Prehistoric animals, such as giant mammoths, mastodons, ground sloths, and bison, were attracted by the swamp's salt and minerals, became trapped in the quagmire, and died. Their remains fossilized, leaving paleontologists a treasure trove of bones to study. Located near Cincinnati, this park stays busy all summer. Visit during the week, or in spring or fall. Security is excellent.

Basics

Operated By: State of Kentucky. **Open:** Year round/closed Dec. 23–Dec. 30. **Site Assignment:** reservations not required, first come first serve. **Registration:** Office. **Fee:** $10. **Parking:** On site.

Facilities

Number of RV Sites: 62. **Number of Tent-Only Sites:** Tent area. **Hookups:** Water, electric (30, 50 amps), sewer. **Each Site:** Grill, water, picnic table. **Dump Station:** Yes. **Laundry:** Yes. **Pay Phone:** Yes. **Rest Rooms and Showers:** Yes. **Fuel:** 5 mi. **Propane:** 5 mi. **Internal Roads:** Paved. **RV Service:** No. **Market:** Yes. **Restaurant:** No. **General Store:** No. **Vending:** Yes. **Swimming Pool:** Yes. **Playground:** Yes. **Other:** Church services (Apr.–Oct.), observation deck, Museum Store. **Activities:** Miniature golf, fishing, boating, basketball, tennis, softball fields, nature trails. **Nearby Attractions:** Inquire at campground. **Additional Information:** State of Kentucky, (859) 384-3522.

Restrictions

Pets: On leash. **Fires:** No. **Alcoholic Beverages:** Not allowed. **Vehicle Maximum Length:** No limit. **Other:** No hunting, rappelling, rock climbing, motorized vehicles & bikes, collecting or digging for artifacts.

To Get There

22 mi. southwest of Covington I-75, go south to KY 338, off US 42/127 and I-71/I-75.

Louisiana

Louisiana is one of America's great cultural melting pots. The state's famous festivals are a lively way for visitors to immerse themselves in the local culture. **Mardi Gras** is the crown jewel of Louisiana festivals. From town to town, folks celebrate Mardi Gras in unique ways. Many cities, including **Shreveport-Bossier,** feature family-oriented Mardi-Gras celebrations. Other noteworthy festivals include **Cajun Fun Fest, New Orleans Jazz & Heritage Festival,** and the **Louisiana Folklife Festival.** Call (800) 947-6711 for a statewide calendar of fairs and festivals.

Throughout history, varied peoples have affected Louisiana history and traditions. Native American habitation dates back thousands of years. Learn about these ancient cultures at various mounds and archaeological sights, including **Poverty Point State Historic Site.** Today, the Tunica-Biloxi, Coushatta, and other tribes make rich contributions to the state's economy and culture.

African Americans in Louisiana contribute greatly to the state's fascinating history. Lavish rice and sugarcane plantations in southeastern Louisiana prospered using slave labor. In the twentieth century, New Orleans' African American community gave birth to jazz. The legendary roots of jazz are said to originate at **Congo Square,** where crowds of slaves once sang and danced to African drum beats.

Folks from outside of Louisiana aren't always aware of the state's Hispanic influences. Even before Hernando de Soto arrived in 1541, other Spanish explorers had seen the mouth of the Mississippi. The present day Isleños community of **St. Bernard Parish** preserve their heritage at the **Isleños Museum.** Vestiges of Spanish colonial culture are also evident throughout **New Orleans'** famous historic districts.

Louisiana is famous for its Cajun culture, which arose from the great Acadian Diaspora of 1755. This tragic phase in Cajun history was brought about when the British asked French-speaking colonists in New Brunswick and Nova Scotia to renounce Catholicism. When families refused to renounce their religion, they were forced to flee. Great numbers of Acadians made their way to southern Louisiana, where their culture thrives. Learn about Acadian culture at numerous museums, including **Acadian Village in Lafayette.**

No discussion of Louisiana is complete without mentioning the food—it's fabulous. Even if you're heading to Louisiana for primitive tent camping, make plans to stop at one of the state's fine Cajun or seafood restaurants. A number of excellent guidebooks detail Louisiana cuisine.

Popular tourist attractions in Louisiana include **Mississippi River Steamboat Cruises. Casinos** draw tourists to Shreveport-Bossier City, Marksville, Kinder, Lake Charles, Baton Rouge, and the New Orleans area. Other worthwhile attractions include: Ark-La-Tex Antique and Classic Vehicle Museum, Sci-Port Discovery Center, Water Town USA, Sports Museum of Champions, Biedenharn Museum and Gardens, **Louisiana Purchase Museum and Gardens,** Northeast Louisiana Children's Museum, Mansfield State Historic Site, Poverty Point State Historic Site, Fort St. Jean Baptiste Historic Site, **Camp Beauregard,** River Oaks Square Arts Center, Frogmore Plantation, Cane River Creole National Historic Park, The Cane River National heritage Area, **Bayou Folk Museum,** Melrose Plantation, World Famous Garden in the Forest, Los Adaes State Historic Site, Lake Charles Carpentier District, DeQuincy Railroad Museum, Chateau des Cocodries, The Zigler Museum, Vermilionville, **Jean Lafitte Acadian Cultural Center,** Children's Museum of Acadiana, Lafayette Natural History Museum, Acadian Memorial, Longfellow-Evangeline State Historic Site, **Louisiana State Arboretum,** Chretien Point Plantation, Shadows-on-the-Teche plantation, Tabasco Factory and Jungle gardens, The Great River Road, Oak Alley Plantation, Laura, Destrehan Plantation, Nottoway Plantation, Houmas House, Tezcuco, Louisiana State Capitol, The Old State Capitol, West Baton Rouge Museum, The USS Kidd, **Port Hudson State Historic Site Civil War Battlefield,** St. Francisville, Rosedown Plantation, and The Myrtles, Audubon State Historic Site.

In the **New Orleans** area, tourist attractions include: The Cabildo, The Presbytere, St. Louis Cathedral, Pontalba Apartments, The Vieux Carré, Top of the Mart, Aquarium of the Americas, Louisiana Superdome, New Orleans Saints, Children's Museum, national D-Day Museum, **Audubon Park, Audubon Zoo,** Warehouse District, cemeteries, Mardi Gras World, German American Museum, Chalmette National Historic Battlefield, Fort Jackson, Rivertown USA, **Abita Brew Pub,** Global Wildlife Center, and Zemurray Gardens.

BASTROP

Chemin-A-Haut State Park

14656 State Park Rd., Bastrop 71220-7078. T: (888) 677-2436; F: (318) 556-7007; www.crt.state.la.us.

★★★★ ★★★★

Beauty: ★★★★ Site Privacy: ★★★★
Spaciousness: ★★★★ Quiet: ★★★★
Security: ★★★★ Cleanliness: ★★★★
Insect Control: ★★★★ Facilities: ★★★

Chemin-A-Haut offers one attractive camping loop. Site size is ample, though privacy varies. The most secluded sites are 11, 12, and 14, in the back of the campground. Though distance between sites varies, all are large and comfortably spaced. Mature trees, including oak, hickory, and pine, shade the campground, and undergrowth provides privacy between sites. Sites feature paved, back-in parking. Chemin-A-Haut is situated on high bluffs overlooking Bayou Bartholomew, and offers a paved walking trail along the water. The large playground and wading pool are a hit with younger children. Older children can cast a line into Big Slough Lake, on the eastern edge of the park. Avoid Chemin-A-Haut on summer and holiday weekends. Summer weather isn't necessarily torturous at this park, so it makes a good mid-week summertime destination. Security is excellent at this very rural park. Gates are locked at night.

BASICS

Operated By: State of Louisiana Dept. of Culture, Recreation & Tourism. **Open:** Year-round. **Site Assignment:** First come, first served, also reservations can be held w/ V or MC (888) 677-1400. If cancelled 15 days or more before the first reserved day then the fee is $10. If cancelled 14 days or less to the first reserved day then the fee is one day's rental of all reserved items. Check-in time is 3 p.m. or later. Check-out time is 11 a.m. or earlier. Stay limit is 15 days. **Registration:** Main office. **Fee:** $12 per night for RV/tent sites, $6 w/ a Golden Access card. **Parking:** 3 car parking at each site/2car & 1 RV.

FACILITIES

Number of Multipurpose Sites: 26. **Hookups:** Electric (30 amps), water. **Each Site:** Tent pad, fire ring, grill, picnic table, lantern hook. **Dump Station:** Yes. **Laundry:** Yes. **Pay Phone:** Yes. **Rest Rooms and Showers:** Yes. **Fuel:** No. **Propane:** No. **Internal Roads:** Paved. **RV Service:** 15 mi. south in Bastrop. **Market:** 7 mi. south in Log Cabin. **Restaurant:** 15 mi. south in Bastrop. **General Store:** 15 mi. south in Bastrop. **Vending:** Beverage only. **Swimming Pool:** Yes. **Playground:** Yes. **Other:** Hiking trails, Baseball field, boat launch, Group lodging. **Activities:** Boat renting, hiking, fishing, field games. **Nearby Attractions:** Poverty Point State Commemorative Area, Lake D'Arbonne State Park, Handy Brake National Wildlife Refuge, Georgia Pacific Wildlife Management Area, Lake Claiborne State Park, Caney Creek Lake State Park. **Additional Information:** Bastrop-Morehouse Tourism Commission, (318) 281-3794.

RESTRICTIONS

Pets: Leash. **Fires:** Fire ring only. **Alcoholic Beverages:** Allowed. **Vehicle Maximum Length:** 60 ft. **Other:** Be familiar w/ all alligator precautions.

TO GET THERE

From Bastrop take US 425 north approx. 10 mi. Turn right onto LA 2229 (State Park Rd.).

BRAITHWAITE

St. Bernard State Park

P.O. Box 534, Violet 70092. T: (888) 677-7823; F: (504) 682-9960; www.crt.state.la.us; st.bernard@crt.state.la.us.

★★★★ ★★★★

Beauty: ★★★★ Site Privacy: ★★★
Spaciousness: ★★★★ Quiet: ★★★★
Security: ★★★★ Cleanliness: ★★★★
Insect Control: ★★ Facilities: ★★★

St. Bernard is situated around a series of man-made lagoons and provides a habitat for alligators, turtles, and other wetlands wildlife. The Mississippi River is across Hwy. 39 from the park, and Chalmette National Historic Park is nearby. Less than one hour from downtown New Orleans, St. Bernard is popular with folks from the Crescent City. It should be avoided on holiday and festival weekends, especially Jazz Fest. Visit in early April or in the fall if you value tranquility. St. Bernard offers one camping loop, with sites partially shaded by a variety of trees. We like the shadier sites, including 16, 22, 45, and 46. Site privacy is not exceptional. Site size varies immensely. Some are 90 feet from their neighbors, while others are only 25 feet from neighbors. All sites offer paved, back-in parking. Remote and gated, security at St. Bernard is excellent.

BASICS

Operated By: State of Louisiana, Dept. of Culture, Recreation, & Tourism. **Open:** Year-round. **Site Assignment:** First come, first served, also reservations can be made w/ a V or MC, Deposit is $12 (888) 677-1400. If cancelled the fee is the deposit ($12). Check-in time is 2 p.m. or later. Check-out time is 1 p.m. or earlier. **Registration:** Ranger's station. **Fee:** $12 per night for RV/tent site. $6 w/ Golden Access Card. **Parking:** 2 vehicle parking at site. Overflow parking is available.

FACILITIES

Number of Multipurpose Sites: 51. **Hookups:** Water, Electric (30 amps). **Each Site:** Picnic table, fire ring, concrete patio, grill. **Dump Station:** Yes. **Laundry:** Yes. **Pay Phone:** Yes. **Rest Rooms and Showers:** Yes. **Fuel:** No. **Propane:** No. **Internal Roads:** Paved. **RV Service:** 5 mi. west in Chalmette. **Market:** Convenience store 0.5 mi. north, grocery 2 mi. west. **Restaurant:** 1 mi. west. **General Store:** K-Mart is 7 mi. west in Chalmette. **Vending:** Beverage only. **Swimming Pool:** Yes (open from Memorial Day–Labor Day). **Playground:** Yes. **Other:** Trails, field for athletics, pavilion. **Activities:** Hiking, boating & fishing less than a mi. from the State Park. **Nearby Attractions:** Bayou Sagnette State Park, Fairview Riverside State Park, Louisiana State Museum, New Orleans & the Historic French Quarter, Chalmette Battlefield-Jean Lafitte National Historic Park & Preserve, Isleno Cultural Center-Jean Lafitte National Historic Park & Preserve, San Bernardo Scenic Byway, Bayou Sauvage National Wildlife Refuge. **Additional Information:** St. Bernard Parish Tourist Commission (888) 278-2054.

RESTRICTIONS

Pets: Leash only. **Fires:** Fire ring. **Alcoholic Beverages:** Allowed. **Vehicle Maximum Length:** 50 ft.

TO GET THERE

From I-10 get on 510 (Hwy. 47) towards Chalmette. Go 6 mi. to the intersection of Hwy. 46 and turn left. Go 7 mi. to Hwy. 39 and turn right to go south. Go 0.5 mi. and the entrance is on the left.

CARENCRO

Bayou Wilderness RV Resort

201 St. Clair Rd., Carencro 70520. T: (337) 896-0598; www.bayouwildernessrvresort.com.

★★★ n/a

Beauty: ★★★ Site Privacy: ★★
Spaciousness: ★★★ Quiet: ★★★★
Security: ★★★ Cleanliness: ★★★★
Insect Control: ★★★ Facilities: ★★★

This quaint RV park is laid out in rows of pull-through sites with gravel parking. Sites are on the small side, and are mostly open. There are trees on the perimeter of the campground, providing shade for a few of the sites. There are no natural privacy barriers. The nicest sites are 15, 16, 33, 34, 46, 47, 54, and 55. These offer views of a small pond with picturesque cypress trees. The park is located in suburban Lafayette. Nearby, you'll find plenty of restaurants, shopping, and tourist attractions. Notable outings include swamp tours in the mammoth Atchafalaya Basin and Acadian Village, a museum of authentic Acadian houses. Bayou Wilderness is relatively safe; there are no gates, but it's in a quiet area. Visit southern Louisiana in spring or fall for pleasant weather.

BASICS

Operated By: George Cormier & Charlie Montgomery. **Open:** Year-round. **Site Assignment:** Deposit, cancellations must be received one & a half weeks before arrival date. reservations are recommended, pick your own site, check in/check out is at noon, payments can be made w/ V or MC. **Registration:** Main office/grocery store. **Fee:** $29–$23. **Parking:** One RV unit & one vehicle per site. Parking area for additional vehicles.

FACILITIES

Number of RV Sites: 122. **Number of Tent-Only Sites:** 0. **Hookups:** Water, electric (30, 50 amps), some have cable. **Dump Station:** Yes. **Laundry:** Yes. **Pay Phone:** Yes. **Rest Rooms and Showers:** Yes. **Fuel:** No. **Propane:** Yes. **Internal Roads:** Gravel, black top. **RV Service:** Limited (3 mi. in south Lafayette). **Market:** On site. **Restaurant:** 3 mi. in Lafayette. **General Store:** Wal-Mart in Lafayette. **Vending:** No. **Swimming Pool:** Yes.

Playground: Yes. **Other:** Tennis court, arcade room, volleyball net, Jacuzzi. **Activities:** Tennis arcade games, volleyball, fishing, shuffleboard, horseshoes. **Nearby Attractions:** Tabasco Plant, Acadian Village, Jean Lafitte National Park, Atchafalaya Basin Boat Tour. **Additional Information:** Bayou Teche Visitors Center (888) 565 5939, big rigs welcome.

Restrictions

Pets: Leash only. **Fires:** Designated areas only. **Alcoholic Beverages:** Allowed. **Vehicle Maximum Length:** 70 ft.

To Get There

From I-10, take exit 1033 onto I-49 North. Go 2.5 mi. to Gloria Switch Rd. (exit 2). Turn right, going east, onto Gloria Switch and travel 2.3 mi. (crossing Moss St. at traffic light) until you come to North Wilderness Trail. Turn left, going north, onto North Wilderness Trail. Travel 0.7 mi. to the entrance on the right.

CHATHAM

Caney Creek Lake State Park

State Rd. No. 1209, Chatham 71226. T: (888) 677-2263; F: (318) 249-2671; www.crt.state.la.us.

RV ★★★★ Tent ★★★★

Beauty: ★★★★★	Site Privacy: ★★★★
Spaciousness: ★★★★★	Quiet: ★★★★
Security: ★★★★★	Cleanliness: ★★★★★
Insect Control: ★★★	Facilities: ★★★

Caney Creek features a lovely camping area, with sites laid out along the lakeshore. Sites vary in size-some are very large. Shadiness also varies-though most are shaded by pine and other species, sites 13–17 are more open. All sites offer paved, back-in parking. Few sites offer privacy. The nicest waterfront sites include 38, 40, 42, 43, and 45. However, the crown jewel of Caney Creek is site 54, with its knockout view of the lake. Boasting numerous record catches, Caney Creek is bass fishin' heaven. The park maintains two boat launches and a fishing pier as well as an attractive swimming beach. Even though it's off the beaten path, Caney Creek is very popular and should be avoided on summer holidays and weekends. Security is excellent. Gates are attended during the day and locked at night.

Basics

Operated By: State of Louisiana Dept. of Culture, Recreation & Tourism (888) 677-1400. **Open:** Year-round. **Site Assignment:** First come, first served, reservations can be held w/ V or MC (888) 677-1400. If reservations are cancelled then the fee is one day's rent. Check-in time is 2 p.m. or later. Check-out time is 1 p.m. or earlier. Stay limit is 15 days. **Registration:** Main office. **Fee:** $12 a night for RV/tent site rental, $6 w/ Golden Access card. **Parking:** 2 car/1 RV & 1 car at each site, overflow parking available.

Facilities

Number of Multipurpose Sites: 73. **Hookups:** Water, electric (30 amps). **Each Site:** Tent pad, grill, fire ring, picnic table. **Dump Station:** Yes. **Laundry:** Yes. **Pay Phone:** Yes. **Rest Rooms and Showers:** Yes. **Fuel:** No. **Propane:** No. **Internal Roads:** Paved. **RV Service:** 35 mi. northeast in West Monroe. **Market:** 6 mi. east in Chatham. **Restaurant:** 6 mi. east in Chatham. **General Store:** 15 mi. west in Jonesboro. **Vending:** No. **Swimming Pool:** No. **Playground:** No. **Other:** Fishing pier, pavilions, boat launch. **Activities:** Picnicking, fishing, boating (bring your own). **Nearby Attractions:** Poverty Point State Commemorative Area, Lake D'Arbonne State Park, Historic Town of Chatham, Lake Claiborne State Park, Jackson Bienville Wildlife Management Area. **Additional Information:** Monroe-West Monroe CVB.

Restrictions

Pets: Leash. **Fires:** Ring. **Alcoholic Beverages:** Yes (none on beach). **Vehicle Maximum Length:** Approx. 72 ft. **Other:** No 3 or 4 wheelers allowed.

To Get There

From Jonesboro go east on LA 4 for 12.8 mi. then turn right onto Lakeshore Dr. State Park Rd. 1209 is on the right, approx. 20 mi. ahead.

COVINGTON

Land-O-Pines

17145 Million Dollar Rd., Covington 70435. T: (985) 892-6023 or (985) 867-8372; F: (985) 898-2072; www.land-o-pines.com; landopines@aol.com.

RV ★★★ Tent ★★★

Beauty: ★★★	Site Privacy: ★★
Spaciousness: ★★★	Quiet: ★★★
Security: ★★★	Cleanliness: ★★★
Insect Control: ★★★	Facilities: ★★★

Land-O-Pines has two things going for it: its location and family-oriented amenities. Here, children enjoy mini-golf, a nice playground, a waterslide and pool, and a duck pond. Adults appreciate the suburban location, with plenty of shopping and restaurants nearby. New Orleans is just across the 26-mile Lake Pontchartrain Causeway. The campground contains residential and overnight sites in two separate areas. The overnight area is laid out in four long rows of back-in campsites. Sites are average sized, with plenty of shady trees. Parking is on grass, and sites are not always well defined. Grassy sites make this park popular with tent campers. The prettiest, quietest sites are on Deer Run Rd., along the back perimeter. Don't visit southern Louisiana in hot, humid late summer. For peachy weather, visit in spring or fall. Security is good–all cars are required to display passes.

Basics

Operated By: Jim Williamson. **Open:** 7 days, all year. **Site Assignment:** First come, first served also reservations. **Registration:** At store, 7 a.m.–7 p.m. Sunday–Thursday, 10 p.m. Friday, 9 p.m. Saturday. **Fee:** $20 (Monday–Thursday & Winter), $25 (Friday–Sunday), $30 (holidays), rates for 5 people, $5 extra per person, 3 under free, senior discount available; cash, check, money order, V, MC, AE, D. **Parking:** Sites plus parking area.

Facilities

Number of Multipurpose Sites: 275 (all sites multi-purpose). **Hookups:** Water, electric (30 amps), some sewer. **Each Site:** Picnic table, fire ring. **Dump Station:** Yes. **Laundry:** Yes. **Pay Phone:** Yes. **Rest Rooms and Showers:** Yes. **Fuel:** Yes. **Propane:** Yes. **Internal Roads:** Gravel. **RV Service:** 10 mi. **Market:** Yes. **Restaurant:** 2 mi. (snack bar on-site). **General Store:** 6 mi. **Vending:** No. **Swimming Pool:** Yes. **Playground:** Yes. **Activities:** Miniature golf, duck pond, water slide, river beach, campground-organized activities weekends, volleyball & basketball courts, game room. **Nearby Attractions:** 17 mi. to New Orleans, Global Wildlife Center, Fontainebleau State Park, Fairview-Riverside State park. **Additional Information:** New Orleans CVB (800) 672-6124, Slidell CVB (504) 646-6426.

Restrictions

Pets: On leash only. **Fires:** In sites, fire rings only. **Alcoholic Beverages:** Okay. **Vehicle Maximum Length:** 35 ft. **Other:** No 4-wheelers or go-carts.

To Get There

From I-12, take Exit 63B, take Hwy. 25 west to Million Dollar Rd. Turn right, and campground is on the left. From New Orleans, take the Causeway/Hwy. 190 which becomes Hwy. 25, to Million Dollar Rd.

DENHAM SPRINGS

Baton Rouge East KOA

7628 Vincent Rd., Denham Springs 70726. T: (225) 664-7281 or (800) 292-8245.

RV ★★★ Tent ★★

Beauty: ★★★	Site Privacy: ★★
Spaciousness: ★★	Quiet: ★★★
Security: ★★★	Cleanliness: ★★★
Insect Control: ★★★	Facilities: ★★

Located in suburban Baton Rouge, this KOA is convenient for touring the State Capitol, the Old State Capitol, and riverboat casinos. KOA is also near famous historic plantations, including Nottoway Plantation, Houmas House, Tezcuco Plantation, and Oak Alley Plantation. The area offers plenty of shopping and restaurants. The campground is underwhelming, with patchy pavement, dirt, gravel, and grass ground cover. Parking spaces are mostly paved. There are both back-in and pull-through spaces. Sites are small and there is little privacy. Most sites are partially shady. We like the sites in the front of the campground, which are tidier than those in the back. Tent campers will appreciate the private bathrooms. The campground is gated, but not fenced, making security iffy. Avoid southern Louisiana in late summer, when it's steamy enough to cook veggies.

Basics

Operated By: Bacot Enterprise. **Open:** 7 days, all year. **Site Assignment:** Sites assigned based on unit; reservations w/ credit card deposit; 24-hour cancellation notice required. **Registration:** In store, seasonal hours. **Fee:** $19 tent, $27 (30 amps), $29 (50 amps). (cash, LA check, V, MC, D, AE). **Parking:** Sites plus lot.

Facilities

Number of RV Sites: 100. **Number of Tent-Only Sites:** 12. **Number of Multipurpose Sites:** 100 (RV sites). **Hookups:** Water, electric (30, 50 amps), sewage, cable. **Each Site:** Picnic table. **Dump Station:** Yes. **Laundry:** Yes. **Pay Phone:** Yes. **Rest Rooms and Showers:** Yes. **Fuel:** No. **Propane:** Yes. **Internal Roads:** Paved & gravel. **RV Service:** Within 2 mi. **Market:** Yes. **Restaurant:** 0.5 mi. **General Store:** 1 mi. **Vending:** Beverages only. **Swimming Pool:** Yes. **Playground:** Yes. **Activities:** Game room, pool table, bicycling & hiking trails, City Park adjacent. **Nearby Attractions:** Plantation homes, USS Kidd, Old State Capitol Museum, Louisiana State Capital, Blue Bayou Water Park, Louisiana State University campus. **Additional Information:** Baton Rouge Conventiona nd Visitors Bureau (225) 383-1825.

Restrictions

Pets: On leash only. **Fires:** In grills, fire rings only (these are not in sites, but scattered around park). **Alcoholic Beverages:** Okay. **Vehicle Maximum Length:** Varies up to 45 ft.

To Get There

Heading West toward Baton Rouge on I-12, take Exit 10 (Denham Springs), turn left at the end of the ramp, and turn right on Vincent Rd. Campground is on the left around the corner. From I-10 (either direction), take the I-12 split, then Exit 10, turn right at the end of the ramp.

DOYLINE

Lake Bistineau State Park

P.O. Box 589, Doyline 71023. T: (888) 677-2478; F: (318) 745-3806; www.la.stateparks.com; lakebistineau@crt.state.la.us.

★★★★ ★★★★

Beauty: ★★★★★ Site Privacy: ★★★★
Spaciousness: ★★★★★ Quiet: ★★★★★
Security: ★★★★ Cleanliness: ★★★★
Insect Control: ★★★ Facilities: ★★★★

The campground at Lake Bistineau consists of one attractive loop. Many sites have lovely views of the lake with its elegant cypress and tupelo trees. Seven sites offer pull-through parking. The rest offer back-in. Parking is paved. Some sites are huge, including number 26, a pull-through with a lake view. Others are close together and offer little privacy. Lake Bistineau is a 200-year-old man-made lake, first created when a goliath log jam caused the Red River to flood. In 1935, a permanent dam was constructed and the lake was enlarged. It now supports black crappie, largemouth bass, yellow bass, bullheads, blue gill, and red ear sunfish. The state park is divided into two areas, each with its own boat launch and swimming pool. The campground is in Area 1. Visit Lake Bistineau in late spring or fall for pleasant weather. Avoid the park on summer weekends and holidays.

Basics

Operated By: Sate Of Louisiana Dept. of Culture, Recreation, & Tourism (888) 677-1400. **Open:** Year-round. **Site Assignment:** First come, first served; V & MC may be used to hold reservations (888) 677-1400. Check-in time is 3 p.m. or later. Check-out time is 11 a.m. or earlier. If cancelled within 48 hours of reserved check-in time then the fee is one day's rent. **Registration:** Main office. **Fee:** $12 for either the tent or RV sites. $6 w/ Golden Access Card. **Parking:** 2 cars or 1 car & 1 RV at each site. Overflow parking is available.

Facilities

Number of Multipurpose Sites: 67. **Hookups:** Water & Electricity (20 & 30 amps). **Each Site:** Tent pad, fire ring, picnic table, lantern hook varies. **Dump Station:** Yes. **Laundry:** Yes. **Pay Phone:** Yes. **Rest Rooms and Showers:** Yes. **Fuel:** No. **Propane:** No. **Internal Roads:** Paved. **RV Service:** 30 mi. northwest in Shreveport. **Market:** 6 mi. north in Doyline. **Restaurant:** 10 mi. north in Doyline. **General Store:** 10 mi. north in Doyline. **Vending:** Beverage only. **Swimming Pool:** Yes. **Playground:** Yes. **Other:** Group lodge, boat launch, athletic field, boat rental. **Activities:** Nature trails, boating, swimming. **Nearby Attractions: Nearby Attractions:** Lake Claiborne State Park, Historic Town of Minden, Kisatche National Forest-Caney Lakes Recreation Area, Trails End Public Golf Course, Loggy Bayou Wildlife Management Area, Ambrose Mountain, Driskoll Mountain, Mt. Lebanon, Bodcau Wildlife Management Area. **Additional Information:** Shreveport/Bossier Convention & Tourist Bureau (888) 45-VISIT.

Restrictions

Pets: Leash. **Fires:** Fire ring only. **Alcoholic Beverages:** Allowed. **Vehicle Maximum Length:** Approx. 40 ft. **Other:** No fireworks, acquaint yourself w/ all alligator precautions.

To Get There

From Shreveport, Take I-20 East to Exit 33 (Haughton/Filmore). Go to the right then take an immediate left on Hwy. 3227, which deadends into Hwy. 164. Take a right on 164 and go about 4–5 mi. until you reach the town of Doyline. Take a right at the flashing caution light (Hwy. 163). Keep straight about 8 mi. Look for Lake Bistineau State Park Area sign to the right. Turn left to enter main gate. Stop at park office on right for further instructions.

FARMERVILLE

Lake D'Arbonne State Park

P.O. Box 236, Farmerville 71241. T: (888) 677-5200; F: (318) 368-8207; www.crt.state.la.us.

★★★★ ★★★★

Beauty: ★★★★★ Site Privacy: ★★★★
Spaciousness: ★★★★ Quiet: ★★★★
Security: ★★★★★ Cleanliness: ★★★★★
Insect Control: ★★★ Facilities: ★★★

The beautiful campground at Lake D'Arbonne is situated in two loops with a fishing pier and boat dock at the campground. The campground is shaded by a lovely stand of loblolly pines. And Sites feature paved, back-in parking. Most sites are larger than average, with a little greenery providing privacy barriers between sites. Sites 24, 28, 44, and 45 enjoy lake views, but are less secluded than some others. For elbow room, head to site 20. The lake is home to gorgeous cypress stands as well as record catches of crappie and bass. The park's well-kept fishing facilities augment the fisherman's experience. This park is also popular with road bikers due to its roads winding through shady hills. Avoid Lake D'Arbonne on summer holidays and weekends and during hot July and Aug. This rural park locks its gates at night, making security excellent.

Basics

Operated By: State of Louisiana Dept. of Culture, Recreation, & Tourism. **Open:** Year-round. **Site Assignment:** First come, first served, Reservations can be held w/ MC or V (888) 677-1400. If cancelled 15 days or more before reserved check-in day the fee is $10. If cancelled 14 days or less before your reserved check-in day then the fee is one day's rental of all reserved items. Check-in time is 2 p.m. or later. Check-out time is 1 p.m. or earlier. 15 day stay limit. **Registration:** Entrance station. **Fee:** $12 a night for RV/tent site, $6 w/ Golden Access card. **Parking:** 2 car/1 RV & 1 car at each site, extra parking available.

Facilities

Number of Multipurpose Sites: 65. **Hookups:** Electric (30 amps), water. **Each Site:** Picnic table, lantern hook, tent pad, grill, fire ring. **Dump Station:** Yes. **Laundry:** Yes. **Pay Phone:** Yes. **Rest Rooms and Showers:** Yes. **Fuel:** No. **Propane:** No. **Internal Roads:** Paved. **RV Service:** 30 mi. southeast in West Monroe. **Market:** 5mi. east in Farmerville. **Restaurant:** 5 mi. east in Farmerville. **General Store:** 5 mi. east in Farmerville. **Vending:** No. **Swimming Pool:** No. **Playground:** Yes. **Other:** Nature trails, tennis courts will be finished in the fall of 2002, fishing piers, volleyball court, horseshoe court. **Activities:** Nature trails, fishing clinic (call for more information), Easter egg hunt, hay rides, tennis starting in the fall of 2002, fishing, picnicking, volleyball, Horseshoe. **Nearby Attractions:** Kisatchie National Forest-Corney Lakes Recreation Area, Lincoln Parish Park, Georgia Pacific Wildlife Management Area, Handy Brake National Wildlife Refuge, Louisiana Purchase Gardens (Berstein Park). **Additional Information:** Union Parish Tourist Commission Bernice (318) 285-9333.

Restrictions

Pets: Leash. **Fires:** Fire ring only. **Alcoholic Beverages:** Allowed. **Vehicle Maximum Length:** Approx. 72 ft.

To Get There

From Farmerville take LA 2 approx. 5 mi. west on the left side.

GARDNER

Kincaid Lake Recreation Area, Kisatchie National Forest

9912 Hwy. 28 West, Boyce 71409. T: (318) 793-9427; F: (318) 793-9430; www.southernregion.fs.fed.us/kisatchie.

 ★★★★★  ★★★★★

Beauty: ★★★★★ Site Privacy: ★★★★
Spaciousness: ★★★★★ Quiet: ★★★★★
Security: ★★★★ Cleanliness: ★★★★★
Insect Control: ★★★ Facilities: ★★★★

The campgrounds at Kincaid Lake Recreation Area are gorgeous. Here, large sites are shaded by a variety of lovely southern yellow pine and other upland hardwoods. Dense growth provides privacy between most sites. All sites feature paved, back-in parking. Most of the sites don't have views of the water in summertime, but site 23 has a gorgeous water view in wintertime. We also like site 29, which is gargantuan. Kisatchie National Forest is not one contiguous tract. Rather, the forest consists of five land units in central and northern Louisiana. Kincaid Lake area includes large group and day use facilities. The man-made lake is stocked with sun perch, bass, and catfish. Security is very good here-gates are locked at night during the summer. Summers are extremely hot and humid in southern Louisiana. For the nicest weather, visit in spring or fall.

Basics

Operated By: USDA Forest Service. **Open:** Year-round. **Site Assignment:** First come, first served, no reservations. **Registration:** Self reservation at fee box. **Fee:** $12 for regular sites, $16 for double sites. **Parking:** At sites, limit 2 vehicles.

Facilities

Number of Multipurpose Sites: 41. **Hookups:** Water, electric (30 amps). **Each Site:** Picnic table, lantern post, fire ring. **Dump Station:** Yes. **Laundry:** No. **Pay Phone:** No. **Rest Rooms and Showers:** Yes. **Fuel:** No. **Propane:** No. **Internal Roads:** Paved. **RV Service:** 13 mi. east in Alexandria. **Market:** 13 mi. east in Alexandria. **Restaurant:** 6 mi. east in Tunks. **General Store:** 5 mi. north in Gardner. **Vending:** No. **Swimming Pool:** No. **Playground:** No. **Other:** Picnic pavilions, trails, boat launch, boat dock, fishing pier, swimming beach. **Activities:** Picnicking, road biking, mountain biking, hiking, nature study, swimming, fishing, boating, automobile touring. **Nearby Attractions:** Louisiana Cowboy Town, Frogmore Cotton Plantation & Gins, Tunica-Biloxi Indian Museum, casinos, Hodges Gardens. **Additional Information:** Alexandria/Pineville Area Convention & Visitor's Bureau (800) 551-9546.

Restrictions

Pets: Leash only. **Fires:** Fire rings only. **Alcoholic Beverages:** Allowed. **Vehicle Maximum Length:** 65 ft.

To Get There

From Alexandria, drive west in LA 28 for 13 mi. Turn left onto LA 121 and drive south for 0.5 mi. Turn right onto Forest Service Rd. 279 and drive south for 6 mi. Turn onto Forest Service Rd. 205, which leads to the campground.

GRAND ISLE

Grand Isle State Park

P.O. Box 741, Grand Isle 70358. T: (225) 787-2559.

Beauty: ★★★ Site Privacy: ★
Spaciousness: ★★★ Quiet: ★★★
Security: ★★★★★ Cleanliness: ★★★
Insect Control: ★★ Facilities: ★★★

Grand Isle's 400-foot fishing pier, ponds, and lagoons provide excellent fishing opportunities. Deep-sea fishing off of Grand Isle is extraordinary, and commercial guide services abound. Birdwatchers appreciate the variety of wetland habitats found at Grand Isle. The campgrounds at Grand Isle are smaller than average, with gravel parking for tent campers and grass parking for . All sites feature back-in parking. Sites are totally open, so come equipped with awnings, umbrellas, and sunscreen. Since all sites are bland, choose your site based on proximity to the beach. Tent campers have better choices; primitive camping is allowed on the beautiful beach. Security is excellent at Grand Isle. The park is excruciatingly remote and it's gated. Avoid Grand Isle in late summer, when it's horribly hot. Also, be sure to arm yourself with insect repellent.

Basics

Operated By: Louisiana State Parks. **Open:** 7 days, all year. **Site Assignment:** No reservations for tent/beach sites. **Registration:** At camp office. **Fee:** $10 per night per vehicle, Golden Access 50% discount (V, MC, cash, money order, LA check). **Parking:** Sites plus overflow.

Facilities

Number of RV Sites: 100. **Number of Tent-Only Sites:** 50 (on beach only). **Hookups:** None. **Each Site:** Picnic table. **Dump Station:** Yes. **Laundry:** No. **Pay Phone:** Yes. **Rest Rooms and Showers:** Yes. **Fuel:** No. **Propane:** No. **Internal Roads:** Paved & gravel. **RV Service:** 100 mi. **Market:** 3 mi. **Restaurant:** 3 mi. **General Store:** 3 mi. **Vending:** In the Park. **Swimming Pool:** No. **Playground:** No. **Other:** Fishing piers, fish-cleaning station. **Activities:** Fishing, crabbing, birding, swimming, nature trail, gulf beaches. **Nearby Attractions:** Fishing rodeos in Grand Isle, charter boats, Wisner Wildlife Management Area, Fort Livingston, 2 hours to New Orleans. **Additional Information:** Grand Isle Tourist Commission (985) 787-2997.

Restrictions

Pets: On leash only. **Fires:** Small okay. **Alcoholic Beverages:** Okay, no glass containers. **Vehicle Maximum Length:** No limit.

To Get There

From US 90 (New Orleans), take LA 1 south to Grand Isle, where Hwy.1 becomes Admiral Craik Dr. The State Park is on the far east end of the island.

HAMMOND

New Orleans/Hammond KOA Kampground

14154 Club Deluxe Rd., Hammond 70403. T: (504) 542-8094.

Beauty: ★★★ Site Privacy: ★★
Spaciousness: ★★★ Quiet: ★★★
Security: ★★★ Cleanliness: ★★★★
Insect Control: ★★★ Facilities: ★★★★

KOA Hammond is much less frenetic than nearby Yogi Bear's and is preferable for couples and seniors who value peace and quiet. The pond is stocked with bass for catch and release fishing, and there's a pleasant walking path circling the pond. Either Baton Rouge or New Orleans can be reached in about an hour. The campground features three long rows of pull-through sites, plus a small tent area. Sites feature paved parking. Some are shady while others are totally open. Sites are average sized and none are very private. Sites along the lake, near the cabins, are picturesque and quiet. Stay away from sites 1–23, which are along the main road and tend to be noisy. Southern Louisiana is like a rice steamer in July and August. Visit in the spring or fall for the nicest weather. Security is fair at this suburban campground—there are no gates.

Basics

Operated By: Surrell Family. **Open:** 7 days, all year. **Site Assignment:** Assigned based on hookups; reservations accepted, especially for holidays & festivals, credit card deposit; 24-hour cancellation for refund (7 days holidays). **Registration:** Camp store, 7 a.m.–7 p.m. **Fee:** $17 tent (dry), $23 electric (30 amps), $25 electric (50 amps), all fees for 2 people, $3 per extra adult, $2 ages 7–17, under 7 free. **Parking:** 1 per site plus overflow.

Facilities

Number of RV Sites: 60. **Number of Tent-Only Sites:** 4. **Hookups:** Water, electric (30, 50 amps), sewer. **Each Site:** Picnic table. **Dump Station:** No. **Laundry:** Yes. **Pay Phone:** Yes. **Rest Rooms and Showers:** Yes. **Fuel:** No. **Propane:** Yes. **Internal Roads:** Paved & gravel. **RV Service:** On call, 3 mi. **Market:** Yes. **Restaurant:** Next door. **General Store:** 3 mi. **Vending:** No. **Swimming Pool:** Yes. **Playground:** Yes. **Other:** Hot tub. **Activities:** Game room, pool table, movie rental, horseshoes, volleyball, basketball, paddle-boat rental, mini-golf, fishing, dog park. **Nearby Attractions:** Swamp tours, plantation tours, alligator farm, 45 mi. to New orleans, 40 mi. to Baton Rouge. **Additional Information:** Tangipahoa Parish Tourist Commission (504) 542-7520, New Orleans CVB (800) 672-6124.

Restrictions

Pets: On leash, except in dog park. **Fires:** Seasonal, limited. **Alcoholic Beverages:** Okay, no glass containers. **Vehicle Maximum Length:** 45 ft.

To Get There

From I-12, take I-55 south to Exit 28, proceed to traffic light, turn left 0.75 mile to the campground.

HOMER

Lake Claiborne State Park

P.O. Box 246, Homer 71040. T: (888) 677-2524; F: (318) 927-2744; www.lastateparks.com; lakeclaiborne@crt.state.la.us.

Beauty: ★★★★★ Site Privacy: ★★★★
Spaciousness: ★★★★ Quiet: ★★★★
Security: ★★★★★ Cleanliness: ★★★★
Insect Control: ★★★ Facilities: ★★★★

This gorgeous park is situated on a peninsula jutting into massive Toledo Bend Reservoir. Across the reservoir is Texas' Sabine National Forest. At North Toledo Bend, recreation revolves around fishing for largemouth bass, catfish, and crappie. For landlubbers, there's a nature trail and an Olympic-sized swimming pool. Although the terrain consists of rolling hills, the campground is pretty flat. The beautiful campground is laid out in two loops containing huge sites. Sites are shaded by a variety of tree species dominated by pine. Privacy is provided by greenery between sites. All parking is paved, back-in style. The most private sites are 29–34. We also like sites 13 and 14, which have partial water views. Avoid North Toledo Bend on holiday weekends and during hot late summer. Otherwise, the campground rarely fills up, making it a good destination for an early summer weekend. Security is excellent at this remote park.

Basics

Operated By: State of Louisiana, Dept. of Culture, Recreation & Tourism (877) 226-7652. **Open:** Year-round. **Site Assignment:** First come, first served, also reservations can be made w/ a V or MC by calling (877) 226-7652. No out of state checks allowed. If reservations are cancelled, the fee is one night's rental. Check-in time is 1 p.m. or later. Check-out time is 1 p.m. or earlier. Stay limit is 15 days. **Registration:** Entrance station. **Fee:** $12 per night for RV/tent sites. $6 w/ a Golden Access card. **Parking:** 2 vehicle parking at each site. Overflow parking is available.

Facilities

Number of Multipurpose Sites: 87. **Hookups:** Water, electric (30, 50 amps). **Each Site:** Picnic table, grill, fire ring, some have lantern hook, tent pad. **Dump Station:** Yes. **Laundry:** Yes. **Pay Phone:** Yes. **Rest Rooms and Showers:** Yes. **Fuel:** No. **Propane:** No. **Internal Roads:** Paved. **RV Service:** Approx. 20 mi. northeast in Homer. **Market:** Approx. 15 mi. northwest in Homer. **Restaurant:** Approx. 15 mi. northwest in Homer. **General Store:** Approx. 15 mi. northwest in Homer. **Vending:** No. **Swimming Pool:** No. **Playground:** Yes. **Other:** Group lodging, boat launch, fishing pier, primitive canoe camp sites available, nature trails. **Activities:** Guided/unguided hiking trails, fishing, boating of all kinds, waterskiing, nature-based programs. **Nearby Attractions:** Poverty Point State Historic Site, Lake Bistineau State Park, Lake D'Arbonne State Park, Historic Town of Homer, Lincoln Parish Park, Kisatchie National Forest-Caney Lakes Recreation Area, Caney Creek Lake State Park, Jackson Bienville Wildlife Management Area, Georgia Pacific Wildlife Management Area. **Additional Information:** Homer Chamber of Commerce.

Restrictions

Pets: Leash only. **Fires:** Ring only. **Alcoholic Beverages:** Allowed. **Vehicle Maximum Length:** 60 ft.

To Get There

From the intersection of Hwy. 79 and Hwy. 146 in Homer, go southeast on Hwy. 146 for 7 mi. and the park entrance will be on the left.

INDEPENDENCE

Indian Creek

53013 West Fontana Rd., Independence 70443. T: (504) 878-6567.

RV ★★★ Tent ★★★

Beauty: ★★★ Site Privacy: ★★★
Spaciousness: ★★★ Quiet: ★★★
Security: ★★★ Cleanliness: ★★★
Insect Control: ★★★ Facilities: ★★★

Indian Creek offers shady sites situated in numerous small sections. Though privacy varies, most sites are on the small side. All sites feature gravel parking. There are both back-in and pull-through sites. Our favorite sites are 86–91, small, wooded, pull-throughs. Families should ask for a site in the front of the park, near the playground, wash house, and other amenities.There's plenty to keep kids busy here, but we don't recommend Indian Creek as a vacation destination. It's better used as a convenient stop over. There are plenty of shops and restaurants nearby. Unfortunately, Indian Creek had an unpleasant smell while we were there. Stay away from southeastern Louisiana in late summer, when the heat and humidity are oppressive. Security is fair. There are no gates, but Indian Creek is in a quiet area.

Basics

Operated By: Bob & Kathy Albright. **Open:** 7 days, all year. **Site Assignment:** First come, first served also reservations. **Registration:** Office in store, 9 a.m.–8 p.m. Sunday–Thursday, 9 a.m.–10 p.m. Friday & Saturday. **Fee:** Primitive $18.50 ($22 holidays), RV sites $24 ($27 holidays), $5 per extra person, max. 7 people. **Parking:** Sites plus overflow.

Facilities

Number of RV Sites: 184. **Number of Tent-Only Sites:** 100 (primitive). **Number of Multipurpose Sites:** 184 (RV sites). **Hookups:** Water, electric (30 amps), some sewer. **Each Site:** Picnic table, grills available. **Dump Station:** Yes. **Laundry:** Yes. **Pay Phone:** Yes. **Rest Rooms and Showers:** Yes. **Fuel:** No. **Propane:** Yes. **Internal Roads:** Gravel. **RV Service:** On call. **Market:** Yes. **Restaurant:** 5 mi. **General Store:** 10 mi. (Wal-Mart), 2 mi. (Piggly Wiggly). **Vending:** Beverages only. **Swimming Pool:** Yes. **Playground:** Yes (2). **Activities:** Fishing pond (catch & release), hiking & biking trails, basketball court, volleyball, horseshoes, paddle-boat & canoe rentals, scheduled activities on weekends. **Nearby Attractions:** Global Wildlife, swamp tours, alligator farm, Aquarium of the Americas, 55 mi. to New Orleans. **Additional Information:** Tangipahoa Parish Tourist Commission (504) 542-7520, New Orleans CVB (800) 672-6124.

Restrictions

Pets: On leash only. **Fires:** Okay. **Alcoholic Beverages:** Okay. **Vehicle Maximum Length:** 50 ft. **Other:** Quiet hours enforced.

To Get There

From I-55, take Exit 41, go 1,000 feet west on Hwy. 40 to Fontana Rd. Turn left, campground is 1.5 mi. on the right.

KINDER

Grand Casino Coushatta Luxury RV Resort At Red Shoes Park

777 Coushatta Dr. P. O. Box 1510, Kinder 70648. T: (888) 867-8727; F: (337) 738-1201; www.gccoushatta.com; sigc.coushatta.com.

RV ★★★★ Tent n/a

Beauty: ★★★ Site Privacy: ★★
Spaciousness: ★★★ Quiet: ★★★★
Security: ★★★★ Cleanliness: ★★★★★
Insect Control: ★★★★ Facilities: ★★★★

The Coushatta Tribe of Louisiana run an extremely tidy campground on a flat piece of land behind their Grand Casino. The swimming pool and other facilities are spotless as well. The drawback here is the overly sanitized landscaping. There are no mature trees to break the park's visual monotony. The campground consists of two main areas, which flank a picturesque fishing pond. Sites are larger than average. Sites are neither shady nor private. Each site has paved parking, a paved patio, and a grassy plot. Most sites are pull-through style. Couples seeking solitude should try for lakeside sites 24–39. Families with children should score a site close to the pool. Security is very good. The park is gated 24-hours a day, but there is no fence around the campground. Avoid southern Louisiana in sticky, hot late summer. For the mildest weather, visit in spring or fall.

Basics

Operated By: Grand Casino Coushatta. **Open:** Year-round. **Site Assignment:** First come, first served, also reservations can be held w/ any major credit card (888) 677-1400. Specific sites may not be reserved. If cancelled 24 hr. or more before the first reserved day then there is no fee. If cancelled within 24 hr. of expected arrival then the fee is the entire cost of using the items that were reserved. Check-in time is 12 p.m. or later. Check-out time is 2 p.m. or earlier. There is no stay limit. **Registration:** Main Lodge. **Fee:** $18.95 plus tax for weekends, $14.95 plus tax for weekdays. **Parking:** 2 vehicle parking at the site. Overflow parking is available.

Facilities

Number of RV Sites: 156. **Number of Tent-Only Sites:** 0. **Hookups:** Electric (30, 50 amps), water. **Each Site:** Fire ring, picnic table. **Dump Station:** Yes. **Laundry:** Yes. **Pay Phone:** Yes. **Rest Rooms and Showers:** Yes. **Fuel:** No. **Propane:** No. **Internal Roads:** Paved. **RV Service:** On call. **Market:** 7 mi. south in Kinder. **Restaurant:** 1 mi. **General Store:** 17 mi. north in Oakdale. **Vending:** Beverage & snack. **Swimming Pool:** Yes. **Playground:** Yes. **Other:** Internet hookup in the main lodge, pier, athletic courts, small group chalets. **Activities:** Volleyball, paddle boating, tennis, shuffleboard, Horse shoes, fishing, basketball. **Nearby**

Attractions: Grand Casino. **Additional Information:** Avoyelles Commission of Tourism (800) 833-4195.

RESTRICTIONS

Pets: Leash. **Fires:** Fire ring that is located behind the main lodge (not 1 per site). **Alcoholic Beverages:** Allowed. **Vehicle Maximum Length:** No limit.

TO GET THERE

Get off I-10 onto Hwy. 165 (Exit 44) north. The park entrance is approx. 35 mi. north on the left side.

LAFAYETTE

KOA–Lafayette

Rte. 2 Box 261, Scott 70583. T: (337) 235-2739; F: (337) 235-2739; www.koa.com.

RV ★★★ Tent ★★

Beauty: ★★★ Site Privacy: ★★
Spaciousness: ★★★ Quiet: ★★
Security: ★★★ Cleanliness: ★★★★
Insect Control: ★★★ Facilities: ★★★

KOA is a good place to stay while touring Lafayette, the heart of Cajun country. This culturally unique region offers excellent restaurants, gorgeous historic homes, and fabulous outdoor recreation. This KOA offers a nightly 20-minute video and cassette-tape tours about the area. The campground is laid out in rows of long narrow sites. Most sites offer pull-through parking, though some offer back-in. Sites are average sized, with gravel parking and concrete patios. Most sites have no grass. There are shady and open sites. Privacy is minimal. This KOA is next to I-10, making many sites way too noisy for our tastes. Numbers 117–124 and 9–16, quieter sites in the back of the park, enjoy a picturesque view of the fishing pond. Avoid southern Louisiana in muggy July and August. Lafayette is a good winter destination. This suburban park has no gates, but the neighborhood is fine.

BASICS

Operated By: Owned by the Alleman Family. **Open:** Year-round. **Site Assignment:** Reservations recommended (800) 562-0809. D, MC, & V are accepted. To receive refund of deposit, cancellation must be made 24 hours in advance. Check in & check out time is 12 noon. There is no stay limit. **Registration:** Main office. **Fee:** From $26–$28 per night plus tax. **Parking:** There is no parking limit. Overflow parking is available.

FACILITIES

Number of RV Sites: 200. **Number of Tent-Only Sites:** 15. **Hookups:** Electric (30, 50 amps), water, sewer, Internet available but not at each site. **Each Site:** Picnic table, fire ring, grill (some sites), & tent pads (some sites). **Dump Station:** Yes. **Laundry:** Yes. **Pay Phone:** Yes. **Rest Rooms and Showers:** Yes. **Fuel:** No. **Propane:** Yes. **Internal Roads:** Paved. **RV Service:** On call. **Market:** 1 mi. **Restaurant:** 1 mi. **General Store:** 9 mi. east in Lafayette. **Vending:** Beverages only. **Swimming Pool:** Yes. **Playground:** Yes. **Other:** Group lodging, athletic field, arcade, fishing pier, mini-golf course. **Activities:** Fishing, mini-golf, basketball, volleyball, paddle boats, arcade games. **Nearby Attractions:** Atchafalaya Basin, Acadian Village & Vermillionville, Art Museum, Planetarium, St. John's Cathedral, Evangeline Downs Horse Racing, Jungle Gardens, Saint Martinville. **Additional Information:** Acadia Parish Convention & Visitors Commission.

RESTRICTIONS

Pets: Leash only. **Fires:** Fire ring only. **Alcoholic Beverages:** Allowed. **Vehicle Maximum Length:** 75 ft.

TO GET THERE

From I-10 going west, take Exit 97, go left over the overpass. Turn onto Apollo Rd., the first road on the right.

LAKE CHARLES

Sam Houston Jones

107 Sutherland Rd., Lake Charles 70611. T: (888) 677-7264; www.lastateparks.com; samhouston@crt.state.la.us.

RV ★★★★ Tent ★★★★

Beauty: ★★★★ Site Privacy: ★★★
Spaciousness: ★★★★ Quiet: ★★★★
Security: ★★★★ Cleanliness: ★★★★
Insect Control: ★★★ Facilities: ★★★

This suburban park is nestled into the West Fork of the Calcasieu River, where it meets the Houston River. Park boat launches provide access to the Gulf of Mexico as well as the river system. Within the park, a series of lagoons provides refuge for alligators, ducks, and geese. Known as one of the finest bird-watching areas in the state, migratory waterfowl are plentiful here in the spring. There are two camping areas at Sam Houston Jones: Area 1 includes pretty sites lining a lagoon-tent sites 16–19 and RV sites 12–21 are especially attractive. Area 2 may be a better choice for families—sites 35 and 37 are near the playground. All sites are shaded by a variety of trees, including cypress in low-lying areas. There are back-in and pull-through sites. Some sites offer gravel parking, others offer paved. Sites are larger than average, but not very private. Gates lock at night, making security good. Avoid muggy late summer in southern Louisiana.

BASICS

Operated By: State of Louisiana Dept. of Culture, Recreation, & Tourism. **Open:** Year-round. **Site Assignment:** Reservations as well as first come, first served. Reservations can be held w/ V or MC (888) 677-1400. Check in time is 2 p.m. Check out time is 1 p.m. If cancelled 15 or more days in advance, fee is $10. If cancelled 14 or less before the first reserved day, fee is one night's rent of all reserved items; Stay limit is 15 days. **Registration:** Entrance station. **Fee:** $12 for both RV & tent sites, $6 w/ a Gold Access card. **Parking:** 2 car parking at site, overflow parking lot.

FACILITIES

Number of RV Sites: 0. **Number of Tent-Only Sites:** 19. **Number of Multipurpose Sites:** 62. **Hookups:** Electric (20, 30 amps), water; 20 RV sites w/ sewer electric & water. **Each Site:** Fire ring, tent pad, some sites have picnic tables. **Dump Station:** Yes. **Laundry:** No. **Pay Phone:** Yes. **Rest Rooms and Showers:** Yes. **Fuel:** No. **Propane:** No. **Internal Roads:** Paved. **RV Service:** Approx. 15 mi. in West Lake. **Market:** 10 mi. north in Moss Bluff. **Restaurant:** 10 mi. north in Moss Bluff. **General Store:** 10 mi. north in Moss Bluff. **Vending:** No. **Swimming Pool:** No. **Playground:** Yes. **Other:** Group lodge, boat launch, nature trails. **Activities:** Boating, hiking, children's weekend nature activities, picnicking, fishing. **Nearby Attractions:** Creole Nature Trail National Scenic Byway, Sabine National Wildlife Refuge, Cameron Prairie National Wildlife Refuge, Lacassine National Wildlife Refuge, Rockefeller Wildlife Refuge. **Additional Information:** Southwest Louisiana/Lake Charles CVB (800) 456-SWLA.

RESTRICTIONS

Pets: On leash. **Fires:** Fire ring only. **Alcoholic Beverages:** Allowed. **Vehicle Maximum Length:** No limit.

TO GET THERE

From I-10, take Exit No. 33 in Lake Charles. Go north on Hwy. 171. At the first light in Moss bluff take a left onto 378. Take a right onto Sam Houston Jones Pkwy.

MADISONVILLE

Fairview-Riverside State Park

P.O. Box 856, Madisonville 70447. T: (504) 845-3318 or (888) 677-3247; www.crt.state.la.us.

RV ★★★ Tent ★★★

Beauty: ★★★★ Site Privacy: ★★★
Spaciousness: ★★★ Quiet: ★★★
Security: ★★★ Cleanliness: ★★★
Insect Control: ★★★ Facilities: ★★★

The nice-looking campground at Fairview-Riverside offers mid-sized sites shaded by moss-laden oaks and other hardwoods. Sites are mid-sized, and there is little foliage to provide privacy between sites. All parking is paved, back-in style. For shade, we like sites near the front of the campground. Popular sites in the back enjoy river views. Fairview-Riverside is an elegant little park nestled into a bend in the Tchefuncte River. Fishing, crabbing, and boating are favorite pastimes here. The historic Otis House (ca. 1880) serves as an elegant reminder of Frank Otis, who, upon his death, donated the park's land to the state in 1961. When we arrived, we were greeted by one of the park's lovely peacocks. Avoid southeastern Louisiana in late summer, when heat and humidity are unbearable. Security is fair at this suburban park; the entrance is gated, but there is no fence around the park.

BASICS

Operated By: Louisiana State Parks. **Open:** 7 days, all year. **Site Assignment:** First come, first served. **Registration:** Park entrance, 6 a.m.–9 p.m. Sunday-Thursday, 6 a.m.–10 p.m. Friday & Saturday. **Fee:** $10 tent, $12 improved; max. 6 people, Golden Access 50% discount. **Parking:** Sites plus parking areas.

Facilities

Number of RV Sites: 81. **Number of Tent-Only Sites:** 20. **Number of Multipurpose Sites:** 81 (RV sites). **Hookups:** Water, electric (20, 30, 50 amps). **Each Site:** Picnic table, grill, fire ring, lantern poles on tent sites. **Dump Station:** Yes. **Laundry:** Yes. **Pay Phone:** Yes. **Rest Rooms and Showers:** Yes. **Fuel:** 0.5 mi. **Propane:** No. **Internal Roads:** Paved. **RV Service:** 30 mi. **Market:** 3 mi. **Restaurant:** 1 mi. **General Store:** 10 mi. **Vending:** No. **Swimming Pool:** No. **Playground:** Yes. **Other:** Boat launch. **Activities:** Fishing, skiing, & water sports, rental pavilions, Otis House Museum, walking trail. **Nearby Attractions:** Fontainebleau State Park, Fort Pike State Commemorative Area, Tammany Trace trail for bicycling, hiking, horseback riding, New Orleans. **Additional Information:** New Orleans CVB (800) 672-6124, Slidell CVB (504) 646-6426.

Restrictions

Pets: On leash only. **Fires:** In fire rings, grills only. **Alcoholic Beverages:** Okay. **Vehicle Maximum Length:** No limit. **Other:** 15-day max. stay.

To Get There

From the east, take I-12 Exit 59 at Mandeville (from the west Exit 57). Take Hwy. 190 south to Hwy. 22. Go west 5 mi., the park is on the right. From New Orleans, take the Causeway/Hwy. 190 north to Hwy. 22.

MANDEVILLE

Fontainebleau State Park

P.O. Box 8925, Mandeville 70470-8925. T: (504) 624-4443 or (888) 677-3668; www.crt.state.la.us.

RV ★★★★ Tent ★★★★

Beauty: ★★★★ Site Privacy: ★★★★
Spaciousness: ★★★★★ Quiet: ★★★★
Security: ★★★★ Cleanliness: ★★★★
Insect Control: ★★★ Facilities: ★★★

Built on a former sugar plantation, Fountainebleau harbors the ruins of an 1829 sugar mill. The park is situated on Lake Ponchartrain, between Bayou Castine and Cane Bayou. Fishermen may try their luck on the lakeshore or on a two-acre brackish pond. The Tammany Trace, an 18-mile multi-use "rail to trail" conversion, is also near the park. The campgrounds at Fountainebleau feature many attractive sites and a few beautiful sites. There are two main areas, "Improved" and "Unimproved." In the improved area, there are huge pull-through sites with refreshing shade cover, including loblolly pine. Dense foliage provides privacy between some sites. The unimproved area contains more hardwoods, such as sweet gum and live oak, and is preferable for tent campers. When we visited Fountainebleau, they had been awarded $9 million for park renovations over the next three years. The park plans to build additional camping facilities. Security is very good at this suburban park. Gates are locked at night. Avoid southern Louisiana in boiling-hot late summer.

Basics

Operated By: Louisiana State Parks. **Open:** 7 days, all year. **Site Assignment:** First come, first served. **Registration:** Ranger station, 7 a.m.–9 p.m. Sunday–Thursday, 7 a.m.–10 p.m. Friday & Saturday. **Fee:** $10 (no hookups), $12 water & electric; Golden Access $6 (cash, LA check, V, MC). **Parking:** Sites plus lots.

Facilities

Number of RV Sites: 132. **Number of Tent-Only Sites:** 200 undesignated primitive sites. **Number of Multipurpose Sites:** 132 (RV sites). **Hookups:** Water, electric (most 30, some 50 amps). **Each Site:** Picnic table (all developed sites, most primitive), grill or fire ring (all developed sites, some primitive). **Dump Station:** Yes. **Laundry:** Yes. **Pay Phone:** Yes. **Rest Rooms and Showers:** Yes. **Fuel:** No. **Propane:** No. **Internal Roads:** Paved. **RV Service:** In Mandeville. **Market:** 2.5 mi. in Mandeville. **Restaurant:** 2.5 mi. in Mandeville. **General Store:** 4 mi. in Mandeville. **Vending:** Beverages only. **Swimming Pool:** Yes. **Playground:** Yes. **Other:** Sailboat launch (shallow). **Activities:** Beach on Lake Ponchartrain, fishing pond, bicycle trail, nature trail, hiking trail, boardwalk, interpretive Ranger programs weekends. **Nearby Attractions:** Swamp tours, antique shopping in Ponchatoula, Tammany Trace bicycling & equestriantrails, Pearl River Wildlife Management Area, New Orleans. **Additional Information:** New Orleans CVB (800) 672-6124.

Restrictions

Pets: On leash only. **Fires:** At sites only. **Alcoholic Beverages:** Okay. **Vehicle Maximum Length:** No limit. **Other:** 15-day max. stay, then 7 days out.

To Get There

From New Orleans, take the Causeway north, across Lake Ponchartrain, then take the first exit onto US 190 East. The park is on the right in 6 mi. From I-12, take Exit 65, then drive 3.5 mi. south to the traffic light at US 190. Turn left and the park is on the right in 2.5 mi.

MARKSVILLE

Paragon RV Resort

124 Earl J. Barbry Sr. Blvd., Marksville 71351. T: (800) 578-7275; www.paragoncasiresort.com.

RV ★★★ Tent ★★★

Beauty: ★★ Site Privacy: ★★
Spaciousness: ★★★ Quiet: ★★★
Security: ★★★ Cleanliness: ★★★★
Insect Control: ★★★★ Facilities: ★★★

Paragon Casino RV Resort is extremely tidy and just as bland. The minimal landscaping is well manicured. The campground consists of 14 rows of pull-through sites plus a few small back-in areas. There are a few saplings scattered around the campground, but no shade or mature trees. All parking is paved. Sites are all the same, so chose your site based on proximity to the pool and other facilities. Paragon offers the usual casino fare, including nice swimming pools and a 24-hour shuttle to and from the campground. Nearby, you can learn about native Tunica-Biloxi history and culture at the Indian Center and Museum and the Marksville State Pre-Historic Indian Park. Avoid southern Louisiana in steamy late summer. Take care of your valuables; Paragon has no gates.

Basics

Operated By: Paragon Casino RV Resort. **Open:** Year-round. **Site Assignment:** Reservation recommended, (800) 946-1946. All major credit cards are accepted. If cancelled 48 hrs. in advance there is no penalty. If cancelled within 48 hrs. of the expected arrival date then the penalty is the fee for one night's stay. Check-in time is 11 p.m. Check-out time is 12 noon. There is a 2-week stay limit. **Registration:** RV Lodge. **Fee:** $12.95 per night for full hookups. **Parking:** 2 vehicles at each site, overflow parking is available.

Facilities

Number of RV Sites: 185. **Number of Tent-Only Sites:** 0. **Hookups:** Sewer, water cable, & electric (20, 30, 50 amps). **Each Site:** Picnic table. **Dump Station:** Yes. **Laundry:** Yes. **Pay Phone:** Yes. **Rest Rooms and Showers:** Yes. **Fuel:** No. **Propane:** No. **Internal Roads:** Paved. **RV Service:** 30 mi. northwest in Alexandria. **Market:** 1 mi. **Restaurant:** 1 mi. **General Store:** 1 mi. **Vending:** Beverage & snack. **Swimming Pool:** Yes. **Playground:** Yes. **Other:** Pool table, volleyball court, shuffleboard, group lodging, Casino. **Activities:** Pool, shuffleboard, horseshoes, volleyball. **Nearby Attractions:** Paragon Casino. **Additional Information:** Avoyelles Commission of Tourism (800) 833-4195.

Restrictions

Pets: Leash only. **Fires:** No fire at site unless in a grill (bring your own). **Alcoholic Beverages:** Allowed. **Vehicle Maximum Length:** 75 ft.

To Get There

From 49 exit onto Hwy. 1 going south. Travel approx. 35 mi. and the entrance to the park is on the left behind the casino.

MINDEN

Caney Lakes Recreation Area, Kisatchie National Forest

3288 Hwy. 795, Homer 71040. T: (318) 927-2061; F: (318) 927-6520; www.southernregion.fs.fed.us/kisatchie.

RV ★★★★ Tent ★★★★

Beauty: ★★★★★ Site Privacy: ★★★★★
Spaciousness: ★★★★★ Quiet: ★★★★★
Security: ★★★★ Cleanliness: ★★★★
Insect Control: ★★★ Facilities: ★★★

The beautiful campground at Caney Lakes Recreation Area includes giant sites with paved, back-in parking. Sites are partially shaded by loblolly and short leaf pine and other species. However, growth is not too thick, a blessing which allows campers to enjoy gorgeous water views. On the Turtle Slide tent loop, we especially like waterfront sites 10, 11, 13, and 15. On the Beaver Dam RV loop, we like waterfront sites 10–15. The Caney Lakes area consists of a number of lakes offering excellent fishing for bass, crappie, bluegill, sand bass, and catfish. Boat launches and docks are available at nearby day-use areas. There is also a seven-mile hiking trail. The area is popular in autumn, when its rolling hills are resplendent with color. Visit on weekdays in summer and fall. Security is very good at Caney-the campground is remote and gated.

BASICS

Operated By: Federal Government Caney Ranger District. **Open:** Year-round. **Site Assignment:** First come, first served. **Registration:** Self register at fee box. **Fee:** $10 for RV sites, $5 for tent sites. **Parking:** At sites.

FACILITIES

Number of RV Sites: 26. **Number of Tent-Only Sites:** 21. **Hookups:** Water, electric. **Each Site:** Picnic table, fire ring, grill, tent pads at tent sites. **Dump Station:** Yes. **Laundry:** No. **Pay Phone:** Yes. **Rest Rooms and Showers:** Yes. **Fuel:** No. **Propane:** No. **Internal Roads:** Paved. **RV Service:** 7 mi. south in Minden. **Market:** 7 mi. south in Minden. **Restaurant:** 7 mi. south in Minden. **General Store:** 7 mi. south in Minden. **Vending:** No. **Swimming Pool:** No. **Playground:** No. **Other:** Hiking trails, volleyball net, boat ramp, dock, swimming beach, picnic area. **Activities:** Hiking, fishing, boating, waterskiing, picnicking. **Nearby Attractions:** Inquire at campground. **Additional Information:** Minden Chamber of Commerce.

RESTRICTIONS

Pets: Leash only. **Fires:** Yes. **Alcoholic Beverages:** Allowed. **Vehicle Maximum Length:** 50 ft.

TO GET THERE

From Shreveport or Monroe take the Minden/Dubberly Exit. Turn left onto Hwy. 79. Keep straight through the traffic light. Follow the signs.

RIVER RIDGE
KOA–New Orleans West

11129 Jefferson Hwy., River Ridge 70123. T: (504) 467-1792; www.koa.com; nowestkoa@comm.net.

RV ★★★	Tent ★★
Beauty: ★★★	Site Privacy: ★★
Spaciousness: ★★★	Quiet: ★★★★
Security: ★★★	Cleanliness: ★★★★
Insect Control: ★★★	Facilities: ★★

Laid out in three long rows of back-in sites plus another small area, this KOA is not the most attractive one we've seen. The roads consist of patchy black-top, red asphalt, and gravel. Most sites have a wee bit of shade and a wee bit of grass All parking is back-in style. Though RV parking is paved, car parking is gravel. Sites are mid-sized, with little privacy. The shadiest sites, 9–105, line an ugly corrugated metal fence. Avoid sites 46–50, which are unattractive. Three words save this place: location, location, location. The campground is about 15 miles from the French Quarter. There are plenty of restaurants and shops in River Ridge and nearby Kenner. Visit the New Orleans area in spring or fall for the nicest weather. Avoid Mardi Gras and other festival weekends if you value serenity. Always make advance reservations for this KOA.

BASICS

Operated By: The Fedderman Family. **Open:** 7 days a week, all year. **Site Assignment:** Reservations recommended, call (800) 562-5110; first come, first served; must use a credit card to guarantee spot (MC,V,AE, D, or cash accepted); will honor requests for specific sites, if possible. **Registration:** At office, also night registration desk. **Fee:** $22–$32. **Parking:** One vehicle per site.

FACILITIES

Number of RV Sites: 97. **Number of Tent-Only Sites:** 6. **Hookups:** Electric, water, most sewer, most cable. **Each Site:** Picnic table. **Dump Station:** Yes. **Laundry:** Yes. **Pay Phone:** Yes. **Rest Rooms and Showers:** Yes. **Fuel:** No. **Propane:** Yes. **Internal Roads:** Paved. **RV Service:** On call. **Market:** On site. **Restaurant:** 0.25 mi. **General Store:** 1.25 mi. **Vending:** Beverages. **Swimming Pool:** Yes. **Playground:** Yes. **Other:** Shuttle to French Quarter, rental cars. **Activities:** Tour service. **Nearby Attractions:** French Quarter, Audubon Zoo & Botanical Gardens, Aquarium of the Americas, Paddlewheel Boats, Superdome, National D-Day Museum, Destrehon Plantation, Rivertown. **Additional Information:** New Orleans CVB (504) 246-5666.

RESTRICTIONS

Pets: On leash only. **Fires:** Not allowed. **Alcoholic Beverages:** At site only. **Vehicle Maximum Length:** 45 ft.

TO GET THERE

Take I-10 to Exit 223A, Williams Blvd. Go south 3 mi. to the dead end at the levy (3rd St. and Kenner) and turn left. The campground is 0.75 mi. ahead on the left.

ROBERT
Yogi Bear's Jellystone Park

P.O. Box 519, Robert 70455. T: (985) 542-1507; F: (985) 345-6629; yogi121@charter.net.

RV ★★★	Tent ★★★
Beauty: ★★★	Site Privacy: ★★
Spaciousness: ★★★	Quiet: ★★
Security: ★★★	Cleanliness: ★★★
Insect Control: ★★★	Facilities: ★★★★

Families with small children wishing to tour New Orleans should consider Yogi Bear's. Though Yogi's carnival-like atmosphere is demanding, the children will love it here. There are excellent play facilities and non-stop activities, including crafts, hayrides, dance contests, and on and on.The park is reasonably attractive, with camping areas surrounding a long narrow fishing lake. Most sites offer gravel back-in parking, though there are also plenty of pull-throughs. Site size is average and each site has a cement patio. Most sites are partially shady, but there is little foliage to provide privacy between sites. We like area P, which has shady sites and its own pool, wash house, playground, and clubhouse. Back-in sites 80–109 are also shady. Yogi stays busy all summer. Visit during the week in the spring or fall to avoid hot weather and swarms of people. Security is poor at this suburban park-there are no gates.

BASICS

Operated By: Mr. Camper Inc. **Open:** Year-round. **Site Assignment:** Reserve w/ cash, in-state checks,V, MC, D (985) 542-1507; first come first served also. If cancelled 24 hours or more before the first reserved day, fee is $10 & the remaining cost for one night (after $10 is subtracted) is held in the form of a rain check. If cancelled 24 hours or less before the time of expected arrival, the fee is $35.There is no stay limit. **Registration:** Ranger's Station. **Fee:** $39 per night for holidays. Mar.–Nov. weekends, & weekdays Jun.–Aug. are $35 per night. Weekdays Mar.–May, & Sep.–Nov. $28 per night. Dec.–Feb. $22 a night. **Parking:** 2 cars per site plus an overflow parking lot.

FACILITIES

Number of Multipurpose Sites: 374. **Hookups:** Water & electric (20, 30 amps), 320 sites w/ sewer hookup. **Each Site:** Tent pad, picnic table. **Dump Station:** Yes. **Laundry:** Yes. **Pay Phone:** Yes. **Rest Rooms and Showers:** Yes. **Fuel:** No. **Propane:** Yes. **Internal Roads:** Slag. **RV Service:** On call. **Market:** 1 mi. **Restaurant:** 1 mi. **General Store:** 10 mi. in Hammond West. **Vending:** Beverage only. **Swimming Pool:** Yes. **Playground:** Yes. **Other:** Group lodging, basketball courts, volleyball nets, baseball field. **Activities:** Rental Boats, horseshoe, volleyball, nature trails, baseball field, fishing, hay rides, arts & crafts, scavenger hunt, hiking trails, canoe races. **Nearby Attractions:** Swamp & Nature walk in Cypress Swamp, shopping at Prime Outlets Gulfport, Old Mandeville Historic & Shopping District. **Additional Information:** Tangipahoa Parish Tourist Commission, (800) 542-7520.

RESTRICTIONS

Pets: Leash. **Fires:** Not allowed. **Alcoholic Beverages:** Allowed. **Vehicle Maximum Length:** 40 ft. **Other:** No motorboats allowed.

TO GET THERE

From interstate 12, get off on Exit 47 and go 3 mi. north to entrance, which will be on the right.

SHREVEPORT
KOA–Shreveport-Bossier City

6510 West 70th St., Shreveport 71129. T: (318) 678-1010.

RV ★★★	Tent ★★
Beauty: ★★★	Site Privacy: ★★
Spaciousness: ★★	Quiet: ★★★
Security: ★★	Cleanliness: ★★★
Insect Control: ★★★	Facilities: ★★

This KOA is laid out in six rows of pull-through sites and three rows of back-in sites. Sites are on the small side of average, and are long and narrow. Most parking is on grass, though a few sites have paved pads. Each site has a concrete picnic area. A few sites are by shaded pine trees, but most sites are completely open. Privacy is nil, as there is no greenery between sites. The quietest sites, 61–78, are in the back of the park, away from the I-20 access road. KOA is located in a western suburb of Shreveport, and is convenient to plenty of restaurants, shops, and casinos. Security is fair, as there is no gate. For the nicest weather, visit the Shreveport-Bossier area in the spring or fall.

Basics

Operated By: Byron Bonewell. **Open:** Year-round. **Site Assignment:** First come, first served also reservations. **Registration:** Reservations (800) 562-1232, office. **Fee:** $26.10–$16.20 (plus tax). **Parking:** 2 vehicle parking per site.

Facilities

Number of RV Sites: 78. **Number of Tent-Only Sites:** 3. **Hookups:** Electric (20, 30, 50 amps), cable, sewer, water. **Each Site:** Water, electric, trash pick up, & picnic tables. **Dump Station:** Yes. **Laundry:** Yes. **Pay Phone:** Yes. **Rest Rooms and Showers:** Yes. **Fuel:** No. **Propane:** Yes. **Internal Roads:** Paved & gravel. **RV Service:** No. **Market:** Less than one mi. **Restaurant:** Less than one mi. **General Store:** Less than 1 mi. **Vending:** No. **Swimming Pool:** Yes. **Playground:** Yes. **Other:** Basketball court, volleyball court, adult lounge, rec hall, hot tub. **Activities:** Basketball, volleyball, fishing. **Nearby Attractions:** The American Rose Center, LA Downs Horse Racing, Riverboat Gambling, Cross Lake, Water Town & Hamel's Amusement Park. **Additional Information:** Bossier/Shreveport Convention & Tourist Bureau.

Restrictions

Pets: Leash only. **Fires:** No. **Alcoholic Beverages:** Not allowed. **Vehicle Maximum Length:** 30 ft.

To Get There

From I-20, take Exit 10 and go south on Pines Rd. Turn right onto West 70th St.

SPRINGFIELD

Tickfaw State Park

27225 Patterson Rd., Springfield 70462-8906. T: (225) 294-5020 or (877) 226-7652 for reservations.

RV ★★★★ Tent ★★★★

Beauty: ★★★★★ Site Privacy: ★★★★
Spaciousness: ★★★★★ Quiet: ★★★★★
Security: ★★★★★ Cleanliness: ★★★★
Insect Control: ★★★ Facilities: ★★★

Bordered on the southwest side by the Tickfaw River, this state park is popular with canoeists. Lucky visitors spot snowy egrets and great blue herons along the river. Convenient to both Baton Rouge and New Orleans, Tickfaw is extremely popular with Louisiana residents. In the area, folks enjoy pick-your-own strawberry, blackberry, and blueberry farms. The campground features huge, beautiful RV sites with varying degrees of shade. All parking is paved, back-in style, with extremely long pads. Shade and privacy vary from site to site. The tent camping area at Tickfaw is fabulous, with shady woods and a little foliage between most sites. We especially liked tent sites 37, 39, 41, 43, and 47. The wash houses at Tickfaw are also nice–they're spacious and brand new. Avoid southern Louisiana when heat and humidity become oppressive in late summer. Security is excellent at Tickfaw. The park is gated and remote.

Basics

Operated By: Louisiana State Parks. **Open:** 7 days, all year. **Site Assignment:** First come, first served also reservations. **Registration:** Fee station at park entrance, 7 a.m.–9 p.m. Sunday–Thursday, 7 a.m.–10 p.m. Friday & Saturday. **Fee:** $10 (tent), $12 (electric & water), Golden Access 50% off. **Parking:** Sites plus overflow.

Facilities

Number of RV Sites: 30. **Number of Tent-Only Sites:** 20. **Number of Multipurpose Sites:** 30 (RV sites, but no tent pads). **Hookups:** Water, electric (RV only, 20, 30, or 50 amps). **Each Site:** Picnic table, grill/fire ring, lantern post, tent pad (tent sites only). **Dump Station:** Yes. **Laundry:** Yes. **Pay Phone:** Yes. **Rest Rooms and Showers:** Yes. **Fuel:** No. **Propane:** No. **Internal Roads:** Paved. **RV Service:** Yes. **Market:** 4 mi. **Restaurant:** 20 minutes to Hammond. **General Store:** 20 min. to Hammond. **Vending:** Yes. **Swimming Pool:** No. **Playground:** (building one currently). **Activities:** Canoe rentals, fishing, elevated boardwalks, Nature Center w/ guided hikes & childrens' activities, hiking trails. **Nearby Attractions:** Turtle & alligator tours, Ponchatoula Historic District, Fairview-Riverside State Park, Global Wildlife Park, 35 mi. to Baton Rouge, 50 mi. to New Orleans. **Additional Information:** Livingston Parish Tourist Commission, New Orleans CVB (800) 672-6124.

Restrictions

Pets: No, except in campers. **Fires:** In sites, rings only (firewood from ground only, no cutting). **Alcoholic Beverages:** Okay. **Vehicle Maximum Length:** Varies. **Other:** Speed limit enforced, rangers always on duty.

To Get There

From I-12, take Exit 32 Albany/Springfield, then go south on LA Hwy. 43 for 2 mi., merge w/ LA Hwy. 42, and go one more mile to the center of Springfield. At the only traffic light, turn right (west) on LA Hwy. 1037, and go 6 mi. to Patterson Rd. (from Woodland Baptist Church). Turn left (south) 1.2 mi. to the park entrance.

ST. JOSEPH

Lake Bruin State Park

Rte. 1 Box 183, St. Joseph 71366. T: (318) 766-3530; www.crt.state.la.us.

RV ★★★★ Tent ★★★★

Beauty: ★★★★★ Site Privacy: ★★★
Spaciousness: ★★★ Quiet: ★★★★
Security: ★★★★ Cleanliness: ★★★★
Insect Control: ★★ Facilities: ★★★★

The pretty campground at this small state park is a real treat. Campers enjoy a view of Lake Bruin, an oxbow lake, formerly part of the Mississippi River. Fishing is excellent here—launches, docks, and three piers support fishermen in their quest for crappie, bluegill, and largemouth bass. The lakeshore is lined with cypress trees, and the sunset over the lake is absolutely gorgeous. The campground is laid out in two areas, each with its own bathhouse. Sites are not outstanding in size or other features. However, the views of Lake Bruin are outstanding. Sumptuous lakefront campsites include numbers 1–20. All sites offer paved back-in style parking. Elegant moss-covered oaks shade campsites, but provide little privacy. Lake Bruin State Park is remote and gated, making it extra secure. Visit in spring or fall for the best weather and the best bass fishin'.

Basics

Operated By: Louisiana State Parks. **Open:** 7 days, all year. **Site Assignment:** First come, first served. **Registration:** Park entrance, 6 a.m.–9 p.m. Sunday–Thursday, 6 a.m.–10 p.m. Friday & Saturday. **Fee:** $12 any site, Golden Access 50% price (cash, LA check, V, MC). **Parking:** Sites plus overflow.

Facilities

Number of RV Sites: 25. **Number of Tent-Only Sites:**. **Number of Multipurpose Sites:** 25 (all sites multipurpose). **Hookups:** Water, electric (5 amps). **Each Site:** Picnic table, grill, fire ring. **Dump Station:** Yes. **Laundry:** Yes. **Pay Phone:** Yes. **Rest Rooms and Showers:** Yes. **Fuel:** No. **Propane:** No. **Internal Roads:** Paved. **RV Service:** 90 mi. in Monroe. **Market:** 3 mi. in St. Joseph. **Restaurant:** 3 mi. in St. Joseph. **General Store:** 45 mi. in Winnsboro. **Vending:** No. **Swimming Pool:** No. **Playground:** Yes. **Other:** Boat launch. **Activities:** Lake swimming, fishing (boat or pier). **Nearby Attractions:** Winter Quarters Commemorative area & Plantation Home, Natchez Trace, Vicksburg casinos, & National Military Park. **Additional Information:** St. Joseph Mayor's Office (318) 766-3713.

Restrictions

Pets: On leash only. **Fires:** In sites, rings only. **Alcoholic Beverages:** Okay. **Vehicle Maximum Length:** 45 ft.

To Get There

From I-20, take US 65 south to LA 128. Turn left (east), then at LA 606 turn left (north). Turn right on LA 604, campground is on the left. From the south, take US 65 north and turn right (east) on LA 128.

ST. JOSEPH

Shiloh's Lake Bruin

Rte. 1 Box 40, Newellton 71357. T: (318) 766-3334.

RV ★★★ Tent ★★★

Beauty: ★★★ Site Privacy: ★★
Spaciousness: ★★★ Quiet: ★★★
Security: ★★★ Cleanliness: ★★★
Insect Control: ★★★ Facilities: ★★★

This private campground gives its members first priority, so call for reservations. Shiloh's offers sites right on the shore of Lake Bruin, an oxbow lake known for its lovely cypress-lined shores and populations of crappie, bluegill, and largemouth bass. The campground at Shiloh's is not as spectacular as the lake. Due to the flat terrain, you can see the water from most sites. Nonetheless, we recommend lakefront sites. Sites are average sized, with pull-through gravel parking. Patches of grass and weeds poke up through the gravel at many sites. Most sites enjoy shady pine and oak trees, but there is little growth to provide privacy buffers between sites. Visit Shiloh's in spring and early summer for the best weather and bass fishing. Avoid this area in late summer when heat and humidity are horrendous. Security at Shiloh's is fair; there are no gates, but the park is extremely remote.

Basics

Operated By: The Pierson Family. **Open:** Year-round. **Site Assignment:** First come, first served; this is a membership park, members receive priority, but it is open to the general public; all credit cards, personal checks, & cash accepted. **Registration:** Main office. **Fee:** $17–$22. **Parking:** At sites & near boat ramp.

Facilities

Number of RV Sites: 84. **Number of Tent-Only Sites:** 20. **Hookups:** Electric, water. **Each Site:** Picnic table. **Dump Station:** Yes. **Laundry:** Yes. **Pay Phone:** Yes. **Rest Rooms and Showers:** Yes. **Fuel:** No. **Propane:** No. **Internal Roads:** Gravel & paved. **RV Service:** On call. **Market:** On site. **Restaurant:** 6.5 mi. either direction. **General Store:** 6.5 mi. either direction. **Vending:** Beverages. **Swimming Pool:** Yes. **Playground:** Yes. **Other:** Mini-golf, boat ramp, boat rentals. **Activities:** Water sports, boating, fishing. **Nearby Attractions:** Ulysses S. Grant's winter quarters, Frogmore Working Plantation, St. Joseph's museums & historical sites, Jerry Lee Lewis Museum. **Additional Information:** St. Joseph City Hall (318) 766-3713.

Restrictions

Pets: Allowed. **Fires:** In fire rings at sites only. **Alcoholic Beverages:** Allowed. **Vehicle Maximum Length:** 40 ft.

To Get There

Located between Natchez and Vicksburg; from I-20 at Tallulah (Exit 171), take I-65 south 29 mi. to LA 607, take a left and bear right on LA 605. Campground is 2,000 yards on the left

ST. MARTINVILLE

Lake Fausse Pointe State Park

5400 Levee Rd., St. Martinville 70582. T: (888) 677-7200; F: (337) 229-2339; www.crt.state.la.us; lakefaussept@crt.state.la.us.

RV ★★★★ Tent ★★★★

Beauty: ★★★★★ Site Privacy: ★★★★
Spaciousness: ★★★★★ Quiet: ★★★★★
Security: ★★★★★ Cleanliness: ★★★★
Insect Control: ★★★ Facilities: ★★★

At 6,000 acres, Lake Fausse Point is one of Lousiana's larger state parks. The park is situated on a peninsula on Lake Fausse Point. Inside the park is a system of streams, complete with canoe trails. The park also maintains walking and hiking trails with varying difficulty levels. The park is built on former swampland. The park is adjacent to the Atchafalaya Basin, a huge swamp that once covered most of the land between The Mississippi River and Bayou Teche. The flat campground consists of two areas along Barrow Pit Canal. Boat docks at the campgrounds provide convenient access to local waters. Sites are large and lovely. Each site features paved, back-in parking plus a gravel picnic area. A variety of hardwoods shade the campground. Unfortunately, there is little foliage between sites. The nicest sites, 27–33, have gorgeous water views and are closest to the docks. Security is excellent at this ultra remote park. Avoid this area in July and August—the heat and humidity are unbearable.

Basics

Operated By: State of Louisiana Dept. of Culture, Recreation & Tourism. **Open:** Year-round. **Site Assignment:** First come, first served, also reservation can be held w/V or MC (888) 677-1400. If cancelled 15 days are more before the first reserved day then the fee is $10. If cancelled 14 days or less before the first reserved day then the fee is one day's rental for all reserved items. Check-in time is 2 p.m. or later. Check-out time is 1 p.m. or earlier. The stay limit is 15 days. **Registration:** Main office. **Fee:** $12 per night for RV/tent site, $6 w/ the Golden Access card. **Parking:** 2 vehicles at each site.

Facilities

Number of Multipurpose Sites: 50. **Hookups:** Water, Electric (20, 30, 50 amps). **Each Site:** Tent pad, fire ring, grill, lantern hook, picnic table. **Dump Station:** Yes. **Laundry:** Yes. **Pay Phone:** Yes. **Rest Rooms and Showers:** Yes. **Fuel:** No. **Propane:** No. **Internal Roads:** Paved. **RV Service:** Approx. 60mi. west in Lafayette. **Market:** Approx. 18 mi. west in St. Martinville. **Restaurant:** Approx. 18mi. west in St. Martinville. **General Store:** Approx. 18mi. west in St. Martinville. **Vending:** Beverage only. **Swimming Pool:** No. **Playground:** Yes. **Other:** Volleyball net, athletic fields, nature trails, boat launch. **Activities:** Business retreats, canoe swamp tours, volleyball, basketball, hiking, fishing, backpacking trails where tent camping is available on the trail, overnight canoe rides where tent camping is available, children's activities. **Nearby Attractions:** Cypremort Point State Park, Longfellow-Evangeline State Historic Site, historic Town of St. Martinville, Historic Town of New Iberia, Plantations along Bayou Teche. **Additional Information:** St. Martin Parish Tourist Commission (888) 565-5939.

Restrictions

Pets: Leash. **Fires:** Fire ring only. **Alcoholic Beverages:** Allowed. **Vehicle Maximum Length:** 62 ft. **Other:** No swimming.

To Get There

From I-10 going south towards Lafayette take Breaux Bridge Town Exit. Turn right onto Hwy. 31 going south and go to St. Martinville. Turn left in St. Martinville onto Hwy. 96 and drive for 3.5 mi. Turn right onto Hwy. 679, drive for 4.3 mi. and then turn left onto Hwy. 3083. Turn right onto Levee Rd. and the park will be 8 mi. south on the right.

VILLE PLATTE

Chicot State Park

3469 Chicot Park Rd., Ville Platte 70586. T: (888) 677-2442; F: (337) 363-2413; www.crt.state.la.us; chicot@crt.state.la.us.

RV ★★★★★ Tent ★★★★★

Beauty: ★★★★★ Site Privacy: ★★★★★
Spaciousness: ★★★★★ Quiet: ★★★★★
Security: ★★★★★ Cleanliness: ★★★★
Insect Control: ★★★★ Facilities: ★★★

Chicot State Park is adjacent to the Louisiana State Arboretum, which offers educational strolls through 300 acres of mature beech-magnolia forest. The Arboretum is home to diverse plants, showcasing species that usually grow in other parts of the state. Chicot State Park maintains extensive fishing, boating, and swimming facilities along the shore of Lake Chicot. There are two camping areas at Chicot. We fell in love with the beautiful South Landing Campground—it's newer, with bigger sites. All of the sites are shaded by gorgeous trees, and feature paved, back-in parking. Some sites are exceptionally large and many are extremely secluded. In South Landing, the largest sites include 24, 26, and 76. Sites 74 and 75 enjoy a gorgeous view of the lake with its majestic cypress and tupelo. Park gates are locked at night, making Chicot extra secure. This area is unbearably hot and humid in late summer. Visit in spring or fall.

Basics

Operated By: State of Louisiana Dept. of Culture, Recreation & Tourism. **Open:** Year-round. **Site Assignment:** First come, first served, reservation can be made w/V or MC (888) 677-1400. If cancelled 15 days or more before the first reserved day the fee is $10. If cancelled 14 days or less before the first reserved day then the fee is one day's rental of all reserved items. Check-in time is 2 p.m. or later. Check-out time is 1 p.m. or earlier. The stay limit is 15 days. **Registration:** Main office at the south entrance. **Fee:** $12 a night for RV/tent site. $6 w/ a Golden Access card. **Parking:** 2 cars/1 RV & 1 car, overflow parking is available.

Facilities

Number of RV Sites: 183. **Number of Tent-Only Sites:** 25. **Hookups:** Electric (30 amps), water. **Each Site:** Tent pad at tent sites only, fire ring, grill, picnic table. **Dump Station:** Yes. **Laundry:** Yes. **Pay Phone:** No. **Rest Rooms and Showers:** Yes. **Fuel:** No. **Propane:** No. **Internal Roads:** Paved. **RV Service:** 6 mi. south in Ville Platte. **Market:** 4 mi. south in Ville Platte. **Restaurant:** 4 mi. south in Ville Platte. **General Store:** 8 mi. south in Ville Platte. **Vending:** Beverage only. **Swimming Pool:** Yes. **Playground:** Yes. **Other:** Nature trails, boat launch, group lodge. **Activities:** Fishing (Florida bass), picnicking, hiking, boating. **Nearby Attractions:** Louisiana State Arboretum, Prairie Acadian Cultural Center-Jean Lafitte National Historical Park & Reserve, Acadian Town of Ville

Platte, Historic town of Opelousas, Historic Town of Washington, Zydeco Cajun Prairie Scenic Byway, Liberal Theatre/City of Eunice, Thistlethwaite Wildlife Management Area. **Additional Information:** Acadia Parish Convention & Visitors Commission (877) 783-2109.

RESTRICTIONS

Pets: Leash. **Fires:** Fire ring only. **Alcoholic Beverages:** Allowed. **Vehicle Maximum Length:** Approx. 65 ft. **Other:** No gray water on the ground.

TO GET THERE

Coming from the north on I-49, exit on LA 106 south. Turn left off LA 106 onto LA 3042 south. Continue to the main entrance.

WESTWEGO

Bayou Segnette State Park

7777 Westbank Expressway, Westwego 70094. T: (504) 736-7140; bayousegnette@crt.state.la.us.

RV ★★★ Tent ★★★

Beauty: ★★★★ Site Privacy: ★★★
Spaciousness: ★★★★ Quiet: ★★★
Security: ★★★ Cleanliness: ★★★★
Insect Control: ★★ Facilities: ★★★

Bayou Segnette lies at the conjunction of two kinds of wetland-swamp and marsh. Plentiful bird species include red-winged blackbirds, Mississippi kites, and bald eagles. Located 30 miles from New Orleans, across the Mississippi River, this suburban park is convenient if you're touring the city on a weekend. However, it's not convenient to New Orleans when rush hour traffic climaxes. Avoid the New Orleans area during festivals, when the city is zoo-like, and late summer, when the heat is unbearable. Security is good here—gates are locked at night. The flat, yet attractive campground offers commodious sites. Most sites have at least a little shade and all parking is paved, back-in style. Privacy varies greatly. We recommend sites 13, 15, 62, and 100 for seclusion. Site No. 7 is recommended for families with children—it's next to the playground and wash house. Site No. 81 is extra shady.

BASICS

Operated By: Louisiana State Parks. **Open:** 7 days a week, all year. **Site Assignment:** Reservations accepted w/ a one night deposit; call (888) 677-2296; V, MC, cash, in-state checks; 2 week notice of cancellation for full refund, otherwise $10 fee. **Registration:** Campground office. **Fee:** $12. **Parking:** 2 vehicles per site, also parking lots.

FACILITIES

Number of Multipurpose Sites: 98. **Hookups:** Electric, water. **Each Site:** Picnic table, fire ring w/ grill. **Dump Station:** Yes. **Laundry:** Yes. **Pay Phone:** Yes. **Rest Rooms and Showers:** Yes. **Fuel:** No. **Propane:** No. **Internal Roads:** Paved. **RV Service:** No. **Market:** No. **Restaurant:** 0.5 mi. east. **General Store:** 0.5 mi. east. **Vending:** No. **Swimming Pool:** Yes. **Playground:** Yes. **Other:** Boat landing, wave pool. **Activities:** Hiking, fishing. **Nearby Attractions:** French Quarter, Audubon Zoo & Botanical Gardens, Aquarium of the Americas, Paddlewheel Boats, Superdome, National D-Day Museum. **Additional Information:** New Orleans CVB (504) 246-5666.

RESTRICTIONS

Pets: On leash only. **Fires:** At site only. **Alcoholic Beverages:** Allowed. **Vehicle Maximum Length:** 50 ft. **Other:** Quiet hours enforced.

TO GET THERE

From New Orleans, take US 90 west over the Greater New Orleans Bridge, which turns into the West Bank Expressway. Continue 8 mi. to flashing caution light and take a left on Drake Ave. There is a sign for the park.

ZWOLLE

North Toledo Bend State Park

P.O. Box 56, Zwolle 71486. T: (888) 677-6400; F: (318) 645-4723; www.crt.state.la.us; toledobend@crt.state.la.us.

RV ★★★★★ Tent ★★★★★

Beauty: ★★★★★ Site Privacy: ★★★★★
Spaciousness: ★★★★★ Quiet: ★★★★★
Security: ★★★★ Cleanliness: ★★★★★
Insect Control: ★★★ Facilities: ★★★★

This gorgeous park is situated on a peninsula jutting into massive Toledo Bend Reservoir. Across the reservoir is Texas' Sabine National Forest. At North Toledo Bend, recreation revolves around fishing for largemouth bass, catfish, and crappie. For landlubbers, there's a nature trail and an Olympic-sized swimming pool. Although the terrain consists of rolling hills, the campground is pretty flat. The beautiful campground is laid out in two loops containing huge sites. Sites are shaded by a variety of tree species dominated by pine. Privacy is provided by greenery between sites. All parking is paved, back-in style. The most private sites are 29–34. We also like sites 13 and 14, which have partial water views. Avoid North Toledo Bend on holiday weekends and during hot late summer. Otherwise, the campground rarely fills up, making it a good destination for an early summer weekend. Security is excellent at this remote park.

BASICS

Operated By: State of Louisiana Dept. of Culture, Recreation & Tourism (888) 677-1400. **Open:** Year-round. **Site Assignment:** First come, first served, also reservations can be held w/ V, MC, (888) 677-1400. No out of state checks are accepted. If cancelled the fee is either $10, or the cost of one night's rent (which ever is largest). Check-in time is 3 p.m. or later. Check-out time is 1 p.m. or earlier. Stay limit is 15 days. **Registration:** Park office. **Fee:** $12 per night for RV/tent site. $6 w/ a Golden Access card. **Parking:** 2 vehicle parking at site.

FACILITIES

Number of Multipurpose Sites: 63. **Hookups:** Water, electric (30 amps). **Each Site:** Tent pad, lantern hook, fire ring, picnic table. **Dump Station:** Yes. **Laundry:** Yes. **Pay Phone:** Yes. **Rest Rooms and Showers:** Yes. **Fuel:** No. **Propane:** No. **Internal Roads:** Paved. **RV Service:** 50 mi. east in Natchitoches. **Market:** 8 mi. east in Zwolle. **Restaurant:** 9 mi. east in Zwolle. **General Store:** 20 mi. east in Many. **Vending:** No. **Swimming Pool:** Yes. **Playground:** Yes. **Other:** Boat launch, fishing pier, athletic field, nature trails, group lodging. **Activities:** Field activities, fishing, picnicking, hiking. **Nearby Attractions:** Fort Jesup State Commemorative Area, Mansfield State Commemorative Area, Rebel State Commemorative Area, Los Adaes State Commemorative Area, Historic town of Natchitoches, Cane River Country, Kisatchie National Forest-Longleaf Vista National Recreation Trail, Sabine Wildlife Refuge, National Fish Hatchery & Aquarium. **Additional Information:** Sabine Parish Tourist & Recreation Commission/Toledo Bend Country, (800) 358-7802.

RESTRICTIONS

Pets: leash. **Fires:** Fire ring only. **Alcoholic Beverages:** Allowed. **Vehicle Maximum Length:** No limit. **Other:** The office is open from 6 a.m.–9 p.m. so check in & out must happen between those times.

TO GET THERE

From I-49, exit onto Hwy. 6 and go west approx. 30 mi. to Many. Turn right on to Hwy. 171 going north. After passing through the town of Zwolle. Take a left onto Hwy. 482. Turn left onto 3229. The entrance to the park is on the left.

Maine

Six moose, four rabbits, a Native American gravesite, and a little bit of Canada: that's what we saw on our campground-to-campground road trip from Rangeley Lake to the Moose River. (They don't call Maine's Route 16 "Moose Alley" for nothing!) From there, we followed the silvery-blue glimmer of Moosehead Lake to spectacular Lily Bay, where Mt. Kineo rises out of a sea (OK, lake) of blue. We took the long way around the lake, since, at 117 square miles, every way is the long way, and set up camp along the shore. Just another day of camping in Maine.

As camping grounds go, Maine is outrageously attractive. Just when you think you've seen the most incredible vista of rockbound coastline, pine-shrouded mountain, or sea-meets-sky, you take another turn in the road and see something even more ahh-inspiring. And we are understating this. Good news for the camper: Maine boasts more than 200 places to take it all in. These vary widely, from upscale camping resorts like **Point Sebago** and **Megunticook-by-the-Sea** with golf courses and gourmet coffee, to rustic retreats (and in Maine, when they say rustic, they mean "the generator goes out at 11 p.m"). Some are so remote, the road in is six suspension-testing miles long; ask 'em if they have a website, and they'll snort, "We don't even have a phone."

Everybody, everybody heads to the south coast and mid-coast regions, for good reason: the beaches and the lobster shacks are there. Count on plenty of traffic in summer, and woe to those who show up in July or August, on a weekend, sans reservation! Keep driving, though, and the glories of Downeast Maine and Acadia await, with a landscape that rivals the most beautiful anywhere.

True Maine insiders know, however, that some of the best camping spots in the state are far from the Atlantic. The **Sebago Lake-Long Lake** chain, in the Western Lakes and Mountains region, offers wonderful lakeside camping, along with boating (many campgrounds offer rentals, or BYOB), fishing, even paddle-wheeler trips. This is camping like you remember it from your childhood, complete with those allowance-busting snack bars. (Hint: come in the fall for the **Fryeburg Fair,** among the best events in Maine.) Heading north, **South Arm** (at Richardson Lake), and **Eustis** (where you'll find an amazing stand of towering red pines, where Benedict Arnold once trod), and **Chain of Ponds** are well worth seeking out. (Just check out our 'best' list.) The Jackman-Moose River area, nudging Canada, is a paradise for sports-loving campers, and everybody who's ever been there loves Greenville, a taste of Montana near Moosehead Lake. Then there's **Katahdin,** and **Caribou**—enough said. Just know that the south coast of Maine is only the beginning.

The following facilities accept payment in checks or cash only:

Bar Harbor Campground, Bar Harbor
Camden Rockport Camping, Rockport
Cupsuptic Campground, Oquossoc
Gray Homestead Campground, Southport
Hermit Island Campground, Small Point
Honey Run Beach & Campground, Peru
Sherwood Forest Campsite, New Harbor
Shore Hills Campground, Boothbay Harbor
Somes Sound Campground, Mt. Desert Island
South Arm Campground, Andover
The Moorings, Searsport
Whispering Pines, East Orland
Wolfeboro Campground, Wolfeboro

ABBOT VILLAGE

Balsam Woods Campground

112 Pond Rd., Abbot Village 04406. T: (207) 876-2731; www.balsamwoods.com; info@balsamwoods.com.

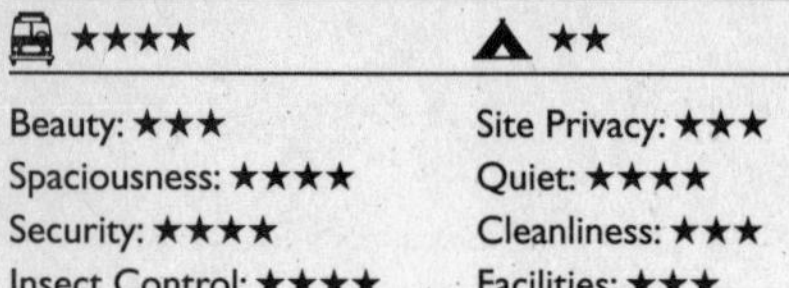

RV ★★★★ Tent ★★

Beauty: ★★★ Site Privacy: ★★★
Spaciousness: ★★★★ Quiet: ★★★★
Security: ★★★★ Cleanliness: ★★★
Insect Control: ★★★★ Facilities: ★★★

Located just 18 miles south of outdoorsy Greenville and Moosehead Lake, Balsam Woods (despite its name) has a totally different vibe. Set in tiny Abbot Village, almost dead-center in the state, the campground has a rural, countryside feel. Freshly-mown grass surrounds a swimming pool and playground area, dotted with picnic tables. Sites in the center of the park are open and grassy, while those at the perimeter are wooded with pines, with plenty of shrubbery buffer for privacy. The property connects with a hiking trail, and the owners will point you toward berry bushes if you want to pick some fresh fruit for dinner. Nothing goes better with Maine blueberries than lobster, and they'll sell you some here. (Shouldn't every Maine campground have its own lobster pound?) Best sites, with hookups, are F3 through 5, and F7, 9, 10, and 11, backing up into the pines. Tenters might find the campsites here too exposed for their taste. In any event, avoid the privies (ugh!) and plan to hike up to the nice, clean rest room behind the rec hall.

BASICS

Operated By: Jay Eberhard. **Open:** Memorial Day–Oct. **Site Assignment:** Reservations recommended. Deposit equal to 1-night stay required for bookings of less than 1 week; 25% deposit for stays of 1 week or longer. Refunds for cancellations w/ 14-day notice. **Registration:** At office. **Fee:** $21–$23 based on family of 4. V, MC (No checks.). **Parking:** At site.

FACILITIES

Number of RV Sites: 50. **Number of Tent-Only Sites:** 0. **Hookups:** Water, electric (30 amps). **Each Site:** Picnic table, fire ring. **Dump Station:** Yes. **Laundry:** Yes. **Pay Phone:** Yes. **Rest Rooms and Showers:** Yes. **Fuel:** No. **Propane:** Yes. **Internal Roads:** Gravel, in good condition. **RV Service:** No. **Market:** 10 mi. south. **Restaurant:** 18 mi. north. **General Store:** Yes. **Vending:** No. **Swimming Pool:** Yes. **Playground:** Yes. **Other:** Rec hall. **Activities:** Hiking, berry picking, horseshoes, volleyball, planned activities. **Nearby Attractions:** Appalachian Trail, Moosehead Lake, S.S. Katahdin steamboat cruises, Moosehead Marine Museum, Eveleth-Crafts-Sheridan Historical House, Lily whitewater rafting, boating, fishing. **Additional Information:** Moosehead Lake Region Chamber of Commerce, (207) 723-4443.

RESTRICTIONS

Pets: Must be leashed, quiet, & cleaned up after. Must not be left unattended. **Fires:** In fire rings only. **Alcoholic Beverages:** Yes. **Vehicle Maximum Length:** 45 ft. **Other:** Maximum of 6 people per campsite.

TO GET THERE

From junction of Rtes. 15 and 16, go 1 mi. north on Rte. 15, then 3 mi. west of Pond Rd. Campground entrance is on the left.

ACADIA NATIONAL PARK

Blackwoods Campground

P.O. Box 177, Bar Harbor 04609. T: (207) 288-3274; www.nps/gov/acad/blackwoods.

RV ★★ Tent ★★★★

Beauty: ★★★ Site Privacy: ★★★★★
Spaciousness: ★★★★★ Quiet: ★★★★
Security: ★★★★★ Cleanliness: ★★★
Insect Control: ★★★ Facilities: ★★

Blackwoods is one of only two campgrounds in Acadia National Park (also see Seawall Campground) and offers a rustic, no frills base for campers exploring the area and visiting park sights and attractions. The woodsy campground is just 5 miles south of popular Bar Harbor and within a ten minute walk to the ocean. Though there are no showers at the campground (there is cold running water), you'll find hot showers and groceries a half-mile down the street. Typical of national park properties, this has roomy sites and lots of privacy. RVs are limited to 35 feet in length and sites are separate from the tent-only area. Evening slide shows and ranger programs are held in the campground amphitheater during July and Aug. This is a great bargain (under $20 a night) for those looking for a traditional camping experience.

BASICS

Operated By: Acadia National Park. **Open:** Year-round. **Site Assignment:** Reservations required mid-June–mid-Sep.; reservations are accepted beginning in Feb. by calling (800) 365-2267 or online (see above website.) Full amount deposit required; cancellations subject to $13.25 service fee; same-day cancellations also subject to 1-night fee; MC, V, no checks. **Registration:** At ranger station on-site. **Fee:** $18. **Parking:** At site.

FACILITIES

Number of RV Sites: 117. **Number of Tent-Only Sites:** 193. **Hookups:** None. **Each Site:** Picnic table, fire ring. **Dump Station:** Yes. **Laundry:** No. **Pay Phone:** Yes. **Rest Rooms and Showers:** Yes, no showers. **Fuel:** No. **Propane:** No. **Internal Roads:** Paved, gravel (good). **RV Service:** No. **Market:** Bar Harbor (5 mi). **Restaurant:** No. **General Store:** No. **Vending:** No. **Swimming Pool:** No. **Playground:** No. **Other:** Amphitheater, group area, island shuttle bus pickup & dropoff, ranger station. **Activities:** Planned park activities, including nature programs, slide shows, & sing-alongs. **Nearby Attractions:** Bar Harbor, Acadia National Park. **Additional Information:** Acadia National Park, P.O. Box 177, Bar Harbor, ME 04609 (207) 288-3338, www.nps/gov/acad. Also, Acadia Information Center, P.O. Box 139, Mount Desert, ME 04660 (207) 667-8550 or (800) 358-8550, www.acadiainfo.com & Bar Harbor Chamber of Commerce, 93 Cottage St., Bar Harbor, ME 04609 (207) 288-5103, www.barharborinfo.com.

RESTRICTIONS

Pets: Must be on a leash, never left unattended. **Fires:** In grills, stoves, & fire rings only. **Alcoholic Beverages:** At site only. **Vehicle Maximum Length:** 35 ft.

TO GET THERE

From junction Rtes. 3 and 233 (in Bar Harbor), go south 5 mi. on Rte. 3; the campground is on the left.

ACADIA NATIONAL PARK

Seawall Campground

P.O. Box 177, Bar Harbor 04609. T: (207) 244-3600; www.nps/gov/acad.

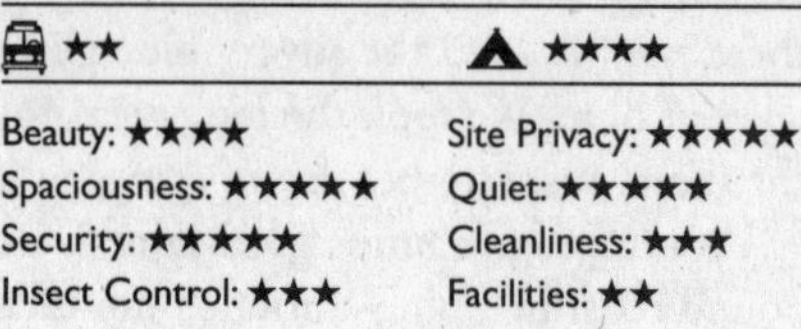

RV ★★ Tent ★★★★

Beauty: ★★★★ Site Privacy: ★★★★★
Spaciousness: ★★★★★ Quiet: ★★★★★
Security: ★★★★★ Cleanliness: ★★★
Insect Control: ★★★ Facilities: ★★

This is one of only two campgrounds in Acadia National Park (also see Blackwoods Campground) and perfect for those who like a traditional, rustic setting. Seawall is just a few miles south of Southwest Harbor on the park's "quiet" side, and within walking distance of the ocean. Showers and a camping supply store are within a half-mile of the campground. Sites are all roomy, situated in the woods along four separate loops. One loop is reserved for RVs only, where cars and trailers are placed on pull-through aisles among the trees. Two loops accommodate drive-in tent sites and another pod is reserved for walk-in tenters, offering the most privacy. We like the granite and boulder rock fire pits with grills at each site and the nightly ranger programs offered in the amphitheater throughout the summer months. For under $20 a night, it's one of the best bargains around but be sure to arrive early in the morning to snag a site.

BASICS

Operated By: Acadia National Park. **Open:** Late-May–late-Sept. **Site Assignment:** first come, first served. **Registration:** At ranger station on site. **Fee:** Drive-in, $18; walk-in, $12. **Parking:** At site or at general lot to walk-in sites.

FACILITIES

Number of RV Sites: 43. **Number of Tent-Only Sites:** 170. **Hookups:** None. **Each Site:** Picnic table & fire ring. **Dump Station:** Yes. **Laundry:** No. **Pay Phone:** Yes. **Rest Rooms and Showers:** Yes, no showers. **Fuel:** No. **Propane:** No. **Internal Roads:** Paved (good). **RV Service:** No. **Market:** Southwest Harbor (4 mi). **Restaurant:** No. **General Store:** No. **Vending:** No. **Swimming Pool:** No. **Playground:** No. **Other:** Amphitheater, group area, island shuttle bus pickup & dropoff, ranger station. **Activities:** Planned park activities, including nature programs, slide shows, & sing-alongs. **Nearby Attractions:** Bar Harbor, Acadia National Park. **Additional Information:** Acadia National Park, P.O. Box 177, Bar Harbor, ME 04609 (207) 288-3338, www.nps/gov/acad. Also, Acadia Information Center, P.O. Box 139, Mount Desert, ME 04660 (207) 667-8550 or (800) 358-8550, www.acadiainfo.com & Bar Harbor Chamber of Commerce, 93 Cottage St., Bar Harbor, ME 04609 (207) 288-5103, www.barharborinfo.com.

RESTRICTIONS

Pets: Must be on a leash, never left unattended. **Fires:** In grills, stoves, & fire rings only. **Alcoholic Beverages:** At site only. **Vehicle Maximum Length:** 35 ft. **Other:** 6 people & 2 small tents or 1 large tent are allowed per site; 1 vehicle per site.

TO GET THERE

From junction Rtes. 102 and 102A, go south 5 mi. on Rte.102A; campground is on the right.

ANDOVER

South Arm Campground

P.O. Box 310, Andover 04216. T: (207) 364-5155 or (978) 465-5427 (winter); www.southarm.com.

RV ★★★★★ Tent ★★★★★

Beauty: ★★★★★ Site Privacy: ★★★★
Spaciousness: ★★ Quiet: ★★★★
Security: ★★★★ Cleanliness: ★★★
Insect Control: ★★ Facilities: ★★★

The owner calls it "Maine's Most Beautiful Campground." No argument here. Set amidst a thousand-acre wilderness area in Western Maine, the campground nudges the south arm of Richardson Lake, with mountains providing a backdrop. Seventeen miles of lakes are accessible here; adventurous campers can choose from remote sites along the lake, reachable only by boat or canoe. The main campground is on a peninsula, with 65 wooded sites set in a loop. At least half of these are on the beach and waterfront. These prime sites require a two-night stay, but you'd want to stay that long anyway. It's a long haul to this campground, and it takes a couple of days to explore the waterways and soak in all the beauty here. Sites 1 through 51 (odd numbers) are shoreside. They're all great, but sites 29A and 29B are set back a bit, with amazing views. Site 31 is beautiful, too. These get snapped up quickly. Off the beach, we like sites 2 through 12 and, especially site 24, near the point. Book early for July and Aug., but don't even consider June, when black flies are out in force. Rainy days, borrow a book, puzzle, game, or novel. For laughs, read the over-the-top prose in their brochure.

BASICS

Operated By: Scott Mitchell. **Open:** May 15–Sept. 15. **Site Assignment:** Reservations recommended. Deposit of 1 nights' fee required; check or cash acceptable. Heavily booked in July & Aug. Refunds for cancellation w/ 1-month notice. **Registration:** At office. **Fee:** $21–$27 for 2 adults & their children under age 18. Wilderness sites, $5 per family/couple. No credit cards. **Parking:** At site.

FACILITIES

Number of RV Sites: 65. **Number of Tent-Only Sites:** 0. **Hookups:** Water, electric (30 amps) Note: Generator goes off at 11 p.m. nightly, comes back on at 6:30 a.m. **Each Site:** Picnic table, fireplace. **Dump Station:** Yes. **Laundry:** Yes. **Pay Phone:** No. **Rest Rooms and Showers:** Yes, coin-op. **Fuel:** No. **Propane:** Yes. **Internal Roads:** Gravel, in fair condition. **RV Service:** No. **Market:** 15 mi. south. **Restaurant:** 15 mi. south. **General Store:** Yes. **Vending:** No. **Swimming Pool:** No. **Playground:** No. **Other:** Marina, boat ramp, dock. **Activities:** Appalachian Trail hiking, fishing, (licenses available), lake swimming, boating (rentals available), boat cruises, planned activities. **Nearby Attractions:** Coose Canyon, White Mountain National Forest, historical museums. **Additional Information:** River Valley Chamber, (207) 364-3241?.

RESTRICTIONS

Pets: Must be leashed, quiet, & cleaned up after. Must not be left unattended. Current rabies vaccination certificate required. **Fires:** In fire rings only. **Alcoholic Beverages:** Yes. **Vehicle Maximum Length:** 35 ft. **Other:** 2-night min. stay for waterfront & beach sites (remote or other sites are available by the day); 3-night min. on holidays.

TO GET THERE

From junction of Rtes. 5 and 120, go 0.5 mi. east on Rte. 120, then 11 mi. north on South Arm Rd. Campground entrance is on the left.

APPLETON

Sennebec Lake Campground

Rte. 131, P.O. Box 602, Appleteon 04862. T: (207) 785-4250; www.sennebeclake.com.

RV ★★★★ Tent ★★★

Beauty: ★★★★ Site Privacy: ★★★
Spaciousness: ★★★ Quiet: ★★★★
Security: ★★★★ Cleanliness: ★★★★★
Insect Control: ★★★ Facilities: ★★★★

This neat, well-kept campsite is set in a rural area in mid-coast Maine, about 12 miles northwest of Camden. It may not be on the ocean, but it's a great spot, with grassy, terraced sites overlooking Lake Sennebec. RV sites are side-by-side along the lakefront; wooded site 72 (electric and water) is the nicest, in our view. Lakeside sites include sites 62 through 73 and 74 through 80. Tent sites are walk-in, with a footpath leading over a stream to a secluded, piney grove. Best tent sites are 94 and 95; beware of lumpy site 93. There's a sandy beach with a float, and they sell bait and fishing gear if you want to have a go at the lake's bass, perch,and pickerel population. We'd be tempted to rent a canoe and paddle around the placid lake. A lodge, overlooking the lake, is the venue for Saturday night dances with live bands. This campground makes a dandy, centralized base for Maine adventures.

BASICS

Operated By: Lorraine & Jim Bender. **Open:** May–Oct. **Site Assignment:** Reservations recommended. 50% deposit required. Refunds for cancellation w/ 14-day notice, minus $10 charge. **Registration:** At office. **Fee:** $19–$28 for 2 adults & up to 3 children under age 18. V, MC. **Parking:** At site.

FACILITIES

Number of RV Sites: 97. **Number of Tent-Only Sites:** 9. **Hookups:** Water, electric (30 amps), sewer, modem access. **Each Site:** Picnic table, fireplace. **Dump Station:** Yes. **Laundry:** Yes. **Pay Phone:** Yes. **Rest Rooms and Showers:** Yes. **Fuel:** No. **Propane:** Yes. **Internal Roads:** Gravel, in good condition. **RV Service:** No. **Market:** 3 mi. south. **Restaurant:** 3 mi. south. **General Store:** Yes. **Vending:** Yes. **Swimming Pool:** No. **Playground:** Yes. **Other:** Rec hall, boat ramp. **Activities:** Lake swimming, fishing (license required), boating (rentals available), basketball, volleyball, planned activities. **Nearby Attractions:** Camden (12 mi. southeast, w/ its harbor, galleries, museums & shops), windjammer fleet, Penobscot Bay cruises, Conway Homestead & Mary Cramer Museum (28th century restored farmhouse & gardens), Camden Hills State Park, Merryspring Park, Owl's Head Transportation Museum, golf. **Additional Information:** Union Chamber, (207) 785-3200.

RESTRICTIONS

Pets: Must be leashed, quiet, & cleaned up after. Must not be left unattended. **Fires:** In fire rings. **Alcoholic Beverages:** At sites only. **Vehicle Maximum Length:** 45 ft. **Other:** 2-night min. stay required in July & Aug.; 3-night min. stay required on holiday weekends.

TO GET THERE

From junction of Rtes. 17 and 131, go 3 mi. north on Rte. 131. Campground entrance is on the right.

BANGOR

Paul Bunyan Campground

1862 Union St., Bangor 04401. T: (207) 941-1177 or (207) 947-3734; www.paulbunyan.com; paulbunyancampground@aol.com.

RV ★★★ Tent ★★

Beauty: ★★★ Site Privacy: ★★★
Spaciousness: ★★★ Quiet: ★★★
Security: ★★★ Cleanliness: ★★★
Insect Control: ★★★ Facilities: ★★★

Of the two campgrounds off the interstate in the Bangor area (also see Pleasant Hill Campground), this one is livelier and a bit noisier, attracting a regular clientele of families during summer weekends and weeklong vacations. The campground offers plenty of entertainment, live bands and DJs, potluck dinners and parades, ice cream socials, contests, and tournaments. There's also free pancake breakfast for campers every Sunday morning throughout the summer. Come fall, the campground calms down a bit, hosting more one-night travelers. The campground feels spacious due to the surrounding fields and expansive public areas, but individual sites are average to small in size. There's a small, separate tent-only area along the road; pull-through, full hookup sites are clustered in the open field toward the back of the campground. There's a pond on the property, aptly dubbed Babe's Bathtub. Don't expect much: it's barely more than a mosquito incubator but small kids have fun tossing stones and navigating paddleboats around its tiny perimeter.

BASICS

Operated By: Dennis & Shirley Hachey. **Open:** May–Oct. **Site Assignment:** Reservations suggested. 1 night deposit required for reservations of 3 days or less, $40 for 4 or more days; 2-week cancellation policy w/ $5 service charge; MC, V, checks. **Registration:** At office. **Fee:** Full hookups, $26 (50 amp), $23 (30 amp); water & electric, $18.50; no hookups, $14, based on 2 adults & 2 children. **Parking:** At site.

Facilities

Number of RV Sites: 77. **Number of Tent-Only Sites:** 18. **Hookups:** Water, electric, sewer (30, 50 amps). **Each Site:** Picnic table, fire ring. **Dump Station:** Yes. **Laundry:** Yes. **Pay Phone:** Yes. **Rest Rooms and Showers:** Yes. **Fuel:** No. **Propane:** Yes. **Internal Roads:** Dirt, gravel (fair). **RV Service:** No. **Market:** Bangor (2 mi). **Restaurant:** No. **General Store:** Yes. **Vending:** No. **Swimming Pool:** Yes. **Playground:** Yes. **Other:** Small pond, paddleboat rentals, picnic shelter, game room, sports field. **Activities:** Swimming, live entertainment, potluck dinners, planned activities, including children's programs, hayrides, socials. **Nearby Attractions:** Bangor, Bar Harbor, Acadia National Park, Maine coast. **Additional Information:** Bangor Regional Chamber of Commerce, 519 Maine St., P.O. Box 1443, Bangor, ME 04402 (207) 947-0307, www.bangorregion.com.

Restrictions

Pets: Must be on a leash, never left unattended. **Fires:** In grills, stoves, & fire rings only. **Alcoholic Beverages:** At site only. **Vehicle Maximum Length:** 40 ft.

To Get There

From I-95, exit 47, go 2.8 mi. west on Rte. 222 (Union St.); campground is on the left.

BAR HARBOR
Bar Harbor Campground

RFD 1, Box 1125, Bar Harbor 04609. T: (207) 288-5185; www.barharborcamping.com.

RV ★★★★★ | Tent ★★★★★

Beauty: ★★★★★	Site Privacy: ★★★★
Spaciousness: ★★★★	Quiet: ★★★★
Security: ★★★	Cleanliness: ★★★★
Insect Control: ★★★	Facilities: ★★★

This is the closet campground to Bar Harbor and one of the prettiest in the area. They like to keep it simple here: all sites are first come, first served. Campers can drive through the campground and select their site and then register. You might have a difficult time choosing; there are plenty of spacious, private spots with sweeping views of Frenchman's Bay. In fact, the entire campground has a roomy, expansive feel. There's a large secluded area for tents and small pop-ups (we like the woodsy privacy in the "s" loop) and a cluster of tent-only ocean view sites (Q1, Q2, and R1-4 are especially nice.) Water and electric sites and full hookups are scattered throughout, many with ocean views. We especially like the swimming pool area at this campground, set high on an point, overlooking the Maine coastline.

Basics

Operated By: Craig Robbins. **Open:** Memorial Day–Columbus Day. **Site Assignment:** First come, first served, cash only. **Registration:** At office. **Fee:** Full hookups, $27; water & electric, $25; no hookups, $20. **Parking:** At site.

Facilities

Number of RV Sites: 155. **Number of Tent-Only Sites:** 145. **Hookups:** Water, electric, sewer (30, 50 amps). **Each Site:** Picnic table, fire ring. **Dump Station:** Yes. **Laundry:** Yes. **Pay Phone:** Yes. **Rest Rooms and Showers:** Yes (coin-op). **Fuel:** No. **Propane:** Yes. **Internal Roads:** Paved, gravel (good). **RV Service:** No. **Market:** Bar Harbor (4 mi). **Restaurant:** No. **General Store:** Yes. **Vending:** Yes. **Swimming Pool:** Yes. **Playground:** Yes. **Other:** Ocean frontage, game room, TV room. **Activities:** Swimming, horseshoes, shuffleboard, basketball. **Nearby Attractions:** Bar Harbor, Acadia National Park. **Additional Information:** Acadia National Park, P.O. Box 177, Bar Harbor, ME 04609 (207) 288-3338, www.nps/gov/acad. Also, Acadia Information Center, P.O. Box 139, Mount Desert, ME 04660 (207) 667-8550 (800) 358-8550, www.acadiainfo.com & Bar Harbor Chamber of Commerce, 93 Cottage St., Bar Harbor, ME 04609 (207) 288-5103, www.barharborinfo.com.

Restrictions

Pets: Must be on a leash, never left unattended. **Fires:** In grills, stoves, & fire rings only. **Alcoholic Beverages:** At site only. **Vehicle Maximum Length:** None. **Other:** No skateboards, rollerblades allowed.

To Get There

From junction Rtes. 102 and 3, go south 5 mi. on Rte. 3; campground is on the left.

BAR HARBOR
Barcadia Campground

RR1 Box 2165, Bar Harbor 04609. T: (207) 288-3520; F: (207) 288-2840; www.campbarcadia.com; barcadia@acadia.net.

RV ★★★★★ | Tent ★★★★

Beauty: ★★★★	Site Privacy: ★★★
Spaciousness: ★★★	Quiet: ★★★
Security: ★★★	Cleanliness: ★★★★
Insect Control: ★★★	Facilities: ★★★★

This pretty property, a stone's throw from Bar Harbor and Acadia National Park, boasts 3,500 feet of oceanfront with stunning panoramic views of the rocky Maine coastline. We love to sit on the oceanfront patio, watch the sun slip to the other side of the world while seals play on off-shore rocks. Another nicety: the campground serves up a traditional fresh lobster dinner nightly during the summer. Campers can rent kayaks on site to explore area waters and coves or sign up for a guided excursion. A variety of tours are available from the campground, ranging from a few hours to all day. There's a rocky oceanfront beach for tidepooling and toe dunking, too. There are plenty of oceanfront sites, a separate tent-only area in the trees (site 405 set on a point overlooking the ocean is primo!) and level, open RV sites clustered near the front, many with ocean views.

Basics

Operated By: Pete & Lynn Desrochers. **Open:** Memorial Day–Columbus Day. **Site Assignment:** Reservations accepted year-round, recommended in Jul.–Aug. 1 day deposit required, 14-day cancellation policy with $10 service charge; MC, V & checks. **Registration:** At office. **Fee:** Full hookups, $39; water & electric, $39 (oceanfront); $38 (premium); $33 (30 amp); $31 (20 amp); tent sites: $39 (large oceanfront); $32 (oceanfront); $30 (premium); $27 (wooded); $19 (tent); based on 2 adults & 2 children under 18. Seventh night is free. **Parking:** At site, 1 vehicle per site.

Facilities

Number of RV Sites: 200. **Number of Tent-Only Sites:** 30. **Hookups:** Water, electric, sewer (20, 30 amps), modem. **Each Site:** Picnic table, fire ring. **Dump Station:** Yes. **Laundry:** Yes. **Pay Phone:** Yes. **Rest Rooms and Showers:** Yes (coin-op). **Fuel:** No. **Propane:** Yes. **Internal Roads:** Paved, gravel (good). **RV Service:** Yes. **Market:** Bar Harbor (2 mi). **Restaurant:** No. **General Store:** Yes. **Vending:** No. **Swimming Pool:** No. **Playground:** Yes. **Other:** Ocean frontage, beach, game room, kayak rentals & guided kayak excursions, boat launch area, sunset viewing patio, free bus shuttle to Bar Harbor, trailer rentals. **Activities:** Swimming, boating, lobster bakes, basketball, volleyball, badminton, horseshoes. **Nearby Attractions:** Bar Harbor, Acadia National Park. **Additional Information:** Acadia National Park, P.O. Box 177, Bar Harbor, ME 04609 (207) 288-3338, www.nps/gov/acad. Also, Acadia Information Center, P.O. Box 139, Mount Desert, ME 04660 (207) 667-8550 (800) 358-8550, www.acadiainfo.com & Bar Harbor Chamber, 93 Cottage St., Bar Harbor, ME 04609 (207) 288-5103, www.barharborinfo.com.

Restrictions

Pets: Must be on a leash, never left unattended. Only 2 dogs per site. **Fires:** In grills, stoves, & fire rings only. **Alcoholic Beverages:** At site only. **Vehicle Maximum Length:** 43 ft.

To Get There

From junction Rtes. 3, 102 and campground road, go southwest on campground road.

BAR HARBOR
Hadley's Point Campground

RFD No. 1, Box 1790, Bar Harbor 04609. T: (207) 288-4808; www.hadleyspoint.com.

RV ★★★ | Tent ★★★

Beauty: ★★★	Site Privacy: ★★★
Spaciousness: ★★★	Quiet: ★★★
Security: ★★★	Cleanliness: ★★★★
Insect Control: ★★★	Facilities: ★★★

This campground, just four miles from the Acadia National Park entrance, is a clean, pleasant base for campers visiting the area. There are plenty of nearby attractions and activities and a public saltwater beach within walking distance of the campground. The plain-jane property offers minimal frills (swimming pool, laundry, ultra clean rest rooms and showers) but you'll have a choice of sites. There's a separate tent-only area with wooded sites and adequate room and privacy. Other sites are located in an open field, ringed in a circle; these don't offer much privacy but they're good for campers who like sunny, open spaces. The staff is exceptionally friendly and come Sunday there's no need to head into town for church, if you're so inclined: church service is held each week at the campground throughout July and Aug.

Basics

Operated By: Robert & Suzanne Baker. **Open:** May 15–Oct. 15. **Site Assignment:** Reservations suggested in Jul.–Aug. $30 deposit for stays of less that 5 days, $50 deposit for stays of 5 days or more, 48-hour cancellation policy, minus $5 service charge, no refunds on holiday weekends; MC, V, checks. **Registration:** At office. **Fee:** Full hookups, $26; water & electric, $23; no hookups, $18, based on a party of 4. **Parking:** At site.

Facilities

Number of RV Sites: 155. **Number of Tent-Only Sites:** 45. **Hookups:** Water, electric, sewer (20, 30 amps). **Each Site:** Picnic table, fire ring. **Dump Station:** Yes. **Laundry:** Yes. **Pay Phone:** Yes. **Rest Rooms and Showers:** Yes (coin-op). **Fuel:** No. **Propane:** Yes. **Internal Roads:** Gravel (good). **RV Service:** No. **Market:** Bar Harbor (5 mi). **Restaurant:** No. **General Store:** Yes. **Vending:** Yes. **Swimming Pool:** Yes. **Playground:** Yes. **Other:** Sunday church service on site. **Activities:** Swimming, horseshoes, shuffleboard. **Nearby Attractions:** Bar Harbor, Acadia National Park. **Additional Information:** Acadia National Park, P.O. Box 177, Bar Harbor, ME 04609 (207) 288-3338, www.nps/gov/acad; Acadia Information Center, P.O. Box 139, Mount Desert, ME, 04660 (207) 667-8550, (800) 358-8550, www.acadiainfo.com & Bar Harbor Chamber, 93 Cottage St., Bar Harbor, ME 04609 (207) 288-5103, www.barharborinfo.com.

Restrictions

Pets: Must be on a leash, never left unattended. **Fires:** In grills, stoves, & fire rings only. **Alcoholic Beverages:** At site only. **Vehicle Maximum Length:** None.

To Get There

From junction Rtes. 102 and 3, go east 3 mi. on Rte. 3, then north 0.25 mi. on Hadley Point Rd.; the campground is on the right.

BAR HARBOR
Mount Desert Narrows

Rte. 3, RR 1, Box 2045B, Bar Harbor 04609. T: (207) 288-4782; www.narrowscamping.com.

RV ★★★★★ Tent ★★★★★

Beauty: ★★★★★ Site Privacy: ★★★★
Spaciousness: ★★★ Quiet: ★★★
Security: ★★★ Cleanliness: ★★★★★
Insect Control: ★★★ Facilities: ★★★★★

This oceanfront campground is one of the most popular in the Bar Harbor/Acadia National Park area for both RVers and tenters, offering modern facilities, a great location, and pretty scenery. You'll find 2,100 feet of shoreline, plenty of oceanfront and ocean view sites, on-site recreation and a free bus shuttle to downtown Bar Harbor. Tenters have their own 25 acre section (first come, first served) and several prime oceanfront sites with sweeping views (sites 14 and 15 are favorites.) Tent site 30 at the end of a point on the shoreline also offers great views and plenty of space. Full hookup sites are set side-by-side near the front of the campground. There are also a handful of water and electric sites and water only sites on the ocean, too. If you're looking for a water and electric hookup, sites 88-94 on the shoreline, can't be beat.

Basics

Operated By: Pat Stanley. **Open:** May–Oct. 25. **Site Assignment:** Reservations accepted year-round, suggested in Jul.–Aug. All sites require a 2 night min. reservation w/ a 3-night min. on holiday weekends; holidays are paid in full & non-refundable. Oceanfront sites have a 3-night min. stay in July & Aug. There are no sewer sites on the ocean. No reservations taken for basic tenting sites; these are first come, first served. $50 deposit for 2 nights, $100 for 3 nights, $150 for 4–7 nights, $200 for 8 or more nights; 30-day cancellation policy w/ a $10 service charge; MC, V, D, checks for reservations; no checks upon arrival. **Registration:** At office. **Fee:** Premium full hookups, $40 (early & late summer) $60 (peak season); premium water, electric (50 amp) phone & cable, $30–$45; water, electric & sewer, $33–$45; best water & electric on ocean, $35–$50; water & electric on ocean, $33–$45; Narrows best water & electric, $28–$35; water & electric, $25–$33; oceanfront tenting, $28–$40; Narrows best tenting, $24–32; Narrows tenting, $20–$23. **Parking:** At site.

Facilities

Number of RV Sites: 219. **Number of Tent-Only Sites:** 20. **Hookups:** Water, electric, sewer (20, 30, 50 amps), cabel TV, modem. **Each Site:** Picnic table, fire ring. **Dump Station:** Yes. **Laundry:** Yes. **Pay Phone:** Yes. **Rest Rooms and Showers:** Yes. **Fuel:** No. **Propane:** Yes. **Internal Roads:** Gravel, dirt (good). **RV Service:** Yes. **Market:** Bar Harbor (4 mi). **Restaurant:** No. **General Store:** Yes. **Vending:** Yes. **Swimming Pool:** Yes. **Playground:** Yes. **Other:** Ocean frontage, entertainment pavilion, game room, shuttle bus service to Bar Harbor, canoe rentals, boat launch. **Activities:** Swimming, boating, horseshoes, basketball, volleyball, planned activities, including hayrides, movies, storytelling, & more. **Nearby Attractions:** Bar Harbor, Acadia National Park. **Additional Information:** Acadia National Park, P.O. Box 177, Bar Harbor, ME 04609 (207) 288-3338, www.nps/gov/acad. Also, Acadia Information Center, P.O. Box 139, Mount Desert, ME 04660 (207) 667-8550 (800) 358-8550, www.acadiainfo.com & Bar Harbor Chamber of Commerce, 93 Cottage St., Bar Harbor, ME 04609 (207) 288-5103, www.barharborinfo.com.

Restrictions

Pets: Must be on a leash, never left unattended. **Fires:** In grills, stoves, & fire rings only. **Alcoholic Beverages:** At site only. **Vehicle Maximum Length:** None.

To Get There

From junction Rtes. 102 and 3, go east 1.5 mi. on Rte. 3; campground is on the left.

BAR HARBOR
Spruce Valley Campground

RR 1, Box 2420, Rte. 102, Bar Harbor 04609. T: (207) 288-5139; www.sprucevalley.com; sprucval@midmaine.com.

RV ★★ Tent ★★★

Beauty: ★★★ Site Privacy: ★★★
Spaciousness: ★★★ Quiet: ★★★★
Security: ★★★ Cleanliness: ★★★
Insect Control: ★★★ Facilities: ★★

This campground, close to Acadia National Park, is best for tenters and smaller trailer campers who prefer peace and quiet to action and activities. It's low-key and family-oriented, complete with country gospel concerts on Saturday evenings during July and Aug. There are the basic conveniences: a pool for warm-day dunks, store and free hot showers, with easy access to Bar Harbor and national park sites. The Acadia National Park Visitor Center is only five miles away. Tent sites have some elbow room, set in the trees for shade and seclusion. Full hookups, including a cluster of 15 or so seasonal renters, are both open or shaded.

Basics

Operated By: Harry & Paula Luhrs. **Open:** May–Oct. **Site Assignment:** Reservations suggested in July–Aug.; 2-night deposit required, 1-night fee charged w/ less than 48-hour notice, $3 service charge for all cancellations. No refunds on holiday reservations; MC, V, D, checks. **Registration:** At office. **Fee:** Full hookups, $27; water & electric, $25; no hookups, $19, based on family of 4, 2 adults & 2 children under 16. **Parking:** 1 vehicle per site.

Facilities

Number of RV Sites: 60. **Number of Tent-Only Sites:** 40. **Hookups:** Water, electric, sewer (30 amps), cable TV. **Each Site:** Picnic table, fire ring. **Dump Station:** Yes. **Laundry:** Yes. **Pay Phone:** Yes. **Rest Rooms and Showers:** Yes. **Fuel:** No. **Propane:** Yes. **Internal Roads:** Gravel, dirt (good). **RV Service:** No. **Market:** Bar Harbor (3 mi). **Restaurant:** No. **General Store:** Yes. **Vending:** Yes. **Swimming Pool:** Yes. **Playground:** Yes. **Other:** Game room, man-made pond, country gospel concerts on Saturday evenings in July-Aug., trailer rentals. **Activities:** Swimming, horseshoes, basketball, volleyball. **Nearby Attractions:** Bar Harbor, Acadia National Park. **Additional Information:** Acadia National Park, P.O. Box 177, Bar Harbor, ME 04609 (207) 288-3338, www.nps/gov/acad. Also, Acadia Information Center, P.O. Box 139, Mount Desert, ME 04660 (207) 667-8550 (800) 358-8550, www.acadiainfo.com & Bar Harbor Chamber, 93 Cottage St., Bar Harbor, ME 04609 (207) 288-5103, www.barharborinfo.com.

Restrictions

Pets: Must be on a leash, never left unattended. **Fires:** In grills, stoves, & fire rings only. **Alcoholic Beverages:** At site only. **Vehicle Maximum Length:** 40 ft.

To Get There

From junction Rtes. 3 and 102, go south 1.5 mi. on Rte. 102; campground is on the left.

BASS HARBOR
Bass Harbor Campground

P.O. Box 122, Rte. 102A, Bass Harbor 04653. T: (207) 244-5857 (800) 327-5857; www.bassharbor.com; info@bassharbor.com.

★★★ ▲ ★★★★

Beauty: ★★★ Site Privacy: ★★★
Spaciousness: ★★★ Quiet: ★★★★
Security: ★★★★ Cleanliness: ★★★
Insect Control: ★★ Facilities: ★★★

Loyal campers return to Bass Harbor Campground year after year, using it as a base to explore Acadia National Park and the surrounding area. Most come for a week or two and appreciate the peace and quiet of the campground, away from the hustle, bustle, and traffic in the Bar Harbor area. Livin' is easy and slower, here; days spent visiting Bass Harbor Lighthouse, biking and hiking area paths, or day trips into Acadia National Park attractions. Full hookups sites are set in rows behind the office and pool area; water and electric and tent sites (some with platforms) are off a loop road in the woods. There's also a separate tent-only area across the street with shaded sites and its own bathhouse and showers.

Basics

Operated By: Mike & Sue Clayton. **Open:** Memorial Day–Columbus Day. **Site Assignment:** Reservations suggested in Jul.–Aug. 1-night deposit, 14-day cancellation policy with $10 service fee; MC, V, D, AE, checks. **Registration:** At office. **Fee:** Full hookups, $30; water, electric, cable, $28; water & electric, $28; no hookups, $23. **Parking:** At site.

Facilities

Number of RV Sites: 94. **Number of Tent-Only Sites:** 36. **Hookups:** Water, electric, sewer (30, 50 amps), cable TV, modem. **Each Site:** Picnic table, fire ring. **Dump Station:** Yes. **Laundry:** Yes. **Pay Phone:** Yes. **Rest Rooms and Showers:** Yes. **Fuel:** No. **Propane:** Yes. **Internal Roads:** Gravel, dirt (good). **RV Service:** No. **Market:** Bass Harbor (1 mi). **Restaurant:** No. **General Store:** Yes. **Vending:** No. **Swimming Pool:** Yes. **Playground:** Yes. **Other:** Cabin, trailer & motor home rentals. **Activities:** Swimming, basketball. **Nearby Attractions:** Bar Harbor, Acadia National Park. **Additional Information:** Acadia National Park, P.O. Box 177, Bar Harbor, ME 04609 (207) 288-3338, www.nps/gov/acad. Also, Acadia Information Center, P.O. Box 139, Mount Desert, ME 04660 (207) 667-8550 (800) 358-8550, www.acadiainfo.com & Bar Harbor Chamber of Commerce, 93 Cottage St., Bar Harbor, ME 04609 (207) 288-5103, www.barharborinfo.com.

Restrictions

Pets: Must be on a leash, never left unattended. **Fires:** In grills, stoves, & fire rings only. **Alcoholic Beverages:** At site only. **Vehicle Maximum Length:** None.

To Get There

From junction Rtes. 102 and 102A, in Southwest Harbor, go south 5 mi. on Rte. 102A; campground is on the right.

BELFAST

The Moorings

191 Searsport Ave., Searsport 04915. T: (207) 338-6860.

★★★ ▲ ★★

Beauty: ★★★ Site Privacy: ★★
Spaciousness: ★★★ Quiet: ★★★
Security: ★★★ Cleanliness: ★★★
Insect Control: ★★★ Facilities: ★★★

The smell of ocean, cool sea breezes, and views of picturesque Penobscot Bay dominate this modest mid-coast Maine campground. There's not a lot happening on this tiny slice of Maine coastline (kids will be bored and teens will die!) There's a small rocky beach, better for walking and beachcombing than swimming, and a small recreation area (volleyball, tetherball, horseshoes.) All sites are in the open, great for ocean viewing, but not very private. The staff lights a bonfire at water's edge each summer evening but most campers are content to relax at the campsite, watch the sun set over the bay and plan the next day's excursions. From here, you have all of mid-coast Maine to explore.

Basics

Operated By: Ben Hill. **Open:** May–Oct. **Site Assignment:** Reservations suggested Jul.–Aug., no deposit requirements, no credit cards, checks. **Registration:** At office. **Fee:** Water & electric, $30; no hookups, $10 per person. **Parking:** At site.

Facilities

Number of RV Sites: 27. **Number of Tent-Only Sites:** 13. **Hookups:** Water, electric (30 amps). **Each Site:** Picnic table, security light. **Dump Station:** Yes. **Laundry:** Yes. **Pay Phone:** No. **Rest Rooms and Showers:** Yes. **Fuel:** No. **Propane:** No. **Internal Roads:** Gravel (good). **RV Service:** No. **Market:** Belfast (.5 mi). **Restaurant:** Yes. **General Store:** No. **Vending:** Yes. **Swimming Pool:** No. **Playground:** Yes. **Other:** Ocean frontage, beach, car rentals on site, game room. **Activities:** Swimming, beachcombing, volleyball, tetherball, horseshoes, basketball. **Nearby Attractions:** Belfast, Searsport, Deer Isle Peninsula, coastal beaches. **Additional Information:** Searsport Economic Development Committee, Reservoir St., Searsport, ME 04974 (207) 54807255, www.searsportme.com.

Restrictions

Pets: Must be on a leash, never left unattended. **Fires:** In grills, stoves only. **Alcoholic Beverages:** At site only. **Vehicle Maximum Length:** None.

To Get There

From Rte. 1 (in Belfast), go north 2.1 mi. beyond bridge over Belfast Harbor; campground is on the right.

BOOTHBAY

Little Ponderosa Campground

R.R. 1, P.O. Box 915, Boothbay 04537. T: (207) 633-2700; www.littleponderoas.com; camp@littleponderosa.com.

★★★★ ▲ ★

Beauty: ★★★★ Site Privacy: ★★★
Spaciousness: ★★★ Quiet: ★★★★
Security: ★★★★★ Cleanliness: ★★★★
Insect Control: ★★★★★ Facilities: ★★★★

Mini-golf and a snack bar—two sure signs that Little Ponderosa caters to the family crowd. Of all the campgrounds in the Boothbay area, this one has the most child-friendly vibe. Saturday night concerts, ice cream sundae nights (Sundays), and non-denominational church services are among the happenings here. Then, there's nearby Boothbay Harbor, a great place to hang out, eat, shop, and take a boat cruise. This nicely-wooded campground is set on a tidal inlet, with a small, squishy-bottomed beach (wear your water shoes) and a swim raft. About one-third of the campsites are situated along the waterfront. Campsites are grass and gravel, set in a loop. The two tent-only sites are fairly exposed; we'd opt for a water/electric site, perhaps 17, 18, or 19, offering more privacy and better views. The best full hookup sites are 63 through 65, backed into the woods. We'd skip site 4, since it's right by the beach path. And Little Ponderosa gets extra points for aggressive insect management: they've installed six "Mosquito Magnets" to rid the place of pesky pests.

Basics

Operated By: Jeff & Allison Lowell. **Open:** May 15–Oct. 15. **Site Assignment:** Reservations recommended. Deposit of 1 nights' fee required. Refund for cancellation w/ 7-day notice, minus 30% service fee. **Registration:** At office. **Fee:** $18–$28 for 2 adults & 2 children. V, MC, D. **Parking:** At site.

Facilities

Number of RV Sites: 95. **Number of Tent-Only Sites:** 2. **Hookups:** Water, electric (20, 30 amps), sewer, modem access. **Each Site:** Picnic table, fire ring. **Dump Station:** Yes. **Laundry:** Yes. **Pay Phone:** Yes. **Rest Rooms and Showers:** Yes, coin-op. **Fuel:** No. **Propane:** Yes. **Internal Roads:** Gravel, in good condition. **RV Service:** No. **Market:** 4 mi. south. **Restaurant:** 2 mi. south. **General Store:** Yes. **Vending:** Yes. **Swimming Pool:** No. **Playground:** Yes. **Other:** Mini-golf, rec hall. **Activities:** Swimming, fishing (no license required), volleyball, horseshoes, boating (canoe & kayak rentals available), planned activities. **Nearby Attractions:** Boothbay Railway Village, Maine Resources Aquarium, Boothbay Harbor restaurants, shops & galleries, deep-sea fishing, whale-watching cruises, golf. **Additional Information:** Boothbay Harbor Region Chamber of Commerce, (207) 633-2353 or (800) 266-8422.

Restrictions

Pets: Must be leashed, quiet, & cleaned up after. Must not be left unattended. **Fires:** In fireplaces only. **Alcoholic Beverages:** At sites only. **Vehicle Maximum Length:** 40 ft. **Other:** Ask on arrival.

To Get There

Take Maine Turnpike to exit 9, then take I-95 to Rte. 1 in Brunswick (exit 22.) Stay on Rte. 1 through Wiscasset, then turn right on Rte. 27 south to Boothbay Harbor Region. Campground is 5 mi. on the right.

BOOTHBAY HARBOR

Shore Hills Campground

Rte. 27, P.O. Box 448, Boothbay 04537. T: (207) 633-4782; www.shorehills.com.

★★★ ▲ ★★★

Beauty: ★★★ Site Privacy: ★★★★
Spaciousness: ★★★ Quiet: ★★★
Security: ★★★★★ Cleanliness: ★★★★
Insect Control: ★★★ Facilities: ★★★

It's very quiet—that's why I keep coming! says Peggy, a happy camper at Shore Hills. That sums it up. Although this wooded, coastal campground is only four miles from bustling, touristy Boothbay Harbor, all is quiet here. The far western edge of this campground sits on the Cross River. The river runs south to the sea. From site 84, guests can take a woodsy walk to the marsh and 'fishing rocks', a great spot to cast a line or just gaze out to the river, where there's bound to be a paddler or two. (Nice touch here: use of canoes is free.) Most sites are back-in, with excellent buffer for privacy. The Family Circle area is wide open, suitable for the largest rigs, while sites 66 and 67 are closest to the water. Site 57, for tenting, boasts awesome views, while hillside site 11 overlooks the marsh, very nice. Some tent sites offer a crushed-rock surface for good drainage in case of rain. All sites have water. Another great feature here, if you hate cruising for a parking place: they'll shuttle-bus you to Boothbay Harbor. This peaceful place caters to an older clientele, many of whom (like Peggy) have been coming for years.

BASICS

Operated By: Peggy Fuller. **Open:** Apr. 15–Columbus Day. **Site Assignment:** Reservations recommended. $15 deposit required. Refunds for cancellations w/ 7-day notice. **Registration:** At office. **Fee:** $16–$28 for 2 adults & 2 children. No credit cards. **Parking:** At site.

FACILITIES

Number of RV Sites: 85. **Number of Tent-Only Sites:** 20. **Hookups:** Water, electric (30, 50 amps), sewer, cable TV. **Each Site:** Picnic table, fire ring. **Dump Station:** Yes. **Laundry:** Yes. **Pay Phone:** Yes. **Rest Rooms and Showers:** Yes, coin-op. **Fuel:** No. **Propane:** Yes. **Internal Roads:** Paved & gravel, in good condition. **RV Service:** No. **Market:** 4 mi. south. **Restaurant:** 4 mi. south. **General Store:** Yes. **Vending:** Yes. **Swimming Pool:** No. **Playground:** Yes. **Other:** Rec hall. **Activities:** Saltwater river fishing, boating (canoes available), swimming (at high tide), horseshoes. **Nearby Attractions:** Boothbay Railway Village, Maine Resources Aquarium, Boothbay Harbor restaurants, shops & galleries, deep-sea fishing, whale-watching cruises, golf. **Additional Information:** Boothbay Harbor Region Chamber of Commerce, (207) 633-2353 or (800) 266-8422.

RESTRICTIONS

Pets: Must be leashed, quiet, & cleaned up after. Must not be left unattended. **Fires:** In fire rings only. **Alcoholic Beverages:** At sites only. **Vehicle Maximum Length:** None. **Other:** 3-day min. stay on holidays.

TO GET THERE

From Portland, take 195 north to Coastal Rte. 1 for 47 mi. From Edgecomb, take Rte. 27 south 8 mi. to campground, on right.

BROWNFIELD
River Run

P.O. Box 90, Brownfield 04010. T: (207) 452-2500; F: (207) 452-2500; www.riverruncanoe.com; canoe@riverruncanoe.com.

RV ★★ Tent ★★★

Beauty: ★★★★ Site Privacy: ★★★★
Spaciousness: ★★★★★ Quiet: ★★★
Security: ★★★★★ Cleanliness: ★★★★
Insect Control: ★★ Facilities: ★

What do you get for your money? Not much in the way of facilities—well, there's a row of porta-potties—but you do get a nice spot on the Saco River, and experienced folks who'll be happy to rent you a canoe and set you up on a paddling trip. When you've had enough of that, or your shoulders give out, stretch out on a strip of sand on one of their private beaches, or jump in for a dip. Besides, you won't get a shower otherwise, if you're tenting. This primitive area is beautifully wooded, except for the grassy field reserved for the largest RVs. Like Woodland Acres Camp 'N' Canoe (see listing), these folks offer shuttle services upstream to put in, then you can paddle downstream, and end up at River Run. Although the camping part of this operation is sort of a sideline to the canoe business, we include it here because this is such a pretty natural area, and the campsites are surprisingly appealing. And cheap. The Moose Crossing and Sandy Pine areas are right on the beach, but no doubt livelier than some other spots; we like Tall Pines, featuring a nice footpath to the beach. Best of all is Big Bend Beach (site 7), secluded, but right on the river. Sites 8, 10, and 11 are peaceful and private. The two campgrounds we've included in this book are the nicest among several along this stretch of river. The people are friendlier at Woodland Acres, but this one's got a great sandy beach. You choose.

BASICS

Operated By: Bob & Joyce Parker. **Open:** Mem. Day–Labor Day. **Site Assignment:** Reservations accepted. No deposit for camping; for canoe rentals, $25 deposit due for canoes reserved for Fri., Sat., or Sun.; 2-week notice required for refund on cancellation. **Registration:** At office. **Fee:** $5 per person; 12 & under, free. V, MC. **Parking:** At site.

FACILITIES

Number of RV Sites: 22. **Number of Tent-Only Sites:** 0. **Hookups:** None. **Each Site:** Picnic table, fire ring. **Dump Station:** No. **Laundry:** No. **Pay Phone:** Yes. **Rest Rooms and Showers:** Yes, No. **Fuel:** No. **Propane:** No. **Internal Roads:** Gravel, in good condition. **RV Service:** No. **Market:** 19 mi. west, in North Conway. **Restaurant:** 8 mi. north, in Fryeburg. **General Store:** No. **Vending:** Yes. **Swimming Pool:** No. **Playground:** No. **Activities:** River fishing (license required), swimming, canoeing. **Nearby Attractions:** Narramissic 19th century working farm, Shawnee Peak Ski Area (hiking, mountain biking), outlet shopping (North Conway, NH). **Additional Information:** Bridgton Lakes Region Chamber of Commerce, (207) 647-3472.

RESTRICTIONS

Pets: Must be leashed, quiet, & under control at all times. **Fires:** In fire rings only. **Alcoholic Beverages:** Yes. **Vehicle Maximum Length:** None. **Other:** Ask on arrival.

TO GET THERE

From Portland, take Rte. 25 west to Rte. 113 north to Rte. 160 north. Campground is 0.75 mi. north of intersection of Rtes. 113 and 160, across the bridge and on the right.

BROWNFIELD
Woodland Acres Camp N Canoe

Rte. 160, R.R. 1, P.O. Box 445, Brownfield 04010. T: (207) 935-2529; www.woodlandacres.com; campcanu@nxi.com.

RV ★★★★ Tent ★★★

Beauty: ★★★ Site Privacy: ★★★
Spaciousness: ★★★★★ Quiet: ★★★★★
Security: ★★★ Cleanliness: ★★★★
Insect Control: ★★ Facilities: ★★★

Just 25 miles from North Conway, New Hampshire, and 45 miles from Portland, this Western Lakes-area campground is a perfect choice for Saco-bound paddlers. The Saco River is a mecca for canoe and kayak enthusiasts, offering a blend of leisurely floats and short stretches of rapids (depending on the trip you choose) and scenery that includes clay cliffs and covered bridges. This peaceful riverfront campground is a great base for exploring the river. Sites are gravel, mostly wooded, and the choicest spots (94 through 104, even numbers) sit alongside the river. If those are taken, ask for something among sites 47 through 50, or 13 and 14, nice and quiet. The paddling is the thing here, and these folks know what they're doing. Bring your own boat, and you can launch it here, or they'll shuttle you to a put-in point on another part of the river. Or, rent one of their canoes or kayaks and have them set you up on a trip lasting two hours or two days (an overnight and wilderness camping along the river) or something in between.

BASICS

Operated By: Chris & Trudy Gantick. **Open:** May 15–Oct. 15. **Site Assignment:** Reservations recommended. Reservations open Jan. 1. 50% deposite required; full payment required for holiday weekends (3 night min. stay required.) Refunds granted for cancellations made 14 days or more prior to arrival date, minus $5 service charge. **Registration:** At office. **Fee:** $22–$30 per night for 2 adults & children under age 18. V, MC, D. **Parking:** At sites or as designated.

FACILITIES

Number of RV Sites: 109. **Number of Tent-Only Sites:** 0. **Hookups:** Water, electric (20, 30 amps), sewer. **Each Site:** Picnic table, fireplace. **Dump Station:** Yes. **Laundry:** Yes. **Pay Phone:** Yes. **Rest Rooms and Showers:** Yes, coin-op. **Fuel:** No. **Propane:** Yes. **Internal Roads:** Gravel (sandy), in good condition. **RV Service:** No. **Market:** 18 mi. west, in North Conway, NH. **Restaurant:** 7 mi. north, in Fryeburg. **General Store:** Yes.

Vending: Yes. **Swimming Pool:** No. **Playground:** Yes. **Other:** Boat ramp, rec hall. **Activities:** Paddling, fishing (license available at general store). **Nearby Attractions:** Narramissic 19th century working farm, Shawnee Peak Ski Area (hiking, mountain biking), outlet shopping (North Conway, NH). **Additional Information:** Bridgton Lakes Region Chamber of Commerce, (207) 647-3472.

Restrictions

Pets: Leashed, quiet, & cleaned up after. Must not be left unattended. $5 per dog per stay. **Fires:** In fireplaces only. **Alcoholic Beverages:** Yes. **Vehicle Maximum Length:** None. **Other:** 7-night min. stay required for river sites during July & Aug.

To Get There

From Maine Turnpike, take exit 11 to Rte. 202 to Rte. 115 west for 3 mi. Connect w/Rte. 35S at junction of Rte. 302 for 9 mi. Turn right onto Rte. 25 West for 2 mi., then go right onto Rte. 113 north. Follow Rte. 113 north 23 mi. into Brownfield. Head right onto Rte. 160. Campground is 0.5 mi. on the left, just before green iron bridge.

BRUNSWICK

Thomas Point Beach

29 Meadow Rd., Brunswick 04011. T: (207) 725-6009 or (877) TPB-4321; www.thomaspointbeach.com; summer@thomaspointbeach.com.

RV ★★★★ Tent ★★★

Beauty: ★★★★ Site Privacy: ★★
Spaciousness: ★★ Quiet: ★★
Security: ★★★★★ Cleanliness: ★★★★★
Insect Control: ★★★ Facilities: ★★★★★

If this pretty, oceanfront spot looks familiar, maybe you've been here before, say, sitting on the lawn at the annual Bluegrass Festival, or the Maine Arts Festival, or, perhaps, the tartaned goings-on of the Maine Highland Games. Set on Thomas Bay in mid-coast Maine, between the towns of Brunswick and Bath, this property is stunning. Manicured green lawns slope to a tidal beach, flanked by lofty pines. No wonder this is a popular site for big community events and festivals. Thomas Point was an old salting bay, used by native people; some of the old salt stones still exist. The property also features odd historic bits like the totem pole from the 1964 World's Fair (when Alaska became a state), millstones, and the handsome old cupola from St. Mary's Church. The public areas, including a pine-panelled rec hall and bathhouse, are extra-nice. Look for pretty, wooded campsites to the right of the main lodge; sites 1 through 3 (RVs only) are among the best. Sites 1 through 64 are set along the marsh, with plenty of tall pines but little privacy; another camping area is located on the other, more forested side of the property. Among these, tent site L is a super spot. This whole area, including sites B through M, give or take, are quiet and wooded.

Basics

Operated By: Patricia Crooker. **Open:** Mid-May–Oct. **Site Assignment:** Reservations recommended. Deposit of 1-day fee required. Full payment due for weekends & holidays. Refunds for cancellations w/ 7-day notice, minus $10 service fee. **Registration:** At office. **Fee:** $20–$25 for 2 adults & 2 children under age 12; additional older child/adult is $5 per night. Shipping/handling fee of $2.50 added to telephone charges. V, MC. **Parking:** At site.

Facilities

Number of RV Sites: 75. **Number of Tent-Only Sites:** 0. **Hookups:** Water, electric (15, 30 amps). **Each Site:** Picnic table, fire ring. **Dump Station:** Yes. **Laundry:** Yes. **Pay Phone:** Yes. **Rest Rooms and Showers:** Yes. **Fuel:** No. **Propane:** No. **Internal Roads:** Gravel, in good condition. **RV Service:** No. **Market:** 7 mi. east. **Restaurant:** 7 mi. east. **General Store:** Yes. **Vending:** Yes. **Swimming Pool:** No. **Playground:** Yes. **Other:** Rec hall. **Activities:** Ocean swimming, ball field. **Nearby Attractions:** Reid State Park, Popham Beach State Park, Morse Mountain Sanctuary, Maine Maritime Museum, Bowdoin College Museum of Art, Peary-MacMillan Arctic Museum, deep-sea fishing. **Additional Information:** Chamber of Commerce of the Bath-Brunswick Region, (207) 725-8797 or (207) 443-9751; www.midcoastmaine.com.

Restrictions

Pets: No. **Fires:** In fire rings only. **Alcoholic Beverages:** At sites only. **Vehicle Maximum Length:** None. **Other:** 14-day max. stay per site.

To Get There

From junction of Rtes. 1 and 24, go 3.75 mi. south on Rte. 24, then 0.5 mi. southeast on Board Rd., then 0.5 mi. east on Meadow Rd. Campground entrance is on the right.

CAMDEN

Camden Hills State Park

280 Belfast Rd., Camden 04843. T: (207) 236-3109 or (207) 236-0849 (off-season); www.state.me.us/doc/prkslands/reserve/htm.

RV ★★★ Tent ★★★★★

Beauty: ★★★★★ Site Privacy: ★★★
Spaciousness: ★★★★ Quiet: ★★★
Security: ★★★★★ Cleanliness: ★★★★★
Insect Control: ★★★ Facilities: ★★★★

Psst. Want to enjoy some of the best views in Maine, or (we'll go out on a limb here) all of New England? Camp here, and drive, or hike to the summit of 800-foot Mt. Battie. From there, climb 26 steps up a stone tower for panoramic views of Penobscot Bay, dotted with sailboats and gem-like islands. You'll feel like you're on top of the (very gorgeous) world. Look for the Edna St. Vincent Millay poem etched on ar rock here, inspired by this spot. There are 25 miles of hiking trails here, including another mountain summit, Mt. Megunticook, elevation 1380 feet. Bring those hiking boots. On one side of the park is Mt. Battie; on the other side is the camping area. Some sites are woody, others are open and grassy. Some, alas, are stony. Site 60L, known as the "Honeymoon Suite," is huge and secluded. We like sites 75M through 81M, on the far side of the property, for tenting. 75M and 81M are real beauties. Good features include new countertops and baby changing stations in the ladies' rest room. Bad features are the black flies, who take over in May.

Basics

Operated By: Maine Dept. of Conservation, Bureau of Parks & Lands. **Open:** May 15–Oct. 15. **Site Assignment:** In spring & fall, camping is on a first-come, first-served basis. For summer stays, reservations open on the first business day in Jan. From June 15 to the night before Labor Day, sites may be reserved for a min. of 2 nights & up to 2 weeks. Reservations recommended in July & Aug., at least 2 weeks in advance. Full payment is charged to credit card when reservation is processed. Refund with $15 cancellation fee. 24 sites are non-reservable, & available on a first-come, first-served basis. **Registration:** At office. **Fee:** $13, Maine residents; $17, non-residents, plus $2 fee if you reserve in advance. V, MC. **Parking:** At sites & hikers lot only.

Facilities

Number of RV Sites: 107. **Number of Tent-Only Sites:** 0. **Hookups:** None. **Each Site:** Picnic table, fireplace. **Dump Station:** Yes. **Laundry:** No. **Pay Phone:** Yes. **Rest Rooms and Showers:** Yes. **Fuel:** No. **Propane:** No. **Internal Roads:** Gravel, in good condition. **RV Service:** No. **Market:** 2 mi.south. **Restaurant:** 2 mi. south. **General Store:** No. **Vending:** No. **Swimming Pool:** No. **Playground:** Yes. **Other:** Rec room. **Activities:** Hiking (25 mi. of trails), scenic drive or hike to summit of Mt. Battie. **Nearby Attractions:** Camden galleries, museums & shops), windjammer fleet, Penobscot Bay cruises, Conway Homestead & Mary Cramer Museum (28th century restored farmhouse & gardens), Camden Hills State Park, Merryspring Park, Owl's Head Transportation Museum, golf, ocean swimming. **Additional Information:** Rockport-Camden-Lincolnville Chamber of Commerce, (207) 236-4404; (800) 223-5459.

Restrictions

Pets: Must be leashed, quiet, & cleaned up after. Must not be left unattended. **Fires:** In fireplaces. **Alcoholic Beverages:** No. **Vehicle Maximum Length:** None. **Other:** No pets on beach.

To Get There

From junction of Rtes. 105 and Rte. 1, go 2 mi. northeast on Rte. 1. Campground entrance is on the left.

CANAAN

Skowhegan/Canaan KOA

P.O. Box 87, Canaan 04924. T: (207) 474-2858 (800) 562-7571 (reservations); www.koa.com; skowkoa@kynd.net.

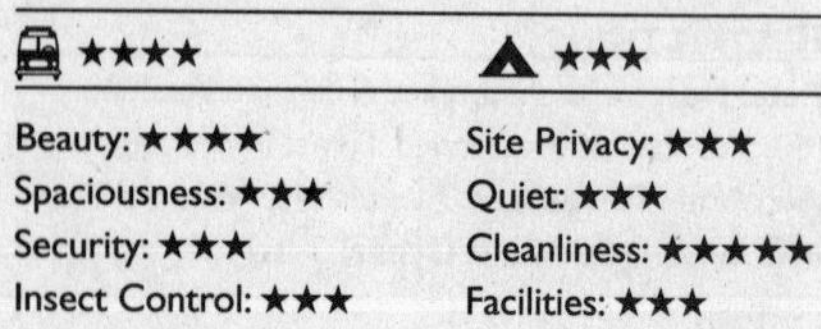

RV ★★★★ Tent ★★★

Beauty: ★★★★ Site Privacy: ★★★
Spaciousness: ★★★ Quiet: ★★★
Security: ★★★ Cleanliness: ★★★★★
Insect Control: ★★★ Facilities: ★★★

This woodsy campground in central Maine is a perfect base for exploring Maine's western lakes and mountains or mid-coastal beaches. There's also whitewater rafting, top-notch stream and lake fishing, hiking and biking, and plenty of good antiquing nearby. The country setting, spread over 60 acres, is pleasant in the summer (try blueberry picking along the trails) and gorgeous in the fall, when the mountains and valleys are awash in fiery hues. Hiking and biking trails take off from the property and, during the summer, there are planned activities to keep families happy. Facilities are white-glove clean, staff helpful and friendly, and atmosphere decidedly low-key. There are 45 spacious pull-throughs, and a separate tent-only area, nestled in the woods. The campground is a pleasant great woods getaway and jumping off point for lots of outdoor recreation.

Basics

Operated By: Tom Kennedy. **Open:** May 15–Oct. 15. **Site Assignment:** Reservations not required; credit card will hold site, 24-hour cancellation policy. **Registration:** At office. **Fee:** Full hookups, $28; water & electric, $26; no hookups, $20, based on 2 adults & 2 children under 10; additional adult, $5; additional child, $3. **Parking:** At site.

Facilities

Number of RV Sites: 86. **Number of Tent-Only Sites:** 14. **Hookups:** Water, electric, sewer (20, 30, 50 amps), cabel TV, modem. **Each Site:** Picnic table, fire ring. **Dump Station:** Yes. **Laundry:** Yes. **Pay Phone:** Yes. **Rest Rooms and Showers:** Yes. **Fuel:** No. **Propane:** Yes. **Internal Roads:** Gravel, dirt (good). **RV Service:** No. **Market:** Skowhegan (10 mi). **Restaurant:** Yes. **General Store:** Yes. **Vending:** Yes. **Swimming Pool:** Yes. **Playground:** Yes. **Other:** Game room, TV room, sports fields, pavilion, nature trails, bike rentals, cabin rentals. **Activities:** Swimming, hiking, biking, softball, volleyball, basketball, horseshoes, badminton, planned activities, including socials, contests, & group hikes. **Nearby Attractions:** western mountains & lakes, midcoast parks & beaches, Bangor. **Additional Information:** Skowhegan Area Chamber of Commerce, 10 Russell St., Skowhegan, ME 04976 (207) 474-3621, www.skowheganchamber.com.

Restrictions

Pets: Must be on a leash, never left unattended. **Fires:** In grills, stoves, & fire rings only. **Alcoholic Beverages:** At site only. **Vehicle Maximum Length:** None.

To Get There

From I-95, exit 36, go north 6 mi. on Rte. 201, then north 7 mi. on Rte. 23, then 0.6 mi. east on Rte. 2; campground is on the right.

CASCO

Point Sebago Golf and Beach Resort

261 Point Sebago Rd., Casco 04015. T: (207) 655-3821 or (800) 655-1232; F: (207) 655-3371; www.pointsebago.com; info@pointsebago.com.

RV ★★★★ | Tent ★★★

Beauty: ★★★★	Site Privacy: ★★
Spaciousness: ★★★★	Quiet: ★★
Security: ★★★★★	Cleanliness: ★★★★★
Insect Control: ★★★	Facilities: ★★★★★

One look at busy Chippy's Pavilion on the beach, and you'd swear you were at a theme park. "Number 32, your onion rings are ready," a voice chirps over the P.A. system. Meanwhile, groups of T-shirt-clad counselors are lining up small fry for scooter races. Just another summer day at Point Sebago, set on southwestern Maine's Lake Sebago, where adults can play golf on one of the finest courses in the state, while the kids chum around with their own kind in an award-winning program, from 9 to 5, if you choose. Kids' programs are split into five groups, by age, and supervised by 40 energetic young counselors. And if you think the fun stops when night falls, you've never been to Point Sebago's Vaudeville Night or the family bonfire. So what's the camping like? Sites are shaded, gravel, and mostly back-in; size and levelness vary. Tents and RVs are intermingled; we noticed that their rental units get the prime spots. If you like to be near the action, sites 801 to 811 are good for RVers, while sites along Red Rd., numbered 601 to 621, are pretty and wooded. Sites 901 to 929 back up into woods and seem fairly quiet. The place is sprawling, people are everywhere, and the place smells like French fries, not woodsmoke. But, how often do you find a camping place with a boutiques, a cybercafe, and great golf?

Basics

Operated By: Larry & Anna Gould. **Open:** May 1–Oct. 31. **Site Assignment:** Reservations recommended. Opens up for following year in mid-June. 50% deposit due within 10 days of making reservation. Refund for cancellation w/ 45-day notice prior to arrival date, minus $25 service charge. **Registration:** At office. **Fee:** $168–$378 per week (during Family Value Weeks) or $280–$420. V, MC, D. **Parking:** At site.

Facilities

Number of RV Sites: 250. **Number of Tent-Only Sites:** 0. **Hookups:** Water, electric (20, 30, 50 amps), sewer. **Each Site:** Picnic table, fireplace. **Dump Station:** Yes. **Laundry:** Yes. **Pay Phone:** Yes. **Rest Rooms and Showers:** Yes. **Fuel:** No. **Propane:** Yes. **Internal Roads:** Gravel, in good condition. **RV Service:** Yes. **Market:** 5 mi. west. **Restaurant:** Yes. **General Store:** Yes. **Vending:** Yes. **Swimming Pool:** No. **Playground:** Yes. **Other:** Cyber cafe, marina, golf (championship course). **Activities:** Lake swimming, golf, tennis, archery, boating (rentals available), boat cruises aboard the Point Sebago Princess, fishing (licenses available), waterskiing (lessons available), mini-golf, basketball, ballfield, shuffleboard, children's program, planned activities. **Nearby Attractions:** Golf, mini-golf, seaplane rides, boat cruises, Songo River Queen paddleboat, Douglas Mountain hiking, Sebago Lake State Park, outlet shopping (North Conway, N.H.). **Additional Information:** Naples Business Assoc., (207) 693-3285.

Restrictions

Pets: Only in one's own unit (not in rentals) & in specific areas. **Fires:** In fireplaces only. **Alcoholic Beverages:** Yes. **Vehicle Maximum Length:** 48 ft. **Other:** 7-day min. stay in peak season (third week of June through Labor Day.).

To Get There

From Maine Turnpike, take exit 8; travel 22 mi. on Rte. 302 to Point Sebago Rd.; proceed left to resort.

CASCO/NAPLES

Sebago Lake State Park

11 Park Access Rd., Casco 04015. T: (207) 693-6321 or (800) 332-1501 (reservations or ME number) or (207) 287-3824 (reservations or out of state); F: (207) 287-6170; www.state.me.us/doc/prkslands/reserve/htm.

RV ★★★ | Tent ★★★

Beauty: ★★★★★	Site Privacy: ★★
Spaciousness: ★★★	Quiet: ★★
Security: ★★★	Cleanliness: ★★★★
Insect Control: ★★★★	Facilities: ★★★★

One of Maine's most beloved recreation areas, Sebago Lake State Park offers campers the opportunity to sleep along the sandy shores of Maine's deepest and second-largest lake. It's a real beauty spot, featuring woodlands of tall pine and oak, bogs and ponds. Weekends in summer book up really early, but you can often luck out with a great lakeside spot during the week (we did). Campsites are set in three sections: Naples Beach, Witch Cove Beach, and a hike-in tenting area near the amphitheater (offering more privacy than the other areas, if you don't mind carrying your gear from a nearby parking lot.) Sites 31M, non-reservable, and 30L, on Naples Beach, are awesome. Lakefront sites on Witch Cove Beach include 138M, 149L, 163M, and 164M (the letters refer to site size, small, medium, large or extra-large.) If you choose to tent at one of these, you probably won't enjoy the quietest night of your life, in spite of the park's supposed 'quiet hours.' If you're in an RV, you won't notice. And you'll no doubt forgive all when you step into the ripply-sand-bottomed lake for that morning swim.

Basics

Operated By: Maine Dept. of Conservation, Bureau of Parks & Lands. **Open:** May 1–Oct. 15. **Site Assignment:** In spring & fall, camping is on a first-come, first-served basis. For summer stays, reservations open on the first business day in Jan. From June 15 to the night before Labor Day, sites may be reserved for a min. of 2 nights & up to 2 weeks. (Note: This park is heavily-visited. For full details on how to best secure a site in season, see website or write to: Dept. of Conservation, Attn: Reservations, 22 SHS, Aug.a, ME 04333.) Full payment is charged to credit card when reservation is processed. Refund with $15 cancellation fee. About 40 sites are non-reservable, & available on a first-come, first-served basis. **Registration:** At office. **Fee:** $13 for Maine residents; $17 for non-residents; $2 extra charge if you reserve in advance. V, MC. **Parking:** At site.

Facilities

Number of RV Sites: 250. **Number of Tent-Only Sites:** 0. **Hookups:** None. **Each Site:** Picnic table, fireplace. **Dump Station:** Yes. **Laundry:** No. **Pay Phone:** Yes. **Rest Rooms and Showers:** Yes. **Fuel:** No. **Propane:** No. **Internal Roads:** Gravel, in good condition. **RV Service:** No. **Market:** 5 mi. north. **Restaurant:** 5 mi. north. **General Store:** No. **Vending:** No. **Swimming Pool:** No. **Playground:** Yes. **Other:** Boat launch. **Activities:** Hiking, lake swimming, ball field, volleyball, interpretive programs. **Nearby Attractions:** Golf, mini-golf, seaplane rides, boat cruises, Songo River Queen paddleboat, Douglas Mountain hiking, outlet shopping (N. Conway, NH). **Additional Information:** Greater Windham Chamber of Commerce, (207) 892-8265; www.windhamchamber.sebagolake.org.

Restrictions

Pets: No. **Fires:** In fire rings only. **Alcoholic Beverages:** No. **Vehicle Maximum Length:** 35 ft. **Other:** 2-week max. stay between last week in June & Labor Day.

To Get There

From junction of Rtes. 302 East and 11/114, go 4 mi. south on Rte. 302 E, then 2.5 mi. west to campground entrance.

DAMARISCOTTA

Lake Pemaquid Camping

P.O. Box 967, Damariscotta 04543. T: (207) 563-5202; lincoln.midcoast.com/~lakepem.

RV ★★★ Tent ★

Beauty: ★★ Site Privacy: ★
Spaciousness: ★ Quiet: ★
Security: ★★★★★ Cleanliness: ★★★
Insect Control: ★★★★★ Facilities: ★★★

A little bit of privacy, a lot of amusements—that's the best way to describe this very popular family campground on Maine's mid-coast, about 50 miles north of Portland. This sprawling place, set on seven-mile Lake Pemaquid, isn't the most manicured campground you'll ever see; piles of dead autumn leaves are still laying around in mid-July. But the families who show up to ride Chucky's Choo-Choo train, swim in the pool, and paddle around in pedal boats don't seem to mind. How often do you see a skate board area at a campground, and outdoor hot tubs? Rustic-style facilities include a restaurant that serves shore dinners. Campsites are wooded with pine, oak, and birch. There's about a mile of lakeside camping. Some sites have boat docks. We'd skip these, though—too crowded—and head for the more peaceful spots along Goose Cove (sites 16 through 18 are nice) and 250 through 253 (not on the water, but pleasant.) You might need a vacation after a visit here, but you're sure to have a good time.

Basics

Operated By: Rebecca Bickmore & Clayton Howard. **Open:** Memorial Day–Columbus Day. **Site Assignment:** Reservations recommended. Deposit of payment in full required for stays of less than 7 days. For longer stays, 50% deposit due. Refund for cancellations w/ 2-week notice, minus $10 service charge. **Registration:** At office. **Fee:** $20–$37 based on 5 people. V, MC, AE, Novus, debit cards. **Parking:** At sites or parking lots only.

Facilities

Number of RV Sites: 290. **Number of Tent-Only Sites:** 0. **Hookups:** Water, electric (20, 30, 50 amps), sewer, modem access. **Each Site:** Picnic table, fire ring. **Dump Station:** Yes. **Laundry:** Yes. **Pay Phone:** Yes. **Rest Rooms and Showers:** Yes, coin-op. **Fuel:** No. **Propane:** Yes. **Internal Roads:** Gravel, in fair condition. **RV Service:** No. **Market:** 5 mi. south. **Restaurant:** Yes. **General Store:** Yes. **Vending:** Yes. **Swimming Pool:** Yes. **Playground:** Yes. **Other:** Boat ramp & slips, rec hall, hot tubs, skate board park, kiddie train ride. **Activities:** Boating (rentals available), fishing (licenses available), tennis, basketball, volleyball, lake swimming, planned activities. **Nearby Attractions:** Ocean beaches, Maine windjammer fleet, Boothbay Railway train rides, golf. **Additional Information:** Damariscotta Region Chamber of Commerce, (207) 563-8340; Damariscotta Region Information Bureau, (207) 563-3176.

Restrictions

Pets: Must be leashed, quiet, & cleaned up after. Must not be left unattended. Not allowed on beach or in pool area. **Fires:** In fireplaces. **Alcoholic Beverages:** At sites only. **Vehicle Maximum Length:** None. **Other:** Lakeside sites available for Saturday to Saturday only during July & Aug. 3-night min. on holidays.

To Get There

Take Maine Turnpike to exit 9, Falmouth/Rte. 1. Follow Rte. 95 to Brunswick, then take Rte. 1 to Bus. Rte. 1. Exit at Damariscotta. Head north from Damariscotta on Bus. Rte. 1 to Biscay Rd. (Turn right after McDonald's.) Follow signs to campground.

DOVER-FOXCROFT

Peaks-Kenny State Park

Rte. 1, P.O. Box 10, Dover-Foxcroft 04426. T: (207) 564-2003; www.state.me.us/doc/parks.htm.

RV ★★ Tent ★★★★

Beauty: ★★★ Site Privacy: ★★★★
Spaciousness: ★★★★ Quiet: ★★★★
Security: ★★★★ Cleanliness: ★★★★
Insect Control: ★★★ Facilities: ★★★

Set right in the heart of the state, about 45 miles northwest of Bangor, maybe 30 miles southeast of Greenville, this state park offers a pleasant day-use beach and picnic area, plus canoe rentals and hiking trails. No wonder it's so popular with families. A porkchop-shaped camping area is set along the south cove of 12-mile Sebec Lake. Trivia note: Benign as the lake looks, it reaches depths up to 160 feet, and divers have discovered shipwrecks here. A grassy slope leads to a nice, wide swimming area, sort of pebbly-bottomed. Most campers can't resist renting a canoe and paddling 'round the coastline. The campground is nicely forested,with big boulders providing rustic seating at some sites. The sites farthest from the beach are but a 10-minute walk to the shore, while the beachside sites aren't quite on the water, but have walking paths to the beach. Some of the choicest include sites 22S, 24S, 56X, and 54X (the letters referring to the size of the site; 'S' as in small, 'X' as in extra-large.) With swimming, canoeing, and nine miles of hiking trails, there's plenty to do here, and there's always the possibility of seeing a moose (though deer are more likely!)

Basics

Operated By: Maine Dept. of Conservation, Bureau of Parks & Lands. **Open:** May 15–Sept. 30. **Site Assignment:** In spring & fall, camping is on a first-come, first-served basis. For summer stays, reservations open on the first business day in Jan. From June 15 to the night before Labor Day, sites may be reserved for a min. of 2 nights & up to 2 weeks. Full payment is charged to credit card when reservation is processed. Refund with $15 cancellation fee. 14 sites are non-reservable, & available on a first-come, first-served basis. Call the reservations line to cancel a reservation more than 3 days in advance. If cancelling less than 3 days in advance, call the park directly. **Registration:** At office. **Fee:** $13, Maine residents; $17, non-residents plus $2 fee if reserving in advance. V, MC. **Parking:** At site.

Facilities

Number of RV Sites: 56. **Number of Tent-Only Sites:** 0. **Hookups:** None. **Each Site:** Picnic table, fire ring. **Dump Station:** Yes. **Laundry:** No. **Pay Phone:** Yes. **Rest Rooms and Showers:** Yes, coin-op. **Fuel:** No. **Propane:** No. **Internal Roads:** Gravel, in good condition. **RV Service:** No. **Market:** 8 mi. south. **Restaurant:** 8 mi. south. **General Store:** No. **Vending:** No. **Swimming Pool:** No. **Playground:** Yes. **Other:** Guarded sand beach. **Activities:** Lake swimming (lifeguards), canoeing (rentals available), hiking trails. **Nearby Attractions:** Blacksmith Shop Museum. **Additional Information:** Southern Piscataquis County Chamber of Commerce, (207) 564-7533.

Restrictions

Pets: Must be leashed, quiet, & cleaned up after. Must not be left unattended. Not allowed on beach. **Fires:** In fire rings only. **Alcoholic Beverages:** No. **Vehicle Maximum Length:** 45 ft. **Other:** 2-week max. stay between last week in June & Labor Day.

To Get There

From Dover-Foxcroft, go 6 mi. north on Rte. 153 (Greeley Landing Rd.), left at State Park Rd.

EAST ORLAND

Balsam Cove

P.O. Box C, Back Ridge Rd., East ORland 04431. T: (207) 469-7771 (800) 469-7771 (reservations); F: (207) 469-0065; www.holidayguide.com/campusa/maine/balsam-cove; c27young@aol.com.

RV ★★★ Tent ★★★

Beauty: ★★★ Site Privacy: ★★★
Spaciousness: ★★★ Quiet: ★★★★
Security: ★★★★ Cleanliness: ★★★
Insect Control: ★★★ Facilities: ★★★

This modest campground, located midway between Bucksport and Ellsworth, (within an hour's drive to Acadia National Park) offers relaxed lakeside camping. Families enjoy the sandy beach area and the warm, shallow waters. There are boats to rent for paddling and fishing and, at night, a campground bonfire for roasting marshmallows. The long drive into the campground, a mile off busy Rte. 1, helps keep the atmosphere subdued and quiet. Sites are a bit helter-skelter placed in rows and loops throughout the property. There are larger pull-through sites near the front of the campground and a handful of beachfront and water view sites. Families may like sites 14-19 across from the swimming area and playground. One of two campgrounds in the area on pristine Toddy Pond (also see Whispering Pines), Balsam Cove offers a few more facilities (laundry, general store) but less rustic charm.

Basics

Operated By: Sharon & Charlie Young. **Open:** Memorial Day–Sept. **Site Assignment:** Reservations suggested in Jul.–Aug. 50 percent deposit required, 14-day cancellation policy with $10 service fee; MC, V, D, checks. **Registration:** At office. **Fee:** Full hookups, $22; waterfront (20 amp), $22; waterfront (no hookups), $19; wooded (30 amp), $20; wooded (20 amp), $19; wooded (no hookups), $17, based on 2 adults & 2 children under 18. **Parking:** At site.

Facilities

Number of RV Sites: 56. **Number of Tent-Only Sites:** 4. **Hookups:** Water, electric (30 amps). **Each Site:** Picnic table, fire ring. **Dump Station:** Yes. **Laundry:** Yes. **Pay Phone:** Yes. **Rest Rooms and Showers:** Yes. **Fuel:** No. **Propane:** No. **Internal Roads:** Gravel (good). **RV Service:** No. **Market:** Bucksport (6 mi). **Restaurant:** No. **General Store:** Yes. **Vending:** Yes. **Swimming Pool:** No. **Playground:** Yes. **Other:** Lake frontage, beach, rowboat, canoe & paddleboat rentals, docks, boat ramp, rec room, group tent area, cabin rentals. **Activities:** Swimming, boating, fishing, basketball, horseshoes. **Nearby Attractions:** Deer Isle Peninsula, Bar Harbor, Acadia National Park. **Additional Information:** Bucksport Bay Area Chamber of Commerce, P.O. Box 1880, 263 Main St., Bucksport, ME 04416-1880 (207) 469-6818 & Acadia Information Center, P.O. Box 139, Mount Desert, ME 04660 (207) 667-8550 or (800) 358-8550, www.acadiainfo.com.

Restrictions

Pets: Must be on a leash, never left unattended. No pets allowed on waterfront sites. 1 pet per site; some breeds not allowed. **Fires:** In grills, stoves, & fire rings only. **Alcoholic Beverages:** At site only. **Vehicle Maximum Length:** 35 ft.

To Get There

From junction Rtes. 1 and 15 (in East Orland), go north 1.7 mi. on Rte. 1, then south 1.5 mi. on Back Ridge Rd.; campground is 1 mi. east on entrance road.

EAST ORLAND

Whispering Pines

US Rte. 1, Gen. Del., East Orland 04431. T: (207) 469-3443; www.campmaine.com/whispering-pines; wpines04431@aol.com.

RV ★★★ Tent ★★★

Beauty: ★★★★	Site Privacy: ★★★★
Spaciousness: ★★★★	Quiet: ★★★★★
Security: ★★★★	Cleanliness: ★★★
Insect Control: ★★★	Facilities: ★★

This small lakeside campground, within commuting distance to Deer Isle Peninsula to the south and Acadia National Park to the north, oozes old-fashioned charm. A stay here is akin to visiting family and friends at their summer cottage and owners Dwight and Sandy Gates do everything they can to make you feel at home. The rustic, woodsy setting, along the shores of Toddy Pond, is scenic and tranquil: birds sing in the pines; loons call at dusk; beavers and otters frolick in the water. "Pond" is a misnomer; it runs 9.7 miles long and 130 feet deep. Relaxing is top activity here, but there's swimming and boating and the fishing, for landlocked salmon, lake trout and bass, is good. ("We're not an entertainment center," owner Sandy readily admits.) There is a handful of seasonal renters, an older clientele who come for the natural setting and peace and quiet. But there are plenty of sites to rent on a nightly basis. Most sites are clustered in the woods but there are a few on the water. Roomy sites B4 and B5, next to the beach, are most popular and are often booked a year in advance.

Basics

Operated By: Dwight & Sandy Gates. **Open:** Memorial Day–Sept. **Site Assignment:** Reservations suggested. $25 deposit, 3-day cancellation policy; no credit cards, checks accepted. **Registration:** At office. **Fee:** $23 for 2 adults; $1 each child; $1 for electricity; $1 for sewer; $3 extra adult. **Parking:** At site.

Facilities

Number of RV Sites: 45. **Number of Tent-Only Sites:** 5. **Hookups:** Water, electric, sewer (20 amps). **Each Site:** Picnic table, fire ring. **Dump Station:** Yes. **Laundry:** No. **Pay Phone:** No. **Rest Rooms and Showers:** Yes. **Fuel:** No. **Propane:** No. **Internal Roads:** Gravel, dirt (fair). **RV Service:** No. **Market:** Bucksport (6 mi). **Restaurant:** No. **General Store:** No. **Vending:** No. **Swimming Pool:** No. **Playground:** Yes. **Other:** Lake frontage, beach, dock, picnic area, game room, canoe, rowboats & bicycles to use (free). **Activities:** Swimming, fishing, boating, volleyball, horseshoes. **Nearby Attractions:** Deer Isle Peninsula, Bar Harbor, Acadia National Park. **Additional Information:** Bucksport Bay Area Chamber of Commerce, P.O. Box 1880, 263 Main St., Bucksport, ME 04416-1880 (207) 469-6818 & Acadia Information Center, P.O. Box 139, Mount Desert, ME 04660 (207) 667-8550 or (800) 358-8550, www.acadiainfo.com.

Restrictions

Pets: Must be on a leash, never left unattended. **Fires:** In grills, stoves, & fire rings only. **Alcoholic Beverages:** At site only. **Vehicle Maximum Length:** None.

To Get There

From junction Rtes. 1 and 15 (in East Orland), go north 2 mi. on Rte. 1; campground is on the right.

ELLSWORTH

Branch Lake Camping Area

180 Hansons Landing Rd., Ellsworth 04605. T: (207) 667-5174; www.campmaine.com.

RV ★★★ Tent ★★★

Beauty: ★★★	Site Privacy: ★★★
Spaciousness: ★★★	Quiet: ★★★
Security: ★★★	Cleanliness: ★★★
Insect Control: ★★★	Facilities: ★★★

This small lakeside campground is located halfway between Ellsworth and Bangor and a short drive to Bar Harbor and Acadia National Park. Set on the shores of 10-mile-long, spring-fed Branch Lake, the campground is a quiet getaway with pretty views of the crystal clear lake dotted with rocky, pine covered islands. Bring your boat (there's dock space if you reserve early) or rent a canoe from the campground. The campground's 175 feet of lake frontage includes a swimming beach and fishing pier. The sites are set randomly throughout the campground, tucked here and there under the trees and around scattered boulders; larger sites are angled in rows, furthest away from the beach area. Tenters may be frustrated. The separate tent area is tiny and has a view of the cluster of RV sites.

Basics

Operated By: Dick & Brenda Graves. **Open:** May–Sept. **Site Assignment:** Reservations suggested, 1 night deposit, 7-day cancellation policy, 2-night min. stay in Jul.–Aug.; MC, V, checks accepted. **Registration:** At office. **Fee:** Full hookups, $25; water & electric, $22, no hookups, $18, based on 2 adults & 3 children under 18. **Parking:** At site.

Facilities

Number of RV Sites: 46. **Number of Tent-Only Sites:** 4. **Hookups:** Water, electric, sewer (30 amps). **Each Site:** Picnic table, fire ring. **Dump Station:** Yes. **Laundry:** No. **Pay Phone:** Yes. **Rest Rooms and Showers:** Yes (coin-op). **Fuel:** No. **Propane:** No. **Internal Roads:** Gravel, dirt (fair). **RV Service:** No. **Market:** Ellsworth (8 mi). **Restaurant:** No. **General Store:** Yes. **Vending:** Yes. **Swimming Pool:** No. **Playground:** Yes. **Other:** Lake frontage, beach, boat launch, boat dock, boat & canoe rentals. **Activities:** Swimming, boating, fishing, horseshoes, potluck dinners. **Nearby Attractions:** Bangor, Bar Harbor, Acadia National Park. **Additional Information:** Ellsworth Area Chamber of Commerce, P.O. Box 267, Ellsworth, ME 04605 (207) 667-5584 & Acadia Information Center, P.O. Box 139, Mount Desert, ME 04660 (207) 667-8550 or (800) 358-8550, www.acadiainfo.com.

Restrictions

Pets: Must be on a leash, never left unattended. 2 dogs per site; some breeds not allowed. **Fires:** In grills, stoves, & fire rings only. **Alcoholic Beverages:** At site only. **Vehicle Maximum Length:** None.

To Get There

From junction Rte. 1 and 1A (in Ellsworth), go northwest 10 mi. on Rte. 1A, then southwest (left) 0.5 mi. on Winkumpaugh Rd., then south 1 mi. on Hanson Landing Rd.; campground is on the left.

ELLSWORTH
Lamoine State Park

RR 2 Box 194, Ellsworth 04605.
T: (207) 667-4778; www.state.me.us/doc/prksInds/lamoine.htm.

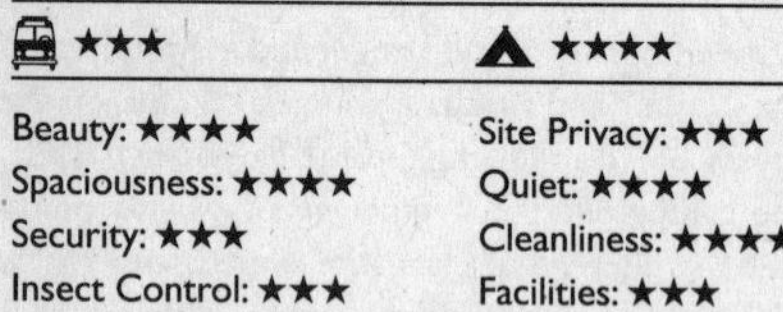

RV ★★★ Tent ★★★★

Beauty: ★★★★ Site Privacy: ★★★
Spaciousness: ★★★★ Quiet: ★★★★
Security: ★★★ Cleanliness: ★★★★
Insect Control: ★★★ Facilities: ★★★

The view of the ocean, the cool ocean breezes (even on the muggiest summer afternoons), the potent scents of evergreen forest blended with the salty tang of the ocean, and the aroma of woodsmoke drifting as the day draws to an end all help to make Lamoine State Park an excellent campground selection. The whole gestalt here is that of being on a windswept, oceanside bluff—which you are. The camping sites, like the park itself, run the gamut from sunny, breezy, spacious, and open and to densely forested, isolated, and tiny. Either way, you can't lose. There's a short path down to the water right across from site 49; and there's also the one-mile Loop Trail for those in need of a little exercise. Take a moment after you've set up your campsite to sit back, draw in a deep breath, and enjoy the sights, sounds, and scents of this oceanside campground.

Basics

Operated By: Maine Dept. of Conservation. **Open:** Mid-May–mid-Oct. **Site Assignment:** Reservations or first come first served. **Registration:** At ranger station. **Fee:** $13–$17; additional $2 per night for reservations. **Parking:** At site.

Facilities

Number of RV Sites: 61. **Number of Tent-Only Sites:** 0. **Hookups:** None. **Each Site:** Fire ring, picnic table. **Dump Station:** No. **Laundry:** No. **Pay Phone:** No. **Rest Rooms and Showers:** Yes. **Fuel:** No. **Propane:** No. **Internal Roads:** Gravel. **RV Service:** No. **Market:** No. **Restaurant:** No. **General Store:** No. **Vending:** No. **Swimming Pool:** No. **Playground:** Yes. **Other:** Boat launch. **Activities:** Boating, swimming, saltwater fishing. **Nearby Attractions:** Arcadia National Park, area lighthouses. **Additional Information:** (207) 941-4014.

Restrictions

Pets: On leash. **Fires:** In fire ring. **Alcoholic Beverages:** At site. **Vehicle Maximum Length:** 30 ft. **Other:** Max. 6 people per party, 14-night max. stay during the summer.

To Get There

The campground is on ME Rte. 184, 8 mi. southeast from Ellsworth.

ELLSWORTH
Patten Pond Camping Resort

1470 Bucksport Rd., Ellsworth 04605. T: (207) 667-7600 or (877) 667-7376; www.pattenpond.com.

RV ★★★★★ Tent ★★★

Beauty: ★★★★ Site Privacy: ★★★
Spaciousness: ★★★ Quiet: ★★★
Security: ★★★★ Cleanliness: ★★★★★
Insect Control: ★★★★ Facilities: ★★★★★

This lively, modern camping resort, a half-hour from Bar Harbor and Acadia National Park, offers an array of activities and top-notch facilities. It's located on pretty Patten Pond, a crystal clear freshwater lake, dotted with rocky islands and flanked by pine tree forests. There's a sandy stretch of beach, a favorite hangout at the campground, with a fishing pier, boat dock, and viewing/sunning deck. When campers are not on the lake, they're buzzing about the campground, taking part in a host of activities: live entertainment, movies, kid's programs, Sunday morning church services, lobster bakes, and more.Most campers use the resort as a base to explore the area, near enough to major attractions but far enough from the summer traffic and commotion of the Bar Harbor area. Sites are uniform throughout the campground, most with three-way hookups, set side-by-side in rows. (No sites are on the water.) There's a separate tenting area that backs up to sparse woods.

Basics

Operated By: Pat Stanley. **Open:** May–Oct. **Site Assignment:** Reservations accepted year-round, suggested in Jul.–Aug. All sites require a 2 night min. reservation, 3-night min. on holiday weekends, $50 deposit required for 3 nights, $75 for 4–7 nights, $100 for 8 nights or more, 14-day cancellation policy with $10 service charge. Holidays are paid in full & non-refundable; MC, V, D, checks accepted for reservations; no checks upon arrival. **Registration:** At office. **Fee:** Full hookups (best, 50 amp), $37 peak, $29 early & late summer; full hookups (50 amp), $35–$28; full hookups (best, 30 amp), $32–$26; full hookup (30 amp), $29–$24; water & electric, $26–$20; best tent, $20–$17; tent, $18–$15, based on 2 adults & 2 children under 18. **Parking:** At site.

Facilities

Number of RV Sites: 113. **Number of Tent-Only Sites:** 37. **Hookups:** Water, electric, sewer (30, 50 amps), modem. **Each Site:** Picnic table, fire ring. **Dump Station:** Yes. **Laundry:** Yes. **Pay Phone:** Yes. **Rest Rooms and Showers:** Yes. **Fuel:** No. **Propane:** Yes. **Internal Roads:** Gravel, dirt (good). **RV Service:** Yes. **Market:** Ellsworth (9 mi). **Restaurant:** No. **General Store:** Yes. **Vending:** No. **Swimming Pool:** No. **Playground:** Yes. **Other:** Lake frontage, beach, fishing pier, dock, paddleboat, sailboat, kayak & canoe rentals, entertainment pavilion, cabin, cottage & apartment rentals, gift store, game room, modem center, car rentals on site. **Activities:** Swimming, boating, fishing, basketball, volleyball, planned activities, including live entertainment, children's programs, lobster bakes. **Nearby Attractions:** Bar Harbor, Acadia National Park. **Additional Information:** Ellsworth Area Chamber of Commerce, P.O. Box 267, Ellsworth, ME 04605 (207) 667-5584 & Acadia Information Center, P.O. Box 139, Mount Desert, ME 04660 (207) 667-8550 or (800) 358-8550, www.acadiainfo.com.

Restrictions

Pets: Must be on a leash, never left unattended. **Fires:** In grills, stoves, & fire rings only. **Alcoholic Beverages:** At site only. **Vehicle Maximum Length:** None.

To Get There

From junction Rtes. 1 and 1A (in Ellsworth), go southwest 7.5 mi. on Rte. 1; campground is on the left.

EUSTIS
Cathedral Pines

P.O. Box 146, Eustis 04936. T: (207) 246-3491.

RV ★★★★★ Tent ★★★★★

Beauty: ★★★★★ Site Privacy: ★★★★★
Spaciousness: ★★★★★ Quiet: ★★★★
Security: ★★★★ Cleanliness: ★★★★
Insect Control: ★★★★ Facilities: ★★★

Northern California has its redwoods; here in Eustis, Maine, the cathedral pines are famous for their lofty beauty. Happily, campers can enjoy this enchanted setting. Located in the rural Western corner of the state, just 26 miles south of the Canadian border, Cathedral Pines is a non-profit campground, and one of the most scenic in all of New England. Funds go to the towns of Stratton and Eustis, who operate the park. The tall, virgin stand of Norway (red) pines is set on the shores of Flagstaff Lake, where there's a private beach for campers, a public beach, and a picnic area. This site was one of Benedict Arnold's stops during his ill-fated march to Quebec City in 1775. The sand and gravel sites are canopied by the gorgeous pines, with buffer provided by low-growing shrubbery. Campsites are set in loops, including a separate area for tents (no water and electric); tent site 69, on the lake, is stunning. Among the water/electric sites, sites 13, 15, 16, 17, and 18 are nice, big, and lakeside. Three-way hookup sites are situated near the campground's entrance. All sites are widely-spaced, spacious, and private, not to mention jaw-droppingly beautiful. Don't miss this one.

Basics

Operated By: Stratton-Eustis Development Corp. **Open:** May 15–Oct. 1. **Site Assignment:** Reservations recommended. No reservations accepted for less than a 2-night stay. Must pay in full within 10 days of making reservation. No refunds for cancellation; credit for future stay only. **Registration:** At office. **Fee:** $15–$20 for 4 people. V, MC. **Parking:** At site.

Facilities

Number of RV Sites: 115. **Number of Tent-Only Sites:** 0. **Hookups:** Water, electric (30 amps), sewer. **Each Site:** Picnic table, fireplace. **Dump Station:** Yes. **Laundry:** Yes. **Pay Phone:** Yes. **Rest Rooms and Showers:** Yes. **Fuel:** No. **Propane:** No. **Internal Roads:** Paved, in good condition. **RV Service:** No. **Market:** 4 mi. south. **Restaurant:** 4 mi. south. **General Store:** Yes. **Vending:** Yes. **Swimming Pool:** No. **Playground:** Yes. **Other:** Boat ramp, rec hall. **Activities:** Lake swimming, fishing (need license), hiking on Appalachian Trail, bicycling, boating (rentals available). **Nearby Attractions:** Moosewatching, Arnold Trail (follows Benedict Arnold's route to Quebec City), Dead River Historical Society Museum, golf, Bigelow Mountain.

Additional Information: Flagstaff Area Business Assoc., (207) 246-4221; www.eustismaine.com.

Restrictions

Pets: Must be leashed, quiet, & cleaned up after. Must not be left unattended. Not allowed in buildings or beaches. $10 refundable deposit required. **Fires:** In fireplaces only. **Alcoholic Beverages:** Yes. **Vehicle Maximum Length:** 40 ft. **Other:** 3-night min. stay on holidays, payable in advance.

To Get There

From Maine Turnpike, take exit 12 (Auburn) to Rte. 4 north. Connect w/Rte. 27 north in Farmington; follow to Eustis. Campground is on the right. (Total mileage from turnpike is 90 mi.)

EUSTIS
Natanis Point Campground

HC73 P.O. Box 270, Eustis 04936. T: (207) 297-2694 or (207) 645-5207 (winter); www.campmaine.com/natanispointcampground or www.geocites.com/yosemite/cabin/3285/index.html.

RV ★★★ Tent ★★

Beauty: ★★★★ Site Privacy: ★★★★
Spaciousness: ★★★ Quiet: ★★★★
Security: ★★★ Cleanliness: ★★★★
Insect Control: ★★★ Facilities: ★★★

We were all set to overlook this tiny, rustic campground, just six miles south of the Canadian border. But, we couldn't, once we realized one could camp here, on the Chain of Ponds, and wake up to gorgeous views of deep-blue water, flanked by pine-sloped mountains. Wooded campsites are set on two loops, overlooking Round Pond and Natanis Pond. We recommend the Natanis Pond side for best views, especially site 6. Sites 3 through 9 are fabulous; you couldn't be closer to the water unless you slept on your boat. Speaking of which, you can park your boat right alongside your tent or RV, and roll it in when you're ready. Sites 32 through 44 are farthest from the water. (Look for the Natanis Memorial just behind site 9; read about the legend of Natanis, a Native American female trapper, in the campground office.) The owners say this campground is at its best in fall, when the foliage season kicks in; however, the cold comes early here, and they drain the water pipes and close the bathhouse in early Oct. Rates drop to $10 per night.

Basics

Operated By: Ken & Sharon Thomas. **Open:** May 15–Oct. 15. **Site Assignment:** Reservations recommended for weekends. 50% deposit required. Refund for cancellation if made 1 week prior to arrival date. **Registration:** At office. **Fee:** $15 per night for 1 to 4 people. V, MC. **Parking:** At site.

Facilities

Number of RV Sites: 63. **Number of Tent-Only Sites:** 0. **Hookups:** Water. **Each Site:** Picnic table, fire ring. **Dump Station:** Yes. **Laundry:** No. **Pay Phone:** Yes. **Rest Rooms and Showers:** Yes. **Fuel:** No. **Propane:** No. **Internal Roads:** Gravel, in good condition. **RV Service:** No. **Market:** 5 mi. north. **Restaurant:** 5 mi. north. **General Store:** Yes. **Vending:** No. **Swimming Pool:** No. **Playground:** Yes. **Other:** Supper building (rec hall). **Activities:** Fishing (license required), pond swimming, boating (kayak & canoe rentals available), volleyball, ATV trails, planned activities. **Nearby Attractions:** Arnold Trail (follows Benedict Arnold's route to Quebec City), Dead River Historical Society Museum, Flagstaff Lake, golf, Bigelow Mountain. **Additional Information:** Flagstaff Area Business Assoc., (207) 246-4221; www.eustismaine.com.

Restrictions

Pets: Must be leashed, quiet, & cleaned up after. Must not be left unattended. **Fires:** In fire rings ony. **Alcoholic Beverages:** At sites only. **Vehicle Maximum Length:** 35 ft.

To Get There

From Maine Turnpike, take exit 12 (Auburn) to Rte. 4 north. Connect w/Rte. 27 North in Farmington; follow Rte. 27 north to Eustis. Stay on Rte. 27 for 17 mi., heading north. Campground is on the left.

FREEPORT
Cedar Haven

39 Baker Rd., Freeport 04032. T: (207) 865-6254 (800) 454-3403 (reservations); www.campmaine.com/cedarhaven; campcedarhaven@yahoo.com.

RV ★★★ Tent ★★★

Beauty: ★★★ Site Privacy: ★★★
Spaciousness: ★★★ Quiet: ★★★
Security: ★★★ Cleanliness: ★★★
Insect Control: ★★★ Facilities: ★★★

This woodsy campground is just two miles from touristy downtown Freeport, but campers feel worlds away. The modest, family-oriented property has a large sports field, a small (0.25-acre) spring-fed swimming pond (usually full of tiny tots at the end of long summer's day) and roomy sites. Tenters will especially enjoy the shaded, private, hillside sites, offering a natural-setting getaway from the busy Freeport area. (Site 38 set back in the woods is a favorite.) Big rig drivers will find four large-size, full hookup sites and extra wide roads for convenience. Most campers spend the day exploring the area (and outlet shopping) and breathe a heavy sigh of relief by the time they reach their site. Nothing fancy here—just a little peace and quiet.

Basics

Operated By: Private operator. **Open:** May–Oct. **Site Assignment:** Reservations suggested; hold w/ credit card during peak season; no shows charged 1-night fee; MC, V, D; no checks. **Registration:** At office. **Fee:** Full hookup, $30; water & electric, $24; no hookups, $18, based on 2 adults & 2 children under 18. **Parking:** At site.

Facilities

Number of RV Sites: 48. **Number of Tent-Only Sites:** 10. **Hookups:** Water, electric, sewer (30 amps), cable TV. **Each Site:** Picnic table, fire ring, trash barrel. **Dump Station:** Yes. **Laundry:** Yes. **Pay Phone:** Yes. **Rest Rooms and Showers:** Yes (coin-op). **Fuel:** No. **Propane:** Yes. **Internal Roads:** Gravel (good). **RV Service:** No. **Market:** Freeport (2 mi). **Restaurant:** No. **General Store:** Yes. **Vending:** No. **Swimming Pool:** No. **Playground:** Yes. **Other:** Sports field, game room, mini-golf, spring-fed pond, beach, cabin rental, group area. **Activities:** Swimming, horseshoes, mini-golf, volleyball, basketball. **Nearby Attractions:** Freeport, outlet shopping, mid-coast parks & beaches. **Additional Information:** Freeport Merchants Assoc., 23 Depot St., Freeport, ME 04032-0452, (207) 865-1212 (800) 865-0881, www.freeportusa.com.

Restrictions

Pets: Must be on a leash, never left unattended. **Fires:** In grills, stoves, & fire rings only. **Alcoholic Beverages:** At site only. **Vehicle Maximum Length:** None.

To Get There

From I-95, exit 20, go, bear right on Rte.125/136 for 0.5 mi, then turn right on Rte. 125 for 0.5 mi, then right on Baker Rd.; campground is on the left.

FREEPORT
Desert Dunes of Maine Campground

95 Desert Rd., Freeport 04032. T: (207) 865-6962; F: (207) 865-1678; www.desertofmaine.com; info@desertofmaine.com.

RV ★★★ Tent ★★★

Beauty: ★★★ Site Privacy: ★★★
Spaciousness: ★★★ Quiet: ★★★
Security: ★★★ Cleanliness: ★★★
Insect Control: ★★★ Facilities: ★★★

This is the only campground we know of in New England that sits next to—and on top of—a desert. The owners of the campground also own the adjacent Desert of Maine attraction, a unique natural phenomenon, drawing close to 50,000 visitors each year. Guided safari and walking tours take visitors across vast sandy dunes. There's a museum, sand art classes, and gemstone hunts for children. Campers have free access to the attraction and most take advantage of it. At the campground, sites are scattered in the trees or up on hills. There's a handful of very nice tent-only sites in the woods with plenty of room and privacy. For extra seclusion, book site T8, the honeymoon site, deep in the woods, set apart from the others. There are also a number of spacious wooded pull-through sites. Though the campground is relatively small, just 50 sites spread on 10 acres, it often feels busy. Not only do tourists funnel through the office/gift store in route to the attraction but the front of the campground, including the picnic area, is often taken over by buses of visitors.

Basics

Operated By: Sid & Carolyn Dobson. **Open:** May–mid-Oct. **Site Assignment:** Reservations suggested, 1-night deposit, 30-day cancellation policy with $5 charge; MC, V, D, AE, no checks. **Registration:** At office. **Fee:** Full hookups, $32; water & electric, $28; no hookups, $20, based on 2 people per site, additional person in RV, $5; additional person in tent, $7; children ages 3–12, $2; ages 13–16, $3. **Parking:** At site.

Facilities

Number of RV Sites: 40. **Number of Tent-Only Sites:** 10. **Hookups:** Water, electric, sewer (20, 30 amps), modem. **Each Site:** Picnic table, fire ring. **Dump Station:** Yes. **Laundry:** Yes. **Pay Phone:** No. **Rest Rooms and Showers:** Yes (coin-op). **Fuel:** No. **Propane:** Yes. **Internal Roads:** Gravel, dirt (good). **RV Service:** No. **Market:** Freeport (6 mi). **Restaurant:** No. **General Store:** Yes. **Vending:** No. **Swimming Pool:** Yes. **Playground:** No. **Other:** Free access to Desert of Maine & discount on tours, group area, picnic area, nature trails. **Activities:** Swimming, horseshoes. **Nearby Attractions:** Desert of Maine, Freeport, mid-coast parks & beaches. **Additional Information:** Freeport Merchants Assoc., 23 Depot St., Freeport, ME 04032-0452; (207) 865-1212 (800) 865-0881; www.freeportusa.com.

Restrictions

Pets: Must be on a leash, never left unattended. **Fires:** In grills, stoves, & fire rings only. **Alcoholic Beverages:** At site only. **Vehicle Maximum Length:** None.

To Get There

From I-95, exit 19, go west 2 mi. on Desert Rd.; campground is on the left.

FREEPORT

Flying Point Campground

10 Lower Flying Point Rd., Freeport 04032. T: (207) 865-4569 (800) 798-4569 (reservations)

RV ★★★ Tent ★★★

Beauty: ★★★★ Site Privacy: ★★★
Spaciousness: ★★★ Quiet: ★★★
Security: ★★★ Cleanliness: ★★★
Insect Control: ★★★ Facilities: ★★

This oceanfront campground, owned by a native and life-long resident of Freeport, overlooks scenic Casco Bay and Maquoit Bay. It boasts 1,200 feet of ocean frontage, with sandy beaches and sweeping views. Couples and families who can forego full hookups, heated pools and planned activities with love this place. Oceanfront sites (nearly half of the sites have ocean frontage) are set in a semi-circle, wrapped around a cove. Other sites are set in a row atop a bluff overlooking the water. There's a wide grassy lawn area in front of the sites that adds to the open, expansive feel of this campground. Water views are everywhere! If you can tear yourself away, downtown Freeport with outlet shopping, restaurants, theater, and more is just a few minutes away.

Basics

Operated By: Hilda Coskery. **Open:** May–Oct. 15. **Site Assignment:** Reservations suggested, 1-night deposit, 1-week cancellation policy; MC, V, no checks. **Registration:** At office. **Fee:** Water & electric, \$23; no hookups, \$17, based on 2 adults & 2 children under 18. **Parking:** At site.

Facilities

Number of RV Sites: 30. **Number of Tent-Only Sites:** 8. **Hookups:** Water, electric (30 amps). **Each Site:** Picnic table, fire ring. **Dump Station:** Yes. **Laundry:** Yes. **Pay Phone:** Yes. **Rest Rooms and Showers:** Yes (coin-op). **Fuel:** No. **Propane:** No. **Internal Roads:** Gravel (good). **RV Service:** No. **Market:** Freeport (3cmi). **Restaurant:** No. **General Store:** No. **Vending:** Yes. **Swimming Pool:** No. **Playground:** No. **Other:** Ocean frontage, beach. **Activities:** Swimming, beachcombing, fishing, volleyball, badminton, horseshoes. **Nearby Attractions:** Freeport, mid-coast parks & beaches. **Additional Information:** Freeport Merchants Assoc., 23 Depot St., Freeport, ME 04032-0452; (207) 865-1212 (800) 865-0881; www.freeportusa.com.

Restrictions

Pets: Must be on a leash, never left unattended. **Fires:** In grills, stoves, & fire rings only. **Alcoholic Beverages:** At site only. **Vehicle Max. Length:** None. **Other:** No mini-bikes or motorcylces.

To Get There

From I-95, exit 29, go north 1 mi. on Rte. 1, then east (right) 3.75 mi. on Bow St. /Lower Flying Point Rd.; campground is on the left.

GEORGETOWN

Camp Seguin

Reid State Park Rd., Georgetown 04548. T: (207) 371-2777; campseguin.com.

RV ★★★ Tent ★★★

Beauty: ★★★★ Site Privacy: ★★
Spaciousness: ★★ Quiet: ★★★
Security: ★★★ Cleanliness: ★★★
Insect Control: ★★ Facilities: ★

What a great surprise! We went to sleep to the sound of the waves crashing over the rocks—pretty sweet. This testimonial comes from a wilderness camper, who stumbled upon this place en route to oceanside Reid State Park, just a quarter-mile up the street. Alas, the state park doesn't offer camping, but Camp Seguin fills the need, with a wonderful location on the rocky shoreline of Sheepscot Bay in mid-coast Maine. It's about an hour from Portland, Boothbay, and Augusta. Campsites are arrayed in a loop, with some right on the water. Many of the tent sites have platforms, a great idea on this rocky spot. Site 17, in the corner and alongside the bay, is semi-secluded, and beautiful. Among the water-and-electric sites, set inland a bit, sites 27 and 28 are the choicest, and most private. Site 29 is the worst; too close to the campground entrance. Facilities are clean but rustic. No matter; most campers spend the day at glorious Reid State Park,with its mile-and-a-half of sandy beaches, ocean swimming and lagoon. The park charges \$2.50 per person, but, for a refundable \$40 deposit, the campground will give you a pass, so you can use the state park for free. (Tip: Bring lots of bug spray; they're fierce around here.)

Basics

Operated By: Betsy & Craig Lane. **Open:** Mid-June-Labor Day. **Site Assignment:** Reservations recommended, 2-night min. stay for reservatons. Walk-ins OK for 1-night stay if space is available. For 2-night stay, payment in full required for deposit; for stays of 1 week or more, 50% of fee due as deposit. Refunds for cancellations w/ 7-day notice, minus \$10 fee. **Registration:** At office. **Fee:** \$23–\$26 for 2 adults & up to 3 children. V, MC, D. **Parking:** At site.

Facilities

Number of RV Sites: 17. **Number of Tent-Only Sites:** 14. **Hookups:** Water, electric (20 amps). **Each Site:** Picnic table, fire ring. **Dump Station:** Yes. **Laundry:** No. **Pay Phone:** Yes. **Rest Rooms and Showers:** Yes, coin-op. **Fuel:** No. **Propane:** No. **Internal Roads:** Gravel, in good to fair condition. **RV Service:** No. **Market:** 14 mi. south. **Restaurant:** 3 mi. east. **General Store:** Yes. **Vending:** No. **Swimming Pool:** No. **Playground:** Yes. **Other:** Rec hall. **Activities:** Fishing. **Nearby Attractions:** Reid State Park, Popham Beach State Park, Morse Mountain Sanctuary, Maine Maritime Museum, Bowdoin College Museum of Art, Peary-MacMillan Arctic Museum, deep-sea fishing. **Additional Information:** Chamber of Commerce of the Bath-Brunswick Region, (207) 725-8797 or (207) 443-9751; www.midcoastmaine.com.

Restrictions

Pets: Must be leashed, quiet, & cleaned up after. Must not be left unattended. **Fires:** In fire rings only. **Alcoholic Beverages:** Yes. **Vehicle Maximum Length:** 27 ft. **Other:** Ask on arrival.

To Get There

From Rte. 1 in Bath, turn right on Rte. 127 south, immediately after crossing Carleton Bridge. Go 12 mi. south, then turn right on Seguinland Rd. (Reid St. Park Rd.) Campground entrance is on the left.

GREENVILLE

Casey's Spencer Bay Camps

P.O. Box 1190, Greenville 04441. T: (207) 695-2801; www.spencerbaycamps.com; casey@caseyspencerbaycamps.com.

RV ★★ Tent ★★

Beauty: ★★ Site Privacy: ★★★
Spaciousness: ★★★★ Quiet: ★★★
Security: ★★★ Cleanliness: ★★
Insect Control: ★★★ Facilities: ★

Want to enjoy the natural splendor of Moosehead Lake, but still have access to full hookups, and on-site motorboat (or canoe) rentals? This campground/cabin operation offers the Maine Sporting Camp Experience in all its rustic glory. So, if a bit of peeling linoleum in the shower house, and a junky-looking storage area don't offend your sensibilities, you'll be quite content here. The spot itself is quite lovely; you reach it via a six-mile gravel road lined with white birch. The drive will put you in the "getting away from it all" frame of mind, especially if you've encountered any moose along the way. Outside of the eyesore of a storage area—smack dab in the middle of things, sad to say—the campsites aren't bad at all. Set around a grassy field housing boat trailers, campsites are fairly wide—mostly 40 feet—with good buffer between sites. Cabins are set around Stevens Point. Some campsites are on the bayside (Spencer Bay), some face Moosehead Lake. Best RV sites are 16, 25, and 7 (awesome), on the bay side; best sites for tents are numbers 5 and 25 (high and dry when it rains.)

Basics

Operated By: Casey & Sarah LaCasce. **Open:** May

15–Oct. 15. **Site Assignment:** Reservations recommended. 50% deposit required. Refunds w/ 30-day notice of cancellation. **Registration:** At office. **Fee:** $18–$22 for 2 adults & their children under age 13. (Age 13 years & older, $4 extra per day.) V, MC. **Parking:** At site.

Facilities

Number of RV Sites: 50. **Number of Tent-Only Sites:** 0. **Hookups:** Water, electric (20 amps), sewer. **Each Site:** Picnic table, fire ring. **Dump Station:** Yes. **Laundry:** No. **Pay Phone:** No. **Rest Rooms and Showers:** Yes, coin-op. **Fuel:** No. **Propane:** No. **Internal Roads:** Gravel, in good condition. **RV Service:** No. **Market:** 18.5 mi. south, in Greenville. **Restaurant:** 18.5 mi. south, in Greenville. **General Store:** Yes. **Vending:** No. **Swimming Pool:** No. **Playground:** No. **Other:** Boat ramp. **Activities:** Lake swimming, fishing (need license), boating (rentals available), hiking trail. **Nearby Attractions:** S.S. Katahdin steamboat cruises, Moosehead Marine Museum, Eveleth-Crafts-Sheridan Historical House, Lily whitewater rafting, boating, fishing, moosewatching at Lazy Tom Bog, Big Squaw Mountain (chairlift & hiking). **Additional Information:** Moosehead Lake Region Chamber of Commerce, (207) 723-4443.

Restrictions

Pets: Must be leashed, quiet, & cleaned up after. Must not be left unattended. $4 per day per pet. **Fires:** In fire rings only. **Alcoholic Beverages:** Yes. **Vehicle Maximum Length:** None. **Other:** Electricity limited to a few hours in the morning & a few hours at night.

To Get There

From Greenville, drive up Kokadjo Rd. 12 mi. north; watch for sign at left marking camp. Turn left. Last 6.5 mi. are a dirt road into camp (watch out for moose.)

GREENVILLE

Lily Bay State Park

HC 76 P.O. Box 425, Greenville 04441. T: (207) 695-2700 or (207) 941-4014 (off-season) or (800) 332-1501 (reservations or in ME) or (207) 287-3824 (reservations or outside ME); F: (207) 287-6170; www.state.me.us/doc/prkslands/reser.

RV ★★★★ Tent ★★★

Beauty: ★★★★★
Site Privacy: ★★★★★
Spaciousness: ★★★★★
Quiet: ★★★★
Security: ★★★
Cleanliness: ★★★
Insect Control: ★★
Facilities: ★

I've waited my whole career for this, says Lily Bay State Park general manager Andy Haskell, spreading his arms to encompass his surroundings. It's easy to see why he's got a big grin on his face. Haskell's realm is a spectacular natural area set on the eastern shore of Moosehead Lake, the largest lake in New England. From the lake, campers look out toward mountain vistas all around, including Mt. Kineo, which seems to spring from the lake itself, rising 800 feet above the water. Campsites are set in two loops, both on the lake. There's Dunn Point, good for families because it's a close walk to the beach and playground, and Rowell Cove, which offers several walk-in tent sites. Plus, at Rowell Cove, tent sites are set closer to the water. Among the choicest sites at Rowell Cove are 20L and 21L, directly on the lake and roomy enough for 30 foot campers. Lake view sites at Dunn Point are those numbered 210, 211, 213, 214, and 215, and 218, 220, 221, and 222. You'll hear the haunting cry of loons at night. If you've brought a kayak or canoe, paddle out to Sugar Island (open to the public.) You knew there had to be a downside, and it's this: No showers and no flush toilets, though the park has an arrangement with Moosehead Family Campground in Greenville, where campers can use the coin-op showers. But if you can handle wilderness camping, it doesn't get better than Lily Bays

Basics

Operated By: Maine Dept. of Conservation, Bureau of Parks & Lands. **Open:** May 1–Oct. 15. **Site Assignment:** In spring & fall, camping is on a first-come, first-served basis. For summer stays, reservations open on the first business day in Jan. From June 15 to the night before Labor Day, sites may be reserved for a min. of 2 nights & up to 2 weeks. Full payment is charged to credit card when reservation is processed. Refund with $15 cancellation fee. 17 sites are non-reservable, & available on a first-come, first-served basis. Call the reservations line to cancel a reservation more than 3 days in advance. If cancelling less than 3 days in advance, call the park directly. **Registration:** At office. **Fee:** $12, Maine residents; $16, non-residents plus $2 fee if you reserve in advance. V, MC. **Parking:** At site.

Facilities

Number of RV Sites: 91. **Number of Tent-Only Sites:** 0. **Hookups:** None. **Each Site:** Picnic table, fireplace. **Dump Station:** Yes. **Laundry:** No. **Pay Phone:** Yes. **Rest Rooms and Showers:** Yes (non-flush), no. **Fuel:** No. **Propane:** No. **Internal Roads:** Gravel, in good condition. **RV Service:** No. **Market:** 9 mi. southwest, in Greenville. **Restaurant:** 9 mi. southwest, in Greenville. **General Store:** No. **Vending:** Yes. **Swimming Pool:** No. **Playground:** Yes. **Other:** Boat ramps, boat docks. **Activities:** Lake swimming, shoreline hiking trail w/ interpretive signage, volleyball, boating, picnicking. **Nearby Attractions:** Moosehead Lake, S.S. Katahdin steamboat cruises, Moosehead Marine Museum, Eveleth-Crafts-Sheridan Historical House, Lily whitewater rafting, boating, fishing, moosewatching at Lazy Tom Bog. **Additional Information:** Moosehead Lake Region Chamber of Commerce, (207) 723-4443.

Restrictions

Pets: Must be leashed, quiet, & cleaned up after. Must have rabies vaccination certificate. Not allowed on beach. **Fires:** In fireplaces only. **Alcoholic Beverages:** No. **Vehicle Maximum Length:** 35 ft. **Other:** 2-week max. stay between last week in June & Labor Day.

To Get There

From Greenville, go 9 mi. northeast on Lily Bay Rd. (also called Kodjako Rd. Campground is on the left.

HERMON

Pleasant Hill Campground

45 Mansell Rd., Hermon 04401. T: (207) 848-5127; www.mint.net/pleasanthill; pleasant@mint.net.

RV ★★★ Tent ★★★

Beauty: ★★★
Site Privacy: ★★★
Spaciousness: ★★★
Quiet: ★★★
Security: ★★★
Cleanliness: ★★★
Insect Control: ★★★
Facilities: ★★★

The name says it all: friendly and pleasant, this rural campground, just outside of Bangor, attracts a wide variety of clientele, from family campers who return year after year for a weekend away to off-the-road travelers in and out in a day. It's situated just a few miles off the main interstate, an hour or so from Acadia National Park and en route to the Canadian Maritime Provinces, making it a favorite stopover for tourists needing a place to lay their heads for the night. Campers find a helpful staff, clean, maintained grounds and a choice of sunny or shaded sites. Pull-through, full hookups are set side-by-side off the main campground road; water and electric sites and tent sites are set in loops nestled in woods or in open, sunny fields. Families will find enough to keep little ones entertained for an evening or two: besides the swimming pool, there's a stocked fishing pond, modest mini-golf course, and game room on site.

Basics

Operated By: Montford family. **Open:** May–Oct. **Site Assignment:** First come, first served; call for reservations to reserve a specific site only. 1-night deposit, 2 week cancellation policy w/ a $7 service fee; MC, V, D, checks. **Registration:** At office. **Fee:** Full hookups, $30.50 (50 amp), $26 (30 amp); water & electirc, $23; water only (tent), $17. **Parking:** At site.

Facilities

Number of RV Sites: 84. **Number of Tent-Only Sites:** 21. **Hookups:** Water, electric, sewer (30, 50 amps). **Each Site:** Picnic table, fire ring. **Dump Station:** Yes. **Laundry:** Yes. **Pay Phone:** Yes. **Rest Rooms and Showers:** Yes. **Fuel:** No. **Propane:** Yes. **Internal Roads:** Gravel, dirt (good). **RV Service:** No. **Market:** Bangor (5 mi). **Restaurant:** No. **General Store:** Yes. **Vending:** No. **Swimming Pool:** Yes. **Playground:** Yes. **Other:** Rec hall, mini golf, stocked fishing pond, adult reading lounge, pavilion. **Activities:** Swimming, fishing, horseshoes, volleyball, mini-golf, basketball. **Nearby Attractions:** Bangor, Bar Harbor, Acadia National Park, Maine coast. **Additional Information:** Bangor Regional Chamber of Commerce, 519 Maine St., P.O. Box 1443, Bangor, ME 04402 (207) 947-0307, www.bangorregion.com.

Restrictions

Pets: On leash, never unattended. **Fires:** In grills, stoves, & fire rings only. **Alcoholic Beverages:** At site only. **Vehicle Maximum Length:** None.

To Get There

From I-95, exit 45; go 5 mi. west on Rte. 222 (Union St.); campground is on the left.

JACKMAN

Moose River Campground

P.O. Box 98, Jackman 04945. T: (207) 668-3341; www.mooserivercampground.com; mooservr@ctel.net.

RV ★★★ Tent ★★

Beauty: ★★★ Site Privacy: ★★
Spaciousness: ★★ Quiet: ★★★★
Security: ★★ Cleanliness: ★★★
Insect Control: ★★★ Facilities: ★★

Nudging the Canadian border in Maine's Moose River Valley, the town of Jackman is a four-season recreational hotspot. In summer, the area draws hikers, rock-climbers, fat-tire bicyclists and whitewater rafting enthusiasts. But, since it's so far north, the crowds never equal the numbers of those at, say, Camden. It's not surprising that Jackman is home to about a half-dozen campgrounds. This one is the nicest, and most family-friendly. ("This campground rocks!" a camper-kid told us—we didn't ask—as we toured the property.) Located in a residential area near Old Mill Dam, the campground is wooded with tall pines and white birch, with campsites set in loops alongside a pond. There's a smaller, stocked fishing pond for kids, with nice grassy banks and benches. A swimming pool and a well-designed play structure add to the family-pleasing amenities. With canoe rentals besides, your bunch will find plenty to do. Sites 12 through 18, at waterside, have no hookups; sites 20 and 21, overlooking a small island, are good sites with electric hookups. Most-secluded site—nice here, since there are so many kids running around—is site 7. A few seasonal sites are grouped together in an inner loop. Rest rooms are no-frills, very basic. This is a good choice for those who want some comforts with their wilderness experience.

BASICS

Operated By: Brian & Cheryl Cousineau. **Open:** May 15–Nov. 1. **Site Assignment:** Reservations accepted. Deposit of 1 nights' fee required. Must give 72-hour notice of cancellation for refund. **Registration:** At office. **Fee:** $14–$19 for 2 adults & 2 children under age 16. V, MC. **Parking:** At site or designated lot.

FACILITIES

Number of RV Sites: 55. **Number of Tent-Only Sites:** 0. **Hookups:** Water, electric (30 amps), sewer, cable TV. **Each Site:** Picnic table, fireplace w/ grill top. **Dump Station:** Yes. **Laundry:** Yes. **Pay Phone:** Yes. **Rest Rooms and Showers:** Yes. **Fuel:** No. **Propane:** No. **Internal Roads:** Gravel, in good condition. **RV Service:** No. **Market:** 2.5 mi. south. **Restaurant:** 2.5 mi. south. **General Store:** Yes. **Vending:** Yes. **Swimming Pool:** Yes. **Playground:** Yes. **Other:** Rec room, boat dock. **Activities:** Fishing (licenses available in town), stocked pond for kid's fishing, boating (rentals available), volleyball, horseshoes, swimming. **Nearby Attractions:** Fishing, hiking, moosewatching. **Additional Information:** Jackman-Moose River Region Chamber of Commerce, (207) 668-417`.

RESTRICTIONS

Pets: Must be leashed, quiet, & cleaned up after. Must not be left unattended. **Fires:** In fireplaces only. **Alcoholic Beverages:** At sites only. **Vehicle Maximum Length:** None. **Other:** 3-night min. stay during holiday weekends.

TO GET THERE

From junction of Rtes. 6/15 and 201, go 2 mi. north on Rte. 201/6, then 1.5 mi. east on Heald Stream Rd. Campground entrance is on the right.

LEEDS

Riverbend Campground

R.R.2, P.O. Box 505, Leeds 04263. T: (207) 524-5711; www.megalink.net/~riverbend; riverbend@megalink.net.

RV ★★★ Tent ★★

Beauty: ★★★ Site Privacy: ★★
Spaciousness: ★★★ Quiet: ★★★
Security: ★★★ Cleanliness: ★★★
Insect Control: ★★★ Facilities: ★★★

Like to bass fish? Crazy for paddling? This might be the campground of your dreams. Set in rural Maine, just west of Augusta, Riverbend is the home of Androscoggin Bass Masters, plus, L.L. Bean uses the campground as a base for its Discovery School canoe and kayak trips. Even without those endorsements, it won't take an outdoors-enthusiast long to discover that the campground boasts easy access to six miles of the Dead River, leading to 3,800-acre Androscoggin Lake, one mile up. The owners are happy to sell you a fishing license and bait, rent you a vessel (canoe or motorboat), and share the best places to haul in the biggest bass. Plus-size RVs occupy a grassy rolling field near the swimming pool (sites 53 and 54, and 57 through 59 are nice), while tents and self-contained units (water, no electric) hug the riverbank. Among these, site 80 is nice and private, overlooking the river. Tenters might find the space a bit wide-open, but if you plan to spend most of the day explore the waterways, who cares?

BASICS

Operated By: Tom & Elaine Gomolka. **Open:** May 1–Sept.30. **Site Assignment:** Reservations recommended. Deposit of 25% required for 2-day stay; full payment required for 1-night stay & holiday weekends. Refund for cancellations w/ 30-day notice, minus $10 fee. **Registration:** At office. **Fee:** $19.50–$23 for a family of 2 adults & up to 4 children age 18 & under. V, MC, D. **Parking:** At site.

FACILITIES

Number of RV Sites: 80. **Number of Tent-Only Sites:** 0. **Hookups:** Water, electric (20, 30 amps). **Each Site:** Picnic table, fire ring. **Dump Station:** Yes. **Laundry:** No. **Pay Phone:** Yes. **Rest Rooms and Showers:** Yes, coin-op. **Fuel:** No. **Propane:** Yes. **Internal Roads:** Gravel, in good condition. **RV Service:** No. **Market:** 11 mi. east, in Winthrop. **Restaurant:** 6 mi. east. **General Store:** Yes. **Vending:** Yes. **Swimming Pool:** Yes. **Playground:** Yes. **Other:** Game room. **Activities:** Fishing (licenses available), boating (rentals available), swimming, planned activities. **Nearby Attractions:** Norlands Living History Museum, Maine State Capitol & Museum, Fort Western, Monmouth Summer Theater. **Additional Information:** Androscoggin Chamber of Commerce, (207) 783-2249; www.androscoggincounty.com.

RESTRICTIONS

Pets: Must be leashed, quiet, & cleaned up after. Must not be left unattended. **Fires:** In fire rings only. **Alcoholic Beverages:** At sites only. **Vehicle Maximum Length:** None. **Other:** No visitors allowed after 8:00 p.m.

TO GET THERE

Take Maine Turnpike north to exit 12 (Auburn), then take Rte. 202 east to Rte. 106 north; follow for 7.5 mi. to campground.

LOVELL

Kezar Lake Camping Area

R.R. 1, P.O. Box 246, Lovell 04051. T: (207) 925-1631 or (888) 925-1631 (reservations); www.kezarlakecamping.com.

RV ★★★ Tent ★★

Beauty: ★★★ Site Privacy: ★★
Spaciousness: ★★ Quiet: ★★
Security: ★★★★★ Cleanliness: ★★★
Insect Control: ★★★ Facilities: ★★

National Geographic named Kezar Lake one of the 10 most beautiful lakes in the world; a British journalist upped that, calling it one of the five loveliest lakes. For whatever that's worth, this is a peachy spot, with azure water, tawny sand, and a backdrop of piney green. Located in Maine's Western Lakes region, this campground sits right on the shoreline, with 400 feet of sandy beach and a variety of wooded campsites. The grass-and-gravel sites, mostly back-in, are a bit packed in, but, nobody spends much time at camp 'til nightfall, when the last child has been coaxed off the beach, the last canoe dragged in for the night. For keeping an eye on the little ones at play, waterfront sites DW3 and 4 and W3 through 7 are good choices. Sites W8 and W9 are winners, too, set back from the beach, but overlooking the lake. We like site L40 because it's backed up into the woods and a tad apart from the rest. Nicest tent sites are T2 and T3, near the marsh (you did pack that insect repellent, no?) Some new sites are being added, near the road and away from the beach; ask about construction activity when you book, if that concerns you.

BASICS

Operated By: Pierce family. **Open:** May 15–Columbus Day. **Site Assignment:** Reservations recommended. May reserve while on site this year for next year. 50% deposit required. Refunds for cancellations if received more than 1 month before arrival, minus $20 service charge. If you book more than 1 month in advance, you must reserve for a full week. **Registration:** At office. **Fee:** $18–$35 for 2 adults & unmarried, dependent children under age 18. V, MC, D, AE. **Parking:** At site or storage area.

FACILITIES

Number of RV Sites: 118. **Number of Tent-Only Sites:** 0. **Hookups:** Water, electric (20, 30 amps). **Each Site:** Picnic table, fireplace. **Dump Station:** Yes. **Laundry:** Yes. **Pay Phone:** Yes. **Rest Rooms and Showers:** Yes, coin-op. **Fuel:** No. **Propane:** Yes. **Internal Roads:** Gravel, in good condition. **RV Service:** No. **Market:** 13 mi. south, in Fryeburg. **Restaurant:** 25 mi. west, in N. Conway, N.H. **General Store:** Yes. **Vending:** Yes. **Swimming Pool:** No. **Playground:** Yes. **Other:** Rec hall, boat ramp. **Activities:** Fishing (license required), boating (rentals available), swimming, volleyball, basketball, planned activities. **Nearby Attractions:** Mt. Sabattus (hiking), outlet shopping (North Conway, N.H.). **Additional Information:** Bridgton Lakes Region Chamber of Commerce, (207) 647-3472.

RESTRICTIONS

Pets: Must be leashed, quiet, & cleaned up after. Must not be left unattended. Not allowed on beach or in public areas. $2 charge per day. **Fires:** In fireplaces only. **Alcoholic Beverages:** At sites only. **Vehicle Maximum Length:** None. **Other:** 3-night min. stay for holidays.

TO GET THERE

From Maine Turnpike, take exit 8, then Rte. 302 through Bridgton. From junction of Rte. 93, continue on Rte. 302 for 4.3 mi. Turn right on Knight's Hill Rd. to Lovell. Go north for 2.5 mi., then turn left at campground sign. Entrance is 3 mi. on the right.

MEDWAY

Katahdin Shadows

P.O. Box 606J, Rte. 157, Medway 04460. T: (207) 746-9349 (800) 794-5267; www.katahdinshadows.com; katshadcamp@midmaine.com.

RV ★★★★ Tent ★★★★★

Beauty: ★★★★★	Site Privacy: ★★★★
Spaciousness: ★★★★	Quiet: ★★★★
Security: ★★★★	Cleanliness: ★★★★
Insect Control: ★★★	Facilities: ★★★★

We love this plush oasis nestled in the vast northern Maine woods, just outside of Baxter State Park. Outdoor enthusiasts have miles of hiking trails, canoeing, whitewater rafting, and some of the best fishing in Maine right outside their doorsteps. The ultra-friendly campground owners provide plenty of tips and information, and will set campers up with outdoor adventure guide and shuttle service. Guided fishing trips take off directly from the campground. Most campers come to play in the great outdoors but save plenty of time for relaxing around the campground. There are lots of nice facilities, here: swimming pool, lounges, sports fields, function hall, and more. On summer weekends, kids can join in a number of planned activities. Tenters looking for quiet and solitude will appreciate "the jungle," a separate, secluded area with plenty of privacy. RVers will like sites 51-56, with full hookups, easy access, and lots of shade. The campground also rents hutniks (8x8 wooded shelters with roll-down doors) and cabins. Added bonus: the campground stays open year-round with miles of cross-country, snowshoe, and snowmobile trails accessible from the property.

BASICS

Operated By: David & Theresa Violette. **Open:** Year-round. **Site Assignment:** Reservations suggested Jul.–Aug.; 1-night deposit, 24-hour cancellation policy; MC, V, checks. **Registration:** At office. **Fee:** Full hookups, $21; water & electric, $19; no hookups, $17, based on 2 adults & 2 children. **Parking:** At site.

FACILITIES

Number of RV Sites: 97. **Number of Tent-Only Sites:** 21. **Hookups:** Water, electric, sewer (30, 50 amps). **Each Site:** Picnic table, fire ring. **Dump Station:** Yes. **Laundry:** Yes. **Pay Phone:** Yes. **Rest Rooms and Showers:** Yes. **Fuel:** No. **Propane:** No. **Internal Roads:** Gravel, dirt (good). **RV Service:** No. **Market:** Medway (within walking distance). **Restaurant:** No. **General Store:** Yes. **Vending:** Yes. **Swimming Pool:** Yes. **Playground:** Yes. **Other:** Game room, sports fields, adult lounge, function hall, guided fishing trips, boat rentals, planned activities, guide & shuttle service to whitewater rafting, kayaking & canoeing. **Activities:** Swimming, boating, fishing, hiking, whitewater rafting, guided excursions. **Nearby Attractions:** Baxter State Park, Penobscot River, Gulf Hagas, Allagash River, Mattawamkeag Wilderness Park. **Additional Information:** Katahdin Area Chamber of Commerce, 1029 Central St., Millinocket, Maine 04462 (207) 723-4443, www.katahdinmaine.com.

RESTRICTIONS

Pets: On leash; never left unattended. **Fires:** In grills, campstoves, & fire rings only. **Alcoholic Beverages:** At site only. **Vehicle Max. Length:** None.

TO GET THERE

From I-95, exit 56, go 1.7 mi. west on Rte. 157; campground is on the right.

MT. DESERT ISLAND

Somes Sound View Campground

86 Hall Quarry Rd., Mt. Desert Island 04660. T: (207) 244-3890; www.mtdesertisland.com.

RV ★★ Tent ★★★

Beauty: ★★★★	Site Privacy: ★★★
Spaciousness: ★★★	Quiet: ★★★★
Security: ★★★	Cleanliness: ★★★
Insect Control: ★★★	Facilities: ★★

This small, quirky campground sits on a rocky saltwater shore and offers tenters and small trailer campers fine views of the ocean and Somes Sound. There's a dock and small beach on the shoreline, and canoe and sailboat rentals from the office, but don't expect much else in the way of services and conveniences. The boulder-strewn, rustic campground is best for those who like their pleasures simple and natural: the sound of the waves, the smell of the ocean, the wind in the trees. The sites vary in size and appeal. Some sites are quite tiny and close to the road; others sit up on flat rock and slabs of granite. Sites 36 and 37 are waterfront with great views but sit almost smack dab in the middle of the road or the public gravel beach, and waterfront sites 30 and 31 barely have enough room for a pup tent. There are also sites looping around an old historic quarry pond, but we find the chainlink fence around quarry unappealing. The best sites are actually off the water where you'll have more room and privacy. We like site 19 and 20 set back in the woods or site 8 set up high on a sunny slab of granite.

BASICS

Operated By: Rudolf & Marilyn Musetti & Rick & Mimi. Mooers. **Open:** Memorial Day–Oct. 15. **Site Assignment:** Reservations suggested in Jul.–Aug., $20 non-refundable deposit. Cash only. **Registration:** At office. **Fee:** Waterfront, $21; wooded, $18; $3 extra for electric hookups. Waterfront sites are tent-only. **Parking:** At site; 1 walk-in site.

FACILITIES

Number of RV Sites: 11. **Number of Tent-Only Sites:** 71. **Hookups:** Water, electric (20, 30 amps). **Each Site:** Picnic table, fire ring. **Dump Station:** Yes. **Laundry:** No. **Pay Phone:** Yes. **Rest Rooms and Showers:** Yes (coin-op). **Fuel:** No. **Propane:** No. **Internal Roads:** Gravel (good). **RV Service:** No. **Market:** Somesville (4mi). **Restaurant:** No. **General Store:** No. **Vending:** Yes. **Swimming Pool:** No. **Playground:** No. **Other:** Boat dock, ocean frontage, sailboat & canoe rentals. **Activities:** Swimming, fishing, boating. **Nearby Attractions:** Bar Harbor, Acadia National Park. **Additional Information:** Acadia National Park, P.O. Box 177, Bar Harbor, ME 04609 (207) 288-3338, www.nps/gov/acad. Also, Acadia Information Center, P.O. Box 139, Mount Desert, ME 04660 (207) 667-8550 (800) 358-8550, www.acadiainfo.com & Bar Harbor Chamber of Commerce, Bar Harbor Chamber of Commerce, 93 Cottage St., Bar Harbor, ME 04609 (207) 288-5103, www.barharborinfo.com.

RESTRICTIONS

Pets: Must be on a leash, never left unattended. **Fires:** In grills, stoves, & fire rings only. **Alcoholic Beverages:** At site only. **Vehicle Maximum Length:** None.

TO GET THERE

From junction Rtes. 198 and 102, in Somesville, go south 2.1 mi. on Rte. 102, then east (left) 1 mi. on Hall Quarry Rd., campground is on the left.

NAPLES

Bay of Naples Family Camping

Rte. 11/114, P.O. Box 240M, Naples 04055. T: (207) 693-6429 or (800) 348-9750 (reservations or outside of ME); www.bayofnaples.com.

RV ★★★ Tent ★★

Beauty: ★★	Site Privacy: ★★
Spaciousness: ★★★	Quiet: ★★★
Security: ★★★★	Cleanliness: ★★★
Insect Control: ★★★★★	Facilities: ★

We'll forgive this campground's rather ramshackle facilities—off-putting as they are—because it's set in such a pretty area. It is located in the Sebago Lake region of southwestern Maine, on the Bay of Naples, set amidst a stand of tall pines. Given the height of the trees, they don't provide much buffer between sites, but the gravel spaces are nicely carpeted with pine needles. Good sites include W6, near the beach, and, for tenters, site 40, offering good tree coverage. The roped-off swimming area here is very large, with two rafts; the Songo River Queen paddleboat cruises right past the beach. The bay accesses the 45-mile Sebago Lake-Long Lake chain of waterways, great for boating. Another plus, for some: the campground adjoins a public golf course. Fishing is another option, but beware the fishing pier if you have mobility issues—it's located down a long, bumpy hill. The attractions of downtown Naples, including an amusement area, and the paddleboat cruise dock, are located nearby, making this a good base for active families.

BASICS

Operated By: James Ruhlin. **Open:** Memorial Day–Columbus Day. **Site Assignment:** Reservations recommended. Deposit of 3 nights' fee required. 3-night min. required for reservations; otherwise, walk-ins accepted. Refunds for cancellation if made within 30 days. **Registration:** At office. **Fee:** $22–$28 for 2 adults & 2 children under age 18. V, MC (accepted for 3 or more nights' stay only). **Parking:** At site.

FACILITIES

Number of RV Sites: 150. **Number of Tent-Only Sites:** 0. **Hookups:** Water, electric (30 amps), sewer. **Each Site:** Picnic table, fireplace. **Dump Station:** Yes. **Laundry:** Yes. **Pay Phone:** Yes. **Rest Rooms and Showers:** Yes, coin-op. **Fuel:** No. **Propane:** Yes. **Internal Roads:** Gravel, in good condition. **RV Service:** No. **Market:** 1 mi. north on Rte. 302. **Restaurant:** 1 mi. north on Rte. 302. **General Store:** No. **Vending:** No. **Swimming Pool:** No. **Playground:** Yes. **Other:** Rec room, dock w/ boat slips. **Activities:** Swimming, boating (rentals available), fishing (license required). **Nearby Attractions:** Golf, mini-golf, seaplane rides, boat cruises, Songo River Queen paddleboat, Douglas Mountain hiking, Sebago Lake State Park, outlet shopping (N. Conway, N.H.). **Additional Information:** Naples Business Assoc., (207) 693-3285.

RESTRICTIONS

Pets: No. **Fires:** In fireplaces only. **Alcoholic Beverages:** Yes. **Vehicle Maximum Length:** None. **Other:** No groups; families & couples only.

TO GET THERE

Take Maine Turnpike north to exit 8, then Rte. 302 for 26 mi. to Naples. Turn left onto Rte. 11/114 for 1 mi. Bay of Naples Campground adjoins golf course.

NAPLES

Four Seasons Family Camping

P.O. Box 927, Rte. 302, Naples 04055. T: (207) 693-6797.

RV ★★★ Tent ★

Beauty: ★★★ Site Privacy: ★★
Spaciousness: ★★ Quiet: ★★★
Security: ★★★★★ Cleanliness: ★★★★
Insect Control: ★★ Facilities: ★★★

Located on 14-mile Long Lake in the Sebago Lake area of southwest Maine, this family campground is set on rolling woodland, alongside a good-sized sandy beach. Some guests bring their boats along, and use the ramp and boat docks. Some waterfront sites have their own docks. Other campers are happy to rent a rowboat, canoe, sailboat or paddleboat. This isn't the best place for tenting in the area, since tent sites sit right alongside a large field, quite exposed, but RVers should be especially happy with site 16A, good-sized, with a water view, and 25, near the beach but tucked into a corner for privacy. Nice features include bike racks and lots of electrical outlets in the ladies' room. Most families (and they stress the family aspect here) come for a week, not a weekend, giving the place a rather lived-in look. Campers here aren't looking for pristine surroundings, however, just a nice, safe place to play outside and enjoy the obvious charms of the Chain of Lakes area.

BASICS

Operated By: Van Der Zee family. **Open:** Mid-May–mid-Oct. **Site Assignment:** Reservations recommended. Deposit of $100 for 1-week stay or full payment in advance for weekend stay or part of week. 14-day notice required for refunds due to cancellation. **Registration:** At office. **Fee:** $22–$37 per family. Includes 2 adults & their unmarried children. V, MC, D. **Parking:** At site.

FACILITIES

Number of RV Sites: 115. **Number of Tent-Only Sites:** 0. **Hookups:** Water, electric (20, 30 amps). **Each Site:** Picnic table, fire ring. **Dump Station:** Yes. **Laundry:** No. **Pay Phone:** Yes. **Rest Rooms and Showers:** Yes, coin-op. **Fuel:** No. **Propane:** No. **Internal Roads:** Gravel, in good condition. **RV Service:** No. **Market:** 3 mi. south & 5 mi. north. **Restaurant:** 3 mi. south & 5 mi. north. **General Store:** Yes. **Vending:** Yes. **Swimming Pool:** Yes. **Playground:** Yes. **Other:** Boat ramp, rec hall. **Activities:** Lake swimming, boating, fishing (license required), volleyball. **Nearby Attractions:** Golf, mini-golf, seaplane rides, boat cruises, Songo River Queen paddleboat, Douglas Mountain hiking, Sebago Lake State Park, outlet shopping (N. Conway, N.H.). **Additional Information:** Greater Windham Chamber of Commerce, (207) 892-8265; www.windhamchamber.sebagolake.org.

RESTRICTIONS

Pets: Must be leashed, quiet & cleaned up after. No pets in rental units. **Fires:** In fire rings only. **Alcoholic Beverages:** Yes. **Vehicle Maximum Length:** None. **Other:** 3-night min. stay required on holiday weekends.

TO GET THERE

Take exit 8 off Maine Turnpike, then Rte. 302W to Naples. Continue 3 mi. to campground sign, on the right.

NEW HARBOR

Sherwood Forest Campsite

Pemaquid Beach, P.O. Box 189, New Harbor 04554. T: (800) 274-1593.

RV ★★★ Tent ★★★

Beauty: ★★★ Site Privacy: ★★★
Spaciousness: ★★★ Quiet: ★★★★
Security: ★★★ Cleanliness: ★★★★
Insect Control: ★★★ Facilities: ★★★

In the party mood? Keep going. "Go to Lake Pemaquid Campground!" owner Marilyn Stooky advises. "You won't be happy here." This wooded campground, about a half-hour's drive from Boothbay Harbor on Maine's mid-coast, is located in the Pemaquid Beach area, but sits inland from the ocean. If you prefer 'quiet and woodsy' to 'crowded and beachy', you 'll be quite content here. This campground has been in the same family for 23 years, with a younger generation poised to take over. Sites are grassy, and set in a loop that starts just beyond the pool, store, and pavilion area, which is bordered by four cabins. Sites are heavily wooded and nicely buffered for privacy; sunlight filters through the dense canopy of foliage on bright summer days. Sites 15E and F, facing a small pond, are pretty, but stay away from 15H, alongside a big brush pile when we visited. Site 15D2 is nestled in woodlands and very private. Sites 9A and 9B sit in a wooded glen, nicely situated. Among the tent sites, the owner recommends sites B, C, and D, set on a cul-de-sac; we like nicely-shaded site 43, which backs into the woods. Outbuildings are fairly rustic, but changes may come as the kids take over.

BASICS

Operated By: Gary & Marilyn Stooky. **Open:** May 1–Oct. 1. **Site Assignment:** Reservations recommended. $25 deposit required. Refunds for cancellations w/ 1-week notice, minus $5 fee. **Registration:** At office. **Fee:** $18–$24 for 2 adults & 2 children. No credit cards. **Parking:** At site.

FACILITIES

Number of RV Sites: 49. **Number of Tent-Only Sites:** 13. **Hookups:** Water, electric (15, 20, 30 amps). **Each Site:** Picnic table, fire ring. **Dump Station:** Yes. **Laundry:** Yes. **Pay Phone:** Yes. **Rest Rooms and Showers:** Yes, coin-op. **Fuel:** No. **Propane:** No. **Internal Roads:** Gravel, in good condition. **RV Service:** No. **Market:** 1 mi. east. **Restaurant:** 1 mi. east. **General Store:** Yes. **Vending:** Yes. **Swimming Pool:** Yes. **Playground:** Yes. **Activities:** Swimming, basketball, boating (may add rentals; pending). **Nearby Attractions:** Pemaquid Point Lighthouse, Boothbay Railway Village, Maine Resources Aquarium, Boothbay Harbor restaurants, shops & galleries, deep-sea fishing, whale-watching cruises, golf. **Additional Information:** Boothbay Harbor Region Chamber of Commerce, (207) 633-2353 or (800) 266-8422.

RESTRICTIONS

Pets: Must be leashed, quiet, & cleaned up after. Must not be left unattended. $1 charge per dog, per day. **Fires:** In fireplaces only. **Alcoholic Beverages:** Yes. **Vehicle Maximum Length:** None. **Other:** 3-day min. stays on July 4th weekend, Old Bristol Days (in Aug., call to confirm dates), & Labor Day.

TO GET THERE

From Bus. Rte. 1 and Rte. 130 in Damariscotta, go 12 mi. south on Rte. 130, then 0.75 mi. west on Snowball Hill Rd., then 800 ft. south on Pemaquid Tr. Entrance is on the left.

NORTH MONMOUTH

Beaver Brook Campground

R.R. 1, P.O. Box 1835, North Monmouth 04265. T: (207) 933-2108 or (207) 622-5231 (off-season); F: (207) 933-3826; www.beaver-brook.com.

Beauty: ★★ Site Privacy: ★★
Spaciousness: ★★ Quiet: ★★
Security: ★★★★★ Cleanliness: ★★★
Insect Control: ★★ Facilities: ★★

Located just 15 miles west of Augusta in south-central Maine, this campground offers a lakeside escape with plenty of action. Woodsy and terraced, this 150-acre property sits on the shore of Androscoggin Lake. They rent all kinds of boats—motorboats, canoes, kayaks, paddleboats—and sell fishing gear and non-resident licenses, all the better to try your luck against small- and large-mouth bass. You might even spot wildlife here; we saw a great blue heron perched on a boulder near the (tiny) beach. Planned activities include goofy stuff like a "Wild & Wacky 'Survivor' Weekend." Among the campsites are 50 seasonals. There's not much buffer between campsites. We'd skip the crowded waterfront camping area, and head out back to the Hemlock Ln.Loop, wooded, quieter, state parkish. Sites 354 through 360 (even numbers) are fairly spacious in this bunch. If you can't resist the waterfront, try sits 216 through 221. For total seclusion, though, you can't beat sites 339, 340, and 341, off in the woods by themselves. One complaint: charging campers $5 each time they launch their boat from the ramp is pretty niggling.

Basics

Operated By: Dick & Jean Parent. **Open:** May 1–Columbus Day. **Site Assignment:** Reservations recommended. Reservation request form available online. 50% of fee due w/ reservation. Must pre-pay in full for holiday weekend stays. Refunds for cancellations if received 14 days prior to arrival date, minus service charge. No refunds for holiday weekend cancellations. **Registration:** At office. **Fee:** $18–$24 for 2 adults & up to 4 children under age 18.V, MC (No checks.). **Parking:** At site.

Facilities

Number of RV Sites: 191. **Number of Tent-Only Sites:** 0. **Hookups:** Water, electric (20, 30 amps). **Each Site:** Picnic table, fire ring. **Dump Station:** Yes. **Laundry:** Yes. **Pay Phone:** Yes. **Rest Rooms and Showers:** Yes. **Fuel:** No. **Propane:** Yes. **Internal Roads:** Gravel, in fair condition. **RV Service:** No. **Market:** 5 mi. north. **Restaurant:** Yes. **General Store:** Yes. **Vending:** Yes. **Swimming Pool:** Yes. **Playground:** Yes. **Other:** Rec hall, boat launch. **Activities:** Boating (rentals available), swimming, fishing (licenses available), volleyball, horseshoes, planned activities. **Nearby Attractions:** Maine State Capitol & Museum, Fort Western, Monmouth Summer Theater. **Additional Information:** Kennebec Valley Chamber of Commerce, (207) 623-4559.

Restrictions

Pets: Must be leashed, quiet, & cleaned up after. Must not be left unattended. **Fires:** In fire rings only. **Alcoholic Beverages:** Yes. **Vehicle Maximum Length:** None. **Other:** 2-week min. stay on weekends in July & Aug. From late June to mid-Aug., prime sites (numbers 100s & 200s) are rented on a Saturday to Saturday basis. 3-night min. on holiday weekends.

To Get There

Take Maine Turnpike to exit 12 (Auburn.) Follow Rte. 202 east 19.5 mi. to Beaver Brook sign. Turn left onto Back St.; follow to end. Turn left on Wilson Pond Rd., follow to end. Look for campground sign.

OLD ORCHARD BEACH
Hid 'n Pines

P.O. Box 647, 8 Cascade Rd., Old Orchard Beach 04064. T: (207) 934-2352; www.mainerec.com/hidnpines; hidnpines@cybertours.com.

RV ★★★ Tent ★★★

Beauty: ★★ Site Privacy: ★★★
Spaciousness: ★★★ Quiet: ★★
Security: ★★★★★ Cleanliness: ★★★
Insect Control: ★★★ Facilities: ★★★

This campground, just minutes from Old Orchard Beach (some folks walk the distance and avoid the parking problems and traffic congestion downtown), really packs 'em in. This large, 250+ site property, bustles with summer vacationers, who head to the beach during the day and crowd into the campground at night. Expect it to be crawling with families, a bit noisy, and congested. Sites are on the smallish side, tucked under pine trees, side-by-side, flanking each side of the campground roads. But there are conveniences: clean bathrooms with free hot showers (nice after a day in the salt-tinged air and ocean waters); heated swimming pool, and a nearby strip mall (you can walk to it) with an ice cream shop and groceries.

Basics

Operated By: Lori Owen. **Open:** Mid-May–Columbus Day. **Site Assignment:** Reservations suggested, $30 deposit, 7-day cancellation notice with $3 service charge; MC, V, no checks. **Registration:** At office. **Fee:** Full hookups, $30.50; water & electric, $27.50; no hookups, $24.50, based on family of 3; additional adults, $5; additional children, ages 3-21, $3. **Parking:** At site, 1 car per site.

Facilities

Number of RV Sites: 200. **Number of Tent-Only Sites:** 50. **Hookups:** Water, electric, sewer (20, 30 amps). **Each Site:** Picnic table, fire ring. **Dump Station:** Yes. **Laundry:** Yes. **Pay Phone:** Yes. **Rest Rooms and Showers:** Yes. **Fuel:** No. **Propane:** Yes. **Internal Roads:** Paved, gravel (good). **RV Service:** No. **Market:** Old Orchard Beach (500 ft.). **Restaurant:** No. **General Store:** No. **Vending:** Yes. **Swimming Pool:** Yes. **Playground:** Yes. **Other:** Game room. **Activities:** Swimming, basketball. **Nearby Attractions:** Old Orchard Beach, southern coast parks & beaches, Portland. **Additional Information:** Old Orchard Beach Chamber of Commerce, First St., Old Orchard Beach, ME 04064 (207) 934-2500 (800) 365-9386; www.oldorchardbeachmaine.com.

Restrictions

Pets: Must be on a leash, never left unattended. Only 1 pet allowed per site. **Fires:** In grills, stoves, & fire rings only. **Alcoholic Beverages:** At site only. **Vehicle Maximum Length:** None. **Other:** No motocycles allowed.

To Get There

From junction, Maine Turnpike and I-195, exit 5, go east 2 mi. on I-195, then east 2 mi. on Rte. 5, then northwest 0.5 mi. on Rte. 98; campground is on the right.

OLD ORCHARD BEACH
Old Orchard Beach Campground

27 Ocean Park Rd., Old Orchard Beach 04064. T: (207) 934-4477; www.gocamping.com; relax@gocamping.com.

RV ★★★ Tent ★★★★

Beauty: ★★★ Site Privacy: ★★★
Spaciousness: ★★★ Quiet: ★★★
Security: ★★★★★ Cleanliness: ★★★
Insect Control: ★★★ Facilities: ★★★

Location, just off the highway and minutes from Old Orchard Beach, makes this campground popular with travelers exploring the southern coast of Maine. Families come for weekends and week-long stays, to vacation at popular Old Orchard Beach. The price is right (particularly when compared to some beach area resorts) and there's the added convenience of the campground shuttle bus. Campers can avoid parking fees and traffic hassles. The campground has modest facilities: clean rest rooms and free showers, two pools, and a kid-friendly arcade room. Most hookup sites are set side-by-side in rows, flanked by woods for shade and privacy. There's a large wooded wilderness area for open tenting (no numbered sites) set in a dense forest apart from the others. Be forewarned: This area is sometimes a magnet for partying groups.

Basics

Operated By: Daigle family. **Open:** May–Columbus Day. **Site Assignment:** Reservations suggested, $25 deposit, 14 day cancellation policy with $10 service charge, 3-night min. stay for holiday weekends; MC, V, D; checks accepted as deposits but not upon arrival. **Registration:** At office. **Fee:** Full hookups, $32; water & electric, $29; no hookups, $25, based on family of 2; additional adults, $7; additional children, ages 3-17, $5. **Parking:** At site.

Facilities

Number of RV Sites: 150. **Number of Tent-Only Sites:** 150. **Hookups:** Water, electric, sewer (20, 30 amps). **Each Site:** Picnic table, fire ring. **Dump Station:** Yes. **Laundry:** Yes. **Pay Phone:** Yes. **Rest Rooms and Showers:** Yes. **Fuel:** No. **Propane:** Yes. **Internal Roads:** Gravel, dirt (good). **RV Service:** No. **Market:** Saco (5 mi). **Restaurant:** No. **General Store:** Yes. **Vending:** No. **Swimming Pool:** Yes. **Playground:** Yes. **Other:** Rec hall, bus shuttles to the beach. **Activities:** Swimming, basketball, horseshoes, volleyball. **Nearby Attractions:** Old Orchard Beach, southern coastal parks & beaches, Portland. **Additional Information:** Old Orchard Beach Chamber of Commerce, First St., Old Orchard Beach, ME 04064 (207) 934-2500 (800) 365-9386; www.oldorchardbeachmaine.com.

Restrictions

Pets: Must be on a leash, never left unattended. Only adults can walk dogs in campground. **Fires:** In grills, stoves, & fire rings only. **Alcoholic Beverages:** At site only. **Vehicle Max. Length:** None.

TO GET THERE

From junction Maine Turnpike and I-195, exit 5, go 2 mi. east on I-195, then east 1,500 feet on Rte. 5; campground is on the right.

OLD ORCHARD BEACH
Paradise Park

P.O. Box 4, Upper Main St., Adelaine Rd., Old Orchard Beach 04064. T: (207) 934-4633; F: (207) 934-8510; www.paradisepark.com.

RV ★★ Tent ★★

Beauty: ★★ Site Privacy: ★★
Spaciousness: ★★ Quiet: ★★
Security: ★★★ Cleanliness: ★★★
Insect Control: ★★★ Facilities: ★★★

The best thing about this busy and often crowded campground is its proximity to popular Old Orchard Beach. Campers are within walking distance to the pier, shopping, amusements, and one of Maine's longest, white sand beaches. If you like the hustle and bustle of tourist-laden, honky-tonk Old Orchard Beach, you're likely to feel right at home at Paradise Park. You'll have close quarters at this campground. Sites are squished together, often close to the road; vehicles are helter-skelter, parked wherever they'll fit. There are a handful of sites ringed around a five-acre bass pond (there are paddleboat races and fishing tournaments for the kids); other sites are clustered in the woods—all tight spaces. If you like friendly folks and a bit of commune living, you'll have fun here. Nice touch: we like the two hot tubs.

BASICS

Operated By: Halle family. **Open:** May 15–Oct. 15. **Site Assignment:** Reservations suggested, $50 deposit, 10-day cancellation policy; MC, V, D, no checks. **Registration:** At office. **Fee:** Full hookups, $32, water & electric, $29; no hookups, $26; waterfront sites, $3 extra, based on 2 people; additional adults, $5; additional children, ages 4-21, $3. **Parking:** At site.

FACILITIES

Number of RV Sites: 162. **Number of Tent-Only Sites:** 15. **Hookups:** Water, electric, sewer (20, 30 amps), cable TV, modem. **Each Site:** Picnic table, fire ring. **Dump Station:** Yes. **Laundry:** Yes. **Pay Phone:** Yes. **Rest Rooms and Showers:** Yes. **Fuel:** No. **Propane:** No. **Internal Roads:** Paved (good). **RV Service:** No. **Market:** Old Orchard Beach (0.5 mi). **Restaurant:** No. **General Store:** Yes. **Vending:** No. **Swimming Pool:** Yes. **Playground:** Yes. **Other:** Pond, paddleboat rentals, hot tubs, game room, rec hall. **Activities:** Swimming, fishing, shuffleboard, basketball, volleyball, horseshoes, planned activities on Saturdays during summer. **Nearby Attractions:** Old Orchard Beach, southern coast parks & beaches, Portland. **Additional Information:** Old Orchard Beach Chamber of Commerce, First St., Old Orchard Beach, ME 04064 (207) 934-2500 (800) 365-9386; www.oldorchardbeachmaine.com.

RESTRICTIONS

Pets: Must be on a leash, never left unattended. **Fires:** In grills, stoves, & fire rings only. **Alcoholic Beverages:** At site only. **Vehicle Max. Length:** None. **Other:** Families & couples only, no singles.

TO GET THERE

From junction Maine Turnpike and I-195, go east 2 mi. on I-195, then north 2 mi. on Rte. 5, then 0.2 mi. west on Adelaine Rd.; campground is at the end of the street.

OLD ORCHARD BEACH
Powder Horn Family Camping Resort

P.O. Box 366, Old Orchard Beach 04064. T: (207) 934-4733 (800) 934-7038 (reservations); www.mainecampgrounds.com; phorn36504@aol.com.

RV ★★★★ Tent ★★★

Beauty: ★★★ Site Privacy: ★★★
Spaciousness: ★★★ Quiet: ★★
Security: ★★★★★ Cleanliness: ★★★★★
Insect Control: ★★★ Facilities: ★★★★★

This giant-size resort in southern Maine is a popular summer vacation destination for New England campers. If you're looking to get away from it all, this is not the place to go. Powder Horn is chockful of nonstop activities and crowds of vacationing families. It's located just minutes from rolicking Old Orchard Beach (the campground offers shuttle bus service to the beach and downtown area), but the pace doesn't slow or calm down much at the campground. The three-pool complex, adjacent to the sports fields and mini golf course, is a hub of activity, especially late afternoon and evening when campers return for the day. There are almost 500 sites, so there's plenty of choice. A number of sites are set in open meadows, with full and partial sun throughout the day. Others, including an open tent-only area, are tucked in oak and pine groves toward the back of the campground, away from the busy front recreation/office area.

BASICS

Operated By: David & Glenna Ahearn. **Open:** Memorial Day–Columbus Day. **Site Assignment:** Reservations suggested, $50 deposit, 7-day cancellation policy with $10 service charge; MC, V, D, no checks. **Registration:** At office. **Fee:** Full hookups (50 amp & cable), $41.50; full hookups (30 amp), $38.50; water & electric, 33.50; no hookups, $28.50, based on 2 people; additional adults, $7; additional children, ages 3-21, $3. **Parking:** At site, 1 vehicle per site; extra vehicles, $3.

FACILITIES

Number of RV Sites: 442. **Number of Tent-Only Sites:** 56. **Hookups:** Water, electric (20, 30, 50 amps), sewer, cable TV, modem. **Each Site:** Picnic table, fire ring. **Dump Station:** Yes. **Laundry:** Yes. **Pay Phone:** Yes. **Rest Rooms and Showers:** Yes. **Fuel:** No. **Propane:** Yes. **Internal Roads:** Paved (good). **RV Service:** No. **Market:** full service store on the premises. **Restaurant:** Yes. **General Store:** Yes. **Vending:** No. **Swimming Pool:** Yes. **Playground:** Yes. **Other:** Game room, shuttle bus to beach, hot tubs, adult lounge, rec room, 18-hole mini-golf course. **Activities:** Swimming, horseshoes, shuffleboard, basketball, mini-golf, planned activities, including children's programs, arts & crafts, contests, live entertainment, dances, socials, & more. **Nearby Attractions:** Old Orchard Beach, southern coast parks & beaches, Portland. **Additional Information:** Old Orchard Beach Chamber, First St., Old Orchard Beach, ME 04064 (207) 934-2500 (800) 365-9386; www.oldorchardbeachmaine.com.

RESTRICTIONS

Pets: Must be on a leash, never left unattended. **Fires:** In grills, stoves, & fire rings only. **Alcoholic Beverages:** At site only. **Vehicle Maximum Length:** None.

TO GET THERE

From junction Maine Turnpike and I-195, exit 5, go east 1.2 mi. on I-195, then north 3 mi. on Rte. 1, then east 2 mi. on Rte. 98; campground is on the left.

OLD ORCHARD BEACH
Wild Acres

179 Saco Ave., Old Orchard Beach 04064. T: (207) 934-2535; F: (207) 934-1947; www.mainecamping.com; wildacres@cyber-tours.com.

RV ★★★★ Tent ★★★★

Beauty: ★★★ Site Privacy: ★★★
Spaciousness: ★★★ Quiet: ★★
Security: ★★★★ Cleanliness: ★★★★
Insect Control: ★★★ Facilities: ★★★★

This is one of southern Maine's bustling mega camping resorts, with more than 500 sites, crowds, and activities galore. Wild Acres is the closest campground to Old Orchard Beach and offers direct ocean access for walking, swimming, and sunbathing. On the property, you'll find more activities than you could possibly do in a weekend, or perhaps, even a week. There are three swimming pools (two adult and one kiddie pool), three hot tubs, an 18-hole mini-golf course, and weekend entertainment. The adult lounge features pool tables, big screen TV and a fieldstone fireplace. Kids have their own rec hall. The landscaping throughout the campground has received special attention (we like the small ponds and fountains scattered throughout the property), and the owner has left several undeveloped areas, adding to the natural ambiance of the resort. Sites are good-sized, shaded or in the open. Pull-through, full hookup sites are set side-by-side near the front of the resort. The tent-only section is nestled in the back of the property, closest to the ocean walk access, with its own nearby pool and playground area.

BASICS

Operated By: Rick Ahearn. **Open:** Memorial Day–Columbus Day. **Site Assignment:** Reservations suggested, $50 credit card deposit, 7-day cancellation policy w/ a $10 service charge. No min. stay Memorial Day weekend, 3-day min. stay on July 4th & Labor Day; MC, V, D, no checks. **Registration:** At office. **Fee:** Full hookups, $38.50; water & electric, $33.50; no hookups, $28.50, based on 2 people, additional adults, $7; children ages 3–21, $3. **Parking:** At site.

Facilities

Number of RV Sites: 455. **Number of Tent-Only Sites:** 45. **Hookups:** Water, electric, sewer (30, 50 amps), cable TV, modem. **Each Site:** Picnic table, fire ring. **Dump Station:** Yes. **Laundry:** Yes. **Pay Phone:** Yes. **Rest Rooms and Showers:** Yes. **Fuel:** No. **Propane:** No. **Internal Roads:** Gravel, dirt (good). **RV Service:** No. **Market:** Saco (2 mi). **Restaurant:** No. **General Store:** Yes. **Vending:** Yes. **Swimming Pool:** Yes. **Playground:** Yes. **Other:** Hot tubs, rec hall, adult lounge, nature trails, stocked fishing pond, 18-hole mini-golf course, entertainment pavilion, access to ocean & beach, tennis courts. **Activities:** Swimming, fishing, beach-combing, tennis, mini-golf, horseshoes, shuffleboard, volleyball. **Nearby Attractions:** Old Orchard Beach, Portland, southern coastal parks & beaches. **Additional Information:** Old Orchard Beach Chamber of Commerce, First St., Old Orchard Beach, ME 04064 (207) 934-2500 (800) 365-9386; www.oldorchardbeachmaine.com.

Restrictions

Pets: Must be on a leash, never left unattended. Some breeds not allowed. **Fires:** In grills, stoves, & fire rings only. **Alcoholic Beverages:** At site only. **Vehicle Maximum Length:** None. **Other:** Skateboards, scooters, & rollerblades not allowed.

To Get There

From Maine Turnpike and I-195, exit 5, go east 2 mi. on I-195, then east 1.5 mi. on Rte. 5; campground is on the right.

OQUOSSOC

Cupsuptic Campground

P.O. Box 326, Rte. 16, Oquossoc 04964. T: (207) 864-5249; www.cupsupticcampground.com; cupsuptic@megalink.net.

RV ★★★ Tent ★★

Beauty: ★★★	Site Privacy: ★★★
Spaciousness: ★★	Quiet: ★★★★
Security: ★★★	Cleanliness: ★★
Insect Control: ★★	Facilities: ★★★

This pleasant, small campground is set in a pine grove on pristine Cupsuptic Lake, just north of Rangeley. A few campsites sit along a sandy beach on the lakeshore, a few others face Toothaker Brook. Twelve sites are set in the woods. If you really like privacy, and you're tenting, rent out an entire island. Some of the choicest spots include DS, V, IV, III, 48, and 50, on the beach, but nicely buffered for privacy. Sites 51 and 52, across Loon Ln.but near the beach, are huge, and great for RVs. Site 23, at the other end of the beach, is an awesome tent site. The rest of that bunch, sites 13 through 29, are fairly open, though. Newly-renovated modern rest rooms, too; just what we like to see. (Look for the flower "bed.") This is a great place to kick back and enjoy the outdoors with little fuss. All you really need is a boat—they'll rent you one—and some fishing gear (look to hook trout or salmon.) Take a day trip to Rangeley Lake, or cruise Rte. 16, a famous moose hang-out. Best time to spot these gangly, cartoony beasts: spring and summer.

Basics

Operated By: Barbara & Danny Gallant. **Open:** May 1–Dec. 1. **Site Assignment:** Reservations recommended (may reserve online.) Deposit of 1- to 2-night fee, depending on length of stay. Refund for cancellation if received within 3 weeks of scheduled arrival, minus $10 fee. **Registration:** At office. **Fee:** $17–$22 for 2 adults & their children under age 18. Wilderness sites, $12. Island sites, $17. No credit cards. **Parking:** At sites or as designated.

Facilities

Number of RV Sites: 55. **Number of Tent-Only Sites:** 0. **Hookups:** Water, electric (15, 30 amps). **Each Site:** Picnic table, fire pit. **Dump Station:** Yes. **Laundry:** No. **Pay Phone:** Yes. **Rest Rooms and Showers:** Yes, coin-op. **Fuel:** No. **Propane:** No. **Internal Roads:** Gravel, in good condition. **RV Service:** No. **Market:** 5 mi. east. **Restaurant:** 5 mi. east. **General Store:** Yes. **Vending:** No. **Swimming Pool:** No. **Playground:** Yes. **Other:** Rec hall. **Activities:** Fishing (licenses available), lake swimming, horseshoes, basketball, boating (rentals available), planned activities. **Nearby Attractions:** Rangeley Lake State Park, Wilhelm Reich Museum, moosewatching, golf, scenic flights. **Additional Information:** Rangeley Lakes Region Chamber of Commerce, (207) 864-5364 or (800) MT-LAKES.

Restrictions

Pets: Must be leashed, quiet, & cleaned up after. Must not be left unattended. Not allowed on beach. Use pet walk area. **Fires:** In fire pits only. **Alcoholic Beverages:** Yes. **Vehicle Maximum Length:** 40 ft. **Other:** Ask on arrival.

To Get There

From junction of Rtes. 16 and 4, go 4.5 mi. northwest on Rte. 16. Campground entrance is on the left.

OQUOSSOC

Black Brook Cove Campground

P.O. Box 319, Oquossoc 04964. T: (207) 486-3828; www.blackbrookcove.com.

RV ★★★ Tent ★★

Beauty: ★★★	Site Privacy: ★★★
Spaciousness: ★★	Quiet: ★★★★
Security: ★★★	Cleanliness: ★★
Insect Control: ★★	Facilities: ★

If your fantasy includes venturing in Maine's backcountry with your own secret weapon, a registered Maine guide, this is your place. Campground owner Jeff LaRochelle is a Maine guide who leads moose- and bear-hunting trips (in season) and fishing expeditions, including fly-in trips to backcountry ponds via seaplane. Even if you don't choose a walk on the wild side, this intimate campground offers a pleasant outdoors experience. It's set on a cove at the southeast end of Aziscohos Lake (stocked with land-locked salmon and brook trout) in Maine's western mountains. Grass and gravel campites are scattered around the property, including some seasonal sites. Only a few sites are set along the waterfront, including site 25 (by itself, and very private), and sites 21 A and B. Not so close to the beach, but very private, area tent sites 10 and 11, backed into the woods. RV sites 26, 27, and 28 are close to the beach and the boat launch. Got the urge to escape? Sixteen remote sites, reachable by boat only, are available on 20-acre Beaver Island. This is the kind of place that's decorated with snapshots of people posing with really big fish.

Basics

Operated By: Janet & Jeff LaRochelle. **Open:** Apr. 15–Nov. 30. **Site Assignment:** Reservations recommended. Full payment required. Refund for cancellation w/ 30-day notice. **Registration:** At office. **Fee:** $15 for 2 adults & their children under age 18. V, MC. **Parking:** At site.

Facilities

Number of RV Sites: 70. **Number of Tent-Only Sites:** 0. **Hookups:** Water, electric (20 amps). **Each Site:** Picnic table, fire ring. **Dump Station:** Yes. **Laundry:** Yes. **Pay Phone:** No. **Rest Rooms and Showers:** Yes, coin-op. **Fuel:** No. **Propane:** Yes. **Internal Roads:** Gravel, in good condition. **RV Service:** No. **Market:** 20 mi. east. **Restaurant:** 20 mi. east. **General Store:** Yes. **Vending:** No. **Swimming Pool:** No. **Playground:** Yes. **Other:** Boat ramp. **Activities:** Boating (rentals available), hiking, guiding hunting & fishing. **Nearby Attractions:** Rangeley Lake State Park, Wilhelm Reich Museum, moosewatching, golf, scenic flights, Appalachian Trail hiking. **Additional Information:** Rangeley Lakes Region Chamber of Commerce, (207) 864-5364 or (800) MT-LAKES.

Restrictions

Pets: Must be leashed, quiet, & cleaned up after. Must not be left unattended. Not allowed in buildings. **Fires:** In fire rings only. **Alcoholic Beverages:** Yes. **Vehicle Maximum Length:** 45 ft. **Other:** Mandatory recycling.

To Get There

From southern Maine, take Rte. 95 north to exit 11 (Gray.) Take Rte. 26 north to Errol, N.H. Take right onto Rte. 16 north; follow for 18-20 mi. and take left onto Lincoln Pond Rd. Campground is on the right.

ORLAND

Shady Oaks

32 Leaches Point, Orland 04472. T: (207) 469-7739; www.shadyoakscampground.com; cuatsorvpk@aol.com.

RV ★★★ Tent ★★

Beauty: ★★	Site Privacy: ★★
Spaciousness: ★★★	Quiet: ★★★
Security: ★★★★★	Cleanliness: ★★★★
Insect Control: ★★★	Facilities: ★★★

Shady Oaks caters to a mature crowd, mostly retirees, who return year after year. It also draws tourists traveling in the area to see the Maine coastline and en route to and from Acadia National Park. Families with young children do okay here; there's a swimming pool, train rides, and kid's crafts. But if you have preteens or teens, forget about it—they'll most likely be miserable. Most sites are too small for our comfort, set out in the open with little privacy.

Most campers here don't seem to mind the cramped, open quarters; they're a friendly bunch eager to meet their neighbors and join in on nightly socials, potluck dinners and pancake breakfasts. The cabins (at a reasonable $30 a night) are a bargain.

Basics

Operated By: Joyce & Don Nelson. **Open:** May–Sept. **Site Assignment:** Reservations suggested in Jul.–Aug.; credit card will hold reservation, no cancellation policy; MC,V, checks. **Registration:** At office. **Fee:** Full hookups, $21; water & electric, $20 based on 2 people per site; additional people, $2. **Parking:** At site, 2 vehicles per site.

Facilities

Number of RV Sites: 55. **Number of Tent-Only Sites:** 0. **Hookups:** Water, electric, sewer (30, 50 amps). **Each Site:** Picnic table, fire ring. **Dump Station:** Yes. **Laundry:** Yes. **Pay Phone:** Yes. **Rest Rooms and Showers:** Yes. **Fuel:** No. **Propane:** Yes. **Internal Roads:** Gravel (good). **RV Service:** Yes. **Market:** Bucksport (1 mi). **Restaurant:** No. **General Store:** Yes. **Vending:** Yes. **Swimming Pool:** Yes. **Playground:** Yes. **Other:** Rec hall, cabin rentals, nature trails. **Activities:** Swimming, trail walking/hiking, horseshoes, planned activities, including potluck suppers, bingo, socials, arts & crafts, & more. **Nearby Attractions:** Bucksport/Searsport, Deer Isle Peninsula, Bar Harbor, Acadia National Park. **Additional Information:** Bucksport Bay Area Chamber of Commerce, P.O. Box 1880, 263 Main St., Bucksport, ME 04416-1880 (207) 469-6818 & Acadia Information Center, P.O. Box 139, Mount Desert, ME 04660 (207) 667-8550 or (800) 358-8550, www.acadiainfo.com.

Restrictions

Pets: No dogs allowed. **Fires:** In grills, stoves, & fire rings only. **Alcoholic Beverages:** At site only. **Vehicle Maximum Length:** None.

To Get There

From junction Rtes.1 and 15 (in Bucksport), go north 1.6 mi. on Rte. 1, then south 0.2 mi. on Leaches Point Rd. (at intersection of Rte. 1, 175 and Leaches Point Rd.); campground is on the left.

ORR'S ISLAND

Orr's Island Campground

45 Bond Point Rd., Orr's Island 04066. T: (207) 833-5595; www.orrsisland.com; camping@orrsisland.com.

RV ★★★★ Tent ★★★★

Beauty: ★★★★★ | Site Privacy: ★★★★
Spaciousness: ★★★★★ | Quiet: ★★★★★
Security: ★★★★★ | Cleanliness: ★★★★
Insect Control: ★★★ | Facilities: ★★★

Orr's Island is quite far out into Casco Bay, but the drive out from Brunswick and over Great Island will melt away any stress. Once you've set up your campsite, take a moment to walk around and drink in the views of Muscongus Bay, Harpswell Cove, and Reed Cove. Close your eyes and feel the breezes and the sunlight washing over you. The open camping sites up on North Bluff offer a view of Harpswell Sound and many feature small stands of trees separating them from their neighbors. Plus, from North and South Bluff, you'll have access to the shore for beachcombing, hanging out on the rocks, or swimming if you're cast of sturdy Scandinavian stock. The Cove Rd. lettered sites are perfectly situated for tents and kayaks—what a stellar combination. After a night spent in one of these sites, you'll have that pleasant ache in your lungs from the fresh salt air.

Basics

Operated By: The Bond Family. **Open:** Memorial Day–mid-Sept. **Site Assignment:** Reservations or first come first served; 2 night min. for advance reservations. **Registration:** At office. **Fee:** $19–$30. **Parking:** At site.

Facilities

Number of RV Sites: 70. **Number of Tent-Only Sites:** 0. **Hookups:** Water, electric, sewer. **Each Site:** Fire ring, picnic table. **Dump Station:** Yes. **Laundry:** Yes. **Pay Phone:** Yes. **Rest Rooms and Showers:** Yes. **Fuel:** No. **Propane:** No. **Internal Roads:** Gravel. **RV Service:** No. **Market:** 0.5 mi. north on Rte. 24. **Restaurant:** No. **General Store:** Ice, soft drinks, camping supplies. **Vending:** No. **Swimming Pool:** No. **Playground:** Yes. **Other:** Recreationsl equipment can be borrowed. **Activities:** Swimming, boating, canoe rental, wild berry picking, bird-watching, games & books. **Nearby Attractions:** L. L. Bean, Boothbay Harbor, movie theater, Reid Sate Park, Popham Beach, Eagle Island. **Additional Information:** Boothbay Harbor Region Chamber of Commerce, (207) 633-2353 or (800) 266-8422.

Restrictions

Pets: On leash. **Fires:** In fire ring. **Alcoholic Beverages:** Yes. **Vehicle Maximum Length:** 40 ft. **Other:** Advance reservations require a 2-night stay.

To Get There

Take Exit 22 off of Rte. 95. This will put you on Rte. #1 between Brunswick and Bath. From Rte. 1 take the Cooks Corner exit for Orr's and Bailey Island. Take Rte. 24 (straight ahead at the traffic light). Follow Rte. 24 the rest of the way. Crossing the first bridge puts you on Great Island. Crossing the second bridge puts you on Orr's Island. Turn right on to Bond Point Rd. (our entrance). A large white ship's wheel (our logo) will be at the turn onto Bond Point Rd. We are approximately 2 mi. from the Orr's Island Bridge, or a total of 11 mi. from Cooks Corner.

OXFORD

Two Lakes Camping Area

P.O. Box 206, Oxford 04270. T: (207) 539-4851; F: (207) 539-4001; www.campmaine.com; twolakes@megalink.net.

RV ★★ Tent ★★

Beauty: ★★ | Site Privacy: ★★
Spaciousness: ★★★★ | Quiet: ★★
Security: ★★★ | Cleanliness: ★★★★
Insect Control: ★★★ | Facilities: ★★

Located in the Western lakes region of southwest Maine, about 35 miles north of Portland, this terraced campground is set on Hogan and Whitney lakes. The 600-foot sandy beach and lake swimming (on Hogan Lake) help make up for the fact that this campground has a somewhat cluttery feel. It's pleasant and wooded, though, with some sites that are fenced in for privacy. Campsites are set on loop roads off Lake View Dr., with seasonal sites lined up along Chipmonk Ln.(that's how they spell it.) Although most people clamor for sites near the lake, the nicest spots, in our view, are on a quiet dead-end road off Moose Run, numbered 103 to 116. These boast some good tree cover between sites, and promise more peace than the busy area near the beach, game room, and boat launch at the other end of the campground. Nice feature: there's a beach for pets, away from the 'people beach.'

Basics

Operated By: Barbara & Dick Varney. **Open:** May 1–Oct. 1. **Site Assignment:** Reservations recommended. 50% deposit required. No refunds for cancellation, but may get credit for future camping. **Registration:** At office. **Fee:** $20–$31 for 2 adults & up to 3 children. V, MC, D. **Parking:** At site.

Facilities

Number of RV Sites: 107. **Number of Tent-Only Sites:** 13. **Hookups:** Water, electric (30 amps), sewer. **Each Site:** Picnic table, fire ring. **Dump Station:** Yes. **Laundry:** Yes. **Pay Phone:** Yes. **Rest Rooms and Showers:** Yes, coin-op. **Fuel:** No. **Propane:** No. **Internal Roads:** Gravel, in good condition. **RV Service:** No. **Market:** 6 mi. north. **Restaurant:** 8 mi. north, on Rte. 26. **General Store:** Yes. **Vending:** Yes. **Swimming Pool:** No. **Playground:** Yes. **Other:** Boat dock, rec hall. **Activities:** Boating (rentals available), fishing (licenses available), volleyball, basketball, horseshoes, mini-golf, planned activities. **Nearby Attractions:** Oxford Plains Speedway. **Additional Information:** Oxford Hills Chamber, (207) 743-228.

Restrictions

Pets: Leashed, quiet, & cleaned up after. Must not be left unattended. No aggressive breeds (ie. Rottweilers, Dobermans, Huskies, Shepherds.). **Fires:** In fireplaces only. **Alcoholic Beverages:** At sites only. **Vehicle Maximum Length:** None. **Other:** 2-day min. stay for reservations. For 1-night stay, call same day to check on availability for walk-ins.

To Get There

From Maine Turnpike, take exit 11 (Gray.) From Gray, take Rte. 26 21 mi. north to Oxford. As you descend hill, slow your speed; campground sign is on the left. Follow road 1 mi. in to lake and lodge.

PALMYRA

Palmyra Golf and RV Resort

147 Lang Hill Rd., Palmyra 04965. T: (207) 938-5677; F: (207) 938-5130; www.palmyra-me.com; palmyra@www.palmyra-me.com.

RV ★★★★★ Tent ★★

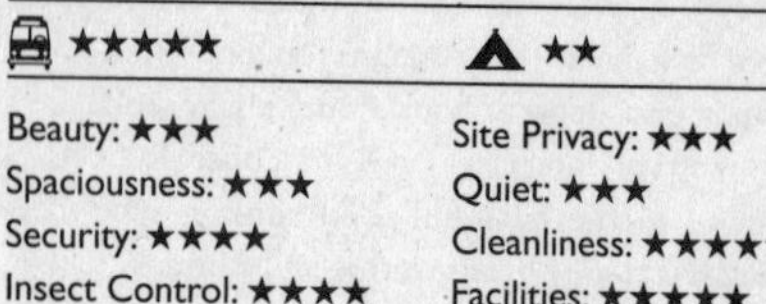

Beauty: ★★★ | Site Privacy: ★★★
Spaciousness: ★★★ | Quiet: ★★★
Security: ★★★★ | Cleanliness: ★★★★★
Insect Control: ★★★★ | Facilities: ★★★★★

If you like to golf, you're going to love this campground in central Maine, with its own 18-hole, 72 par course, pro shop and clubhouse on the premises. Located off the interstate, just south of Bangor, this campground caters to large motor home and RV travelers who enjoy a pampered camping experience. Local golfers use the public course but campers get a discount. There's a driving range and pitch and putt center, too. You'll have a choice of roomy, bigger-than-average open sites, all set in rows off the campground's long, one-way streets. There's also a separate loop of shaded sites behind the office and recreation area. There's plenty of room to spread out in this campground, and the hilly, terraced terrain and views of the golf course add to its expansiveness and beauty.

BASICS

Operated By: Cayer family. **Open:** May 15–Oct. 15. **Site Assignment:** Reservations suggested, no deposit required (if you don't show by 6:30 p.m. of scheduled day of arrival, they rent space) MC, V, D. **Registration:** At office. **Fee:** Full hookups, $24; water & electric, $23 (50 amp); $21.50 (30 amp). **Parking:** At site.

FACILITIES

Number of RV Sites: 143. **Number of Tent-Only Sites:** 4. **Hookups:** Water, electric, sewer (30, 50 amps), modem. **Each Site:** Picnic table, fire ring, light. **Dump Station:** Yes. **Laundry:** Yes. **Pay Phone:** Yes. **Rest Rooms and Showers:** Yes. **Fuel:** No. **Propane:** No. **Internal Roads:** Paved, gravel (good). **RV Service:** No. **Market:** Palmyra (2 mi). **Restaurant:** Yes. **General Store:** Yes. **Vending:** No. **Swimming Pool:** Yes. **Playground:** No. **Other:** 18 hole golf course, pro shop, clubhouse, driving range, function hall, group area. **Activities:** Golf, swimming, horseshoes, volleyball, shuffleboard. **Nearby Attractions:** Bangor, Augusta. **Additional Information:** Bangor Regional Chamber of Commerce, 519 Maine St., P.O. Box 1443, Bangor, ME 04402 (207) 947-0307, www.bangorregion.com.

RESTRICTIONS

Pets: On leash, never left unattended. **Fires:** In grills, stoves, & fire rings only. **Alcoholic Beverages:** At site only. **Vehicle Max. Length:** None.

TO GET THERE

From I-95, exit 39, go west 3 mi. on Rte. 2; campground is on the right.

PERU
Honey Run Beach & Campground

456 East Shore Rd., Peru 04290. T: (207) 562-4913; www.honeyruncampground.com; drjeff@mindspring.com.

RV ★★★★ Tent ★★

Beauty: ★★★ Site Privacy: ★★
Spaciousness: ★★★★ Quiet: ★★★★
Security: ★★★★★ Cleanliness: ★★★★★
Insect Control: ★★★ Facilities: ★★★

Located in a small lakeside community just east of Rumford, Honey Run Beach & Campground is getting a real sprucing up, thanks to new ownership. Formerly more geared to seasonal campers, Honey Run is being reinvented as a vacation destination. Just a handfull of sites are seasonal now. A new pavilion is in place for groups and the family reunion set. Campsites (suitable for big rigs) dot a big, grassy field surrounded by woods. Woodsy sites ring the perimeter of the property, and there are even a few primitive tent sites "up the mountain," as owner Jeff Lennox puts it. OK, so it's not really a mountain, but a climb up the hill would make a dandy work-out and leg-stretch for the road-weary RVer! Another good selling point here: a short but wide, private sandy beach on sparkling Worthley Pond, located across the street. There's enough space for a few sun-bathers, plus some picnic tables and rental canoes and kayaks; good for taking a peek at the houses surrounding the pond and playing the "Would you ever want to move here?" game.

BASICS

Operated By: Jeff Lennox. **Open:** Memorial Day–Labor Day. **Site Assignment:** Reservations suggested. Deposit of first night's fee required. Refund for cancellations w/ 14-day notice. **Registration:** At office. **Fee:** $15–$25. No credit cards. **Parking:** At site.

FACILITIES

Number of RV Sites: 72. **Number of Tent-Only Sites:** 0. **Hookups:** Water, electric (30, 50 amps), sewer. **Each Site:** Picnic table, fire ring. **Dump Station:** Yes. **Laundry:** Yes. **Pay Phone:** Yes. **Rest Rooms and Showers:** Yes. **Fuel:** No. **Propane:** No. **Internal Roads:** Gravel, in good condition. **RV Service:** No. **Market:** 12 mi. north. **Restaurant:** 12 mi. north. **General Store:** Yes. **Vending:** Yes. **Swimming Pool:** No. **Playground:** Yes. **Other:** Rec hall w/ pavilion. **Activities:** Lake swimming, hiking (on hillside trails behind campground), boating (canoe & kayak rentals available). **Nearby Attractions:** Norland's Living History Museum, Appalachian Trail hiking, Black Mountain, Pennacook Falls, Santa's Village, Mt. Blue State Park. **Additional Information:** River Valley Chamber, (207) 364-3241.

RESTRICTIONS

Pets: Must be leashed, quiet, & cleaned up after. Must not be left unattended. **Fires:** In fire rings only. **Alcoholic Beverages:** At sites only. **Vehicle Maximum Length:** None. **Other:** Ask on arrival.

TO GET THERE

Take Maine Turnpike to exit 12 (Auburn.) Follow Rte. 4 north to Rte. 108 west. Follow Rte. 108 for 11 mi., then turn left at Worthley Pond and campground sign. Campground is 3.5 mi. in.

PHIPPSBURG
Meadowbrook Camping

33 Meadowbrook Rd., Phippsburg 04562. T: (207) 443-4967 or (800) 370-CAMP; F: (207) 386-0335; www.meadowbrookme.com; mbcamp@gwi.net.

RV ★★★★ Tent ★★★

Beauty: ★★ Site Privacy: ★★
Spaciousness: ★★ Quiet: ★★★
Security: ★★★ Cleanliness: ★★★★★
Insect Control: ★★★ Facilities: ★★★

This mid-coast campground, located just five miles south of Bath, is wildly popular with RVers, who don't seem to care that the ocean is nowhere in sight. Matter of fact, one of Maine's nicest stretches of sand, Popham Beach State Park, is but a 10-mile drive away, and if you can't wait to swim, there's always the campground's heated pool, surely warmer than the North Atlantic! (About that pool, we think some umbrellas would be a nice touch.) And should you want a shore dinner, you don't have to leave; they sell lobsters, clams, and corn, daily, and will cook it up for you for no extra charge. Campsites, set in loops, are gravel, of varying size. The largest RV sites are in an open, grassy area near the (funky) rec hall and pool area; head farther back into the property, and sites are wooded, nudging toward cliffs and a beaver pond. Sites 77 through 82 overlook a marsh; stay away from 82 if you're tenting, though, since it's on a downhill slope that would be a real mess in the rain. Site 35 is great, with a long approach to a woodsy spot on a hill; site 33 offers great cliffside views, as well, edging a wooded area. Among the tent sites, we'd go for site 73, near the nature trail, built on a platform.

BASICS

Operated By: TLM Enterprises. **Open:** May 1–Oct. 1. **Site Assignment:** Reservations recommended. For less than 1-week stay, full fee required for deposit. For stays of more than 1 week, 10% deposit required. Refunds for cancellations within 7 days, minus $10 service fee. **Registration:** At office. **Fee:** $20–$26 per family. V, MC, D, AE. **Parking:** At site.

FACILITIES

Number of RV Sites: 90. **Number of Tent-Only Sites:** 10. **Hookups:** Water, electric (15, 20, 30, 50 amps). **Each Site:** Picnic table, fireplace. **Dump Station:** Yes. **Laundry:** Yes. **Pay Phone:** Yes. **Rest Rooms and Showers:** Yes. **Fuel:** No. **Propane:** Yes. **Internal Roads:** Gravel, in good to fair condition. **RV Service:** No. **Market:** 5 mi. north. **Restaurant:** 5 mi. north. **General Store:** Yes. **Vending:** No. **Swimming Pool:** Yes. **Playground:** Yes. **Other:** Rec hall, mini-golf. **Activities:** Swimming, mini-golf, mile-long nature trail, basketball, shuffleboard, horseshoes. **Nearby Attractions:** Popham Beach State Park, Morse Mountain Sanctuary, Maine Maritime Museum, Bowdoin College Museum of Art, Peary-MacMillan Arctic Museum, deep-sea fishing. **Additional Information:** Chamber of Commerce of the Bath-Brunswick Region, (207) 725-8797 or (207) 443-9751; www.midcoastmaine.com.

RESTRICTIONS

Pets: Must be leashed, quiet, & cleaned up after. Must not be left unattended. **Fires:** In fireplaces only. **Alcoholic Beverages:** At sites only. **Vehicle Maximum Length:** None. **Other:** 1 vehicle per site.

TO GET THERE

From Rte. 1 in Bath, take Popham Beach exit, Rte. 209. Follow for 2.5 mi., heading south, to Winnegance Store, then turn right and go 3 mi. to campground. Entrance is on right.

POLAND SPRING

Poland Spring Campground

P.O. Box 409, Poland Spring 04274. T: (207) 998-2151; www.polandspringcamp.com; info@polandspringcamp.com.

RV ★★★ Tent ★★

Beauty: ★★★ Site Privacy: ★★★
Spaciousness: ★★★ Quiet: ★★★★
Security: ★★★★ Cleanliness: ★★★★★
Insect Control: ★★★ Facilities: ★★★

The nicest feature of this Western Lakes-area campground: it sits on a pretty, forested pond, dotted with islands. Three-mile-long Lower Range Pond, sandy-bottomed, provides a great swimming hole for campers here. While there isn't much of a beach, the buoyed swimming area is plenty big. Bonus: If you don't like lake swimming, there's a pool. The campground itself is shaded with pines and mixed hardwoods, and campsites are level and woodsy. This campground is better-tended, and the campsites more prepared, than what you'll find at neighboring Two Lakes Camping Area (see listing.) The friendly owners take care of the details that make all the difference: plenty of trash barrels, an inviting picnic grove overlooking the pond, and a nice booklet for campers, chock-full of information about the local area, dining, shopping, and attractions. Campsites are set on spokelike roads, surrounding the activity pod of rec hall, office, store, rest rooms, laundry, game room, and so on. It's quiet, child-friendly, and appealing.

BASICS

Operated By: David & Tami Wight. **Open:** May 1–Columbus Day. **Site Assignment:** Reservations recommended. $30 deposit required for weekend stay; $40 for week-long stay. Refunds for cancellation w/ 7-day notice, minus $5 fee. **Registration:** At office. **Fee:** $19–$25 for 2 adults & up to 3 children. V, MC, D, debit cards. **Parking:** At site.

FACILITIES

Number of RV Sites: 121. **Number of Tent-Only Sites:** 11. **Hookups:** Water, electric (20, 30 amps), sewer, modem. **Each Site:** Picnic table, fire ring. **Dump Station:** Yes. **Laundry:** Yes. **Pay Phone:** Yes. **Rest Rooms and Showers:** Yes, coin-op. **Fuel:** No. **Propane:** Yes. **Internal Roads:** Gravel, in good condition. **RV Service:** No. **Market:** 5 mi. north. **Restaurant:** 1 mi. north; 8 mi. south. **General Store:** Yes. **Vending:** Yes. **Swimming Pool:** Yes. **Playground:** Yes. **Other:** Game room, adult rec room, boat dock. **Activities:** Fishing (licenses available), lake swimming, boating (rentals available), volleyball, planned activities. **Nearby Attractions:** Sabbathday Lake shaker village, Maine Wildlife Park, tourmaline gem mines, golf, hiking at Range Pond State Park. **Additional Information:** Androscoggin County Chamber, (207) 783-2249; www.androscoggincounty.com.

RESTRICTIONS

Pets: Must be leashed, quiet, & cleaned up after. Must not be left unattended. Not allowed in pool, lake, & public areas. **Fires:** In fireplaces only. **Alcoholic Beverages:** Yes. **Vehicle Maximum Length:** 40 ft. **Other:** 2-night min. stay on weekends in July & Aug.; 3-night min. on holidays.

TO GET THERE

From the Maine Turnpike, take exit 11 (Gray.) Follow Rte. 26 north for 12 mi. Turn right on Connor Ln. Entrance is at end of road, 0.5 mi.

RANGELEY

Rangeley Lake State Park

HC 32 P.O. Box 5000, Rangeley 04970. T: (207) 864-3858 or (207) 624-6080 (off-season); www.state.me.us/doc/parks.htm.

RV ★★★★ Tent ★★★★★

Beauty: ★★★★ Site Privacy: ★★★★
Spaciousness: ★★★★ Quiet: ★★★★
Security: ★★★★★ Cleanliness: ★★★★
Insect Control: ★★ Facilities: ★★★

Set in Maine's western mountains region, an area famous for rugged beauty and great fishing, this state park draws nature-loving campers from New England and beyond. The town of Rangeley has several boat rental outfits; bring your boat to the campground and you can launch it for free. Don't forget the fishing license. You'll want to have a go at the trout and land-locked salmon in this icy-cold lake. Should you wish to brave the waters yourself, there's a grassy hill with granite stairs that lead to a marked off, somewhat pebbly swimming area. Campsites are set in a loop on the lakeside, at the opposite end of the park from the day-use area, beach, and boat launch. Well-spaced, offering plenty of privacy, sites are heavily wooded with spruce and fir. Some campsites have footpaths through the trees that lead to the lake. Most desirable sites (closest to the water) are 11M through 21L, even numbers. Letters refer to size of site; 's' is small, 'm' is medium, and so on. Site 42X (as in extra-large) is very private, set off by itself way back in the woods. Besides all the natural beauty you could wish for, this campground boasts another winning attribute, not to be taken lightly in a state park: great showers!

BASICS

Operated By: Maine Dept. of Conservation, Bureau of Parks & Lands. **Open:** May 15–Sept. 30. **Site Assignment:** In spring & fall, camping is on a first-come, first-served basis. For summer stays, reservations open on the first business day in Jan. From June 15 to the night before Labor Day, sites may be reserved for a min. of 2 nights & up to 2 weeks. Full payment is charged to credit card when reservation is processed. Refund with $15 cancellation fee. 10 sites are non-reservable, & available on a first-come, first-served basis. Call the reservations line to cancel a reservation more than 3 days in advance. If cancelling less than 3 days in advance, call the park directly. **Registration:** At office. **Fee:** $13, Maine residents; $17, non-residents, plus $2 fee if reserving in advance. V, MC. **Parking:** At sites & designated lots only.

FACILITIES

Number of RV Sites: 50. **Number of Tent-Only Sites:** 0. **Hookups:** None. **Each Site:** Yes. **Dump Station:** No. **Laundry:** No. **Pay Phone:** Yes. **Rest Rooms and Showers:** Yes. **Fuel:** No. **Propane:** No. **Internal Roads:** Gravel & paved, in good condition. **RV Service:** No. **Market:** 7 mi. northwest. **Restaurant:** 7 mi. northwest. **General Store:** No. **Vending:** No. **Swimming Pool:** No. **Playground:** Yes. **Other:** Boat ramps & slips. **Activities:** Lake swimming, boating, fishing (need license; available in town), ball field, volleyball, horseshoes, hiking, picnicking. **Nearby Attractions:** Wilhelm Reich Museum, moosewatching, golf, scenic flights, Appalachian Trail hiking. **Additional Information:** Rangeley Lakes Region Chamber of Commerce, (207) 864-5364 or (800) MT-LAKES.

RESTRICTIONS

Pets: Must be leashed, quiet, & cleaned up after. Must not be left unattended. **Fires:** In fireplaces only. **Alcoholic Beverages:** No. **Vehicle Maximum Length:** 40 ft. **Other:** 2-week max. stay between last week in June & Labor Day.

TO GET THERE

From junction of Rtes. 16 and 4, go 4 mi. south on Rte. 4, then 5 mi. west on S. Shore Dr., then 1 mi. north to campground.

RAYMOND

Kokatosi Campground

635 Webbs Mills Rd., Raymond 04071. T: (207) 627-4642 or (800) 9-CAMPIN (outside ME); www.maine.com/kokatosi; kokatosi@maine.com.

RV ★★★ Tent ★★★

Beauty: ★★★ Site Privacy: ★
Spaciousness: ★★ Quiet: ★★★
Security: ★★★★★ Cleanliness: ★★★★
Insect Control: ★★ Facilities: ★★★

Whether you're looking for a ride on an antique "Hooterville" fire engine or prefer a freshwater cruise on an eight-seater "Patio Boat," Kokatosi's the place. Located in the Western Lakes region of southwest Maine, on five-mile-long Crescent Lake, this campground offers a "summer camp for families" experience. In fact, this lake-dotted, woodsy area is chock-a-block with summer camps. Most campers can't resist paddling or motoring to Tenney River, a mile-and-a-half away, then on to Panther Pond. The fishing is said to be pretty good, too. The campground offers a rather communal experience; you're bound to get to know your neighbors, since sites don't have much buffer between them (only boulders, in some cases.) About 50 percent of the sites are seasonal, but the transient sites are closest to the beach. RV sites 25, 26, and 28 overlook the lake. Some of the tent sites have platforms and canopies, providing a tree-house effect perched over the lake. Sites 4 through 7 and 11 are among them. A nicely-done rec hall is the scene for country bands and potluck suppers.

BASICS

Operated By: Terri & Neil Southwick. **Open:** May 15–Columbus Day. **Site Assignment:** Reservations recommended. 50% deposit required. Must pay in full for holiday weekends. Refund w/ cancellation w/ 30-day notice, minus $10 fee. No refunds for holiday weekend reservations. **Registration:** At office. **Fee:** $32–$38 for 2 adults & 2 children under age 18. V, MC. **Parking:** At sites & designated lot (tenters).

Facilities

Number of RV Sites: 145. **Number of Tent-Only Sites:** 17. **Hookups:** Water, electric (20, 30 amps), sewer. **Each Site:** Picnic table, fire ring. **Dump Station:** Yes. **Laundry:** Yes. **Pay Phone:** Yes. **Rest Rooms and Showers:** Yes. **Fuel:** No. **Propane:** Yes. **Internal Roads:** Gravel, in good condition. **RV Service:** No. **Market:** 10 mi. east. **Restaurant:** 10 mi. east. **General Store:** Yes. **Vending:** Yes. **Swimming Pool:** No. **Playground:** Yes. **Other:** Rec hall, boat dock. **Activities:** Lake swimming, fishing (license required), boating (rentals available, including 14 ft. motorboats), volleyball, bocces, horseshoes, planned activities. **Nearby Attractions:** Golf, mini-golf, seaplane rides, boat cruises, Songo River Queen paddleboat, Douglas Mountain hiking, Sebago Lake State Park, outlet shopping (N. Conway, NH). **Additional Information:** Gray Business Assoc., (207) 657-7000.

Restrictions

Pets: Must be leashed, quiet, & cleaned up after. Not allowed on beach or in buildings. **Fires:** In fireplaces only. **Alcoholic Beverages:** Yes. **Vehicle Maximum Length:** None. **Other:** 2-day min. stay required; 3-day min. on holidays.

To Get There

From junction of Rtes. 302 and 85, go 6 mi. northeast on Rte. 85. Campground entrance is on the right.

RICHMOND

Augusta/Gardiner KOA

Rte. 1, Box 2410, Richmond 04357. T: (207) 582-5086 (800) 562-1496 (reservations); www.agkoa.homestead.com; augustakoa@hotmail.com.

RV ★★★ Tent ★★★

Beauty: ★★	Site Privacy: ★★★
Spaciousness: ★★★	Quiet: ★★★
Security: ★★★	Cleanliness: ★★★
Insect Control: ★★★	Facilities: ★★★

This centrally-located franchise campground is just off the interstate and a welcome sight for weary travelers. The rural setting offers many shady sites, clean facilities, and a few extras: heated swimming, lake access, rec room and laundry. The lake access is about a quarter-mile walk down the road, where the campground has a dock and launch. A bit inconvenient but good for campers who like to fish (smallmouth bass, perch, pickerel and catfish are abundant.) Campers can bring their boats or rent rowboats and canoes at the office. About 50 percent of the campers are walk-ins, stopping for the night en route to sights and attractions around the state. Most sites are gravel and there are several pull-throughs. Though the facilities are well-maintained, we find the landscaping and general appearance of the individual sites a bit shabby and overgrown.

Basics

Operated By: Al & Lou Maenz. **Open:** Mid-May–mid-Oct. **Site Assignment:** Reservations usually not needed; 1 night deposit; 24-hour cancellation policy; MC, V, D, checks. **Registration:** At office. **Fee:** Full hookups, $27.75; water & electric, $25.75; no hookups, $19.75, based on 2 adults, additional child, ages 5–17, $3; additional adult, $4; ages 5 & under, free. **Parking:** At site.

Facilities

Number of RV Sites: 66. **Number of Tent-Only Sites:** 11. **Hookups:** Water, electric, sewer (30, 50 amps). **Each Site:** Picnic table, fire ring. **Dump Station:** Yes. **Laundry:** Yes. **Pay Phone:** Yes. **Rest Rooms and Showers:** Yes. **Fuel:** No. **Propane:** Yes. **Internal Roads:** Gravel (good). **RV Service:** No. **Market:** Gardiner (7 mi). **Restaurant:** No. **General Store:** Yes. **Vending:** No. **Swimming Pool:** Yes. **Playground:** Yes. **Other:** Lake frontage, dock, canoe & rowboat rentals, cabin rentals, pavilion, game room. **Activities:** Swimming, fishing, boating, volleyball, badminton, basketball, horseshoes. **Nearby Attractions:** mid-coast parks & beaches, western lakes & mountains. **Additional Information:** Kennebec Valley Chamber of Commerce, P.O. Box 676, Augusta, ME 04332-0676 (207) 623-4559, www.info@augustamaine.com.

Restrictions

Pets: Must be on a leash, never left unattended. **Fires:** In grills, stoves, & fire rings only. **Alcoholic Beverages:** At site only. **Vehicle Maximum Length:** None.

To Get There

From I-95, exit 27, go south (toward Richmond) 2.25 mi. on Rte. 201; campground is on the right.

ROCKPORT

Camden Rockport Camping

P.O. Box 639, Rte. 40, Rockport 04856. T: (207) 236-2498 or (888) 842-0592.

RV ★★★ Tent ★★

Beauty: ★★★	Site Privacy: ★★★
Spaciousness: ★★★	Quiet: ★★★★★
Security: ★★★	Cleanliness: ★★★★★
Insect Control: ★★★	Facilities: ★★★

We know where to get the freshest, best, and cheapest lobster around! they whisper conspiratorially at Camden Rockport Camping, and if that's not a selling point, we don't know what is. This quiet, peaceful family campground is located near the bustling seaport towns of Camden and Rockport (thus the name) in mid-coast Maine. You'd never know you were a hop and a skip from tourist-filled streets, shops, and galleries, though. This campground is the quietest one around (quieter than nearby Megunticook By the Sea), since it's off the beaten track—Rte. 1—a bit. The new owners are planning renovations, so we can't offer a complete review. But what probably won't change are the grassy, back-in campsites, with good shade trees dotting the big rig area. Even the tent sites are grassy. They're not super-level, though. Ask for tent site 14, very private and wooded with white birch. The campground is neat as a pin, and boasts nice touches like fresh flowers in the rest room and a rec hall with a kitchen and book exchange.

Basics

Operated By: John & Lori Alexander. **Open:** May 1–Nov. 1. **Site Assignment:** Reservations recommended, especially for July & Aug. Deposit of first nights' fee required. Refund for cancellation w/ 7-day notice, minus $15 fee. **Registration:** At office. **Fee:** $25–$32 for 2 adults & 2 children under age 18. No credit cards. **Parking:** At site.

Facilities

Number of RV Sites: 40. **Number of Tent-Only Sites:** 17. **Hookups:** Water, electric (30, 50 amps), sewer, cable TV. **Each Site:** Picnic table, fire ring. **Dump Station:** Yes. **Laundry:** Yes. **Pay Phone:** Yes. **Rest Rooms and Showers:** Yes. **Fuel:** No. **Propane:** Yes. **Internal Roads:** Gravel, in good condition. **RV Service:** No. **Market:** 3 mi.east. **Restaurant:** 3 mi. east. **General Store:** Yes. **Vending:** Yes. **Swimming Pool:** No (new owners are renovating & may add one; call to inquire). **Playground:** Yes. **Other:** Rec hall (under renovation). **Activities:** Basketball, ball field, horseshoes, volleyball. **Nearby Attractions:** Camden galleries, museums & shops), windjammer fleet, Penobscot Bay cruises, Conway Homestead & Mary Cramer Museum (28th century restored farmhouse & gardens), Camden Hills State Park, Merryspring Park, Owl's Head Transportation Museum, golf, ocean swimming. **Additional Information:** Rockport-Camden-Lincolnville Chamber of Commerce, (207) 236-4404; (800) 223-5459.

Restrictions

Pets: Must be leashed, quiet, & cleaned up after. Must not be left unattended. **Fires:** In fire rings only. **Alcoholic Beverages:** At sites only. **Vehicle Maximum Length:** None. **Other:** No electric heaters. 2-night min. stay on weekends in July & Aug.; 3-night min. stay during Maine Lobster Festival (early Aug.).

To Get There

From junction of Rtes. 1 and 90, go 2 mi. southwest on Rte. 90. Campground entrance is on the left.

ROCKPORT

Megunticook Campground by the Sea

Rte. 1, P.O. Box 375, Rockport 04856. T: (207) 594-2428 or (800) 884-2428; F: (207) 594-0549; www.campgroundbythesea.com.

RV ★★★★ Tent ★★★

Beauty: ★★★★★	Site Privacy: ★★★
Spaciousness: ★★	Quiet: ★★★
Security: ★★★	Cleanliness: ★★★★★
Insect Control: ★★★	Facilities: ★★★★★

As you're enjoying a lobster bake on the oceanfront deck, watching a Maine windjammer schooner sail past on Penobscot Bay, one question might cross your mind: "This is camping?" Oh, yeah, this is camping at Megunticook, a camping resort on mid-coast Maine, just three miles south of Camden. Want freshly-brewed Green Mountain coffee, or pizza delivered to your site? Perhaps a harbor tour on a Downeast cruiser? No problem. Other nice touches include a pool area with a picket fence surrounding it, not that ugly chain-link stuff. A waterfront deck is graced with a tumble of gardens and seating, the perfect place to watch the world—or local lobstermen—go by. Admire Indian Island lighthouse in the distance. A row of rental cabins sits close to busy Rte. 1; we'd head back as far as possible, away from the road and toward the ocean. RV sites 46 through 49, near Vernah Brook, fill the bill. Tent sites are set 'way back, toward the water, nicely level with good surfacing for drainage. Tent site 81 is huge, while site 87 boasts the most privacy, and is closest to the water. This is a classic Maine beauty spot.

BASICS

Operated By: Megunticook Campground By the Sea. **Open:** May 15–Oct. 15. **Site Assignment:** Reservations recommended, Jul.-Oct. Deposit of 1 nights' fee required. Refunds for cancellation w/ 7-day notice, minus $15 fee. **Registration:** At office. **Fee:** $26–$35 for 2 adults & 2 children. V, MC, D. **Parking:** At site.

FACILITIES

Number of RV Sites: 66. **Number of Tent-Only Sites:** 20. **Hookups:** Water, electric (20, 30, 50 amps), sewer, cable TV, phone. **Each Site:** Picnic table, fire ring. **Dump Station:** Yes. **Laundry:** Yes. **Pay Phone:** Yes. **Rest Rooms and Showers:** Yes. **Fuel:** No. **Propane:** No. **Internal Roads:** Gravel, in good condition. **RV Service:** No. **Market:** 2.5 mi. north. **Restaurant:** 3 mi. north. **General Store:** Yes. **Vending:** Yes. **Swimming Pool:** Yes. **Playground:** Yes. **Other:** Game room. **Activities:** Biking (rentals available), kayaking (rentals available), boat cruises on "Loriander," swimming, ball field, croquet, horseshoes, badminton. **Nearby Attractions:** Camden galleries, museums & shops), windjammer fleet, Penobscot Bay cruises, Conway Homestead & Mary Cramer Museum (28th century restored farmhouse & gardens), Camden Hills State Park, Merryspring Park, Owl's Head Transportation Museum, golf. **Additional Information:** Rockport-Camden-Lincolnville Chamber of Commerce, (207) 236-4404; (800) 223-5459.

RESTRICTIONS

Pets: Must be leashed, quiet, & cleaned up after. Must not be left unattended. **Fires:** In fireplaces only. **Alcoholic Beverages:** At sites only. **Vehicle Maximum Length:** None. **Other:** 2-night min. stay required on weekends in July & Aug. 3-night min. stay required on holiday weekends & Aug. 1-5 (Maine Lobster Festival.).

TO GET THERE

From junction of Rtes. 1 and 90 in Rockport, go 2 mi. south on Rte. 1. Campground is on the left.

SACO

Saco/Portland South KOA

814A Portland Rd., Saco 04072. T: (207) 282-0502 (800) 468-6567; www.koa.com.

RV ★★★★★ Tent ★★★★

Beauty: ★★★	Site Privacy: ★★★
Spaciousness: ★★★	Quiet: ★★★★
Security: ★★★★★	Cleanliness: ★★★★★
Insect Control: ★★★	Facilities: ★★★★

This woodsy campground is just two miles from Old Orchard Beach and many of southern Maine's best parks and attractions, and offers a natural, quiet escape from the summer masses. Ultra clean facilities, a family-friendly atmosphere, and lots of added conveniences make this property a favorite with locals and out-of-town travelers alike. Most sites are tucked in a shady, cool virgin forest; tent sites are nestled under old growth pine trees. Recreation fields, pool, office and pavilion areas are clustered in front. We like the porch off the office cabin, with rockers and benches overlooking the pool and playground. The campground also offers discounted tickets to area attractions. Before heading out for the day, feast on a wild blueberry pancake breakfast, offered each day at the campground. Spaghetti dinners and assorted desserts are available in the evening.

BASICS

Operated By: Sylvia & Frank Kelly. **Open:** May–Oct. **Site Assignment:** Reservations suggested, $25 deposit, 24-hour cancellation policy; MC, V, no checks. **Registration:** At office. **Fee:** Full hookups, $34; water & electric, $32; premium tent (w/ water & electric), $30.50; no hookups, $28.50. **Parking:** At site.

FACILITIES

Number of RV Sites: 96. **Number of Tent-Only Sites:** 22. **Hookups:** Water, electric, sewer (20, 30 amps). **Each Site:** Picnic table, fire ring. **Dump Station:** Yes. **Laundry:** Yes. **Pay Phone:** Yes. **Rest Rooms and Showers:** Yes. **Fuel:** No. **Propane:** Yes. **Internal Roads:** Gravel, dirt (good). **RV Service:** No. **Market:** Old Orchard Beach (2 mi). **Restaurant:** No. **General Store:** Yes. **Vending:** No. **Swimming Pool:** Yes. **Playground:** Yes. **Other:** Pavilion, game room, cabin rentals, discount tickets to area attractions. **Activities:** Swimming, basketball, volleyball, horseshoes. **Nearby Attractions:** Old Orchard Beach, southern coast parks & beaches, Portland. **Additional Information:** Old Orchard Beach Chamber of Commerce, First St., Old Orchard Beach, ME 04064 (207) 934-2500 (800) 365-9386; www.oldorchardbeachmaine.com.

RESTRICTIONS

Pets: Must be on a leash, never left unattended. **Fires:** In grills, stoves, & fire rings only. **Alcoholic Beverages:** At site only. **Vehicle Maximum Length:** None.

TO GET THERE

From junction I-95 and I-195, exit 5, go 1.2 mi. east on I-195, then north 1.5 mi. on Rte. 1 (exit 2B); campground is on the left.

SACO

Silver Springs

705 Portland Rd., Saco 04072. T: (207) 283-3880; www.silver-springs.com; silver-springs@cybertours.com.

RV ★★★ Tent ★★

Beauty: ★★	Site Privacy: ★★★
Spaciousness: ★★★	Quiet: ★★★
Security: ★★★★★	Cleanliness: ★★★
Insect Control: ★★★	Facilities: ★★★

Campers looking to get away from the hustle and bustle of Old Orchard Beach and the surrounding area, will find a quiet oasis at Silver Springs campground. The modest facility, less than two miles from Old Orchard Beach, is one of Maine's newest campgrounds. (Though the site, dubbed Goose-fare Hill, and the large home on the property has been around for more than 170 years.) Sites are set side-by-side with a choice of shaded or wooded spaces. You won't find anything extraordinary or fancy at Silver Springs, just a pleasant, economical base to call home while you explore, and an alternative to some of the gigantic, mega camping resorts in the area.

BASICS

Operated By: Michael & Jeanne Glaude. **Open:** May–Columbus Day. **Site Assignment:** Reservations required, 1-night deposit, 10-day cancellation policy w/ a $10 service charge, 3-day min. stay on holidays; MC, V, D, no checks. **Registration:** At office. **Fee:** Full hookups, $34; water & electric, $30; no hookups, $23, based on 2 adults & 2 children under 17. **Parking:** At site.

FACILITIES

Number of RV Sites: 101. **Number of Tent-Only Sites:** 20. **Hookups:** Water, electric, sewer (30, 50 amps), cable TV. **Each Site:** Picnic table, fire ring. **Dump Station:** Yes. **Laundry:** Yes. **Pay Phone:** Yes. **Rest Rooms and Showers:** Yes (coin-op). **Fuel:** No. **Propane:** Yes. **Internal Roads:** Gravel, dirt (good). **RV Service:** No. **Market:** Old Orchard Beach (1.5 mi). **Restaurant:** No. **General Store:** Yes. **Vending:** Yes. **Swimming Pool:** Yes. **Playground:** Yes. **Other:** Game room, on-site motel, cottage rentals. **Activities:** Swimming, horseshoes, basketball, shuffleboard, volleyball. **Nearby Attractions:** Old Orchard Beach, southern coast parks & beaches, Portland. **Additional Information:** Old Orchard Beach Chamber of Commerce, First St., Old Orchard Beach, ME 04064 (207) 934-2500 (800) 365-9386; www.oldorchard-beachmaine.com.

RESTRICTIONS

Pets: Must be on a leash, never left unattended. Only 2 pets allowed per site. **Fires:** In grills, stoves, & fire rings only. **Alcoholic Beverages:** At site only. **Vehicle Maximum Length:** None.

TO GET THERE

From junction Maine Turnpike and I-195, exit 5, go east 1.2 mi. on I-195, then north 0.5 mi. on Rte. 1 (exit 2B); campground is on the right.

SCARBOROUGH

Bayley's

275 Pine Point Rd., Scarborough 04074. T: (207) 883-6043; www.bayleys-camping.com; info@bayleys-camping.com.

RV ★★★★★ Tent ★★★★

Beauty: ★★★	Site Privacy: ★★★
Spaciousness: ★★★	Quiet: ★
Security: ★★★★★	Cleanliness: ★★★★
Insect Control: ★★★	Facilities: ★★★★★

This mega-resort campground in southern coastal Maine is one of the largest in New England. It's a sprawling family resort, spread over 200 acres, with activities to keep everyone entertained. There's professional entertainment four nights a week: bands play, comedians joke, jugglers juggle.there are three swimming pools, three ponds, a full-service restaurant (lobsters anyone?), mini golf, sports fields, and nonstop planned activities morning to night. If that's not enough, campers can hop on the free double decker bus and head to Old Orchard Beach, only a few minutes away. This is probably the best bargain in southern coastal Maine. With 500+ sites, you'll have plenty to choose from. If you're driving a large motor home, the A and C sites are best—shaded, level and easy to pull in and out. They're close to the front office, pool, theater, and restaurant. If you want more privacy, try the V section. If you're a tenter, who prefers to get away from the action, there's a wilderness area in the back of the property. Nature trails, fishing ponds, mini gold, sports fields, and another pool are back even further, and make up one of Maine's largest outdoor activity centers.

Basics

Operated By: Fred & Kathleen Bayley. **Open:** May–Oct. 15. **Site Assignment:** Reservations suggested, stays of 4 days or less must be paid in full; $150 deposit for longer stays, 30 day cancellation policy w/ a $25 service charge. 3-nigh min. stays over Memorial Day & Labor Day weekends, 4-night min. over July 4th holiday; MC,V, no checks. **Registration:** At office. **Fee:** Full hookups (w/ cable TV & AC), $46; full hookups (without AC), $41; water, electric & cable TV (Bayley's Best), $41; water, electric, cable TV, $39, no hookups, $34; 50 amp service is additional $3. **Parking:** At site, 1 vehicle per site (additional vehicle, $5/day).

Facilities

Number of RV Sites: 450. **Number of Tent-Only Sites:** 150. **Hookups:** Water, electric, sewer (30, 50 amps), cable TV, modem. **Each Site:** Picnic table, fire ring. **Dump Station:** Yes. **Laundry:** Yes. **Pay Phone:** Yes. **Rest Rooms and Showers:** Yes. **Fuel:** No. **Propane:** Yes. **Internal Roads:** Gravel (good). **RV Service:** No. **Market:** Old Orchard Beach (2 mi). **Restaurant:** Yes. **General Store:** Yes. **Vending:** Yes. **Swimming Pool:** Yes. **Playground:** Yes. **Other:** 3 ponds (2 stocked fishing ponds), boat dock, hot tubs, mini golf course, boat rentals, outdoor theater, nature trails, bike rentals, complimentary beach bus, trailer rentals, game room, rec hall, sports fields. **Activities:** Swimming, boating, fishing, mini-golf, basketball, volleyball, horseshoes, live entertainment, planned activities, including children's games, fishing derbies, contests, dinners, movies, & more. **Nearby Attractions:** Old Orchard Beach, Portland, southern coastal parks & beaches. **Additional Information:** Old Orchard Beach Chamber of Commerce, First St., Old Orchard Beach, ME 04064 (207) 934-2500 (800) 365-9386; www.oldorchardbeachmaine.com.

Restrictions

Pets: Must be on a leash, never left unattended. Pets not allowed in activity areas; only adults may walk pets in the campground. **Fires:** In grills, stoves, & fire rings only. **Alcoholic Beverages:** At site. **Vehicle Maximum Length:** None. **Other:** No children allowed in hot tubs.

To Get There

From Maine Turnpike (exit 5) and I-195, go east 1.2 mi. on I-195, then north 5 mi. on Rte.1, then east (right) 3 mi. on Rte. 9 (Pine Point Rd.); campground is on right.

SCARBOROUGH

Wassamki Springs

56 Saco St., Scarborough 04074. T: (207) 839-4276; F: (207) 839-2936; www.wassamkisprings.com; wassamkisprings@aol.com.

RV ★★★★ Tent ★★★

Beauty: ★★★★	Site Privacy: ★★★
Spaciousness: ★★★	Quiet: ★★★
Security: ★★★	Cleanliness: ★★★★
Insect Control: ★★★	Facilities: ★★★★

Vacationing families and Maine's summer tourists clamor to this Portland area, activity-based campground. We like that the campground is only a few minutes from Maine's largest city (with restaurants, galleries and historic sites) with quick access to southern coastal beaches, cruises, and attractions. But, if you stay here, you don't have to be in the hub of it all. The property flanks a 30 acre private lake and campers have their own mile-long sandy beach and warm, crystal clear swimming waters. There are boat rentals, family hayrides, group bonfires, and planned activities to keep things entertaining. There's also a trout-stocked fishing pond popular with kids and parents, alike. Facilities are clean and modern and campers have a choice of sites: lakefront, shaded or open (though a little over half of the campground is taken by seasonal renters.) Tent-only sites are few (9) and tucked back away from the lake.

Basics

Operated By: Hillock family. **Open:** May–Columbus Day. **Site Assignment:** Reservations suggested in Jul.–Aug.; $10 per day deposit, holiday weekends paid in full, 2-week cancellation policy, no refunds for holiday weekends; MC,V, D; checks accepted for deposit but not upon arrival. **Registration:** At office. **Fee:** Full hookups (50 amp), $31; full hookups, $29; water & electric, $27; no hookups, $24, base on 2 adults & up to 4 children. **Parking:** At site.

Facilities

Number of RV Sites: 151. **Number of Tent-Only Sites:** 9. **Hookups:** Water, electric, sewer (30, 50 amps), phone, modem. **Each Site:** Picnic table, fire ring. **Dump Station:** Yes. **Laundry:** Yes. **Pay Phone:** Yes. **Rest Rooms and Showers:** Yes. **Fuel:** No. **Propane:** Yes. **Internal Roads:** Gravel, dirt (good). **RV Service:** No. **Market:** Scarborough (0.5 mi). **Restaurant:** Yes. **General Store:** Yes. **Vending:** Yes. **Swimming Pool:** No. **Playground:** Yes. **Other:** Lake frontage, beach, boat rentals, stocked fishing pond, pavilion, game room, sports fields, planned activities. **Activities:** Swimming, boating, fishing, volleyball, horseshoes, basketball, softball. **Nearby Attractions:** Portland, Casco Bay, coastal beaches, Freeport. **Additional Information:** Greater Portland Area Chamber of Commerce, 60 Pearl St., Portland, ME 04101 (207) 772-2811, www.portlandregion.com.

Restrictions

Pets: Must be on a leash; never left unattended. **Fires:** In grills, campstoves, & fire rings only. **Alcoholic Beverages:** At site only. **Vehicle Maximum Length:** None.

To Get There

From I-95 and exit 7A, go 4 mi. west on Rte. 22, then 0.2 mi. east on Saco St.; campground is on the left

SEARSPORT

Searsport Shores Camping Resort

216 W. Main St., Searsport 04974. T: (207) 548-6059; www.campocean.com; camping@ime.net.

RV ★★★★★ Tent ★★★★★

Beauty: ★★★★★	Site Privacy: ★★★★
Spaciousness: ★★★★	Quiet: ★★★★
Security: ★★★★	Cleanliness: ★★★★★
Insect Control: ★★★★	Facilities: ★★★★★

This midcoastal Maine campground, boasting 1,200 feet of scenic ocean shoreline, is one of the top in New England. The views of rocky coastline, picturesque coves, Sears Island (the largest uninhabited, undeveloped island in the state) and open ocean are spectacular. Campers have a long stretch of private beaches to enjoy, ranging from rocky tidepools to water smoothed pebbles to soft sand. Keep meandering and you'll run into Moose Lake State Park, just down the coast, within walking distance from the campground. The grounds include ocean viewing decks and sitting areas, arbors and trellis, and artistic wood carvings. Facilities are top-notch, including new rest rooms and showers, a large rec hall with a library lending area, an array of musical instruments, and an indoor play area for young children. There are hiking and biking trails, kayak and canoe rentals, and a list of planned activities, including old-fashioned lobster bakes on the beach, guided nature walks, children's programs, and more. Sites are spacious and include a separate, large adult-only tenting area overlooking the ocean, affectionately dubbed the "honeymoon suite."

Basics

Operated By: Rosalie & Zaban Koltookian. **Open:** May 15–Oct. 15. **Site Assignment:** Reservations suggested Jul.–Aug. 50 percent deposit for stays less than 1 week, $100 deposit for stays of 1 week or more, 10-day cancellation policy with $15 service fee; sites must be paid in full for holiday weekend reservations & are non-refundable; MC,V, D, checks. **Registration:** At office. **Fee:** Water & electric (premium), $38; water & electric (oceanview), $35; no hookups (premium ocean), $28 (ocean tent), $21. **Parking:** At site.

Facilities

Number of RV Sites: 70. **Number of Tent-Only Sites:** 30. **Hookups:** Water, electric (30 amps). **Each Site:** Picnic table, fire ring. **Dump Station:** Yes. **Laundry:** Yes. **Pay Phone:** Yes. **Rest Rooms and Showers:** Yes. **Fuel:** No. **Propane:** Yes. **Internal Roads:** Gravel (good). **RV Service:** No. **Market:** Searsport (1mi). **Restaurant:** No. **General Store:** Yes. **Vending:** Yes. **Swimming Pool:** No. **Playground:** Yes. **Other:** Ocean frontage, beaches, rec hall, library, patios, ocean viewing sitting areas, group area, biking & walking trails, canoe & kayak rentals, guided kayak lessons & tours, guided tours of Acadia National Park, intrepretive walks on the beach, indoor play center, sports field, cabin rentals. **Activities:** Swimming, fishing, boating, beachcombing, nature walks, baseball, volleyball, horseshoes, basketball, guided tours, planned activities, including potluck suppres, lobster bakes, live entertianment, craft classes, treasure hunts, & more. **Nearby Attractions:** Bucksport, Searsport, Maine coastal beaches, Deer Isle Peninsula, Bar Harbor, Acadia National Park. **Additional Information:** Searsport Economic Development Committee, Reservoir St., Searsport, ME 04974 (207) 54807255, www.searsportme.com & Acadia Information Center, P.O. Box 139, Mount Desert, ME 04660 (207) 667-8550 or (800) 358-8550, www.acadiainfo.com.

Restrictions

Pets: Must be on a leash, never left unattended. 1 pet per site only. **Fires:** In grills, stoves, & fire rings only. **Alcoholic Beverages:** At site only. **Vehicle Maximum Length:** 75 ft.

To Get There

From junction Rtes. 1 and 3 (in Belfast), go north 5 mi. on Rte. 1; campground is on the right.

SMALL POINT

Hermit Island

6 Hermit Island Rd., Phippsburg 04562. T: (207) 443-2101; www.hermitisland.com; info@hermitisland.com.

RV ★ Tent ★★★

Beauty: ★★★★	Site Privacy: ★★★
Spaciousness: ★★	Quiet: ★★
Security: ★★★★	Cleanliness: ★★★
Insect Control: ★★★	Facilities: ★★★

This campground isn't for everyone, but, wow, what a spot. Set on a sandy spit of land in the open Atlantic, bounded by Maine's famously rocky shore, its delicate geography make it suitable for tents, small-to-medium tent trailers, and small pickup trailers only. Here, you can camp amidst sand dunes, with panoramic views of surf and sky, or nestled among groves of young birch or tall spruce. Waterfront sites include some prime spots on Casco Bay, and lower-priced sites on The Branch, an inlet near Small Point Harbor. The farther inland you go, the more breathing room around the campsites (lower prices, too.) Sites at Osprey Point, on the ocean side, perch on hillside dunes; sites 2 and 3 of this bunch offer the most privacy. Branch sites 4 through 12 are really nice, as well. Close to Osprey Point, but inland, value sites 8,10, and 11, at Cross Island and Luff Ln., are woodsy, and a short walk to the beach. Without many frills, save sun, sand, and surf, this campground caters to a young demographic. Kids are everywhere, especially around the store and Kelp Shed, where boat rentals and fishing arrangements are made.

Basics

Operated By: Nicholas Sewall. **Open:** Mid-May–Columbus Day. **Site Assignment:** Reservations recommended from June 15 to Labor Day. Reservations for a weeks' stay or longer are accepted the first business day in Jan. Full fee payable within 30 days of booking. Reservations for less than 1 week are accepted starting Mar. 1; full payment required. Refund for cancellations made w/ at least 72-hour notice, minus 1-day fee. **Registration:** At office. **Fee:** \$27–\$38 for 2 adults & their children or 4 adults, no children. No credit cards. **Parking:** At sites. 1 car per site only.

Facilities

Number of RV Sites: 275. **Number of Tent-Only Sites:** 0. **Hookups:** None. **Each Site:** None. **Dump Station:** No. **Laundry:** Dryers only. **Pay Phone:** Yes. **Rest Rooms and Showers:** Yes. **Fuel:** No. **Propane:** No. **Internal Roads:** Gravel, in good condition. **RV Service:** No. **Market:** 16 mi. north, in Bath. **Restaurant:** 16 mi. north, in Bath. **General Store:** Yes. **Vending:** No. **Swimming Pool:** No. **Playground:** No. **Other:** Rec hall, boat ramp. **Activities:** Ocean swimming, boating (rentals available), saltwater fishing, hiking. **Nearby Attractions:** Popham Beach State Park, Morse Mountain Sanctuary, Maine Maritime Museum, Bowdoin College Museum of Art, Peary-MacMillan Arctic Museum, deep-sea fishing. **Additional Information:** Chamber of Commerce of the Bath-Brunswick Region, (207) 725-8797 or (207) 443-9751; www.midcoastmaine.com.

Restrictions

Pets: Must be leashed, quiet, & cleaned up after. Must not be left unattended. **Fires:** In fire rings only. **Alcoholic Beverages:** At sites only. **Vehicle Maximum Length:** 25 ft. **Other:** Visitor's are not allowed in the campground.

To Get There

From I-95 in Brunswick, take Rte. 1 to Bath, then Rtes. 209 and 216 south to Hermit Island. Campground entrance is on the right.

SOMESVILLE

Mt. Desert Campground

Rte. 198 (Somesville), Mount Desert 04660. T: (207) 244-3710; mdcg@midmaine.com.

RV ★★ Tent ★★★★★

Beauty: ★★★★★	Site Privacy: ★★★★★
Spaciousness: ★★★★★	Quiet: ★★★★
Security: ★★★	Cleanliness: ★★★★★
Insect Control: ★★★	Facilities: ★★

This is traditional camping at its best: quiet, wooded sites on the saltwater shore of scenic Somes Sound on Mount Desert Island. You're in the heart of the island, only 5 miles from with Bar Harbor, Northeast Harbor and Southwest Harbor. The pristine property, nestled in a pine wood forest and perched on a knoll overlooking the water, is a favorite with tenters and small tent trailer campers. (There are only basic water and electric hookups; RVs more than 20 feet long are not allowed.) There's kayaking and canoeing from the campground, salt water fishing and swimming, and guided bird walks and beach strolls in the summer. Pick up a fresh brewed cup of coffee at the Gathering Place in the morning and go back in the afternoon for their homemade ice cream. Sites offer plenty of room and privacy (many tent sites have platforms) but reserve early: many families have been coming here for 25 to 30 years, returning year after year for summer vacation.

Basics

Operated By: Craighead family. **Open:** Mid-June–mid-Sept. **Site Assignment:** Reservations suggested in Jul.–Aug. During Jul.–Aug., waterfront/waterview sites require 1-week stay (Saturday–Saturday), off water sites require 3 night stay. \$40 deposit for reservation for less than a week, \$60 deposit for each week reserved. Deposits are non-refundable; MC, V, checks. **Registration:** At office. **Fee:** Waterfront, \$32; waterview, \$29; off-water platform, \$26; off-water ground, \$24, based on 2 adults & 2 children under 18. **Parking:** At site, 1 vehicle per site.

Facilities

Number of RV Sites: 50. **Number of Tent-Only Sites:** 100. **Hookups:** Water, electric (15 amps). **Each Site:** Picnic table, fire ring. **Dump Station:** No. **Laundry:** No. **Pay Phone:** Yes. **Rest Rooms and Showers:** Yes (coin-op). **Fuel:** No. **Propane:** No. **Internal Roads:** Paved, gravel (good). **RV Service:** No. **Market:** Somesville (5mi). **Restaurant:** No. **General Store:** Yes. **Vending:** Yes. **Swimming Pool:** No. **Playground:** No. **Other:** Saltwater frontage, beach, boat launch, dock, canoe & kayak rentals. **Activities:** Swimming, boating, fishing, guided bird watch & wildlife viewing programs. **Nearby Attractions:** Bar Harbor, Acadia National Park. **Additional Information:** Acadia National Park, P.O. Box 177, Bar Harbor, ME 04609 (207) 288-3338, www.nps/gov/acad. Also, Acadia Information Center, P.O. Box 139, Mount Desert, ME 04660 (207) 667-8550 (800) 358-8550, www.acadiainfo.com & Bar Harbor Chamber of Commerce, 93 Cottage St., Bar Harbor, ME 04609 (207) 288-5103, www.barharborinfo.com.

Restrictions

Pets: No pets allowed in July-Aug. & holiday weekends. **Fires:** In grills, stoves, & fire rings only. **Alcoholic Beverages:** At site only. **Vehicle Maximum Length:** 20 ft. **Other:** 1 tent only on each site (a family w/ an extra tent for chidlren or screenhouse is permissible).

To Get There

From junction Rtes. 233 and 198, go 0.5 mi. on Rte. 198.

SOUTHPORT

Gray Homestead Campground

21 Homestead Rd., Southport 04576. T: (207) 633-4612; graysoceancamping.com; grays@gwi.net.

RV ★★★★ Tent ★★★★

Beauty: ★★★★	Site Privacy: ★★
Spaciousness: ★★★	Quiet: ★★★
Security: ★★★	Cleanliness: ★★★★
Insect Control: ★★★	Facilities: ★★

Finally, a Boothbay-area campground with ocean views! Gray Homestead was once a boarding house for the wealthy; now, the property—still owned by the Gray family— includes a cottage, two apartments, and a small, wooded campground. "People either love it or hate it," says Rachel, a campground employee. "There's nothing to do here, just nature." Big, beautiful nature, as in the Atlantic Ocean. Sounds good to us. There are kayaks, for poking around the peninsula, and owner Steve has a lobster boat. He'll catch lobsters for campers, and they'll cook 'em for you, or they'll lend you a big pot so you can do it yourself. While the campground offers awesome ocean views, and all campsites are a brief walk to the shore, sites tend to be small (and wet, when we visited), better for smaller RVs and pop-ups than tent camping. Site 17C, overlooking the water, is woodsy, with wonderful views. Oceanfront sites go first, naturally. Sites 9A and 9B are pretty, and set back in the woods, while sites 29A through C are nicely secluded for tenters. Sites 23 and 24 (water and electric) are good choices for RVers. Campers are drawn to the rocky point—great for fishing or just basking in the sun.

Basics

Operated By: Steve & Suzanne Gray. **Open:** May 1–Columbus Day. **Site Assignment:** Reservations recommended. 50% deposit required. No refunds for cancellation, but will issue credit for future stay. **Registration:** At office. **Fee:** $19–$27 per campsite. No credit cards. **Parking:** At site.

Facilities

Number of RV Sites: 40. **Number of Tent-Only Sites:** 0. **Hookups:** Water, electric (20, 30 amps). **Each Site:** Picnic table, fire ring. **Dump Station:** Yes. **Laundry:** Yes. **Pay Phone:** Yes. **Rest Rooms and Showers:** Yes, coin-op. **Fuel:** No. **Propane:** No. **Internal Roads:** Gravel, in good condition. **RV Service:** No. **Market:** 4.5 mi. north. **Restaurant:** 2 mi. north. **General Store:** No. **Vending:** Yes. **Swimming Pool:** No. **Playground:** Yes (swings). **Activities:** Boating (kayak rentals), fishing. **Nearby Attractions:** Boothbay Railway Village, Maine Resources Aquarium, Boothbay Harbor restaurants, shops & galleries, deep-sea fishing, whale-watching cruises, golf. **Additional Information:** Boothbay Harbor Region Chamber of Commerce, (207) 633-2353 or (800) 266-8422.

Restrictions

Pets: Must be leashed, quiet, & cleaned up after. Must not be left unattended. **Fires:** In fire rings only. **Alcoholic Beverages:** At sites only. **Vehicle Maximum Length:** 40 ft. **Other:** 3-day min. stay on holidays.

To Get There

From Maine Turnpike, take exit 9 to Coastal Rte. 1, then take exit 22 for Brunswick/Bath. Follow Rte. 1 through Bath and Wiscasset to Rte. 27 south. Follow Rte. 27 to Boothbay Harbor; stay on Rte. 27 through Boothbay to Southport. At second bridge, take a left onto Rte. 238. Campground is 2 mi. on left.

SOUTHWEST HARBOR

Smuggler's Den Campground

P.O. Box 787, Rte. 102, Southwest Harbor 04679. T: (207) 244-3944; F: (207) 244-4072; www.smugglersden.com; smugglersden@acadia.net.

RV ★★★ Tent ★★★★

Beauty: ★★★ | Site Privacy: ★★★
Spaciousness: ★★★★ | Quiet: ★★★★
Security: ★★★★ | Cleanliness: ★★★★
Insect Control: ★★★ | Facilities: ★★★

We like the fact that once we park our car at this campground we never have to get in it again until we leave to go home. There are several hiking trails accessible from the campground, including trails to Long Pond and Echo Lake (one of the best places to swim in the area!) You can walk into lovely Southwest Harbor, if you like, where you'll find supplies, restaurants, galleries, shops, and more. Live lobsters are for sale at the campground store! It's a great base to explore the quiet side of Mount Desert Island and Acadia National Park. We like the airy, sunny sites with views across open fields and mountains in distance. There's a separate group camping area, nestled in the trees, with plenty of elbow room and privacy.

Basics

Operated By: Damaris Smith. **Open:** Memorial Day–Columbus Day. **Site Assignment:** Reservations suggested in Jul.–Aug., accepted for 2 nights or longer, 50% deposit required, 14-day cancellation policy with $15 charge; MC, V & checks. **Registration:** At office. **Fee:** Full hookups, $31.50; water & electric, $27.50; no hookups, $23.50, based on 4 people per site, over 6 years old. **Parking:** At site.

Facilities

Number of RV Sites: 70. **Number of Tent-Only Sites:** 30. **Hookups:** Water, electric, sewer (20, 30 amps). **Each Site:** Picnic table, fire ring. **Dump Station:** Yes. **Laundry:** Yes. **Pay Phone:** Yes. **Rest Rooms and Showers:** Yes. **Fuel:** No. **Propane:** Yes. **Internal Roads:** Gravel, dirt (good). **RV Service:** No. **Market:** Southwest Harbor (0.5 mi). **Restaurant:** No. **General Store:** Yes. **Vending:** Yes. **Swimming Pool:** Yes. **Playground:** Yes. **Other:** Hiking trails, sports field, cabin rentals, group camping area. **Activities:** Swimming, hiking, horseshoes. **Nearby Attractions:** Bar Harbor, Acadia National Park. **Additional Information:** Acadia National Park, P.O. Box 177, Bar Harbor, ME 04609 (207) 288-3338, www.nps/gov/acad. Also, Acadia Information Center, P.O. Box 139, Mount Desert, ME 04660 (207) 667-8550 (800) 358-8550, www.acadiainfo.com & Bar Harbor Chamber of Commerce, 93 Cottage St., Bar Harbor, ME 04609 (207) 288-5103, www.barharborinfo.com.

Restrictions

Pets: On a leash, never left unattended. **Fires:** In grills, stoves, & fire rings only. **Alcoholic Beverages:** At site only. **Vehicle Max. Length:** None.

To Get There

From junction Rtes. 3, 198 and 102, go south 9.5 mi. on Rte. 102; campground is on right.

SOUTHWEST HARBOR

White Birches Campground

195 Seal Cove Rd., Southwest Harbor 04679. T: (207) 244-3797 or (888) 716-0727; www.mainecamper.com; whitebirches@downeast.net.

RV ★★★ Tent ★★★

Beauty: ★★★ | Site Privacy: ★★★
Spaciousness: ★★★★ | Quiet: ★★★
Security: ★★★ | Cleanliness: ★★★
Insect Control: ★★★ | Facilities: ★★★

This modest, no frills campground sits on the doorstep of Acadia National Park, 20 minutes from Bar Harbor and only minutes from Echo Lake, Southwest Harbor and other major sights and attractions. Hiking, biking, kayaking, and swimming are nearby. Most campers use it as a quiet—and economical— base to explore the area. The campground is best for tenters and small pop-up trailer campers who like privacy and elbow room and won't miss the planned activities and evening entertainment offered at other area campgrounds.The campground is divided by Seal Cove Rd. with sites on both sides. Each area offers wooded sites, tucked under pine trees. We like the extra room and privacy of the "b" loop sites, on the opposite side of the street from the office, pool, and play area. Sites 9B-11B are especially nice. But, these sites are also across the street from the campground's only rest rooms and showers, an inconvenient distance away.

Basics

Operated By: Ronald, Jaylene, Melody, & Colton Sanborn. **Open:** May 15–Oct. 15. **Site Assignment:** Reservations accepted year-round, suggested in Jul.–Aug. 1-night non-refundable deposit required for reservation; MC, V & checks. **Registration:** At office. **Fee:** Water & electric, $24; no hookups, $20, based on 2 adults & 2 children under 16. **Parking:** At site, 1 vehicle per site.

Facilities

Number of RV Sites: 15. **Number of Tent-Only Sites:** 45. **Hookups:** Water, electric (20, 30 amps). **Each Site:** Picnic table, fire ring. **Dump Station:** Yes. **Laundry:** Yes. **Pay Phone:** Yes. **Rest Rooms and Showers:** Yes. **Fuel:** No. **Propane:** No. **Internal Roads:** Gravel, dirt (good). **RV Service:** No. **Market:** Southwest Harbor (1.5 mi). **Restaurant:** No. **General Store:** Yes. **Vending:** Yes. **Swimming Pool:** Yes. **Playground:** Yes. **Other:** Cabin rentals. **Activities:** Swimming, tetherball, basketball. **Nearby Attractions:** Bar Harbor, Acadia National Park. **Additional Information:** Acadia National Park, P.O. Box 177, Bar Harbor, ME 04609 (207) 288-3338, www.nps/gov/acad. Also, Acadia Information Center, P.O. Box 139, Mount Desert, ME, 04660 (207) 667-8550, (800) 358-8550, www.acadiainfo.com & Bar Harbor Chamber of Commerce, 93 Cottage St., Bar Harbor, ME 04609 (207) 288-5103, www.barharborinfo.com.

Restrictions

Pets: Must be on a leash, never left unattended. **Fires:** In grills, stoves, & fire rings only. **Alcoholic Beverages:** At site only. **Vehicle Maximum Length:** 35 ft.

To Get There

From junction Rtes. 3 and 102/198, go east 10.5 mi. on Rte. 102 (toward Southwest Harbor), then south (right) 1.2 mi. on Seal Cove Rd.; the campground is on the left.

STANDISH

Family and Friends Campground

140 Richville Rd., Standish 04084. T: (207) 642-2200; www.familynfriends.com; info@familynfriends.com.

RV ★★★ Tent ★★

Beauty: ★★★ Site Privacy: ★★★
Spaciousness: ★★★ Quiet: ★★
Security: ★★★★★ Cleanliness: ★★★
Insect Control: ★★ Facilities: ★★★★

This campground, set in the Sebago Lake area of southwestern Maine, is not on the water, unless you count their swimming pool. But the Sebago-Long Lake chain of lakes, a 42-mile waterway, is just a short hop away. A public boat launch and small beach are less than a mile away. Meanwhile, the campground offers plenty of distractions, from bean-hole dinners (a Maine tradition) to karaoke. A nice log-hewn rec hall, with a fireplace and mounted trophy heads, is a base for activities. They even have hot tubs. The campground is nicely shaded with hemlocks and hardwoods, offering plenty of piney buffer between sites. Little touches provide a pleasant ambience here, such as the stone-banked pond with water fountain, the umbrellaed lounge chairs around the pool, and chipmunk feeders (so, presumably, the critters will leave your goodies alone.) Campsites, which include about 20-some seasonal spots, are set in loops. Tent sites 8, 9,and 10 are nicely backed up into the woods, while RV sites 44 and 46 are very private. Steer clear of sites 12, 15, and 16; too close to the road.

BASICS

Operated By: Joanne & Jim Lavalle. **Open:** Apr. 1–Nov. 1. **Site Assignment:** Reservations recommended. $25 deposit required. Refunds for cancellations w/ 15-day notice. **Registration:** At office. **Fee:** $25 per night for 2 adults & unmarried children under age 18. V, MC, D, AE. **Parking:** At site.

FACILITIES

Number of RV Sites: 65. **Number of Tent-Only Sites:** 0. **Hookups:** Water, electric (30 amps), sewer. **Each Site:** Picnic table, fireplace. **Dump Station:** Yes. **Laundry:** No. **Pay Phone:** Yes. **Rest Rooms and Showers:** Yes. **Fuel:** No. **Propane:** No. **Internal Roads:** Gravel, in good condition. **RV Service:** No. **Market:** 3 mi. north. **Restaurant:** 5 mi. south. **General Store:** Yes. **Vending:** Yes. **Swimming Pool:** Yes. **Playground:** Yes. **Other:** Rec hall, arcade, hot tubs. **Activities:** Swimming, horseshoes, basketball, planned activities. **Nearby Attractions:** Boating (public boat launch is 0.6 mi. away), lake swimming, fishing, Songo River Queen paddlewheeler cruise, Sebago Lake State Park. **Additional Information:** Bridgton Lakes Region Chamber of Commerce, (207) 647-3472.

RESTRICTIONS

Pets: Must be leashed, quiet, & cleaned up after. Must not be left unattended. Not allowed in buildings, lodge, or pool area. **Fires:** In fireplaces only. **Alcoholic Beverages:** Yes. **Vehicle Maximum Length:** 40 ft. **Other:** 3-night min. on holiday weekends.

TO GET THERE

From Maine Turnpike, take exit 7 (mi. 42); follow Rte. 114 northwest through Gorham to intersection of Rte. 35 in Sebago Lake Village. Continue straight on Rte. 114 for 0.75 mi. to campground, on the left.

STEEP FALLS

Acres of Wildlife

Rte. 113/11, P.O. Box 2, Steep Falls 04085. T: (207) 675-CAMP; www.acresofwildlife.com.

RV ★★★★ Tent ★★★★

Beauty: ★★★★ Site Privacy: ★★★
Spaciousness: ★★★★ Quiet: ★★★
Security: ★★★★★ Cleanliness: ★★★
Insect Control: ★★★ Facilities: ★★★★

The long gravel approach to this campground might scare some campers off. To others, it's a sign that they're getting away from it all. Indeed, this southwestern Maine campground, a half-hour from Portland, is its own world of family fun. In summer, the activity schedule is virtually non-stop (we like the water balloon slingshot contest); meanwhile, down at Rainbow Lake, there's swimming, tubing, boating, and fishing, and mini-golf up by the playground and ball field, and a mammoth arcade. Hard to believe this place was once a turkey farm. In that spirit, they still bake turkey pies, but you're more like to see a moose than a turkey lurking around these acres. The fresh baked goods (mostly made here) are a big draw. Savvy muffin-mavens order their breakfast goodies the night before. Campsites (gravel) are clustered around the lake, with a couple rows of seasonal sites set back into the woods. Some tent sites are located in a woodsy wilderness area, as well. We like two-way hookup sites W5 through 8, on the lake, and 61A (if you miss out on the lakeside sites.) Water-only sites B6 through B22 (even numbers) are also lakeside, and really nice.

BASICS

Operated By: Baptista family. **Open:** May 1–Columbus Day. **Site Assignment:** Reservations recommended. For less than 1 week stays in summer season, reserve 30 days in advance. 50% deposit required w/ reservation; refunds for cancellations w/ 30-day notice, minus $10 service charge. **Registration:** At office. **Fee:** $24–$38 for 2 adults & up to 3 children under age 18. V, MC, D, AE. **Parking:** At site (2 cars allowed) or designated lot.

FACILITIES

Number of RV Sites: 200. **Number of Tent-Only Sites:** 0. **Hookups:** Water, electric (30, 50 amps), sewer, cable TV. **Each Site:** Picnic table, fireplace. **Dump Station:** Yes. **Laundry:** Yes. **Pay Phone:** Yes. **Rest Rooms and Showers:** Yes. **Fuel:** No. **Propane:** Yes. **Internal Roads:** Gravel, in good condition. **RV Service:** No. **Market:** 1 mi. east, in Standish. **Restaurant:** Yes. **General Store:** Yes. **Vending:** Yes. **Swimming Pool:** No. **Playground:** Yes. **Other:** Mini-golf, pub, restaurant, rec hall. **Activities:** Fishing (no license required), lake swimming, boating (rentals available), vollyeball, basketball, ball field, bocce, planned activities. **Nearby Attractions:** Songo River Queen paddlewheeler cruise, Sebago Lake State Park, hiking at Douglas Hill, Willbrook Antique Museum, Jones Gallery Glass Museum, Portland. **Additional Information:** Bridgton Lakes Region Chamber of Commerce, (207) 647-3472.

RESTRICTIONS

Pets: Must be leashed, quiet, & cleaned up after. Must not be left unattended. Charge is $5 per night in season. **Fires:** In fireplaces only. **Alcoholic Beverages:** Yes. **Vehicle Maximum Length:** None. **Other:** 3-night min. stay during holiday weekends.

TO GET THERE

From Maine Turnpike, take exit 7A, go left, and follow signs to Rte. 22/114 North (Gorham) on your left. In Gorham, take Rte. 25W on your left, to Rte. 113, on the right. Go 6 mi. on Rte. 113 to campground entrance, then 3 mi. on gravel entrance road.

SURRY

The Gatherings Family Campground

RR 1, Box 4069, Surry 04684. T: (207) 667-8826.

RV ★★ Tent ★★★★

Beauty: ★★★★ Site Privacy: ★★★★
Spaciousness: ★★★★ Quiet: ★★★
Security: ★★★ Cleanliness: ★★★
Insect Control: ★★★ Facilities: ★★

This scenic campground on Union River Bay offers a fabulous slice of Maine's rocky, undeveloped coastline and is best for campers who crave a natural, seaside setting. The campground sites are a bit rustic geared more for campers with tents, small trailers and pop-ups as opposed to larger RVs. You'll get a whiff of the ocean and feel the sea breezes the moment you walk up to the old-fashioned camp quarters. Inside, there's a woodstove for cool Maine nights and a small diner-style restaurant. Outside, there's a wonderful boulder-strewn and pebble oceanside beach and two freshwater fishing ponds. There are a number of fine oceanfront sites with unbeatable views; other sites circle the ponds or loop around the center of the camground in between the ponds and ocean. Rest rooms and shower facilities are clean but dated and the grounds are natural not landscaped but, did we mention the views?

BASICS

Operated By: Rob Salois. **Open:** May 15–Oct. 15. **Site Assignment:** Reservations suggested, 3-night min. stay on waterfront sites, one-half of fee required for deposit, 14-day cancellation policy with $15 service charge; MC, V & checks. **Registration:** At office. **Fee:** Full hookup, $35; waterfront, $45 (30 amp), $42 (20 amp); off oceanfront, $30; no hookups $15–$17. **Parking:** At site.

FACILITIES

Number of RV Sites: 100. **Number of Tent-Only Sites:** 11. **Hookups:** Water, electric, sewer (20, 30 amps). **Each Site:** Picnic table, fire ring. **Dump Station:** Yes. **Laundry:** Yes. **Pay Phone:** Yes. **Rest Rooms and Showers:** Yes (coin-op).

Fuel: No. **Propane:** No. **Internal Roads:** Gravel, dirt (fair). **RV Service:** No. **Market:** Ellsworth (5 mi). **Restaurant:** Yes. **General Store:** Yes. **Vending:** Yes. **Swimming Pool:** No. **Playground:** Yes. **Other:** Ocean frontage, beach, cabin & cottage rentals, 2 fishing ponds. **Activities:** Swimming, fishing, horseshoes. **Nearby Attractions:** mid-coast Maine, Bar Harbor, Acadia National Park. **Additional Information:** Ellsworth Area Chamber of Commerce, P.O. Box 267, Ellsworth, ME 04605 (207) 667-5584 or Acadia Information Center, P.O. Box 139, Mount Desert, ME 04660 (207) 667-8550 or (800) 358-8550, www.acadiainfo.com.

RESTRICTIONS

Pets: Must be on a leash, never left unattended. **Fires:** In grills, stoves, & fire rings only. **Alcoholic Beverages:** At site only. **Vehicle Maximum Length:** 36 ft.

TO GET THERE

From junction Rtes. 1 and 1A, go southwest 0.5 mi. to Rte. 172, then southwest 4 mi.; campground is on the left.

THOMASTON
Saltwater Farm Campground

P.O. Box 165, Thomaston 04861. T: (207) 354-6735; www.midcoast.com/~sfc; sfc@midcoast.com.

RV ★★★ Tent ★★

Beauty: ★★★ Site Privacy: ★★
Spaciousness: ★★ Quiet: ★★★★
Security: ★★★ Cleanliness: ★★★★★
Insect Control: ★★★ Facilities: ★★★

Located in mid-coast Maine, 50 miles east of Brunswick, this small, quiet campground is set on a 35-acre meadow overlooking the St. George River. The bustling Camden-Rockport area is nearby, but this spot is anti-bustle. The main activity here is dropping a line in the river (fishing is said to be terrific) or watching the sun rise over the water. Campsites are open and grassy, with great views of the river. If you've brought a canoe or kayak, launch it here and explore the waterway. A few sites are set along the perimeter of the wooded perimeter of the property, including some tent sites and full hookup spots. There's one huge (unnumbered) riverfront tent site that gets snapped up first; ask for it, they'll know what you mean. Full hookup sites 32 through 35 sit atop the hill, with water views. A few seasonal sites are included in the mix. Things might change, because they're adding some sites. But we're guessing the ambience of the place will remain peaceful and inviting.

BASICS

Operated By: Bruce & Linda Jennings. **Open:** May 15–Oct. 15. **Site Assignment:** Reservations recommended, especially during July & Aug. Deposit of 1 nights' fee required. Refund w/ cancellations within 7 days, minus $5 fee. **Registration:** At office. **Fee:** $20–$28 for 2 adults & up to 3 children. V, MC, D. **Parking:** At site or as directed.

FACILITIES

Number of RV Sites: 33. **Number of Tent-Only Sites:** 7. **Hookups:** Water, electric (50 amps), sewer. **Each Site:** Picnic table, fire ring. **Dump Station:** Yes. **Laundry:** Yes. **Pay Phone:** Yes. **Rest Rooms and Showers:** Yes, coin-op. **Fuel:** No. **Propane:** No. **Internal Roads:** Gravel, in good condition. **RV Service:** No. **Market:** 1.5 mi. west. **Restaurant:** 1.5 mi. west. **General Store:** Yes. **Vending:** Yes. **Swimming Pool:** Yes. **Playground:** Yes. **Other:** 2-hole pitch & putt. **Activities:** Fishing along tidal shore. **Nearby Attractions:** Owl's Head Transportation Museum, Farnsworth Museum & Wyeth Center, Maine Lighthouse Museum, boat cruises, golf. **Additional Information:** Rockland/Thomaston Area Chamber of Commerce, (207) 596-0376; (800) 562-2529.

RESTRICTIONS

Pets: Must be leashed, quiet, & cleaned up after. Must not be left unattended. **Fires:** In fire rings. **Alcoholic Beverages:** Yes. **Vehicle Maximum Length:** None. **Other:** 3-night min. during Maine Lobster Festival (first week in Aug.).

TO GET THERE

Follow I-95 to Maine Turnpike. Exit I-95 at Brunswick, exit 22. Follow Rte. 1 north to Thomaston. Turn right onto Wadsworth St. at the Prison Store. Campground is 1.5 mi. ahead, on left.

TRENTON
Narrows Too

Rte. 3, 1150 Bar Harbor Rd., Trenton 04605. T: (207) 667-4300; www.narrowstoo.com.

RV ★★★★★ Tent ★★★★

Beauty: ★★★★ Site Privacy: ★★★
Spaciousness: ★★★ Quiet: ★★★
Security: ★★★ Cleanliness: ★★★★★
Insect Control: ★★★ Facilities: ★★★★★

In an area blessed with a multitude of fine campgrounds, this oceanfront property remains a standout, especially for campers who like a lot of activities and facilities on site. It has a busy, bustling atmosphere full of families, young couples, and retirees on vacation, here to explore Acadia National Park and the surrounding area. There's plenty to do at the campground: magic shows and movies in the evenings, mini-golf, swimming, and more; most activities and sports fields are clustered in the front of the campground. Head toward the back of the site and you'll have splendid views of the ocean. Days are typically quiet when most campers leave to visit area attractions (there's a free shuttle bus service from the campground to downtown Bar Harbor) but by late afternoon the campground is a hive of activity. You'll have a choice of sites, most are sunny and open, and many have expansive ocean views. There is a cluster of cabins and shaded sites in the woods that offer more privacy (sites 203–206 are favorites), and a separate tenting circle. As expected, most popular sites are on the ocean (sites 311–314 are particularly nice.)

BASICS

Operated By: Pat Stanley. **Open:** Memorial Day–Columbus Day. **Site Assignment:** Reservations accepted year–round, recommended in Jul.–Aug. All sites require a 2 night min. reservation w/ a 3-night min. on holiday weekends; holidays are paid in full & non-refundable. Oceanfront sites are a 3-night min. stay in July & Aug. There are no sewer sites on the ocean. $50 deposit for 2 nights, $100 for 3 nights, $150 for 4–7 nights, $200 for 8 or more nights. 30-day cancellation policy minus a $10 service charge; MC, V, D & checks for reservations; no checks upon arrival. **Registration:** At office. **Fee:** Full hookups, $30 (early & late summer) $45 (peak season); water & electric, $35–$50 (best ocean); $30–$45 (ocean); $23–$35 (narrows best); $22–$32 (narrows choice) & $21–$30 (water/electric); no hookups, $18–$21. **Parking:** At site.

FACILITIES

Number of RV Sites: 120. **Number of Tent-Only Sites:** 12. **Hookups:** Water, electric, sewer (20, 30, 50 amps), cable TV, modem. **Each Site:** Picnic table, fire ring. **Dump Station:** Yes. **Laundry:** Yes. **Pay Phone:** Yes. **Rest Rooms and Showers:** Yes. **Fuel:** No. **Propane:** Yes. **Internal Roads:** Gravel, dirt (good). **RV Service:** No. **Market:** Trenton (1.5 mi). **Restaurant:** No. **General Store:** Yes. **Vending:** No. **Swimming Pool:** Yes. **Playground:** Yes. **Other:** Ocean frontage, rec room, entertainment center, exercise room, reading room, mini golf, free shuttle bus service to Bar Harbor, cabin rentals. **Activities:** Swimming, volleyball, basketball, horseshoes, mini golf, live entertainment & planned activities, including children's programs, arts & crafts, movies, & more. **Nearby Attractions:** Bar Harbor, Acadia National Park. **Additional Information:** Acadia National Park, P.O. Box 177, Bar Harbor, ME 04609 (207) 288-3338, www.nps/gov/acad. Also, Acadia Information Center, P.O. Box 139, Mount Desert, ME, 04660 (207) 667-8550 (800) 358-8550, www.acadiainfo.com & Bar Harbor Chamber of Commerce, 93 Cottage St., Bar Harbor, ME 04609 (207) 288-5103, www.barharborinfo.com.

RESTRICTIONS

Pets: Must be on a leash, never left unattended. **Fires:** In grills, stoves, & fire rings only. **Alcoholic Beverages:** At site only. **Vehicle Maximum Length:** None.

TO GET THERE

From junction Rtes. 230 and 3, go east 200 feet on Rte. 3; campground is on the left.

TRENTON
Timberland Acres

57 Bar Harbor Rd., Trenton 04605. T: (207) 667-3600 or (207) 667-5663.

RV ★★★ Tent ★★

Beauty: ★★ Site Privacy: ★★
Spaciousness: ★★ Quiet: ★★★
Security: ★★★ Cleanliness: ★★★★
Insect Control: ★★★ Facilities: ★★

This large RV park is just outside Bar Harbor and Acadia National Park (15 miles away) and caters to an older, retiree crowd that prefers to stay away from the hustle and bustle surrounding the park. It also draws off-the-road travelers en route to and from the popular vacation area. All sites are uniform and fairly nondescript, set side-by-side in rows. The front sites are blessed with a few trees but most have been snatched up by seasonal renters (there are about 50-60 seasonals at the campground.) The rest of the sites are further back in the campground, a bit cramped for our tastes, and in the open (bring those awnings for shade!) But, there are plenty of convenient pull-throughs, ultra clean facilities, and level, easy hookup sites throughout the campground. On summer weekends, campers can join in planned activities, including arts and crafts projects, bingo tournaments, and socials.

Basics

Operated By: Jim & Elizabeth Awalt. **Open:** May 15–Oct. 15. **Site Assignment:** Reservations suggested in Jul.–Aug., 1-night deposit, 2-week cancellation policy; MC,V & checks. **Registration:** At office. **Fee:** Full hookups, $28 (50 amp), $26 (30 amp); water & electric, $25 (50 amp), $23 (30 amp); no hookups, $20, based on family of 4. **Parking:** At site.

Facilities

Number of RV Sites: 210. **Number of Tent-Only Sites:** 12. **Hookups:** Water, electric, sewer (30, 50 amps). **Each Site:** Picnic table, fire ring. **Dump Station:** Yes. **Laundry:** Yes. **Pay Phone:** Yes. **Rest Rooms and Showers:** Yes (coin-op). **Fuel:** No. **Propane:** Yes. **Internal Roads:** paved. **RV Service:** Yes. **Market:** Ellsworth (2 mi). **Restaurant:** No. **General Store:** Yes. **Vending:** Yes. **Swimming Pool:** Yes. **Playground:** Yes. **Other:** Rec room, pavilion, group area. **Activities:** Swimming, horseshoes, shuffleboard, basketball, volleyball, planned activities, including arts & crafts, bingo, socials, & more. **Nearby Attractions:** Bar Harbor, Acadia National Park. **Additional Information:** Ellsworth Area Chamber of Commerce, P.O. Box 267, Ellsworth, ME 04605 (207) 667-5584 & Acadia Information Center, P.O. Box 139, Mount Desert, ME 04660 (207) 667-8550 or (800) 358-8550, www.acadiainfo.com.

Restrictions

Pets: Must be on a leash, never left unattended. **Fires:** In grills, stoves, & fire rings only. **Alcoholic Beverages:** At site only. **Vehicle Maximum Length:** None.

To Get There

From junction Rtes. 1 and 3 (in Ellsworth), go east 2 mi. on Rte. 3; campground is on the right.

WATERFORD

Papoose Pond Resort & Campground

100 Norway Rd., Rte. 118, Waterford 04088. T: (207) 583-4470; www.papoosepondresort.com; thepond@papoosepondresort.com.

RV ★★★★★ Tent ★★

Beauty: ★★★ Site Privacy: ★★★
Spaciousness: ★★★★ Quiet: ★★
Security: ★★★★ Cleanliness: ★★★★
Insect Control: ★★★ Facilities: ★★★★

The sign at the bathhouse says it all: "Do not use bathhouse sinks for water balloons"! This is definitely a family scene, with a rousing schedule of canoe trips, hayrides, and nightly entertainment. "We're like Beaver Cleaver-ville," says owner Bill Strauss. Set on an 80-acre pond in Western Maine, complete with antique carousel, this place evokes a wholesome, early-60s feel. The only thing lacking: Moms with buoffant hair-dos. Three generations of families have been coming here, to splash in the pond, take out the paddleboats, and roast marshmallows around the campfire. The prime lakeside spots are taken by rental cabins, although BS (beachside) sites 14 through 16, with electric and water, are pretty sweet. Forget the other end of the beach, though; BS sites 4 through 8, plus two on the end, are fairly exposed. Surprise: there's a whole section of campsites across the street, and nestled into the woods. For the sake of peace, quiet, and privacy, we'd opt for any of these, especially sites HB 14 through 16 (they're huge) and HBHM 1 through 11 (ultra-private.) This is definitely a destination campground, great fun for kids.

Basics

Operated By: Strauss family. **Open:** Mid-May–Columbus Day. **Site Assignment:** Reservations recommended. Reservations open 1 year in advance. 50% deposit due for reservations; payment in full due if staying less than 1 week. Refunds for cancellation w/ 30-day notice, minus $15 service fee. $5 service fee charged for each reservation change. **Registration:** At office. **Fee:** $25–$56 for 2 adults & up to 4 children. V, MC. **Parking:** At site.

Facilities

Number of RV Sites: 225. **Number of Tent-Only Sites:** 0. **Hookups:** Water, electric (20, 30 amps), sewer, modem. **Each Site:** Picnic table, fireplace. **Dump Station:** Yes. **Laundry:** Yes. **Pay Phone:** Yes. **Rest Rooms and Showers:** Yes. **Fuel:** No. **Propane:** No. **Internal Roads:** Gravel, in good condition. **RV Service:** No. **Market:** 15 mi. south, in Norway. **Restaurant:** Yes. **General Store:** Yes. **Vending:** Yes. **Swimming Pool:** No. **Playground:** Yes. **Other:** Rec hall, game room, mini-golf, carousel. **Activities:** Mini-golf, lake swimming, tennis, boating (rentals available), fishing, basketball, volleyball, shuffleboard, horseshoes, carousel rides, planned daily activities. **Nearby Attractions:** Mt. Sabattus (hiking), outlet shopping (North Conway, N.H.). **Additional Information:** Bridgton Lakes Region Chamber of Commerce, (207) 647-3472.

Restrictions

Pets: Must be leashed, quiet, & cleaned up after. Must be under control at all times. Not allowed on beach. **Fires:** In fire rings only. **Alcoholic Beverages:** At sites only. **Vehicle Maximum Length:** None. **Other:** 3-night min. on Memorial Day & Labor Day weekends.

To Get There

From Maine Turnpike, take exit 11 (Gray.) From Gray, take Rte.26 north to Norway, then Rte. 118 for 10 mi. west to campground.

WELD

Mount Blue State Park

R.R. 1, P.O. Box 610, Weld 04285. T: (207) 585-2347 or (207) 585-2261 (off-season); www.state.me.us/doc/parks.htm.

RV ★★★ Tent ★★★

Beauty: ★★★ Site Privacy: ★★★
Spaciousness: ★★★ Quiet: ★★★★
Security: ★★★★ Cleanliness: ★★★★
Insect Control: ★★★ Facilities: ★★★★

Gold-panning on the Swift River? Moonlight owl walks? Intriguing ranger-led programs like these are just part of the appeal at this state park, located in mountainous western Maine. The park is split into two areas: a beach and camping area on Lake Webb, and, 14 miles away, 3167-foot Mt. Blue, reachable via hiking trails. If you like to hike, this is your kind of place, with a variety of hikes for all abilities (ask rangers for suggestions.) Campsites are set in three loops, with trails leading to the narrow, sandy beach and big, roped-off swim area. If you're tenting, inquire about a level one, like site 70L; some are pretty bumpy here. Most sites are set far back from the road. Some, like site 22L, even boast their own furnishings—nice, flat boulders that make perfect chairs. Lots of fallen logs are left to nature to deal with here, but campsites are mostly cleared. Site 104X (as in extra-large) has a nice approach, and is great for big rigs. Friday and Saturday evening ranger programs in the amphitheater are worth attending. There's only one shower room at this park, but at least it has plenty of showers.

Basics

Operated By: Maine Dept. of Conservation, Bureau of Parks & Lands. **Open:** May 15–Oct. 1. **Site Assignment:** In spring & fall, camping is on a first-come, first-served basis. For summer stays, reservations open on the first business day in Jan. From June 15 to the night before Labor Day, sites may be reserved for a min. of 2 nights & up to 2 weeks. Full payment is charged to credit card when reservation is processed. Refund with $15 cancellation fee. 26 sites are non-reservable, & available on a first-come, first-served basis. Call the reservations line to cancel a reservation more than 3 days in advance. If cancelling less than 3 days in advance, call the park directly. **Registration:** At office. **Fee:** $13, Maine residents; $17, non-residents; plus $2 fee if reserving in advance. V, MC. **Parking:** At sites or assigned lots.

Facilities

Number of RV Sites: 136. **Number of Tent-Only Sites:** 0. **Hookups:** None. **Each Site:** Picnic table, fireplace. **Dump Station:** Yes. **Laundry:** No. **Pay Phone:** Yes. **Rest Rooms and Showers:** Yes. **Fuel:** No. **Propane:** Yes. **Internal Roads:** Gravel, in good condition. **RV Service:** No. **Market:** 14 mi. southeast. **Restaurant:** 14 mi. southeast. **General Store:** Yes. **Vending:** Yes. **Swimming Pool:** No. **Playground:** Yes. **Other:** Boat ramp, amphitheater, nature center. **Activities:** Bicycling, mountain biking, hiking (multi-use trail & nature trail), boating (rentals available), volleyball, basketball, moosewatching, interpretive programs. **Nearby Attractions:** Mt. Blue (14 mi.), other day hikes. **Additional Information:** Greater Farmington Chamber of Commerce, (207) 778-4215.

Restrictions

Pets: Must be leashed, quiet, & cleaned up after. Must not be left unattended. Not allowed on beach.

Fires: In fire rings only. **Alcoholic Beverages:** No. **Vehicle Maximum Length:** 38 ft. **Other:** 2-week max. stay between last week in June & Labor Day.

To Get There

From junction of Rtes. 156 and 142, go 2.75 mi. north on 156, then 4 mi. west on Shore Rd., then 1 mi. south to campground.

WELLS
Sea Breeze

2073 Post Rd., Wells 04090. T: (207) 646-4301 (888) 792-2177; F: (207) 646-4803.

RV ★★★ Tent ★★

Beauty: ★★ Site Privacy: ★★
Spaciousness: ★★ Quiet: ★★★
Security: ★★★★ Cleanliness: ★★★★
Insect Control: ★★★ Facilities: ★★

There's not much happening at this tranquil campground in southern Maine, just a few miles from downtown Wells. If you have active pre-teens and teens in your bunch, they'll probably be bored—with a capital B (though the campground is on the Wells Trolley line and they can easily head into town.) The campground draws an older, mature crowd, who appreciate the relative peace and quiet and don't crave a lot of activities. There's a full-service market, deli and hot food counter as you enter the property, and two pools—one for the motel and cottages and one for the campground. Sites are basic, set side-by-side in rows off the main road. Trees flank the property, but most sites are in the open. Tenters are placed on multi-purpose sites among the RVs.

Basics

Operated By: Phil & Chun Tumminia. **Open:** Mid-May–mid-Oct. **Site Assignment:** Reservations suggested, 1 night deposit, 14 day cancellation policy, no deposit refunds on holiday & no vacancy nights, 3-night min. stay on holiday weekends; MC, V, D, no checks. **Registration:** At office. **Fee:** Full hookups, $34 (weekday), $38 (weekend); no hookups, $25–$28, based on 4 people per site. **Parking:** At site.

Facilities

Number of RV Sites: 57. **Number of Tent-Only Sites:** 0. **Hookups:** Water, electric, sewer (30, 50 amps), cable TV. **Each Site:** Picnic table, fire ring. **Dump Station:** Yes. **Laundry:** Yes. **Pay Phone:** Yes. **Rest Rooms and Showers:** Yes. **Fuel:** No. **Propane:** Yes. **Internal Roads:** Gravel, dirt (good). **RV Service:** No. **Market:** Wells (1.5 mi). **Restaurant:** Yes. **General Store:** Yes. **Vending:** Yes. **Swimming Pool:** Yes. **Playground:** Yes. **Other:** Motel & cottage rentals. **Activities:** Swimming. **Nearby Attractions:** Old Orchard Beach, Wells Harbor, Ogunquit, Kennebunkport, southern coast parks & beaches, Portland. **Additional Information:** Wells Chamber of Commerce, 136 Post Rd., Rte. 1, Wells, ME 04090 (207) 646-2451; www.wellschamber.org.

Restrictions

Pets: Must be on a leash, never left unattended. **Fires:** In grills, stoves, & fire rings only. **Alcoholic Beverages:** At site only. **Vehicle Maximum Length:** None.

To Get There

From junction Maine Turnpike and Rte. 109, exit 2, go east 1.5 mi. on Rte. 109, then north 1.3 mi. on Rte. 1; campground is on the right.

WELLS
Sea-Vu Campground

Rte. 1, P.O. Box 67, Wells 04090. T: (207) 646-7732; www.sea-vucampground.com; sea-vu@cybertours.com.

RV ★★★ Tent ★★★

Beauty: ★★★ Site Privacy: ★★★
Spaciousness: ★★★ Quiet: ★★★
Security: ★★★★★ Cleanliness: ★★★★
Insect Control: ★★★ Facilities: ★★★

This southern coast campground, with quick and easy access to area parks, beaches, and attractions, boasts picturesque views of the Atlantic Ocean and Wells Harbor. Up front, there's a small fitness area where early morning classes are held throughout the summer. Several rows of seasonal renters stretch from the front office area toward the water. Most sites don't have much of a view but there is a nice seating area overlooking the wide expanse of tidal marshes, inlets, and open ocean. The handful of tent-only sites have ocean views, nestled in a grassy, shaded area in the back. Most campers don't demand much from their stay at Sea-Vu: a clean, friendly place to set up home away from home so they can explore the region. Sea-Vu delivers that.

Basics

Operated By: Dave & Elaine Talevi. **Open:** May–Oct. 15. **Site Assignment:** Reservations suggested, full deposit for 3 nights or less, one-half deposit for 4 nights or more, 14-day cancellation policy; no refunds given for holiday reservations; MC, V, no checks. **Registration:** At office. **Fee:** Full hookups, $41; no hookups (water nearby), $32, based on 2 people, additional people, $4. **Parking:** At site.

Facilities

Number of RV Sites: 262. **Number of Tent-Only Sites:** 8. **Hookups:** Water, electric, sewer (30, 50 amps), cable TV. **Each Site:** Picnic table, fire ring. **Dump Station:** Yes. **Laundry:** Yes. **Pay Phone:** Yes. **Rest Rooms and Showers:** Yes (coin-op). **Fuel:** No. **Propane:** Yes. **Internal Roads:** Paved, gravel (good). **RV Service:** Yes. **Market:** Wells (1 mi). **Restaurant:** Yes. **General Store:** Yes. **Vending:** Yes. **Swimming Pool:** Yes. **Playground:** Yes. **Other:** Game room, fitness center, 18-hole mini-golf course, sports field. **Activities:** Swimming, mini-golf, basketball, volleyball, horseshoes. **Nearby Attractions:** Old Orchard Beach, Wells Harbor, Ogunquit, Kennebunkport, southern coast parks & beaches, Portland. **Additional Information:** Wells Chamber of Commerce, 136 Post Rd., Rte. 1, Wells, ME 04090 (207) 646-2451; www.wellschamber.org.

Restrictions

Pets: Must be on a leash, never left unattended. **Fires:** In grills, stoves, & fire rings only. **Alcoholic Beverages:** At site only. **Vehicle Maximum Length:** None.

To Get There

From junction Maine Turnpike and Rte. 109, exit 2, go east 1.5 mi. on Rte. 109, then north 0.4 mi. on Rte. 1; campground is on the right.

WELLS
Wells Beach Resort Campground

1000 Post Rd., Wells 04090. T: (207) 646-7570 (800) 640-2267 (reservations); www.wells-beach.com.

RV ★★★★ Tent ★★★

Beauty: ★★ Site Privacy: ★★★
Spaciousness: ★★★ Quiet: ★★
Security: ★★★ Cleanliness: ★★★★
Insect Control: ★★★ Facilities: ★★★★

This is one of the nicest campgrounds in the popular Wells Beach area, boasting super clean facilities, modern hookups and level sites, and plenty of amenities for kids and grownups alike— all this in the heart of Maine's southern coastal resort area. What you don't find at the campground, is within easy walking distance: fast food franchises, local restaurants, movie theaters, factory outlet shops, beaches, and more. We like the poolside laundry with an outdoor sitting area and the small fitness room for early morning workouts. There's a choice of open and shaded sites; tent sites come with water, electric and cable TV and are set in the back, flanked by trees. Don't expect much privacy or quiet; it's a busy, activity-oriented place, swarming with southern coastal Maine tourists and vacationing families.

Basics

Operated By: Griffin family. **Open:** May 15–Oct. 15. **Site Assignment:** Reservations suggested, $80 deposit for stays of 3 days or less, $150 deposit for 4 days or more, in full for holiday stays, 14-day cancellation policy w/ a $10 service charge; MC, V, D, no checks. **Registration:** At office. **Fee:** Full hookups (50 amp), $46; (20, 30) amp, $41; water, electric & cable, $38.50, summer weekends may be higher, based on 2 people; additional person, ages 4 & older, $6. **Parking:** At site, 1 vehicle per site.

Facilities

Number of RV Sites: 200. **Number of Tent-Only Sites:** 12. **Hookups:** Water, electric, sewer (20, 30, 50 amps), cable TV, modem. **Each Site:** Picnic table, fire ring. **Dump Station:** Yes. **Laundry:** Yes. **Pay Phone:** Yes. **Rest Rooms and Showers:** Yes. **Fuel:** No. **Propane:** No. **Internal Roads:** Gravel, dirt (good). **RV Service:** No. **Market:** Wells (0.5 mi). **Restaurant:** No. **General Store:** Yes. **Vending:** Yes. **Swimming Pool:** Yes. **Playground:** Yes. **Other:** Fitness center, rec hall, sports fields., 18-hole mini-golf course, pavilion, Wells Trolley Car stop. **Activities:** Swimming, bocce ball, mini-golf, volleyball, basketball, horseshoes. **Nearby Attractions:** Old Orchard Beach, Wells Harbor, Ogunquit, Kennebunkport, southern coast parks &

beaches, Portland. **Additional Information:** Wells Chamber of Commerce, 136 Post Rd., Rte. 1, Wells, ME 04090 (207) 646-2451; www.wellschamber.org.

RESTRICTIONS

Pets: Must be on a leash, never left unattended. Pets are not allowed on tent sites. **Fires:** In grills, stoves, & fire rings only. **Alcoholic Beverages:** At site only. **Vehicle Maximum Length:** None.

TO GET THERE

From junction Maine Turnpike and Rte. 109 (exit 2), go east 1.5 mi. on Rte. 109, then south 1.4 mi. on Rte. 1; campground is on the right.

WISCASSET

Chewonki Campgrounds

P.O. Box 261, Wiscasset 04578. T: (207) 882-7426.

RV ★★★★ Tent ★★★★

Beauty: ★★★★★ Site Privacy: ★★
Spaciousness: ★★★★ Quiet: ★★
Security: ★★★ Cleanliness: ★★★★
Insect Control: ★★ Facilities: ★★★★

Wiscasset calls itself "Maine's Prettiest Village." If you'd like to check out the veracity of that statement, or simply want a pleasant, centralized base for exploring mid-coast Maine, consider this inviting campground. Run by the Brackett family for 25 years, and currently managed by sisters Ann and Pamela, Chewonki Campgrounds overlooks a saltwater inlet of Montsweag Bay. It's a really pretty spot, with rolling hillsides leading to saltmarsh and sea. Watery nooks and crannies beckon paddlers. (When we visited, a large group of kayakers were tent-camping here.) The grassy sites are spacious, with mature trees providing a measure of privacy for some. Sites 10, 10A, and 10B (no hookups) are right on the water, but the best views, we think, are from sites 13 through 16 (water and electricity), overlooking the saltmarsh. Flower plantings add to the sense that this campground is well cared-for; plus, everything from the saltwater-filtered pool area to the rest rooms are super-clean. A downside here: there's a small airport nearby, so you're bound to hear aircraft overhead during the day. By night, they stop flying, so it's peaceful. One look at the star-filled sky, and you'll feel far from the urban hustle and bustle.

BASICS

Operated By: Pamela D. Brackett & Ann Brackett Beck. **Open:** Mid-May–mid-Oct. **Site Assignment:** Reservations recommended. 1-month advance booking in July & Aug. recommended. $25 deposit for stays of 3 days or less; $50 deposit for stays of 4 or more days. Refunds for cancellation w/ 2-week notice, minus $10 service fee. **Registration:** At office. **Fee:** $25–$35 for 2 adults & their unmarried children under 21 years of age. V, MC. **Parking:** At site.

FACILITIES

Number of RV Sites: 47. **Number of Tent-Only Sites:** 0. **Hookups:** Water, electric (20, 30 amps), sewer. **Each Site:** Picnic table, fire ring. **Dump Station:** Yes. **Laundry:** No. **Pay Phone:** Yes. **Rest Rooms and Showers:** Yes, coin-op. **Fuel:** No. **Propane:** No. **Internal Roads:** Gravel, in good condition. **RV Service:** No. **Market:** 2 mi. north. **Restaurant:** 1.5 mi. south. **General Store:** Yes. **Vending:** No. **Swimming Pool:** Yes. **Playground:** Yes. **Other:** Rec hall, tennis courts, boat ramp (for small craft). **Activities:** Boating (canoe & kayak rentals), swimming, volleyball, croquet, nature walk, one-hole golf course. **Nearby Attractions:** Historic village of Wiscasset, Pemaquid Point lighthouse, art museums, Old Jail, boat cruises, deep-sea fishing, antique shops, flea markets. **Additional Information:** Wiscasset Regional Business Assoc., (207) 882-4600; www.wiscassetmaine.com.

RESTRICTIONS

Pets: Must be leashed, quiet, & cleaned up after. Must not be left unattended. **Fires:** In fire rings only. **Alcoholic Beverages:** At sites only. **Vehicle Maximum Length:** None. **Other:** 3-day min. stay on holidays.

TO GET THERE

From Maine Turnpike, take exit 9, Rte. 95 and Rte. 1 to Bath. Follow 7 mi. to Rte. 144, then turn right. Follow signs to campground, 1.5 mi. on right.

YORK HARBOR

Libby's Oceanside Camp

Rte. 1A, P.O. Box 40, York Harbor 03911. T: (207) 363-4171; F: (207) 363-5375; www.libbysoceancamping.com.

RV ★★★★ Tent ★★

Beauty: ★★★★ Site Privacy: ★★
Spaciousness: ★★ Quiet: ★★★
Security: ★★★ Cleanliness: ★★★★★
Insect Control: ★★★★ Facilities: ★★★

Never mind that the sites are a bit tight and that you won't have much privacy: this campground has one of the finest pieces of real estate on the southern coast. Just down the road are multi-million dollar houses; their owners don't have any better views than campers at Libby's. The campground boasts 1,100 feet of ocean frontage, with unsurpassed views of beaches, harbors, coves, and open ocean. On clear days, you can see Nubble Lighthouse, one of the most photographed sights in Maine. There are 45 oceanfront sites. Many are taken by seasonal renters but the owners have been freeing up more and more each year for the transcient crowd. There's access to a rocky beach on one end of the campground, a great place for tidepooling at low tide. At high tide, locals come down with their fishing rods. When we were there, they were casting for stripers from the beach. When you've had enough of "roughing it," head to upscale York Harbor or nearby Ogunquit for gallery hopping and gourmet meals.

BASICS

Operated By: Davidson family. **Open:** May 15–Oct. 15. **Site Assignment:** Reservations accepted for 1 week stays only, Sunday–Sunday; shorter stays are first come, first served. $100 deposit for each week reserved, 14-day cancellation policy; MC, V, D, no checks. **Registration:** At office. **Fee:** Oceanfront sites, $52; all other sites, $42; 50 amp, $2; cable TV, $1.50, based on 2 adults & 2 children under 16, or 3 adults (all sites include sewer, water & 30 amp electric). **Parking:** At site.

FACILITIES

Number of RV Sites: 85. **Number of Tent-Only Sites:** 10. **Hookups:** Water, sewer, electric (20, 30, 50 amps), cable TV. **Each Site:** Picnic table. **Dump Station:** No. **Laundry:** No. **Pay Phone:** Yes. **Rest Rooms and Showers:** Yes. **Fuel:** No. **Propane:** No. **Internal Roads:** Gravel, dirt (good). **RV Service:** No. **Market:** York Harbor (1 mi). **Restaurant:** No. **General Store:** No. **Vending:** Yes. **Swimming Pool:** No. **Playground:** No. **Other:** Hot tub, ocean frontage, beach, activity room. **Activities:** Swimming, saltwater fishing, beachcombing, tidepooling. **Nearby Attractions:** Yok Harbor, York beaches, southern coast parks & beaches, Portsmouth. **Additional Information:** Yorks Chamber of Commerce, One Stonewall Ln., York, ME 03909 (207) 363-4422 (800) 639-2442; www.yorkme.org.

RESTRICTIONS

Pets: Must be on a leash, never left unattended. No pets allowed on the beach; only 2 pets allowed per site. **Fires:** In grills, stoves, & fire rings only. **Alcoholic Beverages:** At site only. **Vehicle Maximum Length:** None.

TO GET THERE

From I-95, exit 4, go east 0.3 mi. on connector road, then south 0.3 mi. on Rte. 1, then north 3 mi. on Rte. 1A; campground is on the right.

Maryland

Dubbed "America in Miniature" by a National Geographic reporter in the 1920s, Maryland boasts the green Allegheny Mountains in the west as well as the tranquil Chesapeake Bay and white-sanded Atlantic beaches along the eastern shore. Consider the culture-rich, metropolitan cities of Baltimore and nearby Washington, D.C., along with myriad historic small towns, and you can see that the reporter's view of Maryland is still accurate.

Cascading streams, hiking trails, lakes ideal for boating, and slopes meant for skiing are prevalent in western Maryland in the Allegheny Mountains. **Deep Creek Lake,** Maryland's largest man-made body of water at six square miles, is a haven for water sports in warmer months. **Wisp Ski & Golf Resort** has more than two dozen slopes and an 18-hole golf course. Part of the **Chesapeake and Ohio Canal National Historical Park**—which includes the **C&O Canal National Park Exhibit Center,** the **C&O Canal Boat Replica,** and the **C&O Canal Paw Paw Tunnel** in **Cumberland**—this region illustrates Maryland's glorious canal era. Though **Gettysburg** is known as the Civil War's bloodiest battle, more than 23,000 men were killed in **Antietam** on September 17, 1862—the deadliest day in the Civil War. More than 350 monuments, plaques, and battlefield amps along eight miles of paved roadways detail the battle's story. The visitors center houses a museum and a 26-minute movie about the battle.

Baltimore is the heart of central Maryland, but it is not the state capital. Nearby Annapolis, home of the United States Naval Academy, has that honor. Shaped by northern and southern traditions, Baltimore served as the nation's capital for two months when Philadelphia was invaded by British troops during the Revolutionary War. In 1814, when the British in turn attacked Baltimore, defenders of Fort McHenry withstood the naval bombardment for 25 hours. When the British ceased fire and gave up, Francis Scott Key noticed the massive American flag still flying above the fort, and this inspired him to compose "The Star-Spangled Banner." Today, the **Fort McHenry National Monument and Historic Shrine** is restored to its War of 1812 appearance. Narrated cruises depart from the fort and explore the surrounding area. Baseball fans will appreciate the Baltimore Orioles at **Camden Yards** and the **Babe Ruth Birthplace and Baseball Center.** The **Edgar Allan Poe House,** the **National Aquarium,** and the **Star-Spangled Banner Flag House and 1812 Museum** are other sites we recommend. Founded in 1649, **Annapolis** is best experienced by Three Centuries Tours of Annapolis, which offers walking tours of the **U.S. Naval Academy** and the historic district led by guides dressed in colonial attire.

In 1791, Maryland officials donated the land that became Washington, D.C. There are many interesting attractions, towns and sites in the Maryland counties that border our nation's capital. **Frederick** is a historic town where museums capture the lives of Civil War heroine Barbara Fritchie and Star-Spangled Banner author Francis Scott Key. **"Olde Towne Gaithersburg," the Clara Barton National Historic Site in Glen Echo, Andrews Air Force Base,** and the **NASA/Goddard Space Flight Visitor Center** are certainly worth exploring before or after venturing to Washington.

Southern Maryland is the most naturally pristine region in the state. Cliffs rise above fossil-strewn beaches. Lighthouses guard the waters of **Chesapeake Bay,** and the fishing is spectacular in the **Patuxent and Potomac Rivers. St. Mary's City,** the area's capital until 1694, features an outdoor museum at the site of the first capitol. The living history complex includes a reconstructed **1676 State House,** a 17th-century tobacco plantation, and a 17th-century inn. Inside the dense forests of 1,460-acre **Calvert Cliffs State Park,** about 600 species of fossils have been discovered around the jutting cliffs overlooking Chesapeake Bay.

Charming villages dot the landscape of Maryland's eastern shore, which includes Chesapeake Bay and the Atlantic Ocean. **Ocean City**—home to white-sand beaches, deep-sea fishing, a three-mile boardwalk, and the **Jolly Roger Amusement Park**—is Maryland's only Atlantic Coast resort town. Many visitors come here not just for the ocean but to explore the **Assateague Island National Seashore,** a 37-mile barrier strand off the eastern shore; large populations of Chincoteague ponies, Sitka deer, and peregrine falcons reside there. The eastern shore is also Maryland's crab country. The blue crab's succulent meat is the essential dish at any of the countless seafood houses along Maryland's coast.

ABINGDON

Bar Harbor RV Park and Marina

4228 Birch Ave., Abingdon 21009. T: (800) 351-CAMP or (410) 679-0880; F: (410) 671-7278; www.barharborrvpark.com.

RV ★★★★ Tent n/a

Beauty: ★★★★★ Site Privacy: ★★★★
Spaciousness: ★★★★ Quiet: ★★★★
Security: ★★★★ Cleanliness: ★★★★
Insect Control: ★★★★ Facilities: ★★★★

Situated on a densely forested peninsula on the Bush River along Chesapeake Bay, Bar Harbor RV Park and Marina is a half-hour northeast of Baltimore's Inner Harbor. The marina, where bald eagles and great blue herons gracefully glide, has boat slips and rowboat, kayak, and pedal boat rentals. Campers who bring their own boat can venture by water to Chesapeake Bay ports, including Baltimore and Annapolis. Sites are shaded and feature full hookups and patios. Some sites are located on the waterfront, and other sites are away from the water. The swimming pool is surrounded with vibrant wildflowers and lush plants. When we were here, many campers were basking in the sun by the pool and casting their lines into Bush River. The aforementioned pedal boat and kayak rentals are also popular.

BASICS

Operated By: Private operator. **Open:** All year. **Site Assignment:** Reservations accepted (MC or V will hold site), walk-ins accepted. **Registration:** At campground office. **Fee:** $31–$34 (VISA, MC). **Parking:** At site.

FACILITIES

Number of RV Sites: 93. **Number of Tent-Only Sites:** None. **Hookups:** Electric (30, 50 amps), cable TV, phone, all sites have full hookups. **Each Site:** Fire ring and picnic table. **Dump Station:** Yes. **Laundry:** Yes. **Pay Phone:** Yes. **Rest Rooms and Showers:** Yes. **Fuel:** No. **Propane:** Yes. **Internal Roads:** Gravel and paved, in good condition. **RV Service:** No. **Market:** Within 2 mi. **Restaurant:** Within 2 mi. **General Store:** Yes. **Vending:** Yes. **Playground:** Yes. **Other:** Bush River. **Activities:** Canoeing, boating, kayaking, boat rentals, fishing, game room, rec hall. **Nearby Attractions:** Baltimore, Camden Yards, Chesapeake Bay, Inner Harbor, Baltimore Zoo, National Aquarium, US Naval Academy, Annapolis, Washington, D.C. **Additional Information:** Baltimore Area Convention and Visitors Assoc., (800) 343-3468, www.baltimore.org.

RESTRICTIONS

Pets: On leash only. **Fires:** At site. **Alcoholic Beverages:** At site. **Vehicle Maximum Length:** 40 ft. **Other:** No tents or screen rooms.

TO GET THERE

From I-95, take Exit 80 and go 1.5 mi. south on Hwy. 543, 2 mi. west on US 40, 0.75 mi. south on Long Bar Rd., and 0.5 mi. east on Baker Ave. Entrance is on the left.

BERLIN

Assateague Island National Seashore, Bayside Campground and Oceanside Campground

7206 National Seashore Ln., Berlin 21811. T: (410) 641-1441 or (800) 365-2267; www.nps.gov/asis/camping.html; christopher_seymour@nps.gov.

RV ★★★ Tent ★★★★

Beauty: ★★★★★ Site Privacy: ★★★★
Spaciousness: ★★★★ Quiet: ★★★★★
Security: ★★★★★ Cleanliness: ★★★★
Insect Control: ★★★ Facilities: ★★★

Operated by the National Park Service, Assateague Island National Seashore has two campgrounds—Bayside and Oceanside. Oceanside walk-in tent sites are provided for tenters who wish to camp 100–200 feet from parking areas. Centrally located facilities include chemical toilets, cold-water showers, and drinking water. Before exploring the island, visit the national park's visitor center, where exhibits and aquariums describe the barrier island environment. Be aware that the barrier island environment can be harsh if you are not prepared. Bring firewood, sunscreen, insect repellent, screen tents for shade, insect protection, and long tent stakes to anchor tents in the sand and wind. Assateague Island National Seashore in Maryland and the Chincoteague National Wildlife Refuge in Virginia (which is located on the island) are federal fee areas. The $5 entrance fee is in effect year round. Also, be sure to observe the wildlife from a distance, especially the renowned Chincoteague ponies, which are known to bite and kick.

BASICS

Operated By: National Park Service. **Open:** All year. **Site Assignment:** Reservations accepted (may be made up to 5 months in advance). Oct. 16–May 14, camping is on a first-come, first-served basis; May 15–Oct. 15, reservations are taken for all campsites. **Registration:** At campground office. **Fee:** $10–$14 (VISA, MC). **Parking:** At designated area.

FACILITIES

Number of RV Sites: 48 (Bayside), 80 (Oceanside). **Number of Tent-Only Sites:** 24 (Oceanside). **Hookups:** None. **Each Site:** Some have fire rings, others have grills. **Dump Station:** Yes. **Laundry:** No. **Pay Phone:** Yes. **Rest Rooms and Showers:** Yes. **Fuel:** No. **Propane:** No. **Internal Roads:** Paved, in good condition. **RV Service:** No. **Market:** Within 7 mi. **Restaurant:** Within 7 mi. **General Store:** No. **Vending:** No. **Playground:** No. **Other:** Assateague Island National Seashore. **Activities:** Saltwater swimming and fishing, hiking trails boating, canoeing. **Nearby Attractions:** Assateague State Park, Chincoteague National Wildlife Refuge. **Additional Information:** Maryland Office of Tourism Development, (800) 543-1036, www.mdisfun.org.

RESTRICTIONS

Pets: On leash only. **Fires:** At site only. **Alcoholic Beverages:** No alcohol permitted. **Vehicle Maximum Length:** 40 ft. **Other:** 14-day max. stay.

TO GET THERE

From Hwy. 376, go 4 mi. southeast on Hwy. 611 and 2 mi. south on Bayberry Drive. Follow signs to campground.

CLARKSBURG

Little Bennett Regional Park Campground

23701 Frederick Rd., Clarksburg 20871. T: (301) 972-9222; www.mc-mncppc.org.

RV ★★★ Tent ★★★★

Beauty: ★★★★ Site Privacy: ★★★★
Spaciousness: ★★★★ Quiet: ★★★★
Security: ★★★★ Cleanliness: ★★★★
Insect Control: ★★★★ Facilities: ★★★

Located in northern Montgomery County, 30 miles north of Washington, D.C. in Clarksburg, the 3,700 forested acres of Little Bennett Regional Park are set amid the tributaries of Little Bennett Creek. The campground has 91 sites, 25 of which have electric hookups. Sites are situated in five loops. Loops D and E, at the north end, are near the amphitheater, laundry facility, nature center, horseshoe pits, and volleyball court. A central dump station is available for self-contained units, but there are no individual water or sewer connections. More than 14 miles of hiking and horseback riding trails wander throughout the park. During winter months, the trails are used as cross country ski trails. A camp store is combined with the registration office. Soda, ice cream, ice, snacks and souvenirs are available. Little Seneca Lake, five miles away in Black Hill Regional Park, also offers boating and fishing.

BASICS

Operated By: Montgomery County. **Open:** Mar. 1–Nov. 30. **Site Assignment:** Reservations and walk-ins accepted. **Registration:** At campground office. **Fee:** $12–$19 (VISA, MC). **Parking:** At site.

FACILITIES

Number of RV Sites: 25. **Number of Tent-Only Sites:** 66. **Hookups:** Electric (20, 30 amps). **Each Site:** Picnic table and grill. **Dump Station:** Yes. **Laundry:** Yes. **Pay Phone:** Yes. **Rest Rooms and Showers:** Yes. **Fuel:** No. **Propane:** No. **Internal Roads:** Paved, in good condition. **RV Service:** No. **Market:** Within 2 mi. **Restaurant:** Within 2 mi. **General Store:** Yes. **Vending:** Yes. **Playground:** Yes. **Other:** Little Bennett Creek. **Activities:** Hiking, horseback riding, horseshoes, volleyball, rec fields, planned activities on weekends. **Nearby Attractions:** Black Hill Regional Park, Baltimore, Washington, D.C. **Additional Information:** Maryland Office of Tourism Development, (800) 543-1036, www.mdisfun.org.

RESTRICTIONS

Pets: On leash only. **Fires:** At site. **Alcoholic Beverages:** No alcohol permitted. **Vehicle Maximum Length:** None. **Other:** 14-day max. stay.

To Get There

From I-270, take Exit 18 and go 0.5 mi. northeast on Hwy. 121, 0.5 mi. north on Hwy. 355, then follow the posted signs. Entrance is on the right.

COLLEGE PARK

Cherry Hill Park

9800 Cherry Hill Rd., College Park 20740.
T: (800) 801-6449 or (301) 937-7116; F: (301) 937-3110; www.cherryhillpark.com; dccamping@aol.com.

★★★★ ★★★★

Beauty: ★★★★	Site Privacy: ★★★★
Spaciousness: ★★★★	Quiet: ★★★★
Security: ★★★★	Cleanliness: ★★★★
Insect Control: ★★★★	Facilities: ★★★★★

Located about seven miles north of Washington, D.C., Cherry Hill Park is convenient (via city bus) to the Washington Area Metrorail (subway), which can take campers to the attractions in our nation's capital; Gray Line tour buses also stop here in season. One of the finest parks in Maryland and the mid-Atlantic, Cherry Hill has two swimming pools, a sauna, a whirlpool, and a large-screen TV lounge (with crackling fireplace in winter). The open and shaded sites are level, and 350 have full hookups. Cherry Hill accommodates 33 pull-throughs. The park is also within a half-hour drive of Baltimore and Annapolis. In nearby College Park, campers can visit the College Park Aviation Museum, located at the world's oldest operating airport; Greenbelt Park, a 1,100-acre wooded area operated by the National Park Service; and the NASA/Goddard Visitor Center, where rockets, capsule and other space-related items are displayed.

Basics

Operated By: Private operator. **Open:** All year. **Site Assignment:** Reservations accepted ($25 deposit required), walk-ins accepted. **Registration:** At campground office. **Fee:** $30–$55 (VISA, MC, D). **Parking:** At site.

Facilities

Number of RV Sites: 360. **Number of Tent-Only Sites:** 50. **Hookups:** Electric (30, 50 amps), cable TV, phone, 350 with full hookups. **Each Site:** Fire ring, picnic table. **Dump Station:** Yes. **Laundry:** Yes. **Pay Phone:** Yes. **Rest Rooms and Showers:** Yes. **Fuel:** No. **Propane:** Yes. **Internal Roads:** Gravel and paved, in good condition. **RV Service:** Yes. **Market:** Within 2 mi. **Restaurant:** On premises. **General Store:** Yes. **Vending:** Yes. **Playground:** Yes. **Other:** Dog-walking service, RV superstore, fishing pond. **Activities:** Swimming, game room, rec hall, sauna, whirlpool, pond fishing, mini-golf, basketball, planned activities, movies, hiking trails, volleyball. **Nearby Attractions:** Baltimore, Annapolis, Washington, D.C., College Park Aviation Museum, Greenbelt Park, NASA/Goddard Visitor Center, University of Maryland. **Additional Information:** Maryland Office of Tourism Development, (800) 543-1036, www.mdisfun.org.

Restrictions

Pets: On leash only. **Fires:** At site. **Alcoholic Beverages:** At site. **Vehicle Maximum Length:** 50 ft. **Other:** $1 for extra vehicle; 1 car is permitted with RV.

To Get There

From I-95, take Exit 25 and go 0.1 mi. south on US 1 and 1 mi. west on Cherry Hill Rd. Entrance is on the left.

CRISFIELD

Janes Island State Park

26280 Alfred Lawson Drive, Crisfield 21817.
T: (410) 968-1565 or (888) 432-2267; F: (410) 968-2515; www.dnr.state.md.us; park-janes-island@dnr.state.md.us.

★★★ ★★★★

Beauty: ★★★★	Site Privacy: ★★★★
Spaciousness: ★★★★	Quiet: ★★★★
Security: ★★★★★	Cleanliness: ★★★★
Insect Control: ★★★★	Facilities: ★★★★

Mostly surrounded by Chesapeake Bay and its inlets, Janes Island State Park features a developed mainland section (where the campground is located) and a portion accessible only by boat. With miles of isolated shoreline and marshes, Janes Island is a place where tranquility reigns. The most exciting part of Janes Island State Park is the canoe trails, which cover 2,900 acres of marshes, beaches, and highlands. Most of the waterways are protected from wind and currents, providing ideal conditions for canoeists of all skill levels. The yellow trail leads to Tangier Sound and the secluded beaches on the west side of the island. Overall, there are six marked trails, all of which begin and end at the marina and boat launch near the campground. Boat slips are available to campers for a small fee. The campground itself is situated along Daugherty Creek Canal. Sites are primarily in three clusters near the water, but not directly along it.

Basics

Operated By: State of Maryland. **Open:** Apr. 1–Oct. 31. **Site Assignment:** Reservations accepted (must be paid in full at time of booking when using credit card), walk-ins accepted. **Registration:** At campground office. **Fee:** $18–$23 (VISA, MC). **Parking:** At site.

Facilities

Number of RV Sites: 104. **Number of Tent-Only Sites:** None. **Hookups:** Electric (20 amps). **Each Site:** Fire ring and picnic table. **Dump Station:** Yes. **Laundry:** Yes. **Pay Phone:** Yes. **Rest Rooms and Showers:** Yes. **Fuel:** No. **Propane:** No. **Internal Roads:** Paved, in good condition. **RV Service:** No. **Market:** Within 2 mi. **Restaurant:** Within 2 mi. **General Store:** Yes. **Vending:** No. **Playground:** Yes. **Other:** Canoe trails. **Activities:** Swimming, fishing, boating, canoeing, boat rentals, planned activities. **Nearby Attractions:** Smith Island and Tangier Island boat cruises, Chesapeake Bay. **Additional Information:** Crisfield Area Chamber of Commerce, (410) 968-2500, www.crisfield.org.

Restrictions

Pets: No pets permitted. **Fires:** At site. **Alcoholic Beverages:** No alcohol permitted. **Vehicle Maximum Length:** 29 ft. **Other:** 14-day max. stay.

To Get There

From Hwy. 54, go 0.1 mi. east on Hwy. 40. Entrance is on the left.

CUMBERLAND

Rocky Gap State Park

12500 Pleasant Valley Rd., Flintstone 21530.
T: (301) 777-2139 or (888) 432-2267; www.dnr.state.md.us; jruark@dnr.state.md.us.

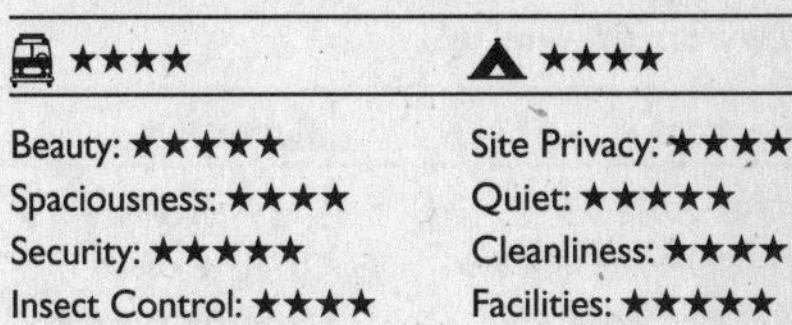

★★★★ ★★★★

Beauty: ★★★★★	Site Privacy: ★★★★
Spaciousness: ★★★★	Quiet: ★★★★★
Security: ★★★★★	Cleanliness: ★★★★
Insect Control: ★★★★	Facilities: ★★★★★

Consisting of 3,000 acres of stunning ridges, valleys, and mountain peaks near Cumberland in western Maryland, Rocky Gap State Park has it all—rugged hiking and mountain biking trails, kayaking and whitewater rafting, fishing and boating on 243-acre Lake Habeeb, the Rocky Gap Lodge and Golf Resort, and a 278-site campground. The lake is fed by Rocky Gap Run, which winds through a mile-long gorge with jutting cliffs, overlooks, and a hemlock forest dense with rhododendron. The campground, where sites are clustered around nine loops, is located at the northeast side of Lake Habeeb. Pets are permitted at the two Ridge loops—one at the northeast tip of the campground and the other at the southeast side. The Rocky Gap Lodge and Golf Resort is at the opposite end of Lake Habeeb. The resort consists of a 220-room lodge, a full-service restaurant overlooking the lake, and an 18-hole Jack Nicklaus–designed golf course.

Basics

Operated By: State of Maryland. **Open:** All year. **Site Assignment:** Reservations and walk-ins accepted. **Registration:** At campground office. **Fee:** $23–$28 (VISA, MC). **Parking:** At site.

Facilities

Number of RV Sites: 250. **Number of Tent-Only Sites:** 28. **Hookups:** Electric (20 amps). **Each Site:** Fire ring and picnic table. **Dump Station:** Yes. **Laundry:** Yes. **Pay Phone:** Yes. **Rest Rooms and Showers:** Yes. **Fuel:** No. **Propane:** No. **Internal Roads:** Paved, in good condition. **RV Service:** No. **Market:** Within 6 mi. **Restaurant:** On premises. **General Store:** Yes. **Vending:** Yes. **Playground:** Yes. **Other:** Lake Habeeb, Rocky Gap Lodge and Golf Resort. **Activities:** Lake swimming and fishing, boat rentals, canoeing, planned activities, hiking trails, golf, kayaking, biking. **Nearby Attractions:** Fort Cumberland Trail, Green Ridge State Forest, The Narrows, George Washington's headquarters, History House, Western Maryland Scenic Railroad, Western Maryland Station Center, Toll Gate House. **Additional Information:** Allegany County Convention and Visitors Bureau, (800) 50-VISIT, www.mdmountainside.com.

RESTRICTIONS

Pets: Allowed in 2 designated loops. **Fires:** At site. **Alcoholic Beverages:** No alcohol permitted. **Vehicle Maximum Length:** 29 ft. **Other:** Pets and fires may not be left unattended.

TO GET THERE

From Cumberland, go 6 mi. east on US 40. Follow signs to park and campground.

DENTON

Martinak State Park

137 Deep Shore Rd., Denton 21629. T: (410) 820-1668 or (888) 432-2267; www.dnr.state.md.us.

RV ★★★★ Tent ★★★★

Beauty: ★★★★ Site Privacy: ★★★★
Spaciousness: ★★★★ Quiet: ★★★★
Security: ★★★★★ Cleanliness: ★★★★
Insect Control: ★★★★ Facilities: ★★★★

Located on the Choptank River and Watts Creek, two miles east of Denton and Maryland's eastern shore, Martinak State Park is surrounded by hardwood and pine forests. A Chesapeake Bay Sportfishing License is required to fish the tidal waters of the river and creek, which teem with bass, perch, sunfish, and catfish. The park has a boat launch, and canoes are available for rent during the summer. Situated north of Watts Creek, the 63-site campground has two loops; the 30 sites of Loop B have electric hookups. A hiking trail winds near the campgrounds and leads to the creek. A well-maintained bathhouse is centrally located in each loop. Though there are no water hookups, a dump station is available for trailer use. Potable water is located around each loop. Martinak rents four camper cabins, as well as a full service cabin which overlooks the Choptank River and is available year round.

BASICS

Operated By: State of Maryland. **Open:** Mar. 29–Dec. 10. **Site Assignment:** Reservations recommended (full payment due at time of booking if using credit card), walk-ins accepted. **Registration:** At campground office. **Fee:** $13–$18 (VISA, MC). **Parking:** At site.

FACILITIES

Number of RV Sites: 60. **Number of Tent-Only Sites:** 3. **Hookups:** Electric (20 amps). **Each Site:** Fire ring, picnic table. **Dump Station:** Yes. **Laundry:** No. **Pay Phone:** Yes. **Rest Rooms and Showers:** Yes. **Fuel:** No. **Propane:** No. **Internal Roads:** Paved, in good condition. **RV Service:** No. **Market:** Within 3 mi. **Restaurant:** Within 3 mi. **General Store:** No. **Vending:** No. **Playground:** Yes. **Other:** Choptank River. **Activities:** Fishing, canoeing, canoe rentals, planned activities, hiking trails. **Nearby Attractions:** Chesapeake Bay, Museum of Rural Life, Chesapeake Bay Maritime Museum, C&D Canal Museum, Plumpton Park Zoo. **Additional Information:** Maryland Office of Tourism Development, (800) 543-1036, www.mdisfun.org.

RESTRICTIONS

Pets: No pets permitted. **Fires:** At site. **Alcoholic Beverages:** No alcohol permitted. **Vehicle Maximum Length:** 30 ft. **Other:** 14-day max. stay.

TO GET THERE

From the business center in Denton, go 1 mi. south on Hwy. 404 and 0.75 mi. on Deep Shore Rd. Entrance is on the left. Follow signs to campground.

DRAYDEN

Dennis Point Marina and Campground

46555 Dennis Point Way, Drayden 20630. T: (301) 994-2288 or (800) 974-2288; F: (301) 994-2253.

RV ★★★ Tent ★★★

Beauty: ★★★★ Site Privacy: ★★
Spaciousness: ★★ Quiet: ★★★
Security: ★★★★ Cleanliness: ★★★★
Insect Control: ★★★★ Facilities: ★★★

In southern Maryland, where the Potomac River meets Chesapeake Bay, fishing, crabbing, and boating are the sports of choice. With full marine service and a boat ramp, Dennis Point Marina and Campground is ideal for campers intent of staying and playing on the water. Located on the western shore of southern Maryland, Dennis Point is on the Potomac River not far from Chesapeake Bay. Sites are shaded and situated along the water. There are 100 full-hookup sites and five pull-throughs. Historic St. Mary's City, the site of Maryland's first settlement in 1634, makes for an interesting afternoon trip from Dennis Point. The outdoor museum depicts life in the 17th century and includes a reconstructed state house, the ship Maryland Dove, a tobacco plantation, and an inn. Nearby Point Lookout State Park features the Confederate Monument, which honors the 3,384 POWs who died in the Point Lookout Prison Camp during the Civil War.

BASICS

Operated By: Gardiner family. **Open:** Apr. 1–Oct. 31. **Site Assignment:** Reservations and walk-ins accepted. **Registration:** At campground office. **Fee:** $20 (VISA, MC). **Parking:** At site.

FACILITIES

Number of RV Sites: 85. **Number of Tent-Only Sites:** 15. **Hookups:** Electric (20, 30 amps). **Each Site:** Picnic table. **Dump Station:** Yes. **Laundry:** Yes. **Pay Phone:** Yes. **Rest Rooms and Showers:** Yes. **Fuel:** Yes. **Propane:** Yes. **Internal Roads:** Gravel, in good condition. **RV Service:** No. **Market:** Within 5 mi. **Restaurant:** On premises. **General Store:** Yes. **Vending:** Yes. **Playground:** Yes. **Other:** Boat ramp, full marine service, fishing pond. **Activities:** Swimming, boating, canoeing, boat rentals, fishing, sports field, badminton, hiking trails, volleyball, horseshoes. **Nearby Attractions:** Potomac River, Chesapeake Bay, Naval Air Test and Evaluation Museum, Historical St. Mary's City, Historic Mt. Carmel Monastery, Port Tobacco, Solomon's Island. **Additional Information:** Maryland Office of Tourism Development, (800) 543-1036, www.mdisfun.org.

RESTRICTIONS

Pets: On leash only. **Fires:** At site. **Alcoholic Beverages:** At site. **Vehicle Maximum Length:** 45 ft. **Other:** Pets and fires may not be left unattended.

TO GET THERE

From Hwy. 5, go 3 mi. west on Hwy. 249, 3 mi. south on Drayden Rd., 3 mi. west on Windmill Point Rd., and 1 mi. on gravel Dennis Point Way. Entrance is at the end.

ELLICOTT CITY

Patapsco Valley State Park

8020 Baltimore National Pike, Ellicott City 21043. T: (410) 461-5005 or (888) 432-2267; www.dnr.state.md.us.

RV ★★★ Tent ★★★★

Beauty: ★★★★ Site Privacy: ★★★★
Spaciousness: ★★★★ Quiet: ★★★★
Security: ★★★★★ Cleanliness: ★★★★
Insect Control: ★★★★ Facilities: ★★★

Stretching 32 miles along the Patapsco River, Patapsco Valley State Park covers 14,000 acres and includes five developed recreational areas, two of which have campgrounds. The Hollofield campground offers tent and RV sites, some of which have electric hookups; the Hilton campground is for tents only. The Patapsco River flows to the Port of Baltimore and empties into the Chesapeake Bay, offering good fishing and boating. Campers here can see the Thomas Viaduct, which is the world's longest multiple-arched stone railroad bridge; walk across the swinging bridge, a 300-foot suspension walkway over the river; hike to Bloede's Dam, the world's first internally housed hydroelectric dam; and gaze at the Patapsco Valley from an overlook near the Hollofield area campground. Pets are prohibited in the Hilton campground, but there is a "pet loop" at the south end of the Hollofield campground. Most of the Hollofield sites are situated in a circle surrounding the camp store, restrooms, and showers.

BASICS

Operated By: State of Maryland. **Open:** Apr.–Oct. **Site Assignment:** Reservations (must be paid in full at time of booking when using credit card), walk-ins accepted. **Registration:** At campground office. **Fee:** $27–$37 (VISA, MC). **Parking:** At site.

FACILITIES

Number of RV Sites: 73. **Number of Tent-Only Sites:** 14. **Hookups:** Electric (20 amps). **Each Site:** Fire ring and picnic table. **Dump Station:** Yes. **Laundry:** No. **Pay Phone:** Yes. **Rest Rooms and Showers:** Yes. **Fuel:** No. **Propane:** No. **Internal Roads:** Gravel, in good condition. **RV Service:** No. **Market:** Within 3 mi. **Restaurant:** Within 3 mi. **General Store:** Yes. **Vending:** No. **Playground:** Yes. **Other:** Patapsco River. **Activities:** Canoeing, river fishing, hiking trails, sports field, bicycling, tubing. **Nearby Attractions:** Cider Mill Farm, Ellicott City B&O Railroad Station Museum. **Additional Information:** Howard County Tourism Council, (800) 288-TRIP, www.howardcountymdtour.com.

RESTRICTIONS

Pets: In Hollofield area pet loop. **Fires:** At site. **Alcoholic Beverages:** No alcohol permitted. **Vehicle Maximum Length:** 29 ft. **Other:** No pets at Hilton area campground.

TO GET THERE

From I-695, take Exit 15 and go 3 mi. west on US 40. Follow signs to Hollofield camping area.

FREDERICK

Gambrill State Park

14039 Catoctin Hollow Rd., Thurmont 21702. T: (301) 271-7574 or (888) 432-2267; www.dnr.state.md.us.

RV: ★★★★ Tent: ★★★★

Beauty: ★★★★★ Site Privacy: ★★★
Spaciousness: ★★★★ Quiet: ★★★★
Security: ★★★★ Cleanliness: ★★★★
Insect Control: ★★★★ Facilities: ★★★

Gambrill State Park is best visited in the spring, when Catoctin Mountain's dogwoods and mountain laurels are in bloom. Of course, considering the breathtaking views in this northwest Maryland park, anytime is a good time to see Gambrill. Three native stone overlooks on the 1,600-foot-high summit of High Knob offer the most stunning vistas, midway between the Mason-Dixon Line and the Potomac River. Two separate areas of Gambrill provide recreational facilities and activities. The Rock Run area, where the campground can be found, is located at the park entrance. The High Knob area is located at the top of Catoctin Mountain. The campground has one major loop with sites surrounding the bathhouse. Six sites have electric hookups. A small pond at the campground has largemouth bass, bluegill, and channel catfish. There are 13 miles of wooded trails, mostly loops that return to the trailhead parking lot just north of the campground on Gambrill Park Rd.

BASICS

Operated By: State of Maryland. **Open:** Apr.–Oct. **Site Assignment:** Reservations (full payment required at time of booking when using credit card), walk-ins accepted. **Registration:** At campground office. **Fee:** $17–$24 (VISA, MC). **Parking:** At site.

FACILITIES

Number of RV Sites: 35. **Number of Tent-Only Sites:** None. **Hookups:** Electric (20 amps). **Each Site:** Fire ring and picnic table. **Dump Station:** Yes. **Laundry:** No. **Pay Phone:** Yes. **Rest Rooms and Showers:** Yes. **Fuel:** No. **Propane:** No. **Internal Roads:** Paved, in good condition. **RV Service:** No. **Market:** Within 6 mi. **Restaurant:** Within 6 mi. **General Store:** No. **Vending:** No. **Playground:** Yes. **Other:** Fishing pond. **Activities:** Fishing, planned activities. **Nearby Attractions:** Monocacy National Battlefield, Brunswick Museum, Barbara Fritchie House and Museum, Francis Scott Key Museum, Rose Hill Manor Children's Museum. **Additional Information:** Tourism Council of Frederick, (800) 999-3613, www.co.frederick.md.us/tour/tourpage.html.

RESTRICTIONS

Pets: On leash only. **Fires:** At site. **Alcoholic Beverages:** No alcohol allowed. **Vehicle Maximum Length:** 30 ft. **Other:** 14-day max. stay.

TO GET THERE

From Frederick, go 6 mi. northwest on US 40 and 0.5 mi. north on Gambrill Pk. Rd. to the Rock Run area. Follow signs to campground.

FREELAND

Morris Meadows Recreation Farm

1523 Freeland Rd., Freeland 21053. T: (410) 329-6636 or (800) 643-7056; F: (410) 357-4089; www.kiz.com; mm@mail.bcpl.lib.md.us.

RV: ★★★★★ Tent: ★★★★★

Beauty: ★★★★★ Site Privacy: ★★★★
Spaciousness: ★★★★ Quiet: ★★★★
Security: ★★★★★ Cleanliness: ★★★★
Insect Control: ★★★★ Facilities: ★★★★★

Located in northern Maryland between Baltimore and Harrisburg (PA), Morris Meadows Recreation Farm is just a few miles south of the Pennsylvania border. In fact, Morris Meadows is central to Baltimore, Washington, D.C., and Annapolis in Maryland, and Gettysburg, Lancaster, and Hershey in Pennsylvania. Morris Meadows is an ideal base for visiting attractions in these cities, but the campground itself is one of the best in the mid-Atlantic. A hiking and biking trail winds through Morris Meadow's rolling hills, and caboose tours are given of the 300-acre farm. Campers have their choice of open and wooded sites, including 75 pull-throughs. The grounds are well-manicured, and facilities here are extremely clean. The museum of antiques and artifacts is truly a treat for adults and children both. The items on display were collected by Clyde and Virginia Morris, among them the Morris family's first recorded land deed, which is written on goat skin and dated December 4th, 1793.

BASICS

Operated By: Morris family. **Open:** All year. **Site Assignment:** Reservations accepted ($35 off for 7-night stay), walk-ins accepted. **Registration:** At campground office. **Fee:** $28–$38 (VISA, MC). **Parking:** At site.

FACILITIES

Number of RV Sites: 250. **Number of Tent-Only Sites:** 12. **Hookups:** Electric (20, 30, 50 amps), cable TV, phone, water, 250 full hookups. **Each Site:** Fire ring and picnic table. **Dump Station:** Yes. **Laundry:** Yes. **Pay Phone:** Yes. **Rest Rooms and Showers:** Yes. **Fuel:** No. **Propane:** Yes. **Internal Roads:** Paved, in good condition. **RV Service:** No. **Market:** Within 4 mi. **Restaurant:** Within 4 mi. **General Store:** Yes. **Vending:** Yes. **Playground:** Yes. **Other:** Museum of antiques and artifacts, caboose tours, fishing pond. **Activities:** Pond fishing, mini-golf, game room, rec hall, driving range, basketball, movies, tennis, planned activities, horseshoes, hiking and biking trails, volleyball. **Nearby Attractions:** Baltimore, Camden Yards, Chesapeake Bay, Inner Harbor, Baltimore Zoo, National Aquarium, US Naval Academy, Annapolis, Washington, D.C. **Additional Information:** Baltimore Area Convention and Visitors Assoc., (800) 343-3468, www.baltimore.org.

RESTRICTIONS

Pets: On leash only. **Fires:** At site. **Alcoholic Beverages:** At site. **Vehicle Maximum Length:** None. **Other:** None.

TO GET THERE

From I-83, take Exit 36 and go 0.25 mi. west on Hwy. 439, 1 mi. north on Hwy. 45, and 3 mi. west on Freeland Rd. Entrance is on the left.

GRANTSVILLE

Big Run State Park

349 Headquarters Ln., Grantsville 21536. T: (301) 895-5453 or (888) 432-2267; www.dnr.state.md.us.

RV: ★★★ Tent: ★★★★

Beauty: ★★★★ Site Privacy: ★★★★
Spaciousness: ★★★★ Quiet: ★★★★
Security: ★★★★ Cleanliness: ★★★★
Insect Control: ★★★ Facilities: ★★★

Situated near the mouth of the Savage River Reservoir in Garrett County, 300-acre Big Run State Park is ideal for campers longing for a rustic outdoor experience. The campground has no showers or electric hookups, and there is no camp store or dump station. Surrounded by the 52,800-acre Savage River State Forest, the park has a boat launch where campers can venture to the Savage River Reservoir. Big Run is the trailhead for Monroe Run, a six-mile pathway that winds through the state forest. Located two miles south of the Pennsylvania border on the western tip of Maryland, Grantsville is also home to the Casselman Bridge, a single-span stone arch built over the Casselman River in 1813. If campers long for more outdoor adventure, Big Run is near New Germany State Park, which is also located within the Savage River State Forest and has a 13-acre lake, hiking trails, and a 37-site campground with cabins.

BASICS

Operated By: State of Maryland. **Open:** All year. **Site Assignment:** First-come, first-served only. **Registration:** At campground office. **Fee:** $10 (VISA, MC). **Parking:** At site.

FACILITIES

Number of RV Sites: 30. **Number of Tent-Only Sites:** None. **Hookups:** None. **Each Site:** Fire ring, picnic table. **Dump Station:** No. **Laundry:** No. **Pay Phone:** No. **Rest Rooms and Showers:** Rest rooms, no showers. **Fuel:** No. **Propane:** No. **Internal Roads:** Paved, in good condition. **RV Service:** No. **Market:** Within 5 mi. **Restaurant:** Within 5 mi. **General Store:** No. **Vending:** No. **Playground:** Yes. **Other:** Savage River Reservoir. **Activities:** Lake and stream fishing, boating, canoeing, hiking trails. **Nearby Attractions:** Casselman Bridge, Savage River State Forest, Spruce Forest Artisan Village, New Germany State Park. **Additional Information:**

Garrett County Chamber of Commerce, (301) 334-1948, www.garrettchamber.com.

RESTRICTIONS

Pets: On leash only. **Fires:** At site. **Alcoholic Beverages:** No alcohol permitted. **Vehicle Maximum Length:** 29 ft. **Other:** 14-day max. stay.

TO GET THERE

From I-68, take Exit 22 and go south on Chestnut Ridge Rd. to New Germany Rd. Follow to Big Run Rd. Follow signs to campground, which is 16 mi. from the I-68 exit.

GREENSBORO

Holiday Park Campground

P.O. Box 277W, Greensboro 21639. T: (410) 482-6797 or (800) 992-6691; F: (410) 482-8348; www.holidaypark.com; sarak@kiz.com.

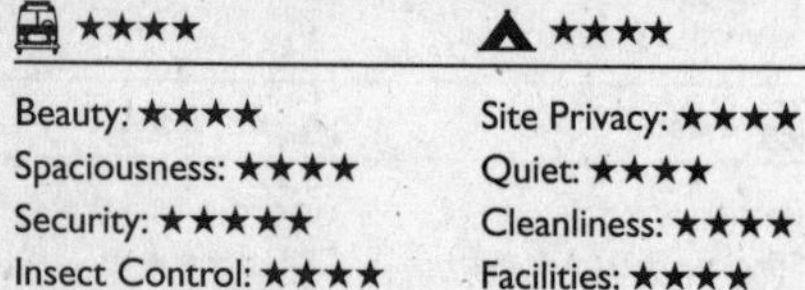

★★★★ ★★★★

Beauty: ★★★★ Site Privacy: ★★★★
Spaciousness: ★★★★ Quiet: ★★★★
Security: ★★★★★ Cleanliness: ★★★★
Insect Control: ★★★★ Facilities: ★★★★

A family-friendly campground with four playgrounds and three pavilions, Holiday Park Campground is situated on the Del-Mar-Va Peninsula at the headwaters of the Choptank River, which flows into Chesapeake Bay in eastern Maryland. Located in Greensboro, Holiday Park offers spacious shaded sites, including 23 pull-throughs. A large game room is stocked with video games, pool tables, and ping pong tables. The swimming pool is large and well-maintained. Campers can paddle on the Choptank in a canoe or a kayak, or just fish the river. Holiday Park is less than five miles west of the Delaware border and about a half-hour drive from Dover, Delaware's capital city. The Delaware Archaeology Museum and the Museum of Small Town Life are intriguing family-oriented attractions in Dover. Tours are offered at the circa-1792 Old State House, which is the second-oldest seat of government in continuous use.

BASICS

Operated By: Private operator. **Open:** Apr. 1–Nov. 15. **Site Assignment:** Reservations and walk-ins accepted. **Registration:** At campground office. **Fee:** $22–$28.50 (VISA, MC). **Parking:** At site.

FACILITIES

Number of RV Sites: 192. **Number of Tent-Only Sites:** 150. **Hookups:** Electric (20, 30, 50 amps), cable TV, water. **Each Site:** Fire ring and picnic table. **Dump Station:** Yes. **Laundry:** Yes. **Pay Phone:** Yes. **Rest Rooms and Showers:** Yes. **Fuel:** No. **Propane:** Yes. **Internal Roads:** Paved and dirt, in good condition. **RV Service:** No. **Market:** Within 5 mi. **Restaurant:** Within 2 mi. **General Store:** Yes. **Vending:** Yes. **Playground:** Yes. **Other:** Three concrete-floored pavilions, Choptank River. **Activities:** Fishing, canoeing, kayaking, mini-golf, rec hall, game room, basketball, shuffleboard, planned activities on weekends, movies, tennis, sports field, badminton, hiking trails, horseshoes, volleyball. **Nearby Attractions:** Choptank River, Del-Mar-Va Peninsula, Chesapeake Bay, Dover (DE), Museum of Small Town Life, Old State House, Delaware Archaeology Museum. **Additional Information:** Maryland Office of Tourism Development, (800) 543-1036, www.mdisfun.org.

RESTRICTIONS

Pets: On leash only. **Fires:** At site. **Alcoholic Beverages:** At site. **Vehicle Maximum Length:** 50 ft. **Other:** None.

TO GET THERE

From Hwy. 313, go 0.25 mi. east on Hwy. 314, 0.1 mi. north on Wothers Rd., 0.75 mi. east on Boyce Mill Rd., and 2 mi. north on Drapers Mill Rd. Entrance is on the left.

HAGERSTOWN

Fort Frederick State Park

11100 Fort Frederick Rd., Big Pool 21711. T: (301) 842-2155 or (888) 432-2267; www.dnr.state.md.us.

★★★ ★★★★

Beauty: ★★★★ Site Privacy: ★★★
Spaciousness: ★★★ Quiet: ★★★★
Security: ★★★★ Cleanliness: ★★★★
Insect Control: ★★★★ Facilities: ★★★

Fort Frederick State Park adjoins the Potomac River, and the Chesapeake and Ohio Canal passes through park grounds. Built in 1756, Fort Frederick was unique because of its large size and strong stone wall. Most other forts of the period were built of wood and earth. Camping at the park is a rustic experience as there are no electric hookups, showers, or dump station. Located at the south end of the park between Big Pool (a lake) and the Potomac River, the campground does have a store. Also, souvenirs and food are sold at Captain Wort's Sutler Shop at the visitors center, where campers can rent rowboats and canoes for use in Big Pool only. The fort is north of the campground and is accessible by road. Exploring the park by foot is simple with two marked pathways, the 0.75-mile Plantation Trail and the 0.3-mile Wetlands Trail.

BASICS

Operated By: State of Maryland. **Open:** Mar. 29–Oct. 29. **Site Assignment:** Reservations accepted May 1–Sept. 30; remaining dates are first come, first served. **Registration:** At campground office. **Fee:** $14 (VISA, MC). **Parking:** At site.

FACILITIES

Number of RV Sites: 29. **Number of Tent-Only Sites:** None. **Hookups:** None. **Each Site:** Fire ring and picnic table. **Dump Station:** No. **Laundry:** No. **Pay Phone:** Yes. **Rest Rooms and Showers:** Rest rooms, no showers. **Fuel:** No. **Propane:** No. **Internal Roads:** Paved, in good condition. **RV Service:** No. **Market:** Within 10 mi. **Restaurant:** Within 8 mi. **General Store:** Yes. **Vending:** No. **Playground:** Yes. **Other:** Fort Frederick. **Activities:** Hiking trails, biking, boating, canoeing, boat rentals, fishing, historical tours. **Nearby Attractions:** Fort Frederick, Antietam National Battlefield, Hagerstown Roundhouse Museum, Washington County Museum of Fine Arts, Harper's Ferry (WV), Chesapeake and Ohio Canal National Historical Park. **Additional Information:** Hagerstown/Washington County Tourism Office, (800) 228-7829, www.marylandmemories.org.

RESTRICTIONS

Pets: No pets permitted. **Fires:** At site. **Alcoholic Beverages:** No alcohol permitted. **Vehicle Maximum Length:** 29 ft. **Other:** 14-day max. stay.

TO GET THERE

From Hagerstown, go 18 mi. west on I-70 to Exit 12 and 1 mi. south on Hwy. 56. Follow signs to the campground.

HAGERSTOWN

Greenbrier State Park

21843 National Pike, Boonsboro 21713. T: (301) 791-4767 or (888) 432-2267; www.dnr.state.md.us.

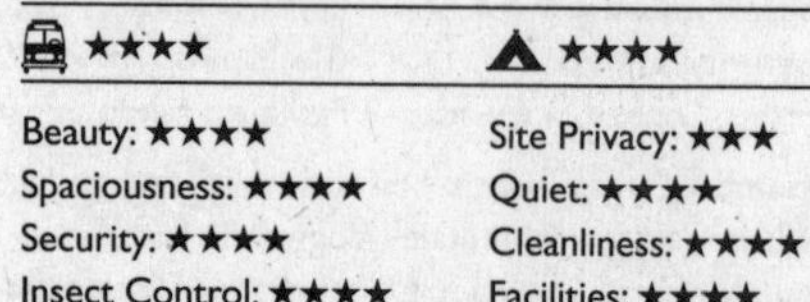

★★★★ ★★★★

Beauty: ★★★★ Site Privacy: ★★★
Spaciousness: ★★★★ Quiet: ★★★★
Security: ★★★★ Cleanliness: ★★★★
Insect Control: ★★★★ Facilities: ★★★★

Ten miles east of Hagerstown, Greenbrier State Park is highlighted by an impressive network of hiking trails and the 42-acre Greenbrier Lake. Greenbrier is nestled in the Appalachian Mountains, and a portion of the Appalachian Trail enters the eastern edge of the park on Bartman's Hill, or South Mountain. Visitors can rent rowboats and canoes at a boat launch on the Greenbrier River. Greenbrier also has a beach and a lifeguard-monitored swimming area. The campground is located south of Greenbrier Lake, and sites are arranged in four loops, each with bathhouses. This campground—which has a dump station, a store, and showers—offers more amenities than the camping area at Fort Frederick State Park. The Dogwood Loop, which is the southernmost cluster of sites, offers the most solitude. All sites on the Cedar Loop, which is near several hiking trails and a hunting area, have electric hookups. A lakeside hiking trail sprouts from the Ash Loop.

BASICS

Operated By: State of Maryland. **Open:** Mar. 29–Oct. 29. **Site Assignment:** Reservations accepted (full payment due at time of booking when using credit card), walk-ins accepted. **Registration:** At campground office. **Fee:** $20–$25 (VISA, MC). **Parking:** At site.

FACILITIES

Number of RV Sites: 165. **Number of Tent-Only Sites:** None. **Hookups:** Electric (20 amps). **Each Site:** Fire ring, picnic table. **Dump Station:** Yes. **Laundry:** No. **Pay Phone:** Yes. **Rest Rooms and Showers:** Yes. **Fuel:** No. **Propane:** No. **Internal Roads:** Gravel and paved, in good condition. **RV Service:** No. **Market:** Within 6 mi. **Restaurant:** Within 4 mi. **General Store:** Yes. **Vending:** Yes. **Playground:** Yes. **Other:** Greenbrier Lake, cabin rentals. **Activities:** Lake fishing and swimming, boating, canoeing, boat rentals, hiking trails, planned activities. **Nearby Attractions:** Fort Frederick, Antietam National Battlefield, Hagerstown Roundhouse Museum, Washington County Museum of Fine Arts, Harper's Ferry (WV), Chesapeake and Ohio Canal National Historical Park. **Additional Information:** Hagerstown/Washington County Tourism Office, (800) 228-7829, www.marylandmemories.org.

Restrictions

Pets: No pets permitted. **Fires:** At site. **Alcoholic Beverages:** No alcohol permitted. **Vehicle Maximum Length:** 29 ft. **Other:** 14-day max. stay.

To Get There

From Hagerstown, go 8 mi. east on US 40. Follow signs to campground.

HAGERSTOWN
KOA—Snug Harbor

11759 Snug Harbor Ln., Williamsport 21795. T: (301) 223-7571 or (800) 562-7607; F: (301) 223-5061; www.gocampingamerica.com/hagerstownkoa; hagkoa@aol.com.

RV ★★★★ Tent ★★★★

Beauty: ★★★★	Site Privacy: ★★★
Spaciousness: ★★★	Quiet: ★★★★
Security: ★★★★★	Cleanliness: ★★★★
Insect Control: ★★★★	Facilities: ★★★★

Nestled on the banks of the historic Conococheague Creek in the rolling hills of western Maryland, KOA—Snug Harbor is convenient to several history-rich Civil War sites, including Gettysburg, Harper's Ferry (WV), and Antietam National Battlefield. Campers have their choice of open and shaded sites, some of which are situated along the creek. There are 20 pull-throughs and 43 full-hookup sites. Guests can cast their lines and paddle a canoe on the creek. The campground has a heated pool, a mini-golf course and wooded hiking trails. A portion of the Appalachian Trail passes near the campground. There are also hiking trails along the Chesapeake and Ohio Canal National Park, and at Fort Frederick and Greenbrier state parks. Of course, many campers use this KOA as a base to visit Civil War sites at Antietam, Harper's Ferry, and even Gettysburg.

Basics

Operated By: John & Judi Durham. **Open:** All year. **Site Assignment:** Reservations accepted (1 night's deposit required), walk-ins accepted. **Registration:** At campground office. **Fee:** $28–$33 (VISA, MC, AE, D). **Parking:** At site.

Facilities

Number of RV Sites: 92. **Number of Tent-Only Sites:** 17. **Hookups:** Electric (20, 30, 50 amps), water, 43 full hookups. **Each Site:** Fire ring and picnic table. **Dump Station:** Yes. **Laundry:** Yes. **Pay Phone:** Yes. **Rest Rooms and Showers:** Yes. **Fuel:** No. **Propane:** Yes. **Internal Roads:** Paved and dirt, in fair condition. **RV Service:** Yes. **Market:** Within 3 mi. **Restaurant:** Within 3 mi. **General Store:** Yes. **Vending:** Yes. **Playground:** Yes. **Other:** Conococheague Creek, cabin rentals. **Activities:** Boating, canoeing, canoe rentals, river fishing, mini-golf, rec hall, game room, badminton, planned activities on weekends, hiking trails, volleyball, horseshoes. **Nearby Attractions:** Fort Frederick, Antietam National Battlefield, Hagerstown Roundhouse Museum, Washington County Museum of Fine Arts, Harper's Ferry (WV), Chesapeake and Ohio Canal National Historical Park, Gettysburg. **Additional Information:** Hagerstown/Washington County Tourism Office, (800) 228-7829, www.marylandmemories.org.

Restrictions

Pets: On leash only, under control. **Fires:** At site. **Alcoholic Beverages:** At site. **Vehicle Maximum Length:** 45 ft. **Other:** No refunds; credits are given.

To Get There

From I-81, go 1.5 mi. west on I-70, 0.25 mi. south on Hwy. 63, 2.5 mi. west on Kemps Mill Rd. Entrance is on the right.

HAGERSTOWN
Yogi Bear's Jellystone Park Williamsport/Hagerstown

16519 Lappans Rd., Williamsport 21795. T: (301) 223-7117 or (800) 421-7116; F: (301) 582-5606; www.jellystonemaryland.com;yogimd@crosslink.net

RV ★★★★ Tent ★★★★

Beauty: ★★★★	Site Privacy: ★★★★
Spaciousness: ★★★★	Quiet: ★★★★★
Security: ★★★★	Cleanliness: ★★★★
Insect Control: ★★★★	Facilities: ★★★★★

Located in western Maryland near Hagerstown, Yogi Bear's Jellystone Park—Williamsport/Hagerstown was named the chain's facility of the year in 2000. The wealth of recreational activities—and the cleanliness and appearance of the facilities—indicate why this honor was bestowed. Though this park is not located along the water like nearby KOA—Snug Harbor, it does have 50-plus acres of forest and meadow trails for hiking and biking. Spacious pull-through sites are located at the northeast side of the campground. A wooded tent-only area is situated at the northwest end. If you prefer to camp near most of the activity centers, the sites along Deer Trail, Piney Woods, and Jellystone Parkway are recommended. This campground has a nice selection of well-maintained cabins for those without an RV or tent. Overall, 60 sites accommodate double and triple slideouts. Guided bus tours of our nation's capital embark from the campground on Saturdays and Sundays in season.

Basics

Operated By: Jellystone Park. **Open:** All year. **Site Assignment:** Reservations accepted (1 night's deposit required, 3-night min. stay on holiday weekends), walk-ins accepted. **Registration:** At campground office. **Fee:** $22–$29 (VISA, MC, D). **Parking:** At site.

Facilities

Number of RV Sites: 131. **Number of Tent-Only Sites:** 28. **Hookups:** Electric (20, 30, 50 amps), phone, water, 78 full hookups. **Each Site:** Fire ring, picnic table. **Dump Station:** Yes. **Laundry:** Yes. **Pay Phone:** Yes. **Rest Rooms and Showers:** Yes. **Fuel:** No. **Propane:** Yes. **Internal Roads:** Gravel and paved, in good condition. **RV Service:** No. **Market:** Within 3 mi. **Restaurant:** Within 3 mi. **General Store:** Yes. **Vending:** Yes. **Playground:** Yes. **Other:** Cabin rentals, Washington, D.C. tours. **Activities:** Kiddie pool plus swimming pool, game room, rec hall, basketball, mini-golf, bike rentals, planned activities, movies, hiking trails, horseshoes, volleyball. **Nearby Attractions:** Fort Frederick, Antietam National Battlefield, Hagerstown Roundhouse Museum, Washington County Museum of Fine Arts, Harper's Ferry (WV), Chesapeake and Ohio Canal National Historical Park, Gettysburg. **Additional Information:** Hagerstown/Washington County Tourism Office, (800) 228-7829, www.marylandmemories.org.

Restrictions

Pets: On leash only. **Fires:** At site. **Alcoholic Beverages:** At site. **Vehicle Maximum Length:** 85 ft. **Other:** No pets permitted in cabins.

To Get There

From I-81, go 1 mi. east on Hwy. 68. Entrance is on the right.

HAVRE DE GRACE
Susquehanna State Park

3318 Rocks Chrome Hill Rd., Jarrettsville 21084. T: (410) 557-7994 or (888) 432-2267; www.dnr.state.md.us.

RV ★★★ Tent ★★★★

Beauty: ★★★★	Site Privacy: ★★★
Spaciousness: ★★★	Quiet: ★★★★
Security: ★★★★	Cleanliness: ★★★★
Insect Control: ★★★★	Facilities: ★★★

Located along the densely forested Susquehanna River Valley at Chesapeake Bay, Susquehanna State Park is home to some of the most popular mountain biking trails in Maryland. Overall, there are 15 miles of marked trails in the park. The boat launch offers access to the river and the headwaters of Chesapeake Bay. Pike, perch, bass, catfish and carp are abundant in the Susquehanna. The campground is divided into the Beechnut and Acorn loops, both of which surround bathhouses with hot showers. Six sites on the Acorn loop have electric hookups. The remnants of the Susquehanna Tidewater Canal can be seen as it parallels the river from Havre de Grace to Wrightsville (PA). Tours of the Rock Run Historic Area are conducted May–September. Susquehanna State Park is also home to the privately-operated Steppingstone Museum, which includes exhibits of antique farm implements, a woodwright's shop, a blacksmith shop, a decoy carving shop, and a restored farm house.

Basics

Operated By: State of Maryland. **Open:** Apr. 26–Oct. 8. **Site Assignment:** Reservations accepted (2-night min. stay required from Memorial Day to Labor Day), walk-ins accepted. **Registration:** At campground office. **Fee:** $16–$21 (VISA, MC). **Parking:** At site.

Facilities

Number of RV Sites: 69. **Number of Tent-Only Sites:** None. **Hookups:** Electric (20 amps). **Each Site:** Fire ring, picnic table. **Dump Station:** No. **Laundry:** No. **Pay Phone:** Yes. **Rest Rooms and Showers:** Yes. **Fuel:** No. **Propane:** No. **Internal Roads:** Paved, in good condition. **RV Service:** No. **Market:** Within 4 mi. **Restaurant:** Within 4 mi. **General Store:** No. **Vending:** No. **Playground:** Yes. **Other:** Susquehanna River, Steppingstone Museum. **Activities:** River fishing and swimming, planned activities, historic buildings, boating, canoeing, hiking trails. **Nearby Attractions:** Concord Point Lighthouse, Decoy Museum, Chesapeake Bay, Baltimore, Wilmington (DE). **Additional Information:** Havre de Grace Chamber of Commerce, (800) 851-7756, www.hdstourism.com.

Restrictions

Pets: On leash only. **Fires:** At site. **Alcoholic Beverages:** At site. **Vehicle Maximum Length:** 29 ft. **Other:** 14-day max. stay.

To Get There

From Havre de Grace, go 3 mi. north on Hwy. 155. Follow signs to the campground.

LA PLATA

Goose Bay Marina and Campground

9365 Goose Bay Ln. P.O. Box 58, Welcome 20693. T: (301) 934-3812 or (301) 932-0885; F: (301) 934-0063; www.goosebaymarina.com; goosepoint@olg.com.

RV ★★★ Tent ★★★

Beauty: ★★★	Site Privacy: ★★
Spaciousness: ★★★	Quiet: ★★★
Security: ★★★★	Cleanliness: ★★★★
Insect Control: ★★★★	Facilities: ★★★

Situated on a sheltered bay adjoining Port Tobacco River and the Potomac River, Goose Bay Marina and Campground has shaded waterfront sites, all which have electric and water hookups. Five sites have full hookups, and there are 46 pull-throughs. Goose Bay's full-service marina has three boat ramps, 250 boat slips, and mechanics on duty. The campgrounds is a short drive from Historic Port Tobacco, one of the oldest continuously inhabited English settlements in North America, first colonized in 1638. Some homes here date to the early 1700s, and there is a reconstructed store and court house. The Port Tobacco Museum, located on the second floor of the court house, has historic exhibits and a half-hour film. Campers who want outdoor adventure away from the water can hike 13 miles of trails at the Doncaster Demonstration Forest outside of La Plate. The 1,477-acre area is thick with red and white oaks, yellow poplar, sweet gum, and pine.

Basics

Operated By: Joe Bowie. **Open:** All year. **Site Assignment:** Reservations and walk-ins accepted. **Registration:** At campground office. **Fee:** $25 (VISA, MC). **Parking:** At site.

Facilities

Number of RV Sites: 90. **Number of Tent-Only Sites:** 15. **Hookups:** Electric (20, 30 amps), phone, water, 5 full hookups. **Each Site:** Fire ring and picnic table. **Dump Station:** Yes. **Laundry:** Yes. **Pay Phone:** Yes. **Rest Rooms and Showers:** Yes. **Fuel:** Yes. **Propane:** Yes. **Internal Roads:** Gravel, in good condition. **RV Service:** Yes. **Market:** Within 6 mi. **Restaurant:** Within 4 mi. **General Store:** Yes. **Vending:** Yes. **Playground:** Yes. **Other:** Potomac River. **Activities:** Swimming, boating, pedal boat rentals, river fishing, hiking trails, basketball, planned activities on weekends, sports field, badminton, horseshoes, volleyball, guided fishing trips. **Nearby Attractions:** Historic Port Tobacco, Doncaster Demonstration Forest, Smallwood State Park, Chesapeake Bay, Washington, D.C. **Additional Information:** Charles County Chamber of Commerce, (301) 645-0558, www.ccccmd.org.

Restrictions

Pets: On leash only. **Fires:** At site. **Alcoholic Beverages:** At site. **Vehicle Maximum Length:** 40 ft. **Other:** General rate for 4 people; additional campers are $1 each.

To Get There

From US 301, go 5.5 mi. west on Hwy. 6, 1.5 mi. south on Blossom Point Rd. and 1 mi. east on Brentland Rd. Entrance is on the right.

LOTHIAN

Duncan's Family Campground

5381 Sands Rd., Lothian 20711. T: (410) 741-9558 or (800) 222-2086; www.welcome.to/duncanscampground; go2duncans@aol.com.

RV ★★★★ Tent ★★★★

Beauty: ★★★	Site Privacy: ★★
Spaciousness: ★★★	Quiet: ★★★
Security: ★★★★	Cleanliness: ★★★★
Insect Control: ★★★★	Facilities: ★★★★

Located a half-hour southeast of Washington, D.C., Duncan's Family Campground is also a half-hour southwest of Annapolis and less than an hour south of Baltimore. Campsites are wooded, and there are 220 pull-throughs. This is a campground that caters to families. Duncan's makes it easy for campers to reach Washington, D.C. The campground offers a shuttle to the nearby DC Metrorail. Also, tour buses depart for DC directly from Duncan's. If you do not take the guided bus tour from the campground, there are numerous guided tours of DC available in the city. Taking either the bus tour from Duncan's or the shuttle to the Metrorail is recommended. Driving in DC is often challenging to say the least, especially for a first-time visitor.

Basics

Operated By: Private operator. **Open:** All year. **Site Assignment:** Reservations accepted (1 night's deposit required), walk-ins accepted. **Registration:** At campground office. **Fee:** $19–$29 (VISA, MC). **Parking:** At site.

Facilities

Number of RV Sites: 237. **Number of Tent-Only Sites:** 45. **Hookups:** Electric (20, 30 amps), phone, water, 120 full hookups. **Each Site:** Picnic tables, grills. **Dump Station:** Yes. **Laundry:** Yes. **Pay Phone:** Yes. **Rest Rooms and Showers:** Yes. **Fuel:** No. **Propane:** Yes. **Internal Roads:** Gravel and paved, in good condition. **RV Service:** No. **Market:** Within 8 mi. **Restaurant:** Within 7 mi. **General Store:** Yes. **Vending:** Yes. **Playground:** Yes. **Other:** Washington, D.C. tours, free shuttle to Metrorail. **Activities:** Swimming, kiddie pool, game room, rec hall, mini-golf, basketball, movies, planned activities on weekends, horseshoes, volleyball, hiking trails. **Nearby Attractions:** Washington, D.C., Six Flags, Chesapeake Bay, Baltimore, Annapolis, US Naval Academy. **Additional Information:** Maryland Office of Tourism Development, (800) 543-1036, www.mdisfun.org.

Restrictions

Pets: On leash only. **Fires:** At site. **Alcoholic Beverages:** At site, under control. **Vehicle Maximum Length:** 50 ft. **Other:** Small pets only.

To Get There

From US 301, go 2 mi. southeast on Hwy. 4, 0.5 mi. on Hwy. 408, and 0.25 mi. north on Sands Rd. Entrance is on the right.

MILLERSVILLE

Capitol KOA

768 Cecil Ave., Millersville 21108. T: (800) 562-0248 or (410) 923-2771; F: (410) 923-3709; www.koa.com; capitolkoa@worldnet.att.net.

RV ★★★★ Tent ★★★★

Beauty: ★★★★	Site Privacy: ★★★
Spaciousness: ★★★	Quiet: ★★★
Security: ★★★★	Cleanliness: ★★★★
Insect Control: ★★★★	Facilities: ★★★★

Located in Millersville, about 10 miles northwest of Annapolis, 20 miles south of Baltimore, and 30 miles northeast of Washington, D.C., Capitol KOA is a rural campground with open and wooded sites, including 69 pull-throughs and 68 full hookups. The campground is centrally located for trips to Baltimore and Annapolis, but as the name suggests, the Capitol KOA especially caters to guests who are visiting Washington, D.C. In fact, the park offers a free shuttle to the DC Metrorail. Guided capital tours embark from the campground daily in season. By car, Washington, D.C. is 30 minutes away, but it is much more convenient and relaxing to catch the shuttle to the Metrorail or buy a ticket for the campground tour bus. The campground also offers weekday shuttles to Baltimore transit stations.

Basics

Operated By: KOA. **Open:** Mar. 25–Oct. 31. **Site Assignment:** Reservations accepted ($35 deposit required), walk-ins accepted. **Registration:** At campground office. **Fee:** $28–$39 (VISA, MC, D). **Parking:** At site.

Facilities

Number of RV Sites: 150. **Number of Tent-Only Sites:** 26. **Hookups:** Electric (20, 30, 50 amps), phone, water, 68 full hookups. **Each Site:** Fire ring and picnic table. **Dump Station:** Yes.

Laundry: Yes. **Pay Phone:** Yes. **Rest Rooms and Showers:** Yes. **Fuel:** No. **Propane:** Yes. **Internal Roads:** Gravel and paved, in good condition. **RV Service:** No. **Market:** Within 2 mi. **Restaurant:** Within 2 mi. **General Store:** Yes. **Vending:** Yes. **Playground:** Yes. **Other:** Washington, D.C. guided tours. **Activities:** Movies, planned activities, game room, rec hall, volleyball, hiking trails, horseshoes, badminton, sports field. **Nearby Attractions:** Washington, D.C., Baltimore, Annapolis, Six Flags, Chesapeake Bay. **Additional Information:** Maryland Office of Tourism Development, (800) 543-1036, www.mdisfun.org.

RESTRICTIONS

Pets: On leash only, under control. **Fires:** At site. **Alcoholic Beverages:** At site. **Vehicle Maximum Length:** 50 ft. **Other:** 14-day max. stay; 1 pet per campsite.

TO GET THERE

From the junction of Hwy. 32, I-97 and Hwy. 3, go 0.5 mi. north on Veterans Hwy. and follow blue campground signs. Entrance is on the right.

NANTICOKE

Roaring Point Waterfront Campground

P.O. Box 80, Nanticoke 21840. T: (410) 873-2553; www.roaringpoint.com.

RV ★★★★ Tent ★★★★

Beauty: ★★★★	Site Privacy: ★★
Spaciousness: ★★★	Quiet: ★★★
Security: ★★★★	Cleanliness: ★★★★
Insect Control: ★★★★	Facilities: ★★★★

Overlooking the Nanticoke River and Tangier Sound, secluded Roaring Point Waterfront offers shaded sites along the waterfront and in a grassy area near the playgrounds, bathhouse, and laundry facilities. Some tent sites have a waterfront view of Tangier Sound, where campers can swim and fish. Crab is king in Maryland, and Roaring Point rents crabbing equipment for use on the 135-foot-long fishing and crabbing pier. Though Roaring Point does not have a swimming pool, it does have a sandy beach and saltwater swimming area. Also, there are many biking-friendly roads in the area surrounding the campground, but be sure to bring your own wheels. The campground rents boats, but not bicycles. Roaring Point is about 15 miles southwest of Salisbury, near points of interest like the Salisbury Zoo and Furnace Town—an 1840s village with blacksmith, broom-making shops, and other historic structures.

BASICS

Operated By: Private operator. **Open:** Apr. 1–Nov. 1. **Site Assignment:** Reservations accepted (deposit of one-third of total fee required), walk-ins accepted. **Registration:** At campground office. **Fee:** $21–$25 (VISA, MC). **Parking:** At site.

FACILITIES

Number of RV Sites: 134. **Number of Tent-Only Sites:** 25. **Hookups:** Electric (20, 30 amps), water, 82 full hookups. **Each Site:** Fire ring and picnic table. **Dump Station:** Yes. **Laundry:** Yes. **Pay Phone:** Yes. **Rest Rooms and Showers:** Yes. **Fuel:** No. **Propane:** Yes. **Internal Roads:** Gravel, in good condition. **RV Service:** No. **Market:** Within 7 mi. **Restaurant:** Within 5 mi. **General Store:** Yes. **Vending:** Yes. **Playground:** Yes. **Other:** Nanticoke River, Tangier Sound. **Activities:** Saltwater swimming and fishing, boating, rowboat and sailboat rentals, basketball, planned activities on weekends, volleyball, hiking trails, horseshoes, badminton, game room, rec hall. **Nearby Attractions:** Smith Island and Tangier Island boat cruises, Ward Museum of Wildfowl Art, Furnace Town, Salisbury City Zoo, Assateague Island National Seashore, Chincoteague National Wildlife Refuge, Chesapeake Bay, Ocean City. **Additional Information:** Maryland Office of Tourism Development, (800) 543-1036, www.mdisfun.org.

RESTRICTIONS

Pets: On leash only. **Fires:** At site. **Alcoholic Beverages:** At site. **Vehicle Maximum Length:** 40 ft. **Other:** Two vehicles in addition to camping unit allowed per campsite; additional vehicles must be parked in storage area.

TO GET THERE

From US 50, go 22 mi. south on Hwy. 349. Entrance is on the right.

OAKLAND

Deep Creek Lake State Park

898 State Park Rd., Swanton 21561. T: (301) 387-5563 or (888) 432-2267; F: (301) 387-4462; www.dnr.state.md.us.

RV ★★★★ Tent ★★★★

Beauty: ★★★★	Site Privacy: ★★★
Spaciousness: ★★	Quiet: ★★★★
Security: ★★★★	Cleanliness: ★★★★
Insect Control: ★★★★	Facilities: ★★★★

Located at the southernmost end of Meadow Mountain on the far western tip of Maryland, Deep Creek Lake State Park features a mile of shoreline along 3,900-acre Deep Creek Lake, the largest lake in Maryland. A boat launch, swimming area, and picnicking area are located along the shore in the park. Meadow Mountain campground is located at the southwest end of the park, near lots of hiking trails and within a short drive of Deep Creek Lake. Sites are clustered around four main loops, each with a bathhouse. The Deep Creek Lake Discovery Center, a new interpretive environmental museum, is nestled on the shore of Deep Creek Lake in the park. The Discovery Center offers hands-on exhibits that showcase the fauna, wildlife, and cultural and historical heritage of western Maryland. Garrett County, where Deep Creek Lake is located, boasts the highest peak in Maryland—3,360-foot Backbone Mountain.

BASICS

Operated By: State of Maryland. **Open:** Mar. 29–Oct. 29. **Site Assignment:** Reservations and walk-ins accepted. **Registration:** At campground office. **Fee:** $22–$27 (VISA, MC). **Parking:** At site.

FACILITIES

Number of RV Sites: 112. **Number of Tent-Only Sites:** None. **Hookups:** Electric (20 amps). **Each Site:** Fire ring and picnic table. **Dump Station:** Yes. **Laundry:** No. **Pay Phone:** Yes. **Rest Rooms and Showers:** Yes. **Fuel:** No. **Propane:** No. **Internal Roads:** Paved, in good condition. **RV Service:** No. **Market:** Within 9 mi. **Restaurant:** Within 9 mi. **General Store:** Yes. **Vending:** Yes. **Playground:** Yes. **Other:** Deep Creek Lake Discovery Center. **Activities:** Lake swimming and fishing, hiking trails, boating, canoeing, rowboat rentals, planned activities. **Nearby Attractions:** Backbone Mountain, Garrett State Forest, Potomac State Forest, Swallow Falls State Park. **Additional Information:** Garrett County Chamber of Commerce, (301) 334-1948, www.garrettchamber.com.

RESTRICTIONS

Pets: Permitted in designated loops. **Fires:** At site. **Alcoholic Beverages:** No alcohol permitted. **Vehicle Maximum Length:** 29 ft. **Other:** 14-day max. stay.

TO GET THERE

From Oakland, go 10 mi. north on US 219 and 2 mi. northeast on Glendale Bridge Rd. Follow signs to campground.

OCEAN CITY

Assateague State Park

7307 Stephen Decatur Hwy., Berlin 21811. T: (410) 641-2120 or (888) 432-2267; www.dnr.state.md.us.

RV ★★★ Tent ★★★★

Beauty: ★★★★★	Site Privacy: ★★
Spaciousness: ★★★	Quiet: ★★★★
Security: ★★★★	Cleanliness: ★★★★
Insect Control: ★★★	Facilities: ★★★★

On Assateague Island—a 37-mile barrier island with stretches of ocean, sand dunes, forests, and marshes—Assateague State Park is Maryland's only ocean park. Bordered on the east by the Atlantic Ocean and on the west by Sinepuxent Bay, the island's two miles of ocean beaches offer swimming, sunbathing, surfing and fishing. Marsh areas support a variety of wildlife, including rare Sika deer and the island's famous wild horses. Sites here are situated around eight main loops with bathhouses. Of the campground's 350 sites, 32 have electric hookups, and most of these are located in the H loop. Assateague Island National Seashore in Maryland and the Chincoteague National Wildlife Refuge in Virginia (which is located on the island) require a $5 federal fee round. Also, be sure to observe the wildlife from a distance—especially the renowned ponies, which are known to bite and kick. Assateague Island National Seashore has two campgrounds—Bayside and Oceanside—operated by the Na-tional Park Service. The state park campground offers electric hookups, while Bayside and Oceanside do not. However, the ocean and natural scenery is more captivating at the national park campgrounds, especially for tent campers.

Basics

Operated By: State of Maryland. **Open:** Mar. 29–Oct. 29. **Site Assignment:** Reservations accepted May 1–Sept. 30, all other days are first come, first served. **Registration:** At campground office. **Fee:** $25–$35 (VISA, MC). **Parking:** At site.

Facilities

Number of RV Sites: 350. **Number of Tent-Only Sites:** None. **Hookups:** Electric (30 amps). **Each Site:** Fire ring and picnic table. **Dump Station:** Yes. **Laundry:** No. **Pay Phone:** Yes. **Rest Rooms and Showers:** Yes. **Fuel:** No. **Propane:** No. **Internal Roads:** Paved, in good condition. **RV Service:** No. **Market:** Within 8 mi. **Restaurant:** Within 8 mi. **General Store:** Yes. **Vending:** Yes. **Playground:** Yes. **Other:** Assateague Island. **Activities:** Saltwater fishing and swimming, boating, hiking trails, planned activities. **Nearby Attractions:** Assateague Island National Seashore, Chincoteague National Wildlife Refuge, Ocean City. **Additional Information:** Maryland Office of Tourism Development, (800) 543-1036, www.mdisfun.org.

Restrictions

Pets: No pets permitted. **Fires:** At site. **Alcoholic Beverages:** No alcohol permitted. **Vehicle Maximum Length:** 29 ft. **Other:** 14-day max. stay.

To Get There

From Ocean City, go 9 mi. south on Hwy. 611. Follow signs to the campground.

OCEAN CITY
Eagle's Nest Camping and Trailer Park

12612 Eagle's Nest Rd., Berlin 21811. T: (410) 213-0097; www.eaglesnestoc.com; eaglesnest@beach-mail.com.

RV ★★★ Tent ★★★

Beauty: ★★★	Site Privacy: ★★
Spaciousness: ★★	Quiet: ★★
Security: ★★★★★	Cleanliness: ★★★★
Insect Control: ★★★★	Facilities: ★★★

Located on Sinepuxent Bay close to Ocean City's bustling boardwalk and inlet beaches, Eagle's Nest Camping and Trailer Park is also near Assateague Island. In fact, from the campground's viewing deck and fishing pier, you can see the wild ponies on Assateague Island as well as Ocean City's towering ferris wheel. The campground has five double rows of sites, as well as a single row of sites at the northern end. Most sites are shaded, many under tall pines. The store, laundromat, office, and rec hall are located near the entrance gate. The beach, pier, boat launch, pool, and lagoon are situated at the western end of the campground. Clusters of sites are located near all of these activity centers, and some are located on the bay.

Basics

Operated By: Fenton family. **Open:** All year. **Site Assignment:** Reservations and walk-ins accepted. **Registration:** At campground office. **Fee:** $27–$34 (VISA, MC, D). **Parking:** At site.

Facilities

Number of RV Sites: 360. **Number of Tent-Only Sites:** 25. **Hookups:** Electric (20, 30 amps), water, cable TV, phone, 190 full hookups. **Each Site:** Picnic table. **Dump Station:** Yes. **Laundry:** Yes. **Pay Phone:** Yes. **Rest Rooms and Showers:** Yes. **Fuel:** No. **Propane:** Yes. **Internal Roads:** Paved, in good condition. **RV Service:** No. **Market:** Within 2 mi. **Restaurant:** Within 2 mi. **General Store:** Yes. **Vending:** Yes. **Playground:** Yes. **Other:** Fishing and crabbing pier, indoor flea market. **Activities:** Saltwater fishing and swimming, boating, canoeing, kayaking, rec hall, game room, boat rentals, basketball, planned activities, horseshoes, volleyball. **Nearby Attractions:** Ocean City boardwalk and beaches, golf course, Assateague Island National Seashore. **Additional Information:** Ocean City Chamber of Commerce, (410) 213-0552, www.oceancity.org.

Restrictions

Pets: On leash only only. **Fires:** Grill or hibachi only. **Alcoholic Beverages:** At site. **Vehicle Maximum Length:** 35 ft. **Other:** Children under 16 must be accompanied by an adult at the swimming pool; clean fish at table provided at boat shack by the bay, not at campsite picnic table.

To Get There

From Hwy. 528, go 1 mi. west on US 50, 1 mi. south on Hwy. 611, and 1 mi. east on Eagle's Nest Rd. Entrance is on the right.

OCEAN CITY
Frontier Town Campground

P.O. Box 691, Ocean City 21843-0691. T: (410) 641-0880 or (800) 228-5590; www.frontiertown.com; info@frontiertown.com.

RV ★★★★ Tent ★★★★

Beauty: ★★★★★	Site Privacy: ★★
Spaciousness: ★★★	Quiet: ★★★
Security: ★★★★★	Cleanliness: ★★★★
Insect Control: ★★★★	Facilities: ★★★★★

Perched along Sinepuxent Bay five minutes from Assateague Island National Seashore, Frontier Town Campground is hands-down the mid-Atlantic's finest family-oriented campground. The campground alone would be attractive to visitors, but Frontier Town also includes a water park, a 38-acre wild west town, and an immaculately landscaped mini-golf course. Sites along AA, BB, and Z lanes are situated on the bay. Sites at the northern end are near the swimming pool, lagoon, marina, basketball and volleyball courts, and the crabbing and fishing pier. The Wild West Show encompasses a 38-acre, circa-1860 recreated western town, with shops, eateries, stage coach, and steam train rides, water park, horseback rides for adults and pony rides for youngsters, gun fights and bank holdups, and Native American ceremonial dancing among other activities. Cowboy Mini-Golf features 18 holes amid a setting of waterfalls and flowers. Lastly, there's a free shuttle from the campground to Ocean City and Assateague Island beaches.

Basics

Operated By: Private operator. **Open:** Apr. 21–Oct. 31. **Site Assignment:** Reservations recommended ($50 per campsite, $25 in spring and fall), walk-ins accepted. **Registration:** At campground headquarters. **Fee:** $21–$43 (VISA, MC). **Parking:** At site.

Facilities

Number of RV Sites: 475. **Number of Tent-Only Sites:** 75. **Hookups:** Electirc (20, 30, 50 amps), water, cable TV, phone, 325 full hookups. **Each Site:** Fire ring and picnic table. **Dump Station:** Yes. **Laundry:** Yes. **Pay Phone:** Yes. **Rest Rooms and Showers:** Yes. **Fuel:** No. **Propane:** Yes. **Internal Roads:** Gravel and paved, in fair condition. **RV Service:** No. **Market:** Within 4 mi. **Restaurant:** On premises. **General Store:** Yes. **Vending:** Yes. **Playground:** Yes. **Other:** Frontier Town Water Park, Frontier Town Wild West Show. **Activities:** Wading pool and swimming pool, boating, canoeing, kayaking, motor boat rentals, mini-golf, saltwater fishing, shuffleboard, basketball, hiking trails, volleyball, horseshoes, planned activities, movies. **Nearby Attractions:** Ocean City boardwalk attractions and beaches, Assateague Island National Seashore, Chincoteague National Wildlife Refuge, golf courses. **Additional Information:** Ocean City Chamber of Commerce, (410) 213-0552, www.oceancity.org.

Restrictions

Pets: On leash only; must have valid rabies tags. **Fires:** At site; 8 am–midnight. **Alcoholic Beverages:** At site, under control. **Vehicle Maximum Length:** 40 ft. **Other:** Quiet time 11 p.m.–8 a.m.; do not leave pets or fires unattended.

To Get There

From Hwy. 528, go 1 mi. west on US 50 and 4 mi. south on Hwy. 611. Entrance is on the left.

OCEAN CITY
Ocean City Campground

105 70th St., Ocean City 21842. T: (410) 524-7601; F: (410) 524-4329; www.occamping.com; occamping@aol.com.

RV ★★★ Tent ★★★

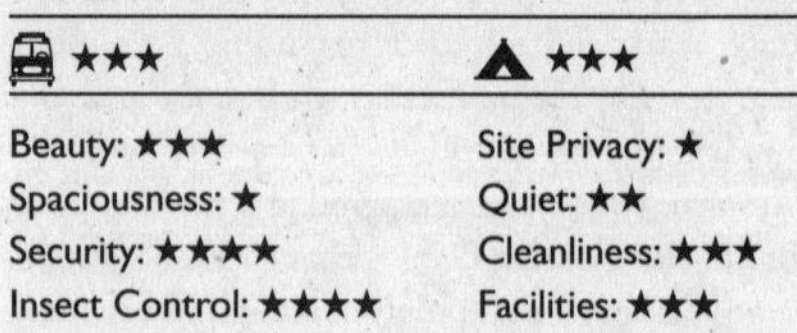

Beauty: ★★★	Site Privacy: ★
Spaciousness: ★	Quiet: ★★
Security: ★★★★	Cleanliness: ★★★
Insect Control: ★★★★	Facilities: ★★★

Campers who love the ocean and prefer the convenience of staying in the middle of Ocean City's attractions will like Ocean City Campground. The campground is just a block and a half from the white-sanded ocean beaches, where lifeguards are stationed every 300 feet. Ocean City has mini-golf courses, water parks, amusement rides, arcades, eateries, and movie theaters among other attractions, many of which are located along the three-mile boardwalk. Ocean City Campground is located across the road from the Atlantic Ocean. With 190 sites on three acres, the campground is crowded, and sites offer little privacy. If you are looking for a park in a tranquil setting with shaded sites, Ocean City Campground is not the answer. It is ideal, though, if you want an urban environment near the Ocean City action. Championship golf courses, succulent seafood restaurants, and deep-sea fishing charters are plentiful in the Ocean City area.

Basics

Operated By: Private operator. **Open:** All year. **Site Assignment:** Reservations accepted (min. 2-night stay, 3 nights on holiday weekends; 2-night non-refundable deposit required, 3-night non-refundable deposit on holiday weekends), walk-ins accepted. **Registration:** At campground office. **Fee:** $32–$54 (VISA, MC, AE). **Parking:** At site.

Facilities

Number of RV Sites: 176. **Number of Tent-Only Sites:** 14. **Hookups:** Electric (30, 50 amps), cable TV, phone, all sites have full hookups. **Each Site:** Picnic table. **Dump Station:** No. **Laundry:** Yes. **Pay Phone:** Yes. **Rest Rooms and Showers:** Yes. **Fuel:** No. **Propane:** No. **Internal Roads:** Paved, in good condition. **RV Service:** No. **Market:** Within 0.25 mi. **Restaurant:** Within 0.25 mi. **General Store:** Yes. **Vending:** No. **Playground:** Yes. **Other:** Boat ramp and dock. **Activities:** Game room, rec hall, saltwater fishing and swimming, boating. **Nearby Attractions:** Ocean City boardwalk attractions and beaches, Assateague Island National Seashore, Chincoteague National Wildlife Refuge, golf courses. **Additional Information:** Ocean City Chamber of Commerce, (410) 213-0552, www.oceancity.org.

Restrictions

Pets: On leash only. **Fires:** In grills only. **Alcoholic Beverages:** At site, under control. **Vehicle Maximum Length:** 34 ft. **Other:** One car allowed per campsite; pets may not be left unattended; no pets in units without air conditioning.

To Get There

From Hwy. 90, go 0.25 mi. north on Hwy. 528. Entrance is on the left.

SCOTLAND

Point Lookout State Park

P.O. Box 48, Scotland 20687. T: (301) 872-5688 or (888) 432-2267; F: (301) 872-5084; www.dnr.state.md.us.

RV ★★★★ Tent ★★★★

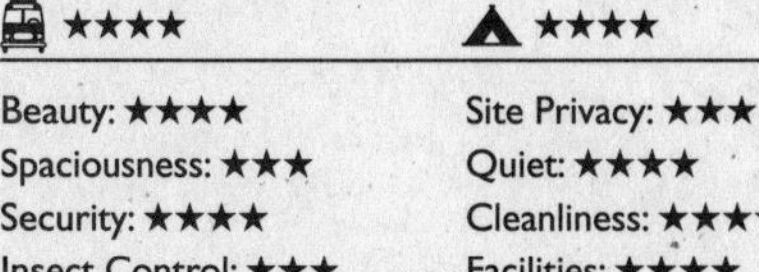

Beauty: ★★★★ Site Privacy: ★★★
Spaciousness: ★★★ Quiet: ★★★★
Security: ★★★★ Cleanliness: ★★★★
Insect Control: ★★★ Facilities: ★★★★

Situated on a peninsula at the confluence of the Potomac River and Chesapeake Bay, southern Maryland's Point Lookout State Park is a haven for water sports and Civil War history. A lighthouse, built in 1830 and now owned by the US Navy, still sits at the tip of the point. The original earthworks and recreated structures of Civl War–era Fort Lincoln are on the river shore near Cornfield Harbor. Of the campground's 143 wooded sites, 26 have full hookups—a pleasant convenience at a park with so many recreational and historical points of interest. Campsites are arranged on five loops which are nestled between Point Lookout Creek (west), Tanner's Creek (east), and Lake Conoy (south). Point Lookout has three fishing areas, including a 710-foot fishing pier; there's also a boat launch, boat rentals, and several hiking trails.

Basics

Operated By: State of Maryland. **Open:** All year. **Site Assignment:** Reservations and walk-ins accepted. **Registration:** At campground office. **Fee:** $18–$25 (VISA, MC). **Parking:** At site.

Facilities

Number of RV Sites: 143. **Number of Tent-Only Sites:** None. **Hookups:** Electric (20, 30 amps), 26 full hookups. **Each Site:** Fire ring, picnic table. **Dump Station:** Yes. **Laundry:** Yes. **Pay Phone:** Yes. **Rest Rooms and Showers:** Yes. **Fuel:** No. **Propane:** No. **Internal Roads:** Paved, in good condition. **RV Service:** No. **Market:** Within 5 mi. **Restaurant:** Within 5 mi. **General Store:** Yes. **Vending:** No. **Playground:** Yes. **Other:** Potomac River, Chesapeake Bay, 2 creeks, lake. **Activities:** Saltwater and freshwater fishing, boating, canoeing, boat rentals, freshwater swimming, hiking trails, planned activities. **Nearby Attractions:** Point Lookout Lighthouse, Civil War Museum, Confederate Cemetery, Potomac River, Chesapeake Bay, Washington, D.C. **Additional Information:** Maryland Office of Tourism Development, (800) 543-1036, www.mdisfun.org.

Restrictions

Pets: In designated loops. **Fires:** At site. **Alcoholic Beverages:** No alcohol permitted. **Vehicle Maximum Length:** 34 ft. **Other:** 14-day max. stay.

To Get There

From Scotland's business center, go 4 mi. south on Hwy. 5. Follow signs to the campground.

THURMONT

Cunningham Falls State Park

14039 Catoctin Hollow Rd., Thurmont 21788. T: (301) 271-7574 or (888) 432-2267; www.dnr.state.md.us.

RV ★★★ Tent ★★★★

Beauty: ★★★★ Site Privacy: ★★★★
Spaciousness: ★★★★ Quiet: ★★★★
Security: ★★★★ Cleanliness: ★★★★
Insect Control: ★★★ Facilities: ★★★★

Nestled in northern Maryland's Catoctin Mountains, Cunningham Falls State Park is named for its 78-foot cascading waterfall, located a half-mile from Big Hunting Creek in the park's Houck Area and accessible by the Falls Trail. There are two main developed sections at Cunningham Falls, the Houck Area and the Manor Area. Camping areas are located in both; Houck has 119 sites and Manor has 31 sites. Each loop has a bathhouse with showers and flush toilets. Campsites with electric hookups are situated in Addison Run Circle and Deer Spring Branch Circle in the Houck Area, and at sites 6–10 and 15–21 in the Manor Area. Drinking water spigots are placed throughout each loop. A dump station is located in the Houck Area near the camp office. There are nine hiking trails which venture through Cunningham Falls and Catoctin Mountain National Park. Big Hunting Creek offers catch-and-release trout fishing and boating.

Basics

Operated By: State of Maryland. **Open:** All year. **Site Assignment:** Reservations accepted May 1–Sept. 30; all other dates are first come, first served. **Registration:** At campground office. **Fee:** $20–$25 (VISA, MC). **Parking:** At site.

Facilities

Number of RV Sites: 171. **Number of Tent-Only Sites:** None. **Hookups:** Electric (30 amps). **Each Site:** Fire ring, picnic table. **Dump Station:** Yes. **Laundry:** No. **Pay Phone:** Yes. **Rest Rooms and Showers:** Yes. **Fuel:** No. **Propane:** No. **Internal Roads:** Paved, in good condition. **RV Service:** No. **Market:** Within 3 mi. **Restaurant:** Within 3 mi. **General Store:** Yes. **Vending:** Yes. **Playground:** Yes. **Other:** Catoctin Furnace, Cunningham Falls. **Activities:** Lake swimming and fishing, boating, canoe rentals, hiking trails, planned activities. **Nearby Attractions:** Catoctin Mountain National Park, Frederick, Monocacy National Battlefield, Francis Scott Key Museum, Harper's Ferry, Hagerstown. **Additional Information:** Tourism Council of Frederick County, (800) 999-3613, www.co.frederick.md.us.

Restrictions

Pets: No pets are permitted. **Fires:** At site. **Alcoholic Beverages:** No alcohol permitted. **Vehicle Maximum Length:** 30 ft. **Other:** 14-day max. stay.

To Get There

To reach the Houck Area from Thurmont, go 3 mi. west on Hwy. 77 and follow signs. To reach the Manor Area from Thurmont, go 3 mi. south on US 15 and follow signs.

WHALEYVILLE

Fort Whaley Campground

11224 Dale Rd., Whaleyville 21872. T: (410) 641-9785; www.fortwhaley.com; info@fortwhaley.com.

RV ★★★★ Tent ★★★★

Beauty: ★★★★ Site Privacy: ★★★
Spaciousness: ★★★ Quiet: ★★★
Security: ★★★★ Cleanliness: ★★★★
Insect Control: ★★★★ Facilities: ★★★★

The sister park to Frontier Town Campground, Fort Whaley Campground is located in Whaleyville, about 10 miles northwest of Ocean City. Fort Whaley campers are granted free admission to Frontier Town's water park and discounted admission to the wild west town. Like Frontier Town, Fort Whaley has a western theme. The swimming pool, mini-golf course, clubhouse and arcade, store, and office are near the park entrance. Sites along E Circle on Rayne Lake are our favorites. The lake is at the eastern end, and three clusters of sites are nearby. Primitive sites along G Lane and water and electric sites on A Lane are closest to most of the activity centers. Fort Whaley is a 15-minute drive from Ocean City's boardwalk attractions and beaches.

Basics

Operated By: Private operator. **Open:** All year. **Site Assignment:** Reservations accepted ($50 deposit required, $25 for spring and fall), walk-ins accepted. **Registration:** At campground office. **Fee:** $16–$28.25 (VISA, MC). **Parking:** At site.

Facilities

Number of RV Sites: 133. **Number of Tent-Only Sites:** 32. **Hookups:** Electric (20, 30, 50 amps), water, cable TV, 64 full hookups. **Each Site:** Fire ring and picnic table. **Dump Station:** Yes. **Laundry:** Yes. **Pay Phone:** Yes. **Rest Rooms and Showers:** Yes. **Fuel:** No. **Propane:** Yes. **Internal Roads:** Gravel and paved, in good condition. **RV Service:** No. **Market:** Within 3 mi. **Restaurant:** Within 3 mi. **General Store:** Yes. **Vending:** Yes. **Playground:** Yes. **Other:** Fishing pond, free admission to Frontier Water Park. **Activities:** Pond fishing, mini-golf, game room, rec hall, pedal boat rentals, basketball, shuffleboard, volleyball, horseshoes, movies, planned activities on weekends, sports field. **Nearby Attractions:** Ocean City boardwalk attractions and beaches, Assateague Island National Seashore, Chincoteague National Wildlife Refuge, Rehoboth Beach (DE). **Additional Information:** Ocean City Chamber of Commerce, (410) 213-0552, www.oceancity.org.

Restrictions

Pets: On leash only, valid rabies tags required. **Fires:** At site. **Alcoholic Beverages:** At site. **Vehicle Maximum Length:** 45 ft. **Other:** Pets and fires may not be left unattended.

To Get There

From US 50, go 0.25 mi. south on Hwy. 610. Entrance is on the left.

WOODBINE

Ramblin' Pines Family Campground

801 Hoods Mill Rd., Woodbine 21797. T: (410) 795-5161 or (800) 550-TREE; www.kiz.com; ramblinpines@juno.com.

RV ★★★★ Tent ★★★★

Beauty: ★★★★ Site Privacy: ★★★
Spaciousness: ★★★★ Quiet: ★★★★
Security: ★★★★★ Cleanliness: ★★★★
Insect Control: ★★★★ Facilities: ★★★★

Located about 45 minutes north of Washington, D.C., a half-hour west of Baltimore, and 20 minutes east of Frederick, Ramblin' Pines Family Campground is the type of park you prefer when looking for a sightseeing home base. The campground is in a rural, tranquil area, and guests have their choice of wooded and open sites, each of which is equipped with a full hookup. Ramblin' Pines can accommodate 15 pull-throughs. Most people know about the multitude of attractions in Washington, D.C. and Baltimore; though lesser known, Frederick is an interesting city in its own right. Monocacy National Battlefield, located three miles south of the town, offers tours at the site of a Union victory in 1864.

Basics

Operated By: Private operator. **Open:** All year. **Site Assignment:** Reservations accepted (2-night min. stay on weekends, 3 nights on holiday weekends), walk-ins accepted. **Registration:** At campground office. **Fee:** $33 (VISA, MC). **Parking:** At site.

Facilities

Number of RV Sites: 184. **Number of Tent-Only Sites:** 16. **Hookups:** Electric (20, 30, 50 amps), phone, water, 200 full hookups. **Each Site:** Fire ring and picnic table. **Dump Station:** Yes. **Laundry:** Yes. **Pay Phone:** Yes. **Rest Rooms and Showers:** Yes. **Fuel:** No. **Propane:** Yes. **Internal Roads:** Gravel and paved, in good condition. **RV Service:** No. **Market:** Within 3 mi. **Restaurant:** Within 3 mi. **General Store:** Yes. **Vending:** Yes. **Playground:** Yes. **Other:** Fishing pond, cabin rentals. **Activities:** Swimming, pond fishing, mini-golf, basketball, game room, rec hall, shuffleboard, planned activities on weekends, hiking trails, volleyball, sports field, horseshoes. **Nearby Attractions:** Frederick, Baltimore, Hagerstown, Harper's Ferry (WV), Washington, D.C. Annapolis, Gettysburg. **Additional Information:** Maryland Office of Tourism Development, (800) 543-1036, www.mdisfun.org.

Restrictions

Pets: On leash only. **Fires:** At site. **Alcoholic Beverages:** At site, under control. **Vehicle Maximum Length:** 50 ft. **Other:** No pets in rental cabins.

To Get There

From I-70, take Exit 76 and go 2.5 mi. north on Hwy. 97 and 0.5 mi. northwest on Hoods Mill Rd. Entrance is on the left.

Massachusetts

What's really special about camping in Massachusetts? No matter where you choose to settle in for the night, you're never too far from great places to sight-see, museum-hop, and soak up the city scene. It takes less than four hours to drive the width of the state—unless you're amazingly unlucky in traffic—so you could wake up in a woodsy rural campground in the **Berkshire Hills** and arrive in **Boston** in time for lunch. Tip: We'd ditch the rig first, and take the car into the city—all the better to navigate those cow paths-turned-cobblestone streets! Happily, there are several campgrounds within a 30-mile radius of the city. Some offer bus tours of Boston, while others are located near the commuter rail line, should you choose not to brave city traffic.

While Massachusetts may not have a huge number of commercial campgrounds, those that do exist are generally clean and well-kept. Also, they tend to be clustered near desirable places to visit. Example: Cape Ann Camp Site, in **Gloucester,** overlooks the salt marshes of the North Shore and is a bike ride away from a lovely ocean beach; close by are fishing villages and art colonies, whale watch tours and sunset boat cruises. All in all, it's a dandy place to enjoy some seaside ambience. **Cape Cod** is home to numerous campgrounds, some chock-full of amenities, others all swaying sea oats and salt air. Even tony **Martha's Vineyard** (shh!) is home to a campground. Besides being surrounded by some of the most dazzling scenery in New England, campers on the Cape and Islands are enjoying it all at a bargain (a word not heard frequently in these parts!)

Fact is, some of the most prime real estate in Massachusetts is open to campers. Twenty-eight state parks offer camping, and the settings are truly spectacular. Settle in for the night behind a sand dune at **Horseneck Beach State Reservation,** just steps away from **Buzzard's Bay.** Farther north, **Salisbury Beach** offers nearly 500 campsites, hugging the Atlantic Coast. These are wildly popular, so reserve early; reserve a site at any state campground by calling the same toll-free number. For a totally different experience, check out the hidden gems in the Western part of the state, the arts-and-theater mecca known as the Berkshires. Besides all the culture you could ask for, this region offers wonderful hiking and paddling, and glorious state parks. Deeply wooded, dotted with sapphire ponds, these campgrounds are a great choice for tent campers or RVers with self-contained units, who consider a pristine natural setting to be the ultimate amenity.

The camping season in Massachusetts generally runs from Memorial Day to Columbus Day.

The following facilities accept payment in checks or cash only:

Coastal Acres Campground, Provincetown
Dune's Edge Campground, Provincetown
Historic Valley Campground, N. Adams
The Old Holbrook Place, Sutton

Campground Profiles

BELLINGHAM
Circle CG Farm

131 North Main St., Bellingham 02019. T: (508) 966-1136; www.hometown.aol.com/cgfrmcamp; cgfrm camp@aol.com.

RV ★★★ | Tent ★

Beauty: ★★ | Site Privacy: ★★
Spaciousness: ★★★ | Quiet: ★★★
Security: ★★★★★ | Cleanliness: ★★★★★
Insect Control: ★★★ | Facilities: ★★★

This Western-themed campground is situated smack-dab in the "golden triangle" of Boston, Providence, and Worcester. Depending on your luck with traffic, it's 35 or 45 minutes from Boston, and 45 minutes from Providence, Rhode Island. But you might feel like you're in the heart of the Smokies, what with the Opry Hall (a funky rec hall with a fake jail), horse corral, and rest rooms designated "Cowboys" and "Cowgirls." Despite the petting animals—horses, a burro, goats—this isn't a particularly child-friendly place. There's no playground and, as a long-time camper put it, "Just not much for kids here." One of the pools is designated for seniors only, while an adult game area is marked for ages 15 and up. The presence of a beauty parlor and guided bus tours provide more evidence that this place is geared to grown-ups. Campsites are arrayed in a series of loops around an open, grassy field; side loops are wooded. Tall pines don't provide much buffer between sites, though. Nicely shaded RV sites (21S through 24S) are set along Six Gun Rd.; on the frog pond, site 91 is a winner. Tents are set along TeePee Ln., a low-lying area that could get very muddy.

BASICS

Operated By: Rob & Linda Daley. **Open:** All year. **Site Assignment:** Reservations suggested. Site preference noted, but not guaranteed. One night's fee required for deposit, check or credit card OK. Refunds issued for cancellation if received one week prior to scheduled arrival date, minus $5 service charge. **Registration:** At office. **Fee:** $31–$33; rate based on two people. Additional person, $5; children under age 1 free. V, MC. **Parking:** At site.

FACILITIES

Number of RV Sites: 138. **Number of Tent-Only Sites:** 20. **Hookups:** Water, electric (20, 30, 50 amps), sewer. **Each Site:** Picnic table, fireplace or grill. **Dump Station:** Yes. **Laundry:** Yes. **Pay Phone:** Yes. **Rest Rooms and Showers:** Yes. **Fuel:** No. **Propane:** Yes. **Internal Roads:** Paved, in good condition. **RV Service:** No. **Market:** 1 mi. north. **Restaurant:** 1 mi. north. **General Store:** Yes. **Vending:** No. **Swimming Pool:** Yes (2). **Playground:** No. **Other:** Mini-golf, beauty parlor, exercise room, rec room. **Activities:** Guided tours to Boston & Cape Cod, planned activities, fishing, swimming, horseshoes, shuffleboard, bocce, petting farm. **Nearby Attractions:** Old Sturbridge Village living history museum, New England Science Center, Ecotarium, Worcester Art Museum, outlet shopping. **Additional Information:** Central Mass. Tourist Council, (508) 755-7400; www.worcester.org.

RESTRICTIONS

Pets: Must be leashed & cleaned up after. Must not be left unattended. Not allowed in or around buildings or pools. **Fires:** In steel rings, 6 p.m.–11:30 p.m. only. **Alcoholic Beverages:** Yes. **Vehicle Maximum Length:** 45 ft. **Other:** Three day min. stay on holiday weekends.

TO GET THERE

Take I-95 to Rte. 495 North to exit 18 (Rte. 126), heading south. Bear left at the light, where Rte. 126 splits. Follow Rte. 126 south 1 mi. to the campground entrance on the left.

BOURNE
Bay View Campgrounds

260 MacArthur Blvd., Rte. 28, Bourne 02532. T: (508) 759-7610; www.bayviewcampground.com.

★★★★ ▲ ★★

Beauty: ★★★★	Site Privacy: ★★★
Spaciousness: ★★★★	Quiet: ★★
Security: ★★★★	Cleanliness: ★★★★★
Insect Control: ★★★	Facilities: ★★★★★

Located on the Upper Cape, just beyond the Bourne Bridge (one of two bridges that connect Cape Cod to the mainland), Bay View is about 60 percent seasonal. Don't let that put you off, though. This is a great spot for RV campers (tenters might find its location near the busy roadway a bit noisy) who want to enjoy the Cape Cod experience without driving the length of the Cape. They also sell tickets here for ferry boats to Martha's Vineyard and Nantucket, a nice convenience. Campsites are level, spacious, and semi-shaded; sites 155 through 160 are especially pleasant, and backed by woods. Number 59 is another good choice, big and level. We'd skip site 169, an elevated site with views of other RV's roofs. There's plenty to do here, from daily planned activities to a really elaborate, state-of-the-art arcade. Nice touches make a difference, including vanity lights around mirrors and a baby changing table in the ladies' room, and good signage and trash bag dispensers throughout the campground. One quibble: the $10 per person guest fee is pretty pricey. Chalk it up to the desirability of the Cape.

BASICS

Operated By: Bay View Campground Inc. **Open:** May 1–Oct. 15. **Site Assignment:** Reservations recommended. Call to reserve after Jan. 10; secure reservation with a non-refundable deposit on Visa or Mastercard. If stay is less than one week, a deposit of one night's fee is required. Otherwise, deposit is generally one night's fee per week of stay. Full balance is required upon arrival in cash, traveler's checks or credit card. **Registration:** At office. **Fee:** $29–$35. Rate based on two adults. Additional children under age 18, $2–$3; additional adult, $8–$10. V, MC. **Parking:** At site.

FACILITIES

Number of RV Sites: 425. **Number of Tent-Only Sites:** 0. **Hookups:** Water, electric (20, 30 amps), sewer, cable TV, modem (in office). **Each Site:** Picnic table, fireplace. **Dump Station:** Yes. **Laundry:** Yes. **Pay Phone:** Yes. **Rest Rooms and Showers:** Yes, coin-op. **Fuel:** No. **Propane:** Yes. **Internal Roads:** Paved, in good condition. **RV Service:** No. **Market:** 3 mi. north. **Restaurant:** Yes. **General Store:** Yes (snack bar). **Vending:** Yes. **Swimming Pool:** Yes (2–3). **Playground:** Yes. **Other:** Rec hall, tennis courts. **Activities:** Swimming, tennis, volleyball, basketball, shuffleboard, horseshoes, ball field, planned activities. **Nearby Attractions:** Cape Cod beaches, boating, fishing, antique shops, golf, scenic bike paths, ferries to Martha's Vineyard & Nantucket. **Additional Information:** Cape Cod Chamber, (888) 33-CAPECOD or (508) 362-3225; www.capecodchamber.org.

RESTRICTIONS

Pets: Must be leashed, quiet, & cleaned up after. Current rabies certificate required upon request. **Fires:** At sites only. **Alcoholic Beverages:** Yes. **Vehicle Maximum Length:** 40 ft. **Other:** Two-night min. stay required on weekends between Memorial Day & Labor Day. Three-night min. stay on holidays. Seven-night min. on July 4th week.

TO GET THERE

Take I-195 or I-495 to Rte. 25, go over Bourne Bridge and continue 1 mi. on Rte. 28 south. Campground entrance is on the right.

BREWSTER
Nickerson State Park

3488 Main St., Rte. 6A, Brewster 02631. T: (508) 896-3491; www.state.ma.us/dem/parks/nick.htm.

★★ ▲ ★★★★

Beauty: ★★★★★	Site Privacy: ★★★
Spaciousness: ★★★★	Quiet: ★★★★
Security: ★★★★	Cleanliness: ★★★
Insect Control: ★★★★	Facilities: ★★★

Self-sufficient, energetic types will adore this state park, located in the mid-Cape area of Cape Cod. You won't find hookups, but you will find acres of piney woods, more reminiscent of the Berkshires than the Cape. The woodsy landscape is dotted with eight freshwater kettle ponds, formed when glaciers retreated from the Cape more than 10,000 years ago. Ponds are stocked with land-locked trout and salmon; marked bike trails connect with 25-mile Cape Cod Rail Trail (rail trail users can park for free). Deep-blue Flax Pond, with a sandy beach, is great for swimming and boating. Hiking trails lead to the beach. For the winter tenting crowd, the park offers yurts (available all year). Campsites are grouped in seven areas. Area 4 is heavily used, since it's close to the beach; sites 41 through 51 (odd numbers) are pretty, and backed by pines. Area 3 is hilly, and not as desirable as Area 2, which boasts wooded water views (especially sites 112 through 120). You'd think the farthest-back camping areas, 6, 6X, and 7 would be quietest, but you'd be wrong; that tends to be Party Central in summer.

BASICS

Operated By: Massachusetts State Parks & Forests. **Open:** All year. **Site Assignment:** Reservations recommended. Reserve up to six months in advance by calling ReserveAmerica at (877) 1-CAMP-MA or online at www.reservamerica.com. 20% of sites are non-reservable, & available for walk-in campers. To change arrival or departure date, or site type, call at least three dayas prior to arrival date. $10 cancellation/transfer fee. No refunds for amounts less than $5. **Registration:** At headquarters. **Fee:** $5–$30, V, MC. **Parking:** At sites or designated parking lots.

FACILITIES

Number of RV Sites: 420. **Number of Tent-Only Sites:** 0. **Hookups:** None. **Each Site:** Picnic table, fireplace. **Dump Station:** Yes. **Laundry:** No. **Pay Phone:** Yes. **Rest Rooms and Showers:** Yes. **Fuel:** No. **Propane:** No. **Internal Roads:** Paved, in good condition. **RV Service:** No. **Market:** 5 mi. east. **Restaurant:** Yes (snack bar). **General Store:** Yes. **Vending:** No. **Swimming Pool:** No. **Playground:** Yes. **Other:** Nature center, amphitheater, boat rentals, bike rentals. **Activities:** Pond swimming, fishing (catch & release) in Higgins Pond, bicycling, boating, hiking. **Nearby Attractions:** Golf, biking (Cape Cod Rail Trail), ocean swimming, pond swimming, boating, tennis, antiquing. **Additional Information:** Cape Cod Chamber, (508) 862-0700 or (888) 33-CAPECOD; www.capecod chamber.org.

RESTRICTIONS

Pets: Must be leashed & cleaned up after. Must not be left unattended. Proof of rabies vaccination required. Not allowed on Flax Pond swimming beach. **Fires:** In fire rings only. **Alcoholic Beverages:** Not permitted. **Vehicle Maximum Length:** 35 ft. **Other:** Must renew by 8 p.m. the night prior to your scheduled check-out. Max. stay is 14 cumulative days between Memorial Day & Labor Day.

TO GET THERE

Take Rte. 6 east to Exit 12. Go left off the ramp. Park is approximately 1 mi. ahead on the left.

BREWSTER
Shady Knoll Campground

1708 Rte. 6A, Brewster 02631. T: (508) 896-3002; www.capecamping.com.

★★ ▲ ★★

Beauty: ★★ Site Privacy: ★★
Spaciousness: ★★ Quiet: ★★★
Security: ★★★★ Cleanliness: ★★★★
Insect Control: ★★★★ Facilities: ★★★★

Location, location, location. This low-key family campground is in mid-Cape, central to Cape Cod attractions, including bay swimming (just a mile away) and the Cape Cod Rail Trail for biking. It has a wholesome feel (maybe because of all the rosy-cheeked cyclists who converge here in summer.) A nice-looking lodge houses the camp store, game room, and small lounge with a fireplace and TV, where they show movies every night during the summer. The (free) showers and bathrooms are roomy and modern. And what's not to like about a place that sells Hawaiian shirts in the campstore? Campsites are mostly shaded, on gravel. Seasonal sites are set apart. Tent sites are clustered in a corner, and fairly exposed. Most appealing tent sites are sites 93 and 94, with plenty of space and no neighbors nearby. RV sites 67 and 68 are level and wooded, while site 82 is set apart by itself for maximum privacy. We'd skip sites 51–52, exposed to a busy thoroughfare. Perhaps not as pretty a place as nearby Sweetwater Forest (see listing), but not bad, either.

Basics

Operated By: Dave & Donna Nussdorfer. **Open:** May 15–Oct. 15. **Site Assignment:** Reservations recommended. 50% deposit required for stays of 5 days or more; all other reservations must be prepaid. No refunds without 14 days' notice. $10 service charge applies to cancellations. Checks OK for advance reservations. **Registration:** At office. **Fee:** $30–$37 for two people; extra unmarried child age 6-18, $2 per night; extra adult, $7.50; age 5 & under free. V, MC, D. **Parking:** At site.

Facilities

Number of RV Sites: 100. **Number of Tent-Only Sites:** 0. **Hookups:** Water, electric (30 amps), sewer. **Each Site:** Picnic table, fireplace. **Dump Station:** Yes. **Laundry:** Yes. **Pay Phone:** Yes. **Rest Rooms and Showers:** Yes. **Fuel:** No. **Propane:** Yes. **Internal Roads:** Gravel, in good condition. **RV Service:** No. **Market:** Just outside campground entrance. **Restaurant:** 1 mi. east on Rte. 6A. **General Store:** Yes. **Vending:** No. **Swimming Pool:** No. **Playground:** Yes. **Other:** Rec room. **Activities:** Bicycling, ball field, nightly movies. **Nearby Attractions:** Golf, biking (Cape Cod Rail Trail), ocean swimming, pond swimming, boating, tennis, antiquing. **Additional Information:** Cape Cod Chamber of Commerce, (508) 862-0700 or (888) 33-CAPECOD; www.capecodcham ber.org.

Restrictions

Pets: Must be leashed & cleaned up after. Must be taken w/you when you leave the campground. Use pet walk located in storage area. Dogs not permitted on beaches. **Fires:** In fireplaces only. **Alcoholic Beverages:** Yes. **Vehicle Maximum Length:** 32 ft. **Other:** Some weekends in July & Aug. may require three-night min. reservation. July 4th week requires four nights.

To Get There

From Sagamore Bridge, follow Rte. 6 to Exit 11. Turn right onto Rte. 137 towards Brewster. Follow Rte. 137 to the end. Campground is directly across Rte. 6A.

BREWSTER

Sweetwater Forest

676 Rte. 124, P.O. Box 1797, Brewster 02631. T: (508) 896-3773; F: (508) 896-2013; www.sweetwaterforest.com; sweeth2orv@aol.com.

RV ★★★ Tent ★★★★

Beauty: ★★★★ Site Privacy: ★★★
Spaciousness: ★★★★ Quiet: ★★★★
Security: ★★★★ Cleanliness: ★★★
Insect Control: ★★★ Facilities: ★★★

Conveniently located in a desirable area of the mid-Cape (Cape Cod), this is the most inviting private campground around. (Brewster is also home to terrific Nickerson State Park.) It has a pleasant feel; campers are greeted with tumbles of blue hydrangea and well-tended plantings, and a winding entrance road skirting oak trees and lofty pines. Set amidst 60 acres of woodland, the property includes Snow's Pond, with a fishing dock and small swimming area. For cyclists, the best feature here may well be the bike path connecting with the Cape Cod Rail Trail, a paved, 25-mile bike path. Rental rowboats and canoes add to the recreation possibilities. Families will have a good time here. Seasonal sites are grouped together to the left of the entrance. Among the rest, sites C6–10 (electric and water) are big, level, and wooded, while site C28B is so big, you could put a house on it. Some tent sites are set alongside a retired cranberry bog. Sites B13–16 are close to a rest room, and a short walk to the pond.

Basics

Operated By: Jim Rylander. **Open:** All year. **Site Assignment:** Reservations recommended; can reserve one year in advance & on-line. $30 deposit required. $15 refund if cancellation occurs two weeks in advance of scheduled arrival. **Registration:** At office. **Fee:** $18–$25 for two adults, plus unmarried children under age 18. V, MC, D. **Parking:** At site.

Facilities

Number of RV Sites: 250. **Number of Tent-Only Sites:** 0. **Hookups:** Water, electric (30 amps), sewer, cable TV. **Each Site:** Picnic table, fireplace. **Dump Station:** Yes. **Laundry:** No. **Pay Phone:** Yes. **Rest Rooms and Showers:** Yes. **Fuel:** No. **Propane:** Yes. **Internal Roads:** Gravel, in good condition. **RV Service:** Yes. **Market:** 3 mi. east. **Restaurant:** 5 mi. east. **General Store:** Yes. **Vending:** Yes. **Swimming Pool:** No. **Playground:** Yes. **Other:** Rec lodge, mini-golf. **Activities:** Boating (rowboat & canoe rentals), hiking, basketball, biking (access to Cape Cod Rail Trail), horseshoes, fishing, planned activities. **Nearby Attractions:** Ocean beaches, freshwater swimming, boating, golf, antiques, Cape Cod Museum of Natural History, charter boat fishing trips, whale-watching cruises. **Additional Information:** Cape Cod Chamber, (508) 862-0700 or (888) 33-CAPECOD; www.capecodchamber.org.

Restrictions

Pets: Must be leashed. Must not be left unattended. Proof of rabies vaccination required. Dog boarding service available. **Fires:** In fireplaces only. **Alcoholic Beverages:** Yes. **Vehicle Maximum Length:** None. **Other:** 2-night min.; 3-night min. on holidays.

To Get There

From Sagamore Bridge, enter Rte. 6. Follow Rte. 6 to Exit 10, Rte. 124. Turn left off ramp, heading north toward Brewster on Rte. 124. Follow Rte. 124 for 2.8 mi. Look for the sign on the left to the campground entrance.

BRIMFIELD

Quinebaug Cove Campsite

49 East Brimfield-Holland Rd., Brimfield 01010. T: (413) 245-9525; www.quinebaugcove.com.

RV ★★★ Tent ★★

Beauty: ★★ Site Privacy: ★★
Spaciousness: ★★★ Quiet: ★★★
Security: ★★★ Cleanliness: ★★★
Insect Control: ★★★ Facilities: ★★★

When someone asks, "Are they biting?" at a campground, they're usually referring to mosquitoes. Not here. At Quinebaug Cove Campsite, avid anglers fish for trout, bass, pickerel, Northern Pike, and perch. (Fishing licenses are available at a nearby Wal-Mart; bait, they'll sell you right here.) The campground, about 10 miles west of Sturbridge, abuts the Brimfield Reservoir and Long Pond. Besides fishing, there's a five-mile canoe trail and a small sandy beach with a swimming area. About 95 percent of the campers here are families. Quinebaug Cove is a privately-owned co-op, or camping club, although one need not be a member to camp here. Set on a series of loop roads, some of the campsites are open, others are shaded. The nicest sites, as you'd expect, are on the waterfront. Sites 908–916B (even numbers), with water and electric, are near the beach, as are tent sites 216–224. Getting around the campground can be tricky; signage is poor. Tent sites are grouped together, on the lower part of the campground, convenient to the snack bar, rec hall, and pool area. Located in a rural area, the campground offers a quiet setting, except (we're guessing) during July 4th week, when a biker's group shows up for their annual camp-out.

Basics

Operated By: Board of Directors. **Open:** All year. **Site Assignment:** Reserve by phone or on web site. Reservations accepted after Jan. 2. Two-night min. on summer weekends; three-night min. on holiday weekends. No refunds for cancellation of campsite with less than seven days' notice. Cancellation fee, $10, V, MC, D. **Registration:** At office. **Fee:** $26–$32. Rates based on two people per night. Extra adult, $6. Extra child (age 3–18), $3. **Parking:** At site or in visitor parking lot.

Facilities

Number of RV Sites: 114. **Number of Tent-Only Sites:** 11. **Hookups:** Water, electric (20, 30 amps), sewer. **Each Site:** Picnic table, fireplace. **Dump Station:** Yes. **Laundry:** Yes. **Pay Phone:** Yes. **Rest Rooms and Showers:** Yes. **Fuel:** No. **Propane:** Yes. **Internal Roads:** Paved & gravel, in fair condition. **RV Service:** No. **Market:** 5 mi. west in Palmer. **Restaurant:** Yes. **General Store:** Yes. **Vending:** Yes. **Swimming Pool:** Yes. **Playground:**

Yes. **Other:** Basketball court, rec hall, boat ramp. **Activities:** Boating (rental canoes & rowboats), swimming (freshwater pond & pool), volleyball, basketball, bocce, shuffleboard, basketball, hayrides, lake fishing, planned activities. **Nearby Attractions:** Old Sturbridge Village living history museum, Six Flags New England theme park, Brimfield Antique Flea Market. **Additional Information:** www.quinebaugcove.com.

RESTRICTIONS

Pets: Must be quiet & leashed at all times. Do not leave pets unattended. Clean up after pets. Must have proof of rabies vaccination. No more than 2 pets per site. **Fires:** In fireplaces only. **Alcoholic Beverages:** Yes. **Vehicle Maximum Length:** 35 ft. **Other:** No electric heaters. No admittance to campground after 9 p.m. Maximum 2 cars & 8 people per site.

TO GET THERE

From the junction of I-84 and Rte. 20, go 3.5 mi. west on Rte. 20, then 0.25 mi. south on Brimfield Rd. Campground entrance is on the left.

BROOKFIELD

Lakeside Resort

13 Hobbs Ave., Brookfield 01506. T: (508) 867-2737 or (800) 320-CAMP; www.camplakeside.com.

RV ★★★ Tent ★★

Beauty: ★★ Site Privacy: ★
Spaciousness: ★★ Quiet: ★★★
Security: ★★★★ Cleanliness: ★★
Insect Control: ★★★ Facilities: ★★

Located just north of Sturbridge in the village of Brookfield, this campground is set on a 540-acre lake. If you agree with the sentiment, "You're not really camping unless you've got your laptop and cable TV," (said by one of the campground's owners, only partially in jest), you'll be very content here. A wilderness escape, it's not. A couple of drawbacks: Grounds and facilities could benefit from some sprucing up, plus, the much-ballyhooed lake is actually across the street, reachable via footpath through a gate. Private homes are set right beside the campground's waterfront clubhouse. Campsites are mostly grassy and level (some are pull-thru.) Look for shaded sites on the perimeter of the property. About one-third are seasonal. Sites beginning with letter 'J' are the most remote, but skip J17 and 18 (near the main entrance.) Most campsites are about 40 feet wide, but packed closely together, making this place a better bet for RVs than for tents. Weekend and holiday activities—scavenger hunts and crafts for the kids, and cook-outs, live music, dances, family movies—enhance the resort-like atmosphere.

BASICS

Operated By: Lakeside Condominiums. **Open:** Apr. 15–Oct. 15. Limited winter camping available by registration. **Site Assignment:** Reservations recommended. Deposit required. **Registration:** At check-in/guest services building. **Fee:** $25-$28 for two persons. Extra fee may be charged on holidays. V, MC, D, AMEX. **Parking:** At site.

FACILITIES

Number of RV Sites: 120. **Number of Tent-Only Sites:** 0. **Hookups:** Water, electric (20, 30, 50 amps), sewer, cable TV, modem. **Each Site:** Picnic table, fireplace. **Dump Station:** Yes. **Laundry:** Yes. **Pay Phone:** Yes. **Rest Rooms and Showers:** Yes, coin op. **Fuel:** No. **Propane:** Yes. **Internal Roads:** Gravel, good condition. **RV Service:** No. **Market:** 1 mi. north. **Restaurant:** 1 mi. north. **General Store:** Yes. **Vending:** Yes. **Swimming Pool:** Yes. **Playground:** Yes. **Other:** Rec hall, club house, boat moorings. **Activities:** Boating (paddle boat & canoe rentals), swimming, fishing, basketball, shuffleboard, volleyball, arcade games, planned activities. **Nearby Attractions:** Old Sturbridge Village living history museum, Brimfield Antique Flea Markets, golf. **Additional Information:** www.camplakeside.com.

RESTRICTIONS

Pets: Quiet, & on leash only. Not left unattended. Must be cleaned up after. Do not walk pets in or around recreational facilities. **Fires:** Fireplaces only. **Alcoholic Beverages:** Sites only. **Vehicle Max. Length:** None. **Other:** Reservations are not assured until confirmation & deposit are received.

TO GET THERE

From junction of I-84 and Rte. 20, head east 2 mi. to Rte. 49. Go north to Rte. 9, then head west 3.9 mi. to Quaboag St. Take left 0.8 mi. to Hobbs Ave. Campground entrance is on the right.

CHARLEMONT

Country Aire Campground

P.O. Box 289, Charlemont 01339. T: (413) 625-2996; www.country-aire-com; dfinn@valinet.com.

RV ★★★ Tent ★

Beauty: ★★★ Site Privacy: ★★
Spaciousness: ★★★★ Quiet: ★★★
Security: ★★★★ Cleanliness: ★★★★
Insect Control: ★★★ Facilities: ★★★

Located in the scenic, outdoorsy Berkshire Hills ("The Berkshires") in Western Massachusetts, Country Aire Campground is a pleasant, if slightly quirky, home away from home. The campground is set behind a motel and golf course, on a wide, grassy meadow bordered by trees. The Berkshire Hills provide a colorful backdrop in autumn. The Deerfield River is right across the street, a favorite destination for fly-fishing, paddling, and rafting. Seasonal sites (numerous) are at the rear and perimeter of the property, while transients are grouped toward the front. Sites are grassy, with a few pull-throughs. The tenting area is located in a separate, nicely shaded spot, not far from the pool. If you want to be away from the crowd, ask for RV sites 27–30, or one of the two tent sites to the left (not right) of the property, near the hiking trail. But you'll end up hanging with fellow campers at the rec hall, where you can order a treat at the snack bar, shoot some pool, or catch up on the latest news. Try one of Country Aire's own private-label vanilla sodas or sign up for the Halloween-in-Aug. party, when little gremlins go trick-or-treating at RVs. (See what we mean by quirky?)

BASICS

Operated By: Doug & Nancy Finn. **Open:** May 1–Dec. 1. **Site Assignment:** Reservations recommended. Deposit of one nights' stay required. Refund w/cancellation if within 7 days of scheduled stay, minus $5 service charge. **Registration:** At office. **Fee:** $20–$25 for two adults/two children. Extra adult, $6; extra child, $3. V, MC. **Parking:** At sites & designated areas.

FACILITIES

Number of RV Sites: 95. **Number of Tent-Only Sites:** 10. **Hookups:** Water, electric (20, 30, 50 amps), sewer, modem. **Each Site:** Picnic table, fire ring. **Dump Station:** Yes. **Laundry:** Yes. **Pay Phone:** Yes. **Rest Rooms and Showers:** Yes, coin-op. **Fuel:** No. **Propane:** Yes. **Internal Roads:** Gravel, good condition. **RV Service:** No. **Market:** 2 mi. west, in Charlemont. **Restaurant:** Yes. **General Store:** Yes. **Vending:** No. **Swimming Pool:** Yes. **Playground:** Yes. **Other:** Game room, picnic pavilion. **Activities:** Basketball, horseshoes, pool table, planned activities. **Nearby Attractions:** Bridge of Flowers, antiques, whitewater rafting & kayaking (Zoar Outdoors). **Additional Information:** Berkshire Hills Visitors Bureau, (413) 443-9186 or (800) 237-5747; www.berkshires.org.

RESTRICTIONS

Pets: Must be leashed, quiet, & cleaned up after. **Fires:** In fire rings only. **Alcoholic Beverages:** Yes. **Vehicle Maximum Length:** None. **Other:** Children under 16 must be accompanied by an adult while using the pool.

TO GET THERE

From I-91, take exit 26, Rte. 2 west, for 13 mi. Campground is on the right, directly behind the Oxbow Motel & Restaurant.

CHARLEMONT

Mohawk Trail State Forest

P.O. Box 7, Rte. 2, Charlemont 01339. T: (413) 339-5504; www.state.ma.us/dem/parks/mhwk.htm.

RV ★★ Tent ★★★★

Beauty: ★★★★ Site Privacy: ★★
Spaciousness: ★★★ Quiet: ★★
Security: ★★★ Cleanliness: ★★★
Insect Control: ★★ Facilities: ★★★

This rustic area, set in the Berkshire Hills in Western Massachusetts, is Bear Country. They've had bear sightings here, so it's wise to heed the advice on the bear flyer you get when you enter the park. The best campsites here are set on the banks of the Cold River. Snag one of these, and you can listen to the rushing water as you drift off to sleep (provided bear nightmares don't keep you awake). The sites are on gravel, and they are close together but buffered by trees. Campsites are set on two loops running alongside the river, with a little string of non-reservable sites at the end of the road. Of the non-reservable sites, numbers 15 through 22 are nice, and close to the river, while 18 and 41 are both good, roomy options for an RV. Sites 46 and 47 are dandy for tenters, with the advantage of an end-of-the-road location. The farther you head back from the river, though, the farther you get from Rte. 2 and the hum of traffic. Reserve a site numbered 23 through 35 if quiet, not water views, are your priority. The showers—just one set serves all, alas—are located near site 24. This is primarily a family camping area, but whitewater paddlers take over when the dam is released. Be sure to grab a trail map when you enter the park; this is a superb area for hiking, with good views from Totem Trail overlook.

Basics

Operated By: Massachusetts Forest & Park Service. **Open:** Mid-Apr.–mid-Oct. **Site Assignment:** Reservations recommended. Reserve up to six months in advance by calling ReserveAmerica at (877) 1-CAMP MA or on-line at www.reservamerica.com. Ten sites non-reservable, set aside for walk-ins on a first-come, first-served basis. To change arrival or departure date, or site type, call at least three days prior to arrival date. $10 cancellation/transfer fee. No refunds for amounts less than $5. **Registration:** At office. **Fee:** Massachusetts residents, $10; non-residents, $12. V, MC. **Parking:** At site.

Facilities

Number of RV Sites: 56. **Number of Tent-Only Sites:** 0. **Hookups:** None. **Each Site:** Picnic table, fireplace. **Dump Station:** No. **Laundry:** No. **Pay Phone:** Yes. **Rest Rooms and Showers:** Yes. **Fuel:** No. **Propane:** No. **Internal Roads:** Gravel, in good condition. **RV Service:** No. **Market:** 4 mi. east, in Charlemont. **Restaurant:** 20–24 mi. east or west, in Greenfield or North Adams. **General Store:** No. **Vending:** Yes. **Swimming Pool:** Yes. **Playground:** No. **Activities:** Canoeing, picnicking, hiking, fishing, swimming, interpretive programs. **Nearby Attractions:** Mass MOCA (Museum of Contemporary Art), Clark Art Museum, Natural Bridge, Bridge of Flowers. **Additional Information:** Berkshire Hills Visitors Bureau, (413) 443-9186 or (800) 237-5747; www.berkshires.org.

Restrictions

Pets: Must be leashed & cleaned up after. Must not be left unattended. Proof of rabies vaccination required. **Fires:** In fireplaces only. **Alcoholic Beverages:** No. **Vehicle Maximum Length:** 35 ft. **Other:** Maximum stay is 14 cumulative days between Memorial Day & Labor Day.

To Get There

From I-91, take Exit 26 (Rte. 2) west to Charlemont. Campground is 4 mi. west of Charlemont Center; entrance is on the right.

CHESTER

Walker Island Camping

No. 27 Rte. 20, Chester 01011. T: (413) 354-2295; shawn1221@aol.com.

RV ★★★★ Tent ★★

Beauty: ★★★	Site Privacy: ★★
Spaciousness: ★★★	Quiet: ★★★
Security: ★★	Cleanliness: ★★★
Insect Control: ★★	Facilities: ★★

This family-friendly campground is located in the Berkshire Hills region of Western Massachusetts. Dead-center in the place is, of all things, a small island, home to a mini golf course, a small beach, a slightly worse-for-wear kiddie playground, and a sports court for bocce, horseshoes, and shuffleboard. Trout-stocked Walker Brook flows around the island, and offers its own recreation possibilities, including fishing and tubing. The brook, abundant trees, and rocky ledges lend a serene aspect to an otherwise rather cluttery place. Campsites are set on three levels, becoming more "wild" the higher you go. On the upper level, campsites are tucked into ledges, offering plenty of seclusion. (Warning: the rest rooms are the non-flush type up there.) Site 68 is a super tent site if you like privacy, while RV sites 49 through 54, near the back entrance, are among the most inviting. There's a lot going on, plus kids everywhere, making this a very different scene than you'll encounter at one of the numerous state park camping areas in the region. Still, it's homey and easy-going.

Basics

Operated By: Shawn Myrick. **Open:** May 1–Oct. 31. **Site Assignment:** Reservations recommended. Deposit equal to one night's stay due w/ reservation. Deposits are refundable w/ min. of one week's notice. **Registration:** At office. **Fee:** $22–$27 for two people per night; extra adult is $5; extra child is $3. V, MC. **Parking:** At site.

Facilities

Number of RV Sites: 70. **Number of Tent-Only Sites:** 15. **Hookups:** Water, electric (30 amps), sewer, cable TV. **Each Site:** Picnic table, fire ring. **Dump Station:** Yes. **Laundry:** Yes. **Pay Phone:** Yes. **Rest Rooms and Showers:** Yes. **Fuel:** No. **Propane:** Yes. **Internal Roads:** Gravel, in good conditon. **RV Service:** No. **Market:** 25 mi. east or west. **Restaurant:** 3 mi. east. **General Store:** No. **Vending:** No. **Swimming Pool:** Yes. **Playground:** Yes. **Other:** Rec hall, game room, mini golf. **Activities:** Swimming, mini golf, tubing, shuffleboard, hiking, fishing, planned activities. **Nearby Attractions:** Norman Rockwell Museum, Tanglewood (music), Jacob's Pillow (dance), Six Flags New England theme park, waterfalls, summer theater, Chesterfield Gorge, golf, horseback riding, boating. **Additional Information:** Berkshire Hills Visitors Bureau, (413) 443-9186 or (800) 237-5747; www.berkshires.org.

Restrictions

Pets: Must be leashed, quiet, & cleaned up after. Must not be left unattended. **Fires:** Fireplaces only. **Alcoholic Beverages:** Yes. **Vehicle Maximum Length:** 40 ft. **Other:** Quiet hours are from 10:00 p.m. until 7:00 a.m.

To Get There

From I-90 (Massachusetts Turnpike), take Exit 3, turn right and proceed for 2 mi. Turn right onto Rte. 20, heading west. Follow Rte. 20 for 17 mi. to Chester. Campground entrance is on the right.

CLARKSBURG

Clarksburg State Park

Middle Rd., Clarksburg 01247. T: (413) 664-8345; www.state.ma.us/dem/parks/clsp.htm.

 ★★  ★★★★★

Beauty: ★★★★★	Site Privacy: ★★★★
Spaciousness: ★★★	Quiet: ★★★
Security: ★★	Cleanliness: ★★★★
Insect Control: ★★	Facilities: ★★★

Set in the far northwest corner of the state, nudging the Vermont border, this densely-forested camping area is beautiful, with secluded, well-spaced campsites. The good looks even extend to the rest rooms, which are nicely landscaped (with usable mirrors, a rarity at state parks) thanks to a recent park beautification program. One of the nicest features here is sparkling Mauserts Pond, a day-use area for swimming, fishing, and picnicking. Campsites are arrayed in a loop near the south end of the pond, but not directly on the waterfront. A scenic hiking trail skirts the pond, great for wildlife watching. The most enticing feature of this park may well be its proximity to the Appalachian Trail. Hikers come here when they want to trek the A.T. and Mt. Greylock (the highest point in the state), the park supervisor tells us. They prefer to camp here rather than at primitive Mt. Greylock so they can take advantage of creature comforts, like hot showers and running water. Only four sites are big enough for 36-footers, so plan ahead. Sites boasting excellent water views include 2, 4, 6, 8, 24, and 25.

Basics

Operated By: Massachusetts State Forests & Parks. **Open:** Memorial Day–Labor Day (perhaps later; call ahead). **Site Assignment:** Reservations may be made up to six months in advance by calling ReserveAmerica at (877) 1 CAMP-MA or online at www.reserveamerica.com. Ten sites are held for walk-ins on a first-come, first-served basis. To change arrival or departure date, or site type, call at least three days prior to arrival date. $10 cancellation/transfer fee. No refunds for amounts less than $5. **Registration:** At office. **Fee:** Mass. residents, $10; non-residents, $12. V, MC. **Parking:** At site.

Facilities

Number of RV Sites: 44. **Number of Tent-Only Sites:** 0. **Hookups:** None. **Each Site:** Picnic table, fireplace. **Dump Station:** No. **Laundry:** No. **Pay Phone:** Yes. **Rest Rooms and Showers:** Yes. **Fuel:** No. **Propane:** No. **Internal Roads:** Paved, in good condition. **RV Service:** No. **Market:** 3 mi. south, in North Adams. **Restaurant:** 3 mi. south, in North Adams. **General Store:** No. **Vending:** No. **Swimming Pool:** No. **Playground:** No. **Other:** Pavilion. **Activities:** Swimming, fishing, picnicking, hiking. **Nearby Attractions:** Mass MOCA (contemporary art museum), Appalachian Trail. **Additional Information:** Berkshire Hills Visitors Bureau, (413) 443-9186 or (800) 237-5747; www.berkshires.org.

Restrictions

Pets: Must be leashed & cleaned up after. Must not be left unattended. Proof of rabies vaccination required. **Fires:** Fireplaces only. **Alcoholic Beverages:** No. **Vehicle Maximum Length:** 36 ft. **Other:** Maximum stay of 14 cumulative days between Memorial Day & Labor Day.

To Get There

Follow Rte. 8 north to Middle Rd. in Clarksburg; follow signs.

DENNISPORT

Campers Haven RV Resort

184 Old Wharf Rd., Dennisport 02639. T: (508) 398-2811; F: (508) 398-3661; www.campershaven.com; camphvn@capecod.net.

RV ★★★ Tent n/a

Beauty: ★★ Site Privacy: ★★
Spaciousness: ★★ Quiet: ★★
Security: ★★★★★ Cleanliness: ★★★★
Insect Control: ★★★ Facilities: ★★

This mid-Cape campground, located on the beach road in Dennisport, has bragging rights to a major amenity: a private sandy beach on Nantucket Sound, right across the street from the campground. Never mind that it's a little, fenced-off thing—it's a beach, with a nice swath of swimmable water which, they say, averages a toasty 80 degrees in the summer. Beyond that, the campground offers open, grassy sites for RVs (no tenting), mostly back-in. Many sites are seasonal. Nice touch: If you're in a class A or class C motor home with no car in tow, they'll shuttle you to local restaurants and ferries. A plethora of planned activities, like sing-alongs and ice cream socials, plus an on-site snack bar, make this a destination park. But, all the attractions of Hyannis, the Cape's biggest town, are just 12 miles away. For all that, it plays to an older crowd. We'd suggest another Cape campground if you have kids in tow.

BASICS

Operated By: Paul & Elaine Peterson. **Open:** May 1–Columbus Day. **Site Assignment:** Reservations recommended. 50% deposit required. Reservations of two nights or less & holidays require payment in full in advance. Deposits for cancellations are refundable, minus a $15 service fee, w/ two weeks' notice. **Registration:** At office. **Fee:** $35–$42 per night for two adults & two children. July 4th & Labor Day weekend, $47 per night, three-night min. V, MC, AE. **Parking:** At sites or by permission only (w/extra charge.).

FACILITIES

Number of RV Sites: 262. **Number of Tent-Only Sites:** 0. **Hookups:** Water, electric (30, 50 amps), sewer, cable TV. **Each Site:** None. **Dump Station:** Yes. **Laundry:** Yes. **Pay Phone:** Yes. **Rest Rooms and Showers:** Yes. **Fuel:** No. **Propane:** No. **Internal Roads:** Paved, in good condition. **RV Service:** No. **Market:** 3 mi. west. **Restaurant:** Yes. **General Store:** Yes. **Vending:** No. **Swimming Pool:** No. **Playground:** Yes. **Other:** Rec hall (pavilion), mini-golf, adult clubhouse w/exercise equipment & hot tub. **Activities:** Swimming (private ocean beach), horseshoes, mini-golf, basketball, shuffleboard, bocce, planned activities. **Nearby Attractions:** JFK Hyannis Museum, Cape Cod Rail Trail, golf, fishing, ferries to islands. **Additional Information:** Cape Cod Chamber, (508) 862-0700 or (888) 33-CAPECOD; www.cape chamber.org.

RESTRICTIONS

Pets: No dogs allowed June 25 to Labor Day. Limit one dog per site when allowed. No outdoor cats. **Fires:** No campfires. **Alcoholic Beverages:** Yes. **Vehicle Maximum Length:** 40 ft. **Other:** No smoking in any of the buildings.

TO GET THERE

Take Rte. 6 to Exit 8. Turn right onto Rte. 134 and go to the end. Turn left onto Lower County Rd. and go 0.5 mi. to Old Wharf Rd. (Look closely; signs are on stone road posts and devilishly hard to read.) Turn right and go 1 mi. to campground, on left.

EAST FALMOUTH

Cape Cod Campresort

176 Thomas Landers Rd., East Falmouth 02536. T: (508) 548-1458; www.resortcamplands.com.

RV ★★★ Tent ★★★

Beauty: ★★★ Site Privacy: ★★
Spaciousness: ★★★ Quiet: ★★★
Security: ★★★★★ Cleanliness: ★★★
Insect Control: ★★ Facilities: ★★★

This campground is actually three entities: a camping club, a camping co-op with some transient and seasonal sites, and the Cape Cod Campresort, with sites available specifically for transient use. Everybody shares the amenities, including a swimming pool, kiddie pool, and clubhouse; otherwise, everybody sticks to their area (marked by signage.) There's a small beach, with a swimming area, on Round Pond. It's a nice-looking place, with campsites nestled in cool pines. Sites are grassy and back-in, carpeted with pine needles. The tenting area is off to one side, just to the right of the office, with tents clustered in a pine grove off a skinny gravel road. Tent site E is especially nice. Among the RV sites, 98 and 99 are very private and set off the road. Site 76 is a winner, too, backed up into the woods. There's not much buffer between campsites. Another quibble: where are the umbrellas alongside the well-used pool area? Compared to nearby Sippewissett Campground (see listing), this one offers more activities for families and a bit more breathing room.

BASICS

Operated By: Cape Cod Campresort. **Open:** Apr. 15–Oct. 15. **Site Assignment:** Reservations recommended. 30% deposit required. No refunds for cancellations occuring 7 days or less prior to scheduled arrival date. **Registration:** At office. **Fee:** $28–$34 based on two people. Extra adult, $6 per night; extra child under age 15, $3 per night. V, MC. **Parking:** At sites & designated parking lots only.

FACILITIES

Number of RV Sites: 200. **Number of Tent-Only Sites:** 0. **Hookups:** Water, electric (30, 50 amps), sewer. **Each Site:** Picnic table, fireplace. **Dump Station:** Yes. **Laundry:** No. **Pay Phone:** Yes. **Rest Rooms and Showers:** Yes. **Fuel:** No. **Propane:** No. **Internal Roads:** Gravel, in good condition. **RV Service:** No. **Market:** 2 mi. east. **Restaurant:** 5 mi. east. **General Store:** Yes. **Vending:** Yes. **Swimming Pool:** Yes. **Playground:** Yes. **Other:** Rec hall. **Activities:** Ball field, swimming, horseshoes, boating (boat rentals). **Nearby Attractions:** Ferries to Martha's Vineyard, Woods Hole aquarium, ocean beaches, Nobska Lighthouse, golf. **Additional Information:** Cape Cod Chamber, (508) 862-0700 or (888) 33-CAPECOD; www.capecodchamber.org.

RESTRICTIONS

Pets: Must be leashed, quiet, & cleaned up after. Proof of rabies vaccination required. $3 charge per day. **Fires:** In fire rings only. **Alcoholic Beverages:** Yes. **Vehicle Maximum Length:** None. Over 30 ft. incurs extra charge of $1 per ft. per night. **Other:** All visitors must register upon entering the park.

TO GET THERE

From Bourne Bridge, take Rte. 28S (second turn off rotary) to next rotary; continue on 28S, then take second exit to Thomas Landers Rd. Take left off ramp. Campground is exactly 2.7 mi. on the right.

EASTHAM

Atlantic Oaks

3700 Rte. 6, Eastham 02642. T: (508) 255-1437 or (800) 332-2267; F: (508) 247-8216; www.capecamp ing.com.

RV ★★★ Tent ★

Beauty: ★★ Site Privacy: ★★
Spaciousness: ★★ Quiet: ★★★
Security: ★★★★★ Cleanliness: ★★★★
Insect Control: ★★★★ Facilities: ★★

Atlantic Oaks, owned by the same family who operates Shady Knoll in Brewster, is located in the town of Eastham on Cape Cod. Eastham is known for its working windmill (visible from Rte. 6), First Encounter Beach (where the pilgrims met the native Wampanoags), and Cape Cod National Seashore's Salt Pond Visitor Center, just one half-mile from the campground. If you're traveling in a big rig, and want to be near the seashore, this one fills the bill. The Cape Cod Rail Trail bike path runs just behind the property. Alas, a motel with a pool and tennis courts is also adjacent to the property; not good if you're traveling with kids, who might be tempted to trespass! Campsites are semi-shaded, on gravel; many are pull-thrus. Theres's not much buffer between sites, though. The prettiest sites back up against the woods and bike trail. These include sites C8, B8, A8, and P4. The T area, off Pine St. , is best for tents. All the basics are covered here. While there's not a lot of atmosphere, the location is great.

BASICS

Operated By: Dave & Donna Nussdorfer. **Open:** May 1–Nov. 1. **Site Assignment:** Reservations recommended. 50% deposit required for stays of 5 days or more; all other reservations must be prepaid. No refunds without 14 days' notice. $10 service charge applies to cancellations. Checks OK for advance reservations. Reservations recommended. **Registration:** At office. **Fee:** $30–$42 for two people. Extra unmarried child age 6-18, $2 per night; extra child age 5 & under, free. Extra adult, $7.50 per night. V, MC, D. **Parking:** At site.

FACILITIES

Number of RV Sites: 100. **Number of Tent-Only Sites:** 0. **Hookups:** Water, electric (30 amps), sewer, cable TV. **Each Site:** Picnic table. **Dump Station:** Yes. **Laundry:** Yes. **Pay Phone:** Yes. **Rest Rooms and Showers:** Yes. **Fuel:** No. **Propane:** Yes. **Internal Roads:** Gravel, in good condition. **RV**

Service: No. **Market:** 4.5 mi. north. **Restaurant:** 0.25 mi. west. **General Store:** Yes. **Vending:** No. **Swimming Pool:** No. **Playground:** Yes. **Other:** Rec room. **Activities:** Horseshoes, bicycling, nightly movies (summer). **Nearby Attractions:** Cape Cod National Seashore Visitor Center, ocean beaches, Cape Cod Rail Trail. **Additional Information:** Cape Cod Chamber of Commerce, (508) 862-0700 or (888) 33-CAPECOD; www.capecodchamber.org.

Restrictions

Pets: Must be leashed & cleaned up after. Must not be left unattended. **Fires:** No open fires. Charcoal grills & campstoves may be used w/caution. **Alcoholic Beverages:** Yes. **Vehicle Maximum Length:** None. **Other:** Minimum stay required for all weekends in July & Aug.

To Get There

From Sagamore Bridge, follow Rte. 6 past the Orleans rotary. Atlantic Oaks is 4 mi. east past rotary, on the left.

ERVING

Erving State Forest

200 East Main St., Erving 01344. T: (978) 544-3939 or (978) 544-7745; www.state.ma.us/dem/parks/ ervf.htm.

RV: ★★ Tent: ★★★

Beauty: ★★★★	Site Privacy: ★★
Spaciousness: ★★	Quiet: ★★★
Security: ★★★	Cleanliness: ★★★★
Insect Control: ★★	Facilities: ★★

Great find: a camping area that stays open into Oct., for the leaf-peeping crowd. The Mohawk Trail is great route for fall color tours, so this campground couldn't be handier. Right off Rte. 2, it's got a great approach: a winding, tree-lined road bordered with lush ferns. Gravel sites are set on both sides of Camp Rd., backed by forest. The centerpiece of the state park is pretty Laurel Lake, stocked with brook trout. There are a few private cottages on the waterfront, but no campsites; campers stay at sites on the other side of the main road, and walk a short distance to picnic areas along the shore. There's a nice beach for campers, and a big buoyed swimming area, complete with lifeguards (sometimes!) Campsites here are not as nice as the surrounding area, but they're adequate, mostly measuring 30 by 30 feet, with mature trees as a buffer between them. Sites 11 and 12 offer a good amount of privacy, since they're spaced far apart. A nice feature here: engaging interpretive programs, such as "Serpent Session" (local snakes) and "Beginnng Birding." A not-so-nice feature: No showers—that's why this park charges only $5 or $6 per night. This may change, however. It is rumored that showers will be coming, if the budget allows. Stay tuned.

Basics

Operated By: Massachusetts State Forests & Parks. **Open:** May–Oct. **Site Assignment:** Reservations may be made up to six months in advance by calling ReserveAmerica at (877) I CAMP-MA or online at www.reserveamerica.com. Ten sites are held for walk-ins on a first-come, first-served basis. To change arrival or departure date, or site type, call at least three days prior to arrival date. $10 cancellation/transfer fee. No refunds for amounts less than $5. **Registration:** At office. **Fee:** Massachusetts residents, $5; non-residents, $6. V, MC. **Parking:** At site.

Facilities

Number of RV Sites: 29. **Number of Tent-Only Sites:** 0. **Hookups:** None. **Each Site:** Picnic table, fireplace. **Dump Station:** No. **Laundry:** No. **Pay Phone:** Yes. **Rest Rooms and Showers:** Yes (non-flush), no showers. **Fuel:** No. **Propane:** No. **Internal Roads:** Paved, in good condition. **RV Service:** No. **Market:** 5 mi. east or west. **Restaurant:** 5 mi. east or west. **General Store:** No. **Vending:** No. **Swimming Pool:** No. **Playground:** No. **Other:** Boat ramp, nature center. **Activities:** Swimming, hiking, boating, fishing (need MA license, available at Wal-Mart in Orange), interpretive programs. **Nearby Attractions:** Mohawk Trail scenic drive, Bridge of Flowers (Shelburne), Historic Deerfield. **Additional Information:** Mohawk Trail Assocation, (413) 743-8127; www.mohawktrail.com.

Restrictions

Pets: Must be leashed & cleaned up after. Must not be left unattended. Proof of rabies vaccination required. **Fires:** In fireplaces only. **Alcoholic Beverages:** No. **Vehicle Maximum Length:** 30 ft. **Other:** Maximum stay is 14 cumulative days between Memorial Day & Labor Day.

To Get There

Take Rte. 2 west to Erving Center. Take immediate left on Church St., exit right, and follow signs.

FALMOUTH

Sippewissett Campground and Cabins

836 Palmer Ave., Falmouth 02540. T: (508) 548-2542 or (800) 957-CAMP; www.sippewissett.com; campcapecod@aol.com.

RV: ★★★ Tent: ★★★★

Beauty: ★★★★	Site Privacy: ★★
Spaciousness: ★★	Quiet: ★★★
Security: ★★★★★	Cleanliness: ★★★
Insect Control: ★★★	Facilities: ★★★

You know you're on Cape Cod when your campground will lend you a lobster pot and lobster crackers, and give you an impromptu lesson on how to boil 'em! It happens here, where the main drawing card (aside from lobster lessons) is close proximity to salt water beaches (one mile away) and ferry boats to Martha's Vineyard. They'll shuttle you to the beach, and ferry dock, for free. They'll also sell you tickets for the ferry. Same price, but less waiting in line at the boat docks. This is the closest campground to the ferry and Wood's Hole. Trivia note: Falmouth is the home of "America the Beautiful" author Katherine Lee Bates. The campground is a quiet, family place, and it feels a bit crowded, except outside the main clusters of campsites. Sites numbered 60 through 64 are most popular, but we prefer the more woodsy and spacious sites 122 through 125. Sites 99 through 103 are pretty, too.

Basics

Operated By: Tessier family. **Open:** May 15–Oct. 15. **Site Assignment:** Reservations recommended. 50% deposit required. Balance is due 30 days prior to arrival date. Checks OK. Full refunds for cancellations made 20 days prior to scheduled arrival date. No refunds for less than 20 day notice. **Registration:** At office. **Fee:** $30–$32 for two people; same rate for families, w/one or two parents & children under age 21. V, MC. **Parking:** At site.

Facilities

Number of RV Sites: 120. **Number of Tent-Only Sites:** 0. **Hookups:** Water, electric (20 amps). **Each Site:** Picnic table, fire ring. **Dump Station:** Yes. **Laundry:** Yes. **Pay Phone:** Yes. **Rest Rooms and Showers:** Yes. **Fuel:** No. **Propane:** No. **Internal Roads:** Gravel, in fair condition. **RV Service:** No. **Market:** 2 mi. south. **Restaurant:** 2 mi. south. **General Store:** Yes. **Vending:** Yes. **Swimming Pool:** No. **Playground:** Yes. **Other:** Rec room. **Activities:** Volleyball. **Nearby Attractions:** Ocean beaches (free shuttles), ferry to Martha's Vineyard, golf, Nobska Lighthouse, Woods Hole aquarium. **Additional Information:** Cape Cod Chamber of Commerce, (508) 862-0700 or (888) 33-CAPECOD; www.capecodchamber.org.

Restrictions

Pets: No dogs. **Fires:** In fire rings only. **Alcoholic Beverages:** Yes. **Vehicle Maximum Length:** 30 ft. **Other:** No animals in cabins.

To Get There

From junction of Rte. 6 and Rte. 28, head south 12.5 mi. on Rte. 28 to Sippewissett exit (Palmer Ave.). Exit right and make immediate left at blinking yellow light. Go 0.5 mi. to campground entrance, on the right.

FOXBORO

Normandy Farms Family Camping Resort

72 West St., Foxboro 02035. T: (508) 543-7600; F: (508) 543-7667; www.normandyfarms.com; camp@normandyfarms.com.

RV: ★★★★★ Tent: ★★★

Beauty: ★★★★★	Site Privacy: ★★★
Spaciousness: ★★★★	Quiet: ★★★★★
Security: ★★★★	Cleanliness: ★★★★
Insect Control: ★★★★★	Facilities: ★★★★★

Wow. The facilities at this four-season camping resort are really something. The timber-beamed rec center is reminiscent of a ski lodge, complete with an 18-plus adult loft and arcade. The lodge overlooks a lovely pool area with two pools. Elsewhere, there's yet another pool and two hot tubs. Campsites are, mostly, located in an open, grassy field, beautifully landscaped and surrounded by woods. The nicest full hookup sites, backing up into the woods, are 801 through 807, 901 through 908, and 1001 through 1008. Test sites are shaded, and set around the perimeter of the park. Best tent sites are T1 through T10, located near the fishing pond. Anywhere, though, there's not much privacy for tenters. This place speaks more to the RVer who's looking for some frills, not a wilderness-seeking tenter. There are lots of daily activities going on in the summer, and during holiday weekends all year, from an Elvis Tribute to ice cream socials. Most of these are free. (Free swim lessons and free water aerobics classes are a nice touch.) The campground runs guided bus trips to the Cape and Boston (30 miles south), very popular with campers.

Basics

Operated By: Daniels family. **Open:** All year. **Site Assignment:** Reservations recommended. May be made by phone, mail, email, or on-line. Reservations line opens Mar. 15 for bookings for the following year. For holidays, book one year in advance; for summer weekends, book at least one month in advance. Two-day min. stay required on weekends; three-to-four day stay required on holiday weekends. Deposit is required within 3 weeks of reservation; secure w/cash, traveler's checks, checks, or credit cards. Refunds for cancellation received one week prior to scheduled arrival date. **Registration:** At office. **Fee:** $32–$48 (late May to Labor Day). V, MC, D. **Parking:** At sites & designated lots only.

Facilities

Number of RV Sites: 400. **Number of Tent-Only Sites:** 23. **Hookups:** Water, electric (20, 30, 50 amps), sewer. **Each Site:** Picnic table, fire ring. **Dump Station:** Yes. **Laundry:** Yes. **Pay Phone:** Yes. **Rest Rooms and Showers:** Yes. **Fuel:** No. **Propane:** Yes. **Internal Roads:** Paved, in good condition. **RV Service:** Yes. **Market:** 6 mi. east, in Mansfield. **Restaurant:** Yes. **General Store:** Yes. **Vending:** Yes. **Swimming Pool:** Yes (3). **Playground:** Yes. **Other:** Hot tubs, rec lodge, 18-hole frisbee golf course. **Activities:** Guided tours to Boston, Plymouth, & Cape Cod, swimming, fishing, volleyball, basketball, soccer field, horseshoes, basketball, planned activities. **Nearby Attractions:** Tweeter Center for the Performing Arts (concerts), CMGI Stadium (football), Edaville Railroad, Plimoth Plantation, Cranberry World Visitors Center, Pilgrim Hall Museum. **Additional Information:** Plymouth County CVB, (508) 747-0100 or (800) 231-1620; www.plymouth-1620.com.

Restrictions

Pets: Must be leashed & cleaned up after. May not be left unattended. **Fires:** In fire rings only. **Alcoholic Beverages:** Yes. **Vehicle Maximum Length:** 45 ft. **Other:** Visitors must pay a fee & are not allowed to bring their pets in.

To Get There

From Boston, take I-93 south to Exit 1, then I-95 south to Exit 9. Take Rte. 1 south for 6.7 mi. to Thurston St. Turn left onto Thurston. Campground is 1.4 mi. on the right.

GLOUCESTER

Cape Ann Camp Site

80 Atlantic St., Gloucester 01930. T: (978) 283-8683; F: (978) 283-5976; www.capeann.com/campsite.

RV: ★★★★ Tent: ★★★

Beauty: ★★★★★ Site Privacy: ★★★★
Spaciousness: ★★★★ Quiet: ★★★★
Security: ★★★ Cleanliness: ★★★
Insect Control: ★★ Facilities: ★★★

Located about an hour's drive north of Boston, this coastal campground overlooks the Jones River salt marsh and the briny bays of the Atlantic Ocean. Salt air, sand dunes, and sea oats beckon at Wingaersheek Beach, a mile away. The lower area of the campground is reserved for sizable RVs; beyond that, a series of loop roads winds up a hill through a woodsy, boulder-studded camping area. Designated areas are set aside for tent campers. Secluded site 330 is a superb choice for tenters, offering the ultimate room-with-a-view: a footpath leads to a rocky ledge with sweeping views of the river, estuaries, and East Gloucester shoreline. For smaller RVs, the electricity-only sites 215E to 217E are pleasant and out-of-the-way. Don't expect much in the way of amenities here; it's just the basics. But the campground's natural beauty, and its superb location, makes up for the lack of frills. During the day, everyone heads out to the beach, or to take in the sights on Cape Ann. Among the options: Gloucester's Rocky Neck, the oldest artists' colony in America, and the arts-flavored town of Rockport—home of the most-painted, most-photographed, fishing shack anywhere, Motif #1.

Basics

Operated By: Matz family. **Open:** May 1–Nov. 1. **Site Assignment:** Reservations recommended. Reserve by phone beginning in Apr. $30 deposit due w/ reservation. Personal checks accepted for deposit only. **Registration:** At office. **Fee:** $20–$28 per day, per car, up to 2 people. Additional person, $1-$6 per day. V, MC. **Parking:** At sites only. 1 vehicle per site.

Facilities

Number of RV Sites: 125. **Number of Tent-Only Sites:** 125. **Hookups:** Water, electric (30, 50 amps), sewer. **Each Site:** Picnic table, fireplace. **Dump Station:** Yes. **Laundry:** No. **Pay Phone:** Yes. **Rest Rooms and Showers:** Yes, coin op. **Fuel:** No. **Propane:** No. **Internal Roads:** Paved & gravel, good conditon. **RV Service:** No. **Market:** 0.5 mi. west. **Restaurant:** 2 mi. south off Rte. 128. **General Store:** Yes. **Vending:** No. **Swimming Pool:** No. **Playground:** No. **Other:** Metered showers, modem in a central location. **Activities:** Swimming at ocean beach, saltwater fishing (no license needed), bike riding. **Nearby Attractions:** Wingaersheek Beach (1 mi. east; discounted parking permit available at campground office), Hammond Castle Museum, whale-watching boat trips, antiquing, Bearskin Neck artists' colony. **Additional Information:** North of Boston CVB, (978) 977-7760 or (800) 742-5306; www.northofboston.org.

Restrictions

Pets: Must be leashed, quiet, & cleaned up after. Must have rabies vaccination certificate. **Fires:** In fireplaces only. **Alcoholic Beverages:** At sites only. **Vehicle Maximum Length:** 45 ft. **Other:** 3-night min. stay for Fri. arrivals, from June 15 through Labor Day. 2-night min. stay for Sat. arrivals during same time period. May require 4-day min. on July 4th & Labor Day weekends. Walk-ins OK if space is available.

To Get There

Take Rte. 129 North to Exit 13. Go northeast on Concord St. for 0.7 mi., then turn right onto Atlantic St. Campground is located 0.5 mi. east; entrance is on the left.

GRANVILLE

Prospect Mountain Campground

P.O. Box 323, 1349 Main Rd., Granville 01034. T: (413) 357-6494; F: (413) 357-6373; www.prospectmtncampground.com; info@prospect mtncampground.com.

RV: ★★★ Tent: ★★★

Beauty: ★★★ Site Privacy: ★★★★
Spaciousness: ★★★★ Quiet: ★★★★★
Security: ★★★ Cleanliness: ★★★★
Insect Control: ★★ Facilities: ★★★★

Located in the rural town of Granville, southwest of Springfield and nudging the Connecticut border, this is a handy base camp for area attractions. Six Flags New England, the region's largest theme park, is a half-hour drive east, and the campground offers good discounts on admission tickets. ($14 off adult ticket prices, at press time.) Sodom Mountain Campground, in Southwick (see listing), is closer, and they, too, offer steeply-discounted tickets to Six Flags. The trade-off here: impeccably-maintained facilities, with nice touches like tent platforms, a nice kiddie playscape, private, bug-free (!) showers, and umbrellaed tables around the swimming pool. Instead of mountain hiking, a la Sodom Mountain, this campground has walking trails, and really gets into the theme stuff, with pig roasts and "Survivor" weekends. The campground boasts a nice spot, at a 1300-foot elevation, with lots of trees and two fishing ponds. The gravel sites are set in loops, with tent sites set at the far end of the property. Tent site T15, on Gaintner Pond, is nice, while the water and electric sites along Peter's Pond, especially sites 64 and 65, are inviting.

Basics

Operated By: Ann Schlosser. **Open:** May 1–Oct. 15. **Site Assignment:** Reservations recommended. 50% deposit required on credit card. No-shows will be charged. Refunds for cancellations w/ two weeks' notice. **Registration:** At office. **Fee:** $24–$28 for two adults & two children. V, MC, AE, D. **Parking:** At site.

Facilities

Number of RV Sites: 200. **Number of Tent-Only Sites:** 0. **Hookups:** Water, electric (30, 50 amps), sewer. **Each Site:** Picnic table, fire ring. **Dump Station:** Yes. **Laundry:** Yes. **Pay Phone:** Yes. **Rest Rooms and Showers:** Yes. **Fuel:** No. **Propane:** Yes. **Internal Roads:** Gravel, in good condition. **RV Service:** No. **Market:** 11 mi. east, in Southwick. **Restaurant:** 11 mi. east, in Southwick. **General Store:** Yes. **Vending:** Yes. **Swimming Pool:** Yes. **Playground:** Yes. **Other:** Rec hall. **Activities:** Swimming, volleyball, basketball, nature trail, paddleboats, planned activities, themed weekends. **Nearby Attractions:** Six Flags New England theme park, Basketball Hall of Fame, Southwick Motocrosse 338, Big E (Eastern States Exposition) fair, late Sept. **Additional Information:** Greater Springfield CVB, (413) 755-1343; www.valleyvisitor.com.

Restrictions

Pets: Must be leashed, quiet, & cleaned up after. Must not be left unattended. Not allowed in cabins or rental trailers. **Fires:** In fire rings only. **Alcoholic Beverages:** At sites only. **Vehicle Maximum Length:** 40 ft. **Other:** Three-night min. stay required on holidays.

To Get There

Take I-90 (Massachusetts Turnpike) to Exit 3, Westfield. Turn right onto Rtes. 10 and 202, follow into Southwick Center. In town, take a right at second light onto Rte. 57 west. Follow Rte. 57 into center of Granville (6.5 mi.) Continue on 57W for another 4.1 mi. Campground is directly off Rte. 57, on the left.

HINGHAM

Wompatuck State Park

Union St., Hingham 02043. T: (781) 749-7160; www.state.ma.us/dem/parks/womp.htm.

RV ★★★★ Tent ★★★★

Beauty: ★★★	Site Privacy: ★★★★★
Spaciousness: ★★★	Quiet: ★★★★
Security: ★★★★	Cleanliness: ★
Insect Control: ★★★★	Facilities: ★★★

This is the closest campground to Boston where campers can enjoy a wilderness experience. Located on the South Shore of Massachusetts, about 19 miles from the city, Wompatuck State Park is a favorite of cycling enthusiasts. The park offers 10 miles of paved bike paths and another 30 miles or so of unpaved multiuse (bike, hike, horseback) trails, winding through lush forests and alongside freshwater ponds. Campsites are set in two areas, one with electric hookups (Camping Area 2), one without (Camping Area 1). Sites along the perimeter road, backed by woodlands, offer the most privacy, especially C-1 through C-14 (with electric hookups). Nearby, sites E-15, 17, and 19, are also nice, and near the rest rooms. In general, the sites in Camping Area 2 are set back farther from the road, more shaded, and more secluded than those in Area 1. Tent campers can use either one. A nice feature of this park is the abundance of fresh water, available at stone washbasins and water fountains scattered throughout the park. There's also collectible spring water, available at Mt. Blue Spring. (Avoid heavily-trafficked campsite X-9, nearest the hiking trail to the spring.) A not-so-nice feature: the rest rooms, where a recent visit revealed missing mirrors, overflowing waste cans and a lack of toilet paper.

Basics

Operated By: Massachusetts State Forests & Parks. **Open:** Mid-Apr.–mid-Oct. **Site Assignment:** Reservations recommended. Reserve up to six months in advance by calling ReserveAmerica at (877) 1-CAMP-MA or online at www.reservamerica.com. Sixty-five sites are non-reservable & held on a first-come, first-served basis. To change arrival or departure date, or site type, call at least three dayas prior to arrival date. $10 cancellation/transfer fee. No refunds for amounts less than $5. **Registration:** At office. **Fee:** Massachusetts residents, $10–$13; non-residents, $12–$15. V, MC. **Parking:** At site.

Facilities

Number of RV Sites: 400. **Number of Tent-Only Sites:** 0. **Hookups:** Electric (20 amps). **Each Site:** Picnic table, fireplace w/ grill top. **Dump Station:** Yes. **Laundry:** No. **Pay Phone:** Yes. **Rest Rooms and Showers:** Yes. **Fuel:** No. **Propane:** No. **Internal Roads:** Paved, in good condition. **RV Service:** No. **Market:** 2.5 mi. north. **Restaurant:** 3.5 mi. north. **General Store:** No. **Vending:** Yes. **Swimming Pool:** No. **Playground:** No. **Other:** Boat ramp. **Activities:** Hiking, bicycling, mountain biking, interpretive programs. **Nearby Attractions:** Boston attractions, golf, South Shore Music Circus (outdoor concerts). **Additional Information:** Greater Boston CVB, (617) 536-4100 or (888) SEE-BOSTON; www.bostonusa.com.

Restrictions

Pets: Must be leashed & cleaned up after. Must not be left unattended. Proof of rabies vaccination required. **Fires:** In fireplaces only. **Alcoholic Beverages:** No. **Vehicle Maximum Length:** 35 ft. **Other:** Two-night min. stay required between Memorial Day & Labor Day. Maximum stay is 14 cumulative days between Memorial Day & Labor Day. No swimming.

To Get There

Follow Rte. 35 to Exit 14; then take Rte. 228 north (left) into Hingham. Turn right on Free St. to campground entrance.

LANESBOROUGH

Hidden Valley Campground

15 Scott Rd., P.O. Box 700, Lanesborough 01237. T: (413) 447-9419 or (877) 392-2267; F: (413) 447-3775; www.campmass.com; hdnvaly@bcn.net.

RV ★★★ Tent ★★★

Beauty: ★★★	Site Privacy: ★★★
Spaciousness: ★★★	Quiet: ★★★
Security: ★★	Cleanliness: ★★★★
Insect Control: ★★★	Facilities: ★★★★

This rural area of the western Berkshires is generously endowed with state parks, but not so rich with good commercial campgrounds. Hidden Valley, nestled at the base of Mt. Greylock, is a happy exception. This campground offers a bit of a natural look (arguably, too natural in spots, where fallen trees interfere with tenting sites), with plentiful trees and big boulders, along with some extras. These include live entertainment, and an inviting rec hall with a wide-screen TV, piano, and ping-pong table. The crowd is mostly seasonal, but 24 to 30 sites are available for transient guests. Unusual and welcoming touches include a full-length mirror and lots of hooks in the rest room; also, tent sites are marked off with logs, and raised on six inches of beach sand, a good move, since water seeps away when it rains. Nice tent sites include numbers 6 and 7, set back with dense tree cover. Numbers 29 and 48 are pretty, secluded RV sites. This campground offers a good blend of amenities and woodsy appeal.

Basics

Operated By: DiLego family. **Open:** May 1–Oct. 31 (may stay open all year; call to check). **Site Assignment:** Reservations recommended; may reserve on-line. Must pay in full when making reservation. A credit card will hold reservation, but no-shows will be charged. Checks accepted for payment if received at least 30 days prior to arrival. Refunds for cancellations made 21 days or more prior to arrival, minus $15 fee. **Registration:** At office. **Fee:** $23, RVs; $18, tents. Rates based on two adults & two children under the age of 18. V, MC, D. **Parking:** At site.

Facilities

Number of RV Sites: 90. **Number of Tent-Only Sites:** 20. **Hookups:** Water, electric (20, 30 amps). **Each Site:** Picnic table, fireplace. **Dump Station:** Yes. **Laundry:** Yes. **Pay Phone:** Yes. **Rest Rooms and Showers:** Yes, coin-op. **Fuel:** No. **Propane:** Yes. **Internal Roads:** Gravel, in fair condition. **RV Service:** No. **Market:** Within 2 mi. south. **Restaurant:** Yes (snack bar). **General Store:** Yes. **Vending:** Yes. **Swimming Pool:** Yes. **Playground:** Yes. **Other:** Rec hall. **Activities:** Swimming, fishing (in private pond), horseshoes, planned activities. **Nearby Attractions:** Tanglewood, Hancock Shaker Village, Mt. Greylock, Norman Rockwell Museum, Mass MOCA (contemporary art), Clark Art Institute, Jacob's Pillow (dance), golf. **Additional Information:** Berkshire Hills Visitors Bureau, (413) 443-9186 or (800) 237-5747; www.berkshires.org.

Restrictions

Pets: 1 pet per RV site. Pets not allowed at tent sites. **Fires:** In fireplaces only. **Alcoholic Beverages:** Yes. **Vehicle Maximum Length:** 38 ft. (5 sites available for big rigs). **Other:** Three-night min. stay on holiday weekends.

To Get There

From Williamstown (Rte. 2), take Rte. 7 south to Lanesborough, 9 mi. Go 3 mi. to the blue camper sign; make an extreme left-hand turn onto N. Main St. Follow for 0.7 mi., then bear left onto Scott Rd. Follow 0.3 mi. to campground.

LEE

October Mountain State Forest

317 Woodland Rd., Lee 01238. T: (413) 243-1778; www.state.ma.us/dem/parks/octm.htm.

RV ★★★ Tent ★★★

Beauty: ★★	Site Privacy: ★★★
Spaciousness: ★★★	Quiet: ★★
Security: ★★★	Cleanliness: ★★★
Insect Control: ★★	Facilities: ★★★

Set on a sunny hillside in the center of Berkshire County, this campground is a good base for enjoying the area's numerous cultural attractions. Tanglewood Music Festival is just six miles away, so this campground offers visitors the chance to hear music under the stars, then return to the park to sleep under the stars (well, sort of!) October Mountain also boasts several miles of hiking paths, including a section of the famous Appalachian Trail. A favorite footpath leads to Schermerhorn Gorge; others lead to lakes and (minor) mountain summits. Trailer sites are set in a loop near the campground entrance. These are mostly open, level, and grassy, with just a bit of shade. Tent sites are grouped together on the second level of the camping area. Site 47 is very secluded, and close to the rest room, and site 40 is also a good, end-of-the-road spot. Stay clear of site 34, on the third level, where an old tank detracts from the beauty of the space. One downside of this park: off-road vehicles are allowed to use the multi-use trails. They're gone by evening, so this shouldn't disturb anyone's sleep. Also, a nearby power plant makes a humming noise. This is most audible near the entrance of the park and the trailer sites, and shouldn't bother tenters, who are sited farther back on the second and third levels of the park. (Trivia note: October Mountain is the largest state forest in Massachusetts.)

BASICS

Operated By: Massachusetts State Forests & Parks. **Open:** Mid-May–mid-Oct. **Site Assignment:** Reservations may be made up to six months in advance by calling ReserveAmerica at (877) I CAMP-MA or online at www.reserveamerica.com. Ten sites are held for walk-ins on a first-come, first-served basis. To change arrival or departure date, or site type, call at least three days prior to arrival date. $10 cancellation/transfer fee. No refunds for amounts less than $5. **Registration:** At office. **Fee:** Massachusetts residents, $10; non-residents, $12 V, MC. **Parking:** At site.

FACILITIES

Number of RV Sites: 50. **Number of Tent-Only Sites:** 0. **Hookups:** None. **Each Site:** Picnic table, fireplace. **Dump Station:** Yes. **Laundry:** No. **Pay Phone:** Yes. **Rest Rooms and Showers:** Yes. **Fuel:** No. **Propane:** No. **Internal Roads:** Paved, in good condition. **RV Service:** No. **Market:** 2 mi. east, in Lee. **Restaurant:** 2 mi. east, in Lee. **General Store:** No. **Vending:** No. **Swimming Pool:** No. **Playground:** No. **Other:** Boat ramp. **Activities:** Hiking, fishing, ATV riding. **Nearby Attractions:** Tanglewood, Jacob's Pillow (dance). **Additional Information:** Berkshire Hills Visitors Bureau, (413) 443-9186 or (800) 237-5747; www.berkshires.org.

RESTRICTIONS

Pets: Must be leashed & cleaned up after. Must not be left unattended. Proof of rabies vaccination required. **Fires:** In fireplaces only. **Alcoholic Beverages:** No. **Vehicle Maximum Length:** 35 ft. **Other:** Pets are not allowed in buildings.

TO GET THERE

From I-90 (Massachusetts Turnpike), take Exit 2, Rte. 20 west. Turn right on Center St., follow signs.

LITTLETON

Boston Northwest/Minuteman KOA

P.O. Box 2122, Littleton 01460. T: (978) 772-0042 or (800) 562-7606 (reservations); F: (978) 772-9332; www.minutemancampground.com; minuteman@ ma.ultranet.com.

 ★★★★ ▲ ★★★★

Beauty: ★★★★★ Site Privacy: ★★★
Spaciousness: ★★★ Quiet: ★★★
Security: ★★★★ Cleanliness: ★★★★★
Insect Control: ★★★ Facilities: ★★★★

A scenic drive, it's not. As you head west on Rte. 2-A, a quarry-lined industrial corridor, you may well be wondering why you'd ever consider camping in such an unlikely area. Then, you spot the KOA sign, and pull into a road flanked by tall white pines. Trees never looked so good! And so it is at Boston Northwest/Minuteman KOA campground, about an hour's drive west of Boston. Not only do the trees provide shade for campsites, but they help muffle the sound of traffic. The heart of the campground is the familiar KOA A-frame with an office, convenience store (very complete, with everything from supplies to souvenirs to rental videos), laundry facility, and rest rooms. A pool and a rec hall are situated nearby. From there, five streets branch out, with a total of 100 campsites. This is definitely an RV camper's scene; just nine sites are designated for tenters, although 25 are multi-use. Seven cabins are sprinkled throughout the property. The park-like setting, plus the pool and (nice) playground make this a good choice for day-tripping families, especially those with the battle sites at Lexington and Concord on their itineraries.

BASICS

Operated By: Ted & Maureen Nussdorfer. **Open:** May 1–week after Columbus Day. **Site Assignment:** Reservations taken all year. Special requests should be made in advance; smaller units can typically book within a week of arrival date. **Registration:** At office. **Fee:** $24–$33 for two adults; extra adult, $5; extra child over age 5, $2. Discounted rates w/ KOA Value Card. V, MC, D. **Parking:** At site.

FACILITIES

Number of RV Sites: 91. **Number of Tent-Only Sites:** 9. **Hookups:** Water, electric (20, 30, 50 amps), sewer. **Each Site:** Picnic table, fire ring. **Dump Station:** Yes. **Laundry:** Yes. **Pay Phone:** Yes. **Rest Rooms and Showers:** Yes. **Fuel:** No. **Propane:** Yes. **Internal Roads:** Paved & gravel, good condition. **RV Service:** No. **Market:** 4 mi. east. **Restaurant:** 1 mi. west. **General Store:** Yes. **Vending:** No. **Swimming Pool:** Yes. **Playground:** Yes. **Other:** Rec hall. **Activities:** Volleyball, horseshoes, videos, planned activities. **Nearby Attractions:** Lexington & Concord historic sites, golf, mini-golf. **Additional Information:** Greater Merrimack Valley CVB, (978) 459-6150 or (800) 443-3332; www.lowell.org.

RESTRICTIONS

Pets: Must be leashed, quiet & cleaned up after. Must not be left unattended. Use enclosed Dog Walk area. **Fires:** In fire rings only. **Alcoholic Beverages:** At sites only. **Vehicle Maximum Length:** 40 ft. **Other:** Maximum stay is 14 days.

TO GET THERE

Take I-495 to Exit 30. Go west on Rte. 2A and Rte. 110 for 2.5 mi. Campground is on the left.

MANSFIELD

Canoe River Campgrounds

137 Mill St., Mansfield 02048. T: (508) 339-6462; F: (508) 339-5237.

★★★ ▲ ★★★

Beauty: ★★ Site Privacy: ★
Spaciousness: ★★ Quiet: ★★★
Security: ★★★★★ Cleanliness: ★★★
Insect Control: ★★★ Facilities: ★★

Compared to nearby Normandy Farms campground, this one is a bargain. Located in southern Massachusetts, halfway between Boston and Cape Cod, Canoe River is geared to families. About half the sites are seasonal—you'll notice a wildly decorated seasonal site just past the campground entrance. The presence of water makes all the difference here, providing a peaceful aspect to the rather closely-packed campsites. The campground is set on a river plateau, with a duck pond (lots of waterfowl), the larger Mill Pond (good for fishing and boating), and access to Canoe River. There's a bit of paddling on the river, but it's fairly overgrown. Sites are grass and gravel, with best tent sites on the river, at a dead end, numbers M4 and M5. Lakeside sites LS9 through 15 are also nice. RVers will like shady sites S5 through S12. This campground is casual, homey, and family-friendly. Ducklings toddle past plastic pink flamingoes. And the snack bar has blast-from-the-past prices—grilled cheese for under a buck, two eggs and toast for $2.15!

BASICS

Operated By: Joe & Emma Gonsalves. **Open:** Apr. 15–Oct. 15. **Site Assignment:** Reservations recommended. Deposit of 1 night's stay required. 2-night min. stay in summer; 3-night min. on holidays. Refunds for cancellation if made within 7 days of scheduled arrival date. **Registration:** At office. **Fee:** $19–$23. Checks, V, MC, D. **Parking:** At site.

FACILITIES

Number of RV Sites: 70. **Number of Tent-Only Sites:** 50. **Hookups:** Water, electric (20, 30 amps), sewer (to come). **Each Site:** Picnic table, fire ring. **Dump Station:** Yes. **Laundry:** Yes. **Pay Phone:** Yes. **Rest Rooms and Showers:** Yes, coin-op. **Fuel:** No. **Propane:** Yes. **Internal Roads:** Gravel, in good condition. **RV Service:** No. **Market:** 3–4 mi., east or west. **Restaurant:** Yes. **General Store:** Yes. **Vending:** Yes. **Swimming Pool:** Yes (2). **Playground:** Yes. **Other:** Rec hall. **Activities:** Boating (rental canoes, rowboats, paddleboats & kayaks), fishing, swimming, planned activities. **Nearby Attractions:** Tweeter Center for the Performing Arts (concerts), CMGI Stadium (football), Edaville Railroad, Plimoth Plantation, Cranberry World Visitors Center, Pilgrim Hall Museum. **Additional Information:** Plymouth County CVB, (508) 747-0100 or (800) 231-1620; www.plymouth-1620.com.

RESTRICTIONS

Pets: Must be leashed, quiet, & cleaned up after. **Fires:** In fire rings only. **Alcoholic Beverages:** Yes. **Vehicle Maximum Length:** 45 ft. **Other:** Limited winter camping.

TO GET THERE

From junction of I-495 and Rte. 123 (Exit 10), go 1 mi. east on Rte. 123, then turn left on Newland St. Go 2.25 mi. north to campground entrance, on left.

MIDDLEBORO

Boston South/Middleboro/ Plymouth KOA

483 Plymouth St., P.O. Box 616, Middleboro 02346. T: (508) 947-6435 or (800) 562-3046 (reservations); www.koa.com; wrnken@ix.netcom.com.

RV ★★ Tent ★

Beauty: ★★ Site Privacy: ★★
Spaciousness: ★★★★ Quiet: ★
Security: ★★★★★ Cleanliness: ★★★★
Insect Control: ★★★ Facilities: ★★★

This urban campground is centrally located, about 15 miles west of Plymouth, 40 miles south of Boston, and about 25 miles northwest of Cape Cod. And there's nearby commuter rail service, from Middleboro to Boston, so you can see the city sights and avoid the awful drive in. That's the good news. The bad news is, this campground is set alongside busy Rte. 44, and not really woodsy enough to muffle the incessant sound of traffic. The least-desirable campsites are, naturally, those closest to the road, including sites numbered in the 100s (except 124 through 132 and 158 through 166, set farther back) and those in the 200s (except 226 through 239 and 258 through 271, same deal.) Sites numbered 500-plus are set back, and might be the best bet for RVers. Tent sites are, mercifully, located in the middle of the campground, which may help with the noise level; still, we wouldn't recommend tent camping here. On the plus side, the place is spanking clean in true KOA style, and the pool is nice, if fairly exposed beside the campground entrance.

Basics

Operated By: Nicholson family. **Open:** Mar. 1–Dec. 1. **Site Assignment:** Reservations recommended. Deposit of $22 required to guarantee deposit for campsites. Cancel by 4 p.m. the day before your arrival date for refund; exceptions may be in effect due to high demand during holidays or special events. **Registration:** At office. **Fee:** $25–$36. V, MC, D. **Parking:** At site.

Facilities

Number of RV Sites: 276. **Number of Tent-Only Sites:** 0. **Hookups:** Water, electric (50 amps), sewer. **Each Site:** Picnic table, fire ring. **Dump Station:** Yes. **Laundry:** Yes. **Pay Phone:** Yes. **Rest Rooms and Showers:** Yes. **Fuel:** No. **Propane:** Yes. **Internal Roads:** Paved, in good condition. **RV Service:** No. **Market:** 3 mi. west on Rte. 44. **Restaurant:** 2.5 mi. west on Rte. 44. **General Store:** Yes. **Vending:** No. **Swimming Pool:** Yes. **Playground:** Yes. **Other:** Rec hall. **Activities:** Guided tours to Boston, Plymouth, & Cape Cod (June 1–Nov. 1), public transportation (commuter rail) to Boston, swimming, horseshoes, volleyball, basketball, bocce, planned activities. **Nearby Attractions:** Edaville Railroad, Tom Thumb Museum, Robbens Museum of Archeology, Eddy Homestead, Plimoth Plantation, Pilgrim Hall Museum, whalewatching, ocean beaches. **Additional Information:** Plymouth County CVB, (508) 747-0100 or (800) 231-1620; www.plymouth-1620.com.

Restrictions

Pets: Leashed only. **Fires:** In fire rings only. **Alcoholic Beverages:** Yes. **Vehicle Maximum Length:** 45 ft. **Other:** No charge for use of modem data port.

To Get There

From I-495, take Exit 6 onto Rte. 44. Head east for 2.5 mi. Entrance is on the left

MONSON

Sunsetview Farm Camping Area

57 Town Farm Rd., Monson 01057. T: (413) 267-9269; F: (413) 267-3163; www.sunsetview.com; camp@sunsetview.com.

RV ★★★ Tent ★★

Beauty: ★★★ Site Privacy: ★
Spaciousness: ★ Quiet: ★★★★
Security: ★★★★★ Cleanliness: ★★★★
Insect Control: ★★★ Facilities: ★★★★

Formerly a dairy farm and apple orchard, Sunsetview has hosted campers for 31 years. Off the beaten path in rural Monson, the campground is located between Sturbridge and Springfield, about six miles from the Massachusetts Turnpike. All recreation facilities, including a softball field, swimming pool, pond, and volleyball pit, are located near the campground's gated entrance. The farther back you head, the more woodsy the campsite. The grassy sites near the beach are tightly packed and the least desirable, in our view. For privacy, the best bet for RVers are sites 20, 20A, and 22A. For tenters, grouped together here at the far end of the property, sites T16 and T11 are set apart from their neighbors; T11 has the advantage of being close to the rest room. Most sites are back-in, some are pull-thru, and many are seasonal. Summer weekends here are jam-packed with activities; we like the Annual Trailer Rodeo (see which Dad can park the best!) This campground offers a country setting with close proximity to the urban areas of Springfield and Worcester (both, a half-hour away).

Basics

Operated By: Carpenter family. **Open:** Apr. 15–Oct. 15. **Site Assignment:** Reservations recommended. A deposit of one night's fee required to hold reservation. Holiday weekends must be paid in full one month prior to arrival. A $5 fee will be charged for all cancelled reservations. Walk-ins accepted for single night stay, if available. **Registration:** At office. $15 refundable deposit due for key to entrance gate. **Fee:** $22–$28. Extra fee for holiday weekends. Rates are for two persons; extra adult (age 18 & up) $2; extra child (age 6 & up), $1. MC, V, D. **Parking:** At site.

Facilities

Number of RV Sites: 160. **Number of Tent-Only Sites:** 20. **Hookups:** Water, electric (30, 50 amps), sewer. **Each Site:** Picnic table, fire ring. **Dump Station:** Yes. **Laundry:** Yes. **Pay Phone:** Yes. **Rest Rooms and Showers:** Yes, coin op. **Fuel:** No. **Propane:** No. **Internal Roads:** Gravel, in good condition. **RV Service:** No. **Market:** In Palmer, 3 mi. north. **Restaurant:** Yes. **General Store:** Yes. **Vending:** No. **Swimming Pool:** Yes. **Playground:** Yes. **Other:** Game room. **Activities:** Basketball, volleyball, ball field, hiking trails, teen area, planned activities. **Nearby Attractions:** Six Flags New England theme park (discounted tickets available), Old Sturbridge Village living history museum, Basketball Hall of Fame. **Additional Information:** Greater Springfield CVB, (413) 787-1548 or (800) 723-1548; www.valleyvisitor.com.

Restrictions

Pets: Must be leashed, quiet, & cleaned up after. Must not be left unattended. Rabies vaccine certificate required. **Fires:** In fire rings only. **Alcoholic Beverages:** At site. **Vehicle Maximum Length:** 45 ft. **Other:** Two night min. stay required in July & Aug.; three night min. on holiday weekends.

To Get There

From junction of I-90 (Massachusetts Turnpike) and Exit 8 (Rte. 32), head south. After entering Monson, take first left onto Fenton Farm Rd. Proceed 0.25 mi., then take a right onto Town Farm Rd. Follow road for 1.5 mi. Campground is on the left.

NORTH ADAMS

Historic Valley Campground

10 Main St., North Adams 01247. T: (413) 662-3198.

RV ★★★ Tent ★★★

Beauty: ★★★ Site Privacy: ★★★
Spaciousness: ★★★ Quiet: ★★★
Security: ★★★ Cleanliness: ★★
Insect Control: ★★★ Facilities: ★★★

This tidy little city-owned campground is tucked away at the end of a city street. If it weren't for the sign, you might not guess it existed. What a nice surprise: the campsites are ringed by woods and a lake, flanked by the lofty hillsides of the Berkshires. There are two beaches here, a municipal beach and a private beach for the camping crowd. Campers are mostly families, with about 30 seasonal sites in the mix. RV sites are back-in and gravel, buffered by trees. Happily, they've left lots of trees in place on the property. Sites 5 and 7 are nice and on the lakefront, while 50 through 52 and 65 through 67 are nicely bordered by woods. We'd skip sites 1 through 7; they're too close to the busy beach pavilion. In general, the perimeter sites are most spacious here. Tenters who don't need electric can choose from among the wilderness sites. (Wilderness I is closest to the lake.) The crumbling fireplaces could use some help. All in all, a pleasant, if busy, camping destination.

Basics

Operated By: City of North Adams. **Open:** May 15–Oct. 15. **Site Assignment:** Reservations recommended; call year-round. All reservations require a full deposit. **Registration:** At office. **Fee:** $12 (wilderness)–$30 (lakefront) No credit cards. **Parking:** At site.

Facilities

Number of RV Sites: 106. **Number of Tent-Only Sites:** 0. **Hookups:** Water, electric (20 amps). **Each Site:** Picnic table, fireplace. **Dump Station:** Yes. **Laundry:** Yes. **Pay Phone:** Yes. **Rest

Rooms and Showers: Yes. **Fuel:** No. **Propane:** No. **Internal Roads:** Gravel, in good condition. **RV Service:** No. **Market:** 2 mi. north. **Restaurant:** 0.5 mi. south, & 2 mi. south (at Adams/North Adams line). **General Store:** Yes. **Vending:** Yes. **Swimming Pool:** No. **Playground:** Yes. **Other:** Rec room, pavilion. **Activities:** Boating on Windsor Lake (rentals available), swimming, horseshoes, volleyball, hiking, ball field. **Nearby Attractions:** Mt. Greylock State Reservation (hiking), Natural Bridge State Park, Hancock Shaker Village, Mass MOCA (contemporary art), Clark Art Institute, Norman Rockwell Museum, summer theater, golf, whitewater canoeing, fishing, horseback riding, Tanglewood (music), Jacob's Pillow (dance). **Additional Information:** Berkshire Hills Visitors Bureau, (413) 443-9186 or (800) 237-5747; www.berkshires.org.

Restrictions

Pets: Dogs & cats permitted; must be leashed at all times. Not allowed on beach, pavilion, or playgrounds. **Fires:** In fireplaces only. **Alcoholic Beverages:** No. **Vehicle Maximum Length:** 40 ft. **Other:** No motorcycles.

To Get There

Follow Rte. 2 (Mohawk Trail) to east side of North Adams. Turn onto East Main St. (look for Ed's Variety), go 0.25 mi. left onto Kemp Ave. Travel 1.5 mi. on Kemp to lake and campground entrance.

NORTH ANDOVER

Harold Parker State Forest

1951 Turnpike Rd., North Andover 01845. T: (978) 686-3391 or (877) I CAMP-MA; F: (978) 689-7504; www.state.ma.us/dem/parks/harp.htm.

 ★★ ▲ ★★★★

Beauty: ★★★★ Site Privacy: ★★★★
Spaciousness: ★★★★ Quiet: ★★★★★
Security: ★★★ Cleanliness: ★★★
Insect Control: ★★ Facilities: ★★

About 25 miles north of Boston, Massachusetts, 3,500-acre Harold Parker State Forest offers a taste of the wilderness with easy access to big-city attractions. A drive into the forest reveals a mix of hardwoods and fragrant pine, studded with nine ponds. Ninety campsites are arrayed in a loop, just to the west of jalapeño-shaped Frye Pond. The most popular sites, for good reason, are those on the waterfront (63–87). If those are taken, site 15 is a good choice, located up a small hill and away from the road. We'd steer clear of sites 52, 54, and 56 if you need proximity to a rest room. Once settled in, you'll enjoy the rustic setting and woodsy hiking trails. (Ask for a trail map when you come in.) If you've brought a kayak or canoe, don't miss a sunset paddle on Frye Pond. The campground opens in mid-Apr., but Apr. tends to be muddy around here. Also beware of mid-May, black fly season. Given the lack of facilities, Harold Parker State Forest is best-suited for tent campers, or self-sufficient RVers looking for a back-to-nature escape. It makes a great base for campers who want to play tourist in bustling Boston and the North Shore, then return to the tranquility of woods and water.

Basics

Operated By: Massachusetts Division of Forests & Parks. **Open:** Mid-Apr.–mid-Oct. **Site Assignment:** Reserve up to 6 months in advance by calling (877) I CAMP-MA or on line at www.reserveamerica.com. If you cancel or change dates or type of site, call (877) 422-6762 at least 3 days prior to arrival. $10 cancellation/transfer fee. Walk-ins welcome if space is available; best time to try is after 11 a.m. check-out period. **Registration:** At office. **Fee:** MA residents, $10; non-residents, $12. Accessible sites available. V, MC. **Parking:** At site.

Facilities

Number of RV Sites: 90. **Number of Tent-Only Sites:** 0. **Hookups:** None. **Each Site:** Picnic table, fireplace, grills (to come). **Dump Station:** Yes. **Laundry:** No. **Pay Phone:** Yes. **Rest Rooms and Showers:** Yes. **Fuel:** No. **Propane:** No. **Internal Roads:** Paved, in good condition. **RV Service:** No. **Market:** 5 mi. east in Middleton. **Restaurant:** 5 mi. east in Middleton. **General Store:** No (firewood for sale at campground office). **Vending:** No. **Swimming Pool:** No. **Playground:** Planned. **Other:** Ball field, basketball court (planned), small beach. **Activities:** 25 mi. of multi-use trails (hiking, biking, bridle), fishing (license required), canoeing, pond swimming, hunting (limited; mostly in fall). **Nearby Attractions:** Witchcraft & maritime-related attractions in Salem, Peabody-Essex Museum, whale-watching boat trips out of Gloucester, Salem, and Newburyport, Lexington & Concord, Boston. **Additional Information:** North of Boston CVB, (978) 977-7760 or (800) 742-5306; www.northofboston.org.

Restrictions

Pets: Must be leashed, quiet, & cleaned up after. Rabies vaccination certificate required. **Fires:** In fireplaces only. **Alcoholic Beverages:** No. **Vehicle Maximum Length:** None. **Other:** 14-day max. cumulative stay from Mem. Day through Labor Day.

To Get There

Take Rte. 495 to Exit 42E to Rte. 114W; follow signs to forest. Go right at camping sign, left at first stop sign. Pass residential area; go left onto Jenkins Rd. Camp office will be on your right.

NORTH TRURO

Horton's Camping Resort

71 Highland Rd., P.O. Box 308, North Truro 02652. T: (508) 487-1220 or (800) 252-7705 (reservations); www.HortonsCampingResort.com; camphrcr@capecod.net.

★★★ ▲ ★★★

Beauty: ★★★ Site Privacy: ★★
Spaciousness: ★★★ Quiet: ★★★
Security: ★★★★ Cleanliness: ★★★★
Insect Control: ★★ Facilities: ★★

Of the three campgrounds in North Truro, this one feels the most inviting. Set on the Outer Cape of Cape Cod, just eight miles from both bustling Provincetown (to the east) and fishing town-turned-artist's-colony Wellfleet (to the west), this campground has an open, pastoral feel. Most sites are grassy, on gravel, and carpeted with pine needles. A section here called 'Wooded Area' is, naturally, woodsy (!), and it's the prettiest area of the property. An interesting feature here: an adult-only section, meant to be peaceful. The best of that bunch is very isolated site 203. Nearby are prime view sites, 173–176. Stand on the hill, and you may see a ribbon of blue ocean. (They claim other 'best view' sites as well, but these are the best!) No campfires allowed, but you can get a permit from the Truro Fire Dept. for a campfire on the beach. Speaking of which, Coast Guard Beach, on the National Seashore, is just a mile away. Walk it, and save money on a parking permit.

Basics

Operated By: Horton family. **Open:** Early May–mid-Oct. **Site Assignment:** Reservations recommended. Three-night min. stay required in season, w/$50 deposit per week for non-hookup sites & $75 per week for hookup sites. No personal checks within 30 days of arrival. No refunds without two-week notice of cancellation. $5 service charge applied to cancellations or alterations to reservation. **Registration:** At office. **Fee:** $19–$28 for one to two people. Extra adult, $8 per night; extra child age 2 to 16, $3. V, MC. **Parking:** At site.

Facilities

Number of RV Sites: 200. **Number of Tent-Only Sites:** 0. **Hookups:** Water, electric (30 amps), sewer. **Each Site:** Picnic tables. **Dump Station:** Yes. **Laundry:** Yes. **Pay Phone:** Yes. **Rest Rooms and Showers:** Yes, coin-op. **Fuel:** No. **Propane:** No. **Internal Roads:** Gravel, in fair condition. **RV Service:** No. **Market:** 12 mi. west. **Restaurant:** 5 mi. west. **General Store:** Yes. **Vending:** No. **Swimming Pool:** No. **Playground:** Yes. **Other:** Volleyball court, winter storage available. **Activities:** Volleyball, horseshoes. **Nearby Attractions:** Cape Cod National Seashore, Cape Cod Light, ocean & bay swimming (1 mi.), golf, hiking, biking, antique shops, fishing, galleries. **Additional Information:** Cape Cod Chamber of Commerce, (508) 862-0700 or (888) 33-CAPECOD; www.capechamber.org.

Restrictions

Pets: No dogs. **Fires:** No open fires. Campstoves, & charcoal grills OK. **Alcoholic Beverages:** Yes. **Vehicle Maximum Length:** 40 ft. **Other:** Children are not allowed at certain sites.

To Get There

From Sagamore Bridge, take Rte. 6 east to Orleans rotary (about 35 mi.). Continue on Rte. 6 to town of Truro, about 13 mi. Approximately 4.5 mi. past the Truro-Wellfleet town line, you'll see the Truro Central School on right. Turn right after school at blue and white 'camping' sign onto South Highland Rd. Campground entrance is 1 mi. on the right after the red bar (campground office and store.)

NORTH TRURO

North Truro Camping Area

46 Highland Rd., P.O. Box 365, North Truro 02652. T: (508) 487-1847; F: (508) 487-9576; www.ntca camping.com; email@ntcacamping.com.

RV ★★ Tent ★★

Beauty: ★★ Site Privacy: ★★
Spaciousness: ★★★ Quiet: ★★★
Security: ★★★ Cleanliness: ★★★★
Insect Control: ★★ Facilities: ★★

Located just north of Truro, one of the most desirable (and sleepiest) towns on the Outer Cape, this hilly campground is dotted with skinny pines that rise out of the sandy soil at odd angles. These provide a nice, sun-dappled effect on bright summer days, but don't provide much privacy between campsites, which are pretty much wall-to-wall with RVs in season. There are no group sites here, but lots of families. Campsites are set in a grid, off a main road. Finding one's way around the one-way streets can be challenging. The most secluded tent sites are 268, 270, and 272, on the far left-hand corner of the property. Tent sites 242, 252, and 254, on the last row of campsites, are also nice, backing up into the woods. Look to the perimeters if you want some privacy. Site 144A (water only) is a good choice, as is 72C (complete hookup.) Tip: Bring your own hand towels for the rest rooms, or drip-dry. This is basically a cheap sleep—two campers can stay with complete hookups and cable TV for $26 a day—and it's close to Provincetown, but quieter.

Basics

Operated By: Edgar Francis. **Open:** Apr. 1–Dec. 31. **Site Assignment:** Reservations recommended. $50 deposit required. Balance due upon arrival. Refunds for cancellation w/ two weeks' notice, minus $5 fee. **Registration:** At office. **Fee:** $9 per person per day; $18 min. Electric (15 amp) & water, $5 per day; complete (30 amp electric), $8 per day. V, MC. **Parking:** At site.

Facilities

Number of RV Sites: 300. **Number of Tent-Only Sites:** 0. **Hookups:** Water, electric (15, 30 amps), sewer, cable TV. **Each Site:** Picnic table. **Dump Station:** Yes. **Laundry:** Yes. **Pay Phone:** Yes. **Rest Rooms and Showers:** Yes, coin-op. **Fuel:** No. **Propane:** Yes. **Internal Roads:** Paved, in good condition. **RV Service:** No. **Market:** 12 mi. west. **Restaurant:** 1 mi. west. **General Store:** Yes. **Vending:** No. **Swimming Pool:** No. **Playground:** No. **Other:** Metered showers, data port. **Activities:** Golf, hiking, biking, beachcombing. **Nearby Attractions:** Cape Cod National Seashore, Cape Cod Light, ocean & bay swimming (1 mi.), golf, hiking, biking, antique shops, fishing, galleries. **Additional Information:** Cape Cod Chamber of Commerce, (508) 862-0700 or (888) 33-CAPECOD; www.capechamber.org.

Restrictions

Pets: Must be leashed. No dogs from June 16 to Labor Day. **Fires:** No open fires. Campstoves, & charcoal grills OK. **Alcoholic Beverages:** Yes. **Vehicle Maximum Length:** None. **Other:** All visitors must register upon entering the park.

To Get There

From Sagamore Bridge, take Rte. 6 east through Truro (about 48 mi.) After passing Truro, watch for sign marked Highland Rd. (Do not turn off at South Highland Rd.) Turn right on Highland Rd. Campground is 0.25 mi. left

OAKHAM

Pine Acres Family Camping Resort

203 Bechan Rd., Oakham 01068. T: (508) 882-9509; F: (508) 882-3302; www.pineacresresort.com.

RV ★★★★★ Tent ★★★★★

Beauty: ★★★★★ Site Privacy: ★★★
Spaciousness: ★★★ Quiet: ★★★★
Security: ★★★★★ Cleanliness: ★★★★★
Insect Control: ★★ Facilities: ★★★★★

This wonderfully appealing campground is located almost dead-center in the state, 15 miles from Worcester and about 50 miles west of Boston. Amidst a small-town New England landscape, this campground is a destination in itself. Set on a pine-shrouded hillside above 70-acre Lake Dean, it's a mini resort-land, with everything from tennis and boating to gourmet coffee and live entertainment. (Even waterskiing, if you bring your own boat.) Operated for 41 years by the Packard family, this place sets the standard, combining natural beauty with loads of amenities and small touches that add up: a porta-potty by the beach, a dog walk, stone fire rings (not the rusty jobs that are all too prevalent.) Campsites are set on loop roads, off a center pod with a lodge, rec hall, store, and so on. About half are seasonal. Site 137, on a hill overlooking the lake, is a fine choice, while sites 78 and 79 face the beach. Ditto sites 89, 93, and 93A. Sites H10 and H11, near wilderness trails, are good for hikers, while site 105, among the tent sites, offers a wooded spot on a hill with lake views. We'd pass on the M sites; too close to the hub of activity. Tip: Don't forget the bug juice!

Basics

Operated By: Oakham Pine Acres, Inc. **Open:** All year. **Site Assignment:** Reservations recommended; three-week advance notice is good. Can reserve on-line. 50% deposit required. Holiday weekends require 3-night min. stay & payment in full w/ reservation. Will try to honor specific site requests, but cannot guarantee site requests for stays of less than 1 week. Refund given for cancellations w/ 30 days' notice, minus $10 fee. If cancelling less than 30 days but at least 7 days prior to arrival, payments will be used as credit for future stay. **Registration:** At office. **Fee:** $17–$42 per family, w/ up to three unmarried children under age 18. V, MC, D. **Parking:** At sites & designated lots only.

Facilities

Number of RV Sites: 300. **Number of Tent-Only Sites:** 0. **Hookups:** Water, electric (20, 30, 50 amps), sewer, cable TV, modems. **Each Site:** Picnic table, fire ring. **Dump Station:** Yes. **Laundry:** Yes. **Pay Phone:** Yes. **Rest Rooms and Showers:** Yes, coin-op. **Fuel:** No. **Propane:** Yes. **Internal Roads:** Paved & gravel, in good condition. **RV Service:** Yes. **Market:** 3 mi. south on Rte. 148. **Restaurant:** Yes. **General Store:** Yes. **Vending:** Yes. **Swimming Pool:** No. **Playground:** Yes. **Other:** Boat ramp, rec hall, adult lounge, tennis court, mini-golf. **Activities:** Fishing (need MA license, available in Rutland), tennis, boating (rentals available), volleyball, horseshoes, ball field, hiking, planned activities. In winter, cross-country skiing, skating, snowmobiling, ice fishing. **Nearby Attractions:** Old Sturbridge Village living history museum, Worcester Art Museum, Worcester Centrum (events), New England Science Center, Quabbin Reservoir, Higgins Armory Museum, Brimfield Flea Markets, apple orchards, golf. **Additional Information:** Central Massachusetts Tourist Council, (508) 755-7400; www.worcester.org.

Restrictions

Pets: Must be leashed, quiet, & cleaned up after. Must not be left unattended. **Fires:** In fire rings only. **Alcoholic Beverages:** Yes. **Vehicle Maximum Length:** 40 ft. **Other:** children must be supervised at all times.

To Get There

From Boston, take Massachusetts Turnpike (I-90) west to Exit 10 (Auburn), then Rte. 20W. Turn right onto Rte. 56N, go through Leicester, then left onto Rte. 122N, and left again onto Rte. 148S. Watch for campground signs on Rte. 148.

PITTSFIELD

Pittsfield State Forest

Cascade St., Pittsfield 01201. T: (413) 442-8992; www.state.ma.us/dem/paraks/pitt.htm.

RV ★★★ Tent ★★★★

Beauty: ★★★★★ Site Privacy: ★★★
Spaciousness: ★★★ Quiet: ★★★★
Security: ★★★★ Cleanliness: ★★★
Insect Control: ★★ Facilities: ★★★

If you don't mind doing without some creature comforts (namely, flush toilets and showers), you'll appreciate the wonderful natural features at this pristine state park located at the far Western edge of the state (Berkshire County.) From late May into June, 65 acres of wild azaleas bloom into a sea of pink blossoms. Two camping areas are clustered nearby, surrounding Berry Pond, the highest natural water body in Massachusetts at 2,150 feet. Fishing enthusiasts have discovered the pond, while hikers enjoy the vista from the top of Berry Mountain, a great place for sunset-watching. Great tent sites in this area include site 7, with good pond views, and sites 9–12, which are roomy, flat, and wooded. The only toilet here is pit-style (non-flush). Follow the loop road, running alongside Parker Brook, and you'll reach the second set of campsites, grouped near a flush toilet. These are pretty and woodsy as well, but set a bit closer together than those at Berry Pond, with less buffer between sites. Site 18 is big, but not very secluded. Hiking trails wind through a variety of forest, and beckon visitors to escape into the woods.

Basics

Operated By: Massachusetts State Forests & Parks. **Open:** May–Oct. **Site Assignment:** Reservations may be made up to six months in advance by calling ReserveAmerica at (877) 1 CAMP-MA or online at www.reserveamerica.com. Some sites are held for walk-ins on a first-come, first-served basis. To change arrival or departure date, or site type, call at least 3 days prior to arrival date. $10 cancellation/transfer fee. No refunds for amounts less than $5. **Registration:** At office. **Fee:** Parker Brook area, $5; Berry Pond area, $4 (no flush toilets) V, MC. **Parking:** At site.

Facilities

Number of RV Sites: 31. **Number of Tent-Only Sites:** 0. **Hookups:** None. **Each Site:** Picnic table, fireplace. **Dump Station:** No. **Laundry:** No. **Pay Phone:** Yes. **Rest Rooms and Showers:** Yes, no showers. **Fuel:** No. **Propane:** No. **Internal Roads:** Paved & gravel, good to fair condition. **RV Service:** No. **Market:** 5 mi. east. **Restaurant:** 5 mi. east. **General Store:** No. **Vending:** No. **Swimming Pool:** No. **Playground:** No. **Other:** Nature center. **Activities:** Hiking (including wheelchair-accessible trail), swimming (in Lulu Pond), bicycling, fishing, horseback riding, interpretive programs. **Nearby Attractions:** Tanglewood (music), Jacob's Pillow (dance), Mt. Greylock, Norman Rockwell Museum. **Additional Information:** Berkshire Hills Visitors Bureau, (413) 443-9186 or (800) 237-5747; www.berkshires.org.

Restrictions

Pets: Must be leashed & cleaned up after. Must not be left unattended. Proof of rabies vaccination required. **Fires:** In fireplaces only. **Alcoholic Beverages:** No. **Vehicle Maximum Length:** 16 ft. **Other:** Paved trail ideal for those in a wheelchair.

To Get There

From the Massachusetts Turnpike (I-90), take Exit 2. At the junction of Rtes. 7 and 20, go west on Rte. 7. Take West St. to Cascade St. Follow signs.

PLAINFIELD
Peppermint Park Camping Resort

169 Grant St., Plainfield 01070. T: (413) 634-5385; peppermintpark.net; pprc@bcn.net.

RV ★★★ Tent ★★

Beauty: ★★ Site Privacy: ★★★★
Spaciousness: ★★★★★ Quiet: ★★★★★
Security: ★★★★★ Cleanliness: ★★★
Insect Control: ★★ Facilities: ★★★

Set in the rural landscape of the Berkshire Hills in Western Massachusetts, Peppermint Park offers a low-key family getaway in summer, and a toasty haven for snowmobilers in winter months. (280 miles of trails are accessible here.) Leaf-peepers descend on the campground in Sep. and Oct. Buffered by trees and shrubs, campsites are mostly grassy and wooded, offering plenty of breathing room. Most sites are set back from the main activities area near the entrance of the campground, except for numbers 122 and 123 and 126–132, which are near the pool area. Campsites are arrayed in two main sections, plus a string of sites running along the perimeter of the property. Sites 27–31 are fairly private and nicely shady. Tent sites are clustered in two sections (with and without water), in close proximity to (pretty basic) rest rooms. Be sure to bring a tarp if you're tenting, and avoid rainy periods if possible; it can get pretty muddy here when it rains. Nice features include a book swap, and an appealing lounger with a stone fireplace. Located within just five miles of another campground, Shady Pines (see listing), Peppermint Park is the quieter of the two.

Basics

Operated By: David & Gale Bulissa. **Open:** All year. **Site Assignment:** Reservations recommended. 50% deposit required; for holidays, must pay in full to reserve. **Registration:** At office. **Fee:** $20–$24, based on two adults & two children. V, MC, D. **Parking:** At site.

Facilities

Number of RV Sites: 125. **Number of Tent-Only Sites:** 75. **Hookups:** Water, electric (20, 30, 50 amps), sewer. **Each Site:** Picnic table, fire ring. **Dump Station:** Yes. **Laundry:** Yes. **Pay Phone:** Yes. **Rest Rooms and Showers:** Yes, coin-op. **Fuel:** No. **Propane:** Yes. **Internal Roads:** Gravel, in fair condition. **RV Service:** No. **Market:** In Adams, 20 mi. west. **Restaurant:** 5 mi. south, in Ashfield. **General Store:** Yes. **Vending:** Yes. **Swimming Pool:** Yes. **Playground:** Yes. **Other:** Pub, hot tub, rec hall. **Activities:** Swimming, horseshoes, hiking, planned activities. **Nearby Attractions:** Mohawk Trail scenic drive, Historic Deerfield, Yankee Candle Factory, Bridge of Flowers, Antique Car Museum, Mount Greylock. **Additional Information:** Berkshire Hills Visitors Bureau, (413) 443-9186 or (800) 237-5747; www.berkshires.org.

Restrictions

Pets: Must be leashed & cleaned up after. Must not be left unattended. **Fires:** Fire rings only. **Alcoholic Beverages:** Yes. **Vehicle Maximum Length:** None. **Other:** A copy of current rabies certificate must be shown upon check-in for all pets.

To Get There

From I-91, take Exit 26 (Greenfield); follow Rte. 2 west to Rte. 112, then south to Rte. 116 north. Continue 6.5 mi. to Bow St. Follow Bow St. 0.75 mi. to campground; entrance is on right.

PLYMOUTH
Ellis Haven Camping Resort

531 Federal Furnace Rd., Plymouth 02360. T: (508) 746-0803; www.ellishaven.com.

RV ★★★ Tent ★★

Beauty: ★★ Site Privacy: ★★
Spaciousness: ★★ Quiet: ★★
Security: ★★★★★ Cleanliness: ★★★★★
Insect Control: ★★★★ Facilities: ★★★

Got teens or pre-teens in your party? You'll win major "props" for bringing them here. Unusual features at this campground include a huge, state-of-the-art arcade, and a tournament-worthy baseball diamond. And that's just the beginning. Set on good-sized Ellis Pond, in a residential area of Plymouth, Ellis Haven offers a day-use picnic area and a private beach. The number of activities at this resort-flavored campground rivals nearby Pinewood Lodge, but this place loses points when it comes to esthetics. Why call a pond "Stupid Duck Pond"? Why all the garish metal signs, every three feet, that read the same thing ("No Fishing")? Why is yellow police tape festooned around Thousand Frog Pond? That said, the camping area isn't bad, with grassy sites amidst plenty of tree coverage. Head to the northwest area of the resort, where you'll get away from the seasonal and permanent-looking set ups (unless you have a fondness for lawn art!) Sites 105 and 106 are nice, overlooking the baseball diamond, but not so close you need beware of fly balls. Amazing to think that this lively place borders its complete opposite, Miles Standish State Forest.

Basics

Operated By: Carreau family. **Open:** May 1–Oct. 1. **Site Assignment:** Reservations recommended. Reservations for two to five nights must be made two weeks prior to arrival date. Four night min. stay required on holidays. Fifty percent deposit required. Payment due in full 30 days prior to arrival. Cancellations made w/15-day notice, full refund minus $10 service charge. Cancellations w/seven day notice, credit available. **Registration:** At office. **Fee:** $25–$38 based on two adults, two children. V, MC, D. **Parking:** At site.

Facilities

Number of RV Sites: 450. **Number of Tent-Only Sites:** 50. **Hookups:** Water, electric (20, 30, 50 amps), sewer. **Each Site:** Picnic table, fireplace. **Dump Station:** Yes. **Laundry:** Yes. **Pay Phone:** Yes. **Rest Rooms and Showers:** Yes. **Fuel:** No. **Propane:** Yes. **Internal Roads:** Gravel, in good condition. **RV Service:** No. **Market:** 3 mi. north, in Plymouth. **Restaurant:** Yes. **General Store:** Yes. **Vending:** Yes. **Swimming Pool:** No. **Playground:** Yes. **Other:** Rec hall, arcade, rental boats, petting zoo. **Activities:** Swimming in Ellis Pond, catch-and-release fishing, paddle boats, basebal, basketball, volleyball, picnicking, arcade games. **Nearby Attractions:** Plimoth Plantation, whale-watching cruises, scenic harbor cruises, Mayflower II, Plymouth National Wax Museum, Pilgrim Hall Museum, winery, Ocean Spray Cranberry World, tours, winery. **Additional Information:** Destination Plymouth, (800) USA-1620 or www.visit-plymouth.com.

Restrictions

Pets: One dog per family. **Fires:** In fireplaces only. **Alcoholic Beverages:** Yes. **Vehicle Maximum Length:** None. **Other:** No teen-aged guests over holiday weekends. Two-night min. stay required except during May & September. Three-night min. stay required on holiday weekends.

To Get There

From Rte. 3 southbound, take exit 6B; turn right at bottom of ramp to Rte. 44W. At second light, take left. At next light, take right onto Federal Furnace Rd. Proceed 3.5 mi. Campground entrance is on the right.

PLYMOUTH
Pinewood Lodge

190 Pinewood Rd., Plymouth 02360. T: (508) 746-3548; www.pinewoodlodge.com.

RV ★★★★★ Tent ★★★★★

Beauty: ★★★ Site Privacy: ★★
Spaciousness: ★★★★ Quiet: ★★★★
Security: ★★★★ Cleanliness: ★★★★★
Insect Control: ★★★★★ Facilities: ★★★★

The tasteful white wooden sign that welcomes guests to Pinewood Lodge is a harbinger of things to come. Run by the Saunders family since 1962 (now operated by the great-grandchildren), this campground is the nicest one in the Plymouth area. Families who stay here while exploring Plimoth Plantation, ten miles away, won't be disappointed. Set amidst the pines on Pinewood Lake, at the end of a dead-end road, the campground boasts 3,000 feet of lake frontage. A private beach is buoyed off for swimming; near the beach there's a playground and rental rowboats and canoes. With its bustling rec room (nice feature: a piano) and activities galore (air hockey tournaments, a pots-and-pans parade), Pinewood Lodge is a destination resort. In summer, that is; in fall, retirees replace kids on bikes and the mood changes completely. Campsites are mostly wooded, carpeted with pine needles, and set fairly close together. Avoid the sites along the main road (beginning with letter D) and head to the East & West Park areas (beginning with letter S.) Nicest sites for tents is the small colony on the opposite side of the park, numbers 14 through 21. Fees are comparable to other area campgrounds, although they charge extra per child, but Pinewood Lodge offers more in the way of cleanliness, amenities, and attention to detail.

BASICS

Operated By: Saunders family. **Open:** May 1–Nov. 1. **Site Assignment:** Reservations recommended. Deposit required equal to one night's stay. $50 deposit required for holiday stay. Deposits refunded w/two-week notice only. $5 service charge applies to cancelled or shortened stays. **Registration:** At office. **Fee:** $23–$33 in season; $20–$30, off-peak. Rates based on two people; extra children age 13-plus, $5; 12 & under, $2. V, MC. **Parking:** At sites & parking lots.

FACILITIES

Number of RV Sites: 230. **Number of Tent-Only Sites:** 20. **Hookups:** Water, electric (20, 30, 50 amps), sewer. **Each Site:** Picnic table, ring. **Dump Station:** Yes. **Laundry:** Yes. **Pay Phone:** Yes. **Rest Rooms and Showers:** Yes, coin-op. **Fuel:** No. **Propane:** Yes. **Internal Roads:** Paved & gravel, in good condition. **RV Service:** Yes. **Market:** 5 mi. east, in Plymouth. **Restaurant:** Yes. **General Store:** Yes. **Vending:** No. **Swimming Pool:** No. **Playground:** Yes. **Other:** Rec hall. **Activities:** Fishing, swimming, boating (rentals available), canoeing, basketball, planned activities. **Nearby Attractions:** Plimoth Plantation, whale-watching cruises, scenic harbor cruises, Mayflower II, Plymouth National Wax Museum, Pilgrim Hall Museum, winery, Ocean Spray Cranberry World, tours, winery. **Additional Information:** Destination Plymouth, (800) USA-1620 or www.visit-plymouth.com.

RESTRICTIONS

Pets: No. **Fires:** In fire rings only. **Alcoholic Beverages:** Yes. **Vehicle Maximum Length:** None. **Other:** Three-night min. stay required on holiday weekends; five-night min. on 4th of July.

TO GET THERE

Take Rte. 3 south to Rte. 44, exit 6B. Take Rte.44 west 3 mi. to Pinewood Rd., turn left to campground entrance.

PROVINCETOWN
Coastal Acres Camping Court

West Vine St. Extension, P.O. Box 593, Provincetown 02657. T: (508) 487-1700; www.coastalacres.com.

RV ★★ Tent ★★★

Beauty: ★★ Site Privacy: ★★
Spaciousness: ★★★★ Quiet: ★★★
Security: ★★ Cleanliness: ★★★
Insect Control: ★★★ Facilities: ★★

If you want to stay within walking distance of Provincetown, on the tip of Cape Cod, this is the place. This campground is set in a residential area in town, so all of P'town's street scene, restaurants, galleries, and charter boats are merely a stroll away. Beaches are close by, as well. Campsites are set in a grid, with the office, store, and rest rooms in the middle. RV sites are open and grassy; biggest sites are 1A through 8. Tent sites are fairly private, set in the pines, with plenty of buffer between sites. Nicest spots are along inland pond—these are lettered, not numbered. Campers are a mix of couples and families. If you want to leave the car behind and explore lively Provincetown and its dazzling beaches, you'll do well here. Bonus: the staff is happy to offer recommendations on restaurants, boat tours, and other attractions, and will happily assist you in making reservations.

BASICS

Operated By: Richard Perry. **Open:** Apr. 1–Nov. 1. **Site Assignment:** Reservations recommended for peak season, Memorial Day to Labor Day. Three-night min. reservation, payable in advance. For one weeks' reservation, three-night deposit required; for two weeks or longer stay, one week deposit required. Refunds granted for cancellations w/one weeks' notice prior to scheduled arrival date, minus $7 service charge. No credit cards. **Registration:** At office. **Fee:** $24–$34 per day for two people; extra adult, $9 per night; extra child $6 per day. No charge for children under age 3. No credit cards. **Parking:** At site only.

FACILITIES

Number of RV Sites: 114. **Number of Tent-Only Sites:** 0. **Hookups:** Water, electric (30 amps). **Each Site:** Picnic table. **Dump Station:** Yes. **Laundry:** No. **Pay Phone:** Yes. **Rest Rooms and Showers:** Yes, coin-op. **Fuel:** No. **Propane:** Yes. **Internal Roads:** Paved, in good condition. **RV Service:** No. **Market:** 1 mi. **Restaurant:** Several within walking distance. **General Store:** Yes. **Vending:** Yes. **Swimming Pool:** No. **Playground:** No. **Other:** Patios, private parking. **Activities:** Biking, horseback riding, boating. **Nearby Attractions:** Cape Cod National Seashore, Provincetown, Pilgrim Monument & Provincetown Museum, Provincetown Repertory Theater, whale watch cruises, charter boats, golf, tennis, hiking, bike trails. **Additional Information:** Cape Cod Chamber of Commerce, (508) 862-0700 or (888) 33-CAPECOD; www.capechamber.org.

RESTRICTIONS

Pets: Must be leashed, quiet, & cleaned up after. **Fires:** No open fires. Campstoves, & charcoal grills OK. **Alcoholic Beverages:** Yes. **Vehicle Maximum Length:** None. **Other:** Minimum of a three night stay when making a reservation.

TO GET THERE

Follow Rte. 6 east to end. Go left on Herring Cove (Rte. 6A), continue to Bradford St. Look for campground sign on the left of Bradford St., just before Seafood Connection. Turn left on West Vine, heading into campground.

PROVINCETOWN
Dunes' Edge Campground

386 Rte. 6, P.O, Box 875, Provincetown 02657. T: (508) 487-9815; F: (508) 487-5918; www.dunes-edge .com.

RV ★★ Tent ★★★

Beauty: ★★★ Site Privacy: ★★
Spaciousness: ★★ Quiet: ★★★★
Security: ★★★ Cleanliness: ★★★
Insect Control: ★★ Facilities: ★★

You'll know you're in Cape Cod when you arrive here; to enter the campground, you drive up a long hill flanked by a huge, sloping sand dune. Aptly-named Dunes' Edge sits in the shadow of Horse's Head, one of Provincetown's tallest hills. This campground sits at the edge of P'town, about a 15-minute walk, so it's more 'country' than 'city', unlike its nearest neighbor, Coastal Acres Camping Court (see listing.) In fact, the brown wood office building with neon-orange lettering reminded us of The Flintstones! It's a five-minute ride by car to two wonderful beaches, Herring Cove and Race Point (expect to pay a $7 parking fee.) Or, take the bike trail to the beach; that's a 20 minute ride or so, depending on your energy level. It's all nicely wooded, and more geared to tenters than RVers. Nice small touches: A full-length mirror, and lots of hooks, in the ladies' room. Campsites are set in a big loop, and a smaller loop with spokes. We'd skip sites 18, 20, 21, 28, and 30, set close to Ground Hog Hill and tightly packed to boot. Nicer tent sites, but harder to get to, are sites 36 through 39. On the other side of the campground, sites 65 and 65A are plenty spacious. Site 71 is a super hilltop spot.

BASICS

Operated By: Miriam Collinson & Jim Buckingham. **Open:** May–late Sept. **Site Assignment:** Reservations accepted, & recommended by Jul., Aug., & holiday weekends (three-night min.) $30 deposit on reservations, payable by check. Two-week notice required for refunds due to cancellation, minus $5 service charge. **Registration:** At office. **Fee:** $25–$34 for two people; extra adult is $10 per night; extra child is $3. No credit cards. **Parking:** At site.

FACILITIES

Number of RV Sites: 15. **Number of Tent-Only Sites:** 85. **Hookups:** Water, electric (20 amps). **Each Site:** Picnic table. **Dump Station:** Yes. **Laundry:** Yes. **Pay Phone:** Yes. **Rest Rooms and Showers:** Yes, coin-op. **Fuel:** No. **Propane:** No. **Internal Roads:** Paved, in good condition. **RV Service:** No. **Market:** 1 mi. north. **Restaurant:** 1 mi. north. **General Store:** Yes. **Vending:** Yes. **Swim-**

ming **Pool:** No. **Playground:** No. **Other:** Modem in central area. **Activities:** Hiking, biking. **Nearby Attractions:** Cape Cod National Seashore, Provincetown, Pilgrim Monument & Provincetown Museum, Provincetown Repertory Theater, whale watch cruises, charter boats, golf, tennis, hiking, bike trails. **Additional Information:** Cape Cod Chamber of Commerce, (508) 862-0700 or (888) 33-CAPECOD; www.capechamber.org.

RESTRICTIONS

Pets: Must be leashed, quiet, & cleaned up after. Must not be left unattended. 1 pet per site. **Fires:** No open fires. Charcoal grills or campstoves OK. **Alcoholic Beverages:** Yes. **Vehicle Maximum Length:** 32 ft. **Other:** 2-week max. & 3-night min. stay.

TO GET THERE

Follow Rte. 6 east to Provincetown. Turn right off Rte. 6 at the blue and white 'seasonal camping' sign, just beyond Mile Marker 116. Campground is on the right.

ROCHESTER

Outdoor World—Gateway to Cape Cod

90 Stevens Rd., Rochester 02770. T: (508) 763-5911 or (800) 588-2221 (reservations); F: (508) 763-2052; www.campoutdoorworld.com.

RV ★★★★ Tent ★★

Beauty: ★★★★	Site Privacy: ★★★
Spaciousness: ★★★	Quiet: ★★★★
Security: ★★★★★	Cleanliness: ★★★★
Insect Control: ★★★	Facilities: ★★★★★

Located about 55 miles south of Boston and 20 miles from the Cape Cod Canal, this membership park is nestled in tall pines at the end of a dead-end road. This is big rig country—you might even see five-wheelers here—so tent campers are likely to feel dwarfed in these surroundings. But RVers will find plenty to like, from pull-thru sites to natural beauty to nice touches, like big umbrellas at poolside. And how often do you find tennis courts at a campground? There's a nice spot to get away from it all, too; a couple of picnic tables overlooking Leonard's Pond, at the end of Whitehorse Rd. (The rusted-out grills at several campsites are a downer, though.) Campsites are set in three sections, with 'A' and 'B' sections closest to the entrance and activities areas, and 'C' section set back, near the tennis courts, basketball court, playground, and, at the very end, the pond and overflow sites. Among the nicest, in our view, are sites A42 through A47, which back up into the woods but are an easy walk to the snack bar, pool, and other facilities. Tent sites are clustered just behind the 'A' section. With so much to do, families will be happy here, in this very resort-like property.

BASICS

Operated By: Resorts USA. **Open:** Mid-Apr.–mid-Oct. **Site Assignment:** Outdoor World is a membership park. Call (800) 222-5557 for information on arranging a visit. or to reserve a campsite. **Registration:** At office. **Fee:** $25 per family. V, MC, D, Amex. **Parking:** At site.

FACILITIES

Number of RV Sites: 180. **Number of Tent-Only Sites:** 8. **Hookups:** Water, electric (30, 50 amps), sewer. **Each Site:** Picnic table, fire ring, grill. **Dump Station:** No. **Laundry:** Yes. **Pay Phone:** Yes. **Rest Rooms and Showers:** Yes. **Fuel:** No. **Propane:** Yes. **Internal Roads:** Gravel, in good condition. **RV Service:** No. **Market:** 5 mi. east. **Restaurant:** Yes. **General Store:** Yes. **Vending:** Yes. **Swimming Pool:** Yes. **Playground:** Yes. **Other:** Game room, rec hall, tennis courts. **Activities:** Tennis, swimming, volleyball, softball, bocce, shuffleboard, horseshoes, canoeing, kayaking, planned activities. **Nearby Attractions:** Edaville Railroad, berry picking, golf, outlet shopping, Plymouth attractions. **Additional Information:** Bristol County CVB, (508) 997-1250 or (800) 288-6263; www.bristol-county.org.

RESTRICTIONS

Pets: Must be leashed, quiet, & cleaned up after. Not permitted in buildings, pavilions, or pool & lake areas. Must not be left unattended. **Fires:** In fireplaces only. **Alcoholic Beverages:** Yes. Must be in a cup when carried off site. **Vehicle Maximum Length:** None. **Other:** Maximum 10 people per campsite (including visitors) at any time.

TO GET THERE

Take I-495 south to junction of Rte. 58, exit 2. Turn right and go to traffic light where Rte. 58 becomes County Rd. Continue south on County Rd. 1.5 mi. to High St. Turn right on High St. and go another 1.5 mi. to Stevens Rd. Turn left onto Stevens Rd., follow signs 0.5 mi. to campground entrance.

SAGAMORE

Scusset Beach State Reservation Camping Area

140 Scusset Beach Rd., Buzzards Bay 02532. T: (508) 888-0859; www.state.ma.us/dem/parks/scus.htm.

RV ★★★ Tent ★★★★

Beauty: ★★★★	Site Privacy: ★★★
Spaciousness: ★★★★	Quiet: ★★★★
Security: ★★★★★	Cleanliness: ★★★
Insect Control: ★★★	Facilities: ★★

Set on Cape Cod Bay on the Upper Cape, Scusset Beach State Reservation is the quietest camping place in the area. The public beach is reachable via a long, looping road; the camping area is set back from the shore, behind the bathhouse, snack bar, and parking lot. The grassy, back-in RV sites are fairly open; scattered low trees provide some buffer between sites, but not much shade. The worst RV sites are numbers 80 through 91, located on an open field right next to the beach parking lot. Anything set back (lower numbers) is much better. Tent sites are surprisingly secluded. While the tent sites (grouped together) are a stroll from the beach, they're tucked away down walking paths, roomy and very private. Each tent site is surrounded by trees. If you're an RVer, don't count on an evening 'round the fire, unless you've brought a campstove; only the tent sites have fireplaces. Only one rest room serves all. This place is low on the frills meter, unless you consider a Cape Cod beach the ultimate amenity.

BASICS

Operated By: Massachusetts State Forests & Parks. **Open:** Apr.–Columbus Day. **Site Assignment:** Reservations recommended. Reserve up to six months in advance by calling ReserveAmerica at (877) I-CAMP MA or online at www.reservamerica.com. To change arrival or departure date, or site type, call at least three dayas prior to arrival date. $10 cancellation/transfer fee. No refunds for amounts less than $5. **Registration:** At office. **Fee:** Massachusetts residents, $17; non-residents, $20. V, MC. **Parking:** At sites or parking lots only.

FACILITIES

Number of RV Sites: 98. **Number of Tent-Only Sites:** 5. **Hookups:** Water, electric (20, 30 amps). **Each Site:** Picnic table (fireplaces at tent sites only). **Dump Station:** Yes. **Laundry:** No. **Pay Phone:** Yes. **Rest Rooms and Showers:** Yes. **Fuel:** No. **Propane:** No. **Internal Roads:** Paved, in good condition. **RV Service:** No. **Market:** 4-5 mi. west in Bourne. **Restaurant:** 2 mi. south. **General Store:** Yes. **Vending:** No. **Swimming Pool:** No. **Playground:** No. **Other:** Interpretive center, fishing pier. **Activities:** Swimming (in Cape Cod Bay), bicycling, volleyball, planned activities. **Nearby Attractions:** Boating, fishing, antique shops, golf, scenic bike paths, ferries to Martha's Vineyard & Nantucket. **Additional Information:** Cape Cod Chamber of Commerce, (888) 33-CAPECOD or (508) 362-3225; www.capecodchamber.org.

RESTRICTIONS

Pets: Must be leashed, quiet, & cleaned up after. Current rabies vaccination certificate required. Posted areas are off-limits to pets. **Fires:** In fireplaces at tent sites only. **Alcoholic Beverages:** No. **Vehicle Maximum Length:** 35 ft. **Other:** Maximum stay is 14 cumulative days between Memorial Day & Labor Day.

TO GET THERE

Follow Rte. 3 to Sagamore Bridge traffic circle, then follow signs to campground.

SALEM

Winter Island Park

50 Winter Island Rd., Salem 01970. T: (978) 745-9430; www.salemweb.com/winterisland; winterisland@cove.com.

RV ★★★ Tent ★★

Beauty: ★★★★	Site Privacy: ★★
Spaciousness: ★	Quiet: ★★
Security: ★★★★	Cleanliness: ★★
Insect Control: ★★★	Facilities: ★★

Talk about a waterfront RV site: at Winter Island Park, you can pull your rig right up alongside the boat ramp and plug in. Any closer, and you'd better sprout a pair of pontoons. Managed by the city of Salem's Park and Recreation Dept., 20-acre Winter Island is a rare thing; a seaside park tucked away in an urban area. Some might call it a hidden gem; if so, it's a rather rough-cut sparkler. The rest rooms could use some attention, and the property has a rather ramshackle feel, with scattered out-buildings that reveal the history of the place. For more than 250 years, the island was a center for commercial fish preparation and boat building. A 1934 Federal-ist-style seaplane hangar is on the property, as are the ruins of Fort Pickering (1799), a colonial fortress. Interpretive signs offer historical details. Just behind the fort is the best tent site, #27, offering shade, seclusion, and close proximity to Waikiki Beach (so named by Coast Guardsmen), a nice crescent of tawny sand on the north end of the park. And how many campgrounds boast a lighthouse on their property? RV sites edge the bustling waterfront, and are also located on a grassy hill inland.

Basics

Operated By: City of Salem. **Open:** May 1–Nov. 1. **Site Assignment:** Reservation line opens on Feb. 1. Deposit of first night's fee required. Refunds issued for cancellation if made 7 days or more prior to arrival date. **Registration:** At office. **Fee:** Tents, $15; RVs, $25–$35. Checks, V, MC. **Parking:** At sites only or as directed.

Facilities

Number of RV Sites: 34. **Number of Tent-Only Sites:** 25. **Hookups:** Water, electric (30, 50 amps). **Each Site:** Picnic table, grill. **Dump Station:** Yes. **Laundry:** No. **Pay Phone:** Yes. **Rest Rooms and Showers:** Yes. **Fuel:** No. **Propane:** No. **Internal Roads:** Gravel, good condition. **RV Service:** No. **Market:** 1 mi. north. **Restaurant:** 1 mi. north on Bridge St. **General Store:** Yes. **Vending:** Yes. **Swimming Pool:** No. **Playground:** Yes. **Other:** Boat ramp. **Activities:** Ocean beach, swimming, boating, walking trail w/interpretive signage, volleyball, picnic shelter (planned). **Nearby Attractions:** Peabody Essex Museum, Salem Willows amusement park, Salem Witch Museum, Witch Dungeon Museum, House of Seven Gables, McIntyre Historic District self-guided walking tour, whale-watching boat cruises, Le Grand David magic show, scenic Marblehead Harbor. **Additional Information:** North of Boston CVB, (978) 977-7760 or (800) 742-5306; www.northofboston.org.

Restrictions

Pets: Must be leashed & cleaned up after. Must show proof of rabies vaccination at check-in. Clean up after pets. Do not leave pets unattended. Pets prohibited on ocean, beach, & in rest rooms. **Fires:** In grills only. **Alcoholic Beverages:** No. **Vehicle Maximum Length:** None. **Other:** Big rigs welcome.

To Get There

From Rte. 128N, take Exit 25A and follow Rte. 114E into Salem. There will be a gas station on your left; go up on overpass and take your first right, then take a right back under the overpass onto Bridge St. Go straight around the rotary until you come to a blinking yellow light. Keep going straight onto island until you reach the first set of working lights. Take that right onto Webb St. Follow Webb all the way until you see a power plant on your right. After passing the power plant, take your first right onto Winter Island Rd. Road leads into park and entrance gate.

SALISBURY
Black Bear Family Campground

54 Main St., Salisbury 01952. T: (978) 462-3183; www.blackbearcamping.com; bbcamping@aol.com.

RV ★★★★ Tent ★★

Beauty: ★★★ Site Privacy: ★★★
Spaciousness: ★★ Quiet: ★★★★
Security: ★★★ Cleanliness: ★★★★
Insect Control: ★★★ Facilities: ★★★★

Despite the menacing appearance of the black bear sculpture at the entrance, the Chouinard family welcomes campers who like a few amenities with their outdoor experience. Although it is located near Salisbury Beach State Reservation, (see listing), this campground offers a completely different experience. The trappings at this suburban campground include two swimming pools, a nice playground area, and a '50s-style rec hall with a pool table and video games. The campground owners operate a pizza shop/bakery next door. The campground is located just south of the New Hampshire border, near the junctions of I-95 and Rte. 1, so it's a handy base for exploring Portsmouth, New Hampshire and Hampton Beach, and it's only three miles from Salisbury Beach. (Bonus: there's a free trolley to the beaches.) Some campsites are shaded, some are open, and some look to be fairly permanent. If your list of campground qualifications reads: 'quiet, family-friendly, and easily accessible to the highway,' Black Bear Family Campground will meet your needs squarely.

Basics

Operated By: Chouinard family. **Open:** May 15–Sept. 30. **Site Assignment:** Reservations accepted year-round. Reservations recommended for Jul. & Aug. For 7 nights or less, payment due in full or 1 weeks' deposit. Refunds only w/cancellation 2 weeks prior to arrival date. Walk-ins & weekenders are welcome & assigned on a space-available basis. (Limited number of sites available for less than 1 week.). **Registration:** At office. **Fee:** Tents, $25–$35. Rate is based on 2 people. Extra adult, $5; extra child under age 18, $1. V, MC. **Parking:** At site. Only 1 car per site.

Facilities

Number of RV Sites: 225. **Number of Tent-Only Sites:** 25. **Hookups:** Water, electric (30, 50 amps), sewer, modem. **Each Site:** Picnic table, fire ring. **Dump Station:** Yes. **Laundry:** Yes. **Pay Phone:** Yes. **Rest Rooms and Showers:** Yes, coin op. **Fuel:** No. **Propane:** No. **Internal Roads:** Gravel, in good condition. **RV Service:** No. **Market:** 1 mi. north. **Restaurant:** Yes. **General Store:** No. **Vending:** No. **Swimming Pool:** Yes. **Playground:** Yes. **Other:** Rec hall. **Activities:** Volleyball, basketball, horseshoes, shuffleboard, pool table, arcade games. **Nearby Attractions:** Ocean beaches, whale-watching cruises, Salisbury Beach amusement area, deep sea fishing charters, golf. **Additional Information:** North of Boston CVB, (978) 977-7760 or (800) 742-5306; www.northofboston.org.

Restrictions

Pets: Small pets permitted if leashed at all times & cleaned up after. **Fires:** In fire rings only. **Alcoholic Beverages:** Sites only. **Vehicle Maximum Length:** None. **Other:** 2 week max. stay for tent campers.

To Get There

From I-95, take Exit 60. At first set of lights, take a left. Campground entrance is 200 feet on the left.

SALISBURY
Rusnik Campground

Rte. 1, Salisbury 01952. T: (978) 462-0551 (summer) or (978) 465-5295 (winter); www.gocampingamer ica.com/rusnik; www.rusnik.com; rusnik2001@ aol.com.

RV ★★★ Tent ★★★

Beauty: ★★★ Site Privacy: ★★
Spaciousness: ★★★ Quiet: ★★★
Security: ★★★★★ Cleanliness: ★★★
Insect Control: ★★ Facilities: ★★★

Located about 40 miles north of Boston, near the border of New Hampshire, Rusnik Family Campground is one of a cluster of campsites near Salisbury Beach and the Atlantic Coast. Salisbury Beach is just three miles away; more upscale Hampton Beach (New Hampshire) is a four-mile jaunt. The inviting, tourist-friendly seaport towns of Portsmouth, New Hampshire and Newburyport, Massachusetts are a close hop away, beckoning vacationers with unique shops, good restaurants, and whale watch boat cruises. With all that going for it, this campground doesn't have to offer much in the way of amenities, although there's a swimming pool (in need of umbrellas for shade) and a pretty basic mini-golf course. Campsites are grouped around an open green. About half are seasonal sites. All sites have water and electricity, and all are back-ins, with some shade and gravel. Site A2 is close to the pool, handy if you're camping with kids who'll use it a lot. Sites E37, 38, and 39 are quiet, and will hold RVs bigger than 40 feet. Site B11 is pretty and wooded. All in all, Rusnik Campground is a quiet and appealing base for sightseeing.

Basics

Operated By: Murray family. **Open:** May 15–Columbus Day. **Site Assignment:** Reservations recommended. Deposit for full amount required to secure reservation (checks OK); refund upon cancellation w/two weeks' notice. **Registration:** At office. **Fee:** $28 for two adults; additional adults, $5 per day; addition children under age 18, $1 daily. V, MC. **Parking:** At site, or designated lot only.

Facilities

Number of RV Sites: 150. **Number of Tent-Only Sites:** 0. **Hookups:** Water, electric (30 amps). **Each Site:** Picnic table, fireplace. **Dump Station:** Yes. **Laundry:** Yes. **Pay Phone:** Yes. **Rest Rooms and Showers:** Yes, coin-op. **Fuel:** No. **Propane:** Yes. **Internal Roads:** Gravel, in good condition. **RV Service:** No. **Market:** 1–2 mi. south, on Rte. 1. **Restaurant:** 1–2 mi. south, on Rte. 1.

General Store: Yes. **Vending:** No. **Swimming Pool:** Yes. **Playground:** Yes. **Other:** Rec hall. **Activities:** Mini-golf, basketball, horseshoes, bocce, volleyball, swimming. **Nearby Attractions:** Salisbury Beach amusement area, whale-watching, ocean beaches, golf, outlet shopping (Kittery, Maine). **Additional Information:** North of Boston CVB, (978) 977-7760 or (800) 742-5306; www.northofboston.org.

Restrictions

Pets: Must be quiet, leashed, & cleaned up after. Must not be left unattended. **Fires:** In fireplaces only. **Alcoholic Beverages:** Yes. **Vehicle Maximum Length:** 40 ft. **Other:** Two night min. stay, from Memorial Day through Labor Day; three night min. on holidays.

To Get There

From I-95 northbound, take exit 58A. Go 2.4 mi. on Rte. 110 east to Rte. 1. Proceed 1 mi. north on Rte. 1 to campground, on left.

SALISBURY

Salisbury Beach State Reservation

P.O. Box 5303, Salisbury 01952. T: (978) 462-4481 or (877) I CAMP MA (reservations); www.state.ma.us/dem/ or www.reserve america.com.

RV ★★★★★ Tent ★★★

Beauty: ★★★★★	Site Privacy: ★★★
Spaciousness: ★★★★	Quiet: ★★★
Security: ★★★	Cleanliness: ★★★★
Insect Control: ★★★	Facilities: ★★★

If this stretch of beach wasn't owned by the state, it would be chock-a-block with high-rise hotels. No wonder Salisbury Beach State Reservation is a favorite of beach-loving campers. It's an "ahh"-inspiring, panoramic vista of sandy shore, lapped by the sparkling waters of the North Atlantic. Located 40 miles north of Boston, at the northeast border of Massachusetts, Salisbury Beach is a destination campground. Why leave, when there's a four-mile ocean beach (swimming permitted), a one-mile river beach, a boardwalk for strolling, fishing gear for rent, and ranger programs in the evenings (in season)? Whether you choose a site alongside the Merrimack River, or a spot near the ocean beach, it's hard to go wrong here. Like a suburban subdivision, campsites are set in rows on "streets" labeled A-H and W-Z, within the park's perimeter loop road. With this set-up, there's not a lot of privacy. Tent campers are likely to feel rather exposed. Sites are grassy, with little shade. The campground is immaculate and well-maintained. You can't beat $20 (or less) per night for an oceanfront setting, and clean rest rooms to boot. While the honky-tonk action of Salisbury Beach (go-carts, skee-ball, dance clubs) is right up the street, it's easy to leave it all behind here.

Basics

Operated By: Massachusetts State Forests & Parks. **Open:** Mid-Apr.–mid-Oct. Limited winter camping available. **Site Assignment:** Reserve up to 6 months in advance by calling (877) I CAMP MA or on line at www.reserveamerica.com. If you cancel or change dates or type of site, call (877) 422-6762 at least 3 days prior to arrival. $10 cancellation/transfer fee. Full payment w/credit card or check required, 30 days prior to arrival. Cancellation fee, $10. 20 percent of campsites reserved for walk-ins. **Registration:** At office. **Fee:** MA residents, $17 w/electric, $14 without. Non-residents, $20–$17. V, MC. **Parking:** At site.

Facilities

Number of RV Sites: 484. **Number of Tent-Only Sites:** 0. **Hookups:** Water, electric (15, 20 amps). **Each Site:** Picnic table, fireplace. **Dump Station:** Yes. **Laundry:** No. **Pay Phone:** Yes. **Rest Rooms and Showers:** Yes. **Fuel:** No. **Propane:** No. **Internal Roads:** Paved, in good condition. **RV Service:** No. **Market:** 4 mi. west. **Restaurant:** Several within 1 mi. **General Store:** Yes. **Vending:** Yes. **Swimming Pool:** No. **Playground:** Yes. **Other:** Boat ramp, boardwalk. **Activities:** Evening ranger programs, swimming, boating, canoeing, fishing in ocean & Merrimack River (ocean fishing prohibited from 10 a.m. to 5 p.m. Rentals & bait available, no license needed). **Nearby Attractions:** Pirate's Fun Park (amusement rides), golf, go-cart track, whale watch boat cruises (out of Newburyport), scenic tours. **Additional Information:** North of Boston CVB, (978) 977-7760 or (800) 742-5306; www.northofboston.org.

Restrictions

Pets: Must be leashed & cleaned up after. Must not be left unattended. Proof of rabies vaccination required at check-in. No pets allowed on ocean, beach, or in rest rooms. **Fires:** Fireplaces only. **Alcoholic Beverages:** No. **Vehicle Maximum Length:** 35 ft. **Other:** Maximum stay is 14 cumulative days between Memorial Day & Labor Day.

To Get There

From junction of I-95 and Rte. 110, head east on Rte. 110 to Rte. 1-A North. Follow signs to state resevation.

SANDWICH

Peters Pond Park Family Camping

185 Cotuit Rd., P.O. Box 999, Sandwich 02563. T: (508) 477-1775; F: (508) 477-1777; www.campcape cod.com; info@peterspond.com.

RV ★★★★ Tent ★

Beauty: ★★	Site Privacy: ★★★
Spaciousness: ★★★	Quiet: ★★
Security: ★★★★★	Cleanliness: ★★★★
Insect Control: ★★	Facilities: ★★★★

This bustling family campground is just seven miles from the Sagamore Bridge, one of two bridges marking the 'entrance' to the vacationland of Cape Cod. And it's definitely a vacation scene here, complete with nightly campfires, a party tent, and kids whooping it up on aqua bikes and paddle boats. The big drawing card here is a 137-acre springfed pond, stocked with salmon, trout and bass, with a nice, sandy beach. (There are actually two beaches, but one is too small to bother with.) Another nice feature: the campground abuts the Rebel Lot Conservation Area, offering good hiking trails. Campsites, with an average width of 40 feet, are set on small side streets, village-like, off a main road. Not quite half the sites are seasonal. A good number of these are set at the far end of the campground. Sites are lined with pine needles or cedar chips and are very level. Best sites on the pond are C21 and 22. Other than those sites, we'd skip the C loop, though; it's pretty crowded. Nice touch: campers get a handy booklet with campground info and map, discounted tickets to area attractions, restaurant menus, etc.

Basics

Operated By: Peters Pond Trust. **Open:** Patriot's Day (mid-Apr.)–Columbus Day. **Site Assignment:** Reservations recommended. Call the Sunday before for weekend reservations during summer season. For each week of camping, a deposit of equal to two-day fee is required. For holiday weekends, deposit is three-day fee. Deposit secures reservation. Checks & credit cards OK for deposit. Cancellation notice of two weeks required for refunds, minus service charge. **Registration:** At office. **Fee:** $27–$40. Rate includes up to four people. V, MC. **Parking:** At site.

Facilities

Number of RV Sites: 452. **Number of Tent-Only Sites:** 0. **Hookups:** Water, electric (20, 30, 50 amps), sewer, cable TV, modem. **Each Site:** Picnic table. **Dump Station:** Yes. **Laundry:** Yes. **Pay Phone:** Yes. **Rest Rooms and Showers:** Yes, coin-op. **Fuel:** No. **Propane:** Yes. **Internal Roads:** Paved, in good condition. **RV Service:** No. **Market:** 5 mi. north. **Restaurant:** Yes (snack bar). **General Store:** Yes. **Vending:** Yes. **Swimming Pool:** No. **Playground:** Yes. **Other:** Rec hall, boat ramp. **Activities:** Lake swimming, boating (rental rowboats, paddleboats, kayaks, aqua cycles), fishing, basketball, ball field, hiking, shuffleboard, volleyball, horseshoes, planned activities. **Nearby Attractions:** Thornton Burgess Museum, Sandwich Glass Museum, Aptucxet Trading Post, ocean beaches, golf. **Additional Information:** Cape Cod Chamber of Commerce, (888) 33-CAPECOD; (508) 862-0700; www.capecodchamber.org.

Restrictions

Pets: Pets welcome from opening day until July 1 & Labor Day until closing. Spruce St. camping area can campers w/pets during July & Aug. Must be leashed; must have rabies vaccination certificate. Must be kept on site in July & Aug. **Fires:** No open fires. **Alcoholic Beverages:** At sites only. **Vehicle Maximum Length:** 45 ft. **Other:** Three-day min. stay on holidays.

To Get There

Take Rte. 3 south to Sagamore Bridge. From bridge, follow Rte. 6 to exit 2, Rte. 130. Turn right, go 3 mi. Turn left at first set of lights, Quaker Meeting House Rd. Turn right at next set of lights (Cotuit Rd.) Then head south 0.5 mi. to campground, on right.

SANDWICH

Shawme-Crowell State Forest

42 Main St., P.O. Box 621, Sandwich 02563.
T: (508) 888-0351;
www.state.ma.us/dem/parks/shrcr.htm.

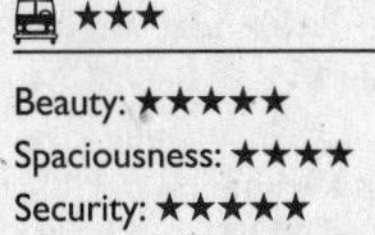

RV ★★★ Tent ★★★★★

Beauty: ★★★★★ Site Privacy: ★★★★★
Spaciousness: ★★★★ Quiet: ★★★★★
Security: ★★★★★ Cleanliness: ★★★★
Insect Control: ★★★ Facilities: ★★★★

Set in Sandwich, the oldest town on Cape Cod, this gorgeous state park camping area is a wonderful option for tent campers and RVers with self-contained units. Campsites are arranged in two loops, Area 1 (hilly, with mixed forest) and Area 2 (piney woods.) Area 1 is closest to the campground entrance and campstore. It's hard to find a bad campsite here. Some have long driveways, though, and would pose a challenge for RVs. Site C26, in Area 1, is pretty and offers easy access for RVs, while site 31 is extra-big. The most appealing sites in Area 1, privacy-wise, are sites C7 and C8, located on a dead end off the main road, but near rest rooms and showers. We prefer pine-scented Area 2, though, especially sites A14 (gorgeous, wide, and near rest rooms and A18. This campground has plenty of rest rooms, by the way, but only one (in Area 2) is open for year-'round campers. Extra bang for your buck: Your camping fee buys you day-use privileges at Scusset Beach State Reservation, located across the Sagamore Bridge. There's camping there, too, but we'd stay here and day-trip to Scusset Beach.

BASICS

Operated By: Massachusetts State Forests & Parks. **Open:** Year-round. **Site Assignment:** Reservations recommended. Reserve up to six months in advance by calling ReserveAmerica at (877) I-CAMP MA or online at www.reservamerica .com. 20 percent of campsites are non-reservable, & available for walk-in campers. To change arrival or departure date, or site type, call at least three dayas prior to arrival date. $10 cancellation/transfer fee. No refunds for amounts less than $5. **Registration:** At office. **Fee:** Massachusetts residents, $10; non-residents, $12. V, MC. **Parking:** At site.

FACILITIES

Number of RV Sites: 285. **Number of Tent-Only Sites:** 0. **Hookups:** None. **Each Site:** Picnic table, fireplace. **Dump Station:** Yes. **Laundry:** No. **Pay Phone:** Yes. **Rest Rooms and Showers:** Yes. **Fuel:** No. **Propane:** No. **Internal Roads:** Paved & gravel, in good condition. **RV Service:** No. **Market:** 5 mi. south. **Restaurant:** 4 mi. east or west. **General Store:** Yes. **Vending:** No. **Swimming Pool:** No. **Playground:** Yes. **Other:** Hunting, horseback riding trails. **Activities:** Biking (on paved roads, mountain bike trails,and along the Cape Cod Canal), fishing (Cape Cod Canal & Cape Cod Bay), hiking, interpretive programs. **Nearby Attractions:** Thornton Burgess Museum, Sandwich Glass Museum, Aptucxet Trading Post, ocean beaches, golf. **Additional Information:** Cape Cod Chamber of Commerce, (888) 33-CAPECOD; (508) 862-0700; www.capecodchamber.org.

RESTRICTIONS

Pets: Must be leashed, quiet, & cleaned up after. Current rabies vaccination certificate required. Posted areas are off-limits to pets. **Fires:** In fireplaces only. **Alcoholic Beverages:** No. **Vehicle Maximum Length:** 35 ft. **Other:** Maximum stay is 14 cumulative days between Memorial Day & Labor Day.

TO GET THERE

Follow Rte. 6 east to exit 1. Turn right at the traffic light onto Rte. 6A, and another right to Rte. 130. Campground entrance is 0.5 mi. on the right.

SAVOY

Shady Pines Campground

547 Loop Rd., Savoy 01256. T: (413) 743-2694; www.shadypinescampground.com; shdypnescg@aol.com.

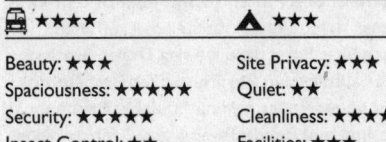

RV ★★★★ Tent ★★★

Beauty: ★★★ Site Privacy: ★★★
Spaciousness: ★★★★★ Quiet: ★★
Security: ★★★★★ Cleanliness: ★★★★
Insect Control: ★★ Facilities: ★★★

Amidst the rolling hills and farmlands of the Berkshires in Western Massachusetts, this campground is a hub of activity. There's often something going on in the adult lounge—perhaps a polka-and-pierogis fest (as when we visited), complete with live entertainment. (Full bar, too.) It's not just a couples scene, though; the fenced-in playground is school-yard sized. Spacious campsites ring a grassy, open area with a ball park, pavilion, swimming pool, and playground. Adjacent to the pavilion is a ten-acre safari field! Somehow, they manage to keep this huge property nicely mown and landscaped; a nice touch is the sand-and-limestone coating on the roads. No mud or dust here. Campsites are semi-wooded or open. Tent sites are clustered in the far right-hand corner of the property, near some rental cabins. These, and RV sites 197 through 202 are in close proximity to walking trails leading to Savoy Mountain. A unique feature here: piped-in music in rest rooms. All in all, a livelier scene than at nearby Peppermint Park Campground (see listing) and—certainly—Windsor State Park.

BASICS

Operated By: Bill & Edna Daniels. **Open:** Year-round. **Site Assignment:** Reservations recommended. Send one-night's fee deposit to reserve. Three-day min. on holiday weekends; reservation will be accepted only w/payment in full. **Registration:** At office. **Fee:** $22 per day, two people; extra children aged 15-18, $3 per day; age 7-14, $2 per day. V, MC. **Parking:** At site.

FACILITIES

Number of RV Sites: 150. **Number of Tent-Only Sites:** 0. **Hookups:** Water, electric (20 amps). **Each Site:** Picnic table, fireplace. **Dump Station:** Yes. **Laundry:** Yes. **Pay Phone:** Yes. **Rest Rooms and Showers:** Yes, coin-op. **Fuel:** No. **Propane:** No. **Internal Roads:** Gravel, in good condition. **RV Service:** No. **Market:** Yes. **Restaurant:** Yes. **General Store:** Yes. **Vending:** No. **Swimming Pool:** Yes. **Playground:** Yes. **Other:** Rec hall, game room, adult lounge (18 & up). **Activities:** Swimming, walking trails, hoursehoes, ball field, planned activities. **Nearby Attractions:** Mt. Greylock, Tanglewood (outdoor concerts), Natural Bridge, Western Gateway Heritage State Park, Mass MOCA (Contemporary Arts museum), Clark Art Institute, Jacob's Pillow (dance). **Additional Information:** Berkshire Hills Visitors Bureau, (413) 443-9186 or (800) 237-5747; www.berkshires.org.

RESTRICTIONS

Pets: Must be leashed & cleaned up after. Must not be left unattended. Walk dogs in woods, away from campsites. **Fires:** Fireplaces only. **Alcoholic Beverages:** Yes. **Vehicle Maximum Length:** 40 ft. **Other:** No motorcycles.

TO GET THERE

From junction of Rte. 8A and Rte. 116, go 3 mi. southeast on Rte. 116, then 0.25 mi. north on Loop Rd. Campground entrance is on the right.

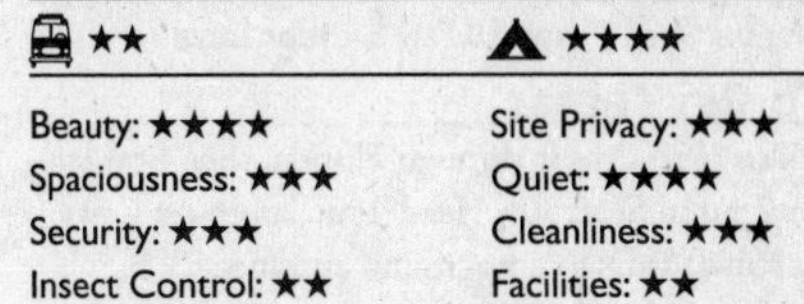

SAVOY/FLORIDA

Savoy Mountain State Forest

260 Central Shaft Rd., Florida 01247. T: (413) 663-8469;
www.state.ma.us/dem/parks/svym.htm.

RV ★★ Tent ★★★★

Beauty: ★★★★ Site Privacy: ★★★
Spaciousness: ★★★ Quiet: ★★★★
Security: ★★★ Cleanliness: ★★★
Insect Control: ★★ Facilities: ★★

A ranger at another state park, with 30 years' experience in the system, deems Savoy Mountain his absolute favorite. It's easy to see why. Located in the Berkshire Hills of Western Massachusetts, this park offers wonderful diversity, with waterfalls, balanced rocks, and scenic vistas galore. Campsites are located in an old apple orchard, which fill the air with scent in springtime. Wooded hills rise in the distance, while fields of moutain laurel are studded with sparkling ponds. Recreational activities including hiking (60 miles of trails), pond swimming, or fishing in trout-stocked North Pond. Campsites, set in a loop, are mostly open and grassy, bordered by trees. Sites 13 through 18, nearest the beach at South Pond, fill up quickly, as do the three nice-looking rustic cabins. Site 43 is fairly open, but near the rest room. Number 29 is very wooded, while sites 21, 22, and 23 are set back for ample privacy. This park offers an inviting wilderness getaway for tent campers and pop-up RVs but note that it's located in bear country (and we saw evidence of same), so practice bear-safe camping.

BASICS

Operated By: Massachusetts State Forests & Parks. **Open:** Mid-May–Columbus Day. **Site Assignment:** Reservations recommended. Reserve up to six months in advance by callingReserveAmerica at (877) I-CAMP-MA or online at www.reservamerica.com. Thirty-six campsites are reservable; nine are non-reservable & held on a first-come, first-served basis. To change arrival or departure date, or site type, call at least three dayas prior to arrival date. $10 cancellation/transfer fee. No refunds for amounts less than $5. **Registration:** At office. **Fee:** Massachusetts residents, $10; non-residents, $12. Log cabins, $25.V, MC. **Parking:** At site.

Facilities

Number of RV Sites: 45. **Number of Tent-Only Sites:** 0. **Hookups:** None. **Each Site:** Picnic table, fireplace. **Dump Station:** No. **Laundry:** No. **Pay Phone:** Yes. **Rest Rooms and Showers:** Yes. **Fuel:** No. **Propane:** No. **Internal Roads:** Paved, in good condition. **RV Service:** No. **Market:** 0.7 mi. north. **Restaurant:** 5 mi. west. **General Store:** No. **Vending:** Yes. **Swimming Pool:** No. **Playground:** No. **Other:** Boat ramp, nature center. **Activities:** Swimming, boating (no gas-powered engines), interpretive programs, fishing. **Nearby Attractions:** Mt. Greylock, Tanglewood (outdoor concerts), Natural Bridge State Park, Western Gateway Heritage State Park, Mass MOCA (contemporary art), Clark Art Institute, Jacob's Pillow (dance). **Additional Information:** Berkshire Hills Visitors Bureau, (413) 443-9186 or (800) 237-5747; www.berkshires.org.

Restrictions

Pets: Must be leashed & cleaned up after. Must not be left unattended. Proof of rabies vaccination required. **Fires:** In fireplaces only. **Alcoholic Beverages:** At site only. **Vehicle Maximum Length:** 16 ft. **Other:** Maximum stay limit is 14 cumulative days between Memorial Day & Labor Day.

To Get There

Follow Rte. 2 west through Florida, then bear left on Central Shaft Rd, Head 4 mi. south on Central Shaft Rd. to campground entrance.

SHELBURNE FALLS

Springbrook Family Camping Area

Patten Rd., Box 52, Shelburne Falls 01370.T: (413) 625-6618; www.springbrookcamping.com; info@ springbrookcamping.com.

RV ★★★ Tent ★★

Beauty: ★★★★	Site Privacy: ★★★
Spaciousness: ★★★★	Quiet: ★★★
Security: ★★★★	Cleanliness: ★★★
Insect Control: ★★★	Facilities: ★★

Set in a quiet farming community along the Mohawk Trail in Western Massachusetts, Springbrook boasts a feature that other area campgrounds can't match: sweeping, high-elevation views of the Holyoke Range to the south, New Hampshire's Mt. Monadnock to the north, and Mt. Wachusett in the middle. Granted, these aren't the Tetons, but this rolling panorama is lovely, especially during fall foliage season. The scenic drive into the campground and tall, fragrant pines add to the ambience here. About half the campsites are seasonal, the other half are transient, and, alas, it's the former who nab best views. There's an open field for those who wish to wander over and enjoy the scenery. Set in a north-south loop along the hillside, sites are spacious, and semi-wooded, with a few pull-thrus. Tents are grouped in a separate area at the western edge of the campground. Tent site F, at the end of the loop, offers the most privacy, although it's a bit far from the rest rooms. For RVs, sites 80 and 82 and 49, 50, and 50A, at the far south end of the property, offer plenty of space. Family-run for 40-plus years, Springbrook is the nicest commercial campground in the area, and a good choice for campers looking for a peaceful escape but more services than they'd find at a nearby state park.

Basics

Operated By: Dean family. **Open:** May 15–Oct. 15. **Site Assignment:** Reservations recommended. Deposit of one night's fee must be received within 7 days. No reservation is confirmed until deposit is received. Three-day min. on holidays; 3-day deposit required. Refunds will be granted w/two week notice of cancellation of if same site can be re-rented. **Registration:** At office. **Fee:** $22–$24 based on two adults w/children under age 17, one car, one camping unit. One day free w/one-week stay.V, MC. **Parking:** At site.

Facilities

Number of RV Sites: 69. **Number of Tent-Only Sites:** 11. **Hookups:** Water, electric (30 amps). **Each Site:** Picnic table, fire ring. **Dump Station:** Yes. **Laundry:** No. **Pay Phone:** Yes. **Rest Rooms and Showers:** Yes, coin-op. **Fuel:** No. **Propane:** Yes. **Internal Roads:** Paved & gravel, fair condition. **RV Service:** No. **Market:** 5 mi. east, at junction of Rte. 2 & I-91. **Restaurant:** 5 mi. east, at junction of Rte. 2 & I-91. **General Store:** Yes. **Vending:** No. **Swimming Pool:** Yes. **Playground:** Yes. **Other:** Rec hall. **Activities:** Volleyball, horseshoes, croquet, shuffleboard, swimming. **Nearby Attractions:** Bridge of Flowers, glacial pot holes, Mohawk Trail scenic drive, golf, Historic Deerfield. **Additional Information:** Berkshire Hills Visitors Bureau, (413) 443-9186 or (800) 237-5747; www.berkshires.org.

Restrictions

Pets: Must be leashed, quiet, & cleaned up after. Proof of rabies vaccination required. **Fires:** In fire rings only. **Alcoholic Beverages:** Sites only. **Vehicle Maximum Length:** 35 ft. **Other:** Quiet hours are from 10:30 p.m. until 7:30 a.m.

To Get There

From I-91, take exit 26 (Greenfield), heading 5.5 mi. west on Rte. 2 to Shelburne Center. Just before the church, turn right (north) onto Little Mohawk Rd. Go 1.5 mi. to Patten District sign, turn left and keep left. Campground entrance is on left.

SOUTH CARVER

Myles Standish State Forest

Cranberry Rd., P.O. Box 66, South Carver 02366.T: (508) 866-2526; www.state.ma.us/dem/parks/ mssf.htm.

RV ★★ Tent ★★★

Beauty: ★★★★★	Site Privacy: ★★★★
Spaciousness: ★★★★	Quiet: ★★★★★
Security: ★★★	Cleanliness: ★★★
Insect Control: ★★	Facilities: ★★★

It's not easy trying to find it-those helpful blue RV road signs seem to be missing at key points along the route-but this immense state forest is worth sleuthing out. Just 40 miles from Boston, Miles Standish State Forest is the largest remaining pine barrens zone in New England, and one of the largest public open spaces in Massachusetts. Soaring pitch pines, scrub oak, and plantations of white and red pine make this a real wilderness escape. Dozens of gem-like ponds dot the landscape. Campsites are clustered near the ponds, with the best ones overlooking Barrett Pond. Camp near Fearing Pond, though, and you get the benefit of a swimming hole; plus, the pond is stocked with trout. Sites 18 and 19 are spectacular; best for RVs are sites 28, 34, and 35, all flat, wooded, and wide, offering great views of Fearing Pond. Beyond swimming and fishing, the park offers more than 90 miles of biking and hiking trails (15 paved for biking), and nature programs daily in season, perhaps a wildflower walk or edible plant hike. At nearly 18,000 acres, the park is big and difficult to navigate. Pay close attention to your map, or you may end up, as we did, face-to-face with the MCI Plymouth correctional facility, located, curiously enough, on park property.

Basics

Operated By: Massachusetts State Forests & Parks. **Open:** Mid-Apr.-Columbus Day. Fully open from Memorial Day-Labor Day; sites limited in off-season. Open-self-contained units only, Nov. 1-Apr. 15. **Site Assignment:** Reservations recommended. Reserve up to six months in advance by calling ReserveAmerica at (877) I-CAMP-MA or online at www.reservamerica.com. Some sites are non-reservable & held on a first-come, first-served basis. Arrive before 11 a.m. to get on waiting list. To change arrival or departure date, or site type, call at least three dayas prior to arrival date. $10 cancellation/transfer fee. No refunds for amounts less than $5. **Registration:** At office. **Fee:** Massachusetts residents, $10; non-residents, $12.V, MC. **Parking:** At sites & parking lots near trailheads.

Facilities

Number of RV Sites: 425. **Number of Tent-Only Sites:** 0. **Hookups:** None. **Each Site:** Picnic table, fireplace. **Dump Station:** Yes. **Laundry:** No. **Pay Phone:** Yes. **Rest Rooms and Showers:** Yes. **Fuel:** No. **Propane:** No. **Internal Roads:** Gravel, in good condition. **RV Service:** No. **Market:** 5 mi. north, in Plymouth. **Restaurant:** 5 mi. north, in Plymouth. **General Store:** No. **Vending:** No. **Swimming Pool:** No. **Playground:** No. **Other:** Interpretive center. **Activities:** Bicycling, boating (no gas-powered engines), hiking, swimming in Fearing Pond & College Pond, fishing (trout-stocked Fearing Pond), interpretive programs, wildlife watching (endangered turtles are seen at East Head Reservoir). **Nearby Attractions:** Plimoth Plantation, whale-watching cruises, scenic harbor cruises, Mayflower II, Plymouth National Wax Museum, Pilgrim Hall Museum, winery, Ocean Spray Cranberry World, tours, winery, Edaville Railroad. **Additional Information:** Destination Plymouth, (800) USA-1620 or www.visit-plymouth.com.

Restrictions

Pets: Must be leashed & cleaned up after. Must not be left unattended. Proof of rabies vaccination required. **Fires:** In fireplaces only. **Alcoholic Beverages:** No. **Vehicle Maximum Length:** 30 ft. **Other:** Maximum stay is 14 cumulative days between Memorial Day & Labor Day.

To Get There

From Rte. 3, take exit 5; head west on Long Pond

Rd. Follow signs to campground; turn right on Alden Rd.

SOUTH CARVER

Shady Acres Family Campground

P.O. Box 128, Carver 02366. T: (508) 866-4040.

RV ★★★ Tent ★★

Beauty: ★★ Site Privacy: ★
Spaciousness: ★★★ Quiet: ★★★★★
Security: ★★★ Cleanliness: ★★★
Insect Control: ★★★★★ Facilities: ★★★

This campground is definitely out-of-the-way; you enter via a twisting road lined with cranberry bogs. In fall, when the bogs are flooded, the berries rise to the surface, looking like pools of scarlet. Split-rail fencing adds a nice country feel. The campground itself is pleasant and quiet, if not very fancy (though improvements are being made to the campstore and office.) Thanks to its location, this campground is far quieter than the nearby KOA just off the highway in Middleboro. Campsites are set in a series of loops, with two lanes of full-hookup sites right in the middle. The six tent sites are right up front, too. An ice cream shop and mini-golf course are set just outside the campground; a game room, rec hall,and swimming pools are set back, overlooking a good-sized pond. Campsites are nicely shaded, but a couple of tall trees between sites don't offer much buffer. We'd avoid the sites surrounding the rec hall—numbers 15–19, 111–115, and 8–10, unless you like camping with a soundtrack of pop music.

BASICS

Operated By: Denise & Joseph Soares. **Open:** Mid-Mar.–mid-Dec. **Site Assignment:** Reservations recommended. Deposit equal to one-night's stay required; check or credit card OK. 72-hour notice required for cancellation refunds. **Registration:** At office. **Fee:** $22–$31. Rate based on two adults & two children. V, MC, D. **Parking:** At site.

FACILITIES

Number of RV Sites: 175. **Number of Tent-Only Sites:** 6. **Hookups:** Water, electric (30, 50 amps), sewer. **Each Site:** Picnic table, fire ring. **Dump Station:** Yes. **Laundry:** Yes. **Pay Phone:** Yes. **Rest Rooms and Showers:** Yes, coin-op. **Fuel:** No. **Propane:** Yes. **Internal Roads:** Gravel, in fair condition. **RV Service:** Yes. **Market:** 8 mi. north. **Restaurant:** Yes. **General Store:** Yes. **Vending:** Yes. **Swimming Pool:** Yes (2). **Playground:** Yes. **Other:** Rec hall, game room, mini-golf. **Activities:** Boating, canoeing, fishing (private pond, no license required), swimming, basketball, planned activities. **Nearby Attractions:** Plimoth Plantation, whale-watching cruises, scenic harbor cruises, Mayflower II, Plymouth National Wax Museum, Pilgrim Hall Museum, winery, Ocean Spray Cranberry World, tours, winery, Edaville Railroad. **Additional Information:** Plymouth County CVB, (508) 747-0100 or (800) 231-1620; www.plymouth-1620.com.

RESTRICTIONS

Pets: Must be leashed, quiet, & cleaned up after. Current rabies vaccination certificate required. **Fires:** In fire rings only. **Alcoholic Beverages:** Yes. **Vehicle Maximum Length:** None. **Other:** Two-night min. stay required on weekends from May to Sep.; three-night min. stay required on holidays.

TO GET THERE

From Rte. 495 north, exit at Rte. 58 north and follow to fork. Bear right onto Tremont St. Campground is on right, about 1 mi. past Post Office.

SOUTH PLYMOUTH

Sandy Pond Campground

834 Bourne Rd., Plymouth 02360. T: (508) 759-9336 (Apr. to Sep.) or off-season (508) 224-3707; www.sandypond.com.

RV ★★ Tent ★★

Beauty: ★★ Site Privacy: ★
Spaciousness: ★ Quiet: ★★
Security: ★★★ Cleanliness: ★★★
Insect Control: ★★★★★ Facilities: ★★

As you drive up to this campground, tucked into a residential area, your first thought might be, "Uh-oh!" Just to the left is a wide-open area, chock-a-block with RVs. Keep driving, though, and you'll realize that was the safari area; among the 300 campsites here are many less-exposed places to pull in for the weekend. Spacious, it's not, but this rather intimate setting has a friendly feel. This is mostly due to the campers, including some seasonal guests, who hang out in groups and meet for campground-run activities like candy bingo, kiddie hayrides, and ice cream socials. A footpath leads to a private, sandy beach, one of the nicest we've seen, on Sandy Pond. Among the tent sites, T-24 and 25 overlook another pond, Covel Pond, but are a hike from the rest rooms. T-6, a corner site, is very secluded. With the RV sites, the higher the number, the farther you are from the action, except for FP-100 to 102 and 78–80 (near well-used horseshoe pits.) One caveat: this campground tends to operate in a rather haphazard fashion. Two rigs on the same site? Two different stories with regard to canoe rental availability? It happens! Therefore, the self-sufficient, easy-going camper is likely to manage best here. Like people? All the better.

BASICS

Operated By: Doonan family. **Open:** Apr. 13–Sept. 30. **Site Assignment:** Reservations recommended. Must be accompanied by 50 percent deposit, received at least one week prior to visit. Refunds issued for cancellation if cancellation occurs at least one week prior to visit. **Registration:** At office. **Fee:** $22–$30 based on family of four (two minor children.) V, MC, D. **Parking:** At site.

FACILITIES

Number of RV Sites: 220. **Number of Tent-Only Sites:** 80. **Hookups:** Water, electric (30, 50 amps), sewer. **Each Site:** Picnic table, fire ring. **Dump Station:** Yes. **Laundry:** Yes. **Pay Phone:** Yes. **Rest Rooms and Showers:** Yes, some coin-op. **Fuel:** No. **Propane:** Yes. **Internal Roads:** Gravel, in good condition. **RV Service:** No. **Market:** 5.5 mi. west on Rte. 6W. **Restaurant:** 5.5 mi.west on Rte. 6W. **General Store:** Yes. **Vending:** Yes. **Swimming Pool:** No. **Playground:** Yes. **Other:** Rec hall. **Activities:** Boating (rentals available), canoeing, hiking, swimming, basketball, planned activities. **Nearby Attractions:** Plimoth Plantation, whale-watching cruises, scenic harbor cruises, Mayflower II, Plymouth National Wax Museum, Pilgrim Hall Museum, winery, Ocean Spray Cranberry World, tours, winery. **Additional Information:** Destination Plymouth, (800) USA-1620 or www.visit-plymouth.com.

RESTRICTIONS

Pets: Must have current rabies certificate. No large or aggressive animals (ie. dobermans, pit bulls, shepherds.) $5 fee per day per dog. No pets on holiday weekends. **Fires:** In fire rings only. **Alcoholic Beverages:** Yes, at sites only. **Vehicle Maximum Length:** None. **Other:** Two-night min. stay, Memorial Day through Labor Day. Three-night min. on holidays. 4th of July min. stay; please inquire.

TO GET THERE

Take Rte. 3 South to exit 3. Right at end of ramp, go 0.2 mi. Head left on Long Pond Rd., go 1.75 mi., turn right at Halfway Pond Rd. Go 0.75 mi. Turn left on Bourne Rd. Follow for 6 mi. to campground (on left.)

SOUTHWICK

Sodom Mountain Campground

P.O. Box 702, Southwick 01077. T: (413) 569-3930; F: (413) 569-2987; www.sodommountain.com.

RV ★★★ Tent ★★★

Beauty: ★★★ Site Privacy: ★★★
Spaciousness: ★★★ Quiet: ★★★★
Security: ★★★★★ Cleanliness: ★★
Insect Control: ★★ Facilities: ★★

Heading to Six Flags New England theme park, or other atttractions in the Springfield area? This campground is a convenient base. Located 12 miles east of Six Flags, it's the closest campground to the park, other than Southwick Acres (owned by the same family, but geared more to seniors and seasonal campers than Sodom Mountain.) Another selling point: they offer discounted tickets to Six Flags—sizable discounts on adult admissions, we found. Factor in your savings on a couple of adult tickets to Six Flags, and it's like you're getting a night of camping for free. Not into wild rides and the whole theme park scene? The campground is located alongside Sodom Mountain, offering marked hiking trails for all abilities. We also sleuthed out Southwick's town beach, on South Pond, with a sandy-bottomed, life-guarded swimming area and lots of picnic tables. The campground offers wooded and open sites, with some pull-thrus. Sites 67A and B are nicest for tents, while site 105 is a shady spot for RVs. The G section is the nicest overall, in our view. The rest room (one serves all) is very basic. Check out the peacock pen near the entrance.

BASICS

Operated By: LaFrance family. **Open:** May 1–Columbus Day. **Site Assignment:** Reservations recommended, especially weekends. 1 nights' fee required for deposit. Refunds for cancellations w/ 2 weeks' notice, minus $7 fee. **Registration:** At office. **Fee:** $29–$38 for 2 adults/2 children. V, MC. **Parking:** At site.

FACILITIES

Number of RV Sites: 165. **Number of Tent-Only Sites:** 15. **Hookups:** Water, electric (30, 50 amps), sewer. **Each Site:** Picnic table, fire ring. **Dump Station:** Yes. **Laundry:** Yes. **Pay Phone:** Yes. **Rest Rooms and Showers:** Yes, coin-op. **Fuel:** No. **Propane:** Yes. **Internal Roads:** Gravel, in good condition. **RV Service:** No. **Market:** 4.1 mi. south on Rte. 202. **Restaurant:** 4.1 mi. south on Rte. 202. **General Store:** Yes. **Vending:** Yes. **Swimming Pool:** Yes. **Playground:** Yes. **Other:** Lodge, game room. **Activities:** Swimming, hiking, shuffleboard, basketball, volleyball. **Nearby Attractions:** Six Flags New England theme park, Basketball Hall of Fame, Southwick Motocrosse 338, Big E (Eastern States Exposition) fair, late Sept., Southwick Town Beach at South Pond. **Additional Information:** Greater Springfield CVB, (413) 755-1343; www.valleyvisitor.com.

RESTRICTIONS

Pets: Must be leashed, quiet, & cleaned up after. Must not be left unattended. Current rabies certificate required. **Fires:** In fire rings only. **Alcoholic Beverages:** At sites or in lodge only. **Vehicle Maximum Length:** 40 ft. **Other:** Two-night min. stay required from June through Aug. Three-night min. plus advance payment in full for holidays.

TO GET THERE

From I-90 (Massachusetts Turnpike), take exit 3. Follow Rte. 202 south to Southwick Center. Go through town, then take Rte. 57 west 3 mi. to South Loomis St. Take a left on South Loomis for 0.25 mi. to campground, on right.

STURBRIDGE
Jellystone Park Sturbridge

P.O. Box 600, Sturbridge 01566. T: (508) 347-9570; F: (508) 347-2336; www.jellystonesturbridge.com; rsmith@jellystonesturbridge.com.

RV: ★★★★ Tent: ★★★

Beauty: ★★★	Site Privacy: ★
Spaciousness: ★★	Quiet: ★★
Security: ★★★★★	Cleanliness: ★★★★
Insect Control: ★★★	Facilities: ★★★★★

If the presence of costumed characters Yogi, Cindy, and Boo Boo Bear don't convince you, perhaps the all-day schedule of kid's activities will—the emphasis here is on family fun. Open year-round, the campground offers non-stop action in summer months, from mini-golf to movies to ice cream-eating contests. Some parents escape to the Bear's Den, a post-and-beam style lounge with a stone fireplace. Campsites are arranged in a series of loops, with the far end devoted to rental cabins. Some sites are pull-thru. The camping area is heavily wooded, but there's not much buffer between sites. Two fairly spacious, pretty sites are 739 and 740, although they're a good trek from the beach, pool, and main building activity hub. The nicest tent sites, grouped together here, are 266 and 267, relatively secluded and leafy, also close to rest rooms, laundry, and the aqua center. (Waterslides, a pool and hot tub; they charge extra for these, which seems rather niggly to us.) This park is on the pricey side, but you get lots of activity, good security, and clean facilities for your money.

BASICS

Operated By: James Leaming, manager. **Open:** May–Oct. **Site Assignment:** Reservations recommended. 50% deposit required. Refund for cancellation w/7 days' notice; beyond 7 days, will transfer deposit to another date for camping. **Registration:** At office. **Fee:** Memorial Day to Labor Day, $40-49. Off-season rates, $26 to $33.50. Extra charge on holiday weekends & weekends in July-Aug. Rates are for two adults at site, per day; extra charge of $3 for children; $5-9 for extra adult. Packages availableV, MC, D, AMEX. **Parking:** At site & designated parking areas only.

FACILITIES

Number of RV Sites: 359. **Number of Tent-Only Sites:** 40. **Hookups:** Water, electric (20, 30 amps), sewer, cable TV. **Each Site:** Picnic tables, fire rings. **Dump Station:** Yes. **Laundry:** Yes. **Pay Phone:** Yes. **Rest Rooms and Showers:** Yes. **Fuel:** No. **Propane:** Yes. **Internal Roads:** Paved & gravel, in fair condition. **RV Service:** No. **Market:** 1 mi. north in Sturbridge. **Restaurant:** Yes. **General Store:** Yes. **Vending:** Yes. **Swimming Pool:** Yes. **Playground:** Yes. **Other:** Mini-golf, aqua center (water slide, hot tub), lounge, game room, petting zoo. **Activities:** Lake swimming, fishing (no license required), boating,pony rides. **Nearby Attractions:** Old Sturbridge Village living history museum. **Additional Information:** Plymouth County CVB, (800) 231-1620; www.plymouth-1620.com.

RESTRICTIONS

Pets: Must be leashed, quiet & cleaned up after. Unattended pets should be left inside trailers. **Fires:** In fire rings only. **Alcoholic Beverages:** Yes. **Vehicle Maximum Length:** 40 ft. **Other:** Air conditioners & electric heaters not allowed unless prior arrangements are made w/office.

TO GET THERE

From junction of I-84 and Rte. 20, go 1 mi. west on I-84 to exit 2, then 0.25 mi. on River Rd. Campground entrance is on the right

STURBRIDGE
Outdoor World Sturbridge Resort

19 Maushapaug Rd., Sturbridge 01566. T: (508) 347-7156; F: (508) 347-3535; www.campoutdoorworld.com.

RV: ★★★★ Tent: ★★★

Beauty: ★★★★	Site Privacy: ★★
Spaciousness: ★★★★	Quiet: ★★★
Security: ★★★★	Cleanliness: ★★★★★
Insect Control: ★★★	Facilities: ★★★★★

Step into the piney lodge or the indoor pool and hot tub area, and you'd think you were on the property of a resort hotel. Such is the oh-so-luxe life that awaits the happy camper at Outdoor World, a membership resort owned by Resorts USA. Set on Pioneer Lake, the resort employs a social director, who arranges things like live music, storyteller visits, and events like a cardboard boat race, chili cook-off, and theme weekends. Campsites ring the lake, with the nicest spots right on the water, including RV sites S-6–S-14 (even numbers) and S-21–23, the most secluded of the bunch. Ask for tent site S18A for best views. Sites B-1–5 are lovely, as well. Steer clear of sites near the busy lodge and pool area. The full hookup sites are more exposed and more tightly packed together than the others. Only two are pull-through. Sites aren't terribly spacious, but campers are generally quiet here, and the wooded surroundings provide a peaceful quality. It's a far less rollicking, more adult atmosphere than that of nearby Jellystone Park.

BASICS

Operated By: Resorts USA. **Open:** Year-round. **Site Assignment:** Outdoor World is a membership park. Call (800) 222-5557 for information on arranging a visit, or to reserve a campsite. **Registration:** At office. **Fee:** $35 in summer, $25 in winter. No extra charge for additional persons. V, MC, D, Amex. **Parking:** At site or designated parking areas.

FACILITIES

Number of RV Sites: 93. **Number of Tent-Only Sites:** 5. **Hookups:** Water, electric (30, 50 amps), sewer, cable TV. **Each Site:** Picnic table, fire ring. **Dump Station:** Yes. **Laundry:** Yes. **Pay Phone:** Yes. **Rest Rooms and Showers:** Yes. **Fuel:** No. **Propane:** Yes. **Internal Roads:** Gravel, in good condition. **RV Service:** No. **Market:** 5 mi. north in Sturbridge. **Restaurant:** 5 mi. north in Sturbridge or 1 mi. south. **General Store:** Yes. **Vending:** Yes. **Swimming Pool:** Yes (indoor). **Playground:** Yes. **Other:** Mini-golf, game room, lounge, hot tub, beach, boat house. **Activities:** Lake swimming, boating (canoes, row boats, paddle boats), lake fishing, mini-golf, basketball, volleyball, horseshoes, hiking trails, movies, planned activities. **Nearby Attractions:** Old Sturbridge Village living history museum. **Additional Information:** Plymouth County CVB, (800) 231-1620; www.plymouth-1620.com.

RESTRICTIONS

Pets: On leash. Pets must accompany owner when leaving campsite or trailer. Owners must clean up after pets. **Fires:** Fire pits only. **Alcoholic Beverages:** Yes. **Vehicle Maximum Length:** 35 ft. **Other:** Limit 10 people per campsite.

TO GET THERE

Take the Massachusetts Turnpike west to I-84 (exit 9); follow I-84 to Mass. exit 1 and turn left off exit. Take first right onto Mashapaug Rd. to campground entrance

STURBRIDGE
Wells State Park

Walker Mountain Rd., P.O. Box 602, Sturbridge 01566. T: (508) 347-9257; www.state.ma.us/dem/ parks/well.htm.

RV: ★★ Tent: ★★★★★

Beauty: ★★★★★	Site Privacy: ★★★★
Spaciousness: ★★★★	Quiet: ★★★★★
Security: ★★★	Cleanliness: ★★★★
Insect Control: ★★	Facilities: ★★★

Among the several campgrounds in the Sturbridge area, this one is the 'wilderness' option. If you can do without hookups, you'll enjoy the Old New England beauty of this property. Criss-crossed with stone walls, Wells State Park is a true beauty spot, heavily wooded with a mix of maples and other deciduous trees. Other natural features include a beaver lodge and dam, vernal pools, and a sandy-bottomed pond. The hiking here is exceptional, offering 9.5 miles of marked scenic trails. The 1.5 mile hike to Carpenter's Rocks leads to a cliff face with east-facing views of the park. Interpretive programs include wildflower walks and beaver pond tours. Campsites are set on upper and lower loops, with each loop surrounding a grassy playing field. The lower loop is closest to Walker Pond. On the upper loop, site 51 is spacious and secluded, as is 27, a campsite set far from the road. The best sites on the lower loop feature water views. Sites 15 and 16 are close together, but near the water. Site 19 is a good waterfront RV site, with pull-thru access. A couple of waterfront sites are held for walk-ins and not reservable, so it may be possible, with luck, to get a prime spot here without planning ahead.

Basics

Operated By: Massachusetts Forest & Park Service. **Open:** May 1–Columbus Day. **Site Assignment:** Reserve up to 6 months in advance through ReserveAmerica by calling (877) CAMP MA or online at www.reserveamerica.com. To change your reservation or site type, or to cancel, you must call at least 3 days prior to your arrival date. $10 cancellation/transfer fee. Refunds for amounts less than $5 cannot be processed. Two night min. stay required on weekends. **Registration:** At park headquarters. **Fee:** Massachusetts residents, $10; non-residents, $12. V, MC. **Parking:** At site & parking lot only.

Facilities

Number of RV Sites: 58. **Number of Tent-Only Sites:** 2. **Hookups:** None. **Each Site:** Picnic table, fireplace w/grill, lantern pole. **Dump Station:** Yes. **Laundry:** No. **Pay Phone:** Yes. **Rest Rooms and Showers:** Yes. **Fuel:** No. **Propane:** No. **Internal Roads:** Gravel, in good condition. **RV Service:** No. **Market:** 2.3 mi. east in Sturbridge. **Restaurant:** 2.3 mi. east in Sturbridge. **General Store:** No. **Vending:** Yes. **Swimming Pool:** No. **Playground:** No. **Other:** Interpretive center. **Activities:** Swimming in Walker Pond, beach, ball fields, basketball court, hiking, biking, equestrian trails, fishing, interpretive programs for children (must be accompanied by an adult). **Nearby Attractions:** Old Sturbridge Village living history museum, Brimfield Flea Markets (various weekends). **Additional Information:** Plymouth County CVB, (508) 747-0100 or (800) 231-1620; www.plymouth-1620.com.

Restrictions

Pets: Pets must be leashed & cleaned up after. Proof of rabies vaccination required. Do not leave pets unattended. **Fires:** Fireplaces only. **Alcoholic Beverages:** No. **Vehicle Maximum Length:** 35 ft. **Other:** Maximum stay is 14 cumulative days between Memorial Day & Labor Day.

To Get There

Take I-90 (Massachusetts Turnpike) to Rte. 20 East. Follow Rte.20E to Rte. 49N, following signs to park access road. Park entrance is 1 mi. north on Rte. 49 (third left).

SUTTON

The Old Holbrook Place

114 Manchaug Rd., Sutton 01590. T: (508) 865-5050.

RV: ★★★★ Tent: ★★

Beauty: ★★★★ Site Privacy: ★★★
Spaciousness: ★★★ Quiet: ★★★★
Security: ★★★★ Cleanliness: ★★★
Insect Control: ★★★ Facilities: ★★★★

Located just south of Worcester on 350-acre Lake Manchaug, The Old Holbrook Place is a tiny gem of a campround. Operating the property since 1946, now on their third generation of guests, the Nelsons are delightfully friendly hosts (Mrs. Nelson was making a shell necklace for a camper kid when we visited, typical of the character here.) The property includes a small picnic grove and a hilly, three-sided sandy beach and swim area with raft. One side is a shallow, baby's crib (wading beach.) Campsites are set along both sides of the camp road, with some along the lake and some along the road. About half are seasonal sites (blessedly lacking in lawn art.) The best tent site is at Big Rock, alongside a boulder. Among the waterfront sites, numbers 16 and 17 boast the best views, and get nice breezes off the lake. They're close to rest rooms, but right next to the boat launch. Site 26 is nice, too, facing a marshy area of the lake. Although the picnic area and beach are open for day use, campers use a private rest room (you get a key upon check-in.) Other nice features: books and puzzles to swap, and nice park benches at waters' edge.

Basics

Operated By: Nelson family. **Open:** Memorial Day–Labor Day. **Site Assignment:** Reservations recommended, at least two weeks in advance. Will try to honor site requests. Deposit required, equal to one night's fee. Deposit is refundable if cancellation is made a week in advance, & if site can be rented. **Registration:** At office. **Fee:** $16–$24 per family (parents & unmarried children.)No credit cards. **Parking:** At site.

Facilities

Number of RV Sites: 66. **Number of Tent-Only Sites:** 0. **Hookups:** Water, electric (20 amps), sewer. **Each Site:** Picnic table, fire ring. **Dump Station:** Yes. **Laundry:** No. **Pay Phone:** Yes. **Rest Rooms and Showers:** Yes. **Fuel:** No. **Propane:** No. **Internal Roads:** Gravel, in good condition. **RV Service:** No. **Market:** 2 mi. west. **Restaurant:** 4 mi. east. **General Store:** Yes. **Vending:** No. **Swimming Pool:** No. **Playground:** No. **Other:** Boat ramp. **Activities:** Boating (rentals available), lake swimming. **Nearby Attractions:** New England Science Center, Ecotarium, Worcester Art Museum, outlet shopping. **Additional Information:** Central Massachusetts Tourist Council, (508) 755-7400; www.worcester.org.

Restrictions

Pets: Must be leashed & cleaned up after. Not allowed on the beach. **Fires:** In fire rings only. **Alcoholic Beverages:** Yes. **Vehicle Maximum Length:** 30 ft. **Other:** Visitors must register upon entering the park.

To Get There

From Rte. 395, take exit 4A, onto Sutton Ave. Head east 3.6 mi., then take second right (after passing white church) to Manchaug Rd. Campground is exactly 1 mi. in from Central Tpk. (Sutton Ave.), on Manchaug Rd. (Second campground you pass.)

TAUNTON

Massasoit State Park

1361 Middleboro Ave., East Taunton 02718. T: (508) 822-7405; www.state.ma.us/dem/parks/mass.htm.

RV: ★★★★ Tent: ★★★★

Beauty: ★★★★ Site Privacy: ★★★
Spaciousness: ★★★★★ Quiet: ★★★★
Security: ★★★ Cleanliness: ★★★
Insect Control: ★★★ Facilities: ★★★

Located about 40 miles south of Boston, this campground boasts a unique feature for a state park: water and electrical hookups. This may explain why campers tend to make a vacation of it, and stay for a whole two weeks. Very popular with local urban dwellers, Massasoit State Park is a cool oasis on a sweltering summer day. Pine carpeted, the gravel and grassy campsites are set in four loops, designated by alphabet. Areas E and G, with hookups, have frontage on Middle Pond. The pond offers a rocky, grassy beach with a small, unguarded swimming area. Site E5 is huge, great for RVs. Section H is for self-contained camping units (no rest rooms), while section C has no electrical hookups. Sites C2 and C3 are fairly secluded tent sites, with good proximity to a rest room. (Shy guys take note: the men's showers are open, not curtained.) There's a nice picnic grove, and fishing, on Big Bearhole Pond (off J Rd.) A hiking trail leads to this peachy spot. Trivia tidbit: Stall Island, on park property, was one of Elizabeth Pole's farms. It is said that she traded "a jacknife and a pot of beans" to Native Americans for 5000 acres of land in 1637.

Basics

Operated By: Massachusetts State Forests & Parks. **Open:** Mid-Apr.–Columbus Day. **Site Assignment:** Reservations recommended. Reserve up to six months in advance by calling ReserveAmerica at (877) I-CAMP MA or online at www.reservamerica.com. 15 sites are non-reservable, & available for walk-in campers. To change arrival or departure date, or site type, call at least three dayas prior to arrival date. $10 cancellation/ transfer fee. No refunds for amounts less than $5. **Registration:** At park headquarters. **Fee:** Massachusetts residents, $10–$15; non-residents, $12–$17. V, MC. **Parking:** At site.

Facilities

Number of RV Sites: 120. **Number of Tent-Only Sites:** 0. **Hookups:** Water, electric (15, 20 amps). **Each Site:** Picnic table, fireplace. **Dump Station:** Yes. **Laundry:** No. **Pay Phone:** Yes. **Rest Rooms and Showers:** Yes. **Fuel:** No. **Propane:** No. **Internal Roads:** Paved, in good condition. **RV Service:** No. **Market:** 3 mi. north on Rte. 44. **Restaurant:** 4–5 mi. northeast. **General Store:**

No. **Vending:** No. **Swimming Pool:** No. **Playground:** No. **Other:** Boat ramp. **Activities:** Hiking, horse trails, bicycling, fishing (MA license available in Middleboro), swimming. **Nearby Attractions:** Edaville Railroad, Battleship Cove, New Bedford Whaling Museum, Plimoth Plantation, Cranberry World Visitors Center, Pilgrim Hall Museum, Fuller Museum of Art. **Additional Information:** Plymouth County CVB, (508) 747-0100 or (800) 231-1620; www.plymouth-1620.com.

RESTRICTIONS

Pets: Must be leashed, quiet, & cleaned up after. Current rabies vaccination certificate required. Posted areas are off-limits to pets. **Fires:** In fireplaces only. **Alcoholic Beverages:** No. **Vehicle Maximum Length:** 40 ft. **Other:** Max. stay is 14 cumulative days between Mem. Day & Labor Day.

TO GET THERE

Follow Rte. 24 south to Rte. 44 (exit 13); heading east, follow signs on Rte. 44 to campground.

TEMPLETON

Otter River State Forest

86 Winchendon Rd., Baldwinville 01436. T: (978) 939-8962; www.state.ma.us/dem/parks/ottr.htm.

RV ★ Tent ★★★

Beauty: ★★★★ Site Privacy: ★★★
Spaciousness: ★★★ Quiet: ★★★★
Security: ★★★ Cleanliness: ★★★★★
Insect Control: ★★ Facilities: ★★

Located in a rural area along Rte. 2, northwest of Boston, Otter River State Forest is notable as the first state forest established in Massachusetts (1915.) Criss-crossed with rivers and streams, this wilderness area offers a clutch of campsites clustered near Beamon Pond. Along with its sister campground, Lake Dennison State Recreation Area, to the north, Otter River is a pleasant place to overnight near the beginning of the Mohawk Trail, a 63-mile scenic drive (and former Native American footpath) that officially starts in Orange. Heavily wooded, and very quiet, Otter River offers good hiking, including a section of the Ware River Rail Trail. Beamon Pond has a small, sandy beach and a concrete fishing bridge. Ranger programs, including kids' crafts, games, nature walks, movies, and bike rides, are run on weekends in summer. Lacking hookups, this campground is best for tent campers and pop-ups. Campsites are mostly gravel, softened with pine needles. Least-desirable sites are numbers 73–78, as they're small and close to the road. Sites 1–27 are open only to self-contained RVs. Site 62 is a great spot, near the beach, as is 81, very secluded on a dead end, but near the beach and showers and a water faucet. There's not a lot of action here, but this campground is a pleasant short-term nature escape, especially if combined with a visit to Lake Dennison State Recreation Area.

BASICS

Operated By: Massachusetts State Parks & Forests. **Open:** Mem. Day–Labor Day. **Site Assignment:** Reservations recommended. Reserve up to 6 months in advance by calling ReserveAmerica at (877) 1-CAMP MA or online at www.reserveamerica.com. About 20 percent of campsites are non-reservable, & available on first-come, first-served basis. To change arrival or departure date, or site type, call at least 3 days prior to arrival date. $10 cancellation/transfer fee. **Registration:** At office. **Fee:** Massachusetts residents, $10; non-residents, $12. V, MC. **Parking:** At site.

FACILITIES

Number of RV Sites: 83. **Number of Tent-Only Sites:** 0. **Hookups:** None. **Each Site:** Picnic table, fireplace. **Dump Station:** No. **Laundry:** No. **Pay Phone:** Yes. **Rest Rooms and Showers:** Yes. **Fuel:** No. **Propane:** No. **Internal Roads:** Paved, good condition. **RV Service:** No. **Market:** 5 mi. north, in Winchendon. **Restaurant:** 5 mi. north, in Winchendon. **General Store:** No. **Vending:** Yes. **Swimming Pool:** No. **Playground:** No. **Other:** Interpretive Center. **Activities:** Hiking, nature walks, campfire programs, fishing, swimming. **Nearby Attractions:** Lake Dennison State Recreation Area, Mohawk Trail scenic drive. **Additional Information:** Central Massachusetts Tourist Council, (508) 755-7400; www.worcester.org.

RESTRICTIONS

Pets: Must be leashed & cleaned up after. Must not be left unattended. Proof of rabies vaccination required. **Fires:** In fireplaces only. **Alcoholic Beverages:** No. **Vehicle Maximum Length:** None (but sites are fairly small, & best for pop-ups & small rigs). **Other:** Maximum stay is 14 cumulative days between Memorial Day & Labor Day.

TO GET THERE

Follow Rte. 2 west to exit 20 (Baldwinville Rd.) to Rte. 202 north; follow signs

WALES

Oak Haven Family Campground

P.O. Box 166, Wales 01081. T: (413) 245-7148; F: (413) 245-4656; www.oakhavencampground.com; oakhaven87@aol.com.

RV ★★★★ Tent ★

Beauty: ★★★ Site Privacy: ★★★
Spaciousness: ★★★★ Quiet: ★★★
Security: ★★★ Cleanliness: ★★★★
Insect Control: ★★★ Facilities: ★★★

Wooded, grassy, and set in a rural area between Worcester and Springfield, Oak Haven has become a summer home-away-from-home for its 80 or so seasonal campers. Campers who join them for the weekend or the week will quickly sense the low-key camaraderie here. St. signs reflect a sense of humor; there's Snob Hill and Rowdy Rd., for example. A comedy hypnotist is likely to show up on the activities schedule. There's a activities director on board to plan kids' stuff. Site sizes vary; some are open, some are shaded. All are back-in, and fairly spacious. Campsites are set in a loop, with the smallest numbers closest to the entrance. Higher numbers are in back, near a good-sized ball field. There are only two rest rooms, so you can bet the that's where the tenters are, although this campground attracts far more RVers than tenters. The ambience of the place is wholesome and well-maintained. Bonus for flea market mavens and collectors: this campground is just five minutes away from Brimfield Flea Markets, New England's largest antique flea market. Events are held on various weekends during spring, summer, and fall.

BASICS

Operated By: Alan & Penny Jalbert. **Open:** May 1–Oct. 15. **Site Assignment:** Reservations accepted year-round; 1 night's fee required as deposit except holidays & Shriner's Benefit weekend, which must be paid in full 1 month in advance. Full refund, less $10 charge, for reservations cancelled before 7 days. **Registration:** At office. **Fee:** $23 –$25. Rates based on 2 people, 1 camping unit & 2 vehicles. Extra adult (18 years & up) $2; children (age 6 & up), $1; air conditioning or electric heat, $3 per day. MC, V. **Parking:** At site.

FACILITIES

Number of RV Sites: 140. **Number of Tent-Only Sites:** 0. **Hookups:** Water, electric (20, 30, 50 amps), sewer. **Each Site:** Picnic table, fireplace. **Dump Station:** Yes. **Laundry:** Yes. **Pay Phone:** Yes. **Rest Rooms and Showers:** Yes (coin-op). **Fuel:** No. **Propane:** Yes. **Internal Roads:** Gravel, in good condition. **RV Service:** No. **Market:** 10 mi. east, in Sturbridge, & 10 mi. west, in Palmer. **Restaurant:** In Sturbridge & Palmer. **General Store:** Yes. **Vending:** Yes. **Swimming Pool:** Yes. **Playground:** Yes. **Other:** Rec hall. **Activities:** Baseball, swimming, volleyball, horseshoes. **Nearby Attractions:** Old Sturbridge Village, Brimfield Flea Markets (various weekends), Norcross Wildlife Sanctuary. **Additional Information:** Greater Springfield CVB, (800) 723-1548; www.valleyvisitor.com.

RESTRICTIONS

Pets: Maximum two dogs per campsite. Dogs must be kept on leash & picked up after. Dogs should not be left unattended. **Fires:** In grills, campstoves, & fireplaces only. **Alcoholic Beverages:** At site only. **Vehicle Maximum Length:** 40 ft. **Other:** Three night min. stay required on holiday weekends.

TO GET THERE

From I-90 (Massachusetts Turnpike), take exit 9 (Sturbridge) to US. 20 W. At the center of Brimfield, take S.R. 19S, 4.5 mi. to center of Wales. Campground will be on your left.

WELFLEET

Maurice's Campground

80 Rte. 6, Unit 1, Wellfleet 02667. T: (508) 349-2029; F: (508) 349-6704; www.mauricescampground.com; stay@mauricescampground.com.

RV ★★★ Tent ★

Beauty: ★★ Site Privacy: ★★
Spaciousness: ★★ Quiet: ★★
Security: ★★★ Cleanliness: ★★★★★
Insect Control: ★★★ Facilities: ★★

Located in Wellfleet on the Outer Cape, 20 miles west of Provincetown, this low-key establishment offers tiny cabins and cottages (toward the front of the property), and campsites for tents, tent trailers, trailers and RVS. Set in a grove of native pines, about half the sites are seasonal. The east side of the campground sits right alongside the Cape Cod Rail Trail bike path. We'd skip tent sites 1 and 2, and RV site 32, since they're right next to the access point of the bike trail, so privacy would be impacted. The rest of the tent sites along the bicycle trail are appealing, though, especially sites 6 through 10. RVers would do well to set up on Anchor Dr. (sites 125–131), nice and spacious, but we'd avoided tightly-packed sites 106–109 and 114–116. Everywhere, tall pine trees don't provide much buffer. In some spots, only a split-rail fence separates you from the next site. On the plus side: within a couple of miles of the campground are beautiful stretches of National Seashore, including Nauset Beach, Coast Guard Beach, and Marconi Beach. (The campground office sells car passes for Wellfleet beaches.)

BASICS

Operated By: Martin Gauthier, manager. **Open:** Mem. Day–Columbus Day. **Site Assignment:** Reservations advised for Jul. & Aug. Deposit for 1–4 days, $25; 5–7 days, $50. Pay in full upon arrival. 2-night min. stay in Jul. & Aug. 48-hour cancellation notice required. Will try to honor specific site requests, but cannot guarantee. **Registration:** At office. **Fee:** $24–$30 for two people. Extra children age 3 to 18, $2 per night; extra adult, $5. V, MC. **Parking:** At site.

FACILITIES

Number of RV Sites: 200. **Number of Tent-Only Sites:** 0. **Hookups:** Water, electric (20, 30 amps), sewer, cable TV. **Each Site:** Picnic tables. **Dump Station:** Yes. **Laundry:** No. **Pay Phone:** Yes. **Rest Rooms and Showers:** Yes, coin-op. **Fuel:** No. **Propane:** Yes. **Internal Roads:** Paved, in good condition. **RV Service:** No. **Market:** Yes. **Restaurant:** Yes. **General Store:** No. **Vending:** No. **Swimming Pool:** No. **Playground:** Yes. **Other:** Rec area, basketball hoop, horseshoe pits. **Activities:** Basketball, horseshoes, bicycling. **Nearby Attractions:** Cape Cod Rail Trail (bike path), Cape Cod National Seashore, Wellfleet Drive-In (movies), Wellfleet Bay Wildlife Sanctuary. **Additional Information:** Cape Cod Chamber, (508) 862-0700 or (888) 33-CAPECOD; www.capecodchamber.org.

RESTRICTIONS

Pets: No. **Fires:** No open fires. Campstoves, & charcoal grills OK. **Alcoholic Beverages:** Yes. **Vehicle Maximum Length:** 32 ft.

TO GET THERE

Follow Rte. 6 east to the Orleans rotary. Then follow Rte. 6 east towards Provincetown for 6 mi. At Eastham/Wellfleet town line, look for Wellfleet Drive-In on left. Campground is 200 yards farther up on the right, just past Maurice's Market.

WESTFORD

Wyman's Beach Family Campground

48 Wyman's Beach Rd., Westford 01886. T: (978) 692-6287; F: (978) 692-4155; www.wymanscamping .com; ewyman@wymanscamping.com.

RV ★★★★ Tent ★★★★

Beauty: ★★★	Site Privacy: ★★★
Spaciousness: ★★	Quiet: ★★★★
Security: ★★	Cleanliness: ★★★
Insect Control: ★★★★★	Facilities: ★★★

Time seems to have stood still at Wyman's Beach campground, 30 miles northwest of Boston. Generations of kids have splashed in sandy-bottomed Long Sought-For Pond, known as, simply, 'the lake.' RVers and tent campers join seasonal campers and cabin-dwellers to relax here on a small campers-only beach, or with the public at a day-use beach. The campground has the feeling of a lakeside resort, with a snack bar, horseshoe pit, playground, even an activity director who leads the kids in arts-and-crafts projects, and theme nights—perhaps a 1950s party (perfect), Hawaiian Night, or bingo. Site sizes vary; some are 25 feet wide, some as big as 60 × 55 feet or so. The most-requested, most-secluded RV site is 81, on a hill, and semi-secluded 117. Best tent sites by far are 129 and 130, roomy and away from the action. Count on plenty of kids, and grandkids, running around, especially on holiday weekends. Sites are grass, back-in, and mostly shaded, set on short side streets and loop streets off the main road. Wyman's Beach campground offers a pleasant lakeshore experience and a central location, with easy access to Lexington and Concord and Boston.

BASICS

Operated By: Wyman family. **Open:** Early May–early Oct. **Site Assignment:** Reserve 2 weeks in advance, by phone or on line. Deposit of 2 days' fee required. Refund w/ 2 week notice prior to arrival date. **Registration:** At office. **Fee:** $20–$24. Fees based on 2 adults per site; for each child over age 5, add $1 per day. V, MC, D. **Parking:** At site.

FACILITIES

Number of RV Sites: 200. **Number of Tent-Only Sites:** 10. **Hookups:** Water, electric (30, 50 amps), sewer. **Each Site:** Picnic table, fire ring. **Dump Station:** Yes. **Laundry:** Yes. **Pay Phone:** Yes. **Rest Rooms and Showers:** Yes, coin op. **Fuel:** No. **Propane:** Yes. **Internal Roads:** Paved & gravel, good condition. **RV Service:** No. **Market:** 5 mi. south. **Restaurant:** 2 mi. west on Rte. 40. **General Store:** Yes. **Vending:** Yes. **Swimming Pool:** No. **Playground:** Yes. **Other:** Rec hall. **Activities:** Pond swimming, arcade games, horseshoes, bocce, volleyball, basketball, shuffleboard, planned activities. **Nearby Attractions:** Butterfly Place, Lowell National Historic Park. **Additional Information:** Greater Merrimack Valley CVB, (978) 459-6150 or (800) 443-3332; www.lowell.org.

RESTRICTIONS

Pets: Must be leashed, quiet & cleaned up after. Must not be left unattended. **Fires:** In fire rings only. **Alcoholic Beverages:** At sites only. **Vehicle Maximum Length:** 40 ft.

TO GET THERE

From I-495, take Exit 35 (Rte. 3N) 4 mi. to Hwy. 40 (Exit 33.) Head west 2.6 mi. to Dunstable Rd. Go north 0.8 mi. Campground is on right.

WESTPORT

Horseneck State Reservation

P.O. Box 328, Westport Point 02791. T: (508) 636-8817 or (508) 636-8816 (off -season); www.state.me.us/dem/parks/hbch.htm.

 ★★★  ★★★

Beauty: ★★	Site Privacy: ★★
Spaciousness: ★★	Quiet: ★★
Security: ★★	Cleanliness: ★
Insect Control: ★★★	Facilities: ★★★

Nudging the Rhode Island border to the west and jutting into Buzzards Bay, Horseneck Beach offers a sublime seacoast setting, with campsites directly on the beach or nestled behind sand dunes. Windswept sea oats and rosa rugosa add to the allure. While the campers' beach is rather rocky, campers get free access to the wide, sandy, public beach to the north. There's not much here in the way of amenities (savvy campers know to bring their own firewood, or they'll have to travel 16-plus miles to the nearest supermarket to get it), and the rest rooms can be really grungy (due to staffing shortages, they say.) But, the seaside location is the draw here. Several campsites are directly on the beach, or right across the road from it, but they can get windy. These sites aren't so good for tenters, but fine for RVers, who sort of parallel-park into them. Even-numbered sites 54–82 sit right on the water's edge; odd-numbered sites 55–81 face the water, too, although the road runs between the campsites and the beach. Avoid site 77; it's oddly tiny. For tenters, sites 97 and 99 sit right behind a dune, but close to the rest rooms and beach path. You're never far from the water here.

BASICS

Operated By: Massachusetts State Forests & Parks. **Open:** Mid-May–mid-Oct. **Site Assignment:** Reservations recommended. Reserve up to 6 months in advance by calling ReserveAmerica at (877) 1-CAMP MA or online at www.reserve america.com. To change arrival or departure date, or site type, call at least 3 dayas prior to arrival date. $10 cancellation/ transfer fee. **Registration:** At office. **Fee:** Massachusetts residents, $12; non-residents, $15. V, MC. **Parking:** At site.

FACILITIES

Number of RV Sites: 100. **Number of Tent-Only Sites:** 0. **Hookups:** None. **Each Site:** Picnic table, fireplace. **Dump Station:** Yes. **Laundry:** No. **Pay Phone:** Yes. **Rest Rooms and Showers:** Yes. **Fuel:** No. **Propane:** No. **Internal Roads:** Gravel, in good condition. **RV Service:** No. **Market:** 16.3 mi. north, on Rte. 88N. **Restaurant:** Yes (snack bar at public beach). **General Store:** No. **Vending:** No. **Swimming Pool:** No. **Playground:** Yes. **Other:** Boat ramp, nature center. **Activities:** Swimming (ocean beach), basketball, volleyball, saltwater fishing, interpretive programs, Jr. ranger program. **Nearby Attractions:** Winery, New Bedford Whaling Museum, Cape Cod. **Additional Information:** Bristol County CVB, (800) 288-6263; www.bristol-county.org.

RESTRICTIONS

Pets: On leash, quiet, & cleaned up after. Rabies vaccination certificate required. Beach & swimming areas are off-limits to pets. **Fires:** In fireplaces only. **Alcoholic Beverages:** No. **Vehicle Maximum Length:** 35 ft. **Other:** 14-day stay limit between Mem. Day & Labor Day.

TO GET THERE

Take I-95W to Rte. 88, exit 10 south. Follow Rte. 88 south for 10 mi. to state reservation. Campground entrance is just past main entrance on right.

Michigan

Outdoor recreation is a way of life in the Wolverine State, especially if it involves a jaunt in your automobile of choice. In the "Motor City" of **Detroit,** Henry Ford and his Model-T gave highway travelers the wheels to hit the road. The state is also home to the original "Big Mac"—the **Mackinac Bridge** that joins Michigan's Lower Peninsula to its rugged Upper Peninsula. Ironically, **Mackinac Island** enforces a "no-cars" ban on its picturesque shores. Visitors take a ferry, catamaran, or plane to the tiny island, often to marvel at the 1887 **Grand Hotel** and its sweeping 600-foot-long white veranda topped by a sky-blue ceiling.

Blessed with two national forests, two national lakeshores, and a national park, Michigan also shares **four Great Lakes** and nearly 100 state parks, as well as magnificent sand dunes. Guarding the shores are more than 100 lighthouses. Despite those guardian lights, the 38,000 square miles of Great Lakes bottomlands are still the final resting place of more than 3,000 shipwrecks, attracting scuba divers and glass-bottomed boats.

For a taste of Dutch heritage, stop by **Holland,** where shopkeepers still scrub cobblestone sidewalks, America's only authentic Dutch windmill still twirls, and a profusion of colorful tulips dazzle visitors each May. To get the feel of Munich, head to **Frankenmuth,** home of **Bronner's Christmas Wonderland.** With a showroom bigger than four football fields, Bronner's is said to be the world's largest Christmas shop.

The cereal capital of the world, **Battle Creek** showcases breakfast food history. **Petoskey** draws rockhounds seeking stone remnants of an extinct coral that inhabited the shallow waters there 350 million years ago. In **Cheboygan,** one of the Great Lakes' largest cattail marshes serves as a nesting site for 54 bird species. **Grand Haven** offers its special singing sands—when walked upon, the small sand particles create a peculiar whistling music. A fish ladder sculpture in **Grand Rapids** helps salmon jump over a six-foot dam to reach their spawning ground.

In **Sault Ste. Marie,** huge freighters pass through the town's greatest attraction, the **Soo Locks.** In winter, icefishing shacks pop up on Michigan waterways as anglers cut through the ice to tempt the fish. With a name that means "heaven," **Ishpeming** has become a well-known ski center. As the largest island in Lake Superior, **Isle Royale** is 99% wilderness. Along with its wealth of activities, Isle Royale is a great place for those seeking solitude and a chance to get closer to Michigan's natural beauty.

The following facilities accept payment in checks or cash only:

- Clearwater Campground, Ortonville
- Cottonwood Resort, Quincy
- Happi Days Campground, Frederic
- Indian Lake Travel Resort, Manistique
- Jerry's Campground, Montague
- Leisure Valley Campground, Decatur
- Rockey's Campground, Albion
- Sandyoak RV Park, Houghton Lake
- Spaulding Lake Campground, Niles
- Trails Campground, Frederic
- Tri-Lakes Trails Campground, Marshall
- Waffle Farm Campground, Coldwater
- Withii Trailer Camp, Harrison

The following facilities have 20 or fewer sites:

- Driftwood Shores Resort & RV Park, Thompson
- Honcho Rest Campground, Elk Rapids
- Jack's Landing Resort, Hillman
- Just-In-Time Campgrounds, Ithaca
- River Pines RV Park & Campground, Ontonagon
- Waterways Campground, Cheboygan
- Whitefish Hill Mobile Home & RV Park, Rapid River

ALBION

Rockey's Campground

19880 27H Mile Rd., Albion 49224. T: (877) 762-5397; F: (517) 857-4455.

★★★★ ★★★

Beauty: ★★★★ Site Privacy: ★★★★
Spaciousness: ★★★★ Quiet: ★★★★
Security: ★★★★ Cleanliness: ★★★★
Insect Control: ★★★★ Facilities: ★★★

A rural campground on a chain of five lakes, Rockey's Campground is located about six-and-a-half miles south of Albion. The secluded campground offers open or shaded sites, with a typical site width of 35 feet. The campground has 50 seasonal campers and and no pull-through sites. A large building is available for groups, and a cement boat ramp is popular with boaters. Sites are level and grassy with gravel pads. The best sites are those closest to the water. Be aware that no large dogs are permitted. Facilities are very clean and well maintained. About half of sites are occupied by seasonals, and many other regulars return year after year, so reservations are recommended. For security measures, owners and staff members seem to keep a close watch on the campground while also being friendly and helpful.

Basics

Operated by: Brian & Vicki Mead. **Open:** May 15–Oct. 1. **Site Assignment:** Reservations w/ 1-night deposit; refund (minus $5) w/ 7-day notice. **Registration:** At campground office. **Fee:** $20 (cash, check). **Parking:** At site.

Facilities

Number of RV Sites: 100. **Number of Tent-Only Sites:** 0. **Hookups:** Electric (20, 30 amps), water. **Each Site:** Picnic table, fire ring. **Dump Station:** Yes. **Laundry:** No. **Pay Phone:** Yes. **Rest Rooms and Showers:** Yes. **Fuel:** No. **Propane:** Yes. **Internal Roads:** Gravel, in good condition. **RV Service:** No. **Market:** 5 mi. south in Albion. **Restaurant:** 5 mi. south in Albion. **General Store:** Yes, limited. **Vending:** Yes. **Swimming Pool:** No. **Playground:** Yes. **Other:** Bass Lake, sandy beach, lake swimming, game room, mini-golf, boat ramp, sports field, horseshoes, rental cottage. **Activities:** Swimming, fishing, boating (rental rowboats, canoes available), scheduled weekend activities. **Nearby Attractions:** Whitehouse Nature Center, antiques, Albion's Historic Walkway, Albion College Observatory, Bobbitt Visual Arts Center, children's museum, Star Commonwealth, golf, Brueckner Museum & Gladstone Cottage. **Additional Information:** Greater Albion Chamber of Commerce, (517) 629-5533.

Restrictions

Pets: No large dogs. **Fires:** Fire ring only. **Alcoholic Beverages:** Permitted. **Vehicle Maximum Length:** None.

To Get There

From the junction of I-94 and 28 Mile Rd., take Exit 121 and drive 7 mi. north on 28 Mile Rd. Roads are mostly wide and well maintained w/ adequate shoulders.

ALLEGAN

Tri-Ponds Family Camp Resort

3687 Dumont Rd., Allegan 49010. T: (616) 673-4740

★★★★ ★★★★

Beauty: ★★★ Site Privacy: ★★★★
Spaciousness: ★★★★ Quiet: ★★★★
Security: ★★★★ Cleanliness: ★★★★
Insect Control: ★★★★ Facilities: ★★★★

Circling several small ponds in Allegan, Tri-Ponds Family Camp Resort offers open and shaded campsites. Sites are level with a typical site width of 35 feet. The campground has 26 seasonal campers and eight pull-through sites. An activities and crafts director is on staff and worship services are held on Sunday. No license is necessary to fish in the ponds. The campground is well maintained and clean, with a great deal of attention put into keeping bathrooms and shower facilities in tip-top shape. Security is good with owners who make sure the campground is safe and quiet for campers.

Basics

Operated by: Paul & Dotty VanDrunen. **Open:** May 1–Oct. 31. **Site Assignment:** Reservations w/ 1-night deposit; refund w/ 2-week notice. **Registration:** At campground office. **Fee:** $24 (cash, check, credit cards). **Parking:** At site.

Facilities

Number of RV Sites: 86. **Number of Tent-Only Sites:** 15. **Hookups:** Electric (20, 30 amps), water, sewer. **Each Site:** Picnic table, fire ring. **Dump Station:** Yes. **Laundry:** Yes. **Pay Phone:** Yes. **Rest Rooms and Showers:** Yes. **Fuel:** No. **Propane:** No. **Internal Roads:** Paved, in good condition. **RV Service:** No. **Market:** 2 mi. **Restaurant:** 2 mi. **General Store:** Yes. **Vending:** Yes. **Swimming Pool:** No. **Playground:** Yes. **Other:** Pond, swimming beach, rec hall, horseshoes, hiking trails, volleyball, sports field, activities & craft director. **Activities:** Swimming, fishing, scheduled activities. **Nearby Attractions:** Golf, antiques, bowling, horseback riding, Old Jail Museum, orchards, parks, Allegan State Game Area, arts & crafts, skiing. **Additional Information:** Allegan Area Chamber of Commerce, (616) 673-2479.

Restrictions

Pets: Leash only. **Fires:** Fire ring only. **Alcoholic Beverages:** Not permitted. **Vehicle Maximum Length:** None.

To Get There

From the junction of Hwy. 222 and Hwy. 40/89, drive 3 mi. northwest on Hwy. 40/89, then 2 mi. north on 36th St., then 0.5 mi. west on Dumont Rd. Roads are mostly wide and well maintained w/ narrow shoulders in places. Dumont Rd. is paved but only in fair condition.

ALPENA

Campers Cove RV Park

5005 Long Rapids Rd., Alpena 49707. T: (888) 306-3708; www.camperscovecampground.com.

 ★★★★  ★★★★

Beauty: ★★★★ Site Privacy: ★★★★
Spaciousness: ★★★★ Quiet: ★★★★
Security: ★★★★ Cleanliness: ★★★★
Insect Control: Yes Facilities: ★★★★

Located on a lake seven miles west of Alpena, Campers Cove RV Park has 45 waterfront sites. Sites are mostly grassy and shaded with a typical site width of 50 feet. Some sites have places to tie up boats on the inland waterway for easy access to Thunder Bay River. A sauna is available by request only and takes half an hour to heat. No children ages 12 and under are permitted in the sauna unless accompanied by an adult. The indoor heated pool has adults-only swim times. Laid out in a series of loops, the campground has level sites with 15 seasonal campers and ten pull-throughs. Rustic tent sites are in a separate area with more green space and privacy. Speed limit is 5.6 mph and quiet times are 11 p.m. to 8 a.m. Security measures include one entrance/exit road, owners who live on site, and regular patrols of the campground.

Basics

Operated by: Bruce, Jo, & Jill Canady. **Open:** May 1–Oct. 1. **Site Assignment:** Reservations w/ $25 deposit; refund (minus $5) w/ 15-day notice. Deposits made a year in advance are non refundable. **Registration:** At campground office. **Fee:** $27 (cash, check, credit cards). **Parking:** At site.

Facilities

Number of RV Sites: 80. **Number of Tent-Only Sites:** 20. **Hookups:** Electric (20, 30, 50 amps), water, sewer, cable TV, phone. **Each Site:** Picnic table, fire ring. **Dump Station:** Yes. **Laundry:** Yes. **Pay Phone:** Yes. **Rest Rooms and Showers:** Yes. **Fuel:** No. **Propane:** Yes. **Internal Roads:** Paved/gravel, in good condition. **RV Service:** No. **Market:** 7 mi. east in Alpena. **Restaurant:** 7 mi. east in Alpena. **General Store:** Yes. **Vending:** Yes. **Swimming Pool:** Yes. **Playground:** Yes. **Other:** Lake Winyah, sauna, game room, TV lounge, pavilion, mini-golf, shuffleboard, basketball, volleyball, nature area, stocked fishing pond, badminton, sports field, coin games, boat ramp, boat dock. **Activities:** Swimming, boating (rental canoes, kayaks, paddleboats, & rowboats available), biking (rental bicyles, fun cycles, & electric scooters available), fishing. **Nearby Attractions:** Wildlife sanctuary, planetarium, golf, museums, historic homes, dinosaur gardens, charter boat fishing, lighthouses, beaches, underwater park, diving, rockhound areas, sinkholes, antiques. **Additional Information:** Alpena Area CVB, (800) 4-ALPENA.

Restrictions

Pets: Leash only. **Fires:** Fire ring only. **Alcoholic Beverages:** Permitted. **Vehicle Maximum Length:** None.

To Get There

From the junction of US 23 and Long Rapids Rd., drive 6 mi. west on Long Rapids Rd. (Johnson St.). Roads are wide and well maintained w/ broad shoulders.

BELMONT

Grand Rogue Campgrounds Canoe & Tube Livery

6400 West River Dr., Belmont 49306. T: (616) 361-1053; F: (616) 972-1071; www.grandrogue.com.

RV ★★★★ Tent ★★★★

Beauty: ★★★★ Site Privacy: ★★★★
Spaciousness: ★★★★ Quiet: ★★★★
Security: ★★★★ Cleanliness: ★★★★
Insect Control: ★★★★ Facilities: ★★★

Located on the Grand and Rogue Rivers in Belmont, Rogue River Campgrounds Canoe & Tube Livery is minutes away from Grand Rapids attractions. Sites are grassy and partly shaded with a typical site width of 40 feet. The campground is adjacent to an 18-hole golf course and lighted driving range. Located in a secluded lake and riverside setting, the campground offers canoe and tube trips from one to four hours long. Be aware that alcohol is not permitted on paddlesport trips. The campground also has a tour train that runs along the river and through 75 acres of wooded trails. A large pavilion is available for use to campers. Campground staff is friendly and helpful, escorting campers to sites upon check-in. They will help park the camping unit or park it for you.

Basics

Operated by: Tom & Joan Briggs. **Open:** May 1–Oct. 15. **Site Assignment:** Reservations w/ $26 deposit; refund (minus $2) w/ 5-day notice. **Registration:** At campground office. **Fee:** $24 (cash, check, credit cards). **Parking:** At site.

Facilities

Number of RV Sites: 82. **Number of Tent-Only Sites:** 10. **Hookups:** Electric (20, 30 amps), water, phone. **Each Site:** Picnic table, fire ring. **Dump Station:** Yes. **Laundry:** Yes. **Pay Phone:** Yes. **Rest Rooms and Showers:** Yes. **Fuel:** No. **Propane:** No. **Internal Roads:** Gravel, in good condition. **RV Service:** No. **Market:** 3 mi. **Restaurant:** 3 mi. **General Store:** Yes, limited. **Vending:** Yes. **Swimming Pool:** No. **Playground:** Yes. **Other:** Lake, river, pavilion, horseshoes, sports field, boat ramp, float trips, golf, basketball, hiking trails, volleyball. **Activities:** Swimming, fishing, boating (rental canoes, kayaks available), scheduled weekend activities. **Nearby Attractions:** Gerald B. Ford Museum, Fredrick Meijer Gardens, zoo, Michigan Adventure Amuseument Park, Roger B. Chaffee Planetarium, golf, tennis, rivers & lakes, antiques, Wooden Shoe Factory. **Additional Information:** Grand Rapids/Kent County CVB.

Restrictions

Pets: Leash only. **Fires:** Fire ring only. **Alcoholic Beverages:** Not on river activities. **Vehicle Maximum Length:** None.

To Get There

From north junction of I-96 and US 131, take Exit 91 and drive 1.5 mi. north on US 131, then 4 mi. east on West River Dr. Roads are mostly wide and well maintained w/ adequate shoulders.

BENTON HARBOR

Benton Harbor/St. Joseph KOA

3527 Coloma Rd., Riverside 49084. T: (616) 849-3333; www.koa.com; bhstjoekoa@qtm. net.

RV ★★★★ Tent ★★★★

Beauty: ★★★ Site Privacy: ★★★
Spaciousness: ★★★★ Quiet: ★★★★
Security: ★★★★ Cleanliness: ★★★★
Insect Control: ★★★★ Facilities: ★★★★

With easy interstate access and a big roster of activities, Benton Harbor/St. Joseph KOA is a popular camping spot. Reservations are recommended, especially for busy weekends and peak season. The area is known for having a festival almost every summer and early fall weekend. The campground offers level, grassy sites with a choice of open or shaded. The typical site width is 45 feet. The campground has 12 seasonal campers and 16 pull-through sites. A small pond offers a chance to dunk a worm, but don't count on catching much. Lake Michigan is only five minutes away with great fishing and other water activities. The hot tub is a nice touch, but sometimes it gets crowded. Quiet time is enforced beginning at 11 p.m., and rowdy people can be ejected. Security is also good with regular patrols and owners who keep a close watch on the campground. The goal is to have a nice, family-oriented campground, and it seems to be working at Benton Harbor/St. Joseph KOA.

Basics

Operated by: Ginter & Ursela Bansen. **Open:** Apr. 15–Oct. 15. **Site Assignment:** Reservations w/ 1-night deposit; refunds (minus $5) w/ 3-day notice. **Registration:** At campground office. **Fee:** $30 (cash, check, credit cards). **Parking:** At site.

Facilities

Number of RV Sites: 115. **Number of Tent-Only Sites:** 18. **Hookups:** Electric (20, 30 amps), water, sewer. **Each Site:** Picnic table, fire ring. **Dump Station:** Yes. **Laundry:** Yes. **Pay Phone:** Yes. **Rest Rooms and Showers:** Yes. **Fuel:** No. **Propane:** Yes. **Internal Roads:** Paved, in good condition. **RV Service:** No. **Market:** 3 mi. west. **Restaurant:** 3 mi. west. **General Store:** Yes. **Vending:** Yes. **Swimming Pool:** Yes. **Playground:** Yes. **Other:** Fishing pond, sauna, hot tub, rental cabins, tennis, basketball, volleyball, shuffleboard, mini-golf, movies, rec hall, badminton, sports field, hiking trails, horseshoes. **Activities:** Swimming, fishing, hiking, scheduled activities. **Nearby Attractions:** Lake Michigan, fruit farms, charter boats, golf, Deer Forest, Curious Kids' Museum, Krasl Art Center, nature center, wineries, atomic plants, tennis, historic walking tour, antiques, arts & crafts. **Additional Information:** St. Joseph Today, (616) 982-0032.

Restrictions

Pets: Leash only. **Fires:** Fire ring only. **Alcoholic Beverages:** Permitted. **Vehicle Max. Length:** None. **Other:** Only 1 sleeping unit per site.

To Get There

From the junction of I-196 and Coloma-Riverside Rd., take Exit 4 and drive 1 block east on Coloma-Riverside Rd. Roads are wide and well maintained w/ broad shoulders.

BENZONIA

Vacation Trailer Park

2080 Benzie Hwy., Benzonia 49616. T: (800) 482-5101; F: (231) 882-4687; www.vacationtrailer.com; vacation@benzie.com.

RV ★★★★ Tent ★★★

Beauty: ★★★★ Site Privacy: ★★★★
Spaciousness: ★★★★ Quiet: ★★★★
Security: ★★★★ Cleanliness: ★★★★
Insect Control: ★★★★ Facilities: ★★★★

Nestled into the natural beauty of the Betsie River, Vacation Trailer Park offers camping and activities on the designated scenic river. Located less than a mile from West Benzonia, the campground is rolling and grassy with a typical site width of 30 feet. Vacation Trailer Park has 20 seasonal campers and five pull-through sites with a choice of open or shaded. A canoe livery service lets you rent a canoe and paddle down the Betsie River right past your camp site. The best sites for RVs are right on the river. Tents are permitted on any sites except the river ones to prevent erosion and problems with water pipes. Vacation Trailer Sales is located only 100 yards up the road and carries a complete line of RV parts and accessories. The campground general store also has a nice selection of fishing and hunting supplies. The campground provides 24-hour security with night managers on site and regular patrols of the campground.

Basics

Operated by: Bill & Betty Workman. **Open:** Mar. 1–Dec. 1. **Site Assignment:** Reservations w/ 1-night deposit; no refund but camping credit for 1 year. **Registration:** At campground office. **Fee:** $25 (cash, check, credit cards). **Parking:** At site.

Facilities

Number of RV Sites: 100. **Number of Tent-Only Sites:** 0. **Hookups:** Electric (20, 30, 50 amps), water, sewer, cable TV. **Each Site:** Picnic table, fire ring. **Dump Station:** Yes. **Laundry:** Yes. **Pay Phone:** Yes. **Rest Rooms and Showers:** Yes. **Fuel:** No. **Propane:** No. **Internal Roads:** Gravel, in good condition. **RV Service:** Yes. **Market:** 0.25 mi. north to West Benzonia. **Restaurant:** 0.25 mi. north to West Benzonia. **General Store:** Yes. **Vending:** Yes. **Swimming Pool:** Yes. **Playground:** Yes. **Other:** Betsie River, rec room, coin games, boat docks, fishing guide, fish-cleaning station, basketball, badminton, horseshoes, canoe launch area, rental RVs, rental cabins, hiking trails, volleyball, sports field. **Activities:** Swimming, hiking, fishing, boating (rental canoes, kayaks available), float trips. **Nearby Attractions:** Lake Michigan, Crystal Mountain, Point Betsie Lighthouse, marinas, golf, downhill ski runs, snowmobile & cross-country ski trails, antiques, arts & crafts, Benzie Area Historical Museum, Gwen Frostic Prints. **Additional Information:** Benzie Area Visitors Bureau, (800) 882-5801.

Restrictions

Pets: Leash only. **Fires:** Fire ring only. **Alcoholic

Beverages: At sites only. **Vehicle Maximum Length:** None.

To Get There

From south junction of Hwy. 115 and US 31, drive 1 mi. north on US 31. Roads are wide and well maintained w/ broad shoulders.

BROOKLYN

Greenbriar Golf & Camping

14820 Wellwood, Brooklyn 49230. T: (517) 592-6952; www.michcampgrounds.com/greenbriar.

RV ★★★★ Tent ★★★

Beauty: ★★★★ Site Privacy: ★★★
Spaciousness: ★★★ Quiet: ★★★★
Security: ★★★★ Cleanliness: ★★★★
Insect Control: ★★★★ Facilities: ★★★

The name says it all. Greenbriar Golf & Camping offers golf and camping with an 18-hole golf course and watered fairways. Located five minutes from Michigan International Speedway in Brooklyn, the campground is also near Wampler's Lake and Irish Hills attractions. With a rolling, grassy terrain, the campground offers a choice of open or shaded sites with a typical site width of 30 feet. There are ten pull-throughs and 15 seasonals. A children's fishing pond provides catch-and-release fishing. Golf and camping packages are available. A pavilion and clubhouse are comfortable gathering spots. Facilities are clean and well maintained. Grounds are nicely landscaped and mowed, as would be expected for a golf course.

Basics

Operated by: Arthur & Thelma Babian. **Open:** Apr. 1–Nov. 1. **Site Assignment:** Reservations w/ 1-night deposit; refund (minus $5) w/ 7-day notice. **Registration:** At campground office. **Fee:** $30 (cash, check, credit cards). **Parking:** At site.

Facilities

Number of RV Sites: 82. **Number of Tent-Only Sites:** 18. **Hookups:** Electric (20, 30, 50 amps), water. **Each Site:** Picnic table, fire ring. **Dump Station:** Yes. **Laundry:** Yes. **Pay Phone:** Yes. **Rest Rooms and Showers:** Yes. **Fuel:** No. **Propane:** No. **Internal Roads:** Gravel, in good condition. **RV Service:** No. **Market:** 1 mi. **Restaurant:** 1 mi. **General Store:** Yes. **Vending:** Yes. **Swimming Pool:** Yes. **Playground:** Yes. **Other:** 18-hole golf course, club house, children's fishing pond, pavilion, game room, putting green, basketball, horseshoes, volleyball, sports field. **Activities:** Golf, swimming, fishing. **Nearby Attractions:** Irish Hills, Michigan International Speedway, Irish Hills Towers, Mystery Hill, Prehistoric Forest, St. Joseph's Shrine, Stagecoach Stop, Cambridge Historical Park, Hidden Lake Gardens, state parks, antiques. **Additional Information:** Jackson County Visitors Bureau, (517) 764-4440.

Restrictions

Pets: Leash only. **Fires:** Fire ring only. **Alcoholic Beverages:** Permitted. **Vehicle Maximum Length:** None.

To Get There

From the junction of US 12 and Hwy. 124, drive 1.5 mi. north on Hwy. 124 to Wellwood Rd. Roads are wide and well maintained w/ broad shoulders.

BUCHANAN

Fuller's Resort & Campground on Clear Lake

1622 East Clear Lake Rd., Buchanan 49107. T: (616) 695-3785; F: (616) 695-4066; www.fullersresort.com; justjeffmc@aol.com.

RV ★★★ Tent ★★★

Beauty: ★★★★ Site Privacy: ★★★
Spaciousness: ★★★ Quiet: ★★★★
Security: ★★★★ Cleanliness: ★★★
Insect Control: ★★★★ Facilities: ★★★

Fuller's Resort & Campground on Clear Lake offers a quiet country setting. Located in Buchanan, the campground has 110 seasonal campers, so it is best to make reservations. Sites are level and mostly shaded, with four pull-throughs and a typical site width of 30 feet. The campground features an eight-acre spring-fed lake with 400 feet of clean sandy beach. The best sites are closest to the lake. A primitive area for tents offers more green space and privacy. A rental log cabin nestled in the woods features a fieldstone fireplace. Two modern cottages can be rented right on the lakeside. A shaded picnic area is a nice addition. A family-oriented campground under strict supervision, Fuller's Resort boasts 16 flavors of ice cream in its concession stand.

Basics

Operated by: Jeff & Rene McNeil. **Open:** Apr. 15–Oct. 15. **Site Assignment:** Reservations w/ 1-night deposit; refund (minus $5) w/ 2-week notice. **Registration:** At campground office. **Fee:** $20 (cash, check, credit cards). **Parking:** At site.

Facilities

Number of RV Sites: 140. **Number of Tent-Only Sites:** 30. **Hookups:** Electric (20, 30 amps), water, sewer. **Each Site:** Picnic table, fire ring. **Dump Station:** Yes. **Laundry:** Yes. **Pay Phone:** Yes. **Rest Rooms and Showers:** Yes. **Fuel:** No. **Propane:** Yes. **Internal Roads:** Gravel, in good condition. **RV Service:** No. **Market:** 3 mi. **Restaurant:** 3 mi. **General Store:** Yes. **Vending:** Yes. **Swimming Pool:** No. **Playground:** Yes. **Other:** Clear Lake, sandy beach, rental log cabins & cottages, recreation barn, coin games, boat ramp, basketball, sports field, horseshoes, volleyball. **Activities:** Swimming, fishing, boating (rental rowboats, canoes, & paddleboats available), scheduled weekend activities. **Nearby Attractions:** Amish Acres, golf, antiques, Berrien County Museum, Deer Forest, Bear Cave, Apple Valley Market, nature center, zoo, Kamm's Brewery, musuems, Andrews University. **Additional Information:** Buchanan Area Chamber of Commerce, (616) 695-3291.

Restrictions

Pets: Leash only. **Fires:** Fire ring only. **Alcoholic Beverages:** Permitted. **Vehicle Maximum Length:** None.

To Get There

From the junction of US 12 and Bakertown Rd., drive 2 mi. north on Bakertown Rd., then 1 mi. west on Elm Valley, then 1 mi. northwest on East Clear Lake Rd. Roads are mostly wide and in fair condition w/ narrow shoulders in spots.

BYRON

Myers Lake United Methodist Campground

10575 Silver Lake Rd., Byron 48418. T: (800) 994-5050; F: (810) 266-6037; www.michcampgrounds.com/myerslake; myerslak@shianet.org.

RV ★★★ Tent ★★★

Beauty: ★★★★ Site Privacy: ★★★★
Spaciousness: ★★★★ Quiet: ★★★★
Security: ★★★★ Cleanliness: ★★★
Insect Control: ★★★ Facilities: ★★★

Located on the banks of a 100-acre lake in Byron, Myers Lake United Methodist Campground offers good, clean, family fun in a quiet rural facility. The campground features family, group, and church camping in an alcohol-free environment. Sites are mostly grassy and shaded, with a typical site width of 30 feet. The campground has only 18 water and electric sites; the rest are electric-only, so reservations are recommended. The best RV sites are the lakeview ones with 50 amp electricity and water hookups. The sites overlook the clear, spring-fed lake and nature trail. Special sites with 20 amp electricity for tenters, overlooking the lake and outdoor chapel, are also available on holiday weekends. The lake has a 75 hp limit. Centrally located near the cities of Brighton, Flint, and Lansing, the campground is owned by the United Methodist Church, but is open to the public. Basic safety and security rules are enforced, but few campers seem to need to be reminded. Church services are held on Sunday.

Basics

Operated by: Detroit Conference, The United Methodist Church. **Open:** May 1–Oct. 15. **Site Assignment:** Reservations w/ 1-night deposit; refund (minus $5) w/ 3-day notice. **Registration:** At campground office. **Fee:** $25 (cash, check, credit cards). **Parking:** At site.

Facilities

Number of RV Sites: 126. **Number of Tent-Only Sites:** 0. **Hookups:** Electric (20, 30, 50 amps), water. **Each Site:** Picnic table, fire ring. **Dump Station:** Yes. **Laundry:** Yes. **Pay Phone:** Yes. **Rest Rooms and Showers:** Yes. **Fuel:** No. **Propane:** Yes. **Internal Roads:** Gravel, in good condition. **RV Service:** No. **Market:** 5 mi. **Restaurant:** 5 mi. **General Store:** Yes. **Vending:** Yes. **Swimming Pool:** No. **Swimming Pool:** No. **Playground:** Yes. **Other:** Myers Lake, sandy beach, rec hall, pavilion, coin games, boat dock, boat ramp, basketball, sports field, horseshoes, volleyball, tetherball, softball, rental cabins. **Activities:** Swimming, fishing, boating (rental pontoons, rowboats, kayaks, & paddleboats available), scheduled weekend activities. **Nearby Attractions:** Children's Museum, Crossroads Village & Huckleberry Railroad, *Genesee Belle* cruises, Flint Cultural Center, Genesee Recreation Area, Alfred P. Sloan Museum, Flint Institute of Arts,

Longway Planetarium, golf, antiques, arts & crafts. **Additional Information:** Flint Area CVB, (800) 253-5468.

RESTRICTIONS

Pets: Leash only. **Fires:** Fire ring only. **Alcoholic Beverages:** Not permitted. **Vehicle Maximum Length:** None.

TO GET THERE

From the junction of US 23 and Silver Lake Rd., take Linden-Fenton Exit 79 and drive 10 mi. west on Silver Lake Rd. Road is mostly wide and well maintained w/ narrow shoulders in places.

CADILLAC

Camp Cadillac

10621 East 34 Rd., Cadillac 49601. T: (800) 927-3124; F: (231) 775-9724; www.campcadillac.com; vcs@netonecom.net.

RV ★★★★ Tent ★★★★

Beauty: ★★★★ Site Privacy: ★★★★
Spaciousness: ★★★★ Quiet: ★★★★
Security: ★★★★ Cleanliness: ★★★★
Insect Control: ★★★★ Facilities: ★★★★

Adjacent to state forest land, Camp Cadillac has the privacy and feel of a park with the conveniences of a modern campground. Located two miles east of Cadillac, the campground offers level, grassy, and mostly shaded sites with a typical site width of 45 feet. Laid out in a series of loops, the rural campground has nine pull-through sites. A large roster of activities, including the popular barrel train and petting zoo, makes this a favorite spot for families. Friendly owners, sparkling-clean rest rooms, and a nice family atmosphere keeps campers coming back. Many people also use Camp Cadillac as a base to enjoy all the area has to offer. The best RV sites are by the pool and facilities. The best tent sites are in the more wooded, private areas. Security measures include owners who live on site and keep a close watch on the campground.

BASICS

Operated by: Tim & Angie Vaughan. **Open:** Apr. 15–Oct. 15. **Site Assignment:** Reservations w/ 1-night deposit; refund (minus $5) w/ 7-day notice. **Registration:** At campground office. **Fee:** $30 (cash, check, credit cards). **Parking:** At site.

FACILITIES

Number of RV Sites: 105. **Number of Tent-Only Sites:** 10. **Hookups:** Electric (20, 30, 50 amps), water, sewer, phone. **Each Site:** Picnic table, fire ring. **Dump Station:** Yes. **Laundry:** Yes. **Pay Phone:** Yes. **Rest Rooms and Showers:** Yes. **Fuel:** No. **Propane:** Yes. **Internal Roads:** Gravel, in good condition. **RV Service:** No. **Market:** 2 mi. west in Cadillac. **Restaurant:** 2 mi. west in Cadillac. **General Store:** Yes, limited. **Vending:** Yes. **Swimming Pool:** Yes. **Playground:** Yes. **Other:** Clam river, petting zoo, rec hall, coin games, pond fishing, basketball, movies, badminton, sports field, horseshoes, hiking trails, volleyball, rental cabins, rental RVs. **Activities:** Swimming, hiking, fishing, scheduled activities. **Nearby Attractions:** Johnny's Wild Game & Fish Park, golf, hunting, bike path, walkway, scenic drives, pontoon boat rides, natural history museum, Shay Steam Locomotive, historic walking tour, antiques, arts & crafts, Shrine of the Pines. **Additional Information:** Cadillac Area Visitors Bureau, (800) 225-2537.

RESTRICTIONS

Pets: Leash only; 1 dog per site. **Fires:** Fire ring only. **Alcoholic Beverages:** At sites only. **Vehicle Maximum Length:** None. **Other:** No extra tents on same site.

TO GET THERE

From north junction of Hwy. 55 and US 131, drive 2.4 mi. north on US 131, then 2 mi. east on East Boon Rd./E 34 Rd. Roads are mostly wide and well maintained w/ adequate shoulders.

CEDAR SPRING

Lakeside Camp Park

13677 White Creek Ave., Cedar Springs 49319. T: (616) 696-1735

RV ★★★★ Tent ★★★

Beauty: ★★★★ Site Privacy: ★★★★
Spaciousness: ★★★★ Quiet: ★★★★
Security: ★★★★ Cleanliness: ★★★★
Insect Control: ★★★★ Facilities: ★★★★

Located 17 miles north of Grand Rapids, Lakeside Camp Park offers convenience and easy access from the interstate. In a suburban setting, the campground features a five-acre private lake with a nice sandy swimming beach and off-shore raft and fishing dock. The lake is stocked annually with trout, bass, catfish, perch, and panfish. No fishing license is required. Laid out in a series of loops, the campground has grassy, level, lakeside sites with a typical site width of 30 feet. Sites offer a choice of open or shaded, with nine pull-throughs and 62 seasonal campers in a separate area from daily or weekend campers. The best sites are closest to Lake Waller. A recreation building has seating for 80 and can be used by small or large groups camping at Lakeside. A speed limit of 7.5 mph is enforced and owners keep a close watch on the campground for security.

BASICS

Operated by: Richard & Diane Lupico. **Open:** May 1–Oct. 1. **Site Assignment:** Reservations w/ 1-night deposit; refund w/ 2-week notice. **Registration:** At campground office. **Fee:** $21 (cash, check, credit cards). **Parking:** At site.

FACILITIES

Number of RV Sites: 155. **Number of Tent-Only Sites:** 0. **Hookups:** Electric (20, 30 amps), water, sewer. **Each Site:** Picnic table, fire ring. **Dump Station:** Yes. **Laundry:** Yes. **Pay Phone:** Yes. **Rest Rooms and Showers:** Yes. **Fuel:** No. **Propane:** No. **Internal Roads:** Gravel, in good condition. **RV Service:** No. **Market:** One block. **Restaurant:** One block. **General Store:** Yes. **Vending:** Yes. **Swimming Pool:** No. **Playground:** Yes. **Other:** Waller Lake, swimming beach, volleyball, basketball, game room, golf range, coin games, pavilion, boat ramp, badminton, sports field. **Activities:** Swimming, fishing, boating (rental rowboats, kayaks, & paddleboats available), scheduled weekend activities. **Nearby Attractions:** Grand Rapids, golf, botanical gardens, pro baseball, Van Andel Museum, Gerald Ford Museum, Old Kent Baseball Stadium, antiques. **Additional Information:** Cedar Springs Chamber of Commerce, (616) 696-3260.

RESTRICTIONS

Pets: Leash only. **Fires:** Fire ring only. **Alcoholic Beverages:** Permitted. **Vehicle Maximum Length:** None.

TO GET THERE

From the junction of US 31 and Hwy. 46, take Exit 104 and drive 100 yards east on Hwy. 46, then 0.25 mi. south on White Creek Ave. Roads are wide and well maintained w/ adequate shoulders.

CEDARVILLE

Cedarville RV Park Campground

634 Grove St., Cedarville 49719. T: (800) 906-3351; www.michcampgrounds.com/cedarville; cedarr@northernway.net.

RV ★★★★ Tent ★★★★

Beauty: ★★★★ Site Privacy: ★★★
Spaciousness: ★★★ Quiet: ★★★★
Security: ★★★★ Cleanliness: ★★★★
Insect Control: ★★★★ Facilities: ★★★★

Located on the shores of Lake Huron in the midst of Les Cheneaux Islands, Cedarville RV Park Campground offers beautiful views. The campground also has seven deep-water docks and 35 other boat docks, as well as a boat launch. A fish-cleaning building helps give the campground its sparkling facilities. Just three blocks away from downtown Cedarville, the campground offers level, mostly open sites, with a typical site width of 25 feet. There are 9 pull-throughs and 12 seasonal campers. Reservations are recommended during prime vacation time since the campground is a popular spot with water sports enthusiasts, as well as campers visiting the local attractions. Security measures include owners who live on site and keep a close watch on the campground. Although they won't tolerate any misbehavior, owners are very friendly and helpful.

BASICS

Operated by: Jon & Sharrie Steinbach. **Open:** May 1–Oct. 31. **Site Assignment:** Reservations w/ 1-night deposit; refund (minus $7.50) w/ 1-week notice. **Registration:** At campground office. **Fee:** $22 (cash, check, credit cards). **Parking:** At site.

FACILITIES

Number of RV Sites: 75. **Number of Tent-Only Sites:** 2. **Hookups:** Electric (20, 30, 50 amps), water, sewer. **Each Site:** Picnic table, fire ring. **Dump Station:** Yes. **Laundry:** Yes. **Pay Phone:** Yes. **Rest Rooms and Showers:** Yes. **Fuel:** No. **Propane:** No. **Internal Roads:** Gravel, in good condition. **RV Service:** No. **Market:** 6 blocks. **Restaurant:** 4 blocks. **General Store:** No. **Vending:** No. **Swimming Pool:** No. **Playground:** No. **Other:** Lake Huron, rec hall, boat dock, boat ramp, rental cabins, fish-cleaning building. **Activities:** Swimming, fishing, boating (rental rowboats & kayaks available). **Nearby Attractions:** Castle Rock, Mackinac Bridge, Mackinac Island, Mackinaw City, Deer Ranch, golf, casino, Fort

De Baude Indian Museum, Marquette Mission Park & Museum of Ojibwa Culture, New France Discovery Center & Father Marquette National Memorial, Soo Locks, Ft. Millimackinac, Tahqomen Falls. **Additional Information:** St. Ignace Tourism Assoc., (800) 338-6660.

Restrictions

Pets: Leash only. **Fires:** Fire ring only. **Alcoholic Beverages:** Permitted. **Vehicle Maximum Length:** None.

To Get There

From the junction of I-75 and Hwy. 134, take Exit 359 and drive 17 mi. east on Hwy. 134 through Cedarville, then 1 block south on Lake St. Roads are well maintained w/ adequate shoulders.

CHAMPION

Michigamme Shores Campground Resort

Box 6, Champion 49814. T: (906) 339-2116; www.michigammeshores.com.

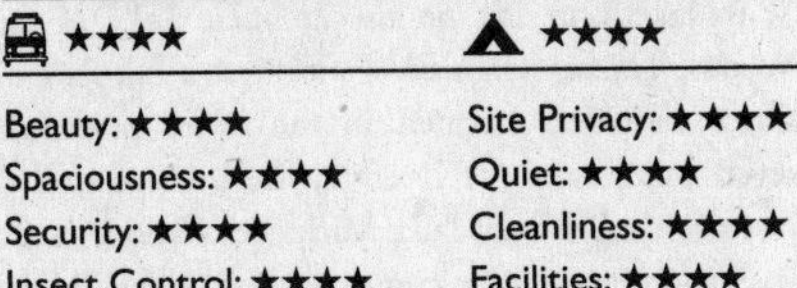

RV ★★★★ Tent ★★★★

Beauty: ★★★★ Site Privacy: ★★★★
Spaciousness: ★★★★ Quiet: ★★★★
Security: ★★★★ Cleanliness: ★★★★
Insect Control: ★★★★ Facilities: ★★★★

Michigamme Shores Campground Resort has a great location—two-and-a-half miles west of Champion, on the shores of Lake Michigamme, in the heart of Upper Michigan's moose country. Facilities are very clean and well maintained, showing close attention to detail. Sites are mostly gravel and shaded, with a typical site width of 30 feet and eight pull-throughs. A separate area for tents provides more green space and privacy. The best sites are as close to the lake. Lake Michigamme encompasses 4,360 acres, or almost seven square miles. The lake has more than 20 islands and depths of 50 feet. Michigamme Shores is the closest resort to moose country, and winter sports enthusiasts can catch cross-country ski trails right at the campground. Miles of groomed trails through the UP's snow-covered backcountry are available for snowmobiling or skiing. Hunters have access to some of the best hunting in the UP. Hikers can enjoy the wilderness and a bevy of animals and birds.

Basics

Operated by: Woody & Pat Taylor. **Open:** All year. **Site Assignment:** Reservations w/ 1-night deposit; refund w/ 2-week notice. **Registration:** At campground office. **Fee:** $26 (cash, check, credit cards). **Parking:** At site.

Facilities

Number of RV Sites: 80. **Number of Tent-Only Sites:** 20. **Hookups:** Electric (20, 30, 50 amps), water, sewer. **Each Site:** Picnic table, fire ring. **Dump Station:** Yes. **Laundry:** Yes. **Pay Phone:** Yes. **Rest Rooms and Showers:** Yes. **Fuel:** No. **Propane:** Yes. **Internal Roads:** Paved, in good condition. **RV Service:** No. **Market:** 2 mi. east in Champion. **Restaurant:** 2 mi. east in Champion. **General Store:** Yes. **Vending:** Yes. **Swimming Pool:** No. **Playground:** Yes. **Other:** Michigamme Lake, sandy beach, rec hall, coin games, basketball, tennis, badminton, sports field, horseshoes, hiking trails, volleyball, boat dock,. **Activities:** Swimming, fishing, boating (rental canoes, rowboats, motorboats, pontoons, paddleboats available), hiking. **Nearby Attractions:** Walking tours, Historical Museum, Marquette Maritime Mueum, Presque Isle Park, Upper Peninsula Children's Museum, golf, waterfalls, ghost towns, Pictured Rocks National Lakeshore, rock hounding, Copper Harbor & Keweenaw Peninsula. **Additional Information:** Marquette County CVB.

Restrictions

Pets: Leash only. **Fires:** Fire ring only. **Alcoholic Beverages:** Permitted. **Vehicle Maximum Length:** None.

To Get There

From west edge of Champion, drive 2.5 mi. west on US 41/Hwy. 28. Roads are wide and well maintained w/ broad shoulders.

CHEBOYGAN

Waterways Campground

P.O. Box 262, Cheboygan 49721. T: (888) 882-7066

RV ★★★ Tent ★★★

Beauty: ★★★ Site Privacy: ★★★
Spaciousness: ★★★ Quiet: ★★★★
Security: ★★★★ Cleanliness: ★★★★
Insect Control: None Facilities: ★★★

One of the newest campgrounds on the inland waterway, Waterways Campground is nestled on the shores of the Cheboygan River. Located two miles south of Cheboygan, the campground offers level sites arranged in upper and lower levels. Sites are grassy with gravel parking spots and have a typical site width of 30 feet. The campground has 11 seasonal campers, mostly open sites, and ten pull-throughs. Bouquets of fresh-cut flowers in the clean bathroom are a nice touch. Apple trees are scattered around the property, which is located across from a marina. A tent area is separate from RVs and offers more privacy and green space. The best RV sites are 42–50 because they are in the back of the campground, offer full hookup, and have cable TV. The speed limit is five mph and security measures include one entrance/exit road, one-way streets, owners who live on site, and regular campground patrols.

Basics

Operated by: Ron & Jan Ramsey. **Open:** May 1–Nov. 1. **Site Assignment:** Reservations w/ 1-night deposit; refund w/ 48-hour notice. **Registration:** At campground office. **Fee:** $23 (cash, check, credit cards). **Parking:** At site.

Facilities

Number of RV Sites: 50. **Number of Tent-Only Sites:** Tent area. **Hookups:** Electric (30, 50 amps), water, sewer, cable TV. **Each Site:** Picnic table, fire ring. **Dump Station:** Yes. **Laundry:** No. **Pay Phone:** No. **Rest Rooms and Showers:** Yes. **Fuel:** No. **Propane:** No. **Internal Roads:** Gravel, in good condition. **RV Service:** No. **Market:** 2 mi. north in Cheboygan. **Restaurant:** 2 mi. north in Cheboygan. **General Store:** Yes. **Vending:** Yes. **Swimming Pool:** No. **Playground:** Yes. **Other:** Cheboygan River, horseshoes, game room, recreation field, boat ramp, boat dock, basketball, badminton, hiking trails, volleyball. **Activities:** Fishing, boating (rental pontoon, rowboats, paddleboats available), scheduled weekend activities. **Nearby Attractions:** Opera House, golf, archery range, Cross of the Woods Shrine, Mackinaw City, Mackinac Island, museums, antiques, beaches, state & city parks, 42 mi. of continuous inland waterway. **Additional Information:** Cheboygan Area Chamber of Commerce, (800) 968-3302.

Restrictions

Pets: Leash only. Large or multiple pets must have prior approval. **Fires:** Fire ring only. **Alcoholic Beverages:** Permitted. **Vehicle Maximum Length:** None.

To Get There

From the junction of Hwy. 27 and Hwy. 33, drive 0.25 mi. south on Hwy. 33. Roads are wide and well maintained w/ broad shoulders.

COLDWATER

Waffle Farm Campground

790 North Union Rd., Coldwater 49036. T: (517) 278-4315; www.wafflefarm.com.

RV ★★★★ Tent ★★★★

Beauty: ★★★★ Site Privacy: ★★★★
Spaciousness: ★★★★ Quiet: ★★★★
Security: ★★★★ Cleanliness: ★★★★
Insect Control: None Facilities: ★★★★

A lakeside campground with open and shaded sites, Waffle Farm Campground got its name from the owner's grandmother, Myra Waffle, who started the camping business in 1925 with primitive camping and two wooden boats for rent. The camp sites are now spread over more than one-and-a-half miles of water frontage, mainly Craig Lake and part of Morrison Lake. The two lakes are part of a group totaling over 1,074 acres known as the Randall-Morrison Chain. The campground has 240 seasonal campers, 25 pull-throughs, and a typical site width of 30 feet. Seasonal campers are mostly in a separate area from other campsites. Tent campers have a section with more green space and privacy. Quiet hours are 11 p.m. to 8 a.m. Speed limit is 10 mph, a bit fast for a family campground. Security includes a guard on weekends.

Basics

Operated by: Loyd Green Jr. & Family. **Open:** Apr. 15–Oct. 15. **Site Assignment:** Reservations w/ $20 deposit; refund (minus $5) w/ 7-day notice. **Registration:** At campground office. **Fee:** $24 (cash, check). **Parking:** At site.

Facilities

Number of RV Sites: 370. **Number of Tent-Only Sites:** 25. **Hookups:** Electric (20, 30, 50 amps), water, sewer. **Each Site:** Picnic table, fire spot. **Dump Station:** Yes. **Laundry:** No. **Pay Phone:** Yes. **Rest Rooms and Showers:** Yes. **Fuel:** Yes. **Propane:** Yes. **Internal Roads:** Gravel, in good condition. **RV Service:** No. **Market:** 3 mi. south in Coldwater. **Restaurant:** 3 mi. south in Coldwater. **General Store:** Yes. **Vending:** Yes.

Swimming Pool: No. **Playground:** Yes. **Other:** Lake, swimming beach, pavilion, arcade, mini golf, driving range, fish-cleaning stand, club area, boat ramp, boat landing, rental cottages, rec room, sports field, hiking trails. **Activities:** Swimming, fishing, hiking, boating (rental rowboats, paddleboats available). **Nearby Attractions:** Bowling, golf, summer theater, Branch County Historical Society, antiques, drive-in theaters, motor speedway, historic homes, museums, arts & crafts shops. **Additional Information:** Branch County Tourism Bureau, (800) 968-9333.

Restrictions

Pets: Leash only. **Fires:** Fire ring only. **Alcoholic Beverages:** Permitted. **Vehicle Maximum Length:** None.

To Get There

From the junction of I-69 and US 12, drive 3.5 mi. north on I-69, take Exit 16, then 2.75 mi. west on Jonesville Rd., then 0.75 mi. north on Union City Rd. Roads are well maintained w/ broad shoulders.

DECATUR

Leisure Valley Campground

40851 CR 669, Decatur 49045. T: (616) 423-7122

RV ★★★★ Tent ★★★

Beauty: ★★★★	Site Privacy: ★★★★
Spaciousness: ★★★★	Quiet: ★★★★
Security: ★★★★	Cleanliness: ★★★★
Insect Control: ★★★★	Facilities: ★★★★

A grassy campground with open and shaded sites, Leisure Valley Campground is located three miles south of Decatur. Sites are level with a typical site width of 35 feet. The campground has 30 seasonal campers. A clubhouse with a kitchen is available. Campsites are adjacent to a small lake and five ponds. The lake is stocked with bass, bluegill, and perch. The best camp sites are closest to the water. A small island is a nice picnic spot. Facilities are very clean and well maintained, and the owners provide security for this quiet, family-oriented place.

Basics

Operated by: Gale & Josie Congdon. **Open:** Apr. 1–Oct. 31. **Site Assignment:** Reservations w/ 1-night deposit; refund (minus $5) w/ 7-day notice. **Registration:** At campground office. **Fee:** $20 (cash, check). **Parking:** At site.

Facilities

Number of RV Sites: 108. **Number of Tent-Only Sites:** 0. **Hookups:** Electric (20, 30 amps), water, sewer, phone. **Each Site:** Picnic table, fire ring. **Dump Station:** Yes. **Laundry:** Yes. **Pay Phone:** Yes. **Rest Rooms and Showers:** Yes. **Fuel:** No. **Propane:** Yes. **Internal Roads:** Gravel, in good condition. **RV Service:** No. **Market:** 2 mi. north in Decatur. **Restaurant:** 2 mi. north in Decatur. **General Store:** Yes. **Vending:** Yes. **Swimming Pool:** Yes. **Playground:** Yes. **Other:** Swimming lake, rec hall, pavilion, coin games, boat dock, mini golf, basketball, shuffleboard, badminton, horseshoes, volleyball, hiking trails, rental trailers. **Activities:** Swimming, fishing, boating (rental canoes, rowboats, paddleboats available), scheduled weekend activities, hiking. **Nearby Attractions:** Golf, stock car racing, winery tours, playhouses, Palisades Nuclear Plant, Deer Forest, antiques, arts & crafts. **Additional Information:** Decatur Chamber of Commerce, (616) 423-7014.

Restrictions

Pets: Leash only. **Fires:** Fire ring only. **Alcoholic Beverages:** Permitted. **Vehicle Maximum Length:** None.

To Get There

From the junction of Hwy. 51 and George St., drive 3 mi. south on George St., then 0.25 mi. west on Valley Rd. Roads are mostly wide and well maintained w/ adequate shoulders. Access road is in fair condition.

DECATUR

Oak Shores Campground

86882 CR 215, Decatur 49045. T: (616) 423-7370; www.michcampgrounds.com/oakshores/decatur.

RV ★★★★ Tent ★★★★

Beauty: ★★★	Site Privacy: ★★★★
Spaciousness: ★★★★	Quiet: ★★★★
Security: ★★★★	Cleanliness: ★★★
Insect Control: ★★★★	Facilities: ★★★★

Located on a private 75-acre lake in Decatur, Oak Shores Campground offers a choice of sites ranging from full sun to full shade. Sites are level and grassy with a typical site width of 30 feet. There are 95 seasonal campers and 30 pull-through sites. The best sites are closest to Knickerbocker Lake. A separate primitive tent area provides more green space and privacy. Along with other playgrounds, Oak Shores offers a fenced-in Little Tykes playground with more size-appropriate equipment. A large rec hall is available for dancing and club activities. Owners provide security measures and try to make sure the campground maintains a peaceful, family-oriented atmosphere. From all the camping families that keep returning, their efforts must be working.

Basics

Operated by: Joe & Mary Lou Schantz. **Open:** Apr. 15–Oct. 15. **Site Assignment:** Reservations w/ 1-night deposit; refund (less $5) w/ 2-week notice. **Registration:** At campground office. **Fee:** $25 (cash, check, credit cards). **Parking:** At site.

Facilities

Number of RV Sites: 220. **Number of Tent-Only Sites:** 10. **Hookups:** Electric (20, 30 amps), water, sewer, phone. **Each Site:** Picnic table, fire ring. **Dump Station:** Yes. **Laundry:** Yes. **Pay Phone:** Yes. **Rest Rooms and Showers:** Yes. **Fuel:** No. **Propane:** Yes. **Internal Roads:** Gravel, in good condition. **RV Service:** No. **Market:** 5 mi. **Restaurant:** 5 mi. **General Store:** Yes. **Vending:** Yes. **Swimming Pool:** Yes. **Playground:** Yes. **Other:** Knickerbocker Lake, sandy beach, coin games, rental cabins & travel trailers, sports field, whirlpool, game room, adult game room, pavilion, tennis, shuffleboard, rec hall, horseshoes, volleyball, basketball. **Activities:** Swimming, fishing, boating (rental canoes, kayaks, rowboats, paddleboats available), scheduled weekend activities. **Nearby Attractions:** Golf, stock car racing, winery tours, playhouses, Palisades Nuclear Plant, Deer Forest, antiques, arts & crafts. **Additional Information:** Decatur Chamber of Commerce, (616) 423-7014.

Restrictions

Pets: Small pets only; on leash. **Fires:** Fire ring only. **Alcoholic Beverages:** Permitted. **Vehicle Maximum Length:** None.

To Get There

From the junction of I-94 and Hwy. 51, take Exit 56 and drive 10 mi. southwest on Hwy. 51, then 0.25 mi. north on CR 215. Roads are mainly wide and well maintained w/ adequate shoulders.

DECATUR

Timber Trails RV Park

84981 47H St., Decatur 49045. T: (616) 681-9836

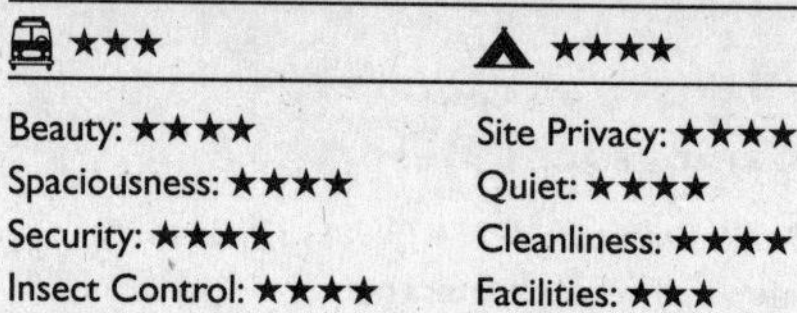

RV ★★★ Tent ★★★★

Beauty: ★★★★	Site Privacy: ★★★★
Spaciousness: ★★★★	Quiet: ★★★★
Security: ★★★★	Cleanliness: ★★★★
Insect Control: ★★★★	Facilities: ★★★

With lakefront sites on the 289-acre Lake of the Woods, Timber Trails RV Park offers a full slate of water activities. Located in the lower peninsula seven miles north of Decatur, the campground is just a few miles from Lake Michigan. Campsites are level and grassy with a choice of open or shade. The best sites are on the lakefront. The typical site width is 30 feet, and the campground has three pull-through sites. Group RV and tent sites are available. Facilities are clean and well maintained, and the location is scenic. Those facts are all the good news. The bad news is that most of the campsites are taken by seasonal campers. About 25 sites are available for non-seasonal campers, so reservations are recommended. Note that pets are not allowed.

Basics

Operated by: Gary & Deborah Douglas. **Open:** May 1–Sept. 30. **Site Assignment:** Reservations w/ 1-night deposit; refund w/ 14-day notice. **Registration:** At campground office. **Fee:** $22 (cash, check, credit cards). **Parking:** At site.

Facilities

Number of RV Sites: 107. **Number of Tent-Only Sites:** 10. **Hookups:** Electric (20, 30 amps), water. **Each Site:** Picnic table, fire ring. **Dump Station:** Yes. **Laundry:** Yes. **Pay Phone:** Yes. **Rest Rooms and Showers:** Yes. **Fuel:** No. **Propane:** Yes. **Internal Roads:** Gravel, in good condition. **RV Service:** None. **Market:** 6 mi. north in Decatur. **Restaurant:** 6 mi. north in Decatur. **General Store:** Yes, limited. **Vending:** Yes. **Swimming Pool:** No. **Playground:** Yes. **Other:** Lake of the Woods, sandy beach, volleyball, horseshoes, shuffleboard, game room, boat dock, sports field, badminton, boat slips. **Activities:** Swimming, fishing, boating (rental rowboats, canoes, paddleboats available). **Nearby Attractions:** Golf, stock car racing, winery tours, playhouses, Palisades Nuclear Plant, Deer Forest, antiques, arts & crafts. **Additional Information:** Decatur Chamber, (616) 423-7014.

Restrictions

Pets: No pets allowed. **Fires:** Fire ring only. **Alcoholic Beverages:** Permitted. **Vehicle Maximum Length:** None.

To Get There

From the junction of I-94 and Hwy. 51, take Exit 56 and drive 8 mi. south on Hwy. 51, then 0.75 mi. north on 47H St. Roads are mostly wide and well maintained w/ broad shoulders.

DORR

Hungry Horse Campground

2016 142nd St., Dorr 49323. T: (616) 681-9836; www.hungryhorsecampground.com; hhorse@accn.org.

RV ★★★★ Tent ★★★★

Beauty: ★★★★ Site Privacy: ★★★★
Spaciousness: ★★★★ Quiet: ★★★★
Security: ★★★★ Cleanliness: ★★★★
Insect Control: ★★★★ Facilities: ★★★★

Located 15 miles south of Grand Rapids in Dorr, Hungry Horse Campground offers a quiet rural setting. Laid out in a series of loops, the campground has level, grassy sites with a choice of open or shade. The typical site width is 30 feet, and the campground has 30 seasonal campers and 31 pull-through sites. Hungry Horse is nicely landscaped with flower beds, hanging baskets, and many perennial and annual flowers. Someone has a green thumb and spends a great deal of time keeping the grounds in tip-top shape. The playground with wooden structures is a nice addition. A heated wading pool is also popular with smaller youngsters. Rules are enforced to keep the campground well maintained and quiet. For example, long hair on swimmers in the swimming pool must be braided or tied back. Bicycles can be ridden on campground roads only, and quiet hours are enforced from 10 a.m. to 8 p.m. Motorcycles and all terrain vehicles also can't be ridden in the campgrounds. A ten mph speed limit is enforced but seems a bit high for such a family-oriented facility.

Basics

Operated by: Norm & Nancy Fifelski. **Open:** May 1–Oct. 1. **Site Assignment:** Reservations w/ 1-night deposit; refund (minus $10) w/ 3-day notice. **Registration:** At campground office. **Fee:** $28 (cash, check, credit cards). **Parking:** At site.

Facilities

Number of RV Sites: 85. **Number of Tent-Only Sites:** 5. **Hookups:** Electric (20, 30 amps), water, sewer. **Each Site:** Picnic table, fire ring. **Dump Station:** Yes. **Laundry:** Yes. **Pay Phone:** Yes. **Rest Rooms and Showers:** Yes. **Fuel:** No. **Propane:** Yes. **Internal Roads:** Paved/gravel, in good condition. **RV Service:** No. **Market:** 3 mi. east. **Restaurant:** 3 mi. east. **General Store:** Yes. **Vending:** Yes. **Swimming Pool:** Yes. **Playground:** Yes. **Other:** Pavilion, rec room, shuffleboard, badminton, sports field, horseshoes, hiking trails, volleyball, coin games, wading pool. **Activities:** Swimming, hiking, scheduled weekend activities. **Nearby Attractions:** Gerald B. Ford Museum, Fredrick Meijer Gardens, zoo, Michigan Adventure Amusement Park, Roger B. Chaffee Planetarium, golf, tennis, rivers & lakes, antiques, Wooden Shoe Factory. **Additional Information:** Grand Rapids/Kent County CVB, (800) 678-9859.

Restrictions

Pets: Leash only. **Fires:** Fire ring only. **Alcoholic Beverages:** At sites only. **Vehicle Maximum Length:** None.

To Get There

From the junction of US 131 and 142nd Ave., take Exit 68 and drive 4 mi. west on 142nd Ave. Roads are wide and well maintained w/ adequate shoulders.

ELK RAPIDS

Honcho Rest Campground

8988 Cairn Hwy., Elk Rapids 49629. T: (231) 264-8548; F: (231) 264-6849.

RV ★★★ Tent n/a

Beauty: ★★★ Site Privacy: ★★★
Spaciousness: ★★★ Quiet: ★★★
Security: ★★★★ Cleanliness: ★★★★
Insect Control: ★★★★ Facilities: ★★★

Located on the east shore of Bass Lake in Elk Rapids, Honcho Rest Campground offers a choice of shaded or open sites with a typical site width of 30 feet. Honcho Rest has 25 seasonal campers and two pull-through sites. Campsites have cement pads and patios. Across the street is a nine-hole golf course and Elk Lake. One mile away is Lake Michigan. The campground is clean and well maintained with seasonal spots also kept attractive. The number of seasonal campers does seem to continue growing, so reservations are recommended. Security measures are good with a main gate that is closed from 11 p.m. to 6 a.m.

Basics

Operated by: Robert & Johanna Wilder. **Open:** May 1–Oct. 15. **Site Assignment:** Reservations w/ 1-night deposit; refund w/ 2-week notice. **Registration:** At campground office. **Fee:** $26 (cash, check, credit cards). **Parking:** At site.

Facilities

Number of RV Sites: 50. **Number of Tent-Only Sites:** 0. **Hookups:** Electric (20, 30, 50 amps), water, sewer, cable TV. **Each Site:** Picnic table, fire ring. **Dump Station:** Yes. **Laundry:** Yes. **Pay Phone:** Yes. **Rest Rooms and Showers:** Yes. **Fuel:** No. **Propane:** Yes. **Internal Roads:** Gravel, in good condition. **RV Service:** No. **Market:** Two blocks. **Restaurant:** Two blocks. **General Store:** No. **Vending:** Yes. **Swimming Pool:** No. **Playground:** Yes. **Other:** Bass Lake, boat dock, sports field. **Activities:** Swimming, fishing, boating (rental rowboats, canoes available). **Nearby Attractions:** Golf course, Lake Michigan, Elk Lake, marina, Guntzviller's Spirit of the Woods Museum, antiques, arts & crafts, fishing, swimming, watersports. **Additional Information:** Elk Rapids Chamber of Commerce, (231) 264-8202.

Restrictions

Pets: Leash only. **Fires:** Fire ring only. **Alcoholic Beverages:** Permitted. **Vehicle Maximum Length:** None. **Other:** No tents allowed.

To Get There

From the junction of US 31 and Ames St. in Elk Rapids, drive 1.25 mi. southeast on Ames St. Roads are wide and well maintained w/ adequate shoulders.

FENWICK

Snow Lake Kampground

644 East Snow Lake Rd., Fenwick 48834. T: (517) 248-3224

RV ★★★★ Tent ★★★★

Beauty: ★★★★ Site Privacy: ★★★★
Spaciousness: ★★★★ Quiet: ★★★★
Security: ★★★★ Cleanliness: ★★★★
Insect Control: ★★★★ Facilities: ★★★★

Located 28 miles from Grand Rapids in Fenwick, Snow Lake Kampground is a Christian family resort. The rural campground has open or shaded sites with a typical site width of 40 feet. The campground has 200 seasonal campers so reservations are recommended. Sites are mostly gravel with 25 pull-throughs. A new rally area features a new bathhouse and an enclosed pavilion. Facilities are very clean and well maintained. A nice touch is a kiddie pool for youngsters who might be too small for the regular heated pool. Sunday church services are held in the Little Church in the Wildwood. The best sites are those closest to Snow Lake. Owners keep a close watch on the campground and provide security measures. Without being nagging or intrusive, owners also enforce guidelines to keep Snow Lake Kampground a clean, quiet, safe, family-oriented facility.

Basics

Operated by: Ronald & Marie Sellers. **Open:** May 1–Oct. 1. **Site Assignment:** Reservations w/ 1-night deposit; refund w/ 5-day notice. **Registration:** At campground office. **Fee:** $28 (cash, check, credit cards). **Parking:** At site.

Facilities

Number of RV Sites: 252. **Number of Tent-Only Sites:** 5. **Hookups:** Electric (20, 30, 50 amps), water, sewer, phone. **Each Site:** Picnic table, fire ring. **Dump Station:** Yes. **Laundry:** Yes. **Pay Phone:** Yes. **Rest Rooms and Showers:** Yes. **Fuel:** No. **Propane:** No. **Internal Roads:** Gravel, in good condition. **RV Service:** No. **Market:** 3 mi. north. **Restaurant:** On site. **General Store:** Yes. **Vending:** Yes. **Swimming Pool:** Yes. **Playground:** Yes. **Other:** Snow Lake, rec room, coin games, wading pool, boat dock, mini-golf, basketball, shuffleboard, sports field, horseshoes, volleyball, pavilion. **Activities:** Swimming, fishing, boating (rental rowboats, kayaks, paddleboats available), scheduled weekend activities. **Nearby Attractions:** Gerald B. Ford Museum, Fredrick Meijer Gardens, zoo, Michigan Adventure Amusement Park, Roger B. Chaffee Planetarium, golf, tennis, rivers & lakes, antiques, Wooden Shoe Factory. **Additional Information:** Grand Rapids/ Kent County CVB, (800) 678-9859.

Restrictions

Pets: Leash only. **Fires:** Fire ring only. **Alcoholic Beverages:** Not permitted. **Vehicle Maximum Length:** 40 ft.

To Get There

From the junction of Hwy. 57 and Hwy. 66, drive 3 mi. south on Hwy. 66, then 0.75 mi. east on

Snow Lake Rd. Roads are mostly wide and well maintained w/ adequate shoulders.

FRANKENMUTH
Frankenmuth Jellystone Park

1339 Weiss St., Frankenmuth 48734. T: (989) 652-6668; F: (989) 652-3461; www.frankenmuthjellystone.com.

RV ★★★★ Tent ★★★★

Beauty: ★★★★ Site Privacy: ★★★★
Spaciousness: ★★★★ Quiet: ★★★★
Security: ★★★★★ Cleanliness: ★★★★★
Insect Control: Yes Facilities: ★★★★★

Located in the heart of the number one tourist attraction in Michigan, Frankenmuth Jellystone Park is a popular spot with reservations recommended. A bonus is that it's possible to park at the campground and walk to many attractions. It is 1,000 yards to Bronner's Christmas Wonderland and three-quarter mile to most shopping areas. There are sidewalks from the park to downtown. Laid out in a series of loops, sites are mostly open, level, and grassy with concrete pads or gravel to park on. The campground has no seasonal campers. The typical site width is 30 feet, and there are 48 pull-through sites. Cleanliness and security are tops. Security measures include a card-coded gate, ranger patrols, and an owner who lives on site. The downside to the campground's convenient location is that it must abide by city ordinances concerning campfires. So if you enjoy spending a quiet evening by your private campfire, this is not the place. Campers are welcome to use charcoal or gas grills at their sites but wood campfires are permitted only in designated rings off the sites. Community campfire rings are located between the rec hall and bathrooms and next to the pool.

Basics

Operated by: Erv Banes. **Open:** All year. **Site Assignment:** Reservations w/ $35 deposit; refund (minus $5) w/ 7-day notice. **Registration:** At campground office. **Fee:** $40 (cash, credit cards). **Parking:** At site.

Facilities

Number of RV Sites: 250. **Number of Tent-Only Sites:** 20. **Hookups:** Electric (20, 30, 50 amps), water, sewer. **Each Site:** Picnic table. **Dump Station:** Yes. **Laundry:** Yes. **Pay Phone:** Yes. **Rest Rooms and Showers:** Yes. **Fuel:** No. **Propane:** Yes. **Internal Roads:** Paved, in great condition. **RV Service:** No. **Market:** Next door. **Restaurant:** Next door. **General Store:** Yes. **Vending:** Yes. **Swimming Pool:** Yes. **Playground:** Yes. **Other:** Game room, hot tub, activity room, rec hall, snack bar, mini golf, pavilion, rental cabins, coin games, basketball, badminton, movies, horseshoes, volleyball. **Activities:** Swimming, scheduled activities. **Nearby Attractions:** Bronner's Christmas Wonderland, golf, paddlewheel boat, winery, antiques, arts & crafts, Bavarian shops, cheese haus, Military & Space Museum. **Additional Information:** Frankenmuth Chamber of Commerce, (800) FUN-TOWN.

Restrictions

Pets: Leash only. **Fires:** Designated community fire rings only. **Alcoholic Beverages:** At sites only. **Vehicle Maximum Length:** None. **Other:** Children under 16 not permitted in hot tub. Limit of one guest family per site per day. Guests are not permitted on holiday & Halloween event weekends.

To Get There

From the junction of I-75 and M-83 (Birch Run Rd.), take Exit 136, drive 2 mi. east on Birch Run Rd., drive 5 mi. north on Gera Rd., drive 1 block north on Weiss St. Roads are wide and well maintained w/ broad shoulders.

FRANKENMUTH
Pine Ridge RV Campground

11700 Gera Rd., Birch Run 48415. T: (989) 624-9029

RV ★★★ Tent n/a

Beauty: ★★★ Site Privacy: ★★★
Spaciousness: ★★★★ Quiet: ★★★★
Security: ★★★★ Cleanliness: ★★★★
Insect Control: None Facilities: ★★★

Located about four miles south of Frankenmuth, Pine Ridge RV Campground has the benefit of being conveniently close to "Little Bavaria" without being restricted under city campfire codes. Individual campsites are permitted to have wood campfires in fire rings. Laid out in a series of loops, the campground is mostly shaded with mature trees. Sites are grassy with gravel parking spots. The campground has 150 pull-through sites and no seasonal campers. Tents are not permitted. The best site is 61, but it is often reserved a year or two in advance. This end site has a beautiful yard with tall trees, offers pull-through access, and is a quiet spot. Site 147 is also popular because it is across from the clubhouse. The typical site width is 40 feet. Security measures are great with a card-coded gate, a manager who lives on site, and regular patrols of the campground.

Basics

Operated by: Norman Wooten. **Open:** Apr. 15–Nov. 15. **Site Assignment:** Reservations w/ 1-night deposit; refund w/ 7-day notice. **Registration:** At campground office. **Fee:** $30 (cash, check, credit cards). **Parking:** At site.

Facilities

Number of RV Sites: 201. **Number of Tent-Only Sites:** 0. **Hookups:** Electric (20, 30, 50 amps), water, sewer. **Each Site:** Picnic table, fire ring. **Dump Station:** Yes. **Laundry:** Yes. **Pay Phone:** Yes. **Rest Rooms and Showers:** Yes. **Fuel:** No. **Propane:** Yes. **Internal Roads:** Paved/gravel, in good condition. **RV Service:** No. **Market:** Walking distance. **Restaurant:** Walking distance. **General Store:** Yes, limited. **Vending:** No. **Swimming Pool:** No. **Playground:** Yes. **Other:** Pavilion, rec hall, basketball, volleyball. **Activities:** None. **Nearby Attractions:** Bronner's Christmas Wonderland, golf, paddlewheel boat, winery, antiques, arts & crafts, Bavarian shops, cheese haus, Military & Space Museum. **Additional Information:** Frankenmuth Chamber, (800) FUN-TOWN.

Restrictions

Pets: Leash only. **Fires:** Fire ring only. **Alcoholic Beverages:** At sites only. **Vehicle Maximum Length:** None. **Other:** No tents allowed.

To Get There

From the junction of I-75 and M-83 (Birch Run Rd.), take Exit 136 and drive 2 mi. east on Birch Run Rd., then 0.4 mi. north on Gera Rd. Roads are wide and well maintained w/ broad shoulders.

FREDERIC
Happi Days Campground

7486 West Batterson Rd., Frederic 49733. T: (989) 348-6115; hapidays@freeway.net.

RV ★★ Tent ★★

Beauty: ★★ Site Privacy: ★★
Spaciousness: ★★ Quiet: ★★★★
Security: ★★★ Cleanliness: ★★
Insect Control: ★★ Facilities: ★★

Happi Days Campground has so much potential. It's in a great location with a lot to do in the area. Sites are level and shaded in a quiet wooded area surrounded by pines and hardwoods. The roads to it are good. You can walk next door for a home-cooked breakfast or lunch in the comfortable Happi Days Diner, which has an interesting collection of 1950s memorabilia, including old 45 records, photos of Elvis, James Dean, Marilyn Monroe, and much more. The campground has a friendly owner (who is also the diner's cook). Laid out in a loop, the campground has one seasonal camper, 30 pull-through sites, and 2 group camping areas. Security is good, with an owner who lives on site and provides regular patrols of the campground. However, Happi Days Campground needs a good cleaning.

Basics

Operated by: Gilmar Smith. **Open:** All year. **Site Assignment:** Reservations w/ 1-night deposit; refund w/ 7-day notice. **Registration:** At campground office. **Fee:** $18 (cash, check). **Parking:** At site.

Facilities

Number of RV Sites: 40. **Number of Tent-Only Sites:** 50. **Hookups:** Electric (50 amps), water. **Each Site:** Picnic table, fire ring. **Dump Station:** Yes. **Laundry:** Yes. **Pay Phone:** No. **Rest Rooms and Showers:** Yes. **Fuel:** No. **Propane:** Yes. **Internal Roads:** Dirt, in fair condition. **RV Service:** No. **Market:** 8 mi. south in Grayling. **Restaurant:** Next door. **General Store:** No. **Vending:** No. **Swimming Pool:** No. **Playground:** Yes. **Other:** Horseshoes, volleyball, rental cabins. **Activities:** None. **Nearby Attractions:** Au Sable River, fishing, canoeing, hunting, Wellington Farm Park, state parks, golf, fish hatchery, bowling, antiques, arts & crafts. **Additional Information:** Grayling Area Visitors Council, (800) 937-8837.

Restrictions

Pets: Leash only. **Fires:** Fire ring only. **Alcoholic Beverages:** Permitted. **Vehicle Maximum Length:** None.

To Get There

From the junction of I-75 and Hwy. 93, take Exit 259 and drive 1.5 mi. west on Hwy. 93, then 4 mi. north on Old 27, then 1 block west on Batterson Rd. Roads are wide and well maintained w/ broad shoulders.

FREDERIC
Trails Campground

4066 Old 27 N., Frederic 49733. T: (517) 348-8692

RV ★★★ Tent ★★★

Beauty: ★★★ Site Privacy: ★★★
Spaciousness: ★★★ Quiet: ★★★★
Security: ★★★★ Cleanliness: ★★★★★
Insect Control: None Facilities: ★★

Trails Campground offers a quiet little place at a low price. It has few activities, but the campground is very clean and would be a nice spot to stay while enjoying all the recreational opportunities in the Au Sable River area. Laid out in a series of loops, the campground offers grassy, level sites with a choice of shade or open. There are 18 seasonal campers and no pull-through sites. Mature white pines, red pines, aspens and maples add a woodland effect. Located two miles south of Frederic, the campground has well maintained, decorated bathrooms, including shower stalls with woodland scenes and nice wooden counters. The best tent sites are in the back against the woods where there is more privacy and green space. Security measures include one entrance/exit road and owners who live on site and patrol the campground.

BASICS

Operated by: Jim & Ruth Thompson. **Open:** All year. **Site Assignment:** Reservations w/ no deposit. **Registration:** At campground office. **Fee:** $18 (cash, check). **Parking:** At site.

FACILITIES

Number of RV Sites: 40. **Number of Tent-Only Sites:** 23. **Hookups:** Electric (20 amps), water. **Each Site:** Picnic table, fire ring. **Dump Station:** Yes. **Laundry:** Yes. **Pay Phone:** Yes. **Rest Rooms and Showers:** Yes. **Fuel:** No. **Propane:** No. **Internal Roads:** Dirt, in good condition. **RV Service:** No. **Market:** 8 mi. south in Grayling. **Restaurant:** 2 mi. north in Frederic. **General Store:** No. **Vending:** Yes. **Swimming Pool:** No. **Playground:** Yes. **Other:** Horseshoes, volleyball. **Activities:** None. **Nearby Attractions:** Au Sable River, fishing, canoeing, hunting, Wellington Farm Park, state parks, golf, fish hatchery, bowling, antiques, arts & crafts. **Additional Information:** Grayling Area Visitors Council, (800) 937-8837.

RESTRICTIONS

Pets: Leash only. **Fires:** Fire ring only. **Alcoholic Beverages:** Permitted. **Vehicle Maximum Length:** None.

TO GET THERE

From the junction of I-75 and Hwy. 93, take Exit 259, drive 1.5 mi. west on Hwy. 93, then 4 mi. north on Old 27. Roads are wide and well maintained w/ broad shoulders.

GAYLORD
Gaylord Michaywe Wilderness Resort

5101 Campfires Parkway, Gaylord 49735. T: (517) 939-8723

 ★★★  ★★★

Beauty: ★★★ Site Privacy: ★★★
Spaciousness: ★★★ Quiet: ★★★
Security: ★★★★ Cleanliness: ★★★
Insect Control: No Facilities: ★★★

Nestled in 80 acres of birch, aspen, and pine, Gaylord Michaywe is bordered by the north branch of the Au Sable River. Laid out in a series of loops, the campground has 40 pull-through sites and a typical site width of 35 feet. The campground offers level, shaded, riverside sites. A five mph speed limit is strictly enforced with first-time offenders kicked out. "Kids always have right of way," campground rules state. Quiet hours are from 10 p.m. to 8 a.m. In season, campers can pick morel mushrooms, wild strawberries, raspberries, blueberries, and blackberries on the property. Security includes a traffic control gate, one entrance/exit, an owner who lives on site, and regular patrols of the campground.

BASICS

Operated by: John Dohan. **Open:** May 1–Oct. 15. **Site Assignment:** Reservations w/ 1-night deposit; refund w/ 7-day notice. **Registration:** At campground office. **Fee:** $33 (cash, check, credit cards). **Parking:** At site.

FACILITIES

Number of RV Sites: 120. **Number of Tent-Only Sites:** 3. **Hookups:** Electric (20, 30, 50 amps), water, sewer. **Each Site:** Picnic table, fire ring. **Dump Station:** Yes. **Laundry:** Yes. **Pay Phone:** Yes. **Rest Rooms and Showers:** Yes. **Fuel:** No. **Propane:** Yes. **Internal Roads:** Gravel, in good condition. **RV Service:** No. **Market:** 3 mi. west in Gaylord. **Restaurant:** 3 mi. west in Gaylord. **General Store:** Yes. **Vending:** Yes. **Swimming Pool:** Yes. **Playground:** Yes. **Other:** Au Sable River, golf driving nets, rental cabins, mini golf, basketball, volleyball, rental cabins, game room, child-sitting service, horseshoes, shuffleboard, sports field, hiking trails. **Activities:** Swimming, fishing, scheduled weekend activities. **Nearby Attractions:** Golf, bowling, ice skating, Bottle Cap Museum, canoeing, horseback riding, elk viewing, Otsego County Historical Museum, antiques. **Additional Information:** Gaylord Area Information Center, (800) 345-8621.

RESTRICTIONS

Pets: Leash only. **Fires:** Fire ring only. **Alcoholic Beverages:** At sites only. **Vehicle Maximum Length:** None.

TO GET THERE

From the junction of I-75 and Old 27, take Exit 279 and drive 2 mi. south on Old 27, then 0.5 mi. east on Charles Brink Rd. Roads are wide and well maintained w/ broad shoulders.

GRAYLING
River Park Campground and Trout Pond

2607 Peters Rd., Grayling 49738. T: (888) 517-9092; F: (517) 348-1638; www.riverparkcampground.com; riverpark@voyager.net.

RV ★★★★ Tent ★★★

Beauty: ★★★ Site Privacy: ★★★★
Spaciousness: ★★★★ Quiet: ★★★★
Security: ★★★★ Cleanliness: ★★★★
Insect Control: ★★★★ Facilities: ★★★

Surrounded by hundreds of acres of state land, River Park Campground and Trout Pond is located on the east branch of the Au Sable River in Grayling. The campground offers level, grassy, shaded spots with a wealth of pine, maple, and oak trees. The typical site width is 40 feet. River Park has 40 seasonal campers and no pull-through sites. Laid out in a series of loops, the campground has a separate area for tent campers with more green space and privacy. The trout pond is stocked two or three times each summer with rainbow trout. No throwbacks are allowed—you have to keep what you catch and pay 40 cents per inch for the fish. Most of the trout measure from 10 inches up to 21 inches. River Park is open year-round and attracts winter enthuiasts who like being able to snowmobile from their campsite or ski out of the campground. Water is turned off at individual campsites during the winter, but the bathhouse is kept heated and open. Security includes owners who live on site, one entrance/exit road, and regular camp patrols.

BASICS

Operated by: Dennis & Maureen Fyock. **Open:** All year. **Site Assignment:** Reservations w/ 1-night deposit; refund w/ 7-day notice. **Registration:** At campground office. **Fee:** $20 (cash, check, credit cards). **Parking:** At site.

FACILITIES

Number of RV Sites: 58. **Number of Tent-Only Sites:** 10. **Hookups:** Electric (30 amps), water. **Each Site:** Picnic table, fire ring. **Dump Station:** Yes. **Laundry:** Yes. **Pay Phone:** Yes. **Rest Rooms and Showers:** Yes. **Fuel:** No. **Propane:** Yes. **Internal Roads:** Paved, in good condition. **RV Service:** No. **Market:** 6 mi. south in Grayling. **Restaurant:** 6 mi. south in Grayling. **General Store:** Yes, limited. **Vending:** No. **Swimming Pool:** No. **Playground:** Yes. **Other:** Au Sable River, shuffleboard, horseshoes, rec hall, sports field, coin games, basketball, shuffleboard, fishing pond. **Activities:** Swimming, fishing. **Nearby Attractions:** Wellington Farm Park, state parks, golf, fish hatchery, bowling antiques, arts & crafts, fishing, canoeing, hunting. **Additional Information:** Grayling Area Visitors Council, (800) 937-8837.

RESTRICTIONS

Pets: Leash only. **Fires:** Fire ring only. **Alcoholic Beverages:** Permitted. **Vehicle Maximum Length:** None.

TO GET THERE

From the junction of US 41 and 10th Ave., drive behind the K-Mart Shopping Center. Roads are wide and well maintained w/ broad shoulders.

GRAYLING
Yogi Bear's Jellystone Park Camp-Resort

370 West Four Mile Rd., Grayling 49738. T: (989) 348-2157; www.michcampground.com/yogibears.

RV ★★★★ Tent ★★★

Beauty: ★★★★ Site Privacy: ★★★★
Spaciousness: ★★★★ Quiet: ★★★★

Security: ★★★★ Cleanliness: ★★★★
Insect Control: ★★★★ Facilities: ★★★★

With easy access to the interstate and a widely recognized name, Yogi Bear's Jellystone Park Camp-Resorts in Grayling, is a popular stopping spot. The campground also is a destination for families because of its large roster of recreational activities. Located in a wooded, rural setting, the campground is laid out in a series of loops and offers grassy, mostly shaded sites. The typical site width is 45 feet, and the campground has 130 seasonal campers and no pull-through sites. Quiet hours are enforced from 11 p.m. to 8 a.m. and the campground doesn't allow ATVs anywhere in the campground or in adjacent private property. Security measures include a five mph speed limit, one entrance/exit road, owners who live on site, and patrols of the campground.

Basics

Operated by: Gregory & Marlene Schoo. **Open:** May 1–Sept. 31. **Site Assignment:** Reservations w/ 1-night deposit; refund w/ 7-day notice. **Registration:** At campground office. **Fee:** $32 (cash, check, credit cards). **Parking:** At site.

Facilities

Number of RV Sites: 230. **Number of Tent-Only Sites:** 0. **Hookups:** Electric (20, 30 amps), water, sewer. **Each Site:** Picnic table, fire ring. **Dump Station:** Yes. **Laundry:** Yes. **Pay Phone:** Yes. **Rest Rooms and Showers:** Yes. **Fuel:** No. **Propane:** No. **Internal Roads:** Dirt, in good condition. **RV Service:** No. **Market:** 10 mi. north in Grayling. **Restaurant:** 10 mi. north in Grayling. **General Store:** Yes. **Vending:** Yes. **Swimming Pool:** Yes. **Playground:** Yes. **Other:** Mini Golf, coin games, outdoor cartoon theatre, shuffleboard, horseshoes, rec hall, game room, sports field, rental cabins, hiking trails, horseshoes. **Activities:** Swimming, hiking, scheduled activities. **Nearby Attractions:** Au Sable River, fishing, canoeing, hunting, Wellington Farm Park, state parks, golf, fish hatchery, bowling, antiques, arts & crafts, horseback riding. **Additional Information:** Grayling Area Visitors Council, (800) 937-8837.

Restrictions

Pets: Leash only. **Fires:** Fire ring only. **Alcoholic Beverages:** At sites only. **Vehicle Maximum Length:** 32 ft.

To Get There

From the junction of I-75 and Four Mile Rd., take Exit 251 and drive 4.5 mi. east on Four Mile Rd. Roads are wide and well maintained w/ broad shoulders.

HARRISON
Countryside Campground

805 Byfield Dr., Harrison 48625.T: (989) 539-5468; country@glccomputers.com.

RV ★★★ Tent ★★

Beauty: ★★★ Site Privacy: ★★★
Spaciousness: ★★★ Quiet: ★★★
Security: ★★★★ Cleanliness: ★★★★
Insect Control: None Facilities: ★★★

Located one mile west of Harrison, Countryside Campground has a nice combination of town conveniences and country peacefulness. Laid out in a series of loops, the campground has four seasonal campers, 20 pull-through sites, and a typical site width of 35 feet. A major plus is the campground's proximity to 20 lakes within 20 miles. Situated on rolling hills with a forest of pine trees, the campground offers a choice of shaded or open spots. Sites are grassy and level. The best sites are 14–24 because they surround a wooded area and offer more privacy. Pull-through sites also are popular because of their convenience. Families with children often prefer sites 8–13 located near the playground and swimming pool. Security measures include one-way roads past the office and owners who keep a close eye on the campground.

Basics

Operated by: Bob & Sylvia Kern. **Open:** May 1–Oct. 15. **Site Assignment:** Reservations w/ 1-night deposit; refund w/ 2-week notice. **Registration:** At campground office. **Fee:** $21 (cash, check, credit cards). **Parking:** At site.

Facilities

Number of RV Sites: 55. **Number of Tent-Only Sites:** 0. **Hookups:** Electric (30 amps), water, sewer. **Each Site:** Picnic table, fire ring. **Dump Station:** Yes. **Laundry:** Yes. **Pay Phone:** Yes. **Rest Rooms and Showers:** Yes. **Fuel:** No. **Propane:** No. **Internal Roads:** Gravel, in good condition. **RV Service:** No. **Market:** Yes, limited. **Restaurant:** Two blocks. **General Store:** 1.5 mi. south in Harrison. **Vending:** Yes. **Swimming Pool:** Yes. **Playground:** Yes. **Other:** Rental cabins, horseshoes, volleyball, basketball, badminton, sports field, rental bikes. **Activities:** Swimming. **Nearby Attractions:** Golf, cambling casino, river rafting, hunting, hiking, canoeing, boating, fishing, museums, antiques, Amish area. **Additional Information:** Clare County CVB, (800) 715-3550.

Restrictions

Pets: Leash only. **Fires:** Fire ring only. **Alcoholic Beverages:** At sites only. **Vehicle Maximum Length:** None.

To Get There

From the junction of Business 27 and Hwy. 61 in Harrison, drive 0.75 mi. west on Hwy. 61/Main St., then 0.25 mi. north on Byfield Dr. Roads are wide and well maintained w/ broad shoulders.

HARRISON
Wilson State Park

910 North First St., Harrison 48625.T: (517) 539-3021; www.michigandnr.com.

RV ★★★ Tent ★★★★

Beauty: ★★★★ Site Privacy: ★★★
Spaciousness: ★★★ Quiet: ★★★
Security: ★★★★ Cleanliness: ★★★
Insect Control: Yes Facilities: ★★

Located in Harrison, Wilson State Park is known for its sandy beach on Budd Lake and its muskie fishing. The campground also is unusual because it is in town and provides easy access to local attractions, restaurants, and shops. The campground is right across the street from the county fairground. Reservations are a must during fair time (the last weekend of July and first week of Aug.). Sites are grassy and mostly shaded with no seasonal campers and four pull-through sites. The best sites for RVs are 25 because it is big, 125 because it overlooks the lake, and 134 because it is a pull-through close to the beach. Tents are permitted on any sites. Because of the lake and woods, the campground is quiet despite its location off such a busy street. Park rangers also ensure that the noise level at campsites is kept down so as not to disturb other campers. Security is tops with one entrance/exit road, a state park sticker required on vehicles, and regular patrols by park rangers and county police.

Basics

Operated by: State of Michigan. **Open:** Apr. 1–Dec. 1. **Site Assignment:** Reservations are accepted w/ a $2 fee; refund w/ 48-hour notice. **Registration:** At campground office. **Fee:** $14 (cash, check, credit cards). **Parking:** At site.

Facilities

Number of RV Sites: 160. **Number of Tent-Only Sites:** 0. **Hookups:** Electric (30 amps). **Each Site:** Picnic table, fire ring. **Dump Station:** Yes. **Laundry:** No. **Pay Phone:** Yes. **Rest Rooms and Showers:** Yes. **Fuel:** No. **Propane:** No. **Internal Roads:** Paved/gravel, in good condition. **RV Service:** No. **Market:** Next door. **Restaurant:** Next door. **General Store:** No. **Vending:** Yes. **Swimming Pool:** No. **Playground:** Yes. **Other:** Budd Lake, swimming beach, pavilion, boating ramp, fishing lake, horseshoes, volleyball, recreation field, rental cabin. **Activities:** Swimming, fishing, boating. **Nearby Attractions:** Golf, gambling casino, river rafting, hunting, hiking, caoeing, museums, antiques, Amish area. **Additional Information:** Clare County CVB, (800) 715-3550.

Restrictions

Pets: Leash only. **Fires:** Fire ring only. **Alcoholic Beverages:** At sites only. **Vehicle Maximum Length:** 40 ft. **Other:** 15-day stay limit.

To Get There

From US 27, take the Harrison exit, drive 3.5 mi. west. Roads are wide and well maintained w/ broad shoulders.

HARRISON
Withii Trailer Camp

1820 Hampton Rd., Harrison 48625.T: (989) 539-3128

RV ★★ Tent ★★★

Beauty: ★★★ Site Privacy: ★★★
Spaciousness: ★★★★ Quiet: ★★★★
Security: ★★★★ Cleanliness: ★★★★
Insect Control: Yes Facilities: ★★

Located one mile north of Harrison, Withii Trailer Park has 20 lakes within a 20 miles proximity. The campground itself offers little recreation or activities, but the area is rich in swimming, boating, hiking, hunting and fishing. Laid out in a horseshoe, the campground has 50 seasonal campers and ten pull-through sites. Spots are grassy, level, and mostly shaded with a typical site width of 40 feet. Under the same ownership since 1970, the campground also has several mobile homes in an adjoining park.

Campers are asked not to walk between the mobile homes since they are private residences. Showers are well maintained and clean with private dressing rooms. Safety and security measures include a five mph speed limit, no riding of motorized vehicles in the park, no generators permitted, and children under age ten are not allowed in rest rooms unless accompanied by an adult. Although the campground is open year-round, be prepared for frigid cold and deep snow during winter. No fires are permitted when fire rings are hidden by snow, and roads are kept open "to the best of our ability" during winter seasons.

Basics

Operated by: Allen & Pat Tomes. **Open:** All year. **Site Assignment:** Reservations w/ 1-night deposit; refund w/ 2-week notice. **Registration:** At campground office. **Fee:** $20 (cash). **Parking:** At site.

Facilities

Number of RV Sites: 88. **Number of Tent-Only Sites:** 6. **Hookups:** Electric (20, 30, 50 amps), water, sewer. **Each Site:** Picnic table, fire ring. **Dump Station:** Yes. **Laundry:** No. **Pay Phone:** No. **Rest Rooms and Showers:** Yes. **Fuel:** No. **Propane:** No. **Internal Roads:** Gravel, in good condition. **RV Service:** No. **Market:** 1 mi. south in Harrison. **Restaurant:** 1 mi. south in Harrison. **General Store:** No. **Vending:** No. **Swimming Pool:** No. **Playground:** Yes. **Other:** Horseshoes, recreation field. **Activities:** None. **Nearby Attractions:** Golf, gambling casino, river rafting, hunting, hiking, canoeing, boating, fishing, musuems, antiques, Amish area. **Additional Information:** Clare County CVB, (800) 715-3550.

Restrictions

Pets: Leash only. **Fires:** Fire ring only. **Alcoholic Beverages:** At sites only. **Vehicle Maximum Length:** 35 ft. **Other:** No bare feet in rest rooms.

To Get There

From the junction of Hwy. 61 and Business US 27, drive 1.25 mi. north on Business US 27, then 200 yards west on Hampton Rd. Roads are wide and well maintained w/ broad shoulders.

HASTINGS

Whispering Waters Campground & Canoe Livery

1805 North Irving Rd., Hastings 49058. T: (800) 985-7019; F: (616) 945-8722; www.michcampgrounds.com/whisperingwaters; whisper@iserv.net.

RV ★★★★ Tent ★★★★

Beauty: ★★★★	Site Privacy: ★★★★
Spaciousness: ★★★★	Quiet: ★★★★
Security: ★★★★	Cleanliness: ★★★★
Insect Control: ★★★★	Facilities: ★★★★

A river runs through it. Whispering Waters Campground & Canoe Livery is is a wooded rolling campground on the high bank of the Thornapple River. Located in South Central Michigan in Hastings, the campground offers level, mostly shaded sites with a typical site width of 35 feet. The campground has 20 seasonal campers and 20 pull-through sites. A tent area on the river offers more green space and privacy. No motors are permitted on the river. A huge front porch at the campground building is a nice gathering spot, as is a commons area that features comfortable chairs, a microwave, TV, and library. Basic regulations for safety and security are enforced, including no alcohol on the river. The campground also doesn't tolerate rowdy behavior.

Basics

Operated by: Roger & Uta Wilmont. **Open:** Last Friday of Apr. through first Sunday of Oct. **Site Assignment:** Reservations w/ 1-night deposit; refund (minus $5) w/ 2-week notice. **Registration:** At campground office. **Fee:** $24 (cash, check, credit cards). **Parking:** At site.

Facilities

Number of RV Sites: 115. **Number of Tent-Only Sites:** 3. **Hookups:** Electric (20, 30, 50 amps), water, sewer, phone. **Each Site:** Picnic table, fire ring. **Dump Station:** Yes. **Laundry:** Yes. **Pay Phone:** Yes. **Rest Rooms and Showers:** Yes. **Fuel:** No. **Propane:** Yes. **Internal Roads:** Gravel, in good condition. **RV Service:** No. **Market:** 3 mi. **Restaurant:** 3 mi. **General Store:** Yes. **Vending:** Yes. **Swimming Pool:** Yes. **Playground:** Yes. **Other:** Thornapple River, swimming beach, rec room, pavilion, shuffleboard, badminton, sports field, horseshoes, hiking trails, volleyball, rental cabins, adults room. **Activities:** Swimming, fishing, hiking, boating (rental canoes available), scheduled weekend activities. **Nearby Attractions:** Riding ranch, golf, hot air ballooning, Gilmore Car Museum, Cheesbrough Rake Factory, Gun Lake, skydiving school, state parks, Kalamazoo Air Zoo, Historic Charleton Park Village & Museum. **Additional Information:** Barry County Chamber, (616) 945-2454.

Restrictions

Pets: Leash only. **Fires:** Fire ring only. **Alcoholic Beverages:** At sites only. **Vehicle Maximum Length:** None.

To Get There

From the west junction of Hwy. 43 and Hwy. 37, drive 3 mi. north on Hwy. 37, then 0.5 mi. north on Irving Rd. Roads are mostly wide and well maintained w/ adequate shoulders.

HILLMAN

Jack's Landing Resort

5966 Tennis Rd., Hillman 49746. T: (517) 742-4370; www.jackslanding.com.

RV ★★★ Tent ★★★

Beauty: ★★★★	Site Privacy: ★★★
Spaciousness: ★★★	Quiet: ★★★
Security: ★★★★	Cleanliness: ★★★
Insect Control: Yes	Facilities: ★★★

Located seven miles southeast of Hillman, Jack's Landing Resort has a beautiful view of Fletcher Pond. But don't let the name fool you. The "pond" offers 9,000 acres of premier fishing for pike, bass, and panfish. Wildlife viewing includes sights of eagles, osprey, loons and many ducks. The campground has level, open or shaded sites. It has no pull-throughs. From Jan. 4–Mar. 18, the campground offers ice fishing, with heated ice fishing shanties and a snow plow to keep the area open. The best RV site is 25 because it offers 50 amp hookup. The best tent site is 44 because it is set back in the woods and offers more privacy. Security measures include a five mph speed limit, one entrance/exit road, an owner who lives on site, and occasional campground patrols.

Basics

Operated by: Dean & Annie Robinson. **Open:** May 1–Oct. 31. **Site Assignment:** Reservations w/ 1-night deposit; refund w/ 7-day notice. **Registration:** At campground office. **Fee:** $22 (cash, check, credit cards). **Parking:** At site.

Facilities

Number of RV Sites: 14. **Number of Tent-Only Sites:** 16. **Hookups:** Electric (20, 30, 50 amps), water. **Each Site:** Picnic table, fire ring. **Dump Station:** Yes. **Laundry:** No. **Pay Phone:** Yes. **Rest Rooms and Showers:** Yes. **Fuel:** Yes. **Propane:** Yes. **Internal Roads:** Gravel, in fair condition. **RV Service:** No. **Market:** 7 mi. west in Hillman. **Restaurant:** On site. **General Store:** Yes. **Vending:** Yes. **Swimming Pool:** No. **Playground:** Yes. **Other:** Fletcher Pond, marina, bar, rental cabins, lodge rooms, boat slips, boat launch, sports field, horseshoes, hiking trails, fish-cleaning hut. **Activities:** Fishing, swimming, boating (rental motorboats, pontoons available), hiking. **Nearby Attractions:** Golf, charter boat fishing, Lake Huron, elk viewing, Pigeon River Country State Forest, lighthouses, antiques, shipwreck sanctuary, museums, historic homes. **Additional Information:** Hillman Area Chamber of Commerce, (517) 742-3739.

Restrictions

Pets: Leash only. **Fires:** Fire ring only. **Alcoholic Beverages:** Permitted. **Vehicle Maximum Length:** None.

To Get There

From the junction of Hwy. 451 and Hwy. 32, drive 2 mi. east on Hwy. 32, then 5 mi. south on Jack's Landing Rd. The highway is wide and well maintained w/ broad shoulders but Jack's Landing Rd. is bumpy gravel.

HILLMAN

Lyons' Landing & Campground

24553 Landing Rd., Hillman 49746. T: (517) 742-4756

RV ★★ Tent ★★★★

Beauty: ★★★★	Site Privacy: ★★★
Spaciousness: ★★★	Quiet: ★★★
Security: ★★★	Cleanliness: ★★★
Insect Control: None	Facilities: ★★

Fishing reigns at Lyons' Landing, eight miles northeast of Hillman. No wonder, the campground is located on a 8,970-acre reservoir. A dam built in 1930 to generate electric power went through an area where the Upper South Branch of the Thunder Bay River ran through a large swamp. The result was an ideal fish habitat among flooded timber stumps and a dark bottom. Fletcher's is famous for its northern pike and largemouth bass. Because it is shallow, about seven to ten feet deep with some deeper creekbeds, the water warms up quickly to give an early start to bass fishing. Campground sites are grassy, open, and shaded with 30 pull-throughs and a typical site width of 35 feet. No swimming is allowed, nor are jet skis or water skis. Security includes one entrance, owners who live on site, and "no hesitation at calling law enforcement, if needed," according to campground rules.

Basics

Operated by: Craig & Cathy Lyons. **Open:** All year. **Site Assignment:** Reservations w/ 1-night deposit; refund w/ 7-day notice. **Registration:** At campground office. **Fee:** $12 (cash, check, credit cards). **Parking:** At site.

Facilities

Number of RV Sites: 75. **Number of Tent-Only Sites:** 10. **Hookups:** Electric (20, 30 amps). **Each Site:** Picnic table, fire ring. **Dump Station:** Yes. **Laundry:** No. **Pay Phone:** Yes. **Rest Rooms and Showers:** Yes. **Fuel:** No. **Propane:** No. **Internal Roads:** Gravel, in fair condition. **RV Service:** No. **Market:** 8 mi. northeast in Hillman. **Restaurant:** 8 mi. northeast in Hillman. **General Store:** Yes. **Vending:** No. **Swimming Pool:** No. **Playground:** Yes. **Other:** Fletcher's Floodwaters, pavilion, boat ramp, boat dock, shuffleboard, sports field, horseshoes, volleyball, fish-cleaning hut, heated ice shanties in winter. **Activities:** Fishing, boating (rental boats available). **Nearby Attractions:** Golf, charter boat fishing, Lake Huron, elk viewing, Pigeon River Country State Forest, lighthouses, antiques, shipwreck sanctuary, museums, historic homes. **Additional Information:** Hillman Area Chamber of Commerce, (517) 742-3739.

Restrictions

Pets: Leash only. **Fires:** Fire ring only. **Alcoholic Beverages:** Permitted. **Vehicle Maximum Length:** None.

To Get There

From Hillman, drive 4 mi. southwest on Hwy. 32, then 3 mi. south on Farrier Rd., then 1 mi. east on Landing Rd. Highway is wide and well maintained w/ broad shoulders. Landing Rd. is bumpy gravel.

HOLLAND
Oak Grove Resort Campgrounds

2011 Ottawa Beach Rd., Holland 49424. T: (616) 399-9230; www.michcampgrounds.com/oakgrove.

RV ★★★★ Tent n/a

Beauty: ★★★★ Site Privacy: ★★★★
Spaciousness: ★★★★ Quiet: ★★★★
Security: ★★★★ Cleanliness: ★★★★★
Insect Control: ★★★★ Facilities: ★★★★

Oak Grove Resort Campground fills the wish list many campers have of the ideal spot to visit. Located within walking distance of Lake Macatawa and Lake Michigan beaches, the Holland campground is in the midst of a wealth of vacation recreation. Oak Grove itself is sparkling-clean, well arranged, friendly, secure, and a pleasure to visit. Beautiful landscaping touches such as flowers, shrubs, and mowed sites show close attention to detail. A large 24 × 50 heated pool and hot tub are a nice treat for those not ready to jump into the cold waters of Lake Michigan. The campground is also one mile before Holland State Park and offers access to miles of paved bike trails. Sites are level, wooded, and mostly shaded, with a typical site width of 35 feet. All sites have full hookups, and there are 80 seasonal campers. Mid-May brings the annual Tulip Festival, a glorious event which means reservations are strongly recommended for the campground. Be aware that no tents are allowed. Also note that the office building is closed on Sunday and that the security gate closes each night at 10 p.m.

Basics

Operated by: Ron & Betty, Rod & Maria VandenBerg. **Open:** May 1–Oct. 1. **Site Assignment:** Reservations w/ 1-night deposit; refund (minus $10) w/ 2-week notice. **Registration:** At campground office. **Fee:** $36 (cash, check, credit cards). **Parking:** At site.

Facilities

Number of RV Sites: 135. **Number of Tent-Only Sites:** 0. **Hookups:** Electric (30, 50 amps), water, sewer, cable TV. **Each Site:** Picnic table, fire ring. **Dump Station:** Yes. **Laundry:** Yes. **Pay Phone:** Yes. **Rest Rooms and Showers:** Yes. **Fuel:** No. **Propane:** No. **Internal Roads:** Paved, in good condition. **RV Service:** No. **Market:** Two blocks. **Restaurant:** Two blocks. **General Store:** Yes. **Vending:** Yes. **Swimming Pool:** Yes. **Playground:** Yes. **Other:** Rec hall, hiking trails, rental cabins, whirlpool, horseshoes, basketball. **Activities:** Swimming, hiking. **Nearby Attractions:** Lake Macatawa, Lake Michigan, bike trails, Cappon House Museum, De Klomp Wooden Shoe & Delftware Factory, Dutch Village, Holland Museum, tulip gardens, Windmill Island, antiques, arts & crafts. **Additional Information:** Holland Area CVB, (800) 506-1299.

Restrictions

Pets: Leash only. **Fires:** Fire ring only. **Alcoholic Beverages:** Not permitted. **Vehicle Maximum Length:** None. **Other:** No tents allowed.

To Get There

From the junction of US 31 and Lakewood Blvd., drive 1.5 mi. west on Lakewood Blvd., then 1.5 mi. west on Douglas, then 3 mi. west on Ottawa Beach Rd. Roads are mostly wide and well maintained w/ adequate shoulders.

HOLLY
Yogi Bear's Jellystone Park Camp-Resort

7072 East Grange Hall Rd., Holly 48442. T: (248) 634-8621; F: (248) 634-3177; www.michcampgrounds.com/jellystone-holly; lsyogi@megsinet.net.

RV ★★★★ Tent ★★★

Beauty: ★★★ Site Privacy: ★★★★
Spaciousness: ★★★★ Quiet: ★★★★
Security: ★★★★ Cleanliness: ★★★★
Insect Control: None Facilities: ★★★★

Easy access off I-75 is a major draw for this campground, as is a long list of activities provided for campers. An activities director keeps fun times rolling with a creative list of activities for all ages. One unusual activity invites visitors to "fine tune" their campers by comparing notes on how to repair or fix up a camper and where to visit, when to camp, and what to see. Located three miles east of Holly, Yogi Bear's Jellystone Park of Holly offers shaded grassy sites with gravel parking spots. Laid out in a series of loops, the campground has 30 seasonal campers, 40 pull-through sites, and a typical site width of 30 feet. The campground is open all year but has limited winter facilities and would appeal to only the hardiest campers. One time it might be fun to brave the cold would be for the annual Dickens Olde Fashioned Christmas Festival in Holly during weekends in late Nov. and throughout Dec. But be prepared for frigid weather and possible snow. The speed limit is 7.5 mph and quiet times are 11 p.m. to 8 a.m.

Basics

Operated by: Leon & Sandy Sterling. **Open:** All year. **Site Assignment:** Reservations w/ 1-night deposit; refund (minus $5) w/ 7-day notice. **Registration:** At campground office. **Fee:** $33 (cash, check, credit cards). **Parking:** At site.

Facilities

Number of RV Sites: 146. **Number of Tent-Only Sites:** 40. **Hookups:** Electric (20, 30 amps), water. **Each Site:** Picnic table, fire ring. **Dump Station:** Yes. **Laundry:** Yes. **Pay Phone:** Yes. **Rest Rooms and Showers:** Yes. **Fuel:** No. **Propane:** Yes. **Internal Roads:** Paved/gravel, in good condition. **RV Service:** No. **Market:** 3 mi. west in Holly. **Restaurant:** 3 mi. west in Holly. **General Store:** Yes. **Vending:** Yes. **Swimming Pool:** Yes. **Playground:** Yes. **Other:** Arcade, mini-golf, rental cabins, kiddie train, bumper boats, T-Rex, bounce house, power wheels, basketball, rental bikes, horseshoes, movies, activities director, adults room. **Activities:** Swimming, scheduled activities. **Nearby Attractions:** Children's Museum, Huckleberry Railroad, paddlewheeler, museums, Longway Planetarium, Flint River, antiques, golf, arts & crafts. **Additional Information:** Holly Chamber, (248) 634-1900.

Restrictions

Pets: Leash only. **Fires:** Fire ring only. **Alcoholic Beverages:** Permitted. **Vehicle Maximum Length:** None. **Other:** No check-ins after 9 p.m.

To Get There

From junction of I-75 and Grange Hall Rd., take Exit 101 and drive 100 yards east on Grange Hall Rd. Roads are wide and well maintained with broad shoulders.

HOPKINS
East Lake Camping

3091 Weick Dr., Hopkins 49328. T: (616) 793-7177

RV ★★★ Tent ★★★

Beauty: ★★★★ Site Privacy: ★★★
Spaciousness: ★★★ Quiet: ★★★★
Security: ★★★★ Cleanliness: ★★★★
Insect Control: ★★★ Facilities: ★★★

Located midway between Grand Rapids, Holland, and Kalamazoo, East Lake Camping offers family camping in the hills around East Lake. The quiet country setting outside Hopkins features camping sites from rustic to full hookups. The campground has open and shaded sites on a hilly terrain. The best sites are closest to the large lake. East Lake Camping has 59 seasonal campers, a typical site width of 30 feet, and seven pull-through sites. Chapel services are offered on Sunday. The lake has a nice sandy beach for swimmers and is a good place to fish and boat. Owners enforce basic regulations to keep the campground safe, quiet, and family-oriented, while still maintaining a friendly atmosphere.

Basics

Operated by: Greg & Catherine Miller. **Open:** May 1–Oct. 1. **Site Assignment:** Reservations w/ 1-night deposit; refund (minus $5) w/ 7-day notice. **Registration:** At campground office. **Fee:** $23 (cash, check, credit cards). **Parking:** At site.

Facilities

Number of RV Sites: 109. **Number of Tent-Only Sites:** 1. **Hookups:** Electric (20, 30, 50 amps), water, sewer. **Each Site:** Picnic table, fire ring. **Dump Station:** Yes. **Laundry:** Yes. **Pay Phone:** Yes. **Rest Rooms and Showers:** Yes. **Fuel:** No. **Propane:** No. **Internal Roads:** Gravel, in good condition. **RV Service:** No. **Market:** 1 mi. **Restaurant:** 1 mi. **General Store:** Yes. **Vending:** Yes. **Swimming Pool:** No. **Playground:** Yes. **Other:** East Lake, sandy beach, pavilion, coin games, rec room, basketball, shuffleboard, sports field, horseshoes, boat ramp, boat dock, volleyball, hiking trail, rental RVs, rental cabin. **Activities:** Swimming, hiking, fishing, boating (rental rowboats, kayaks, paddleboats available), scheduled weekend activities. **Nearby Attractions:** Gerald B. Ford Museum, Fredrick Meijer Gardens, zoo, Michigan Adventure Amusement Park, Roger B. Chaffee Planetarium, golf, tennis, rivers & lakes, antiques, Wooden Shoe Factory. **Additional Information:** Grand Rapids/ Kent County CVB, (800) 678-9859.

Restrictions

Pets: Leash only. **Fires:** Fire ring only. **Alcoholic Beverages:** Permitted. **Vehicle Maximum Length:** 35 ft.

To Get There

From US 131, take Wayland Exit 64 and drive 3 mi. west on 135th Ave., then 2.5 mi. south on 18th St., then 2.5 mi. west on 130th Ave. to Weick Dr. Roads are mostly wide and well maintained w/ narrow shoulders in spots.

HOUGHTON LAKE
Houghton Lake Travel Park

370 Cloverleaf Ln., Houghton Lake 48629. T: (989) 422-3931; www.houghtonlaketravelpark.com.

RV ★★★ Tent ★★★

Beauty: ★★★ Site Privacy: ★★★
Spaciousness: ★★★ Quiet: ★★★★
Security: ★★★★ Cleanliness: ★★★★
Insect Control: None Facilities: ★★★

Houghton Lake Travel Park offers easy access to Michigan's largest inland lake. Houghton Lake is ten miles long and six miles wide with a 31-mile shoreline. The campground offers open, level sites. All sites are pull-throughs and there are 21 seasonal campers. Tent sites are in a rustic section with more green space and privacy. A tradition of the travel park, located 12 miles south of Frederic, is the train ride. Sports enthusiasts and vacationers have replaced the loggers and commercial anglers who once were the vital elements of Houghton Lake. The village is the core of a year-round resort area that borders the lake. Summer brings boaters and water skiers. Winter attracts snow skiers. Fishing knows no season. The rural campground closes in Oct., so it is not available for the winter season of ice fishing and snowmobiling.

Basics

Operated by: Ron & Jo Seim. **Open:** Apr. 1–Oct. 15. **Site Assignment:** Reservations w/ 1-night deposit; refund w/ 7-day notice. **Registration:** At campground office. **Fee:** $23 (cash, check, credit cards). **Parking:** At site.

Facilities

Number of RV Sites: 60. **Number of Tent-Only Sites:** 20. **Hookups:** Electric (20, 30 amps), water, sewer. **Each Site:** Picnic table, fire ring. **Dump Station:** Yes. **Laundry:** Yes. **Pay Phone:** Yes. **Rest Rooms and Showers:** Yes. **Fuel:** No. **Propane:** Yes. **Internal Roads:** Gravel, in good condition. **RV Service:** No. **Market:** 12 mi. north in Frederic. **Restaurant:** 12 mi. north in Frederic. **General Store:** Yes. **Vending:** Yes. **Swimming Pool:** Yes. **Playground:** Yes. **Other:** Rec room, rental cabins, sports field, horseshoes, volleyball. **Activities:** Swimming. **Nearby Attractions:** Houghton Lake, fishing, golf, amusement parks, mini-golf, Merritt Speedway, Firemans Memorial, antiques, arts & crafts. **Additional Information:** Houghton Lake Chamber of Commerce, (800) 248-5253.

Restrictions

Pets: Leash only. **Fires:** Fire ring only. **Alcoholic Beverages:** Permitted. **Vehicle Maximum Length:** None.

To Get There

From the junction of US 27 and Hwy. 55, drive 220 yards east on Hwy. 55, then south on Cloverleaf Ln. Roads are wide and well maintained w/ broad shoulders.

HOUGHTON LAKE
Sandyoak RV Park

2757 Owens Rd., Houghton Lake 48629. T: (800) 323-0220

RV ★★★★ Tent n/a

Beauty: ★★★ Site Privacy: ★★★
Spaciousness: ★★★★ Quiet: ★★★★
Security: ★★★★ Cleanliness: ★★★★
Insect Control: None Facilities: ★★★★

Located in the town of Houghton Lake, Sandyoak RV Park is a resort with camping lots for sale or rent. No tents are allowed. The campground has 183 seasonal campers and no pull-through sites. Laid out in a series of loops, the park has an indoor heated pool, two heated bathhouses, and two laundries. Sites are mostly grassy and shaded with a typical site width of 40 feet. A large clubhouse with kitchen facilities is available for gatherings. Speed limit is ten mph, a bit high especially in the playground areas. Most permanent sites are well maintained and decorated. To keep the park attractive, the association has a rule that the sales and rental agent has the right to refuse the registration of any trailer that would be "detrimental to the general appearance" of the park. They also have the right to instruct that such trailers must be removed from the park by the owner.

Basics

Operated by: Sandyoak Village Assoc. **Open:** All year. **Site Assignment:** Reservations w/ 1-night deposit; refund w/ 2-week notice. **Registration:** At campground office. **Fee:** $22 (cash, check). **Parking:** At site.

Facilities

Number of RV Sites: 227. **Number of Tent-Only Sites:** 0. **Hookups:** Electric (30 amps), water, sewer, cable TV. **Each Site:** Picnic table, fire ring. **Dump Station:** No. **Laundry:** Yes. **Pay Phone:** Yes. **Rest Rooms and Showers:** Yes. **Fuel:** No. **Propane:** No. **Internal Roads:** Paved, in good condition. **RV Service:** No. **Market:** 1 block. **Restaurant:** 1 block. **General Store:** No. **Vending:** No. **Swimming Pool:** Yes. **Playground:** Yes. **Other:** Clubhouse, horseshoes, shuffleboard, basketball, sales office, spa, rec hall, game room, recreation field, hiking trails. **Activities:** Swimming, hiking, scheduled activities. **Nearby Attractions:** Houghton Lake, fishing, golf, amusement parks, mini-golf, Merritt Speedway, Firemans Memorial, antiques, arts & crafts. **Additional Information:** Houghton Lake Chamber of Commerce, (800) 248-5253.

Restrictions

Pets: Leash only; max. of 2 per site. **Fires:** Fire rings only; must be extinguished w/ water before retiring for night. **Alcoholic Beverages:** At sites only. **Vehicle Maximum Length:** None. **Other:** Children under 12 not permitted in hot tub.

To Get There

From the junction of US 27 and Hwy. 55, drive 6 mi. east on Hwy. 55 (West Houghton Lake Dr.), then 1 block south on Owens Dr. Roads are wide and well maintained w/ broad shoulders.

HOUGHTON LAKE
Wooded Acres Family Campground

997 Federal Ave., Houghton Lake 48629. T: (989) 422-3413; www.woodedacrescampground.net; ddietzel@freeway.net.

RV ★★★★ Tent ★★★

Beauty: ★★★ Site Privacy: ★★★
Spaciousness: ★★★ Quiet: ★★★
Security: ★★★★ Cleanliness: ★★★★
Insect Control: None Facilities: ★★★★

Located in a large resort area in Houghton Lake, Wooded Acres Family Campground offers open and secluded sites in a wooded area. Laid out in a series of loops, the campground has 30 seasonal campers, 30 pull-through sites and a typical site width of 30 feet. The best RV sites are 77–88 because they offer full hookups. The best tent site is 14 because it is well shaded, large, and offers more privacy. Security measures include one entrance/ exit, owners who live on site, and campground patrols. As the name indicates, Wooded Acres has a wealth of trees and enforces rules to keep them. Cutting any standing timber or vegetation is prohibited. If a tree branch is in the way of a camper, staff employees should be notified to deal with the problem. Violation of the regulation results in a $100 fine. For safety and quietness, snowmobiles, motorcycles, scooters, mopeds, and three- and four-wheelers are not allowed to be ridden in the park. Golf carts also are prohibited, except for use by elderly people or those with disabilities. The campground is well maintained and features an antique John Deere Tractor theme.

Basics

Operated by: Dave & Tina Dietzel. **Open:** All year. **Site Assignment:** Reservations w/ 1-night deposit; refund (minus $5) w/ 7-day notice. **Registration:** At campground office. **Registration:** At campground office. **Fee:** $28 (cash, check, credit cards). **Parking:** At site.

Facilities

Number of RV Sites: 72. **Number of Tent-Only Sites:** 30. **Hookups:** Electric (30, 50 amps), water, sewer. **Each Site:** Picnic table, fire ring. **Dump Station:** Yes. **Laundry:** Yes. **Pay Phone:** No. **Rest Rooms and Showers:** Yes. **Fuel:** No. **Propane:** Yes. **Internal Roads:** Gravel, in good condition. **RV Service:** No. **Market:** 2 mi. north in Houghton Lake. **Restaurant:** 2 mi. north in Houghton Lake. **General Store:** Yes, limited. **Vending:** No. **Swimming Pool:** Yes. **Playground:** Yes. **Other:** Pavilion, rental cabin, gameroom, basketball, volleyball, shuffleboard, horseshoes, fishing pond, sports field. **Activities:** Swimming, fishing. **Nearby Attractions:** Houghton Lake, fishing, amusement parks, mini-golf, Merritt Speedway, golf, Firemans Memorial, antiques, arts & crafts. **Additional Information:** Houghton Lake Chamber of Commerce, (800) 248-5253.

Restrictions

Pets: Leash only. **Fires:** Fire ring only. **Alcoholic Beverages:** Permitted. **Vehicle Maximum Length:** 40 ft.

To Get There

From the junction of US 27 and Hwy. 55, drive 2 mi. east on Hwy. 55, then 1 mi. south on Loxley. Roads are wide and well maintained w/ broad shoulders.

INDIAN RIVER

Indian River RV Resort & Campground

561 North Straits Hwy., Indian River 49749. T: (888) 792-CAMP; www.michcampgrounds.com/indianriver; ircgrest@email.msn.com.

RV: ★★★★ Tent: ★★★★

Beauty: ★★★★	Site Privacy: ★★★★
Spaciousness: ★★★★	Quiet: ★★★★
Security: ★★★★	Cleanliness: ★★★★★
Insect Control: ★★★★★	Facilities: ★★★★

Just minutes from I-75, Indian River RV Resort & Campground offers convenience in the heart of the Inland Waterways and the gateway to Mackinaw City. Located in Indian River, the campground offers shaded level sites with a typical site width of 45 feet. Sites are mostly gravel with 75 pull-throughs. Tent sites are in an area offering more green space and privacy. A large pavilion is handy for groups and family gatherings. Facilities are so sparkling-clean that they must be attended to more often than the customary once a day. Owners provide security and enforce simple regulations to keep the campground safe, quiet, and comfortable, while still being friendly.

Basics

Operated by: Don & Nancy Schlickau. **Open:** Apr. 15–Nov. 1. **Site Assignment:** Reservations w/ 1-night deposit; refund w/ 2-week notice. **Registration:** At campground office. **Fee:** $25 (cash, check, credit cards). **Parking:** At site.

Facilities

Number of RV Sites: 120. **Number of Tent-Only Sites:** 17. **Hookups:** Electric (20, 30 amps), water, sewer, cable TV. **Each Site:** Picnic table, fire ring. **Dump Station:** Yes. **Laundry:** Yes. **Pay Phone:** Yes. **Rest Rooms and Showers:** Yes. **Fuel:** No. **Propane:** Yes. **Internal Roads:** Gravel, in good condition. **RV Service:** No. **Market:** Less than 1 mi. **Restaurant:** Less than 1 mi. **General Store:** Yes. **Vending:** Yes. **Swimming Pool:** Yes. **Playground:** Yes. **Other:** Pavilion, rental cabins, coin games, rec hall, horseshoes, basketball, volleyball, badminton, sports field, hiking trials. **Activities:** Swimming, hiking, scheduled weekend activities. **Nearby Attractions:** Mackinac Island, golf, casino, Cross in the Woods, Lake Michigan, beaches, dunes, ferry, Old Mill Creek State Historic Park, Fort Michilimackinac, antiques, scenic drives, arts & crafts, Mackinac Bridge, Mackinac Bridge Museum. **Additional Information:** Greater Mackinaw City Area Chamber of Commerce, (800) 814-0160.

Restrictions

Pets: Leash only. **Fires:** Fire ring only. **Alcoholic Beverages:** Permitted. **Vehicle Maximum Length:** 45 ft.

To Get There

From the junction of I-75 North and Hwy. 27, take Exit 313 and drive 1.5 mi. north on Hwy. 27. Roads are wide and well maintained w/ broad shoulders.

INDIAN RIVER

Yogi Bear's Jellystone Park Camp-Resort

2201 E M-68, Indian River 49749. T: (231) 238-8259; www.gocampingamerica.com/yogiindianriver; jellystoneindianriver@gocampingamerica.com.

RV: ★★★★ Tent: ★★★★

Beauty: ★★★★	Site Privacy: ★★★★
Spaciousness: ★★★★	Quiet: ★★★★
Security: ★★★★★	Cleanliness: ★★★★
Insect Control: ★★★★	Facilities: ★★★★

Campers usually know what they will find when they pull into a Yogi Bear's Jellystone Park. Facilities and security are top-notch. Activities are abundant and well organized. Rest rooms and showers are sparkling-clean, and the grounds are well maintained. But the Indian River Yogi Bear's has an extra surprise. The heated swimming pool is in the shape of Michigan with a road map on the bottom. That nice touch shows the attention to detail this campground goes to make a visit special. The campground offers level, wooded sites with a typical site width of 30 feet. There are 36 pull-through sites. Tent sites are in a rustic area with more green space and privacy. The campgrounds is in the heart of Northern Michigan with all its attractions and reservations are strongly recommended. Rangers are on hand for security and to answer questions or lend a helping hand to campers.

Basics

Operated by: Clark & Barbara Tallman & Fred Jana. **Open:** May 15–Sept. 15. **Site Assignment:** Reservations w/ 1-night deposit; refund (minus $5) w/ 7-day notice. **Registration:** At campground office. **Fee:** $35 (cash, check, credit cards). **Parking:** At site.

Facilities

Number of RV Sites: 156. **Number of Tent-Only Sites:** 24. **Hookups:** Electric (20, 30, 50 amps), water, sewer. **Each Site:** Picnic table, fire ring. **Dump Station:** Yes. **Laundry:** Yes. **Pay Phone:** Yes. **Rest Rooms and Showers:** Yes. **Fuel:** No. **Propane:** Yes. **Internal Roads:** Paved/gravel, in good condition. **RV Service:** No. **Market:** 3 mi. west in Indian River. **Restaurant:** 3 mi. west in Indian River. **General Store:** Yes. **Vending:** Yes. **Swimming Pool:** Yes. **Playground:** Yes. **Other:** Mini-golf, nature trails, pavilion, outdoor theater, tetherball, horseshoes, bocce ball, volleyball, shuffleboard, game room, rental cabins, basketball, activities director, snack bar, coin games, sports field. **Activities:** Swimming, hiking, scheduled activities. **Nearby Attractions:** Mackinac Island, golf, casino, Cross in the Woods, Lake Michigan, beaches, dunes, ferry, Old Mill Creek State Historic Park, Fort Michilimackinac, antiques, scenic drives, arts & crafts, Mackinac Bridge, Mackinac Bridge Museum. **Additional Information:** Greater Mackinaw City Area Chamber of Commerce, (800) 814-0160.

Restrictions

Pets: Leash only. **Fires:** Fire ring only. **Alcoholic Beverages:** Permitted. **Vehicle Maximum Length:** 40 ft.

To Get There

From I-75, take Indian River Exit 310, drive 4 mi. east on Hwy. 68. Roads are wide and well maintained w/ broad shoulders.

INTERLOCHEN

Interlochen State Park

M 137, Interlochen 49643. T: (231) 276-9511; www.michigandnr.com.

RV: ★★★ Tent: ★★★★

Beauty: ★★★★	Site Privacy: ★★★
Spaciousness: ★★★	Quiet: ★★★★
Security: ★★★★	Cleanliness: ★★★
Insect Control: ★★★	Facilities: ★★

Established in 1919, Interlochen State Park was the first campground in Michigan's state park system. The campground, 14 miles southwest of Traverse

City, is nestled among one of the state's few remaining stands of virgin pine. Located between two lakes, the park offers a rustic campground with 72 sites along Green Lake and a modern campground with 428 sites at Duck Lake. In addition to enjoying a natural setting, watersports, and recreation, campers can attend summer concerts given by premier entertainers next door at Interlochen National Music Camp. Walking trails lead from the campground to the cultural center. Modern campsites with electricity at Duck Lake have rest rooms with flush toilets. The Duck Lake campground offers two loops of campsites on each side of the day-use area with its park store, volleyball, video arcade, beach, and swimming area. But boat launch ramps are provided on both lakes. As usual, the rest rooms could be better maintained. The tree-lined shores of Green Lake offers rustic camping. Duck Lake sites are mostly gravel, with a typical site width of 30 feet and five pull-through sites. Security is great with a 24-hour attendant and regular campground patrols.

Basics

Operated by: State of Michigan. **Open:** Apr. 15–Nov. 1. **Site Assignment:** Reservations w/ 1-night deposit; refund (minus $5) w/ 1-week notice. Call (800) 44-PARKS. **Registration:** At campground office. **Fee:** $17, plus $4 a day or $20 a season for state park sticker fee. **Parking:** At site.

Facilities

Number of RV Sites: 428. **Number of Tent-Only Sites:** 72. **Hookups:** Electric (30 amps). **Each Site:** Picnic table, fire ring. **Dump Station:** Yes. **Laundry:** No. **Pay Phone:** Yes. **Rest Rooms and Showers:** Yes. **Fuel:** No. **Propane:** No. **Internal Roads:** Paved/gravel, in good condition. **RV Service:** No. **Market:** 4 mi. **Restaurant:** 4 mi. **General Store:** Yes. **Vending:** Yes. **Swimming Pool:** No. **Playground:** Yes. **Other:** Duck Lake, Green Lake, coin games, swimming beach, boat ramp, horseshoes, game room, sports field, display of 1890s logging era. **Activities:** Swimming, fishing, boating (rental rowboats available). **Nearby Attractions:** Canoe livery, Grand Traverse Bay, Sleeping Bear Sand Dunes, casino, golf, outlet mall, cherry orchards, winter sports, Old Mission, museums, wineries. **Additional Information:** Interlochen Chamber of Commerce, (231) 276-7141.

Restrictions

Pets: Leash only. **Fires:** Fire ring only. **Alcoholic Beverages:** Permitted. **Vehicle Maximum Length:** 30 ft. **Other:** 15-day stay limit.

To Get There

From the junction of US 31 and M-137, drive 2 mi. south on M-137. Roads are wide and well maintained w/ adequate shoulders.

ITHACA

Just-In-Time Campgrounds

8421 Earl Pierce Rd., Ithaca 48847. T: (989) 875-2865; F: (989) 875-4464; www.justintimecampgrounds.com; cal@justintimecampgrounds.com.

 ★★★ ▲ ★★★

Beauty: ★★★ Site Privacy: ★★★
Spaciousness: ★★★ Quiet: ★★★
Security: ★★★ Cleanliness: ★★★
Insect Control: None Facilities: ★★★

Just-In-Time Campgrounds is a beautiful little nook about seven miles east of Ithaca. An abundance of trees and a spring-fed lake add to the rural setting. But a sandpit across from the lake stands out like a sore thumb. The campground offers a choice of shaded or open sites, some backing up into the woods or situated right on the lake. Nicely maintained grass adds to the beauty. The campground has 29 seasonal campers and no pull-through sites. No license is needed for fishing in Lake Earl. No outboard motors are permitted on the lake, and the campground has only a few boats to rent, so it is best to bring your own, including required life preservers. Be aware that the water outside the roped-in swimming area is very deep and dangerous. No swimming or wading is permitted outside the roped-in area. No lifeguard is on duty, and swimmers are urged to never swim alone. Children must always be accompanied by an adult when swimming. No pets are allowed at the campground.

Basics

Operated by: Cal & Roxie Claxton. **Open:** May 1–Oct. 15. **Site Assignment:** Reservations w/ 1-night deposit; refunds w/ 7-day notice. **Registration:** At campground office. **Fee:** $25 (cash, check, credit cards). **Parking:** At site.

Facilities

Number of RV Sites: 50. **Number of Tent-Only Sites:** 0. **Hookups:** Electric (30 amps), water, sewer. **Each Site:** Picnic table, fire ring. **Dump Station:** Yes. **Laundry:** No. **Pay Phone:** Yes. **Rest Rooms and Showers:** Yes. **Fuel:** No. **Propane:** Yes. **Internal Roads:** Gravel, in good condition. **RV Service:** No. **Market:** 7 mi. west in Ithaca. **Restaurant:** 7 mi. west in Ithaca. **General Store:** Yes, limited. **Vending:** Yes. **Swimming Pool:** No. **Playground:** Yes. **Other:** Lake Earl, swimming beach, rental cabins. **Activities:** Swimming, fishing, boating (electric motors only, rental rowboats available). **Nearby Attractions:** Golf, hiking, horseback riding, charter boats, historic downtown, antiques, arts & crafts, museums. **Additional Information:** Travel Michigan, (888) 784-7328.

Restrictions

Pets: Not permitted. **Fires:** Fire ring only. **Alcoholic Beverages:** Permitted. **Vehicle Maximum Length:** 40 ft.

To Get There

From the junction of US 27 and Washington Rd., drive 7 mi. east on Washington Rd., then 2 mi. south on Ransom, then 0.5 mi. east on Pierce Rd. Roads are wide and well maintained w/ broad shoulders, except for Pierce Rd. which is a rough gravel surface.

LAKE LEELANAU

Lake Leelanau RV Park

3101 Lake Shore Dr., Lake Leelanau 49653. T: (231) 256-7236; F: (231) 256-7238; www.lakeleelanaurvpark.com; donrrman@aol.com.

 ★★★★ ▲ ★★★

Beauty: ★★★★ Site Privacy: ★★★★
Spaciousness: ★★★★ Quiet: ★★★★
Security: ★★★★ Cleanliness: ★★★★
Insect Control: ★★★★ Facilities: ★★★★

Check out all the boats and fishing gear at Lake Leelanau RV Park and you'll know one of the main draws for this campground. Located on 700 feet of frontage on the shores of Lake Leelanau, the campground offers easy access to 21 miles of clear waters for boating, fishing, and other water activities. The campground also has a boat launch, gas pump, and 98 boat docks available for rent. A safe sandy beach with large shallow swimming area attracts big and little swimmers. Sites are mostly grassy and scattered among trees. Lakefront sites are mostly open and grassy with a concrete pad and patio. Laid out in a series of loops, the campground has a typical site width of 30 feet, 116 seasonal campers, and 15 pull-through sites. Paved roads make it easy to maneuver RVs and boat trailers in the campground. An extra is the free pipe organ concerts every Sunday evening, played on the 3,576-pipe, 62-rank pipe organ right in the office.

Basics

Operated by: Donald & Marilyn Wilson. **Open:** May 1–Oct. 15. **Site Assignment:** Reservations w/ 1-night deposit; refund (minus $5) w/ 7-day notice. **Registration:** At campground office. **Fee:** $35 (cash, check, credit cards). **Parking:** At site.

Facilities

Number of RV Sites: 196. **Number of Tent-Only Sites:** 0. **Hookups:** Electric (20, 30, 50 amps), water, sewer, cable TV. **Each Site:** Picnic table, fire ring. **Dump Station:** Yes. **Laundry:** Yes. **Pay Phone:** Yes. **Rest Rooms and Showers:** Yes. **Fuel:** Yes. **Propane:** Yes. **Internal Roads:** Paved, in good condition. **RV Service:** No. **Market:** 3 mi. **Restaurant:** 3 mi. **General Store:** Yes. **Vending:** Yes. **Swimming Pool:** No. **Playground:** Yes. **Other:** Lake Leelanau, sandy beach, badminton, sports field, horseshoes, volleyball, boat dock, boat ramp, marina. **Activities:** Swimming, fishing, boating (rental motorboats, pontoons, canoes, paddleboats, seadoos available), scheduled activities. **Nearby Attractions:** Historic Fishtown, orchards, wineries, Manitou Island, excursion boats, Sleeping Bear Dunes, beaches, golf, casino, Interlochen Music Camp. **Additional Information:** Leelanau Peninsula Chamber of Commerce, (231) 256-9895.

Restrictions

Pets: Leash only. **Fires:** Fire ring only. **Alcoholic Beverages:** Permitted. **Vehicle Maximum Length:** None.

To Get There

From the junction of Hwy. 204 and CR 643, drive 3.5 mi. south on CR 643. Roads are mostly wide and well maintained w/ adequate shoulders.

LUDINGTON

Crystal Lake Best Holiday Trav-L-Park

1884 West Hansen Rd., Scottville 49454. T: (231) 757-4510

 ★★★★ ▲ ★★★

Beauty: ★★★ Site Privacy: ★★★★
Spaciousness: ★★★★ Quiet: ★★★★
Security: ★★★★ Cleanliness: ★★★★
Insect Control: ★★★★ Facilities: ★★★★

A rural lakeside campground near Ludington, Crystal Lake Best Holiday Trav-L-Park offers secluded sites with a choice of shade or open. The typical site width is 30 feet. There are 30 seasonal campers and no pull-through sites. A nice plus is that children camp free. The wooded campground also has a very clean, tiled bathroom which must see more than the usual once-a-day cleaning. The lake has a nice sandy walk-out beach, that is also kept very clean. The best sites, of course, are as close to the lake as possible. Security measures include owners who keep a close watch on the campground to make sure it stays a clean, quiet, family-oriented facility. Their efforts seem to be working.

Basics

Operated by: The Purcells. **Open:** Apr. 1–Nov. 1. **Site Assignment:** Reservations w/ 1-night deposit; refund (minus $5) w/ 7-day notice. **Registration:** At campground office. **Fee:** $26 (cash, check, credit cards). **Parking:** At site.

Facilities

Number of RV Sites: 160. **Number of Tent-Only Sites:** 0. **Hookups:** Electric (20, 30 amps), water, sewer. **Each Site:** Picnic table, fire ring. **Dump Station:** Yes. **Laundry:** Yes. **Pay Phone:** Yes. **Rest Rooms and Showers:** Yes. **Fuel:** No. **Propane:** Yes. **Internal Roads:** Paved/gravel, in good condition. **RV Service:** No. **Market:** 3 mi. west. **Restaurant:** 3 mi. west. **General Store:** Yes. **Vending:** Yes. **Swimming Pool:** No. **Playground:** Yes. **Other:** Crystal Lake, sandy beach, rec hall, coin games, boat dock, fishing lake, mini-golf, basketball, badminton, sports field, horseshoes, hiking trails, volleyball, snack bar, ice cream parlor. **Activities:** Swimming, hiking, fishing, boating (rental rowboats, canoes, kayaks, paddleboats), scheduled weekend activities. **Nearby Attractions:** Lake Michigan, Pere Marquette River, harbor, SS *Badger* cruises, beaches, dunes, antiques, scenic drives, arts & crafts, White Pine Village, golf, tennis, charter fishing, lighthouse, seaplane rides. **Additional Information:** Ludington Area CVB, (800) 542-4600.

Restrictions

Pets: Leash only. **Fires:** Fire ring only. **Alcoholic Beverages:** Permitted. **Vehicle Maximum Length:** Inquire ahead.

To Get There

From west junction of US 10 and US 31, drive 3 mi. east on US 10/31, then 1.5 mi. north on Stiles Rd. and 0.5 mi. east on Hansen Rd. Roads are generally wide and well maintained w/ narrow shoulders in spots.

LUDINGTON
Poncho's Pond

5335 West Wallace Rd., Ludington 49431. T: (888) 308-6602; F: (231) 845-5538; www.poncho.com.

 ★★★★★  ★★★★

Beauty: ★★★★ Site Privacy: ★★★★★
Spaciousness: ★★★★★ Quiet: ★★★★
Security: ★★★★★ Cleanliness: ★★★★★
Insect Control: ★★★★★ Facilities: ★★★★★

Poncho's Pond has a well-deserved reputation for a quality place to stay. Located in Ludington, only two miles from Lake Michigan beaches, Poncho's isn't content to rest on its laurels. The friendly owners keep a close watch on maintenance and are always looking for ways to improve the campground. Cleanliness is tops as are the lighted, paved roads. The campground boasts two pools—one for children and families, the other for adults, along with an adult spa. Laid out in a series of loops, the campground has a typical site width of 35 feet, 55 seasonal campers, and 68 pull-through sites. Located in the center of the park is a pleasant three-acre pond stocked with fish to keep young anglers happy. Sites are mostly open and level, with the most popular ones being by the pond. Each lot has cable TV at no extra charge. For security, owners live on site and make sure the campground is secure. Even though the owners of Poncho's Pond and nearby Vacation Station have the same last name, they are not related. Both have top-notch facilities.

Basics

Operated by: Robert Smith Jr. & Nancy Smith. **Open:** Apr. 1–Oct. 31. **Site Assignment:** Reservations w/ 1-night deposit; refund w/ 7-day notice. **Registration:** At campground office. **Fee:** $32 (cash, check, credit cards). **Parking:** At site.

Facilities

Number of RV Sites: 202. **Number of Tent-Only Sites:** 8. **Hookups:** Electric (30, 50 amps), water, sewer, cable TV, phone. **Each Site:** Picnic table, fire ring. **Dump Station:** Yes. **Laundry:** Yes. **Pay Phone:** Yes. **Rest Rooms and Showers:** Yes. **Fuel:** No. **Propane:** Yes. **Internal Roads:** Paved, in good condition. **RV Service:** No. **Market:** 2 blocks. **Restaurant:** 2 blocks. **General Store:** Yes. **Vending:** Yes. **Swimming Pool:** Yes. **Playground:** Yes. **Other:** Pond, rec hall, pavilion, coin games, spa, basketball, movies, badminton, sports field, horseshoes, volleyball, club house. **Activities:** Swimming, fishing, boating (rental paddleboats available), scheduled activities. **Nearby Attractions:** Lake Michigan, Pere Marquette River, harbor, SS *Badger* cruises, illuminated cross, beaches, dunes, antiques, scenic drives, arts & crafts, White Pine Village, golf, tennis, charter fishing, lighthouse, seaplane rides. **Additional Information:** Ludington Area CVB, (800) 542-4600.

Restrictions

Pets: Leash only. **Fires:** Fire ring only. **Alcoholic Beverages:** Permitted. **Vehicle Maximum Length:** None.

To Get There

From the junction of US 31 and US 10, drive 2 mi. west on US 10. Roads are wide and well maintained w/ broad shoulders.

LUDINGTON
Vacation Station RV Park

4895 West US 10, Ludington 49431. T: (877) 856-0390; F: (616) 843-8897; www.vacationstationrv-park.com; camp@vacationstationrvpark.com.

★★★★★ ★★★★

Beauty: ★★★★ Site Privacy: ★★★★★
Spaciousness: ★★★★★ Quiet: ★★★★★
Security: ★★★★★ Cleanliness: ★★★★★
Insect Control: ★★★★★ Facilities: ★★★★★

Ask a camping family to create their dream campground, and this might be it. That's what the Smith family did in 1997. Vacation Station RV Park in Ludington offers the tops in convenience, clean facilities, and activities. Plus, the owners are friendly and want campers to enjoy their stay. Located on one of the state's most beautiful shorelines, the campground has a quiet, natural setting with a "neighborhood" feel. Adjacent to a family fun park, the campground is within walking distance of restaurants and shopping. Vacation Station has lighted paved roads, a choice of open or shaded sites, and exceptionally clean rest rooms and showers. A nice touch is flowers in the rest rooms and attention to detail that means more than a daily cleaning. The rural campground has a typical site width of 40 feet, 50 seasonal campers in a secluded area away from overnight campers, and 16 pull-through sites. A clubhouse overlooks a private pond with a fountain. Security includes an on-site manager and regular patrols of the campground.

Basics

Operated by: The Smith Family. **Open:** Apr. 1–Oct. 31. **Site Assignment:** Reservations w/ credit card; refund (minus $5) w/ 7-day notice. **Registration:** At campground office. **Fee:** $33 (cash, check, credit cards). **Parking:** At site.

Facilities

Number of RV Sites: 150. **Number of Tent-Only Sites:** 0. **Hookups:** Electric (20, 30, 50 amps), water, sewer, phone, cable TV. **Each Site:** Picnic table, fire ring. **Dump Station:** Yes. **Laundry:** Yes. **Pay Phone:** Yes. **Rest Rooms and Showers:** Yes. **Fuel:** No. **Propane:** Yes. **Internal Roads:** Paved, in good condition. **RV Service:** No. **Market:** Across the street. **Restaurant:** Across the street. **General Store:** Yes. **Vending:** Yes. **Swimming Pool:** Yes. **Playground:** Yes. **Other:** Fishing pond, snack bar, game room, adult spa, rec hall, coin games, basketball, movies, badminton, sports field, horseshoes, volleyball. **Activities:** Swimming, boating, fishing, (rental paddleboats available), scheduled activities. **Nearby Attractions:** Lake Michigan, Pere Marquette River, harbor, SS *Badger* cruises, illuminated cross, beaches, dunes, antiques, scenic drives, arts & crafts, White Pine Village, golf, tennis, charter fishing, lighthouse, seaplane rides. **Additional Information:** Ludington Area CVB, (800) 542-4600.

Restrictions

Pets: Leash only. **Fires:** Fire ring only. **Alcoholic Beverages:** At sites only. **Vehicle Maximum Length:** None.

To Get There

From west junction of US 31/10, drive 0.9 mi. west on US 10. Roads are wide and well maintained w/ broad shoulders.

MACKINAW CITY

Mackinaw Mill Creek Camping

P.O. Box 728, Mackinaw City 49701.T: (231) 436-5584; F: (208) 246-4350; www.campmackinaw.com; office@campmackinaw.com.

RV ★★★★ Tent ★★★★

Beauty: ★★★★ Site Privacy: ★★★★
Spaciousness: ★★★★ Quiet: ★★★★
Security: ★★★★ Cleanliness: ★★★★
Insect Control: ★★★★ Facilities: ★★★★

The beautiful view of Mackinac Bridge is reason enough to try this campground. But there is so much more to make a camper happy. Located in Mackinaw City, Mackinaw Mill Creek Camping has more than one mile of shoreline, which means more campers get lakeside spots. Just five minutes from Mackinac Island ferry docks, the campground offers free shuttles to the ferries. Laid out in a series of loops, the campground has level, grassy sites. It offers a choice of shaded or open sites, with a typical site width of 25 feet. There are 20 seasonal campers and no pull-through sites. Reservations are recommended, especially on busy weekends. Quiet time from 10 p.m. to 9 a.m. is enforced, with no generators allowed at any time in the campground. No motorbikes of any kind are permitted. Speed limit is five mph. Security measures include a manager who lives on site and provides regular patrols of the campground.

BASICS

Operated by: Richard & Rose Rogala. **Open:** May 1–Oct. 31. **Site Assignment:** Reservations w/ 1-night deposit; refund w/ 7-day notice. **Registration:** At campground office. **Fee:** $20 (cash, check, credit cards). **Parking:** At site.

FACILITIES

Number of RV Sites: 525. **Number of Tent-Only Sites:** 75. **Hookups:** Electric (30 amps), water, sewer, Internet. **Each Site:** Picnic table, fire ring. **Dump Station:** Yes. **Laundry:** No. **Pay Phone:** Yes. **Rest Rooms and Showers:** Yes. **Fuel:** No. **Propane:** Yes. **Internal Roads:** Paved/gravel, in good condition. **RV Service:** No. **Market:** 2 mi. north in Mackinaw City. **Restaurant:** 2 mi. north in Mackinaw City. **General Store:** Yes. **Vending:** Yes. **Swimming Pool:** Yes. **Playground:** Yes. **Other:** Lake Huron, rental cabins, rec hall, basketball, boat pier, foor bridge, mini-golf, coin games, sports field, hiking trails, badminton. **Activities:** Swimming, fishing, boating, hiking, local tours. **Nearby Attractions:** Mackinac Island, golf, casino, Lake Michigan, beaches, Olde Mill State Historic Park, Fort Michilamackinac, antiques, scenic drives, arts & crafts, Mackinac Bridge, Mackinac Bridge Museum. **Additional Information:** Greater Mackinaw City Area Chamber of Commerce, (800) 814-0160.

RESTRICTIONS

Pets: Leash only. **Fires:** Fire ring only. **Alcoholic Beverages:** At sites only. **Vehicle Maximum Length:** None. **Other:** No camping motorcyclists. Do not feed seagulls, Canadian geese or swans as their droppings may damage the finish on cars or campers.

TO GET THERE

From I-75, take Exit 338 and drive 0.2 mi. south past Ramada Inn, then 2.5 mi. east and south on US 23. Roads are wide and well maintained w/ broad shoulders.

MACKINAW CITY

Tee Pee Campground

P.O. Box 10, Mackinaw City 49701.T: (231) 436-5391; www.teepeecampground.com; gjcooley@ triton.net.

RV ★★★★ Tent ★★★★

Beauty: ★★★★ Site Privacy: ★★★★
Spaciousness: ★★★★ Quiet: ★★★★
Security: ★★★★ Cleanliness: ★★★★
Insect Control: ★★★ Facilities: ★★★

Location is everything, and Tee Pee Campground has a terrific location. On Lake Huron in Mackinaw City, the campground has an excellent view of Mackinac Bridge and Mackinac Island. Some lucky campers can be lulled to sleep by the sounds of the lake lapping the shore. Nightly beach campfires give a friendly atmosphere to the campground owned by the same family since 1969. Tee Pee is a ten-minute walk from downtown attractions. Laid out in a horseshoe, the campground offers level, mostly shaded sites, a typical site width of 35 feet, six pull-through sites, and eight seasonal campers. Another plus is free shuttle service to ferry boats and a casino. The most popular sites are close to the lake. Reservations are recommended, especially for busy weekends. Quiet hours starting at 10 p.m. are enforced, as is a 5 mph speed limit. Security includes a resident manager and regular camp patrols.

BASICS

Operated by: Gene & Jo Cooley. **Open:** May 15–Oct. 15. **Site Assignment:** Reservations w/ 1-night deposit; refund (minus $5) w/ 48-hour notice. **Registration:** At campground office. **Fee:** $22 (cash, check, credit cards). **Parking:** At site.

FACILITIES

Number of RV Sites: 100. **Number of Tent-Only Sites:** 0. **Hookups:** Electric (20, 30 amps), water. **Each Site:** Picnic table, fire ring. **Dump Station:** Yes. **Laundry:** No. **Pay Phone:** Yes. **Rest Rooms and Showers:** Yes. **Fuel:** No. **Propane:** No. **Internal Roads:** Gravel, in good condition. **RV Service:** No. **Market:** 0.5 mi. northwest in Mackinaw City. **Restaurant:** 0.5 mi. northwest in Mackinaw City. **General Store:** Yes, limited. **Vending:** Yes. **Swimming Pool:** No. **Playground:** Yes. **Other:** Lake Huron, swimming beach, rec room, coin games, basketball, badminton, sports field, volleyball, horseshoes, bonfire pit, boat dock. **Activities:** Swimming, fishing, boating, local tours. **Nearby Attractions:** Mackinac Island, golf, casino, Lake Michigan, beaches, dunes, ferry, Old Mill Creek State Historic Park, Fort Michilimackinac, antiques, scenic drives, arts & crafts, Mackinac Bridge & Museum. **Additional Information:** Greater Mackinaw City Area Chamber, (800) 814-0160.

RESTRICTIONS

Pets: Leash only. **Fires:** In fire ring. **Alcoholic Beverages:** Permitted. **Vehicle Max. Length:** 38 ft.

TO GET THERE

From the junction of I-75 and US 23, drive 1 mi. southeast on US 23. Roads are wide and well maintained w/ broad shoulders.

MANISTIQUE

Indian Lake Travel Resort

HCO1 Box 3286, Manistique 49854.T: (906) 341-2807

RV ★★★★ Tent ★★★

Beauty: ★★★★ Site Privacy: ★★★★
Spaciousness: ★★★★ Quiet: ★★★★
Security: ★★★★ Cleanliness: ★★★★
Insect Control: ★★★★ Facilities: ★★★★

Located six miles west of Manistique, in the heart of the Hiawatha National Forest, Indian Lake Travel Resort is popular for its water attractions. Surrounded by trees, the campground is also quiet and clean. Situated on the southwest shore of Indian Lake, the campground has level, mowed-grass sites with a choice of open or shaded. A safe sandy beach is a nice spot for swimming. The typical site width is 35 feet. The campground has seven seasonal campers and four pull-through sites. The campground charges no fee to launch boats of registered guests. The best sites are closest to Indian Lake. Rates at about $15 are very reasonable for such a popular tourism area.

BASICS

Operated by: Richard & Jeanette Ellis. **Open:** May 1–Oct. 15. **Site Assignment:** Reservations w/ 1-night deposit; refund w/ 7-day notice. **Registration:** At campground office. **Fee:** $20 (cash, check). **Parking:** At site.

FACILITIES

Number of RV Sites: 58. **Number of Tent-Only Sites:** 0. **Hookups:** Electric (20, 30 amps), water, sewer. **Each Site:** Picnic table, fire ring. **Dump Station:** Yes. **Laundry:** Yes. **Pay Phone:** Yes. **Rest Rooms and Showers:** Yes. **Fuel:** Yes. **Propane:** Yes. **Internal Roads:** Gravel, in good condition. **RV Service:** No. **Market:** 3 mi. **Restaurant:** 3 mi. **General Store:** Yes, limited. **Vending:** Yes. **Swimming Pool:** No. **Playground:** Yes. **Other:** Indian Lake, rec hall, sandy beach, boat ramp, badminton, sports field, horseshoes, hiking trails, volleyball, boat dock. **Activities:** Swimming, fishing, boating (rental rowboats available). **Nearby Attractions:** Lake Michigan, lighthouse, maritime museum, golf, fish hatchery, state parks, antiques, Seney Wildlife Refuge, Big Spring, Siphon Bridge, snowmobile trails, casino, scenic drive. **Additional Information:** Schoolcraft County Chamber of Commerce, (906) 341-5010.

RESTRICTIONS

Pets: Leash only. **Fires:** Fire ring only. **Alcoholic Beverages:** Permitted. **Vehicle Maximum Length:** None.

TO GET THERE

From the junction of US 2 and Hwy. 149, drive 3.75 mi. northwest on Hwy. 149, then 0.5 mi. north on CR 455. Roads are mostly wide and well maintained w/ adequate shoulders.

MARSHALL
Tri-Lakes Trails Campground

219 Perrett Rd., Marshall 49068. T: (616) 781-2297

★★★ ★★★

Beauty: ★★★★ Site Privacy: ★★★
Spaciousness: ★★★★ Quiet: ★★★
Security: ★★★★ Cleanliness: ★★★★
Insect Control: Yes Facilities: ★★★

Tri-Lakes Trails Campground has the natural beauty and economic price to make it a popular place for campers who may prefer the tradeoffs of amenities for price and more natural ambience. The public announcement service is a noisy distraction on a quiet day. Located five miles south of Marshall, Tri-Lake Trails has three lakes and a nice nature trail through virgin timber. Sites are open, shaded, and grassy, with 160 seasonals and no pull-through sites. The typical site width is 40 feet, most popular spots are by the lake. Speed limit is six mph. The entrance to the campground is beautiful, like a state park with a good road and woods on both sides. A sign along the way does note that "if you don't like rules and common courtesy, pleasure turn around here."

Basics

Operated by: Jack & Jean Gladstone, Jack & Doris Sebring, Bob & Faye Sebring. **Open:** May 1–Oct. 1. **Site Assignment:** Reservations w/ 1-night deposit; refund w/ 7-day notice. **Registration:** At camp office. **Fee:** $18 (cash, check). **Parking:** At site.

Facilities

Number of RV Sites: 300. **Number of Tent-Only Sites:** 22. **Hookups:** Electric (30 amps), water. **Each Site:** Picnic table, fire ring. **Dump Station:** Yes. **Laundry:** No. **Pay Phone:** Yes. **Rest Rooms and Showers:** Yes. **Fuel:** No. **Propane:** Yes. **Internal Roads:** Mostly paved, in great condition. **RV Service:** No. **Market:** 5 mi. north in Marshall. **Restaurant:** 5 mi. north in Marshall. **General Store:** Yes, limited. **Vending:** Yes. **Swimming Pool:** No. **Playground:** Yes. **Other:** Lake, pond, swimming beach, pavilion, activity barn, hiking trails, shuffleboard, mini golf, horseshoes, recreation field, boat dock, badminton, volleyball. **Activities:** Swimming, fishing, boating (rental rowboats available), scheduled weekend activities. **Nearby Attractions:** Historic homes, golf, antiques, arts & crafts shops, museums. **Additional Information:** Marshall Area Chamber of Commerce, (800) 877-5163.

Restrictions

Pets: Leash only. **Fires:** Fire ring only. **Alcoholic Beverages:** Permitted. **Vehicle Maximum Length:** None. **Other:** No scooters, skate-boards or roller blades permitted. Small motors only on lake.

To Get There

From the junction of I-94 and I-69, drive 5.75 mi. south on I-69, take Exit 32, then 1.25 mi. east on F Dr. South, then 0.25 mi. south on Old US 27, then 0.75 mi. west on Perrett Rd. Roads are wide and well maintained w/ generally good shoulders, but entrance is through a residential neighborhood. Campground signs ask campers to limit trips through neighborhood and also to be aware of speed traps.

MEARS
Hide-A-Way Campground

9671 West Silver Lake Rd., Mears 49436. T: (231) 873-4428; F: (231) 873-0402; www.hideawaycampground.com; generalinfo@hideawaycampground.com.

★★ ★★

Beauty: ★★★ Site Privacy: ★★★
Spaciousness: ★★★ Quiet: ★★★
Security: ★★★ Cleanliness: ★★
Insect Control: ★★ Facilities: ★★

Hide-A-Way Campground has so much going for it. Located in Mears, it is close to Lake Michigan, Silver Lake attractions, and sand dunes. There is enough natural beauty and outdoor activity to keep most campers happy. But the campground itself needs some work. The sand dunes about a quarter mile away make the campground a handy base for "duners," and the campground can get crowded when the sand dune meets are going on. Campsites are mostly shaded, with a typical site width of 30 feet. Some sites are level. A 340-foot water slide is a popular attraction. The water slide is open to the public and has discounts and some free time for Hide-A-Way campers.

Basics

Operated by: Dan & Laurie Kolosci. **Open:** May 1–Oct. 1. **Site Assignment:** Reservations w/ 1-night deposit; refund w/ 2-week notice. No 1-night reservations. **Registration:** At camp office. **Fee:** $28 (cash, check, credit cards). **Parking:** At site.

Facilities

Number of RV Sites: 175. **Number of Tent-Only Sites:** 38. **Hookups:** Electric (20, 30 amps), water. **Each Site:** Picnic table, fire ring. **Dump Station:** Yes. **Laundry:** Yes. **Pay Phone:** Yes. **Rest Rooms and Showers:** Yes. **Fuel:** No. **Propane:** Yes. **Internal Roads:** Paved/gravel, in fair condition. **RV Service:** No. **Market:** 2 mi. **Restaurant:** 2 mi. **General Store:** Yes. **Vending:** Yes. **Swimming Pool:** Yes. **Playground:** Yes. **Other:** Game room, sports field, water slide, rental units. **Activities:** Swimming. **Nearby Attractions:** Lake Michigan, sand dune, state parks, golf, fruit farms, harbor, riverboats, lighthouse, antiques, gemstone factory, arts & crafts. **Additional Information:** Oceana County Tourism Bureau, (616) 873-3982.

Restrictions

Pets: Leash only. **Fires:** Fire ring only. **Alcoholic Beverages:** Permitted. **Vehicle Maximum Length:** None.

To Get There

From the junction of US 31 and Shelby Rd., drive 5 mi. west on Shelby Rd., then 4.5 mi. north on Scenic Dr. Roads are mostly wide and well maintained w/ narrow shoulders in places.

MEARS
Sandy Shores Campground & Resort

8595 West Silver Lake, Mears 49436. T: (231) 873-3003; F: (231) 873-2142.

★★★★ ★★★

Beauty: ★★★★ Site Privacy: ★★★★
Spaciousness: ★★★★ Quiet: ★★★★
Security: ★★★★ Cleanliness: ★★★★
Insect Control: ★★★★ Facilities: ★★★★

Located in a sand dune recreation area in Mears, Sandy Shores Campground & Resort is a wonderful spot to enjoy all the area activities. Right next to Silver Lake State Park, the campground is on a good fishing lake with a large sandy beach for swimming. Sites are level and grassy with a choice of open or shade. The typical site width is 40 feet. The campground has 140 seasonal campers and 11 pull-through sites. Rest rooms and showers are very clean and well maintained, which must be the result of more than once-a-day attention. Reservations are recommended since about two-thirds of the campground is filled with seasonal campers. Security measures are top-notch with owners who live on the premises. The campground's central location in the midst of such a popular resort area also means that local law enforcement officials will be patrolling.

Basics

Operated by: Jerry & Chris Klepper. **Open:** May 1–Oct. 1. **Site Assignment:** Reservations w/ 1-night deposit; refund (minus $5) w/ 7-day notice. **Registration:** At campground office. **Fee:** $30 (cash, check, credit cards). **Parking:** At site.

Facilities

Number of RV Sites: 210. **Number of Tent-Only Sites:** 0. **Hookups:** Electric (30 amps), water, sewer. **Each Site:** Picnic table, fire ring. **Dump Station:** Yes. **Laundry:** Yes. **Pay Phone:** Yes. **Rest Rooms and Showers:** Yes. **Fuel:** No. **Propane:** Yes. **Internal Roads:** Paved/gravel, in good condition. **RV Service:** No. **Market:** Less than 1 mi. **Restaurant:** Less than 1 mi. **General Store:** Yes. **Vending:** Yes. **Swimming Pool:** Yes. **Playground:** Yes. **Other:** Silver Lake, badminton, volleyball, boat dock, marina, rental cottage. **Activities:** Swimming, fishing, boating (rental rowboats, canoes, sailboats, paddleboats available). **Nearby Attractions:** Lake Michigan, sand dunes, state parks, golf, fruit farms, harbor, riverboats, lighthouse, antiques, gemstone factory, arts & crafts. **Additional Information:** Oceana County Tourism Bureau, (616) 873-3982.

Restrictions

Pets: Leash only. **Fires:** Fire ring only. **Alcoholic Beverages:** Permitted. **Vehicle Maximum Length:** None.

To Get There

From the junction of US 31 and Shelby Rd., drive 5 mi. west on Shelby Rd., then 4 mi. north on Scenic Dr., then 0.5 mi. east on Silver Lake Rd. Roads are well maintained w/ adequate shoulders.

MEARS
Silver Lake Yogi Bear's Jellystone Park Camp-Resort

8239 West Hazel Rd., Mears 49436. T: (616) 873-4502; www.campjellystone.com; silveryogi@yahoo.com.

Beauty: ★★★ Site Privacy: ★★★★
Spaciousness: ★★★★ Quiet: ★★★
Security: ★★★★ Cleanliness: ★★★★
Insect Control: ★★★★ Facilities: ★★★★

Located near a large sand dune area and next door to an amusement center, Silver Lake Yogi Bear's Jellystone Park Camp-Resort has enough activities to keep anyone busy. The campground itself boasts a big slate of things to do. Just a quarter mile away is Silver Lake, one mile is the dunes, and two miles away is Lake Michigan Beach and a lighthouse. Next door are a slide, go-carts, adventure golf, bumper boats, an arcade, and dune buggy rentals. The campground offers open or shaded sites with a typical site width of 40 feet. There are 40 seasonal campers. Rest rooms and showers are cleaned often to keep up with all the children and sand lovers. The heated pool is a refreshing change from the cold Lake Michigan swimming beach. Security measures include regular campground patrols. Reservations are strongly recommended.

Basics

Operated by: Craig & Lorie Cihak. **Open:** Apr. 15–Oct. 15. **Site Assignment:** Reservations w/ 1-night deposit; refund w/ 2-week notice. **Registration:** At campground office. **Fee:** $34 (cash, check, credit cards). **Parking:** At site.

Facilities

Number of RV Sites: 200. **Number of Tent-Only Sites:** 23. **Hookups:** Electric (20, 30 amps), water, sewer, phone. **Each Site:** Picnic table, fire ring. **Dump Station:** Yes. **Laundry:** Yes. **Pay Phone:** Yes. **Rest Rooms and Showers:** Yes. **Fuel:** No. **Propane:** No. **Internal Roads:** Paved/gravel, in good condition. **RV Service:** No. **Market:** 1 mi. **Restaurant:** 1 mi. **General Store:** Yes. **Vending:** Yes. **Swimming Pool:** Yes. **Playground:** Yes. **Other:** Rec hall, pavilion, coin games, fishing pond, mini-golf, basketball, shuffleboard, movies, horseshoes, volleyball, rental trailers, rental cabins, sports field. **Activities:** Swimming, fishing, scheduled activities. **Nearby Attractions:** Lake Michigan, sand dunes, state parks, golf, fruit farms, harbor, riverboats, lighthouse, antiques, gemstone factory, arts & crafts. **Additional Information:** Oceana County Tourism Bureau, (616) 873-3982.

Restrictions

Pets: Leash only. **Fires:** Fire ring only. **Alcoholic Beverages:** Permitted. **Vehicle Maximum Length:** None.

To Get There

From US 31, take Hart Exit and drive 5.5 mi. west on Polk Rd./56th Ave./Fox Rd., then 0.5 mi. west on Hazel Rd. Roads are wide and well maintained w/ adequate shoulders.

MIDLAND

River Ridge Campground

1989 West Pine River Rd., Breckenridge 48615. T: (800) 647-2267

RV ★★★★ Tent ★★★★

Beauty: ★★★★ Site Privacy: ★★★★
Spaciousness: ★★★★ Quiet: ★★★★
Security: ★★★★ Cleanliness: ★★★★
Insect Control: ★★★★ Facilities: ★★★★

A wooded campground with some open sites on Pine River, River Ridge Campground offers two important camping ingredients—quiet and cleanliness. Located in Breckenridge, the campground also has a scenic river and plenty of activities to keep campers happy. Good fishing can be found in the river or the spring-fed pond where no license is required. Campsites are level with a typical site width of 30 feet. There are 30 seasonal campers and 10 pull-through sites. The best sites are alongside the river. Swimmers have a choice between the heated pool, pond, or river. An added water plus is the spa. Security includes a traffic control gate and owners who keep a close watch on the campground.

Basics

Operated by: Dan & Louella Staley. **Open:** May 1–Oct. 15. **Site Assignment:** Reservations w/ 1-night deposit; refund w/ 7-day notice. **Registration:** At office. **Fee:** $20 (check, credit). **Parking:** At site.

Facilities

Number of RV Sites: 150. **Number of Tent-Only Sites:** 12. **Hookups:** Electric (20, 30, 50 amps), water, sewer, phone. **Each Site:** Picnic table, fire ring. **Dump Station:** Yes. **Laundry:** Yes. **Pay Phone:** Yes. **Rest Rooms and Showers:** Yes. **Fuel:** No. **Propane:** Yes. **Internal Roads:** Gravel, in good condition. **RV Service:** No. **Market:** 6 mi. north. **Restaurant:** 6 mi. north. **General Store:** Yes, limited. **Vending:** No. **Swimming Pool:** Yes. **Playground:** Yes. **Other:** Pine River, rec hall, pavilion, coin games, spa, basketball, badminton, sports field, horseshoes, volleyball, rental cabins. **Activities:** Swimming, fishing, boating (rental kayaks, paddleboats, tubes available). **Nearby Attractions:** Bowling, mini-golf, hiking trails, outdoor concert park, farmers' market, Alden B. Down Home & Studio, Chippewa Nature Center, Dow Gardens, antiques, arts & crafts, golf, casino. **Additional Information:** Midland County CVB, (888) 464-3526.

Restrictions

Pets: Leash only; indoor pets only. **Fires:** Fire ring only. **Alcoholic Beverages:** At sites only. **Vehicle Maximum Length:** None.

To Get There

From the junction of Hwy. 20 and Meridian Rd., drive 3 mi. south on Meridian Rd., then 4.5 mi. west on Pine River Rd. Roads are mostly wide and well maintained w/ narrow shoulders in spots.

MIDLAND

Valley Plaza RV Park

5221 Bay City Rd., Midland 48642. T: (517) 496-2159; www.valleyplazaresort.com.

RV ★★★ Tent n/a

Beauty: ★★★ Site Privacy: ★★★★
Spaciousness: ★★★★ Quiet: ★★★
Security: ★★★★ Cleanliness: ★★★★
Insect Control: ★★★★ Facilities: ★★★★

Campers can get spoiled at Valley Plaza RV Park with all the luxury features in the recreation complex. Located five miles south of Midland, the campground is behind a recreation complex that includes a motel, restaurant, theatre, bowling alley, health club, tanning beds, indoor mini-golf, arcade, and more. This is not an out-in-the-country kind of campground. It is more like an open space with trees that still have a bunch of growing to do to provide shade. Sites are mostly open with a typical site width of 30 feet. There are 12 seasonal campers and 55 pull-through sites. The campground has a three-acre lake with a sandy beach and seasonal water sports. Sites are within a well-illuminated and fenced area, ensuring privacy. Be aware that no tents are permitted. Many campers come to enjoy the facilities at the campground as well as those at the recreation complex. Security is tops with a security patrol that keeps a close eye on the area.

Basics

Operated by: Jason Raponis. **Open:** Mar. 1–Nov. 1. **Site Assignment:** Reservations w/ 1-night deposit; refund (minus $5) w/ 7-day notice. **Registration:** At campground office. **Fee:** $25 (cash, check, credit cards). **Parking:** At site.

Facilities

Number of RV Sites: 96. **Number of Tent-Only Sites:** 0. **Hookups:** Electric (20, 30, 50 amps), water, sewer. **Each Site:** Picnic table, fire ring. **Dump Station:** Yes. **Laundry:** No. **Pay Phone:** Yes. **Rest Rooms and Showers:** Yes. **Fuel:** Yes. **Propane:** Yes. **Internal Roads:** Paved, in good condition. **RV Service:** No. **Market:** 5 mi. north in Midland. **Restaurant:** Walking distance. **General Store:** Yes. **Vending:** Yes. **Swimming Pool:** Yes. **Playground:** Yes. **Other:** Lake, rec hall, pavilion, coin games, wading pool, sauna, whirlpool, fishing pond, mini golf, basketball, badminton, horseshoes, volleyball, boat dock, adults room, sports field. **Activities:** Swimming, fishing, boating (rental paddleboats, kayaks available), scheduled activities. **Nearby Attractions:** Bowling, mini-golf, hiking trails, outdoor concert park, farmers' market, Alden B. Down Home & Studio, Chippewa Nature Center, Dow Gardens, antiques, arts & crafts, golf, casino. **Additional Information:** Midland County CVB, (888) 464-3526.

Restrictions

Pets: Leash only. **Fires:** Fire ring only. **Alcoholic Beverages:** Permitted. **Vehicle Maximum Length:** None. **Other:** No tents allowed.

To Get There

From the junction of I-75 and US 10, take Exit 162B and drive 10 mi. west on US 10 to Bay City Rd. exit, then drive 0.1 mi. west on Bay City Rd. Roads are wide and well maintained w/ broad shoulders.

MILAN

KC Campground

14048 Sherman Rd., Milan 48160. T: (734) 439-1076

RV ★★★ Tent ★★★

Beauty: ★★★ Site Privacy: ★★★
Spaciousness: ★★★ Quiet: ★★★
Security: ★★★★ Cleanliness: ★★★
Insect Control: ★★★ Facilities: ★★★

A rural campground with mostly shaded sites in a grassy meadow, KC Campground is located three miles east of Milan. The best sites are along a very small pond used for swimming. The campground has a typical site width of 30 feet, with 20 seasonal campers and 15 pull-through sites. Laid out in a series of loops, the campground has separate tent areas with more green space and privacy. Quiet time between 10 p.m. and 8 a.m. is enforced, and no motorcyles, minibikes, or ATVs are allowed. Reservations are recommended during the annual Milan Bluegrass Festival in Aug. The festival draws top names in Bluegrass entertainment. Security measures at the campground include an owner and manger who live on site, one entrance/exit road, and regular patrols of the campground.

Basics

Operated by: Mark & Peggy Ann Gaynier. **Open:** May 1–Oct. 31. **Site Assignment:** Reservations w/ 1-night deposit; refund w/ 72-hour notice. **Registration:** At campground office. **Fee:** $20 (cash, check, credit cards). **Parking:** At site.

Facilities

Number of RV Sites: 100. **Number of Tent-Only Sites:** 50. **Hookups:** Electric (20, 30 amps), water. **Each Site:** Picnic table, fire ring. **Dump Station:** Yes. **Laundry:** No. **Pay Phone:** No. **Rest Rooms and Showers:** Yes. **Fuel:** No. **Propane:** Yes. **Internal Roads:** Gravel, in good condition. **RV Service:** No. **Market:** 3 mi. west in Milan. **Restaurant:** 3 mi. west in Milan. **General Store:** Yes, limited. **Vending:** No. **Swimming Pool:** No. **Playground:** Yes. **Other:** Swimming pond, rec hall, volleyball, basketball, horseshoes, sports field. **Activities:** Swimming. **Nearby Attractions:** Golf, Cabela's, Cedar Point, Toledo Center of Science & Industry, Greenfield Village, Monroe County Historical Museum, River Raisin Battlefield, Sauders Farm & Craft Village, zoo, Yankee Air museum, antiques. **Additional Information:** Monroe County Convention & Tourism Bureau, (800) 252-3011.

Restrictions

Pets: Leash only. **Fires:** Fire ring only. **Alcoholic Beverages:** At sites only. **Vehicle Maximum Length:** 54 ft.

To Get There

From the junction of US 23 and Plank Rd., take Exit 25 and drive 1.5 mi. southeast on Plank Rd., then 1 mi. east Sherman Rd. Roads are mostly wide and well maintained, but Plank Rd. has narrow shoulders, and the access road is bumpy and gravel.

MONROE

Harbortown RV Resort

14931 LaPlaisance Rd., Monroe 48161. T: (734) 384-4700; www.harbortownrv.com.

RV ★★★★ Tent ★

Beauty: ★★★	Site Privacy: ★★★
Spaciousness: ★★★	Quiet: ★★
Security: ★★★★★	Cleanliness: ★★★★★
Insect Control: ★★★★★	Facilities: ★★★★★

Opened in spring of 2000, Harbortown RV Resort is a state-of-the-art facility in Monroe, that includes Time Out Family Recreation Center. Bring plenty of coins for the activities. Offering easy access from I-75, the campground is only one mile from Lake Erie and all its water sports. Laid out in a series of loops, the campground offers level, open, paved sites with a typical site width of 30 feet. There are 105 pull-throughs. Facilities are new and squeaky clean. A full-time staff must be at work constantly to keep the campground in such tip-top shape. Security is great; it doesn't seem likely anyone would enter or exit without being seen. Tents are permitted, but there is no separate section for them. Tent campers must pay the regular fee for an RV site. Harbortown seems like a campground of the future. There are several opportunities for improvement, however. One would be the addition of propane for sale; it's not easy to find nearby. Another would be the need for some shade trees; that will come with time when the landscaping has a chance to mature. The last is the installation of a hedge or other sound buffer next to the train tracks bordering one edge of the campground.

Basics

Operated by: Private Operator. **Open:** All year. **Site Assignment:** Reservations w/ 1-night deposit; refund w/ 2-week notice. **Registration:** At campground office. **Fee:** $32 (cash, check, credit cards). **Parking:** At site.

Facilities

Number of RV Sites: 250. **Number of Tent-Only Sites:** 0. **Hookups:** Electric (20, 30, 50 amps), water, sewer, phone, cable TV. **Each Site:** Picnic table, fire ring. **Dump Station:** Yes. **Laundry:** Yes. **Pay Phone:** Yes. **Rest Rooms and Showers:** Yes. **Fuel:** No. **Propane:** No. **Internal Roads:** Paved, in good condition. **RV Service:** No. **Market:** Next door. **Restaurant:** Next door. **General Store:** Yes. **Vending:** Yes. **Swimming Pool:** Yes. **Playground:** Yes. **Other:** Rec hall, coin games, mini-golf, movies, horseshoes, volleyball, go-karts, 18-hole golf course, sports field, rental cabins, batting cages. **Activities:** Swimming, scheduled activities. **Nearby Attractions:** Cabela's, outlet mall, Lake Erie, Vietnam War Memorial, Heck Park, historic tours, Monroe County Historical Museum, River Raisin Battlefield Visitor Center, antiques, arts & crafts, Navarre-Anderson Trading Post Complex. **Additional Information:** Monroe County Convention & Tourism Bureau, (800) 252-3011.

Restrictions

Pets: Leash only. **Fires:** Fire ring only. **Alcoholic Beverages:** Permitted. **Vehicle Maximum Length:** None.

To Get There

From the junction of I-75 and Laplaisance Rd., take Exit 11 and drive 0.5 mi. west on Laplaisance Rd. Roads are wide and well maintained w/ broad shoulders.

MONTAGUE

Jerry's Campground

4540 Dowling St., Montague 49437. T: (231) 894-4903

RV ★★★★ Tent ★★★★

Beauty: ★★★	Site Privacy: ★★★
Spaciousness: ★★★	Quiet: ★★★★
Security: ★★★★	Cleanliness: ★★★★
Insect Control: ★★★★	Facilities: ★★★

Although the campground offers little activities of its own, it does provide a fish-cleaning hut and complimentary fish freezing. That tells you what the major draw is. Jerry's Campground in Montague, is across from beautiful White Lake and two blocks from the public boat launch. It is also at the south end of the Montague/Hart Bike Trail. Most people use Jerry's Campground as a base to enjoy area activities. Golf is nearby, and shops and dining are within walking distance. A campground in town, Jerry's has mostly open, flat, grassy sites with a typical site width of 30 feet. The campground has 25 seasonal campers and 21 pull-through sites. Quiet hours from 10 p.m. to 7 a.m. are enforced. Security measures are good with patrols and local police always close at hand.

Basics

Operated by: Jerry Woller. **Open:** Late Apr.–late Oct. **Site Assignment:** Reservations w/ 1-night deposit; refund w/ 7-day notice. **Registration:** At campground office. **Fee:** $20 (cash, check). **Parking:** At site.

Facilities

Number of RV Sites: 51. **Number of Tent-Only Sites:** 4. **Hookups:** Electric (30 amps), water, sewer, cable TV. **Each Site:** Picnic table, grill. **Dump Station:** Yes. **Laundry:** No. **Pay Phone:** Yes. **Rest Rooms and Showers:** Yes. **Fuel:** No. **Propane:** No. **Internal Roads:** Gravel, in good condition. **RV Service:** No. **Market:** 1 mi. **Restaurant:** Walking distance. **General Store:** No. **Vending:** Yes. **Swimming Pool:** No. **Playground:** Yes. **Other:** Pavilion, horseshoes, fish-cleaning station. **Activities:** None. **Nearby Attractions:** Lake Michigan, White Lake, marinas, Michgan's Adventure Amusement Park, White River Lighthouse Museum, golf, bike trail, mini-golf, world's largest weather vane, bike trail. **Additional Information:** White Lake Area Chamber of Commerce, (800) 879-9702.

Restrictions

Pets: Leash only. **Fires:** Grills only. **Alcoholic Beverages:** Permitted. **Vehicle Max. Length:** None.

To Get There

From the junction of US 31 and Business 31, take Whitehall-Montague Exit and drive 2.25 mi. west on Business 31. Roads are wide and well maintained w/ broad shoulders.

MT. PLEASANT

Shardi's Hide-Away

340 North Loomis Rd., Mt. Pleasant 48858. T: (517) 773-4268

RV ★★★ Tent ★★★

Beauty: ★★★	Site Privacy: ★★★
Spaciousness: ★★★	Quiet: ★★★
Security: ★★★	Cleanliness: ★★★
Insect Control: None	Facilities: ★★★

A rural campground in a semi-wooded setting, Shardi's Hide-Away is located six miles east of Mt.

Pleasant. Sites are level, mostly shaded and with a typical site width of 25 feet. There are no seasonal campers and the campground has eight pull-through sites. The campground is a popular place for deer hunters and campers who enjoy mushroom and berry picking. The playground features a big wooden boat and a jeep which are hits with youngsters. The ten mph speed limit is rather high, but traffic generally travels slower because of the gravel and dirt road. Reservations are highly recommended during festival times—Apr. for the Maple Syrup Festival, May for the Highland Scottish Festival, July for the Bluegrass Festival and Antique Engine Show, and Aug. for the Isabella County Fair.

Basics

Operated by: The Miller Family. **Open:** All year. **Site Assignment:** Reservations w/ 1-night deposit; no refunds**Registration:** At campground office. **Registration:** At campground office. **Fee:** $22 (cash, check, credit cards). **Parking:** At site.

Facilities

Number of RV Sites: 102. **Number of Tent-Only Sites:** 10. **Hookups:** Electric (20, 30, 50 amps), water, sewer. **Each Site:** Picnic table, fire ring. **Dump Station:** Yes. **Laundry:** No. **Pay Phone:** No. **Rest Rooms and Showers:** Yes. **Fuel:** No. **Propane:** No. **Internal Roads:** Gravel/dirt, in fair condition. **RV Service:** No. **Market:** 6 mi. west in Mt. Pleasant. **Restaurant:** 6 mi. west in Mt. Pleasant. **General Store:** Yes. **Vending:** No. **Swimming Pool:** Yes. **Playground:** Yes. **Other:** Pavilion, rental cabins, hiking trails, shuffleboard, volleyball, horseshoes, sand hill, basketball, tetherball, fishing pond, badminton, recreation field. **Activities:** Swimming, fishing, hiking. **Nearby Attractions:** Gambling casino, horse & car race tracks, golf, canoeing, tubing, fishing, antiques, farmers market. **Additional Information:** Mt. Pleasant Area CVB, (800) 772-4433.

Restrictions

Pets: Leash only. **Fires:** Fire ring only. **Alcoholic Beverages:** Permitted. **Vehicle Maximum Length:** None.

To Get There

From the junction of US 27 and Hwy. 20, drive 3.5 mi. east on Hwy. 20, then 2.5 mi. north on Loomis Rd. Roads are wide and well maintained w/ broad shoulders, except for Loomis Rd. which is a rough gravel surface.

MUNISING

Wandering Wheels Campground

P.O. Box 419, Munising 49862. T: (906) 387-3315; F: (906) 387-3315; www.wanderingwheels.com; vbragg@up.net.

RV: ★★★★ Tent: ★★★

Beauty: ★★★★	Site Privacy: ★★★★
Spaciousness: ★★★★	Quiet: ★★★★
Security: ★★★★	Cleanliness: ★★★★
Insect Control: ★★★★	Facilities: ★★★★

Wandering Wheels Campground, three-and-a-half miles east of Munising, is surrounded by scenic attractions and activities. The campground is quite nice in and of itself. Sites are level, secluded, and mostly wooded. About half are grassy and half are dirt. The typical site width is 40 feet and the campground has 44 pull-through sites. Free showers in the sparkling- clean facilities are a nice plus. Wandering Wheels also has camping cabins with gas fireplaces that cost about $40 for up to four persons, which is cheaper than most motels and far more pleasant. Reservations are recommended for the campsites and cabins. Security is good, with owners keeping a close eye on the campground.

Basics

Operated by: Dennis & Vickie Bragg. **Open:** May 1–Oct. 15. **Site Assignment:** Reservations w/ 1-night deposit; refund w/ 7-day notice. **Registration:** At campground office. **Fee:** $26 (cash, check, credit cards). **Parking:** At site.

Facilities

Number of RV Sites: 88. **Number of Tent-Only Sites:** 12. **Hookups:** Electric (20, 30, 50 amps), water, sewer, phone, cable TV. **Each Site:** Picnic table, fire ring. **Dump Station:** Yes. **Laundry:** Yes. **Pay Phone:** Yes. **Rest Rooms and Showers:** Yes. **Fuel:** No. **Propane:** Yes. **Internal Roads:** Gravel, in good condition. **RV Service:** No. **Market:** Less than 1 mi. **Restaurant:** Next door. **General Store:** Yes. **Vending:** Yes. **Swimming Pool:** Yes. **Playground:** Yes. **Other:** Rec room, coin games, basketball, badminton, sports field, horseshoes, volleyball, rental cabins. **Activities:** Swimming. **Nearby Attractions:** Waterfalls, Pictured Rocks National Lakeshore, golf, Alger Underwater Preserve, boat tours, shipwreck tours, glass bottom boat tours, snowmobiling. **Additional Information:** Munising Visitors Bureau, (906) 387-2138.

Restrictions

Pets: Leash only. **Fires:** Fire ring only. **Alcoholic Beverages:** Permitted. **Vehicle Maximum Length:** None.

To Get There

From town, drive 3.5 mi. east on Hwy. 28. Roads are wide and well maintained w/ broad shoulders.

NILES

Spaulding Lake Campground

2305 Bell Rd., Niles 49120. T: (616) 684-1393; F: (616) 684-4065.

RV: ★★★★ Tent: ★★★

Beauty: ★★★★	Site Privacy: ★★★★
Spaciousness: ★★★★	Quiet: ★★★★
Security: ★★★★	Cleanliness: ★★★★
Insect Control: ★★★★	Facilities: ★★★★

On the Indiana/Michigan border in Niles, Spaudling Lake Campground is a good base to cover a wide area, including Amish country in Northern Indiana. The campground has three man-made ponds, one for swimming and two for fishing. Just five miles north of South Bend, Spaulding Lake is the closest campground to Notre Dame. No fishing license is required at the spring-fed, stocked pond. Sites are level and grassy, with a typical site width of 30 feet. The campground has 15 seasonal campers and 44 pull-through sites. Be aware that the campground does not permit alcohol anywhere on the premises. The campground and facilities are clean and well maintained. Rules and security measures are enforced. The goal is a family-oriented campground where people feel comfortable camping. Spaulding Lake Campground is always busy, so the owners must be achieving their goal.

Basics

Operated by: Nolan & Virginia Spaulding. **Open:** Apr. 1–Oct. 15. **Site Assignment:** Reservations w/ 1-night deposit; refund (minus $5) w/ 7-day notice. **Registration:** At campground office. **Fee:** $20 (cash, check). **Parking:** At site.

Facilities

Number of RV Sites: 120. **Number of Tent-Only Sites:** 0. **Hookups:** Electric (20, 30, 50 amps), water, sewer, cable TV, phone. **Each Site:** Picnic table, fire ring. **Dump Station:** Yes. **Laundry:** Yes. **Pay Phone:** Yes. **Rest Rooms and Showers:** Yes. **Fuel:** No. **Propane:** Yes. **Internal Roads:** Gravel, in good condition. **RV Service:** No. **Market:** 3 mi. **Restaurant:** 3 mi. **General Store:** Yes. **Vending:** Yes. **Swimming Pool:** No. **Playground:** Yes. **Other:** Swimming lake, fishing lake, rec hall, coin games, trout stream, basketball, shuffleboard, bandminton, sports field, pavilion, horseshoes, volleyball, hiking trails. **Activities:** Swimming, fishing, hiking. **Nearby Attractions:** Amish Country, Fort St. Joseph Museum, historic homes, antiques, arts & crafts, Fernwood Botanic Garden & Nature Center, Notre Dame. **Additional Information:** Four Flags Area Council on Tourism, (616) 684-7444.

Restrictions

Pets: Leash only. **Fires:** Fire ring only. **Alcoholic Beverages:** Not permitted. **Vehicle Maximum Length:** None. **Other:** No outside firewood permitted.

To Get There

From the junction of US 12 and Hwy. 51, drive 0.25 mi. south on Hwy. 51, then 2 mi. east on Bell Rd. Roads are generally wide and well maintained w/ adequate shoulders.

ONTONAGON

River Pines RV Park & Campground

600 River Rd., Ontonagon 49953. T: (800) 424-1520; www.ontonagonmi.com/riverpines; gladorp@up.net.

RV: ★★★★ Tent: ★★★★

Beauty: ★★★★	Site Privacy: ★★★★
Spaciousness: ★★★★	Quiet: ★★★★
Security: ★★★★	Cleanliness: ★★★★
Insect Control: ★★★★	Facilities: ★★★★

A little gem along the Ontonagon River, River Pines RV Park & Campground offers great facilities with sparkling-clean rest rooms. Located outside Ontonagon, the campground has open or shaded level sites, with a typical site width of 35 feet. Laid out in a series of loops, the campground has 30 pull-through sites. A separate tent section in the woods allows more green space and privacy. A four-season campground, River Pines features easy access to 500 miles of snowmobile trails and five major ski hills within a 60-mile radius. Winter group housing in available in the main building for those frigid, snowy Michigan winters. The best RV sites are in the pine tree section. Walleye and salmon fishing are popular in the river by the campground. With only 32 sites, reservations are strongly recommended from June through Sept. Security includes owners who live on the site and keep a close watch on the campground.

Basics

Operated by: Dot Phillips & Gladys Chamberlain. **Open:** All year. **Site Assignment:** Reservations w/ 1-night deposit; refund w/ 7-day notice. **Registration:** At campground office. **Fee:** $21 (cash, check, credit cards). **Parking:** At site.

Facilities

Number of RV Sites: 30. **Number of Tent-Only Sites:** 2. **Hookups:** Electric (20, 30, 50 amps), water, sewer, phone, cable TV. **Each Site:** Picnic table, fire ring. **Dump Station:** Yes. **Laundry:** Yes. **Pay Phone:** Yes. **Rest Rooms and Showers:** Yes. **Fuel:** No. **Propane:** Yes. **Internal Roads:** Gravel, in good condition. **RV Service:** No. **Market:** 1 mi. east in Ontonagon. **Restaurant:** 1 mi. east in Ontonagon. **General Store:** Yes, limited. **Vending:** Yes. **Swimming Pool:** No. **Playground:** Yes. **Other:** Rec hall, coin games, boat dock, fishing river, basketball, bandminton, sports field, horseshoes, volleyball. **Activities:** Fishing, boating (rental canoe, rowboats, paddleboats, motorboats available). **Nearby Attractions:** Ontonagon River, 45 waterfalls, Porcupine Mountains State Park, sailing, backpacking, hiking, Presque Isle Falls, Lake of the Clouds, golf, antiques, arts & crafts, Ontonagon County Historical Museum. **Additional Information:** Ontonagon County Chamber, (906) 884-4735.

Restrictions

Pets: Leash only. **Fires:** Fire ring only. **Alcoholic Beverages:** Permitted. **Vehicle Maximum Length:** None.

To Get There

From the junction of US 45 and Hwy. 64, drive 0.25 mi. south on Hwy. 64, then 0.5 mi. east on River Rd. Roads are mostly wide and well maintained w/ adequate shoulders.

ORTONVILLE

Clearwater Campground

1140 South M-15, Ortonville 48462. T: (248) 627-3820

RV ★★★ Tent ★★★

Beauty: ★★★	Site Privacy: ★★★
Spaciousness: ★★★	Quiet: ★★★
Security: ★★★★	Cleanliness: ★★★
Insect Control: ★★★	Facilities: ★★★

A lakeside campground with open and shaded sites, Clearwater Campground is located in Ortonville. Laid out in a series of loops, the campground has a typical site width of 25 feet. It has 30 seasonal campers and eight pull-through sites. All sites have full hookup, and tents are not allowed on any of the full hookup sites. Tents are permitted only in the primitive area which offers more green space and privacy. Quiet time from 10 p.m. to 8 a.m. is enforced, as is a five mph speed limit. No minibikes, off-road bikes or similar vehicles are permitted in the park. The campground also has a rule that any RV that is detrimental to the appearance of the park may be refused registration. The campground manager decides what constitutes a detrimental appearance. Security measures include a resident manager and a gate that requires a card pass to enter.

Basics

Operated by: Mike & Christie Neadow & Mark & Michaelanne Reis. **Open:** Apr. 15–Oct. 15. **Site Assignment:** Reservations w/ 1-night deposit; refund w/ 7-day notice. **Registration:** At camp office. **Fee:** $25 (cash, check). **Parking:** At site.

Facilities

Number of RV Sites: 209. **Number of Tent-Only Sites:** 15. **Hookups:** Electric (30, 50 amps), water, sewer, cable TV, phone. **Each Site:** Picnic table, fire ring. **Dump Station:** Yes. **Laundry:** Yes. **Pay Phone:** Yes. **Rest Rooms and Showers:** Yes. **Fuel:** No. **Propane:** Yes. **Internal Roads:** Paved, in good condition. **RV Service:** No. **Market:** 0.25 mi. north in Ortonville. **Restaurant:** Across the street. **General Store:** Yes, limited. **Vending:** Yes. **Swimming Pool:** No. **Playground:** Yes. **Other:** Swimming lake, pavilion, mini tolf, sports field, horseshoes. **Activities:** Swimming, fishing, boating (electric motors only), scheduled weekend activities. **Nearby Attractions:** Children's Museum, Huckleberry Railroad, paddlewheeler, museums, Longway Planetarium, Flint River, antiques, golf, arts & crafts. **Additional Information:** Holly Chamber of Commerce, (248) 634-1900.

Restrictions

Pets: Leash only; 1 pet per site. **Fires:** Fire ring only. **Alcoholic Beverages:** Permitted. **Vehicle Maximum Length:** None. **Other:** Tents permitted only on primitive sites.

To Get There

From the junction of I-75 and Hwy. 15, take Exit 91 and drive 6.2 mi. north on Hwy. 15. Roads are wide and well maintained w/ broad shoulders.

PENTWATER

Whispering Surf Camping Resort

7070 South Lake Shore Dr., Pentwater 49449. T: (231) 869-5050; F: (231) 869-5935; www.denaliseed.com/wsurf; wsurf@denaliseed.com.

RV ★★★ Tent ★★★★

Beauty: ★★★★	Site Privacy: ★★★★
Spaciousness: ★★★★	Quiet: ★★★★
Security: ★★★★	Cleanliness: ★★★★
Insect Control: ★★★★	Facilities: ★★★

One of Michigan's oldest continuously operating resorts, Whispering Surf Camping Resort got its start in 1913. But the campground is not outdated. Full hookups and modern facilities are available, along with free hot showers. Located four miles north of Pentwater, between Bass Lake and Lake Michigan, Whispering Surf is forested with oak, pine, and white birch trees. Tucked in the North Woods, the campground offers shaded sites and a private beach. Sites are mostly grassy with a typical site width of 35 feet. There are 20 seasonals that maintain their sites nicely. It's an eight-mile walk to Lake Michigan and its white "singing sands." The campground has a rustic tent area for more green space and privacy. A fishing license is required to fish in the lake. The turn-of-the-century pavilion is now used for recreation and as a meeting place for groups. It is one of the few such pavilions remaining in Michigan.

Basics

Operated by: Reginald Yaple. **Open:** May 15–Oct. 15. **Site Assignment:** Reservations w/ 1-night deposit; refund w/ 2-week notice. **Registration:** At campground office. **Fee:** $26 (cash, check, credit cards). **Parking:** At site.

Facilities

Number of RV Sites: 65. **Number of Tent-Only Sites:** 20. **Hookups:** Electric (20, 30 amps), water, sewer. **Each Site:** Picnic table, fire ring. **Dump Station:** Yes. **Laundry:** No. **Pay Phone:** Yes. **Rest Rooms and Showers:** Yes. **Fuel:** No. **Propane:** No. **Internal Roads:** Gravel, in good condition. **RV Service:** No. **Market:** 1 mi. **Restaurant:** 1 mi. **General Store:** Yes, limited. **Vending:** Yes. **Swimming Pool:** No. **Playground:** Yes. **Other:** Bass Lake, boat dock, game room, rec hall, pavilion, coin games, swimming beach, horseshoes, boat ramp. **Activities:** Swimming, fishing, boating (rental canoe, paddleboats available) scheduled weekend activities. **Nearby Attractions:** Hart-Montague Bike Trail, state parks, White Pine Village, Rose Hawley Museum, lighthouses, Shrine of the Pines, English Double-Decker Bus Tour, historic homes, antiques, Lake Michigan Carferry. **Additional Information:** Pentwater Chamber of Commerce, (231) 869-4150.

Restrictions

Pets: Leash only. **Fires:** Fire ring only. **Alcoholic Beverages:** Permitted. **Vehicle Maximum Length:** None.

To Get There

From north junction US 31 and Business US 31, drive 0.75 mi. west on Business US 31, then 1 mi. north on Lake Shore Dr. Roads are mostly wide and well maintained w/ adequate shoulders.

PETERSBURG

Monroe County KOA Kampground

US 23 at Exit 9, Petersburg 49270. T: (734) 856-4972; F: (734) 856-8224; www.koa.com.

RV ★★★★ Tent ★★★★

Beauty: ★★★★	Site Privacy: ★★★★
Spaciousness: ★★★★	Quiet: ★★★★
Security: ★★★★	Cleanliness: ★★★★★
Insect Control: Yes	Facilities: ★★★★

Nestled in maple, oak, and pine trees, Monroe County KOA Kampground is nine miles north of the Ohio line. Sites are grassy and mostly shaded. Laid out in a series of loops, the campground has a typical site width of 35 feet and 47 pull-through sites. There are no seasonal campers. A two-acre sandy-beach swimming lake is a popular draw. The beach is cleaned and dragged several times a week.

The lake has two aerators putting oxygen in the lake year-round. Quiet hours are from 11 p.m. to 7 a.m., when no radio, TV or voices are to be heard beyond each camping site. No subwoofers on car stereos are allowed at any time. No golf carts or generators are allowed. Security includes traffic control gates and owners who live on the site and provide campground patrols.

Basics

Operated by: Ray & Donna Crots. **Open:** Apr. 13–Oct. 13. **Site Assignment:** Reservations w/ $50 deposit; refund (less half) w/ 48-hour notice. **Registration:** At campground office. **Fee:** $30 (cash, check, credit cards). **Parking:** At site.

Facilities

Number of RV Sites: 230. **Number of Tent-Only Sites:** 50. **Hookups:** Electric (20, 30, 50 amps), water, sewer. **Each Site:** Picnic table, fire ring. **Dump Station:** Yes. **Laundry:** Yes. **Pay Phone:** Yes. **Rest Rooms and Showers:** Yes. **Fuel:** No. **Propane:** Yes. **Internal Roads:** Gravel, in good condition. **RV Service:** No. **Market:** 5 mi. south in Lambertville. **Restaurant:** 5 mi. south in Lambertville. **General Store:** Yes. **Vending:** Yes. **Swimming Pool:** No. **Playground:** Yes. **Other:** Rec hall, fishing lake, mini golf, shuffleboard, tetherball, basketball, horseshoes, baseball, trout pond, volleyball, club room, rental cabins, water slides, sandy beach, coin games, food wagon. **Activities:** Swimming, fishing, boating (rental rowboats, canoes, kayaks, paddleboats available), schedule weekend activities. **Nearby Attractions:** Golf, Cabela's, Cedar Point, Toledo Center of Science & Industry, Greenfield Village, Monroe Co. Historical Museum, River Raisin Battlefield, Sauders Farm & Craft Village, Toledo Zoo, Yankee Air Museum, antiques. **Additional Information:** Monroe County Convention & Tourism Bureau, (800) 252-3011.

Restrictions

Pets: Leash only, $2 extra. **Fires:** Fire rings only; must be extinguished by 11 p.m. **Alcoholic Beverages:** At sites only. **Vehicle Maximum Length:** 40 ft.

To Get There

From the junction of US 23 and Hwy. 50, drive 9 mi. south on US 23, then 200 yards southeast on Summerfield Rd., then 10 yards east on Tunnicliffe Rd. Roads are wide and well maintained w/ broad shoulders.

PETERSBURG

Pirolli Park

6030 Sylvania-Petersburg Rd., Petersburg 49270. T: (734) 279-1487

RV ★★★ Tent ★★★

Beauty: ★★★	Site Privacy: ★★★
Spaciousness: ★★★	Quiet: ★★★
Security: ★★★★	Cleanliness: ★★★
Insect Control: Yes	Facilities: ★★★

When leaving Pirolli Park, visitors are not only bade farewell and asked to drive safely, they are also given directions to US 23. Every major stop also has signs directing travelers to the main road. More campgrounds should pick up on that useful idea. Laid out in a series of loops, the campground has 45 seasonal campers, 20 pull-through sites and a typical site width of 30 feet. Sites are level and mostly shaded. Located two miles south of Petersburg, the campground does not allow outside firewood to be brought into the area because of infectious tree diseases such as Dutch Elm Disease and because of gypsy moths. Firewood is for sale at the campground. Scheduled activities include such creative themes as cowboys-and-Indians weekend (where children make their own Native American headdress and get an Native American name), grandparents weekend, and law enforcement weekends. Security includes one entrance/exit road, owners who live on site, and regular campground patrols.

Basics

Operated by: James & Pat Pirolli. **Open:** All year. **Site Assignment:** Reservations w/ 1-night deposit; refund w/ 7-day notice. **Registration:** At camp office. **Fee:** $29 (check, credit). **Parking:** At site.

Facilities

Number of RV Sites: 200. **Number of Tent-Only Sites:** 50. **Hookups:** Electric (20, 30, 50 amps), water, sewer. **Each Site:** Picnic table, fire ring. **Dump Station:** Yes. **Laundry:** Yes. **Pay Phone:** Yes. **Rest Rooms and Showers:** Yes. **Fuel:** No. **Propane:** Yes. **Internal Roads:** Paved/gravel, in good condition. **RV Service:** No. **Market:** 2 mi. north in Petersburg. **Restaurant:** 2 mi. north in Petersburg. **General Store:** Yes, well equipped, also sells beer, wine & liquor. **Vending:** Yes. **Swimming Pool:** No. **Playground:** Yes. **Other:** Swimming lake, fishing lake, sports field, horseshoes, volleyball, pavilion, rec hall, driving range, pavilion. **Activities:** Swimming, fishing, scheduled weekend activities. **Nearby Attractions:** Golf, Cabela's, Cedar Point, Toledo Center of Science & Industry, Greenfield Village, Monroe Co. Historical Museum, River Raisin Battlefield, Sauder Farm & Craft Village, Toledo Zoo, Yankee Air Museum, antiques. **Additional Information:** Monroe County Convention & Tourism Bureau, (800) 252-3011.

Restrictions

Pets: Leash only, no rottweilers, chows, pitbulls, dobermans, German Shepherds are allowed. **Fires:** Fire ring only. **Alcoholic Beverages:** At sites only. **Vehicle Maximum Length:** 50 ft.

To Get There

From the junction of US 23 and Summerfield Rd., take Exit 9, drive 0.25 mi. north on Summerfield Rd., then 1.5 mi. west on Teal Rd., then 1.5 mi. southwest on Ida Center Rd., then 0.25 mi. south on Sylvania-Petersburg Rd. Roads are generally wide and well maintained w/ broad shoulders, sometimes becoming narrow shoulders.

PETERSBURG

Totem Pole Park

16333 Lulu Rd., Petersburg 49270. T: (800) 227-2110; F: (734) 279-2113; totem@cass.net.

RV ★★★ Tent ★★★

Beauty: ★★★	Site Privacy: ★★★
Spaciousness: ★★★	Quiet: ★★★★
Security: ★★★★	Cleanliness: ★★★★
Insect Control: None	Facilities: ★★★

A rural campground with open and shaded sites, Totem Pole Park is located three miles east of Petersburg. Laid out in a series of loops, the campground has 65 seasonal campers, 13 pull-through sites, and a typical site width of 35 feet. A nice playground features a wooden train and wooden fort. No motors are allowed on the lake, nor are metal, wooden or fiberglass boats. The lake area closes at dark. Most popular RV sites are the 13 pull-throughs. The best tent sites are 120–130 which are grassy and wooded, and offer more privacy. The speed limit is five mph, and no off-road vehicles such as motorcyles and ATVs are allowed.The campground adjoins state game land and offers a sandy bottom lake for swimming. Security includes one entrance/exit road and owners who live on site and offer patrols of the campground.

Basics

Operated by: Carl & Joyce Laming. **Open:** Apr. 15–Oct. 15. **Site Assignment:** Reservations w/ 1-night deposit; refund (minus $5) w/ 7-day notice. **Registration:** At campground office. **Fee:** $24 (cash, check, credit cards). **Parking:** At site.

Facilities

Number of RV Sites: 119. **Number of Tent-Only Sites:** 11. **Hookups:** Electric (30, 50 amps), water, sewer. **Each Site:** Picnic table, fire ring. **Dump Station:** Yes. **Laundry:** No. **Pay Phone:** Yes. **Rest Rooms and Showers:** Yes. **Fuel:** No. **Propane:** No. **Internal Roads:** Gravel, in good condition. **RV Service:** No. **Market:** 10 mi. north in Dundee. **Restaurant:** 3 mi. west in Petersburg. **General Store:** Yes. **Vending:** Yes. **Swimming Pool:** No. **Playground:** Yes. **Other:** Swimming beach, pond fishing, basketball, horseshoes, sand volleyball, rental cabins, shuffleboard, pavilion, sports field. **Activities:** Swimming, fishing, scheduled weekend activities. **Nearby Attractions:** Golf, Cabela's, Cedar Point, Toledo Center of Science & Industry, Greenfield Village, Monroe Co. Historical Museum, River Raisin Battlefield, Sauders Farm & Craft Village, zoo, Yankee Air Museum, antiques. **Additional Information:** Monroe County Convention & Tourism Bureau, (800) 252-3011.

Restrictions

Pets: Leash only. **Fires:** Fire ring only. **Alcoholic Beverages:** Permitted. **Vehicle Maximum Length:** None.

To Get There

From the junction of US 23 and Summerfield Rd., take Exit 9, drive 2.5 mi. north on Summerfield Rd., then 0.25 mi. west on Lulu Rd. Summerfield Rd. is paved but bumpy; Lulu Rd. has a rough gravel surface.

PETOSKEY

Petoskey KOA

1800 North US 31, Petoskey 49770. T: (800) 933-1574; www.petoskeykoa.com; petkoa@msn.com.

RV ★★★★★ Tent ★★★★

Beauty: ★★★★★	Site Privacy: ★★★★★
Spaciousness: ★★★★★	Quiet: ★★★★★

Security: ★★★★★ Cleanliness: ★★★★★
Insect Control: ★★★★★ Facilities: ★★★★★

In a vacation wonderland, Petoskey KOA is a camper's dream. Facilities are top-notch, cleanliness is A+, activities are varied and many, security and safety measures are excellent, and the folks who run the campground are friendly and hardworking. Campers return again and again to this Petoskey campground, and begin to feel part of the Rose family. Laid out in a series of loops, the campground offers level, open, and shaded sites in sloping and level terrain. There are 31 pull-through sites. Nice landscaping and attention to detail make Petoskey KOA a pleasure to see. No mats or carpets are permitted on grass or ground to keep the area nice. A recreation and activities director has a wealth of programs, including nature programs to educate as well as entertain. A gazebo kitchen with electric cooking burners, sinks, and picnic tables is a welcome facility for campers. A Fun Bus makes it easy to catch the shuttle and leave your car at home or parked with the camper. Security measures include a card-coded gate. A speed limit of five mph is enforced.

Basics

Operated by: The Rose Family. **Open:** Apr. 27–Oct. 15. **Site Assignment:** Reservations w/ 1-night deposit; refund w/ 2-week notice. **Registration:** At campground office. **Fee:** $30 (cash, check, credit cards). **Parking:** At site.

Facilities

Number of RV Sites: 169. **Number of Tent-Only Sites:** 6. **Hookups:** Electric (20, 30, 50 amps), water, sewer, phone, cable TV. **Each Site:** Picnic table, fire ring. **Dump Station:** Yes. **Laundry:** Yes. **Pay Phone:** Yes. **Rest Rooms and Showers:** Yes. **Fuel:** No. **Propane:** Yes. **Internal Roads:** Paved/gravel, in good condition. **RV Service:** No. **Market:** 1 mi. **Restaurant:** 1 mi. **General Store:** Yes. **Vending:** Yes. **Swimming Pool:** Yes. **Playground:** Yes. **Other:** Hot tub, horseshoes, rec hall, sports field, rental cabins, game room, movies, rental cottages, coin games, volleyball, nature classes, recreation & activities director, local tours, rental cottages, shuttle bus, rental cars. **Activities:** Swimming, schedule activities. **Nearby Attractions:** Golf, marina, go-carts, bike trails, horseback riding, Lake Michigan Beach, Mackinac Island, casino, Tunnel of Trees Drive, historic Bay View, Little Traverse Bay, antiques, Little Traverse Historical Museum. **Additional Information:** Petoskey/Harbor Springs/ Boyne County Visitors Bureau, (800) 845-2828.

Restrictions

Pets: Leash only. **Fires:** In fire ring. **Alcoholic Beverages:** Permitted. **Vehicle Max. Length:** None.

To Get There

From the junction of Hwy. 119 and US 31, drive 1 mi. north on US 31. Roads are wide and well maintained w/ broad shoulders.

PORT HURON

Fort Trodd Family Campground Resort

6350 Lapeer Rd., Clyde 48049. T: (810) 987-4889

 ★★★★ ▲ n/a

Beauty: ★★★★ Site Privacy: ★★★★
Spaciousness: ★★★★ Quiet: ★★★★
Security: ★★★★ Cleanliness: ★★★★★
Insect Control: ★★★★★ Facilities: ★★★★

A campground can't get much more convenient than Fort Trodd Family Campground Resort, just a stone's throw from I-69. The grassy campground is nicely landscaped with a typical site width of 30 feet. Situated beside a 40-acre, spring-fed lake, the campground has three swimming beaches. The lake is stocked with largemouth bass and northern pike. Air-conditioned camping cabins for rent on an island are a nice addition. Located six miles west of Port Huron, the campground has 65 seasonal sites and 26 pull-throughs. Sites are a mix of paved, gravel, or grass with open or shade. Be aware that no tents are allowed. Facilities are sparkling-clean and well maintained. A group camping area is available with a pavilion. Security measures include a card-coded security gate.

Basics

Operated by: Tom & Kathy Hess. **Open:** May 1–Sept. 30. **Site Assignment:** Reservations w/ 1-night deposit; refund w/ 7-day notice. **Registration:** At campground office. **Fee:** $28 (cash, check, credit cards). **Parking:** At site.

Facilities

Number of RV Sites: 185. **Number of Tent-Only Sites:** 0. **Hookups:** Electric (20, 30, 50 amps), water, sewer. **Each Site:** Picnic table, fire ring. **Dump Station:** Yes. **Laundry:** Yes. **Pay Phone:** Yes. **Rest Rooms and Showers:** Yes. **Fuel:** No. **Propane:** No. **Internal Roads:** Paved, in good condition. **RV Service:** No. **Market:** Two blocks. **Restaurant:** Two blocks. **General Store:** Yes. **Vending:** Yes. **Swimming Pool:** No. **Playground:** Yes. **Other:** Lake Tomka, 3 swimming beaches, rental cabin, pavilion, rec hall, coin games, basketball, shuffleboard, tennis, badminton, sports field, horseshoes, hiking trials, volleyball. **Activities:** Swimming, hiking, fishing, boating (rental canoes, kayaks, paddleboats available), scheduled weekend activities. **Nearby Attractions:** Parks, Fort Gratiot Lighthouse, Huron Lightship Museum, historic district, antiques, arts & crafts, golf, Port Huron Museum, Canadian International Border. **Additional Information:** Blue Water Area CVB, (800) 852-4242.

Restrictions

Pets: Leash only. **Fires:** Fire ring only. **Alcoholic Beverages:** Permitted. **Vehicle Maximum Length:** None. **Other:** No tents allowed.

To Get There

From the junction of I-69 and Barth Rd., take Exit 194 and drive 500 feet north on Barth Rd. Roads are wide and well maintained w/ broad shoulders.

PORT HURON

Port Huron KOA

5111 Lapeer Rd., Kimball 48074. T: (810) 987-4070; www.koa.com/where/mi; phkoa@aol.com.

 ★★★★ ▲ ★★★★

Beauty: ★★★★ Site Privacy: ★★★★
Spaciousness: ★★★★ Quiet: ★★★
Security: ★★★★★ Cleanliness: ★★★★
Insect Control: ★★★★ Facilities: ★★★★★

Just a stone's throw from the Canadian border, Port Huron KOA is a combination amusement park/ campground. Located five miles west of Port Huron, the campg has enough activities to keep anyone hopping from morning into the night. Many activities like hayrides, train rides and movies are free but many others will need a ready supply of coins. Air conditioned rest rooms, a western town and two swimming pools are nice touches, as are the 1–6 passenger rental bikes. Sites are mostly level with a choice of open or heavily shaded. The campground has 56 pull-throughs and a typical site width of 42 feet. A separate area for tents allows for more privacy and green space. The best sites depend on what the goal of the camper is—if it's to enjoy all the activities with children, then sites close to the recreation are best; if it's to get some peace and commune with nature, then stay as far away from the recreation as possible.

Basics

Operated by: Private Operator. **Open:** Apr. 1–Oct. 31. **Site Assignment:** Reservations w/ 1-night deposit; refund w/ 2-week notice. **Registration:** At campground office. **Fee:** $28 (cash, check, credit cards). **Parking:** At site.

Facilities

Number of RV Sites: 313. **Number of Tent-Only Sites:** 33. **Hookups:** Electric (20, 30, 50 amps), water, sewer, phone, cable TV. **Each Site:** Picnic table, fire ring. **Dump Station:** Yes. **Laundry:** Yes. **Pay Phone:** Yes. **Rest Rooms and Showers:** Yes. **Fuel:** No. **Propane:** No. **Internal Roads:** Paved/gravel, in good condition. **RV Service:** No. **Market:** 1 mi. **Restaurant:** 1 mi. **General Store:** Yes. **Vending:** Yes. **Swimming Pool:** Yes. **Playground:** Yes. **Other:** Adventure golf, batting cages, bumper boats, game room, Western Town, go-kart track, soccer, tennis, in-line skating rink, sports shop, Pursuit Park Paint Ball, rental cottages, train rides, pavilion, coin games, sports field, horseshoes, hiking trails, volleyball, basketball, baseball. **Activities:** Swimming, hiking, scheduled activities, movies. **Nearby Attractions:** Parks, Fort Gratiot Lighthouse, Huron Lightship Museum, historic district, antiques, arts & crafts, golf, Port Huron Museum, Canadian International. **Additional Information:** Blue River Area CVB, (800) 852-4242.

Restrictions

Pets: Leash only. **Fires:** Fire ring only. **Alcoholic Beverages:** Permitted. **Vehicle Maximum Length:** None.

To Get There

From the junction of I-69 and Wadhams Rd., take Exit 196 and drive 0.5 mi. north on Wadhams Rd., then 0.25 mi. east on Lapeer Rd. Roads are mostly wide and well maintained w/ adequate shoulders.

QUINCY

Cottonwood Resort

801 West Wildwood Rd., Quincy 49082. T: (517) 639-4415

 ★★★★ ▲ ★★★★

Beauty: ★★★★ Site Privacy: ★★★
Spaciousness: ★★★ Quiet: ★★★★
Security: ★★★ Cleanliness: ★★★★
Insect Control: None Facilities: ★★★

Marble Lake is the centerpiece of Cottonwood Resort, located eight miles southeast of Coldwater. The lake leads into Branch County's Chain of Lakes, offering 2,500 acres of water in six lakes for fishing and water activities. A rural campground with shaded level sites, Cottonwood has 78 of its sites occupied by seasonal campers, leaving 15 for short-term campers. The typical site width is 25 feet, and the campground has four pull-throughs. Quiet time is 11 p.m. to 7 a.m., and the speed limit is five mph. The campground offers easy access from the interstate but, be sure to check that a site is available before planning to stop. Owners live on site to help with security measures.

Basics

Operated by: Barney & Eunice Pohl, Roy, Darla & Bailey Pohl. **Open:** May 1–Oct. 15. **Site Assignment:** Reservations w/ 1-night deposit; refund w/ 7-day notice. **Registration:** At campground office. **Fee:** $24 (cash, check). **Parking:** At site.

Facilities

Number of RV Sites: 93. **Number of Tent-Only Sites:** 4. **Hookups:** Electric (30 amps), water, sewer. **Each Site:** Picnic table, fire ring. **Dump Station:** Yes. **Laundry:** No. **Pay Phone:** Yes. **Rest Rooms and Showers:** Yes. **Fuel:** No. **Propane:** Yes. **Internal Roads:** Gravel, in good condition. **RV Service:** No. **Market:** 8 mi. northwest in Coldwater. **Restaurant:** 8 mi. northwest in Coldwater. **General Store:** Yes, limited. **Vending:** Yes. **Swimming Pool:** No. **Playground:** Yes. **Other:** Marble Lake, swimming beach, rental cottages, horseshoes, rec hall, video games, volleyball, boat ramp, sports field. **Activities:** Swimming, fishing, boating (rental fishing boats available). **Nearby Attractions:** Bowling, golf, summer theater, Branch County Historical Society, antiques, drive-in theaters, motor speedway, historic homes, museums, arts & crafts shops. **Additional Information:** Branch County Tourism Bureau, (800) 969-9333.

Restrictions

Pets: Leash only. **Fires:** Fire ring only. **Alcoholic Beverages:** Permitted. **Vehicle Maximum Length:** None.

To Get There

From the junction of I-69 and US 12; drive 4.75 mi. east on US 12, then 2.25 mi. south on Main St. and Ray Quincy Rd., then 1 mi. west on Wildwood Rd. Roads are wide and well maintained w/ broad shoulders.

RAPID RIVER

Whitefish Hill Mobile Home & RV Park

8455 US 2, Rapid River 49878. T: (800) 476-6515; whtfish@up.net.

RV ★★★ Tent ★★

Beauty: ★★★ Site Privacy: ★★★
Spaciousness: ★★★ Quiet: ★★★
Security: ★★★ Cleanliness: ★★★★
Insect Control: ★★★★ Facilities: ★★★

An RV area in a mobile home park, Whitefish Hill Mobile Home & RV Park is just one-and-a-half miles from access waters to Little Bay De Noc. Located two miles east of Rapid River, the campground offers open, level, grassy sites with eight pull-throughs. The typical site width is 30 feet. A nice benefit is facilities that are open 24 hours a day. The focal point of the park is an old barn that houses an office, showers, small kitchen, and activity room. The campground is a popular base for fishing and hunting. Whitefish Hill opens earlier in the season and stays open later than many other campgrounds, which makes it handy for outdoor enthusiasts who want a home base that is modern rather than rustic. Security includes owners who live on site and keep an eye on the campground.

Basics

Operated by: Ed & Pat Violette. **Open:** Apr. 30–Nov. 30. **Site Assignment:** Reservations w/ 1-night deposit; refund w/ 7-day notice. **Registration:** At campground office. **Fee:** $25 (cash, check, credit cards). **Parking:** At site.

Facilities

Number of RV Sites: 23. **Number of Tent-Only Sites:** 2. **Hookups:** Electric (30, 50 amps), water, sewer, cable TV, phone. **Each Site:** Picnic table, fire ring. **Dump Station:** Yes. **Laundry:** Yes. **Pay Phone:** Yes. **Rest Rooms and Showers:** Yes. **Fuel:** No. **Propane:** No. **Internal Roads:** Paved/gravel, in good condition. **RV Service:** No. **Market:** 1 mi. **Restaurant:** 1 mi. **General Store:** No. **Vending:** Yes. **Swimming Pool:** No. **Playground:** Yes. **Other:** Game room, rental RVs, sports field, horseshoes, basketball, sauna, fish-cleaning station. **Activities:** None. **Nearby Attractions:** Little Bay De Noc, fishing, swimming, boating, scenic drives, Lake Michigan, Delta County Historical Museum, Sandpoint Lighthouse, antiques, arts & crafts. **Additional Information:** Delta County Area Chamber of Commerce, (888) 335-8264.

Restrictions

Pets: Leash only. **Fires:** Fire ring only. **Alcoholic Beverages:** Permitted. **Vehicle Maximum Length:** None.

To Get There

From US 2 and US 41, drive 2.5 mi. east on US 2. Roads are wide and well maintained w/ adequate shoulders.

ROSCOMMON

Higgins Hills RV Park

3800 West Federal Hwy., Roscommon 48653. T: (800) 478-8151; www.michcampgrounds.com/higginshills; snow@snowshoecenter.com.

RV ★★★★ Tent ★★★★

Beauty: ★★★★ Site Privacy: ★★★★
Spaciousness: ★★★★ Quiet: ★★★★
Security: ★★★★ Cleanliness: ★★★★
Insect Control: ★★★★ Facilities: ★★★★

Location is everything, and Higgins Hills RV Park certainly has it. With easy access to I-75 and US 27, the campground is in a large lake resort area. Year-round activities abound, and Higgins Hills is open all year with limited facilities in the winter. One mile east of Higgins Hills, the campground offers level, shaded sites with a typical site width of 30 feet. There are 35 seasonal campers and 32 pull-through sites. The campground has abundant natural hardwoods and pine trees, deer, and other wildlife. It's only minutes to Higgins Lake and Au Sable River, and there are groomed snowmobile trails as well as cross-country and downhill skiing. The campground also is home to the Michigan Snowshoe Center, which offers a large selection of snowshoes and sporting equipment. Facilities are very clean, and owners provide on-site security.

Basics

Operated by: The Carr Family. **Open:** All year. **Site Assignment:** Reservations w/ 1-night deposit; refund w/ 7-day notice. **Registration:** At campground office. **Fee:** $25 (cash, check, credit cards). **Parking:** At site.

Facilities

Number of RV Sites: 92. **Number of Tent-Only Sites:** 8. **Hookups:** Electric (20, 30 amps), water, sewer, phone. **Each Site:** Picnic table, fire ring. **Dump Station:** Yes. **Laundry:** Yes. **Pay Phone:** Yes. **Rest Rooms and Showers:** Yes. **Fuel:** No. **Propane:** Yes. **Internal Roads:** Gravel, in good condition. **RV Service:** No. **Market:** 1 mi. **Restaurant:** 1 mi. **General Store:** Yes. **Vending:** Yes. **Swimming Pool:** No. **Playground:** Yes. **Other:** Rec room, coin games, basketball, shuffleboard, badminton, sports field, volleyball, horseshoes, hiking trails, rental cabins, rental RVs. **Activities:** Hiking, scheduled weekend activities. **Nearby Attractions:** Higgins Lake, AuSable River, fishing, canoeing, hunting, Wellington Farm Park, state parks, golf, fish hatchery, bowling, antiques, arts & crafts. **Additional Information:** Higgins Lake-Roscommon Chamber of Commerce, (989) 275-8760.

Restrictions

Pets: Leash only. **Fires:** In fire ring. **Alcoholic Beverages:** Permitted. **Vehicle Max. Length:** None.

To Get There

From the junction of I-75 and Old Hwy. 76, take Exit 244 and drive 1.25 mi. west on Old Hwy. 76. Roads are wide and well maintained w/ adequate shoulders.

SAULT ST. MARIE

Soo Locks Campground & RV Park

1001 East Portage Ave., Sault Ste. Marie 49783. T: (906) 632-3191

RV ★★★★ Tent ★★★

Beauty: ★★★ Site Privacy: ★★★
Spaciousness: ★★★ Quiet: ★★★★
Security: ★★★★ Cleanliness: ★★★★
Insect Control: ★★★★ Facilities: ★★★

Watch the freighters travel through Soo Locks from your campsite at Soo Locks Campground & RV

Park in Sault Ste. Marie. With sites on St. Mary's River, the facility is the closest campground to the locks. Sites are mostly open and grassy, with a typical site width of 25 feet. Campers also can walk to the locks and watch ships pass through. Restaurants and other facilities are within one block. The campground has ten pull-through sites. Complimentary coffee is a nice welcoming touch. Facilities are very clean and well maintained, and owners provide good security. The best sites are closest to the river. Be aware that the area can be quite cold in May and in Oct. when the campground is open. The camping experience is definitely worth it, but be sure and bring plenty of warm blankets and clothing if camping during those times.

BASICS

Operated by: Bob & Helen Collia. **Open:** May 1–Oct. 20. **Site Assignment:** Reservations w/ 1-night deposit; refund (minus $5) w/ 2-week notice. **Registration:** At campground office. **Fee:** $23 (cash, check, credit cards). **Parking:** At site.

FACILITIES

Number of RV Sites: 100. **Number of Tent-Only Sites:** 0. **Hookups:** Electric (20, 30 amps), water. **Each Site:** Picnic table, fire ring. **Dump Station:** Yes. **Laundry:** Yes. **Pay Phone:** Yes. **Rest Rooms and Showers:** Yes. **Fuel:** No. **Propane:** No. **Internal Roads:** Paved/gravel, in good condition. **RV Service:** No. **Market:** 1 block. **Restaurant:** 1 block. **General Store:** Yes. **Vending:** Yes. **Swimming Pool:** No. **Playground:** Yes. **Other:** St. Mary's River, boat dock, rec room, coin games, adults room. **Activities:** Fishing, boating, boat tours. **Nearby Attractions:** Soo Locks, Locks Park Historic Walkway, Johnston Homestead, Museum Ship Valley Camp, River of History Museum, dinner cruises, boat tours, Tower of History, casino. **Additional Information:** Sault Area Chamber of Commerce & Convention & Bureau, (800) 647-2858.

RESTRICTIONS

Pets: Leash only. **Fires:** Fire ring only. **Alcoholic Beverages:** Permitted. **Vehicle Maximum Length:** None.

TO GET THERE

From the junction of I-75 and Easterday, take Exit 394 and drive 10.1 mi. west on Easterday, then 3 mi. north and east on Portage. Roads are wide and well maintained w/ adequate shoulders.

SMYRNA
Double R Ranch Camping Resort

4424 Whites Bridge Rd., Smyrna 48887. T: (800) 734-3575; www.doubleranch.com; rrranch@path-waynet.com.

★★★★ ★★★★

Beauty: ★★★★ Site Privacy: ★★★★
Spaciousness: ★★★★ Quiet: ★★★★
Security: ★★★★ Cleanliness: ★★★★
Insect Control: ★★★★ Facilities: ★★★★

Double R Ranch Resort Campground is a ranch, resort, and campground with so much going for it, it's hard to know where to start. As a resort, it has a full slate of activities, like two heated swimming pools as well as a river and a variety of water sports. As a ranch, it has horses and one of West Michigan's best trail rides over hills, along forest paths, and fording streams, plus a bunkhouse where guests can enjoy the Wild West without roughing it. As a campground, it features camping by the river. Sites are mostly grassy and level, with a typical site width of 40 feet. The campground has ten seasonal sites and ten pull-throughs. Located 20 miles from Grand Rapids, the campground has a choice of open or shaded sites. The best sites are the wooded ones along Flat River. The Ironhorse golf course alone draws plenty of golfers with its 3,365-yard championship golf course.

BASICS

Operated by: Richard & Mary Reeves. **Open:** May 1–Sept. 15. **Site Assignment:** Reservations w/ $25 deposit; refund w/ 2-week notice. **Registration:** At campground office. **Fee:** $25 (cash, check, credit cards). **Parking:** At site.

FACILITIES

Number of RV Sites: 100. **Number of Tent-Only Sites:** 0. **Hookups:** Electric (20, 30 amps), water, sewer. **Each Site:** Picnic table, fire ring. **Dump Station:** Yes. **Laundry:** Yes. **Pay Phone:** Yes. **Rest Rooms and Showers:** Yes. **Fuel:** No. **Propane:** No. **Internal Roads:** Gravel, in good condition. **RV Service:** No. **Market:** 2 mi. **Restaurant:** 2 mi. **General Store:** Yes. **Vending:** Yes. **Swimming Pool:** Yes. **Playground:** Yes. **Other:** Flat River, rec hall, rec room, coin games, boat ramp, float trips, basketball, horseback riding trails, badminton, sports field, horseshoes, hiking trails, volleyball, snack bar, adult lounge, rental chalets, motel, 9-hole golf course. **Activities:** Swimming, fishing, golf, hiking, boating (rental canoes available), horseback riding (rental horses available), tubing, scheduled weekend activities. **Nearby Attractions:** Gerald B. Ford Museum, Fredrick Meijer Gardens, zoo, Michigan Adventure Amusement Park, Roger B. Chaffee Planetarium, golf, tennis, rivers & lakes, antiques, Wooden Shoe Factory. **Additional Information:** Grand Rapids/Kent County CVB, (800) 678-9859.

RESTRICTIONS

Pets: Leash only. **Fires:** Fire ring only. **Alcoholic Beverages:** Permitted. **Vehicle Maximum Length:** None.

TO GET THERE

From the junction of Hwy. 91 and Hwy. 44, drive 100 yards west on Hwy. 44, then 3 mi. south on White Bridge Rd. Roads are wide and well maintained w/ adequate shoulders.

ST. IGNACE
Castle Rock Mackinac Trail Campark

2811 Mackinac Tr., St. Ignace 49781. T: (800) 333-8754; www.stignace.com/lodging/castlecamp.

★★★★ ★★★★

Beauty: ★★★★ Site Privacy: ★★★★
Spaciousness: ★★★★ Quiet: ★★★★
Security: ★★★★ Cleanliness: ★★★★
Insect Control: ★★★★ Facilities: ★★★★

The sunsets alone are worth a night at Castle Rock Mackinac Trail Campark. Sites are nestled between landscaped trees on Lake Huron with half a mile of lake frontage in view of Mackinac Island. Campsites are available on or off the beach. Castle Rock provides the only beach camping on Lake Huron with a Mackinac Island view. The campground features 2,000 feet of sandy beach. Sites are level and grassy with a typical site width of 30 feet. There are six pull-throughs and a choice of open or shaded. Less than a mile from the St. Ignace city limits, the campground is next to a federal forest with trails and bird-watching. A nearby casino and a ferry service for Mackinac Island offer free shuttle service from the campground. The most popular sites are on the beach. Reservations are strongly recommended. Security includes careful watches of the campground, along with the assistance of local law officials, if necessary.

BASICS

Operated by: Charles & Delores Muscott. **Open:** May 15–Oct. 10. **Site Assignment:** Reservations w/ $10 deposit; refund w/ 3-day notice. **Registration:** At campground office. **Fee:** $20 (cash, check, credit cards). **Parking:** At site.

FACILITIES

Number of RV Sites: 65. **Number of Tent-Only Sites:** 15. **Hookups:** Electric (20, 30, 50 amps), water, sewer. **Each Site:** Picnic table, fire ring. **Dump Station:** Yes. **Laundry:** Yes. **Pay Phone:** Yes. **Rest Rooms and Showers:** Yes. **Fuel:** No. **Propane:** No. **Internal Roads:** Paved/gravel, in good condition. **RV Service:** No. **Market:** Two blocks. **Restaurant:** Two blocks. **General Store:** Yes. **Vending:** Yes. **Swimming Pool:** No. **Playground:** Yes. **Other:** Sandy beach, rec room, fishing pond, coin games, boat ramp, boat dock, badminton, sports field, horseshoes, volleyball, free casino shuttle, free ferry shuttle. **Activities:** Swimming, fishing, boating, local tours. **Nearby Attractions:** Castle Rock, Mackinac Bridge, Mackinac Island, Mackinaw City, Deer Ranch, ice arena, golf, casino, Fort De Baude Indian Museum, Marquette Mission Park & Museum of Ojibwa Culture, New France Discovery Center & Father Marquette National Memorial, Soo Locks, Ft. Michillimackinac, Tahqomenon Falls. **Additional Information:** St. Ignace Tourism Assoc., (800) 338-6660.

RESTRICTIONS

Pets: Leash only. **Fires:** Fire ring only. **Alcoholic Beverages:** Permitted. **Vehicle Maximum Length:** None.

TO GET THERE

From I-75, take Exit 348, drive 0.25 mi. south, then 0.25 mi. north on Mackinac Tr. Roads are wide and well maintained w/ broad shoulders.

ST. IGNACE
St. Ignace/Mackinac Island KOA

1242 US 2 West, St. Ignace 49781. T: (906) 643-9303; www.koa.com/where/mi; simikoa@sault.com.

★★★★ ★★★★

Beauty: ★★★★ Site Privacy: ★★★★
Spaciousness: ★★★★ Quiet: ★★★★

Security: ★★★★ Cleanliness: ★★★★★
Insect Control: ★★★★ Facilities: ★★★★

Located in the heart of Michigan vacationland, St. Ignace-Mackinac Island KOA offers easy access to I-75 and quality facilities. Sites are grassy, wooded, and secluded, with a typical site width of 50 feet, and 82 pull-throughs. Campers are greeted with a travel info packet when they register, and the friendly staff is very helpful in recommending local attractions. The campground has its own attractions—a free Indian museum and a wildlife zoo featuring a live fox, bobcat, peacock, and deer. Campers are invited to hand-feed the deer and take photos. The campground also offers free shuttles to the island ferries and casino. A separate rustic tent area provides more green space and privacy. Campground facilities are very clean, and landscaping shows extra attention to detail.

Basics

Operated by: Private Operator. **Open:** May 1–Oct. 31. **Site Assignment:** Reservations w/ 1-night deposit; refund w/ 3-day notice. **Registration:** At office. **Fee:** $28 (check, credit). **Parking:** At site.

Facilities

Number of RV Sites: 140. **Number of Tent-Only Sites:** 60. **Hookups:** Electric (20, 30 amps), water, sewer, phone. **Each Site:** Picnic table, fire ring. **Dump Station:** Yes. **Laundry:** Yes. **Pay Phone:** Yes. **Rest Rooms and Showers:** Yes. **Fuel:** No. **Propane:** No. **Internal Roads:** Gravel, in good condition. **RV Service:** No. **Market:** 1 mi. **Restaurant:** 1 mi. **General Store:** Yes. **Vending:** Yes. **Swimming Pool:** Yes. **Playground:** Yes. **Other:** Rec room, coin games, rental cabins, mini golf, badminton, sports field, hiking trails. **Activities:** Swimming, hiking, local tours, free shuttle to ferry & casino. **Nearby Attractions:** Castle Rock, Mackinac Island, Mackinaw City, Deer Ranch, ice arena, golf, casino, Fort De Baude Indian Museum, Marquette Mission Park & Museum of Ojibwa Culture, New France Discovery Center & Father Marquette National Memorial, Soo Locks, Ft. Michilli-mackinac, Tahqomenon Falls. **Additional Information:** St. Ignace Tourism Assoc., (800) 338-6660.

Restrictions

Pets: Leash only. **Fires:** Fire ring only. **Alcoholic Beverages:** Permitted. **Vehicle Maximum Length:** Inquire ahead.

To Get There

From the junction of I-75 and US 2, take Exit 344B and drive 2 mi. west on US 2. Roads are wide and well maintained w/ broad shoulders.

THOMPSON

Driftwood Shores Resort & RV Park

US 2, Thompson 49854. T: (800) 788-3111; www.wmallory.com; wmallory@up.net.

RV ★★★★ Tent n/a

Beauty: ★★★★ Site Privacy: ★★★★
Spaciousness: ★★★★ Quiet: ★★★★
Security: ★★★★ Cleanliness: ★★★★★
Insect Control: ★★★★★ Facilities: ★★★

For the right kind of camper, Driftwood Shores Resort & RV Park is a sparkling gem. Located on Lake Michigan six miles west of Manistique, the campground offers 500 feet of shoreline and a sandy beach with complimentary float tubes. The campground caters to campers ages 55 and up but is open to anyone. What campers won't find are coin games, playgrounds, and activities aimed at children. What campers will find is peaceful surroundings, great fishing and birding, and benches, swings, and gliders overlooking the lake. Campers also are welcome to complimentary videos and all the free driftwood they can burn. The campground got its name from the wealth of driftwood that continues to wash up on its shores. The driftwood is the legacy of a sawmill that used to be nearby in the 1880s. It closed in the 1930s, but the driftwood keeps coming, enough for campers to take home as souvenirs, artists to gather up for painting and carving, and still enough left over for campfires. A huge stone fireplace is available for everyone to enjoy. Security measures include owners who live on site and offer regular patrols of the campground.

Basics

Operated by: Bill & Diane Mallory. **Open:** May 1–Oct. 31. **Site Assignment:** Reservations w/ full pay; refund w/ 2-week notice. **Registration:** At campground office. **Fee:** $18 (cash, check, credit cards). **Parking:** At site.

Facilities

Number of RV Sites: 23. **Number of Tent-Only Sites:** 0. **Hookups:** Electric (30, 50 amps), water. **Each Site:** Picnic table, fire ring. **Dump Station:** Yes. **Laundry:** Yes. **Pay Phone:** Yes. **Rest Rooms and Showers:** Yes. **Fuel:** No. **Propane:** No. **Internal Roads:** Gravel, in good condition. **RV Service:** No. **Market:** 2 mi. **Restaurant:** 2 mi. **General Store:** No. **Vending:** No. **Swimming Pool:** No. **Playground:** No. **Other:** Lake Michigan, sandy beach, sports field, rental cabins, rental lodge rooms. **Activities:** Swimming, fishing, boating. **Nearby Attractions:** Lighthouse, maritime musem, golf, fish hatchery, state parks, antiques, Seney Wildlife Refuge, Big Spring, Siphon Bridge, snowmobile trails, casino, scenic drive. **Additional Information:** Schoolcraft County Chamber of Commerce, (906) 341-5010.

Restrictions

Pets: Leash only. **Fires:** Fire ring only. **Alcoholic Beverages:** Permitted. **Vehicle Maximum Length:** None.

To Get There

From the junction of Hwy. 149 and US 2 and Little Harbor Rd., drive 0.5 mi. south on Thompson Rd. Roads are mainly wide and well maintained w/ adequate shoulders.

TIPTON

Ja Do Campground

5603 US 12, Tipton 49287. T: (517) 431-2111; F: (517) 431-2390; www.michcampgrounds.com/jado.

RV ★★★ Tent ★★★

Beauty: ★★★ Site Privacy: ★★★★
Spaciousness: ★★★★ Quiet: ★★★★
Security: ★★★★ Cleanliness: ★★★★
Insect Control: ★★★★ Facilities: ★★★

Nestled in rolling hills in Tipton, Ja Do Campground offers open and shaded sites with a typical site width of 50 feet. Laid out in a series of loops, the campground has primitive sites with more green space and privacy for tent campers. The campground has 30 seasonal campers. A stocked fishing pond set in the woods has a nature trail leading to it. Quiet hours are 11 p.m. to 7 a.m., when all children must be at sites. No loud music is allowed at any time. Motorcycles, ATVs, minibikes, and scooters cannot be ridden in the campground. No bike riding is allowed after dark. Speed limit is ten mph, a bit high for such a family-friendly campground. Security is good, with owners keeping a close watch.

Basics

Operated by: Doug & Kay Miller. **Open:** May 1–Oct. 15. **Site Assignment:** Reservations w/ 1-night deposit; refund (minus $5) w/ 5-day notice. **Registration:** At campground office. **Fee:** $23 (cash, check, credit cards). **Parking:** At site.

Facilities

Number of RV Sites: 100. **Number of Tent-Only Sites:** 30. **Hookups:** Electric (30, 50 amps), water, sewer, phone. **Each Site:** Picnic table, fire ring. **Dump Station:** Yes. **Laundry:** Yes. **Pay Phone:** Yes. **Rest Rooms and Showers:** Yes. **Fuel:** No. **Propane:** Yes. **Internal Roads:** Gravel, in good condition. **RV Service:** No. **Market:** 1 mi. **Restaurant:** 1 mi. **General Store:** Yes, limited. **Vending:** Yes. **Swimming Pool:** No. **Playground:** Yes. **Other:** Pond, basketball, horseshoes, hiking trails, volleyball. **Activities:** Fishing. **Nearby Attractions:** Michigan International Speedway, Irish Hills, golf, Mystery Hill, mini-golf, waterskiing, Prehistoric Forest, museums, St. Joseph's Shrine, Stagecoach Stop USA, Irish Hills Towers. **Additional Information:** Lenawee Conference & Visitors Bureau, (800) 682-6580.

Restrictions

Pets: Leash only. **Fires:** Fire ring only. **Alcoholic Beverages:** Permitted. **Vehicle Maximum Length:** 40 ft.

To Get There

From the junction of US 12 and Hwy. 52, drive 4.5 mi. west on US 12. Roads are wide and well maintained w/ adequate shoulders.

TRAVERSE CITY

Holiday Park Campground

4860 US 31 South, Traverse City 49864. T: (231) 943-4410; www.michcampgrounds.com/holidaypark.

RV ★★★★ Tent ★★★★

Beauty: ★★★★ Site Privacy: ★★★★
Spaciousness: ★★★★ Quiet: ★★★★
Security: ★★★★ Cleanliness: ★★★★
Insect Control: ★★★★ Facilities: ★★★★

Nestled in a forest on the shores of Silver Lake, Holiday Park Campground offers quiet, level campsites with a choice of open or shade. Laid out in a loop, the campground has a typical site width of 35 feet, with 16 pull-throughs. Located seven miles south of

Traverse City, the campground is open year-round with limited facilities in the winter. The best sites are on the lakefront—sites 66–75—which have full hookups. Other sites also are available on the lake, where campers can see some grand sunsets. A sandy beach offers nice swimming. Facilities are clean and well maintained and feature such landscaping touches as a split-rail fence and flower beds.

BASICS

Operated by: Private operator. **Open:** All year. **Site Assignment:** Reservations w/ 1-night deposit; refund w/ 7-day notice. **Registration:** At camp office. **Fee:** $35 (check, credit). **Parking:** At site.

FACILITIES

Number of RV Sites: 154. **Number of Tent-Only Sites:** 0. **Hookups:** Electric (20, 30 amps), water, sewer, phone. **Each Site:** Picnic table, fire ring. **Dump Station:** Yes. **Laundry:** Yes. **Pay Phone:** Yes. **Rest Rooms and Showers:** Yes. **Fuel:** No. **Propane:** Yes. **Internal Roads:** Paved/gravel, in good condition. **RV Service:** No. **Market:** 3 mi. **Restaurant:** 3 mi. **General Store:** Yes. **Vending:** Yes. **Swimming Pool:** No. **Playground:** Yes. **Other:** Silver Lake, sandy beach, boat ramp, boat dock, basketball, badminton, horseshoes, volleyball, sports field. **Activities:** Swimming, fishing, boating (rental rowboats, kayaks, paddleboats). **Nearby Attractions:** Grand Traverse Bay, Interlochen Music Camp, Sleeping Bear Sand Dunes, casinos, golf, outlet mall, cherry orchards, beaches, winter sports, Old Mission, parks, replica schooner, museums, wineries. **Additional Information:** Traverse City CVB, (800) 872-8377.

RESTRICTIONS

Pets: Leash only. **Fires:** In fire ring. **Alcoholic Beverages:** Permitted. **Vehicle Max. Length:** None.

TO GET THERE

From south junction Hwy. 37 and US 31, drive 1 mi. west on US 31. Roads are wide and well maintained w/ adequate shoulders.

TRAVERSE CITY

Timber Ridge Campground

4050 Hammond Rd., Traverse City 49686. T: (800) 909-2327; www.michcampgrounds.com/timberridge; timberrg@traverse.net.

RV ★★★★ Tent ★★★★

Beauty: ★★★★ Site Privacy: ★★★★
Spaciousness: ★★★★ Quiet: ★★★★
Security: ★★★★ Cleanliness: ★★★★
Insect Control: ★★★★ Facilities: ★★★★

A secluded resort campground six miles east of Traverse City, Timber Ridge Campground offers gently rolling terrain. Sites are level and mostly shaded, with a typical site width of 30 feet. The campground has 43 pull-throughs and tent sites that have more green space and privacy. A lodge with a color TV, games, and fireplace is a nice amenity, especially in the winter when the area can get very cold and snow-covered. Open all year with limited facilities in the winter, the campground offers winter sports such as lighted ski trails. Timber Ridge also conducts learn-to-ski cross-country clinics throughout the season. The property borders over 60,000 acres of state land and trail systems for biking, hiking, and cross-country skiing. Reservations are recommended, particularly in July during the annual Traverse City Cherry Festival.

BASICS

Operated by: Private operator. **Open:** All year. **Site Assignment:** Reservations w/ 1-night deposit; refund (minus $10) w/ 5-day notice. **Registration:** At office. **Fee:** $38 (check, credit). **Parking:** At site.

FACILITIES

Number of RV Sites: 202. **Number of Tent-Only Sites:** 29. **Hookups:** Electric (20, 30 amps), water, sewer, phone. **Each Site:** Picnic table, fire ring. **Dump Station:** Yes. **Laundry:** Yes. **Pay Phone:** Yes. **Rest Rooms and Showers:** Yes. **Fuel:** No. **Propane:** Yes. **Internal Roads:** Paved/gravel, in good condition. **RV Service:** No. **Market:** 2 mi. **Restaurant:** 2 mi. **General Store:** Yes. **Vending:** Yes. **Swimming Pool:** Yes. **Playground:** Yes. **Other:** Wading pool, rec hall, pavilion, coin games, mini golf, basketball, shuffleball, movies, badminton, sports field, horseshoes, hiking trails, volleyball, rental cabins. **Activities:** Swimming, hiking, scheduled activities, winter sports. **Nearby Attractions:** Grand Traverse Bay, Interlochen Music Camp, Sleeping Bear Sand Dunes, casinos, golf, outlet mall, cherry orchards, beaches, winter sports, Old Mission, parks, replica schooner, museums, wineries. **Additional Information:** Traverse City CVB, (800) 872-8377.

RESTRICTIONS

Pets: Leash only. **Fires:** Fire ring only. **Alcoholic Beverages:** Not permitted. **Vehicle Maximum Length:** None.

TO GET THERE

From south junction US 31 and Hwy. 72, drive 5 mi. east on Hwy. 31/72, then 2 mi. south on Four Mile Rd., then 2 mi. east on Hammond Rd. Roads are mostly wide and well maintained w/ narrow shoulders in places.

TRAVERSE CITY

Traverse City South KOA

4050 Hammond Rd., Traverse City 49686. T: (800) 249-3203; F: (231) 947-5457; www.traversecitykoa.com; gtcamping@coslink.net.

RV ★★★★ Tent ★★★★

Beauty: ★★★★ Site Privacy: ★★★★
Spaciousness: ★★★★ Quiet: ★★★★
Security: ★★★★ Cleanliness: ★★★★
Insect Control: ★★★★ Facilities: ★★★★

Located 15 miles south of Traverse City, the Traverse City South KOA is a family campground in a quiet country setting. Sites are level and grassy with a choice of open or shaded. The typical site width is 30 feet, and the campground has eight pull-throughs. Rest rooms are very clean; someone must check on them more than the usual once a day to keep them so spiffy. A wading pool is a popular spot with toddlers and their parents. The campground is a good base for Traverse City attractions, but it is also a destination campground for families. Owners keep a close watch on the campground for security and safety measures, but they are also friendly and helpful and seem to enjoy what they are doing.

BASICS

Operated by: Dave, Cathy, Stacy & Jamie Kuebler. **Open:** May 1–Oct. 15. **Site Assignment:** Reservations w/ 1-night deposit; refund w/ 2-week notice. **Registration:** At campground office. **Fee:** $30 (cash, check, credit cards). **Parking:** At site.

FACILITIES

Number of RV Sites: 110. **Number of Tent-Only Sites:** 8. **Hookups:** Electric (20, 30, 50 amps), water, sewer, phone. **Each Site:** Picnic table, fire ring. **Dump Station:** Yes. **Laundry:** Yes. **Pay Phone:** Yes. **Rest Rooms and Showers:** Yes. **Fuel:** No. **Propane:** Yes. **Internal Roads:** Gravel, in good condition. **RV Service:** No. **Market:** 3 mi. south in Buckley. **Restaurant:** 3 mi. south in Buckley. **General Store:** Yes. **Vending:** Yes. **Swimming Pool:** Yes. **Playground:** Yes. **Other:** Rec room, rental cabins, wading pool, coin games, basketball, movies, badminton, sports field, horseshoes, volleyball, snack bar, petting farm, hiking trails, snack bar. **Activities:** Swimming, hiking, scheduled activities. **Nearby Attractions:** Grand Traverse Bay, Interlochen Music Camp, Sleeping Bear Sand Dunes, casinos, golf, outlet mall, cherry orchards, beaches, winter sports, Old Mission, parks, replica schooner, museums, wineries. **Additional Information:** Traverse City CVB, (800) 872-8377.

RESTRICTIONS

Pets: Leash only. **Fires:** In fire ring. **Alcoholic Beverages:** Permitted. **Vehicle Max. Length:** None.

TO GET THERE

From the junction of US 31 and Hwy. 37, drive 10 mi. south on Hwy. 37. Roads are wide and well maintained w/ broad shoulders.

VICKSBURG

Oak Shores Resort Campground

13496 28th St., Vicksburg 49097. T: (800) 583-0662; oakshoresresort@aol.com.

RV ★★★★ Tent ★★★★

Beauty: ★★★ Site Privacy: ★★★★
Spaciousness: ★★★★ Quiet: ★★★★
Security: ★★★★ Cleanliness: ★★★★
Insect Control: ★★★★ Facilities: ★★★★

Located halfway between Chicago and Detroit, Oak Shores Resort Campground in Vicksburg, is a popular stopping point as well as a destination in itself. Situated on Thrall Lake—a natural lake with a large sandy beach—Oak Shores is shaded by many beautiful mature oak trees. The rural campground has mostly grassy, level sites with a typical site width of 30 feet. There are 20 seasonal campers. Sites are modern or rustic with a group camping area. A heated rec hall is a nice option for groups. The best sites are closest to the lake. No motors are allowed on the lake. Facilities are clean and well maintained. Owners keep a close watch on the campground and provide security to keep it a family-oriented facility.

BASICS

Operated by: Warren & Janet Wright. **Open:** May 1–Oct. 15. **Site Assignment:** Reservations w/ 1-night deposit; refund w/ 2-week notice. **Registra-**

tion: At campground office. **Fee:** $24 (cash, check, credit cards). **Parking:** At site.

Facilities

Number of RV Sites: 117. **Number of Tent-Only Sites:** 20. **Hookups:** Electric (20, 30, 50 amps), water, sewer. **Each Site:** Picnic table, fire ring. **Dump Station:** Yes. **Laundry:** Yes. **Pay Phone:** Yes. **Rest Rooms and Showers:** Yes. **Fuel:** No. **Propane:** Yes. **Internal Roads:** Gravel, in fair condition. **RV Service:** No. **Market:** 5 mi. **Restaurant:** 5 mi. **General Store:** Yes. **Vending:** Yes. **Swimming Pool:** Yes. **Playground:** Yes. **Other:** Thrall Lake, sandy beach, rec hall, camping cabins, baseball, pavilion, hiking trails, game room, volleyball, basketball, badminton, horseshoes, boat ramp, boat dock. **Activities:** Swimming, fishing, boating (rental canoes, kayaks & paddleboats available). **Nearby Attractions:** Golf, antiques, Kalamazoo Aviation History Museum, Kalamazoo Institute of Arts, nature center, Kalamazoo Valley Museum, wineries. Gilmore Classic Car Museum, zoo. **Additional Information:** Kalamazoo County CVB, (800) 222-6363.

Restrictions

Pets: Leash only. **Fires:** Fire ring only. **Alcoholic Beverages:** Permitted. **Vehicle Maximum Length:** None.

To Get There

From I-94, take Exit 80 and drive 9 mi. south on Sprinkle Rd., then 2 mi. east on V Ave. Roads are mostly wide and well maintained w/ adequate shoulders.

WATERS

Headwaters Camping & Cabins

11687 Headwaters Court, Waters 49797. T: (989) 705-2066

RV ★★★ Tent ★★★

Beauty: ★★★ Site Privacy: ★★★★
Spaciousness: ★★★★ Quiet: ★★★★
Security: ★★★★ Cleanliness: ★★★★★
Insect Control: None Facilities: ★★★

Headwaters Court Camping & Cabins offers level, grassy sites with gravel parking spots on Bradford Lake. Located two miles south of Water, the campground also shows what a little creativity can do to brighten bathrooms. A "stone" floor and little critters painted on the walls make Headwaters' bathrooms more attractive and outdoorsy. Laid out in one big loop, the campground has five seasonals and seven pull-through sites. Sites are mostly open, with some situated right on a canal so boats can be left docked conveniently close to campsites. A welcoming extra is a free pancake breakfast every Sunday during the summer. Speed limit is five mph, and quiet hours are 10 p.m. to 9 a.m. Snowmobiling is a popular sport at the campground during winter. Security measures include one entrance/exit road, owners who live on site, and regular patrols of the campground.

Basics

Operated by: Steve & Kimi Kwapis. **Open:** All year. **Site Assignment:** Reservations w/ 1-night deposit; refund w/ 7 day notice. **Registration:** At campground office. **Fee:** $21 (cash, check, credit cards). **Parking:** At site.

Facilities

Number of RV Sites: 76. **Number of Tent-Only Sites:** 4. **Hookups:** Electric (30, 50 amps), water, sewer. **Each Site:** Picnic table, fire ring. **Dump Station:** Yes. **Laundry:** No. **Pay Phone:** No. **Rest Rooms and Showers:** Yes. **Fuel:** No. **Propane:** No. **Internal Roads:** Gravel, in good condition. **RV Service:** No. **Market:** 2 mi. north in Waters. **Restaurant:** 2 mi. north in Waters. **General Store:** No. **Vending:** Yes. **Swimming Pool:** No. **Playground:** Yes. **Other:** Bradford Lake, swimming beach, boat ramp, volleyball, horseshoes, shuffleboard, boat dock, rental cabins, pavilion,. **Activities:** Swimming, fishing, boating, scheduled weekend activities. **Nearby Attractions:** Au Sable River, golf, bowling, ice skating, Bottle Cap Museum, canoeing, horseback riding, elk viewing, antiques, arts & crafts. **Additional Information:** Grayling Area Visitors Council, (800) 937-8837.

Restrictions

Pets: Leash only, proof of immunizations required. **Fires:** Fire ring only. **Alcoholic Beverages:** Permitted. **Vehicle Maximum Length:** None. **Other:** No check in after 10 p.m.

To Get There

From I-75, take Exit 270, drive 0.25 mi. west on Marlett Rd., then 2 mi. south on Old 27, then 0.1 mi. west on Headwaters Court. Roads are wide and well maintained w/ broad shoulders.

ZEELAND

Dutch Treat Camping & Recreation

10300 Gordon, Zeeland 49464. T: (616) 772-4303

RV ★★★★ Tent ★★★

Beauty: ★★★ Site Privacy: ★★★★
Spaciousness: ★★★★ Quiet: ★★★★
Security: ★★★★ Cleanliness: ★★★★
Insect Control: ★★★★ Facilities: ★★★★

Right in the heart of vacationland, Dutch Treat Camping in Zeeland, offers level sites by a small pond. The campground has level sites with a choice of open or shaded sites and a typical site width of 35 feet. There are 15 seasonal campers and 44 pull-through sites. Rustic tent sites offer more green space and privacy. During May, millions of beautiful tulips provide a floral display in this western Michigan city settled by Dutch immigrants. Reservations are recommended during the annual tulip festival. Dutch Treat facilities are clean and well maintained. Most sites are grassy, but some gravel ones are available. A large deck around the heated pool is a nice bonus. A large recreation shelter is heated or air conditioned and provides a welcome spot during extreme weather. Church services are offered on Sundays. Owners make sure the campground is well monitored to maintain a friendly family atmosphere.

Basics

Operated by: Nelson Reimersma. **Open:** Apr. 1–Nov. 1. **Site Assignment:** Reservations w/ 1-night deposit; refund (minus $5) w/ 2-week notice. **Registration:** At campground office. **Fee:** $24 (cash, check, credit cards). **Parking:** At site.

Facilities

Number of RV Sites: 105. **Number of Tent-Only Sites:** 15. **Hookups:** Electric (20, 30, 50 amps), water, sewer, phone. **Each Site:** Picnic table, fire ring. **Dump Station:** Yes. **Laundry:** Yes. **Pay Phone:** Yes. **Rest Rooms and Showers:** Yes. **Fuel:** No. **Propane:** No. **Internal Roads:** Paved, in good condition. **RV Service:** No. **Market:** Two blocks. **Restaurant:** Two blocks. **General Store:** Yes, limited. **Vending:** Yes. **Swimming Pool:** Yes. **Playground:** Yes. **Other:** Pond, horseshoes, rec hall, sports field, coin games, basketball, badminton, volleyball, game room. **Activities:** Swimming, fishing, boating (rental paddleboats available). **Nearby Attractions:** Lake Macatawa, Lake Michigan, bike trails, Cappon House Museum, De Klomp Wooden Shoe & Delftware Factory, Dutch Village, Holland Museum, tulip gardens, Windmill Island, antiques, arts & crafts. **Additional Information:** Holland Area CVB, (800) 506-1299.

Restrictions

Pets: Leash only. **Fires:** Fire ring only. **Alcoholic Beverages:** Permitted. **Vehicle Maximum Length:** None.

To Get There

From the junction of Hwy. 31 and East/West Business I-196, drive 2.2 mi. east on I-96, then 0.25 mi. east on Gordon. Roads are wide and well maintained w/ broad shoulders.

Minnesota

The "land of 10,000 lakes" isn't just bragging. In fact, Minnesota actually has more than 15,000 lakes and just about any known water-related activity. It also is the reputed home of Babe the Blue Ox, sidekick to that legendary lumberman, Paul Bunyan. Don't be surprised to see Babe and Paul statues along the roadsides.

Eastern timber wolves can be found at **Voyageurs National Park,** home of one of the last colonies of eastern timber wolves left in the continental United States. To appreciate hardships settlers faced, visit the **Walnut Grove** museum with memorabilia from resident Laura Ingalls Wilder, author of the "Little House on the Prairie" books. For history, towns like **New Ulm** have an unmistakable European accent in their shops, restaurants, festivals, and breweries. Shoppers flock from around the world for the huge **Mall of America** in **Bloomington.**

With such a wealth of outdoor activities, it's appropriate that America's first snowmobile was created in Minnesota. More than 15,000 miles of snowmobile trails in state recreation areas also make winter a popular outdoor time. Ice fishing, as highlighted in the movie "Grumpy Old Men," keeps away winter boredom for dedicated anglers. One of the first rivers in the nation to be granted the Wild and Scenic designation, the **St. Croix** has an outstandingly beautiful shoreline. To preserve the natuarl beauty of the area, the **Boundary Waters Canoe Area Wilderness,** part of Superior National Forest, has banned motorized boats on most of its more than 2,500 lakes. With a name meaning "lake with river flowing through," **Bemidji's Paul Bunyan Bike Trail** is a popular route for bicycling, skating, and snowmobiling.

Throughout Minnesota are cities with curious points of interest of their own. The **Runestone Museum** is located in **Alexandria** where mystery surounds the rock found in a Minnesota farmer's field in 1898. Carvings on the rock tell the tale of a Viking voyage that ended in tragedy in 1362. Known as Spam Town USA, **Austin** pays homage to its world famous meat product, and in **Duluth,** an unusual elevator bridge is 386 feet long and spans the canal entrance to Duluth Harbor. Located near the navigational headwaters of the Mississippi River, the city of **Grand Rapid** was the birthplace of Judy Garland and offers its own yellow brick road to her historic home. The **Mayo Clinic** in **Rochester** is known for its advanced technologies and pioneering discoveries in the world of medicine. The twin cities of **Minneapolis** and **St. Paul** have distinctive personalities and enough attractions to keep folks returning time after time.

The following facilities accept payment in checks or cash only:

Camp Waub-O-Jeeg, Taylors Falls
Forest Heights RV Park, Hibbing
Gull Lake Campground, Bemidji
Hidden Valley Campground, Preston
Money Creek Haven, Houston
Pioneer Campsite, Wabasha
Red Fox Campground & RV Park, Moose Lake
Sherwood Forest Campground, Gilbert
Silver Lake RV Park, Rochester
Vagabond Village, Park Rapids

The following facilities have 20 or fewer sites:

Charles A. Lindbergh State Park, Little Falls
Country Campground, Detroit Lakes
Doty's Riverview RV Park, Pine River
Forest Heights RV Park, Hibbing
Hidden Valley Campground, Preston
Interstate State Park, Taylors Falls
Nodak Lodge, Bena
Shores of Leech Lake Campground & Marina, Walker
Silver Rapids Lodge, Ely
Sugar Bay Campground/Resort, Grand Rapids
Sullivan's Resort & Campground, Brainerd
Upper Cullen Resort & Campground, Nisswa

ALBERT LEA

Albert Lea- Austin KOA Kampground

Rte. 3, Box 15, Hayward 56043. T: (507) 373-5170

RV ★★★ Tent ★★

Beauty: ★★★ Site Privacy: ★★★
Spaciousness: ★★★★ Quiet: ★★
Security: ★★★★ Cleanliness: ★★★★
Insect Control: None Facilities: ★★★★

Many a traveling camper must have breathed a sigh of relief to see the Albert Lea-Austin KOA Kampground from the interstate. In fact, the campground is so close to the highway that only a patch of grass and a barrier of trees separates the two. Convenience, cleanliness, and security attract repeat campers. Though it's not a particularly scenic place and there are almost no scheduled activities, the campground is a welcome overnight rest for weary travelers hoping to enjoy the area attractions. The campground offers large (45 × 60), open, gravel sites, at least half of which are pull-through. RVs would fare much better than tent campers. Though the campground is surrounded by serene farm fields and a golf course is next door, the noise of the interstate is inescapable.

BASICS

Operated by: Mike & Sharon Calow. **Open:** Apr. 20–Oct. 15. **Site Assignment:** Reservations w/ 1-night deposit; refund w/ notice by 4 p.m. the day before arrival. **Registration:** At campground office. **Fee:** $28 (cash, check, credit cards). **Parking:** At site.

FACILITIES

Number of RV Sites: 100. **Number of Tent-Only Sites:** 23. **Hookups:** Electric (30 amp), water, sewer. **Each Site:** Picnic table, fire ring. **Dump Station:** Yes. **Laundry:** Yes. **Pay Phone:** Yes. **Rest Rooms and Showers:** Yes. **Fuel:** No. **Propane:** Yes. **Internal Roads:** Gravel, in good condition. **RV Service:** No. **Market:** 3 mi. west in Hayward. **Restaurant:** 7 mi. west in Albert Lea. **General Store:** Yes. **Vending:** Yes. **Swimming Pool:** Yes. **Playground:** Yes. **Other:** Nature trail, volleyball, horseshoes, game room, recreation field. **Activities:** Swimming, scheduled activities on holiday weekends. **Nearby Attractions:** Golf, Cabelo's, Mall of America, Story Lady Doll & Toy Museum, Freeborn County Museum & Historical Village, nature center, lake. **Additional Information:** Albert Lea—Freeborn County CVB, (800) 345-8414.

RESTRICTIONS

Pets: Leash only. **Fires:** Fire ring only. **Alcoholic Beverages:** Permitted. **Vehicle Maximum Length:** None.

TO GET THERE

From the junction of I-35 and I-90, take Exit 166 and drive 8 mi. east on I-90, then 0.5 mi. northeast on CR 46. Roads are wide and well maintained w/ broad shoulders.

ALBERT LEA

Hickory Hills Campground

Rte. 1, Box 166A, Albert Lea 56007. T: (866) 233-3680; F: (507) 852-2068; www.hickoryhillscampground.com; daveklug@smig.net.

RV ★★★ Tent ★★

Beauty: ★★★ Site Privacy: ★★★
Spaciousness: ★★★ Quiet: ★★★★
Security: ★★★★ Cleanliness: ★★★
Insect Control: Yes Facilities: ★★★

In 1999, Hickory Hills Campground got new owners, and they've been working hard to fix it up. Showers and rest rooms have been fixed up, and the campground area has been regularly weeded and mowed. Located in a rural area with shaded, wooded sites, the campground is off the beaten path and has little outside noise. The only noise would be whatever the campers bring with them, and the owners try to keep that to a minimum. Sites are generally 30 × 60 with about 12 pull-through sites. At 35 × 84, the swimming pool is bigger than those at most campgrounds. Sites 1 and 10 are the most popular RV sites because they are the first in the park, located near the playground, and offer easy access to campground amenities. Tent sites are separated from RVs, but not enough to provide much privacy. With one entrance/exit and owners who live on site and patrol the area, security is very good. Also, it would be hard to imagine anyone driving all the way out to Hickory Hills on those gravel roads for any reason other than camping.

BASICS

Operated by: Dave & Cheri Klug. **Open:** Apr. 15–Oct. 15. **Site Assignment:** Reservations accepted w/ no desposit; holiday weekends require $10 deposit. **Registration:** At campground office. **Fee:** $22 (cash, check, credit cards). **Parking:** At site.

FACILITIES

Number of RV Sites: 94. **Number of Tent-Only Sites:** 5. **Hookups:** Electric (20, 30 amps), water. **Each Site:** Picnic table, fire ring. **Dump Station:** Yes. **Laundry:** Yes. **Pay Phone:** Yes. **Rest Rooms and Showers:** Yes. **Fuel:** No. **Propane:** No. **Internal Roads:** Gravel, rough in some spots. **RV Service:** No. **Market:** 7 mi. north in Albert Lea. **Restaurant:** 7 mi. north in Albert Lea. **General Store:** Yes. **Vending:** No. **Swimming Pool:** Yes. **Playground:** Yes. **Other:** Hiking trail, horseshoes, game room, recreation field, volleyball, mini-golf. **Activities:** Swimming, hiking, scheduled activities on weekends & holdiays such as karaoke, treasure hunt, sock hop dance, hog roast. **Nearby Attractions:** Lake, Freeborn County Museum & Historical Village, Story Lady Doll & Toy Museum, golf, aquatic center. **Additional Information:** Albert Lea-Freeborn County CVB, (900) 345-8414.

RESTRICTIONS

Pets: Leash only. **Fires:** Fire ring only. **Alcoholic Beverages:** Permitted. **Vehicle Maximum Length:** None.

TO GET THERE

From the junction of I-90 and Hwy. 13/69, take Exit 154 and drive 9.75 mi. south on Hwy. 69, then follow signs for 1.5 mi. on gravel roads. Gravel roads are wide but rough in spots.

ALEXANDRIA

Eden Acres Resort

5181 Fish Hook Dr. Southwest, Alexandria 56308. T: (320) 763-7434

RV ★★ Tent ★

Beauty: ★★★ Site Privacy: ★★★
Spaciousness: ★★★ Quiet: ★★★
Security: ★★★★ Cleanliness: ★★★
Insect Control: None Facilities: ★★★

Located on the eastern shore of beautiful Lake Mary, Eden Acres Resort offers great fishing, fun swimming (when the lake water is warm enough), and other water activities. Many people come for the great fishing, and they usually aren't disappointed. Spring and fall are best for walleyes and crappies (running large at one to two pounds.). Sunfish are abundant from late June through early Aug. Northerns and bass are always waiting and put up a good fight. Unfortunately, only 7 of the 60 campground sites are not occupied by seasonals. Reservations are necessary and require a four-night minimum stay. Tents are allowed on the available sites—but it might not be much fun to be surrounded by RVs unless the tenter is really dedicated to fishing and lake activities.

BASICS

Operated by: Ron & Pat Meyers. **Open:** Apr. 15–Oct. 15. **Site Assignment:** Reservations recommended w/ a 4-night min. stay. **Registration:** At campground office. **Fee:** $25 (cash, check, credit cards). **Parking:** At site.

FACILITIES

Number of RV Sites: 60. **Number of Tent-Only Sites:** 0. **Hookups:** Electric (50 amp), water, sewer. **Each Site:** Some picnic tables. **Dump Station:** Yes. **Laundry:** Yes. **Pay Phone:** Yes. **Rest Rooms and Showers:** Yes. **Fuel:** Yes. **Propane:** No. **Internal Roads:** Gravel, in good condition. **RV Service:** No. **Market:** 5 mi. northeast in Alexandria. **Restaurant:** 5 mi. northeast in Alexandria. **General Store:** Yes. **Vending:** No. **Swimming Pool:** No. **Playground:** Yes. **Other:** Sandy beach on Lake Mary, swim area w/ raft, volleyball, horseshoes, paddleboat, lodge w/ TV, gameroom, video games, pinball, boats, motors, pntoon, boat lifts, boat launch. **Activities:** Fishing, swimming, boating (rentals available). **Nearby Attractions:** Golf, tennis, theater, shopping mall, antique stores, amusement park, Runestone Museum. **Additional Information:** Alexandria Lakes Area Chamber of Commerce, (800) 245-2539.

RESTRICTIONS

Pets: Leash only. **Fires:** Fire ring only. **Alcoholic Beverages:** Permitted. **Vehicle Maximum Length:** 40 ft. **Other:** Must stay 4-night min.

To Get There

Take Exit 100 on I-94, drive 1.75 mi. west on Hwy. 27W, drive 1 mi. east on Lake Mary Rd. Lake Mary Rd. is gravel, in good condition.

ALEXANDRIA

Sun Valley Resort and Campground

10045 State Hwy. 27, Alexandria 56308. T: (320) 886-5417; F: (320) 886-5217; www.alexandriamn.com/sunvalley; sunvalley@rea-alp.com.

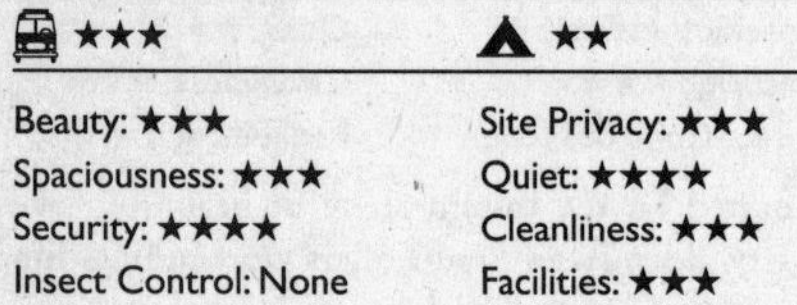

RV ★★★ Tent ★★

Beauty: ★★★ Site Privacy: ★★★
Spaciousness: ★★★ Quiet: ★★★★
Security: ★★★★ Cleanliness: ★★★
Insect Control: None Facilities: ★★★

Located on Mill Lake, Sun Valley Resort and Campground has all but 30 of its sites occupied by seasonal campers, but the seasonals are generally located in clumps away from the unoccupied sites. And, 15 of the most requested lakeside sites have been reserved for non-seasonal campers. Tent campers are not separated from RV campers. The campground is typically used as a destination for campers rather than as an overnight spot for travelers. The rural campground—located away from the main resort—offers level, open, and shaded sites. A well stocked bait and tackle shop offers fishing licenses and freezer service. Swimmers use the heated pool or the lake for water recreation. Conveniently, the campground offers a babysitting service.

Basics

Operated by: Jeff & Lori Carstensen. **Open:** May 1–Oct. 1. **Site Assignment:** Reservations w/ $20 fee; no refund. **Registration:** At campground office. **Fee:** $22 (cash, check, credit card). **Parking:** At site.

Facilities

Number of RV Sites: 74. **Number of Tent-Only Sites:** 0. **Hookups:** Electric (20, 30, 50 amps), water, sewer. **Each Site:** Picnic table, fire ring. **Dump Station:** Yes. **Laundry:** Yes. **Pay Phone:** Yes. **Rest Rooms and Showers:** Yes. **Fuel:** Yes. **Propane:** No. **Internal Roads:** Gravel, narrow in good condition. **RV Service:** No. **Market:** 7 mi. east in Alexandria. **Restaurant:** 7 mi. east in Alexandria. **General Store:** Yes. **Vending:** No. **Swimming Pool:** Yes. **Playground:** Yes. **Other:** Mill Lake, tennis court, mini-golf, bait & tackle shop, boat launch, piers, basketball, horseshoes, volleyball, shuffleboard, rec hall. **Activities:** Fishing, swimming, boating (rental motorboats, canoes, rowboats & paddleboats available). **Nearby Attractions:** Golf, downhill & cross-country skiing, snowmobiling, ice fishing, Runestone Museum, Fort Alexandria Agricultural Exhibit. **Additional Information:** Alexandria Lakes Area Chamber of Commerce, (800) 245-2539.

Restrictions

Pets: Leash only, $2 daily fee or $10 per week. **Fires:** Fire ring only. **Alcoholic Beverages:** Permitted. **Vehicle Maximum Length:** 32 ft. **Other:** 3-day min. for holidays.

To Get There

From the junction of I-94 and Hwy. 27, take Exit 100, drive 5 mi. west on Hwy. 27. Roads are wide and well maintained w/ broad shoulders.

ALTURA

Whitewater State Park

Rte. 1, Box 256, Altura 55910. T: (507) 932-3007; www.dnr.state.mn.us.

RV ★★ Tent ★★★★

Beauty: ★★★★ Site Privacy: ★★★★
Spaciousness: ★★★★ Quiet: ★★★★
Security: ★★★★ Cleanliness: ★★★
Insect Control: None Facilities: ★★

Established in 1919, Whitewater State Park is one of the most popular Minnesota state parks because of its dolomite cliffs, trout streams, hardwood forests, and noticeable lack of mosquitos. The absence of the pesky insects isn't because of vigilant spraying. Rather, it is the result of the fast-moving streams which don't give mosquitos a chance to breed. Located two miles south of Elba, the campground's screens of trees and plants keep it naturally quiet. Do note that the park gate is closed from 10 p.m. to 8 a.m., except to registered campers, and quiet time begins at 10 p.m. each night. The RV sites are mostly grassy and shady, with five pull-throughs. Size width varies from 15 to 30 feet. In addition to 55 tent camping sites, Whitewater also has four hike-in sites and a primitive area that can accommodate 100 tent campers. Tent campers have an edge at this wilderness campground: the tent sites outnumber the RV sites. Though rattlesnake sightings are rare, reptiles do live within the park. Hikers should report any sightings to the park office.

Basics

Operated by: State of Minnesota. **Open:** All year. **Site Assignment:** Reservations w/ 1-night fee plus $7.25 non-refundable service charge; refunds (minus $5 & $7.25 service charge) w/ 3-day notice. **Registration:** At campground office. **Fee:** $15 (cash, check, credit cards). **Parking:** At site.

Facilities

Number of RV Sites: 47. **Number of Tent-Only Sites:** 59. **Hookups:** Electric (20, 30, 50 amps). **Each Site:** Picnic table, fire ring. **Dump Station:** Yes. **Laundry:** No. **Pay Phone:** Yes. **Rest Rooms and Showers:** Yes. **Fuel:** No. **Propane:** No. **Internal Roads:** Paved, gravel, in good condition. **RV Service:** No. **Market:** 2 mi. north in Elba. **Restaurant:** 2 mi. north in Elba. **General Store:** No. **Vending:** Yes. **Swimming Pool:** No. **Playground:** No. **Other:** Whitewater River, swimming beach, volleyball, horseshoes, hiking trails, ski touring trails, naturalist, interpretive center, visitor center, handicapped accessible fishing pier. **Activities:** Hiking, fishing, swimming, cross-country ski trails, interpretive programs. **Nearby Attractions:** Mayo Clinic, art center, Mayowood Mansion, golf, Olmsted County History Center, Root River State Trail, scenic drives. **Additional Information:** Rochester CVB, (800) 634-8277.

Restrictions

Pets: Leash only. **Fires:** Fire ring only. **Alcoholic Beverages:** Not permitted. **Vehicle Maximum Length:** 50 ft. **Other:** Vehicle permits of $20 per year or $4 per day are required to enter all Minnesota state parks; 14 day stay-limit.

To Get There

From Elba, drive 2 mi. south on Hwy. 74. Roads are wide and well maintained w/ broad shoulders.

AUSTIN

Beaver Trails Campgrounds

21943 630th Ave. No. 1, Austin 55912. T: (507) 584-6611; F: (507) 584-6661; www.beavertrails.com; camping@beavertrails.com.

RV ★★★★ Tent ★★★★

Beauty: ★★★ Site Privacy: ★★★★
Spaciousness: ★★★★ Quiet: ★★★★
Security: ★★★★ Cleanliness: ★★★
Insect Control: None Facilities: ★★★★

Beaver Trails Campgrounds is four campgrounds in one. The Lodge Area is where the action is and is a favorite with families and children. As a result, it is a little noisier and crowded. The Quiet Area offers large sites (30 × 78), plenty of grass and trees, and some primitive sites. The Group Area can accommodte any size group and features pavilions for gatherings. The wooded Trails End Area has pack-in sites, chemical toilets, and plenty of solitude. It would be the best pick for tent campers. The campground is blessed with grassy, level sites each with its own tree. A big bonus for RV campers is that most of the sites are pull-throughs. It may have been unusual, but at the time of our visit, one of the campground's toilets was out of order and another wouldn't flush. With a campground this size, having two unusable toilets isn't pleasant.

Basics

Operated by: Bill & Carol Sheely. **Open:** Apr. 15–Oct. 15. **Site Assignment:** Reservations w/ $10 deposit; refund w/ 1-week notice, 2 week notice on holidays. **Registration:** At campground office. **Fee:** $26 (cash, check, credit cards). **Parking:** At site.

Facilities

Number of RV Sites: 267. **Number of Tent-Only Sites:** 13. **Hookups:** Electric (20, 30, 50 amps), water, sewer. **Each Site:** Picnic table, fire ring. **Dump Station:** Yes. **Laundry:** Yes. **Pay Phone:** Yes. **Rest Rooms and Showers:** Yes. **Fuel:** No. **Propane:** Yes. **Internal Roads:** Gravel/paved in good condition. **RV Service:** No. **Market:** 8 mi. west in Austin. **Restaurant:** 8 mi. west in Austin. **General Store:** Yes. **Vending:** Yes. **Swimming Pool:** Yes. **Playground:** Yes. **Other:** Dance hall, shuffleboard, game room, ping-pong room, volleyball, meeting room, big screen TV, pavilion, hiking trails, badminton, horseshoes, snack bar, small animal zoo, outdoor stage, mini-golf, fish pond, coin games, wading pool. **Activities:** Swimming, fishing, canoeing (rental canoes & pedal boats available), movies, activities every weekend, such as karaoke, line dancing, Christmas inJuly, kid's crafts, train rides, story time. **Nearby Attractions:** Nature center, historical center, cave, Spam Museum, historic homes, skate park, golf, bowling, snowmobile trails, speedway, hockey rink. **Additional Information:** Austin CVB, (800) 444-5713.

Restrictions

Pets: Leash only. **Fires:** Fire ring only. **Alcoholic Beverages:** Permitted. **Vehicle Maximum Length:** None.

To Get There

From the junction of US 218 and I-90, drive 7.5 mi. east on I-90, take Exit 187, drive 25 yards south on CR 20. Roads are wide and well maintained w/ broad shoulders.

BEMIDJI

Bemidji KOA

5705 Hwy. 2 West, Bemidji 56601.T: (218) 751-1792; bemidjikoa.com; kamp@bemidjikoa.com.

RV ★★★★ Tent ★★★★

Beauty: ★★★★ Site Privacy: ★★★★
Spaciousness: ★★★★ Quiet: ★★★★
Security: ★★★★ Cleanliness: ★★★★
Insect Control: Yes Facilities: ★★★★

Located in the heart of the Northwoods county, two miles west of Bemidji, this KOA has five area lakes within four miles. Tall pine, spruce, fir, and white birch trees offer shade. The campground has 28 pull-throughs, and the typical site width is 20 feet.The RV sites have a gravel pad for parking. Laid out in a loop, the rural campground has a well-stocked store and a 24-hour laundry. Primitive tent sites are situated away from the RV sites in a wooded area. Summer temperatures are generally cool with daytime highs in the 70s and 80s. It can snow in May and Oct. The owner lives on site and offers regular patrols. As a friendly touch, the campground shows free movies every night and offers free popcorn in the pavilion. Every morning, free coffee is offered in the store.

Basics

Operated by: Keith & Mary Davidson. **Open:** May 1–Oct. 15. **Site Assignment:** Reservations w/ 1-night deposit; refund w/ 7-day notice. **Registration:** At campground office. **Fee:** $28 (cash, check, credit cards). **Parking:** At site.

Facilities

Number of RV Sites: 100. **Number of Tent-Only Sites:** 11. **Hookups:** Electric (30, 50 amps), water, sewer, cable TV. **Each Site:** Picnic table, fire ring. **Dump Station:** Yes. **Laundry:** Yes. **Pay Phone:** Yes. **Rest Rooms and Showers:** Yes. **Fuel:** No. **Propane:** Yes. **Internal Roads:** Gravel, in good condition. **RV Service:** No. **Market:** 4 mi. east in Bemidji. **Restaurant:** 2 mi. east in Bemidji. **General Store:** Yes. **Vending:** No. **Swimming Pool:** Yes. **Playground:** Yes. **Other:** Mini-golf, video game room, book exchange, badminton, sports field, horseshoes, hiking trails, volleyball, rental cabins. **Activities:** Swimming, hiking, biking (rental bikes available), scheduled weekend activities. **Nearby Attractions:** Mississippi River, Paul Bunyan & Babe the Blue Ox statues, amusement parks, water slide, logging camp, fishing, golf. **Additional Information:** Bemidji Area Tourist Information, (800) 458-2223.

Restrictions

Pets: Leash only. **Fires:** Fire ring only. **Alcoholic Beverages:** Permitted. **Vehicle Maximum Length:** None.

To Get There

From the junction of US 71 and US 2, drive 2.5 mi. west on US 2. Road is wide and well maintained w/ broad shoulders.

BEMIDJI

Gull Lake Campground

Rte. 1 Box 28, Tenstrike 56683.T: (218) 586-2842; www.resortwebonline.com/gulllakecampground.

RV ★★★★ Tent ★★★★

Beauty: ★★★★ Site Privacy: ★★★★
Spaciousness: ★★★★ Quiet: ★★★★
Security: ★★★★ Cleanliness: ★★★★
Insect Control: ★★★★ Facilities: ★★★★

Overlooking Gull Lake just north of Bemidji, this campground offers 3,000 feet of lakeshore. Sites are grassy with a choice of open or shaded areas. The typical site width is a generous 45 feet, and the campground has six pull-throughs. Naturally, the best camping spots are closest to the water. Fishing is a popular pasttime here, and a clean, screened-in fish-cleaning house is located on site. Rest room and laundry facilities are very clean. Priding itself on being a quiet, family-oriented campground, Gull Lake takes measures to keep the facility safe and comfortable. The owners keep a close watch on the campground and set the mood for a friendly stay.

Basics

Operated by: Wes & Karen Nelson. **Open:** May 15–Oct. 1. **Site Assignment:** Reservations w/ 1-night deposit; refund w/ 7-day notice. **Registration:** At campground office. **Fee:** $20 (cash, check). **Parking:** At site.

Facilities

Number of RV Sites: 71. **Number of Tent-Only Sites:** 21. **Hookups:** Electric (20, 30 amps), water, sewer. **Each Site:** Picnic table, fire ring. **Dump Station:** Yes. **Laundry:** Yes. **Pay Phone:** Yes. **Rest Rooms and Showers:** Yes. **Fuel:** Yes. **Propane:** Yes. **Internal Roads:** Gravel, in good condition. **RV Service:** No. **Market:** 5 mi. south. **Restaurant:** 5 mi. south. **General Store:** Yes. **Vending:** Yes. **Swimming Pool:** Yes. **Playground:** Yes. **Other:** Gull Lake, boat ramp, fish-cleaning house, rec room, coin games, horseshoes, shuffleboard, badminton, volleyball, sports field. **Activities:** Swimming, fishing, boating (rental fishing boats, canoes, paddleboats, rowboats available), scheduled weekend activities. **Nearby Attractions:** Mississippi River, Paul Bunyan & the Blue Ox statues, amusement parks, water slide, logging camp, fishing, golf, antiques, arts & crafts. **Additional Information:** Bemidji Area Tourist Information, (800) 458-2223.

Restrictions

Pets: Leash only. **Fires:** Fire ring only. **Alcoholic Beverages:** Permitted. **Vehicle Maximum Length:** None.

To Get There

From West Junction US 2 and US 71, drive 10.5 mi. north on US 71, then 6 mi. north on CR 23. Roads are mostly wide and well maintained w/ narrow shoulders in spots.

BENA

Nodak Lodge

15080 Nodak Dr., Bena 56626.T: (800) 752-2758; www.nodaklodge.com; nodaks@means.net.

RV ★★★ Tent ★★

Beauty: ★★★ Site Privacy: ★★★
Spaciousness: ★★★ Quiet: ★★★
Security: ★★★ Cleanliness: ★★★
Insect Control: None Facilities: ★★★

A lakeside RV area in a mobile home park, Nodak Lodge offers water recreation activities galore with fishing as a highlight. Charter boats and whole- or half-day launch fishing is available as are fishing guides. The marina features a large harbor with plenty of docking space and has boat rentals, a fish-cleaning house, gas, oil, and live bait. Dock boys are on hand to assist in the marina area and will clean and package a daily catch for a small fee. As often happens in a popular campground, all the full hookup sites are occupied by seasonals. The sites are grassy, level, and open with few trees, and the typical site width is 30 feet. There are no scheduled activities at this campground. The best RV site is B3 because it is bigger and has shade. Tent campers will like Nodak Lodge for its outdoor activities but might not like being clumped with RVs and mobile homes.

Basics

Operated by: Bob & Shirley Kline. **Open:** May 1–Oct. 1. **Site Assignment:** Reservations, no deposit necessary. **Registration:** At campground office. **Fee:** $20 (cash, check, credit cards). **Parking:** At site.

Facilities

Number of RV Sites: 10. **Number of Tent-Only Sites:** 0. **Hookups:** Electric (30), water. **Each Site:** Picnic table, fire ring. **Dump Station:** Yes. **Laundry:** Yes. **Pay Phone:** Yes. **Rest Rooms and Showers:** Yes. **Fuel:** Yes. **Propane:** No. **Internal Roads:** Dirt, in fair condition. **RV Service:** No. **Market:** 20 mi. east in Deer River. **Restaurant:** 20 mi. east in Deer River. **General Store:** Yes. **Vending:** No. **Swimming Pool:** Yes. **Playground:** Yes. **Other:** Lake Winnibigoshish, tanning bed, marina, boat docks, fish-cleaning house, lodge, snack bar, game room, sports field, horseshoes, volleyball. **Activities:** Fishing, swimming, boating (rental motor boats, canoes & paddleboats available). **Nearby Attractions:** Hunting, hiking, mountain biking, fish-angling houses, fish-spearing houses, snowmobile trails, cross-country & downhill skiing.

Additional Information: Grand Rapids CVB, (800) 472-6366.

Restrictions

Pets: Leash only, $5 fee per day. **Fires:** Fire ring only. **Alcoholic Beverages:** Permitted. **Vehicle Maximum Length:** 40 ft.

To Get There

From the junction of CR 8 and US 2, drive 0.5 mi. west on US 2. Roads are wide and well maintained w/ broad shoulders.

BIG LAKE

Shady River Campground

21353 CR 5, Big Lake 55309. T: (612) 263-3705; www.shadyriver.com; shadyriver@hotmail.com.

RV ★★ Tent ★★

Beauty: ★★★ Site Privacy: ★★★
Spaciousness: ★★★★ Quiet: ★★★
Security: ★★ Cleanliness: ★★
Insect Control: ★★★ Facilities: ★★

Maple trees provide a cooling canopy at Shady River Campground located outside the town of Big Lake. The campground offers level, grassy sites with some open spots in a secluded rural location. The campground has a typical site width of 45 feet. Some sites are available on Elk River at a cost of $2 extra. Activities center around the river and include fishing, boating, and swimming. If you happen to drive through in Sept., you might be able to enjoy the annual pot-luck and pig roast. The cost is only $1, and if you bring your own utensils and something to drink, you can enjoy a festive dinner while making new friends with fellow campers.

Basics

Operated by: Dick & Arlyce Hewett. **Open:** May 1–Oct. 1. **Site Assignment:** Reservations w/ 1-night deposit; refund w/ 7-day notice. **Registration:** At campground office. **Fee:** $20 (cash, check, credit cards). **Parking:** At site.

Facilities

Number of RV Sites: 75. **Number of Tent-Only Sites:** 0. **Hookups:** Electric (20, 30, 50 amps), water, sewer. **Each Site:** Picnic table, fire ring. **Dump Station:** Yes. **Laundry:** Yes. **Pay Phone:** Yes. **Rest Rooms and Showers:** Yes. **Fuel:** No. **Propane:** Yes. **Internal Roads:** Gravel, in fair condition. **RV Service:** No. **Market:** 2 mi. south. **Restaurant:** 2 mi. south. **General Store:** Yes, limited. **Vending:** Yes. **Swimming Pool:** No. **Playground:** Yes. **Other:** Elk River, rec room, horseshoes, volleyball. **Activities:** Swimming, fishing, boating (rental canoes, tubes & paddleboats available). **Nearby Attractions:** Sherburne National Wildlife Refuge, Sand Dunes State Forest, Munsinger & Clemens Gardens, Oliver H. Kelley living history farm, scenic drives, golf, horseback riding, antiques, arts & crafts. **Additional Information:** Big Lake Chamber of Commerce, (877) 363-0549.

Restrictions

Pets: Leash only. **Fires:** Fire ring only. **Alcoholic Beverages:** Permitted. **Vehicle Maximum Length:** None.

To Get There

From the junction of Hwy. 25 and US 10, drive 2 blocks east on US 10, then 2 mi. north on CR 5. Roads are mostly wide and well maintained w/ adequate shoulders.

BRAINERD

Don and Mayva's Crow Wing Lake Campground

2393 Crow Wing Camp Rd., Brainerd 56401. T: (218) 829-6468; www.brainerd.net/~cwcamp; cwcamp@brainerd.net.

RV ★★★★ Tent ★★★★

Beauty: ★★★★ Site Privacy: ★★★★
Spaciousness: ★★★★ Quiet: ★★★★
Security: ★★★★ Cleanliness: ★★★★
Insect Control: None Facilities: ★★★★

Nestled in 40 wooded acres on the shores of 400-acre Crow Wing Lake, Don and Mayva's Crow Wing Lake Campground offers plenty of mature oak tree shade, grassy sites, and RV locations with large concrete patios. The campstore is well stocked, including a snack bar and bait section. The campground has 40 seasonal sites, leaving 60 for visiting campers. The typical site width is 30 feet, and the campground has 16 pull-throughs. While tent campers are definitely in the minority, they are provided with separate grassy, wooded sites. Started in 1970 by the Kottke's, the campground is well organized and well maintained. Concrete patios and designated parking spots help keep the grass in good condition. The campground of the security is ensured with only one entrance road that passes the office, owners who live on site, and a regular area patrol. Quiet hours—which means no radios, generators or loud voices—are strictly enforced from 10 p.m. to 8 a.m., even on weekends. Reservations are strongly recommended as the campground fills up quickly on weekends and holidays. Weekday camping is recommended for those who like to avoid the crowds.

Basics

Operated by: Don & Mayva Kottke. **Open:** May 1–Oct. 1. **Site Assignment:** Reservations accepted w/ $30 deposit; refunds (minus $5) w/ 7-day notice. 2-night min. for weekends; 3-night min. for holidays. **Registration:** At campground office. **Fee:** $29 (cash, check, credit cards). **Parking:** At site.

Facilities

Number of RV Sites: 90. **Number of Tent-Only Sites:** 10. **Hookups:** Electric (30, 50 amps), water, sewer. **Each Site:** Picnic table, fire ring. **Dump Station:** Yes. **Laundry:** Yes. **Pay Phone:** Yes. **Rest Rooms and Showers:** Yes. **Fuel:** Yes. **Propane:** No. **Internal Roads:** Gravel, in good condition. **RV Service:** No. **Market:** 10 mi. north in Brainerd. **Restaurant:** 5 mi. south in Port Ripley. **General Store:** Yes. **Vending:** Yes. **Swimming Pool:** Yes. **Playground:** Yes. **Other:** Crow Wing Lake, fish-cleaning house, boat launch, Frisbee golf, bankshot basketball, shuffleboard, badminton, softball, horseshoes, volleyball, nature trail, rec room, coin games,. **Activities:** Swimming, hiking, fishing, boating (rental motorboats, canoes, paddleboats, rowboats, pontoon boats available). **Nearby Attractions:** Raceway, casino, golf, Mille Lacs Indian Museum, Paul Bunyan Amusement Center, antique stores, art galleries, historic homes, Lindbergh State Park, Lindbergh Home & Interpretive Center. **Additional Information:** Brainerd Lakes Area Chamber of Commerce, (800) 450-2838.

Restrictions

Pets: Leash only. **Fires:** Fire ring only. **Alcoholic Beverages:** Permitted. **Vehicle Maximum Length:** None.

To Get There

From the junction of Hwys 18, 371 and 210, drive 11.5 mi. south on Hwy. 371. Roads are wide and well maintained w/ broad shoulders.

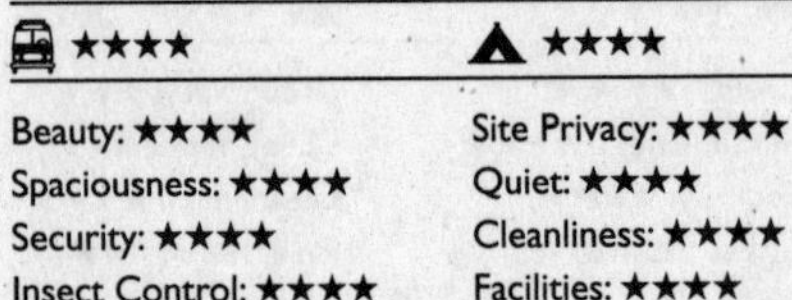

BRAINERD

Sullivan's Resort and Campground

7685 CR 127, Brainerd 56401. T: (888) 829-5697; F: (218) 828-8785; www.sullivansresort.com; vacation@sullivansresort.com.

RV ★★★★ Tent ★★★★

Beauty: ★★★★ Site Privacy: ★★★★
Spaciousness: ★★★★ Quiet: ★★★★
Security: ★★★★ Cleanliness: ★★★★
Insect Control: ★★★★ Facilities: ★★★★

Take a look at beautiful North Long Lake and the clean facilities at Sullivan's Resort and Campground, and you'll know why so many campers find their way to this spot located just three-and-a-half miles from the Paul Bunyan State Trail. The trail's first 50 miles are paved for bicycling, hiking, and skating. The campground's North Long Lake is seven miles long and three miles wide with 5,998 acres of clean, clear water. Shallow, sandy shores make the lake ideal for children and adults who like to play in the water. To accent the natural water attractions, Sullivan's also has a heated indoor-pool, a sauna, and a hot tub. Sullivan's has 16 seasonal campers, so reservations are recommended for those who wish to camp on the remaining sites. The campground has partly shaded sites on grassy, level ground along the lake. The typical site width is 30 feet, and there are no pull-throughs available.

Basics

Operated by: Lowell & Dee Sullivan. **Open:** May 1–Oct. 1. **Site Assignment:** Reservations w/ $50 non-refundable deposit. **Registration:** At campground office. **Fee:** $29 (cash, check, credit cards). **Parking:** At site. One car per site. Extra cars must be registered & parked in extra parking area.

Facilities

Number of RV Sites: 50. **Number of Tent-Only Sites:** 0. **Hookups:** Electric (20, 30, 50 amps), water, sewer. **Each Site:** Picnic table, fire ring. **Dump Station:** Yes. **Laundry:** Yes. **Pay Phone:** Yes. **Rest Rooms and Showers:** Yes. **Fuel:** Yes. **Propane:** Yes. **Internal Roads:** Gravel, in good condition. **RV Service:** No. **Market:** 8 mi. east in Brainerd. **Restaurant:** 8 mi. east in Brainerd. **Gen-**

eral Store: Yes. **Vending:** Yes. **Swimming Pool:** Yes. **Playground:** Yes. **Other:** North Long Lake, hot tub, rec room, coin games, boat dock, boat ramp, fish-cleaning house, sandy beach, fish freezing service, shuffleboard, horseshoes, volleyball, recreation field, rental cabins, large retreat home. **Activities:** Fishing, swimming, boating (rental kayaks, pontoons, motor boats, canoes, paddleboats available). **Nearby Attractions:** Paul Bunyan Bike Trail, cross-county skiing, snowmobiling, Brainerd International Raceway, antiques, arts & crafts, Crow Wing County Historical Society Museum, golf, Paul Bunyan Amusement Center. **Additional Information:** Brainerd Lakes Area Chamber of Commerce, (800) 450-2838.

Restrictions

Pets: No pets allowed. **Fires:** Fire ring only. **Alcoholic Beverages:** Permitted. **Vehicle Maximum Length:** None. **Other:** Tents & screen houses must be moved every 2–3 days on the same site; doormats & rugs not allowed on site.

To Get There

From the junction of Hwy. 210 and Hwy. 371, drive 7.5 mi. north on Hwy. 371, then 2.25 mi. northeast on CR 115, then 1 mi. east on CR 127. Roads are mostly wide and well maintained w/ adequate shoulders.

BRANDON

Kamp Kappy Family Resort and Campgrounds

13110 Devils Lake Rd. Northwest, Brandon 56315. T: (800) 845-2566; www.rea-alp.com/~bkampkap; bkampkap@rea-alp.com.

RV: ★★★ Tent: ★★★★

Beauty: ★★★★	Site Privacy: ★★★
Spaciousness: ★★★★	Quiet: ★★★★
Security: ★★★★	Cleanliness: ★★★
Insect Control: None	Facilities: ★★★

Third and fourth generations are now visiting the almost 100-year-old Kamp Kappy. Located on Devils Lake one-and-a-half miles north of Brandon, the campground has no highway or trains running by it to disturb the quiet. The only noise is what campers bring with them, and the owners work to keep that minimal. Part of a chain of lakes leading to the Minnesota River, Devils Lake is a 300-acre natural lake. Because the lake is small and stocked well, it is a relatively easy lake to fish, even in weather that would typically keep folks off most other lakes. The campground offers a fish-cleaning house with three sinks and plenty of freezer space for daily catches. The sandy swimming beach gradually slopes out to a swim dock, and the swimming area is marked with buoys. Sites are level, grassy, and shaded in this wooded lakeside campground. The typical site width is 40 feet, and the best RV sites are 1A and 2A because they provide slightly bigger pull-through spaces. Tent campers have a separate area overlooking the lake that is protected by an unobtrusive security light. With one dead-end access road, owners who live on the campground, and regular campground patrols, campers are likely to feel quite safe.

Basics

Operated by: Ray & Sharalyn Berndt. **Open:** May 1–Oct. 1. **Site Assignment:** Reservations w/ 1-night deposit; refunds (minus $15 fee) w/ 30-day notice. **Registration:** At campground office. **Fee:** $20 (cash, check, credit cards). **Parking:** At site.

Facilities

Number of RV Sites: 50. **Number of Tent-Only Sites:** 14. **Hookups:** Electric (15, 20, 30 amps), water, sewer. **Each Site:** Picnic table, fire ring. **Dump Station:** Yes. **Laundry:** No. **Pay Phone:** Yes. **Rest Rooms and Showers:** Yes. **Fuel:** Yes. **Propane:** No. **Internal Roads:** Gravel, in good condition. **RV Service:** No. **Market:** 1.5 mi. south in Brandon. **Restaurant:** 1.5 mi. south in Brandon. **General Store:** Yes. **Vending:** Yes. **Swimming Pool:** No. **Playground:** Yes. **Other:** Devils Lake, sandy beach, Ray's R/C Land (radio control hobby shop), horseshoes, volleyball, badminton, basketball, rec room, fish-cleaning facility, pavilion, boat ramp, boat dock, sports field. **Activities:** Swimming, fishing, boating (rental motorboats, pontoons, canoes & paddleboats available). **Nearby Attractions:** Golf, tennis, Runestone Museum, Fort Alexandria Agricultural Exhibit. **Additional Information:** Alexandria Lakes Area Chamber of Commerce, (800) 245-2539.

Restrictions

Pets: Leash only, $10 per pet per stay. **Fires:** Fire ring only. **Alcoholic Beverages:** Permitted. **Vehicle Maximum Length:** 35 ft.

To Get There

From the junction of I-94 and CR 7, take Exit 90 and drive 4 mi. north on CR 7, then 0.5 mi. west on access road. Roads are wide and well maintained w/ adequate shoulders.

CASS LAKE

Stony Point Resort Campground and RV Park

P.O. Box 518, Cass Lake 56633. T: (800) 332-6311; F: (218) 335-2680; www.stonyptresortcasslake.com; stonypt@paulbunyan.net.

RV: ★★★★ Tent: ★★★★

Beauty: ★★★★	Site Privacy: ★★★★
Spaciousness: ★★★★	Quiet: ★★★★
Security: ★★★★	Cleanliness: ★★★★
Insect Control: Yes	Facilities: ★★★★

Known as the "Little Venice of the North," Stony Point has a 2,000-foot winding boat canal. that keeps campers within close proximity to their boats. The campground is located two miles east of Cass Lake which is connected with seven other lakes. This is a nice stop for avid boaters. Located on the lake, the campsites are mostly shaded, level, and grassy with concrete patios. The typical site width is 35 feet, and there are 28 pull-throughs. The campground also has mobile homes and many seasonals. Tent sites are in a separate area for more privacy. The restaurant and lounge offers a complete menu and salad bar, as well as catering services for picnics and other events. The marina offers fish-cleaning, fish freezing, and fish packing. Security measures are good with owners who live on site, regular patrols, and surveillance cameras.

Basics

Operated by: Delbert & Kay Gangelhoff, Karen & Jim Bowley. **Open:** May 1–Oct. 15. **Site Assignment:** Reservations w/ 1-night deposit; refunds w/ 7-day notice. **Registration:** At campground office. **Fee:** $24 (cash, check, credit cards). **Parking:** At site.

Facilities

Number of RV Sites: 165. **Number of Tent-Only Sites:** 10. **Hookups:** Electric (30, 50 amps), water, sewer. **Each Site:** Picnic table, fire ring. **Dump Station:** Yes. **Laundry:** Yes. **Pay Phone:** Yes. **Rest Rooms and Showers:** Yes. **Fuel:** Yes. **Propane:** Yes. **Internal Roads:** Gravel, in good condition. **RV Service:** No. **Market:** 2 mi. west in Cass Lake. **Restaurant:** On site. **General Store:** Yes. **Vending:** Yes. **Swimming Pool:** No. **Playground:** Yes. **Other:** Lake, boat canal, rec room, marina, concrete patios, restaurant & bar, video games, pavilion, recreation field, basketball, badminton, horseshoes, hiking trails, volleyball, fish-cleaning house. **Activities:** Swimming, boating (rental pontoon boats, kayaks, canoes, paddleboats, motor boats available), hiking, fishing, hunting. **Nearby Attractions:** Lakes, Native American burial grounds, logging museum, wildlife park, scenic drives, golf, tennis, bingo, casino, summer theater. **Additional Information:** Bemidji Area Tourist Information Center, (800) 458-2223, ext. 100.

Restrictions

Pets: Leash only. **Fires:** Fire ring only. **Alcoholic Beverages:** Permitted. **Vehicle Maximum Length:** None.

To Get There

From the junction of Hwy. 371 and US 2, drive 2 mi. east on US 2. Roads are wide and well maintained w/ broad shoulders.

CLOQUET

Cloquet/Duluth KOA

1479 Old Carlton Rd., Cloquet 55720. T: (800) KOA-9506

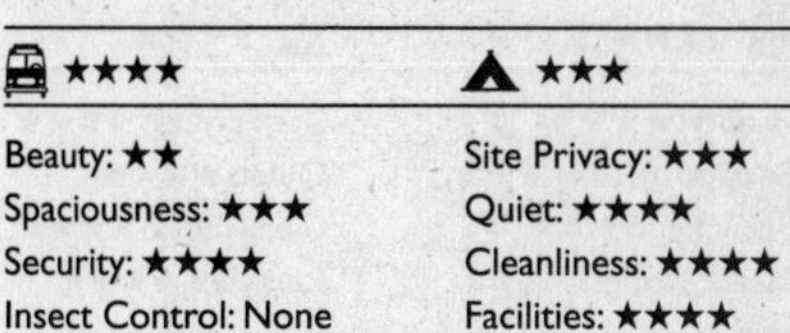

RV: ★★★★ Tent: ★★★

Beauty: ★★	Site Privacy: ★★★
Spaciousness: ★★★	Quiet: ★★★★
Security: ★★★★	Cleanliness: ★★★★
Insect Control: None	Facilities: ★★★★

Travelers on their way through the Cloquet and Duluth area are often pleased to find the Cloquet/Duluth KOA. It is very clean, offers good facilities, and is conveniently located near major roads. It is not much of a destination campground, however. Campers don't stop here planning to spend several days at the campground. The activities are rather skimpy, and it doesn't provide much in the way of natural beauty. Sites are level, open, and shaded, and 30 feet is the average site width. Most RV sites are gravel, and 27 are pull-throughs. The most requested RV sites are 1–10 because they offer full hookup and pull-through access. Tent sites are scattered throughout the campground. Security is provided by owners who live on the grounds providing regular patrols, and local police also keep an eye on the campground.

BASICS

Operated by: Bill, Barbara, Bob, & Linde Higton. **Open:** May 1–Oct. 15. **Site Assignment:** Reservations w/ 1-night deposit; refunds w/ 5-day notice. **Registration:** At campground office. **Fee:** $25 (cash, check, credit cards). **Parking:** At site.

FACILITIES

Number of RV Sites: 50. **Number of Tent-Only Sites:** 9. **Hookups:** Electric (30, 50 amps), water, sewer. **Each Site:** Picnic table, fire ring. **Dump Station:** Yes. **Laundry:** Yes. **Pay Phone:** Yes. **Rest Rooms and Showers:** Yes. **Fuel:** No. **Propane:** Yes. **Internal Roads:** Gravel, in good condition. **RV Service:** No. **Market:** 1 mi. south in Cloquet. **Restaurant:** 3 mi. south in Cloquet. **General Store:** Yes. **Vending:** Yes. **Swimming Pool:** Yes. **Playground:** Yes. **Other:** Hot tub, horseshoes, volleyball, game room, badminton, basketball, rec hall, recreation field, TV room. **Activities:** Swimming, biking (rental bikes available), Saturday night hayride, weekly ice cream social. **Nearby Attractions:** Zoo, depot museum, harbor cruises, casino, paper mill tour, train rides, charter fishing, agate hounding, Congdon Mansion, canal park. **Additional Information:** Cloquet Area Chamber of Commerce, (800) 554-4350.

RESTRICTIONS

Pets: Leash only. **Fires:** Fire ring only. **Alcoholic Beverages:** Permitted. **Vehicle Maximum Length:** 40 ft.

TO GET THERE

From the junction of I-35 and Hwy. 45, take Exit 239 and drive 2 mi. south on Hwy. 45, then 0.25 mi. west on CR 3. Roads are wide and well maintained w/ broad shoulders

COKATO LAKE

Cokato Lake Campground

2945 CR 4 Southwest, Cokato 55321. T: (320) 286-5779

RV ★★★★ Tent ★★★★

Beauty: ★★★★ Site Privacy: ★★★★
Spaciousness: ★★★★ Quiet: ★★★★
Security: ★★★★ Cleanliness: ★★★★
Insect Control: None Facilities: ★★★★

Located beside Cokato Lake on a hilly terrain, this campground offers mostly shaded, grassy sites with a typical site width of 25 feet. There are 12 pull-through sites, and some open spots for campers concerned about satellite TV reception. Laid out in a series of loops, the campground has 100 seasonal campers. Quiet hours are enforced from 11 p.m. to 8 a.m. when all children must remain at sites and radios must be off. Mini-bikes, ATVs, and gas golf carts are not allowed on the grounds. The swimming pool is closed on Mondays for maintenance. The speed limit is ten mph, rather high for a family campground, and campers are asked to limit driving after dark. Security includes owners who live on site and a security gate.

BASICS

Operated by: Brent & Kathryn Helmke. **Open:** May 1–Oct. 1. **Site Assignment:** Reservations w/ 1-night deposit; refunds (minus $5) w/ 7-day notice. **Registration:** At campground office. **Fee:** $25 (cash, check, credit cards). **Parking:** At site.

FACILITIES

Number of RV Sites: 202. **Number of Tent-Only Sites:** 23. **Hookups:** Electric (20, 30, 50 amps), water, sewer. **Each Site:** Picnic table, fire ring. **Dump Station:** Yes. **Laundry:** Yes. **Pay Phone:** Yes. **Rest Rooms and Showers:** Yes. **Fuel:** No. **Propane:** Yes. **Internal Roads:** Gravel, in good condition. **RV Service:** No. **Market:** 3 mi. south in Cokato. **Restaurant:** 3 mi. south in Cokato. **General Store:** Yes. **Vending:** Yes. **Swimming Pool:** Yes. **Playground:** Yes. **Other:** Rental cabins & cottages, chapel, Cokato Lake, game room, mini-golf, tennis, softball, volleyball, rec hall, pavilion, boat ramp, boat dock. **Activities:** Swimming, fishing, boating (rental rowboats, canoes, paddleboats & motorboats available, scheduled weekend activities. **Nearby Attractions:** Charles A. Lindberg House & History Center, Ellingson Car Museum, Minnesota Baseball Hall of Fame, St. John's Benedictine Abbey, golf, antiques, arts & crafts shops. **Additional Information:** St. Cloud Area CVB, (800) 264-2940.

RESTRICTIONS

Pets: Leash only. **Fires:** In fire ring. **Alcoholic Beverages:** Permitted. **Vehicle Max. Length:** 40 ft.

TO GET THERE

From the junction of US 12 and CR 4, drive 3 mi. northeast on CR 4. Roads are wide and well maintained w/ broad shoulders.

DETROIT LAKES

Country Campground

13639 260th Ave., Detroit Lakes 56501. T: (800) 898-7901; www.lakesnet.net/ccdl; ccdl@lakesnet.net.

RV ★★★★ Tent ★★★★

Beauty: ★★★★ Site Privacy: ★★★★
Spaciousness: ★★★★ Quiet: ★★★★
Security: ★★★★ Cleanliness: ★★★★
Insect Control: ★★★★ Facilities: ★★★

Little touches are what make Country Campground such an inviting place to stay. The entrance is welcoming with a trellis, old wagon-wheel, flowers, and statues of friendly critters. Other bits of landscaping around the campground are also pleasant. Located one mile south of Detroit Lakes, which has a mile-long beach, Country Campground offers level, grassy sites along Glawe Lake. The typical site width is 40 feet, and there are 14 pull-through sites. A well-organized gift shop with dolls, wood carvings, ceramics, and hand-blown glass is a plus. Another attraction is a fenced-in children's area complete with swing sets, sandbox, and toys. A dock with a love seat swing is a popular spot. Security measures include owners who keep a close watch on the campground.

BASICS

Operated by: Elwood & Lois Orner. **Open:** May 1–Oct. 15. **Site Assignment:** Reservations w/ 1-night deposit; refund w/ 7-day notice. **Registration:** At campground office. **Fee:** $20 (cash, check, credit cards). **Parking:** At site.

FACILITIES

Number of RV Sites: 30. **Number of Tent-Only Sites:** 4. **Hookups:** Electric (30 amps), water, sewer. **Each Site:** Picnic table, fire ring. **Dump Station:** Yes. **Laundry:** No. **Pay Phone:** Yes. **Rest Rooms and Showers:** Yes. **Fuel:** No. **Propane:** Yes. **Internal Roads:** Gravel, in good condition. **RV Service:** No. **Market:** 1 mi. north in Detroit Lakes. **Restaurant:** 1 mi. north in Detroit Lakes. **General Store:** Yes, limited. **Vending:** Yes. **Swimming Pool:** No. **Playground:** Yes. **Other:** Pavilion, fishing lake, recreation building, softball, basketball, horseshoes, volleyball, lounge, gift shop, croquet. **Activities:** Fishing, boating (paddleboats & canoes available). **Nearby Attractions:** Swimming, golf, two amusement parks, boating, snowmobiling, cross-country skiing, downhill skiing, Becker County Museum, 412 lakes, scenic drives, Tamarac National Wildlife Refuge. **Additional Information:** Detroit Lakes Regional Chamber of Commerce & Tourism Bureau, (800) 542-3992.

RESTRICTIONS

Pets: Leash only. **Fires:** Fire ring only. **Alcoholic Beverages:** Permitted. **Vehicle Maximum Length:** None.

TO GET THERE

From the junction of US 10 and US 59., drive south 2.2 mi. on US 50 to CR 22, then drive south 0.5 mi. to West Lake Dr., then 1.2 mi. to 260th Ave., south 0.8 mi. Roads are mostly wide and well maintained w/ adequate shoulders.

ELY

Silver Rapids Lodge

459 Kawishiwi Trail, Ely 55731. T: (800) 950-9425; F: (218) 365-3540; wwwsilverrapidslodge.com; rapids@northernet.com.

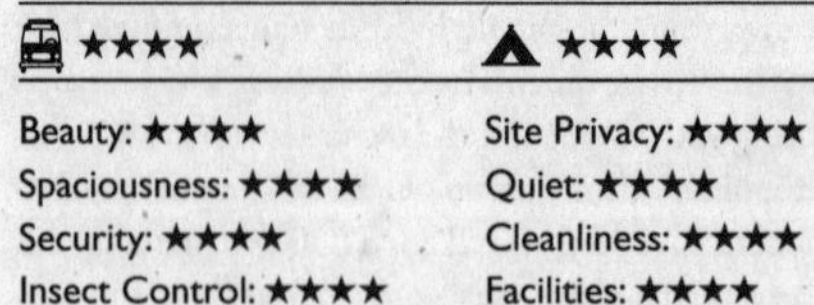

RV ★★★★ Tent ★★★★

Beauty: ★★★★ Site Privacy: ★★★★
Spaciousness: ★★★★ Quiet: ★★★★
Security: ★★★★ Cleanliness: ★★★★
Insect Control: ★★★★ Facilities: ★★★★

At the gateway to the Boundary Waters, Silver Rapids Lodge has enough year-round outdoor activities to keep any sporting enthusiast happy. Silver Rapids has a nature and fishing guide on hand and rents a variety of boats for fishing, as well as equipment for winter sports (camping facilites are limited in the winter). Snowmobiles, skis, snowshoes, and portable ice-fishing houses are available for rent. Silver Rapids ski trails link into the Ely Hidden Valley and Mesabi ski trail system. One of the prettiest sights is the Friday and Saturday night lantern-skiing. The Tomahawk snowmobile trail system leads right to Silver Rapids' front door. The trail is groomed twice a week and offers some of the most picturesque scenery around. Camping sites are semi-wooded with pine trees and overlook a river and lake scenery. Sewer sites are on a hillside. The typical site width is 30 feet, and the campground has no pull-through sites. Security measures include owners who live on site and patrol the campground.

BASICS

Operated by: Bryan & Pam Klubbin. **Open:** All year. **Site Assignment:** Reservations w/ 1-night deposit; refund w/ 60-day notice. **Registration:** At campground office. **Fee:** $30 (cash, check, credit cards). **Parking:** At site.

FACILITIES

Number of RV Sites: 39. **Number of Tent-Only Sites:** 2. **Hookups:** Electric (20, 30 amps), water, sewer. **Each Site:** Picnic table, fire ring. **Dump Station:** Yes. **Laundry:** Yes. **Pay Phone:** Yes. **Rest Rooms and Showers:** Yes. **Fuel:** Yes. **Propane:** Yes. **Internal Roads:** Gravel, in good condition. **RV Service:** No. **Market:** 5 mi. southwest in Ely. **Restaurant:** Adjacent. **General Store:** Yes, limited. **Vending:** Yes. **Swimming Pool:** No. **Playground:** Yes. **Other:** White Iron Lake, swimming beach, whirlpool, boat ramp, rec room, marina, coin games, basketball, shuffleboard, horseshoes, hiking trails, rental cabins, retreat house, suites. **Activities:** Swimming, fishing (rental portable ice-fishing house available), hiking, boating (rental pontoons, canoes, kayaks, paddleboats, motorboats available), scheduled activities. **Nearby Attractions:** Boundary Waters Canoe Area Wilderness, Ely/Winton History Museum, International Wolf Center, scenic drives, arts & crafts, antiques, snowmobiling, cross-country skiing, bowling, mini-golf, Dorothy Molter Museum. **Additional Information:** Ely Chamber of Commerce, (800) 777-7281.

RESTRICTIONS

Pets: Leash only. **Fires:** Fire ring only. **Alcoholic Beverages:** Permitted. **Vehicle Maximum Length:** None.

TO GET THERE

From the junction of Hwy. 1 and Hwy. 169, drive 1.75 mi. northeast on Hwy. 169, then 3 mi. east on CR 58 and CR 16. Roads are mostly wide and well maintained w/ narrow shoulders in spots.

FARIBAULT

Camp Faribo

21851 Bagley Ave., Faribault 55021. T: (800) 689-8453

RV ★★★★ Tent ★★★

Beauty: ★★★★ Site Privacy: ★★★
Spaciousness: ★★★ Quiet: ★★★★
Security: ★★★★ Cleanliness: ★★★★
Insect Control: ★★★★ Facilities: ★★★★

An open, grassy campground with level sites, Camp Faribo is a handy camping spot if you plan to visit nearby attractions. Many campers come year after year to visit area attractions and to enjoy the activities at the campground. Camp Faribo is about 45 minutes from the Mall of America and the Minnesota Zoo and is close to ten lakes. The campground has a typical site width of 25 feet and has 20 pull-throughs. With only nine seasonal campers, the campground has plenty of room for visitors. The most popular sites are close to the heated swimming pool and the facilities. The owners keep a close watch on the campground to keep it quiet and family oriented.

BASICS

Operated by: Chuck & Fern Kubalsky. **Open:** Apr. 15–May 15. **Site Assignment:** Reservations w/ 1-night deposit; refund (minus $5) w/ 15-day notice. **Registration:** At campground office. **Fee:** $22 (cash, check, credit cards). **Parking:** At site.

FACILITIES

Number of RV Sites: 71. **Number of Tent-Only Sites:** 0. **Hookups:** Electric (20, 30, 50 amps), water, sewer. **Each Site:** Picnic table, fire ring. **Dump Station:** Yes. **Laundry:** Yes. **Pay Phone:** Yes. **Rest Rooms and Showers:** Yes. **Fuel:** No. **Propane:** Yes. **Internal Roads:** Gravel, in good condition. **RV Service:** No. **Market:** 2 mi. north. **Restaurant:** 2 mi. north. **General Store:** Yes. **Vending:** Yes. **Swimming Pool:** Yes. **Playground:** Yes. **Other:** Rec hall, coin games, shuffleboard, sports field, horseshoes, volleyball. **Activities:** Swimming. **Nearby Attractions:** Historic walking tours, Alexander Faribault House, Episcopal Cathedral, Faribault Woolen Mill, Ivan Whillock Studio, Rice County Museum of History, Mall of America, Minnesota Zoo, 10 lakes. **Additional Information:** Faribault Area Chamber of Commerce, (800) 658-2354.

RESTRICTIONS

Pets: Leash only. **Fires:** Fire ring only. **Alcoholic Beverages:** Permitted. **Vehicle Maximum Length:** None.

TO GET THERE

From the junction of I-35 and Hwy. 60, take Exit 56, drive 500 ft. east on Hwy. 60, then 1.5 mi. south on Western Ave. Roads are wide and well maintained w/ adequate shoulders.

GILBERT

Sherwood Forest Campground

Box 548, Gilbert 55741. T: (800) 403-1803

RV ★★★ Tent ★★★

Beauty: ★★★ Site Privacy: ★★
Spaciousness: ★★ Quiet: ★★★
Security: ★★★★ Cleanliness: ★★★
Insect Control: None Facilities: ★★

Because it is located a couple of blocks from the main street of Gilbert, the Sherwood Forest Campground offers easy access on good paved roads. The campground is on a hill with the beach and Lake Ore-Be-Gone spread out below. It is a good walk downhill from the campsites to the beach. Wooden plank steps have been built to make scaling down the hill easier for campers. The 140-acre lake is a huge mine pit lake resulting from the natural flooding of three iron-ore mines. The lake is popular for waterskiing, fishing, boating, and swimming. The Mesabi Trail runs directly past the campground. Laid out in a series of loops, the campground offers mostly grassy, open sites with an average width of 30 feet. The nine pull-through sites measure 24 × 100. Security is good—the campground is two blocks from the police station and city police patrol every hour. Showers and rest rooms have a code number given only to campers, so non-campers can't use the facilities.

BASICS

Operated by: City of Gilbert. **Open:** May 1–Oct. 31. **Site Assignment:** Reservations accepted w/ $10 deposit; no refund but deposit can be applied to later visit. **Registration:** At campground office. **Fee:** $15 (cash, check). **Parking:** At site.

FACILITIES

Number of RV Sites: 43. **Number of Tent-Only Sites:** 8. **Hookups:** Electric (30 amp), water, sewer. **Each Site:** Picnic table, fire ring. **Dump Station:** Yes. **Laundry:** No. **Pay Phone:** Yes. **Rest Rooms and Showers:** Yes. **Fuel:** No. **Propane:** No. **Internal Roads:** Paved, in good condition. **RV Service:** No. **Market:** 4 mi. north in Virginia. **Restaurant:** 3 blocks in Gilbert. **General Store:** No. **Vending:** No. **Swimming Pool:** No. **Playground:** Yes. **Other:** Lake Ore-Be-Gone, boat ramp, dock, swimming beach, volleyball, baseball field, hiking trail, picnic shelters. **Activities:** Swimming, fishing, boating, hiking. **Nearby Attractions:** Hockey Hall of Fame, water skiing, golf, skiing, Mesabi Trail, shops, Iron Range Historical Society, Iron World USA, Giant's Ridge ski & summer recreation area. **Additional Information:** City of Gilbert, (218) 749-3837.

RESTRICTIONS

Pets: Leash only. **Fires:** Fire ring only. **Alcoholic Beverages:** At sites only. **Vehicle Maximum Length:** None.

TO GET THERE

From the junction of US 53 and SR 37 East, drive 3 mi. east on SR 37 to Wisconsin Ave. (in town,) then drive 0.5 mi. southeast on Wisconsin Ave.

GRAND RAPIDS

Sugar Bay Campground/Resort

21812 Moose Point Rd., Cohasset 55721. T: (218) 326-8493

RV ★★★ Tent ★★

Beauty: ★★★★ Site Privacy: ★★★
Spaciousness: ★★★★ Quiet: ★★★★
Security: ★★★★ Cleanliness: ★★★★
Insect Control: None Facilities: ★★★

Campers who have seen the campground exit sign on the highway often pull in to Sugar Bay frustrated and tired. Since the state won't post a mileage sign for the campground, many campers who have turned off hoping to find a convenient night's rest are often a bit angry. It is almost a 14 mile trip from the highway to the campground. But it is worth it for a quiet night's sleep. The campground is small, well maintained, and clean. Sites are level, grassy, and some are shady with three pull-throughs and a typical site width of 40 feet. Baby trees are planted around the site. The Pokegama Lake campground features water activities and many repeat customers because of them. Bait and groceries are not sold at Sugar Bay, so be sure to take what you need, or you might have to drive 20 miles round trip to get it.

Basics

Operated by: Jim & Sandy Holasek. **Open:** May 11–Oct. 31. **Site Assignment:** Reservations w/ 1-night deposit; refunds w/ 7-day notice. **Registration:** At campground office. **Fee:** $17 (cash, check, credit cards). **Parking:** At site.

Facilities

Number of RV Sites: 23. **Number of Tent-Only Sites:** 0. **Hookups:** Electric (20, 30, 50 amps), water, sewer. **Each Site:** Picnic table, fire ring. **Dump Station:** Yes. **Laundry:** No. **Pay Phone:** No. **Rest Rooms and Showers:** Yes. **Fuel:** Yes. **Propane:** No. **Internal Roads:** Gravel, in good condition. **RV Service:** No. **Market:** 10 mi. east in Grand Rapids. **Restaurant:** 8 mi east in Grand Rapids. **General Store:** Yes. **Vending:** No. **Swimming Pool:** No. **Playground:** No. **Other:** Pokegama Lake, boat ramp, boat dock, horseshoes, cement patios, marina. **Activities:** Swimming, fishing, boating (rental motor boats, paddleboats & pontoons available). **Nearby Attractions:** Golf, Forest History Center, Otasca Heritage Center, Judy Garland Birthplace, Children's Discovery Museum. **Additional Information:** Grand Rapids Convention & Visitors Center, (800) 472-6366.

Restrictions

Pets: Leash only, restricted to campsite. **Fires:** Fire ring only. **Alcoholic Beverages:** Permitted. **Vehicle Maximum Length:** 40 ft.

To Get There

From the junction of US 2 and US 169S, drive 7.5 mi. south on US 169, then 6 mi. west and north on CR 17, then 0.25 mi. east on CR 239. Roads are wide and well maintained w/ broad shoulders.

HIBBING
Forest Heights RV Park

2240 East 25th St., Hibbing 55746. T: (218) 263-5782

★★ ▲ ★

Beauty: ★★	Site Privacy: ★★
Spaciousness: ★★	Quiet: ★★
Security: ★★★	Cleanliness: ★★★
Insect Control: Yes	Facilities: ★★

An urban campground located behind a mobile home park, Forest Heights RV Park would be a good place for travelers who are passing through or staying for a brief time to enjoy local attractions. The campground is not, however, a destination that most would consider for a camping experience. The campground has better infrastructure than most campgrounds—paved streets, curbs, and gutters, and sidewalks leading up to camping sites. Most of the sites are level, open, and grassy with six pull-throughs and a typical width of 35 feet. For RVs, it would be like staying in a mobile home park. For tents, it would be more like camping out in someone's backyard. The price, convenience, and city amenities are attractive. On-site activities are lacking, but Forest Heights does not pretend to be a camping resort.

Basics

Operated by: Alvin & Allayne Glover. **Open:** May 1–Oct. 31. **Site Assignment:** Reservation w/ 1-night deposit; no refund. **Registration:** At campground office. **Fee:** $18 (cash, check). **Parking:** At site.

Facilities

Number of RV Sites: 44. **Number of Tent-Only Sites:** 6. **Hookups:** Electric (20, 30, 50 amps), water, sewer. **Each Site:** Picnic table, grill. **Dump Station:** Yes. **Laundry:** Yes. **Pay Phone:** No. **Rest Rooms and Showers:** Yes. **Fuel:** No. **Propane:** No. **Internal Roads:** Paved, in good condition. **RV Service:** No. **Market:** 1 mi. south in Hibbing. **Restaurant:** 1 mi. south in Hibbing. **General Store:** No. **Vending:** No. **Swimming Pool:** No. **Playground:** No. **Other:** Rec hall, sports field. **Activities:** None. **Nearby Attractions:** Swimming lake & park, First Settlers Museum, Hull Ruse Mahoning Mine, Greyhound Bus Origin Center, Paulucci Space Theatre. **Additional Information:** Hibbing Area Chamber of Commerce, (900) 444-2246.

Restrictions

Pets: Leash only. **Fires:** Grills only. **Alcoholic Beverages:** Permitted. **Vehicle Maximum Length:** None.

To Get There

From the junction of Hwy. 37 and US 169/Hwy. 73, drive 1 mi. north on US 169/Hwy. 73, then 1 mi. east on 25th St.

HINCKLEY
Grand Casino Hinckley RV Resort

Rte. 3, Box 14, Hinckley 55037. T: (800) 995-GRAND; F: (952) 449-7785; www.grandcasinosminnesota.com.

★★★★★ ▲ n/a

Beauty: ★★★	Site Privacy: ★★★
Spaciousness: ★★★	Quiet: ★★★★
Security: ★★★★★	Cleanliness: ★★★★★
Insect Control: None	Facilities: ★★★★★

Grand Casino RV Resort is the best money can buy. A full-time cleaning staff keeps the rest rooms, showers, grounds, and other facilities spotless. The interior roads are better than you find in some towns. The grass is manicured like a golf course. The recreation options are excellent and suited to all ages. The security is outstanding—the campground office is open 24 hours a day, the campgrounds are well-lit and patrolled, and access is through a manned locked gate where visitors need an access code to enter. If you want to gamble and enjoy the pool and other amenities, it is well worth a visit. The Grand Casino Hinckley is open 24 hours a day with blackjack tables and more than 2,000 slot machines, big-name entertainment acts from Las Vegas to Nashville, four restaurants, and an all-you-can-eat buffet. But, if you want to sit under a shade tree and commune with nature, this is not the place. Laid out in a series of loops, the campground is basically a big paved field with baby trees. The typical site width is 35 feet. All 222 sites have full hookup, and all sites are back-ins. Tent campers are out of luck. Tents are allowed only as an auxiliary unit.

Basics

Operated by: The Mille Lacs Band of Ojibwe. **Open:** All year. **Site Assignment:** Reservation w/ 1-night deposit; refund w/ 7-day notice. **Registration:** At campground office. **Fee:** $16 (cash, check, credit cards). **Parking:** At site.

Facilities

Number of RV Sites: 222. **Number of Tent-Only Sites:** 0. **Hookups:** Electric (30, 50 amps), water, sewer, cable TV. **Each Site:** Picnic table, fire ring, light, patio. **Dump Station:** Yes. **Laundry:** Yes. **Pay Phone:** Yes. **Rest Rooms and Showers:** Yes. **Fuel:** No. **Propane:** No. **Internal Roads:** Paved, in excellent condition. **RV Service:** No. **Market:** 2 mi. west in Hinckley. **Restaurant:** Next door. **General Store:** Yes. **Vending:** Yes. **Swimming Pool:** Yes. **Playground:** Yes. **Other:** Casino, free shuttle to casino, lodge, performers in outdoor amphitheater & Silver Sevens Lounge, volleyball, horseshoes, game room, Kids Quest Activity Center, rec room, whirlpool, golf, badminton, video games, shuffleboard, basketball, recreation field, adults room. **Activities:** Gambling, swimming, golf. **Nearby Attractions:** Fire Museum, state trails, scenic drives, flea market, antique shops, historical sites. **Additional Information:** Hinckley CVB, (800) 996-4566.

Restrictions

Pets: Leash only. **Fires:** Fire ring only. **Alcoholic Beverages:** Permitted. **Vehicle Maximum Length:** 60 ft. **Other:** Tents are permitted as an auxiliary unit only.

To Get There

From the junction of I-35 and Hwy. 48, drive 1 mi. east on Hwy. 48. Roads are wide and well maintained w/ broad shoulders.

HINCKLEY
St. Croix Haven Campground

Rte. 3 Box 385, Hinckley 55037. T: (320) 655-7989; www.worman.com/haven.

★★★★ ▲ ★★★★

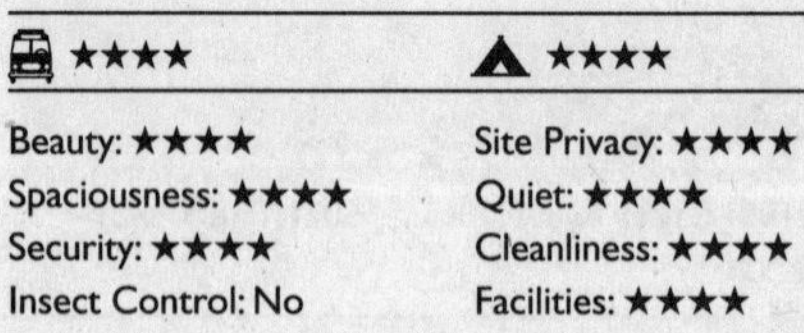

Beauty: ★★★★	Site Privacy: ★★★★
Spaciousness: ★★★★	Quiet: ★★★★
Security: ★★★★	Cleanliness: ★★★★
Insect Control: No	Facilities: ★★★★

St. Croix Haven Campground has a major advantage over other campgrounds—it is laid out in a series of cul de sac patterns each with six sites. This arrangement provides for more spacious, private sites, particularly with several trees spaced between the sites. Located five miles west of Danbury, the campground offers a natural setting with level, grassy, and gravel sites, but no pull-throughs. Tent sites are in a special grassy section. The most popular RV sites are 27–44 because they are close to the pool and the bathroom. The heated indoor pool offers three seasons of swimming. A well-stocked campstore and a deluxe, all-carpeted adult lounge with a split rock fireplace, sundeck, and color TV add to the facilities. Security measures are good with one entrance past the office, owners who live on site, adequate lights, and campground patrol. Now, if the campground just had sewer hookups and some pull-throughs, it would be even better.

BASICS

Operated by: Jerry & Joy Holt. **Open:** May 1–Oct. 22. **Site Assignment:** Reservations w/ 2-night deposit, refunds w/ 7-day notice. **Registration:** At campground office. **Fee:** $23 (cash, check, credit cards). **Parking:** At site.

FACILITIES

Number of RV Sites: 92. **Number of Tent-Only Sites:** 20. **Hookups:** Electric (20, 30, 50 amps), water. **Each Site:** Picnic table, fire ring. **Dump Station:** Yes. **Laundry:** Yes. **Pay Phone:** Yes. **Rest Rooms and Showers:** Yes. **Fuel:** No. **Propane:** No. **Internal Roads:** Gravel, in good condition. **RV Service:** No. **Market:** 5 mi. east in Danbury. **Restaurant:** 5 mi. east in Danbury. **General Store:** Yes. **Vending:** No. **Swimming Pool:** Yes. **Playground:** Yes. **Other:** St. Croix River, game room, horseshoes, badminton, volleyball, covered pavilion, adult lounge, sundeck, private card rooms, sports field, hiking trail. **Activities:** Swimming, fishing, free firetruck rides, canoeing (rental canoes available), innertube floats (rental intertubes available, biking (rental bikes available), scheduled weekend activities. **Nearby Attractions:** Casino, Fire Museum, golf, state trails, scenic drives, flea market, antique shops, historical sites. **Additional Information:** Hinckley CVB, (800) 996-4566.

RESTRICTIONS

Pets: Leash only. **Fires:** Fire ring only. **Alcoholic Beverages:** Permitted. **Vehicle Maximum Length:** None. **Other:** Friends & visitors must register at the campground office & pay a $3 fee.

TO GET THERE

From the junction of I-35 and Hwy. 48, drive 23.5 mi. est on Hwy. 48, then 1 mi. north on CR 173. Roads are wide and well maintained w/ broad shoulders.

HINCKLEY

St. Croix State Park

Rte. 3, Box 450, Hinckley 55037. T: (320) 384-6591; www.dnr.state.mn.us.

RV: ★★	Tent: ★★★★
Beauty: ★★★★	Site Privacy: ★★★★
Spaciousness: ★★★★	Quiet: ★★★★
Security: ★★★★	Cleanliness: ★★★
Insect Control: None	Facilities: ★★

Located 15 miles east of Hinckley, St. Croix State Park is Minnesota's largest state park. Situated along the St. Croix River, the park covers over 33,000 acres of forests, meadows, marshes, and streams. The park was established in 1943 after being developed by the National Park Service as a demonstration area. It lives up to its reputation as a popular recreational spot. The park offers 127 miles of hiking trails, 75 miles of horse trails, 6 miles of paved trails, 80 miles of groomed snowmobile trails, and 6 miles of ski trails. The RV sites are gravel and rather small at 15 × 60. They are mostly shaded with no pull-through sites available. Tent sites include two pack-in sites, ten primitive canoe campsites, and a primitive group camp for up to 200 campers. Tent campers have more room and privacy in their wilderness setting.

BASICS

Operated by: State of Minnesota. **Open:** All year. **Site Assignment:** Reservations w/ 1-night fee plus $7.25 non-refundable service charge. Refunds (minus $5 fee & $7.25 service charge) w/ 3-day notice. **Registration:** At campground office. **Fee:** $15 (Cash, check, credit cards). **Parking:** At site.

FACILITIES

Number of RV Sites: 42. **Number of Tent-Only Sites:** 170. **Hookups:** Electric (30 amps). **Each Site:** Picnic table, fire ring. **Dump Station:** Yes. **Laundry:** No. **Pay Phone:** Yes. **Rest Rooms and Showers:** Yes. **Fuel:** No. **Propane:** No. **Internal Roads:** Paved/gravel, in good condition. **RV Service:** No. **Market:** 22 mi. north in Hinckley. **Restaurant:** 22 mi. north in Hinckley. **General Store:** Yes. **Vending:** Yes. **Swimming Pool:** No. **Playground:** Yes. **Other:** Lake w/ sandy beach, hiking trail, bike trail, interpretive center, horse camp area, enclosed picnic shelter, canoe landings. **Activities:** Swimming, fishing, hiking, boating (rental canoes available), biking (rental bikes available), year-round interpretive programs. **Nearby Attractions:** Casino, Fire Museum, golf, state trails, scenic drives, flea market, antique shops, historical sites. **Additional Information:** Hinckley CVB, (800) 996-4566.

RESTRICTIONS

Pets: Leash only. **Fires:** Fire ring only. **Alcoholic Beverages:** Not permitted. **Vehicle Maximum Length:** 66 ft. **Other:** Vehicle permits of $20 per year or $4 per day are required to enter all Minnesota state parks; 14-day stay limit.

TO GET THERE

From the junction of I-35 and Hwy. 48, take the Hinckley exit, drive 15 mi. east on Hwy. 48, then 5 mi. south on CR 22. Roads are wide and well maintained w/ broad shoulders.

HOUSTON

Money Creek Haven

18502 County 26, Houston 55943. T: (507) 896-3544

RV: ★★★	Tent: ★★★
Beauty: ★★★	Site Privacy: ★★★
Spaciousness: ★★★★	Quiet: ★★★
Security: ★★★	Cleanliness: ★★★
Insect Control: None	Facilities: ★★★

The campsite's 40th birthday will be celebrated in 2002 by the same man who started it. About half the sites at Money Creek Haven are occupied by seasonals. The on-site restaurant serves several hundred people every morning with a big country breakfast. The restaurant offers mostly fast-food the rest of the day. The campground offers primarily shaded, grassy sites in a rural setting. The typical site size is 50 × 50 with a mix of back-in and pull-through sites. The best sites for RVs are in the B section, which offers full hookups, easy access, lots of shade, and a location by the pool. Tents are not well screened for privacy from RV campers. Be aware that no one is allowed in the swimming pool after dark.

BASICS

Operated by: Allen Fitting. **Open:** Apr. 15–Oct. 15. **Site Assignment:** Reservations w/ 1-night deposit; refunds w/ 5-day notice. **Registration:** At camp office. **Fee:** $20 (cash, check). **Parking:** At site.

FACILITIES

Number of RV Sites: 185. **Number of Tent-Only Sites:** 12. **Hookups:** Electric (20, 30 amps), water, sewer. **Each Site:** Picnic table, fire ring. **Dump Station:** Yes. **Laundry:** Yes. **Pay Phone:** Yes. **Rest Rooms and Showers:** Yes. **Fuel:** No. **Propane:** No. **Internal Roads:** Paved/gravel, in good condition. **RV Service:** No. **Market:** 6 mi. south in Houston. **Restaurant:** On site. **General Store:** Yes. **Vending:** Yes. **Swimming Pool:** Yes. **Playground:** Yes. **Other:** Game room w/ video & pool tables, horseshoes, volleyball, fishing pond, badminton, hiking trails, recreation field. **Activities:** Swimming, fishing, hiking, no scheduled activities. **Nearby Attractions:** Golf, snowmobile, farm tours, art & antique shops, scenic drives, nature center. **Additional Information:** Bluff Country Regional CVB, (800) 428-2030.

RESTRICTIONS

Pets: Leash only. **Fires:** Fire ring only. **Alcoholic Beverages:** Permitted. **Vehicle Maximum Length:** None.

TO GET THERE

From the junction of I-90 and Hwy. 76, drive 8 mi. south on Hwy. 76, then 0.25 mi. west on Hwy. 26. Roads are wide and well maintained w/ broad shoulders.

ISLE

South Isle Family Campground

39002 Hwy. 47, Isle 56342. T: (320) 676-8538; www.ecenet.com/~sifcamp; sifcamp@ecenet.com.

RV: ★★★	Tent: ★★★
Beauty: ★★★	Site Privacy: ★★★
Spaciousness: ★★★	Quiet: ★★★
Security: ★★★	Cleanliness: ★★★
Insect Control: None	Facilities: ★★★

Family owned and operated since 1991, South Isle Family Campground is located two miles south of Isle. The rural campground is surrounded by woods, marsh land, and prairie grass areas. The typical campsite width is 40 feet, and the campground has 30 pull-throughs. However, all the full hookup sites are occupied by seasonals. Sites are grassy and shaded to semi shaded. A separate area for tent campers offers privacy and more natural amenities. The campground is known for its R/C airplane airstrip where hobbyists can fly their remote control airplanes and curious bystanders can watch.

Basics

Operated by: Wally & Sue Heise. **Open:** May 1–Oct. 1. **Site Assignment:** Reservations w/ $25 deposit, $50 deposit on holiday weekends; refund (minus $3 fee) w/ 7-day notice. **Registration:** At campground office. **Fee:** $22 (cash, credit cards). **Parking:** At site.

Facilities

Number of RV Sites: 120. **Number of Tent-Only Sites:** 9. **Hookups:** Electric (20, 30, 50 amps), water. **Each Site:** Picnic table, fire ring. **Dump Station:** Yes. **Laundry:** Yes. **Pay Phone:** Yes. **Rest Rooms and Showers:** Yes. **Fuel:** No. **Propane:** No. **Internal Roads:** Gravel, in good condition. **RV Service:** No. **Market:** Yes. **Restaurant:** 2 mi. north in Isle. **General Store:** 2 mi. north in Isle. **Vending:** Yes. **Swimming Pool:** Yes. **Playground:** Yes. **Other:** Kids fishing pond w/ free paddleboat to use, horshoes, Frisbee golf course, shuffleboard, nature trails, basketball, volleyball, softball, tetherball, badminton, TV lounge & video game area. **Activities:** Swimming. hiking, scheduled weekend activities. **Nearby Attractions:** Golf, Mille Lacs Lake, Soo Line Bicycle Trail, Mille Lacs Grand Casino, craft & antique shops, museums, Father Hennepin State Park. **Additional Information:** Mille Lacs Area Tourism Council, (888) 350-2692.

Restrictions

Pets: Leash only, $3 a day if more than 1 dog. **Fires:** Fire ring only. **Alcoholic Beverages:** Permitted. **Vehicle Maximum Length:** None. **Other:** Daily rates are based on 2 people; children under age 4 are free; additional children are $1.50 per day; additional adults are $2.50 per day; visitors are $2.50 per day.

To Get There

From town, drive 2 mi. south on Hwy. 47. Road is in good shape.

KELLIHER

Rogers' Campground & RV Park

HC78 Box 20, Kelliher 56650. T: (800) 678-1871; www.rogerscg.net; funn@rogerscg.net.

RV ★★★ Tent ★★★

Beauty: ★★★ Site Privacy: ★★★
Spaciousness: ★★★ Quiet: ★★★
Security: ★★★ Cleanliness: ★★★
Insect Control: ★★★ Facilities: ★★★

Located on the Upper Red Lake in Kelliher, Rogers' Campground provides lakeside access. The remote campground offers mostly open campsites that enjoy the lakeside breeze. More shaded sites are offered in the back. The typical site width is 25 feet. Laid out in a series of loops, the campground has four pull-through sites and 20 seasonal campers. Shotley Brook winds its way through the center of the campground, making many on-the-water campsites. Over 800 feet of sandy beach is available on Upper Red Lake, a very shallow lake with no drop-off making it a nice swimming beach. A private concrete boat ramp and protected harbor add to the boating activities. To protect the peace and quiet, as well as the abundant wildlife—including an active eagle's nest on the property—no ATVs are allowed in the campground. Though only the most hearty would want to camp in northern Minnesota during the winter, the campground provides some wintertime amenities. Available for rent are several cabins and ice-fishing shacks. Owners also have three snowplows to make the campground passable for winter campers.

Basics

Operated by: Jerry & Joani Barthel. **Open:** All year. **Site Assignment:** Reservations w/ 1-night deposit; refund (minus $5) w/ 2-week notice. **Registration:** At campground office. **Fee:** $18 (cash, check, credit cards). **Parking:** At site.

Facilities

Number of RV Sites: 74. **Number of Tent-Only Sites:** 0. **Hookups:** Electric (20, 30 amps), water, sewer. **Each Site:** Picnic table, fire ring. **Dump Station:** Yes. **Laundry:** Yes. **Pay Phone:** Yes. **Rest Rooms and Showers:** Yes. **Fuel:** No. **Propane:** No. **Internal Roads:** Gravel, in good condition. **RV Service:** No. **Market:** 14 mi. southeast in Kelliher. **Restaurant:** 14 mi. southeast in Kelliher. **General Store:** Yes, limited. **Vending:** Yes. **Swimming Pool:** No. **Playground:** Yes. **Other:** Upper Red Lake, swimming beach, hiking trails, fish-cleaning house, sports field, croquet, pavilion, tetherball, volleyball, basketball, horseshoes, rec room, boat dock, boat ramp, badminton, rental houses. **Activities:** Swimming, fishing, hiking, boating (rental tubes, paddleboats & kayaks available), scheduled weekend activities. **Nearby Attractions:** Mississippi River, Paul Bunyan & Babe the Blue Ox statues, water parks, water slide, logging camp, fishing, golf, antiques, arts & crafts. **Additional Information:** Bemidji Area Tourist Information, (800) 458-2223.

Restrictions

Pets: Leash only. **Fires:** Fire ring only. **Alcoholic Beverages:** Permitted. **Vehicle Maximum Length:** None.

To Get There

From the junction of CR 36 and Hwy. 72, drive 9 mi. north on Hwy. 72, then 5 mi. west on CR 23, then 0.75 mi. north on access road. Roads are mostly wide and well maintained w/ adequate shoulders.

LAKE ITASCA

Itasca State Park

HC 05 Box 4, Lake Itasca 56470. T: (218) 266-2100; www.dnr.state.mn.us.

RV ★★★ Tent ★★★★

Beauty: ★★★★ Site Privacy: ★★★★
Spaciousness: ★★★ Quiet: ★★★★
Security: ★★★★ Cleanliness: ★★★
Insect Control: None Facilities: ★★★

Itasca State Park really offers two campgrounds—Bear Paw Campground along the shores of Lake Itasca and Pine Ridge Campground, originally the 1930s Civilian Conservation Corps Camp. Both campgrounds have shady, back-in sites with a typical site size of 15 × 60 feet. Some sites have 40-foot widths. During the off season, Pine Ridge Campground is open for rustic winter camping with pit toilets; water is available at the park headquarters. For those looking for solitude, 11 year-round back country campsites are accessible via one- to five-mile hikes. These sites offer fire rings and pit toilets but no water supply, and campers must carry out their garbage. Itasca also offers group camps with a staff cabin, dining hall with kitchen, modern toilet facility, and a tent area for up to 75 people. What Itasca State Park lacks in camping amenities, it makes up for in beauty and recreational opportunities.

Basics

Operated by: State of Minnesota. **Open:** May 15–Oct. 15. **Site Assignment:** Reservations w/ 1-night deposit; refund (minus $5 fee) w/ 3-day notice. A non-refundable $7.25 reservation fee is charged per camping reservation. **Registration:** At campground office. **Fee:** $15 (cash, check, credit cards), plus $4 day park fee or $20 for season permit. **Parking:** At site.

Facilities

Number of RV Sites: 100. **Number of Tent-Only Sites:** 135. **Hookups:** Electric (20, 30 amps). **Each Site:** Picnic table, fire ring. **Dump Station:** Yes. **Laundry:** No. **Pay Phone:** Yes. **Rest Rooms and Showers:** Yes. **Fuel:** No. **Propane:** No. **Internal Roads:** Paved/gravel, in good condition. **RV Service:** No. **Market:** 3 mi. north to Lake Itasca. **Restaurant:** Douglas Lodge at park. **General Store:** No. **Vending:** Yes. **Swimming Pool:** No. **Playground:** Yes. **Other:** Hiking trails, hostel, sandy beach, bike trail, several lakes, lodges, cabins, tour boat, gift shop, visitor center, lodge, amphitheatre, boat landing, fire tower, interpretive center. **Activities:** Swimming, fishing, hiking, biking, (rental bikes available), boating (rental pontoons, paddleboat, canoe & fishing boats available), naturalist programs, workshops. **Nearby Attractions:** Scenic drives, historic sites. **Additional Information:** Minnesota Office of Tourism, (800) 657-3700.

Restrictions

Pets: Leash only. **Fires:** Fire ring only. **Alcoholic Beverages:** Not permitted. **Vehicle Maximum Length:** 60 ft. **Other:** 14-day stay limit.

To Get There

From Park Rapids, drive 20 mi. north on US 71. Road is fair condition w/ often narrow shoulders.

LANESBORO

Eagle Cliff Campground and Lodging

Rte. 1, Box 344, Lanesboro 55949. T: (507) 467-2598

RV ★★★ Tent ★★★★

Beauty: ★★★★ Site Privacy: ★★★
Spaciousness: ★★★ Quiet: ★★★★
Security: ★★★★ Cleanliness: ★★★★★
Insect Control: None Facilities: ★★★

Located in a valley with bluffs rising on one side and the Root River running on another, Eagle Cliff Campground and Lodging is a great place for river activities. It has a useful rinse area to keep the river water and dirt out of spotless showers and bathroom facilities. The wilderness campground has no scheduled activities or swimming pool, thereby allowing the river to be the center of recreation. All sites are grassy and level, and there are no gravel or paved sites. Many RV sites are open with young trees too little to provide shade. The typical site width is 45 feet with a dozen pull-throughs. A special section by the river has been set aside for tent campers, and, unlike many campgrounds, Eagle Cliff has more tent sites than RV sites. Visiting during the week would be best because the campground quickly fills on weekends. Reservations are recommended.

Basics

Operated by: Naber family. **Open:** Apr. 1–Dec. 1. **Site Assignment:** Reservations w/ 1-night deposit; refunds w/ 2-weeks notice. **Registration:** At campground office. **Fee:** $19 (cash, check, credit cards). **Parking:** At site.

Facilities

Number of RV Sites: 62. **Number of Tent-Only Sites:** 88. **Hookups:** Electric (20, 30, 50), water, sewer. **Each Site:** Picnic table, fire ring. **Dump Station:** Yes. **Laundry:** Yes. **Pay Phone:** Yes. **Rest Rooms and Showers:** Yes. **Fuel:** No. **Propane:** No. **Internal Roads:** Gravel, in good condition. **RV Service:** No. **Market:** 3 mi. west in Lanesboro. **Restaurant:** 3 mi. west in Lanesboro. **General Store:** Yes. **Vending:** Yes. **Swimming Pool:** No. **Playground:** Yes. **Other:** River rinse-off area, game room, horseshoes, volleyball, canoe landing, recreation field. **Activities:** Hunting, fishing, boating (rental kayaks, canoes & tubes available), biking (rental bikes available), hiking. **Nearby Attractions:** Golf, scenic drives, petting zoo, Amish tours. **Additional Information:** Lanesboro Office of Visitor Information, (800) 944-2670.

Restrictions

Pets: Leash only. **Fires:** Fire ring only. **Alcoholic Beverages:** Permitted. **Vehicle Maximum Length:** 40 ft. **Other:** No check-in after 11 p.m. You will be charged if your dog digs holes.

To Get There

From the junction of US 52 and Hwy. 16, drive 9 mi. east on Hwy. 16.

LITTLE FALLS

Charles A. Lindbergh State Park

P.O. Box 364, Little Falls 56345. T: (320) 616-2525; www.dnr.state.mn.us.

RV ★★ Tent ★★★★

Beauty: ★★★★	Site Privacy: ★★★★
Spaciousness: ★★★★	Quiet: ★★★★
Security: ★★★★	Cleanliness: ★★★
Insect Control: None	Facilities: ★★

This state park was established in 1931 when 110 acres were donated to the state in memory of Charles A. Lindbergh, Sr. World renowned for his trans-Atlantic solo flight in 1927, Lindbergh lived his boyhood years in the house by the park overlooking the Mississippi River. Water and woodland activities are a major attraction in the state park. The Pike Creek meanders through and empties into the Mississippi River in the southern part of the park. Located one-and-a-half miles south of Little Falls, the campground's sites are mostly shaded and level with back-ins and no pull-throughs. The most popular RV sites are 1, 3, 7, 9, 10, 11, and 12 because they offer electricity and are next to Pike Creek. Tent sites are in a separate loop. Also, there is one hike-in site and one site available by canoe. Security is great with one access road, a security gate which is closed from 10 p.m. to 8 a.m. except to registered campers, and regular patrols by park rangers and city police.

Basics

Operated by: State of Minnesota. **Open:** All year. **Site Assignment:** First come, first served; no reservations accepted. **Registration:** At campground office. **Fee:** $15 (cash, check, credit cards). **Parking:** At site.

Facilities

Number of RV Sites: 15. **Number of Tent-Only Sites:** 23. **Hookups:** Electric (30 amps). **Each Site:** Picnic table, fire ring. **Dump Station:** Yes. **Laundry:** No. **Pay Phone:** No. **Rest Rooms and Showers:** Yes. **Fuel:** No. **Propane:** No. **Internal Roads:** Paved, in good condition. **RV Service:** No. **Market:** No. **Restaurant:** 1.5 mi. north in Little Falls. **General Store:** 1.5 mi. north in Little Falls. **Vending:** No. **Swimming Pool:** No. **Playground:** Yes. **Other:** Picnic area, enclosed shelters, hiking & skiing trails, boat ramp, ranger station. **Activities:** Fishing, hiking, boating (rental canoes available). **Nearby Attractions:** Charles A. Lindbergh House State Historic Site, Weyerhaeuser Museum, Minnesota Military Museum, Pine Grove Park & Zoo, bowling, golf, horseback riding, tennis. **Additional Information:** Little Falls CVB, (800) 325-5916.

Restrictions

Pets: Leash only. **Fires:** Fire ring only. **Alcoholic Beverages:** "3.2" beer only. **Vehicle Maximum Length:** 50 ft. **Other:** Vehicle permits of $20 per year or $4 per day are required to enter all Minnesota state parks; 14-day stay limit.

To Get There

From the junction of Hwy. 27 and CR 52, drive 1.5 mi. southwest on CR 52. Roads are wide and well maintained w/ broad shoulders.

LITTLE FALLS

Fletcher Creek Campground

20771 Hwy. 371, Little Falls 56345. T: (800) 337-9636

RV ★★ Tent ★★★

Beauty: ★★★	Site Privacy: ★★
Spaciousness: ★★	Quiet: ★★★
Security: ★★★★★	Cleanliness: ★★
Insect Control: None	Facilities: ★★

Mississippi River canoe trips set Fletcher Creek Campground apart from other camping experiences. The campground provides shuttle service, a canoe, paddles, and life jackets for an eight-mile river trip for $15 per person. It usually takes people two to three hours to make the entire trip. If that isn't long enough, the campground also offers 16 mile trips for $25. Those trips usually take five to six hours. The shuttle service takes campers up the river where they paddle canoes back down to the campground landing. Canoe rental is available at $3.50 per hour with a maximum cost of $25 per day. The campground offers semi-wooded and open sites with 15 pull-throughs. The typical site width is 25 feet. The most popular RV sites are 1–7 by the creek, and the sites in Bunny Hollow are most attractive to tent campers because of the privacy and shade. Security is tops at the campground—there is one entrance and the campground is patrolled by the owner who is a former policeman.

Basics

Operated by: Dennis Heise. **Open:** May 1–Oct. 31. **Site Assignment:** Reservations; no deposit required except for holiday weekends ($10); refund w/ 30-day notice. **Registration:** At campground office. **Fee:** $20 (cash,check, credit cards). **Parking:** Fire rings only.

Facilities

Number of RV Sites: 35. **Number of Tent-Only Sites:** 20. **Hookups:** Electric (20, 30, 50 amps), water, sewer. **Each Site:** Picnic table, fire ring. **Dump Station:** Yes. **Laundry:** Yes. **Pay Phone:** No. **Rest Rooms and Showers:** Yes. **Fuel:** No. **Propane:** No. **Internal Roads:** Gravel, in good condition. **RV Service:** No. **Market:** 6 mi. south in Little Falls. **Restaurant:** 3 mi. south in Little Falls. **General Store:** Yes. **Vending:** No. **Swimming Pool:** Yes. **Playground:** Yes. **Other:** Fletcher Creek, mini-golf, volleyball, badminton, horseshoes, sports field, rec room. **Activities:** Fishing, swimming, canoeing (rental canoes available). **Nearby Attractions:** Charles A. Lindbergh House State Historic Site, Weyerhaeuser Museum, Minnesota Military Museum, Pine Grove Park & Zoo, bowling, golf, horseback riding, tennis. **Additional Information:** Little Falls CVB, (800) 325-5916.

Restrictions

Pets: Leash only. **Fires:** Fire ring only. **Alcoholic Beverages:** Permitted. **Vehicle Maximum Length:** 40 ft.

To Get There

From the junction of US 10 and Hwy. 371, drive 6 mi. south on Hwy. 371. Roads are wide and well maintained w/ broad shoulders.

MOOSE LAKE

Red Fox Campground and RV Park

P.O. Box 356, Moose Lake 55767. T: (800) 569-4181

RV ★★★ Tent ★★★

Beauty: ★★★	Site Privacy: ★★★
Spaciousness: ★★★	Quiet: ★★★
Security: ★★★★	Cleanliness: ★★★
Insect Control: None	Facilities: ★★★

Red Fox Campground and RV Park offers easy access from I-35, two miles south of Moose Lake. But it also is easy to drive past it. The campground is located behind a Conoco gas station, which serves as a convenience and fast-food store for campers. The campground features a typical site width of 30 feet but the sites are long. Site 34 is 100 feet long, and sites 19 and 20 are 90 feet long. The shortest site length is 45 feet. Sites are level, shady, and grassy with 11 pull-throughs. A separate tent site sets tent campers off from RVs for more privacy. The campground has very good security measures—a manager lives on site, visitors must leave by 10 p.m., and city police patrol the grounds regularly.

Basics

Operated by: Bob & Bena Adamczak. **Open:** May 15–Oct. 15. **Site Assignment:** Reservations accepted w/ $15 deposit; refund (minus a $3 fee) w/ week notice. **Registration:** At campground office. **Fee:** $23.50 (cash, check). **Parking:** At site.

Facilities

Number of RV Sites: 36. **Number of Tent-Only Sites:** 50. **Hookups:** Electric (30, 50 amps), water. **Each Site:** Picnic table, fire ring. **Dump Station:** Yes. **Laundry:** Yes. **Pay Phone:** No. **Rest Rooms and Showers:** Yes. **Fuel:** No. **Propane:** No. **Internal Roads:** Gravel, narrow but good condition. **RV Service:** No. **Market:** 2 mi. north in Moose Lake. **Restaurant:** 2 mi. north in Moose Lake. **General Store:** No. **Vending:** No. **Swimming Pool:** No. **Playground:** Yes. **Other:** Pond w/ sandy beach, basketball, recreation building, putting green, horseshoes, group picnic area, hiking trails, volleyball, mini-golf. **Activities:** Swimming, fishing, hiking. **Nearby Attractions:** Casinos, state park, whitewater rafting, bike trails, golf, bowling, State Agate Center. **Additional Information:** Duluth Convention & Visitors Center, (800) 438-5884.

Restrictions

Pets: Leash only. **Fires:** Fire ring only. **Alcoholic Beverages:** At sites only. **Vehicle Maximum Length:** None.

To Get There

From the junction of I-35 and Hwy. 73, take Exit 214, drive 500 ft. west behind Conoco gas station. Road is wide and well maintained w/ broad shoulders.

NISSWA
Fritz's Resort and Campground

P.O. Box 803, Nisswa 56468. T: (218) 568-8988; www.fritzresort.com; fritzrst@uslink.net.

RV: ★★★★ Tent: ★★

Beauty: ★★★★	Site Privacy: ★★★
Spaciousness: ★★★	Quiet: ★★★
Security: ★★★★	Cleanliness: ★★★★
Insect Control: None	Facilities: ★★★★

Fritz's Resort and Campground offers easy access and a nice roster of activities, as many campers have already discovered. All but 25 RV sites are occupied by seasonal campers. Call ahead to be sure a site is open before pulling in. Also be aware that pets are not allowed from Memorial Day to Labor Day. The rural campground is well organized in a series of loops with level, shaded sites, cement patios, and 15 pull-throughs. The typical site width is 25 feet. Tent campers are sort of left out with only three sites available, but they are well shaded. Being so close to the highway, two-and-a-half miles north of Nisswa, it's inevitable that traffic noise would creep in a bit. Lake Edna is a beautiful attraction, and the beach is groomed every morning by a maintenance team to keep it that way. The best RV sites are 1–4 around the rec hall because they are pull-throughs and roomy at 60 × 100. Security is good with owners who live on site, a regular campground patrol, and city police driving through the area.

Basics

Operated by: Richard & Jane Geike. **Open:** May 1–Oct. 1. **Site Assignment:** Reservations w/ $30 deposit; refund (minus $10) w/ 21 day notice. **Registration:** At campground office. **Fee:** $24 (cash, check, credit cards). **Parking:** At site.

Facilities

Number of RV Sites: 70. **Number of Tent-Only Sites:** 3. **Hookups:** Electric (30, 50 amps), water, sewer. **Each Site:** Picnic table, fire ring. **Dump Station:** Yes. **Laundry:** Yes. **Pay Phone:** Yes. **Rest Rooms and Showers:** Yes. **Fuel:** Yes. **Propane:** Yes. **Internal Roads:** Paved, in good condition. **RV Service:** No. **Market:** 2.5 mi. south in Nisswa. **Restaurant:** 2.5 mi. south in Nisswa. **General Store:** Yes. **Vending:** No. **Swimming Pool:** No. **Playground:** Yes. **Other:** Lake Edna, sandy beach, rec hall, pool tables, ping pong, shuffleboard, 9-hole golf course, snack bar, adult room, fish-cleaning house, tennis court. **Activities:** Swimming, fishing, boating (rental motorboats, pontoons, canoes, paddleboats available). **Nearby Attractions:** Cross-country skiing, snowmobiling, raceway, Crow Wing County Historical Society, Paul Bunyan Amusement Center, Paul Bunyan Trail. **Additional Information:** Brainerd Lakes Area Chamber of Commerce, (800) 450-2838.

Restrictions

Pets: Pets will be allowed in campgrounds only before Memorial weekend & after Labor Day; $3 per day for each pet. **Fires:** Fire ring only. **Alcoholic Beverages:** Permitted. **Vehicle Maximum Length:** None.

To Get There

From Nisswa, drive 1.5 mi. north on Hwy. 371

NISSWA
Upper Cullen Resort and Campground

P.O. Box 72, Nisswa 56468. T: (218) 963-2249; www.uppercullen.com; lakefun@uslink.net.

RV: ★★★ Tent: ★★★

Beauty: ★★★	Site Privacy: ★★★
Spaciousness: ★★★	Quiet: ★★★★
Security: ★★★★	Cleanliness: ★★★
Insect Control: None	Facilities: ★★★

A rural lakeside facility, Upper Cullen Resort and Campground is a peaceful family place. Located on the eastern shore of the Upper Cullen Lake, five miles east of Nisswa, the secluded, heavily wooded campground features nature in abundance. Arranged in a series of loops, the campground has well-shaded level sites but no pull-throughs. The quiet surroundings and outdoor activities would probably appeal to tent campers. But there is no area set off for tents; tent sites are interspersed among RVs. Security is good with only one entrance to the campground, owners who live on site, and regular patrols. Reservations are recommended as the campground is very popular in June, July, and Aug.

Basics

Operated by: Bruce & Donna Galles. **Open:** May 1–Oct. 1. **Site Assignment:** Reservations w/ 2-night deposit; refund if site re-rented. **Registration:** At campground office. **Fee:** $24 (cash, check, credit cards). **Parking:** At site.

Facilities

Number of RV Sites: 43. **Number of Tent-Only Sites:** 7. **Hookups:** Electric (20, 30 amps), water, sewer. **Each Site:** Picnic table, fire ring. **Dump Station:** Yes. **Laundry:** Yes. **Pay Phone:** Yes. **Rest Rooms and Showers:** Yes. **Fuel:** Yes. **Propane:** No. **Internal Roads:** Gravel, narrow but in good condition. **RV Service:** No. **Market:** 5 mi. west in Nisswa. **Restaurant:** 5 mi. west in Nisswa. **General Store:** Yes. **Vending:** No. **Swimming Pool:** No. **Playground:** Yes. **Other:** Upper Cullen Lake, sandy beach, horseshoes, shuffleboard, badminton, volleyball, basketball, tetherball, boat ramp, game room, nature trails, boat ramp, boat dock. **Activities:** Swimming, fishing, boating (rental motorboats, canoes, paddleboats & pontoons), hayrides, scheduled activities. **Nearby Attractions:** Cross-country skiing, snowmobiling, raceway, Crow Wing County Historical Society Museum, Paul Bunyan Amusement Center, Paul Bunyan Trail. **Additional Information:** Brainerd Lakes Area Chamber of Commerce, (800) 450-2838.

Restrictions

Pets: Leash only. **Fires:** Fire ring only. **Alcoholic Beverages:** Permitted. **Vehicle Maximum Length:** 40 ft.

To Get There

From downtown Nisswa, drive 2.25 mi. east on CR 18, then 2.5 mi. north on Old Hwy. 18. Roads are wide and well maintained w/ broad shoulders.

OGILVIE
Hilltop Family Campground

2186 Empire St., Ogilvie 56358. T: (320) 272-4300; www.hilltopcampground.com; hilltop@ncis.

RV: ★★★ Tent: ★★★

Beauty: ★★★	Site Privacy: ★★★
Spaciousness: ★★★★	Quiet: ★★★★
Security: ★★★	Cleanliness: ★★★
Insect Control: None	Facilities: ★★★

Located six miles south of Ogilvie, Hilltop Family Campground offers spacious, wooded sites near a lake. The typical site width is 40 feet. Tent campers can use any sites, but there is no primitive area. The general store has limited stock, and all of the full hookup sites are occupied by the 80seasonals.

Laid out in a series of loops, the campground has grassy sites—there are no concrete RV pads—and shade from Norway pines and other hardwood trees. The rural campground has 12 pull-through sites. Day visitors pay a $3 fee and must leave by 10 p.m. Quiet hours, including no radio playing, are between 11 p.m. and 8 a.m. No one under age 16 is allowed in the spa pool or spa area. Also, children under 14 must be accompanied by an adult at the swimming pool. Although the campground speed limit is ten mph, the owners ask that campers walk instead of drive around the campground because of children playing.

Basics

Operated by: John & Dot Forrest. **Open:** May 1–Oct. 1. **Site Assignment:** Reservations w/ 1-night deposit; refunds w/ 10-day notice. **Registration:** At campground office. **Fee:** $26 (cash, check, credit cards). **Parking:** At site.

Facilities

Number of RV Sites: 123. **Number of Tent-Only Sites:** 0. **Hookups:** Electric (20, 30, 50 amps), water. **Each Site:** Picnic table, fire ring. **Dump Station:** Yes. **Laundry:** Yes. **Pay Phone:** Yes. **Rest Rooms and Showers:** Yes. **Fuel:** No. **Propane:** No. **Internal Roads:** Gravel, in fair condition. **RV Service:** No. **Market:** 6 mi. south to Ogilvie. **Restaurant:** 6 mi. south to Ogilvie. **General Store:** Yes. **Vending:** No. **Swimming Pool:** Yes. **Playground:** Yes. **Other:** Fish-cleaning house, boat parking, rec hall, library, snack area, electronic games, pool table, spa tub, volleyball, basketball, softball, horseshoes,hiking trails. **Activities:** Swimming, hiking. **Nearby Attractions:** Fishing & boating across road on Ann Lake, golf,. **Additional Information:** St. Cloud Area CVB, (800) 264-2940.

Restrictions

Pets: Leash only, $3 per pet per day. **Fires:** Fire ring only. **Alcoholic Beverages:** Permitted. **Vehicle Maximum Length:** None.

To Get There

From the junction of Hwy. 23 and Hwy. 47, drive 5 mi. north on Hwy. 47, then 0.75 mi. east on CR 90, then 0.25 mi. south on Empire St. Roads are narrow and in fair condition w/ narrow shoulders.

ORTONVILLE

Lakeshore RV Park & Fruit Farm

Rte. 1 Box 95, Ortonville 56278. T: (800) 9FOR-FUN; F: (320) 839-3701; www.lakeshorervpark.com; mrd-dragt@maxminn.com.

RV ★★★★ Tent ★★★★

Beauty: ★★★★ Site Privacy: ★★★★
Spaciousness: ★★★★ Quiet: ★★★★
Security: ★★★★ Cleanliness: ★★★★★
Insect Control: ★★★★ Facilities: ★★★★

A winning combination for campers is at Lakeshore RV Park and Fruit Farm. Located three miles north of Ortonville, the campground on the shores of Big Stone Lake offers level, prepared sites in a working apple orchard. The campground has a typical site width of 30 feet and 30 pull-through sites with a choice of open or shaded. Cleanliness is tops and it's a pleasure to see such sparkling rest room facilities. Apples are available to be picked starting in Sept. A separate primitive area for tents allows more green space and privacy. The mini-golf course is an unusually challenging one, with such toughies as Adam's Rib and the Apple and the Worm in the Dutchman's Rock Garden. Security measures are good with owners who keep a close eye on the campground to make sure it is quiet, clean, and family-oriented.

Basics

Operated by: Dennis, Carol, Steve & Colette Dragt. **Open:** Apr. 15–Oct. 15. **Site Assignment:** Reservations w/ 1-night deposit; refund w/ 7-day notice. **Registration:** At campground office. **Fee:** $22 (cash, check, credit cards). **Parking:** At site.

Facilities

Number of RV Sites: 40. **Number of Tent-Only Sites:** 15. **Hookups:** Electric (30, 50 amps), water, sewer. **Each Site:** Picnic table, fire ring. **Dump Station:** Yes. **Laundry:** Yes. **Pay Phone:** Yes. **Rest Rooms and Showers:** Yes. **Fuel:** No. **Propane:** Yes. **Internal Roads:** Gravel, in good condition. **RV Service:** No. **Market:** 3 mi. south in Ortonville. **Restaurant:** 3 mi. south in Ortonville. **General Store:** Yes, limited. **Vending:** Yes. **Swimming Pool:** Yes. **Playground:** Yes. **Other:** Big Stone Lake, arcade, hot tub, boat ramp, train rides, rec room, mini-golf, pavilion, sports field, volleyball, boat dock. **Activities:** Swimming, fishing, boating (rental excursion boat, bumper boats, pontoons, charter fishing, paddleboats available). **Nearby Attractions:** Golf, excursion boats, scenic drives, antiques, arts & crafts, wildlife refuge, mahogany granite quarries. **Additional Information:** Big Stone Lake Area Chamber of Commerce, (800) 568-5722.

Restrictions

Pets: Leash only. **Fires:** Fire ring only. **Alcoholic Beverages:** Permitted. **Vehicle Maximum Length:** None.

To Get There

From the junction of US 12 and Hwy. 7, drive 3 mi. north on Hwy. 7. Roads are wide and well maintained w/ broad shoulders.

PARK RAPIDS

Spruce Hill Campgrounds

17404 Driftwood Ln., Park Rapids 56470. T: (218) 732-3292

RV ★★★ Tent ★★★

Beauty: ★★★ Site Privacy: ★★★
Spaciousness: ★★★ Quiet: ★★★★
Security: ★★★ Cleanliness: ★★★
Insect Control: None Facilities: ★★★

Tall evergreen, poplar, and oak trees offer abundant shade at this wilderness campground overlooking Long Lake. Located two miles east of Park Rapids, Spruce Hill Campground is primarily a destination. Campers come here for the lake fishing, swimming, and boating. There are 25 seasonal sites, five pull-throughs, and the typical site width is 35 feet. Laid out in a series of loops, the campground has grassy sites with patios for RVs. The best RV sites are 11–14 because they are all pull-throughs, they are the biggest, and they overlook the lake. The best tent sites are the ones backing up to the woods away from RVs with more shade and privacy. Quiet time is enforced between 10 p.m. and 8 a.m. The owners live on site, keeping an eye on security and safety. The posted speed limit is five mph and the owners mean it.

Basics

Operated by: John & Judi Nelson. **Open:** May 1–Oct. 1. **Site Assignment:** Reservations w/ 1-night deposit; refund w/ 14-day notice. **Registration:** At campground office. **Fee:** $25 (cash, check, credit cards). **Parking:** At site.

Facilities

Number of RV Sites: 50. **Number of Tent-Only Sites:** 7. **Hookups:** Electric (30 amps), water, sewer. **Each Site:** Picnic table, fire ring. **Dump Station:** Yes. **Laundry:** No. **Pay Phone:** Yes. **Rest Rooms and Showers:** Yes. **Fuel:** No. **Propane:** No. **Internal Roads:** Gravel, in good condition. **RV Service:** No. **Market:** 2 mi. west in Park Rapids. **Restaurant:** 2 mi. west in Park Rapids. **General Store:** Yes. **Vending:** No. **Swimming Pool:** No. **Playground:** Yes. **Other:** Long Lake, volleyball, basketball, game room, boat ramp, sports field. **Activities:** Swimming, fishing, boating (rental motorboats, pontoons, canoes, paddleboats available). **Nearby Attractions:** Itasca State Park, historic sites, antiques, arts & crafts shops, golf, tennis, horseback riding, go carts, Heartland Trail. **Additional Information:** Park Rapids Area Chamber of Commerce, (800) 247-0054.

Restrictions

Pets: Leash only. **Fires:** Fire ring only. **Alcoholic Beverages:** Permitted. **Vehicle Maximum Length:** None.

To Get There

From the junction of US 71 and Hwy. 34, drive 2 mi. east on Hwy. 34, then 1 mi. south on West Long Lake Rd., then 0.5 mi. east on access road. Roads are wide and well maintained w/ broad shoulders.

PARK RAPIDS

Vagabond Village

HC06, Box 381A, Park Rapids 56470. T: (218) 732-5234; www.vagabondvillage.com; gocamping@vagabondvillage.com.

RV ★★★★ Tent ★★★★

Beauty: ★★★★ Site Privacy: ★★★★
Spaciousness: ★★★★ Quiet: ★★★★
Security: ★★★★ Cleanliness: ★★★★
Insect Control: Yes Facilities: none

Surrounded by birch and pine trees, Vagabond Village Campground overlooks Potato Lake with views of hills and water. Located eight miles north of Park Rapids, the campground has level, mostly open sites with a typical site width of 50 feet. Laid out in a series of loops, Vagabond Village has ten pull-through sites and 35 seasonal campers. Most RVs prefer the bigger sites near the facilities. Tents usually like F section best, because it is more private with green space and separated from RVs. Several outside shelters are popular for group gatherings and family reunions. A nice soda fountain serves old-fashioned ice cream and other treats. Security measures include owners who live on site, regular campground patrols, a gate, and surveillance cameras.

Basics

Operated by: The Nelson Family. **Open:** May 15–Oct. 1. **Site Assignment:** Reservation w/ $30 deposit; refund (minus $5) w/ 15-day notice. **Registration:** At campground office. **Fee:** $28 (cash, check). **Parking:** At site.

Facilities

Number of RV Sites: 125. **Number of Tent-Only Sites:** 3. **Hookups:** Electric (20, 30, 50 amps), water, sewer. **Each Site:** Picnic table, fire ring. **Dump Station:** Yes. **Laundry:** Yes. **Pay Phone:** Yes. **Rest Rooms and Showers:** Yes. **Fuel:** No. **Propane:** Yes. **Internal Roads:** Gravel/dirt, in good condition. **RV Service:** No. **Market:** 8 mi. south in Park Rapids. **Restaurant:** 8 mi. south in Park Rapids. **General Store:** Yes, limited. **Vending:** Yes. **Swimming Pool:** Yes. **Playground:** Yes. **Other:** Potato Lake, volleyball, hiking trails, horseshoes, sports field, bandminton, tennis, rec hall, pavilion, boat ramp, boat dock, croquet, game room, soda fountain, pavilions. **Activities:** Swimming, fishing, boating (rental motorboats, pontoons, paddleboats, canoes available), hiking, scheduled weekend activities. **Nearby Attractions:** Itasca State Park, tennis, horseback riding, golf, go-carts, Heartland Trail, antiques, historic sites, arts & crafts shops. **Additional Information:** Park Rapids Area Chamber of Commerce, (800) 247-0054.

Restrictions

Pets: Leash only. **Fires:** Fire ring only. **Alcoholic Beverages:** Permitted. **Vehicle Maximum Length:** 50 ft.

To Get There

From the junction of Hwy. 34 and US 71, drive 7.25 mi. north on US 71, then 6 mi. east on CR 40, then 0.5 mi. on access road. Roads are wide and well maintained w/ broad shoulders.

PINE CITY

Pokegama Lake RV Park and Golf Course

Rte. 4, Box 54, Pine City 55063. T: (800) 248-6552; F: (320) 629-5400.

RV ★★★ Tent ★★★

Beauty: ★★★ Site Privacy: ★★★
Spaciousness: ★★★ Quiet: ★★★
Security: ★★★★ Cleanliness: ★★★★
Insect Control: None Facilities: ★★★

Pokegama Lake RV Park and Golf Course is a nice family place with many activities. In fact, it is so popular that 97 of the full-hookup sites are taken by seasonals. That leaves 15 full hookup sites and 26 with water and electric for visiting RVs. Reservations are strongly recommended for the campground six miles north of Pine City. Most people come for the golfing, swimming, fishing, and boating. The fish-cleaning house is located away from campers—but yet is convenient- and is kept very clean with a garbage disposal at the bottom of the fish-cleaning counter. Campsites are both open and wooded with 30 pull-throughs. The typical site width is 25 feet with the campground laid out in a series of loops. A welcome respite for adults is a modular adult recreation center that does not allow anyone under age 18.

Basics

Operated by: Bill & Shirl Woischke. **Open:** May 1–Oct. 1. **Site Assignment:** Reservations w/ $10 deposit; refund w/ 7-day notice; 3-night min. on holiday weekends w/ $40 deposit; refund w/ 14-day notice. **Registration:** At campground office. **Fee:** $21 (cash, check, credit cards). **Parking:** At site.

Facilities

Number of RV Sites: 138. **Number of Tent-Only Sites:** 30. **Hookups:** Electric (20, 30 amps), water, sewer. **Each Site:** Picnic table, fire ring. **Dump Station:** Yes. **Laundry:** No. **Pay Phone:** No. **Rest Rooms and Showers:** Yes. **Fuel:** No. **Propane:** No. **Internal Roads:** Paved, in good condition. **RV Service:** No. **Market:** 6 mi. south in Pine City. **Restaurant:** 0.5 mi. south in Pokegama Lake. **General Store:** Yes. **Vending:** No. **Swimming Pool:** Yes. **Playground:** Yes. **Other:** Pokegama Lake, lounge area w/ color TV, rec room, video games, pool tables, screened picnic shelter, adult recreation center, horseshoes, volleyball, basketball, fish-cleaning house, boat harbor, boat ramps, boat docks, 9-hole golf. **Activities:** Golfing, swimming, fishing, boating skiing, scheduled activities on holiday weekends. **Nearby Attractions:** North West Company Fur Post, supper club in walking distance, antique shops, scenic drives, museum. **Additional Information:** Pine City Area Chamber of Commerce, (320) 629-3861.

Restrictions

Pets: Leash only. **Fires:** Fire ring only. **Alcoholic Beverages:** At sites only. **Vehicle Maximum Length:** 40 ft.

To Get There

From the junction of I-35 and CR 11, take Exit 171 and drive 4 mi. west on CR 11, then 1 block south on access road. Roads are wide and well maintained w/ broad shoulders

PINE RIVER

Doty's Riverview RV Park

3040 16th Ave. Southwest, Pine River 56474. T: (218) 587-4112

RV ★★★ Tent ★★★

Beauty: ★★★ Site Privacy: ★★★
Spaciousness: ★★★ Quiet: ★★★★
Security: ★★★★ Cleanliness: ★★★★
Insect Control: None Facilities: ★★

Doty's Riverview RV Park has two big natural attractions going for it—the Pine River and the Paul Bunyan Trail. Doty's is the closest campground—right across the street—to the 100-mile-long trail that runs from Brainerd to Bemidji. The trail is popular for biking, rollerblading, jogging, walking, and snowmobiling. Located two miles south of Pine River, the campground also offers easy access to the river. Canoes can be rented at the campground, for a trip that starts in the Arvig Creek that flows through the campground and leads into the Pine River and then into White Fish Lake. As avid campers, the Dotys opened the campground next to their home in 1990. RV sites are grassy with cement patios and mostly shady by pine, oak, and elm trees. The typical site width is 30 feet and the campground has three pull-throughs. Tent sites are separate from RVs and provide more privacy and shade. The best RV sites are 1–9 because they are on the east side and get better satellite TV reception, and sites 11, 19, and 20 because they are on the west side and get more shade in the afternoon. Firewood is provided free. Think maybe a small washer and dryer could be squeezed in somewhere?

Basics

Operated by: Bob & Twyla Doty. **Open:** May 1–Oct. 1. **Site Assignment:** Reservations w/ no deposit. **Registration:** At campground office. **Fee:** $16. **Parking:** At site.

Facilities

Number of RV Sites: 26. **Number of Tent-Only Sites:** 4. **Hookups:** Electric (30 amps), water, sewer. **Each Site:** Picnic table, fire ring. **Dump Station:** Yes. **Laundry:** No. **Pay Phone:** No. **Rest Rooms and Showers:** Yes. **Fuel:** No. **Propane:** No. **Internal Roads:** Gravel, in fair condition. **RV Service:** No. **Market:** 2 mi. north in Pine River. **Restaurant:** 2 mi. north in Pine River. **General Store:** No. **Vending:** No. **Swimming Pool:** No. **Playground:** Yes. **Other:** Rec hall, ping pong, pool table, horseshoes, volleyball, badminton,. **Activities:** Fishing, canoeing (rental canoes available), biking. **Nearby Attractions:** Paul Bunyan Trail, Paul Bunyan Amusement Center, raceway, Crow Wing County Historical Society, cross-country skiing, snow. **Additional Information:** Pine River Area Chamber of Commerce, (800) BUNYAN..

Restrictions

Pets: Leash only. **Fires:** In fire ring. **Alcoholic Beverages:** Permitted. **Vehicle Max. Length:** None.

To Get There

From the junction of Hwy. 371 and CR 44, drive 0.25 mi. east on CR 44. Roads are wide and well maintained w/ broad shoulders.

PIPESTONE

Pipestone RV Campground

919 North Hiawatha Ave., Pipestone 56164. T: (507) 825-2455; rvcmpgrd@rconnect.com.

RV ★★★ Tent ★★★

Beauty: ★★★ Site Privacy: ★★★
Spaciousness: ★★★ Quiet: ★★★
Security: ★★★★ Cleanliness: ★★★
Insect Control: None Facilities: ★★★

Pipestone RV Campground offers level, grassy sites with crushed stone for RV pads. The typical site width is 35 feet and the rural campground has 24 pull-throughs. A fully stocked campstore also features complimentary morning coffee and a good selection of souvenirs and crafts. Most of the sites are shaded with tall oak trees. The most popular RV sites are 1–24 because they offer full service. Tenters favor sites in the back where it is more rustic and away from RVs. Located in Pipestone, the campground doesn't have any seasonal campers. It does offer large camping teepees for rent that kids seem to love to sleep in with their parents. Security is good with owners who live on the premises and regular patrols by city police.

BASICS

Operated by: Carl & Nancy Cowan. **Open:** May–Oct. **Site Assignment:** Reservations w/ $10 fee; refunds w/ 24-hour notice. **Registration:** At campground office. **Fee:** $24 (cash, check, credit cards). **Parking:** At site.

FACILITIES

Number of RV Sites: 53. **Number of Tent-Only Sites:** 13. **Hookups:** Electric (20, 30 amps), water, sewer. **Each Site:** Picnic table, fire ring. **Dump Station:** Yes. **Laundry:** Yes. **Pay Phone:** Yes. **Rest Rooms and Showers:** Yes. **Fuel:** No. **Propane:** No. **Internal Roads:** Gravel, in good condition. **RV Service:** No. **Market:** 7 blocks south in Pipestone. **Restaurant:** 7 blocks south in Pipestone. **General Store:** Yes. **Vending:** No. **Swimming Pool:** Yes. **Playground:** Yes. **Other:** Horseshoes, rental teepees, volleyball, tetherball, enclosed pavilion, rec hall, sports field. **Activities:** Swimming. **Nearby Attractions:** Across the street from Pipestone National Monument & Hiawatha Pageant Grounds, antiques, crafts. **Additional Information:** Pipestone Area CVB, (800) 336-6125.

RESTRICTIONS

Pets: Leash only. **Fires:** Fire ring only. **Alcoholic Beverages:** Permitted. **Vehicle Maximum Length:** None.

TO GET THERE

From the junction of Hwy. 23 and Hwy. 30, drive 0.25 mi. west on Hwy. 30, then 1.25 mi. north on Hiawatha Ave. Roads are wide and well maintained w/ broad shoulders.

PRESTON

Hidden Valley Campground

Rte. 1, Box 56, Preston 55965. T: (507) 765-2467; www.hiddenvalleycampground.com; info@hiddenvalleycampground.com.

RV ★★★ Tent ★★★

Beauty: ★★★★ Site Privacy: ★★★
Spaciousness: ★★★★ Quiet: ★★★★
Security: ★★★★ Cleanliness: ★★★★
Insect Control: None Facilities: ★★

Located on the edge of Preston, Hidden Valley Campground has two major recreation attractions going for it—the Root River and the 65-mile-long Root River Bike Trail. Nestled in a valley of willows, oaks, and pines, the campground is bordered by a well-stocked trout stream. In the same family since 1968, the campground is kept wooded and shady by a tree-planting program which sees about 50–100 trees planted every year. Laid out in a series of loops, the campground has mostly grassy, shady, large sites with no pull-through sites. The typical site width is 50 feet. The most popular RV sites are the 16 along the river. Tent sites are separate from RVs, in a more wooded, primitive area that offers more privacy. About three-and-a-half miles of hiking trails take hikers through the pine woods and ravines to the bluff. Quiet and security measures are good with a 10 p.m. quiet time, an owner who lives on site, regular patrols, plus swing-throughs from city police and county sheriff deputies. Changes are being implemented that should improve campground facilities, including a central building, more services, and more sites.

BASICS

Operated by: Tim & Stef Bestor. **Open:** Apr. 15–Oct. 15. **Site Assignment:** Reservations w/ no deposit. **Registration:** At campground office. **Fee:** $15 (cash, check). **Parking:** At site.

FACILITIES

Number of RV Sites: 37. **Number of Tent-Only Sites:** 8. **Hookups:** Electric (30 amps), water. **Each Site:** Picnic table, fire ring. **Dump Station:** Yes. **Laundry:** No. **Pay Phone:** No. **Rest Rooms and Showers:** Yes. **Fuel:** No. **Propane:** No. **Internal Roads:** Gravel, in good condition. **RV Service:** No. **Market:** 0.5 mi. west in Preston. **Restaurant:** 0.5 mi. west in Preston. **General Store:** No. **Vending:** No. **Swimming Pool:** No. **Playground:** Yes. **Other:** Root River, swimming beach, sports field, horseshoes, volleyball, hiking trails, basketball. tetherball, softball. **Activities:** Swimming, fishing, canoeing (rental canoes available), hiking. **Nearby Attractions:** State park, Amish community, scenic drives, historic sites, antique & craft shops. **Additional Information:** Preston Area Tourism Assoc., (888) 845-2100.

RESTRICTIONS

Pets: Leash only. **Fires:** Fire pits only. **Alcoholic Beverages:** Permitted. **Vehicle Maximum Length:** None.

TO GET THERE

From north junction of Hwy. 16 and US 52, drive 2 mi. south on Hwy. 16/US 52 to bridge, then 0.25 mi. north on gravel road. Roads are wide and well maintained w/ good shoulders.

PRESTON

Old Barn Resort

Rte. 3 Box 57, Preston 55965. T: (800) 552-2512; F: (507) 467-2382; www.bluffcountry.com.

RV ★★★★ Tent ★★★★

Beauty: ★★★★ Site Privacy: ★★★★
Spaciousness: ★★★ Quiet: ★★★★
Security: ★★★★ Cleanliness: ★★★★
Insect Control: None Facilities: ★★★★

A big four-story white barn is the hub for the Old Barn Resort. Built in 1884 by Edward Allis of Allis-Chalmers, the barn was restored in 1988 to house a bar and grill, banquet rooms, and a 44-bed hostel. The campground is located in a scenic valley in Historic Bluff County, right on the Root River State Trail. The campsites are mostly open and level with a typical site width of 30 feet. A few pull-through sites are available. Favorite sites for RVs are A4 and A19 because they are on the ends and quieter. Tent campers like F1 and G1 because they offer more shade. The heated pool is a nice combination of indoor/outdoor, with a roof that lets the sunshine in and sides that can be opened for an outdoor feeling. The Old Barn books up quickly and recommends reservations be made three to four months in advance for holidays and two nights in advance for summer weekends.

BASICS

Operated by: Doug & Shirley Brenner. **Open:** Apr. 1–Nov. 1. **Site Assignment:** Reservations accepted w/ 1-night deposit; refund w/ 2-week notice; reservations require 2-night min. for weekends & 3-night min. for holidays. **Registration:** At campground office. **Fee:** $25.50 (cash, check, credit cards). **Parking:** At site.

FACILITIES

Number of RV Sites: 130. **Number of Tent-Only Sites:** 40. **Hookups:** Electric (30, 50 amps), water, sewer. **Each Site:** Picnic table, fire ring. **Dump Station:** Yes. **Laundry:** Yes. **Pay Phone:** Yes. **Rest Rooms and Showers:** Yes. **Fuel:** No. **Propane:** No. **Internal Roads:** Gravel, in fair condition. **RV Service:** No. **Market:** 3 mi. southwest in Preston. **Restaurant:** On site. **General Store:** Yes. **Vending:** Yes. **Swimming Pool:** Yes. **Playground:** Yes. **Other:** Golf course, Root River, hiking trail, game room, horseshoe, volleyball, basketball, sports field. **Activities:** Hiking, golf, swimming, fishing, biking (rental bikes available), boating (rental canoes & inner tubes available). **Nearby Attractions:** State park, Amish community, scenic drives, historic sites, antique & craft shops. **Additional Information:** Preston Area Tourism Assoc., (888) 845-2100.

RESTRICTIONS

Pets: Leash only. **Fires:** Fire ring only. **Alcoholic Beverages:** Permitted. **Vehicle Maximum Length:** None.

TO GET THERE

From the junction of US 52 and CR 17 (Apple Orchard Rd.) at west edge of town, drive 3 mi. east on CR 17, then 1 mi north on gravel road. Gravel road is bumpy, in fair condition.

RICHMOND

El Rancho Manana

27302B Ranch Rd., Richmond 56368. T: (320) 597-2740; F: (320) 597-2740.

RV ★★★★ Tent ★★★★

Beauty: ★★★★ Site Privacy: ★★★★
Spaciousness: ★★★★ Quiet: ★★★★
Security: ★★★★★ Cleanliness: ★★★★
Insect Control: None Facilities: ★★★★

Campers don't have to go out West to experience a ranch setting. El Rancho Manana, ten miles north of Cold Springs, offers 1,208 acres of campground, riding stable, pastures, lake, pond and riding trails on a working ranch. The rural, rolling, lakeside campground is out in the middle of nowhere, no houses around. Seasonal campers have reserved 28 of the campsites. The wilderness setting offers mostly shady, grassy sites but there are some gravel and open RV sites available. The typical site width is 45 feet and the campground has 60 pull-throughs. Secluded tent sites are available in the woods and by the lake. The quiet family campground has rules that are enforced to preserve the peace and security. A gate has been installed and all campers are asked for a $20 deposit or drivers license in return for a security card, which will be returned at time of departure. Visitors must leave the campground by 10 p.m. Quiet hours are from 11 p.m. to 10 a.m. and all radios must be turned off between 10 p.m. and 10 a.m. The speed limit is five mph. The owners live on the campground and provide regular patrols. But it is hard to imagine that anyone would want to drive all that way back those rough, dusty gravel roads unless they want to camp and enjoy the recreation.

BASICS

Operated by: Ward family. **Open:** May 15–Sept. 30. **Site Assignment:** Reservations w/ 2-night deposit; refunds w/ 2-week notice. **Registration:** At campground office. **Fee:** $28 (cash, check, credit cards). **Parking:** At site.

FACILITIES

Number of RV Sites: 115. **Number of Tent-Only Sites:** 30. **Hookups:** Electric (20, 30, 50 amps), water, sewer. **Each Site:** Picnic table, fire ring. **Dump Station:** Yes. **Laundry:** Yes. **Pay Phone:** Yes. **Rest Rooms and Showers:** Yes. **Fuel:** Yes. **Propane:** Yes. **Internal Roads:** Gravel/dirt, in good condition. **RV Service:** No. **Market:** 10 mi. south in Cold Springs. **Restaurant:** 10 mi. south in Cold Springs. **General Store:** Yes. **Vending:** Yes. **Swimming Pool:** No. **Playground:** Yes. **Other:** Rec hall, horse stables, game room, hiking trails, horse trails, horseshoes, volleyball, baseball, sandy swimming beach, Long Lake, shelter, boat landing, boat docks, mountain biking trails, badminton. **Activities:** Swimming, fishing, boating (rental rowboats, pontoons,canoes, paddleboats available), hayrides, hiking, mountain biking, horseback riding (rental horses available), planned activities. **Nearby Attractions:** Golf, historic sites, museums, Minnesota Baseball Hall of Fame, antique shops, art galleries. **Additional Information:** St. Cloud Area CVB, (800) 264-2940.

RESTRICTIONS

Pets: Leash only. **Fires:** Fire ring only. **Alcoholic Beverages:** At sites only. **Vehicle Maximum Length:** None. **Other:** A $20 deposit or drivers license in return for a security card to operate security gate; deposit or license will be returned at time of departure.

TO GET THERE

From the junction of I-94 and CR 9, take Exit 153 and drive 8.5 mi. south on CR 9, then 0.5 mi. east on Manana Rd., then 2 mi. north on Ranch Rd. Roads are wide and well maintained w/ good shoulders. Ranch Rd. is rough gravel and can stir up a lot of dust.

ROCHESTER
Rochester KOA

5232 65th Ave Southeast, Rochester 55904. T: (507) 288-0785

RV ★★★★ Tent ★★

Beauty: ★★★ Site Privacy: ★★★★
Spaciousness: ★★★★ Quiet: ★★★★
Security: ★★★★ Cleanliness: ★★★★★
Insect Control: None Facilities: ★★★★

Rochester KOA is a nice, clean, well-run, friendly, safe place to stay. It is not particularly pretty but that is not the owners' fault. They have done what they could to make it attractive, including having exceptionally clean bathrooms. But the natural beauty just isn't there. The open, rural campground is conveniently located just a quarter mile from I-90 and features level sites mostly 30 feet wide. The most popular sites are 4–16 with full hookup. A separate grassy tent site offers privacy, but tents must be moved daily by noon to protect the grass. The campground is mostly used for overnight stays by RVs on their way to or from somewhere. For that, it fits the need perfectly.

BASICS

Operated by: Roger & Barb Philip. **Open:** Mar. 15–Oct. 31. **Site Assignment:** Reservations accepted w/ 1-night deposit; refund (minus $5 fee) w/ 2-day notice, 1-week notice on holidays. **Registration:** At campground office. **Fee:** $28 (cash, credit cards). **Parking:** At site.

FACILITIES

Number of RV Sites: 73. **Number of Tent-Only Sites:** 20. **Hookups:** Electric (30 amp), water, sewer. **Each Site:** Picnic table, fire ring. **Dump Station:** Yes. **Laundry:** Yes. **Pay Phone:** Yes. **Rest Rooms and Showers:** Yes. **Fuel:** No. **Propane:** Yes. **Internal Roads:** Gravel, in good condition. **RV Service:** No. **Market:** 6 mi. north in Rochester. **Restaurant:** 6 mi. north in Rochester. **General Store:** Yes. **Vending:** Yes. **Swimming Pool:** Yes. **Playground:** Yes. **Other:** Volleyball, basketball, badminton, game room, horseshoes, rec hall, recreation field. **Activities:** Swimming, no scheduled activities except an ice cream social on Sat. nights from Memorial Day to Labor Day. **Nearby Attractions:** Mayo Clinic, park, art center, Mayowood Mansion, Olmsted County History Center, Root River State Trail, scenic drive, shopping center. **Additional Information:** Rochester CVB, (800) 634-8277.

RESTRICTIONS

Pets: Leash only. **Fires:** Fire ring only. **Alcoholic Beverages:** Permitted. **Vehicle Maximum Length:** None. **Other:** Camper visitors may stay only 1 hour & may not use any facilities including pool, playground, or rest rooms.

TO GET THERE

From the junction of I-90 and US 52, take Exit 218, drive 0.25 mi. south on US 52, then 500 ft. east on 54th St. Southeast, then 100 ft. north on 65th Ave. Roads are wide and well maintained w/ broad shoulders.

ROCHESTER
Silver Lake RV Park

1409 North Broadway, Rochester 55906. T: (507) 289-6412

RV ★★★ Tent n/a

Beauty: ★★ Site Privacy: ★★★
Spaciousness: ★★★ Quiet: ★★★★
Security: ★★★★★ Cleanliness: ★★★★★
Insect Control: None Facilities: ★★

Silver Lake RV Park is a metro facility used mainly by family and patients at the Mayo Clinic and other medical facilities. The Rochester City Bus Lines picks up passengers less than a block from the campground entrance and arrives at the Mayo Clinic in seven to nine minutes. Each campground guest receives a complimentary round-trip bus ticket and additonal tickets may be purchased at the campground at a discounted price of $1.60 per round trip. Taxi and wheelchair van services also are available. Cleanliness and security are tops. The campground is surrounded by a privacy fence and chain-link fence, there is only one entrance, and city police patrol the area. Rest rooms and showers have combination locks with the combination given to guests when they check in. Private phones may be available upon request and the campground office takes messages and delivers them to guests as soon as possible. The campground is surprisingly quiet to be the midst of a city. It also is easy to miss the turn in on a busy street.

BASICS

Operated by: Silver Lake RV Park Inc. **Open:** Apr. 1–Nov. 1. **Site Assignment:** Reservations recommended, no deposit required. **Registration:** At campground office. **Fee:** $29 (cash, check). **Parking:** At site.

FACILITIES

Number of RV Sites: 58. **Number of Tent-Only Sites:** 0. **Hookups:** Electric (30, 50 amps), water, sewer, cable TV. **Each Site:** Picnic table. **Dump Station:** No. **Laundry:** Yes. **Pay Phone:** Yes. **Rest Rooms and Showers:** Yes. **Fuel:** No. **Propane:** No. **Internal Roads:** Paved, in good condition. **RV Service:** No. **Market:** Across the street. **Restaurant:** Next door. **General Store:** No. **Vending:** No. **Swimming Pool:** No. **Playground:** No. **Other:** River, horseshoes. **Activities:** Fishing. **Nearby Attractions:** Mayo Clinic,walking & bike trail, movie theaters, shopping center, restaurants, historic homes, museums, park. **Additional Information:** Rochester CVB, (800) 634-8277.

RESTRICTIONS

Pets: Leash only. **Fires:** Not permitted in city limits. **Alcoholic Beverages:** Permitted. **Vehicle Maximum Length:** None. **Other:** No tents allowed.

TO GET THERE

From the junction of Hwy. 14 and US 63, drive 2.3 mi. north on US 63. Roads are wide and well maintained w/ broad shoulders.

ROYALTON
Two Rivers Park

P.O. Box 137, Royalton 56373. T: (320) 584-5125

RV ★★★★ Tent ★★★★

Beauty: ★★★★ Site Privacy: ★★★★
Spaciousness: ★★★★ Quiet: ★★★★
Security: ★★★★ Cleanliness: ★★★★
Insect Control: None Facilities: ★★★

Two Rivers Park is located three miles south of Royalton, on a peninsula formed by the waters of the Mississippi and Platte Rivers. Not surprisingly, the campground is popular for water activities, especially its inner tube float trips. Starting with a shuttle bus trip to the beginning point, you can lean back in a huge inner tube and float three-and-a-half miles back to the park through the beautiful Platte River Valley. The relaxing trip takes about two hours and costs $7 a person, children age five and under are free. Laid out in a series of loops, the landscaped campground offers grassy shaded sites with 20 pull-throughs. The typical site width is among the largest in any campground—60 feet. From water front to high bluff and whispering pine sites, tent campers have a wonderful choice of places. Security and safety measures are good—the campground has one access road and owners live on site and provide regular patrols. Quiet time is from 11 p.m. to 8 a.m., visitors must leave by 10 p.m., the playground closes at dusk, no bike riding after dark, and children must be on site by 10 p.m. The posted speed limit is "as fast as a child can walk." With all it has going for it, the campground has one pesky flaw—no laundry facilities for all those wet and dirty clothes from river activities.

BASICS

Operated by: Bernie & Pat Palmer. **Open:** May 15–Sept. 15. **Site Assignment:** Reservations w/ full payment; 3-night min. on holiday weekends; refunds (minus $5 fee) w/ 7-day notice. **Registration:** At campground office. **Fee:** $20 (cash, check, credit cards). **Parking:** At site.

FACILITIES

Number of RV Sites: 60. **Number of Tent-Only Sites:** 20. **Hookups:** Electric (20, 30 amps), water. **Each Site:** Picnic table, fire ring. **Dump Station:** Yes. **Laundry:** No. **Pay Phone:** No. **Rest Rooms and Showers:** Yes. **Fuel:** No. **Propane:** Yes. **Internal Roads:** Paved/gravel, in good condition. **RV Service:** No. **Market:** 3 mi. north in Royalton. **Restaurant:** 3 mi. north in Royalton. **General Store:** Yes. **Vending:** Yes. **Swimming Pool:** No. **Playground:** Yes. **Other:** Game room, tubing shuttle bus, volleyball, mini-golf, badminton, basketball, croquet, chucker golf, boat launch, recreation field, shelter building, boat ramp, horseshoes, hiking trails. **Activities:** Fishing, river swimming, boating, agate hunting, inner tube float trips, planned activities. **Nearby Attractions:** Golf, zoo, bowling, roller skating, water slide, museums, tennis, skeet shoot, game farm, go-cart tracks. **Additional Information:** Little Falls CVB, (800) 325-5916.

RESTRICTIONS

Pets: Leash only. **Fires:** Fire ring only. **Alcoholic Beverages:** Permitted. **Vehicle Maximum Length:** None. **Other:** No jet skis, personal watercraft allowed.

TO GET THERE

From the junction of US 10 and CR 40, drive 100 ft. southwest on CR 40, then 1 mi. south on CR 73, then 0.5 mi. west on 145th St. Roads are wide and well maintained w/ good shoulders.

SAVAGE
Town & Country Campground

12630 Boone Ave. South, Savage 55378. T: (612) 445-1756; www.townandcountrycampground.com.

RV ★★★★ Tent ★★★★

Beauty: ★★★★ Site Privacy: ★★★★
Spaciousness: ★★★★ Quiet: ★★★★
Security: ★★★★ Cleanliness: ★★★★
Insect Control: ★★★★ Facilities: ★★★★

Town & County Campground in Savage, has done a good job of providing "city close and country quiet." Conveniently located 18 miles southwest of Minneapolis, Town & Country is surprisingly quiet and homey for being so close to a metro area. Attractive landscaping, including bushes and flowers, adds to the welcoming atmosphere. There's even Eagle Creek for quiet walks and a big shade tree on the playground—a nice change from campgrounds whose playgrounds are sitting right out in the broiling sun. Sites are level, grassy, shaded, or open with a typical site width of 35 feet. Laid out in a series of loops, the campground has 15 pull-through sites and five seasonal campers. Security is great with owners who keep a close eye on the site. A speed limit of five mph is enforced, as is quiet time from 10 p.m. to 7 a.m. Be aware that campfires are not permitted on individual sites, but there is a community fire ring available with wood provided.

BASICS

Operated by: David & Jill Olmstead. **Open:** Apr. 1–Nov. 1. **Site Assignment:** Reservations w/ $25 deposit; refund w/ 48-hour notice. **Registration:** At campground office. **Fee:** $28 (cash, check, credit cards). **Parking:** At site; 1 car per site only.

FACILITIES

Number of RV Sites: 82. **Number of Tent-Only Sites:** 10. **Hookups:** Electric (20, 30, 50 amps), water, sewer, phone, cable TV. **Each Site:** Picnic table. **Dump Station:** Yes. **Laundry:** Yes. **Pay Phone:** Yes. **Rest Rooms and Showers:** Yes. **Fuel:** No. **Propane:** No. **Internal Roads:** Paved, in good condition. **RV Service:** No. **Market:** Couple of blocks. **Restaurant:** Couple of blocks. **General Store:** Yes, limited. **Vending:** Yes. **Swimming Pool:** Yes. **Playground:** Yes. **Other:** Spa, game room, storm shelter, sports field, stream, coin games, basketball. **Activities:** Swimming. **Nearby Attractions:** Mall of America, Minnesota Zoo, Mississippi River cruises, casino, Minnesota Children's Zoo, Murphy's Landing Historic Village, Fort Snelling State Park, horse racing, auto racing, antiques, gold, horseback riding. **Additional Information:** Greater Minneapolis Convention & Visitors Assoc., (800) 445-7412.

RESTRICTIONS

Pets: Leash only; extra fee of $1 per pet. **Fires:** In community fire ring only; not at individual sites. **Alcoholic Beverages:** Permitted. **Vehicle Maximum Length:** None. **Other:** Motorcycles & motorbikes not to be ridden, except to & from site.

TO GET THERE

From the junction of I-35W and Hwy. 13S, take Exit 38 and drive 4.5 mi. west on Hwy. 13S, then 500 ft. south on Hwy. 13, then 0.5 mi. west on 126th St. to Boone Ave. Roads are mostly wide and well maintained w/ adequate shoulders.

ST. CHARLES
Lazy D Campground

R. R. 1, Box 252, Altura 55910. T: (507) 932-3098; www.lazyd-camping-trailrides.com.

RV ★★★ Tent ★★★★

Beauty: ★★★★ Site Privacy: ★★★★
Spaciousness: ★★★★ Quiet: ★★★★
Security: ★★★ Cleanliness: ★★★
Insect Control: None Facilities: ★★★

A river runs through Lazy D Campground. And it's filled with trout. That's one reason the campground is popular. Another is that is offers horseback rides and other equestrian treats and the horses are on site. Located in the wilderness bluff country on the Middle Branch of the Whitewater River, the campground has spacious (40 × 50 the smallest) level, grassy sites. RV and tent sites are both available alongside the stream. The campground is mowed and the spring-fed water flows fast so mosquitos aren't a problem. What is a problem for some is the lack of a laundry and no pull-through sites.

BASICS

Operated by: Mark & Betty Thoreson. **Open:** Apr. 1–Dec. 1. **Site Assignment:** Reservations w/ 1-night deposit; refunds w/ 7-day notice. **Registration:** At campground office. **Fee:** $17 (cash, check, credit cards). **Parking:** At site.

FACILITIES

Number of RV Sites: 65. **Number of Tent-Only Sites:** 25. **Hookups:** Electric (20, 30, 50 amps), water, sewer. **Each Site:** Picnic table, fire ring. **Dump Station:** Yes. **Laundry:** No. **Pay Phone:** Yes. **Rest Rooms and Showers:** Yes. **Fuel:** No. **Propane:** No. **Internal Roads:** Gravel, in good condition. **RV Service:** No. **Market:** 8 mi. south in St. Charles. **Restaurant:** 2 mi. north in Elba. **General Store:** Yes. **Vending:** Yes. **Swimming Pool:** Yes. **Playground:** Yes. **Other:** Game room, volleyball, basketball, tether ball, horseshoes, antique carriage museum, trout stream, recreation field. **Activities:** Fishing, swimming, horseback riding (horses on site), pony rides, hay rides, trail rides, inner tubing, covered wagon rides, sleigh rides. **Nearby Attractions:** Aquatic center, golf, fire tower, hiking trails, beach, Historic Marnach House. **Additional Information:** Rochester CVB, (800) 634-8277.

RESTRICTIONS

Pets: Leash only. **Fires:** In fire ring. **Alcoholic Beverages:** Permitted. **Vehicle Max. Length:** None.

To Get There

From the junction of I-90 and Hwy. 74, take Exit 233, drive 8.5 mi. north on Hwy. 74, then 150 yards west on CR 139.

ST. CLOUD

St. Cloud Campground and RV Park

2491 2nd St. Southeast, St. Cloud 56304. T: (800) 690-7045; F: (320) 202-8990; stcloudcampgrd@aol.com.

★★★★ ★★★★

Beauty: ★★★★ Site Privacy: ★★★★
Spaciousness: ★★★★ Quiet: ★★★★
Security: ★★★★★ Cleanliness: ★★★★★
Insect Control: Yes Facilities: ★★★★

St. Cloud Campground and RV Park plays host to many camping club rallys. That's one indication of what a well run, popular facility it is. Another indication is to visit, drive through, stay, and see why it is one of the best in the state. Laid out in a series of loops, the campground offers a mix of gravel and grassy, shaded and open RV sites with a typical site width of 30 feet and 40 pull-throughs at 35 × 70. As campers check in, a guide escorts them to their site, shows them where the hookup is, and makes sure the sewer site is correctly attached to the RV. Just a little over a mile outside St. Cloud, the campground is in a quiet country setting. Tent campers have several different sites separated from RVs, as well as a primitive area offering more room and privacy. Security is tops with an owner who lives on site, regular patrols, Workkampers who live in each row of campsites and keep an eye on their area, and county sheriff patrols coming through for rounds.

Basics

Operated by: Jim & Dana Reed. **Open:** May 1–Oct. 15. **Site Assignment:** Reservations w/ no deposit. **Registration:** At campground office. **Fee:** $23.50 (cash, check, credit cards). **Parking:** At site.

Facilities

Number of RV Sites: 88. **Number of Tent-Only Sites:** 17. **Hookups:** Electric (30, 50 amps), water, sewer. **Each Site:** Picnic table, fire ring. **Dump Station:** Yes. **Laundry:** Yes. **Pay Phone:** Yes. **Rest Rooms and Showers:** Yes. **Fuel:** No. **Propane:** Yes. **Internal Roads:** Gravel, in good condition. **RV Service:** No. **Market:** 2 mi. west in St. Cloud. **Restaurant:** 2 mi. west in St. Cloud. **General Store:** Yes. **Vending:** No. **Swimming Pool:** Yes. **Playground:** Yes. **Other:** Hiking trails, volleyball, basketball, badminton, croquet, lodge, book exchange, pool table, electronic games, heated rally center building w/ kitchenette, game room. **Activities:** Swimming, hiking. **Nearby Attractions:** Charles A. Lindberg House & History Center, Ellingson Car Museum, Minnesota Baseball Hall of Fame, Munsinger Gardens & Clemens Gardens, Stearn's County Heritage Center, St. John's Benedictine Abbey. **Additional Information:** St. Cloud Area CVB, (800) 264-2940.

Restrictions

Pets: Leash only. **Fires:** Fire ring only. **Alcoholic Beverages:** Permitted. **Vehicle Maximum Length:** None.

To Get There

From the junction of US 10 and Hwy. 23, drive 1 block east on Hwy. 23 to lights at 14th Ave., drive south 1 block, then east 1 mi. Roads are wide and well maintained w/ broad shoulders.

STURGEON LAKE

Timberline Campground

9152 Timberline Rd., Sturgeon Lake 55783. T: (218) 372-3272

★★★★ ★★★★

Beauty: ★★★★ Site Privacy: ★★★★
Spaciousness: ★★★★ Quiet: ★★★★
Security: ★★★★ Cleanliness: ★★★★★
Insect Control: None Facilities: ★★★★

Set in a rural river valley six miles south of Moose Lake, Timberline Campground offers RV sites in a variety of sizes, from 28 × 50 to 50 × 100. The grounds are well maintained and guests are welcome to hunt for agates and pick wild berries in the campground and surrounding area. Sites are generally shaded and often covered with pine needles. More than half the sites are occupied by seasonals, many of whom have landscaped their sites and added personal touches. RV sites 165–168 and 181–184 are most desirable. They are larger, more private sites. The campground is quiet with a natural buffer of pine trees and noise-softening pine needle carpet. Tents have a separate section with some privacy from RV campers. Security is tops—the campground has one access road which is monitored, the owners live on site, and the grounds are patrolled.

Basics

Operated by: Jeff & Sue Floding. **Open:** May 1–Sept. 30. **Site Assignment:** Reservations accepted w/ $20 deposit; refund (minus $4) w/ 5-day notice. **Registration:** At campground office. **Fee:** $25 (cash, check, credit). **Parking:** At site.

Facilities

Number of RV Sites: 76. **Number of Tent-Only Sites:** 19. **Hookups:** Electric (20, 30, 50 amps), water, sewer. **Each Site:** Picnic table, fire ring. **Dump Station:** Yes. **Laundry:** Yes. **Pay Phone:** Yes. **Rest Rooms and Showers:** Yes. **Fuel:** No. **Propane:** No. **Internal Roads:** Paved/gravel, in good condition. **RV Service:** No. **Market:** 6 mi. north in Moose Lake. **Restaurant:** 4 mi. east in Sturgeon Lake. **General Store:** Yes. **Vending:** Yes. **Swimming Pool:** Yes. **Playground:** Yes. **Other:** Screened shelter pavilion, bike path, hiking path, snack bar, video game room, 3-hole golf course, Moose River, horseshoe, basketball, volleyball, rec room, sports field, river beach, innertube launch. **Activities:** Swimming, fishing, hiking, shuttle canoe service, boating (rental paddleboats available, berry picking, agate hunting, biking (rental bikes available), tubing (rental tubes available), Saturday night movies, scheduled activities. **Nearby Attractions:** Casinos, museums, golf, state trails, scenic drives, flea market, antique shops, historical sites. **Additional Information:** Hinckley CVB, (800) 996-4566.

Restrictions

Pets: Leash only. **Fires:** Fire ring only. **Alcoholic Beverages:** Permitted. **Vehicle Maximum Length:** None. **Other:** Visitors are charged $5 per person per day.

To Get There

From the junction of I-35 and CR 46, take Exit 209, drive 2.25 mi. west on CR 46 (through business district) to Timberlane Rd., drive north 0.75 mi. on Timberlane. Roads are wide and well maintained w/ broad shoulders.

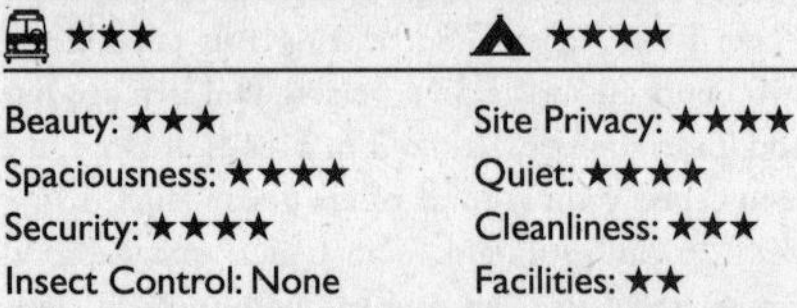

TAYLORS FALLS

Camp Waub-O-Jeeg

2185 Chisago St., Taylors Falls 55084. T: (651) 465-5721; www.taylorsfalls.com/waubojeeg.

★★★ ★★★★

Beauty: ★★★ Site Privacy: ★★★★
Spaciousness: ★★★★ Quiet: ★★★★
Security: ★★★★ Cleanliness: ★★★
Insect Control: None Facilities: ★★

Once you get there, Camp Waub-O-Jeeg is a nice quiet place to stay. But driving an RV on some of those roads is a bit tricky. CR 16 is wide and well maintained with mostly broad shoulders, but it is a curvy scenic road. The real test is the steep narrow hill leading from the campground office into the campground. Since the campground is atop a hill, the main access road is paved but it is steep, narrow, and winding with a pull-off lane in case a vehicle is coming down while another is going up. Very narrow, rough, gravel roads lead into the campsites. But it really feels like camping once you arrive. Sites are secluded on wooded, rolling terrain with level, prepared shaded spots. The typical site width is 20 feet with no pull-throughs. The sites seem bigger and more private because of all the trees surrounding them. Tent campers in particular will appreciate the privacy and wilderness setting. Security measures are good with a gate that is closed at night, owners who live on site and patrol, and regular patrols by local police. Located five miles west of Taylors Falls, the campground got its unusual name from a brave Chippewa war leader born about 1747.

Basics

Operated by: Ron & Beth Egge. **Open:** Apr. 15–Oct. 15. **Site Assignment:** Reservations w/ 1-night deposit; refund w/ 48-hour notice. **Registration:** At campground office. **Fee:** $21 (cash, check). **Parking:** At site.

Facilities

Number of RV Sites: 25. **Number of Tent-Only Sites:** 45. **Hookups:** Electric (30 amps), water. **Each Site:** Picnic table, fire ring. **Dump Station:** Yes. **Laundry:** No. **Pay Phone:** No. **Rest Rooms and Showers:** Yes. **Fuel:** No. **Propane:** No. **Internal Roads:** Gravel, in fair condition. **RV Service:** No. **Market:** 5 mi. east in Taylors Falls. **Restaurant:** 5 mi. east in Taylors Falls. **General Store:** Yes. **Vending:** No. **Swimming Pool:** No. **Playground:** Yes. **Other:** St. Croix River, pavilion, shuffleboard, badminton, horseshoes, hiking trail, volleyball. **Activ-**

ities: Swimming, fishing, hiking. **Nearby Attractions:** Scenic drives, Wild Mountain, art shops, antique stores, historic homes, skiing, snowboarding, Wildlife Educational Center, golf, rock climbing. **Additional Information:** Taylors Falls Chamber of Commerce, (80) 447-4958.

RESTRICTIONS

Pets: Leash only. **Fires:** Fire ring only. **Alcoholic Beverages:** At sites only. **Vehicle Maximum Length:** 30 ft.

TO GET THERE

From the junction of Hwy. 95 and CR 16, drive 2 mi. north on CR 16.

TAYLORS FALLS

Interstate State Park

P.O. Box 254, Taylors Falls 55084. T: (651) 465-5711; www.dnr.state.mn.us.

RV ★★ Tent ★★★★

Beauty: ★★★★★ Site Privacy: ★★
Spaciousness: ★★ Quiet: ★★★
Security: ★★★★ Cleanliness: ★★★
Insect Control: None Facilities: ★★

Few private campgrounds can compete with the natural beauty of city, state, and national parks. Interstate State Park is one of the most beautiful in Minnesota. However, few public parks can compete with the facilities offered at private campgrounds—such as water and sewer hookups, laundry, general store, and heated swimming pool. That's the case with Interstate State Park. And enough campers must find the beauty and recreational activities more important than the comfort amenities because this campground is often packed. Folks know a good thing when they see it. Establihsed in 1895, it is the oldest state park in both Wisconsin and Minnesota, and is located on the border of Taylors Falls in Minnesota and St. Croix Falls in Wisconsin. The park is best known for the towering rocky gorge which forms the dalles of the river and for the glacial potholes that are the deepest in the world. Laid out in a loop, the campground offers shady, level, back-in sites—no pull-throughs. Both RV and tent sites are right on the river, with sites 5–23 offering the best view. Swimming is prohibited because of the drop-offs, deep channel, and strong current.

BASICS

Operated by: State of Minnesota. **Open:** Mar. 1–Dec. 1. **Site Assignment:** Reservations w/ 1-night fee plus $7.25 non-refundable service charge; refunds (minus $5 fee & $7.25 service charge) w/ 3-day notice. **Registration:** At campground office. **Fee:** $15 (cash, check, credit cards). **Parking:** At site.

FACILITIES

Number of RV Sites: 22. **Number of Tent-Only Sites:** 15. **Hookups:** Electric (30, 50 amps). **Each Site:** Picnic table, fire ring. **Dump Station:** Yes. **Laundry:** No. **Pay Phone:** Yes. **Rest Rooms and Showers:** Yes. **Fuel:** No. **Propane:** No. **Internal Roads:** Paved, in good condition. **RV Service:** No. **Market:** 2 mi. north in Taylors Falls. **Restaurant:** 2 mi. north in Taylors Falls. **General Store:** No. **Vending:** Yes. **Swimming Pool:** No. **Playground:** No. **Other:** St. Croix River, nature store, picnic shelters, hiking trail, visitor center, volleyball. **Activities:** Fishing, hiking, boating (rental canoes available). **Nearby Attractions:** Scenic drives, Wild Mountain, art shops, antique stores, historic homes, skiing, snowboarding, Wildlife Educational Center, golf, rock climbing,. **Additional Information:** Taylors Falls Chamber of Commerce, (800) 447-4958.

RESTRICTIONS

Pets: Leash only. **Fires:** Fire ring only. **Alcoholic Beverages:** "3.2" beer only. **Vehicle Maximum Length:** 50 ft. **Other:** Vehicle permits of $20 per year or $4 per day are required to enter all Minnesota state parks; 14-day stay limit.

TO GET THERE

From Taylors Falls, drive 1.5 mi. south on US 8. Road is wide and well maintained w/ broad shoulders.

TAYLORS FALLS

Wildwood RV Park and Campground

P.O. Box 235, Taylors Falls 55084. T: (800) 447-4958; www.wildmountain.com; camp@wildmountain.com.

RV ★★★ Tent ★★

Beauty: ★★ Site Privacy: ★★
Spaciousness: ★★★ Quiet: ★★★
Security: ★★★★ Cleanliness: ★★
Insect Control: No Facilities: ★★★

Location is everything. Wildwood RV Park and Campground, three miles east of Taylors Falls, is expensive for what it offers but it is located in a favorite tourist area. With easy access to Hwy. 95, the campground has level, mostly shaded sites with a mix of gravel and grassy areas and 30 pull-throughs. The typical site width is 30 feet. The campground has 33 seasonal campers. Many overnight campers stop by for the convenience after seeing the campground signs on the highway. Security is good with a manager that lives on site, a gate that is closed at night, and regular patrols. The $20 fee for tent sites is rather steep for what a tent camper gets—little privacy or distance from RV campers.

BASICS

Operated by: Raedeke family. **Open:** May 1–Oct. 15. **Site Assignment:** Weekend reservations require a 2-night stay & $35 deposit; refund w/ 14-day notice. **Registration:** At campground office. **Fee:** $25 (cash, check, credit cards). **Parking:** At site.

FACILITIES

Number of RV Sites: 78. **Number of Tent-Only Sites:** 60. **Hookups:** Electric (20, 30, 50 amps), water, sewer. **Each Site:** Picnic table, fire ring. **Dump Station:** Yes. **Laundry:** No. **Pay Phone:** Yes. **Rest Rooms and Showers:** Yes. **Fuel:** No. **Propane:** No. **Internal Roads:** Gravel, in fair condition. **RV Service:** No. **Market:** 8 mi. east in St. Croix. **Restaurant:** 3 mi. west in Taylors Falls. **General Store:** Yes. **Vending:** Yes. **Swimming Pool:** Yes. **Playground:** Yes. **Other:** Mini-golf, wading pool, mountain bike trails, game room, basketball, horseshoes, free shuttles to Taylors Falls Canoe Rental 7 days a week. **Activities:** Swimming. **Nearby Attractions:** Scenic drives, Wild Mountain, art shops, antique stores, historic homes, skiing, snowboarding, Wildlife Educational Center, golf, rock climbing. **Additional Information:** Taylors Falls Chamber of Commerce, (800) 447-4958.

RESTRICTIONS

Pets: Leash only, plus $4.70 fee. **Fires:** Fire ring only. **Alcoholic Beverages:** Permitted. **Vehicle Maximum Length:** 40 ft.

TO GET THERE

From the junction of Hwy. 95 and US 8, drive 3 mi. west on US 8 and 95. Road is wide and well maintained w/ broad shoulders.

WABASHA

Pioneer Campsite

130 Pioneer Dr., Wabasha 55981. T: (651) 565-2242

RV ★★★ Tent ★★★

Beauty: ★★★ Site Privacy: ★★★
Spaciousness: ★★★ Quiet: ★★★
Security: ★★★ Cleanliness: ★★★
Insect Control: None Facilities: ★★★

A rural campground with access to the Mississippi River, Pioneer Campsite is four-and-a-half miles east of Wabasha. The campground offers a choice of shaded or open, grassy or sandy sites, with a typical site width of 35 feet. There are 20 pull-through sites and 183 seasonal campers. The grounds are somewhat hilly with plenty of trees, lots of birds, and bird feeders. "Behold the beauty of the Lord," a campground sign says. Church services are offered on Sundays. Laid out in a series of loops, Pioneer Campsites has a separate area for tent campers for more green space and privacy. Security measures include owners who live on site and provide patrols of the campgrounds.

BASICS

Operated by: Ray & Lorraine Logan. **Open:** Aptil 15–Oct. 15. **Site Assignment:** Reservations w/ 1-night deposit; refund w/ 7-day notice. **Registration:** At campground office. **Fee:** $24 (cash, check). **Parking:** At site.

FACILITIES

Number of RV Sites: 240. **Number of Tent-Only Sites:** 7. **Hookups:** Electric (20, 30, 50 amps), water, sewer. **Each Site:** Picnic table, fire ring. **Dump Station:** Yes. **Laundry:** Yes. **Pay Phone:** Yes. **Rest Rooms and Showers:** Yes. **Fuel:** No. **Propane:** No. **Internal Roads:** Paved/gravel, in good condition. **RV Service:** No. **Market:** 4.5 mi. west in Wabasha. **Restaurant:** 4.5 mi. west in Wabasha. **General Store:** Yes, limited. **Vending:** Yes. **Swimming Pool:** Yes. **Playground:** Yes. **Other:** Rec hall, recreation game, coin games, river, mini-golf, basketball, sports field, horseshoes, hiking trails, volleyball, boat ramp. **Activities:** Swimming, hiking, fishing, boating (rental canoes, rowboats available). **Nearby Attractions:** Mississippi River, toy museum, golf, Arrowhead Bluffs Museum, antiques, historic sites, arts & crafts shops. **Additional Information:** Wabasha Area Chamber of Commerce, (800) 565-4158.

Restrictions

Pets: Leash only. **Fires:** Fire ring only. **Alcoholic Beverages:** Permitted. **Vehicle Maximum Length:** 40 ft.

To Get There

From the junction of Hwy. 60 and US 61, drive 4 mi. south on US 61, then 0.75 mi. north on CR 30, then 2.5 mi. east on CR 24, then 0.25 mi. east on Prairie Ln. Roads are wide and well maintained w/ broad shoulders but you have to go through a residential area to get to the campground.

WALKER

Moonlight Bay Resort and Campground on Leech Lake

6409 Wedgewood Rd., Northwest, Walker 56484. T: (888) 973-7078; F: (218) 547-3047; www.fishandgame.com/moonlight.

RV ★★★ Tent ★★

Beauty: ★★★★	Site Privacy: ★★
Spaciousness: ★★	Quiet: ★★★
Security: ★★★	Cleanliness: ★★★
Insect Control: None	Facilities: ★★★

First off, all but 20 of the campground sites at Moonlight Bay Resort and Campground on Leech Lake are occupied by seasonals. That's what happens when a campground has a pretty setting, a nice restaurant with an eating deck overlooking the lake, good access, and a lot of water activities. The campground is built on a hill that runs down to the lake, so most campers have a nice view of the lake. Sites are level with concrete pads to park on. But some of the tiered sites have to be backed onto down a bit of a grade and that might not be a pleasant experience for some squeamish drivers—particularly if the ground is wet. Located five miles north of Walker, the campground's typical site width is 25 feet and most of the area is wooded with giant pine trees. Leech Lake is a famous fishing spot with its walleye, northern, perch, and muskie. Campers can bring a boat and launch it at the concrete ramp or have the campground launch it. The resort also has ample space to dock a boat after a day of fishing. Live bait and other fishing necessities are sold at the tackle shop. A golf course and driving range are right across the street. The best RV sites are 57 and 65 because they offer easy access and are bigger at 50 × 75. Tent sites are mingled among RVs.

Basics

Operated by: Al & Diane Sproessig. **Open:** May 1–Oct. 1. **Site Assignment:** Reservations w/ $15 deposit; no refunds; credit will be given for following year if 60-day notice given. **Registration:** At campground office. **Fee:** $20 (cash, check, credit cards). **Parking:** At site.

Facilities

Number of RV Sites: 107. **Number of Tent-Only Sites:** 10. **Hookups:** Electric (30, 50 amps), water, sewer, cable TV. **Each Site:** Picnic table, fire ring. **Dump Station:** Yes. **Laundry:** No. **Pay Phone:** Yes. **Rest Rooms and Showers:** Yes. **Fuel:** Yes. **Propane:** Yes. **Internal Roads:** Paved, in good condition. **RV Service:** No. **Market:** 5 mi. south in Walker. **Restaurant:** On site. **General Store:** Yes. **Vending:** No. **Swimming Pool:** Yes. **Playground:** Yes. **Other:** rec room, boat dock, boat ramp, marina, horseshoes, hiking trails, volleyball, video game room, croquet, shuffleboard. **Activities:** Fishing, swimming, boating (rental motor boats, canoes, paddleboats, kayaks available), scheduled weekend activities. **Nearby Attractions:** Golf, hunting, birdwatching, snowmobiling, skiing, horseback riding, antique & craft shops, Museum of Natural History, Sugar Point Battle Monument, Itasca State Park. **Additional Information:** Leech Lake Area Chamber of Commerce, (800) 833-1118.

Restrictions

Pets: Leash only, $6 fee per day. **Fires:** Fire ring only. **Alcoholic Beverages:** Permitted. **Vehicle Maximum Length:** 40 ft. **Other:** 3-day min. stay on holidays.

To Get There

From the junction of Hwy. 34, Hwy. 200 and Hwy. 371, drive 5.5 mi. north on Hwy. 371, then 0.5 mi. east on access road. Roads are wide and well maintained w/ broad shoulders.

WALKER

Shores of Leech Lake Campground and Marina

Box 327, Walker 56484. T: (218) 547-1819; www.shoresofleechlake.com.

RV ★★★★ Tent ★

Beauty: ★★★★	Site Privacy: ★★★
Spaciousness: ★★★	Quiet: ★★★★
Security: ★★★★	Cleanliness: ★★★
Insect Control: Yes	Facilities: ★★★★

The best sites in Shores of Leech Lake Campground and Marina are on the water—not just the shoreline but on the actual lake itself. Covered boat slips with water and electric hookups make this a wonderful place for people who want to camp on their boats. Some of the 20- to 30-foot floating bungalows have homesteaded this harbor for more than a decade. Nestled deep in the Chippewa National Forest, Leech Lake is the third largest lake in Minnesota. Except for the eagles, mosquitoes, deer, bear, and fireflies who make their home here, midweek sailors often have this 20-mile-wide, 23-mile-long body of water to themselves. Many lakefront campground sites are occupied by seasonal campers. Sites have a typical width of 30 feet, are shaded and level with eight pull-throughs. Only one site is set aside for tent campers. The campground located three miles north of Walker, has a full service marina with gas, bait, ice, marine power, pump-out station, boat, and motor rentals. A comfortable lodge offers sandwiches, pizza, beer, wine, and free coffee.

Basics

Operated by: Mitch & Mara Loomis. **Open:** May 1–Oct. 15. **Site Assignment:** Reservations for 3-night min. w/ 1-night deposit; refund w/ 14-day notice. **Registration:** At campground office. **Fee:** $24 (cash, check, credit cards). **Parking:** At site.

Facilities

Number of RV Sites: 47. **Number of Tent-Only Sites:** 1. **Hookups:** Electric (30 amp), water, sewer, cable TV, phone. **Each Site:** Picnic table, fire ring. **Dump Station:** Yes. **Laundry:** Yes. **Pay Phone:** Yes. **Rest Rooms and Showers:** Yes. **Fuel:** Yes. **Propane:** No. **Internal Roads:** Dirt, rough & narrow. **RV Service:** No. **Market:** 2.5 mi. south in Walker. **Restaurant:** 2.5 mi. south in Walker. **General Store:** Yes. **Vending:** Yes. **Swimming Pool:** No. **Playground:** Yes. **Other:** Leech Lake, fish-cleaning house, sandy beach, basketball court, hiking trails, boat ramp, boat dock, rec room, lodge. **Activities:** Swimming, fishing, boating, hiking, (rental canoes, sailboats, paddleboats, motor boats available). **Nearby Attractions:** Golf, hunting, birdwatching, snowmobiling, skiing, horseback rides, antique & craft stores, Museum of Natural History, Sugar Point Battle Monument, Itasca State Park. **Additional Information:** Leech Lake Area Chamber of Commerce, (800) 833-1118.

Restrictions

Pets: Leash only, $10 fee per night. **Fires:** Fire ring only. **Alcoholic Beverages:** Permitted. **Vehicle Maximum Length:** None.

To Get There

From the junction of Hwy. 34 and Hwy. 200/371, drive 2.5 mi. north on Hwy. 371, then 0.5 mi. east on access road. Roads are wide and well maintained w/ good shoulders.

WASECA

Kiesler's Campground

Box 503B, Waseca 56093. T: (800) 533-4642, ext. 5; www.kieslers.com; camp@kieslers.com.

RV ★★★★ Tent ★★★★

Beauty: ★★★★	Site Privacy: ★★★★
Spaciousness: ★★★★	Quiet: ★★★★
Security: ★★★★	Cleanliness: ★★★★
Insect Control: None	Facilities: ★★★★

If you played from sunup to sundown, you probably wouldn't run out of things to do at Kiesler's Campground. Recreation choices are everywhere, including a 2,000-square-foot heated swimming pool with a gigantic enclosed slide and a heated wading pool, along with a nice lake for fishing and swimming. A wood chip base on the playground makes it both cleaner for children and less painful if they fall. Laid out in a series of loops, the rural campground offers a tree on every site, gravel pads for RVs, and a typical site width of 40 feet. Not surprisingly, Kiesler's has 80 seasonal campers. Surprisingly, it has only ten pull-throughs. Although tents can be put on any site, most tenters seem to prefer the east area of the park which is more wooded and away from RVs. Security measures are good with owners who live on site, regular patrols, and a traffic control gate that requires a pass to enter.

BASICS

Operated by: Steve Kiesler. **Open:** Apr. 15–Oct. 1. **Site Assignment:** Reservations accepted w/ $30 deposit, $50 on holidays; refund (minus $5 fee) w/ 7-day notice. **Registration:** At campground office. **Fee:** $33 (cash, check, credit cards). **Parking:** At site.

FACILITIES

Number of RV Sites: 280. **Number of Tent-Only Sites:** 17. **Hookups:** Electric (30, 50 amps), water, sewer, cable TV. **Each Site:** Picnic table, fire ring. **Dump Station:** Yes. **Laundry:** Yes. **Pay Phone:** Yes. **Rest Rooms and Showers:** Yes. **Fuel:** No. **Propane:** Yes. **Internal Roads:** Gravel, in good condition. **RV Service:** No. **Market:** 1.5 mi. west in Waseca. **Restaurant:** Within walking distance. **General Store:** Yes. **Vending:** Yes. **Swimming Pool:** Yes. **Playground:** Yes. **Other:** Volleyball, shuffleboard, horseshoes, mini-golf, game room, basketball, wading pool, hiking trails, recreation building, boat docks, lake. **Activities:** Swimming, fishing, hiking, boating (rental motorboats available), scheduled weekend activities. **Nearby Attractions:** Cabela's, Heritage Halls Museum, golf, antique & craft shops, Mall of America, Farmamerica. **Additional Information:** Owatonna Area Convention & Tourism, (800) 423-6466.

RESTRICTIONS

Pets: Leash only but encourage campers to leave pets at home. **Fires:** Fire ring only. **Alcoholic Beverages:** Permitted. **Vehicle Maximum Length:** 40 ft. **Other:** All visitors must register as day campers at $4 per person per day.

TO GET THERE

From the junction of US 14 and Hwy. 13, drive east 1.5 mi. Roads are wide and well maintained w/ broad shoulders.

WINONA
Prairie Island Campground

1120 Prairie Island Rd., Winona 55987. T: (507) 452-4501

RV ★★ Tent ★★★

Beauty: ★★★ Site Privacy: ★★★
Spaciousness: ★★★ Quiet: ★★★
Security: ★★★★ Cleanliness: ★★★
Insect Control: None Facilities: ★★

Located on the banks of the Mississippi River, one-and-a-half miles north of Winona, Missouri, Prairie Island Campground is surrounded by city park land including hiking trails and a deer park. Five golf courses are located within a 25-mile radius. Arranged in a series of loops, the sites are level, grassy, and mostly shaded with 20 pull-throughs. The typical site width is 40 feet. Tent sites have some privacy away from RV sites. Security is great—resident managers live on site, the entrance gate is closed at night, and the campground is patrolled. Like all riverfront campgrounds, however, the site sometimes floods. It doesn't happen every year, but it is best to check for flood conditions before planning an overnight stay.

BASICS

Operated by: City of Winona. **Open:** Apr. 1–Nov. 1. **Site Assignment:** Reservations accepted; no deposit. **Registration:** At campground office. **Fee:** $15 (cash, check, credit cards). **Parking:** At site.

FACILITIES

Number of RV Sites: 86. **Number of Tent-Only Sites:** 90. **Hookups:** Electric (20, 30, 50 amps). **Each Site:** Picnic table, fire ring. **Dump Station:** Yes. **Laundry:** No. **Pay Phone:** Yes. **Rest Rooms and Showers:** Yes. **Fuel:** No. **Propane:** No. **Internal Roads:** Paved, in good condition. **RV Service:** No. **Market:** 1.5 mi. south in Winona. **Restaurant:** 1.5 mi. south in Winona. **General Store:** Yes. **Vending:** No. **Swimming Pool:** No. **Playground:** Yes. **Other:** Mississippi River, sandy beach, boat launch, game room, walking trails, putting green, video/paperback library, recreation field, fish-cleaning station. **Activities:** Fishing, swimming, hiking, boating (rental canoes available), planned weekend activities. **Nearby Attractions:** River boat cruises, aquatic park, 208-ft. water slide, Steamboat Center, ice arena, golf, Winona County Historical Museum, antique & art shops. **Additional Information:** Winona Area Chamber of Commerce CVB, (800) 657-4972.

RESTRICTIONS

Pets: Leash only. **Fires:** Fire ring only. **Alcoholic Beverages:** Permitted. **Vehicle Maximum Length:** None.

TO GET THERE

From the junction of US 61 and Pelzer St., drive northeast 1.5 mi. on Pelzer to Prairie Island Rd., drive 1 mi. east on Prairie Island Rd. Roads are wide and well maintained w/ broad shoulders.

WINONA
Winona KOA

Rte. 6, Box 181, Winona 55987. T: (877) 454-2267

RV ★★★ Tent ★★★

Beauty: ★★★ Site Privacy: ★★★
Spaciousness: ★★★ Quiet: ★★★
Security: ★★★ Cleanliness: ★★★
Insect Control: None Facilities: ★★★

Located in hilly country eight miles south of Winona, the Winona KOA is a rural campground with sites on three levels of the hillside. A metal staircase leads up to the office and playroom. The third tier of campsites has a steep hill going up to it. The different levels of campground allow for more privacy and a better view. The campground attracts a lot of local campers—there are 27 seasonal campers—as well as travelers on their way to the Wisconsin Dells. Campsites are generally shady with mature oak trees, level, and grassy. The typical site width is 30 feet and the campground has 12 pull-throughs. Most sites have gravel pads for RVs. Tent sites have more trees, grass, and greenery. For security, the owner lives on site and patrols the campground.

BASICS

Operated by: Gordie & Ann Rasmussen. **Open:** Apr. 15–Oct. 15. **Site Assignment:** Reservations w/ no deposit. **Registration:** At campground office. **Fee:** $24 (cash, check, credit cards). **Parking:** At site.

FACILITIES

Number of RV Sites: 60. **Number of Tent-Only Sites:** 12. **Hookups:** Electric (20, 30, 50 amps), water. **Each Site:** Picnic table, fire ring. **Dump Station:** Yes. **Laundry:** Yes. **Pay Phone:** Yes. **Rest Rooms and Showers:** Yes. **Fuel:** No. **Propane:** Yes. **Internal Roads:** Paved/gravel, in good condition. **RV Service:** No. **Market:** 8 mi. north in Winona. **Restaurant:** 4 mi. south in Pickwick. **General Store:** Yes. **Vending:** Yes. **Swimming Pool:** Yes. **Playground:** Yes. **Other:** Mississippi River, rec room, pavilion, boat ramp, boat dock, sports field, hiking trails, horseshoes, volleyball, marina. **Activities:** Swimming, fishing, hiking, boating (rental canoes available), planned weekend activities. **Nearby Attractions:** Museums, Polish Cultural Institute, golf, boating, aquatic center, antique shops, art galleries, ice arena. **Additional Information:** Winona CVB, (800) 657-4972.

RESTRICTIONS

Pets: Leash only. **Fires:** Fire ring only. **Alcoholic Beverages:** Permitted. **Vehicle Maximum Length:** None.

TO GET THERE

From the junction of Hwy. 43 and US 61/14, drive 6 mi. south and east on US 61/14. Roads are wide and well maintained w/ broad shoulders.

Mississippi

Visitors to Mississippi can explore a rich cultural heritage. As the home of the Delta blues, legend has it that bluesman Robert Johnson sold his soul to the Devil in southern Mississippi. Writers such as Eudora Welty and Nobel laureate William Faulkner immortalized the struggles of fictional Mississippians. Today, much of Mississippi's drama occurs in the casinos that dot the Gulf Coast and the Mississippi River.

Mississippi historical sites span centuries. The **Phau Indian Mounds** in the northeast corner of the state were maintained by ancient nomadic Indians until roughly 1200 AD. Antebellum Mississippi enjoyed a thriving economy based on cotton and slave labor. **Natchez** was at one time purported to have the most millionaires outside of New York City. Many of Natchez's pre-Civil War buildings were spared desecration in the Civil War because of the city's early surrender to the Union forces. Scores of these historic buildings and lavish mansions are open for touring today.

Confederate president Jefferson Davis grew up near **Woodville** in southern Mississippi and retired to **Biloxi** after being acquitted of Federal treason charges.

The fortified port city of **Vicksburg** was the focus of one of the bloodiest and most dramatic campaigns of the Civil War. In the spring and summer of 1863, battles were fought at various sites in west central Mississippi. The campaign culminated in the 47-day siege of Vicksburg, and its capitulation on July 4, 1863. With this victory, the Union gained control of the lower Mississippi River while severing confederate transport and communication with Louisiana, Arkansas and Texas. Learn more at the 1700-acre **Vicksburg National Military Park.**

Think of Mississippi's geography in terms of five regions: the Hills Region lies in the northeast corner of the state and is traced on the eastern side by the Tennessee–Tombigbee Waterway. The flatter-than-a-pancake Delta Region in the northwestern part of the state is bounded by the Mississippi River on its western side. The Capitol/River region in the southwest corner of the state contains the historically and culturally significant cities of Natchez, Vicksburg, and **Jackson.** The central eastern Pines region contains prairies and hills as well as piney forests. Finally, the Coastal region of the southeast is enjoying a tourism boom due to its newly established gaming industry.

The **Natchez Trace Parkway** may have originated as long as 8,000 years ago, as a migratory path for buffalo. Today the historic roadway begins in Natchez and terminates in Nashville, Tennessee. The Trace is designated and maintained as a scenic parkway, with campgrounds and attractions.

Outdoors enthusiasts will find plenty to do in Mississippi, such as freshwater fishing, boating, skiing, and swimming on some of the most surprisingly gorgeous lakes in the southeast. There is also deep-sea fishing, plenty of hunting, hiking, biking, and paddling. Golfers also fare well in Mississippi, where casinos have augmented respected older courses with some exciting new ones.

Popular attractions in Mississippi include: **Bienville National Forest, Beauvoir-Jefferson Davis Home and Presidential Library, DeSoto National Forest,** Native American mounds, plantations and historic buildings, **Gulf Islands National Seashore,** the state capitol in Jackson, **Grand Village of the Natchez Indians, The Old Spanish Fort and Museums,** Elvis Presley's birthplace in **Tupelo** and the **Elvis Presley Center and Museum,** the **Jimmie Rodgers Museum.**

The following facilities accept payment in checks or cash only:

Plantation Park, Natchez

ABERDEEN

Blue Bluff

20051 Blue Bluff Rd., Aberdeen 39730. T: (662) 369-2832 or (877) 444-6777; F: (662) 369-0232; www.reserveusa.com.

RV ★★★★ Tent ★★★★

Beauty: ★★★★ Site Privacy: ★★★★
Spaciousness: ★★★★ Quiet: ★★★
Security: ★★★★★ Cleanliness: ★★★★
Insect Control: ★ Facilities: ★★★

Named for the 80-foot clay and limestone bluffs bordering the park on the eastern side, the campground at Blue Bluff is quite attractive. The campground is laid out in two loops. Most sites are spacious, but sites found in pairs feel small and exposed. Gorgeous tree cover provides shade to all sites. A few sites are secluded, but most are open to their neighbors. The most secluded sites (good honeymoon suites) are 53 and 65. Sites 66–92 include some waterfront sites with nice views. Site 45 wins the beauty pageant with its breathtaking view. Sites 1–32, while nicely wooded, tend to be closer together than the rest. Most sites offers back-in parking; all parking is paved.

Basics

Operated By: US Army Corps of Engineers. **Open:** Year-round. **Site Assignment:** First come, first served; reservations accepted through the National Recreation Reservation Service (NRRS) at (877) 444-6777 or www.reserveusa.com. Reservations can be made up to 240 days in advance, full payment required upon making reservation; credit card preferred (V, MC, D, AE), or pay by money order if at least 21 days in advance of arrival. $10 fee for cancellation or change of site or dates. Cancellation within three days of arrival charged first night, no-show charged $20 plus first night. **Registration:** Gatehouse or night access lane. **Fee:** $16 for waterfront or sewer, $14 for basic. **Parking:** At site, limit 2 vehicles per site, fee for extra vehicles.

Facilities

Number of Multipurpose Sites: 92. **Hookups:** Water, electric (30, 50 amps), 2 w/ sewer. **Each Site:** Picnic table, fire ring, grill, lantern post, impact pad. **Dump Station:** Yes. **Laundry:** Yes. **Pay Phone:** Yes. **Rest Rooms and Showers:** Yes. **Fuel:** No. **Propane:** No. **Internal Roads:** Paved. **RV Service:** 1.5 mi. northwest in Aberdeen. **Market:** 1.5 mi. northwest in Aberdeen. **Restaurant:** 1.5 mi. northwest in Aberdeen. **General Store:** 20 mi. north in Armory. **Vending:** Beverages only. **Swimming Pool:** No. **Playground:** Yes. **Other:** Boat launch, fishing piers, boat ramp, boat docks, fish cleaning station. **Activities:** Swimming beach, hiking trail, volleyball & tennis courts. **Nearby Attractions:** Aberdeen Pilgrimage Antebellum home tours, Blue Bluff River Festival. **Additional Information:** Aberdeen Chamber of Commerce, (662) 369-6488.

Restrictions

Pets: Leash only. **Fires:** Allowed, fire rings only. **Alcoholic Beverages:** Allowed (no glass bottles). **Vehicle Maximum Length:** 50 ft. **Other:** Title 36 regulations posted.

To Get There

From Columbus, drive 30 mi. north on US 45 to Aberdeen. In downtown Aberdeen, at the intersection of Commerce and Meridian, turn northeast onto Meridian. Cross the railroad tracks and the bridge, then take the first right. The campground is on the left.

BAY ST. LOUIS

Casino Magic RV Park

711 Casino Magic Dr., Bay St. Louis 39520. T: (800) 5-MAGIC-5 or ext. 4802; F: (228) 463-4008; www.casimagic.com.

RV ★★★★ Tent n/a

Beauty: ★★★★ Site Privacy: ★★★
Spaciousness: ★★★★ Quiet: ★★★★
Security: ★★★★ Cleanliness: ★★★★
Insect Control: ★★★★ Facilities: ★★★★

Attractive Casino Magic has large sites laid out in two loops that flank the office and washhouse. Few sites are shady. Sites 45, 47, 49, and 50 are shady and roomy, with nice views of the golf course. Sites 4, 5, 7, and 9 enjoy a pleasant view of marshy bayou with ducks and water lilies. All sites feature paved parking, and most have back-in parking. Guests either walk to the casino or take the free 24-hour shuttle. The campground is about one mile from a beach on Bay St. Louis and about 15 miles from beaches on the Gulf of Mexico. Bay St. Louis is an energetic little town with plenty of dining and entertainment. There are no gates at Casino Magic, but the park is patrolled by casino security personnel 24 hours a day. Avoid southern Mississippi in the hot, humid summer months.

Basics

Operated By: Casino Magic. **Open:** Year-round. **Site Assignment:** Sites assigned; reservations strongly recommended, credit card deposit; 24-hour cancellation notice required for refund; reservations held until 6 p.m. **Registration:** Office (24-hours weekends), late-comers check for instructions at office. **Fee:** $21 for weekdays, $23 for weekends (cash, V, MC, AE, D); Players Club discounts. **Parking:** At sites, not on grass.

Facilities

Number of RV Sites: 100. **Number of Tent-Only Sites:** 0. **Number of Multipurpose Sites:** None. **Hookups:** Water, electric (30, 50 amps), sewer, cable TV. **Each Site:** Grill, picnic table. **Dump Station:** No. **Laundry:** Yes. **Pay Phone:** Yes. **Rest Rooms and Showers:** Yes. **Fuel:** No. **Propane:** No. **Internal Roads:** Paved. **RV Service:** On call mechanic. **Market:** 0.5 mi. **Restaurant:** Several at the casiNo. **General Store:** 15 mi. in Gulfport. **Vending:** Yes. **Swimming Pool:** No (hotel access). **Playground:** No. **Other:** Boat launch, pavilion. **Activities:** Free shuttle to casinos (walking distance), The Bridges 18-hole golf course. **Nearby Attractions:** John C. Stennis Space Center, Gulfport boat & bayou tours, Marine Life Oceanarium, Wildlife Management Areas, Bay St. Louis antique shopping. **Additional Information:** Mississippi Gulf Coast CVB, (228) 896-6699.

Restrictions

Pets: Leash only. **Fires:** Allowed, grills only. **Alcoholic Beverages:** At site only. **Vehicle Maximum Length:** 45 ft. **Other:** One-week stay limit.

To Get There

From I-10, take exit 13 and drive 5 mi. south on State Hwy. 603 to US 90. Turn east and drive on US 90 for 2 mi. Turn left (north) on Blue Meadow Rd. Casino Magic Dr. is 0.5 mi. on the right.

BILOXI

Mazalea Travel Park

8220 West Oaklawn Rd., Biloxi 39532. T: (228) 392-8575; F: (228) 392-4502; wmsentr@aol.com.

RV ★★★★ Tent ★★★

Beauty: ★★★★ Site Privacy: ★★★★
Spaciousness: ★★★★ Quiet: ★★★★
Security: ★★★★ Cleanliness: ★★★★
Insect Control: ★★ Facilities: ★★

Mazalea is 9 miles from the beach and 8 miles from outlet malls. There are over a dozen casinos in Biloxi and scores of restaurants. Tourist attractions include Beauvoir, the retirement home of Jefferson Davis, and art galleries and museums. The campground is adjacent to I-10, making it a cinch to tool around Biloxi. However, this urban locale is cause for security concerns given the park's lack of gates. Snowbirds like to winter at Mazalea, and families flock here in the spring, summer, and fall. Try to visit in spring or fall in order to avoid the heat.

Basics

Operated By: Williams family. **Open:** Year-round. **Site Assignment:** Sites usually assigned; reservations recommended, no deposit; receive credit toward future stay w/ early departure. **Registration:** Camp store. **Fee:** $20–$22 (cash, check, V, MC, D). **Parking:** At site, in parking lot.

Facilities

Number of RV Sites: 134. **Number of Tent-Only Sites:** 5. **Number of Multipurpose Sites:** RV sites can be multipurpose in the off-season only. **Hookups:** Water, electric (30, 50), sewer, cable. **Each Site:** Picnic table. **Dump Station:** Yes. **Laundry:** Yes. **Pay Phone:** Yes. **Rest Rooms and Showers:** Yes. **Fuel:** No. **Propane:** Yes. **Internal Roads:** Paved. **RV Service:** 7 mi. east in D'Iberville. **Market:** Camp store, Wal-Mart 5 mi. east in D'Iberville. **Restaurant:** 3 mi. west in Gulfport. **General Store:** Camp store, Wal-Mart 5 mi. east in D'Iberville. **Vending:** Yes. **Swimming Pool:** No. **Playground:** Yes. **Other:** Activities building. **Activities:** Shuffleboard, horseshoes, winter potluck gatherings. **Nearby Attractions:** Biloxi casinos, museums, outlet shopping, beach within 8 mi. **Additional Information:** Mississippi Gulf Coast CVB, (228) 896-6699.

Restrictions

Pets: Leash only. **Fires:** Not allowed. **Alcoholic Beverages:** At site only. **Vehicle Maximum Length:** 45 ft.

To Get There

From I-10, take exit 41 (Woolmarket Rd.). The campground is 300 yards south on the right.

BILOXI

Parker's Landing

7577 East Oaklawn Rd., Biloxi 39532. T: (228) 392-7717; F: (228) 392-7717; www.woodalls.com; parkersland@aol.com.

RV ★★★★	Tent ★★★
Beauty: ★★★★	Site Privacy: ★★★
Spaciousness: ★★★	Quiet: ★★★
Security: ★★★	Cleanliness: ★★★★
Insect Control: ★★	Facilities: ★★★

Convenient to numerous casinos, restaurants, and tourist attractions, Parker's Landing is located eight miles from the beach in Biloxi. This tidy, urban campground straddles Parker's Creek and maintains a boat ramp. This park doesn't offer the wide assortment of entertainment facilities found at many private campgrounds. There are two camping areas. The older section includes mid-sized sites, which are long, thin, and sandwiched together. Some sites in the older section are open. Others, including sites 64–76 and 50–58, are nicely shaded by pine, cedar, and oak. Newer sites across the creek are completely open and provide parking for two additional vehicles at each site. All parking is paved, and there are pull-through and back-in sites. Parker's Landing is adjacent to I-10 and has no gates, making security marginal. Try to plan a visit for spring or fall.

Basics

Operated By: Elva & Dennis O'Brian. **Open:** Year-round. **Site Assignment:** Reservations recommended, credit card deposit; 3-day cancellation policy for refund on Holidays. **Registration:** Office. **Fee:** $16–$22 (cash, check, V, MC, AE). **Parking:** At sites, in parking lot.

Facilities

Number of RV Sites: 130. **Number of Tent-Only Sites:** 5. **Number of Multipurpose Sites:** 12. **Hookups:** Water, electric (30, 50 amps), sewer, cable. **Each Site:** Picnic table. **Dump Station:** No. **Laundry:** Yes. **Pay Phone:** Yes. **Rest Rooms and Showers:** Yes. **Fuel:** No. **Propane:** Yes. **Internal Roads:** Paved. **RV Service:** 7 mi. east in D'Iberville. **Market:** Camp store, Wal-Mart 5 mi. east in D'Iberville. **Restaurant:** 5 mi. east in D'Iberville. **General Store:** 5 mi. east in D'Iberville. **Vending:** Beverages only. **Swimming Pool:** Yes. **Playground:** No. **Other:** Fire rings by the creek, boat ramp, banquet hall, lodge, gift shop. **Activities:** Creek fishing. **Nearby Attractions:** Biloxi casinos, Beauvoir Jefferson Davis home, museums, outlet shopping, beach within 7 mi. **Additional Information:** Mississippi Gulf Coast CVB, (228) 896-6699.

Restrictions

Pets: Leash only. **Fires:** Creekside fire-rings only. **Alcoholic Beverages:** Allowed. **Vehicle Maximum Length:** 45 ft.

To Get There

From I-10, take exit 41 (Woolmarket Rd.). The campground is just south of the interstate on the right.

COLUMBUS

DeWayne Hayes Campground

7934 Barton Ferry Rd., Columbus 39701. T: (662) 434-6939 or (877) 444-6777 for reservations; F: (662) 434-9346, Mar. through Oct. only; www.reserveusa.com.

RV ★★★★	Tent ★★★★
Beauty: ★★★★★	Site Privacy: ★★★
Spaciousness: ★★★★★	Quiet: ★★★★
Security: ★★★★★	Cleanliness: ★★★★
Insect Control: ★	Facilities: ★★★

This area was named after Pfc Loyd DeWayne Hayes, who died at the age of 20 while helping with preparations for the Tennessee-Tombigbee Waterway. Though less wooded, DeWayne Hayes campground has nicer waterfront sites than nearby Town Creek. Sites on the right-hand side of the main road often have water views. The nicest of these are sites 3–36 and 70–92. Site 91 is exceptionally lovely. All sites are large with ample space between neighbors. All are nicely shaded, although there is little privacy between sites. Parking is paved, and most sites are back-ins. Of the pull-throughs, lackluster number 66 is the largest. Day-use facilities are extensive at this rural recreation area. Prepare for monster mosquitoes, and avoid visiting during hot, humid late summer. Excellent destinations when the weather is mild, the campgrounds along the Tennessee-Tombigbee Waterway rarely fill to capacity. Gates lock at night, making this park extremely secure.

Basics

Operated By: US Army Corps of Engineers. **Open:** Year-round. **Site Assignment:** First come, first served; reservations accepted through the National Recreation Reservation Service (NRRS) at (877) 444-6777 or www.reserveusa.com. Reservations can be made up to 240 days in advance, full payment required upon making reservation; credit card preferred (V, MC, D, AE), or pay by money order if at least 21 days in advance of arrival. $10 fee for cancellation or change of site or dates. Cancellation within three days of arrival charged first night, no-show charged $20 plus first night. **Registration:** Gatehouse. **Fee:** $18 for waterfront & sewer, $16 for waterfront or sewer, $14 for water & electric, $8 for primitive tent site. **Parking:** At site, limit 2 vehicles, fee for extra vehicles.

Facilities

Number of RV Sites: 0. **Number of Tent-Only Sites:** 10. **Number of Multipurpose Sites:** 100. **Hookups:** Water, electric (50 amps), 25 w/ sewer. **Each Site:** Picnic table, fire ring, concrete pad, grill, lantern pole. **Dump Station:** Yes. **Laundry:** Yes. **Pay Phone:** Yes. **Rest Rooms and Showers:** Yes. **Fuel:** No. **Propane:** No. **Internal Roads:** Paved. **RV Service:** 5 mi. east in Columbus. **Market:** 7 mi. east in Columbus. **Restaurant:** 5 mi. east in Columbus. **General Store:** 5 mi. east in Columbus. **Vending:** Beverages only. **Swimming Pool:** No. **Playground:** Yes. **Other:** Boat launch, fish cleaning station, picnic shelters, group campfire ring, wildlife viewing area. **Activities:** Cypress Swamp Nature Trail, swimming beach, fishing, volleyball, tennis, hiking. **Nearby Attractions:** Columbus & West Point within 5 mi., Mississippi State University, Tombigbee National Forest, Lake Lowndes State Park. **Additional Information:** Columbus Chamber of Commerce, (662) 327-7796.

Restrictions

Pets: Leash only. **Fires:** Allowed, fire rings only. **Alcoholic Beverages:** Allowed. **Vehicle Maximum Length:** 50 ft.

To Get There

From Columbus, take US 45 north for 4 mi. to the junction of MS Hwys. 50 and 373. Turn left and follow 373 north for 1.5 mi. to Stenson Creek Rd. and turn left. Drive 2 mi. to Barton's Ferry Rd. Turn left to the entrance.

COLUMBUS

Lake Lowndes State Park

3319 Lake Lowndes Rd., Columbus 39702. T: (662) 328-2110; F: (662) 241-7683; www.mdwfp.com; lowndesl@ayrix.net.

RV ★★★	Tent ★★★
Beauty: ★★★★	Site Privacy: ★★★
Spaciousness: ★★★	Quiet: ★★★
Security: ★★★	Cleanliness: ★★★★
Insect Control: ★★	Facilities: ★★★★

Situated on 150-acre Lake Lowndes, this state park offers an interesting variety of activities. The small lake is stocked with catfish, crappie, bass, and bream.The campground consists of thee main loops situated in a shady stand of trees dominated by loblolly pine and various oak species. Site size is average, and there is little foliage between sites to provide privacy. All parking is back-in–style and paved. The nicest sites are situated along the lake. There is only one washhouse serving 50 sites, so we anticipate lines for potties on crowded holiday weekends. Located six miles from Columbus, home of Mississippi State University, this campground is busier on fall football weekends. Try visiting in late spring when Mississippi weather is at its best. Security is fair at this rural park, where gates were not locked and night-time patrolling was sporadic when we visited.

Basics

Operated By: Mississippi Dept. of Wildlife, Fisheries & Parks. **Open:** Year-round. **Site Assignment:** First come, first served; reservations accepted, $15 first night deposit, nonrefundable. **Registration:** Ranger makes rounds in the evening. **Fee:** $14 for full hookup (first night $15 w/ reservation), $13 for water & electric, $9 for tent, seniors, disabled (cash, V, MC, D). **Parking:** At site, in lot.

Facilities

Number of RV Sites: 0. **Number of Tent-Only Sites:** 12 primitive. **Number of Multipurpose Sites:** 50. **Hookups:** Water, electric (30, 50 amps), some w/ sewer. **Each Site:** Picnic table, grill. **Dump Station:** Yes. **Laundry:** Yes. **Pay Phone:** Yes. **Rest Rooms and Showers:** Yes. **Fuel:** No. **Propane:** No. **Internal Roads:** Paved. **RV Service:** 20 mi. north in Columbus. **Market:** Camp store (in season only), 1 mi. west in Columbus. **Restaurant:** 1 mi. west in Columbus. **General Store:** Camp store (in season only), 2.5 mi. north in Columbus. **Vending:** Yes. **Swimming Pool:** No. **Playground:** Yes.

Other: Pool table, ping pong table, nature trail, picnic sites, swimming beach, bike trail, equestrian trail, visitor's center, meeting rooms, video games, marina, boat ramp. **Activities:** Disc golf, walking track, boat rentals, tennis, volleyball, basketball, soccer, softball, fishing. **Nearby Attractions:** Over 100 antebellum homes, Historic Downtown Columbus, river ferry, Tennessee-Tombigbee Waterway, art & family festivals. **Additional Information:** Columbus Visitor Information, (662) 329-1191.

Restrictions

Pets: Leash only. **Fires:** Campsites only. **Alcoholic Beverages:** Not allowed. **Vehicle Maximum Length:** No limit.

To Get There

Take I-82 to Columbus. Take the Least Oaks exit and drive south on State Hwy. 69. Turn east onto Lake Lowndes Rd. The park is 10 mi. southeast of Columbus.

COLUMBUS

Town Creek Campground

3606 West Plymouth Rd., Columbus 39701-9504. T: (662) 327-2142; F: (662) 328-8766; sam.usace.army.mil/op/rec/tenn-tom/camp.html; janalie.m.graham@sam.usacc.army.mil.

RV ★★★★ Tent ★★★★

Beauty: ★★★★ Site Privacy: ★★★★
Spaciousness: ★★★★★ Quiet: ★★★★★
Security: ★★★★ Cleanliness: ★★★★★
Insect Control: ★ Facilities: ★★★

Yet another lovely impoundment of the Tennessee-Tombigbee River system, Columbus Lake offers excellent fishing, and Town Creek Recreation Area offers excellent amenities for anglers. Within the recreation area, small Kennedy Lake provides additional fishing opportunities, as well as a sandy swimming beach with sundeck. Many campsites boast serene lake views. Site size varies, with lakefront sites often smaller than their upland counterparts. Some sites are totally shady and secluded, while others are only partially shaded and open to neighbors. The campground is laid out in two loops and a spur with paved, back-in parking spaces. There are two attractive pull-through sites, 73 and 78, in the back of the campground. Other beautiful sites include 34, 36, 70, 71, 75, and 83–94. At this very rural campground, security is fine. However, mosquitoes are extremely annoying along the low-lying Tenn-Tom Waterway. Bring plenty of insect repellent. Avoid this area in steamy late summer.

Basics

Operated By: Army Corps of Engineers. **Open:** Year-round. **Site Assignment:** 60% reserveable, 40% first come, first served. **Registration:** At office. **Fee:** $8–$18. **Parking:** at site, 2 vehicles.

Facilities

Number of RV Sites: 100. **Number of Tent-Only Sites:** 110. **Hookups:** Electric (30, 50 amps). **Each Site:** Concrete pads, lantern posts, grills, fire ring, picnic table, access to boat ramp. **Dump Station:** Yes. **Laundry:** Yes. **Pay Phone:** Yes. **Rest Rooms and Showers:** Yes. **Fuel:** No. **Propane:** No. **Internal Roads:** Paved. **RV Service:** 10 mi. **Market:** Nearby. **Restaurant:** Nearby. **General Store:** Nearby. **Vending:** Yes. **Swimming Pool:** No. **Playground:** Yes. **Other:** Fish-cleaning station, disabled-accessible. **Activities:** Swim beach, multi use park fields, picnic pavilions, nature & hiking trails.

Restrictions

Pets: On leash only. **Fires:** Fire ring. **Alcoholic Beverages:** Allowed but not on beach. **Vehicle Maximum Length:** No limit. **Other:** 24 hour attendant.

To Get There

From Columbus, take Hwy. 45 N to junction w/ Hwy. 50 W, turn left, follow Hwy. 50 W past Hwy. 50 Waterway Bridge. Intersection is approximately 2 mi. west of bridge. Turn north, follow signs.

DENNIS

Piney Grove Campground

82 Bay Springs Resource Rd., Dennis 38838. T: (662) 728-1134; www.reserveusa.com.

RV ★★★★ Tent ★★★★

Beauty: ★★★★★ Site Privacy: ★★★★
Spaciousness: ★★★★★ Quiet: ★★★★
Security: ★★★★★ Cleanliness: ★★★★★
Insect Control: ★ Facilities: ★★★

Piney Grove is typical of the Corps of Engineers campgrounds found along the Tennessee-Tombigbee Waterway; it has incredibly beautiful campsites. All sites are commodious, with ample shade provided by loblolly pine and various hardwoods. Most campsites are afforded plenty of privacy by screening foliage. The peninsular campground contains sites in three main areas. With views of Bay Springs Lake, the area containing sites 55–81 boasts some of the most gorgeous sites in the state. Secluded and picturesque, sites 64 and 75 are absolutely fabulous. All sites have paved parking and a large gravel picnic area. Most sites are back-in. There are 10 pull-throughs sites, the nicest of which is number 113. Situated in the rural, rolling hills of northeast Mississippi, this park locks its gates at night, making it extremely secure. Rarely crowded, it's safe to visit here on summer weekends if you can stand the heat and mosquitoes.

Basics

Operated By: US Army Corps of Engineers. **Open:** Mid-Mar.–mid-Nov. **Site Assignment:** First come, first served; reservations accepted through the National Recreation Reservation Service (NRRS) at (877) 444-6777 or www.reserveusa.com. Reservations can be made up to 240 days in advance, full payment required upon making reservation; credit card preferred (V, MC, D, AE), or pay by money order if at least 21 days in advance of arrival; $10 fee for cancellation or change of site or dates; cancellation within three days of arrival charged first night; no-show charged $20 & first night. **Registration:** Gatehouse, gate locks at 10 p.m. **Fee:** $18 for waterfront site, $16 for non-waterfront site; 8 people max. **Parking:** At site, limit 3 vehicles, fee for extra vehicles.

Facilities

Number of RV Sites: 0. **Number of Tent-Only Sites:** 10 primitive-boat access only (island). **Number of Multipurpose Sites:** 142. **Hookups:** Water, electric (20, 30, 50 amps). **Each Site:** Grill, picnic table, fire ring, lantern pole. **Dump Station:** Yes. **Laundry:** Yes. **Pay Phone:** Yes. **Rest Rooms and Showers:** Yes. **Fuel:** No. **Propane:** No. **Internal Roads:** Paved. **RV Service:** 30 mi. east in Red Bay, AL. **Market:** 25 mi. west in Booneville. **Restaurant:** 25 mi. west in Booneville. **General Store:** 25 mi. west in Booneville. **Vending:** Beverages only. **Swimming Pool:** No. **Playground:** Yes. **Other:** Boat ramp, fishing piers, fish-cleaning station, amphitheater, swimming beach, picnic shelter. **Activities:** Multi-use game courts, nature trails, fishing, swimming, campfire programs in-season. **Nearby Attractions:** Tishomingo State Park, Brices Cross Roads National Battlefield Site, Chickasaw Village, Tupelo, Birthplace of Elvis Presley, Tennessee-Tombigbee Waterway. **Additional Information:** Tupelo CVB, (662) 842-4521.

Restrictions

Pets: Leash only. **Fires:** Grills, fire rings. **Alcoholic Beverages:** Not allowed. **Vehicle Maximum Length:** Sites vary (see www.reserveusa.com for site specifications). **Other:** 14-day stay limit.

To Get There

From Tupelo, take the Natchez Trace Parkway northeast 36 mi. to the first exit after crossing the Tennessee-Tombigbee Waterway. Take this exit (Bay Springs Lake) and turn left on Tishomingo CR 1. Drive 0.75 mi. to Mississippi Hwy. 4 and turn left. Drive 1 mi. and turn right on Prentiss CR 3501. Continue 7 mi. to the park. From the intersection of State Hwys. 4 and 30 in Booneville, take State Hwy. 30 east 11 mi. to Burton, and turn right on CR 3501. Follow for 3 mi. and turn left at the sign for Piney Grove Recreation Area.

ENID

Wallace Creek Campground Enid Lake

P.O. Box 10, Enid 38927. T: (662) 563-4571 or (877) 444-6777 for reservations; www.reserveusa.com.

RV ★★★★ Tent ★★★★

Beauty: ★★★★ Site Privacy: ★★★★
Spaciousness: ★★★★ Quiet: ★★★★
Security: ★★★ Cleanliness: ★★★★★
Insect Control: ★★★★ Facilities: ★★★

The Enid Lake area includes verdant rolling hills, blue water, and extensive recreational facilities. Fishing is spectacular here—Enid Lake holds the world's record for largest crappie. With the newest wash-houses and largest sites, Wallace Creek is the most appealing campground at Enid Lake. A few choice sites, including 26, 28, 41, 71, 90, 91, and 92, have views of the lake. All campsites at Wallace Creek are spacious and shady, though few are secluded. All parking is paved. Most sites offer back-in parking. Security at Wallace Creek is fair; the campground is very close to I-55, and there are no locked gates at night, although rangers patrol regularly and Enid is in a rural location.

Basics

Operated By: US Army Corps of Engineers.

Open: All year, some seasonal. **Site Assignment:** First come, first served; reservations accepted through the National Recreation Reservation Service (NRRS) at (877) 444-6777 or www.reserveusa.com. Reservations can be made up to 240 days in advance, full payment required upon making reservation; credit card preferred (V, MC, D, AE), or pay by money order if at least 21 days in advance of arrival. $10 fee for cancellation or change of site or dates. Cancellation within three days of arrival charged first night, no-show charged $20 plus first night. **Registration:** Self-registration, booth registration. **Fee:** $10–$15 (cash, V, MC, D, AE). **Parking:** At site, in parking lot.

Facilities

Number of RV Sites: 0. **Number of Tent-Only Sites:** 16. **Number of Multipurpose Sites:** 235. **Hookups:** Water, electric (50 amps). **Each Site:** Picnic table, grill, fire ring, lantern pole. **Dump Station:** Yes. **Laundry:** No. **Pay Phone:** Yes. **Rest Rooms and Showers:** Yes. **Fuel:** No. **Propane:** No. **Internal Roads:** Paved. **RV Service:** 21 mi. south in Grenada. **Market:** 13 mi. north Batesville. **Restaurant:** 1 mi. at Enid Dam. **General Store:** 1 mi. at Enid Dam. **Vending:** No. **Swimming Pool:** No (at the State Park). **Playground:** Yes. **Other:** Boat launches, motorcycle trail, picnic shelters, amphitheater, swimming beach, scenic overlook, information center. **Activities:** Fishing, boating (boat rentals at State Park), swimming, hiking, equestrian trail. **Nearby Attractions:** George Payne Cossar State Park, Holly Springs National Forest, attractions in Oxford, Tunica & Memphis. **Additional Information:** Panola Partnership/ Chamber of Commerce, (662) 563-3126.

Restrictions

Pets: Leash only. **Fires:** Fire rings only. **Alcoholic Beverages:** Allowed (dry county for beer, wet for liquor). **Vehicle Maximum Length:** 40 ft. **Other:** Title 36 regulations posted.

To Get There

From I-55, take exit 233. Proceed 1 mi. east on CR 36. The recreation area is well-marked.

FULTON

Whitten Park Campground (formerly Fulton Campground)

82 Bay Springs Resource Rd., Dennis 38838. T: (662) 862-7070; www.reserveusa.com.

RV: ★★★★ Tent: ★★★★

Beauty: ★★★★★ Site Privacy: ★★★★
Spaciousness: ★★★★ Quiet: ★★★★★
Security: ★★★★★ Cleanliness: ★★★★★
Insect Control: ★★ Facilities: ★★★

Whitten Park is extremely pretty. The campground is laid out in three loops, each of which has a few waterfront sites. Sites 10, 11, and 12 have pretty water views. Close to the playground, 27 and 28 are excellent choices for families. Sites 42 and 46, the only pull-throughs at Whitten Park, are extremely large. Parking is paved, and sites are shaded by dense woods with foliage providing site privacy. On the property, the Jamie L. Whitten Historical Center features exhibits on the area's economic development. One focus is the Tennessee-Tombigbee Waterway, the largest Corps of Engineers project in history. Built mainly for navigation, the "Ten-Tom" connects the lower Tennessee Valley to the Gulf of Mexico, is five times longer than the Panama Canal, and required moving one third more earth. Security is excellent at this remote, gated campground. This campground rarely fills up, making it a good choice for summer weekend camping.

Basics

Operated By: US Army Corps of Engineers. **Open:** Year-round. **Site Assignment:** First come, first served; reservations accepted through the National Recreation Reservation Service (NRRS) at (877) 444-6777 or www.reserveusa.com. Reservations can be made up to 240 days in advance, full payment required upon making reservation; credit card preferred (V, MC, D, AE), or pay by money order if at least 21 days in advance of arrival. $10 fee for cancellation or change of site or dates. Cancellation within three days of arrival charged first night, no-show charged $20 plus first night. **Registration:** Gatehouse (gates lock at 10 p.m.). **Fee:** $16 for waterfront, $14 for non-waterfront; fee includes 8 people (cash, personal check, V, MC, D, AE). **Parking:** At sites, in parking lots.

Facilities

Number of Multipurpose Sites: 61. **Hookups:** Water, electric (30, 50 amps). **Each Site:** Picnic table, fire ring, grill, lantern pole. **Dump Station:** Yes. **Laundry:** Yes. **Pay Phone:** Yes. **Rest Rooms and Showers:** Yes. **Fuel:** No. **Propane:** No. **Internal Roads:** Paved. **RV Service:** 25 mi. east in Red Bay. **Market:** 2 mi. south in Fulton. **Restaurant:** 2 mi. south in Fulton. **General Store:** Wal-Mart 2 mi. south in Fulton. **Vending:** Beverages only. **Swimming Pool:** No. **Playground:** Yes. **Other:** Boat ramp, fish-cleaning station, fishing piers, boat docks, picnic shelters, information center, Jamie L. Whitten Historical Center. **Activities:** Multi-use courts, swimming (swimming beach for campground use only), fishing, nature trails. **Nearby Attractions:** Bean's Ferry Pottery, Tennessee-Tombigbee Waterway, Elvis Presley Birthplace in Tupelo, Tupelo National Battlefield, Oren Dunn Museum. **Additional Information:** Tupelo CVB, (800) 533-0611.

Restrictions

Pets: Leash only. **Fires:** Fire rings only. **Alcoholic Beverages:** Not allowed. **Vehicle Maximum Length:** No limit. **Other:** Title 36 regulations posted.

To Get There

From the intersection of US 78 and MS Hwy. 25 (16 mi. north of Tupelo), take Hwy. 25 north 200 yards. Turn north on Access Rd./Johnny Rankin Memorial Hwy. and drive 4.5 mi. The campground is on the left, inside the Jamie L. Whitten Historical Center and Park.

GRENADA

North Graysport Campground, Grenada Lake

P.O. Box 903, Grenada 38901-0903. T: (662) 226-8963; www.reserveusa.com.

RV: ★★★★ Tent: ★★★★

Beauty: ★★★★ Site Privacy: ★★★★
Spaciousness: ★★★★ Quiet: ★★★
Security: ★★★ Cleanliness: ★★★★
Insect Control: ★★★ Facilities: ★★★★

The 63,000-acre Grenada Lake is the largest lake in Mississippi, and there is plenty of recreation available here. Stop by the Visitor Center (located on scenic Hwy. 333) to get information on what's available. The North Graysport Campground is one of nine on Grenada Lake. It offers generous sites, with lovely shade provided by mature loblolly pine, short-leaf pine, red cedar, and various oak species. However, there is little privacy between sites. All parking is paved, back-in style. There are no waterfront sites, and many sites are far from the washhouses. Opt for a site near the "facilities." Security is fair at this rural campground which doesn't lock its gates at night. Also, the campground gets incredibly crowded in the summer and should be avoided particularly on holiday weekends.

Basics

Operated By: Us Army Corps of Engineers in conjunction w/ Mississippi Dept. of Wildlife, Fisheries & Parks. **Open:** Year-round. **Site Assignment:** First come, first served; reservations accepted for three night min., w/ $15 nonrefundable first night deposit. **Registration:** Gatehouse. **Fee:** $13 ($15 first night w/ reservation), $10 seniors. **Parking:** At site (preferably not to exceed 3 vehicles).

Facilities

Number of RV Sites: 0. **Number of Tent-Only Sites:** 30 (some w/ electric & water in the area). **Number of Multipurpose Sites:** 158. **Hookups:** Water, electric (30, 50 amps). **Each Site:** Picnic table, grill, fire ring, lantern pole, some tent pads. **Dump Station:** Yes. **Laundry:** Yes. **Pay Phone:** Yes. **Rest Rooms and Showers:** Yes. **Fuel:** No. **Propane:** No. **Internal Roads:** Paved. **RV Service:** 5 mi. south in Grenada. **Market:** 7 mi. south in Grenada. **Restaurant:** 7 mi. south in Grenada. **General Store:** 8 mi. south in Grenada (Wal-Mart). **Vending:** Beverages only. **Swimming Pool:** No. **Playground:** Yes. **Other:** Boat launches, picnic area, visitor center, picnic shelters. **Activities:** Several swimming beaches, fishing, boating, amphitheater. **Nearby Attractions:** Historic Grenada, walking & driving tours, Confederate Cemetery, Cocchuma Archery Range, Hugh White State Park. **Additional Information:** Grenada Tourism Commission, (800) 373-2571.

Restrictions

Pets: Leash only. **Fires:** Fire ring only. **Alcoholic Beverages:** Allowed. **Vehicle Maximum Length:** 50 ft.

To Get There

From I-55, take exit 206 and drive east on State Hwy. 8 about 3.5 mi. Turn north on scenic route 333 toward Grenada Dam. Turn left on Toe Rd., next to the dam, and the gatehouse is at the foot of the dam.

GULFPORT

Baywood Campground-RV Park

1100 Cowan Rd., Gulfport 39507. T: (228) 896-4840 or (888) 747-4840; F: (228) 604-1739; www.woodalls.com; wmsentr@aol.com.

RV ★★★ Tent ★★

Beauty: ★★★ Site Privacy: ★★★
Spaciousness: ★★ Quiet: ★★★
Security: ★★ Cleanliness: ★★★
Insect Control: ★★★ Facilities: ★★

One mile from the beach, eight miles from outlet malls, and within easy driving distance of a dozen casinos, Baywood's location is excellent. The campground at Baywood offers mostly back-in parking. Most parking is paved, and the rest is gravel. Sites are on the small side with little privacy. Spanish moss–laden hardwoods provide shade. The campground is laid out in two main areas. Families should look for a site convenient to the pool and playground, such as site 93 or 94. Couples seeking solitude should head to the back and choose a site numbering in the 50's or 60's. This urban campground offers few security measures, as there are no gates. Watch your belongings. We don't recommend Gulf Coast touring in the height of summer, when the heat is unbearable. Winter is also problematic due to the migration of the venerable snowbirds. Visit in the autumn for maximum peace and quiet.

BASICS

Operated By: Marshall J. Williams. **Open:** Year-round. **Site Assignment:** First come, first served; reservations accepted, no deposit required. **Registration:** Office, late-comers register next morning. **Fee:** $24 for pull-through, $23 for back-in; prices for 2 adults & 2 children, $2 per extra person; Good Sam & AAA discounts available (cash, personal check, V, MC). **Parking:** At site, in designated areas (2 vehicles, max.).

FACILITIES

Number of Multipurpose Sites: 114. **Hookups:** Water, electric (30, 50 amps), sewer, cable. **Each Site:** Picnic table. **Dump Station:** Yes. **Laundry:** Yes. **Pay Phone:** Yes. **Rest Rooms and Showers:** Yes. **Fuel:** No. **Propane:** Yes. **Internal Roads:** Paved. **RV Service:** 7 mi. east in Biloxi. **Market:** 0.25 mi. **Restaurant:** 0.25 mi. **General Store:** 0.25 mi. **Vending:** Yes. **Swimming Pool:** Yes. **Playground:** Yes. **Activities:** Fishing pond, recreation center. **Nearby Attractions:** Biloxi, Gulf beaches, Gulf Island national Seashore, Beauvoir Jefferson Davis Home, Barrier Islands, cruises, casinos. **Additional Information:** Mississippi Gulf Coast, CVB (228) 896-6699.

RESTRICTIONS

Pets: Leash only. **Fires:** Allowed, grills only (bring your own). **Alcoholic Beverages:** Allowed, sites only. **Vehicle Maximum Length:** 45 ft. (sites vary). **Other:** No aggressive dogs.

TO GET THERE

From I-10, take exit 38 and drive south 3 mi. on Cowan Lorraine Rd. The park entrance is on the left.

HATTIESBURG

Paul B. Johnson State Park

319 Geiger Lake Rd., Hattiesburg 39401. T: (601) 582-7721; www.mdwfp.com.

RV ★★★★ Tent ★★★★

Beauty: ★★★★ Site Privacy: ★★★
Spaciousness: ★★★ Quiet: ★★★★
Security: ★★★★ Cleanliness: ★★★★
Insect Control: ★★★★ Facilities: ★★★

Paul B. Johnson State Park offers back-in campsites situated in one area and 22 pull-through sites in another area. We recommend the back-in area. The pull-through area is crowded and far less attractive. For a nice view of 300-acre Lake Geiger, try back-in sites 15-18 and 65, 67, 69, 71, 77, 78, 80, 85, and 84. These sites are shaded by a variety of tree species, including loblolly, longleaf, and short-leaf pine. All parking is paved. Less than two hours from New Orleans, this park is popular with Crescent City–slickers and should be avoided on summer holidays and weekends. In the summer, this park becomes so hot and humid that you could steam veggies on your car hood. Although the park's surroundings are rural, Hattiesburg businesses are only 15–20 miles away. Park gates are not locked at night, but rangers patrol regularly.

BASICS

Operated By: Mississippi Dept. of Wildlife, Fisheries & Parks. **Open:** All year (office closed Christmas). **Site Assignment:** Some first come, first served; designated sites available for reservation, w/ $15 non-refundable first night deposit. **Registration:** Ranger checks in. **Fee:** $14 for full hookup, $13 for water & electric, $9 for primitive tent sites or seniors. **Parking:** At site, limit 2 vehicles.

FACILITIES

Number of RV Sites: 0. **Number of Tent-Only Sites:** 50 (primitive area, undesignated). **Number of Multipurpose Sites:** 108. **Hookups:** Water, electric (30, 50 amps), sewer in 50 sites. **Each Site:** Picnic table, grill. **Dump Station:** Yes. **Laundry:** Yes. **Pay Phone:** Yes. **Rest Rooms and Showers:** Yes. **Fuel:** No. **Propane:** No. **Internal Roads:** Paved. **RV Service:** 22 mi. north in Hattiesburg. **Market:** 15 mi. north in Hattiesburg. **Restaurant:** 3.5 mi. north in Hattiesburg. **General Store:** 15 mi. north in Hattiesburg. **Vending:** Yes. **Swimming Pool:** No. **Playground:** Yes. **Other:** Boat ramp, lake beach, picnic pavilions, group camp, group camp swim area. **Activities:** Fishing, swimming, paddle boat rentals in-season, fishing boat & canoe rentals year-round, water sports, nature trail. **Nearby Attractions:** Historic Hattiesburg, Camp Shelby Armed Forces Museum, Black Creek, Wildlife Management Areas, University of Southern Mississippi. **Additional Information:** Hattiesburg Chamber of Commerce, (601) 268-3220.

RESTRICTIONS

Pets: 6-ft. leash only. **Fires:** Allowed. **Alcoholic Beverages:** Not allowed. **Vehicle Maximum Length:** 40 ft. **Other:** No metal detectors.

TO GET THERE

From I-59, take exit 59 (Lucedale/Mobile/Hwy. 98 East). Drive 3.5 mi. on Hwy. 98 east to the Hwy. 49/Mississippi Gulf Coast exit. Take Hwy. 49 south 8.5 for mi. The park is on the right.

HERNANDO

South Abutment Campground, Arkabutla Lake

3905 Arkabutla Dam Rd., Coldwater 38618. T: (601) 562-6261 or (877) 444-6777 for reservations; F: (601) 562-8972; www.reserveusa.com.

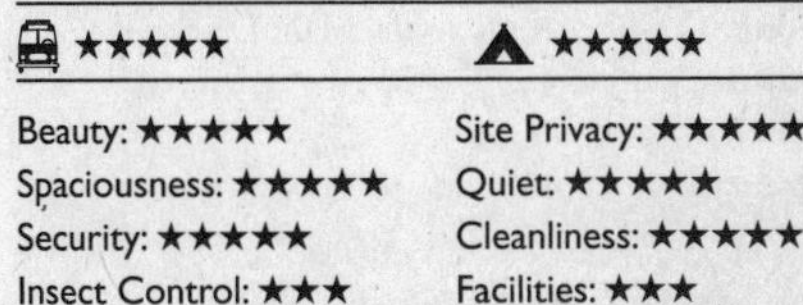

RV ★★★★★ Tent ★★★★★

Beauty: ★★★★★ Site Privacy: ★★★★★
Spaciousness: ★★★★★ Quiet: ★★★★★
Security: ★★★★★ Cleanliness: ★★★★★
Insect Control: ★★★ Facilities: ★★★

Often less crowded than Enid and Sardis Lakes, Arkabutla Lake also has extensive recreational facilities. Fishermen find catfish, bream, white bass, black bass, and some of the largest crappie in the southeast. All three campgrounds at Arkabutla have nice-looking, commodious sites. We prefer the South Abutment campground; it is the least frequented of the three and has the most spacious washhouse. Sites at south Abutment are shady, and most are secluded. All campsites at Lake Arkabutla have paved parking. There are two pull-throughs at Hernando Point; other sites offer back-in parking. Security at this rural recreation area is fair; gates do not lock, but law enforcement patrols throughout the night.

BASICS

Operated By: US Army Corps of Engineers. **Open:** Year-round. **Site Assignment:** First come, first served; reservations accepted through the National Recreation Reservation Service (NRRS) at (877) 444-6777 or www.reserveusa.com. Reservations can be made up to 240 days in advance, full payment required upon making reservation; credit card preferred (V, MC, D, AE), or pay by money order if at least 21 days in advance of arrival. $10 fee for cancellation or change of site or dates. Cancellation within three days of arrival charged first night, no-show charged $20 plus first night. **Registration:** Entrance stations. **Fee:** $8–$18 (V, MC, D). **Parking:** At site.

FACILITIES

Number of Multipurpose Sites: 234. **Hookups:** Water, electric (20, 30 amps). **Each Site:** Picnic table, grill, fire ring. **Dump Station:** Yes. **Laundry:** No. **Pay Phone:** Yes. **Rest Rooms and Showers:** Yes. **Fuel:** No. **Propane:** No. **Internal Roads:** Paved. **RV Service:** 40 mi. north in Memphis. **Market:** 15 mi. southeast in Coldwater. **Restaurant:** 5 mi. south in Arkabutla. **General Store:** 15 mi. southeast in Coldwater. **Vending:** No. **Swimming Pool:** No. **Playground:** Yes. **Other:** Boat launch,

36,000 acres, beaches, primitive equestrian trails, picnic areas & shelters, nature trails. **Activities:** Fishing, hunting, swimming, hunting, hiking, wind-sailing, volleyball, fall festival. **Nearby Attractions:** Attractions in Tunica & Memphis; Beale St., Mud Island, Graceland. **Additional Information:** Hernando Chamber of Commerce, (662) 429-9055; or Senatobia Chamber of Commerce, (662) 562-8715.

Restrictions

Pets: Leash only. **Fires:** Allowed, sites only. **Alcoholic Beverages:** Not allowed. **Vehicle Maximum Length:** No limit.

To Get There

From I-55, take exit 271 (Coldwater) and go west on State Hwy. 306 for 2 mi. Turn left onto US 51 and go south for 1 mi. to Coldwater. At the four-way stop, turn right and go west on Scenic Rte. 304 for 10 mi. to Arkabutla, where 304 turns north. Continue 5 mi. to the Main Dam and office.

JACKSON
LeFleur's Bluff State Park

2140 Riverside Dr., Jackson 39202. T: (601) 987-3923; F: (601) 354-6930; www.mdwfp.com.

★★★★ ★★★★

Beauty: ★★★★ Site Privacy: ★★★★
Spaciousness: ★★★★ Quiet: ★★★★
Security: ★★★★ Cleanliness: ★★★★
Insect Control: ★ Facilities: ★★★★★

This family-oriented park is building the state's largest playground. A small fishing lake is stocked with bass, bream, catfish and crappie. The campground is attractive, although you can see suburban neighborhoods from your campsite. Site size is ample, and there are plenty of shady loblolly pines. Parking is on back-in, paved pads. About half of the sites are lakefront. Of these, 6, 7, 12, and 14 are recommended because of their views and proximity to the washhouses. All sites are situated on one loop. Security is very good at this suburban state park; gates are locked at night and attended during the day. When we visited, we were eaten by mosquitoes, and the rangers told us that ants and bees are also problematic. Bring insect repellent.

Basics

Operated By: Mississippi Dept. of Wildlife, Fisheries & Parks. **Open:** All year (frequent closings in the spring due to flooding). **Site Assignment:** First come, first served; 5 sites available for reservation for 2 night min., $15 nonrefundable first night deposit. **Registration:** Gatehouse, ranger checks in (code required to enter after gate closes-call ahead). **Fee:** $13, $10 seniors. **Parking:** At site, in parking lot, limit 2 vehicles.

Facilities

Number of Multipurpose Sites: 30. **Hookups:** Water, electric (50 amps). **Each Site:** Picnic table, grill. **Dump Station:** Yes. **Laundry:** No. **Pay Phone:** Yes. **Rest Rooms and Showers:** Yes. **Fuel:** No. **Propane:** No. **Internal Roads:** Gravel, limestone. **RV Service:** 6 mi. west in Jackson. **Market:** 2 mi. north in Jackson. **Restaurant:** 1 mi. east in Flowood. **General Store:** 3 mi. north in Jackson. **Vending:** Beverages only. **Swimming Pool:** No. **Playground:** Yes. **Other:** Clubhouse, picnic area & pavilion, lodge, meeting rooms. **Activities:** Fishing (trolling motors only), boat rentals year-round, nature trails, 9-hole golf course, driving range, tennis, disc golf. **Nearby Attractions:** Jim Buck Ross Mississippi Agriculture & Forestry Museum, National Agricultural Aviation Museum, Mississippi Governors Mansion, Museum of Art, Natural Science Museum, Mississippi Sports Hall of Fame, Old Capital Museum. **Additional Information:** Jackson CVB, (800) 354-7695 or (601) 960-1891, www.visitjackson.com.

Restrictions

Pets: Leash only. **Fires:** Allowed. **Alcoholic Beverages:** Not allowed. **Vehicle Maximum Length:** 50 ft.

To Get There

From I-55, take exit 98B and drive east on Lakeland Dr. to the second traffic light. Turn right, and the campground is straight ahead.

JACKSON
Timberlake Campground and RV Park

143 Timberlake Dr., Brandon 39047. T: (601) 992-9100; F: (601) 919-0219.

★★★ ★★★

Beauty: ★★★ Site Privacy: ★★
Spaciousness: ★★★★ Quiet: ★★★★
Security: ★★★ Cleanliness: ★★★★
Insect Control: ★★★ Facilities: ★★★

Built on mammoth Ross Barnett Reservoir, Timberlake is enjoyed by anglers. As at Le Fleur State Park, neighboring homes are visible from your campsite. Families will find that the two parks maintain different yet qualitatively comparable recreational facilities. Built on a peninsula, most sites are leased residentially. For overnighters, RV sites N1–N66 are in a shadier, older portion of the park. Sites N1–N8 are popular lakefront sites and cannot be reserved. Sites N67–N108 are newer, completely tree-less, and available for reservations. Sites are large with paved, back-in parking. Even when trees provide shade, there is little privacy. The exceptions are the shadier and more private tent and pop-up areas.

Basics

Operated By: Pearl River Valley Water Supply District. **Open:** Year-round. **Site Assignment:** First come, first served; designated sites available for reservation, one night deposit, 3 day notice for refund. **Registration:** Office, late-comers register the next day. **Fee:** $17 for full hookups, $15 for water & electric, $12 for tent site, $2 discount for seniors, fee includes 4 people, $1 per extra person (cash, personal check, V, MC, AE, D). **Parking:** At sites.

Facilities

Number of RV Sites: 0. **Number of Tent-Only Sites:** 18. **Number of Multipurpose Sites:** 126. **Hookups:** Water, electric (20, 30, 50 amps), sewer in 108 sites. **Each Site:** Picnic table, grill. **Dump Station:** Yes. **Laundry:** Yes. **Pay Phone:** Yes. **Rest Rooms and Showers:** Yes. **Fuel:** No. **Propane:** No. **Internal Roads:** Paved. **RV Service:** 15 mi. north in Gloudtstat. **Market:** 1 mi. in Brandon. **Restaurant:** 1 mi. in Brandon. **General Store:** 0.25 mi. in Brandon. **Vending:** Yes. **Swimming Pool:** Yes. **Playground:** Yes. **Other:** Boat ramp, fishing dock, recreation room. **Activities:** Game room, tennis, boating, skiing, fishing, bicycling & hiking trails. **Nearby Attractions:** Jim Buck Ross Mississippi Agriculture & Forestry Museum/ National Agricultural Aviation Museum, Mississippi Governors Mansion, Museum of Art, Natural Science Museum, Mississippi Sports Hall of Fame, Old Capital Museum. **Additional Information:** Jackson CVB, (800) 354-7695 or (601) 960-1891, www.visitjackson.com.

Restrictions

Pets: Leash only. **Fires:** Allowed, grills only (need permission for ground fire). **Alcoholic Beverages:** Not allowed. **Vehicle Maximum Length:** 45 ft. (sites vary). **Other:** No mobile homes.

To Get There

From I-55, take exit 98B and drive east 3.2 mi. on Lakeland Dr. East. Turn left on Old Fannin Rd. and go 3 mi. The park is on the left.

MCCOMB
Percy Quinn State Park

1156 Camp Beaver Dr., McComb 39648. T: (601) 684-3938; F: (601) 249-4382; www.mdwfp.com; pqspark@telepak.net.

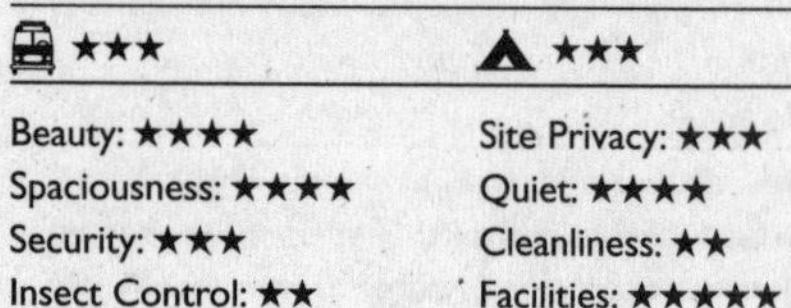

★★★ ★★★

Beauty: ★★★★ Site Privacy: ★★★
Spaciousness: ★★★★ Quiet: ★★★★
Security: ★★★ Cleanliness: ★★
Insect Control: ★★ Facilities: ★★★★★

With its mild southern climate, Percy Quinn State Park makes a good late fall or early spring destination. Its extensive recreational facilities make it popular with the city folk from "N'awlins"—avoid it like the plague on holiday weekends. This nice-looking campground features various-sized sites shaded by loblolly pine and magnolia. All parking is back-in and paved. Site privacy also varies. Sites 83–91 are recommended if you value elbow room and seclusion. If you prefer a water-view site, make a reservation for site 56 or 58. Site 100 is adjacent to the less-crowded North Swimming Beach, making it a good choice for families.

Basics

Operated By: Mississippi Dept. of Wildlife, Fisheries & Parks. **Open:** Year-round. **Site Assignment:** Most sites first come, first served; 27 sites (w/ 50 amp hookup) available for reservation, 2 night min. (3-night min. on holidays), $15 nonrefundable first night's deposit. **Registration:** Ranger station at entrance gate, late-comers set up & register the next morning. **Fee:** $13 for RV sites, $10 for seniors; $9 for primitive tent sites (cash, personal check, V, MC). **Parking:** At site, in parking lot (2 vehicles, max.).

FACILITIES

Number of RV Sites: 0. **Number of Tent-Only Sites:** 22 (primitive). **Number of Multipurpose Sites:** 100. **Hookups:** Water, electric (30, 50 amps, 50 amps in reserved sites only). **Each Site:** Picnic table, grill, primitive sites include fire ring & lantern pole. **Dump Station:** Yes. **Laundry:** Yes. **Pay Phone:** Yes. **Rest Rooms and Showers:** Yes. **Fuel:** No. **Propane:** No. **Internal Roads:** Paved. **RV Service:** 12 mi. east in McComb. **Market:** Camp store in season, 6 mi. north in McComb. **Restaurant:** 6 mi. north in McComb. **General Store:** Camp store in season, 0.25 mi. **Vending:** Beverages only. **Swimming Pool:** Yes (in day-use area, for a fee). **Playground:** Inquire at campground. **Other:** Marina, boat launch, picnic area & pavilions, lodge & meeting rooms, chapel. **Activities:** Swimming beach, fishing, boat rentals available, nature trail, archery range, 27-hole golf course, tennis, game room, (multipurpose fields at group site only), mini golf. **Nearby Attractions:** Copiah County, Homochitto & Marion County Wildlife Management Areas, Homochitto National Forest. **Additional Information:** Pike County Chamber of Commerce, (601) 684-2291, www.pikeinfo.com.

RESTRICTIONS

Pets: Leash only. **Fires:** Allowed, fire rings & grills only. **Alcoholic Beverages:** Allowed, sites only. **Vehicle Maximum Length:** 40 ft. (sites vary). **Other:** 14-night stay limit.

TO GET THERE

From I-55, take exit 13 and turn west on Fernwood Rd. Follow Fernwood Rd. until it ends and turn right on State Hwy. 48. Look for the park on the left. The park is 1 mi. from the interstate.

MERIDIAN

Meridian East Toomsuba KOA

3953 KOA Campground Rd., Toomsuba 39364.
T: (601) 632-1684; F: (601) 632-9493;
www.koa.com; koakamp@mississippi.net.

RV ★★★ Tent ★★★

Beauty: ★★★★	Site Privacy: ★★★
Spaciousness: ★★★	Quiet: ★★★★
Security: ★★★	Cleanliness: ★★★★
Insect Control: ★★★	Facilities: ★★★

Situated in a shady grove dominated by loblolly pine, this is an incredibly attractive KOA. Sites at this rural campground are mid-sized and offer gravel parking. Roughly 25% of the sites offer pull-through parking. The prettiest RV campsites (sites 26–29) are the shady back-ins flanking the group tent area. All of the tent sites are nice looking, and some have tent pads. Children will especially like the pool, water slide, and other recreation here. In Meridian, children will enjoy the historic Dentzel Carousel, which has been in operation since 1909. Although there is no gate, this KOA is off the beaten path, making security fair. Avoid visiting Meridian during the hot, humid southern summer. Also avoid this campground on holiday weekends, when its facilities make it popular with families.

BASICS

Operated By: Mike & Shirley Groseclose. **Open:** Year-round. **Site Assignment:** Sites assigned; reservations recommended during summer season & holidays, credit card deposit required for reservation, cancel by 4 p.m. the day before arrival for refund. **Registration:** Store, self-registration at night. **Fee:** $28 for full hookups (50 amps), $25 (30 amps), $23 for water & electric, $20 for tent site, fee includes 2 people, $3 per extra adult, $2 per extra child. **Parking:** At site, in parking lot.

FACILITIES

Number of RV Sites: 0. **Number of Tent-Only Sites:** 6. **Number of Multipurpose Sites:** 43. **Hookups:** Water, electric (30, 50 amps), sewer. **Each Site:** Picnic table, fire ring, (tent sites have tent pads). **Dump Station:** Yes. **Laundry:** Yes. **Pay Phone:** Courtesy phones. **Rest Rooms and Showers:** Yes. **Fuel:** No. **Propane:** Yes. **Internal Roads:** Gravel. **RV Service:** 12 mi. southwest in Meridian. **Market:** Grocery on site, supermarket 12 mi. southwest in Meridian. **Restaurant:** Snack bar on site & 12 mi. southwest in Meridian. **General Store:** On site & 12 mi. southwest in Meridian. **Vending:** No. **Swimming Pool:** Yes. **Playground:** Yes. **Other:** Pavilion, snack bar. **Activities:** 550-ft. ground water slide, game room, horseshoes, tetherball, basketball. **Nearby Attractions:** Jimmie Rodgers Museum, Peavey Museum, Antebellum homes, Highland Park, Dentzel Carousel, Dunn's Falls in Enterprise, Hamasa Shrine Temple Theater. **Additional Information:** Meridian Chamber of Commerce, (601) 693-1306.

RESTRICTIONS

Pets: Leash only (clean-up enforced). **Fires:** Allowed, tent sites only. **Alcoholic Beverages:** Allowed, sites only. **Vehicle Maximum Length:** 60 ft. (sites vary). **Other:** Visitors must register at the office.

TO GET THERE

Campground is 12 mi. east of Meridian. From I-59, take exit 165 (Toomsuba). Drive south 1.5 mi. and turn right on KOA Campground Rd. The campground is 1.5 mi. ahead on the right.

MERIDIAN

Twitley Branch Camping Area, Okatibee Lake

9200 Hamrick Rd. North, Collinsville 39325.
T: (601) 626-8431; F: (601) 626-8750;
www.reserveusa.com.

RV ★★★★ Tent ★★★★

Beauty: ★★★★★	Site Privacy: ★★★
Spaciousness: ★★★★	Quiet: ★★★★
Security: ★★★★★	Cleanliness: ★★★★
Insect Control: ★★★★	Facilities: ★★★★

Twitley Branch is preferable to nearby Okatibee Water Park campground for both tent and RV campers. There are plenty of activities for all ages at Okatibee Lake, including a water park. About 4,000 acres of forest are available for hunting. The attractive campground features large to huge sites shaded by loblolly pine, black gum, and various oak species. Parking is on gravel and back-in –style. The exceptions are three huge, paved pull-throughs. There is little foliage to provide privacy between sites. Two loops have hookups. Although all lakefront sites are pretty, sites 32–36 on the Black Gum Loop are exceptional for their size and shadiness. The Cypress Loop has no hookups, but it is near a lovely stand of cypress.

BASICS

Operated By: US Army Corps of Engineers. **Open:** Year-round. **Site Assignment:** First come, first served; 38 sites available for reservation through the National Recreation Reservation Service (NRRS) at (877) 444-6777 or www.reserve usa.com. Reservations can be made up to 240 days in advance, full payment required upon making reservation; credit card preferred (V, MC, D, AE), or pay by money order if at least 21 days in advance of arrival. $10 fee for cancellation or change of site or dates. Cancellation within three days of arrival charged first night, no-show charged $20 & first night. **Registration:** Gatehouse, no late registration. **Fee:** $16 for waterfront sites, $14 for non-waterfront sites, $10 for primitive tent sites, fees include 8 people. **Parking:** At site, in parking lot.

FACILITIES

Number of RV Sites: 0. **Number of Tent-Only Sites:** 12 (primitive). **Number of Multipurpose Sites:** 65. **Hookups:** Water, electric (30 amps). **Each Site:** Picnic table, fire ring, grill, lantern pole. **Dump Station:** Yes. **Laundry:** Yes. **Pay Phone:** Yes. **Rest Rooms and Showers:** Yes. **Fuel:** No. **Propane:** No. **Internal Roads:** Paved. **RV Service:** 10 mi. south in Meridian. **Market:** 3 mi. west in Collinsville. **Restaurant:** 10 mi. south in Meridian. **General Store:** 3 mi. west in Collinsville. **Vending:** Beverages. **Swimming Pool:** No. **Playground:** Yes. **Other:** Boat ramps, boat rentals at marina, foot trails, Okatibee Water Park (lodge, playground, water slide, beaches, picnic shelter), beaches, picnic facilities, scenic overlook, amphitheater. **Activities:** Swimming, waterskiing, bank fishing, hunting. **Nearby Attractions:** Mississippi Grand Opera House, Dunn's Falls in Enterprise, Bonita Lakes City Park & golf course, Sam Dale Historic Site. **Additional Information:** Meridian Chamber of Commerce, (601) 693-1306.

RESTRICTIONS

Pets: Leash only (no pets on the beach). **Fires:** Allowed, fire rings only. **Alcoholic Beverages:** Allowed, at sites only (not allowed on the beach). **Vehicle Maximum Length:** No limit. **Other:** 2 weeks stay limit within 30 days, limit 8 people per campsite.

TO GET THERE

From I-20, take exit 150 and drive north on Hwy. 19 for 8.5 mi. Turn right onto Twitley Branch Rd. and drive 2 mi. to Hamrick Rd. Turn right and drive about 0.75 mi. to the park entrance.

MORTON

Roosevelt State Park

2149 Hwy. 13 South, Morton 38117. T: (601) 732-6316; F: (601) 732-6317; www.mdwfp.com; roosevelt@localink4.com.

RV ★★★★★ Tent ★★★★★

Beauty: ★★★★★ Site Privacy: ★★★★★
Spaciousness: ★★★★★ Quiet: ★★★★★
Security: ★★★ Cleanliness: ★★★★
Insect Control: ★★ Facilities: ★★★★★

Set in the rolling hills of Bienville National Forest, Roosevelt State Park is one of the most beautiful state parks in Mississippi. The park has plenty of recreation for families. The 160-acre Shadow Lake is stocked with bream, crappie, bass, and catfish. Waterskiing is allowed in summertime, making the park noisier during the day. Commodious sites are shaded by lovely loblolly pine and other species. Plenty of foliage provides privacy between sites. Campsites feature back-in, paved parking. Both camping areas have drop-dead gorgeous lakefront sites. At the old campground, sites 13–15 and 24–28 are choice. At the new campground, snag a site in the 40's, 50's, 80's, or 90's. Security is fair at rural Roosevelt State Park. There are no gates, and the park is close to I-20, but rangers cruise regularly. Folks from Jackson reach the park in under one hour, making it extremely popular. If you're looking for nice weather and solitude, visit in spring or fall.

BASICS

Operated By: Mississippi Dept. of Wildlife, Fisheries, & Parks. **Open:** Year-round. **Site Assignment:** Most sites first come, first served; limited sites available for reservation w/ $15 nonrefundable first night deposit. **Registration:** Gate, after-hours ranger will check in. **Fee:** $14 for full hookups, $13 for water & electric, $9 for primitive tent sites (cash, checks, V, MC). **Parking:** At site, in lot.

FACILITIES

Number of RV Sites: 0. **Number of Tent-Only Sites:** 28 (primitive area). **Number of Multipurpose Sites:** 109. **Hookups:** Water, electric (30, 50 amps), 28 sites w/ sewer. **Each Site:** Picnic table, grill, burn-out area. **Dump Station:** Yes. **Laundry:** Yes. **Pay Phone:** Yes. **Rest Rooms and Showers:** Yes. **Fuel:** No. **Propane:** No. **Internal Roads:** Paved. **RV Service:** 32 mi. west in Jackson. **Market:** 2 mi. north in Morton. **Restaurant:** 12 mi. east in Forest. **General Store:** 12 mi. east in Forest. **Vending:** Yes. **Swimming Pool:** Yes (seasonal). **Playground:** Yes. **Other:** Full time catering service for groups, picnic area, pavilions, meeting rooms, group lodge, lodge, picnic facilities, gift shop, amphitheater. **Activities:** Fishing, fishing boat & paddle boat rentals in-season, water slide, swimming, skiing, tennis, softball, nature trail, video games. **Nearby Attractions:** Bienville National Forest, several wildlife management areas, Shockaloe riding trails, Natchez Trace National Scenic Trail. **Additional Information:** Morton Chamber, (601) 732-6135.

RESTRICTIONS

Pets: Leash only. **Fires:** Allowed, sites only (except under burn ban). **Alcoholic Beverages:** Not allowed. **Vehicle Maximum Length:** 32 ft.

TO GET THERE

The park is located 32 mi. east of Jackson. From I-20, take exit 77 and head north on MS Hwy. 13 for 0.25 mi. The entrance to the park is on the left.

NATCHEZ

Plantation Park

1 Frederick Rd., Natchez 39120. T: (601) 442-5222.

RV ★★★ Tent n/a

Beauty: ★★★ Site Privacy: ★★★
Spaciousness: ★★★ Quiet: ★★★
Security: ★★★ Cleanliness: ★★★
Insect Control: ★★ Facilities: ★★

This quiet, semi-residential RV park is conveniently located if you plan on to tour historic Natchez. Just before the Civil War, over half of the millionaires in the United States had homes in Natchez. Most of these antebellum mansions survived the war and are open for touring in the spring and fall. Call the Natchez Convention and Visitors Bureau, and plan to visit while the tours are in progress. Plantation Park offers mid-sized sites with plenty of shade, but there is little privacy between sites. All sites offer paved back-in parking. Most of the overnight sights are parallel to Mississippi Hwy. 61. The nicest sites are even numbers 19–31, which are quieter than the other overnight sites. Security at Plantation is fair to good; there is no gate, but the park is in a rural area. Since the swimming pool is the only recreational facility, there's not much here to keep children occupied.

BASICS

Operated By: Plantation Park. **Open:** Year-round. **Site Assignment:** First come, first served; reservations accepted w/ first night deposit (by check, no credit cards), cancel 2 weeks in advance for refund, $5 cancellation fee. **Registration:** Office, late-comers register next morning. **Fee:** $21 for 2 people; $2 per extra person (cash, personal checks only). **Parking:** At site.

FACILITIES

Number of Multipurpose Sites: 45. **Hookups:** Water, electric (30, 50 amps), sewer, cable. **Each Site:** Picnic table, concrete patio. **Dump Station:** No. **Laundry:** Yes. **Pay Phone:** Yes. **Rest Rooms and Showers:** Yes. **Fuel:** No. **Propane:** No. **Internal Roads:** Paved. **RV Service:** 63 mi. east in McComb. **Market:** Camp store, 3 mi. north in Natchez. **Restaurant:** 3 mi. north in Natchez. **General Store:** Camp store, Wal-Mart 5 mi. west in Natchez. **Vending:** Beverages only. **Swimming Pool:** Yes. **Playground:** No. **Activities:** Swimming. **Nearby Attractions:** Historic downtown Natchez, Grand Village of the Natchez Indians, Natchez Trace National Scenic Trail, Jefferson Military College. **Additional Information:** Natchez Visitor Reception Center, (800) 647-6724 or (601) 446-6345, www.natchez.ms.us.

RESTRICTIONS

Pets: Leash only. **Fires:** At campsite. **Alcoholic Beverages:** Allowed. **Vehicle Max. Length:** 70 ft.

TO GET THERE

From the intersection of US 61 and US 84 in Natchez, drive south on US 61 for 3.4 mi. The park entrance is on the left.

OCEAN SPRINGS

Camp Journey's End

7501 Hwy. 57, Ocean Springs 39565. T: (228) 875-2100; www.campjourneys-end.com; info@campjourneys-end.com.

RV ★★★★ Tent ★★★

Beauty: ★★★★ Site Privacy: ★★★
Spaciousness: ★★★★ Quiet: ★★★★
Security: ★★★ Cleanliness: ★★★★
Insect Control: ★★★★ Facilities: ★★★

This is an attractive campground with an uncommonly welcoming staff. On property is "Liberty," a 350-year old live oak tree. Adjacent to the park is Fort Bayou River with its speckled trout. The park maintains a boat ramp and dock. Camp Journey's End is seven miles from the beach and within 35 miles of the casinos, attractions, and restaurants in Biloxi. The campground is one large grid, featuring mid-sized sites and back-in parking. Popular sites 62–73 and 80–91 have paved parking. Other sites may have grass, gravel, or sand parking. Most sites are partially shady, while a few are totally open. Shady sites include 58–61, 74–79, and 99–108. Bathhouses are nicer than average. Camp Journeys End is popular with retirees during the winter and families during the summer and spring. Plan an autumn visit to avoid crowds. The park is right next to I-20 and has no gate; security is not fantastic.

BASICS

Operated By: Craig & Linda Orrison. **Open:** Year-round. **Site Assignment:** First come, first served; reservations accepted, credit card deposit; no charge w/ 24-hour notice of cancellation. **Registration:** Office. **Fee:** $19–$28 for 2 people, $2 for additional children, $3 for adults. **Parking:** At site, in parking lot.

FACILITIES

Number of RV Sites: 118. **Number of Tent-Only Sites:** 15. **Number of Multipurpose Sites:** 10. **Hookups:** Water, electric (30, 50 amps), sewer, cable. **Each Site:** Picnic tables at most sites, grills, fire rings on request. **Dump Station:** Yes. **Laundry:** Yes. **Pay Phone:** Yes. **Rest Rooms and Showers:** Yes. **Fuel:** No. **Propane:** Yes. **Internal Roads:** Paved. **RV Service:** On call. **Market:** Camp store, 5 mi. south in Ocean Springs. **Restaurant:** Barbecue on site, 1 mi. south in Ocean Springs. **General Store:** Camp store, 5 mi. south in Ocean Springs. **Vending:** Yes. **Swimming Pool:** Yes. **Playground:** Yes. **Other:** Boat launch, 18 mi. of waterway, pier, duck pond. **Activities:** Fishing, boating, horseshoes, basketball, seasonal organized activities. **Nearby Attractions:** Ocean Springs art museums, 11 mi. to Biloxi casinos, Beauvoir Jefferson Davis home, 60 mi. to Mobile, 90 mi. to New Orleans. **Additional Information:** Mississippi Gulf Coast CVB, (228) 896-6699.

RESTRICTIONS

Pets: Leash only. **Fires:** Allowed, fire rings only. **Alcoholic Beverages:** Allowed. **Vehicle Maximum Length:** 40 ft.

To Get There

The campground is 11 mi. east of Biloxi and 20 mi. west of the Alabama state line. From I-10, take exit 57. Drive north on MS Hwy. 57 for 0.25 mi. to the campground.

OCEAN SPRINGS

Davis Bayou Campground, Gulf Islands National Seashore

3500 Park Rd., Ocean Springs 39564. T: (228) 875-3962; F: (228) 872-2954; www.nps.gov.

RV ★★★★ Tent ★★★★

Beauty: ★★★★ Site Privacy: ★★★
Spaciousness: ★★★★ Quiet: ★★★★
Security: ★★★★ Cleanliness: ★★★
Insect Control: ★★ Facilities: ★★★

Gulf Island National seashore consists of 11 geographically distinct units stretching from West Ship Island, MS to Santa Rosa Island, FL. Davis Bayou Recreation Area nestles into the suburban mainland and has no beach. Visitors enjoy the bayou via the boat ramp and fishing pier. The beach is four miles away at Ocean Springs. The small, very pretty campground consists of two loops. The smaller loop (sites 11–19) contains the nicest sites. Sites 12 and 13 are especially gorgeous. These sites are afforded shade and privacy by ample woods, and they include views of the salt marsh. Most sites are wooded with little foliage between them. Site size varies widely, but all are adequate. Parking is paved and back-in–style. Coastal Mississippi can be excruciatingly hot in the summer. Try to plan a visit in spring or fall. Patrolled by rangers all night, security at this national park is good.

Basics

Operated By: National Park Service. **Open:** Year-round. **Site Assignment:** First come, first served. **Registration:** Office or self-registration. **Fee:** $16 for electric, $14 for water only (cash, personal check, V, MC, D). **Parking:** At sites & parking areas.

Facilities

Number of Multipurpose Sites: 51. **Hookups:** Water, electric (50 amps). **Each Site:** Picnic table, grill. **Dump Station:** Yes. **Laundry:** No. **Pay Phone:** Yes. **Rest Rooms and Showers:** Yes. **Fuel:** No. **Propane:** No. **Internal Roads:** Paved. **RV Service:** No. **Market:** No. **Restaurant:** 0.5 mi. west. **General Store:** 1.5 mi. east. **Vending:** No. **Swimming Pool:** No. **Playground:** Yes. **Other:** Boat launches, visitor center, fishing pier, picnic area. **Activities:** Fishing, boating, kayaking, walking trails, bicycle trails; no swimming due to alligators. **Nearby Attractions:** Beaches, museums, boat tours, 4 mi. to Biloxi casinos, 75 mi. to New Orleans. **Additional Information:** Mississippi Gulf Coast CVB, (228) 896-6699.

Restrictions

Pets: Leash only. **Fires:** Grills only. **Alcoholic Beverages:** Allowed (no glass containers). **Vehicle Maximum Length:** 45 ft. **Other:** No swimming due to alligators.

To Get There

From the west, take I-10 to Ocean Springs and exit at Tucker Rd. Take Tucker Rd. south 5–7 mi. to US 90. Head east (left) on 90 and proceed 5–7 mi. The park is on the right, and the campground is 2 mi. inside the Seashore area on the right. From the east, take I-10 to the Fontainebleau exit. Take State Hwy. 57 south to US 90 west, and the Seashore is on the left.

SARDIS

John W. Kyle State Park

Rte. 1 Box 115, Sardis 38666. T: (662) 487-1345; F: (662) 487-0409; www.mdwfp.com; johnkyle@panola.com.

RV ★★★ Tent ★★★

Beauty: ★★★ Site Privacy: ★★★
Spaciousness: ★★★ Quiet: ★★
Security: ★★★ Cleanliness: ★★★
Insect Control: ★★★ Facilities: ★★★★

John W. Kyle State Park offers some of the best freshwater fishing in the southeast. Best known for prize bass, Sardis Reservoir also has huge crappie. The campground is nice-looking, but families have as many as four vehicles per site, making it crowded and congested. Children, boats, and trucks make the park noisy too. Avoid John W. Kyle on summer weekends and especially on holiday weekends. Situated in a shady stand of mature red oak trees, sites are average-sized. There is little privacy between sites. Both of the camping areas have a few lakefront sites, such as sites 87–90 and 284–287. Of these, site 90 is the top choice for its spaciousness and lovely view.

Basics

Operated By: Mississippi Dept. of Wildlife, Fisheries & Parks. **Open:** Year-round. **Site Assignment:** First come, first served; 13 sites available for reservation for 3-night min. w/ $15 nonrefundable first night deposit. **Registration:** Gatehouse. **Fee:** $13, $10 for seniors (cash, check, V, MC). **Parking:** At site.

Facilities

Number of Multipurpose Sites: 201. **Hookups:** Water, electric (30, 50 amps). **Each Site:** Picnic table, grill, some w/ tent pads, some w/ fire rings. **Dump Station:** Yes. **Laundry:** Yes. **Pay Phone:** Yes. **Rest Rooms and Showers:** Yes. **Fuel:** No. **Propane:** No. **Internal Roads:** Paved. **RV Service:** 8 mi. west in Sardis. **Market:** 8 mi. southwest in Batesville. **Restaurant:** 8 mi. southwest in Batesville. **General Store:** 8 mi. southwest in Batesville. **Vending:** Beverages only. **Swimming Pool:** Yes. **Playground:** Yes. **Other:** Boat launch, snack bar, pavilion, lodge, recreation building, picnic area, 18-hole golf course. **Activities:** Swimming beach, nature trail, playing fields, tennis, water sports, fishing, boat rentals. **Nearby Attractions:** Tunica casinos, Holly Springs National Forest, University of Mississippi in Oxford, 40 mi. to Memphis. **Additional Information:** Sardis Chamber of Commerce, (662) 487-3451.

Restrictions

Pets: On leash. **Fires:** Fire ring. **Alcoholic Beverages:** At site. **Vehicle Max. Length:** 32 ft. standard.

To Get There

From I-55, take exit 252 onto State Hwy. 315 and drive east for 7 mi. The park entrance is on right.

TUNICA

Grand Casino RV Resort

111 Resort Village Rd., Robinsonville 38664. T: (800) 946-4946; F: (662) 357-3208; www.grandcasis.com.

RV ★★★ Tent n/a

Beauty: ★★ Site Privacy: ★★
Spaciousness: ★★★ Quiet: ★★★★
Security: ★★★★ Cleanliness: ★★★★
Insect Control: ★★★ Facilities: ★★★★

The RV resort at Grand Casino Tunica won't win any beauty contests, but it does offer casino patrons a clean, livable place to park their campers. Couples will appreciate the park's attempt to maintain quiet by corralling families with children into a separate area. Families will enjoy the spacious pool and playground. Resort privileges include access to the 18-hole golf course (call for greens fees) and sporting clays. Bus service to and from the casino is provided 24 hours a day. Security (a serious concern at casinos) is good; while not fenced, the campground is gated at all times. The campground is a long walk from the casino and is patrolled by security guards. Tunica is much safer than Las Vegas or Atlantic City—at this rural gaming Mecca, casinos tower over vast acres of flat croplands.

Basics

Operated By: Grand Casino, Inc. **Open:** Year-round. **Site Assignment:** First come, first served; reservations accepted, no deposit, 24-hour notice for cancellation. **Registration:** Lodge. **Fee:** $19. **Parking:** At site, in parking lot.

Facilities

Number of RV Sites: 200. **Number of Tent-Only Sites:** 0. **Number of Multipurpose Sites:** None. **Hookups:** Water, electric (20, 30, 50 amps), sewer, cable. **Each Site:** Picnic table, concrete pads. **Dump Station:** No. **Laundry:** Yes. **Pay Phone:** Yes. **Rest Rooms and Showers:** Yes. **Fuel:** No. **Propane:** Yes. **Internal Roads:** Paved. **RV Service:** 15 mi. north in Southaven. **Market:** 15 mi. north in Southaven. **Restaurant:** In casino. **General Store:** 15 mi. north in Southaven. **Vending:** No. **Swimming Pool:** Yes. **Playground:** Yes. **Other:** Lounge. **Activities:** Casino, volleyball, horseshoes, basketball, shuffleboard, sports green, sporting clays, 18-hole golf course, video arcade, Kids Quest (hands-on activity center). **Nearby Attractions:** Sporting clays, outlet shopping, 15 mi. to Memphis, Beale St., Mud Island, Graceland. **Additional Information:** Tunica CVB, (888) 4-TUNICA.

Restrictions

Pets: Allowed. **Fires:** Grills only. **Alcoholic Beverages:** Allowed (no glass bottles). **Vehicle Maximum Length:** No limit.

To Get There

From Memphis, take I-55 to exit 7 (3rd St./ Vicksburg). Take US 61 south 19 mi. to the Tunica Resort on the right. Pass the first entrance, then pass the visitors center and outlet malls and take the next entrance on the right. Pass the golf course, and turn left at the traffic light into the RV park. From Jackson, take I-55 to Hernando, then take State Hwy. 304 west about 17 miles to US 61 North. The resort is 5 mi. on the left (west).

TUPELO

Tombigbee State Park

264 Cabin Dr., Tupelo 38804. T: (662) 842-7669; F: (662) 840-5594; www.mdwfp.com.

RV ★★★ Tent ★★★

Beauty: ★★★ Site Privacy: ★★
Spaciousness: ★★★ Quiet: ★★★
Security: ★★★ Cleanliness: ★★★
Insect Control: ★★ Facilities: ★★★

This small state park is not as attractive as other Mississippi state parks. We prefer it over private campgrounds in the area for its recreational facilities and seclusion. The campground offers mid-sized sites with paved back-in parking. Most sites enjoy partial shade, but there is no foliage between sites to provide privacy. Trees include a variety of pine and hardwoods. Sites are laid out in a large oval with bathhouses in the middle. Here, each site looks just like its neighbor, so choose yours based on location. Tombigbee State Park maintains extensive facilities for large groups, as well as a fishing lake stocked with bass, bream, and catfish. The park never locks its gates, but it is fairly remote, making security fair. The area around Tupelo tends to be moist and low-lying; mosquitoes and summer heat can be unbearable, so plan accordingly.

BASICS

Operated By: Mississippi Dept. of Wildlife, Fisheries & Parks. **Open:** Year-round. **Site Assignment:** First come, first served; 3 sites available for reservation, 2 night min., w/ $15 nonrefundable first night deposit. **Registration:** Office, ranger will collect in the evenings. **Fee:** $13 for full hookups ($15 first night if reserved), $12 for water & electric, $8 for primitive tent site, $10 for seniors or disabled. **Parking:** At site.

FACILITIES

Number of RV Sites: 0. **Number of Tent-Only Sites:** 4. **Number of Multipurpose Sites:** 20. **Hookups:** Water, electric (20, 30 amps), 6 sites w/ sewer. **Each Site:** Picnic table, grill, fire ring, some lantern poles. **Dump Station:** Yes. **Laundry:** Yes. **Pay Phone:** Yes. **Rest Rooms and Showers:** Yes. **Fuel:** No. **Propane:** No. **Internal Roads:** Paved. **RV Service:** 35 mi. south in Aberdeen. **Market:** 4 mi. toward Plantersville. **Restaurant:** 4 mi. toward Plantersville. **General Store:** Wal-Mart 10 mi. west in Tupelo. **Vending:** Yes. **Swimming Pool:** No. **Playground:** Yes. **Other:** Picnic area, pavilions, visitor center, group lodge & dining hall, meeting rooms. **Activities:** Fishing, boating (rentals available, paddle boats in-season), nature trail, game room, disc-golf course. **Nearby Attractions:** Natchez Trace National Scenic Trail, Birthplace of Elvis Presley in Tupelo, Tupelo Civil War Battlefield, Tennessee-Tombigbee Waterway, Wildlife Management Areas. **Additional Information:** Tupelo CVB, (800) 533-0611.

RESTRICTIONS

Pets: On leash. **Fires:** In fire ring. **Alcoholic Beverages:** No. **Vehicle Maximum Length:** 40 ft.

TO GET THERE

From Tupelo, go south on Main St./State Hwy. 6. Stay on Hwy. 6 south until Plantersville, then turn left and drive east on State Park Rd. The park is 3 mi. east of Plantersville (6 mi. from Tupelo).

VICKSBURG

Magnolia RV Park

211 Miller St., Vicksburg 39180. T: (601) 631-0388; F: (601) 631-0013; magnoliarv@aol.com.

RV ★★ Tent ★

Beauty: ★★ Site Privacy: ★
Spaciousness: ★★ Quiet: ★★
Security: ★ Cleanliness: ★★★
Insect Control: ★★★ Facilities: ★★

We chose to include this completely treeless RV park because of its location and its tidy rest rooms. Situated in urban Vicksburg, the park is a convenient choice if you're touring Vicksburg National Military Park. There are four rows of pull-through campsites at Magnolia. All sites are completely open. Sites 50–66 are bordered by trees to the north, making them slightly more attractive but not any shadier. All sites are small, and all parking is on gravel. Security is poor, as this park is not gated and is surrounded by urban development. Avoid visiting this historic Mississippi River town in the summer, when heat and humidity become unbearable.

BASICS

Operated By: Dino & Sheryl Ross. **Open:** Year-round. **Site Assignment:** Sites assigned; reservations recommended fall & spring, credit card deposit; cancel by 2 p.m. arrival day for refund. **Registration:** Camp store, after hours registration instructions posted. **Fee:** $20 for 50 amps, $18 for 30 amps, $11 for tent sites; prices for 4 people, $1 per extra person; Good Sam, FMCA, AAA, AARP, Escapees RV Club discounts. **Parking:** At sites, in gravel pads only.

FACILITIES

Number of RV Sites: 66. **Number of Tent-Only Sites:** 4.5 acres of primitive area. **Number of Multipurpose Sites:** None. **Hookups:** Water, electric (20, 30, 50 amps), sewer. **Each Site:** Picnic table. **Dump Station:** No. **Laundry:** Yes. **Pay Phone:** Yes. **Rest Rooms and Showers:** Yes. **Fuel:** No. **Propane:** No. **Internal Roads:** Gravel. **RV Service:** 45 mi. east in Jackson. **Market:** 0.5 mi. in Vicksburg. **Restaurant:** 0.5 mi. in Vicksburg. **General Store:** Camp store (w/ limited RV supplies). **Vending:** Beverages only. **Swimming Pool:** Yes. **Playground:** Yes. **Other:** Meeting room, free casino shuttle. **Activities:** Game room, basketball. **Nearby Attractions:** Casinos, Civil War Battlefield, National Military Cemetery, Biedenharm Coca-Cola Museum, Historic Downtown Vicksburg, Gray & Blue Naval Musem. **Additional Information:** Vicksburg CVB, (601) 636-9421 or (800) 221-3536.

RESTRICTIONS

Pets: Leash only. **Fires:** In your own grill **Alcoholic Beverages:** At site. **Vehicle Max. Length:** None.

TO GET THERE

From I-20, take exit 1B and drive south on US 61 for 1 mi. Turn right onto Miller St. The park is on the right.

WAVELAND

Buccaneer State Park

1150 South Beach Blvd., Waveland 39576. T: (228) 467-3822; F: (228) 467-1598; www.mdwfp.com; buccaneer@intu.net.

RV ★★★ Tent ★★★

Beauty: ★★★★ Site Privacy: ★★★
Spaciousness: ★★★ Quiet: ★★
Security: ★★★ Cleanliness: ★
Insect Control: ★★★★ Facilities: ★★★★

Children delight in the recreation and folklore here. Legend says that French buccaneer Jean Lafitte buried his loot here in the late 1700s. Lafitte did in fact live in the nearby "Old Pirate House." When we visited, the park and campground both needed a serious cleaning. The campground property includes seven areas. The most spacious and heavily wooded is the loop containing sites 105–149. Even-numbered sites 112–124 have a lovely view of the salt marsh. In other areas, site size and shadiness vary. All sites feature paved, back-in parking.

BASICS

Operated By: Mississippi Dept. of Wildlife, Fisheries & Parks. **Open:** All year. **Site Assignment:** First come, first served; 25 full hookup sites available for reservation w/ 2-night min. & $15 deposit. **Registration:** Office at park entrance, late comers register the next morning. **Fee:** $9–$14 (cash, personal checks, V, MC). **Parking:** At sites.

FACILITIES

Number of Multipurpose Sites: 386. **Hookups:** Water, electric (20, 30, 50 amps), some w/ sewer. **Each Site:** Grill, picnic table, some w/ tent pad. **Dump Station:** Yes. **Laundry:** Yes. **Pay Phone:** Yes. **Rest Rooms and Showers:** Yes. **Fuel:** No. **Propane:** No. **Internal Roads:** Paved. **RV Service:** 25 mi. east in Gulfport. **Market:** 5 mi. in Waveland. **Restaurant:** 3 mi. in Waveland. **General Store:** Yes. **Vending:** Beverages only. **Swimming Pool:** Yes. **Playground:** Yes. **Other:** Amphitheater, picnic pavilions, multi-purpose court, activity building. **Activities:** Nature trails, disc-golf, tennis, basketball, arcade, beach, fishing, Buccaneer Bay Waterpark (open May–Sept.). **Nearby Attractions:** John C. Stennis Space Center in Bay St. Louis, Marine Life Oceanarium in Gulfport, Bayou & boat tours, Gulf Islands National Seashore. **Additional Information:** Mississippi Gulf Coast CVB, (228) 896-6699.

RESTRICTIONS

Pets: Leash only. **Fires:** Allowed, in designated areas. **Alcoholic Beverages:** Allowed (moderation). **Vehicle Maximum Length:** No limit. **Other:** 14-day stay limit summer season.

TO GET THERE

From I-10, take exit 13 and drive south on State Hwy. 603 about 7 mi. to the coast. Turn right on Beach Blvd. and drive west just over 4 mi. The park is on the right.

Missouri

Missouri is a state with history—there's no mistaking it. The Pony Express was headquartered here, Lewis and Clark took a little trip through the state, and Kansas City hosted the Dred Scott slavery trial that triggered the Civil War. Along with the American Indian roots of the state, all of this adds up to a wealth of reasons to visit Missouri. And the growing number of tourists is reflected in the number of campgrounds and RV parks built to serve their needs.

For RVers seeking top-notch resorts, the **Kansas City** area is the place to go. Many visitors come to Kansas City for the casinos, amusement parks, or a dash of culture. Others may pine for a photo of the Arch in **St. Louis.** And for some, Missouri means **Branson**—home to dozens of theaters that host big-name entertainers in extravagant shows. These are all legitimate destinations, but so much more of Missouri lies in the natural places—and you don't have to tunnel underground in The Cave State to find them.

Rockhounds and fortune-seekers alike will want to visit **Crater of Diamonds State Park,** where visitors can keep whatever gems they uncover. The **Trail of Tears State Park** near **Cape Girardeau** is *de rigeur* for anyone wishing to understand the state's history. And if you really *do* want to visit a cave, **Meramec State Park** near **Sullivan** is a fine place to look for hidden adventure.

One not-so-hidden treasure is the **Mark Twain National Forest,** which covers much of the southeastern part of the state. Similarly evident is the **Ozark Mountains** region, where scenic hills offer free roller-coaster rides. The **Harry S. Truman Reservoir** is an enormous complex of lakes that will appeal to water sports enthusiasts, anglers, and campers. You don't have to go to the big cities in Missouri to enjoy this state; its green places have as much to offer as its metropolitan centers.

The following facilities accept payment in checks or cash only:

Ballard's Campground, Carthage
Glenwood Park, Branson
McCullough Park Campground, Chillicothe
Missouri Park Campground, Mountain Grove
Peculiar Park Place, Peculiar
Pine Trails RV Ranch, Monett
Stadium RV Park, Independence
Thousand Hills State Park, Kirksville
Traveler's Park Campground, Springfield

The following facilities feature 20 sites or fewer:

Pheasant Acres Campground, St James

Campground Profiles

BRANSON

Glenwood Park

1550 Fall Creek Rd., Branson 65616. T: (417) 334-7024.

RV ★★★ Tent ★★★

Beauty: ★★★ Site Privacy: ★★★
Spaciousness: ★★ Quiet: ★★★★
Security: ★★★★ Cleanliness: ★★★★
Insect Control: ★★★★ Facilities: ★★★

Laid out in a figure eight, this campground packs in a lot of sites (mostly back-ins) and at times suffers from a lack of room. The inner side of the first loop (sites in 10s–30s) feels cramped: although there are some long sites (75 feet), the width is restricted to 24 feet. An unsightly storage shed impinges on the space of sites 38 and 39, making them less desirable. Sites 42–44 are very petite sites (25 × 25 feet) in the southeast corner. Sites 49–54, by contrast, are larger (75 feet) back-ins that feel roomier. These are undoubtedly the sites de choix, being nicely shaded and secluded feeling. Sites 55–61 in the same corner are the same size as these latter sites, but can accommodate only about 45 feet because of the angle at which an RV has to back in. Hidden in their own little clearing in the woods, sites 65–67 are cute but large enough only for a van or a pop-up. Despite the cramped feel of a number of sites, this is a decent stop for anyone visiting Branson for even a couple of days. The campground is within a short drive of many of the attractions and has shaded sites that can keep summer campers cool.

BASICS

Operated By: Carol & Kyle Taylor. **Open:** Mar. 15–Nov. 15. **Site Assignment:** Depending on site availability; verbal reservations OK w/ a contact phone number. **Registration:** In office; late arrivals select available site & pay in the morning. **Fee:** RV $22 (full), $20 (water, electric); tent $16; checks, V, MC, D. **Parking:** At site.

FACILITIES

Number of RV Sites: 62. **Number of Tent-Only Sites:** Undesignated sites. **Hookups:** Water, sewer, electric (30, 50 amp). **Each Site:** Picnic table. **Dump Station:** Yes. **Laundry:** Yes. **Pay Phone:**

Yes. **Rest Rooms and Showers:** Yes. **Fuel:** No. **Propane:** No. **Internal Roads:** Paved. **RV Service:** No. **Market:** 1.25 mi. west. **Restaurant:** Across street. **General Store:** No. **Vending:** Yes. **Swimming:** No. **Playground:** No. **Other:** Close to attractions, easy access. **Activities:** Fishing, boating, swimming, hiking, wine-tasting, shows, tours, train rides. **Nearby Attractions:** Bull Shoals Lakes, Table Rock, Taneycomo, Branson Scenic Railway, Silver Dollar City, Talking Rocks Cavern, wineries. **Additional Information:** Branson Chamber of Commerce, (417) 334-4136, (417) 334-4137.

RESTRICTIONS

Pets: On leash only, cleaned up after. **Fires:** In grills. **Alcoholic Beverages:** At sites. **Vehicle Maximum Length:** None.

TO GET THERE

From the junction of Hwy. 65 and Hwy. 76, turn west onto Hwy. 76 (Main St.) and go 1.1 mi. Turn left onto Fall Creek Rd. The campground is on left.

CAMDENTON

Heavenly Days Resort and Campground

Rte. 71 Box 799, Camdenton 65020. T: (573) 873-5325; www.funlake.com/accommodations/heavenlydays; heavenlycg@socket.net.

RV ★★★★ Tent ★★★★

Beauty: ★★★★★	Site Privacy: ★★★
Spaciousness: ★★★	Quiet: ★★★★
Security: ★★★★	Cleanliness: ★★★★
Insect Control: ★★★	Facilities: ★★★

This lakeside campground has tiered sites with attractive stone and cement retaining walls, as well as nice grass and trees. All RV sites have cement tracks to drive onto. Site 1 really is *the one* site, located on a promontory overlooking the lake. Sites 2–4 are very nice 60-foot back-ins. Sites 5–14 are back-ins that range from 30 to 45 feet. Of these, 5–9 are in the parking area for the office, and 14 is adjacent to a trash dumpster, making it least desirable. Sites 17–22, located on a tier above the tenting area, are 60-foot back-ins. The road leading down to sites 24–31 is very steep and in poor condition. However, the drive is worth the effort, as these sites rival site 1 in quality. Situated right on the water, they are extremely attractive. The problem with this area is the lack of space: sites seem stacked one upon the other. However, if you can tolerate the lack of space, these sites are very pleasant. The tenting area is an open grassy field. There are a couple of tall shade trees for protection. The rest rooms are very clean and spacious but, oddly, have windows (and no curtains) at eye-level running the entire length of the front. This may put off campers who prefer more privacy. Overall, Heavenly Days has some excellent sites for both tenters and RVers, and can be an exceptional stay for either.

BASICS

Operated By: Chip. **Open:** Apr.–Oct. **Site Assignment:** Depending on site availability; reservations require check deposit, 2 weeks cancellation policy. **Registration:** In office; late arrivals ring bell. **Fee:** RV $21–$23, tent $19; checks, V, MC, D. **Parking:** At site.

FACILITIES

Number of RV Sites: 29. **Number of Tent-Only Sites:** 4. **Hookups:** Water, sewer, electric (30 amp). **Each Site:** Picnic table, fire pit. **Dump Station:** No (sewer at all sites). **Laundry:** Yes. **Pay Phone:** Yes. **Rest Rooms and Showers:** Yes. **Fuel:** No. **Propane:** No. **Internal Roads:** Gravel. **RV Service:** No. **Market:** 3 mi. to Greenview. **Restaurant:** 3 mi. to Greenview. **General Store:** No. **Vending:** No. **Swimming:** Yes (lake). **Playground:** Yes. **Other:** Shuffleboard, arcade games, picnic area, pavilion. **Activities:** Fishing, boating. **Nearby Attractions:** Bridal Cave. **Additional Information:** Camdenton Area Chamber of Commerce, (800) 769-1004, (573) 346-2676.

RESTRICTIONS

Pets: On leash, cleaned up after. **Fires:** In grills. **Alcoholic Beverages:** At sites. **Vehicle Maximum Length:** 50 ft.

TO GET THERE

From the junction of Hwy. 54 and Hwy. 5/7, go north on Hwy. 5/7 8.8 mi. Turn left onto Hwy. 7 and go 0.6 mi. Turn left onto Hwy. EE and go 3.1 mi. Stay to the left at the fork in the road and go 2.8 mi. Turn right at the sign into the entrance.

CAMERON

Down Under Camp Resort

8074 Northeast County Hwy. H, Turney 64493. T: (800) 221-6056 or (816) 632-3695; www.campdownunder.com.

RV ★★★★ Tent ★★★★★

Beauty: ★★★★	Site Privacy: ★★★
Spaciousness: ★★★	Quiet: ★★★★★
Security: ★★★★★	Cleanliness: ★★★★
Insect Control: ★★★★	Facilities: ★★★★

Sites in this huge campground are scattered, undeveloped spaces with grass-and-gravel mix and a fair number of trees. Sites A1–A5, north of Kanga Lake, are full-hookup back-ins. Site 27 is a large (90 feet) pull-through, while 28–28 are much smaller (30–45 feet). These sites are mostly open, without the cover of shade trees. Sites 60–69 are 70-foot pull-throughs with little shade. A small gazebo lies next to site 65. Sites 70–74, 81, and 82 are 30-foot back-ins that lie right next to the pool. These sites see a large amount of foot traffic. The best sites in the campground are 87–100 and 120, which are located right on the lake. They are grassy and without much shade (except for 96 and 97). These sites are 45-foot back-ins, although a larger rig could overhang slightly, due to the sites' open end. Sites 104–110 are open grassy sites that face lush vegetation. They are very nice, but the grassy strip they lie on suffers from some degree of slope, and campers will have to take time to level their rig. The nicest tent sites are T3–T5, which lie right on the lake (but also on the entrance road). The grass here is very suitable for tenting. The showers are clean and spacious, if a little primitive. The rest rooms are also clean, and, on the whole, the facilities are quite comfortable. A fun campground that offers activities for the whole family in a pleasant environment.

BASICS

Operated By: Bonnie Beck. **Open:** All year (limited services Apr.–Nov.). **Site Assignment:** Upon registration; reservations recommended, credit card or check required for reservation more than 7 days (lose $5 to cancell); less than 7 days, lose one night's deposit. **Registration:** In office; late arrivals use drop box. **Fee:** RV $25 (full), $23 (water, electric), $20 (electric); tent $18; checks, V, MC. **Parking:** At site.

FACILITIES

Number of RV Sites: 120. **Number of Tent-Only Sites:** 26. **Hookups:** Water, sewer, electric (20, 30, 50 amp). **Each Site:** Picnic table, grill. **Dump Station:** Yes. **Laundry:** Yes. **Pay Phone:** Yes. **Rest Rooms and Showers:** Yes. **Fuel:** No. **Propane:** Yes. **Internal Roads:** Gravel. **RV Service:** No. **Market:** 8 mi. west. **Restaurant:** 8 mi. west. **General Store:** Yes. **Vending:** Yes. **Swimming:** Pool. **Playground:** Yes. **Other:** RV parts, modem, lake, mini-golf, pavilion, snack bar, game room, cabin on lake. **Activities:** Fishing, paddle boating, swimming, shuffleboard. **Nearby Attractions:** Worlds of Fun. **Additional Information:** Cameron Chamber of Commerce, (816) 632-2005.

RESTRICTIONS

Pets: On leash, cleaned up after. **Fires:** In grills. **Alcoholic Beverages:** At sites. **Vehicle Maximum Length:** None. **Other:** No fireworks, children under 14 years in pool must be supervised by adult within pool fence.

TO GET THERE

From Hwy. I-35 (Exit 48), turn east onto Hwy. 69 and go 2.5 mi. Turn right onto H and go 1.1 mi. Turn right at the sign into the entrance.

CAPE GIRARDEAU

Trail of Tears State Park

429 Moccasin Springs, Jackson 63755. T: (573) 334-1711.

RV ★★★★ Tent ★★★★★

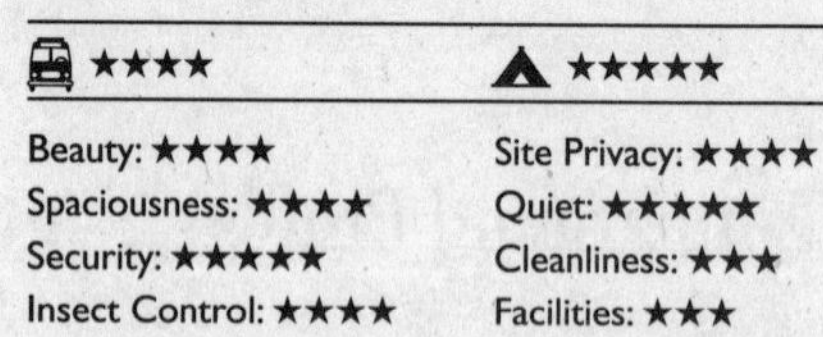

Beauty: ★★★★	Site Privacy: ★★★★
Spaciousness: ★★★★	Quiet: ★★★★★
Security: ★★★★★	Cleanliness: ★★★
Insect Control: ★★★★	Facilities: ★★★

This state parks contains the only campground in Missouri that lies on the Mississippi River (named, appropriately, Mississippi River Campground), as well as one primitive campground (Boutin Campground). The Mississippi River Campground has electric sites close to the river bank. Sites 4–10 back to the river. Site 13 is a handicapped site that lies in a corner against a forested backdrop. Sites 14–19 back to woods as well, and are all well-shaded. There is only one unisex toilet in this campground and the bathhouse is within 0.25 mi. Boutin Campground has forested primitive sites. Site 20 is by far the longest pull-through (140 feet). Site 30 is located across from the bathhouse and the Camp Hosts, which is normally a benefit, but the dump station is also right next to it. Sites 47, 51, 52, and

54 are more isolated, being located at the end of a roundbout in the internal road. Boutin is a wonderful campground with a historical element that families will appreciate, and with plenty of recreational facilities appreciated by any camper.

Basics

Operated By: Missouri Dept. of Natural Resources. **Open:** All year. **Site Assignment:** First come, first served; no reservations. **Registration:** In office; fees also collected by Camp Hosts. **Fee:** RV $15 (full), $12 (water, electric); tent $7; checks, V, MC, D. **Parking:** At site.

Facilities

Number of RV Sites: 18. **Number of Tent-Only Sites:** 35. **Hookups:** Water, sewer, electric (30 amp). **Each Site:** Picnic table, fire pit. **Dump Station:** Yes. **Laundry:** Yes. **Pay Phone:** Yes. **Rest Rooms and Showers:** Yes. **Fuel:** No. **Propane:** No. **Internal Roads:** Paved. **RV Service:** No. **Market:** 15 mi. south. **Restaurant:** 15 mi. south. **General Store:** No. **Vending:** No. **Swimming:** Yes (lake). **Playground:** Yes. **Other:** Boat ramp, exhibits. **Activities:** Fishing, boating, swimming, hiking, tours. **Nearby Attractions:** Trail of Tears, Bollinger Mill State Historic Site, Cape Rock. **Additional Information:** Cape Girardeau CVB, (800) 777-0068, (573) 335-1631.

Restrictions

Pets: On leash, cleaned up after. **Fires:** In grills. **Alcoholic Beverages:** At sites. **Vehicle Maximum Length:** None. **Other:** Gates locked at 10 p.m.

To Get There

From the junction of Broadway and Hwy. 177 in town, turn north onto Hwy. 177 and go 11.8 mi. (Be sure to turn right at tyhe 11.7 mi. mark.) Take first right into park.

CARTHAGE

Ballard's Campground

13965 Ballard Loop, Carthage 64836. T: (417) 359-0359; F: (417) 359-0359; wswwgoff@yahoo.com.

RV ★★★ Tent ★★★

Beauty: ★★★★	Site Privacy: ★★★★
Spaciousness: ★★★★	Quiet: ★★★
Security: ★★★★★	Cleanliness: ★★★★
Insect Control: ★★★★	Facilities: ★★★

While the highway passes on one side of this campground, the other three sides are surrounded by forest, giving it a natural, almost wilderness, feel. Ballard's is arranged in three rows of paired sites that are slightly tiered but level. Sites 1–6, 13–18, and 21–26 are 85-foot pull-throughs, while 7–12 and 19–20 are 75-foot pull-throughs. Most sites are very well shaded, but 10 and 25 are exceptions. Outside sites 12, 22, 24, and 26 seem a little short on space. They require parking at the edge of the internal road and sharing the picnic space on the far side of the neighboring site. Site 7 is close to the fishing pond, and site 12 is at the edge of the property, which makes it a little more private. The nicest site is probably 21—everything just seems to coalesce nicely here: it is well-shaded, grassy, far from the entrance, and facing mostly forest. The tent area is in a large open space next to the pond, with trees around the perimeter. The grass is very nice, but there is little shade or protection from the elements. The rest rooms are spacious and mostly clean, with modern facilities. A nice campground that feels further away from it all than its convenient location belies.

Basics

Operated By: William & Wanda Goff. **Open:** All year. **Site Assignment:** Depend on availability; no reservations. **Registration:** In office; late arrivals pay in morning. **Fee:** RV $12 (full), $11 (water, electric); tent $10; no credit, but check. **Parking:** At site.

Facilities

Number of RV Sites: 30. **Number of Tent-Only Sites:** Undesignated sites. **Hookups:** Water, sewer, electric (30 amp). **Each Site:** Picnic table, fire pit. **Dump Station:** Yes. **Laundry:** Yes. **Pay Phone:** Yes. **Rest Rooms and Showers:** Yes. **Fuel:** No. **Propane:** Yes. **Internal Roads:** Gravel. **RV Service:** No. **Market:** 5 mi. northeast. **Restaurant:** 2 mi. south. **General Store:** Yes. **Vending:** Yes. **Swimming:** No. **Playground:** No. **Other:** Fishing pond w/ pavilion. **Activities:** Fishing (catch & release). **Nearby Attractions:** Precious Moments Chapel. **Additional Information:** Carthage CVB, (417) 358-2373.

Restrictions

Pets: On leash only, cleaned up after. **Fires:** In grills. **Alcoholic Beverages:** At sites. **Vehicle Maximum Length:** None.

To Get There

From Hwy. I-44, take Exit 18A. On the south side of the highway overpass, go 0.3 mi. on Hwy. Alt 71.

CHARLESTON

Sams Camping

Beasly Park Rd., P.O. Box 357, Charleston 63834. T: (573) 683-6362 or (573) 683-6415.

RV ★★★ Tent ★★

Beauty: ★★	Site Privacy: ★★★
Spaciousness: ★★★	Quiet: ★★★
Security: ★★★★	Cleanliness: ★★★
Insect Control: ★★★★	Facilities: ★★★

This campground has grassy/gravel pull-through sites laid out in strips. Sites A–T are in two rows that run perpendicular to the road. J and T are right on the road and closest to the entrance. J has a large sign, light post, and fire hydrant that encroach on its space. Sites A–G are well shaded, particularly D–F, but not B. Sites 1–8 are in a strip along the south edge of the campground, facing an agricultural field. Contiguous with 1–8, sites 9–16 run along the eastern edge, facing truck parking and commercial buildings. Site 16 is closest to the road, but not as close as J and T. All of these sites are 72 × 21-foot pull-throughs. Tenting is permitted in a field of open grass, but is not overly comfortable. The rest rooms are clean, but could use some brightening up. An acceptable overnight stay, but not comfortable enough to warrant a special trip.

Basics

Operated By: Donald Sams. **Open:** All year. **Site Assignment:** Depending on site availability; no reservations. **Registration:** In office; late arrivals use drop box. **Fee:** 2 people $15, 4 people $17, 6 people $19. **Parking:** At site.

Facilities

Number of RV Sites: 36. **Number of Tent-Only Sites:** Undesignated sites. **Hookups:** Water, sewer, electric (20, 30, 50 amp). **Dump Station:** No (sewer at all sites). **Laundry:** No. **Pay Phone:** Yes. **Rest Rooms and Showers:** Yes. **Fuel:** No. **Propane:** No. **Internal Roads:** Gravel. **RV Service:** No. **Market:** Less than 0.25 mi. north. **Restaurant:** Less than 0.25 mi. north. **General Store:** No. **Vending:** Yes. **Swimming:** No. **Playground:** No. **Other:** Fish in city lake across street. **Activities:** Fishing. **Nearby Attractions:** Big Oak Tree State Park. **Additional Information:** Charleston Chamber, (573) 683-6509.

Restrictions

Pets: On leash, cleaned up after. **Fires:** In grills. **Alcoholic Beverages:** At sites. **Vehicle Maximum Length:** None.

To Get There

From Hwy. 57 (Exit 10), turn south and take the first left after the off-ramp onto Beasly Park Rd. Go 0.2 mi. and then turn right at the sign into the entrance.

CHILLICOTHE

McCullough Park Campground

13248 Liv 216, Chillicothe 64601. T: (816) 646-2735.

RV ★★★★ Tent ★★★★

Beauty: ★★★★★	Site Privacy: ★★★★
Spaciousness: ★★★★★	Quiet: ★★★★★
Security: ★★★★★	Cleanliness: ★★★★
Insect Control: ★★★★★	Facilities: ★★★

Most sites in this campground are forested, making for cooler summer days. The main campground is in the wooded area to the north of the office. This is a slice of forest with a farm flavor. (None of the sites are designated by anything other than an open area with an electrical outlet for several sites, and the owners often provide extention cords for additional electric sites, so a description of individual sites is neither possible nor helpful in this case.) The undeveloped sites to the east of the office are tenter or pop-up heaven, but not convenient for large rigs or tows. Larger RVs should head towards the "big rig section" on the hill to the northwest of the office. It's an open field with trees around the perimeter and huge sites with room for wide turns. Again, the sites are not numbered, but are indicated by the presence of the hookups. Tenting is unlimited in lush, beautiful grass and a thick forest canopy overhead. The rest room is smallish but comfortable and clean. With the exception of the bluegrass festival held here every year, this is a quiet campground secluded in the woods. It is absolutely a haven for tenters, and the section for large RVs ensures that all campers can enjoy their stay here.

Basics

Operated By: Don McCullough. **Open:** All year (limited service Nov.–Mar.). **Site Assignment:** Upon registration; verbal reservations OK. **Registration:** In office; late arrivals select available site & pay in the morning. **Fee:** RV $18 (full), $15 (water, electric); tent $12; no credits cards, but checks. **Parking:** At site.

Facilities

Number of RV Sites: 300. **Number of Tent-Only Sites:** 30. **Hookups:** Water, sewer, electric (30 amp). **Each Site:** Can get table from owners. **Dump Station:** Yes. **Laundry:** No. **Pay Phone:** Yes. **Rest Rooms and Showers:** Yes. **Fuel:** No. **Propane:** No. **Internal Roads:** Gravel. **RV Service:** No. **Market:** 4 mi. south. **Restaurant:** 4 mi. south. **General Store:** No. **Vending:** No. **Swimming:** No. **Playground:** No. **Other:** Firewood. **Activities:** Special events (including bluegrass festival), old-time harvest. **Nearby Attractions:** Pershing State Park, Poosey Conservation Area, Bunch Hollow Conservation Area. **Additional Information:** Chillicothe Area Chamber of Commerce, (660) 646-4050.

Restrictions

Pets: On leash only, cleaned up after. **Fires:** In grills. **Alcoholic Beverages:** At sites, restricted during events. **Vehicle Maximum Length:** None.

To Get There

From the junction of Hwy. 36 and Hwy. 65, turn north onto Hwy. 65 and go 7.4 mi. Turn right onto the gravel road and go 0.3 mi. Turn left at the sign into the entrance.

CLINTON

Harry S. Truman Dam and Reservoir (Sparrowfoot Park)

150 Southeast 450 Rd., Clinton 64735. T: (877) 444-6777, or Visitor's center (660) 438-2216, or park (660) 885-7546; www.reserveusa.com.

RV ★★★★ Tent ★★★★

Beauty: ★★★★	Site Privacy: ★★★★
Spaciousness: ★★★	Quiet: ★★★★
Security: ★★★★	Cleanliness: ★★★★
Insect Control: ★★★★	Facilities: ★★★

A lakeside campground, this park has sites laid out in two large loops. Loop A itself has two loops in a figure 8. Most sites in this loop are somewhat shaded, but not forested. Sites on the inside of the loop back to dense vegetation, while sites on the outside back to more open vegetation. Sites A13 and A14 are entirely unshaded. Prime sites closest to the lake include A15–A21, of which A17–A19 have the best views. Site A22, a 90-foot pull-through, is just across from A20 and A21 but does not include the prime-site price tag. Site 33 is just as close to the toilets as 32, but likewise does not cost as much as the more expensive site. Sites 28–48 back to other sites and are thus less private. Sites along the northeast edge and 16–21 do not back to any other sites. Site A50 is a 105-foot pull-through, and sites A59–62 are closest to the rest rooms in the second loop of Loop A. In Loop B, site B1 is a prime site due to its proximity to the rest rooms, but is much too close to the road for comfort. Even-numbers 2–16 back to dense vegetation, which makes them very attractive. Sites B15, 18, and 20 are just as close to the water access area as B16, 17, and 19, but are not priced like prime sites. Sites B19 and 20 may, in fact, suffer from an inordinate amount of passing foot traffic. The rest rooms and showers are basic but functional. During off-season, only pit toilets are available—no showers, flush toilets, or laundry. Overall, an attractive campground that offers plenty of recreation facilities and pleasant spots for campers.

Basics

Operated By: Army Corps of Engineers. **Open:** All year (limited services Oct. 16–Apr. 14). **Site Assignment:** First come, first served; no reservations. **Registration:** In office; late arrivals select available site from sign-in sheet in booth & pay in the morning. **Fee:** RV $16 (prime), $14 (electric); tent $10, off-season $6; V, MC, AE, D, DC. **Parking:** At site.

Facilities

Number of RV Sites: 93. **Number of Tent-Only Sites:** 19. **Hookups:** Electric (20, 30 amp). **Each Site:** Picnic table, fire pit, lantern pole. **Dump Station:** Yes. **Laundry:** Yes. **Pay Phone:** No. **Rest Rooms and Showers:** Yes. **Fuel:** No. **Propane:** No. **Internal Roads:** Paved. **RV Service:** No. **Market:** 5 mi. to Clinton. **Restaurant:** 5 mi. to Clinton. **General Store:** No. **Vending:** No. **Swimming:** Yes (lake). **Playground:** Yes. **Other:** Picnic area, beach. **Activities:** Fishing, boating, swimming, ATV riding. **Nearby Attractions:** Henry County Museum & Cultural Arts Center. **Additional Information:** Clinton Chamber of Commerce, (660) 885-8168.

Restrictions

Pets: On leash only, cleaned up after. **Fires:** In grills. **Alcoholic Beverages:** At sites. **Vehicle Maximum Length:** None.

To Get There

From the junction of Hwy. 7 and Hwy. 13 by hospital, turn south onto Hwy. 13 and go 7 mi. Turn left onto southeast 450 and go 1.2 mi. Turn right at the sign into the entrance.

COLUMBIA

Cottonwoods RV Park

5170 Oakland, Columbia 65202. T: (573) 474-2747; F: (573) 474-0946; cottonwoodrv@aol.com.

RV ★★★★★ Tent ★★★★

Beauty: ★★★★	Site Privacy: ★★★★
Spaciousness: ★★★★	Quiet: ★★★★
Security: ★★★★★	Cleanliness: ★★★★★
Insect Control: ★★★★	Facilities: ★★★★★

Like most RV parks in the area, Cottonwoods does not offer much shade. This is where the similarity with most other campgrounds ends, however, as this is a fantastic, upscale resort that will appeal to all RV campers. It features extremely well-tended landscaping, with grass and trees on three sides and buildings to the east. Strips of grassy sites run east to west, with monthlies (1–23) located at the southern end. All sites are 27 feet wide, and overnight spaces are 60–65 feet. pull-throughs. (Sites 70–97 are doubles that meet end to end and measure 110 feet—slightly less than the rest of the sites.) Although it is difficult to pick a "best" site, campers may prefer the middle area (roughly 32–43, 52–63, 74–80, 87–93), as it is furthest from the entry road, does not face any buildings, has very nice trees and grass, and is close to the rest rooms. Tent sites are at the entrance of the park. They have beautiful grass but—again—no shade, and feel somewhat like an afterthought in an RV park. Rest rooms and showers are exceptionally clean and comfortable. This RV park caters to the upscale urban camper. It is extremely comfortable by any standards, and campers of any kind will enjoy a stay here.

Basics

Operated By: Buster & Loretta Candle (owners), Gary Lynch (mgr.). **Open:** All year. **Site Assignment:** Upon registration; credit card required for reservation, 24-hours cancellation policy. **Registration:** In office; late arrivals use drop box. **Fee:** RV $25 (50 amp), $22 (30 amp), $20 (water, electric); tent $18; checks, V, MC, D. **Parking:** At site.

Facilities

Number of RV Sites: 100. **Number of Tent-Only Sites:** 6. **Hookups:** Water, sewer, electric (20, 30, 50 amp). **Each Site:** Picnic table. **Dump Station:** Yes. **Laundry:** Yes. **Pay Phone:** Yes. **Rest Rooms and Showers:** Yes. **Fuel:** No. **Propane:** Yes. **Internal Roads:** Gravel. **RV Service:** No. **Market:** 4 mi. south. **Restaurant:** 2 mi. south. **General Store:** Yes. **Vending:** Yes. **Swimming:** Pool. **Playground:** Yes. **Other:** Meeting room, game room, antique mall, gift shop, modem, pool table, exercise equipment, pet walk, small & large pavilions. **Activities:** Biking, hiking, basketball, horseshoes, swimming. **Nearby Attractions:** Katy Trail State Park, Rockbridge State Park. **Additional Information:** Columbia Chamber of Commerce, (573) 875-1231.

Restrictions

Pets: On leash only, cleaned up after. **Fires:** In grills. **Alcoholic Beverages:** At sites. **Vehicle Maximum Length:** None. **Other:** No refunds.

To Get There

From Hwy. I-70 (Exit 128A), turn north onto PP and take entrance to Hwy. 63. Go 3 mi., then turn right onto Oakland Gravel Rd. Turn right off the ramp, then left onto Starke Ln. Go 0.4 mi., then turn right at the sign into the entrance.

DANVILLE

Kan-Do Kampground RV Park

99 Hwy. TT, Montgomery City 63361. T: (573) 564-7993; kando@ktis.net.

RV ★★★★★ Tent ★★★★★

Beauty: ★★★★	Site Privacy: ★★★★
Spaciousness: ★★★★	Quiet: ★★★★
Security: ★★★★	Cleanliness: ★★★★★
Insect Control: ★★★★	Facilities: ★★★★

This campground is laid out in a loop, with all sites on the outside and a large grassy field on the inside. All sites are pull-throughs, some of them enormous (11 is 140 feet, 2–9 and 15–26 are 120 feet), and all well shaded. In fact, you really can't go wrong with any site in the park. Sites with full hookups are located along the south side of the campground. Sites 1 and 27–29 are seasonal. Tent sites are equally well shaded and have a mix of grass, gravel, and dirt. The rest room is small but immaculate. Kan-Do is a campground that all campers will enjoy, and spacious enough to meet the demands of any sized rig.

Basics

Operated By: Debbie & Randy Bohnsac. **Open:** Apr. 15–Oct. 15 (otherwise limited services). **Site Assignment:** Upon registration; credit card required for reservation, 4-days cancellation policy. **Registration:** In office; late arrivals use drop box. **Fee:** RV $20 (50 amp), $17 (30 amp), $13 (water, electric); tent $11. **Parking:** At site.

Facilities

Number of RV Sites: 35. **Number of Tent-Only Sites:** 12. **Hookups:** Water, sewer, electric (30, 50 amp). **Each Site:** Picnic table, fire pit. **Dump Station:** No (sewer at all sites). **Laundry:** Yes. **Pay Phone:** Yes. **Rest Rooms and Showers:** Yes. **Fuel:** No. **Propane:** Yes. **Internal Roads:** Gravel. **RV Service:** No. **Market:** 7 mi. northeast. **Restaurant:** 5 mi. east. **General Store:** Yes. **Vending:** No. **Swimming:** Pool. **Playground:** Yes. **Other:** Fishing pond, recreation fields, pavilion. **Activities:** Volleyball, swimming, fishing. **Nearby Attractions:** Graham Cave State Park. **Additional Information:** Columbia Chamber of Commerce, (573) 874-1132.

Restrictions

Pets: On leash, cleaned up after. **Fires:** In grills. **Alcoholic Beverages:** At sites. **Vehicle Maximum Length:** None. **Other:** Visitors must purchase day pass.

To Get There

From Hwy. I-70 (Exit 170), turn north onto Hwy. 161 and then take the first left onto West Service Rd. at the dead-end sign. Go 1 mi., then turn right at the sign into the entrance.

DONIPHAN

Rocky River Resort

304 West Jefferson, Doniphan 63935. T: (800) 748-7672 or (573) 996-7171; F: (573) 996-4018.

RV: ★★★★	Tent: ★★★★
Beauty: ★★★★	Site Privacy: ★★★★
Spaciousness: ★★★★	Quiet: ★★★
Security: ★★★★★	Cleanliness: ★★★
Insect Control: ★★★★	Facilities: ★★★

Hidden in the forest, Doniphan has wooded, grassy back-ins and pull-throughs, as well as a tenting area. This campground abuts the Current River, and the focus is squarely on float trips. Sites 1–18 are 60 × 55-foot back-ins along the entrance road. Sites 6–9 are located across from a play area, and 13–15 are across from a pavilion, which may increase traffic past these sites. Sites 19–34 are situated around the "Teardrop" area. These are 50-foot back-ins, best for tenters or smaller RVs (such as pop-ups), as the dirt road can be difficult to navigate. Closest to the river access area are sites 23–27. The rest of the sites (35–51) are forested, comfortable, and spacious. Site 35, across from the Snack Shack, has one open side that is not forested. The tenting area is secluded and close to the river on the western edge of the campground. The rest rooms are reasonably modern and clean, aside from paint flaking off the floors. There are several porta-potties throughout the campground in addition to the rest rooms. A fun campground geared towards floating on the river; a great destination for families.

Basics

Operated By: Bill & Virginia. **Open:** All year. **Site Assignment:** Upon registration; credit card or check deposit for reservation (credit, but no refunds, given). **Registration:** In office; late arrivals select available site & pay in the morning. **Fee:** RV $17, tent $4/person; checks, V, MC, AE, D. **Parking:** At site.

Facilities

Number of RV Sites: 51. **Number of Tent-Only Sites:** 6. **Hookups:** Water, sewer, electric (30, 50 amp), cable. **Each Site:** Picnic table, fire pit. **Dump Station:** Yes. **Laundry:** No. **Pay Phone:** No. **Rest Rooms and Showers:** Yes. **Fuel:** No. **Propane:** No. **Internal Roads:** Gravel. **RV Service:** No. **Market:** 0.25 mi. east. **Restaurant:** 0.25 east. **General Store:** Yes. **Vending:** No. **Swimming:** No. **Playground:** Yes. **Other:** Tube rentals. **Activities:** Tubing. **Nearby Attractions:** Current River. **Additional Information:** Doniphan Chamber of Commerce: (573) 996-2212.

Restrictions

Pets: On leash, cleaned up after, no pit bulls or rottweilers. **Fires:** In grills. **Alcoholic Beverages:** At sites, no bottles. **Vehicle Maximum Length:** None. **Other:** 2 vehicles per site, visitors must check in.

To Get There

From the junction of Hwy. 21 and Hwys. 142 and 160, go 0.85 mi. west on 21/142/160. Take last left turn on east side of bridge and go 0.35 mi. on Jefferson (which is not signed). Turn right at the sign into the entrance.

EAGLEVILLE

I-35 RV Park

Exit 106, P.O. Box 56, Eagleville 64442. T: (660) 867-3377; F: (660) 867-3377; theoasis@grm.net.

RV: ★★★	Tent: ★★★
Beauty: ★★★	Site Privacy: ★★★
Spaciousness: ★★	Quiet: ★★★
Security: ★★★★	Cleanliness: ★★★
Insect Control: ★★★★	Facilities: ★★

Sites in this campground are laid out in one big loop, with pull-throughs in a strip on the west side, and back-ins in a strip on the east side. Pull-through sites range 75–85 feet in length and average 22 feet in width. Back-ins are 45 feet long before the site begins to slope. Site 1 is next to the office, and may receive registration traffic passing by. Sites 7 and 8 are closest to the rest rooms, while 9 and 10 are closest to the entrance. The nicest site is 18, closest to a tree with a seat below it. The tenting area is to the south, near the rest rooms. There is good grass cover for these sites, and a communal fire pit. The rest rooms are primitive but decent. The shower is a cement room with plastic sheeting that renders it waterproof. Some campers may find this setup a little bizarre and uncomfortable. With residences to the west and north and a semi-industrial area to the east, this campground has a slightly urban feel, but the pretty farmland to the south makes up somewhat for the lacking beauty. Overall, an acceptable stay but not an important destination.

Basics

Operated By: Michael & Betty Sanchez. **Open:** All year. **Site Assignment:** First come, first served; verbal reservations OK. **Registration:** In office; late arrivals use drop box. **Fee:** RV $15 (pull-through), $13 (back-in); tent $8, checks. **Parking:** At site.

Facilities

Number of RV Sites: 22. **Number of Tent-Only Sites:** Undesignated sites. **Hookups:** Water, sewer, electric (20, 30, 50 amp). **Dump Station:** Yes. **Laundry:** No. **Pay Phone:** Yes. **Rest Rooms and Showers:** Yes. **Fuel:** No. **Propane:** No. **Internal Roads:** Gravel. **RV Service:** No. **Market:** 3 mi. east. **Restaurant:** 3 blocks east. **General Store:** No. **Vending:** No. **Swimming:** No. **Playground:** No. **Other:** Snack shop, RV supplies, close to town square, covered picnic pavilion. **Activities:** Horseshoes. **Nearby Attractions:** Grand Trace Conservation Area. **Additional Information:** Cameron Chamber of Commerce, (816) 632-2005.

Restrictions

Pets: On leash, cleaned up after. **Fires:** In communal fire ring. **Alcoholic Beverages:** At sites. **Vehicle Maximum Length:** None. **Other:** Pay before occupying site.

To Get There

From Hwy. I-35 (Exit 106), turn west and go 0.4 mi. Turn left at the sign into the entrance.

EMINENCE

Jacks Fork Campground

P.O. Box 188, Eminence 65466. T: (800) 333-5628 or (800) 365-2537 or (800) 522-5736; www.currentrivercanoe.com.

RV: ★★★★	Tent: ★★★★★
Beauty: ★★★★	Site Privacy: ★★★★
Spaciousness: ★★★★★	Quiet: ★★★
Security: ★★★★	Cleanliness: ★★★
Insect Control: ★★★	Facilities: ★★★★

This natural campground lies along a river and is geared towards floating and canoe trips. Sites 1–21 are in a forested strip along the entrance road. These grassy sites have water and electricity, and back to lush vegetation. Along the same entrance road, sites 22–29 are much more open and not quite as nice as the first 21 sites. Grassy sites with no hookups, sites 37–40, 46, and 47 lie along the river. They contain lots of vegetation and a fair number of trees, which makes them quite comfortable. One row back from the river, sites 41–45 are spacious and with lots of shade. Similar to these are sites 50–55 in another row further back. Pull-through sites with river access include 41–45. Sites 102–129 are in a loop at the north end of the campground. Of these, sites 105–108 are right on the river, 114–115 are in a shaded corner, while 129 contains a little stand of young trees that give some amount of shade. Right at the entrance to the loop are sites 102, 127, and 128. They are right under a number of shade trees, but all other sites in this loop are very open. The rest rooms are in an aging wooden building, the showers are coin-operated. Jacks Fork makes for a decent stay for RVers who can snag a site with hookups (or don't mind going without electricity and using their facilities), and is a great place for tenters to camp.

Basics

Operated By: Gene & Eleanor Maggard. **Open:** Apr. 15–Oct. 15. **Site Assignment:** Depending on site availability; credit card required for reservations (credit certificates given but no refunds). **Registration:** In office; late arrivals pick available site & settle in the morning. **Fee:** Sun.–Thu. $5/person, Fri.–Sat. $6/person, electricity $5/night. **Parking:** At site.

Facilities

Number of RV Sites: 133. **Number of Tent-Only Sites:** 0. **Hookups:** Water, electric (30, 50 amp). **Each Site:** Picnic table, grill, trees. **Dump Station:** Yes. **Laundry:** No. **Pay Phone:** No. **Rest Rooms and Showers:** Yes. **Fuel:** No. **Propane:** No. **Internal Roads:** Gravel. **RV Service:** No. **Market:** 0.5 mi. to Eminence. **Restaurant:** 0.5 mi. to Eminence. **General Store:** Yes. **Vending:** Yes. **Swimming:** Yes (river). **Playground:** Yes. **Other:** Cabins, pavilion. **Activities:** Swimming, canoeing, volleyball, fishing. **Nearby Attractions:** Angenvine Conservation Area, Peck Ranch Conservation Area, Ozarck National Scenic Riverways, Mark Twain National Forest. **Additional Information:** Eminence Chamber of Commerce, (573) 226-3318.

Restrictions

Pets: On leash, cleaned up after. **Fires:** In grills. **Alcoholic Beverages:** At sites. **Vehicle Maximum Length:** None. **Other:** Campground divided into noisy & quiet sections.

To Get There

From the junction of Hwy. 19 and Hwy. 106, go 0.4 mi. east on Hwy. 106. Turn left at the sign into the campground.

GRAVOIS MILLS

Gravois Creek Campground

P.O. Box 167, Gravois Mills 65037. T: (800) 573-CAMP or (573) 372-3211; F: (573) 372-3212; www.gravoiscreek.com; camp@gravoiscreek.com.

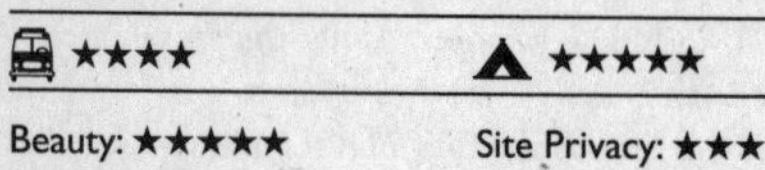

Beauty: ★★★★★	Site Privacy: ★★★
Spaciousness: ★★★	Quiet: ★★★★
Security: ★★★★★	Cleanliness: ★★★★
Insect Control: ★★★★	Facilities: ★★★★

Gravois Creek is a rural campground with a wilderness feel and very attractive landscaping, including grape vines on a trellis in front of the rest rooms, flowering trees, and woods on all four sides. The creek lies to the northeast and is accessible from the campground. Most sites are shaded, making this an exceptional camping area. Sites 1–4 are 75-foot pull-throughs, 7–13 are larger (85 feet) and well shaded, and 15–22 are even bigger (90 feet) and hidden amidst trees. Down by the creek are sites suitable for tents or pop-ups. Sites furthest to the east are electric sites wrapped by bushes and hidden under shade trees. For tenters and those RVs that can fit, this is an excellent place to camp. The area to the north of the office—a beautiful grassy field with loads of shade—is strictly for tents (no cars allowed). The showers are individual units, and the rest rooms are small but very clean. This campground is a shade-lovers paradise (a rare thing in the area).

Basics

Operated By: Johnny Keller. **Open:** Mar.–Nov. **Site Assignment:** Depending on site availability; credit card required for reservation, 48-hours cancellation policy. **Registration:** In office; late arrivals use drop box. **Fee:** RV $18 (full), $16 (water, electric); tent $11; checks, V, MC, D. **Parking:** At site.

Facilities

Number of RV Sites: 35. **Number of Tent-Only Sites:** Undesignated sites. **Hookups:** Water, sewer, electric (20, 30, 50 amp), cable. **Each Site:** Picnic table, grill or fire pit. **Dump Station:** Yes. **Laundry:** Yes. **Pay Phone:** Yes. **Rest Rooms and Showers:** Yes. **Fuel:** No. **Propane:** No. **Internal Roads:** Gravel. **RV Service:** No. **Market:** 2 mi. south. **Restaurant:** 1 mi. south. **General Store:** Yes. **Vending:** No. **Swimming:** Yes (stream). **Playground:** Yes. **Other:** Cabins, firewood, pet area, creek. **Activities:** Fishing, swimming. **Nearby Attractions:** Free public boat ramp. **Additional Information:** Lake of The Ozarks West Chamber of Commerce, (573) 374-5500.

Restrictions

Pets: On leash, cleaned up after, not in cabins. **Fires:** In grills. **Alcoholic Beverages:** At sites. **Vehicle Maximum Length:** None. **Other:** No fireworks.

To Get There

From the north city limits, go 1.7 mi. north on Hwy. 5. Turn right at the sign into the entrance.

HANNIBAL

Injun Joe Campground

14113 Clemens Dr., New London 63459. T: (573) 985-3581.

RV ★★★★	Tent ★★★★
Beauty: ★★★★	Site Privacy: ★★★
Spaciousness: ★★★	Quiet: ★★★
Security: ★★★★★	Cleanliness: ★★★
Insect Control: ★★★★	Facilities: ★★★★

A sure hit with families, Injun Joe offers swimming, go karts, plays, and many more recreation facilities. Most sites are back-ins, with an average size of 55 feet. Sites 8–35 are laid out in a loop and back to woods as do sites 101–107. Sites 130–133 are located along the entrance road and may receive more passing traffic. Site 107 is in the furthest corner, with pleasant views to two sides. Sites 139–144 back to sites 1–7 so closely that detract from the privacy of both sets of sites. The tenting area is a large field with quite a number of trees. There is a picnic shelter and decent grass covering. Most natural and woodsy is the area to the southwest. The rest room is extremely small for such a large campground, with one toilet for every 45 RV campers. It is clean and modern, but you may have to wait in line for a while during the morning rush hour. It is hard not to have a great time in Injun Joe, and families would do well to spend a few days enjoying the recreation facilities on offer.

Basics

Operated By: Clarence & Ann Steinman. **Open:** All year. **Site Assignment:** Upon registration; credit card or check required for reservation, 2-weeks cancellation policy. **Registration:** In office. **Fee:** RV $19 (full), $17 (water, electric); tent $15; checks, V, MC, D. **Parking:** At site.

Facilities

Number of RV Sites: 168. **Number of Tent-Only Sites:** Undesignated sites. **Hookups:** Water, sewer, electric (20, 30, 50 amp). **Each Site:** Picnic table on concrete slab, grill. **Dump Station:** Yes. **Laundry:** Yes. **Pay Phone:** Yes. **Rest Rooms and Showers:** Yes. **Fuel:** No. **Propane:** No. **Internal Roads:** Gravel. **RV Service:** No. **Market:** 2 mi. south. **Restaurant:** On site. **General Store:** Yes. **Vending:** No. **Swimming:** Pool. **Playground:** Yes. **Other:** Dog walk, lakes, go karts, water slide, mini-golf, batting cage, amphitheater, game room. **Activities:** Fishing, swimming, plays, go-karting. **Nearby Attractions:** Mark Twain Cave, Sawyer's Creek Fun Park, Riverview Park, Mark Twain Outdoor Theater. **Additional Information:** Hannibal CVB, (573) 221-2477.

Restrictions

Pets: On leash, cleaned up after. **Fires:** In grills. **Alcoholic Beverages:** At sites. **Vehicle Maximum Length:** 40 ft. **Other:** No ATVs.

To Get There

From the junction of Hwy. 36 and Hwy. 61, turn south onto Hwy. 61 and go 6.5 mi. Turn right. (Look for the statue and sign for Clemens Landing.) Go 2 blocks past the residences into the campground.

HAYTI

Hayti-Portageville KOA

2824 MO State East Outer Rd., Portageville 63873. T: (800) KOA-0965 or (573) DJW-1580; F: (573) DJW-0965; www.koa.com.

RV ★★★★	Tent ★★★★
Beauty: ★★★	Site Privacy: ★★★★
Spaciousness: ★★★★	Quiet: ★★★

Security: ★★★★ Cleanliness: ★★★★★
Insect Control: ★★★★ Facilities: ★★★★★

This campground is surrounded on three sides by agricultural land (with the highway on the fourth side), which lends it a rural feel. A large number of trees throughout the park make the sites comfortable, even when the sun is boring down. Situated in five rows, sites are a combination of gravel and grass, with a predominance of pull-throughs. Sites 1–7 are 45-foot back-ins close to the playground area. The rest of the sites are 70–75-foot pull-throughs, whose desirability more or less depends on personal taste (proximity to rest rooms, etc.). Several exceptionally good sites are the end sites (31, 41, 39, 49) of the last two rows, as these are furthest from the highway and seem to have more space. The tent sites are located in the southwest corner on grassy ground cover and have loads of trees. The tenting area is so spacious that each tent can be pitched under a different tree. The laundry is small but clean and contains an exercise bike. The rest rooms are very clean, and the showers (individual units) are immaculate and have air conditioning. A very comfortable campground with great facilities.

Basics

Operated By: Dan & Joyce Webb. **Open:** All year. **Site Assignment:** Upon registration; credit card required for reservations, $20 non-refundable deposit. **Registration:** In office; late arrivals use drop box. **Fee:** RV $24 (full), $22 (water, electric); tent $19. **Parking:** At site.

Facilities

Number of RV Sites: 49. **Number of Tent-Only Sites:** 20. **Hookups:** Water, sewer, electric (30, 50 amp). **Each Site:** Picnic table, grill. **Dump Station:** Yes. **Laundry:** Yes. **Pay Phone:** Yes. **Rest Rooms and Showers:** Yes. **Fuel:** No. **Propane:** Yes. **Internal Roads:** Gravel. **RV Service:** No. **Market:** 7 mi. north or south. **Restaurant:** 7 mi. north or south. **General Store:** Yes. **Vending:** Yes. **Swimming:** Pool. **Playground:** Yes. **Other:** Cabins, game room, snack bar, kitchen, modem. **Activities:** Swimming. **Nearby Attractions:** Mississippi River. **Additional Information:** Hayti Chamber of Commerce, (573) 359-0632.

Restrictions

Pets: On leash, cleaned up after, no vicious breeds (pit bulls, rottweilers) outside of vehicles. **Fires:** In fire rings. **Alcoholic Beverages:** At sites. **Vehicle Maximum Length:** None. **Other:** No smoking in buildings.

To Get There

From Hwy. I-55, take Exit 27. Turn onto the service road on the east side of the highway (East Outer Rd.) and go 3 mi. Turn left at the sign into the campground.

INDEPENDENCE

Stadium RV Park

10021 East US Hwy. 40, Independence 64055. T: (816) 353-0242; F: (816) 358-4226.

 ★★★  n/a

Beauty: ★★ Site Privacy: ★★★
Spaciousness: ★★ Quiet: ★★★
Security: ★★★★ Cleanliness: ★★★
Insect Control: ★★★★ Facilities: ★★★

A renovated mobile-home park, this campground still has a few scattered tenants (mostly on the east side), although the management is slowly converting to all RVs. Stadium is surrounded by residential areas and has a definite urban feel. Sites are not consistently numbered, and finding any one particular spot is difficult. Most sites are 30–36 feet long and 25 feet wide. Two sites on the south edge can take vehicles of at least 45 feet in length, but not with tows. Sites feel a little cramped, especially for rigs with slideouts. The laundry is old and in need of a good scrubbing and paint job. The rest rooms are likewise a little past prime, though acceptable. Larger rigs in particular might want to skip this campground altogether.

Basics

Operated By: Sarah Donahue. **Open:** All year. **Site Assignment:** Upon registration; check deposit required for reservation, 24-hours cancellation policy. **Registration:** In office; late arrivals go to house. **Fee:** RV $20. **Parking:** At site.

Facilities

Number of RV Sites: 58. **Number of Tent-Only Sites:** 0. **Hookups:** Water, sewer, electric (30, 50 amp). **Dump Station:** No (sewer at all sites). **Laundry:** Yes. **Pay Phone:** No. **Rest Rooms and Showers:** Yes. **Fuel:** No. **Propane:** No. **Internal Roads:** Gravel. **RV Service:** No. **Market:** 0.5 mi. east or west. **Restaurant:** In front. **General Store:** No. **Vending:** Yes. **Swimming:** No. **Playground:** Yes. **Activities:** Tours of KC, visiting museums, golf, theater, shopping. **Nearby Attractions:** Harry S. Truman Coutroom & Office, Kansas City. **Additional Information:** Independence Dept. of Tourism, (816) 325-7111.

Restrictions

Pets: On leash, cleaned up after, keep indoors. **Fires:** In grills. **Alcoholic Beverages:** At sites. **Vehicle Maximum Length:** None.

To Get There

From Hwy. I-70 (Exit 10), turn north onto Sterling Ave. and go 0.2 mi. Turn right onto Hwy. 40 and go 0.8 mi. Turn left at the sign into the entrance. (Beware of the hard curb.) The office is on the left.

KIRKSVILLE

Thousand Hills State Park

Rte. 3 Box 126, Kirksville 63501. T: (660) 665-6995; www.mostateparks.com.

RV: ★★★★ Tent: ★★★★

Beauty: ★★★★ Site Privacy: ★★★
Spaciousness: ★★★ Quiet: ★★★★
Security: ★★★★ Cleanliness: ★★★★
Insect Control: ★★★★ Facilities: ★★★

Although there are currently three campgrounds in this state park, campground 2 is slated to be remodeled and will be closed in 2002. Campground 1 has grassy sites (mostly back-ins) that back to forest. This is a large, popular place, and sites go quickly during high season. They range from 30 feet to more than 80 feet. Sites 28–35 are located on a separate road from the others, affording a little more privacy. Sites 36, 48, 50, 57, and 58 are paved pull-throughs. Site 66 is closest to the bathhouse. Campground 3 is smaller and not quite as popular. However, with the closing of campground 2, it is likely to be just as packed. Site 13 is located right at the entrance, which makes it less desirable. Contrary to this, sites 15–17 are located on a separate road and are thus more private. Site 18 is a large pull-through. The rest room here is less developed than the bathhouse in campground 1, but still decent. This campground makes a wonderful destination for RVers and campers who wish to recreate on the water or learn about the local natural environment.

Basics

Operated By: Missouri Dept. of Natural Resources. **Open:** All year (limited services Nov.–Mar.). **Site Assignment:** First come, first served, no reservations. **Registration:** Ranger will collect fees at site. **Fee:** RV $15 (full), $12 (water, electric); tent $7; checks, but no credit cards. **Parking:** At site.

Facilities

Number of RV Sites: 50. **Number of Tent-Only Sites:** 8. **Hookups:** Electric (30, 50 amp). **Each Site:** Picnic table, grill, lantern post. **Dump Station:** Yes. **Laundry:** Yes. **Pay Phone:** Yes. **Rest Rooms and Showers:** Yes. **Fuel:** No. **Propane:** No. **Internal Roads:** Paved. **RV Service:** No. **Market:** Junction of Hwy. 6 & 63. **Restaurant:** Junction of Hwy. 6 & 63. **General Store:** Yes. **Vending:** Yes. **Swimming:** Yes (lake). **Playground:** Yes. **Other:** Amphitheater, cabins, petroglyphs, picnic area, mountain-biking trails, boat rentals, fishing licenses. **Activities:** Fishing, boating, swimming, hiking, mountain biking, nature activities. **Nearby Attractions:** Still National Osteopathic Museum, Big Creek, Sugar Creek. **Additional Information:** Kirksville Area Chamber: (660) 665-3766.

Restrictions

Pets: On leash, cleaned up after. **Fires:** In grills. **Alcoholic Beverages:** At sites. **Vehicle Maximum Length:** None.

To Get There

From the junction of Hwy. 63 and Hwy. 6, turn west onto Hwy. 6 and go 3.3 mi. Turn left onto Hwy. 157. Go 1.7 mi. to first campground.

LAMAR

Lamar KOA

240 Southeast 1st Ln., Lamar 64739. T: (417) 682-9600; F: (417) 682-3504; www.camplamar.com; lamarmo@mykoa.com.

RV: ★★★★ Tent: ★★★

Beauty: ★★★ Site Privacy: ★★★★★
Spaciousness: ★★★★★ Quiet: ★★★★
Security: ★★★★ Cleanliness: ★★★★★
Insect Control: ★★★★ Facilities: ★★★★★

Although Lamar KOA is surrounded to the south and east by woods, there are few trees within the campground itself. Those that are inside the campground are young and offer little shade. All sites are grassy pull-throughs with gravel drives, averaging 75 × 50 feet—a decent size by any standard. Sites with the best views of the woods and the pond are 9, 16, 20, and 25. Site 9, in the southeast corner, is the overall nicest, being closest to the pond and furthest from the entrance and pool traffic. Tent spaces are completely open—no shade at all. The sites are crushed gravel pads that include a lantern pole. There is a very nice kitchen (and grills) in the pavilion for tenters' use. The rest rooms and showers are individual units by the pool. They are modern and extremely clean and spacious—some of the nicest rest rooms that can be found on the road. Lamar KOA is a relatively new campground, and some work is still underway. It promises to be an excellent stay in the future. One consideration to keep in mind, especially if travelling in summer, is the lack of shade trees.

Basics

Operated By: Bill & Shari Emmerling. **Open:** Mar. 1–Nov. 1. **Site Assignment:** Depending on site availability; credit card required for reservation, 24-hours cancellation policy. **Registration:** In office; late arrivals use drop box. **Fee:** RV $25 (full), $22 (water, electric), $20 (electric); tent $18; checks for small amounts, V, MC, AE, D. **Parking:** At site.

Facilities

Number of RV Sites: 31. **Number of Tent-Only Sites:** 6. **Hookups:** Water, sewer, electric (50 amp). **Each Site:** Picnic table, fire pit. **Dump Station:** Yes. **Laundry:** Yes. **Pay Phone:** Yes. **Rest Rooms and Showers:** Yes. **Fuel:** No. **Propane:** Yes. **Internal Roads:** Gravel. **RV Service:** No. **Market:** 3 mi. north. **Restaurant:** 2 mi. north. **General Store:** Yes. **Vending:** Yes. **Swimming:** Pool. **Playground:** Yes. **Other:** Fishing pond, pavilion w/ kitchen, communal fire ring. **Activities:** Volleyball, fishing. **Nearby Attractions:** Harry S. Truman Birthplace State Historic Site. **Additional Information:** Lamar Chamber of Commerce, (417) 682-3595.

Restrictions

Pets: On leash, cleaned up after, not in cabins. **Fires:** In grills. **Alcoholic Beverages:** At sites. **Vehicle Maximum Length:** None.

To Get There

From the junction of Hwy. I-44 and Hwy. 160, turn east onto Hwy. 160 and go to first set of traffic lights. Trun right onto Outer Rd. and go 1.9 mi. Turn left at the sign into the entrance.

LEBANON

Lebanon KOA

18376 Campground Rd., Phillipsburg 65722. T: (800) KOA-3424 or (417) 532-3422; F: (417) 588-7084; www.koa.com; lebanonkoa@socket.net.

 ★★★★  ★★★★

Beauty: ★★★★ Site Privacy: ★★★★
Spaciousness: ★★★ Quiet: ★★★★
Security: ★★★★ Cleanliness: ★★★★★
Insect Control: ★★★★ Facilities: ★★★★★

Long pull-throughs are the name of the game in this campground. There is no need to unhook any towed vehicles, as there is sure to be a site that can accommodate the longest rigs on the road. Sites 16–19B (RV sites start at 16) are 70 feet long, while the neighboring ones (in the 20s–40s) average 75 feet. Sites 50–52 are the "big boys" of the campground, measuring 100–120 feet. Site 52—the longest and very well shaded—is the nicest in the entire campground. Site 50 is unshaded and therefore less desirable. Tent sites have crushed gravel inside a tent pad surrounded by logs, and nice thick grass. Unfortunately, there is little shade offered to tent sites. (Tent sites T1–T3, along the entrance road, are shaded, but receive all of the incoming and outgoing traffic from the campground.) Billing itself as an "overnight park," this campground with easy on/off access from the highway offers much more than what that label might suggest. In fact, it's nice enough for an extended stay for either RVers or tenters.

Basics

Operated By: Dennis & Kelly Szymanski. **Open:** Mar. 31–Dec. 31. **Site Assignment:** Upon registration; credit card required for reservation, 24-hours cancellation policy (by 4 p.m. the day before). **Registration:** In office; late arrivals use drop box. **Fee:** RV $26 (full), $21 (water, electric); tent $18; checks, V, MC, D. **Parking:** At site.

Facilities

Number of RV Sites: 48. **Number of Tent-Only Sites:** 5. **Hookups:** Water, sewer, electric (50 amp). **Each Site:** Picnic table, fire pit. **Dump Station:** Yes. **Laundry:** Yes. **Pay Phone:** Yes. **Rest Rooms and Showers:** Yes. **Fuel:** No. **Propane:** Yes. **Internal Roads:** Gravel. **RV Service:** Next door. **Market:** 7 mi. east. **Restaurant:** 4 mi. east. **General Store:** Yes. **Vending:** No. **Swimming:** Pool. **Playground:** Yes. **Other:** Cabins, video games, modem, fishing hole. **Activities:** Basketball, volleyball, ping pong, breakfasts & dinners, ice cream socials on weekends, fishing. **Nearby Attractions:** Branson, Springfield, Mansfield, Meramec Caverns, Laura Ingalls Wilder Home, Bennett Springs State Park. **Additional Information:** Lebanon Chamber of Commerce, (417) 588-3256.

Restrictions

Pets: On leash, cleaned up after. **Fires:** In grills. **Alcoholic Beverages:** At sites. **Vehicle Maximum Length:** None.

To Get There

From Hwy. I-44 (Exit 123), turn south and take the first left after the highway ramp onto Outer Rd. East. Go 3 mi. and turn right at the sign into the entrance.

LESTERVILLE

Parks Bluff Campground

P.O. Box 24, Lesterville 63654. T: (573) 637-2290; F: (573) 637-2342.

 ★★★  ★★★★

Beauty: ★★★★ Site Privacy: ★★★
Spaciousness: ★★★ Quiet: ★★★★★
Security: ★★★★★ Cleanliness: ★★★★
Insect Control: ★★★★ Facilities: ★★★

Campers looking for fun on the river or in an ATV have come to the right place, but those who are looking for a quiet time should probably look elsewhere. (One indication of this is that quiet time begins at midnight.) Sites 1–4 and A–K are located in an open field surrounded by bushes and trees. These sites can accommodate a rig of any size, but cannot be pulled through unless the campground were completely empty. Most other electric sites are in a forested patch just off the Mud Pit (used for 4-wheeling). Sites 23–30 are 60-foot back-ins adjacent to the pit. Across the internal road are loads of tenting spaces. These are mostly dirt with some grass, and back thick vegetation. Many of the sites have short paths that lead to the river. There is also unlimited tenting possible along the southeast edge of the property by the river's edge. The restroom building is primitive, but the facilities are decent; the three showers are all open. Parks Bluff is geared more towards tenters than RVs (view the lack of hookups other than electric), but anyone in search of fun on the river will enjoy their stay here.

Basics

Operated By: Jayme Parks. **Open:** May–Sept. **Site Assignment:** RV sites upon registration, tent sites first come, first served; credit card or check deposit for reservation, 7-days cancellation policy. **Registration:** In office; late arrivals check in w/ guard at gate. **Fee:** $3 adult, $2 child, $3 hookup; checks, V, MC, D. **Parking:** At site.

Facilities

Number of RV Sites: 30. **Number of Tent-Only Sites:** Undesignated sites. **Hookups:** Electric (30 amp). **Each Site:** Picnic table, fire pit. **Dump Station:** No. **Laundry:** No. **Pay Phone:** Yes. **Rest Rooms and Showers:** Yes. **Fuel:** No. **Propane:** No. **Internal Roads:** Dirt. **RV Service:** No. **Market:** 9 mi. to Centerville. **Restaurant:** Less than 1 mi. west. **General Store:** Yes. **Vending:** No. **Swimming:** Yes (river). **Playground:** No. **Activities:** Floating, 4-wheeling, volleyball. **Nearby Attractions:** Black River, Johnsons Shut-Ins State Park, Taum Sauk State Park. **Additional Information:** Missouri Dept. of Natural Resources, (800) 334-6946.

Restrictions

Pets: On leash, cleaned up after. **Fires:** In grills. **Alcoholic Beverages:** At sites, no glass. **Vehicle Maximum Length:** None. **Other:** No vehicles in river.

To Get There

From the junction of Hwy. 49 North and Hwy. 21/49/72, turn east onto Hwy. 21/49/72 and go 2.8 mi. Turn right at the sign into the entrance.

LIBERTY

Miller's Kampark

145 1/2 North Stewart Rd., Liberty 64068. T: (800) 272-7578 or (816) 781-7724.

 ★★★ n/a

Beauty: ★★ Site Privacy: ★★★
Spaciousness: ★★ Quiet: ★★
Security: ★★★★ Cleanliness: ★★★
Insect Control: ★★★★ Facilities: ★★★

A number of towns in the Kansas City area have campgrounds. This one has the advantage of being relatively close to the city; however, it is really only an overnighter, and not a great place for tenters. (Tent sites are possible in 25 and 26, which are gravel sites; 25 is at least shaded.) The inner strip in the park has 60-foot pull-throughs. A strip along the south has 45-foot back-ins that back to trees and a fence. There are 30-foot back-ins on the east side of the park as well as a strip along the north side. The laundry facility is clean and roomie, and the rest rooms and showers are somewhat primitive but clean. The floors are untrated cement, and the stalls only contain half doors. This RV park is a middling stop for RVers, but tenters will want to move on. There is some amount of choice in the area, including campgrounds in Independence, Kansas City, and Oak Grove, that may be more suited for tenters.

Basics

Operated By: Richard & Barb Gercken. **Open:** All year. **Site Assignment:** Upon registration; credit card required for reservation, 24-hours cancellation policy. **Registration:** In office; late arrivals use drop box. **Fee:** RV $21 (50 amp), $20 (30 amp), $18 (water, electric); checks, V, MC, D. **Parking:** At site.

Facilities

Number of RV Sites: 48. **Number of Tent-Only Sites:** 0. **Hookups:** Water, sewer, electric (30, 50 amp). **Each Site:** Picnic tables. **Dump Station:** Yes. **Laundry:** Yes. **Pay Phone:** Yes. **Rest Rooms and Showers:** Yes. **Fuel:** No. **Propane:** Yes. **Internal Roads:** Gravel. **RV Service:** No. **Market:** 0.25 mi. west. **Restaurant:** 0.25 mi. west. **General Store:** Yes. **Vending:** Yes. **Swimming:** Pool. **Playground:** Yes. **Other:** Rec hall, close to Wal-Mart. **Activities:** Basketball, swimming, horseshoes. **Nearby Attractions:** Kansas City, Historic Liberty Jail, Jesse James Bank Museum, casinos, Worlds of Fun. **Additional Information:** CVB of Kansas City, (800) 767-7700, (816) 221-5242.

Restrictions

Pets: On leash, cleaned up after. **Fires:** In grills. **Alcoholic Beverages:** At sites. **Vehicle Maximum Length:** None.

To Get There

From Hwy. I-35 (Exit 17), turn south onto Hwy. 291 and go 1 mi. Turn right onto Stewart Rd. and go 0.25 mi. Turn left, then right at the sign into the entrance.

MACON

Long Branch Lake State Park

30174 Visitor Center Rd., Macon 63552. T: (660) 385-2108.

RV ★★★★ Tent ★★★★★

Beauty: ★★★★★ Site Privacy: ★★★★
Spaciousness: ★★★★ Quiet: ★★★★★
Security: ★★★★★ Cleanliness: ★★★★
Insect Control: ★★★★ Facilities: ★★★★

Sites in this campground are divided between electric and primitive. Those with electrical hookups are numbered 1–40, and those without any hookups, 41–83. Most sites are 65-foot back-ins. Sites located on the outside of the loop are open, while those on the inside are more forested. Site 1 is right next to the entrance, 10 is next to the restrooms. Sites 12 and 13 and 19 and 20 are doubles. The nicest site is 52, which is located at the end of a roundabout, surrounded by lush vegetation, and offers views of the lake. Site 53, also secluded, is adjacent to a lake access area, and 78–80 are next to a boat access area. Sites 54–62 are walk-in tent sites hidden in thick woods. Site 30 is a long (120 feet) pull-through located next to the entrance for easy access. Site 40, all on its own, is located near the entrance and the RV dump. The rest rooms and showers are clean, roomy, and modern. This is a great campground for those who like to get out into the wild , but it also offers modern amenities for maximum comfort.

Basics

Operated By: Missouri Dept. of Natural Resources. **Open:** All year (limited facilities Nov.–Mar. 31). **Site Assignment:** First come, first served; no reservations. **Registration:** On-season, fees collected at sites; off-season, register in visitor center; late arrivals select available site & pay in the morning. **Fee:** RV $15 (full), $12 (water, electric); tent $7; checks, V, MC, D. **Parking:** At site.

Facilities

Number of RV Sites: 40. **Number of Tent-Only Sites:** 43. **Hookups:** Water, electric (30 amp). **Each Site:** Picnic table, fire pit, lantern pole. **Dump Station:** Yes. **Laundry:** No. **Pay Phone:** No. **Rest Rooms and Showers:** Yes. **Fuel:** No. **Propane:** No. **Internal Roads:** Paved. **RV Service:** No. **Market:** 4.5 mi. east. **Restaurant:** 3 mi. east. **General Store:** Yes. **Vending:** Yes. **Swimming:** Yes (lake). **Playground:** Yes. **Activities:** Fishing, boating, swimming, hiking. **Nearby Attractions:** Thomas Hill Reservoir. **Additional Information:** Macon Economic Development Corp., (660) 385-5627.

Restrictions

Pets: On 6-ft. leash, cleaned up after. **Fires:** In grills. **Alcoholic Beverages:** At sites. **Vehicle Maximum Length:** None. **Other:** Max. 6 people/site.

To Get There

From the junction of Hwy. 63 and Hwy. 36, turn west onto Hwy. 36 and go 2.1 mi. Exit to the right at the sign, then take the first left onto Visitor Center Rd. Go 2.6 mi., then turn right into the campground.

MARSHALL

Lazy Days Campground

Rte. 1 Box 66, Marshall 65340. T: (660) 879-4411; F: (660) 879-4396.

RV ★★★ Tent ★★★

Beauty: ★★★ Site Privacy: ★★★
Spaciousness:0★★★ Quiet: ★★
Security: ★★★★ Cleanliness: ★★★★
Insect Control: ★★★★ Facilities: ★★★

This rural campground is surrounded on three sides by woods, with some residences to the north, and some commercial buildings to the southwest. There are three sections: the 30-amp sites (1–20), the 50-amp sites (21–35), and the tent area. Sites 1–4 are 60-foot pull-throughs in the 30-amp section, site 5 is a little shorter (50 feet). Sites 6–14, 17, and 18 are 75-foot pull-throughs, while 19 and 20 are shorter (50 feet). Sites 8, 12, 14, 16, and 17 have nice shade trees. The 50-amp section is a large open field that can accommodate rigs of any size. (Sites 31 and 32 share a shed that limits them to about 50 feet.) All of these sites are pull-throughs. The tent sites are likewise in a huge open field. While it offers lush grass to all tent campers, there are only two trees and two picnic tables. The rest rooms are fairly clean, but the showers are much less comfortable—the flaking paint and stained walls during our visit were a bit of a shock. The cement building that houses them looks somewhat worn. As it is, this campground is adequate, though not very quiet.

Basics

Operated By: The Younger Family. **Open:** All year. **Site Assignment:** Depending on site availability; verbal reservations OK. **Registration:** In office; late arrivals use drop box. **Fee:** RV $15 (full), tent $10; checks, V, MC, AE, D. **Parking:** At site.

Facilities

Number of RV Sites: 35. **Number of Tent-Only Sites:** 55. **Hookups:** Water, sewer, electric (30, 50 amp). **Each Site:** Picnic table, grill. **Dump Station:** Yes. **Laundry:** Yes. **Pay Phone:** Yes. **Rest Rooms and Showers:** Yes. **Fuel:** No. **Propane:** Yes. **Internal Roads:** Gravel. **RV Service:** No. **Market:** 8 mi. north. **Restaurant:** Onsite. **General Store:** Yes. **Vending:** Yes. **Swimming:** Pool. **Playground:** Yes. **Other:** Modem, rec room, video games, fish pond, breakfasts. **Activities:** Fishing, basketball, Fri. night prime rib night. **Nearby Attractions:** Van Meter State Park. **Additional Information:** Marshall Chamber of Commerce, (660) 886-3324.

Restrictions

Pets: On leash, cleaned up after. **Fires:** In grills. **Alcoholic Beverages:** At sites. **Vehicle Maximum Length:** None.

To Get There

From Hwy. I-70 (Exit 78B), follow off-ramp onto Hwy. 65, and take the first right. Go 0.6 mi. and turn right at the sign into the entrance.

MOBERLY

Thompson Campground

Rothwell Park Rd., Moberly 65270. T: (660) 670-4522 or (660) 263-6757.

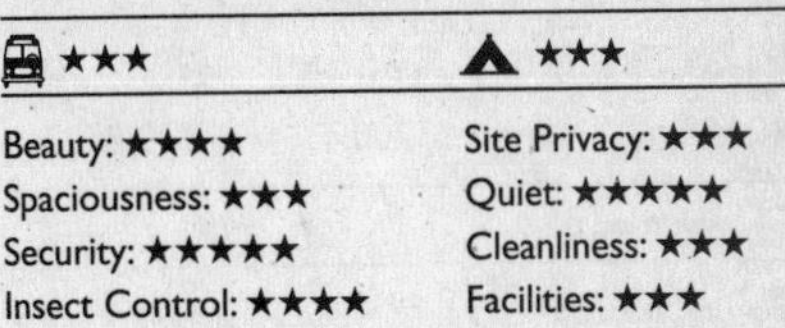

RV ★★★ Tent ★★★

Beauty: ★★★★ Site Privacy: ★★★
Spaciousness: ★★★ Quiet: ★★★★★
Security: ★★★★★ Cleanliness: ★★★
Insect Control: ★★★★ Facilities: ★★★

This park has RV sites in a strip of 12 spaces, with two RVs designated per site. None of the sites are numbered. Sounds confusing? The setup is apparently just as confusing to the people who run the park, as they are not even sure of the number of RVs that the park can accommodate. However, this is a nice little park surrounded on three sides by woods, and is worth the minor hassle the site numbers may cause. Although sites are 90 feet in length, the slope from which nearly all of them suffer cuts the usable length down to about 70 feet. (Sites to the south are more level, but are adjacent to stored equipment and piles of miscellaneous stuff.) The tenting area is just as confusing as the RV section. In fact, there is no indication anywhere of the location of the tent area. It is, for the record, just to the north of the internal road, facing the RV sites. The thick grass and tree coverage make for comfortable camping, but the primitive toilet and lack of sink and showers is a severe drawback for tenters—as are the almost inescapable security lights. (Still, at this price, who can complain?) Police and ranger patrols ensure that the campground is secure throughout the night. Thompson is nicer for RVs than for tents, although the cheap price makes it worthwhile for any camper on a budget.

Basics

Operated By: City of Moberly. **Open:** All year. **Site Assignment:** First come, first served; no reservations. **Registration:** Wait for ranger to collect fees. **Fee:** $8 (water, electric), $3 tent; checks. **Parking:** At site.

Facilities

Number of RV Sites: 24. **Number of Tent-Only Sites:** Undesignated sites. **Hookups:** Water, electric (30 amp). **Each Site:** Picnic table. **Dump Station:** Yes. **Laundry:** No. **Pay Phone:** No. **Rest Rooms and Showers:** Rest rooms; no shower. **Fuel:** No. **Propane:** No. **Internal Roads:** Gravel. **RV Service:** No. **Market:** 1 mi. northeast. **Restaurant:** 1 mi. northeast. **General Store:** No. **Vending:** No. **Swimming:** Pool. **Playground:** Yes. **Other:** Jogging trails, group shelters, lake, pool, recreation field, boat ramp. **Activities:** Fishing, boating, swimming, field sports, basketball, archery. **Nearby Attractions:** Mark Twain Birthplace State Historic Area. **Additional Information:** Chamber of Commerce Moberly Area, (660) 263-6070.

Restrictions

Pets: On leash, cleaned up after. **Fires:** In grills. **Alcoholic Beverages:** At sites, subject to public drinking ordinance if outside sites. **Vehicle Maximum Length:** None.

To Get There

From the junction of Hwy. 63 and Hwy. 24, turn west on Hwy. 24 and go 3 mi. Turn right onto Rothwell Park Rd. Turn right at the sign into the entrance.

MONETT

Pine Trails RV Ranch

40 Hwy. 60, Monett 65708. T: (417) 235-8682.

RV ★★★★ Tent n/a

Beauty: ★★★★ Site Privacy: ★★★★★
Spaciousness: ★★★★ Quiet: ★★★★
Security: ★★★★★ Cleanliness: ★★★★★
Insect Control: ★★★★ Facilities: ★★

This small RV park in the pine trees has 80 × 33-foot pull-throughs laid out in two rows. To the northeast is forest, and to the northwest are open fields creating a very quiet and peaceful atmosphere. Site 1 is slightly easier to get in and out of. (This is true of the lower numbers in general.) Site 21 has a larger grassy area than other sites, but, in general, all the sites are of a uniform quality. Unabashedly oriented towards older folks, this campground provides a very low-key and quiet place to camp. Note the lack of rest rooms, which disqualifies tents and RVs that are not self-contained.

Basics

Operated By: Frank & Sandy Theser. **Open:** All year. **Site Assignment:** Upon registration; verbal reservations OK. **Registration:** In office; late arrivals use drop box. **Fee:** RV $19 (50 amp), $17 (30 amp); no credits cards, but checks. **Parking:** At site.

Facilities

Number of RV Sites: 21. **Number of Tent-Only Sites:** 0. **Hookups:** Water, sewer, electric (30, 50 amp). **Each Site:** Picnic table. **Dump Station:** Yes. **Laundry:** No. **Pay Phone:** No. **Rest Rooms and Showers:** No. **Fuel:** No. **Propane:** No. **Internal Roads:** Gravel. **RV Service:** No. **Market:** 3 mi. west. **Restaurant:** 3 mi. west. **General Store:** No. **Vending:** No. **Swimming:** No. **Playground:** No. **Other:** Modem, picnic area, close to attractions, pet walk area. **Activities:** Hiking, shows (in Branson), fishing, boating. **Nearby Attractions:** Roaring River State Park, Mark Twain National Forest, Branson, Springfield. **Additional Information:** Monett Chamber of Commerce, (417) 235-7919.

Restrictions

Pets: On leash, cleaned up after. **Fires:** In common fire ring. **Alcoholic Beverages:** At sites. **Vehicle Maximum Length:** None. **Other:** Keep satellite dish on gravel.

To Get There

From the junction of Hwy. 37 and Hwy. 60, turn east onto Hwy. 60 and go 3 mi. Turn left at the sign into the entrance.

MOUNTAIN GROVE

Missouri Park Campground

2325 Missouri Park Dr., Mountain Grove 65711. T: (417) 926-4104 or (417) 926-6237; mopark@getgoin.net.

RV ★★★★ Tent ★★★★

Beauty: ★★★★ Site Privacy: ★★★★
Spaciousness: ★★★ Quiet: ★★★★
Security: ★★★★ Cleanliness: ★★★★
Insect Control: ★★★★ Facilities: ★★★★

This campground has a combination of overnight RV spaces and mobile homes. Sites 1–9 are right at the entrance. These are 90-foot gravel pull-throughs just south of the mobile-home area. Site 2 has some shade, but the others in this strip are all open. The rest of the RV sites lie west, in a forested area, with sites 1–10 being the most forested. Sites 2, 4, and 6 are 95–120-foot pull-throughs; 16 and 18 are also very long. The back-ins in this area range from 35 to 45 feet in length. (Most of the sites are not numbered, which makes it difficult to find the proper site, especially in the nothern part of the loop, 12–18.) The tenting area is a large grassy field that can take any number of tents. The grass cover is healthy, but because the area is slightly sloped, tenting in some areas becomes difficult; there is also a lack of shade in the entire field. The rest rooms are clean and comfortable, with air conditioning, new countertops, and brand-new tile laid on the floor. A woodsy, comfortable campground.

Basics

Operated By: Paul & Christine Gasperson. **Open:** All year (limited services Jan.–Feb.). **Site Assignment:** Depending on site availability; verbal reservations OK. **Registration:** In office; late arrivals use drop box. **Fee:** RV $20 (full), $15 (water, electric); tent $12; no credits, but checks. **Parking:** At site.

Facilities

Number of RV Sites: 30. **Number of Tent-Only Sites:** Undesignated sites. **Hookups:** Water, sewer, electric (30, 50 amp). **Dump Station:** No (sewer at all sites). **Laundry:** Yes. **Pay Phone:** Yes. **Rest Rooms and Showers:** Yes. **Fuel:** No. **Propane:** No. **Internal Roads:** Gravel. **RV Service:** No. **Market:** 3 mi. to Exit 95. **Restaurant:** 3 mi. to Exit 95. **General Store:** Yes. **Vending:** No. **Swimming:** Pool. **Playground:** No. **Other:** Fishing lake, game room w/ pool table. **Activities:** Swimming, fishing, hiking. **Nearby Attractions:** Laura Ingles Wilder's Home, Mark Twain NF **Additional Information:** Mountain Grove Chamber, (417) 926-4135.

Restrictions

Pets: On leash, cleaned up after. **Fires:** In grills. **Alcoholic Beverages:** At sites. **Vehicle Maximum Length:** None.

To Get There

From Hwy. 65 (Business 60 Hwy. Exit, which is Mountain Grove's westernmost exit), go north over the highway overpass and take the service road 1.2 mi. Turn right onto Missouri Park Dr. and then left into the campground.

NOEL

Elk River Floats Wayside Campground

P.O. Box 546, Noel 64854. T: (417) 475-3230 or (417) 475-3561; www.missouri2000.net/wayside; wayside@netins.net.

RV ★★★ Tent ★★★★

Beauty: ★★★★★ Site Privacy: ★★
Spaciousness: ★★★ Quiet: ★★★
Security: ★★★★★ Cleanliness: ★★★
Insect Control: ★★★★ Facilities: ★★★

The "open camping" policy of this campground means that once you pay for a site, you can go and pick any site you want to occupy. Therefore, sites are not numbered, as they are not assigned. You can also camp as close to the water as you like. The first designated sites are near the office, on the southwest edge. These are gravel/grass full hookup sites with some shade. Open-ended, they can take rigs of any size but are restricted to a tight 16 -foot width. Sites along the western edge are the best—level, grassy, and shady. The downside is that the highway lies just on the other side of a wooded strip from these sites. Other full hookup sites are found on the penninsula. They are rather open and receive a fair amount of passing traffic, but are close to the water. The tip of the penninsula is a more secluded area that is great for such groups as family reunions. Tenters can pitch a tent anywhere they like, right up to the water's edge, if they prefer. The rest rooms are a little rough, made of cement and wood and lacking both windows and external doors. Showers are located only in the red office building. These are spacious cement stalls that remind one of YMCA showers—minus the lockers. Elk River is a water fun–oriented campground, geared more towards a younger crowd. It is definitely a destination for groups, although couples will also enjoy a stay here. Those looking for a quiet time should look elsewhere. One note of caution: the highway coming into the park has overhanging cliffs that could present a danger to large rigs.

Basics

Operated By: Rod & Rence Lett. **Open:** Apr.–Oct. **Site Assignment:** First come, first served; no reservations. **Registration:** In office; late arrivals select site & pay in the morning during the week, see person at the gate on weekends. **Fee:** RV $16 (full), $6 person, $3 electric, $6 RV hookups; V, MC, D, no checks. **Parking:** At site.

Facilities

Number of RV Sites: 98. **Number of Tent-Only Sites:** Undesignated sites. **Hookups:** Water, sewer, electric (30 amp). **Each Site:** Picnic tables at some sites. **Dump Station:** Yes. **Laundry:** No. **Pay Phone:** At motel next door. **Rest Rooms and Showers:** Yes. **Fuel:** No. **Propane:** No. **Internal Roads:** Gravel. **RV Service:** No. **Market:** 0.25 mi. east. **Restaurant:** 0.25 mi. west. **General Store:** No. **Vending:** No. **Swimming:** Yes (river). **Playground:** Yes. **Other:** Boat rentals, paddleboats, tubes. **Activities:** Floating, boating, swimming, fishing. **Nearby Attractions:** Grand Lake (OK), Bluff Dwellers Cave, Branson, Table Rock Lake, Bass Pro Shop. **Additional Information:** Joplin Area Chamber of Commerce, (417) 624-1996.

Restrictions

Pets: On leash, cleaned up after, prefer no large breeds. **Fires:** In grills. **Alcoholic Beverages:** At sites, no glass or styrofoam on river. **Vehicle Maximum Length:** None. **Other:** No fireworks.

To Get There

From the junction of Hwy. 59 and Hwy. 90, turn wast onto Hwy. 90 and go 0.1 mi. Take first right into campground.

OAK GROVE

Kansas City East KOA

303 Northeast 3rd St. P.O. Box 191, Oak Grove 64075. T: (800) 562-7507 or (816) 690-6660; F: (816) 690-6660; www.koa.com; kckoa@yahoo.com.

RV: ★★★★ | Tent: ★★★

Beauty: ★★★	Site Privacy: ★★★
Spaciousness: ★★★	Quiet: ★★★
Security: ★★★★	Cleanliness: ★★★★
Insect Control: ★★★★	Facilities: ★★★★

Under new management, this campground may introduce new services or procedures than those described below. As of today, it has several rows of large pull-throughs: 1–10 are unshaded 70-foot sites, 18–26 are unshaded 54-foot sites, and 27–33 are shaded 90-foot sites. Sites 42–47 are head-to-head pull-throughs along the east edge. These sites are well shaded, but as a consequence of being doubles, they offer less room and privacy. Sites 54–68 along the south edge are back-ins that back to trees and other vegetation. These are mostly well-shaded sites. Sites 71–73 are located in the shaded northwest corner and are comfortable and grassy. Sites T1 and T2 are located in the southeast corner, and back to a hedge. They have decent grass and cool shade. Other tent sites (38–41) are located to the north of sites 42–43. The rest rooms and showers are somewhat old but still clean and comfortable. Although slightly better for RVers than for tents, this campground is a decent stay with loads of facilities for all.

Basics

Operated By: Mary & Melvin Lueck. **Open:** All year. **Site Assignment:** Depending on site availability; credit card required for reservation but not charged. **Registration:** In office; late arrivals use drop box in laundry. **Fee:** RV $28 (full), $25 (water, electric); tent $20; checks, V, MC, D. **Parking:** At site.

Facilities

Number of RV Sites: 73. **Number of Tent-Only Sites:** 14. **Hookups:** Water, sewer, electric (30, 50 amp). **Each Site:** Picnic table, fire pit. **Dump Station:** Yes. **Laundry:** Yes. **Pay Phone:** Yes. **Rest Rooms and Showers:** Yes. **Fuel:** No. **Propane:** Yes. **Internal Roads:** Gravel. **RV Service:** No. **Market:** Less than 1 mi. southwest. **Restaurant:** Less than 1 mi. southwest. **General Store:** Yes. **Vending:** Yes. **Swimming:** Pool. **Playground:** Yes. **Other:** Mini golf, dog walk, cabins, game room, pool table, horseshoes. **Activities:** Volleyball, basketball, swimming. **Nearby Attractions:** Worlds of Fun, Truman Library, Truman Home, casinos. **Additional Information:** CVB of Greater Kansas City, (800) 767-7700, (816) 221-5242.

Restrictions

Pets: On leash, cleaned up after. **Fires:** In grills. **Alcoholic Beverages:** At sites. **Vehicle Maximum Length:** None.

To Get There

From Hwy. I-70 (Exit 28), turn north onto H and go 0.25 mi. Turn right onto 3rd St. and go 2 blocks to the entrance on the right.

OZARK

Ozark RV Park

320 North 20th St., Ozark 65721. T: (417) 581-3203; chickenfoot@pcis.net.

RV: ★★ | Tent: n/a

Beauty: ★	Site Privacy: ★★★
Spaciousness: ★★★	Quiet: ★★★
Security: ★★★	Cleanliness: ★★★★
Insect Control: ★★★★	Facilities: ★

Ozark RV park is surrounded by commercial development, which unfortunately detracts heavily from the environment. These unshaded sites are all grassy pull-throughs ranging from 60 feet (21–28) to 70 feet (1–14), laid out in three rows. As the park is surrounded by roads on three sides, the least desirable sites are closest to the edges. Better sites are somewhere in the middle (9–13). Site 14 has the largest strip of grass, but is closest to the external road to the south. There are no rest rooms or showers, so self-contained vehicles are the only kind possible. The one advantage that the park has is proximity to restaurants and other commercial sites. As such, it makes a fair overnight stop.

Basics

Operated By: Jeanne Siler. **Open:** All year. **Site Assignment:** Upon registration; credit card required for reservation, 24-hours cancellation policy. **Registration:** Use drop box. **Fee:** RV $18 (full), $15 (water, electric). **Parking:** At site.

Facilities

Number of RV Sites: 28. **Number of Tent-Only Sites:** 0. **Hookups:** Water, sewer, electric (30, 50 amp), cable. **Dump Station:** No. **Laundry:** No. **Pay Phone:** No. **Rest Rooms and Showers:** No. **Fuel:** No. **Propane:** No. **Internal Roads:** Gravel. **RV Service:** No. **Market:** Less than 0.5 mi. east. **Restaurant:** Less than 0.25 mi. east. **General Store:** No. **Vending:** Yes. **Swimming:** No. **Playground:** No. **Activities:** Musical shows, shopping, hiking. **Nearby Attractions:** Springfield, Branson, Mark Twain National Forest. **Additional Information:** Ozark Chamber of Commerce, (417) 581-6139.

Restrictions

Pets: On leash, cleaned up after. **Fires:** In grills. **Alcoholic Beverages:** At sites. **Vehicle Maximum Length:** None.

To Get There

From Hwy. 65 (Nixa/Hwy. 14 Exit), turn west onto Hwy. 14. Go through the light and take the first left, then an immediate left into the park.

PECULIAR

Peculiar Park Place

22901 Southeast Outer Rd., Peculiar 64078. T: (816) 779-6300; F: (816) 779-6303.

RV: ★★★★★ | Tent: n/a

Beauty: ★★★★	Site Privacy: ★★★★
Spaciousness: ★★★★	Quiet: ★★★
Security: ★★★★★	Cleanliness: ★★★★★
Insect Control: ★★★★	Facilities: ★★★★

Although only open since August 2000, this RV park is already a beautiful place to camp. The landscaping includes rocks, plants, trees, brick and wood on the office building, and a bricked patio and stenciled cement table for each site. Sites 1–10 are 75-foot pull-throughs that have a very nice view of the highway and the woods beyond. Sites 11 and 12 are located in a beautiful grassy spot with an attractive rock retaining wall behind, while 13–18 back to woods, also with very pleasant landscaping. Sites 19–28 are 90-foot unshaded pull-throughs that overlook sites 1–10 and share the same view. Sites 29–34 are 70-foot pull-throughs, 39–51 are 90-foot pull-throughs. Like 13–18, 35–38 also back to some nice woods. Planned improvements to the park include a paved road, as well as many recreation facilities. The rest rooms are absolutely top-notch—some of the best of any campground on the road. They are tiled, modern, and at least as comfortable as at home. Although tenters will have to find another place to camp, RVers would be well advised to mark this park on their itinerary. It is the nicest RV park in the Kansas City area, and is destined only to get better.

Basics

Operated By: Frosty & Gail. **Open:** All year. **Site Assignment:** Upon registration; verbal reservations OK. **Registration:** In office; late arrivals call phone number on door 24 hrs. **Fee:** RV $24 (50 amp), $22 (30 amp); checks OK, no credit cards. **Parking:** At site.

Facilities

Number of RV Sites: 61. **Number of Tent-Only Sites:** 0. **Hookups:** Water, sewer, electric (20, 30, 50 amp). **Each Site:** Picnic table, brick patio, fire pit. **Dump Station:** Yes. **Laundry:** Yes. **Pay Phone:** Yes. **Rest Rooms and Showers:** Yes. **Fuel:** No. **Propane:** Yes. **Internal Roads:** Gravel. **RV Service:** No. **Market:** 2 mi. west. **Restaurant:** 2 mi. west. **General Store:** No. **Vending:** No. **Swimming:** No. **Playground:** No. **Other:** Pet walk, gift shop, gazebo; planned facilities include pavilion, bandstand, putting green, dance floor, hot tub. **Activities:** Wildlife-viewing, hiking, potlucks. **Nearby Attractions:** Branson, Kansas City. **Additional Information:** CVB of Greater Kansas City, (800) 767-7700, (816) 221-5242.

Restrictions

Pets: On leash, cleaned up after, small or medium-sized dogs only. **Fires:** In grills. **Alcoholic Beverages:** At sites. **Vehicle Maximum Length:** None.

To Get There

From Hwy. 71 (Peculiar Exit), turn east onto J and take first right after highway off-ramp onto East Outer Rd. Go 1.5 mi. and turn left at the sign into the entrance.

PERRYVILLE

Perryville/Cape Girardeau KOA

89 KOA Ln., Perryville 63775. T: (800) 562-5304 or (573) 547-8303; F: (573) 547-7422; www.koa.com.

RV ★★★★★ Tent ★★★★★

Beauty: ★★★★ Site Privacy: ★★★★
Spaciousness: ★★★ Quiet: ★★★
Security: ★★★★ Cleanliness: ★★★★★
Insect Control: ★★★★ Facilities: ★★★★★

Sites in this campground are arranged in rows A–K. All rows but A and B are hidden amongst shade trees which makes them more desirable. Row A contains 65-foot pull-throughs, rows B–J have 72-foot pull-throughs. Sites A1 and B1 are next to a residence, and C1 and D1 are next to an unattractive shed. Sites J4 and J5 and F1 have large pieces of electrical hardware that encroach on their space. Sites F8 and F9 and E9 and E10 are less shaded than others around them. Aside from these few shortcomings, you really can't go wrong with any of the sites in this park. For a more wilderness feel, try rows H–K. They are less developed and are further back in the woods. Row K has 52-foot back-ins that back to the forest surrounding the campground. The best sites in any row (especially C–J) are close to the middle (for example, 3–6). Tent sites are 45 feet wide, with plenty of depth, grassy, and forested—ideal for a tenter. The rest rooms are clean, spacious, and very private. This campground is comfortable for any style of camping and offers plenty to do. A great place to bring kids.

Basics

Operated By: Mary Ann Abernathy. **Open:** All year. **Site Assignment:** Depending on site availability; verbal reservations OK. **Registration:** In office; late arrivals use drop box. **Fee:** RV $25 (full), $23 (water, electric); tent $19; checks, V, MC, AE, D. **Parking:** At site.

Facilities

Number of RV Sites: 92. **Number of Tent-Only Sites:** 10. **Hookups:** Water, sewer, electric (30, 50 amp). **Each Site:** Picnic table, grill. **Dump Station:** Yes. **Laundry:** Yes. **Pay Phone:** Yes. **Rest Rooms and Showers:** Yes. **Fuel:** No. **Propane:** Yes. **Internal Roads:** Gravel. **RV Service:** No. **Market:** 1 mi. east. **Restaurant:** 1 mi. east. **General Store:** Yes. **Vending:** Yes. **Swimming:** Pool. **Playground:** Yes. **Other:** Mini-golf, cabins, tipis, pavilions, pet walk, game room, sun deck, accommodates groups, fishing pond. **Activities:** Campfires, Sat. kids' events, Chirstmas in July, fishing (catch & release). **Nearby Attractions:** Hometown of Popeye the Sailor (Chester, IL), Hostoric St. Genevieve (oldest town west of the Mississippi), St. Mary's seminary. **Additional Information:** Perryville Chamber of Commerce, (573) 547-6062.

Restrictions

Pets: On leash, cleaned up after. **Fires:** In grills. **Alcoholic Beverages:** At sites. **Vehicle Maximum Length:** None. **Other:** Catch & release fishing.

To Get There

From Hwy. I-55 (Exit 129), turn west onto Hwy. 51 and take the first right after the highway overpass (Outer Rd. North). Go 1.4 mi., then turn left at the sign into the entrance.

PLATTE CITY

Basswood Country Inn and RV Resort

15880 Interurban Rd., Platte City 64079. T: (800) 242-2775 or (816) 858-5556; F: (816) 858-5556; www.basswoodresort.com; info@basswoodresort.com.

RV ★★★★★ Tent ★★★★

Beauty: ★★★★ Site Privacy: ★★★
Spaciousness: ★★★ Quiet: ★★★★
Security: ★★★★★ Cleanliness: ★★★★★
Insect Control: ★★★★ Facilities: ★★★★★

Rarely does an RV "resort" live up to the excellence its name promises. However, Basswood is an exception; it's a smooth operation and a guaranteed great stay for both RVers and tenters. Besides the usual facilites, there are stocked fishing lakes, modem access, and room at the inn for those who need a change of pace. The two areas named "Tent A" and "Tent B" on the map handed out to you are misleading—these are all RV spaces. Tent A has 51-foot cement slabs in pull-throughs sites, while Tent B has 30-foot gravel back-ins. Of these sites, 8 and 21 are particularly well shaded. South of this is the real tenting area. These are grassy, shaded sites, very comfortable for tents. Site A is above the lake and across the interior road, B and C are right on the lake. These are the best tent sites, as they are closest to the lake and more isolated. Sites D–T are in rows to the west of this area. These are grass-and-dirt sites but lack any real shade. (There are only decorative trees and shrubs.) Sites D–L on the east side are 33 × 45 feet, while M–T are 25 × 36 feet. The big-rig area is located to the extreme west, in a hollow surrounded by trees and dirt cliffs. Sites 75 and 76 are 35-foot back-ins, but the rest of the sites are much larger. Sites 77–97 and 120–129 are 75 × 30-foot gravel pull-throughs. The rest rooms are individual units with shower, toilet, and sink. They are all very modern, extremely comfortable, and with air conditioning.

Basics

Operated By: John Pottie. **Open:** All year. **Site Assignment:** Upon registration; credit card required for reservation, 7-days cancellation policy. **Registration:** In office; late arrivals knock on night window. **Fee:** RV $26 (full), tent $18. **Parking:** At site.

Facilities

Number of RV Sites: 58. **Number of Tent-Only Sites:** 20. **Hookups:** Water, sewer, electric (30, 50 amp), phone. **Each Site:** Picnic table, grill, fire pit. **Dump Station:** No (sewer at all sites). **Laundry:** Yes. **Pay Phone:** Yes. **Rest Rooms and Showers:** Yes. **Fuel:** No. **Propane:** Yes. **Internal Roads:** Gravel/paved. **RV Service:** On-call. **Market:** 6 mi. west. **Restaurant:** 5 mi. west. **General Store:** Yes. **Vending:** Yes. **Swimming:** Pool. **Playground:** Yes. **Other:** Athletic field, meeting facilities, fishing lakes, games, cottage, inn, trails, covered picnic shelter, modem. **Activities:** Fishing, boating, swimming, hiking. **Nearby Attractions:** Alldredge Orchards, Guy B. Park Conservation Area, Platte Falls Conservation Area, "Pumpkins, Etc.", Fulk's Tree Farm, Shiloh Springs Golf Course. **Additional Information:** Platte City Chamber of Commerce: www.plattecitymo.com.

Restrictions

Pets: On leash, cleaned up after. **Fires:** In grills. **Alcoholic Beverages:** At sites. **Vehicle Maximum Length:** None. **Other:** No washing or working on vehicles.

To Get There

From Hwy. I-29 (Exit 18), turn east onto Hwy. 92 and go 3.5 mi. Turn left onto Winan Ave. and go 1.7 mi. to the stop sign. Turn left onto Interurban Hwy. and go 0.3 mi. Turn left at the sign onto Basswood Lake Rd. and drive up to the office.

REVERE
Battle of Athens State Historical Site Campground

RR 1 Box 26, Revere 63465. T: (660) 877-3871; F: (600) 877-1202.

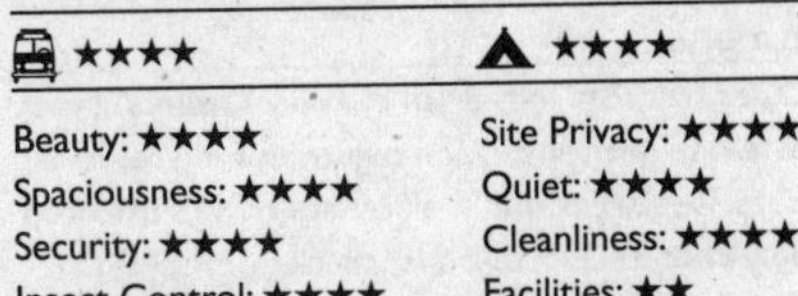

RV ★★★★ Tent ★★★★

Beauty: ★★★★ Site Privacy: ★★★★
Spaciousness: ★★★★ Quiet: ★★★★
Security: ★★★★ Cleanliness: ★★★★
Insect Control: ★★★★ Facilities: ★★

Located southwest of the historical site, this campground has all forested sites located in lush vegetation. Sites are back-ins that average 65–75 feet. Sites 1–4 are located on a separate road that branches off the main road right at the entrance. Sites 1 and 4 are the nicest in the campground, as they are more secluded than the others. Sites 14 and 18 are very close together and lack privacy. Sites 26 and 27 are doubles, best suited for groups that need two adjacent sites. The three rest rooms in the campground all have pit toilets and no showers or running water. An attractive campground, but rather short on facilities—especially for tent campers.

Basics

Operated By: Missouri Dept. of Natural Resources. **Open:** All year. **Site Assignment:** First come, first served; no reservations. **Registration:** Camp Host will collect fees at sites. **Fee:** RV $15 (full), $12 (water, electric); tent $7; checks, V, MC, D. **Parking:** At site.

Facilities

Number of RV Sites: 15. **Number of Tent-Only Sites:** 14. **Hookups:** Electric (30 amp). **Each Site:** Picnic table, fire pit. **Dump Station:** No. **Laundry:** No. **Pay Phone:** Yes. **Rest Rooms and Showers:** Rest rooms; no shower. **Fuel:** No. **Propane:** No. **Internal Roads:** Paved. **RV Service:** No. **Market:** 10 mi. to Farmington. **Restaurant:** 10 mi. to Farmington. **General Store:** No. **Vending:** No. **Swimming:** No. **Playground:** Yes. **Other:** Lake. **Activities:** Fishing, boating, hiking. **Nearby Attractions:** Des Moines River, Mark Twain Birthplace Museum, Thousand Hills. **Additional Information:** Kirksville Chamber of Commerce, (660) 665-3766.

Restrictions

Pets: On leash, cleaned up after. **Fires:** In grills. **Alcoholic Beverages:** At sites. **Vehicle Maximum Length:** None.

To Get There

From the junction of Hwy. 81 and Hwy. CC, turn east onto Hwy. CC and go 4 mi. Turn left onto gravel road and continue to park entrance.

SEDALIA
Countryside Adult/Senior RV Park

5464 South Limit Ave., Sedalia 65301. T: (660) 827-6513 or (660) 827-3735; F: (660) 826-9471; rvpark@murlin.com.

RV ★★★ Tent n/a

Beauty: ★★★★ Site Privacy: ★★★
Spaciousness: ★★★ Quiet: ★★★
Security: ★★★★ Cleanliness: ★★★★
Insect Control: ★★★★ Facilities: ★★★

The owners of this campground are normally out during the day, but sites available for overnighters are posted on the door to the office. Sites 19–22, 27, and 28 are (at least nominally) pull-throughs. It is, however, difficult to see how sites 21–25 could be pull-throughs without driving over the grassy patch that borders them on one side (and looks more like landscaping than a driveway). Sites are on a large gravel area and measure 100 feet in length. Sites 1–13, on the east side, back to woods and residences. Sites 14–20 are against the southern edge and back to woods and the office. The large open field to the northwest that looks so enticing is used only during the summer fair in Sedalia. Overnighters must select from open sites on the gravel. The rest rooms are individual units that include showers. These are all very clean and comfortable. This campground is a decent stop for overnighters, although many may wish they could camp out on the grass instead.

Basics

Operated By: Linda Alcorn. **Open:** All year. **Site Assignment:** First come, first served; reservations required for more than 5 days. **Registration:** In house. **Fee:** RV $19 (full), $17 (water, electric). **Parking:** At site.

Facilities

Number of RV Sites: 27. **Number of Tent-Only Sites:** 0. **Hookups:** Water, sewer, electric (30, 50 amp), cable. **Each Site:** Picnic table. **Dump Station:** Yes. **Laundry:** Yes. **Pay Phone:** Yes. **Rest Rooms and Showers:** Yes. **Fuel:** No. **Propane:** No. **Internal Roads:** Gravel. **RV Service:** No. **Market:** Less than 5 mi. north. **Restaurant:** Less than 5 mi. north. **General Store:** No. **Vending:** Yes. **Swimming:** No. **Playground:** No. **Other:** Modem hookup, pavilion. **Activities:** Self-guiding tours. **Nearby Attractions:** Bothwell Lodge, Silver Dollar City. **Additional Information:** Sedalia Area Chamber, (800) 827-5295, (660) 826-2222.

Restrictions

Pets: On leash, cleaned up after. **Fires:** In grills. **Alcoholic Beverages:** At sites. **Vehicle Maximum Length:** None.

To Get There

From the junction of Hwy. 50 and Hwy. 65, turn south onto Hwy. 65 and go 2.8 mi. Turn right at the sign into the entrance and follow the gravel drive around to the house.

SIKESTON
Hinton Park

2860 East Malone, Sikeston 63801. T: (800) 327-1457 or (573) 471-1457.

RV ★★★ Tent ★★

Beauty: ★★ Site Privacy: ★★★★
Spaciousness: ★★★★ Quiet: ★★★
Security: ★★★★★ Cleanliness: ★★★★
Insect Control: ★★★★ Facilities: ★★★

Hinton Park has long pull-throughs laid out in rows of gravel and grassy sites. Sites 1–26, located on the east edge of the property, are 90 × 30 feet. They are sandwiched between mobile homes to the west and an industrial field to the east. Site 1 is slightly shorter (75 feet), but is adjacent to a pleasant agricultural field to the south. Other sites, some unnumbered, lie in rows to the southwest of the office. As they are in a large open field, there is no size restriction to the vehicles that can occupy these sites. Site 16 has a nice shade tree, and 8 and 13 are next to a row of pretty bushes. Tenting is possible on a large grassy field off the highway. While there is plenty of room, the location is not conducive to quiet. The rest-room facilities are clean and modern, but the walls and floors are unattractive cement. (Tile would help the appearance of cleanliness.) This is a fine campground, but better suited for RVers than tenters.

Basics

Operated By: Mark Hinton. **Open:** All year. **Site Assignment:** Upon registration; check deposit required for reservation, 24-hours cancellation policy. **Registration:** In office; late arrivals use drop box. **Fee:** RV $17, tent $9; checks, V, MC. **Parking:** At site.

Facilities

Number of RV Sites: 46. **Number of Tent-Only Sites:** Undesignated sites. **Hookups:** Water, sewer, electric (30, 50 amp), cable. **Each Site:** Picnic table. **Dump Station:** Yes. **Laundry:** Yes. **Pay Phone:** Yes. **Rest Rooms and Showers:** Yes. **Fuel:** No. **Propane:** Yes. **Internal Roads:** Gravel. **RV Service:** No. **Market:** 3 mi. west. **Restaurant:** 0.6 mi. west. **General Store:** No. **Vending:** No. **Swimming:** No. **Playground:** No. **Other:** Modem/phone at every site, free shuttle to Lambert's Cafe (home of the "throwed roll"). **Activities:** Hiking, fishing. **Nearby Attractions:** Big Oak Tree State Park. **Additional Information:** Charleston Chamber, (573) 683-6509.

Restrictions

Pets: On leash, cleaned up after, keep in RV. **Fires:** In grills. **Alcoholic Beverages:** At sites. **Vehicle Maximum Length:** None.

To Get There

From the junction of Hwy. I-55 and Hwy. 62, turn east onto Hwy. 62 and go 0.4 mi. Turn right at the sign into the entrance.

SPRINGFIELD
Travelers Park Campground

425 South Trailview Rd., Springfield 65802. T: (417) 866-4226.

RV ★★★★ Tent ★★★★

Beauty: ★★★★★ Site Privacy: ★★★★
Spaciousness: ★★★★★ Quiet: ★★★
Security: ★★★★ Cleanliness: ★★★★
Insect Control: ★★★★ Facilities: ★★★

This campground is surrounded by trees, and some of the sites have tree cover, providing desirable shade in the summer months. Sites are unnumbered, making it a little hard to figure out which site is which. Four RV sites in the northwest corner are completely forested, which makes them very desirable. On the north side of the campground are 72-foot back-ins that back to fields with a natural, "wild," feel. Five sites in the middle of the campground are 90–110-foot pull-throughs with loads of space. The two westernmost sites are well shaded and are some of the most desirable sites in the entire park. In the southeast corner are RV sites in an open field that can accommodate rigs of any size. In the same corner are tent sites with exceptionally nice grass and a number of large shade trees.

Basics

Operated By: Winfred & Maxine Short. **Open:** All year. **Site Assignment:** Upon registration; verbal reservations OK. **Registration:** In office; late arrivals select available site & pay in the morning or use drop box. **Fee:** RV $19 (full), tent $14; no credits cards, but checks. **Parking:** At site.

Facilities

Number of RV Sites: 33. **Number of Tent-Only Sites:** Undesignated sites. **Hookups:** Water, sewer, electric (30 amp). **Each Site:** Picnic table. **Dump Station:** No (sewer at all sites). **Laundry:** Yes. **Pay Phone:** No. **Rest Rooms and Showers:** Yes. **Fuel:** No. **Propane:** No. **Internal Roads:** Gravel. **RV Service:** Next door. **Market:** 4 mi. east. **Restaurant:** 4 mi. east. **General Store:** Yes. **Vending:** No. **Swimming:** Pool. **Playground:** No. **Other:** Game room. **Activities:** Golf. **Nearby Attractions:** Bass Pro Shop, golf course, tours, Dy Center, Fantastic Caverns, Japanese Stroll Garden. **Additional Information:** Springfield CVB Tourist Information Center, (800) 678-8767, (417) 881-5300.

Restrictions

Pets: On leash, cleaned up after. **Fires:** In grills. **Alcoholic Beverages:** At sites. **Vehicle Maximum Length:** 42 ft. **Other:** See rule sheet.

To Get There

From Hwy. I-44 (Exit 72), on west side of Hwy. overpass, take the first left onto Outer Rd. and go 0.5 mi. The campground is at the end of this dead-end road.

ST. JAMES

Pheasant Acres

20279 Hwy. 8, St. James 65559. T: (573) 265-5149; F: (573) 265-6900; pheasant@tigernet.missouri.org.

RV ★★★★ Tent ★★★★

Beauty: ★★★★★	Site Privacy: ★★★★★
Spaciousness: ★★★★	Quiet: ★★★★★
Security: ★★★★★	Cleanliness: ★★★★★
Insect Control: ★★★★	Facilities: ★★

RV sites in this campground are back-ins that range from 36 to 54 feet in length and are 35 feet wide. Sites 1–10 are in a strip along the west side. These sites are well shaded and back to a line of trees. In front of these spaces is a grassy field with some lovely flowers, bushes, and other vegetation. Site 10 has a large amount of space and is furthest from the entrance. Sites 12–18 are located on the inner loop of the internal road. All of these sites are quite decent. Sites 19–21 lie between the rest rooms and a barn. They are a little less roomy, but back to woods and are otherwise comfortable. The tenting area lies under magnificent oaks and has a thick grass cover. The area is surrounded on two sides by woods, but, on the downside, there is some slope. The rest rooms are located in a mobile home near the tenting area. It is very clean and comfortable, and the showers even have a large dry area for clothes and a towel.

Basics

Operated By: Chuck & Diana Kesler. **Open:** All year. **Site Assignment:** Depending on site availability; verbal reservations OK. **Registration:** In office; late arrivals use drop box. **Fee:** RV $15 (full), $12 (electric); tent $10. **Parking:** At site.

Facilities

Number of RV Sites: 20. **Number of Tent-Only Sites:** 5. **Hookups:** Water, sewer, electric (30 amp). **Each Site:** Picnic table, grill. **Dump Station:** No (sewer at all sites). **Laundry:** No. **Pay Phone:** No. **Rest Rooms and Showers:** Yes. **Fuel:** No. **Propane:** No. **Internal Roads:** Gravel. **RV Service:** No. **Market:** 5 mi. west. **Restaurant:** 2 mi. east or west. **General Store:** No. **Vending:** No. **Swimming:** No. **Playground:** No. **Other:** Borders conservation area, wood, pavilion. **Activities:** Hiking, float trips, basketball. **Nearby Attractions:** Wineries, Maramec Spring Park, Maramec Museum. **Additional Information:** Rolla Chamber of Commerce, (573) 364-3577.

Restrictions

Pets: On leash, cleaned up after. **Fires:** In grills. **Alcoholic Beverages:** At sites. **Vehicle Maximum Length:** 40 ft. **Other:** Quiet enforced.

To Get There

From Hwy. I-44 (Exit 195), turn south and go 5.5 mi. east. Turn left at the sign into the entrance. (Campers would be advised to drive slowly, as the sign is small and the entrance a little narrow.)

ST. JOSEPH

AOK Overnite Kampground

12430 CR 360, St. Joseph 64505. T: (816) 324-4263 or (816) 324-7808; jhun213@aol.com.

RV ★★★ Tent ★★★

Beauty: ★★★	Site Privacy: ★★★
Spaciousness: ★★★	Quiet: ★★★
Security: ★★★★	Cleanliness: ★★
Insect Control: ★★★★	Facilities: ★★★

Laid out in a giant loop, this campground has RV and tent sites near a fishing lake. The nicest rows of RV sites are the closest to the lake (1–6 and 7–14). The lower-numbered row contains 75-foot pull-through sites, while one row in from the lake contains 60-foot pull-throughs. Sites with nice shade trees include 5–8, 10, 12, and 14. Sites 15–22 range from 60 to 90 feet, with lower numbers being larger sites. Sites 23–28 are adjacent to a mobile-home park making them less desirable. The row of sites to the east (43–50) consists of grassy 75-foot back-ins that back to woods and residences. The tent area has very thick grass, which is excellent for tenting, but there are no shade trees. The rest rooms and shower appear neglected. This is too bad, as the campground would benefit from a nicer rest room. As it is, this campground is adequate if you need to spend a night near St. Joseph.

Basics

Operated By: Jody & Jan Hundley. **Open:** All year. **Site Assignment:** Upon registration; no reservations. **Registration:** In office; late arrivals use drop box. **Fee:** RV $15, tent $10; checks, V, MC, AE, D. **Parking:** At site.

Facilities

Number of RV Sites: 50. **Number of Tent-Only Sites:** Undesignated sites. **Hookups:** Water, sewer, electric (20, 30, 50 amp). **Each Site:** Picnic table. **Dump Station:** Yes. **Laundry:** Yes. **Pay Phone:** Yes. **Rest Rooms and Showers:** Yes. **Fuel:** No. **Propane:** No. **Internal Roads:** Gravel. **RV Service:** No. **Market:** 3 mi. south. **Restaurant:** 3 mi. south. **General Store:** No. **Vending:** Yes. **Swimming:** Pool. **Playground:** Yes. **Other:** Lake, limited groceries, pavilion. **Activities:** Fishing, volleyball, horseshoes. **Nearby Attractions:** Jesse James Museum, St. Joseph Museum, Pony Express Stables Museum, casinos. **Additional Information:** St. Joseph CVB, (800) 785-0360, (816) 233-6688.

Restrictions

Pets: On leash, cleaned up after. **Fires:** In grills. **Alcoholic Beverages:** At sites. **Vehicle Maximum Length:** 45 ft.

To Get There

From Hwy. 29/71 (Exit 53), turn north onto 71 Business and go 0.3 mi. to the second left (across the highway) onto the (gravel) Rd. 360. Go 0.4 mi. to the campground. The office is on the left.

ST. LOUIS

St. Louis RV Park

900 North Jefferson P.O. Box 7663, St. Louis 63106. T: (800) 878-3330 or (314) 241-3330; F: (314) 241-4823; www.stlouisrvpark.com.

RV ★★★ Tent n/a

Beauty: ★★	Site Privacy: ★★★
Spaciousness: ★★	Quiet: ★★★
Security: ★★★★★	Cleanliness: ★★★★★
Insect Control: ★★★★	Facilities: ★★★

Some like it paved. St. Lous RV park consists entirely of a paved lot, with a hedge running around the perimeter. Three rows of 55 × 20-foot pull-throughs lie in the middle of the park (1–15, 16–31, and 32–48). The lower numbers of each row have the best view of downtown and the Arch. The rest of the sites are back-ins in a ring around the campground. These sites are 36 × 20 feet, with the possibility of rigs sticking out somewhat due to the large amount of space in the interior road. Most of these sites back to the hedge. Sites 81 and 82 in the northwest corner are two of the most desirable, containing a grassy patch, bushes, and even a shade tree. Sites 59 and 60 in the northeast corner come close, but do not have a tree on the grass patch they share. Probably the single nicest site, however, is 97 in the southwest corner. This site has extra space, a shade tree, and a flower pot, and is close to the rest rooms, which are absolutely immaculate. Showers are self-contained units that are a bit older than the rest rooms and contain no fan, but are otherwise comfortable. This is a decent RV park for folks who like ultra-developed parks. It offers nice views of the Arch, but the addition of shade trees would improve it immensely.

Basics

Operated By: Mary & George Hudson. **Open:** Mar. 1–Nov. 15. **Site Assignment:** Upon registration; credit card required for reservation, 24-hours cancellation policy. **Registration:** In office; late arrivals must call in advance to get into the security gate. **Fee:** RV $31 (50 amp), $29 (30 amp). **Parking:** At site.

Facilities

Number of RV Sites: 100. **Number of Tent-Only Sites:** 0. **Hookups:** Water, sewer, electric (30, 50 amp). **Dump Station:** Yes. **Laundry:** Yes. **Pay Phone:** Yes. **Rest Rooms and Showers:** Yes. **Fuel:** No. **Propane:** No. **Internal Roads:** Paved. **RV Service:** No. **Market:** 2 mi. southwest. **Restaurant:** 1 mi. southeast. **General Store:** Yes. **Vending:** No. **Swimming:** Pool. **Playground:** No. **Other:** Meeting room, observation deck, e-mail access, dog walk area, close to downtown (15 blocks), view of Arch. **Activities:** Visiting museums, shopping, tours, riverboat cruises, theater. **Nearby Attractions:** St. Louis Art Museum, St. Louis Zoo, Forest Park, Gateway Arch, St. Louis Science Center. **Additional Information:** St. Louis Visitors Center: (314) 241-1764.

Restrictions

Pets: On leash, cleaned up after. **Fires:** In grills. **Alcoholic Beverages:** At sites. **Vehicle Maximum Length:** None.

To Get There

From Hwy. I-55 (Exit 207C: Lafayette Ave.), turn left at the light. Go 0.6 mi., then turn right onto Jefferson. Go 1.7 mi. on Jefferson, then turn right onto Dr. Martin Luther King, left onto 23rd St., then right at the sign into the entrance.

SULLIVAN

Native Experience Adventure Campground

1451 East Springfield, Sullivan 63080. T: (573) 468-8750.

RV: ★★★★ | Tent: ★★★★★

Beauty: ★★★★	Site Privacy: ★★★★
Spaciousness: ★★★★	Quiet: ★★★★
Security: ★★★★★	Cleanliness: ★★★★★
Insect Control: ★★★★	Facilities: ★★★★★

More than just a campground, Native Experience is a philosophy. New proprietor Keith Campbell envisions creating a natural and ecologically-sustainable campground where travelers and adventurers converge for shared experiences. (However, as the campground is new, many of the services proposed are not yet in operation.) The campground is situated on Historic Rte. 66 and close to a number of recreation areas, which attracts travelers and adventurers alike. All sites are well shaded, with grassy sites laid out in a loop. Sites 1–17 are 75–100-foot pull-throughs (the largest are sites 10–17). Sites 19 and 20 are even longer, at 120 feet and 80 feet respectively. Running in a row from north to south, sites 24–36 are 50 × 36-foot back-ins. (Sites 22 and 23 can pull through if the opposite site is vacant.) The tenting area is north of RV site 36. Surrounded on all sides by woods, the area is also well forested and protects tenters from both sun and rain. All tent sites are located on the inside of the looped interior road. Campers are encouraged to enjoy a "native experience" in Sullivan, and should feel free to ask the knowledgeable owner about natural recreation opportunities in the area.

Basics

Operated By: Keith Campbell. **Open:** All year. **Site Assignment:** Depending on site availability; verbal reservations OK. **Registration:** In office; late arrivals use drop box. **Fee:** RV $20 (full), $18 (electric); tent $15. **Parking:** At site.

Facilities

Number of RV Sites: 36. **Number of Tent-Only Sites:** 10. **Hookups:** Water, sewer, electric (30 amp). **Each Site:** Picnic table, fire pit. **Dump Station:** Yes. **Laundry:** Yes. **Pay Phone:** Yes. **Rest Rooms and Showers:** Yes. **Fuel:** No. **Propane:** Yes. **Internal Roads:** Gravel. **RV Service:** No. **Market:** 2 mi. west (at I-44). **Restaurant:** 2 mi. west (at I-44). **General Store:** Yes. **Vending:** No. **Swimming:** Pool. **Playground:** Yes. **Other:** Dog walk, cabin, adventure tours. **Activities:** Caving, swimming, hiking, kayaking, biking. **Nearby Attractions:** Meremac State Park, Rte. 66. **Additional Information:** Sullivan Area Chamber of Commerce, (573) 468-3314.

Restrictions

Pets: On leash, cleaned up after. **Fires:** In grills. **Alcoholic Beverages:** At sites. **Vehicle Maximum Length:** None. **Other:** No ATVs/dirt bikes, no generators.

To Get There

From Hwy. I-44 (Exit 226), turn south onto Hwy. 185 and go 0.25 mi. Turn left onto Service Rd. (first left after gas station complex) and go 1.4 mi. Turn left at the sign into the entrance.

WILLIAMSVILLE

Lake Wappapello State Park

HC 2 Box 2349, Williamsville 63966. T: (573) 222-8139 or (573) 222-8773 or (573) 222-8562.

RV: ★★★★ | Tent: ★★★★★

Beauty: ★★★★★	Site Privacy: ★★★★★
Spaciousness: ★★★★★	Quiet: ★★★★★
Security: ★★★★★	Cleanliness: ★★★★
Insect Control: ★★★	Facilities: ★★★★

This state park offers two campgrounds—one by the lake and the other perched on a ridge in the woods. All sites in the lakeside campground are grassy, shaded sites with cement slabs and a view of the lake. Closest to the lake are 57, 58, 63, 65, and 67–73. Sites 55 and 74 are furthest from the lake and have more of a forested feel than a lakeside feel. Sites 65, 71, 74, and 79 are 75-foot pull-throughs. Sites 61 and 62 are 60-foot doubles. The ridgeside campground has 60-foot gravel back-ins that back to forest as well as some collossal (110 feet) pull-throughs, such as 38. The east side of this campground has a partial view of the lake, while the west side is pure forest. Sites 7 and 8 are doubles. The remotest sites are 23 and 24, which are located at the end of a roundabout. Lake Wappapello State Park offers the best of both worlds: forest and lakeside sites. Both those wishing to play in the water and those wishing to relax in the shade will find it an appealing campsite.

Basics

Operated By: Missouri Dept. of Natural Resources. **Open:** All year (limited services Nov.–Mar.). **Site Assignment:** First come, first served; currently no reservations, may begin reservation system in 2002. **Registration:** Fees will be collected by ranger. **Fee:** $12 (water, electric), $7 tent; checks, V, MC, D. **Parking:** At site, do not park on grass (boat or trailer OK).

Facilities

Number of RV Sites: 37. **Number of Tent-Only Sites:** 43. **Hookups:** Electric (30 amp). **Each Site:** Picnic table, grill, lantern post. **Dump Station:** Yes. **Laundry:** Yes. **Pay Phone:** Yes. **Rest Rooms and Showers:** Yes. **Fuel:** No. **Propane:** No. **Internal Roads:** Paved. **RV Service:** No. **Market:** 16 mi. to Poplar Bluff. **Restaurant:** 5 mi. to Chaonia Landing. **General Store:** No. **Vending:** No. **Swimming:** Yes (lake). **Playground:** Yes. **Other:** 3 boat ramps, 8 cabins, amphitheater, firewood, picnic shelters, horse trails, hiking trails. **Activities:** Fishing, boating, swimming, horseback riding, hiking. **Nearby Attractions:** Lake Wappapello. **Additional Information:** Poplar Bluff Chamber of Commerce, (573) 785-7761.

Restrictions

Pets: On leash, cleaned up after. **Fires:** In grills. **Alcoholic Beverages:** At sites, no glass bottles. **Vehicle Maximum Length:** None. **Other:** No fireworks, no digging, no metal detectors, no hunting, visitors must leave by 10 p.m., no breaking of tree limbs.

To Get There

From the junction of Hwy. 67 and Hwy. 172, turn east onto Hwy. 172 and go 8 mi. Turn left at the T in the road at the 4.4 mile mark, and right at the 5.5 mile mark.) The office is on the left.

Montana

As with much of the US, Montana was first inhabited by Native Americans, including the Arapaho, Assiniboine, and Cheyenne. French trappers made inroads into the land as early as 1740, followed some years later by the Lewis and Clark Expedition in 1805.

Most of what is now Montana was turned over to the United States in the Louisiana Purchase of 1803. The Jesuits and various trading companies attempted to form permanent settlements here, but not until gold was discovered in the 1860s did great numbers of people begin to settle in the area. The wide open land in the eastern parts of the state drew another type of pioneer who helped settle the land—the cattle farmer.

The settling of Montana did not go easy. Native Americans did not give up their land willingly; pioneers appropriating Native American land were under constant threat of raids, which did not abate until the Wounded Knee Massacre in 1890. Settlers then caused their own strife, as rancher fought rancher during the infamous range wars in the late 1800s.

In the twentieth century, drilling for oil joined mining as a major source of revenue for the state, but enough people also recognized the need to preserve natural resources. In addition to Glacier National Park, many state parks and historic sites were created to preserve Montana's natural and cultural heritage.

Montana is comprised of six different regions, each with a distinct history and recreational offerings. The most western region, **Glacier Country,** is home to **Glacier National Park,** the **Flathead Indian Reservation,** and the town of Missoula, seen by many as the cultural, retail, and medical hub of western Montana. Home of the **University of Montana,** Missoula is the gateway to the Flathead and Bitterroot valleys. Numerous festivals are held in this region, including the famous **Testicle Festival,** an off-kilter culinary homage to mountain oysters (i.e. bulls bullocks).

The adjacent **Gold Country** is similar in geography to Glacier Country. The many mountains and valleys create a beautiful landscape, and numerous recreational possibilities abound, from hiking the **Continental Divide Trail** to skiing down spectacular slopes. The two largest towns in this region, Butte and Helena (Big Sky's capital), originated as mining towns. Many attractions in this area still reflect that heritage, including **Butte's World Museum of Mining** where visitors can see an authentic reproduction of an 1890s mining camp and can visit the numerous ghost towns around Helena.

To the west of Gold Country is Montana's most famous region, **Yellowstone Country**. While over 4 million people visit the nation's first national park each year, few venture north of the park, much to their loss. Those who do will find Bozeman. Located in the Gallatin valley, this city is a significant agricultural center as well as home to the largest university in Montana's system. Several annual festivals enliven this college town, including the **Montana Winter Fair** and the **Sweet Pea Festival.** The region also hosts two key ski resorts—**Bridger Bowl** and **Big Sky.**

For those interested in raft trips, **Russell Country** is the place to visit. Rivers of all difficulty are paddled here, including the Madison, Gallatin, Yellowstone and the river that carried Lewis and Clark across the state, the Missouri. Lewis and Clark's progress west was stymied at the "great falls" along the Missouri, site now of Montana's third largest city. **Great Falls** is known as the Electric City for its many hydroelectric dams. While here, visitors can swing by the **Lewis and Clark National Historic Trail Interpretive Center** or by **Malmstrom Air Force Base,** location of the nation's first Minuteman Missile Complex.

Much of Lewis and Clark's journey through Montana passed through the Missouri River Country. This region is home to **Fort Belknap** and **Fort Peck Indian Reservations** as well as the 1.1 million-acre **Charles M. Russell National Wildlife Refuge.** Also known as the Montana Badlands, this area was once a lush wetland where dinosaurs roamed, but now provides a wealth of fossils from the dry landscape.

Located in the southeastern part of the state, **Custer Country** is probably most famous for one of the worst US military defeats. The Battle of Little Bighorn, sometimes referred to as Custer's Last Stand, took place not far from present day **Billings**. While other towns arose (and died) because of mining, Billings' existence is due to the railroad. Today it is a major shipping point for cattle and other agricultural products as well as home of **Montana State University-Billings.** Cultural offerings include the **Yellowstone Art Museum** and the **Western Heritage Museum.**

The following facilities accept payment in checks or cash only:

Canyon RV & Campground, Hungry Horse

Glacier National Park, West Glacier

Shady Grove RV Park & Campground, Cut Bank

Campground Profiles

ALDER

Alder/Virginia City KOA

P.O. Box 103, Alder 59710. T: (406) 842-5677 or (800) 562-1898; F: (406) 842-5564; www.koa.com; twernt@3rivers.net.

RV ★★★ Tent ★★★

Beauty: ★★★ Site Privacy: ★★★
Spaciousness: ★★★ Quiet: ★★★★
Security: ★★★★ Cleanliness: ★★★
Insect Control: ★★★ Facilities: ★★★

Over one hundred years ago, people visited this valley for one reason—gold. Not far from this KOA campground, Alder Gulch was one of the largest producers of gold in Montana. Modern-day visitors can still pan for gold or search for semi-precious stones while using this campground as a base. This campground is small, with 32 RV sites (hookups include electric, water, sewer, and some phones) and 18 tent-only sites. The sites are all grass. A daily pancake breakfast and ice cream social are available, and Sundays are steak nights. Several accessible rivers means outstanding fishing, and the campground is located in the heart of elk country—good news for hunters. Those leaning more toward history may want to visit nearby Virginia and Nevada City. Visitors can wander through an historic logcabin village, or take an "historic" stage coach or steam engine ride through the landscape. Several festivals and gatherings occur locally, including Gold Rush Fever Days and the Cowboy & Indian Western Antique & Collectible Trade Show, so reservations are recommended far in advance.

BASICS

Operated By: Ed & Andy. **Open:** All year. **Site Assignment:** Reservations (800) 562-1898. **Registration:** In general store. **Fee:** Tent $20, RV $23–$28. **Parking:** At site.

FACILITIES

Number of RV-Only Sites: 32. **Number of Tent-Only Sites:** 18. **Hookups:** Electric (20, 30 amps), water, sewer, phone. **Each Site:** Picnic tables, grated fire pits. **Dump Station:** Yes. **Laundry:** Yes. **Pay Phone:** Yes. **Rest Rooms and Showers:** Yes. **Fuel:** Yes. **Propane:** Yes. **Internal Roads:** Gravel. **RV Service:** Sheridan. **Market:** Sheridan. **Restaurant:** Sheridan. **General Store:** Yes. **Vending:** In store only. **Swimming Pool:** No. **Playground:** Yes. **Other:** 1 cabin. **Activities:** Fishing (rainbow & brown trout), volleyball, horseshoes, hiking, rock hunting. **Nearby Attractions:** 9 mi. west of Virginia City, Nevada City, Museums, gold panning, tours. **Additional Information:** Virginia City Chamber of Commerce, (800) 829-2969.

RESTRICTIONS

Pets: On leash. **Fires:** Fire pits only. **Alcoholic Beverages:** Yes. **Vehicle Max. Length:** None.

TO GET THERE

Located 0.25 mi. east of Alder on Hwy. 287.

BELT

Fort Ponderosa Family Campground and RV Park

568 Armington Rd., Belt 59412. T: (406) 277-3232; F: (406) 277-3309; shilo@3rivers.net.

RV ★★★★ Tent ★★★

Beauty: ★★★★ Site Privacy: ★★★
Spaciousness: ★★★ Quiet: ★★★★
Security: ★★★★ Cleanliness: ★★★★
Insect Control: ★★★★ Facilities: ★★★★

Fort Ponderosa Family Campground and RV Park is conveniently located directly off I-90 in Belt. The campground is situated on seven acres, with large shade trees and a blue ribbon trout stream. The campsites are level, gravel, and offered in both pullthrough and back-in. The grass is green and well kept. In addition to the campsites, there are several mobile homes as well as the owner's home. Facilities include a large playground, pavilion, five-hole golf coarse, and room for children to play and ride bicycles. While it is well used, the campground is nice and peaceful. The community of Belt is a short drive from Great Falls, and there are a variety of outdoor activities in the area. Summer days are warm, the evenings cool, and the owner offers delightful conversation.

BASICS

Operated By: Jack Wiederrick. **Open:** May 1–Dec. 1. **Site Assignment:** By reservation. **Registration:** In camp office. **Fee:** Tent $16.75, RV $19–$25. **Parking:** At site.

FACILITIES

Number of RV-Only Sites: 45. **Number of Tent-Only Sites:** 20. **Hookups:** Electric (30 amps), water, sewer. **Each Site:** Picnic table. **Dump Station:** Yes. **Laundry:** Yes. **Pay Phone:** Yes. **Rest Rooms and Showers:** Yes. **Fuel:** No. **Propane:** Yes. **Internal Roads:** Gravel, in good condition. **RV Service:** 20 mi. west in Great Falls. **Market:** 2 mi. in town. **Restaurant:** 2 mi. in town. **General Store:** Yes w/ gift shop. **Vending:** Just the store. **Swimming Pool:** No. **Playground:** Yes. **Other:** 2 covered pavilions, 1 w/ BBQ, gift shop. **Activities:** Mini golf, swimming in Belt Creek, fishing (German, brown, & rainbow trout). **Nearby Attractions:** More fly fishing, fishing guide services, float trips, horseback riding, Smith River, Fort Benton, Great Falls, Sluice Box hiking Area, Clark National Forest, Memorial Falls. **Additional Information:** Great Falls Chamber of Commerce, (406) 761-4434.

RESTRICTIONS

Pets: On leash. **Fires:** In fire rings only. **Alcoholic Beverages:** Yes. **Vehicle Max. Length:** None.

TO GET THERE

20 mi. southeast on Hwys. 87/89 (Armington Jct.) then 1 mi. north (follow signs).

BILLINGS

Yellowstone River RV Park & Campground

309 Garden Ave., Billings 59101. T: (406) 259-0878 or (800) 654-0878; F: (406) 248-1416; yellowstoneriver@hotmail.com.

RV ★★★★ Tent ★★★

Beauty: ★★★★ Site Privacy: ★★★★
Spaciousness: ★★★★ Quiet: ★★★★
Security: ★★★★ Cleanliness: ★★★★
Insect Control: ★★★ Facilities: ★★★

Often called the "Magic City," Billings is where the rustic adventure of the Wild West and the conveniences of a modern city converge. The town provides a number of activities for the passing traveler. The city is surrounded by six mountain ranges and offers a fine view of Montana scenery. Located on the Yellowstone River, this campground is beautifully landscaped, and all sites are arranged in rows and most are shaded. Sites are spacious, and the RV sites are separated from the tent sites but with little distinction. The nice lawn, clean surroundings, and quiet stillness contribute to a pleasing experience. River access and a nature trail compliment the campground, and amenities make this a more than comfortable stay. A large on-site antique display is a unique addition for avid collectors and curious visitors. Be sure to visit historical area attractions to give yourself a taste of the area's rich past.

BASICS

Operated By: Doug & Judy Barnes. **Open:** Apr.–Oct. **Site Assignment:** Reservations recommended. **Registration:** In general store. **Fee:** Tent $23.88, RV $29.08–$32.20 per 2 people, extra person $4. **Parking:** At site.

FACILITIES

Number of RV-Only Sites: 85. **Number of Tent-Only Sites:** 21. **Hookups:** Electric (20, 30, 50 amps), water, sewer. **Each Site:** Picnic table. **Dump Station:** Yes. **Laundry:** Yes. **Pay Phone:** Yes. **Rest Rooms and Showers:** Yes. **Fuel:** Less than 1 mi. **Propane:** Less than 1 mi. **Internal Roads:** Gravel. **RV Service:** Local service. **Market:** Locally. **Restaurant:** Several possibilities in Billings. **General Store:** Yes. **Vending:** General store only. **Swimming Pool:** No. **Playground:** Yes. **Other:** Arcade, gift shop, river access, Internet data port, recreation area. **Activities:** Nature walk, fishing, horseshoes. **Nearby Attractions:** Little Bighorn Battlefield National Monument, Pompeys Pillar National Historic Landmark, Beartooth Mountain Pass/Red Lodge, Bighorn Canyon National

Recreation Area/Yellowtail Dam. **Additional Information:** Billings Chamber, (406) 245-4111.

RESTRICTIONS

Pets: Leash only. **Fires:** No open fires. **Alcoholic Beverages:** Yes. **Vehicle Maximum Length:** None. **Other:** Good Sam, AAA, KOA, AARP, plus a other clubs discount.

TO GET THERE

From I-90 Exit 450, go west on SR-3 (S 27th St.) 0.2 mi., then left onto State Ave., left on to Sugur Ave., left onto Garden Ave. (total distance from I-90 is 3 mi.).

BOZEMAN

Bozeman KOA

81123 Gallatin Rd., Bozeman 59718. T: (406) 587-3030; F: (406) 582-9351; www.koa.com.

RV ★★★ Tent ★★

Beauty: ★★★	Site Privacy: ★★★
Spaciousness: ★★★	Quiet: ★★★
Security: ★★★★	Cleanliness: ★★★
Insect Control: ★★★	Facilities: ★★★

This campground is located within the Bozeman city limits, and it offers neither a purely wilderness experience nor a purely citified experience. A view of distant mountains, a trickling creek behind the on-site cabins, and a small collection of mature trees characterize the nature experience here, but it is quite accessible to the city. This campground works best as a base camp to explore Bozeman and the surrounding area. Nearby Gallatin Canyon provides some favored hiking, and proximity to Yellowstone Park, Lewis and Clark Caverns, and Red Rock Mine makes for some nice day trips. The 100 RV sites are more spacious than the 22 tent sites, and the tent sites sit cramped together, offering little privacy or shade. Sites L6–L11 and M1–M4 are arranged in rows, and all sites are grassy. Keep in mind that Bozeman is home to Montana State University, so avoid the area during graduation, unless of course, you are attending the graduation.

BASICS

Operated By: Marvin Linde. **Open:** Apr.–Oct. 31. **Site Assignment:** Reservation. **Registration:** In camp store. **Fee:** Tent $26, RV $34–$36 per 2 people, extra person $3, children under 5 free. **Parking:** At site.

FACILITIES

Number of RV-Only Sites: 100. **Number of Tent-Only Sites:** 22. **Number of Multipurpose Sites:** 50. **Hookups:** Electric (30, 50 amps), water, sewer. **Each Site:** Picnic table. **Dump Station:** Yes. **Laundry:** Yes. **Pay Phone:** Yes. **Rest Rooms and Showers:** Yes. **Fuel:** No. **Propane:** Yes. **Internal Roads:** Gravel, in good condition. **RV Service:** In Bozeman. **Market:** In town. **Restaurant:** There are several in town. **General Store:** Yes. **Vending:** No, only in store. **Swimming Pool:** No, however they are next door to the indoor hot springs & pools. **Playground:** Yes. **Other:** Recreation Hall, cabins, camper kitchen, 15 cabins, & a creek. **Activities:** Swimming (next door), horseshoes, volleyball, basketball, fun cycles, mountain biking. **Nearby Attractions:** Museum of the Rockies, Yellowstone Park, Lewis & Clark Caverns. **Additional Information:** Bozeman Chamber of Commerce, (406) 586-5421.

RESTRICTIONS

Pets: On leash. **Fires:** In fire pits only. **Alcoholic Beverages:** Yes. **Vehicle Max. Length:** None.

TO GET THERE

I-90 (Exit 298) then 7 mi. south on Hwy. 85

CAMERON

Madison River Cabins & RV

1403 Hwy. 287 North, Cameron 59720. T: (406) 682-4890; F: (406) 682-4890; www.madison-river.com; cabins@madison-river.com.

RV ★★★★ Tent ★★★★

Beauty: ★★★★★	Site Privacy: ★★★
Spaciousness: ★★★	Quiet: ★★★★
Security: ★★★★	Cleanliness: ★★★★★
Insect Control: ★★★★	Facilities: ★★★★★

A small but quaint family-run campground, Madison River Cabins & RV is nestled in the beautiful Madison Valley directly on the banks of the Madison River. This park makes for a very cozy, romantic get away or a great base for serious anglers. The campground is within easy reach of many famous trout streams—Madison, Gallatin, Beaverhead, and Henry's Fork Rivers. Each of the twelve unique cabins and RV sites has no shade, but they do offer great views of the adjacent Madison River and the distant mountains. The sites are level, have gravel parking spurs with some grassy areas, and have full-hookups. The Crazy Lady Outpost offers a variety of fishing supplies, licenses, and a large assortment of groceries. In addition, it houses the laundry facilities and rest rooms. The rest rooms and showers are the cleanest and best maintained of any campground in the state. Madison River Cabins and RV is less than an hour from the west entrance to Yellowstone National Park.

BASICS

Operated By: Carol Salisbury. **Open:** Apr.–Oct. **Site Assignment:** By reservation. **Registration:** In fly shop. **Fee:** RV $19–$25. **Parking:** At site.

FACILITIES

Number of RV-Only Sites: 9. **Number of Tent-Only Sites:** Open tent area. **Hookups:** Electric (30 amps), water, sewer. **Each Site:** Picnic table. **Dump Station:** Yes. **Laundry:** Yes. **Pay Phone:** Yes. **Rest Rooms and Showers:** Yes. **Fuel:** No, 6 mi. south. **Propane:** No, 6 mi. south. **Internal Roads:** Gravel, in good condition. **RV Service:** Limited mobile service. **Market:** 35 mi. in either direction. **Restaurant:** Steak house next door. **General Store:** Crazy Lady Outpost: rustic lodge fly shop w/ fishing tack, supplies, gift items & groceries. **Vending:** No. **Swimming Pool:** No. **Playground:** Only a swing. **Other:** 12 fully furnished & unique cabins, all cabins & RV sites over look the Madison River, restaurant next door. **Activities:** Fly fishing & riverfront activities. **Nearby Attractions:** More fly fishing, fishing guide services, float trips, horseback riding, Yellowstone National Park, golf, hot springs, Historic Virginia City. **Additional Information:** Virginia City Chamber of Commerce, (800) 829-2969.

RESTRICTIONS

Pets: On leash. **Fires:** In fire rings only. **Alcoholic Beverages:** Yes. **Vehicle Max. Length:** None.

TO GET THERE

On Hwy. 287 north between Virginia City and West Yellowstone.

CARDWELL

Cardwell Store & RV Park

770 Hwy. 2 East, Cardwell 59721. T: (406) 287-5092; F: (406) 287-5092.

RV ★★★ Tent ★★★

Beauty: ★★★	Site Privacy: ★★★★
Spaciousness: ★★★★	Quiet: ★★★★
Security: ★★★	Cleanliness: ★★★
Insect Control: ★★★	Facilities: ★★★

Cardwell Store and RV Campground is located between Whitehall and Three Forks, directly off I-90. This simple campground is great for over night stays. It offers extra large, spacious sites, all of them pull-throughs arranged in a horseshoe configuration. They each have a level, gravel parking spur, full hook-ups, and a light post. To the east of the RV sites is a separate tent area with water and one cabin on the bank of a nice size stocked fishing pond. There is a large day use and picnic area, with lots of room for children to play. The grounds are well kept, and the rest rooms are clean. The campground has a large store, with fuel and movies to rent for the evening. The staff is friendly and inviting. There are many attractions in the area, including the Lewis and Clark Caverns.

BASICS

Operated By: Kipp & Dawn Huckaba. **Open:** All year, but the utilities are off Nov.–Feb. 28. **Site Assignment:** By reservation or walk-in. **Registration:** In camp store. **Fee:** Tent $10, RV $16–$18 per unit. **Parking:** At site.

FACILITIES

Number of RV-Only Sites: 36. **Number of Tent-Only Sites:** 10. **Hookups:** Electric (30, 50 amps), water, sewer. **Each Site:** Picnic table, light post. **Dump Station:** Yes. **Laundry:** Yes. **Pay Phone:** Yes. **Rest Rooms and Showers:** Yes. **Fuel:** Yes. **Propane:** Yes. **Internal Roads:** Gravel, in good condition. **RV Service:** 30 mi. west in Butte. **Market:** Whitehall. **Restaurant:** In Whitehall. **General Store:** Yes. **Vending:** Store only. **Swimming Pool:** No. **Playground:** No. **Other:** All pull-through sites, 1 cabin, stocked fishing pond, recreation area, picnic area, 1 tepee, movie rentals. **Activities:** Hiking, biking, fishing (trout), volleyball, horseshoes, small casino. **Nearby Attractions:** Lewis & Clark Caverns State Park, Madison Buffalo Jump State Park, Museum of the Rockies, Deer Lodge NF, hunting & fishing outfitters. **Additional Information:** Whitehall Chamber, (406) 287-2260.

RESTRICTIONS

Pets: On leash. **Fires:** Tent area only. **Alcoholic Beverages:** Yes. **Vehicle Maximum Length:** 60 ft. **Other:** Group max 5 to a site.

TO GET THERE

I-90 Exit 256 on the east frontage road.

CHOTEAU

Choteau KOA

85 MT Hwy. 221, Choteau 59422. T: (406) 466-2615; F: (406) 466-5635; www.koa.com; rulonkoa@montana.com.

 ★★★ 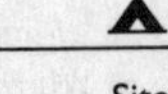 ★★★

Beauty: ★★★ Site Privacy: ★★★
Spaciousness: ★★★ Quiet: ★★★★
Security: ★★★★ Cleanliness: ★★★
Insect Control: ★★★ Facilities: ★★★

Located 20 miles east of the Rocky Mountains on the Rocky Mountain Front, Choteau KOA is a great base camp for exploring the area. Campers are in easy reach of the one million acre Bob Marshall Wilderness and the Teton Spring Creek Bird Preserve. Those interested in dinosaurs should visit the Old Trail Museum in town, where visitors learn about the vast inland sea that covered this area 80 million years ago; if time permits, go on a dinosaur dig at Egg Mountain, available Jun.–Aug.

BASICS

Operated By: Shelly & Larry Rulon. **Open:** Apr. 1–Nov. 15. **Site Assignment:** By reservation. **Registration:** In camp store. **Fee:** Tent $17, RV $17-$23 per 2 people, extra person $2, children under 3 stay free. **Parking:** At site.

FACILITIES

Number of RV-Only Sites: 55. **Number of Tent-Only Sites:** 15. **Hookups:** Electric (20, 30, 50 amps), water, sewer. **Each Site:** Picnic tables, fire pits. **Dump Station:** Yes. **Laundry:** Yes. **Pay Phone:** Yes. **Rest Rooms and Showers:** Yes. **Fuel:** No, 1 mi. in town. **Propane:** No. **Internal Roads:** Gravel. **RV Service:** Limited service in town. **Market:** In town. **Restaurant:** In town. **General Store:** Yes. **Vending:** Yes. **Swimming Pool:** No, but the public pool is less than 1 mi. **Playground:** 2 playgrounds. **Other:** 2 cabins, 3 tepees, a tent village, and data port. **Activities:** Mini-golf, horseshoes, large common area for games, game room, 9 hole golf course next door. **Nearby Attractions:** Fishing (Eureka Lake, Teton River), dinosaur digs, Bob Marshall Wilderness Complex, Old Trail Museum, Teton Spring Creek Bird Preserve. **Additional Information:** Choteau Chamber of Commerce, (800) 823-3866.

RESTRICTIONS

Pets: On leash. **Fires:** In fire rings (fires may be prohibited due to dry weather; please ask management before starting any open fires). **Alcoholic Beverages:** Yes. **Vehicle Max. Length:** None.

TO GET THERE

From I-15 Exit 290, go west on US-89 for 40 mi., then bear right (west) on US-287 and follow in to Choteau. From Choteau, go east at the blinking light, 0.75 mi. on Hwy. 221.

COLUMBIA FALLS

La Salle RV Park

5618 Hwy. 2 West, Columbia Falls 59912. T: (406) 892-4668; F: (406) 892-4773.

 ★★★  ★★★

Beauty: ★★★ Site Privacy: ★★★
Spaciousness: ★★★ Quiet: ★★★★
Security: ★★★★ Cleanliness: ★★★★
Insect Control: ★★★★ Facilities: ★★★

Conveniently located off Hwy 2 about 5 miles southwest of Columbia Falls, the La Salle RV Park is a comfortable, clean, and well maintained campground with excellent service and friendly smiles. The seven acre property is divided into three areas: RV, tent, and cabins. The main entrance road is paved and loops around several rows of RV sites. Each RV site has a lush lawn and a level gravel parking pad. The tent area is in the back of the property with large sites divided by well-kept shrubs. In addition, there are 5 simple sleeping cabins. The campground is only 14 miles outside of Kalispell and 15 miles from the west entrance to Glacier National Park. The camping prices are one of the most reasonable in the area. The days are warm in the summer and evenings are cool. The owners live year-round on site and are always there to assist.

BASICS

Operated By: Gordon, Carolynn & Andy Beloit. **Open:** All year. **Site Assignment:** Reservations recommended May–Oct., held w/ a credit card. **Registration:** In office/general store. **Fee:** Tent $15, RV $17–$20 per 4 people, extra person $2 (cash, credit, checks). **Parking:** At site.

FACILITIES

Number of RV-Only Sites: 52. **Number of Tent-Only Sites:** 8. **Hookups:** Electric (20, 30, 50 amps), water, sewer. **Each Site:** Picnic table, grated fire pits (tent sites, cabins). **Dump Station:** Yes. **Laundry:** Yes. **Pay Phone:** Yes. **Rest Rooms and Showers:** Yes. **Fuel:** 2 mi. northeast in Columbia Falls. **Propane:** 2 mi. northwest in Columbia Falls. **Internal Roads:** Paved & gravel. **RV Service:** 11 mi. south in Kalispell. **Market:** 2 mi. northeast in Columbia Falls. **Restaurant:** 2 mi. northeast in Columbia Falls. **General Store:** Yes. **Vending:** Yes. **Swimming Pool:** No. **Playground:** Yes. **Other:** 5 cabins, 1 tepee, lobby w/ color TV & Internet. **Activities:** Volleyball, basketball, horseshoes, group outings. **Nearby Attractions:** Glacier National Park 20 mi., water slides, go-kart tracks, fishing (rainbow trout, white fish), Hungry Horse Dam, Whitefish Lake, boating, whitewater rafting. **Additional Information:** Columbia Falls Area Chamber, (406) 892-2072.

RESTRICTIONS

Pets: Leash only. **Fires:** In fire pit only (fires maybe prohibited due to weather; please ask management before starting any fire.). **Alcoholic Beverages:** Yes. **Vehicle Max. Length:** 65 ft.

TO GET THERE

11 mi. northeast of Kalispell directly off Hwy. 2.

CONRAD

Pondera RV Park

510 South Maryland, Conrad 59425. T: (406) 278-5724; F: (406) 278-7644; www.conradrv.com; mail@conradrv.com.

 ★★★  ★★

Beauty: ★★★ Site Privacy: ★★★
Spaciousness: ★★★ Quiet: ★★★
Security: ★★★ Cleanliness: ★★★
Insect Control: ★★★ Facilities: ★★★

Pondera RV Park is located in the center of Conrad, across from the city park. Pondera RV Park is a full-service facility with all the amenities looked for in an RV park. The sites are level and gravel. There is some grass and a few shade trees. Sites are close together and there are a few mobile homes. The area seems fairly quiet, and the park across the street has several activities: an Olympic-size public pool, large play ground, tennis courts and picnic areas. The campground is convenient to local restaurants, shopping, and repair. The Lewis and Clark Trail runs through Conrad, and the campground is not far from Glacier National Park, Great Falls, or Lake Holter Recreation Area. The area is very dry in the summer, and days can be very warm. This campground is not staffed during the day, and the owners show up around 4p.m.. There is a number on the bulletin board for emergencies.

BASICS

Operated By: Ralph & Gladys Dunahoo. **Open:** All year. **Site Assignment:** By reservation or walk-in. **Registration:** The camp office. **Fee:** $18–$20 per unit. **Parking:** At site.

FACILITIES

Number of RV-Only Sites: 52. **Number of Tent-Only Sites:** 10. **Hookups:** Electric (30 amps), water, sewer, cable, phone. **Each Site:** Some picnic tables. **Dump Station:** Yes. **Laundry:** Yes. **Pay Phone:** Yes. **Rest Rooms and Showers:** Yes. **Fuel:** Less than 1 mi. **Propane:** Less than 1 mi. **Internal Roads:** Gravel, in good condition. **RV Service:** Limited local service. **Market:** In town. **Restaurant:** In town. **General Store:** No. **Vending:** Yes. **Swimming Pool:** Public pool across the street. **Playground:** Located across the street in city park. **Other:** Internet data port, across from the Conrad Municipal Park: pavilions, grills, pool, tennis, & other activities. **Activities:** Park, pool, tennis, volleyball, horseshoes. **Nearby Attractions:** Golf, bowling, movies, dinosaur digs, hiking, fishing, an hour drive to Glacier National Park, community theater, horseback riding. **Additional Information:** Conrad Chamber, (406) 278-7791.

RESTRICTIONS

Pets: On leash. **Fires:** No open fires. **Alcoholic Beverages:** Yes. **Vehicle Max. Length:** 60 ft.

TO GET THERE

Take Exit 339 off of I-15 and enter Conrad, Montana. Follow Main St. 11 Blocks. Turn Right on 7th. Go 1.5 blocks and look to your left.

CORAM

North American RV Park & Yurt Village

P.O. Box 130449, Coram 59913. T: (406) 387-5800 or (800) 704-4266; F: (406) 387-5888; narvpark@montana.com.

★★★ ★★

Beauty: ★★★ Site Privacy: ★★★
Spaciousness: ★★★ Quiet: ★★★★
Security: ★★★ Cleanliness: ★★★
Insect Control: ★★★★ Facilities: ★★★★

Located a few miles from the west entrance of Glacier National Park in the small community of Coram is the North American RV Park. This campground is ideal for those campers looking for a convenient base camp with up-to-date modern amenities. North America RV Park offers its patrons a clean, well-maintained facility with large, gravel, pull-through sites at the base of a huge mountain. There are few trees and little shade, but the satellite television reception is great. There is plenty of additional parking, and this campground caters to extra large motor coaches with tows. The tent sites lie along the back of the property in a sparsely grassy area by the mountain. The campground also has two rental yurts. Since this campground is in a valley with few trees, summer days can be very warm though the evenings tend to be very cool. The park office is open daily and there are also camp hosts to assist with any needs that may arise.

Basics

Operated By: Curt & Susan Sholar. **Open:** Apr.–Oct. **Site Assignment:** Reservations recommended. **Registration:** In camp office. **Fee:** Tent $17.50, RV $18.50–$24.50 per 4 people, extra person $3, Good Sam Club. (cash, credit, checks). **Parking:** At site.

Facilities

Number of RV-Only Sites: 101. **Number of Tent-Only Sites:** 12. **Hookups:** Electric (30, 50 amps), water, sewer, cable, phone. **Each Site:** Picnic table. **Dump Station:** Yes. **Laundry:** Yes. **Pay Phone:** Yes. **Rest Rooms and Showers:** Yes. **Fuel:** In Coram or West Glacier. **Propane:** In Coram or West Glacier. **Internal Roads:** Gravel. **RV Service:** 14 mi. southwest in Columbia Falls. **Market:** In Coram or West Glacier. **Restaurant:** In Coram or West Glacier. **General Store:** No. **Vending:** Yes. **Swimming Pool:** No. **Playground:** Yes. **Other:** 2 yurts (a circular, Mongolian-style domed tent w/ a plywood floor, sleeps 4–6 people). **Activities:** Picnic area, volleyball, horseshoes, North American Wildlife Museum. **Nearby Attractions:** Glacier National Park, House of Mystery, Hungry Horse Dam, golf, fishing tours, white water rafting, helicopter tours. **Additional Information:** Columbia Falls Area Chamber, (406) 892-2072.

Restrictions

Pets: Leash only. **Fires:** Fire pits only (fires may be prohibited due to dry weather; please ask management before starting any fires.). **Alcoholic Beverages:** Yes. **Vehicle Maximum Length:** None.

To Get There

Off US 2 about 5 mi. south of West Glacier.

CUT BANK

Shady Grove RV Park & Campground

P.O. Box 691, Cut Bank 59427. T: (406) 336-2475; F: (406) 336-2475; shdygrov@northerntel.net.

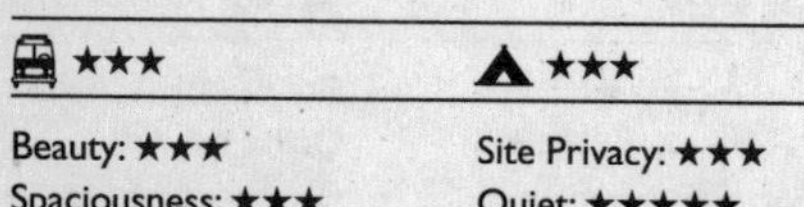

Beauty: ★★★ Site Privacy: ★★★
Spaciousness: ★★★ Quiet: ★★★★★
Security: ★★★★ Cleanliness: ★★★★
Insect Control: ★★★★ Facilities: ★★★

Located on the east side of Glacier National Park in the flat farmland of Montana is Shady Grove RV Park and Campground. The air is sweet and the grass is green. There are beautiful mature trees that surround the property, and a feeling of home and family pervades the campground. The campsites form a circular perimeter around the property, with the Bomar's home in the center. There are clean and well-maintained facilities, and a small playground. All the sites are back-in but roomy in size and length. The tent sites are on lush grass and are well spaced for privacy. The park is a wonderful place to enjoy the stars on a cloudless night. The weather is typical of high desert, and is very dry in the summer. There are no open fires allowed in the campground. For extra security, the gates are closed in the evening. It is 30 miles to the east entrance of Glacier National Park.

Basics

Operated By: Larry & Carole Bomar. **Open:** May 1–Oct. 1. **Site Assignment:** Reservations recommended, held w/ a credit card. **Registration:** Larry & Carole's home. **Fee:** Tent $12, RV $15 per 2 people, extra adult $2, Child 3–12 $1, under 3 stay free. (cash & check only). **Parking:** At site.

Facilities

Number of RV-Only Sites: 19. **Number of Tent-Only Sites:** 10. **Number of Multipurpose Sites:** 10. **Hookups:** Electric (20, 30 amps), water, sewer. **Each Site:** Picnic table. **Dump Station:** No. **Laundry:** No. **Pay Phone:** Yes. **Rest Rooms and Showers:** Yes. **Fuel:** 6 mi. east in Cut Bank. **Propane:** 6 mi. east in Cut Bank. **Internal Roads:** Gravel & grass. **RV Service:** 100 mi. in Great Falls. **Market:** 6 mi. east in Cut Bank. **Restaurant:** 6 mi. east in Cut Bank. **General Store:** No. **Vending:** Drinks & ice available at owners' home. **Swimming Pool:** No. **Playground:** Yes. **Activities:** Play Area, horseshoes, large open field great for playing ball. **Nearby Attractions:** Glacier National Park. **Additional Information:** www.visitmontana.com.

Restrictions

Pets: Leash only, some large breed restrictions. **Fires:** No open fires. **Alcoholic Beverages:** In campers only. **Vehicle Max. Length:** None.

To Get There

Directly off Hwy. 2, 6 mi. west of Cut Bank.

DEER LODGE

Indian Creek RV Campground

745 Maverick Ln., Deer Lodge 59722. T: (406) 846-3848; www.indiancreekcampground.com; indiancreek@montana.com.

★★★ ★★★

Beauty: ★★★★ Site Privacy: ★★★
Spaciousness: ★★★ Quiet: ★★★
Security: ★★★★ Cleanliness: ★★★
Insect Control: ★★★ Facilities: ★★★

Indian Creek RV Campground is a great location for travelers with extra large motor-coaches or towed vehicles. Situated in the scenic Deer Lodge area, this park is less than an hour away from Yellowstone National Park. The campground offers level sites, 50 amp service, modem service and cable TV. There is a large recreation lodge with laundry, very well maintained rest rooms, and lounge. The campground sits on the banks of the Yellowstone River, and the view is spectacular. The staff is friendly and welcoming, and the climate is dry and breezy. In addition to Yellowstone, the Deer Lodge area has fine dinning, shopping, hot springs and much more. This is a wonderful place to mountain bike or hike. Indian Creek has a tendency to fill up early, so reservations are highly recommended.

Basics

Operated By: Flicker Oil Company. **Open:** Apr. 15– Oct. 15. **Site Assignment:** By reservation. **Registration:** In camp office. **Fee:** Tent $13.52, RV $17–$19. **Parking:** At site.

Facilities

Number of RV-Only Sites: 50. **Number of Tent-Only Sites:** Open tent area. **Hookups:** Electric (30 amps), water, sewer, cable, phone. **Each Site:** Picnic table. **Dump Station:** Yes. **Laundry:** Yes. **Pay Phone:** Yes. **Rest Rooms and Showers:** Yes. **Fuel:** Next door. **Propane:** Yes. **Internal Roads:** Gravel, in good condition. **RV Service:** Mobile service from Butte. **Market:** In town. **Restaurant:** In town. **General Store:** Small w/ a few drinks. **Vending:** Just the store. **Swimming Pool:** No. **Playground:** Yes. **Activities:** Hiking, biking, enjoying views of Mt. Powell. **Nearby Attractions:** Grant-Kohrs Ranch National Historic Site, the Old Montana Prison Museum Complex. **Additional Information:** Deer Lodge Chamber of Commerce, (406) 846-2094.

Restrictions

Pets: On leash. **Fires:** No open fires. **Alcoholic Beverages:** Yes. **Vehicle Maximum Length:** 45 ft. w/tow. **Other:** Good Sam, KOA, discounts.

To Get There

From I-90 Exit 184, go west on I-90 Bus 0.25 mi., make a left on Access Rd., follow signs 0.5 mi. down access road to 745 Maverick Ln.

ELMO

Arrowhead Resort

76076 Hwy. 93, Elmo 59915. T: (406) 849-5545; F: (406) 849-5545, ext. 51; www.webtize.com/arrowhead; arohed1_2@yahoo.com.

★★★ ★★★

Beauty: ★★★★ Site Privacy: ★★★
Spaciousness: ★★★ Quiet: ★★★★
Security: ★★★★ Cleanliness: ★★★★★
Insect Control: ★★★★ Facilities: ★★★★

Situated on Flathead Lake, the largest natural freshwater lake west of the Mississippi, Arrowhead Resort is a perfect retreat if you are looking for a quiet atmosphere in a pristine setting. Flathead Lake is fed by melting glaciers in the nearby Glacier National Park. Only 15 miles north of Polson, Arrowhead Resort overlooks Chief Cliff Mountain and Wild Horse Island. Arrowhead Resort is a delightfully manicured resort offering 40 pull-through grass sites, a swimming beach, and a marina. The breeze off the lake creates pleasant summer days and cool evenings. Charles and Ronnie Smith, the proprietors, live on site throughout the season and are there to assist in any way.

Basics

Operated By: E. Charles & Ronnie Smith. **Open:** May 1–Sept. 30. **Site Assignment:** Reservations recommended, $16.50 Non-refundable deposit if less than 1 week, $25 deposit for more than 1 week. **Registration:** In camp office. **Fee:** Tent $12.50, RV $19.50–$20.50. **Parking:** At site.

Facilities

Number of RV-Only Sites: 40. **Number of Tent-Only Sites:** 2. **Hookups:** Electric (30, 50 amps), water, sewer. **Each Site:** Picnic table, some grills. **Dump Station:** Yes. **Laundry:** No. **Pay Phone:** You may use office phone. **Rest Rooms and Showers:** Yes. **Fuel:** 1 mi. in Elmo. **Propane:** 1 mi. in Elmo. **Internal Roads:** Gravel. **RV Service:** 25 mi. north in Kalispell. **Market:** 13 mi. south in Polson. **Restaurant:** 13 mi. south in Polson. **General Store:** No. **Vending:** In office, drinks & ice. **Swimming Pool:** No, you may swim in lake. **Playground:** No. **Other:** Marina, boat launch, boat rentals. **Activities:** Fishing, boating, waterskiing, jet skiing, parasailing. **Nearby Attractions:** Charter fishing trips, hunting, hiking, backpacking, Flathead Lake State Park. **Additional Information:** Polson Chamber of Commerce, (406) 883-5971.

Restrictions

Pets: Leashed only. **Fires:** In fire pits only. **Alcoholic Beverages:** Yes. **Vehicle Maximum Length:** None.

To Get There

Located on Hwy. 93, 13 mi. north of Polson at the 76 mi. marker.

GARDINER

Yellowstone RV Park

P.O.Box 634, Gardiner 59030. T: (406) 848-7496; F: (406) 848-7496; www.visitmt.com.

RV ★★★ Tent ★★

Beauty: ★★★ | Site Privacy: ★★
Spaciousness: ★★ | Quiet: ★★★
Security: ★★★★ | Cleanliness: ★★★
Insect Control: ★★★ | Facilities: ★★★

Situated at the north entrance to Yellowstone National Park in breathtaking Paradise Valley, the Yellowstone RV Park is adjacent to the only park entrance open year-round. All sites look over the Yellowstone River, and because there are very few trees, each site has good views of the surrounding landscape. The park stays packed most of the year, so reserve way ahead of time. The mix of back-ins and pull-throughs is on level, gravel sites, organized in an oval shape. Locally, the town of Gardiner has many places to eat and shop. The park is 5 miles away from Mammoth Hot Springs and 55 miles away from Old Faithful

Basics

Operated By: Venture West. **Open:** May 1–Nov. 1. **Site Assignment:** By reservation. **Registration:** In camp office. **Fee:** Tent $15–$21.50, RV $21.50–$30.50 per 6 people, extra person $4. **Parking:** At site.

Facilities

Number of RV-Only Sites: 46. **Number of Tent-Only Sites:** 10. **Hookups:** Electric (30 amps), water, sewer, cable. **Each Site:** Picnic table. **Dump Station:** Yes. **Laundry:** 2 laundry areas. **Pay Phone:** Yes. **Rest Rooms and Showers:** Yes. **Fuel:** In town. **Propane:** In town. **Internal Roads:** Gravel, in good condition. **RV Service:** Mobile RV Service (406) 646-9084. **Market:** In town. **Restaurant:** In town. **General Store:** No. **Vending:** Drinks. **Swimming Pool:** No. **Playground:** No. **Other:** Located on the Yellowstone River Basin. **Activities:** Hiking, biking, fishing. **Nearby Attractions:** Yellowstone National Park, casino, trading post, shopping, fishing tours, park tours, Old Faithful, Roosevelt Arch. **Additional Information:** Gardiner Chamber of Commerce, (406) 848-7971, gardinerchamber@gomontana.com.

Restrictions

Pets: On leash. **Fires:** No open fires, grills in tent area. **Alcoholic Beverages:** Yes. **Vehicle Maximum Length:** 50 ft. **Other:** Good Sam, AAA, AARP, discounts.

To Get There

On US 89S 1.3 mi. from the north gate to Yellowstone National Park.

GLENDIVE

Glendive RV Park and Campground

201 California St., Glendive 59330. T: (406) 377-6721; www.glendivervpark.com; larry@midrivers.com.

RV ★★★ Tent ★★★

Beauty: ★★★ | Site Privacy: ★★★
Spaciousness: ★★★ | Quiet: ★★★
Security: ★★★ | Cleanliness: ★★★
Insect Control: ★★★ | Facilities: ★★★

Located 33 miles west of the North Dakota border, Glendive offers the last bit of civilization before leaving the sprawling desert-like scenery of eastern Montana. Just a quick exit from I-94, this campground might be a convenient stop as you journey to the next state. The chain-link fence, hodge-podge of buildings, and patchy grass found at the entrance are not aesthetically pleasing, but, luckily, the campsites are not located in close view. Sites 1–18 are arranged in three rows and are the farthest from the interstate. However, they are not as spacious as sites 19–52, which are arranged in a horseshoe pattern. The inner horseshoe, sites 19–31, hug the playground, and sites 19 and 33 catch any incoming traffic. The separate tent area places tent campers closest to the interstate and hides them among occasional trees and sparse ground cover. Not far from the camp, Makoshika State Park (makoshika is the Sioux name for "bad lands") captures the subtle desert scenery of sandstone and sage, and is an interesting contrast to the Yellowstone experience. If you happen through during spring, be sure to catch the annual Buzzard Days festival celebrating the return of the turkey vultures.

Basics

Operated By: Larry Phillips. **Open:** Apr. 1–Dec. 1. **Site Assignment:** By reservation. **Registration:** In camp office. **Fee:** Tent $14, RV $21–$25 per 2 people, extra person charge $2, children under age 5 stay free. **Parking:** At site.

Facilities

Number of RV-Only Sites: 52. **Number of Tent-Only Sites:** 10. **Hookups:** Electric (20, 30, 50 amps), water, sewer, phone. **Each Site:** Picnic tables, fire pits. **Dump Station:** Yes. **Laundry:** Yes. **Pay Phone:** Yes. **Rest Rooms and Showers:** Yes. **Fuel:** Less than 1 mi. **Propane:** No. **Internal Roads:** Gravel, in good condition. **RV Service:** MIles City (70 mi.). **Market:** In town. **Restaurant:** On site. **General Store:** Yes. **Vending:** Yes. **Swimming Pool:** Yes. **Playground:** Yes. **Other:** On the Yellowstone River, 2 cabins w/ refrigerators, hot plates, running water, air-conditioning, cable TV, exercise bar, Internet data port. **Activities:** Horseshoes, basketball, volleyball, swimming, fishing, badminton. **Nearby Attractions:** Yellowstone River, boating, fishing, agate hunting, Makoshika State Park, self-guided walking tour of Glendive's downtown historic district. **Additional Information:** Glendive Chamber of Commerce, (406) 365-5601.

Restrictions

Pets: On leash. **Fires:** In fire pits only. **Alcoholic Beverages:** Yes. **Vehicle Maximum Length:** None. **Other:** Good Sam Park.

To Get There

North of I-94 Exit 215; you can see campground from the interstate.

HARDIN

Hardin KOA

RR 1, Hardin 59034. T: (406) 665-1635 or (800) 562-1635; www.koa.com; hardinkoa@aol.com.

RV ★★★ Tent ★★★

Beauty: ★★★ | Site Privacy: ★★★
Spaciousness: ★★★ | Quiet: ★★★★
Security: ★★★★ | Cleanliness: ★★★★
Insect Control: n/a | Facilities: ★★★

Hardin KOA is the perfect place for campers who have a taste for history. Within easy driving distance is Pompey's Pillar, a large, solitary plateau offering panoramic views of the surrounding countryside. The remnants of Native Americans pictographs can be found here, as well as the signature of Captain William Clark of Lewis and Clark fame. Also nearby is the Little Bighorn National Monument, site of the brutal battle between Custer's 7th Cavalry and the Sioux Indians. The 58 RV sites and 10 tent-only sites lie on mostly flat ground with minimal shade. Activities within camp include swimming, horseshoes, volleyball, and nightly movies during the summer. This camp fills up quickly during Little Big Horn Days each summer, so call ahead.

Basics

Operated By: Warren D. Hardy. **Open:** Apr. 1–Oct. 1. **Site Assignment:** By reservation. **Registration:** In camp store. **Fee:** Tent $15, RV $20.50–$21.50 per 2 people, extra person $1.50, children under 3 free. **Parking:** At site.

Facilities

Number of RV-Only Sites: 58. **Number of Tent-Only Sites:** 10. **Hookups:** Electric (30, 50 amps), water, sewer, cable. **Each Site:** Picnic table. **Dump Station:** Yes. **Laundry:** Yes. **Pay Phone:** Yes. **Rest Rooms and Showers:** Yes. **Fuel:** No. **Propane:** Yes. **Internal Roads:** Gravel, in good condition. **RV Service:** In Billings. **Market:** In town. **Restaurant:** There are several in town. **General Store:** Yes. **Vending:** No. **Swimming Pool:** Yes w/ hot tub. **Playground:** Yes. **Other:** 6 cabins, hot tub, snack bar, nightly summer BBQs. **Activities:** Swimming, horseshoes, volleyball, basketball, nightly summer movies. **Nearby Attractions:** Fishing (Big Horn River), Big Horn Nat'l Monument, Little Big Horn Days June 20–25. **Additional Information:** Hardin Chamber, (406) 665-1672.

Restrictions

Pets: On leash. **Fires:** In fire pits only. **Alcoholic Beverages:** Yes. **Vehicle Maximum Length:** Limited sites for very large RVs.

To Get There

I-90 Exit 495, go north 1.5 mi. on Hwy. 47

HAVRE

Havre RV Park

1415 First St., Havre 59501. T: (406) 265-8861 or (800) 278-8861; www.havremt.com/duck-inn/havre_rv_park.htm

RV ★★★ Tent ★★★

Beauty: ★★★	Site Privacy: ★★★
Spaciousness: ★★★	Quiet: ★★
Security: ★★★	Cleanliness: ★★★
Insect Control: ★★★	Facilities: ★★★

The Havre Campground, located in downtown Havre, is owned in conjunction with the Emporium Food and Fuel Store (Conoco), The Best Western Hotel, and The Duck Inn Restaurant and Casino. All of Havre Campground sites have concrete parking pads with full hookups and 50 amp service. They are configured in a large paved oval, surrounded by green grass and a wooden privacy fence. The only real drawback to this park is the railroad tracks that run behind the property. All campground guests are invited to use the pool, spa, sauna, and exercise room at the hotel, and rest rooms and shower are located inside the store. The campground office is located inside a refurbished train caboose and oversees the gate into the park. The restaurant serves three meals a day and is moderately priced. The Havre community offers tours of its downtown area and has an enriching history to share.

Basics

Operated By: Private Operator. **Open:** All year. **Site Assignment:** By reservation. **Registration:** In office. **Fee:** Tent $14, RV $27. **Parking:** At site.

Facilities

Number of RV-Only Sites: 50. **Number of Tent-Only Sites:** Open tent area. **Hookups:** Electric (20, 30, 50 amps), water, sewer. **Each Site:** Concrete parking pad, picnic tables. **Dump Station:** Yes. **Laundry:** Yes. **Pay Phone:** Yes. **Rest Rooms and Showers:** Yes. **Fuel:** Yes. **Propane:** Yes. **Internal Roads:** Paved. **RV Service:** Limited service in town. **Market:** In town. **Restaurant:** On site. **General Store:** Large Conoco. **Vending:** Yes. **Swimming Pool:** No, but free use of the pool & spa at the Best Western Great Northern Inn. **Playground:** Yes. **Other:** Emporium Food & Fuel Store (Conoco), saloon, The Best Western, The Duck Inn Restaurant, a small casino, & all sites have concrete parking pad w/ full hookups & 50 amp service. **Activities:** Casino, swim, spa, picnic, exercise room, sauna (located at the Best Western). **Nearby Attractions:** Bears Paw Mountains & battle field, Havre Beneath the Streets w/ daily tours of the town, Beaver Creek Park, several reservoirs w/ excellent fishing & boating. **Additional Information:** Havre Chamber, (406) 265-4383.

Restrictions

Pets: On leash. **Fires:** No open fires. **Alcoholic Beverages:** Yes. **Vehicle Max. Length:** None.

To Get There

From Hwy. 2, go east at 14th Ave

HELENA

Helena Campground & RV Park

5820 North Montana Ave., Helena 59602. T: (406) 458-4714; F: (406) 458-6001; www.helenacampgroundrvpark.com; info@helenacampgroundrvpark.com.

RV ★★★ Tent ★★

Beauty: ★★★	Site Privacy: ★★★
Spaciousness: ★★★★	Quiet: ★★★
Security: ★★★	Cleanliness: ★★★★
Insect Control: ★★★★	Facilities: ★★★

Welcome to the Capital city of Helena. The Helena Campground and RV Park is a mere three miles outside the city limits and is a comfortable vacation spot for those visitors wishing to visit the city and surrounding area. The campground is configured in rows containing both pull-through and back-in sites, which are well groomed with trailer pads. Tent sites have nice lawn areas, but are small with little privacy. There is also a tent corral with electricity and water, and a few cabins. During the peak season patrons may enjoy an all-you-can-eat breakfast, ice cream socials, and a dip in the pool. Canyon Ferry and Hauser Lakes are close by with tours and boating. The weather in Helena is dry and warm in the summer, with temperatures dropping in the evening. The campground has good security with someone always on the clock.

Basics

Operated By: Robert Dunlop. **Open:** Mar. 1–Oct. 31. **Site Assignment:** By reservation, w/ first night deposit. $5 cancellation fee. **Registration:** In camp office. **Fee:** Tent $22-23, RV $22–$29 per 2 people, extra person $6 children under 3 free, ac/heat $2 extra per night. **Parking:** Yes, extra vehicle $5.

Facilities

Number of RV-Only Sites: 100. **Number of Tent-Only Sites:** 29. **Hookups:** Electric (30, 50 amps), water, sewer. **Each Site:** Picnic tables, some grills, some fire pits. **Dump Station:** Yes. **Laundry:** Yes. **Pay Phone:** Yes. **Rest Rooms and Showers:** Yes. **Fuel:** In Helena. **Propane:** In Helena. **Internal Roads:** Paved & gravel. **RV Service:** In Helena. **Market:** In Helena. **Restaurant:** In Helena. **General Store:** Yes. **Vending:** In general store only. **Swimming Pool:** Yes (very large, open Memorial Day–Labor Day). **Playground:** Yes. **Other:** All tent sites have water, 3 cabins, tent village, recreation room, breakfast. **Activities:** Game room, swimming, fun cycles. **Nearby Attractions:** State Capitol Building, Holter Museum of Art, Boulder Hot Springs, St. Helena Cathedral, Elkhorn Ghost Town, Holter Lake & Recreation Area. **Additional Information:** Helena Chamber, (406) 444-2654, (800)743-5362 or www.helenachamber.com.

Restrictions

Pets: On leash. **Fires:** In fire pits or grills only (fires may be restricted due to dry weather; please ask management before starting any fire.). **Alcoholic Beverages:** Yes. **Vehicle Maximum Length:** None. **Other:** Good Sam, AAA, & 30% discount to cyclist w/o vehicle.

To Get There

From I-15, take Lincoln Rd. Exit 200 (SR-279) west, take a left onto Montana Ave. Park is located 3 mi. down on your right.

HUNGRY HORSE

Canyon RV & Campground

9540 Hwy. 2 East, Hungry Horse 59919. T: (406) 387-9393; F: (406)387-9394; www.montanacampground.com; canyonrv@montanacampground.com.

RV ★★★ Tent ★★★

Beauty: ★★★★	Site Privacy: ★★★
Spaciousness: ★★	Quiet: ★★★★
Security: ★★★★	Cleanliness: ★★★★
Insect Control: ★★★	Facilities: ★★★

Only ten minutes away from the western entrance to Glacier National Park on the Flat Head River is Canyon RV & Campground. Canyon RV & Campground enjoys river frontage, great for trout fishing, and panoramic views of the snow-capped mountains. It is conveniently located near many of the attractions in the Hungry Horse–West Glacier area, including golf, the Hungry Horse Dam, and glacier helicopter tours. The campground is configured in a large loop with both back-in and pull-through sites. Sites, however, are relatively close together and tent sites lack privacy and shade. The air is crisp and dry, but be prepared for the cold any day of the year. The foliage is spectacular in the late spring, early summer, and the sunsets are magnificent. The owners stay on property during the operating season and are there to assist in any way.

Basics

Operated By: Steve & Dee Brown. **Open:** May 1–Sept. 30. **Site Assignment:** Reservations held w/ a credit card number. **Registration:** In general store. **Fee:** Tent $16, RV $16–$22 per 2 people, extra person $3 (cash & checks). **Parking:** At site.

Facilities

Number of RV-Only Sites: 51. **Number of Tent-Only Sites:** 10. **Hookups:** Electric (20, 30, 50 amps), water, sewer. **Each Site:** Picnic table, some grills. **Dump Station:** Yes. **Laundry:** No.

Pay Phone: Yes. **Rest Rooms and Showers:** Yes. **Fuel:** In Hungry Horse. **Propane:** In Hungry Horse. **Internal Roads:** Gravel. **RV Service:** In Hungry Horse, and there is a mobile service. **Market:** In Hungry Horse. **Restaurant:** In Hungry Horse. **General Store:** Yes. **Vending:** General store only. **Swimming Pool:** No. No swimming in the Flathead River. **Playground:** No. **Other:** 6 cabins & 1 tepee, central fire ring. **Activities:** Fishing (bull trout, white fish, rainbow trout), horseshoes, hiking. **Nearby Attractions:** Glacier National Park, House of Mystery, North American Wildlife Museum, go karts, helicopter tours, white water rafting, fishing tours. **Additional Information:** Columbia Falls Area Chamber, (406) 892-2072.

Restrictions

Pets: Leash only. **Fires:** Fire ring only (fires maybe prohibited due to dry weather, please ask management before starting any fire.). **Alcoholic Beverages:** No alcoholic beverages allowed. **Vehicle Maximum Length:** 45 ft. plus.

To Get There

Directly off Hwy. 2 in Hungry Horse, 18 mi. northeast of Kalispell.

HUNGRY HORSE

Mountain Meadow Campground

P.O. Box 190442, Hungry Horse 59919. T: (406) 387-9125; F: (406) 387-9126; www.mmrvpark.com; camp@mmrvpark.com.

RV: ★★★★★ Tent: ★★★★

Beauty: ★★★★★	Site Privacy: ★★★★
Spaciousness: ★★★★	Quiet: ★★★★★
Security: ★★★★	Cleanliness: ★★★★★
Insect Control: ★★★★	Facilities: ★★★★★

Welcome to one of the most beautiful and pristine campgrounds in Montana. Located only a few short miles from the west entrance to Glacier National Park and the Hungry Horse Dam is Mountain Meadow Campground. High atop a mountain peak with a spectacular view of the Glacier Mountains, one finds cozy wooded camping sites, cabins with all the modern luxuries of a full service campground, and the rustic ambiance only nature can share. Large Douglas firs and cedars canopy each site and lend their sweet aroma to the air. The roads are wide, the sites are large, most are pull-through, and the trees are groomed. Tent sites are secluded and private. There is a large well-stocked fishing pond and large picnic area. The air is crisp and the breeze is inviting. Several nice restaurants are in walking distance as well as outfitters and helicopter tours. The office is staffed daily and security is good.

Basics

Operated By: Dan & Sue Hussion. **Open:** May 1–Oct. 1. **Site Assignment:** Reservations recommended w/ credit card number. **Registration:** In general store. **Fee:** Tent $16.50, RV $21.50–$24.50 per 4 people, extra child $1.50, adult $3.(cash, credit, checks). **Parking:** At site.

Facilities

Number of RV-Only Sites: 51. **Number of Tent-Only Sites:** 11. **Hookups:** Electric (30, 50 amps), water, sewer. **Each Site:** Picnic table, grated fire pits. **Dump Station:** Yes. **Laundry:** Yes. **Pay Phone:** Yes. **Rest Rooms and Showers:** Yes. **Fuel:** In Coram. **Propane:** In Coram. **Internal Roads:** Graded dirt & sand, smooth & in excellent condition. **RV Service:** 10 mi. southwest in Columbia Falls. **Market:** In town. **Restaurant:** In town. **General Store:** Yes. **Vending:** Yes. **Swimming Pool:** No. **Playground:** Yes. **Other:** 2 cabins, stocked rainbow trout lake over looking the mountains, swings, modem hookup in the office. **Activities:** Fishing (rainbow trout), swing, hiking, biking. **Nearby Attractions:** 9 mi. from Glacier National Park, Hungry Horse Dam, Lion Lake, horseback riding, fly-fishing tours, white water rafting, helicopter tours. **Additional Information:** Columbia Falls Area Chamber of Commerce, (406) 892-2072.

Restrictions

Pets: Leash-only. **Fires:** Fire pits only (fires may be prohibited due to weather: please ask management before starting any fires.). **Alcoholic Beverages:** Yes. **Vehicle Maximum Length:** 45 ft plus. **Other:** Good Sam & AAA honored.

To Get There

Located directly off Hwy. 2 in Hungry Horse

HUNGRY HORSE

Timber Wolf Resort

9105 Hwy. 2 East, Hungry Horse 59919. T: (406) 847-9653 or (877) 846-9653; F: (406) 387-9654; www.timberwolfresort.com; elek@timberwolfresort.com.

RV: ★★★★ Tent: ★★★★

Beauty: ★★★★★	Site Privacy: ★★★
Spaciousness: ★★★	Quiet: ★★★★★
Security: ★★★★	Cleanliness: ★★★★
Insect Control: ★★★★	Facilities: ★★★★★

Nestled in a 20-acre forest only nine miles from the west entrance to Glacier National Park, Timber Wolf Resort is a true jewel. Timber Wolf offers a full service campground with excellent amenities, including a beautiful large gazebo with three barbeque grills, bike rentals, and a new playground. The campground has hiking trails and bike trails that connect to those in Glacier National Park. Timber Wolf offers large gravel sites, both pull-through and back-in, with a natural forest floor and shade. In addition, they offer 15 beautiful camping cabins, a small bed and breakfast, and wonderfully secluded tent sites. The campground, while offering large sites, is not designed for huge (45 ft. plus) RVs. The resort is open year-round and the owners reside on the property. The winters are long, cold, and snowy, and the summers too short, but beautiful.

Basics

Operated By: Rob & Tracy Elek. **Open:** All year. **Site Assignment:** Reservations recommended. **Registration:** In general store or at the Elek's residence. **Fee:** Tent $16, RV $18–$23 (cash, credit, checks). **Parking:** At site.

Facilities

Number of RV-Only Sites: 24. **Number of Tent-Only Sites:** 10. **Hookups:** Electric (30, 50 amps), water, sewer. **Each Site:** Picnic table, grated fire pits. **Dump Station:** No. **Laundry:** No. **Pay Phone:** Yes. **Rest Rooms and Showers:** Yes. **Fuel:** In Hungry Horse. **Propane:** In Hungry Horse. **Internal Roads:** Gravel. **RV Service:** 10 mi. southwest in Columbia Falls. **Market:** In Hungry Horse. **Restaurant:** In Hungry Horse. **General Store:** Yes. **Vending:** Yes. **Swimming Pool:** No. **Playground:** Yes. **Other:** Large gazebo w/ 3 gas BBQs, bed & breakfast, cabins. **Activities:** Hiking, horseshoes. **Nearby Attractions:** 9 mi. from Glacier National Park, Hungry Horse Dam, House of Mystery, helicopter tours, fly fishing (bull trout, rainbow trout), whitewater rafting,cross-country skiing, Big Mountain Ski Resort. **Additional Information:** Columbia Falls Area Chamber, (406) 892-2072.

Restrictions

Pets: Leash only (Please note that the owners have a beautiful, well-behaved & friendly retriever that has free reign of the property, but guestss pets must be on leash.). **Fires:** Fire pits only; fires may be prohibited due to weather: please ask management before starting any fires. **Alcoholic Beverages:** Yes. **Vehicle Maximum Length:** 45 ft.

To Get There

Located directly off Hwy. 2 in Hungry Horse, 20 mi. northeast of Kalispell.

LIVINGSTON

Paradise Valley KOA

163 Pine Creek Rd., Livingston 59047. T: (406) 222-0992 or (800) 562-2805; F: (402) 222-5911; www.koa.com; liv.koa@ycsi.net.

RV: ★★★ Tent: ★★★

Beauty: ★★★★★	Site Privacy: ★★★
Spaciousness: ★★★	Quiet: ★★★★
Security: ★★★★	Cleanliness: ★★★
Insect Control: ★★★	Facilities: ★★★★

The drive on I-90 to this KOA offers a pleasant combination of Montana's subtle sloping hills, expansive plains, distant cragged mountains, and towering pines, marking a transition in the journey toward Yellowstone National Park. On your way into Paradise Valley, you'll pass a sign that reads, "Don't get the gumps. It's only a few more bumps to KOA." Rest assured your camping experience here will keep you gump free. Located 8 miles south of Livingston, the campground is nestled at the foot of the Absaroka Mountains on the banks of the winding Yellowstone River. This KOA provides well-maintained, semi-private sites surrounded by huge cottonwood, Douglas fir, and quaking aspen. The campground offers the usual KOA comforts complete with morning coffee and inexpensive breakfasts. Yellowstone is a short 35 miles away, but you might find yourself tempted to enjoy the area attractions: challenge yourself to a white water rafting trip, enjoy a quiet fly fishing adventure, or hike one of the scenic trails.

Basics

Operated By: Terry & Diane Devine. **Open:** May 1–Oct. 15. **Site Assignment:** By reservation. **Registration:** In camp store. **Fee:** Tent $15–19, RV $23–$30 per 2 people, extra person $2.50, children under 7 free. **Parking:** At site.

Facilities

Number of RV-Only Sites: 47. **Number of Tent-Only Sites:** 22. **Hookups:** Electric (30, 50 amps), water, sewer. **Each Site:** Picnic table. **Dump Station:** Yes. **Laundry:** Yes. **Pay Phone:** Yes. **Rest Rooms and Showers:** Yes. **Fuel:** No. **Propane:** Yes. **Internal Roads:** Gravel, in good condition. **RV Service:** In Bozeman. **Market:** In town. **Restaurant:** There are several in town. **General Store:** Yes. **Vending:** Only in store. **Swimming Pool:** Indoor w/ hot tub. **Playground:** Yes. **Other:** 23 cabins, 1 cottage, hot tub, snack bar, pavilion. **Activities:** Swimming, horseshoes, volleyball, basketball, fun cycles, mountain biking, rafting (outfitters next door). **Nearby Attractions:** Yellowstone National Park, Scenic drives, horseback riding, hot springs, guided park tours, fly fishing trips, Yellowstone Gateway Museum. **Additional Information:** Livingston Chamber of Commerce, (406) 222-0850.

Restrictions

Pets: On leash. **Fires:** In fire pits only. **Alcoholic Beverages:** Yes. **Vehicle Maximum Length:** Limited sites for very large RVs.

To Get There

I-90 Exit 333 towards Yellowstone, go south 10 mi. on Hwy. 89 to Yellowstone Rd.

LIVINGSTON

Yellowstone's Edge RV Park

3502 Hwy. 89, Livingston 59047. T: (406) 333-4036 or (800) 865-7322; F: (406) 333-4052; www.mtrv.com; edge@mtrv.com.

RV: ★★★★★ Tent: ★★★★

Beauty: ★★★★	Site Privacy: ★★★★
Spaciousness: ★★★★	Quiet: ★★★★★
Security: ★★★★	Cleanliness: ★★★★★
Insect Control: ★★★★	Facilities: ★★★★★

As its name implies, Yellowstone's Edge RV Park is situated on the Yellowstone River, one of the longest free-flowing rivers in the United States and a great fly fishing destination to boot. The park's 81 RV and 13 tent-only sites don't have much in the way of shade, but they have great views of the river and surrounding landscape. Sites are close together, but with many return folks, this means the park is quite a friendly and neighborly place. The RV sites are divided evenly between pull-through and back-in, with electric, water, sewer, and phone hookups available. Tent sites have grass pads with picnic tables available at some. This is a great alternative to staying in Yellowstone, which is only a 35-mile drive south. Other activities within easy driving distance include Chico Hot Springs, Museum of the Rockies, Lewis and Clark Caverns, and Virginia City. Staying closer to camp, campers have the option to hike, fish, mountain bike, or play volleyball.

Basics

Operated By: Chan & Pam Libbey. **Open:** May 1–Oct. 15. **Site Assignment:** By reservation. **Registration:** In camp store. **Fee:** Tent $16.50, RV $28.50 per 2 people. **Parking:** At site.

Facilities

Number of RV-Only Sites: 81. **Number of Tent-Only Sites:** 13. **Hookups:** Electric (30, 50 amps), water, sewer, phone. **Each Site:** Picnic table. **Dump Station:** No, all sites are on sewers. **Laundry:** Yes. **Pay Phone:** Yes. **Rest Rooms and Showers:** Yes. **Fuel:** 5 mi. south in Immigrant. **Propane:** Yes. **Internal Roads:** Gravel, in good condition. **RV Service:** In Bozeman. **Market:** In Livingston. **Restaurant:** There are several towards Bozeman. **General Store:** Yes. **Vending:** Yes. **Swimming Pool:** No. **Playground:** No. **Other:** Large lodge, recreation room, game room, 1 river suite, central fire ring, modem. **Activities:** Hiking, fishing (Yellowstone River), mountain biking, volleyball, game room, book exchange. **Nearby Attractions:** 36 mi. from the North Gate to Yellowstone National Park, scenic drives, horseback riding, hot springs, guided park tours, fly-fishing trips, Yellowstone Gateway Museum. **Additional Information:** Livingston Chamber of Commerce, (406) 222-0850.

Restrictions

Pets: On leash. **Fires:** No open fires. **Alcoholic Beverages:** Yes. **Vehicle Max. Length:** Up to 90 ft. w/tow. **Other:** Good Sam discount, group rates.

To Get There

Directly off Hwy. 89 in S. Livingston

POLSON

Polson/ Flathead Lake KOA

200 Irvine Flats Rd., Polson 59860. T: (406) 883-2151 or (800) 562-2130; F: (406) 883-0151; www.flatheadlakekoa.com; polsonkoa@bigsky.net.

RV: ★★★★★ Tent: ★★★★

Beauty: ★★★★★	Site Privacy: ★★★
Spaciousness: ★★★	Quiet: ★★★★
Security: ★★★★	Cleanliness: ★★★★★
Insect Control: ★★★★	Facilities: ★★★★★

Built atop a hill, peering over the Flathead Lake is the Polson/Flathead Lake KOA. The view is magnificent and the air is crisp and cool. This KOA offers exceptional service and a lovely, clean, and well maintained property. Campsites offer level, gravel camping spurs, both back-in and pull-through, some lawn, and a terrific panoramic view of the Mission Mountains. There is a separate tent area, and if you prefer, there are sites in a tent village with water. The Polson KOA has a charming pool, spa, and snack bar. The Polson Koa is conveniently located to Glacier National Park and the National Bison Range. The Polson area has several places to rent boats or jet skis and offers outfitter services. The Flathead Lake is one of the largest naturally fed lakes in the country and offers recreation for every member of the family.

Basics

Operated By: Paul & Carlisa London. **Open:** Apr. 1–Oct. 15. **Site Assignment:** By reservation. **Registration:** In camp store. **Fee:** Tent $18.50–$20, RV $24–$32 per 2 people, extra person $5., children under 6 stay free. **Parking:** At site.

Facilities

Number of RV-Only Sites: 52. **Number of Tent-Only Sites:** 6. **Hookups:** Electric (30, 50 amps), water, sewer. **Each Site:** Picnic table. **Dump Station:** Yes. **Laundry:** Yes. **Pay Phone:** Yes. **Rest Rooms and Showers:** Yes. **Fuel:** No. **Propane:** Yes. **Internal Roads:** Gravel, in good condition. **RV Service:** Limited in town. **Market:** In town. **Restaurant:** There are several in town. **General Store:** Yes. **Vending:** No, only in store. **Swimming Pool:** Indoor w/ hot tub. **Playground:** Yes. **Other:** 6 cabins, 1 cottage, hot tub, snack bar, pavilion, camp kitchen, tent village, central fire ring, adult-only hot tub, pancake breakfast weekends & holidays. **Activities:** Swimming, horseshoes, volleyball, day tours. **Nearby Attractions:** Flathead Lake, great fishing & boating, boat rental, Wild Horse Island, several museums, short drive to Glacier National Park, The Polson Princess (50-ft. tour boat), whitewater float trips, guided fishing trips. **Additional Information:** Polson Chamber of Commerce, (406) 883-5969.

Restrictions

Pets: On leash. **Fires:** In fire pits only. **Alcoholic Beverages:** Yes. **Vehicle Maximum Length:** Limited sites for very large RVs.

To Get There

Half-mile north of Polson, just off Hwy. 93.

POLSON/FLATHEAD LAKE AREA

Flathead Lake State Park

490 North Meridian, Kalispell 59901. T: (406) 752-5501; www.fwp.state.mt.us/parks; dmonger@state.mtFla.

RV: ★★★ Tent: ★★★

Beauty: ★★★★	Site Privacy: ★★★
Spaciousness: ★★★	Quiet: ★★★
Security: ★★★★	Cleanliness: ★★★
Insect Control: ★★★	Facilities: ★★★

The Flathead Lake State Park consists of six areas and five campgrounds around the outer circumference of Flathead Lake. Flathead Lake is one of the largest natural lakes in the world with the Flathead River as its major tributary. Montana's Department of Fish, Wildlife and Parks operates these park units as well as several islands around this magnificent lake. The campgrounds are semi-developed with paved parking pads and great waterfront access. Finley Point is the only waterfront site with hookups. All of the sites are large back-in parking spaces. Yellow Bay is intended for tent camping only. It is the smallest and most private of the areas with only five camping sites. Each of the areas has entrance gates, water access, boat ramps, and someone on staff or a host at all times. The weather is cool in the evening and there is always a breeze.

Basics

Operated By: Montana Fish, Wildlife & Parks. **Open:** May–Sept. **Site Assignment:** Self serve & by reservation, (406) 751-7577. **Registration:** At park entrance. **Fee:** $8–$16 depending on residency & camp site. **Parking:** At site.

Facilities

Number of RV-Only Sites: 16. **Number of Tent-Only Sites:** 4 in Yellowbay. **Number of Multipurpose Sites:** 20 to 40 each in the other campgrounds. **Hookups:** Electric (30 amps), water (Finley Point Campground only). **Each Site:** Picnic table, fire pit or grill. **Dump Station:** In Wayfarers. **Laundry:** No. **Pay Phone:** In Wayfarers & Big

Arm. **Rest Rooms and Showers:** Yes, but only in Wayfarers, Yellow Bay, & Big Arm (these are coin operated showers, 25 cents per 3 minutes.). **Fuel:** No. **Propane:** No. **Internal Roads:** Paved. **RV Service:** Kalispell. **Market:** Polson or Kalispell. **Restaurant:** Polson or Kalispell. **General Store:** No. **Vending:** No. **Swimming Pool:** No, but you may swim in the lake. **Playground:** No. **Other:** Group camping, interpretive programs, boat launches, covered picnic areas, horse trails, Wild Horse Island accessible by boat. **Activities:** Swimming, fishing, hiking, waterskiing. **Nearby Attractions:** Ninepipes Museum, North America Wildlife Museum, Glacier National Park. **Additional Information:** Polson Chamber, (406) 883-5970.

RESTRICTIONS

Pets: On leash. **Fires:** In approved pits & grills. **Alcoholic Beverages:** Yes. **Vehicle Max. Length:** 51 ft. **Other:** 7 day limit, you may purchase a MT state passport, which waives entrance fees.

TO GET THERE

The Flathead State Park Units each have there own entrance. The entrances are all located around the perimeter of Flathead Lake. They are located either off US 93 or SR 35. For exact directions to the campground or area of your choice, please visit the web sight.

SILVER STAR

Jefferson River Guest Ranch and Campground

5162 State Hwy 41, Silver Star 59751. T: (406) 684-5225

RV ★★★ Tent ★★★★★

Beauty: ★★★★	Site Privacy: ★★★
Spaciousness: ★★★	Quiet: ★★★
Security: ★★★★	Cleanliness: ★★★★
Insect Control: ★★★★	Facilities: ★★★

Less than 30 miles from historic Virginia City, this campground is a beautiful 75-acre working ranch. Located on the Jefferson River, there are 15 RV sites. For tenters, the ranch offers open tenting most anywhere on the ranch. If you left your RV or tent at home, two fully-furnished cabins are available for rent (probably best to call ahead for reservations, especially in summer). The friendly folks who own the campground also own the Four Rivers Fishing Company. The campground, located on a half-mile stretch of the scenic and trout-rich Jefferson River, is a prime stop for trout fisherman.

BASICS

Operated By: Greg & Janet Smith. **Open:** Apr. 1–Nov. 1. **Site Assignment:** By reservation, open tenting. **Registration:** In camp office or self registration. **Fee:** Tent $10, RV $15. **Parking:** At site.

FACILITIES

Number of RV-Only Sites: 15. **Number of Tent-Only Sites:** Open tent area. **Hookups:** Electric (30, 50 amps), water, sewer. **Each Site:** Picnic table, fire pits. **Dump Station:** No. **Laundry:** Yes, at the courtesy of the host. **Pay Phone:** Courtesy phone available. **Rest Rooms and Showers:** Yes. **Fuel:** About 2 mi. in Silver Star. **Propane:** No. **Internal Roads:** Combination of gravel & packed dirt. **RV Service:** In Butte. **Market:** In Twin Bridges. **Restaurant:** 10 mi. in either direction. **General Store:** No. **Vending:** Yes. **Swimming Pool:** No, but you may swim in river. **Playground:** No. **Other:** Located on Jefferson River. **Activities:** Blue-ribbon fly fishing, quilting, book exchange, mt. biking. **Nearby Attractions:** Horseback riding, Virginia City, hunting, gold panning, biking. **Additional Information:** Whitehall Chamber, (406) 287-2260.

RESTRICTIONS

Pets: Leash only. **Fires:** Fire pits only (fires may be prohibited due to dry weather: please ask management before starting any fire.). **Alcoholic Beverages:** Yes. **Vehicle Maximum Length:** 40 ft. **Other:** 14 day limit Memorial Day–Labor Day.

TO GET THERE

Located between I-90 and I-15 on Hwy. 41.

ST. MARY

Johnson's Campground & RV Park

HC 72 10 St. Mary Rte., Browing 59417. T: (406) 732-4207; F: (406) 732-4453; www.glacierinfo.com & click on St. Mary.

RV ★★★ Tent ★★★

Beauty: ★★★	Site Privacy: ★★★
Spaciousness: ★★★	Quiet: ★★★★
Security: ★★★	Cleanliness: ★★★
Insect Control: ★★★	Facilities: ★★★

Upon a hilltop directly adjacent to the east entrance to Glacier National Park is Johnson Campground and RV Park. East of the Continental Divide, the St. Mary's area offers a diversified high desert terrain and hot summer days. The campground sits atop a large hill overlooking the peaks of Logan Pass and circles back down the hill into a small grass and sand valley where there are several tent sites. The larger RV sites are located on top of the hill in an open clearing with a panoramic view of Glacier. The internal roads are gravel and dirt, which may hinder mobility into sites provided for smaller RVs and 5th wheelers. The campground has a very natural appearance and sites tend to be a bit rustic. In addition to the campground, there is a café, a covered picnic area with a grill, and a small motel. Someone is always on staff to assist with any need.

BASICS

Operated By: Johnson Family. **Open:** May–Oct. **Site Assignment:** Reservations recommended w/1 night deposit. **Registration:** In general store. **Fee:** Tent $14, RV $18–$25 per 2 people, extra person $3.50. Children under 12 stay free. (cash, credit, check) members of Good Sam. **Parking:** At site.

FACILITIES

Number of RV-Only Sites: 42. **Number of Tent-Only Sites:** 75. **Number of Multipurpose Sites:** 42. **Hookups:** Electric (20, 30 amps), water, sewer. **Each Site:** Picnic table, some fire pits. **Dump Station:** Yes. **Laundry:** Yes. **Pay Phone:** Yes. **Rest Rooms and Showers:** Yes. **Fuel:** Next door. **Propane:** Yes. **Internal Roads:** Gravel. **RV Service:** 50 mi. west in Kalispell. **Market:** 1 mi. southeast in St. Mary. **Restaurant:** In St. Mary, or on property. **General Store:** Yes. **Vending:** Yes. **Swimming Pool:** No. **Playground:** Yes. **Other:** 1 cabin, covered pavilion w/ kitchen facilities & 2 barbeque grills, small motel, cafe. **Activities:** Horseshoe pit, hiking, biking. **Nearby Attractions:** Glacier National Park (east entrance), hiking, backpacking, guided tours of the park, interpretive programs, helicopter tours, ballon tours. **Additional Information:** www.glacierinfo.com & click St. Mary.

RESTRICTIONS

Pets: Leash only. **Fires:** Fire pits only (fires may be prohibited due to weather; please ask management before starting any fire.). **Alcoholic Beverages:** At site only. **Vehicle Maximum Length:** Call ahead for details.

TO GET THERE

Located in the heart of St. Mary on Hwy. 89, 0.25 mi. from the east entrance to Glacier National Park, (15 mi. northwest of Browing).

ST. MARY

St. Mary-Glacier Park KOA

106 West Shore, St. Mary 59417. T: (406)732-4122 or (800) 562-1504; F: (406) 732-4327; www.goglacier.com, www.koa.com; wsbrooke@goglacier.com.

RV ★★★ Tent ★★★

Beauty: ★★★	Site Privacy: ★★★
Spaciousness: ★★★	Quiet: ★★★★
Security: ★★★	Cleanliness: ★★★★
Insect Control: ★★★	Facilities: ★★★★

Directly at the east gate of Glacier and Waterton International Parks sits St. Mary KOA. The campground is an ideal base for families wishing to visit the national parks. Scenic Going-to-the-Sun Road is only a few miles away. St. Mary KOA is a full service modern campground with all the amenities including canoe, paddleboat, and kayak rentals. There are barbeque dinners in the evenings and pancakes for breakfast. The campground is large, but sites are small with little privacy between. Tent sites are in fields of aspen but a fair walk from the facilities. There is a nice hot tub with a spectacular mountain view. However, it is in close proximity to the dump. The weather is warm and dry in the summer on the eastern side of the Continental Divide. The altitude is high, so the air may seem a bit thin. The view is spectacular and the staff is friendly.

BASICS

Operated By: Will & Susan Brook. **Open:** May–Oct. **Site Assignment:** Reservations recommended, held w/ credit card number. **Registration:** In gift shop. **Fee:** Tent $21.95, RV $29.95–$36.95 plus 10% tax per 2 people.(cash, credit, checks) KOA value card 10% discount. **Parking:** At site.

FACILITIES

Number of RV-Only Sites: 60. **Number of Tent-Only Sites:** 64. **Number of Multipurpose Sites:** 10. **Hookups:** Electric (30, 50 amps), water, sewer. **Each Site:** Picnic table, some grated fire pits. **Dump Station:** Yes. **Laundry:** Yes. **Pay Phone:** Yes. **Rest Rooms and Showers:** Yes. **Fuel:** No.

Propane: Yes. **Internal Roads:** Gravel. **RV Service:** 126 mi. southeast in Great Falls. **Market:** In St. Mary. **Restaurant:** In St. Mary or on the property. **General Store:** Yes. **Vending:** General store only. **Swimming Pool:** No, but 2 hot tubs. **Playground:** Yes. **Other:** 25 camp cabins, 2 cottages, game room, gift shop, outdoor barbeque restaurant, 2 hot tubs, canoe rental, bike rental, car rental, group sites, Internet dataport in the gift shop. **Activities:** Fish (rainbow trout), canoe, bike, hike, game room, horseshoes, volleyball. **Nearby Attractions:** Glacier National Park (2 mi. from east entrance), hiking trails, mountain bike trails, horseback riding, nightly interpretive programs in Glacier. **Additional Information:** www.goglacier.com, www.koa.com.

RESTRICTIONS

Pets: Leash only. **Fires:** Fire pits only (fire may be prohibited due to weather; please ask camp staff before starting any fire). **Alcoholic Beverages:** Yes. **Vehicle Maximum Length:** None.

TO GET THERE

From Hwy. 89 in St. Mary, look for huge KOA sign; turn down West Shore, and the KOA sits on the right hand side 1 mi. down.

ST. REGIS

Campground St. Regis

Drawer 8, St. Regis 59866. T: (406) 649-2470 or (888) 247-8734; www.campgroundstregis.com; moose@campgroundstregis.com.

RV ★★★★ Tent ★★★★

Beauty: ★★★★★	Site Privacy: ★★★★
Spaciousness: ★★★★	Quiet: ★★★★
Security: ★★★★	Cleanliness: ★★★★★
Insect Control: ★★★★	Facilities: ★★★★

Campground St. Regis is conveniently located off I-90 on the frontage road in St. Regis. This family oriented campground is nestled in a wooded setting, offering activities for all. Campground St. Regis is surrounded by mountains and is only a few miles from the St. Regis River. This campground offers large, spacious, shaded sites with some pull-throughs as long as 75 ft. They provide a large heated pool, game room, and video rentals. The weather offers summer days averaging in the 70s and evenings in the low 40s. There are two golf courses in the area, along with white water rafting, horseback riding, hunting, antique stores, and lots of fishing. St. Regis is the western gateway to the National Bison Range and the Flathead Lake Area.

BASICS

Operated By: Gail Pierce & Tom Satterthwaite. **Open:** Apr. 16–Oct. 15. **Site Assignment:** Reservations recommended. **Registration:** In general store. **Fee:** Tent $17, RV $22. **Parking:** At site.

FACILITIES

Number of Multipurpose Sites: 75. **Hookups:** Electric (20, 30, 50 amps), water, sewer, phone, Internet. **Each Site:** Picnic table, some fire pits. **Dump Station:** Yes. **Laundry:** Yes. **Pay Phone:** Yes. **Rest Rooms and Showers:** Yes. **Fuel:** 1 mi. in St. Regis. **Propane:** Yes. **Internal Roads:** Gravel. **RV Service:** 24 mi. east in Superior. **Market:** In St. Regis. **Restaurant:** In St. Regis. **General Store:** Yes. **Vending:** General store only. **Swimming Pool:** Yes (Memorial Day–Labor Day). **Playground:** Yes. **Other:** Game room, video rental, fax service, horse boarding (must make reservations). **Activities:** Swimming, horseshoes, biking, hiking. **Nearby Attractions:** Fishing (St. Regis River or Flathead Lake), boating, hunting, golf, whitewater rafting, casinos. **Additional Information:** Montana Visitors Information, (406) 649-2290.

RESTRICTIONS

Pets: Leash only. **Fires:** Fire pits only. **Alcoholic Beverages:** Yes. **Vehicle Maximum Length:** None. **Other:** Good Sam & KOA discount.

TO GET THERE

I-90 Exit 33, go north to 4-way and turn left onto Mullan Rd. Go 0.75 mi. and turn left on Little Joe Rd. Go 0.5 mi. and turn right on Frontage Rd.; campground is 0.5 mi. on right. There are excellent signs directing you from interstate exit.

ST. REGIS

St. Regis KOA

105 Old Hwy. 10 East, St. Regis 59866. T: (406) 649-2122 or (800)562-4670; www.koa.com; koastregis@blackfoot.net.

RV ★★★ Tent ★★

Beauty: ★★★	Site Privacy: ★★★
Spaciousness: ★★★	Quiet: ★★★
Security: ★★★★	Cleanliness: ★★★
Insect Control: ★★★★	Facilities: ★★★★

Conveniently located on the frontage road directly off I-90 in St. Regis, the St. Regis KOA is a unique experience. Of all the campgrounds in this book, the St. Regis KOA is the only campground with a "Caution Rabbit Crossing" sign at the entrance gate. The campground is full (I mean hundreds) of free-range domestic rabbits. There are paths and crossings and cute little shelters, all built for the rabbits. The facility itself is well maintained and clean. They offer all the modern amenities including a pool and driving range. There is a historic mining camp on the property to visit or use as a camping site. There is a camping kitchen, snack bar, and modem data port. The sites are a combination of grass and gravel, and there is a need for some leveling. The weather is comfortable in the summer and cold in the winter. There is someone on security duty around the clock.

BASICS

Operated By: John & Louise Cochran. **Open:** All year. **Site Assignment:** Reservations recommended. **Registration:** In general store. **Fee:** Tent $16–$20, RV $27–$29 per 2 people, extra person $3. **Parking:** At site.

FACILITIES

Number of RV-Only Sites: 66. **Number of Tent-Only Sites:** 21. **Hookups:** Electric (30, 50 amps), water, sewer. **Each Site:** Picnic tables, some lantern poles. **Dump Station:** Yes. **Laundry:** Yes. **Pay Phone:** Yes. **Rest Rooms and Showers:** Yes. **Fuel:** 1 mi. in St. Regis. **Propane:** Yes. **Internal Roads:** Gravel. **RV Service:** 24 mi. east in Superior. **Market:** In St. Regis. **Restaurant:** In St. Regis. **General Store:** Yes. **Vending:** General store only. **Swimming Pool:** Yes (Memorial Day weekend–September 15). **Playground:** Yes. **Other:** Cabins, camp kitchen w/grill & microwave, historic mining camp (tent area), snack bar, dataport. **Activities:** Golf driving range, nature trails, fishing, hunting. **Nearby Attractions:** St. Regis River, golf, Flathead Lake, horseback riding. **Additional Information:** Montana Visitors Information, (406) 649-2290.

RESTRICTIONS

Pets: Leash only. **Fires:** Fire pits only. **Alcoholic Beverages:** Yes. **Vehicle Maximum Length:** None. **Other:** There are domestic rabbits all over this KOA, please watch for them on the road.

TO GET THERE

I-90, Exit 33 in St. Regis, go north to 4 way, turn right on Frontage Rd., KOA is 1 mi. on your left.

THREE FORKS

Three Forks KOA

P.O. Box 15, Three Forks 59752. T: (406) 285-3611 or (800) 562-9752; www.koa.com.

RV ★★★★ Tent ★★★

Beauty: ★★★★	Site Privacy: ★★★
Spaciousness: ★★★	Quiet: ★★★
Security: ★★★★	Cleanliness: ★★★★
Insect Control: ★★★	Facilities: ★★★★

Nestled in a panoramic setting, this KOA is a very pleasant park indeed. The RV and tent sites are adequately sized, with lovely views of the countryside. Security is above average and the grounds are well maintained. Each site offers parking, picnic tables and fire pits, and some RV sites with full hookups. The campground also offers a good many family activities, including a petting zoo, ice cream parlor, and a pool table. For those guests on a working vacation, dataports are available. Nearby, there are golf courses, the Lewis and Clark Caverns, and the Headwater Heritage Museum, just to list a few. Reservations are recommended, however, because finding a place in the peak season is difficult.

BASICS

Operated By: Tom Glorvigen. **Open:** Apr. 15–Oct. 15. **Site Assignment:** Reservations recommended. **Registration:** In general store. **Fee:** Tent $18, RV $22–$24 per 2 persons, extra person $3. **Parking:** At site.

FACILITIES

Number of RV-Only Sites: 56. **Number of Tent-Only Sites:** 21. **Hookups:** Electric (30, 50 amps), water, sewer. **Each Site:** Picnic tables, fire pits. **Dump Station:** Yes. **Laundry:** Yes. **Pay Phone:** Yes. **Rest Rooms and Showers:** Yes. **Fuel:** 1 mi. by I-90. **Propane:** 1 mi. by I-90. **Internal Roads:** Gravel. **RV Service:** 32 mi. in E. Bozeman. **Market:** 3 mi. in Three Fork. **Restaurant:** There are a few in town. **General Store:** Yes. **Vending:** General store only. **Swimming Pool:** Yes w/a slide. **Playground:** Yes. **Other:** Cabins, petting zoo (chickens & horses), ice cream, dataport. **Activities:** Volleyball, pool table, nature trails, fishing w/water access. **Nearby Attractions:** Headwater Heritage Museum, golf, Lewis & Clark Caverns, fishing, the Madison, Jefferson, & Missouri Rivers, fishing, hunting, & float trip outfitters. **Additional Information:** Montana Visitors Info, (406) 649-2290.

Restrictions

Pets: Leash only. **Fires:** Fire pits only. **Alcoholic Beverages:** Yes. **Vehicle Max. Length:** None.

To Get There

I-90 Exit 274 follow signs to KOA, less than 1 mi.

WEST GLACIER

Glacier Campground

P.O. Box 447, West Glacier 59936. T: (406) 387-5689 or (888) 387-5689; www.glaciercampground.com.

RV ★★★★ Tent ★★★★

Beauty: ★★★★★	Site Privacy: ★★★★
Spaciousness: ★★★★	Quiet: ★★★★
Security: ★★★★	Cleanliness: ★★★★★
Insect Control: ★★★★	Facilities: ★★★

Just outside the gates of Glacier National Park is Glacier Campground. This delightful campground is nestled in a mountain clearing surrounded by 40 acres of wooded area. The air is crisp and the view is spectacular. The campground consists of 175 wooded sites that are private, spacious and large enough for easy mobility. Sites are both back-in and pull-through, with gravel parking pads. The natural fir and pines stand tall, and overhanging branches do not seem to be a problem. Tent sites are private and offer a rustic ambiance. The campground is convenient to numerous lakes and rivers, restaurants, ski resorts, and other area activities. The weather is typical of high altitude areas, with dramatic temperature drops in the evening. The campground is staffed around the clock, with the office and lodge open daily.

Basics

Operated By: George & Kathleen Flint. **Open:** May 15–Sept. 30. **Site Assignment:** Reservations recommended held w/a credit card number. **Registration:** In general store. **Fee:** Tent $17, RV $22 per 2 people, extra child ages 5–11, $1., extra adult $1.50(cash, credit, checks). **Parking:** At site.

Facilities

Number of RV-Only Sites: 50. **Number of Tent-Only Sites:** 50. **Number of Multipurpose Sites:** 75. **Hookups:** Electric (20, 30 amps), water, sewer. **Each Site:** Picnic tables, grated fire pits. **Dump Station:** Yes. **Laundry:** Yes. **Pay Phone:** Yes. **Rest Rooms and Showers:** Yes. **Fuel:** In West Glacier. **Propane:** Yes. **Internal Roads:** Mostly paved, some well-graded gravel. **RV Service:** Mobile Service ask in office. **Market:** In West Glacier. **Restaurant:** Next door & in West Glacier. **General Store:** Yes. **Vending:** General Store only. **Swimming Pool:** No. **Playground:** Yes. **Other:** Pavilion w/kitchen facilities, 5 cabins, level tent pads, beautiful rustic Lodge w/round central fire place & recreation room, large screen TV, area where large dogs may run. **Activities:** Horseshoes, volleyball, basketball, picnic area. **Nearby Attractions:** Glacier National Park, world class fly-fishing (Dolly Verden trout, eastern brook trout, western slope native cut throat, bull trout), white water rafting, helicopter tours, scenic drives, fishing tours, horseback riding, House of Mystery, North American Wildlife Museum. **Additional Information:** Columbia Falls Area Chamber, (406) 892-2072, Glacier National Park (406) 888-7800, or www.areaparks.com.

Restrictions

Pets: Leash only. **Fires:** Fire pits only (fires may be restricted due to dry weather; please ask management before starting any fire.). **Alcoholic Beverages:** Yes. **Vehicle Maximum Length:** 45 ft.-plus.

To Get There

Located directly off Hwy. 2 in West Glacier.

WEST GLACIER

Glacier National Park

Park Headquarters, West Glacier 59936. T: (406) 888-7800; F: (406) 888-7808; www.nps.gov/glac/home.htm; glac_info@nps.gov.

RV ★★★ Tent ★★★★

Beauty: ★★★★★	Site Privacy: ★★★
Spaciousness: ★★★	Quiet: ★★★
Security: ★★★★	Cleanliness: ★★★★
Insect Control: ★★★★	Facilities: ★★★★

Welcome to one of America's most pristine and biodiverse parks. Glacier National Park stretches over a million acres, crosses the Continental Divide, and is home too over 1,000 species of plants and some of the largest and smallest animals found below the Arctic Circle. Glacier National Park offers over 1,000 campsites in varying terrain. You may chose the mature Western Red Cedar and Hemlock Forests found in the west, to rolling grasslands and aspens found in the east. In order to preserve the natural setting and protect its wildlife inhabitants, Glacier National Park does not offer full hookup facilities. There are several dump stations located throughout the park. Most of Glacier's campgrounds are designed in loops, with an amphitheater somewhere in the middle offering evening interpretive programs. The weather in Glacier National Park varies from the east to the west, with more rain in the west, and warmer days in the east. Temperatures in the summer average high 70s for the day and drop into the low 40s during the evening. Remember, however, it can snow any day of the year. Camphosts attend to most campground areas, and rangers are on duty 24 hours a day.

Basics

Operated By: US National Park Service. **Open:** All year, most campsites are open May–the end of Sept.; there is primitive winter camping available. **Site Assignment:** 2 of the 13 campgrounds are reservable (Fish Creek on the west & St Mary on the east); the rest are on a first come basis; (800) 365-2267 or reservations.nps.gov. **Registration:** Register at information bulletin board for the selected campground, only pay 1 night at a time (see camp host for assistance). **Fee:** $12–$17 per night (cash or check). **Parking:** At site.

Facilities

Number of Multipurpose Sites: 13 campgrounds vehicle-accessible w/ a total of 1,019 sites, 2 reservable campgrounds (Fish Creek & St. Mary) 328 sites. **Hookups:** Potable water. **Each Site:** Picnic table, grated fire pits. **Dump Station:** Yes. **Laundry:** Yes, located at the Swift Current Motor Inn in the Many Glacier area of the park also in West Glacier & St. Mary right outside the park gate. **Pay Phone:** Yes in designated service areas, but not individual campgrounds. **Rest Rooms and Showers:** There are rest rooms in all the campgrounds w/many campgrounds having flush toilets. Showers may be taken at the Swiftcurrent Motor Inn in the Many Glacier Area, or the Rising Sun Motor Inn in the Rising Sun Area (purchase shower tokens at any camp store or front desk). **Fuel:** There is no fuel in the park; you may purchase fuel in West Glacier (west entrance) or St. Mary (east entrance), also in Babb, MT; Waterton, Alberta; and Browning, MT. **Propane:** No. **Internal Roads:** Paved, gravel, & dirt. **RV Service:** In West Glacier. **Market:** Apgar, Lake McDonald, West Glacier, St. Mary, or Waterton. **Restaurant:** There are 8 restaurants located in the park, or West Glacier, & St. Mary. **General Store:** There are 10 gift shops/camp stores in the area. **Vending:** Yes in designated service areas, but not in individual campgrounds. **Swimming Pool:** No, but there are lakes & streams available for swimming. **Playground:** No. **Other:** Several boat launches, boat rentals (Lake McDonald, Apgar, Many Glaciers, Two Medicine), picnic areas, amphitheaters, 6 hotels, 10 gift shops, camera & film development shop, 3 visitor centers, many more primitive hike-in camp sites, ATM machines (Apgar, Lake McDonald Lodge, Many Glacier, St. Mary, West Glacier), backcountry lodging (Granite Park Chalet, must have a reservation, (406) 387-5654 or www.ptinet/sperrychalet), worship services (check schedule for the ampitheather & denomination of your choice.). **Activities:** Scenic boat tours (Lake McDonald, Many Glacier, Rising Sun, Two Medicine), 700 mi. of maintained hiking trails & backpacking (permit required), bicycling (only permitted on roadways), horseback riding (Many Glacier & Lake McDonald), interpretive bus tours, scenic Going-to-the-Sun Road (vehicle or vehicle combinations may not be longer than 21 ft. × 8 ft. wide between Avalanche Campground & the Sun Point parking area, the park does offer shuttle service), stream fishing (western slope native cut throat, bull trout, lake trout), world class fly-fishing (Dolly Varden trout, eastern brook trout, arctic grayling), 1–7 day guided backpacking & hiking tours, interpretive programs nightly at the many amphitheaters in the park. **Nearby Attractions:** Whitewater rafting, balloon rides, helicopter tours. **Additional Information:** www.glacierparkinc.com, www.americanparks.net/glaciernationalpark.htm.

Restrictions

Pets: Leashed, or crated only. Pets are not permitted on trails, along lake shores, or in backcountry. **Fires:** In fire pits only; fires maybe restricted due to dry weather; please always ask park official before starting any fire. **Alcoholic Beverages:** Yes w/discretion. **Vehicle Maximum Length:** Apgar 40 ft., Many Glacier, Fish Creek, St. Mary, Two Medicine 35 ft., Avalanche 26 ft., Sprague Creek 21ft. (no tow-in units). **Other:** 7-day limit per camp site; 8 people max. to a site; no more than 2 tents per site; group sites are available; special bike-camping sites are also available for $3 per night per person.

To Get There

West entrance is located off Hwy. 2 in West Glacier 23 mi. northeast of Kalispell; East entrance is located off Hwy. 89 in St. Mary, 17 mi. north of Browning. You may also enter the park in Waterson, Alberta, or off Hwy. 89 in Babb, MT.

WEST YELLOWSTONE
Lionshead RV Resort

1545 Targhee Pass Hwy., West Yellowstone 59758. T: (406) 646-7662

RV ★★★ Tent ★★★

Beauty: ★★★ Site Privacy: ★★★
Spaciousness: ★★★ Quiet: ★★★
Security: ★★★ Cleanliness: ★★
Insect Control: ★★★ Facilities: ★★

Lionshead has a little of everything, including a Super 8 Motel, casino, restaurants, and, of course, an RV park. Located on Denny Creek, the park offers excellent views of the surrounding mountains, and it's only eight miles west of Yellowstone Entrance. With a few exceptions, most of the 168 RV sites are pull-through, with electric, water, and sewer hookups available. Gravel roads wind between the grassy sites, but none of them are overly spacious or too cramped. Outdoor activities include anything imaginable, from whitewater rafting and mountain biking to horseback riding and fishing; winter visitors can cross-country ski or rent one of the resort's snowmobiles to explore the adjacent meadows. For enthusiastic hikers, the Continental Divide National Scenic Trail is close by.

Basics

Operated By: Private Operator. **Open:** Call ahead for details. **Site Assignment:** First come, first served. **Registration:** In camp office. **Fee:** $16–$27.50. **Parking:** At site.

Facilities

Number of RV-Only Sites: 168. **Number of Tent-Only Sites:** 26. **Hookups:** Electric (20, 30, 50 amps), water, sewer. **Each Site:** Picnic table, fire pits in tent sites. **Dump Station:** No. **Laundry:** Yes. **Pay Phone:** Yes. **Rest Rooms and Showers:** Yes. **Fuel:** Yes. **Propane:** Yes. **Internal Roads:** Gravel. **RV Service:** On site (the local RV mobile service is based from this campground). **Market:** In West Yellowstone. **Restaurant:** In West Yellowstone or on site. **General Store:** Yes. **Vending:** Yes. **Swimming Pool:** No. **Playground:** Yes. **Other:** Super 8 Hotel, dance hall, restaurant. **Activities:** Dances, fishing, hiking, book exchange, pool room. **Nearby Attractions:** Yellowstone National Park, IMAX, whitewater rafting, museums, shopping, Grizzly Discovery Center. **Additional Information:** West Yellowstone Chamber of Commerce, (406) 646-7701.

Restrictions

Pets: On leash only. **Fires:** Inquire at campground. **Alcoholic Beverages:** Inquire at campground. **Vehicle Maximum Length:** Call ahead for details.

To Get There

7 mi. west of West Yellowstone on Hwy 20.

WEST YELLOWSTONE
Yellowstone Park/West Entrance KOA

P.O. Box 348, West Yellowstone 59758. T: (406) 646-7606 or (800) 562-7591; F: (406) 646-7606; www.koa.com/where/wy/26122.htm; ypkoa@aol.com.

RV ★★★★ Tent ★★★

Beauty: ★★★★ Site Privacy: ★★★
Spaciousness: ★★★ Quiet: ★★★
Security: ★★★★ Cleanliness: ★★★★
Insect Control: ★★★ Facilities: ★★★★

The perfect base camp for exploring Yellowstone's two million acres, Yellowstone Park KOA offers 166 RV sites and 73 tent-only sites within 6 miles of the west entrance. The newly paved road provides easy access throughout the grounds. Pancake breakfast and a chuckwagon dinner are available daily, in season (mid-June to Labor Day). There's not much campers can't do outside of camp, including hiking, whitewater rafting, and horseback riding. Camp activities include mini-golf, basketball, and horseshoes. Bike rentals are also available. Nearby attractions include the Yellowstone IMAX Theater, Grizzly Discovery Center and Wolf Preserve, and Museum of Yellowstone. A new indoor pool and spa provide comfort for those relaxing after a day of adventuring.

Basics

Operated By: Marvin & Carol Linde. **Open:** May 22–Oct. 1. **Site Assignment:** Reservations highly recommended. **Registration:** General Store. **Fee:** Tent $33, RV $27–$43. **Parking:** At site.

Facilities

Number of RV-Only Sites: 166. **Number of Tent-Only Sites:** 73. **Number of Multipurpose Sites:** 3. **Hookups:** Electric (30, 50 amps), water, sewer. **Each Site:** Picnic table, grated fire pits, some concrete patios. **Dump Station:** Yes. **Laundry:** Yes. **Pay Phone:** Yes. **Rest Rooms and Showers:** Yes. **Fuel:** No. **Propane:** Yes. **Internal Roads:** Paved. **RV Service:** Local service. **Market:** West Yellowstone. **Restaurant:** West Yellowstone (pancake breakfast & BBQ dinners served on site). **General Store:** Yes. **Vending:** Yes. **Swimming Pool:** Indoor pool & hot tub. **Playground:** Yes. **Other:** 58 cabins, camping kitchen, gifts, fresh fudge, Internet data port. **Activities:** Mini-golf, fun cycle & bike rentals, fishing, basketball, game room, Yellowstone tours. **Nearby Attractions:** Yellowstone National Park, IMAX, Museums, Grizzly Discovery Center, white water rafting, Teton Aviation Center, Yellowstone Historic Center. **Additional Information:** West Yellowstone Chamber, (406) 646-7701.

Restrictions

Pets: On leash. **Fires:** In fire pits only. **Alcoholic Beverages:** Yes. **Vehicle Maximum Length:** None.

To Get There

From West Yellowstone, go east 5 mi. on US 20 to the campground entrance.

WHITE SULPHUR SPRINGS
Conestoga Campground

P.O.Box 508, White Sulphur Springs 59645. T: (406) 547-3890; F: (406) 547-3638; www.ccmemberships.com; info@ccmemberships.com.

RV ★★★ Tent ★★★

Beauty: ★★★ Site Privacy: ★★★
Spaciousness: ★★★ Quiet: ★★★★
Security: ★★★★ Cleanliness: ★★★
Insect Control: ★★★ Facilities: ★★★

This privately-owned campground is surrounded by the Big Belt, Little Belt, and Castle Mountains, and offers some of the most magnificent views in North America. While the site facilities are average, the campground's strongest selling point is its location. The campground is nestled between Yellowstone National Park and Glacier National Park, and provides easy access to these national treasures. The campground is also in close proximity to the world-famous Smith River along with numerous mountain lakes and streams filled with various species of fish. The locals boast that this unspoiled part of Montana has more elk and deer than people. There are more than 860 miles of hiking trails in seven mountain ranges. The campground is open from Apr. through Nov., and reservations can be made by phone.

Basics

Operated By: Roy & Linda Reich. **Open:** May 15–Oct. 15. **Site Assignment:** By reservation. **Registration:** In camp office. **Fee:** $21–$25 per 2 people, extra person $3 (special rate plans apply-members). **Parking:** At site.

Facilities

Number of RV-Only Sites: 41. **Number of Tent-Only Sites:** Open tent area. **Hookups:** Electric (20, 30, 50 amps), water, sewer. **Each Site:** Picnic tables. **Dump Station:** Yes. **Laundry:** Yes. **Pay Phone:** Yes. **Rest Rooms and Showers:** Yes. **Fuel:** No, 1 mi. in town. **Propane:** No. **Internal Roads:** Gravel. **RV Service:** Limited service in Townsend. **Market:** In town. **Restaurant:** In town. **General Store:** Yes. **Vending:** Yes. **Swimming Pool:** No. **Playground:** Yes. **Other:** Trout pond, all pull-through sites 25 x 80 ft., water in tent area, free shuttle service to many area activities. **Activities:** Games, picnicking, fishing. **Nearby Attractions:** Golf, teen center, hot mineral baths, many fishing & rafting outfitters, big game hunting, skiing, boating, several museums, Old Fort Logan. **Additional Information:** Meagher County Chamber of Commerce, (406) 547-2250.

Restrictions

Pets: On leash. **Fires:** No open fires. **Alcoholic Beverages:** Yes. **Vehicle Max. Length:** None. **Other:** This is a special membership RV park, please refer to their website or call for more information.

To Get There

66 mi. from I-90 Exit 340, head northeast on US 89 for 57 mi., then go north on US 12 for 9 mi., left onto SR 360 go 0.25 mi. and left or south on 8th Ave. Sw to entrance.

WHITEFISH
Whitefish-Glacier KOA Kampground

5121 Hwy. 93S, Whitefish 59937. T: (406) 862-4242 or (800) 562-8734; F: (406) 862-8967; www.koa.com; whitefishkoa@netscape.net.

RV ★★★★ Tent ★★★★

Beauty: ★★★★ Site Privacy: ★★★
Spaciousness: ★★★ Quiet: ★★★
Security: ★★★★ Cleanliness: ★★★★
Insect Control: ★★★★ Facilities: ★★★★★

Whitefish-Glacier KOA is a superb campground with amenities and activities for the entire family. Nestled in a scenic forest atmosphere two miles south of Whitefish, this campground is located in the Rocky Mountains, near Glacier National Park, the Flathead River, Whitefish Lake, and Big Mountain Ski Resort. The campground offers large comfortable sites, both pull-through and back-in. Tent sites are available in the woods or on a more open lawn area. The park features a large family entertainment center with an indoor/outdoor pool, game room, and pizzeria. The area is famous for its skiing and fishing, and has an abundance of hiking and biking trails (the campground rents bikes). In addition the campground has 10 cabins and a huge recreation hall that accommodates up to 500 people. The weather is cool through late June, so remember to pack warm. The campground offers 24-hour security and the staff is very friendly. Summers fill up quickly, so make reservations as far in advance as possible.

Basics

Operated By: Walt Staves. **Open:** All year. **Site Assignment:** Reservations recommended Apr.–Oct. held w/credit card number. **Registration:** In general store. **Fee:** Tent $20–$24 RV $25.50–$34.50 per 2 people, extra adult $4, children under 17 stay free. KOA Value card discount, & Good Sam honored (cash, credit, checks). **Parking:** At site.

Facilities

Number of RV-Only Sites: 15. **Number of Tent-Only Sites:** Open tent area. **Hookups:** Electric (30, 50 amps), water, sewer. **Each Site:** Picnic table, fire pits. **Dump Station:** No. **Laundry:** Yes, at the courtesy of the host. **Pay Phone:** Courtesy phone available. **Rest Rooms and Showers:** Yes. **Fuel:** About 2 mi. in Silver Star. **Propane:** No. **Internal Roads:** Combination of gravel & packed dirt. **RV Service:** In Butte. **Market:** In Whitefish. **Restaurant:** Buffalo Bob's Pizza Place on property; also in Kalispell or Whitefish. **General Store:** Yes. **Vending:** In restaurant or general store only. **Swimming Pool:** Yes, indoor w/child wading pool (open year-round). **Playground:** Yes. **Other:** Recreation center w/game room, 10 cabins, hot tub, restaurant. **Activities:** Paddle boats, volleyball, horseshoes, basketball, fun cycles, game room, hiking. **Nearby Attractions:** Big Mountain Ski Resort, Whitefish Lake, 18 mi. from Glacier National Park, boating, fishing (whitefish, cut throat), cross-country skiing, snowmobile trails, waterskiing, windsurfing. **Additional Information:** Whitefish Chamber, (406) 862-3501.

Restrictions

Pets: Leash only. **Fires:** Fire pits only (fires may be prohibited due to dry weather: please ask management before starting any fire.). **Alcoholic Beverages:** Yes. **Vehicle Maximum Length:** 40 ft. **Other:** 14 day limit Memorial Day–Labor Day.

To Get There

Located directly off Hwy. 93, 4 mi. south of Whitefish.

WHITEHALL
Pipestone Campground

41 Bluebird Ln., Whitehall 59759. T: (406) 287-5224

RV ★★★ Tent ★★★

Beauty: ★★★ Site Privacy: ★★★
Spaciousness: ★★★ Quiet: ★★★★
Security: ★★★ Cleanliness: ★★★
Insect Control: ★★★ Facilities: ★★★

Located 16 miles east of Butte, just off of I-90, Pipestone Campground has 75 sites that offer a mix of pull-throughs and back-ins, some with complete hookups. The grounds are mostly open with a few scattered trees that provide little shade. Visitors will want to make sure to take advantage of the outdoor hot tub with a view of the snow-capped mountains. Activities such as horseshoes, swimming, tetherball and volleyball can help pass the time time. Those wanting to explore Butte will find several museums and interpretive centers dedicated to mining, including the World Museum of Mining, the Mineral Museum, and the Anselmo Mine Yard.

Basics

Operated By: Dan & Dianna Graves. **Open:** Apr. 1–Oct. 15. **Site Assignment:** Reservations accepted. **Registration:** In general store. **Fee:** $17.25–$21.75. **Parking:** At site.

Facilities

Number of RV-Only Sites: 75. **Number of Tent-Only Sites:** Open tent area. **Hookups:** Electric (20, 30, 50 amps), water, sewer, phone. **Each Site:** Picnic tables, some fire pits. **Dump Station:** Yes. **Laundry:** Yes. **Pay Phone:** Yes. **Rest Rooms and Showers:** Yes. **Fuel:** No. **Propane:** Yes. **Internal Roads:** Gravel, in good condition. **RV Service:** 18 mi. west in Butte. **Market:** 5 mi. east in Whitehall. **Restaurant:** 5 mi. east in Whitehall. **General Store:** Yes. **Vending:** Yes. **Swimming Pool:** Yes. **Playground:** Yes. **Other:** Cabins, RV wash, game room, mail service, large adult spa, Internet data port on pay phone. **Activities:** Swimming, campfires, volleyball, tetherball, horseshoes. **Nearby Attractions:** Fishing (rainbow trout), hunting, float trips, fishing tours. **Additional Information:** Whitehall Chamber of Commerce, (406) 287-2260.

Restrictions

Pets: On leash. **Fires:** In fire pits only (fires may be restricted due to weather; please ask management before starting any open fires.). **Alcoholic Beverages:** Yes. **Vehicle Maximum Length:** None.

To Get There

I-90 Exit 241, 16 mi. east of Butte, can be seen from interstate.

WOLF CREEK
Lake Holter Recreation Area

1383 Beartooth Rd., Wolf Creek 59648. T: (406) 494-5059; F: (406) 235-4314; www.mt.blm.gov.

RV ★★★ Tent ★★★

Beauty: ★★★ Site Privacy: ★★★
Spaciousness: ★★★ Quiet: ★★★
Security: ★★★ Cleanliness: ★★★
Insect Control: ★★★ Facilities: ★★★

Approximately 35 miles north of Helena, the highlight of this recreation area is its proximity to Holter Lake. With 56 grassy sites located on the lake, there is a good chance you might be able to enjoy some lakefront camping. The area provides plenty of opportunity for recreational activities, including hiking, horseback riding, and fishing. Gravel access and interior roads, scant landscaping, a propensity for high winds, and sparsely wooded surrounding hills make this campground wanting of scenery. However, this might well be a worthwhile stop for any avid fisher. Lake Holter, located on the Missouri River, is home to walleye, and the "Mighty Mo," known worldwide for its dry fly-fishing, runs wild with brown and rainbow trout. Definitely, this is a destination spot for a pleasing fishing experience.

Basics

Operated By: Bureau of Land Management. **Open:** All year. **Site Assignment:** First come, first served. **Registration:** Self serve. **Fee:** $8 per unit. **Parking:** At site.

Facilities

Number of Multipurpose Sites: 140. **Hookups:** Water. **Each Site:** Picnic tables, fire pits. **Dump Station:** Yes at Holter Lake Lodge for a fee. **Laundry:** No. **Pay Phone:** Yes. **Rest Rooms and Showers:** Rest rooms only. **Fuel:** No. **Propane:** No. **Internal Roads:** Gravel. **RV Service:** Limited local service. **Market:** In town. **Restaurant:** Next door. **General Store:** No. **Vending:** No. **Swimming Pool:** No, but there is a beach on the lake. **Playground:** Yes. **Other:** Lake access, covered pavilion, lodge, 3 designated swimming areas, 2 multi-laned boat ramps, docks w/about 60 slips. **Activities:** Swimming, fishing, boating, jet skiing, waterskiing. **Nearby Attractions:** Several vacation ranches, blue ribbon fishing, the state capital, horseback riding, natural hot springs, ghost towns, Helena. **Additional Information:** Helena Chamber of Commerce, (406) 442-4120.

Restrictions

Pets: On leash. **Fires:** In fire pits only. **Alcoholic Beverages:** Yes. **Vehicle Maximum Length:** None. **Other:** 14 day stay limit.

To Get There

Take Exit 226 at Wolf Creek and follow Recreation Frontage Rd. northeast about 3 mi., then 2 mi. east on gravel road.

Nebraska

A motor coach, a bike, and a good horse are the best ways to experience Nebraska, America's gateway to the west. The most famous stories of adventure and transcontinental travel take you through the byways of Nebraska. Fur traders of the past navigated through this high plains state to avoid the mountain passes of Colorado as they ventured toward the Pacific. Famous trails such as the **Lewis and Clark, Oregon,** and **Mormon Trails** pass through this state. Nebraska was used for the first transcontinental railroad, as well as the Pony Express. Nebraska in many ways is a living museum. Every scenic byway tells a story and adds another piece to the puzzle of our American heritage. From the **Great Platte River Road Archway** to the famous **Oregon Trail Chimney Rock** landmark, the past comes alive.

Nebraska is also an outdoor enthusiast's paradise. The rivers and streams of Nebraska offer a variety of adventures. Whether you enjoy paddling, rafting, waterskiing, or sitting on the dock, there is a river for you, and if you are a serious angler, the waters of Nebraska are full of walleye, trout, and bass. If you enjoy biking and are looking for a wide-open scenic route, look no further. Nebraska has hundreds of miles of biking trails. You can pedal complete sections of the **Cowboy Trail** linking **Norfolk** and **Chadron,** or bike along the Platte River. And if you are an equestrian the trails are equally limitless. There are professional outfitters throughout the state, and the Nebraska state parks are wonderful base camps.

The state offers more than just the ruggedness of the west, however. There is a refined side of Nebraska as well—one devoted to the fine arts, offering world-class art museums of frontier paintings, sculptured gardens, symphonies, and theatre.

Recreational camping is the best way to see and experience the adventures Nebraska has to offer. The majority of full-service campgrounds are located of I-80, but you have to venture away from the interstate to fully appreciate the landscape and history. For impressive vistas of sweeping natural beauty, Nebraska state parks and recreation areas are some of the best in the country.

Campground Profiles

ASHLAND

Eugene T. Mahoney State Park

28500 West Park Hwy., Ashland 68003. T: (402) 944-2523; F: (402) 944-7604; www.ngpc.state.ne.us; etmsp@ngpc.state.ne.us.

RV ★★★ Tent ★★★

Beauty: ★★★ Site Privacy: ★★★
Spaciousness: ★★★ Quiet: ★★★★
Security: ★★★★ Cleanliness: ★★★
Insect Control: ★★★ Facilities: ★★

Offering large, shady sites near Owen Marina Lake, camping in Eugene T. Mahoney State Park can be enjoyed year-round. It is easily accessible due to its I-80 location midway between Lincoln and Omaha. For campers who don't want to travel far for activities, this is the place to be, with everything from a water slide to a new virtual reality game room within the park. Winter recreation pursuits include ice skating from Nov. through Mar. in the Pavilion, fishing in the 10-acre, trout-stocked US West Lake, and downhill sledding. The centrally located theatre provides family fun with melodramas that run from Memorial Day weekend thru early November. Next door to the park is the new Strategic Air and Space Museum, the nation's foremost facility of its kind, with aircraft and missile exhibits.

Basics

Operated By: Nebraska Game & Parks Commission. **Open:** All year. **Site Assignment:** First come, first served. **Registration:** Self-serve registration kiosks. **Fee:** $11–$12 depends on site & amenities, plus vehicle entrance fee. **Parking:** At site.

Facilities

Number of RV-Only Sites: 149. **Number of Tent-Only Sites:** 24. **Hookups:** Electric (20, 30 amps), water. **Each Site:** Picnic tables, fire pit. **Dump Station:** Yes, there is also a boat pump out on the marina. **Laundry:** Yes. **Pay Phone:** Yes. **Rest Rooms and Showers:** Yes. **Fuel:** Boat fuel only at the marina. **Propane:** No. **Internal Roads:** Paved. **RV Service:** 17 mi. in Elkhorn. **Market:** In Ashland. **Restaurant:** Peter Kiewit Lodge on site, the mariana, or in Ashland. **General Store:** The marina is open Memorial Day through Labor Day. **Vending:** Yes. **Swimming Pool:** Yes. **Playground:** Yes. **Other:** 51 cabin, 40 room lodge w/ full-service restaurant, water slide, hiking trails, 10 picnic shelters, one w/ electricity, fish-cleaning station, full service marina, Kountz Memorial Theater, observation tower, visitor center, indoor activity center, boat rental. **Activities:** Swimming, water slide, mini-golf, boating, fishing, hiking, arts & crafts, rock climbing simulator, indoor playground, hunting simulator, ball simulator, ice skating, picnics, driving range. **Nearby Attractions:** Gavins Point Dam, Lewis & Clark Visitor Center, The National Fish Hatchery, Lakeview Golf Course. **Additional Information:** Gretna Chamber of Commerce, (402) 332-3535.

Restrictions

Pets: On leash. **Fires:** In grills or fire pits only. **Alcoholic Beverages:** No alcoholic beverages allowed. **Vehicle Maximum Length:** 45 ft. **Other:** Nebraska State Park passes honored.

To Get There

From I-80 Exit 426, go northwest on W. Park Hwy. then bear right on Park Dr.

CHADRON

Chadron State Park

15951 Hwy. 385, Chadron 69337-7353. T: (308) 432-6167; F: (308)432-6102; www.ngpc.state.ne.us; chadronsp@ngpc.state.ne.us.

 ★★★  ★★★

Beauty: ★★★ Site Privacy: ★★★
Spaciousness: ★★★ Quiet: ★★★★
Security: ★★★★ Cleanliness: ★★★
Insect Control: ★★★ Facilities: ★★

Situated near the Nebraska National Forest, Chadron State Park guarantees exceptional scenery. The fees are very reasonable, and there are no reservations required. The sites for both RVs and tents are average sized, with picnic tables and fire pits. The campground offers only adequate privacy, but there's lots of peace and quiet. As for activities available, Chadron has some very unusual and interesting pastimes for the family. There is an old-time fur trade demonstration, and arts and crafts, as well as archery, tennis, and a buffalo stew cookout by appointment. Nearby, guests will find the Dawes County Historical Museum, biking, and golf.

Basics

Operated By: Nebraska Game & Parks Commission. **Open:** All year. **Site Assignment:** First come, first served. **Registration:** Self-serve registration kiosks. **Fee:** $3–$12 depends on site & amenities, plus vehicle entrance fee. **Parking:** At site.

Facilities

Number of RV-Only Sites: 70. **Number of Tent-Only Sites:** 18. **Hookups:** Electric (20, 30 amps), water. **Each Site:** Picnic tables, fire pit. **Dump Station:** Yes. **Laundry:** Yes. **Pay Phone:** Yes. **Rest Rooms and Showers:** Yes. **Fuel:** No. **Propane:** No. **Internal Roads:** Paved. **RV Service:** In town. **Market:** In town. **Restaurant:** There is a large variety of restaurant in town. **General Store:** Yes. **Vending:** Yes. **Swimming Pool:** Yes. **Playground:** Yes. **Other:** 22 cabins, hiking trails, biking trails, horseback riding, fishing pond, large picnic shelter w/ electricity, several hundred picnic tables & grills. **Activities:** Archery, horseback riding, old time fur trade demonstration, arts & crafts, Jeep rides, volleyball, tennis, fishing, Buffalo Stew Cookouts by appointment. **Nearby Attractions:** Museum of the fur trade, Nebraska National Forest, Dawes County Historical Museum, biking, golf. **Additional Information:** Chadron Chamber, (308) 432-4401.

Restrictions

Pets: On leash. **Fires:** In grills or fire pits only. **Alcoholic Beverages:** No alcoholic beverages allowed. **Vehicle Maximum Length:** 45 ft. **Other:** Nebraska State Park passes honored.

To Get There

From Chadron, take South Hwy. 385 for 8.4 mi., turn right on to park road.

CRAWFORD

Fort Robinson State Park

P.O.Box 392, Crawford 69339-0392. T: (308) 665-2900; F: (308)665-2906; www.ngpc.state.ne.us; ftrobsp@ngpc.state.ne.us.

★★★ ★★★

Beauty: ★★★ Site Privacy: ★★★
Spaciousness: ★★★ Quiet: ★★★★
Security: ★★★★ Cleanliness: ★★★
Insect Control: ★★★ Facilities: ★★

Fort Robinson State Park is a place in western tradition, made famous by men such Walter Reed and Red Cloud. The fort was established in 1874 as an active military post and remained so for the next 74 years. Today, Fort Robinson State Park is a living museum. Train, horseback, and jeep tours help tell of this western heritage. The park greets its visitors with resort-like accommodations with lodging and modern camping available. The internal roads are paved, and the campground offers large, paved camping spurs, well separated from neighbors. The park works hard at keeping the facilities clean and the lawn manicured. There are variety of activities taking place in the park and the surrounding area. Camping is on a first come, first served basis, so be sure to arrive early in order to get a site. There is full restaurant service in the Fort Robinson Inn during the summer. All visitor mush register at the entrance gate and pay an entrance fee.

Basics

Operated By: Nebraska Game & Parks Commission. **Open:** The park is open year-round, camping Apr.–Nov. **Site Assignment:** First come, first served. **Registration:** Self-serve registration kiosks. **Fee:** $8–$12 depends on site & amenities, plus vehicle entrance fee. **Parking:** At site.

Facilities

Number of RV-Only Sites: 100. **Number of Tent-Only Sites:** 25. **Hookups:** Electric (20, 30, 50 amps), water. **Each Site:** Picnic tables, fire pit. **Dump Station:** Yes. **Laundry:** Yes. **Pay Phone:** Yes. **Rest Rooms and Showers:** Yes. **Fuel:** No. **Propane:** No. **Internal Roads:** Paved. **RV Service:** 60 mi. in Scottsbluff. **Market:** In Crawford. **Restaurant:** At the lodge, or Sutler's Store on site (Memorial Day through Labor Day) or in town. **General Store:** Yes, Sutler's Store, Mem. Day–Labor Day. **Vending:** Yes. **Swimming Pool:** Yes. **Playground:** Yes. **Other:** 35 cabins, 22-room lodge w/ restaurant, hiking trails, 4 picnic shelters, one w/ electricity, Fort Robinson Museum, trailside museum, meeting facilities, historic tours, bike rentals, over 100 picnic tables & grills, modern horse stable (boarding available). **Activities:** Swimming, boating, fishing, hiking, horseback riding, (22,000 acres of horse trails), Jeep rides, Craft Center, horse drawn tour train, stagecoach rides, pony rides, rodeo. **Additional Information:** Chadron Chamber, (308) 432-4401.

Restrictions

Pets: On leash. **Fires:** In grills or fire pits only. **Alcoholic Beverages:** No alcoholic beverages allowed. **Vehicle Maximum Length:** 45 ft. **Other:** Nebraska State Park passes honored.

To Get There

Off US 20 about 8 mi. west of Crawford.

CROFTON

Lewis and Clark State Recreation Area

5473 897 Rd., Crofton 68730-3290. T: (402) 388-4169; F: (402) 388-4696; www.ngpc.state.ne.us; lcsra@ngpc.state.ne.us.

Beauty: ★★★ Site Privacy: ★★★
Spaciousness: ★★★ Quiet: ★★★★
Security: ★★★★ Cleanliness: ★★★
Insect Control: ★★★ Facilities: ★★

Straddling the northeast border with South Dakota, Lewis and Clark Lake offers a good place to fish and relax. On the Nebraska side of the lake, the recreation area is roughly divided into five parts. The Weigand-Burbach area is the most developed, featuring most of the campsites (electric hookups, pull-throughs, some tent camping, etc.), a full-service marina, convenience store, swimming beach, and other amenities. This is the first choice of most campers. Bloomfield is smaller and more secluded, with about 30 campsites with electric hookups, modern and primitive rest rooms, and a boat ramp; this is an acceptable second option if Weigand-Burbach is full or if you just want fewer neighbors. The Miller Creek and South Shore areas are primitive camping only, offering primitive rest rooms and boat ramps. The Deep Water area is nothing more than an access point with a parking lot.

Basics

Operated By: Nebraska Game & Parks Commission. **Open:** Year-round. **Site Assignment:** First come, first served. **Registration:** Self-serve registration kiosks, a few sites are reservable. **Fee:** $3–$12, plus vehicle entrance fee. **Parking:** At site.

Facilities

Number of RV-Only Sites: 150. **Number of Tent-Only Sites:** 45. **Number of Multipurpose Sites:** 50. **Hookups:** Electric (20, 30 amps), water. **Each Site:** Picnic tables, fire pit. **Dump Station:** Yes, there is also a boat pump out on the marina. **Laundry:** Yes. **Pay Phone:** Yes. **Rest Rooms and Showers:** Yes. **Fuel:** Boat fuel only at the marina. **Propane:** No. **Internal Roads:** Paved. **RV Service:** 10 mi. in Yankton, SD. **Market:** In Yankton, SD. **Restaurant:** There is one restaurant in Crofton, but there are several in Yankton, SD. **General Store:** The marina is open Memorial Day through Labor Day. **Vending:** Yes. **Swimming Pool:** Yes. **Playground:** Yes. **Other:** Swimming beach, 5 cabins, 4 boat ramps, 16 docks, 80 boat slips, boat fuel, marina, fish-cleaning station, picnic shelter w/electricity, over 200 picnic table & grills. **Nearby Attractions:** Gavins Point Dam, Lewis & Clark Visitor Center, the National Fish Hatchery, Lakeview Golf Course. **Additional Information:** Bloomfield City Clerk, (402) 373-4396.

Restrictions

Pets: On leash. **Fires:** In grills or fire pits only. **Alcoholic Beverages:** No alcoholic beverages allowed. **Vehicle Maximum Length:** 45 ft. **Other:** Nebraska State Park passes honored.

To Get There

From Crofton, drive north on Rte. 121 for 15 mi. Park entrance is on the left.

GOTHENBURG

Gothenburg KOA

P.O.Box 385, Gothenburg 69139. T: (308) 537-7387 or (800) 562-1873; www.koa.com.

Beauty: ★★ Site Privacy: ★★
Spaciousness: ★★ Quiet: ★★★
Security: ★★★ Cleanliness: ★★★
Insect Control: ★★★ Facilities: ★★★

This KOA campground is located off I-80 Exit 211, a quarter of a mile south on Hwy. 47. This KOA is best used as an overnight stop. The RV and tent sites are not very spacious or private, and the facilities are merely adequate. However, the sites are nicely shaded with trees, and the Platte River provides excellent opportunities for fishing. The Campground is situated in close proximity to the Pony Express Station, Buffalo Bill's Guest Ranch. and the Sod House Museum. The campground is open from March to November, with sites assigned in advance through either phone or web reservations. KOA discount member rates apply.

Basics

Operated By: Private operator. **Open:** Mar. 15–Nov. 15. **Site Assignment:** By reservation. **Registration:** At convenience store. **Fee:** Tent $16–$20 RV $20–$28. per 2 people. **Parking:** At site.

Facilities

Number of RV-Only Sites: 33. **Number of Tent-Only Sites:** 15. **Number of Multipurpose Sites:** 14. **Hookups:** Electric (20, 30, 50 amps), water, sewer. **Each Site:** Picnic tables, few grills. **Dump Station:** Yes. **Laundry:** Yes. **Pay Phone:** Yes. **Rest Rooms and Showers:** Yes. **Fuel:** Yes. **Propane:** Yes. **Internal Roads:** Combination of gravel & pavement. **RV Service:** 33 mi. in North Platte. **Market:** Local. **Restaurant:** Local. **General Store:** Yes. **Vending:** General Store only. **Swimming Pool:** Yes. **Playground:** Yes. **Other:** Cabins, nature trail, Internet data port. **Activities:** Horseshoes, nature walk, swimming. **Nearby Attractions:** Pony Express Station, Sod House Museum. **Additional Information:** Gothenburg Chamber, (308) 537-3505.

Restrictions

Pets: On leash. **Fires:** No open fires, charcoal fires in grills only. **Alcoholic Beverages:** Yes. **Vehicle Maximum Length:** None.

To Get There

Off I-80 Exit 211, 0.25 mi. south on Hwy. 47.

HASTINGS

Hastings Campground

302 East 26th St., Hastings 68901. T: (402) 462-5621; F: (402) 461-3892; billgilliland@inebraska.com.

RV ★★★ Tent ★★★

Beauty: ★★★ Site Privacy: ★★★
Spaciousness: ★★★ Quiet: ★★★
Security: ★★★★ Cleanliness: ★★★
Insect Control: ★★★ Facilities: ★★★

Located on the north edge of town, Hastings Campground has a semi-rural location situated among the cornfields. The 48 RV sites have hookups available, and the 15 tent-only sites round out the campground's offerings. There isn't any shade, but the owners have planted numerous trees to improve this new campground for future years. There are numerous outdoor recreation areas within easy driving distance (many located along the I-80 corridor), though most are fairly small. Hastings' main draws are its cultural and sports offerings. Numerous softball tournaments occur here, including the state championships, and the nearby Champions Sports and Recreation Center offers fun for the family as well as fitness buffs. Hastings also has the only symphony between Lincoln and Denver, and the Hastings Museum offers explorations into cultural and natural history, as well as an IMAX theater and planetarium. And those who remember drinking Kool-Aid as kids will by happy to know that the sweet, summer concoction got its start here.

Basics

Operated By: Bill & Dorothy Gilliland. **Open:** Year-round. **Site Assignment:** By reservation, held on credit card number. **Registration:** Camp Office. **Fee:** Tent $16.75, RV $18.90–$22.16 per unit (cash, credit, check). **Parking:** At site.

Facilities

Number of RV-Only Sites: 48. **Number of Tent-Only Sites:** 15. **Hookups:** Electric (20, 30, 50 amps), water, sewer, cable tv. **Each Site:** Picnic tables. **Dump Station:** Yes. **Laundry:** Yes. **Pay Phone:** Yes. **Rest Rooms and Showers:** Yes. **Fuel:** No. **Propane:** No. **Internal Roads:** Gravel. **RV Service:** On site or 25 mi. in Grand Island. **Market:** In town. **Restaurant:** In town. **General Store:** Yes. **Vending:** No. **Swimming Pool:** Yes & two hot tubs. **Playground:** Yes. **Other:** TV room, RV wash, wild flower garden, arcade room, 3 cabins, horseshoes, storm shelter. **Activities:** Swimming, coin games, horseshoes. **Nearby Attractions:** Hastings Fun Park, Imax, Pioneer Village. **Additional Information:** Hastings Chamber of Commerce, (402) 462-4159.

Restrictions

Pets: On leash. **Fires:** In grills or fire pits only. **Alcoholic Beverages:** Yes. **Vehicle Maximum Length:** None. **Other:** Good Sam, AAA, KOA.

To Get There

From I-80 Exit 312, go south on US 34 for 14.6 mi., turn left into South Shore Dr., and continue east on CR 80 (East 26th St.) about 300 yards.

HENDERSON

Prairie Oasis

913 Rd. B, Henderson 68371. T: (402) 723-4310; prairie@telcoweb.net.

RV ★★★ Tent ★★★

Beauty: ★★★ Site Privacy: ★★
Spaciousness: ★★ Quiet: ★★★
Security: ★★★ Cleanliness: ★★★
Insect Control: ★★★ Facilities: ★★★

Located in Henderson, the Prairie Oasis is a pleasant and relaxing campground, especially at night. The campground offers 70 full-service pull-through sites, all of which are level and gravel. The campsites have nice lawns, and there are several large shade trees on the property. There is an open area used to accommodate larger RVs. A separate tent area is next to a swing set, with lush grass and good shade. There is a lake for fishing on the property, and four lakeside tent sites. The campground has one cabin, a small store, and a recreation room. The weather here is dry but comfortable most of the time. There are several historic attractions to see in the area. The campground staff is friendly and helpful, and fuel service is just around the corner.

Basics

Operated By: Jacque & Valerie Stunich. **Open:** Apr.–Oct. **Site Assignment:** By reservation, held on credit card number. **Registration:** Camp Office. **Fee:** $18–$24 per two people. **Parking:** At site.

Facilities

Number of RV-Only Sites: 58. **Number of Tent-Only Sites:** 16. **Hookups:** Electric (20, 30, 50 amps), water, sewer. **Each Site:** Picnic tables, some grills. **Dump Station:** Yes. **Laundry:** Yes. **Pay Phone:** Yes. **Rest Rooms and Showers:** Yes. **Fuel:** No. **Propane:** No. **Internal Roads:** Gravel, in fair condition. **RV Service:** 30 mi. west in Grand Island. **Market:** 9 mi. east of York. **Restaurant:** 9 mi. east in York. **General Store:** Yes. **Vending:** No. **Swimming Pool:** No. **Playground:** Yes. **Other:** Fishing pond, camp store, free morning coffee. **Activities:** Fishing, volleyball, horseshoes, softball. **Nearby Attractions:** Lake View Park, golf. **Additional Information:** Henderson Chamber of Commerce, (402) 723-4228.

Restrictions

Pets: On leash. **Fires:** In grills or fire pits only. **Alcoholic Beverages:** Yes. **Vehicle Maximum Length:** None. **Other:** FMCA discount.

To Get There

Off I-80 Exit 342, go 3 mi. south on Rte. 93A to Henderson. Rte. 93A becomes 17th St. through Henderson, then Rd. B as you leave downtown. Campground is on the right.

LINCOLN

Camp A Way

200 Ogden Rd., Lincoln 68521. T: (402) 476-2282 or 866 -719-CAMP; www.camp-a-way.com; jqueen@neb.rr.com.

RV ★★★ Tent ★★★

Beauty: ★★★ Site Privacy: ★★
Spaciousness: ★★ Quiet: ★★★
Security: ★★★ Cleanliness: ★★★★
Insect Control: ★★★ Facilities: ★★★

Located in the heart of Lincoln, Camp A Way is a pleasant metropolitan campground. Camp A Way is also a full-service RV park with an array of amenities. The campground offers 50-amp service, free cable, and phone hookups. There are plenty of large shade trees and nice-sized camping sites. Many of the sites are a combination of dirt and gravel, so some are more level than others. There are two sets of rest rooms in the campground; the set closest to the office is well kept and clean, whereas those in the rear needed some attention when we visited. Lincoln is the capital of Nebraska and a cultural center for the state. The community offers a variety of events, festivals, and celebrations, as well as fine restaurants, shopping, historical sites, and a zoo. There is also wonderful fishing and hiking in the area. The staff at Camp A Way is very welcoming.

Basics

Operated By: Jacque & Valerie Stunich. **Open:** Year-round. **Site Assignment:** By reservation, held on credit card number. **Registration:** Camp office. **Fee:** Tent $18, RV $18–$26.50 per 2 people, extra adult $2. (cash, credit, check). **Parking:** At site.

Facilities

Number of RV-Only Sites: 73. **Number of Tent-Only Sites:** 5. **Number of Multipurpose Sites:** 8. **Hookups:** Electric (20, 30, 50 amps), water, sewer, tv, phone. **Each Site:** Picnic tables, some grills & fire rings. **Dump Station:** Yes. **Laundry:** Yes. **Pay Phone:** Yes. **Rest Rooms and Showers:** Yes. **Fuel:** No. **Propane:** No. **Internal Roads:** Gravel, in good condition. **RV Service:** Local service. **Market:** Local. **Restaurant:** Local. **General Store:** Yes. **Vending:** Yes. **Swimming Pool:** Yes. **Playground:** Yes. **Activities:** Game room, swimming, basketball, horseshoes. **Nearby Attractions:** State Capitol Building, Devaney Center, zoo, National Museum of Roller Skating, Sheldon Art Gallery. **Additional Information:** Lincoln Chamber of Commerce, (402) 436-2350.

Restrictions

Pets: On leash. **Fires:** In grills or fire pits only. **Alcoholic Beverages:** Yes. **Vehicle Maximum Length:** None.

To Get There

Off I-80 Exit 401, corner of 1st and Superior St.

LINCOLN

Branched Oak State Recreation Area

RR 2 Box 61, Raymond 68428. T: (402) 783-3400; F: (402) 783-0361; www.ngpc.state.ne.us; kinnamon@ngpc.state.ne.us.

RV ★★★ Tent ★★★

Beauty: ★★★ Site Privacy: ★★★
Spaciousness: ★★★ Quiet: ★★★★
Security: ★★★★ Cleanliness: ★★★
Insect Control: ★★★ Facilities: ★★

The largest of the Salt Valley areas, Branched Oak has nine camping areas spread out around a lake which stretches for almost four miles. Sites in the new campground are set in a straight line overlooking the lake. Trees are behind the sites, but they're too far away to provide much in the way of shade. Visitors with horses can use the three-mile multi-use trail on the south side of Branched Oak Lake and camp with their horses in Area 3. The 800-acre dog trail (about a mile from Area 9) has championship events, so call ahead for a schedule to avoid the crowds. Anglers will enjoy the variety of fish found in the lake, including bluegill, largemouth bass, and catfish. The recreation area is also classified as a wildlife management area, so hunters arrive in the fall to hunt pheasants, quail, doves, and ducks.

Basics

Operated By: Nebraska Game & Parks Commission. **Open:** Year-round. **Site Assignment:** First come, first served. **Registration:** Self-serve registration kiosks, or by reservation, $3 fee. **Fee:** $3–$12, plus vehicle entrance fee. **Parking:** At site.

Facilities

Number of RV-Only Sites: 206. **Number of Tent-Only Sites:** 287. **Number of Multipurpose Sites:** 71. **Hookups:** Electric (20, 30 amps), water. **Each Site:** Picnic tables, fire pit. **Dump Station:** Yes. **Laundry:** No. **Pay Phone:** Yes. **Rest Rooms and Showers:** Yes in areas one, four & at the pool. **Fuel:** Yes. **Propane:** Yes. **Internal Roads:** Paved. **RV Service:** in Lincoln. **Market:** in Lincoln. **Restaurant:** On site at the Marine or in Lincoln. **General Store:** Yes at the Marina. **Vending:** Yes. **Swimming Pool:** Yes. **Playground:** Yes. **Other:** 9 boat ramps, 49 fishing, 41 picnic shelters w/ over 600 picnic tables & grills. **Activities:** Fishing (walleye, blue gill, blue catfish, largemouth bass), boating, waterskiing, hiking, biking. **Nearby Attractions:** Lincoln Nebraska, shopping, golf, museums, movies. **Additional Information:** Lincoln Chamber of Commerce, (402) 436-2350.

Restrictions

Pets: On leash. **Fires:** In grills or fire pits only. **Alcoholic Beverages:** No alcoholic beverages allowed. **Vehicle Maximum Length:** 45 ft. **Other:** Nebraska State Park passes honored.

To Get There

From I-80 Exit 388, go north on SR 103 for 5.5 mi., then east on US 34 for 1 mi. Take NW 140 St. for 6 mi. and then turn right (east) onto West Branched Oak Rd. for 1.6 mi. and follow signs into park.

NIOBRARA

Niobrara State Park

P.O.Box 226, Niobrara 68760-0226. T: (402) 857-3373; F: (402) 857-3420; www.ngpc.state.ne.us; nsp@ngpc.state.ne.us.

RV ★★★ Tent ★★★★

Beauty: ★★★ Site Privacy: ★★★
Spaciousness: ★★★ Quiet: ★★★★
Security: ★★★★ Cleanliness: ★★★
Insect Control: ★★★ Facilities: ★★

Niobrara State Park is situated at the confluence of the Niobrara and Missouri Rivers on Nebraska's northeastern border. Visitors at this park have an opportunity to sample a wide range of outdoor recreation, including horseback trail rides, hiking, and fishing. The park offers numerous opportunities to observe wildlife such as white-tailed deer, wild turkeys, beavers, muskrats, and mink. The camping area extends along three miles of an extremely hilly, winding, one-way road, and it's interspersed with stands of elm, hackberry, and ash. Many sites are situated on elevated hills adjacent to the Niobrara River. The park is open year-round, although modern facilities, including cabins, are open from mid-April through mid-November. Reservations for all campsites may be made up to one year in advance.

Basics

Operated By: Nebraska Game & Parks Commission. **Open:** Year-round. **Site Assignment:** First come, first served. **Registration:** Self-serve registration kiosks. **Fee:** $8–$12 plus vehicle entrance fee. **Parking:** At site.

Facilities

Number of RV-Only Sites: 69. **Number of Tent-Only Sites:** 50. **Hookups:** Electric (20, 30 amps), water. **Each Site:** Picnic tables, fire pit. **Dump Station:** Yes. **Laundry:** Yes. **Pay Phone:** Yes. **Rest Rooms and Showers:** Yes. **Fuel:** No. **Propane:** No. **Internal Roads:** Paved. **RV Service:** 30 mi. in Yanton, SD. **Market:** In town. **Restaurant:** In town. **General Store:** No. **Vending:** Yes. **Swimming Pool:** Yes. **Playground:** Yes. **Other:** 19 cabins, hiking trails, 9 picnic shelters, two w/ electricity, over 160 acres open for horseback riding, over 100 picnic tables & grills, 3 boat ramps, mountain bike trails, hiking trails. **Activities:** Swimming, boating, fishing, hiking, horseback riding, (160 acres of horse trails), guided float trips. **Nearby Attractions:** Smith Falls, golf, Ashfall State Historic site. **Additional Information:** Creighton Area Chamber of Commerce, (402) 358-3737.

Restrictions

Pets: On leash. **Fires:** In grills or fire pits only. **Alcoholic Beverages:** No alcoholic beverages allowed. **Vehicle Maximum Length:** 45 ft. **Other:** Nebraska State Park passes honored.

To Get There

The campground is about 3 mi. west of Niobrara on SR 12.

PONCA

Ponca State Park

88119 Spur 26-E, Ponca 68770. T: (402) 755-2284; F: (402) 755-2593; www.ngpc.state.ne.us; poncasp@ngpc.state.ne.us.

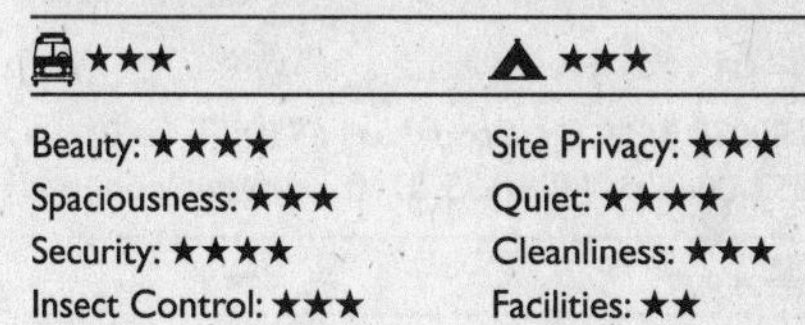

RV ★★★ Tent ★★★

Beauty: ★★★★ Site Privacy: ★★★
Spaciousness: ★★★ Quiet: ★★★★
Security: ★★★★ Cleanliness: ★★★
Insect Control: ★★★ Facilities: ★★

As you would expect from a state-operated park in this area, Ponca State Park is well run and situated in the midst of gorgeous scenery. The fees are very reasonable, and the available sites medium sized. Even though the camping area is fairly large, the sites still afford privacy and quiet for all guests. The biggest surprise regarding this park is the list of activities. Over and above the usual, Ponca offers golf, archery, waterskiing, hunting, and a special fishing clinic for the children on Sundays. The surrounding area isn't a disappointment either. Nearby, visitors to the park can hike the Lewis and Clark Trail; hunt deer, turkey, or duck; or stop by the Mid America Air Museum. Overall, this is a wonderful place to stay, and reservations are not required.

Basics

Operated By: Nebraska Game & Parks Commission. **Open:** Mid-Apr.–mid-Nov. **Site Assignment:** First come, first served. **Registration:** Camp Office. **Fee:** $8 without hookups, $11–$12 w/ hookups, plus vehicle fee. **Parking:** At site.

Facilities

Number of RV-Only Sites: 75. **Number of Tent-Only Sites:** 72. **Number of Multipurpose Sites:** 10. **Hookups:** Electric (20, 30, 50 amps), water. **Each Site:** Picnic tables, fire pit. **Dump Station: Yes. **Laundry:** No. **Pay Phone:** Yes. **Rest Rooms and Showers:** Yes. **Fuel:** No. **Propane:** No. **Internal Roads:** Paved in good condition. **RV Service:** 14 mi. in Sioux City. **Market:** Local or Sioux City. **Restaurant:** There are two restaurants in Ponca, or Sioux City. **General Store:** No. **Vending:** Yes. **Swimming Pool:** Yes (you may not swim in the river). **Playground:** Yes. **Other:** Lodge, 14 modern cabins, covered picnic shelters, boat ramps, scenic overlook, horse barn, horse trails, hiking trails, biking trails, golf course. **Activities:** Swimming, horseback riding, golf, fishing, hiking, organized activities Memorial weekend through Labor day, children fishing clinics on Sunday, boating, canoeing, rafting, waterskiing & tubing, archery range, outdoor education naturalist program. **Nearby Attractions:** Missouri River, Lewis & Clark Trail w/ 17 mi. of hiking trails, deer, pheasant, duck & turkey hunting, Mid America Air Museum, Sgt Floyd River Museum. **Additional Information:** Ponca Chamber of Commerce, (402) 755-2224.

Restrictions

Pets: Yes, w/ a 6 ft.- or under leash. **Fires:** In approved areas & fire pit. **Alcoholic Beverages:** No alcoholic beverages allowed in the State Park. **Vehicle Maximum Length:** 45 ft. **Other:** Annual vehicle passes accepted.

To Get There

From I-29 Exit 144B, go west on US 75, which becomes US 20. Turn right on SR 12 go 12.5 mi. and follow signs into park (campground is 32.5 mi. from Sioux City and I-29).

SCOTTSBLUFF

Scottsbluff KOA

180037 KOA Dr., Scottsbluff 69361. T: (800) 562-0845 or (308)635-3760; www.koa.com.

RV ★★★ Tent ★★★

Beauty: ★★★	Site Privacy: ★★★
Spaciousness: ★★	Quiet: ★★★★
Security: ★★★★	Cleanliness: ★★★
Insect Control: ★★★	Facilities: ★★★

This KOA is rather small by comparison to others we've visited, but it still offers all the amenities of the larger campgrounds. The scenery is not spectacular by any means, but the property is pleasant and fairly clean. The RV and tent sites are small to average, but despite this fact, they still manage to provide a little privacy and a lot of quiet. Quite a few of the RV sites offer full hookups, and all sites come with picnic tables, grills, and fire pits. As a bonus to the guests, amenities on the premises include a dataport, game room, recreation room, and nature trails. Nearby, visitors can enjoy the Agate Fossil Beds, Fort Laramie, North Platte Valley Museum, or the local zoo.

Basics

Operated By: Private Operator. **Open:** Apr. 15–Oct. **Site Assignment:** By reservation. **Registration:** Camp Office. **Fee:** Tent $16–$18 RV $20–$26 per 2 people (cash or credit). **Parking:** At site.

Facilities

Number of RV-Only Sites: 22. **Number of Tent-Only Sites:** 6. **Number of Multipurpose Sites:** 17. **Hookups:** Electric (20, 30, 50 amps), water, sewer. **Each Site:** Picnic tables, few grills & fire pits. **Dump Station:** Yes. **Laundry:** Yes. **Pay Phone:** Yes. **Rest Rooms and Showers:** Yes. **Fuel:** No. **Propane:** Yes. **Internal Roads:** Combination of gravel & pavement. **RV Service:** Local service. **Market:** Local. **Restaurant:** Local. **General Store:** Yes. **Vending:** General Store only. **Swimming Pool:** Yes. **Playground:** Yes. **Other:** Cabins, nature trail, Internet data port, recreation room. **Activities:** Game room, swimming, volleyball, basketball, horseshoes. **Nearby Attractions:** Scottsbluff National Monument, Agate Fossil Beds, North Platte Valley Museum, Fort Laramie, the zoo. **Additional Information:** Gothenburg Chamber of Commerce, (308) 537-3505.

Restrictions

Pets: On leash. **Fires:** In fire pits only. **Alcoholic Beverages:** Yes. **Vehicle Maximum Length:** None.

To Get There

From I-80 Exit 59, take SR 17 north 0.2 mi. to SR 19. Follow SR 19 2 mi., then go north on US 30 for 0.3 mi. to US 385. Follow US 385 for 40 mi., then take US 26 west for another 42 mi. to KOA.

WACO

Double Nickel Campground

I-80 & Waco, Waco 68460. T: (402) 728-5558

RV ★★★ Tent ★★★

Beauty: ★★★	Site Privacy: ★★
Spaciousness: ★★	Quiet: ★★★
Security: ★★★	Cleanliness: ★★★
Insect Control: ★★★	Facilities: ★★★

The Double Nickel Campground is located one block south of I-80 in Waco. It is a moderately sized, privately owned facility with a lounge and meeting rooms attached. The campground has 103 sites that are basically gravel parking spurs with hookups. The area does have some grass and a fishing pond. There is a pool, a playground, and mini-golf. The internal roads were a bit rutty when we visited. However, the facilities in the campground were clean, though not manicured. The staff are friendly and helpful, and there are movies to rent. The park is quiet and seems genuinely family oriented. You can see the interstate from most campsites, and there is the possibility you may have to level out. The weather is dry here, and days in the summer are long and hot.

Basics

Operated By: Craig & Shannon Runge. **Open:** Year-round. **Site Assignment:** By reservation, held on credit card number. **Registration:** Camp Office. **Fee:** Tent $16, RV $22–$24 per 2 people, extra person $1.50 (cash, credit, checks). **Parking:** At site.

Facilities

Number of Multipurpose Sites: 103. **Hookups:** Electric (20, 30, 50 amps), water, sewer. **Each Site:** Picnic tables. **Dump Station:** Yes. **Laundry:** Yes. **Pay Phone:** Yes. **Rest Rooms and Showers:** Yes. **Fuel:** No. **Propane:** No. **Internal Roads:** Gravel, in poor condition. **RV Service:** 35 mi. east Lincoln. **Market:** 8 mi. east in York. **Restaurant:** 8 mi. east in York. **General Store:** Yes. **Vending:** No. **Swimming Pool:** Yes. **Playground:** Yes. **Other:** Storm shelter, adult lounge (serve alcohol), mini-golf, fishing pond, videos, indoor meeting room. **Activities:** Swimming, fishing, videos, horseshoes. **Nearby Attractions:** Bruce L. Anderson Recreation Area, Kirkpatrick Wildlife Basin. **Additional Information:** York Chamber of Commerce, (402) 362-5531.

Restrictions

Pets: On leash. **Fires:** In grills or fire pits only. **Alcoholic Beverages:** Yes. **Vehicle Maximum Length:** None.

To Get There

Off I-80 Exit 360, the campground is 1 block south of Waco.

WATERLOO

Two Rivers State Recreation Area

27702 F St., Waterloo 68069-7012. T: (402) 359-5165; F: (402) 359-9040; www.ngpc.state.ne.us.

RV ★★★ Tent ★★★

Beauty: ★★★	Site Privacy: ★★★
Spaciousness: ★★★	Quiet: ★★★★
Security: ★★★★	Cleanliness: ★★★
Insect Control: ★★★	Facilities: ★★

Adjacent to the Platte River just off NE 92 near Venice, Two Rivers State Recreation Area offers a wide range of campsites in five campgrounds, with primitive camping in two areas and sites for small groups in a third. Campgrounds are located near the river or one of the five ponds. This is a popular spot for canoe-campers travelling the 55-mile segment of the Platte River. Due to the location, most sites enjoy peace and quiet with deer, rabbits, and foxes often spotted. For campers who enjoy fishing, this is one of the few spots in the state that offers trout fishing. A wheelchair-accessible pier is provided. Railroad buffs will delight in ten cabooses donated by the Union Pacific Railroad, remodeled and restored, and now used as lodging in the park.

Basics

Operated By: Nebraska Game & Parks Commission. **Open:** Apr.–Oct. **Site Assignment:** First come, first served. **Registration:** Self-serve registration kiosks. **Fee:** $8–$12 depends on site & amenities, plus vehicle entrance fee. **Parking:** At site.

Facilities

Number of RV-Only Sites: 93. **Number of Tent-Only Sites:** 39. **Number of Multipurpose Sites:** 63. **Hookups:** Electric (20, 30 amps), water. **Each Site:** Picnic tables, fire pit. **Dump Station:** Yes. **Laundry:** No. **Pay Phone:** Yes. **Rest Rooms and Showers:** Yes. **Fuel:** No. **Propane:** No. **Internal Roads:** Paved. **RV Service:** Local service. **Market:** In town. **Restaurant:** In town. **Gen-**

eral Store: Yes. **Vending:** Yes. **Swimming Pool:** No, but there is a swimming beach w/ showers. **Playground:** Yes. **Other:** 10 Union Pacific train cabooses converted into cabins (no pets in cabooses), hiking trails, 2 picnic shelters, 2 w/ electricity, over 100 picnic tables & grills, boat ramps, 5 ponds, Platte River access, pull & take trout lake, mountain bike trails, hiking trails, fish cleaning station. **Activities:** Swimming, boating, fishing, hiking. **Nearby Attractions:** Strategic Air Command Museum. **Additional Information:** Elkhorn Chamber of Commerce, (402) 289-2678.

Restrictions

Pets: On leash. **Fires:** In grills or fire pits only. **Alcoholic Beverages:** No alcoholic beverages allowed. **Vehicle Maximum Length:** 45 ft. **Other:** Nebraska State Park passes honored.

To Get There

From I-80 Exit 445 (in Omaha) go west on US 275 for 10.8 mi.; US 275 becomes SR 92, so continue for 2 mi., then turn left on CR 96 (S. 26th St), go 1 mi. and turn right onto CR 49 (F St.) into park.

WOODRIVER

Woodriver Motel and Campground

11774 South Hwy. 11, Woodriver 68883.
T: (308) 583-2256

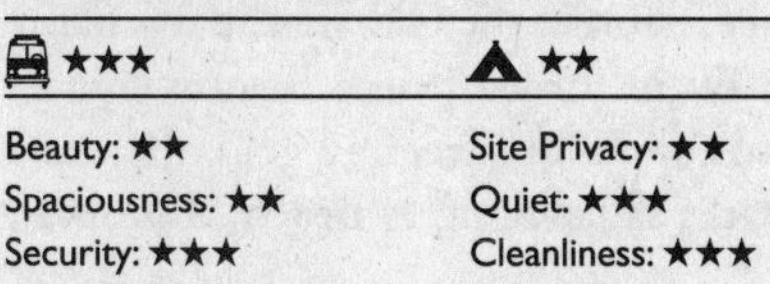

RV ★★★ Tent ★★

Beauty: ★★ Site Privacy: ★★
Spaciousness: ★★ Quiet: ★★★
Security: ★★★ Cleanliness: ★★★
Insect Control: ★★★ Facilities: ★★★

The Wood River Motel and Campground is conveniently located off I-80 in Woodriver. This campground is ideal for those people traveling through and looking for a comfortable, clean, simple place to spend the night. The Wood River Campground is located behind a truck stop and the Wood River Motel, and it offers well-spaced concrete parking spurs, separated by a lawn. There are a total of 30 sites, most of which are pull-throughs, each having its own lamp post. In addition, there are a few grills and an open tent area. The campground has a small playground, fishing pond, and clean facilities. There is a restaurant in the truck stop, and there's vending in the motel. The campground is open year-round, with the utilities turned off in the winter. The motel is privately run, and the owners live on the property. You must drive by the motel office in order to enter the RV park.

Basics

Operated By: Deb Gerlach. **Open:** Year-round (water off in the winter). **Site Assignment:** By reservation. **Registration:** Motel front desk. **Fee:** Tent $9.50, RV $13.75 per unit (cash or credit). **Parking:** At site.

Facilities

Number of Multipurpose Sites: 30. **Hookups:** Electric (20, 30, 50 amps), water, sewer. **Each Site:** Picnic tables, few grills. **Dump Station:** Yes. **Laundry:** Yes. **Pay Phone:** Yes. **Rest Rooms and Showers:** Yes. **Fuel:** Next door. **Propane:** Next door. **Internal Roads:** Combination of gravel & pavement. **RV Service:** 18 mi. in Grand Island. **Market:** Local. **Restaurant:** Local. **General Store:** Truckstop next door. **Vending:** Yes. **Swimming Pool:** No. **Playground:** Yes. **Other:** 26 room motel. **Activities:** Fishing pond. **Nearby Attractions:** It is 17 mi. to Grand Island or Hastings. **Additional Information:** Grand Island Chamber of Commerce, (308) 382-9210.

Restrictions

Pets: On leash. **Fires:** No open fires, charcoal fires in grills only. **Alcoholic Beverages:** Yes. **Vehicle Maximum Length:** None.

To Get There

Off I-80 Exit 300, merge left off Hwy. 11; the campground is behind the truck stop.

Nevada

Nevada is much more than just Las Vegas, though the state has no shortage of casino RV parks combining parking-lot camping and hookups with buffets, entertainment, and gaming. Within an hour of Las Vegas, nature lovers can begin experiencing another Nevada, where livestock and wild burros wander across roads and ancient Native American petroglyphs hide among red rock formations that hold their own with the best in the American West.

High mountains and high deserts present winter sports opportunities, the best known being around **Lake Tahoe** and **Carson City.** High elevations also mean summer opportunities to escape the searing desert heat outside the air-conditioned casinos, though weekend reservations are needed to edge out locals fleeing Las Vegas for the cool juniper and pine forests of **Spring Mountain National** and **Lee Canyon Recreation Areas.**

Nevada has 200 isolated mountain ranges snaking north and south among its equally numerous desert valleys. Small government campgrounds and attractive lakes and reservoirs present summer recreation and winter possibilities like helicopter skiing and ice fishing. There are numerous amenities and hookups in cities like **Fallon, Hawthorne, Winnemucca, Ely,** and **Elko.** But the best of the northern and central mountain ranges are the province of self-sufficient campers seeking out the more primitive campgrounds to experience nature in all its raw ruggedness and isolated beauty.

The folded, rippled, uplifted, and otherwise intriguingly contorted and colorfully banded sedimentary and metamorphic mountain ranges are more than just geologic curiosities. Indeed, camping in Nevada is often a history lesson in the Old West, particularly the boom-and-bust economics of mining. A pathetic failure of a gold miner named Mark Twain turned it into literary gold in "Roughing It." Though Nevada's many working mines produce everything from gypsum and copper to silver and gold, there is a widespread legacy of old gold, silver, mercury, and tungsten mines and ghost towns near places as far-flung as **Beatty, Tonopah, Gabbs, Ely, Elko, Pioche,** and **Carson City.**

Nevada is also a state with incredible manmade lakes like **Lakes Mead** and **Mohave** south of Las Vegas, which are popular for fishing, houseboats, and water sports. Natural lakes in the middle of the desert are not a mirage. **Walker Lake** is a still-shrinking remnant of ancient Lake Lahontan, which once filled Nevada's desert valleys and left ancient Native Americans living along a shoreline that is now mountaintops.

Campground Profiles

AMARGOSA VALLEY

Longstreet Inn, Casino, RV Park & Golf Club

HCR 70 Box 559, Amargosa Valley 89020.
T: (702) 372-1777; F: (702) 372-1280;
www.longstreetinn.com.

RV ★★★ Tent ★★

Beauty: ★★★	Site Privacy: ★★★★
Spaciousness: ★★★★	Quiet: ★★★★
Security: ★★★★	Cleanliness: ★★★★★
Insect Control: ★★★★	Facilities: ★★★★★

An isolated stopping post for those crossing Death Valley Junction, Longstreet is far enough from Beatty's RV parks on US 95 to provide relative solitude. The 25-foot-wide spaces are meant to accommodate anything on the road, and snag Furnace Creek traffic. The gravel RV park with its few scraggly trees looks out over a small golf course towards Death Valley's Funeral Mountains. Sharp eyes can detect the ridge where the old Tidewater & Tonopah Railroad ran. The casino, with its pool and large freeform rock firewater reservoir (often mistaken for the pool), acts as a protective backdrop and is the source of all amenities here. Nearby Ash Meadows National Wildlife Refuge, designated a "Wetland of International Importance," contains "fossil water," an endangered pup fish, and 24 plant and animals found nowhere else in the world. There are no tables or grills (fire hazard), and tent campers need air mattresses.

BASICS

Operated By: Longstreet Inn, Casino, RV Park & Golf Club. **Open:** All year. **Site Assignment:** First come, first served. **Registration:** At hotel front desk in casino. **Fee:** $16 (VISA, MC, AE, D, DC, CB). **Parking:** At site.

FACILITIES

Number of RV Sites: 52. **Number of Tent-Only Sites:** 0. **Hookups:** Electric (50 amp), water, sewer, cable TV, phone (16 sites). **Each Site:** Varies. **Dump Station:** Yes. **Laundry:** Yes. **Pay Phone:** Yes. **Rest Rooms and Showers:** Yes. **Fuel:** No. **Propane:** No. **Internal Roads:** Gravel, dusty but good. **RV Service:** No. **Market:** In casino. **Restaurant:** In casino. **General Store:** Yes. **Vending:** Yes. **Swimming:** In hotel pool. **Playground:** No. **Other:** 9-hole par-28 golf course, jacuzzi. **Activities:** Gambling. **Nearby Attractions:** Death Valley, Ash Meadows National Wildlife Refuge. **Additional Information:** Ash Meadows NWR, (775) 372-5435.

RESTRICTIONS

Pets: On leash under owner's control. **Fires:** No. **Alcoholic Beverages:** Allowed. **Vehicle Maximum Length:** 75 ft.

To Get There

From junction of US Hwy. 95 at Lathrop Wells, go 7 mi. south on NV Hwy. 373.

BEATTY

Bailey's Hot Springs

U.South Hwy. 95, Beatty 89003. T: (775) 553-2395.

RV ★★★ Tent ★★★

Beauty: ★★★ Site Privacy: ★★★★
Spaciousness: ★★★★ Quiet: ★★★★
Security: ★★★ Cleanliness: ★★★
Insect Control: ★★★ Facilities: ★★

One of five RV parks in Beatty, Bailey's is the only campground with hot springs (available for day-use visitors), though it is also furthest from the casinos and markets. Beatty's RV parks are all along the highway, but traffic is relatively light at night. Tent campers on the lawns here are protected by reeds and can fall asleep to the sound of running creek water (which irrigates local farms). The campground is shady, breezy, and friendly. Most here are regulars and word-of-mouth customers stopping for a night or two of hot-spring use, coming and going from Death Valley. The adjacent corral houses the owner's breeding horses, and the view across the highway is BLM land (OK to hike) and Death Valley mountain ranges. Only weekly customers get sewer hookups because of the high water table from the spring and the underground Amargosa River.

Basics

Operated By: Sharon Patton. **Open:** All year. **Site Assignment:** First come, first served. **Registration:** In office (an RV). **Fee:** $12. **Parking:** At site.

Facilities

Number of RV Sites: 14. **Number of Tent-Only Sites:** Undesignated sites. **Hookups:** Electric (30 amp), water. **Each Site:** Varies. **Dump Station:** No. **Laundry:** No. **Pay Phone:** Yes. **Rest Rooms and Showers:** Yes. **Fuel:** No. **Propane:** No. **Internal Roads:** Gravel, good. **RV Service:** No. **Market:** Beatty, 5 mi. **Restaurant:** Beatty, 5 mi. **General Store:** No. **Vending:** No. **Swimming:** Hot springs. **Playground:** No. **Other:** Central picnic area w/ BBQ. **Activities:** Soaking in hot springs. **Nearby Attractions:** Death Valley, Rhyolite ghost town, Amargosa Valley, Goldfield. **Additional Information:** Beatty Chamber of Commerce, (775) 553-2424.

Restrictions

Pets: On leash under owner's control. **Fires:** Yes (in fire ring only). **Alcoholic Beverages:** Allowed. **Vehicle Maximum Length:** 30 ft. **Other:** High water table limits sewage discharge.

To Get There

Go 5 mi. north of Beatty on US Hwy. 95.

BOULDER CITY

Boulder Beach

601 Nevada Hwy., Boulder City 89005. T: (702) 293-8907; F: (702) 293-8936; www.nps.gov/lame/home.html.

RV ★★★ Tent ★★★

Beauty: ★★★★★ Site Privacy: ★★★★
Spaciousness: ★★★ Quiet: ★★★★★
Security: ★★★ Cleanliness: ★★★★★
Insect Control: ★★★★ Facilities: ★★

Boulder Beach shares the same scenic Lake Mead desert landscape as Las Vegas Bay, which is seven miles to the north along the Lakeshore Scenic Drive. The park's Alan Bible Visitor Center is nine miles southwest and Hoover Dam is five miles southeast, making this an especially good choice for first-time visitors getting acquainted with the area. Unlike Las Vegas Bay, there is swimming here. South of Hoover Dam the waters flow through Black Canyon, a prime bighorn sheep viewing area, and become Lake Mohave. Another 20 miles south on US Hwy. 93 (a route leading to the South Rim of the Grand Canyon) is Willow Beach, a 1,500-year-old Native American trading site known for petroglyphs and fine fishing. Those wanting Boulder Beach with hookups can check into the adjacent Lakeshore Trailer Village (See Appendix), which has 80 "transient" spaces with cable TV among the 215 mobile homes.

Basics

Operated By: National Park Service. **Open:** All year. **Site Assignment:** First come, first served. **Registration:** Self-pay entrance fee station. **Fee:** $10. **Parking:** At site.

Facilities

Number of RV Sites: 142. **Number of Tent-Only Sites:** 0. **Hookups:** None. **Each Site:** Table, grill. **Dump Station:** Yes. **Laundry:** Yes. **Pay Phone:** Yes. **Rest Rooms and Showers:** Yes (shower fee at trailer village). **Fuel:** No (boat fuel only). **Propane:** No. **Internal Roads:** Paved, good. **RV Service:** No. **Market:** Boulder City, 6 mi. **Restaurant:** Boulder City, 6 mi. **General Store:** Yes. **Vending:** Yes. **Swimming:** In lake at own risk. **Playground:** No. **Other:** Partial handicap access, motel, boat launch. **Activities:** Boating, fishing. **Nearby Attractions:** Lake Mead, Las Vegas, Henderson, Hoover Dam. **Additional Information:** Lakeshore Trailer Village, (702) 293-2540; Lake Mead Resort, (800) 752-9669, (702) 293-3484; Lake Mead Cruises, (702) 293-6180.

Restrictions

Pets: On leash under owner's control. **Fires:** Yes. **Alcoholic Beverages:** Allowed. **Vehicle Maximum Length:** 30 ft. **Other:** 30-day max. stay.

To Get There

From Boulder City, go 6 mi. northeast on NV Hwy. 166 (Lakeshore Rd.).

BOULDER CITY

Katherine Campground

601 Nevada Hwy., Boulder City 89005. T: (520) 754-3272 (Katherine Camp) or (702) 293-8906 (Alan Bible Visitors Center); www.nps.gov/lame/home.html.

RV ★★★★ Tent ★★★★

Beauty: ★★★★ Site Privacy: ★★★★
Spaciousness: ★★★★ Quiet: ★★★★
Security: ★★★★ Cleanliness: ★★★★
Insect Control: ★★★ Facilities: ★★★★

About five miles north of Bullhead City and Laughlin's casinos, in the Lake Mead National Recreation Area, Katherine is divided into five smaller campgrounds with solar power, paved roads, and gravel sites separated by oleanders, eucalyptus, and palms. Though the Park Service does not provide hookups, a private concessionaire (Lake Mojave Resort and Marina) offers sites with hookups ($18; register at motel), along with a trailer village, motel, marina, houseboat rentals, restaurant, and lounge. A favorite of Californians, on a recent three-day holiday weekend Katherine was overrun by 44,000 visitors. A warning to the wise: those who didn't snag a campsite on the Thursday prior to the holiday were backed up in a two-hour line of cars, only to be turned away. But when the crowds abate, Katherine offers enough true desert relaxation and water to make the rest of the world seem like memories from a distant planet.

Basics

Operated By: National Park Service (also separate Lake Mojave Resort & Marina concession). **Open:** All year. **Site Assignment:** First come, first served; no reservations (except groups). **Registration:** At entrance kiosk. **Fee:** $10 ($5 w/ Golden Age & Golden Access passes; cash only). **Parking:** At site.

Facilities

Number of RV Sites: 173. **Number of Tent-Only Sites:** 0. **Hookups:** None (private Lake Mojave Resort & Marina concession offers sites w/ hookups). **Each Site:** Table, grill. **Dump Station:** Yes. **Laundry:** Yes. **Pay Phone:** Yes. **Rest Rooms and Showers:** Yes. **Fuel:** Yes. **Propane:** Yes. **Internal Roads:** Paved, in good condition. **RV Service:** Limited; better in Bullhead City or Laughlin. **Market:** Yes. **Restaurant:** Yes. **General Store:** Yes. **Vending:** Yes. **Swimming:** No. **Playground:** No. **Activities:** House boat rentals, full marina, fishing. **Nearby Attractions:** Laughlin casinos & outlet shopping. **Additional Information:** Lake Mohave Resort, (520) 754-3245 or (800) 752-9669.

Restrictions

Pets: Must be kept on 6-ft. leash and not left alone. **Fires:** Yes (in grills only). **Alcoholic Beverages:** In designated areas. **Vehicle Maximum Length:** 25 ft. **Other:** 30-day stay limit, NRA entry fee must also be paid.

To Get There

From junction of Hwy. 95 and Hwy. 68, north of Bullhead City, go west 0.25 mi. on Hwy. 68, then north 3 mi. on Katherine Rd.

CALIENTE

Young's RV Park

P.O. Box 84, Caliente 89008. T: (775) 726-3418.

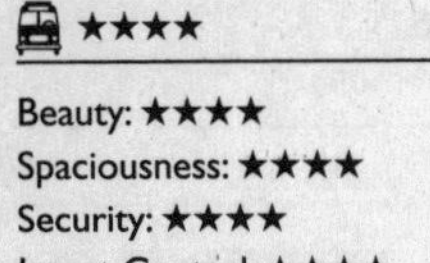
RV ★★★★ Tent ★★★★

Beauty: ★★★★ Site Privacy: ★★★★
Spaciousness: ★★★★ Quiet: ★★★★
Security: ★★★★ Cleanliness: ★★★★
Insect Control: ★★★★ Facilities: ★★★

For travelers between Las Vegas and Great Basin National Park on US Hwy. 93, Young's is the only intermediate stop with full hookups. Young's is also a popular stopping place for migrating snowbirds, who like the poplar, cottonwood, and elm trees, as well as the grass strips between the three gravel rows. Tent campers share a large grassy area with a few tables. The campground can be a bit tricky to locate, as the sign for the dirt turnoff road on the southwest edge of Caliente says "Young's" in tiny black letters easily missed. Look instead for the big blue letters saying "RV Park" above the large red arrow to spot the turnoff. About half the park's business comes from the sign whose tiny white letters advertise full hookups and showers. Except for the Union Pacific train rumbling through at night, it is fairly quiet because highway traffic slows to 25 mph entering town.

Basics

Operated By: Chad & Brenda Young. **Open:** All year. **Site Assignment:** First come, first served. **Registration:** In office. **Fee:** $13.50. **Parking:** At site.

Facilities

Number of RV Sites: 27. **Number of Tent-Only Sites:** Undesignated sites. **Hookups:** Electric (20, 30 amp), water, sewer. **Each Site:** Table. **Dump Station:** Yes. **Laundry:** Yes. **Pay Phone:** Yes. **Rest Rooms and Showers:** Yes. **Fuel:** No. **Propane:** No. **Internal Roads:** Gravel, good. **RV Service:** No. **Market:** Caliente. **Restaurant:** Caliente. **General Store:** No. **Vending:** No. **Swimming:** No. **Playground:** No. **Activities:** Historic buildings tour. **Nearby Attractions:** Several state parks, Pioche Boot Hill Cemetery, Caliente train depot. **Additional Information:** Caliente Chamber of Commerce, (775) 726-3129; Nevada Div. of State Parks Regional Visitors Center, (775) 728-4460.

Restrictions

Pets: On leash under owner's control. **Fires:** Yes. **Alcoholic Beverages:** Allowed. **Vehicle Maximum Length:** 60 ft.

To Get There

From US Hwy. 93 near the bridge at the southwest outskirts of Caliente, turn down the gravel road running between the BLM building and the Lincoln County shops.

CARSON CITY

Davis Creek Regional Park

25 Davis Creek Rd., Carson City 89704. T: (775) 849-1825.

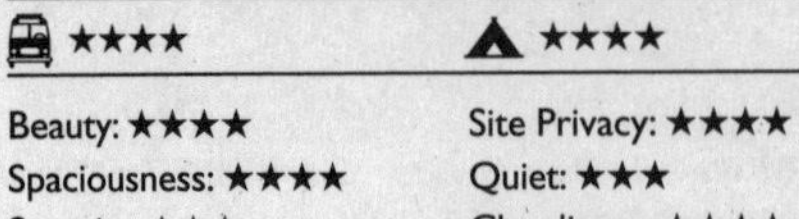
RV ★★★★ Tent ★★★★

Beauty: ★★★★ Site Privacy: ★★★★
Spaciousness: ★★★★ Quiet: ★★★
Security: ★★★ Cleanliness: ★★★★
Insect Control: ★★★ Facilities: ★★

An attractive area where pine forests meet sagebrush desert on the eastern slope of the Sierra Nevada Mountains in the Washoe Valley north of Carson City, Davis Creek Regional Park features a picnic area surrounding a three-acre pond. The pond, used for ice skating in winter, was once an ice source for Virginia City. The park, once part of the 4,000-acre Winters Ranch known for its racetrack and horse breeding in the early 1900s, has separate North and South Campgrounds for tents and RVs that can be reserved by groups. Granite boulders line the perimeter, tall ponderosa pines provide shade and whiffs of vanilla scent, and pine needles carpet the campground. The Ophir Creek Trail leads from the campground through steep canyons, mountain creeks, and boulder fields to Price Lake and Tahoe Meadows. Reno's gaming and entertainment is only 21 miles away.

Basics

Operated By: Washoe County Parks & Recreation Dept. **Open:** All year. **Site Assignment:** First come, first served; group reservations. **Registration:** Self-pay fee station. **Fee:** $11 (cash or check only). **Parking:** At site.

Facilities

Number of RV Sites: 19. **Number of Tent-Only Sites:** 44. **Hookups:** None. **Each Site:** Table, fire ring. **Dump Station:** Yes. **Laundry:** No. **Pay Phone:** Yes. **Rest Rooms and Showers:** Yes. **Fuel:** No. **Propane:** No. **Internal Roads:** Paved, excellent. **RV Service:** No. **Market:** Carson City, 12 mi. **Restaurant:** Carson City, 12 mi. **General Store:** No. **Vending:** No. **Swimming:** Pool at Bowers Mansion Regional Park, 1 mi. **Playground:** No. **Other:** Wheelchair-accessible site, amphitheather, pond. **Activities:** Horseback riding, fishing, boating, ice skating. **Nearby Attractions:** Bowers Mansion, Lake Tahoe. **Additional Information:** Carson Valley Chamber of Commerce & Visitors Authority, (800) 727-7677, www.carsonvalleynv.org.

Restrictions

Pets: On leash under owner's control. **Fires:** Yes (only in fire pits, no fires when danger is high in summer). **Alcoholic Beverages:** Allowed. **Vehicle Maximum Length:** 30 ft. **Other:** No firearms or patio torches, food must be locked from bears, no amplified music.

To Get There

Go 12 mi. north from Carson City on US 395 and 0.5 mi. southwest on Old US Hwy. 395.

CARSON CITY

Washoe Lake State Park

4855 East Lake Blvd., Carson City 89704. T: (775) 687-4319; F: (775) 684-8053; www.state.nv.us/stparks.

 ★★★★  ★★★★

Beauty: ★★★★ Site Privacy: ★★★★★
Spaciousness: ★★★★ Quiet: ★★★★
Security: ★★★★ Cleanliness: ★★★★
Insect Control: ★★★★ Facilities: ★★★

Six-foot tall sagebrush teeming with quail and sand dunes stand between the two campground loops and Washoe Lake, while the backdrop is forested mountains in one direction and low rocky hills that turn golden in summer in the other. Loop B (sites 25–49) is at a slightly higher elevation than Loop A (sites 1–24) and has more glimpses of the lake over the sand dunes. A few tables are sheltered, but the mostly small trees have yet to grow tall enough to provide much shade. Site 37 is wheelchair accessible and one of the few sites with a tall cottonwood tree for shade and a good lake view. The lake's willows and cattails were used for basketry by the Washo Indians thousands of years ago, and provide good migratory bird-watching habitat today. Carson City is 5 miles south and Reno only 18 miles to the north.

Basics

Operated By: Nevada State Parks. **Open:** All year. **Site Assignment:** First come, first served; group area requires reservations. **Registration:** Self-pay fee station. **Fee:** $10 (cash or check only). **Parking:** At site.

Facilities

Number of RV Sites: 47. **Number of Tent-Only Sites:** 2. **Hookups:** None. **Each Site:** Table, fire ring. **Dump Station:** Yes. **Laundry:** No. **Pay Phone:** Yes. **Rest Rooms and Showers:** Yes. **Fuel:** No. **Propane:** No. **Internal Roads:** Paved, excellent. **RV Service:** No. **Market:** Carson City, 6 mi. **Restaurant:** Carson City, 6 mi. **General Store:** No. **Vending:** No. **Swimming:** Lake. **Playground:** No. **Other:** Boat launch, windsocks, equestrian & wildlife viewing areas, day-use picnic tables & grills. **Activities:** Hang gliding, fishing, hunting, boating, bird-watching, golf. **Nearby Attractions:** Virginia City, historic areas, museums. **Additional Information:** Carson City Chamber of Commerce, (775) 882-1565, www.carsoncity-chamber.com.

Restrictions

Pets: On leash at all times (except in wetlands during hunting season). **Fires:** Yes (in grills only, no wood collection, firewood sold). **Alcoholic Beverages:** Allowed. **Vehicle Maximum Length:** 45 ft. **Other:** 7-day limit per 30-day period.

To Get There

From US Hwy. 395 exit 42 north of Carson City, go 2 mi. east on East Lake Blvd.

COTTONWOOD COVE

Cottonwood Cove

P.O. Box 123, Searchlight 89046. T: (702) 293-8907; F: (702) 293-8936; www.nps.gov/lame/home.html.

 ★★★★ Tent ★★★★★

Beauty: ★★★★★ Site Privacy: ★★★★★
Spaciousness: ★★★★ Quiet: ★★★★★

Security: ★★★★★ Cleanliness: ★★★★★
Insect Control: ★★★ Facilities: ★★★★★

Like Katherine near Bullhead City, AZ, Cottonwood Cove is a very popular Lake Mohave destination that begins filling up on Thursday for long weekends. At peak times consider instead a reservation at the Forever Resorts (call (800) 255-5561; www.foreverresorts.com) trailer village (30, 50 amp hookups) and camp out amongst the mobile homes. Tent campers will like having a whole loop area of their own, an unusual arrangement in the Lake Mead National Recreation Area. The gray desert beauty and solitude of the location should provide solace against holiday crowds. The ranger station has a cactus garden with several cholla species and a good display of area history, ranging from local railroad spikes to minerals. It is only 14 miles (west) to Searchlight and a roadside casino with 10-cent coffee. Like the rest of the Lake Mead National Recreation Area, Lake Mohave life revolves around the water and boating.

Basics

Operated By: National Park Service. **Open:** All year. **Site Assignment:** First come, first served. **Registration:** Self-pay entrance fee station. **Fee:** $10. **Parking:** At site.

Facilities

Number of RV Sites: 100. **Number of Tent-Only Sites:** 45. **Hookups:** None. **Each Site:** Table, fire pit. **Dump Station:** Yes. **Laundry:** Yes. **Pay Phone:** Yes. **Rest Rooms and Showers:** Yes. **Fuel:** Yes. **Propane:** Yes. **Internal Roads:** Paved, good. **RV Service:** No. **Market:** At marina. **Restaurant:** At marina. **General Store:** Yes. **Vending:** Yes. **Swimming:** In lake at own risk. **Playground:** No. **Other:** Boat launch, motel. **Activities:** Boating, canoeing, fishing. **Nearby Attractions:** Laughlin. **Additional Information:** Cottonwood Cove Marina & Resort, (702) 297-1464, www.foreverresorts.com.

Restrictions

Pets: On leash under owner's control. **Fires:** Yes. **Alcoholic Beverages:** Allowed in moderation; problems will result in arrest. **Vehicle Maximum Length:** 30 ft. **Other:** No loaded firearms or fireworks, no disturbing plants or rocks or archaeological features.

To Get There

Take NV Hwy. 164 between Laughlin and Las Vegas, and at Searchlight go east for 14 mi. on Cottonwood Cove Rd.

ELKO
Valley View RV Park

6000 East Idaho St. (Hwy. 40 East), Elko 89801. T: (775) 753-9200.

RV ★★★ Tent ★★★

Beauty: ★★★ Site Privacy: ★★★
Spaciousness: ★★★★ Quiet: ★★★
Security: ★★★★ Cleanliness: ★★★★
Insect Control: ★★★★ Facilities: ★★★★

Just down the road from the Hilton and the bare gravel Double Dice RV Park, Valley View at least offers some attractive patches of grass, a friendly family feel, and the best campsite prices in town. The word of mouth here is good, and repeat customers stop by regularly for three to five days. Families settling in for longer stays let their kids pick up the school bus at the bus stop in front. The owners are amiable, and Valley View seems like a friendly little town where people have the time to stop and chat. There is some noise from the highway being nearby, but the trees provide an offset and a snack bar should soon be in operation to lessen the need for trips into town. All in all, a pleasant alternative to Nevada's prevalent casino RV parking lots and about as good as they come in this remote area.

Basics

Operated By: Elaine Poirier. **Open:** All year. **Site Assignment:** First come, first served. **Registration:** Office. **Fee:** $9 tent; $15 RV (V, MC). **Parking:** At site.

Facilities

Number of RV Sites: 100. **Number of Tent-Only Sites:** Undesignated sites. **Hookups:** Electric (30, 50 amp), water, sewer, phone (modem), cable TV. **Each Site:** Grills & tables in tent area only. **Dump Station:** Yes. **Laundry:** Yes. **Pay Phone:** Yes. **Rest Rooms and Showers:** Yes. **Fuel:** No. **Propane:** No. **Internal Roads:** Paved, good. **RV Service:** No. **Market:** Elko, 3 mi. **Restaurant:** Elko, 1 mi. **General Store:** No. **Vending:** Yes. **Swimming:** At park in town. **Playground:** Yes. **Other:** Mail delivery, school-bus pickup, dog walk. **Activities:** Fishing, hunting, biking, golf, baseball, bird-watching. **Nearby Attractions:** Ruby Mountains, Lamoille Canyon, Jarbridge Wilderness, ghost towns. **Additional Information:** Elko Chamber of Commerce, (775) 738-7135, www.elko-nevada.com.

Restrictions

Pets: On leash and/or contained at all times. **Fires:** Yes. **Alcoholic Beverages:** Allowed. **Vehicle Maximum Length:** 55 ft. **Other:** Children must have adult supervision at all times.

To Get There

From US I-80 Exit 303, go 3 mi. east on Idaho St. (Hwy. 40).

ELY
Cave Lake State Park

P.O. Box 761, Ely 89301. T: (775) 728-4467; www.state.nv.us/stparks.

RV ★★ Tent ★★★★

Beauty: ★★★★ Site Privacy: ★★★★
Spaciousness: ★★★ Quiet: ★★★★★
Security: ★★★★ Cleanliness: ★★★★
Insect Control: ★★★ Facilities: ★★

The road to Elk Flat and Lake View Campgrounds in Cave Lake State Park is lined with typical Great Basin big sagebrush and rabbitbrush, but the campgrounds are heavily wooded with pinyon pines and junipers. The surrounding Humboldt-Toiyabe National Forest is a prime elk habitat with scenic upthrusts, narrow canyons, and shallow caves. Elk Flat (16 sites) is newer and more spacious, but closes with the snows and cold weather between mid-October and early May. Lake View remains open year-round for ice fishing, ice skating, and other winter sports, but you need to bring your own water then and without 4WD there is a risk of being stuck a day or two waiting for the snow plows. Large vehicles may need to camp at the roadside turnouts (which are overflow areas and trailheads for streams with native brown trout), as the tight campground turns have trapped large RVs (necessitating towing).

Basics

Operated By: Nevada State Parks. **Open:** All year. **Site Assignment:** First come, first served. **Registration:** Self-pay fee station. **Fee:** $12 (cash or check only). **Parking:** At site.

Facilities

Number of RV Sites: 34. **Number of Tent-Only Sites:** 0. **Hookups:** None. **Each Site:** Table, grill, fire pit. **Dump Station:** Yes. **Laundry:** No. **Pay Phone:** No. **Rest Rooms and Showers:** Yes. **Fuel:** No. **Propane:** No. **Internal Roads:** Gravel, good. **RV Service:** No. **Market:** Ely, 14 mi. **Restaurant:** Ely, 14 mi. **General Store:** No. **Vending:** No. **Swimming:** Lake. **Playground:** No. **Other:** Boat ramp, 1 wheelchair-accessible site. **Activities:** Winter sports, fishing, crawdading, boating, horseback riding. **Nearby Attractions:** Ward Charcoal Ovens, Great Basin National Park, Ely museum, historic railroad. **Additional Information:** Ely Ranger District, (702) 289-3031, www.fs.fed.us; White Pine County Chamber of Commerce, (702) 289-8877.

Restrictions

Pets: On leash. **Fires:** Yes. **Alcoholic Beverages:** Allowed. **Vehicle Maximum Length:** 24 ft. **Other:** 5 trout limit, 5 mph (flat wake) motorized boat speed limit, no snowmobiles, after 10 p.m. children under 18 years must be under the supervision of a parent or legal guardian.

To Get There

From Ely, go 8 mi. south on US Hwy. 93 and 7 mi. east on NV Hwy. 486 (Success Summit Rd.).

ELY
Ward Mountain Campground

350 8th St., P.O. Box 539, Ely 89301. T: (702) 289-3031; www.fs.fed.us.

RV ★★★★ Tent ★★★★★

Beauty: ★★★★★ Site Privacy: ★★★★★
Spaciousness: ★★★★ Quiet: ★★★★
Security: ★★★★ Cleanliness: ★★★★
Insect Control: ★★★ Facilities: ★★

When the hunger for open space is strong enough that Ely's rustic KOA and Valley View (no relation to the one in Elko) RV Parks and even the free promo hookups at the Holiday Inn casino will no longer do, Ward Mountain's large, wide (site 29 is 38-feet wide and 126-feet long) spaces deep in the pines and junipers may be the perfect remedy. Large RVs have their own private loop (sites 22–29) with a huge parking area near the South Trailhead. Two loops with smaller sites are on either side of the RV loop. Though Ward Mountain is popular for group picnics, it rarely reaches 50% occupancy (usually at Ely special event). Typically, a half dozen campers a night share the three loops, which are on the German and Swiss tourist routes for doing the national parks between San Francisco and Denver.

Basics

Operated By: Humboldt-Toiyabe National Forests Ely Ranger District. **Open:** All year. **Site Assignment:** First come, first served; day-use picnic area reservations. **Registration:** Self-pay fee station. **Fee:** $4 (cash or check only). **Parking:** At site.

Facilities

Number of RV Sites: 29. **Number of Tent-Only Sites:** 0. **Hookups:** None. **Each Site:** Table, grill, fire ring. **Dump Station:** No. **Laundry:** No. **Pay Phone:** No. **Rest Rooms and Showers:** No showers, pit toilets. **Fuel:** No. **Propane:** No. **Internal Roads:** Gravel, well maintained. **RV Service:** No. **Market:** Ely, 6 mi. **Restaurant:** Ely, 6 mi. **General Store:** No. **Vending:** No. **Swimming:** No. **Playground:** Yes (baseball field). **Other:** Amphitheater. **Activities:** Baseball. **Nearby Attractions:** Ward Charcoal Ovens, Cave Lake State Park, Great Basin National Park, museum, historic railroad. **Additional Information:** White Pine County Chamber of Commerce, (702) 289-8877.

Restrictions

Pets: On leash under owner's control. **Fires:** Yes. **Alcoholic Beverages:** Allowed. **Vehicle Maximum Length:** 126 ft. **Other:** 14-day limit, no saddle or pack animals, no water Oct. 16–May 20.

To Get There

From Ely, go 6 mi. southwest on US Hwy. 6 and 1 mi. on gravel road (FR 10439) turnoff.

GABBS

Berlin Ichthyosaur State Park

HC Box 61200, Austin 89310. T: (775) 964-2440; F: (775) 964-2012; www.state.nv.us/stparks.

RV ★★★ Tent ★★★★

Beauty: ★★★★	Site Privacy: ★★★★★
Spaciousness: ★★★	Quiet: ★★★★★
Security: ★★★★	Cleanliness: ★★★★
Insect Control: ★★★	Facilities: ★★★

An unusual combination of ghost town and aquatic dinosaur fossil site, Berlin Ichthyosaur State Park is relatively remote, even by Nevada standards. Nevada mining towns have a history of boom and bust, with miners carting off the scarce wood and moving to the next site when the ore plays out. What makes Berlin unique is the intact nature of the town. Summer weekends the rangers even run some of the old mining equipment. The ichthyosaur fossils were first exposed by erosion, not miners, and the 50-foot-long specimens in the fossil shelter are among the world's largest. The campsites pose a back-in challenge for trailers, but each site is very private and screened from the others by tall junipers and pines. Seven miles to the north along a gravel road, the historic mercury-mining town of Ione clings to life with a few prospectors, a bar, and several RV sites with hookups.

Basics

Operated By: Nevada State Parks. **Open:** All year. **Site Assignment:** First come, first served; group reservations required. **Registration:** Self-pay fee station. **Fee:** $3–$7 ($7 April 1–Oct. 31; $3 Nov. 1–Mar. 30; cash or check only). **Parking:** At site.

Facilities

Number of RV Sites: 14. **Number of Tent-Only Sites:** 0. **Hookups:** None. **Each Site:** Sheltered table, grill, fire ring. **Dump Station:** Yes. **Laundry:** No. **Pay Phone:** No. **Rest Rooms and Showers:** No showers. **Fuel:** No. **Propane:** No. **Internal Roads:** Gravel, good. **RV Service:** No. **Market:** Tonopah, 77 mi. **Restaurant:** Gabbs, 23 mi. **General Store:** No. **Vending:** No. **Swimming:** No. **Playground:** No. **Other:** Drinking water (mid-Apr.–Oct.). **Activities:** Fossil, mine- & ghost-town exploration. **Nearby Attractions:** Ghost towns. **Additional Information:** Ione Mercantile (RV hookups), (775) 847-0571.

Restrictions

Pets: On leash. **Fires:** Yes (in designated fire containers or commercial stoves/fireplaces only). **Alcoholic Beverages:** Allowed. **Vehicle Maximum Length:** 25 ft. **Other:** No horses without permit, no metal detectors, no loaded firearms, no wood gathering.

To Get There

From Gabbs, go 23 mi. east on NV Hwy. 844 (last 4 mi. are gravel).

GREAT BASIN NATIONAL PARK

Lower & Upper Lehman Creek Campgrounds

100 Great Basin National Park, Baker 89311. T: (775) 234-7331; www.nps.gov/grba; grbainterpretation@nps.gov.

RV ★★★★ Tent ★★★★★

Beauty: ★★★★★	Site Privacy: ★★★★★
Spaciousness: ★★★★	Quiet: ★★★★★
Security: ★★★★	Cleanliness: ★★★★
Insect Control: ★★★	Facilities: ★

One of the eight least visited National Parks in the nation, Great Basin's four campgrounds usually fill up only on weekends and holidays like Memorial Day, Labor Day, 4th of July, and Utah Pioneer Days (July). Lower Lehman campsites offer ample privacy where the desert sagebrush, greasewood, and rabbitbrush give way to evergreen pines and aspens in this vast park that includes alpine meadows, cool streams, Lehman Caves, and nineteenth-century mining remnants like Osceola Ditch. Lower Lehman Creek (six pull-through sites) and sites 1–8 of Upper Lehman Creek are best for RVs and trailers. Upper Lehman has tent-only sites, and the road narrows too much for all but the smallest trailers on the secluded loop with sites 17–24. Wheeler Peak Campground, further up a steep (8% grade) scenic road, is not recommended for long vehicles. However, four miles of sagebrush-lined dirt road lead to Baker Campground, which has seven pull-through sites.

Basics

Operated By: National Park Service. **Open:** All year. **Site Assignment:** First come, first served. **Registration:** Self-pay fee station. **Fee:** $10 (cash or check only). **Parking:** At site.

Facilities

Number of RV Sites: 25. **Number of Tent-Only Sites:** 9. **Hookups:** None. **Each Site:** Table, fire ring. **Dump Station:** Yes. **Laundry:** No. **Pay Phone:** Yes (Visitor Center). **Rest Rooms and Showers:** No showers. **Fuel:** No. **Propane:** No. **Internal Roads:** Paved, rough w/ ruts, pot holes. **RV Service:** No. **Market:** Baker, 5 mi. **Restaurant:** Baker, 5 mi. (Park cafe has limited hours). **General Store:** No. **Vending:** No. **Swimming:** No. **Playground:** No. **Other:** Ranger-led summer programs. **Activities:** Cave tours, horseback riding. **Nearby Attractions:** Baker Archaeological Site, Johnson Lake Mining District. **Additional Information:** White Pine Chamber of Commerce, (775) 289-8877; Great Basin Assoc., (775) 234-7270.

Restrictions

Pets: On leash under owner's physical control at all times. **Fires:** Yes (only in metal fire rings, no collecting of firewood, which is sold 24 hours in Baker). **Alcoholic Beverages:** Allowed. **Vehicle Maximum Length:** 35 ft. **Other:** No fireworks.

To Get There

From junction of NV Hwys. 487 & 488 in Baker, go 5 mi. west on NV Hwy. 488.

HENDERSON

Las Vegas Bay Campground

601 Nevada Hwy., Boulder City 89005. T: (702) 293-8907; F: (702) 293-8936; www.nps.gov/lame/home.html.

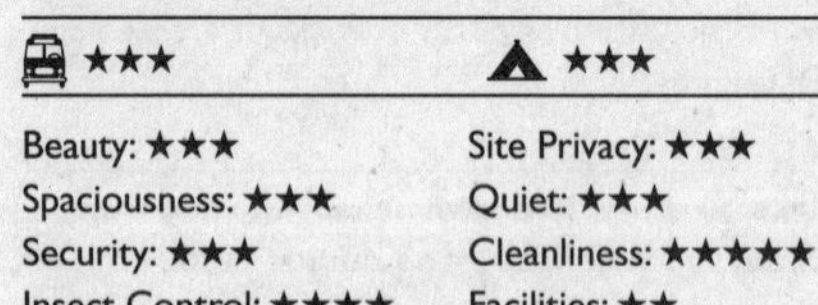

RV ★★★ Tent ★★★

Beauty: ★★★	Site Privacy: ★★★
Spaciousness: ★★★	Quiet: ★★★
Security: ★★★	Cleanliness: ★★★★★
Insect Control: ★★★★	Facilities: ★★

A small, very relaxing campground, Las Vegas Bay combines Lake Mead water recreation with nearness to the Henderson and Las Vegas casino strips. The 650-slip marina does not rent houseboats or allow swimming, but many campsites have marina or lake views. Landscaping is the Lake Mead National Recreation Area standard of palms, oleanders, and eucalyptus. The gray desert backdrop is greened up some by the creosote bush desert wash plant community of rabbit brush, brittle brush, and mesquite. One loop houses both tents and RVs, so a steady hum of diesel generators can often be heard until the quiet hours, 10 p.m. to 6 a.m. There are plenty of picnic tables to make this part of a day trip from

Las Vegas, possibly stopping off at the Ethel M chocolate factory and cactus garden en route to Hoover Dam. However, even picnic table use requires the same $5 entry fee and $10 charge as overnight camping.

BASICS

Operated By: National Park Service. **Open:** All year. **Site Assignment:** First come, first served. **Registration:** Self-pay entrance fee station. **Fee:** $10. **Parking:** At site.

FACILITIES

Number of RV Sites: 86. **Number of Tent-Only Sites:** 0. **Hookups:** None. **Each Site:** Table, grill. **Dump Station:** Yes. **Laundry:** No. **Pay Phone:** Yes. **Rest Rooms and Showers:** Yes. **Fuel:** No (boat fuel only). **Propane:** No. **Internal Roads:** Paved, good. **RV Service:** No. **Market:** Henderson, 8 mi. **Restaurant:** At marina. **General Store:** Yes. **Vending:** No. **Swimming:** No. **Playground:** No. **Other:** Boat ramp, marina, partial handicap access. **Activities:** Fishing, boating. **Nearby Attractions:** Lake Mead, Las Vegas, Henderson, Hoover Dam. **Additional Information:** Las Vegas Bay Marina, (702) 565-9111.

RESTRICTIONS

Pets: On leash under owner's control. **Fires:** Yes. **Alcoholic Beverages:** Allowed. **Vehicle Maximum Length:** Not specified. **Other:** 30-day max. stay.

TO GET THERE

From Henderson, go 9 mi. northeast on NV 146.

LAKE MEAD NATIONAL RECREATION AREA
Callville Bay

601 Nevada Hwy., Boulder City 89005. T: (702) 293-8906; www.nps.gov/lame/home.html.

RV ★★★ | Tent ★★★

Beauty: ★★★★ | Site Privacy: ★★★
Spaciousness: ★★★ | Quiet: ★★★★
Security: ★★★★ | Cleanliness: ★★★★
Insect Control: ★★★ | Facilities: ★★★★

A 589-slip boating and water recreation site on the huge desert lake created when Hoover Dam was built, Callville Bay offers access to Lake Mead and proximity to Las Vegas Territory casinos. Low desert foothills surround the campsites, which are jammed close together and separated from each other by tall poisonous oleanders (watch young kids closely). The nearby marina offers ample facilities and rentals for water fun. RV hookups can be found across the street at Callville Bay Resort (operated by Forever Resorts; (800) 255-5561), which caters to mobile-home residents. A word of warning: Though near the lake, the area is still desert, and summer temperatures in locked vehicles can reach 130° F in 30 minutes. So, don't leave pets in locked vehicles. For more impressive desert scenery and red rocks, continue east on NV Hwy. 167 towards Echo Bay or head inland to Valley of Fire State Park.

BASICS

Operated By: National Park Service. **Open:** All year. **Site Assignment:** First come, first served. **Registration:** Self-pay station at entrance. **Fee:** $10 ($5 Golden Age/Access). **Parking:** At site.

FACILITIES

Number of RV Sites: 80. **Number of Tent-Only Sites:** 0. **Hookups:** None. **Each Site:** Sheltered table, grill. **Dump Station:** Yes. **Laundry:** Yes. **Pay Phone:** Yes. **Rest Rooms and Showers:** Yes. **Fuel:** Yes. **Propane:** Yes. **Internal Roads:** Paved, good condition. **RV Service:** No. **Market:** At nearby marina. **Restaurant:** At nearby marina. **General Store:** No. **Vending:** Yes. **Swimming:** In lake at own risk. **Playground:** No. **Other:** Boat & houseboat rentals, launch ramp, yacht club, trailer village. **Activities:** Boating, fishing. **Nearby Attractions:** Las Vegas, Hoover Dam, Lost City Museum, Valley of Fire State Park. **Additional Information:** Callville Bay Resort, (702) 565-8958 or (800) 255-5561; Alan Bible Visitor Center (NPS), (702) 293-8990.

RESTRICTIONS

Pets: On leash under handler's control. **Fires:** Grills only, no ground fires. **Alcoholic Beverages:** Allowed at site. **Vehicle Maximum Length:** Not specified. **Other:** 30-day limit, noon checkout, 8 people & 2 vehicles or 4 motorcycles per site.

TO GET THERE

From North Las Vegas go east on Lake Mead Blvd. (NV Hwy. 147) 12 mi., then northeast on NV Hwy. 167 (Northshore Scenic Dr.) for 8 mi. and south at Callville Bay turnoff for 4 mi.

LAKE MEAD NATIONAL RECREATION AREA
Echo Bay

601 Nevada Hwy., Boulder City 89005. T: (702) 293-8906; www.nps.gov/lame/home.html.

RV ★★★ | Tent ★★★★★

Beauty: ★★★★ | Site Privacy: ★★★★
Spaciousness: ★★★★ | Quiet: ★★★★
Security: ★★★★ | Cleanliness: ★★★★
Insect Control: ★★ | Facilities: ★★★★

After the Overton Beach tent campground flooded out four years ago, Echo Bay became the northernmost tent campground along Lake Mead. The sites are small and best for car camping, but nearby Echo Bay RV Park has large pull-through sites. More RV sites are also available 18 miles north at Overton Beach Resort. Echo Bay is a good place to stake tents because it combines access to water fun on Lake Mead with nearness to the red-rock formations of Valley of Fire State Park. Two widely separated loops (designated upper and lower) function like separate campgrounds with their own entrances and fee stations. The lower loop has several advantages. It is closer to the marina, has taller oleanders between sites, shady cottonwood and olive trees, and a ranger station perched on a ledge overlooking the campground. The upper loop has smaller oleanders, eucalyptus, small olives, and palms.

BASICS

Operated By: National Park Service. **Open:** All year. **Site Assignment:** First come, first served. **Registration:** Self-pay entrance fee station. **Fee:** $10 ($5 Golden Age/Access). **Parking:** At site.

FACILITIES

Number of RV Sites: 155. **Number of Tent-Only Sites:** 0. **Hookups:** None. **Each Site:** Table, fire ring. **Dump Station:** Yes. **Laundry:** Yes. **Pay Phone:** Yes. **Rest Rooms and Showers:** Yes (shower fee at trailer village). **Fuel:** Yes. **Propane:** Yes. **Internal Roads:** Paved, excellent. **RV Service:** No. **Market:** At marina. **Restaurant:** At marina. **General Store:** No. **Vending:** No. **Swimming:** In lake at own risk. **Playground:** No. **Other:** Houseboat & watercraft rentals, motel. **Activities:** Boating, fishing. **Nearby Attractions:** Las Vegas, Hoover Dam, Lost City Museum (Overton), Valley of Fire State Park. **Additional Information:** Alan Bible Visitor Center (NPS), (702) 293-8990; Seven Crowns Resorts, (702) 394-4000.

RESTRICTIONS

Pets: On leash under owner's control. **Fires:** Yes (in grills only). **Alcoholic Beverages:** Allowed; disorderly conduct and/or public intoxication will result in arrest. **Vehicle Maximum Length:** Not specified. **Other:** 30-day max. stay.

TO GET THERE

From junction of NV Hwys. 147 & 167, go 32 mi. northeast on Hwy. 167 and then 5 mi. east on Echo Bay Rd.

LAKE MEAD NATIONAL RECREATION AREA
Echo Bay RV Park

HC30 Box 30, Overton 89040. T: (702) 394-4000 or (800) 752-9669 (reservations); www.sevencrown.com.

RV ★★★★ | Tent n/a

Beauty: ★★★★ | Site Privacy: ★★★★
Spaciousness: ★★★★ | Quiet: ★★★★
Security: ★★★★ | Cleanliness: ★★★★
Insect Control: ★★★ | Facilities: ★★★★

Pleasant desert living amongst eucalyptus trees best sums up Echo Bay RV Park, which is geared for larger rigs that don't fit into the nearby Echo Bay campground. Some sites have views of Lake Mead, and the nearby marina beckons with water play rentals ranging from houseboats and fishing gear to water skiis, sea-doos, and knee boards. The sites lack tables and grills, but most people are too busy at the lake to even notice the occasional bighorn sheep wandering into the RV park for water during the day. It is harder to miss the wild burros wandering in at night. The campground is further from the water than the one at Overton Beach Marina. But Echo Bay RV Park has a rustic charm that makes Overton seem like a lakeside parking lot.

BASICS

Operated By: Seven Crowns Resorts. **Open:** All year. **Site Assignment:** First come, first served; reservations advised for peak times. **Registration:**

At motel in marina. **Fee:** $12–$18 (V, MC, AE). **Parking:** At site.

FACILITIES

Number of RV Sites: 58. **Number of Tent-Only Sites:** 0. **Hookups:** Electric (30, 50 amp), water, sewer. **Each Site:** Wood posts. **Dump Station:** Yes. **Laundry:** Yes. **Pay Phone:** Yes. **Rest Rooms and Showers:** Yes. **Fuel:** Yes. **Propane:** Yes. **Internal Roads:** Paved, weathered. **RV Service:** No. **Market:** At Echo Bay Marina. **Restaurant:** At Echo Bay Marina. **General Store:** No. **Vending:** Yes. **Swimming:** In lake at own risk. **Playground:** No. **Other:** Houseboat, watercraft & water sport rentals, moorage slips, dry storage, motel, airstrip. **Activities:** Boating, fishing. **Nearby Attractions:** Las Vegas, Lost City Museum (Overton), Roger Springs, Valley of Fire State Park. **Additional Information:** Alan Bible Visitor Center (NPS), (702) 293-8990, www.nps.gov/lame/home.html.

RESTRICTIONS

Pets: On leash under owner's control. **Fires:** Yes. **Alcoholic Beverages:** Allowed. **Vehicle Maximum Length:** 45 ft.

TO GET THERE

From junction of NV Hwys. 147 & 167, go 32 mi. northeast on Hwy. 167 and then 5 mi. east on Echo Bay Rd.

LAKE TAHOE

Zephyr Cove RV Park & Campground

760 Hwy. 50, Zephyr Cove 89448. T: (775) 589-4981; F: (775) 588-9627; www.tahoedixie2.com; zcr-campground@aramark.com.

RV ★★★★ Tent ★★★★

Beauty: ★★★★	Site Privacy: ★★★★
Spaciousness: ★★★★	Quiet: ★★★★
Security: ★★★★	Cleanliness: ★★★★
Insect Control: ★★★★	Facilities: ★★★★

A National Forest Service campground that stretches far back from the trolley stop fronting US Hwy. 50, Zephyr Cove's coveted boulder-strewn, walk-in tent sites must keep foodstuffs locked from black bears that roam across the street from beaches and water recreation. Pull-through sites book up quickly and are closest to the highway, which means more road noise and lake views. There are also good lake views from the 47 walk-in tent sites, especially 45–53, but 32–43 and 54–57 are more secluded among the campground's tall ponderosa pine trees. The drive-in tent sites, 1–10, and RV sites like 117–120 are also attractively situated among the tall ponderosa pines and boulders. Weekends, particularly in summer, the campground books solid and reservations are a necessity. Besides Lake Tahoe's casinos, Zephyr Cove Resort has beaches, an operational Mississippi River Paddleboat, the M.S. Dixie II, stables with horses, and a restaurant across the street from the campground.

BASICS

Operated By: Aramark. **Open:** All year. **Site Assignment:** First come, first served; reservations advised. **Registration:** Office/trailer at entrance. **Fee:** $32 RV, $22 tent (V, MC, AE). **Parking:** At site; parking areas for walk-in tent sites.

FACILITIES

Number of RV Sites: 94. **Number of Tent-Only Sites:** 57. **Hookups:** Electric (30, 50 amp), water, sewer, cable TV, phone (modem, unlimited Internet access). **Each Site:** Table, fire pit. **Dump Station:** Yes. **Laundry:** Yes. **Pay Phone:** Yes. **Rest Rooms and Showers:** Yes. **Fuel:** No. **Propane:** No. **Internal Roads:** Paved, good. **RV Service:** No. **Market:** Stateline, 2 mi. **Restaurant:** Across street. **General Store:** Yes. **Vending:** Yes. **Swimming:** Lake. **Playground:** No. **Other:** Cabins, lodge accommodations, stables, marina, Mississippi River paddleboat. **Activities:** Boating, fishing, horseback riding, winter sports, gambling. **Nearby Attractions:** Incline Village ski slopes. **Additional Information:** Forest Service (Lake Tahoe), www.r5.fs.fed.us/ltbmu; Lake Tahoe Visitors Authority, (530) 544-5050. www.virtualtahoe.com.

RESTRICTIONS

Pets: On leash under owner's control. **Fires:** Yes (no higher than 1 ft. above fire ring or after 11 p.m., $50 fine for ground fires, firewood for sale). **Alcoholic Beverages:** Allowed. **Vehicle Maximum Length:** No limit. **Other:** No kegs, loud music, or generators.

TO GET THERE

At the Zephyr Cove stoplight on US Hwy. 50.

LAS VEGAS

Silverton Hotel Casino RV Park

3333 Blue Diamond Rd., Las Vegas 89139. T: (702) 263-7777 or (800) 588-7711; F: (702) 897-4208; www.silvertoncasino.com.

RV ★★★★ Tent n/a

Beauty: ★★★	Site Privacy: ★★★
Spaciousness: ★★★★	Quiet: ★★★
Security: ★★★★★	Cleanliness: ★★★★
Insect Control: ★★★★	Facilities: ★★★★★

With a sizeable pine tree, tan gravel, and a small wood fence separating each site, Silverton is one of the most pleasant Las Vegas casino RV parks. Indeed, it is proof that sites can be squeezed close together without resembling a parking lot. The casino itself has Old West charm and a friendly, laid-back feel more like rural Nevada than modern Las Vegas. The restaurant has timber and leather chairs and cafeteria-style buffets at prices reminiscent of the Strip of long ago, plus a 10% senior discount and sugar-free deserts for the health conscious. The 45-foot back-in and 70-foot pull-through sites are far enough from the highway that only the loudest of trucks plying the I-15 are bothersome. Shuttle buses run to the Tropicana on the Strip and to the factory outlet stores from this island of sanity just southwest of the international airport.

BASICS

Operated By: Silverton Hotel Casino RV Park. **Open:** All year. **Site Assignment:** First come, first served; reservations accepted. **Registration:** Office. **Fee:** $17–$23 (V, MC, AE, D, DC). **Parking:** At site.

FACILITIES

Number of RV Sites: 460. **Number of Tent-Only Sites:** 0. **Hookups:** Electric (30, 50 amp), water, sewer, cable TV, phone (modem). **Each Site:** Table, grill, 12-ft. wide concrete pad. **Dump Station:** Yes. **Laundry:** Yes. **Pay Phone:** Yes. **Rest Rooms and Showers:** Yes. **Fuel:** No. **Propane:** Yes. **Internal Roads:** Paved, excellent. **RV Service:** No. **Market:** Las Vegas, 3 mi. **Restaurant:** Casino, adjacent. **General Store:** Yes. **Vending:** Yes. **Swimming:** Pool. **Playground:** No. **Other:** Whirlpool, horseshoes, pet area, airport shuttle, free USA Today newspaper. **Activities:** Horseback riding, golf, gun range. **Nearby Attractions:** Red Rock Canyon, Death Valley. **Additional Information:** Las Vegas Convention & Visitors Authority, (702) 892-0711, www.lasvegas24hours.com.

RESTRICTIONS

Pets: On leash under owner's control (cannot be left alone at night). **Fires:** Yes (in charcoal containers or hibachis only, no open fires). **Alcoholic Beverages:** Allowed. **Vehicle Maximum Length:** 70 ft. **Other:** No skateboards, drugs or generator use.

TO GET THERE

From US I-15, go west 0.25 mi. on NV Hwy. 160 (Blue Diamond Rd.).

LAUGHLIN

Riverside RV Park

P.O. Box 500, Laughlin 89029. T: (800) 227-3849 or (702) 298-2535.

RV ★★★ Tent n/a

Beauty: ★★★	Site Privacy: ★★★★
Spaciousness: ★★★★	Quiet: ★★★★
Security: ★★★★	Cleanliness: ★★★★
Insect Control: ★★★	Facilities: ★★★★

Across the street from Don Laughlin's Riverside Resort Hotel and Casino, at the north edge of Casino Dr., across the river from Bullhead City, AZ, is a nicely terraced alternative to the informal camping prevalent in casino parking lots here. The terraces add a sense of privacy and a view, but are too unstable for walking or child's play. However, children can use two swimming pools and play the latest coin games in the casino kids arcade. Cable TV, phone, and modem hookups are among the other comforts. Besides casino entertainment, outlet stores and a bank are next door. Sellouts are the rule when special events come to town, so reservations are advised three weeks in advance (no cancellation penalties). Bullhead City across the river also has several conventional RV parks to choose from, albeit sans casinos, and there are more isolated casino RV parks north and south of here (See appendix).

BASICS

Operated By: Don Laughlin's Riverside Resort Hotel & Casino. **Open:** All year. **Site Assignment:** First come, first served; reservations highly recommended. **Registration:** At office. **Fee:** $17 (V, MC, AE, D). **Parking:** At site.

Facilities

Number of RV Sites: 740. **Number of Tent-Only Sites:** 0. **Hookups:** Electric (30, 50 amps), cable TV, phone. **Each Site:** Varies. **Dump Station:** Yes. **Laundry:** Yes. **Pay Phone:** Yes. **Rest Rooms and Showers:** Yes. **Fuel:** Nearby. **Propane:** Yes. **Internal Roads:** Paved, excellent condition. **RV Service:** No. **Market:** Next door. **Restaurant:** Yes (across street, at casino). **General Store:** No. **Vending:** Yes. **Swimming:** Yes. **Playground:** No. **Other:** Boat ramp, casino shuttles. **Activities:** Casino has bowling, movies, auto museum, Kids Kastle. **Nearby Attractions:** Casinos, outlet stores, river boating, fishing. **Additional Information:** Laughlin Visitor Center, (702) 298-3321 or (800) 4-LAUGHLIN

Restrictions

Pets: 2 per rig; must be kept attended on leash. **Fires:** In approved containers only. **Alcoholic Beverages:** Nevada state law prevails. **Vehicle Maximum Length:** Not specified (tries to accommodate, 20-ft. width most common). **Other:** Firearms & firecrackers prohibited.

To Get There

From Laughlin Civic Drive and Colorado River bridge, go 0.25 mi. south on Casino Dr.

LEE CANYON RECREATION AREA

McWilliams & Dolomite Campgrounds

HCR 38, P.O. Box 451, Las Vegas 89124. T: (702) 872-0156 or (800) 328-6226 or (877) 444-6777 (Reserve America or reservations only); F: (702) 872-0018; www.thousandtrails.com.

RV ★★★★ Tent ★★★★

Beauty: ★★★★ Site Privacy: ★★★★★
Spaciousness: ★★★★ Quiet: ★★★★★
Security: ★★★★ Cleanliness: ★★★★★
Insect Control: ★★★★ Facilities: ★

When summer temperatures are hitting 110° F in Las Vegas, the locals are fleeing to their reserved sites here under the tall ponderosa pines for long, cool (7–85° F) three-day mountain weekends. In winter this Humboldt Toiyabe National Forest area is a bustling ski and snowboard resort. At McWilliams, 1–9 are double sites reservable for families (240 days in advance); loop sites 26–40 are reservable single sites; sites 10–25 on a long hilly straightaway are first-come first-serve. Both McWilliams and Dolomite Campgrounds are exceptionally well maintained by Thousand Trails Inc. under a special use permit granted by the Humboldt Toiyabe National Forest. A totally separate entity, National Recreation Reservation Service, handles phone and Internet (www.reserveusa.com) reservations. For tent site reservations, request McWilliams, which has only a few 34-foot sites. Big vehicles do best at adjacent Dolomite (20 reservable sites), which accommodates 40-foot vehicles.

Basics

Operated By: Thousand Trails Inc. **Open:** May–Sept. (weather permitting). **Site Assignment:** First come, first served; weekend, holiday reservations advised. **Registration:** Self-pay entrance fee station. **Fee:** $13 ($20 double sites; $30 triple sites). **Parking:** At site.

Facilities

Number of RV Sites: 70. **Number of Tent-Only Sites:** 0. **Hookups:** None. **Each Site:** Table, fire ring, grill. **Dump Station:** Yes. **Laundry:** No. **Pay Phone:** Yes. **Rest Rooms and Showers:** No showers. **Fuel:** No. **Propane:** No. **Internal Roads:** Paved, good condition. **RV Service:** No. **Market:** Las Vegas, 35 mi. **Restaurant:** Kyle Canyon, 15 mi. **General Store:** No. **Vending:** No. **Swimming:** No. **Playground:** No. **Other:** Double & triple sites, helicopter pad, large picnic areas nearby. **Activities:** Boating, skiing, winter sports. **Nearby Attractions:** Las Vegas, Mt. Charleston trails, Lee Canyon Ski & Snowboard Resort. **Additional Information:** Humboldt Toiyabe National Forest, (702) 873-8800, www.fs.fed.us.htnf.

Restrictions

Pets: On leash at all times. **Fires:** Yes (firewood sold). **Alcoholic Beverages:** Allowed (provided no boisterous behavior). **Vehicle Maximum Length:** 34 ft. (McWilliams), 40 ft. (Dolomite). **Other:** $5 per extra vehicle at family sites, no tree chopping.

To Get There

From US Hwy. 95 20 mi. north of Las Vegas, go west 15 mi. on NV Hwy. 156 (Lee Canyon Rd.).

OVERTON

Overton Beach Marina

HCR 30, Box 7, Overton 89040. T: (702) 394-4040; F: (702) 394-4124; www.overtonbeachmarina.com.

RV ★★★★ Tent n/a

Beauty: ★★★★ Site Privacy: ★★★★
Spaciousness: ★★★★ Quiet: ★★★★
Security: ★★★★ Cleanliness: ★★★★
Insect Control: ★★★ Facilities: ★★★★

Well run by a National Park Service concessionaire inside Lake Mead National Recreation Area, the Overton Beach Marina RV park is a boater's paradise. The campground itself is down a short road (dirt and paved patches alternate) separated by a quarter mile stretch of swimming beach and a boat launch from the busy Marina, where there is a store, gas station, fish cleaner, restaurant, lounge, motel, and ranger station. The middle of the three rows of RV sites accommodates the largest vehicles. Each site is attractively separated by a low wooden fence and has its own cottonwood tree. Many sites also enjoy at least a partial lake view. Most sites also have room to park a trailer with a boat. Indeed, life here centers around the lake and lovely marina. It is hard to go wrong here, but best to call ahead and reserve a site.

Basics

Operated By: Overton Beach Marina. **Open:** All year. **Site Assignment:** First come, first served; reservations accepted. **Registration:** Inside Marina store. **Fee:** $18 (V, MC). **Parking:** At site.

Facilities

Number of RV Sites: 41. **Number of Tent-Only Sites:** 0. **Hookups:** Electric, water, sewer. **Each Site:** Table, grill, cottonwood tree, low wood fence. **Dump Station:** Yes. **Laundry:** Yes. **Pay Phone:** Yes. **Rest Rooms and Showers:** Yes. **Fuel:** Yes. **Propane:** No. **Internal Roads:** Pavement, worn in spots. **RV Service:** No. **Market:** Overton, 8 mi. **Restaurant:** At Marina. **General Store:** Yes. **Vending:** Yes. **Swimming:** In lake at own risk. **Playground:** No. **Other:** House boat, boat & slip rentals, launch ramp, fish cleaner, motel, boat storage. **Activities:** boating, fishing. **Nearby Attractions:** Lost City Museum, Valley of Fire State Park. **Additional Information:** Alan Bible Visitor Center (NPS), (702) 293-8990.

Restrictions

Pets: On leash under handler's control. **Fires:** Grills only. **Alcoholic Beverages:** Allowed. **Vehicle Maximum Length:** 65 ft.

To Get There

From junction of NV Hwys. 167 & 169, go 4 mi. south on Overton Beach Rd.

OVERTON

Valley of Fire State Park

P.O. Box 515, Overton 89040. T: (702) 397-2621; F: (702) 397-2088; www.state.nv.us/stparks.

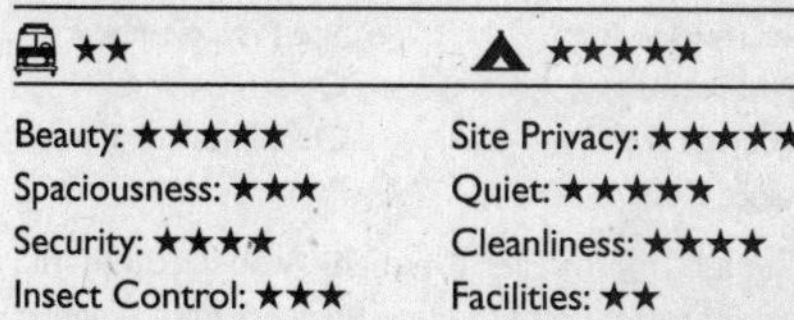

RV ★★ Tent ★★★★★

Beauty: ★★★★★ Site Privacy: ★★★★★
Spaciousness: ★★★ Quiet: ★★★★★
Security: ★★★★ Cleanliness: ★★★★
Insect Control: ★★★ Facilities: ★★

Nevada's first state park, Valley of Fire, began with 1930s CCC sandstone cabins and now has two campgrounds, Atlatl Rock and Arch Rock, scenically hidden amongst twisted, weathered, and black-stained orange-and-red sandstone formations. Atlatl Rock Campground has a shower building, a loop with 19 campsites (one is wheelchair accessible) and a smaller loop with three more isolated walk-in sites for those craving more wilderness. One Atlatl Rock site is big enough for anything on the road, but most are car camping size. Arch Rock Campground is even more secluded amongst the eroded red rocks, and its sites accommodate Tiogas, but nothing much larger. Camping among the red sandstone formations with birds, jack rabbits, and other desert wildlife (shake the boots for scorpions) is a real Nevada wilderness experience, with rock art and red rocks changing color with the sun's movement.

Basics

Operated By: Nevada State Parks. **Open:** All year. **Site Assignment:** First come, first served; reservations required for group areas. **Registration:** Self-pay fee station at campground. **Fee:** $12 (cash or check). **Parking:** At site (48); nearby for 3 walk-in sites.

Facilities

Number of RV Sites: 48. **Number of Tent-Only Sites:** 3. **Hookups:** None. **Each Site:** Table, grill or fire ring, tent pad. **Dump Station:** Yes. **Laundry:** No. **Pay Phone:** Yes. **Rest Rooms and Showers:** Yes. **Fuel:** No. **Propane:** No. **Internal Roads:** Gravel, good condition. **RV Service:** No. **Market:** Overton. **Restaurant:** Overton Beach Marina. **General Store:** No. **Vending:** No. **Swimming:** No. **Playground:** No. **Other:** Shelter over tables at many sites. **Activities:** Picnic areas. **Nearby Attractions:** Lake Mead National Recreation Area, Lost City Museum. **Additional Information:** Overton Chamber of Commerce, (702) 397-2193.

Restrictions

Pets: On leash under handler's control. **Fires:** Yes (only in grills, fire rings). **Alcoholic Beverages:** No public intoxication. **Vehicle Maximum Length:** (see description). **Other:** 2 vehicles & 8 persons per site, disturbing human artifacts or nature is a criminal offense.

To Get There

Exit I-15 at NV Hwy. 169 (Exit 75), and go 18 mi. east.

PANACA

Cathedral Gorge State Park

P.O. Box 176, Panaca 89042. T: (775) 728-4460; F: (775) 728-4469; www.state.nv.us/stparks.

RV ★★★★ Tent ★★★★

Beauty: ★★★★ Site Privacy: ★★★★
Spaciousness: ★★★★ Quiet: ★★★★
Security: ★★★★ Cleanliness: ★★★★
Insect Control: ★★★ Facilities: ★★

Though mostly an overnight stop because the turnoff is right off US Hwy. 93, Cathedral Gorge is beautifully surrounded by white, tan, and buff colored eroding clay and siltstone cliffs and spires from a million-year-old lakebed known as the Panaca Formation. The badland cliffs are fronted by desert scrub loaded with black-tailed jackrabbits and the occasional rattler. Snowbirds on their spring and fall migration journeys often stop here, and if their timing is lucky snag one of the two large pull-through sites (the other 20 sites are mostly 24–30 feet). With Russian olive trees providing shade, this is actually a very relaxing stop and far enough from the highway that noise is not a factor. Advantages to overnighters include being nearer to historic towns (Caliente, Pioche, Panaca) and the main highway (US 93) than either Echo Canyon or Spring Valley State Parks, which require roundtrips down NV Hwy. 322.

Basics

Operated By: Nevada State Parks. **Open:** All year. **Site Assignment:** First come, first served; group site reservation only. **Registration:** Self-pay entrance fee station. **Fee:** $12. **Parking:** At site.

Facilities

Number of RV Sites: 22. **Number of Tent-Only Sites:** 0. **Hookups:** None. **Each Site:** Sheltered table, grill. **Dump Station:** Yes. **Laundry:** No. **Pay Phone:** Yes. **Rest Rooms and Showers:** Yes. **Fuel:** No. **Propane:** No. **Internal Roads:** Gravel, good. **RV Service:** No. **Market:** Panaca, 2 mi. **Restaurant:** Panaca, 2 mi. **General Store:** No. **Vending:** No. **Swimming:** No. **Playground:** No. **Other:** Wheelchair accessible. **Activities:** Bird-watching. **Nearby Attractions:** Bullionville Cemetery, Caliente, Pioche, Echo Canyon, Spring Valley. **Additional Information:** Panaca District Ranger, (775) 728-4467.

Restrictions

Pets: On leash under owner's control. **Fires:** Yes (bring own firewood). **Alcoholic Beverages:** Allowed (if quiet & not drunk). **Vehicle Maximum Length:** 40 ft. **Other:** No guns.

To Get There

Go 2 mi. north of Panaca to park turnoff.

PIOCHE

Echo Canyon State Park

Star Rte. Box 295, Pioche 89043. T: (775) 962-5103; www.state.nv.us/stparks.

RV ★★ Tent ★★★★★

Beauty: ★★★★★ Site Privacy: ★★★★★
Spaciousness: ★★ Quiet: ★★★★
Security: ★★★★ Cleanliness: ★★★★
Insect Control: ★★ Facilities: ★

Hot summers and cool winters prevail at this high-desert park 12 miles east of the Nevada-Utah border. The campground itself is just across the road from earthen Echo Dam, where the reservoir is a mix of cold and warm waters favorable to largemouth bass, rainbow and brown trout, and white crappie. A drive across the dusty earthen dam leads to group campsites, some less developed near the water's edge and one with a restroom perched atop a windy hill surveying surrounding alfalfa farms. Individual campsites on the opposite side of the road from the reservoir offer plenty of privacy in the shade of pines, Russian olives, cottonwood, and sage. There is only one 40-foot pull-through site, making this more a secluded retreat for tent campers. RVs over 32 feet will find more spots continuing east through Ursine to Spring Valley State Park.

Basics

Operated By: Nevada State Parks. **Open:** All year. **Site Assignment:** First come, first served; group area may be reserved. **Registration:** Self-pay entrance fee station. **Fee:** $8. **Parking:** At site.

Facilities

Number of RV Sites: 34. **Number of Tent-Only Sites:** 0. **Hookups:** None. **Each Site:** Sheltered table, grill, fire ring. **Dump Station:** Yes. **Laundry:** No. **Pay Phone:** Yes. **Rest Rooms and Showers:** No showers. **Fuel:** No. **Propane:** No. **Internal Roads:** Gravel, slippery. **RV Service:** No. **Market:** Pioche, 12 mi. **Restaurant:** Pioche, 12 mi. **General Store:** No. **Vending:** No. **Swimming:** In reservoir at own risk. **Playground:** No. **Other:** Boat launch, fish cleaning station, picnic tables. **Activities:** Boating, fishing, bird-watching. **Nearby Attractions:** Spring Valley State Park, Pioche Boot Hill Cemetery. **Additional Information:** Pioche Chamber of Commerce, (775) 962-5544.

Restrictions

Pets: On leash under owner's control. **Fires:** Yes (firewood sold). **Alcoholic Beverages:** Allowed. **Vehicle Maximum Length:** 40 ft. **Other:** 14-day max. stay, occasional winter snow.

To Get There

From Pioche, go 4 mi. east on NV Hwy. 322 and then 8 mi. east on NV Hwy. 323.

RACHEL

Quik-Pik Mini Mart & Campground

HCR 61 Box 23, Rachel 89001. T: (775) 729-2529.

RV ★★★ Tent ★★★

Beauty: ★★★ Site Privacy: ★★★★
Spaciousness: ★★★★ Quiet: ★★★★
Security: ★★★★ Cleanliness: ★★★★
Insect Control: ★★★★ Facilities: ★★

The only stopping place on the Extraterrestrial Highway (NV Hwy. 375), so named because it leads the world in UFO sightings, the 22-year-old town of Rachel is a major motorcycle stopping place, as heading west the next gas is 110 miles away in Tonopah. Rachel's 3,000 acres of high-protein alfalfa trucked to California dairies are overshadowed by its proximity to Area 51. ET buffs believe that the US government's super-secret weapons development center around usually dry Groom Lake houses the remains of space aliens from the 1947 Roswell, NM, crash. The lady and her son running the store, gas station, and RV park are skeptics, but they'll sell you alien T-shirts and souvenirs to take home. The trailer park itself has 22 spots filled by permanent residents. The 10 available spaces across from the Rachel Senior Center Thrift Store are gravel with a bit of desert brush.

Basics

Operated By: Fay Day. **Open:** All year. **Site Assignment:** First come, first served. **Registration:** At mini-mart. **Fee:** $12. **Parking:** At site.

Facilities

Number of RV Sites: 10. **Number of Tent-Only Sites:** 0. **Hookups:** Electric (20, 30 amp), water, sewer. **Each Site:** Gravel. **Dump Station:** Yes. **Laundry:** Yes. **Pay Phone:** Yes. **Rest Rooms and Showers:** Yes. **Fuel:** Yes. **Propane:** Yes. **Internal Roads:** Gravel, good. **RV Service:** No. **Market:** At Mini Mart (limited; Tonopah, 110 mi.). **Restaurant:** In Rachel. **General Store:** Yes. **Vending:** No. **Swimming:** No. **Playground:** No. **Activities:** UFO-watching. **Nearby Attractions:** Area 51. **Additional Information:** Little A'Le Inn, (702) 729-2515.

Restrictions

Pets: On leash under owner's control. **Fires:** No. **Alcoholic Beverages:** Allowed. **Vehicle Maximum Length:** Any size.

To Get There

From triple junction of US Hwy. 93 and NV Hwys. 318 & 375, go west 36 mi. on NV Hwy. 375.

RED ROCK CANYON NATIONAL CONSERVATION AREA

13 Mile Campground

HCR 33 Box 5500, Las Vegas 89124. T: (702) 363-1921; www.redrockcanyon.blm.gov.

RV ★★★ Tent ★★★★

Beauty: ★★★★ Site Privacy: ★★★★
Spaciousness: ★★★★ Quiet: ★★★★
Security: ★★★★ Cleanliness: ★★★★
Insect Control: ★★★ Facilities: ★★

Watch for wildlife when driving Blue Diamond Road between Las Vegas and Red Rock Canyon, as cottontail rabbits, wild horses, and burros dart onto the highway in this National Conservation Area that is so incongruously close to the glitzy Vegas strip. During the sizzling summer months only about 25% of 13 Mile Campground's loops are open. Nevertheless, people come here to camp in the cool evening hours and leave to do their hiking by 6 a.m., before the desert temperatures once again soar. Tent campers will appreciate the 25 walk-in sites and the level gray gravel pads widely dispersed among the low desert scrub, though red-rock views are lacking. The Visitor Center has vending machines, a botanical display, and excellent exhibits explaining the shallow sea origins of nearby gypsum mines and how the area's stunning red rocks formed from 180-million-year-old iron oxide-tinged sand dunes.

Basics

Operated By: BLM. **Open:** All year. **Site Assignment:** First come, first served; 5 group sites require advance reservation. **Registration:** Self-pay fee station. **Fee:** $10 (cash or check only). **Parking:** At site; parking area for walk-in sites.

Facilities

Number of RV Sites: 70. **Number of Tent-Only Sites:** 25. **Hookups:** None. **Each Site:** Table, grill, fire ring. **Dump Station:** No. **Laundry:** No. **Pay Phone:** No. **Rest Rooms and Showers:** No showers. **Fuel:** No. **Propane:** No. **Internal Roads:** Gravel, good. **RV Service:** No. **Market:** Las Vegas, 17 mi. **Restaurant:** Bonnie Springs, 7 mi. **General Store:** No. **Vending:** No. **Swimming:** No. **Playground:** No. **Other:** Visitor Center, gift shop. **Activities:** Horseback riding, biking, rock climbing. **Nearby Attractions:** Las Vegas casinos. **Additional Information:** Friends of Red Rock Canyon, (702) 255-8743.

Restrictions

Pets: On leash under owner's control. **Fires:** Yes (no open fires). **Alcoholic Beverages:** Allowed. **Vehicle Maximum Length:** 40 ft. **Other:** Do not feed or touch wild burros (they kick & bite).

To Get There

From Las Vegas go 20 mi. west on NV Hwy. 159 (Blue Diamond Rd.).

SILVER SPRINGS

Fort Churchill State Historic Park

US Hwy. 50, Silver Springs 89429. T: (775) 577-2345; www.state.nv.us/stparks.

RV ★★★ Tent ★★★★

Beauty: ★★★★ Site Privacy: ★★★★
Spaciousness: ★★★★ Quiet: ★★★★
Security: ★★★★ Cleanliness: ★★★★
Insect Control: ★★★★ Facilities: ★★★

After three white male kidnappers were killed and their outpost burned by local American Indians to free two of their girls held hostage, a volunteer group of white settlers declared all-out war and were routed near Pyramid Lake in 1860. Government troops were called in from California and Fort Churchill was constructed to guard the Pony Express and serve as a base for anti–American Indian expeditions. Fort Churchill was abandoned in 1869, and all that remains now are some old adobe ruins that can be explored, a cemetery, some relics, and an interpretive center. A scenic trail network connecting up with Lahontan State Recreation Area is an on-going state project. The campground at Fort Churchill, which is reached via a gravel road crossing a one-lane wood bridge, has large cottonwood trees shading widely dispersed campsites with good views of the surrounding low rolling hills and cattle grazing in pastures.

Basics

Operated By: Nevada State Parks. **Open:** All year. **Site Assignment:** First come, first served; group reservation required. **Registration:** Self-pay fee station. **Fee:** $7 (cash or check only). **Parking:** At site.

Facilities

Number of RV Sites: 20. **Number of Tent-Only Sites:** 0. **Hookups:** None. **Each Site:** Table, fire ring. **Dump Station:** Yes. **Laundry:** No. **Pay Phone:** Yes. **Rest Rooms and Showers:** No showers. **Fuel:** No. **Propane:** No. **Internal Roads:** Gravel, good. **RV Service:** No. **Market:** Lahontan, 5 mi. **Restaurant:** Silver Springs, 9 mi. **General Store:** No. **Vending:** Yes. **Swimming:** No. **Playground:** No. **Other:** Museum, cemetery, wheelchair-accessible site. **Activities:** Boating, water sports, horseback riding, bird-watching, hunting. **Nearby Attractions:** Virginia City, Carson City, Reno. **Additional Information:** Lyon County Information Center, (775) 463-2246, www.telenet.net/lyontour.

Restrictions

Pets: On leash. **Fires:** Yes (only in fire rings, bring own firewood or approved stove). **Alcoholic Beverages:** Allowed. **Vehicle Maximum Length:** 30 ft. **Other:** Do not climb on the ruins, 14-day stay limit.

To Get There

From junction of US Hwys. 50 & Alt 95, go 8 mi. south on Alt 95 and 1 mi. west on Old Fort Churchill Rd.

SILVER SPRINGS

Lahontan State Recreation Area/ Silver Springs Beach

16799 Lahontan Dam, Fallon 89406. T: (775) 577-2226 or (775) 867-3500; www.state.nv.us/stparks.

RV ★★★ Tent ★★★★

Beauty: ★★★★ Site Privacy: ★★★★
Spaciousness: ★★★★ Quiet: ★★★★
Security: ★★★★ Cleanliness: ★★★★
Insect Control: ★★★ Facilities: ★★★

A 17-mile-long reservoir with 69 miles of shoreline, Lahontan State Recreation Area offers unlimited beach camping on the sand right up to the water's edge, and a small number of designated sites shaded by tall cottonwood trees. Beach 7 has designated campsites, some with lake views and a few large enough to accommodate any vehicle on the road. Large diesel trucks have camped here, and there is no limit on what can be driven onto the beaches. However, the undesignated beach camping sites have no facilities other than restrooms, not even shade. Just beyond Beach 7 the pavement ends and a sign says "Where the pavement ends and the fun begins," which is where a vendor offers horse rides across Lahontan's varied terrain. Additional designated campsites are available about 25 miles northeast on the Carson River near Lahontan Dam and the park headquarters in Fallon.

Basics

Operated By: Nevada State Parks. **Open:** All year. **Site Assignment:** First come, first served. **Registration:** Entrance kiosk. **Fee:** $8 (V, MC). **Parking:** At site.

Facilities

Number of RV Sites: 29. **Number of Tent-Only Sites:** 0. **Hookups:** None. **Each Site:** Table, fire ring. **Dump Station:** Yes. **Laundry:** No. **Pay Phone:** Yes. **Rest Rooms and Showers:** Yes. **Fuel:** No. **Propane:** No. **Internal Roads:** Paved, excellent. **RV Service:** No. **Market:** Lahontan, 1 mi. **Restaurant:** Silver Springs, 5 mi. **General Store:** No. **Vending:** No. **Swimming:** Lake. **Playground:** No. **Other:** Boat launch, horseback ride vendor, wheelchair-accessible site. **Activities:** Boating, water sports, bird watching. **Nearby Attractions:** Virginia City, Carson City, Reno. **Additional Information:** Lahontan Trails (horse rides), (775) 577-4696.

Restrictions

Pets: On leash. **Fires:** Yes. **Alcoholic Beverages:** Allowed. **Vehicle Maximum Length:** No limit. **Other:** No ATVs.

To Get There

From junction of US Hwys. 50 & Alt 95, go 4 mi south on US Hwy. Alt 95 and 1.5 mi. east on Fir St.

SPRING MOUNTAIN NATIONAL RECREATION AREA

Hilltop Campground

HCR 38, P.O. Box 451, Las Vegas 89124. T: (702) 872-0156 or (800) 328-6226 or (877) 444-6777 (Reserve America or reservations only); F: (702) 872-0018; www.thousandtrails.com.

RV: ★ Tent: ★★★★

Beauty: ★★★★★ Site Privacy: ★★★★★
Spaciousness: ★★ Quiet: ★★★★★
Security: ★★★★ Cleanliness: ★★★★
Insect Control: ★★★★ Facilities: ★

Midway between Lee Canyon and Kyle Canyon on a twisting mountain highway with gnarled bristlecone pines and spectacular views into distant canyons, Hilltop Campground is the most remote area campground and the only one with showers (coin-operated; often inoperative). The entrance from NV Hwy. 158 forks, with one road leading to Spring Mountain Youth Camp Correctional Facility and the adjacent Hilltop Exit sporting a warning sign for the tire shredders that will ruin the day of those entering the wrong way. Like Lee Canyon, 60% of the sites among the gnarled hillside pines here are reserved in advance on hot Vegas weekends. Sites have either forest views or views deep into the valleys below. Reserve sites 9–11,13,14, and 16–18 for the best valley views (not for those afraid of heights). Sites 25–30 (no reservations) are among the most private looking into the forest. Nearby Mahogany Grove has two group sites.

BASICS

Operated By: Thousand Trails Inc. **Open:** May 15–Oct. 15 (weather permitting). **Site Assignment:** First come, first served. **Registration:** Self-pay entrance fee station. **Fee:** $13 ($20 double sites; $30 triple sites). **Parking:** At site.

FACILITIES

Number of RV Sites: 35. **Number of Tent-Only Sites:** 0. **Hookups:** None. **Each Site:** Table, grill, fire ring. **Dump Station:** No. **Laundry:** No. **Pay Phone:** No. **Rest Rooms and Showers:** Yes. **Fuel:** No. **Propane:** No. **Internal Roads:** Paved, excellent condition. **RV Service:** No. **Market:** Las Vegas, 35 mi. **Restaurant:** Kyle Canyon, 6 mi. **General Store:** No. **Vending:** No. **Swimming:** No. **Playground:** No. **Other:** Tire shredders at exit. **Activities:** Archery range. **Nearby Attractions:** Mt. Charleston, Lee Canyon, Las Vegas. **Additional Information:** Humboldt Toiyabe National Forest, (702) 873-8800, www.fs.fed.us.htnf; Spring Mountains Assoc., (702) 896-7213.

RESTRICTIONS

Pets: On leash under owner's control. **Fires:** Yes. **Alcoholic Beverages:** Allowed. **Vehicle Maximum Length:** 25 ft. **Other:** No fireworks.

TO GET THERE

From junction of US Hwy. 95 & NV Hwy. 157 north of Las Vegas, go 17 mi. west on Hwy. 157 and then 6 mi. northwest on NV Hwy. 158.

SPRING MOUNTAIN NATIONAL RECREATION AREA

Kyle Canyon & Fletcher View Campgrounds

HCR 38, P.O. Box 451, Las Vegas 89124. T: (702) 872-0156 or (800) 328-6226 or (877) 444-6777 (Reserve America or reservations only); F: (702) 872-0018; www.thousandtrails.com.

RV: ★★★★ Tent: ★★★★

Beauty: ★★★★ Site Privacy: ★★★★★
Spaciousness: ★★★★ Quiet: ★★★★
Security: ★★★★ Cleanliness: ★★★★
Insect Control: ★★★ Facilities: ★

Nestled alongside a dry creek bed with shady oaks and ponderosa pines, Kyle Canyon and Fletcher View Campgrounds are closer to Las Vegas than Hilltop, Dolomite, and McWilliams Campgrounds. All five campgrounds attract the same weekenders seeking to beat the Vegas summer heat by fleeing to the mountains. The dozen Fletcher View sites are very spread out, relatively spacious (most can squeeze in 36–40-foot vehicles) and cannot be reserved in advance. In contrast, 10 of the 25 Kyle Canyon sites, which are closer together, can be reserved, and often are booked up well in advance (beginning Friday night) on summer weekends. Picnics are also popular, and the Visitors Centers has hiking. Less than a mile down the road is Kyle Canyon RV Camp, which lacks toilets but can hold 15 self-contained vehicles as an overflow area or be reserved as a group area.

BASICS

Operated By: Thousand Trails Inc. **Open:** May–Sept. (weather permitting). **Site Assignment:** First come, first served; 60% of sites reservable. **Registration:** Self-pay entrance fee station. **Fee:** $13. **Parking:** At site.

FACILITIES

Number of RV Sites: 37. **Number of Tent-Only Sites:** 0. **Hookups:** None. **Each Site:** Table, grill, fire ring. **Dump Station:** No. **Laundry:** No. **Pay Phone:** Yes. **Rest Rooms and Showers:** No showers. **Fuel:** No. **Propane:** No. **Internal Roads:** Gravel, good. **RV Service:** No. **Market:** Las Vegas, 23 mi. **Restaurant:** Kyle Canyon. **General Store:** No. **Vending:** No. **Swimming:** No. **Playground:** No. **Other:** Wheelchair-accessible sites, hotel, picnic area. **Activities:** Hiking, winter sports. **Nearby Attractions:** Lee Canyon Ski Area, Mt. Charleston, Las Vegas. **Additional Information:** Humboldt Toiyabe National Forest, (702) 873-8800, www.fs.fed.us.htnf; Spring Mountains Assoc., (702) 896-7213.

RESTRICTIONS

Pets: On leash under owner's control. **Fires:** Yes. **Alcoholic Beverages:** Allowed. **Vehicle Maximum Length:** 36 ft.

TO GET THERE

From junction of US Hwy. 95 & NV Hwy. 157 north of Las Vegas, go 18 mi. west on Hwy. 157.

TONOPAH

The Station House

P.O. Box 1351, 1100 Erie St., Tonopah 89049. T: (775) 482-9777.

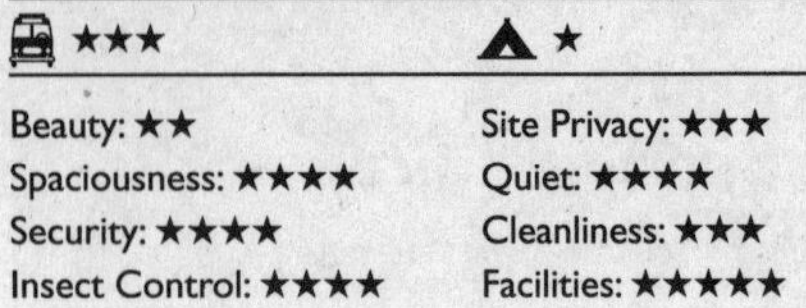

RV: ★★★ Tent: ★

Beauty: ★★ Site Privacy: ★★★
Spaciousness: ★★★★ Quiet: ★★★★
Security: ★★★★ Cleanliness: ★★★
Insect Control: ★★★★ Facilities: ★★★★★

Halfway between Las Vegas and Reno, Tonopah is a boom-and-bust mining town (the copper mine is currently going bust and buildings are getting boarded up) best known for its Air Force testing range where the F-117A Blackhawk stealth fighter was secretly test flown on moonless nights. The Station House is a friendly small town Old West casino complex where the back of the small rear parking lot has back-in spaces with hookups. There is some competition from the Bang Club Casino down the street, where the sign on the adjacent gravel lot invites self-contained RVs and trucks to park for free. But with the exception of the funky Twister trailer park, these are the only hookups in town and for 93 miles. In winter people even pitch their tents on the asphalt, plug in their heaters and use the facilities. The casino's Old West facade helps mitigate the asphalt ambiance.

BASICS

Operated By: The Station House. **Open:** All year. **Site Assignment:** First come, first served; reservations advised for special-event weekends. **Registration:** At hotel desk inside casino. **Fee:** $16.08 (V, MC, AE, D, DC). **Parking:** At site.

FACILITIES

Number of RV Sites: 18. **Number of Tent-Only Sites:** 0. **Hookups:** Electric (20, 30 amp), water, sewer. **Each Site:** Blacktop space. **Dump Station:** Yes. **Laundry:** Yes. **Pay Phone:** Yes. **Rest Rooms and Showers:** Yes. **Fuel:** Yes (nearby). **Propane:** No. **Internal Roads:** Paved, good. **RV Service:** No. **Market:** On the property. **Restaurant:** In casino. **General Store:** Yes. **Vending:** Yes. **Swimming:** No. **Playground:** Yes. **Other:** 24-hour casino, slot machine museum, clothing store, wheelchair accessible. **Activities:** Gambling, video arcade for kids, Tues.–Sun. live band, Monday night big-screen footbal. **Nearby Attractions:** Tonopah Historic Mining Park, Central Nevada Museum. **Additional Information:** Tonopah Chamber of Commerce, (775) 482-3859.

RESTRICTIONS

Pets: On leash under owner's control; not allowed in hotel. **Fires:** No. **Alcoholic Beverages:** Allowed. **Vehicle Maximum Length:** 44 ft. **Other:** All spots are back-in.

TO GET THERE

Go 0.25 mi. south on US Hwy. 95 from the junction of US Hwys. 95 & 6.

URSINE

Spring Valley State Park

Star Rte. Box 201, Pioche 89043. T: (775) 962-5102; www.state.nv.us/stparks.

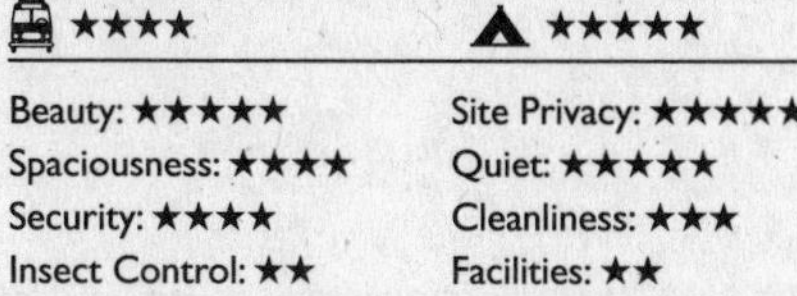

RV ★★★★ Tent ★★★★★

Beauty: ★★★★★ Site Privacy: ★★★★★
Spaciousness: ★★★★ Quiet: ★★★★★
Security: ★★★★ Cleanliness: ★★★
Insect Control: ★★ Facilities: ★★

Horsethief Gulch Campground is the most developed of Spring Valley State Park's two campgrounds, with 36 sites just west of Eagle Valley Reservoir where paved NV Hwy. 322 ends after winding through several miles of tall gray spires reminiscent of Great Basin National Park to the north. Two miles north of Horsethief Gulch via a dirt road is the primitive six-site Ranch Campground (tables, grills, restroom). Many RVs skip the park fees altogether and park on nearby BLM land (a big turnout loop just before the paved road ends), mooching free showers at the park while swimming, fishing, and boating at the reservoir. The upper loop at Horsethief Gulch has a large pull-through site and is particularly private thanks to many large junipers (a source of rot resistant wood in NV's early days) growing amongst the singleleaf pinons (edible nuts), big sagebrush (state flower), and rubber rabbitbrush (winter jackrabbit food).

Basics

Operated By: Nevada State Parks. **Open:** All year. **Site Assignment:** First come, first served; group site reservations. **Registration:** Self-pay entrance fee station. **Fee:** $12. **Parking:** At site.

Facilities

Number of RV Sites: 42. **Number of Tent-Only Sites:** 0. **Hookups:** None. **Each Site:** Sheltered table, grill, fire ring. **Dump Station:** Yes. **Laundry:** No. **Pay Phone:** Yes. **Rest Rooms and Showers:** Yes. **Fuel:** No. **Propane:** No. **Internal Roads:** Gravel, good. **RV Service:** No. **Market:** Pioche, 18 mi. **Restaurant:** Pioche, 18 mi. **General Store:** No. **Vending:** No. **Swimming:** In reservoir at own risk. **Playground:** No. **Other:** Boat launch, fish cleaning station, 2 wheelchair-accessible sites. **Activities:** Boating, fishing. **Nearby Attractions:** Pioche, Echo Canyon, Cathedral Gorge. **Additional Information:** Pioche Chamber of Commerce, (775) 962-5544.

Restrictions

Pets: On leash under owner's control. **Fires:** Yes. **Alcoholic Beverages:** Allowed. **Vehicle Maximum Length:** 40 ft. **Other:** Firewood collection prohibited.

To Get There

From Pioche, go 18 mi. northeast on NV Hwy. 322 through the town of Ursine until the paved road ends.

WALKER LAKE

Sportsman's Beach Recreation Site

1535 Hot Springs Rd., Suite 330, Carson City 89706. T: (775) 885-6000; www.blm.gov.

RV ★★★ Tent ★★★

Beauty: ★★★★★ Site Privacy: ★★★★
Spaciousness: ★★★★ Quiet: ★★★
Security: ★★ Cleanliness: ★★★
Insect Control: ★★★ Facilities: ★★

One of Nevada's few natural desert freshwater lakes, Walker Lake's wave-cut shoreline has been steadily shrinking for several thousand years since the climate began warming at the end of the last Ice Age. Closest to the roadside at Sportsman's Beach are 16 lake-view campsites with sheltered tables on cement pads. Switchbacks wend down to campsites even closer to the lake. The cluster of campsites numbered 17–21 just above the boat ramp have the most vehicle parking, and small stake-like signs documenting lake water levels indicate that this area was underwater in the 1940s. Sites 22–32 have narrow circular pull-through areas capable of accommodating boats and narrow vehicles well over 30 feet in length. More primitive beach camping (restrooms only; bring your own tables, chairs and stoves) is available less than a mile north via badly rutted roads at Tamarack and 20 Mile Beaches.

Basics

Operated By: BLM. **Open:** All year. **Site Assignment:** First come, first served. **Registration:** Self-pay fee station. **Fee:** $4–$6 ($4 primitive sites; $6 developed sites; cash or check only). **Parking:** At site.

Facilities

Number of RV Sites: 34. **Number of Tent-Only Sites:** 0. **Hookups:** None. **Each Site:** Sheltered table, fire ring. **Dump Station:** Yes. **Laundry:** No. **Pay Phone:** No. **Rest Rooms and Showers:** No showers. **Fuel:** No. **Propane:** No. **Internal Roads:** Paved road needing patching turns to gravel. **RV Service:** No. **Market:** Hawthorne, 12.5 mi. south. **Restaurant:** Paiute reservation truck stop, 5 mi. north. **General Store:** No. **Vending:** No. **Swimming:** In lake at own risk. **Playground:** No. **Other:** Boat ramp. **Activities:** Boating, fishing, bird-watching. **Nearby Attractions:** Ghost towns. **Additional Information:** Mineral County Chamber of Commerce, (775) 945-5896.

Restrictions

Pets: On leash. **Fires:** Yes (only in fire ring). **Alcoholic Beverages:** Allowed. **Vehicle Maximum Length:** 28 ft. **Other:** 14 day limit.

To Get There

From Hawthorne, go 12.5 mi. north on US 95.

WINNEMUCCA

Hi-Desert RV Park

5575 East Winnemucca Blvd., Winnemucca 89455. T: (775) 623-4513 or (800) 699-3959; F: (775) 625-4329; www.hi-desertrv.com; Camp@hi-desertrv.com.

RV ★★★★ Tent ★★★★

Beauty: ★★★★ Site Privacy: ★★★★
Spaciousness: ★★★★ Quiet: ★★★★
Security: ★★★★ Cleanliness: ★★★★
Insect Control: ★★★★ Facilities: ★★★★

Winnemucca is a good stopping place between Reno and Salt Lake City or Boise, and Hi-Desert is an attractive alternative to the casino parking lots. Poplar and walnut trees provide shade, grassy strips separate each site, and attractive white-bulb fixtures sit atop black lamp poles. The highway is nearby, but the rustling of tree leaves in the wind helps muffle the occasional motorcycle or truck at this well-maintained park. The tent area is grass, and conveniently located near the store and pool. The gift shop has an interesting selection of knives sheathed in python, alligator, and rattlesnake skin cases, plus gambling machines to satisfy casino urges. Heading east there is not another good RV park until Elko, as Battle Mountain has been suffering from low gold prices and the miners living in the RV Parks there have moved on.

Basics

Operated By: Connie Sasser. **Open:** All year. **Site Assignment:** First come, first served; reservations advised May–Aug. **Registration:** Office. **Fee:** $16 tent; $22.50 RV (V, MC, AE, D. **Parking:** At site.

Facilities

Number of RV Sites: 137. **Number of Tent-Only Sites:** 11. **Hookups:** Electric (20, 30, 50 amp), water, sewer, cable TV. **Each Site:** Table. **Dump Station:** Yes. **Laundry:** Yes. **Pay Phone:** Yes. **Rest Rooms and Showers:** Yes. **Fuel:** No. **Propane:** Yes. **Internal Roads:** Paved, good. **RV Service:** No. **Market:** Winnemucca, 2 mi. **Restaurant:** Winnemucca, 0.3 mi. **General Store:** Yes. **Vending:** Yes. **Swimming:** Pool. **Playground:** Yes. **Other:** Grills in tent area, dog walk, free shuttle to town, whirlpool, tetherball, volleyball, horseshoes. **Activities:** Golf, bowling, gambling, hunting, fishing, biking. **Nearby Attractions:** Buckaroo Hall of Fame, Paradise Valley. **Additional Information:** Winnemucca Convention Center, (775) 623-5071, (800) 962-2638, www.winnemucca.com.

Restrictions

Pets: On leash under owner's control. **Fires:** Yes (no open fires, only in grills). **Alcoholic Beverages:** Allowed. **Vehicle Maximum Length:** 61 ft. **Other:** Children must be under adult supervision & in campsites by 10 p.m.

To Get There

From US I-80, take Exit 180 west 0.8 mi.

New Hampshire

From coastal beaches, freshwater lakes, northern forests, rolling hills and valleys, and towering mountains, New Hampshire offers campers a diverse landscape, rich in scenic beauty and cultural heritage. The state boasts more than 150 private campgrounds, ranging from rustic sites to resort-style properties, and some of the finest state parks in the nation. Visitors to the Granite State can set up camp on an ocean beach or along the shorelines of a pristine lake; you can camp amid acres of dense pine forest dotted with meandering rivers, cascades, and waterfalls, or in the shadows of New England's tallest mountains. Campgrounds can also be found near the state's top tourist attractions and just outside its bustling cities and resort towns.

The southwest region of the state, dominated by **Mount Monadnock** (the most climbed mountain in North America!) is often called New Hampshire's quiet corner. Campers will find scenic backroads leading to woodlands, lakes, valley villages, and historic sites. It's the perfect place to get away from it all.

The New Hampshire Lakes Region, nestled in the center of the state, is dotted with 273 lakes and ponds, including **Lake Winnipesaukee,** the state's largest. As expected, campers in this region will find that recreation centers around the water: fishing, swimming, and boating are popular pursuits.

The south central region of the state is home to its largest cities: **Manchester, Nashua,** and **Concord,** where campers have museums, theaters, and shopping malls to visit. Just outside the cities, campgrounds are nestled in a rural landscape of rolling hills, fields, and farms.

Campground choices abound in the popular northern White Mountains region. This region encompasses the 780,000-acre **White Mountain National Forest,** the **Kancamagus National Scenic Byway,** 6,288-foot **Mt. Washington** (the tallest mountain in the Northeast), more than 100 waterfalls, and thousands of miles of rivers, streams, and trails. Campers have a delightful blend of busy resort towns (like **North Conway, Lincoln,** and **North Woodstock**), quaint villages and wide expanses of back-to-nature wilderness to explore. Campgrounds in the area run the gamut from small, tucked-away properties to spacious, amenity-laden resorts.

New Hampshire has a mere 18 miles of Atlantic coastline and only one state park campground with oceanfront property. But several top-notch campgrounds are clustered in surrounding inland towns, some set in rural areas, others along freshwater rivers and tidal marshlands. All have quick access to the historic seaport city of **Portsmouth,** ocean beaches and parks (much of the coastline is public land), and popular seacoast attractions.

One very nice bonus for campers visiting small and condensed New Hampshire: no matter where you set up camp, the mountains, lakes, cities, attractions, and ocean, all are just a short drive away.

The following facilities accept payment in checks or cash only:

Beech Hill, Twin Mountain

Wakeda Family Campground, Hampton Falls

The following facilities feature 20 or fewer sites:

Cannon Mountain RV Park, Laconia

Twin Mountain Motor Court & RV Park, Twin Mountain

ALBANY

Jigger Johnson Campground

Kancamagus Hwy., Albany 03818. T: (603) 447-5448.

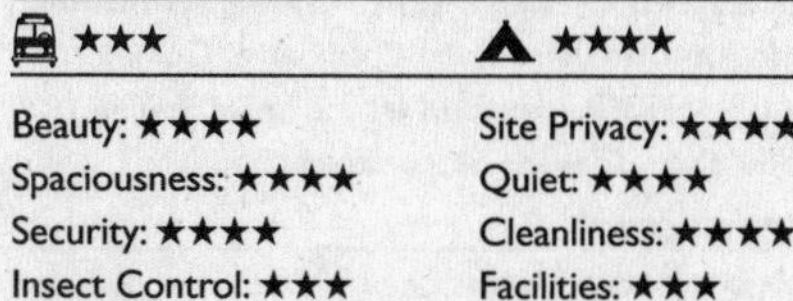

RV ★★★ Tent ★★★★

Beauty: ★★★★ Site Privacy: ★★★★
Spaciousness: ★★★★ Quiet: ★★★★
Security: ★★★★ Cleanliness: ★★★★
Insect Control: ★★★ Facilities: ★★★

Jigger Johnson is the largest campground on the Kancamagus, and the only campground along the Kanc that has coin-operated hot showers. Most of the sites along the northeastern end of the campground, near the banks of the Swift River, are spacious and set amid fairly dense forest. There is a series of interpretive programs on Saturday evenings throughout the summer, focusing on a particular aspect of the local flora and fauna, and the campground is very close to some classic White Mountain hiking. The trail that leads down to the banks of the Swift River intersects with a trail that runs along the backside of the campground. This mellow trail follows the Swift both upstream and downstream for quite a distance, passing some beautiful bends in the river and traveling through delightful aromatic groves of birch and pine. It's a great hike to do with kids because it's relatively flat, and there are all sorts of wonderful things to see and experience.

BASICS

Operated By: US Forest Service. **Open:** Late May–mid-Oct. **Site Assignment:** First come first served. **Registration:** Select site, then pay at self-service fee station. **Fee:** $15. **Parking:** At site.

FACILITIES

Number of RV Sites: 76. **Number of Tent-Only Sites:** 0. **Hookups:** None. **Each Site:** Fire ring, picnic table. **Dump Station:** No. **Laundry:** No. **Pay Phone:** No. **Rest Rooms & Showers:** Yes. **Fuel:** No. **Propane:** No. **Internal Roads:** Paved. **RV Service:** No. **Market:** No. **Restaurant:** No. **General Store:** No. **Vending:** No. **Swimming Pool:** No. **Playground:** No. **Activities:** Fishing, hiking, scenic byway. **Nearby Attractions:** Historic Russell-Colbath, an 1830s homestead. **Additional Information:** North Conway Chamber of Commerce, (603) 356-3171.

RESTRICTIONS

Pets: On leash. **Fires:** In fire ring. **Alcoholic Beverages:** At site. **Vehicle Maximum Length:** 2 vehicles per site. **Other:** 8 people per site; 14-day stay limit.

TO GET THERE

From Lincoln, follow Kancamagus Hwy. to campground on left. From Conway, follow Kancamagus Hwy. to campground on right, shortly after Bear Notch Rd., also on right.

ASHLAND

Ames Brook Campground

104 Winona Rd., Ashland 03217. T: (603) 968-7998; amsbrkcg@lr.net.

RV ★★★ Tent ★★★

Beauty: ★★★ Site Privacy: ★★★
Spaciousness: ★★★ Quiet: ★★★★
Security: ★★★ Cleanliness: ★★★
Insect Control: ★★★ Facilities: ★★★

If all you're looking for is a clean, pleasant base to explore the New Hampshire Lakes region and beyond, you can't go wrong here. This rural campground, minutes from downtown Ashland and Lake Winnipesaukee, has flat sites, rectangular sandy swatches laid out in a row, all carved out of the woods. Alas, the campground doesn't have much of a personality, a row of semi-permanent-looking seasonals crowd the front of the campground; further back in the woods, you'll find the narrow, barely-there Ames Brook winding through a small section of the campground. If you like to sleep to the sound of babbling water, request sites numbers 50 to 52. A small row of full hookup sites are also along the brook. We like the library of books and magazines the owners keep in the office and laundromat area; nice touch. The campground offers a quieter, more natural setting than its neighborhood Yogi Bear's Jellystone Park, but with fewer activities and facilities.

BASICS

Operated By: Barbara Marion. **Open:** Memorial Day–Columbus Day. **Site Assignment:** Reservations suggested, one-half of scheduled stay required as deposit, must cancel within 5 days of scheduled visit, MC, V, D, & personal checks accepted. **Registration:** At office. **Fee:** Full hookup, $29; water & electric, $27; no hookup, $22, based on two adults; children 10–17 years are additional $2, extra adult is $6. **Parking:** At site, one vehicle per site.

FACILITIES

Number of RV Sites: 56. **Number of Tent-Only Sites:** 0. **Hookups:** Water, electric, sewer (30 amps), cable TV. **Each Site:** Table, fire ring. **Dump Station:** Yes. **Laundry:** Yes. **Pay Phone:** Yes. **Rest Rooms & Showers:** Yes. **Fuel:** No. **Propane:** Yes. **Internal Roads:** Gravel, dirt (fair). **RV Service:** No. **Market:** Ashland (1 mi). **Restaurant:** No. **General Store:** Yes. **Vending:** No. **Swimming Pool:** Yes. **Playground:** Yes. **Other:** Small book library, game room, activities hall. **Activities:** Swimming, croquet, basketball. **Nearby Attractions:** Lake Winnipesaukee, Squam Lake, Weirs Beach, outlet shopping, antiquing, quick access to the White Mountain area. **Additional Information:** Greater Laconia/Weirs Beach Chamber of Commerce, 11 Veterans Square, Laconia, NH 03246 (603) 524-5531.

RESTRICTIONS

Pets: Must be on a leash, never left unattended. **Fires:** In grills, stoves, & fire rings only. **Alcoholic Beverages:** At site only. **Vehicle Maximum Length:** None. **Other:** Two tents or one trailer per site; no boats parked on site but may be parked in lot.

TO GET THERE

From I-93, exit 24, go 0.75 mi. south on Rte. 3, then 0.25 mi. south on Rte. 132, then 0.5 mi. south on Winona Rd. campground is on the right.

ASHLAND

Yogi Bear's Jellystone Park

P.O. Box 1926, Ashland 03217. T: (603) 968-9000; www.jellystonenh.com; yogi@jellystonenh.com.

RV ★★★★ Tent ★★

Beauty: ★★ Site Privacy: ★★
Spaciousness: ★★ Quiet: ★★
Security: ★★★ Cleanliness: ★★★★
Insect Control: ★★★ Facilities: ★★★★★

If you're looking for a little peace and quiet, don't even think about coming here. This franchise property is a "happening place," for campers who like a jam-packed, bustling schedule of activities and very close neighbors. The campground features major events throughout the summer, with concerts, dances, parades, contests, and more. This, in addition to the daily schedule of arts and crafts, hayrides, workshops, bingo.whew! We get tired just reading the list and watching the families scurry from event to event. Most sites are small and in the open, with little privacy. The property is set on the pretty Pemigawasset River, but an annoying and unattractive fence separates you from the view. There's a small beach area and a fishing dock. But, if you want to get away from it all, you'll have to rent a boat and paddle the river. Otherwise, let the kids go meet Yogi and BooBoo while you join the country line dancing lessons-right before the ice cream social! Lots of people, especially families, love this place.

BASICS

Operated By: Jane, Marvin, & Erma Cohen. **Open:** Memorial Day–Columbus Day. **Site Assignment:** Reservations strongly urged; full deposit for 2-3 day stay, 50 percent for longer stays. Refunds, less $5 w/ 14 day notice. MC, V, D, & personal checks accepted. **Registration:** At office. **Fee:** Full hookup, $49; water & electric, $45; no hookup, $42, based on two people per site, children, ages 2–17 are $2; grandparents, $6; additional adults, $22.50. **Parking:** At site, one vehicle per site.

FACILITIES

Number of RV Sites: 255. **Number of Tent-Only Sites:** 20. **Hookups:** Water, electric, sewer (20, 30 amps). **Each Site:** Table, fire ring. **Dump Station:** Yes. **Laundry:** Yes. **Pay Phone:** Yes. **Rest Rooms & Showers:** Yes (coin-op). **Fuel:** No. **Propane:** No. **Internal Roads:** Paved (good). **RV Service:** Yes. **Market:** Ashland (2 mi). **Restaurant:** Yes. **General Store:** Yes. **Vending:** Yes. **Swimming Pool:** Yes. **Playground:** Yes. **Other:** Water playground, hot tub, river frontage, boat dock, indoor & outdoor theaters, teen rec hall, arcade, canoe, rowboat, & kayak rentals, 19-hole mini-golf, day trip information center babysitting referral service, ice cream shop, cabin rentals. **Activities:** Swimming, fishing, boating, basketball, mini-golf, horseshoes, shuffleboard, bolleyball, softball, bocci ball, planned activities including dance workshops, arts & crafts, concerts, live entertainment, hayrides, movies, & more. **Nearby Attractions:** Lake Winnipesaukee, Squam Lake, Weirs Beach, outlet shopping, antiquing, quick access to the White Mountain area. **Additional Information:** Greater Laconia/ Weirs Beach Chamber of Commerce, 11 Veterans Square, Laconia, NH 03246 (603) 524-5531.

Restrictions

Pets: Strongly discouraged; must be on a leash, never left unattended & not allowed in most public areas. **Fires:** In grills, stoves, & fire rings only. **Alcoholic Beverages:** Must be in cup or glass if carried off site. **Vehicle Maximum Length:** 35 ft. **Other:** No motor bikes.

To Get There

From I-93, exit 23, go 0.5 mi. east on Rte. 104, then 4 mi. north on Rte. 132; campground is on the left

BARNSTEAD

Sun River Campground

Rte. 28, P.O. Box 7, Center Barnstead 03225. T: (603) 269-3333; www.ucampnh.com/sunriver; sun river@worldpath.net.

RV ★★ Tent ★★★

Beauty: ★★★	Site Privacy: ★★★
Spaciousness: ★★★	Quiet: ★★★★
Security: ★★★	Cleanliness: ★★★★
Insect Control: ★★★	Facilities: ★★★

This modest, rural campground will appeal to those looking for quiet days and nights and simple outdoor fun. The campground, nestled in thick woods, along two miles of the meandering Suncook River, has spacious, shaded sites (average width is about 40 feet.) Bring your fishing pole; there's state stocked fishing in the river for trout, bass, pickerel, and perch. The beach is a tiny patch of sand near a pool in the river, ringed by trees-a picturesque place to wet your feet or for the kids to take a dunk. The sites along the river are best but we'd avoid the ones near the beach (site 43 particularly), where you might not get the peace and quiet you crave. Many visitors use the campground as a base to explore the area, heading to southern New Hampshire attractions or north into the mountains.

Basics

Operated By: Keith & Nancy Bainton. **Open:** May 15–Oct. 15. **Site Assignment:** Reservations suggested. One half of amount due w/ reservation; one week cancellation notice for deposit return. MC, V, AE, & personal checks accepted. **Registration:** At office. **Fee:** Water & electric, $22; no hookups, $18, based on two adults & two children. **Parking:** At site, one vehicle per site.

Facilities

Number of RV Sites: 63. **Number of Tent-Only Sites:** 7. **Hookups:** Water, electric (20, 30 amps). **Each Site:** Picnic table, fire ring. **Dump Station:** Yes. **Laundry:** Yes. **Pay Phone:** Yes. **Rest Rooms & Showers:** Yes. **Fuel:** No. **Propane:** No. **Internal Roads:** Gravel, dirt (fair). **RV Service:** No. **Market:** Barnstead (5 mi.). **Restaurant:** No. **General Store:** Yes. **Vending:** No. **Swimming Pool:** No. **Playground:** Yes. **Other:** Two mi. of river frontage, rec hall, beach, group area, pop-up & trailer rentals. **Activities:** Swimming, stocked fishing, ping pong, horseshoes, basketball, volleyball, pot luck suppers, marshmallow roasts on the beach, walking club & story hours. **Nearby Attractions:** Concord, NH International Speedway, quick access to Lakes Region & Seacoast area, antiquing. **Additional Information:** Greater Concord Chamber of Commerce, 244 North Main St., Concord, NH 03301-5078, (603) 224-2508.

Restrictions

Pets: Must be on a leash, never left unattended, not allowed on the beach. **Fires:** In grills, stoves, & fire rings only. **Alcoholic Beverages:** At site only. **Vehicle Maximum Length:** None. **Other:** No bike riding after dusk, no mini bikes or all terrain vehicles allowed.

To Get There

From junction of Rtes. 4/202 & 28, go 12 miles north on Rte. 28; campground is on the right.

BARRINGTON

Ayers Lake Farm

557 Rte. 202, Barrington 03825. T: (603) 335-1110 (603) 332-5940; www.ucampnh.com/ayerslake.

RV ★★★ Tent ★★★★

Beauty: ★★★★	Site Privacy: ★★★
Spaciousness: ★★★	Quiet: ★★★★
Security: ★★★★★	Cleanliness: ★★★★
Insect Control: ★★★	Facilities: ★★★

When we first drove up to the campground, we thought we'd arrived at a very pretty New England country inn. The office is in a beautiful, historic farmhouse, with sweeping lawns and gardens reaching to the water. The campground itself is just south of the farmhouse, with nearly all the sites nestled in a semi-circle along the shoreline. There's a pretty beach on Ayers Lake, and 15 secluded acres of pine forest, fields, and shorefront. It's located between New Hampshire's mountains and ocean, only a short 30- to 45-minute drive to either if you'd like to explore. But you'll be tempted to stay put. That's the good news. The bad news: Only a few sites are available on any given night throughout the season; most are taken by returning seasonal renters who obviously love this place. Call ahead and see if you get lucky. Also, check into the campground's more secluded cottage rentals on the property.

Basics

Operated By: Bedford family. **Open:** Memorial Day–Columbus Day. **Site Assignment:** Reservations suggested, 50 percent deposit, 3 days paid in advance for holiday weekends, two weeks notice for refund of deposit. **Registration:** At office. **Fee:** Full hookups, $29; waterside, $34; waterfront, $32, no hookups, $25. **Parking:** At site.

Facilities

Number of RV Sites: 47. **Number of Tent-Only Sites:** 3. **Hookups:** Water, electric, sewer (20, 30 amps). **Each Site:** Picnic table, fire ring. **Dump Station:** Yes. **Laundry:** No. **Pay Phone:** Yes. **Rest Rooms & Showers:** Yes. **Fuel:** No. **Propane:** No. **Internal Roads:** Dirt (good). **RV Service:** No. **Market:** Barrington (5 mi). **Restaurant:** No. **General Store:** No. **Vending:** No. **Swimming Pool:** No. **Playground:** Yes. **Other:** Lake frontage, beach, boat ramp, cottage rentals, canoe & rowboat rentals, psorts field. **Activities:** Swimming, boating, fishing, horseshoes. **Nearby Attractions:** New Hampshire seacoast beaches, historic town of Portsmouth, quick access to Lakes region, antiquing. **Additional Information:** Barrington Chamber of Commerce, P.O. Box 363, Barrington, NH 03825, (603) 664-2200; also visit www. SeacoastNH.com.

Restrictions

Pets: Must be on a leash, never left unattended. Pets are not allowed on beach or playground. **Fires:** In grills, stoves, & fire rings only. **Alcoholic Beverages:** At site only. **Vehicle Maximum Length:** 32 ft. **Other:** No power boats can be landed, launched or docked in the campground.

To Get There

From junction Hwy. 16 (Spaulding Turnpike) and US 202, go 5 mi. southwest on US 202; campground is on the right

BARRINGTON

Barrington Shores

70 Hall Rd., Barrington 03825. T: (603)664-9333; www.barringtonshores.com; bashores@world path.net.

RV ★★★★ Tent ★★★

Beauty: ★★★★	Site Privacy: ★★★
Spaciousness: ★★★	Quiet: ★★★
Security: ★★★★★	Cleanliness: ★★★★
Insect Control: ★★★	Facilities: ★★★

Remember busy summer days spent at the lakeside cottage? There was boating, and fishing, and races to the raft. In the evening, there were bonfires and marshmallow roasts. If you're looking for that classic lake vacation, for a fraction of the cost, head to Barrington Shores. This hilly campground on pretty Swain's Lake offers freshwater lake swimming, fishing, boating, and lots of planned activities. There are plenty of lake views from the tiered sites, two large, sandy beaches, boat ramp (many campers bring their own), and dock. This is a busy place with a festive atmosphere, perfect for hot, summer days. The roads are a bit of a maze, but we like the sandy sites and field stone fire pits. Try to avoid sites 116 and 117 right off a road, but 121 and 122 on the lake and with water and electric are especially nice; sites 69–73, with full service, overlook the lake and have a bit of room around them.

Basics

Operated By: Don & Gail Ziemba. **Open:** Mid-May–late-Sept. **Site Assignment:** Reservations recommended; holiday weekends/three-night stay or less requires payment in full, longer stays a 50% deposit; two-week notice for full refund, less $5 processing fee. **Registration:** At office. **Fee:** Waterfront w/ water, electric, & waterview w/water, electric, cable, $32; waterview w/water & electric, $29; full-service, $30; rates are based on 2 adluts & up to 3 children under 18; additional child is $2 per night; additional adult is $10 per night. Maximum four adults per site. **Parking:** At site; 1 vehicle per site.

FACILITIES

Number of RV Sites: 137. **Number of Tent-Only Sites:** 5. **Hookups:** Water, electric, sewer (20, 30, 50 amps), cable TV, phone. **Each Site:** Picnic table, fireplace. **Dump Station:** Yes. **Laundry:** Yes. **Pay Phone:** Yes. **Rest Rooms & Showers:** Yes (coin-op). **Fuel:** No. **Propane:** Yes. **Internal Roads:** Dirt, gravel (fair). **RV Service:** No. **Market:** Lee (2 mi). **Restaurant:** No. **General Store:** Yes. **Vending:** No. **Swimming Pool:** No. **Playground:** Yes. **Other:** Game room, safari field for rallies, two lakeside beaches, cottage & cabin rentals. **Activities:** Boat rentals, basketball, fishing, swimming, planned activities on weekends. **Nearby Attractions:** New Hampshire & southern Maine beaches, Portsmouth, factory outlet shopping, golf courses, waterpark, Strawbery Banke historic museum, Seacoast Science Center, antique shops. **Additional Information:** Barrington Chamber of Commerce, P.O. Box 363, Barrington, NH 03825, (603) 664-2200; also visit www.SeacoastNH.com.

RESTRICTIONS

Pets: Must be on a leash & never left unattended. No pets in cottage or cabins. **Fires:** In grills, stoves, & fire rings. **Alcoholic Beverages:** At site only. **Vehicle Maximum Length:** 40 ft. **Other:** No bicycle riding after dark.

TO GET THERE

From I-95, take Spaulding Turnpike (Rte. 16) in Portsmouth to exit 6W (Rte. 4). Follow Rte. 4 to Lee traffic circle & the junction of Rtes. 4 & 125. Take Rte. 125 north 2.5 mi.; take left onto Beauty Hill Rd. Go 1 mi., take left onto Hall Rd., 1 mi. to campground.

BARTLETT

Passaconaway Campground

Rte. 12, Kancamagus Hwy., Bartlett 03812.
T: (603) 447-5448.

RV ★★★ | Tent ★★★★

Beauty: ★★★★	Site Privacy: ★★★★★
Spaciousness: ★★★★	Quiet: ★★★★
Security: ★★★★	Cleanliness: ★★★★
Insect Control: ★★★	Facilities: ★★★

Of all the campgrounds along the Kancamagus, Passaconaway is probably most conducive to RVs, though there are no hookups. The spacious sites are well suited to larger groups or families with kids, and the relatively central location along the Kancamagus Hwy. puts you in a good spot if you're not sure what part of the Kanc you want to explore first. You'll be close to Rocky Gorge, Sabbaday Falls, the Swift River picnic area, and the myraid trailheads spread out along the length of this superlative stretch of road. The forest separating the individual sites at Passaconaway is fairly dense, which provides a nice sense of seclusion and helps make this an extremely quiet campground. All you'll hear is an occasional vehicle zipping past on the Kanc and the soft rush of the wind in the evergreens, punctuated by the chatter of the forest birds and animals. There's a trailhead right next to site 18; the campground host is located at site 19. Site 10 or site 24.

BASICS

Operated By: US Forest Service. **Open:** Mid-May–mid-Oct. **Site Assignment:** First come first served; no reservations. **Registration:** Select site, then pay at self-service fee station. **Fee:** $14. **Parking:** At site.

FACILITIES

Number of RV Sites: 33. **Number of Tent-Only Sites:** 0. **Hookups:** None. **Each Site:** Fire ring, picnic table. **Dump Station:** No. **Laundry:** No. **Pay Phone:** No. **Rest Rooms & Showers:** No. **Fuel:** No. **Propane:** No. **Internal Roads:** Paved. **RV Service:** No. **Market:** No. **Restaurant:** No. **General Store:** No. **Vending:** No. **Swimming Pool:** No. **Playground:** No. **Activities:** Fishing, hiking, picnicking, scenic byway. **Nearby Attractions:** Historic Russell-Colbath, an 1830s homestead. **Additional Information:** North Conway Chamber of Commerce, (603) 356-3171.

RESTRICTIONS

Pets: On leash. **Fires:** In fire ring. **Alcoholic Beverages:** At site. **Vehicle Maximum Length:** 2 vehicles per site. **Other:** 8 people per site; 14-day stay limit.

TO GET THERE

Passaconaway Campground is almost in the center of the Kancamagus Hwy. From Lincoln, follow the Kancamagus Hwy. for 16 mi. to campground on left. From Conway, follow Kancamagus Hwy. for 15 mi. to campground on right.

BRENTWOOD

3 Ponds Campground

146 North Rd., Brentwood 03833. T: (603) 679-5350; www.3pondscampground.com.

RV ★★★ | Tent ★★★

Beauty: ★★★	Site Privacy: ★★
Spaciousness: ★★★	Quiet: ★★★★
Security: ★★★	Cleanliness: ★★★★
Insect Control: ★★★	Facilities: ★★★

If our grandma owned a campground this is probably what it would look like: a sweep of perfectly manicured lawn (think golf course quality) stretching to the banks of three pristine, spring-fed ponds, a white gazebo perched on the banks, ham and bean suppers and afternoon cribbage games. Though only 20 to 30 miles from southern New Hampshire's major attractions, this campground sits off the main drag at the end of a residential street, making it feel a bit out of the way. The property has a friendly, quiet and wholesome appeal with just enough conveniences to make it pleasant, enough outdoor scenery to feel like camping. Most sites are perched in open on a grassy knoll—not a lot of privacy but with good views of the water. If you want more privacy, head to the back of campground where you'll have more space and shade.

BASICS

Operated By: Clarence & Claire Hibbard. **Open:** May 15–Oct. 1. **Site Assignment:** First-come, first-served, reservations recommended on weekends; MC, V, personal checks accepted. **Registration:** At office. **Fee:** $25. **Parking:** At site.

FACILITIES

Number of RV Sites: 136. **Number of Tent-Only Sites:** 0. **Hookups:** Water, electric, sewer (20, 30 amps). **Each Site:** Picnic table, fire ring. **Dump Station:** Yes. **Laundry:** Yes. **Pay Phone:** Yes. **Rest Rooms & Showers:** Yes. **Fuel:** No. **Propane:** No. **Internal Roads:** Dirt (fair). **RV Service:** No. **Market:** Raymond (5 mi). **Restaurant:** No. **General Store:** Yes. **Vending:** Yes. **Swimming Pool:** No. **Playground:** Yes. **Other:** Three spring-fed ponds, sandy beach w/swimming area, safari field, adult gazebo on lake, paddleboat rentals, game room. **Activities:** Swimming, fishing, boating, horsehoes, softball, volleyball, basketball, planned activities. **Nearby Attractions:** Portsmouth, New Hampshire beaches, Canobie Lake Park. **Additional Information:** Greater Portsmouth Chamber of Commerce, P.O. Box 239, Portsmoutn, NH 03801 (603) 436-3988; also visit www.SeacoastNH.com.

RESTRICTIONS

Pets: Must be on a leash, never left unattended. **Fires:** In grills, stoves, & fire rings only. **Alcoholic Beverages:** At site only. **Vehicle Maximum Length:** 40 ft. **Other:** Ask on arrival.

TO GET THERE

From junction Rte. 101 and 125 (in Epping), go south 1 mi. on Rte. 125 to Rockingham County Complex Rd., then east 1 mi. to entrance.

CAMBRIDGE

Umbagog Lake Campground

181 North, Errol 03579. T: (603) 482-7795 (603) 271-3628 (reservations); F: (603) 271-2629; www.nhparks.state.nh.us; nhcampres@dred. state.nh.us.

RV ★★★ | Tent ★★★★

Beauty: ★★★★	Site Privacy: ★★★★
Spaciousness: ★★★★	Quiet: ★★★★
Security: ★★★★	Cleanliness: ★★★
Insect Control: ★★	Facilities: ★★

This unique, rustic campground in New Hampshire's Great North Woods region offers wilderness sites on remote islands, in addition to its woodsy, lakeside base camp. If you're looking to get away from it all, and enjoy a more natural, wilderness experience, this campground has plenty to offer. The base camp is situated on the shores of still-wild Lake Umbagog, and is popular with canoeists, kayakers, and anglers. In recent years, outdoor enthusiasts have come for its peace and quiet and wildlife watching. Herons, osprey, loons, moose, deer, beavers, and bald eagles are often spotted. The base camp includes 38 spacious sites, some with two-way hookups, clustered in loops from the shoreline. For a more private, remote camping experience, reserve one of the island sites. Transportation, for a nominal fee, can be arranged to these sites. Though, to really appreciate this spot, you'll want to explore in your own boat.

BASICS

Operated By: New Hampshire Division of Parks & Recreation. **Open:** Mid-May–mid-Oct. **Site**

Assignment: Reservations suggested & must be made through central reservations (603) 271-3628. Reservations must be made at least seven days in advance; $3 non-refundable fee for each reservation. 24-hour cancellation policy w/$10 service fee. MC,V, D; no personal checks. **Registration:** At office. **Fee:** Water & electric, $24; no hookups, $20. **Parking:** At site, no parking at remote wilderness sites (boat access only).

Facilities

Number of RV Sites: 38. **Number of Tent-Only Sites:** 30. **Hookups:** Water, electric (15, 20 amps). **Each Site:** Picnic table, fire ring. **Dump Station:** Yes. **Laundry:** No. **Pay Phone:** No. **Rest Rooms & Showers:** Yes. **Fuel:** No. **Propane:** No. **Internal Roads:** Dirt, gravel (fair). **RV Service:** No. **Market:** Errol (7 mi). **Restaurant:** No. **General Store:** Yes. **Vending:** No. **Swimming Pool:** No. **Playground:** Yes. **Other:** Boat launch, boat slips, canoe rentals, cabin rentals, transportation to remote sites. **Activities:** Swimming, boating, fishing, wildlife watching. **Nearby Attractions:** Connecticut Lakes, Rangley & Sadlleback Mountain area of Maine. **Additional Information:** North Country Chamber of Commerce, P.O. Box 1, Colebrook, NH 03576, (603) 237-8939 or Northern White Mountains Chamber of Commerce, 164 Main St., P.O. Box 298, Berlin, NH 03570, (603) 752-6060.

Restrictions

Pets: Must be on a leash; never left unattended. **Fires:** In grills, campstoves, & fire rings only. **Alcoholic Beverages:** At site only. **Vehicle Maximum Length:** None. **Other:** 30 wilderness campsites are accessible by water only; transportation available.

To Get There

From junction Rtes. 16 and 26 (in Errol), go east 7 mi. on Rte. 26; campground is on the right.

CHICHESTER

Hillcrest Campground

78 Dover Rd., Chichester 03234. T: (603) 798-5124 or (508) 695-7391 (winter); www.ucampnh.com/hillcrest; hilcrest@tiac.net.

RV ★★★★ Tent ★★★★

Beauty: ★★★	Site Privacy: ★★★★
Spaciousness: ★★★★	Quiet: ★★★
Security: ★★★★★	Cleanliness: ★★★★★
Insect Control: ★★★	Facilities: ★★★★★

The living is easy at this central New Hampshire campground, one of the prettiest in the area. It also offers plenty of conveniences, including a centralized location and on-site amenities. The hilly campground site features towering pine tree woods and a picturesque pond, with a sandy cove beach. The mostly shaded sites, nestled in the woods, are adequately spaced (about 30 feet in average width) and level. The campground is popular with families, who enjoy the organized activities, the large, modern pool, fishing and boating on the pond, and nature trails. Tenters will like the private and spacious Honeymoon site or No. 10, overlooking the pond. There's also a safari field for larger groups with its own pavilion and recreational hall. Forget your gear? Rent one of the eight heated cabins flanking the front of the campground. During the busy summer months, there's a plethora of planned activities to keep you busy, including dances, dinners, children's activities and games, hayrides, fishing tournaments, bingo, and more.

Basics

Operated By: Potter family. **Open:** May–mid-Oct. **Site Assignment:** Reservations recommended. One night deposit required, one week cancellation notice. **Registration:** At office. **Fee:** Full hookup w/cable, $30; water & electric w/cable, $28; water & electric, $27; no hookups, $24. **Parking:** At site, one vehicle per site.

Facilities

Number of RV Sites: 138. **Number of Tent-Only Sites:** 9. **Hookups:** Water, electric, sewer (20, 30 amps), cable TV. **Each Site:** Picnic table, fire ring. **Dump Station:** Yes. Laundry: Yes. **Pay Phone:** Yes. **Rest Rooms & Showers:** Yes (coin-op). **Fuel:** No. **Propane:** No. **Internal Roads:** Paved, gravel (good). **RV Service:** No. **Market:** Epsom (2 mi). **Restaurant:** Yes. **General Store:** Yes. **Vending:** No. **Swimming Pool:** Yes. **Playground:** Yes. **Other:** Small pond, group area, mini-golf, rec room, arcade, boat rentals, nature trails, pavillion, cabin rentals. **Activities:** Swimming, boating, fishing, volleyball, badminton, mini-golf, horseshoes, organized activities throughout Jul.–Aug., including arts & crafts, contests, dances, hayrides, dinners, bingo, & more. **Nearby Attractions:** Concord, NH International Speedway, quick access to Lakes Region & Seacoast area, antiquing. **Additional Information:** Greater Concord Chamber of Commerce, 244 North Main St., Concord, NH 03301-5078, (603) 224-2508.

Restrictions

Pets: Must be on a leash, never left unattended. **Fires:** In grills, stoves, & fire rings only. **Alcoholic Beverages:** At site only. **Vehicle Maximum Length:** 40 ft.

To Get There

From junction Rtes. 4/202 and 28, go west 2 mi. on Rte. 4; campground is on the right

CONWAY

The Beach Camping Area

P.O. Box 1007, Rte. 16, North Conway 03818. T: (603) 447-2723; www.ucampnh.com/thebeach; beachcampingarea@yahoo.com.

RV ★★★ Tent ★★★

Beauty: ★★★	Site Privacy: ★★
Spaciousness: ★★★	Quiet: ★★
Security: ★★★	Cleanliness: ★★★
Insect Control: ★★★	Facilities: ★★

If you have to be in the middle of the action, close to North Conway attractions and outlet shopping, here's one of your choices. (Also see the Eastern Slope Campground and Saco River Camping.) All are on the Saco River, very busy and often noisy. The sites at this campground are set side-by-side in rows. The corner river sites are the best, numbers 1 through 7A, offering a little more room and scenery. Be warned that some of the river sites don't offer access or much of a water view of the river, though you will have beach grass and dunes as your backdrop as opposed to another tent or trailer. The tent-only section, ringed by trees and flanked by the Saco River, offers more privacy than other sites. There's a nice sandy beach area and classic cool water swimming hole, offering a refreshing place to dip and dunk after a busy day touring the area. The rec hall, with a few arcade games, is a dreary afterthought; the laundry is a basic one machine facility. Still, it's clean, economical, and if you're like most of campers here, you'll be off early in the morning exploring the area—or outlet shopping!

Basics

Operated By: Jeff & Stephanie Moore. **Open:** Mid-May–mid-Oct. **Site Assignment:** Reservations suggested, deposit of $30 per weekend, long holiday weekends (three day min. stay) paid in full. 14 day cancellation policy. MC,V, & personal checks accepted. **Registration:** At office. **Fee:** Full hookups, $25, full hookup water sites, $27; water & electric, $23–$25; no hookups, $20–$22. **Parking:** At site.

Facilities

Number of RV Sites: 114. **Number of Tent-Only Sites:** 7. **Hookups:** Water, electric, sewer (20, 30 amps). **Each Site:** Picnic table, fire ring. **Dump Station:** Yes. **Laundry:** Yes. **Pay Phone:** Yes. **Rest Rooms & Showers:** Yes. **Fuel:** No. **Propane:** Yes. **Internal Roads:** Dirt, gravel (good). **RV Service:** No. **Market:** Conway (2 mi). **Restaurant:** No. **General Store:** Yes. **Vending:** No. **Swimming Pool:** No. **Playground:** Yes. **Other:** Rec hall, sports field, river frontage, beach. **Activities:** Swimming, fishing. **Nearby Attractions:** North Conway, White Mountains, outlet shopping. **Additional Information:** Greater Conway Village Area Chamber of Commerce, P.O. Box 1019, Conway, NH 03818, (603) 447-2639; also Mount Washington Valley Chamber of Commerce, P.O. Box 2300, North Conway, NH 03860, (800) 521-2137.

Restrictions

Pets: On leash, must never be left unattended. Pets not allowed on the beach or in buildings. **Fires:** In grills, stoves, & fire rings . **Alcoholic Beverages:** At site only. **Vehicle Maximum Length:** 40 ft.

To Get There

From junction Rtes. 16 and 113, go north 1.5 mi. on Rte. 16; campground is on the left.

CONWAY

Eastern Slope Camping Area

P.O. Box 1127, Conway 03818. T: (603) 447-5092; www.ucampnh.com/easternslope.

RV ★★★ Tent ★★★

Beauty: ★★★	Site Privacy: ★★
Spaciousness: ★★★	Quiet: ★★★
Security: ★★★	Cleanliness: ★★★
Insect Control: ★★★	Facilities: ★★

This place can really rock and roll on summer weekends when vacationing families head to North Conway and the White Mountains for fun, fun, fun. During the day, the campground is quiet and peaceful; most campers are visiting area attractions or pursuing outdoor activities (hiking, biking, rock climbing, kayaking, and canoeing are all readily accessible.) By late afternoon when folks return, the campground comes alive. The property sites have two personalities: there's the fairly congested side-by-side, row after row of sites in the center of the campground. These sites are under a pine tree cover but back-to-back rows don't offer much privacy. Ringing the beach and playground area are much more secluded and spacious sites. Our favorites: sites one-12 along the river. For recreation, there are two swimming holes with sandy beaches, sports fields, and lots of comraderie around the bonfire.

Basics

Operated By: Danie & Valerie Boatwright. **Open:** Memorial Day–Columbus Day. **Site Assignment:** Reservations suggested, three night deposit, 14-day cancellation policy w/$5 service charge, MC,V, & personal checks accepted. **Registration:** At office. **Fee:** Full hookups, $25.95; sites 1–32A, 53, 54, $31.95; sites 33–39, $30.95; sites 40–71, $28.95; sites 72–215, $23.95, based on one or two adults & three children under 13. **Parking:** At site.

Facilities

Number of RV Sites: 204. **Number of Tent-Only Sites:** 6. **Hookups:** Water, electric, sewer (20, 30 amps). **Each Site:** Picnic table, fire ring. **Dump Station:** Yes. **Laundry:** No. **Pay Phone:** Yes. **Rest Rooms & Showers:** Yes. **Fuel:** No. **Propane:** No. **Internal Roads:** Paved (good). **RV Service:** No. **Market:** North Conway (0.5 mi). **Restaurant:** No. **General Store:** Yes. **Vending:** Yes. **Swimming Pool:** No. **Playground:** Yes. **Other:** River frontage, beach, sports field, canoe rentals. **Activities:** Swimming, horseshoes, shuffleboard, softball. **Nearby Attractions:** Storyland, Santa's Village, Six Gun City, North Conway, White Mountains, outlet shopping. **Additional Information:** Greater Conway Village Area Chamber, P.O. Box 1019, Conway, NH 03818, (603) 447-2639; also Mount Washington Valley Chamber, P. O. Box 2300, North Conway, NH 03860, (800) 521-2137.

Restrictions

Pets: Must be on a leash, never left unattended. Pets not allowed at beach area. **Fires:** In grills, stoves, & fire rings only. **Alcoholic Beverages:** At site only. **Vehicle Maximum Length:** 38 ft.

To Get There

From junctions Rte. 16 and 113, go 1 mi. north on Rte. 16; campground is on the left

DEERING

Oxbow Campground

8 Oxbow Rd., Deering 03244. T: (603) 464-5952; www.ucampnh.com/oxbow; oxbow@conknet.com.

RV ★★★ Tent ★★★

Beauty: ★★★★ Site Privacy: ★★★★
Spaciousness: ★★★★ Quiet: ★★★
Security: ★★★★★ Cleanliness: ★★★
Insect Control: ★★★ Facilities: ★★★

This peaceful, outdoors-oriented campground in southwestern New Hampshire, less than a mile from downtown Hillsboro, is a favorite among local campers and vacationing families. There are three brook-fed ponds on the property: a three-acre, boating pond (people-powered boats only), a one-acre, sandy bottom swimming pond, and a 0.3-acre catch and release stocked fishing pond (no license needed.) Sites on the property vary from deeply wooded for those who like privacy, to open for sun worshipers. All sites have plenty of space; average width is about 55 feet. More than 140 acres of the campground are open for hiking. The Welcome Hall is especially nice, with reading and video libraries, puzzle making and card-playing tables. The Pine Pavillion, on the beach overlooking the swimming pond, is also a favorite gathering spot.

Basics

Operated By: John Ramsey. **Open:** May–Columbus Day. **Site Assignment:** Reservations suggested, 1-4 day stay, $20 deposit; 1-2 week stay, $50 deposit; 3 weeks or longer, $100 deposit; three day min. stay on holiday weekends. Three to 13 days cancellation notice, deposit returned less $50; 14 day notice, deposit returned less $10; no refunds for reservations for three week stays or longer. MC,V, & personal checks accepted. **Registration:** At office. **Fee:** Full hookups, $27; electric, $24; no hookups, $21; waterfront sites, $3 extra; based on two adults & two children under 18. **Parking:** At site.

Facilities

Number of RV Sites: 86. **Number of Tent-Only Sites:** 13. **Hookups:** Water, electric, sewer (20, 30 amps), cable TV, modem. **Each Site:** Picnic table, fire ring. **Dump Station:** No. **Laundry:** Yes. **Pay Phone:** Yes. **Rest Rooms & Showers:** Yes (coin-op). **Fuel:** No. **Propane:** Yes. **Internal Roads:** Gravel, dirt (fair). **RV Service:** No. **Market:** Hillsboro (0.5 mi). **Restaurant:** No. **General Store:** Yes. **Vending:** No. **Swimming Pool:** No. **Playground:** Yes. **Other:** 3 ponds, beach areas, rec hall, pavillion, sports field, hiking trails, cabin rentals. **Activities:** Swimming, fishing, boating, shuffleboard, volleyball, basketball, horseshoes, planned activities on summer weekends,. **Nearby Attractions:** Hillsboro, Concord, state parks, lakes & fishing streams. **Additional Information:** Greater Concord Chamber, 244 North Main St., Concord, NH 03301-5078, (603) 224-2508.

Restrictions

Pets: Must have up to date vaccinations, kept on a leash, never left unattended. **Fires:** In grills, stoves, & fire rings only. **Alcoholic Beverages:** No more than one beverage per person open at any time. **Vehicle Maximum Length:** None.

To Get There

From junction Rtes. 202, 9 and 149, go south 0.75 mi. on Rte. 149; campground is on the left

EAST WAKEFIELD

Lake Ivanhoe Inn & RV Resort

631 Acton Ridge Rd., East Wakefield 03830. T: (603) 522-8824; F: (603) 522-9235; www.lakeivanhoe.com; office@lakeivanhoe.com.

RV ★★★ Tent ★★★

Beauty: ★★★ Site Privacy: ★★★
Spaciousness: ★★★★ Quiet: ★★★★
Security: ★★★ Cleanliness: ★★★
Insect Control: ★★★ Facilities: ★★

If your idea of the perfect getaway is to get away from it all, this campground could be for you. (Though within an hour's drive, you can be in the White Mountains or on the seacoast of Maine.) This campground, set off the main drag, is pleasantly quiet and relaxing. There's a small historic inn on the property and a 100-foot long private, sandy beach across the street for campers. About half the campground is taken by summer seasonal renters who seem content with the slow life: a morning paddle on the lake, an afternoon nap, bingo at night. Lake pleasures seem to dominate, here. There's swimming, boating and fishing on spring-fed 120-acre Lake Ivanhoe, one of 11 lakes in the Wakefield area. Facilities are clean but basic (chem toilets.) Seasonal renters and large rigs are placed up front, while tenters head to the shaded, back portion of the property.

Basics

Operated By: Ann & Tony Bettencourt. **Open:** Mid-May–Columbus Day. **Site Assignment:** Reservations suggested, a 50 percent deposit is required, 14 day notice for refund of deposit. Two night min. on weekends. MC,V, & personal checks accepted. **Registration:** At office. **Fee:** Full hookup, $35; water & electric, $31; no hookups, $23–$27. **Parking:** At site.

Facilities

Number of RV Sites: 69. **Number of Tent-Only Sites:** 6. **Hookups:** Water, electric, sewer (20, 30 amps), cable TV, modem. **Each Site:** Picnic table, fire ring. **Dump Station:** Yes. **Laundry:** Yes. **Pay Phone:** Yes. **Rest Rooms & Showers:** Yes. **Fuel:** No. **Propane:** Yes. **Internal Roads:** Dirt, gravel (fair). **RV Service:** No. **Market:** Wakefield (1 mi). **Restaurant:** No. **General Store:** Yes. **Vending:** No. **Swimming Pool:** No. **Playground:** Yes. **Other:** Lake frontage & beach, canoe & paddleboat rentals, adult rec hall, game room, sports field, safari area. **Activities:** Swimming, boating, horseshoes, badminton, volleyball, shuffleboard, planned activities on weekends including hayrides, bingo, socials. **Nearby Attractions:** Lake Winnipesaukee, Lakes region attractions. **Additional Information:** Lakes Region Assoc., Rte. 104, P.O. Box 430, New Hampton, NH 03252, (603) 744-8664.

Restrictions

Pets: Must be on a leash, never left unattended. Pets are not allowed on the beach. **Fires:** In grills, stoves, & fire rings only. **Alcoholic Beverages:** At site only. **Vehicle Maximum Length:** None.

To Get There

From junction Rtes. 16 and Wakefield Rd., go 0.5 mi. east on Wakefield Rd. to Rte. 152, then 2.5 mi. north to Acton Ridge Rd., then 1.2 mi. east; campground is on the left.

EPSOM
Circle 9 Ranch

Windymere Dr., P.O. Box 282, Epsom 03234.
T: (603) 736-9656;
www.circle9campground.com;
circle9rch@aol.com.

RV ★★★★★ Tent ★★

Beauty: ★★ Site Privacy: ★★
Spaciousness: ★★★ Quiet: ★★
Security: ★★★★★ Cleanliness: ★★★★★
Insect Control: ★★★★ Facilities: ★★★★★

If you're looking for a hootin' and hollerin' time, head to Circle 9, New Hampshire's nod to the west. This popular campground, minutes from downtown Concord and the New Hampshire International Speedway, features live country and western music every Saturday night in its well-known entertainment and commercial bingo center. If you don't meet your fellow campers on the dance floor, you surely will at the campsite, where big rigs are perched side-by-side in an open central area. There's not a lot of space at individual sites; average width is about 20 feet. We prefer the more private, shaded sites in the back of the campground, clustered around two small ponds or in the woods—and farthest away from the dance hall. Site No. 59 is popular with tenters. You'll find all the amenities here, but not a lot of peace and quiet. Come here for the location and the action.

BASICS

Operated By: Warren & Sheila Rich. **Open:** Year-round. **Site Assignment:** Reservations recommended, MC, V, D, AE, personal checks accepted. Sites must be paid in full during Jul. & Aug., no money returned for cancellations. **Registration:** At office. **Fee:** Full hookup, premium sites, $30; trailer & motor homes, $28; tents & pop-ups, $23, based on two adults & two children. **Parking:** At site, one vehicle per site.

FACILITIES

Number of RV Sites: 113. **Number of Tent-Only Sites:** 12. **Hookups:** Water, electric, sewer (30, 50 amps), cable TV, modem. **Each Site:** Picnic table, fire ring. **Dump Station:** Yes. **Laundry:** Yes. **Pay Phone:** Yes. **Rest Rooms & Showers:** Yes (coin-op). **Fuel:** No. **Propane:** Yes. **Internal Roads:** Paved, gravel (good). **RV Service:** Yes. **Market:** Epsom (1 mi). **Restaurant:** Yes. **General Store:** Yes. **Vending:** Yes. **Swimming Pool:** Yes. **Playground:** Yes. **Other:** Adult-only hot tub, large entertainment center, live country music & western band performances, rec hall, arcade, function hall, pond, safari area. **Activities:** Saturday night concerts & dances, basketball, pond fishing, swimming, horseshoes, commercial bingo. **Nearby Attractions:** Concord, NH International Speedway, quick access to Lakes Region & Seacoast area, antiquing. **Additional Information:** Greater Concord Chamber of Commerce, 244 North Main St., Concord, NH 03301-5078, (603) 224-2508.

RESTRICTIONS

Pets: Must be on a leash, never left unattended. No dogs on holiday weekends; no dogs allowed w/visitors. **Fires:** In grills, stoves, & fire rings only. **Alcoholic Beverages:** At site & at entertainment center. **Vehicle Maximum Length:** 45 ft.

TO GET THERE

From junction Rtes. 2/202 and 28, go south 0.25 mi. on Rte. 28, then south 0.25 mi. to Windymere Dr.; the campground is on the right.

EPSOM
Epsom Valley Campground

990 Suncook Valley Hwy., Epsom 03234. T: (603) 736-9758 or (978) 658-4396 (winter); www.ucampnh.com/epsomvalley.

RV ★★★ Tent ★★★

Beauty: ★★★ Site Privacy: ★★★
Spaciousness: ★★★ Quiet: ★★★★
Security: ★★★ Cleanliness: ★★★★
Insect Control: ★★ Facilities: ★★★

You'll find none of the thrills and frills of some of the more modern campgrounds at Epsom Valley. Come here to settle in the woods, swim in the Suncook River, cast a lure in a rock-strewn river pool. Shaded sites are set under tall pine trees about 25 feet from one another. Not a lot of room, but the woods offer some privacy. There are also a number of open, grassy sites for those who prefer the sun. Activities are centered around simple pleasures: paddling a canoe on the river; fishing from the banks; tossing horseshoes, or playing a game of mini-golf. Most visitors will take time to explore the area; the campground is centrally located, an hour's drive from the seacoast, New Hampshire lakes region, or the mountains. Holiday and race weeks (New Hampshire International Speedway in Loudon is just up the road) are busy and the atmosphere becomes a bit more bustling and noisy, especially with groups filling the campground's Safari Field area.

BASICS

Operated By: John & Dwyna Arvanitis. **Open:** Memorial Day–Oct. 12. **Site Assignment:** Reservations suggested. 2 day min. stay during holiday weekends & race weeks. Deposit at your discretion. **Registration:** At office. **Fee:** Full hookups, $25; water & electric, $22; no hookups, $19, based on two adults, two children. **Parking:** At site, one vehicle per site.

FACILITIES

Number of RV Sites: 67. **Number of Tent-Only Sites:** 3. **Hookups:** Water, electric, sewer (20, 30 amps). **Each Site:** Picnic table, fire ring. **Dump Station:** Yes. **Laundry:** No. **Pay Phone:** Yes. **Rest Rooms & Showers:** Yes (coin-op). **Fuel:** No. **Propane:** No. **Internal Roads:** Gravel, dirt (fair). **RV Service:** No. **Market:** Epsom (1 mi). **Restaurant:** No. **General Store:** No. **Vending:** Yes. **Swimming Pool:** No. **Playground:** Yes. **Other:** Recreational field, baseball diamond, mini-golf course, canoe & paddleboat rentals, safari field. **Activities:** fishing, swimming, horseshoes, volleyball, canoeing, potluck dinners on weekends. **Nearby Attractions:** NH International Speedway, Concord, quick access to Lakes Region & Seacoast area, antiquing. **Additional Information:** Greater Concord Chamber of Commerce, 244 North Main St., Concord, NH 03301-5078, (603) 224-2508.

RESTRICTIONS

Pets: Must be on a leash, never left unattended, not allowed beach. One pet per site. **Fires:** In grills, stoves, & fire rings only. **Alcoholic Beverages:** At site only. **Vehicle Maximum Length:** 34 ft.

TO GET THERE

From junction Rtes. 4/202 and 28, go 0.25 mi. north on Rte. 28; campground is on the right.

EPSOM
Lazy River Campground

427 Goboro Rd., Epsom 03234. T: (603) 798-5900.

RV ★★★ Tent ★★★

Beauty: ★★★ Site Privacy: ★★★
Spaciousness: ★★★ Quiet: ★★★★
Security: ★★★ Cleanliness: ★★★
Insect Control: ★★ Facilities: ★★★

One of the clusters of campgrounds in the Concord area, this rural, riverside property offers more activities than its neighbor up the street (Epsom Valley) and a bit more space to roam. Though, it lacks some of its neighbor's picturesque, woodsy scenery. There's swimming in the Suncook River or take a dip in one of the two pools (one of them is a children's pool.)On holiday weekends, families join in a host of activities, including dances, water balloon tosses, and arts and crafts.You have a choice of wooded, open field sites, or riverfront sites. We like site No. 1 on the river, or site No. 91A, which is larger than most. (The average site width is about 35 feet, so all have a bit of space around them.) If you're traveling in a group, try to rent sites 53–58. These campsites are set off by themselves, situated on a point along the river. This campground, as most in the area, fills up fst during the popular Loudon race car weeks. If you're looking to miss the crowds avoid these summer events (times vary); if you're heading to the races, reserve well in advance, often up to a year.

BASICS

Operated By: Smith family (Ken, Barb, Duane, & Kenny). **Open:** May–Sept. **Site Assignment:** Reservations recommended; 2-day min. stay during holiday weekends & race week. One night deposit required, no fee for cancellation. MC, V, & personal checks accepted. **Registration:** At office. **Fee:** Full hookups, $28; water & electric, $24, based on two adults & three children. **Parking:** At site, one vehicle per site.

FACILITIES

Number of RV Sites: 109. **Number of Tent-Only Sites:** 0. **Hookups:** Water, electric, sewer (20, 30 amps). **Each Site:** Picnic table, fire ring, phone hookup. **Dump Station:** Yes. **Laundry:** Yes. **Pay Phone:** Yes. **Rest Rooms & Showers:** Yes (coin-op). **Fuel:** No. **Propane:** No. **Internal Roads:** Dirt (fair). **RV Service:** No. **Market:** Epsom (0.5 mi). **Restaurant:** No. **General Store:** No. **Vending:** No. **Swimming Pool:** Yes (two).

Playground: Yes. **Other:** Rec hall, arcade, canoe rentals, riverfront beach, group area. **Activities:** Volleyball, fishing, canoeing, swimming, horseshoes, ping pong, pool, planned activities on holiday weekends including dances, contests, arts & crafts. **Nearby Attractions:** Concord, NH International Speedway, quick access to New Hampshire Lakes Region & Seacoast areas, antiquing. **Additional Information:** Greater Concord Chamber of Commerce, 244 North Main St., Concord, NH 03301-5078, (603) 224-2508.

Restrictions

Pets: Must be on a leash, never left unattended. **Fires:** In grills, stoves, & fire rings only. **Alcoholic Beverages:** At site only. **Vehicle Maximum Length:** 35 ft.

To Get There

From junction of Rtes. 4/202 & 28, go 2 mi. north on Rte. 28, then 0.5 mi. east on Depot Rd.; campground is on the right.

EXETER

Exeter Elms

188 Court St., Exeter 03833. T: (603) 778-7631; www.ucampnh.com/exeterelms; cwaleryszak@aol.com.

RV: ★★★ Tent: ★★★★

Beauty: ★★★	Site Privacy: ★★★★
Spaciousness: ★★★★	Quiet: ★★★★
Security: ★★★★★	Cleanliness: ★★★
Insect Control: ★★	Facilities: ★★★

We like the spacious, woodsy feel of this rural campground, set far off the main road, along the Exeter River. The level sites are spacious and private; average width is about 50 feet and most are nestled in trees for extra seclusion with river frontage or views. Many waterfront sites have banks that drop off into deep water so parents with young children may have to keep an eye out; but we particularly like the fact that, unlike some campgrounds, here, there are no annoying, unattractive fences to detract from the natural beauty of the setting. The campground offers a separate wooded tent-only area, but, if you prefer sun and open spaces, you'll have plenty to choose from, too. You'll find a variety of campground activities, plus fishing and canoeing on the river. The town of Portsmouth and the Seacoast region is less than a half-hour's drive away.

Basics

Operated By: Eric & Carol Waleryszak. **Open:** May 15–Sept. 15. **Site Assignment:** Reservations recommended; 50% deposit; refund given if cancelled two weeks prior to check-in, minus 10% processing fee; three-day min. stay on Memorial Day & Labor Day weekends; four-day min. over Jul. 4th. **Registration:** At office. **Fee:** $21, tents; $27 w/water, electric; $31, full hookup. **Parking:** At site.

Facilities

Number of RV Sites: 202. **Number of Tent-Only Sites:** 50. **Hookups:** Water, electric, sewer (15, 30, 50 amps). **Each Site:** Picnic table, fire ring. **Dump Station:** Yes. **Laundry:** Yes. **Pay Phone:** Yes. **Rest Rooms & Showers:** Yes. **Fuel:** No. **Propane:** No. **Internal Roads:** Dirt, gravel (good). **RV Service:** No. **Market:** Exeter (3 mi.). **Restaurant:** No. **General Store:** Yes. **Vending:** Yes. **Swimming Pool:** Yes. **Playground:** Yes. **Other:** Game room, boat rentals, one-mi. river frontage w/access & beach area, recreation field. **Activities:** Swimming, fishing, boating, planned activities w/full-time rec. director, volleyball, basketball, shuffleboard. **Nearby Attractions:** New Hampshire & southern Maine beaches, Portsmouth, Exeter, factory outlet shopping, golf courses, waterpark, Strawbery Banke historic museum, Seacoast Science Center, antique shops. **Additional Information:** Exeter Area Chamber of Commerce, 120 Water St., Exeter, NH 03833, (603) 772-2411; also visit www.SeacoastNH.com.

Restrictions

Pets: Must be on a leash, never left unattended. **Fires:** In grills, stoves, & fire rings only. **Alcoholic Beverages:** At site only. **Vehicle Maximum Length:** 40 ft. **Other:** No all terrain vehicles.

To Get There

From junction Rtes. 111 and 108, go 1.5 mi. south on Rte. 108 to entrance; campground is on the left

FRANCONIA

Lafayette Campground

Rte. 3, Franconia Notch State Park, Franconia 03580. T: (603) 823-9513; F: (603) 823-7214; www.nhparks.state.nh.us; nhcampres@dred.state.nh.us.

RV: ★ Tent: ★★★★★

Beauty: ★★★★	Site Privacy: ★★★★
Spaciousness: ★★★★	Quiet: ★★★
Security: ★★★	Cleanliness: ★★★
Insect Control: ★★	Facilities: ★★

This rustic state park campground sits in gorgeous Franconia Notch State Park, surrounding by mountains, streams, and hiking trails. It's best for campers who like to rough it a bit, tenters and pop-up trailers take up the majority of sites. The campground draws lots of outdoorsy types and backpackers, who come to play in the mountains. There are several popular hiking trails that leave directly from the campground and state park attractions, including The Basin, Profile Lake, Old Man in the Mountains, and The Flume are all close by. The woodsy sites, set on hilly terrain and along the Pemigewasset River, are generously spaced with plenty of privacy, but no hookups. Added bonus: new rest rooms with hot showers.

Basics

Operated By: New Hampshire Division of Parks & Recreation. **Open:** Mid-May–mid-Oct. **Site Assignment:** Reservations suggested. Half the sites can be reserved, half are set aside on a first come, first served basis. Call Reservation Center (603) 271-3628 from Jan.–early Oct., Mon.–Fri. or via email, www.nhparks.state.nh.us. Payment is due within seven days of making reservation. Each reservation is subject to a $3 non-refundable reservation fee. Refunds requests must be received in writing by the reservation office within 14 days of scheduled arrival & are handled on a case by case basis, subject to a $10 handling fee & may be subject to a penalty of a one night cmaping fee. MC, V; no personal checks. **Registration:** At office. **Fee:** $16, based on 2 adults & children under 18. Each additional adult is half the site fee w/a max. of 5 adults per site. **Parking:** At site.

Facilities

Number of RV Sites: 98. **Number of Tent-Only Sites:** 0. **Hookups:** None. **Each Site:** Picnic table, fire ring. **Dump Station:** No. **Laundry:** No. **Pay Phone:** Yes. **Rest Rooms & Showers:** Yes (coin-op). **Fuel:** No. **Propane:** No. **Internal Roads:** Dirt, gravel (fair). **RV Service:** No. **Market:** Lincoln (10 mi). **Restaurant:** No. **General Store:** Yes. **Vending:** No. **Swimming Pool:** No. **Playground:** No. **Other:** River frontage, hiking trails. **Activities:** Swimming, hiking. **Nearby Attractions:** Franconia Notch State Park, White Mountains. **Additional Information:** Franconia Notch Chamber of Commerce, P.O. Box 780, Franconia, NH 03580, (800) 237-9007.

Restrictions

Pets: Not allowed. **Fires:** In grills, stoves, & fire rings only. **Alcoholic Beverages:** At site only. **Vehicle Maximum Length:** None. **Other:** Ask on arrival.

To Get There

Take Lafayette Campground Exit off Rte. 3, Franconia Notch Parkway

FRANCONIA NOTCH STATE PARK

Cannon Mountain RV Park

P.O. Box 1856, Concord 03302. T: (603) 823-8800, (603) 271-3628 (reservations); F: (603) 271-2747; www.nhparks.state.nh.us; nhcampres@dred.state.nh.us.

RV: ★★★★ Tent: na

Beauty: ★★★★	Site Privacy: ★★★
Spaciousness: ★★★	Quiet: ★★★
Security: ★★★	Cleanliness: ★★★★
Insect Control: ★★★	Facilities: ★★★★

The campground itself is meager, only seven sites, stuck in a row at the back of a parking lot. Yet, if you want to camp here you better reserve a spot well in advance—up to a year! The setting, in Franconia Notch State Park, is gorgeous. You'll camp at the base of pristine Echo Lake, elevation 1,931 feet, surrounded by views of Mt. Lafayette and Cannon Mountain. From here, you can walk to the shoreline for boating, swimming, and fishing, take an aerial tram ride to the 4,180-foot summit of Cannon Mountain, visit the New England Ski Museum and the Old Man in the Mountain Museum, and access a handful of popular hiking trails. You can also walk to the Cannon Mountain Ski Resort facilities, including its cafeteria, shops, and restaurant. All this, without ever having to get back in your vehicle. Another bonus: The campground is open all year (though there's no electric or water hookups after mid-Oct.) Reserve now for next year.

Basics

Operated By: New Hampshire Division of Parks & Recreation. **Open:** Year-round. **Site Assignment:** Reservations suggested & must be made through central reservation office (603) 271-3628). Reservations must be made at least seven days in advance; $3 non-refundable reservation fee for each reservation. 24-hour cancellation fee w/$10 service charge. MC, V, D; no personal checks. **Registration:** At office. **Fee:** $24. **Parking:** At site.

Facilities

Number of RV Sites: 7. **Number of Tent-Only Sites:** 0. **Hookups:** Water, electric, sewer (20, 30 amps). **Each Site:** Picnic table. **Dump Station:** Yes. **Laundry:** No. **Pay Phone:** Yes. **Rest Rooms & Showers:** Yes. **Fuel:** No. **Propane:** No. **Internal Roads:** Paved, gravel (good). **RV Service:** No. **Market:** Franconia (3 mi). **Restaurant:** No. **General Store:** No. **Vending:** No. **Swimming Pool:** No. **Playground:** Yes. **Other:** Access to Franconia Notch State Park & Cannon Ski Resort facilities, boat launch. **Activities:** Swimming, boating, fishing, skiing, hiking, aerial tram. **Nearby Attractions:** Franconia Notch State Park, White Mountains attractions. **Additional Information:** Franconia Notch Chamber of Commerce, P.O. Box 780, Franconia, NH 03580, (800) 237-9007.

Restrictions

Pets: No pets allowed. **Fires:** No. **Alcoholic Beverages:** At site only. **Vehicle Maximum Length:** None.

To Get There

At junction of Franconia Notch State Parkway and Echo Lake

GILFORD

Ellacoya State Beach & RV Park

Rte. 11, P.O. Box 7277, Gilford 03247. T: (603) 293-7821, (603) 271-3628 (reservations); F: (603) 271-2629; www.nhparks.state.nh.us; nhcampres@dred.state.nh.us.

RV: ★★★ Tent: n/a

Beauty: ★★★	Site Privacy: ★★★
Spaciousness: ★★★	Quiet: ★★★
Security: ★★★★★	Cleanliness: ★★★
Insect Control: ★★★	Facilities: ★★8

Come summer, it seems that everyone in New Hampshire (and beyond) wants to get on Lake Winnipesaukee, the state's largest lake. Camping here is one way to do it. This small RV campground sits on the southwest shore of the lake, and boasts a 600-foot-long sandy beach, with views of the surrounding Sandwich and Ossipee mountains. Campers must share the space with hordes of day visitors, but come sunset, you'll have it—and the spectacular views— to yourself. Sites all have three-way hookups and are set in rows; amenities are basic (bathouse, small camp store, showers.) But, it's tough to beat this shoreline location, in the heart of the Lakes region.

Basics

Operated By: New Hampshire Division of Parks & Recreation. **Open:** Early-May–mid-Oct. **Site Assignment:** Reservations suggested & must be made through central reservation office (603) 271-3628); two sites left open on a first-come, first-served basis. Reservations must be made at least seven days in advance; $3 non-refundable reservation fee for each reservation. 24-hour cancellation policy w/$10 service charge. MC, V, D; no personal checks. **Registration:** At office. **Fee:** $35. **Parking:** At site.

Facilities

Number of RV Sites: 38. **Number of Tent-Only Sites:** 0. **Hookups:** Water, electric, sewer (20, 30 amps). **Each Site:** Picnic table. **Dump Station:** No. **Laundry:** Yes. **Pay Phone:** Yes. **Rest Rooms & Showers:** Yes. **Fuel:** No. **Propane:** No. **Internal Roads:** Gravel, dirt (fair). **RV Service:** No. **Market:** Laconia (5 mi). **Restaurant:** No. **General Store:** Yes. **Vending:** No. **Swimming Pool:** No. **Playground:** No. **Other:** Lake frontage, beach, boat launch, canoe rentals. **Activities:** Swimming, boating, fishing, volleyball. **Nearby Attractions:** Weirs Beach, Lakes region attractions. **Additional Information:** Greater Laconia/Weirs Beach Chamber of Commerce, 11 Veterans Square, Laconia, NH 03246, (603) 524-5531.

Restrictions

Pets: No pets allowed. **Fires:** In communal firepit only. **Alcoholic Beverages:** At site only. **Vehicle Maximum Length:** None. **Other:** No tents allowed.

To Get There

From junction of I-93 and US 3 at Belmont, take US 3 north 9 mi.; turn east on NH 118 and then east on NH 110 to Ellacoya Beach.

GLEN

Glen Ellis Family Campground

P.O. Box 397, Glen 03838. T: (603) 383-4567; www.glenelliscampground.com.

RV: ★★★★★ Tent: ★★★★★

Beauty: ★★★★★	Site Privacy: ★★★★
Spaciousness: ★★★★★	Quiet: ★★★★
Security: ★★★★★	Cleanliness: ★★★★★
Insect Control: ★★★	Facilities: ★★★★★

This is top-notch, upscale camping at its finest. Here, campers have the beauty, scenery and economics of outdoor living with the comforts, amenities and services of a resort. Glen Ellis is one of our favorite places to camp. The campground, in New Hampshire's picturesque White Mountains area, lies in the shadows of the Presidential mountain range, nestled between the Ellis and Saco rivers. Facilities, including a large pool, sports fields, laundramat (open to the public), store, playground, and tennis courts are top-of-the-line, immaculately clean and finely landscaped. There are sweeping fields and spacious public areas, offering lots of room to romp and roam. Sites are spacious too, many with river frontage, offering both shade and sun at each site. There are two riverfront beaches for dunks in cool mountain waters (the pool is heated), a few planned activities on Saturday evenings, and White Mountain attractions and outdoor activities at your doorstep. Set your camp on riversite 56, our favorite (if you'd like hookups look at sites 86–100 on the Saco River or 33–51 on the Ellis River) and you won't want to leave.

Basics

Operated By: Richard & Dick Goff. **Open:** Memorial Day–Columbus Day. **Site Assignment:** Reservations required, one-night deposit; 14-day cancellation policy. **Registration:** At office. **Fee:** Waterfront sites, $24; all other sites, $22, $2 charge for electricity, air conditioning, & sewer, based on two adults & children under 18. **Parking:** At site.

Facilities

Number of RV Sites: 130. **Number of Tent-Only Sites:** 73. **Hookups:** Water, electric, sewer (20, 30 amps). **Each Site:** Picnic table, fire ring. **Dump Station:** Yes. **Laundry:** Yes. **Pay Phone:** Yes. **Rest Rooms & Showers:** Yes (coin-op). **Fuel:** No. **Propane:** No. **Internal Roads:** Gravel, dirt (good). **RV Service:** No. **Market:** Gorham (0.5 mi). **Restaurant:** No. **General Store:** Yes. **Vending:** No. **Swimming Pool:** Yes. **Playground:** Yes. **Other:** Rec hall, river frontage & beaches on two rivers, tennis courts, sports fields. **Activities:** Swimming, tubing, basketball, volleyball, baseball, tennis, planned activities on Saturday evening during summer. **Nearby Attractions:** Storyland, Santa's Village, Six Gun City, White Mountains, North Conway. **Additional Information:** Mount Washington Valley Chamber of Commerce, P.O. Box 2300, North Conway, NH 03860, (800) 521-2137.

Restrictions

Pets: No dogs allowed. **Fires:** In grills, stoves, & fire rings only. **Alcoholic Beverages:** At site only. **Vehicle Maximum Length:** 40 ft.

To Get There

From junction Rtes. 16 and 302, go west 0.2 mi. on 302; campground is on the left

GORHAM

Timberland

P.O. Box 303, Gorham 03581. T: (603) 466-3872; www.ucampnh.com/timberland.

RV: ★★★ Tent: ★★★

Beauty: ★★★	Site Privacy: ★★★
Spaciousness: ★★★	Quiet: ★★★★
Security: ★★★★★	Cleanliness: ★★★
Insect Control: ★★★	Facilities: ★★★

This campground is a favorite relaxing stopover for those traveling in New Hampshire's northern White Mountains region. Transcient campers who come for a night or two as they tour New England's top attractions make up the bulk of the summer clientele. In fall, the campground becomes a destination, a great place to view New Hampshire's northern fall foliage show. Set in the shadows of the Presidential mountain range, the campground offers shady rows of sites, ultra clean facilities and plenty of convenient full hookup pull-throughs. Nice touches: a 30-minute show on nearby attractions is shown each evening in the rec hall and an adult-only lounge offers a quiet place to read, play cards, watch TV or just relax. Kids have a pool, rec room and sports fields to keep them happily amused.

BASICS

Operated By: Jeff & Sue Davis. **Open:** May–Oct. 20. **Site Assignment:** Reservations suggested, one night deposit, seven day cancellation policy, no refunds on holiday weekends, personal checks accepted. **Registration:** At office. **Fee:** Full hookups (w/cable TV), $24; water & electric (20 amp), $21; no hookups, $18, based on two adults per site, additional child, ages 6-17, $1.50; additional adult, $3. **Parking:** At site.

FACILITIES

Number of RV Sites: 77. **Number of Tent-Only Sites:** 35. **Hookups:** Water, electric, sewer (20, 30 amps), cable TV. **Each Site:** Picnic table, fire ring. **Dump Station:** Yes. **Laundry:** Yes. **Pay Phone:** Yes. **Rest Rooms & Showers:** Yes (coin-op). **Fuel:** No. **Propane:** No. **Internal Roads:** Gravel, dirt (good). **RV Service:** No. **Market:** Gorham (4 mi). **Restaurant:** No. **General Store:** Yes. **Vending:** No. **Swimming Pool:** Yes. **Playground:** Yes. **Other:** Adult-only lounge, rec hall. **Activities:** Swimming, badminton, volleyball, horseshoes, croquet, basketball. **Nearby Attractions:** Santa's Village, Six Gun City, Storyland, White Mountains, North Conway, outlet shopping. **Additional Information:** Mount Washington Valley Chamber of Commerce, P.O. Box 2300, North Conway, NH 03860, (800) 521-2137.

RESTRICTIONS

Pets: Must be on a leash, never left unattended. **Fires:** In grills, stoves, & fire rings only. **Alcoholic Beverages:** At site only. **Vehicle Maximum Length:** None.

TO GET THERE

From junction Rtes. 16 and 2, go 4.5 miles on Rte. 2; campground is on the left

GREENFIELD

Greenfield State Park Campground

P.O. Box 203, Greenfield 03047. T: (603) 547-3497, (603) 271-3628; F: (603) 547-8361; www.nhparks.state.nh.us.

RV ★★★ Tent ★★★★★

Beauty: ★★★★	Site Privacy: ★★★★
Spaciousness: ★★★★	Quiet: ★★★
Security: ★★★	Cleanliness: ★★★
Insect Control: ★★★	Facilities: ★★★

If you like a lot of elbow room and a woodsy, natural setting, you can't beat this lovely state park campground in southern New Hampshire. The wind in the trees, the heavy smell of pine, a crystal clear lake and plenty of room to roam are enticing features of this 401-acre oasis. We like the extra large sites, all nestled in the woods, and the separate "campers beach." Day visitors and picnickers have their own lake front area, which means campers don't have to share their own slice of sandy beach and swimming area on pretty Otter Lake. Bring your hiking boots and fishing poles: There are nature trails meandering through the woods and skirting Beaver, Mud, and Hogback Ponds, and canoes for rent at the lakeside general store.

BASICS

Operated By: New Hampshire Division of Parks & Recreation. **Open:** May–Columbus Day. **Site Assignment:** Reservations suggested, must be made at least seven days in advance of stay; full payment due, plus $3 non-refundable reservation fee. Seven day cancellation policy. Some sites not reservable but available first come, first served. MC, V accpeted; no personal checks. **Registration:** At office. **Fee:** $16, based on two adults & dependent children under 18. Each additional adult is half the site fee. **Parking:** At site, two cars per site.

FACILITIES

Number of RV Sites: 252. **Number of Tent-Only Sites:** 0. **Hookups:** None. **Each Site:** Picnic table, fire ring. **Dump Station:** Yes. **Laundry:** No. **Pay Phone:** Yes. **Rest Rooms & Showers:** Yes (coin-op). **Fuel:** No. **Propane:** No. **Internal Roads:** Gravel, dirt (good). **RV Service:** No. **Market:** Greenfield (1 mi). **Restaurant:** No. **General Store:** Yes. **Vending:** No. **Swimming Pool:** No. **Playground:** No. **Other:** Lake frontage, beach, nature trails, boat launch, boat rentals. **Activities:** Swimming, boating, fishing, hiking. **Nearby Attractions:** Manchester, Concord, Monadnock State Park. **Additional Information:** Manchester Chamber of Commerce, 889 Elm St., Manchester, NH 03101, (603) 434-7438 or Greater Peterborough Chamber of Commerce, P.O. Box 401, Peterborough, NH 03458, (603) 924-7234.

RESTRICTIONS

Pets: Pets are allowed on designated sites only. Must be on a leash, never left unattended. **Fires:** In grills, stoves, & fire rings only. **Alcoholic Beverages:** At site only. **Vehicle Maximum Length:** None.

TO GET THERE

From junction Rtes. 31 and 136, go west i mi. on Rte. 136; campground is on the right

HAMPTON

Tidewater Campground

160 Lafayette Rd., Hampton 03842. T: (603) 926-5474.

RV ★★★ Tent ★★

Beauty: ★★★	Site Privacy: ★★
Spaciousness: ★★	Quiet: ★★★★
Security: ★★★★★	Cleanliness: ★★★
Insect Control: ★★★	Facilities: ★★★★

This campground, just minutes from Hampton Beach, draws a steady return of vacationing families. There's also a fairly entrenched neighborhood of seasonal renters; more than 140 of its 228 sites are taken by people who've set up their home away from home here. The remaining sites are mainly filled by folks with children, who come to explore the New Hampshire seacoast. Many stay for at least a week or two. Sites vary: there's a section of tent-only sites plopped in the open right behind the office; more attractive sites (16J–16P) back up to an expanse of marsh grasses and tidal water; still others (95C–95H) sit back from busy and noisy Rte. 1. In all, it's a clean, relatively quiet and economical base in the area.

BASICS

Operated By: Wallace Shaw Sr. **Open:** May 15–Oct. 15. **Site Assignment:** Reservations required, min. stay three nights in Jul.–Aug., $50 deposit, full refund w/30 day notice, camping credit towards current year w/15-29 day notice, no refund or credit w/14 days or less. MC, V, personal checks accepted for advance reservations only. **Registration:** At office. **Fee:** Full hookup, $31; electric, $28; no hookups, $26; based on two adults & three children (2–17 years). **Parking:** At site.

FACILITIES

Number of RV Sites: 190. **Number of Tent-Only Sites:** 38. **Hookups:** Water, electric, sewer (20, 30, 50 amps). **Each Site:** Picnic table, fire ring. **Dump Station:** Yes. **Laundry:** No. **Pay Phone:** Yes. **Rest Rooms & Showers:** Yes (coin-op). **Fuel:** No. **Propane:** No. **Internal Roads:** Dirt, gravel (fair). **RV Service:** No. **Market:** Hampton (1 mi). **Restaurant:** No. **General Store:** Yes. **Vending:** No. **Swimming Pool:** Yes. **Playground:** Yes. **Other:** Rec hall, playing field, arcade. **Activities:** basketball, horseshoes. **Nearby Attractions:** Portsmouth, Hampton Beach, New Hampshire seacoast, Odiorne State Park, deep sea fishing, whale-watching. **Additional Information:** Hampton Beach Chamber of Commerce, 490 Lafayette Rd., Hampton, NH 03843, (603) 926-8717; also visit www.seacoastnh.com.

RESTRICTIONS

Pets: no dogs. **Fires:** In grills, stoves, & fire rings only. **Alcoholic Beverages:** At site only. **Vehicle Maximum Length:** 40 ft. **Other:** No weekend visitors, no motocycles.

TO GET THERE

From I-95 take exit 2, Rt. 101 east towards Hampton Beach, take second right (1.5 mi) on Rte. 1 south; campground is on the right.

HAMPTON BEACH

Hampton Beach State RV Park

P.O. Box 606, Rye Beach 03871. T: (603) 926-8990; www.nhparks.state.nh.us.

RV ★★★★ Tent NA

Beauty: ★★★★	Site Privacy: ★★
Spaciousness: ★★★	Quiet: ★★★
Security: ★★★★	Cleanliness: ★★★★
Insect Control: ★★★	Facilities: ★★

The New Hampshire seacoast is a mere 18 miles long (though full of fine state parks and beaches along the way) and this is the only campground on its shoreline. This state park campground, for RVs only, offers few conveniences and fewer comforts. The sites are basic; RVs are set side-by-side on open gravel sites with little privacy and no shade. The office is in a public-works-style building that sits next to a huge parking lot, used for overflow campsites (no hookups in this area.) But the view! Cast your eyes to the east and you'll see swaying sea grasses, a stretch of sugar white beach and the Atlantic Ocean beyond. To your south, is a wide, picturesque tidal inlet. There are sandy paths to th beach and to the state park next door (with a store, rest rooms, and cold showers.) Smack dab on Hampton Beach, you can't beat the locale—or the price—of this real estate. You'll need to reserve one year in advance to get a site for anytime during the summer months.

Basics

Operated By: NH Division of Parks & Recreation. **Open:** Apr.–Thanksgiving. **Site Assignment:** Reservations required through Reservation Center at (603)271-3628. Reservations can also be made via email at www.nhparks.state.nh.us. Minimum two night stay, three nights on holiday weekends & for a max. of 14 days in a 30-day period. Overflow area accommodates 30 RVs (no hookups) on a first-come, first-served basis. MC,V. **Registration:** At office. **Fee:** $35. **Parking:** At site.

Facilities

Number of RV Sites: 58. **Number of Tent-Only Sites:** 0. **Hookups:** Water, electric, sewer (30 amps). **Each Site:** Picnic table, fire ring. **Dump Station:** Yes. **Laundry:** No. **Pay Phone:** Yes. **Rest Rooms & Showers:** Yes, cold showers. **Fuel:** No. **Propane:** No. **Internal Roads:** Gravel (good). **RV Service:** No. **Market:** Hampton (1 mi). **Restaurant:** No. **General Store:** Yes. **Vending:** No. **Swimming Pool:** No. **Playground:** No. **Other:** Boat ramp, direct access to ocean, pavillion & state park adjacent to campground. **Activities:** Ocean swimming, fishing, beach combing. **Nearby Attractions:** Hampton Beach, whale-watching, saltwater fishing, Porstmouth, New Hampshire oceanfront state parks. **Additional Information:** Hampton Beach Chamber of Commerce, 490 Lafayette Rd., Hampton, NH 03843, (603) 926-8717; also NH Division of Parks & Recreation, P.O. Box 1856, Concord, NH 03302-1856, (603) 271-3556, fax (603)271-2629, www.nhparks.state.nh.us.

Restrictions

Pets: Must be on a leash, never left unattended. **Fires:** In grills, stoves, & fire rings only. **Alcoholic Beverages:** At site only. **Vehicle Maximum Length:** None. **Other:** There are often high winds in this area. Use of awnings, fires, etc. may be restricted.

To Get There

From I-95 take exit 2, Rte. 101 east towards Hampton Beach. Follow signs to Hampton Beach. Campground is located on Rte. 1A just south of the main part of Hampton Beach near the Seabrook-Hampton town line.

HAMPTON FALLS

Wakeda Family Campground

Rte. 88, Hampton Falls 03844. T: (603) 772-5274; www.wakedacampground.com.

RV: ★★★ Tent: ★★★

Beauty: ★★★ Site Privacy: ★★★
Spaciousness: ★★★ Quiet: ★★★
Security: ★★★★ Cleanliness: ★★★
Insect Control: ★★★ Facilities: ★★★

This family-friendly campground in the New Hampshire seacoast, offers the best of two worlds: far enough from the maddening crowds and traffic of seacoast beaches and attractions but close enough (only 20–30 minutes) for convenient day trips. The ride back and forth is pleasant, too: you'll pass farms, you-pick-it-orchards, and the sprawling lawns and meandering fieldstone walls of new and historic homes. The campground is a mile off the road, its own large neighborhood of seasonal renters and vacationing families. It's quiet (especially considering that there are more than 400 sites here) and spread out. The kids will like the 18-hole mini-golf course, but miss not having a swimming pool. The adults will appreciate the small hut serving coffee with bagels and donuts on the weekends (nice touch, we think.) There's a variety of sites, open and shaded, all about the same size (average width is about 35 feet.) If you like a bit more privacy and extra space, consider sites 32–47 and 16 East.

Basics

Operated By: Terry Savage, Jan Humbleton & Karen Bark. **Open:** May 15–Oct. 1. **Site Assignment:** Reservations suggested. No deposit required. No credit cards, personal checks accepted. **Registration:** At office. **Fee:** Full hookup w/50 amp, $35; full w/30 amp, $29.50; full w/20 amp, $28.50; water w/30 amp, $27.50; water w/20 amp, $24.50; no hookups, $21.50. All fees based on two adults & three children or less. **Parking:** At site.

Facilities

Number of RV Sites: 300. **Number of Tent-Only Sites:** 108. **Hookups:** Water, electric, sewer (20, 30, 50 amps). **Each Site:** Picnic table, fire ring. **Dump Station:** Yes. **Laundry:** Yes. **Pay Phone:** Yes. **Rest Rooms & Showers:** Yes (coin-op). **Fuel:** No. **Propane:** No. **Internal Roads:** Paved, gravel (good). **RV Service:** No. **Market:** Hampton (5 mi). **Restaurant:** Yes, small coffee shop. **General Store:** Yes. **Vending:** No. **Swimming Pool:** No. **Playground:** Yes. **Other:** Pavillion, 18-hole mini-golf course, game room, arcade, group facilities, camping cabins, 0.5 court basketball. **Activities:** Mini-golf, horseshoes, vollyeball, badminton, basketball, planned activities (ice cream bar, pancake breakfasts) on weekends. **Nearby Attractions:** Portsmouth, seacoast beaches including Hampton Beach, whale-watching, saltwater fishing. **Additional Information:** Hampton Beach Chamber of Commerce, 490 Lafayette Rd., Hampton, NH 03843, (603) 926-8717.

Restrictions

Pets: Must be on a leash, never left unattended. **Fires:** In grills, stoves, & fire rings only. **Alcoholic Beverages:** At site only. **Vehicle Maximum Length:** 40 ft.

To Get There

From I-95, take exit 1 (Kingston-Seabrook). Bear right off ramp, turn left at Rte. 1. Go 1 0.5 mi. and take a left on Rte. 88; campground is 4 miles on left.

HANCOCK

Seven Maples Campground

24 Longview Rd., Hancock 03449. T: (606) 525-3321; www.sevenmaples.com; sevenmaples@monad.net.

RV: ★★★ Tent: ★★★

Beauty: ★★ Site Privacy: ★★★
Spaciousness: ★★★ Quiet: ★★★★
Security: ★★★ Cleanliness: ★★★
Insect Control: ★★★ Facilities: ★★★

This modest campground, tucked in the quiet southwestern corner of New Hampshire, is best for campers who like their pleasures simple and their getaways restful. The pastoral woods setting, framed by grand stand of maple trees, is particularly scenic in the fall. The campground sits on the grounds of an historic 19th-century farm; campers can still walk along side old stone walls built during the 1800s to clear pastures. Within walking distance is the historic town of Hancock, considered one of prettiest towns in New England. Visiting this area is like taking a step back in time. Campground facilities, befitting its setting, are not fancy, but adequate. There are a few welcome concessions to the 20th century: hot showers, heated pool, and small general store. Sites are tucked in the woods or in open pastures. Tenters have sites among the hookups or head to the campground's new open wilderness area.

Basics

Operated By: Dave & Tina Gullotti. **Open:** Mid-May–Columbus Day. **Site Assignment:** Reservations suggested. One night deposit for stays of less than one week; three night deposit for stays of one week or more; holiday weekends payment in full ;min. three nights on holiday weekends. Two week cancellation policy. MC, V, & personal checks accepted. **Registration:** At office. **Fee:** Full hookups, $29; water & electric, $26; no hookups, $21; wilderness sites, $17, based on family of four. **Parking:** At site.

Facilities

Number of RV Sites: 91. **Number of Tent-Only Sites:** 34. **Hookups:** Water, electric, sewer (20, 30 amps). **Each Site:** Picnic table, fire ring. **Dump Station:** Yes. **Laundry:** No. **Pay Phone:** Yes. **Rest Rooms & Showers:** Yes (coin-op). **Fuel:** No. **Propane:** Yes. **Internal Roads:** Gravel, dirt (good). **RV Service:** No. **Market:** Hancock (2 mi). **Restaurant:** No. **General Store:** Yes. **Vending:** Yes. **Swimming Pool:** Yes. **Playground:** Yes. **Other:** Safari group area, sports court, pond. **Activities:** Swimming, hiking, horseshoes, planned activities & theme weekends. **Nearby Attractions:** Monadnock State Park, historic Hancock, Manchester, Keene. **Additional Information:** Manchester Chamber of Commerce, 889 Elm St., Manchester, NH 03101, (603) 434-7438 or Greater Peterborough Chamber of Commerce, P.O. Box 401, Peterborough, NH 03458, (603) 924-7234.

Restrictions

Pets: Must be on a leash, have current vaccinations, never left unattended. **Fires:** In grills, stoves, & fire rings only. **Alcoholic Beverages:** At site only. **Vehicle Maximum Length:** None.

To Get There

From junction Rtes. 202 and 123, go northwest 2 mi. on Rte. 123, then north 1 mi. on Rte. 137, then north 0.3 mi. on Longview Rd.; campground is on the left

HENNIKER

Keyser Pond Campground

47 Old Concord Rd., Henniker 03242. T: (603) 428-7741; F: (603) 428-8701; www.keyserpond.com; jolly@conknet.com.

RV ★★★ Tent ★★★

Beauty: ★★★★ Site Privacy: ★★★
Spaciousness: ★★★ Quiet: ★★★
Security: ★★★ Cleanliness: ★★★★
Insect Control: ★★★ Facilities: ★★★

This relaxed and friendly campground in the south central region of New Hampshire is one of two favorites in the area. (Also see Mile-Away listing.) Both are very popular with families, but this is our pick of the two. We like the low-key, slow-paced style of this woodsy destination, sitting on the shores of pretty Keyser Pond. We also like the views from the large, sandy beach and from the waterfront sites: glistening waters surrounded by rolling hills carpeted in dense pine forests. (There is little development along the shoreline.) Days are spent pursuing old-fashioned pleasures, like swim races to a raft, canoe paddles, early morning fishing outings and marshmallow roasts and sing-alongs around the communal campfire circle. There are planned activities and socials offered on summer weekends, too.

Basics

Operated By: Cal & Jolly Kimball. **Open:** May 15–Oct. 15. **Site Assignment:** Reservations suggested, one night deposit, three day cancellation policy MC,V, D accepted, no personal checks. **Registration:** At office. **Fee:** Waterfront, $30; full hookups, waterfront, $32; full hookups, $27; water & electric, $25; water, $20, based on two adults & their children under 18. **Parking:** At site.

Facilities

Number of RV Sites: 107. **Number of Tent-Only Sites:** 9. **Hookups:** Water, electric, sewer (20, 30 amps). **Each Site:** Picnic table, fire ring. **Dump Station:** Yes. **Laundry:** Yes. **Pay Phone:** Yes. **Rest Rooms & Showers:** Yes (coin-op). **Fuel:** No. **Propane:** Yes. **Internal Roads:** Gravel (good). **RV Service:** No. **Market:** Henniker (4.5 mi). **Restaurant:** No. **General Store:** Yes. **Vending:** No. **Swimming Pool:** No. **Playground:** Yes. **Other:** Lake frontage, beach, boat rentals, mini golf course, rec hall, trailer rentals. **Activities:** Swimming, boating, fishing, horseshoes, shuffleboard, volleyball, badminton, planned activities on summer weekends. **Nearby Attractions:** Henniker, Concord, Lakes region. **Additional Information:** Greater Concord Chamber of Commerce, 244 North Main St., Concord, NH 03301-5078, (603) 224-2508 or New London/Lake Sunapee Region Chamber of Commerce, P.O. Box 532, New London, NH 03257, (603) 536-6575.

Restrictions

Pets: Must be on a leash, never left unattended. **Fires:** In grills, stoves, & fire rings only. **Alcoholic Beverages:** At site only. **Vehicle Maximum Length:** None.

To Get There

From junction Rtes. 202 and 127 and Old Concord Rd., go south 300 yards on Old Concord Rd.; campground is on the right

HENNIKER

Mile Away Campground

41 Old West Hopkinton Rd., Henniker 03242. T: (603) 428-7616, (800) 787-4679 (reservations); www.ucampnh.com/mi.-away.

RV ★★★★ Tent ★★★

Beauty: ★★★ Site Privacy: ★★★
Spaciousness: ★★★ Quiet: ★★★
Security: ★★★ Cleanliness: ★★★★
Insect Control: ★★★ Facilities: ★★★

This well-kept, woodsy campground in the south central region of New Hampshire is one of two favorites in the area (Also see Keyser Pond campground listing.) Both are popular with families and great places to stay. Mile-Away is located on state-stocked French's Pond (trout anglers may want to pack their fly rods) with a picturesque sandy beach area, and a long shallow slope prefect for young swimmers. There are boat rentals and plenty of planned activities offered on weekends throughout the summer. This campground is one of the few in the state that stays open throughout the winter months, with cross country and snowmobile trails accessible from the property, ice skating on the pond and alpine skiing nearby. There are several summer seasonal renters, most clustered near the rec hall and office and toward the beach area. The rest of the sites, mostly shaded with water and electric hookups, are scattered in loops on good-sized lots (average width is about 50 feet.)

Basics

Operated By: Kate Tenney. **Open:** Memorial Day–Columbus Day. **Site Assignment:** Reservations suggested, one night deposit; no shows forfeit deposit, MC,V, & personal checks accepted. **Registration:** At office. **Fee:** Full hookups, $33; water & electric, $26; based on four people. **Parking:** At site.

Facilities

Number of RV Sites: 156. **Number of Tent-Only Sites:** 14. **Hookups:** Water, electric, sewer (20, 30, 50 amps). **Each Site:** Picnic table, fire ring. **Dump Station:** Yes. **Laundry:** Yes. **Pay Phone:** Yes. **Rest Rooms & Showers:** Yes (coin-op). **Fuel:** No. **Propane:** Yes. **Internal Roads:** Gravel, dirt (good). **RV Service:** No. **Market:** Henniker (3 mi). **Restaurant:** No. **General Store:** Yes. **Vending:** No. **Swimming Pool:** No. **Playground:** Yes. **Other:** Pond, beach, boat dock, boat rentals, mini-golf, rec hall, game room, pavillion, safari field. **Activities:** Swimming, boating, fishing, hiking, ice skating, cross country skiing, snowmobiling, shuffleboard, basketball, horseshoes, mini golf, badminton, volleyball, planned activities on summer weekends, including socials, bingo, crafts & games. **Nearby Attractions:** Henniker, Lake Sunapee. **Additional Information:** Greater Concord Chamber of Commerce, 244 North Main St., Concord, NH 03301-5078, (603) 224-2508 or New London/Lake Sunapee Region Chamber of Commerce, P.O. Box 532, New London, NH 03257, (603) 536-6575.

Restrictions

Pets: Must be on a leash, never left unattended. **Fires:** In grills, stoves, & fire rings only. **Alcoholic Beverages:** At site only. **Vehicle Maximum Length:** None.

To Get There

From junction I-89 and Rte. 202 (exit 5), go west 5 mi. on Rte. 202, then northeast 1 mi. on Old West Hopkinton Rd.; campground is on the left

JEFFERSON

Lantern Motor Inn & Campground Resort

P.O. Box 97, Rte. 2, Jefferson 03583. T: (603) 586-7151; www.thelanternresort.com.

RV ★★★ Tent ★★★

Beauty: ★★★ Site Privacy: ★★
Spaciousness: ★★★ Quiet: ★★
Security: ★★★ Cleanliness: ★★★★★
Insect Control: ★★★ Facilities: ★★★★★

It's directly across the street from Santa's Village, minutes from Six Gun City and Storyland (New Hampshire's most popular kiddie amusement park attractions) and, as you'd expect, crawling with kids. This campground is a magnet for families and does a nice job of welcoming them and keeping them entertained. The setting is pretty, nestled in the meadows and woods at the foot of the Presidential mountain range. At the end of the day, you'll have stunning views of the sun setting over the craggy mountaintops. Of course, the kids will be too busy to notice: there are two full-size pools (one with piped in underwater music) and a wading pool for young tykes, a large playground and two hot tubs. There are planned activities running from 10 a.m. to 9 p.m. each day, including old-fashioned fun like haywagon rides, face painting, and sing-alongs. At the on-site motor inn, a nightly children's movie is shown followed by a general audience movie (both free.) Everything is clean, bathrooms immaculate. The sites are basic, set in rows, all similar in size (average width is about 35 feet). The tent-only area in the front of the campground backs up to woods facing an open field. Big rigs will find a number of super large, pull-through sites for added ease and convenience.

Basics

Operated By: John & Norma Ahern. **Open:** May 15–Oct. 15. **Site Assignment:** Reservations suggested, one night deposit, seven day cancellation policy, MC,V, D, AE; no personal checks. **Registration:** At office. **Fee:** Full hook up, super sites, $35; full hookups, $32; water & electric, $27, no hookups, $22, based on a family of four. **Parking:** At site.

Facilities

Number of RV Sites: 76. **Number of Tent-Only Sites:** 15. **Hookups:** Water, electric, sewer (30, 50 amps). **Each Site:** Picnic table, fire ring. **Dump Station:** Yes. **Laundry:** Yes. **Pay Phone:** Yes. **Rest Rooms & Showers:** Yes. **Fuel:** No. **Propane:** Yes. **Internal Roads:** Gravel, dirt (good). **RV Service:** No. **Market:** Lancaster (8 mi). **Restaurant:** No. **General Store:** Yes. **Vending:** No. **Swimming Pool:** Yes. **Playground:** Yes. **Other:** Game room, video arcade, trailer rentals, wading pool & two hot tubs, activity tent, on-site motor inn. **Activities:** Swimming, planned activities including hayrides, arts & crafts, contests, kid's programs, & more. **Nearby Attractions:** Santa's Village, Six Gun City, Storyland, North Conway, White Mountains, outlet shopping. **Additional Information:** Mount Washington Valley Chamber of Commerce, P.O. Box 2300, North Conway, NH 03860, (800) 521-2137.

Restrictions

Pets: Must be on a leash, never left unattended. **Fires:** In grills, stoves, & fire rings only. **Alcoholic Beverages:** At site only. **Vehicle Maximum Length:** None.

To Get There

From junction Rtes. 2 and 116, go west 0.5 mi. on Rte.2; campground is on the right

LACONIA
Gunstock Campground

Rte. 11A, P.O. Box 1307, Laconia 03247. T: (603) 293-4341, (800) 486-7862 or ext 502; F: (603) 293-4318; www.gunstock.com; camping@gunstock.com.

RV ★★★★ Tent ★★★★

Beauty: ★★★★ Site Privacy: ★★★
Spaciousness: ★★★ Quiet: ★★★
Security: ★★★★ Cleanliness: ★★★★
Insect Control: ★★★ Facilities: ★★★★★

Within a few minutes drive are three mountain ranges, dozens of sparkling lakes (including the Granite State's largest—Lake Winnipesaukee) and a slew of attractions. But, there's no need to ever leave the campground property; we rarely venture out once we've pounded in the stakes. Outside your doorstep (or tent flap) is a top notch year-round resort, complete with a mountain sports center, equestrian center, swimming pools, skate park, archery center, restaurant, and more. In winter, there's cross country and downhill skiing, tubing, nature programs, and snowshoeing. The property also boasts several ponds and a good-sized lake. The campground is large, with more than 250 sites, and often bustling with activity (especially during New Hampshire's popular Race Weeks held in the summer.) Sites are set in rows; the lakeview sites are the prettiest, if you can get one.

Basics

Operated By: Laconia County. **Open:** Year-round. **Site Assignment:** Reservations suggested & can be made one year in advance. Reservations require a two-night stay, $20 nonrefundable deposit in addition to a $2 reservation fee. Holiday stays must be paid in advance & may require three-night min. stay. MC, V, D, AE; no personal checks. **Registration:** At office. **Fee:** Full hookups, $30; water & electric, $28; no hookups, $24. **Parking:** At site.

Facilities

Number of RV Sites: 111. **Number of Tent-Only Sites:** 139. **Hookups:** Water, electric, sewer (20, 30 amps). **Each Site:** Picnic table, fire ring. **Dump Station:** Yes. **Laundry:** Yes. **Pay Phone:** Yes. **Rest Rooms & Showers:** Yes. **Fuel:** No. **Propane:** Yes. **Internal Roads:** Gravel, dirt (good). **RV Service:** No. **Market:** Gilford (4 mi). **Restaurant:** Yes. **General Store:** Yes. **Vending:** Yes. **Swimming Pool:** Yes. **Playground:** Yes. **Other:** Mountain sports center, mountain bike center, skate park, equestrian center, group areas, conference center, ski resort, trails, rec hall, ponds & lake access, cabin rentals. **Activities:** Swimming, boating, hiking, horseback riding, archery, biking, alpine & cross country skiing, planned programs. **Nearby Attractions:** Lake Winnipesaukee, Lakes region attractions. **Additional Information:** Greater Laconia/Weirs Beach Chamber of Commerce, 11 Veterans Square, Laconia, NH 03246, (603) 524-5531 or Meredith Area Chamber of Commerce, P.O. Box 732, Meredith, NH 03253-0732, (603) 279-6121.

Restrictions

Pets: Must be on a leash; never left unattended. **Fires:** In grills, campstoves, & fire rings only. **Alcoholic Beverages:** At site only. **Vehicle Maximum Length:** None.

To Get There

From junction Rtes. 16 (Spaulding Turnpike) and 11, go 15 mi. north on Rte. 11, then 12 mi. north on Rte. 11A; Gunstock resort and campground is on the left.

LANCASTER
Mountain Lake Campground

P.O. Box 475, Rte. 3, Lancaster 03584. T: (603) 788-4509; www.greatnorthwoods.org/mountainlake; mtnlake@ncia.net.

RV ★★★ Tent ★★★

Beauty: ★★★ Site Privacy: ★★★
Spaciousness: ★★★ Quiet: ★★★★
Security: ★★★★ Cleanliness: ★★★★
Insect Control: ★★★ Facilities: ★★★

This Lancaster campground in the northern White Mountains, close to Santa's Village, Franconia Notch State Park and other popular atttractions, is suited to families who prefer a quieter, lakeside locale. Situated on the pristine 25-acre Mountain Lake, campers have access to a sandy beach, two boat docks and rental boats (paddleboats, canoes and kayaks.) Campers can also bring their own boats, though no power motors are allowed on the lake. Fishing for perch, bass, pickerel and sunfish is good and a favorite pasttime at the campground. Families will enjoy the short nature trail that runs through the property, skirting a frog pond and tadpole stream. There's also a giant size chess and checker game to play, sports fields, and a rec hall. Level RV sites are set on a hill; the tent area is below towards the lake. There are a number of waterfront sites with water and electric (sites 76-80 are favorites); site 23 is nicely tucked in the woods for extra privacy. We'd stay away from sites 1-15, if you can; they're too close to the road for our liking. Looking for something different? You can rent the teepee on site; the rustic cabins are nice, too.

Basics

Operated By: Lois & Geert Pesman. **Open:** May–Oct. **Site Assignment:** Reservations suggested in Jul.–Aug., $25 deposit, 7 day cancellation policy, MC, V, & personal checks accepted. **Registration:** At office. **Fee:** Full hookups, $23; water & electric, $20.50; no hookups, $18. **Parking:** At site.

Facilities

Number of RV Sites: 100. **Number of Tent-Only Sites:** 1. **Hookups:** Water, electric, sewer (30 amps), cable TV. **Each Site:** Picnic table, fire ring. **Dump Station:** Yes. **Laundry:** Yes. **Pay Phone:** Yes. **Rest Rooms & Showers:** Yes. **Fuel:** No. **Propane:** Yes. **Internal Roads:** Dirt, gravel (good). **RV Service:** No. **Market:** Lancaster (4 mi). **Restaurant:** No. **General Store:** Yes. **Vending:** No. **Swimming Pool:** Yes. **Playground:** Yes. **Other:** Lake frontage, beach, boat rentals, boat docks, rec hall, cabin rentals. **Activities:** Swimming, boating, fishing, shuffleboard, basketball, volleyball, horseshoes. **Nearby Attractions:** Santa's Village, Six Gun City, Storyland, White Mountains, Franconia Notch State Park. **Additional Information:** Northern White Mountains Chamber of Commerce, 164 Main St., P.O. Box 298, Berlin, NH 03570, (603) 752-6060, also Franconia Notch Chamber of Commerce, P.O. Box 780, Franconia, NH 03580, (800) 237-9007; Mount Washington Valley Chamber of Commerce, P.O. Box 2300, North Conway, NH 03860, (800) 521-2137.

Restrictions

Pets: No pit bulls. Certain breeds, including german shepard, rotweiller, & doberman are not allowed during summer months. All pets must be on a leash under 10 ft. long, never left unattended. Pets are not allowed in public buildings, on swimming beach, or docks. **Fires:** In grills, stoves, & fire rings only. **Alcoholic Beverages:** At site only. **Vehicle Maximum Length:** 38 ft.

To Get There

From junction Rtes. 3 and 2, go south 4 mi. on Rte. 3; campground is on the right.

LANCASTER
Roger's Family Camping Resort & Motel

10 Roger's Campground Rd., Lancaster 03584. T: (603) 788-4885; F: (603) 788-3697; www.rogerscamgroundandmotel.usrc.net.

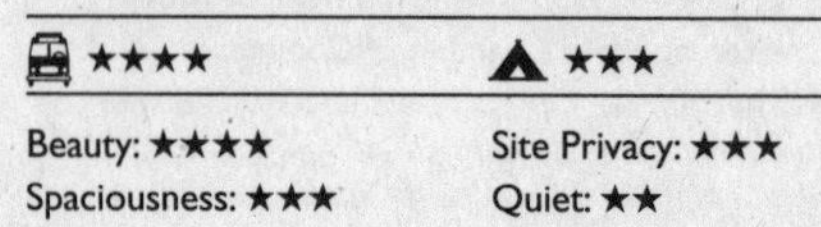

RV ★★★★ Tent ★★★

Beauty: ★★★★ Site Privacy: ★★★
Spaciousness: ★★★ Quiet: ★★

Security: ★★★★★ Cleanliness: ★★
Insect Control: ★★★ Facilities: ★★★★★

Located halfway between Lancaster and Jefferson in the scenic northern White Mountains area, Roger's is New Hampshire's largest campground with 400 sites (not including a large safari group area.) The backdrop is splendid: rolling foothills, forested valleys and craggy summits of the Presidential mountain range surround the campground. There are plenty of nearby attractions and outdoor activities at your doorstep but most campers come to stay put for awhile. This is a destination campground with lots of on-site facilities: hot tub, swimming pool with waterslide, kiddie pool, tennis courts, mini-golf, nature trails, on-site restaurant and a host of planned activities and live entertainment. Kids will love the huge barn-turned-arcade/billiards room and upstairs TV room. RV sites are all pull-throughs, set side-by-side in rows of grassy sites. The tenting area is separate, set behind the pool and motel area, backed by woods. We find the campsites and some facilities a bit bedraggled; it'd all look better with a little sprucing up.

Basics

Operated By: Crosby Peck/Interlocks Property North. **Open:** May 1–Oct. 15. **Site Assignment:** Reservations suggested, one-half of stay required for deposit, 14 day cancellation policy, MC, V, D, AE & personal checks accepted. **Registration:** At office. **Fee:** Full hookups, $26; water & electric, $21; electric, $20; no hookups, $19, based on two people, additional adult, $5; additional child, $3. **Parking:** At site.

Facilities

Number of RV Sites: 300. **Number of Tent-Only Sites:** 100. **Hookups:** Water, electric, sewer (30 amps), modem. **Each Site:** Picnic table, fire ring. **Dump Station:** Yes. **Laundry:** Yes. **Pay Phone:** Yes. **Rest Rooms & Showers:** Yes. **Fuel:** No. **Propane:** Yes. **Internal Roads:** Dirt, gravel (fair). **RV Service:** Yes. **Market:** Lancaster (3 mi). **Restaurant:** Yes. **General Store:** Yes. **Vending:** Yes. **Swimming Pool:** Yes. **Playground:** Yes. **Other:** Cabin & trailer rentals, on-site motel, mini-golf, arcade, waterslide, rec hall, TV room, hot tub, wading pool, tennis courts, safari field, nature trail, sports field. **Activities:** Swimming, tennis, hiking, softball, volleyball, mini-golf, basketball, shuffleboard, horseshoes. **Nearby Attractions:** Santa's Village, Six Gun City, Storyland, White Mountains, Franconia Notch State Park. **Additional Information:** Northern White Mountains Chamber of Commerce, 164 Main St. , P.O. Box 298, Berlin, NH 03570, (603) 752-6060, also Franconia Notch Chamber of Commerce, P.O. Box 780, Franconia, NH 03580, (800) 237-9007; Mount Washington Valley Chamber of Commerce, P.O. Box 2300, North Conway, NH 03860, (800) 521-2137.

Restrictions

Pets: Must be on a leash, never left unattended. Pets are allowed in motel units, cabin or trailer rentals. **Fires:** In grills, stoves, & fire rings. **Alcoholic Beverages:** At site only. **Vehicle Max. Length:** None.

To Get There

From junction Rtes. 2 and 3, go 2 mi. east on Rte. 2; campground is on the right

LEBANON

Mascoma Lake Campground

92 US Rte. 4A, Lebanon 03766. T: (603) 448-5076, (800) 769-7861; www.mascomalake.com; camping@mascomalake.com.

RV: ★★★★ Tent: ★★★★

Beauty: ★★★★ Site Privacy: ★★★
Spaciousness: ★★★ Quiet: ★★★
Security: ★★★ Cleanliness: ★★★
Insect Control: ★★★ Facilities: ★★★★

If you're in the mood for old-fashioned pleasures (think: sunsets across the lake, early morning canoe paddles, and sing-alongs around a bonfire), you'll enjoy your stay at this lakeside campground. It's situated in the "quiet corner" of New Hampshire (though there are plenty of those!) straddling the Vermont border. Campground activity centers around pretty Mascoma Lake, with plenty of boating (there are canoe, kayak and paddleboat rentals) swimming, fishing, and lots of lounging on the sandy beach. Campsites are terraced, many overlooking the lake, with a bit of elbow room; average site width is about 35 feet. Type A, active types can happily busy with planned events on the weekend and sports activities, or a trip to nearby attractions (covered bridges, Quechee Gorge, and antiquing are favorites.)

Basics

Operated By: Carol & Dave Hill. **Open:** May–Oct. **Site Assignment:** Reservations suggested; one night deposit, holiday weekends paid in full; 14-day cancellation policy w/$5 service fee. MC, V. **Registration:** At office. **Fee:** Full hookups, $28; water & electric, $25; no hookups, $22. **Parking:** At site.

Facilities

Number of RV Sites: 82. **Number of Tent-Only Sites:** 18. **Hookups:** Water, electric, sewer (20, 30 amps), modem. **Each Site:** Picnic table, fire ring. **Dump Station:** Yes. **Laundry:** Yes. **Pay Phone:** Yes. **Rest Rooms & Showers:** Yes. **Fuel:** No. **Propane:** Yes. **Internal Roads:** Gravel, dirt (good). **RV Service:** No. **Market:** Lebanon (3 mi). **Restaurant:** No. **General Store:** Yes. **Vending:** Yes. **Swimming Pool:** No. **Playground:** Yes. **Other:** Lake frontage, beach, rec hall, boat dock, boat rentals, sports field, planned activities. **Activities:** Swimming, boating, fishing, hiking. **Nearby Attractions:** Hanover, Dartmouth, Sunapee, Quechee Gorge, covered bridges, antiquing. **Additional Information:** Greater Lebanon Chamber of Commerce, 2 Whipple Place, P.O. Box 97, Lebanon, NH 03766, (603) 448-1203.

Restrictions

Pets: Must be on a leash; never left unattended. **Fires:** In grills, campstoves, & fire rings only. **Alcoholic Beverages:** At site only. **Vehicle Maximum Length:** 35 ft.

To Get There

From I-89 and exit 17, go east 2 mi. on Rte. 4, then south 0.75 mi. on Rte. 4A; campground is on right.

LEE

Ferndale Acres

132 Wednesday Hill Rd., Lee 03824. T: (603) 659-5082 (May-Sept.) or, (603) 623-2351 (Oct.-Apr.); www.ferndaleacres.com; fac132.com.

RV: ★★★ Tent: ★★

Beauty: ★★★ Site Privacy: ★★
Spaciousness: ★★ Quiet: ★★★
Security: ★★★ Cleanliness: ★★
Insect Control: ★★★ Facilities: ★★★

This plain Jane is a bit off the beaten path, set in the middle of a former farmer's field along the Lamprey River. The natural setting is pretty enough but, alas, the best sites, along the river, are taken by a core of regulars who rent for the season. Some of these trailers, including an old beat-up bus, look like they've been around for awhile. Tenters and pop-up campers can pick from a handful of shaded sites in the woods, flanking the property. Still, there is plenty for families to do here, including fishing in the river, swimming in the pool, video games, bonfires, dances, and a plethora of planned activities. Adults have their own recreational hall, often with a disc jockey and potluck dinner. Many visitors use the campground as a base to explore Portsmouth and the Seacoast region (about 0.5-hour's drive away.)

Basics

Operated By: Walter & Lorraine George. **Open:** May 15–Sept. 15. **Site Assignment:** First-come, first-served; hold w/credit card or one-day deposit reservations required on holiday weekends & must be paid in full prior to arrival; MC, V, AE & personal checks accepted. **Registration:** At office. **Fee:** $25 for a family of 2, $1 extra per child, $5 extra per adult. **Parking:** At site.

Facilities

Number of RV Sites: 138. **Number of Tent-Only Sites:** 12. **Hookups:** Water, electric, sewer (30 amps). **Each Site:** Picnic table, fire ring. **Dump Station:** No. **Laundry:** Yes. **Pay Phone:** Yes. **Rest Rooms & Showers:** Yes (coin-op). **Fuel:** No. **Propane:** No. **Internal Roads:** Dirt (fair). **RV Service:** No. **Market:** Lee (5 mi.). **Restaurant:** No. **General Store:** Yes. **Vending:** Yes. **Swimming Pool:** Yes. **Playground:** Y. **Other:** Game room, adult rec. hall, river access. **Activities:** Planned activities on weekends, fishing, boat rentals, horseshoes, volleyball, baseball, basketball. **Nearby Attractions:** New Hampshire & southern Maine beaches, Portsmouth, factory outlet shopping, University of New Hampshire, antique shops. **Additional Information:** Greater Portsmouth Chamber of Commerce, P.O. Box 239, Portsmoutn, NH 03801, 603-436-3988; also visit www.SeacoastNH.com.

Restrictions

Pets: Must be on a leash, never left unattended. **Fires:** In grills, stoves, & fire rings only. **Alcoholic Beverages:** At site only. **Vehicle Maximum Length:** 36 ft. **Other:** No motorbikes.

To Get There

From junctions Rte. 4 and 155; go 2.5 mi. south on

Rte. 155, then 1.5 mi. east on Wednesday Hill Rd., then 1 mi. south on entry road

LINCOLN

Hancock Campground

Kancamagus Hwy., Lincoln 03251.T: (603) 447-5448.

RV ★★★ Tent ★★★

Beauty: ★★★★ Site Privacy: ★★★
Spaciousness: ★★★★ Quiet: ★★★★
Security: ★★★ Cleanliness: ★★★★
Insect Control: ★★★ Facilities: ★★★

Hancock Campground is one of two along the Kancamagus that is open all year, and great for those looking to ski on the cheap, with a dash of added adventure. Most all the sites are nicely forested, fairly spacious, well spaced apart, and set within a beautiful birch grove. Right across the street from Hancock is a trail that takes you up and over Potash Knob and Big Coolidge Mountain. Hancock is the campground on the Kancamagus that is closest to civilization, only five miles east of Lincoln, where you can grab a pizza or see a movie if need a little diversion. Another diversionary tactic is to take the short path to the East Branch of the Pemigewasset River (between sites 43 and 45 on the outer side of the loop) and drop a hook in the water. There are also a few spots where you can drop yourself in the water, but be careful. Even late in the summer, that water can be mighty chilly.

BASICS

Operated By: US Forest Service. **Open:** All year. **Site Assignment:** First come first served; no reservations. **Registration:** Select site, then pay at self-service fee station. **Fee:** $16. **Parking:** At site.

FACILITIES

Number of RV Sites: 37. **Number of Tent-Only Sites:** 40. **Hookups:** None. **Each Site:** Fire ring, picnic table. **Dump Station:** No. **Laundry:** No. **Pay Phone:** No. **Rest Rooms & Showers:** Yes. **Fuel:** No. **Propane:** No. **Internal Roads:** Gravel. **RV Service:** No. **Market:** No. **Restaurant:** No. **General Store:** No. **Vending:** No. **Swimming Pool:** No. **Playground:** No. **Other:** Unique swimming hole, Upper Lady's Bath. **Activities:** Swimming fishing, hiking, picnicking, scenic byway. **Nearby Attractions:** Whale's Tale Water Park, White Mountain Motor Sports Park, Lost River Reservation. **Additional Information:** Lincoln-Woodstock Chamber of Commerce, (603) 745-6621, www.lincolnwoodstock.com.

RESTRICTIONS

Pets: On leash. **Fires:** In fire ring. **Alcoholic Beverages:** At site. **Vehicle Maximum Length:** 2 vehicles per site. **Other:** 8 people per site; 14-day stay limit.

TO GET THERE

From Lincoln, follow Kancamagus Hwy. to campground on right. It's the first campground you'll come to. From Conway, follow Kancamagus Hwy. to Hancock campground on left. From this side, it will be the last campground you come to.

LISBON

Littleton/Lisbon KOA

2154 Rte. 302, Lisbon 03585.T: (603) 838-5525, (800) 562-5836 (reservations); www.koa.com.

RV ★★★★ Tent ★★★

Beauty: ★★★ Site Privacy: ★★★
Spaciousness: ★★★ Quiet: ★★★
Security: ★★★ Cleanliness: ★★★★★
Insect Control: ★★★ Facilities: ★★★★

This campground is a popular stopover and weekend destination for travelers exploring the scenic Franconia Notch area and beyond. Upon check-in, campers are given a helpful brochure detailing six one-day itineraries, all within an hour of the campground. Conveniently located, the Littleton/Lisbon KOA also offers some nice touches: an adult-only hot tub, frontage on the Ammonoosuc River with swimming holes and pebble beaches (bring your own tubes or kayaks; stocked fishing with license, too), white-glove clean bath facilities and—our favorite—meal delivery! The campground owners work with a local Italian restaurant (pizza, sandwiches, pasta, salads); pick from the menu in the office and the campground will deliver your meal for a nominal fee. Large pull-through sites are clustered in the middle of the property, while tent-only sites back up to the trees and the river. Full hookups are contained in a small loop behind the office and store. All sites are very tidy and uniform.

BASICS

Operated By: Judy & Mike Sullivan. **Open:** First weekend in May–mid-Oct. **Site Assignment:** Reservations suggested in Jul.–Aug., one night deposit, 24-hour cancellation policy, three day min. stay on holiday weekends, MC,V, & personal checks accepted. **Registration:** At office. **Fee:** Full hookups, $31; water & electric, $28; no hookups, $25, based on two adults, additional child, 17 years & under, $2; additional adult, $5. **Parking:** At site.

FACILITIES

Number of RV Sites: 43. **Number of Tent-Only Sites:** 17. **Hookups:** Water, electric, sewer (30 amps), cable TV, modem. **Each Site:** Picnic table, fire ring. **Dump Station:** Yes. **Laundry:** Yes. **Pay Phone:** Yes. **Rest Rooms & Showers:** Yes. **Fuel:** No. **Propane:** Yes. **Internal Roads:** Gravel (good). **RV Service:** No. **Market:** Littleton (5 mi). **Restaurant:** No. **General Store:** Yes. **Vending:** No. **Swimming Pool:** Yes. **Playground:** Yes. **Other:** Adult-only hot tub, river frontage, bike rentals, cabin rentals. **Activities:** Swimming, fishing, horseshoes, basketball. **Nearby Attractions:** White Mountains, Franconia Notch State Park. **Additional Information:** Littleton Area Chamber of Commerce, P.O. Box 105, 120 Main St. , Littleton, NH 03561, (603) 444-6561; Franconia Notch Chamber of Commerce, P.O. Box 780, Franconia, NH 03580, (800) 237-9007.

RESTRICTIONS

Pets: Must be on a leash, never left unattended. **Fires:** In grills, stoves, & fire rings only. **Alcoholic Beverages:** At site only. **Vehicle Maximum Length:** 40 ft.

TO GET THERE

From I-93, exit 42, go southwest 5.5 mi. on Rte. 302; campground is on the left.

LITTLETON

Crazy Horse Campground

778 Hilltop Rd., Littleton 03561.T: (603) 444-2204, (800) 639-4107; F: (603) 444-0776; www.ucampnh.com/crazyhorse; crazyhorse@conriver.net.

RV ★★★ Tent ★★★★

Beauty: ★★★★ Site Privacy: ★★★
Spaciousness: ★★★ Quiet: ★★★★
Security: ★★★★ Cleanliness: ★★★★
Insect Control: ★★★ Facilities: ★★★

Looking to get away from it all? This White Mountain–area campground offers a picturesque, serene escape, especially appealing to tent campers and outdoor enthusiasts. That's not to say there isn't lots to do in the area: From here you can visit Franconia Notch State Park attractions or head east to the busy North Conway area—easy day trips, if you're looking for some action. But you might be tempted to stay close to the campground, where you'll find hiking and biking trails, planned activities, and a number of nature programs conducted throughout the summer by the New Hampshire Audubon Society. Also nearby is 12-mile long Moore Lake, with a sandy beach, canoe rentals, and good fishing.The tent-only area is separate and remote, tucked in the woods, with the White Mountains as a backdrop (sites C88–96 are especially nice). Full-hookup sites for larger rigs are clustered in loops near the front, with plenty of shade and level ground.

BASICS

Operated By: Barbara & Joseph DiPierre. **Open:** Year-round. **Site Assignment:** Reservations suggested; one night deposit, 48 hour cancellation policy, 4-day cancellation policy for holiday weekends. MC,V, no personal checks. **Registration:** At office. **Fee:** Full hookups, $25; water & electric, $23; no hookups, $20. **Parking:** At site.

FACILITIES

Number of RV Sites: 112. **Number of Tent-Only Sites:** 48. **Hookups:** Water, electric, sewer (30, 50 amps), modem. **Each Site:** Picnic table, fire ring. **Dump Station:** Yes. **Laundry:** Yes. **Pay Phone:** Yes. **Rest Rooms & Showers:** Yes. **Fuel:** No. **Propane:** Yes. **Internal Roads:** Gravel, dirt (fair). **RV Service:** No. **Market:** Littleton (2 mi). **Restaurant:** No. **General Store:** Yes. **Vending:** Yes. **Swimming Pool:** Yes. **Playground:** Yes. **Other:** Boat rentals, rec hall, pavillion, lake access, trailer, teepee & tent rentals. **Activities:** Swimming, boating, fishing, volleyball, horseshoes, basketball, biking, hiking, planned activities, NH Audubon programs, winter activities nearby including skiing, snowmobiling, **Nearby Attractions:** White Mountain attractions, Franconia State Park. **Additional Information:** Littleton Area Chamber of Commerce, P.O. Box 105, 120 Main St. , Littleton, NH 03561, (603) 444-6561.

RESTRICTIONS

Pets: Must be on a leash; never left unattended; current rabies certificate. Pets not allowed in rental units. **Fires:** In grills, campstoves, & fire rings only. **Alcoholic Beverages:** At site only. **Vehicle Maximum Length:** None.

TO GET THERE

From junction I-93 and Rte. 135 (exit 43), go south 100 yards on Rte. 135, then northwest (right) 1 mi. on Rte. 135/18, then north (right) 1.5 mi. on Hilltop Rd.; campground is on the right

MEREDITH

Clearwater Campground

26 Campground Rd., Meredith 03253. T: (603) 279-7761; www.clearwatercampground.com; info@clearwatercampground.com.

RV ★★★ Tent ★★★

Beauty: ★★★★ Site Privacy: ★★★
Spaciousness: ★★★ Quiet: ★★★
Security: ★★★★★ Cleanliness: ★★★★
Insect Control: ★★★★ Facilities: ★★★★

This centrally located Lakes-region campground, just minutes off the highway, is a water-lover's paradise. The property bumps up to pretty Pemigewasset Lake, with its own sandy beach, boat launch, slips, and dock. There's plenty of recreation off the water, too, with planned activities, play areas, a rec room, and more. It's easier to get to a number of popular attractions in the area and to explore the region from this base. Still, many campers, especially those with kids in tow, are content to stick around and enjoy the lake and campground activities. Most of the sites are on nicely wooded lots that loop off the main roads; only a handful have water views. The most requested site is site 125 next to a huge granite boulder. It's very picturesque, but we found it a bit busy, next to the docks and beach area. Bigger rigs should consider the Meredith Woods RV resort across the street, owned by the same family.

BASICS

Operated By: John & Sue Mackie. **Open:** May 18–Oct. 9. **Site Assignment:** Reservations recommended, $100 per week deposit is required for holiday period; three nights or less require full payment in advance. Cancellation policy: deposits refunded up to one week before arrival. Minimum stays are often required during summer & holiday weekends. V, MC, D, AE & personal checks accepted. **Registration:** At office. **Fee:** $33, no hookups; $34, electric & water; $37 electric, water, sewer, & cable. From May 18-Jun. 14 (excluding Memorial Day weekend) & from Sept. 3-Oct. 9, fees are $20–$23 per night. **Parking:** At site.

FACILITIES

Number of RV Sites: 146. **Number of Tent-Only Sites:** 4. **Hookups:** Water, electric, sewer (20, 30, 50 amps), cable TV. **Each Site:** Picnic table, fire ring, trash barrel. **Dump Station:** Yes. **Laundry:** Yes. **Pay Phone:** Yes. **Rest Rooms & Showers:** Yes. **Fuel:** No. **Propane:** No. **Internal Roads:** Paved, gravel (good). **RV Service:** No. **Market:** Meredith (2 mi). **Restaurant:** No. **General Store:** Yes. **Vending:** No. **Swimming Pool:** No. **Playground:** Yes. **Other:** Lake frontage, beach area, self-guided nature walk, boat rentals, boat dock, launching & slips, recreation pavilion, trailor & cabin rentals, rec rooms w/library, arcade games, TV. **Activities:** Swimming, boating, ping pong, shuffleboard, planned activities. **Nearby Attractions:** Lake Winnepesaukee, Squam Lake, Weirs Beach, scenic railroad, golf courses, hiking trails. **Additional Information:** Meredith Area Chamber of Commerce, P.O. Box 732, Meredith, NH 03253-0732, (603) 279-6121 or Lakes Region Assoc., Rte. 104, P.O. Box 430, New Hampton, NH 03252, (603) 744-8664.

RESTRICTIONS

Pets: Must be on a leash, never left unattended. **Fires:** In grills, stoves, & fire rings only. **Alcoholic Beverages:** At site. **Vehicle Maximum Length:** 35 ft. **Other:** No motorcycles.

TO GET THERE

From I-93, exit 23 (Meredith); go 3 mi. east on Rte. 104; campground is on the right.

MEREDITH

Harbor Hill

189 Rte. 25 East, Meredith 03253. T: (603) 279-6910; www.ucampnh.com; hhcamp@cyberportal.net.

RV ★★★ Tent ★★★★

Beauty: ★★★ Site Privacy: ★★★★
Spaciousness: ★★★★ Quiet: ★★★★
Security: ★★★★★ Cleanliness: ★★★★
Insect Control: ★★★ Facilities: ★★★

Location, location, location. You can't beat Harbor Hill's location if you want to explore New Hampshire's popular Lakes region. The campground is a short distance to the shores of Squam Lake (where *On Golden Pond* was filmed), Lake Winnipesaukee (New Hampshire's largest freshwater lake), and to rollicking Weirs Beach. It's especially popular with families who want a quiet, relaxing place to come home to after a day of exploring area beaches and attractions.

BASICS

Operated By: Barbara Palm. **Open:** Memorial Day–Columbus Day. **Site Assignment:** Reservations suggested, 50 percent deposit, 3-day deposit for holiday weekends, cancellations made less than 7 days before scheduled arrival, the deposit is held as raincheck for a future stay within the same year subject to availability & a $10 service charge. MC, V, & personal checks accepted. **Registration:** At office. **Fee:** Full hookups, $30; water & electric, $28; no hookup, $24. **Parking:** At site, 1 vehicle per site.

FACILITIES

Number of RV Sites: 107. **Number of Tent-Only Sites:** 33. **Hookups:** Water, electric, sewer (20, 30, 50 amps). **Each Site:** Picnic table, fire ring. **Dump Station:** Yes. **Laundry:** Yes. **Pay Phone:** Yes. **Rest Rooms & Showers:** Yes (coin-op). **Fuel:** No. **Propane:** Yes. **Internal Roads:** Paved, gravel (good). **RV Service:** No. **Market:** Meredith (2 mi). **Restaurant:** No. **General Store:** Yes. **Vending:** Yes. **Swimming Pool:** Yes. **Playground:** Yes. **Other:** Rec hall, arcade, cabin rentals, sport court. **Activities:** Swimming, basketball. **Nearby Attractions:** Lake Winnipesaukee, Squam Lake, Weirs Beach, fishing, boating, quick access to White Mountain area. **Additional Information:** Meredith Chamber of Commerce, P.O. Box 732, Meredith, NH 03253-0732, (603) 279-6121.

RESTRICTIONS

Pets: Must be on a leash, never left unattended. **Fires:** In grills, stoves, & fire rings. **Alcoholic Beverages:** At site only. **Vehicle Maximum Length:** 40 ft.

TO GET THERE

Rt. 93, exit 23, Rt. 104 east go 12 mi. to Rt. 3, then left on Rt. 3 to Rt. 25 east; campground is 1.5 mi. on right

MEREDITH

Meredith Woods

26 Campground Rd., Meredith 03253. T: (603) 279-5449; www.ucampnh.com/meredithwoods; meredithwoods@worldnet.att.net.

RV ★★★★ Tent na

Beauty: ★★★ Site Privacy: ★★★
Spaciousness: ★★★ Quiet: ★★★
Security: ★★★★★ Cleanliness: ★★★★
Insect Control: ★★★★★ Facilities: ★★★★★

This year-round RV park is a miniature gated neighborhood of rigs. It's RV heaven, smack-dab in the middle of New Hampshire's popular Lakes region. You won't find much in the way of scenic beauty at this campground: all sites are level, gravel or sandy plots, flanked by a few trees and bushes scattered in between for foliage and privacy. It's all very clean and orderly, albeit a bit bland. The most extraordinary feature of this park is the large (and plush by campground standards) recreational center with a heated indoor pool and hot tub, TV social room, and game room. All the facilities are new and modern. Another bonus: Meredith Woods campers have access to the beach, boating, and all other programs and facilities at Clearwater Campground, across the street. (But not vice versa.)

BASICS

Operated By: Mackie family. **Open:** Year-round. **Site Assignment:** Reservations recommended, $75 deposit per each week of scheduled stay; reservations of 3 nights or less & holiday reservations require full payment in advance. Deposits are refundable up to 7 days of arrival. **Registration:** At office. **Fee:** $37, summer; $23–$33, early spring & winter, based on two adults & 3 children under age of 18; additional adults, $10; additional children, $1. **Parking:** At site, one vehicle per site.

FACILITIES

Number of RV Sites: 101. **Number of Tent-Only Sites:** 0. **Hookups:** Water, electric (50 amps), sewer, cable TV, phone. **Each Site:** Picnic table, fire ring, trash can. **Dump Station:** No, all sites have sewer. **Laundry:** Yes. **Pay Phone:** Yes. **Rest Rooms & Showers:** Yes. **Fuel:** No.

Propane: No. **Internal Roads:** Paved (good). **RV Service:** No. **Market:** Meredith (2 mi). **Restaurant:** No. **General Store:** Yes. **Vending:** No. **Swimming Pool:** Yes. **Playground:** Yes. **Other:** indoor pool & hot tub, TV social room & game room, boat docking by reservation, canoe rack space available; guests also have use of all activities & facilities at Clearwater Campground, across the street, including lake frontage, beach area, self-guided nature walk, boat rentals, boat dock, launching & slips, recreation pavillion, trailor & cabin rentals, rec rooms w/library, arcade games. **Activities:** Swimming, boating, hiking, ping pong, shuffleboard, planned activities. **Nearby Attractions:** Lake Winnipesaukee, Squam Lake, Weirs Beach, quick access to White Mountain region. **Additional Information:** Meredith Area Chamber of Commerce, P.O. Box 732, Meredith, NH 03253-0732, (603) 279-6121.

Restrictions

Pets: Must be on a leash, never left unattended. **Fires:** In grills, stoves, & fire rings only. **Alcoholic Beverages:** At site nly. **Vehicle Maximum Length:** 40 ft. **Other:** limit of 7 people per site on an overnight basis, no more than 4 of whom can be adults; limit of 1 RV per site.

To Get There

From I-93, exit 23 (Meredith), go 3 mi. east on Rte. 104; campground is on the left

MILTON

Mi-Te-Jo Campground

P.O. Box 830, Townhouse Rd., Milton 03851. T: (603) 652-9022; www.mi-te-jo.com; mitejo@worldpath.net.

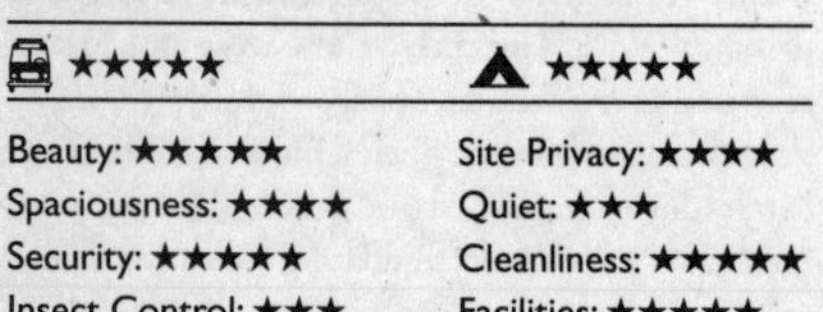

★★★★★ ▲ ★★★★★

Beauty: ★★★★★	Site Privacy: ★★★★
Spaciousness: ★★★★	Quiet: ★★★
Security: ★★★★★	Cleanliness: ★★★★★
Insect Control: ★★★	Facilities: ★★★★★

This top-notch lakeside campground, less than one hour from the White Mountains to the north and ocean beaches to the east, is a real gem. There's lots of easy day trips from here, but there is little reason to leave. In fact, most campers rent summer sites a week at a time, Saturday to Saturday. This is a true destination/vacation campground, with plenty of outdoor pleasures. There are two sandy beaches on Northeast Pond. "Pond" is an understatement: 770 acres of fresh water feed into another 371-acre pond. Swimming and fishing are top pursuits, and many campers choose to bring their own boats to park in slips or at the docks ($5 per day charge.) There are lots of nice sites on the water (sites A–D are especially nice); sites 111, 112, and 0 are favorites, too, overlooking the lake. But you really can't go wrong here. Landscaping throughout the campground is well-done; facilities are clean, modern, and top-of-the-line.

Basics

Operated By: Gary & Susan Marique. **Open:** May 15–Columbus Day. **Site Assignment:** Reservations recommended; required during Jul.–Aug., 50 percent deposit, cancel within 14 days to avoid $20 service charge MC, V, & personal checks accepted. **Registration:** At office. **Fee:** Premium sites w/full hookup, $34; premium sites w/water & electric, $31; vacation sites w/full hookup, $29; vacation sites w/water & electric, $26, based on two adults & their children ages 18 & under. **Parking:** At site.

Facilities

Number of RV Sites: 179. **Number of Tent-Only Sites:** 0. **Hookups:** Water, electric, sewer (30 amps), modem. **Each Site:** Picnic table, fire ring. **Dump Station:** Yes. **Laundry:** Yes. **Pay Phone:** Yes. **Rest Rooms & Showers:** Yes (coin-op). **Fuel:** No. **Propane:** Yes. **Internal Roads:** Dirt (good). **RV Service:** No. **Market:** Milton (1 mi). **Restaurant:** No. **General Store:** Yes. **Vending:** Yes. **Swimming Pool:** No. **Playground:** Yes. **Other:** Two beaches, 1900 ft. of lake frontage, skateboard park, ballfield, pavillion, rec hall, boat slips, docks, cabin rentals, canoe, kayak & paddleboat rentals, arcade. **Activities:** Swimming, boating, fishing, bocci, horseshoes, basketball, volleyball, skateboarding. **Nearby Attractions:** New Hampshire seacoast, Portsmouth, quick access to Lakes region & Lake Winnipesaukee, antiquing, hiking. **Additional Information:** Lakes Region Assoc., Rte. 104, P.O. Box 430, New Hampton, NH 03252, (603) 744-8664, fax (603) 744-8659, or visit www.lakesregion.org.

Restrictions

Pets: Must be on a leash, never left unattended. Pets are not allowed on the beaches or in cabins. **Fires:** In grills, stoves, & fire rings only. **Alcoholic Beverages:** Responsible consumption. **Vehicle Maximum Length:** None. **Other:** Sites are limited to seven campers of which only four may be adults. One RV per site.

To Get There

Rte. 16 (Spaulding Turnpike), exit 17, go 0.75 mi. east on Rte. 75, then 3.5 mi. north on Rte. 125. Turn right on Townhouse Rd.; the campground is 1 mi. on the left

MOULTONBORO

Long Island Bridge Campground

HCR 62, Box 455, Center Harbor 03226. T: (603) 253-6053.

★★★ ▲ ★★★

Beauty: ★★★★	Site Privacy: ★★★
Spaciousness: ★★★	Quiet: ★★★★
Security: ★★★	Cleanliness: ★★★
Insect Control: ★★★	Facilities: ★★★

Here's your chance to get your own slice of pricey Lake Winnipesaukee waterfront real estate, if only for a few nights. This campground rests on the shores of New Hampshire's largest (and very popular) freshwater lake. Only 15 minutes from Center Harbor, the campground is nestled in a cove, away from the hustle and bustle of many of the busier spots on the lake. (Note: the campground is next to a large marina, so you're likely to see some boat traffic.) Campers have access to a lovely, sandy stretch of beach and, if you reserve well in advance, a choice of sites along the shore facing picturesque Long Island and the setting sun. The rest of the sites and facilities are on a hilly terrace across the street. You won't see much, if any, of the lake from these sites (and those with water views have already been snatched up by long-time seasonal renters), but most of the available sites are spacious and ringed with trees for privacy. There are some open, grassy sites, too, for those who prefer the sun. We like the waterfront sites the best, of course, but sites 55, 55A, and 55B are roomy and private. This campground is a great base to explore the area and enjoy the lake.

Basics

Operated By: Watson family. **Open:** May 15–Oct. 15. **Site Assignment:** Reservations suggested, one night deposit, refunded on a 2 week notice, MC, V, personal checks accepted. **Registration:** At office. **Fee:** Full hookup, $25; water & electric, $23; no hookus, $21; waterfront, $28, based on one family (mother, father & unmarried children) per site. **Parking:** At site.

Facilities

Number of RV Sites: 100. **Number of Tent-Only Sites:** 12. **Hookups:** Water, electric, sewer (20, 30 amps). **Each Site:** Picnic table, fire ring. **Dump Station:** Yes. **Laundry:** Yes. **Pay Phone:** Yes. **Rest Rooms & Showers:** Yes (coin-op). **Fuel:** No. **Propane:** No. **Internal Roads:** Dirt (fair). **RV Service:** No. **Market:** Moultonborough (7 mi). **Restaurant:** No. **General Store:** Yes. **Vending:** No. **Swimming Pool:** No. **Playground:** Yes. **Other:** Lake frontage, beach, boat rentals, **Activities:** Swimming, boating, fishing, basketball, volleyball, horseshoes. **Nearby Attractions:** Lake Winnipesaukee, Squam Lake, Weirs Beach, outlet shopping, antiquing. **Additional Information:** Wolfeboro Chamber of Commerce, P.O. Box 547, 32 Central Ave., Wolfeboro, NH 03894, (603) 569-2200.

Restrictions

Pets: Must be on a leash, never left unattended. Pets not allowed at waterfront sites or beach area (pets are generally not encouraged here). **Fires:** In grills, stoves, & fire rings nly. **Alcoholic Beverages:** At site nly. **Vehicle Maximum Length:** None.

To Get There

From the junction of Rtes. 3 and 25 (in Meredith), go 7 mi. northeast on Rte. 25, then 6.5 mi. south on Moultonboro Neck Rd.; the campground is on the left

NEW BOSTON

Friendly Beaver Campground

Old Coach Rd., New Boston 03070. T: (603) 487-5570; www.friendlybeaver.com; info@friendlybeaver.com.

★★★★★ ▲ ★★★

Beauty: ★★★	Site Privacy: ★★★
Spaciousness: ★★★	Quiet: ★★★
Security: ★★★★	Cleanliness: ★★★★★
Insect Control: ★★★	Facilities: ★★★★★

We love the facilities at this southern New Hampshire campground; they rival many high-end resorts. A stay at Friendly Beaver is certainly not "roughing it." There's a three-pool outdoor complex, including a children's pool, sports pool (water basketball, anyone?), swim pool, and hot tubs. Next door is the adult-only rec hall and indoor pool complex. Kids have their own rec hall—a huge space with an upstairs activity area, large-screen TV, and games. There are plenty of planned activities for adults and children throughout summer weekends, too. Despite the size and resort-style facilities, the campground remains quite friendly, almost quaint. Seasonal renters are spread throughout the major areas of the campground; transient campers are clustered in a separate circle (full hookups available) in open, sunny sites. Special note: the campground is open year-round, with nearby skiing, ice fishing, and snowmobiling in the winter.

Basics

Operated By: Christine & Tom Quirk. **Open:** Year-round. **Site Assignment:** Reservations suggested, full payment required as deposit. Three night min. stay during holidays. 14-day cancellation notice, w/a $10 service charge; 7-13 day notice, camoing credit for the same year, 6 days notice or less, no refund or credit. MC, V, & personal checks accepted for deposit; no personal checks accepted upon arrival. **Registration:** At office. **Fee:** Full hookups, $36; water & electric, $33; no hookups, $31, based on 2 adults & 2 children under 18. **Parking:** At site.

Facilities

Number of RV Sites: 166. **Number of Tent-Only Sites:** 7. **Hookups:** Water, electric, sewer (30, 50 amps). **Each Site:** Picnic table, fire ring. **Dump Station:** Yes. **Laundry:** Yes. **Pay Phone:** Yes. **Rest Rooms & Showers:** Yes. **Fuel:** No. **Propane:** No. **Internal Roads:** Gravel, dirt (good). **RV Service:** No. **Market:** Goffstown (15 mi). **Restaurant:** No. **General Store:** Yes. **Vending:** Yes. **Swimming Pool:** Yes. **Playground:** Yes. **Other:** Adult rec hall & lounge, game room, hiking, biking & snowmobiling trails, outdoor patios & decks, safaria field, hot tubs, sports field, pavillion. **Activities:** Swimming, basketball, volleyball, horseshoes, hiking, biking, snowmobiling, planned activities, including pony rides, arts & crafts, children's programs, socials, contests, dances, live entertainment, & more. **Nearby Attractions:** Manchester, Concord, Crotched Mountain. **Additional Information:** Manchester Chamber of Commerce, 889 Elm St., Manchester, NH 03101, (603) 434-7438.

Restrictions

Pets: Must be on a leash, never left unattended. **Fires:** In grills, stoves, & fire rings only. **Alcoholic Beverages:** At site only. **Vehicle Maximum Length:** None.

To Get There

From the junction of Rtes. 77, 136, and 13, go south 100 feet on Rte. 13, then west 2 mi. on Old Coach Rd.; campground is on the right

NEW HAMPTON

Twin Tamarack

Rte. 104, P.O. Box 121, New Hampton 03256.
T: (603) 279-4387; www.minbiz.org/tamarack; bevsands@juno.com.

RV ★★★★ Tent ★★★

Beauty: ★★★	Site Privacy: ★★★
Spaciousness: ★★★	Quiet: ★★
Security: ★★★★★	Cleanliness: ★★★★
Insect Control: ★★★	Facilities: ★★★★

This large, activity-oriented campground in the Lakes region is popular with families and groups. On warm, sunny days, campers gather around the pool, located up front next to the recreational hall and office. Or they head across the street to the sandy beach area on Pemigewasset Lake to swim in spring-fed waters or go boating. Evenings are filled with special events and activities (movies, music, and socials.) There's ping pong, video games, pool, hayrides, fishing contests, and more to keep even the most active in your brood busy and happy. The boulder-strewn, hilly grounds and scattered woods add visual interest, but don't expect too much privacy. Many sites are small, close to the road, and each other. But it's a "more the merrier" attitude here, perfect for social, friendly campers and traveling groups.

Basics

Operated By: Laurie Osuchowski. **Open:** Memorial Day–Columbus Day. **Site Assignment:** Reservations suggested, take credit card to reserve site & charges one night's fee if cancelled less than 24 hours before arrival unless site is resold. Groups of four sites or more require nonrefundable $75 deposit. MC, V, D, personal checks not accepted on arrival but can be used to reserve a site. **Registration:** At office. **Fee:** Full hookup, $34; water & electric, $30, based on a family of four or two adults. **Parking:** At site.

Facilities

Number of RV Sites: 256. **Number of Tent-Only Sites:** 0. **Hookups:** Water, electric, sewer (30, 50 amps). **Each Site:** Picnic table, fire ring. **Dump Station:** Yes. **Laundry:** Yes. **Pay Phone:** Yes. **Rest Rooms & Showers:** Yes. **Fuel:** No. **Propane:** Yes. **Internal Roads:** Gravel, dirt (good). **RV Service:** No. **Market:** New Hampton (3 mi). **Restaurant:** No. **General Store:** Yes. **Vending:** Yes. **Swimming Pool:** Yes. **Playground:** Yes. **Other:** Hot door hot tub, sports courts, canoe & boat rentals, lake access, boat launch, rec room, arcade, group safari area. **Activities:** Swimming, boating, fishing, basketball, horseshoes, volleyball, planned activities, including arts & crafts, fishing derbies, movies, hayrides, dances & socials. **Nearby Attractions:** Lake Winnipesaukee, Squam Lake, Weirs Beach, quick access to White Mountain region. **Additional Information:** Greater Laconia/Weirs Beach Chamber of Commerce, 11 Veterans Square, Laconia, NH 03246, (603) 524-5531.

Restrictions

Pets: Must be on a leash, never left unattended. **Fires:** In grills, stoves, & fire rings only. **Alcoholic Beverages:** At site only. **Vehicle Maximum Length:** 40 ft. **Other:** Motorcycles not allowed.

To Get There

From I-93, exit 23, go 2.5 mi. east on Rte. 104; campground is on the left.

NEWFIELDS

Great Bay Campground

56 Rte. 108, P.O. Box 390, Newfields 03856.
T: (603) 778-0226; www.nebsnow.com/greatbay; greatbay@ttic.net.

RV ★★★ Tent ★★★

Beauty: ★★★	Site Privacy: ★★
Spaciousness: ★★	Quiet: ★★★
Security: ★★★	Cleanliness: ★★★
Insect Control: ★★	Facilities: ★★★

If you're an angler, with your own boat, you're going to love this campground, situated on the tidal water Squamscott River. It has its own boat launch and is the only private campground in the state located on a saltwater river. Extra bonus: no fishing license is required if you're casting from campground shores. With a boat, campers have access to pristine Great Bay, and beyond, to the ocean. Anglers fill the campground when the stripers and bluefish are running, but this is also a popular summer spot for area families and those visiting the Seacoast region. Unfortunately, most riverfront sites are taken by a cramped cluster of seasonal rentals, but you'll find a good selection of shady, level sites on the property. There's also a wooded tent-only section, nestled in the pines off the water (mosquitoes and black flies can be a nuisance.) This is a good base and destination campground both; when you're not on the water or visiting area attractions, there are planned suppers, dances, and other activities.

Basics

Operated By: Pat Elderly. **Open:** May 15–Oct. 1. **Site Assignment:** Reservations required; deposits required: 1–3 days, full amount; 4–7 days, a 3-day deposit; 8–30 days, a 7-day deposit. Cancellations: full refund 7 days before arrival, 75%, 5-6 days before arrival; 50%, 3–4 days before arrival; no refund, 0–2 days before arrival. V, MC, D, AE & personal checks accepted. **Registration:** At office. **Fee:** No hookups, $19; water & electric, $23; water, electric, sewer, $28. Rates based on two adults & their under 18 children or grandchildren per site. **Parking:** At site.

Facilities

Number of RV Sites: 68. **Number of Tent-Only Sites:** 17. **Hookups:** Water, electric, sewer (20, 30, 50 amps). **Each Site:** Picnic table, fire ring. **Dump Station:** Yes. **Laundry:** Yes. **Pay Phone:** Yes. **Rest Rooms & Showers:** Yes (coin-op). **Fuel:** Yes. **Propane:** Yes. **Internal Roads:** Gravel, dirt (good). **RV Service:** No. **Market:** Newmarket (5 mi). **Restaurant:** No. **General Store:** Yes. **Vending:** Yes. **Swimming Pool:** Yes. **Playground:** Yes. **Other:** Game room, separate tent-only area, tidal river access, small beach area, boat rentals, boat ramp. **Activities:** Swimming, salt water fishing, boating, volleyball, tetherball, basketball, planned activities. **Nearby Attractions:** New Hampshire & southern Maine beaches, Portsmouth, Exeter, factory outlet shopping, golf courses, waterpark, Strawbery Banke historic museum, Seacoast Science Center, antique shops. **Additional Information:** Greater Portsmouth Chamber of Commerce, P.O. Box 239, Portsmoutn,

NH 03801, (603) 436-3988; also visit www.SeacoastNH.com.

RESTRICTIONS

Pets: Must be on a leash, never left unattended. No pit bulls or rotweillers allowed. **Fires:** In grills, stoves, & fire rings only. **Alcoholic Beverages:** At site. **Vehicle Maximum Length:** 44 ft. **Other:** Maximum 28-day stay for tenters.

TO GET THERE

From I-95 and Rte. 101 (exit 2), go west on Rte. 101 for 3.5 mi. to Rte. 108, then go 4 mi. north on Rte. 101 to entrance (entrance is at the Citgo gas station).

NEWPORT

Crow's Nest

529 S. Main St., Newport 03773. T: (603) 863-6170; www.crowsnestcampground; camping@crowsnestcampground.com.

RV ★★★ Tent ★★★

Beauty: ★★★ Site Privacy: ★★★
Spaciousness: ★★★ Quiet: ★★★
Security: ★★★ Cleanliness: ★★★
Insect Control: ★★★ Facilities: ★★★

Located in the Lake Sunapee region, Crow's Nest Campground is a favorite with families and anglers in the summer and snowmobilers and skiers in the winter. It is one of the few campgrounds in New Hampshire that remains open when the mercury drops. The property flanks the meandering Sugar River, with plenty of spots for trout fishing and hot summer day dunks. (Those who prefer a less natural swimming experience can take advantage of the campground's heated pool and kid-friendly wading pool.) There's also a spring-fed pond on the property. In winter, there's downhill and cross country skiing nearby, sledding, and snowmobiling (trails are directly accessible from the campground). You'll have a choice of open, wooded, pond, and riverfront sites. The more primitive tent sites are located near the pond with a convenient footpath to the river. Full hookup sites are set in rows near the front of the campground with easy access to the rec hall and office (both heated in the winter.) Our favorites sites are 56–65, with water and electric, set on the riverbank.

BASICS

Operated By: Howie & Kathy Neuberger. **Open:** May 15–Oct. 15 & Dec. 1–Apr. 1. **Site Assignment:** Reservations suggested; stay of one night requires full deposit; two or more nights, 50% deposit; holiday stays paid in full. 14 day cancellation policy w/a $5 service fee. No refunds for holiday stays. MC, V, D; no personal checks. **Registration:** At office. **Fee:** Full hookups (50 amp), $27; full hookup (30 amp), $25; water & electric (riverfront) $25; water & electric, $22; no hookups, $20, based on two adults & three children. **Parking:** At site.

FACILITIES

Number of RV Sites: 84. **Number of Tent-Only Sites:** 11. **Hookups:** Water, electric, sewer (20, 30, 50 amps), modem. **Each Site:** Picnic table, fire ring. **Dump Station:** Yes. **Laundry:** Yes. **Pay Phone:** Yes. **Rest Rooms & Showers:** Yes (coin-op). **Fuel:** No. **Propane:** Yes. **Internal Roads:** Gravel, dirt (good). **RV Service:** No. **Market:** Newport (2 mi). **Restaurant:** No. **General Store:** Yes. **Vending:** Yes. **Swimming Pool:** Yes. **Playground:** Yes. **Other:** Pond & river frontage, group area, mini-golf, bike rentals, sports fields, rec hall, RV, cabin & tent rentals, planned activities, including arts & crafts, socials, & themed weekends. **Activities:** Swimming, fishing, basketball, biking, mini-golf, badminton, horseshoes, volleyball, snowmobiling. **Nearby Attractions:** Lake Sunapee, Dartmouth, Hanover. **Additional Information:** Greater Lebanon Chamber of Commerce, 2 Whipple Place, P.O. Box 97, Lebanon, NH 03766, (603) 448-1203.

RESTRICTIONS

Pets: Must be on a leash; never left unattended. No pets in rental units. **Fires:** In grills, campstoves, & fire rings only. **Alcoholic Beverages:** At site only. **Vehicle Maximum Length:** None.

TO GET THERE

From the junction of I-89 and Rte. 103 (exit 9), go west 22 mi. on Rte. 103, then south 2 mi. on Rte. 10; campground is on the right.

NEWPORT

Loon Lake

P.O. Box 345, Reed's Hill Rd., Newport 03773. T: (603) 863-8176; www.camploonlake.com; fnguilmette@turbont.net.

RV ★★★ Tent ★★★

Beauty: ★★★ Site Privacy: ★★★
Spaciousness: ★★★ Quiet: ★★★
Security: ★★★★★ Cleanliness: ★★★★
Insect Control: ★★★ Facilities: ★★★★

We used to go to Lake Sunapee to vacation, one camper told us. "But it got a bit too busy and crowded for us. Now, we come here, where the pace is a bit slower and more relaxing." These were the sentiments we heard again and again during our visits to Loon Lake Campground. New Hampshire's popular Lake Sunapee is just 15 minutes away, but many campers are content to set up camp here and stay put. Who can blame them? The campground setting is beautiful: 750 acres of pine forest surrounding a mile-long freshwater lake. There are canoes, kayaks, and paddleboats to rent (gasoline motors are not allowed on Loon Lake), a sandy beach for lounging, and plenty of campground activities for the active (mini-golf, sports fields, planned events—even a small fitness room, if you must). There are several sites overlooking the lakeshore; others are placed in loops with plenty of shade and adequate privacy.

BASICS

Operated By: Fred & Nancy Guilmette. **Open:** Mid-May–mid-Oct. **Site Assignment:** Reservations suggested; one night deposit; 30 day cancellation notice; less than 30 day notice, campers receive rain check for future stay within the same year w/a $10 service fee. MC, V; no personal checks. **Registration:** At office. **Fee:** Full hookups, $26 (lakeview), $28; water & electric, $24; no hookups, $20, based on two adults & unmarried children under 18. **Parking:** At site.

FACILITIES

Number of RV Sites: 92. **Number of Tent-Only Sites:** 10. **Hookups:** Water, electric, sewer (20, 30 amps). **Each Site:** Picnic table, fire ring. **Dump Station:** Yes. **Laundry:** Yes. **Pay Phone:** Yes. **Rest Rooms & Showers:** Yes. **Fuel:** No. **Propane:** Yes. **Internal Roads:** Gravel, dirt (good). **RV Service:** No. **Market:** Newport (2 mi). **Restaurant:** No. **General Store:** Yes. **Vending:** Yes. **Swimming Pool:** No. **Playground:** Yes. **Other:** Lake frontage, beach, boat rentals, sports field, rec hall, game room, fitness room, mini-golf course, group area, cabin & tent rentals, planned activities, including arts & crafts, contests, socials, theme weekends. **Activities:** Swimming, boating, fishing, mini-golf, horseshoes. **Nearby Attractions:** Lake Sunapee, Dartmouth, Hanover. **Additional Information:** Greater Lebanon Chamber of Commerce, 2 Whipple Place, P.O. Box 97, Lebanon, NH 03766, (603) 448-1203.

RESTRICTIONS

Pets: Must be on a leash; never left unattended. **Fires:** In grills, campstoves, & fire rings only. **Alcoholic Beverages:** At site only. **Vehicle Maximum Length:** None.

TO GET THERE

From the junction of I-89 and Rte. 103 (exit 9), go north 19 mi. on Rte. 103, then west 1.5 mi. on Rte. 103/11, then north 2.5 mi. on Reeds Mill Rd.; campground is on the left.

NORTH CONWAY

Saco River Camping

P.O. Box 546, Rte. 16, North Conway 03860. T: (603) 356-3360; www.sacorivercamping.com.

RV ★★★ Tent ★★★

Beauty: ★★★ Site Privacy: ★★
Spaciousness: ★★ Quiet: ★★
Security: ★★★★★ Cleanliness: ★★★
Insect Control: ★★★ Facilities: ★★★

In the heart of North Conway, this campground is best suited for families who don't mind a bit of noise and commotion. Like other campgrounds in the area, this one can be action-packed, crowded, and bustling. There's room to roam in the sweeping fields and play areas (look for the horses that are kept on site; kids get pony rides, too), but individual sites don't offer much privacy. Most are laid out side-by-side in long rows, flanking each side of road. They do a nice job of entertaining the kids here, with a full-time activity planner offering a large menu of daily programs. Expect evening bonfires, sing-alongs, hayrides, and more. There's also a small beach on the Saco River for swimming and rock skipping.

BASICS

Operated By: John & Don McClure. **Open:** May 1– Oct. 15. **Site Assignment:** Reservations suggested, one night deposit, two week cancellation policy, MC, V, & personal checks accepted. **Registration:** At office. **Fee:** Full hookups, $25; full hookups (riverfront), $27; water & electric, $21; water &

electric (riverfront), $23; no hookups, $19. **Parking:** At site.

Facilities

Number of RV Sites: 120. **Number of Tent-Only Sites:** 20. **Hookups:** Water, electric, sewer (20, 30 amps). **Each Site:** Picnic table, fire ring. **Dump Station:** Yes. **Laundry:** Yes. **Pay Phone:** Yes. **Rest Rooms & Showers:** Yes (coin-op). **Fuel:** No. **Propane:** Yes. **Internal Roads:** Gravel, paved (good). **RV Service:** No. **Market:** North Conway (0.25 mi). **Restaurant:** No. **General Store:** Yes. **Vending:** Yes. **Swimming Pool:** No. **Playground:** Yes. **Other:** Game room, river frontage, canoe rentals, group safari area. **Activities:** Swimming, boating, softball, horseshoes, planned activities including children's programs, arts & crafts, contests, hayrides, & more. **Nearby Attractions:** North Conway, White Mountains, outlet shopping. **Additional Information:** Greater Conway Village Area Chamber of Commerce, P.O. Box 1019, Conway, NH 03818, (603) 447-2639.

Restrictions

Pets: Must be on a leash, never left unattended. **Fires:** In grills, stoves, & fire rings only. **Alcoholic Beverages:** At site only. **Vehicle Maximum Length:** None.

To Get There

From the junction of Rtes. 16 and 302 south, go north 0.25 mi. on Rte. 16/302; campground is on the left.

NORTH WOODSTOCK

Lost River Valley Campground

951 Lost River Rd., Rte. 112, North Woodstock 03262. T: (603) 745-8321, (800) 370-678 (reservations); www.lostriver.com.

RV ★★★★ Tent ★★★★★

Beauty: ★★★★	Site Privacy: ★★★★★
Spaciousness: ★★★★★	Quiet: ★★★★
Security: ★★★★★	Cleanliness: ★★★★★
Insect Control: ★★★	Facilities: ★★★★

We've dubbed this campground, "The Rivers Run Through It." Located on the site of a turn-of-the-century lumber mill (an authentic water wheel still churns), the scenic property is surrounded on three sides by national forest and situated between the Lost River and Walker Brook. It's hard to believe that you're only minutes off the highway and near many of New Hampshire's White Mountains and Franconia Notch State Park attractions. Large sites have been sensitively carved out of the boulder-strewn deep-woods setting, many with river or brook frontage. Recreation areas, including a swimming pond, beach area, playground, and sports fields, are situated across the street. Crossing the street may be an issue for families with small children, but the set-up keeps the campground sites quiet, more natural, and pristine. You'll go to sleep to the sound of running waters.

Basics

Operated By: Nancy Simmons. **Open:** May 15–Columbus Day. **Site Assignment:** First come, first served w/reservations accepted for three nights stay or longer, three-day deposit or 50 percent for stays of a week or more, 14 day cancellation policy w/$15 service charge. MC, V, D & personal checks accepted. **Registration:** At office. **Fee:** Full hookups, $31.50; water & electric, $26 (wooded), $30 (brookfront); water only, $22 (wooded), $26.50 (brookfront), based on two adults per site, one camp unit & one car per site, additional children, ages 17 & under, $2; additional adult, $8; limit of four adults per site. **Parking:** At site.

Facilities

Number of RV Sites: 100. **Number of Tent-Only Sites:** 32. **Hookups:** Water, electric, sewer (20, 30, 50 amps). **Each Site:** Picnic table, fire ring, water. **Dump Station:** Yes. **Laundry:** Yes. **Pay Phone:** Yes. **Rest Rooms & Showers:** Yes. **Fuel:** No. **Propane:** Yes. **Internal Roads:** Dirt, gravel (good). **RV Service:** No. **Market:** North Woodstock (4 mi). **Restaurant:** No. **General Store:** Yes. **Vending:** Yes. **Swimming Pool:** No. **Playground:** Yes. **Other:** River frontage, beach area, kayak & paddleboat rentals, rec hall, TV/reading room, game room, sports court, tennis court. **Activities:** Swimming, boating, fishing, badminton, tennis, basketball, volleyball. **Nearby Attractions:** Franconia Notch State Park, The Flume, Lost River Gorge, Clark's Trading Post, hiking, biking. **Additional Information:** Lincoln-Woodstock Chamber of Commerce, P.O. Box, 358, Kancamagus Hwy., Lincoln, NH 03251, (603) 745-6621; Franconia Notch Chamber of Commerce, P.O. Box 780, Franconia, NH 03580, (800) 237-9007.

Restrictions

Pets: Must be on a leash, never left unattended. **Fires:** In grills, stoves, & fire rings only. **Alcoholic Beverages:** At site only. **Vehicle Maximum Length:** 32 ft.

To Get There

From I-93, exit 32, go 3.5 mi. west on Rte. 112; campground is on the left.

NOTTINGHAM

Pawtuckaway State Park

128 Mountain Rd., Nottingham 03290. T: (603) 895-3031; F: (603) 895-2061; www.nhparks.state.nh.us; info@nhparks.state.nh.us.

RV ★★★ Tent ★★★★★

Beauty: ★★★★	Site Privacy: ★★★★
Spaciousness: ★★★★	Quiet: ★★★
Security: ★★★	Cleanliness: ★★★★
Insect Control: ★★★	Facilities: ★★★

This state park gem in the south central region of New Hampshire is one of our favorite lakeside destinations. Woods and water dominate the scenery and outdoor activities. Forested, primitive-style campsites are clustered on islands dotting pristine Pawtuckaway Lake. Our favorites are the sites on Horse Island (check out sites 16, 41-46, and 67-69 on the island points with great water views), but you can hardly go wrong here—all are spacious and private. This is a popular spot for day visitors; we like that overnight campers have a separate area, removed from the daytime crowds and school and scout groups. There are boat rentals for exploring the lake (fishing is decent, too) and miles of hiking trails. Pack a lunch and head to the top of 908-foot South Mountain, with great views from its summit fire tower. Or walk the Fundy Trail bordering Burnhams Marsh in early morning or evening for a glimpse of beavers, deer, and great herons.

Basics

Operated By: New Hampshire Division of Parks & Recreation. **Open:** Mid-May–Columbus Day. **Site Assignment:** Reservations suggested by calling Reservation Center (603) 271-3628 from Jan. through early Oct. Reservations must be made seven days in advance of stay, paid in full. Seven day cancellation policy w/a $3 service charge. A number of sites are left open on a first-come, first-served basis. MC, V; no personal checks. **Registration:** At office. **Fee:** Waterview sites on Horse Island & Neals Cove (tents only), $22; Big Island (inland), $16; Big Island (waterview), $22; based on two adults & dependent children under 18. **Parking:** At site.

Facilities

Number of RV Sites: 192. **Number of Tent-Only Sites:** 0. **Hookups:** None. **Each Site:** Picnic table, fire ring. **Dump Station:** No. **Laundry:** No. **Pay Phone:** Yes. **Rest Rooms & Showers:** Yes. **Fuel:** No. **Propane:** No. **Internal Roads:** Dirt, gravel (good). **RV Service:** No. **Market:** Raymond (4 mi). **Restaurant:** No. **General Store:** Yes. **Vending:** No. **Swimming Pool:** No. **Playground:** No. **Other:** Lake frontage, beach, boat rentals, boat launch, hiking trails, group areas. **Activities:** Swimming, hiking, biking, boating, fishing. **Nearby Attractions:** Concord, Manchester, coastal beaches & attractions. **Additional Information:** Greater Concord Chamber of Commerce, 244 North Main St., Concord, NH 03301-5078, (603) 224-2508 or Manchester Chamber of Commerce, 889 Elm St., Manchester, NH 03101, (603) 434-7438.

Restrictions

Pets: No. **Fires:** In grills, stoves, & fire rings only. **Alcoholic Beverages:** At site only. **Vehicle Maximum Length:** None.

To Get There

From the junction of Rtes. 101 and 107 (exit 5 in Raymond), go north 3.5 mi. on Rte. 107, then 0.2 mi. west on Rte. 27, then 1 mi. north on Rte. 156; campground is on the left

OSSIPEE

Westward Shores

P.O. Box 308, 110 Nichols Rd., West Ossipee 03890. T: (603) 539-6445; www.wwscamp.com; wwscamp@landmarknet.net.

RV ★★★★ Tent ★

Beauty: ★★★	Site Privacy: ★★★
Spaciousness: ★★★	Quiet: ★★★
Security: ★★★★★	Cleanliness: ★★★
Insect Control: ★★★	Facilities: ★★★★

This destination getaway rests on shores of Ossipee Lake, with 1,800 feet of natural sandy beach and a full-service marina on site. Watery pleasures—

swimming, boating, and fishing—reign here. You'll find all the supplies you need, including a fleet of boats to rent. Fishing for bass, perch, salmon, and trout is a big draw; Lovell River, one of New England's top trout streams, flows into Ossipee Lake. Families like the gradually sloping, sandy swimming area and the planned activities throughout the summer months. There's also a large rec hall for dances, bingo, and socials, and tennis courts (free to campers). This year-round destination welcomes snowmobilers, cross country skiers, and ice fishers in the winter. You'll have to reserve early to get a site in the summer; most are taken by seasonal renters, so only about 20 are reserved for overnighters. We especially like this campground in the fall, when the surrounding mountain ranges and valleys are ablaze with color, and the lake is still warm enough to enjoy.

Basics

Operated By: Jim & Patti Gray. **Open:** Year-round. **Site Assignment:** Reservations required, one-night stay deposit, 24-hour cancellation policy. MC,V, & personal checks accepted. **Registration:** At gatehouse. **Fee:** $35 (all sites have full hookups). **Parking:** At site.

Facilities

Number of RV Sites: 260. **Number of Tent-Only Sites:** 0. **Hookups:** Water, electric, sewer (20, 30 amps), cable TV. **Each Site:** Picnic table, fire ring. **Dump Station:** Yes. **Laundry:** No. **Pay Phone:** Yes. **Rest Rooms & Showers:** Yes (coin-op). **Fuel:** No. **Propane:** No. **Internal Roads:** Dirt, gravel (good). **RV Service:** No. **Market:** Ossipee (2 mi). **Restaurant:** Yes. **General Store:** Yes. **Vending:** No. **Swimming Pool:** No. **Playground:** Yes. **Other:** Rec hall, marina, launching ramp, boat slips, lake frontage, private beach, boat rentals (including power boats, jet skis, pontoons), cabin rentals, game room, tennis courts, pavillion. **Activities:** Swimming, boating, fishing, snowmobiling, ice skating, tennis, basketball, volleyball, planned activities including arts & crafts, children's games, socials. **Nearby Attractions:** North Conway, White Mountains. **Additional Information:** Greater Conway Village Area Chamber of Commerce, P.O. Box 1019, Conway, NH 03818, (603) 447-2639; also Mount Washington Valley Chamber of Commerce, P.O. Box 2300, North Conway, NH 03860, (800) 521-2137.

Restrictions

Pets: Must be on a leash, never left unattended. **Fires:** In grills, stoves, & fire rings only. **Alcoholic Beverages:** At site only. **Vehicle Maximum Length:** 32 ft.

To Get There

From the junction of Rtes. 25 and 16, go 8 mi. north on Rte. 16; campground is on the right.

RAYMOND

Pine Acres

74 Freetown Rd., P.O. Box 364, Raymond 03077. T: (603) 895-2519; www.pineacresrecreation.com; camping@pineacresrecreation.com.

RV ★★★★★ Tent ★★★★

Beauty: ★★★★	Site Privacy: ★★★
Spaciousness: ★★★	Quiet: ★★★
Security: ★★★★	Cleanliness: ★★★
Insect Control: ★★★	Facilities: ★★★★★

This busy, action-packed campground is a mini-resort, popular with vacationing families. It's within a half-hour's drive to New Hampshire's coastal beaches to the east and the Lakes region to the north. But why leave? Most campers don't; they stay to play on the on-site waterslides, swim, fish and boat in the pond, order burgers, fries, and sundaes from Big Daddy's snack bar, and join in non-stop activities (think bingo, hayrides, karoake, crafts, races, contests). This large campground has a natural side, too, as it flanks the pretty Lamprey River. There's a good-sized sandy beach and a wide, still-water section of the river. Most sites are nicely shaded and spaced about 30 feet from one another. Tenters will like sites A1–A4 near the beach. There are cabin and RV rentals on site, too.

Basics

Operated By: John, Tracy & Stanley Shea. **Open:** May–Nov. **Site Assignment:** Reservations recommended; min. stay five nights in Jul. & Aug. (but check two weeks prior to arrival & they may fit you in for less nights) Cancellation policy: 30 days notice, full refund minus $10 service fee; 9–29 day notice, camping credit toward current year; 9 days notice, no refund or credit. MC,V, D. **Registration:** At office. **Fee:** $34, full hookup; $31, water & electric; $26, no hookup; weekends & holidays an additional $5 per night. Based on a family of 5, 2 adults, 3 children. **Parking:** At site, 2 vehicles per site.

Facilities

Number of RV Sites: 400. **Number of Tent-Only Sites:** 0. **Hookups:** Water, electric, sewer (20, 50 amps). **Each Site:** Picnic table, fire ring. **Dump Station:** Yes. **Laundry:** Yes. **Pay Phone:** Yes. **Rest Rooms & Showers:** Yes (coin-op). **Fuel:** Yes. **Propane:** Yes. **Internal Roads:** Paved, gravel (good). **RV Service:** No. **Market:** Raymond (2 mi). **Restaurant:** Yes. **General Store:** Yes. **Vending:** Yes. **Swimming Pool:** No. **Playground:** Yes. **Other:** Dual flume waterslide, 18-hole mini-golf, river frontage, beach area, boat rentals, teen rec. hall, adult rec. hall, trailor & cabin rentals, mountain bike rentals, full-time activities director. **Activities:** Swimming, boating, basketball, horseshoes, softball,volleyball, lake & river fishing, planned activities, special themed weekends. **Nearby Attractions:** New Hampshire beaches, Portsmouth, Strawbery Banke museum. **Additional Information:** Greater Portsmouth Chamber of Commerce, P.O. Box 239, Portsmoutn, NH 03801, (603) 436-3988; also visit www.SeacoastNH.com.

Restrictions

Pets: Must be on a leash, never left unattended. **Fires:** In grills, stoves, & fire rings only. **Alcoholic Beverages:** At site only. **Vehicle Maximum Length:** 40 ft. **Other:** Ask on arrival.

To Get There

From the junction of Rtes. 101 and 107/102, go south 1 mi. on Rte. 107/102; campground is on the left.

RICHMOND

Shir-Roy Camping Area

100 Athol Rd., Richmond 03470. T: (603) 239-4768.

RV ★★★ Tent ★★★★

Beauty: ★★★★	Site Privacy: ★★★
Spaciousness: ★★★	Quiet: ★★★★
Security: ★★★	Cleanliness: ★★★
Insect Control: ★★★	Facilities: ★★★

This woodsy, rustic campground on pretty, 42-acre, spring-fed Wheeler Pond has been around since 1956. The first time we visited, it was a cool summer night (not unusual for New England) and a warm, roaring log fire was burning in the massive fieldstone fireplace in the main building. This is also where the office and recreational room are housed and where the popular campground potluck dinners are held. Walk out the door, and footsteps away is a 200-foot sandy beach, a kiddie playground, and boats to rent. At night, bring a long stick and marshmallows to roast; there are campfires on the beach. Sounds like summer camp, huh? It feels like it, too. This rustic gem always takes us back to nostalgic, carefree summer days of our youth. Today, families return to share a similar experience with their children and grandchildren. Most of the sites are tucked into the woods, scattered in pods behind the recreation area. Only a handful of sites have lake views, but most are only a short walk away from the beach. The most spacious and private sites are in the "R" section, nestled in the northwest corner of the property. Of the campgrounds in the quiet Monadnock region of New Hampshire, this one is our sentimental favorite.

Basics

Operated By: Shirley Heise. **Open:** Memorial Day–Columbus Day. **Site Assignment:** Reservations suggested, 50 percent deposit or min. 3 day deposit for holiday weekends, 14 day cancellation notice for return of deposit. MC,V, & personal checks accepted. **Registration:** Office. **Fee:** Full hookup, $24; electric only, $23; no hookup, $20, based on one family (husband,wife & unmarried children) per site. **Parking:** At site, one vehicle per site.

Facilities

Number of RV Sites: 106. **Number of Tent-Only Sites:** 2. **Hookups:** Water, electric, sewer (20, 30 amps). **Each Site:** Picnic table, fire ring. **Dump Station:** Yes. **Laundry:** Yes. **Pay Phone:** Yes. **Rest Rooms & Showers:** Yes. **Fuel:** No. **Propane:** No. **Internal Roads:** Gravel, dirt (fair). **RV Service:** No. **Market:** Winchester (7 mi). **Restaurant:** No. **General Store:** Yes. **Vending:** No. **Swimming Pool:** No. **Playground:** Yes. **Other:** Rec. hall, 200 ft. of frontage on spring-fed pond, beach, dock, canoe, rowboat & paddleboat rentals, trailer rentals, group camping area, game room, athletic field. **Activities:** Swimming, fishing, boating, volleyball, horseshoes, potluck suppers. **Nearby Attractions:** Mt. Monadnock, historic towns of Keene, Jaffrey & Peterborough, covered bridges, hiking, antiquing. **Additional Information:** Greater Keene Chamber of Commerce, 48 Central Square, Keene, NH 03431, (603) 352-1303.

RESTRICTIONS

Pets: Must be on a leash, never left unattended. **Fires:** In grills, stoves, & fire rings only. **Alcoholic Beverages:** At site only. **Vehicle Maximum Length:** None.

TO GET THERE

From the junction of Rtes. 10 and 119 (in WInchester), go 6 mi. east on Rte. 119, then 0.5 mi. south on Rte. 32; the campground is on the left.

SOUTH HAMPTON

Tuxbury Pond Camping Area

88 Whitehall Rd., South Hampton 03827.
T: (603) 394-7660, (800) 585-7660; F: (603) 394-7114; www.holipub.com/tuxbury; tuxburypondcamp@aol.com.

RV ★★★★ Tent ★★★

Beauty: ★★★★ Site Privacy: ★★★
Spaciousness: ★★★ Quiet: ★★★
Security: ★★★★★ Cleanliness: ★★★★
Insect Control: ★★★ Facilities: ★★★★★

This high-energy, action-packed campground is a magnet for vacationing families and a longtime favorite among repeat summer visitors. Located in the popular Hampton Beach area, there's plenty to do on and off this property. The campground is located on a freshwater pond with swimming, boat rentals, and fishing. There's a boat ramp, too, and some campers bring their own boats in tow. (There's a 40-horsepower limit.) Sports fields, rec rooms, mini-golf, two swimming pools, and a variety of planned activities keep youngsters busy while parents relax. There's even a snack bar on the premises for quick meals and munchies. There are many seasonal sites and lots of big rigs, all for campers drawn to the campground for its many facilities and recreation.

BASICS

Operated By: Richard Smith. **Open:** Mother's Day–Columbus Day. **Site Assignment:** Reservations suggested; 50 percent deposit, seven day cancellation policy. MC,V; no personal checks. **Registration:** At office. **Fee:** Full hookups, $31; water & electric, $29, based on two adults & two children. **Parking:** At site.

FACILITIES

Number of RV Sites: 180. **Number of Tent-Only Sites:** 0. **Hookups:** Water, electric (20, 30, 50 amps), sewer, cable TV, modem in office. **Each Site:** Picnic table, fire ring. **Dump Station:** Yes. **Laundry:** Yes. **Pay Phone:** Yes. **Rest Rooms & Showers:** Yes. **Fuel:** No. **Propane:** Yes. **Internal Roads:** Gravel, dirt (good). **RV Service:** No. **Market:** South Hampton (3 mi). **Restaurant:** Yes. **General Store:** Yes. **Vending:** Yes. **Swimming Pool:** Yes. **Playground:** Yes. **Other:** Pond, beach, boat rentals, game room, rec hall, mini-golf, pavillion, group area, sports fields, snack bar. **Activities:** Swimming, boating, fishing, mini-golf, softball, basketball, volleyball, horseshoes, planned activities. **Nearby Attractions:** Hampton Beach, Massachusett's North Shore, Portsmouth, coastal beaches. **Additional Information:** Hampton Beach Area Chamber of Commerce, 490 Lafayette Rd., Hampton, NH 03843, (603) 926-8717.

RESTRICTIONS

Pets: Must be on a leash; never left unattended. **Fires:** In grills, campstoves, & fire rings only. **Alcoholic Beverages:** At site only. **Vehicle Maximum Length:** 40 ft.

TO GET THERE

From the junction of I-495 and Rte. 150 (exit 54 in Amesbury, MA), go 0.8 mi. north on Rte. 150, then 0.5 mi. northwest on Highland St. , then 1.5 mi. west on Lions Mouth Rd., then 1 mi. on Newton road; campground is on the left.

TAMWORTH

Tamworth Camping Area

P.O. Box 99, Depot Rd., Tamworth 03886.
T: (603) 323-8031, (800) 274-8031 (reservations); www.tamworthcamping.com; tamworthcampingarea.rscs.net.

RV ★★★ Tent ★★★★

Beauty: ★★★ Site Privacy: ★★★
Spaciousness: ★★★★ Quiet: ★★★
Security: ★★★★★ Cleanliness: ★★★
Insect Control: ★★★ Facilities: ★★★

This pretty riverside campground has been around since 1967 and keeps on improving. Just 30 minutes from popular North Conway and White Mountain area attractions, the campground is close enough for convenient day trips yet away from the hustle and bustle. It boasts about 1,900 feet of Swift River frontage and a pretty, sandy-bottom swimming area perfect for fishing, wading, and river tubing. The 18 river sites, with water and electric hookups, are the most spacious and scenic; reserve them early. We especially like sites 8, 10, and 12. There's also an open group-tent area, nestled in a meadow filled with blueberries and views of Mt. Whittier and the Ossipee Mountains. Families also like the weekend activities that may include arts and crafts, make-your-own-sundae parties, hayrides, and more.

BASICS

Operated By: Dana & Laurie Bonica. **Open:** May 15–Columbus Day. **Site Assignment:** Reservations suggested; two night min. stay for riverfront sites. 50 percent deposit, 100 percent deposit during holiday weekends & motorcycle rally weeks. 14 day cancellation policy w/$5 service fee. MC,V, & personal checks accepted. **Registration:** At office. **Fee:** Full hookups, $33; water & electric, $29; water & electric on river, $33; water, $24; no hookups, $22. **Parking:** At site.

FACILITIES

Number of RV Sites: 87. **Number of Tent-Only Sites:** 13. **Hookups:** Water, electric, sewer (20, 30 amps). **Each Site:** Picnic table, ring. **Dump Station:** Yes. **Laundry:** Yes. **Pay Phone:** Yes. **Rest Rooms & Showers:** Yes (coin-op). **Fuel:** No. **Propane:** Yes. **Internal Roads:** Dirt, gravel (good). **RV Service:** No. **Market:** Ossipee (6 mi). **Restaurant:** No. **General Store:** Yes. **Vending:** No. **Swimming Pool:** No. **Playground:** Yes. **Other:** Rec hall, pavillion, group area, crafts cabin, lending library, 9-hole mini golf course, sports field. **Activities:** Swimming, volleyball, basketball, horseshoes, softball, shuffleboard, badminton, fishing, planned activities, including arts & crafts, hayrides, dances, & more. **Nearby Attractions:** Attitash Bear Peak, Weirs Beach, Story Land, Conway Scenic Railroad, North Conway, quick access to White Mountains. **Additional Information:** Greater Conway Village Area Chamber of Commerce, P.O. Box 1019, Conway, NH 03818, (603) 447-2639.

RESTRICTIONS

Pets: Must be on a leash, never left unattended. **Fires:** In grills, stoves, & fire rings only. **Alcoholic Beverages:** In a responsible manner. **Vehicle Maximum Length:** None. **Other:** Ask on arrival.

TO GET THERE

From the junction of Rtes. 25 and 16, go 0.5 mi. north on Rte. 16 to Depot Rd., then 3 mi. west; campground is on the left

TAMWORTH

White Lake State Park

Rte. 16, Tamworth 03886. T: (603) 323-7350 (information) (603) 271-3628 (reservations); www.nhparks.state.nh.us.

RV ★ Tent ★★★★★

Beauty: ★★★★★ Site Privacy: ★★★★
Spaciousness: ★★★★ Quiet: ★★★
Security: ★★★★★ Cleanliness: ★★★★
Insect Control: ★★★ Facilities: ★★

This is New Hampshire's most popular state park and campground for several good reasons. First, there's the lake: gorgeous White Lake, clear, sandy-bottomed, and ringed by picturesque mountains. The state owns all the property you can see surrounding the lake, so there's no development. The shallow, gradually sloping swimming area is popular with families with young children. There's also a lifeguard on duty. The campground sites are rustic (no hookups) but spacious and private, nestled in trees; a handful are on the water. Sites are divided into two separate campground pods, one on each side of the beach and park picnic and day-use area. Both have paths to the large, natural-sand beach. There's also a two-mile walking trail around the lake through the Pitch Pine National Natural Landmark, one of the most virginal stands of northern pitch pines in North America. Recently, the state has upgraded the park, putting in new showers, rest rooms, and bathouse; these are uncommonly nice for state park campground facilities. Only downside: this gets plenty of day-use visitors, so the beach can get crowded.

BASICS

Operated By: New Hampshire Division of Parks & Recreation. **Open:** Mid-May–Columbus Day. **Site Assignment:** Reservations are suggested but 25 sites are set aside on first-come, first-served basis. Call Reservation Center (603) 271-3628 from Jan. through early Oct., Monday through Friday or via email, www.nhparks.state.nh.us. Payment is due within seven days of making reservation. Refunds requests must be received in writing by the reservation office within 14 days of scheduled arrival & are handled on a case by case basis, subject to a $10 handling fee & may be subject to a penalty of a one night cmaping fee. MC,V are accepted. **Registration:** At office. **Fee:** $16; $22, waterview, based on two adults & children under the age of 18. Each additional adult is half the site fee, max. 5 adults per site. **Parking:** At site.

FACILITIES

Number of RV Sites: 200. **Number of Tent-Only Sites:** 0. **Hookups:** None. **Each Site:** Picnic table, fire ring. **Dump Station:** Yes. **Laundry:** No. **Pay Phone:** Yes. **Rest Rooms & Showers:** Yes (coin-op). **Fuel:** No. **Propane:** No. **Internal Roads:** Gravel (good). **RV Service:** No. **Market:** Tamworth (1 mi). **Restaurant:** No. **General Store:** Yes. **Vending:** Yes. **Swimming Pool:** No. **Playground:** Yes. **Other:** Lake frontage, beach, lifeguards, kayak, canoe & paddleboat rentals, playfield, hiking trails. **Activities:** Swimming, hiking, boating. **Nearby Attractions:** North Conway, White Mountains, Craword Notch Scenic Railroad, outlet shopping. **Additional Information:** Greater Conway Village Area Chamber of Commerce, P.O. Box 1019, Conway, NH 03818, (603) 447-2639.

RESTRICTIONS

Pets: Not allowed. **Fires:** In grills, stoves, & fire rings only. **Alcoholic Beverages:** Not allowed. **Vehicle Maximum Length:** None. **Other:** No car stereos allowed.

TO GET THERE

From the junction of Rtes. 16 and 25, go north 1.25 mi; campground is on the left.

TWIN MOUNTAIN
Beech Hill Campground

P.O. Box 129, Twin Mountain 03595. T: (603) 846-5561; www.beechhill.com; bousquin@ncia.net.

RV ★★★★ Tent ★★★★★

Beauty: ★★★★ Site Privacy: ★★★★★
Spaciousness: ★★★★★ Quiet: ★★★★
Security: ★★★★ Cleanliness: ★★★
Insect Control: ★★★ Facilities: ★★★★

We love the spaciousness, privacy, and location of this campground in the White Mountains. Beech Hill caters to folks who like to explore area attractions during the day and return to a lot of elbow room, outdoor scenery, an indoor pool, and planned activities in the evening. The campground is also a favorite with hikers who have some of New Hampshire's best trails nearby (including trails to the summit of Mount Washington, New England's highest peak). Each site is surrounded by trees for privacy; the tent-only sites are especially roomy and secluded. Our favorites: sites 26A–26D. RVers looking for full hookups will like sites 50, 90, and 91. But, really, you can't go wrong here.

BASICS

Operated By: Ed & Linda Bousquin. **Open:** May 15–Oct. 15. **Site Assignment:** Reservations suggested, one night deposit, 10 day cancellation policy, no credit cards, personal checks accepted. **Registration:** At office. **Fee:** Full hookups, $28, water & electric, $26, no hookups, $22, based on two adults & three children under 14. **Parking:** At site.

FACILITIES

Number of RV Sites: 93. **Number of Tent-Only Sites:** 38. **Hookups:** Water, electric, sewer (15, 30 amps). **Each Site:** Picnic table, fire ring. **Dump Station:** Yes. **Laundry:** Yes. **Pay Phone:** Yes. **Rest Rooms & Showers:** Yes. **Fuel:** No. **Propane:** Yes. **Internal Roads:** Dirt, gravel (good). **RV Service:** No. **Market:** Littleton (12 mi). **Restaurant:** No. **General Store:** Yes. **Vending:** No. **Swimming Pool:** Yes. **Playground:** Yes. **Other:** Rec hall, game room, hiking trails, cabin rentals. **Activities:** Swimming, basketball, volleyball, planned activities on summer weekends. **Nearby Attractions:** White Mountains, Franconia Notch State Park. **Additional Information:** Franconia Notch Chamber of Commerce, P.O. Box 780, Franconia, NH 03580, (800) 237-9007; also Twin Mountain Chamber of Commerce, (800) 245-TWIN.

RESTRICTIONS

Pets: Must be on a leash, never left unattended. **Fires:** In grills, stoves, & fire rings only. **Alcoholic Beverages:** At site only. **Vehicle Maximum Length:** None.

TO GET THERE

From the junction of Rtes. 3 and 302, go west 1.8 mi. on Rte. 302; campground is on the right.

TWIN MOUNTAIN
Living Water Campground

P.O. Box 158, Rte. 302 East, Twin Mountain 03595. T: (603) 846-5513; www.livingwatercampground.com.

RV ★★★ Tent ★★★★

Beauty: ★★★★ Site Privacy: ★★★★
Spaciousness: ★★★ Quiet: ★★★★★
Security: ★★★★★ Cleanliness: ★★★★★
Insect Control: ★★★ Facilities: ★★★

This campground is clean, clean, clean, in more ways than one. "Alcohol-free camping, Experience the Difference!" is their motto, and the owners go the extra mile to ensure a "clean, quiet, family atmosphere." Rules are heavily enforced: absolutely no alcohol, no pets, no radios, no rowdy behavior, quiet time—and they mean quiet—by 10 p.m. "We're only after a niche market, and when they find us, they like it," says owner Jack Catalano. They're very upfront and forward about the rules when taking reservations and when campers check in. If you like a few wine coolers or bottle of ale around the campfire, you better look elsewhere. The campground is located in the center of popular White Mountain attractions set along the Ammonoosuc River. Most families head out during the day to explore the area and return in late afternoon to wade in the river, swim in the pool, and watch the sun set over the mountains. Both open, grassy sites and shaded, wooded sites are available; full hookups are clustered in a half-circle behind the office.

BASICS

Operated By: Jack Catalano. **Open:** Memorial Day–Columbus Day. **Site Assignment:** Reservations suggested, one inght deposit, 48-hour cancellation policy. MC,V; no personal checks. **Registration:** At office. **Fee:** Full hookups, $32; water & electric (30 amp), $30; water & electric (20 amp), $28; no hookups, $26, riverfront sites add $2, based on two persons, additional child 4-11, $1; additional child 12-17, $2; additional adult, family member, $6; additional adult, non-family member, $10. **Parking:** At site.

FACILITIES

Number of RV Sites: 45. **Number of Tent-Only Sites:** 35. **Hookups:** Water, electric, sewer (30 amps). **Each Site:** Picnic table, fire ring. **Dump Station:** Yes. **Laundry:** Yes. **Pay Phone:** Yes. **Rest Rooms & Showers:** Yes (coin-op). **Fuel:** Yes. **Propane:** No. **Internal Roads:** Dirt, gravel (good). **RV Service:** No. **Market:** Littleton (9 mi). **Restaurant:** No. **General Store:** Yes. **Vending:** No. **Swimming Pool:** Yes. **Playground:** Yes. **Other:** Rec hall, river frontage, on-site motel. **Activities:** Swimming, fishing, tetherball, basketball, badminton, volleyball, horseshoes. **Nearby Attractions:** White Mountains, Franconia Notch State Park. **Additional Information:** Franconia Notch Chamber of Commerce, P.O. Box 780, Franconia, NH 03580, (800) 237-9007; Twin Mountain Chamber of Commerce, (800) 245-TWIN.

RESTRICTIONS

Pets: Not allowed. **Fires:** In grills, stoves, & fire rings only. **Alcoholic Beverages:** Not allowed. **Vehicle Maximum Length:** None. **Other:** Lots of restrictions that are strongly enforced: musical instruments & singing must be kept at at low volumes & not permitted after 10 pm or before 7 am; radios, TVs, CD players, etc. permitted only w/earphones; minibikes, scooters, ATVs not permitted.

TO GET THERE

From the junction of Rtes. 3 and 302, go east 1000 feet on Rte. 302; campground is on the right.

TWIN MOUNTAIN
Tarry Ho Campground & Cottages

P.O. Box 369, Rte. 302, Twin Mountain 03595. T: (603) 846-5577; www.tarryho.com; tarryho@loa.com.

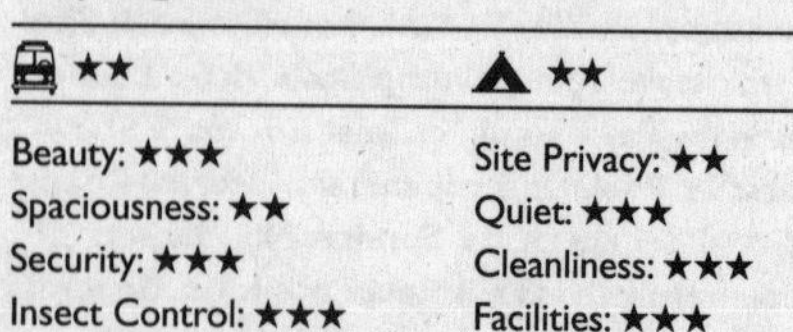

RV ★★ Tent ★★

Beauty: ★★★ Site Privacy: ★★
Spaciousness: ★★ Quiet: ★★★
Security: ★★★ Cleanliness: ★★★
Insect Control: ★★★ Facilities: ★★★

We include this campground mainly for its location in the heart of the White Mountains and New Hampshire's popular attractions. It's an excellent base, and the mountain views from the sites are lovely. The campground is relatively small compared to others in the area, sites are a bit cramped, and rest room and showers dated. Still, you have all you need to call home: a small general store for essentials, sports courts, playground, and a swimming pool and river to cool off in at the end of the day. Tenters have better choices in the area (see Beech Hill Campground); tent sites are tiny and clustered near the road, but RVers will find 35 full hookups. Friendly staff, free showers, and free coffee on Saturday mornings are nice touches.

BASICS

Operated By: Bob & Jo Dean. **Open:** Year-round, closed Apr. & Oct. 15-Nov. 15. **Site Assignment:** Reservations suggested, two nights deposit, 14 day cancellation policy, no refunds on weekend & holiday reservations. MC, V, D & personal checks accepted. **Registration:** At office. **Fee:** Full hookups, $27; river sites, $27; water & electric, $24; no hookups, $20, based on two adults & two children to 15 years or three adults. **Parking:** At site, one vehicle per site.

FACILITIES

Number of RV Sites: 47. **Number of Tent-Only Sites:** 8. **Hookups:** Water, electric, sewer (30 amps). **Each Site:** Picnic table, fire ring. **Dump Station:** Yes. **Laundry:** No. **Pay Phone:** Yes. **Rest Rooms & Showers:** Yes. **Fuel:** No. **Propane:** No. **Internal Roads:** Dirt (fair). **RV Service:** No. **Market:** Twin Mountain (0.5 mi). **Restaurant:** No. **General Store:** Yes. **Vending:** No. **Swimming Pool:** Yes. **Playground:** Yes. **Other:** River access, rec hall. **Activities:** Swimming, fishing, tubing, volleyball, basketball, horseshoes. **Nearby Attractions:** White Mountains, Franconia Notch State Park. **Additional Information:** Franconia Notch Chamber of Commerce, P.O. Box 780, Franconia, NH 03580, (800) 237-9007; Twin Mountain Chamber of Commerce, (800) 245-TWIN.

RESTRICTIONS

Pets: Must be on a leash, never left unattended. **Fires:** In grills, stoves, & fire rings only. **Alcoholic Beverages:** At site only. **Vehicle Maximum Length:** None. **Other:** Ask on arrival.

TO GET THERE

From the junction of Rtes. 3 and 302, go 7 mi. west on Rte. 302; campground is on the left.

TWIN MOUNTAIN

Twin Mountain KOA

P.O. Box 148, Twin Mountain 03595. T: (603) 846-5559; F: (603) 846-7762; ucampnh.com/twinmountain; campkoa@ncia.net.

RV ★★★★ Tent ★★★

Beauty: ★★★★ Site Privacy: ★★★
Spaciousness: ★★★ Quiet: ★★★★
Security: ★★★ Cleanliness: ★★★★★
Insect Control: ★★★ Facilities: ★★★★

The last time we visited this White Mountain area campground was in the fall, and the surrounding forest of towering pine, poplar, maple, and birch was ablaze with fiery autumn hues. The summit of Mount Washington, visible from our site, had a fresh dusting of powdery white snow. You'll have wonderful mountain views, quick access to outdoor activities (biking, hiking, rock climbing, fishing, boating), and plenty of on-site amenities (swimming pool, planned activities, free movies) at this franchise campground. Most campers explore the surrounding area attractions (check out the popular moose-watching tours in nearby Gorham) before returning to the campground in late afternoon. The facilities and sites are ultra-clean, and the atmosphere friendly and relaxed. For something different, reserve the "kamping kaboose." Where else can you camp in an authentic 19th-century train caboose?

BASICS

Operated By: Barbara & Steve Rabesa. **Open:** May 15–Oct. 15. **Site Assignment:** Reservations suggested; one night deposit, holiday weekends paid in full; seven day cancellation policy w/$10 service fee. MC, V, no personal checks. **Registration:** At office. **Fee:** Full hookups, $32; water & electric, $27.50; no hookups, $25, based on two people; additionl adults, $6; additional children, ages 3-17, $2. **Parking:** At site.

FACILITIES

Number of RV Sites: 30. **Number of Tent-Only Sites:** 30. **Hookups:** Water, electric, sewer (30, 50 amps), cable TV, modem. **Each Site:** Picnic table, fire ring. **Dump Station:** Yes. **Laundry:** Yes. **Pay Phone:** Yes. **Rest Rooms & Showers:** Yes. **Fuel:** No. **Propane:** Yes. **Internal Roads:** Gravel, dirt (good). **RV Service:** No. **Market:** Twin Mountain (2 mi). **Restaurant:** No. **General Store:** Yes. **Vending:** Yes. **Swimming Pool:** Yes. **Playground:** Yes. **Other:** Rec hall, amphitheater, nature trails, cabin & caboose rentals, group area. **Activities:** Swimming, hiking, biking, volleyball, badminton, horseshoes. **Nearby Attractions:** Moose tours, fishing, boating, Storyland, Conway Scenic Railroad, Mount Washington Auto Rd. **Additional Information:** Twin Mountain Chamber of Commerce, Twin Mountain, NH 03595, (800) 245-TWIN.

RESTRICTIONS

Pets: Must be on a leash, never left unattended. Pets not allowed in rental units. **Fires:** In grills, stoves, & fire rings only. **Alcoholic Beverages:** At site. **Vehicle Maximum Length:** None.

TO GET THERE

From the junction of Rtes. 3 and 302, go north 2 mi. on Rte. 3, then north 1 mi. on Rte. 115; campground is on the right.

TWIN MOUNTAIN

Twin Mountain Motor Court & RV Park

P.O. Box 104B, Rte. 3, Twin Mountain 03595. T: (603) 846-5574, (800) 332-8946; www.ucampnh.com/twinmountain.rvpark.

RV ★★★ Tent n/a

Beauty: ★★★ Site Privacy: ★★★
Spaciousness: ★★★ Quiet: ★★★★
Security: ★★★ Cleanliness: ★★★★
Insect Control: ★★★ Facilities: ★★★

If you're a self-contained big-rig driver looking for ease and convenience, this campground is a great base when traveling in the White Mountains area. Large 25 × 85–foot sites, all pull-throughs, cater to large RVs; sites are easy to pull in and out of, and all have four-way hookups. Outside, you'll find panoramic views of the mountains, including Mount Washington, Twin Mountains, and Mt. Haystack. There's an outdoor swimming pool for a refreshing dip at the end of the day, or head to the Ammonoosuc River, which flanks the rear of the campground. Bring your fishing rod; the Ammonoosuc is famous for its elusive trout.

BASICS

Operated By: John & Dotty Barber. **Open:** May 15–Oct. 15. **Site Assignment:** Reservations suggested, one night deposit, seven day cancellation policy, MC, V, D & personal checks accepted. **Registration:** At office. **Fee:** $28. **Parking:** At site.

FACILITIES

Number of RV Sites: 18. **Number of Tent-Only Sites:** 0. **Hookups:** Water, electric, sewer (30 amps), cable TV, modem. **Each Site:** Picnic table. **Dump Station:** No. **Laundry:** Yes. **Pay Phone:** Yes. **Rest Rooms & Showers:** No. **Fuel:** No. **Propane:** No. **Internal Roads:** Gravel (good). **RV Service:** No. **Market:** Littleton (8 mi). **Restaurant:** No. **General Store:** Yes. **Vending:** No. **Swimming Pool:** Yes. **Playground:** Yes. **Other:** River frontage, hiking trails, rec hall, cottage rentals. **Activities:** Swimming, hiking, badminton, horseshoes, basketball, volleyball. **Nearby Attractions:** White Mountains, Franconia Notch State Park. **Additional Information:** Franconia Notch Chamber of Commerce, P.O. Box 780, Franconia, NH 03580, (800) 237-9007; Twin Mountain Chamber of Commerce, (800) 245-TWIN.

RESTRICTIONS

Pets: Must be on a leash, never left unattended. Pets not allowed in cottages. **Fires:** In campground communal bonfire site only. **Alcoholic Beverages:** At site only. **Vehicle Maximum Length:** None.

TO GET THERE

From the junction of Rtes. 302 and 3, go 1 mi. south on Rte. 3; campground is on the right.

WARREN

Moose Hillock Campground

RFD 1, Box 96, Rte. 118 North, Warren 03279. T: (603) 764-5294; www.moosehillock.com.

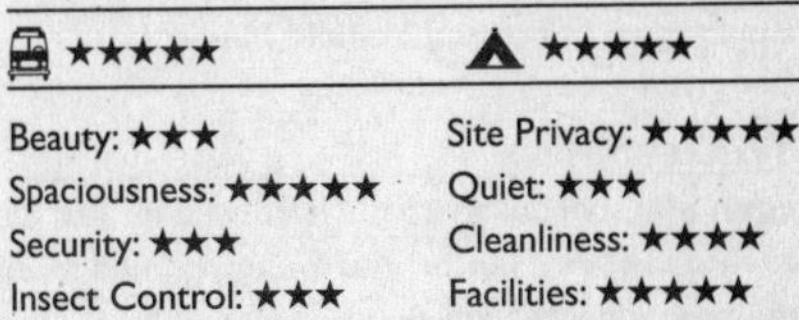

RV ★★★★★ Tent ★★★★★

Beauty: ★★★ Site Privacy: ★★★★★
Spaciousness: ★★★★★ Quiet: ★★★
Security: ★★★ Cleanliness: ★★★★
Insect Control: ★★★ Facilities: ★★★★★

Campers with kids in tow will find everything they need—and more!—at this action-packed, family-friendly campground. This place is always squirming with smiling kids—zipping down the waterslide at the themed "Blue Lagoon" swimming pool, fishing the stocked pond, shooting pool, playing games in the large post-and-beam barn turned rec hall, or joining in the organized games, treasure hunts, and arts-and-crafts activities. Nearby are miles of mountain biking and hiking trails. (Two trails leave right from the campground.) Most families come to stay and play and (for the adventurous) to climb nearby Mt. Moosilauke, one of New Hampshire's 4,000-footers. Facilities are top-notch, and most sites are adequately spaced for elbow room and privacy. Families with young children tend to cluster around the lower loop, close to the pool and playground. RVers wanting more privacy and peace and quiet should select one of the very large full hookup sites that back up to the national forest. Tenters have their own woodsy, private area.

BASICS

Operated By: Ed & Robin Paradis. **Open:** Mid-May –mid-Sept. **Site Assignment:** Reservations suggested. Deposit of full amount for stays of three days or less, 50 percent for stays of one week or longer. 14 day cancellation policy w/$5 service fee. Reservations cancelled 7-14 days prior to scheduled arrival receive 50 percent of deposit; no refunds of deposit for cancellations less than 7 days notice. MC,V, & personal checks accepted. **Registration:** At office. **Fee:** Full hookups, $31 (midweek) $34 (Friday, Saturday & holidays); water & electric, 28–$31; no hookups, $25–$28. **Parking:** At site.

FACILITIES

Number of RV Sites: 195. **Number of Tent-Only Sites:** 25. **Hookups:** Water, electric, sewer. **Each Site:** Picnic table, fire ring. **Dump Station:** Yes. **Laundry:** Yes. **Pay Phone:** Yes. **Rest Rooms & Showers:** Yes (coin-op). **Fuel:** No. **Propane:** Yes. **Internal Roads:** Dirt, gravel (fair). **RV Service:** No. **Market:** Warren (5 mi). **Restaurant:** Yes. **General Store:** Yes. **Vending:** Yes. **Swimming Pool:** Yes. **Playground:** Yes. **Other:** Rec hall, game room, cabin rentals, pavillion, Chapel service, river access, stocked fishing pond, nature trails. **Activities:** Swimming, volleyball, horseshoes, tetherball, basketball, fishing, hiking planned activities including live entertainment, arts & crafts, contests, socials, & more. **Nearby Attractions:** White Mountains, Franconia Notch State Park, Mt. Moosilauke. **Additional Information:** Lincoln-Woodstock Chamber of Commerce, P.O. Box 358, Kancamagus Hwy., Lincoln, NH 03251, (603) 745-6621; also Franconia Notch Chamber of Commerce, P.O. Box 780, Franconia, NH 03580, (800) 237-9007.

RESTRICTIONS

Pets: Must be on a leash, never left unattended. **Fires:** In grills, stoves, & fire rings only. **Alcoholic Beverages:** At site only. **Vehicle Maximum Length:** None.

TO GET THERE

From I-93, exit 26, go 25 mi. northwest on Rte. 25 to Rte. 118, then north 1 mi. to campground road; campground is 0.5 mi. ahead.

WEARE

Cold Springs Camp Resort

22 Wildlife Dr., Weare 03281. T: (603) 529-2528; F: (603) 529-1155; www.coldspringscamp resort.com; coldspr@gsinet.net.

 ★★★★★ ▲ ★★★★

Beauty: ★★★ Site Privacy: ★★★
Spaciousness: ★★★ Quiet: ★★★
Security: ★★★★★ Cleanliness: ★★★★★
Insect Control: ★★★ Facilities: ★★★★★

This high-energy, activity-based campground is one of the top choices for families in the southern New Hampshire region. This is primarily a destination campground. Though the mountains to the north and ocean to the east are just an hour-and-a-half drive away, most folks are content to stay put once they've set up camp. They come to Cold Springs for a quick getaway, to relax at their sites, take part in weekend activities, and use the facilities. There really is no need to leave: everything we wanted was right here. The three-pool complex, complete with hot tubs and waterfall, is the action spot at this property. There's an adult-only pool, a family fun pool for all ages, and another for folks six years and older. There's also a beach area along a slow-moving river if you prefer a more natural and tranquil setting. About half the sites located in the back of the campground are taken by seasonal renters. But there are plenty more to choose from if you wish to come for the weekend or week. Sites are fairly uniform in size and appearance. All are set in level, gravel clearings flanked by trees with an average width of about 25 feet. Tenters have few choices, but we liked sites 147 and 148, set in the woods and backing up to a small (often dry in the summer) creek.

BASICS

Operated By: Bob Silva. **Open:** May–early Oct. **Site Assignment:** Reservations suggested, one night deposit, holiday stays paid in full, 7 day cancellation policy w/$20 service charge. MC,V, D accepted, no personal checks. **Registration:** At office. **Fee:** Full hookups (w/cable), $36; full hookups, $34; water & electric, $32, based on two people; additional adult, $6; additional children under 16, $2. **Parking:** At site.

FACILITIES

Number of RV Sites: 400. **Number of Tent-Only Sites:** 10. **Hookups:** Water, electric, sewer (30, 50 amps), cable TV, modem. **Each Site:** Picnic table, fire ring. **Dump Station:** Yes. **Laundry:** Yes. **Pay Phone:** Yes. **Rest Rooms & Showers:** Yes (coin-op). **Fuel:** No. **Propane:** Yes. **Internal Roads:** Paved (good). **RV Service:** Yes. **Market:** Weare (1 mi). **Restaurant:** Yes. **General Store:** Yes. **Vending:** Yes. **Swimming Pool:** Yes. **Playground:** Yes. **Other:** Hot tubs, river frontage, beach, pavillions, adult, teen & children's rec halls, trailer rentals. **Activities:** Swimming, shuffleboard, basketball, volleyball, horseshoes, planned activities, including children's & adult programs, contests, socials, dances, live entertainment, & more. **Nearby Attractions:** Manchester, Concord. **Additional Information:** Manchester Chamber of Commerce, 889 Elm St., Manchester, NH 03101, (603) 434-7438.

RESTRICTIONS

Pets: Must be on a leash, never left unattended. Pets are not allowed in beach area. **Fires:** In grills, stoves, & fire rings only. **Alcoholic Beverages:** At site only. **Vehicle Maximum Length:** None.

TO GET THERE

From the junction of Rte. 149 and 114, go southeast 1 mi. on Rte. 114, then east 0.25 mi. on Barnard Hill Rd.; campground is on the right.

WENTWORTH

Pine Haven Campground

P.O. Box 43, Wentworth 03282. T: (603) 786-2900 (information) (800) 370-PINE (reservations); www.pinehavencampground.com; rebele@cyberportal.net.

★★★★ ▲ ★★★★

Beauty: ★★★★ Site Privacy: ★★★★
Spaciousness: ★★★★ Quiet: ★★★
Security: ★★★★ Cleanliness: ★★★★
Insect Control: ★★★ Facilities: ★★★★

If you like the sound of rustling woods and moving waters, you're going to love this pristine campground at the base of the White Mountains. It sits in the quiet and quaint Wentworth area, halfway between popular Lincoln and North Woodstock, with 3,000 feet of frontage on the South Branch of the Baker River. There's a classic river swimming hole for dunks in the clear, cold mountain waters; there's also a heated pool. Families not only flock here for the scenery and clean outdoor living, but also for the daily activities offered throughout July and Aug. These are moonlight swims, horseshoe tournaments, archery, hayrides, crafts, and more. Sites are spacious and nicely tucked in the woods for privacy. Tenters have choice spots along the river; M5 and M6 are our favorites, as is R1. The campground is also popular with rock climbers who come to scale the giant boulders and rock walls in nearby Rumney.

BASICS

Operated By: Rebele family. **Open:** May 15–Oct. 15. **Site Assignment:** Reservations highly suggested. Payment in full for stays of three days or less; or three day deposit for stays longer than three days. Must cancel within 14 days of arrival for deposit refund minus $10 charge. **Registration:** At office. **Fee:** Full hookups, $29; water & electric, $27; no hookups, $25, basedon two adults & their children under the age of 18. **Parking:** At site.

FACILITIES

Number of RV Sites: 67. **Number of Tent-Only Sites:** 35. **Hookups:** Water, electric, sewer (20, 50 amps). **Each Site:** Picnic table, fire ring. **Dump Station:** Yes. **Laundry:** Yes. **Pay Phone:** Yes. **Rest Rooms & Showers:** Yes. **Fuel:** No. **Propane:** Yes. **Internal Roads:** Dirt, gravel (good). **RV Service:** No. **Market:** Wentworth (0.5 mi). **Restaurant:** No. **General Store:** Yes. **Vending:** No. **Swimming Pool:** Yes. **Playground:** Yes. **Other:** Rec hall, kayak & canoe rentals, river frontage, river swimming, game room, cabin rentals. **Activities:** Swimming, boating, basketball, horseshoes, archery, planned activities throughout the summer including arts & crafts, hayrides, moonlight swims, game nights. **Nearby Attractions:** quick access to White Mountains & Lakes region, hiking, rock climbing, antiquing. **Additional Information:** Lincoln-Woodstock Chamber of Commerce, P.O. Box 358, Kancamagus Hwy., Lincoln, NH 03251, (603) 745-6621.

RESTRICTIONS

Pets: Must be on a leash, never left unattended.

Fires: In grills, stoves, & fire rings only. **Alcoholic Beverages:** At site only. **Vehicle Maximum Length:** 40 ft. **Other:** Four night min. reservation Jul. & Aug.

To Get There

On I-93, take exit 26, go 12 mi. west on Rte. 25; campground is on the left.

WENTWORTH

Swain Brook Campground

P.O. Box 157, Beech Hill Rd., Wentworth 03282. T: (603) 764-5537; www.swainbrook.com; swainbrook1@aol.com.

RV ★★★★ Tent ★★★★★

Beauty: ★★★★★ Site Privacy: ★★★★
Spaciousness: ★★★★ Quiet: ★★★★
Security: ★★★★ Cleanliness: ★★★★
Insect Control: ★★★ Facilities: ★★★★

Nature lovers and outdoor enthusiasts will think they've died and gone to heaven when they check into this modest campground in New Hampshire's quiet countryside. You'll be about 12 miles from a major city (Plymouth to the southeast and Lincoln to the northeast) but at the doorstep of your own private nature preserve. The campground encompasses 417 acres—65 acres of campground and 352 acres of forest, waterfalls, cascades, and swimming holes. There are four miles of hiking trails on the property, with mountain vistas, rest areas, and fishing and swimming spots along the way. Swain Brook is the largest of five mountain brooks in the campground, dropping 520 feet in elevation over a 116-mile stretch. Elevation on the property ranges from 650 feet to 1,290 feet, so bring your hiking boots—and your fishing pole, as the deep hole at the bottom of Freedom Falls is a favorite with campground anglers. The rustic, wilderness sites are our favorites, though RV campers will find a cluster of nicely-spaced, shaded back-in sites near the front of the campground.

Basics

Operated By: Swain Brook Campground, Inc. **Open:** May–Oct. **Site Assignment:** Reservations suggested; 14-day cancellation policy w/a $10 service fee. MC,V; no personal checks. **Registration:** At office. **Fee:** Full hookup, $25; water & electric (on brook), $27; water & electric, $23; no hookups, $19 (on pond or brook), $22, based on two adults & two children. **Parking:** At site.

Facilities

Number of RV Sites: 18. **Number of Tent-Only Sites:** 30. **Hookups:** Water, electric, sewer (30 amps). **Each Site:** Picnic table, fire ring. **Dump Station:** Yes. **Laundry:** No. **Pay Phone:** Yes. **Rest Rooms & Showers:** Yes (coin-op). **Fuel:** No. **Propane:** No. **Internal Roads:** Gravel, dirt (fair). **RV Service:** No. **Market:** Lincoln (12 mi). **Restaurant:** No. **General Store:** Yes. **Vending:** No. **Swimming Pool:** No. **Playground:** Yes. **Other:** nature park, trails, river & pond frontage, swimming holes, mini-golf, trailer, tent & teepee rentals, library, rec hall. **Activities:** Swimming, hiking, biking, mini-golf, horseshoes, tetherball. **Nearby Attractions:** Lincoln, Plymouth, North Woodstock, Mt. Moosilauke, Franconia State Park. **Additional Information:** Lincoln-Woodstock Chamber of Commerce, P.O. Box 358, Kancamagus Hwy., Lincoln, NH 03251, (603) 745-6621 or Greater Plymouth Chamber of Commerce, P.O. Box 65, Plymouth, NH 03264, (800) 386-3678.

Restrictions

Pets: Must be on a leash; never left unattended. **Fires:** In grills, stoves, & fire rings only. **Alcoholic Beverages:** At site only. **Vehicle Maximum Length:** None. **Other:** No motorcycles allowed.

To Get There

From the junction of I-93 and Rte. 25 (exit 26), go west 16.5 mi. on Rte. 25, then west 1 mi. on Beech Hill Rd.; campground is on the left.

WEST OSSIPEE

Chocorua Camping Village

P.O. Box 118C, West Ossipee 03890. T: (603) 323-8536, (800)237-8642 (reservations); www.chocoruacamping.com; info@chocoruacamping.com.

RV ★★★★ Tent ★★★★

Beauty: ★★★★ Site Privacy: ★★★★
Spaciousness: ★★★★ Quiet: ★★★
Security: ★★★★★ Cleanliness: ★★★★
Insect Control: ★★★ Facilities: ★★★★★

A pretty setting on the shores of Moore's Pond and the Chocorua River, a central locale, 30 minutes to North Conway and the White Mountains, and an award-winning activities program have made this campground a top choice for families vacationing in the area. There's plenty to do at the campground: swimming and boating on the pond, hiking the four miles of nature paths, and biking the trails throughout the property. There are also lots of sports, free movies in the small theater, and planned activities three times a day. Kids have a wide choice of entertainment, from flower planting, mushroom hunts, and arts and crafts to bonfires, sing-alongs, and parades. For more sedate pleasures, there's a piano in the rec hall, lending library, and a deck and picnic area overlooking the pond. All of the terraced campground sites are generously spaced; as expected, waterfront sites are the most popular.

Basics

Operated By: Shirley & Lee Spencer. **Open:** May–Columbus Day. **Site Assignment:** Reservations suggested. Deposit of one-half fee required, 14 day cancellation policy w/10 percent service charge. MC,V, & personal checks accepted. **Registration:** At office. **Fee:** Full hookups & waterfront, $34 (3 nights or less) $32 (4 nights or more); water & electric, $28–$26; no hookups, $24–$22. **Parking:** At site.

Facilities

Number of RV Sites: 126. **Number of Tent-Only Sites:** 4. **Hookups:** Water, electric, sewer (20, 30 amps). **Each Site:** Picnic table, fire ring. **Dump Station:** Yes. **Laundry:** Yes. **Pay Phone:** Yes. **Rest Rooms & Showers:** Yes (coin-op). **Fuel:** No. **Propane:** Yes. **Internal Roads:** Gravel, dirt (good). **RV Service:** No. **Market:** Ossipee (2 mi). **Restaurant:** No. **General Store:** Yes. **Vending:** Yes. **Swimming Pool:** No. **Playground:** Yes. **Other:** Lake & river frontage,group safari area, rec hall, movie theater, craft shop, nature trails, cabin rentals, game room, rowboat & canoe rentals. **Activities:** Swimming, fishing, boating, basketball, volleyball, horseshoes, hiking, planned activities including arts & crafts, nature walks, day hikes, sing-alongs, movies, & more. **Nearby Attractions:** Attitash Bear Peak, Story Land, Conway Scenic Railroad, North Conway, quick access to White Mountains. **Additional Information:** Greater Conway Village Area Chamber of Commerce, P.O. Box 1019, Conway, NH 03818, (603) 447-2639; also Mount Washington Valley Chamber of Commerce, P.O. Box 2300, North Conway, NH 03860, (800) 521-2137.

Restrictions

Pets: Must be on a leash, never left unattended. No rotweillers, pit bulls, dobermans, german shepards; one dog per site. **Fires:** In grills, stoves, & fire rings only. **Alcoholic Beverages:** At site only. **Vehicle Maximum Length:** 35 ft. **Other:** Ask on arrival.

To Get There

From the junction of Rtes. 25 and 16, go 3 mi. north on Rte. 16; campground is on the right.

WEST SWANZEY

Swanzey Lake Camping Area

P.O. Box 115, 88 East Shore Rd., West Swanzey 03469. T: (603) 352-9880; www.swanzeylake.com; lobo@top.monad.net.

RV ★★★ Tent ★★★

Beauty: ★★★ Site Privacy: ★★★
Spaciousness: ★★★ Quiet: ★★★
Security: ★★★★ Cleanliness: ★★
Insect Control: ★★ Facilities: ★★

This campground in the quiet Monadnock region offers a rustic, woodsy getaway. The office is in an old summer camp house overlooking pretty, spring-fed Swanzey Lake. Out front, there's a beach and swimming area ("Race you to the raft!") and boat dock. The campsites are across the streeet, nestled in a dense pine forest. Bring your bug repellent. Most vacationers come to get away from it all, to swim and fish in the lake, and to hike; there are plenty of trails nearby, including New Hampshire's popular Mt.Monadnock. Some of the campground facilities are a bit worn, but new owners have been gradually fixing things up since they bought the place a few years ago.

Basics

Operated By: Bill Whitcomb & Jill Amadon. **Open:** May–Oct. **Site Assignment:** Reservations suggested. One-night deposit, seven day cancellation notice required. MC,V, personal checks accepted. **Registration:** At office. **Fee:** Full hookups, $24; electric & water, $22; no hookups, $18. **Parking:** At site, one car per site.

Facilities

Number of RV Sites: 60. **Number of Tent-Only

Sites: 48. **Hookups:** Water, electric, sewer (20, 30 amps). **Each Site:** Picnic table, fire ring. **Dump Station:** Yes. **Laundry:** Yes. **Pay Phone:** Yes. **Rest Rooms & Showers:** Yes (coin-op). **Fuel:** No. **Propane:** Yes. **Internal Roads:** Dirt (fair). **RV Service:** No. **Market:** Keene (7 mi). **Restaurant:** No. **General Store:** Yes. **Vending:** No. **Swimming Pool:** No. **Playground:** Yes. **Other:** Boat rentals, function field, rec hall, dock, boat moorings & storage. **Activities:** lake swimming, fishing, boating, horseshoes, volleyball. **Nearby Attractions:** Mt. Monadnock, historic towns of Keene, Jaffrey & Peterborough, covered bridges, hiking, antiquing. **Additional Information:** Greater Keene Chamber of Commerce, 48 Central Square, Keene, NH 03431, (603) 352-1303.

Restrictions

Pets: Must be on a leash, must remain at site, never left unattended. **Fires:** In grills, stoves, & fire rings only. **Alcoholic Beverages:** At site only. **Vehicle Maximum Length:** 35 ft. **Other:** No mini bikes or all terrain vehicles.

To Get There

From the junction of Rtes. 12 and 32, go 5 mi. south on Rte. 32, then 2 mi. south on Swanzey Lake Rd., then 0.5 mi. north on East Shore Rd.; campground is on left.

WOLFEBORO

Wolfeboro Campground

61 Haines Hill Rd., Wolfeboro 03894. T: (603) 569-9881.

RV ★★ Tent ★★★

Beauty: ★★★	Site Privacy: ★★★
Spaciousness: ★★★	Quiet: ★★★★
Security: ★★★	Cleanliness: ★★★
Insect Control: ★★★	Facilities: ★★

The charm of this rustic, old-fashioned campground is in what it doesn't have: no arcade games, no swimming pools, no planned evening activities and get-togethers. Instead, you'll camp in the woods with a little elbow room and go to sleep to the sounds of crickets in the fields and wind in the trees. Tenters have their own area for extra privacy. The facilities are unsurprisingly a bit dated, but they are clean and well kept. The campground's been around for more than 30 years, and most visitors are repeat guests who eschew the busy and developed atmosphere of some of today's more modern campgrounds. "When I go camping, I want to hear the sounds of the woods, to relax outside," one long-time camper told us. "I don't need all that fancy stuff. Might as well stay in the city if I want arcade games and parties." Still, those who want a little action need only travel a couple of miles; the campground is only a few minutes from historic Wolfeboro on the shores of Lake Winnipesaukee, and it's a great base, albeit rustic, for exploring the area.

Basics

Operated By: Warren Hamilton. **Open:** May 15–Oct. 15. **Site Assignment:** Reservations suggested. Deposit not necessary. No credit cards, personal checks accepted. **Registration:** At office. **Fee:** Water & electric, $19; no hookups, $18, based on family of two adults & two children. **Parking:** At site.

Facilities

Number of RV Sites: 50. **Number of Tent-Only Sites:** 10. **Hookups:** Water, electric, sewer (20, 30 amps). **Each Site:** Picnic table, fire ring. **Dump Station:** Yes. **Laundry:** No. **Pay Phone:** Yes. **Rest Rooms & Showers:** Yes (coin-op). **Fuel:** No. **Propane:** Yes. **Internal Roads:** Dirt (fair). **RV Service:** No. **Market:** Wolfeboro (5 mi). **Restaurant:** No. **General Store:** Yes. **Vending:** No. **Swimming Pool:** No. **Playground:** No. **Other:** Rec hall, open sports field. **Activities:** Croquet, horseshoes, ping pong, badminton, volleyball. **Nearby Attractions:** Lake Winnipesaukee, Squam Lake, Weirs Beach, outlet shopping, antiquing. **Additional Information:** Wolfeboro Chamber of Commerce, P.O. Box 547, 32 Central Ave., Wolfeboro, NH 03894, (603) 569-2200.

Restrictions

Pets: Must be on a leash, never left unattended. **Fires:** In grills, stoves, & fire rings. **Alcoholic Beverages:** At site only. **Vehicle Maximum Length:** 32 ft.

To Get There

From the junction of Rte. 109 and Rte. 28, go north 4.5 mi. on Rte. 28, then 0.25 mi. east on Haines Rd.; campground is on the right.

New Jersey

Though New Jersey is the most densely populated state in the nation—with more than 1,000 people per square mile—that figure is misleading. About two-thirds of the population lives in the northern section of the state, within 30 miles of New York City. You may be surprised to learn that much of New Jersey is composed of tree-lined 18th-century towns; more than 800 lakes and ponds; and 100-plus rivers and streams, many of which are teeming with trout. The Jersey Shore includes beautifully preserved Cape May and longtime resort areas Atlantic City and Ocean City.

The coast of New Jersey stretches about 130 miles from Cape May in the south to Sandy Hook in the north. **Avon, Spring Lake, Bay Head,** and **Point Pleasant Beach** are among the resort towns found along the coast. The nation's oldest seashore resort, **Cape May** is surrounded by the Atlantic Ocean and Delaware Bay. The entire town is a National Historic Landmark, with more than 600 Victorian homes and buildings lining the streets. Cape May has four miles of beaches, a 1.5-mile promenade, and a three-block area of shops and restaurants. There are several guided tours in Cape May that take visitors along the beaches and through historic homes. If you find a shiny rock on the shores of Delaware Bay, you've most likely got a "Cape May diamond"—unfortunately not a real diamond, but actually pure quartz rounded by the waves. Each year, millions of migratory birds flock to **Cape May Point State Park,** where the 157-foot Cape May Lighthouse, circa 1859, is open for tours.

Even before the casinos arrived in 1977, **Atlantic City** was a popular resort. Now it's one of the country's most visited destinations, with more than 37 million visitors annually. The boardwalk at Atlantic City was the first of its kind; Alexander Boardman created the walkway of wooden planks, originally called "Boardman's Walk" and later shortened to "Boardwalk." From the **Trump Taj Mahal** and **Trump Plaza** to the **Sands** and **Bally's Park Place,** Atlantic City has a wide selection of casinos and hotels, most of which are located on the boardwalk along with a multitude of restaurants, shops, and attractions. Highlights include the **Atlantic City Historical Museum** and the amusements on **Steel Pier.** The sparkling $300-million **Atlantic City Convention Center** has a 12,000-room hotel, shops, theaters, and eateries, and it hosts the Miss America Pageant every September. Other Atlantic City attractions include **Storybook Land,** an amusement park with more than 50 children's storybook-n-themed buildings; and **Lucy the Elephant,** a six-story elephant-shaped building in **Margate** built in 1881.

Other Jersey Shore areas include **Sandy Hook,** home to the **Lifesaving Museum** and **Fort Hancock and Sandy Hook Museum;** the **Highlands,** where the twin towers of **Twin Lights Historic Site** were built in 1862; **Monmouth Park,** the famous thoroughbred race track; and **Ocean Grove,** a town with well-preserved Victorian homes and buildings.

Northern New Jersey encompasses the old industrial towns of Hoboken and Jersey City, but a surprising amount of the region is rural. Much of it is in the **Skylands,** which includes the **Delaware Water Gap National Recreation Area** and the 7,200-acre **Great Swamp National Wildlife Refuge.** The **Appalachian Trail** passes through the Delaware Water Gap, which stretches for 37 miles on both sides of the Delaware River, forming the border of New Jersey and Pennsylvania. Though **Hoboken** and **Jersey City** are not exactly meccas of tourism, the latter has 1,200-acre **Liberty State Park,** which faces the Statue of Liberty and boasts stunning views of Manhattan.

Central New Jersey sports **Princeton,** home of **Princeton University** and **Princeton Battlefield State Park; Camden,** located across the Delaware River from Philadelphia; **New Brunswick,** where **Rutgers University** is situated; and **Trenton,** the state's capital.

In southeast New Jersey, the **Pine Barrens** includes the 100,000-acre **Wharton State Forest,** the 40,000-acre **Edwin B. Forsythe National Wildlife Refuge,** and **Batsto Village,** a restored 19th-century settlement.

The following facilities accept payment in checks or cash only:

The Depot Travel Park, West Cape May

ABSECON

Shady Pines Camping Resort

443 S. 6th Ave., Absecon 08201. T: (609) 652-1516 or (800) 352-4917; F: (609) 652-7750.

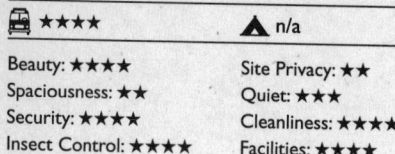

RV ★★★★ Tent n/a

Beauty: ★★★★ Site Privacy: ★★
Spaciousness: ★★ Quiet: ★★★
Security: ★★★★ Cleanliness: ★★★★
Insect Control: ★★★★ Facilities: ★★★★

Every site has a full hookup at Shady Pines Camping Resort, located six miles north of Atlantic City's casinos, boardwalk, and beach. As the name implies, sites are shaded by mature pines. The terrain here is flat and sandy, and sites are spacious and level. Campers can rent economy cars at Shady Pines and join the 37 million annual visitors who flock to the row of casinos along the beach. The boardwalk features amusement piers lined with shops, eateries, museums, and entertainment. If you need a break from the ringing of slot machines and the crowds along the boardwalk, head to the Edwin B. Forsythe National Wildlife Refuge, a 40,000-acre sanctuary with interpretive trails and a self-guided driving tour route. As exhilarating as Atlantic City can be, after a while it's a relief to leave the city and surround yourself with the sounds of nature.

BASICS

Operated By: Jay and Carol Waters. **Open:** Mar. 15–Oct. 15. **Site Assignment:** Reservations accepted (7-day notice required for refund), walk-ins accepted. **Registration:** At campground office. **Fee:** $31 (VISA, MC). **Parking:** At site.

FACILITIES

Number of RV Sites: 140. **Number of Tent-Only Sites:** None. **Hookups:** Electric (20, 30 amps), phone, all sites have full hookups. **Each Site:** Fire ring and picnic table. **Dump Station:** Yes. **Laundry:** Yes. **Pay Phone:** Yes. **Rest Rooms and Showers:** Yes. **Fuel:** Yes. **Propane:** Yes. **Internal Roads:** Paved, in good condition. **RV Service:** No. **Market:** Within 1 mi. **Restaurant:** Within 1 mi. **General Store:** No. **Vending:** Yes. **Playground:** Yes. **Other:** Rentals cars available. **Activities:** Swimming, shuffleboard, horseshoes, rec hall. **Nearby Attractions:** Atlantic City casinos, boardwalk and beach. **Additional Information:** Atlantic City Convention and Visitors Authority, (800) ACVISIT, www.atlanticcitynj.com.

RESTRICTIONS

Pets: On leash only. **Fires:** At site. **Alcoholic Beverages:** At site. **Vehicle Maximum Length:** 40 ft. **Other:** None.

TO GET THERE

From US 9, go 1.5 mi. west on US 30 and 1.5 mi. north on 6th Ave. Entrance is on the left.

ANDOVER

Panther Lake Camping Resort

6 Panther Lake Rd., Andover 07821. T: (973) 347-4440 or (800) 543-2056; F: (973) 347-6402; www.njcamping.com/pantherlakehome; panther@njcamping.com.

RV ★★★★ Tent ★★★★

Beauty: ★★★★ Site Privacy: ★
Spaciousness: ★★ Quiet: ★★★
Security: ★★★★ Cleanliness: ★★★★
Insect Control: ★★★★ Facilities: ★★★★

The 45-acre Panther Lake is the centerpiece of Panther Lake Camping Resort in northern New Jersey. The 160-acre campground is adorned with forests and meadows on the rolling hills of the New Jersey Skylands region, so there are open and wooded sites, including 300 full hookups. The lake, complete with sandy beach, is situated on the southwest side of the campground, while the pond and swimming pool are in the southeast section. Clusters of sites are located along and near both areas as well as between the two. An adults-only whirlpool is located next to the swimming pool. The 70,000-acre Delaware Water Gap National Recreation Area and the 7,000-acre Great Swamp National Wildlife Refuge offer excellent hiking, fishing, boating, and other recreational opportunities. A day trip to New York City is feasible from Panther Lake; the Big Apple is about a 1.5-hour drive east.

BASICS

Operated By: Private operator. **Open:** Apr. 1–Nov. 1. **Site Assignment:** Reservations and walk-ins accepted. **Registration:** At campground office. **Fee:** $28–$35 (VISA, MC). **Parking:** At site.

FACILITIES

Number of RV Sites: 400. **Number of Tent-Only Sites:** 35. **Hookups:** Electric (15, 20, 30 amps), water, 300 full hookups. **Each Site:** Picnic table and fire ring. **Dump Station:** Yes. **Laundry:** Yes. **Pay Phone:** Yes. **Rest Rooms and Showers:** Yes. **Fuel:** No. **Propane:** Yes. **Internal Roads:** Gravel and paved, in good condition. **RV Service:** No. **Market:** Within 5 mi. **Restaurant:** Within 3 mi. **General Store:** Yes. **Vending:** Yes. **Playground:** Yes. **Other:** Panther Lake. **Activities:** Lake swimming, lake and pond fishing, boating, canoeing, boat rentals, mini-golf, rec hall, game room, shuffleboard, tennis, planned activities on weekends, horseshoes, volleyball. **Nearby Attractions:** Delaware Water Gap National Recreation Area, Great Swamp National Wildlife Refuge, Duke Gardens, Lakota Wolf Preserve, Space Farms Zoo and Museum. **Additional Information:** Skylands Tourism Council of New Jersey, (800) 4SKYLAND, www.state.nj.us/travel.

RESTRICTIONS

Pets: On leash only. **Fires:** At site only. **Alcoholic Beverages:** At site only. **Vehicle Maximum Length:** 40 ft. **Other:** Check-in and check-out time is 2 p.m. There is a half-day charge for early arrival or late departure, vacancy permitting.

TO GET THERE

From CR 517, go 1.5 mi. south on US 206. Entrance is on the left.

BAYVILLE

Cedar Creek Campground

1052 Rte. 9, Bayville 08721. T: (732) 269-1413; F: (732) 269-0455; www.cedarcreeknj.com; mngr@cedarcreeknj.com.

RV ★★★★ Tent ★★★★

Beauty: ★★★★ Site Privacy: ★★★
Spaciousness: ★★★ Quiet: ★★★★
Security: ★★★★ Cleanliness: ★★★★
Insect Control: ★★★★ Facilities: ★★★★

Located on the eastern side of central New Jersey, Cedar Creek Campground's is close to both the Atlantic Ocean and the Pine Barrens—home to one million acres of pine forests. Of course, location is not the only amenity at Cedar Creek. The campground has an on-site canoe livery, and there are guided canoe and kayak excursions on Barnegat Bay and along Cedar Creek. Wooded sites on sandy terrain are spacious. There are 20 pull-throughs and 100 full-hookup sites. Island Beach State Park is a short drive away across Barnegat Bay. The park is situated along the Atlantic Ocean and features 1,900 acres of sand dunes, saltwater marshes, and freshwater bogs. A canoe float on Barnegat Bay and Cedar Creek, a hike at Island Beach State Park, and a drive through the Pine Barrens will change your impression of New Jersey for the better.

BASICS

Operated By: Debra Fleming. **Open:** All year. **Site Assignment:** Reservations recommended, walk-ins accepted. **Registration:** At campground office. **Fee:** $27–$37 (VISA, MC). **Parking:** At site.

FACILITIES

Number of RV Sites: 220. **Number of Tent-Only Sites:** 45. **Hookups:** Electric (20, 30, 50 amp), phone, water, 100 full hookups. **Each Site:** Fire ring and picnic table. **Dump Station:** Yes. **Laundry:** Yes. **Pay Phone:** Yes. **Rest Rooms and Showers:** Yes. **Fuel:** No. **Propane:** Yes. **Internal Roads:** Gravel and paved, in good condition. **RV Service:** No. **Market:** Within 2 mi. **Restaurant:** Within 2 mi. **General Store:** Yes. **Vending:** Yes. **Playground:** Yes. **Other:** Cabin and RV rentals. **Activities:** Canoeing, kayaking, planned activities on weekends, game room, rec hall, badminton, horseshoes, volleyball. **Nearby Attractions:** Island Beach State Park, Toms River, Barnegat Light Museum, Deep Cut Gardens, Six Flags Great Adventure and Wild Safari, Longstreet Farm, Point Pleasant Beach. **Additional Information:** Shore Region Tourism Council, (732) 544-9300, www.state.nj.us/travel.

RESTRICTIONS

Pets: On leash only. **Fires:** At site. **Alcoholic Beverages:** At site. **Vehicle Maximum Length:** None. **Other:** Pets may not be left unattended.

TO GET THERE

From Garden State Parkway, take Exit 80 and go 5 mi. south on US 9. Follow signs to entrance.

BRANCHVILLE

Harmony Ridge Campground

23 Risdon Dr., Branchville 07826. T: (973) 948-4941; F: (973) 948-5253; www.harmonyridge.com; harmony@nac.net.

RV ★★★ Tent ★★★★

Beauty: ★★★★ Site Privacy: ★★★
Spaciousness: ★★★ Quiet: ★★★★

Security: ★★★★ Cleanliness: ★★★★★
Insect Control: ★★★★ Facilities: ★★★

Perched in the Kittatiny Mountains in northern New Jersey, the 160-acre Harmony Ridge Campground includes colorful flower gardens, three lakes, and several hiking trails. Chances are you will see a deer, wild turkey, raccoon, or bald eagle—or maybe a few of each. Some sites are clustered around the three lakes, including island sites in the center of the eastern lake. Tent sites are located on the western side of the campground. The office resembles an old-fashioned barn, complete with antique farm tools. The volleyball court is lined with sand brought from Cape May. The Space Wild Animal Farm and Museum is located about 10 miles north in Sussex. Here, you will find a zoo and a village of buildings stocked with historic exhibits, including antique cars, motorcycles, carriages, and wagons.

BASICS

Operated By: Ed Risdon. **Open:** All year. **Site Assignment:** Reservations accepted (cancellations with at least 72 hours notice will receive credit vailid for 1 year depending on availability), walk-ins accepted. **Registration:** At campground office. **Fee:** $11 per person (VISA, MC, AE). **Parking:** At site.

FACILITIES

Number of RV Sites: 225. **Number of Tent-Only Sites:** 50. **Hookups:** Electric (20, 30 amps), water. **Each Site:** Stone fireplace. **Dump Station:** Yes. **Laundry:** Yes. **Pay Phone:** Yes. **Rest Rooms and Showers:** Yes. **Fuel:** No. **Propane:** Yes. **Internal Roads:** Gravel, in fair condition. **RV Service:** Yes, limited. **Market:** Within 2 mi. **Restaurant:** Within 2 mi. **General Store:** Yes. **Vending:** Yes. **Playground:** Yes. **Other:** Pond. **Activities:** Pond swimming and fishing, game room, mini-golf, basketball, shuffleboard, badminton, volleyball, horseshoes, hiking trails, rec hall. **Nearby Attractions:** Appalachian Trail, Waterloo Village, Delaware Water Gap National Recreation Area, Space Wild Animal Farm and Museum, High Point State Park, Stokes State Forest, Kittatiny Mountains. **Additional Information:** Skylands Tourism Council of New Jersey, (800) 4SKYLAND, www.state.nj.us/travel.

RESTRICTIONS

Pets: On leash only, under control. **Fires:** At site. **Alcoholic Beverages:** At site. **Vehicle Maximum Length:** None. **Other:** None.

TO GET THERE

From CR 521, go 0.5 mi. north on US 206, 2 mi. east and south on CR 636, and 1 mi. east on Mattison Reservoir Ave. Entrance is on the left.

BRANCHVILLE

Kymer's Camping Resort

69 Kymer Rd., Branchville 07826. T: (973) 875-3167 or (800) 526-2267; F: (973) 875-3183; www.njcamping.com; kymers@njcamping.com.

★★★★ ★★★★

Beauty: ★★★★ Site Privacy: ★★
Spaciousness: ★★★ Quiet: ★★★★
Security: ★★★★ Cleanliness: ★★★★
Insect Control: ★★★★ Facilities: ★★★★

Like Harmony Ridge Campground, Kymer's Camping Resort is nestled in the Kittatiny Mountains, close to the Appalachian Trail. The 200-acre campground is similar in size to Harmony Ridge, and both places offer similar amenities and clean facilities. While Harmony Ridge has waterfront sites on three lakes, Kymer's has a lake with no waterfront sites. What Kymer's does have is a vast menu of recreational opportunities, including mini-golf, tennis, and basketball. On weekends, Kymer's is often the scene of special events such as bingo and country and western music entertainment. Most full-hookup sites are situated at the north end of the campground, while a small cluster of sites is located in the center. The group of sites with water and electric hookups on the western side is secluded from the rest of the campground; these sites are near the lake, swimming pool, store and most activity centers. For outdoor adventure, nearby Stokes State Forest is located on the Kittatiny Ridge. The mountain view is spectacular from Sunrise Mountain, and the natural gorge Tillman Ravine can be found in the southern part of the forest.

BASICS

Operated By: Kymer family. **Open:** Apr. 1–Nov. 1. **Site Assignment:** Reservations accepted (2-night min. stay required), walk-ins accepted. **Registration:** At campground office. **Fee:** $24–$27 (VISA, MC). **Parking:** At site.

FACILITIES

Number of RV Sites: 250. **Number of Tent-Only Sites:** None. **Hookups:** Electric (20, 30 amps), water, 111 full hookups. **Each Site:** Picnic table and fire ring. **Dump Station:** Yes. **Laundry:** Yes. **Pay Phone:** Yes. **Rest Rooms and Showers:** Yes. **Fuel:** No. **Propane:** No. **Internal Roads:** Gravel and paved, in good condition. **RV Service:** No. **Market:** Within 5 mi. **Restaurant:** Within 5 mi. **General Store:** Yes. **Vending:** Yes. **Playground:** Yes. **Other:** Pond. **Activities:** Fishing, rec hall, game room, swimming, mini-golf, planned activities on weekends, tennis, basketball, sports field, horseshoes, volleyball. **Nearby Attractions:** Waterloo Village, Appalachian Trail, High Point State Park and Franklin Mineral Museum, Delaware Water Gap National Recreation Area, Space Wild Animal Farm and Museum, Stokes State Forest, Kittatiny Mountains. **Additional Information:** Skylands Tourism Council of New Jersey, (800) 4SKYLAND, www.state.nj.us/travel.

RESTRICTIONS

Pets: On leash only. **Fires:** At site. **Alcoholic Beverages:** At site. **Vehicle Maximum Length:** 35 ft. **Other:** Quiet time 11 p.m.–7 a.m.

TO GET THERE

From I-80, take Exit 34B and go 16 mi. north on SR 15, 2 mi. north on SR 206, 5 mi. northeast on CR 519, and 1 mi. west on Kymer Rd. Entrance is on the right.

BUENA

Buena Vista Camping Park

775 Harding Hwy., Buena 08310. T: (856) 697-5555; F: (856) 697-3855; www.bvcp.com.

 ★★★★ ★★★★

Beauty: ★★★★ Site Privacy: ★
Spaciousness: ★★ Quiet: ★★★
Security: ★★★★★ Cleanliness: ★★★★
Insect Control: ★★★★ Facilities: ★★★★

Centrally located between Atlantic City and Philadelphia, Buena Vista Camping Park is a place that kids—and kids at heart—will not want to leave. In addition to a miniature zoo with exotic animals, the 175-acre campground features a 40-foot double waterslide, a spacious swimming pool, a kiddie pool, and a mini-golf course. Just those would keep most children entertained, but Buena Vista offers much more for families. An amusement area features child-friendly carnival rides, a trampoline, and a 30-foot "dry" slide. Admission is free at the campground's antique museum, which is stocked with old cars, farm equipment and artifacts. Most sites provide little privacy, but they are situated under mature woodlands, so there is plenty of shade on sticky summer days. Buena Vista's variety of fun things for the family to do compensate for the lack of privacy the sites offer. Buena Vista is located about 30 miles northwest of Atlantic City—away from the crowds, but close enough if boardwalk excitement is your goal.

BASICS

Operated By: Private operator. **Open:** All year. **Site Assignment:** Reservations and walk-ins accepted. **Registration:** At campground office. **Fee:** $25–$39 (VISA, MC). **Parking:** At site.

FACILITIES

Number of RV Sites: 700. **Number of Tent-Only Sites:** None. **Hookups:** Electric (20, 30, 50 amps), water, phone, 200 full hookups. **Each Site:** Fire ring and picnic table. **Dump Station:** Yes. **Laundry:** Yes. **Pay Phone:** Yes. **Rest Rooms and Showers:** Yes. **Fuel:** No. **Propane:** Yes. **Internal Roads:** Gravel and paved, in good condition. **RV Service:** No. **Market:** Within 4 mi. **Restaurant:** Within 4 mi. **General Store:** Yes. **Vending:** Yes. **Playground:** Yes. **Other:** Water slide, cabin rentals. **Activities:** Wading pool, lake swimming, water slide, boat rentals, pond fishing, mini-golf, zoo, basketball, shuffleboard, game room, rec hall, movies, sports field, hiking trails, volleyball. **Nearby Attractions:** Atlantic City, Ocean City, Cape May, Philadelphia. **Additional Information:** Greater Atlantic City Region Tourism, (609) 652-7777, www.state.nj.us/travel.

RESTRICTIONS

Pets: On leash only. **Fires:** At site. **Alcoholic Beverages:** At site. **Vehicle Maximum Length:** 40 ft. **Other:** None.

TO GET THERE

From Hwy. 54, go 0.1 mi. east on Hwy. 40. Entrance is on the left.

CAPE MAY

Beachcomber Camping Resort

462 W. Seashore Rd., Cape May 08204. T: (609) 886-6035 or (800) 233-0150; F: (609) 886-0289; www.beachcombercamp.com; info@beachcombercamp.com.

 ★★★★★  ★★★★★

Beauty: ★★★★ Site Privacy: ★★
Spaciousness: ★★ Quiet: ★★★
Security: ★★★★★ Cleanliness: ★★★★★
Insect Control: ★★★★ Facilities: ★★★★★

Four miles north of Cape May, and the same distance south of Wildwoods, Beachcomber Camping Resort is the premiere park in southern New Jersey. On the New Jersey Cape, Beachcomber has two spring-fed lakes for fishing and swimming, three adult pools, and three kiddie pools. An adults-only clubhouse, a new playground, and two laundromats are some of the other amenities. Site offerings range from water and hookups for pop-up campers and tents to the "Ultra VIP" site area, which accommodates RVs up to 48 feet long and includes full hookups, a concrete pad, a lamp post and a fence. These tree-canopied sites are close to the resort's central activity hub. Classic car and motorcycle shows and remote-controlled boat and dune buggy races are among the events hosted here. Seven- and ten-day packages entice campers with vouchers for dolphin-watch boat trips, railroad excursions to the zoo, and passes to see Elvis in concert. We think this Elvis is an impersonator, but you never know.

BASICS

Operated By: Brodesser family. **Open:** Apr. 15–Oct. 31. **Site Assignment:** Reservations recommended (3-day min. stay in July and Aug., and on holiday weekends), walk-ins accepted. **Registration:** At campground office. **Fee:** $20–$44 (VISA, MC, D). **Parking:** At site.

FACILITIES

Number of RV Sites: 530. **Number of Tent-Only Sites:** 60. **Hookups:** Electric (30, 50, 100 amps), cable TV, phone, water, 337 full hookups. **Each Site:** Fire ring and picnic table. **Dump Station:** Yes. **Laundry:** Yes. **Pay Phone:** Yes. **Rest Rooms and Showers:** Yes. **Fuel:** No. **Propane:** Yes. **Internal Roads:** Gravel and paved, in good condition. **RV Service:** No. **Market:** Within 1.5 mi. **Restaurant:** Within 1.5 mi. **General Store:** Yes. **Vending:** Yes. **Playground:** Yes. **Other:** Private lake, lakefront cabin rentals. **Activities:** Lake swimming and fishing, boat rentals, wading pool, 3 swimming pools, basketball, shuffleboard, planned activities, movies, horseshoes, volleyball, game room, rec hall, canoeing, kayaking. **Nearby Attractions:** Historic Cape May boat and walking tours, Victorian Cape May, Point Lighthouse and Park, Cold Spring Village, Cape May beaches, Wildwood amusement parks, Cape May County Park & Zoo, Cape May–Lewes (DE) Ferry, Atlantic City. **Additional Information:** Cape May Chamber of Commerce, (609) 884-9562, www.capemaychamber.com.

RESTRICTIONS

Pets: On leash only, 1 pet per site. **Fires:** At site. **Alcoholic Beverages:** At site. **Vehicle Maximum Length:** 38 ft. **Other:** Pets may not be left unattended.

TO GET THERE

From Hwy. 47, go 1 mi. south on US 9 and follow signs to entrance, which is on the left.

CAPE MAY
Cape Island Campground

709 Rte. 9, Cape May 08204. T: (800) 437-7443 or (609) 884-5777; F: (609) 884-5777; www.capeisland.com; info@capeisland.com.

RV ★★★★ Tent ★★★★

Beauty: ★★★★ Site Privacy: ★★★★
Spaciousness: ★★★ Quiet: ★★★★
Security: ★★★★★ Cleanliness: ★★★★★
Insect Control: ★★★★ Facilities: ★★★★

Cape Island Campground has 475 sites situated on 175 acres; many of these sites are separated by shrubbery, so campers have plenty of privacy. Few parks in southern New Jersey offer as much privacy as Cape Island. Overall, there are 310 full hookups and 17 pull-throughs. Since Cape May is a major tourist destination, parking can be a hassle at many of the attractions. The Cape May Seashore Line Railroad, which has a stop across from the campground, transports passengers from Cape May Court House across the Cape May Canal to the city of Cape May. Cape Island is also across the street from Cold Spring Historic Village, a replica circa-1870 living farm village. Cape May Point Lighthouse is also nearby, as are the beaches. The Cape May–Lewes (DE) Ferry takes passengers on a 16-mile, 70-minute voyage across Delaware Bay. Be sure to take your Dramamine before embarking if oceangoing travel makes you sick. Believe us, you will not regret it.

BASICS

Operated By: Private operator. **Open:** May 1–Sept. 30. **Site Assignment:** Reservations recommended, walk-ins accepted. **Registration:** At campground office. **Fee:** $36–$38 (VISA, MC). **Parking:** At site.

FACILITIES

Number of RV Sites: 455. **Number of Tent-Only Sites:** 20. **Hookups:** Electric (20, 30 amps), water, phone, 310 full hookups. **Each Site:** Picnic table and fire ring. **Dump Station:** Yes. **Laundry:** Yes. **Pay Phone:** Yes. **Rest Rooms and Showers:** Yes. **Fuel:** No. **Propane:** Yes. **Internal Roads:** Gravel, in good condition. **RV Service:** Yes. **Market:** Within 0.5 mi. **Restaurant:** Within 0.25 mi. **General Store:** Yes. **Vending:** Yes. **Playground:** Yes. **Other:** Pavilion. **Activities:** Game room, rec hall, swimming, wading pool, mini-golf, basketball, shuffleboard, planned activities, tennis, horseshoes, sports field, volleyball. **Nearby Attractions:** Historic Cape May boat and walking tours, Victorian Cape May, Point Lighthouse and Park, Cold Spring Village, Cape May beaches, Wildwood amusement parks, Cape May County Park & Zoo, Cape May–Lewes (DE) Ferry, Atlantic City. **Additional Information:** Cape May Chamber of Commerce, (609) 884-9562, www.capemaychamber.com.

RESTRICTIONS

Pets: On leash only. **Fires:** At site. **Alcoholic Beverages:** At site. **Vehicle Maximum Length:** None. **Other:** Pets may not be left unattended.

TO GET THERE

From Hwy. 109, go 0.5 mi. north on US 9. Entrance is on the right.

CAPE MAY
Holly Shores

491 Rte. 9, Cape May 08204. T: (609) 886-1234 or (877) 49-HOLLY; www.hollyshores.com; camping@algorithms.com.

RV ★★★★ Tent ★★★★

Beauty: ★★★★ Site Privacy: ★
Spaciousness: ★★ Quiet: ★★★
Security: ★★★★ Cleanliness: ★★★★
Insect Control: ★★★★ Facilities: ★★★★

A Holiday Trav-L-Park, Holly Shores is situated between Cape May and the Wildwoods. Along with lots of recreational activities, the campground has a full menu of theme weekends and special events throughout the season, including our favorite—the Gilligan's Island Survivor's Weekend, when campers dress as their favorite character. Call us old-fashioned, but we prefer Mary Ann over Ginger. Keep in mind that the swimming pool area, store, game room, and basketball courts are at the southern end, while the tennis, volleyball, and bocce ball courts, as well as the nature trail are at the northern end. Sites along the pool loop are ideal if you prefer to be near most of the activity centers. The campground has 181 full hookups but no pull-throughs. Cape May Point Lighthouse and Victorian Cape May are among our favorite attractions in the Cape May area, which is about four miles south of Holly Shores.

BASICS

Operated By: Robinson family. **Open:** Apr. 15–Oct. 31. **Site Assignment:** Reservations accepted (stay 6 nights, get 7th night free), walk-ins accepted. **Registration:** At campground office. **Fee:** $25–$39 (VISA, MC). **Parking:** At site.

FACILITIES

Number of RV Sites: 300. **Number of Tent-Only Sites:** None. **Hookups:** Electric (20, 30, 50 amps), water, cable TV, phone, 181 full hookups. **Each Site:** Fire ring and picnic table. **Dump Station:** Yes. **Laundry:** Yes. **Pay Phone:** Yes. **Rest Rooms and Showers:** Yes. **Fuel:** No. **Propane:** Yes. **Internal Roads:** Gravel and paved, in good condition. **RV Service:** Yes. **Market:** Within 2 mi. **Restaurant:** Within 2 mi. **General Store:** Yes. **Vending:** Yes. **Playground:** Yes. **Other:** Shuffleboard courts are lighted. **Activities:** Swimming, wading pool, whirlpool, game room, rec hall, shuffleboard, tennis, planned activities, movies, horseshoes, hiking trails, sports field, volleyball, basketball. **Nearby Attractions:** Historic Cape May boat and walking tours, Victorian Cape May, Point Lighthouse and Park, Cold Spring Village, Cape May beaches, Wildwood amusement parks, Cape May County Park & Zoo, Cape May–Lewes (DE) Ferry, Atlantic City. **Additional Information:** Cape May Chamber, (609) 884-9562, www.capemaychamber.com.

RESTRICTIONS

Pets: On leash only. **Fires:** At site. **Alcoholic Beverages:** At site. **Vehicle Maximum Length:** 45 ft. **Other:** Pets may not be left unattended.

TO GET THERE

From Hwy. 47, go 1.25 mi. south on US 9. Entrance is on the left.

CAPE MAY
Seashore Campsites

720 Seashore Rd., Cape May 08204. T: (609) 884-4010 or (800) 313-2267; www.seashorecampsites.com; inquire@seashorecampsites.com.

★★★★ ★★★★

Beauty: ★★★★ Site Privacy: ★
Spaciousness: ★★ Quiet: ★★★
Security: ★★★★ Cleanliness: ★★★★
Insect Control: ★★★★ Facilities: ★★★★

Wooded sites, a heated pool, and a filtered lake solely for swimming are among the features of Seashore Campsites, located close to the beaches in Cape May. Seashore has its own beach at the lake; the campground is open all year, but facilities are only fully operational Apr. 15–Oct. 31. Like most campgrounds in the Cape May area, July and Aug. are the busiest months at Seashore. Three-night stays are required during this time. If you do not like crowds but want to see Cape May during warmer months, consider visiting in June or Sept. The restored homes of Victorian Cape May are nearby, and there are several tours that detail the history behind these homes. Cold Spring Village, another attraction close to the campground, recreates an 1870 south Jersey farm village, where blacksmiths, weavers, potters, broommakers, and bakers ply their trades.

BASICS
Operated By: Private operator. **Open:** Apr. 15–Oct. 31. **Site Assignment:** Reservations accepted (recommended in July and Aug., when there is a 3-night min. stay), walk-ins accepted. **Registration:** At campground office. **Fee:** $28–$34 (VISA, MC, AE, D). **Parking:** At site.

FACILITIES
Number of RV Sites: 632. **Number of Tent-Only Sites:** 68. **Hookups:** Electric (20, 30, 50 amps), cable TV, water, 375 full hookups. **Each Site:** Fire ring and picnic table. **Dump Station:** Yes. **Laundry:** Yes. **Pay Phone:** Yes. **Rest Rooms and Showers:** Yes. **Fuel:** No. **Propane:** Yes. **Internal Roads:** Paved, in good condition. **RV Service:** No. **Market:** Within 1 mi. **Restaurant:** Within 1 mi. **General Store:** Yes. **Vending:** No. **Playground:** Yes. **Other:** Filtered swimming lake. **Activities:** Tennis, basketball, lake swimming, water slide, mini-golf, badminton, horseshoes, volleyball, rec halls, shuffleboard, planned activities, movies, game room. **Nearby Attractions:** Historic Cape May boat and walking tours, Victorian Cape May, Point Lighthouse and Park, Cold Spring Village, Cape May beaches, Wildwood amusement parks, Cape May County Park & Zoo, Cape May–Lewes (DE) Ferry, Atlantic City. **Additional Information:** Cape May Chamber, (609) 884-9562, www.capemaychamber.com.

RESTRICTIONS
Pets: On leash. **Fires:** At site. **Alcoholic Beverages:** Not permitted. **Vehicle Maximum Length:** 40 ft. **Other:** Proof of shots required for pets.

TO GET THERE
From Hwy. 47, go 3 mi. south on US 9, 0.1 mi. west over train tracks and 0.1 mi. north on Hwy. 626. Entrance is on the left.

CAPE MAY COURT HOUSE
Big Timber Lake Camping Resort

116 Swainton-Goshen Rd., Cape May Court House 08210. T: (609) 465-4456 or (800) 542-CAMP; F: (609) 465-7468; www.bigtimberlake.com; btlcamp@bellatlantic.net.

★★★★ ★★★★

Beauty: ★★★★ Site Privacy: ★★
Spaciousness: ★★ Quiet: ★★★
Security: ★★★★ Cleanliness: ★★★★
Insect Control: ★★★★ Facilities: ★★★★

Two freshwater lakes—one for swimming and the other for fishing—adorn the grounds of Big Timber Lake Camping Resort, located in Cape May Court House near the ocean beaches. This campground is "families only"; the owners define a family as a husband, wife, and unmarried children. Only one family is allowed to stay at each site. A small cluster of full hookup sites are situated along the southwestern end of the swimming lake. The fishing lake, which is just north of the swimming lake, borders the basketball, shuffleboard, and bocce ball courts, as well as the horseshoe pits. Though no sites are directly on the fishing lake, several sites are within sight of it. Located northwest of Cape May, Cape May Court House is home to the Cape May County Park and Zoo. The town, like Cape May, has its share of immaculate Victorian-style homes. The nearby Leaming's Run Gardens has 20 acres of lush lawns, ponds, and gardens, each with a different theme.

BASICS
Operated By: Menz family. **Open:** Apr. 15–Oct. 15. **Site Assignment:** Reservations accepted (deposit required to hold site), walk-ins accepted. **Registration:** At campground office. **Fee:** $29–$41 (VISA, MC, D). **Parking:** At site.

FACILITIES
Number of RV Sites: 515. **Number of Tent-Only Sites:** 100. **Hookups:** Electric (20, 30, 50 amps), cable TV, phone, water, 375 full hookups. **Each Site:** Fire ring and picnic table. **Dump Station:** Yes. **Laundry:** Yes. **Pay Phone:** Yes. **Rest Rooms and Showers:** Yes. **Fuel:** No. **Propane:** Yes. **Internal Roads:** Gravel and paved, in good condition. **RV Service:** No. **Market:** Within 2 mi. **Restaurant:** Within 2 mi. **General Store:** Yes. **Vending:** Yes. **Playground:** Yes. **Other:** Cabin rentals, fishing pond. **Activities:** Pond fishing, game room, mini-golf, sports field, rec hall, basketball, shuffleboard, movies, volleyball, badminton. **Nearby Attractions:** Cape May County Historical Museum, Cape May County Park and Zoo, Leaming's Run Gardens, Historic Cape May boat and walking tours, Victorian Cape May, Point Lighthouse and Park, Cold Spring Village, Cape May beaches, Wildwood amusement parks, Cape May–Lewes (DE) Ferry, Atlantic City. **Additional Information:** Cape May County Chamber of Commerce, (609) 465-7181, www.cmccofc.com.

RESTRICTIONS
Pets: On leash only. **Fires:** At site. **Alcoholic Beverages:** At site. **Vehicle Maximum Length:** None. **Other:** No guests permitted after 10 p.m. unless prior arrangement are made with office.

TO GET THERE
From Garden State Parkway, take Exit 13 and go 0.5 mi. west, 1 mi. south on US 9, and 1 mi. west on CR 646. Entrance is on the right.

CAPE MAY COURT HOUSE
Hidden Acres Campground

1142 W. Rte. 83, Cape May Court House 08210. T: (609) 624-9015 or (800) 874-7576; www.hiddenacrescampground.com; springer@bellatlantic.net.

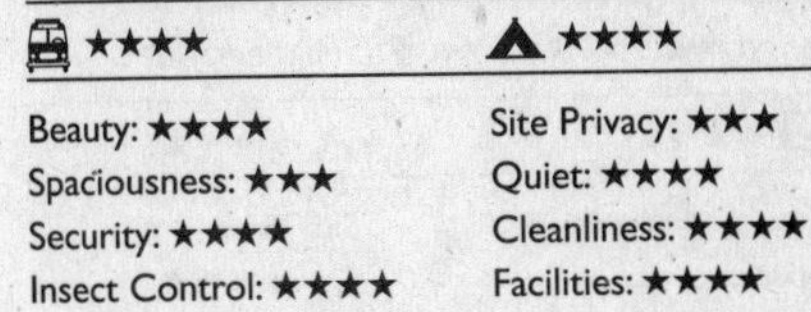

★★★★ ★★★★

Beauty: ★★★★ Site Privacy: ★★★
Spaciousness: ★★★ Quiet: ★★★★
Security: ★★★★ Cleanliness: ★★★★
Insect Control: ★★★★ Facilities: ★★★★

Located between Cape May Court House and Clermont, Hidden Acres Campground is an ideal base for exploring Cape May, the Wildwoods, and even Atlantic City. Set amid forests of pine and laurel, Hidden Acres features 300 shaded sites on flat, sandy ground. Half of the sites offer full hookups, while the other half have water and electric hookups. The Atlantic Ocean is less than 10 minutes away, but you do not have to leave the campground to enjoy the water. Hidden Acres has a filtered swimming lake and a white-sanded beach. Few people leave Cape May without strolling along the beach and visiting the 157-foot-tall Cape May Lighthouse, which was built in 1859. We recommend that, before you leave the Cape May area, take a whale-watching cruise. Cape May Whale Watcher guarantees the sighting of a whale or dolphin; if you do not see either, you receive credit for another trip.

BASICS
Operated By: Joyce Springer. **Open:** Apr. 1–Oct. 31. **Site Assignment:** Reservations accepted (3-day min. stay on holidays), walk-ins accepted. **Registration:** At campground office. **Fee:** $29–$33 (VISA, MC, D). **Parking:** At site.

FACILITIES
Number of RV Sites: 200. **Number of Tent-Only Sites:** 100. **Hookups:** Electric (20, 30, 50 amps), cable TV, phone, water, 100 full hookups. **Each Site:** Picnic table and fire ring. **Dump Station:** Yes. **Laundry:** Yes. **Pay Phone:** Yes. **Rest Rooms and Showers:** Yes. **Fuel:** No. **Propane:** Yes. **Internal Roads:** Paved and dirt, in fair condition. **RV Service:** No. **Market:** Within 2 mi. **Restaurant:** Within a half-mile. **General Store:** Yes. **Vending:** No. **Playground:** Yes. **Other:** Freshwater lake with beach. **Activities:** Lake swimming, basketball, shuffleboard, mini-golf, game room, rec hall, horseshoes, badminton. **Nearby Attractions:** Cape May County Historical Museum, Cape May County Park and Zoo, Leaming's Run Gardens, Historic Cape May boat and walking tours, Victorian Cape May, Point Lighthouse and Park, Cold Spring

Village, Cape May beaches, Wildwood amusement parks, Cape May–Lewes (DE) Ferry, Atlantic City. **Additional Information:** Cape May County Chamber, (609) 465-7181, www.cmccofc.com.

Restrictions

Pets: On leash. **Fires:** At site. **Alcoholic Beverages:** At site. **Vehicle Maximum Length:** None.

To Get There

From US 9, go 0.5 mi. west on Hwy. 83. Entrance is on the right.

CAPE MAY COURT HOUSE

North Wildwood Camping Resort

240 W. Shell Bay Ave., Cape May Court House 08210. T: (609) 465-4440; F: (609) 465-5605; www.nwcamp.com; nwcr@bellatlantic.net.

RV ★★★★ Tent ★★★★

Beauty: ★★★★	Site Privacy: ★
Spaciousness: ★★	Quiet: ★★★
Security: ★★★★★	Cleanliness: ★★★★
Insect Control: ★★★★	Facilities: ★★★★

Located 10 minutes north of Cape May, North Wildwood Camping Resort is just a few minutes from Stone Harbor and North Wildwood beaches. A well-kept park with wooded sites on flat, sandy grounds, North Wildwood does not have the same variety of recreational facilites as some campgrounds in the area. Campers looking for a clean and comfortable place to stay while visiting Cape May and the Wildwoods—those who do not require filtered swimming lakes, fishing ponds, and multiple pools—will find North Wildwood to their liking. This does not mean the campground is without recreation, as it does have a pool and athletic courts. All of the activity centers (including the pool) are located along Shell Bay Ave. at the southern end of North Wildwood. Full hookup sites stretch from the center to the far western end. Primitive, wooded tent sites are located at the far north end of the campground near the paintball field.

Basics

Operated By: Richard and Bonnie Lynch. **Open:** Apr. 1–Oct. 15. **Site Assignment:** Reservations recommended (3-night min. stay required in July and Aug. and on holiday weekends), walk-ins accepted. **Registration:** At campground office. **Fee:** $25–$33 (VISA, MC). **Parking:** At site.

Facilities

Number of RV Sites: 260. **Number of Tent-Only Sites:** 120. **Hookups:** Electric (20, 30 amps), cable TV, water, 125 full hookups. **Each Site:** Fire ring and picnic table. **Dump Station:** Yes. **Laundry:** Yes. **Pay Phone:** Yes. **Rest Rooms and Showers:** Yes. **Fuel:** No. **Propane:** Yes. **Internal Roads:** Gravel and paved, in fair condition. **RV Service:** Yes. **Market:** Within 2 mi. **Restaurant:** Within 2 mi. **General Store:** Yes, limited. **Vending:** Yes. **Playground:** Yes. **Other:** Pavilion. **Activities:** Tennis, horseshoes, shuffleboard, rec hall, planned activities, swimming. **Nearby Attractions:** Cape May County Historical Museum, Cape May County Park and Zoo, Leaming's Run Gardens, Historic Cape May boat and walking tours, Victorian Cape May, Point Lighthouse and Park, Cold Spring Village, Cape May beaches, Wildwood amusement parks, Cape May–Lewes (DE) Ferry, Atlantic City. **Additional Information:** Cape May County Chamber of Commerce, (609) 465-7181, www.cmccofc.com.

Restrictions

Pets: On leash. **Fires:** At site. **Alcoholic Beverages:** At site. **Vehicle Maximum Length:** None. **Other:** Pets and fires must be attended at all times.

To Get There

From Garden State Parkway, take Exit 9 and go 1 mi. west on Shell Bay Ave. Entrance is on the right.

CHATSWORTH

Wading Pines Camping Resort

85 Godfrey Bridge Rd., Chatsworth 08019. T: (609) 726-1313 or (888) 726-1313; F: (609) 726-1413; www.wadingpines.com; wadingpines@wadingpines.com.

RV ★★★★ Tent ★★★★

Beauty: ★★★★	Site Privacy: ★★
Spaciousness: ★★★	Quiet: ★★★★
Security: ★★★★★	Cleanliness: ★★★★
Insect Control: ★★★★	Facilities: ★★★★

Located deep in the million-acre Pine Barrens—or Pinelands, if you prefer—Wading Pines Camping Resort is situated along the Wading River. The campground has a private hiking and picnicking island ("Fantasy Island") on the river; campers can also fish in the river or the stocked pond, or swim in the river and the pool. Children are entertained by the "Jersey Devil," the campground train that winds around Wading Pines. A cluster of inviting full-hookup sites surrounds the fishing lake on the southeast side. The row of sites at the far western end of the campground (away from the activity centers) is also pleasant. Some sites that border the fishing lake are also along the river, though there are no sites on the river near Fantasy Island. The island is accessed by footbridge or swimming from the beach. Activity centers, including the swimming pool and the riverside beach, are situated on the northeast end of the campground.

Basics

Operated By: Mark and Margie Rogers. **Open:** Mar. 1–Dec. 15. **Site Assignment:** Reservations accepted (2-night min. stay required for weekends), walk-ins accepted. **Registration:** At campground office. **Fee:** $26–$30 (VISA, MC, AE, D). **Parking:** At site.

Facilities

Number of RV Sites: 283. **Number of Tent-Only Sites:** 17. **Hookups:** Electric (20, 30 amps), cable TV, phone, water, 130 full hookups. **Each Site:** Fire ring and picnic table. **Dump Station:** Yes. **Laundry:** Yes. **Pay Phone:** Yes. **Rest Rooms and Showers:** Yes. **Fuel:** No. **Propane:** Yes. **Internal Roads:** Dirt, in good condition. **RV Service:** No. **Market:** Within 9 mi. **Restaurant:** Within 7 mi. **General Store:** Yes. **Vending:** Yes. **Playground:** Yes. **Other:** Stocked fishing lake, train rides. **Activities:** Swimming, volleyball, canoeing, kayaking, canoe and kayak rentals, game room, rec hall, lake and river fishing, basketball, planned activities on weekends, shuffleboard, tennis, movies, horseshoes, badminton, hiking trails. **Nearby Attractions:** Pine Barrens, Wading River, Island Beach State Park, Atlantic City, Barnegat Lighthouse State Park, wineries. **Additional Information:** New Jersey Office of Travel & Tourism, (800) JERSEY7, www.state.nj.us/travel.

Restrictions

Pets: On leash only. **Fires:** At site. **Alcoholic Beverages:** At site. **Vehicle Maximum Length:** None. **Other:** No pets in cabins, proof of rabies vaccination required.

To Get There

From Hwy. 72, go 13 mi. south on CR 563 and 0.75 mi. north at campground sign. Entrance is on the left.

CLARKSBORO

Timberlane Campground

117 Timberlane Rd., Clarksboro 08020. T: (856) 423-6677; F: (856) 423-5096; www.timberlanecampground.com; timberlane@home.com.

RV ★★★★ Tent ★★★★

Beauty: ★★★	Site Privacy: ★★
Spaciousness: ★★	Quiet: ★★★
Security: ★★★★	Cleanliness: ★★★★
Insect Control: ★★★★	Facilities: ★★★★

A suburban campground where ducks and swans gracefully paddle on a shimmering pond, Timberlane Campground is located in Clarksboro, about 15 minutes from Independence Hall and other history-rich attractions in downtown Philadelphia. Covering 20 acres, Timberlane offers open and wooded sites, including 51 pull-throughs. This is an ideal base for a family vacation in Philadelphia. The restrooms, laundry room, and playground are new. The lounge has a TV and a fireplace. Not all the fun near Timberlane is limited to Philly. In Camden, the New Jersey State Aquarium contains one of the nation's largest open ocean tanks. At the aquatic nursery, you can touch sharks, stingrays, and starfish in special tanks. Literature buffs will want to visit the Walt Whitman House State Historic Site; it was the poet's last residence before his death in 1892.

Basics

Operated By: Delores Goess. **Open:** All year. **Site Assignment:** Reservations recommended, walk-ins accepted. **Registration:** At campground office. **Fee:** $24–$34 (VISA, MC). **Parking:** At site.

Facilities

Number of RV Sites: 91. **Number of Tent-Only Sites:** 14. **Hookups:** Electric (20, 30, 50 amps), cable TV, phone, water, 72 full hookups. **Each Site:** Picnic table and fire ring. **Dump Station:** Yes. **Laundry:** Yes. **Pay Phone:** Yes. **Rest Rooms and Showers:** Yes. **Fuel:** No. **Propane:** Yes. **Internal Roads:** Gravel and paved, in good condition. **RV Service:** Yes. **Market:** Within 1.5 mi. **Restaurant:** Within 1.5 mi. **General Store:** RV supplies. **Vending:** Yes. **Playground:** Yes. **Other:** Cabin rentals, batting cages. **Activities:** Game room, rec hall, pond fishing, basketball, shuffleboard, horseshoes, volleyball, pool, kiddie pool. **Nearby Attractions:** Philadelphia, New Jersey State Aquarium, Sesame

Place, Delaware Memorial Bridge, Garden State Race Track, Rutgers University. **Additional Information:** Delaware River Region Tourism, (856) 414-0805, www.state.nj.us/travel.

RESTRICTIONS

Pets: On leash only. **Fires:** At site. **Alcoholic Beverages:** At site. **Vehicle Maximum Length:** None. **Other:** No pets permitted in cabins.

TO GET THERE

From I-295, take Exit 18 and go 0.75 mi. east on Timberlane Rd. Entrance is on the right.

CLERMONT

Driftwood Camping Resort

1955 Rte. 9 and Rte. 83, Clermont 08210.
T: (609) 624-1899 or (800) 624-3743; F: (609) 624-1915; www.gocampingamerica.com; driftwoodresort@gocampingamerica.com.

RV ★★★★ Tent ★★★★

Beauty: ★★★	Site Privacy: ★
Spaciousness: ★★★	Quiet: ★★★
Security: ★★★★★	Cleanliness: ★★★★
Insect Control: ★★★★	Facilities: ★★★★

From Driftwood Camping Resort, casino tours embark for Atlantic City about 40 miles north, but you do not need to leave the campground for excitement. Located midway between Atlantic City and Cape May, Driftwood has a wide selection of shaded sites, including primitive tent sites and 400 full hookups. The campground's freshwater lake has a soft-sand beach. Linksters will enjoy the Pine Barrens Golf Club, a beautiful 27-hole course named one of the "Top 10 New Golf Courses in America" by The Golfer Magazine in 1997. Driftwood has an RV sales and service center with new motor homes, park models, fifth wheels, and travel trailers and they stock a large inventory of RV parts and accessories. Driftwood is a short drive from attractions and beaches in the Wildwoods and Cape May, both of which are less than a half-hour drive south.

BASICS

Operated By: Robertson family. **Open:** Apr. 15–Oct. 15. **Site Assignment:** Reservations accepted (1 night's deposit required), walk-ins accepted. **Registration:** At campground office. **Fee:** $28-$36 (VISA, MC, AE, D). **Parking:** At site.

FACILITIES

Number of RV Sites: 680. **Number of Tent-Only Sites:** 20. **Hookups:** Electric (20, 30, 50 amps), cable TV, phone, water, 400 full hookups. **Each Site:** Fireplace and picnic table. **Dump Station:** Yes. **Laundry:** Yes. **Pay Phone:** Yes. **Rest Rooms and Showers:** Yes. **Fuel:** No. **Propane:** Yes. **Internal Roads:** Paved and dirt, in fair condition. **RV Service:** Yes. **Market:** Within 3 mi. **Restaurant:** Within 3 mi. **General Store:** Yes. **Vending:** Yes. **Playground:** Yes. **Other:** Private lake with beach, RV and cabin rentals. **Activities:** Lake swimming, pool, 3 playgrounds, basketball, tennis, rec hall, game room, horseshoes, volleyball, casino tours. **Nearby Attractions:** Cape May County Historical Museum, Cape May County Park and Zoo, Leaming's Run Gardens, Historic Cape May boat and walking tours, Victorian Cape May, Point Lighthouse and Park, Cold Spring Village, Cape May beaches, Wildwood amusement parks, Cape May–Lewes (DE) Ferry, Atlantic City. **Additional Information:** Cape May County Chamber of Commerce, (609) 465-7181, www.cmccofc.com.

RESTRICTIONS

Pets: On leash only, under control. **Fires:** At site. **Alcoholic Beverages:** At site. **Vehicle Maximum Length:** 40 ft. **Other:** None.

TO GET THERE

From Hwy. 83, go 0.25 mi. south on US 9. Entrance is on the right.

COLUMBIA

Camp Taylor Campground

85 Mount Pleasant Rd., Columbia 07832.
T: (908) 496-4333 or (800) 545-9662; www.camptaylor.com.

RV ★★★★ Tent ★★★★

Beauty: ★★★★	Site Privacy: ★★★★
Spaciousness: ★★★★	Quiet: ★★★★★
Security: ★★★★	Cleanliness: ★★★★
Insect Control: ★★★★	Facilities: ★★★★

Adjacent to the 72,000-acre Delaware Water Gap National Recreation Area, Camp Taylor Campground is situated on 350 acres of densely forested mountain ridges in the northern New Jersey Skylands region. The Delaware Water Gap is accessible from hiking trails at the campground, and the Appalachian Trail is nearby. One of the most fascinating campground attractions anywhere is Camp Taylor's Lakota Wolf Preserve, where you can observe packs of tundra, timber, and Arctic wolves. Informal talks about the wolves are presented, and guided wildlife photography sessions are available. Sites are located on both sides of Mount Pleasant Rd., though most sites are on the northern side. The row of sites near the wildlife pens are popular, especially if you do not mind the occasional howling of wolves. A cluster of primitive tenting sites are on the northwest side, secluded from the rest of the campground.

BASICS

Operated By: Taylor family. **Open:** All year. **Site Assignment:** Reservations accepted (reservations required Oct. 15–May 1), walk-ins accepted. **Registration:** At front building. **Fee:** $19–$23 (VISA, MC, AE, D). **Parking:** At site.

FACILITIES

Number of RV Sites: 150. **Number of Tent-Only Sites:** 20. **Hookups:** Electric (20, 30 amps), water. **Each Site:** Picnic table. **Dump Station:** Yes. **Laundry:** No. **Pay Phone:** Yes. **Rest Rooms and Showers:** Yes. **Fuel:** No. **Propane:** Yes. **Internal Roads:** Gravel, in good condition. **RV Service:** No. **Market:** Within 2 mi. **Restaurant:** Within 4 mi. **General Store:** Yes, limited. **Vending:** Yes. **Playground:** Yes. **Other:** Lakota Wolf Preserve located on the premises. **Activities:** Lake swimming (no fishing), game room, rec hall, volleyball, hiking trails, boat rentals, mini-golf, planned activities on weekends, badminton, sports field. **Nearby Attractions:** Lakota Wolf Preserve, Hope Historic Village, Delaware Water Gap, High Point State Park, Land of Make Believe, Space Farms Zoo and Museum. **Additional Information:** Skylands Tourism Council of New Jersey, (800) 4SKYLAND, www.state.nj.us/travel.

RESTRICTIONS

Pets: On leash only. **Fires:** At site. **Alcoholic Beverages:** At site. **Vehicle Maximum Length:** 38 ft. **Other:** One pet permitted per campsite.

TO GET THERE

From I-80, go 3.5 mi. north on Hwy. 94, 0.5 mi. west on Benton Rd., 0.2 mi. north on Frog Pond Rd., 1.5 mi. north on Wishing Well Rd., and 0.5 mi. south on Mount Pleasant Rd. Entrance is on the right.

EGG HARBOR CITY

Holly Acres RV Park

218 Frankfurt Ave., Egg Harbor City 08215.
T: (609) 965-2287 or (800) 2RVCAMP; www.kiz.com/bestholiday.

RV ★★★★ Tent n/a

Beauty: ★★★★	Site Privacy: ★★★
Spaciousness: ★★★	Quiet: ★★★★
Security: ★★★★★	Cleanliness: ★★★★
Insect Control: ★★★★	Facilities: ★★★★

Located about 20 miles northwest of Atlantic City, Holly Acres RV Park is a short drive to the casino and the boardwalk attractions, yet it is far enough away to avoid the crowds. The RV-only campsites are open and wooded. The pool and arts and crafts center are located near the office close to the entrance. A cluster of sites in the center of the campground are near the pool, mini-golf course, and most of the other activity centers. The fishing pond is nestled amid fragrant pines at the northern end of Holly Acres. Renault Winery is a short drive from the campground, as is Historic Smithville, a restored 18th-century village where streets are lined with specialty shops and eateries. Horse-drawn carriage rides, train rides, and an old-fashioned carousel are among the attractions. Animal lovers will enjoy the Marine Mammal Stranding Center and Museum and the Edwin B. Forsythe National Wildlife Refuge.

BASICS

Operated By: Holiday Trav-L-Park. **Open:** May 1–Sept. 30. **Site Assignment:** Reservations accepted ($25 for 2-night stay), walk-ins accepted. **Registration:** At campground office. **Fee:** $27–$30 (VISA, MC, D). **Parking:** At designated area.

FACILITIES

Number of RV Sites: 175. **Number of Tent-Only Sites:** None. **Hookups:** Electric (20, 30, 50 amps), water, cable TV, 125 full hookups. **Each Site:** Picnic table and fire ring. **Dump Station:** Yes. **Laundry:** Yes. **Pay Phone:** Yes. **Rest Rooms and Showers:** Yes. **Fuel:** No. **Propane:** Yes. **Internal Roads:** Gravel, in good condition. **RV Service:** No. **Market:** Within 4 mi. **Restaurant:** Within 3 mi. **General Store:** Yes. **Vending:** Yes. **Playground:** Yes. **Other:** Fishing pond. **Activities:** Pond fishing, blueberry picking, rec hall, game room, swimming, wading pool, mini-golf, shuffleboard, planned activities on weekends, volleyball, badminton, horseshoes. **Nearby Attractions:** Atlantic City, Story Book

Land, Sea Life Museum, Edwin B. Forsythe National Wildlife Refuge. **Additional Information:** Greater Atlantic City Region Tourism, (609) 652-7777, www.state.nj.us/travel.

Restrictions

Pets: On leash. **Fires:** At site. **Alcoholic Beverages:** At site. **Vehicle Maximum Length:** None. **Other:** Mini-bikes and motor bikes notpermitted.

To Get There

From Hwy. 50, go 2 mi. east on US 30 and 1.5 mi. north on Frankfurt Ave. Entrance is on the left.

ELMER

Yogi Bear's Jellystone Park at Tall Pines Resort

49 Beal Rd., Elmer 08318. T: (800) 252-2890 or (856) 451-7479; F: (856) 455-3378; www.tallpines.com; tallpines@jnlk.com.

RV: ★★★★ Tent: ★★★★

Beauty: ★★★★ Site Privacy: ★★
Spaciousness: ★★★ Quiet: ★★★
Security: ★★★★★ Cleanliness: ★★★★
Insect Control: ★★★★ Facilities: ★★★★★

Spacious, shaded sites under towering pines define the landscape of Yogi Bear's Jellystone Park at Tall Pines Resort. The campground is located in Elmer—about 40 miles south of Philadelphia—yet Tall Pines is still a comfortable drive to Atlantic City, the Wildwoods, and Cape May. Children will like the playground, hayrides, and fire engine rides. Most of the activity centers—including the pool, mini-golf course, and camp store—are in the middle of the campground. Conveniently, the lake is along Cohansey Creek, providing campers with ample water-related activities in one area. A cluster of full-hookup sites and water-electric sites are on the southwest side of the lake. A row of primitive tenting sites are located a short distance from the lake on Cohansey Creek. Tall Pines also has attractive lodges, chalets, and cottages for rent.

Basics

Operated By: Rick and Leigh Frederick. **Open:** All year. **Site Assignment:** Reservations accepted (required in July and Aug. and on holiday weekends), walk-ins accepted. **Registration:** At campground office. **Fee:** $25–$38 (VISA, MC). **Parking:** At site.

Facilities

Number of RV Sites: 254. **Number of Tent-Only Sites:** 8. **Hookups:** Electric (20, 30 amps), cable TV, water, 190 full hookups. **Each Site:** Fire ring and picnic table. **Dump Station:** Yes. **Laundry:** Yes. **Pay Phone:** Yes. **Rest Rooms and Showers:** Yes. **Fuel:** No. **Propane:** Yes. **Internal Roads:** Dirt, in good condition. **RV Service:** No. **Market:** Within 8 mi. **Restaurant:** Within 6 mi. **General Store:** Yes. **Vending:** Yes. **Playground:** Yes. **Other:** Lake Jellystone. **Activities:** Lake swimming and fishing, stream fishing, wading pool, boating, canoeing, kayaking, boat rentals, mini-golf, basketball, planned activities, movies, bike rentals, horseshoes, badminton, volleyball, hiking trails, sports field. **Nearby Attractions:** Philadelphia, New Jersey State Aquarium, Delaware River, Delaware Bay, Wildwoods, Cape May, Atlantic City. **Additional Information:** Delaware River Region Tourism, (856) 414-0805, www.state.nj.us/travel.

Restrictions

Pets: On leash only. **Fires:** At site. **Alcoholic Beverages:** At site. **Vehicle Maximum Length:** 40 ft. **Other:** No pets in rental units.

To Get There

From Hwy. 40, go 6 mi. southwest on CR 635 and a half-mile east on Beal Rd. Entrance is on right.

HAMMONTON

Indian Branch Park Campground

2021 Skip Morgan Dr., Hammonton 08037. T: (609) 561-4719 or (800) 974-2287.

RV: ★★★ Tent: ★★★

Beauty: ★★★★ Site Privacy: ★★
Spaciousness: ★★★ Quiet: ★★★★
Security: ★★★★ Cleanliness: ★★★★
Insect Control: ★★★★ Facilities: ★★★

Located in the New Jersey Pine Barrens, between Philadelphia and Atlantic City just off the Atlantic City Expressway, Indian Branch Park Campground offers a Christian-oriented environment popular for church group outings. Chapel services are held in the longhouse on Sunday morning from Memorial Day to Labor Day. Sites along Indian Lake are a favorite among repeat guests due to their separate swimming and boating areas; these sites require reservations. Covering 100,000 acres of the Pine Barrens, nearby Wharton State Forest is the largest single forest in the New Jersey state park system. Picnic areas, fishing, hiking trails, and a nature center surround the park's visitors center in Atsion. Historic Batsto Village, a restored 19th-century settlement, is located at the southwestern tip of the forest. Indian Branch is ideally located for campers who want to explore Philadelphia (about 35 miles northwest) and Atlantic City (25 miles southeast).

Basics

Operated By: Lawrence Morgan. **Open:** May 1–Sept. 30. **Site Assignment:** Reservations required for lakefront sites, walk-ins accepted for all other sites. **Registration:** At campground store. **Fee:** $18–$34 (VISA, MC, D). **Parking:** At site.

Facilities

Number of RV Sites: 214. **Number of Tent-Only Sites:** None. **Hookups:** Electric (20, 30 amps), water, 160 full hookups. **Each Site:** Fire ring and picnic table. **Dump Station:** Yes. **Laundry:** Yes. **Pay Phone:** Yes. **Rest Rooms and Showers:** Yes. **Fuel:** No. **Propane:** Yes. **Internal Roads:** Gravel and paved, in good condition. **RV Service:** Yes. **Market:** Within 1.5 mi. **Restaurant:** Within a half-mile. **General Store:** Yes. **Vending:** Yes. **Playground:** Yes. **Other:** Indian Lake. **Activities:** Lake swimming, boating, boat rentals, rec hall, canoeing, fishing, shuffleboard, sports field, horseshoes, volleyball. **Nearby Attractions:** Atlantic City, Story Book Land, Sea Life Museum, Edwin B. Forsythe National Wildlife Refuge, Philadelphia, New Jersey State Aquarium. **Additional Information:** Greater Atlantic City Region Tourism, (609) 652-7777, www.state.nj.us/travel.

Restrictions

Pets: On leash only. **Fires:** At site. **Alcoholic Beverages:** Not permitted. **Vehicle Maximum Length:** 40 ft. **Other:** Mini-bikes and ATVs are not permitted.

To Get There

From Atlantic City Expressway, go 2 mi. south on Hwy. 54 and 3.5 mi. east on US 322. Entrance is on the left.

HOPE

Triplebrook Family Camping Resort

58 Honey Run Rd., Hope 07825. T: (888) 343-CAMP or (908) 459-4079; www.triplebrook.com; info@triplebrook.com.

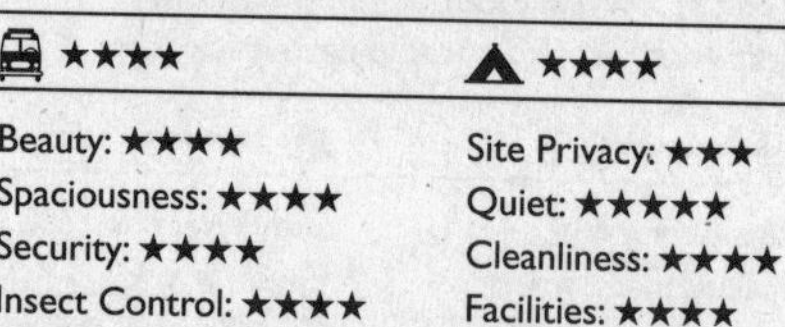

RV: ★★★★ Tent: ★★★★

Beauty: ★★★★ Site Privacy: ★★★
Spaciousness: ★★★★ Quiet: ★★★★★
Security: ★★★★ Cleanliness: ★★★★
Insect Control: ★★★★ Facilities: ★★★★

Chickens fly (or at least attempt to fly) and cow dung is art at Triplebrook Family Camping Resort in Hope—and campers flock here to see both. Located in the Kittatiny Mountains, Triplebrook is set on a 250-acre working farm seven miles from the Delaware Water Gap National Recreation Area in the New Jersey Skylands. Many sites are wooded, and most are situated at the northern end. The campground hosts several entertaining special events throughout the year, including Hillbilly Weekend, the International Chicken Flying Meet, and Bovine Day. On Bovine Day, cow-dung sculpting and cow-chip throwing contests are held. On any day, campers can see chickens, emus, horses, and other farm animals, and watch feedings. The campground's trading post is stocked with groceries, sundries, and RV and camping supplies.

Basics

Operated By: Brenda and George James. **Open:** All year. **Site Assignment:** Reservations required Dec. 1–Mar. 31; walk-ins accepted during other months; 2-night min. stay required for reservations. **Registration:** At campground office. **Fee:** $28–$31 (VISA, MC, AE, D). **Parking:** At site.

Facilities

Number of RV Sites: 217. **Number of Tent-Only Sites:** None. **Hookups:** Electric (20, 30, 50 amps), water, phone, 110 full hookups. **Each Site:** Picnic table. **Dump Station:** Yes. **Laundry:** Yes. **Pay Phone:** Yes. **Rest Rooms and Showers:** Yes. **Fuel:** No. **Propane:** Yes. **Internal Roads:** Gravel and paved, in fair condition. **RV Service:** Yes. **Market:** Within 4 mi. **Restaurant:** Within 4 mi. **General Store:** Yes. **Vending:** Yes. **Playground:** Yes. **Other:** Cabin rentals. **Activities:** Basketball, tennis, game room, sports field, rec hall, canoeing, kayaking, fishing, mini-golf, movies, hiking trails, boat rentals. **Nearby Attractions:** Delaware Water Gap National Recreation Area, Appalachian Trail, Land of Make Believe, Lakota Wolf Preserve, Space Wild Animal Farm, Moravian Village of Hope. **Additional Information:** Skylands Tourism Council of New Jersey, (800) 4SKYLAND, www.state.nj.us/travel.

RESTRICTIONS

Pets: No pets allowed. **Fires:** At site. **Alcoholic Beverages:** At site. **Vehicle Maximum Length:** None. **Other:** No electric bug zappers.

TO GET THERE

From I-80, take Exit 12 and go 1 mi. south on CR 521, 3 mi. west on CR 609, 1 mi. north on Nightingale Rd., and 0.5 mi. east on Honey Run Rd. Entrance is on the left.

JACKSON

Butterfly Camping Resort

360 Butterfly Rd., Jackson 08527. T: (732) 928-2107; F: (732) 928-1106; www.butterflycamp1.com.

RV ★★★★ Tent ★★★★

Beauty: ★★★★ Site Privacy: ★★★
Spaciousness: ★★ Quiet: ★★
Security: ★★★★ Cleanliness: ★★★★
Insect Control: ★★★★ Facilities: ★★★★

Adjacent to Butterfly Bogs State Wildlife Refuge, Butterfly Camping Resort attracts many visitors because of its proximity to Six Flags Great Adventure Theme Park and Wild Safari. The campground offers discount tickets to Six Flags for its guests. Butterfly features private, shaded sites, including eight pull-throughs. The activity centers are located near the entrance at the southern end. There are four long clusters of sites stretching south to north. Six Flags features a 350-acre drive-through safari with more than 1,200 free-roaming animals from six continents and a 125-acre theme park with rollercoasters, rides, and live shows. Island Beach State Park is about 20 minutes east of Butterfly Camping Resort. This unspoiled barrier beach separating Barnegat Bay from the Atlantic Ocean is a must-see, with 1,900 acres of sand dunes, freshwater bogs, and saltwater marshes.

BASICS

Operated By: Don and Patty Letho. **Open:** Apr. 1–Oct. 31. **Site Assignment:** Reservations accepted (3-night min. stay on holiday weekends), walk-ins accepted. **Registration:** At campground store. **Fee:** $28–$30 (VISA, MC). **Parking:** At site.

FACILITIES

Number of RV Sites: 135. **Number of Tent-Only Sites:** 70. **Hookups:** Electric (20, 30, 50 amps), phone, water, 80 full hookups. **Each Site:** Fire ring and picnic table. **Dump Station:** Yes. **Laundry:** Yes. **Pay Phone:** Yes. **Rest Rooms and Showers:** Yes. **Fuel:** No. **Propane:** Yes. **Internal Roads:** Gravel and dirt, in good condition. **RV Service:** No. **Market:** Within 2.5 mi. **Restaurant:** Within 2.5 mi. **General Store:** Yes. **Vending:** Yes. **Playground:** Yes. **Other:** Cabin rentals. **Activities:** Lake fishing, boating, canoeing, kayaking, mini-golf, basketball, volleyball, badminton, horseshoes, sports field, shuffleboard, game room, rec hall, planned activities, movies. **Nearby Attractions:** Six Flags Great Adventure and Wild Safari, Island Beach State Park, Barnegat Light Museum, Deep Cut Gardens, Longstreet Farm, Atlantic Ocean beaches. **Additional Information:** Shore Region Tourism Council, (732) 544-9300, www.state.nj.us/travel.

RESTRICTIONS

Pets: On leash only. **Fires:** At site. **Alcoholic Beverages:** At site. **Vehicle Maximum Length:** None. **Other:** Fires may not be left unattended; no pit bulls, Dobermans, or rottweilers allowed.

TO GET THERE

From I-195, take Exit 21 and go 3.5 mi. south on CR 527, 5.25 mi. east on CR 528, and 0.5 mi. north on Butterfly Rd. Entrance is on the left.

JACKSON

Indian Rock RV Resort and Campground

920 W. Veterans Hwy. (Rte. 528), Jackson 08527. T: (732) 928-0034 or (800) 442-4954 (NJ only); www.indianrockresort.com; info@indianrockresort.com.

RV ★★★★ Tent ★★★★

Beauty: ★★★★ Site Privacy: ★★
Spaciousness: ★★ Quiet: ★★★★
Security: ★★★★★ Cleanliness: ★★★★
Insect Control: ★★★★ Facilities: ★★★★

Located within an hour's from midtown Manhattan, Philadelphia, and the Jersey Shore, Indian Rock RV Resort and Campground is a good base for day trips to the aforementioned areas and nearby Six Flags. A snack bar is open on weekends, and the campground store is well stocked. Sites here are spacious and set among pine and oak trees; most of the sites are east and north of the activity centers, though a cluster of sites near the entrance is convenient to the children's catch-and-release fishing pond. During Oct., Indian Rock becomes a "frightening" place with its Jersey Devil Hayride. Country-western line dancing is held every Friday night from 8 p.m. to midnight on the expansive dance floor. Even the beginner's lessons offered on the first Friday of each month would not help us move any better, but perhaps they can help you.

BASICS

Operated By: Private operator. **Open:** All year. **Site Assignment:** Reservations accepted (2-night min. stay June 29–July 10), walk-ins accepted. **Registration:** At campground office. **Fee:** $30–$35 (VISA, MC). **Parking:** At site.

FACILITIES

Number of RV Sites: 210. **Number of Tent-Only Sites:** None. **Hookups:** Electric (20, 30 amps), phone, water, 90 full hookups. **Each Site:** Fire ring and picnic table. **Dump Station:** Yes. **Laundry:** Yes. **Pay Phone:** Yes. **Rest Rooms and Showers:** Yes. **Fuel:** No. **Propane:** Yes. **Internal Roads:** Dirt, in fair condition. **RV Service:** No. **Market:** Within 10 mi. **Restaurant:** Within 10 mi. **General Store:** Yes. **Vending:** Yes. **Playground:** Yes. **Other:** Cabin rentals. **Activities:** Pond fishing, game room, pool, mini-golf, basketball, planned activities on weekends, movies, hiking trails, badminton, hiking trails, volleyball, rec hall, arts & crafts center. **Nearby Attractions:** Six Flags Great Adventure and Wild Safari, Island Beach State Park, Barnegat Light Museum, Deep Cut Gardens, Longstreet Farm, Atlantic Ocean beaches. **Additional Information:** Shore Region Tourism Council, (732) 544-9300, www.state.nj.us/travel.

RESTRICTIONS

Pets: Under 25 pounds, at campsite. **Fires:** At site. **Alcoholic Beverages:** No alcohol allowed. **Vehicle Maximum Length:** 40 ft. **Other:** Fires must be out by midnight.

TO GET THERE

From I-95, take Exit 16B and go 1 mi. southeast on CR 537, 4.5 mi. south on CR 571, and 1.5 mi. west on CR 528. Entrance is on the right.

JACKSON

Timberland Lake Campground

P.O. Box 48, Jackson 08527. T: (732) 928-0500 or (609) 758-2235; www.timberlandlakecampground.com.

RV ★★★★ Tent ★★★★★

Beauty: ★★★ Site Privacy: ★★★
Spaciousness: ★★★ Quiet: ★★★★
Security: ★★★★★ Cleanliness: ★★★★
Insect Control: ★★★★ Facilities: ★★★

A five-acre lake is the centerpiece of Timberland Lake Campground, which is located in Jackson (not to be confused with Timberlane Campground in Clarksboro). Sites are set on the eastern and western sides of the lake, which is wide at the southern end but narrows to the north. The fishing pier is located at the southern end, across the lake from the beach, the store, and most of the activity centers. A cluster of sites here is ideal for campers who want to be near the action, but we recommend the lakeside sites on both sides of the lake at the northern end. These are more spacious and more peaceful, since they are away from the activity centers. Timberland Lake offers three-, four-, and five-night packages, as well as discounted tickets to Six Flags. In late Mar., Timberland Lake offers a free camping weekend for guests who rake leaves for two hours (advance reservations required).

BASICS

Operated By: William and Kathleen Elliott. **Open:** Mar. 1–Dec. 1. **Site Assignment:** Reservations accepted (1-night deposit required), walk-ins accepted. **Registration:** At campground office. **Fee:** $30 (VISA, MC, D). **Parking:** At site.

FACILITIES

Number of RV Sites: 200. **Number of Tent-Only Sites:** None. **Hookups:** Electric (20, 30 amps), water, phone, cable TV. **Each Site:** Fire ring and picnic table. **Dump Station:** Yes. **Laundry:** No. **Pay Phone:** Yes. **Rest Rooms and Showers:** Yes. **Fuel:** No. **Propane:** Yes. **Internal Roads:** Dirt, in fair condition. **RV Service:** Yes. **Market:** Within 1 mi. **Restaurant:** Within 1 mi. **General Store:** Yes. **Vending:** Yes. **Playground:** Yes. **Other:** Timberland Lake. **Activities:** Canoeing, kayaking, boat rentals, lake fishing, mini-golf, game room, planned activities, movies, hiking trails, horseshoes, shuffleboard, volleyball, rec hall. **Nearby Attractions:** Six Flags Great Adventure and Wild Safari, Island Beach State Park, Barnegat Light Museum, Deep Cut Gardens, Longstreet Farm, Atlantic

Ocean beaches. **Additional Information:** Shore Region Tourism Council, (732) 544-9300, www.state.nj.us/travel.

RESTRICTIONS

Pets: On leash only, at campsite. **Fires:** At site. **Alcoholic Beverages:** At site. **Vehicle Maximum Length:** None. **Other:** None.

TO GET THERE

From I-195, take Exit 16 and go 3 mi. west on CR 537, 0.25 mi. south on Hawkins Rd., and 0.5 mi. east on Reed Rd. Entrance is on the right.

JACKSON

Tip Tam Camping Resort

301 Brewers Bridge Rd., Jackson 08527. T: (877) TIP-TAMI or (732) 363-4036; F: (732) 363-8240; www.tiptam.com; tiptam@aol.com.

RV ★★★★ Tent ★★★★

Beauty: ★★★★ Site Privacy: ★
Spaciousness: ★★ Quiet: ★★★★
Security: ★★★★★ Cleanliness: ★★★★
Insect Control: ★★★★ Facilities: ★★★★

Featuring shaded sites in a colorful grove, Tip Tam Camping Resort offers discount tickets and packages to nearby Six Flags in Jackson. Most sites have full hookups, though the campground does not accommodate pull-throughs. RVers with big rigs may be more satisfied with Butterfly Camping Resort or Timberland Lake Campground, both of which accommodate pull-throughs. Children are kept happy with swimming races, scavenger and treasure hunts, mini-golf tournaments, and coloring contests. Team trivia matches, children's olympics, candy bar bingo, and weekends honoring mothers and fathers on their respective holidays are also hosted at Tip Tam. With savvy planning, a memorable family vacation can include a day each at Six Flags, Philly, New York City, Island Beach State Park, Cape May, and the Wildwoods.

BASICS

Operated By: Guglielmelli family. **Open:** Apr. 15–Sept. 30. **Site Assignment:** Reservations accepted (10-day cancellation notice required, 3-night min. stay on holiday weekends), walk-ins accepted. **Registration:** At campground office. **Fee:** $30–$31 (VISA, MC, D). **Parking:** At site.

FACILITIES

Number of RV Sites: 200. **Number of Tent-Only Sites:** 15. **Hookups:** Electric (20, 30 amps), water, cable TV, 168 full hookups. **Each Site:** Fire ring and picnic table. **Dump Station:** Yes. **Laundry:** Yes. **Pay Phone:** Yes. **Rest Rooms and Showers:** Yes. **Fuel:** No. **Propane:** Yes. **Internal Roads:** Gravel and paved, in fair condition. **RV Service:** No. **Market:** Within 1.5 mi. **Restaurant:** Within 1.5 mi. **General Store:** Yes. **Vending:** No. **Playground:** Yes. **Other:** Amphitheater, cabin rentals. **Activities:** Game room, 2 rec halls, 2 pools, planned activites, mini-golf, volleyball, horseshoes, shuffleboard, basketball, sports field. **Nearby Attractions:** Six Flags Great Adventure and Wild Safari, Island Beach State Park, Barnegat Light Museum, Deep Cut Gardens, Longstreet Farm, Atlantic Ocean beaches. **Additional Information:** Shore Region Tourism Council, (732) 544-9300, www.state.nj.us/travel.

RESTRICTIONS

Pets: At site only. **Fires:** At site. **Alcoholic Beverages:** At site. **Vehicle Maximum Length:** 35 ft. **Other:** No pets permitted in rental units.

TO GET THERE

From I-195, take Exit 21 and go 0.25 mi. south on CR 527, 6 mi. east on CR 526, and 2 mi. south on Brewers Bridge Rd. Entrance is on the left.

JERSEY CITY

Liberty Harbor RV Park

11 Marin Blvd., Jersey City 07302. T: (201) 386-7500 or (800) 646-2066; F: (201) 451-0812.

RV ★★★ Tent ★★★

Beauty: ★★★★★ Site Privacy: ★
Spaciousness: ★ Quiet: ★★
Security: ★★★★ Cleanliness: ★★★★
Insect Control: ★★★★ Facilities: ★★★

The tragic destruction of the World Trade Center towers certainly altered the Manhattan skyline, but the view of the Statue of Liberty, Ellis Island and New York City from Liberty Harbor is still breathtaking. Situated on the Hudson River at a full-service marina, the park offers fishing on the Hudson and a boarding site for the New York Waterway Ferry, which goes across the Hudson into New York City. Daily bus tours embark from the campground to New York City Apr. 15–Nov. 15, and the subway to Manhattan is just five minutes away. The campground is best suited as a base for visiting New York City. Sites are crowded and offer no privacy. Fishing is the lone activity, though nearby 60-acre Liberty State Park has nature trails and observation points along an area that is mostly a salt marsh. The state park has a swimming pool and an impressive display of flags, including the Stars and Stripes.

BASICS

Operated By: Private operator. **Open:** All year. **Site Assignment:** Reservations and walk-ins accepted. **Registration:** At campg office. **Fee:** $50 per family (VISA, MC, AE, D). **Parking:** At site.

FACILITIES

Number of RV Sites: 60. **Number of Tent-Only Sites:** None. **Hookups:** Electric (30, 50 amps), water, phone. **Each Site:** Water and electric hookups. **Dump Station:** Yes. **Laundry:** Yes. **Pay Phone:** Yes. **Rest Rooms and Showers:** Yes. **Fuel:** No. **Propane:** No. **Internal Roads:** Gravel, in good condition. **RV Service:** No. **Market:** Within 2 mi. **Restaurant:** On premises. **General Store:** No. **Vending:** No. **Playground:** No. **Other:** Marina and boat dock on Hudson River. **Activities:** Fishing. **Nearby Attractions:** New York City, Statue of Liberty, Liberty State Park, ferry to New York City. **Additional Information:** Shore Region Tourism Council, (732) 544-9300, www.state.nj.us/travel.

RESTRICTIONS

Pets: On leash. **Fires:** No fires allowed. **Alcoholic Beverages:** At site. **Vehicle Max. Length:** 45 ft.

TO GET THERE

From New Jersey Turnpike, take Exit 14C and follow signs to Grand St.; you will encounter 3 consecutive left turns. Go 0.25 mi. on Marin Blvd. Entrance is at the end.

MARMORA

Whippoorwill Campground

810 S. Shore (US 9), Marmora 08223. T: (609) 390-3458 or (800) 424-8275; www.campwhippoorwill.com; campoceancitynj@aol.com.

RV ★★★★ Tent ★★★★

Beauty: ★★★★ Site Privacy: ★★
Spaciousness: ★★ Quiet: ★★★
Security: ★★★★★ Cleanliness: ★★★★
Insect Control: ★★★★ Facilities: ★★★★

Located three miles from Ocean City, Whippoorwill Campground offers level, wooded sites and a family atmosphere. Most of the non-seasonal sites are nestled in the center of the campground around a bathhouse and laundry facility. The Olympic-sized swimming pool is located across from the camp store and office northwest of the entrance, but most of the activity centers, including basketball, volleyball, and tennis courts, are positioned on the southeast side near Rte. 9. From the Work Party Weekend in early Apr. (when campers earn a free stay by performing clean-up tasks for four hours) to the Pig Roast Finale in early Sept., Whippoorwill has several entertaining theme weekends. If you like canned meat, the Spam Fest will whet your appetite with an assortment of creative dishes. If you have a more discriminating palate, there are lots of eateries along the two-mile boardwalk in Ocean City.

BASICS

Operated By: Tom and Cindy Swank. **Open:** Apr. 1–Nov. 1. **Site Assignment:** Reservations recommended (2-night min. stay required, payment in full required for holiday weekends), walk-ins accepted. **Registration:** At campground office. **Fee:** $37 (VISA, MC, D). **Parking:** At site.

FACILITIES

Number of RV Sites: 288. **Number of Tent-Only Sites:** 50. **Hookups:** Electric (20, 30, 50 amps), cable TV, water, 226 full hookups. **Each Site:** Fire ring and picnic table. **Dump Station:** Yes. **Laundry:** Yes. **Pay Phone:** Yes. **Rest Rooms and Showers:** Yes. **Fuel:** No. **Propane:** Yes. **Internal Roads:** Paved, in good condition. **RV Service:** No. **Market:** Within 15 mi. **Restaurant:** Within 15 mi. **General Store:** Yes. **Vending:** Yes. **Playground:** Yes. **Other:** Cabin rentals. **Activities:** Tennis, volleyball, game room, planned activities, basketball, horseshoes, rec hall, kiddie pool. **Nearby Attractions:** Ocean City boardwalk and beaches, Atlantic City, Cape May, the Wildwoods. **Additional Information:** New Jersey Office of Travel and Tourism, (800) JERSEY7, www.state.nj.us/travel.

RESTRICTIONS

Pets: On leash only. **Fires:** At site. **Alcoholic Beverages:** No alcohol permitted. **Vehicle Maximum Length:** None. **Other:** No pets permitted in rental units.

To Get There

From Garden State Parkway, take Exit 25 and go 1 block west and 1.5 mi. south on US 9. Entrance is on the right.

MAYS LANDING

Winding River Campground

6752 Weymouth Rd., Mays Landing 08330. T: (609) 625-3191; F: (609) 625-7460; www.gocampingamerica.com/windingrivernj; windingrivernj@gocampingamerica.com.

RV ★★★★ Tent ★★★★

Beauty: ★★★★ Site Privacy: ★★★
Spaciousness: ★★★ Quiet: ★★★★
Security: ★★★★ Cleanliness: ★★★★
Insect Control: ★★★★ Facilities: ★★★★

Egg Harbor River cuts through Winding River Campground, where sites are set among mature, lush woodlands near Mays Landing in southern New Jersey. Most sites have full hookups. Cooled by a gentle breeze beneath a forested canopy, campers can relax on lawn chairs beside the river. Winding River is a half-hour from the boardwalk and beaches of Atlantic City. Ocean City, the Wildwoods, and Cape May are located to the south. The allure of Egg Harbor River is what draws many campers to Winding River. The campground has a swimming pool, but outdoor enthusiasts head for the river, where canoes, kayaks, and inner tubes are available for rent. Guided canoe floats ranging from two to six hours depart from Winding River. Adirondack-style cabins are available for campers without RVs and tents. The rustic-looking cabins have two double-decker, built-in bunks, restrooms, a kitchen, and a screened dining area.

Basics

Operated By: Al and Therese Horsey. **Open:** May 1–Oct. 15. **Site Assignment:** Reservations accepted (3-night min. stay on holiday weekends), walk-ins accepted. **Registration:** At campground office. **Fee:** $22–$28 (VISA, MC, D). **Parking:** At site.

Facilities

Number of RV Sites: 133. **Number of Tent-Only Sites:** 29. **Hookups:** Electric (30 amps), water, 105 full hookups. **Each Site:** Fire ring and picnic table. **Dump Station:** Yes. **Laundry:** Yes. **Pay Phone:** Yes. **Rest Rooms and Showers:** Yes. **Fuel:** No. **Propane:** Yes. **Internal Roads:** Dirt, in fair condition. **RV Service:** No. **Market:** Within 8 mi. **Restaurant:** Within 4 mi. **General Store:** Yes. **Vending:** No. **Playground:** Yes. **Other:** Cabin rentals. **Activities:** Tubing, canoeing, kayaking, boating, badminton, game room, river fishing, basketball, rec hall, volleyball, planned activities on weekends. **Nearby Attractions:** Atlantic City, Cape May, Ocean City, Story Book Land, the Wildwoods. **Additional Information:** Greater Atlantic City Region Tourism, (609) 652-7777, www.state.nj.us/travel.

Restrictions

Pets: On leash only. **Fires:** At site in fire ring. **Alcoholic Beverages:** At site. **Vehicle Maximum Length:** 39 ft. **Other:** No pets in rental units.

To Get There

From Hwy. 50 and Hwy. 40 in Mays Landing, go 4 mi. north on CR 559. Entrance is on the right.

MAYS LANDING

Yogi Bear's Jellystone Park Camp Resort

1079 W. 12th Ave., Mays Landing 08330. T: (800) 355-0264 or (609) 476-2811; F: (609) 476-2811; www.atlanticcityjellystone.com; yogibear@erols.com.

RV ★★★★ Tent ★★★★

Beauty: ★★★★ Site Privacy: ★★
Spaciousness: ★★ Quiet: ★★★
Security: ★★★★ Cleanliness: ★★★★
Insect Control: ★★★★ Facilities: ★★★★

In Mays Landing, located a half-hour northwest of Atlantic City, Yogi Bear's Jellystone Park Camp Resort and Winding River Campground are the two main camping choices. Both campgrounds are clean and well-maintained, but each serves a different purpose. With its Egg Harbor River location and amenities, Winding River is a destination in itself. Though it has some recreation options, Jellystone is best used as a base for trips to Atlantic City, Ocean City, Cape May, and Philadelphia. Shower and restroom facilities are extremely clean here. The campground has open and wooded sites on flat ground. Rental units include cabins (with ceiling fans and cable TV) and trailers with room for six people. Themed events include the "No Talent Needed Weekend," when daring campers attempt to sing, dance, and perform. Audience members recommend we stick to writing and forego a career in stand-up comedy.

Basics

Operated By: Yogi Bear's Jellystone Park. **Open:** Apr. 1–Nov. 1. **Site Assignment:** Reservations accepted (7-day notice required for refund), walk-ins accepted. **Registration:** At campground office. **Fee:** $22–$31 (VISA, MC, D). **Parking:** At site.

Facilities

Number of RV Sites: 130. **Number of Tent-Only Sites:** 20. **Hookups:** Electric (20,30, 50 amps), cable TV, phone, water, 139 full hookups. **Each Site:** Fire ring and picnic table. **Dump Station:** Yes. **Laundry:** Yes. **Pay Phone:** Yes. **Rest Rooms and Showers:** Yes. **Fuel:** No. **Propane:** Yes. **Internal Roads:** Gravel and dirt, in fair condition. **RV Service:** No. **Market:** Within 3 mi. **Restaurant:** Within 2 mi. **General Store:** Yes. **Vending:** Yes. **Playground:** Yes. **Other:** Cabin and trailer rentals. **Activities:** Pond fishing, kiddie pool, game room, rec hall, mini-golf, basketball, planned activities, movies, horseshoes, badminton, volleyball. **Nearby Attractions:** Atlantic City, Cape May, Ocean City, Story Book Land, the Wildwoods. **Additional Information:** Greater Atlantic City Region Tourism, (609) 652-7777, www.state.nj.us/travel.

Restrictions

Pets: On leash only. **Fires:** At site. **Alcoholic Beverages:** At site. **Vehicle Maximum Length:** 40 ft. **Other:** Pets not permitted in rental units.

To Get There

From Hwy. 40, go 0.5 mi. south on Hwy. 50, 4 mi. west on 11th Ave., 0.25 mi. north on Beach St., and 0.1 mi. east on 12th Ave. Entrance is on the right.

NEW GRETNA

Timberline Lake Camping Resort

P.O. Box 278, New Gretna 08224. T: (609) 296-7900; F: (609) 296-8927; www.timberlinelake.homestead.com

RV ★★★★ Tent ★★★

Beauty: ★★★★ Site Privacy: ★★★
Spaciousness: ★★★★ Quiet: ★★★★
Security: ★★★★★ Cleanliness: ★★★★
Insect Control: ★★★★ Facilities: ★★★★

Located about 20 miles northwest of the 24-hour excitement of Atlantic City, Timberline Lake Camping Resort is nestled in the Pine Barrens around a 30-acre private lake. Some sites are open, but many are wooded and lakeside. The campground can accommodate 10 pull-throughs. Canoes and kayaks are available for rent. Families flock to the TV lounge, which has a deck and a playroom. Timberline's location north of Atlantic City is convenient to the boardwalk and the casinos, as well as the scenery of Island Beach State Park, an unspoiled barrier island separating Barnegat Bay from the Atlantic Ocean. The park boasts more than 1,900 acres of sand dunes, saltwater marshes, and freshwater bogs.

Basics

Operated By: William McGourley. **Open:** All year. **Site Assignment:** Reservations and walk-ins accepted. **Registration:** At campground office. **Fee:** $24–$28 (VISA, MC). **Parking:** At site.

Facilities

Number of RV Sites: 158. **Number of Tent-Only Sites:** None. **Hookups:** Electric (20, 30, 50 amps), cable TV, phone, water, 68 full hookups. **Each Site:** Fire ring and picnic table. **Dump Station:** Yes. **Laundry:** Yes. **Pay Phone:** Yes. **Rest Rooms and Showers:** Yes. **Fuel:** No. **Propane:** No. **Internal Roads:** Dirt, in good condition. **RV Service:** No. **Market:** Within 8 mi. **Restaurant:** Within 4 mi. **General Store:** Yes. **Vending:** Yes. **Playground:** Yes. **Other:** Timberline Lake. **Activities:** Lake swimming and fishing, basketball, rec hall, game room, boating, canoeing, kayaking, boat rentals, planned activities on weekends, volleyball, horseshoes. **Nearby Attractions:** Atlantic City, Barnegat Light Museum, Island Beach State Park, Story Book Land, Edwin B. Forsythe National Wildlife Refuge. **Additional Information:** Greater Atlantic City Region Tourism, (609) 652-7777, www.state.nj.us/travel.

Restrictions

Pets: On leash only. **Fires:** At site. **Alcoholic Beverages:** At site. **Vehicle Maximum Length:** 35 ft. **Other:** Proof of rabies shots required for pets.

To Get There

From US 9, go 4 mi. west on CR 679. Entrance is on the left.

NEWTON

Green Valley Beach Family Campground

68 Phillips Rd., Newton 07860. T: (973) 383-4026; F: (973) 383-1291; www.greenvalleybeach.com.

RV ★★★★ Tent ★★★★

Beauty: ★★★★ Site Privacy: ★
Spaciousness: ★★ Quiet: ★★★★
Security: ★★★★★ Cleanliness: ★★★★
Insect Control: ★★★★ Facilities: ★★★★

Located in the foothills of the Kittatiny Mountains in northwest New Jersey's Sussex County, Green Valley Beach Family Campground is convenient to lots of family-oriented attractions, including Space Farms Zoo and Museum and Wild West City. Of course, with a 3.5-acre lake for fishing and swimming, an Olympic-sized swimming pool, and a rec hall where live entertainment is hosted and free movies are shown, there is plenty to do without leaving the grounds. Ideal for families who want to be in the center of the action, a cluster of sites is situated between a pond and the lake on the southwest end of the campground. The pool fronts the lake near the entrance. The recreation hall and the pavilion border the lake. Full hookup sites at the northwest tip offer the most privacy away from activity centers. The Delaware Water Gap National Recreation Area is a 15-minute drive to the west. Green Valley is also near Skylands Park, home of the New Jersey Cardinals, the St. Louis Cardinals Single-A affiliate in the New York–Penn League.

Basics

Operated By: Private operator. **Open:** Apr. 15–Oct. 15. **Site Assignment:** Reservations accepted (2-night stay required on weekends, 3 nights on holiday weekends), walk-ins accepted. **Registration:** At campground office. **Fee:** $26–$28 (VISA, MC, D). **Parking:** At site.

Facilities

Number of RV Sites: 235. **Number of Tent-Only Sites:** 15. **Hookups:** Electric (15, 20, 30 amps), cable TV, phone, water, 180 full hookups. **Each Site:** Fire ring and picnic table. **Dump Station:** Yes. **Laundry:** Yes. **Pay Phone:** Yes. **Rest Rooms and Showers:** Yes. **Fuel:** No. **Propane:** Yes. **Internal Roads:** Gravel and paved, in good condition. **RV Service:** No. **Market:** Within 4 mi. **Restaurant:** Within 2 mi. **General Store:** Yes. **Vending:** Yes. **Playground:** Yes. **Other:** Private lake. **Activities:** Lake fishing and swimming, game room, rec hall, canoeing, kayaking, boat rentals, planned activities, sports field, horseshoes, volleyball. **Nearby Attractions:** Delaware Water Gap National Recreation Area, Village of Waterloo, Sterling Hill Mine, Wild West City, Kittatiny Valley State Park, Lakota Wolf Preserve, Land of Make Believe, Space Farms Zoo and Museum, Great Swamp National Wildlife Refuge. **Additional Information:** Skylands Tourism Council of New Jersey, (800) 4SKYLAND, www.state.nj.us/travel.

Restrictions

Pets: On leash only. **Fires:** At site. **Alcoholic Beverages:** At site. **Vehicle Maximum Length:** 35 ft. **Other:** All daily visitors must leave the campground by 10 p.m.

To Get There

From US 206, go 0.5 mi. west on CR 611 and follow signs 1 mi. south to the entrance, which is on the left.

OCEAN VIEW

Frontier Campground

84 Tyler Rd., Ocean View 08230. T: (609) 390-3649 or (800) 277-4109; F: (609) 390-0673; www.frontiercampground.com; frontiercampground@prodigy.net.

RV ★★★★ Tent ★★★★

Beauty: ★★★★ Site Privacy: ★★★
Spaciousness: ★★★ Quiet: ★★★★
Security: ★★★★ Cleanliness: ★★★★
Insect Control: ★★★★ Facilities: ★★★★

Located between Ocean City and Sea Isle City on the Jersey Cape, Frontier Campground is a short drive from the ocean beaches. Adorned with evergreens, hardwoods, and wild laurel, the campground is also a half-hour north of Cape May and a half-hour south of Atlantic City. Frontier offers wooded and open sites amid rolling hills. Tall shrubs separate many sites, offering good privacy. Recreational opportunities are minimal here; most campers stay at Frontier because the facilities are clean and well-maintained, and the campground is centrally located between Atlantic City, Ocean City, the Wildwood, and Cape May. Ocean City is the closest of these destinations at about 10 miles north of Frontier. Actually an island nestled between Great Egg Harbor and the Atlantic Ocean, Ocean City has eight miles of beaches and two-plus miles of boardwalk and related points of interest. The boardwalk sports various attractions and amusements, including an enclosed auditorium.

Basics

Operated By: George Reagan. **Open:** Mid-Apr.–mid-Oct. **Site Assignment:** Reservations recommended (1-night deposit required), walk-ins accepted. **Registration:** At A-frame house. **Fee:** $23–$30 (VISA, MC, AE, D). **Parking:** At site.

Facilities

Number of RV Sites: 196. **Number of Tent-Only Sites:** 9. **Hookups:** Electric (20, 30, 50 amps), cable TV, phone, water, 130 full hookups. **Each Site:** Fire ring and picnic table. **Dump Station:** Yes. **Laundry:** Yes. **Pay Phone:** Yes. **Rest Rooms and Showers:** Yes. **Fuel:** No. **Propane:** Yes. **Internal Roads:** Dirt, in good condition. **RV Service:** No. **Market:** Within 1 mi. **Restaurant:** Within 1 mi. **General Store:** Yes. **Vending:** Yes. **Playground:** Yes. **Other:** Furnished tree houses available for rent. **Activities:** Rec hall, saltwater fishing, basketball, badminton, horseshoes, volleyball. **Nearby Attractions:** Ocean City, Atlantic City, the Wildwoods, Cape May. **Additional Information:** New Jersey Office of Travel and Tourism, (800) JERSEY7, www.state.nj.us/travel.

Restrictions

Pets: Not allowed. **Fires:** At site. **Alcoholic Beverages:** Not allowed. **Vehicle Max. Length:** 40 ft.

To Get There

From Garden State Parkway, take Exit 25 and go 3.5 mi. west on Hwy. 631 and 1.5 mi. south on Hwy. 616. Entrance is on the right.

OCEAN VIEW

Ocean View Resort Campground

2555 Rte. 9, Ocean View 08230. T: (609) 624-1675; www.ovresort.com; ovr@worldnet.att.net.

RV ★★★★ Tent ★★★★

Beauty: ★★★★ Site Privacy: ★
Spaciousness: ★★★ Quiet: ★★★
Security: ★★★★★ Cleanliness: ★★★★
Insect Control: ★★★★ Facilities: ★★★★★

At Ocean View Resort Campground, more than 1,175 sites are set in groves of oak, cedar, and pine on 180 acres, just outside of Ocean View, south of Atlantic City, and north of Cape May. The boardwalk and beaches of Ocean City are 10 minutes away; Atlantic City and Cape May are each about a half-hour drive. Yet Ocean View Resort campers can be entertained without leaving the grounds. You can swim, ride a pedal boat, or bask in the sun on the sandy beach at the spring-fed Trail's End Lake. Or you can fish for largemouth bass and hybrid striped bass at Greenbriar Pond. Kids flock to the fully-equipped playground and the game room building with video games, pool tables, air hockey, and skee ball. The expansive club house hosts craft shows, flea markets, movies, and dances. Each of Ocean View's sites has full hookups. Most are wooded, and some are situated along the lake. Obviously, with more than 1,175 sites on 180 acres, privacy is at a minimum, though the sites are spacious.

Basics

Operated By: Private operator. **Open:** Apr. 14–Sept. 24; open weekends only in Apr., May, and after Labor Day. **Site Assignment:** Reservations recommended; July–Aug., min. 3-night stay, walk-ins accepted. **Registration:** At campground office. **Fee:** $37–$45 (VISA, MC, D). **Parking:** At site.

Facilities

Number of RV Sites: 1,175. **Number of Tent-Only Sites:** 40. **Hookups:** Electric (20, 30, 50 amps), cable TV, phone, 1,175 full hookups. **Each Site:** Fire ring and picnic table. **Dump Station:** No. **Laundry:** Yes. **Pay Phone:** Yes. **Rest Rooms and Showers:** Yes. **Fuel:** No. **Propane:** Yes. **Internal Roads:** Paved, in good condition. **RV Service:** Yes. **Market:** Within 3 mi. **Restaurant:** Within 3 mi. **General Store:** Yes. **Vending:** Yes. **Playground:** Yes. **Other:** Freshwater lake with beaches, stocked fishing pond. **Activities:** Lake swimming, wading pool, game room, rec hall, pedal boat rentals, boating, pond fishing, mini-golf, basketball, shuffleboard, planned activities, movies, tennis, badminton, sports field, volleyball. **Nearby Attractions:** Ocean City, Atlantic City, the Wildwoods, Cape May. **Additional Information:** New Jersey Office of Travel and Tourism, (800) JERSEY7, www.state.nj.us/travel.

Restrictions

Pets: On leash only. **Fires:** At site. **Alcoholic Beverages:** At site. **Vehicle Maximum Length:** 40 ft. **Other:** No motor bikes are buses permitted.

To Get There

From Garden State Parkway, take Exit 17 and go 0.25 mi. west on CR 625 and 0.25 mi. north on US 9. Entrance is on the left.

OCEAN VIEW

Pine Haven Campground

P.O. Box 606, Ocean View 08230. T: (609) 624-3437; F: (609) 624-0246; www.pinehavennj.com; dpb1@avaloninternet.net.

RV ★★★ Tent ★★★

Beauty: ★★★★ Site Privacy: ★★
Spaciousness: ★★ Quiet: ★★★★
Security: ★★★★ Cleanliness: ★★★★
Insect Control: ★★★★ Facilities: ★★★

Shaded by forests of pine and oak trees in the Ocean View area, Pine Haven Campground offers wooded sites, all which have full hookups or water and electric hookups. Pine Haven has two freshwater lakes—one for fishing and the other for swimming. The swimming lake is surrounded by a sandy beach. The fishing lake is stocked with bass, sunfish, and catfish. Pine Haven hosts mother-daughter and father-son fishing contests. Most of the activity centers—including the mini-golf course, pool, basketball and volleyball courts, game room, and swimming lake—are near the entrance at the north of Pine Haven. The camp store and deli/snack bar are also in this area. The fishing lake is near the center, and sites are located north and south of the lake. Water and electric sites at the southeast tip offer the most privacy, and they are not far from the lake.

Basics

Operated By: Private operator. **Open:** Apr. 1–Sept. 30. **Site Assignment:** Reservations accepted (4-night min. stay in July and Aug., 3-night min. stay on Memorial Dal and Labor Day weekends), walk-ins accepted. **Registration:** At campground office. **Fee:** $29–$33 (VISA, MC, AE, D). **Parking:** At site.

Facilities

Number of RV Sites: 625. **Number of Tent-Only Sites:** None. **Hookups:** Electric (20, 30, 50 amps), water, 400 full hookups. **Each Site:** Picnic table. **Dump Station:** Yes. **Laundry:** Yes. **Pay Phone:** Yes. **Rest Rooms and Showers:** Yes. **Fuel:** No. **Propane:** Yes. **Internal Roads:** Gravel and dirt, in good condition. **RV Service:** No. **Market:** Within 3 mi. **Restaurant:** Within 3 mi. **General Store:** Yes. **Vending:** Yes. **Playground:** Yes. **Other:** Fishing lake, swimming lake. **Activities:** Lake fishing and swimming, pedal boat rentals, rec hall, game room, mini-golf, shuffleboard, planned activities, volleyball, horseshoes, sports field. **Nearby Attractions:** Ocean City, Atlantic City, the Wildwoods, Cape May. **Additional Information:** New Jersey Office of Travel and Tourism, (800) JERSEY7, www.state.nj.us/travel.

Restrictions

Pets: On leash only. **Fires:** At site. **Alcoholic Beverages:** At site. **Vehicle Maximum Length:** 40 ft. **Other:** Rates apply for family of 4; additional guests are extra.

To Get There

From Hwy. 50, go 4.5 mi. south on US 9. Entrance is on the right.

OCEAN VIEW

Sea Grove Camping Resort

2665 Rt. 9, Ocean View 08230. T: (609) 624-3529 or (800) 432-6629; F: (609)-624-1435; www.seagroveresort.com; sgresort@aol.com.

RV ★★★★ Tent ★★★★

Beauty: ★★★★ Site Privacy: ★
Spaciousness: ★★ Quiet: ★★★★
Security: ★★★★ Cleanliness: ★★★★
Insect Control: ★★★★ Facilities: ★★★★

Though the beaches of Sea Isle City are a short drive away, and Ocean City is about 15 minutes to the north, sometimes a simple afternoon by the pool is what you want on a vacation. Unlike many of the campgrounds in the Ocean View/Sea Isle City area, Sea Grove does not have a private lake. Many campers head for Sea Isle City's beaches when they are not by the pool. Sea Grove's sites are wooded, but none accommodate pull-throughs. Sea Grove has one- and two-bedroom cabins and park models for rent if you choose to leave your RV or tent at home. If you decide to visit Cape May, a 20-minute drive to the south, hop aboard the Cape May–Lewes (DE) Ferry. The 16-mile, 70-minute journey across Delaware Bay leads to Lewes, which is not far from Rehoboth Beach.

Basics

Operated By: Private operator. **Open:** Apr. 1–Nov. 1. **Site Assignment:** Reservations accepted; 1-night deposit required, 3-night stay required on holiday weekends and June 22–Sept. 3; walk-ins accepted. **Registration:** At campground office. **Fee:** $20–$35 (VISA, MC). **Parking:** At site.

Facilities

Number of RV Sites: 182. **Number of Tent-Only Sites:** 8. **Hookups:** Electric (20, 30, 50 amps), water, 135 full hookups. **Each Site:** Picnic table. **Dump Station:** Yes. **Laundry:** Yes. **Pay Phone:** Yes. **Rest Rooms and Showers:** Yes. **Fuel:** No. **Propane:** Yes. **Internal Roads:** Gravel and paved, in good condition. **RV Service:** No. **Market:** Within 3 mi. **Restaurant:** Within 3 mi. **General Store:** Yes. **Vending:** Yes. **Playground:** Yes. **Other:** Cabin and park model rentals. **Activities:** Swimming, horseshoes, volleyball, rec hall, game room, planned activities, sports field. **Nearby Attractions:** Ocean City, Atlantic City, the Wildwoods, Cape May. **Additional Information:** New Jersey Office of Travel and Tourism, (800) JERSEY7, www.state.nj.us/travel.

Restrictions

Pets: On leash only. **Fires:** At site. **Alcoholic Beverages:** At site. **Vehicle Maximum Length:** 35 ft. **Other:** No camping motorcycles allowed.

To Get There

From CR 550, go 0.5 mi. north on US 9. Entrance is on the left.

PORT REPUBLIC

Thousand Trails–Chestnut Lake

631 Old New York Rd., Port Republic 08241. T: (609) 652-1005 or (800) 288-7245; F: (228) 497-8722; www.thousandtrails.com; member_services@1000trails.com.

RV ★★★★ Tent ★★★★

Beauty: ★★★★ Site Privacy: ★★★
Spaciousness: ★★★ Quiet: ★★★★
Security: ★★★★★ Cleanliness: ★★★★
Insect Control: ★★★★ Facilities: ★★★★

This Thousand Trails park is centered around pristine Chestnut Lake, located in Port Republic about 15 miles northwest of Atlantic City. Like Outdoor World parks, Thousand Trails properties are clean and well-maintained. And like most Thousand Trails parks, Chestnut Lake is in a rural location secluded from the hustle and bustle of Jersey Shore tourism. The campground accommodates 102 pull-throughs, and most sites are open. The lake is the focus of activity during warmer months. Chestnut Lake is about a 20-minute drive from Atlantic City's boardwalk, beaches, and casinos. Storybook Land—which features 50-plus buildings and displays depicting children's stories, live animals, rides, and a playground area —is also about 20 minutes away in Atlantic City. The Edwin B. Forsythe National Wildlife Refuge is only a 10-minute drive from the campground. This 40,000-acre refuge includes an eight-mile drive through wetlands and uplands where more than 200 species of birds may be observed.

Basics

Operated By: Thousand Trails. **Open:** May 1–Oct. 15. **Site Assignment:** Reservations and walk-ins accepted. **Registration:** At campground office. **Fee:** $20 per vehicle (VISA, MC, AE, D). **Parking:** At site.

Facilities

Number of RV Sites: 175. **Number of Tent-Only Sites:** 38. **Hookups:** Electric (30, 50 amps), water, 55 full hookups. **Each Site:** Grill and picnic table. **Dump Station:** Yes. **Laundry:** Yes. **Pay Phone:** Yes. **Rest Rooms and Showers:** Yes. **Fuel:** No. **Propane:** Yes. **Internal Roads:** Gravel and paved, in good condition. **RV Service:** No. **Market:** Within 8 mi. **Restaurant:** Within 6 mi. **General Store:** Yes. **Vending:** Yes. **Playground:** Yes. **Other:** Chestnut Lake. **Activities:** Swimming, canoeing, kayaking, fishing, mini-golf, basketball, shuffleboard, horseshoes, rec hall, game room. **Nearby Attractions:** Ocean City, Atlantic City, the Wildwoods, Cape May. **Additional Information:** New Jersey Office of Travel and Tourism, (800) JERSEY7, www.state.nj.us/travel.

Restrictions

Pets: On leash only. **Fires:** At site. **Alcoholic Beverages:** At site. **Vehicle Maximum Length:** None. **Other:** None.

To Get There

From Garden State Parkway, take Exit 48 and turn right onto US 9, follow US 9.25 mi., then go 0.5 mi. west on CR 575. Entrance is on the right.

SEA ISLE CITY

Outdoor World—Lake and Shore Campground

545 Corson Tavern Rd., Ocean View 08230. T: (800) 222-5557; www.campoutdoorworld.com; mbrsrvs@ptd.net.

RV ★★★★ Tent ★★★★

Beauty: ★★★★ Site Privacy: ★★★
Spaciousness: ★★★ Quiet: ★★★★
Security: ★★★★ Cleanliness: ★★★★
Insect Control: ★★★★ Facilities: ★★★★★

Central to Cape May, the Wildwoods, Ocean City, and Atlantic City, Outdoor World—Lake and Shore Campground is located outside of Ocean View near the Jersey Shore. Outdoor World campgrounds are typically clean and well-maintained, and this one is no different. All but 25 sites have full hookups. Recreational opportunities are plentiful here, with options like mini-golf, an indoor waterpark, outdoor pool, kiddie pool, whirlpool, and a 12-acre lake for fishing and swimming. Pedal boats are also available for rent. The campground has a full slate of special events throughout the year. Lake and Shore is about 10 minutes north of another Outdoor World campground, Sea Pines, which has similar recreational facilities and site features. Both are good bases for Jersey Shore vacations. Lake and Shore is a few minutes closer to Ocean City and Atlantic City, while Sea Pines is a few minutes closer to the Wildwoods and Cape May.

BASICS

Operated By: Outdoor World. **Open:** All year. **Site Assignment:** Reservations required; 2-week notice for the public, no advance notice required for Outdoor World members. **Registration:** At campground office. **Fee:** $30 (VISA, MC, AE, D). **Parking:** At designated area.

FACILITIES

Number of RV Sites: 426. **Number of Tent-Only Sites:** 25. **Hookups:** Electric (30, 50 amps), cable TV, phone, 426 full hookups. **Each Site:** Fire ring and picnic table. **Dump Station:** Yes. **Laundry:** Yes. **Pay Phone:** Yes. **Rest Rooms and Showers:** Yes. **Fuel:** No. **Propane:** Yes. **Internal Roads:** Paved and dirt, in good condition. **RV Service:** No. **Market:** Within 3 mi. **Restaurant:** Within 3 mi. **General Store:** Yes. **Vending:** Yes. **Playground:** Yes. **Other:** Private lake, indoor waterpark. **Activities:** Lake fishing and swimming, wading pool, whirlpool, canoeing, kayaking, pedal boat rentals, game room, rec hall, mini-golf, basketball, shuffleboard, planned activities, horseshoes, hiking trails, sports field, volleyball. **Nearby Attractions:** Ocean City, Atlantic City, the Wildwoods, Cape May. **Additional Information:** New Jersey Office of Travel and Tourism, (800) JERSEY7, www.state.nj.us/travel.

RESTRICTIONS

Pets: On leash only. **Fires:** At site. **Alcoholic Beverages:** At site, under control. **Vehicle Maximum Length:** None. **Other:** Pets may not be leftunattended.

TO GET THERE

From Garden State Parkway, take Exit 17 and go 0.25 mi. west on CR 625, 0.5 mi. north on US 9, 1 mi. west on CR 550, and 0.25 mi. north on Corson Tavern Rd. Look for posted sign.

SUSSEX

Beaver Hill Campground

P.O. Box 353, Sussex 07461. T: (800) 229-CAMP or (973) 827-0670; F: (973) 827-8957; www.beaverhill.com; beaverhill@nac.net.

RV ★★★★ Tent ★★★★

Beauty: ★★★★ Site Privacy: ★★
Spaciousness: ★★★ Quiet: ★★★★
Security: ★★★★ Cleanliness: ★★★★
Insect Control: ★★★★ Facilities: ★★★★

Located in the Skylands region of northern New Jersey, where the Kittatiny Mountains offer a contrast to the Jersey Shore beaches, Beaver Hill Campground has shaded sites amid well-manicured lawns. If you are fortunate, you will arrive at Beaver Hill during the Hawaiian Luau weekend when campers dance Hawaiian style and partake in a pig roast. Beaver Hill is near several interesting family-oriented attractions, such as Space Farms Zoo and Museum, a combination of exotic animals and historical museums; Sterling Hill Mine, where tours of a former zinc mine are offered; Mountain Creek, a waterpark; and Wild West City, which recreates a 19th-century town in—you guessed it—the Wild West. The campground is also a short drive from Skylands Park, home of the New Jersey Cardinals, the Single-A affiliate of the St. Louis Cardinals.

BASICS

Operated By: Private operator. **Open:** May 1–Nov. 15. **Site Assignment:** Reservations accepted (3-day min. stay on holiday weekends). **Registration:** At log cabin. **Fee:** $23–$28 (VISA, MC, D). **Parking:** At site.

FACILITIES

Number of RV Sites: 135. **Number of Tent-Only Sites:** None. **Hookups:** Electric (20, 30 amps), phone, water, 63 full hookups. **Each Site:** Fire ring and picnic table. **Dump Station:** Yes. **Laundry:** Yes. **Pay Phone:** Yes. **Rest Rooms and Showers:** Yes. **Fuel:** No. **Propane:** Yes. **Internal Roads:** Paved and dirt, in good condition. **RV Service:** No. **Market:** Within 3 mi. **Restaurant:** Within 1 mi. **General Store:** Yes. **Vending:** No. **Playground:** Yes. **Other:** RV rentals, fishing pond. **Activities:** Pond fishing, game room, rec hall, basketball, sports field, mini-golf, planned activities on weekends, hiking trails, badminton. **Nearby Attractions:** Delaware Water Gap National Recreation Area, Village of Waterloo, Sterling Hill Mine, Wild West City, Kittatiny Valley State Park, Lakota Wolf Preserve, Land of Make Believe, Space Farms Zoo and Museum, Great Swamp National Wildlife Refuge. **Additional Information:** Skylands Tourism Council of New Jersey, (800) 4 SKYLAND, www.state.nj.us/travel.

RESTRICTIONS

Pets: On leash only, $1 extra per night. **Fires:** At site. **Alcoholic Beverages:** At site. **Vehicle Maximum Length:** 40 ft. **Other:** Fires and pets may not be left unattended.

TO GET THERE

From CR 565, go 3 mi. south on Hwy. 23, 1 mi. south on Hwy. 94, 2 mi. west on Beaver Spring Run Rd., and 0.5 mi. south on Big Spring Rd. Entrance is on the left.

SUSSEX

Pleasant Acres Farm Campground

61 DeWitt Rd., Sussex 07461. T: (800) 722-4166; F: (973) 702-1551; www.pleasantacres.com; info@pleasantacres.com.

RV ★★★★★ Tent n/a

Beauty: ★★★★★ Site Privacy: ★★★
Spaciousness: ★★★★ Quiet: ★★★★
Security: ★★★★★ Cleanliness: ★★★★
Insect Control: ★★★★ Facilities: ★★★★★

Guests at Pleasant Acres Farm Campground typically do not make the rounds to the many nearby attractions; they are too busy enjoying the campground itself. A working farm where campers can pet baby animals, participate in pig chases and cow milking, and take a horse-drawn hayride around the lush hills, Pleasant Acres is one of our favorite places in the mid-Atlantic. Sites are open and shaded; no tents are permitted, except for RV campers who want to pitch a tent on their site. Meals, entertainment, and recreation are included in the basic campsite price here. Though the farm attractions are a big draw, Pleasant Acres also has an Olympic-sized swimming pool, a kiddie pool, a mini-golf course, a three-acre fishing lake, basketball and volleyball courts, and several nature trails in the mountains. Scheduled free meals are offered on weekdays in July and Aug. You can work up an appetite shearing sheep and chasing pigs.

BASICS

Operated By: Richard Denman. **Open:** All year. **Site Assignment:** Reservations recommended ($20 deposit required, 3-night min. stay required on holiday weekends), walk-ins accepted. **Registration:** At campground office. **Fee:** $32 (VISA, MC, D). **Parking:** At site.

FACILITIES

Number of RV Sites: 300. **Number of Tent-Only Sites:** None. **Hookups:** Electric (20, 30, 50 amps), phone, water, 289 full hookups. **Each Site:** Fire ring and picnic table. **Dump Station:** Yes. **Laundry:** Yes. **Pay Phone:** Yes. **Rest Rooms and Showers:** Yes. **Fuel:** No. **Propane:** Yes. **Internal Roads:** Paved, in good condition. **RV Service:** Yes. **Market:** Within 4 mi. **Restaurant:** Within 4 mi. **General Store:** Yes. **Vending:** Yes. **Playground:** Yes. **Other:** Working farm, fishing pond. **Activities:** Swimming, wading pool, whirlpool, fishing, mini-golf, basketball, planned activities, movies, sports field, volleyball, horseshoes, hiking trails, pig chases, cow milking, hiking trails. **Nearby Attractions:** Delaware Water Gap National Recreation Area, Village of Waterloo, Sterling Hill Mine, Wild West City, Kittatiny Valley State Park, Lakota Wolf Preserve, Land of Make Believe, Space Farms Zoo and Museum, Great Swamp National Wildlife Refuge. **Additional Information:** Skylands Tourism

Council of New Jersey, (800) 4SKYLAND, www.state.nj.us/travel.

RESTRICTIONS

Pets: On leash only. **Fires:** At site. **Alcoholic Beverages:** At site. **Vehicle Maximum Length:** 40 ft. **Other:** No tents are permitted, though RV campers can use a tent on their site.

TO GET THERE

From Hwy. 284, go 5 mi. north on Hwy. 23 and 1 mi. east on DeWitt Rd. Entrance is on the right.

SWAINTON

Outdoor World— Sea Pines Campground

P.O. Box 1535 Rte. 9, Swainton 08210. T: (609) 465-4517 or (800) 222-5557; F: (609) 465-2369; www.campoutdoorworld.com; mbrsrvs@ptd.net.

RV ★★★★ Tent ★★★★

Beauty: ★★★★★ Site Privacy: ★★
Spaciousness: ★★ Quiet: ★★★★
Security: ★★★★ Cleanliness: ★★★★
Insect Control: ★★★★ Facilities: ★★★★★

Located south of Outdoor World's Lake and Shore Campground near Sea Isle City, Outdoor World—Sea Pines Campground features wooded sites, 300 of which have full hookups. There are no pull-through sites. Like at most Outdoor World campgrounds, there are a wide assortment of recreational opportunities. Campers can fish and kayak in the private lake, take a dip in the swimming pool, and play mini-golf. Sea Pines does not have an indoor waterpark as Lake and Shore does. With the glitz of Atlantic City, the tradition of Ocean City, and the Victorian charm of Cape May, the Wildwoods are sometimes forgotten by travelers making vacation plans to the Jersey Shore. However, Wildwood's two-mile-long boardwalk is scenic and inviting, as is the five-mile-long beach it shares with neighboring North Wildwood and Wildwood Crest.

BASICS

Operated By: Outdoor World. **Open:** May 19–Sept. 19. **Site Assignment:** Reservations and walk-ins accepted. **Registration:** At campground office. **Fee:** $25 per family (VISA, MC, AE, D). **Parking:** At site.

FACILITIES

Number of RV Sites: 541. **Number of Tent-Only Sites:** 8. **Hookups:** Electric (30, 50 amps), water, 300 full hookups. **Each Site:** Fire ring and picnic table. **Dump Station:** Yes. **Laundry:** Yes. **Pay Phone:** Yes. **Rest Rooms and Showers:** Yes. **Fuel:** No. **Propane:** Yes. **Internal Roads:** Gravel and dirt, in good condition. **RV Service:** No. **Market:** Within 3 mi. **Restaurant:** Within 3 mi. **General Store:** Yes. **Vending:** Yes. **Playground:** Yes. **Other:** Private lake. **Activities:** Swimming, lake fishing, wading pool, canoeing, kayak, boat rentals, rec hall, game room, mini-golf, basketball, shuffleboard, planned activites, movies, sports field, horseshoes, volleyball. **Nearby Attractions:** Wildwoods boardwalk and beaches, Ocean City, Cape May, Cape May County Park and Zoo, Victorian Cape May tours, Historic Cold Spring Village, Cape May–Lewes (DE) Ferry, Atlantic City. **Additional Information:** New Jersey Office of Travel and Tourism, (800) JERSEY7, www.state.nj.us/travel.

RESTRICTIONS

Pets: On leash only. **Fires:** At site. **Alcoholic Beverages:** At site. **Vehicle Maximum Length:** 40 ft. **Other:** None.

TO GET THERE

From Garden State Parkway, take Exit 13 and go 0.25 mi. west on CR 601 and 0.25 mi. south on US 9. Entrance is on the right.

TUCKERTON

Atlantic City North Family Campground

P.O. Box 242 Stage Rd., Tuckerton 08087. T: (609) 296-9163 or (888) 229-9776; www.members.aol.com/campacn.contact.htm; campacn@aol.com.

RV ★★★★ Tent ★★★★

Beauty: ★★★★ Site Privacy: ★★
Spaciousness: ★★ Quiet: ★★★★
Security: ★★★★ Cleanliness: ★★★★
Insect Control: ★★★★ Facilities: ★★★★

Set in the Pine Barrens of New Jersey, 15 minutes west of Long Beach Island and a half-hour north of Atlantic City, Atlantic City North Family Campground is ideal for visitors who want to experience both sides of the Jersey Shore. The campground provides free passes to Long Beach Island in season and a free van service to Atlantic City to campers who stay at least two nights. For dog owners, a dog-walking path winds around the outskirts of the campground. The swimming pool and the main building—which houses the camp store, rec hall, lounge, rest rooms, showers, laundry room, and snack bar—are located west of campground's main entrance. Sites surround the pool and main building in circular rows. Other site clustes are located east of the main entrance. These sites are more spacious and are away from the activity centers. Tent sites are located at the far western end, beyond the circular rows of RV sites that surround the pool and main building.

BASICS

Operated By: Private operator. **Open:** All year. **Site Assignment:** Reservations accepted (2-night min. stay in July and Aug.), walk-ins accepted. **Registration:** At campground office. **Fee:** $25–$35 (VISA, MC, D). **Parking:** At site.

FACILITIES

Number of RV Sites: 119. **Number of Tent-Only Sites:** 33. **Hookups:** Electric (30, 50 amps), water, phone, 65 full hookups. **Each Site:** Fire ring and picnic table. **Dump Station:** Yes. **Laundry:** Yes. **Pay Phone:** Yes. **Rest Rooms and Showers:** Yes. **Fuel:** No. **Propane:** Yes. **Internal Roads:** Gravel, in good condition. **RV Service:** No. **Market:** Within 4 mi. **Restaurant:** Within 4 mi. **General Store:** Yes. **Vending:** Yes. **Playground:** Yes. **Other:** Cabin rentals. **Activities:** Swimming, wading pool, mini-golf, basketball, rec hall, game room, shuffleboard, planned activities, movies, horseshoes, badminton, hiking trails, volleyball. **Nearby Attractions:** Long Beach Island; Atlantic City casinos, boardwalk, and beach. **Additional Information:** Atlantic City Convention and Visitors Authority, (800) ACVISIT, www.atlanticcitynj.com.

RESTRICTIONS

Pets: On leash only. **Fires:** At site. **Alcoholic Beverages:** At site. **Vehicle Maximum Length:** 40 ft. **Other:** Max. of 1 camping unit and 6 people per campsite.

TO GET THERE

From Garden State Parkway, take Exit 58 and go about 50 ft. east on CR 539, 4 mi. south on Poormans Parkway, and 0.5 mi. east on Stage Rd. Entrance is on the right.

WEST CAPE MAY

The Depot Travel Park

800 Broadway, West Cape May 08204. T: (609) 884-7075; F: (609) 884-7075.

RV ★★★★ Tent ★★★★

Beauty: ★★ Site Privacy: ★
Spaciousness: ★★ Quiet: ★★
Security: ★★★★ Cleanliness: ★★★★
Insect Control: ★★★★ Facilities: ★★★★

If you are looking for a campground with loads of swimming pools, sports courts, clubhouses, and private lakes, the Depot Travel Park in West Cape May is not for you. This campground has little on-site recreation, but it is located just blocks from Cape May's beaches, shops, and historic district. Sunbathing, ocean swimming, fishing, sightseeing boats, seafood restaurants, antique and gift shops, and the boardwalk are all a few minutes away on foot. Cape May Beach is one mile away, and the Washington Street Victorian Mall, with three blocks of charming shops and sidewalk cafes, is within a few blocks of the Depot. Sites are open and offer little privacy; a cluster of sites surrounds a small wooded area at the northern end of the campground.

BASICS

Operated By: Glen Reeve. **Open:** May 1–Sept. 30. **Site Assignment:** Reservations accepted (full payment due upon check-in), walk-ins accepted. **Registration:** At campground office. **Fee:** $24 (no credit cards accepted). **Parking:** At site.

FACILITIES

Number of RV Sites: 135. **Number of Tent-Only Sites:** None. **Hookups:** Electric (20, 30 amps), water. **Each Site:** Picnic table. **Dump Station:** Yes. **Laundry:** No. **Pay Phone:** Yes. **Rest Rooms and Showers:** Yes. **Fuel:** No. **Propane:** Yes. **Internal Roads:** Paved, in good condition. **RV Service:** No. **Market:** Within 0.25 mi. **Restaurant:** Within 0.25 mi. **General Store:** No. **Vending:** No. **Playground:** Yes. **Other:** Located near the beach and Victorian Cape May. **Activities:** Horseshoes. **Nearby Attractions:** Victorian Cape May tours, Cape May beaches, Cape May–Lewes (DE) Ferry, Historic Cold Spring Village, Cape May County Park and Zoo. **Additional Information:** Cape May Chamber of Commerce, (609) 884-5508, www.capemaychamber.com.

RESTRICTIONS

Pets: On leash only. **Fires:** At site. **Alcoholic Beverages:** No alcohol permitted. **Vehicle Maximum Length:** None. **Other:** No cleaning of fish permitted on campground premises, no washing of vehicles allowed, electric heaters and electric water heaters not allowed.

TO GET THERE

From Hwy. 109, go 0.2 mi. west on US 9 and 2 mi. south on Seashore Rd. Entrance is on the right.

WEST CREEK

Sea Pirate Campground

P.O. Box 271 Rte. 9, West Creek 08092. T: (800) 822-CAMP; F: (609) 296-8385; www.seapiratecamp.com; seapiratecamp@shorenetworks.com.

RV ★★★★ Tent ★★★★

Beauty: ★★★★ Site Privacy: ★★★
Spaciousness: ★★★★ Quiet: ★★★★
Security: ★★★★★ Cleanliness: ★★★★
Insect Control: ★★★★ Facilities: ★★★★

Located eight miles west of Long Beach Island, and about a half-hour north of Atlantic City near West Creek, Sea Pirate Campground definitely caters to families. The park has a fishing pond stocked with bass, basketball and volleyball courts, and an assortment of scheduled activities, including ceramics, arts and crafts, and hayrides. Campers can rent a 14- or 16-foot John boat to explore the creek, which winds through a natural estuary leading into Little Egg Harbor Bay. Most of the activity centers—including the pool, basketball court, and softball field—are located near the entrance. A building housing the arcade, game room, and store is near the center. Sites are located across the street from the ice cream parlor, snack bar, and activity centers, as well as all around the arcade building. Wooded sites near the fishing pond at the northwestern tip of the campground are recommended for campers who crave solitude.

BASICS

Operated By: Private operator. **Open:** May 1–Oct. 1. **Site Assignment:** Reservations accepted (4-night min. stay June 26–Labor Day), walk-ins accepted. **Registration:** At campground office. **Fee:** $26–$35 (VISA, MC). **Parking:** At site.

FACILITIES

Number of RV Sites: 193. **Number of Tent-Only Sites:** 6. **Hookups:** Electric (20, 30, 50 amps), cable TV, phone, water, 84 full hookups. **Each Site:** Fire ring and picnic table. **Dump Station:** Yes. **Laundry:** Yes. **Pay Phone:** Yes. **Rest Rooms and Showers:** Yes. **Fuel:** No. **Propane:** Yes. **Internal Roads:** Gravel, in good condition. **RV Service:** No. **Market:** Within 5 mi. **Restaurant:** Within 5 mi. **General Store:** Yes. **Vending:** No. **Playground:** Yes. **Other:** RV and cabin rentals, fishing pond. **Activities:** Swimming, boating, canoeing, kayaking, boat rentals, rec hall, game room, fishing, basketball, planned activities, movies, sports field, volleyball, horseshoes. **Nearby Attractions:** Long Beach Island; Atlantic City casinos, boardwalk, and beaches. **Additional Information:** Atlantic City Convention and Visitors Authority, (800) ACVISIT, www.atlanticcitynj.com.

RESTRICTIONS

Pets: On leash only. **Fires:** At site. **Alcoholic Beverages:** No alcohol permitted. **Vehicle Maximum Length:** 40 ft. **Other:** Pets and fires may not be left unattended.

TO GET THERE

From Hwy. 72, go 5 mi. south on US 9. Entrance is on the left.

New Mexico

Lucky are those about to visit New Mexico for the first time. The epitome of the Southwest, New Mexico presents a striking, sun-baked beauty that peeks out in a bloom of purple flowers in the desert, in the shocking red of dried chilies hanging from a brown adobe house, or in the reds, yellows, and blacks of Indian blankets on sale in the marketplace. Just look at Georgia O'Keefe's life work for a glimpse into this living gallery. You practically expect to see cattle skulls bleaching by the highway as you pass.

But it's not all desert. **Taos** hosts world-class skiing, the railroad in **Chama** winds through sheer mountains, and the forest around **Gila National Monument** looks like a lost slice of Colorado. The extremes of Mother Nature's handiwork can be found in New Mexico—**Carlsbad Caverns, White Sands, Capulin Volcano National Monument**—as well as some very impressive man-made creations—the **Very Large Assembly** radio telescope at **Datil,** the **Gila Cliff Dwellings,** and of course, the (perhaps *space*-man-made) attractions in **Roswell.** RVers will be happy to note that these attractions are generally served by well-maintained roads, and camping opportunities abound.

Camping in New Mexico is a pleasure. Prices are much more reasonable than at many resorts in Arizona, and the bounty of attractions makes an exciting destination possible at the end of practically every travel day. In addition to the numerous places to see within the state, many visitors use New Mexico as a stepping stone to the country for which it was named. **Las Cruces** is a convenient stop on the way down I-25 toward **El Paso** and points more foreign. But you don't need to travel to a foreign country to find a meaningful travel experience. Whether you stay for a week or a winter, New Mexico will surprise you like those chilies in your green sauce.

The following facilities accept payment in checks or cash only:

- Bluewater Lake State Park, Prewitt
- Bosque Birdwatcher's RV Park, San Antonio
- Buckhorn RV Park, Buckhorn
- Capulin RV Park, Capulin
- Casas Adobes RV Park, Mimbres
- Ideal RV Park, Clovis
- Manzano's RV Park, Silver City
- Ramblin' Rose RV Park, Santa Rosa
- Rodeo RV Park, Rodeo
- Summerlan RV Park, Raton
- Trail's End RV Park, Jemez Springs
- Ute Lake State Park, Logan
- Vado RV Park, Vado
- Wagon Wheel RV Park, Deming
- Wagon Wheel RV Park, Portales
- West Lake RV Park, Eagle Nest

The following facilities feature 20 sites or fewer:

- Buckhorn RV Park, Buckhorn
- Casas Adobes RV Park, Mimbres
- Coyote Creek State Park, Angelfire
- Manzano Mountains State Park, Mountainair
- Rodeo RV Park, Rodeo
- Trail's End RV Park, Jemez Springs

Campground Profiles

ABIQUIU

Riana Campground

Abiquiu Lake Project Office P.O. Box 290, Abiquiu 87510. T: (505) 685-4371; F: (505) 685-4647; www.spa.usace.army.mil/abiquiu; cespa-od-ab@spa02.usace.army.mil.

 ★★★★ ★★★★★

Beauty: ★★★★★ Site Privacy: ★★★★

Spaciousness: ★★★★ Quiet: ★★★★★

Security: ★★★★ Cleanliness: ★★★★

Insect Control: ★★★★ Facilities: ★★

Laid out in several loops, Riana offers sites above the reservoir—some with excellent views. Sites 1–15 are mostly 60–75-foot back-ins with electric hookups. These sites have extra space for a boat or second vehicle. Sites 9 and 10 are pull-throughs (actually "pull-alongsides") that are 90 feet in length. Sites 13 and 15 have the best views, but are just above the playground. Sites 16–30 are located in a fenced-in parking area. Each site is 36 × 30 feet with a camping area beside. The fences make it difficult for larger rigs to back into some of these sites (such as 25–30). Sites 16 and 17 are pull-throughs similar to 9 and 10. Sites 18–20 have the best views. The remaining sites are primitive or walk-in sites. The RV sites are 45–55-foot back-ins with wonderful views of the reservoir. Sites 40–54 are walk-in tent sites inside a fenced-in area. Each site has a 12 × 12-foot crushed gravel pad for a tent. Sites 47–50 have nice desert views. There are porta-potties for tenters' use in this area. Riana is a pretty (but rather primitive) campground that offers lake recreation and fun for the entire family.

Basics

Operated By: US Army Corps of Engineers. **Open:** All year. **Site Assignment:** First come, first served; reservations made through ReserveAmerica (www.reserveusa.com, (877) 444-6777). **Registration:** At gate; camp host will come around to sites in morning in case of late arrivals. **Fee:** $17 (water, electric), primitive $10, walk-in tent $5; checks, V, MC, AE, D. **Parking:** At site, overflow parking.

Facilities

Number of RV Sites: 39. **Number of Tent-Only Sites:** 15. **Hookups:** Electric (30, 50 amp). **Each Site:** Covered picnic table, grill, lantern pole. **Dump Station:** Yes. **Laundry:** No. **Pay Phone:** Yes. **Rest Rooms and Showers:** Yes. **Fuel:** No. **Propane:** No. **Internal Roads:** Paved. **RV Service:** No. **Market:** 8 mi. south to Abiquiu. **Restaurant:** 8 mi. south to Abiquiu. **General Store:** No. **Vending:** No. **Swimming:** Yes (reservoir). **Playground:** Yes. **Other:** Picnic area. **Activities:** Fishing, boating, swimming, hiking. **Nearby Attractions:** Ghost Ranch Conference Center, Georgia O'Keefe house in Abiquiu. **Additional Information:** Española Chamber of Commerce, (505) 753-2831.

Restrictions

Pets: On leash, cleaned up after. **Fires:** In grills. **Alcoholic Beverages:** At sites. **Vehicle Maximum Length:** None.

To Get There

From the junction of Hwy. 84 and Hwy. 96 (about 7 mi. north of town), turn west onto Hwy. 96 and go 1.3 mi. Turn right at the sign into the entrance.

ALAMOGORDO

Alamogordo KOA

412-24th St., Alamogordo 88310. T: (800) KOA-3992 or (505) 437-3003; F: (505) 437-1493.

RV ★★★★★ Tent ★★★

Beauty: ★★★★	Site Privacy: ★★★★★
Spaciousness: ★★★★	Quiet: ★★★★
Security: ★★★★	Cleanliness: ★★★★
Insect Control: ★★★★	Facilities: ★★★★★

This campground boasts beautiful landscaping as well as mountain vistas to the east (especially sites 48–63). A small section of ratty fencing to the south that conceals a mobile-home park does insult the view, but can be mostly ignored. Pull-throughs are level and long (60 × 30 feet), while back-ins are a spacious 32 × 30 feet. The smaller back-ins close to the pool (65–67) have nice grass and trees and are still pleasant spots to camp. Tent sites are away from the RV sites, along the southwest side of the office on a strip of grass with plenty of tree coverage. However, parking is directly behind the sites, where a row of RVs in storage compete for space. The laundry facility is large, clean, and modern, with lots of machines, loads of space, and a raft of magazines. Rest rooms are also large, clean, well lit, and tastefully decorated. Playground facilities are well maintained and safe. Overall, this is a great destination in a great location for visiting the White Sands National Monument, and even Carlsbad Caverns and Mexico.

Basics

Operated By: Ken and Judy Bonnell. **Open:** All year. **Site Assignment:** Upon registration; credit card required for reservation, must cancel within 24 hours for refund. **Registration:** In office; late arrivals use drop box. **Fee:** RV up to $30 (depending on hookups), tent $18. **Parking:** At site.

Facilities

Number of RV Sites: 65. **Number of Tent-Only Sites:** 10. **Hookups:** Water, sewer, electric (15, 30, 50 amp), cable. **Each Site:** Cement table, cement privacy wall, tree, lamp, grill. **Dump Station:** Yes. **Laundry:** Yes. **Pay Phone:** Yes. **Rest Rooms and Showers:** Yes. **Fuel:** No. **Propane:** Yes. **Internal Roads:** Paved. **RV Service:** No. **Market:** 1 mi. **Restaurant:** 2 blocks. **General Store:** Yes. **Vending:** No. **Swimming:** Pool. **Playground:** Yes. **Other:** 2 cabins, pool open May 15–Sept. 15. **Activities:** Swimming. **Nearby Attractions:** White Sands National Monument, White Sands Missle Range/Trinity site, Texas, Mexico. **Additional Information:** Alamogordo Chamber of Commerce, (800) 826-0294, (505) 437-6120.

Restrictions

Pets: On leash. **Fires:** None. **Alcoholic Beverages:** At sites. **Vehicle Maximum Length:** None.

To Get There

From Hwy. 54/70 (White Sands Blvd.), turn east onto 24th St. in town. Go 0.2 mi. on 24th St., then turn right at the sign into the entrance. The office lies straight ahead.

ALBUQUERQUE

Albuquerque Central KOA

12400 Skyline Rd. Northeast, Albuquerque 87123. T: (505) 296-2729; F: (505) 296-3354; www.koa.com; albuquerque@koa.net.

RV ★★★★ Tent ★★★

Beauty: ★★★	Site Privacy: ★★★
Spaciousness: ★★★	Quiet: ★★★
Security: ★★★★	Cleanliness: ★★★★★
Insect Control: ★★★★	Facilities: ★★★★★

This is an enormous campground with rows and rows of RV sites. Sites 1–15 are 35-foot sites that back to a fence and residential area. D row, which contains the best sites (28–44), is in the middle of the campground, away from the road and the highway on the other side. Sites 33–36 are close to the rest rooms, and 35 is well shaded. The rows containing sites 45–74 are in the second-best area. West of this area is a sea of RVs: five rows of RV sites (81–169) packed in together. Sites 81–88, along the southwest fence, are 60-foot back-ins. Sites 98–148 are 70 × 33-foot pull-throughs—large enough for any rig, but placed like dozens of pawns on a chessboard. Sites 149–169 are 30-foot back-ins along the west wall that back to apartments close by. End sites on the north side (113 and 130) are close to both the pet run and the highway, and are therefore less desirable. The "Tent Village" is a fenced-in dirt area with one shade tree. While it might work out if a large group were camping together, it feels cramped for campers who do not know each other. There are, in fact, two tenting areas, one of which has a shaded bench and table per tent site, and one that does not. Neither is particularly roomy, and campers may feel hemmed in by the fencing. This is a gigantic campground, and one may feel somewhat like an anonymous log moving through a sawmill. The facilities, however, are clean and comfortable, and the campground offers a safe and comfortable (if crowded) environment.

Basics

Operated By: Frank De Turo. **Open:** All year. **Site Assignment:** Upon registration; credit card required for reservation, 24-hours cancellation policy. **Registration:** In office; late arrivals use drop box. **Fee:** RV $39 (full, 50 amp), $37 (full, 30 amp), $34 (water, electric); tent $26; V, MC, AE, D. **Parking:** At site.

Facilities

Number of RV Sites: 206. **Number of Tent-Only Sites:** 25. **Hookups:** Water, sewer, electric (30, 50 amp). **Each Site:** Picnic table. **Dump Station:** Yes. **Laundry:** Yes. **Pay Phone:** Yes. **Rest Rooms and Showers:** Yes. **Fuel:** No. **Propane:** Yes. **Internal Roads:** Paved. **RV Service:** Mobile. **Market:** 0.25 mi. north. **Restaurant:** 0.25 mi. north. **General Store:** Yes. **Vending:** Yes. **Swimming:** Pool. **Playground:** Yes. **Other:** Cabin, modem, 1 phone site, rec hall, mini-golf, video games, RV rentals. **Activities:** Swimming, golf. **Nearby Attractions:** Balloon Fiesta (first Sun. in Oct.). **Additional Information:** Albuquerque Chamber of Commerce, (505) 764-3700.

Restrictions

Pets: On leash, cleaned up after. **Fires:** In grills. **Alcoholic Beverages:** At sites. **Vehicle Maximum Length:** None.

To Get There

From Hwy. I-40 (Exit 166), turn south onto Juan Tabo Blvd. and go 0.25 mi. Turn left onto Skyline Rd. and go 0.35 mi. Turn left at the sign into the entrance.

ANGEL FIRE

Sierra Bonita Cabins and RV Park

P.O. Box 963, Angel Fire 87710. T: (800) 942-1556 or (505) 387-5508; www.sierrabonita.com; sierrabonita@bigfoot.com.

RV ★★★★ Tent ★★★★

Beauty: ★★★★★	Site Privacy: ★★★
Spaciousness: ★★★	Quiet: ★★★★
Security: ★★★★	Cleanliness: ★★★★★
Insect Control: ★★★★	Facilities: ★★★

This park consists of one strip of open-ended back-ins. The open field in which these sites are located allows for any size of rig. Most sites are 22 feet wide and back to the road about 50 feet away. Site 1, in the northwest corner, is closest to the bathhouse. Site 11 in the southwest corner seems a little cramped (there is a fence on one side). The park is located in a valley, which means that sunrise is slightly later and sunset slightly earlier—this may make for a chilly morning or evening. The location is absolutely gorgeous, with forested hills on all sides. The park abuts a fishing area that guests may use. The showers are individual unisex units that are very clean and comfortable. The rest rooms are also individual units, and likewise very clean. This park is much more secluded than the RV park in town, although it requires longer drive to get to. However, the drive is absolutely worth the extra effort, and this is a campground that many people return to year after year.

Basics

Operated By: Dale Powell. **Open:** May 15–Oct. 15. **Site Assignment:** First come, first served; credit card required for reservation, 1 week cancellation policy. **Registration:** In office; late arrivals select available site and pay in the morning. **Fee:** $13 (water, electric); checks, V, MC, D. **Parking:** At site.

Facilities

Number of RV Sites: 11. **Number of Tent-Only Sites:** 0. **Hookups:** Water, electric (20, 30 amp). **Each Site:** Picnic table, fire pit. **Dump Station:** Yes. **Laundry:** Yes. **Pay Phone:** Yes. **Rest Rooms and Showers:** Yes. **Fuel:** No. **Propane:** No. **Internal Roads:** Dirt. **RV Service:** No. **Market:** 17 mi. north or south. **Restaurant:** 17 mi. north or south. **General Store:** Yes. **Vending:** No. **Swimming:** No. **Playground:** No. **Other:** Cabins, group shelter. **Activities:** Fishing, scenic drives through Coyote Creek Canyon. **Nearby Attractions:** Harold Brock fishing area, Coyote Creek State Park. **Additional Information:** New Mexico State Parks Division, (888) NM-PARKS.

Restrictions

Pets: On leash, cleaned up after. **Fires:** In grills. **Alcoholic Beverages:** At sites, not in group shelter. **Vehicle Maximum Length:** None.

To Get There

From the junction of Hwy. 64 and Hwy. 434, turn south onto Hwy. 434 and go 10.8 mi. Turn right at the junction with Hwy. 120 to stay on Hwy. 434 and go a further 8.2 mi. The office is on the right, up a flight of stairs.

ARTESIA

Artesia RV Park

201 West Hermosa Dr., Artesia 88210. T: (505) 746-6184; www.artesiarv.com; artesiarv@swcinternet.net.

RV: ★★★★ Tent: ★★★

Beauty: ★★ Site Privacy: ★★★★★
Spaciousness: ★★★★★ Quiet: ★★★★
Security: ★★★★★ Cleanliness: ★★★★★
Insect Control: ★★★★ Facilities: ★★★

This is a rather simple but comfortable campground with open gravel spaces divided into undefined rows. Sites 1–5 to the northwest average 45 × 34 feet. Sites 6–13 (in two rows) are also 45 feet in length. Site 13 is located against a shed, which makes it less desirable, but 10 has a trellis with plants growing up it, and 9 and 12 have trees. (The trees that dot the park are not large enough to provide shade, but add to the overall attractiveness.) Sites B1–10 and A1–10 in the middle of the park are doubles about 75 feet long but only 12 feet wide. End sites A6 and B10 are the widest (30 feet), since they do not share a site. Site 14 in the southwest corner is adjacent to a wooden storage shed, and is thus less desirable. Sites 16–21 along the southern edge are for long-term residents. The tent area is a grassy strip to the east of the RV sites. While there are a few covered tables and two grills, it is obvious that this park is more RV- than tent-oriented. The horseshoes at one end of the tent area could make for a rude awakening to an unlucky tent camper on that side. The rest rooms and showers are wonderfully clean and extremely spacious. This is a park that RVers will enjoy thoroughly, although tenters may wish to move on.

Basics

Operated By: Ken, Wayne, and Mary Floyd. **Open:** All year. **Site Assignment:** Upon registration; verbal reservations OK. **Registration:** In office; late arrivals use drop box. **Fee:** RV $18 (full), tent $15; checks, V, MC. **Parking:** At site.

Facilities

Number of RV Sites: 42. **Number of Tent-Only Sites:** 10. **Hookups:** Water, sewer, electric (30, 50 amp), cable, phone. **Dump Station:** Yes. **Laundry:** Yes. **Pay Phone:** Yes. **Rest Rooms and Showers:** Yes. **Fuel:** No. **Propane:** No. **Internal Roads:** Gravel. **RV Service:** No. **Market:** 3 mi. west. **Restaurant:** 0.25 mi. south. **General Store:** No. **Vending:** No. **Swimming:** No. **Playground:** No. **Other:** Modem, pet walk. **Activities:** Fishing, boating, swimming, hiking, tours to Carlsbad Caverns, horseshoes. **Nearby Attractions:** Brantly Lake State Park, Carlsbad Caverns, Roswell. **Additional Information:** Artesia Chamber of Commerce, (505) 746-2744.

Restrictions

Pets: On leash, cleaned up after. **Fires:** In grills. **Alcoholic Beverages:** At sites. **Vehicle Maximum Length:** 40 ft.

To Get There

From the junction of Hwy. 82 and Hwy. 285, turn south onto Hwy. 285 and go 1 mi. to Hermosa Drive. Turn right onto Hermosa Dr. and go 0.1 mi. Turn left at the sign into the entrance.

AZTEC

Aztec Ruins RV Park

312 Ruins Rd., Aztec 87410. T: (505) 334-3160; F: (505) 334-3160; rrrv@outbounds.net.

RV: ★★ Tent: ★★★

Beauty: ★★★ Site Privacy: ★★★
Spaciousness: ★★★ Quiet: ★★★★
Security: ★★★★ Cleanliness: ★★★
Insect Control: ★★★ Facilities: ★

Like many RV parks in this area, Aztek Ruins does not offer many services: there are no rest rooms, no laundry, no phone. In fact, there is not much to this park than a place to spend a night. However, the trees around the park (and the few inside), as well as the grassy sites, make it slightly nicer than the RV parks in the neighboring towns of Farmington and Kirtland. (This RV park abuts a trailer park to the north, which seems quiet enough and should not pose a problem to RVers.) As an added bonus, the pull-through sites are 85 feet long, with a possibility of sticking out even further, since the internal road is so wide. Tenters have it a little better. The tent sites are on an "island" by the river that has loads of trees, grass, and other vegetation. (Be sure to take the hill down into the tenting area slowly—it's steep.) The tenting experience would benefit from rest rooms and showers, but otherwise the park is a wild, comfortable place to tent. (Tenters in need of a potty might consider the Aztec Public Library at 201 West Chaco St.)

Basics

Operated By: Dave Hare. **Open:** All year. **Site Assignment:** Depending on availability. **Registration:** In office; late arrivals knock on door of manager. **Fee:** RV $15, tent $6. **Parking:** At site.

Facilities

Number of RV Sites: 24. **Number of Tent-Only Sites:** 5. **Hookups:** Water, sewer, electric (30, 50 amp). **Dump Station:** Yes. **Laundry:** No. **Pay Phone:** No. **Rest Rooms and Showers:** No. **Fuel:** No. **Propane:** No. **Internal Roads:** Dirt. **RV Service:** No. **Market:** 2 mi. into Aztec. **Restaurant:** 2 mi. into Aztec. **General Store:** No. **Vending:** No. **Swimming:** No. **Playground:** No. **Activities:** Sightseeing, swimming, boating, fishing. **Nearby Attractions:** Aztec Ruins National Monument, Navajo Lake (23 mi.). **Additional Information:** Aztec Chamber of Commerce and Visitors Center, (505) 334-9551.

Restrictions

Pets: On leash, cleaned up after; ask about other restrictions. **Fires:** In grills; subject to seasonal bans. **Alcoholic Beverages:** At sites. **Vehicle Maximum Length:** None.

To Get There

From the junction of Hwy. 550 and Hwy. 516 (Main St. in town), go 0.6 mi. southwest on 550. Turn right onto Ruins Rd. Go 0.3 mi., then turn right at the sign into the campground. The office is on the left.

BERNARDO

Kiva RV Park and Horse Motel

21 Old Hwy. 60 West, Bernardo 87006. T: (877) 374-KIVA or (505) 861-0693; kivarv@juno.com.

RV: ★★★ Tent: ★★★

Beauty: ★★★ Site Privacy: ★★★★★
Spaciousness: ★★★★★ Quiet: ★★
Security: ★★★★ Cleanliness: ★★★
Insect Control: ★★★★ Facilities: ★★★

Smack dab in the middle of wildlife sanctuaries, this campground emphasizes horses and horseback riding. These unnumbered sites are gravel pull-throughs that are designated as 56 feet long, but can accommodate much larger rigs than this. Sites are very wide (40 feet), with a logged-in patch of grass and bushes between each site. Eastern end sites are not defined on the east side and are therefore extremely large. There is a beautiful desert rock garden at the west edge of the campground, containing flagstones, trellises with grapes, and a fountain. The rest rooms are almost Zen-like in simplicity, but very clean (other than the chipped linoleum and cement floor). Tenting is possible on grassy areas around the park. The best area is in the northeast corner, where there are two stone pads sunk into the ground. This is a fairly nice campground, but geared more towards horse enthusiasts than your average overnighter.

Basics

Operated By: Bob and Diane Wiltshire. **Open:** All year. **Site Assignment:** First come, first served; credit card required for reservation, 24 hours cancellation policy. **Registration:** In office; late arrivals use drop box. **Fee:** RV $18 (full), tent $5; checks, V, MC, D. **Parking:** At site.

Facilities

Number of RV Sites: 26. **Number of Tent-Only Sites:** Undesignated sites. **Hookups:** Water, sewer, electric (20, 30, 50 amp). **Dump Station:** No (sewer at all sites). **Laundry:** Yes. **Pay Phone:** Yes. **Rest Rooms and Showers:** Yes. **Fuel:** No. **Propane:** Yes. **Internal Roads:** Gravel. **RV Service:** No. **Market:** 5 mi. into town. **Restaurant:** 5 mi. into town. **General Store:** No. **Vending:** No. **Swimming:** No. **Playground:** No. **Other:** Horse facilities. **Activities:** Horseback riding, next to 280,000 acres of wildlife reserve. **Nearby Attractions:** Riley Ghost Town. **Additional Information:** Socorro Chamber, (505) 835-0424.

Restrictions

Pets: On leash, cleaned up after. **Fires:** In grills. **Alcoholic Beverages:** At sites. **Vehicle Maximum Length:** None.

To Get There

From Hwy. I-25 (Exit 175): on the north side of the highway, take the first left turn and then turn left into the campground.

BUCKHORN

Buckhorn RV Park

7656 Hwy. 180 West, Buckhorn 88025. T: (505) 535-2995.

RV: ★★★★ Tent: ★★★

Beauty: ★★★	Site Privacy: ★★★
Spaciousness: ★★★	Quiet: ★★★★
Security: ★★★★	Cleanliness: ★★★★
Insect Control: ★★★★	Facilities: ★★

Sites in this campground are laid out in two rows and numbered 1–10 and A–I. All sites in this field are open-ended, roughly 90 feet long. There are mobile homes around the entire perimeter of this campground. Sites on the east side (A–I) are 24 feet wide pull-throughs under willow trees. Site I is next to a mobile home. The nicest sites are A–C, as they are closest to the rest rooms and away from the mobile homes. On the west side, sites 1–10 are open-ended, 20-foot-wide back-ins. These sites are entirely unshaded and not as nice as the pull-through spaces. Site 10 lies next to some buildings. The rest rooms are small but clean and comfortable. This is a decent stop for a short stay, and is conveniently located near some interesting areas, such as the Catwalk.

Basics

Operated By: Dave and Polli Morgan. **Open:** All year. **Site Assignment:** First come, first served; verbal reservations OK. **Registration:** In house or store; late arrivals use drop box at manager's house. **Fee:** RV $15 (full), tent $10; checks, but no credits cards. **Parking:** At site.

Facilities

Number of RV Sites: 19. **Number of Tent-Only Sites:** Undesignated sites. **Hookups:** Water, sewer, electric (30, 50 amp). **Dump Station:** No (sewer at all sites). **Laundry:** Yes. **Pay Phone:** Yes. **Rest Rooms and Showers:** Yes. **Fuel:** No. **Propane:** No. **Internal Roads:** Gravel. **RV Service:** No. **Market:** 10 mi. to Gila. **Restaurant:** Next door. **General Store:** Yes. **Vending:** Yes. **Swimming:** No. **Playground:** No. **Activities:** Bird-watching, fishing, hiking. **Nearby Attractions:** Mogollon ghost town, Glenwood Catwalk, Bill Evans Lake, Silver City. **Additional Information:** Silver City Grant County Chamber, (505) 538-3785.

Restrictions

Pets: On leash, cleaned up after. **Fires:** In grills. **Alcoholic Beverages:** At sites. **Vehicle Maximum Length:** None.

To Get There

From Hwy. 180, 0.25 mi. west of the town sign, on the south side of the highway.

CAPULIN

Capulin Camp and RV Park

P.O. Box 68, Capulin 88414. T: (505) 278-2921.

RV: ★★★ Tent: ★★★

Beauty: ★★★	Site Privacy: ★★★
Spaciousness: ★★	Quiet: ★★★
Security: ★★★★	Cleanliness: ★★★★
Insect Control: ★★★★	Facilities: ★★★

This campground has one row of back-ins and one row of pull-throughs. Sites 1–10 are 60-foot back-ins along the north edge that back to trees behind which is the highway. Sites 11–29 are 50-foot pull-throughs that can pull in sideways for extra space if one site is not large enough. Eastern end site 11 has the most space (33 feet wide) compared to the others (15 feet wide). Sites 13 and 14 and 15 and 16 share large shade trees. All other pull-through sites are unshaded, except for 29, which is right up against a copse of trees. (In fact, it is so close that the space is somewhat cramped because of its location.) Tenting is possible wherever there is grass (which is mostly to the south or east, next to sites 11 or 12). While the grass cover is quite adequate, the campground itself is not really tent-oriented, and there are no other facilities (such as table or fire pit) for tenters' use. The rest rooms are clean and comfortable. This campground is a very nice spot to stay at for a few days, and the Capulin Volcano National Monument is well worth checking out.

Basics

Operated By: Donna Shewbert. **Open:** All year. **Site Assignment:** First come, first served; verbal reservations OK. **Registration:** In office; late arrivals use drop box. **Fee:** RV $18 (50 amp), $16 (30 amp), tent $10; checks, but no credits cards. **Parking:** At site.

Facilities

Number of RV Sites: 29. **Number of Tent-Only Sites:** Undesignated sites. **Hookups:** Water, sewer, electric (30, 50 amp). **Dump Station:** Yes. **Laundry:** Yes. **Pay Phone:** 1 block. **Rest Rooms and Showers:** Yes. **Fuel:** No. **Propane:** No. **Internal Roads:** Gravel. **RV Service:** No. **Market:** 0.25 mi. east. **Restaurant:** 0.25 mi. east. **General Store:** No. **Vending:** No. **Swimming:** No. **Playground:** No. **Other:** Cards and picnicking in the garage. **Activities:** Cards, hiking, swimming, boating, fishing. **Nearby Attractions:** Sugarite Canyon State Park, Capulin Volcano National Monument, Folsom Man Site, Clayton Lake State Park. **Additional Information:** Clayton Chamber, (505) 374-9253.

Restrictions

Pets: On leash, cleaned up after. **Fires:** In grills. **Alcoholic Beverages:** At sites. **Vehicle Maximum Length:** None.

To Get There

From the junction of Hwy. 325 and Hwy. 64/87, turn east onto Hwy. 64/87 and go 0.1 mi. Turn right at the sign into the entrance.

CARLSBAD

Carlsbad RV Park and Campground

4301 National Parks Hwy., Carlsbad 88220. T: (505) 885-6333; F: (505) 885-0784; www.carlsbadrvpark.com; camping@cavement.net.

RV: ★★★★ Tent: ★★★

Beauty: ★★★	Site Privacy: ★★★★
Spaciousness: ★★★★	Quiet: ★★★★
Security: ★★★★	Cleanliness: ★★★★★
Insect Control: ★★	Facilities: ★★★★★

Located on the southwest side of town (towards the caverns as you leave Carlsbad), this campground has got it all: pool, laundry, RV servicing, and activities galore. On top of that, facilities are super-clean and spacious. Sites are level and long (60 feet), with some extra-wide spaces (45 feet) for slideouts. Most RV sites have trees, with the exception of A4–A6. End site B31 is perhaps the most desirable site, with a large shade tree, extra space, and an easy in/out. Tent sites are level, but with a thin grass coverage. Tent sites 33 and 39 have good, large trees, and the unmarked site in the extreme northeast corner has extra room, being on the end of a row and backing onto a grassy field. Normal tent sites are 40 × 40 feet, a comfortable size. However, tent sites would be greatly improved if the trees were away from the road instead of right up against it. Owners of large dogs will be happy with the 3 acre off-leash area, where horses have even been let out to roam! Large camping groups can likewise be accommodated with the meeting room that can hold over one hundred people and includes a kitchen. Carlsbad makes a wonderful stop for those exploring the caverns or making their way to Texas or even Mexico.

Basics

Operated By: Eddie and Sammie Herrington. **Open:** All year. **Site Assignment:** Upon registration; verbal reservations OK, necessary in summer; cancel within 24 hours for refund. **Registration:** In office; late arrivals use drop box. **Fee:** RV $20, tent $15. **Parking:** At site.

Facilities

Number of RV Sites: 96. **Number of Tent-Only Sites:** 36. **Hookups:** Water, sewer, electric (30, 50 amp), cable. **Each Site:** Tent sites: picnic table, grill. **Dump Station:** Yes. **Laundry:** Yes. **Pay Phone:** Yes. **Rest Rooms and Showers:** Yes. **Fuel:** No. **Propane:** No. **Internal Roads:** Gravel, in good condition. **RV Service:** Yes. **Market:** 1.5 mi. in Carlsbad. **Restaurant:** 3 blocks. **General Store:** Yes. **Vending:** Yes. **Swimming:** Heated indoor pool. **Playground:** Yes. **Other:** Cabins, rec room, group meeting room (100-plus person) w/ kitchen, dog walk, free charcoal and gas grills, RV storage, juke box. **Activities:** Summer holiday potlucks, ping pong, video games, swimming, air hockey. **Nearby Attractions:** Carlsbad Caverns, Sitting Bull Falls, Living Desert. **Additional Information:** Carlsbad CVB, (800) 221-1224, (505) 887-6516.

Restrictions

Pets: On leash. **Fires:** In fire rings or grills. **Alcoholic Beverages:** Prefer none. **Vehicle Maximum Length:** 60 ft.

To Get There

From the junction of Hwy. 62/180 and Hwy. 285, go 1.7 mi. south on Hwy. 62/180. Turn west at the sign into the campground. The office is straight ahead.

CARRIZOZO

Sands RV Park and Motel

South Hwy. 54, P.O. Box 957, Carrizozo 88301. T: (800) 81SANDS or (505) 648-2989; F: (505) 648-4029.

RV ★★★ Tent ★★

Beauty: ★★★	Site Privacy: ★★
Spaciousness: ★★	Quiet: ★★
Security: ★★★★	Cleanliness: ★★★
Insect Control: ★★★★	Facilities: ★★★

Laid out in two rows, these RV sites are located close to a railway, and it gets very noisy when a train passes (just across the road). All sites are open-ended pull-throughs 15 feet wide and 75 feet (or so) long. Site 14 is blocked by a tree, so there is no way to pull through. End site 18 is also blocked by a tree, but has loads more space than any other site. The nicest site in the park is 15, which is very well shaded. Sites 19–21, situated to the west at 90° from the other sites, have cement slabs to park on, and are divided by short cement walls. The rest room is one unisex unit that is clean and comfortable. This park, under new management, makes a decent overnight stop, but need not make anyone's destination list.

Basics

Operated By: Steve and Gwen Dunne. **Open:** All year. **Site Assignment:** First come, first served; no reservations. **Registration:** In office, 24 hours. **Fee:** RV $15; checks, V, MC, AE, CB. **Parking:** At site.

Facilities

Number of RV Sites: 21. **Number of Tent-Only Sites:** Undesignated sites. **Hookups:** Water, sewer, electric (30, 50 amp), cable. **Dump Station:** No (sewer at all sites). **Laundry:** Yes. **Pay Phone:** No. **Rest Rooms and Showers:** Yes. **Fuel:** No. **Propane:** No. **Internal Roads:** Gravel. **RV Service:** No. **Market:** 0.1 mi. north. **Restaurant:** less than 0.25 mi. north. **General Store:** No. **Vending:** Yes. **Swimming:** No. **Playground:** No. **Other:** Rec center within walking distance. **Activities:** Fishing, boating. **Nearby Attractions:** Benito Lake, Valley of Fires, Ruidoso. **Additional Information:** Ruidoso Chamber of Commerce, (505) 257-7395.

Restrictions

Pets: On leash, cleaned up after. **Fires:** In grills. **Alcoholic Beverages:** At sites. **Vehicle Maximum Length:** None.

To Get There

From the junction of Hwy. 380 and Hwy. 54, turn south onto Hwy. 54 and go 0.8 mi. Turn right at the sign into the entrance.

CHAMA

Rio Chama RV Park

182 North State Hwy. 17, P.O. Box 706, Chama 87520. T: (505) 756-2303.

RV ★★★★★ Tent ★★★★★

Beauty: ★★★★★	Site Privacy: ★★★★★
Spaciousness: ★★★★	Quiet: ★★★★
Security: ★★★★★	Cleanliness: ★★★★
Insect Control: ★★★	Facilities: ★★

This lovely campground is loaded with trees, sits next to the Rio Chama River, and has beautiful RV and tent sites. The Cumbres and Toltec Scenic Railway passes within a stone's throw of the east border—which may or may not be an attraction to some campers. (There is only one run per day, entailing two passes of the campground.) Pretty much any site is highly desirable, with the possible exception of A6, which is right at the entrance. Site 39 has no shade tree but receives shade from the trees in neighboring sites. Pull-throughs are a good 65 feet in length, while back-ins average 42 feet. All sites are nearly 30 feet in width, which makes them comfortably spacious. The tenting area is absolutely gorgeous: it contains lush grass, large sites, and plenty of trees. A barbed-wire fence runs the length of the area, making it quite secure. Site 5 is the least desirable, as it contains a telephone pole and the communal wash basin. Any other tent site is well worth the price of admission. This campground is a popular destination—many seniors return year after year to meet old friends—and justifiably so.

Basics

Operated By: Harry and Kathy Tate. **Open:** May–Oct. **Site Assignment:** Upon registration; for reservations, write to the campground between Oct. and May, call between May and Oct. **Registration:** In office; late arrivals wake up manager for site assignment. **Fee:** RV $20 (full, 50 amp), $18 (full, 30 amp), $16 (water, electric); tent $12; V, MC. **Parking:** At site.

Facilities

Number of RV Sites: 98. **Number of Tent-Only Sites:** 14. **Hookups:** Water, sewer, electric (30, 50 amp). **Each Site:** Picnic table, fire ring/grill, many trees. **Dump Station:** Yes. **Laundry:** No. **Pay Phone:** Yes. **Rest Rooms and Showers:** Yes. **Fuel:** No. **Propane:** No. **Internal Roads:** Gravel. **RV Service:** No. **Market:** 2 mi. into Chama. **Restaurant:** 0.25 mi. **General Store:** No. **Vending:** Limited in office. **Swimming:** No. **Playground:** No. **Other:** Rio Chama River, covered shelter and stage, RV storage, notice board, railroad passes park (twice daily). **Activities:** Pot lucks, ice-cream socials, coffee and doughnuts on weekends, horseback riding, fishing. **Nearby Attractions:** Cumbres and Toltec Scenic Railroad, Rio Chama River. **Additional Information:** Chama Valley Chamber, (800) 477-0149, (505) 756-2306.

Restrictions

Pets: On leash, cleaned up after, always attended outside. **Fires:** In ring/grill between 4–10 p.m. **Alcoholic Beverages:** At sites. **Vehicle Maximum Length:** None. **Other:** No generators.

To Get There

From the junction of Hwy. US 84/64 and Hwy. 17, go 1.8 mi. north on Hwy. 17. Turn right (east) at the sign into the campground entrance. The office is in a boxcar on the right.

CIMARRON

Ponil Campground

P.O. Box 323, Cimarron 87714. T: (505) 376-2700; F: (505) 376-2700.

RV ★★★★ Tent ★★★

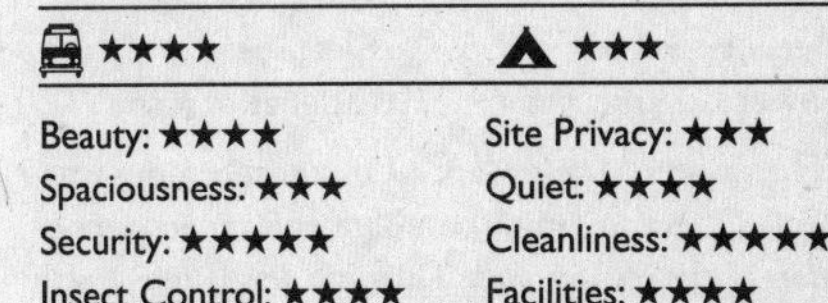

Beauty: ★★★★	Site Privacy: ★★★
Spaciousness: ★★★	Quiet: ★★★★
Security: ★★★★★	Cleanliness: ★★★★★
Insect Control: ★★★★	Facilities: ★★★★

There is a tangible feeling of community amongst campers in Ponil. The sites in this park contribute to this feeling, as they are not all clearly delineated, and there is not a lot of space between them. However, there are spaces to accommodate a rig of any size. Sites in the northeast corner (in a somewhat separated nook) are very well shaded. Sites along the north and northwest edge back to trees. Sites in the southwest (along the entrance) back to an open grassy field where deer and elk are seen in the morning. These sites can pull through. The space around them is enough for each camper to do his or her own thing, but also lends itself to meeting and interacting with neighbors—one of the best reasons to travel. Tenting is possible in the open field in front of the house. There is one large tree and a hedge along the perimeter of the property that blocks out the road. This is a favorite destination for cub scouts and for RVers who wish to meet other campers in a lovely and quiet setting.

Basics

Operated By: Butch and Lawana Whitten. **Open:** All year. **Site Assignment:** Depending on site availability; verbal reservations OK. **Registration:** At manager's trailer; late arrivals select available site and pay in the morning. **Fee:** RV $15 (full), tent $10; checks, but no credits cards. **Parking:** At site.

Facilities

Number of RV Sites: 36. **Number of Tent-Only Sites:** Undesignated sites. **Hookups:** Water, sewer, electric (30 amp). **Dump Station:** Yes. **Laundry:** Yes. **Pay Phone:** Yes. **Rest Rooms and Showers:** Yes. **Fuel:** No. **Propane:** No. **Internal Roads:** Gravel. **RV Service:** No. **Market:** 1.5 mi. south. **Restaurant:** 1 mi. south. **General Store:** No. **Vending:** No. **Swimming:** No. **Playground:** Yes. **Other:** Rec room. **Activities:** Singing twice weekly, hiking, wildlife-viewing. **Nearby Attractions:** Cimarron Canyon State Park, Maxwell National Wildlife Reserve, Ponil River at edge of campground. **Additional Information:** Cimarron Chamber of Commerce, (505) 376-2417.

Restrictions

Pets: On leash, cleaned up after. **Fires:** In grills. **Alcoholic Beverages:** At sites. **Vehicle Maximum Length:** None.

To Get There

From the junction of Hwy. 58 and Hwy. 64, turn east onto Hwy. 64 and go 1 mi. Turn left at the sign into the entrance.

CLAYTON

Meadowlark KOA

P.O. Box 366, Clayton 88415. T: (800) 562-9507 or (505) 374-9508.

RV ★★★★ Tent ★★★★

Beauty: ★★★★	Site Privacy: ★★★★
Spaciousness: ★★★★	Quiet: ★★★★
Security: ★★★★	Cleanliness: ★★★★★
Insect Control: ★★★★	Facilities: ★★★★

The sites in Meadowlark KOA are enormous (easily 100 feet in length) and are able to accommodate a rig of any size. They are level, open, and grassy, with decent space (30 feet) between each one. The campground is surrounded by trees (except to the south), but there are not a lot of shade trees within the campground itself. The best RV sites are end sites 7, 14, 21, 27, and 33, which are endowed with larger trees and much more space. The least desirable sites are the back-ins along the eastern edge—not only because they are smaller (24 × 30 feet) and require backing in, but because they are close to the dog walk area. Indeed, sites 109 and 110 (100 and 101 on the map) are right on top of the dog walk area and contain a pooper scooper and trash bin. Sites 50–80 to the north are also less desirable, as they contain unsightly stumps (one has to wonder why the trees were cut down!) and are closer to the manager's house and the office buildings. Tent sites along the western edge are situated in front of a row of trees (which supply a canopy of shade), and are a roomy 24 × 40 feet. Those tent sites at the north side of the campground have much smaller trees, and back to a residential area, which makes them not nearly as nice as the former. The rest room and showers are modern, spacious, and spotless. They are simply, but nicely, decorated. The laundry is likewise clean and roomy. This is a campground that is worthwhile finding, whether camping in an RV or a tent.

Basics

Operated By: Chuck and Sue Richardson. **Open:** Mar. 1–Oct. 31. **Site Assignment:** Upon registration; credit card required for reservation, 24 hours cancellation policy. **Registration:** In office; late arrivals use drop box. **Fee:** RV $20 (full), tent $16. **Parking:** At site.

Facilities

Number of RV Sites: 65. **Number of Tent-Only Sites:** 12. **Hookups:** Water, sewer, electric (30, 50 amp), cable. **Each Site:** Picnic table, grill, shrubs for privacy. **Dump Station:** Yes. **Laundry:** Yes. **Pay Phone:** Yes. **Rest Rooms and Showers:** Yes. **Fuel:** No. **Propane:** Yes. **Internal Roads:** Gravel. **RV Service:** No. **Market:** 8 blocks northwest. **Restaurant:** 6 blocks northwest. **General Store:** Yes. **Vending:** No. **Swimming:** No. **Playground:** Yes. **Other:** 2 cabins, game room, pet walk area. **Activities:** Hiking, tetherball. **Nearby Attractions:** Clayton State Park, Capulin Mountain National Monument, dinosaur tracks. **Additional Information:** Clayton Chamber of Commerce, (505) 374-9253.

Restrictions

Pets: On leash, cleaned up after. **Fires:** In grills. **Alcoholic Beverages:** At sites. **Vehicle Maximum Length:** None.

To Get There

From the junction of Hwy. 56/64/412 and Hwy. 87, go 0.7 mi. south on Hwy. 87 (East). Turn left at the sign onto Spruce, and go 0.35 mi. to the entrance. Turn right at the sign.

CLOVIS

Ideal RV Park

1051 NM 311, Clovis 88101. T: (505) 791-3177 or (505) 799-2315; F: (505) 791-3177; idealrv@zianet.com.

RV ★★★ Tent n/a

Beauty: ★★★	Site Privacy: ★★★
Spaciousness: ★★★★	Quiet: ★★★★
Security: ★★★	Cleanliness: ★★★
Insect Control: ★★★	Facilities: ★★★

Ideal is a shady campground with loads of trees: there are trees at nearly every site, and a row of trees along the north perimeter, beyond which lies agricultural land. The downside are the mobile homes to the east and along part of the south side—they detract about as much as the trees add. Sites are 60-foot long pull-throughs, 33 feet wide, level and grassy. However, most sites are not clearly marked: only those closest to the laundry have numbers. The laundry facility is large and well-lit, with a cute row of flowers planted around the outside. The rest rooms within are clean except for the floors (including inside the showers), which, during our visit, were peeling paint and in need of a scrub. The site that could be 14 (6 sites east of the laundry on the north side) has a nice tree and a little extra space. The least desirable sites are on the ends closest to the mobile homes—again, unnumbered. According to its proprietor, the park is only in its second year of operation and hopefully it will see some improvement in the coming years. As it stands today, it is a campground of extremes, with its deficiencies offsetting its attributes.

Basics

Operated By: Rickey and Mindy Boddy. **Open:** All year. **Site Assignment:** First come, first served; verbal reservations OK. **Registration:** In office; late arrivals use drop box. **Fee:** $14. **Parking:** At site.

Facilities

Number of RV Sites: 20. **Number of Tent-Only Sites:** 0. **Hookups:** Water, sewer, electric (30, 50). **Each Site:** Tree. **Dump Station:** No (sewer at all sites). **Laundry:** Yes. **Pay Phone:** No. **Rest Rooms and Showers:** Yes. **Fuel:** No. **Propane:** No. **Internal Roads:** Gravel. **RV Service:** No. **Market:** 7 mi. east to Clovis. **Restaurant:** 7 mi. east to Clovis. **General Store:** No. **Vending:** No. **Swimming:** No. **Playground:** No. **Other:** Close to Cannon Air Force Base. **Activities:** Clovis Music Festival. **Nearby Attractions:** Blackwater Draw Museum. **Additional Information:** Clovis/Curry County Chamber of Commerce, (505) 763-3435.

Restrictions

Pets: On leash. **Fires:** In grills/pits (unless burn ban in effect). **Alcoholic Beverages:** At sites. **Vehicle Maximum Length:** None.

To Get There

From the junction of Hwy. 70 and Hwy. 60/84, turn west onto Hwy. 60/84 (first street north of the bridge) and drive 7.2 mi. to Hwy. 311. Turn right onto Hwy. 311 and drive 0.5 mi., then turn right at the sign into the entrance. The office is on the right.

COLUMBUS

Pancho Villa State Park

P.O. Box 450, Columbus 88029. T: (505) 531-2711; F: (505) 531-2115.

RV ★★★★★ Tent ★★★★

Beauty: ★★★★★	Site Privacy: ★★★★★
Spaciousness: ★★★★★	Quiet: ★★★★
Security: ★★★★	Cleanliness: ★★★★
Insect Control: ★★★★	Facilities: ★★★

Columbus is a small town, and despite proximity to the highway and the town, the park still retains a desert-wilderness feel. On top of this, the park management obviously puts a lot of work into maintenance, which brings out the beauty of the natural environment. Large rigs will love this park, as all but four sites are pull-throughs—and those four are large enough (60 feet) to "parallel park" instead of backing in, if so desired. Sites 1–4 are 150-foot pull-throughs along the eastern edge of the campground (by the highway). Sites

22–25 are the same, but across an internal drive, and 26–34 are further south. Sites 5–10 are located on a gigantic, open gravel road that can fit any rig in practically any direction. Sites 10–16 are nicer than the eastern side, since they are further from the highway. Sites 58–61 are developed back-in sites (no electricity) that measure 60 × 60 feet. The best area to camp in is the western side, as it is further from the highway and the entrance. However, any site in this park is a beautiful place to camp. Tent sites are located on a patch of thick grass that looks rather out of place in this desert campground, but offers nice camping. The rest rooms are attractively modeled and both clean and spacious. This is a wonderful campground with natural sites that tenters and RVers will enjoy.

Basics

Operated By: New Mexico State Park Division. **Open:** All year. **Site Assignment:** First come, first served; reservations by credit card or check, no refunds. **Registration:** At pay station. **Fee:** Primitive site $8, developed site $10, water, electric $14; checks, but no credit cards. **Parking:** At site.

Facilities

Number of RV Sites: 80. **Number of Tent-Only Sites:** Undesignated sites. **Hookups:** Electric (20, 30 amp). **Each Site:** Picnic table, fire pit. **Dump Station:** Yes. **Laundry:** No. **Pay Phone:** Yes. **Rest Rooms and Showers:** Yes. **Fuel:** No. **Propane:** No. **Internal Roads:** Paved. **RV Service:** No. **Market:** 0.25 mi. north. **Restaurant:** 0.25 mi. north. **General Store:** No. **Vending:** No. **Swimming:** No. **Playground:** Yes. **Other:** Rec hall, picnic pavilion, botanical gardens, museum. **Activities:** Tours to Mexico, rock-hounding. **Nearby Attractions:** Mexico, El Paso, Rockhound State Park. **Additional Information:** New Mexico State Parks Division, (888) NM-PARKS.

Restrictions

Pets: On leash, cleaned up after. **Fires:** In grills. **Alcoholic Beverages:** At sites. **Vehicle Maximum Length:** None.

To Get There

From the junction of Hwy. 11 and Hwy. 9, turn southwest onto Hwy. 9 and go 0.1 mi. Turn left at the sign into the entrance.

DATIL

Eagle Guest Ranch

P.O. Box 68, Datil 87821. T: (505) 772-5612.

RV ★★★★ Tent ★★

Beauty: ★★★★ Site Privacy: ★★★★
Spaciousness: ★★★★ Quiet: ★★★★
Security: ★★★★ Cleanliness: ★★★
Insect Control: ★★★★ Facilities: ★★

This RV park is located behind a cafe, motel, gas station, and crafts store. The campground is very undeveloped, with grass and dirt spaces. Some of the sites (especially 1–4) are overgrown with weeds, and the campground itself needs a good picking-up. Sites 1–14 are 45-foot back-ins laid out along the highway. Sites 1–3 are very well shaded, site 10 is unshaded, and sites 7 and 8 are used by long-term residents. Pull-throughs include 15 and 16 (40 feet) and 20–22 (150 feet). Sites 12 and 14 and 17 and 18 can be used as pull-throughs if the accompanying site is unoccupied. Sites 24 and 25 are 75-foot back-ins, and 26 is a well shaded 45-foot pull-through. Both 25 and 26 have a rather rough road. Tenting is possible wherever there is grass (which is pretty much anywhere around the campground), but a shade tree is hard to come by. As there are no showers, tenters will have a rougher time than self-contained units. Likewise, the rest rooms in the store are closed from 9 p.m. and all day Sunday. There are many campgrounds in the area, but they do not offer hookups. In fact, this may very well be the only campground within 50 miles to offer hookups of any kind. Tenters may have a better stay at a National Forest campground, as these are sure to provide showers.

Basics

Operated By: Carol Coker. **Open:** All year. **Site Assignment:** First come, first served; no reservations. **Registration:** In store; late arrivals select available site and pay in the morning. **Fee:** RV $12 (full), tent $6; V, MC, AE, D, DC, CB. **Parking:** At site.

Facilities

Number of RV Sites: 25. **Number of Tent-Only Sites:** Undesignated sites. **Hookups:** Water, sewer, electric (20, 50 amp). **Dump Station:** No. **Laundry:** No. **Pay Phone:** Yes. **Rest Rooms and Showers:** No (rest rooms in store). **Fuel:** Yes. **Propane:** No. **Internal Roads:** Dirt. **RV Service:** No. **Market:** 34 mi. to Magdalena. **Restaurant:** On-site. **General Store:** Yes. **Vending:** No. **Swimming:** No. **Playground:** No. **Other:** Cafe, motel. **Activities:** Rock-climbing, fishing, boating, hunting. **Nearby Attractions:** Thompson Canyon, VLA, Quemado Lake. **Additional Information:** Socorro Chamber of Commerce, (505) 835-0424.

Restrictions

Pets: On leash, cleaned up after. **Fires:** In grills. **Alcoholic Beverages:** At sites. **Vehicle Maximum Length:** None.

To Get There

Located at the intersection of Hwy. 12 and Hwy. 60 in Datil.

DEMING

Wagon Wheel RV Park

2801 East Motel Dr., Deming 88030. T: (505) 546-8650.

RV ★★★★ Tent ★★★

Beauty: ★★★ Site Privacy: ★★★
Spaciousness: ★★★★ Quiet: ★★★
Security: ★★★★ Cleanliness: ★★★
Insect Control: ★★★★ Facilities: ★★★

Laid out in three rows of sites, this campground has very attractive landscaping using bushes, trees, and flowers. Sites 1–11 are 45-foot back-ins in the southeast corner. Site 12 is secluded by trees and a fence and has good shade. In the eastern row, sites 13–28 are 60-foot pull-throughs. Sites in the northern section (21–28) are bare gravel. Sites 29–51 in the middle row are open-ended pull-throughs averaging 60 × 21 feet. Site 29, in front of the office, may receive registration traffic. Sites 31, 34, and 39 are very well shaded. Sites in the northern section (44–51) are bare gravel. The western row (sites 56–72) has back-ins along the fence (sites 56–63) and 60-foot pull-throughs (64–72). All sites can be used for tenting, although 1–12 are probably the best. The rec room and Jacuzzi are comfortable, although the campground gets crowded in winter, and you may have to wait to use these facilities. The rest rooms are OK, but could use a deep cleaning. Priding itself on being the least expensive campground in the area, this is a very nice destination for RVers for a short stay or even over the winter.

Basics

Operated By: Dan Wagner. **Open:** All year. **Site Assignment:** Depending on site availability; verbal reservations OK. **Registration:** In office; late arrivals use drop box. **Fee:** RV $11 (full), tent $11; no credits cards, but checks. **Parking:** At site.

Facilities

Number of RV Sites: 73. **Number of Tent-Only Sites:** 0. **Hookups:** Water, sewer, electric (20, 30, 50 amp), cable, phone. **Each Site:** Picnic table. **Dump Station:** No (sewer at all sites). **Laundry:** Yes. **Pay Phone:** Yes. **Rest Rooms and Showers:** Yes. **Fuel:** No. **Propane:** No. **Internal Roads:** Gravel. **RV Service:** No. **Market:** 1.25 mi. west. **Restaurant:** Less than 0.25 mi. west. **General Store:** No. **Vending:** Yes. **Swimming:** No (Jacuzzi). **Playground:** No. **Other:** RV supplies, clubhouse w/ kitchen, game room, movies, gift shop, modem. **Activities:** Planned activities in winter, rock-hounding, hiking. **Nearby Attractions:** Rockhound State Park, City of Rocks State Park. **Additional Information:** Deming Chamber of Commerce, (505) 546-2674.

Restrictions

Pets: On leash, cleaned up after. **Fires:** In grills. **Alcoholic Beverages:** At sites (not in clubhouse). **Vehicle Maximum Length:** None.

To Get There

From Hwy. I-10 (Exit 85), turn south onto Motel Dr. and go 1.2 mi. Turn right at the sign into the entrance.

DWYER

Faywood Hot Springs

165 Hwy. 61, HC 71 Box 1240, Dwyer 88034. T: (505) 536-9663; www.faywood.com.

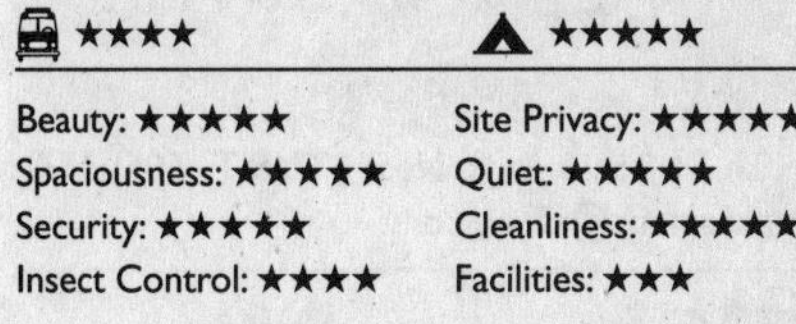

RV ★★★★ Tent ★★★★★

Beauty: ★★★★★ Site Privacy: ★★★★★
Spaciousness: ★★★★★ Quiet: ★★★★★
Security: ★★★★★ Cleanliness: ★★★★★
Insect Control: ★★★★ Facilities: ★★★

Let's put this out upfront: this natural campground in the desert wilderness will most likely appeal to folks with an adventurous heart. The public clothing-optional areas are certainly not for everyone. That being said, it's a wonderful campground with beautiful, if undeveloped, sites somewhat scattered about the property. Site 7–16 are pull-throughs located along the northern edge. Site 7 is located next to the caretaker's mobile home. Site 10 is extra wide (40 feet compared to 21 feet). One of the nicest spots, 18, lacks shade but is an extremely large back-in that commands a gorgeous view. Sites 23–26 in the southwest corner are surrounded by vegetation and are therefore very private. Tent sites 4–6 are sandy sites surrounded by vegetation. These are the nicest, most private sites. The other tent sites are mixed in amongst the RV sites. The rest rooms are pit toilets scattered around the campground, and the shower is outdoors, only partially concealed. This campground may appeal most to tenters and the adventurous Airstream crowd, but is a beautiful slice of desert wilderness that should not be missed.

BASICS

Operated By: Elon Yurwit and Wanda Fuselier. **Open:** All year. **Site Assignment:** First come, first served; credit card required for reservation, 2 days cancellation policy. **Registration:** In office; no late arrivals, gate locked at 10 p.m. **Fee:** RV $27 (full), tent $15; V, MC. **Parking:** At site.

FACILITIES

Number of RV Sites: 21. **Number of Tent-Only Sites:** 12. **Hookups:** Water, sewer, electric (20, 30, 50 amp). **Dump Station:** Yes. **Laundry:** No. **Pay Phone:** No. **Rest Rooms and Showers:** Yes. **Fuel:** No. **Propane:** No. **Internal Roads:** Gravel. **RV Service:** No. **Market:** Convenience store 12 mi. north to Hurley, supermarket 24 mi. north or south. **Restaurant:** 12 mi. north to Hurley. **General Store:** No. **Vending:** No. **Swimming:** No (hot springs). **Playground:** No. **Other:** 1,200 acres of hiking, drinks and some grocery items, cabins, tipi, shaded picnic pavilion, clothing required/optional areas. **Activities:** Horseback riding, birding, hiking, biking, stargazing. **Nearby Attractions:** City of Rocks State Park, Gila National Monument, Las Cruces. **Additional Information:** Deming Chamber of Commerce, (505) 546-2674.

RESTRICTIONS

Pets: On leash, cleaned up after. **Fires:** In grills. **Alcoholic Beverages:** At sites. **Vehicle Maximum Length:** None.

TO GET THERE

From the junction of Hwy. 180 and Hwy. 61, go north on Hwy. 61 1.6 mi. Turn left onto a very nondescript gravel road (with small sign) and follow it to the office.

EAGLE NEST

West Lake RV Park

HCR 71 Box 6, Eagle Nest 87718. T: (505) 377-PARK; gplenz@afweb.com.

RV ★★★★ Tent n/a

Beauty: ★★★★	Site Privacy: ★★★
Spaciousness: ★★	Quiet: ★★★★
Security: ★★★★	Cleanliness: ★★★★★
Insect Control: ★★★★	Facilities: ★

This campground is located in a valley surrounded by mountains, with lake views and access to lake. Sites are laid out in a semi-circle around the perimeter of the property. Sites are open-ended back-ins, but limited to about 45 × 25 feet. Sites 1–12 are located along the wooden fence to the north. Site 1 is quite small (30 × 25 feet), and 11–13, in the corner, seem somewhat hemmed in. Sites 13–18 are laid out along the east side, overlooking the lake. These sites (minus 13 and 18) are the nicest sites. Sites 19–28, along the south side, overlook fields, cabins, and the lake. Site 18 and 19 are slightly blocked by one another. In an area with a number of RV parks, this campground offers nice lake views. Any one of the RV parks in the area are a great place to be when the weather elsewhere is climbing into the 90s, as this place stays cool all year.

BASICS

Operated By: Phil and Glenda Lenz. **Open:** May 1–Oct. 31. **Site Assignment:** Depending on site availability; verbal reservations OK. **Registration:** In office; late arrivals select available site and pay in the morning. **Fee:** RV $19; checks, but no credits cards. **Parking:** At site.

FACILITIES

Number of RV Sites: 28. **Number of Tent-Only Sites:** 0. **Hookups:** Water, sewer, electric (30, 50 amp). **Each Site:** Covered picnic table. **Dump Station:** No (sewer at all sites). **Laundry:** Yes. **Pay Phone:** No. **Rest Rooms and Showers:** No. **Fuel:** No. **Propane:** No. **Internal Roads:** Gravel. **RV Service:** No. **Market:** 12 mi. to Angel Fire. **Restaurant:** 1.5 mi. east. **General Store:** No. **Vending:** No. **Swimming:** No. **Playground:** No. **Other:** Covered pavilion, views, cool weather. **Activities:** Fishing, boating, fish fry Fri., potlucks. **Nearby Attractions:** Cimarron Canyon State Park, DAV Vietnam Veterans National Memorial. **Additional Information:** Eagle Nest Chamber of Commerce, (505) 377–2420.

RESTRICTIONS

Pets: On leash, cleaned up after. **Fires:** In common grill. **Alcoholic Beverages:** At sites. **Vehicle Maximum Length:** 42 ft.

TO GET THERE

From the junction of Hwy. 38 and Hwy. 64, turn west onto Hwy. 64 and go 1.5 mi. Turn left at the sign into the entrance.

EDGEWOOD

Red Arrow Edgewood RV Park

P.O. Box 1750, Edgewood 87015. T: (505) 281-0893.

RV ★★★ Tent ★★

Beauty: ★★★	Site Privacy: ★★★
Spaciousness: ★★★	Quiet: ★★★
Security: ★★★★	Cleanliness: ★★★
Insect Control: ★★★★	Facilities: ★★★

Basically a large, open desert area, Red Arrow Edgewood has a natural, back-to-earth feel. There is an attractive garden with bench and fountain at the entrance. However, the campground itself is in need of some attention. While most visitors (especially RVers) may not even notice, those who poke around a little (or use the tenting area) will soon begin to find the stored equipment, piles of wood and tree limbs. The RV section itself is mainly clean. Consisting of lettered rows of sites, this park has long back-ins and pull-throughs that can accommodate most rigs—even with tows. Rows A and M have 75-foot pull-throughs. While row A is unshaded, a few sites in row M (11 and 12) are shaded. Rows B, BD, and P have 60-foot back-ins. Rows B and BD are a little nicer; P abuts a junky yard. The tent area to the northwest is—to say the least—a disappointment. The nicest site has a good view of a billboard, while the other tent sites are located next to piles of wood and other debris. The rest rooms, likewise, need only a few basic repairs to be of better service. While the campground itself has the potential to be utterly charming, the lack of maintenance detracts from the experience.

BASICS

Operated By: Jerry and Lory Veckert. **Open:** All year. **Site Assignment:** Upon registration; verbal reservations OK. **Registration:** In office; late arrivals use drop box. **Fee:** RV $22 (full), tent $15; checks, V, MC, AE, D. **Parking:** At site.

FACILITIES

Number of RV Sites: 40. **Number of Tent-Only Sites:** 5. **Hookups:** Water, sewer, electric (30, 50 amp). **Each Site:** Some tables. **Dump Station:** Yes. **Laundry:** Yes. **Pay Phone:** Yes. **Rest Rooms and Showers:** Yes. **Fuel:** No. **Propane:** No. **Internal Roads:** Gravel. **RV Service:** No. **Market:** 0.25 mi. west. **Restaurant:** 0.5 mi. west. **General Store:** No. **Vending:** No. **Swimming:** Pool. **Playground:** Yes. **Activities:** Tours to Albuqurque. **Nearby Attractions:** Rte. 66. **Additional Information:** Albuquerque Chamber, (505) 764-3700.

RESTRICTIONS

Pets: On leash, cleaned up after. **Fires:** In grills. **Alcoholic Beverages:** At sites. **Vehicle Maximum Length:** None.

TO GET THERE

From Hwy. I-40 (Exit 187), turn south onto Hwy. 334 and go 1 block to the 4-way stop. Turn left onto Historic Rte. 66 (Hwy. 333E) and go 0.5 mi. east on Hwy. 333. Turn left at the sign into the entrance.

EL MORRO

El Morro RV Park

Rte. 2 Box 44, Ramah 87321. T: (505) 783-4612; www.elmorrow-nm.com; elmorrow@elmorrow-nm.com.

RV ★★★ Tent ★★★★

Beauty: ★★★★	Site Privacy: ★★★
Spaciousness: ★★★★	Quiet: ★★★★
Security: ★★★★	Cleanliness: ★★★
Insect Control: ★★★★	Facilities: ★★★

This is a wilderness campground with the highway directly to the north. Sites are not all numbered, and the only distinction between a tent or

RV site is the existence or lack of hookups. Sites 1 and 3 are 60-foot back-ins that back slightly into the woods. Sites 2 and 4 are 45-foot back-ins that are slightly sloped. Sites on the inside of the loop are 54-foot back-ins (including 7). The site furthest west on the outside of the loop (possibly 9) is a 65-foot back-in. Site 10 is the largest, at 75 feet. This is a dirt back-in with trees around the site, but the site itself is not shaded. Sites 15 and 16 are overgrown with weeds. Sites that back to the highway include 10, 16, and 19, as well as some unnumbered sites on the north side of the loop. Tent sites include three in the southwest corner, on the inside of the loop. Tent site 35 is the best, as it offers a space under a tree. Neither the roads nor the sites themselves are in especially good condition. The sites are mostly dirt, and many are overgrown. On the plus side, there are excellent views of a rocky outcropping, and the campground is located only one mile from the El Morro National Monument.

Basics

Operated By: Louis Gross. **Open:** All year. **Site Assignment:** First come, first served; no reservations. **Registration:** In cafe; late arrivals select available site and pay in the morning. **Fee:** RV $10 (full), tent $7; V, MC. **Parking:** At site.

Facilities

Number of RV Sites: 27. **Number of Tent-Only Sites:** 6. **Hookups:** Water, sewer, electric (20, 30 amp). **Each Site:** Picnic table. **Dump Station:** No. **Laundry:** No. **Pay Phone:** Yes. **Rest Rooms and Showers:** Yes. **Fuel:** No. **Propane:** No. **Internal Roads:** Gravel/dirt. **RV Service:** No. **Market:** Small, 5 mi. southwest; large, 15 mi. to Vine Hill. **Restaurant:** 15 mi. to Vine Hill. **General Store:** No. **Vending:** No. **Swimming:** No. **Playground:** No. **Other:** Cafe, cabins, trails. **Activities:** Hiking, caving. **Nearby Attractions:** El Morro National Monument, Bandera Crater and Ice Caves, Cibola National Forest. **Additional Information:** Grants Chamber of Commerce, (505) 287-4802.

Restrictions

Pets: On leash, cleaned up after. **Fires:** In grills. **Alcoholic Beverages:** At sites. **Vehicle Maximum Length:** None.

To Get There

From Hwy. I-40 (Exit 81), turn southwest onto Hwy. 53 and go 40 mi. Turn left at the sign (near mile marker 46) into the entrance.

ELEPHANT BUTTE

Lakeside RV Park

107 Country Club Blvd., P.O. Drawer 981, Elephant Butte 87935. T: (800) 808-5848 or (505) 744-5996; F: (505) 744-4903; www.lakeside.com; lakeside@riolink.com.

RV ★★★★★ Tent n/a

Beauty: ★★★★ Site Privacy: ★★★★★
Spaciousness: ★★★★★ Quiet: ★★★★
Security: ★★★★★ Cleanliness: ★★★★★
Insect Control: ★★★★ Facilities: ★★★★

This RV park is not only the closest park to the lake, but is a beautiful place to camp to boot. Laid out in three tiers, the park uses natural desert landscaping (rocks, cacti) to beautiful effect. In the lowest tier, sites 2–8 are open-ended back-ins (roughly 55 × 22 feet) situated around the office. The uppermost tier contains sites large enough for a vehicle and boat. These open-ended pull-throughs (sites 20–26 and 36–41) are about 70 × 30 feet. Sites 27–30 are 45-foot back-ins. Sites 42–50 deserve special mention, as they are located around the Native Garden, a gorgeous display of alow, rocks, and cacti. Of these sites, 44 and 47 have the best shade. These are by far the most beautiful sites in the park. In the middle tier are 54-foot back-ins that back to either a fence and the first tier (on the west side) or to a hedge and the road (on the east side). Two hosts live in the campground, ensuring that the park remains secure at all times. The rest rooms are absolutely spotless and nicely decorated. The showers are likewise clean and very comfortable. This is an RV park that deserves a special visit, not only for the surrounding beauty, but for the care and maintenance given to the park itself.

Basics

Operated By: Mary and Dave Amaral. **Open:** All year. **Site Assignment:** Upon registration; credit card required for reservation, no refunds. **Registration:** In office; late arrivals select available site and pay in the morning. **Fee:** Back-ins $20, pull-throughs $22–26; checks, V, MC, D. **Parking:** At site.

Facilities

Number of RV Sites: 50. **Number of Tent-Only Sites:** 0. **Hookups:** Water, sewer, electric (30, 50 amp), cable. **Dump Station:** Yes. **Laundry:** Yes. **Pay Phone:** Yes. **Rest Rooms and Showers:** Yes. **Fuel:** No. **Propane:** No. **Internal Roads:** Gravel. **RV Service:** No. **Market:** 5 mi. to Truth or Consequences. **Restaurant:** 0.5 mi. to Elephant Butte. **General Store:** No. **Vending:** No. **Swimming:** Yes (lake). **Playground:** No. **Other:** Lounge, phone hookups, BBQ pits. **Activities:** Organized activities (in winter), potlucks, doughnuts on Wednesday morning, boating, fishing, swimming. **Nearby Attractions:** Ghost towns, Truth or Consequences, Elephant Butte State Park. **Additional Information:** Elephant Butte Chamber of Commerce, (505) 744-9101.

Restrictions

Pets: On leash, cleaned up after, no barking. **Fires:** In grills. **Alcoholic Beverages:** At sites. **Vehicle Maximum Length:** None.

To Get There

From Hwy. I-25 (Exit 83): from the east side of the highway, go straight east on Hwy. 95 for 3.6 mi. Turn right onto Country Club Blvd., and go 0.1 mi. Turn right onto Water Ave. and take the first right into the park.

ESPAÑOLA

Cottonwood RV Park

Rte. 3 Box 245, Española 87532. T: (505) 753-6608; F: (505) 753-3858.

RV ★★★ Tent ★★★

Beauty: ★★★★ Site Privacy: ★★★
Spaciousness: ★★★ Quiet: ★★★★
Security: ★★★★★ Cleanliness: ★★★
Insect Control: ★★★★ Facilities: ★★★

RV sites in this campground are laid out in one continuous row from the entrance at the south end to the furthest site to the north. They are, however, broken up into three tiers, with a fourth tier for tents right at the entrance. Sites 1–12 on the first tier are 30-foot sites (1–6 are pull-throughs, 7–12 are back-ins). All spaces are 25 feet wide. Sites 2 and 10 are well shaded, site 12 lies next to and above a house. On the second tier, site 13 is used by a long-term guest, and 14 is the smallest site at 40 feet. The rest of the sites are 70-foot pull-throughs. Sites 17–20 have the best shade. Site 22 has only 45 feet of usable space before it begins to slope. On the lowest tier, 23 requires an excruciatingly tight turn on the sloped road from the second tier and should be avoided by larger rigs. Sites 30–33 share a large shade tree, and 30 is the overall nicest (and shadiest) site. Site 32 looks unusable, and the tree there prevents 31 from being a true pull-through. This level is the nicest area, as it is surrounded by vegetation and offers the most shade. The tent sites are located in a dirt area sheltered by tree. There is one BBQ and a cement fire pit with seats for communal use. The rest rooms need a good cleaning, and the stalls (at least in the men's room) do not have doors. This campground is equally nice for tenters as for RVers.

Basics

Operated By: Art Martinez. **Open:** All year. **Site Assignment:** Upon registration; credit card required for reservation, 48 hours cancellation policy. **Registration:** In restaurant; late arrivals select available site and pay in the morning. **Fee:** RV $19 (full), tent $15; checks, V, MC, D. **Parking:** At site.

Facilities

Number of RV Sites: 37. **Number of Tent-Only Sites:** Undesignated sites. **Hookups:** Water, sewer, electric (30, 50 amp). **Dump Station:** No (sewer at all sites). **Laundry:** Yes. **Pay Phone:** Yes. **Rest Rooms and Showers:** Yes. **Fuel:** No. **Propane:** No. **Internal Roads:** Gravel. **RV Service:** No. **Market:** 2 mi. north. **Restaurant:** On-site. **General Store:** No. **Vending:** No. **Swimming:** No. **Playground:** No. **Other:** Discount on meal or free margarita upon registration. **Activities:** Fishing, gambling, visiting pueblos. **Nearby Attractions:** Pueblos, Santa Fe Opera, casinos. **Additional Information:** Española Chamber of Commerce, (505) 753-2831.

Restrictions

Pets: On leash, cleaned up after. **Fires:** In grills. **Alcoholic Beverages:** At sites. **Vehicle Maximum Length:** None.

To Get There

From the junction of Hwy. 30 and Hwy. 84/285, turn east onto Hwy. 84/285 and go 2 mi. Turn left into the restaurant complex and register in the restaurant.

FARMINGTON

Dad's RV Park

202 East Pinon St., Farmington 87401. T: (888) 326-DADS or (505) 564-2222.

RV ★★ Tent n/a

Beauty: ★ Site Privacy: ★★★
Spaciousness: ★★★ Quiet: ★★★
Security: ★★★★★ Cleanliness: ★★★
Insect Control: ★★★★ Facilities: ★

This RV park is an enclosed gravel area in the middle of an urban setting. The fence is locked at night for added security. The park is close to services that a traveler might need, and its proximity makes it a popular place to stay for visitors to the city's hospital. However, there is little else to recommend here. The sites are flat and open. There is one tree in the park, shared by sites 8 and 9. These two sites, along with 10, are clustered together and slightly set apart from the rest of the sites, which makes them slightly more private. The rest of the sites are located in a strip. They all are pull-throughs designed for self-contained units. The laundry, in the red "barn" by the manager's house, is small but comfortable and clean. Dad's would benefit from shade trees and rest room facilities. RVers who are not equipped (or willing) to stay in a park without rest rooms or shade trees should press on—possibly to Aztec.

Basics

Operated By: Regina Ingram. **Open:** All year. **Site Assignment:** Upon registration; credit card or check required for reservation, 8–12 hours cancellation policy. **Registration:** In office at back of park, 24 hours. **Fee:** RV $15; V, MC, D. **Parking:** At site.

Facilities

Number of RV Sites: 13. **Number of Tent-Only Sites:** 0. **Hookups:** Water, sewer, electric (30 amp). **Each Site:** Picnic table. **Dump Station:** No (sewer at all sites). **Laundry:** Yes. **Pay Phone:** Yes. **Rest Rooms and Showers:** No. **Fuel:** No. **Propane:** No. **Internal Roads:** Gravel. **RV Service:** No. **Market:** 9 blocks. **Restaurant:** 4 blocks. **General Store:** No. **Vending:** No. **Swimming:** No. **Playground:** No. **Activities:** Golf, sightseeing. **Nearby Attractions:** Aztec Ruins National Monument, Bisti/De-Na-Zin Wilderness Area. **Additional Information:** Farmington CVB, (800) 448-1240, (505) 326-7602.

Restrictions

Pets: On leash, cleaned up after. **Fires:** None. **Alcoholic Beverages:** None. **Vehicle Maximum Length:** 45 ft.

To Get There

From the junction of Hwys. 64 (Murray St.) and 371 (Pinon St.), go 1 mi. east on Pinon. Turn left at the sign into the entrance. The office is at the very back of the park.

FORT SUMNER

Valley View Mobile Home and RV Park

Rte. 1 Box 36, 1401 East Sumner, Fort Sumner 88119. T: (505) 355-2380; www.billythekid.nv.switchboard.net; btkmuseum@plateautel.net.

RV ★★ Tent n/a

Beauty: ★★ Site Privacy: ★★★
Spaciousness: ★★★★ Quiet: ★★★
Security: ★★ Cleanliness: ★★★
Insect Control: ★★★ Facilities: ★★

Valley View has super-long sites (80-foot pull-throughs and back-ins), but, alas, little else for which to recommend it. The trees visible from the campground help elevate the beauty of this park from its urban setting, but the mobile homes inside detract in equal measure. The three (unnumbered) back-ins in the southeast corner have a hedge along the east side, and there is a row of trees along the south side, making these three back-ins much nicer than the rest of the sites. The pull-throughs in the middle of the park are long, level, and grassy, but quite open. They are, however, clearly numbered, which is not the case for the back-ins. The least desirable site is undoubtedly 19, barely 30 feet from a mobile home to the south. Other sites are a good 40 feet wide. Be advised that there are no showers, no toilets, no dump station. Drivers of long rigs may welcome the spacious sites, but those looking for more than a parking space should look elsewhere. Tenters might consider nearby Lake Sumner.

Basics

Operated By: Don and Lula Sweet. **Open:** All year. **Site Assignment:** First come, first served; verbal reservations OK, please call to cancel. **Registration:** Wait for someone to collect fee, after 10 p.m. use drop box. **Fee:** $15, subject to change without notice. **Parking:** At site.

Facilities

Number of RV Sites: 37. **Number of Tent-Only Sites:** 0. **Hookups:** Water, sewer, electric (30, 50 amp), cable. **Each Site:** 1–2 trees. **Dump Station:** No (sewer at all sites). **Laundry:** No. **Pay Phone:** No. **Rest Rooms and Showers:** No. **Fuel:** No. **Propane:** No. **Internal Roads:** Dirt. **RV Service:** No. **Market:** 1 mi. west. **Restaurant:** Across street. **General Store:** No. **Vending:** No. **Swimming:** No. **Playground:** No. **Activities:** Visiting sites/museums. **Nearby Attractions:** Billy the Kid Museum, Billy the Kid's Grave. **Additional Information:** Da Baca/Ft. Sumner County Chamber of Commerce, (505) 355-7705.

Restrictions

Pets: On leash. **Fires:** In own grills. **Alcoholic Beverages:** Prefer none, but in RV unit OK. **Vehicle Maximum Length:** None.

To Get There

From the junction of Hwy. 60 and Hwy. 84, go 0.8 mi. east on Hwy. 60/84 and turn right at the sign. Take the immediate left into the campground and select a spot.

GALLUP

Gallup KOA

2925 West Hwy. 66, Gallup 87301. T: (505) 865-5021; F: (505) 865-5021; www.koa.com; koagallup@cnetco.com.

RV ★★★★ Tent ★★★

Beauty: ★★★ Site Privacy: ★★★★
Spaciousness: ★★★★ Quiet: ★★★★
Security: ★★★★★ Cleanliness: ★★★★★
Insect Control: ★★★★ Facilities: ★★★★★

This campground is laid out in five rows of pull-throughs with two rows of tent sites behind them, and one row of back-ins along the eastern wall. Sites 1–12 and 15–30 are 70-foot gravel sites, slightly shorter (60 feet) on the ends. Sites 31–48 are 65-foot sites, while 49–69 and 70–91 are slightly shorter (54 feet and 60 feet). Back-ins 122–141 are 30-foot sites, best suited for pop-ups or vans. The best RV sites are those on the eastern edge (1, 15, 31, 49, and 70), as these face into trees and hills beyond. The tent sites at the end of the park are 24 × 27-foot open sites. Trees are mostly small and scarce. The best tent sites are 23 and 25, which share a larger tree. The rest rooms and showers are exceptionally clean and comfortable. The electric eye at the gate alerts the owners of all incoming guests, ensuring the safety of the park. A very comfortable campground that campers of all types will enjoy.

Basics

Operated By: Charles Diaz. **Open:** All year. **Site Assignment:** Upon registration; verbal reservations OK. **Registration:** In office. **Fee:** RV $27 (full), $25 (water, electric); tent $21; checks, V, MC, D. **Parking:** At site.

Facilities

Number of RV Sites: 120. **Number of Tent-Only Sites:** 16. **Hookups:** Water, sewer, electric (30, 50 amp). **Each Site:** Picnic table. **Dump Station:** Yes. **Laundry:** Yes. **Pay Phone:** Yes. **Rest Rooms and Showers:** Yes. **Fuel:** No. **Propane:** Yes. **Internal Roads:** Paved. **RV Service:** No. **Market:** 1 mi. west. **Restaurant:** On-site. **General Store:** Yes. **Vending:** No. **Swimming:** Pool. **Playground:** Yes. **Other:** Cabins, modem. **Activities:** Swimming, rodeos, American Indian dances. **Nearby Attractions:** Historic Rte. 66, Red Rock State Park, Inter-Tribal Indian Ceremonial. **Additional Information:** Gallup Mc Kinley City Chamber, (505) 722-2228.

Restrictions

Pets: On 6-ft. leash, cleaned up after, use dog walk. **Fires:** In grills. **Alcoholic Beverages:** At sites. **Vehicle Max. Length:** None. **Other:** No groups.

To Get There

From Hwy. I-40 (Exit 16), turn east onto Rte. 66 and go 1 mi. Turn right at the sign into entrance.

GRANTS

Lavaland RV Park

1901 East Santa Fe Ave., Grants 87020. T: (505) 287-8665; F: (505) 285-5181; lavaland@7cities.net.

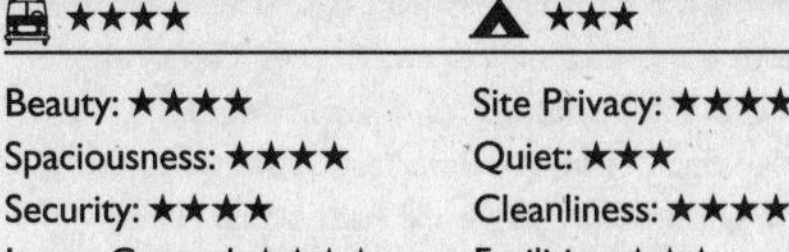

★★★★ ★★★

Beauty: ★★★★ Site Privacy: ★★★★
Spaciousness: ★★★★ Quiet: ★★★
Security: ★★★★ Cleanliness: ★★★★
Insect Control: ★★★★ Facilities: ★★★

Sites in Lavaland are laid out in four rows. Sites are 60 feet long and 30 feet wide. Sites 1–11 are back-ins along the western edge that back to a retaining wall with trees and a fence. Sites 11 and 12 at the end do not have shade trees. In the middle of the campground, sites 12–27 and 28–39 are pull-throughs. Site 39 is located next to the dump station and is thus less desirable. On the east side, sites 40–51 face the highway and hills in the distance. These pull-throughs as well as the road they lie on are rougher in spots (especially 48) than the other rows of pull-throughs. The tenting area is in the southeast corner by the entrance. These dirt sites have nice desert views, and some are shaded. The rest rooms and showers are clean, but there is no window, so the room is pitch black when the light is not on. (Be sure to turn on the light before the door closes!) Lavaland is an attractive campground that will appeal to many campers—a little better to RVers than to tenters.

Basics

Operated By: Fidel and Leticia Duenas. **Open:** All year. **Site Assignment:** Upon registration; credit card required for reservation, 48 hours cancellation policy. **Registration:** In office; late arrivals use drop box. **Fee:** RV $16 (full), tent $14; V, MC, D. **Parking:** At site.

Facilities

Number of RV Sites: 51. **Number of Tent-Only Sites:** Undesignated sites. **Hookups:** Water, sewer, electric (30, 50 amp). **Each Site:** Picnic table, grill. **Dump Station:** Yes. **Laundry:** Yes. **Pay Phone:** Yes. **Rest Rooms and Showers:** Yes. **Fuel:** No. **Propane:** No. **Internal Roads:** Gravel. **RV Service:** No (minor repairs). **Market:** 0.25 mi. at I-40. **Restaurant:** 0.25 mi. at I-40. **General Store:** No. **Vending:** Yes. **Swimming:** No. **Playground:** No. **Other:** Studio rooms, gift shop. **Activities:** Caving, hiking. **Nearby Attractions:** Visitor center within walking distance, Mine Museum, ice caves, Acoma Sky City, Cibola Natioanl Forest. **Additional Information:** Grants Chamber, (505) 287-4802.

Restrictions

Pets: On leash, cleaned up after, no big dogs outside. **Fires:** In grills. **Alcoholic Beverages:** At sites. **Vehicle Maximum Length:** 60 ft.

To Get There

From Hwy. I-40 (Exit 85), from the south side of the highway, turn south and take the first right onto Jurassic Ct., then take the first right into the campground.

HOBBS

Harry McAdams Park

5000 Jack Gomez Blvd., Hobbs 88240. T: (505) 392-5845.

 ★★★  ★★★★

Beauty: ★★★★ Site Privacy: ★★★★
Spaciousness: ★★★★ Quiet: ★★★★
Security: ★★★★ Cleanliness: ★★★★
Insect Control: ★★★ Facilities: ★★

Six miles northwest of Hobbs, near the College of the Southwest, the Harry McAdams Park is divided into north and south, each with a different flavor. The north campground is more primitive with regards to hookups (only three sites have full hookups), but contains the rest room facilities and sits on prettier grounds. Sites are 54-foot back-ins with enough space on all sides to accommodate a large family with children. Sites inside the loop share an interior common grounds, while those on the outside of the loop back onto an expansive grassy area. Site 9 on the outside loop is situated somewhat away from the rest and backs onto a field that runs toward the day area a few hundred yards away. The grass is lush and extremely well maintained—be forewarned that crews get under way early to avoid the hot sun of afternoon. The rest room facilities are acceptably clean and spacious, with showers in a separate curtained-off area. The south campground is an open field with a strip of sites down a central road. The field is humongous, but does receive some airplane noise. Campsites here are more minimalist, with a table and young tree that does not provide shade. (An exception is the tree in sites 21/23.) These pull-through sites, virtually unlimited in size, are not your traditional pull-throughs: when leaving, you pull out into the field, turn around, and come back through your site. The south campground rates lower on beauty and quiet, and would rate higher on facilities due to the hookups, although the rest rooms are a block away in the north campground. For those seeking a quiet escape (and can forego full hookups for a night), Harry McAdams (especially the north side) is an extremely pleasant and comfortable place to stay.

Basics

Operated By: Rudy and Lorraine. **Open:** All year. **Site Assignment:** First come, first served. **Registration:** At self-pay station. **Fee:** Site $7, electricity $11. **Parking:** At site.

Facilities

Number of RV Sites: 62. **Number of Tent-Only Sites:** 0. **Hookups:** Water, sewer, electric (30 amp). **Each Site:** North campground: Picnic shelter w/ table, trees, grill; South campground: picnic table. **Dump Station:** Yes. **Laundry:** No. **Pay Phone:** Yes. **Rest Rooms and Showers:** Yes. **Fuel:** No. **Propane:** No. **Internal Roads:** Paved, in perfect condition. **RV Service:** No. **Market:** 6 mi. to Hobbs. **Restaurant:** 2 mi. towards Hobbs. **General Store:** No. **Vending:** Yes. **Swimming:** No. **Playground:** Yes. **Other:** 2 trout-stocked ponds, day use area. **Activities:** Volleyball, horseshoes, fishing. **Nearby Attractions:** Blackwater Draw Museum, Old Fort Sumner Museum, Billy the Kid Museum. **Additional Information:** Hobbs Chamber of Commerce, (800) 658-6291, (505) 397-3202.

Restrictions

Pets: On leash. **Fires:** In grills. **Alcoholic Beverages:** At sites. **Vehicle Maximum Length:** None. **Other:** No generators, 1 camp vehicle, plus 1 other vehicle per site.

To Get There

From Hwy. 18 (between Hobbs and Lovington), turn west onto Jack Gomez. (Much more visible than the street sign are the two signs at the street entrance on the west side for the Hobbs Industrial Air Park.) Go 0.8 mi. on Jack Gomez behind a police station, then turn right into the campground. All guests must register at the pay station here. To get to the south campground, continue on Jack Gomez through the stop sign and into the area marked Hobbs Army Air Base. Make the first left into the campground, then return to the north campground to register.

JEMEZ SPRINGS

Trail's End RV Park

37695 Hwy. 126, Jemez Springs 87025. T: (505) 829-4072; F: (505) 829-4072; trailsendrv@hotmail.com.

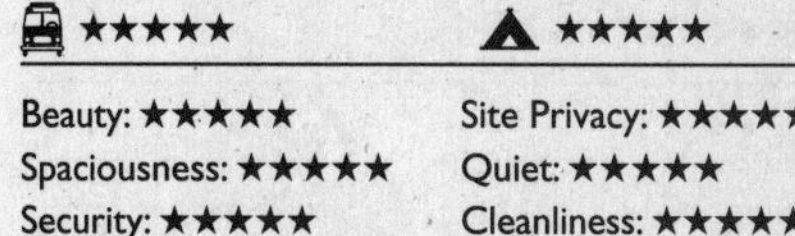

★★★★★ ★★★★★

Beauty: ★★★★★ Site Privacy: ★★★★★
Spaciousness: ★★★★★ Quiet: ★★★★★
Security: ★★★★★ Cleanliness: ★★★★★
Insect Control: ★★★★★ Facilities: ★★

Trail's End offers the only full hookups in the area. But even if that weren't the case, it would well be worth a visit. The area is gorgeous, and the campground takes full advantage of the forest where it lies. Sites are left in a natural condition, and there are flowers planted amongst the pines. Sites 1–7 are gravel back-ins located up-slope from the office. Site 1 is one of the longest, at 55 feet. Smaller sites (30 feet) include 3–9. Sites 8–17 are located along the southern side. Of these, 11 is a 70-foot pull-through (of which only 60 feet are usable, due to the slope), and 17 is likewise quite long (65 feet). Sites 12, 13, and 15 are 45-foot back-ins. Closest to the entrance (which makes for the easiest in and out), but also located just off the highway is site 16, which is a 60-foot pull-through. (Some of the sites have a slightly smaller usable length due to the slope.) Tenting is possible in sites 18 and 19, but, with 50,000 acres of national forest surrounding the campground and offering free camping, even the owner asks why a tenter would pay to camp. The rest room, although small, is brand-spanking new, with further facilities under construction. An absolutely gorgeous campground that is not to be missed by RVers.

Basics

Operated By: Steve McMahon. **Open:** All year. **Site Assignment:** Upon registration; verbal reservations OK. **Registration:** In office; no arrivals after 9 p.m. **Fee:** RV $22 (full), $20 (water, electric); tent $12; checks, no credits cards. **Parking:** At site.

Facilities

Number of RV Sites: 14. **Number of Tent-Only Sites:** 2. **Hookups:** Water, sewer, electric (30 amp). **Each Site:** Picnic table, grill. **Dump Station:** No (sewer at all sites). **Laundry:** No. **Pay Phone:** No. **Rest Rooms and Showers:** Toilet; no shower. **Fuel:** No. **Propane:** No. **Internal Roads:** Gravel. **RV Service:** No. **Market:** 1 mi. south. **Restaurant:** 1 mi. south. **General Store:** No. **Vending:** No. **Swimming:** No. **Playground:** Yes. **Other:**

Surrounded by national forest. **Activities:** Fishing, hiking, horseback riding, hunting. **Nearby Attractions:** Soda Dam, Santa Fe, Albuquerque, hot springs, Fenton Lake State Park, Santa Fe National Forest, Jemez Pueblo, Zia Pueblo. **Additional Information:** Los Alamos Chamber, (505) 662-8105.

RESTRICTIONS

Pets: On leash, cleaned up after. **Fires:** In grills. **Alcoholic Beverages:** At sites. **Vehicle Maximum Length:** 38 ft.

TO GET THERE

From the junction of Hwy. 550 and Hwy. 4, turn north onto Hwy. 4 and go 26.5 mi. (8.1 mi. north of Jemez Springs National Monument). Turn left onto Hwy. 126 and go 5 mi. to the campground.

KIRTLAND

Paramount RV Park

4336 US Hwy. 64, Kirtland 87417. T: (505) 598-9824; F: (505) 598-6515.

RV: ★★ Tent: n/a

Beauty: ★	Site Privacy: ★★★
Spaciousness: ★★★	Quiet: ★★
Security: ★★★★★	Cleanliness: ★★★★
Insect Control: ★★★★	Facilities: ★

This RV park is a large gravel area with no defined sites (other than hookups). As a result, both back-ins and pull-throughs can accommodate a rig of any size, which, along with the security fence and gate, is pretty much the main draw to this park. You know you can get any vehicle inside, and you won't be bothered once there. Apart from this, the park does not stand out, save for some distant views of buttes to the south. Back-ins 1–8 have some low shrubs and so could be called a little prettier, but they back directly to the highway, which makes them closer to the traffic noise. Site 25 is right next to the office and seems more cramped and busy because of this. All sites are level but very open—RVers will have to roll out the awning here.

BASICS

Operated By: James and Darlene Stewart. **Open:** All year. **Site Assignment:** Depending on site availability; check required for reservation, 24 hours cancellation policy. **Registration:** In office; late arrivals use drop box. **Fee:** RV $16 (full, cable), $12 (water, electric); no credits cards, but checks. **Parking:** At site.

FACILITIES

Number of RV Sites: 24. **Number of Tent-Only Sites:** 0. **Hookups:** Water, sewer, electric (30, 50 amp). **Dump Station:** No. **Laundry:** No. **Pay Phone:** No. **Rest Rooms and Showers:** No. **Fuel:** No. **Propane:** No. **Internal Roads:** Gravel. **RV Service:** No. **Market:** 1 mi. **Restaurant:** 1 mi. **General Store:** No. **Vending:** No. **Swimming:** No. **Playground:** No. **Other:** Dog walk. **Activities:** Sightseeing. **Nearby Attractions:** Navajo Reservation, Aztec Ruins, Four Corners. **Additional Information:** Farmington Chamber, (505) 325-0279.

RESTRICTIONS

Pets: On leash, cleaned up after. **Fires:** In grills; subject to seasonal bans. **Alcoholic Beverages:** At sites. **Vehicle Maximum Length:** None.

TO GET THERE

From the junction of Hwy. 64 and the only stop light in town, go 1.3 mi. east on Hwy. 64. Turn left into the entrance. (Look for the sign at the top of the hill.) Turn into paved road, follow it to the back of the park, then take the first left at the sign into the campground. The office is on the right.

LAS CRUCES

Best View RV Park

814 Weinrich Rd., Las Cruces 88005. T: (800) 526-6555 or (505) 526-6555; F: (505) 526-9421; www.bestviewrvpark.com; bvrvpark@zianet.com.

RV: ★★★★★ Tent: ★★★★

Beauty: ★★★★	Site Privacy: ★★★
Spaciousness: ★★★	Quiet: ★★★★
Security: ★★★★★	Cleanliness: ★★★★
Insect Control: ★★★★	Facilities: ★★★★★

Southwest of Las Cruces and toward the airport, this campground commands a view of the town with its agricultural areas, plentiful trees, and the Organ Pipe Mountain behind that really lives up to its name. The campground is laid out in a giant "L" shape, with back-ins around the perimeter and pull-throughs inside. Pull-throughs average 62 feet in length, with sites 60–61 slightly longer (65 feet), which makes them among the best sites available—certainly for longer rigs. Back-ins are roughly the same length as pull-throughs, although there are some much smaller sites to accommodate vans/pop-ups near the tent and cabin area. All sites are level and mostly open. The tent area is short of tables and grills, with only a bare ground covering of grass. (Grass does not grow well in the area.) However, there are enough trees for ample protection from above. Tent sites are generally flat, with a slight slope in sites 75 and 80. The second tent (and RV) area near the cabins is close to the road, with the attendant traffic sounds. The southwest corner above the cabins contains a slightly scruffy residence, but that is the only detraction from the beauty of this campground. The rest room and shower facilities are quite clean. Overall, this is a great camping experience for both RVers and tenters, with a "best view" from nearly all of the sites.

BASICS

Operated By: Steve and Keri Perry. **Open:** All year. **Site Assignment:** Upon registration; reservations require credit card, cancel up to 7 p.m. day of arrival. **Registration:** In office; late arrivals use drop box. **Fee:** Full $22, water, electric $17.50, tent $14.50. **Parking:** At site.

FACILITIES

Number of RV Sites: 84. **Number of Tent-Only Sites:** 14. **Hookups:** Water, sewer, electric (30, 50 amp). **Each Site:** Picnic table, grill, tree. **Dump Station:** Yes. **Laundry:** Yes. **Pay Phone:** Yes. **Rest Rooms and Showers:** Yes. **Fuel:** No. **Propane:** Yes. **Internal Roads:** Paved. **RV Service:** No. **Market:** 5 mi. northeast to Las Cruces. **Restaurant:** 5 mi. northeast to Las Cruces. **General Store:** Yes. **Vending:** Yes. **Swimming:** Pool (May–Sept.). **Playground:** Yes. **Other:** 4 acres RV storage, 4 cabins, dog walk. **Activities:** Hiking. **Nearby Attractions:** White Sands National Monument, Mesilla, City of Rocks State Park. **Additional Information:** Las Cruces CVB, (800) 343-7827, (505) 541-2444.

RESTRICTIONS

Pets: On leash, cleaned up after. **Fires:** In grills. **Alcoholic Beverages:** At sites. **Vehicle Maximum Length:** None.

TO GET THERE

From I-25, take Exit 6B, turn west onto Main St., and drive 2.4 mi. to Picachio St. Turn right onto Picachio and drive 5.2 mi. Turn left at the sign, then take the second immediate left into the campground. The office is right at the entrance.

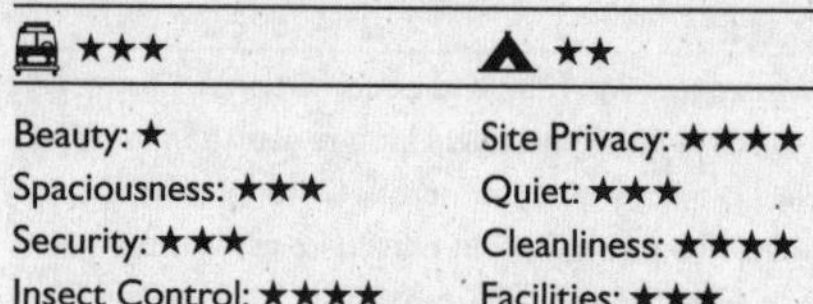

LAS VEGAS

Vegas RV Overnite Park

504 Harris Rd., Las Vegas 87701. T: (505) 425-5640; vegasrv@zialink.com.

RV: ★★★ Tent: ★★

Beauty: ★	Site Privacy: ★★★★
Spaciousness: ★★★	Quiet: ★★★
Security: ★★★	Cleanliness: ★★★★
Insect Control: ★★★★	Facilities: ★★★

Take it from the business card of this park: this is a storage business with an RV park attached. There are storage units to the north and east, mobile homes to the west, and residences and commercial development to the south. None of these add to the attractiveness of the campground. Sites are laid out in four rows. Sites in row A are 54 × 33 feet, sites in row B are 65 × 33 feet, and sites in row C are 70 × 33 feet. All of these are pull-throughs. Back-ins in Row D are 48 × 30 feet. These sites are right next to the storage units. Tenting sites are also located in this area. While there is decent grass cover, there is no shade—a problem endemic to the entire park. There is also very little landscaping, aside from the bench and vegetation next to C1—which prevents the use of a grill at this site. The northeast corner (sites C6–11) is the nicest section, as it is furthest from the office and road. End site C11 is right off the road, and can therefore accommodate larger rigs but does get more passing traffic. The rest rooms are clean, but the showers do not have a lip to hold back the water. As a result, the entire rest room gets drenched with every shower.

BASICS

Operated By: Mark Shubert. **Open:** All year. **Site Assignment:** Upon registration; credit card required for reservation, 24 hours cancellation policy. **Registration:** In office; late arrivals use drop box. **Fee:** RV $18 (full), $13 (water, electric); tent $11; checks, V, MC. **Parking:** At site.

FACILITIES

Number of RV Sites: 40. **Number of Tent-Only Sites:** 0. **Hookups:** Water, sewer, electric (30 amp), cable. **Dump Station:** No (sewer at all sites).

Laundry: No. **Pay Phone:** Yes. **Rest Rooms and Showers:** Yes. **Fuel:** No. **Propane:** No. **Internal Roads:** Gravel. **RV Service:** No. **Market:** Less than 0.25 mi. south. **Restaurant:** Less than 0.25 mi. south. **General Store:** No. **Vending:** No. **Swimming:** No. **Playground:** No. **Other:** Phone hookups for long-term guests. **Activities:** Fishing, boating, swimming, hiking. **Nearby Attractions:** Storrie Lake State Park, historic downtown, Pecos National Monument, Santa Fe Trail, Ft. Union. **Additional Information:** Las Vegas Chamber of Commerce, (505) 425-8631.

RESTRICTIONS

Pets: On leash, cleaned up after. **Fires:** In grills. **Alcoholic Beverages:** At sites. **Vehicle Maximum Length:** 58 ft.

TO GET THERE

From Hwy. I-25 (Exit 347), turn south onto Grand Ave. and go 1.2 mi. Turn right onto Mills Ave. and go 0.7 mi. Turn right onto 7th St. and go 1.1 mi. north. Turn right before the sign and take the second left into the campground.

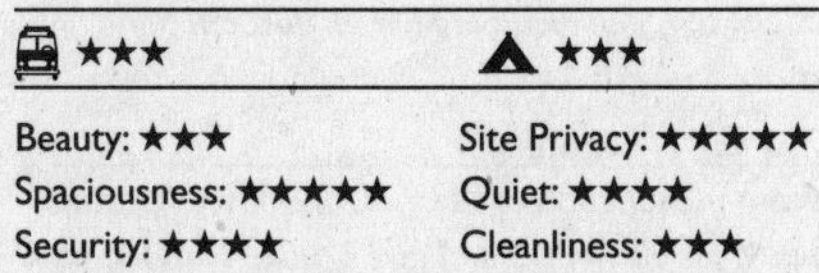

LOGAN

Ute Lake State Park

P.O. Box 52, Logan 88426. T: (877) 664-7787 or (888) NM-PARKS or (505) 487-2284; www.icampnm.com.

RV ★★★ Tent ★★★

Beauty: ★★★ Site Privacy: ★★★★★
Spaciousness: ★★★★★ Quiet: ★★★★
Security: ★★★★ Cleanliness: ★★★
Insect Control: ★★★ Facilities: ★★

There are two campgrounds (Zia and Yucca) in this desert-setting state park. Zia Campground is closest to the office and contains the reservable sites. The outside of this looped campground contains 95-foot pull-throughs (all odd numbers), while the inside contains 35-foot back-ins (all even numbers), which are separated one from the other by large boulders and trees. Sites with the best lake views are 11, 13, and 15. Those closest to the rest rooms are 17, 18, 20, and 21. To the south of this loop is an area of primitive sites that offer sheltered picnic tables and grills. The southernmost sites are grassy, shaded, and open to the lake. (The rest of the sites are open to the blazing sun.) Yuccan Campground has absolutely the largest pull-throughs you'll ever see (165 × 65 feet)—obviously built with the boater in mind. Sites are in two rows along a gravel drive. Sites on the south side (57–72) have a view of the lake and are closest to the lake access area (by 72), but there is no boat ramp there. Instead, this road provides access to the dispersed tent camping along the bank of the lake. While there is no shade nor grass, the upside is that you can practically roll out of your tent into the lake if you want. The bathhouse, located east of Yucca Campground, is clean, comfortable, and very spacious. There are further campgrounds on the north and south sides of the lake, but the two described are easier to access and enjoyable by anyone looking for fun on a lake.

BASICS

Operated By: New Mexico State Park Division. **Open:** May 15–Sept. 15. **Site Assignment:** First come, first served; reservations by credit card or check, no refunds. **Registration:** At pay station. **Fee:** Primitive site $8, developed site $10, hookup $4; checks, V, MC, D. **Parking:** At site.

FACILITIES

Number of RV Sites: 77. **Number of Tent-Only Sites:** 57. **Hookups:** Water, electric (30 amp). **Each Site:** Picnic table, grill, fire pit. **Dump Station:** Yes. **Laundry:** No. **Pay Phone:** Yes. **Rest Rooms and Showers:** Yes. **Fuel:** No. **Propane:** No. **Internal Roads:** Paved. **RV Service:** No. **Market:** 2.5 mi. east. **Restaurant:** 2.5 mi. east. **General Store:** Yes. **Vending:** No. **Swimming:** Yes (lake). **Playground:** Yes. **Other:** Trails, boat ramp, baseball field. **Activities:** Fishing, boating, swimming, hiking. **Nearby Attractions:** Ute Lake. **Additional Information:** State Park Office, (505) 487-2284.

RESTRICTIONS

Pets: On leash, cleaned up after. **Fires:** In grills. **Alcoholic Beverages:** At sites. **Vehicle Maximum Length:** None.

TO GET THERE

From the junction of Hwy. 54 and Hwy. 540, turn west onto Hwy. 540 and go 2.4 mi. Turn left at the sign into the entrance.

LORDSBURG

Lordsburg KOA

1501 Lead St., Lordsburg 88045. T: (800) 562-5772 or (505) 542-8003; www.koa.com.

RV ★★★★ Tent ★★★★

Beauty: ★★★ Site Privacy: ★★★★★
Spaciousness: ★★★★★ Quiet: ★★★
Security: ★★★★ Cleanliness: ★★★★★
Insect Control: ★★★★ Facilities: ★★★★★

This campground with mountain views in all directions offers all 60-foot (or larger) pull-throughs laid out in eight rows. Rows 1 and 2 (sites 1–4 and 14–17) are open-ended sites that can easily accommodate 60 feet, and are 33 feet wide. These sites are closest to the facilities. Rows 4–7 are slightly larger than 60 feet and contain the remotest sites to the southwest. (The single remotest site is 54 in row 7.) Row 8 runs perpendicular to rows 1–7 on the south edge of the property. The longest pull-throughs (90 feet) are located in this row. Of these sites, the least desirable are 5 (faces a mobile home) and 9 (faces a dumpster). Sites 58–63, along the north edge, are electric sites only. These are grassier, however, and quite nice. Tent sites occupy sites 1–3 of row 3, and T4 of row 4. These walled-in sites are 33 × 22 feet and offer a square of dirt for a tent. Site 3 has the communal wash basin and trash recepticle. There is also group tenting along the north edge by the cabins. A camping kitchen for tenters is located next to the basketball court. Lordsburg is a very nice campground that both RVers and tenters will enjoy.

BASICS

Operated By: Marin and Naty. **Open:** All year. **Site Assignment:** Upon registration; credit card required for reservation, 24 hours cancellation policy. **Registration:** In office; late arrivals use drop box. **Fee:** RV $22 (full), $20 (water, electric); tent $17; checks, V, MC, D. **Parking:** At site.

FACILITIES

Number of RV Sites: 62. **Number of Tent-Only Sites:** 5. **Hookups:** Water, sewer, electric (30, 50 amp). **Each Site:** Picnic table (tent sites: picnic table, grill, lantern pole). **Dump Station:** Yes. **Laundry:** Yes. **Pay Phone:** Yes. **Rest Rooms and Showers:** Yes. **Fuel:** No. **Propane:** No. **Internal Roads:** Gravel. **RV Service:** No. **Market:** Less than 0.25 mi. on Main St. **Restaurant:** Less than 0.25 mi. on Main St. **General Store:** Yes. **Vending:** Yes. **Swimming:** Pool. **Playground:** Yes. **Other:** Dog walk, cabins, covered pavilion, rec room. **Activities:** Swimming, basketball, badminton, horseshoes, hiking, visiting ghost towns. **Nearby Attractions:** Shakespeare Ghost Town, Gila National Forest. **Additional Information:** Lordsburg-Hidalgo Chamber of Commerce, (505) 542-9864.

RESTRICTIONS

Pets: On leash, cleaned up after. **Fires:** In grills. **Alcoholic Beverages:** At sites. **Vehicle Maximum Length:** None.

TO GET THERE

From Hwy. I-10 (Exit 22), from the south side of the highway, go 1 block south on Main to Maple St. and turn right. Follow Maple (which curves to the left) and go 0.3 mi. Continue straight on into the campground.

MAYHILL

Rio Penasco RV Camp

P.O. Box 47, Mayhill 88339. T: (505) 687-3715; ejnutt@pvtnetworks.net.

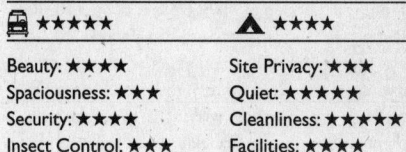

RV ★★★★★ Tent ★★★★

Beauty: ★★★★ Site Privacy: ★★★
Spaciousness: ★★★ Quiet: ★★★★★
Security: ★★★★ Cleanliness: ★★★★★
Insect Control: ★★★ Facilities: ★★★★

Just to the south of Mayhill, Rio Penasco is surrounded on all sides by trees and verdant hills along the entire eastern perimeter. Laid out as a giant circle with rows cut inside, the campground boasts gigantic (70 feet long) pull-throughs as well as a few back-ins around the office area. (These are the least desirable sites, assigned last when the park is full. Sites 3 and 4 are especially prone to registration traffic, being smack dab in front of the office.) The best site by a long shot is 13, which is a huge pull-through well apart from the rest, under an enormous willow, and open to the hills and creek to the east. Second place goes to 9, which is similar in every way to 13, but is sided by site 8, which detracts only slightly from its desirability. Sites are all a level grassy/gravel mix, long enough to accommodate pretty much anything, but a little on the narrow side (22 feet wide). Should this concern you at all, however, the rest room and laundry facilities will ease your mind a hundredfold. These are the nicest rest room facilities you are likely to find on your journey—no matter where you are destined. Tastefully decorated with handicrafts, they are carpeted, immaculate, and as comfortable as those at home. Likewise, the laundry facility is spacious and clean, and contains a small, carpeted rec room with sofa, table, games, puzzles, magazines, and more handicrafts. Situated in a gorgeous setting in the tiny mountain town of Mayhill near Cloudcroft, this campground is a splendid destination for return visits.

Basics

Operated By: John and Emily Nutt. **Open:** All year. **Site Assignment:** Depending on availability; credit card or check for reservations, reservations required June–Aug. **Registration:** In office; late arrivals use drop box or settle in morning. **Fee:** RV $13.50, tent $10. **Parking:** At site.

Facilities

Number of RV Sites: 32. **Number of Tent-Only Sites:** Undesignated sites. **Hookups:** Water, sewer, electric (30 amp). **Each Site:** Picnic table. **Dump Station:** No (sewer at all sites). **Laundry:** Yes. **Pay Phone:** Yes. **Rest Rooms and Showers:** Yes. **Fuel:** No. **Propane:** Yes. **Internal Roads:** Gravel, in good condition. **RV Service:** No. **Market:** 1 mi. to Mayhill. **Restaurant:** 1 mi. to Mayhill. **General Store:** Yes. **Vending:** No. **Swimming:** No. **Playground:** No. **Other:** RV supplies, creek, pavilion, rec room. **Activities:** Nightly entertainment in pavilion, fishing, games. **Nearby Attractions:** Cloudcroft, Weed (historic logging town). **Additional Information:** Cloudcroft Chamber of Commerce, (505) 682-2733.

Restrictions

Pets: On leash, cleaned up, no barking. **Fires:** In grills or fire ring in pavilion. **Alcoholic Beverages:** None. **Vehicle Maximum Length:** None. **Other:** Christian atmosphere (no swearing).

To Get There

From the junction of Hwy. 82 and Hwy. 130 (Rio Penasco Rd.), turn west onto Rio Penasco Rd., cross bridge and take the first left at the sign into the campground. (This turn may be a little tricky for large rigs. For those wishing to avoid the turn, there is another entrance/exit just to the west of this one.) The office is to the right of the first entrance.

MIMBRES

Casas Adobes RV Park

Rte. 15 Box 2540, Mimbres 88049. T: (505) 536-9599.

RV ★★★★ Tent ★★★★

Beauty: ★★★★ Site Privacy: ★★★★
Spaciousness: ★★★ Quiet: ★★★★
Security: ★★★★ Cleanliness: ★★★★
Insect Control: ★★★★ Facilities: ★★

All sites in this campground are 72 × 24-foot pull-throughs laid out in a straight line bordering the highway 60 feet away. There are mountain views to the north and south. Most sites are quite well-shaded. Site 3 is extra wide to accommodate a long-term guest. Site 11 is closest to the bath house. There are Camp Hosts in sites 8 and 9. End site 20 is next to mobile homes, but end site 1 has a fence, extra space, and larger trees, making it the most desirable site. Tenting is possible in sites 12 and 13, which are roped off from RVs. These sites have fine gravel and sparse grass, and loads of shade from trees. There is also an open tenting area to the southwest. The rest rooms and showers are in a carpeted mobile home, and are both clean and very comfortable. This campground makes a very nice stop for both RVers and tenters.

Basics

Operated By: Aaron and Wandra Emerson. **Open:** All year. **Site Assignment:** First come, first served; verbal reservations OK. **Registration:** Pay station at entrance. **Fee:** RV $12 (full), tent $6; checks, but no credits cards. **Parking:** At site.

Facilities

Number of RV Sites: 19. **Number of Tent-Only Sites:** Undesignated sites. **Hookups:** Water, sewer, electric (50 amp), phone. **Each Site:** Garbage can. **Dump Station:** No (sewer at all sites). **Laundry:** No (within 0.5 mi.). **Pay Phone:** No. **Rest Rooms and Showers:** Yes. **Fuel:** No. **Propane:** No (within 0.25 mi.). **Internal Roads:** Gravel. **RV Service:** No. **Market:** 25 mi. to Silver City. **Restaurant:** 0.5 mi. north. **General Store:** No. **Vending:** No. **Swimming:** No. **Playground:** No. **Activities:** Hiking, scenic drives. **Nearby Attractions:** Gila Cliff Dwellings National Monument, Gila National Forest. **Additional Information:** Silver City Grant County Chamber of Commerce, (505) 538-3785.

Restrictions

Pets: On leash, cleaned up after. **Fires:** In grills. **Alcoholic Beverages:** None. **Vehicle Maximum Length:** None.

To Get There

From the junction of Hwy. 180 and Hwy. 152, turn north onto Hwy. 152 and go 14.3 mi. east. Turn left onto Hwy. 35 and go 1.5 mi. Turn left at the sign into the entrance.

MOUNTAINAIR

Manzano Mountains State Park

HC 66 Box 202, Mountainair 87036. T: (505) 847-2820.

RV ★★★★ Tent ★★★★

Beauty: ★★★★★ Site Privacy: ★★★★★
Spaciousness: ★★★★ Quiet: ★★★★★
Security: ★★★★ Cleanliness: ★★★★★
Insect Control: ★★★★ Facilities: ★★

Laid out in a loop, this small campground is located in a forest at the foot of the Manzano Mountains. Sites are all back-ins, ranging from 30 feet (1 and 3) to 70 feet (6). Some sites (1, 6, 7, 10, and 12) have covered shelters, while others (11–16) offer electrical hookups. Site 7 seems particularly spacious, as does 16. Sites 9 and 10 are next to the access for overflow camping, which is normally closed, but may increase traffic by these two sites when open. Site 8 is a 60-foot site, completely hidden in trees. Sites 4 and 5 are tent-only sites, but a tenter would be happy at any of these sites. Although the sites are not grassy, nearly all offer overhanging tree cover, making tenting comfortable in this park. The rest rooms are clean and modern. The nearby Red Canyon National Forest campground (accessed by turning right at the entrance to this state park) is only slightly larger at around 50 sites, but offers no hookups. Tenters may find it an acceptable alternative, but RVers will prefer the Manzano Mountains campground due to the electrical hookups.

Basics

Operated By: New Mexico State Park Division. **Open:** All year. **Site Assignment:** First come, first served; reservations by credit card or check, no refunds. **Registration:** At pay station. **Fee:** Primitive site $8, developed site $10, water, electric $14; checks, but no credit cards. **Parking:** At site.

Facilities

Number of RV Sites: 18. **Number of Tent-Only Sites:** 0. **Hookups:** Electric (20, 30 amp). **Each Site:** Picnic table, grill, fire pit. **Dump Station:** Yes. **Laundry:** No. **Pay Phone:** In office. **Rest Rooms and Showers:** Yes. **Fuel:** No. **Propane:** No. **Internal Roads:** Gravel. **RV Service:** No. **Market:** Small: Mountainair (16 mi.); large: Sturgess (26 mi.). **Restaurant:** 16 mi. to Mountainair. **General Store:** No. **Vending:** No. **Swimming:** No. **Playground:** No. **Other:** Group shelter, backs to national forest. **Activities:** Hiking, visiting ruins, horseshoes. **Nearby Attractions:** Salinas Pueblo Ruins. **Additional Information:** New Mexico State Parks Division, (888) NM-PRKS.

Restrictions

Pets: On leash, cleaned up after. **Fires:** In grills. **Alcoholic Beverages:** At sites. **Vehicle Maximum Length:** None.

To Get There

From the junction of Hwy. 60 and Hwy. 55, turn north onto Hwy. 55 and go 12.4 mi. Turn left onto Hwy. 31 and go 2.4 mi. Continue straight ahead to enter the park.

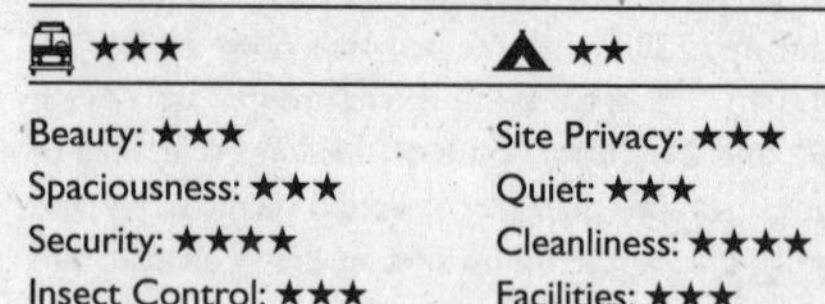

PORTALES

Wagon Wheel RV Park

42699 US 70, Portales 88130. T: (505) 356-3700.

RV ★★★ Tent ★★

Beauty: ★★★ Site Privacy: ★★★
Spaciousness: ★★★ Quiet: ★★★
Security: ★★★★ Cleanliness: ★★★★
Insect Control: ★★★ Facilities: ★★★

On the wall outside the rest rooms is a collage of notes from previous satisfied customers attesting to their contentment with this quiet and "pease-ful" campground. The grounds are quite clean and peaceful, although some traffic noise from the highway does reach the park. The campground is laid out in two rows, the lettered strip sporting more grass and thus being generally a little nicer. While most trees are too thin to provide shade, the tree at sites 7 and 8 is an exception. Sites are level pull-throughs that vary in length from 45 to 56 feet. Site 11 is at the shortest extreme (45 feet) and has no tree, making it the least desirable RV site. Tent sites in the southeast corner have good grass, and the possible use of a row of small trees along the back fence. Behind these sites is a pleasant farm with geese and a pond. The rest rooms are reasonably clean and comfortable with a nice wood decor. The campground, likewise, is comfortable and clean, but may not quite live up to the letters it boasts on the walls.

Basics

Operated By: Birl and Sue Gray. **Open:** All year. **Site Assignment:** First come, first served. **Registration:** In office; late arrivals use drop box (most often no one in office); verbal reservations OK. **Fee:** RV $16, tent $14; checks are OK, but no credit cards. **Parking:** At site.

Facilities

Number of RV Sites: 21. **Number of Tent-Only Sites:** 4. **Hookups:** Water, sewer, electric (20, 30, 50 amp). **Each Site:** Most have trees, some picnic tables. **Dump Station:** Yes. **Laundry:** Yes. **Pay Phone:** No. **Rest Rooms and Showers:** Yes. **Fuel:** No. **Propane:** No. **Internal Roads:** Gravel, in good condition. **RV Service:** No. **Market:** 2.5 mi. southwest. **Restaurant:** 5 mi. southwest. **General Store:** No. **Vending:** No. **Swimming:** No. **Playground:** No. **Other:** Basketball hoop. **Activities:** Basketball. **Nearby Attractions:** Blackwater Draw Museum. **Additional Information:** Roosevelt County Chamber of Commerce, (800) 635-8036, (505) 356-8541.

Restrictions

Pets: On leash, cleaned up, no barking, not tied up outside. **Fires:** Talk to manager. **Alcoholic Beverages:** At sites. **Vehicle Maximum Length:** 55 ft. **Other:** No generators; do not park vehicle next to RV.

To Get There

From the junction of Hwy. 70 and Hwy. 206 in town, drive 4.2 mi. north on Hwy. 70. Turn east at the sign (at mile marker 427) into the campground. The office is at the entrance.

PREWITT

Bluewater Lake State Park

Lake Rte. Box 3419, Prewitt 87045. T: (505) 876-2391 or (505) 876-2318.

RV ★★★★ Tent ★★★★★

Beauty: ★★★★★ Site Privacy: ★★★★
Spaciousness: ★★★★★ Quiet: ★★★★★
Security: ★★★★ Cleanliness: ★★★★
Insect Control: ★★★★ Facilities: ★★★

There are four major campgrounds in this state park (Canyonside, Lakeside, Northpoint, and Creek Overlook), offering everything from waterfront camping to hillside sites with a view. Canyonside Campground, to the southeast of the ranger station, has the only electric sites in the park. Reservable sites are E1–E6, which are 57-foot back-ins. The Campground host is located at E7. Sites E9 and E10 are doubles (75 feet and 60 feet), while E11 and E13 are huge (100-foot and 150-foot) pull-throughs. This campground also has the only showers. Lakeside Campground (which ought really to be called "Lake Overlook") has primitive sites with a view (although Pinon Cliff Campground is better).The road in is rough and steep—no place for a large RV. Northpoint Campground likewise has primitive sites and a rough road that ends at the lake. There is no real road between sites. For the best views (but, again, primitive sites), go to Creek Overlook Campground. This campground offers dirt sites amidst trees. There are beautiful vistas of rocky bluffs, the grassy creek area, and woods below. The rest rooms and showers (in Canyonside Campground) are clean and decently large. This state park caters to tenters, but RVers who don't mind forgoing water and sewer hookups (let alone cable!) will enjoy the beautiful views and outdoor recreation opportunities this park affords.

Basics

Operated By: New Mexico State Park Division. **Open:** All year. **Site Assignment:** First come, first served; reservations by credit card or check, no refunds. **Registration:** At pay station. **Fee:** Primitive site $8, developed site $10, electric $14; checks, but no credit cards. **Parking:** At site.

Facilities

Number of RV Sites: 14. **Number of Tent-Only Sites:** 106. **Hookups:** Electric (20, 30 amp). **Each Site:** Picnic table, fire pit. **Dump Station:** Yes. **Laundry:** No. **Pay Phone:** Yes. **Rest Rooms and Showers:** Yes. **Fuel:** No. **Propane:** No. **Internal Roads:** Gravel. **RV Service:** No. **Market:** 25 mi. Grants. **Restaurant:** 25 mi. Grants. **General Store:** No. **Vending:** No. **Swimming:** No. **Playground:** Yes. **Other:** Boat ramp. **Activities:** Fishing, boating, swimming, hiking. **Nearby Attractions:** Red Rock State Park. **Additional Information:** New Mexico State Parks Division, (888) NM-PARKS.

Restrictions

Pets: On leash, cleaned up after. **Fires:** In grills. **Alcoholic Beverages:** At sites. **Vehicle Maximum Length:** None.

To Get There

From Hwy. I-40 (Exit 63), turn south onto Hwy. 412 and go 5.9 mi. to the entrance of the park.

RATON

Summerlan RV Park

1900 South Cedar St., Raton 87740. T: (505) 445-9536; F: (505) 445-9536.

RV ★★★★ Tent ★★★

Beauty: ★★★ Site Privacy: ★★★
Spaciousness: ★★★ Quiet: ★★★
Security: ★★★★ Cleanliness: ★★★★
Insect Control: ★★★★ Facilities: ★★★★

Sites in this campground are laid out in Rows A, B, and C. Western end sites (A1 and 2, B1 and 2, C1 and 2) share large shade trees. Sites B9, C5–8, and C15 are well shaded, but A4–8 are mostly unshaded. Rows A and B are pull-throughs, while Row C has only back-ins. Tenting is possible behind the RV sites. (There is a bridge between the two areas at site C9.) There is thick grass, but not much shade. There is, however, a covered pavilion for tenters' use. The rest rooms are simple, with painted cement walls, but quite clean and spacious. This is a decent campground for a short stay, and there is long-term RV storage for those who do not want to haul their rig back home at the end of the season. Tenters will also enjoy this campground, although the addition of shade trees would make the tenting experience much better.

Basics

Operated By: Buddy, Linda, and Tim Bryant. **Open:** All year. **Site Assignment:** Upon registration; credit card required for reservation, 24 hours cancellation policy. **Registration:** In office; late arrivals use drop box. **Fee:** RV $21.50 (full), tent $14.50; checks, but no credits cards. **Parking:** At site.

Facilities

Number of RV Sites: 45. **Number of Tent-Only Sites:** Undesignated sites. **Hookups:** Water, sewer, electric (30, 50 amp), cable. **Each Site:** Picnic table. **Dump Station:** No (sewer at all sites). **Laundry:** Yes. **Pay Phone:** Yes. **Rest Rooms and Showers:** Yes. **Fuel:** No. **Propane:** Yes. **Internal Roads:** Gravel. **RV Service:** Yes. **Market:** 0.75 mi. west. **Restaurant:** Across street. **General Store:** No. **Vending:** No. **Swimming:** No. **Playground:** Yes. **Other:** Storage, covered pavilion. **Activities:** Horseshoes, hiking. **Nearby Attractions:** Sugarite Canyon State Park, Capulin Volcano National Monument. **Additional Information:** Cimarron Chamber of Commerce, (505) 376-2417.

Restrictions

Pets: On leash, cleaned up after. **Fires:** In grills. **Alcoholic Beverages:** At sites. **Vehicle Maximum Length:** None.

To Get There

From Hwy. I-25 (Exit 451), from the east side of the highway, take the immediate right into 1900 Cedar St. and go 0.2 mi. Turn right at the sign into the entrance.

RODEO

Rodeo RV Park and Country Store

P.O. Box 80, Rodeo 88056. T: (505) 557-2266.

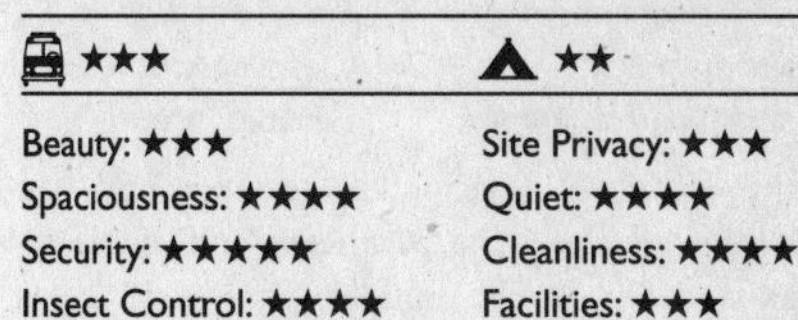

RV ★★★ Tent ★★

Beauty: ★★★ Site Privacy: ★★★
Spaciousness: ★★★★ Quiet: ★★★★
Security: ★★★★★ Cleanliness: ★★★★
Insect Control: ★★★★ Facilities: ★★★

This campground consists of an open gravel lot next to a residence and a store. Sites are open-ended pull-throughs that can accommodate a rig of any length, but are only 18 feet wide. Laid out in a single row, site 9 lies closest to the entrance (next to a fence and stored equipment), while site 1 is furthest from the entrance. There is a number of vehicles, along with stored equipment, scattered around the campground, making it less attractive than it would otherwise be. Tenting is possible anywhere, as there is crushed gravel all around the campground. This campground is OK for an overnight stay for RVers, but the motel right next door (that also has RV spaces) might be better for tenters. It is only slightly more expensive ($1 more for tenters, $2 more for RVers), and of roughly the same quality.

Basics

Operated By: Marianne and Edward Gullot. **Open:** All year. **Site Assignment:** First come, first served; verbal reservations OK. **Registration:** In store; late arrivals select available site and pay in the morning. **Fee:** RV $10 (full), tent $5; checks, but no credits cards. **Parking:** At site.

Facilities

Number of RV Sites: 9. **Number of Tent-Only Sites:** Undesignated sites. **Hookups:** Water, sewer, electric (20, 30 amp). **Dump Station:** No (sewer at all sites). **Laundry:** No. **Pay Phone:** No. **Rest Rooms and Showers:** Yes. **Fuel:** No. **Propane:** No. **Internal Roads:** Gravel. **RV Service:** No (some small repairs). **Market:** 0.25 mi. north. **Restaurant:** 0.1 mi. north. **General Store:** Yes. **Vending:** No. **Swimming:** No. **Playground:** No. **Activities:** World-class bird-watching, hiking, hunting. **Nearby Attractions:** Chiracahua Gallery, Wachuka Mountains, Geronimo Surrender Monument, Wonderland of Rock, Natural History Museum Research Center. **Additional Information:** Lordsburg-Hidalgo Chamber of Commerce, (505) 542-9864.

Restrictions

Pets: On leash, cleaned up after. **Fires:** In grills. **Alcoholic Beverages:** At sites. **Vehicle Maximum Length:** None.

To Get There

From the junction of Hwy. 9 and Hwy. 80, turn south onto Hwy. 80 and go 5.8 mi. into Rodeo. Turn left at the sign into the entrance.

ROSWELL

Trailer Village RV Campground

1706 East 2nd, Roswell 88201. T: (505) 623-6040; F: (505) 623-6040.

RV ★★★ Tent ★★★

Beauty: ★★★ Site Privacy: ★★★
Spaciousness: ★★★★ Quiet: ★★★★
Security: ★★★★ Cleanliness: ★★★★
Insect Control: ★★★★ Facilities: ★★★

Laid out in an L-shape this campground has back-ins all along the perimeter, and a row of pull-throughs in the middle. Sites 1–13 back against a fence and residences. All of these but 5 are well-shaded. Sites 14–19 turn the corner towards the southwest. These are 42-foot back-ins against the fence. Sites 20–27 back to a fence along the south side, beyond which lies a farm. Site 27 is a little narrower than other sites, and fenced on three sides. Sites 29–45 are smaller back-ins (30 feet) that back to a field beyond the fence. Of these, 30 has the most shade. The pull-throughs sites in the middle of the park all have a shade tree except 48. End site 46 has a larger grassy area than the other sites. The tent sites are the same as RV sites 1–5. These offer a thin grass covering and little shade. As the name suggests, this "campground" is RV-oriented, but it is not really a camping destination.

Basics

Operated By: Private Operator. **Open:** All year. **Site Assignment:** Depending on site availability; credit card required for reservation, 24 hours cancellation policy. **Registration:** In office; late arrivals use drop box. **Fee:** RV $17.50 (full), tent $17.50; V, MC, D. **Parking:** At site.

Facilities

Number of RV Sites: 53. **Number of Tent-Only Sites:** 5. **Hookups:** Water, sewer, electric (30, 50 amp), cable. **Dump Station:** No (sewer at all sites). **Laundry:** Yes. **Pay Phone:** Yes. **Rest Rooms and Showers:** Yes. **Fuel:** No. **Propane:** No. **Internal Roads:** Gravel. **RV Service:** No. **Market:** 8 blocks west. **Restaurant:** 14 blocks west. **General Store:** No. **Vending:** No. **Swimming:** No. **Playground:** No. **Other:** Modem. **Activities:** Swimming, visiting museums, boating, watching wildlife. **Nearby Attractions:** Bitter Lake National Wildlife Reserve, Bottomless Lakes State Park, International UFO Museum and Research Center. **Additional Information:** Roswell Chamber of Commerce, (505) 623-5695.

Restrictions

Pets: On leash, cleaned up after, 2 pets of max. 20 lbs/RV. **Fires:** In grills. **Alcoholic Beverages:** At sites. **Vehicle Maximum Length:** None. **Other:** See rule sheet.

To Get There

From the junction of Hwy. 285 and Hwy. 70/380, turn east onto Hwy. 380 (2nd St. in town) and go 1.4 mi. Turn right at the sign into the entrance.

RUIDOSO

Tall Pines RV Park

1800 Sudderth Dr., Ruidoso 88345. T: (877) 957-5233 or (505) 257-5233; F: (505) 630-0712; www.tallpinesrv.com; info@tallpinesrv.com.

RV ★★★★ Tent n/a

Beauty: ★★★★ Site Privacy: ★★★
Spaciousness: ★★★ Quiet: ★★★
Security: ★★★★ Cleanliness: ★★★★
Insect Control: ★★★★ Facilities: ★★★★

This campground is divided into three sections: an upper, middle, and lower tier. The lower tier is located on the same level as the office and entrance. Lower-numbered sites back to woods on the west side, and to a fence on the south side. Sites 17–32 are 60-foot back-ins that also back to woods. Sites 33–38 are 45-foot back-ins, and 39–43 are 78-foot pull-throughs. In the middle tier, sites 49 and 50 are slightly secluded in a wooded patch along the road. Site 61, to the west, is also slightly secluded. The sites in this section 61–76) are 75-foot pull-throughs. The lower level is coated by the river, and is the nicest area to camp in. Sites 51–57 back to sites in the middle tier, but sites 58–60 back to the river, making these the most desirable sites in the park. The rest room in the rec building is a decent facility, but if you happen to find the one in the laundry, you will not be as pleased. That rest room seems to be an afterthought, stuck in an old furnace room, with one toilet and no sink. This campground is a popular spot for campers, and choice sites may be occupied by guests staying for several weeks. However, it is definitely worth the trip.

Basics

Operated By: Private operator. **Open:** All year. **Site Assignment:** Upon registration; credit card required for reservation, 48 hours cancellation policy. **Registration:** In office; late arrivals use drop box. **Fee:** RV $37 (33 w/ discount); checks, V, MC, AE, D. **Parking:** At site, lots of extra parking.

Facilities

Number of RV Sites: 74. **Number of Tent-Only Sites:** 0. **Hookups:** Water, sewer, electric (30, 50 amp), cable. **Dump Station:** Yes. **Laundry:** Yes. **Pay Phone:** Yes. **Rest Rooms and Showers:** Toilets; no shower. **Fuel:** No. **Propane:** No. **Internal Roads:** Gravel. **RV Service:** No. **Market:** 1.5 mi. west. **Restaurant:** Across street. **General Store:** No. **Vending:** Yes. **Swimming:** No. **Playground:** No. **Other:** Downtown within walking distance, modem, rec building. **Activities:** Fishing, golf. **Nearby Attractions:** Casinos, horse races. **Additional Information:** Ruidoso Chamber of Commerce, (505) 257-7395.

Restrictions

Pets: On leash, cleaned up after. **Fires:** In grills. **Alcoholic Beverages:** At sites. **Vehicle Maximum Length:** 45 ft.

To Get There

From the junction of Hwy. 70 and Hwy. 48 (Sudderth Dr. in town), turn west onto Sudderth Dr. and go 2.1 mi. Turn right at the sign into the entrance.

SAN ANTONIO

Bosque Birdwatcher's RV Park

1481 NM Rd. 1, San Antonio 87832. T: (505) 835-1366.

RV ★★★ Tent ★★

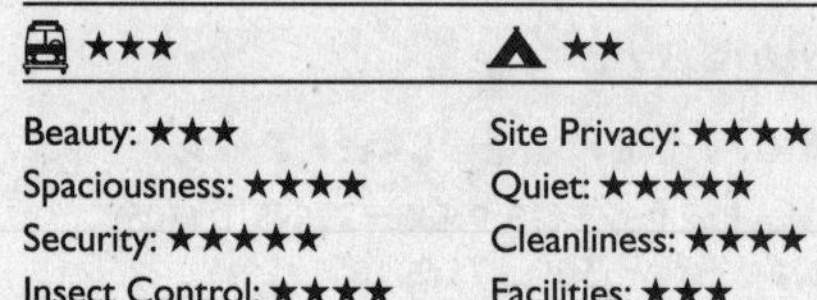

Beauty: ★★★ Site Privacy: ★★★★
Spaciousness: ★★★★ Quiet: ★★★★★
Security: ★★★★★ Cleanliness: ★★★★
Insect Control: ★★★★ Facilities: ★★★

Surrounded by national wildlife refuge land, this campground has undeveloped (mostly dirt) sites and natural gardens and landscaping, using rocks and local plants. Sites around the house are unnumbered and finding them can be at times a confusing task. There is one small site behind the house under a shade tree, and one long pull-through under a row of shade trees to the south of the house. These sites are the nicest, as they are very well-shaded and have character. The rest of the sites are in a gravel clearing to the west of the house. The south row has 60 × 30-foot pull-throughs, while the north row has larger (90 × 30 feet) sites. The north row has some amount of shade at each site, but the south row is unshaded. Tenting is possible along the north edge of the gravel lot. There is sparse grass and no shade, making for rather barren camping. The rest rooms are rather simple but spotless and very comfortable. This is a reasonable stop for RVers, and a great convenience for bird-watchers, but tenters will likely want to move on.

Basics

Operated By: Jackie and Billy Trujillo. **Open:** All

year. **Site Assignment:** Upon registration; verbal reservations OK. **Registration:** In office; late arrivals select available site and pay in the morning. **Fee:** RV $17.50 (full), tent $10; no credits cards, but checks. **Parking:** At site.

Facilities

Number of RV Sites: 30. **Number of Tent-Only Sites:** Undesignated sites. **Hookups:** Water, sewer, electric (20, 30, 50 amp). **Dump Station:** No (sewer at all sites). **Laundry:** No. **Pay Phone:** No. **Rest Rooms and Showers:** Yes. **Fuel:** No. **Propane:** No. **Internal Roads:** Gravel. **RV Service:** No. **Market:** 13 mi. north. **Restaurant:** 3 mi. north. **General Store:** No. **Vending:** No. **Swimming:** No. **Playground:** No. **Other:** 2 phone hookups, modem. **Activities:** Bird-watching. **Nearby Attractions:** Bosque del Apache National Wildlife Refuge. **Additional Information:** Socorro Chamber of Commerce, (505) 835-0424.

Restrictions

Pets: On leash, cleaned up after. **Fires:** In grills. **Alcoholic Beverages:** At sites. **Vehicle Maximum Length:** None.

To Get There

From Hwy. I-40 (Exit 139), turn east onto Hwy. 380 from the east side of the highway, and go 0.55 mi. Turn right onto Hwy. 1 and go 3.1 mi. (Go 0.1 mi. past the billboard.) Turn right at the sign into the entrance.

SAN JOSE

Pecos River Campground

HCR 73 Box 30, San Jose 87565. T: (505) 421-2211; F: (505) 421-3660; campground@pleateautel.net.

RV: ★★★★ Tent: ★★★★★

Beauty: ★★★★ Site Privacy: ★★★
Spaciousness: ★★★★ Quiet: ★★★★★
Security: ★★★★★ Cleanliness: ★★★★
Insect Control: ★★★★ Facilities: ★★★

This wilderness campground with a typical "southwest" flavor is pretty in a somewhat austere way. There is sparse grass and low trees, but also beautiful mountain views. An additional plus: all sites are long pull-throughs. Sites in the middle row average 65 feet, while those in the west row average 70 feet and those in the east row 78 feet. Sites 3, 5, 7, 10, and 12 are double width. Site 1 has somewhat more space, but is not as large as a double-width site. There are some really nice views of national forest in the west row, and other views from sites 12, 36, and 37. The tenting area is located in the northeast corner. This area has sparse grass cover but loads of juniper bushes and a scenic overlook to the north. The nicest site, at the very northern tip, has a covered picnic table and great views. This is an attractive campground that tenters and RVers alike will enjoy.

Basics

Operated By: Glen and Nina Post. **Open:** All year. **Site Assignment:** Depending on site availability; verbal reservations OK. **Registration:** In office; late arrivals use drop box. **Fee:** $10, $15, $20, depending on site size. **Parking:** At site.

Facilities

Number of RV Sites: 37. **Number of Tent-Only Sites:** 10. **Hookups:** Water, sewer, electric (30, 50 amp). **Dump Station:** No (sewer at all sites). **Laundry:** Yes. **Pay Phone:** Yes. **Rest Rooms and Showers:** Yes. **Fuel:** No. **Propane:** No. **Internal Roads:** Gravel. **RV Service:** No. **Market:** 24 mi. north. **Restaurant:** 5 mi. southeast. **General Store:** Yes. **Vending:** Yes. **Swimming:** No. **Playground:** Yes. **Other:** Meeting room, 1000-plus videos for rental, hunting and fishing licenses, borders national forest. **Activities:** Fishing, ATV riding, hiking. **Nearby Attractions:** Rte. 66, Pecos River. **Additional Information:** Las Vegas Chamber of Commerce, (505) 425-8631.

Restrictions

Pets: On leash, cleaned up after. **Fires:** In grills. **Alcoholic Beverages:** At sites. **Vehicle Maximum Length:** None. **Other:** See rule sheet.

To Get There

From Hwy. I-25 (Exit 319), on the north side of the highway, take the first left. Turn left at the sign into the entrance.

SANTA FE

Santa Fe Skies RV Park

14 Browncastle Ranch, Santa Fe 87505. T: (877) 565-0451; www.santafeskiesrvpark.com; sfskysrv@swcp.com.

RV: ★★★★★ Tent: n/a

Beauty: ★★★★★ Site Privacy: ★★★★
Spaciousness: ★★★★ Quiet: ★★★★★
Security: ★★★★ Cleanliness: ★★★★★
Insect Control: ★★★★ Facilities: ★★★★

Although this campground is brand-new and still under construction, one thing that will not change as new facilities are added are the gorgeous 360-degree views for which the campground is named. There are, in essence, two mini-campgrounds contained in this park. The first has an RV park feel to it, with sites laid out in rows of gravel strips with a small strip of vegetation. These are 70 × 25-foot pull-throughs. Sites 1–10 are back-ins along the western edge. The second section of this park lies on Yucca, and has a more "campground" feel to it. Sites are 45–54 × 42-foot back-ins separated by wild-growing bushes. Sites 1–22 back to a wooden fence. The sites with the best views face north on top of a slight hill on Yucca: 24–28, J, and K. The rest rooms are provisionally located in a mobile home, but the new bathhouse was already under construction in 2001. The existing rest rooms are individual unisex units that are absolutely immaculate and very comfortable. Hopefully, these units herald what is to come. Even with construction still underway, this campground promises to be a destination to return to annually, and the owners will hopefully maintain their current level of quality.

Basics

Operated By: John Brown. **Open:** All year. **Site Assignment:** Upon registration; credit card required for reservation (July-Oct.), 48 hours cancellation policy. **Registration:** In office; late arrivals select available site and pay in the morning. **Fee:** RV $25 (full), $20 (water, electric); checks, V, MC. **Parking:** At site.

Facilities

Number of RV Sites: 98. **Number of Tent-Only Sites:** 0. **Hookups:** Water, sewer, electric (30, 50 amp), instant phone. **Dump Station:** Yes. **Laundry:** Yes. **Pay Phone:** Yes. **Rest Rooms and Showers:** Yes. **Fuel:** No. **Propane:** No. **Internal Roads:** Gravel. **RV Service:** On-call. **Market:** 5 mi. north. **Restaurant:** 5 mi. north. **General Store:** Yes. **Vending:** No. **Swimming:** No. **Playground:** No. **Other:** Modem, views. **Activities:** Tours, shopping, opera, music. **Nearby Attractions:** Hyde Memorial State Park, Tesuque Pueblo, galleries, Georgia O'Keefe Museum. **Additional Information:** Santa Fe CVB, (800) 777-CITY, (505) 984-6760.

Restrictions

Pets: On leash, cleaned up after. **Fires:** In grills. **Alcoholic Beverages:** At sites. **Vehicle Maximum Length:** None.

To Get There

From Hwy. I-25 (Southbound Exit 276, Northbound Exit 276A): on the north side of the highway, follow the signs for Hwy. 14, then cross Hwy. 14 and go 0.5 mi. Turn left at the sign into the entrance.

SANTA ROSA

Ramblin' Rose RV Park

602 Black St., Santa Rosa 88435. T: (505) 472-3820.

RV: ★★★ Tent: n/a

Beauty: ★★ Site Privacy: ★★★
Spaciousness: ★★★ Quiet: ★★
Security: ★★★★ Cleanliness: ★★★★
Insect Control: ★★★★ Facilities: ★★

This is an urban RV park with a bit of an unfortunate location. To the east is ugly industrial area, and the train passes very close by on the west side, making for both unattractive and noisy surroundings. In addition, the site numbers are either out of whack or missing, making for a confusing time in finding a particular site. Sites 1–3, in the southwest corner by the office, are 60-foot back-ins. There is a strip of 6 sites along the south side that are approximately 60-foot pull-throughs. In the middle of the park, sites 6–12 are 45-foot sites, while 12 is 30 feet. These sites are right in front of the office, and are not very attractive. The unnumbered site at the tip of the "island" in the parking lot in front of the office is arguably the most spacious site, but not very private. Look to 6–12 or 5–10 by the train for more privacy. This RV park is an acceptable overnighter. Tenters will have to look elsewhere for camping regardless.

Basics

Operated By: Rosie Pruitt. **Open:** All year. **Site Assignment:** First come, first served; no reservations. **Registration:** In office; late arrivals select available site and pay in the morning or use drop box. **Fee:** RV $15; no credits cards, but checks. **Parking:** At site.

Facilities

Number of RV Sites: 32. **Number of Tent-Only Sites:** 0. **Hookups:** Water, sewer, electric (30, 50 amp), cable. **Dump Station:** No (sewer at all sites). **Laundry:** No. **Pay Phone:** Yes. **Rest Rooms and Showers:** Yes. **Fuel:** No. **Propane:** No. **Internal Roads:** Gravel/paved. **RV Service:** No. **Market:** 6 blocks north. **Restaurant:** 6 blocks north. **General Store:** No. **Vending:** No. **Swimming:** No. **Playground:** No. **Activities:** Fishing, boating, swimming, hiking. **Nearby Attractions:** Santa Rosa Lake State Park. **Additional Information:** Santa Rosa Chamber of Commerce, (505) 472-3763.

Restrictions

Pets: On leash, cleaned up after. **Fires:** In grills. **Alcoholic Beverages:** At sites. **Vehicle Maximum Length:** None.

To Get There

From Hwy. I-40 (Exit 275), turn west onto Hwy. 54/84 and to 1.3 mi. Turn left at the sign for Vaughn onto Hwy. 54 and go 0.2 mi. Turn right at the sign into the entrance.

SILVER CITY

Manzano's RV Park

103 Flury Ln., Silver City 88061. T: (505) 538-0918.

RV: ★★★★★ Tent: n/a

Beauty: ★★★★★
Site Privacy: ★★★★★
Spaciousness: ★★★★★
Quiet: ★★★★★
Security: ★★★★★
Cleanliness: ★★★★★
Insect Control: ★★★★
Facilities: ★★★

In this campground, natural beauty reigns. There are flowers, trees, native plants, and rocks, and the campground itself is surrounded by trees. Site 1, a 90-foot back-in by the entrance, is nicely mostly hidden by bushes. Site 2 is smaller (75 feet) and more open, but has attractive landscaping. Sites 4 and 6 and 5 and 7 are pull-throughs that flow into each other, and are easily 80 feet each. Sites 8–13 are 60–80-foot back-ins. In the middle island, site 14 (on the west side) is laid out along the internal road, and can accommodate a rig of any size. In the southwest corner of the island, site 15 is easily the widest site (45 feet wide), but only 40 feet in length. 16, on the other hand, is the shortest pull-through, at 40 feet. Sites 17 and 18, located behind the office, are 60-foot back-ins that are situated quite close together. This is a delightfully natural campground that RVers will enjoy much more than the nearby competition. (Tenters, however, may find the KOA the best choice, as Manzano's does not take tents.)

Basics

Operated By: E.C. Manzano. **Open:** All year. **Site Assignment:** First come, first served; verbal reservations OK. **Registration:** In house; late arrivals select an available site and pay in the morning. **Fee:** RV $16; no credits cards, but checks. **Parking:** At site.

Facilities

Number of RV Sites: 18. **Number of Tent-Only Sites:** 0. **Hookups:** Water, sewer, electric (20, 30, 50 amp). **Each Site:** Picnic table. **Dump Station:** No (sewer at all sites). **Laundry:** Yes. **Pay Phone:** Yes. **Rest Rooms and Showers:** Yes. **Fuel:** No. **Propane:** No. **Internal Roads:** Gravel. **RV Service:** No. **Market:** 1 mi. towards Silver City. **Restaurant:** 1 mi. towards Silver City. **General Store:** No. **Vending:** No. **Swimming:** No. **Playground:** No. **Other:** Quiet, views. **Activities:** Hiking. **Nearby Attractions:** City of Rocks State Park, Gila National Forest. **Additional Information:** Old West Country Chamber of Commerce, (505) 538-0061.

Restrictions

Pets: On leash, cleaned up after. **Fires:** In grills. **Alcoholic Beverages:** At sites. **Vehicle Maximum Length:** 45 ft. **Other:** Pick up cigarette butts.

To Get There

From the junction of Hwy. 90 and Hwy. 180, turn east onto Hwy. 180 and go 3.8 mi. Turn left onto Kirkland Rd. and go 0.3 mi. to Flury Ln. Turn right and go 0.4 mi. straight into the campground.

TAOS

Monte Bello RV Park

24819 Hwy. 64 West, El Prado 87529. T: (505) 751-0774; F: (505) 751-0675; www.taosmontebellorvpark.com; monte@taosnet.com.

RV: ★★★★ Tent: ★★★

Beauty: ★★★★★
Site Privacy: ★★★★
Spaciousness: ★★★★★
Quiet: ★★★
Security: ★★★★
Cleanliness: ★★★★★
Insect Control: ★★★★
Facilities: ★★★★

This is a brand new campground with parts still under construction. There are three rows of unshaded sites, but with wonderful views of the mountains and spectacular sunrises and sunsets. Both the campground and the sites themselves are left in a natural state, without being overly developed. All sites are 80 × 40-foot pull-throughs. End site 7 (to the north) has extra space to the side, as does 14, but this latter is next to the playground. Site 19 is next to the tenting sites. The best sites are on the northern or eastern end (7 and 19), as they are furthest from the highway and have the best views. The tent sites to the northeast are 25 × 40-foot spaces of dirt and sparse grass. Although there are currently only 4 tent sites, more are planned for the future. This campground looks like it will become a top-notch campground when all of the facilities are in place. It is already a very nice place to stay.

Basics

Operated By: John and Concha Torres. **Open:** All year. **Site Assignment:** Depending on site availability; credit card required for reservation, $10 deposit, no refund. **Registration:** In store; late arrivals select available site and pay in the morning. **Fee:** RV $25 (full), $21 (water, electric); tent $13; V, MC. **Parking:** At site.

Facilities

Number of RV Sites: 19. **Number of Tent-Only Sites:** 4. **Hookups:** Water, sewer, electric (20, 30, 50 amp). **Each Site:** Picnic table. **Dump Station:** Yes. **Laundry:** Yes. **Pay Phone:** Yes. **Rest Rooms and Showers:** Yes. **Fuel:** No. **Propane:** No. **Internal Roads:** Gravel. **RV Service:** No. **Market:** 5 mi. to Taos. **Restaurant:** 3 mi. to Taos. **General Store:** Yes. **Vending:** No. **Swimming:** No. **Playground:** Yes. **Other:** Dog walk, walking trail, modem, sunrises/sunsets. **Activities:** Children's activities, skiing, scenic drives, mountain biking, rafting, walking tours, galleries. **Nearby Attractions:** Taos, Rio Grande Gorge Bridge, Taos Pueblo, Kit Carson State Historic Park. **Additional Information:** Taos Chamber of Commerce, (505) 758-3873.

Restrictions

Pets: On leash, cleaned up after. **Fires:** In grills. **Alcoholic Beverages:** At sites. **Vehicle Maximum Length:** None.

To Get There

From the junction of Hwy. 522, 150, and 64, turn west onto Hwy. 64 and go 2.25 mi. Turn right at the sign into the entrance.

TUCUMCARI

Mountain Rd. RV Park

1700 Mountain Rd., Tucumcari 88401. T: (505) 461-9628.

RV: ★★★ Tent: ★★★

Beauty: ★★★
Site Privacy: ★★★
Spaciousness: ★★★
Quiet: ★★★★
Security: ★★★★
Cleanliness: ★★★★
Insect Control: ★★★★
Facilities: ★★★

This campground has 4 rows of open-ended pull-throughs. Sites are only about 45 × 28 feet, although rigs can stick out somewhat from there. Sites are mostly of a uniform quality, without much to distinguish one from the other. Site 59 is given over to long-term residents. Site 60 is a little cramped compared to the other sites. The best sites are 50–55, which face mostly fields, and are located away from the entrance and the mobile homes. The tent sites are in an area to the southwest. This area has a decent grass covering and two large shade trees for protection from the sun. The adjacent fields make for attractive surroundings. This campground makes for an agreeable overnight stay, and is fine for even longer.

Basics

Operated By: Jackie O'Brien. **Open:** All year. **Site Assignment:** Depending on site availability; no reservations. **Registration:** In office; late arrivals use drop box. **Fee:** RV $18 (full), tent $10; checks, V, MC, D. **Parking:** At site.

Facilities

Number of RV Sites: 60. **Number of Tent-Only Sites:** 6. **Hookups:** Water, sewer, electric (30, 50 amp). **Each Site:** Picnic table. **Dump Station:** No (sewer at all sites). **Laundry:** Yes. **Pay Phone:** Yes. **Rest Rooms and Showers:** Yes. **Fuel:** No. **Propane:** No. **Internal Roads:** Gravel. **RV Service:** No. **Market:** less than 8 mi. to Tucumcari. **Restaurant:** less than 8 mi. to Tucumcari. **General Store:** No. **Vending:** No. **Swimming:** No. **Play-

ground: Yes. **Other:** RV supplies. **Activities:** Fishing, boating, swimming, hiking, visiting museums, cheese sampling. **Nearby Attractions:** Mesalands Dinosaur Museum, Tucumcari Historical Museum, Tucumcari Mountain Cheese Museum, Conchas Lake State Park. **Additional Information:** Tucumcari Chamber of Commerce, (505) 461-1694.

RESTRICTIONS

Pets: On leash, cleaned up after. **Fires:** In grills. **Alcoholic Beverages:** At sites. **Vehicle Maximum Length:** None.

TO GET THERE

From Hwy. I-40 (Exit 333), from the north side of the highway, turn north onto Hwy. 54 and go 0.3 mi. Turn left at the sign into the entrance.

VADO

Vado RV Park

16201 Las Alturas Ave., Vado 88072. T: (505) 233-2573.

RV ★★★ Tent ★

Beauty: ★★★ Site Privacy: ★★★
Spaciousness: ★★★ Quiet: ★★★★
Security: ★★★★ Cleanliness: ★★★
Insect Control: ★★★★ Facilities: ★★★★

Laid out in 7 strips of pull-throughs with plenty of space at the back, this campground can accommodate vehicles of any length. The average size of a site is 30 × 45 feet, but the internal road is quite wide and can allow for longer vehicles. (As a last resort, super-long vehicles such as semis can be parked in the back, but without hookups.) There is a potential for some very attractive landscaping in the front that seems, unfortunately, to have been abandoned. The views at the back of the park (to the east) are also very nice, but sabotaged by a storage shed and miscellaneous equipment parked or piled around it. The proximity of the highway to row G makes these sites the least desirable, but not drastically so. End sites (those with the highest numbers) in all rows are also less desirable, due to their "view" of the storage unit. The most favorable sites are those along row A, as they are furthest from the highway and abut a desert with views of the mountains. Tent sites are located in a small enclosed section in front of the laundry facility at the end of row D. There is enough space to fit 6–8 tents comfortably, but only one table and no fire pit or grill. The rest room facilities are slightly shabby (cracked mirror, unsightly flystrip, paper on the floor) but comfortable. A huge convenience for guests is the clubhouse at the east boundary of the property. Open to guests, the clubhouse has a full kitchen (including fridge and microwave), sofas, board games, free coffee, and TV. This is a worthwhile visit made all the more comfortable by its numerous facilities.

BASICS

Operated By: Ruth and Shane Brisco. **Open:** All year. **Site Assignment:** Upon registration; verbal reservations OK. **Registration:** In office; late arrivals use drop box. **Fee:** RV $16, tent $6; no credit cards, checks OK. **Parking:** At site.

FACILITIES

Number of RV Sites: 73. **Number of Tent-Only Sites:** Undesignated sites. **Hookups:** Water, sewer, electric (20, 30 amp). **Each Site:** Picnic table, 1–2 trees, concrete slab. **Dump Station:** Yes. **Laundry:** Yes. **Pay Phone:** Yes. **Rest Rooms and Showers:** Yes. **Fuel:** No. **Propane:** No. **Internal Roads:** Dirt. **RV Service:** No. **Market:** 1 mi. into town. **Restaurant:** 0.5 mi. into town. **General Store:** Yes. **Vending:** Yes. **Swimming:** Pool. **Playground:** No. **Other:** Pet walk area, clubhouse. **Activities:** Board games, TV. **Nearby Attractions:** Organ Mountains, City of Rocks State Park, White Sands National Monument, Mexico. **Additional Information:** Las Cruces CVB, (800) 343-7827, (505) 541-2444.

RESTRICTIONS

Pets: On leash. **Fires:** In grills. **Alcoholic Beverages:** At sites. **Vehicle Maximum Length:** None.

TO GET THERE

From I-10, take Exit 155 and turn east. Turn right onto the frontage road and drive 0.4 mi. Turn left at the sign into the campground. The office is straight ahead.

WHITE'S CITY

AAA White's City RV Park

17 Carlsbad Caverns Highway, White's City 88268. T: (800) CAVERNS or (505) 785-2291; www.whitescity.com (keyword "caverns").

RV ★★★ Tent ★★

Beauty: ★★★ Site Privacy: ★★★
Spaciousness: ★★★ Quiet: ★★★★
Security: ★★★★ Cleanliness: ★★★
Insect Control: ★★★★ Facilities: ★★★

Located a block west of the Registration Lobby, this campground is made up of blocks of individual campgrounds, making effectively four different campgrounds. The RV sites closest to the road are average 32 × 36 feet in size, for both back-ins and pull-throughs. (Longer sites further south and west can accommodate vehicles up to 60 feet in length.) Sites are open and level on a gravel lot. Sites J–P sit atop a bit of an embankment, but are otherwise level. Sites around the perimeter abut a dried stream bed filled with cacti and bushes, and most benefit from a mature shade tree, making these sites (127–142) most desirable. The least desirable sites (R–Y) are situated along the road and exit, and are not clearly labeled. Site R is particularly open to road traffic. Rest room facilities are unisex rooms with an open toilet and shower. The laundry facility is modern and clean, with a counter for folding clothes and table and bench for killing time while your clothes get done. Tent sites, separated from the RV sites by 100 yards, are located on a loop with a grassy field on the interior. Sites on the inside of the loop have ample tree coverage and those in the middle back to the common area, making them potentially double the size of end sites. Tent sites on the outside of the loop have no trees, and are restricted to 30 × 40 feet. The rest room facilities here are less modern and less clean, and the shower is not closed off. The playground area occupies the most lush patch of grass in the entire park, with several large trees providing enough shade for families to picnic while the children play. Tenters may be green with envy at the sight of this patch of grass, but RVers will find this an acceptable base of operations for tours into Carlsbad, or a jumping-off point to Texas and beyond.

BASICS

Operated By: Tom Dugger. **Open:** All year. **Site Assignment:** First come, first served. **Registration:** In registration lobby; late arrivals ring bell. **Fee:** RV/tent $22. **Parking:** At site.

FACILITIES

Number of RV Sites: 92. **Number of Tent-Only Sites:** 40. **Hookups:** Water, sewer, electric (30 amp). **Each Site:** Picnic table, grill, shared shelter, most have trees. **Dump Station:** Yes. **Laundry:** Yes. **Pay Phone:** Yes. **Rest Rooms and Showers:** Yes. **Fuel:** Yes. **Propane:** No. **Internal Roads:** Paved, gravel. **RV Service:** No. **Market:** Yes. **Restaurant:** Yes. **General Store:** Yes. **Vending:** Yes. **Swimming:** Pool. **Playground:** Yes. **Other:** Security gate, post office, shops. **Activities:** Tennis, volleyball, basketball. **Nearby Attractions:** Carlsbad Caverns. **Additional Information:** Carlsbad CVB, (800) 221-1224, (505) 887-6516.

RESTRICTIONS

Pets: On leash. **Fires:** In grills/pits. **Alcoholic Beverages:** At sites. **Vehicle Maximum Length:** None. **Other:** Water park is not part of RV park. No overnight parking within 5 mi. radius (if not in campground).

TO GET THERE

From Hwy. 62/180, turn west onto Carlsbad Caverns Highway, then take the first left into the Old West complex. Resister in the Registration Lobby.

New York

First thoughts of New York State evoke visions of the bright lights, mammoth skyscrapers, Broadway shows, trendy restaurants, world-class museums, and non-stop energy of New York City. After all, there is no place in the United States quite like it. Yet New York City is just the southeastern tip of New York State. New York, in fact, is an outdoor enthusiast's paradise. There is Niagara Falls; the gorge in Genesee country, called the Grand Canyon of the east; the Finger Lakes region; the Thousand Islands of the St. Lawrence River; the Catskill Mountains, where Rip Van Winkle slept; the forested peaks and shining lakes of the Adirondack Mountains; the bluffs along the Hudson Valley; and the mineral baths of Saratoga Springs. Even Cooperstown, home of the National Baseball Hall of Fame and Museum, has Otsego Lake.

Even after the tragic destruction of the World Trade Center towers, **New York City** is a place every American should visit at least once. Of course, though one trip will only permit you to see a fraction of what the most populous city in the nation has to offer, you can at least whet your appetite for another visit. Before venturing to New York City, visit the NYC & Company Convention and Visitors Bureau website at www.nycvisit.com. This will help you plan your trip. The organization has an information center at 810 7th Ave. and 53rd St. in Manhattan. Just exploring **Manhattan** can take days. Your best bet is taking a comprehensive tour that hits multiple sites. There are several specialized tours in Manhattan and other tours explore the other boroughs (**Queens, Harlem, Staten Island,** and **Brooklyn**).

Stretching 120 miles from Queens and Brooklyn on the western shore to the dunes of Montauk Point State Park, **Long Island** is mostly a resort area with white-sanded beaches, secluded bays and coves, and thick woods. Prominent Long Island destinations include **Jones Beach State Park; Shelter Island,** home to the **Mashomack Nature Preserve;** the trendy **Hamptons,** a beach retreat for the rich and famous; and **Montauk,** where you will find **Montauk Point State Park** and the 1795 **Montauk Lighthouse.**

Victorian cottages with stone fences, opulent mansions, and small towns define the Hudson Valley, the area south of Albany that follows the Hudson River between the Catskill Mountains and the Connecticut state border. Heading north from New York City, the lower Hudson Valley includes picturesque and historic towns like **Nyack, Goshen, Tarrytown,** and **West Point,** home of the **U.S. Military Academy.** In the mid-Hudson Valley, the **Samuel F. B. Morse Historic Site** is found near **Poughkeepsie. Hyde Park** features the **Franklin D. Roosevelt Home National Historic Site,** where FDR is buried; the **Eleanor Roosevelt National Historic Site,** better known as Val-Kill; and the **Vanderbilt Mansion National Historic Site.** In the upper Hudson Valley are the classic Americana downtown of Hudson, as well as the **Shaker Museum and Library** about 20 miles north.

The Catskills refers to both the mountain range and a region of small towns and resorts north and west of the Hudson Valley. The Hudson River borders the Catskills on the eastern side and the Delaware River on the southwest border with Pennsylvania. There are also numerous streams and nature trails, making the Catskills a favorite destination for fishing, boating, and hiking. Part of the Appalachians, the Catskills include the **Catskill Park** and the **Catskill Forest Preserve.**

Albany, New York's capital, is near the confluence of the Hudson and Mohawk rivers in Mohawk Valley. Famous for its Victorian homes, pristine gardens, and lavish spas, **Saratoga Springs** is home to **Saratoga Spa State Park.** Located on the banks of Otsego Lake, **Cooperstown** is the home of the **National Baseball Hall of Fame and Museum,** but it also has the **Fenimore Art Museum** and the **Farmers Museum and Village Crossroads.**

Covering six million acres, **Adirondack Park** is the main feature of the Adirondack Mountains in northern New York. The **Adirondack Forest Preserve** makes up 40% of the park, which includes the state's highest peak, the 5,344-foot **Mt. Marcy.** Within the park are 46 mountains more than 4,000 feet high; 2,800 lakes and ponds; 6,000 miles of rivers, and more than 2,000 miles of hiking trails. **Lake George, Lake Champlaign,** and **Lake Placid** are resort areas offering bountiful outdoor activities. **Fort Ticonderoga,** built in 1755 and an integral part of the Revolutionary War, is located in the Lake George area. The village of **Blue Mountain Lake** not only has the 2,000-foot-high peak overlooking the lake, but it is also the home of the **Adirondack Museum,** a complex of 22 historic buildings.

Located at the head of the St. Lawrence River on the U.S.–Canada border and extending more than 50 miles downstream from Lake Ontario, the Thousand Islands region actually consists of more than 1,800 islands ranging in size from small rocks to five miles wide and 20 miles long. Stretching seven miles between the New York and Ontario mainlands, the **Thousand Islands Bridge**

and Highway crosses many of the isles and channels. **Alexandria Bay** is the main resort town of the Thousand Islands, which also has a multitude of other small towns, state parks, and boat tours.

The Finger Lakes region encompasses 11 finger-shaped lakes such as **Seneca, Cayuga,** and **Keuka,** as well as countless breathtaking natural sites like the gorges and waterfalls of **Watkins Glen State Park. Syracuse** and **Rochester,** which both have pleasant museums and attractions, are also located near the Finger Lakes.

New York's second-most visited attraction (besides New York City) is **Niagara Falls.** Located in western New York, Niagara Falls can be viewed on either the American or Canadian side. The famous Maid of the Mist boat tour is a must if you visit the falls. **Buffalo,** New York's second-largest city, is 20 miles from Niagara Falls. The **Buffalo and Erie County Naval and Military Park,** an assortment of Frank Lloyd Wright homes, and the **Original American Kazoo Factory** are among the most interesting attractions in Buffalo.

The following facilities accept payment in checks or cash only:

Belvedere Lake Resort, Cherry Valley
Frost Ridge Recreation Area Campground, LeRoy
Lazy K RV Ranch, Cleveland
Merry Knoll 1000 Islands Campground, Clayton
Oleana Family Campground, Copake

Campground Profiles

ALBION
Lakeside Beach State Park

Rte. 18, Waterport 14571. T: (716) 682-4888 or (800) 456-CAMP; www.nysparks.state.ny.us.

RV ★★★ Tent ★★★★

Beauty: ★★★★ Site Privacy: ★★★★
Spaciousness: ★★★★ Quiet: ★★★
Security: ★★★ Cleanliness: ★★★★
Insect Control: ★★★★ Facilities: ★★★

Located along the rocky shores of Lake Ontario, Lakeside Beach State Park offers postcard-worthy panoramic views of the lake, surrounding farms, and fruit orchards. Each site is equipped with an electric hookup. Though there are no tent-only sites here, tent campers will like the Lakeside Beach experience—especially on a summer night, when the cool, refreshing breeze gently blows from Lake Ontario. There is a general store, laundry facilities, and hot showers. Though no swimming is allowed because of the steep banks, there is still lots to do within the park boundaries. Recreation areas include softball diamonds, horseshoe pits, several playgrounds, and two basketball courts. Hikers, mountain bikers, and cross-country skiers flock to the four miles of multi-use trails that wind through the park. Anglers cast their lines into Lake Ontario. The park is centrally located between Niagara Falls (about 50 miles southwest) and Rochester (about 35 miles southeast). If you prefer camping in warmer weather, visit this campground during the late spring and throughout the summer. It can be rather cool in Apr. and Oct., and Lake Ontario is famous for its enormous snowfalls.

BASICS

Operated By: State of New York. **Open:** Apr.–Oct. **Site Assignment:** Reservations and walk-ins accepted. **Registration:** At campground office. **Fee:** $13 (VISA, MC). **Parking:** At site.

FACILITIES

Number of RV Sites: 274. **Number of Tent-Only Sites:** None. **Hookups:** Electric (20 amps). **Each Site:** Picnic table. **Dump Station:** Yes. **Laundry:** Yes. **Pay Phone:** Yes. **Rest Rooms and Showers:** Yes. **Fuel:** No. **Propane:** No. **Internal Roads:** Paved, in good condition. **RV Service:** No. **Market:** Within 10 mi. **Restaurant:** Within 10 mi. **General Store:** Yes. **Vending:** Yes. **Playground:** Yes. **Other:** Near Lake Ontario. **Activities:** Fishing, sports field, rec hall, biking, hiking trails, skiing, canoeing, boating. **Nearby Attractions:** Lake Ontario, Niagara Falls, Rochester. **Additional Information:** New York Division of Tourism, (800) CALL-NYS, www.ilovenystate.ny.us.

RESTRICTIONS

Pets: On leash only. **Fires:** At site. **Alcoholic Beverages:** No alcohol permitted. **Vehicle Maximum Length:** 30 ft. **Other:** 14-day max. stay.

TO GET THERE

From Albion, go 10 mi. north on Hwy. 98 and 2 mi. west on Lake Ontario Pkwy. Follow signs to campground.

ALEXANDRIA BAY
Grass Point State Park

42247 Grassy Point Rd., Alexandria Bay 13607. T: (315) 686-4472 or (800) 456-CAMP; www.nysparks.state.ny.us.

RV ★★★ Tent ★★★★

Beauty: ★★★★ Site Privacy: ★★★
Spaciousness: ★★★ Quiet: ★★★★
Security: ★★★★ Cleanliness: ★★★★
Insect Control: ★★★ Facilities: ★★★★

Don't be deceived by the name—New York's Thousand Islands region actually consists of 1,800 green islands divided by intricate waterways. These islands range in size from a few square inches to several miles in length. Alexandria Bay is the resort center of the Thousand Islands region, and Grass Point State Park is one of several area state parks. Grass Point is located on a point of land that projects into the American Channel of the St. Lawrence River, known for some of the best fishing in the country. There's also a swimming beach, a boat launch, and a marina. Fishing in the St. Lawrence River and hunting for waterfowl in season are among the outdoor recreational opportunities. The park has a long fishing pier where anglers can fish in deep waters and sightseers can marvel at stunning views of the St. Lawrence. Unlike Keewaydin State Park, which is also located in Alexandria Bay, Grass Point offers sites with electric hookups. Keewaydin has fewer sites and is quieter, but Grass Point is more scenic for tent and RV campers alike.

BASICS

Operated By: State of New York. **Open:** May–Sept. **Site Assignment:** Reservations and walk-ins accepted. **Registration:** At campground office. **Fee:** $13 (VISA, MC). **Parking:** At site only.

FACILITIES

Number of RV Sites: 75. **Number of Tent-Only Sites:** None. **Hookups:** Electric (20 amps). **Each Site:** Picnic table. **Dump Station:** Yes. **Laundry:** No. **Pay Phone:** Yes. **Rest Rooms and Showers:** Yes. **Fuel:** No. **Propane:** No. **Internal Roads:** Paved, in good condition. **RV Service:** No. **Market:** Within 6 mi. **Restaurant:** Within 6 mi. **General Store:** Yes. **Vending:** Yes. **Playground:** Yes. **Other:** Pavilion. **Activities:** Swimming, boating, canoeing, hiking trails, river fishing. **Nearby Attractions:** Thousand Islands Skydeck, Lake Ontario, St. Lawrence River, Boldt Castle, Ogdensburg, Oswego,

Fort Ontario, H. Lee White Marine Museum. **Additional Information:** St. Lawrence County Chamber of Commerce, (315) 386-4000, slccoc@northnet.org.

Restrictions

Pets: On leash only. **Fires:** At site only. **Alcoholic Beverages:** No alcohol permitted. **Vehicle Maximum Length:** 35 ft. **Other:** 14-day max. stay.

To Get There

From Alexandria Bay, go 6 mi. south on SR 12 After the ranger station, cabins are to the left and camping is to the right.

ALEXANDRIA BAY

Keewaydin State Park

P.O. Box 247, Alexandria Bay 13607. T: (800) 456-CAMP or (315) 482-3331; www.nysparks@state.ny.us.

RV ★★★ Tent ★★★★

Beauty: ★★★★ Site Privacy: ★★★★
Spaciousness: ★★★★ Quiet: ★★★★
Security: ★★★★ Cleanliness: ★★★★
Insect Control: ★★★★ Facilities: ★★★

Located one mile west of Alexandria Bay, Keewaydin State Park is situated along the St. Lawrence River in New York's Thousand Islands region. The park's terrain includes steep, rocky outcroppings between the campground's 41 sites and the shoreline, providing vantage points for watching the ocean-going vessels traversing the St. Lawrence. If you want an electric hookup, nearby Grass Point State Park has it; however, Keewaydin is quieter and more private, especially for tent campers The swimming pool is within walking distance of the campground; and there's a marina and a boat launch for boaters and anglers. Ice fishing, snowshoeing, and cross-country skiing are popular during the winter, when the campground is closed. The Boldt Castle, located on Heart Island, is an interesting side trip from Keewaydin. George C. Boldt, proprietor of the Waldorf-Astoria in New York City, began construction on a turreted stone castle in 1900—a $2.5 million gift to his wife. When Boldt's wife died in 1904, construction was halted and the castle was never finished. Tours of the castle and the grounds are given mid-May–mid-Oct.

Basics

Operated By: State of New York. **Open:** May–Labor Day. **Site Assignment:** Reservations and walk-ins accepted. **Registration:** At campground office. **Fee:** $13 (VISA, MC). **Parking:** At site.

Facilities

Number of RV Sites: 41. **Number of Tent-Only Sites:** None. **Hookups:** None. **Each Site:** Picnic table. **Dump Station:** No. **Laundry:** No. **Pay Phone:** Yes. **Rest Rooms and Showers:** Yes. **Fuel:** No. **Propane:** No. **Internal Roads:** Paved, in good condition. **RV Service:** No. **Market:** Within 2 mi. **Restaurant:** Within 2 mi. **General Store:** Yes. **Vending:** Yes. **Playground:** Yes. **Other:** Marina and boat launch. **Activities:** Boating, fishing, hiking trails, canoeing, swimming. **Nearby Attractions:** Thousand Islands Skydeck, Lake Ontario, St. Lawrence River, Boldt Castle, Ogdensburg, Oswego, Fort Ontario, H. Lee White Marine Museum. **Additional Information:** St. Lawrence County Chamber of Commerce, (315) 386-4000, slccoc@northnet.org.

Restrictions

Pets: On leash only. **Fires:** At site. **Alcoholic Beverages:** No alcohol permitted. **Vehicle Maximum Length:** 35 ft. **Other:** 14-day max. stay.

To Get There

From Alexandria Bay, go 1 mi. west on SR 12. Follow signs to campground.

AUSABLE CHASM

Ausable River Campsite

P.O. Box 276, Keeseville 12944. T: (518) 834-9379; www.ausablerivercampsite.com; ausablerivcamp@aol.com.

RV ★★★ Tent ★★★★

Beauty: ★★★★ Site Privacy: ★★★
Spaciousness: ★★★ Quiet: ★★★
Security: ★★★★ Cleanliness: ★★★★
Insect Control: ★★★★ Facilities: ★★★

The Ausable River Campsite is located on 130 acres along the Ausable River within the Adirondack Park. Most of the 102 sites are open, and there are 12 pull-throughs. Some sites are situated along the river, and campers can even cast their line from their site. The section of tent sites offers the most privacy in the park; RV sites are open. Ceramic classes are offered, movies are shown, and there is an adults-only lounge. Children enjoy the pirate ship playground, but families who like to spend extensive time at a campground may prefer the nearby KOA, which has a mini-golf course and a tennis court among other recreational opportunities. However, Ausable River Campsite's facilities are cleaner, and campers who do not require mini-golf and tennis will be happy. Ausable Chasm is the main draw to the area. A 1.5-mile-long gorge, Ausable Chasm ranges from 20 to 50 feet wide, and its rocky walls rise as high as 200 feet above the Ausable River. Tours include a raft ride followed by a 0.75-mile-long self-guided walking tour before reaching the bus for the return trip. The tour offers stunning views. Be sure to wear comfortable clothing, and be aware that the self-guided walking tour includes many stairs to climb. Ausable River Campsite is also just three miles from Lake Champlain and the ferry that transports passengers to Vermont.

Basics

Operated By: Private operator. **Open:** May 15–Oct. 11. **Site Assignment:** Reservations and walk-ins accepted. **Registration:** At campground office. **Fee:** $20–$28 (VISA, MC). **Parking:** At site.

Facilities

Number of RV Sites: 90. **Number of Tent-Only Sites:** 12. **Hookups:** Electric (20, 30, 50 amps), water, 94 full hookups. **Each Site:** Fire ring, picnic table. **Dump Station:** Yes. **Laundry:** Yes. **Pay Phone:** Yes. **Rest Rooms and Showers:** Yes. **Fuel:** No. **Propane:** No. **Internal Roads:** Gravel, in fair condition. **RV Service:** No. **Market:** Within 3 mi. **Restaurant:** Within 3 mi. **General Store:** Yes. **Vending:** Yes. **Playground:** Yes. **Other:** Located on Ausable River. **Activities:** Swimming, canoeing, river and pond fishing, planned activities on weekends, sports field, horseshoes, volleyball. **Nearby Attractions:** Ausable Chasm, Lake Placid, Lake Champlaign, Fort Ticonderoga, ferry to Vermont, Whiteface Mountain, Adirondack Park. **Additional Information:** New York Division of Tourism, (800) CALL-NYS, www.iloveny.state.ny.us.

Restrictions

Pets: On leash only. **Fires:** At site. **Alcoholic Beverages:** At site. **Vehicle Maximum Length:** 40 ft. **Other:** None.

To Get There

From I-87, take Exit 34 and go 0.25 mi. west on Hwy. 9N and 0.75 mi. south on entry road. Entrance is on the left.

AUSABLE CHASM

KOA—Ausable Chasm

P.O. Box 390, Ausable Chasm 12911. T: (800) 562-9105 or (518) 834-9990; F: (518) 834-1104; www.koa.com.

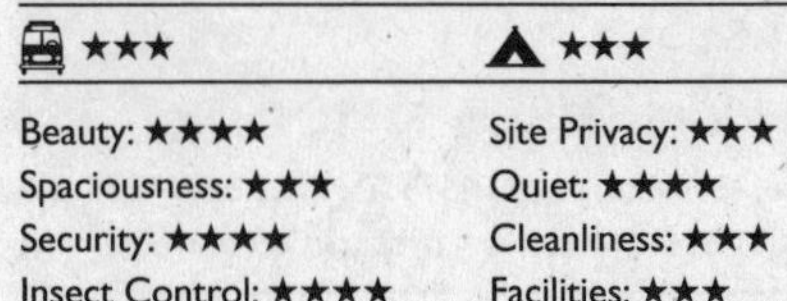

RV ★★★ Tent ★★★

Beauty: ★★★★ Site Privacy: ★★★
Spaciousness: ★★★ Quiet: ★★★★
Security: ★★★★ Cleanliness: ★★★
Insect Control: ★★★★ Facilities: ★★★

Located near the Ausable Chasm in Adirondack Park, KOA—Ausable Chasm offers spacious wooded sites, including 80 pull-throughs. Ausable Chasm boasts one of the most popular campgrounds in the KOA chain, mostly because of its proximity to the Ausable Chasm itself. The multitude of pull-through sites makes this KOA convenient for RVers. Families will not be disappointed with the extensive selection of activities here. Facilities here are acceptable but not as well-kept as those at the Ausable River Campsite. This campground is especially ideal for travelers who want to be near the Ausable Chasm boat ride and tour. A 1.5-mile-long gorge, Ausable Chasm ranges from 20 to 50 feet wide, and its rocky walls rise as high as 200 feet above the Ausable River. Tours include a raft ride followed by a 0.75-mile-long self-guided walking tour before reaching the bus for the return trip. Lake Champlaign is just three miles away from the campground, as are the ferries that carry passengers across the lake to Vermont. Other attractions near the campground include Santa's Workshop, where the magic of Christmas springs to life in rides, shows, and entertainment; High Falls Gorge, overlooking the Ausable River; and Frontier Town, a recreated 19th-century town with action-packed shows and rodeo.

Basics

Operated By: KOA. **Open:** May 19–Oct. 15. **Site Assignment:** Reservations and walk-ins accepted. **Registration:** At campground office. **Fee:** $25–$30 (VISA, MC). **Parking:** At site.

Facilities

Number of RV Sites: 103. **Number of Tent-Only Sites:** 46. **Hookups:** Electric (20, 30, 50 amps), water, 35 full hookups. **Each Site:** Fire ring, picnic table. **Dump Station:** Yes. **Laundry:** Yes. **Pay Phone:** Yes. **Rest Rooms and Showers:** Yes. **Fuel:** No. **Propane:** Yes. **Internal Roads:** Dirt, in fair condition. **RV Service:** No. **Market:** Within 5 mi. **Restaurant:** Within 3 mi. **General Store:** Yes. **Vending:** Yes. **Playground:** Yes. **Other:** None. **Activities:** Rec room, swimming, mini-golf, shuffleboard, planned activities, tennis, badminton, sports field, horseshoes, hiking trails, volleyball. **Nearby Attractions:** Ausable Chasm, Lake Placid, Lake Champlaign, Fort Ticonderoga, ferry to Vermont, Whiteface Mountain, Adirondack Park. **Additional Information:** New York Division of Tourism, (800) CALL-NYS, www.iloveny.state.ny.us.

Restrictions

Pets: On leash only. **Fires:** At site. **Alcoholic Beverages:** At site. **Vehicle Maximum Length:** None. **Other:** None.

To Get There

From US 9, go 800 ft. east on Hwy. 373. Entrance is on the left.

AUSTERLITZ

Woodland Hills Campground

386 Fog Hill Rd., Austerlitz 12017. T: (518) 392-3557; F: (518) 392-5557; www.whcg.net; whcg@whcg.net.

RV: ★★★★ Tent: ★★★

Beauty: ★★★★ Site Privacy: ★★★
Spaciousness: ★★★ Quiet: ★★★★
Security: ★★★★ Cleanliness: ★★★★
Insect Control: ★★★★ Facilities: ★★★★

Nestled in the Berkshires near the Massachusetts border in southeastern New York, Woodland Hills Campground has 206 open and shaded sites, including 149 full hookups—a definite plus for RVers. This is a campground with peaceful surroundings, though many sites offer little privacy. A private lake is located in the center of the campground, and the sites surround it. There are small clusters of sites bordering both sides of the lake, and larger clusters are located away from the lake on all sides of the park. The lake is a serene and peaceful place where campers can rent pedal boats and swim. The campground also has a fishing pond. Woodland Hills is a short drive to Tanglewood and Lebanon Valley Speedway. Catskill Park and Albany are within 40 miles and make interesting day trips for Woodland Hills campers. Consisting of 705,500 acres, Catskill Park boasts some of the wildest terrain south of Maine. The park has more than 200 miles of marked hiking trails. The capitol of New York, Albany is home to the New York State Museum, Schuyler Mansion State Historic Site, and Rensselaerville among other attractions.

Basics

Operated By: Rich and Nancy Hreschak. **Open:** May 15–Oct. 8. **Site Assignment:** Reservations recommended, walk-ins accepted. **Registration:** At campground office. **Fee:** $18–$25 (VISA, MC, D). **Parking:** At site.

Facilities

Number of RV Sites: 190. **Number of Tent-Only Sites:** 16. **Hookups:** Electric (20, 30 amps), water, phone, 149 full hookups. **Each Site:** Fire ring, picnic table. **Dump Station:** Yes. **Laundry:** Yes. **Pay Phone:** Yes. **Rest Rooms and Showers:** Yes. **Fuel:** No. **Propane:** Yes. **Internal Roads:** Gravel, in good condition. **RV Service:** No. **Market:** Within 4 mi. **Restaurant:** Within 4 mi. **General Store:** Yes. **Vending:** Yes. **Playground:** Yes. **Other:** Private lake. **Activities:** Lake swimming, pond fishing, game room, rec hall, boating, canoeing, pedal boat rentals, basketball, playground, badminton, sports field, horseshoes, volleyball. **Nearby Attractions:** Catskill Park, Albany, Lebanon Valley Speedway, Tanglewood, Berkshire Mountains. **Additional Information:** New York Division of Tourism, (800) CALL-NYS, www.iloveny.state.ny.us.

Restrictions

Pets: On leash only. **Fires:** At site. **Alcoholic Beverages:** At site. **Vehicle Maximum Length:** 40 ft. **Other:** None.

To Get There

From I-90, take Exit B-3 and go 2 mi. south on Hwy. 22, 0.5 mi. west on Middle Rd., and 0.75 mi. north on Fog Hill Rd. Entrance is on the left.

AVERILL PARK

Alps Family Campground

1928 NY 43, Averill Park 12018. T: (518) 674-5565; alpscamp@capital.net.

RV: ★★★★ Tent: ★★★★

Beauty: ★★★★ Site Privacy: ★★★
Spaciousness: ★★★ Quiet: ★★★★
Security: ★★★★ Cleanliness: ★★★★
Insect Control: ★★★★ Facilities: ★★★★

Located 15 miles west of the Massachusetts border and about 20 miles southwest of the Vermont border, Alps Family Campground in Averill Park is an ideal base for campers interested in exploring nearby Albany and venturing into Massachusetts and Vermont. This is a clean and quiet campground, and most sites are shaded by mature trees; however, there are only three pull-throughs, which is a minus for RVers on crowded spring and autumn weekends. Open all year, Alps has activities for campers no matter the weather. There's a fishing pond, a swimming pool, basketball and volleyball courts, and hiking trails. Indoors, Alps has a teen center and a game room. The campground also features a spacious adult pavilion with fireplace. During the summer, the campground hosts live entertainment in the courtyard, hayrides, and softball games. In Albany, in addition to the architectural and historical treasures such as the state capitol and the Crailo State Historic Site, visitors can embark on scenic cruises on the Hudson River with Dutch Apple Cruises.

Basics

Operated By: Private operator. **Open:** All year. **Site Assignment:** Reservations and walk-ins accepted. **Registration:** At campground office. **Fee:** $22–$27 (VISA, MC). **Parking:** At site.

Facilities

Number of RV Sites: 79. **Number of Tent-Only Sites:** 21. **Hookups:** Electric (20, 30 amps), phone, water, 40 full hookups. **Each Site:** Fire ring, picnic table. **Dump Station:** Yes. **Laundry:** Yes. **Pay Phone:** Yes. **Rest Rooms and Showers:** Yes. **Fuel:** No. **Propane:** Yes. **Internal Roads:** Gravel, in fair condition. **RV Service:** No. **Market:** Within 3 mi. **Restaurant:** Within 3 mi. **General Store:** Yes. **Vending:** Yes. **Playground:** Yes. **Other:** Adult pavilion with fireplace. **Activities:** Pond and stream fishing, game room, rec hall, swimming, basketball, shuffleboard, planned activities on weekends, badminton, sports field, horseshoes, hiking trails, volleyball. **Nearby Attractions:** Junior Museum, Troy, Albany, New York State Capitol, New York State Museum. **Additional Information:** Albany County CVB, (800) 258-3582, www.albany.org.

Restrictions

Pets: On leash only. **Fires:** At site. **Alcoholic Beverages:** At site. **Vehicle Maximum Length:** 40 ft. **Other:** None.

To Get There

From Hwy. 66, go 3 mi. southeast on Hwy. 66/Hwy. 43 and 1.5 mi. southeast on Hwy. 43. Entrance is on the left.

BATAVIA

Lei-Ti Campground

9979 Francis Rd., Batavia 14020. T: (716) 343-8600 or (800) 445-3484; F: (716) 345-0713; www.leiti.com; leiti@leiti.com.

RV: ★★★★ Tent: ★★★★

Beauty: ★★★★ Site Privacy: ★★★★
Spaciousness: ★★★★ Quiet: ★★★★
Security: ★★★★ Cleanliness: ★★★★
Insect Control: ★★★★ Facilities: ★★★★

Located in western New York—west of Rochester and east of Buffalo—the Lei-Ti Campground is a haven for recreation. This rural campground has open and shaded sites, including seven pull-throughs and 85 full hookups. The wooded RV and tent sites are especially inviting and more private than the open sites. Lei-Ti RV Sales and Service is located on-site, so RV campers have access to a full-time mechanic. At Lei-Ti, children will enjoy the petting zoo, two playgrounds, hayrides, a mini-golf course, and a video arcade. Lei-Ti Lake has a sandy beach, and boat rentals are available. Birdwatchers and nature enthusiasts will like the nearby Iroquois National Wildlife Refuge, where waterfowl migrate in massive numbers, especially during the spring. The refuge has several hiking trails and scenic overlooks. Since Batavia is quiet in all seasons, some campers use Lei-Ti as a base for ventures to Niagara Falls, located about 40 miles west.

Basics

Operated By: Private operator. **Open:** All year. **Site Assignment:** Reservations and walk-ins accepted. **Registration:** At campground office. **Fee:** $20–$26 (VISA, MC, D). **Parking:** At site.

FACILITIES

Number of RV Sites: 221. **Number of Tent-Only Sites:** 12. **Hookups:** Electric (20, 30 amps), water, phone, 85 full hookups. **Each Site:** Fire ring, picnic table. **Dump Station:** Yes. **Laundry:** Yes. **Pay Phone:** Yes. **Rest Rooms and Showers:** Yes. **Fuel:** No. **Propane:** Yes. **Internal Roads:** Gravel and paved, in good condition. **RV Service:** Yes. **Market:** Within 5 mi. **Restaurant:** Within 3 mi. **General Store:** Yes. **Vending:** Yes. **Playground:** Yes. **Other:** Lei Ti Lake. **Activities:** Lake swimming, boating, boat rentals, bike rentals, rec hall, equipped pavilion, game room, mini-golf, lake fishing, basketball, canoeing, shuffleboard, planned activities on weekends, movies, tennis, badminton, hiking trails, sports field, horseshoes, volleyball. **Nearby Attractions:** Batavia Downs, Six Flags Darien Lake, Holland Land Office Museum, Iroquois National Wildlife Refuge, Le Roy House, Niagara Falls, Rochester. **Additional Information:** Genesee County Chamber of Commerce, (800) 622-2686, www.iinc.com/gencounty.

RESTRICTIONS

Pets: On leash only. **Fires:** At site. **Alcoholic Beverages:** At site. **Vehicle Maximum Length:** 45 ft. **Other:** At least one person in party must be 21 or older to reserve site.

TO GET THERE

From Hwy. 5, go 2.5 mi. southeast on Hwy. 63, 0.5 mi. south on Shepherd Rd., 0.75 mi. west on Putnam Rd., and 2 mi. south on Francis Rd. Entrance is on the left.

BATH

Hickory Hills Family Camping Resort

7531 Mitchellsville Rd., Bath 14810. T: (607) 776-4345 or (800) 760-0947; F: (607) 776-9218; www.hickoryhillcampresort.com; hickory5@ptd.net.

RV ★★★★ Tent ★★★★

Beauty: ★★★★	Site Privacy: ★★★
Spaciousness: ★★★	Quiet: ★★★★
Security: ★★★★	Cleanliness: ★★★★★
Insect Control: ★★★★	Facilities: ★★★★★

Located in western New York, Hickory Hills Family Camping Resort is one of the finest and cleanest campgrounds in the mid-Atlantic region. The campground has open and shaded sites, including 35 pull-throughs. Sites with water and electric hookups near the pond are ideal for RVers, as are the full-hookup sites scattered about the park. Tenters will like the "Rustic Village" perched at Hickory Hill's north tip. These sites are in a quiet part of the campground, but they are away from the activity centers. We like any campground that offers therapeutic massage—Hickory Hills has licensed therapists performing deep-tissue massages, sports massages, and Swedish massages among other options. Campers can also participate in Tai Chi, yoga, water aerobics, and kickboxing. Often, Hickory Hill campers venture to nearby Corning, where the Corning Glass Center features the Corning Museum of Glass, which has more than 25,000 striking objects on display; the Hall of Science and Industry, which explores the glassmaking industry; and the Steuben Factory, where craftspeople transform molten glass into fine crystal. Nature enthusiasts flock to Watkins Glen State Park, a short drive from Hickory Hills. Within the park, Watkins Glen Gorge drops about 400 feet in two miles, and features 18 waterfalls and a bridge that spans the glen 165 feet above the water.

BASICS

Operated By: Randy Lehman and Janet Opila-Lehman. **Open:** May 1–Oct. 30. **Site Assignment:** Reservations recommended (1-night deposit required), walk-ins accepted. **Registration:** At campground store. **Fee:** $25–$29 (VISA, MC, D). **Parking:** At site.

FACILITIES

Number of RV Sites: 208. **Number of Tent-Only Sites:** 5. **Hookups:** Electric (20, 30, 50 amps), cable TV, phone, water, 155 full hookups. **Each Site:** Picnic tables and fire rings. **Dump Station:** Yes. **Laundry:** Yes. **Pay Phone:** Yes. **Rest Rooms and Showers:** Yes. **Fuel:** No. **Propane:** Yes. **Internal Roads:** Gravel, in good condition. **RV Service:** No. **Market:** Within 3 mi. **Restaurant:** Within 3 mi. **General Store:** Yes. **Vending:** Yes. **Playground:** Yes. **Other:** Cabin and cottage rentals. **Activities:** Rec hall, hiking trails, sports field, skating area, mini-golf, pond fishing, basketball, shuffleboard, planned activities, movies, volleyball. **Nearby Attractions:** National Warplane Museum, National Soaring Museum, Sonnenberg Gardens and Mansion, Corning Museum of Glass, Rockwell Museum, Historic Corning, Greyton H. Taylor Wine Museum, Watkins Glen Gorge, Watkins Glen Farm Sanctuary. **Additional Information:** Corning Chamber of Commerce, (607) 936-4686, www.corning-chamber.org.

RESTRICTIONS

Pets: On leash only. **Fires:** At site. **Alcoholic Beverages:** At site. **Vehicle Maximum Length:** None. **Other:** Two vehicles allowed per campsite.

TO GET THERE

From Hwy. 17, take Exit 38 and go 1 mi. east and north on Hwy. 54 and 2 mi. north on Haverling St. Entrance is on the left.

BRIDGEWATER

Lake Chalet Campground and Motel

Rte. 8 Box 22, Bridgewater 13313. T: (315) 822-6074; F: (315) 822-3267; www.gocampingamerica.com/lakechalet.

RV ★★★ Tent ★★★

Beauty: ★★★	Site Privacy: ★★★
Spaciousness: ★★★	Quiet: ★★★★
Security: ★★★★	Cleanliness: ★★★★
Insect Control: ★★★★	Facilities: ★★★

Located between Cooperstown and Utica in central New York, Lake Chalet Campground and Motel is a place where campers fish and swim in a private six-acre lake, cast their lines into a shaded and stocked brook, and explore more than 10,000 acres of forest laced with trails. Lake Chalet has both open and shaded sites; all sites are grassy. Some RV sites overlook the lake. Tent sites are situated in a secluded part of the campground between the lake and a gurgling brook—the perfect relaxing harmony for a peaceful night's sleep. Though there is no swimming pool, Lake Chalet has a spacious, sandy beach where campers can bask in the sun or swim in the lake. There are also log cabins and a Swiss-style efficiency motel overlooking the lake. In nearby Utica, children will like the Utica Zoo and the Children's Museum. Cooperstown is home to the National Baseball Hall of Fame, a must-see for fans of our national pastime. Here, the history of baseball's players, stadiums, teams, and figures are brought to life with interactive displays and lively exhibits.

BASICS

Operated By: Joe and Martha Pcola. **Open:** May 1–Oct. 15. **Site Assignment:** Reservations and walk-ins accepted. **Registration:** At campground office. **Fee:** $20–$23 (VISA, MC, AE, D). **Parking:** At site.

FACILITIES

Number of RV Sites: 22. **Number of Tent-Only Sites:** 28. **Hookups:** Electric (20, 30, 50 amps), phone, water. **Each Site:** Fireplace, picnic table. **Dump Station:** Yes. **Laundry:** Yes. **Pay Phone:** Yes. **Rest Rooms and Showers:** Yes. **Fuel:** No. **Propane:** No. **Internal Roads:** Gravel, in good condition. **RV Service:** No. **Market:** Within 2 mi. **Restaurant:** Within 2 mi. **General Store:** Yes. **Vending:** Yes. **Playground:** Yes. **Other:** Slovak Lake. **Activities:** Lake swimming and fishing, game room, boating, canoeing, pedal boat rentals, basketball, badminton, horseshoes, volleyball, sports field. **Nearby Attractions:** Bridgewater 1240 BMX Track, National Baseball Hall of Fame, Utica Brewery, Utica Zoo, Erie Canal Village, Turning Stone Casino, Madison Bouckville Antique Fair and Shops, Unadilla International motocross races, Holy Trinity Russian Monastery, Auriesville Martyrs Shrine. **Additional Information:** Oneida County CVB, (315) 724-7221, www.oneidacounty-cvb.com.

RESTRICTIONS

Pets: On leash only. **Fires:** At site. **Alcoholic Beverages:** At site. **Vehicle Maximum Length:** 40 ft.

TO GET THERE

From US 20, go 1 mi. north on Hwy. 8. Entrance is on the left.

BYRON

Southwoods RV Resort

6749 Townline Rd., Byron 14422. T: (716) 548-9002.

RV ★★★★ Tent ★★★★

Beauty: ★★★★	Site Privacy: ★★
Spaciousness: ★★	Quiet: ★★★
Security: ★★★★	Cleanliness: ★★★★
Insect Control: ★★★★	Facilities: ★★★★

Just minutes from Six Flags Darien Lake and a short drive from from Rochester, Southwoods RV Resort has open and wooded sites, including 80 full hookups and 60 pull-throughs. This campground is nestled in a pastoral country setting, but sites offer little privacy. For linksters, there is a six-hole amateur golf course. Southwoods also has a swimming pool and hiking trails among other recreational activities. Rochester, home to Seneca Park Zoo and the Susan B. Anthony House, is 30 miles east. Niagara Falls is less than an hour's drive west. Some campers use Southwoods as a base to explore nearby Letchworth State Park, called the Grand Canyon of the East by locals. At Letchworth, cliffs rise as high as 600 feet, and there are three waterfalls. Located in Avon, the Genesee Country Village and Museum is an interesting day trip from Southwoods. The recreated village depicts 19th-century life in the Genesee River valley with 57 period buildings.

Basics

Operated By: Private operator. **Open:** May 1–Nov. 1. **Site Assignment:** Reservations and walk-ins accepted. **Registration:** At campground office. **Fee:** $21 (VISA, MC). **Parking:** At site.

Facilities

Number of RV Sites: 144. **Number of Tent-Only Sites:** None. **Hookups:** Electric (20, 30, 50 amps), phone, water, 80 full hookups. **Each Site:** Fire ring, picnic table. **Dump Station:** Yes. **Laundry:** Yes. **Pay Phone:** Yes. **Rest Rooms and Showers:** Yes. **Fuel:** No. **Propane:** Yes. **Internal Roads:** Gravel, in good condition. **RV Service:** No. **Market:** Within 5 mi. **Restaurant:** Within 5 mi. **General Store:** Yes. **Vending:** Yes. **Playground:** Yes. **Other:** Six-hole golf course. **Activities:** Game room, swimming, rec hall, golf, basketball, planned activities on weekends, badminton, sports field, horseshoes, hiking trails, volleyball. **Nearby Attractions:** Six Flags Darien Lake, Rochester, Seneca Park Zoo, Genesee Country Village and Museum, Niagara Falls, Finger Lakes. **Additional Information:** Greater Rochester Visitors Assoc., (800) 677-7282, www.visitrochester.com.

Restrictions

Pets: On leash only. **Fires:** At site. **Alcoholic Beverages:** At site. **Vehicle Maximum Length:** None.

To Get There

From I-90, take Exit 47 and go 3.5 mi. north on Hwy. 19 and 4.5 mi. west on Hwy. 262. Entrance is on the left.

CALEDONIA

Genesee Country Campground

40 Flint Hill Rd. P.O. Box 100, Caledonia 14423. T: (716) 583-4200; F: (716) 538-9253; www.gocampingamerica.com/geneseecountry; jaka40@juno.com.

RV ★★★ Tent ★★★

Beauty: ★★★★	Site Privacy: ★★★
Spaciousness: ★★★	Quiet: ★★★★
Security: ★★★★	Cleanliness: ★★★★
Insect Control: ★★★	Facilities: ★★★

Like Southwoods RV Resort, Genesee Country Campground is convenient to Rochester, Niagara Falls, and Letchworth State Park. And, like Southwoods, Genesee Country has a golf course—this one a Par-3. Genesee Country has 100 grassy and wooded sites, 50 of which have electric and water hookups, and 50 which have no hookups. As far as campsties are concerned for RVers and tenters, Genesee Country and Southwoods are even—though the nod for recreational facilities goes to Southwoods. Campers looking to cool off on a sweltering summer day should look elsewhere; there is no swimming pool here. Of course, there are plenty of swimming holes to be found in the Finger Lakes region, and Genesee Country is near Six Flags Darien Lake. The campground is not far from Genesee Country Village and Museum in Avon, as well as a multitude of museums in Rochester, including the Rochester Museum and Science Center and the Strong Museum, a family favorite where children can appear on a television screen with Sesame Street characters.

Basics

Operated By: Private operator. **Open:** May 1–Oct. 31. **Site Assignment:** Reservations and walk-ins accepted. **Registration:** At campground office. **Fee:** $18–$22 (VISA, MC). **Parking:** At site.

Facilities

Number of RV Sites: 50. **Number of Tent-Only Sites:** 50. **Hookups:** Electric (20, 30 amps), water, phone. **Each Site:** Fire ring, picnic table. **Dump Station:** Yes. **Laundry:** Yes. **Pay Phone:** Yes. **Rest Rooms and Showers:** Yes. **Fuel:** No. **Propane:** Yes. **Internal Roads:** Gravel, in good condition. **RV Service:** No. **Market:** Within 3 mi. **Restaurant:** Within 3 mi. **General Store:** Yes. **Vending:** Yes. **Playground:** Yes. **Other:** Par-3 golf course. **Activities:** Golf, basketball, game room, rec hall, planned activities, sports field, hiking trails, horseshoes. **Nearby Attractions:** Rochester, Niagara Falls, Letchworth State Park, Six Flags Darien Lake, Finger Lakes. **Additional Information:** Greater Rochester Visitors Assoc., (800) 677-7282, www.visitrochester.com.

Restrictions

Pets: On leash only. **Fires:** At site. **Alcoholic Beverages:** At site. **Vehicle Maximum Length:** None.

To Get There

From Hwy. 36N in Caledonia, go 3 mi. west on Hwy. 5 and 0.5 mi. northeast on Flint Hill Rd. Entrance is on the left.

CAMBRIDGE

Lake Lauderdale Campground

744 County Rte. 61, Cambridge 12816. T: (518) 677-8855; www.lakelauderdalecampgrnd.com.

RV ★★★★ Tent ★★★★

Beauty: ★★★★	Site Privacy: ★★★
Spaciousness: ★★★	Quiet: ★★★★
Security: ★★★★	Cleanliness: ★★★★
Insect Control: ★★★★	Facilities: ★★★★

Located in eastern New York just minutes from the Vermont border, Lake Lauderdale Campground is convenient to many places. Historic and scenic Saratoga Springs and Saratoga National Historical Park are about 20 miles west. Albany is less than an hour's drive southwest. Lake George and the southeastern tip of Adirondack Park is less than an hour's drive northwest. The campground's proximity to several attractions is a consolation for what it doesn't have—no swimming pool or sites that accommodate pull-throughs or double slideouts. Trout fishing in the nearby Battenkill River and the leisurely Battenkill Scenic Train Ride are recommended activities for campers. A short drive from the campground will lead to the springs, mineral baths, and geysers of Saratoga Springs. At Saratoga National Historical Park, visitors can see where American forces defeated the British in two skirmishes in 1777.

Basics

Operated By: Private operator. **Open:** May 1–Oct. 15. **Site Assignment:** Reservations and walk-ins accepted. **Registration:** At campground office. **Fee:** $16–$19 (VISA, MC). **Parking:** At site.

Facilities

Number of RV Sites: 60. **Number of Tent-Only Sites:** 15. **Hookups:** Electric (20, 30, 50 amps), water, phone, 17 full hookups. **Each Site:** Fire ring, picnic table. **Dump Station:** Yes. **Laundry:** Yes. **Pay Phone:** Yes. **Rest Rooms and Showers:** Yes. **Fuel:** No. **Propane:** Yes. **Internal Roads:** Gravel, in fair condition. **RV Service:** Yes. **Market:** Within 4 mi. **Restaurant:** Within 5 mi. **General Store:** Yes. **Vending:** Yes. **Playground:** Yes. **Other:** Cabin and trailer rentals. **Activities:** Game room, basketball, shuffleboard, planned activities on weekends, sports field, horseshoes, badminton, hiking trails, hayrides. **Nearby Attractions:** Battenkill Scenic Train Ride, Battenkill River (trout fishing), Saratoga Springs, Saratoga National Historical Park, Arlington and Manchester (VT), Lake George, Albany. **Additional Information:** New York Division of Tourism, (800) CALL-NYS, www.iloveny.state.ny.us.

Restrictions

Pets: On leash only, under control. **Fires:** At site. **Alcoholic Beverages:** At site. **Vehicle Maximum Length:** None.

To Get There

From Hwy. 372, go 4.5 mi. north on Hwy. 22 and 0.75 mi. east on CR 61. Entrance is on the right.

CAMPBELL

Camp Bell Campground

8700 SR 415 P.O. Box 463, Campbell 14821. T: (607) 527-3301 or (800) 587-3301; F: (607) 527-3720; www.campbellcampground.com; info@campbellcampground.com.

RV ★★★★ Tent ★★★★

Beauty: ★★★	Site Privacy: ★★
Spaciousness: ★★★★	Quiet: ★★★
Security: ★★★★	Cleanliness: ★★★★
Insect Control: ★★★★	Facilities: ★★★★

Located in New York's Finger Lakes region between Bath and Corning, Camp Bell Campground is nestled outside of the town of Campbell (hence "Camp Bell"). Camp Bell is an ideal place to relax with a group. There are comfortable club facilities, a spacious rec hall, and a 60-foot heated swimming pool. Campers have their choice of open or shaded sites, all which have electric and water hookups. Most sites are spacious, but privacy is limited. RVers like Camp Bell because the park can accommodate any size rig. The glass center of Corning is about 15 miles southeast of Camp Bell. The Rockwell Museum, which houses the largest collection of American Western art in the east, is also located in Corning. Watkins Glen State Park and Seneca Lake are about a half-hour's drive to the east. Watkins Glen Gorge is surely a sight to behold, and tour boats offer cruises along Seneca Lake. Seneca Lake is known for its 22 wineries, many of which offer tastings and tours.

Basics

Operated By: Private operator. **Open:** May 1–Oct. 15. **Site Assignment:** Reservations recommended (especially on holiday weekends), walk-ins accepted. **Registration:** At campground office. **Fee:** $24–$27 (VISA, MC, D). **Parking:** At site.

Facilities

Number of RV Sites: 111. **Number of Tent-Only Sites:** None. **Hookups:** Electric (20, 30 amps), cable TV, phone, water. **Each Site:** Fire ring, picnic table. **Dump Station:** Yes. **Laundry:** Yes. **Pay Phone:** Yes. **Rest Rooms and Showers:** Yes. **Fuel:** No. **Propane:** Yes. **Internal Roads:** Gravel, in good condition. **RV Service:** No. **Market:** Within 4 mi. **Restaurant:** Within 4 mi. **General Store:** Yes. **Vending:** Yes. **Playground:** Yes. **Other:** Cabin rentals. **Activities:** Rec hall, game room, sports field, planned activities on weekends, basketball, horseshoes, volleyball, swimming. **Nearby Attractions:** Watkins Glen State Park, Corning Glass Center, Rockwell Museum, Harris Hill Soaring Museum. **Additional Information:** Schuyler County Chamber of Commerce, (800) 607-4552, www.schuylerny.com.

Restrictions

Pets: On leash only. **Fires:** At site. **Alcoholic Beverages:** At site. **Vehicle Maximum Length:** None. **Other:** None.

To Get There

From Hwy. 17, take Exit 41 and go 0.5 mi. east on Hwy. 333 and 0.75 mi. northwest on Hwy. 415. Entrance is on the left.

CANANDAIGUA

KOA—Canandaigua/Rochester

5374 Farmington Town Line Rd., Farmington 14425. T: (800) KOA-0533 or (716) 398-3582; F: (716) 398-3954; www.koa.com; syl@frontiernet.net.

RV: ★★★★ Tent: ★★★★

Beauty: ★★★ Site Privacy: ★★★
Spaciousness: ★★★ Quiet: ★★★★
Security: ★★★★ Cleanliness: ★★★★
Insect Control: ★★★★ Facilities: ★★★★

The westernmost of the Finger Lakes, Canandaigua Lake is a haven for outdoor recreation, and the KOA—Canandaigua/Rochester is an ideal base for it. The campground has open and shaded sites, including 36 pull-throughs. This KOA has a swimming pool, a water park, a fishing pond, pedal boat rentals, and a mini-golf course. Sonnenberg Gardens is a worthy side trip in Canandaigua. The 50-acre Victorian garden estate includes the 1887 mansion, a conservatory, and nine formal gardens. Canandaigua is one of the 11 Finger Lakes. The region is graced with numerous glens and gorges with plunging streams, creating a photographer's paradise. Overall, there are 25 state parks in the Finger Lakes region, and plenty of opportunities for hiking, fishing, and boating, among other diversions. As the name implies, this campground is also near Rochester, about 35 miles southeast.

Basics

Operated By: KOA. **Open:** Apr. 1–Nov. 1. **Site Assignment:** Reservations and walk-ins accepted. **Registration:** At campground office. **Fee:** $30–$36 (VISA, MC, AE, D). **Parking:** At site.

Facilities

Number of RV Sites: 90. **Number of Tent-Only Sites:** 20. **Hookups:** Electric (20, 30, 50 amps), water, phone, 40 full hookups. **Each Site:** Picnic tables. **Dump Station:** Yes. **Laundry:** Yes. **Pay Phone:** Yes. **Rest Rooms and Showers:** Yes. **Fuel:** No. **Propane:** Yes. **Internal Roads:** Gravel, in good condition. **RV Service:** No. **Market:** Within 4 mi. **Restaurant:** Within 1 mi. **General Store:** Yes. **Vending:** Yes. **Playground:** Yes. **Other:** Cabin rentals. **Activities:** Pond fishing, pedal boat rentals, water park, sports field, mini-golf, game room, rec hall, movies, planned activities on weekends, shuffleboard, horseshoes. **Nearby Attractions:** Canandaigua Lake, Finger Lakes, Finger Lakes Race Track, Sonnenberg Gardens, wineries. **Additional Information:** Finger Lakes Assoc., (800) 548-4386, www.fingerlakes.org.

Restrictions

Pets: On leash only. **Fires:** At site. **Alcoholic Beverages:** At site. **Vehicle Maximum Length:** None. **Other:** None.

To Get There

From I-90, take Exit 44 and go 4 mi. south on Hwy. 332 and 1 mi. east on Farmington Town Line Rd. Entrance is on the left.

CATSKILL

Indian Ridge Campsites

HC 2 Box 23, Leeds 12451. T: (518) 943-3516; lorgo3516@aol.com.

RV: ★★★ Tent: ★★★

Beauty: ★★★★ Site Privacy: ★★★
Spaciousness: ★★★ Quiet: ★★★★
Security: ★★★★ Cleanliness: ★★★★
Insect Control: ★★★★ Facilities: ★★★★

Near the eastern entrance to the Catskill Mountains resort area, Indian Ridge Campsites is set in a mountain valley overlooking its private pond. Most sites here are wooded, though some are open. There are 10 pull-through sites. Indian Ridge offers a family tenting area. Tent sites here are secluded—even more so than the RV sites, only some of which have privacy. There's a swimming pool, a walking trail, and a children's fishing pond, along with other activities like basketball and volleyball. The Catskill area is an ideal place for children who enjoy animals. Visitors may feed tame deer, antelope, llamas, and other exotic animals (some of which are rare or endangered) at the Catskill Game Farm. Turtles, alligators, and crocodiles are among the featured residents at Ted Martin's Reptile Adventure. The Zoom Flume Waterpark is also a popular family-oriented attraction in Catskill. Outdoor enthusiasts flock to the 287,989-acre Catskill Forest Preserve, where Slide Mountain is the highest point at 4,180 feet. The preserve has hiking trails and three fishing streams.

Basics

Operated By: Private operator. **Open:** May 1–Oct. 25. **Site Assignment:** Reservations and walk-ins accepted. **Registration:** At campground headquarters. **Fee:** $22–$25 (VISA, MC, AE). **Parking:** At site.

Facilities

Number of RV Sites: 45. **Number of Tent-Only Sites:** 25. **Hookups:** Electric (20, 30 amps), phone, water. **Each Site:** Fire ring, picnic table. **Dump Station:** Yes. **Laundry:** Yes. **Pay Phone:** Yes. **Rest Rooms and Showers:** Yes. **Fuel:** No. **Propane:** Yes. **Internal Roads:** Gravel, in good condition. **RV Service:** No. **Market:** Within 3 mi. **Restaurant:** Within 3 mi. **General Store:** Yes. **Vending:** Yes. **Playground:** Yes. **Other:** Children's fishing pond. **Activities:** Pond fishing, game room, rec hall, swimming, basketball, planned activities on weekends, volleyball, horseshoes, badminton, walking trail. **Nearby Attractions:** Catskill Mountains, Catskill Game Farm, Zoom Flume Waterpark. **Additional Information:** Greene County Promotion Dept., (800) 355-CATS, www.greene-ny.com.

Restrictions

Pets: On leash only, under control. **Fires:** At site. **Alcoholic Beverages:** At site. **Vehicle Maximum Length:** 33 ft. **Other:** None.

To Get There

From I-87, take Exit 21 and go 0.25 mi. west on Hwy. 23B and 0.5 mi. north on Forest Hill Ave. Entrance is on the right.

CHAUTAUQUA

Camp Chatauqua Camping Resort

P.O. Box 100, Stow 14785. T: (716) 789-3435 or (800) 578-4849; F: (716) 789.4415; www.campchautauqua.com; info@campchautauqua.com.

RV: ★★★★★ Tent: ★★★★★

Beauty: ★★★★★ Site Privacy: ★★★
Spaciousness: ★★★ Quiet: ★★★★
Security: ★★★★★ Cleanliness: ★★★★
Insect Control: ★★★★ Facilities: ★★★★★

Located on Chautauqua Lake in western New York, Camp Chautauqua Camping Resort is one of the nicest in New York and the mid-Atlantic. Some of the 250 sites are located along the shoreline, and all sites are within a five-minute walk of the lake. This is one of New York's finest parks because of the cleanliness of its facilities and the abundance of recreational opportunities. RVers are especially catered to with 114 pull-through sites. The campground has boat rentals, a boat dock, and a beach. The world-famous Chautauqua Institution, a lakeside summer retreat for the arts, education, religion, and recreation, is only minutes away from Camp Chautauqua. You can catch a performance by the Chatauqua Symphony Orchestra and other arts organizations at the amphitheater, listen to a lecture by a well-known speaker, and stroll through Palestine Park, a model of the Holy Land. Fans of I Love Lucy will not want to miss the Lucy-Desi Museum in nearby Jamestown. Campers who like hitting the links should bring their clubs to Camp Chautauqua; there are 20 golf courses within 45 minutes of the campground.

Basics

Operated By: Private operator. **Open:** All year. **Site Assignment:** Reservations accepted (traveler's rates available for overnight stays), walk-ins accepted. **Registration:** At campground office. **Fee:** $30–$32.50 (VISA, MC, D). **Parking:** At site.

Facilities

Number of RV Sites: 225. **Number of Tent-Only Sites:** 25. **Hookups:** Electric (20, 30, 50 amps), cable TV, phone, water, 125 full hookups. **Each Site:** Fire ring, picnic table. **Dump Station:** Yes. **Laundry:** Yes. **Pay Phone:** Yes. **Rest Rooms and Showers:** Yes. **Fuel:** Yes. **Propane:** Yes. **Internal Roads:** Gravel, in good condition. **RV Service:** Yes. **Market:** Within 3 mi. **Restaurant:** Within 3 mi. **General Store:** Yes. **Vending:** Yes. **Playground:** Yes. **Other:** Boat dock, animal petting farm. **Activities:** Swimming in pool and lake, wading pool, game room, boat rentals, sports field, tennis, basketball, volleyball, horseshoes, boating, fishing, planned activities on weekends, badminton. **Nearby Attractions:** Chautauqua Lake, Chautauqua Belle and Summer Wind excursion boats, Chautauqua Institution. **Additional Information:** New York Division of Tourism, (800) CALL-NYS, www.iloveny.state.ny.us.

Restrictions

Pets: On leash only. **Fires:** At site. **Alcoholic Beverages:** At site. **Vehicle Maximum Length:** None. **Other:** One pet per campsite.

To Get There

From I-86, take Exit 8 and go 3 mi. north on Hwy. 394. Follow signs to campground.

CHERRY VALLEY

Belvedere Lake Resort

270 Gage Rd., Cherry Valley 13320. T: (607) 264-8182; F: (607) 264-9343; www.gocampingamerica.com/belvedereny; belvdere@telenet.net.

 ★★★★  ★★★★

Beauty: ★★★★ Site Privacy: ★★★
Spaciousness: ★★★ Quiet: ★★★★
Security: ★★★★ Cleanliness: ★★★★
Insect Control: ★★★★ Facilities: ★★★★

Located about 10 miles northeast of Cooperstown and the National Baseball Hall of Fame and Museum, Belvedere Lake Resort is an ideal base for campers interested in exploring the history of Cooperstown and the natural splendor of Lake Otsego. The 25-acre Belvedere Lake is tranquil and beautiful, and the campground has spacious open and shaded sites. The best sites are situated along the lake. Recreational opportunities include a mini-golf course; a 9-hole, Par 3 golf course; fishing, swimming, and boating at the lake; and a petting zoo and playground for the children. Fire truck rides, hayrides, bingo contests, and ice cream socials are among the special events that are regularly held at Belvedere Lake Resort, which also hosts live entertainment in season. If you are not traveling with your RV or your tent, the campground has seven octagon-shaped, two-bedroom cottages for rent that overlook the lake. Tents are also available.

Basics

Operated By: Private operator. **Open:** May 1–Oct. 15. **Site Assignment:** Reservations and walk-ins accepted. **Registration:** At campground office. **Fee:** $22–$29. **Parking:** At site.

Facilities

Number of RV Sites: 160. **Number of Tent-Only Sites:** None. **Hookups:** Electric (20, 30 amps), water, 120 full hookups. **Each Site:** Fire ring, picnic table. **Dump Station:** Yes. **Laundry:** Yes. **Pay Phone:** Yes. **Rest Rooms and Showers:** Yes. **Fuel:** No. **Propane:** Yes. **Internal Roads:** Gravel and paved, in good condition. **RV Service:** No. **Market:** Within 6 mi. **Restaurant:** Within 6 mi. **General Store:** Yes. **Vending:** Yes. **Playground:** Yes. **Other:** Belvedere Lake. **Activities:** Lake swimming and fishing, boating, canoeing, boat rentals, mini-golf, rec hall, planned activities on weekends, tennis, sports field, hiking trails, horseshoes, volleyball. **Nearby Attractions:** Cherry Valley Museum, National Baseball Hall of Fame and Museum, Farmers Museum and Village Crossroads, Lake Otsego Boat Tours, Fenimore Art Museum. **Additional Information:** Cooperstown Chamber of Commerce, (607) 547-9983, www.cooperstownchamber.org.

Restrictions

Pets: On leash only. **Fires:** At site. **Alcoholic Beverages:** At site, under control. **Vehicle Maximum Length:** 40 ft. **Other:** No cash refunds.

To Get There

From Hwy. 54, go 4 mi. south on Hwy. 166, 0.5 mi. southeast on Hwy. 165, 0.1 mi. east on CR 57, and 0.75 mi. north on Gage Rd. Entrance is on the left.

CLAYTON

Merry Knoll 1000 Islands Campground

38115 Rte. 12E, Clayton 13624. T: (315) 686-3055; www.merryknollcampground.com; mryknoll@gisco.net.

 ★★★ ▲ ★★★

Beauty: ★★★ Site Privacy: ★★
Spaciousness: ★★ Quiet: ★★★
Security: ★★★★ Cleanliness: ★★★★
Insect Control: ★★★★ Facilities: ★★★

From the sundeck at Merry Knoll 1000 Islands Campground, you can watch mammoth ocean-bound vessels float along the St. Lawrence River. Located near Clayton, seven miles from the stunning Thousand Islands International Bridge and 12 miles from Alexandria Bay, Merry Knolls has open and shaded riverside sites, including 12 pull-throughs. Anglers can drop their lines from the campground's fishing pier, and boating enthusiasts can bring their own watercraft or rent a 14-foot aluminum boat. Rental cabins, each with a double bed and bunk beds, are located in a shaded area near the bathhouse. Near Merry Knolls, Uncle Sam Boat Tours offers 40-mile cruises of the Thousand Islands through American and Canadian waters, with stops at Boldt Castle and Alexandria Bay. Three state parks are also in the vicinity, offering fishing, boating, hiking and picnicking.

Basics

Operated By: Jim, Joanne, and Baxter. **Open:** May 15–Oct. 15. **Site Assignment:** Reservations and walk-ins accepted. **Registration:** At campground office. **Fee:** $23–$24). **Parking:** At site.

Facilities

Number of RV Sites: 77. **Number of Tent-Only Sites:** 10. **Hookups:** Electric (20, 30, 50 amps), phone, water, 77 full hookups. **Each Site:** Fire ring, picnic table. **Dump Station:** Yes. **Laundry:** Yes. **Pay Phone:** Yes. **Rest Rooms and Showers:** Yes. **Fuel:** No. **Propane:** No. **Internal Roads:** Paved, in good condition. **RV Service:** No. **Market:** Within 4 mi. **Restaurant:** Within 4 mi. **General Store:** Yes. **Vending:** Yes. **Playground:** Yes. **Other:** St Lawrence River. **Activities:** Swimming, boating, canoeing, game room, rec hall, boat rentals, river fishing, basketball. **Nearby Attractions:** Thousand Islands, Thousand Islands Museum, Antique Boat Museum, Boldt Castle. **Additional Information:** Clayton Chamber of Commerce, (800) 252-9806, www.thousandislands.com/clayton.

Restrictions

Pets: On leash only. **Fires:** At site. **Alcoholic Beverages:** At site. **Vehicle Maximum Length:** None. **Other:** None.

To Get There

From Hwy. 12, go 2.5 mi. southwest on Hwy. 12E. Entrance is on the right.

CLEVELAND

Lazy K RV Ranch

965 Stonebarn Rd. P.O. Box 507, Cleveland 13042. T: (315) 675-8100 or (888) 381-6415; F: (315) 675-8860; www.gocampingamerica.com/lazykrvranch.

★★★ ▲ ★★★

Beauty: ★★★★ Site Privacy: ★★★
Spaciousness: ★★★ Quiet: ★★★★
Security: ★★★★ Cleanliness: ★★★★
Insect Control: ★★★★ Facilities: ★★★★

Located near Oneida Lake and 20 miles northeast of Syracuse in north-central New York, Lazy K RV Ranch offers level and wooded campsites on 200 acres of tranquil woodlands accessible by several hiking trails. Ninety-two of the sites handle pull-throughs. Tent sites are located near many of the hiking trails. If you enjoy the water, Lazy K an ideal place to camp. The campground itself has a 50-acre pond for fishing, rowboating, and canoeing. Two miles away is a boat launch on Oneida Lake. Children will like the well-equipped playground, wagon rides, and the kidde-sized pool. The outdoor activities and natural splendor of Oneida Lake, the thrill rides of Sylvan Beach Amusement Park, and the history-rich Erie Canal Village are among the attractions close to Lazy K. If you are captivated by the 24-hour excitement of slot machines and craps, Turning Point Casino is nearby. Operated by the Oneida Indian Nation, Turning Point was the first legalized gambling casino in New York.

BASICS

Operated By: Lew and Dolores Kraeuter. **Open:** May 15–Oct. 15. **Site Assignment:** Reservations recommended, walk-ins accepted. **Registration:** At campground office. **Fee:** $18–$26). **Parking:** At site.

FACILITIES

Number of RV Sites: 100. **Number of Tent-Only Sites:** 20. **Hookups:** Electric (15, 30 amps), water, 36 full hookups. **Each Site:** Fire ring, picnic table. **Dump Station:** Yes. **Laundry:** Yes. **Pay Phone:** Yes. **Rest Rooms and Showers:** Yes. **Fuel:** No. **Propane:** No. **Internal Roads:** Dirt and gravel, in good condition. **RV Service:** No. **Market:** Within 2 mi. **Restaurant:** Within 2 mi. **General Store:** Yes. **Vending:** Yes. **Playground:** Yes. **Other:** 50-acre pond stocked with bass. **Activities:** Pond fishing, game room, rec hall, hiking trails, planned activities on weekends, horseshoes, volleyball. **Nearby Attractions:** Sylvan Beach Amusement Park, Oneida Lake, Stonebarn Castle, Turning Stone Casino, Erie Canal Village, Fort Rickey Children's Discovery Zoo, Syracuse. **Additional Information:** Syracuse Convention and Visitors Bureau, (800) 234-4797, www.visitsyracuse.org.

RESTRICTIONS

Pets: On leash only. **Fires:** At site. **Alcoholic Beverages:** At site. **Vehicle Maximum Length:** None. **Other:** Fires are monitored duing extended dry weather.

TO GET THERE

From Cleveland, go 2.5 mi. east on Hwy. 49, 0.25 mi. north on Hall Rd., and 0.1 mi. east on Stonebarn Rd. Entrance is on the left.

COOPERSTOWN

Beaver Valley Campground

Box 704, Cooperstown 13326. T: (800) 726-7314; www.beavervalleycampground.com; camp@telenet.net.

 ★★★★ ▲ ★★★★

Beauty: ★★★★ Site Privacy: ★★★
Spaciousness: ★★★ Quiet: ★★★★
Security: ★★★★ Cleanliness: ★★★★
Insect Control: ★★★★ Facilities: ★★★★

Beaver Valley is home to Cooperstown Baseball Camp, which uses the campground's two pristine baseball fields. Nestled amid wooded hills and dotted with open meadows, Beaver Valley has open and shaded sites, 17 of which accommodate pull-throughs. Sites on the south end offer greater privacy than those at the north end. Tent sites along Beaver Pond are ideal. This is a campground where you wish you were a kid. Few children can resist the timber playground, which has a track ride, tire swing, sheltered sandbox, and traditional swings. The centerpiece of the fenced pre-school play area is a castle. There is fishing and boating on Beaver Pond Lake, and a fossil pit for aspiring young archeologists. You can even feed carrots to the Sadie the pony and Tannin the cow. For campers without RVs or tents, Beaver Valley has three modular homes located in a secluded area in the campground. There are also seven one-room cabins situated in a row at the edge of the baseball fields.

BASICS

Operated By: Private operator. **Open:** May 15–Oct. 15. **Site Assignment:** Reservations and walk-ins accepted. **Registration:** At campground office. **Fee:** $31 (VISA, MC). **Parking:** At site.

FACILITIES

Number of RV Sites: 95. **Number of Tent-Only Sites:** 20. **Hookups:** Electric (20, 30 amps), water, phone. **Each Site:** Fire ring, picnic table. **Dump Station:** Yes. **Laundry:** Yes. **Pay Phone:** Yes. **Rest Rooms and Showers:** Yes. **Fuel:** No. **Propane:** Yes. **Internal Roads:** Gravel, in good condition. **RV Service:** No. **Market:** Within 5 mi. **Restaurant:** Witin 5 mi. **General Store:** Yes. **Vending:** Yes. **Playground:** Yes. **Other:** Beaver Pond Lake. **Activities:** Swimming, game room, fishing, boating, canoeing, boat rentals, bike rentals, basketball, planned activities on weekends, sports field, horseshoes, hiking trails, volleyball. **Nearby Attractions:** Cooperstown Dreams Park, National Baseball Hall of Fame and Museum, Otsego Lake, Farmers Museum and Village Crossroads, Fenimore Art Museum. **Additional Information:** Cooperstown Chamber of Commerce, (607) 547-9983, www.cooperstownchamber.org.

RESTRICTIONS

Pets: On leash only. **Fires:** At site. **Alcoholic Beverages:** At site. **Vehicle Maximum Length:** None. **Other:** Rabies certificate for pet must be presented upon arrival.

TO GET THERE

From Hwy. 80 in Cooperstown, go 4 mi. south on Hwy. 28 and 2.25 mi. west on Seminary Rd. Entrance is on the left.

COOPERSTOWN

Cooperstown Shadow Brook Campground

2149 County Rd. 31, Cooperstown 13326. T: (607) 264-8431 or (888) 806-2267; www.cooperstowncamping.com; shadowbr@telenet.net.

 ★★★★★ ▲ ★★★★★

Beauty: ★★★★★ Site Privacy: ★★★
Spaciousness: ★★★ Quiet: ★★★★
Security: ★★★★ Cleanliness: ★★★★★
Insect Control: ★★★★ Facilities: ★★★★

Featuring 100 sites that surround a spring-fed stocked pond, Shadow Brook Campground is one of the nicest campgrounds in New York. Though it does not offer the on-site baseball excitement that Beaver Valley does, Shadow Brook has plenty to recommend it. Colorful landscaped grounds, a heated pool with an inviting sun deck, an abundance of activities, clean facilities, and serene mountain scenery are among the features that attract campers here. In the middle of the campground, sites are available on the north and south sides of the pond. If you want to camp near the water but away from the center of the campground and the pond, sites are available along the actual Shadow Brook on the campground's northeast tip. New "cozy cabins" are available for rent as well. Weekend fun includes big-screen movies, hayrides, and dances. The National Baseball Hall of Fame and Museum and Cooperstown Dreams Park are a short drive away.

BASICS

Operated By: Private operator. **Open:** May 18–Sept. 30. **Site Assignment:** Reservations accepted (1-night deposit required), walk-ins accepted. **Registration:** At campground office. **Fee:** $28–$35 (VISA, MC, D). **Parking:** At site.

FACILITIES

Number of RV Sites: 90. **Number of Tent-Only Sites:** 10. **Hookups:** Electric (20, 30 amps), water, phone, 15 full hookups. **Each Site:** Fire ring, picnic table. **Dump Station:** Yes. **Laundry:** Yes. **Pay Phone:** Yes. **Rest Rooms and Showers:** Yes. **Fuel:** No. **Propane:** Yes. **Internal Roads:** Paved, in good condition. **RV Service:** No. **Market:** Within 5 mi. **Restaurant:** Within 5 mi. **General Store:** Yes. **Vending:** Yes. **Playground:** Yes. **Other:** Spring-fed stocked pond. **Activities:** Game room, rec hall, fishing, planned activities on weekends, movies, dances, boat rentals, sports field, boating. **Nearby Attractions:** Cooperstown Dreams Park, National Baseball Hall of Fame and Museum, Otsego Lake, Farmers Museum and Village Crossroads, Fenimore Art Museum. **Additional Information:** Cooperstown Chamber of Commerce, (607) 547-9983, www.cooperstownchamber.org.

RESTRICTIONS

Pets: On leash only. **Fires:** At site. **Alcoholic Beverages:** At site. **Vehicle Maximum Length:** None. **Other:** Reservations & 5-night min. stay required June 30–Aug. 22.

TO GET THERE

From Cooperstown, at Main St. take Hwy. 80E and go 10.75 mi. north, 4 mi. east on Hwy. 20, and 1 mi. south on CR 31. Entrance is on the right.

COOPERSTOWN
KOA—Cooperstown

P.O. Box 786, Cooperstown 13326. T: (315) 858-0236 or (800) 562-3402; www.koa.com; coopkoa@telenet.net.

RV ★★★★ Tent ★★★★

Beauty: ★★★ Site Privacy: ★★
Spaciousness: ★★★ Quiet: ★★★★
Security: ★★★★ Cleanliness: ★★★★
Insect Control: ★★★★ Facilities: ★★★★

Convenient to the National Baseball Hall of Fame Museum, Otsego Lake, and the history-rich village of Cooperstown, KOA—Cooperstown is a comfortable base to visit the many area attractions. Mini-golf, swimming, hiking and basketball are among the activities at the campground, which is ideal for RVers with 58 pull-throughs and 27 full hookups. Sites are open and shaded, and facilities here are clean. The National Baseball Hall of Fame and Museum, of course, is the destination of many campers here. Our favorite is the exhibit on beloved ballparks, but the displays on baseball's greatest moments, the World Series and the All-Star Game are about equally fascinating. Did you know that, though Pete Rose is banned from the sport and not eligible for the hall of fame, baseball's all-time hits leader has a museum devoted to him on Cooperstown. Other area attractions that are inviting to families but not widely known are the Lolly Pop Farm and Petting Zoo, the Petrified Creates Museum of Natural History and the Cooperstown Fun Park, home of the Hamburger Hall of Fame.

BASICS

Operated By: KOA. **Open:** Apr 15–Oct. 15. **Site Assignment:** Reservations recommended, walk-ins accepted. **Registration:** At campground office. **Fee:** $28–$35 (VISA, MC, AE, D). **Parking:** At site.

FACILITIES

Number of RV Sites: 106. **Number of Tent-Only Sites:** 28. **Hookups:** Electric (20, 30 amps), water, phone, 27 full hookups. **Each Site:** Fire ring, picnic table. **Dump Station:** Yes. **Laundry:** Yes. **Pay Phone:** Yes. **Rest Rooms and Showers:** Yes. **Fuel:** No. **Propane:** Yes. **Internal Roads:** Gravel, in good condition. **RV Service:** No. **Market:** Within 6 mi. **Restaurant:** Within 8 mi. **General Store:** Yes. **Vending:** Yes. **Playground:** Yes. **Other:** Cabin rentals. **Activities:** Swimming, game room, mini-golf, planned activities on weekends, basketball, movies, badminton, hiking trails, horseshoes, volleyball, rec hall. **Nearby Attractions:** Cooperstown Dreams Park, National Baseball Hall of Fame and Museum, Otsego Lake, Farmers Museum and Village Crossroads, Fenimore Art Museum. **Additional Information:** Cooperstown Chamber of Commerce, (607) 547-9983, www.cooperstownchamber.org.

RESTRICTIONS

Pets: On leash only. **Fires:** At site. **Alcoholic Beverages:** At site. **Vehicle Maximum Length:** None.

TO GET THERE

From Hwy. 28, go 11 mi. north on Hwy. 80E, 0.5 mi. west on US 20, and 1 mi. north and west on paved road with signs leading to campground. Entrance is on the left.

COOPERSTOWN
Meadow-Vale Campsites

505 Gilbert Lake Rd., Mt. Vision 13810. T: (607) 293-8802 or (800) 701-8802; F: (607) 293-8213; www.cooperstown.com/ad/mvale.htm; meadowvale@dmcom.net.

RV ★★★ Tent ★★★

Beauty: ★★★★ Site Privacy: ★★★
Spaciousness: ★★★ Quiet: ★★★★
Security: ★★★★ Cleanliness: ★★★★
Insect Control: ★★★ Facilities: ★★★★

Everywhere you look from the grounds of Meadow-Vale Campsites, there are towering woods and rolling green hills, which in the distance resemble a patchwork quilt. Meadow-Vale is a peaceful campground with a 2.5-acre natural lake, where campers can fish and explore with rented canoes and pedal boats. Each RV site has electric and water hookups. Tent sites are located in a wooded area and offer more privacy than RV sites. The campground has a mini-golf course, but if you are a serious golfer, there are three full-size courses in the area. If you still have energy to spare after boating and swimming at Otsego Lake and exploring Cooperstown, you can tackle the physical fitness trail. With 16 exercise stations along the way, you are sure to get a vigorous workout. An expansive croquet court, nature trails, horseshoe pits, and basketball and volleyball courts are other recreational options. Bingo and pot luck suppers are among Meadow-Vale's special events.

BASICS

Operated By: Private operator. **Open:** May 1–Oct. 15. **Site Assignment:** Reservations and walk-ins accepted. **Registration:** At campground office. **Fee:** $25 (VISA, MC). **Parking:** At site.

FACILITIES

Number of RV Sites: 96. **Number of Tent-Only Sites:** 14. **Hookups:** Electric (15, 20, 30 amps), water, phone. **Each Site:** Fire ring, picnic table. **Dump Station:** Yes. **Laundry:** Yes. **Pay Phone:** Yes. **Rest Rooms and Showers:** Yes. **Fuel:** No. **Propane:** Yes. **Internal Roads:** Gravel, in good condition. **RV Service:** No. **Market:** Within 7 mi. **Restaurant:** Within 5 mi. **General Store:** Yes. **Vending:** Yes. **Playground:** Yes. **Other:** Meadow-Vale Lake. **Activities:** Swimming, boating, boat rentals, pond fishing, pavilion, game room, mini-golf, basketball, planned activities on weekends, movies, badminton, sports field, hiking trails, volleyball, canoeing. **Nearby Attractions:** Cooperstown Dreams Park, National Baseball Hall of Fame and Museum, Otsego Lake, Farmers Museum and Village Crossroads, Fenimore Art Museum. **Additional Information:** Cooperstown Chamber, (607) 547-9983, www.cooperstownchamber.org.

RESTRICTIONS

Pets: On leash only. **Fires:** At site. **Alcoholic Beverages:** At site. **Vehicle Maximum Length:** 40 ft.

TO GET THERE

From Hwy. 80, go 2.5 mi. south on Hwy. 28, 7.5 mi. west on CR 11, 4 mi. southwest on CR 14, and 0.25 mi. south on Gilbert Lake Rd. Entrance is on the right.

COOPERSTOWN
Yogi Bear's Jellystone Park at Crystal Lake

111 E. Turtle Lake Rd., Garrattsville 13342. T: (607) 965-8265 or (800) 231-1907; www.cooperstown-jellystone.com; coopyogi@ascent.net.

RV ★★★★ Tent ★★★★

Beauty: ★★★★ Site Privacy: ★★★★
Spaciousness: ★★★ Quiet: ★★★★
Security: ★★★★ Cleanliness: ★★★★★
Insect Control: ★★★★ Facilities: ★★★★

Located centrally between the National Baseball Hall of Fame and Museum in Cooperstown and the National Soccer Hall of Fame in Oneonta (where there is also a Single-A minor league baseball team), Yogi Bear's Jellystone Park at Crystal Lake is certainly an all-star in the franchise's vast league of campgrounds. There are open and shaded sites, including 40 full hookups. The campground's most attractive sites are located along 35-acre Crystal Lake. The lake offers campers fishing and boating opportunities, but no swimming is allowed. Sites on the north side of Crystal Lake offer more privacy than those on the south side, which is near the traffic of County Rd. 17. Full hookup sites are located on the southeast side of the campground near a nature trail. Non-RVers and tenters need not fret; cabins, cottages, and trailers are available for rent.

BASICS

Operated By: Reinard family. **Open:** May 1–Sept. 30. **Site Assignment:** Reservations recommended (2-night deposit required, 3 on holidays), walk-ins accepted. **Registration:** At campground office. **Fee:** $28–$35 (VISA, MC). **Parking:** At site.

FACILITIES

Number of RV Sites: 220. **Number of Tent-Only Sites:** 16. **Hookups:** Electric (30 amps), water, phone, 40 full hookups. **Each Site:** Fire ring, picnic table. **Dump Station:** Yes. **Laundry:** Yes. **Pay Phone:** Yes. **Rest Rooms and Showers:** Yes. **Fuel:** No. **Propane:** Yes. **Internal Roads:** Paved, in good condition. **RV Service:** No. **Market:** Within 4 mi. **Restaurant:** Within 6 mi. **General Store:** Yes. **Vending:** Yes. **Playground:** Yes. **Other:** Crystal Lake. **Activities:** Swimming, game room, rec hall, boating, canoeing, boat rentals, lake fishing, basketball, planned activities, movies, bingo, trolley, tennis, badminton, volleyball, hiking trails, sports field, horseshoes. **Nearby Attractions:** National Soccer Hall of Fame, Cooperstown Dreams Park, National Baseball Hall of Fame and Museum, Otsego Lake, Farmers Museum and Village Crossroads, Fenimore Art Museum. **Additional Information:** Cooperstown Chamber of Commerce, (607) 547-9983, www.cooperstownchamber.org.

Restrictions

Pets: On leash only, under control. **Fires:** At site. **Alcoholic Beverages:** At site. **Vehicle Maximum Length:** None. **Other:** Two pets per campsite.

To Get There

From Hwy. 28, go 10.75 mi. west on Hwy. 80, 5.75 mi. south on CR 16, 0.75 mi. north on Hwy. 51, and 1 mi. west on CR 17. Entrance is on the left.

COPAKE

Oleana Family Campground

2236 CR 7, Copake 12516. T: (518) 329-2811; www.oleanacampground.com; ole@taconic.net.

RV ★★★★ Tent ★★★★

Beauty: ★★★★ Site Privacy: ★★
Spaciousness: ★★ Quiet: ★★★★
Security: ★★★★★ Cleanliness: ★★★★
Insect Control: ★★★ Facilities: ★★★

Oleana Family Campground is nestled in the Hudson Valley between the Catskill Mountains and the Berkshires, two hours north of New York City and near the Massachusetts and Connecticut borders. All sites here have full hookups, and there are 50 pull-throughs. With 350 sites, Oleana is crowded in some areas with little privacy. Some sites along Cree Pass at the far north tip of the campground offer more space and some privacy. You can fish and swim in the campground's lake. Children will enjoy the fire truck rides and hayrides. Remember the Seinfeld episode when George was bullied by the Van Buren Boys, who named the gang after the eighth President of the United States? Even if you don't, you still may enjoy the Martin Van Buren State Historic Site in nearby Kinderhook. The American Museum of Firefighting in Hudson is also an interesting afternoon venture.

Basics

Operated By: Bill and Claudia Storey. **Open:** All year. **Site Assignment:** Reservations and walk-ins accepted. **Registration:** At campground office. **Fee:** $20–$25. **Parking:** At site.

Facilities

Number of RV Sites: 350. **Number of Tent-Only Sites:** None. **Hookups:** Electric (15, 20, 30), phone, all sites have full hookups. **Each Site:** Fire ring, picnic table. **Dump Station:** Yes. **Laundry:** Yes. **Pay Phone:** Yes. **Rest Rooms and Showers:** Yes. **Fuel:** No. **Propane:** Yes. **Internal Roads:** Gravel, in good condition. **RV Service:** No. **Market:** Within 2 mi. **Restaurant:** Within 2 mi. **General Store:** Yes. **Vending:** Yes. **Playground:** Yes. **Other:** Lake. **Activities:** Lake swimming and fishing, boating, planned activities on weekends, volleyball, horseshoes, game room, sports field, rec hall, tennis. **Nearby Attractions:** Catamount Ski Mountain, American Museum of Firefighting, Clermont State Historic Site, Martin Van Buren National Historic Site. **Additional Information:** Columbia County Chamber of Commerce, (800) 724-1846 www.columbiacountyny.org.

Restrictions

Pets: On leash only. **Fires:** At site. **Alcoholic Beverages:** At site. **Vehicle Maximum Length:** None. **Other:** Max. 4 adults per campsite.

To Get There

West of Copake, the campground is located at the junction of Hwy. 7 and Hwy. 7A.

CORINTH

Alpine Lake Camping Resort

78 Heath Rd., Corinth 12822. T: (518) 654-6260; F: (518) 654-7652; www.alpinelakecamping.com.

RV ★★★★ Tent ★★★★

Beauty: ★★★★ Site Privacy: ★★
Spaciousness: ★★★ Quiet: ★★★★
Security: ★★★★ Cleanliness: ★★★★
Insect Control: ★★★★ Facilities: ★★★★★

Located near Lake George, Lake Luzerne, and Saratoga Springs in the lush Adirondack Forest, Alpine Lake Camping Resort is a truly giant campground. Each RV site accommodates double slide-outs, and there are 300 pull-throughs. Few sites here offer privacy, but campers do not seem to mind, especially since there is so much to do. The campground's centerpiece is the namesake Alpine Lake, a beautiful private lake where campers can boat, fish, swim, and bask in the sun on a sandy beach. Alpine Lake Resort has two swimming pools, two pavilions, lighted tennis courts, hiking trails, a gift shop, and even a day-use kennel among other amenities. South of Alpine Lake, Saratoga Springs is known for its mineral baths. The Great Escape and Splashwater Kingdom Fun Park is New York's largest theme park with 120 rides, including roller coasters, a river raft adventure, and a water park. At the Fort William Henry Museum, visitors can see a rebuilt French and Indian War–era stockade.

Basics

Operated By: Sandwick family. **Open:** May 1–Sept. 30. **Site Assignment:** Reservations and walk-ins accepted. **Registration:** At campground office. **Fee:** $31–$35 (VISA, MC). **Parking:** At site.

Facilities

Number of RV Sites: 450. **Number of Tent-Only Sites:** 50. **Hookups:** Electric (30, 50 amps), cable TV, phone, all sites have full hookups. **Each Site:** Fire ring, picnic table. **Dump Station:** Yes. **Laundry:** Yes. **Pay Phone:** Yes. **Rest Rooms and Showers:** Yes. **Fuel:** No. **Propane:** Yes. **Internal Roads:** Paved, in good condition. **RV Service:** Yes. **Market:** Within 3 mi. **Restaurant:** Within 3 mi. **General Store:** Yes. **Vending:** Yes. **Playground:** Yes. **Other:** Alpine Lake. **Activities:** Lake swimming and fishing, game room, rec hall, boating, canoeing, boat rentals, basketball, planned activities on weekends, movies, tennis, sports field, badminton, horseshoes, hiking trails, volleyball. **Nearby Attractions:** Lake George, Saratoga Springs, Lake Luzerne, Prospect Mountain, Fort William Henry, Water Slide World, Great Escape & Splash Water Kingdom Fun Park. **Additional Information:** Lake George Chamber of Commerce, (800) 705-0059, www.lakegeorgevillage.com.

Restrictions

Pets: On leash only. **Fires:** At site. **Alcoholic Beverages:** At site. **Vehicle Maximum Length:** None. **Other:** No skateboards.

To Get There

From Corinth, go 1.25 mi. south on Hwy. 9N and 1.25 mi. east on Heath Rd. Entrance is on the left.

CORNING

Ferenbaugh Campsites

4121 SR 414, Corning 14830. T: (607) 962-6193; ferencamp@aol.com.

RV ★★★★ Tent ★★★★

Beauty: ★★★★ Site Privacy: ★★★★
Spaciousness: ★★★ Quiet: ★★★★
Security: ★★★ Cleanliness: ★★★★
Insect Control: ★★★★ Facilities: ★★★★

Covering 275 acres and located five miles from Corning, Ferenbaugh Campsites is set in a valley bursting with colo in the spring and the fall. The campground has many wooded and creekside sites—offering welcomed privacy—and 30 pull-throughs. Campers without RVs or tents will relish the spacious, clean cabins that overlook Post Creek. Ferenbaugh is just a few minutes from the Corning Glass Center. If you are interested in the crafting and history of glass, this is a must-see. The center includes the Corning Museum of Glass, which contains a vast collection of 26,000 glass items; the Hall of Science and Industry, which features hands-on exhibits about technology; and the Steuben Glass Factory, where you can watch glass blowers transform molten glass into gifts and collectibles. In Corning's historic Market Street area, the Rockwell Museum displays a large collection of American Western art.

Basics

Operated By: Private operator. **Open:** Apr. 15–Oct. 15. **Site Assignment:** Reservations and walk-ins accepted. **Registration:** At campground headquarters. **Fee:** $20–$29 (VISA, MC, D). **Parking:** At site.

Facilities

Number of RV Sites: 145. **Number of Tent-Only Sites:** 18. **Hookups:** Electric (20, 30, 50 amps), water, cable TV, phone, 33 full hookups. **Each Site:** Fire ring, picnic table. **Dump Station:** Yes. **Laundry:** Yes. **Pay Phone:** Yes. **Rest Rooms and Showers:** Yes. **Fuel:** No. **Propane:** Yes. **Internal Roads:** Gravel, in good condition. **RV Service:** No. **Market:** Within 5 mi. **Restaurant:** Within 5 mi. **General Store:** Yes. **Vending:** Yes. **Playground:** Yes. **Other:** Trout stream, stocked pond. **Activities:** Fishing, mini-golf, hiking trails, game room, sports field, planned activities on weekends, volleyball, badminton, horseshoes. **Nearby Attractions:** Corning Glass Center, Rockwell Museum, Watking Glen State Park, Watkins Glen International Speedway, Harris Hill Soaring Museum, National War Plane Museum, Seneca Lake wineries. **Additional Information:**

Corning Chamber of Commerce, (607) 936-4686, www.corning-chamber.org.

RESTRICTIONS

Pets: On leash only. **Fires:** At site. **Alcoholic Beverages:** At site. **Vehicle Maximum Length:** None. **Other:** None.

TO GET THERE

From I-86, take Exit 46 and go 5 mi. north on Hwy. 414. Entrance is on the right.

DANSVILLE

Sugar Creek Glen Campground

P.O. Box 143W, Dansville 14437. T: (716) 335-6294; www.crosswinds.net/~sugarcreekglen.

RV ★★★★ Tent ★★★★

Beauty: ★★★★★ Site Privacy: ★★★
Spaciousness: ★★★ Quiet: ★★★★
Security: ★★★★ Cleanliness: ★★★★
Insect Control: ★★★★ Facilities: ★★★★

Located in east central New York, Sugar Creek Glen Campground is less than two hours from Niagara Falls, but it has 15 acres of natural beauty on its own grounds. Sugar Creek Glen is in fact a shady glen with five cascading waterfalls, including one that is lighted for nighttime viewing. There are several hiking trails that meander through the glen and offer spectacular views of the waterfalls. Sites are shaded and wooded, and many are along Sugar Creek. RVers and tenters alike can camp in the summer with shelter from the hot sun. Most campers venture here because of the waterfalls and hiking trails, but the campground does have a full menu of family-oriented activites. Sugar Creek Glen is convenient to the Finger Lakes region; Conesus Lake and Canandaigua Lake are closest to the campground. Letchworth State Park with its Genesee River Gorge is a rewarding day trip for campers. The park has three waterfalls, one of which is 107 feet high

BASICS

Operated By: Alice and Bob Klos. **Open:** Apr. 27–Oct. 14. **Site Assignment:** Reservations and walk-ins accepted. **Registration:** At campground office. **Fee:** $20–$26 (VISA, MC). **Parking:** At site.

FACILITIES

Number of RV Sites: 109. **Number of Tent-Only Sites:** 26. **Hookups:** Electric (15, 30 amps), water. **Each Site:** Fire ring, picnic table. **Dump Station:** Yes. **Laundry:** No. **Pay Phone:** Yes. **Rest Rooms and Showers:** Yes. **Fuel:** No. **Propane:** No. **Internal Roads:** Gravel and dirt, in good condition. **RV Service:** No. **Market:** Within 5 mi. **Restaurant:** Within 5 mi. **General Store:** Yes. **Vending:** Yes. **Playground:** Yes. **Other:** Five waterfalls on grounds; one is lighted. **Activities:** River swimming, game room, rec hall, hiking trails, fishing, basketball, badminton, volleyball. **Nearby Attractions:** Niagara Falls, Letchworth State Park, Finger Lakes. **Additional Information:** Finger Lakes Assoc., (800) 548-4386, www.fingerlakes.org.

RESTRICTIONS

Pets: On leash only. **Fires:** At site. **Alcoholic Beverages:** At site. **Vehicle Maximum Length:** 30 ft.

TO GET THERE

From I-390, take Exit 4 and go about 500 ft. south on Hwy. 36 and 4 mi. southwest on Poag's Hole Rd. Entrance is at the end.

DARIEN CENTER

Skyline Camping Resort

10933 Townline Rd., Darien Center 14040. T: (716) 591-2021 or (800) 724-3619; F: (716) 591-2022; www.skylinervresort.com.

RV ★★★★ Tent ★★★★

Beauty: ★★★★ Site Privacy: ★★
Spaciousness: ★★ Quiet: ★★★★
Security: ★★★★★ Cleanliness: ★★★★
Insect Control: ★★★★ Facilities: ★★★★

Located 40 miles east of Niagara Falls and five minutes from Six Flags Darien Lake, Skyline Camping Resort sits atop a ridge in the rolling, forested hills of western New York. Sites are wooded and open. We especially like the privacy and the fragrant aroma around the sites in the Pine Woods area. These shaded sites are situated amid Scotch and Austrian Pine trees. Sites at the northwest side of the pond offer little privacy, but they have a good view of the water and are near activity centers. Campers can fish in the six-acre private pond that teems with largemouth bass. Skyline has a large pavilion for live entertainment, dances, bingo, and movies. Skyline also has an RV sales and service center, so you are in luck if your RV is running rough. In addition to Darien Lake, Six Flags Darien Lake, and Niagara Falls, Buffalo and Rochester are other potential day trip destinations for Skyline campers.

BASICS

Operated By: Tybor family. **Open:** Apr. 15–Oct. 15. **Site Assignment:** Reservations and walk-ins accepted. **Registration:** At campground office. **Fee:** $23 (VISA, MC, D). **Parking:** At site.

FACILITIES

Number of RV Sites: 250. **Number of Tent-Only Sites:** 25. **Hookups:** Electric (20, 30 amps), water. **Each Site:** Picnic table. **Dump Station:** Yes. **Laundry:** No. **Pay Phone:** Yes. **Rest Rooms and Showers:** Yes. **Fuel:** No. **Propane:** Yes. **Internal Roads:** Gravel, in good condition. **RV Service:** Yes. **Market:** Within 3 mi. **Restaurant:** Within 3 mi. **General Store:** Yes. **Vending:** Yes. **Playground:** Yes. **Other:** Six-acre private fishing lake. **Activities:** Fishing, swimming, mini-golf, game room, rec hall, basketball, shufleboard, planned activities on weekends, tennis, badminton, sports field, horseshoes, volleyball. **Nearby Attractions:** Darien Lake, Six Flags Darien Lake, Niagara Falls, Rochester, Buffalo. **Additional Information:** New York Division of Tourism, (800) CALL-NYS, www.iloveny.state.ny.us.

RESTRICTIONS

Pets: On leash only. **Fires:** At site. **Alcoholic Beverages:** At site. **Vehicle Maximum Length:** None.

TO GET THERE

From Hwy. 77, go 4 mi. east on US 20 and 1 mi. south on Townline Rd. Entrance is on the left.

DAVENPORT

Beaver Spring Lake Campground

Rte. 23 Box 64, Davenport 13750. T: (607) 278-5293; bslcg@catskill.net.

RV ★★★★ Tent ★★★★

Beauty: ★★★★ Site Privacy: ★★★
Spaciousness: ★★ Quiet: ★★★★
Security: ★★★★ Cleanliness: ★★★★
Insect Control: ★★★★ Facilities: ★★★★

Located 20 miles southeast of Cooperstown and 15 miles east of Oneonta, Beaver Spring Lake Campground is a tranquil place where campers fish and boat in the 15-acre lake. The campground has 12 pull-throughs among its open and shaded sites. For venturing onto the lake, there are rowboats, pedal boats, and canoes for rent. Beaver Spring Lake also has a game room, a clean and well-equipped pavilion, a swimming pool, and playground among other facilities. Many campers use Beaver Spring Lake as a base for a visit to Cooperstown—and not just to see the National Baseball Hall of Fame and other baseball attractions. The Fenimore Art Museum houses memorabilia from author James Fenimore Cooper, who wrote *The Last of the Mohicans.*

BASICS

Operated By: Bob and Betty. **Open:** Apr. 15–Nov. 30. **Site Assignment:** Reservations and walk-ins accepted. **Registration:** At campground office. **Fee:** $25 (VISA, MC). **Parking:** At site.

FACILITIES

Number of RV Sites: 104. **Number of Tent-Only Sites:** 20. **Hookups:** Electric (15, 20, 30 amps), water, 70 full hookups. **Each Site:** Fire ring, picnic table. **Dump Station:** Yes. **Laundry:** Yes. **Pay Phone:** Yes. **Rest Rooms and Showers:** Yes. **Fuel:** No. **Propane:** Yes. **Internal Roads:** Gravel and dirt, in fair condition. **RV Service:** No. **Market:** Within 2 mi. **Restaurant:** Within 2 mi. **General Store:** Yes. **Vending:** Yes. **Playground:** Yes. **Other:** Beaver Spring Lake. **Activities:** Fishing, boating, game room, sports field, boat rentals, planned activities on weekends, badminton, horseshoes, volleyball. **Nearby Attractions:** National Soccer Hall of Fame, Cooperstown Dreams Park, National Baseball Hall of Fame and Museum, Otsego Lake, Farmers Museum and Village Crossroads, Fenimore Art Museum. **Additional Information:** Cooperstown Chamber of Commerce, (607) 547-9983, www.cooperstownchamber.org.

RESTRICTIONS

Pets: On leash only. **Fires:** At site. **Alcoholic Beverages:** At site. **Vehicle Maximum Length:** 40 ft. **Other:** None.

TO GET THERE

From Davenport, head east on Hwy. 23. Entrance is on the left.

DEWITTVILLE

Chautauqua Heights Camping Resort

5652 Thumb Rd., Dewittville 14728. T: (716) 386-3804; F: (716) 386-3043; www.chautauquahgts.com; contact@chautauquahgts.com.

RV ★★★★ Tent ★★★★

Beauty: ★★★★ Site Privacy: ★★★
Spaciousness: ★★★ Quiet: ★★★★
Security: ★★★★★ Cleanliness: ★★★★
Insect Control: ★★★★ Facilities: ★★★★

Chautauqua Heights Camping Resort has 142 open and wooded sites on 150 acres in western New York, near Lake Erie and the Pennsylvania border. With its proximity to Lake Erie and Allegheny State Park, Chautauqua Heights is a haven for outdoor enthusiasts. Each site accommodates a double slideout, and there are 40 pull-throughs. The campground is a half-mile from Chautauqua Lake and a short drive to the Chautauqua Institution, a 215-acre center for religion, recreation, education, and the arts. The gated institution, designated a National Historic District, began as a Sunday-school-teachers' training camp. About 1,000 people live here year-round, but the population swells to more than 10,000 during the summer. Entertainment and lectures at the amphitheater, performances by the Chautauqua Opera Company at Norton Memorial Hall, and boating and fishing on the lake are among the activities here.

BASICS

Operated By: Bill Perry. **Open:** Apr. 15–Oct. 15. **Site Assignment:** Reservations and walk-ins accepted. **Registration:** At campground office. **Fee:** $20–$25 (VISA, MC, AE, D). **Parking:** At site.

FACILITIES

Number of RV Sites: 132. **Number of Tent-Only Sites:** 10. **Hookups:** Electric (20, 30, 50 amps), water, phone, 117 full hookups. **Each Site:** Fire ring, picnic table. **Dump Station:** Yes. **Laundry:** Yes. **Pay Phone:** Yes. **Rest Rooms and Showers:** Yes. **Fuel:** No. **Propane:** Yes. **Internal Roads:** Gravel, in good condition. **RV Service:** No. **Market:** Within 1 mi. **Restaurant:** Within 1 mi. **General Store:** Yes. **Vending:** Yes. **Playground:** Yes. **Other:** Cottage and cabin rentals. **Activities:** Swimming, basketball, game room, rec hall, movies, horseshoes, hiking trails, volleyball. **Nearby Attractions:** Chautauqua Institution, Chautauqua Belle steamboat, Chautauqua Lake, Midway Park, Allegheny State Park. **Additional Information:** Chautauqua-Allegheny Region, (800) 242-4569, www.chautauqua-allegheny.org.

RESTRICTIONS

Pets: On leash only. **Fires:** At site. **Alcoholic Beverages:** At site. **Vehicle Maximum Length:** 40 ft. **Other:** Check-in is 4 p.m.; $1 added for early check-in.

TO GET THERE

From Chautauqua, go 0.5 mi. east on Hwy. 430. Entrance is on the left.

DEXTER

Black River Bay Campground

P.O. Box 541, Dexter 13634-0541. T: (315) 639-3735; www.blackriverbaycamp.com; laura@blackriverbaycamp.com.

RV ★★★★ Tent ★★★★

Beauty: ★★★★ Site Privacy: ★★
Spaciousness: ★★ Quiet: ★★★★
Security: ★★★★ Cleanliness: ★★★★
Insect Control: ★★★★ Facilities: ★★★★

The raging whitewater of Black River Canyon. The world-class fishing on Lake Ontario. The natural splendor of the Thousand Islands. Black River Bay Campground is near all of it. Guided whitewater rafting excursions in Black River Canyon start and embark from the campground. Fishing trips on Lake Ontario, which is one mile by boat from Black River Bay, lead to dramatic catch stories of muskie, salmon, small and largemouth bass, brown trout and lake trout, and northern pike. We like the campsites located along the Black River, especially sites 16–19, which have a good view of Squaw Island. Alexandria Bay, the resort center of the Thousand Islands, is not far from Black River Bay. Points of interest in the area include the Thousand Islands Skydeck, which offers stunning views of the islands between the spans of the Thousand Islands International Bridge, and Boldt Castle, the 19th century creation of hotel magnate George C. Boldt.

BASICS

Operated By: Laura Todd. **Open:** May 1–Oct. 15. **Site Assignment:** Reservations and walk-ins accepted. **Registration:** At campground office. **Fee:** $14–$19 (VISA, MC). **Parking:** At site.

FACILITIES

Number of RV Sites: 150. **Number of Tent-Only Sites:** 50. **Hookups:** Electric (20, 30 amps), water, phone, 75 full hookups. **Each Site:** Fire ring, picnic table. **Dump Station:** Yes. **Laundry:** Yes. **Pay Phone:** Yes. **Rest Rooms and Showers:** Yes. **Fuel:** Yes. **Propane:** Yes. **Internal Roads:** Gravel, in good condition. **RV Service:** No. **Market:** Within 5 mi. **Restaurant:** Within 5 mi. **General Store:** Yes. **Vending:** Yes. **Playground:** Yes. **Other:** Boat docks and boat launch. **Activities:** Boating, canoeing, boat rentals, river fishing, planned activites on weekends, horseshoes, volleyball, game room, rec hall. **Nearby Attractions:** Thousand Islands, Lake Ontario, Black River. St. Lawrence River, Alexandria Bay, American Maple Museum, Long Point State Park. **Additional Information:** Watertown Chamber of Commerce, (315) 788-4400, www.watertownny.com.

RESTRICTIONS

Pets: On leash only. **Fires:** At site. **Alcoholic Beverages:** At site. **Vehicle Maximum Length:** 35 ft. **Other:** Quiet hours 10 p.m.–7 a.m.

TO GET THERE

From I-81, take Exit 46 and go 6 mi. west on Rte. 12F and 0.25 mi. on Foster Park Rd. Entrance is on the right.

DUANE

Deer River Campsite

HCR 01 Box 101A, Malone 12953. T: (518) 483-0060; www.deerrivercampsite.com; deeriver@westelcom.com.

RV ★★★★ Tent ★★★★

Beauty: ★★★★ Site Privacy: ★★★
Spaciousness: ★★★★ Quiet: ★★★★
Security: ★★★★★ Cleanliness: ★★★★
Insect Control: ★★★★ Facilities: ★★★★★

Located near Malone at the edge of the northern section of Adirondack Park, Deer River Campsite features wooded and spacious sites, some of which accommodate double slideouts and pull-throughs, and some of which are set on the 1.5-mile lake. The campground has clean rest rooms and showers, a laundry facility, and a cafe. Campers can fish and swim in the lake. Rowboats, canoes, and pedal boats are available for rent. The six-million-acre Adirondack Park encompasses New York's largest mountain range, itself ribboned with rippling streams that cut through towering peaks, winding wilderness trails, and unspoiled forests mirrored in shiny lakes and ponds. There are 750 miles of marked trails wandering through pine and spruce forests and along the numerous streams and lakes. Whiteface Mountain, Lake Placid, and Saranac Lake are within an hour's drive south of Deer River.

BASICS

Operated By: Janine Paddock. **Open:** May 1–Oct. 1. **Site Assignment:** Reservations and walk-ins accepted. **Registration:** At campground office. **Fee:** $19–$23 (VISA, MC, D). **Parking:** At site.

FACILITIES

Number of RV Sites: 78. **Number of Tent-Only Sites:** 6. **Hookups:** Electric (30 amps), water, phone, 12 full hookups. **Each Site:** Fire ring, picnic table. **Dump Station:** Yes. **Laundry:** Yes. **Pay Phone:** Yes. **Rest Rooms and Showers:** Yes. **Fuel:** No. **Propane:** Yes. **Internal Roads:** Gravel, in good condition. **RV Service:** No. **Market:** Within 3 mi. **Restaurant:** On premises. **General Store:** Yes. **Vending:** Yes. **Playground:** Yes. **Other:** Deer River. **Activities:** Lake swimming and boating, boat rentals, game room, rec hall, lake fishing, basketball, planned activities on weekends, movies, volleyball, hiking trails, horseshoes, sports field, badminton. **Nearby Attractions:** Adirondack Park, Whiteface Mountain, Lake Placid, Saranac Lake, Six Nations Indian Museum, Akwesasne Mohawk Casin, Ausable Chasm, Adirondack Visitors Center, St. Lawrence Seaway Locks, Laura Ingalls Wilder Home. **Additional Information:** New York Division of Tourism—The Adirondacks, (800) 487-6867. www.iloveny.state.ny.us.

RESTRICTIONS

Pets: On leash only. **Fires:** At site. **Alcoholic Beverages:** At site. **Vehicle Maximum Length:** 35 ft. **Other:** Overnight visitors must register by 8 p.m.

TO GET THERE

From Hwy. 30, go 1.5 mi. west on CR 14 (Red Tavern Rd.). Entrance is on the left.

ELLENVILLE
Skyway Camping Resort

P.O. Box 194, Greenfield Park 12435. T: (845) 647-5747 or (800) 447-5992; www.skywaycamping.com; skywaymail@skywaycamping.com.

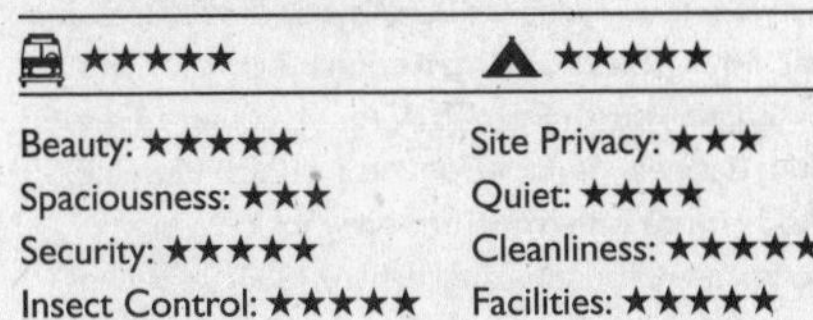
RV ★★★★★ Tent ★★★★★

Beauty: ★★★★★ Site Privacy: ★★★
Spaciousness: ★★★ Quiet: ★★★★
Security: ★★★★★ Cleanliness: ★★★★★
Insect Control: ★★★★★ Facilities: ★★★★★

The Catskill Mountains are just two hours north of New York City, but it seems like a world away. That is the feeling you get at Skyway Camping Resort, six miles west of Ellenville near the southeastern edge of Catskill Park. RVers and tenters will feel like they are staying at a resort hotel. The immaculate three-story clubhouse, a well-equipped workout room, an Olympic-sized solar-heated pool and whirlpool, a pond for fishing and boating, and tennis and handball courts are among the amenities at this campground—one of the best in the Catskills. Luxury trailers with full baths rent for $115 a night. Located north and west of the Hudson Valley, the Catskills are bordered by the Hudson and Delaware rivers. Skyway is not far from Minnewaska State Park, which has numerous trails for hiking, biking, cross-country skiing, and snowshoeing. The Fort Delaware Museum of Colonial History in nearby Narrowsburg is open during summer months.

BASICS
Operated By: Holiday Trav-L-Park. **Open:** May 1–Columbus Day. **Site Assignment:** Reservations and walk-ins accepted. **Registration:** At campground office. **Fee:** $38 (VISA, MC, AE, D). **Parking:** At site.

FACILITIES
Number of RV Sites: 145. **Number of Tent-Only Sites:** 45. **Hookups:** Electric (20, 30 amps), water, phone, cable TV, 149 full hookups. **Each Site:** Fire ring, picnic table. **Dump Station:** Yes. **Laundry:** Yes. **Pay Phone:** Yes. **Rest Rooms and Showers:** Yes. **Fuel:** No. **Propane:** Yes. **Internal Roads:** Gravel and paved, in good condition. **RV Service:** No. **Market:** Within 5 mi. **Restaurant:** Within 5 mi. **General Store:** Yes. **Vending:** Yes. **Playground:** Yes. **Other:** Three-story clubhouse, professional exercise room. **Activities:** Swimming, whirlpool, tennis, handball, boating, boat rentals, lake fishing, basketball, sports field, badminton, planned activities, hiking trails, volleyball, horseshoes. **Nearby Attractions:** Catskill Park, Lake Superior State Park, Delaware & Hudson Canal Linear Park, Minisink Battleground Park, Stone Arch Bridge Historical Park, Fort Delaware Museum of Colonial History. **Additional Information:** New York Division of Tourism—The Catskills, (800) NYS-CATS, www.iloveny.state.ny.us.

RESTRICTIONS
Pets: On leash only. **Fires:** At site. **Alcoholic Beverages:** At site. **Vehicle Maximum Length:** None. **Other:** None.

TO GET THERE
From US 209, go 5 mi. west on Hwy. 52 and 1 mi. south on Skyway RV Rd. Entrance is on the left.

ELLENVILLE
Yogi Bear's Jellystone Park at Birchwood Acres

P.O. Box 482, Woodridge 12789. T: (845) 434-4743 or (800) 552-4724; F: (845) 436-7239; www.nyjellystone.com; nyyogi@aol.com.

RV ★★★★★ Tent ★★★★★

Beauty: ★★★★★ Site Privacy: ★★
Spaciousness: ★★★ Quiet: ★★★★
Security: ★★★★ Cleanliness: ★★★★★
Insect Control: ★★★★ Facilities: ★★★★★

Located eight miles west of Ellenville near the southeastern edge of Catskill Park, Yogi Bear's Jellystone Park at Birchwood Acres rivals nearby Skyway Camping Resort. This 150-acre campground has a nice swimming pool and whirlpool and a central sports complex with softball, basketball, paddleball, tennis, shuffleboard, and horseshoes. There is a well-maintained playground, plus wagon rides with Yogi and fire truck rides for the children. The five-acre lake is stocked with bass and bluegill. Campsites are partially wooded. There are 136 double slideout sites, but no pull-throughs. If you want to stay near the lake, the swimming pool, the adult lounge, basketball and volleyball courts, and other activity centers, we recommend the cluster of sites at the southeast end of the campground. Lodge rentals and RV sites at the northern tip of the campground are away from the activity centers and offer more tranquility.

BASICS
Operated By: Jellystone Park. **Open:** May 1–Columbus Day. **Site Assignment:** Reservations and walk-ins accepted. **Registration:** At campground office. **Fee:** $37–$42 (VISA, MC). **Parking:** At site.

FACILITIES
Number of RV Sites: 227. **Number of Tent-Only Sites:** 25. **Hookups:** Electric (20, 30 amps), phone, cable TV, water, 136 full hookups. **Each Site:** Fire ring, picnic table. **Dump Station:** Yes. **Laundry:** Yes. **Pay Phone:** Yes. **Rest Rooms and Showers:** Yes. **Fuel:** No. **Propane:** Yes. **Internal Roads:** Gravel and paved, in good condition. **RV Service:** No. **Market:** Within 6 mi. **Restaurant:** Within 5 mi. **General Store:** Yes. **Vending:** Yes. **Playground:** Yes. **Other:** Cabin, lodge and trailer rentals. **Activities:** Swimming, whirlpool, boating, boat rentals, game room, rec hall, lake fishing, movies, shuffleboard, basketball, planned activities, volleyball, tennis, sports field, horseshoes. **Nearby Attractions:** Catskill Park, Minnewaska State Park, Delaware & Hudson Canal Linear Park, Minisink Battleground Park, Stone Arch Bridge Historical Park, Fort Delaware Museum of Colonial History. **Additional Information:** New York Division of Tourism—The Catskills, (800) NYS-CATS, www.iloveny.state.ny.us.

RESTRICTIONS
Pets: On leash only, under control. **Fires:** At site. **Alcoholic Beverages:** At site. **Vehicle Maximum Length:** None.

TO GET THERE
From US 209, go 8 mi. west on Hwy. 52 and 0.5 mi. south on Martinfield Rd. Entrance is on the left.

ENDICOTT
Pine Valley RV Park and Campground

600 Boswell Hill Rd., Endicott 13760. T: (607) 785-6868; www.pinevalleycampground.com; pinevalley@baka.com.

RV ★★★★ Tent ★★★

Beauty: ★★★★ Site Privacy: ★
Spaciousness: ★★ Quiet: ★★★★
Security: ★★★★ Cleanliness: ★★★★
Insect Control: ★★★★ Facilities: ★★★★

Nestled in the rolling hills that overlook Binghamton, Pine Valley Campground is located outside of Endicott, which forms the Triple Cities with Binghamton and Johnson City. The open and wooded sites are situated around a six-acre lake in the center of the campground. Sites in sections A and D offer more space than other sections. Privacy is virtually non-existent here. Sites along the lake are extremely popular. There are 18 golf courses and several shopping malls in the area. Though Pine Valley is located near Endicott, most of the area's attractions are found in Binghamton. Some campers also use Pine Valley as a base for day trips in Cooperstown and Corning.

BASICS
Operated By: Private operator. **Open:** May 1–Oct. 15. **Site Assignment:** Reservations accepted (3-day min. stay on holiday weekend), walk-ins accepted. **Registration:** At campground office. **Fee:** $20–$25 (VISA, MC, D). **Parking:** At site.

FACILITIES
Number of RV Sites: 102. **Number of Tent-Only Sites:** 13. **Hookups:** Electric (20, 30, 50 amps), phone, water, 47 full hookups. **Each Site:** Fire ring, picnic table. **Dump Station:** Yes. **Laundry:** Yes. **Pay Phone:** Yes. **Rest Rooms and Showers:** Yes. **Fuel:** No. **Propane:** Yes. **Internal Roads:** Gravel, in fair condition. **RV Service:** No. **Market:** Within 3 mi. **Restaurant:** Within 3 mi. **General Store:** Yes. **Vending:** Yes. **Playground:** Yes. **Other:** Lodge. **Activities:** Lake swimming and fishing, boat rentals, planned activities on weekends, canoeing, boating, hiking trails, horseshoes, volleyball, sports field. **Nearby Attractions:** Binghamton, Ross Park Zoo, Chenango Valley State Park, Discovery Center of the Southern Tier, Roberson Museum and Science Center, Kopernik Space Education Center, Finch Hollow Nature Center. **Additional Information:** Broome County Convention and Visitors Bureau, (800) 836-6740, www.specentera.net/broomechamber.

RESTRICTIONS

Pets: On leash only. **Fires:** At site. **Alcoholic Beverages:** At site. **Vehicle Maximum Length:** 45 ft. **Other:** Check-in/out time is 3 p.m.; early arrivals and late departures are charged $3 per hour.

TO GET THERE

From Hwy. 17, take Exit 67N and go 6 mi. north on Hwy. 26, 1 block northwest on Maple Dr., and 1 mi. west on Boswell Hill Rd. Entrance is on the left. Owners of RVs taller than 12 feet should call for alternative directions.

FLORIDA

Black Bear Campground

P.O. Box 22, Florida 10921. T: (845) 651-7717 or (888) 867-2267; www.blackbearcampground.com; topcamp@warwick.net.

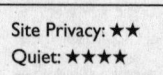

 ★★★ ▲ ★★★

Beauty: ★★★★ Site Privacy: ★★
Spaciousness: ★★ Quiet: ★★★★
Security: ★★★★ Cleanliness: ★★★★
Insect Control: ★★★★ Facilities: ★★★★

Located in Orange County in the Hudson Valley, Black Bear Campground is an hour northwest of New York City. With its rural location on a mountaintop plateau, (within 15 miles of the Appalachian Trail), Black Bear's environment is very tranquil, and you can tour New York City by boarding a tour bus that departs from the campground. Black Bear has level, open, and shaded sites, including 10 pull-throughs. Neither RV nor tent sites offer much privacy, but they are well-kept. The large swimming pool, mini-golf course, basketball court, and arcade are among the activity centers. New York City is not the only worthwhile destination for Black Bear campers. The oldest horse-racing venue in the country and the Hall of Fame of the Trotter are located six miles away. Brotherhood Winery, the oldest winery in America, is 10 miles away, as is Museum Village, a restored village from 1850.

BASICS

Operated By: Howard Smith. **Open:** All year. **Site Assignment:** Reservations accepted ($20 deposit required), walk-ins accepted. **Registration:** At campground office. **Fee:** $24–$27 (VISA, MC). **Parking:** At site.

FACILITIES

Number of RV Sites: 160. **Number of Tent-Only Sites:** 20. **Hookups:** Electric (20, 30, 50 amps), cable TV, phone, water, 109 full hookups. **Each Site:** Fire ring, picnic table. **Dump Station:** Yes. **Laundry:** Yes. **Pay Phone:** Yes. **Rest Rooms and Showers:** Yes. **Fuel:** No. **Propane:** Yes. **Internal Roads:** Paved, in good condition. **RV Service:** No. **Market:** Within 2 mi. **Restaurant:** Within 1.5 mi. **General Store:** Yes. **Vending:** Yes. **Playground:** Yes. **Other:** Cabin and trailer rentals. **Activities:** Game room, rec hall, sports field, basketball, mini-golf, planned activities, badminton, horseshoes. **Nearby Attractions:** New York City, West Point (US Military Academy), Appalachian Trail, Orange County Fairgrounds, Orange County Speedway, Museum Village in Orange County, Harness Racing & Hall of Fame, Brotherhood Winery, Storm King Art Center, Museum of the Hudson Highlands, Harriman State Park. **Additional Information:** New York Division of Tourism—Hudson Valley, (800) 762-8687, www.iloveny.state.ny.us.

RESTRICTIONS

Pets: On leash only. **Fires:** At site, out by midnight. **Alcoholic Beverages:** At site. **Vehicle Maximum Length:** None. **Other:** Check-in time 10 a.m.–10 p.m.

TO GET THERE

From Hwy. 17, take Exit 124 and go 5 mi. southwest on Hwy. 17A, 0.5 mi. south on Hwy. 94/17A, 1 block west on Bridge St., 1 block south on Highland Ave., and 0.75 mi. southwest on Wheeler Rd. Entrance is on the left.

FRANKLINVILLE

Triple R Camping Resort

3491 Bryant Hill Rd., Franklinville 14737. T: (716) 676-3856; F: (716) 676-3856; www.triplercamp.com; triprcamp@aol.com.

★★★★ ▲ ★★★★

Beauty: ★★★★ Site Privacy: ★★★
Spaciousness: ★★★ Quiet: ★★★★
Security: ★★★★★ Cleanliness: ★★★★★
Insect Control: ★★★★ Facilities: ★★★★

Situated in the foothills of the Allegheny Mountains in western New York, Triple R Camping Resort is an hour south of Buffalo and Niagara Falls. Two swimming pools, volleyball and basketball courts, a fishing pond, a mini-golf course, and 50 acres of hiking trails through a wooded hillside are among the recreational offerings here. There are also wagon rides and live entertainment on holiday weekends. The open and wooded sites are spacious; there are 14 pull-throughs. RV sites around the pools are very spacious, as are the sites that border the woods near the tenting area, which is nestled amid mature trees and not far from hiking trails. The campground is a short drive from Allegheny State Park, which covers 64,000 acres and is the largest state park in New York. The nearby Seneca-Iroquois National Museum in Salamanca is another interesting attraction. The museum has numerous exhibits on the Seneca Indians, who lived in New York 10,000 years ago.

BASICS

Operated By: Don and Lori Evans. **Open:** Apr. 15–Oct. 15. **Site Assignment:** Reservations recommended (1-night deposit required; reservations required on holiday weekends), walk-ins accepted. **Registration:** At campground office. **Fee:** $21–$24 (VISA, MC, AE, D). **Parking:** At site.

FACILITIES

Number of RV Sites: 130. **Number of Tent-Only Sites:** 15. **Hookups:** Electric (30, 50 amps), water, phone, cable TV, 118 full hookups. **Each Site:** Fire ring, picnic table. **Dump Station:** Yes. **Laundry:** Yes. **Pay Phone:** Yes. **Rest Rooms and Showers:** Yes. **Fuel:** No. **Propane:** Yes. **Internal Roads:** Gravel, in good condition. **RV Service:** Yes. **Market:** Within 1.5 mi. **Restaurant:** Within 1.5 mi. **General Store:** Yes. **Vending:** Yes. **Playground:** Yes. **Other:** RV rentals. **Activities:** Game room, sports field, mini-golf, basketball, planned activities on weekends, hiking trails, volleyball, horseshoes, rec hall, fishing. **Nearby Attractions:** Allegany State Park, Letchworth State Park, Amish country, Freedom Raceway, Seneca-Iroquois National Museum. **Additional Information:** New York Division of Tourism—Chautauqua-Allegheny, (800) 242-4569, www.iloveny.state.ny.us.

RESTRICTIONS

Pets: On leash only. **Fires:** At site. **Alcoholic Beverages:** At site. **Vehicle Maximum Length:** None. **Other:** All dogs must stay inside vehicle or tent at night.

TO GET THERE

From Hwy. 98, go 1 mi. north on Hwy. 16/98, 1.5 mi.west on Elm St., and 0.3 mi. southwest on Bryant Hill Rd. Entrance is on the left.

GARDINER

Yogi Bear's Jellystone Park Camp Resort at Lazy River

50 Bevier Rd., Gardiner 12525. T: (845) 255-5193 or (800) 610-3433; F: (845) 255-2259; www.gocampingamerica.com/yogigardiner; yogibear1@msn.com.

★★★★★ ▲ ★★★★★

Beauty: ★★★★★ Site Privacy: ★★★
Spaciousness: ★★★ Quiet: ★★★★
Security: ★★★★★ Cleanliness: ★★★★★
Insect Control: ★★★★ Facilities: ★★★★★

Located 90 minutes northwest of New York City in the Mid-Hudson Valley, Yogi Bear's Jellystone Park Camp Resort at Lazy River has been named on the of top 10 in its chain. The campground has riverfront, meadow, and wooded RV sites, 30 of which accommodate pull-throughs. Sites on the river at the east side of the park are away from the noise of the activity centers but have less space than riverfront sites at the center of the park. Most riverfront sites are more spacious than the clusters of sites at the center of the campground. Boo Boo's Toddler Playground and the Pirate Ship Playground are kid favorites. If you stay on a weekend and savor fresh fruit, you are in luck. On Saturday mornings, the fresh produce wagon travels throughout the campground offering its tempting inventory. New York City is a popular day trip destination for campers. The Franklin D. Roosevelt Home National Historic Site, the Eleanor Roosevelt National Historic Site, and the Vanderbilt Mansion National Historic Site—all in the Hyde Park area—are a short drive away. Of course, the highlight for some campers (especially the younger ones) will be the visits from Yogi Bear and Boo Boo.

BASICS

Operated By: John and Heidi Lawrence and Glen

and Tammy Bracklow. **Open:** Apr. 27–Oct. 18. **Site Assignment:** Reservations recommended, walk-ins accepted. **Registration:** At campground store. **Fee:** $33–$39 (VISA, MC, D). **Parking:** At site.

Facilities

Number of RV Sites: 175. **Number of Tent-Only Sites:** 10. **Hookups:** Electric (20, 30, 50 amps), water, phone, 80 full hookups. **Each Site:** Fire ring, picnic table. **Dump Station:** Yes. **Laundry:** Yes. **Pay Phone:** Yes. **Rest Rooms and Showers:** Yes. **Fuel:** No. **Propane:** Yes. **Internal Roads:** Gravel, in good condition. **RV Service:** Yes, limited. **Market:** Within 2 mi. **Restaurant:** Within 3 mi. **General Store:** Yes. **Vending:** Yes. **Playground:** Yes. **Other:** Cabin and RV rentals. **Activities:** Volleyball, rec hall, game room, sports field, mini-golf, planned activities, shuffleboard, boating, whitewater rafting, movies, hiking trails, river fishing. **Nearby Attractions:** New York City, West Point (US Military Academy), Franklin D. Roosevelt Home National Historic Site, Eleanor Roosevelt National Historic Site, Vanderbilt Mansion National Historic Site, Hudson River tours. **Additional Information:** New York Division of Tourism—Hudson Valley, (800) 762-8687, www.iloveny.state.ny.us.

Restrictions

Pets: On leash only. **Fires:** At site. **Alcoholic Beverages:** At site. **Vehicle Maximum Length:** None. **Other:** Fires must be out by 11 p.m.

To Get There

From Hwy. 208, go 2.5 mi. west on Hwy. 44/55, 0.2 mi. south on Albany Post Rd., and 0.5 mi. east on Bevier Rd. Entrance is at the end.

GASPORT

Niagara Hartland RV Park and Campground

2383 Hartland Rd., Gasport 14067. T: (716) 795-3812 or (800) 571-4829.

RV: ★★★★	Tent: ★★★★
Beauty: ★★★★	Site Privacy: ★★★
Spaciousness: ★★★	Quiet: ★★★★
Security: ★★★★	Cleanliness: ★★★★
Insect Control: ★★★★	Facilities: ★★★★

Located in Niagara County near Niagara Falls and Lake Ontario, Niagara Hartland RV Park and Campground offers spacious, grassy sites. There are 75 full hookups and 14 pull-throughs. With the spring-fed lake—where campers can swim, fish, and use rented pedal boats—there is no shortage of outdoor recreation. Anglers can also drop their lines in Lake Ontario, which is just 10 miles away. Niagara Falls and its multitude of tours, including the famous Maid of the Mist boat excursion, is about a half-hour drive from Hartland. Devil's Hole State Park offers a good view of the lower falls, and Niagara Reservation State Park provides views of the main falls. At Prospect Point, there is a 282-foot-high observation tower. An elevator takes passengers to the gorge below and the Maid of the Mist boarding point.

Basics

Operated By: Private operator. **Open:** May 15–Oct. 15. **Site Assignment:** Reservations and walk-ins accepted. **Registration:** At campground office. **Fee:** $23 (VISA, MC, D). **Parking:** At site.

Facilities

Number of RV Sites: 78. **Number of Tent-Only Sites:** 22. **Hookups:** Electric (20, 30, 50 amps), water, phone, 75 full hookups. **Each Site:** Fire ring, picnic table. **Dump Station:** Yes. **Laundry:** Yes. **Pay Phone:** Yes. **Rest Rooms and Showers:** Yes. **Fuel:** No. **Propane:** No. **Internal Roads:** Gravel and paved, in good condition. **RV Service:** No. **Market:** Within 5 mi. **Restaurant:** Within 4 mi. **General Store:** Yes. **Vending:** Yes. **Playground:** Yes. **Other:** Spring-fed lake. **Activities:** Fishing, lake swimming, boating, canoeing, pedal boat rentals, game room, rec hall, planned activities on weekends, badminton, sports field, horseshoes, volleyball, basketball. **Nearby Attractions:** Niagara Falls, Lake Ontario, Aquarium of Niagara Falls, Artpark, Devil's Hole State Park, Fort Niagara State Park, Niagara Reservation State Park, Maid of the Mist tours, Prospect Point Observation Tower. **Additional Information:** New York Division of Tourism—Greater Niagara, (800) 338-7890, www.iloveny.state.ny.us.

Restrictions

Pets: On leash only, under control. **Fires:** At site. **Alcoholic Beverages:** At site. **Vehicle Maximum Length:** None. **Other:** None.

To Get There

From Hwy. 104, go 3.75 mi. north on Hartland Rd. Entrance is on the right.

GILBOA

Country Roads Campground

Kingsley Rd., Gilboa 12076. T: (518) 827-6397; www.countryroadscampground.com; countryroads@gocampingamerica.com.

RV: ★★★	Tent: ★★★
Beauty: ★★★★	Site Privacy: ★★★
Spaciousness: ★★★	Quiet: ★★★★
Security: ★★★★	Cleanliness: ★★★
Insect Control: ★★★★	Facilities: ★★★

Perched on a hilltop in the northern Catskill Mountains—in the skies at an elevation of 2,175 feet—Country Roads Campground is a peaceful campground with an extensive menu of outdoor recreation in the vicinity, including horseback riding, fishing, and hiking. Most of the park features wooded sites, but there are a cluster of open, grassy sites at the southeastern side. Events such as corn roasts, pot luck suppers, bingo, and live entertainment are hosted in the pavilion. Minekill State Park and Minekill Falls are a recommended excursion for Country Roads campers. Located on the Hudson River about 50 miles southeast of Gilboar, Catskill is the scene of numerous family-oriented attractions. Choices include the Zoom Flume Waterpark, known as the largest of its kind in the Catskills, and Catskill Game Farm, where children can feed tame deer, antelope, llamas, and other exotic animals.

Basics

Operated By: Diane and Art Keil. **Open:** May 15–Columbus Day. **Site Assignment:** Reservations recommended, walk-ins accepted. **Registration:** At A-frame house. **Fee:** $20–$23 (VISA, MC, D). **Parking:** At site.

Facilities

Number of RV Sites: 80. **Number of Tent-Only Sites:** 20. **Hookups:** Electric (20, 30, 50 amps), water, phone, 40 full hookups. **Each Site:** Fire ring, picnic table. **Dump Station:** Yes. **Laundry:** Yes. **Pay Phone:** Yes. **Rest Rooms and Showers:** Yes. **Fuel:** No. **Propane:** Yes. **Internal Roads:** Gravel, in good condition. **RV Service:** No. **Market:** Within 11 mi. **Restaurant:** Within 3 mi. **General Store:** Yes. **Vending:** Yes. **Playground:** Yes. **Other:** None. **Activities:** Swimming, whirlpool, game room, rec hall, planned activities on weekends, sports field, badminton, horseshoes, volleyball. **Nearby Attractions:** Catskill Park, Catskill Game Farm, Hunter Mountain, Howe Caverns, Zoom Flune Waterpark, Mine Kill Falls, Carson City Wild West Town, Cooperstown and National Baseball Hall of Fame and Museum. **Additional Information:** Greene County Promotion Dept., (800) 355-CATS, www.greene-ny.com.

Restrictions

Pets: On leash only, keep quiet. **Fires:** At site, confined to fire ring. **Alcoholic Beverages:** At site. **Vehicle Maximum Length:** 40 ft. **Other:** None.

To Get There

From Hwy. 23, go 3 mi. north on Hwy. 30, 1.75 mi. east on Hwy. 990V, and follow signs for 3.25 mi. north. Entrance is on the left.

HERKIMER

KOA—Herkimer Diamond Campground

5661 SR 5, Herkimer 13350. T: (315) 891-7355 or (800) 562-0897; F: (315) 891-3099; www.herkimerdiamond.com; diamonds@ntcnet.com.

RV: ★★★★	Tent: ★★★★
Beauty: ★★★★	Site Privacy: ★★
Spaciousness: ★★	Quiet: ★★★★
Security: ★★★★	Cleanliness: ★★★★
Insect Control: ★★★★	Facilities: ★★★★

Located about 20 miles from the southwest tip of Adirondack Park in Herkimer, KOA—Herkimer Diamond Campground is well-maintained and offers a lot to do without leaving the area. There is a choice of level open or wooded sites, including 18 pull-throughs. The campground is located on West Canada Creek, where campers can fish and swim. There is also a disc golf area, a mini-golf course, and hiking trails among other activities. Diamond prospecting is the name of the game at the Herkimer Diamond Mines, which claims it is the only place in the world where you can prospect for diamonds like this. Hammers are provided, but power tools are not permitted, so you have to find your gem through old-fashioned elbow grease. You can also learn about diamonds and minerals at the geological museum or dine at the Crystal Chandelier Restaurant. This KOA can be used as a base for ventures to Adirondack Park, Cooperstown, and Utica.

Basics

Operated By: KOA. **Open:** Apr. 15–Nov. 1. **Site Assignment:** Reservations recommended (1-night deposit required), walk-ins accepted. **Registration:** At campground office. **Fee:** $22–$29 (VISA, MC, AE, D). **Parking:** At site.

Facilities

Number of RV Sites: 107. **Number of Tent-Only Sites:** 22. **Hookups:** Electric (20, 30, 50 amps), water, cable TV, phone, 22 full hookups. **Each Site:** Fire ring, picnic table. **Dump Station:** Yes. **Laundry:** Yes. **Pay Phone:** Yes. **Rest Rooms and Showers:** Yes. **Fuel:** No. **Propane:** Yes. **Internal Roads:** Gravel, in good condition. **RV Service:** No. **Market:** Within 7 mi. **Restaurant:** On premises. **General Store:** Yes. **Vending:** Yes. **Playground:** Yes. **Other:** Interactive museum, rock and gem gift shop. **Activities:** Diamond prospecting, game room, rec hall, sports field, trout fishing, movies, disc golf, mini-golf, horseshoes, hiking trails, volleyball, planned activities on weekends, river swimming. **Nearby Attractions:** Herkimer Diamond Mines, Herkimer Home State Historic Site, Adirondack Park, Utica, National Baseball Hall of Fame and Museum, Cooperstown, Remington Gun Museum. **Additional Information:** Herkimer County Chamber of Commerce, (315) 866-7820, www.herkimercounty-info.com.

Restrictions

Pets: On leash only. **Fires:** At site. **Alcoholic Beverages:** At site. **Vehicle Maximum Length:** None. **Other:** None.

To Get There

From Hwy. 5, go 7 mi. north on Hwy. 28. Entrance is on the right.

HINCKLEY

Trail's End Campground

P.O. Box 60, Hinckley 13352. T: (315) 826-7220; F: (315) 826-3626; www.trailend.com; info@trailend.

RV ★★★★ Tent ★★★★

Beauty: ★★★★ Site Privacy: ★★★
Spaciousness: ★★ Quiet: ★★★★
Security: ★★★★★ Cleanliness: ★★★★
Insect Control: ★★★★ Facilities: ★★★★

Located in the Adirondack foothills near Old Forge, Trail's End Campground is situated on seven-mile-long Hinckley Lake. This well-kept campground has a beach, a boat launch, and a fishing pond among other features. Sites alongside the pond and the lake are especially pleasant. Trail's End has just three pull-throughs. Hinckley Lake is the center of attention here; the campground's beach is for campers only Monday–Friday, but it is open to the public on Saturday and Sunday. Trail's End rents boats and ATVs. Raquette Lake and Blue Mountain Lake—both with a variety of hiking, fishing, and boating opportunities—are a short drive away from the campground. Water Safari, in nearby Old Forge, has several slides and pools. The Old Forge Hardware Store offers an entire city block of housewares, books, handmade furniture, and, of course, hardware.

Basics

Operated By: Private operator. **Open:** May 1–Oct. 15. **Site Assignment:** Reservations required. **Registration:** At campground office. **Fee:** $20–$30 (VISA, MC). **Parking:** At site.

Facilities

Number of RV Sites: 84. **Number of Tent-Only Sites:** 12. **Hookups:** Electric (15, 20, 30 amps), water, 25 full hookups. **Each Site:** Fire ring, picnic table. **Dump Station:** Yes. **Laundry:** Yes. **Pay Phone:** Yes. **Rest Rooms and Showers:** Yes. **Fuel:** No. **Propane:** Yes. **Internal Roads:** Dirt and sand, in good condition. **RV Service:** No. **Market:** Within 10 mi. **Restaurant:** Within 3 mi. **General Store:** Yes. **Vending:** Yes. **Playground:** Yes. **Other:** Hinckley Lake. **Activities:** Fishing, boating, boat rentals, hiking trails, planned activities on weekends, canoeing, lake swimming, shuffleboard, sports field, horseshoes, volleyball. **Nearby Attractions:** Adirondack Park, Utica Zoo, Adirondack Scenic Railroad, Blue Mountain Lake, Water Safari Water Park, Old Forge. **Additional Information:** New York Division of Tourism—Adirondacks, (800) 487-6867, www.iloveny.state.ny.us.

Restrictions

Pets: On leash only. **Fires:** At site, confined to fire pit. **Alcoholic Beverages:** At site. **Vehicle Maximum Length:** None. **Other:** No more than two pets per campsite.

To Get There

From Hwy. 12, go 4 mi. east on Hwy. 365 and 3 mi. southeast on CR 151. Follow signs. Entrance is at the end.

HOUGHTON

Camping at Mariposa Ponds

Box 4, Houghton 14744. T: (716) 567-4211; F: (716) 567-8211; www.mariposaponds.com; mariposa@houghton.edu.

RV ★★★★ Tent ★★★★

Beauty: ★★★★ Site Privacy: ★★★
Spaciousness: ★★★ Quiet: ★★★★
Security: ★★★★ Cleanliness: ★★★★
Insect Control: ★★★★ Facilities: ★★★★

Butterflies and songbirds share forests of hickory, maple, oak, and beech at Camping at Mariposa Ponds in Houghton, a town about midway between Letchworth State Park and Allegheny State Park in western New York. "Mariposa," the owners tell us, is Spanish for butterfly, and this campground is a haven for these colorful and beautiful creatures. Five butterfly gardens at Mariposa Ponds host plants like butterfly weed, butterfly bush, coreopsis, and purple coneflowers, attracting monarchs, white admirals, fritillaries, and hummingbirds. Hiking trails at the campground meander through lush stands of pines and hardwoods. Largemouth bass, perch, and sunfish are among the residents in the fishing pond. Sites here are open and wooded. Tenting is permitted; however, there are no tent-only sites. The lodge has an indoor swimming pool, a game room, and a landscaped patio. Nearby Moss Lake Nature Sanctuary, operated by the Nature Conservancy, is a bog where fish, turtles, birds and other wildlife live amid rare carnivorous plants.

Basics

Operated By: Dave and Trudi Schwert. **Open:** May 1–Oct. 15. **Site Assignment:** Reservations accepted (stay 6 nights, 7th night free), walk-ins accepted. **Registration:** At campground office. **Fee:** $20–$23 (VISA, MC, D). **Parking:** At site.

Facilities

Number of RV Sites: 75. **Number of Tent-Only Sites:** None. **Hookups:** Electric (30 amps), 66 full hookups. **Each Site:** Fire ring, picnic table. **Dump Station:** Yes. **Laundry:** No. **Pay Phone:** Yes. **Rest Rooms and Showers:** Yes. **Fuel:** No. **Propane:** Yes. **Internal Roads:** Gravel, in good condition. **RV Service:** No. **Market:** Within 4 mi. **Restaurant:** Within 3 mi. **General Store:** Yes. **Vending:** Yes. **Playground:** Yes. **Other:** Lodge, cabin rentals. **Activities:** Indoor swimming, game room, rec hall, pond fishing, basketball, planned activities on weekends, horseshoes, sports field, hiking trails, volleyball. **Nearby Attractions:** Letchworth State Park, Allegany State Park, Moss Lake Nature Sanctuary, Genesee River, Seneca-Iroquois National Museum. **Additional Information:** New York Division of Tourism—Chautauqua-Allegheny, (800) 242-4569, www.iloveny.state.ny.us.

Restrictions

Pets: On leash only. **Fires:** At site. **Alcoholic Beverages:** At site. **Vehicle Maximum Length:** 40 ft. **Other:** No pets in rental cabins.

To Get There

Hrom Hwy. 243, go 3 mi. north on Hwy. 19, 0.25 mi. west on Houghton College Rd., and 1.5 mi. west on Centerville Rd. Entrance is on the right.

ITHACA

Spruce Row Campsite and RV Resort

2271 Kraft Rd., Ithaca 14850. T: (607) 387-9225; F: (607) 387-9225; www.campgrounds.com/sprucerow; sprucerow@clarityconnect.com.

RV ★★★★ Tent ★★★★

Beauty: ★★★★ Site Privacy: ★
Spaciousness: ★★ Quiet: ★★★
Security: ★★★★ Cleanliness: ★★★★
Insect Control: ★★★★ Facilities: ★★★★

Perched on a hill above the southern end of Cayuga Lake just north of downtown Ithaca, Spruce Row Campsite and RV Resort has open and shaded sites, 30 of which handle pull-throughs. Sites along Willow Creek and in the walnut grove are particularly inviting. Though it looks unusual, the 70 × 130 swimming pool is roomy and refreshing. Nature walks, hayrides, live entertainment, and the popular fall pig roast are among the activities hosted at Spruce Row. Cayuga Lake, one of the Finger Lakes, has an abundance of hiking and water sports opportunities. Four state parks—Robert H. Treman, Allan H. Treman, Buttermilk Falls, and Taughannock Falls—are located in the Ithaca area. Several wineries are situated along the Cayuga Wine Trail, including Six Mile Creek Vineyard in Ithaca. The campuses of Cornell University and Ithaca College overlook Cayuga Lake and are open for tours.

BASICS

Operated By: Harry Weber. **Open:** May 1–Columbus Day. **Site Assignment:** Reservations recommended (1-night deposit required), walk-ins accepted. **Registration:** At campground office. **Fee:** $21–$26 (VISA, MC, D). **Parking:** At site.

FACILITIES

Number of RV Sites: 202. **Number of Tent-Only Sites:** 30. **Hookups:** Electric (20, 30 amps), phone, water, 42 full hookups. **Each Site:** Fire ring, picnic table. **Dump Station:** Yes. **Laundry:** No. **Pay Phone:** Yes. **Rest Rooms and Showers:** Yes. **Fuel:** No. **Propane:** Yes. **Internal Roads:** Gravel and paved, in good condition. **RV Service:** No. **Market:** Within 2 mi. **Restaurant:** Within 2 mi. **General Store:** Yes. **Vending:** Yes. **Playground:** Yes. **Other:** Cabin and RV rentals. **Activities:** Game room, sports field, boating, boat rentals, pond fishing, planned activities on weekends, mini-golf, bike rentals, basketball, badminton, horseshoes, shuffleboard, hiking trails, volleyball. **Nearby Attractions:** Watkins Glen, Cornell University, Ithaca College, Buttermilk Falls, Taughannock Falls, Cayuga Wine Trail, Sciencenter, Cayuga Lake. **Additional Information:** Ithaca/Tompkins County Convention and Visitors Bureau, (800) 284-8422, www.ithaca.ny.us/commerce.

RESTRICTIONS

Pets: On leash only. **Fires:** At site. **Alcoholic Beverages:** At site. **Vehicle Maximum Length:** None. **Other:** Keep dogs in designated dog walk areas.

TO GET THERE

From Hwy. 13, go 7 mi. northwest on Hwy. 96, 0.5 mi. north on Jacksonville Rd., and 1.25 mi. east on Kraft Rd. Entrance is on the right.

LAKE GEORGE
Adirondack Camping Village

Box 406, Lake George 12845. T: (518) 668-5226; F: (518) 668-4256; www.adirondackcampingvillage.com; info@adirondackcampingvillage.com.

RV ★★★★	Tent ★★★★
Beauty: ★★★★	Site Privacy: ★★★
Spaciousness: ★★	Quiet: ★★★★
Security: ★★★★★	Cleanliness: ★★★★
Insect Control: ★★★★	Facilities: ★★★★

Located in Adirondack Park at the northern edge of Lake George Village, the Adirondack Camping Village is situated on a forested mountain and has level, open, and wooded sites. Tent sites are located at the campground's northern end. RV sites along the woods where the Possum Run Nature Trail cuts through are private and serene. The campground is within five minutes of Lake George and the village. A heated swimming pool, a wading pool, a fishing pond, and scenic hiking trails are some of the campground's recreational offerings. The Lake George Trolley stops at the campground and takes passengers to Lake George Village. Boat tours on Lake George are popular. So is swimming at Million Dollar Beach. Water Slide World and the Great Escape and Splashwater Kingdom Fun Park offer thrills for families. The Fort William Henry Museum, a replica of the 1755 stockade, details the area's French and Indian War heritage.

BASICS

Operated By: Private operator. **Open:** May 15–Oct. 1. **Site Assignment:** Reservations and walk-ins accepted (10% discount to Canadians). **Registration:** At campground office. **Fee:** $24–$29 (VISA, MC). **Parking:** At site.

FACILITIES

Number of RV Sites: 125. **Number of Tent-Only Sites:** 25. **Hookups:** Electric (15, 20, 30 amps), water, 50 full hookups. **Each Site:** Fire ring, picnic table. **Dump Station:** Yes. **Laundry:** Yes. **Pay Phone:** Yes. **Rest Rooms and Showers:** Yes. **Fuel:** No. **Propane:** No. **Internal Roads:** Gravel and paved, in good condition. **RV Service:** No. **Market:** Within 2 mi. **Restaurant:** Within 2 mi. **General Store:** Yes. **Vending:** Yes. **Playground:** Yes. **Other:** None. **Activities:** Game room, rec hall, swimming, wading pool, basketball, pond fishing, hiking trails, movies, planned activities, sports field, horseshoes, volleyball, shuffleboard. **Nearby Attractions:** Lake George, Fort William Henry Museum, The Great Escape and Splashwater Kingdom Fun Park, Lake George boat tours, Water Slide World, Prospect Mountain, Lake George Battlefield Picnic Area, Lake George Dinner Theater, Lake George Action Park. **Additional Information:** Lake George Chamber of Commerce, (800) 705-0059, www.lakegeorgevillage.com.

RESTRICTIONS

Pets: On leash only. **Fires:** At site. **Alcoholic Beverages:** At site. **Vehicle Maximum Length:** 35 ft. **Other:** None.

TO GET THERE

From I-87, take Exit 22 and go 1.5 mi. on US 9. Entrance is on the right.

LAKE GEORGE
KOA—Lake George/Saratoga

P.O. Box 533, Lake George 12845. T: (800) KOA-2618 or (518) 696-2615; www.koa.com.

RV ★★★	Tent ★★★
Beauty: ★★★★	Site Privacy: ★★
Spaciousness: ★★★	Quiet: ★★★★
Security: ★★★★	Cleanliness: ★★★★
Insect Control: ★★★★	Facilities: ★★★

Located near Lake Luzerne and Lake George, KOA—Lake George/Saratoga is aptly named since it is also convenient to Saratoga Springs and Saratoga National Historical Park. Situated amid pines that top 100 feet, the campground has seven pull-throughs among its 85 sites. Typically, guests here use the campground as a base for visiting attractions in Lake George and Saratoga Springs areas. Outdoor recreation is plentiful at Lake George and Lake Luzerne. Saratoga Spa State Park, with its mineral baths and performing arts center, is a much visited site in Saratoga Springs. The area is also rich in Revolutionary War historical attractions such as Saratoga National Historical Park and Fort Ticonderoga. Located between Lake George and Lake Champlaign, Fort Ticonderoga was the site of the Continental Army's first victory in 1775. Today, the recreated fort houses a museum that displayes weapons, artwork, and artifacts representing the daily life of soldiers once stationed there.

BASICS

Operated By: KOA. **Open:** May 1–Sept. 15. **Site Assignment:** Reservations and walk-ins accepted. **Registration:** At campground office. **Fee:** $26–$36 (VISA, MC, D). **Parking:** At designated area.

FACILITIES

Number of RV Sites: 75. **Number of Tent-Only Sites:** 10. **Hookups:** Electric (15, 20, 30 amps), water, 45 full hookups. **Each Site:** Fire ring, picnic table. **Dump Station:** Yes. **Laundry:** Yes. **Pay Phone:** Yes. **Rest Rooms and Showers:** Yes. **Fuel:** No. **Propane:** No. **Internal Roads:** Gravel, in good condition. **RV Service:** No. **Market:** Within 6 mi. **Restaurant:** Within 4 mi. **General Store:** Yes. **Vending:** Yes. **Playground:** Yes. **Other:** Fishing stream. **Activities:** Fishing, game room, rec hall, basketball, movies, sports field, badminton, horseshoes, volleyball. **Nearby Attractions:** Lake George, Fort William Henry Museum, The Great Escape and Splashwater Kingdom Fun Park, Lake George boat tours, Water Slide World, Prospect Mountain, Lake George Battlefield Picnic Area, Lake George Dinner Theater, Lake George Action Park. **Additional Information:** Lake George Chamber of Commerce, (800) 705-0059, www.lakegeorgevillage.com.

RESTRICTIONS

Pets: On leash only. **Fires:** At site. **Alcoholic Beverages:** At site. **Vehicle Maximum Length:** None.

TO GET THERE

From I-87, take Exit 21 and go 8.5 mi. southwest on Hwy. 9N. Entrance is on the left.

LAKE GEORGE
Lake George Campsite

1053 Rt. 9, Queensbury 12804. T: (800) 542-2292 or (518) 798-6218; www.lgcamp.com; info@lgcamp.com.

RV ★★★★	Tent ★★★★
Beauty: ★★★★	Site Privacy: ★★★★
Spaciousness: ★★★	Quiet: ★★★★
Security: ★★★★	Cleanliness: ★★★★
Insect Control: ★★★★	Facilities: ★★★★

Located near Lake George Village, Lake George Campsite is the closest campground to the Great Escape and Splashwater Kingdom Fun Park. Billed as New York's largest theme park, the Great Escape has more than 120 rides, live shows, and a storybook-themed children's area. The water park includes a massive wave pool, water slides, and Adventure River. Lake George Campsite does not have the same abundance of activities that some of the other area campgrounds possess, but its proximity to family-oriented attractions and the village itself makes it an ideal base for a Lake George vacation. The campground does have a swimming pool, a well-stocked store, clean restrooms and showers, and basketball and volleyball courts. It also sells discount tickets to many Lake George attractions, and a bus transports campers to Lake George beaches, boat tours, and other sites.

Basics

Operated By: Private operator. **Open:** All year. **Site Assignment:** Reservations accepted (1-night deposit required), walk-ins accepted. **Registration:** At campground office. **Fee:** $24–$32 (VISA, MC, D). **Parking:** At site.

Facilities

Number of RV Sites: 206. **Number of Tent-Only Sites:** 40. **Hookups:** Electric (20, 30 amps), water, cable TV, phone, 58 full hookups. **Each Site:** Fire ring, picnic table. **Dump Station:** Yes. **Laundry:** Yes. **Pay Phone:** Yes. **Rest Rooms and Showers:** Yes. **Fuel:** No. **Propane:** Yes. **Internal Roads:** Gravel and paved, in good condition. **RV Service:** Yes. **Market:** Within 2 mi. **Restaurant:** Within 2 mi. **General Store:** Yes. **Vending:** Yes. **Playground:** Yes. **Other:** None. **Activities:** Game room, basketball, horseshoes, volleyball, basketball, rec hall, badminton. **Nearby Attractions:** Lake George, Fort William Henry Museum, The Great Escape and Splashwater Kingdom Fun Park, Lake George boat tours, Water Slide World, Prospect Mountain, Lake George Battlefield Picnic Area, Lake George Dinner Theater, Lake George Action Park. **Additional Information:** Lake George Chamber of Commerce, (800) 705-0059, www.lakegeorgevillage.com.

Restrictions

Pets: On leash only. **Fires:** At site. **Alcoholic Beverages:** At site. **Vehicle Maximum Length:** None. **Other:** None.

To Get There

From I-87S, take Exit 20 and go 1 mi. south on US 9. Entrance is on the right.

LAKE GEORGE

Lake George Escape Resort

P.O. Box 431, Lake George 12845. T: (800) 327-3188 or (518) 623-3207; www.lakegeorgeescape.com; info@lakegeorgeescape.com.

RV: ★★★★★ | Tent: ★★★★★

Beauty: ★★★★ | Site Privacy: ★★★
Spaciousness: ★★★ | Quiet: ★★★
Security: ★★★★★ | Cleanliness: ★★★★★
Insect Control: ★★★★★ | Facilities: ★★★★★

In the Adirondacks—and throughout New York—few campgrounds can match the beauty and amenities of the Lake George Escape Camping Resort. Located six miles from Lake George Village, Lake George Escape features a large fishing pond and several sites along the Schroon River. Covering 148 acres of woods and meadows and a mile of riverbank, Lake George Escape is a haven for RVers and tenters alike. The 324 RV sites include 50 pull-throughs. The campground has 193 tent sites situated along the pond, the river, and in the towering pine woods. You can fish, swim, inner tube in the Schroon River, which flows to the Hudson River. Canoes and rowboats are available for rent. You do not have to leave the campground to satisfy your hunger, since the new Alfresco serves breakfast, lunch, and dinner. A free shuttle transports campers to attractions in Lake George Village.

Basics

Operated By: Private operator. **Open:** May 15–Columbus Day. **Site Assignment:** Reservations recommended (1-night deposit for 3 nights or less, $85 for 4 nights or more), walk-ins accepted. **Registration:** At campground office. **Fee:** $19–$46 (VISA, MC, AE, D). **Parking:** At site.

Facilities

Number of RV Sites: 324. **Number of Tent-Only Sites:** 193. **Hookups:** Electric (20, 30, 50 amps), water, cable TV, phone, 214 full hookups. **Each Site:** Fire ring, picnic table. **Dump Station:** Yes. **Laundry:** Yes. **Pay Phone:** Yes. **Rest Rooms and Showers:** Yes. **Fuel:** No. **Propane:** Yes. **Internal Roads:** Paved, in good condition. **RV Service:** No. **Market:** Within 2 mi. **Restaurant:** On premises. **General Store:** Yes. **Vending:** Yes. **Playground:** Yes. **Other:** Schroon River. **Activities:** River swimming, canoeing, boating, boat rentals, river and pond fishing, mini-golf, shuffleboard, golf, planned activities, movies, tennis, badminton, sports field, horseshoes, hiking trails, volleyball, game room, rec hall. **Nearby Attractions:** Lake George, Fort William Henry Museum, The Great Escape and Splashwater Kingdom Fun Park, Lake George boat tours, Water Slide World, Prospect Mountain, Lake George Battlefield Picnic Area, Lake George Dinner Theater, Lake George Action Park. **Additional Information:** Lake George Chamber of Commerce, (800) 705-0059, www.lakegeorgevillage.com.

Restrictions

Pets: On leash only, under control. **Fires:** At site. **Alcoholic Beverages:** At site. **Vehicle Maximum Length:** None. **Other:** Pets cannot be left unattended at campsite.

To Get There

From I-87, take Exit 23 and go 0.25 mi. east on Diamond Point Rd. and 0.75 mi. north on E. Schroon River Rd. Entrance is on the left.

LAKE GEORGE

Lake George RV Park

74 SR 149 Dept. W, Lake George 12845-3501. T: (518) 792-3775; F: (518) 792-5923; www.lakegeorgervpark.com; info@lakegeorgervpark.com.

RV: ★★★★★ | Tent: n/a

Beauty: ★★★★★ | Site Privacy: ★★★
Spaciousness: ★★★ | Quiet: ★★★★
Security: ★★★★★ | Cleanliness: ★★★★★
Insect Control: ★★★★★ | Facilities: ★★★★★

Like Lake George Escape Camping Resort, the Lake George RV Park is an immaculate campground with beautiful surroundings and a multitude of amenities. Lake George RV Park; however, does not have tent-only sites, though campers can pitch a tent next to their RV. Sites are level and wooded, and there are 250 pull-throughs. The cluster of sites on the western end of campground is close to the pedal boat and fishing pond, as well as the indoor pool, snack bar, game room, and adult lounge. Sites on the eastern side are near the creek and the athletic area, which includes a softball field, volleyball and basketball courts, and a bocce ball area. There are three miles of paved bike trails; bicyclists can also ride trails to Lake George and Glens Falls. A trolley takes passengers from Lake George RV Park to the assortment of Lake George attractions. The campground offers discount tickets to many attractions.

Basics

Operated By: David King. **Open:** May 4–Oct. 8. **Site Assignment:** Reservations recommended (required for holiday weekends), walk-ins accepted. **Registration:** At lodge. **Fee:** $33–$45 (VISA, MC, AE, D). **Parking:** At site.

Facilities

Number of RV Sites: 350. **Number of Tent-Only Sites:** None. **Hookups:** Electric (20, 30, 50 amps), cable TV, phone, all sites have full hookups. **Each Site:** Fire ring, picnic table. **Dump Station:** Yes. **Laundry:** Yes. **Pay Phone:** Yes. **Rest Rooms and Showers:** Yes. **Fuel:** No. **Propane:** Yes. **Internal Roads:** Paved, in good condition. **RV Service:** No. **Market:** Within 4.5 mi. **Restaurant:** Within 0.5 mi. **General Store:** Yes. **Vending:** Yes. **Playground:** Yes. **Other:** RV rentals. **Activities:** Two swimming pools (one indoor), game room, rec hall, wading pool, pedal boat rentals, pond and stream fishing, basketball, planned activities, movies, badminton, tennis, sports field, horseshoes, hiking trails, volleyball. **Nearby Attractions:** Lake George, Fort William Henry Museum, The Great Escape and Splashwater Kingdom Fun Park, Lake George boat tours, Water Slide World, Prospect Mountain, Lake George Battlefield Picnic Area, Lake George Dinner Theater, Lake George Action Park. **Additional Information:** Lake George Chamber of Commerce, (800) 705-0059, www.lakegeorgevillage.com.

Restrictions

Pets: On leash only. **Fires:** At site, confined to fire ring. **Alcoholic Beverages:** At site. **Vehicle Maximum Length:** None. **Other:** Pets may not be left unattended.

To Get There

From I-87, take Exit 20 Northway and go 0.75 mi. north on Hwy. 149/US 9 and 0.5 mi. east on Hwy. 149. Entrance is on the right.

LAKE GEORGE
Ledgeview Village RV Park

321 SR 149, Lake George 12845. T: (518) 798-6621 or (888) 353-5936; F: (518) 798-2315; www.ledgeview.com; info@ledgeview.com.

RV ★★★★ Tent n/a

Beauty: ★★★★ Site Privacy: ★★
Spaciousness: ★★★ Quiet: ★★★★
Security: ★★★★★ Cleanliness: ★★★★
Insect Control: ★★★★ Facilities: ★★★★

Though Ledgeview Village RV Park does not have the amenities of nearby Lake George RV Park, Ledgeview is still a good base for exploring Lake George and area attractions. These campsites are spacious, level, and wooded, and there are 17 pull-throughs. No tents are permitted. The store is well-stocked; and the laundromat, restrooms, and showers are clean. The swimming pool, playground, store, and recreational areas are located near the entrance of the park, and sites are situated along the streets behind them. Fort William Henry Museum, Million Dollar Beach, and the water parks are some of Lake George's better-known attractions—along with the lake itself. For breathtaking scenery, take a drive along the Veternas Memorial Highway (a toll road) to the top of 2,021-foot-high Prospect Mountain. There are hiking trails and picnic sites at the summit, where you can see Lake George, Vermont's Green Mountains, and New Hampshire's White Mountains.

BASICS

Operated By: Hughes family. **Open:** May 1–Columbus Day. **Site Assignment:** Reservations accepted (2-night deposit required), walk-ins accepted. **Registration:** At campground office. **Fee:** $27–$30 (VISA, MC). **Parking:** At site.

FACILITIES

Number of RV Sites: 133. **Number of Tent-Only Sites:** None. **Hookups:** Electric (30, 50 amps), water, cable TV, phone, 132 full hookups. **Each Site:** Fire ring, picnic table. **Dump Station:** Yes. **Laundry:** Yes. **Pay Phone:** Yes. **Rest Rooms and Showers:** Yes. **Fuel:** No. **Propane:** No. **Internal Roads:** Paved, in good condition. **RV Service:** No. **Market:** Within 3 mi. **Restaurant:** Within 2 mi. **General Store:** Yes. **Vending:** Yes. **Playground:** Yes. **Other:** Pavilion. **Activities:** Game room, rec hall, basketball, bike rentals, badminton, shuffleboard, volleyball. **Nearby Attractions:** Lake George, Fort William Henry Museum, The Great Escape and Splashwater Kingdom Fun Park, Lake George boat tours, Water Slide World, Prospect Mountain, Lake George Battlefield Picnic Area, Lake George Dinner Theater, Lake George Action Park. **Additional Information:** Lake George Chamber of Commerce, (800) 705-0059, www.lakegeorgevillage.com.

RESTRICTIONS

Pets: No pets permitted. **Fires:** At site. **Alcoholic Beverages:** At site. **Vehicle Maximum Length:** None.

TO GET THERE

From I-87, take Exit 20 Northway and go 0.75 mi. north on Hwy. 149/US 9 and 1.5 mi. east on Hwy. 149. Entrance is on the left.

LAKE GEORGE
Mohawk Camping on Lake George

3144 Lake Shore Dr., Lake George 12845. T: (518) 668-2760; www.mohawkcampground.com; info@mohawkcampground.com.

RV ★★★ Tent ★★★

Beauty: ★★★★ Site Privacy: ★
Spaciousness: ★ Quiet: ★★★
Security: ★★★★ Cleanliness: ★★★★
Insect Control: ★★★★ Facilities: ★★★

Nestled in the densely forested Adirondack Preserve, Mohawk Camping on Lake George is the only private campground directly located on the lake. Sites are wooded, and Mohawk has a private beach on the lake where campers can swim and fish. The drawback here is that the sites lack privacy and spaciousness. Though the campground does not have a boat launch or dock, campers can bring canoes, rafts, or small beachable boats. Rowboats are also available for rent. Mohawk has a rec hall and a game room, but most of its recreation is centered on the beach. The 32-mile-long Lake George has 365 islands. Its water is crystal clear, and its shoreline is lush and forested. A boat cruise is an ideal way to experience the natural splendor of this lake. Several tour boats depart from Beach Rd., which is on the southern shore opposite Fort William Henry. Choices range from one-hour sightseeing tours to dinner cruises.

BASICS

Operated By: Private operator. **Open:** May 25–Sept. 4. **Site Assignment:** Reservations accepted (10% discount for 7 nights or more), walk-ins accepted. **Registration:** At campground office. **Fee:** $21–$34 (VISA, MC, AE, D). **Parking:** At site.

FACILITIES

Number of RV Sites: 75. **Number of Tent-Only Sites:** 2. **Hookups:** Electric (20 amps), water, phone, 17 full hookups. **Each Site:** Picnic table, grill. **Dump Station:** No. **Laundry:** Yes. **Pay Phone:** Yes. **Rest Rooms and Showers:** Yes. **Fuel:** No. **Propane:** No. **Internal Roads:** Gravel and paved, in fair condition. **RV Service:** No. **Market:** Within 3 mi. **Restaurant:** Within 2 mi. **General Store:** Yes. **Vending:** No. **Playground:** Yes. **Other:** Lake George. **Activities:** Lake swimming, game room, rec hall, canoeing, rowboat rentals, lake fishing. **Nearby Attractions:** Lake George, Fort William Henry Museum, The Great Escape and Splashwater Kingdom Fun Park, Lake George boat tours, Water Slide World, Prospect Mountain, Lake George Battlefield Picnic Area, Lake George Dinner Theater, Lake George Action Park. **Additional Information:** Lake George Chamber of Commerce, (800) 705-0059, www.lakegeorgevillage.com.

RESTRICTIONS

Pets: No pets allowed. **Fires:** At site. **Alcoholic Beverages:** At site. **Vehicle Maximum Length:** 30 ft. **Other:** None.

TO GET THERE

From I-87, take Exit 22 Northway and go 1 mi. north on Hwy. 9N. Entrance is on the right.

LEROY
Frost Ridge Recreation Area Campground

8101 Conlon Rd., LeRoy 14482. T: (716) 768-4883 or (716) 594-2304; F: (716) 594-2304; frostridge58@aol.com.

RV ★★★ Tent ★★★

Beauty: ★★★★ Site Privacy: ★★★
Spaciousness: ★★ Quiet: ★★★
Security: ★★★ Cleanliness: ★★★★
Insect Control: ★★★★ Facilities: ★★★★

Located about 16 miles southwest of Rochester, Frost Ridge Recreation Area Campground is known for its proximity to challenging ski slopes and for its tasty sourdough pancakes (served with maple syrup to campers on Sunday mornings). The campground is dotted with apple trees, and there are 10 pull-through sites. Frost Ridge has hiking trails on its grounds, but the most inviting outdoor recreation is in the surrounding area. Options include Letchworth State Park, the home of Genesee River Gorge or the "Grand Canyon of the East"; the outdoor recreation of Hamlin Beach State Park; and Genesee County Village and Museum. In Rochester, you can visit the Susan B. Anthony House and the George Eastman House (the founder of Kodak). Frost Ridge is also an hour's drive from Niagara Falls.

BASICS

Operated By: Private operator. **Open:** All year. **Site Assignment:** Reservations and walk-ins accepted. **Registration:** At campground office. **Fee:** $20. **Parking:** At site.

FACILITIES

Number of RV Sites: 116. **Number of Tent-Only Sites:** 15. **Hookups:** Electric (15, 20, 30, 50 amps), phone, water, 21 full hookups. **Each Site:** Fire ring, picnic table. **Dump Station:** Yes. **Laundry:** No. **Pay Phone:** Yes. **Rest Rooms and Showers:** Yes. **Fuel:** No. **Propane:** Yes. **Internal Roads:** Gravel, in good condition. **RV Service:** No. **Market:** Within 4 mi. **Restaurant:** Within 5 mi. **General Store:** Yes. **Vending:** Yes. **Playground:** Yes. **Other:** Large recreation building. **Activities:** Game room, rec hall, basketball, sports field, hiking trails, horseshoes. **Nearby Attractions:** Jell-O Museum, Rochester, Lake Ontario, Letchworth State Park, Hamlin Beach State Park, Rochester Museum and Science Center, Genesee Country Village and Museum, Susan B. Anthony House, University of Rochester, George Eastman House, International Museum of Photography and Film. **Additional Information:** Greater Rochester Visitors Assoc., (800) 677-7282, www.visitrochester.com.

RESTRICTIONS

Pets: On leash only. **Fires:** At site. **Alcoholic Beverages:** At site. **Vehicle Maximum Length:** 60 ft.

TO GET THERE

From I-90, take Exit 47 and go 0.5 mi. south on

Hwy. 19, 1 mi. east on North Rd., and 0.25 mi. south on Conlon Rd. Entrance is on the left.

LEROY

Timberline Lake Park

8150 Vallance Rd., LeRoy 14482. T: (716) 768-6635; timcamp@localnet.com.

RV ★★★ Tent ★★★

Beauty: ★★★★ Site Privacy: ★★
Spaciousness: ★★ Quiet: ★★★
Security: ★★★★ Cleanliness: ★★★★
Insect Control: ★★★ Facilities: ★★★★

Timberline Lake Park's proximity to Rochester (16 miles southwest) places it near culture- and history-rich museums such as the Rochester Museum and Science Center, the Susan B. Anthony House, and the (Kodak founder) George Eastman House. However, you do not have to leave LeRoy to experience a slice of Americana—the town is home to the Jell-O Museum. Here, you can learn about the history of Jell-O, purchase Jell-O items in the gift shop, and learn new Jell-O recipes. A clean campground with open and shady sites, including 10 pull-throughs, Timberline Lake Park is an ideal stopover for travelers heading for the Finger Lakes, Niagara Falls, or Rochester. Campers can fish in Timberline Lake, swim in the pool, or shoot hoops at the basketball court. Hamlin Beach State Park and Letchworth State Park are nearby recreation options. With the recreational opportunities available on what is actually a pond, Timberline Lake may be more appealing to families than Frost Ridge, unless it is winter and campers want to go skiing.

BASICS

Operated By: Skip and Lil Norris. **Open:** Apr. 1–Dec. 15. **Site Assignment:** Reservations and walk-ins accepted. **Registration:** At campground headquarters. **Fee:** $20–$23 (VISA, MC). **Parking:** At site.

FACILITIES

Number of RV Sites: 175. **Number of Tent-Only Sites:** 25. **Hookups:** Electric (20, 30, 50 amps), water, phone, 80 full hookups. **Each Site:** Fire ring, picnic table. **Dump Station:** Yes. **Laundry:** Yes. **Pay Phone:** Yes. **Rest Rooms and Showers:** Yes. **Fuel:** No. **Propane:** Yes. **Internal Roads:** Gravel, in good condition. **RV Service:** No. **Market:** Within 5 mi. **Restaurant:** Within 3 mi. **General Store:** Yes. **Vending:** Yes. **Playground:** Yes. **Other:** Timberline Lake. **Activities:** Game room, rec hall, swimming, lake fishing, basketball, horseshoes, sports field. **Nearby Attractions:** Jell-O Museum, Rochester, Lake Ontario, Letchworth State Park, Hamlin Beach State Park, Rochester Museum and Science Center, Genesee Country Village and Museum, Susan B. Anthony House, University of Rochester, George Eastman House, International Museum of Photography and Film. **Additional Information:** Greater Rochester Visitors Assoc., (800) 677-7282, www.visitrochester.com.

RESTRICTIONS

Pets: On leash only. **Fires:** At site only. **Alcoholic Beverages:** At site only. **Vehicle Maximum Length:** None.

TO GET THERE

From I-90, take Exit 47 and go 0.1 mi. north on I-490, 0.1 mi. southwest on Hwy. 19, and 1 mi. east on Vallance Rd. Entrance is on the right.

LEWISTON

KOA—Niagara Falls North

1250 Pletcher Rd., Youngstown 14174. T: (716) 754-8013 or (800) 562-8715; F: (716) 754-8013; www.koa.com; nfnorthkoa@aol.com.

RV ★★★★ Tent ★★★★

Beauty: ★★★★ Site Privacy: ★
Spaciousness: ★★ Quiet: ★★
Security: ★★★ Cleanliness: ★★★★
Insect Control: ★★★ Facilities: ★★★★

Wooded and peaceful with open and shaded sites, KOA—Niagara Falls North serves as an uncrowded home base for campers who want to explore Niagara Falls. There are 18 pull-through sites, and guided tours of Niagara Falls embark from the campground. Niagara Reservation State Park offers views of the falls from several points. The 282-foot-high Prospect Point Observation Tower is adjacent to American Falls, and the elevator transports guests to the famous Maid of the Mist boat tour. Other great views can be found at Whirlpool State Park and Goat Island. Nearby attractions include Fantasy Island, an 80-acre theme park, and the Aquarium at Niagara Falls, where more than 2,000 marine creatures reside. For a fun day trip, take a 1.5-hour drive to Toronto, where points of interest include Ontario Place, the Canadian National Exhibition, Ontario Science Center, Toronto Zoo, and Casaloma Castle.

BASICS

Operated By: KOA. **Open:** Apr. 1–Oct. 15. **Site Assignment:** Reservations and walk-ins accepted. **Registration:** At campground office. **Fee:** $29–$35 (VISA, MC, D). **Parking:** At site.

FACILITIES

Number of RV Sites: 84. **Number of Tent-Only Sites:** 25. **Hookups:** Electric (20, 30, 50 amp), phone, water, 18 full hookups. **Each Site:** Fire ring, picnic table. **Dump Station:** Yes. **Laundry:** Yes. **Pay Phone:** Yes. **Rest Rooms and Showers:** Yes. **Fuel:** No. **Propane:** Yes. **Internal Roads:** Gravel, in good condition. **RV Service:** No. **Market:** Within 3 mi. **Restaurant:** Within 3 mi. **General Store:** Yes. **Vending:** Yes. **Playground:** Yes. **Other:** Cabin rentals. **Activities:** Game room, rec hall, swimming, basketball, bike rentals, horseshoes, volleyball. **Nearby Attractions:** Niagara Falls Convention and Visitors Bureau, (800) 421-5223, www.nfcvb.com. **Additional Information:** Niagara Falls, Aquarium of Niagara Falls, Artpark, Devil's Hole State Park, Fantasy Island, Fort Niagara State Park, Niagara Reservation State Park, Prospect Point Observation Tower, Maid of the Mist tours, Whirlpool State Park, Wintergarden, Fatima Shrine.

RESTRICTIONS

Pets: On leash only. **Fires:** At site. **Alcoholic Beverages:** At site. **Vehicle Maximum Length:** None.

TO GET THERE

From I-90, take Exit 25B and go 3 mi. north on Robert Moses Pkwy. and 1.75 mi. east on Pletcher Rd. Entrance is on the left.

LONG ISLAND

Eastern Long Island Kampground

P.O. Box 89, Greenport 11944. T: (631) 477-0022; www.greenport.com/kampground; mydon1@aol.com.

RV ★★★ Tent ★★★

Beauty: ★★★ Site Privacy: ★★
Spaciousness: ★★ Quiet: ★★★★
Security: ★★★★ Cleanliness: ★★★★
Insect Control: ★★★★ Facilities: ★★★

Dotted with charming villages, vineyards, and white-sand beaches, Long Island's North Fork is a tranquil place where outdoor enthusiasts and wine connoisseurs are in heaven. Located in Greenport, on Little Peconic Bay, Eastern Long Island Kampground has level, open, and wooded sites for RVers and tenters. Bay beaches are nearby, and bike rentals are available at the campground, which offers a full roster of planned activities for adults and children both. Long Island has 14 full-scale wineries, many of which are located in the North Fork. Nearby Shelter Island is home to the Mashomack Nature Preserve and its hiking trails. The historic seaport village of Greenport has lots of restaurants and shops. At nearby Orient Point, you can take a ferry to New London (CT) and test your luck at Foxwoods Casino. Mohegan Sun Casino is not far from Foxwoods.

BASICS

Operated By: Myron and Donna. **Open:** Apr. 15–Columbus Day. **Site Assignment:** Reservations recommended (full payment required), walk-ins accepted. **Registration:** At campground office. **Fee:** $27–$33 (VISA, MC, AE, D). **Parking:** At site.

FACILITIES

Number of RV Sites: 98. **Number of Tent-Only Sites:** 50. **Hookups:** Electric (20, 30, 50 amps), water, phone, 43 full hookups. **Each Site:** Fire ring, picnic table. **Dump Station:** Yes. **Laundry:** Yes. **Pay Phone:** Yes. **Rest Rooms and Showers:** Yes. **Fuel:** No. **Propane:** No. **Internal Roads:** Paved, in good condition. **RV Service:** No. **Market:** Within 5 mi. **Restaurant:** Within 3 mi. **General Store:** Yes. **Vending:** Yes. **Playground:** Yes. **Other:** RV rentals. **Activities:** Game room, sports field, rec hall, planned activities on weekends, volleyball, horseshoes, fishing, boating, badminton. **Nearby Attractions:** Mashomack Nature Preserve, Long Island Sound, Shelter Island, Orient Point State Park, wineries, Splish Splash Water Park. **Additional Information:** New York Division of Tourism - Long Island, (800) FUNONLI, www.iloveny.state.ny.us.

RESTRICTIONS

Pets: On leash only. **Fires:** At site. **Alcoholic Beverages:** At site. **Vehicle Maximum Length:** 40 ft.

To Get There

From Hwy. 25, go 1 mi. west on CR 48/Old 27, which is North Rd. Entrance is on the right.

MASSENA

Massena International Kampground

84 Country Rte. 42 Exit, Massena 13662. T: (315) 769-9483; www.woodalls.com/a/00396_massena.htm; miklara@northweb.com.

RV ★★★ Tent ★★★★

Beauty: ★★★★ Site Privacy: ★★
Spaciousness: ★★★ Quiet: ★★★
Security: ★★★★★ Cleanliness: ★★★★★
Insect Control: ★★★★ Facilities: ★★★

Located along Grasse River, a short drive or canoe float from where the Grasse meets the St. Lawrence River, Massena International Kampground is a place where campers can explore the St. Lawrence Seaway, display their dancing skills, and test their luck at a nearby casino and bingo center. With its proximity to the Grasse and St. Lawrence Rivers and Lake St. Lawrence, this campground attracts boaters, anglers, and hikers. Sites here are open and shaded, and they offer views of the Grasse. Though there are no pull-through sites, each of Massena's RV sites accommodate double slideouts. Some Massena campers take day trips to Montreal and Ottawa, Canada's capital city.

Basics

Operated By: Private operator. **Open:** May 1–Oct. 15. **Site Assignment:** Reservations and walk-ins accepted. **Registration:** At campground office. **Fee:** $21–$26 (VISA, MC, AE, D). **Parking:** At site.

Facilities

Number of RV Sites: 115. **Number of Tent-Only Sites:** 16. **Hookups:** Electric (15, 30 amps), water, cable TV, phone, 68 full hookups. **Each Site:** Picnic table, grill. **Dump Station:** Yes. **Laundry:** Yes. **Pay Phone:** Yes. **Rest Rooms and Showers:** Yes. **Fuel:** No. **Propane:** Yes. **Internal Roads:** Gravel, in good condition. **RV Service:** No. **Market:** Within 6 mi. **Restaurant:** Within 6 mi. **General Store:** Yes. **Vending:** Yes. **Playground:** Yes. **Other:** Grasse River. **Activities:** Swimming, wading pool, game room, rec hall, canoeing, river fishing, planned activities on weekends, volleyball, badminton, horseshoes, sports field. **Nearby Attractions:** Robert Moses State Park, Eisenhower Lock, FDR Power Dam & Visitor's Center, St. Regis Mohawk Indian Reservation, Thousand Islands Boat Tours, Ottawa, Frederic Remington Museum, Akwesasne Mohawk Casino. **Additional Information:** New York Division of Tourism—Thousand Islands, (800) 847-5263, www.iloveny.state.ny.us.

Restrictions

Pets: On leash only. **Fires:** At site. **Alcoholic Beverages:** At site. **Vehicle Maximum Length:** None. **Other:** None.

To Get There

From Hwy. 56, go 6 mi. east on Hwy. 37. Follow signs for 0.5 mi. northeast. Entrance is at the end.

MECHANICVILLE

Deer Run Campground

P.O. Box 120 Rte. 67, Schaghticoke 12154. T: (518) 664-3265; dcampground@aol.com.

RV ★★★★★ Tent n/a

Beauty: ★★★★ Site Privacy: ★★
Spaciousness: ★★★ Quiet: ★★★★
Security: ★★★★★ Cleanliness: ★★★★★
Insect Control: ★★★★ Facilities: ★★★★★

Perched on a green plateau overlooking the Hoosic River, Deer Run Campground is certainly a treasure for families and nature seekers. The grounds are colorful, and the facilities are well-maintained and clean. There are three swimming pools and a kiddie pool, plus two enclosed pavilions with fireplaces. Volleyball, basketball, and bocce ball courts can also be found on the grounds. Situated in the woods, Deer Run is solely an RV park; no tents are permitted. Located about 30 miles from the southeast tip of Adirondack Park and about the same distance west of the Vermont and Massachusetts borders, Deer Run is convenient to attractions in Saratoga Springs and Albany. If Deer Run's fresh air and three swimming pools do not refresh you, certainly the mineral baths of Saratoga Spa State Park will.

Basics

Operated By: Doug and Jacklyn Dyer. **Open:** May 1–Oct. 15. **Site Assignment:** Reservations and walk-ins accepted. **Registration:** At campground office. **Fee:** $32 (VISA, MC). **Parking:** At site.

Facilities

Number of RV Sites: 369. **Number of Tent-Only Sites:** None. **Hookups:** Electric (30 amps), cable TV, phone, all sites have full hookups. **Each Site:** Fire ring, picnic table. **Dump Station:** Yes. **Laundry:** Yes. **Pay Phone:** Yes. **Rest Rooms and Showers:** Yes. **Fuel:** No. **Propane:** Yes. **Internal Roads:** Gravel and paved, in good condition. **RV Service:** No. **Market:** Within 3 mi. **Restaurant:** Within 1 mi. **General Store:** Yes. **Vending:** Yes. **Playground:** Yes. **Other:** Fishing pond and animal sanctuary. **Activities:** Fishing, game room, three swimming pools, wading pool, movies, planned activities on weekends, mini-golf, basketball, sports field, badminton, hiking trails, volleyball, horseshoes. **Nearby Attractions:** Saratoga Springs, Albany, Adirondack Park, Saratoga Spa State Park, Saratoga National Historical Park. **Additional Information:** Saratoga County Chamber of Commerce, (518) 584-3255, www.saratoga.org.

Restrictions

Pets: On leash only, rabies certificate required for dogs. **Fires:** At site. **Alcoholic Beverages:** At site. **Vehicle Maximum Length:** None. **Other:** No electric heaters permitted.

To Get There

From I-87, take Northway Exit 9 and go 2.25 mi. north on Hwy. 4/Hwy. 32, 1.25 mi. east on Hwy. 67, and 1.5 mi. north on Deer Run Dr. Entrance is on the left.

MEXICO

Yogi Bear's Jellystone Park Campground

601 CR 16, Mexico 13114. T: (800) 248-7096 or (315) 963-7096; www.jellystonecny.com; campyogi@dreamscape.com.

RV ★★★★ Tent ★★★★

Beauty: ★★★★ Site Privacy: ★★
Spaciousness: ★★ Quiet: ★★★★
Security: ★★★★★ Cleanliness: ★★★★
Insect Control: ★★★★ Facilities: ★★★★

At Yogi Bear's Jellystone Park in Mexico, campers can swim in the pool, test their putting skills on the mini-golf course, and play shuffleboard under the lights, among other activities. Located 35 miles north of Syracuse, the campground is just two miles from Lake Ontario, where it has a private boat dock and boat launch. At the campground, there is a lounge for adults and a play room for toddlers. Sites are open and shaded, and there are 15 pull-throughs. The sites are well-maintained, but they offer little privacy, and some are cramped. Ideal for a day trip, Syracuse has its share of natural and cultural attractions. Beaver Lake Nature Center, Burnet Park Zoo, the Erie Canal Museum, and New York State Canal cruises are some of the more interesting things to do in the city.

Basics

Operated By: Yogi Bear's Jellystone Park. **Open:** Apr. 15–Oct. 25. **Site Assignment:** Reservations recommended (2-night stay required on weekends), walk-ins accepted. **Registration:** At campground headquarters. **Fee:** $20–$32 (VISA, MC, D). **Parking:** At site.

Facilities

Number of RV Sites: 92. **Number of Tent-Only Sites:** 32. **Hookups:** Electric (20, 30 amps), water, phone, 22 full hookups. **Each Site:** Fire ring, picnic table. **Dump Station:** Yes. **Laundry:** Yes. **Pay Phone:** Yes. **Rest Rooms and Showers:** Yes. **Fuel:** No. **Propane:** Yes. **Internal Roads:** Gravel, in good condition. **RV Service:** No. **Market:** Within 5 mi. **Restaurant:** Within 3 mi. **General Store:** Yes. **Vending:** Yes. **Playground:** Yes. **Other:** Little Salmon River. **Activities:** River fishing, swimming, rec hall, game room, bike rentals, basketball, shuffleboard, planned activities, movies, sports field, volleyball, horseshoes. **Nearby Attractions:** Lake Ontario, Little Salmon River, Syracuse. **Additional Information:** Syracuse Convention and Visitors Bureau, (800) 234-4797, www.syracusecvb.org.

Restrictions

Pets: On leash only. **Fires:** At site. **Alcoholic Beverages:** At site. **Vehicle Maximum Length:** None. **Other:** No pets allowed in rental units.

To Get There

From I-81, take Exit 34 and go west on to Rt. 104 into Mexico, turn right onto CR 16, and go 3 mi. Entrance is on the left.

MT. MORRIS

Letchworth State Park

1 Letchworth State Park, Castile 14427. T: (716) 493-3600 or (800) 456-CAMP; www.nysparks.state.ny.us.

RV ★★★ Tent ★★★

Beauty: ★★★★ Site Privacy: ★★★
Spaciousness: ★★★ Quiet: ★★★★
Security: ★★★★ Cleanliness: ★★★
Insect Control: ★★★ Facilities: ★★★

At Letchworth State Park in western New York, the raging whitewater of the Genesee River roars through deep canyons and over three waterfalls. No wonder it is called the "Grand Canyon of the East." Sites here are wooded; a separate camping area features cabins for rent. Seventeen miles of the 14,344-acre park include the Genesee River Gorge. Cliffs rise as high as 600 feet, and one of the three waterfalls is 107 feet high. Overall, 66 miles of hiking trails can be found in the park, which is also a center for fishing, whitewater rafting, and even hot-air ballooning. Breakfast, lunch, and dinner are served at the nearby Glen Iris Inn. The park also has a conference center for group retreats. If you can pull yourself away from the natural splendor, the William Pryor Letchworth Museum displays Native American artifacts and captivating photos of the park.

BASICS

Operated By: State of New York. **Open:** May 9–Oct. 25. **Site Assignment:** Reservations and walk-ins accepted. **Registration:** At campground office. **Fee:** $16 (VISA, MC). **Parking:** At designated area.

FACILITIES

Number of RV Sites: 270. **Number of Tent-Only Sites:** None. **Hookups:** Electric (20, 30 amps). **Each Site:** Fire ring, picnic table. **Dump Station:** Yes. **Laundry:** Yes. **Pay Phone:** Yes. **Rest Rooms and Showers:** Yes. **Fuel:** No. **Propane:** No. **Internal Roads:** Paved, in good condition. **RV Service:** No. **Market:** Within 7 mi. **Restaurant:** Within 5 mi. **General Store:** Yes. **Vending:** Yes. **Playground:** Yes. **Other:** Cabin rentals. **Activities:** Fishing, swimming, canoeing, rec hall, planned activities, sports field, volleyball, hiking trails. **Nearby Attractions:** Genesee River Gorge, William Pryor Letchworth Museum, Rochester, Genesee Country Village and Museum, Conesus Lake. **Additional Information:** Greater Rochester Visitors Assoc., (800) 677-7282, www.visitrochester.com.

RESTRICTIONS

Pets: On leash only. **Fires:** At site. **Alcoholic Beverages:** At site, no kegs. **Vehicle Maximum Length:** 30 ft. **Other:** Dogs require rabies certificate.

TO GET THERE

From I-390, take Exit 7 and go 2 mi. southwest on Hwy. 408, 2 mi. north on Hwy. 36, and 6 mi. south on the main park road. Entrance is on the left.

NATURAL BRIDGE

KOA—Natural Bridge/ Watertown

Box 71 A Rte. 3, Natural Bridge 13665. T: (800) 562-478 or (315)644-4880; F: (315) 644-4017; www.koa.com; fxlkoa@northnet.org.

RV ★★★★ Tent ★★★★

Beauty: ★★★★ Site Privacy: ★★
Spaciousness: ★★★ Quiet: ★★★★
Security: ★★★★ Cleanliness: ★★★★
Insect Control: ★★★★ Facilities: ★★★★

Set under towering pines, east of Adirondack Park and west of Watertown, KOA—Natural Bridge/ Watertown is an ideal base for whitewater rafting on the Black River and exploring the Thousand Islands (about 30 miles northwest). Many sites are shaded here, but some are open. The campground accommodates 37 pull-throughs. The swimming pool is located indoors, which is especially welcome when it is cold or raining. Bingo, pancake breakfasts, scavenger hunts, and moonlight madness sales are a sampling of the events. Alexandria Bay, located 30 miles northwest of the campground, is the center for Thousand Islands activities. This is where you will find Boldt Castle, the Thousand Islands Skydeck, and many offer boat tours of the region. Watertown, a short drive west of the campground, is home to Long Point State Park, the American Maple Museum, and Sci-Tech Center, a hands-on science and technology museum for children.

BASICS

Operated By: KOA. **Open:** Apr. 1–Nov. 1. **Site Assignment:** Reservations (3-day advance cancellation notice required), walk-ins accepted. **Registration:** At campground office. **Fee:** $25–$29 (VISA, MC, D). **Parking:** At site.

FACILITIES

Number of RV Sites: 55. **Number of Tent-Only Sites:** 13. **Hookups:** Electric (20, 30, 50 amps), water, 29 full hookups. **Each Site:** Fire ring, picnic table. **Dump Station:** Yes. **Laundry:** Yes. **Pay Phone:** Yes. **Rest Rooms and Showers:** Yes. **Fuel:** No. **Propane:** Yes. **Internal Roads:** Gravel, in fair condition. **RV Service:** No. **Market:** Within 10 mi. **Restaurant:** Within 7 mi. **General Store:** Yes. **Vending:** Yes. **Playground:** Yes. **Other:** Cabin rentals. **Activities:** Indoor swimming, game room, rec hall, planned activities on weekends, badminton, sports field, hiking trails, horseshoes, volleyball. **Nearby Attractions:** Thousand Islands boat tours, Boldt Castle, Fort Drum military reservation, whitewater rafting on Black River, Adirondack Park, Alexandria Bay, Long Point State Park, Sci-Tech Center in Watertown. **Additional Information:** New York Division of Tourism—Thousand Islands, (800) 847-5263, www.iloveny.state.ny.us.

RESTRICTIONS

Pets: On leash only. **Fires:** At site. **Alcoholic Beverages:** At site. **Vehicle Maximum Length:** None.

TO GET THERE

From I-81, take Exit 48 and go 7 mi. east on Hwy. 342, 7 mi. east on Hwy. 3, 5 mi. east on Hwy. 3A, and 6 mi. east on Hwy. 3. Entrance is on the left.

NEWBURGH

KOA—Newburgh/ New York City North

P.O. Box 134D, Plattekill 12568. T: (845) 564-2836 or (800) 562-7220; F: (845) 564-2852; www.koa.com; nnycnkoa@aol.com.

RV ★★★★★ Tent ★★★★★

Beauty: ★★★★ Site Privacy: ★★★
Spaciousness: ★★★★ Quiet: ★★★★
Security: ★★★★ Cleanliness: ★★★★
Insect Control: ★★★★ Facilities: ★★★★★

Situated in the Hudson Valley, the 65 forested acres of KOA—Newburgh/New York City North offer lovely mountain views, new playgrounds, two swimming pools, a fishing pond, and a nature trail. This is the closest KOA campground to New York City, and guided tours of the Big Apple depart from the campground. Campers have their choice of wooded sites, which are spacious and private. There are 20 pull-throughs. The campground even offers a dog-walking service. The Hudson Valley is renowned for its lavish homes and wineries, many of which are open for tours. In nearby Hyde Park, you can see the Franklin D. Roosevelt National Historic Site and the Eleanor Roosevelt National Historic Site. Minnewaska State Park is a short drive away; hiking and bridle trails lead to mountain lakes, waterfalls, and beautiful overlooks. "The Gunks" at Minnewaska is a popular rock-climbing area.

BASICS

Operated By: KOA. **Open:** Apr. 1–Oct. 31. **Site Assignment:** Reservations accepted (2-night min. stay on weekends), walk-ins accepted. **Registration:** At campground office. **Fee:** $33–$39 (VISA, MC, D). **Parking:** At site.

FACILITIES

Number of RV Sites: 140. **Number of Tent-Only Sites:** 10. **Hookups:** Electric (20, 30, 50 amps), water, cable TV, phone, 90 full hookups. **Each Site:** Fire ring, picnic table. **Dump Station:** Yes. **Laundry:** Yes. **Pay Phone:** Yes. **Rest Rooms and Showers:** Yes. **Fuel:** No. **Propane:** Yes. **Internal Roads:** Paved, in good condition. **RV Service:** No. **Market:** Within 6 mi. **Restaurant:** Within 4 mi. **General Store:** Yes. **Vending:** Yes. **Playground:** Yes. **Other:** New York City tours. **Activities:** Shuffleboard, mini-golf, planned activities, movies, game room, rec hall, swimming, pond fishing, bike rentals, sports field, badminton, horseshoes, basketball, hiking trails, volleyball. **Nearby Attractions:** Newburgh, West Point (US Military Academy), Franklin D. Roosevelt National Historic Site, Eleanor Roosevelt National Historic Site, Washington's Headquarters State Historic Site, Hudson River cruises, New York City. **Additional Information:** Orange County Chamber, (914) 562-5100, www.orangeny.org.

RESTRICTIONS

Pets: On leash only, under control. **Fires:** At site.

Alcoholic Beverages: At site. **Vehicle Maximum Length:** None.

To Get There

From I-84, take Exit 7N and go 4 mi. north on Hwy. 300, 5 mi. north on Hwy. 32, and 0.5 mi. northeast on Freetown Hwy. Entrance is on left.

NIAGARA FALLS

KOA—Niagara Falls

P.O. Box 509, Grand Island 14072. T: (800) KOA-0787 or (716) 773-7583; F: (716) 773-8014; www.koa.com; djrkoa@buffnet.net.

RV ★★★★ Tent ★★★★

Beauty: ★★★★ Site Privacy: ★★
Spaciousness: ★★ Quiet: ★★★
Security: ★★★★ Cleanliness: ★★★★
Insect Control: ★★★★ Facilities: ★★★★

Location is certainly an amenity at KOA—Niagara Falls—along with its 462 sites, heated pool, and ponds where campers can fish and pedal boat. Set on Grand Island, this KOA is seven miles from Niagara Falls and 10 miles from Buffalo. The campground is also next to Fantasy Island, an 80-acre theme park with roller coasters, live shows, a water park, and a western town. A train at the campground transports passengers to Fantasy Island. There is no shortage of open and shaded sites here. Though Niagara Falls is the main attraction for many campers, a day in nearby Buffalo is worthwhile. New York's second-largest city has several Frank Lloyd Wright houses. The Buffalo & Erie County Botanical Gardens and the Buffalo & Erie County Naval & Military Park are interesting attractions. Sites are well-kept here, but privacy and space are lacking.

Basics

Operated By: KOA. **Open:** Apr. 1–Oct. 31. **Site Assignment:** Reservations and walk-ins accepted. **Registration:** At campground headquarters. **Fee:** $25–$39 (VISA, MC, D). **Parking:** At site.

Facilities

Number of RV Sites: 362. **Number of Tent-Only Sites:** 100. **Hookups:** Electric (20, 30, 50 amps), water, phone, 162 full hookups. **Each Site:** Fire ring, picnic table. **Dump Station:** Yes. **Laundry:** Yes. **Pay Phone:** Yes. **Rest Rooms and Showers:** Yes. **Fuel:** No. **Propane:** Yes. **Internal Roads:** Gravel, in good condition. **RV Service:** No. **Market:** Within 3 mi. **Restaurant:** Within 2 mi. **General Store:** Yes. **Vending:** Yes. **Playground:** Yes. **Other:** Niagara Falls tours embark from campground. **Activities:** Pond fishing, game room, rec hall, basketball, movies, planned activities, bike rentals, badminton, horseshoes, volleyball. **Nearby Attractions:** Niagara Falls, Buffalo, Fort Niagara State Park, Fantasy Island, Buffalo & Erie County Naval & Military Park, Buffalo Zoological Gardens, Niagara River and Lake Erie boat cruises. **Additional Information:** Niagara Falls Convention and Visitors Bureau, (800) 421-5223, www.nfcvb.com.

Restrictions

Pets: On leash only, under control. **Fires:** At site. **Alcoholic Beverages:** At site. **Vehicle Maximum Length:** None.

To Get There

From I-190, take Exit N19 and go 0.5 mi. east on Whitehaven Rd. and 0.75 mi. north on Hwy. 324. Entrance is on the left.

NORTH HUDSON

Yogi Bear's Jellystone Park at Paradise Pines

Box 180, North Hudson 12855. T: (518) 532-7493 or (800) 232-5349; F: (518) 532-0535; www.paradisepines.com; office@paradisepines.com.

RV ★★★★ Tent ★★★★

Beauty: ★★★★ Site Privacy: ★★
Spaciousness: ★★★ Quiet: ★★★
Security: ★★★★ Cleanliness: ★★★★
Insect Control: ★★★★ Facilities: ★★★★

Located along the Schroon River amid the fragrant trees that give the campground its name, Yogi Bear's Jellystone Park and Paradise Pines rests beneath the Adirondack Mountains. Lake George, Lake Placid, Lake Champlaign, Ausable Chasm, and the Vermont border are all within an hour's drive. Many sites are shaded by pines, others are open. Not all sites are located along the Schroon River, but riverside sites are quieter. Sites along the river on the campground's southwest side are near activity centers. For more solitude, stay at a riverside site on the northwest side. Campers can swim in the Schroon, and there are rowboats, canoes, and kayaks available for rent. The store here is more like a miniature supermarket where you can stock your basket and then enjoy a picnic by the river.

Basics

Operated By: Mike and Gina Lenhard. **Open:** May 1–Oct. 20. **Site Assignment:** Reservations accepted (1-night deposit required for 2-night stay), walk-ins accepted. **Registration:** At campground office. **Fee:** $27–$43 (VISA, MC, D). **Parking:** At designated area.

Facilities

Number of RV Sites: 125. **Number of Tent-Only Sites:** 15. **Hookups:** Electric (20, 30, 50 amps), water, cable TV, phone, 105 full hookups. **Each Site:** Fire ring, picnic table. **Dump Station:** Yes. **Laundry:** Yes. **Pay Phone:** Yes. **Rest Rooms and Showers:** Yes. **Fuel:** No. **Propane:** Yes. **Internal Roads:** Gravel and paved, in good condition. **RV Service:** No. **Market:** Within 3 mi. **Restaurant:** Within 1 mi. **General Store:** Yes. **Vending:** Yes. **Playground:** Yes. **Other:** Schroon River, cabin and trailer rentals. **Activities:** Swimming, game room, rec hall, wading pool, river swimming, whirlpool, canoeing, kayaking, boat rentals, mini-golf, fishing, bike rentals, basketball, planned activities, movies, shuffleboard, sports field, horseshoes, volleyball. **Nearby Attractions:** Adirondack Park, Lake George, Vermont, Lake Placid, Fort Ticonderoga, Ausable Chasm. **Additional Information:** New York Division of Tourism—Adirondacks, (800) 487-6867, www.iloveny.state.ny.us.

Restrictions

Pets: On leash only, 1 dog per site. **Fires:** At site. **Alcoholic Beverages:** At site. **Vehicle Maximum Length:** None. **Other:** Visitors may not bring pets.

To Get There

From I-87, take Exit 29 and go about 750 ft. east on Blue Ridge Rd. Entrance is on the left.

NORTH JAVA

Yogi Bear's Jellystone Park at Rolling Pines

5204 Youngers Rd., North Java 14113. T: (716) 457-9644 or (800) 232-4039; www.rollingpines.com; info@rollingpines.com.

RV ★★★★ Tent ★★★★

Beauty: ★★★★ Site Privacy: ★★★
Spaciousness: ★★★ Quiet: ★★★★
Security: ★★★★ Cleanliness: ★★★★
Insect Control: ★★★★ Facilities: ★★★★

Like much of the state, the lush forests and hills of western New York are especially vibrant during the spring and fall. Yogi Bear's Jellystone Park at Rolling Pines is an ideal place to observe this splendor. You can fish and pedal boat the pond, explore the hilly trails by foot or mountain bike, or take a dip in the heated swimming pool. There is a full slate of activities for children and adults both. The cluster of sites tucked between the fishing pond and the swimming pools on the eastern side are ideal if you prefer proximity to recreation. Sites on the far northern side of the campground are away from the bustle of activity centers. If you don't have an RV or tent, trailers and attractive one-bedroom chalets are available for rent. Letchworth State Park and Conesus Lake are the nearest major natural attractions. Buffalo is about an hour's drive away.

Basics

Operated By: Yogi Bear's Jellystone Park. **Open:** May 1–Oct. 31. **Site Assignment:** Reservations accepted (full deposit required for 2- and 3-night stays, 50% required for longer stays), walk-ins accepted. **Registration:** At campground office. **Fee:** $20–$34 (VISA, MC). **Parking:** At site.

Facilities

Number of RV Sites: 160. **Number of Tent-Only Sites:** 40. **Hookups:** Electric (15, 20, 30 amps), water, 40 full hookups. **Each Site:** Fire ring, picnic table. **Dump Station:** Yes. **Laundry:** Yes. **Pay Phone:** Yes. **Rest Rooms and Showers:** Yes. **Fuel:** No. **Propane:** Yes. **Internal Roads:** Gravel and paved, in fair condition. **RV Service:** No. **Market:** Within 3 mi. **Restaurant:** Within 2 mi. **General Store:** Yes. **Vending:** Yes. **Playground:** Yes. **Other:** Fishing pond. **Activities:** Swimming, boating, pedal boat rentals, game room, rec hall, fishing, mini-golf, planned activities on weekends, badminton, sports field, horseshoes, hiking trails, volleyball. **Nearby Attractions:** Niagara Falls, Buffalo, Letchworth State Park, Conesus Lake, Lake Erie. **Additional Information:** New York

Division of Tourism—Greater Niagara, (800) 338-7890, www.iloveny.state.ny.us.

Restrictions

Pets: On leash only. **Fires:** At site. **Alcoholic Beverages:** At site. **Vehicle Maximum Length:** None. **Other:** Visitors may not bring pets.

To Get There

From North Java, go 2.25 mi. south on Hwy. 98, 1.5 mi. east on Pee Dee Rd., and 0.75 mi. south on Youngers Rd. Entrance is on the right.

OLD FORGE

Old Forge Camping Resort

P.O. Box 51 Rte. 28, Old Forge 13420. T: (315) 369-6011 or (800) CAMPING; F: (315) 369-2506; www.oldforgecamping.com; info@oldforgecamping.com.

RV ★★★★ Tent ★★★★

Beauty: ★★★★ Site Privacy: ★★★
Spaciousness: ★★★ Quiet: ★★★★
Security: ★★★★ Cleanliness: ★★★★
Insect Control: ★★★★ Facilities: ★★★★

Located on the western end of Adirondack Park, near the Fulton Chain of Lakes, Old Forge Camping Resort is a year-round campground in the Adirondack Mountains with 123 acres and its own lake. Sites are spacious and wooded, and the campground is within a mile of the village of Old Forge, where 28-mile boat cruises float along the Fulton Chain of Lakes. Though Old Forge does not have a swimming pool, it does have Serene Lake, where campers can swim, fish, or enjoy the water aboard a rented rowboat, canoe, or pedal boat. The nearby Enchanted Forest is a 60-acre water park that also has amusement rides and circus performances. Since the campground is open all year, you can enjoy the winter wonderland in cold months. In the region, there are 500 miles of groomed trails for snowmobiling, cross-country and alpine skiing, and snowshoeing.

Basics

Operated By: Private operator. **Open:** All year. **Site Assignment:** Reservations recommended (1-night deposit required), walk-ins accepted. **Registration:** At campground office. **Fee:** $23–$37 (VISA, MC, D). **Parking:** At site.

Facilities

Number of RV Sites: 205. **Number of Tent-Only Sites:** 47. **Hookups:** Electric (20, 30, 50 amps), water, phone, 90 full hookups. **Each Site:** Fire rings, picnic tables. **Dump Station:** Yes. **Laundry:** Yes. **Pay Phone:** Yes. **Rest Rooms and Showers:** Yes. **Fuel:** Yes. **Propane:** Yes. **Internal Roads:** Gravel and paved, in good condition. **RV Service:** No. **Market:** Within 1 mi. **Restaurant:** Within 1 mi. **General Store:** Yes. **Vending:** Yes. **Playground:** Yes. **Other:** Serene Lake. **Activities:** Lake swimming and fishing, basketball, rec hall, game room, boating, boat rentals, movies, horseshoes, hiking trails, volleyball. **Nearby Attractions:** Adirondack Scenic Railroad, Old Forge Lake Cruise, Enchanted Forest and Water Safari, McCauley Mountain, Adirondack Park, Forest Industries Exhibit Hall, Raquette Lake. **Additional Information:** New York Division of Tourism—Adirondacks, (800) 487-6867, www.iloveny.state.ny.us.

Restrictions

Pets: On leash only. **Fires:** At site. **Alcoholic Beverages:** At site. **Vehicle Maximum Length:** None.

To Get There

From Old Forge, go 1 mi. north on Hwy. 28. Entrance is on the left.

PHELPS

Cheerful Valley Campground

1412 Rte. 14, Phelps 14532. T: (315) 781-1222; www.gocampingamerica.com/cheerfulvalley; cheerfulvalley@cny.net.

RV ★★★★ Tent ★★★★

Beauty: ★★★★ Site Privacy: ★★★
Spaciousness: ★★★ Quiet: ★★★★
Security: ★★★★ Cleanliness: ★★★★
Insect Control: ★★★★ Facilities: ★★★★

Blessed with beautiful weeping willow trees and the serenity of the Canandaigua, Cheerful Valley Campground is located in the Geneva area in the heart of the Finger Lakes region. The campground is nestled in a valley—thus the name Cheerful Valley—where open and shaded sites include 35 pull-throughs. Campers can fish in the river and swim in the spacious pool. Dances and ice cream socials are among the events held at the party pavilion. Outlets malls are within five minutes of the campground, and Cheerful Valley has occasional on-site flea markets. The Finger Lakes are the main draw here: fishing, boating, and hiking opportunities abound. Cheerful Valley is located on the Canandaigua, and Seneca and Cayuga Lakes are not far. The region boasts several wineries; Applewood Winery is a short drive from Cheerful Valley. Lake Ontario and Sodus Point and Bay are 18 miles away.

Basics

Operated By: Carl and Grace Carlson. **Open:** May 1–Sept. 1. **Site Assignment:** Reservations and walk-ins accepted. **Registration:** At campground office. **Fee:** $25–$30 (VISA, MC). **Parking:** At site.

Facilities

Number of RV Sites: 80. **Number of Tent-Only Sites:** 20. **Hookups:** Electric (20, 30 amps), phone, water, 30 full hookups. **Each Site:** Fire ring, picnic table. **Dump Station:** Yes. **Laundry:** Yes. **Pay Phone:** Yes. **Rest Rooms and Showers:** Yes. **Fuel:** No. **Propane:** Yes. **Internal Roads:** Gravel and paved, in good condition. **RV Service:** No. **Market:** Within 2 mi. **Restaurant:** Within 2 mi. **General Store:** Yes. **Vending:** Yes. **Playground:** Yes. **Other:** Party pavilion. **Activities:** Game room, sports field, rec hall, fishing, shuffleboard, fire truck rides, planned activities, horseshoes, volleyball. **Nearby Attractions:** Rochester, Syracuse, Seneca Lake, Cayuga Lake, Canandaigua Lake, Lake Ontario, Sodus Point and Bay, Finger Lakes outlets. **Additional Information:** New York Division of Tourism—Finger Lakes, (800) 548-4386, www.iloveny.state.ny.us.

Restrictions

Pets: On leash only. **Fires:** At site. **Alcoholic Beverages:** At site. **Vehicle Maximum Length:** 36 ft.

To Get There

From I-90, take Exit 42 and go 0.5 mi. north on Hwy. 14. Entrance is on the left.

POLAND

West Canada Creek Campsites

12275 SR 28, Poland 13431. T: (315) 826-7390 or (888) 461-2267; F: (315) 826-5239; ajswiger@aol.com.

RV ★★★★ Tent ★★★★

Beauty: ★★★★ Site Privacy: ★★
Spaciousness: ★★ Quiet: ★★★★
Security: ★★★★ Cleanliness: ★★★★
Insect Control: ★★★★ Facilities: ★★★★

West Canada Creek is angler heaven, so it's natural that West Canada Creek Campsites near Poland serves as an angler's sanctuary. Five miles from the southwest tip of Adirondack Park and 10 miles northeast of Utica, the campground is situated along West Canada Creek and features level open and shaded sites. Bait and licenses are sold at the campground. If you crave something sweet, stroll to the Lil' Caboose Ice Cream Station on the premises. The 24-hour Turning Stone Casino is a short drive from the campground. Utica has a zoo and a children's museum. Cooperstown (home of the National Baseball Hall of Fame and Museum) and Otsego Lake are an hour south of West Canada Creek. We learned that many campers prefer to remain at the campground, though—the fishing at West Canada Creek is that good.

Basics

Operated By: Private operator. **Open:** Apr. 15–Oct. 15. **Site Assignment:** Reservations accepted (10-day notice required for refunds), walk-ins accepted. **Registration:** At campground office. **Fee:** $28–$32 (VISA, MC, D). **Parking:** At site.

Facilities

Number of RV Sites: 56. **Number of Tent-Only Sites:** 12. **Hookups:** Electric (20, 30, 50 amps), cable TV, phone, water, 38 full hookups. **Each Site:** Fire ring, picnic table. **Dump Station:** Yes. **Laundry:** Yes. **Pay Phone:** Yes. **Rest Rooms and Showers:** Yes. **Fuel:** No. **Propane:** Yes. **Internal Roads:** Gravel, in good condition. **RV Service:** No. **Market:** Within 10 mi. **Restaurant:** Within 8 mi. **General Store:** Yes. **Vending:** Yes. **Playground:** Yes. **Other:** Ice cream parlor, West Canada Creek. **Activities:** River swimming and fishing, planned activities on weekends, game room, rec hall, horseshoes, hiking trails, volleyball, badminton, basketball, canoeing, canoe rentals. **Nearby Attractions:** Turning Stone Casino, Utica, Adirondack Park, Herkimer Diamond Mines, Utica Zoo, F.X. Matt Brewing Co., Utica Children's Museum. **Additional Information:** Oneida County Convention and Visitors Bureau, (315) 724-7221, www.oneidacountycvb.com.

Restrictions

Pets: On leash only. **Fires:** At site. **Alcoholic Bev-

erages: At site. **Vehicle Maximum Length:** 40 ft. **Other:** None.

To Get There

From I-90, take Exit 31 and go 11 mi. north on Hwy. 8. Entrance is on the left.

PORTAGEVILLE

Four Winds Campground

7350 Tenefly Rd., Portageville 14536. T: (716) 493-2794 or (877) 777-8655; 4winds@wycol.com.

RV ★★★★ Tent ★★★★

Beauty: ★★★★ Site Privacy: ★★★
Spaciousness: ★★ Quiet: ★★★★
Security: ★★★★ Cleanliness: ★★★★
Insect Control: ★★★★ Facilities: ★★★★

Located three miles from Letchworth State Park, Four Winds Campground draws campers interested in exploring the Genesee River Gorge, Niagara Falls, Buffalo, or Rochester. This Por-tageville campground has does not have a pool, but there is a pond for fishing and swimming. Four Winds is definitely tranquil enough to hear the gentle wind blow; its rural location is quite peaceful. Sites are open and partially shaded, and there are 10 pull-throughs. You can whet your appetite on the campground's hilly and forested hiking trails, but the best hiking is within the 14,344 acres of Letchworth. Bring your camera along; there are cliffs that rise as high as 600 feet, plus three waterfalls, one of which is 107 feet high. Rochester is about an hour north of Four Winds. Niagara Falls and Buffalo are a little more than an hour northwest. The campground is also within an hour of Canandaigua Lake and the Finger Lakes region.

Basics

Operated By: Private operator. **Open:** May 4–Oct. 13. **Site Assignment:** Reservations and walk-ins accepted. **Registration:** At campground office. **Fee:** $24–$26 (VISA, MC, D). **Parking:** At site.

Facilities

Number of RV Sites: 125. **Number of Tent-Only Sites:** 25. **Hookups:** Electric (20, 30, 50 amps), phone, water, 94 full hookups. **Each Site:** Fire ring, picnic table. **Dump Station:** Yes. **Laundry:** Yes. **Pay Phone:** Yes. **Rest Rooms and Showers:** Yes. **Fuel:** No. **Propane:** Yes. **Internal Roads:** Gravel, in good condition. **RV Service:** No. **Market:** Within 8 mi. **Restaurant:** Within 6 mi. **General Store:** Yes. **Vending:** Yes. **Playground:** Yes. **Other:** Pond. **Activities:** Pond swimming, fishing, game room, rec hall, shuffleboard, planned activities on weekends, hiking trails, volleyball, sports field, horseshoes, hiking trails, volleyball. **Nearby Attractions:** Letchworth State Park, Rochester, Niagara Falls, Buffalo, Conesus Lake, Lake Erie . **Additional Information:** New York Div. of Tourism—Greater Niagara, (800) 338-7890, www.iloveny.state.ny.us.

Restrictions

Pets: On leash only, under control. **Fires:** At site. **Alcoholic Beverages:** At site. **Vehicle Maximum Length:** None.

To Get There

From Hwy. 436, go 0.25 mi. north on Hwy. 19A, 1.75 mi. west on Griffith Rd., and 1.25 mi. south on Tenefly Rd. Entrance is on the right.

PULASKI

Brennan Beach RV Park

Rte. 3, Pulaski 13142. T: (888) 891-5979 or (315) 298-2242; www.woodalls.com/a/00373_brennanbeach.html; brennanbeach@prodigy.net.

RV ★★★★ Tent ★★★★

Beauty: ★★★★ Site Privacy: ★
Spaciousness: ★★ Quiet: ★★★
Security: ★★★★★ Cleanliness: ★★★★
Insect Control: ★★★★ Facilities: ★★★★

Overall, Brennan Beach RV Park has more than 1,100 sites, making it the largest campground in New York and one of the largest in the northeast United States. There are two swimming pools, two recreation halls and a recreation center, two tennis courts, an indoor mini-golf course, shuffleboard courts, playgrounds, and basketball and volleyball courts. Relaxing on the beach is a favorite pastime here, and it is easy to do since the white sands stretch a half-mile. Not all sites here are used at once; there are seasonal sections. You can drop your line in Lake Ontario and the nearby Salmon River. Craft classes and dances are scheduled here, and the campground also offers bingo games and flea markets. This is truly a campground where you can remain on-site for your entire stay—unless you choose to fish in the Salmon River or drive an hour south to Syracuse.

Basics

Operated By: Private operator. **Open:** May 1–Oct. 15. **Site Assignment:** Reservations accepted (2-night min. stay), walk-ins accepted. **Registration:** At campground office. **Fee:** $24–$29 (VISA, MC, AE, D). **Parking:** At site.

Facilities

Number of RV Sites: 400. **Number of Tent-Only Sites:** 700. **Hookups:** Electric (20, 30, 50 amps), cable TV, phone, water, 296 full hookups. **Each Site:** Picnic table. **Dump Station:** Yes. **Laundry:** Yes. **Pay Phone:** Yes. **Rest Rooms and Showers:** Yes. **Fuel:** No. **Propane:** Yes. **Internal Roads:** Gravel and paved, in good condition. **RV Service:** No. **Market:** Within 5 mi. **Restaurant:** Within 3 mi. **General Store:** Yes. **Vending:** Yes. **Playground:** Yes. **Other:** Lake Ontario. **Activities:** Lake swimming and fishing, wading pool, mini-golf, game room, rec hall, boating, canoeing, basketball, shuffleboard, planned activities, tennis, horseshoes, volleyball. **Nearby Attractions:** Lake Ontario, Salmon River, Syracuse. **Additional Information:** New York Division of Tourism, (800) CALL-NYS, www.iloveny.state.ny.us.

Restrictions

Pets: On leash only. **Fires:** At site. **Alcoholic Beverages:** At site. **Vehicle Maximum Length:** None.

To Get There

From Hwy. 13, go 1 mi. north on Hwy. 3 and follow signs for 0.5 mi. west on entry road. Entrance is on the left.

RED CREEK

Holiday Harbor Resort Campground and Marina

9415 Blind Sodus Bay Rd., Red Creek 13143. T: (315) 947-5244; F: (315) 947-5065; www.lakeontario.net/holidayharbor; holiday1@redcreek.net.

RV ★★★★ Tent ★★★★

Beauty: ★★★★ Site Privacy: ★★
Spaciousness: ★★★ Quiet: ★★★
Security: ★★★★ Cleanliness: ★★★★
Insect Control: ★★★★ Facilities: ★★★★

Located on Lake Ontario's Blind Sodus Bay, Holiday Harbor Resort Campground and Marina is sheltered in a small harbor. The campground includes a 900-foot-long beach on Lake Ontario and a boat ramp and dock along the bay. Grassy bayside sites are popular, and all sites have a view of the lake or the bay. The campground rents rowboats, and guided fishing trips are available. In nearby Fair Haven, you can drive the New York Seaway Trail, a 454-mile roadway that parallels Lake Erie, the Niagara River, the St. Lawrence River, and Lake Ontario. The route passes through villages, towns, and many historic points. Interpretive signs along the way mark 42 different War of 1812 sites. Holiday Harbor is 15 miles southwest of Oswego, where Lake Ontario meets the mouth of the Oswego River. Fair Haven Beach State Park and the Fort Ontario State Historic Site, built by the British in 1755, are among Oswego's attractions.

Basics

Operated By: Robert Schneider. **Open:** Apr. 1–Oct. 20. **Site Assignment:** Reservations accepted (recommended on July and Aug. weekends), walk-ins accepted. **Registration:** At the old farm house. **Fee:** $15–$25 (VISA, MC). **Parking:** At site.

Facilities

Number of RV Sites: 100. **Number of Tent-Only Sites:** 22. **Hookups:** Electric (15, 20, 30 amps), phone, water, 80 full hookups. **Each Site:** Fire ring, picnic table. **Dump Station:** Yes. **Laundry:** No. **Pay Phone:** Yes. **Rest Rooms and Showers:** Yes. **Fuel:** No. **Propane:** No. **Internal Roads:** Gravel, in good condition. **RV Service:** Yes, limited. **Market:** Within 2.5 mi. **Restaurant:** Within 2.5 mi. **General Store:** Yes. **Vending:** Yes. **Playground:** Yes. **Other:** Cottage rentals, boat dock. **Activities:** Game room, rec hall, boat rentals, lake fishing, hiking trails, horseshoes, boating, canoeing. **Nearby Attractions:** Lake Ontario, Oswego, Fair Haven Beach State Park, Syracuse, Rochester. **Additional Information:** Fair Haven Chamber of Commerce, (315) 947-6037, www.fairhavenny.com.

Restrictions

Pets: On leash only. **Fires:** At site. **Alcoholic Beverages:** At site. **Vehicle Maximum Length:** 70 ft.

To Get There

From Fair Haven, go 1 mi. west on Hwy. 104A and 3 mi. north on Blind Sodus Bay Rd. Entrance is on the left.

ROSCOE

Russell Brook Campsite

101 Russell Brook Rd., Roscoe 12776. T: (607) 498-5416; www.russellbrook.com; russellbrook@citlink.net.

RV ★★★ Tent ★★★

Beauty: ★★★★ Site Privacy: ★★★
Spaciousness: ★★★ Quiet: ★★★★
Security: ★★★★ Cleanliness: ★★★★
Insect Control: ★★★★ Facilities: ★★★★

High in the Catskill Mountains, Russell Brook Campsites is surrounded by nature's splendor—15,000 acres packed with hiking trails and fishing spots. Located in southeastern New York, Russell Brook is situated on the southwestern tip of Catskill Park. Sites are scattered among tall evergreens along Russell Brook and through the center of the campground. There are two tent-only sections which are secluded from the RV section. At the campground, anglers can cast their lines into Russell Brook (there are two children's fishing ponds as well). For other challenges, the Beaverkill is just a few minutes away. Willowemoc and Little Beaverkill are both a 10-minute drive from Russell Brook. Binghamton is about an hour west; attractions there include Ross Park Zoo, the Roberson Museum and Science Center, and the Discovery Center of the Southern Tier.

Basics

Operated By: Doris and Charlie. **Open:** May 1–Dec. 10. **Site Assignment:** Reservations accepted (1-night deposit required), walk-ins accepted. **Registration:** At campground office. **Fee:** $22–$25 (VISA, MC). **Parking:** At site.

Facilities

Number of RV Sites: 90. **Number of Tent-Only Sites:** 50. **Hookups:** Electric (20 amps), water. **Each Site:** Fire ring, picnic table. **Dump Station:** Yes. **Laundry:** Yes. **Pay Phone:** Yes. **Rest Rooms and Showers:** Yes. **Fuel:** No. **Propane:** Yes. **Internal Roads:** Fair, gravel and dirt roads. **RV Service:** No. **Market:** Within 3 mi. **Restaurant:** Within 3 mi. **General Store:** Yes. **Vending:** Yes. **Playground:** Yes. **Other:** Russell Brook, fishing ponds. **Activities:** Fishing, swimming, hiking trails, game room, rec hall, planned activities, basketball, horseshoes. **Nearby Attractions:** Catskill Park, Catskill Fly Fishing Center and Museum, Delaware & Ulster Railway, Delaware County Fair. **Additional Information:** New York Division of Tourism—Catskills, (800) NYS-CATS, www.iloveny.state.ny.us.

Restrictions

Pets: On leash only. **Fires:** At site. **Alcoholic Beverages:** At site. **Vehicle Maximum Length:** 40 ft. **Other:** Max. 6 people per site.

To Get There

From Hwy. 17, take Exit 93 and go 0.1 mi. west on Old Hwy. 17 and 0.75 mi. on Russell Brook Rd. Entrance is on the left.

SAUGERTIES

Rip Van Winkle Campground

14 Robinson St., Saugerties 12477. T: (914) 246-8334 or (800) 842-6316; ripvanwinkle@prodigy.net.

RV ★★★★ Tent ★★★★

Beauty: ★★★★ Site Privacy: ★★★
Spaciousness: ★★★★ Quiet: ★★★★
Security: ★★★★★ Cleanliness: ★★★★
Insect Control: ★★★★ Facilities: ★★★★

Rip Van Winkle, legend says, slept somewhere in the Catskills for 20 years. His namesake campground is perfect as a base for Hudson River excursions and outdoor adventures in the Cat-skills. The campground has a mile of frontage on Plattekill Creek, where campers can swim and fish for trout. Catskill Game Farm and Zoom Flume Waterpark are located in nearby Catskill. The arts colony of Woodstock and the town of Saugerties are not far from Rip Van Winkle. Woodstock was originally chosen as the site for the famous 1969 music festival. When the event grew larger than expected, it was moved 40 miles southwest to a farmer's field outside of Bethel. Cortina Valley Ski Area is in Saugerties, where the Hudson River meets Esopus Creek. The Overlook Observatory, where you can gaze at the stars, is located between Saugerties and Woodstock.

Basics

Operated By: Private operator. **Open:** May 1–Sept. 30. **Site Assignment:** Reservations accepted (7-day advance notice required for refund), walk-ins accepted. **Registration:** At campground office. **Fee:** $24–$29 (VISA, MC, D). **Parking:** At site.

Facilities

Number of RV Sites: 120. **Number of Tent-Only Sites:** 50. **Hookups:** Electric (20, 30, 50 amps), water, phone, 36 full hookups. **Each Site:** Fire ring, picnic table. **Dump Station:** Yes. **Laundry:** Yes. **Pay Phone:** Yes. **Rest Rooms and Showers:** Yes. **Fuel:** No. **Propane:** Yes. **Internal Roads:** Gravel, in good condition. **RV Service:** No. **Market:** Within 3 mi. **Restaurant:** Within 3 mi. **General Store:** Yes. **Vending:** Yes. **Playground:** Yes. **Other:** Plattekill Creek. **Activities:** River fishing and swimming, hiking trails, volleyball, badminton, sports field, horseshoes. **Nearby Attractions:** Cortina Valley Ski Area, Opus 40 and Quarryman's Museum, Catskill Park, Catskill Game Farm, Zoom Flume Waterpark, Hudson River, Howe Caverns, Franklin D. Roosevelt National Historic Site, Eleanor Roosevelt National Historic Site. **Additional Information:** New York Division of Tourism—Catskills, (800) NYS-CATS, www.iloveny.state.ny.us.

Restrictions

Pets: On leash only. **Fires:** At site. **Alcoholic Beverages:** At site. **Vehicle Maximum Length:** 40 ft.

To Get There

From I-87, take Exit 20 and go 0.1 mi. south on Hwy. 32, 2 mi. west on Hwy. 212, and 0.5 mi. north at Centerville Fork on CR 35. Entrance is on the left.

ST. JOHNSVILLE

Crystal Grove Diamond Mine and Campground

161 County Hwy. 114, St. Johnsville 13452. T: (518) 568-2914 or (800) KRY-DIAM; F: (847) 556-0208; www.crystalgrove.com; fun@crystalgrove.com.

RV ★★★★ Tent ★★★★

Beauty: ★★★ Site Privacy: ★
Spaciousness: ★★ Quiet: ★★★
Security: ★★★★ Cleanliness: ★★★★
Insect Control: ★★★★ Facilities: ★★★

Set in the foothills of the Adirondacks, Crystal Grove Campground is located adjacent to a mine where—with some work—you may walk away with a sparkling diamond. The prizes are Herkimer diamonds, which are world-famous quartz crystals found only in specific locations in New York State. These unusually clear, brilliant crystals began forming millions of years ago and are highly sought after. Campers can bring their own shovel, hammer, and chisel, or they can rent tools from Crystal Grove. There is also a rock and mineral shop near the mine. This is a small campground with just 35 sites, all of which are wooded and located along a stream. The diamond mine is Crystal Grove's main draw, though the campground is not completely devoid of activites. It does have basketball and volleyball courts and a horseshoes pit. About 10 miles from the southern tip of Adirondack Park, Crystal Grove is 30 miles east of Utica and 30 miles north of Cooperstown.

Basics

Operated By: Private operator. **Open:** Apr. 15–Oct. 15. **Site Assignment:** Reservations recommended (1-night deposit required), walk-ins accepted. **Registration:** At campground office. **Fee:** $20–$24 (VISA, MC, D). **Parking:** At designated area.

Facilities

Number of RV Sites: 25. **Number of Tent-Only Sites:** 10. **Hookups:** Electric (15, 30 amps), phone, water. **Each Site:** Fire ring, picnic table. **Dump Station:** Yes. **Laundry:** No. **Pay Phone:** Yes. **Rest Rooms and Showers:** Yes. **Fuel:** No. **Propane:** No. **Internal Roads:** Gravel and dirt, in fair condition. **RV Service:** No. **Market:** Within 4 mi. **Restaurant:** Within 4 mi. **General Store:** No. **Vending:** No. **Playground:** Yes. **Other:** Crystal Grove Diamond Mine. **Activities:** Stream fishing, volleyball, horseshoes, basketball, sports field, rec hall. **Nearby Attractions:** Howe Caverns, Cooperstown, National Baseball Hall of Fame and Museum, Otsego Lake, Remington Gun Museum, Adirondack Park. **Additional Information:** New York Division of Tourism, (800) CALL-NYS, www.iloveny.state.ny.us.

Restrictions

Pets: On leash only. **Fires:** At site. **Alcoholic Beverages:** At site. **Vehicle Maximum Length:** None. **Other:** No pets allowed in mines.

To Get There

From St. Johnsville, go 0.75 mi. on Division St. and 3.75 mi. northeast on Lassellville Rd. Entrance is on the right.

VERONA

The Villages at Turning Stone RV Park

5218 Patrick Rd. P.O. Box 126, Verona 13478. T: (800) 771-7711; www.turning-stone.com.

RV ★★★★★ Tent n/a

Beauty: ★★★★ Site Privacy: ★
Spaciousness: ★★★ Quiet: ★★★★
Security: ★★★★ Cleanliness: ★★★★★
Insect Control: ★★★★★ Facilities: ★★★★★

Once you arrive on the grounds of the Villages of Turning Stone RV Park, you may not depart until your vacation is over—and you may not leave with your shirt. After all, this lavish destination revolves around the action-packed casino games, high-stakes bingo, and prize fights. Seven eateries, a resort hotel, an inn, trendy shops, three golf courses, a driving range and putting green, and an on-site golf academy are just a few of the many facilities available. The park also has a convenience store and a laundromat. All sites here are paved and have full hookups, and there are 50 pull-throughs. The cluster of sites at the southeast end of the campground are near the boating pond, store, arcade, and most of the athletic courts. Sites at the far northern tip are quieter and are near the deep woods hiking trail.

Basics

Operated By: Villages at Turning Stone. **Open:** Apr. 1–Nov. 30. **Site Assignment:** Reservations and walk-ins accepted. **Registration:** At campground headquarters. **Fee:** $23–$34 (VISA, MC, AE, D). **Parking:** At site.

Facilities

Number of RV Sites: 175. **Number of Tent-Only Sites:** None. **Hookups:** Electric (20, 30, 50 amps), cable TV, phone, all sites have full hookups. **Each Site:** Fire ring, picnic table. **Dump Station:** Yes. **Laundry:** Yes. **Pay Phone:** Yes. **Rest Rooms and Showers:** Yes. **Fuel:** Yes. **Propane:** Yes. **Internal Roads:** Paved, in good condition. **RV Service:** No. **Market:** Within 2 mi. **Restaurant:** At the resort. **General Store:** Yes. **Vending:** Yes. **Playground:** Yes. **Other:** Casino, shops, hotel. **Activities:** Swimming, whirlpool, wading pool, game room, rec hall, pedal boat rentals, pond fishing, golf, driving range, putting green, basketball, planned activities on weekends, movies, tennis, hiking trails, horseshoes. **Nearby Attractions:** Utica, Oneida Lake, Cooperstown, National Baseball Hall of Fame and Museum. **Additional Information:** New York Division of Tourism, (800) CALL-NYS www.iloveny.state.ny.us.

Restrictions

Pets: On leash. **Fires:** At site. **Alcoholic Beverages:** At site. **Vehicle Maximum Length:** None.

To Get There

From I-90, take Exit 33 and go 1.5 mi. south on Hwy. 365. Entrance is on the right.

WARRENSBURG

Lake George/Schroon Valley Resort

1730 Schroon River Rd., Warrensburg 12885. T: (518) 494-2451 or (800) 958-CAMP; F: (518) 494-4715; www.lakegeorgecamping.com; reservations@lakegeorgecamping.com.

RV ★★★★ Tent ★★★★

Beauty: ★★★★★ Site Privacy: ★★
Spaciousness: ★★★ Quiet: ★★★★
Security: ★★★★★ Cleanliness: ★★★★★
Insect Control: ★★★★ Facilities: ★★★★★

Situated along the Schroon River not far from Lake George and Lake George Village, the Lake George/Schroon Valley Resort is a tranquil campground under white pines, birches, and maples in the Adirondacks. Some sites are open; others are wooded and located on the river, where campers fish for northern pike and rainbow trout when not inner-tubing. Sites on the northeast side are on the river and near many of the recreational facilities. On display is a restored 1931 Covered Wagon RV, which campground managers say was built in Detroit and registered as New York State's first RV trailer. In nearby Lake George Village, you can take a boat tour of the lake, visit Fort William Henry Museum, and frolic at the Great Escape and Splashwater Kingdom Fun Park. The latter has more than 120 rides, including roller coasters, a storybook-themed children's area, and an expansive water park.

Basics

Operated By: Private operator. **Open:** Mother's Day–Columbus Day. **Site Assignment:** Reservations accepted (camp 6 nights and 7th night is free), walk-ins accepted. **Registration:** At campground office. **Fee:** $23–$34 (VISA, MC). **Parking:** At site.

Facilities

Number of RV Sites: 140. **Number of Tent-Only Sites:** None. **Hookups:** Electric (20, 30 amps), phone, water, 48 full hookups. **Each Site:** Fire ring, picnic table. **Dump Station:** Yes. **Laundry:** Yes. **Pay Phone:** Yes. **Rest Rooms and Showers:** Yes. **Fuel:** No. **Propane:** Yes. **Internal Roads:** Gravel, in good condition. **RV Service:** No. **Market:** Within 2 mi. **Restaurant:** Within 2 mi. **General Store:** Yes. **Vending:** Yes. **Playground:** Yes. **Other:** Cabin and trailer rentals, Schroon River. **Activities:** Swimming, game room, rec hall, canoeing, float trips, bike rentals, fishing, basketball, planned activities on weekends, movies, badminton, sports field, volleyball, horseshoes. **Nearby Attractions:** Lake George, Fort William Henry Museum, Great Escape and Splashwater Kingdom Fun Park, Prospect Mountain State Parkway, Lake George boat excursions, Water Slide World, Adirondack Park. **Additional Information:** New York Division of Tourism—Adirondacks, (800) 487-6867, www.iloveny.state.ny.us.

Restrictions

Pets: On leash only. **Fires:** At site. **Alcoholic Beverages:** At site. **Vehicle Maximum Length:** None. **Other:** No refunds for early departures.

To Get There

From I-87, take Exit 24 and go 50 yards east and 0.75 mi. south on Schroon River Rd. Entrance is on the left.

WATKINS GLEN

KOA—Watkins Glen/Corning

P.O. Box 228, Watkins Glen 14891. T: (607) 535-7404 or (800) KOA-7430; F: (607) 535-7474; www.watkinsglenkoa.com; mail@watkinsglenkoa.com.

RV ★★★★ Tent ★★★★

Beauty: ★★★★ Site Privacy: ★★★
Spaciousness: ★★★ Quiet: ★★★★
Security: ★★★★ Cleanliness: ★★★★
Insect Control: ★★★★ Facilities: ★★★★

South of Watkins Glen and Seneca Lake, KOA—Watkins Glen/Corning is in the heart of central New York's Finger Lakes region. Amenities are plentiful here. A trout stream cuts through the campground's northern end; campers can fish in the stream and in a stocked pond. From Memorial Day to Labor Day, a breakfast buffet is served on Saturday and Sunday. Full hookup sites at the northern tip of the campground are near the trout stream. A cluster of forested tent sites on the northeast side are a short walk from the fishing pond. Nearby Watkins Glen State Park has 19 waterfalls and stunning canyon views from well-marked trails. Cruises of Seneca Lake embark from the Watkins Glen area. Twenty-two wineries dot the hillsides around the lake, and each of them offer tastings and tours. South of the campground, Corning is home to the Corning Glass Center and historic district with shops and cafes.

Basics

Operated By: Cam and Paul Friesch. **Open:** Apr. 22–Nov. 1. **Site Assignment:** Reservations recommended (1-night deposit required), walk-ins accepted. **Registration:** At A-frame office. **Fee:** $24–$32 (VISA, MC, AE, D). **Parking:** At site.

Facilities

Number of RV Sites: 106. **Number of Tent-Only Sites:** 9. **Hookups:** Electric (20, 30, 50 amps), cable TV, phone, water, 56 full hookups. **Each Site:** Fire ring, picnic table. **Dump Station:** Yes. **Laundry:** Yes. **Pay Phone:** Yes. **Rest Rooms and Showers:** Yes. **Fuel:** No. **Propane:** Yes. **Internal Roads:** Gravel, in good condition. **RV Service:** No. **Market:** Within 5 mi. **Restaurant:** Within 5 mi. **General Store:** Yes. **Vending:** Yes. **Playground:** Yes. **Other:** Fishing pond, cabin and cottage rentals. **Activities:** Mini-golf, movies, rec hall, game room, pond fishing, sports field, bike rentals, hiking trails, horseshoes. **Nearby Attractions:** Watkins Glen, Seneca Lake boat cruises, Montour Falls, Watkins Geln State Park, Seneca Lake winery tours, Watkins Glen International Speedway, Corning Glass Center. **Additional Information:** Schuyler County Chamber of Commerce, (800) 607-4552, www.schuylerny.com.

Restrictions

Pets: On leash only. **Fires:** At site. **Alcoholic Bev-

erages: At site. **Vehicle Maximum Length:** None. **Other:** Check-in and check-out is 1 p.m.

To Get There

From Hwy. 14, go 4.5 mi. south on Hwy. 414. Entrance is on the left.

WILMINGTON
KOA—Lake Placid/ Whiteface Mountain

Rte. 86 and Fox Farm Rd., Wilmington 12997. T: (800) 562-0368 or (518) 946-7878; F: (518) 946-2172; www.koa.com; koa@whiteface.net.

RV ★★★★ Tent ★★★★

Beauty: ★★★★★	Site Privacy: ★★★★
Spaciousness: ★★★★	Quiet: ★★★★★
Security: ★★★★	Cleanliness: ★★★★
Insect Control: ★★★★	Facilities: ★★★★★

Shaded by behemoth white birches and pines, KOA—Lake Placid/Whiteface Mountain is nestled along the Ausable River at the base of Whiteface Mountain in the northeast section of Adirondack Park. Sites are spacious, level, and wooded, and there are 82 pull-throughs. Bikes are available for rent, as are canoes, kayaks, and tubes for use on the Ausable River. Special events include bingo, movies, and ice cream socials. With its location at the base of Whiteface Mountain, the campground is near many hiking trails and fishing spots, some of which are accessible from the grounds. Mt. Marcy, New York's highest peak at 5,344 feet, is one of the mountains that surround nearby Lake Placid, a Winter Olympics hot spot. High Falls Gorge and Ausable Chasm are must-see natural treasures nearby. For a refreshing drive, venture along the Whiteface Mountain Memorial Highway, a five-mile toll road that leads to the peak's summit, where you can see Lake Placid, the St. Lawrence River, and Vermont.

Basics

Operated By: KOA. **Open:** Apr. 1–Nov. 1. **Site Assignment:** Reservations and walk-ins accepted. **Registration:** At campground office. **Fee:** $20–$35 (VISA, MC, D). **Parking:** At site.

Facilities

Number of RV Sites: 165. **Number of Tent-Only Sites:** 50. **Hookups:** Electric (20, 30, 50 amps), cable TV, phone, water, 48 full hookups. **Each Site:** Fire ring, picnic table. **Dump Station:** Yes. **Laundry:** Yes. **Pay Phone:** Yes. **Rest Rooms and Showers:** Yes. **Fuel:** No. **Propane:** Yes. **Internal Roads:** Gravel and dirt, in fair condition. **RV Service:** No. **Market:** Within 3 mi. **Restaurant:** Within 1 mi. **General Store:** Yes. **Vending:** Yes. **Playground:** Yes. **Other:** Cabin and cottage rentals. **Activities:** Swimming, canoeing, boat rentals, river fishing, mini-golf, basketball, rec hall, game room, bike rentals, planned activities, movies, tennis, hiking trails, horseshoes. **Nearby Attractions:** Lake Placid, Ausable River, Whiteface Mountain, High Falls Gorge, Whiteface Mountain Memorial Highway, Ausable Chasm, Whiteface Mountain Ski Center, Santa's Home Workshop, Lake Placid Center for the Arts. **Additional Information:** Whiteface Mountain Regional Visitors Bureau, (888) WHITEFACE, www.whiteface.net.

Restrictions

Pets: On leash only. **Fires:** At site. **Alcoholic Beverages:** At site. **Vehicle Maximum Length:** None. **Other:** None.

To Get There

From Hwy. 431, go 2 mi. southwest on Hwy. 86 and 0.25 mi. east on Fox Farm Rd. Entrance is on the left.

WILMINGTON
North Pole Campground and Motor Inn

P.O. Box 68, Wilmington 12997. T: (800) 245-0228 or (518) 946-7733; www.northpoleresorts.com; info@northpoleresorts.com.

RV ★★★★ Tent ★★★★

Beauty: ★★★★★	Site Privacy: ★★★
Spaciousness: ★★★	Quiet: ★★★★★
Security: ★★★★	Cleanliness: ★★★★
Insect Control: ★★★★	Facilities: ★★★★★

Located at the base of Whiteface Mountain along the banks of the Ausable River, North Pole Campground and Motor Inn has two sections for RV and tent campers. The campground's original spot, along the Ausable River, features few sites directly on the river, but all sites are shaded and just a short walk away from the river. Activity centers are situated near the entrance at the south end. Sites lead north from the campground entrance to the river. North Pole's new 100-acre "wilderness area" is located across the street and features spacious, secluded sites for tenters and pull-through sites for RVers. The network of hiking and mountain biking trails connects to state park trails at Whiteface Mountain. For those without an RV or tent, North Pole has a motel located at the campground, as well as cabins and cottages for rent. Campers can rent rowboats, canoes or pedal boats for use on the Ausable River.

Basics

Operated By: Carmelitano family. **Open:** All year. **Site Assignment:** Reservations and walk-ins accepted. **Registration:** At campground office. **Fee:** $23–$29 (VISA, MC, D). **Parking:** At site.

Facilities

Number of RV Sites: 85. **Number of Tent-Only Sites:** 40. **Hookups:** Electric (30, 50 amps), cable TV, phone, water, 40 full hookups. **Each Site:** Fire ring, picnic table. **Dump Station:** Yes. **Laundry:** Yes. **Pay Phone:** Yes. **Rest Rooms and Showers:** Yes. **Fuel:** No. **Propane:** Yes. **Internal Roads:** Paved, in good condition. **RV Service:** No. **Market:** Within 4 mi. **Restaurant:** Within 4 mi. **General Store:** Yes. **Vending:** Yes. **Playground:** Yes. **Other:** On-site motel; cabins and cottages available for rent. **Activities:** Swimming, canoeing, boating, boat rentals, rec hall, game room, fishing, mini-golf, basketball, planned activities on weekends, movies, sports field, horseshoes, hiking trails, volleyball. **Nearby Attractions:** Lake Placid, Ausable River, Whiteface Mountain, High Falls Gorge, Whiteface Mountain Memorial Highway, Ausable Chasm, Whiteface Mountain Ski Center, Santa's Home Workshop, Lake Placid Center for the Arts. **Additional Information:** Whiteface Mountain Regional Visitors Bureau, (888) WHITEFACE, www.whiteface.net.

Restrictions

Pets: On leash only, under control. **Fires:** At site. **Alcoholic Beverages:** At site. **Vehicle Maximum Length:** 50 ft. **Other:** One vehicle and one camping unit per site.

To Get There

From Hwy. 431, go 0.25 mi. southwest on Hwy. 86. Entrance is on the left.

North Carolina

With a wide variety of recreational activities to be had from the western mountain region, through the central Heartland, and to the eastern coastal region, North Carolina is a camper's delight. In the Mountains region of North Carolina, you'll find two ranges of the Southern Appalachians, the Blue Ride Mountains, and the Great Smoky Mountains. Here, there are 43 peaks that reach 6,000 feet, and **Mt. Mitchell,** at 6,684 feet, is the highest peak in the eastern United States. Enjoy your camping experience by engaging in the limitless activities available in the mountains: fly-fish for trout in the Great Smoky Mountains on **Kerr** or **Falls Lake;** rock climb or hike at **Table Rock, Looking Glass Rock,** or **Linville Gorge** in Pisgah National Forest; or enjoy exciting white-water rafting on the **Nantahala** and **Pidgeon Rivers.** Along the 252 miles of the **Blue Ridge Parkway** located in North Carolina, you will find five campgrounds, so be sure to stop to enjoy some of the outdoor adventure offered in this area. The **Land of Waterfalls** in the **Pisgah National Forest** offers some breathtaking scenery, and camping in the Great Smoky Mountains might afford you a scenic ride on the railroad to enjoy unsurpassed views of the area.

Also known as the Piedmont and home of America's first gold rush, the Heartland of North Carolina bustles with the state's largest urban areas. Its rolling plains, smooth lakes, meandering rivers, and romantic lagoons provide scenic camping experiences and plenty of water recreation. Be sure to explore the banks and waters of the **Lumber River,** one of North Carolina's four rivers designated as a National Wild and Scenic River. **Lake Norman,** boasting 32,500 acres of water, provides ample opportunity for campers hoping to swim and boat—it's especially nice on those hot, lazy summer days. The **Roanoke Canal Trail** is an excellent stop, with nicely preserved nineteenth-century canal construction and seven miles of unique hiking trails with views of old bridges and steps carved in the earth.

Venture to the Coast where you'll enjoy 300 miles of beach interrupted only by quiet inlets. The history here is rich and inspiration is strong. It was here that Sir Walter Raleigh established the first English Settlement and the Wright Brothers experienced their first flight on the sandy beaches of **Kitty Hawk** in 1903. The city of **New Bern** is known as the birthplace of Pepsi, first marketed as "Brad's Drink." Perhaps you can enjoy a sip of the bubbly drink (does it taste different here?) while enjoying the coastal scenery: historic lighthouses, coasts of islands rising from the water, and graceful seabirds skimming the surface of the sea. Scuba diving proves to be a particularly unusual experience in the "Graveyard of the Atlantic" where you can explore the remains of over 2,000 ships. And it is on the coast where the **Croatan National Forest** offers an excellent stop for campers looking for a wide variety of outdoor activities. Be sure, too, to visit the **Cape Hatteras National Seashore,** where you can enjoy a number of attractions including the Cape Hatteras Lighthouse, which, at 208 feet tall, is the tallest lighthouse in the country.

Campground Profiles

ALBEMARLE

Morrow Mountain State Park

49104 Morrow Mountain Rd., Albemarle 28001.
T: (704) 982-4402; F: (704) 982-5323;
ncsparks.net; momo@vnet.net.

RV ★★★★ Tent ★★★★

Beauty: ★★★★★	Site Privacy: ★★★
Spaciousness: ★★★★	Quiet: ★★★★
Security: ★★★★	Cleanliness: ★★★★★
Insect Control: ★★★★	Facilities: ★★★★

The campground at Morrow Mountain is situated on gently rolling terrain shaded by pine trees and various hardwoods. Pine straw softens the ground. Many sites enjoy views of pleasant fields, but with little greenery between sites, privacy is minimal. Sites are large, with gravel parking. Most offer back-in parking, though there are couple of pull-through sites. Loop C is recommended for RVs—sites tend to be flatter, with greater maneuverability. Morrow Mountain is the only state park in North Carolina with a swimming pool. For fisherfolk, Lake Tillery supports crappie, largemouth bass, striped bass, white bass, perch, bluegill, and catfish. The park is located in the gentle Uwharrie Mountains and includes 16 miles of hiking trails and 16 miles of equestrian trails. When we visited, we saw neither hide nor hair of rangers or staff, making security a bit iffy. But the park is extremely remote. Visit anytime except summer weekends and holidays.

BASICS

Operated By: North Carolina State Parks. **Open:** All year except Christmas. **Site Assignment:** First come, first served, campers can pick desirable site if the site is vacant. **Registration:** At the campsite. **Fee:** Site w/ no hookups is $12 per night, $10 for senior citizens (62 years of age). **Parking:** 2 vehicle parking at each site.

FACILITIES

Number of Multipurpose Sites: 106. **Hookups:** None. **Each Site:** Picnic table, grill, fire ring, lantern hook, tent pad. **Dump Station:** Yes. **Laundry:** No. **Pay Phone:** Yes. **Rest Rooms and Showers:** Yes. **Fuel:** No. **Propane:** No. **Internal Roads:** Paved. **RV Service:** Approx. 30 mi. in Charlotte. **Market:** 7 mi. west in Albemarle. **Restaurant:** 7 mi. west in

Albemarle. **General Store:** 8 mi. west in Albemarle. **Vending:** No (concession stand during the summer months). **Swimming Pool:** Yes (open Jun. 1–Labor Day). **Playground:** No. **Other:** Group lodging, fishing deck, boat launch, amphitheater, primitive camp sites. **Activities:** Boat rental, horseback riding, picnicking, fishing. **Nearby Attractions:** Afro-American Cultural Center, Brem House Artisans Gallery, Charlotte Museum of History, Mint Museum of Art, Paramount's Carowinds Water & Theme Park. **Additional Information:** Charlotte CVB, (704) 334-2282.

Restrictions

Pets: Leash only. **Fires:** Fire ring & in other designated areas. **Alcoholic Beverages:** Not allowed. **Vehicle Maximum Length:** None.

To Get There

From Albemarle, travel 6 mi. east on NC 740. Follow Morrow Mountain Rd. into the park.

APEX

Crosswinds Campground, Jordan Lake State Recreation Area

280 State Park Rd., Apex 27502. T: (919) 362-0586; F: (919) 362-1621; ncparks.net; jordan.lake@ncmail.net.

RV ★★★★ Tent ★★★★

Beauty: ★★★★	Site Privacy: ★★★★★
Spaciousness: ★★★★★	Quiet: ★★★★
Security: ★★★★★	Cleanliness: ★★★
Insect Control: ★★★★	Facilities: ★★★

Crosswinds has one advantage over nearby Poplar Point: it's smaller. Otherwise, these two campgrounds are comparable. Crosswinds features incredibly large sites amid hills. And double sites (designed for two families to share) are gargantuan. Sites are densely wooded, with plenty of undergrowth providing privacy between sites. Most sites have back-in parking, though there are a handful of pull-through sites. Parking pads are gravel, and each site has a pea gravel picnic area. Our favorite sites in Area A (18, 19, 22, 46, and 47) have pristine lake views. Families should head for sites 36–39 in Area B, which are convenient to the beach. In Area C, we like sites 19 and 21. Recreation revolves around Jordan Lake, which is known for its teeming crappie, catfish, and bass. Crosswinds locks its gates at night. Though it feels extremely rural, it's only about 20 miles from Raleigh. The campground stays busy in the summer. Visit in spring or fall for solitude.

Basics

Operated By: NC State Parks. **Open:** All year. **Site Assignment:** First come, first served. Reservations can be made if staying 7 nights or more, (919) 362-0586. Cash & checks are accepted. Cancel 2 weeks before the expected arrival date without penalty. Stay limit is 2 weeks. **Registration:** Campground office. **Fee:** Site w/ no hookups is $12 per night, $10 for senior citizens (62 years of age). $17 for sites w/ water & electric, $14 for senior citizens. **Parking:** 2 vehicles at each site, overflow parking available.

Facilities

Number of Multipurpose Sites: 177 total, 129 w/ water & electric. **Hookups:** Electric (30 amps), water. **Each Site:** Lantern pole, picnic table, fire ring, grill, trash can. **Dump Station:** Yes. **Laundry:** No. **Pay Phone:** Yes. **Rest Rooms and Showers:** Yes. **Fuel:** No. **Propane:** No. **Internal Roads:** Paved & gravel. **RV Service:** 6 mi. east in Pittsboro. **Market:** 6 mi. east in Pittsboro. **Restaurant:** 6 mi. in Pittsboro. **General Store:** 1 mi. **Vending:** No. **Swimming Pool:** No. **Playground:** No. **Other:** Boat ramps. **Activities:** Fishing, boating, educational activities, hiking. **Nearby Attractions:** African American Cultural Complex, North Carolina Art Museum, Mordecai Historic Park, Exploris, JC Raulston Arboretum. **Additional Information:** Greater Raleigh CVB, (919) 831-2887.

Restrictions

Pets: Leash only. **Fires:** Allowed. **Alcoholic Beverages:** Not allowed. **Vehicle Maximum Length:** None.

To Get There

From the US1 and US 64 junction, go west on US 64.

APEX

Poplar Point Campground, Jordan Lake State Recreation Area

280 State Park Rd., Apex 27502. T: (919) 362-0586; F: (919) 362-1621; ncparks.net; jordan.lake@ncmail.net.

RV ★★★★ Tent ★★★★

Beauty: ★★★★	Site Privacy: ★★★★★
Spaciousness: ★★★★★	Quiet: ★★★★
Security: ★★★★★	Cleanliness: ★★★
Insect Control: ★★★★	Facilities: ★★★

Mammoth Poplar Point offers sites very much like those at Crosswinds. Both campgrounds feature large sites amongst lovely hills. Most sites are very shady, with plenty of greenery to provide privacy between neighbors. The majority of parking is back-in style, though there are a few sites with pull-through parking. Parking spaces are gravel, with a pea gravel picnic area at each site. Our favorite lake views are at sites C3–C35, F12, F15, F17, F19. Loop E offers picturesque sites near a small pond (E9, E10, E14, and E15 are the nicest). Tent campers should head to E50–E55. RV campers craving a big, gorgeous pull-through should head for E98. Amenities at Poplar Point are also comparable to those at Crosswinds. However, the beach is more likely to be crowded here because there are so many more sites. Security is good—the campground is gated. To avoid throngs of people, visit mid-week or in spring or autumn.

Basics

Operated By: NC State Parks. **Open:** Mar.–Nov. **Site Assignment:** First come, first served. Reservations can be made if staying 7 nights or more, (919) 362-0586. Cash & checks are accepted. If cancelled 2 weeks before expected arrival there is no penalty. Stay limit is 2 weeks. **Registration:** Camp office. **Fee:** Site w/ no hookups is $12 per night, $10 for senior citizens (62 years of age). $17 for sites w/ water & electric, $14 for senior citizens. **Parking:** 2 vehicles at each site, overflow parking available.

Facilities

Number of Multipurpose Sites: 580 total, 361 have electric. **Hookups:** Electric (30 amps). **Each Site:** Lantern pole, picnic table, fire ring, grill, trash can. **Dump Station:** Yes. **Laundry:** No. **Pay Phone:** Yes. **Rest Rooms and Showers:** Yes. **Fuel:** No. **Propane:** No. **Internal Roads:** Paved & gravel. **RV Service:** Approx. 6 mi. east in Pittsboro. **Market:** Approx. 6 mi. east in Pittsboro. **Restaurant:** Approx. 6 mi. east in Pittsboro. **General Store:** 1 mi. **Vending:** No. **Swimming Pool:** No. **Playground:** No. **Other:** Boat ramps. **Activities:** Boating, fishing, canoeing, cultural history programs, hiking. **Nearby Attractions:** African American Cultural Complex, North Carolina Art Museum, Mordecai Historic Park, Exploris, JC Raulston Arboretum. **Additional Information:** Greater Raleigh CVB, (919) 831-2887.

Restrictions

Pets: Leash only. **Fires:** Allowed. **Alcoholic Beverages:** Not allowed. **Vehicle Maximum Length:** None.

To Get There

Go 10 mi. west on US 64 to Wilsonville, then go 2 mi. south on Hwy 1008.

BALSAM

Moonshine Creek Campground

Box 10 Dark Ridge Road 28707. T: (828) 586-6666; www.moonshinecreekcampground.com; moonshinecreek@hotmail.com.

RV ★★★★ Tent ★★★★

Beauty: ★★★★★	Site Privacy: ★★★
Spaciousness: ★★★	Quiet: ★★★★
Security: ★★★★	Cleanliness: ★★★★
Insect Control: ★★★★	Facilities: ★★

Balsam is a sweet little town, with restaurants as close as Waynesville and plenty of mountain recreation nearby. The Blue Ridge Parkway intersects the town, making Balsam a good camping choice for motor tourists. Drive east about ten miles to Richland Balsam, the highest point on the Blue Ridge Parkway (elev. 6,047 feet). The campground offers small, picturesque sites laid out along Moonshine Creek. Tree cover is lovely. Gravel parking pads overwhelm some sites to the extent that there is little natural ground cover. Our favorite creekside sites, 14, 16, 18, and 20, are nicely situated but have no grass. Other nice sites include 8, which is more spacious than most, and 9–12. Balsam's cool mountain weather is heavenly in the summer. For the least hassled touring, plan a mid-week visit. Security is fine here. There is no gate but the park is extremely remote.

Basics

Operated By: Mack & Janet McDonald. **Open:** Apr.–Nov. **Site Assignment:** Deposit must be received 7 days prior to reservation; 7-day notice on cancellations for refund; V, MC, check, cash, money order. **Registration:** In office. **Fee:** RV is $24/day, tent is $20/day. **Parking:** At site.

FACILITIES

Number of RV Sites: 59. **Number of Tent-Only Sites:** 30. **Number of Multipurpose Sites:** 0. **Hookups:** Water, sewer, electric (30 amps). **Each Site:** Water, electric, fire ring, picnic table. **Dump Station:** Yes. **Laundry:** Yes. **Pay Phone:** Yes. **Rest Rooms and Showers:** Yes. **Fuel:** No. **Propane:** Yes. **Internal Roads:** Gravel, entrance is asphalt. **RV Service:** 5 mi. toward Waynesville. **Market:** 5 mi. toward Waynesville. **Restaurant:** 5 mi. toward Waynesville. **General Store:** 5 mi. toward Waynesville. **Vending:** No. **Swimming Pool:** No. **Playground:** No. **Other:** Grocery store. **Activities:** Planned cook outs. **Nearby Attractions:** Appalachian Trail, biltmore House, Blowing Rock, Blue Ridge Pkwy., Cherohala Skyway, Cherokee Bear Zoo, Cherokee Corn Maze, Cherokee Indian Museum, Cherokee Indian Reservation, Chimney Rock Park, Deep Creek tubes, Fields of the Wood, Fontana Lake and Dam, Ghost Town in Maggie Valley, Grand Father Mountain, Great Smoky Mountain National Park, Harra's Cherokee Casino, Joyce Kilmer Memorial Forest, Linville Caverns, Mountain Farm & Museum, Moutain Waters Scenic Byway, Nantahala National Forest, Nantahala River Rafting, Oconaluftee Indian Village, Pisgah National Forest, Santa's Land Fun Park & Zoo, Soco Gardens Zoo, Smoky Mountain Country Club, Tribal Bingo, Tsali Trail, Unto These Hills Outdoor Drama.

RESTRICTIONS

Pets: Allowed. **Fires:** Fire rings only. **Alcoholic Beverages:** At site only. **Vehicle Maximum Length:** None.

TO GET THERE

From Cherokee: Drive south on US 441, then northeast on US 74/23. Follow signs to campground.

BUXTON

Cape Woods Campground and Cabins

47649 Buxton Back Rd, Buxton, NC 27920. T: (252)995-5850; F: (252)995-3732; www.Capewoods.com.

RV ★★★ Tent ★★★

Beauty: ★★★★
Spaciousness: ★★★
Security: ★★★★
Insect Control: ★★★
Site Privacy: ★★
Quiet: ★★★★
Cleanliness: ★★★★
Facilities: ★★

Campers who prefer full hookups and wish to tour Cape Hatteras National Seashore are in luck. Attractive Cape Woods is located centrally on Hatteras Island, just a few miles from the Wright Brothers National Memorial, including the first airstrip, site of Orville Wright's historic 1903 flight. The swimming beach at the national seashore is less than five miles from the campground. The park includes back-in sites with grass parking and paved patios at each site. Most sites are average size, though some are long and narrow. Shadiness varies from site to site, though most are partially shady. Since the campground is inland and treed, it stays a little cooler than the national park campgrounds. There is no seclusion. Sites are differentiated by their amenities, so choose your site based on the hookups you need. Security is excellent at Cape Woods. The campground is gated at all times. Avoid Cape Hatteras on summer weekends. Bring bug spray in the summer.

BASICS

Operated By: Kevin & Laurie Morris. **Open:** All year. **Site Assignment:** Encourage reservations. **Registration:** Office. **Fee:** $26–$33. **Parking:** At site.

FACILITIES

Number of RV Sites: 135. **Number of Tent-Only Sites:** 11. **Number of Multipurpose Sites:** 0. **Hookups:** Water, electric (50 amps), septic, cable. **Each Site:** Water, electric (50 amps). **Dump Station:** Yes. **Laundry:** Yes. **Pay Phone:** No. **Rest Rooms and Showers:** Yes. **Fuel:** No. **Propane:** Yes. **Internal Roads:** Gravel. **RV Service:** Nearby. **Market:** No. **Restaurant:** No. **General Store:** Yes. **Vending:** Yes. **Swimming Pool:** Yes. **Playground:** Yes. **Activities:** Game room, volleyball, horseshoes, fising. **Nearby Attractions:** NPS Cape Hatteras Lighthouse, Ocracoke Island, 2 mi. from beach.

RESTRICTIONS

Pets: Allowed. **Fires:** Fire pits on some sites. **Alcoholic Beverages:** Allowed. **Vehicle Maximum Length:** None.

TO GET THERE

From Atlanta: I-85 North towards Greenville, take I-40 East toward Raleigh, take Raleigh Chapel Hill Expressway (it becomes Wade Ave.) Turn right onto ramp. Merge onto I-440 North, Take Exit No. 13B toward Rocky Mount/Wilson. In Buxton, bear left at Centura Bank. Buxton Back Rd. is 1 mi. on the left.

CAPE HATTERAS

Cape Point

Route 1 Box 675, Manteo 27954. T: (252) 473-2111; www.nps.gov./caha.

RV ★★★ Tent ★★★

Beauty: ★★★
Spaciousness: ★★★★
Security: ★★★
Insect Control: ★★★
Site Privacy: ★★
Quiet: ★★★★
Cleanliness: ★★★★
Facilities: ★

This is the least attractive of the Cape Hatteras National Seashore campgrounds. However, this campground is quieter than Oregon inlet because it's further from the main road. Also, sites are larger and more open than at Oregon. Cape Point is completely flat. Sites feature paved, back-in parking and paved picnic table pads. There is no shade or privacy. Vegetation consists of natural marsh grasses that grow on the campground borders. Choose your site based on proximity to beach path or potties. Security is passable; the gates are not locked at night, the area is extremely quiet. Cape Point campers can walk a quarter mile to the beach, through attractive grasses and dunes. Or drive to the Cape Hatteras Lighthouse. At 208 feet, it's the tallest in the United States. There are also hiking trails and fishing piers nearby. Visit Cape Hatteras on weekdays if possible. Prepare to battle insects in the summertime.

BASICS

Operated By: National Park Service. **Open:** May 25–Sept. 2. **Site Assignment:** First come, first served only. Check-out time is noon. Stay limit is 2 weeks. **Registration:** Entrance office. **Fee:** $18, 50% off the price to the holders of a Golden Access/Age card. **Parking:** 2 vehicle parking at each site, overflow parking is available.

FACILITIES

Number of Multipurpose Sites: 202. **Hookups:** None. **Each Site:** Picnic table, grill. **Dump Station:** Yes. **Laundry:** No. **Pay Phone:** Yes. **Rest Rooms and Showers:** Yes. **Fuel:** No. **Propane:** No. **Internal Roads:** Paved. **RV Service:** Approx. 3 mi. north in Buxton. **Market:** Approx. 3 mi. north in Buxton. **Restaurant:** Approx. 3 mi. north in Buxton. **General Store:** Approx. 3 mi. north in Buxton. **Vending:** No. **Swimming Pool:** No. **Playground:** No. **Activities:** Fishing, picnicking, hiking. **Nearby Attractions:** Currituck Beach Lighthouse, Elizabethan Gardens, Engineer Research Development Center, Frisco Native American Museum, Wright Brother's National monument, Lost Colony. **Additional Information:** Outer Banks Visitor's Bureau, (252) 473-2138.

RESTRICTIONS

Pets: Leash only. **Fires:** In grill. **Alcoholic Beverages:** Not allowed. **Vehicle Maximum Length:** 35 ft.

TO GET THERE

From Norfolk, Virginia take 64 going south. Turn onto 168 going south. 168 will turn into 158 and then into NC12. Stay on NC12 going south and the park will be on the Left.

CAPE HATTERAS

Hatteras Sands

BOX 295, Hatteras 27943. T: (252) 986-2422; F: (252) 986-2647; www.hatterassands.com; hatsandscg@aol.com.

RV ★★★ Tent ★★

Beauty: ★★★
Spaciousness: ★★
Security: ★★★★★
Insect Control: ★★★
Site Privacy: ★★
Quiet: ★★★★
Cleanliness: ★★★★
Facilities: ★★★

Hatteras Sands is laid out in two areas surrounded by canals where folks enjoy fishing and crabbing. Each section has its own 24-hour security gate, making the park extremely safe. Other facilities are attractive and clean. The campground's location is excellent—it's in the heart of Hatteras, convenient to restaurants, attractions, and the Ocracoke Ferry. Explore the natural beauty of the coast on a day trip to Ocracoke Island. Hatteras is a popular summer destination and should be avoided on summer holidays and weekends. The campground is totally flat and has no shady trees. Manicured grass and shrubs add some life to the landscape. Campsites are tidy, with paved parking and a paved patio at each site. There are both back-in and pull-though sites. Sites are tiny and offer no privacy. Families should head for sites A1–A9, near the playground and pool area (which includes a children's pool). Couples prefer sites in section B, which is quiet.

BASICS

Operated By: The Williams family. **Open:** Mar. 1–Nov. 31. **Site Assignment:** First come, first served is available but reservations are recommended, (252) 986-2422; V, MC are accepted. If cancelled within 10 days to the expected arrival date, the fee is $10 plus the deposit. Rain checks are available. The check-in & check-out time is 12 noon. **Registration:** Main office. **Fee:** Sites w/ water, sewer, electric, & cable range $35.95–$47.95. Sites w/ water & electric range $32.95–$44.95. Sites w/ no hookups range $28.95–$36.95. (All depending on season.) **Parking:** 2 vehicles at each site, overflow parking is available.

FACILITIES

Number of RV Sites: 100. **Number of Tent-Only Sites:** 20. **Number of Multipurpose Sites:** None. **Hookups:** Water, electric (30, 50 amps), cable, sewer. **Each Site:** Picnic table. **Dump Station:** Yes. **Laundry:** Yes. **Pay Phone:** Yes. **Rest Rooms and Showers:** Yes. **Fuel:** No. **Propane:** No. **Internal Roads:** Paved. **RV Service:** 1 mi. **Market:** 19 mi. north in Avon. **Restaurant:** 1 mi. **General Store:** 75 mi. north in Southern Shores (large chain store). **Vending:** Beverage only. **Swimming Pool:** Yes. **Playground:** Yes. **Other:** Canals, group meeting facilities, club house. **Activities:** Paddle boats, crabbing, fishing, picnicking. **Nearby Attractions:** Ocracoke Island Ferry, Fishing Fleet, Hatteras Museum, Lost colony, Wright Memorial, Nags Head Dunes. **Additional Information:** Outer Banks Visitor's Bureau, (800) 446-6262.

RESTRICTIONS

Pets: Leash only. **Fires:** No open pit (bring your own grill). **Alcoholic Beverages:** Allowed. **Vehicle Maximum Length:** 36 ft.

TO GET THERE

From Raleigh take Hwy. 64 to the east coast where ts intersects w/ Hwy. 12. Take Hwy. 12 south and go through Cape Hatterasa and the entrance will be on the right.

CAPE HATTERAS

Ocracoke

Route 1 Box 675, Manteo 27954. T: (252) 473-2111; www.nps.gov/caha.

RV: ★★★★ Tent: ★★★★

Beauty: ★★★★★ Site Privacy: ★★
Spaciousness: ★★★★ Quiet: ★★★★★
Security: ★★★★★ Cleanliness: ★★★★
Insect Control: ★★★ Facilities: ★

Beautiful Ocracoke campground is bounded by gentle natural dunes and native grasses. It is flatter than the campground at Oregon Inlet, allowing for nicer views. We recommend this quiet campground for tent campers. Ocracoke can be reached by ferry only. Once you're on the island, you can explore the beaches once frequented by Blackbeard, or check out the oldest operating lighthouse in North Carolina (built ca. 1823). Many sites on the outside perimeter of the campground are nestled into the dunes. Sites D23, D25, and D27 are especially comfortable for tent campers. RV campers should head for sites B3, D33, D35, and D37, which offer both privacy and long parking pads. If you prefer open sites, there are plenty to choose from. Sites contain back-in parking, paved parking as well as grassy areas. Site size is ample, though spacing between sites varies. Security is excellent; Ocracoke Island is nearly deserted at night. Come prepared to battle insects. Visit midweek for peace and quiet.

BASICS

Operated By: National park service. **Open:** Apr. 13–Oct. 8. **Site Assignment:** First come, first served only accept between May 15–Sept. 17, reservations can be made at (800) 365-CAMP. V, MC, D are accepted. If cancelled prior to the expected date of arrival the fee is $13.65. If cancelled on the expected day of arrival the fee is $13.65 plus 1 night's stay ($17). Check-out time is 12 noon. Stay limit is 14 days. **Registration:** Main office at campground. **Fee:** $17 per night, 50% off for holders of a Golden Age/Access card. **Parking:** 2 vehicle parking at each site.

FACILITIES

Number of Multipurpose Sites: 136. **Hookups:** None. **Each Site:** Picnic table, grill. **Dump Station:** Yes. **Laundry:** No. **Pay Phone:** Yes. **Rest Rooms and Showers:** Yes (no heated showers). **Fuel:** No. **Propane:** No. **Internal Roads:** Paved. **RV Service:** 1 mi. **Market:** 15 mi. north in Hatteras (must take ferry). **Restaurant:** 15 mi. north in Hatteras (must take ferry). **General Store:** 15 mi. north in Hatteras (must take ferry). **Vending:** No. **Swimming Pool:** No. **Playground:** No. **Activities:** Picnicking, fishing. **Nearby Attractions:** Currituck Beach Lighthouse, Elizabethan Gardens, Engineer Research Development Center, Frisco Native American Museum, Wright Brother's National monument, Lost Colony. **Additional Information:** Outer Banks Visitor's Bureau, (252) 473-2138.

RESTRICTIONS

Pets: Leash only. **Fires:** In grill & on the beach under the high tide line 100 ft. away from vegetation. **Alcoholic Beverages:** Not allowed. **Vehicle Maximum Length:** 35 ft. **Other:** Longer than normal tent stakes are recommended.

TO GET THERE

From Norfolk, Virginia take 64 South. Turn onto 168 South. 168 turns into 158 and then into NC 12. Stay on NC 12 going south and the campground will be on the left.

CAPE HATTERAS

Oregon Inlet

Route 1 Box 675, Manteo 27954. T: (252) 473-2111; www.nps.gov/caha.

RV: ★★★★ Tent: ★★★★

Beauty: ★★★★★ Site Privacy: ★★★
Spaciousness: ★★★★ Quiet: ★★★
Security: ★★★ Cleanliness: ★★★★
Insect Control: ★★★ Facilities: ★

Oregon Inlet is the most attractive of the Cape Hatteras National Seashore campgrounds. It's also the closest to civilization, with quaint private beach houses as little as two miles away. The Wright Brothers National Memorial, including the first flight airstrip, is about 20 miles north. The Bodie Island Lighthouse, built in 1872, is just a few miles north of Oregon Inlet. The campground consists of three loops, built amongst pleasant dunes. Sites are large, with an some privacy provided by the dunes and grasses. Back-in parking spaces may be paved or packed sand. Our favorite sites, 2, 19, 21, and 23, are the most private because they're recessed into the dunes. We also like sites along the back of loops B and C, which are the furthest from Hwy. 12. Oregon Inlet is the most popular of the National Seashore campgrounds, and should be avoided on busy summer weekends. Security is fair—the gates are not closed at night.

BASICS

Operated By: National park service. **Open:** Apr. 13–Oct. 8. **Site Assignment:** First come, first served. Check-out time is 12 noon. Stay limit is 2 weeks. **Registration:** Entrance station. **Fee:** $17 per night, 50% for holders of a Golden Age/Access card. **Parking:** 2 vehicles at each site, overflow parking is available.

FACILITIES

Number of Multipurpose Sites: 120. **Hookups:** None. **Each Site:** Picnic table, grill. **Dump Station:** Yes. **Laundry:** No. **Pay Phone:** Yes. **Rest Rooms and Showers:** Yes. **Fuel:** No. **Propane:** No. **Internal Roads:** Paved. **RV Service:** 5 mi. north in Nags Head. **Market:** 17 mi. north in Manteo. **Restaurant:** 17 mi. north in Manteo. **General Store:** 17 mi. north in Manteo. **Vending:** No. **Swimming Pool:** No. **Playground:** No. **Other:** Group lodging is available for groups w/ 7–30 members. **Activities:** Picnicking, fishing. **Nearby Attractions:** Currituck Beach Lighthouse, Elizabethan Gardens, Engineer Research Development Center, Frisco Native American Museum, Wright Brother's National monument, Lost Colony. **Additional Information:** Outer Banks Visitor's Bureau, (252) 473-2138.

RESTRICTIONS

Pets: Leash only. **Fires:** Grill only. **Alcoholic Beverages:** Not allowed. **Vehicle Maximum Length:** 35 ft.

TO GET THERE

From Norfolk, Virginia take 64 South. Turn onto 168 South. 168 turns into 158 and then into NC 12. Stay on NC 12 going south and the campground will be on the left.

CAROLINA BEACH

Carolina Beach State Park

P.O. Box 475, Carolina Beach 28428. T: (910) 458-8206; F: (910) 458-6350; www.ncsparks.com; Carolina.Beach@ncmail.net.

RV: ★★★★ Tent: ★★★★

Beauty: ★★★★★ Site Privacy: ★★★★★
Spaciousness: ★★★★★ Quiet: ★★★★

Security: ★★★★ Cleanliness: ★★★★
Insect Control: ★★★ Facilities: ★★★

Carolina Beach is a tent camper's dream-come-true. Intrepid RV campers also appreciate the beauty of this campground, even if they must forego hookups for a few days. Sites are commodious and lovely, with a thick understory providing privacy between them. Campsites enjoy the shade of longleaf pine, turkey oak, and live oak. Parking is on gravel and packed sand, and all sites offer back-in parking. The best sites are on the outside of the camping loops. The park is located in a densely developed suburb of Wilmington, at the conjunction of the Cape Fear River and the Intracoastal Waterway. A marina and fishing deck serve anglers and boaters. Swimmers will have to drive a few miles, to the Atlantic Ocean beach at Fort Fisher State Recreation Area. Before you leave Carolina Beach, check out the exhibit on carnivorous plants in the exhibit hall (species found in the park include Venus flytraps, pitcher plants, butterworts, and bladderworts). Security is fair—gates are locked at night, but attended during the day. Avoid visiting on summer weekends.

Basics

Operated By: NC State Parks. **Open:** All year except Christmas. **Site Assignment:** First come, first served policy, stay limit is 2 weeks. **Registration:** Marina office. **Fee:** $12 per night. **Parking:** 2 vehicle parking at each site.

Facilities

Number of RV Sites: 0. **Number of Tent-Only Sites:** 83. **Number of Multipurpose Sites:** 83. **Hookups:** None. **Each Site:** Picnic table, grill. **Dump Station:** Yes. **Laundry:** Yes. **Pay Phone:** Yes. **Rest Rooms and Showers:** Yes. **Fuel:** Sold for boats only. **Propane:** No. **Internal Roads:** Paved. **RV Service:** 15 mi. north in Wilmington. **Market:** 2 mi. south in Carolina Beach. **Restaurant:** 2 mi. south in Carolina Beach. **General Store:** 2 mi. south in Carolina Beach. **Vending:** Marina store. **Swimming Pool:** No. **Playground:** No. **Other:** Boat launch, trails. **Activities:** Boat rental, picnicking, hiking, fishing. **Nearby Attractions:** Winter boat cruises. **Additional Information:** Cape Fear Coast CVB, (910) 341-4029.

Restrictions

Pets: Leash only, not inside buildings. **Fires:** Grill only. **Alcoholic Beverages:** Not allowed. **Vehicle Maximum Length:** Call ahead for details.

To Get There

From Wilmington take NC 421 10 mi. south. Follow signs to entrance.

CHARLOTTE
Carowinds

P.O. Box 410289, Charlotte 28241. T: (800) 888-4386; www.carowinds.com.

RV ★★★ Tent ★★

Beauty: ★★★ Site Privacy: ★★
Spaciousness: ★★★ Quiet: ★★★
Security: ★★★ Cleanliness: ★★
Insect Control: ★★★★ Facilities: ★★★

Near Paramount's Carowinds theme park, this large campground is laid out in four main areas, with average-sized sites. Most are long and narrow, and sandwiched together very tightly. Some sites are partially shady, but many are totally open. There are both back-in and pull-through sites. All have paved parking. The RV area is totally flat and boring. The biggest sites are 201–207. The tent area is slightly more attractive, but not recommended due to poor safety. There are no gates, and suburban Carowinds is full of teenagers. The pool and mini-golf are a minor consolation to the dreariness of the campground. Parents will be glad to know that lifeguards are on duty during pool hours (children under ten must be accompanied by an adult nonetheless). Visit the theme park during the week for less-hassled touring.

Basics

Operated By: Paramount's Carowinds. **Open:** All year. **Site Assignment:** Reservations recommended. $10 deposit, Cancellation: 48 hours in advance. Payment methods: V, MC, D, AM, & travelers checks, personal checks w/ ID. **Registration:** Office. **Fee:** Call ahead for details. **Parking:** 1 car per site; overflow parking available.

Facilities

Number of RV Sites: 150. **Number of Tent-Only Sites:** 50-plus. **Number of Multipurpose Sites:** 0. **Hookups:** Water, sewer, electric (20, 30 amps). **Each Site:** Picnic table, grill. **Dump Station:** Yes. **Laundry:** Yes. **Pay Phone:** Yes. **Rest Rooms and Showers:** Yes. **Fuel:** No. **Propane:** No. **Internal Roads:** Paved. **RV Service:** 5 mi. **Market:** 5 mi. **Restaurant:** 5 mi. **General Store:** 5 mi. **Vending:** No. **Swimming Pool:** Yes. **Playground:** Yes. **Other:** Tram service to & from park. **Activities:** Mini golf, volleyball, set-ups, game room, grocery store, picnic tables, transportation to park, shuffleboard, horseshoes. **Nearby Attractions:** Charolette Motor Speedway, Charolette coliseum, Cricket Arena, Charolette Convention Center, Ericsson Stadium.

Restrictions

Pets: Allowed. **Fires:** Not allowed. **Alcoholic Beverages:** At site only. **Vehicle Maximum Length:** None. **Other:** No skateboards or rollerblades.

To Get There

From I-77, take Exit 90. Go west on Carowinds Blvd toward Spartanburg. Turn right on Catawba Trace. The campground is on the left.

CHEROKEE
Cherokee KOA

92 KOA Kampground 12D, Cherokee 28719. T: (828)497-9711.

RV ★★★★ Tent ★★★

Beauty: ★★★ Site Privacy: ★★★
Spaciousness: ★★★ Quiet: ★★★
Security: ★★★★★ Cleanliness: ★★★
Insect Control: ★★★★ Facilities: ★★★★

The KOA in Cherokee is an attractive campground nestled between the Raven Fork River and a narrow trout pond. Sites are on the small side, and this campground is extremely popular. If you value breathing space, KOA Cherokee is not for you. Sites are mostly shady, with paved parking. There are both back-in and pull-through sites. Our favorite sites are those along the river and pond—they have the prettiest views and tend to be the shadiest. The fishing pond is stocked twice a week in season. The recreational facilities here are very good—and very crowded. With 300 campsites, there should be more than one swimming pool and playground. To avoid the vacationing masses, visit during the week in summer and fall. Security is excellent. With gates attended at all times, the park is nearly impenetrable.

Basics

Operated By: KOA. **Open:** All year. **Site Assignment:** Reservations required 30 days in advance; Pay in full at time of reservation; $50 cancellation fee. **Registration:** Kamping Kottage. **Fee:** RV $25–$50, tent w/ no hookup $20–$40, Kamping Kabins $34–$99. **Parking:** On site.

Facilities

Number of RV Sites: 300. **Number of Tent-Only Sites:** 107. **Number of Multipurpose Sites:** 0. **Hookups:** Cable, electric (30 amps). **Each Site:** None. **Dump Station:** No. **Laundry:** Yes. **Pay Phone:** No. **Rest Rooms and Showers:** Yes. **Fuel:** Yes. **Propane:** No. **Internal Roads:** Paved. **RV Service:** Yes. **Market:** on site. **Restaurant:** On site. **General Store:** Yes. **Vending:** Inquire at campground. **Swimming Pool:** Yes. **Playground:** Yes. **Other:** Hot tub. **Activities:** Tennis, basketball, horseshoes, fishing, white-water rafting. **Nearby Attractions:** Inquire at campground.

Restrictions

Pets: Yes. **Fires:** Only in designated areas. **Alcoholic Beverages:** Allowed. **Vehicle Maximum Length:** Call ahead for details.

To Get There

Take Cherokee North 441 to park boundary then take Big Cove Rd.

CHEROKEE
Great Smoky Mountains National Park Smokemont Campground

Address: 107 Park Headquarters Rd., Gatlinburg 37738. T: (865) 436-1200; F: (865) 436-1204; www.nps.gov/grsm.

RV ★★★★ Tent ★★★★

Beauty: ★★★★ Site Privacy: ★★★
Spaciousness: ★★★★ Quiet: ★★★★
Security: ★★★ Cleanliness: ★★★★
Insect Control: ★★★★★ Facilities: ★★★

Situated in a flat river valley, Smokemont is the largest campground in Great Smoky Mountains National Park. It's popular with hikers, who may choose from day or overnight hikes originating at Smokemont. Anglers enjoy the Oconaluftee River, which runs alongside the campground. Automobile touring is another popular pastime—Smokemont is just a few miles from the southern terminus of the Blue Ridge Parkway. Nearby, the town of Cherokee offers casinos, kitsch, and Native American culture and crafts. The long, slender campground includes a large multipurpose camping area as well as an RV-only loop. Sites are on the large side of average, with paved parking. In the RV-only area, sites have back-in parking. In the multipurpose area, there are both back-in and pull-through sites. Though there are some open sites in the RV loop, most sites are deliciously shady and fairly private. For beauty, the nicest sites are 8–18, in the back of the multi-purpose area. Smokemont Campground stays packed on summer and fall weekends. Visit during the week. Security is fair—there are no gates.

Basics

Operated By: National Park Service. **Open:** All year. **Site Assignment:** First come, first served; reservations accepted for May 15–Oct. 31 up to 5 months in advance, w/ full deposit; $13.25 cancellation fee w/ at least 24-hour notice, otherwise first night plus fee charged; reservations made by calling (800) 365-CAMP or at reservations.nps.gov (personal check, money order, V, D, MC). **Registration:** Self-registration. **Fee:** $14–$17 for up to 6 people, 2 tents or 1 tent & 1 RV (cash only for off-season self-registration). **Parking:** At site (2 vehicles).

Facilities

Number of RV Sites: 43. **Number of Tent-Only Sites:** 18. **Number of Multipurpose Sites:** 140. **Hookups:** None. **Each Site:** Picnic table, fire ring, grill, tent pad. **Dump Station:** Yes. **Laundry:** No. **Pay Phone:** Yes. **Rest Rooms and Showers:** Rest rooms, no showers. **Fuel:** No. **Propane:** No. **Internal Roads:** Paved. **RV Service:** No. **Market:** 8 mi. in Cherokee. **Restaurant:** 8 mi. in Cherokee. **General Store:** 20 mi. in Waynesville. **Vending:** No. **Swimming Pool:** No. **Playground:** No. **Other:** Amphitheater, picnic areas, horse trails, interpretive trails. **Activities:** Hiking, fishing, horseback riding, canoeing, backcountry hiking, ranger programs (seasonal). **Nearby Attractions:** Pisgah National Forest, Eastern Cherokee Indian Reservation, Cataloochee Ski Area, Gatlinburg, Pigeon Forge, Dollywood, Asheville. **Additional Information:** Pigeon Forge Visitor Information, (865) 453-5700; Park Information, (865) 436-1200; Asheville Area Chamber of Commerce, (828) 258-6101.

Restrictions

Pets: On leash only. **Fires:** In fire rings only. **Alcoholic Beverages:** Allowed. **Vehicle Maximum Length:** 35 ft.

To Get There

From US Hwy 441, drive north to Newfound Gap Rd. Smokemont campground is on the right approximately 4 mi. off the highway.

CHEROKEE

Yogi in the Smokies

317 Galamore Bridge Rd., Cherokee, NC 28719. T: (828) 497-9151.

Beauty: ★★★★	Site Privacy: ★★★
Spaciousness: ★★★	Quiet: ★★★
Security: ★★★★	Cleanliness: ★★★
Insect Control: ★★★★	Facilities: ★★★

This Jellystone resort doesn't offer as much recreation as its Gatlinburg counterpart, but it is attractive and kid-oriented. Planned recreation in the summer and fall includes live bands, fishing contests, and costume parties. The playground and pool are aged, but adequate. The campground includes sites in two main areas, which hug a bend in the Raven Fork River. Sites are on the small side. Parking is on packed dirt, grass, and gravel—it's a bit messy. There are both pull-through and back-in sites. Most sites are nicely shaded. Our favorite sites, 114–134E, line the river. Other nice sites include 213–235, which have full hookups and are large and heavily wooded. Security is fair at Yogi's. There are no gates, but the park is very remote. Avoid Cherokee on summer and fall weekends, when hordes of automobiles create gridlock on Cherokee roads.

Basics

Operated By: Bruce & Sharon Daughters. **Open:** Mar.–Oct. **Site Assignment:** Reservations accepted, 2-day cancellation notice required for deposit refund. **Registration:** Office. **Fee:** RV $22–$31, primitive tent $20. **Parking:** On site.

Facilities

Number of RV Sites: 192. **Number of Tent-Only Sites:** 8. **Number of Multipurpose Sites:** 0. **Hookups:** Water, sewer, cable, electric (20, 30 amps). **Each Site:** Picnic table. **Dump Station:** Yes. **Laundry:** Yes. **Pay Phone:** Yes. **Rest Rooms and Showers:** Yes. **Fuel:** No. **Propane:** Yes. **Internal Roads:** Gravel. **RV Service:** No. **Market:** No. **Restaurant:** No. **General Store:** Yes. **Vending:** Yes. **Swimming Pool:** Yes. **Playground:** Yes. **Other:** Arcade. **Activities:** Fishing, tubing, horseshoes, theatre, hiking, mountain biking. **Nearby Attractions:** Great Smoky Mtn. National Park, Dollywood, Ghost Town in the Sky, Pigeon Forge, Mingo Falls, Museum of Cherokee Indians.

Restrictions

Pets: Yes. **Fires:** Fire rings. **Alcoholic Beverages:** Allowed. **Vehicle Maximum Length:** 46 ft.

To Get There

Take I-40 to Exit No. 27 onto Hwy. 74 West, then to Exit No. 74 onto Hwy. 441 North; 6.5 mi. north of Cherokee. Follow the signs.

DANBURY

Hanging Rock State Park

P.O. Box 278, Danbury 27016. T: (336) 593-8480; F: (336) 593-9166; www.rthcarolinaout-doors.com; ncs1220@interpath.com.

 ▲ ★★★★★

Beauty: ★★★★★	Site Privacy: ★★★★★
Spaciousness: ★★★★★	Quiet: ★★★★★
Security: ★★★★★	Cleanliness: ★★★★★
Insect Control: ★★★★	Facilities: ★★★★

Hanging Rock contains 18 miles of easy to strenuous hiking trails, may leading to picturesque waterfalls. There's also a 12-acre lake equipped with a swimming beach for sun-lovers and stocked with bass and bream for fishermen. At the north end of the park, a boat launch provides access to the Dan River for canoeing, tubing, or fishing for small mouth bass and catfish. The campground is laid out in two loops on a gentle mountain ridge. Campsites are lovely; most are extremely large and secluded. Mature trees shade the sites and dense foliage provides a natural barrier between neighbors. Although the park is very popular, the campground is quiet due to adequate spacing between sites. Sites have gravel back-in parking. We especially like sites 8 and 32 for RVs and sites 1 and 4 for tent campers. Security is excellent. Hanging Rock is extra remote and gated. Avoid this park on busy summer and fall weekends.

Basics

Operated By: NC State Parks. **Open:** All year except Christmas Eve & Christmas Day. **Site Assignment:** First come, first served. Pay w/ in-state check or cash. Check-out time is 3 p.m. **Registration:** At campsite; camp ranger will come by to register. **Fee:** $12–$18 per night. **Parking:** 2 vehicles per site.

Facilities

Number of Multipurpose Sites: 73. **Hookups:** None. **Each Site:** Picnic table, tent pad, fire ring, grill. **Dump Station:** No. **Laundry:** No. **Pay Phone:** Yes. **Rest Rooms and Showers:** Yes. **Fuel:** No. **Propane:** No. **Internal Roads:** Paved. **RV Service:** Winston-Salem. **Market:** In Danbury approx. 5 mi. northeast. **Restaurant:** In Danbury approx. 5 mi. northeast. **General Store:** In Danbury approx. 5 mi. northeast. **Vending:** Beverage & Snack from June 1–Labor Day. **Swimming Pool:** Swimming at park lake June 1–Labor Day, extra fee. **Playground:** No. **Other:** Group lodging available, trails. **Activities:** Hiking, rock climbing, picnicking, fishing, Natural & Cultural History Programs, Museum exhibits. **Nearby Attractions:** Diggs Gallery at Winton-Salem State University, Historic Bethabara Park, Old Salem. **Additional Information:** Stokes County EDC, (336) 983-8468.

Restrictions

Pets: Leash only, attended at all times by responsible adult. **Fires:** Fire ring only. **Alcoholic Beverages:** Not allowed. **Vehicle Maximum Length:** Call ahead for details. **Other:** Max 6 people per site, each site must have at least 1 adult (18 or older), all tent must be on tent pads, visitors out of the park by closing time.

To Get There

From Danbury, take Hwy. 889 going north, go approx. 4 mi. and turn left onto Hanging Rock Rd.

EMERALD ISLE

Holiday Trav-L-Park Resort

9102 Coast Guard Rd., Emerald Isle 28594. T: (252) 354-2250; F: (252) 354-3870; www.htpresort.com; htpresort@mail.clis.co.

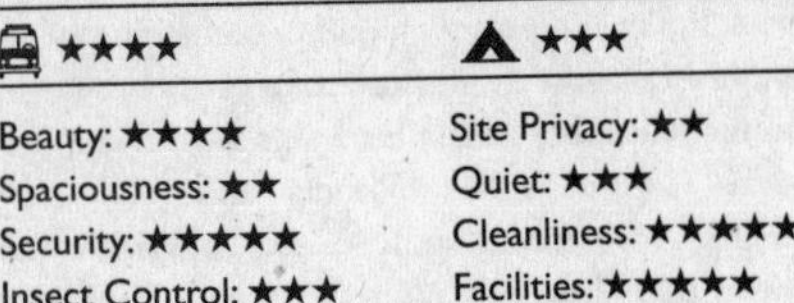

Beauty: ★★★★ Site Privacy: ★★
Spaciousness: ★★ Quiet: ★★★
Security: ★★★★★ Cleanliness: ★★★★★
Insect Control: ★★★ Facilities: ★★★★★

This attractive park is right on the Atlantic Ocean. Holiday Trav-L-Park has extremely nice pools, playgrounds, and other amenities, as well as planned activities in the summer. The most unique amenity is the park's gourmet food and wine shop. Nearby attractions include Fort Macon, a five-sided fort built between 1826 and 1834, and the historic town of Beaufort, including buildings dating back to 1709. The campground is laid out in five long rows of back-in and pull-through sites, terminating at the Atlantic Ocean. Sites in the back, near the ocean, have nice views of the dunes. Landscaping is very tidy, with shady trees in the front of the campground, near the store and pool. Sites are small, with grass parking. Choose your site based on desired location. Security is excellent. Holiday Trav-L-Park is located in an urban resort area, and is conscientious about camper safety. Visit in spring or fall for peace. Avoid the park on crowded summer weekends.

Basics

Operated By: Watson family. **Open:** Feb. 15–Dec. 5. **Site Assignment:** Reservations recommended, (252) 354-2250. No out-of-state checks allowed, MC,V accepted. If cancelled less than 7 days before the reserved check-in day, the deposit is nonrefundable. There is no check-in time, check-out time is 2 p.m. **Registration:** Check in station. **Fee:** Call ahead for details. **Parking:** 2 vehicles per RV site, 1vehicle per tent, overflow parking is available.

Facilities

Number of RV Sites: 375. **Number of Tent-Only Sites:** 30. **Number of Multipurpose Sites:** 0. **Hookups:** Tent sites have no hookups. 115 of the RV are seasonal, 19 of the RV sites have water, electric (20, 30, 50 amps), cable. The rest of the RV sites have full hookups. **Each Site:** Picnic table. **Dump Station:** Yes. **Laundry:** Yes. **Pay Phone:** Yes. **Rest Rooms and Showers:** Yes. **Fuel:** No. **Propane:** Yes. **Internal Roads:** Paved. **RV Service:** 2 mi. west in Cedarpoint. **Market:** 1 mi. **Restaurant:** 1 mi. **General Store:** 20 mi. north east in Morehead. **Vending:** Beverage & snack. **Swimming Pool:** Yes. **Playground:** Yes. **Other:** Rec. hall, no group lodging. **Activities:** Live entertainment, church service, Bible school, kid's cook-out, bingo, sandcastle competitions, arts & crafts, kite flying. **Nearby Attractions:** Lamb Amphitheater. **Additional Information:** Carteret County Tourism Development, (252) 726-8148.

Restrictions

Pets: Leash only. **Fires:** No open fires (bring your own grill). **Alcoholic Beverages:** Allowed. **Vehicle Maximum Length:** 45 ft. **Other:** No pets allowed in tenting area, call for more information, (252) 354-2250.

To Get There

Take Hwy. 58 going east through Emerald Isle. Go over the high-rise bridge and at the first stop light after the bridge take a right. The park will be on the left.

FLAT ROCK

Lakewood RV Resort

495 Ballenger Rd, Flat Rock 28731. T: (888) 819-4200; lakewood@brinet.com.

RV ★★★ Tent ★

Beauty: ★★★ Site Privacy: ★★
Spaciousness: ★★★ Quiet: ★★★
Security: ★★★ Cleanliness: ★★★★
Insect Control: ★★★★ Facilities: ★★★

Lakewood is just outside of Hendersonville, convenient to shopping and restaurants. Hendersonville is a good place to stay if you would like to tour Asheville and the mountain towns beyond Brevard. Many shops and buildings in historic downtown Hendersonville are on the National Register of Historic Places. The park is about 50 percent residential, and offers mid-sized campsites with gravel parking and concrete patios. Most sites are open, although a few sites contain young trees. There is little privacy. The campground is laid out in five blocks of back-in sites plus a few rows of pull-through sites. Sites 1–9 in section C are the flattest and most spacious. Security is fair—there is no gate at this small-town campground. To avoid crowds, visit Hendersonville during the week in the summer and autumn.

Basics

Operated By: Phil De Masso. **Open:** All year. **Site Assignment:** Reservations one week in advance. **Registration:** Office. **Fee:** RV, starting at $25, tent, starting at $20. **Parking:** At site.

Facilities

Number of RV Sites: 100. **Number of Tent-Only Sites:** Use field. **Number of Multipurpose Sites:** 0. **Hookups:** Electric (30, 100 amps). **Each Site:** Concrete pad for table. **Dump Station:** Yes. **Laundry:** Yes. **Pay Phone:** Yes. **Rest Rooms and Showers:** Yes. **Fuel:** No. **Propane:** Yes. **Internal Roads:** Paved. **RV Service:** On site. **Market:** on site. **Restaurant:** On site. **General Store:** On site. **Vending:** Inquire at campground. **Swimming Pool:** Yes. **Playground:** No. **Other:** TV lounge, pool table, club house. **Activities:** Shuffleboard, ping pong, horseshoes, fishing pond. **Nearby Attractions:** Inquire at campground.

Restrictions

Pets: Allowed. **Fires:** Allowed. **Alcoholic Beverages:** Only at picnic areas & lakeside. **Vehicle Maximum Length:** None.

To Get There

Take I-26 to Exit 22 (Upward Rd), Proceed 0.2 mi. to Ballenger Rd. and turn left. Entrance is 0.3 mi. on the right.

FRANKLIN

Country Woods

60 Country Woods Drive, Franklin 28734. T: (828) 524-4339; F: (828) 524-4339; www.kiz.com/countrywoods; cwoodsrv@dnet.net.

 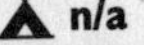 n/a

Beauty: ★★★★ Site Privacy: ★★★
Spaciousness: ★★★ Quiet: ★★★★
Security: ★★★★ Cleanliness: ★★★★★
Insect Control: ★★★★ Facilities: ★★★

The friendly owners of Country Woods operate an attractive and extremely tidy sites on a terraced mountainside. Sites are small, but picturesque. Sites are nicely wooded. Many have wooden decks or concrete patios. Parking is gravel. Most sites feature back-in parking, but there are a few pull-through sites. Our favorite sites are 18, a large pull-through, and 57, a picturesque wooded campsite in the back of the park. Many sites offer views of the surrounding Black Mountains. Though Country Woods' amenities aren't extensive, they are well maintained and inviting. Franklin is a lovely town, with numerous boutiques and fishing and tubing on the Little Tennessee River. Security is fine here—there are no gates, but Franklin is a very nice town. Avoid the mountains on summer and fall weekends. Instead, visit during the week.

Basics

Operated By: Darold & Marilyn Long. **Open:** Call ahead for details. **Site Assignment:** May cancel on day of arrival except during Oct. or July. **Registration:** Office. **Fee:** $20/day. **Parking:** 1 car at site, additional parking if necessary.

Facilities

Number of RV Sites: 72. **Number of Tent-Only Sites:** 0. **Number of Multipurpose Sites:** 0. **Hookups:** Water, 30 amps electric, sewer, cable. **Each Site:** Picnic table, fire ring. **Dump Station:** Yes. **Laundry:** Yes. **Pay Phone:** Yes. **Rest Rooms and Showers:** Yes. **Fuel:** No. **Propane:** No. **Internal Roads:** Gravel & paved. **RV Service:** 1.5 mi. northwest in Aberdeen. **Market:** 1.5 into city. **Restaurant:** 1.5 into city. **General Store:** 1.5 into city. **Vending:** No. **Swimming Pool:** No. **Playground:** No. **Other:** Gathering room, library, club house, waling trails. **Activities:** Horseshoes, park ket togethers. **Nearby Attractions:** Antique shops, gem mining, hiking rails, waterfalls, Scottish Tartan Museum, Granklin Gem Show, Wayah Bald, Great Smoky Mountain National Park, Blue Ridge Pkwy., the town of Cherokee, Harrah's Casino, Biltmore House, Smoky Mountain Train Ride.

Restrictions

Pets: Allowed. **Fires:** Fire rings only. **Alcoholic Beverages:** At site only. **Vehicle Maximum Length:** 40 ft. **Other:** Motorized bikes may be used for transportaion into & out of park only.

To Get There

Located on US 441/23, 2 mi. south of the intersection of 441/23 and Hwy. 64.

FRANKLIN

Standing Indian

90 Sloan Rd., Franklin 28734. T: (828) 524-6441; www.cs.unca.edu/nfsnc.

RV ★★★★ Tent ★★★★

Beauty: ★★★★★ Site Privacy: ★★★★
Spaciousness: ★★★★★ Quiet: ★★★★
Security: ★★★★ Cleanliness: ★★★★
Insect Control: ★★★★★ Facilities: ★★★

This beautiful campground is laid out in five loops, with sites offering varying levels of shade and privacy. Some sites are set in areas densely wooded by yellow birch and sugar maple, while others are flatter and more open. Almost all sites are very large. Most of the multipurpose sites have paved parking, while others, recommended for tent campers only, have gravel parking. Four sites offer pull-through parking. The rest are back-in style. RV campers should choose from sites 1–54. Tent campers should head for sites 55 –84. Recreation in the area is outstanding. Several hiking trails are accessible from the park, including one that connects with a portion of the Appalachian Trail. Folks also like to fish for native brook trout (rainbow and brown) in the Nantahala River and Kimsey Creek. For a real treat, visit in late May or June, when the rhododendrons are blooming. Security is fine at this remote campground.

Basics

Operated By: USDA Forest Service. **Open:** Call ahead for details. **Site Assignment:** First come, first served. **Registration:** Office. **Fee:** Call ahead for details. **Parking:** Yes.

Facilities

Number of RV Sites: 65. **Number of Tent-Only Sites:** 16. **Number of Multipurpose Sites:** 0. **Hookups:** None. **Each Site:** Picnic table, fire grate, lantern post, tent pad. **Dump Station:** No. **Laundry:** No. **Pay Phone:** Yes. **Rest Rooms and Showers:** Yes. **Fuel:** No. **Propane:** No. **Internal Roads:** Paved. **RV Service:** No. **Market:** No. **Restaurant:** No. **General Store:** Yes. **Vending:** No. **Swimming Pool:** No. **Playground:** No. **Activities:** Hiking, fishing, river swimming.

Restrictions

Pets: Allowed. **Fires:** Allowed. **Alcoholic Beverages:** Inquire at campground. **Vehicle Maximum Length:** Call ahead for details.

To Get There

From Franklin, drive on 64 West approx. 13 mi. to West Old Murphy Rd. Turn left and travel approx. 3 mi. to Standing Indian.

HENDERSON

Hibernia

269 Glass House Rd., Henderson 27356.
T: (252) 438-7791; F: (252) 438-7582; www.unc.edu/parkproject/kelahi; kerr.lake@ncmail.net.

RV: ★★★★★ Tent: ★★★★★

Beauty: ★★★★★ Site Privacy: ★★★★★
Spaciousness: ★★★★★ Quiet: ★★★★★
Security: ★★★★ Cleanliness: ★★★★★
Insect Control: ★★★ Facilities: ★★★

Hibernia is a gorgeous campground with numerous lakefront sites. Sites are huge, with your choice open sites or heavily wooded sites. Often the open sites provide stunning views of Kerr Lake, the banks of which are fortified with either concrete walls, rocks, or other materials to prevent erosion. Parking is on aged gravel, and the campground includes mostly back-in sites. For RVs we recommend Area 2, which has hookups and a newer washhouse. Other recommendations are amazingly lovely sites 43 and 44 in Area 1. Recreation at mammoth Kerr Lake revolves around lake swimming, sailing, boating, and fishing for crappie, channel catfish, and various bass species. There are limited foot paths for walkers and hikers. Hibernia is extremely remote, with gates locked at night, making security very good. Visit anytime except for summer holidays and weekends. Also avoid special-event weekends, such as the Governor's Cup Invitational Regatta and various bass tournaments.

Basics

Operated By: NC Division of Parks & Recreation. **Open:** All year except Christmas. **Site Assignment:** First come, first served; reservations can be made at (252) 438-7791. Cash & checks are accepted. If cancelled 2 weeks before expected arrival there is no penalty. Stay limit is 2 weeks. **Registration:** Main office at campground. **Fee:** Site w/ no hookups is $12 per night, $10 for senior citizens (62 years of age). $17 for sites w/ electric, $14 for senior citizens. **Parking:** 2 vehicle parking at each site.

Facilities

Number of Multipurpose Sites: 141. **Hookups:** Electric (30 amps). **Each Site:** Some have picnic table, fire ring, grill. **Dump Station:** Yes. **Laundry:** No. **Pay Phone:** Yes. **Rest Rooms and Showers:** Yes. **Fuel:** No. **Propane:** No. **Internal Roads:** Paved. **RV Service:** 15 mi. south in Henderson. **Market:** 15 mi. south in Henderson. **Restaurant:** 15 mi. south in Henderson. **General Store:** 2 mi. from park entrance in Henderson. **Vending:** Beverage only. **Swimming Pool:** No. **Playground:** Yes. **Other:** Group camping available, boat ramp, trails. **Activities:** Fishing, picnicking, boating, hiking, canoeing, natural & cultural history programs. **Nearby Attractions:** Steele Creek & Satterwhite Point. **Additional Information:** Vance County Tourism, (252) 438-5873.

Restrictions

Pets: Leash only. **Fires:** Designated areas only. **Alcoholic Beverages:** Not allowed. **Vehicle Maximum Length:** 40 ft.

To Get There

From I-85 take Exit 214 and get onto NC 39. Travel approx. 12.5 mi. north on NC 39 and turn right onto Hibernia Rd.

HIGHLANDS

Sassafras Gap

5920 Walhalla Road, Highlands 28741. T: (800) 815-2259; F: (828) 526-3032; www.kiz.com/sassafrasgap; sassa@direcpc.com.

RV: ★★★ Tent: ★★★

Beauty: ★★★ Site Privacy: ★★★
Spaciousness: ★★★ Quiet: ★★★★
Security: ★★★ Cleanliness: ★★★
Insect Control: ★★★★ Facilities: ★★★

This funky little campground is something of an anomaly in tony Highlands, a town known for its annual Chamber Music Festival. Down-home Sassafras Gap hosts live bluegrass and folk music events. Adventurous souls should consider a trip down the Chattooga Wild and Scenic River. The campground offers RV campsites laid out in eight rows descending a hillside. Most sites feature gravel pull-through parking and enjoy a little shade. RV sites at the top of the hill, including 19, 33, 34, 48, and 59, are the prettiest. There are two tent areas in the back of the campground, both of which are shady, secluded, and nice-looking. Although the bathrooms are notably spacious and clean, the landscaping is very untidy, with long grass and patchy gravel. Security is fair—there are no gates, but the campground is in the middle of nowhere. Visit during the week in summer and fall.

Basics

Operated By: Steve Potts. **Open:** Apr.–Oct. **Site Assignment:** $20 deposit or reserve w/ credit card; MC, V, D, AE, cash, check. Must cancel 5 days in advance for refund. **Registration:** In office. **Fee:** $15–$26. **Parking:** At site.

Facilities

Number of RV Sites: 77. **Number of Tent-Only Sites:** 21. **Number of Multipurpose Sites:** 0. **Hookups:** Water, sewer, electric (30, 50 amps), cable. **Each Site:** Tables, fire rings, trash pickup. **Dump Station:** No. **Laundry:** Yes. **Pay Phone:** Yes. **Rest Rooms and Showers:** Yes. **Fuel:** No. **Propane:** Yes. **Internal Roads:** Paved & gravel. **RV Service:** 4 mi. toward Highlands. **Market:** on site. **Restaurant:** 5 mi. toward Highlands. **General Store:** 5 mi. toward Highlands. **Vending:** Yes. **Swimming Pool:** No. **Playground:** Yes. **Activities:** 2 ponds & pavilion, gameroom, horseshoes. **Nearby Attractions:** Highland Playhouse, National Wild & Scenic Chattooga River, Highlands Botanical Gardens & Nature Center, whitewater rafting, Whiteside Mountain & Yellow Mountain, tubing, Dry Falls, canoeing, Whitewater Falls, kayaking, Glen Falls, fishing, Foothills Trail, horseback riding, Bartram Trail, golf.

Restrictions

Pets: Allowed. **Fires:** Fire rings only. **Alcoholic Beverages:** At site only. **Vehicle Maximum Length:** 45 ft.

To Get There

Located 5 mi. south of Highlands, near wild and scenic Chattooga River.

JACKSON SPRINGS

Travel Resorts of America

1059 Sycamore Ln., Jackson Springs, NC 27281. T: (910) 652-5559; F: (910) 652-2411; services@travelresorts.com.

RV: ★★★★ Tent: n/a

Beauty: ★★★★★ Site Privacy: ★★
Spaciousness: ★★★ Quiet: ★★★★★
Security: ★★★★ Cleanliness: ★★★★★
Insect Control: ★★★★ Facilities: ★★★★

Travel Resorts of America is a lovely flat campground situated in a stand of towering pine trees with pine straw ground cover. Picturesque Lake Sycamore is stocked with bass. Manicured landscaping adds to the natural beauty of the setting, and recreational amenities are excellent. This park is preferred over the Heritage for couples who seek solitude. It's also closer to most of the golf courses than the Heritage. The campground is laid out in rows of back-in sites, with large chunky gravel parking pads. Sites are average sized, with little privacy. The quietest sites, 1–12, are the furthest from Sycamore Lane and the closest to the bath house. Security is fine. There is no gate, but the neighborhood is spotless. Avoid this area during golf tournaments. For the best deals on greens fees and the least crowds, visit in the winter—but prepare for cold weather.

BASICS

Operated By: Travel Resorts of America. **Open:** All year. **Site Assignment:** Reservations required. **Registration:** Office. **Fee:** Call ahead for details. **Parking:** Yes.

FACILITIES

Number of RV Sites: 136. **Number of Tent-Only Sites:**. **Number of Multipurpose Sites:** 0. **Hookups:** Water, electric (30, 50 amps). **Each Site:** Water. **Dump Station:** Yes. **Laundry:** No. **Pay Phone:**. **Rest Rooms and Showers:** Yes. **Fuel:** Yes. **Propane:** Yes. **Internal Roads:** Paved & gravel. **RV Service:** Yes. **Market:** Nearby. **Restaurant:** Nearby. **General Store:** Yes. **Vending:** Inquire at campground. **Swimming Pool:** Yes. **Playground:** Yes. **Activities:** Boating, basketball, fishing. **Nearby Attractions:** Rockingham Speedway, Stoneybrook Steeplechase.

RESTRICTIONS

Pets: Allowed. **Fires:** Only in designated areas. **Alcoholic Beverages:** Inquire at campground. **Vehicle Maximum Length:** None.

TO GET THERE

From south US I-95, take Hwy. 501 north to Aberdeen, NC. Turn right onto Roseland Rd. Continue until it ends, turn right onto Sycamore Ln., 3 mi. to entrance.

LINVILLE FALLS

Linville Falls Campground

Mile Post 316.4, Linville 28646. T: (828) 298-0398.

RV ★★★★ | Tent ★★★★

Beauty: ★★★	Site Privacy: ★★★
Spaciousness: ★★★★	Quiet: ★★★
Security: ★★★★★	Cleanliness: ★★★★★
Insect Control: ★★★★★	Facilities: ★★★

Linville falls is an excellent choice for nature nuts. Nearby Linville Gorge Wilderness Area is beloved for its fantastic rock formations and dramatic waterfalls. Grandfather Mountain, a privately owned park that was designed by the United Nations as an International Biosphere Reserve, is about 15 miles north of the campground. Like other Blue Ridge Parkway campgrounds, Linville Falls offers separate tent and RV sites interspersed on two loops. Situated in a flat river valley, most sites are shaded by white pine and a variety of hardwoods. Parking is paved, back-in style. The nicest sites are on Loop A, next to picturesque Linville River. Security is good—there are no gates, but the campground is in a remote location. The Blue Ridge Parkway experiences outrageous traffic on summer and fall weekends. If you can't live without gorgeous fall foliage, tour the parkway mid-week.

BASICS

Operated By: National Park Service. **Open:** Call ahead for details. **Site Assignment:** First come, first served. **Registration:** Office. **Fee:** $12. **Parking:** Yes.

FACILITIES

Number of RV Sites: 20. **Number of Tent-Only Sites:** 50. **Number of Multipurpose Sites:** 0. **Hookups:** None. **Each Site:** Picnic table, fireplace. **Dump Station:** Yes. **Laundry:** No. **Pay Phone:** Yes. **Rest Rooms and Showers:** Yes. **Fuel:** No. **Propane:** No. **Internal Roads:** Paved. **RV Service:** No. **Market:** No. **Restaurant:** No. **General Store:** Yes. **Vending:** Inquire at campground. **Swimming Pool:** No. **Playground:** No. **Activities:** Hiking, fishing. **Nearby Attractions:** Linville Gorge, Linville Caverns, Gem Mountain.

RESTRICTIONS

Pets: Allowed. **Fires:** Allowed. **Alcoholic Beverages:** Inquire at campground. **Vehicle Maximum Length:** Call ahead for details.

TO GET THERE

Follow the Blueridge Pkwy. to mile post 316.4. Follow signs to campground.

MARION

Hidden Valley Campground and Waterpark

1210 Deacon Dr., Marion 28752. T: (828) 652-7208.

RV ★★★★ | Tent ★★★★

Beauty: ★★★★	Site Privacy: ★★★
Spaciousness: ★★★★	Quiet: ★★★
Security: ★★★★	Cleanliness: ★★★
Insect Control: ★★★★	Facilities: ★★★★

Hidden Valley is built into a gorgeous mountainside, leading down to a pond. The campground would be exceptionally beautiful, if not for obtrusive telephone lines and poor road conditions. The water park and playground are appreciated by children, and the park is convenient to the quaint towns of Black Mountain and Chimney Rock. Hidden Valley has uncommonly large campsites for a private campground. Some sites are totally open, including our favorite pull-through sites, B9–B13. Others are nicely shaded, including our favorite back-in sites, B1–B8. These back-in sites enjoy a pretty view across the valley. Tent sites T5–T8 are wooded and private. The rest of the tent sites should be avoided. Hidden Valley is extremely popular on summer and fall weekends. For fewer crowds, visit mid-week. The campground is only about three miles from I-40, but it has a rural feel. There are no gates, making security fair.

BASICS

Operated By: Private operator. **Open:** Apr. 1–Nov. 1. **Site Assignment:** Reservations accepted, w/ a nonrefundable deposit. **Registration:** Office. **Fee:** $18 Tent, $20–$22 RV. **Parking:** At site.

FACILITIES

Number of RV Sites: 62. **Number of Tent-Only Sites:** 9. **Number of Multipurpose Sites:** 0. **Hookups:** Water, sewer, electric (20, 30 amps). **Each Site:** Picnic table, grill on the tent sites. **Dump Station:** Yes. **Laundry:** Yes. **Pay Phone:** Yes. **Rest Rooms and Showers:** Yes. **Fuel:** No. **Propane:** No. **Internal Roads:** Gravel. **RV Service:** Nearby. **Market:** Nearby. **Restaurant:** Nearby. **General Store:** Yes. **Vending:** Yes. **Swimming Pool:** Yes. **Playground:** Yes. **Other:** Snack bar. **Activities:** Waterslide, mini-golf, paddle boats, game room, fishing, volleyball, basketball, horseshoes, shuffleboard. **Nearby Attractions:** Black Mountain, Chimney Rock.

RESTRICTIONS

Pets: Allowed. **Fires:** Fire rings only. **Alcoholic Beverages:** Not in public areas. **Vehicle Maximum Length:** None.

TO GET THERE

Take I-40 to Exit 86, then north on Hwy 226, follow the signs for 2.5 mi.

MOCKSVILLE

Lake Myers RV Resort

150 Fred Lanier Rd., Mocksville 27028. T: (336) 492-7736.

RV ★★★ | Tent ★★★

Beauty: ★★★★	Site Privacy: ★★
Spaciousness: ★★	Quiet: ★★★
Security: ★★★★	Cleanliness: ★★★
Insect Control: ★★★	Facilities: ★★

This attractive campground is set on gentle hills with lovely trees. Though the crowd is older and more residential on weekdays, Lake Myers is inundated by families on the weekends. Why not? Extensive recreation includes two 400-foot water boggans, two Olympic-sized pools, and numerous playgrounds throughout the park. Campsites are small and feel crowded when they're full. Most are shaded by gorgeous hardwoods. Ground cover is gravel. There isn't any grass or pine straw, just gravel. Most sites offer back-in parking, though there are some pull-through sites. Tent campers enjoy their own playground and washhouse, but tent sites are sandwiched between two busy roads. Mocksville is convenient to attractions in Winston-Salem and Lexington. Security is excellent at this rural park. The front gate is attended on weekends and closed at night.

BASICS

Operated By: Private operator. **Open:** Mar.–Nov. (Some sites are opened all year, ask about discounts.) **Site Assignment:** Deposit must be made within 1 week from date of reservation. Deposit will be returned if reservation is cancelled 1 week in advance. **Registration:** Office. **Fee:** $25–$27 per night (Nov.–Feb.). **Parking:** At site.

FACILITIES

Number of RV Sites: 425.**Hookups:** Electric (30 amps), sewer, cable (free), water. **Pay Phone:** Yes. **Rest Rooms and Showers:** Yes. **Fuel:** No. **Propane:** LP Gas. **Internal Roads:** Paved & gravel. **RV Service:** I-40 Exit 150 (15 min. from Lake Myers). **Market:** Nearby. **Restaurant:** Nearby. **General Store:** On site. **Vending:** Inquire at campground. **Swimming Pool:** Yes. **Playground:** Yes. **Other:** Sidewalk café, rec hall, recreation building, pool tables. **Activities:** Paddle boating, canoeing, firewood, fishing, skating, mini-golf, game room, horseshoes, shuffleboard. **Nearby Attractions:** Old Salem, R. J. Reynolds Tobacco Co., Joseph Schitz Brewery, Tanglewood Park.

RESTRICTIONS

Pets: Leash. **Fires:** Allowed. **Alcoholic Beverages:** Keep alcohol concealed. **Vehicle Maximum Length:** Call ahead for details. **Other:** Cars should not be used for transportation within the park. No lake swimming. No motor bikes.

TO GET THERE

Exit I-40 at US Hwy. 64 (Exit 168) (Mocksville Junction) and turn north.

MORGANTON

Steel Creek Park

7081 NC 181, Morganton 28655. T: (828) 433-5660.

RV ★★★★ Tent ★★★★

Beauty: ★★★★ Site Privacy: ★★
Spaciousness: ★★★ Quiet: ★★★★
Security: ★★★★ Cleanliness: ★★★★
Insect Control: ★★★★ Facilities: ★★★★

Steel Creek is a lovely campground situated in a flat mountain valley. Sites fan out from a huge grassy field, and many have lovely views of the surrounding southernmost portion of the Blue Ridge Mountains. Most sites are partially shady. RV sites generally have gravel parking, while tent and pop-up sites usually have grass parking. There are both pull-through and back-in sites. Sites are on the small side, but the setting is so open that we didn't feel penned in. Choose your site based on location and amenities. Families will want to camp closer to the beach, while couples may want to seek a quieter site away from the recreation. Steel Creek has very nice recreational facilities, especially for children. The Blue Ridge Parkway is about 15 miles north, and other tourist attractions are within 30 miles. There is no gate, but it's very remote. So, security is good.

BASICS

Operated By: The Loven family. **Open:** Apr. 1–Nov. 1. **Site Assignment:** First come, first served; reservations for groups only. **Registration:** Main building. **Fee:** $25 per night for up to 4 people, $5 for each additional person. **Parking:** On site.

FACILITIES

Number of RV Sites: 168. **Number of Tent-Only Sites:** 65. **Number of Multipurpose Sites:** 0. **Hookups:** Water, electric (30, 50 amps), sewer. **Each Site:** None. **Dump Station:** Yes. **Laundry:** Yes. **Pay Phone:** Yes. **Rest Rooms and Showers:** Yes. **Fuel:** No. **Propane:** Yes. **Internal Roads:** Paved. **RV Service:** Morganton. **Market:** Morganon. **Restaurant:** Morganton. **General Store:** Morganton. **Vending:** Yes. **Swimming Pool:** No. **Playground:** Yes. **Other:** Beach by creek w/ swimming area. **Activities:** Fishing, game room, horseshoes, mini-golf, waterslide, hiking. **Nearby Attractions:** Mt. Mitchell, Grandfather Mountain, Linville Falls, Linville Cavern, Table Rock.

RESTRICTIONS

Pets: Allowed. **Fires:** Allowed. **Alcoholic Beverages:** Not allowed. **Vehicle Maximum Length:** 45 ft.

TO GET THERE

13 mi. north of Morganton, south on 181 from Linville.

MURPHY

Hanging Dog

201 Woodland Dr., Murphy 28906. T: (828) 837-5152; www.cs.unca.edu/nfsnc.

RV ★★★★ Tent ★★★★

Beauty: ★★★★ Site Privacy: ★★★★
Spaciousness: ★★★★ Quiet: ★★★★
Security: ★★★★ Cleanliness: ★★★★
Insect Control: ★★★★ Facilities: ★★★

This attractive campground is laid out in four loops, with grass and gravel back-in parking. Site size is ample but not huge. Many sites offer plenty of shade, compliments of pine and various oak species. Privacy varies, with wooded sites at the end of loop A tending to be the most private. Our favorite sites are on loop B, which offers views of 6,120-acre Hiwassee Lake. The lake is known for catches including northern pike, bass, and musky. There are also trout streams in the area. Murphy, a charming town, is home to the worthwhile Cherokee County Historical Museum. Security is good at this extremely remote campground. Visit in late spring to enjoy the blooming rhododendrons. Or visit on weekdays in the fall for leaf peeping.

BASICS

Operated By: USDA Forest Service. **Open:** May–Oct. **Site Assignment:** First come, first served. **Registration:** Self-registration on site. **Fee:** $8. **Parking:** At site.

FACILITIES

Number of RV Sites: 60. **Number of Tent-Only Sites:** 9. **Number of Multipurpose Sites:** 0. **Hookups:** None. **Each Site:** Picnic table, fire ring, tent pad, lantern post. **Dump Station:** No. **Laundry:** No. **Pay Phone:** Yes. **Rest Rooms and Showers:** Yes. **Fuel:** No. **Propane:** No. **Internal Roads:** Paved. **RV Service:** No. **Market:** No. **Restaurant:** No. **General Store:** No. **Vending:** No. **Swimming Pool:** No. **Playground:** No. **Activities:** Boating, hiking, fishing. **Nearby Attractions:** Inquire at campground.

RESTRICTIONS

Pets: Allowed. **Fires:** In fire ring. **Alcoholic Beverages:** At site. **Vehicle Maximum Length:** Call ahead for details. **Other:** 14-day stay limit.

TO GET THERE

From Murphy, take Brown Rd. (NC 1326) northwest for 5 mi. Turn left at campground sign. The campground is straight ahead.

NEWPORT

Water's Edge RV Park

1463 Hwy. 24, Newport 28570. T: (252) 247-0494; F: (252) 247-0494; www.watersedge-rvpark.com; rvpark@mail.clis.com.

RV ★★★ Tent ★★

Beauty: ★★★ Site Privacy: ★★
Spaciousness: ★★ Quiet: ★★★★
Security: ★★★ Cleanliness: ★★★★
Insect Control: ★★ Facilities: ★★

Attractive Water's Edge is located in a suburban area just outside of Morehead City. The park lies along the Bogue Sound and maintains a fishing pier and a laid-back community atmosphere. The park is convenient to area beaches and other attractions. Take a day trip to the historic town of Beaufort, with buildings pre-dating the town's incorporation in 1723. The long, narrow campground consists of mainly back-in sites. Site size varies from small to average. Parking is on a messy mixture of gravel and grass, and shade and privacy vary from site to site. The shadiest sites are along the park boundaries, on both sides. But our favorite sites are in section C, and have views of Bogue sound. Long-term and short-term campers share the same areas. The land and landscaping, with marsh grasses and cattails, are gorgeous. Unfortunately, there are quite a few junky buildings in view. There are no gates, making security at Water's Edge fair. Visit in late spring or fall for peace and quiet.

BASICS

Operated By: Singleton Family. **Open:** All year. **Site Assignment:** Reservations recommended (252) 247-5709. MC,V,AE are accepted. There is no penalty for a cancellation more than 24 hrs. in advance. If cancelled within 24 hrs. of expected arrival date then the deposit is non refundable. Check-in time is 12 noon. Check-out time is 11 a.m. For tent sites the stay limit is 2 weeks. **Registration:** Main office. **Fee:** Full hookup per night is $25, water & electric hookup is $20 per night. The weekly rate is stay six nights & get the seventh night free. $250 monthly rate for RV site plus the bill for the water & electric hookup. **Parking:** 2 vehicles per site, overflow parking is available.

FACILITIES

Number of RV Sites: 72. **Number of Tent-Only Sites:** 14. **Number of Multipurpose Sites:** None. **Hookups:** RV sites have water, electric (20, 30 amps), sewer; tent sites have water & electric (20, 30 amps); some sites w/ no hookups. **Each Site:** Picnic table. **Dump Station:** No. **Laundry:** No. **Pay Phone:** No. **Rest Rooms and Showers:** Yes. **Fuel:** No. **Propane:** No. **Internal Roads:** Paved. **RV Service:** On call. **Market:** 1 mi. **Restaurant:** 3 mi. west in Newport. **General Store:**

approx. 3.5 mi. east in Newport. **Vending:** No. **Swimming Pool:** No. **Playground:** No. **Other:** Fishing pier, athletic field, no group lodging. **Activities:** Picnicking, boat rentals. **Nearby Attractions:** Maritime Museum, NC Aquarium, 19th cent. Fort Macon, Beaufort Historic Site, Blackbeard's stomping grounds. **Additional Information:** Carteret CountyTourism Development Bureau, (252) 726-8148.

RESTRICTIONS

Pets: Leash only. **Fires:** In designated area, not on site. **Alcoholic Beverages:** Allowed. **Vehicle Maximum Length:** None.

TO GET THERE

Go east on US 70 for 3 mi. after the city of Havelock. Go 3 stop lights and then turn right onto Hibbs Rd. Go 3 mi. and take a left onto Hwy. 24. Go 1 mi. and turn right into the entrance of the park.

ROARING GAP

Stone Mountain State Park

3042 Frank Parkway, Roaring Gap 28668.
T: (336) 957-8185; stonemtn@infoave.net.

RV ★★★★ Tent ★★★★

Beauty: ★★★★ Site Privacy: ★★★★
Spaciousness: ★★★★ Quiet: ★★★★
Security: ★★★★★ Cleanliness: ★★★★★
Insect Control: ★★★★ Facilities: ★★★★

Stone Mountain State Park is beloved by nature enthusiasts, though it offers a wide range of activities. For the adventurous, there's rock climbing on the park's namesake, a 600-foot gray granite inselberg. Mellower folks can reach the top of Stone Mountain by a short but strenuous hiking trail. Other park activities include trout fishing in mountain streams. The campground consists of two loops, with gravel parking. Sites are shaded by white pine, red ample, and various oak species. A thick understory provides privacy between most sites. Site size is moderate, but there is plenty of space between sites. For tent campers, we recommend sites on the first loop, which tend to be more wooded. For RV campers, we recommend sites 20, 26, and 27, on the second loop. Stone Mountain is extremely secure—it's remote and gates are locked at night. This park stays cool in late summer, making it a great mid-week summer destination.

BASICS

Operated By: State of North Carolina. **Open:** All year. **Site Assignment:** First come, first served Reservations for groups only. **Registration:** Office. **Fee:** $8–$12 per night. **Parking:** On site.

FACILITIES

Number of RV Sites: 37. **Number of Tent-Only Sites:** 6. **Number of Multipurpose Sites:** 0. **Hookups:** None. **Each Site:** Picnic table, grill, tent pad. **Dump Station:** Yes. **Laundry:** No. **Pay Phone:** Yes. **Rest Rooms and Showers:** Yes. **Fuel:** No. **Propane:** No. **Internal Roads:** Paved & gravel. **RV Service:** Yes. **Market:** Nearby. **Restaurant:** Nearby. **General Store:** Inquire at campground. **Vending:** Inquire at campground. **Swimming Pool:** No. **Playground:** Inquire at campground. **Other:** Waterfalls, mountain cultural exhibit, Hutchingson Homestead. **Activities:** Trout fishing, rock climbing, hiking.

RESTRICTIONS

Pets: Allowed. **Fires:** Allowed. **Alcoholic Beverages:** Inquire at campground. **Vehicle Maximum Length:** None.

TO GET THERE

From the south: Take US Hwy. 21 to SR 1002, go 4.5 mi. to John P. Frank Pkwy. From the west: Take NC 18 north and turn right on SR 1002, follow SR 1002 to the John P. Frank Pkwy.

RODANTHE

Cape Hatteras KOA Kampgound

Cape Hatteras National Seashore on Hwy. 12 Box 100, Rodanthe 27968. T: (252) 987-2307; F: (252) 987-2535; www.koa.com; capehkoa@pinn.net.

RV ★★★ Tent ★★★

Beauty: ★★★ Site Privacy: ★★
Spaciousness: ★★★ Quiet: ★★
Security: ★★★ Cleanliness: ★★★★
Insect Control: ★★★ Facilities: ★★★

KOA and nearby Camp Hatteras are comparable in most respects. The KOA has nicer washrooms, but Camp Hatteras has a nicer tent-only area. The flat campground is laid out in a giant grid, comprised of both back-in and pull-through sites. Sites are small, and there are no natural privacy barriers. There's also no shade. Although some sites are near the beach, tall dunes obscure views of the Atlantic Ocean. Since there is little resolution between sites, we recommend choosing a site based on proximity to the beach (back of the park), or proximity to pool (front of the park). Cape Hatteras KOA offers planned children's activities and nice recreational facilities. The small town of Rodanthe is adjacent to Pea Island National Wildlife Refuge, a birdwatcher's Mecca. Other popular outings include taking the ferry to Ocracoke Island. Security is fair—there are no gates, but Rodanthe is a safe little town. Don't visit on busy summer weekends.

BASICS

Operated By: KOA, Inc. **Open:** Mar. 1–Dec 1. **Site Assignment:** Reservations recommended (800) 562-5268. All major credit cards are accepted. If cancelled 24 hrs. in advance then there is no penalty. If cancelled after 4 p.m. of the day before expected arrival the penalty is no refund on the deposit. Check-in time is 1 p.m. Check-out time is 12 p.m. Out-of-state checks can be used to make reservations only. There is no stay limit. **Registration:** Main office. **Fee:** Call ahead for details. **Parking:** 2 vehicles at each site, overflow parking is available.

FACILITIES

Number of RV Sites: 324. **Number of Tent-Only Sites:** 36. **Number of Multipurpose Sites:** Some of the RV sites can be used as tent sites. **Hookups:** Water, electric (30, 50 amps), sewer (some). **Each Site:** Picnic table, some have shelters. **Dump Station:** Yes. **Laundry:** Yes. **Pay Phone:** Yes. **Rest Rooms and Showers:** Yes. **Fuel:** No. **Propane:** Yes. **Internal Roads:** Paved. **RV Service:** On call. **Market:** 17 mi. south in Avon. **Restaurant:** 1 mi. **General Store:** 40 mi. north in Kitty Hawk. **Vending:** Beverage only. **Swimming Pool:** Yes. **Playground:** Yes. **Other:** Fishing pier, bike rental, water wars, volleyball court, basketball court, group lodging, horseshoe game area. **Activities:** Picnicking, fishing, volleyball, & basketball. **Nearby Attractions:** Cape Hatteras Lighthouse, Wright Brothers Monument, Elizabethan Gardens, free ferry from Cape Hatteras to Ocracoke Island. **Additional Information:** Outer Banks Visitors Bureau, (252) 473-2138.

RESTRICTIONS

Pets: Leash only. **Fires:** Only below high tide line on the beach. **Alcoholic Beverages:** Allowed. **Vehicle Maximum Length:** None. **Other:** No golf carts allowed.

TO GET THERE

From Virginia Beach take I-64 to Hwy. 168 south. From Hwy. 168 turn onto 158 south. Go through Nagshead NC and turn onto Hwy. 12 going south. The park is 0.25 mi. down the road on the ocean side.

SOUTHMONT

High Rock Lake Marina and Campground

P.O. Box 815, Southmont 27351-0346. T: (336) 798-1196; F: (336) 798-2026; www.gocampingamerica.com/highroads/; highrock@gocampingamerica.com.

RV ★★★★ Tent ★★★★

Beauty: ★★★★★ Site Privacy: ★★★★
Spaciousness: ★★★ Quiet: ★★★
Security: ★★★★ Cleanliness: ★★★★
Insect Control: ★★★ Facilities: ★★★★

This attractive campground is situated on a peninsula on High Rock Lake. Most sites are rented on a seasonal/long term basis, but there are usually a few short-term sites available. Site size is ample, but not huge. Most sites are very shady, and there are often a few trees between sites. Parking is on gravel. There are both pull-through and back-in spaces, and sites are often misrepresented on the park map. Nice looking pull-through sites 77–82, are more likely to be available for short-term campers. Tent sites have a lovely view of the lake, but they are preposterously small. We don't recommend the tent sites. The campground offers boat dockage (fees apply), and other excellent amenities for anglers. Fishing in High Rock Lake is excellent, and usually not too crowded. Avoid this campground on summer holidays. Security is fine here—there are no gates, but the campground is rurally located.

BASICS

Operated By: Lynn & Stephany Farguhar, Owners. **Open:** All year. **Site Assignment:** Reservations reccomended, 2 week cancellation. **Registration:** Office. **Fee:** RV $22–$25 (daily), $154–$175 (weekly); tent $20 (daily), $125 (weekly). **Parking:** 1 vehicle per site, extra overflow area.

Facilities

Number of RV Sites: 101. **Number of Tent-Only Sites:** 5. **Number of Multipurpose Sites:** 0. **Hookups:** Water, electric (30, 50 amps). **Each Site:** Cable TV, trash pickup, picnic table, fire ring. **Dump Station:** Yes. **Laundry:** Yes. **Pay Phone:** Yes. **Rest Rooms and Showers:** Yes. **Fuel:** Yes. **Propane:** Yes. **Internal Roads:** Main paved, some gravel. **RV Service:** 7 mi., Lexington. **Market:** 7 mi. Lexington. **Restaurant:** 7 mi., Lexington. **General Store:** 7 mi., Lexington. **Vending:** Yes. **Swimming Pool:** Yes. **Playground:** Yes. **Other:** Snack bar, game room. **Activities:** Fishing pier, boat rental, waterskiing. **Nearby Attractions:** "RCR Promotions," Welcome Center, Nascar Racing, NC Zoo at Asheboro, Furniture Discovery Center, Furniture Capitol of the World. Lexington BBQ festival (October), Historic Old Salem, Southeast Old Thresher's Reunion (July), Carowinds, Emerald Pointe Water Park.

Restrictions

Pets: Allowed. **Fires:** Fire rings only. **Alcoholic Beverages:** Yes, only covered containers. **Vehicle Maximum Length:** 50 ft. **Other:** No bike riding after dark, no skateboards or rollerblades allowed. Disorderly behavior, profanity, any firearms (including liscensed concealed weapons), illegal drugs, fireworks, & intoxication are strictly prohibited. No swimming in the lake.

To Get There

From Salisbury take I-85 (US 52) 15 mi. to Exit 91. Exit onto SR 8. Head south on SR 8 for 8 mi.

SPRUCE PINE

Bear Den Campground

600 Bear Den Mountain Rd., Spruce Pine 28777. T: (828) 765-2888; F: (828) 765-2864; www.bear-den.com; bearden@M-Y.net.

RV ★★★★★ Tent ★★★★★

Beauty: ★★★★★	Site Privacy: ★★★★★
Spaciousness: ★★★★	Quiet: ★★★★★
Security: ★★★★★	Cleanliness: ★★★★★
Insect Control: ★★★★★	Facilities: ★★★★

Bear Den is fabulous. The campground is laid out in four areas nestled into a mountainside right off the Blue Ridge Parkway. Excellent amenities include five playgrounds and a picturesque swimming lake. There's also fishing in the creek bordering the park. Hikers enjoy easy access to miles of trails managed by the National Park Service and US Forest Service. Sites at Bear Den aren't huge, but most feel very private due to the confluence of natural vegetation and thoughtful landscaping; almost all sites are refreshingly wooded with greenery between sites. Parking is on pea gravel and there are back-in and pull-through sites. If your rig fits, go for a pull-through site, as they tend to be more private. Our favorite sites in areas A and B are those on the outside of the loops. In area D, sites 15 and 16 are huge. Security is fine. There are no gates, but the area is pretty remote. The mountain towns that dot the Blue Ridge Parkway in this area are uniformly quaint and worth exploring.

Basics

Operated By: Moody Family. **Open:** Apr.–Oct. **Site Assignment:** 1-night deposit for reservations; 90% of deposit is refundable if reservation cancelled 7 days in advance; V, MC, D, AE. **Registration:** In office. **Fee:** $27–$58. **Parking:** At site.

Facilities

Number of RV Sites: 44. **Number of Tent-Only Sites:** 100. **Number of Multipurpose Sites:** 0. **Hookups:** Water, sewer, electric (30 amps). **Each Site:** Water, electric, fire rings, picnic tables. **Dump Station:** Yes. **Laundry:** Yes. **Pay Phone:** Yes. **Rest Rooms and Showers:** Yes. **Fuel:** No. **Propane:** Yes. **Internal Roads:** Gravel & paved. **RV Service:** 15 mi. toward Spruce Pine. **Market:** on site. **Restaurant:** 15 mi. toward Spruce Pine. **General Store:** 15 mi. toward Spruce Pine. **Vending:** No. **Swimming Pool:** No. **Playground:** Yes. **Other:** Golf cart rentals, store, game room, fire wood, ATM, swimming lake, & nature trails. **Activities:** Pool table, basketball, volleyball, horseshoes, badminton, shuffleboard, ping pong, square dancing, Sunday church services, pinball, video games, canoe & paddleboat rentals. **Nearby Attractions:** Gemstone mining, mini golf, climbing wall, go carts, Mt. Mitchell, golf, Linville Caverns, Linville Gorge, Whitewater rafting, Blue Ridge Pkwy., Grandfather Mtn., Little Switzerland, Museum of NC, Fishing, Blowing Rock, Roan Mtn., Tweetsie Railroad.

Restrictions

Pets: Allowed. **Fires:** Fire rings only. **Alcoholic Beverages:** Not permitted. **Vehicle Maximum Length:** None.

To Get There

Going north from junction Hwy. 226, it is 6 mi. to mile post 324.8, Bear Den Mtn. Rd. Turn right. Going south from junction Hwy. 221, it is 5.3 mi. to Bear Den Overlook, milepost 323. Travel another 1.8 mi. to Bear Den Mtn. Rd. (mile post 324.8). Turn left.

STATESVILLE

Midway Campground

Rt. 4 Box 199 B, Statesville 28677. T: (888) 754-4809 (704) 546-7615; F: (704) 546-7615; www.kiz.com/midway; rljenkins@conninc.com.

RV ★★★ Tent ★★★

Beauty: ★★★★	Site Privacy: ★★★
Spaciousness: ★★★	Quiet: ★★★
Security: ★★★	Cleanliness: ★★★★
Insect Control: ★★★★	Facilities: ★★★

Midway is an attractive campground situated on a hillside sloping down to fishing pond teeming with catfish. Sites are on the small side, but nicely spaced. Most sites are shady, though privacy is not optimal. Parking is on gravel. Most parking pads are back-in, though there are a few very long pull-through sites that can accommodate big rigs. The prettiest sites, 19–24, enjoy views of the pond. The pool is large enough for lap swimmers, and recreation areas are also nicely appointed. Midway has no gates, and is close to I-40 in a rural area, making security fair. South of Statesville is mammoth Lake Norman, offering fishing and boating opportunities. Many buildings in downtown Statesville are on the National Register of Historic Places. For the nicest weather, visit Statesville in late spring or fall.

Basics

Operated By: Randy & Jocelyn Jenkins. **Open:** All year. **Site Assignment:** Reservations are suggested for holidays & weekends; deposit is based on length of stay; full refund is given on deposit only if cancelled at least 1 week ahead of time; Accepted methods of payment include MC, AE, V. **Registration:** In office. **Fee:** RV is $28–$33/day, tent is $25/day. **Parking:** Yes.

Facilities

Number of RV Sites: 60. **Number of Tent-Only Sites:** 13. **Number of Multipurpose Sites:** 0. **Hookups:** Water, sewer, electric (20, 30, 50 amps). **Each Site:** Picnic tables, fire rings. **Dump Station:** Yes. **Laundry:** Yes. **Pay Phone:** Yes. **Rest Rooms and Showers:** Yes. **Fuel:** No. **Propane:** Yes. **Internal Roads:** Paved & gravel. **RV Service:** Exit 170 on I-40. **Market:** On site. **Restaurant:** 7 mi. from town. **General Store:** 7 mi. from town. **Vending:** No. **Swimming Pool:** Yes. **Playground:** Yes. **Other:** Game room, ATM machine, modem connection. **Activities:** Basketball, badminton, horseshoes, mini-golf, volleyball, paddleboats, fishing lake, pavillion, Sunday church services. **Nearby Attractions:** Mall.

Restrictions

Pets: Yes. **Fires:** Fire rings only. **Alcoholic Beverages:** At site only. **Vehicle Maximum Length:** None.

To Get There

Heading east on I-40, take Exit 162. Turn right. Go 0.25 mi. and turn left on Camground Rd. 0.25 mi. to Campground. Heading west on I-40, take Exit 162. Turn left and go 0.5 mi. to Camground Rd. Turn left. Go 0.25 mi. to campground.

SWANNANOA

Asheville East KOA

P.O. Box 485, Swannanoa 28778. T: (800) KOA-5907; F: (704) 686-7758; www.koakampgrounds.com/where/nc/33116.htm.

RV ★★★★ Tent ★★★★

Beauty: ★★★★	Site Privacy: ★★★★
Spaciousness: ★★★★	Quiet: ★★★
Security: ★★★	Cleanliness: ★★★★
Insect Control: ★★★★	Facilities: ★★★★

The Asheville East KOA is laid out in numerous sections dissected by the Swannanoa River. There are also two ponds adding to the visual appeal of the property. Both the river and the ponds are open for trout fishing (no license required for the ponds). Though site size and privacy vary, most are slightly larger than average. Tree cover ranges from dense to totally open. Parking is on gravel, grass, or dirt, and all sites are back-in style. Our favorite RV sites are found in Section D—these are lakeside, with picturesque views of water lilies. Section G contains shady tent sites. Security is fair; the campground has no gates. Avoid this area on summer and autumn weekends. KOA is a good place to stay if you plan on touring the lovely city of Asheville as well as the wilderness areas east of Black Mountain. A day at the Biltmore Estate, America's largest privately-owned home, is worth inflated admissions prices.

Basics

Operated By: KOA. **Open:** All year. **Site Assignment:** Reservations recommended. Must cancel 7 days in advance during hohlidays & 2 days in advance during non-holidays to refund deposit. Requested campsites are not guaranteed. Deposit is 1-night rent or can be held w/ a credit card. **Registration:** Payment accepted is V, MC, local checks, travelers checks, or cash. **Fee:** RV site is $24–$28/day. **Parking:** 1 vehicle & camping unit per site. Additional vehicle parking is available.

Facilities

Number of RV Sites: 225. **Number of Tent-Only Sites:**. **Number of Multipurpose Sites:** 0. **Hookups:** Water, sewer, electric (20, 30, 50 amps), cable. **Each Site:** Water & electric. **Dump Station:** Yes. **Laundry:** Yes. **Pay Phone:** Yes. **Rest Rooms and Showers:** Yes. **Fuel:** No. **Propane:** Yes. **Internal Roads:** Gravel & dirt. **RV Service:** 10 mi. toward Asheville. **Market:** 2 mi. toward SwannaNoa. **Restaurant:** 10 mi. toward Ashville. **General Store:** 10 mi. toward Asheville. **Vending:** Yes. **Swimming Pool:** Yes. **Playground:** Yes. **Activities:** 2 fishing lakes, trout stream, game room, mini-golf, bicycle rentals, pavilion, basketball, horseshoes, boat rentlas, paddle boat rentals, ping pong, walking trail, firewood. **Nearby Attractions:** Maggie Valley, Ridgecrest/Montreat, River Rafting, Horseback Riding, WNC Nature Center.

Restrictions

Pets: Allowed. **Fires:** Fire rings only. **Alcoholic Beverages:** At site only. **Vehicle Maximum Length:** None.

To Get There

From I-40, take Exit 59. Go north for 1 block to signal (US 70). Turn right and drive tow miles.

TUCKASEGEE

Singing Waters Camping Resort

1006 Trout Creek Rd., Tuckasegee 28783.
T: (828) 293-5872; F: (828) 293-3325;
www.kiz.com/singingwaters; sngwtrs@dnet.net.

RV ★★★★ Tent ★★★★

Beauty: ★★★★ Site Privacy: ★★★
Spaciousness: ★★★ Quiet: ★★★★
Security: ★★★★ Cleanliness: ★★★★
Insect Control: ★★★★ Facilities: ★★★

This pretty campground is tucked into a wooded mountain valley, with sites alongside bubbling Trout Creek. With an elevation of 3,000 feet, Singing Waters stays cool, making it an excellent summertime destination—just avoid visiting on busy holidays. Their refreshing natural swimming pond is just the thing to escape summer heat. The campground consists of back-in sites beautifully shaded by mature white pine trees. Parking, on a mixture of pine bark mulch and pine straw, is luxurious. Sites are medium sized, and a little greenery provides privacy. The nicest sites, 28–32, are in the back of the campground along the creek. Two tent sites, 48 and 49, offer raised tent pads and covered picnic tables. More traditional tent camping sites are also available. Security is fine here; there are no gates but the park is off the beaten path. Halfway between Sylva and Cashiers, Singing Waters is in the heart of Pisgah National Forest.

Basics

Operated By: Cooper family. **Open:** Full hookups are open from Mar.–Dec. Partial hookups are open May–Oct. **Site Assignment:** Reservations recommended, (828) 293-5872. AE, MC, D are accepted. If cancelled within 7 days of the expected arrival date the deposit is nonrefundable. Check-in time is 2 p.m. Check-out time is 12 noon. **Registration:** Registration office. **Fee:** $28–$24 campsites, $26 for full hookups for 2 people. Each additional child (6–17 yrs. old) is $2 more. Each additional adult is $5 more. **Parking:** 2 vehicle parking at each site, overflow parking is available.

Facilities

Number of RV Sites: 42. **Number of Tent-Only Sites:** 21. **Number of Multipurpose Sites:** None. **Hookups:** Water, electric (20, 30, 50 amps), 42 sites w/ sewer, water & electric (20, 30, 50 amps). **Each Site:** Picnic table, fire ring, grill. **Dump Station:** No. **Laundry:** Yes. **Pay Phone:** Yes. **Rest Rooms and Showers:** Yes. **Fuel:** No. **Propane:** No. **Internal Roads:** Gravel. **RV Service:** On call. **Market:** 10 mi. south in Cashiers. **Restaurant:** 3 mi. south Cashiers. **General Store:** 17 mi. north in Sylva. **Vending:** Beverage. **Swimming Pool:** No (swimming is OK in pond). **Playground:** Yes. **Other:** Pond, basketball court, volleyball net, trails, rec room, pavilion, no group lodging. **Activities:** Hiking, basketball, volleyball, indoor games. **Nearby Attractions:** Blue Ridge Pkwy., Great Smoky Mountains National Park, Nantahala National Forest, Qualla-Cherokee Indian Reservation, Harrah's Cherokee Casino, Great Smoky Mountains Railway, Ghost Town in the Sky, Biltmore Estates, white-water rafting, golf, gem mining, boating & fishing, crafts & antique shops. **Additional Information:** Jackson County Chamber of Commerce, (828) 586-2155.

Restrictions

Pets: Leash only. **Fires:** Fire pit only. **Alcoholic Beverages:** At site only. **Vehicle Maximum Length:** 45 ft.

To Get There

On I-40 from Ashville take Exit 27 onto Smoky Mountain Expressway west. Take Exit 85 and go west. Take a left at the second light and go 17 mi. south on Hwy. 107 to sign for Park. Turn left onto Trout Creek Rd. Go 1 mi. east. The entrance is on the right.

WAKE FOREST

Holly Point State Recreational Area

13304 Creedmoor Rd., Wake Forest 27587.
T: (919) 676-1027; F: (919) 676-2954;
www.ncsparks.net; Falls.lake@ncmail.net.

RV ★★★★★ Tent ★★★★★

Beauty: ★★★★★ Site Privacy: ★★★★★
Spaciousness: ★★★★★ Quiet: ★★★★★
Security: ★★★★ Cleanliness: ★★★★
Insect Control: ★★★★ Facilities: ★★★

The gorgeous campsites at Holly Point are similar to those at Jordan Lake in terms of size and design. Campers can choose between ultra-private sites set in the woods, or more open sites with fantastic lake views. Sites are gargantuan, with plenty of space between neighbors. Most sites offer pull-through parking, though there are a few back-in spaces. Parking pads are gravel, and need some attention—most had grass growing in them. The prettiest sites are 166 (a huge, gorgeous pull-through), 121–126 (open sites with lake views), and 58, 59, 65, and 66 (on a peninsula, with gorgeous views). Fishing is excellent at Falls Lake. Artificial reefs and underwater fish shelters support bass, crappie, and catfish populations. For hikers, part of the North Carolina Mountains-to-Sea-Trail winds through the park. Though the park feels rural, it's in the Raleigh/Wake Forest suburbs. Security is fine. Gates are not attended during the day, but they are locked at night. Avoid the popular park on summer holidays and weekends.

Basics

Operated By: NC State Parks. **Open:** All year except Christmas Eve & Christmas Day. **Site Assignment:** Campers may choose their own site. Reservations have to be made 2 weeks in advance for a min. of a 7-night stay. Must give 2-week notice of cancellation. Cash or check payments are accepted. Max. stay is 2 weeks. **Registration:** During peak season at entrance station. Other times the ranger will come to the site. **Fee:** Non-hookup site is $12 per night. A site w/ hookups is $17 per night. Doubles range $24–$34 per night. **Parking:** 2 vehicles per site.

Facilities

Number of RV Sites: 87. **Number of Tent-Only Sites:** 62. **Number of Multipurpose Sites:** 7 double w/ electric & water, 2 double w/ water. **Hookups:** Water, electric (20, 30 amps). **Each Site:** Picnic table, fire ring, grill, lantern hook, tent pad. **Dump Station:** Yes. **Laundry:** No. **Pay Phone:** Yes. **Rest Rooms and Showers:** Yes. **Fuel:** No. **Propane:** No. **Internal Roads:** Paved. **RV Service:** Approx. 15 mi. south in Raleigh. **Market:** Approx. 6 mi. north in Wake Forest. **Restaurant:** Appox. 15 mi. south in Raleigh. **General Store:** Approx. 2 mi. north in Wake Forest. **Vending:** No. **Swimming Pool:** No. **Playground:** Yes. **Other:** Group camping, boat ramp, trails. **Activities:** Boating, fishing, hiking. **Nearby Attractions:** Diggs Gallery at Winston-Salem State University, Historic Bethabara Park, Museum of Anthropology, Old Salem. **Additional Information:** Greater Raleigh CVB, (919) 834-2887.

Restrictions

Pets: Leash only. **Fires:** Designated areas only. **Alcoholic Beverages:** Not allowed. **Vehicle Maximum Length:** 40 ft.

To Get There

From Hwy. 98 turn onto New Light Rd. and go south. Follow the signs.

WAVES

Camp Hatteras

P.O. Box 10, Waves 27968. T: (252) 987-2777; F: (252) 987 2733; www.camphatteras.com; camphatteras7@cs.com.

RV ★★★ Tent ★★★

Beauty: ★★★ | Site Privacy: ★★
Spaciousness: ★★ | Quiet: ★★
Security: ★★★★ | Cleanliness: ★★★★
Insect Control: ★★★ | Facilities: ★★★★

Camp Hatteras is situated on a narrow piece of Hatteras Island and maintains two main camping areas along Hwy. 12, one on each side of the road. The largest area is on the same side as the pool and office, and includes some sites near the Atlantic Ocean. Across the highway, a smaller section includes tent-only sites with pretty views of Pamlico Sound. The recreation and facilities at Camp Hatteras are very nice. Unfortunately, Camp Hatteras offers miserably small campsites, situated in a series of loops. Sites feature paved, back-in parking. There is no shade. Views of the ocean are obscured by dunes. Families should choose their site based on proximity to facilities and the beach. Sites along the perimeter of the park are likely to be a little quieter. Security is very good. The campground is gated and attended at all times. Avoid Hatteras Island on summer holidays and weekends, when masses of people flock here.

Basics

Operated By: Jett Ferebee. **Open:** All year. **Site Assignment:** Reservations are recommended, (252) 987-2777. MC, AE, D, V are accepted. There in no penalty for cancellation a week in adavance. If cancelled within a week of expected arrival day then the deposit is nonrefundable. Check-in & check-out time is 12 noon. **Registration:** Guardhouse. **Fee:** Winter rates are $29.95 per night for full hookups, $24.95 for tent. Summer rates are $55.95 per night for full hookups, 32.95 per night for tent sites. **Parking:** 2 vehicle at site, overflow parking is available.

Facilities

Number of RV Sites: 300. **Number of Tent-Only Sites:** 70. **Number of Multipurpose Sites:** None. **Hookups:** RV sites have cable, sewer, electric (30, 50 amps), water; tent sites have water, electric (30, 50 amps); 60 sites w/ no hookups. **Each Site:** Picnic tables, pads for RV sites. **Dump Station:** No. **Laundry:** Yes. **Pay Phone:** Yes. **Rest Rooms and Showers:** Yes. **Fuel:** No. **Propane:** No. **Internal Roads:** Paved. **RV Service:** On call. **Market:** 18 mi. south in Avon. **Restaurant:** 1 mi. **General Store:** K-Mart 32 mi. north in Kill Devil Hills. **Vending:** Beverage & snack. **Swimming Pool:** Yes. **Playground:** Yes. **Other:** Marina Area, boat ramp (small boats), mini-golf course, arcade. **Activities:** Golfing, wind surfing, sailing, shuffleboard, tennis, arcade games, recreational activities. **Nearby Attractions:** Elizabethan Gardens, Lost colony Drama, Cape Hatteras Lighthouse, Pea Island National Refuge, NC Aquarium, Wright Brothers Memorial. **Additional Information:** Outer Banks Visitors Bureau, (252) 473-2138.

Restrictions

Pets: Leash only. **Fires:** On beach only. **Alcoholic Beverages:** At sites only. **Vehicle Maximum Length:** 45 ft. **Other:** Family-oriented park.

To Get There

From Virginia beach take Rte. 168 south to Rte. 158 East. Exit onto Rte. 12 South. Turn left into park

WHISPERING PINES

The Heritage

Sadler Family, The Heritage 28387. T: (910) 949-3433; F: (910) 949-5538; www.theheritagenc.com.

RV ★★★★ Tent ★★★★

Beauty: ★★★★★ | Site Privacy: ★★★★
Spaciousness: ★★★★ | Quiet: ★★★★
Security: ★★★★ | Cleanliness: ★★★★
Insect Control: ★★★ | Facilities: ★★★★

The owners of the Heritage are nice folks. Small and inviting, this campground is preferable to nearby Travel Resorts of America if you're traveling with children. The picturesque lake is outfitted with a fun swimming beach and stocked with game fish. Although the park is in a rural location, the golf courses of Pinehurst and its environs are a short drive away. The campground is laid out in five long rows, including both pull-through and back-in sites. Parking is on packed sand and pine straw. Lovely tree cover includes tall southern pines, dogwood, and various oak species. Privacy is good, with a little foliage between most sites. Sites are on the large side of average. Sites 39 and 40 are excellent—secluded and lakefront. Try not to visit the Heritage during a major golf tournament. Security is fine—there are no gates, but the driveway leading to the campground is about a mile long.

Basics

Operated By: Lee Sadler. **Open:** All year. **Site Assignment:** Reservations accepted. **Registration:** Office. **Fee:** Call ahead for details. **Parking:** At ofice.

Facilities

Number of RV Sites: 56. **Number of Tent-Only Sites:**. **Number of Multipurpose Sites:** 0. **Hookups:** Water, electric (30, 50 amps). **Each Site:** Water, electric, fire rings. **Dump Station:** Yes. **Laundry:** Dryer only. **Pay Phone:** In office. **Rest Rooms and Showers:** Yes. **Fuel:** Nearby. **Propane:** Nearby. **Internal Roads:** Gravel. **RV Service:** Nearby. **Market:** Nearby. **Restaurant:** Nearby. **General Store:** Nearby. **Vending:** Yes. **Swimming Pool:** No. **Playground:** Yes. **Other:** Beach by lake w/ swimming area. **Activities:** Fishing, hiking, boating, horseshoes, volleyball, croquet, shuffleboard, basketball, petting farm.

Restrictions

Pets: Yes. **Fires:** In fire ring. **Alcoholic Beverages:** Not in public areas. **Vehicle Maximum Length:** None. **Other:** Children must be attended at all times; check out is at 2 p.m.

To Get There

From Raleigh: Take US Hwy. 1 to Vass, turn right at first stoplight onto Union Church Rd., go 4 mi. and turn onto Heritage Farm Rd., go 1 mi. and turn left into The Heritage. From Southern Pines and Rockingham: Take US Hwy. 1 to Vass, turn left onto Carthage Rd., go 3.5 mi. and turn right onto Heritage Farms Rd., go 0.5 mi. and turn right into The Heritage.

WILKESBORO

Bandits Roost Park, W. Kerr Scott Reservoir

P.O. Box 182, Wilkesboro 28697-0182. T: (336) 921-3390; F: (336) 931-2330; www.saw.usace.army.mil; jory.triplett@usace.army.mil.

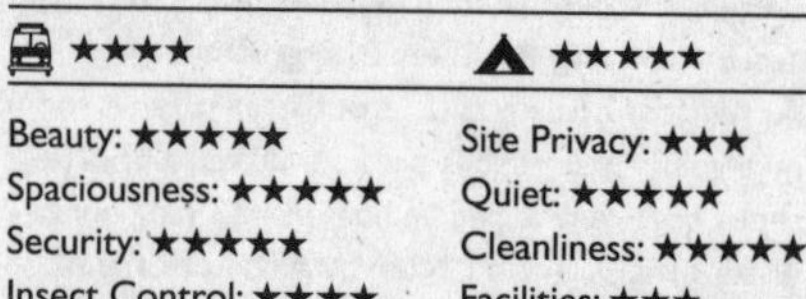

RV ★★★★ Tent ★★★★★

Beauty: ★★★★★ | Site Privacy: ★★★
Spaciousness: ★★★★★ | Quiet: ★★★★★
Security: ★★★★★ | Cleanliness: ★★★★★
Insect Control: ★★★★ | Facilities: ★★★

This gorgeous campground features an amazing tent area. Tent campers are treated to stunning views of W. Kerr Scott Reservoir from huge secluded sites. RV campers have good choices too: there are delightfully secluded sites on Loop B, surrounded by white pine, Virginia pine, and oak trees, or choose an open site with a fabulous view of the lake. We like stunning pull-through sites 24–28, which are situated on a peninsula. Sites 32–35 are also very nice. All sites have gravel parking, with pea gravel picnic areas. Though site size varies, most are large. Bandits Roost is extremely remote, and is gated and guarded, making security outstanding. This area experiences mild summers, making it a good destination in spring, summer, and fall. Just avoid visiting on holiday weekends. Near Bandits Roost are day-use areas and the Skyline Marina, which offers boat launches and other fishing facilities. The reservoir is stocked with crappie, bluegill, catfish, and largemouth and striped hybrid bass.

Basics

Operated By: US Army Corps of Engineers. **Open:** Apr. 1–Oct. 31. **Site Assignment:** 60% of the site can be reserved (877) 444-6777, MC, V are accepted; the other 40% are first come first served. If cancelled the fee is $10 plus the first nights fee.

Check-in time is 4 p.m.The check-out time is 3 p.m. There is a 14-day stay limit. **Registration:** Entrance station. **Fee:** $16 per night for a RV site, $12 for a tent site; $8 & $6 w/ a Golden Age or Golden Access card. **Parking:** 2 vehicle parking at each site, overflow parking is available.

FACILITIES

Number of RV Sites: 42. **Number of Tent-Only Sites:** 42. **Number of Multipurpose Sites:** 0. **Hookups:** Water, electric (30 amps) at RV site, tent sites have no hookups. **Each Site:** Picnic table, fire ring, tent pad, lantern hook. **Dump Station:** Yes. **Laundry:** No. **Pay Phone:** Yes. **Rest Rooms and Showers:** Yes. **Fuel:** No. **Propane:** No. **Internal Roads:** Paved. **RV Service:** 6 mi. north in Wilkesboro. **Market:** 6 mi. south in Wilkesboro. **Restaurant:** 6 mi. south in Wilkesboro. **General Store:** 5 mi. south in Wilkesboro. **Vending:** No. **Swimming Pool:** No. **Playground:** Yes. **Other:** Boating ramp, trails, group lodging. **Activities:** Picnicking, hiking, fishing, basketball, activities in the amphitheater. **Nearby Attractions:** Blue Ridge Pkwy., river rafting. **Additional Information:** Wilkes Chamber of Commerce.

RESTRICTIONS

Pets: Leash only. **Fires:** Fire ring only. **Alcoholic Beverages:** Not allowed. **Vehicle Maximum Length:** No limit. **Other:** Fishing is state regulated.

TO GET THERE

From I-77, exit onto 421 north, then exit onto Hwy. 268 going west, the park is 6 mi. on the right.

WILKESBORO

Doughton Park Campground

45356 Blue Ridge Parkway 28644. T: (336) 372-4499; www.blueridgeparkway.org.

RV ★★★★ Tent ★★★★

Beauty: ★★★★	Site Privacy: ★★★
Spaciousness: ★★★	Quiet: ★★★
Security: ★★★★	Cleanliness: ★★★★★
Insect Control: ★★★★★	Facilities: ★★★

Doughton Park is the largest recreation area on the Blue Ridge Parkway, and offers plenty of mileage for hikers in the summer and cross-country skiers in the winter. We like the lodge's restaurant for a break from campsite cooking. Nearby, Stone Mountain State Park offers numerous rock climbing routes to the top of the park's namesake. The campground at Doughton is separated into six loops, some for RV campers, others for tent campers. There are both heavily wooded and more open sites, so take your pick. Sites are average sized, with varying levels of privacy. Tent campers seeking private sites should go for walk-in sites 23–33. RV campers looking for solitude should head to the back of the campground. Though there are no gates, security is excellent at this isolated campground. Even though this is a less-trafficked part of the Blue Ridge Parkway, it's best to visit mid-week during summer and fall.

BASICS

Operated By: National Park Service. **Open:** Call ahead for details. **Site Assignment:** First come, first served. **Registration:** Office. **Fee:** Call ahead for details. **Parking:** Yes.

FACILITIES

Number of RV Sites: 25. **Number of Tent-Only Sites:** 110. **Number of Multipurpose Sites:** 0. **Hookups:** None. **Each Site:** Picnic table, fireplace. **Dump Station:** Yes. **Laundry:** No. **Pay Phone:** Yes. **Rest Rooms and Showers:** Yes. **Fuel:** Yes. **Propane:** No. **Internal Roads:** Paved. **RV Service:** No. **Market:** No. **Restaurant:** Yes. **General Store:** Yes. **Vending:** Inquire at campground. **Swimming Pool:** No. **Playground:** No. **Activities:** Hiking, fishing. **Nearby Attractions:** Cumberland Knob, Brinegar Cabin.

RESTRICTIONS

Pets: Allowed. **Fires:** Allowed. **Alcoholic Beverages:** Inquire at campground. **Vehicle Maximum Length:** Call ahead for details.

TO GET THERE

From intersection of US 21 and Blue Ridge Pkwy., drive south to mile post 239, or from intersection of NC 18 and Blue Ridge Pkwy., drive north to mile post 239.

WILLIAMSTON

Green Acres Camping Resort

1679 Green Acres Rd., Williamston 27892. T: (252) 792-3939; F: (252) 792-3939; www. martincounty nc.com/mc/greeneacres; bgreene@coastalnet.com.

RV ★★★ Tent n/a

Beauty: ★★★★	Site Privacy: ★★
Spaciousness: ★★★	Quiet: ★★★
Security: ★★★	Cleanliness: ★★★★
Insect Control: ★★★	Facilities: ★★★★

It's a good thing there's plenty to do here—the area around Williamston is completely agricultural. Activities at Green Acres include par-3 golf and fishing in a pretty pond stocked with bream and catfish. Green Acres also offers planned activities. The campground is arranged in two areas. Three rows of sites hug the pond. Sites 1–21 line the pond, and are the most level and picturesque in the park. On the other side of the park, seven rows of sites fan out from the office and other buildings. Looking for shade and quiet? Head for sites 87, 100, 116, 136, and 149. There are both back-in and pull-through sites with packed sand, pine straw, and grass parking. Sites are on the small side of average. Most are partially shady, but none are secluded. Avoid Green Acres on busy summer weekends and holidays; for peace and quiet, plan a mid-week visit. Security is fine at this extremely remote campground.

BASICS

Operated By: The Greene family. **Open:** All year. **Site Assignment:** Reservations are recommended, (888) 792-3939. MC, V, D are accepted. No penalty if cancelled 24 hrs. or more before expected arrival date. If cancelled within the 24 hrs. of the expected arrival date the deposit is nonrefundable. Check-in & check-out time is 2 p.m. **Registration:** Entrance office. **Fee:** $18–$22. **Parking:** 2 vehicle parking at each site, overflow parking is available.

FACILITIES

Number of RV Sites: 100. **Number of Tent-Only Sites:** 75. **Number of Multipurpose Sites:** all. **Hookups:** Water, electric (30 amps), sewer (at 100 sites). **Each Site:** Picnic table, fire ring. **Dump Station:** Yes. **Laundry:** Yes. **Pay Phone:** Yes. **Rest Rooms and Showers:** Yes. **Fuel:** No. **Propane:** Yes. **Internal Roads:** Gravel & dirt. **RV Service:** 25 mi. south in Washington. **Market:** 5 mi. north in Williamston. **Restaurant:** 5 mi. north in Williamston. **General Store:** 5 mi. north in Williamston. **Vending:** Beverage & snack. **Swimming Pool:** Yes. **Playground:** Yes. **Other: Other:** Game room, club house, amphitheater, tennis court, volleyball net, mini & 3-par golf course, no group lodging, live entertainment, church services. **Activities:** Horseshoes, golf, tennis badmitten, bingo, volleyball boat rental. **Nearby Attractions:** The Outer Banks. **Additional Information:** Martin County T&TA, (252) 792-6605.

RESTRICTIONS

Pets: Leash only. **Fires:** Must be contained. **Alcoholic Beverages:** Yes, at sites only. **Vehicle Maximum Length:** 40 ft.

TO GET THERE

US 64 east of Raleigh take Exit 514 onto US 17. Go 4.2 mi. south and turn right onto Roger's Elementary School Rd. going west and travel 1 mi.

North Dakota

Although generally considered a Plains state, North Dakota offers a varied terrain loaded with unique opportunities for prospective campers to take advantage of the outdoors. After all, camping is said to be the most popular recreational activity within the state! In addition to its flat, rolling landscape, North Dakota has **four state forests** that are ideal habitats for moose and deer. The state is rich in wildlife and contains over **60 wildlife refuges,** more than any other state. Animals native to the state range from wild horses, sheep, bison, white-tailed deer, and eagles

North Dakota is divided into distinct geological areas: The Missouri Plateau, The Red River Valley, and the Drift Prairie. The Missouri Plateau is sculpted with colorful canyons, gorges, ravines, bluffs and buttes, while the Red River Valley and Drift Prairie serve as fertile farmlands. Added to the geological mix are North Dakota's numerous state parks and forests. Most of North Dakota's 18 state parks have camping and picnicking facilities. **Theodore Roosevelt National Park** is located in northwestern North Dakota and is one of six national parks found in the state

North Dakota is also filled with rivers and lakes, 171 to be exact. The major rivers are the Missouri, which flows south into the Mississippi, and the Red, which forms the border between North Dakota and Minnesota. Consequently, there are countless opportunities for fishing, boating, and waterfowl gazing. It is said that more ducks reproduce in North Dakota than anywhere in the nation.

The state's largest city is Fargo, which offers many of the modern conveniences while maintaining its rustic, western charm. Other prominent cities include **Bismark,** the capital, **Grand Forks,** home of the **University of North Dakota,** and **Pembina,** home of the newest state museum.

North Dakota is heaven on earth for lovers of the outdoors and is one of the most diverse wildlife areas in the country. In terms of camping, the state's only drawback is its winters, which are cold and long, to say the least! However, it is the ideal spot for winter activities such as snowmobiling, skiing, fishing, sledding, and skating.

The following facility features 20 or fewer sites:

Sportsmen's Centennial Park, Garrison

Campground Profiles

ARVILLA

Turtle River State Park

3084 Park Ave., Arvilla 58214. T: (701) 594-4445; F: (701) 594-2556; www.ndparks.com; trsp@stste.nd.us.

RV ★★★ Tent ★★★

Beauty: ★★★	Site Privacy: ★★★
Spaciousness: ★★★	Quiet: ★★★★
Security: ★★★★	Cleanliness: ★★★
Insect Control: ★★	Facilities: ★★

In the eastern part of the state, not far from Grand Forks, campers can find a nice mix of river recreation and mountain fun. Typical of nature-oriented camping in this climate, the time of year absolutely defines the vacation, with cross-country skiing in winter and water fun in the summer (mountain bikers ride whenever they will). This is a family place, and kids can even borrow fishing gear from the park office to try their luck in the rainbow trout–stocked Turtle River. The campground is fairly attractive, with average-sized back-in sites and varying privacy. The facilities are nothing special, but are totally adequate for both RV and tent campers (although facilities are limited during the off-season). We recommend this campground for families.

Basics

Operated By: The North Dakota Parks & Recreation Dept. **Open:** Year round, but the water is off Oct.–May in the campground. **Site Assignment:** By reservation in the summer, first come Oct.–Apr. **Registration:** At the entrance gate. **Fee:** $7 w/ no hookup, $12 w/ electric plus a $4 entrance fee per vehicle or annual park pass. **Parking:** At site.

Facilities

Number of Multipurpose Sites: 125. **Hookups:** Electric (30 amps), water. **Each Site:** Picnic table, grated fire pits. **Dump Station:** Yes. **Laundry:** No. **Pay Phone:** Yes. **Rest Rooms and Showers:** Yes. **Fuel:** No. **Propane:** No. **Internal Roads:** Paved. **RV Service:** 22 mi. in Grand Forks. **Market:** In Arvilla. **Restaurant:** In Arvilla or Grand Forks. **General Store:** Yes. **Vending:** Yes. **Swimming Pool:** No. **Playground:** Yes, several. **Other:** Camp Store, paved nature trails, 6 cabins, picnic shelters, 6 mi. of groomed cross-country ski trails. **Activities:** Hiking, fishing (rainbow trout), biking, sledding, cross-country skiing, wildlife viewing, special park programs. **Nearby Attractions:** Grand Forks 22 mi. east, golf. **Additional Information:** ND Parks & Recreation Dept., (701) 328-5357.

Restrictions

Pets: On leash. **Fires:** In fire pits or grills only; fires may be restricted due to weather conditions; please ask management before starting any open fires.

Alcoholic Beverages: Yes. **Vehicle Maximum Length:** None.

To Get There

22 mi. west of Grand Forks directly off of Hwy. 2; there are excellent signs.

BISMARK

Bismark KOA

3720 Centennial Rd., Bismark 58501. T: (701) 222-2662; www.koa.com; bismkoa@aol.com.

RV ★★★★★ Tent ★★★★★

Beauty: ★★★★★ Site Privacy: ★★★★★
Spaciousness: ★★★★★ Quiet: ★★★★
Security: ★★★★ Cleanliness: ★★★★
Insect Control: ★★★ Facilities: ★★★★

Located just ten minutes from the state capitol, the Heritage Center, and the museums and art galleries of Bismarck, this KOA offers a comfortable camping experience. The 20-acre campground is spacious, and a nicely wooded area provides both site privacy and relaxing shade for activity wearied campers. Arranged in rows, most sites offer proximity to some campground amenity. Sites 1–10 border the playing fields but are close to nearby Centennial Road. Though they are closest to the frequented dog walk area, sites 71–78 are on the perimeter of the campground, farthest from the access road, and offer one of the only views of land without campers. Sites 100–115 offer a similar experience except that the tent campground occupies the adjacent "wilderness." With relatively mild summer temperatures, Bismarck is a nice family destination. The city itself provides a busy schedule of summertime activities, including a softball tournament, rodeo, United Tribes International Pow-Wow, and Folkfest. Depending on whether or not you plan to participate in the festivities or avoid the crowds, be sure to check dates for events before making plans to camp.

Basics

Operated By: Don & Pam Mueller. **Open:** May–Oct. **Site Assignment:** By reservation. **Registration:** In general store. **Fee:** Tent $15, RV $17–$20 per 2 people, $3. extra people, under 6 stay free. **Parking:** Limited.

Facilities

Number of RV-Only Sites: 80. **Number of Tent-Only Sites:** 34. **Number of Multipurpose Sites:** 0. **Hookups:** Electric (20, 30, 50 amps), water, sewer. **Each Site:** Picnic tables. **Dump Station:** Yes. **Laundry:** Yes. **Pay Phone:** Yes. **Rest Rooms and Showers:** Yes. **Fuel:** No, in town. **Propane:** No, in town. **Internal Roads:** Gravel. **RV Service:** In town. **Market:** In town. **Restaurant:** In town. **General Store:** Yes. **Vending:** Yes. **Swimming Pool:** Yes. **Playground:** Yes. **Other:** Picnic shelter, 4 cabins, jogging area, dataport by office. **Activities:** Swimming, basketball, volleyball, horseshoes, tennis, game room. **Nearby Attractions:** State Capital, Dakota Zoo, Heritage Center, Museums, golf, Fort Abraham Lincoln. **Additional Information:** www.koa.com.

Restrictions

Pets: On leash. **Fires:** 1 central fire ring. **Alcoholic Beverages:** Yes, in site only. **Vehicle Maximum Length:** None.

To Get There

From I-94, take Exit 276 (Eckelson) and go south less than 0.25 mi. on the left.

BOTTINEAU

Lake Metigoshe State Park

No. 2 Lake Metigoshe State Park Rd., Bottineau 58318. T: (701) 263-4651 office; www.ndparks.com; lmsp@state.nd.us.

RV ★★★★ Tent ★★★★

Beauty: ★★★★ Site Privacy: ★★★★
Spaciousness: ★★★★ Quiet: ★★★★
Security: ★★★★ Cleanliness: ★★★
Insect Control: ★★★ Facilities: ★★

Situated in the scenic Turtle Mountains on the shores of Lake Metigoshe, this campground was constructed by the Works Progress Administration (WPA) in the 1930s. The park's rolling hills, aspen forests, and small lakes make the site one of the most popular vacation spots in North Dakota. Lake Metigoshe is noted for its northern pike, walleye, and perch. The Old Oak Trail, a National Recreation Trail, is also found within the park's boundaries. The park has both modern and primitive camping, as well as picnic areas. The RV sites are spacious and private, providing a wonderful feeling of tranquility. Winter provides opportunities for snowmobiling, skating, sledding, and ice fishing. The park is open year-round, although water is turned off from October through May in the campground. The sites are assigned by reservation during the summer and first come first served from Oct. through Apr.

Basics

Operated By: The North Dakota Parks & Recreation Dept. **Open:** Year round, but the water is off Oct.–May in the campground. **Site Assignment:** By reservation in the summer, first come Oct.–Apr. **Registration:** At the entrance gate. **Fee:** $7 w/ no hookup, $12 w/ 30 amp, $14 w/ 50 amp. plus a $4 entrance fee per vehicle or annual park pass. **Parking:** At site.

Facilities

Number of Multipurpose Sites: 130. **Hookups:** Electric (30 amps), water. **Each Site:** Picnic table, grated fire pits. **Dump Station:** Yes. **Laundry:** No. **Pay Phone:** Yes. **Rest Rooms and Showers:** Yes. **Fuel:** No. **Propane:** No. **Internal Roads:** Paved. **RV Service:** 55 mi. South in Minot, ND. **Market:** There are 3 in town. **Restaurant:** There are several in town. **General Store:** No. **Vending:** Yes. **Swimming Pool:** No, but there is a lake front beach. **Playground:** Yes, several. **Other:** 3 year-round cabins, group dorms (total cap. 120), kitchen, dining hall & auditorium, swim beach, boat ramp, fishing dock, picnic shelters, seasonal naturalist, canoe rentals, warming House, cross-country ski & snowshoe rentals. **Activities:** Hiking, fishing (walleye, chinook, trout, pike), boating, skiing, ice fishing in the winter, wildlife viewing, special park programs, cross-country skiing, sledding, mountain biking. **Nearby Attractions:** International Peace Garden, downhill & cross-country ski areas, Peace Garden State Snowmobile Trail, Golf courses, Turtle Mountains, J. Clark Salyer & Lords Lake National Wildlife Refuges, State Scenic Byway. **Additional Information:** ND Parks & Recreation Dept. (701) 328-5357.

Restrictions

Pets: On leash, but not on beach or public picnic areas. **Fires:** In fire pits or grills only; fires may be restricted due to weather conditions; please ask management before starting any open fires. **Alcoholic Beverages:** Yes. **Vehicle Maximum Length:** None.

To Get There

14 mi. northeast of Bottineau. From SR 5 go north on Lake Rd. 10.2 mi., make a right on SR 43 for 6.1 mi., then follow signs into park.

CAVALIER

Graham's Island State Park

152 South Duncan Dr., Devils Lake 58301. T: (701) 766-4015; F: (701) 766-4311; www.ndparks.com; dlsp@state.nd.us.

RV ★★★★ Tent ★★★★

Beauty: ★★★★ Site Privacy: ★★★★★
Spaciousness: ★★★★ Quiet: ★★★★
Security: ★★★★ Cleanliness: ★★★
Insect Control: ★★ Facilities: ★★

Of the three state parks on Devils Lake, this is the largest and most developed. Naturally, water sports are a big draw, and you can even do some serious ice fishing for yellow perch in the winter. Other catches in the warmer months may include walleye, northern pike and white bass. While you're tromping through the oak, ash, elm, and aspen in the surrounding hills, you may partake of some deer, wild turkey and other small game. The camping facilities are nothing spectacular, but they are certainly sufficient for RVs and tents, with plenty of recreation for all ages—with emphasis on nature appreciation, of course. The back-in sites vary in size, and the facilities are more limited in the winter, but with a little planning this would be a lovely destination anytime. The setting is rural, about nine miles from the town of Devils Lake, and near plenty of other diversions. Security is good, and privacy is superb at this campground. Take your parka or your swimsuit and enjoy.

Basics

Operated By: The North Dakota Parks & Recreation Dept. **Open:** Year round, but the water is off Oct.–May in the campground. **Site Assignment:** By reservation in the summer, (800) 807 4723 first come Oct.–Apr. **Registration:** At the entrance gate. **Fee:** $7 w/ no hookup, $12 w/ electric plus a $4 entrance fee per vehicle or annual park pass. **Parking:** At site.

Facilities

Number of Multipurpose Sites: 70. **Hookups:** Electric (30 amps), water. **Each Site:** Picnic table, grated fire pits. **Dump Station:** Yes. **Laundry:** No. **Pay Phone:** Yes. **Rest Rooms and Showers:** Yes. **Fuel:** No. **Propane:** No. **Internal Roads:** Paved.

RV Service: Devils Lake. **Market:** Devils Lake. **Restaurant:** Devils Lake. **General Store:** Yes, Grahams Island. **Vending:** Yes. **Swimming Pool:** No. **Playground:** Yes, several. **Other:** Boat ramp (Grahams Island & Black Tiger Bay), picnic shelter, hiking trails (Grahams Island) & Sivert Thompson Activities Center (Grahams Island). **Activities:** Boating, fishing (walleye, northern pike, perch, & white bass), hiking, biking, self guided nature tours, interpretive programming, playgrounds, swimming, snowmobiling, cross-country skiing, & ice fishing. **Nearby Attractions:** Fort Totten State Historic Site, Sully's Hill National Game Preserve, Historic Downtown Devils Lake. **Additional Information:** ND Parks & Recreation Dept., (701) 328-5357.

Restrictions

Pets: On leash. **Fires:** In fire pits or grills only; fires may be restricted due to weather conditions; please ask management before starting any open fires. **Alcoholic Beverages:** Yes. **Vehicle Maximum Length:** None.

To Get There

To get to Grahams Island State Park, take Hwy. 2 north to Hwy. 19 south to Grahams Island Rd. Continue south on Grahams Island Rd. to park entrance. Shelvers Grove State Recreation Area is 3 miles east of Devils Lake on Hwy. 2.

CAVALIER

Icelandic State Park

13571 Hwy. 5, Cavalier 58220. T: (701) 265-4561; F: (701) 265-4443; www.ndparks.com; isp@state.nd.us.

RV ★★★ Tent ★★★

Beauty: ★★★	Site Privacy: ★★★
Spaciousness: ★★★	Quiet: ★★★★
Security: ★★★★	Cleanliness: ★★★
Insect Control: ★★	Facilities: ★★

It's not as cold as you think. But, then, neither is Iceland. Actually, this state park celebrates and preserves natural splendor and pioneer history, at the same time providing a good variety of recreation. In the northeastern corner of the sate, this rural spot on Lake Renwick offers plenty of water sports, and the northern pike are abundant. In the winter, plan to do your fishing through a hole in the ice (okay, it gets pretty cold). This is a well-rounded campground, with average facilities (that are more limited in the winter), comfortable for RVs and tents, relatively quiet, and secure. The medium-sized back-in sites offer a decent amount of privacy, and the old oak trees provide a good bit of shade, especially in the picnic area. Family-friendly recreation and wonderful wildlife viewing make this a delightful vacation spot. Depending on the crowd, this is a quiet, remote, secure campground where you can expect a peaceful and fun vacation.

Basics

Operated By: The North Dakota Parks & Recreation Dept. **Open:** Year round, but the water is off Oct.–May in the campground. **Site Assignment:** By reservation in the summer, (800) 807 4723 first come Oct.–Apr. **Registration:** At the entrance gate. **Fee:** $7 w/ no hookup, $12 w/ electric plus a $4 entrance fee per vehicle or annual park pass. **Parking:** At site.

Facilities

Number of Multipurpose Sites: 165. **Hookups:** Electric (30 amps), water. **Each Site:** Picnic table, grated fire pits. **Dump Station:** Yes. **Laundry:** No. **Pay Phone:** Yes. **Rest Rooms and Showers:** Yes. **Fuel:** No. **Propane:** No. **Internal Roads:** Paved. **RV Service:** In Cavalier. **Market:** In Cavalier. **Restaurant:** In Cavalier. **General Store:** No. **Vending:** Yes. **Swimming Pool:** No. **Playground:** Yes, several. **Other:** Boat ramp, picnic shelter, visitors center, historic buildings, historic artifacts, meeting room, & cabin. **Activities:** Boating, shore & ice fishing (northern pike), hiking, biking, self guided nature tours, interpretive programming, playgrounds, swimming, & artifacts exhibits on area's settlement. **Nearby Attractions:** Pembina County Historical Museum, Patton's Isle of Memories, Frostfire Mountain Ski Resort, golf, snowmobile trail, & scenic byway. **Additional Information:** ND Parks & Recreation Dept., (701) 328-5357.

Restrictions

Pets: On leash. **Fires:** In fire pits or grills only; fires may be restricted due to weather conditions; please ask management before starting any open fires. **Alcoholic Beverages:** Yes. **Vehicle Maximum Length:** None.

To Get There

Icelandic State Park is located 5 mi. west of Cavalier on Hwy. 5.

ECKELSON

Prairie Haven

10121 36th St. Southeast, Eckelson 58481. T: (701) 646-2267; www.prairie-haven.com; prairhvn@ictc.com.

RV ★★★ Tent ★★★

Beauty: ★★★	Site Privacy: ★★★
Spaciousness: ★★★	Quiet: ★★★
Security: ★★★	Cleanliness: ★★★
Insect Control: ★★★	Facilities: ★★★

The onsite spring-fed lake, more aptly called a pond, compliments the quiet serenity of this park-like campground and offers a quaint experience slightly reminiscent of Thoreau's Walden. Sites here are spacious and most can accommodate double slide-outs. Though mature trees give ample shade and the uninterrupted grassy sites provide an expanse of pleasing green, the lack of bushes and trees between sites offers little privacy. Perhaps this is a ploy of hosts and owners Biff and Claudine Flowers to encourage guests to make new friends, but if you like eating dinner alone, you may have to venture elsewhere. The rustic architecture of the general store and one-room cabin add to the country ambiance of the campground. This campground offers a simple, pleasing experience to both RV and tent-campers alike and is a nice overnight stop.

Basics

Operated By: Biff & Claudine Flowers. **Open:** May–Oct. **Site Assignment:** By reservation. **Registration:** In general store. **Fee:** Tent $15, RV $17–$20 per 2 people, $3 extra person, under age 6 stay free. **Parking:** Limited.

Facilities

Number of Multipurpose Sites: 31. **Hookups:** Electric (20, 30, 50 amps), water, sewer. **Each Site:** Picnic tables. **Dump Station:** Yes. **Laundry:** Yes. **Pay Phone:** Yes. **Rest Rooms and Showers:** Yes. **Fuel:** Yes. **Propane:** No, 8 mi. in Sandborn. **Internal Roads:** Gravel. **RV Service:** 15 mi. in Jamestown. **Market:** 15 mi. in Jamestown. **Restaurant:** Snacks on property, or in Jamestown. **General Store:** Yes. **Vending:** Store Only. **Swimming Pool:** No. **Playground:** Yes. **Other:** Spring-fed lake, 2 cabins. **Activities:** Fishing, basketball, volleyball, horseshoes. **Nearby Attractions:** Inquire at campground. **Additional Information:** www.prairie-haven.com.

Restrictions

Pets: On leash. **Fires:** 1 central fire ring. **Alcoholic Beverages:** Yes, in site only. **Vehicle Maximum Length:** None.

To Get There

From I-94, take Exit 276 (Eckelson) and go south less than 0.25 mi. on the left.

EPPING

Lewis and Clark State Park

119th Rd. Northwest, Epping 58843. T: (701) 859-3071; F: (701) 859-3001; www.ndparks.com; lcsp@stste.nd.us.

RV ★★★★ Tent ★★★★

Beauty: ★★★★	Site Privacy: ★★★★
Spaciousness: ★★★★	Quiet: ★★★★
Security: ★★★★	Cleanliness: ★★★★
Insect Control: ★★★	Facilities: ★★★

A rural spot on an upper bay of the mighty Lake Sakakawea, this state park is of course named for the famous explorers, and you can find commemorations of the Lewis and Clark expedition here and there. In the northwest part of the state, this setting offers a striking view of the rugged buttes of the Badlands. Water sports and wildlife viewing are major draws, and the fishing is terrific as well. In addition to the healthy supply of walleye, sauger, and northern pike, you might occasionally discover a pallid sturgeon or a paddle-fish. This is a great place for tent and RV camping, with adequate facilities (although they are limited in the winter). As is the case with many state parks, this is a beautiful place to spend a vacation, with privacy, space and peace defining the campground, and a great variety of recreation for all ages in and around the park. History buffs and nature lovers alike will love it here.

Basics

Operated By: The North Dakota Parks & Recreation Dept. **Open:** Year round, but the water is off Oct.–May in the campground. **Site Assignment:** By reservation in the summer, first come Oct.–Apr. **Registration:** At the entrance gate. **Fee:** $7 w/ no hookup, $12 w/ electric plus a $4 entrance fee per vehicle, or annual park pass. **Parking:** At site.

Facilities

Number of Multipurpose Sites: 87. **Hookups:** Electric (30 amps), water. **Each Site:** Picnic table, grated fire pits. **Dump Station:** Yes, (there is also a marina dump for boats). **Laundry:** No. **Pay Phone:** Yes. **Rest Rooms and Showers:** Yes. **Fuel:** Yes, located at the marina. **Propane:** No. **Internal Roads:** Paved. **RV Service:** 19 mi. southeast of Williston. **Market:** 19 mi. southeast of Williston. **Restaurant:** In Garrison or snack bar at the marina. **General Store:** Yes, located at the marina. **Vending:** Yes at the marina. **Swimming Pool:** No. **Playground:** Yes, several. **Other:** Full service marina with ramps, fish cleaning station, picnic shelters, lake front beach, picnic area with grills, nature trails, slip rentals. **Activities:** Hiking, fishing (walleye, sauger, & northern pike), boating, skiing, ice fishing (perch & walleye), wildlife viewing, special park programs. **Nearby Attractions:** Buffalo Trail Museum, Fort. Buford, Fort Union. **Additional Information:** ND Parks & Recreation Dept., (701) 328-5357.

Restrictions

Pets: On leash. **Fires:** In fire pits or grills only; fires may be restricted due to weather conditions; please ask management before starting any open fires. **Alcoholic Beverages:** Yes. **Vehicle Maximum Length:** None.

To Get There

The park is 19 mi. southeast of Williston on Hwy. 1804; turn on CR 15 and it is mi. down on the left. There is excellent signage from Hwy. 1804.

GARRISON
Fort Stevenson State Park

1252-A 41st. Ave. Northwest, Garrison 58540. T: (701) 337-5576; F: (701) 337-5313; www.ndparks.com; fssp@stste.nd.us.

RV ★★★★ Tent ★★★★

Beauty: ★★★★	Site Privacy: ★★★★
Spaciousness: ★★★★	Quiet: ★★★★
Security: ★★★★	Cleanliness: ★★★
Insect Control: ★★★	Facilities: ★★

Located in the center of the state, on the eastern end of giant Lake Sakakawea, this park is a fisher person's paradise. Plenty of other water sports and nature appreciation is available to campers here, but the park hosts several annual fishing tournaments, and is known as the "walleye capital of North Dakota." Accordingly, the marina and fishing-related facilities outshine those in the campground, but both RVs and tents should be comfortable here. The facilities are more limited in the winter, but the park is fun year-round. Just a few miles from the small town of Garrison, the park is in a rural area, and its remoteness enhances the security as well as the general quiet and privacy. This is a typically lovely campground for a state park, and all ages should enjoy the experience, just so long as you're not trying to escape fishing folks.

Basics

Operated By: The North Dakota Parks & Recreation Dept. **Open:** Year-round, but the water is off Oct.–May in the campground. **Site Assignment:** By reservation in the summer, first come Oct.–Apr. **Registration:** At the entrance gate. **Fee:** $7 w/ no hookup, $12 w/ 30 amp, $14 w/ 50 amp. plus a $4 entrance fee per vehicle or annual park pass. **Parking:** At site.

Facilities

Number of RV-Only Sites: 107. **Number of Tent-Only Sites:** 35. **Number of Multipurpose Sites:** 0. **Hookups:** Electric (30, 50 amps), water. **Each Site:** Picnic table, grated fire pits. **Dump Station:** Yes, (there is also a marina dump for boats). **Laundry:** No. **Pay Phone:** Yes. **Rest Rooms and Showers:** Yes. **Fuel:** Yes, located at the marina. **Propane:** No. **Internal Roads:** Paved. **RV Service:** 4 mi. North in Garrison. **Market:** 4 mi. north in Garrison. **Restaurant:** In Garrison or snack bar at the marina. **General Store:** Yes, located at the marina. **Vending:** Yes at the marina. **Swimming Pool:** No, but there is a lakefront beach. **Playground:** Yes, several. **Other:** Full service marina with high & low water ramps, boat rentals, pavilions with grill, 3 cabins, lake front beach, picnic area with grills, meeting facilities, arboretum, prairie dog town. **Activities:** Hiking, fishing (walleye, chinook, trout, pike), boating, skiing, ice fishing in the winter, wildlife viewing, special park programs, cross-country skiing, in season bow hunting for white tail deer. **Nearby Attractions:** Broste Rock Museum, White Shield Powwow, golf, tennis. **Additional Information:** ND Parks & Recreation Dept., (701) 328-5357.

Restrictions

Pets: On leash, but not on beach or public picnic areas. **Fires:** In fire pits or grills only; fires may be restricted due to weather conditions; please ask management before starting any open fires. **Alcoholic Beverages:** Yes. **Vehicle Maximum Length:** None.

To Get There

Garrison is located on Hwy. 37, and the park is 4 mi. south on CR 15 on Lake Sakakawea's north shore.

GARRISON
Sportsmen's Centennial Park

P.O. Box 98, Garrison 58540. T: (701) 337-5377; www.visitmcleancounty.com.

RV ★★★ Tent ★★★

Beauty: ★★★★	Site Privacy: ★★★
Spaciousness: ★★★	Quiet: ★★★★
Security: ★★★★	Cleanliness: ★★★
Insect Control: ★★	Facilities: ★

Since it was only created in 1989, this park is still being developed and tweaked by its McLean County operators. However simple, its wide-open spaces make it a very attractive and peaceful property. Set near the shore of Lake Sakakawea, the campground's boat ramp and dock make it a good place for anglers, and there is a stocked trout pond ideal for younger fisherfolk. The park is adjacent to the DeTobriand Game Management Area, which makes the campground an ideal overnight stop for visiting hunters and wildlife enthusiasts. The hiking trail offers the typical North Dakota vistas of rolling plains and vaulted skies. Though facilities and amenities are sparse, the youth of the park means that they are relatively new and in good condition.

Basics

Operated By: McLean County Park Board, overseen by COE **Open:** Apr.–late Oct., depends on weather. **Site Assignment:** By reservation. **Registration:** In general store. **Fee:** $8 no hookups, $10 with hookups. **Parking:** At site.

Facilities

Number of RV-Only Sites: 20. **Number of Tent-Only Sites:** 0. **Number of Multipurpose Sites:** 90. **Hookups:** Electric (20, 30 amps), water. **Each Site:** Picnic table. **Dump Station:** No. **Laundry:** No. **Pay Phone:** Yes. **Rest Rooms and Showers:** Yes. **Fuel:** No. **Propane:** No. **Internal Roads:** Gravel. **RV Service:** Inquire at campground. **Market:** Garrison. **Restaurant:** Garrison. **General Store:** Yes. **Vending:** Yes. **Swimming Pool:** No (Lakefront beach with life guard). **Playground:** Yes. **Other:** Fish cleaning station, picnic shelters & 2 boat ramps. **Activities:** Softball, volleyball, boating, waterskiing, fishing, hiking, swimming, & biking. **Nearby Attractions:** Inquire at campground. **Additional Information:** McLean County Park Board.

Restrictions

Pets: On leash. **Fires:** In fire pits or grills only; fires may be restricted due to weather conditions, please ask management before starting any open fires. **Alcoholic Beverages:** Yes. **Vehicle Maximum Length:** None. **Other:** No garbage facilities, much carry out all garbage.

To Get There

One mi. west of the junction of Hwy. 37 and Hwy. 83, then 2 mi. south and 1 mi. west.

JAMESTOWN
Frontier Fort Campground

P.O. Box 143, Jamestown 58402-0143. T: (701) 252-7492

RV ★★★ Tent ★★★

Beauty: ★★★	Site Privacy: ★★★
Spaciousness: ★★★	Quiet: ★★★
Security: ★★★	Cleanliness: ★★★
Insect Control: ★★★	Facilities: ★★★

Frontier Fort is a solid middle-of-the-road campground attached to a small Western-themed tourist attraction called Frontier Village. Despite Frontier Village's general tackiness, it's hard not to marvel at the World's Largest Buffalo (a 26-foot-tall, 46-foot-long, 60-ton concrete behemoth). There's even a pair of normal-sized live buffalo you can hand-feed behind the gift shop. Depending as it does almost completely on traveling flocks of older RVers, facilities are limited at this campground during the off-season. Twenty-eight of the campsites are sizable pull-throughs. Besides Frontier Village attractions, there is little to see here.

Basics

Operated By: Tanata Enterprises Inc. (Charley, Liz, & Jim). **Open:** Year round. **Site Assignment:** By reservation. **Registration:** In general store. **Fee:** Tent $8.50, RV $16.50. **Parking:** At site.

Facilities

Number of RV-Only Sites: 46. **Number of Tent-Only Sites:** 0. **Number of Multipurpose Sites:** 20. **Hookups:** Electric (20, 30, 50 amps), water, sewer. **Each Site:** Picnic table. **Dump Station:** Yes. **Laundry:** Yes. **Pay Phone:** Yes. **Rest Rooms and Showers:** Yes. **Fuel:** No, but in town. **Propane:** No, but in town. **Internal Roads:** Combination pavement & gravel in good condition. **RV Service:** In town. **Market:** In Jamestown. **Restaurant:** On site, & in Jamestown. **General Store:** Yes. **Vending:** Yes. **Swimming Pool:** No. **Playground:** No. **Other:** Museum, bar, small zoo, buffalo, Village Trader Gift Shoppe. **Activities:** Museum, zoo, electronic gaming (adults only). **Nearby Attractions:** Frontier Village, old west stagecoach ride, dinner theater.

Restrictions

Pets: On leash. **Fires:** In fire pits or grills only; fires may be restricted due to weather conditions; please ask management before starting any open fires. **Alcoholic Beverages:** Yes. **Vehicle Maximum Length:** None. **Other:** RV clubs welcome.

To Get There

From I-94 take Exit 258, Go north on US 281 (about 0.5 mi.) to first stop light, then east on 17th St. entrance on right.

JAMESTOWN

Jamestown KOA

3605 80th Ave. South, Jamestown 58401-9511. T: (701) 252-6262; F: (701) 252-6249; www.rv.camping.com/nd/jamestownkoa or www.koa.com; ahc@pocketmail.com.

RV ★★★★ Tent ★★★★

Beauty: ★★★★	Site Privacy: ★★★★
Spaciousness: ★★★★	Quiet: ★★★★
Security: ★★★★	Cleanliness: ★★★
Insect Control: ★★	Facilities: ★★★

While this KOA offers the usual amenities and abundant opportunities for play, including bocci ball, tetherball, heated pool, and disc golf, it lacks anything particularly unique. Though the RV sites are spacious, the landscaping and design are modest. All RV sites are gravel, and sites1–6 are best if you are looking for a nicely shaded spot. Sites 1–18 are closest to the play equipment, and sites 19–36 are closer to the lodge and rest rooms. Smart planning places the play area and lodge between the sites and the frontage road to act as a buffer. Tent sites, designated separately from the RV sites, offer the most secluded and wooded experience. A nice feature is a half-mile walking trail on the perimeter of the campground. Jamestown, only two miles away, pays homage to the legendary buffalo and frontier spirit with its National Buffalo Museum and the World's Largest Buffalo and Frontier Village. This is a nice overnight stop to someplace else, but is probably not a destination for an extended stay.

Basics

Operated By: Ann Case. **Open:** May 1–Oct. 1. **Site Assignment:** By reservation (800) 562-6350, held on credit card number. **Registration:** In the general store. **Fee:** Tent $20., RV $25–$27 per 2 people, $3 per extra person. **Parking:** At site.

Facilities

Number of RV-Only Sites: 48. **Number of Tent-Only Sites:** 20. **Number of Multipurpose Sites:** 0. **Hookups:** Electric (20, 30, 50 amps), water, sewer, cable. **Each Site:** Picnic table. **Dump Station:** Yes. **Laundry:** Yes. **Pay Phone:** Courtesy phone. **Rest Rooms and Showers:** Yes. **Fuel:** No. **Propane:** No. **Internal Roads:** Gravel. **RV Service:** Jamestown. **Market:** Jamestown. **Restaurant:** Jamestown. **General Store:** Yes. **Vending:** Yes. **Swimming Pool:** Yes (Jun. 15–Aug. 15). **Playground:** Yes. **Other:** Cabins, gameroom. **Activities:** Tetherball, disc golf, bocci ball, basketball, horseshoes, & nature walk. **Nearby Attractions:** National Buffalo Museum & live herd, world's largest buffalo & frontier village. **Additional Information:** Jamestown Chamber of Commerce, (701) 252-4830.

Restrictions

Pets: On leash. **Fires:** In fire pits or grills only; fires may be restricted due to weather conditions; please ask management before starting any open fires. **Alcoholic Beverages:** Yes. **Vehicle Maximum Length:** None.

To Get There

I-94 to Exit 256, then west on South Frontage Rd. 1 mi.

LARIMORE

Larimore Dam Recreation Area and Campground

P.O. Box 268, Larimore 58251-0268. T: (701) 343-2078

RV ★★★★ Tent ★★★★

Beauty: ★★★★	Site Privacy: ★★★★
Spaciousness: ★★★★	Quiet: ★★★★
Security: ★★★★	Cleanliness: ★★★★
Insect Control: ★★	Facilities: ★★★

This pretty and well-run campground makes a good headquarters for exploring the nearby Grand Forks area. Anglers will relish the chance to fish for trout, bluegill, bullhead, walleye, and largemouth bass in the waters of the Turtle River. Other recreational options abound, of course. Campers can hike or bike the nature trails; there's even a paved bike path running from the town of Larimore to the dam itself, which makes for a good day trip in either direction. Seasonally, visitors can relax on the campground beach in warmer months, or enjoy snow sledding during the winter.

Basics

Operated By: Private operator. **Open:** Apr.–late Oct., depends on weather. **Site Assignment:** By reservation. **Registration:** In general store. **Fee:** $8 no hookups, $10 with hookups. **Parking:** At site.

Facilities

Number of Multipurpose Sites: 114. **Hookups:** Electric (20, 30 amps), water. **Each Site:** Picnic table, fire pits. **Dump Station:** Yes. **Laundry:** No. **Pay Phone:** Yes. **Rest Rooms and Showers:** Yes. **Fuel:** No. **Propane:** No. **Internal Roads:** Combination pavement & gravel in good condition. **RV Service:** Grand Forks. **Market:** In Larimore. **Restaurant:** In Larimore. **General Store:** Yes. **Vending:** Yes. **Swimming Pool:** No, but there is swimming beach. **Playground:** Yes. **Other:** Picnic shelters, Myra Arboretum, a gazebo, fishing dock, nature trail. **Activities:** Softball, volleyball, boating, waterskiing, fishing, hiking, swimming, & biking. **Nearby Attractions:** Inquire at campground.

Restrictions

Pets: On leash. **Fires:** In fire pits or grills only; fires may be restricted due to weather conditions; please ask management before starting any open fires. **Alcoholic Beverages:** Yes. **Vehicle Maximum Length:** None. **Other:** No garbage facilities, must carry out all garbage.

To Get There

Located 30 mi. west of Grand Forks on Hwy. 4.

MANDAN

Fort Lincoln State Park

4480 Fort Lincoln Rd., Mandan 58554. T: (701) 663-9571; F: (701) 633-9234; www.ndparks.com; falsp@stste.nd.us.

RV ★★★ Tent ★★★

Beauty: ★★★	Site Privacy: ★★★
Spaciousness: ★★★	Quiet: ★★★★
Security: ★★★★	Cleanliness: ★★★
Insect Control: ★★	Facilities: ★★

This state park is interesting for both its military and Native American commemorative sites. What with Little Big Horn and Custer battle reminders, and the reconstructed On-A-Slant Indian Village, the cultural history here is intriguing. The view of the Missouri River from the trails is stunning, offering a full panorama in some places. The recreational opportunities include hiking, rainbow trout fishing, and wildlife viewing, with snowmobiling and cross-country skiing in the winter. Campers will find typical facilities for a state park, average-sized back-in sites and decent privacy, comfortable but not luxurious. It is a fairly quiet and secure campground, pleasant and generally peaceful. Keep in mind that facilities are limited in the winter, and bring along a history and/or anthropology friend to enhance your culturally enriching camping vacation.

Basics

Operated By: The North Dakota Parks & Recreation Dept. **Open:** Year round, but the water is off Oct.–May in the campground. **Site Assignment:** By reservation in the summer, (800) 807 4723 first come Oct.–Apr. **Registration:** At the entrance gate. **Fee:** $7 w/ no hookup, $12 w/ electric plus a

$4 entrance fee per vehicle or annual park pass. **Parking:** At site.

Facilities

Number of Multipurpose Sites: 95. **Hookups:** Electric (30 amps), water. **Each Site:** Picnic table, grated fire pits. **Dump Station:** Yes. **Laundry:** No. **Pay Phone:** Yes. **Rest Rooms and Showers:** Yes. **Fuel:** No. **Propane:** No. **Internal Roads:** Paved. **RV Service:** 7 mi. north in Mandan. **Market:** 7 mi. north in Mandan. **Restaurant:** 7 mi. north in Mandan. **General Store:** Yes, in the commissary. **Vending:** Yes. **Swimming Pool:** No. **Playground:** Yes, several. **Other:** Camp Store, paved nature trails, 2 cabins, picnic shelters, trail riding concession, state snowmobile trailhead, On-a-Slant Mandan village Earthlodges & other historical buildings including the Custer House & commissary, museum, cross-country ski trails. **Activities:** Tours of Fort Lincoln, snowmobiling, Hiking, fishing (rainbow trout), biking, sledding, cross-country skiing, wildlife viewing, special park programs. **Nearby Attractions:** Grand Forks 22 mi. east, golf. **Additional Information:** ND Parks & Recreation Dept., (701)328-5357.

Restrictions

Pets: On leash. **Fires:** In fire pits or grills only; fires may be restricted due to weather conditions; please ask management before starting any open fires. **Alcoholic Beverages:** Yes. **Vehicle Maximum Length:** None.

To Get There

From I-94 Exit 152 go south on Sunset Dr. to Main St.; take a left on Main St. to 6th Ave.; then right on 6th Ave. 7 mi. to Fort Abraham Lincoln State Park.

MINOT

Minot KOA

5261 Hwy. 52 East, Minot 58701. T: (701) 839-7400; www.koa.com.

RV ★★★ Tent ★★★

Beauty: ★★★	Site Privacy: ★★★
Spaciousness: ★★★	Quiet: ★★★★
Security: ★★★★	Cleanliness: ★★★
Insect Control: ★★	Facilities: ★★★

This campground is really lovely, set in rolling hills and meadowland. The grounds are well manicured, clean and on-site security is great. Each site is medium to average size, which gives the guests privacy and quiet. It's somewhat smaller than other KOAs we've seen, with only 49 RV sites and 17 tent sites. However, we don't think this takes away from the campground at all. There are still all the amenities of the larger facilities, even a laundry, but without the crowd you'd find at a big park. There are plenty of things to do on site, as well as in town, but some of the more interesting attractions are Roosevelt Park and Zoo and Pioneer Village.

Basics

Operated By: Jerry & Sandy Boe. **Open:** Apr. 15–Oct. 15. **Site Assignment:** By reservation (800) 562-7421, held on credit card number. **Registration:** In the general store. **Fee:** Tent $15., RV $19–$21 per 2 people. **Parking:** At site.

Facilities

Number of RV-Only Sites: 49. **Number of Tent-Only Sites:** 17. **Number of Multipurpose Sites:** 0. **Hookups:** Electric (30 amps), water, sewer. **Each Site:** Picnic table. **Dump Station:** Yes. **Laundry:** Yes. **Pay Phone:** Yes. **Rest Rooms and Showers:** Yes. **Fuel:** No. **Propane:** No. **Internal Roads:** Gravel. **RV Service:** Minot. **Market:** Minot. **Restaurant:** There are several in town. **General Store:** Yes. **Vending:** Yes. **Swimming Pool:** No, but there is swimming at the Roosevelt Park & Zoo. **Playground:** Yes. **Other:** Cabins, gameroom. **Activities:** Mini-golf, go-carts, movies. **Nearby Attractions:** Roosevelt Park & Zoo, golf, Pioneer Village. **Additional Information:** Minot Chamber of Commerce, (701) 852-6000.

Restrictions

Pets: On leash. **Fires:** In fire pits or grills only; fires may be restricted due to weather conditions; please ask management before starting any open fires. **Alcoholic Beverages:** Yes. **Vehicle Maximum Length:** None.

To Get There

Go 2.25 mi. southeast on Hwy. 52 from Minot.

WILLISTON

Prairie Acres RV Park

2008 University Ave., Williston 58801. T: (701) 572-4860; jloomer@dia.net.

RV ★★★ Tent n/a

Beauty: ★★★	Site Privacy: ★★★
Spaciousness: ★★★	Quiet: ★★★★
Security: ★★★	Cleanliness: ★★★★
Insect Control: ★★★	Facilities: ★★★

Prairie Acres RV Park is located on the Montana, North Dakota line one mile west of Williston, ND. Prairie Acres offers a rural setting overlooking crop fields and summer wildflowers. All of Prairie Acres sites are grass, level, and pull-through, set on a large rectangular open lawn with few trees. The area is great for observing the stars and watching the summer evening lightning. Prairie Acres caters exclusively to people in RVs wishing to escape to a quiet and restful environment, no tenting allowed. Prairie Acres offers full service hookups with 50-amp receptacles, but there are no public rest rooms, showers, or laundry. This is a simple well-groomed campground for those visitors wishing for a comfortable nights sleep. There are no bells and whistles, just friendly people, and peace. The spring is cool, and the summer dry. The wind blows constantly.

Basics

Operated By: Orville C. Loomer. **Open:** May–Oct. **Site Assignment:** First come, first served. **Registration:** In camp office. **Fee:** $12. **Parking:** At site.

Facilities

Number of RV-Only Sites: 29. **Number of Tent-Only Sites:** 0. **Number of Multipurpose Sites:** 0. **Hookups:** Electric (30, 50 amps), water, sewer. **Each Site:** Picnic table. **Dump Station:** Yes. **Laundry:** No. **Pay Phone:** No. **Rest Rooms and Showers:** No. **Fuel:** No. **Propane:** No. **Internal Roads:** Paved. **RV Service:** 0.25 mi. in Williston. **Market:** In Williston. **Restaurant:** In Williston. **General Store:** No. **Vending:** No. **Swimming Pool:** No. **Playground:** No. **Activities:** Inquire at campground. **Nearby Attractions:** Fort Union Trading Post National Historic Site, The James Memorial Center for the Visual Arts, Williston Community Center w/ indoor pool. **Additional Information:** Williston Area Chamber of Commerce, (701) 572-3767.

Restrictions

Pets: On leash. **Fires:** No open fires**Alcoholic Beverages:** Yes. **Vehicle Maximum Length:** None.

To Get There

One mile west of Williston on Hwy. 2.

Ohio

With a name meaning "great" in Iroquois, Ohio has a big reputation to live up to. And it does that quite easily. From Lake Erie on its northern border to the Ohio River on its southern, the Buckeye State offers a treasure trove of water recreation. But wait, there's a lot more than water sports! **Hocking State Forest** and **Hocking Hills State Park** in southern Ohio, for example, add climbing and rappelling on 99 acres of sheer rock faces and challenging cliffs, including climbs from 20 to 120 feet.

Ohio's 72 state parks offer 57 campgrounds and recreation galore. At **Mohican State Park** near **Mansfield,** Clear Fork River is stocked with more than 100,000 brown trout for a fishing fantasy. **Cleveland** has one of the nation's largest park systems with its 100-mile chain of city parks, known as the "Emerald Necklace." For an unusual adventure, try scuba diving adjacent to downtown Cleveland where a **freshwater reef** has been created by the remains of the demolished Cleveland Municipal Stadium. In **Sandusky,** the 364-acre **Cedar Point Amusement Park** features 60 rides, including 13 spine-tingling roller coasters. See the stars at **Akron's Civil Theatre,** where the blinking stars and floating clouds are simulated on the ceiling. At the **Hale Farm and Village,** travel back in time to the mid-1800s as craftsmen and village residents portray life as it was in Ohio's Western Reserve. Historic **Sauder Village** in **Archbold** and **Roscoe Village** in **Coshocton** likewise celebrate the past.

Called "the most beautiful of America's inland cities" by Winston Churchill, **Cincinnati** saved its famed railroad station, **Union Terminal,** and turned it into several museums and an OMNIMAX theater. Nearby **Lebanon** evokes an unusual Colonial atmosphere, and **Waynesville** is renowned for its antique shops. In its 100 acres, **Fort Ancient** contains a pre-historic earthwork built by the Hopewell Indians. Stop in **Columbus** to see one of the nation's largest collections of reptiles at the **Columbus Zoo,** as well as the first gorilla born in captivity. In **Dayton,** check out where Orville and Wilbur Wright first dreamed of flying in and visit the **United States Air Force Museum.**

Hinckley has the dubious honor every March 15th of welcoming home squadron after squadron of buzzards returning from winter in the Smoky Mountains. If you prefer more variety, about 110 kinds of birds are known to nest in Hocking Hills State Park in **Logan. Put-In-Bay** on **South Bass Island** is known for its fish hatcheries, wineries, and caves, while **COSI Toledo** is a hands-on center that makes learning science fun.

The following facilities accept payment in checks or cash only:

Camp Qtokee, Sidney
Carthage Gap Campground, Athens
Chippewa Valley Campground, Seville
Hidden Acres Campground, West Salem
The Landings Family Campground, Marietta
Pin-Oak Acres, Leavittsburg
Poor Farmer's Campground, Piqua
Scenic Hills RV Park, Berlin
Shady Lake Campground, Findlay
Town & Country Camp Resort, West Salem

The following facility features 50 or fewer sites:

Blue Lagoon Campground, Butler

ASHLAND

Hickory Lakes Campground

23 Township Rd. 1300 Meyers Rd., West Salem 44287. T: (419) 869-7587; F: (419) 869-5007; www.gocampingamerica.com/hickorylakesoh; hickory lake@bright.net.

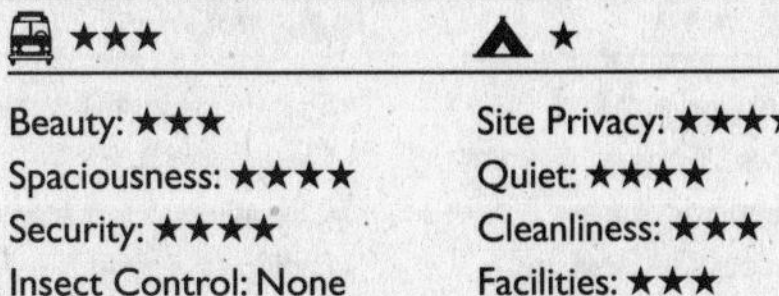

RV ★★★ Tent ★

Beauty: ★★★ Site Privacy: ★★★★
Spaciousness: ★★★★ Quiet: ★★★★
Security: ★★★★ Cleanliness: ★★★
Insect Control: None Facilities: ★★★

Hickory Lakes Campground is pleasant and serene with ponds, trees, meadows, and a sandy bottom swimming lake, although some of the seasonal campers need to repair and tidy up their sites. Owners should understand that as a rule, seasonal RVs must be 1982 or newer. However, it is not the age but the level of disrepair and poor maintenance of some of the seasonal sites that mar the campground's beauty. Located 15 miles east of Ashland, Hickory Lakes offers shaded or open sites surrounding a lake. There are 100 seasonal campers and 14 pull-through sites. Camping areas are grassy with gravel parking spots, and most sites are shaded by a tree. The best RV sites are C17–19 and C21–23, all overlooking the pond. Speed limit is five mph, and children 17 and younger must be on their sites by 10 p.m. Security measures are tops, with one entrance/exit road, a security gate requiring a coded card, surveillance cameras, owners who live on site, and regular campground patrols.

BASICS

Operated by: Randy & Karen Burkhead. **Open:** May 1–Oct. 15. **Site Assignment:** Reservations w/ 1-night deposit; refund w/ 7-day notice. **Registration:** At campground office. **Fee:** $22 (cash, check, credit cards). **Parking:** At site.

FACILITIES

Number of RV Sites: 200. **Number of Tent-Only Sites:** 0. **Hookups:** Electric (20, 30, 50 amps), water. **Each Site:** Picnic table, fire ring. **Dump Station:** Yes. **Laundry:** Yes. **Pay Phone:** Yes. **Rest Rooms and Showers:** Yes. **Fuel:** No. **Propane:** Yes. **Internal Roads:** Gravel, in good condition. **RV Service:** No. **Market:** 15 mi. west in Ashland. **Restaurant:** 15 mi. west in Ashland. **General Store:** Yes. **Vending:** Yes. **Swimming Pool:** No. **Playground:** Yes. **Other:** Swimming lake, 3 fishing lakes, horseshoes, pavilion, recreation barn, rental cabins, coin games, hiking trail, volleyball, basketball, sports field. **Activities:** Swimming, fishing, hiking, scheduled weekend activities. **Nearby Attractions:** Golf, Ashland College, canoeing, Sea World, antiques, reservoir, Amish country, Cedar Point, outlet mall, Carousel Park, Living Bible Museum. **Additional Information:** Ashland Area Chamber of Commerce, (419) 281-4584.

RESTRICTIONS

Pets: Leash only. **Fires:** Fire ring only. **Alcoholic Beverages:** Permitted. **Vehicle Maximum Length:** None. **Other:** No working caravans.

TO GET THERE

From the junction of I-71 and US 250, take Exit 186 and drive 6 mi. east on US 250, then 1 mi. north on Township Rd. 63, then 0.5 mi. east on Township Rd. 1300. US 250 is wide and well maintained w/ broad shoulders. Township Rds. 63 and 1300 are well maintained but narrow and winding w/ narrow shoulders. The campground entrance is over a dam between two ponds.

ATHENS

Carthage Gap Campground

22575 Brimstone Rd., Coolville 45723. T: (740) 667-3072

RV ★★★★ Tent ★★★

Beauty: ★★★★ Site Privacy: ★★★★
Spaciousness: ★★★★ Quiet: ★★★★
Security: ★★★★ Cleanliness: ★★★★
Insect Control: None Facilities: ★★★★

A rural campground by a lake, Carthage Gap Campground has the little touches that make camping a pleasure, including friendly owners. The campground is well maintained, right down to such niceties as a clean, pleasantly decorated laundry room. Sites are level, with a choice of open or shaded. Located ten miles west of Athens, the campground has 100 seasonal campers and 30 pull-through sites. The typical site width is 40 feet. No license or fee is required for campers to use the fishing lake. Many weekends feature campground-wide meals, such as a corn roast, bean soup supper, pancake breakfast and ice cream and dessert social. Security measures include one entrance/exit road, owners who live on site, and the presence of four local policemen as seasonal campers.

BASICS

Operated by: Gloyd & Nina McDermott. **Open:** Apr. 15–Nov. 1. **Site Assignment:** Reservations w/ 1-night deposit; no refunds but will honor the deposit for a year. **Registration:** At campground office. **Fee:** $22 (cash, check). **Parking:** At site.

FACILITIES

Number of RV Sites: 135. **Number of Tent-Only Sites:** 0. **Hookups:** Electric (20, 30, 50 amps), water, sewer. **Each Site:** Picnic table, fire ring. **Dump Station:** Yes. **Laundry:** Yes. **Pay Phone:** Yes. **Rest Rooms and Showers:** Yes. **Fuel:** No. **Propane:** Yes. **Internal Roads:** Gravel, in good condition. **RV Service:** No. **Market:** 10 mi. east in Athens. **Restaurant:** 10 mi. east in Athens. **General Store:** No. **Vending:** Yes. **Swimming Pool:** No. **Playground:** Yes. **Other:** Swimming lake, fishing lake, basketball, volleyball, horseshoes, pavilion, hiking trails. **Activities:** Swimming, fishing, hiking, scheduled weekend activities. **Nearby Attractions:** Cave, golf, Ohio Univ., museums, historic homes, Fenton Glass Factory, antiques, arts & crafts. **Additional Information:** Athens Area Chamber of Commerce, (740) 594-2251.

RESTRICTIONS

Pets: Leash only. **Fires:** Fire ring only. **Alcoholic Beverages:** Permitted. **Vehicle Maximum Length:** None.

TO GET THERE

From the junction of Hwy. 7 and US 50, drive 3.5 mi. west on US 50, then 0.5 mi. north on CR 56. US 50 is wide and well maintained w/ broad shoulders. CR 56 is wide and well maintained w/ narrow shoulders. A steep, narrow, gravel hill leads into the campground.

AURORA

Yogi Bear's Jellystone Park Camp-Resort

3392 State Rte. 82, Mantua 44255. T: (800) 344-YOGI; www.jellystoneohio.com.

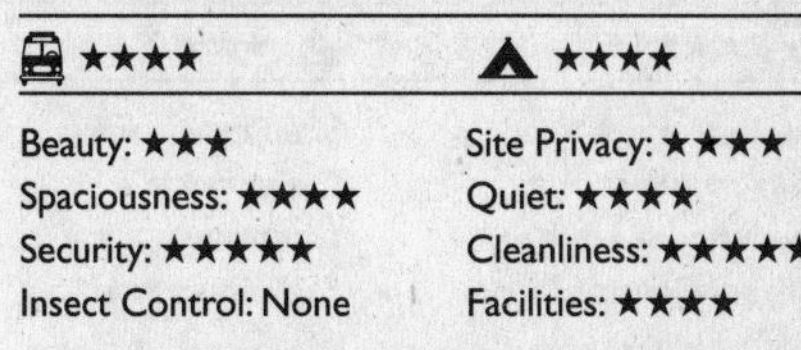

RV ★★★★ Tent ★★★★

Beauty: ★★★ Site Privacy: ★★★★
Spaciousness: ★★★★ Quiet: ★★★★
Security: ★★★★★ Cleanliness: ★★★★★
Insect Control: None Facilities: ★★★★

Pull into a Yogi Bear's Jellystone Park Camp-Resort and you know what to expect—clean facilities, good security, a family atmosphere, and plenty of activities. That's what the Yogi Bear four miles east of Aurora offers. The campground also has a great location—ten minutes from Sea World and Six Flags Ohio, ten minutes from the Ohio Turnpike, and a half hour from Cleveland. Situated on a 50-acre spring-fed lake, Yogi Bear's has 110 seasonal campers, an activities director, and a typical site width of 33 feet. Most popular RV sites are the 40 pull-throughs with full hookups. Although tents can be placed on any site, tent campers seem to prefer the rustic area with no hookups and more privacy. Laid out in a series of loops, the campground has mostly grassy, open sites, and trees are scarace. Security is tops, with an entrance gate manned 24 hours a day, along with regular patrols of the campground.

BASICS

Operated by: Yogi Bear's Jellystone Park Camp-Resorts. **Open:** May 1–Oct. 15. **Site Assignment:** Reservations w/ 1-night deposit; refunds w/ 7-day notice. **Registration:** At campground office. **Fee:** $44 (cash, credit cards). **Parking:** At site.

FACILITIES

Number of RV Sites: 310. **Number of Tent-Only Sites:** 115. **Hookups:** Electric (30, 50 amps), water, sewer. **Each Site:** Picnic table, fire ring. **Dump Station:** Yes. **Laundry:** Yes. **Pay Phone:** Yes. **Rest Rooms and Showers:** Yes. **Fuel:** No. **Propane:** Yes. **Internal Roads:** Paved/gravel, in good condition. **RV Service:** No. **Market:** 4 mi. west in Aurora. **Restaurant:** 4 mi. west in Aurora. **General Store:** Yes. **Vending:** Yes. **Swimming Pool:** Yes. **Playground:** Yes. **Other:** Lake, swimming beach, game room, snack bar, rental cottages & cabins, mini-golf, pavilion, coin games, wading pool, boat ramp, boat dock, basketball, shuffleboard, sports field, volleyball, hiking trails. **Activities:** Swimming, fishing, electric motors only boating (rental rowboats, paddlebaots, canoes, kayaks available), hiking, scheduled activities. **Nearby Attractions:** Sea World, Six Flags, golf, museums, antiques, historic homes, arts & crafts shops, outlet stores. **Additional Information:** Portage County Visitor & Convention Bureau, (800) 648-6342.

RESTRICTIONS

Pets: Leash only. **Fires:** Fire ring only. **Alcoholic Beverages:** At sites only. **Vehicle Maximum Length:** 40 ft.

To Get There

From the junction of Hwy. 306 and Hwy. 82, drive 4 mi. east on Hwy. 82. Roads are wide and well maintained w/ broad shoulders.

BATAVIA

East Fork State Park

P.O. Box 119, Bethel 45106. T: (513) 724-6521; www.dnr.state.oh.us/odnr/parks.

RV ★★★ Tent ★★★

Beauty: ★★★★ Site Privacy: ★★
Spaciousness: ★★ Quiet: ★★★★
Security: ★★★★ Cleanliness: ★★★
Insect Control: None Facilities: ★★★

One of the largest camping areas in the state, East Fork State Park offers 416 sites for either RVs or tents. Thirty-one seasonal sites are also available, as is a 17-site equestrian camp. Located 15 miles southwest of Williamsburg and 25 mi. from Cincinnati, the park's terrain includes both rugged hills and open meadows. There are 2,160 acres of water and unlimited-horsepower boating, with access available at five launch ramps. For sport fishing, East Fork is stocked with hybrid striper and as well as largemouth and smallmouth bass, bluegill, and crappie. East Fork has a 1,200-foot swimming beach. Campsites are 18 × 30, with most under a canopy of mature beech, sugar maple, and white oak. There are no pull-through sites. Park rangers provide security with regular patrols from a nearby ranger station.

Basics

Operated by: State of Ohio. **Open:** All year. **Site Assignment:** First come, first served. No reservations. **Registration:** At campground office. **Fee:** $17 (cash, check, credit cards). **Parking:** At site.

Facilities

Number of RV Sites: 416. **Number of Tent-Only Sites:** 0. **Hookups:** Electric (30 amps). **Each Site:** Picnic table, fire ring. **Dump Station:** Yes. **Laundry:** No. **Pay Phone:** Yes. **Rest Rooms and Showers:** Yes. **Fuel:** No. **Propane:** No. **Internal Roads:** Paved, in good condition. **RV Service:** No. **Market:** 15 mi. northeast in Williamsburg. **Restaurant:** 15 mi. northeast in Williamsburg. **General Store:** Yes. **Vending:** Yes. **Swimming Pool:** No. **Playground:** Yes. **Other:** William H. Harsha Lake, swimming beach, boat ramp, amphitheater, horseshoes, pavilion, horseback riding trails, hiking trails, rental camps, rental RVs. **Activities:** Swimming, boating, fishing, hiking, scheduled activities. **Nearby Attractions:** Golf, museums, historic homes, zoo, Kings Island amusement park, conservatory, antiques. **Additional Information:** Clermont County CVB, (800) 796-4282.

Restrictions

Pets: Leash only, pet camping area; $1 per pet a day, max. 2 pets. **Fires:** Fire ring only. **Alcoholic Beverages:** Not permitted. **Vehicle Maximum Length:** 35 ft. **Other:** 14-day stay limit.

To Get There

From the junction of I-275 and Hwy. 32, drive 10 mi. east on Hwy. 32, then 0.25 mi. south on Half Acre Rd., then 500 feet east on access road. Roads are wide and well maintained w/ broad shoulders.

BELLVILLE

Honeycreek Valley Campground

1219 Honeycreek Rd. West, Bellville 44813. T: (419) 886-2777

RV ★★★ Tent ★★★

Beauty: ★★★ Site Privacy: ★★★
Spaciousness: ★★★ Quiet: ★★★★
Security: ★★★★ Cleanliness: ★★★
Insect Control: Yes Facilities: ★★★

A county campground on a lake, Honeycreek Valley Campground offers level ground with a choice of open or shaded sites. Located in a valley with forests rising around it, the quiet campground is graced with vibrant autumn foliage and flowering dogwoods in the spring. Three miles west of Bellville, the campground has a typical site width of 30 feet, 30 seasonal campers, and 25 pull-through sites. Laid out in tiers, the campground has a five mph speed limit and enforces quiet hours between 11 p.m. and 9 a.m. Fishing is catch and release only. Security includes a one-road loop, an owner who lives on site, and regular campground patrols.

Basics

Operated by: Mike Romano. **Open:** May 1–Oct. 15. **Site Assignment:** Reservations w/ 1-night deposit; refund w/ 7-day notice. **Registration:** At campground office. **Fee:** $20 (cash, check, credit cards). **Parking:** At site.

Facilities

Number of RV Sites: 50. **Number of Tent-Only Sites:** 35. **Hookups:** Electric (30 amps), water, sewer. **Each Site:** Picnic table, fire ring. **Dump Station:** Yes. **Laundry:** Yes. **Pay Phone:** Yes. **Rest Rooms and Showers:** Yes. **Fuel:** No. **Propane:** No. **Internal Roads:** Gravel, in fair condition. **RV Service:** Yes. **Market:** 3 mi. east in Bellville. **Restaurant:** 3 mi. east in Bellville. **General Store:** Yes. **Vending:** Yes. **Swimming Pool:** No. **Playground:** Yes. **Other:** Swimming lake, pavilion, fishing lake, nature trails, horseshoes, volleyball, softball, coin games, sports field. **Activities:** Swimming, fishing, hiking, boating (rental paddleboats available), scheduled weekend activities. **Nearby Attractions:** Living Bible Museum, Johnny Appleseed Monument, Richland Carousel Park, state forest, covered bridge, Amish country, Mid Ohio Sports Car Course, golf, antiques, arts & crafts, Kingwood Center, B & O Bike Trail. **Additional Information:** Mansfield-Richland Area Chamber, (419) 522-3211.

Restrictions

Pets: Leash only. **Fires:** Fire ring only. **Alcoholic Beverages:** At sites only. **Vehicle Maximum Length:** None.

To Get There

From the junction of I-71 and Hwy. 97, drive 3 mi. east on Hwy. 97, then 1.5 mi. south on Hwy. 13, then 2 mi. west on Honey Creek Rd. Hwy. 97 and Hwy. 13 are wide and well maintained w/ broad shoulders. Honey Creek Rd. is a country road, mainly gravel, winding, and narrow w/ narrow shoulders.

BELLVILLE

Yogi Bear's Jellystone Park Camp-Resort

SR 546 at Black Rd., Bellville 44813. T: (419) 886-CAMP

RV ★★★ Tent ★★★

Beauty: ★★★ Site Privacy: ★★★★
Spaciousness: ★★★★ Quiet: ★★★★
Security: ★★★ Cleanliness: ★★★★
Insect Control: Yes Facilities: ★★★

Yogi Bear's Jellystone Park Mansfield, located eight miles south of Bellville, features rolling terrain along a lake. Laid out in a series of loops, the campground has 80 seasonal campers (some sites in not very good shape), three pull-through sites, and an average site width of 45 feet. Sites are level and grassy, with a choice of shaded or open. The entrance is a nice welcome to the campground with a fence, flowers, and ivy climbing a trellis. Security is provided by owners who live on site. Speed limit is 10.5 mph, high for a Yogi Bear facility. Quiet hours are 11 p.m. to 8 a.m. and minors age 18 and under are not permitted on the park grounds after 7:30 p.m. without adult supervision. Best RV sites are by the lake. Best tent sites are in a rustic area by the woods that affords more green space and privacy.

Basics

Operated by: Bill Bings. **Open:** Apr. 15–Oct. 28. **Site Assignment:** Reservations w/ 1-night deposit; refund w/ 7-day notice. **Registration:** At campground office. **Fee:** $27 (cash, check, credit cards). **Parking:** At site.

Facilities

Number of RV Sites: 175. **Number of Tent-Only Sites:** 30. **Hookups:** Electric (30, 50 amps), water, sewer. **Each Site:** Picnic table, fire ring. **Dump Station:** Yes. **Laundry:** Yes. **Pay Phone:** Yes. **Rest Rooms and Showers:** Yes. **Fuel:** No. **Propane:** Yes. **Internal Roads:** Gravel, in good condition. **RV Service:** None. **Market:** 8 mi. north in Bellville. **Restaurant:** 8 mi. north in Bellville. **General Store:** Yes. **Vending:** Yes. **Swimming Pool:** No. **Playground:** Yes. **Other:** Swimming beach, pavilion, rental cabins, volleyball, game room, outdoor theater, horsehoes, stocking fishing lake, boat ramp, boat dock, recreation field. **Activities:** Swimming, fishing, boating (rental rowboats, canoes & paddleboats available), scheduled activities. **Nearby Attractions:** Amish Country, Mid-Ohio Race Track, golf, Mohican Forest, canoeing, plant tours, Malabar Farm State Park, Living Bible Museum, Richland Carousel Park, ski resorts, Ohio State Reformatory. **Additional Information:** Mansfield-Richland Area Chamber of Commerce, (419) 522-3211.

Restrictions

Pets: Leash only. **Fires:** Fire ring only. **Alcoholic Beverages:** At sites only. **Vehicle Maximum Length:** None. **Other:** Bass & catfish under 15 inches must be returned to the lake immediately.

To Get There

From the junction of I-71 and Hwy. 97, take Exit 165 and drive 1.5 mi. southeast on Hwy. 97, then

3 mi. west on Mock Rd., then 4 mi. south on Hwy. 546, then 0.25 mi. southwest on Black Rd. Roads are wide and well maintained but have narrow shoulders in spots.

BERLIN

Scenic Hills RV Park

4483 TR 367, Millersburg 44654. T: (330) 893-3258

RV ★★★★ Tent n/a

Beauty: ★★★ Site Privacy: ★★★★
Spaciousness: ★★★★ Quiet: ★★★★
Security: ★★★★ Cleanliness: ★★★★
Insect Control: None Facilities: ★★★

Because there are so many nearby attractions here in the heart of Amish country, Scenic Hills RV Park offers little on-site recreation. Located one mile east of Berlin, the campground accepts full-hookup units only. No tents are allowed. The campground offers open sites on a grassy hilltop with sunrise and sunset views. Scenic Hills has 12 seasonal campers and 40 pull-through sites, with a typical site width of 40 feet. The campground has no rest rooms. A craft shop and store are located on the grounds. Sites are laser leveled to assure easier parking for RVs and easy access for big rigs. Security and safety measures include a five-mph speed limit and owners who live nearby and keep a close eye on the campground.

Basics

Operated by: Sam & Mary Hershberger. **Open:** Apr. 1–Nov. 1. **Site Assignment:** Reservations w/ 1-night deposit; refund w/ 7-day notice. **Registration:** At campground office. **Fee:** $20 (cash, check). **Parking:** At site.

Facilities

Number of RV Sites: 88. **Number of Tent-Only Sites:** 0. **Hookups:** Electric (20, 30, 50 amps), water, sewer, phone. **Each Site:** Picnic table, fire ring. **Dump Station:** Yes. **Laundry:** No. **Pay Phone:** Yes. **Rest Rooms and Showers:** No. **Fuel:** No. **Propane:** Yes. **Internal Roads:** Gravel, in good condition. **RV Service:** No. **Market:** 1 mi. west in Berlin. **Restaurant:** 1 mi. west in Berlin. **General Store:** Yes. **Vending:** No. **Swimming Pool:** No. **Playground:** No. **Other:** Sports field, horseshoes. **Activities:** None. **Nearby Attractions:** Amish country, Wendell August Forge, arts & crafts, antiques, Behalt cyclorama, Rolling Ridge Ranch, Schrock's Amish Farm, scenic drives. **Additional Information:** Holmes County Chamber of Commerce & Tourism Bureau, (330) 674-3975.

Restrictions

Pets: Leash only. **Fires:** Fire ring only. **Alcoholic Beverages:** At sites only. **Vehicle Maximum Length:** None.

To Get There

From the junction of US 62 and Hwy. 39, drive 1 mi. east on Hwy. 39, then 0.25 mi. south on TR 367. Roads are wide and well maintained w/ mostly broad shoulders.

BLANCHESTER

Stonelick State Park

2895 Lake Dr., Pleasant Plain 45162. T: (513) 625-7544; F: (513) 625-7526; www.dnr.state.oh.us/odnr/parks; stonelick.parks@dnr.state.oh.us.

RV ★★★ Tent ★★★★

Beauty: ★★★★ Site Privacy: ★★★
Spaciousness: ★★★ Quiet: ★★★★
Security: ★★★★ Cleanliness: ★★★
Insect Control: None Facilities: ★★★

Tucked away in the rolling highlands six miles southwest of Blanchester, Stonelick State Park was originally created in 1950 as a wildlife area for local sporting enthusiasts. Now the area is operated by the state and offers a variety of outdoor recreational activities centered around a 200-acre lake. The woodland campground setting offers mostly grassy, shady sites. The typical site size is 15 × 40 feet with no pull-throughs. Laid out in a series of loops, Stonelick offers six non-electric sites for tent campers, although tents and RVs are permitted on any of the sites. Four Rent-A-Camp units consisting of a tent, dining canopy, cooler, cook stove and other equipment can be rented during the summer months by reservation. The lake is well known for catches of bass, bluegill, crappie and catfish. A valid Ohio hunting and/or fishing license is required. There is a laundry facility. Campground security is great, with a ranger-controlled access station and regular patrols.

Basics

Operated by: State of Ohio. **Open:** All year. **Site Assignment:** First come, first served. No reservations. **Registration:** At campground office. **Fee:** $15 (cash, check, credit cards). **Parking:** At site.

Facilities

Number of RV Sites: 109. **Number of Tent-Only Sites:** 6. **Hookups:** Electric (50 amps). **Each Site:** Picnic table, fire ring. **Dump Station:** Yes. **Laundry:** Yes. **Pay Phone:** Yes. **Rest Rooms and Showers:** Yes. **Fuel:** No. **Propane:** Yes. **Internal Roads:** Paved, in good condition. **RV Service:** No. **Market:** 6 mi. northeast in Blanchester. **Restaurant:** 6 mi. northeast in Blanchester. **General Store:** Yes. **Vending:** Yes. **Swimming Pool:** No. **Playground:** Yes. **Other:** Stonelick lake, beach, boat launch, amphitheater, hiking trail, rental camper units. **Activities:** Swimming, fishing, boating (electric motors only), hiking, schedule activities. **Nearby Attractions:** Kings Island Amusement Park, Blue Jacket outdoor drama, Wilmington College, antqiues, museums. **Additional Information:** Clinton County CVB, (877) 4-A-VISIT.

Restrictions

Pets: Leash only, pet camping area; $1 per night per pet, max. of 2 pets. **Fires:** Fire pits only. **Alcoholic Beverages:** Not permitted. **Vehicle Maximum Length:** 35 ft. **Other:** 14-day stay limit.

To Get There

From the junction of Hwy. 28 and Hwy. 133, drive 6 mi. southwest on Hwy. 133, then 1.5 mi. south on Hwy. 727. Roads are wide and well maintained w/ good shoulders.

BLUFFTON

Twin Lakes Park

3506 Township Rd. 34, Bluffton 45817. T: (419) 477-5255; twinlakes@turbosurf.net.

RV ★★★ Tent ★★★

Beauty: ★★★ Site Privacy: ★★★
Spaciousness: ★★★ Quiet: ★★★
Security: ★★★ Cleanliness: ★★★
Insect Control: Yes Facilities: ★★★

A grassy campground on two lakes, Twin Lakes Park offers level, wooded, and open sites. Located five miles north of Bluffton, the campground's typical site has a width of 30 feet. There are 50 seasonals and three pull-through sites. Situated near I-75, the campground is subject to some noise from vehicles whizzing past. The best RV sites are by the lake or near the facilities. Tent sites are in a separate area with more greenery and privacy. A flea market, where campers set-up is free, is a popular event that takes place the last Saturday of each month, May through Aug. Safety measures include a 5.5-mph speed limit and speed bumps. Security includes one entrance/exit through a card-coded gate, owners who live on site, and regular patrols.

Basics

Operated by: Bob & Elaine Harris. **Open:** All year. **Site Assignment:** Reservations w/ 1-night deposit; refunds "if you name appears in the Findlay Courier obituary columns.". **Registration:** At campground office. **Fee:** $30 (cash, check, credit cards). **Parking:** At site.

Facilities

Number of RV Sites: 85. **Number of Tent-Only Sites:** 10. **Hookups:** Electric (30, 50 amps), water, sewer. **Each Site:** Picnic table, fire ring. **Dump Station:** Yes. **Laundry:** No. **Pay Phone:** Yes. **Rest Rooms and Showers:** Yes. **Fuel:** No. **Propane:** Yes. **Internal Roads:** Paved, in good condition. **RV Service:** No. **Market:** 5 mi. south in Bluffton. **Restaurant:** 5 mi. south in Bluffton. **General Store:** Yes, limited. **Vending:** Yes. **Swimming Pool:** No. **Playground:** Yes. **Other:** Swimming lake, fishing lake, volleyball, horseshoes, shuffleboard, basketball, shelter house, game room, volleyball, sandy beach, sports field. **Activities:** Swimming, fishing, boating (rental rental rowboats, canoe, paddleboats available), scheduled weekend activities. **Nearby Attractions:** Golf, antiques, museums, historic homes, arts & crafts shops, motorsports park, Children's Garden, skating arena, Neil Armstrong Air & Space Museum, Indian Lake. **Additional Information:** Lima/Allen County CVB, (888) 222-6075.

Restrictions

Pets: Leash only; $2 for first pet, $3 for additional. Must provide proof current vaccinations for pets. **Fires:** Fire ring only. **Alcoholic Beverages:** Permitted. **Vehicle Maximum Length:** None. **Other:** No hunting of frogs or turtles, limit of 2 bass.

To Get There

From the junction of I-75 and Hwy. 235, take Exit 145 and drive 0.1 mi. south on Hwy. 235, then 0.5 mi. east on Township Rd. 34. The roads are wide and well maintained w/ broad shoulders.

BOWLING GREEN

Fire Lake Camper Park

13630 West Kramer Rd., Bowling Green 43402. T: (419) 352-1185; www.gocampingamerica.com.

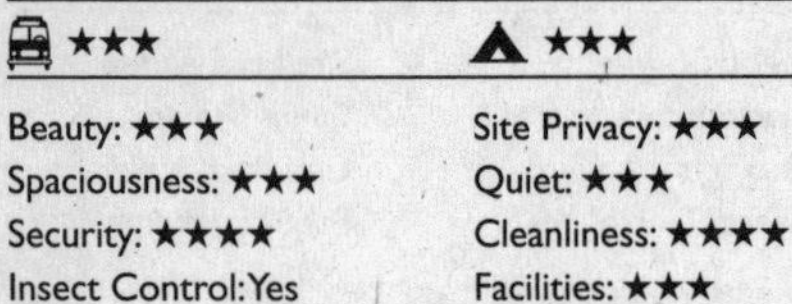

RV ★★★ Tent ★★★

Beauty: ★★★ Site Privacy: ★★★
Spaciousness: ★★★ Quiet: ★★★
Security: ★★★★ Cleanliness: ★★★★
Insect Control: Yes Facilities: ★★★

A rural campground by an eight-acre lake, Fire Lake Camper Park offers open and shaded sites with easy access to the interstate. Some highway traffic noise can be heard at the far end of the campground. Sites are grassy with gravel pads for parking. The campground has 45 seasonal campers and five pull-through sites. Many sites are right on the lake, and most offer a lake view. A design flaw affecting a number of sites is the positioning of vehicle parking berween the lake and the campsites. Typical site width is 30 feet. The campground is adjacent to the Slippery Elm Trail, a 23-mile trail that is free and open to the public for biking, walking, running, skating, horseback riding, and rollerblading. The trail, which is also wheelchair accesible, is a beautiful natural corridor converted from an unused railroad track. Bikes are available for rent at the campground. Security measures include owners who live on site, one entrance/exit road (with an enforced five-mph speed limit), and regular campground patrols.

Basics

Operated by: Martin & Jennifer Gladieux. **Open:** Apr. 15–Oct. 15. **Site Assignment:** Reservations w/ 1-night deposit; refunds w/ 7-day notice. **Registration:** At campground office. **Fee:** $22 (cash, check, credit cards). **Parking:** At site.

Facilities

Number of RV Sites: 96. **Number of Tent-Only Sites:** 20. **Hookups:** Electric (30 amps), water. **Each Site:** Picnic table, fire ring. **Dump Station:** Yes. **Laundry:** Yes. **Pay Phone:** Yes. **Rest Rooms and Showers:** Yes. **Fuel:** No. **Propane:** Yes. **Internal Roads:** Paved/gravel, in good condition. **RV Service:** No. **Market:** 3 mi. north in Bowling Green. **Restaurant:** 3 mi. north in Bowling Green. **General Store:** Yes. **Vending:** Yes. **Swimming Pool:** No. **Playground:** Yes. **Other:** Lake, swimming beach, rental cabins, basketball, volleyball, pavilion, rec room, boat dock, sports field, rental bikes. **Activities:** Swimming, catch-&-release fishing, boating (rental kayaks & paddleboats available), scheduled weekend activities. **Nearby Attractions:** Bowling Green State University, Slippery Elm Trail, museum, Sauder Historic village, golf, antiques, mill, canal boat, passenger train, Toledo Zoo. **Additional Information:** Greater Toledo CVB, (800) 243-4667.

Restrictions

Pets: Leash only. **Fires:** Fire ring only. **Alcoholic Beverages:** At sites only. **Vehicle Maximum Length:** None.

To Get There

From the junction of I-75 and US 6, take Exit 179 and drive 1.5 mi. west on US 6, then 0.5 mi. south on Hwy. 25, then 0.5 mi. west on Kramer Rd. Roads are wide and well maintained w/ broad shoulders.

BROOKVILLE

Dayton Tall Timbers KOA Resort

7796 Wellbaum Rd., Brookville 45309. T: (937) 833-3888; daytonkoa@aol.com.

RV ★★★★ Tent ★★★

Beauty: ★★★★ Site Privacy: ★★★★
Spaciousness: ★★★★ Quiet: ★★★★
Security: ★★★★★ Cleanliness: ★★★★★
Insect Control: None Facilities: ★★★★★

Dayton Tall Timbers Resort KOA has all the large and small touches that make camping a pleasure. Laid out in a series of loops, the campground is grassy with gravel parking spots and concrete patios. The semi-wooded facility offers a choice of open or shaded sites. The typical site width is 30 feet, and the campground has 20 seasonal campers and 150 pull-through sites. Little ponds, gazebos, flowers, brick walkways, benches, and a covered bridge add to the beauty. A well-stocked general store also features craft and souvenir items. A spring-fed fishing lake has bass, bluegill, perch, crappie, and catfish. No mini-bikes, mopeds or golf carts are allowed. Modest swimwear is required, i.e., no revealing bikinis or thongs. Alcoholic beverages are permitted at campsites, but tables should be kept free of open containers. Speed limit is five mph. Security measures include owners who live on site, one entrance/exit road, and regular campground patrols.

Basics

Operated by: Jim & Jane Rose. **Open:** Apr. 1–Nov. 1. **Site Assignment:** Reservations w/ 1-night deposit; refund (minus $5) w/ 7-day notice. **Registration:** At campground office. **Fee:** $32 (cash, check, credit cards). **Parking:** At site.

Facilities

Number of RV Sites: 235. **Number of Tent-Only Sites:** 0. **Hookups:** Electric (20, 30, 50 amps), water, sewer, modem. **Each Site:** Picnic table, fire ring. **Dump Station:** Yes. **Laundry:** Yes. **Pay Phone:** Yes. **Rest Rooms and Showers:** Yes. **Fuel:** No. **Propane:** Yes. **Internal Roads:** Paved/gravel, in good condition. **RV Service:** No. **Market:** 3 mi. west in Brookville. **Restaurant:** 3 mi. west in Brookville. **General Store:** Yes. **Vending:** Yes. **Swimming Pool:** Yes. **Playground:** Yes. **Other:** Petting zoo, basketball, horseshoes, mini golf, game room, picnic shelter, hiking trail, volleyball, rental cabins, badminton, fishing lake, coin games, pavilion, sports field. **Activities:** Swimming, boating (rental paddleboats available), fishing, hiking, scheduled activities. **Nearby Attractions:** Golf, US Air Force Museum, Sunwatch Indian Village, Wright Cycle Company Shop, Dayton Art Institute, Packard Museum, historic homes, musuems, outdoor drama, Paramount Kings Island Theme Park, Museum of Discovery. **Additional Information:** Dayton & Montgomery County CVB, (800) 221-8235.

Restrictions

Pets: Leash only. **Fires:** Fire ring only. **Alcoholic Beverages:** At sites only. **Vehicle Maximum Length:** None.

To Get There

From the junction of I-70 and Hwy. 49N, take Exit 24 and drive 0.5 mi. north on Hwy. 49, then 0.5 mi. west on Pleasant Plains Rd., then 0.25 mi. south on Wellbaum Rd. Roads are wide and well maintained w/ broad shoulders.

BUCKEYE LAKE

Buckeye Lake KOA

P.O. Box 972, Buckeye Lake 43008. T: (740) 928-0706; buckeyekoa@aol.com.

RV ★★★★ Tent ★★★★

Beauty: ★★★★ Site Privacy: ★★★★
Spaciousness: ★★★★ Quiet: ★★★★
Security: ★★★★ Cleanliness: ★★★★
Insect Control: Yes Facilities: ★★★★

Located 23 miles east of Columbus, Buckeye Lake KOA offers shady, level sites. The campground has ten seasonals, 102 pull-through sites, and a typical site width of 35 feet. Our favorite RV sites are the full-hookup ones. The best tent sites are in the primitive area at the rear of the campground, with more trees and privacy. Some tenters prefer the sites with full hookup or water and electric, but the tradeoff is a little less privacy and green space. Because it is convenient to the interstate and offers easy access, the campground is popular with campers visiting Columbus attractions. No outside firewood is permitted in the campground in order to prevent tree diseases, but firewood is for sale at the campground. A small gift shop is a nice touch. The campground provides on-site security 24/7.

Basics

Operated by: Preble Family. **Open:** Apr. 2, Oct. 31. **Site Assignment:** Reservations w/ 1-night deposit; refund w/ 7-day notice. **Registration:** At campground office. **Fee:** $38 (cash, check, credit cards). **Parking:** At site.

Facilities

Number of RV Sites: 177. **Number of Tent-Only Sites:** 28. **Hookups:** Electric (20, 30, 50 amps), water, sewer, phone, cable TV. **Each Site:** Picnic table, fire ring. **Dump Station:** Yes. **Laundry:** Yes. **Pay Phone:** Yes. **Rest Rooms and Showers:** Yes. **Fuel:** No. **Propane:** Yes. **Internal Roads:** Gravel, in good condition. **RV Service:** No. **Market:** 2 mi. south. **Restaurant:** 2 mi. south. **General Store:** Yes. **Vending:** Yes. **Swimming Pool:** Yes. **Playground:** Yes. **Other:** Rec hall, pavilion, coin games, mini-golf, basketball, shuffleboard, movies, badminton, sports field, horseshoes, hiking trails, volleyball, rental cabins. **Activities:** Swimming, hiking, scheduled weekend activities. **Nearby Attractions:** Golf, musuems, Columbus Zoo, botanical garden & conservatory, German Village, Ohio Statehouse, COSI Columbus, antiques, Ohio State Univ., museums, historic homes. **Additional Information:** Greater Columbus CVB, (800) 345-4386.

Restrictions

Pets: Leash only. **Fires:** Fire rings only, no outside wood can be brought in. **Alcoholic Beverages:** At sites only. **Vehicle Maximum Length:** None.

To Get There

From the junction of I-70 and Hwy. 79, take Exit 129A, then drive 1.5 mi. south on Hwy. 79. Roads are wide and well maintained w/ broad shoulders.

BUTLER
Blue Lagoon Campground

1597 SR 97 East, Butler 44822. T: (419) 883-3888; bluelagooncg@aol.com.

RV ★★★ Tent ★★★

Beauty: ★★★ Site Privacy: ★★★★
Spaciousness: ★★★★ Quiet: ★★★★
Security: ★★★★ Cleanliness: ★★★★
Insect Control: None Facilities: ★★★

Nestled in the foothills of the Appalachian Mountains along Clear Fork River, Blue Lagoon Campground offers level, open sites with a typical site width of 50 feet. Located three miles west of Butler, the campground has one seasonal camper and two pull-through areas. A five-mph speed limit and quiet hours between 11 p.m. and 8 a.m. are enforced. The river is stocked by the Ohio Division of Natural Resources with trout and 26 other species of fish. The property is the only full-facility campground with direct access to the Richland B & O Bike Trail, an 18-mile paved multi-use trail. Open year-round during daylight hours and accessible to people with disabilities, the trail is off-limits to motorized vehicles and horseback riding. Security measures at the campground include owners who live on site and locked bathroom facilities. Campers pay a $5 deposit to get a bathroom key.

Basics

Operated by: David & Linda Chalut. **Open:** May 1–Oct. 15. **Site Assignment:** Reservations w/ 1-night deposit; refund (minus $4) w/ 7-day notice. **Registration:** At campground office. **Fee:** $22 (cash, credit cards). **Parking:** At site.

Facilities

Number of RV Sites: 27. **Number of Tent-Only Sites:** 17. **Hookups:** Electric (20, 30 amps), water, sewer. **Each Site:** Picnic table, fire ring. **Dump Station:** Yes. **Laundry:** Yes. **Pay Phone:** No. **Rest Rooms and Showers:** Yes. **Fuel:** No. **Propane:** Yes. **Internal Roads:** Paved, in good condition. **RV Service:** No. **Market:** 3 mi. east in Butler. **Restaurant:** 3 mi. east in Butler. **General Store:** Yes. **Vending:** No. **Swimming Pool:** No. **Playground:** Yes. **Other:** Swimming pond, fishing river, volleyball, rental cabin, tetherball, horseshoes, basketball. **Activities:** Swimming, fishing. **Nearby Attractions:** Living Bible Museum, Johnny Appleseed Monument, Richland Carousel Park, state forest, covered bridge, Amish country, Mid-Ohio Sports Car Course, golf, antiques, arts & crafts, Kingwood Center. **Additional Information:** Mansfield-Richland Area Chamber of Commerce, (419) 522-3211.

Restrictions

Pets: Leash only, $1 per pet. **Fires:** Fire rings only; fires must be extinguished before retiring for night. **Alcoholic Beverages:** Permitted. **Vehicle Maximum Length:** None. **Other:** RV outdoor mats larger than 2 × 3 ft. are not permitted.

To Get There

From the junction of I-71 and Hwy. 97, take Exit 165 and drive 7.7 mi. east on Hwy. 97. Roads are wide and well maintained w/ broad shoulders.

BUTLER
Butler Mohican KOA

6918 Bunker Hill Rd. South, Butler 44822. T: (419) 883-3314; F: (419) 883-3149; www.koa.com/where/oh/35134.htm; ButlerMohicanKOA@aolcom.

RV ★★★ Tent ★★★

Beauty: ★★★ Site Privacy: ★★★★
Spaciousness: ★★★★ Quiet: ★★★★
Security: ★★★★ Cleanliness: ★★
Insect Control: None Facilities: ★★★

A quiet country campground, Butler Mohican KOA is semi wooded with a choice of open or shaded sites. The rental cabins look new, but the rest of the campground could use some cleaning and fixing up. Located eight miles east of Butler, the campground has five seasonal campers, 15 pull-through sites, and a typical site width of 35 feet. Quiet time from 10:30 p.m. to 8:30 a.m. is enforced. No generators or loud music are allowed at any time. Speed limit is ten mph. Fishing in Broken Arrow Lake is from dawn to dusk only, and all fish must be released when caught. Swimming and wading are not permitted in the lake. Security measures include one entrance/exit road, surveillance cameras, and owners who live on the site.

Basics

Operated by: Kevin & Cathy Wies. **Open:** Apr. 1–Nov. 1. **Site Assignment:** Reservations w/ $25 deposit; refund (minus $5) w/ 3-day notice. **Registration:** At campground office. **Fee:** $25 (cash, check, credit cards). **Parking:** At site.

Facilities

Number of RV Sites: 57. **Number of Tent-Only Sites:** 33. **Hookups:** Electric (20, 30, 50 amps), water, sewer. **Each Site:** Picnic table, fire ring. **Dump Station:** Yes. **Laundry:** Yes. **Pay Phone:** Yes. **Rest Rooms and Showers:** Yes. **Fuel:** No. **Propane:** No. **Internal Roads:** Gravel, in good condition. **RV Service:** No. **Market:** 8 mi. west in Butler. **Restaurant:** 8 mi. west in Butler. **General Store:** Yes. **Vending:** No. **Swimming Pool:** Yes. **Playground:** Yes. **Other:** Broken Arrow Lake, rental cabins, pavilion, game room, basketball, horseshoes, coin games, hiking trails. **Activities:** Swimming, fishing, hiking, scheduled weekend activities. **Nearby Attractions:** Living Bible Museum, Johnny Appleseed Monument, Richland Carousel Park, state forest, covered bridge, Amish country, Mid Ohio Sports Car Course, golf, antiques, arts & crafts, Kingwood Center, B & O Bike Trail. **Additional Information:** Mansfield-Richland Area Chamber of Commerce, (419) 522-3211.

Restrictions

Pets: Leash only. **Fires:** Fire ring only. **Alcoholic Beverages:** Permitted. **Vehicle Maximum Length:** None.

To Get There

From the junction of Hwy. 95 and Hwy. 97, drive 3.5 mi. east on Hwy. 97, then 2 mi. south on Bunkerhill Rd. Hwy. 97 is wide and well maintained with generally broad shoulders. Bunkerhill Rd. is a winding country road with narrow shoulders.

CAMBRIDGE
Hillview Acres Campground

66271 Wolfs Den Rd., Cambridge 43725. T: (740) 439-3348

RV ★★★ Tent ★★★

Beauty: ★★★★ Site Privacy: ★★★★
Spaciousness: ★★★★ Quiet: ★★★★
Security: ★★★★ Cleanliness: ★★
Insect Control: None Facilities: ★★★

Hillview Acres Campground looks like a state park except the roads aren't paved. Located one mile east of Cambridge, the campground has a wealth of natural beauty—rolling hillsides, old forests, and ponds. The campground itself is clean and well maintained but needs a new shower and bathroom facility. The ten-mph speed limit also could be cut in half because the campground has such steep narrow hills and so many youngsters playing outdoors. Sitting atop a hill, the campground is quiet with no highway noise. Campers have a choice of shaded or open sites; the hills are beautiful in autumn foliage. Laid out in a series of loops well separated from each other, the campground has a typical site width of 33 feet. There are 70 seasonal campers and seven pull-through sites. Quiet time is from 11 p.m. to 7 a.m., and no "foul" music is permitted at any time. Security measures here include one entrance/exit road, owners who live on site, and regular patrols of the campground.

Basics

Operated by: John & Nancy Walker. **Open:** Apr. 15–Oct. 31. **Site Assignment:** Reservations w/ 1-night deposit; refunds w/ 48-hour notice. **Registration:** At campground office. **Fee:** $20 (cash, check, credit cards). **Parking:** At site.

Facilities

Number of RV Sites: 145. **Number of Tent-Only Sites:** 25. **Hookups:** Electric (30 amps), water. **Each Site:** Picnic table, fire ring. **Dump Station:** Yes. **Laundry:** No. **Pay Phone:** Yes. **Rest Rooms and Showers:** Yes. **Fuel:** No. **Propane:** No. **Internal Roads:** Gravel, in good condition. **RV Service:** No. **Market:** 1 mi. west in Cambridge. **Restaurant:** 1 mi. west in Cambridge. **General Store:** Yes. **Vending:** No. **Swimming Pool:** Yes. **Playground:** Yes. **Other:** Rec room, pavilion, coin games, catch-&-release fishing pond, basketball, badminton, sports field, horseshoes, hiking trails, volleyball. **Activities:** Swimming, fishing, hiking, scheduled weekend activities. **Nearby Attractions:** State parks, golf, antiques, art glass factories, museums, Living Word outdoor drama, Hopalong Cassidy Museum, riding stable, Amish country. **Additional Information:** Cambridge CVB, (800) 933-5480.

Restrictions

Pets: Leash only. **Fires:** Fire ring only. **Alcoholic Beverages:** Permitted. **Vehicle Maximum Length:** None.

To Get There

From the junction of I-77 and US 22, drive 4 mi. east on US 22, then 0.25 mi. south on Wolf's Den Rd. US 22 is wide and well maintained w/ mostly broad shoulders. Wolf's Den Rd. is narrow and winding w/ steep hills.

CAMBRIDGE

Spring Valley Campground

8000 Dozer Rd., Cambridge 43725. T: (740) 439-9291

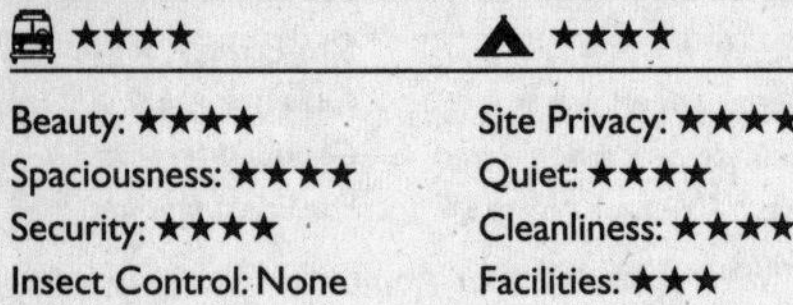

RV ★★★★ Tent ★★★★

Beauty: ★★★★ Site Privacy: ★★★★
Spaciousness: ★★★★ Quiet: ★★★★
Security: ★★★★ Cleanliness: ★★★★
Insect Control: None Facilities: ★★★

With easy access off the interstate, Spring Valley Campground is surprisingly quiet. The grassy campground is cushioned by beautiful hills and woods. Level sites include 21 pull-throughs and a typical site width of 35 feet. Most sites have trees, but there are some open sites. There are also 65 seasonal campers. The well-maintained campground has a five-mph speed limit and quiet time beginning at 11 p.m. Sunday through Friday and at midnight on Saturday. The 3.5-acre lake is stocked with bass, crappie, and bluegill. It also has a beach area, slides, and diving boards, as well as a separate swimming pool. Security includes one entrance/exit road and owners who live on site.

Basics

Operated by: Hlads family. **Open:** Apr. 1–Nov. 1. **Site Assignment:** Reservations w/ $10 deposit, not refundable or transferable. **Registration:** At campground office. **Fee:** $23 (cash, check, credit cards). **Parking:** At site.

Facilities

Number of RV Sites: 180. **Number of Tent-Only Sites:** 50. **Hookups:** Electric (30, 50 amps), water, sewer, cable TV. **Each Site:** Picnic table, fire ring. **Dump Station:** Yes. **Laundry:** No. **Pay Phone:** Yes. **Rest Rooms and Showers:** Yes. **Fuel:** No. **Propane:** Yes. **Internal Roads:** Gravel, in good condition. **RV Service:** No. **Market:** 1 mi. in any direction. **Restaurant:** 1 mi. in any direction. **General Store:** Yes. **Vending:** Yes. **Swimming Pool:** Yes. **Playground:** Yes. **Other:** Lake, pavilion, rental cabins, basketball, rec room, coin games, badminton, sports field, horseshoes, hiking trails, volleyball. **Activities:** Swimming, fishing, hiking, scheduled weekend activities. **Nearby Attractions:** State parks, golf, antiques, art glass factories & museums, Living Word outdoor drams, museums, Hopalong Cassidy Museum, riding stable, Amish country. **Additional Information:** Cambridge Visitors & Convention Bureau, (800) 933-5480.

Restrictions

Pets: Leash only. **Fires:** Fire ring only. **Alcoholic Beverages:** Not permitted. **Vehicle Maximum Length:** None.

To Get There

From the junction of I-77 and I-70, drive 1 mi. west on I-70. Take Exit 178, then 50 yards south on Hwy. 209, then 1 mi. west on Dozer Rd. Roads are wide and well maintained w/ broad shoulders.

CANTON

Bear Creek Resort Ranch KOA

3232 Downing St. Southwest, East Sparta 44626. T: (330) 484-3901

RV ★★★★ Tent ★★★★

Beauty: ★★★★ Site Privacy: ★★★★
Spaciousness: ★★★★ Quiet: ★★★★
Security: ★★★★ Cleanliness: ★★★★★
Insect Control: None Facilities: ★★★★

A hilly campground with level sites, Bear Creek Ranch Resort offers a western flair. Horses and ponies are available, and the campground provides miles of wooded horse trails. Located three miles south of Canton, the campground has grassy sites with gravel parking spots, along with a choice of open or shaded sites. The campground has 12 seasonal campers, 42 pull-through sites, and a typical site width of 35 feet. The facility is very clean and well maintained, including such touches as a live ivy plant, curtains, and wallpaper border in the bathroom. The most popular sites for tents and RVs both are alongside the lake and in the woods. No generators or loud radios are permitted, and quiet times are between 11 p.m. and 8 a.m. Speed limit is ten mph—rather high for such a child-pleasing campground. Security includes owners who live on site and provide regular patrols.

Basics

Operated by: Lee & Carol Soehnlen. **Open:** All year. **Site Assignment:** Reservations w/ 1-night deposit; refund w/ 1-day notice. **Registration:** At campground office. **Fee:** $28 (cash, credit cards). **Parking:** At site.

Facilities

Number of RV Sites: 782. **Number of Tent-Only Sites:** 30. **Hookups:** Electric (50 amps), water, sewer. **Each Site:** Picnic table, fire ring. **Dump Station:** Yes. **Laundry:** Yes. **Pay Phone:** Yes. **Rest Rooms and Showers:** Yes. **Fuel:** No. **Propane:** Yes. **Internal Roads:** Paved/gravel, in good condition. **RV Service:** No. **Market:** 3 mi. north in Canton. **Restaurant:** 3 mi. north in Canton. **General Store:** Yes. **Vending:** Yes. **Swimming Pool:** Yes. **Playground:** Yes. **Other:** Catch-&-release fishing pond, rental cabins, pavilion, mini golf, activities field, basketball, volleyball, badminton, tetherball, horseshoes, game room, coin games, horseback riding trails. **Activities:** Swimming, fishing, horseback riding (rental horses available), boating (rental paddleboat available), scheduled weekend activities. **Nearby Attractions:** Pro Football Hall of Fame, golf, Canton Classic Car Museum, antiques, arts & crafts, McKinley Museum of History, Science & Industry, McKinley National Memorial, historic homes, Amish community. **Additional Information:** Canton/Stark County CVB.

Restrictions

Pets: Leash only. **Fires:** Fire ring only. **Alcoholic Beverages:** At sites only. **Vehicle Maximum Length:** None.

To Get There

From the junction of 1-77 and Fohl Rd., take Exit 99, drive 3 mi. south on Sherman Church Rd., then 1 mi. east on Haut Rd. Roads are wide and well maintained w/ mostly broad shoulders.

DELAWARE

Alum Creek State Park Campground

3615 South Old State Rd., Delaware 43015. T: (740) 548-4039

RV ★★★★ Tent ★★★★

Beauty: ★★★★ Site Privacy: ★★★★
Spaciousness: ★★★★ Quiet: ★★★★
Security: ★★★★ Cleanliness: ★★★★
Insect Control: None Facilities: ★★★

For beauty, it is hard to beat most state parks. At Alum Creek State Park Campground, the surroundings include mature forests of maple, oak, elm, and locust trees, along with a huge inland beach, lovely lake and pond, and a variety of hiking trails. Sites are mostly shaded and level with no pull-throughs. There are also no seasonal campers. RVs or tents have access to any site. The most popular areas are on G road because of its proximity to the beach, and the ends of B, G, L, and K roads because they are premium sites near the lake. Security includes a gatehouse, campground office, and regular patrols by campground officers.

Basics

Operated by: State of Ohio. **Open:** All year. **Site Assignment:** First come, first served. No reservations. **Registration:** At campground office. **Fee:** $17 (cash, check, credit cards). **Parking:** At site.

Facilities

Number of RV Sites: 297. **Number of Tent-Only Sites:** 0. **Hookups:** Electric (15 amps). **Each Site:** Picnic table, fire ring. **Dump Station:** Yes. **Laundry:** No. **Pay Phone:** Yes. **Rest Rooms and Showers:** Yes. **Fuel:** No. **Propane:** No. **Internal Roads:** Paved, in good condition. **RV Service:** No. **Market:** 6 mi. east in Delaware. **Restaurant:** 6 mi. east in Delaware. **General Store:** Yes. **Vending:** Yes. **Swimming Pool:** No. **Playground:** Yes. **Other:** Swimming lake, beach, nature trails, fishing lake, amphitheater, pond, basketball, volleyball, horseshoes, boat dock, boat ramp, horse trails, sports field. **Activities:** Swimming, fishing, hiking, boating (rental boats available), scheduled activities. **Nearby Attractions:** Golf, Ohio Statehouse, Ohio State University, science museum, zoo, German Village, museums, historic homes, antiques, arts & crafts, tennis, baseball, horse racing. **Additional Information:** Greater Columbus CVB, (800) 800) 345-4386.

Restrictions

Pets: Leash only, pet camping area, $1 fee per pet per day. **Fires:** Fire ring only. **Alcoholic Beverages:** Not permitted. **Vehicle Maximum Length:** 35 ft. **Other:** 14-day stay limit.

To Get There

From the junction of I-71 and Hwy. 36/37, drive 1 mi. west on Hwy. 36/37. Road is wide and well maintained w/ broad shoulders.

DELAWARE

Cross Creek Camping Resort

3190 South Old State Rd., Delaware 43015. T: (740) 549-2267; www.alumcreek.com.

RV ★★★★ Tent ★★★★

Beauty: ★★★★ Site Privacy: ★★★★
Spaciousness: ★★★★ Quiet: ★★★★
Security: ★★★★ Cleanliness: ★★★★★
Insect Control: Yes Facilities: ★★★★

Ringed by woods, Cross Creek Camping Resort offers shaded or open spots on level sites. The campground is grassy with gravel parking spaces. Located five miles southeast of Delaware, the campground has 30 seasonal campers, 11 pull-through sites, and a typical site width of 35 feet. The facility is well maintained, with sparkling restrooms,that have curtains on both the shower the dressing room. A whimsical touch is a fire hydrant painted like a dog. Security and safety measures include a five-mph speed limit, speed bumps, a traffic control gate, and a manager who lives on site and patrols the campground. Open year-round, Cross Creek Camping Resort is a popular winter stopover for campers because of its proximity to Columbus and because water hookups are available at the campground in the winter.

BASICS

Operated by: Steve Cross. **Open:** All year. **Site Assignment:** Reservations w/ 1-night deposit; refund w/ 7-day notice. **Registration:** At campground office. **Fee:** $28 (cash, check, credit cards). **Parking:** At site.

FACILITIES

Number of RV Sites: 179. **Number of Tent-Only Sites:** 21. **Hookups:** Electric (30, 50 amps), water, sewer. **Each Site:** Picnic table, fire ring. **Dump Station:** Yes. **Laundry:** Yes. **Pay Phone:** Yes. **Rest Rooms and Showers:** Yes. **Fuel:** No. **Propane:** Yes. **Internal Roads:** Paved, in good condition. **RV Service:** No. **Market:** 5 mi. northwest in Delaware. **Restaurant:** 5 mi. northwest in Delaware. **General Store:** Yes. **Vending:** Yes. **Swimming Pool:** Yes. **Playground:** Yes. **Other:** Pavilion, shuffleboard, basketball, tennis, horseshoes, club house, game room, fishing pond, billiards, coin games, movies, volleyball, badminton. **Activities:** Swimming, fishing, hiking, scheduled activities. **Nearby Attractions:** Golf, Ohio Statehouse, Ohio State University, science museum, Columbus Zoo, German Village, museums, historic homes, antiques, arts & crafts, tennis, baseball, horse racing. **Additional Information:** Greater Columbus CVB, (800) 345-4386.

RESTRICTIONS

Pets: Leash only. **Fires:** Fire ring only. **Alcoholic Beverages:** At sites only. **Vehicle Maximum Length:** None.

TO GET THERE

From the junction of I-71, US 36, and Hwy. 37, take Exit 131 and drive 3 mi. west on US 36/Hwy. 37, then 3 mi. south on Lackey Rd. Roads are wide and well maintained w/ broad shoulders.

FINDLAY

Shady Lake Campground

11506 Township Rd. 101, Findlay 45840. T: (419) 423-3490

RV ★★★ Tent ★★★

Beauty: ★★ Site Privacy: ★★★
Spaciousness: ★★★ Quiet: ★★★
Security: ★★★ Cleanliness: ★★
Insect Control: Yes Facilities: ★★★

A rural lakeside campground with open and shaded sites, Shady Lake Campground offers easy access from the interstate. Located three miles north of Findlay, the campground has 70 seasonal campers and five pull-through sites. The typical site width is 35 feet. Quiet hours are from 10 p.m. to 8 a.m. and children under 18 years of age are to be at their campsite at sundown, unless accompanied by an adult. A maximum of two sets of lights is permitted per campsite, and they must be turned off upon retiring for the night. Security lights and Christmas lights are not permitted. All fish are catch and release except bluegill. Speed limit is five mph and includes bicycles. A railroad track runs along one side of the campground, detracting somewhat from the camping experience.

BASICS

Operated by: Terry & Claudia Rowland. **Open:** Apr. 15–Oct. 15. **Site Assignment:** Reservations w/ 1-night deposit; refunds w/ 7-day notice. **Registration:** At campground office. **Fee:** $17 (cash, check). **Parking:** At site.

FACILITIES

Number of RV Sites: 130. **Number of Tent-Only Sites:** 20. **Hookups:** Electric (30 amps), water. **Each Site:** Picnic table, fire ring. **Dump Station:** Yes. **Laundry:** No. **Pay Phone:** Yes. **Rest Rooms and Showers:** Yes. **Fuel:** No. **Propane:** Yes. **Internal Roads:** Gravel, in good condition. **RV Service:** No. **Market:** 3 mi. south in Findlay. **Restaurant:** 3 mi. south in Findlay. **General Store:** Yes, limited. **Vending:** Yes. **Swimming Pool:** No. **Playground:** Yes. **Other:** Lake, pavilion, swimming beach, shuffleboard, sports field, horseshoes, volleyball. **Activities:** Swimming, fishing, boating (rental rowboats, canoes & paddleboats available). **Nearby Attractions:** Golf, museums, canal boat, passenger train, antiques, Toledo Zoo, boauems, antiques, arts & crafts shops. **Additional Information:** Greater Toledo CVB, (800) 243-4667.

RESTRICTIONS

Pets: Leash only. **Fires:** Fire ring only. **Alcoholic Beverages:** Permitted. **Vehicle Maximum Length:** None.

TO GET THERE

From the junction of US 224 and I-75, drive 2 mi. north on I-75, take Exit 161, drive 0.5 mi. east on Township Rd 99, then 1.5 mi. north on CR 220, then 0.5 mi. west on Township Rd 101. Roads are wide and well maintained w/ broad shoulders.

GALENA

Berkshire Lake Campground

1848 Alexander Rd., Galena 43021. T: (740) 965-2321

RV ★★★ Tent n/a

Beauty: ★★★ Site Privacy: ★★★
Spaciousness: ★★★ Quiet: ★★★★
Security: ★★★★ Cleanliness: ★★★
Insect Control: None Facilities: ★★★

A tradition since 1966, Berkshire Lake Campgrounds is still run by its original owner and now attracts the grandchildren of some old-time campers. The campground also has an action committee composed of veteran Berkshire campers to coordinate and oversee activities and help support campground improvements. Sites are mostly grassy and shaded, with 175 seasonal campers and eight pull-throughs. No tents are allowed. Laid out in a series of loops, the campground has a fishging-only lake (no swimming or boating). A ten-mph speed limit is enforced, as are quiet hours from midnight until 8 a.m. Security measures here include a gate, an owner who lives on site, and regular patrols of the campground.

BASICS

Operated by: Bill Davis. **Open:** All year. **Site Assignment:** Reservations w/ 1-night deposit; refund w/ 7-day notice. **Registration:** At campground office. **Fee:** $21 (cash, check, credit cards). **Parking:** At site.

FACILITIES

Number of RV Sites: 350. **Number of Tent-Only Sites:** 0. **Hookups:** Electric (30 amps), water, sewer. **Each Site:** Picnic table, fire ring. **Dump Station:** No. **Laundry:** Yes. **Pay Phone:** Yes. **Rest Rooms and Showers:** Yes. **Fuel:** No. **Propane:** Yes. **Internal Roads:** Gravel, in fair condition. **RV Service:** Yes. **Market:** 6 mi. northeast in Sunbury. **Restaurant:** 6 mi. northeast in Sunbury. **General Store:** Yes. **Vending:** No. **Swimming Pool:** Yes. **Playground:** Yes. **Other:** Mini golf, basketball, horseshoes, volleyball, game room, meeting room, lake, sports field, coin games. **Activities:** Swimming, fishing, scheduled weekend activities. **Nearby Attractions:** Golf, Ohio Statehouse, Ohio State University, science museum, Columbus Zoo, German Village, museums, historic homes, antiques, arts & crafts, tennis, baseball, horse racing. **Additional Information:** Greater Columbus CVB, (800) 345-4386.

RESTRICTIONS

Pets: Leash only. **Fires:** Fire ring only. **Alcoholic Beverages:** Not permitted. **Vehicle Maximum Length:** 40 ft. **Other:** No tents allowed.

TO GET THERE

From the junction of I-71 and Hwy. 36/37, drive 0.25 mi. east on Hwy. 36/37, then 3 mi. south on South Galena Rd. (CR 34), then 0.5 mi. southwest on Alexander. Bear left at the 5-way stop. Roads are wide and well maintained w/ broad shoulders, except for some narrow shoulders on South Galena Rd.

GENEVA-ON-THE-LAKE

Indian Creek Camping Resort

4710 Lake Rd. East, Geneva-on-the Lake 44041. T: (440) 466-8191; F: (440) 466-6900; www.indiancreekresort.com.

RV ★★★★★ Tent ★★★★★

Beauty: ★★★★★ Site Privacy: ★★★★★
Spaciousness: ★★★★★ Quiet: ★★★★★
Security: ★★★★★ Cleanliness: ★★★★★
Insect Control: None Facilities: ★★★★★

Make up a list of what the ideal campground would have. Then drive to Geneva-on-the-Lake ; chances are that dream facility would be waiting at the Indian Creek Camping Resort. In addition to the beautiful non-denominational chapel (services every Sunday), there's also an "automatic external defibrillator" to save a life in the event of cardiac arrest. Then there's the two heated swimming pools—one for adults only and one for families. The tiled bathrooms are so clean they gleam. The grass is well manicured, and the folks are friendly. Sites are level and grassy, shaded or open, and with a typical site width of a generous 45 feet. A full-service restaurant, Farone's, and the Step Above Lounge offer a good choice of food and drink. Security includes a traffic control gate and owners who live on site and don't miss much that goes on in the campground. Not surprisingly, about half the camping sites are taken by seasonal campers, which means it is a good idea to book a reservation.

BASICS

Operated by: The Andrus family. **Open:** All year, limited facilities in the winter. **Site Assignment:** Reservations w/ 1-night deposit; refund w/ 7-day notice. **Registration:** At campground office. **Fee:** $34 (cash, check, credit cards). Parking: At site.

FACILITIES

Number of RV Sites: 553. **Number of Tent-Only Sites:** 30. **Hookups:** Electric (20, 30, 50 amps), water, sewer, phone, cable TV. **Each Site:** Picnic table, fire ring. **Dump Station:** Yes. **Laundry:** Yes. **Pay Phone:** Yes. **Rest Rooms and Showers:** Yes. **Fuel:** Yes. **Propane:** Yes. **Internal Roads:** Paved/gravel, in good condition. **RV Service:** No. **Market:** 4 mi. east in Geneva-On-The-Lake. **Restaurant:** On site. **General Store:** Yes. **Vending:** Yes. **Swimming Pool:** Yes. **Playground:** Yes. **Other:** Chapel, baseball, volleyball, shuffleboard, game room, horseshoes, pavilions, fishing lake, coin games, sports field, hiking trails, restaurant & lounge. **Activities:** Swimming, fishing, hiking, scheduled activities, local tours. **Nearby Attractions:** Lake Erie, boat races, roller skating, Lake Farmpark, golf, summer concerts, antiques, state parks, historic homes, scenic drives, covered bridges. **Additional Information:** Ashtabula County CVB, (800) 337-6746.

RESTRICTIONS

Pets: Leash only. **Fires:** Fire ring only. **Alcoholic Beverages:** Permitted. **Vehicle Maximum Length:** None.

TO GET THERE

From the junction of I-90 and Hwy. 45, take Exit 223 and drive 6 mi. north on Hwy. 45, then 4 mi. west on Hwy. 531. Roads are wide and well maintained w/ broad shoulders.

HILLSBORO

Rocky Fork State Park

9800 North Shore Dr., Hillsboro 45133. T: (937) 393-3210; www.dnr.state.oh.us/odnr/parks.

RV ★★★★ Tent ★★★★

Beauty: ★★★★ Site Privacy: ★★★
Spaciousness: ★★★ Quiet: ★★★★
Security: ★★★★ Cleanliness: ★★★★
Insect Control: None Facilities: ★★★★

At last, a state campground with full hookups. But you have to be fast to get one of those sites. Rocky Fork State Park has only 20 full hookups (sites 301–320), and folks are waiting in line for those precious spots. Located four miles east of Hillsboro, Rocky Fork State Park is a paradise for outdoor recreation enthusiasts. Unlimited horsepower boating allows for excellent skiing on the lake, which also provides catches of bass, muskellunge, and walleye. A scenic gorge, dolomite caves, and natural wetlands add to the beauty. Two large public beaches with changing booths and bathhouses are located on the north and south sides of the lake. A short hiking trail near the campground takes nature lovers to an observation station where excellent birdwatching can be enjoyed. Laid out in a series of loops, the grassy campground offers shaded and open sites with an average size of 12 × 35 feet. There are no pull-through sites. Park rangers provide security and regular patrols.

BASICS

Operated by: State of Ohio. **Open:** All year. **Site Assignment:** First come, first served. No reservations. **Registration:** At campground office. **Fee:** $20 (cash, check, credit cards). **Parking:** At site.

FACILITIES

Number of RV Sites: 148. **Number of Tent-Only Sites:** 82. **Hookups:** Electric (30 amps), water, sewer. **Each Site:** Picnic table, fire ring. **Dump Station:** Yes. **Laundry:** Yes. **Pay Phone:** Yes. **Rest Rooms and Showers:** Yes. **Fuel:** No. **Propane:** Yes. **Internal Roads:** Paved, in good condition. **RV Service:** No. **Market:** 4 mi. west in Hillsboro. **Restaurant:** Restaurant on site. **General Store:** Yes. **Vending:** No. **Swimming Pool:** No. **Playground:** Yes. **Other:** Rocky Fork Lake, swimming beach, boat launch, hiking trails, marinas, amphitheater, basketball, volleyball, horseshoes, mini-golf, boat dock. **Activities:** Swimming, fishing, boating (rental fishing boats & pontoons available), hiking, scheduled activities. **Nearby Attractions:** Nature sanctuary, Fort Hill Indian mounds, museums, Serpent Mound, golf, Kings Island amusement park. **Additional Information:** Highland County CVB, (937) 393-4883.

RESTRICTIONS

Pets: Leash only, in pet camping areas; $1 per night per pet, max. of 2 pets. **Fires:** Fire ring only. **Alcoholic Beverages:** Not permitted. **Vehicle Maximum Length:** 35 ft. **Other:** 14-day stay limit.

TO GET THERE

From Hillsboro, drive 3.5 mi. east on SR 124 to North Shore Dr., then 1 mi. northeast. Roads are wide and well maintained w/ broad shoulders.

JACKSON

Deerland Resort

974 Standpipe Rd., Jackson 45640. T: (740) 286-6422; F: (740) 286-1995.

RV ★★★★ Tent ★★★★

Beauty: ★★★★ Site Privacy: ★★★★
Spaciousness: ★★★★ Quiet: ★★★★
Security: ★★★★ Cleanliness: ★★★★
Insect Control: Yes Facilities: ★★★

Deerland Resort offers a country setting with rolling hills and a beautiful lake. But the resort lacks one popular recreation that campers often seek—there is no swimming. Located two miles south of Jackson, the campground is arranged in tiers overlooking the lake. The campground has 35 seasonals, and all the sites are pull-throughs. Sites are open or shaded, with the best tent sites by the water and dam. A fee is charged for fishing. The resort has four pages of rules and regulations, including notice that children under the age of 18 must be at their sites during curfew from 11 p.m. to 8 a.m. unless accompanied by an adult. Curfew violators will be escorted back to their sites, a report will be filed with the resort manager, and second-time offenders will be required to leave Deerland Resort. A five-mph speed limit also is enforced. Security measures include a one-way road and traffic control gate.

BASICS

Operated by: Marge & Bill Parks. **Open:** Apr. 1–Nov. 1. **Site Assignment:** Reservations w/ 1-night deposit; refund w/ 7-day notice. **Registration:** At campground office. **Fee:** $24 (cash, check, credit cards). **Parking:** At site.

FACILITIES

Number of RV Sites: 79. **Number of Tent-Only Sites:** 15. **Hookups:** Electric (30, 50 amps), water, sewer. **Each Site:** Picnic table, fire ring. Dump Station: Yes. **Laundry:** Yes. **Pay Phone:** Yes. **Rest Rooms and Showers:** Yes. **Fuel:** No. **Propane: No. Internal Roads:** Gravel, in fair condition. RV Service: No. Market: 2 mi. north in Jackson. **Restaurant:** 2 mi. north in Jackson. **General Store:** No. **Vending:** Yes. **Swimming Pool:** No. **Playground:** Yes. **Other:** Fishing lake, rec room, coin games, mini golf, basketball, shuffleboard, horseshoes, hiking trails, volleyball, rental paddleboats, rental cabins, banquet facilities. **Activities:** Fishing, hiking. **Nearby Attractions:** Noah's Ark Animal Farm, antiques, arts & crafts, gold, Bob Evans Original Farm, Splash Down Water Park, wildlife area. Additional Information: Jackson Area Chamber of Commerce, (740) 286-2722.

RESTRICTIONS

Pets: Leash only. **Fires:** Fire ring only. **Alcoholic Beverages:** Permitted. **Vehicle Maximum Length:** None.

TO GET THERE

From the junction of Hwy. 32 and US 35, drive 3

mi. southeast on US 35, then 1 mi. west on CR 55. Hwy. 32 is wide and well maintained w/ broad shoulders. CR 55 is wide and well maintained w/ narrow shoulders.

JACKSON

Yogi Bear's Jellystone Park Camp-Resort

1527 McGiffins Rd., Jackson 45640. T: (800) 282-2167; www.placesohio.com/yogibear.

RV ★★★ Tent ★

Beauty: ★★★ Site Privacy: ★★★
Spaciousness: ★★★ Quiet: ★★★
Security: ★★★★ Cleanliness: ★★★★
Insect Control: None Facilities: ★★★

Yogi Bear's Jellystone Park Camp-Resort offers level, gravel sites along a fishing lake with very few trees. Most sites are open, and some have concrete patios. Arranged in a loop around the four-acre lake, the campground has 30 seasonal campers, 25 pull-through sites, and a typical site width of 25 feet. Located five miles east of Jackson and adjacent to Noah's Ark Animal Farm, the campground is right next to the main highway. Fishing is not included in the camping rate; it costs $9 per adult (age 13 and up) to fish for 12 hours with two poles. Children ages 4–12 cost $6 for one pole for 12 hours. The fishing ticket is void if you leave the lake. There is a limit of four catfish under ten pounds per trip. All fish ten pounds and over must be returned back to the lake. A 5.5-mph speed limit and quiet times from 11 p.m. to 8 a.m. are enforced. Security measures include one-way roads, owners who live on site, and regular patrols of the campground.

BASICS

Operated by: Dan & Edna Byler. **Open:** All year. **Site Assignment:** Reservations w/ 1-night deposit; refund w/ 14-day notice. **Registration:** At campground office. **Fee:** $22 (cash, check, credit cards). **Parking:** At site.

FACILITIES

Number of RV Sites: 79. **Number of Tent-Only Sites:** 0. **Hookups:** Electric (30, 50 amps), water, sewer. **Each Site:** Picnic table, fire ring. **Dump Station:** Yes. **Laundry:** Yes. **Pay Phone:** Yes. **Rest Rooms and Showers:** Yes. **Fuel:** No. **Propane:** Yes. **Internal Roads:** Paved/gravel, in good condition. **RV Service:** No. **Market:** 5 mi. west in Jackson. **Restaurant:** 5 mi. west in Jackson. **General Store:** Yes. **Vending:** Yes. **Swimming Pool:** Yes. **Playground:** Yes. **Other:** Fast food restaurant, pay lake, rental cabins, horseshoes, basketball, volleyball, tetherball, shuffleboard, pavilion, mini golf. **Activities:** Swimming, fishing, scheduled weekend activities. **Nearby Attractions:** Noah's Ark Animal Farm, antiques, arts & crafts, golf, Bob Evans Original Farm, Splash Down Water Park, wildlife area. **Additional Information:** Jackson Area Chamber of Commerce, (740) 286-2722.

RESTRICTIONS

Pets: Leash only. **Fires:** Fire ring only. **Alcoholic Beverages:** Not permitted. **Vehicle Maximum Length:** None. **Other:** Rental cabins are non-smoking & require a $50 deposit.

TO GET THERE

From the junction of US 35 and Hwy. 32, drive 5 mi. east on Hwy. 32. Roads are wide and well maintained w/ broad shoulders.

LATHAM

Long's Retreat Family Resort

50 Bell Hollow Rd., Latham 45646. T: (937) 588-3725; www.longsretreat.com.

RV ★★★ Tent ★★★

Beauty: ★★★ Site Privacy: ★★★
Spaciousness: ★★★★ Quiet: ★★★★
Security: ★★★★ Cleanliness: ★★★
Insect Control: None Facilities: ★★★

Long's Retreat Family Resort is built around a lake and offers a wide array of water activities and other recreation. Two giant 300- and 350-foot water slides, a hydrotube slide, raindrop, diving boards, and sandy beach make the lake a popular place. Located five miles west of Latham, Ohio, Long's Retreat has open and shaded sites on rolling terrain. Most of the shade is from woods on the perimeter of the campground. Sites are level, with 300 seasonal campers, 75 pull-throughs, and a typical site width of 40 feet. The best RV sites are in area B because of the pine trees, proximity to facilities, and scenic views. Although those sites lack water hookups, many RV campers choose the benefits over that disadvantage. The best tent sites are in areas A or E because they are located on a peninsula on the lake where campers can fish almost from their campsite. Security includes an owner who lives on site and patrols by the local deputy sheriffs department.

BASICS

Operated by: Eric Long. **Open:** All year. **Site Assignment:** No reservations; first come, first served. **Registration:** At campground office. **Fee:** $16 (cash, check, credit cards). **Parking:** At site.

FACILITIES

Number of RV Sites: 350. **Number of Tent-Only Sites:** 100. **Hookups:** Electric (30 amps), water, sewer. **Each Site:** Picnic table, fire ring. **Dump Station:** Yes. **Laundry:** Yes. **Pay Phone:** Yes. **Rest Rooms and Showers:** Yes. **Fuel:** No. **Propane:** Yes. **Internal Roads:** Paved, in good condition. **RV Service:** No. **Market:** 3 mi. east in Latham. **Restaurant:** 3 mi. east in Latham. **General Store:** Yes. **Vending:** Yes. **Swimming Pool:** No. **Playground:** Yes. **Other:** Swimming lake, sandy beach, giant waterslide, go-carts, mini-golf, arcade, rental cabins, basketball, fishing lake, go-kart track, mini golf, tennis, game room, recreation field, badminton, hiking trails, volleyball. **Activities:** Swimming, fishing, hiking, boating (electric motors only, rental canoes, paddleboats available), scheduled weekend activities. **Nearby Attractions:** Fort Hill State Memorial & Nature Preserve, Indian mounds, museums, golf, Serpent Mound, Kings Island amusement park, Octagonal Schoolhouse, antiques. **Additional Information:** Highland County CVB, (937) 393-4883.

RESTRICTIONS

Pets: Leash only. **Fires:** Fire ring only. **Alcoholic Beverages:** Permitted. **Vehicle Maximum Length:** None.

TO GET THERE

From the junction of Hwy. 41 and Hwy. 124, drive 5.25 mi. east on Hwy. 124, then 0.1 mi. northwest on Bell Hollow Rd. Roads are wide and well maintained w/ broad shoulders.

LEAVITTSBURG

Pin-Oak Acres

4063 Eagle Creek Rd., Leavittsburg 44430. T: (216) 898-8559

RV ★★★ Tent ★★★

Beauty: ★★★ Site Privacy: ★★★
Spaciousness: ★★★ Quiet: ★★★
Security: ★★★ Cleanliness: ★★★
Insect Control: Yes Facilities: ★★★

A rural campground in a semi-wooded area, Pin-Oak Acres Family Camping offers level sites laid out in a series of loops. Located five miles east of Leavittsburg, the campground has 12 pull-through sites and a typical site width of 35 feet. The swimming lake is chemically treated, so it is almost like a swimming pool separate from the fishing lake. Sites are grassy, with a choice of open or shaded. The best RV sites are 69–78 in the rear of the campground, where it is quieter, has full hookups, and backs into the woods. Sites 1–17 also are favorites because they are on a creek. The primitive area has the best tent sites because it is more wooded and offers privacy. Security measures include one-way roads and owners who live on site and keep an eye on the campground.

BASICS

Operated by: Ray & Ele Price. **Open:** May 1–Oct. 15. **Site Assignment:** Reservations w/ 1-night deposit; no refunds. **Registration:** At campground office. **Fee:** $13 (cash). **Parking:** At site.

FACILITIES

Number of RV Sites: 81. **Number of Tent-Only Sites:** 40. **Hookups:** Electric (30 amps), water, sewer. **Each Site:** Picnic table, fire ring. **Dump Station:** Yes. **Laundry:** Yes. **Pay Phone:** No. **Rest Rooms and Showers:** Yes. **Fuel:** No. **Propane:** No. **Internal Roads:** Gravel, in fair condition. **RV Service:** No. **Market:** 5 mi. east in Leavittsburg. **Restaurant:** 5 mi. east in Leavittsburg. **General Store:** No. **Vending:** No. **Swimming Pool:** No. **Playground:** Yes. **Other:** Swimming lake, fishing pond, horseshoes, pavilion, game room, coin games, basketball, volleyball, hiking trails, sports field, jogging area. **Activities:** Swimming, fishing, hiking, scheduled weekend activities. **Nearby Attractions:** Golf, covered bridge, Geauga Lake, coliseum, reservoir, Sea World, cheese factory, water mill, Hale Farm, Packard Music Hall, antiques. **Additional Information:** Youngstown CVB, (800) 447-8201.

RESTRICTIONS

Pets: Leash only. **Fires:** Fire ring only. **Alcoholic Beverages:** At sites only. **Vehicle Maximum Length:** 38 ft.

To Get There

From the junction of Ohio Turnpike and Hwy. 5, take Exit 14/209, drive 0.2 mi. west on Hwy. 5, then 3.5 mi. north on Newton Falls-Braceville Rd., then 0.5 mi. east on Eagle Creek Rd. Roads are generally wide and well maintained but have narrow shoulders in spots.

LIMA

Sun Valley Family Campgrounds

9779 Faulkner Rd., Harrod 45850. T: (419) 648-2235

RV ★★★ Tent ★★★

Beauty: ★★ Site Privacy: ★★★
Spaciousness: ★★★ Quiet: ★★★
Security: ★★★★ Cleanliness: ★★★
Insect Control: Yes Facilities: ★★★

A rural campground with level, shaded sites, Sun Valley Campgrounds has only 31 sites available for overnight campers, so reservations are required. The rest of the RV sites are used by 211 seasonal campers. Laid out in a series of loops, the campground, located five miles northeast of Westminster, offers a typical site width of 30 feet and one pull-through. Speed limit is five mph, and quiet time is from 11 p.m. to 8 a.m. A lifeguard is on duty in the swimming area, and children ages 12 and under must have a parent to sign them in. Only two-person tents may be set up on lots with campers and must be approved by the office first. Tent-camping sites are located in the primitive area, which offers more green space and privacy. Security measures include one entrance/exit road, a coded traffic gate, and regular campground patrols.

Basics

Operated by: Richard Williams & Darrel Reed. **Open:** Apr.–Oct. **Site Assignment:** Reservations required w/ non-refundable $15 fee. **Registration:** At campground office. **Fee:** $19 (cash, check, credit cards). **Parking:** At site.

Facilities

Number of RV Sites: 242. **Number of Tent-Only Sites:** 50. **Hookups:** Electric (20, 30, 50 amps), water, sewer. **Each Site:** Picnic table, fire ring. **Dump Station:** Yes. **Laundry:** Yes. **Pay Phone:** Yes. **Rest Rooms and Showers:** Yes. **Fuel:** No. **Propane:** Yes. **Internal Roads:** Gravel, in good condition. **RV Service:** No. **Market:** 5 mi. southwest in Westminster. **Restaurant:** 5 mi. southwest in Westminster. **General Store:** Yes, limited. **Vending:** Yes. **Swimming Pool:** No. **Playground:** Yes. **Other:** Volleyball, shuffleboard, horseshoes, game room, pavilion, video games, fishing lake, outdoor stage & dance floor, biking trails, sports field. **Activities:** Swimming, fishing, boating (electric motors only), scheduled weekend activities. **Nearby Attractions:** Golf, antiques, museums, historic homes, arts & crafts, motorsports park, Children's Garden, skating arena, Neil Armstrong Air & Space Museum, Indian Lake. **Additional Information:** Lima/Allen County CVB, (888) 222-6075.

Restrictions

Pets: Leash only. **Fires:** Fire ring only. **Alcoholic Beverages:** Permitted. **Vehicle Maximum Length:** None.

To Get There

From the junction of Hwy. 309 and Hwy. 117, drive 9 mi. southeast on Hwy. 117, then 2 mi. north on Phillips Rd., then 0.75 mi. east on Faulkner Rd. Roads are wide and well maintained; Phillips Rd. has mostly good shoulders; Faulkner Rd. has narrow shoulders. Be careful not to miss the turnoff on Faulker Rd.; it is in the middle of a cemetery.

LOUDONVILLE

Camp Toodik Family Campground, Cabins, & Canoe Livery

770 TR 462, Loudonville 44842. T: (419) 994-3835; F: (419) 994-4093; www.camptoodik.org; mrtoodik@aol.com.

RV ★★★★ Tent ★★★★

Beauty: ★★★★ Site Privacy: ★★★★
Spaciousness: ★★★★ Quiet: ★★★★
Security: ★★★★ Cleanliness: ★★★★
Insect Control: ★★★★ Facilities: ★★★★

Located in the foothills of the Appalachian Mountains, four miles north of Loudonville, Camp Toodik Family Campground, Cabins, & Canoe Livery offers beautiful, rolling, grassy terrain overlooking a river valley. Sites are level and mostly shaded, with three pull-through sites and a typical site width of 45 feet. The campground is convenient to the interstate and to the largest Amish settlement in the Midwest. A big plus at the campground is its convenience for canoeing and kayaking. Campground personnel will take canoers or kayakers upstream for a quiet scenic float back to the campground. Campground restrooms are not only very clean but also have the added luxury touch of matted floors. For tenters, the campground offers great, shaded sites right on the river. Security and safety measures include a traffic control gate and owners who keep a close eye on the campground.

Basics

Operated by: Britt & Nancy Young. **Open:** Apr. 1–Nov. 1. **Site Assignment:** Reservations w/ 1-night deposit; refund w/ 7-day notice. **Registration:** At campground office. **Fee:** $40 (cash, check, credit cards). **Parking:** At site.

Facilities

Number of RV Sites: 172. **Number of Tent-Only Sites:** 16. **Hookups:** Electric (20, 30, 50 amps), water, sewer, phone. **Each Site:** Picnic table, fire ring. **Dump Station:** Yes. **Laundry:** Yes. **Pay Phone:** Yes. **Rest Rooms and Showers:** Yes. **Fuel:** No. **Propane:** Yes. **Internal Roads:** Gravel, in good condition. **RV Service:** No. **Market:** 4 mi. south in Loudonville. **Restaurant:** 4 mi. south in Loudonville. **General Store:** Yes. **Vending:** Yes. **Swimming Pool:** Yes. **Playground:** Yes. **Other:** Rec hall, pavilion, coin games, river/pond fishing, mini-golf, basketball, shuffleboard, movies, badminton, sports field, horseshoes, hiking trails, volleyball, rental cabins, rental tent trailers. **Activities:** Swimming, hiking, fishing, canoeing, kayaking (rental canoes, kayaks available), scheduled activities. **Nearby Attractions:** Amish Country, Mid-Ohio Race Track, golf, Mohican Forest, plant tours, Malabar Farm State Park, Living Bible Museum, Richland Carousel Park, ski resorts, Ohio State Reformatory. **Additional Information:** Mansfield-Richland Area Chamber of Commerce, (419) 522-3211.

Restrictions

Pets: Leash only. **Fires:** Fire ring only. **Alcoholic Beverages:** Permitted. **Vehicle Maximum Length:** None.

To Get There

From the junction of Hwy. 3 and Hwy. 39/60, drive 2.5 mi. southeast on Hwy. 39/60, then 0.75 mi. north on Township Rd. 462. Roads are wide and well maintained w/ broad shoulders.

MARIETTA

The Landings Family Campground

P.O. Box 220, Reno 45773. T: (740) 373-6180

RV ★★★ Tent ★★★

Beauty: ★★★ Site Privacy: ★★★
Spaciousness: ★★★ Quiet: ★★★★
Security: ★★★★ Cleanliness: ★★★
Insect Control: None Facilities: ★★★

Don't even consider dropping by the Landings and finding an open campsite. Reservations are a must. With 103 seasonal campers, the campground has only five sites available for short-term visitors. And that number seems to dwindle with each passing year. Located five miles north of Marietta, the campground has over 1,200 feet of Ohio River frontage. Look at all the boat trailers and big boats, and you'll know what the main draw is for this campground. Campers by the river have a beautiful view; campers back in the field are not so lucky. Sites are mostly open, but some shade is available. The speed limit is ten mph, and quiet time starts at 11 p.m. each night. Security includes a one-way road, an owner who lives on site, and regular patrols of the campgrounds.

Basics

Operated by: David Cook. **Open:** Apr. 1–Nov. 1. **Site Assignment:** Reservations w/ 1-night deposit; refunds w/ 7-day notice. **Registration:** At campground office. **Fee:** $21 (cash, check). **Parking:** At site.

Facilities

Number of RV Sites: 108. **Number of Tent-Only Sites:** 75. **Hookups:** Electric (20, 30 amps), water, sewer. **Each Site:** Picnic table, fire ring. **Dump Station:** Yes. **Laundry:** No. **Pay Phone:** Yes. **Rest Rooms and Showers:** Yes. **Fuel:** No. **Propane:** No. **Internal Roads:** Gravel, in good condition. **RV Service:** No. **Market:** 5 mi. south in Marietta. **Restaurant:** 5 mi. south in Marietta. **General Store:** No. **Vending:** No. **Swimming Pool:** Yes. **Playground:** Yes. **Other:** Ohio River, boat ramp, horseshoes. **Activities:** Swimming, fishing, boating, waterskiing. **Nearby Attractions:** Showboat, Museum of the Northwest Territory, Ohio River museum, historic homes, Harmar Village, Mound Cemetery, trolley tours, stern-wheeler cruises, golf, antiques. **Additional Information:** Marietta/Washington County CVB, (800) 288-2577.

Restrictions

Pets: Leash only. **Fires:** Fire ring only. **Alcoholic Beverages:** Permitted. **Vehicle Maximum Length:** 40 ft.

To Get There

From the junction of I-77 and SR 7, take Exit 1 and drive 3 mi. north on SR 7. Roads are wide and well maintained w/ broad shoulders.

MT. GILEAD

Mt. Gilead Campground

SR 95, Mt. Gilead 43338. T: (419) 768-3428

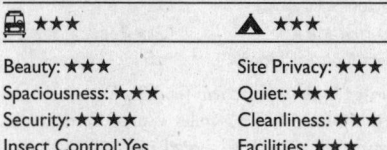

RV ★★★ Tent ★★★

Beauty: ★★★ Site Privacy: ★★★
Spaciousness: ★★★ Quiet: ★★★
Security: ★★★★ Cleanliness: ★★★
Insect Control: Yes Facilities: ★★★

Located three miles west of Chesterville, Mt Gilead Campground offers open or shaded sites, most of them grassy with gravel parking spots. Arranged in a series of loops, the campground has 40 seasonal campers, 154 pull-through sites, and a typical site width of 27 feet. No generators are permitted, and quiet hours are from 10 p.m. to 8 a.m. The best sites for tents are 21 and 141–147 because they are more level and are located in the back of the campground with more green space and privacy. The best RV sites are 32–35 and 125–31 because they are bigger and closer to the facilities. Security measures include an entrance past the office, an owner who lives on site, and regular patrols of the campground.

Basics

Operated by: Chris Hansen. **Open:** Apr. 1–Oct. 31. **Site Assignment:** First come, first served; no reservations. **Registration:** At campground office. **Fee:** $26 (cash, check, credit cards). **Parking:** At site.

Facilities

Number of RV Sites: 154. **Number of Tent-Only Sites:** 40. **Hookups:** Electric (30, 50 amps), water, sewer. **Each Site:** Picnic table, fire ring. **Dump Station:** Yes. **Laundry:** Yes. **Pay Phone:** Yes. **Rest Rooms and Showers:** Yes. **Fuel:** No. **Propane:** Yes. **Internal Roads:** Gravel, in fair condition. **RV Service:** No. **Market:** 3 mi. east in Chesterville. **Restaurant:** 0.5 mi. east toward Chesterville. **General Store:** Yes. **Vending:** No. **Swimming Pool:** Yes. **Playground:** Yes. **Other:** Fishing pond, game room, pavilion, horseshoes, volleyball, recreation field. **Activities:** Swimming, fishing, boating (rental paddleboats available), scheduled weekend activities. **Nearby Attractions:** Golf, flea markets, antiques, Living Bible Museum, carousel park, Amish village, state forest, covered bridge. **Additional Information:** Mansfield-Richland Area Chamber of Commerce, (419) 522-3211.

Restrictions

Pets: Leash only. **Fires:** Fire ring only. **Alcoholic Beverages:** Permitted. **Vehicle Maximum Length:** None.

To Get There

From the junction of I-71 and US 95, take Exit 151 and drive 0.5 mi. west on US 95. Roads are wide and well maintained w/ broad shoulders.

PEEBLES

Mineral Springs Lake Resort

162 Bluegill Rd., Peebles 45660. T: (937) 587-3132

RV ★★★ Tent ★★★★

Beauty: ★★★★ Site Privacy: ★★★
Spaciousness: ★★★★ Quiet: ★★★
Security: ★★★★ Cleanliness: ★★★
Insect Control: None Facilities: ★★★

A rural campground adjoining a pretty lake, Mineral Springs Lake Resort has natural beauty but could fix up its entranceway. It's a shame one of the first things a visitor sees on entering is a clump of dumpsters and recycling bins. Located two miles southeast of Peebles, the campground has 240 seasonal campers, 12 pull-through sites, and a typical site width of 50 feet. The wooded campground offers mostly shaded sites on its rolling terrain. The best sites are by the lake. The speed limit is ten mph, rather high especially with so many golf carts in use. Security measures include owners who live on site, surveillance cameras, and a gate. Rates are very reasonable for such a nice campground with a good array of activities.

Basics

Operated by: Robin Waddell. **Open:** Apr. 1–Nov. 1. **Site Assignment:** Reservations w/ 1-night deposit; refund w/ 7-day notice. **Registration:** At campground office. **Fee:** $18 (cash, check, credit cards). **Parking:** At site.

Facilities

Number of RV Sites: 280. **Number of Tent-Only Sites:** 100. **Hookups:** Electric (20, 30 amps), water, sewer. **Each Site:** Picnic table, fire ring. **Dump Station:** Yes. **Laundry:** Yes. **Pay Phone:** Yes. **Rest Rooms and Showers:** Yes. **Fuel:** No. **Propane:** Yes. **Internal Roads:** Paved/gravel, in good condition. **RV Service:** No. **Market:** 2 mi. northwest in Peebles. **Restaurant:** 2 mi. northwest in Peebles. **General Store:** Yes. **Vending:** Yes. **Swimming Pool:** No. **Playground:** Yes. **Other:** Swimming lake, basketball, mini golf, volleyball, crazy cars, surf bikes, mountain bikes, horseshoes, fishing lake, rec room, pavilion, coin games, boat ramp, boat dock, hiking trails. **Activities:** Swimming, fishing, hiking, boating (electric motors only; rental paddleboats, canoes, rowboats available). **Nearby Attractions:** Diving quarry, Serpent Mound, Davis Memorial, Amish community, caves, Tecumseh outdoor drama, golf, historic homes, antiques, arts & crafts. **Additional Information:** Adams County Travel & Visitors Bureau, (877) 687-7446.

Restrictions

Pets: Leash only. **Fires:** Fire ring only. **Alcoholic Beverages:** At sites only. **Vehicle Maximum Length:** None.

To Get There

From the junction of Hwy. 41 and Hwy. 32 at the south edge of town, drive 1.25 mi. east on Hwy. 32, then 2 mi. south on Steam Furnace Rd., then 2 mi east on Mineral Springs Rd. Hwy. 32 is wide and well maintained w/ broad shoulders. Steam Furnace Rd. is winding w/ some narrow shoulders at points. Mineral Springs Rd. is generally well maintained w/ narrow shoulders.

PIQUA

Poor Farmer's Campground

7211 North Lostcreek-Shelby Rd., Fletcher 45326. T: (937) 368-2449; poorfarmersrv.com.

RV ★★ Tent ★★

Beauty: ★★★ Site Privacy: ★★★
Spaciousness: ★★★ Quiet: ★★★★
Security: ★★★ Cleanliness: ★★★
Insect Control: None Facilities: ★★

A rural campground associated with RV sales and service, Poor Farmer's Campground is located nine miles east of Piqua. Sites are grassy, open, and shaded with a typical site width of 35 feet. Arranged in a series of loops, the campground has 120 seasonal sites and 16 pull-throughs. Speed limit is five mph; violators will be warned once, then they will have to park at the camp office and walk to and from their site. To help provide quiet, safety, and a better camping experience, seasonals are not allowed to mow their lots on Friday evening, Saturday, or Sunday. Nor are campers allowed to hang out laundry on Fridays, Saturdays, or Sundays.

Basics

Operated by: Steve & Patty Springer. **Open:** All year. **Site Assignment:** Reservations w/ no deposit. **Registration:** At campground office. **Fee:** $15 (cash, check). **Parking:** At site.

Facilities

Number of RV Sites: 500. **Number of Tent-Only Sites:** 0. **Hookups:** Electric (20, 30 amps), water. **Each Site:** Picnic table, fire ring. **Dump Station:** Yes. **Laundry:** No. **Pay Phone:** Yes. **Rest Rooms and Showers:** Yes. **Fuel:** No. **Propane:** Yes. **Internal Roads:** Gravel, in good condition. **RV Service:** Yes. **Market:** 9 mi. west in Piqua. **Restaurant:** 9 mi. west in Piqua. **General Store:** No. **Vending:** Yes. **Swimming Pool:** No. **Playground:** Yes. **Other:** Shelter, pond, wildlife area, creek, basketball, horseshoes, volleyball, museum of antique tractors & farm machinery, hiking trails. **Activities:** Hiking, fishing, scheduled weekend activities. **Nearby Attractions:** Woods reserve & sanctuary, golf, historic farmstead, Piatt Castles, Kiser Lake, Air Force Museum, antiques, arts & crafts. **Additional Information:** Miami County Visitors & Convention Bureau, (800) 348-8993.

Restrictions

Pets: Leash only but no large dogs permitted "at management discretion.". **Fires:** Fire ring only. **Alcoholic Beverages:** Not permitted. **Vehicle Maximum Length:** None.

To Get There

From the junction of I-75 and US 36, take Exit 82 and drive 6 mi. east on US 36, then 0.75 mi. south on Lost Creek-Shelby Rd. US 36 is wide and well maintained w/ broad shoulders. Lost Creek-Shelby Rd. is well maintained w/ narrow shoulders.

PORT CLINTON
East Harbor State Park

1169 North Buck Rd., Lakeside-Marblehead 43440. T: (419) 734-5857; F: (419) 734-1473; www.dnr.state.oh.us/odnr/parks; east.harbor.parks@dnr.state.oh.us.

RV ★★★ Tent ★★★★

Beauty: ★★★★ Site Privacy: ★★★
Spaciousness: ★★★ Quiet: ★★★★
Security: ★★★★ Cleanliness: ★★★
Insect Control: None Facilities: ★★★

Situated on a peninsula stretching into the waters of Lake Erie, East Harbor State Park has the largest campground in the Ohio State Park system. Laid out in a series of loops, the campground offers level sites with a choice of open or shaded. Located eight miles west of Port Clinton, Ohio, the campground is part of the 1,152-acre state park. A 1,500-foot sand beach is popular with swimmers. East Harbor lies on the fringe of Ohio's prairie marsh zone, home of more wildlife than any other type of habitat in the state. Hundreds of migrating songbirds rest here before winging north across the lake. The campground has 142 pull-through sites and welcomes big rigs. Lake Erie offers unlimited-horsepower boating opportunities, including a full-time boat mechanic, boat supplies, boat storage, and a restaurant. East Harbor's seven-mile hiking trail system leads through the many different habitats within the park. Park rangers provide security patrols and check on entering motorists.

Basics

Operated by: State of Ohio. **Open:** All year. **Site Assignment:** First come, first served. No reservations. **Registration:** At campground office. **Fee:** $17 (cash, check, credit cards). **Parking:** At site.

Facilities

Number of RV Sites: 366. **Number of Tent-Only Sites:** 204. **Hookups:** Electric (20, 30, 50 amps). **Each Site:** Picnic table, fire ring. **Dump Station:** Yes. **Laundry:** Yes. **Pay Phone:** Yes. **Rest Rooms and Showers:** Yes. **Fuel:** No. **Propane:** No. **Internal Roads:** Paved, in good condition. **RV Service:** No. **Market:** 8 mi. east in Port Clinton. **Restaurant:** 8 mi. east in Port Clinton. **General Store:** Yes, limited. **Vending:** Yes. **Swimming Pool:** No. **Playground:** Yes. **Other:** Swimming lake, fishing lake, pavilion, rec room, boat ramp, boat dock, sports field, hiking trails, volleyball, rental RVs, rental tents, nature center. **Activities:** Swimming, boating (rental boats available), hiking, fishing, scheduled activities. **Nearby Attractions:** Lake Erie, ferry, Put-in-Bay, Kelley's Island, lighthouse, winery, golf, Cedar Point Amusement Park, antiques, boating. **Additional Information:** Ottawa County Visitors Bureau, (800) 441-1271.

Restrictions

Pets: Leash only; $1 fee per pet per day. **Fires:** Fire ring only. **Alcoholic Beverages:** Not permitted. **Vehicle Maximum Length:** None. **Other:** 14-day stay limit.

To Get There

From the junction of Hwy. 2 and Hwy. 269, drive 4 mi. north on Hwy. 269. Roads are wide and well maintained w/ broad shoulders.

PORT CLINTON
Tall Timbers Campground Resort

340 Christy Chapel Rd., Port Clinton 43452. T: (419) 732-3938; www.OnLakeErie.com/TallTimbers.

RV ★★★ Tent ★★★

Beauty: ★★★ Site Privacy: ★★★
Spaciousness: ★★★ Quiet: ★★★
Security: ★★★★ Cleanliness: ★★★
Insect Control: None Facilities: ★★★

Nestled in a woods near the shores of Lake Erie, Tall Timbers Campground Resort is in the heart of a popular recreation area and is the walleye fishing capital of the world. Not surprisingly, many of the campers who visit Tall Timbers come for all the area attractions. But the campground has a goodly number of recreation opportunities itself. Located in Port Clinton, the campground has 300 seasonal campers, five pull-through sites, and a typical site width of 30 feet. Laid out in a series of loops, the campground offers grassy, shaded, and open sites. The best RV sites are the pull-throughs; the best tent sites are 1–39, which offer water and electric hookups in an area by a pond. The primitive camping area is also a favorite with tenters because it is separated from RVs and has more grass and trees. Security and safety measures include a five-mph speed limit, one entrance/exit road, a manager who lives on site, and patrols of the campground.

Basics

Operated by: Dave & Cindy Young. **Open:** May 1–Oct. 31. **Site Assignment:** Reservations w/ 1-night deposit; refund w/ 7-day notice. **Registration:** At campground office. **Fee:** $25 (cash, check, credit cards). **Parking:** At site.

Facilities

Number of RV Sites: 409. **Number of Tent-Only Sites:** 24. **Hookups:** Electric (30 amps), water. **Each Site:** Picnic table, fire ring. **Dump Station:** Yes. **Laundry:** Yes. **Pay Phone:** Yes. **Rest Rooms and Showers:** Yes. **Fuel:** No. **Propane:** No. **Internal Roads:** Gravel, in fair condition. **RV Service:** No. **Market:** 1 mi. east. **Restaurant:** 1 mi. east. **General Store:** Yes. **Vending:** Yes. **Swimming Pool:** No. **Playground:** Yes. **Other:** Swimming pond, game room, fishing pond, fish cleaning facility, sports field, volleyball, basketball, horseshoes, pavilion, activity director. **Activities:** Swimming, fishing, weekend activities. **Nearby Attractions:** Lake Erie, ferry, Put-in-Bay, Kelley's Island, lighthouse, winery, golf, Cedar Point Amusement Park, antiques, boating, museums, historic homes. **Additional Information:** Ottawa County Visitors Bureau, (800) 441-1271.

Restrictions

Pets: Leash only. **Fires:** Fire ring only. **Alcoholic Beverages:** At sites only. **Vehicle Maximum Length:** 40 ft.

To Get There

From the junction of Hwy. 2 and Hwy. 53, drive 1.25 mi. north on Hwy. 53, then 1.5 mi. west on Hwy. 163, then 0.25 mi. south on Christy Chapel Rd. Roads are wide and well maintained w/ generally broad shoulders.

PORTSMOUTH
Shawnee State Park

4404 State Rte. 125, Portsmouth 45663. T: (740) 858-4561; www.dnr.state.oh.us/odnr/parks.

RV ★★★★ Tent ★★★★

Beauty: ★★★★ Site Privacy: ★★★
Spaciousness: ★★★ Quiet: ★★★★
Security: ★★★★ Cleanliness: ★★★
Insect Control: None Facilities: ★★★

Located in the Applachian foothills near the banks of the Ohio River 15 miles east of Portsmouth, Shawnee State Park is nestled in the 63,000-acre Shawnee State Forest. Once the hunting grounds of the Shawnee Indians, the region is one of the most picturesque in the state, featuring erosion-carved valleys and wooded hills. The rugged beauty of the area has earned it the nickname "The Little Smokies." Shawnee State Forest is the largest of Ohio's 19 state forests and contains impressive stands of oak, hickory, sassafras, buckeye, black gum, pitch pine, and Virginia pine. It also includes a 42-mile backpack trail with primitive campsites, over 70 miles of bridle trails, a horse campground, an 8,000-acre wilderness area, and five small fishing lakes. Laid out in a series of loops, the campground offers paved pads for RVs with back-in site sizes of 25 × 40 feet. Sites are a mix of shaded and open. A ranger station and regular campground patrols provide security.

Basics

Operated by: State of Ohio. **Open:** All year. **Site Assignment:** First come, first served. No reservations. **Registration:** At campground office. **Fee:** $17 (cash, check, credit cards). **Parking:** At site.

Facilities

Number of RV Sites: 104. **Number of Tent-Only Sites:** 3. **Hookups:** Electric (20, 30, 50 amps). **Each Site:** Picnic table, fire ring. **Dump Station:** Yes. **Laundry:** Yes. **Pay Phone:** Yes. **Rest Rooms and Showers:** Yes. **Fuel:** No. **Propane:** No. **Internal Roads:** Paved, in good condition. **RV Service:** No. **Market:** 15 mi. west in Portsmouth. **Restaurant:** At lodge on site. **General Store:** Yes. **Vending:** Yes. **Swimming Pool:** No. **Playground:** Yes. **Other:** Roosevelt Lake, Turkey Creek Lake, Bear Lake, swimming beach, pavilion, golf, horseback riding trails, hiking trails, horseshoes, volleyball, boat ramp, rental cottages, lodge, mini-golf, tennis, shuffleboard. **Activities:** Swimming, fishing, electric motorboating (rental rowboats & canoes available), biking (rental bikes available), scheduled activities. **Nearby Attractions:** Serpent Mound, antiques, floodwall murals, Ohio River, museums, historic homes, raceway. **Additional Information:** Portsmouth Area CVB, (740) 353-1116.

Restrictions

Pets: Leash only, in pet camping area. Fee $1 per day per pet, max. 2 pets. **Fires:** Fire ring only. **Alcoholic Beverages:** Not permitted. **Vehicle Maximum Length:** 35 ft. **Other:** 14-day stay limit.

To Get There

From the junction of US 52 and State Rd. 125, drive 6 mi. north on SR 125. Roads are wide and well maintained w/ usually good shoulders. SR 125 is very hilly and curving.

SEVILLE

Chippewa Valley Campground

8809 Lake Rd., Seville 44273. T: (330) 769-2090

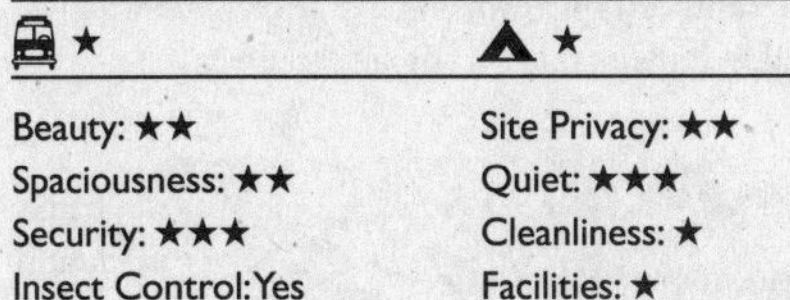

RV ★ Tent ★

Beauty: ★★ Site Privacy: ★★
Spaciousness: ★★ Quiet: ★★★
Security: ★★★ Cleanliness: ★
Insect Control: Yes Facilities: ★

Chippewa Valley Campgrounds has a handy location, right off the interstate, five miles northest of Seville. It also has the nice trees and grass that make a good campground, though when we visited, the entrance road was poorly tended and passed by some unsightly buildings. Laid out in a series of loops, the campground has 25 seasonal campers, 40 pull-through sites, and a 13-acre stocked lake. Sites are mostly grassy and shaded. Traffic from the interstate is audible in front parts of the campground. The speed limit is ten mph—"three strikes and you are removed from the park with no refund," rules state. Quiet hours are from 11 p.m. to 8 a.m. Children are not to be permitted on other sites unless invited. Security measures include an entrance gate that is locked from 10 p.m. to 8 a.m. Seasonal campers have a card to open the gate, but overnight campers don't. To enter, overnight campers have to park their vehicles by the gate and get the manager to let them in. A manager lives on site and patrols the campground.

Basics

Operated by: Guillermo Carrasco. **Open:** May 1–Oct. 31. **Site Assignment:** Reservations w/ 1-night deposit; refund w/ 7-day notice. **Registration:** At campground office. **Fee:** $21 (cash, check). **Parking:** At site.

Facilities

Number of RV Sites: 160. **Number of Tent-Only Sites:** 40. **Hookups:** Electric (30, 50 amps), water, sewer. **Each Site:** Picnic table, fire ring. **Dump Station:** No. **Laundry:** No. **Pay Phone:** Yes. **Rest Rooms and Showers:** Yes. **Fuel:** No. **Propane:** No. **Internal Roads:** Paved/gravel, in poor condition. **RV Service:** No. **Market:** 5 mi. southeast in Seville. **Restaurant:** 5 mi. southeast in Seville. **General Store:** No. **Vending:** Yes. **Swimming Pool:** No. **Playground:** Yes. **Other:** Pavilion, rec room, basketball, tennis, baseball, shuffleboard, horseshoes, lake. **Activities:** Fishing, swimming. **Nearby Attractions:** Amish country, golf, Pro Football Hall of Fame, Rock & Roll Hall of Fame, Sea World, Cleveland Zoo, antiques, arts & crafts, museums, historic homes. **Additional Information:** Medina County CVB, (800) 860-2943.

Restrictions

Pets: Leash only. No pitbulls, dobermans or rottweillers permitted. **Fires:** Fire ring only. **Alcoholic Beverages:** Permitted. **Vehicle Maximum Length:** None.

To Get There

From the junction of I-76 and I-71, take Exit 209, drive west 0.2 mi. on US 224 to CR 19, then north 0.2 mi. Roads are wide and well maintained w/ broad shoulders.

SEVILLE

Maple Lakes Recreational Park

4275 Blake Rd., Seville 44273. T: (330) 336-2251; F: (330) 334-8042; www.maplelakes.com; maplelk@gte.net.

RV ★★★ Tent ★★

Beauty: ★★★ Site Privacy: ★★★★
Spaciousness: ★★★★ Quiet: ★★★★
Security: ★★★★ Cleanliness: ★★★★
Insect Control: None Facilities: ★★★

A grassy campground on hilly terrain, Maple Lakes Recreational Park offers both open and shaded spots. A steep hill leads into the campground. The speed limit is ten mph, but speed bumps slow it down even more. Arranged in a series of loops, the campground has 150 seasonal campers, ten pull-through sites, and a typical site width of 35 feet. Level campsites are grassy with gravel parking spots. Be aware that pets must be kept on campsites; no dog-walking is allowed. Quiet hours are enforced between 11 p.m. and 8:30 a.m. With the woods surrounding it, autumn would be a peak time to view the changing foliage—but the campground closes Oct. 1, just as the leaves are showing their colors. Security includes a gate, owners who live on site, and regular patrols of the campground.

Basics

Operated by: Romeyn family. **Open:** Apr. 1–Oct. 1. **Site Assignment:** Reservations w/ 1-night deposit; refund w/ 7-day notice. **Registration:** At campground office. **Fee:** $25 (cash, check, credit cards). **Parking:** At site.

Facilities

Number of RV Sites: 225. **Number of Tent-Only Sites:** 0. **Hookups:** Electric (30, 50 amps), water, sewer. **Each Site:** Picnic table, fire ring. **Dump Station:** Yes. **Laundry:** Yes. **Pay Phone:** Yes. **Rest Rooms and Showers:** Yes. **Fuel:** No. **Propane:** Yes. **Internal Roads:** Paved/gravel, in good condition. **RV Service:** No. **Market:** 3 mi. south in Seville. **Restaurant:** 3 mi. south in Seville. **General Store:** Yes. **Vending:** Yes. **Swimming Pool:** Yes. **Playground:** Yes. **Other:** Game room, pavilion, fishing lake, badminton, coin games, horseshoes, volleyball, basketball, ball field. **Activities:** Swimming, fishing, scheduled weekend activities. **Nearby Attractions:** Amish country, golf, Pro Football Hall of Fame, Rock & Roll Hall of Fame, Sea World, Cleveland Zoo, antiques, arts & crafts, museums, historic homes. **Additional Information:** Medina County CVB, (800) 860-2943.

Restrictions

Pets: Leash only. Pets cannot be walked in campground, have to be transported to pet area. **Fires:** Fire ring only. **Alcoholic Beverages:** At sites only. **Vehicle Maximum Length:** None. **Other:** No working transient caravans.

To Get There

From the junction of I-76 and Hwy. 3, drive 1 mi. northeast on Hwy. 3, then 1 mi. east on CR 118 (Blake Rd.). Roads are wide and well maintained but have narrow shoulders in spots.

SHREVE

Whispering Hills Recreation

P.O. Box 607, Shreve 44676. T: (800) 992-2435; F: (330) 567-3299; www.whisperinghillsrvpark.com; WHRI@bright.net.

RV ★★★★ Tent ★★★★

Beauty: ★★★ Site Privacy: ★★★
Spaciousness: ★★★ Quiet: ★★★★
Security: ★★★★ Cleanliness: ★★★★
Insect Control: None Facilities: ★★★★

Located on rolling hills deep in the heart of Amish country, three miles south of Shreve, Whispering Hills Recreation is a destination campground. Most folks come here for vacations or brief getaways to enjoy the large array of recreational opportunities. Two big draws are the olympic-sized swimming pool and the Ol' Smokehaus Restaurant (serving homecooked food, Amish baked goods, and Ruth's famous apple dumplings). The country campground has 85 seasonals, an average site size of 25 × 45, ten pull-throughs, and a tree on almost every site. Laid out in a series of loops, the campground is mostly grassy and quiet with natural tree buffers. The most popular RV sites are the six with pull-throughs and sewer hookups. A separate tent section allows for more privacy away from RVs. Security measures include owners who live on site, regular patrols, and random patrols from the local sheriff's department.

Basics

Operated by: Ruth Murray Saurer. **Open:** Apr. 15–Oct. 15. **Site Assignment:** Reservations w/ $25 deposit; refund (minus $5) w/ 48-hour notice. **Registration:** At campground office. **Fee:** $29 (cash, check, credit cards). **Parking:** At site.

Facilities

Number of RV Sites: 300. **Number of Tent-Only Sites:** 40. **Hookups:** Electric (30, 50 amps), water, sewer. **Each Site:** Picnic table, fire ring. **Dump Station:** Yes. **Laundry:** Yes. **Pay Phone:** Yes. **Rest Rooms and Showers:** Yes. **Fuel:** No. **Propane:** Yes. **Internal Roads:** Paved/gravel, in good condition. **RV Service:** No. **Market:** 3 mi. north in Shreve. **Restaurant:** on site. **General Store:** Yes. **Vending:** Yes. **Swimming Pool:** Yes. **Playground:** Yes. **Other:** Fishing lake, mini-golf, volleyball, hiking trails, basketball, rec room, pavilion, coin games, boat dock, sports field, RV rentals, cabin rentals. **Activities:** Swimming, fishing, boating (electric motors only), church services, free entertainment, scheduled weekend activities. **Nearby

Attractions: Golf, antiques, arts & crafts shops, nature preserve, railroad museum, Toy & Hobby Museum, wildlife area. **Additional Information:** Wayne County CVB (800) 362-6474.

Restrictions

Pets: Leash only. **Fires:** Fire ring only. **Alcoholic Beverages:** Permitted. **Vehicle Maximum Length:** None.

To Get There

From the junction of US 30 and SR 3, drive 1.8 mi. southwest on SR 3 to SR 226, then 8.2 mi. south to SR 514, then 2 mi. south. The roads are generally in good condition w/ adequate shoulders.

SIDNEY

Camp Qtokee

2686 St. Rte. 29, Sidney 45365. T: (937) 492-7324

RV ★ Tent ★

Beauty: ★★ Site Privacy: ★★
Spaciousness: ★★ Quiet: ★★
Security: ★★★ Cleanliness: ★★
Insect Control: None Facilities: ★★

Camp Otokee has two major things going for it—easy access from the interstate and signs pointing the way. Maintained as a camping getaway and recreation spot for the local Eagles organization, Camp Otkoee welcomes non-member campers and would be a handy place to stay. Built on a lake on the north edge of Sidney, the campground has 90 seasonal campers, leaving 30 sites for visiting campers. Sites are mostly shaded and grassy, with 36 pull-throughs. No gas motors are allowed on the lake, and all game fish are to be released. A separate primitive tent area is set off from RVs, with no vehicles driving in or out of the area after dark unless it is an emergency. Also, all vehicles on campground property must be licensed and driveable at all times. Quiet hours are 11 p.m. to 8 a.m., and the speed limit is five mph. Security measures include one entrance/exit, a manager who lives on site, and regular campground patrols.

Basics

Operated by: Sidney Eagles FOE 1403. **Open:** All year. **Site Assignment:** Reservations w/ 1-night deposit; refund w/ 7-day notice. **Registration:** At campground office. **Fee:** $19 (cash, check). **Parking:** At site.

Facilities

Number of RV Sites: 120. **Number of Tent-Only Sites:** 7. **Hookups:** Electric (30, 50 amps), water. **Each Site:** Picnic table, fire ring. **Dump Station:** Yes. **Laundry:** No. **Pay Phone:** No. **Rest Rooms and Showers:** Yes. **Fuel:** No. **Propane:** No. **Internal Roads:** Gravel, in good condition. **RV Service:** No. **Market:** 2 mi. south in Sidney. **Restaurant:** 2 mi. south in Sidney. **General Store:** No. **Vending:** Yes. **Swimming Pool:** No. **Playground:** Yes. **Other:** Swimming beach, rec hall, video games, basketball, volleyball, horseshoes, ping pong. **Activities:** Swimming, fishing, boating (rental rowboats, paddleboats, canoes available). **Nearby Attractions:** Woods reserve & sanctuary, golf, historic farmstead, museums, antiques, Piatt Castles, Air Force Museum, arts & crafts shops. **Additional Information:** Miami County Visitors & Convention Bureau, (800) 348-8993.

Restrictions

Pets: Leash only. **Fires:** Fire ring only. **Alcoholic Beverages:** Permitted. **Vehicle Maximum Length:** None.

To Get There

From the junction of I-75 and SR 29, take Exit 93 and drive 0.4 mi. northwest on SR 29. Roads are wide and well maintained w/ broad shoulders. Gravel road leading into campground is narrow.

VAN BUREN

Pleasant View Recreation

12611 Township Rd. 218, Van Buren 45889. T: (419) 299-3897

RV ★★★★ Tent ★★★★

Beauty: ★★★ Site Privacy: ★★★★
Spaciousness: ★★★★ Quiet: ★★★★
Security: ★★★★ Cleanliness: ★★★★
Insect Control: None Facilities: ★★★★

The name of this campground lets campers know what to expect—enough recreation possibilities to keep children and adults happy. A rural campground one mile off I-75 in Van Buren, Pleasant View Recreation offers both open and wooded sites with 40 pull-throughs. As often happens, seasonals have 230 of the campground sites, leaving 70 for overnight campers. Sites are level, with a typical site width of 32 feet. The speed limit is five mph with speed bumps. The best RV sites are in Campers Loop because they offer full hookups and are near the pond. Tent sites are in a separate area by the pond with more green space and privacy. Laid out in a series of loops, the campground is a bargain with rates running from $15 to $22 for a family of two adults, two children, and one vehicle. Additional children are $1, adults are $2, and vehicles are $1. Security measures include a card-coded traffic gate, owners who live on site, and occasional campground patrols.

Basics

Operated by: Dan & Kathy Gant. **Open:** All year. **Site Assignment:** Reservations w/ 1-night deposit; refunds w/ 7-day notice. **Registration:** At campground office. **Fee:** $22 (cash, check, credit cards). **Parking:** At site.

Facilities

Number of RV Sites: 300. **Number of Tent-Only Sites:** 45. **Hookups:** Electric (30, 50 amps), water, sewer. **Each Site:** Picnic table, fire ring. **Dump Station:** Yes. **Laundry:** Yes. **Pay Phone:** Yes. **Rest Rooms and Showers:** Yes. **Fuel:** No. **Propane:** Yes. **Internal Roads:** Paved/gravel, in good condition. **RV Service:** No. **Market:** 5 mi. northwest in North Baltimore. **Restaurant:** 5 mi. northwest in North Baltimore. **General Store:** Yes. **Vending:** Yes. **Swimming Pool:** Yes. **Playground:** Yes. **Other:** Fishing pond, adult card room, mini golf, dance hall, game room, restaurant, horseshoes, baseball, sports field, volleyball, basketball, shuffleboard, coin games, tennis, badminton. **Activities:** Swimming, fishing, boating (rental paddleboats available), scheduled weekend activities. **Nearby Attractions:** Historic courthouse, golf, nature preserve, equestrian farm, motor sports park, Ghost Town, museums, Little Red Schoolhouse, planetarium, Riverside Train. **Additional Information:** Findlay CVB, (419) 423-3315.

Restrictions

Pets: Leash only. **Fires:** Fire ring only. **Alcoholic Beverages:** Permitted. **Vehicle Maximum Length:** None.

To Get There

From the junction of I-75 and Hwy. 613, take Exit 164, drive 0.75 mi. east on Hwy. 613, then 0.25 mi. southeast on Township 218. Roads are wide and well maintained w/ broad shoulders.

WAPAKONETA

Glacier Hill Lakes

11675 Wapak-Freyburg Rd., Wapakoneta 45895. T: (419) 738-3005

RV ★★★ Tent ★★

Beauty: ★★★ Site Privacy: ★★★
Spaciousness: ★★★ Quiet: ★★
Security: ★★★★ Cleanliness: ★★★★
Insect Control: None Facilities: ★★★

A rural campground on hilly terrain, Glacier Hill Lakes is centered around its two lakes. With 180 seasonal campers, the campground accepts no reservations for its remaining 50 RV sites, so be sure to have a back-up plan ready. Sites are open or shaded, with 24 pull-throughs and a typical site width of 40 feet. Some major utility lines and towers run through the campground, and in some areas campers can hear the lines buzzing. A ten-mph speed limit seems a bit high with so many children around, but the speed is lessened by speed bumps. Security measures include an owner who lives on site, regular patrols, and a card-coded traffic gate.

Basics

Operated by: Earl Wuebbenhorst. **Open:** All year. **Site Assignment:** First come, first served; no reservations. **Registration:** At campground office. **Fee:** $21 (cash, check, credit cards). **Parking:** At site.

Facilities

Number of RV Sites: 230. **Number of Tent-Only Sites:** 15. **Hookups:** Electric (30, 50 amps), water, sewer. **Each Site:** Picnic table, fire ring. **Dump Station:** Yes. **Laundry:** No. **Pay Phone:** Yes. **Rest Rooms and Showers:** Yes. **Fuel:** No. **Propane:** Yes. **Internal Roads:** Gravel, in good condition. **RV Service:** Yes. **Market:** 3 mi. northwest in Wapakoneta. **Restaurant:** 3 mi. northwest in Wapakoneta. **General Store:** Yes. **Vending:** Yes. **Swimming Pool:** No. **Playground:** Yes. **Other:** Swimming lake, shelter house, horseshoes, volleyball, fishing lake, pavilion, sports field, boating lake (no motors allowed). **Activities:** Swimming, fishing, some scheduled activities, boating (rental canoes, rowboats, paddleboats available). **Nearby Attractions:** Neil Armstrong Air & Space Museum, Ohio

Caverns, Piatt Castle, train displays, bicycle museum, antiques, US Air Force Museum, Indian Lake, golf. **Additional Information:** Wapakoneta Area Chamber of Commerce (419) 738-2911.

Restrictions

Pets: Leash only. **Fires:** Fire ring only. **Alcoholic Beverages:** Permitted. **Vehicle Maximum Length:** None.

To Get There

From the junction of I-75 and US 33, take Exit 110 and drive 0.5 mi. east on US 33, then 0.75 mi. southeast on Wapak-Fisher Rd. (CR 33A), then 2 mi. south on Wapak-Freyburg Rd. The roads are wide and well maintained w/ broad shoulders

WAPAKONETA

Wapakoneta/Lima South KOA

14719 Cemetery Rd., Wapakoneta 45895.
T: (419) 738-6016; www.koa.com;
wapakkoa@bright.net.

RV ★★★★ Tent ★★★★

Beauty: ★★★★	Site Privacy: ★★★★
Spaciousness: ★★★★	Quiet: ★★★
Security: ★★★★	Cleanliness: ★★★★
Insect Control: Yes	Facilities: ★★★★

Wapakoneta/Lima East KOA offers easy interstate access, clean facilities, and comfortable amenities. Located close to I-75 one mile east of Wapa-koneta, the campground has to contend with some traffic noise. Under new ownership since 2001, the campground has level grassy sites with gravel for parking. The typical site width is 27 feet, with a typical site length of 70 feet. There are 50 pull-through sites and no seasonal campers. The speed limit is eight mph, quiet hours are 10:30 p.m. to 8 a.m., and generators are not permitted at any time. The best RV sites are 1, 3, and 5 because they are bigger and have more grass. The best tent site is 44 because it has more trees and shade. Security includes owners who live on site, regular patrols, and a coded gate. Security gates are closed between 11 p.m. and 6 a.m.

Basics

Operated by: John & Debbie Schuettler. **Open:** Feb. 30–Dec. 3. **Site Assignment:** Reservations w/ 1-night deposit; refund w/ 7-day notice. **Registration:** At campground office. **Fee:** $33 (cash, credit cards). **Parking:** At site.

Facilities

Number of RV Sites: 68. **Number of Tent-Only Sites:** 6. **Hookups:** Electric (30, 50 amps), water, cable TV. **Each Site:** Picnic table, fire ring. **Dump Station:** Yes. **Laundry:** Yes. **Pay Phone:** Yes. **Rest Rooms and Showers:** Yes. **Fuel:** No. **Propane:** Yes. **Internal Roads:** Gravel, in good condition. **RV Service:** No. **Market:** 1 mi. west in Wapakoneta. **Restaurant:** 1 mi. west in Wapakoneta. **General Store:** Yes. **Vending:** Yes. **Swimming Pool:** Yes. **Playground:** Yes. **Other:** Club room, basketball, volleyball, horseshoes, pavilion, rental cabins, coin games, sports field, rental bikes. **Activities:** Swimming. **Nearby Attractions:** Neil Armstrong Air & Space Museum, Ohio Caverns, Piatt Castle, train displays, bicycle museum, antiques, US Air Force Museum, Indian Lake, golf. **Additional Information:** Wapakoneta Area Chamber of Commerce, (419) 738-2911.

Restrictions

Pets: Leash only. **Fires:** Fire ring only. **Alcoholic Beverages:** Permitted. **Vehicle Maximum Length:** None.

To Get There

From I-75, take northbound Exit 110 or southbound Exit 111, drive east to first intersection, then 0.75 mi. north on Cemetery Rd., past membership resort. Roads are wide and well maintained w/ broad shoulders.

WAYNESVILLE

Caesar Creek State Park

8570 East State Rte. 73, Waynesville 45068.
T: (513) 897-3055; www.ohiostateparks.org.

RV ★★★ Tent ★★★

Beauty: ★★★★	Site Privacy: ★★★
Spaciousness: ★★★	Quiet: ★★★
Security: ★★★★	Cleanliness: ★★★
Insect Control: None	Facilities: ★★★

For beauty, natural amenities, naturalist programs, roads, and maintenance, it's usually hard to beat a state park. But for facilities like water hookups and laundries, state parks are often at the bottom of the scale. Caesar Creek State Park has all the pluses you would expect, as well as the minuses often found at a state-run park. The 2,830-acre Caesar Creek Lake was created in 1978 when Caesar's Creek, which empties into the Little Miami River, was dammed by the Army Corps of Engineers for flood control and as a water resource. Legend has it that the creek was named for a runaway slave called Cezar who camped on its banks and lived with a local Native American tribe. Popular for waterskiing, pleasure boating, swimming, and fishing, Caesar Creek Lake offers a huge beach and four boat ramps. A pioneer village, visitors center, and a wealth of nature center programs are also big draws. Located ten miles east of Waynesville, Caesar Creek State Park Campground offers sites with electricity which can be used by either tents or RVs. An equestrian camp with 25 sites is available for overnight trail rides. The typical site size is 12 × 35 feet. Guests have a choice of shaded or open sites, but no pull-throughs are available. Park rangers provide security patrols and check on entering motorists.

Basics

Operated by: State of Ohio. **Open:** All year. **Site Assignment:** First come, first served. No reservations. **Registration:** At campground office. **Fee:** $17 (cash, check, credit cards). **Parking:** At site.

Facilities

Number of RV Sites: 287. **Number of Tent-Only Sites:** 0. **Hookups:** Electric (30 amps). **Each Site:** Picnic table, fire ring. **Dump Station:** Yes. **Laundry:** No. **Pay Phone:** Yes. **Rest Rooms and Showers:** Yes. **Fuel:** No. **Propane:** Yes. **Internal Roads:** Paved, in good condition. **RV Service:** No. **Market:** 10 mi. west in Waynesville. **Restaurant:** 10 mi. west in Waynesville. **General Store:** Yes. **Vending:** Yes. **Swimming Pool:** No. **Playground:** Yes. **Other:** Caesar Creek lake, swimming beach, boat ramp, pavilion, horseback riding trails, horseshoes, hiking trails, nature center, wildlife area, rental RVs. **Activities:** Swimming, fishing, boating, hiking, scheduled activities. **Nearby Attractions:** Antiques, arts & crafts shops, skydiving, Kings Island amusement park, bike trails, pioneer village, golf, Quaker meeting house, Blue Jacket outdoor drama. **Additional Information:** Warren County CVB, (800) 433-1072.

Restrictions

Pets: Leash only, pet camping area; $1 fee extra per pet per day, max. of 2 pets. **Fires:** Fire ring only. **Alcoholic Beverages:** Not permitted. **Vehicle Maximum Length:** 35 ft. **Other:** 14-day stay limit.

To Get There

From Waynesville, drive 8 mi. east on SR 73 to SR 380, then drive 3 mi. north to Center Rd., then 1 mi. west. Roads are wide and well maintained w/ broad shoulders.

WAYNESVILLE

Spring Valley Frontier Campground

9580 Collett Rd., Waynesville 45068. T: (937) 862-4510; www.gocampingamerica.com;
nlineen@aol.com.

RV ★★★ Tent ★★

Beauty: ★★	Site Privacy: ★★
Spaciousness: ★★★	Quiet: ★★★
Security: ★★★★	Cleanliness: ★★★
Insect Control: None	Facilities: ★★★

Located off the beaten path eight miles north of Waynesville, Spring Valley Frontier Campground is a wooded, rural property with 45 seasonal campers in the back half. Typical site width is 30 feet, with three pull-through sites. Laid out in a series of loops, the campground is mostly shaded by mature sycamore, ash, and walnut trees. Sites are grassy, with crushed limestone for RV pads. Tent sites are separated from RVs, offering more privacy and natural surroundings. Campsites tend to fill up quickly, particularly with RV clubs, so it is advisable to call ahead. Security measures include one access road that goes past the office and owners who live on the premises. A five-mph speed limit is enforced, and the campground has speed bumps to slow down traffic.

Basics

Operated by: Paul & Nancy Lineen. **Open:** All year. **Site Assignment:** Reservations w/ no deposit. **Registration:** At campground office. **Fee:** $22 (cash, credit cards). **Parking:** At site.

Facilities

Number of RV Sites: 75. **Number of Tent-Only Sites:** 22. **Hookups:** Electric (30, 50 amps), water, sewer. **Each Site:** Picnic table, fire ring. **Dump Station:** Yes. **Laundry:** Yes. **Pay Phone:** Yes. **Rest Rooms and Showers:** Yes. **Fuel:** No. **Propane:** Yes. **Internal Roads:** Paved/gravel, in fair condition. **RV Service:** No. **Market:** 8 mi. south in Waynesville. **Restaurant:** 8 mi. south in Waynesville. **General Store:** Yes. **Vending:** Yes. **Swimming Pool:** Yes. **Playground:** Yes. **Other:** Mini-golf, shelter house, rec hall, basketball, rental cabins, rental mobile homes. **Activities:** Swimming. **Nearby Attractions:** Antiques, arts & crafts shops, skydiving, Kings Island amusement park, bike trail, pioneer village, Caesar Creek State Park, canoe livery, wildlife area, golf, Blue Jacket outdoor drama. **Additional Information:** Warren County CVB, (800) 433-1072.

RESTRICTIONS

Pets: Leash only. **Fires:** Fire ring only. **Alcoholic Beverages:** Permitted. **Vehicle Maximum Length:** None.

TO GET THERE

From the junction of I-75 and US35E, take exit 52B, drive 16 mi. east on US 35 Bypass, then 7 mi. south on US 42, then 1.75 mi. east on Roxanna, New Burlington Rd., then 0.75 mi. south on Pence Jones Rd., then 0.2 mi. west on Collett Rd. Roads are often narrow and twisty w/ poor shoulders.

WEST SALEM

Hidden Acres Campground

P.O. Box 40, West Salem 44287. T: (419) 853-4687

RV ★★★ Tent ★★★

Beauty: ★★★★ Site Privacy: ★★★★
Spaciousness: ★★★★ Quiet: ★★★★
Security: ★★★ Cleanliness: ★★★★
Insect Control: None Facilities: ★★★

Located two-and-a-half miles south of West Salem, Hidden Acres Campground offers level, grassy sites, mostly shaded by mature trees. Some open sites are available right on a lake. Laid out in a series of loops, the campground has 110 seasonal campers, two pull-through sites, and a typical site width of 35 feet. Attractive touches include a gazebo, water fountain, and wooden fishing pier. The camp store offers fast food; on weekends, the also serve special dishes such as chili or sauerkraut and kielbasa. A five-mph speed limit and quiet time from 11 p.m. to 9 a.m. are enforced. An unusual rule forbids perming or coloring of hair in the restrooms. An extra fee of $2 per pole is charged for fishing in the stocked lake, but there is a small pond where fishing is free. Hidden Acres is in back of a small mobile home park.

BASICS

Operated by: Jim & Ginger Kovacich, Jim & Sandy Whittlesey. **Open:** Apr. 15–Oct. 15. **Site Assignment:** Reservations w/ 1-night deposit; refund w/ 7-day notice. **Registration:** At campground office. **Fee:** $24 (cash, check). **Parking:** At site.

FACILITIES

Number of RV Sites: 180. **Number of Tent-Only Sites:** 0. **Hookups:** Electric (30, 50 amps), water, sewer. **Each Site:** Picnic table, fire ring. **Dump Station:** Yes. **Laundry:** No. **Pay Phone:** No. **Rest Rooms and Showers:** Yes. **Fuel:** No. **Propane:** Yes. **Internal Roads:** Paved/gravel, in good condition. **RV Service:** No. **Market:** 2.5 mi. north in West Salem. **Restaurant:** 1.5 mi. north in West Salem. **General Store:** Yes. **Vending:** No. **Swimming Pool:** Yes. **Playground:** Yes. **Other:** Fishing lake, shuffleboard, basketball, game room, horseshoes, shelter house, sports field, volleyball. **Activities:** Fishing, swimming, boating (rental paddleboats available). **Nearby Attractions:** State Parks, antiques, golf, museums, historic homes, arts & crafts. **Additional Information:** Ashland Area Chamber of Commerce (419) 281-4584.

RESTRICTIONS

Pets: Leash only, proof immunization required. **Fires:** Fire ring only. **Alcoholic Beverages:** At sites only. **Vehicle Maximum Length:** None. **Other:** No working caravans permitted. Max. stay for tents is 7 days. Electric heaters are prohibited.

TO GET THERE

From the junction of Hwy. 301 and US 42, drive 3 mi. west on US 42, then 200 yards south on Township Rd 810. Roads are wide and well maintained w/ broad shoulders.

WEST SALEM

Town & Country Camp Resort

7555 Shilling Rd., West Salem 44287. T: (419) 853-4550

RV ★★★★ Tent ★★★★

Beauty: ★★★★ Site Privacy: ★★★★
Spaciousness: ★★★★ Quiet: ★★★★
Security: ★★★★ Cleanliness: ★★★★
Insect Control: None Facilities: ★★★★

Town & Country Camp Resort is only two miles south of West Salem, but it has a definite country feel. Sites are grassy with gravel parking spots, and campers have a choice of shaded or open sites. Several lakes and a woods add to the country atmosphere. Laid out in a series of loops, the campground has 120 seasonal campers and ten pull-through sites. All sites have sewer connections so there is no dump station. A five-mph speed limit is enforced, as is quiet time from 11 p.m. to 8 a.m. No license is required for fishing in the campground lakes, and there is no limit on bluegills. Bass must be at least 12 inches with a limit of four per day, and catfish must be returned to the lake. Security measures include owners who live on site, a security gate, and regular patrols of the campgrounds.

BASICS

Operated by: Don & Linda Castella. **Open:** Apr. 1–Oct. 31. **Site Assignment:** Reservations accepted without deposit, except on holidays. Holiday reservations w/ 1-night deposit; refunds w/ 7-day notice. **Registration:** At campground office. **Fee:** $25 (cash, check). **Parking:** At site.

FACILITIES

Number of RV Sites: 200. **Number of Tent-Only Sites:** 25. **Hookups:** Electric (30 amps), water, sewer. **Each Site:** Picnic table, fire ring. **Dump Station:** No. **Laundry:** Yes. **Pay Phone:** Yes. **Rest Rooms and Showers:** Yes. **Fuel:** No. **Propane:** Yes. **Internal Roads:** Gravel, in good condition. **RV Service:** No. **Market:** 2 mi. north in West Salem. **Restaurant:** 2 mi. north in West Salem. **General Store:** Yes, limited. **Vending:** Yes. **Swimming Pool:** Yes. **Playground:** Yes. **Other:** Fishing lake, game room, pavilion, softball, horseshoes, basketball, volleyball. **Activities:** Swimming, fishing, scheduled activities. **Nearby Attractions:** State parks, antiques, golf, museums, historic homes, arts & crafts. **Additional Information:** Ashland Area Chamber of Commerce, (419) 281-4584.

RESTRICTIONS

Pets: Leash only. **Fires:** Fire ring only. **Alcoholic Beverages:** Must be kept in covered containers. **Vehicle Maximum Length:** 40 ft. **Other:** No working caravans are permitted.

TO GET THERE

From the junction of I-71 and SR 539, take Exit 198, drive 1 mi. northwest on SR 539 to Shilling Rd., drive 1 mi. north. SR 539 is a good road, well maintained w/ broad shoulders. The entry road is paved, but it's also narrow, hilly, and twisting w/ a narrow squeeze past a farm silo.

WILMINGTON

Cowan Lake State Park

729 Beechwood Rd., Wilmington 45177. T: (937) 289-2105; www.dnr.state.oh.us/odnr/parks.

RV ★★★ Tent ★★★

Beauty: ★★★★ Site Privacy: ★★★
Spaciousness: ★★★ Quiet: ★★★★
Security: ★★★★ Cleanliness: ★★★
Insect Control: None Facilities: ★★★

Located five miles west of Wilmington, Cowan Lake State Park has a 700-acre lake as a centerpiece. The lake is very popular for sailboats and pontoon boats. The lake has a ten-horsepower limit on motors. The Cowan Lake region was once a stronghold of the Miami and Shawnee Indians. Cowan Creek was named for the area's first surveyor, John Cowan. A dam was completed across Cowan Creek in 1950, and in 1968, Cowan Lake was dedicated as a state park. Campground sites are suitable for tents or RVs. Four sites are wheelchair accessible. Pet camping is offered on designated sites. Unlike many state campgrounds, Cowan Lake offers laundry facilities. Most sites are shaded by a beech and maple forest, and the average site size is 14 × 40 feet. There are no pull-through sites. Security is good, with park rangers who patrol and monitor motorists at a park gate.

BASICS

Operated by: State of Ohio. **Open:** All year. **Site Assignment:** First come, first served. No reservations. **Registration:** At campground office. **Fee:** $17 (cash, check, credit cards). **Parking:** At site.

FACILITIES

Number of RV Sites: 237. **Number of Tent-Only Sites:** 18. **Hookups:** Electric (50 amps). **Each Site:** Picnic table, fire ring. **Dump Station:** Yes. **Laundry:** Yes. **Pay Phone:** Yes. **Rest Rooms and Showers:** Yes. **Fuel:** No. **Propane:** No. **Internal Roads:** Paved, in good condition. **RV Service:**

No. **Market:** 5 mi. east in Wilmington. **Restaurant:** 5 mi. east in Wilmington. **General Store:** Yes. **Vending:** Yes. **Swimming Pool:** No. **Playground:** Yes. **Other:** Cowan Lake, beach, boat dock, boat ramp, hiking trails, pavilion, horseshoes, game room, mini-golf, mountain bike trail, rental cabins. **Activities:** Swimming, fishing, hiking, low-speed boating (rental canoes, motorboats available), scheduled activities. **Nearby Attractions:** Kings Island amusement park, Blue Jacket outdoor drama, antiques, covered bridge, pottery, pheasant farm, Wilmington College, rails-to-trails recreational trail. **Additional Information:** Clinton County CVB, (877) 4-A-VISIT.

Restrictions

Pets: Leash only. Pet camping area, $1 fee per pet per day. **Fires:** Fire ring only. **Alcoholic Beverages:** Not permitted. **Vehicle Maximum Length:** 35 ft. **Other:** 14-day stay limit.

To Get There

From Wilmington, drive 3 mi. south on US 68 to Dalton Rd., then 1.5 mi. Roads are wide and well maintained w/ broad shoulders.

WILMINGTON

Thousand Trails-Wilmington

1786 State Rd. 380, Wilmington 45177. T: (800) 334-9103; F: (937) 655-8065; www.1000trails.com.

RV ★★★★ Tent ★★★★

Beauty: ★★★	Site Privacy: ★★★★
Spaciousness: ★★★★	Quiet: ★★★★
Security: ★★★★★	Cleanliness: ★★★★★
Insect Control: None	Facilities: ★★★★

Thousand Trails—Wilmington is part of a nationwide network of 57 campground resorts for members of a private camping club. Membership options with annual dues allow members to camp at every preserve in the system or choose only a favorite region. Non-members are allowed a get-acquainted visit. Located seven miles west of Wilmington, the campground is on a preserve of gently rolling land surrounding a lake. The typical site width is 40 feet, and the campground has two pull-throughs. Sites are mostly shaded by mature oak, maple, and ash trees. Members have access to such extras as an iron and ironing board in the laundry and canoes and paddleboats on the small lake. The campground has 40 rally sites and ten tent sites in a wooded area with water hookups. Three stocked ponds are for catch-and-release fishing only. Quiet time is enforced from 11 p.m. to 8 a.m., as is a five-mph speed limit. Security is excellent, with a gate that requires a code to get in, a manager on site, and regular patrols.

Basics

Operated by: Thousand Trails Inc. **Open:** May 1–Oct. 31. **Site Assignment:** Reservations w/ 1-night deposit; refund w/ 24-hour notice. **Registration:** At campground office. **Fee:** $25 (cash, check, credit cards). **Parking:** At site.

Facilities

Number of RV Sites: 164. **Number of Tent-Only Sites:** 10. **Hookups:** Electric (30 amps), water, sewer. **Each Site:** Picnic table, fire ring. **Dump Station:** Yes. **Laundry:** Yes. **Pay Phone:** Yes. **Rest Rooms and Showers:** Yes. **Fuel:** No. **Propane:** Yes. **Internal Roads:** Paved/gravel, in good condition. **RV Service:** No. **Market:** 10 mi. east in Wilmington. **Restaurant:** 7 mi. east in Wilmington. **General Store:** Yes. **Vending:** Yes. **Swimming Pool:** No. **Playground:** Yes. **Other:** Adult lodge, basketball, campfire circle, family lodge, horseshoe, meeting room, mini-golf, shuffleboard, wading pool, whirlpool, tennis, volleyball, hiking trail, fishing pond, rental trailers. **Activities:** Swimming, fishing, hiking, electric motorboating (free canoes, paddleboats available), scheduled weekend activities. **Nearby Attractions:** Kings Island amusement park, pottery, Blue Jacket outdoor drama, pheasant farm, Wilmington College, antiques, covered bridge, rails-to-trails recreational trail. **Additional Information:** Clinton County CVB, (877) 4-A-VISIT.

Restrictions

Pets: Leash only. **Fires:** Fire ring only. **Alcoholic Beverages:** Permitted. **Vehicle Maximum Length:** None. **Other:** 14-day stay limit.

To Get There

From the junction of I-71 and Hwy. 73, take Exit 45, drive 0.25 mi. east on Hwy. 73, then 1.5 mi. south on Hwy. 380. Roads are wide and well maintained w/ broad shoulders.

Oklahoma

Oklahoma is a real slice of American bread. There's nobody more down-to-earth than a native Oklahoman working the land, having coffee with friends before a hard day's work, or going to church to start the week. And nobody's more hospitable. This is wave-at-your-neighbor-as-you-drive-past country, and strangers are greeted with the same friendly wave.

Many of Oklahoma's visitor-friendly towns line I-35, which bisects the state. The panhandle of Oklahoma (from the New Mexico border to about Canton Lake) does not offer much to travelers, and any Oklahoman will tell you: *nobody* comes to Oklahoma in the dead of summer. July and August are months for exploring the other 49 states. But spring and fall are beautiful—and popular—times to visit. **Tulsa** is a modern city with a history, **Bartlesville** is home to a 3,500-acre wildlife preserve, **Grove** has a reconstructed village from the nineteenth century, and you can still get your kicks on (Historic) **Route 66.**

And of course, there's **Oklahoma City.** Oklahoma City lies at the crossroads of I-35, I-40, and I-44, ensuring that visitors from any surrounding state can get there. And well they should. Oklahoma City might strike you at first as the fitting home of the **National Cowboy Hall of Fame,** but promenade through the skywalks of downtown for another view. Take in the **Air Space Museum,** the **Crystal Bridge at Myriad Gardens,** the **Civic Center** that spans six blocks in the heart of downtown, and the touching **Oklahoma City National Memorial.** The impression you take with you of the city—and quite likely the state for which it was named—will be of a complex embroidery waiting to be unraveled. Don't believe the Board of Tourism signs that claim, "Oklahoma is OK!" It's much better than that.

The following facilities accept payment in checks or cash only:

Big Cedar RV Park, Big Cedar
Big Cedar RV Park, Big Cedar
Bridgeport RV Park, Eufaula
Elk Run RV Park, Elk City
Moneka Park, Waurika
Rockin' Horse RV Park, Spiro
Sawyer RV Park, Sawyer
Simmons RV Park, Durant
Wink's RV Park, Clinton
Woodland Camper Park, Tonkawa

The following facilities feature 20 sites or fewer:

Cherokee Riverside Campground, Disney
Corky's Get & Go, Woodward
Oak Hill RV Park, Davis
Sawyer RV Park, Sawyer

Campground Profiles

ANADARKO

Indian City USA

P.O. Box 695, Anadarko 73005. T: (405) 247-5661; F: (405) 247-2467; www.indiancityusa.com; indiancty@aol.com.

RV ★★★ Tent ★★★

Beauty: ★★★ Site Privacy: ★★★
Spaciousness: ★★★★ Quiet: ★★★★★
Security: ★★★★ Cleanliness: ★★
Insect Control: ★★★ Facilities: ★★

This campground is set up in two tiers. The top tier is an open gravel lot surrounded on the perimeter by trees, but containing a row of only 4 shade trees down the middle. The (unnumbered) sites that have shade trees are the more desirable sites. The lower tier to the west is a nicer area, but requires negotiating a tight hairpin turn just where the road is most damaged. These are all grassy sites with cement one-piece picnic tables. While still quite open, there are more shade trees here than in the upper tier. (Be sure to drive carefully on the lower tier, as the grass is rather choppy and uneven.) There are unlimited tenting possibilities in the grassy field to the west of the RV park, and even in the woods around it. The grass is great for tents, but there are no trees whatsoever in the field. The rest room itself is clean, but appears rather old and worn. The floors are stained and could use a retiling. One gets the impression of a very nice campground that only needs a helping hand to make it really sparkle. As it is, it's a decent place to spend the night, and offers touristy attractions for those interested in Native American culture.

BASICS

Operated By: George Moran. **Open:** All year. **Site Assignment:** First some, first served; verbal reservations OK. **Registration:** In Indian City. (Late arrivals select an available site & settle in the morning.) **Fee:** RV $13.12, tent $9.98. **Parking:** At site.

FACILITIES

Number of RV Sites: 65. **Number of Tent-**

Only Sites: Undesignated sites. **Hookups:** Water, sewer, electric (30 amps). **Each Site:** Picnic tables on lower tier. **Dump Station:** Yes. **Laundry:** No. **Pay Phone:** No. **Rest Rooms and Showers:** Yes. **Fuel:** No. **Propane:** No. **Internal Roads:** Paved, but in disrepair. **RV Service:** No. **Market:** 2 mi. in Anadarko. **Restaurant:** 1 block. **General Store:** No. **Vending:** Yes. **Swimming:** Pool. **Playground:** Yes. **Other:** None. **Activities:** Guided tours of American Indian villages. **Nearby Attractions:** Indian City USA, Indian City Museum, American Indian dancing, National Hall of Fame for Famous American Indians, Anadarko Philomathic Pioneer Museum, Southern Plains Indian Museum & Crafts Center. **Additional Information:** Anadarko Chamber of Commerce, (405) 247-6651.

Restrictions

Pets: On leash, cleaned up after. **Fires:** In grills. **Alcoholic Beverages:** At sites. **Vehicle Maximum Length:** None.

To Get There

From the junction of Hwys. 8, 9, and 62, go 2.3 mi. south on Hwy. 8. Turn left at the sign onto the paved road and go 0.3 mi. Turn right into the campground or continue up the road 0.2 mi. to register in Indian City.

ARDMORE

Ardmore/Marietta KOA

Rte. 1 Box 640, Ardmore 73448. T: (800) KOA-5893 or (580) 276-2800.

RV ★★★★ Tent ★★★★

Beauty: ★★★★ Site Privacy: ★★★★
Spaciousness: ★★★★ Quiet: ★★★
Security: ★★★★ Cleanliness: ★★★★★
Insect Control: ★★★★ Facilities: ★★★★

Built on a slope, this campground has levelled pull-throughs 84 × 25 feet in size. There is a distinct farm feeling on the campground, and it is surrounded on the south by a farm, on the west by trees, and the north by an open field with trees in the distance. The most desirable sites are 15, 16, and 21–26, which all have shade trees. The other sites are in the open to a greater or lesser extent. Tenting is possible on the grassy field to the west of the RV sites, or—better yet—in the field to the north, where a handful of shade trees provide coverage. The rest rooms and showers are extremely clean, although the floor is slightly peeling (but not dirty). The laundry room is equally clean and spacious, and very well decorated. This is a small but very nice campground. Tenters and RVers alike will enjoy a stay here.

Basics

Operated By: Jery Burns. **Open:** All year. **Site Assignment:** Assigned upon registration; credit card required for reservation. **Registration:** In office. (Late arrivals use drop box in laundry.) **Fee:** RV $22 (full), $20 (water, electric), tent $16. **Parking:** At site.

Facilities

Number of RV Sites: 26. **Number of Tent-Only Sites:** Undesignated sites. **Hookups:** Water, sewer, electric (30, 50 amps). **Each Site:** Picnic table, grill. **Dump Station:** Yes. **Laundry:** Yes. **Pay Phone:** Yes. **Rest Rooms and Showers:** Yes. **Fuel:** No. **Propane:** Yes. **Internal Roads:** Gravel. **RV Service:** No. **Market:** 6 mi. south to Marietta. **Restaurant:** 6 mi. south to Marietta. **General Store:** Yes. **Vending:** No. **Swimming:** No. **Playground:** Yes. **Other:** Game room, 2 cabins. **Activities:** Volleyball, fishing, boating. **Nearby Attractions:** Arbuckle Mountains, Eliza Cruce Hall Doll Collection, Tucker Tower Nature Center, Charles B. Goddard Center for the Visual & Performing Arts. **Additional Information:** Ardmore Chamber of Commerce, (580) 223-7765.

Restrictions

Pets: On leash, cleaned up after. **Fires:** In grills. **Alcoholic Beverages:** At sites. **Vehicle Maximum Length:** None.

To Get There

From I-35, take Exit 21. Turn west onto Oswalt and go 0.1 mi. Turn left at the sign onto the dirt entrance road.

BARTLESVILLE

Riverside RV Resort

1211 Southeast Adams Blvd., Bartlesville 74003. T: (888) 572-1241 or (918) 336-6431; F: (918) 336-3892; riversidervrst@aol.com.

RV ★★★ Tent ★★★

Beauty: ★★★ Site Privacy: ★★★
Spaciousness: ★★ Quiet: ★★★★
Security: ★★★★ Cleanliness: ★★★
Insect Control: ★★★★ Facilities: ★★★

Located in a residential area, this campground features some attractive landscaping using flowers, bricks around some of the sites, and a fountain, but it also looks a little run-down. Sites 1–14 are in the northwest corner, along the entrance. These sites (especially 1–8) are closest to the pool. Sites 15–19, in the middle of the campground, are pull-throughs 65 × 21 feet, and 20–23, in the same area, are pull-throughs 60 × 21 feet. All of these sites but 21 are well-shaded. Other 65-foot pull-throughs are 49–53 in the southeast corner. Sites 55–60, also in the southeast corner, are slightly shorter, at 60 feet. Any of these are a decent stay, depending on the length of site required for your vehicle. These sites are closest to the river, but are still up and off the bank. Tenting is allowed along the river bank. While shaded, these sites do not have abundant room for a tent—let alone recreating or relaxing at your site. The rest rooms and showers, individual units located in the office building, are tidy and nicely decorated. Both the rest rooms and the (small) laundry are clean. While adequate, this park is, as the name implies, better for RVs than tents—although it hardly lives up to the title "resort."

Basics

Operated By: Dave & Joyce Butler. **Open:** All year. **Site Assignment:** Assigned upon registration; verbal reservations OK. **Registration:** In office. (Late arrivals pay in morning.) **Fee:** RV $16 (full), tent $6 (checks, no credit cards). **Parking:** At site.

Facilities

Number of RV Sites: 70. **Number of Tent-Only Sites:** Undesignated sites. **Hookups:** Water, sewer, electric (20, 30, 50 amps), cable. **Dump Station:** Yes. **Laundry:** Yes. **Pay Phone:** Yes. **Rest Rooms and Showers:** Yes. **Fuel:** No. **Propane:** Yes. **Internal Roads:** Gravel. **RV Service:** No. **Market:** Less than 0.5 mi. west. **Restaurant:** 1.5 mi. east. **General Store:** No. **Vending:** Yes. **Swimming:** Pool. **Playground:** No. **Other:** Dataport, pavilion, river. **Activities:** Swimming, fishing. **Nearby Attractions:** Caney River, Woolaroc Ranch Museum. **Additional Information:** Bartlesville Area CVB, (800) 364-8708 or (918) 336-8708.

Restrictions

Pets: On leash, cleaned up after. **Fires:** In grills. **Alcoholic Beverages:** Inside RV only. **Vehicle Maximum Length:** 70 ft. **Other:** None.

To Get There

From the junction of Hwy. 75 and Hwy. 60 West (Pawhuska/Ponca City Exit), turn west onto Hwy. 60 and go 1.6 mi. to Quapaw Ave. Turn left onto Quapaw Ave. and take the first left into the campground.

BEAVER

Beaver Dunes State Park

P.O. Box 1190, Beaver 73932. T: (405) 625-3373; F: (405) 625-3525; www.otrd.state.ok.us; rstrpark@otrd.state.ok.us.

RV ★★★ Tent ★★★★

Beauty: ★★★★ Site Privacy: ★★★
Spaciousness: ★★★★ Quiet: ★★★★
Security: ★★★ Cleanliness: ★★★★
Insect Control: ★★ Facilities: ★★★

Just a mile and a half north of town, this campground offers primitive sites and electrical hookups for campers who like to get close to nature. There are campsites right at the water's edge (although no swimming is permitted), as well as furth up on shore. (Sites are not numbered.) There are seven huge pull-throughs (85 feet long) to the north of the "comfort station" (rest rooms and showers), which are the best bet for anything longer than 22 feet. There are, however, no shade trees in these sites. Following the one-way road, you come across three 27-foot back-ins that have covered picnic tables. One of these sites has water. Just to the southeast of the comfort station are four primitive sites: two are right on the lake, while the other two are on either side of the building. These are attractive sites, with nice tree coverage and good views of the lake and the bridge. However, they receive foot traffic to and from the rest rooms and cars drive past to reach other campsites. Perhaps the nicest campsite of all is the first one you see when you enter the campground. It is right on the water, has soft sand (on a bit of a slope), and some tree shade. The biggest drawback is that you must park above the site on the road, and walk down to the campsite, making RV parking at this site impossible. The "comfort station" is very spacious and clean, although the cement building itself seems a little old. This is a fine campground for those seeking to sleep out in nature, and has enough variety to satisfy pretty much any tastes.

Basics

Operated By: Oklahoma State Parks. **Open:** All year. **Site Assignment:** First come, first served; no reservations. **Registration:** In office, or ranger will collect at site. **Fee: Hookups:** $13, primitive: $7 (V & MC). **Parking:** At (or near) site.

Facilities

Number of RV Sites: 7. **Number of Tent-Only Sites:** 10. **Hookups:** Water, electric (30 amps). **Each Site:** Picnic table, grill/pit. **Dump Station:** Yes. **Laundry:** No. **Pay Phone:** In office (collect or calling card only). **Rest Rooms and Showers:** Yes. **Fuel:** No. **Propane:** No. **Internal Roads:** Paved. **RV Service:** No. **Market:** 1 mi. to Beaver. **Restaurant:** 1 mi. to Beaver. **General Store:** No. **Vending:** No. **Swimming:** No. **Playground:** Yes. **Other:** Picnic pavillion, wildlife. **Activities:** Hiking, ATV riding, volleyball, horseshoes, children's fishing. **Nearby Attractions:** Sand dunes, lake. **Additional Information:** Beaver County Chamber of Commerce, (580) 625-4726.

Restrictions

Pets: On leash, cleaned up after. **Fires:** In grills; subject to bans. **Alcoholic Beverages:** Beer only. **Vehicle Maximum Length:** None. **Other:** No swimming, ATV regulations.

To Get There

From the junction of Hwy. 64/270 and Hwy. 23, turn right onto Hwy. 23/270, and go 4.9 mi. south. Turn right at the sign into the campground, or left to get to the office.

BIG CEDAR

Big Cedar RV Park

0.3 mi. west of US Hwy. 259 on SH63, Big Cedar 74939. T: (918) 651-3271; www.big-cedar.net; rlsand50@yahoo.com.

RV ★★★★ Tent ★★★

Beauty: ★★★★ Site Privacy: ★★★★
Spaciousness: ★★★★ Quiet: ★★★★★
Security: ★★★★★ Cleanliness: ★★★★★
Insect Control: ★★★ Facilities: ★★★

This rural campground is surrounded by lush woods and forested hills to the north and east. It has a down-home, farmy atmosphere and grassy pull-through sites laid out in rows. Sites are a lengthy 75 feet and a uniform 24 feet wide. The most desirable sites are the lowest in number (1–6), as these are furthest from the highway and closest to the "Bath Barn". Site 1 contains a tree, but is not itself shaded. Sites 12 and 13 share a small shed that impinges slightly on their space. The tenting area is an open field on the south and east sides of the RV sites. There is a very nice grass cover, which will appeal to tenters, and one large tree, but otherwise the tenting area is quite open. The laundry is very spacious and clean and contains two small showers (normally not used). The facilities in the "Bath Barn" are self-contained units that include nicely decorated rest rooms with a vanity and showers. All facilities are kept immaculate. Although this is a small campground, it is worthy as a destination, and its family-run atmosphere will make all visitors feel comfortable.

Basics

Operated By: Bob & Carolyn Sanders. **Open:** All year. **Site Assignment:** First come, first served; verbal reservations OK. **Registration:** In office. (Late arrivals use drop box.) **Fee:** RV (30 amps) or tent $10, RV (50 amps): $12 (checks, no credit cards). **Parking:** At site.

Facilities

Number of RV Sites: 21. **Number of Tent-Only Sites:** Undesignated sites. **Hookups:** Water, sewer, electric (30, 50 amps). **Each Site:** Picnic table. **Dump Station:** Yes. **Laundry:** Yes. **Pay Phone:** No (0.3 mi. away). **Rest Rooms and Showers:** Yes. **Fuel:** No (0.3 mi. away). **Propane:** No (0.3 mi. away). **Internal Roads:** Gravel. **RV Service:** No. **Market:** 30 mi. to Taliniha. **Restaurant:** 5 mi. in Big Cedar. **General Store:** No. **Vending:** No. **Swimming:** No. **Playground:** No. **Other:** None. **Activities:** Hiking, scenic drives, wildlife watching. **Nearby Attractions:** Winding Stair National Wildlife Reserve. **Additional Information:** Talihina Chamber of Commerce, (918) 567-3434.

Restrictions

Pets: On leash, cleaned up after. **Fires:** In grills. **Alcoholic Beverages:** At sites. **Vehicle Maximum Length:** None.

To Get There

From the junction of Hwy. 63 and Hwy. 259, go 0.35 mi. west on Hwy. 63. Turn left at the sign into the entrance. The office is the green building on the left.

BROKEN BOW

Reiger RV Park

Rte. 4 Box 27, Hwy. 259 North, Broken Bow 74728. T: (800) 550-6521 or (580) 494-6553; F: (580) 494-6553; www.hochatownjunction.com; HJ-Resorts@pine-net.com.

RV ★★★ Tent n/a

Beauty: ★★★★ Site Privacy: ★★★★
Spaciousness: ★★★ Quiet: ★★★
Security: ★★★★ Cleanliness: ★★★★
Insect Control: ★★★★ Facilities: ★★

This campground is carved into the forest, and the road into the campground is as rough as you might expect. However, the campground itself is quite pretty and worth the cautious drive. Sites are grassy and basically level, although longer pull-throughs are shortened from 95 feet to a useable 50 feet by a slope at both ends (1–6). The nicest sites include 20, which is in a shaded corner to the northeast; 24, which is in a shaded corner separated from all other sites by a wall of pines; and 25–27, which are in a clearing surrounded by lush vegetation. These sites are all 75-foot back-ins. Sites 4–6 along the south strip are also nice and long. (Note that you must drive around the entire campground to get to these spaces.) The least desirable sites are 1–3, 7–9, and an unnumbered site by the shed, at all of which campers may find the noise from the nearby go-carts annoying. This is a very nice campground located on some beautiful land, and only needs a rest room to come very highly recommended.

Basics

Operated By: Stan Zimmerman. **Open:** All year. **Site Assignment:** Flexible, depending on availability. Credit card required for reservation; refund requires 24-hours notice. **Registration:** In store. (Late arrivals find on-site manager.) **Fee:** $12 (checks, V, MC, AE, D). **Parking:** At site.

Facilities

Number of RV Sites: 27. **Number of Tent-Only Sites:** 0. **Hookups:** Water, sewer, electric (35 amps). **Dump Station:** No (sewer at all sites). **Laundry:** No. **Pay Phone:** Yes. **Rest Rooms and Showers:** No. **Fuel:** No. **Propane:** No. **Internal Roads:** Dirt/gravel. **RV Service:** No. **Market:** 6 mi. south. **Restaurant:** Less than 1 mi. south. **General Store:** No. **Vending:** Yes. **Swimming:** No. **Playground:** No. **Other:** Go carts, mini golf, cabins, fly shop, casting pond. **Activities:** Scuba diving, fishing, swimming, golf. **Nearby Attractions:** Broken Bow Lake. **Additional Information:** Broken Bow Chamber of Commerce, (800) 528-7337 or (580) 584-3393.

Restrictions

Pets: On leash, cleaned up after. **Fires:** In grills. **Alcoholic Beverages:** At sites. **Vehicle Maximum Length:** None. **Other:** No fireworks.

To Get There

From the junction of Hwy. 70 and Hwy. 259, go 6.4 mi. north on Hwy. 259. Turn left into "The Cedar Chest" complex. Register in the store.

CLAYTON

Clayton Lake State Park

Rte. 1 Box 33-10, Clayton 74536. T: (918) 569-7981; www.touroklahoma.com/Pages/stateparks/parks/cllspbig.html; rsrtpark@otrd.state.ok.us.

RV ★★★ Tent ★★★★★

Beauty: ★★★★ Site Privacy: ★★★★
Spaciousness: ★★★ Quiet: ★★★★
Security: ★★★★ Cleanliness: ★★★
Insect Control: ★★★ Facilities: ★★

This state park is divided up into 2 Areas. Area 1 has a boat ramp and lake access, with RV sites to the north. RVers should take note that the road is steep and broken in places, and drivers should take it slowly. As you drive in, it can be a little confusing as to where the RV sites are (look for the sign that says "RV Area"), but note that the tent sites (to the southeast of the office) are all forested and have some degree of slope to them, whereas the RV sites are all on a level, open strip. These sites are all large back-ins with an open area to pull in, allowing a rig of any size to park here. There is only one (unnumbered) site that has a table, grill, and tree—the rest do not have these features. Area 2 is designated the "assigned camping" area. These are also large (75-foot) back-ins that any RV should be able to fit into. The first site is right at the entrance, and is therefore less desirable. Further from the water, but with excellent views, are sites E3 and E4. There is a small gated area away from the rest of the sites that has gravel sites and 50-foot back-ins. The sites in this area are all open but surrounded by forest. The rest room facilities are clean and modern, as are the showers. This park offers a nice getaway on a lake, with shaded spots that are fine for RVs and ideal for tents.

Basics

Operated By: Oklahoma State Parks. **Open:** All year. **Site Assignment:** Assigned upon registration; verbal reservations OK. **Registration:** In office. (Late arrivals select an available site & pay in the morning.) **Fee:** RV $14 (water, electric), tent $7. **Parking:** At site.

Facilities

Number of RV Sites: 55. **Number of Tent-Only Sites:** 0. **Hookups:** Water, electric. **Each Site:** Picnic table, grill. **Dump Station:** Yes. **Laundry:** No. **Pay Phone:** No. **Rest Rooms and Showers:** Yes. **Fuel:** No. **Propane:** No. **Internal Roads:** Paved. **RV Service:** No. **Market:** 5 mi. north. **Restaurant:** 2 mi. north. **General Store:** No. **Vending:** No. **Swimming:** Lake. **Playground:** Yes. **Other:** Covered pavilion. **Activities:** Swimming, boating, fishing, hiking, wildlife watching. **Nearby Attractions:** Talimena State Park, McGee Creek State Park. **Additional Information:** Choctaw County Chamber Of Commerce, (580) 326-7511.

Restrictions

Pets: On leash, cleaned up after. **Fires:** In grills. **Alcoholic Beverages:** At sites. **Vehicle Maximum Length:** None.

To Get There

From the junction of Hwy. 2 and Hwy. 271, turn south onto Hwy. 271 and go 4.4 mi. Turn right at the sign into the entrance. Area 1 is to the right, Area 2 lies straight ahead.

CLINTON

Wink's RV Park

1410 Neptune, Clinton 73601.T: (580) 323-1664.

RV ★★★★ Tent ★★★★

Beauty: ★★★★ Site Privacy: ★★★★
Spaciousness: ★★★★ Quiet: ★★★★
Security: ★★★★ Cleanliness: ★★★★★
Insect Control: ★★ Facilities: ★★★

This campground is divided into 3 tiers, providing a very different experience in the top tier than in the bottom two. The top tier contains all open back-ins averaging 40 × 18 feet. These sites are all level, but do not have shade, picnic tables, or grills. This makes for an unmistakably "urban" camping experience. However, the lower two tiers have beautiful campsites with huge shade trees and beautiful grass. These sites are all pull-throughs that average 35 feet in length, although there are much larger ones on the lower tier. The best sites are 11–13 and 33–39, as they are practicall enveloped in shade trees and face a nice grassy area. Less nice is site 14, which seems clipped and looks out over junked autos in the neighboring yard. Sites 49 and 50 are the largest, as they are not delineated in size, but are rather spaces in a grassy field that could accommodate a rig of any size. These sites are separated from the others, as are sites 43–45, which offers more privacy. The rest rooms and showers are spacious and clean, but have two flaws: the toilets are only separated by a curtain, and there is no space to hold clothes inside each individual shower. These are rather small faults, however, and the overall camping experience is excellent.

Basics

Operated By: Winston & Ruthelma Hoffman. **Open:** All year. **Site Assignment:** Assigned upon registration; verbal reservations OK. **Registration:** In office. (Late arrivals use drop box.) **Fee:** RV, tent (2 people): $18, tent (1 person): $10. **Parking:** At site.

Facilities

Number of RV Sites: 65. **Number of Tent-Only Sites:** 0. **Hookups:** Water, sewer, electric (20, 30, 50 amps). **Dump Station:** No (sewer at all sites). **Laundry:** Yes. **Pay Phone:** Yes. **Rest Rooms and Showers:** Yes. **Fuel:** No. **Propane:** No. **Internal Roads:** Gravel. **RV Service:** No. **Market:** 0.75 mi. north. **Restaurant:** 0.5 mi. north. **General Store:** No. **Vending:** No. **Swimming:** No. **Playground:** Yes. **Other:** Basketball net. **Activities:** Visiting museums, basketball. **Nearby Attractions:** Oklahoma Rte. 66 Museum. **Additional Information:** Clinton Chamber of Commerce, (800) 759-1397 or (580) 323-2222.

Restrictions

Pets: On leash, cleaned up after. **Fires:** In grills. **Alcoholic Beverages:** At sites. **Vehicle Maximum Length:** None.

To Get There

From the junction of I-40 (Exit 65A) and Historic Rte. 66, go 0.3 mi. south on Rte. 66. Turn right at the sign into the campground. The office is on the right.

COLBERT

Sherrard RV and KOA Kampground

411 Sherrard St., Colbert 74733.T: (800) KOA-2485 or (580) 296-2485.

RV ★★★★ Tent ★★★★

Beauty: ★★★★ Site Privacy: ★★★★
Spaciousness: ★★★★ Quiet: ★★★
Security: ★★★★ Cleanliness: ★★★★
Insect Control: ★★★★ Facilities: ★★★★

Half RV sales and servicing, half campground, the Sherrard complex has much to offer the RV camper. The sites open to overnighters are on the west side of the park. (The sites to the north, 1–50 and 107–111 are reserved for monthly customers.) These sites are all 75-foot grassy pull-throughs arranged in rows (61–98) and two small groups on their own (53–56 and 101–106). Most every site is well-shaded, although 64, 65, and 76 are not, and sites 101 and 104 have a single shade tree at the edge of their space. Sites 102, 103, 105, and 106 have several large shade trees each. The row numbered in the 80s has the most developed sites, with cement slabs, and the best sites in the park are on this row: 86–88. These three sites face a row of trees (that cover an RV storage area), and are furthest from the service building. Sites 66–68 are also very nice—they are closest to the attractive tenting area. The least desirable sites are 51–56, which are out in a field by the cabins and the park entrance. 54 and 56 are so close to the RVs for sale in the adjacent lot that you could put your hand out your window and touch them. Sites 51 and 52 are also less nice, being located on the parking lot next to the office. The tenting area is just west of the pool in a very well-shaded area with good grass. The rest rooms are clean and modern, but a touch "used" looking. This is a superb RV park that has much to offer the RVer, and is fine for the tent camper, too.

Basics

Operated By: Carolyn Work. **Open:** All year. **Site Assignment:** Assigned upon registration; verbal reservations OK. **Registration:** In office. (Late arrivals use drop box.) **Fee:** RV $17.50 (full), $15.50 (electric), tent $13.95. **Parking:** At site.

Facilities

Number of RV Sites: 48. **Number of Tent-Only Sites:** 6. **Hookups:** Water, sewer, electric (30, 50 amps). **Each Site:** Picnic table, tree. **Dump Station:** Yes. **Laundry:** Yes. **Pay Phone:** Yes. **Rest Rooms and Showers:** Yes. **Fuel:** Yes. **Propane:** Yes. **Internal Roads:** Paved. **RV Service:** Yes. **Market:** 1 mi. to Colbert. **Restaurant:** 1 mi. to Colbert. **General Store:** Yes. **Vending:** No. **Swimming:** Pool. **Playground:** Yes. **Other:** TV lounge, pet walk area, recreation room with pool table. **Activities:** Fishing, swimming, boating. **Nearby Attractions:** Denison Dam, boat shows, antique shops, Lake Texoma State Park. **Additional Information:** Durant Chamber of Commerce, (580) 924-0848.

Restrictions

Pets: On leash, cleaned up after. **Fires:** In grills. **Alcoholic Beverages:** At sites. **Vehicle Maximum Length:** None. **Other:** Rule sheet on back of site map.

To Get There

From the junction of Hwy. 75/69 and Hwy. 91, turn west onto Hwy. 91 and take the first right onto Sherrard Dr. Go 0.25 mi. and turn left at the sign into the entrance. Follow the road straight ahead to the office.

DAVIS

Oak Hill RV Park

P.O. Box 515, Davis 73030. T: (580) 369-5270.

RV ★★★ Tent ★★

Beauty: ★★★ Site Privacy: ★★★
Spaciousness: ★★★★ Quiet: ★★★
Security: ★★★★ Cleanliness: ★★★
Insect Control: ★★★★ Facilities: ★★

Despite its location immediately behind a gas station and store, this park has some nice landscaping (flowers and trees) that liven up what would otherwise be an open grassy field. While surrounded by the highway to the east, by the store to the south, and a lumber company to the west, this campground has a definite "get-away" feel, enhanced by the trees that surround it in the distance. The best thing about this park, though, is the size of its sites. There are eleven back-ins 70 × 34 feet and five 115-foot pull-throughs. Of the back-ins, the best are sites 5, 8 and 9, which have large shade trees (which the others lack). For those who require pull-throughs, site 13 has the only shade trees, and has them in spades. All the other pull-throughs are open to the sun. (Site 13 is also close to a grassy section of field and abuts a thicket of vegetation, making it an attractive RV site.) Tenting is possible, they say, but not worth the price unless you are hard-pressed for a spot. For RVers, don't let the proximity of the gas station scare you off—this is a nice, hidden RV park that offers a decent overnight stay.

BASICS

Operated By: Rick McElhaney. **Open:** All year. **Site Assignment:** First come, first served; no reservations. **Registration:** In store. (Late arrivals select an available site & settle in the morning.) **Fee:** $14 (V, MC, AE, D). **Parking:** At site.

FACILITIES

Number of RV Sites: 16. **Number of Tent-Only Sites:** 0. **Hookups:** Water, sewer, electric (30 amps). **Dump Station:** Yes. **Laundry:** No. **Pay Phone:** Yes. **Rest Rooms and Showers:** Yes (no shower). **Fuel:** Yes. **Propane:** No. **Internal Roads:** Gravel. **RV Service:** No. **Market:** 2.5 mi. east (limited on-site). **Restaurant:** 2.5 mi. east (limited on-site). **General Store:** Yes. **Vending:** Yes. **Swimming:** No. **Playground:** No. **Other:** 2 picnic tables. **Activities:** Hiking, swimming. **Nearby Attractions:** Arbuckle Wilderness, Turner Falls Park. **Additional Information:** Davis Chamber of Commerce, (580) 369-2402.

RESTRICTIONS

Pets: On leash, cleaned up after. **Fires:** In grills. **Alcoholic Beverages:** At sites. **Vehicle Maximum Length:** None.

TO GET THERE

From the junction of I-35 (Exit 55) and Hwy. 7, go west on Hwy. 7 to the first right (into the gas station/store). The campground is behind the store.

DISNEY

Cherokee State Park (Riverside Campground)

P.O. Box 220, Disney 74340. T: (918) 782-9830.

RV ★★★ Tent ★★★★★

Beauty: ★★★★★ Site Privacy: ★★★★
Spaciousness: ★★★★★ Quiet: ★★★★★
Security: ★★★★★ Cleanliness: ★★
Insect Control: ★★★ Facilities: ★★★

As the name implies, Riverside Campground lies along the banks of the Grand River, where fishing is the name of the game. The campground is situated on a penninsula, surrounded on three sides by water. Packed-dirt RV sites are on the east side of the campground, on the inside of the internal looped road. While all sites are technically back-ins, it is possible to pull through on 3, which the camp host encourages for larger rigs. This site, like 2 and 4, is 100 feet in length. (Not all site numbers are visible. Starting at the camp host site, RV sites increase in number counter-clockwise.) Sites 17 and 18 are next in size (90 feet), while 10 is still a generous 75 feet. The rest of the sites average 65 feet in length. Of these, 12 and 13 are very close together, and can be used by groups who wish to camp close together. The RV sites with the best views of the river are 2–10; higher numbers look out over the "inland" portion of the river between the campground and shore. Tent sites are located to the west, by the boat ramp. These sites are also mostly dirt, but they have excellent tree cover. Tent sites right on the banks of the river tend to be grassier. Site 26 is particularly secluded. The rest room at the entrance is quite simple and "state park–clean". The bathhouses at the west end are old and peeling, and probably do not benefit from regular maintenance. However, this should not discourage those who enjoy state parks, as this one is quite nice—especially for fishermen.

BASICS

Operated By: Oklahoma State Parks. **Open:** All year. **Site Assignment:** First come, first served; no reservations. **Registration:** With camp host. (Late arrivals see camp host in morning.) **Fee:** RV $14 (water, electric), tent $7 (checks, V, MC, AE, D). **Parking:** At site.

FACILITIES

Number of RV Sites: 18. **Number of Tent-Only Sites:** 50. **Hookups:** Water, electric (30 amps). **Each Site:** Picnic table, grill, fire pit. **Dump Station:** Yes. **Laundry:** No. **Pay Phone:** No. **Rest Rooms and Showers:** Yes. **Fuel:** No. **Propane:** No. **Internal Roads:** Paved. **RV Service:** No. **Market:** 2.5 mi. to Langley. **Restaurant:** less than 1 mi. to Disney. **General Store:** No. **Vending:** No. **Swimming:** Lake. **Playground:** Yes (at Lakeside campground). **Other:** Boat ramp, golf course, pavilions. **Activities:** Swimming, boating, fishing, tours of dam. **Nearby Attractions:** Grand River, Pensacola Dam, Har-Ber Village, Will Rogers Memorial Rodeo. **Additional Information:** Grove Area Chamber of Commerce, (918) 786-9079.

RESTRICTIONS

Pets: On leash, cleaned up after. **Fires:** In grills. **Alcoholic Beverages:** Beer only. **Vehicle Maximum Length:** None. **Other:** Prefer no glass containers.

TO GET THERE

From Hwy. 28, cross the dam to the west of Disney (into Langley). Veer left after the large Grand River Dam (Langley side). Take the first left after the electric station (where Hwy. 82A ends). Turn left onto Broadway Ave. and go 1.5 mi. Turn left at the sign into the entrance.

DURANT

Simmons RV Park

Rte. 1 Box 50, Mead 74701. T: (580) 924-3091; coysimmons@hotmail.com.

RV ★★★ Tent ★★★

Beauty: ★★★★ Site Privacy: ★★★
Spaciousness: ★★ Quiet: ★★
Security: ★★★★ Cleanliness: ★★★
Insect Control: ★★★ Facilities: ★★★

This is a cute urban park on a residential property with very attractive landscaping. Flowers, bushes, some trees, and rustic farm equipment perk up the grounds. Sites are in strips along the outside of the internal road. All sites are open, grassy, and very level. Sites 1–9E on the east side are all 45-foot back-ins with no shade. Sites in row C are 60-foot pull-throughs by the laundry, and are quite good sites due to their length and location. Less desirable sites are 1–5W, which are just off the highway. The best sites are 8–11, which have the most amount of shade and are furthest from the highway.

BASICS

Operated By: Coy Simmons. **Open:** All year. **Site Assignment:** Assigned upon registration; verbal reservations OK. **Registration:** In office. (Late arrivals settle in the morning). **Fee:** RV $12 (full), tent $12. **Parking:** At site.

FACILITIES

Number of RV Sites: 34. **Number of Tent-Only Sites:** Undesignated sites. **Hookups:** Water, sewer, electric (20, 30 amps). **Dump Station:** Yes. **Laundry:** Yes. **Pay Phone:** Yes. **Rest Rooms and Showers:** Yes. **Fuel:** No. **Propane:** No. **Internal Roads:** Gravel. **RV Service:** No. **Market:** 3.5 mi. east. **Restaurant:** 3.5 mi. east. **General Store:** No. **Vending:** No. **Swimming:** No. **Playground:** No. **Other:** Covered pavilion w/ BBQ grill, patio. **Activities:** Basketball, swimming, boating. **Nearby Attractions:** Lake Texacoma Recreational Area. **Additional Information:** Durant Chamber of Commerce, (580) 924-0848.

RESTRICTIONS

Pets: On leash, cleaned up after. **Fires:** In grills. **Alcoholic Beverages:** At sites. **Vehicle Maximum Length:** None.

TO GET THERE

From Hwy. 75/69, take the Hwy. 70 exit. Turn west onto Hwy. 70 and go 3.8 mi. Turn left at the sign (somewhat difficult to see). The office is in the house at the back.

EL RENO

Best Western

2701 South Country Club Rd., El Reno 73036. T: (800) 263-3844 or (405) 262-6490; F: (405) 262-3844.

RV: ★★★★ Tent: n/a

Beauty: ★★★ Site Privacy: ★★★
Spaciousness: ★★★ Quiet: ★★★★
Security: ★★★★ Cleanliness: ★★★★★
Insect Control: ★★★★ Facilities: ★★★★

This RV park contains three rows of sites, the first two of which (sites 1–9 and 10–18) are 60-foot pull-throughs, and the final row of which contains 80-foot pull-throughs (19–23) and 40-foot pull-throughs (24–26). All sites are cement with a strip of grass and bushes in between them. Although mostly concrete, the park is quite attractive: there are 2 flowering bushes and a large rock at the end of each of the grassy strips. The park itself is bordered on the east and south by large bushes (although there is less attractive commercial development to the north and west). Although there is not a large amount of room between most sites (which average 18 feet wide), there are a few extra-wide spaces that are 21 feet wide. The best sites are in the north/northeast corner (especially 9, 18, and 26, which have extra grassy space and a tree). Site 18 has the largest grassy section. The less desirable sites are 10 and (especially) 19, which are next to a commercial building. The laundry, rest rooms, and showers are all very clean and spacious, making this a very decent stop that only needs a little more room between sites to make for an even better stay.

Basics

Operated By: Sadhna Kelly. **Open:** All year. **Site Assignment:** Assigned upon registration. Reservations can be made using credit card; cancel before 6 p.m. the day of arrival. **Registration:** In office (24 hours). **Fee:** RV $22 (checks, V, MC, AE, D, DC). **Parking:** At site.

Facilities

Number of RV Sites: 26. **Number of Tent-Only Sites:** 0. **Hookups:** Water, sewer, electric (30, 50 amps), cable. **Each Site:** Picnic table. **Dump Station:** No (sewer at all sites). **Laundry:** Yes. **Pay Phone:** Yes. **Rest Rooms and Showers:** Yes. **Fuel:** Next door. **Propane:** No. **Internal Roads:** Gravel. **RV Service:** No. **Market:** Less than 0.25 mi. **Restaurant:** Across street. **General Store:** No. **Vending:** Yes. **Swimming:** Pool. **Playground:** Yes. **Other:** Dataport. **Activities:** Fishing, boating, swimming. **Nearby Attractions:** Downtown trolley, antique stores, Lake El Reno, golf course, Lucky Star Casino, Oklahoma City. **Additional Information:** El Reno Chamber of Commerce, (405) 262-1188.

Restrictions

Pets: On leash, cleaned up after. **Fires:** In grills. **Alcoholic Beverages:** At sites. **Vehicle Maximum Length:** None.

To Get There

From I-40 (Exit 123): on the south side of the highway, turn left into the Best Western complex.

ELK CITY

Elk Run RV Park

Rte. 1 Box 161, Elk City 73644. T: (580) 225-4888.

RV: ★★★ Tent: ★★★

Beauty: ★ Site Privacy: ★★★★
Spaciousness: ★★★★ Quiet: ★★★
Security: ★★★★ Cleanliness: ★★★★
Insect Control: ★★★★ Facilities: ★★★

Unfortunately for this campground, the panhandle of Oklahoma does not have many pretty features to make it an attractive destination, and this park reflects that reality all too well. The commercial development to the south and a parking lot and building to the east make for less-than-spectacular views. The sites themselves are rather roomy, which makes up somewhat for the surroundings. Row A, to the south by the office, has 2 60-foot back-ins and 3 90-foot back-ins. Row B, sites 7–18 to the east, has 105-foot back-ins, while Rows C–E contain 90-foot pull-throughs. None of the sites has a real shade tree, although there are a few smaller trees and bushes around the park. Tenters can camp anywhere on the open grass (mostly to the east) at the back of the park. These sites, like the RV sites, have no shade, and they are situated next to a chain link fence that surrounds a parking lot on the other side. The rest room and showers are very clean, but the toilet in the men's room does not have a curtain or separator of any kind, which can make some campers feel awkward. The park is an acceptable overnight stay, but if you are after a scenic campground, you'll have to push on.

Basics

Operated By: Ed Tremblay. **Open:** All year. **Site Assignment:** Assigned upon registration; verbal reservations OK. **Registration:** In office. (Late arrivals select an available site & pay in the morning.) **Fee:** RV $16 (full), tent $6 (checks, no credits cards). **Parking:** At site.

Facilities

Number of RV Sites: 39. **Number of Tent-Only Sites:** 20. **Hookups:** Water, sewer, electric (30, 50 amps), cable. **Dump Station:** No (sewer at all sites). **Laundry:** Yes. **Pay Phone:** Yes. **Rest Rooms and Showers:** Yes. **Fuel:** Next door. **Propane:** No. **Internal Roads:** Gravel. **RV Service:** No. **Market:** 2 mi. south. **Restaurant:** Across street. **General Store:** No. **Vending:** Yes. **Swimming:** No. **Playground:** No. **Other:** Easy on/off from highway, close to gasoline & restaurants. **Activities:** Hiking. **Nearby Attractions:** National Rte. 66 Museum, Elk City Old Town Museum Complex, Black Kettle National Grasslands. **Additional Information:** Elk City Chamber of Commerce, (800) 280-0207 or (580) 225-0207.

Restrictions

Pets: On leash, cleaned up after. **Fires:** In grills. **Alcoholic Beverages:** At sites. **Vehicle Maximum Length:** None. **Other:** See rule sheet.

To Get There

From I-40 (Exit 41), turn north at the light onto Hwy. 34 and then turn right just past the gas station complex. The drive leads straight into the park.

ENID

High Point RV Park

2700 North Van Buren Box 0, Enid 73703. T: (580) 234-1726; F: (580) 234-5081; highpoint@characterlink.net.

RV: ★★★★★ Tent: ★★★

Beauty: ★★★★ Site Privacy: ★★★★★
Spaciousness: ★★★★★ Quiet: ★★★★★
Security: ★★★★★ Cleanliness: ★★★★
Insect Control: ★★★★ Facilities: ★★★

This RV park contains sites in three distinct locations. Closest to the office is the "Custer Circle"—a unique and really neat way of parking RVs: in a circle. Pull-through sites 73–92 form the inner circle, with 35–72 (all long-term sites) forming an outside ring. These pull-throughs are 105 × 45 feet—large enough for the largest rigs with slide-outs. In addition, all sites are separated by rows of hedges and have shade trees, making them both private and comfortable. These sites are by far the best in the entire park. The two other locations are to the west of the office, outside the main park entrance. On the south side are 18 102-foot back-ins that are enclosed by hedges. These sites are somewhat shaded, but many are occupied by long-term residents and mobile homes. The final area is to the northwest of the office. Laid out in two rather indistinct rows, these sites are shaded, gravel pull-throughs of varying lengths. Sites 2–6 are the largest at 105 feet, while 9–18 are 54 feet in length. Sites 17 and 18 are close to the road and share an oil pump, which makes these sites distinctly less desirable. Tenters can camp in an open grassy space in this last area. There is not much shade to protect tenters, and the grass is likewise rather sparse. This is much more of an RV-oriented park, and those who can "circle the wagons" will pass an extremely enjoyable stay here.

Basics

Operated By: Robert Stewart. **Open:** All year. **Site Assignment:** Assigned upon registration; verbal reservations OK. **Registration:** In office. (Late arrivals use drop box or pay in morning.) **Fee:** RV $17 (full), tent $5 (checks, V, MC, AE, D, DC.) **Parking:** At site.

Facilities

Number of RV Sites: 60. **Number of Tent-Only Sites:** Undesignated sites. **Hookups:** Water, sewer, electric (30, 50 amps), instant phone. **Dump Station:** Yes. **Laundry:** Yes. **Pay Phone:** Yes. **Rest Rooms and Showers:** Yes. **Fuel:** End of block. **Propane:** No. **Internal Roads:** Gravel. **RV Service:** Call-in. **Market:** 0.25 mi. south. **Restaurant:** 0.25 mi. south. **General Store:** No. **Vending:** No. **Swimming:** No. **Playground:** No. **Other:** RV supplies, storm shelter, clubhouse. **Activities:** Visiting museums, fishing, boating, swimming, hiking. **Nearby Attractions:** Museum of the Cherokee Strip, Railroad Museum of Oklahoma, Great Salt

Plains State Park. **Additional Information:** Greater Enid Chamber of Commerce, (888) 229-2443 or (580) 237-2494.

RESTRICTIONS

Pets: On leash, cleaned up after. **Fires:** In grills. **Alcoholic Beverages:** At sites. **Vehicle Maximum Length:** None.

TO GET THERE

From the junction of Hwy. 81 and Hwy. 60, go north on 81/60 for 2.2 mi. Turn left at the sign into the entrance.

EUFAULA

Bridgeport RV Park

Rte. 6 Box 379, Eufaula 74432. T: (918) 689-5177; bkent@icok.net.

RV: ★★★ Tent: n/a

Beauty: ★★★ Site Privacy: ★★★★
Spaciousness: ★★★★ Quiet: ★★★
Security: ★★★★★ Cleanliness: ★★★★★
Insect Control: ★★★★ Facilities: ★★★

The setting for this campground is somewhat rural, with woods bordering the north, west, and south. Sites are laid out in four rows. Row A has 60-foot back-ins that back to the highway to the east, and are the least desirable for this fact. The 60-foot pull-throughs in Row C (in the middle of the park) have most of the shade trees—all but 2. The 60-foot pull-throughs in Row D contain arguably the best sites (in the southwest corner), which are next to the woods, and furthest from the highway and the entrance but do not have any shade. The electric eye on the gate and the on-site manager make this campground extremely secure, while the immaculate rest rooms in both the bathhouse and the clubhouse ensure that guests will be comfortable. This campground is geared toward overnighters and clubs—sometimes filling to capacity with the latter. Phone ahead to ensure that there are spaces, as this is a good campground that can make a nice destination or just a one-night stay.

BASICS

Operated By: Bill & Cindy Kent. **Open:** Mar. 1–Oct. 31. **Site Assignment:** Flexible, depending on site availability; verbal reservations OK. **Registration:** In office. (Late arrivals select an available site & pay in the morning.) **Fee:** RV $17 (checks, no credits cards). **Parking:** At site.

FACILITIES

Number of RV Sites: 53. **Number of Tent-Only Sites:** 0. **Hookups:** Water, sewer, electric (30 amps). **Each Site:** Picnic table. **Dump Station:** No (sewer at all sites). **Laundry:** Yes. **Pay Phone:** Yes. **Rest Rooms and Showers:** Yes. **Fuel:** No. **Propane:** No. **Internal Roads:** Gravel. **RV Service:** Call-in. **Market:** 6 mi. to Eufaula. **Restaurant:** 1 mi. south. **General Store:** Yes. **Vending:** No. **Swimming:** No. **Playground:** No. **Other:** Clubhouse (with kitchen), storm shelter, electric eye on gate. **Activities:** Fishing, boating, swimming, golfing. **Nearby Attractions:** Lake Eufaula, 2 golf courses, Whole Hawg Day. **Additional Information:** Eufaula Chamber of Commerce, (918) 689-2791.

RESTRICTIONS

Pets: On leash, cleaned up after. **Fires:** In grills. **Alcoholic Beverages:** At sites. **Vehicle Maximum Length:** None.

TO GET THERE

From the junction of Hwy. 69 and Hwy. 150 (Fountainhead state Park Exit): on the northwest side of the highway overpass, turn left onto the frontage road, then immediately left onto Bridgeport Rd. Turn right at the sign into the entrance.

GORE

MarVal Family Resort

Rte. 1 Box 314M, Gore 74435. T: (918) 489-2295; F: (918) 489-2671; www.marvalresort.com; marvalre@crosstel.net.

RV: ★★★★ Tent: ★★★★★

Beauty: ★★★★ Site Privacy: ★★
Spaciousness: ★★★ Quiet: ★★★★
Security: ★★★★★ Cleanliness: ★★★★
Insect Control: ★★★★ Facilities: ★★★★

This campground is positively huge, with sites scattered from the river up to the entrance drive. Assuming availability, there is truly a site for any camper's tastes. (Note that aside from H, the lettered sites to the west and south of the pool are seasonal sites, and not for overnight use.) Sites 102–108 are 70-foot back-ins right along the riverbank, where a camper could put a canoe or small boat into the water, while 400–408 are back-ins close to the swimming access area. Across from these sites, 216–219 also offer proximity to the swimming beach. Sites 110–112, in the northeast corner, are 60-foot pull-throughs that are one row away from the water's edge. Fishermen will want to camp in sites 410–415, which are back-ins (as long as 75 feet) that run along the bank of the trout pond. Sites 207–215 are are smaller back-ins (45 feet long), suitable for a pop-up. Some very nice, more developed, back-ins are 510–518, which have a concrete pad and wooden walkway on one side. These sites back to a row of trees, beyond which is a huge open field. A large field in the southeast corner provides more than enough tenting space, although only one site (22) has a large shade tree. (18 has several much smaller trees.) This field has excellent grass, and is surrounded by woods, lending it a nice wild feel. The rest rooms are individual unisex units that are very clean and modern. The showers are also very clean and cozy, if a little compact. This campground guarantees water fun for all ages, and should be a definite destination for families.

BASICS

Operated By: Val & Marc Marcum, Dan & Leia Nosalek, Lynn & Gary Cleek. **Open:** All year. **Site Assignment:** Most sites by reservation; credit card required. No holiday cancellations. **Registration:** In office. (No late arrivals. Gates locked at 10 p.m.) **Fee:** $15–27; varies widely by season & day of week. **Parking:** At site.

FACILITIES

Number of RV Sites: 111. **Number of Tent-Only Sites:** 14. **Hookups:** Water, sewer, electric (30, 50 amps). **Each Site:** Picnic table. **Dump Station:** Yes. **Laundry:** Yes. **Pay Phone:** Yes. **Rest Rooms and Showers:** Yes. **Fuel:** No. **Propane:** No. **Internal Roads:** Gravel. **RV Service:** No. **Market:** 1.25 mi. south. **Restaurant:** 1 mile south. **General Store:** Yes. **Vending:** Yes. **Swimming:** Pool, river. **Playground:** Yes. **Other:** Mini golf, basketball, cabins, snack bar, trout fishing, horseback riding, events with activities director, recreation field. **Activities:** Volleyball, fishing, swimming. **Nearby Attractions:** Cherokee Courthouse. **Additional Information:** Gore Chamber, (918) 489-2534.

RESTRICTIONS

Pets: On leash, cleaned up after. **Fires:** In grills. **Alcoholic Beverages:** At sites. **Vehicle Maximum Length:** None. **Other:** No ATVs.

TO GET THERE

From I-40 Exit 287, turn north onto Hwy. 100 and go 5.9 mi. Turn right onto Gore Landing Rd. and go 0.2 mi. Turn left onto Marval Ln. and go straight into the campground.

GROVE

Cedar Oaks RV Resort

1550 83rd St., Grove 74344. T: (800) 880-8884 or (918) 786-4303; F: (918) 786-4303.

RV: ★★★★★ Tent: n/a

Beauty: ★★★★★ Site Privacy: ★★★★
Spaciousness: ★★★★ Quiet: ★★★★★
Security: ★★★★★ Cleanliness: ★★★★★
Insect Control: ★★★★ Facilities: ★★★★★

This RV park lives up to the standards implied by the word "resort." Sites are highly developed, averaging 30 feet wide, with nice grassy sections next to paved strips. The park is divided into two sections: the main park to the north and a smaller loop to the south. In the main section, sites 1–17 lie along the entrance road, and have nothing to recommend them (besides being in a nice park). Sites 18–31 back to the first 17 sites, and like them are 58-foot back-ins without any outstanding features. Sites 32–45 and 50–63 are 65-foot pull-throughs in the middle of the park that have decent views of the lake when the park is mostly empty. 46–49 and 74–76 are 51-foot back-ins located in a strip along the north edge. 76 is a good alternative to one of the pull-throughs, as it commands a very nice view of the lake. The most exquisitie sites, however, are 64–73. These are 65-foot pull-throughs facing the lake. End site 73 has an enormous grassy section adjacent to it. The southern section of the park contains sites 77–110 in a large loop. These are all 45-foot back-ins on the outside of the loop. (The inside will contain some enormous 100-foot pull-throughs, but they are as-yet unfinished.) Sites 88–96 have the best views, while 80–86 are closest to the bathhouse. All facilities are sparkling clean, and the park has a security guard for peace of mind. Campers in this resort can count on a comfortable and secure stay.

Basics

Operated By: The Coats Family. **Open:** All year. **Site Assignment:** Assigned upon registration (verbal reservations "highly recommended"). **Registration:** In office. (Late arrivals use drop box.) **Fee:** $19.50 (checks, V, MC). **Parking:** At site.

Facilities

Number of RV Sites: 126. **Number of Tent-Only Sites:** 0. **Hookups:** Water, sewer, electric (30, 50 amps). **Each Site:** Picnic table. **Dump Station:** Yes. **Laundry:** Yes. **Pay Phone:** Yes. **Rest Rooms and Showers:** Yes. **Fuel:** No. **Propane:** No. **Internal Roads:** Paved/gravel. **RV Service:** No. **Market:** 1.5 mi. over bridge. **Restaurant:** Less than 0.5 mi. southeast. **General Store:** Yes. **Vending:** No. **Swimming:** Lake. **Playground:** No. **Other:** Dock, boat ramps, private cove, meeting rooms (with kitchen), RV & boat storage, dataport, pavilion. **Activities:** Boating, swimming, fishing, shuffleboard, horseshoes. **Nearby Attractions:** Har-Ber Village. **Additional Information:** Grove Area Chamber of Commerce, (918) 786-9079.

Restrictions

Pets: On leash, cleaned up after. **Fires:** In grills. **Alcoholic Beverages:** At sites. **Vehicle Maximum Length:** None.

To Get There

From the junction of Hwy. 10 North and Hwy. 59 North, turn northwest onto Hwy. 59 and go 3.2 mi. Turn left at the sign into the entrance.

GUTHRIE

Pioneer RV Park

1601 Seward Rd., Guthrie 73044. T: (405) 282-3557; F: (405) 282-5376.

RV ★★★★ Tent ★★★

Beauty: ★★★★	Site Privacy: ★★★★
Spaciousness: ★★★★	Quiet: ★★★★
Security: ★★★★	Cleanliness: ★★★★
Insect Control: ★★★★	Facilities: ★★★

Laid out in strips, this campground offers grassy pull-throughs throughout the park and back-ins along the eastern edge. These back-ins (1–12) back to a chain-link fence, beyond which lie green agricultural fields. Sites 13–21 are 70-foot pull-throughs on the eastern side of the park, and 24–30 are 75-foot pull-throughs dead in the middle. Being an end site, 21 has a more generous amount of space and a shade tree, which make it one of the nicest sites in the park. To the west lie two rows of 70-foot pull-throughs, of which the southernmost strip (37–48) has slightly nicer sites due to their proximity to the tenting area and the view to the south. (The best views are from 30 and 36.) Site 32 has extremely limited space due to the landscaping and a fountain that encroaches on this space. Tenting is permitted on a strip along the southern edge of the campground. There is nice grass, but no real shade. RVers will be pleased with this campground, and tenters will enjoy a pleasant enough stay at this park.

Basics

Operated By: Bill & Sue True. **Open:** All year. **Site Assignment:** Assigned upon registration. Reservations require credit card; cancellation requires one week's notice. **Registration:** In office. (Late arrivals pay in morning.) **Fee:** RV $17.50 (full), tent $10. (checks, V, MC). **Parking:** At site.

Facilities

Number of RV Sites: 63. **Number of Tent-Only Sites:** 4. **Hookups:** Water, sewer, electric (30, 50 amps). **Each Site:** Picnic table. **Dump Station:** No (sewer at all sites). **Laundry:** Yes. **Pay Phone:** Yes. **Rest Rooms and Showers:** Yes. **Fuel:** No. **Propane:** Yes. **Internal Roads:** Gravel. **RV Service:** No. **Market:** 6 mi. north. **Restaurant:** 6 mi. north. **General Store:** Yes. **Vending:** Yes. **Swimming:** No. **Playground:** No. **Other:** Clubhouse. **Activities:** Tours to Oklahoma City, visiting museums. **Nearby Attractions:** Scottish Rite Temple, State Capital Publishing Museum, Oklahoma City. **Additional Information:** Guthrie CVB, (800) 299-1889 or (405) 282-1947.

Restrictions

Pets: On leash, cleaned up after. **Fires:** In grills. **Alcoholic Beverages:** At sites. **Vehicle Maximum Length:** None.

To Get There

From I-35 Exit 151, go 0.55 mi. Turn right at the sign into the campground.

GUYMON

Southwind RV Park

3941 Southwest Hwy. 54, Rte. 3 Box 52-A, Guymon 73942. T: (877) 861-8103 or (580) 338-7415; swindrv@ptsi.net.

RV ★★★ Tent ★★

Beauty: ★★★	Site Privacy: ★★★★
Spaciousness: ★★★★	Quiet: ★★★
Security: ★★★★	Cleanliness: ★★★
Insect Control: ★★★★	Facilities: ★★★

This campground is arranged in rows of odd and even numbered pull-through sites. The odd numbered sites in the row on the east side are 36 45 feet, while the even numbered sites to the west are longer: 36 × 65 feet. The best sites are odd numbers 3–23, as they are longer, they face an agricultural field, they are located away from the mobile homes, and they have larger trees. The least desirable sites are the even numbered sites 2–18, which are shorter pull-throughs next to the manager's mobile home and the office, which brings registration traffic right past these sites. There are mobile homes at the southwest end, and some in the campground itself (27, 29). The tent area has a thin grass covering over hard dirt. There is only one site under tree coverage—the rest are out in the open and have no shade whatsoever. There is also scattered equipment and a shed in this area, making it less attractive. However, tent sites are well removed from the road, which makes them feel more private. The rest room and showers are modern and clean. The TV lounge has a greenhouse with an absolutely monster-sized agave cactus. RVers will enjoy this campground slightly more than tenters, who may want to check out one of the region's state parks.

Basics

Operated By: Eddy Ainsworth. **Open:** All year. **Site Assignment:** Assigned upon registration. Verbal reservations OK, unless arriving after 6 pm, which requires a credit card. Same day cancellation before 6 p.m. for refund. **Registration:** In office. (Late arrivals use drop box.) **Fee:** RV $17 (30 amps), $20 (50 amps), tent $9 (V, MC, D). Senior discount of $2. **Parking:** At site.

Facilities

Number of RV Sites: 40. **Number of Tent-Only Sites:** 10. **Hookups:** Water, sewer, electric (30, 50 amps). **Each Site:** Tree, a few picnic tables. **Dump Station:** No (sewer at all sites). **Laundry:** Yes. **Pay Phone:** Yes. **Rest Rooms and Showers:** Yes. **Fuel:** No. **Propane:** Cylinder exchange. **Internal Roads:** Dirt/gravel. **RV Service:** No. **Market:** 1.75 mi. northeast. **Restaurant:** 1 mile northeast. **General Store:** No. **Vending:** No. **Swimming:** No. **Playground:** Yes. **Other:** Dataport, city water, TV lounge. **Activities:** Visiting museums, fishing, boating, swimming. **Nearby Attractions:** Large rodeo (May 1), museums, Optima Lake. **Additional Information:** Guymon Chamber of Commerce, (580) 338-3376.

Restrictions

Pets: On leash, cleaned up after. **Fires:** In grills. **Alcoholic Beverages:** At sites. **Vehicle Maximum Length:** 65 ft. **Other:** No generators, additional charge for more than 2 people.

To Get There

From the junction of Hwy. 3/136/412 and Hwy. 54, turn onto Hwy. 54 West and go 1.3 mi. southwest. (Keep your eyes peeled for the sign on the left-hand side.) Turn left at the sign onto the dirt road entrance.

HINTON

Red Rock Canyon State Park

P.O. Box 502, Hinton 73047. T: (800) 654-8240 or (405) 542-6344; F: (405) 542-6342; www.touroklahoma.com; redrockcanyon@hintonnet.net.

RV ★★★★ Tent ★★★★★

Beauty: ★★★★★	Site Privacy: ★★★★
Spaciousness: ★★★★	Quiet: ★★★★★
Security: ★★★★	Cleanliness: ★★★
Insect Control: ★★★	Facilities: ★★★

Stunning views of red canyon walls and campsites smothered in shade trees: if that sounds unattractive to you, stay away from this campground. But everyone else should definitely make a stop here! This campground has sites divided into Areas 1–4. Area 1 has water and electric sites right up against the canyon walls. There are loads of trees, but some sites have only dirt and no grass. The section of the road leading to 5–7 is in disrepair, and may present a challenge. Sites 11–18 are 40–65-foot grassy back-ins, while 8 could fit a rig of any size. Some sites are not perfectly level. This area is also used for rappelling on the rocks, and therefore it sees a fair amount of day traffic. Area 2 offers group camping with 45-foot back-ins. These sites are more open, with shade trees around the perimeter. Area 3 has full hookups and open 50-foot back-ins in an area separated from the road. All sites have concrete slabs and grass, and some have shade trees. This is the easiest place for RVs to camp, as it involves the least amount of turns or technical driving. Area 4 is for overflow camping, but is used even when the other areas are not all full. These are the furthest sites in, and are less developed. These grassy, shaded sites are well off the road, but also have some degree of slope. Sites at the extreme south end (in the 50s and 60s) are in an open field with little shade. The rest rooms are small but quite clean. This is a beautiful campground that will appeal to the whole family, whether in an RV or tents.

Basics

Operated By: Oklahoma State Park. **Open:** All year. **Site Assignment:** First come, first served; no reservations. **Registration:** Can register in office. Fees collected at sites. **Fee:** RV $17 (full), $14 (water, electric), tent $7. **Parking:** At site.

Facilities

Number of RV Sites: 52. **Number of Tent-Only Sites:** 32. **Hookups:** Water, sewer, electric (30, 50 amps). **Each Site:** Picnic table, grill. **Dump Station:** Yes. **Laundry:** No. **Pay Phone:** Yes. **Rest Rooms and Showers:** Yes. **Fuel:** No. **Propane:** No. **Internal Roads:** Paved, gravel. **RV Service:** No. **Market:** 6 mi. in Hinton. **Restaurant:** 6 mi. in Hinton. **General Store:** No. **Vending:** No. **Swimming:** Pool. **Playground:** Yes. **Other:** None. **Activities:** Swimming, rappelling, rockhounding, volleyball, hiking, horseback riding. **Nearby Attractions:** Ft Cobb State Park, Crowder Lake State Park. **Additional Information:** Hinton Chamber of Commerce, (405) 542-6428.

Restrictions

Pets: On leash, cleaned up after. **Fires:** In grills. **Alcoholic Beverages:** At sites. **Vehicle Maximum Length:** None. **Other:** 14 days max. stay limit, no amplified music.

To Get There

From I-40, take Exit 101 and turn south onto Hwy. 2/281. Go 5.2 mi. then turn left at the sign into the entrance. The entrance road is steep and winding.

KINGFISHER

Sleepee Hollo RV Park

918 North Main, Kingfisher 73750. T: (405) 375-5010.

RV ★★★★ Tent ★★★

Beauty: ★★★★	Site Privacy: ★★★★
Spaciousness: ★★★★	Quiet: ★★★
Security: ★★★★	Cleanliness: ★★★★
Insect Control: ★★★★	Facilities: ★★★

Farms surround this campground to the north, west, and south, giving it a rural feel. Sites are grassy and level pull-throughs, many of which are not numbered. Sites 1–7 are all super-long (105–120-foot) pull-throughs, all but one of which are well-shaded. A row of unnumbered back-in sites to the south range in length from 45 feet (in the southeast corner) to 90 feet (in the southwest corner). One RV site just in front of the office is a shady, all-grass site that is quite attractive. The rest of the sites to the west and north are unnumbered sites on an open grassy field. These are huge back-ins, ranging from 45 feet to 90 feet long. There is a potential to pull-through on some sites, if neighboring sites are vacant. Tenters have a huge open space to the west in which to pitch a tent. The field is grassy, but has no shade trees. This is an attractive campground with lots of trees inside, and farms with cattle surround the perimeter. It makes a nice stop for any kind of camper, although is slightly better for RVs than tents.

Basics

Operated By: Joe Farrell. **Open:** All year. **Site Assignment:** Assigned upon registration; verbal reservations OK. **Registration:** In office. (Late arrivals select an available site & pay in the morning.) **Fee:** RV $19.50 (50 amps), $16.50 (30 amps), tent $8. **Parking:** At site.

Facilities

Number of RV Sites: 29. **Number of Tent-Only Sites:** Undesignated sites. **Hookups:** Water, sewer, electric (30, 50 amps). **Dump Station:** Yes. **Laundry:** Yes. **Pay Phone:** Yes. **Rest Rooms and Showers:** Yes. **Fuel:** No. **Propane:** No. **Internal Roads:** Gravel. **RV Service:** No. **Market:** 2 mi. south. **Restaurant:** 2 mi. south. **General Store:** No. **Vending:** Yes. **Swimming:** No. **Playground:** No. **Other:** Basement for entertainment or storm shelter, pet walk area. **Activities:** Hiking, tours, biking. **Nearby Attractions:** Chisolm Trail Museum & Governor Seay Mansion, Oklahoma City. **Additional Information:** Kingfisher Chamber of Commerce, (405) 375-5176.

Restrictions

Pets: On leash, cleaned up after. **Fires:** In grills. **Alcoholic Beverages:** At sites. **Vehicle Maximum Length:** None.

To Get There

From the junction of Hwy. 33 and Hwy. 81, go 0.8 mi. north on Hwy. 81. Turn left at the sign into the entrance.

LAWTON

Lawton Campground

3701 Southwest 11th St., Lawton 73501. T: (580) 355-1293.

RV ★★★ Tent ★★★

Beauty: ★★★	Site Privacy: ★★★
Spaciousness: ★★★	Quiet: ★★★★
Security: ★★★★	Cleanliness: ★★★★
Insect Control: ★★★	Facilities: ★★★

This is a new campground (less than two years old), and consequently still a little unfinished. While it may be rustic in style, however, fixtures are brand-new and clean. Laid out in three strips, sites are unnumbered and a little difficult to locate. There are four full hookups near the rest rooms (the red barn next to the house) and two sites just east of the barn under a large shade tree. These two are the nicest sites in the park, due to the overhanging tree. Apart from these, the rest of the sites are undelineated spaces in a grassy field. There is little to distinguish one from the other save for the hookups, but this does allow for a rig of any size to occupy pretty much any site. All sites are very level and grassy, and the setting is quiet and rural. Tenting is allowed in the southern portion of the central and eastern strips. The grass ground covering is excellent, and there are trees for protection to the eastern side. This small campground has a very homey feel, and will only get better as it becomes more established.

Basics

Operated By: Pat Reynolds. **Open:** All year. **Site Assignment:** Flexible, depending on availabilitiy; verbal reservations OK. **Registration:** In office. (Late arrivals use drop box in bath house). **Fee:** RV $12 (full), $9 (water, electric), tent $6. **Parking:** At site.

Facilities

Number of RV Sites: 30. **Number of Tent-Only Sites:** 0. **Hookups:** Water, sewer, electric (30 amps). **Dump Station:** No. **Laundry:** No. **Pay Phone:** No. **Rest Rooms and Showers:** Yes. **Fuel:** No. **Propane:** No. **Internal Roads:** Gravel. **RV Service:** No. **Market:** 2.5 mi. north. **Restaurant:** 2 mi. north. **General Store:** No. **Vending:** No. **Swimming:** No. **Playground:** No. **Other:** Easy access off the interstate, golf course next door. **Activities:** Golf, visiting museums. **Nearby Attractions:** Fort Sill Military Reservation, Museum of the Great Plains, Wichita Mountains National Wildlife Refuge. **Additional Information:** Lawton Chamber of Commerce & Industry, (800) 872-4540 or (580) 355-3541.

Restrictions

Pets: On leash, cleaned up after. **Fires:** In grills. **Alcoholic Beverages:** At sites. **Vehicle Maximum Length:** None.

To Get There

From I-44, take Exit 33. Go 0.7 mi. north on 11th St. Turn right into the gravel entrance across from Coobs St. (just south of the golf course). The office is in the house on the left.

MUSKOGEE

Crossroads RV Park

P.O. Box 95-5, Porter 74454. T: (918) 686-9104; F: (918) 683-8685.

RV ★★★ Tent ★★★

Beauty: ★★★	Site Privacy: ★★★
Spaciousness: ★★★★	Quiet: ★★★
Security: ★★★★	Cleanliness: ★★★★
Insect Control: ★★★★	Facilities: ★★★

As this RV park has numerous long-term residents, a sign indicates to all visitors that only sites 1–17 and B1–8 are for overnighters. Sites 1–17 are all large gravel sites in the north part of the park. Sites 1–10 are open-ended pull-throughs that can fit a rig of any size. End site 10 has a grassy space, which the other sites lack. In a row slightly east of the first strip, sites 11–17 are open-ended back-ins that can reasonably accomodate about 50–60 feet before encroaching on the (undefined) gravel drive. Sites

B1-8 are in the southeast corner of the park. All of these sites are open-ended pull-throughs that can take RVs of almost any size (with the exception of B8, which is somewhat restricted in size due to its proximity to another site.) All other sites in the park are for long-term guests or mobile homes. This is a good overnight stay for RVers—more so than for tenters—but lacks a certain something to make it as a destination.

Basics

Operated By: Janie Burwell. **Open:** All year. **Site Assignment:** Assigned upon registration; verbal reservations OK. **Registration:** In office. (Late arrivals use drop box.) **Fee:** RV $14 (full), tent $7. **Parking:** At site.

Facilities

Number of RV Sites: 25. **Number of Tent-Only Sites:** 5. **Hookups:** Water, sewer, electric (30, 50 amps). **Each Site:** Picnic table, grill. **Dump Station:** Yes. **Laundry:** Yes. **Pay Phone:** Yes. **Rest Rooms and Showers:** Yes. **Fuel:** No. **Propane:** No. **Internal Roads:** Gravel. **RV Service:** No. **Market:** 7 mi. to Muskogee. **Restaurant:** 6 mi. to Muskogee. **General Store:** Yes. **Vending:** Yes. **Swimming:** No. **Playground:** No. **Other:** Pavilion. **Activities:** Fishing, boating, swimming, hiking. **Nearby Attractions:** Ataloa Lodge Museum, Five Civilized Tribes Museum, Sequoya Bay State Park. **Additional Information:** Muskogee Convention & Tourism, (918) 684-6363.

Restrictions

Pets: On leash, cleaned up after. **Fires:** In grills. **Alcoholic Beverages:** At sites. **Vehicle Maximum Length:** None.

To Get There

From the junction of Hwy. 16/62 and Hwy. 69, go north on Hwy. 69 for 4.8 mi. (2 mi. north of the Arkansas River). At the junction with Hwy. 51B, turn right and go striaght into the campground.

OKLAHOMA CITY

Sands Motel

721 South Rockwell Ave., Oklahoma City 73128. T: (405) 787-7353.

★★★ n/a

Beauty: ★★	Site Privacy: ★★★
Spaciousness: ★★★	Quiet: ★★★
Security: ★★★	Cleanliness: ★★
Insect Control: ★★★★	Facilities: ★★★

Located behind (to the south of) the office, RV sites in this park are operated in conjunction with a motel. There are 6 rows in all, and not all sites are numbered, which makes finding your site potentially difficult. Row 1 contains 60-foot pull-throughs next to the motel. (There is a possibility of sticking out to about 70 feet.) Sites B and C share an electricity pylon that encroaches on their space. Row 3 has probably the nicest sites, which are all nicely shaded. However, the pull-throughs are a little shorter in this row (54 feet long). Row 4 contains 40-foot back-ins that back to a culvert and an unsightly storage shed. The southernmost sites, in Row 6, back to a fence, which adds to their security and privacy, but G also abuts a storage shed. This RV park is an acceptable overnight stay, and the pool makes for pleasant recreation, but it is not a destination.

Basics

Operated By: Sands Motel. **Open:** All year. **Site Assignment:** Assigned upon registration; no reservations. **Registration:** In office (24 hours). **Fee:** RV $13.90. **Parking:** At site.

Facilities

Number of RV Sites: 34. **Number of Tent-Only Sites:** 0. **Hookups:** Water, sewer, electric (30, 50 amps). **Dump Station:** No (sewer at all sites). **Laundry:** Yes. **Pay Phone:** Yes. **Rest Rooms and Showers:** Yes. **Fuel:** No. **Propane:** No. **Internal Roads:** Gravel/dirt. **RV Service:** No. **Market:** 0.5 mi. east. **Restaurant:** 2 mi. east. **General Store:** Yes. **Vending:** No. **Swimming:** Pool. **Playground:** Yes. **Activities:** Golf, tennis, tours, theater, swimming, basketball, automobile racing, horse racing, shopping. **Nearby Attractions:** Crystal Bridge at Myriad Botanical Gardens, National Cowboy Hall of Fame & Western Heritage Center, Oklahoma City Art Museum, Oklahoma City National Memorial. **Additional Information:** Oklahoma City Convention & Tourism Bureau, (800) 225-5652 or (405) 297-8912.

Restrictions

Pets: On leash, cleaned up after. **Fires:** In grills. **Alcoholic Beverages:** At sites. **Vehicle Maximum Length:** None. **Other:** No busses.

To Get There

From I-40 Exit 143 (Rockwell Ave.), turn south onto Rockwell Ave. On the south side of the highway interchange, take the first right into the motel parking lot.

PONCA CITY

Snyder's RV Park

3171 West North Ave., Ponca City 74601. T: (580) 762-4686.

★★★ n/a

Beauty: ★★	Site Privacy: ★★★
Spaciousness: ★★★	Quiet: ★★★★
Security: ★★★★	Cleanliness: ★★★
Insect Control: ★★★★	Facilities: ★★★

As there are no rest rooms, this RV park accepts only rigs that are self-contained. RV sites are located behind the store, in two small rows. All sites are level, gravel sites, and all but 10 are well-shaded. Site 7 is next to a shed, making it slightly less desirable. Sites are often occupied by road crews and other long-term guests, so a phone call would be worthwhile before arriving. The store really jumps around lunch time, and this is not the best time to check in, as all staff will be busy. This park is a functional stop that offers convenience services (gas, food, etc.), but won't likely become a repeat destination for most travelers.

Basics

Operated By: Dave Snyder. **Open:** All year. **Site Assignment:** Flexible, depending on site availability; verbal reservations OK. **Registration:** In store. (Late arrivals select an available site & pay in the morning.) **Fee:** RV $12. **Parking:** At site.

Facilities

Number of RV Sites: 10. **Number of Tent-Only Sites:** 0. **Hookups:** Water, sewer, electric (20, 30, 50 amps), cable. **Dump Station:** Yes. **Laundry:** No. **Pay Phone:** Yes. **Rest Rooms and Showers:** No. **Fuel:** Yes. **Propane:** No. **Internal Roads:** Gravel. **RV Service:** No. **Market:** 3 mi. east. **Restaurant:** Limited on-site; 2 mi. east. **General Store:** Yes. **Vending:** No. **Swimming:** No. **Playground:** No. **Other:** ATM, sandwiches. **Activities:** Fishing, boating, swimming, hiking. **Nearby Attractions:** Kaw Lake, Marland Estate Mansion, Ponca City Cultural Center. **Additional Information:** Ponca City Area Chamber of Commerce, (580) 765-4400.

Restrictions

Pets: On leash, cleaned up after. **Fires:** In grills. **Alcoholic Beverages:** At sites. **Vehicle Maximum Length:** None.

To Get There

From the junction of Hwy. 60 and Hwy. 156, turn south onto Hwy. 156 (toward Marland) and go 0.4 mi. Turn left onto North Ave. and go 0.85 mi. Turn left at the sign into the entrance.

SALLISAW

Lakeside RV Park

P.O. Box 1414, Sallisaw 74955. T: (918) 775-7522; F: (918) 775-0457.

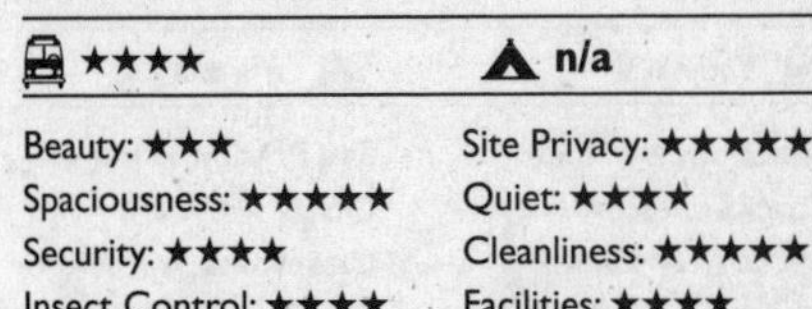

★★★★ n/a

Beauty: ★★★	Site Privacy: ★★★★★
Spaciousness: ★★★★★	Quiet: ★★★★
Security: ★★★★	Cleanliness: ★★★★★
Insect Control: ★★★★	Facilities: ★★★★

With woods to the north, east, and west, this campground has a definite rural feel, despite the numerous residences in close proximity to it. Sites are arranged in two rows of pull-throughs, with back-ins along the east and west sides. (Sites 21–28 to the west are reserved for long-term guests.) Back-ins 1–6 on the eastern edge of the campground are 60 × 45 feet. Site 6 is closest to the (covered) pool, whereas end sites 1 and 11 are furthest from the entrance and closest to the woods to the north, making these the nicest overnight spots. The eastern strip of pull-throughs boasts some incredibly long sites that range in length from 75 feet (13) to 90 feet (14) to 105 feet (15). End site 20 is slightly shorter, at 65 feet. The rec room is comfortable and tastefully furnished, and the rest rooms (individual unisex units) would look great in anyone's home. One small drawback is that the coin-op shower runs for only four minutes per quarter. All facilities are clean and incredibly comfy, making this a very pleasant stay. (Note that there is an overt Christian theme to the park, with pamphlets, iconography, and other religious paraphernalia scattered throughout.)

Basics

Operated By: Paula & Mike Mouzakis. **Open:** Mar. 15–Nov. 15. **Site Assignment:** Assigned upon registration, but flexible; verbal reservations OK. **Reg-**

istration: In office. (Late arrivals use drop box.) **Fee:** RV $18 (50 amps), $16 (30 amps). **Parking:** At site.

Facilities

Number of RV Sites: 28. **Number of Tent-Only Sites:** 0. **Hookups:** Water, sewer, electric (30, 50 amps). **Each Site:** Picnic table. **Dump Station:** No (sewer at all sites). **Laundry:** Yes. **Pay Phone:** No. **Rest Rooms and Showers:** Yes. **Fuel:** No. **Propane:** Yes. **Internal Roads:** Gravel. **RV Service:** No. **Market:** 7 mi. to Sallisaw. **Restaurant:** 2 blocks. **General Store:** Across street. **Vending:** No. **Swimming:** Pool. **Playground:** No. **Other:** Rec room (w/ TV & chairs), pavilion. **Activities:** Board games. **Nearby Attractions:** Fourteen Flags Museum, Sequoyah's Home site. **Additional Information:** Sallisaw Chamber of Commerce, (918) 775-2558.

Restrictions

Pets: On leash, cleaned up after. **Fires:** In grills. **Alcoholic Beverages:** At sites. **Vehicle Maximum Length:** None.

To Get There

From I-40 Exit 308, turn south onto Hwy. 59 and go 7.2 mi. Turn left at the sign into the campground.

SAWYER

Sawyer RV Park

HC 66 Box 1430, Sawyer 74756. T: (580) 326-0830.

RV ★★★★★ Tent ★★★★

Beauty: ★★★★★ Site Privacy: ★★★★
Spaciousness: ★★★★ Quiet: ★★★★★
Security: ★★★★★ Cleanliness: ★★★★★
Insect Control: ★★★★ Facilities: ★★★★

Surrounded by forest and pasture land, this campground has both a wilderness and an on-the-farm feel. The campground is very pretty (there are flowers and a small white fence that run along the entryway), and is located just one mile from the Hugo Lake Recreation Area. Sites are back-ins arranged on the outside of a loop. Sites 1–8 are 40-foot back-ins, while sites 14–17 can accommodate an RV of any size. Sites 10 and (especially) 11 have the best shade in the park and can likewise accommodate a big rig. Sites 1–4 have grassy patches but little shade. The rest room facility is a small individual rest room and shower in the laundry. All facilities are kept extremely clean. This is definitely one of the nicest parks in the region. Although small, it is a deserving destination for RV campers. Even campers who don't take advantage of the nearby Hugo Lake facilities will enjoy a stay at this park.

Basics

Operated By: Jan Park. **Open:** All year. **Site Assignment:** Flexible, depending on availability; verbal reservations OK. **Registration:** In office (trailer 13). **Fee:** $15 (checks, no credit cards). **Parking:** At site.

Facilities

Number of RV Sites: 19. **Number of Tent-Only Sites:** 0. **Hookups:** Water, sewer, electric (30 amps). **Each Site:** Picnic table. **Dump Station:** No (sewer at all sites). **Laundry:** Yes. **Pay Phone:** No. **Rest Rooms and Showers:** Yes. **Fuel:** No. **Propane:** No. **Internal Roads:** Gravel. **RV Service:** No. **Market:** 12 mi. to Hugo. **Restaurant:** 12 mi. to Hugo. **General Store:** No. **Vending:** No. **Swimming:** No. **Playground:** No. **Other:** 6 overflow sites, wildlife. **Activities:** Swimming, boating, fishing. **Nearby Attractions:** Hugo Lake, Raymond Gary State Park. **Additional Information:** Choctaw County Chamber of Commerce, (580) 326-7511.

Restrictions

Pets: On leash, cleaned up after. **Fires:** In grills. **Alcoholic Beverages:** At sites ("party elsewhere"). **Vehicle Maximum Length:** None. **Other:** No refunds.

To Get There

From the junction of Hwy. 70 and Hwy. 147, turn north onto Hwy. 147 and go 2.6 mi. Turn at the sign for Virgil Point Park.

SEMINOLE

Round-Up RV Park

Rte. 3 Box 285F, Seminole 74868. T: (405) 382-7957.

RV ★★★ Tent n/a

Beauty: ★★★ Site Privacy: ★★★
Spaciousness: ★★★ Quiet: ★★★
Security: ★★★ Cleanliness: ★★★
Insect Control: ★★★★ Facilities: ★★★

Although this park is located in an urban setting, it has some features (such as flowering bushes and a wooden fence) that make it more attractive. In addition, each site has a shade tree, which makes a stay there more comfortable than it would otherwise be (especially in late summer). The restaurant parking lot (as well as the highway) lies to the west of the park, residences border it in the southeast and northeast, and a fishing pond (with a pretty pavilion) sits to the east. The RV sites, all pull-throughs, average 75 × 30 feet in size. End sites 1 and 14 are closest to the pond (1 is right next to the pavilion and its two grills), while end sites 13 and 27 are closest to the parking lot. The best area is in the middle of the south row (sites 19–22, more or less), which faces an open field and is away from both the entrance and the residences. The rest rooms are air conditioned, but rather small and basic. They also seem to suffer from some amount of neglect. Nevertheless, this park and its very nice restaurant make for quite a decent overnight stop.

Basics

Operated By: Larry Kinslow. **Open:** All year. **Site Assignment:** First come, first served; no reservations. **Registration:** In restaurant. (Late arrivals use drop box.) **Fee:** RV $14.10 (checks, V, MC, AE, D). **Parking:** At site.

Facilities

Number of RV Sites: 27. **Number of Tent-Only Sites:** 0. **Hookups:** Water, sewer, electric (50 amps). **Each Site:** Picnic table. **Dump Station:** Yes. **Laundry:** No. **Pay Phone:** Yes. **Rest Rooms and Showers:** Yes. **Fuel:** No. **Propane:** No. **Internal Roads:** Gravel. **RV Service:** No. **Market:** 7 mi. in town. **Restaurant:** On site. **General Store:** No. **Vending:** No. **Swimming:** No. **Playground:** Yes. **Other:** Fishing pond (catch & release), dog walk, covered pavilion with 2 grills. **Activities:** Fishing, festivals. **Nearby Attractions:** Jasmine Moran Children's Museum, festivals. **Additional Information:** Seminole Chamber of Commerce, (405) 382-3640.

Restrictions

Pets: On leash, cleaned up after. **Fires:** In grills. **Alcoholic Beverages:** At sites. **Vehicle Maximum Length:** None.

To Get There

From I-40 (Exit 200): on the south side of the highway, go 0.2 mi. south on Hwy. 99 to the 2nd commercial complex. Turn left at the sign for the restaurant into the entrance.

SPIRO

Rockin' Horse RV Park

Rte. 1 Box 267, Spiro 74959. T: (918) 962-2524.

RV ★★★ Tent ★★★

Beauty: ★★★ Site Privacy: ★★★★
Spaciousness: ★★★ Quiet: ★★★★
Security: ★★★★ Cleanliness: ★★★
Insect Control: ★★★★ Facilities: ★★

This rural campground has grassy RV sites situated along a loop. Not all sites are numbered. Sites 2–7 are gravel pull-throughs without any shade. Sites 10 and 15 are 75-foot pull-throughs, while end site 12 is a 60-foot pull-through. Sites 21 and those to either side of 21 are 60-foot back-ins that back to a grassy field and then to woods. These are the nicest sites due to the grass and the natural surroundings. One site (possibly 16) in the southeast corner is exceptionally spacious. Tenting is possible in the field to the south of the RV sites. Tent sites have thick grass but no shade. The one rest room and one shower are acceptably clean. Please note that the campground has recently been sold to new owners, and any number of changes may be expected.

Basics

Operated By: Jack & Jeanie. **Open:** All year. **Site Assignment:** Assigned upon registration; verbal reservations OK. **Registration:** In office. (Late arrivals use drop box.) **Fee:** RV $15 (full), tent $8 (checks). **Parking:** At site.

Facilities

Number of RV Sites: 22. **Number of Tent-Only Sites:** Undesignated sites. **Hookups:** Water, sewer, electric (30 amps). **Dump Station:** No (sewer at all sites). **Laundry:** Yes. **Pay Phone:** No. **Rest Rooms and Showers:** Yes. **Fuel:** No. **Propane:** No. **Internal Roads:** Gravel. **RV Service:** No. **Market:** Less than 1 mi. east. **Restaurant:** Less than 1 mi. east. **General Store:** No. **Vending:** Yes. **Swimming:** No. **Playground:** No. **Other:** Storm shelter, RV & boat storage. **Activities:** Fishing, boating, swimming, hiking. **Nearby Attractions:** Spiro Mounds Archaeological State Park, Robert S. Kerr

Lake. **Additional Information:** Spiro Area Chamber of Commerce, (918) 962-3816.

RESTRICTIONS

Pets: On leash, cleaned up after. **Fires:** In grills. **Alcoholic Beverages:** At sites. **Vehicle Maximum Length:** None.

TO GET THERE

From the junction of Main St. and Hwy. 9/271, turn west onto Hwy. 271 and go 1.2 mi. Turn right at the sign into the entrance.

TALEQUAH

Diamondhead Resort

12081 Hwy. 10, Talequah 74464. T: (800) 722-2411 or (918) 456-4545.

★★★ ★★★★

Beauty: ★★★★ Site Privacy: ★★★
Spaciousness: ★★★★ Quiet: ★★★★★
Security: ★★★★★ Cleanliness: ★★★
Insect Control: ★★★ Facilities: ★★★

All of the RV sites here are situated in a row in the northwest portion of the campground. These grassy, undeveloped sites are unnumbered. Counting from the southwest by the gravel road, sites 1–10 and 12–16 are under large shade trees, which make them more attractive. Sites 11–22 could conceivably be pull-throughs, if the campground is relatively empty, but 1–10 back to trees and cannot be anything other than back-ins. However, since the field in which they sit is so large, these sites can take a rig of any size. There are loads of tenting sites, none of which are numbered. Since the campground is so natural and is surrounded by woods and the river, this is an ideal site for tenting. Restroom facilities are basic, and rather small for such a large campground. The building they are housed in needs a good cleaning, but the facilities themselves are well maintained. Note that campers who stay here are expected to take float trips, making this campground somewhat unusual. However, this seems to be a common restriction among "float" campgrounds in the area (which has many).

BASICS

Operated By: Joyce Eastham. **Open:** Apr. 1–Oct. 1. **Site Assignment:** First come, first served; verbal reservations OK. **Registration:** In office, or with guard (nights & weekends). **Fee:** RV $15 (electric), tent $10, car (V, MC, D). **Parking:** At site.

FACILITIES

Number of RV Sites: 22. **Number of Tent-Only Sites:** Undesignated sites. **Hookups:** Electric (30 amps). **Each Site:** Picnic table, grill. **Dump Station:** Yes. **Laundry:** No. **Pay Phone:** No. **Rest Rooms and Showers:** Yes. **Fuel:** No. **Propane:** No. **Internal Roads:** Gravel. **RV Service:** No. **Market:** 7 mi. to Talequah. **Restaurant:** 3 mi. towards Talequah. **General Store:** Yes. **Vending:** No. **Swimming:** River. **Playground:** No. **Other:** Canoe rentals. **Activities:** Canoe floating, volleyball, basketball. **Nearby Attractions:** Fishing. **Additional Information:** Talequah Area Chamber of Commerce, (800) 456-4860 or (918) 456-3742.

RESTRICTIONS

Pets: On leash, cleaned up after. **Fires:** In grills. **Alcoholic Beverages:** At sites. **Vehicle Maximum Length:** None. **Other:** Only floaters may stay in campground. No glass or styrofoam on or near river.

TO GET THERE

From the junction of Hwy. 51/62/82 and Hwy. 10 in town by Wal-Mart, go northeast on Hwy. 10/51/62/82 for 2.2 mi. Turn right onto Downing St. (3rd light) and go 1.9 mi. Turn left onto Scenic Hwy. 10 and go 5.3 mi. Turn right at the sign into the entrance. (Follow the gravel road to the back of the campground for electrical sites.)

TONKAWA

Woodland Camper Park

16600 West South Ave., Tonkawa 74653. T: (580) 628-2062.

★★★ ★★★

Beauty: ★★★ Site Privacy: ★★★
Spaciousness: ★★★ Quiet: ★★★
Security: ★★★★ Cleanliness: ★★★
Insect Control: ★★★★ Facilities: ★★★

Just off the interstate, this campground is bordered by a gas station to the west and fields to the north and south. Mostly unnumbered, sites range from 75 feet (east row) to 95 feet (west row) long. They are all undeveloped grassy sites, averaging 40 feet wide. The least desirable sites are the end sites to the south, which are closest to the highway (especially the southeast end site, which also has no shade tree). The most desirable site, in the northeast corner, has a large shade tree, abuts a field, and is furthest from the highway. There is an enormous area where tenting is possible. The best tent site is in front of the house, under a large shade tree (unfortunately, closer to the road). The rest rooms and showers are passable, but there was paint flaking from the shower stalls during our visit, and the floor is unpainted cement. This campground is mainly an overnighter, about equally decent for tenters and RVers.

BASICS

Operated By: Gary & Jo Wood. **Open:** All year. **Site Assignment:** Flexible, depending on site availability; verbal reservations OK. **Registration:** In office. (Late arrivals use drop box.) **Fee:** RV $14 (full), tent $8. **Parking:** At site.

FACILITIES

Number of RV Sites: 38. **Number of Tent-Only Sites:** Undesignated sites. **Hookups:** Water, sewer, electric (30 amps). **Dump Station:** Yes. **Laundry:** No. **Pay Phone:** Across street. **Rest Rooms and Showers:** Yes. **Fuel:** No. **Propane:** No. **Internal Roads:** Paved. **RV Service:** No. **Market:** 2 mi. east. **Restaurant:** Across street. **General Store:** Across street. **Vending:** No. **Swimming:** No. **Playground:** No. **Other:** None. **Activities:** Boating, swimming, fishing. **Nearby Attractions:** Ponca City, Great Salt Plains State State Park. **Additional Information:** Tonkawa Chamber of Commerce, (580) 628-2220.

RESTRICTIONS

Pets: On leash, cleaned up after. **Fires:** In grills. **Alcoholic Beverages:** At sites. **Vehicle Maximum Length:** None.

TO GET THERE

From I-35 (Exit 214): on the west side of the highway, go 0.15 mi. west. Turn right at the sign into the entrance.

TULSA

Tulsa Northeast KOA

19605 East Skelly Dr., Catoosa 74015. T: (800) KOA-7657 or (918) 266-4227; www.koa.com/where/OK/36106.htm.

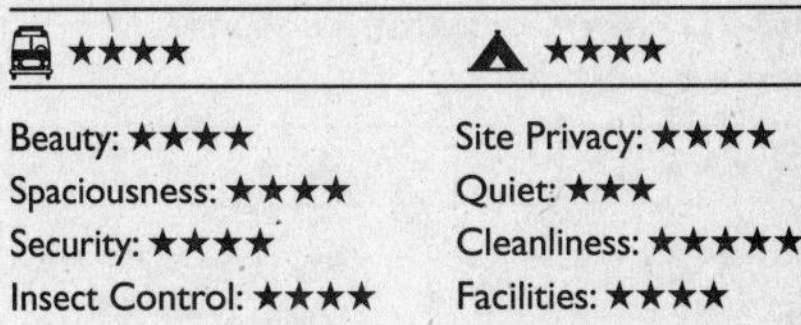

★★★★ ★★★★

Beauty: ★★★★ Site Privacy: ★★★★
Spaciousness: ★★★★ Quiet: ★★★
Security: ★★★★ Cleanliness: ★★★★★
Insect Control: ★★★★ Facilities: ★★★★

This campground offers open grassy sites in the front section and more shaded sites behind the office. All sites are pull-throughs. The front section has 75-foot sites that are roomier than most of the sites in the back (24 feet wide versus 18 feet wide). Northern end sites (116, 130, 143, 153, 163, 177, 191, and 205) are closest to the entrance road and are therefore less desirable. End sites closer to the office (112 and 158 especially) receive more passing traffic from registering campers. Of the southern sites, the two rows (the 40s and 50s) directly behind the office are the widest and most suitable for rigs with slide-outs. Of the remaining sites, 10 and 16 in the eastern side are closest to a storage shed. Sites in the southwestern corner (77, 84, 91, 98, 104, 100) are furthest from the entrance and the office. Tent sites are directly behind the office, in a strip of grassy sites. The rest rooms and showers are absolutely spotless and very comfortable. This campground makes a great home base for exploring Tulsa and its environs.

BASICS

Operated By: Private operator. **Open:** All year. **Site Assignment:** Assigned upon registration Credit card required for reservation; 24-hours cancellation policy. **Registration:** In office. (Late arrivals use drop box.) **Fee:** RV $24 (full), $20 (water, electric), tent $18. **Parking:** At site.

FACILITIES

Number of RV Sites: 118. **Number of Tent-Only Sites:** 9. **Hookups:** Water, sewer, electric (30, 50 amps). **Each Site:** Picnic table, grill. **Dump Station:** Yes. **Laundry:** Yes. **Pay Phone:** Yes. **Rest Rooms and Showers:** Yes. **Fuel:** No. **Propane:** Yes. **Internal Roads:** Gravel. **RV Service:** No. **Market:** 3 blocks south. **Restaurant:** 0.25 mi. south. **General Store:** Yes. **Vending:** Yes. **Swimming:** Pool. **Playground:** Yes. **Other:** Cabins, pet walk, dataport, rec room, video games. **Activities:** Swimming, volleyball, fishing, boating, swimming, tours, golf, softball/baseball, horse racing. **Nearby Attractions:** Trail of Tears, amusement parks, casinos, lakes, Tulsa Zoo. **Additional Information:** Tulsa CVB, (800) 558-3311 or (918) 585-1201.

RESTRICTIONS

Pets: On leash, cleaned up after. **Fires:** In grills. **Alcoholic Beverages:** At sites. **Vehicle Maximum Length:** None.

TO GET THERE

From I-44 (Exit 240A: 193rd Ave.), turn north onto 193rd Ave. and go 0.15 mi. Turn right at the sign into the entrance. Follow the entrance road past the trucking companies. Turn right at the sign into the campground.

WAURIKA

Moneka Park

1645 South 101st Ave., Tulsa 74128. T: (580) 963-2111; www.lasr.net/lasr/oklahoma/waurika/body.html.

RV ★★★ Tent ★★★★

Beauty: ★★★★ Site Privacy: ★★★★
Spaciousness: ★★★★ Quiet: ★★★★★
Security: ★★★ Cleanliness: ★★★★
Insect Control: ★★ Facilities: ★★

Sites in this wilderness campground are situated around a loop. Depending on your preference, you can select a site on the outside of the loop (on the right side), nestled into the forest, or on the more open inside of the loop (left side). (Inside sites 12–23 at the south end are also totally forested.) Sites on the west side of the loop (1, 4, 6, and odd 7–17) have short footpaths to the creek. Sites 3 and 36–38 offer the best opportunity to recreate in the grassy field. Less desirable sites are 12 and 13, located at the intersection of two internal roads and therefore sunject to road traffic. Sites 18–20 are apt to receive more passing foot traffic due to the proximity of the hiking trail between 18 and 19. Perhaps the only downside to this beautiful campground is that the rest rooms are small (one non-flush toilet) and only naturally lit, but they are clean. This campground is a quiet and fun destination for RVers and tenters alike, as long as you can stand getting back to basics a little.

BASICS

Operated By: Army Corps of Engineers. **Open:** Mar. 1–Oct. 31. **Site Assignment:** First come, first served; no reservations. **Registration:** At pay station. **Fee:** $8. **Parking:** At site.

FACILITIES

Number of RV Sites: 38. **Number of Tent-Only Sites:** 0. **Hookups:** None. **Each Site:** Picnic table, grill, wooden "prep table" by grill. **Dump Station:** No. **Laundry:** No. **Pay Phone:** No. **Rest Rooms and Showers:** Yes (No showers). **Fuel:** No. **Propane:** No. **Internal Roads:** Paved. **RV Service:** No. **Market:** 8 mi. to Waurika. **Restaurant:** 8 mi. to Waurika. **General Store:** No. **Vending:** No. **Swimming:** Lake. **Playground:** No. **Other:** Hiking trail. **Activities:** Hiking, swimming, boating, fishing. **Nearby Attractions:** Waurika Lake, Beaver Creek Trail. **Additional Information:** Waurika Chamber of Commerce, (580) 228-2081.

RESTRICTIONS

Pets: On leash, cleaned up after. **Fires:** In grills. **Alcoholic Beverages:** At sites. **Vehicle Maximum Length:** None.

TO GET THERE

From the junction of Hwy. 70 and Hwy. 5, turn west onto Hwy. 5 and go 5.3 mi. Turn right at the wooden sign for Waurika Lake. Go 0.9 mi. (past the Project Office and Information Center), and veer left when the road starts along the lake. Go 0.8 mi. and turn left into the campground.

WOODWARD

Corky's Get and Go

802 Northwest Hwy. 270, Woodward 73801. T: (405) 254-9161.

RV ★★★ Tent ★★

Beauty: ★★★ Site Privacy: ★★★
Spaciousness: ★★★ Quiet: ★★
Security: ★★★ Cleanliness: ★★★★
Insect Control: ★★★★ Facilities: ★★

An RV park managed in conjunction with a convenience store, this park has 2 rows of 5 back-in sites. Sites 1–5 are directly behind the store, while 6–10 back to a residential area. All sites are open and level, measure 40 × 25 feet, and have excellent grass. Site 6 has a nice shade tree, making it the most desirable. Sites 8 and 9 share a smaller tree, but are a better pick than the other treeless sites. Sites 1 and 10 (especially 1) are least desirable, as they border a city street. Site 1 also has the RV dump station next to it. While there may be several long-term guests in the numbered sites, campers who only want to stay one night and can afford to forgo hookups can park in the field that abuts the RV park at no cost. Tenting is possible in the field, which has a very nice grass floor. There is no charge for tents, assuming that no hookups are used. If Corky's park is full, there is a motel right next door that offers overnight RV parking spaces, but these are on a tar surface and do not have any shade trees.

BASICS

Operated By: Corky Chestnut. **Open:** All year. **Site Assignment:** First come, first served; verbal reservations OK. **Registration:** In convenience store (5p.m.–midnight). (Late arrivals select an available site & settle in the morning.) **Fee:** $10 (free for no hookups) (V, MC, AE, D). **Parking:** At site, in field for no hookups.

FACILITIES

Number of RV Sites: 10. **Number of Tent-Only Sites:** 0. **Hookups:** Water, sewer, electric (30 amps). **Dump Station:** Yes. **Laundry:** No. **Pay Phone:** Yes. **Rest Rooms and Showers:** Rest rooms in convenience store. **Fuel:** Yes. **Propane:** No. **Internal Roads:** Gravel. **RV Service:** No. **Market:** 1.5 mi. southeast. **Restaurant:** 0.5 mi. southeast. **General Store:** Yes. **Vending:** Yes. **Swimming:** No. **Playground:** No. **Other:** None. **Activities:** Visiting museums. **Nearby Attractions:** Plains Indians & Pioneers Museum, Southern Plains Range Research Station. **Additional Information:** Woodward Chamber of Commerce, (800) 364-5352 or (580) 256-7411.

RESTRICTIONS

Pets: On leash, cleaned up after. **Fires:** In grills. **Alcoholic Beverages:** At sites. **Vehicle Maximum Length:** 45 ft.

TO GET THERE

From the junction of Hwys 3/15/183/270/412, go 0.3 mi. north on Hwy. 270 (Old Fort Supply Rd.). Turn right at the Conoco sign into Corky's Convenience Store.

Oregon

Like its northern neighbor, Oregon exhibits amazing variety in terms of climates and ecosystems. Much of the I-5 corridor has plenty of rain, big forests and beautiful mountains. The **Cascade Range** divides the state into a temperate year-round wonderland on the west side and a forbidding desert on the east. Nearing the California border, the terrain morphs into arid, rolling hills.

West of the Cascade Mountains are the I-5 cities of **Portland, Salem,** and **Eugene,** and the Highway 101 coastline. State government and community involvement impact regional culture, making it surprisingly isolated. Portland resonates with cosmopolitan yet blue-collar vibes, combining fine arts venues, communities of foreign nationals, and funky things to do. Driving south down I-5, the next city is Salem, the surprisingly conservative capital of the state. The scenery along northern I-5—a mixture of forests, farms, and mountains—continues south past Eugene, home of the **University of Oregon** and one of the most liberal, earthy, scholarly concentrations of people of any city on the west coast.

The forestlands surrounding the I-5 corridor between Portland and **Roseburg** (the rafting capital of Oregon) are indescribable. **Mt. Hood** and the Umpqua River Valley (OR 38 to the coast from I-5) have must see status for all travelers.

Another area not to be missed is the coast. Hwy 101 runs the length of the coast to California with cut-throughs to I-5 every 60 to 100 miles. Starting in **Astoria,** the Oregon coast offers huge surf breaking against high rock cliffs and gnarled rock formations off shore. Rocky tidal pools at almost any beach hold all types of ecological wonders. During spring break and summer, traffic jams on two-lane 101 can get hairy. Oregon state parks litter the whole drive; make sure to see **Oswald West.** Another point of interest, **Newport** has an aquarium, an oceanography satellite of OSU, an enormous fishing fleet, a brewery, and a wax museum. South of **North Bend** and the **Oregon Dunes,** tourist traffic drops off, although the blue collar shipping, fishing, and logging villages have a certain charm to them and are worth seeing if time permits.

Driving east from Portland, I-84 follows the Columbia through the **Columbia River Gorge National Scenic Area.** Large rock formations, mountains, and, of course, the river make the drive appealing. Continuing on past the gorge, the scenery changes into flat, high-altitude plains and rolling hills along the Columbia and Snake Rivers. Eastern Oregon has very low population density and not many attractions, but there's plenty of beautiful scenery in both snowy winter and boiling summer weather.

The central part of the state has the second-largest tourism draw after the I-5 corridor (including the coast, the gorge and Mount Hood). In the **Bend-Sisters** area, recreation attractions include skiing, rafting, horseback riding, stream fishing, and drinking.

Driving south from Bend on Highway 97, day trips abound. Recreation comes in one flavor: outdoors. Lakes, national forests, and volcanoes sum up the attractions between Bend and **Klamath Falls.**

The following facilities accept payment in checks or cash only:

Bastendorff Beach Campground, Coo's Bay
Cinder Hill Campground, Bend
Columbia River RV Park, Portland
Diamond Lake Campground, Diamond Lake
Harbor Vista Campground, Florence
Paulina Lake Campground, Bend
Portland-Dayton RV Park, Portland
Princess Creek Campground, Cascade Summit
Richardson Park, Eugene

The following facilities feature 20 or fewer sites:

Eagle Creek Campground, Bonneville
Elk Lake Campground, Detroit
Illahe Campground, Gold Beach
Riverside Campground, Sisters
Saddle Mountain State Park, Cannon Beach

ASHLAND

Glenyan Campground of Ashland

5310 Hwy. 66, Ashland 97520. T: (541) 488-1785

RV ★★★ Tent ★★★

Beauty: ★★★ Site Privacy: ★
Spaciousness: ★★ Quiet: ★★★
Security: ★ Cleanliness: ★★★
Insect Control: ★★ Facilities: ★★★

Glenyan Campground, located in a scenic rural area six miles east of I-5, greets guests with a small pond shaded by medium-sized trees. The grounds, foliated with small cedars and shrubs, huge oaks and pines, birch, elm, willow, and thick blackberry brambles, sit nestled in the scruffy, rolling farmland foothills of the southern cascades. Sites within the campground contain a mixture of grass, moss, dirt, and very fine-grit gravel (about the size of kitty litter). All preferred sites back up to a gently flowing, clear stream and beyond that a lightly wooded hill. The stream helps to mask road noise in the sites arranged along it. Choice RV sites include 45–49 and 28–35. The best tent sites, 2–5, 39, D, E, and G, have some privacy; the RV sites do not. Avoid RV sites 58–63 and 26–15 as they catch the brunt of noise from a nearby road. The spring, summer, and fall necessitate reservations in this older park with well kept facilities; vacancies are more common in winter, despite relatively mild weather. The older game room has one large pool table and some classic arcade games.

BASICS

Operated By: Glenyan Campground. **Open:** All year. **Site Assignment:** First come, first served; reservation (required deposit is 1 night's stay; refund w/ 48-hours notice plus $2 cancellation fee). **Registration:** Office, after hours at drop box or in morning when office opens. **Fee:** Full $22, electric/cable $21, tent $17.50; fee covers 2 people, extra person $2; V, MC, cash. **Parking:** At site.

FACILITIES

Number of RV-Only Sites: 78. **Number of Tent-Only Sites:** 20. **Hookups:** Electric (20, 30 amps), water, sewer, cable. **Each Site:** Picnic table, fire ring. **Dump Station:** Yes. **Laundry:** Yes. **Pay Phone:** Yes. **Rest Rooms and Showers:** Yes. **Fuel:** No. **Propane:** Yes. **Internal Roads:** Paved. **RV Service:** No. **Market:** 4 mi. west in Ashland. **Restaurant:** 4 mi. west in Ashland. **General Store:** Yes. **Vending:** No. **Swimming Pool:** Yes. **Playground:** No. **Other:** Game room, meeting hall (capacity 40), horseshoes, badminton. **Activities:** Blackberry picking, bird-watching. **Nearby Attractions:** Emigrant Lake Recreation Area (across the street from campground; has a water slide), Oregon Shakespearean Festival (Feb.–Oct.), Britt Music Festival (summer), cabaret theater, Pacific Northwest Museum of Natural History. **Additional Information:** Ashland Chamber of Commerce, (541) 482-3486.

RESTRICTIONS

Pets: No more than 2, leash only. **Fires:** Fire pit/grill only. **Alcoholic Beverages:** Site only. **Vehicle Maximum Length:** 60 ft. **Other:** No clotheslines; only commercial RV awnings; quiet hours 10 p.m.–7 a.m.; no RV washer/dryer usage; no firearms.

TO GET THERE

From I-5 take Exit 14; drive 3.2 mi. southeast on Hwy. 66; Entrance is on right

ASTORIA

Astoria/Warrenton/Seaside KOA

1100 Northwest Ridge Rd., Hammond 97121. T: (503)861-2606 or (800)562-8506 for reservations; F: (503) 861-3209; www.koa.com; astoriakoa@aol.com.

RV ★★★ Tent ★★

Beauty: ★★ Site Privacy: ★★
Spaciousness: ★★ Quiet: ★★★
Security: ★★★ Cleanliness: ★★★
Insect Control: ★★ Facilities: ★★★★

Astoria/Warrenton/Seaside KOA, just across the street from gorgeous Fort Stevens State Park and south of Astoria a few miles off Hwy. 101, offers a bounty of family recreational activities within the property. These include a large, nice indoor pool, sandy playgrounds, an arcade with 14 machines and an Internet access terminal (20 cents a minute), nine holes of mini-golf in good condition, and a paved basketball court with opposing goals; all of these on top of regular and varying planned activities. The most visually appealing, flat, spacious sites on the property, the deluxe sites (sections B, C, D, E) have some foliage-generated privacy. The small number of grassy tent sites lack privacy, and this also applies to the rest of the RV sites: when full they create an almost treeless city of trailers. Sites J11–36 and sites K13–38 are quiet and isolated from the rest of the grounds along a lane ending in a cul-de-sac, but have the same privacy problems.

BASICS

Operated By: Recreational Adventures Campgrounds. **Open:** All year (some seasonal sites). **Site Assignment:** First come, first served; reservation (required deposit is 1 night's fee, 3 nights on holidays; refund w/ 24 hours notice, 1 week notice for holidays). **Registration:** At the office, after hours drop in front of office. **Fee:** Deluxe $37, water/electric/sewer $32, water/electric $30, tent village (w/ electricity) $25, tent w/ no hookups $23; fee covers 2 people, additional adults $3.95 per day, children ages 6–17 $2.95, children under age 5 free; off-season/weekday rates are $3 less; V, MC, D, cash. **Parking:** At site, limited off site.

FACILITIES

Number of RV-Only Sites: 230. **Number of Tent-Only Sites:** 26. **Hookups:** Electric (20, 30, 50 amps), water, sewer, cable, phone. **Each Site:** Picnic table, fire ring. **Dump Station:** No. **Laundry:** Yes. **Pay Phone:** Yes. **Rest Rooms and Showers:** Yes. **Fuel:** No. **Propane:** Yes. **Internal Roads:** Paved & grave. **RV Service:** No. **Market:** 5 mi. north in Astoria. **Restaurant:** 5 mi. North in Astoria. **General Store:** Yes. **Vending:** Yes. **Swimming Pool:** Yes. **Playground:** Yes. **Other:** Indoor Pool & hot tub, arcade, outdoor electric stoves w/full sized sinks, volleyball court, basketball court, horseshoes, stage, mini-golf, rec room, outdoor pavilion, fish cleaning station, bike rental, pancake house (open summers), board game & movie rentals. **Activities:** Multiple planned activities. **Nearby Attractions:** Columbia River Maritime Museum, Fort Clatsop National Memorial, Fort Stevens State Park, Flavel House Museum. **Additional Information:** Astoria-Warrenton Chamber of Commerce, (503) 325-6311 or www.oldoregon.com

RESTRICTIONS

Pets: On leash only. **Fires:** In fire pits, grills only. **Alcoholic Beverages:** At site. **Vehicle Maximum Length:** 60 ft. **Other:** 3 night min. stay on blackout dates: Crab Festival Weekend (end of Apr.), Memorial Day, Fourth of July week, Labor Day, All weekends in July & Aug.

TO GET THERE

After Astoria Suzuki Dealership on Hwy. 101, take next right on unmarked road with an ODOT KOA sign. Drive west 0.8 mi. and dead-end on S. Main St. Turn left and drive 0.2 mi., then take a right on Delaura Beach Rd. which turns into Ridge Rd. Follow for 3 mi.; entrance on the right across from state park.

BAKER CITY

Mountain View RV Park

2845 Hughs Ln., Baker City 97814. T: (541) 523-4824

RV ★★★ Tent ★★

Beauty: ★★★ Site Privacy: ★
Spaciousness: ★★ Quiet: ★★★
Security: ★★★ Cleanliness: ★★★★
Insect Control: ★★ Facilities: ★★★

Baker City has many RV parks, but none have faux-wild-west store-fronts like Mountain View RV Park's. The park is actually in better shape than appearances initially suggest; the facilities behind the facades are well maintained. Sites sit closer together than in some other parks. Mountain View has tall, older deciduous trees shading sites from the intense summer sun (trees are hard to find in eastern Oregon). The trees and grass below them create a kind of quaint park feel. Some sites have very limited views of the mountains on the horizon, limited by the perimeter fencing and older trees overhead. On one perimeter the park has a grassy tenting area; the sites have shade but like other sites on the grounds they lack privacy. RV sites on the perimeter provide good accomodations due to an absence of neighbors to the rear. The park stays open year-round, but winters bring extreme cold.

BASICS

Operated By: Mt. View RV Park. **Open:** All year. **Site Assignment:** On arrival, reservation (required deposit is 1 night's fee; refund w/ 24 hours notice). **Registration:** At office, after hours night box at office. **Fee:** Full $22, tent $19; fee covers 2 people, extra person $2, extra child (ages 3–12) $1; Units using air-conditioning, 50 amp units, & units longer than 34 ft. add $1; V, MC, cash. **Parking:** At site, off site.

Facilities

Number of RV-Only Sites: 88. **Number of Tent-Only Sites:** 10. **Hookups:** Electric (20, 30, 50 amps), water, sewer, cable. **Each Site:** Picnic table. **Dump Station:** Yes. **Laundry:** Yes. **Pay Phone:** Yes. **Rest Rooms and Showers:** Yes. **Fuel:** No. **Propane:** Yes. **Internal Roads:** Paved. **RV Service:** No. **Market:** A few mi. away in Baker City. **Restaurant:** A few mi. away in Baker City. **General Store:** Yes, open seasonally. **Vending:** No. **Swimming Pool:** Yes. **Playground:** Yes. **Other:** Meeting room (reservable), indoor Jacuzzi. **Activities:** Inquire at campground. **Nearby Attractions:** Hell's Canyon, Hells Canyon National Scenic Byway, horseback riding, llama pack trips, Snake River Reservoirs (3), watersports, Alder House Museum. **Additional Information:** Baker County Visitor & Convention Bureau, (541) 523-3356.

Restrictions

Pets: On leash only. **Fires:** No fires. **Alcoholic Beverages:** At site. **Vehicle Maximum Length:** 73 ft.

To Get There

From I-84 Exit 302, turn south on North Cedar Dr. and follow for 0.7 mi. Turn right on Hughes Ln., drive 1 mi. and turn left into campground.

BEND

Bend Kampground

63615 North Hwy. 97, Bend 97701. T: (541) 382-7738 or for reservations (800) 323-8899

RV ★★★ Tent ★★

Beauty: ★★★ Site Privacy: ★
Spaciousness: ★★★ Quiet: ★★
Security: ★★ Cleanliness: ★★★★
Insect Control: ★★ Facilities: ★★★

Quick access to the greater Bend area and recreational facilities describe the advantages of staying at Bend Kampground, located just a few minutes northwest of Bend between Hwy. 97 and Hwy. 20. The irrigated campground consists of several rows of sites, all without privacy. The older, marginally maintained facilities within the grounds include a small arcade and a pool. The best gravel full hookup sites, pull-throughs 61–67, have grass perimeters and a little shade from the high desert sun. Back-in sites 18–24 have views of the distant mountains to the west. The worst RV sites, 40–47, consist of an area covered solely in gravel. The best grass tent sites within the grounds, letters H–K, have some shade but no privacy. Most tent sites have picnic tables with small, wall-less shelters, providing a canopy for diners from the blazing sun and infrequent rain. The usually cloudless summers here can be hot, winters bring good skiing conditions.

Basics

Operated By: Bend Kampground. **Open:** All year. **Site Assignment:** On arrival, reservation (deposit & refund policy varies depending on time of year & local events). **Registration:** At convenience store. **Fee:** Full $28, water/electric $24, tent $18; fee covers 2 people, extra adult $3, extra child (ages 3–18) $2; V, MC, cash. **Parking:** At site.

Facilities

Number of RV-Only Sites: 79. **Number of Tent-Only Sites:** 21. **Hookups:** Electric (30, 50 amps), water, sewer, cable. **Each Site:** Picnic table. **Dump Station:** Yes. **Laundry:** Yes. **Pay Phone:** Yes. **Rest Rooms and Showers:** Yes. **Fuel:** Yes. **Propane:** Yes. **Internal Roads:** Paved. **RV Service:** No. **Market:** 1 mile south. **Restaurant:** 1 mi. south. **General Store:** Yes. **Vending:** No. **Swimming Pool:** Yes. **Playground:** Yes. **Other:** Deli, horseshoes, volleyball, fishing pond (catch & release), tether ball, basketball, arcade. **Activities:** Swimming, fishing. **Nearby Attractions:** Pilot Butte, Deshutes Brewery, regional rodeos, national forests, all types of outdoor sports, horseback riding. **Additional Information:** Bend Chamber of Commerce, (541) 382-3221.

Restrictions

Pets: On leash only. **Fires:** Fire pits only. **Alcoholic Beverages:** At site. **Vehicle Maximum Length:** None.

To Get There

Located at north end of Bend on Hwy. 97, 0.25 mi. north of Mountain View Mall.

BEND

Cinder Hill Campground

P.O. Box 989, Bend 97709. T: (541) 383-4000; F: (541) 383-4700; www.fs.fed.us/r6/centraloregon/recinfo/camping/cinderhill.html.

RV ★★★ Tent ★★★★

Beauty: ★★★★ Site Privacy: ★★★
Spaciousness: ★★★ Quiet: ★★★★★
Security: ★★ Cleanliness: ★★★
Insect Control: ★★ Facilities: ★

Cinder Hill Campground, located at the end of the main access road passing through Newberry National Volcanic Monument, provides a wilderness camping environment easily accessible to larger rigs. Most sites sit situated along an avenue with loops branching from this straightaway. The start of the avenue has some of the best sites, numbered 1–16 and 34–40, and the area containing these has a low site density, some shade from evergreens, and some privacy from foliage. Site density increases as one travels deeper into the campground. Some sites have views of East Lake, and the best sites, numbers 27–33, have obscured views that avoid the late day glare plaguing many of the lakefront sites with unobstructed views. Sites numbered 65 and higher sit closer together than those in the front of the grounds. Facilities here are limited. Summers are hot but provide good fishing and swimming.

Basics

Operated By: High Lake Contractors. **Open:** May–Oct. **Site Assignment:** On arrival only. **Registration:** At self pay station. **Fee:** Regular site $10, premium site (usually paved, marked on site signpost) $12; cash. **Parking:** At site.

Facilities

Number of Multipurpose Sites: 110. **Hookups:** None. **Each Site:** Picnic table, fire ring. **Dump Station:** No. **Laundry:** No. **Pay Phone:** No. **Rest Rooms and Showers:** Rest rooms only. **Fuel:** No. **Propane:** No. **Internal Roads:** Paved. **RV Service:** No. **Market:** 30 mi. west. **Restaurant:** 30 mi. west. **General Store:** No. **Vending:** No. **Swimming Pool:** No. **Playground:** No. **Other:** Boat ramp (2), hiking trails. **Activities:** Swimming, fishing, hiking, biking, boating, watching bubbles surface in the lake. **Nearby Attractions:** Bend, Deschutes National Forest, hiking, biking, boating, ecotourism. **Additional Information:** Bend Chamber of Commerce, (541) 382-3221.

Restrictions

Pets: On leash only (max. length 6 ft.). **Fires:** Fire pits only. **Alcoholic Beverages:** At site. **Vehicle Maximum Length:** 45 ft. **Other:** 14-day max. stay limit, Unlawful to clean fish in lakes or streams.

To Get There

From Bend, drive 23.5 mi. south on Hwy. 97, then 12.9 mi. east on Rd. 21 marked as leading to Newberry Caldera; Paulina, East Lakes.

BEND

Crown Villa RV Park

60801 Brosterhouse Rd., Bend 97702. T: (541) 388-1131

RV ★★★★★ Tent ★

Beauty: ★★★★ Site Privacy: ★★
Spaciousness: ★★★★ Quiet: ★★★
Security: ★★ Cleanliness: ★★★★★
Insect Control: ★★ Facilities: ★★★★★

Crown Villa RV Park, off the Hwy. 97/20 Business Loop in Bend, provides a quiet, suburban setting for travelers. Not endowed with many in-house recreational activities, this park has more of an adult feel. The enormous, adjacent RV sites give the impression of camping on a golf course with ponderosa pines providing partial shade. The one common building, a club house and covered porch is equipped with an array of propane grills. There's no privacy between sites, but site sizes make up for this. The best full hookup sites within the grounds, designated 447–458 and 461–471, back up to a fairway-like grassy area; many other sites have similar backyards but these have the largest. On the other hand, sites 601–610 provide a contrast to the rest of the park, as they make up an area of open gravel with electric hookups only. The park also has several tent sites in different areas, also open but with grass surfaces. Both fair weather and winter weather recreation abound in Bend.

Basics

Operated By: Crown Villa. **Open:** All year. **Site Assignment:** On arrival, reservation (required deposit is 1 night's fee; refund w/ 24-hours notice repayed w/ credits for future stay). **Registration:** At office. **Fee:** Full $38.50, electric/cable $33, dry $23, tent $19.25; V, MC, cash. **Parking:** At site.

Facilities

Number of RV-Only Sites: 131. **Number of Tent-Only Sites:** 16. **Hookups:** Electric (30, 50 amps), water, sewer, cable. **Each Site:** Picnic table. **Dump Station:** No. **Laundry:** Yes. **Pay Phone:** Yes. **Rest Rooms and Showers:** Yes. **Fuel:** No. **Propane:** Yes. **Internal Roads:** Paved. **RV Service:** No. **Market:** 2 mi. west on 97. **Restaurant:** 2 mi. west on 97. **General Store:** No. **Vending:** Yes. **Swimming Pool:** No. **Playground:** Yes. **Other:** Club house w/ TV, kitchen, covered BBQ area w/ propane grills (Non-commercial), horseshoes, volleyball, basketball, storage. **Activities:** Lounging. **Nearby Attractions:** City parks, Pilot Butte, Mt. Bachelor (Year-round skiing), Benham Falls, Newberry National Volcanic Monument, Oregon High Desert Museum, every type of outdoor recreation. **Additional Information:** Bend Chamber of Commerce, (541) 382-3221.

Restrictions

Pets: On leash only, no fighting breeds. **Fires:** No open fires. **Alcoholic Beverages:** At site. **Vehicle Maximum Length:** None. **Other:** Only newer (or well maintained) RVs allowed.

To Get There

Driving south on Hwy. 97, turn left on Brosterhouse Rd. (at traffic light near Hollywood Video), follow for 0.8 mi. Brosterhouse turns right (but is poorly marked) just after the Bend Trap Club on the left, continue to follow this road for 0.9 mi., park entrance is on the right.

BEND

Paulina Lake Campground

P.O. Box 989, Bend 97709. T: (541) 383-4001; F: (541) 383-4701; www.fs.fed.us/r6/central oregon/recinfo/camping/paulinalake.html.

RV: ★★★ Tent: ★★★

Beauty: ★★★★	Site Privacy: ★★
Spaciousness: ★★★	Quiet: ★★★★★
Security: ★★	Cleanliness: ★★★
Insect Control: ★★	Facilities: ★

Paulina Lake Campground, located within Newberry National Volcanic Monument, offers a rustic camping experience. No sites within this wilderness area campground have hookups of any sort. Some sites have paved while others have gravel surfaces, and all sites can accept a tent or RV; for tenting one can set up in the flat dirt area just off the parking area of each site. Sites are situated along several loops. Sites sit fairly close together with little privacy for RVs, but some privacy for tents generated by random trees and bushes. The longest sites, 38–53, sit in the back of the campground, near the lake with partial views of the lake and mountains on the opposite shore. Contrary to Forest Service estimates there are a few sites that can take rigs up to 45 feet long. The camground really doesn't have any objectively undesirable sites. Within Newberry National Volcanic Monument there exist four campgrounds, this one and Cinder Hill have the highest capacity for longer rigs. Of the other grounds, Little Crater consists of almost totally lakefront sites along a single straight-away in a secluded cove, East Lake has a mixture of sites positioned around a single loop.

Basics

Operated By: High Lake Contractors for National Forest Service. **Open:** May–Oct. **Site Assignment:** First come, first served. **Registration:** At self pay station. **Fee:** Regular site $10, premium site (usually paved, marked on site signpost) $12; cash. **Parking:** At site.

Facilities

Number of Multipurpose Sites: 68. **Hookups:** None. **Each Site:** Picnic table, fire ring. **Dump Station:** No. **Laundry:** No. **Pay Phone:** No. **Rest Rooms and Showers:** Rest room Only. **Fuel:** No. **Propane:** No. **Internal Roads:** Paved. **RV Service:** No. **Market:** 30 mi. west. **Restaurant:** 30 mi. west. **General Store:** No. **Vending:** No. **Swimming Pool:** No. **Playground:** No. **Other:** Boat ramp, hiking trails. **Activities:** Hiking, biking, swimming, fishing, basking in the sun. **Nearby Attractions:** hiking, biking, fishing, golf, ecotourism in the Bend area, rock climbing. **Additional Information:** Bend Chamber, (541) 382-3221.

Restrictions

Pets: On leash only (max. length 6 ft.). **Fires:** Fire pits only. **Alcoholic Beverages:** At site. **Vehicle Maximum Length:** 45 ft. (listed smaller, but their are some sites w/ larger lengths). **Other:** 14 day max. stay limit, Unlawful to clean fish in lakes or streams.

To Get There

From Bend, drive 23.5 mi. south on Hwy. 97, then 12.9 mi. east on Rte. 21 marked as leading to Newberry Caldera; Paulina, East Lakes.

BONNEVILLE

Eagle Creek Campground

902 Roscoe Ave. Suite 200, Head River 97031. T: (541) 308-1700

RV: ★★★ Tent: ★★★

Beauty: ★★★★	Site Privacy: ★★★★
Spaciousness: ★★★	Quiet: ★★★★
Security: ★★★	Cleanliness: ★★★★
Insect Control: ★★★	Facilities: ★★★

This campground sits just east of the Bonneville Dam. The campground can be easily missed by many Columbia Gorge travelers whose eyes are directed riverward to the massive plant that provides hydroelectric power to the metropolitan areas farther west. Despite its proximity to this hulking tribute to human engineering, Eagle Creek offers a woodsy setting amidst true fir, western red cedar, and hemlock, and provides access to some beautiful walks high above the river in the Columbia Wilderness. The nearby busy freeway quickly fades into oblivion as Eagle Creek Trail leaves the end of FSR 241 beside the campground and follows Eagle Creek for 13 miles to Wahtum Lake and the intersection with Pacific Crest National Scenic Trail. Along the way the trail passes high cliffs along Eagle Creek and waterfalls too numerous to mention. Several other trails and Forest Service roads lead off very near the campground to other points within the Columbia Wilderness.

Basics

Operated By: Mount Hood National Forest. **Open:** May–Oct. **Site Assignment:** First come, first served. **Registration:** self-registration on site. **Fee:** $10. **Parking:** At site.

Facilities

Number of RV-Only Sites: 17. **Number of Tent-Only Sites:** 0. **Hookups:** No. **Each Site:** Picnic table, fire ring & grill. **Dump Station:** No. **Laundry:** No. **Pay Phone:** No. **Rest Rooms and Showers:** Yes. **Fuel:** No. **Propane:** No. **Internal Roads:** Call ahead for details. **RV Service:** No. **Market:** No. **Restaurant:** No. **General Store:** No. **Vending:** No. **Swimming Pool:** No. **Playground:** No. **Activities:** Hiking. **Nearby Attractions:** Cascade Locks, Fort Dalles Museum, Crown Pointe Vista House & Observatory. **Additional Information:** Mt. Hood National Forest, (541) 308-1700.

Restrictions

Pets: On leash only. **Fires:** In fire rings only. **Alcoholic Beverages:** Allowed. **Vehicle Maximum Length:** 22 ft.

To Get There

From Portland, drive 33 mi. east on I-84 to the campground, it is 2 mi. past the town of Bonneville, just off of the interstate.

CANNON BEACH

RV Resort At Cannon Beach

P.O. Box 219, Cannon Beach 97110. T: (503) 436-2231 or (800) 847-2231; www.cbrvresort.com; info@cbrvresort.com.

RV: ★★★★★ Tent: n/a

Beauty: ★★★★	Site Privacy: ★★★
Spaciousness: ★★★	Quiet: ★★★
Security: ★★★	Cleanliness: ★★★★
Insect Control: ★★	Facilities: ★★★★

Just off of 101 on the west side of Cannon Beach sits the RV Resort at Cannon Beach. This well kept campground with plenty of trees provides a quiet escape from the bustle of the nearby resort town. The park has spacious, paved sites surrounded by grass and shaded by medium sized pines, maples and oaks. Quiet can be found in the back of the park in pull-through sites 84–89 and back-in sites 27–35 and 97–100. The campground has good views of the surrounding evergreen dotted hills, and on rainy days, beautiful patches of clouds and mist drift serenely around the tops of these hills. The indoor hot tub is big enough to accomodate a family reunion, and the rec room has two pool tables. This campground has a unique advantage of easy access; a city shuttle stops at the entrance to pick up tourists every half hour, with stops throughout the Cannon Beach area. Best times to visit are just before or after the on season in summer.

Basics

Operated By: RV Resort at Cannon Beach. **Open:** All year. **Site Assignment:** First come, first served; reservation (required deposit is 1st night's stay; refund w/ 72 hours notice). **Registration:** At mini-mart, after hours pay in morning. **Fee:** Summer $34, spring & fall $27, winter $23; fee covers 2 people & 2 vehicles, extra person (age 5 or older) $3, extra vehicle $3; V, MC, cash. **Parking:** At site.

Facilities

Number of RV-Only Sites: 100. **Number of Tent-Only Sites:** 0. **Hookups:** Electric (30, 50 amps), water, sewer, cable, central data port. **Each Site:** Picnic table, fire ring. **Dump Station:** No. **Laundry:** Yes. **Pay Phone:** Yes. **Rest Rooms and Showers:** Yes. **Fuel:** Yes. **Propane:** Yes. **Internal Roads:** Paved. **RV Service:** No. **Market:** Across 101 in Cannon Beach. **Restaurant:** Across 101 in Cannon Beach. **General Store:** Yes. **Vending:** No. **Swimming Pool:** Yes. **Playground:** Yes. **Other:** Reservable meeting room w/ TV, hot tub, basketball court, horseshoe pit, mini-storage, game room w/ 2 pool tables & 3 arcade games, free shuttle to Cannon Beach. **Activities:** Free hot dog roast Saturdays in summer, Thanksgiving potluck. **Nearby Attractions:** Beaches, Haystack Rock, Tillimook Rock Lighthouse, Sandcastle Day. **Additional Information:** Cannon Beach Visitor's Information Center, (503) 436-2623.

Restrictions

Pets: On leash only. **Fires:** Fire pits only. **Alcoholic Beverages:** At site. **Vehicle Maximum Length:** 60 ft. **Other:** Max. 8 people per site.

To Get There

From Hwy. 101, Campground is across from 2nd Cannon Beach Exit, turn (south bound-left) onto Sunset Blvd. After 200 feet turn left into entrance.

CANNON BEACH

Saddle Mountain State Park

P.O. Box 681, Cannon Beach 97110. T: (503) 368-5943

RV: n/a Tent: ★★

Beauty: ★★ Site Privacy: ★★★
Spaciousness: ★★ Quiet: ★★
Security: ★★ Cleanliness: ★
Insect Control: ★★★ Facilities: ★★★

Want to enjoy the beach, see the mountains, and not get trampled by the crowds? Saddle Mountain is the answer. You have the best of both worlds at Saddle Mountain because you'll be less than 15 miles from the nearest coastal attractions of Cannon Beach and Seaside, well away from the crowded Coast Highway corridor, and only a 2.6-mile hike from superb views atop the highest peak in northwestern Oregon. Add to that a campground (albeit primitive) that is for tent campers only and nearly 3,000 acres of forests, with meadows, and creeks that you'll share with a number of woodland critters and several rare and endangered plant species. Saddle Mountain was a haven for certain species of plant life during the Ice Age, and much of the flora that has evolved today high on the flanks of this 3,283-foot peak is not found anywhere else. Alpine wildflowers put on one of the best shows of colors in the region in early to mid-June.

Basics

Operated By: Oregon State Parks & Recreation. **Open:** Apr.–Oct. (depending on snow). **Site Assignment:** First come, first served, no reservations. **Registration:** self-registration on site. **Fee:** $10. **Parking:** At site.

Facilities

Number of RV-Only Sites: 0. **Number of Tent-Only Sites:** 10. **Hookups:** None. **Each Site:** Picnic table, fire pit, piped water. **Dump Station:** No. **Laundry:** No. **Pay Phone:** No. **Rest Rooms and Showers:** Vault toilets. **Fuel:** No. **Propane:** No. **Internal Roads:** Call ahead for details. **RV Service:** No. **Market:** No. **Restaurant:** No. **General Store:** No. **Vending:** No. **Swimming Pool:** No. **Playground:** No. **Activities:** Hiking. **Nearby Attractions:** Del Rey Beach, Hug Point, Arcadia Beach. **Additional Information:** Cannon Beach Visitor's Information Center, (503) 436-2623.

Restrictions

Pets: On leash only. **Fires:** In fire rings only. **Alcoholic Beverages:** Allowed. **Vehicle Maximum Length:** None. **Other:** No accommodations for RVs or trailers, but self-contained units are allowed in the parking lot.

To Get There

Turn north on Saddle Mountain Rd. off of US 26 about 1.5 mi. east of Necanicum Junction. Drive 7 mi. to the campground.

CASCADE LOCKS

Ainsworth State Park Campground

P.O. Box 100, Corbett 97019. T: (503) 695-2301 or (503) 695-2261; www.oregonstateparks.org.

RV: ★★★ Tent: ★★★

Beauty: ★★★★ Site Privacy: ★★
Spaciousness: ★★ Quiet: ★
Security: ★★ Cleanliness: ★★★
Insect Control: ★★ Facilities: ★★★

Ainsworth State Park, in the Columbia River Scenic Area east of Portland off I-84, provides a scenic location on the Oregon side of the gorge. This beautiful wooded campground has paved, terraced pull-throughs and a row of paved back-ins under the shade of cottonwoods and out-of-place coastal pines. The more spacious terraced sites, numbered A1–13, have tree-obscured views of surrounding cliffs. Facilities are limited in scope, and like all campgrounds in the gorge, train tracks run past the park to the north of the grounds. Still, Ainsworth is the quietest state park in the gorge. The few walk-in tent sites provide little privacy from other tenters, but are positioned away from the rest of the grounds. The loudest sites, the paved back-ins, sit closest to the railroad tracks, numbered B1-32.

Basics

Operated By: Oregon State Parks & Recreation. **Open:** Mar. 16–the end of Oct. **Site Assignment:** First come, first served. **Registration:** At self pay station. **Fee:** Full $20, walk-in tent $13; V, MC, check, cash. **Parking:** At site.

Facilities

Number of RV-Only Sites: 42. **Number of Tent-Only Sites:** 5. **Hookups:** Electric (20, 30 amps), water, sewer, cable. **Each Site:** Picnic table, fire ring. **Dump Station:** Yes. **Laundry:** No. **Pay Phone:** No. **Rest Rooms and Showers:** Yes. **Fuel:** No. **Propane:** No. **Internal Roads:** Paved. **RV Service:** No. **Market:** 10 mile east in Cascade Locks. **Restaurant:** 10 mi. east in Cascade Locks. **General Store:** No. **Vending:** No. **Swimming Pool:** No. **Playground:** Yes. **Other:** Small Amphitheater, hiking trails. **Activities:** Seasonal interpretive programs, hiking, picnicking. **Nearby Attractions:** Bonneville Dam, Columbia Gorge Interpretive Center, Cascade Locks, hiking trails, Multnomah Falls. **Additional Information:** Portland Oregon Visitor's Assoc., 1-87-Portland.

Restrictions

Pets: On leash only (max. length 6 ft.). **Fires:** Fire pits only. **Alcoholic Beverages:** At site. **Vehicle Maximum Length:** 55 ft. **Other:** No firewood collecting.

To Get There

From I-84 Exit 35 turn right (south) off of ramp, access road dead-ends after 0.2 mi.; turn left and drive 0.2 mi.; entrance to campground is on the left marked with a sign.

CASCADE LOCKS

Cascade Locks KOA

841 Northwest Forest Ln., Cascade Locks 97014. T: (541) 374-8668

RV: ★★★ Tent: ★★★

Beauty: ★★★ Site Privacy: ★
Spaciousness: ★★★ Quiet: ★
Security: ★★ Cleanliness: ★★★
Insect Control: ★★ Facilities: ★★★

Cascade Locks KOA, located just a few miles off I-84 in the riverside hamlet of Cascade Locks, provides quick access to nearby manmade and natural wonders. Located in the heart of the Columbia River Gorge, this campground lacks views of the actual gorge, but has a view of its surrounding hills in Oregon. The wooded park, heavily shaded and colored by tall green Douglas firs, mossy oaks, and maples, sits next to a wood mill whose slight yet constant hum does not distract the peace-seeking camper as much as the nearby railroad track. The RV sites, both paved and gravel, afford little privacy, nor do the tent sites with the minimal exception of T21 and T16. Sites are arranged in a hodgepodge of rows, and the best RV sites with a view, 61–65 and 68–71, sit near the pool. The game room has several early-1990s video games. The playground has several pieces of equipment but also gets muddy.

Basics

Operated By: Cascade Locks KOA. **Open:** Feb.–Nov. **Site Assignment:** First come, first served; reservation (required deposit is 1 night's fee; refund w/ 72 hours notice). **Registration:** At office, after hours at drop box in front of office. **Fee:** Full: $28, water/electric: $27, tent $16; fee covers 2 people, extra person $3; V, MC, AE, D, check, cash. **Parking:** At site.

Facilities

Number of RV-Only Sites: 77. **Number of Tent-Only Sites:** 30. **Hookups:** Electric (20, 30,

50 amps), water, sewer, cable. **Each Site:** Picnic table, fire ring. **Dump Station:** Yes. **Laundry:** Yes. **Pay Phone:** Yes. **Rest Rooms and Showers:** Yes. **Fuel:** No. **Propane:** Yes. **Internal Roads:** Paved & gravel. **RV Service:** No. **Market:** 1 mile west. **Restaurant:** 1 mi. west. **General Store:** Yes. **Vending:** Yes. **Swimming Pool:** Yes. **Playground:** Yes. **Other:** Hot tub, rental cabins, arcade, meeting room. **Activities:** swimming, hot tubbing. **Nearby Attractions:** Cascade Locks, Bonneville Dam, Bridge of the Gods, The Sternwheeler, Columbia Gorge Scenic Highway. **Additional Information:** Portland Oregon Visitor's Assoc. 1-87-Portland.

Restrictions

Pets: On leash only, no more than 2 dogs. **Fires:** Fire pits only. **Alcoholic Beverages:** At site only. **Vehicle Maximum Length:** None. **Other:** No operating of mini bikes or dirt bikes; No fireworks or firearms.

To Get There

From I-84 Exit 44, the off-ramp becomes an unnamed road. Drive 0.75 mi. on this road and then turn left on Forest Ln. Follow Forest Ln. for 1 mi.; the entrance is on the left.

CASCADE SUMMIT

Princess Creek Campground

P.O. Box 208, Crecent 97733. T: (541) 433-3200; F: (541) 433-3224; www.fs.fed.us/r6/central oregon/recinfo/camping/princesscreek.html.

RV ★★★ Tent ★★★★

Beauty: ★★★★★ Site Privacy: ★★★
Spaciousness: ★★★ Quiet: ★★★★
Security: ★ Cleanliness: ★★★
Insect Control: ★★ Facilities: ★

Princess Creek Campground, off Hwy. 58 and on the shores of Odell Lake, provides a no-frills alternative to camping in the area. The grounds don't have flush toilets, but there is potable water. Shaded by tall firs, the campground has a woodland feel and easy access to the lake. Organized into two loops, with sites on both sides of the road, the best dirt sites sit on the shoreline and just across the access road to the shore. These are numbered 12–32. Sites not on or near the lakefront sit near Hwy. 58, a road heavily traveled during the day but quiet at night. Summers provide the best time to visit, with fishing and good weather.

Basics

Operated By: Recreation Resource Management. for National Forest Service. **Open:** May–Oct. (weather permitting). **Site Assignment:** On arrival. **Registration:** At self pay station. **Fee:** Regular site $10, Lakefront $12, second vehicle $12; in-state check, cash. **Parking:** At site.

Facilities

Number of Multipurpose Sites: 45. **Hookups:** None. **Each Site:** Picnic table, fire ring. **Dump Station:** No. **Laundry:** No. **Pay Phone:** No. **Rest Rooms and Showers:** Non flush, No showers. **Fuel:** No. **Propane:** No. **Internal Roads:** Paved. **RV Service:** No. **Market:** 7 mi. east on Hwy. 58. **Restaurant:** 7 mi. east on Hwy. 58. **General Store:** No. **Vending:** No. **Swimming Pool:** No. **Playground:** No. **Other:** Boat ramp. **Activities:** Fishing, boating, hiking. **Nearby Attractions:** Inquire at campground. **Additional Information:** www.fs.fed.us/r6/centraloregon/recinfo/camping/princesscreek.html.

Restrictions

Pets: On leash only (max. length 6 ft.). **Fires:** Fire pits only per fire conditions. **Alcoholic Beverages:** At site. **Vehicle Maximum Length:** 50 ft. **Other:** Harvest dead & down wood only, no chainsaw operation, no fish cleaning in lake, 14 day stay limit.

To Get There

From Hwy. 58 westbound, entrance on left between mile 63 and mile 65.

CASCADE SUMMIT

Shelter Cove Resort and Marina

West Odell Lake Rd., Cascade Summit 97425. T: (541) 433-2548; www.sheltercoveresort.com; sheltercov@coinet.com.

RV ★★★ Tent ★★★

Beauty: ★★★★★ Site Privacy: ★★
Spaciousness: ★★★ Quiet: ★★★★
Security: ★★ Cleanliness: ★★★
Insect Control: ★★ Facilities: ★★★

Shelter Cove Resort and Marina, on the shore of Odell Lake in the Central Cascades and off Hwy. 58, provides excellent fishing opportunities in a quiet, shady, woodland setting. The grounds house many seasonal travelers that stay and fish the lake all summer. Semi private gravel and dirt sites within the grounds sit off three loops, but the best sites 29–33 and 38–47 lack good views of the lake, though they have more individual privacy than the rest of the sites. Sites 5–8A have good views of the lake and some privacy but sit near a high traffic area (for fishermen rush hour equals dawn). Avoid sites 9–12 and 23–28, they have a cramped feel without much privacy. Common areas have an open, spacious feel and the scenery is both lovely and rustic. In late July and early August, expect to see thru-hikers in the area coming off the Pacific Crest Trail. Summer necessitates reservations, walk up availability doesn't really exist here.

Basics

Operated By: Shelter Cove Resort on Forest Service land. **Open:** Apr. 1–Oct. 30 or first snow fall. **Site Assignment:** On arrival, reservations highly recommended (required deposit is 1 night's stay or a third of stays longer than 4 days; refund less $10 w/ 10-days notice or 30-days notice for stays 2 weeks or longer). **Registration:** At office during business hours only unless w/ a reservation, w/ reservation info left outside. **Fee:** Non-electric RV or tent $12; extra sleeping units $10 (non-electric) or $19 (electric); moorage $10 per day; V, MC, AE, D, check, cash. **Parking:** At site, limited off site.

Facilities

Number of Multipurpose Sites: 20. **Number of RV-Only Sites:** 40. **Number of Tent-Only Sites:** 0. **Hookups:** Electric (30 amps). **Each Site:** Picnic table, fire ring. **Dump Station:** Yes. **Laundry:** Yes. **Pay Phone:** Yes. **Rest Rooms and Showers:** Yes. **Fuel:** No. **Propane:** Yes. **Internal Roads:** Gravel. **RV Service:** No. **Market:** 9 mi. east. **Restaurant:** 9 mi. east. **General Store:** Yes. **Vending:** No. **Swimming Pool:** No. **Playground:** No. **Other:** Large fish freezer for storage of catch, fish cleaning station, power boat rentals, horseshoes, community fire pit, marine gasoline, boat launch, tons of moorage. **Activities:** Fishing, hiking, boating, cross country skiing in winter, occasional planned activities. **Nearby Attractions:** Fishing, hiking, boating, skiing, city of Eugene, lots of wilderness, Deshutes National Forest. **Additional Information:** Klamath County Dept. of Tourism, (800) 445-6732.

Restrictions

Pets: On leash only. **Fires:** Fire pits only. **Alcoholic Beverages:** Not allowed inside public buildings. **Vehicle Maximum Length:** None. **Other:** Quiet hours 10 p.m.–6 a.m.

To Get There

From Hwy. 58 west bound, turn left between mile 62 and 63 onto West Odell Lake Access Rd., drive 2 mi. and the entrance is on the left.

CHILOQUIN

Head of the River Campground

38500 Hwy. 97 North, Chiloquin 97624. T: (541) 783-4001

RV ★★★ Tent ★★

Beauty: ★★★★ Site Privacy: ★★
Spaciousness: ★★★★ Quiet: ★★★★
Security: ★★ Cleanliness: ★★★
Insect Control: ★★★ Facilities: ★★★

This campground is one of those little-known, out-of-the-way camping spots locals are afraid to trumpet because some sly, outdoor writer might include it in a guidebook. Located in the Winema National Forest, Visitors are more likely to encounter wildlife than fellow campers while staying at these rustic sites. Drinking water should be carried-in; otherwise, treat water available from the Williamson River. There is not much out here on this tableland of ponderosa pine, lodgepole pine, and assorted conifers except excellent trout fishing in the Williamson River and a crazy contingent of Forest Service roads that wander around the numerous buttes and flats. This area is relatively dry year-round. However, there is enough groundwater seeping to the surface from natural springs that wildflowers, such as fireweed, foxglove, lupine, and dandelion, line the banks of tiny creeks that quickly dry up after spring.

Basics

Operated By: Winema National Forest, Klamath Ranger District. **Open:** May–Oct. (depending on weather). **Site Assignment:** First come, first served, no reservations. **Registration:** not necessary. **Fee:** none. **Parking:** At site.

Facilities

Number of RV-Only Sites: 6. **Number of Tent-Only Sites:** 0. **Hookups:** No. **Each Site:** Picnic table, fire grill. **Dump Station:** No. **Laundry:** No.

Pay Phone: No. **Rest Rooms and Showers:** Vault toilets. **Fuel:** No. **Propane:** No. **Internal Roads:** Call ahead for details. **RV Service:** No. **Market:** No. **Restaurant:** No. **General Store:** No. **Vending:** No. **Swimming Pool:** No. **Playground:** No. **Activities:** Fishing, hunting, hiking. **Nearby Attractions:** Inquire at campground. **Additional Information:** Klamath County Dept. of Tourism, (800) 445-6730.

Restrictions

Pets: On leash only. **Fires:** In fire rings only. **Alcoholic Beverages:** Allowed. **Vehicle Maximum Length:** 30 ft.

To Get There

Take Sprague River Hwy. northeast out of Chiloquin. Take a left onto Williamson River Hwy. at a about the 5-mi. point. Turn left onto FS 4648 the campground is 1 mi. on the left.

CHILOQUIN

The Waterwheel Campground

200 Williamson River Dr., Chiloquin 97624. T: (541) 783-2738

RV: ★★★ | Tent: ★★

Beauty: ★★★ | Site Privacy: ★
Spaciousness: ★★ | Quiet: ★★
Security: ★★ | Cleanliness: ★★★★
Insect Control: ★★ | Facilities: ★★★

The Waterwheel Campground, on Hwy. 97 in the sparse outskirts of rural Chiloquin, offers an excellent location on the Williamson River for fishing and day trips to Crater Lake. The property is laid out in several parallel rows of sites. The best gravel full hookups sit in the middle of the park with some shade, pull-throughs numbered 1–6. There are some riverfront water/electric sites with nice views of the river and surrounding countryside, but not much shade. The grounds come complete with decorative, antiquated farm equipment. Located across a small bridge over the clear, brown-bottomed river stands a small island for tent camping, novel but not particularly flat in the shadiest areas of the island. Summers here can be intensely hot so plan for a high sun magnitude or visit at the beginning of the summer for the best experience.

Basics

Operated By: The Waterwheel Campground. **Open:** All year. **Site Assignment:** On arrival, reservation (required deposit is 1 night's fee; refund w/ 48-hours notice). **Registration:** At office, after hours drop in front of office. **Fee:** Full $22, water/electric $19, tent $16; fee covers 2 people, extra person (age 5 or older) $1.50. **Parking:** At site.

Facilities

Number of RV-Only Sites: 28. **Number of Tent-Only Sites:** 6. **Hookups:** Electric (30, 50 amps), water, sewer. **Each Site:** Picnic table, fire ring. **Dump Station:** Yes. **Laundry:** Yes. **Pay Phone:** Yes. **Rest Rooms and Showers:** Yes. **Fuel:** No. **Propane:** Yes. **Internal Roads:** Gravel. **RV Service:** No. **Market:** 4 mi. north. **Restaurant:** Across street. **General Store:** Yes. **Vending:** Yes. **Swimming Pool:** No. **Playground:** Yes. **Other:** Horseshoes, boat ramp, fish cleaning station, rec room, boat dock. **Activities:** Fishing, boating. **Nearby Attractions:** Crater Lake National Park, city of Klamath Falls, fishing, boating. **Additional Information:** Klamath County Dept. of Tourism, (800) 445-6730.

Restrictions

Pets: On leash only. **Fires:** Fire pits only. **Alcoholic Beverages:** At site. **Vehicle Maximum Length:** 88 ft. **Other:** Quiet hours 10 p.m.–9 a.m., do not park on roadways.

To Get There

From Hwy. 97 (north-bound turn left) between mile 251 and 253 onto Williamson River Dr., entrance to park immediately on left.

COO'S BAY

Bastendorff Beach Campground

181 South Broadway, Coos Bay 97420. T: (541) (888) 5353; www.co.coos.or.us/ccpark/main.html.

RV: ★★★ | Tent: ★★★★

Beauty: ★★★ | Site Privacy: ★★★
Spaciousness: ★★ | Quiet: ★★★★
Security: ★ | Cleanliness: ★★★
Insect Control: ★★ | Facilities: ★★

Situated on the Pacific Ocean, this campground might be the perfect spot for recreation and relaxation. This 89-acre park provides easy access to the most desirable forms of natural entertainment. Navigate one of the scenic rivers or hike in the deep wilderness forest nearby. Catch a glimpse of a passing pod of whales as you enjoy the beaches and the ocean view. You will find great lake and river fishing and a convenient station to clean all of your day's catch. With picnic shelters, kitchens, and a large fire pit for grilling, you are sure to find plenty of the amenities you need to feel at home. Don't forget to let the kids visit the unique playground area. With a variety of activities along the spectrum of outdoor interests, this campground makes a great place for a family vacation, reunion, or group event.

Basics

Operated By: Coos County Parks & Recreation. **Open:** All year. **Site Assignment:** First come, first served. **Registration:** At self pay station by vending machines. **Fee:** Water/electric $14, tent $10; extra vehicle $5; cash, check. **Parking:** At site.

Facilities

Number of RV-Only Sites: 56. **Number of Tent-Only Sites:** 25. **Hookups:** Electric (20, 30 amps), water, sewer, cable. **Each Site:** Picnic table, fire pit. **Dump Station:** Yes. **Laundry:** No. **Pay Phone:** Yes. **Rest Rooms and Showers:** Yes. **Fuel:** No. **Propane:** No. **Internal Roads:** Paved. **RV Service:** No. **Market:** 5 mi. north in Florence. **Restaurant:** 5 mi. North in Florence. **General Store:** No. **Vending:** Yes. **Swimming Pool:** No. **Playground:** No. **Other:** Basketball goal, horseshoe pit, pavilion w/ view of ocean, cabins, fish cleaning station. **Activities:** Hiking, picnicking, cleaning fish, horseshoes, basketball. **Nearby Attractions:** Charter fishing, Myrtlewood factories & shops, The Mill Resort & Casino, Oregon Dunes National Recreation Area, ATV rentals. **Additional Information:** Bay Area Chamber of Commerce, (800) 824-8486.

Restrictions

Pets: On leash only. **Fires:** Fire pits only. **Alcoholic Beverages:** At site. **Vehicle Maximum Length:** 45 ft. **Other:** Check out by 2 p.m.

To Get There

From Hwy. 101 in downtown Coo's Bay, turn west (right from 101 southbound) onto Commercial Ave. Veer left when road forks at Dairy Queen, then immediatly right onto Central Ave. Drive 0.3 mi. and turn right at a yellow caution flasher; the road becomes Ocean Blvd. Drive 2.6 mi. to a red light, where the road dead ends; turn left onto Newmark Ave. Drive 0.5 mi.; at a yellow caution flasher turn left onto Empire Blvd. Continue 7 mi. on through Charleston. Turn right at a big sign for the park and the entrance is on the right atop the hill.

CRATER LAKE NATIONAL PARK

Manzama Campground

P.O.Box 158, Crater Lake 97604. T: (541) 594-2511 ex. 3705; www.crater-lake.com.

RV: ★★★ | Tent: ★★★★★

Beauty: ★★★★★ | Site Privacy: ★★★
Spaciousness: ★★★ | Quiet: ★★★★
Security: ★★ | Cleanliness: ★★★★
Insect Control: ★★ | Facilities: ★★★

Manzama Campground, concessionaire campground to Crater Lake National Park, has an excellent location for exploring all of the park's natural wonders. The campground is laid out in seven loops backing up to a canyon. There are a few sites with electric hookups, but most have no hookups. RV sites are pull-throughs (tent sites are back-ins) parallel, rather than perpendicular, to access roads. All sites have lots of room and some privacy. The campground has a very natural feel with lots of shade and foliage. Loops C and D have the best RV sites with lots of shade and some particularly large intrasite areas. The tenter-only G loop provides privacy for tenters with buffering shrubs and shady pines. RV-loop parking areas have gravel surfaces, while soft dirt is the rule for tents sites. Be aware that sites on the back perimeters of all loops sit on the edge of the canyon.

Basics

Operated By: Estey Corp. for National Park Service. **Open:** Jun.–n–Sept. (snow melt–snow fall). **Site Assignment:** First come, first served. **Registration:** At kiosk, after hours pay in morning. **Fee:** RV $17, RV w/ electric $19, tent $15; fee covers 2 people, extra adult (18 or older) $3.50, max. site occupancy is 6 adults; V, MC, cash. **Parking:** At site.

Facilities

Number of RV-Only Sites: 84. **Number of Tent-Only Sites:** 143. **Hookups:** Electric (30 amps). **Each Site:** Picnic table, fire ring. **Dump Station:** Yes. **Laundry:** Yes. **Pay Phone:** Yes. **Rest Rooms and Showers:** Yes. **Fuel:** Yes. **Propane:** No. **Internal Roads:** Narrow paved. **RV Service:** No. **Market:** On site, limited groceries. **Restaurant:** 7 mi. North. **General Store:** Yes. **Vending:** No. **Swimming Pool:** No. **Playground:** No. **Other:** Amphitheater (interpretive programs). **Activities:** Hiking, interpretive programs, Jr. Ranger programs. **Nearby Attractions:** City of Klamath Falls, hiking, fishing, boating, National Park programs & facilities. **Additional Information:** Klamath County Dept. of Tourism, (800) 445-6728.

Restrictions

Pets: On leash only, not allowed on any trails. **Fires:** Fireplaces only. **Alcoholic Beverages:** At site. **Vehicle Maximum Length:** 42 ft. **Other:** Store food & food paraphernalia in vehicles Do not leave any food or cookware in open.

To Get There

From the south entrance of the National Park (Hwy. 62), the campground is on the right just past the entrance gate

DETROIT

Elk Lake Campground

HC 73 Box 320, Mill City 97360. T: (503) 854-3366

RV ★★★★ Tent ★★★

Beauty: ★★★★★ Site Privacy: ★★★★
Spaciousness: ★★★★★ Quiet: ★★★★★
Security: ★★★ Cleanliness: ★★★★
Insect Control: ★★★ Facilities: ★★★

The word "foolhardy" may come to mind as you find yourself at the junction that leads to this gem of a spot in Willamette National Forest, about ten miles above the small, historic burg of Detroit. The road is decidedly rough but not impassable. As long as your exhaust system and oil pan sit high and secure, you should be okay. Elk Lake's campsites are strung along the shore of the lake. Tall stands of Douglas fir and western hemlock share the land with white fir, birches, Oregon grape, ferns, and trillium to offer a prime collection of natural cover. This campground may be tough to get to, but once you're there, peaceful Elk Lake makes for a terrific base camp while you enjoy the recreational options. For anyone who brings a boat into this remote area, Elk Lake is a nice spot to take in lazy kayaking or canoeing.

Basics

Operated By: Willamette National Forest. **Open:** Jul.–Sept. **Site Assignment:** First come, first served, no reservations. **Registration:** not necessary. **Fee:** none. **Parking:** At site, in parking lot, 4x4 recommended.

Facilities

Number of RV-Only Sites: 14. **Number of Tent-Only Sites:** 0. **Hookups:** No. **Each Site:** Picnic table, fire pit w/ grill. **Dump Station:** No. **Laundry:** No. **Pay Phone:** No. **Rest Rooms and Showers:** Vault toilets. **Fuel:** No. **Propane:** No. **Internal Roads:** Call ahead for details. **RV Service:** No. **Market:** No. **Restaurant:** No. **General Store:** No. **Vending:** No. **Swimming Pool:** No. **Playground:** No. **Activities:** Fishing, hiking, non-motorized boating. **Nearby Attractions:** Battle Ax Mt., Mount Beachie. **Additional Information:** (503) 854-3366.

Restrictions

Pets: On leash only. **Fires:** In fire rings only. **Alcoholic Beverages:** Allowed. **Vehicle Maximum Length:** None. **Other:** No low clearance RVs, no trash collection, fishing license required.

To Get There

From Detroit, drive north on FS 46 for 4.5 mi. to FS 4697. Follow this for 10 mi. to the campground. Stay to the left fork where FS 4697 and FS 4696 intersect at about 8 mi. The last 2 mi. are extremely rough.

DIAMOND LAKE

Diamond Lake Campground

2020 Toketee Ranger Station Rd., Idleyld Park 97447. T: (541) 498-2531; www.fs.fed.us/r6/umpqua/rec/cmp_gnd/cg3diaml.html.

RV ★★★ Tent ★★★★

Beauty: ★★★★★ Site Privacy: ★★★
Spaciousness: ★★★ Quiet: ★★★★
Security: ★★ Cleanliness: ★★★★
Insect Control: ★★ Facilities: ★

Diamond Lake Campground, located about ten minutes off Hwy. 230 on the shores of Diamond Lake, provides a particularly beautiful view of the summer sunset over the lake and mountains opposite the campground. This huge National Forest Campground covers over three miles of shoreline, but only has about six showers per gender, although more claim to be in the works and the existing ones are free (a rarity in campgrounds on publicly owned lands). The campground is organized into several loops diverging from a main access road which runs the span of the grounds. Sites have no hookups and can accept either a tent or RV. The best gravel-parking sites are on L loop with less site density, more shade, seclusion, and beautiful views. This is followed by K loop, which offers better than average space between sites. Loops M and G have the highest density with more open sites.

Basics

Operated By: National Forest Service. **Open:** May 15–Oct. 31 (weather permitting). **Site Assignment:** First come, first served; reservation (required deposit is 1 night's fee; refund w/ 72-hours notice less a $10 service charge. **Registration:** At office/entrance gate; After hours see notice posted at window, pay in morning. **Fee:** Regular site $10, shoreline $15, multiparty $20; cash upon arrival. **Parking:** At site, limited off site.

Facilities

Number of Multipurpose Sites: 238. **Hookups:** None. **Each Site:** Picnic table; Fire ring. **Dump Station:** Yes. **Laundry:** No. **Pay Phone:** Yes. **Rest Rooms and Showers:** Yes. **Fuel:** No. **Propane:** No. **Internal Roads:** Paved. **RV Service:** No. **Market:** Small, nearby. **Restaurant:** Nearby, at a hotel. **General Store:** No. **Vending:** No. **Swimming Pool:** No. **Playground:** No. **Other:** Paved bike trails, Amphitheater, fish cleaning stations, boat ramp. **Activities:** Hiking, fishing, boating, biking, interpretive programs on weekends. **Nearby Attractions:** Crater Lake National Park, Douglas County Museum, Umpqua Valley Wineries, Roseburg, rafting, fishing, biking, covered bridges. **Additional Information:** Douglas County Information, (541) 672-3311.

Restrictions

Pets: On leash only (max. length 6 ft.). **Fires:** Fire pits only. **Alcoholic Beverages:** At site. **Vehicle Maximum Length:** 40 ft. **Other:** Quiet hours 10 p.m.–6 a.m.

To Get There

Located 80 mi. east of Roseburg on Hwy. 138, turn right onto Rd. 4795 (Diamond Lake Loop) at the north entrance to Diamond Lake Recreation Area. Proceed 2.5 mi. to the campground entrance. Diamond Lake may also be accessed via Hwy. 230 from Medford, or Hwy. 97 from Klamath Falls and Bend.

DIAMOND LAKE

Diamond Lake RV Resort

3500 Diamond Lake Loop, Diamond Lake 97731. T: (541) 793-3318; F: (541) 793-3088. www.diamondlakervpark.com.

RV ★★★ Tent n/a

Beauty: ★★★★ Site Privacy: ★
Spaciousness: ★★ Quiet: ★★★★
Security: ★★ Cleanliness: ★★★
Insect Control: ★★ Facilities: ★★

Diamond Lake RV Park, off of Hwy. 230 right at the 138/230 junction, offers full hookups in a beautiful natural recreation area. Sites sit in several lettered sections, some on islands and some on loops. The grounds are ungroomed, with some grass but more dirt. There exists a reasonable amount of shade provided by firs and pines, and the grounds retain the woodland feel characteristic of the area. All sites have gravel parking surfaces, but some have potholes and hills. The nicest back-in sites sit in section W, particularly sites 1–7 and 31–34. The whole section has the most space as well as good foliage for privacy and shade. The worst sections, H and F, have a cramped feel with not as much shade. There is a laundry facility, but it is quite basic.

Basics

Operated By: Diamond Lake RV Park on National Forest Service land. **Open:** May–Oct. 1. **Site Assignment:** On arrival, reservation (required deposit is 1 night's stay or $25 for an extended stay; refund less $3 w/ 48-hours notice). **Registration:** At office. **Fee:** Full $23.20; fee covers 2 people, extra adult $2, extra child (ages 2–15) $1, max. site occupancy is1 family or 6 people; V, MC, cash. **Parking:** At site.

Facilities

Number of RV-Only Sites: 100. **Number of Tent-Only Sites:** 0. **Hookups:** Electric (30, 50

amps), water, sewer. **Each Site:** Picnic table, grated fire pits. **Dump Station:** Yes. **Laundry:** Yes. **Pay Phone:** Yes. **Rest Rooms and Showers:** Yes. **Fuel:** No. **Propane:** Yes. **Internal Roads:** Narrow paved. **RV Service:** No. **Market:** Across street. **Restaurant:** Across street. **General Store:** No. **Vending:** No. **Swimming Pool:** No. **Playground:** No. **Other:** Movie rentals, horseshoes, BBQ grills for loan (charcoal). **Activities:** Inquire at campground. **Nearby Attractions:** Diamond Lake, Crater Lake National Park, Umpqua National Forest, river rafting (Roseburg), fishing, city of Klamath Falls. **Additional Information:** Douglas County Information, (541) 672-3311.

Restrictions

Pets: On leash only, no loud or vicious dogs. **Fires:** Fire pits only. **Alcoholic Beverages:** At site. **Vehicle Maximum Length:** 45 ft. **Other:** No tents, check w/ office before cutting firewood.

To Get There

The campground is located 80 mi. east of Roseburg on Hwy. 138, or 85 mi. from Medford on Hwys. 62 and 230. The north entrance of Crater Lake National Park is 6 mi. south of Diamond Lake.

DIAMOND LAKE

Thielsen View Campground

2020 Toketez Ranger Station Rd., Idlewyld Park 97447. T: (541) 498-2531; www.fs.fed.us/r6/umpqua/rec/cmp_gnd/cg3diaml.html.

RV ★★★★ Tent ★★★★

Beauty: ★★★★★ Site Privacy: ★★★★
Spaciousness: ★★★★★ Quiet: ★★★★★
Security: ★★★★ Cleanliness: ★★★★★
Insect Control: ★★★ Facilities: ★★★

With two other campgrounds across scenic Diamond Lake that can accommodate several hundred campers between them, chances are you won't find yourself alone out in this remote territory. However, this spacious campground offers a relatively private stay. Diamond Lake is an immensely popular area, particularly for trout fishermen, who troll the lake's crystalline waters. Great fishing notwithstanding, Diamond Lake's popularity can be attributed to a number of other factors. For starters, it is one of the largest natural lakes in Oregon. Add to this its proximity to some spectacular mountain scenery, and follow that up with blissfully warm, dry summer weather. Last but not least, factor in the proximity of Crater Lake National Park to the south. The area is a fantastic natural playgrounds that can turn the most resolute vacation planner into a miserable heap of indecision. The facilities here are limited, as is the norm in this national forest, but you won't need to spend a lot of time in the campground.

Basics

Operated By: Umpqua National Forest. **Open:** May 15–Sept. 15. **Site Assignment:** First come, first served, no reservation. **Registration:** self-registration on site. **Fee:** $9. **Parking:** At site.

Facilities

Number of Multipurpose Sites: 60. **Hookups:** Water. **Each Site:** Picnic table, fire ring & grill. **Dump Station:** No. **Laundry:** No. **Pay Phone:** No. **Rest Rooms and Showers:** Vault toilets. **Fuel:** No. **Propane:** No. **Internal Roads:** Gravel **RV Service:** No. **Market:** No. **Restaurant:** No. **General Store:** No. **Vending:** No. **Swimming Pool:** No. **Playground:** No. **Activities:** Hiking, fishing, hunting, bird-watching, biking, canoeing, kayaking. **Nearby Attractions:** Crater Lake, North Umpqua River. **Additional Information:** Douglas County Information, (541) 672-3311.

Restrictions

Pets: On leash only. **Fires:** In fire rings only. **Alcoholic Beverages:** Allowed. **Vehicle Maximum Length:** 30 ft.

To Get There

From Roseburg and I-5, take SR 138 east/southeast to Clearwater (about 50 mi.), at Clearwater the road leaves the North Umpqua and parallels Clearwater River. At the intersection with FS 4795, turn right and go around the north end of Diamond Lake to find the campground.

EUGENE

Eugene Kamping World RV Park

90932 South Stuart Way, Coburg 97408. T: (541) 343-4832 or (800)343-3008; F: (541) 343-5313.

RV ★★ Tent ★★

Beauty: ★★ Site Privacy: ★
Spaciousness: ★★ Quiet: ★★
Security: ★★ Cleanliness: ★★
Insect Control: ★★ Facilities: ★★★

Eugene Kamping World RV Park, located ten minutes north of downtown Eugene, provides vistas of the high, rolling hills on the eastern edge of the Willamette Valley. The grounds consist of a triangular arrangement with several rows of sites. The interior of the grounds lacks vegetation save the grass in between sites and a few flowering hardwoods, but the views from pull-through section D and pull-through sites C7–13 distract one's attention from the meager groundcover. The aforementioned paved sections have water and electric hookups. The best full hookup sites (paved) are E6–11. The lumpy grass and dirt tent sites T2–8 have some privacy created by wooden fences, the remainder of tent sites are in an open field. Essential facilities stay clean and well maintained.

Basics

Operated By: Eugene Kamping World. **Open:** All year. **Site Assignment:** First come, first served; reservation (required deposit is 1 night's stay; refund w/ 24-hours notice). **Registration:** At office, after hours at night drop box in front of office. **Fee:** Full $22, water/electric $19.50, tents $15; fee covers 2 people & 2 vehicles, extra person (age 5 or older) $1.50, extra vehicle $1; V, MC, cash. **Parking:** At site.

Facilities

Number of RV-Only Sites: 110. **Number of Tent-Only Sites:** 40. **Hookups:** Electric (20, 30, 50 amps), water, sewer, cable. **Each Site:** Picnic table. **Dump Station:** Yes. **Laundry:** Yes. **Pay Phone:** Yes. **Rest Rooms and Showers:** Yes. **Fuel:** No. **Propane:** Yes. **Internal Roads:** Paved, gravel. **RV Service:** No. **Market:** 2 mi. north in Coburg. **Restaurant:** 2 mi. North in Coburg. **General Store:** Yes. **Vending:** Yes. **Swimming Pool:** No. **Playground:** Yes. **Other:** Volleyball court, basketball half court, central data port, mini golf, tetherball, horseshoes. **Activities:** Use of local recreational facilities. **Nearby Attractions:** Oregon Coast Lighthouses, The 20 Covered Bridges of Lane County, wineries, University of Oregon, Shelton-McMurphy-Johnson House. **Additional Information:** Convention & Visitors Assoc. of Lane County Oregon (800) 547-5445.

Restrictions

Pets: On leash only. **Fires:** Communal fire pits only. **Alcoholic Beverages:** At site only. **Vehicle Maximum Length:** None. **Other:** No tarps or other mats on the grass, no on-site vehicle repair.

To Get There

From I-5 Exit 199 (southbound turn right) onto Van Duyn Rd. Drive 0.25 mi. west to South Stuart Way (marked with Eugene Camping World Sign), turn left and drive 1 block to entrance.

EUGENE

Richardson Park

90064 Coburg Rd., Eugene 97408. T: (541) 682-2000; www.co.lane.or.us/parks.

RV ★★★★ Tent ★★★

Beauty: ★★★ Site Privacy: ★★★
Spaciousness: ★★ Quiet: ★★★
Security: ★ Cleanliness: ★★★★
Insect Control: ★★ Facilities: ★★★

Richardson Park Campground, located in a quiet, rural county park 20 minutes west of Eugene and 8 miles off of Hwy. 99, offers very private sites and nearby access to a wide array of water sports. The enormous and marina-plentiful Fern Ridge Reservoir creates the eastern boundary of the county park. The campground is separated into two sections by a main access road and organized into several loops within each section. There is an eclectic mix of sites here, some private and some not. The best sites, 12, 13, 15, and 17–24, have privacy created by a dense mix of lime-green, moss encrusted pines, oaks, firs, and a thick bramble of secondary growth. Other sites stand totally open and adjacent. Those to avoid include 56–60 and 72–84. All paved sites have an area that will accommodate a tent, but there are no formal tent sites within the park. Winters mix mild and cold weather; summer brings better weather and is the best time to travel here.

Basics

Operated By: Lane County Parks Division. **Open:** Apr. 15–Oct. 15. **Site Assignment:** First come, first served; reservation (541) 935-2005), (required deposit is 1 night's stay plus $10 non-refundable reservation fee; refund w/ 72-hours notice). **Registration:** At office, after hours see camp host. **Fee:** $16; xtra vehicle (more than 1 unit & 1 car) $5; cash, check. **Parking:** At site.

Facilities

Number of Multipurpose Sites: 88. **Number**

of RV-Only Sites: 0. **Number of Tent-Only Sites:** 0. **Hookups:** Electric (30, 50 amps), water. **Each Site:** Picnic table, fire ring. **Dump Station:** Yes. **Laundry:** No. **Pay Phone:** Yes. **Rest Rooms and Showers:** Yes. **Fuel:** No. **Propane:** No. **Internal Roads:** Paved. **RV Service:** No. **Market:** 5 mi. west in Venita. **Restaurant:** 5 mi. west in Venita. **General Store:** No. **Vending:** No. **Swimming Pool:** No. **Playground:** Yes. **Other:** Small Amphitheater, boat & jet ski rentals, boat launch, short hiking trails, horseshoe pits, a lake. **Activities:** Swimming, fishing, boating, various planned activities during high volumes. **Nearby Attractions:** Fern Ridge Reservoir, The Bridges of Lane County, wineries, hiking trails, whitewater rafting, art & cultural events. **Additional Information:** Convention & Visitors Assoc. of Lane County Oregon, (800) 547-5445.

Restrictions

Pets: On leash only (max. length 6 ft.). **Fires:** At site. **Alcoholic Beverages:** At site only. **Vehicle Maximum Length:** None. **Other:** Vehicles must be parked on paved surfaces; site max. 8 people; 2-week stay limit.

To Get There

From I-5 Exit 194B, drive 3 mi. west on Hwy. 105/126 to West Eugene/Florence Exit for 99N/126W/6th Ave. Continue on 6th Ave for 5.2 mi., then turn left onto Clear Lake Rd. just after Beltline Hwy. underpass. Follow Clear Lake Rd. for 5 mi. to the entrance on the right.

FLORENCE

Harbor Vista Campground

3040 Delta Hwy. North, Eugene 97408. T: (541) 997-5987; www.co.lane.or.us/parks/harbor/harbor.htm.

RV: ★★★ Tent: n/a

Beauty: ★★★	Site Privacy: ★★★
Spaciousness: ★★	Quiet: ★★★★
Security: ★★	Cleanliness: ★★★
Insect Control: ★★	Facilities: ★★★

Harbor Vista Campground off of Hwy. 101 in residential Florence is distinguished by the seclusion of it's 38 water and electric sites from the outside world. Many of the deep, narrow, non-adjacent sites sit totally buffered on three sides by thick groves of woody deciduous shrubs including rhododendron. The paved sites sit on a loop and a roundabout. The roundabout has the most secluded sites, numbered 32, 34, and 35. The worst sites have little or no privacy, numbered 2–5 and 10–13. The grounds sit on a ridge overlooking the north jetty and a small, driftwood littered beach. None of this can be seen from any of the good sites due to thick vegetation, but there is a covered lookout on the ridge at the edge of the park. Spring and summer bring the best weather and flowers.

Basics

Operated By: Lane Co. Parks. **Open:** All year. **Site Assignment:** First come, first served; reservation (required deposit is 1 night's stay plus $10 non-refundable reservation fee; refund w/ 72-hours notice). **Registration:** At self pay station. **Fee:** $16, extra vehicle (more than 1 vehicle & 1 car) $5; cash, check. **Parking:** At site.

Facilities

Number of RV-Only Sites: 38. **Number of Tent-Only Sites:** 0. **Hookups:** Electric (20, 30, 50 amps), water. **Each Site:** Picnic table. **Dump Station:** Yes. **Laundry:** No. **Pay Phone:** Yes. **Rest Rooms and Showers:** Yes. **Fuel:** No. **Propane:** No. **Internal Roads:** Paved. **RV Service:** No. **Market:** 4 mi. east in Florence. **Restaurant:** 4 mi. east in Florence. **General Store:** No. **Vending:** No. **Swimming Pool:** No. **Playground:** Yes. **Other:** Coastal viewing area. **Activities:** hiking, picnicking. **Nearby Attractions:** Oregon Dunes National Recreation Area, Sea Lion Caves, Heceta Head Lighthouse, Oregon Coast Aquarium, beaches. **Additional Information:** Florence Chamber of Commerce, (541) 997-3128 or (800) 524-4864.

Restrictions

Pets: On leash only (max. length 6 ft.). **Fires:** Fire pits or grills only. **Alcoholic Beverages:** At site. **Vehicle Maximum Length:** 40 ft. **Other:** No firearms, fireworks; reservations must be made 14 days prior to arrival date.

To Get There

From Hwy. 101, southbound turn right onto Rhododendron (at light 1 block south of Safeway Grocery in Florence). Drive 3.8 mi. on Rhododendron, then turn left onto Jetty Rd. and drive for 1 block. Entrance is on right.

FLORENCE

Jessie M. Honeyman Memorial State Park Campground

84505 Hwy. 101 South, Florence 97439. T: (541) 997-3641 or (800) 551-6949; www.oregonstateparks.org.

RV: ★★★★ Tent: ★★★★★

Beauty: ★★★★★	Site Privacy: ★★★
Spaciousness: ★★★	Quiet: ★★★
Security: ★★	Cleanliness: ★★★★
Insect Control: ★★	Facilities: ★★★

Jessie M. Honeyman Memorial State Park Campground, located on Hwy. 101 a few minutes south of Florence, has a camping area as big as the name is long. The heavily forested park has many semi-private sites. Unfortunately most full hookup sites lack privacy. These make up the section open to ATVs in the winter (H loop). Further, avoid C loop with it's close proximity to the highway, and sites 283–299. The rest of the campground receives shade from tall cedars and firs, and gains privacy from the dense groves of huckleberry, salal, and rhododendron. As it is with most Oregon publicly owned camping property, the grounds have a very natural, woodland appearance. Tent sites and RV sites differ very little; both have paved parking and a flat side area of dirt and moss. The best time to visit is late spring when the rhododendron are in bloom all over the Florence area.

Basics

Operated By: Oregon State Parks & Recreation. **Open:** All year (some seasonal areas). **Site Assignment:** First come, first served; reservation (required deposit is 1 night plus non refundable reservation fee; refund w/ 48-hours notice). **Registration:** At entrance gate or self pay station. **Fee:** Full $20, water/electric $19, tent $16; V, MC, check, cash. **Parking:** At site.

Facilities

Number of RV-Only Sites: 166. **Number of Tent-Only Sites:** 191. **Hookups:** Electric (20, 30 amps), water, sewer, cable. **Each Site:** Picnic table, fire ring. **Dump Station:** Yes. **Laundry:** No. **Pay Phone:** Yes. **Rest Rooms and Showers:** Yes. **Fuel:** No. **Propane:** No. **Internal Roads:** Paved. **RV Service:** No. **Market:** 5 mi. north in Florence. **Restaurant:** 5 mi. North in Florence. **General Store:** Yes. **Vending:** No. **Swimming Pool:** No. **Playground:** No. **Other:** Kayak & paddle boat rentals, reservable meeting hall, reservable outdoor pavilion, boat ramp (day use), pedestrian dune access. **Activities:** Fishing, hiking, lake swimming, interpretive programs, boating, sand boarding, winter dune buggy & ATV access. **Nearby Attractions:** Sea Lion Caves, Oregon Dunes National Recreation Area, the covered bridges of Lane County, Haceta Head Lighthouse. **Additional Information:** Florence Chamber of Commerce, (541) 997-3128 or (800) 524-4864.

Restrictions

Pets: On leash only (max. length 6 ft.). **Fires:** Fire pits only. **Alcoholic Beverages:** At site only. **Vehicle Maximum Length:** 50 ft. **Other:** Max. stay 14 days in winter, 10 days in summer.

To Get There

Located 3 mi. south of Florence on Hwy. 101. Driving southbound, entrance is on right. Upon entering park, road forks; take left fork and pay attention to one-way signs; follow this road into the campground.

FORT KLAMATH

Crater Lake Resort Fort Creek Campground

P.O. Box 457, Fort Klamath 97626. T: (541) 381-2349; F: (541) 381-2343; www.craterlakeresort.com; CrtrLkRst@aol.com.

RV: ★★★★ Tent: ★★★

Beauty: ★★★★	Site Privacy: ★
Spaciousness: ★★	Quiet: ★★★★
Security: ★	Cleanliness: ★★★★
Insect Control: ★★	Facilities: ★★

Crater Lake Resort, the closest private land campground to the south entrance of the National Park, has a quaint, country feel. The park has few recreational opportunities on site due to it's location, though it does have several canoes free to use for patrons wanting to explore the nearby creek. The best RV sites in the park sit on Fort Creek, numbered 12–23. The tenting area has no delineated sites, but can fit quite a few tents and has lots of grass and shade. The whole park has an open feel, with little sense of privacy. The worst sites sit on the edge of Hwy. 62 and are subject to infrequent but irritating road noise. In the summer, mosquitos breed in nearby creeks and the weather is hot, so consider visiting during the late spring or early fall.

BASICS

Operated By: Crater Lake Resort. **Open:** Apr 1–Nov 1. **Site Assignment:** On arrival, reservation (required deposit is 1 night's fee; refund w/ 2-weeks notice). **Registration:** At office, after hours ring bell outside office. **Fee:** Full $20, water/electric $18, tent $5 per person; RV fee covers 2 people, extra person $2; V, MC, cash, personal check. **Parking:** At site, limited off site.

FACILITIES

Number of RV-Only Sites: 23. **Number of Tent-Only Sites:** 40. **Hookups:** Electric (30, 50 amps), water, sewer. **Each Site:** Picnic table. **Dump Station:** No. **Laundry:** Yes. **Pay Phone:** Yes. **Rest Rooms and Showers:** Yes. **Fuel:** No. **Propane:** No. **Internal Roads:** Gravel. **RV Service:** No. **Market:** 2 mi. northwest in Fort Klamath. **Restaurant:** 2 mi. Northwest in Fort Klamath. **General Store:** Yes. **Vending:** Yes. **Swimming Pool:** No. **Playground:** Yes. **Other:** Volleyball, horseshoes, canoes (free to guests), basketball, air hockey, ping pong, fooseball, meeting hall. **Activities:** Fishing, canoeing, swimming (in creek, cold). **Nearby Attractions:** Crater Lake National Park, Williamson River, Collier Logging Museum, fish hatchery, Agency lake. **Additional Information:** Klamath County Dept. of Tourism, (800) 445-6731.

RESTRICTIONS

Pets: On leash only. **Fires:** Fire pits only. **Alcoholic Beverages:** At site. **Vehicle Maximum Length:** None.

TO GET THERE

Located a few miles southeast of town on Hwy. 62, located at mile marker 92.

GOLD BEACH

Illahe Campground

29279 Ellensburg Ave., Gold Beach 97444.
T: (541) 247-3600; www.fs.fed.us/r6/siskiyou

RV: ★★★★ Tent: ★★★★

Beauty: ★★★★	Site Privacy: ★★★★
Spaciousness: ★★★★	Quiet: ★★★
Security: ★★★★★	Cleanliness: ★★★★★
Insect Control: ★★★★	Facilities: ★★★

Just past the wilderness section of the Rogue River lies Illahe Campground. Nearby competitor campgrounds provide water access, and thus draw the greater crowds. But at Illahe, where a short, rough trail leads to a rugged shoreline, the relative inaccessibility of the river keeps the crowds away-that is, as long as you don't come from mid-June, when the jet boat racers take over the area, through the end of July. Campsites at Illahe have a thick buffer of vegetation that gives the sites a feeling of solitude. The area near the campground entrance is grassy and open, dotted with a few apple and plum trees. Campground hosts encourage guests to take the fruit when it ripens, because if the campers don't get it, the bears likely will. (Sensible campers will store food out of sight and out of reach of the critters.)

BASICS

Operated By: Gold Beach Ranger District, Siskiyou National Forest. **Open:** All year. **Site Assignment:** First come, first served, no reservations. **Registration:** self-registration on site. **Fee:** $5. **Parking:** At site.

FACILITIES

Number of RV-Only Sites: 14. **Number of Tent-Only Sites:** 0. **Hookups:** None. **Each Site:** Picnic table, fire ring. **Dump Station:** No. **Laundry:** No. **Pay Phone:** No. **Rest Rooms and Showers:** Yes. **Fuel:** No. **Propane:** No. **Internal Roads:** Call ahead for conditions. **RV Service:** No. **Market:** No. **Restaurant:** No. **General Store:** No. **Vending:** No. **Swimming Pool:** Yes. **Playground:** No. **Activities:** Hiking, boating, swimming. **Nearby Attractions:** Whitewater rafting on the Rogue River. **Additional Information:** Siskiyou National Forest, (541) 858-2200.

RESTRICTIONS

Pets: On leash only. **Fires:** In fire rings only. **Alcoholic Beverages:** Allowed. **Vehicle Maximum Length:** 22 ft.

TO GET THERE

From Gold Beach, turn east on Jerry's Flat Rd. north of town and on the south side of the Rogue River. Follow it as it turns into FSR 33 for 35 mi. At the junction after crossing the river, where Agness is left and Powers is straight, veer right on CR 375. Illahe Campground is 2 mi. on the right.

GRANT'S PASS

Riverpark RV Resort

2956 Rogue River Hwy., Grants Pass 97527.
T: (541) 479-0046 or (800) 677-8857; F: (541) 471-1448; www.mullendesign.com; info@mullendesign.com.

RV: ★★★★ Tent: n/a

Beauty: ★★★★	Site Privacy: ★
Spaciousness: ★★★	Quiet: ★★★
Security: ★★	Cleanliness: ★★★★
Insect Control: ★★	Facilities: ★★★

On the banks of the Rogue River just a couple of miles south of Downtown Grants Pass travelers find an outdoor art museum, or is it an RV park? It's actually both; the owner/operator/avid sculptor of Riverpark RV Resort uses metal and wood to fill his campground with sculptures demonstrating both down home crafty and contemporary artsy styles. The flat concrete sites shaded by tall mossy hardwoods have grass perimeters, and the grounds have some garden-like qualities including a large number of rose bushes in the public areas. Riverpark RVs 20 sites, numbered 5–24, are on the bank of a calm stretch of the Rogue, and of these numbers 5–12 sit furthest from a nearby road. On the negative side, all sites lack privacy. Avoid sites 25–29 and J–Q; these are located too close to the office, dump station, and entrance. Winters here stay mild; summer usually brings crowds and some hot days.

BASICS

Operated By: Riverpark RV Resort. **Open:** All year. **Site Assignment:** First come, first served; reservation (required deposit is 1 night's stay; refund w/ 24-hours notice). **Registration:** At office, after hours follow instructions on office door. **Fee:** $22; fee covers 2 people, extra person $3. **Parking:** At site.

FACILITIES

Number of RV-Only Sites: 47. **Number of Tent-Only Sites:** 0. **Hookups:** Electric (20, 30 amps), water. **Each Site:** Picnic table, trash can. **Dump Station:** Yes. **Laundry:** Yes. **Pay Phone:** Yes. **Rest Rooms and Showers:** Yes. **Fuel:** No. **Propane:** No. **Internal Roads:** Paved. **RV Service:** No. **Market:** 3 mi. north in Grant's Pass. **Restaurant:** 3 mi. North in Grant's Pass. **General Store:** No. **Vending:** No. **Swimming Pool:** No. **Playground:** No. **Other:** Horseshoe pit, tennis court, sculptures. **Activities:** Swimming, fishing, tennis, horseshoes. **Nearby Attractions:** The Applegate Trail Interpretive Center, Hellgate Jetboat Excursions, rafting, fishing, golf, museums. **Additional Information:** Grants Pass Visitor Information, (800) 547-5927.

RESTRICTIONS

Pets: On leash only, limit 2 dogs. **Fires:** No open fires. **Alcoholic Beverages:** At site. **Vehicle Maximum Length:** None. **Other:** No vehicle washing.

TO GET THERE

From I-5 Exit 55, drive 1.8 mi. west on Hwy. 199, turn left and drive 0.2 mi. south on Parkdale Dr. Then turn left onto Rogue River Hwy. and follow it for 2 mi. to the entrance on the left.

GRESHAM

Oxbow Park

3010 Southeast Oxbow Pkwy., Gresham 97080.
T: (503) 663-4708

RV: ★★★★ Tent: ★★★★

Beauty: ★★★★★	Site Privacy: ★★★★
Spaciousness: ★★★★	Quiet: ★★★★
Security: ★★★★★	Cleanliness: ★★★★
Insect Control: ★★★★	Facilities: ★★★

Oxbow Park sets a prime example of what a metropolitan park can and should be. The grounds are a sprawling 1,000 acres of dense forests, grassy clearings, sandy riverbanks, and sheer canyon walls. Old-growth forest alone covers 180 acres. Native salmon spawn within a quarter-mile of camping areas on Sandy River, known as the top-rated winter steelhead stream in Oregon. Wildlife abounds in the park, and a full-time naturalist employed year-round, is busiest in summer with a heavy schedule of public and private programs. The first order of business once you get settled into your site is to explore the trails on foot. There are roughly 15 miles of trails that follow Sandy River and wind throughout the park. Even at the height of the summer season, you'll be amazed at how quickly you can find seclusion.

BASICS

Operated By: Multnomah County Parks. **Open:** All year. **Site Assignment:** First come, first served, no reservations. **Registration:** daily fee collected each night, 1-time fee-enter park. **Fee:** $10. **Parking:** At site.

Facilities

Number of RV-Only Sites: 0. **Number of Tent-Only Sites:** 45. **Hookups:** None. **Each Site:** Picnic table, freestanding barbecue pit. **Dump Station:** No. **Laundry:** No. **Pay Phone:** Yes. **Rest Rooms and Showers:** Vault toilets. **Fuel:** No. **Propane:** No. **Internal Roads:** Call ahead for details. **RV Service:** No. **Market:** No. **Restaurant:** No. **General Store:** No. **Vending:** No. **Swimming Pool:** Yes. **Playground:** Yes. **Other:** equestrian area, group camps, interpretive programs. **Activities:** Hiking, horseback riding trails, fishing boating (non-motorized watercraft only). **Nearby Attractions:** Crown Point Vista House. **Additional Information:** County info line, 503.823.4000 or www.co.multnomah.or.us

Restrictions

Pets: No. **Fires:** In fire rings only. **Alcoholic Beverages:** not permitted. **Vehicle Maximum Length:** 35 ft. **Other:** No ATVs, guns or fireworks.

To Get There

Take the Wood Village Exit 16 off I-84 in Gresham. Go south to Division St., turn left and continue to Oxbow Parkway. From here follow the signs down to the park.

HUNTINGTON

Farewell Bend State Recreation Area

23751 Old Hwy. 30, Huntington 97907. T: (541) 869-2365 or (800) 551-6949 or reservations (800) 452-5687; www.oregonstateparks.org/park7.php.

RV ★★★★ Tent ★★

Beauty: ★★★★ Site Privacy: ★★★
Spaciousness: ★★ Quiet: ★★★
Security: ★ Cleanliness: ★★★
Insect Control: ★ Facilities: ★★★

Farewell Bend State Park is set on an irrigated, flat arm of the Snake River, and it makes a great stopover for whitewater rafters on their way to Idaho or Utah. The campground has two sections, A and B; both campgrounds have sites on the river. Sites A42–A52 (even numbers only) have shade and some privacy; section B has three premium sites on the river with gas grills and patios but without cover from the intense sun. The tenting area has 45 drive in "primitive" sites with lots of shade, but no privacy or protection from occasional road noise. Remember that sites near the water receive, at times, copious amounts of wind, and that the high altitude summer sun here will burn skin very quickly. Winters in this part of Oregon are long and cold. Call before arrival to make sure the area has not flooded, as this is a recurring problem.

Basics

Operated By: Oregon State Parks & Recreation. **Open:** All year. **Site Assignment:** On arrival, reservation (required deposit is 1 night plus non refundable reservation fee; refund w/ 48-hours notice). **Registration:** At self pay station. **Fee:** Electric $15, preferred electric $17, tepee $27, covered wagon $27; extra vehicle $7; V, MC, cash. **Parking:** At site.

Facilities

Number of RV-Only Sites: 91. **Number of Tent-Only Sites:** 45. **Hookups:** Electric (20, 30 amps), water, sewer. **Each Site:** Picnic table, fire ring. **Dump Station:** Yes. **Laundry:** No. **Pay Phone:** Yes. **Rest Rooms and Showers:** Yes. **Fuel:** No. **Propane:** No. **Internal Roads:** Paved. **RV Service:** No. **Market:** East in Pendleton. **Restaurant:** East in Pendleton. **General Store:** No. **Vending:** No. **Swimming Pool:** No. **Playground:** No. **Activities:** Boating, fishing, relaxing, bird-watching, interpretive programs. **Nearby Attractions:** Snake River Reservoirs, watersports, Ontario. **Additional Information:** Ontario Chamber of Commerce, (541) 889-8012.

Restrictions

Pets: On leash only (max. length 6 ft.). **Fires:** Fire pits only. **Alcoholic Beverages:** At site. **Vehicle Maximum Length:** 40 ft.

To Get There

From I-84 Exit 353, eastbound turn right onto Hwy. 30, to park entrance, 1 mi.

KLAMATH FALLS

Klamath Falls KOA

3435 Shasta Way, Klamath Falls 97603. T: (541) 884-4644 or (800) 562-9036; www.koa.com.

RV ★★★ Tent ★★★

Beauty: ★★ Site Privacy: ★
Spaciousness: ★★ Quiet: ★
Security: ★★★ Cleanliness: ★★★
Insect Control: ★★ Facilities: ★★★

Klamath Falls KOA, located in southeast Klamath Falls a few minutes off the 97 business loop, affords quick access to municipal attractions. The grounds have several rows of sites, and back up to the levee of an irrigation canal. All of the flat, privacy lacking sites have partial views of nearby arid, rolling hills. The best RV sites, full hookup pull-throughs 30–47, have grass islands and a little shade provided by birch and other hardwoods. Tent sites 72–84 have grass surfaces, lots of shade, and also back up to the levee. There are also some grass water/electric and no hookup multi-use sites with a good amount of shade. The worst sites within the park, numbers 5–9, have no shade or grass. The pool within the campground is small but adequate, while the laundry is enormous. Visit during the mild fall or spring months, summers bring hot, arid weather and intense sunlight.

Basics

Operated By: Klamath Falls KOA. **Open:** All year. **Site Assignment:** On arrival, reservation (required deposit is 1 night's stay; refund w/ 72-hours notice). **Registration:** At office, after hours at drop box in front of office. **Fee:** Full $25 (50 amp add $2), water/electric $23, RV w/ no hookups $21, tent $20; fee covers 2 people, extra adult (age 10 or older) $3, extra child (age 6–9) $2, max. site occupancy is 6 people; V, MC, cash. **Parking:** At site.

Facilities

Number of RV-Only Sites: 63. **Number of Tent-Only Sites:** 19. **Hookups:** Electric (30, 50 amps), water, sewer, cable. **Each Site:** Picnic table. **Dump Station:** Yes. **Laundry:** Yes. **Pay Phone:** Yes. **Rest Rooms and Showers:** Yes. **Fuel:** Yes. **Propane:** Yes. **Internal Roads:** Gravel, some deteriorating pavement. **RV Service:** No. **Market:** 1 block away. **Restaurant:** 1 Block away. **General Store:** Yes. **Vending:** Yes. **Swimming Pool:** Yes. **Playground:** Yes. **Other:** Game room (a few mid-1980s era games, ping pong), meeting room, horseshoes, volleyball, jogging trail on top of levee. **Activities:** swimming. **Nearby Attractions:** Crater Lake National Park, Klamath County Museum, Favell Museum, Upper Klamath Lake, Lava Beds National Monument, hunting. **Additional Information:** Klamath County Dept. of Tourism, (800) 445-6733.

Restrictions

Pets: On leash only, no fighting breeds. **Fires:** No open fires. **Alcoholic Beverages:** Sites only. **Vehicle Maximum Length:** None.

To Get There

From Hwy. 97 Jct. with Hwy. 97 Business/Hwy. 39 in north Klamath Falls, drive 2.7 mi. south on Hwy. 97 Business. Turn right on Washburn Way. Drive 0.8 mi. and turn left at intersection with Schlotzki's Deli onto Shasta Way. Continue 0.5 mi. and KOA entrance is on the left.

KLAMATH FALLS

Lake of the Woods Resort

950 Harriman Rte., Klamath Falls 97601. T: (541) 949-8300; F: (541) 949-8229; www.lakeofthewoods.com; lowresort@earthlink.net.

RV ★★★★ Tent ★★★

Beauty: ★★★★ Site Privacy: ★
Spaciousness: ★★ Quiet: ★★★★★
Security: ★ Cleanliness: ★★★★
Insect Control: ★★ Facilities: ★★★★

Lake of the Woods Resort, a few minutes off of Hwy. 140 and 40 miles north of Klamath Falls, provides a variety of outdoor recreational activities for all seasons. The campground area has open, flat sites on several islands, and a few sites on the perimeter. The best dirt tent sites, A–E, sit on the perimeter near the back of the campground while the best wood chip surfaced RV full hookups, 3–9, sit on one of the islands. Tent sites F–M and RV sites 10–20 have a more disorganized and crowded feel. The whole resort stays very shady with a large number of old firs and pines towering overhead. The campground and the common areas of the resort have a very spacious, open, woodland feel. The marina rents a variety of boats including pontoon boats and even a sail boat. While the camp area has no scenic views, the common areas, beaches and restaurant have beautiful, peaceful vistas of the Lake of the Woods and its far, wooded shores. Any time of the year makes a good time to visit, as the grounds provide year-round recreation opportunities.

Basics

Operated By: Lake of the Woods Resort for the National Forest Service **Open:** All year. **Site Assignment:** On arrival, reservation (required deposit is 50% of stay upon making reservation, 100% due 30 days before arrival; refund w/ 10-days notice less $15 cancellation fee). **Registration:** At office. **Fee:** RV $14, tent $12, extra vehicle $4, pets $5;V, MC, cash. **Parking:** At site.

Facilities

Number of RV-Only Sites: 23. **Number of Tent-Only Sites:** 23. **Hookups:** Electric (30 amps), water, sewer. **Each Site:** Picnic table, fire pit. **Dump Station:** Yes. **Laundry:** Yes. **Pay Phone:** Yes. **Rest Rooms and Showers:** Yes. **Fuel:** Yes. **Propane:** Yes. **Internal Roads:** Dirt w/ wood chips. **RV Service:** No. **Market:** In Klamath Falls. **Restaurant:** On site. **General Store:** Yes. **Vending:** No. **Swimming Pool:** No. **Playground:** No. **Other:** Marina w/ supplies, horseshoes, amphi-theater, restaurant & bar, beach, boat rentals (an assortment of powered & Non), mountain bike rentals, moorage, movie rentals,VCR rentals, BBQ rentals, hiking & biking trails, lake swimming area, ice skate rentals, snowshoe rentals. **Activities:** Swimming, hiking, biking, fishing, boating, dining, occasional planned activities, cross country skiing, snowshoeing, ice skating, snow mobiling. **Nearby Attractions:** City of Klamath Falls, Upper Klamath Lake, Crater Lake National Park, boating, winter sports, fishing, hiking. **Additional Information:** Klamath County Dept. of Tourism, (800) 445-6734.

Restrictions

Pets: On leash only. **Fires:** Fire pits only. **Alcoholic Beverages:** Not in public buildings. **Vehicle Maximum Length:** None. **Other:** No cutting of firewood.

To Get There

Between mile 37 and mile 39 on Hwy. 140, turn (westbound-left) onto Dead Indian Memorial Dr. Follow 1 mi. and then turn right onto an unnamed road marked with "Resort" ODOT sign. This road dead ends into the resort.

KLAMATH FALLS

Rocky Point Resort

28121 Rocky Point Rd., Klamath Falls 97601. T: (541) 356-2287; F: (541) 356-2222; www.rockypointoregon.com; rvoregon@aol.com.

RV ★★★ Tent ★★

Beauty: ★★★★★	Site Privacy: ★★
Spaciousness: ★★	Quiet: ★★★★
Security: ★	Cleanliness: ★★★
Insect Control: ★★	Facilities: ★★★

Rocky Point Resort, off of Hwy. 140 a half hour northwest of Klamath Falls, offers a quiet lakeside retreat. Located on Upper Klamath Lake, the resort rents both powered and non-powered boats for fishing or sightseeing. The small campground has a cramped feeling, but houses some nice shaded pull-throughs, numbered 1–4, with partial views of the beautiful lake, it's offshore marshes, and the arid, partially forested hills on the far shore. Shaded back-in sites 12–15 have the best lake views, sitting on an access road just off the main area of the grounds. The restaurant has beautiful views from both the dining room and outside porch. RV sites have gravel, and tent sites have dirt surfaces. Although the main tent sites, 30–33, sit on the lake's edge they have no privacy or shade. Additionally, avoid unattractive and shadeless sites 25–28, which also lack hookups.

Basics

Operated By: Rocky Point Resort on NFS leased land. **Open:** Apr. 1–Nov. 1. **Site Assignment:** On arrival, reservation (required deposit is 50% of reservation; refund w/ 2 weeks notice). **Registration:** At office, after hours pay in morning. **Fee:** Full $20, water/electric $18, tent $14; fee covers 2 people, extra person $2, max. site occupancy is 4 adults or 1 family of 5; pets $1;V, MC, cash, check. **Parking:** At site.

Facilities

Number of RV-Only Sites: 29. **Number of Tent-Only Sites:** 5, **Hookups:** Electric (30 amps), water, sewer. **Each Site:** Picnic table, fire ring. **Dump Station:** Yes. **Laundry:** Yes. **Pay Phone:** Yes. **Rest Rooms and Showers:** Yes. **Fuel:** No. **Propane:** No. **Internal Roads:** Gravel. **RV Service:** No. **Market:** 40 mi. south in Klamath Falls. **Restaurant:** On site. **General Store:** Yes. **Vending:** No. **Swimming Pool:** No. **Playground:** No. **Other:** Ping pong, horseshoes, boat rentals (powered & non), boat launch, basketball, restaurant, moorage. **Activities:** Fishing, boating, swimming. **Nearby Attractions:** Crater Lake National Park, Favell Museum of Western Art & Native American Artifacts, rodeos, theatre, golf, Collier State Park & Logging Museum. **Additional Information:** Klamath County Dept. of Tourism, (800) 445-6729.

Restrictions

Pets: On leash only. **Fires:** Fire pits only. **Alcoholic Beverages:** At site. **Vehicle Maximum Length:** 40 ft. **Other:** Clean all game & fish in the fish-cleaning station.

To Get There

From Hwy. 140, turn right on Rocky Point Rd. between mile 43 and mile 45; follow road for 2.8 mi. When road forks take right fork; entrance to resort is on the left just past fork.

LA GRANDE

Hot Lake RV Resort

65182 Hot Lake Ln., La Grande 97850. T: (541) 922-2699

RV ★★★★ Tent ★★

Beauty: ★★★★	Site Privacy: ★
Spaciousness: ★★★	Quiet: ★★★★
Security: ★	Cleanliness: ★★
Insect Control: ★★	Facilities: ★★

Hot Lake RV Resort, located in a peacefully scenic area, has some of the best views in Eastern Oregon. The park sits in a very flat area in a valley. From the campground, guests have views of the surrounding grassy, golden brown, rolling hills, complete with a train visible miles away. Save the occasional, distant train noises, the campground is quiet; there being nothing around to generate noise. Gravel sites on the perimeters have the best views, these include sites 82–100 and 40–49. The totally unobscured views from these sites provide enchanting, big sky sunsets and, at night, a stunning view of the heavens. With an organizational scheme of parallel rows, the RV section has some large pull-throughs, but the section lacks shade or privacy. The grassy tent area sits across a nearby stream, shaded by small, deciduous trees, but also lacks intersite privacy. The pool area needs more upkeep than it receives. Visit right before or after summer for the best weather conditions, summers here can be scorching.

Basics

Operated By: Hot Lake Campground. **Open:** All year. **Site Assignment:** On arrival, reservation. **Registration:** At office, after hours see drop by office. **Fee:** Full $24, tent $12; fee covers 2 people, extra adult $2, children free;V, MC, Cash. **Parking:** At site.

Facilities

Number of RV-Only Sites: 100. **Number of Tent-Only Sites:** Open tent area. **Hookups:** Electric (20, 30 amps), water, sewer. **Each Site:** None. **Dump Station:** No. **Laundry:** Yes. **Pay Phone:** Yes. **Rest Rooms and Showers:** Yes. **Fuel:** No. **Propane:** No. **Internal Roads:** Gravel. **RV Service:** No. **Market:** 5 mi. away in La Grande. **Restaurant:** 5 mi. away in La Grande. **General Store:** Yes (seasonal hours). **Vending:** No. **Swimming Pool:** Yes. **Playground:** No. **Other:** Spa. **Activities:** Inquire at campground. **Nearby Attractions:** Golf, Anthony Lakes Mt. Resort & Recreation Area, Winom-Frazier Off Highway Vehicle Trail Complex, Spout Springs Ski Area. **Additional Information:** Union County Chamber of Commerce, (541) 963-8588.

Restrictions

Pets: On leash only. **Fires:** No fires. **Alcoholic Beverages:** At site. **Vehicle Maximum Length:** None. **Other:** No washing vehicles in park.

To Get There

From I-84 Exit 265, drive 4.8 mi. east on Hwy. 203 South. The campground is listed by a small ODOT sign. Pass the sign, turn right onto Hot Lake Ln. (gravel); drive 0.5 mi. to the campground.

LINCOLN CITY

Lincoln City KOA Campground

5298 Northeast Park Ln., Otis 97368. T: (541) 994-2961; F: (541) 994-9454.

RV ★★★★ Tent ★★★

Beauty: ★★★	Site Privacy: ★★
Spaciousness: ★★★	Quiet: ★★★★
Security: ★★	Cleanliness: ★★★★★
Insect Control: ★★	Facilities: ★★★

Lincoln City KOA Kampground, a few miles off of 101 just north of Lincoln city, offers a quiet and serene retreat from surrounding beach culture. The grounds, shaded by pine and fir trees, and bordered on one side by a stream and all other sides by dense blackberry brambles, possess both terraced and field-set gravel pull-through and back-in sites. The terraced sites provide more of a feeling of spaciousness than the field sites. The best back-ins, 23–36 (some full hookup, some water/electric), and the best pull-throughs, 8–16, rise up the terraced hill to the entrance. None of the sites afford much privacy. Preferable tent sites, numbers 51–63, lie along the clear, gently flowing stream at the edge of the field. Many water/electric sites double as tent sites (be wary of sites where leaky motor homes have previously parked). Avoid the trailer city–like sites numbered 64–87. The playground here is large and well equipped and the grounds are very quiet.

Basics

Operated By: Lincoln City KOA. **Open:** All year. **Site Assignment:** First come, first served; reservation (required deposit is 1 night's stay; refund w/ 24 hrs notice). **Registration:** At office, after hours in drop box in front of office. **Fee:** Full $25, water/electric $23, tent $20; fee covers 2 people, extra person $3, max. site occupancy is 6; V, MC, AE, D, cash. **Parking:** At site.

Facilities

Number of RV-Only Sites: 56. **Number of Tent-Only Sites:** 15. **Hookups:** Electric (20, 30 amps), water, sewer, cable. **Each Site:** Picnic table. **Dump Station:** Yes. **Laundry:** Yes. **Pay Phone:** Yes. **Rest Rooms and Showers:** Yes. **Fuel:** No. **Propane:** Yes. **Internal Roads:** Gravel. **RV Service:** No. **Market:** 5 mi. west in Lincoln City. **Restaurant:** 5 mi. west in Lincoln City. **General Store:** Yes. **Vending:** Yes. **Swimming Pool:** No. **Playground:** Yes. **Other:** Horseshoes, game room, volleyball, basketball, tetherball. **Activities:** Berry picking, ice cream socials & other planned activities, wildlife viewing (elk). **Nearby Attractions:** Devil's Lake, beaches, Cascade Head Scenic Research Area, charter fishing, whale-watching. **Additional Information:** Lincoln City Chamber of Commerce, (541) 994-3070.

Restrictions

Pets: On leash only. **Fires:** Fire pits only. **Alcoholic Beverages:** At site only. **Vehicle Maximum Length:** 60 ft. **Other:** No multi-room tents; no hanging tarps from trees; Don't drive through unoccupied sites; Quiet hours 10 p.m. to 6 a.m.

To Get There

Headed south on Hwy. 101: Just past Faith Baptist church, 1 mi. south of the junction of Hwy. 18 and US 101, turn left onto East Devil's Lake Rd. and follow for 1 mi.; turn left on Park Ln. The entrance is on the right.

MANZANITA/NEHALEM

Nehalem Bay State Park

9500 Sandpiper Ln., Nehalem 97131. T: (503) 368-5154 or (800) 551-6949; www.oregonstateparks.org.

 ★★★★ ▲ ★★★

Beauty: ★★★★ Site Privacy: ★★★
Spaciousness: ★★ Quiet: ★★★★
Security: ★★ Cleanliness: ★★★
Insect Control: ★★ Facilities: ★★★

Nehalem Bay State Park, positioned in between the tiny villages of Nehalem and Manzanita, makes up for its lack of commerce with access to natural beauty. Campers need hike only a few hundred feet over the dunes to find themselves on beautiful, narrow, driftwood covered beaches of the great blue Pacific. The campground, divided into six loops, sits in a grove of short coastal pines that provide privacy for the sites. There are no official tent sites, save those reserved for coastal thru-hikers and bikers, but all of the campground sites have flat grassy areas to accommodate a tent. Sites vary significantly in width, and all have flat, paved areas for RVs. Avoid sites F41, F43, E34, E36, E40, E42, D36, D38, C38, C40, C47, B24, B34, B36, A25, and A27 as they are next to beach access trails (high traffic). Sacrificing some privacy, C43–46, B24–33, and A17–24 have the best views of the lovely, undeveloped surrounding coastal hills.

Basics

Operated By: Oregon State Parks & Recreation. **Open:** All year. **Site Assignment:** First come, first served; reservation (required deposit is 1 night plus nonrefundable reservation fee; refund w/ 48-hours notice). **Registration:** At entrance gate or self pay station. **Fee:** $21, extra vehicle (more than 1 unit & 1 vehicle) $7; V, MC, cash. **Parking:** At site.

Facilities

Number of Multipurpose Sites: 277. **Hookups:** Electric (20, 30 amps), water. **Each Site:** Picnic table, fire ring. **Dump Station:** Yes. **Laundry:** No. **Pay Phone:** Yes. **Rest Rooms and Showers:** Yes. **Fuel:** No. **Propane:** No. **Internal Roads:** Paved. **RV Service:** No. **Market:** 5 mi. north in Manzanita. **Restaurant:** 5 mi. North in Manzanita. **General Store:** No. **Vending:** No. **Swimming Pool:** No. **Playground:** Yes. **Other:** Amphitheater, horse camp, boat launch, beach, airstrip, non-motorized traveler camp. **Activities:** Nightly interpretive programs, day time Jr. Ranger programs, other various planned activities (all above listed are seasonal). **Nearby Attractions:** Oswald West State Park, Nehalem Bay Winery, bike rentals. **Additional Information:** Nehalem Bay Area Chamber of Commerce, (503) 355-2335.

Restrictions

Pets: On leash only (max. length 6 ft.). **Fires:** Fire pits only. **Alcoholic Beverages:** At site only. **Vehicle Maximum Length:** 50 ft. **Other:** Quiet hours 10 p.m.–6 a.m.; stay away from driftwood on the beach, it can cause drowning.

To Get There

From Hwy. 101, turn right at the Texaco near Nehalem, drive 0.3 mi. to first stop, then turn right. Drive another 1.4 mi. to next stop and turn right into the park entrance. Drive 1 mi. and turn right at the wooden sign.

MAUPIN

Bear Creek Campground

16400 Champion Way, Sandy 97055. T: (503) 622-7674; www.reserveusa.com/nrrs/or/brsg.

★★★ ▲ ★★★★

Beauty: ★★★★★ Site Privacy: ★★
Spaciousness: ★★★★ Quiet: ★★★★
Security: ★ Cleanliness: ★★★
Insect Control: ★★ Facilities: ★

Bear Creek Campground, a National Forest Service Campground off Hwy. 26 in the southeast corner of the Mt. Hood National Forest, offers a quiet wooded respite to the weary traveler. This campground has facilities just above the primitive line, which is code for non-flush toilets. Still, the little campground has some charm, being a good distance away from anything but the trees. Gravel back-in sites with no hookups make up the whole of the campground with the exception of one pull-through. The campground is shaded, but not canopied, by tall spruce and pine, and sometimes receives visits from bears and stray livestock. Sites 12-20 sit the furthest from any roads, the grounds do get the occasional noise from passing vehicles on nearby, but lightly-traveled, Hwy. 216. The best time to visit has to be the summer months when the nearby rafting season is in full swing. The campground can get full on the weekends from people trying to escape the tourist bustle of Maupin.

Basics

Operated By: 1000 Trails for the National Forest Service. **Open:** Maintained mid-May–mid-Sept. **Site Assignment:** Walkup, reservation. **Registration:** W/ host; at self pay station if host not available. **Fee:** $10, extra vehicle $5. **Parking:** At site.

Facilities

Number of Multipurpose Sites: 21. **Hookups:** None. **Each Site:** Picnic table, fire ring. **Dump Station:** No. **Laundry:** No. **Pay Phone:** No. **Rest Rooms and Showers:** Non-flush only. **Fuel:** No. **Propane:** No. **Internal Roads:** Paved. **RV Service:** No. **Market:** 7 mi. east on 216. **Restaurant:** 24 mi. east in Maupin. **General Store:** No. **Vending:** No. **Swimming Pool:** No. **Playground:** No. **Activities:** Hiking. **Nearby Attractions:** Rafting on the Deschutes from Maupin, Mt. Hood National Forest, Mt. Hood, Portland. **Additional Information:** Mt. Hood Area Chamber of Commerce, (888) 622-4822.

Restrictions

Pets: On leash only. **Fires:** Fire pits only. **Alcoholic Beverages:** At site. **Vehicle Maximum Length:** 32 ft. **Other:** Collecting of dead & down wood allowed, no chainsaw operation within campground, No off road vehicles allowed in campground.

To Get There

From junction of Hwy. 26 and Hwy. 216 (72 mi. east of Sandy), take Hwy. 216 east and follow for 4 mi. Turn right at sign for Bear Creek Campground just before a ranger station; drive 0.1 mi. on a gravel road. Entrance is on right.

MCKENZIE BRIDGE

Trail Bridge Campground

57600 McKenzie Hwy., McKenzie Bridge 97413. T: (541) 822-3381; www.fs.fed.us/r6/willamette.

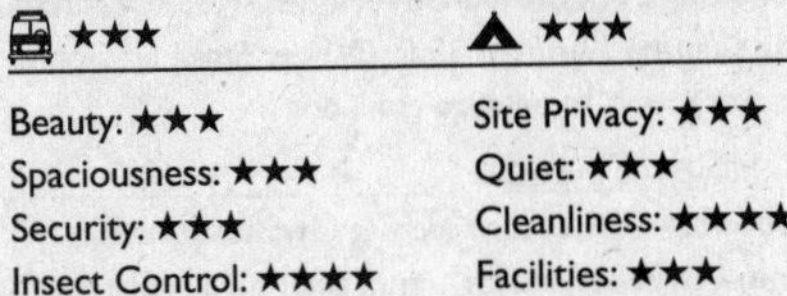

★★★ ★★★

Beauty: ★★★ Site Privacy: ★★★
Spaciousness: ★★★ Quiet: ★★★
Security: ★★★ Cleanliness: ★★★★
Insect Control: ★★★★ Facilities: ★★★

Think of Trail Bridge as the ultimate scenic drive, complete with campground. You can make it as short as 130 miles if your starting point is Redmond, or quite a bit longer if you are coming from points west and want to make more than a frenetic weekend of it. The drive takes you along one of Oregon's most prized trout streams, over two historic and scenic mountain passes, through a diverse assortment of picturesque landscapes ranging from alpine meadows to high desert grasslands, past many unusual geologic formations, across two of the state's largest national forests, and between two designated wildernesses. Trail Bridge Campground is located on Trail Bridge Reservoir, a small depository of McKenzie River headwaters and a good stopping point in the journey. Flowing pure and cold out of Clear Lake (a natural lava-dam lake just west of lava beds contained within Mount Jefferson Wilderness), the McKenzie River attracts both the drift boat community and vast numbers of rafters, kayakers, and canoeists who appreciate the McKenzie's gentle grade. The campground is split almost evenly between RV- and tent-only sites. Each site has a picnic table, a fire grill, and electricity, but there are no other hookups or special amenities. Rest rooms and showers are adequate, without frills.

BASICS

Operated By: Willamette National Forest. **Open:** May–Oct. **Site Assignment:** First come, first served. **Registration:** self-registration. **Fee:** $6. **Parking:** At site.

FACILITIES

Number of RV-Only Sites: 21. **Number of Tent-Only Sites:** 26. **Hookups:** None. **Each Site:** Picnic table, fire grill, electricity. **Dump Station:** No. **Laundry:** No. **Pay Phone:** No. **Rest Rooms and Showers:** Yes. **Fuel:** No. **Propane:** No. **Internal Roads:** Call ahead. **RV Service:** No. **Market:** No. **Restaurant:** No. **General Store:** No. **Vending:** No. **Swimming Pool:** Yes. **Playground:** No. **Activities:** Fishing, boating, hiking, picnicking. **Nearby Attractions:** Trout fishing. **Additional Information:** Willamette NF, (541) 822-3381.

RESTRICTIONS

Pets: On leash only. **Fires:** In fire rings only. **Alcoholic Beverages:** Allowed. **Vehicle Maximum Length:** None. **Other:** Must follow local fishing regulations.

TO GET THERE

Take SR 126 from Eugene or Redmond to McKenzie Bridge. Follow this road north until it becomes SR 26 in McKenzie Bridge. Continue driving to Trail Bridge Reservoir and campground.

MEACHAM

Emmigrant Springs State Park

P.O.Box 85, Meacham 97859. T: (541)983-2277 or (800) 551-6949 or for horse camp or cabin reservations (800) 452-5687; www.oregonstateparks.org/park23.php.

★★★ ★★★

Beauty: ★★★★★ Site Privacy: ★★
Spaciousness: ★★ Quiet: ★★★★
Security: ★ Cleanliness: ★★★
Insect Control: ★★ Facilities: ★★★

Emmigrant Springs State Park in eastern Oregon, makes a beautiful base for exploring the area or just taking a night off of the interstate. Unlike many campgrounds in the region, this semi-arid, high altitude location has shade; sites sit underneath towering ponderosa pines and other evergreens. Although quiet, the area still has a close proximity to the interstate, making some sites louder than others. Sites B14–B5 and A18–A26 have the most protection from this noise. Sites have a mixture of gravel and paved surfaces, and all lack privacy. The park has an amphitheater and horse camp, but surrounding recreation outside the park is limited. Because of the higher altitude, the park has a milder climate than the surrounding desert, so a coat might be necessary when staying the night. And remember, eastern Oregon has cold weather nine months of the year.

BASICS

Operated By: Oregon State Parks & Recreation. **Open:** Mar.–Nov. **Site Assignment:** On arrival, reservation (required deposit is1 night plus non refundable reservation fee; refund w/ 48-hours notice). **Registration:** At self pay station. **Fee:** Full $15, tent $13, extra vehicle $7; V, MC, cash, check. **Parking:** At site.

FACILITIES

Number of RV-Only Sites: 18. **Number of Tent-Only Sites:** 33. **Hookups:** Electric (20, 30 amps), water, sewer. **Each Site:** Picnic table, fire ring. **Dump Station:** Yes. **Laundry:** No. **Pay Phone:** Yes. **Rest Rooms and Showers:** Yes. **Fuel:** No. **Propane:** No. **Internal Roads:** Paved. **RV Service:** No. **Market:** Pendleton, 26 mi. west. **Restaurant:** Pendleton, 26 mi. west. **General Store:** No. **Vending:** No. **Swimming Pool:** No. **Playground:** No. **Other:** Amphitheater, horse camp. **Activities:** Interpretive programs during summer. **Nearby Attractions:** Trees. **Additional Information:** Pendleton Chamber of Commerce, (541) 276-7411.

RESTRICTIONS

Pets: On leash only (max. length 6 ft.). **Fires:** Fire pits only. **Alcoholic Beverages:** At site. **Vehicle Maximum Length:** 40 ft. **Other:** Bikes not permitted on hiking trails.

TO GET THERE

From I-84 Exit 234 (eastbound), drive straight towards Meacham, 0.8 mi, and turn left into the park.

NETARTS

Cape Lookout State Park

13000 Whiskey Creek Rd. West, Tillamook 97141. T: (503) 842-4981

★★★ ★★★★

Beauty: ★★★★★ Site Privacy: ★★★★
Spaciousness: ★★★ Quiet: ★★★★
Security: ★★★★ Cleanliness: ★★★★★
Insect Control: ★★★ Facilities: ★★★

Situated on one of the most scenic capes in the Northwest, Cape Lookout State Park is located just south of Netarts on the Three Capes Scenic Dr. that encompasses two other magnificent headlands (Cape Meares on the north and Cape Kiwanda on the south). These are also state parks but are limited to day-use activities. Collectively these three areas cover more than 2,500 acres of coastal rain forest, sheer cliffs, wide sandy beaches and dunes, narrow spits, rocky points and outcroppings, protected bays, and estuaries. To accommodate the sizable numbers of seashore enthusiasts, the well-maintained and efficiently designed Cape Lookout State Park offers a whopping 185 tent sites and 54 RV sites, many of which are accessible all year. In addition, it offers hikers and bikers a separate area not far from the central camping grounds. Group camps are also available, as well as a meeting hall.

BASICS

Operated By: Oregon State Parks & Recreation. **Open:** All year. **Site Assignment:** First come, first served; reservation. **Registration:** self registration on site. **Fee:** $13–$20. **Parking:** At site.

FACILITIES

Number of RV-Only Sites: 54. **Number of Tent-Only Sites:** 185. **Hookups:** Water, electric, sewer. **Each Site:** Picnic table, fire pit & grill, piped water, shade trees. **Dump Station:** Yes. **Laundry:** No. **Pay Phone:** Yes. **Rest Rooms and Showers:** Yes. **Fuel:** 10 mi. (in Tillamook). **Propane:** 10 mi. (in Tillamook). **Internal Roads:** Call ahead for details. **RV Service:** No. **Market:** 10 mi. (in Tillamook). **Restaurant:** 10 mi. (in Tillamook). **General Store:** 10 mi. (in Tillamook). **Vending:** No. **Swimming Pool:** No. **Playground:** No. **Other:** 10 rental units, firewood. **Activities:** Beachcombing, hiking, walking, fishing, evening & historic programs. **Nearby Attractions:** Tillamook Cheese Factory. **Additional Information:** Information: (503) 842-4981 or (503) 842-3182.

RESTRICTIONS

Pets: On leash only. **Fires:** In fire rings only. **Alcoholic Beverages:** Allowed. **Vehicle Maximum Length:** None.

TO GET THERE

From Tillamook, drive southwest on Netarts Hwy. and follow signs the entire way for Cape Lookout State Park, total distance from Tillamook is 10 mi.

NEWPORT

Pacific Shores Motorcoach Resort

6225 North Coast Hwy. 101, Newport 97365. T: (541)265-3750 or (800)333-1583; www.outdoor-resorts.com; stay@pacificshoresrv.com.

RV ★★★★ Tent n/a

Beauty: ★★★ Site Privacy: ★
Spaciousness: ★★★ Quiet: ★★
Security: ★★★★★ Cleanliness: ★★★★★
Insect Control: ★★ Facilities: ★★★★★

Pacific Shores Motor coach Resort, on the northern edge of Newport and the coastal side of Hwy. 101, is a newly renovated family oriented beach resort. Many of the individual sites are privately owned but rented out when not occupied. The well equipped facilities include a large indoor pool, several saunas, a hilly chip-and-putt six-hole golf area (with maintained grass) and a three story high viewing tower to watch whales playing off the coast. The park sits on cliffs above the beach and has beach access. The best (and also most expensive) sites, numbered 141, 161–168, 185, and 186, have a view of the Pacific and an outcropping to the south, finishing with a lighthouse. Additionally, sites 26–34 have a view slightly obscured by tall pines. Particular sites to avoid, located next to Hwy. 101, include 1–16, 237–252, and 76–93. The spacious, paved, grass bordered, shadeless sites have wide access roads. Summer months make up the busiest and best time to visit.

BASICS

Operated By: Outdoor Resorts of America, Inc. **Open:** All year. **Site Assignment:** On arrival, reservation (required deposit is 1 night's stay; refund w/ cancel before 1 p.m. on arrival date). **Registration:** At office, after hours at guardhouse. **Fee:** Main $35, clubhouse $45, view $55; fee covers 4 people, extra person $5; cash, check; V, MC. **Parking:** At site.

FACILITIES

Number of RV-Only Sites: 203. **Number of Tent-Only Sites:** 0. **Hookups:** Electric (20, 30, 50 amps), water, sewer, cable. **Each Site:** Picnic table. **Dump Station:** No. **Laundry:** Yes. **Pay Phone:** Yes. **Rest Rooms and Showers:** Yes. **Fuel:** No. **Propane:** No. **Internal Roads:** Paved (wide). **RV Service:** No. **Market:** 2 mi. south in Newport. **Restaurant:** 2 mi. south in Newport. **General Store:** Yes. **Vending:** Yes. **Swimming Pool:** Yes. **Playground:** Yes. **Other:** 2 hot tubs, 3 saunas, 6 hole chip & putt golf, arcade (w/ 2 pool tables), reservable large meeting room, enclosed viewing tower. **Activities:** Bingo, weekly dinners, occasional live entertainment, wine & cheese socials, salt water swimming & fishing. **Nearby Attractions:** Yaquina Head Lighthouse, beaches, Oregon Coast Aquarium, Historic Bayfront, Ripley's Believe it or Not, Undersea Gardens, The Wax Works. **Additional Information:** Newport Chamber of Commerce, (800) 262-7844.

RESTRICTIONS

Pets: On leash only, no more than 2 per site. **Fires:** Communal fire pit only. **Alcoholic Beverages:** At site. **Vehicle Maximum Length:** None. **Other:** Min. Vehicle Length 25 ft., no 5th wheels, motorcoaches only, towed secondary vehicles ok.

TO GET THERE

From southbound on Hwy. 101, park is located on right-hand side just north of Newport City limits and 3 mi. north of Hwy. 101 junction with Hwy. 20.

ONTARIO

Lake Owyhee State Park

P.O.Box 247, Adrian 97901. T: (541) 339-2331; www.oregonstateparks.org/park14.php.

RV ★★★ Tent ★★

Beauty: ★★★★★ Site Privacy: ★
Spaciousness: ★★★ Quiet: ★★★★★
Security: ★ Cleanliness: ★★★
Insect Control: ★★ Facilities: ★

Lake Owyhee State Park, located in the absolute middle of nowhere in the desert, eastern-central part of the state, provides a scenic and quiet place to spend a few days. The park can only be accessed by *small* rigs and cars, the road is too narrow and treacherous for anything longer than 25 feet. Created by a dam, the artificial lake plays host to fishing, summer water sports, and provides irrigation to nearby farmers. The campground's location, far from agrarian, sits in what was once a lush canyon. Downstream from the dam (on the way to the campground) the canyon still has such a look and feel. The area before the dam provides some of the most interesting and beautiful scenery in the surrounding area. The state park has two campgrounds, one with water/electric hookups and one with no hookups. All sites have good views of the surrounding, arid, sage-covered, red hills. The campground has little shade, and no privacy; the summer sun here packs a punch. Also, the remote location means no services and lots of bugs. Visit during late spring or late summer for the best conditions; reiterating: *do not attempt this trip in a large rig or during freezing weather; the road has steep, treacherous curves without guardrails.*

BASICS

Operated By: Oregon State Parks & Recreation. **Open:** Mid Apr.–Oct. (weather permitting). **Site Assignment:** On arrival. **Registration:** At self pay station. **Fee:** Water/electric $15, tent $13, overflow or primitive $10, extra vehicle $7; V, MC (cash preferred as credit machine is unreliable). **Parking:** At site.

FACILITIES

Number of RV-Only Sites: 80. **Number of Tent-Only Sites:** 10. **Hookups:** Electric (20, 30 amps), water. **Each Site:** Picnic table, fire ring. **Dump Station:** Yes. **Laundry:** No. **Pay Phone:** No. **Rest Rooms and Showers:** Yes. **Fuel:** Marine only (Seasonal). **Propane:** No. **Internal Roads:** Paved, gravel. **RV Service:** No. **Market:** 30 mi. north. **Restaurant:** 30 mi. North. **General Store:** Yes (seasonal). **Vending:** No. **Swimming Pool:** No. **Playground:** No. **Other:** Boat ramp. **Activities:** Boating, fishing, swimming, hiking, wildlife viewing. **Nearby Attractions:** Hiking, fishing, swimming, boating, wildlife viewing. **Additional Information:** State Park, (541) 339-2331.

RESTRICTIONS

Pets: On leash only (max. length 6 ft.). **Fires:** Fire pits only; small fires only, pay attention to wildfire conditions. **Alcoholic Beverages:** At site. **Vehicle Maximum Length:** 25 ft. **Other:** Small fires only, pay attention to wildfire conditions.

TO GET THERE

From Hwy. 201, turn west at Owyhee Junction onto Owyhee Ave. for 5 mi., then turn south (left) onto Owyhee Dam Cutoff Rd. for 22 mi. to the park. *Warning:* Parts of this road are steep and narrow with sharp corners, and with limited visibility. Please use caution.

PACIFIC CITY

Cape Kiwanda RV Park

P.O.Box 129, Pacific City 97135. T: (503) 965-6230; F: (503) 965-6235; www.pacificcity.net/capekiwandarvpark; capekiwanda@oregoncoast.com.

RV ★★ Tent ★★

Beauty: ★★ Site Privacy: ★
Spaciousness: ★★ Quiet: ★★★
Security: ★ Cleanliness: ★★
Insect Control: ★★ Facilities: ★★

Cape Kiwanda RV Park across from Haystack Rock and a few miles off of 101 in Pacific City provides a modest resting place amidst great natural beauty. Across the street the public beach has tidal pools, colorful sedimentary rock cliffs, a giant sand dune to climb, and the majestic, monolithic Haystack Rock offshore. The campground has flat, adjacent gravel sites surrounded by more gravel and sand, lots of yard junk (all that's missing is a ceramic gnome) and backs up to evergreen-forested hills. The property has few trees and therefore little shade. The best RV sites are A12–14 because they have a view of the rock, and 112, 113 for their size. Courtyard sites 5, 6, and 7 also have good distant views but are visually appalling at short range. The tent sites are flat and grassy and back up to the forest at the rear of the park, but the only ones with any privacy at all are T12–15.

BASICS

Operated By: Cape Kiwanda RV Park. **Open:** All year, some seasonal areas. **Site Assignment:** First come, first served; reservation (required deposit is 1 night's stay; refund w/ 48-hours notice). **Registration:** At office, after hours at drop outside office. **Fee:** Full $25, water/electric $23, tent $16; V, MC, cash. **Parking:** At site.

FACILITIES

Number of RV-Only Sites: 168. **Number of Tent-Only Sites:** 22. **Hookups:** Electric (30, 50 amps), water, sewer, cable. **Each Site:** Picnic table. **Dump Station:** Yes. **Laundry:** Yes. **Pay Phone:** Yes. **Rest Rooms and Showers:** Yes. **Fuel:** No. **Propane:** Yes. **Internal Roads:** Gravel. **RV Service:** No. **Market:** South in Pacific City. **Restaurant:** South in Pacific City. **General Store:** Yes. **Vending:** Yes. **Swimming Pool:** No. **Playground:** Yes. **Other:** Reservable rec room w/ kitchen, shuffleboard. **Activities:** Bingo, crafts (seasonal & on demand). **Nearby Attractions:** Haystack Rock, beaches, fishing, hang gliding. **Additional Information:** Pacific City Chamber of Commerce, (503) 965-6161.

Restrictions

Pets: On leash only. **Fires:** Fire rings only. **Alcoholic Beverages:** At site only. **Vehicle Maximum Length:** None.

To Get There

From Hwy. 101, turn west off 101 onto Three Capes Scenic Dr. (Brooten Rd.) just south of Cloverdale and follow for 2 mi. to a blinking red light. Turn left onto Pacific Ave, drive 2 blocks and then turn right onto Cape Kiwanda Dr. Follow for 0.4 mi.; entrance is on the right.

PENDELTON

Mountain View RV Park

1375 Southeast 3rd, Pendleton 97801. T: (541) 276-1041 or (866) 302-3311; F: (541) 966-8820; rvpdt@oregontrail.net.

RV ★★★★ Tent ★

Beauty: ★★★★
Site Privacy: ★
Spaciousness: ★★★
Quiet: ★★
Security: ★★★★
Cleanliness: ★★★★
Insect Control: ★★
Facilities: ★★★

Mountain View RV Park in Pendleton has nice vistas and easy interstate access. Arranged in several parallel rows, the newer part has flat, paved, grass bordered sites, both with and without views. Unfortunately none of the sites have any shade or privacy. The best RV sites sit on a perimeter, numbers 52–70, that have an open view of the golden, rolling hills and dry flatlands to the south. The huge sky in this part of the countryside makes the scenery particularly impressive. The tenting section consists of a small grassy area with little shade and no intersite privacy. The park has very limited in-house recreation, but makes a good base for exploring the area or for stopping overnight on the long trek through eastern Oregon. Winters here bring extremely cold temperatures and summers just the opposite; late Spring and early fall provide the most comfortable climate.

Basics

Operated By: Mt. View RV Park. **Open:** All year. **Site Assignment:** On arrival, reservation (required deposit is 1 night stay; refund w/ 24-hours notice). **Registration:** At office, after hours at drop or pay in morning. **Fee:** Premium $25, full $22, tent $15; fee covers 2 peopl, extra person (age 6 or older) $2; V, MC, check, cash. **Parking:** At site, limited off site.

Facilities

Number of RV-Only Sites: 100. **Number of Tent-Only Sites:** 6. **Hookups:** Electric (30, 50 amps), water, sewer, cable. **Each Site:** Picnic table. **Dump Station:** Yes. **Laundry:** Yes. **Pay Phone:** Yes. **Rest Rooms and Showers:** Yes. **Fuel:** No. **Propane:** Yes. **Internal Roads:** Paved. **RV Service:** No. **Market:** North in Pendleton. **Restaurant:** North in Pendelton. **General Store:** No. **Vending:** No. **Swimming Pool:** No. **Playground:** Yes. **Other:** Meeting room (reservable), storage. **Activities:** Watching the sky. **Nearby Attractions:** All types of outdoor sports, casino gambling, Tamastslikt Cultural Institute (confederated tribes). **Additional Information:** Pendleton Chamber of Commerce, (541) 276-7411.

Restrictions

Pets: On leash only (max. quantity 2; max. weight 40 lbs.each). **Fires:** No open fires. **Alcoholic Beverages:** At site. **Vehicle Maximum Length:** None. **Other:** Max. 6 people per site.

To Get There

From I-84 Exit 210, (eastbound turn right), turn south from the exit ramp and drive 1 block. Turn right on SE Nye and drive a short distance, turning right on SE 3rd St. This road dead-ends into the RV park after 0.2 mi.

PENDLETON

Wildhorse RV Park

72781 Hwy. 331, Pendleton 97801. T: (541) 966-1891

RV ★★★ Tent ★★

Beauty: ★★★
Site Privacy: ★
Spaciousness: ★★★
Quiet: ★★★
Security: ★
Cleanliness: ★★★★
Insect Control: ★★
Facilities: ★★★

Wild Horse Resort, in Pendleton, makes a great place to camp for the gambling enthusiast. Located on reservation lands, the campground operates in conjunction with the casino down the road. The flat setting has an enormous canvas of a sky, but not much in the way of shade, or for that matter high growing foliage. Most RV sites have paved surfaces but all lack privacy; the resort has a basic layout of parallel rows over a grassy field. Wild Horse has a tenting section consisting of a grassy area but sites lack borders, shade, or privacy. The facilities within walking distance of campsites have a good maintenance schedule, but are few in number. And of course a shuttle runs between the campground and the closest recreation, as mentioned above, the casino. The campground provides services all year but winters here bring bitter cold.

Basics

Operated By: Wild Horse Resort. **Open:** All year. **Site Assignment:** On arrival, reservation (required deposit is during events $50; refund w/ 10-days notice). **Registration:** At office, after hours drop in office door. **Fee:** 30 amp or tent $19, 50 amp $21; V, MC, cash. **Parking:** At site, limited off site.

Facilities

Number of RV-Only Sites: 100. **Number of Tent-Only Sites:** Open tent area. **Hookups:** Electric (30, 50 amps), water, sewer. **Each Site:** Picnic table. **Dump Station:** Yes. **Laundry:** Yes. **Pay Phone:** Yes. **Rest Rooms and Showers:** Yes. **Fuel:** No. **Propane:** No. **Internal Roads:** Paved. **RV Service:** No. **Market:** In Pendleton. **Restaurant:** Next door at Casino. **General Store:** No. **Vending:** Yes. **Swimming Pool:** Yes. **Playground:** No. **Other:** Free continental breakfast, casino. **Activities:** Gambling. **Nearby Attractions:** Pendleton Underground Tours, Pendleton Woolen Mills, Tamastslikt Cultural Institute, Pendleton Round-Up, Happy Canyon Hall of Fame, Umatilla County Historical Society Museum. **Additional Information:** Pendleton Chamber of Commerce, (541) 276-7411.

Restrictions

Pets: On leash only. **Fires:** No fires. **Alcoholic Beverages:** Not allowed. **Vehicle Maximum Length:** None. **Other:** No tents in RV sites.

To Get There

From I-84 Exit 216, turn north and drive 0.7 mi.; the casino is on the right. Turn right at the casino and drive past the casino; campground entrance is on the right.

PORT ORFORD

Bandon-Port Orford KOA

46612 Hwy. 101, Langlois 97450. T: (541) 348-2358; www.koacampgrounds.com/where/or/37116.htm.

RV ★★★ Tent ★★★★

Beauty: ★★★★
Site Privacy: ★★★
Spaciousness: ★★★
Quiet: ★★★
Security: ★
Cleanliness: ★★
Insect Control: ★★
Facilities: ★★★

Bandon-Port Orford KOA, ten miles north of Port Orford on Hwy. 101, offers both quiet, wooded sites for smaller vehicles and family-oriented recreation. The older grounds, canopied by fir, pine, and the occasional cedar, have good intersite privacy due to dense, low lying groves of green vegetation including huckleberries. Not suited for huge rigs, the gravel and grass sites are not uniformaly flat and the facilities are older but in good condition. The sites sit in rows lettered A–F, the quietest of which have numbers greater than four. The best tent sites sit near the back, numbered A10–12, and the best RV sites sit in the middle, water/electric pull-throughs B5–7 and full hookup pull-throughs E7 and E11. The best time to visit the shady campground is during the warm summers. Near the coast, beach access requires a 15-minute drive at the shortest distance.

Basics

Operated By: Bandon -Port Orford KOA. **Open:** All year. **Site Assignment:** First come, first served; reservation (24 hour cancellation policy, 1-week on holidays). **Registration:** At office, after hours at drop box. **Fee:** Full $28, water/electric $26, tent $22; fee covers 2 people & 2 vehicles, extra person $3, max. site occupancy is 8 people per site, extra vehicle $5; V, MC, D, cash, check. **Parking:** At site.

Facilities

Number of RV-Only Sites: 36. **Number of Tent-Only Sites:** 30. **Hookups:** Electric (20, 30 amps), water, sewer, cable. **Each Site:** Picnic table, fire ring. **Dump Station:** Yes. **Laundry:** Yes. **Pay Phone:** Yes. **Rest Rooms and Showers:** Yes. **Fuel:** No. **Propane:** Yes. **Internal Roads:** Gravel. **RV Service:** No. **Market:** 10 mi. south in Port Orford. **Restaurant:** 10 mi. south in Port Orford. **General Store:** Yes. **Vending:** Yes. **Swimming Pool:** Yes. **Playground:** Yes. **Other:** Basketball goal, volleyball net, horseshoe pit, arcade, rec room. **Activities:** (On seasonal demand) pancake breakfast every morning, ice cream social & train ride every night, line dancing, berry picking. **Nearby Attractions:** Cape Blanco Lighthouse, whale-watching, charter fishing, cranberry bogs. **Additional Information:** Greater Port Orford North Curry Chamber of Commerce, (541) 332-8055.

Restrictions

Pets: On leash only. **Fires:** In fire pits only. **Alcoholic Beverages:** At site only. **Vehicle Maximum Length:** 36 ft. **Other:** No pets in rest rooms.

To Get There

The grounds are located 10 mi. north of Port Orford between Bandon and Port Orford on the western side of the highway (south bound turn right), marked by large sign.

PORT ORFORD

Cape Blanco State Park

P.O. Box 1345, Port Orford 97465. T: (541) 332-6774; www.prd.state.or.us.

RV ★★★ Tent ★★★★

Beauty: ★★★★★ Site Privacy: ★★★
Spaciousness: ★★★★ Quiet: ★★★
Security: ★★★★ Cleanliness: ★★★★★
Insect Control: ★★★ Facilities: ★★★

This state park covers 1,895 acres of forested headlands and wildflower fields that flood the area with color in late spring and early summer. The lush vegetation of Cape Blanco is kept green by the year-round temperate marine climate that brings in half of the total annual precipitation between December and February. This makes it an ideal place to enjoy during the off-season and to avoid at peak times. The summer tourist season along the Oregon Coast-all 360 miles of it-is lovely weatherwise, and the scenery is consistently spectacular, but it is one of those experiences you could learn to hate. There is little relief from the crowds, campgrounds fill up quickly (including Cape Blanco), and the main north/south route (US 101) is one long, nearly unbroken procession of RVs and trailers.

Basics

Operated By: Oregon State Parks & Recreation. **Open:** All year. **Site Assignment:** First come, first served, no reservations. **Registration:** In camp office. **Fee:** $18. **Parking:** At site.

Facilities

Number of RV-Only Sites: 54. **Number of Tent-Only Sites:** 54. **Hookups:** Electric. **Each Site:** Picnic table, fire grill, electricity. **Dump Station:** Yes. **Laundry:** Yes. **Pay Phone:** Yes. **Rest Rooms and Showers:** Yes. **Fuel:** No. **Propane:** Yes. **Internal Roads:** Call ahead for details. **RV Service:** Yes. **Market:** No. **Restaurant:** No. **General Store:** Yes. **Vending:** No. **Swimming Pool:** Yes. **Playground:** No. **Other:** 4 reservable log cabins, horse camping. **Activities:** Fishing, hiking, horseback riding. **Nearby Attractions:** Oregon Islands National Refuge, Dunes of Bandon, New river, Blacklock point, Tower Rock, Oregon Coast Trail, lighthouses. **Additional Information:** Port Orford Chamber of Commerce, (541) 332-8055 or www.portorfordregion.com.

Restrictions

Pets: On leash only. **Fires:** In fire rings only. **Alcoholic Beverages:** not permitted. **Vehicle Maximum Length:** None.

To Get There

From Port Orford, drive north on US 101 to Cape Blanco Hwy., and then go 5 mi. west to the state park campground.

PORT ORFORD

Historic Arizona Beach RV Park

36939 Hwy. 101, Port Orford 97465. T: (541) 332-6491

RV ★★★★ Tent ★★★

Beauty: ★★★★★ Site Privacy: ★
Spaciousness: ★★★ Quiet: ★★★
Security: ★★★ Cleanliness: ★★★
Insect Control: ★★ Facilities: ★★

There are campgrounds in the Port Orford and Gold Beach Area with nicer facilities and shadier sites than those found at Historic Arizona Beach RV Park, located on Hwy. 101 between the two cities. However, Arizona Beach is the only park in the area, and possibly on the Oregon Coast, with beach back-ins. The grounds consist of two sections on either side of 101 with an underpass connecting them, and the east side backs up to steep wooded coastal hills. But on the west side sit 38 water/electric sites at sea level, five or so feet off a narrow, gray sand beach. The grass and dirt sites, numbered 112–165, have breathtaking views of the big, crashing Pacific surf and surrounding hills, and very easy beach access. The RV sites on either side lack privacy; some beach side tent sites have privacy, numbered 6–10. The park, located right across the street from Prehistoric Gardens (plaster dinosaurs), recently changed hands and the new management has plans for facility improvement. Late spring is less crowded than summer, summer has better weather.

Basics

Operated By: Arizona Beach RV Park. **Open:** All Year (but up–owner). **Site Assignment:** Reservable (required deposit is 1 night's stay; refund w/ 7-days notice), first come first served. **Registration:** At office, after hours see office window for varying directions. **Fee:** Waterfront $26, other RV $23, tent $16; V, MC, check, cash. **Parking:** At site, off site parking ample.

Facilities

Number of RV-Only Sites: 125. **Number of Tent-Only Sites:** 30. **Hookups:** Electric (20, 30 amps), water, sewer. **Each Site:** Picnic table, fire ring. **Dump Station:** Yes. **Laundry:** Yes. **Pay Phone:** Yes. **Rest Rooms and Showers:** Yes. **Fuel:** No. **Propane:** Yes. **Internal Roads:** Dirt & gravel. **RV Service:** No. **Market:** North or south 15 mi. in Bandon or Port Orford. **Restaurant:** North or south 15 mi. in Bandon or Port Orford. **General Store:** Yes. **Vending:** Yes. **Swimming Pool:** No. **Playground:** Yes. **Other:** Large reservable rec room, basketball goal, chipping range, horseshoes, tide pools(on beach), beach, discount tickets to Prehistoric Gardens, crab nets, fishing equipment rentals. **Activities:** Fishing, crabbing, golfing, body boarding, surfing, planned activities, gold panning, berry picking, whale-watching (seasonal & inconsistent). **Nearby Attractions:** Prehistoric Gardens, Bandon Cheese Factory, golf, charter fishing, cranberry bogs. **Additional Information:** Bandon Chamber of Commerce, (541) 347-9616.

Restrictions

Pets: On leash only. **Fires:** Fire pits only, no beach fires. **Alcoholic Beverages:** At site. **Vehicle Maximum Length:** None. **Other:** No gathering, cutting of firewood; no mechanized vehicles on beach.

To Get There

Entrance marked by large sign on east side of Hwy. 101, 14 mi. north of Gold Beach, opposite from Prehistoric Gardens. If you can see a big green Tyrannosaurus Rex in your side view mirrors, you missed it.

PORTLAND

Columbia River RV Park

10649 Northeast 13th Ave., Portland 97211. T: (503) 285-4397 or (888) 366-7725; F: (503) 285-4397.

RV ★ Tent n/a

Beauty: ★ Site Privacy: ★
Spaciousness: ★★ Quiet: ★
Security: ★★★ Cleanliness: ★★★★
Insect Control: ★★ Facilities: ★★

Columbia River RV Park, situated just off of I-5 and a short walk from its wide namesake river, is not a family-oriented park. If more than four people travel with you (no breaks for kids) you *have* to a second site. This new, defoliated park has flat paved sites and close proximity to downtown Portland, but no privacy. Sites arrangement consists of a perimeter surrounding parallel rows divided by access roads. Small sections of grass separate the sites. Sites 129–145 and 98–114 get the least public road noise; sites 24–68 get the most. Worse than traffic or frequent commercial jets from nearby Portland International Airport are the Air National Guard fighter jets breaking the sound barrier right over the property, no site has immunity from frequent aerial auditory assault. The park sits in a hole and does not have a good view of anything. On the bright side, the campground has good hookups and is located within easy striking distance of Portland.

Basics

Operated By: Columbia River RV Park. **Open:** All year. **Site Assignment:** First come, first served; reservation. **Registration:** At office, after hours at drop box by office. **Fee:** $22; fee covers 2 people, xtra person $2, max. site occupancy is 4 people; cash, check, no credit. **Parking:** At site.

Facilities

Number of RV-Only Sites: 152. **Number of Tent-Only Sites:** 0. **Hookups:** Electric (20, 30, 50 amps), water, sewer, cable. **Each Site:** Concrete pad. **Dump Station:** Yes. **Laundry:** Yes. **Pay**

Phone: Yes. **Rest Rooms and Showers:** Yes. **Fuel:** No. **Propane:** No. **Internal Roads:** Paved. **RV Service:** No. **Market:** 2 mi. west in Jantzen Beach. **Restaurant:** 2 mi. west in Jantzen Beach. **General Store:** No. **Vending:** Yes. **Swimming Pool:** No. **Playground:** No. **Other:** Reservable Rec room w/ a kitchen. **Activities:** Inquire at campground. **Nearby Attractions:** Saturday Market, Children's Museum, The Grotto, Sternwheeler Columbia Gorge, Portland Art Museum. **Additional Information:** Portland Oregon Visitor's Assoc. 1-87-PORTLAND.

Restrictions

Pets: On leash only, under 20 lbs. **Fires:** No open fires. **Alcoholic Beverages:** At site. **Vehicle Maximum Length:** None. **Other:** Only RV models ten years or younger; no boats or tow dolly's.

To Get There

From I-5 Exit 307 to Marine Dr. East. Follow Marine Dr. east for 1.4 mi. to 13th Ave.; entrance is on the right across from the yacht club.

PORTLAND

Janzen Beach RV Park

1503 North Hayden Island Dr, Portland 97217. T: (503) 289-7626 or (800) 443-7248

RV: ★★ Tent: n/a

Beauty: ★★	Site Privacy: ★
Spaciousness: ★★	Quiet: ★
Security: ★★★	Cleanliness: ★★★
Insect Control: ★★	Facilities: ★★★

Jantzen Beach RV Park, in Northwest Portland just off I-5, is located on Hayden Island, a short walk away from public transit, and adjacent to a well kept trailer park. The flat, paved sites are delineated manicured grass, shrubs and trees. Many of the trees flower in the spring, but theylack sufficient height to provide much of shade. The RV section has two distinctly different areas. The first area, sites 801–844 and A–D, makes up two cramped and unattractive rows back to back. The second consists of comparatively more spacious sites. The best sites, 903–922 and 859–871, have the most isolation from the surrounding noise of the city. These sites may or may not be available depending on demand for monthly accommodations. Although security is marginal, the convenient urban location's only real downfall, found directly overhead, is one of Portland International's Exit corridors. You can expect a low altitude jumbo jet screaming over about once every ten minutes during busier times of day.

Basics

Operated By: Jantzen Beach RV Park. **Open:** All year. **Site Assignment:** First come, first served; reservation (required deposit is 1 night's stay; refund w/ 24-hours notice). **Registration:** At office, after hours pay in morning. **Fee:** back-in $24, pull-through $26, fee covers 2 people, extra person $1; V, MC, cash, check. **Parking:** At site.

Facilities

Number of RV-Only Sites: 169. **Number of Tent-Only Sites:** 0. **Hookups:** Electric (20, 30, 50 amps), water, sewer, cable, central data port. **Each Site:** Picnic table. **Dump Station:** Yes. **Laundry:** Yes. **Pay Phone:** Yes. **Rest Rooms and Showers:** Yes. **Fuel:** No. **Propane:** No. **Internal Roads:** Paved. **RV Service:** No. **Market:** 1 mile east by interstate. **Restaurant:** Across Hayden Island Dr. **General Store:** Yes. **Vending:** Yes. **Swimming Pool:** Yes. **Playground:** Yes. **Other:** basketball court, rec room, pool table. **Activities:** swimming, frolicking. **Nearby Attractions:** Burnside Park, Powell's Bookstore, Oregon Zoo, brewpubs, Vancouver, Columbia River gorge.

Restrictions

Pets: On leash only. **Fires:** No open fires. **Alcoholic Beverages:** At site only. **Vehicle Maximum Length:** None.

To Get There

From I-5 Exit 308, drive 0.5 mi. west on Hayden Island Dr.; entrance is on the right across from a large strip mall.

PORTLAND

Mt. Hood Village

65000 East Hwy. 26, Welches 97067. T: (503) 622-4011; www.mthoodvillage.com; mhoodv@mthoodvillage.com.

RV: ★★★★ Tent: ★★

Beauty: ★★★	Site Privacy: ★
Spaciousness: ★★	Quiet: ★★★
Security: ★★★★★	Cleanliness: ★★★★
Insect Control: ★★	Facilities: ★★★★★

Mt. Hood Village, located on Hwy. 26 southeast of Portland, offers an amazing number of resort amenities within close proximity to the scenic National Forest Area. These facilities include, among others, a large indoor pool, tons of exercise equipment, resident massage therapists, and a very large lodge and outdoor pavilion for meetings of all sizes. The campground has several different sections offering different hookups, and these sections all have outdoorsy names. The best gravel, back-in, full-hookup sites can be found in Vine Maple Hollow, numbered 82–100; these adjacent sites, shaded by birch and pine, offer the most seclusion from the rest of the busy grounds. Conversely, the worst sites also sit in this section near a high traffic area of the park, numbered 8–50. There exist some quality water/electric sites, numbers 38–70, in the section deemed Hemlock Meadows; these sites are perhaps the shadiest on the property. All sections within the park make an attempt at maintaining the wooded feel of the surrounding country-side. The grounds only have slim opportunities for tent camping, with the tent sites consisting of gravel and crushed shale.

Basics

Operated By: Grayco Resources, Inc. **Open:** All year. **Site Assignment:** On arrival, reservation (required deposit is 1 night's fee; refund w/ 48-hours notice of reservation). **Registration:** At entrance gate, after hours use phone at gate-call attendant. **Fee:** Full $32, water/electric $29, group tent $40, tent $20; fee covers 6 people w/ 1 unit & 1 vehicle, extra vehicle $2 per stay; V, MC, D, AE, personal checks, cash. **Parking:** At site, some off site.

Facilities

Number of RV-Only Sites: 361. **Number of Tent-Only Sites:** 18. **Hookups:** Electric (20, 30, 50 amps), water, sewer, cable. **Each Site:** Picnic table, fire ring. **Dump Station:** Yes. **Laundry:** Yes. **Pay Phone:** Yes. **Rest Rooms and Showers:** Yes. **Fuel:** Yes. **Propane:** Yes. **Internal Roads:** Paved & gravel. **RV Service:** No. **Market:** 2 mi. east on 26. **Restaurant:** On site for breakfast, lunch. **General Store:** Yes. **Vending:** Yes. **Swimming Pool:** Yes. **Playground:** Yes. **Other:** Game room (no video games, indoor pool, indoor hot tub (large), saunas (1 per gender, small), cardio room, freeweight room, fireside room (small meeting room), lodge (enormous meeting room), huge outdoor pavilion w/ tables & tents, basketball, volleyball (sand), cabins, cottages, pedal carts (2 & 4 person), massage therapy. **Activities:** Weekend planned activities, swimming, ping-pong, pool, foos ball, fishing, use of facilities. **Nearby Attractions:** Mt. Hood National Forest, Portland, winter sports. **Additional Information:** Mt. Hood Area Chamber of Commerce, (888) 622-4822.

Restrictions

Pets: On leash only. **Fires:** Fire pits only. **Alcoholic Beverages:** At site, not allowed inside common areas. **Vehicle Maximum Length:** None. **Other:** Washing vehicles allowed in site w/ biodegradable soap.

To Get There

Take I-84 East to Exit 16 (Wood Village, Gresham, Mt. Hood). Drive south about 6 mi., then turn left (east) onto Burnside St. Burnside turns into Hwy. 26 East in about 1 mi. Take Hwy. 26 through the town of Sandy. About 15 mi. East of Sandy, the entrance will be on the right.

PORTLAND

Pheasant Ridge RV Park

8275 Southwest Elligsen Rd., Wilsonville 97070. T: (503) 682-7829 or (800) 532-7829; F: (503) 682-9043; www.pheasantridge.com; terri@pheasantridge.com.

RV: ★★★ Tent: ★★

Beauty: ★★★	Site Privacy: ★★
Spaciousness: ★★★	Quiet: ★★
Security: ★★	Cleanliness: ★★★★
Insect Control: ★★	Facilities: ★★★★

Pheasant Ridge RV Park, one-half hour south of Portland on I-5, provides a good place for people wanting to daytrip to surrounding areas. The terraced sites climb a hill to views of the surrounding developed hill country, providing a feeling of inter-site spaciousness. Young pines also scale the hill alongside the paved, grass-enclosed sites. The pines afford a sense of privacy but not much shade. Sites with the best view sit at the top of the grounds, numbered 86–90 and 104–109. The campground was approved for its compliance with the Americans with Disabilities Act (although dumpsters are a long hike from most sites) and the indoor hot tub has a Hoyer lift for disabled access; the indoor pool does not. Several groups meet at the grounds in the rec room and open their doors to visitors, and these include (although schedules vary) a barbershop quartet on Tuesday nights, a men's Sunday morning prayer group, and a women's Wednesday morning craft and sewing circle.

Basics

Operated By: Pheasant Ridge RV Park. **Open:** All year. **Site Assignment:** First come, first served; reservation (deposit 1 night's stay; refund w/ 24-hours notice). **Registration:** At office, after hours ring bell. **Fee:** $27 plus $1 per person; V, MC, checks. **Parking:** At site 1.

Facilities

Number of RV-Only Sites: 130. **Number of Tent-Only Sites:** 0. **Hookups:** Electric (20, 30, 50 amps), water, sewer. **Each Site:** Picnic table. **Dump Station:** No. **Laundry:** Yes. **Pay Phone:** Yes. **Rest Rooms and Showers:** Yes. **Fuel:** No. **Propane:** Yes. **Internal Roads:** Paved. **RV Service:** No. **Market:** North up I-5 3 mi. **Restaurant:** North up I-5 3 mi. **General Store:** Yes. **Vending:** Yes. **Swimming Pool:** Yes. **Playground:** No. **Other:** Hoyer lift for hot tub, exercise room, horseshoe pit, hot tub. **Activities:** BBQs & various planned activities. **Nearby Attractions:** End of the Oregon Trail Interpretive Center, wineries, Powell's Bookstore, Wilsonville Family Fun Center. **Additional Information:** Portland Oregon Visitor's Assoc. 1-87-PORTLAND.

Restrictions

Pets: On leash only, no larger than 40 lbs, no more than 2. **Fires:** No open flames. **Alcoholic Beverages:** At site. **Vehicle Maximum Length:** 45 ft. **Other:** No skateboards.

To Get There

From I-5 Exit 286, drive 0.25 mi. east on Elligsen Rd.; entrance is on the left.

PORTLAND

Portland Fairview RV Park

21401 Northeast Sandy Blvd., Fairview 97024. T: (503) 661-1047 or (877) 777-1047; F: (503) 665-4643; portlandrv@aol.com.

RV ★★★ Tent n/a

Beauty: ★★★	Site Privacy: ★
Spaciousness: ★★★	Quiet: ★
Security: ★★	Cleanliness: ★★★★
Insect Control: ★★	Facilities: ★★★★

The common areas of Portland Fairview RV Park, located about 15 minutes east of Portland off I-84 in the suburb of Fairview, are graces with flowers in the spring and early summer. Within this well manicured but shadeless park one finds flowering white pear trees, purple heather, camellias, a couple of low lying rose hedges, and several varieties of carefully shaped conifers. The grounds have five terraced levels providing views of the surrounding developed hill country. A clear stream cascading gently over rocks into a pond shaded by weeping willows is a visual focal point. Up a hill from the pond sit the prettiest (although not the quietest) sites, numbered 215-220. These shady sites can accommodate small RVs (around 25 ft). The campground's only shortcoming is the active railroad track 20 feet off the back perimeter. Sites 385–396 and 399–407 have the quietest views of the hills. None of the paved, grass bordered sites have visual privacy.

Basics

Operated By: Commonwealth Investors, Inc. **Open:** All year. **Site Assignment:** First come, first served; reservation (deposit to guarantee: 1 night's stay; refund w/ 24-hours notice). **Registration:** At office, after hours at drop in office door. **Fee:** $25.44; fee covers 2 people, extra person $1.06; 7th night stay free w/ 6 nights paid in advance; V, MC, check, cash. **Parking:** At site.

Facilities

Number of RV-Only Sites: 407. **Number of Tent-Only Sites:** 0. **Hookups:** Electric (20, 30, 50 amps), water, sewer, cable. **Each Site:** Picnic table. **Dump Station:** No. **Laundry:** Yes. **Pay Phone:** Yes. **Rest Rooms and Showers:** Yes. **Fuel:** No. **Propane:** No. **Internal Roads:** Paved. **RV Service:** No. **Market:** 5 mi. east in Troutdale. **Restaurant:** 5 mi. east in Troutdale. **General Store:** No. **Vending:** Yes. **Swimming Pool:** Yes. **Playground:** Yes. **Other:** Reservable rec room & log cabin meeting room rentals, basketball court, horseshoes, pool table, hot tub, exercise room. **Activities:** Inquire at campground. **Nearby Attractions:** The Columbia River Gorge National Scenic Area, Classical Chinese Garden, Oregon Museum of Science & Industry, Mt. Hood. **Additional Information:** Portland Oregon Visitor's Assoc. 1-87-PORTLAND.

Restrictions

Pets: On leash only, limit 2 dogs. **Fires:** No open fires. **Alcoholic Beverages:** Not allowed. **Vehicle Maximum Length:** 45 ft. **Other:** No tents; bicycles allowed only on paved streets; only camping units appearing 20 years or younger are allowed, no tents.

To Get There

From I-84 Exit 14, drive 0.25 mi. north on 207th St.; this dead-ends into Sandy Blvd. Turn right on Sandy and drive another 0.25 mi.; entrance is on the left.

PORTLAND

Portland-Dayton RV Park

16205 Southeast Kreder Rd., Dayton 97114. T: (503) 864-2233; www.sites.onlinemac.com/pdrp/rv-park; pdrp@macnet.com.

RV ★★★ Tent n/a

Beauty: ★★	Site Privacy: ★
Spaciousness: ★★★	Quiet: ★★
Security: ★★	Cleanliness: ★★★★
Insect Control: ★★	Facilities: ★★★

Portland-Dayton RV Park, just off of Hwy. 99 West on the Hwy. 18 bypass, has a location close to the local wineries halfway between Portland and Salem. The landscaped grounds have a long way to grow; the young trees do not provide much shade or privacy, but location plus free corn more than makes up for this. The owner of the grounds plants corn in an adjacent field in several cycles every summer, and guests can pick it free of charge. The best back-in sites, numbered 10–25, sit adjacent to this field and wrap around the back perimeter of the park. Most of the park consists of row after row of pull-throughs surrounded by a four-sided block of back-ins. All sites are paved and surrounded by well-kept grass. Within walking distance of the grounds flows the Yamhill River. The trip to downtown Dayton is further but still possible on foot.

Basics

Operated By: Portland-Dayton RV Park. **Open:** All year. **Site Assignment:** First come, first served; reservation (no deposit required). **Registration:** At office, after hours drop in office door. **Fee:** $25.44; fee covers 2 people, extra person $2; 7th night stay free w/ 6 nights paid in advance; check, cash. **Parking:** At site.

Facilities

Number of RV-Only Sites: 190. **Number of Tent-Only Sites:** 0. **Hookups:** Electric (30, 50 amps), water, sewer, cable. **Each Site:** Picnic table. **Dump Station:** No. **Laundry:** Yes. **Pay Phone:** Yes. **Rest Rooms and Showers:** Yes. **Fuel:** No. **Propane:** No. **Internal Roads:** Paved. **RV Service:** No. **Market:** 4 mi. south in Dayton. **Restaurant:** 4 mi. south in Dayton. **General Store:** Yes. **Vending:** No. **Swimming Pool:** Yes. **Playground:** No. **Other:** Exercise-rec-meeting room, horseshoe pit, corn field. **Activities:** Potlucks, corn picking, gold panning. **Nearby Attractions:** Wineries, Portland. **Additional Information:** Portland Oregon Visitor's Assoc. 1-87-PORTLAND.

Restrictions

Pets: On leash only; small or medium dogs limit 2. **Fires:** No open fires. **Alcoholic Beverages:** At site. **Vehicle Maximum Length:** 40 ft. **Other:** Exercise equipment for adults only, no firearms, fireworks.

To Get There

Southbound on 99W, take first Hwy. 18 Exit for Dayton, drive 0.75 mi. Entrance on left.

PORTLAND

Roamers Rest RV Park

17585 Southwest Pacific Hwy., Tualatin 97062. T: (503) 692-6350 or (877) 4RV-PARK; F: (503) 691-6998.

RV ★★★★ Tent n/a

Beauty: ★★★	Site Privacy: ★
Spaciousness: ★★	Quiet: ★★★
Security: ★★	Cleanliness: ★★★★
Insect Control: ★★	Facilities: ★★★★

Southwest of Portland, in between the city and wine country on the Tualatin River, is Roamers Rest RV Park. The lower level of the park, a rectangular perimeter of sites with a central road, lays on a bank of the slow moving murky green river. Lush green ferns, cedars, oak, and cottonwood climb a steep hill from the river sites to a small alternate section of the grounds. The latter section has thick growth on three sides; the former has 25 waterfront sites. Also on the grounds are some protected wetlands that consist of ponds surrounded by cattails. These house many different species of birds, making the park popular for avid bird-watchers. The best sites for bird-watching, numbered 34–29, sit across from one marshy pond. Portland public transit stops nearby, providing access to many parts of the city.

Basics

Operated By: Roamer's Rest RV Park, LLC. **Open:** All year. **Site Assignment:** First come, first served; reservation (required deposit is 1 night's stay; refund w/ 24-hours notice. **Registration:** At office, after hours pay in morning. **Fee:** Full $24; fee covers 2 people, xtra person (age 5 or older) $2; V, MC, cash. **Parking:** At site, no parking on internal roads.

Facilities

Number of RV-Only Sites: 93. **Number of Tent-Only Sites:** 0. **Hookups:** Electric (20, 30, 50 amps), water, sewer, cable, phone. **Each Site:** Pavement. **Dump Station:** No. **Laundry:** Yes. **Pay Phone:** Yes. **Rest Rooms and Showers:** Yes. **Fuel:** No. **Propane:** No. **Internal Roads:** Paved. **RV Service:** No. **Market:** North on Hwy. 99. **Restaurant:** North on Hwy. 99. **General Store:** No. **Vending:** Yes. **Swimming Pool:** No. **Playground:** No. **Other:** Loaner books, protected wetlands. **Activities:** Bird-watching, fishing. **Nearby Attractions:** Portland Rose Gardens, Japanese Gardens, World Forestry Center Museum, Oregon Zoo, wineries. **Additional Information:** Portland Oregon Visitor's Assoc. 1-87-PORTLAND.

Restrictions

Pets: On leash only, no more than 2 dogs per site. **Fires:** No open fires. **Alcoholic Beverages:** At site. **Vehicle Maximum Length:** 40 ft. **Other:** No skates, skateboards, generators, or vehicle maintenance.

To Get There

From I-5 Exit 292 (junction with Hwy. 217), drive 2 mi. north on Hwy. 217 then 5 mi. south on Hwy. 99W; entrance is on the right just past the Tualatin River.

PROSPECT
Natural Bridge Campground

47201 Hwy. 62, Prospect 97536. T: (541) 560-3623

RV ★★★★ Tent ★★★★

Beauty: ★★★★★ Site Privacy: ★★★★★
Spaciousness: ★★★ Quiet: ★★★★
Security: ★★★★ Cleanliness: ★★★★★
Insect Control: ★★★★ Facilities: ★★★

Natural Bridge is so named for the unique feature adjacent to it. It is at this point that the upper Rogue disappears from sight and runs underground for 200 feet. The campground sits virtually on top of water flowing beneath it. Natural Bridge is one of several campgrounds in the vicinity that is located on the banks of the Rogue or on small creeks that feed it. Given its proximity to Crater Lake, this area can be quite busy in the summertime, with the larger, more developed campsites filling up first. The surrounding Rogue River National Forest is characterized by dense forests of Douglas fir and sugar pine that soften the contours of the high plateau upon which the forests grow. This rugged land is full of thick vegetation, laced with over 450 miles of trails within the national forest. Getting lost can happen easily. Make sure you have a good topographic or Forest Service map with you when you head out for lonely and distant spots.

Basics

Operated By: Rogue River National Forest. **Open:** May–Oct. **Site Assignment:** First come, first served, no reservations. **Registration:** not necessary. **Fee:** None. **Parking:** At site.

Facilities

Number of RV-Only Sites: 16. **Number of Tent-Only Sites:** 0. **Hookups:** No. **Each Site:** Picnic table, fire pit w/ grill. **Dump Station:** No. **Laundry:** No. **Pay Phone:** No. **Rest Rooms and Showers:** Vault toilets. **Fuel:** No. **Propane:** No. **Internal Roads:** Call ahead for details. **RV Service:** No. **Market:** No. **Restaurant:** No. **General Store:** No. **Vending:** No. **Swimming Pool:** No. **Playground:** No. **Activities:** Hiking, backpacking. **Nearby Attractions:** Rogue River. **Additional Information:** Information: (541) 560-3623 May–early Nov.

Restrictions

Pets: On leash only. **Fires:** In fire rings only. **Alcoholic Beverages:** Allowed. **Vehicle Maximum Length:** 22 ft.

To Get There

Travel northeast on SR 62 (about 32 mi. from Medford), from the Prospect turnoff. Continue north on SR 62 another 12 mi. or so to FS 300; turn left and the campground is 1 mi. in.

SALEM
Phoenix RV Park

4130 Silverton Rd. Northeast, Salem 97305. T: (503) 581-2497 or (800) 237-2497; F: (503) 391-2705; phoenixRVPK@aol.com.

RV ★★★★ Tent n/a

Beauty: ★ Site Privacy: ★
Spaciousness: ★★★ Quiet: ★★
Security: ★★★ Cleanliness: ★★★★★
Insect Control: ★★ Facilities: ★★★

Phoenix RV Park, located just off I-5 on the northeast side of Salem has the feel of a newly developed suburban community. The young campground occupies an L-shaped field of large paved sites surrounded by juvenile shrubs, small trees, and very well maintained grass. The sites come minus shade or privacy, but the convenient location more than makes up for this. The newly furbished, spacious, indoor facilities include two large laundry rooms and a kitchen. One would be hard pressed to find a campground with better access to Metropolitan Salem. The grocery store and RV service on either side of the grounds, as well as nearby bus routes only add to the park's convenient location. The campground is surrounded by privacy fencing and has night security. Sites 25-41 and 47-71 stay surprisingly quiet considering the urban location. The rec room has a Stairmaster, treadmill, two pinball games, and an assortment of jigsaw puzzles.

Basics

Operated By: Phoenix RV Park. **Open:** All year. **Site Assignment:** First come, first served; reservation (required deposit is 1 night's stay; refund w/ 24-hours notice). **Registration:** At office, after hours at drop box outside office. **Fee:** $25; fee covers 2 people, extra person (age 3 or older) $2. **Parking:** At site.

Facilities

Number of RV-Only Sites: 107. **Number of Tent-Only Sites:** 0. **Hookups:** Electric (20, 30, 50 amps), water, sewer, cable. **Each Site:** Picnic table. **Dump Station:** No. **Laundry:** Yes. **Pay Phone:** Yes. **Rest Rooms and Showers:** Yes. **Fuel:** No. **Propane:** Yes. **Internal Roads:** Paved (wide). **RV Service:** No (next door). **Market:** Next door. **Restaurant:** 0.25 mi. east. **General Store:** Yes. **Vending:** Yes. **Swimming Pool:** No. **Playground:** Yes. **Other:** Multipurpose room. **Activities:** Watching traffic from park entrance. **Nearby Attractions:** State Capital, Silvercreek Falls, antique shops, Hallie Ford Museum of Art/Willamette University, Marion County Historical Society Museum. **Additional Information:** Salem Convention & Visitor's Assoc., (503) 581-4325 or (800) 874-7012.

Restrictions

Pets: On leash only (max. length 6 ft.), no fighting breeds; dogs over 25 lbs must be approved by mgmt. **Fires:** No open fires or charcoal. **Alcoholic Beverages:** At site. **Vehicle Maximum Length:** None. **Other:** No motor or generator usage, no fireworks or lethal weapons, no parking anywhere other than registered sites, no clotheslines, no business operations legal or otherwise without approval of mgmt.

To Get There

From I-5 Exit 256, drive 0.25 mi. east on Market St., then turn left on Lancaster Dr. Follow for 1.25 mi. then turn right onto Silverton Rd. Entrance is on the right after 1 block.

SALEM
Salem Campground and RV

3700 Hagers Grove Rd. Southeast, Salem 97301. T: (800) 826-9605 or (800) 825-9605; F: (503) 581-9945.

RV ★★★ Tent ★

Beauty: ★★ Site Privacy: ★
Spaciousness: ★★ Quiet: ★
Security: ★★ Cleanliness: ★★★
Insect Control: ★★ Facilities: ★★★

In the southeast corner of Salem, just off I-5 in what used to be a walnut grove, stands Salem Campground and RV. The convenient location consists of a grassy field with paved sites, and has some shade but no intersite privacy. The shade-providing trees consist primarily of poplar and walnut trees. Unfortunately walnut gathering can prove difficult as the local squirrels provide worthy competition with the winning advantages of reach and speed. The campground, which offers easy access to Cascade Gateway Park, features a swimming hole and a couple of fishing ponds. Tent sites sit on a beautifully flat, shady, grassy knoll. right next to the interstate. A grove of trees and the tent sites buffer much of the RV section from the interstate. The best RV sites are in areas A, B, C, D, E, and F; the sections D, E, and F have more shade but are closer to the interstate. Quieter sections A, B, and C have a good view of Home Depot. Sections G-K have smaller sites and lack visual appeal. Avoid them. Summers bring warmer weather, more metropolitan events, and crowds; visit during the late spring.

Basics

Operated By: Salem Campground and RVs. **Open:** All year. **Site Assignment:** first come first served; reservation (required deposit is 1 night's stay to guarantee space; refund w/ 48-hours notice). **Registration:** At office, after hours at drop box outside office. **Fee:** Full $21, water/electric $20, RV w/ no hookups $14, tent-only sites $15, fee covers 2 people, extra person (age 3 or older) $2; V, MC, D, cash. **Parking:** At site.

Facilities

Number of RV-Only Sites: 185. **Number of Tent-Only Sites:** 32. **Hookups:** Electric (20, 30, 50 amps), water, sewer, central data port. **Each Site:** Picnic table. **Dump Station:** Yes. **Laundry:** Yes. **Pay Phone:** Yes. **Rest Rooms and Showers:** Yes. **Fuel:** No. **Propane:** Yes. **Internal Roads:** Paved. **RV Service:** No. **Market:** 0.25 mile northwest. **Restaurant:** 0.25 mi. Northwest. **General Store:** Yes. **Vending:** Yes. **Swimming Pool:** No. **Playground:** Yes. **Other:** Basketball court, game room, trail under interstate to Cascade Park (has fishing, swimming). **Activities:** swimming, fishing in Cascade Park. **Nearby Attractions:** Adelman Peony Gardens, Oregon Garden, Bush House Museum, Jensen Arctic Museum, wineries. **Additional Information:** Salem Convention & Visitor's Assoc., (503) 581-4325 or (800) 874-7012.

Restrictions

Pets: On leash only, no fighting breeds. **Fires:** No open fires, charcoal in tent area only. **Alcoholic Beverages:** At site. **Vehicle Maximum Length:** None. **Other:** No repairing or washing of vehicles, no parking in grass, no tents in hookup sites, no laundry hanging, no tarps or canopies draped over RVs or cars.

To Get There

From I-5 Exit 253, drive 0.25 mi. west on Hwy. 22, then turn left on Lancaster Dr. Follow for 0.25 mi. and turn right on Hager's Grove Rd., which dead-ends into the park.

SISTERS
Black Butte Resort

25635 Southwest FSR 1419, Camp Sherman 97730. T: (541)595-6514 or (877)595-6514; F: (541) 595-5971; www.blackbutte-resort.com; almills@myexcel.com.

RV: ★★★★ Tent: ★★

Beauty: ★★★★	Site Privacy: ★
Spaciousness: ★★	Quiet: ★★★★
Security: ★	Cleanliness: ★★★★
Insect Control: ★★	Facilities: ★★★

Black Butte Resort, located west of Sisters off Hwy. 20, offers a serene setting within a resort community centered on fly-fishing and outdoor activities. The small campground consists of a grass field shaded by aspens, birch, and pine with a beautiful, unobstructed view of the butte providing the campground's name. Facilities are basic, but the campgrounds proximity to outdoor recreation and the cities of Sister and Bend, increase its appeal. Sites are distributed along both sides of a loop road. The best of the gravel and dirt sites sit on the back perimeter, numbered 3–8, with lots of shade but no view of the butte. Nearby are a reservation-only five star restaurant and a general store with a small selection of quality wines. No-hookup sites 23 and 24 A and B are less spacious back-ins, but have the best views of the nearby butte.

Basics

Operated By: Black Butte Resort. **Open:** All year. **Site Assignment:** On arrival, reservation (required deposit is 1 night's stay; refund w/ 14-days notice). **Registration:** At office, after hours pay in morning. **Fee:** Full $24, water/electric $19, dump station use $5; fee covers 2 people, extra person (age 6 or older) $3. **Parking:** At site.

Facilities

Number of RV-Only Sites: 31. **Number of Tent-Only Sites:** 0. **Hookups:** Electric (30, 50 amps), water, sewer. **Each Site:** Picnic table. **Dump Station:** Yes. **Laundry:** Yes. **Pay Phone:** No. **Rest Rooms and Showers:** Yes. **Fuel:** No. **Propane:** No. **Internal Roads:** Gravel. **RV Service:** No. **Market:** 0.1 mile east (Well stocked convenience store). **Restaurant:** 0.1 mi. east (5 star, reservations only). **General Store:** No. **Vending:** No. **Swimming Pool:** No. **Playground:** No. **Other:** Horseshoe pit, meeting room (w/ kitchen, electric organ), book & game loans. **Activities:** Hiking, biking (trails across road from park). **Nearby Attractions:** Deshutes National Forest, hiking, fishing, boating, city of Sisters, city of Bend, horseback riding, Sisters Rodeo. **Additional Information:** Sisters Area Chamber of Commerce, (541) 549-0251.

Restrictions

Pets: On leash only. **Fires:** Fire pits only. **Alcoholic Beverages:** At site. **Vehicle Maximum Length:** 40 ft. (call if over 40 for availability). **Other:** Laundry closed Sundays from noon to 4 p.m.

To Get There

From Hwy. 20 westbound, turn right on Forest Service road marked Camp Sherman-Metolius River. This turn is located between mile 91 and 92 about 15 minutes west of Sisters. Follow this road for 2.5 miles, when road forks take the left fork and drive 2.6 miles on FR 1419. This road continues through a stop, goes right at the stop sign. The park entrance is on the right.

SISTERS
Mountain Shadow RV Park

540 Hwy. 20 West, Sisters 97759. T: (541)549-7275

RV: ★★★ Tent: n/a

Beauty: ★★	Site Privacy: ★
Spaciousness: ★★	Quiet: ★★
Security: ★★★	Cleanliness: ★★★★
Insect Control: ★★	Facilities: ★★

Mountain Shadow RV Park on Hwy. 20 sits just east of the quaint town of Sisters adjacent to a Comfort Inn. The park is laid out in several sets of parallel rows, plus sites around the perimeter of, a very flat field. The newer park lacks shade, privacy, or views, but has well maintained facilities, easily navigable access roads, an indoor pool, and possibly the largest rest rooms of any RV park in Oregon. Tenting is not allowed within the park. All sites have full hookups with nightly phone service available for an extra fee. The best of the paved, grass-bordered sites, back-ins numbered 1–16 and 76–84, are on the boundary of the park. Mountain Shadow also has some exceptionally long pull-throughs, numbered 60-75. Avoid the trailer-city like setting of back-in sites 17–42. Since the park is open year-round, those willing to camp in the winter can sample a variety of snow sports nearby.

Basics

Operated By: Choice Hotels, inc. **Open:** All year. **Site Assignment:** On arrival, reservation (required deposit is 1 night's stay; refund w/ 24-hours notice). **Registration:** At office, after hours pay in morning. **Fee:** $27.95, phone add $3; fee covers 3 adults, extra adult $3; D, AM, V, MC, cash. **Parking:** At site.

Facilities

Number of RV-Only Sites: 105. **Number of Tent-Only Sites:** 0. **Hookups:** Electric (20, 30, 50 amps), water, sewer, cable, phone. **Each Site:** Picnic table, grill riser. **Dump Station:** No. **Laundry:** Yes. **Pay Phone:** Yes. **Rest Rooms and Showers:** Yes. **Fuel:** No. **Propane:** No. **Internal Roads:** Paved. **RV Service:** No. **Market:** 2 mi. east. **Restaurant:** Next door. **General Store:** No. **Vending:** Yes. **Swimming Pool:** Yes. **Playground:** No. **Other:** Hot tub, wading pool, meeting/TV room w/ kitchen, horseshoes, 2 covered picnic pavilions. **Activities:** Swimming. **Nearby Attractions:** Paintball, rock climbing, rafting, boating, anything related to outdoor sports Bend or Sisters has it, Deshutes Brewing Company (Bend), horseback riding, Sisters Rodeo (first weekend in Jun.). **Additional Information:** Sisters Area Chamber, (541) 549-0251.

Restrictions

Pets: On leash only. **Fires:** Off ground in portable fire place, grills only. **Alcoholic Beverages:** At site. **Vehicle Maximum Length:** None. **Other:** Rest rooms closed between 10 p.m.–7 a.m.

To Get There

Located on Hwy. 20, 1 mi. northeast of Sisters; entrance is on left if driving northbound.

SISTERS
Riverside Campground

P.O. Box 249, Sisters 97759. T: (541) 549-7700

RV: ★★★ Tent: ★★★

Beauty: ★★★★	Site Privacy: ★★★
Spaciousness: ★★★★	Quiet: ★★★★

Security: ★★★ Cleanliness: ★★★
Insect Control: ★★★ Facilities: ★★★

Ah, the magical and mysterious Metolius. Welling up clear and bright from a tiny underground spring at the base of Black Butte, the river provides one of the finest trout habitats around before emptying into Lake Billy Chinook. The number of campgrounds on or near the Metolius is staggering, and are there primarily to serve the abundance of anglers. In addition to Riverside, there are Camp Sherman, Allingham, Smiling River, Pine Rest, Gorge, Allen Springs, Pioneer Ford, and Lower Bridge. Dominating the landscape in various stages of geologic splendor are the snowcapped peaks to the west. In order from north to south, they are Mount Jefferson, Mount Washington, North Sister, Middle Sister, South Sister, and last but not least even with its forlorn name, Broken Top. Highlights of a stay at Riverside Campground include short walks to Metolius Spring and Jack Creek Spring, the Metolius River Canyon near Camp Sherman, and the Wizard Falls Fish Hatchery.

Basics

Operated By: Concessionaire. **Open:** Apr.–Oct. **Site Assignment:** First come, first served, no reservations. **Registration:** self-registration on site. **Fee:** $8. **Parking:** At access road, about 200–400 yards from the campground.

Facilities

Number of RV-Only Sites: 16. **Number of Tent-Only Sites:** 0. **Hookups:** No. **Each Site:** Picnic table, fire grill. **Dump Station:** No. **Laundry:** No. **Pay Phone:** No. **Rest Rooms and Showers:** Vault toilets. **Fuel:** No. **Propane:** No. **Internal Roads:** Call ahead for details. **RV Service:** No. **Market:** No. **Restaurant:** No. **General Store:** No. **Vending:** No. **Swimming Pool:** No. **Playground:** No. **Activities:** Fishing, biking, hiking. **Nearby Attractions:** Mountains, lakes. **Additional Information:** Information: (541) 549-2111.

Restrictions

Pets: On leash only. **Fires:** In fire rings only. **Alcoholic Beverages:** Allowed. **Vehicle Maximum Length:** 21 ft. **Other:** 14 day limit on stay.

To Get There

Take SR 126/US 20 (Santiam Hwy.) north of Sisters to its intersection with FS 14 (Camp Sherman Rd.). Turn right, and follow FS 14 around the base of Black Butte to FS 900. The camp is less than 1 mi. north on this road.

SISTERS

Sisters/Bend KOA

67667 Hwy. 20 West, Bend 97701. T: (541) 549-3021 or reservations (800)562-0363; F: (541) 549-8144.

RV: ★★★★ Tent: ★★★

Beauty: ★★★★ Site Privacy: ★★
Spaciousness: ★★ Quiet: ★★★
Security: ★★ Cleanliness: ★★★★
Insect Control: ★★ Facilities: ★★★★

From the frontal appearance, Sisters/Bend KOA located on Hwy. 20 doesn't look very attractive. But upon closer examination, one finds quality facilities. Within the grounds there is an eclectically themed nine-hole mini-golf course, a pool with a beautiful surrounding deck, and a movie room complete with the biggest of big screen TVs and surround sound. The office/store also rents DVDs and videocassettes. In the camping area one finds many low juniper trees, adding a musty, pine fragrance to the air. Some areas have grass, but for the most part there is little cover. Sites are arranged in parallel rows. The full hookup area consists of gravel surfaces; tent sites 17–19 and 5–8 have grass while 92–100 have dirt surfaces. Avoid tent sites 92–94 as they sit near a road; the general overflow area also sits near Hwy. 20. Sites afford little privacy or shade.

Basics

Operated By: Sisters/Bend KOA. **Open:** Closed Jan.–Feb. **Site Assignment:** On arrival, reservation (required deposit is 1 night's stay; refund less $10 service charge: 24-hours notice. **Registration:** At office, after hours drop located out front of office. **Fee:** Full $29, water/electric $28, dry $25; fee covers 2 people, extra adult $9, children 4–17 $2, students 18–20 $3; extra vehicle $1; V, MC, cash. **Parking:** At site.

Facilities

Number of RV-Only Sites: 100. **Number of Tent-Only Sites:** 20. **Hookups:** Electric (20, 30, 50 amps), water, sewer. **Each Site:** Picnic table, fire ring (overflow section lacks these). **Dump Station:** Yes. **Laundry:** Yes. **Pay Phone:** Yes. **Rest Rooms and Showers:** Yes. **Fuel:** No. **Propane:** Yes. **Internal Roads:** Gravel. **RV Service:** No. **Market:** 4 mi. west in Sisters. **Restaurant:** 4 mi. west in Sisters. **General Store:** Yes. **Vending:** Yes. **Swimming Pool:** Yes. **Playground:** Yes. **Other:** 9-hole mini golf, ping pong, volleyball, basketball, spa, movie room, fishing pond, movie/DVD rental, deli. **Activities:** Swimming, fishing, nightly movies. **Nearby Attractions:** Sisters Rodeo (first weekend Jun.), Camp Sherman, fly-fishing, rafting, horseback riding, hiking, Deshutes National Forest, Bend. **Additional Information:** Sisters Area Chamber of Commerce, (541) 549-0251.

Restrictions

Pets: On leash only, not allowed on grass & some sections of park. **Fires:** Fire pits only. **Alcoholic Beverages:** At site. **Vehicle Maximum Length:** None. **Other:** Tie dogs to own RV only, must be attended.

To Get There

Located 3 mi. southeast of Sisters on Hwy. 20; westbound, entrance on left.

STANFIELD

Pilot RV Park

2125 Hwy. 395 South, Stanfield 97875. T: (541) 779-2136

RV: ★★ Tent: n/a

Beauty: ★ Site Privacy: ★
Spaciousness: ★★★ Quiet: ★★
Security: ★★★ Cleanliness: ★★★★
Insect Control: ★★ Facilities: ★

Pilot RV in Stanfield has convenient access from the interstate and all the truckin'-culture a camper could ever want, but little else. As a place to pull in late and leave early, Pilot RV works perfectly. The campground has perimeter fencing and sits adjacent to a truck stop providing limited, but always open, services. Because of it's location, ambient noise does exist but nothing of the magnitude of, say, an RV park in north-central Portland. The sites themselves have flat, paved surfaces and wide, grass borders but no shade or privacy. Though the park is open year-round, be mindful that in this region winters often bring freezing weather and the peak of summer can be sweltering.

Basics

Operated By: Pilot RV. **Open:** All year. **Site Assignment:** On arrival, reservation. **Registration:** At office or self pay station. **Fee:** Full $18; fee covers 2 people, extra person $5; V, MC, cash. **Parking:** At site.

Facilities

Number of RV-Only Sites: 40. **Number of Tent-Only Sites:** 0. **Hookups:** Electric (20, 30, 50 amps), water, sewer, cable. **Each Site:** Picnic table. **Dump Station:** Yes. **Laundry:** Yes. **Pay Phone:** Yes. **Rest Rooms and Showers:** Yes. **Fuel:** Yes. **Propane:** No. **Internal Roads:** Paved. **RV Service:** No. **Market:** North on Hwy. 395. **Restaurant:** North on Hwy. 395. **General Store:** Yes. **Vending:** Yes. **Swimming Pool:** No. **Playground:** No. **Other:** Truck stop. **Activities:** Inquire at campground. **Nearby Attractions:** Pendleton. **Additional Information:** Pendleton Chamber of Commerce, (541) 276-7411.

Restrictions

Pets: On leash only. **Fires:** No fires. **Alcoholic Beverages:** At site. **Vehicle Maximum Length:** 40 ft.

To Get There

From I-90 Exit 188, drive north to Pilot Station

WARM SPRINGS

Kah Nee Ta Resort

P.O.Box K, Warm Springs 97761. T: (541) 553-1112 or (800) 554-4SUN; F: (541) 553-1071; www.Kah-Nee-TaResort.com; margos@bendnet.com.

RV: ★★★★★ Tent: n/a

Beauty: ★★★★ Site Privacy: ★
Spaciousness: ★★ Quiet: ★★★★
Security: ★★★★★ Cleanliness: ★★★★★
Insect Control: ★★ Facilities: ★★★★★

Ka-Nee-Ta resort, twenty minutes east of Warm Springs, is among the best destination parks in the Northwest. An astounding array of recreational activities operated under the resort's dominion, and shuttles every half hour to move visitors to and fro, provide plenty of incentive for an extended stay. Facilities include a top-notch health spa, an enormous pool, a water slide, horse stables with trail rides, and a casino; the facilities are well maintained and frequently crowded. No tents are allowed on the property, but the RV section has 51 flat, paved, full hookup spaces. The only slightly unattractive sites are number 18-26 (even numbers only) for their lack of surrounding grass. The rest have nice grassy areas, well manicured and creating an oasis-like feel in the middle of the high desert. Unfortunately there is little shade. Without an RV, lodging options include a hotel and concrete-floored tepees (your own bedding is required for the latter). Early summer provides the most opportune time to visit, August especially can reach temperatures up to and over 100 degrees Fahrenheit.

Basics

Operated By: Confederated Tribes of Warm Springs. **Open:** All year. **Site Assignment:** On arrival, reservation (required deposit is 1 night's stay; refund w/ 72-hours). **Registration:** At office (village gate); after hours at lodge front desk. **Fee:** Full $38, tepee $70 ($50 refundable deposit on tepees); fee covers 2 people plus 1 unit & 1 car, extra person (age 7 or older) $6, extra vehicle $5; 2 night min. on weekends, 3 on holidays; V, MC, AE, D, check, cash. **Parking:** At site, limited off site.

Facilities

Number of RV-Only Sites: 51. **Number of Tent-Only Sites:** 0. **Hookups:** Electric (30, 50 amps), water, sewer, cable. **Each Site:** None. **Dump Station:** Yes. **Laundry:** Yes. **Pay Phone:** Yes. **Rest Rooms and Showers:** Yes. **Fuel:** No. **Propane:** Yes. **Internal Roads:** Paved. **RV Service:** No. **Market:** 11 mi. west in Warm Springs. **Restaurant:** 1 mi. east at resort lodge. **General Store:** Yes. **Vending:** Yes. **Swimming Pool:** Yes. **Playground:** Yes. **Other:** Arcade, mini-golf ($6 adults, $3 kids & seniors), basketball, picnic pavilion (small), huge pool, water slide, 2 small spas, kiddie pool, golf course, horseback riding ($20/person), kayaking trips ($20/person), tennis, bike rentals, shuttles around resort every half hour, arts & crafts, planned activities, volleyball, full service health spa, Indian Head Casino, gear rentals for most activities. **Activities:** Hiking, biking, horseback riding, swimming, relaxing, kayaking, gambling. **Nearby Attractions:** Outside of the resort, not much save National Forests, Native Cultural Events & Museum at Warm Springs. **Additional Information:** Ka Nee Ta Resort, (541) 553-1112.

Restrictions

Pets: On leash only (campground only). **Fires:** Pits only. **Alcoholic Beverages:** In areas where children are not present. **Vehicle Maximum Length:** 73 ft. **Other:** Be culturally sensitive; Fires here can get out of hand very quickly, keep even cigarette butts under control.

To Get There

From Hwy. 26 West in Warm Springs, turn right on Rte. 3 (marked with a big Kah-Nee-Tah sign, just after Texaco, westbound). Drive 10 mi. on Rte. 3; at bottom of a hill with lots of switchbacks, turn right onto Rte. 8 (marked with a large Kah-Nee-Tah sign). Drive 1.5 mi. and the entrance is on the right. There is an alternate route about 15 minutes northwest of Warm Springs that ends up in the same place and is marked in a similar way.

WINCHESTER BAY

Eel Creek Campground

855 Hwy. 101, Reedsport 97467. T: (541) 271-3611; www.reserveusa.com.

RV ★★★★ Tent ★★★★

Beauty: ★★★★★	Site Privacy: ★★★★★
Spaciousness: ★★★★	Quiet: ★★★★★
Security: ★★★★	Cleanliness: ★★★★
Insect Control: ★★★	Facilities: ★★★

Eel Creek is just one of many campgrounds that are clustered in the Florence/Reedsport/Coos Bay stretch of US 101. Heavy vegetation helps absorb traffic sounds and provides lovely secluded, sandy-bottomed sites. Though no sires are designated "tent-only," tenters are free to choose from among the campgrounds all-purpose sites. Ocean breezes help keep insects to a minimum. Aside from its vegetation-lush private sites, Eel Creek's strongest selling point is the absence of off-road vehicle access to the dunes. If you want peace and quiet as part of your dunes experience, make sure you're not hiking in an area where they rent dune buggies. Eel Creek backs up against some of the largest dunes in the 46-mile-long protected beach. Always shifting, always changing, there are dunes that reach as high as 600 feet. Slog your way to the top of one of these monsters and look out over a most spectacular sight. Headquarters for Oregon Dunes National Recreation Area is right on US 101 at the junction of State Rte. 38 in Reedsport. This is a well-stocked information bureau. The exhibits are worth a look, too.

Basics

Operated By: Siuslaw National Forest, Oregon Dunes National Recreation Area. **Open:** May 14–Sept. 15. **Site Assignment:** First come, first served; reservation during the summer. **Registration:** self-registration or camp host collects. **Fee:** $13. **Parking:** At site.

Facilities

Number of Multipurpose Sites: 52. **Number of RV-Only Sites:** 0. **Number of Tent-Only Sites:** 0. **Hookups:** No. **Each Site:** Picnic table, fire grill. **Dump Station:** No. **Laundry:** No. **Pay Phone:** No. **Rest Rooms and Showers:** Yes. **Fuel:** No. **Propane:** No. **Internal Roads:** Call ahead for details. **RV Service:** No. **Market:** No. **Restaurant:** No. **General Store:** No. **Vending:** No. **Swimming Pool:** No. **Playground:** No. **Activities:** Hiking, beach. **Nearby Attractions:** Dean Creek Elk Viewing Area. **Additional Information:** Information: (541) 271-3611.

Restrictions

Pets: On leash only. **Fires:** In fire rings only. **Alcoholic Beverages:** Allowed. **Vehicle Maximum Length:** 35 ft.

To Get There

From Reedsport, drive south on US 101 for 12 mi. The campground entrance is on the ocean side.

YACHATS

Cape Perpetua Scenic Area

P.O. Box 274, Yachats 97498. T: (541) (563) 3211

RV ★★★ Tent ★★★

Beauty: ★★★★★	Site Privacy: ★★
Spaciousness: ★★★	Quiet: ★★★★
Security: ★★★★	Cleanliness: ★★★★
Insect Control: ★★★★	Facilities: ★★★

Both Cape Perpetua and the nearby town of Yachats (pronounced yah hots) have long been the vacation destination favored by Oregonians who choose the small town's relative seclusion amidst some of the coast's most awe-inspiring scenery. The Cape Perpetua Campground is actually two campgrounds managed by the Forest Service (as is the rest of the Scenic Area). Both are quite close to the Visitor Center, and the only difference between them is that one is an individual-site complex and the other accommodates groups of up to 50 people. Privacy is not great—mostly provided by spruce with little ground cover. On the other hand, the ocean breezes blow right through and keep insects to a minimum. Cape Perpetua is an enormously popular whale-watching spot in the wintertime. Although the campgrounds are not open, the visitor center has interpretive programs for the whale-watching crowd. The Cape Perpetua Viewpoint 800 feet above the sea provides a bird's-eye look in all directions over this breathtaking panorama.

Basics

Operated By: Concessionaire, under contract w/ Siuslaw National Forest. **Open:** May–Oct. **Site Assignment:** First come, first served, no reservations. **Registration:** self registration on site. **Fee:** $12–$14. **Parking:** At site.

Facilities

Number of RV-Only Sites: 38. **Number of Tent-Only Sites:** 0. **Hookups:** No. **Each Site:** Picnic table, fire grill, electricity. **Dump Station:** No. **Laundry:** No. **Pay Phone:** Yes. **Rest Rooms and Showers:** Yes. **Fuel:** No. **Propane:** No. **Internal Roads:** Call ahead for details. **RV Service:** No. **Market:** No. **Restaurant:** No. **General Store:** No. **Vending:** No. **Swimming Pool:** No. **Playground:** No. **Other:** Group camping. **Activities:** Hiking, biking, tide pool walks. **Nearby Attractions:** Visitor's center, whale-watching, Devil's Churn, Captain Cook's Chasm. **Additional Information:** Information: (541) 563-3211.

Restrictions

Pets: On leash only. **Fires:** In fire rings only. **Alcoholic Beverages:** Allowed. **Vehicle Maximum Length:** 22 ft.

To Get There

From Yachats, drive 3 mi. south on US 101. The entrance is on the non- ocean side.

Pennsylvania

Pennsylvania has helped shape America's history since England's Charles II granted Quaker statesman William Penn leadership in the territory that is now Pennsylvania. Philadelphia, the nation's first capital, is where the Declaration of Independence was written. Valley Forge to the west and present-day Bucks County to the east are where George Washington crossed the Delaware River. On the south shore of Presque Isle Bay near Erie, Commodore Oliver Hazard Perry built his fleet, set sail, and defeated British troops in the Battle of Lake Erie in 1813. Gettysburg, the scene of perhaps the most famous battle on U.S. soil, is rich with Civil War history.

A city that makes tasty cheese steaks and hoagie sandwiches, **Philadelphia** blends Colonial heritage with world-class museums, performing arts, and architecture. An ideal starting point for a visit to Philadelphia is the Historic District, which includes **Independence National Historic Park.** West of the Delaware River, the 45-acre park features **Independence Hall** and **Liberty Bell Pavilion** among other historical buildings. The 8,700-acre **Fairmount Park** features the **Philadelphia Museum of Art, Philadelphia Zoo,** and 18th-century mansions authentically preserved and furnished.

Northeast of Philadelphia in Bucks County, the **Washington Crossing Historic Park** is where George Washington and 2,400 soldiers crossed the Delaware River on Christmas night in 1776 and marched into Trenton. There, they surprised Hessian mercenaries and captured the city. **Washington Crossing State Park** is across the river in New Jersey.

Northwest of Philadelphia, **Valley Forge National Historic Park** is the site of the Continental army's encampment from December 1777–June 1778, when British troops occupied Philadelphia. **Washington Headquarters, Washington Memorial Chapel,** and the **Museum of the Valley Forge Historical Society** are among the attractions here.

Southwest of Philadelphia, the rolling countryside of Brandywine Valley is adorned with charming villages, gardens, museums, chateau estates, and historic sites. Brandywine Valley straddles the Pennsylvania and Delaware border, so its attractions extend into Delaware. The Pennsylvania side features **Brandywine Battlefield State Historic Park,** 1,050-acre **Longwood Gardens,** and the **Brandywine River Museum** among other points of interest.

Located in the southeastern section of the state, Pennsylvania Dutch Country is home to an expansive population of Amish, Mennonites, and Brethren. The region has several small villages offering crafts, handmade furniture, and homemade delicacies. Lancaster is the heart of Pennsylvania Dutch Country, and many of the area's best shops, museums, and restaurants are located there. Other Dutch Country destinations worth exploring include **Strasburg, Strasburg Railroad** and the **Railroad Museum of Pennsylvania,** and the **Reading** area, which is graced with the 2,400-acre **Hawk Mountain Sanctuary** and the **Daniel Boone Homestead.** Dutch Country is best seen on the back roads, where shops and villages are less crowded and the Amish can be seen working their fields on antique farm machinery.

About 55 miles southwest of Lancaster, **Gettysburg** is a quiet town with a load of history. **Gettysburg National Military Park,** which surrounds the town, is dotted with stores and homes much like it was during the Civil War. You can take a self-guided driving tour, but your visit will be more memorable if you hire a licensed battlefield guide. Must-see sites include **Cemetery Ridge,** the **Soldiers National Cemetery,** and **National Tower,** which offers a battlefield view from 307 feet.

Also in south central Pennsylvania, the state capital of **Harrisburg** is set on the shores of the Susquehanna River. East of Harrisburg, **Hershey** is renowned for **Hersheypark,** the 90-acre amusement park which includes **Chocolate World,** the **Hershey Museum, Hershey Gardens,** and **ZooAmerica.** At **Three Mile Island Visitor Center,** you can learn how the nuclear plant operates. In **York,** tour the **Harley-Davidson plant** and explore the **Rodney Gott Antique Motorcycle Museum.**

There was a time when **Pittsburgh** was a polluted city where the air was blackened by coal smoke. Pittsburgh still retains its iron- and steel-making heritage, but like Philadelphia, the city has undergone a renaissance. Situated at the Three Rivers—the Ohio, Monongahela, and Allegheny—the city offers lots of culture, architecture, and history. The **Andy Warhol Museum, Carnegie Science Center, Pittsburgh Children's Museum,** and **Pittsburgh Zoo and National Aviary** are interesting sites. Not far from Pittsburgh, the wooded and hilly Laurel Highlands features whitewater rafting on the Youghiogheny River, the 1,700-foot Youghiogheny River Gorge at **Ohiopyle State Park,** and two Frank Lloyd Wright architectural treasures in **Fallingwater** and **Kentuck Knob.**

Northern Pennsylvania is more natural and remote than the rest of the state. **Erie,** a port town located on the southern shore of Lake Erie, is home to **Presque Isle State Park,** the **Erie Maritime Museum,** and **Discovery Square.** The 797-square-mile

Allegheny National Forest, the 301-foot-high **Kinzua Railroad Bridge,** and the town of **Scranton** are visitor favorites. Southeast of Scranton, the **Pocono Mountains** have 2,400 square miles of peaks, waterfalls, lakes, streams, and resort towns. A popular place for honeymooners, the Poconos are also a camper's haven—especially campers who like to fish, boat, swim, and hike.

The following facilities accept payment in checks or cash only:

BelvedeBald Eagle State Park (Russel P. Letterman Campground), Howard

Buttercup Woodlands Campground, Butler

Kittatinny Campgrounds, Barryville

Mount Pocono Campground and Resort, Mount Pocono

Campground Profiles

ADAMSTOWN
Shady Grove Campground

264 W. Swartzville Rd., Adamstown 19501. T: (717) 484-4225; www.shadygrove campground.com; shadygrove@redrose.net.

RV ★★★ Tent ★★★

Beauty: ★★★★ Site Privacy: ★★
Spaciousness: ★★ Quiet: ★★★
Security: ★★★ Cleanliness: ★★★
Insect Control: ★★★ Facilities: ★★★★

In the heart of Lancaster County's Pennsylvania Dutch Country, Shady Grove Campground is as tranquil as the lush Amish and Mennonite farms that surround it. There are three pull-throughs and 30 double slideout sites. The campground's rolling landscape has wooded and open sites, and even though most of Shady Grove is situated on rolling terrain, level camping sites are available. Of the 96 RV sites, 90 have full hookups. Children will especially like the swimming pool and the expansive playground. No license is required to fish at the spring-fed, three-acre lake, and paddle boats can be rented. This is a pleasant and peaceful place to stay while exploring Dutch Country and visiting the outlet malls in nearby Reading.

BASICS

Operated By: Doug and Julia Nolan. **Open:** Apr. 1–Nov. 1. **Site Assignment:** Reservations accepted, require 1st night's deposit; otherwise first come, first served. **Registration:** At campground headquarters. **Fee:** $23 (VISA, MC, D). **Parking:** At site.

FACILITIES

Number of RV Sites: 96. **Number of Tent-Only Sites:** None. **Hookups:** Electric (20, 30 amps), cable TV, phone, 90 full hookups. **Each Site:** Fire ring, picnic table. **Dump Station:** Yes. **Laundry:** Yes. **Pay Phone:** Yes. **Rest Rooms and Showers:** Yes. **Fuel:** Yes. **Propane:** Yes. **Internal Roads:** Gravel, in good condition. **RV Service:** No. **Market:** Within 1 mi. **Restaurant:** Within 1 mi. **General Store:** Yes, limited. **Vending:** Yes. **Playground:** Yes. **Other:** On-site game room, spring-fed 3-acre lake, cabins. **Activities:** Basketball, volleyball, rec room, horseshoes, fishing, rental boats and pedal boats. **Nearby Attractions:** Pennsylvania Dutch Country and Lancaster County, antique markets, Reading outlet malls. **Additional Information:** Pennsylvania Dutch CVB, (800) PADUTCH, www.padutchcountry.com.

RESTRICTIONS

Pets: On leash only. **Fires:** No. **Alcoholic Beverages:** At site. **Vehicle Maximum Length:** None. **Other:** Check-in at 2 p.m., check-out at 1 p.m.

TO GET THERE

Take Exit 21 on I-76. Go 1.2 mi. north on SR 272 and 0.5 mi. northwest on SR 897.

ADAMSTOWN
Sill's Family Campground

1906 Bowmansville Rd. P.O. Box 566, Adamstown 19501. T: (717) 484-4806; F: (717) 484-6132; campsills@aol.com.

RV ★★★★ Tent ★★★

Beauty: ★★★ Site Privacy: ★★
Spaciousness: ★★ Quiet: ★★★★
Security: ★★★★ Cleanliness: ★★★
Insect Control: ★★★★ Facilities: ★★★

Located 15 miles northeast of Lancaster, in Pennsylvania Dutch Country where well-kept farmhouses and barns dot the rolling terrain, Sill's Family Campground is a haven for campers seeking shelter from the sweltering sun. Many sites are shaded, and part of the park is wooded. There are 20 sites that accommodate pull-throughs and 25 that suit double slideouts. The location of Sill's is ideal for travelers interested in Pennsylvania Dutch Country attractions, but there are few activities other than swimming, badminton, horseshoes, volleyball, and softball. Shady Grove Campground, also in Adamstown, has a spring-fed lake, which offers campers more recreational opportunities. Both Sill's and Shady Grove are comfortable base camps when visiting Dutch Country attractions.

BASICS

Operated By: Russ South. **Open:** Apr. 1–Oct. 31. **Site Assignment:** Reservations recommended. **Registration:** At campground headquarters. **Fee:** $20 (VISA, MC, D). **Parking:** At site.

FACILITIES

Number of RV Sites: 140. **Number of Tent-Only Sites:** 20. **Hookups:** Electric (20, 30 amps), cable TV, Internet, water, 100 full hookups. **Each Site:** Picnic table, fire ring. **Dump Station:** Yes. **Laundry:** Yes. **Pay Phone:** Yes. **Rest Rooms and Showers:** Yes. **Fuel:** No. **Propane:** Yes. **Internal Roads:** Gravel and paved, in good condition. **RV Service:** No. **Market:** Within 2 mi. **Restaurant:** Within 2 mi. **General Store:** Yes. **Vending:** Yes. **Playground:** Yes. **Other:** The campground has a traffic control gate. **Activities:** Game room, rec room, softball diamond, badminton, horseshoes, volleyball. **Nearby Attractions:** Pennsylvania Dutch Country, Lancaster County, antique markets, Maple Grove Racetrack, Reading outlet malls, Valley Forge. **Additional Information:** Pennsylvania Dutch CVB, (800) PADUTCH, www.padutchcountry.com.

RESTRICTIONS

Pets: On leash. **Fires:** At site. **Alcoholic Beverages:** At site. **Vehicle Maximum Length:** 45 ft. **Other:** None.

TO GET THERE

Take Exit 21 (junction of I-76 & SR-272). Head north on SR-272 to Bowmansville Rd. Head east for 0.5 mi. Campground is on the left.

ASHFIELD
Bake Oven Campground

P.O. Box 269 SR-895, Ashfield 18212. T: (570) 386-2911; www.homestead.com/ bakeovencampground; bakeoven@ptd.net.

RV ★★★ Tent ★★★

Beauty: ★★★★ Site Privacy: ★★
Spaciousness: ★★ Quiet: ★★★
Security: ★★★ Cleanliness: ★★★★
Insect Control: ★★★ Facilities: ★★★★

Located midway between Snyders and Bowmansville on St. Rte. 895, Bake Oven Campground is situated at the entrance of the Pocono Mountains' western region. Some sites are shaded, and the most picturesque sites are streamside. Fifteen gravel sites and 15 grass sites are available, as are three pull-throughs and 10 double slideouts. The stream on the Bake Oven grounds is stocked with trout, increasing the likelihood of lively fish stories. The swimming pool is new. Bake Oven is not fancy, but it is a clean, quiet, and relaxing place to absorb the atmosphere of the Poconos.

BASICS

Operated By: Private operator. **Open:** All year. **Site Assignment:** Reservations accepted; walk-ins accepted first-come, first-served basis. **Registration:** At campground headquarters. **Fee:** $22 (VISA, MC, D). **Parking:** At site.

FACILITIES

Number of RV Sites: 130. **Number of Tent-Only Sites:** None. **Hookups:** Electric (20, 30 amps), water, 100 full hookups. **Each Site:** Fire ring, picnic table. **Dump Station:** Yes. **Laundry:** Yes. **Pay Phone:** Yes. **Rest Rooms and Showers:** Yes. **Fuel:** No. **Propane:** Yes. **Internal Roads:** Gravel, in good condition. **RV Service:** No. **Market:** Within 3 mi. **Restaurant:** Within 3 mi. **General Store:** Yes. **Vending:** Yes. **Playground:** Yes. **Other:** Planned activities are scheduled on weekends only. **Activities:** Stream fishing, badminton, basketball, horseshoes, hiking trails, volleyball, rec room, coin games, playground, sports field. **Nearby Attractions:** Beltzville Lake, Allentown Fair, Allentown. **Additional Information:** Pocono Mountains Vacation Bureau, (800) POCONOS, www.800poconos.org.

RESTRICTIONS

Pets: On leash only. **Fires:** At site. **Alcoholic Beverages:** At site. **Vehicle Maximum Length:** 40 ft. **Other:** The campground is partially handicapped accessible.

TO GET THERE

From I-76, take Exit 34 (US 209); go 1.5 mi. south on US 209. Go 3 mi. southeast on SR-248 and 5 mi. west on SR-895. Campground entrance is on the left.

BARRYVILLE

Kittatinny Campgrounds

102 Kittatinny Ct., Dingmans Ferry 18328. T: (570) 828-2338; F: (570) 828-2165; www.kittatinny.com.

RV ★★★ Tent ★★★★

Beauty: ★★★★ Site Privacy: ★★★★
Spaciousness: ★★★★ Quiet: ★★★★
Security: ★★★★ Cleanliness: ★★★★
Insect Control: ★★★★ Facilities: ★★★

Outdoor adventure is the name of the game at Kittatinny Campgrounds. Located close to the Pennsylvania border along the crystal-clear waters of the Delaware River, Kittatinny has more than 320 sites spread over 250 wooded acres. Sites 901–960, located along the Delaware River on the campground's southeastern end, are among the most inviting. Upon request, campers can stay at sites in a non-alcohol section. With the river, a stream teeming with trout, mountin trails to explore, and 252 sites with no hookups, Kittatinny is especially ideal for tent campers who long to be one with nature. Kittatinny's headquarters is located in Dingman's Ferry, PA. The campground in Barryville is convenient to Kittatinny's whitewater rafting trips. Kittatinny also offers relaxing canoe trips, kayak rentals, and tube rentals. For adventure of a different sort, try paintball. Kittatinny's combat fields are situated on a mountain top and overlook the Delaware River. You can combine adventure with history in Barryville, which is home to the Fort Delaware Museum of Colonial History and the Zane Grey Museum.

BASICS

Operated By: Kittatinny Canoes. **Open:** Apr. 15–Oct. 15. **Site Assignment:** Reservations and walk-ins accepted. **Registration:** At campground headquarters. **Fee:** $7 per site ($10 per person). **Parking:** At site.

FACILITIES

Number of RV Sites: 72. **Number of Tent-Only Sites:** 250. **Hookups:** Electric (15, 20 amps), water. **Each Site:** Fire ring, picnic table. **Dump Station:** Yes. **Laundry:** Yes. **Pay Phone:** Yes. **Rest Rooms and Showers:** Yes. **Fuel:** No. **Propane:** No. **Internal Roads:** Gravel and paved, in good condition. **RV Service:** No. **Market:** Within 3 mi. **Restaurant:** Within 3 mi. **General Store:** Yes. **Vending:** Yes. **Playground:** Yes. **Other:** 1,000 canoe rentals. **Activities:** Canoeing, swimming, boating, river and stream fishing, badminton, sports field, hiking trails, horseshoes, volleyball, rec hall. **Nearby Attractions:** Delaware River, whitewater rafting, Fort Delaware Museum of Colonial History, Zane Grey Museum. **Additional Information:** Kittatinny Canoes, (800) FLOAT-KC, www.kittatinny.com.

RESTRICTIONS

Pets: On leash only. **Fires:** At site. **Alcoholic Beverages:** At site. **Vehicle Maximum Length:** 40 ft. **Other:** None.

TO GET THERE

From Hwy. 55, go 2 mi. northwest on Hwy. 97. Entrance is on the right.

BEDFORD

Friendship Village Campground

348 Friendship Village, Bedford 15522. T: (814) 623-1677 or (800) 992-3528; F: (814) 623-3076; www.bedfordcounty.net/camping/friendship; camping@nb.net.

RV ★★★★ Tent ★★★★

Beauty: ★★★★ Site Privacy: ★★★
Spaciousness: ★★★ Quiet: ★★★★
Security: ★★★★ Cleanliness: ★★★★★
Insect Control: ★★★★ Facilities: ★★★★★

In Bedford County, it seems like the covered bridges outnumber the stoplights. With this in mind, it's good that Friendship Village offers plenty of amenities and activities for families. Located midway between Pittsburgh and Harrisburg—not far from historic Bedford—Friendship Village has a full slate of planned activities, not counting the recreation menu that ranges from basketball and volleyball to mini-golf and fishing. Many sites are shaded or partially shaded. There are 44 pull-through sites, many of which are open. The best sites are along the trout-stocked stream. The tent sites are grassy and comfortable.

BASICS

Operated By: Ken and Darla Rhodes. **Open:** All year. **Site Assignment:** Reservations encouraged, first-come, first-served accepted. **Registration:** At campground headquarters. **Fee:** $22 (VISA, MC, D). **Parking:** At site.

FACILITIES

Number of RV Sites: 155. **Number of Tent-Only Sites:** 20. **Hookups:** Electric (20, 30, 50 amps), cable TV, phone, water, 98 full hookups. **Each Site:** Fire ring, picnic table. **Dump Station:** Yes. **Laundry:** Yes. **Pay Phone:** Yes. **Rest Rooms and Showers:** Yes. **Fuel:** No. **Propane:** Yes. **Internal Roads:** Gravel and paved, in good condition. **RV Service:** No. **Market:** Within 1 mi. **Restaurant:** Within 1 mi. **General Store:** Yes. **Vending:** Yes. **Playground:** Yes. **Other:** Cabins available for rent Friendship Village has a full slate of planned activities; check website for details. **Activities:** Rec hall, coin games, boating, canoeing, mini-golf, rowboat and paddleboat rentals, fishing, basketball, shuffleboard, sports field, horseshoes, volleyball. **Nearby Attractions:** Old Bedford Village, the Bison Corral, Fort Bedford Museum, Blue Knob Ski Resort, Shawnee Lake, Raystown Lake, Historic Bedford, covered bridges. **Additional Information:** Bedford County Visitors Bureau, (877) BC-GUIDE, www.bedford-county.net.

RESTRICTIONS

Pets: On leash only. **Fires:** At site. **Alcoholic Beverages:** At site. **Vehicle Maximum Length:** 50 ft. **Other:** Pets and smoking are not permitted in cabins.

TO GET THERE

From I-76, take Exit 11 and head south 1 mi. on US 220, then west on Rte. 30 to Friendship Village Rd. Campground is 0.25 mi.

BELLEFONTE

Bellefonte/State College KOA

2481 Jacksonville Rd., Bellefonte 16823. T: (814) 355-7912 or (800) 562-8127; www.koacampgrounds.com; bellkoa@aol.com.

RV ★★★★ Tent ★★★★

Beauty: ★★★★ Site Privacy: ★★
Spaciousness: ★★ Quiet: ★★★
Security: ★★★★ Cleanliness: ★★★★
Insect Control: ★★★★ Facilities: ★★★★

With postcard perfect mountain views and lots of amenities, Bellefonte/State Collage KOA is a comfortable place for your RV and tent. There are many grassy sites. Of the 100 RV sites, 18 accommodate pull-throughs and 26 accommodate slide-outs. The campground is especially popular during the summer (considering all the outdoor activities nearby) and during college football season when the Penn State Nittany Lions play in Happy Valley. The free pancakes on Sunday are certainly a welcome bonus.

BASICS

Operated By: KOA. **Open:** Apr. 1–Nov. 15. **Site Assignment:** Reservations and first-come, first-served accepted. **Registration:** At campground headquarters. **Fee:** $25 (VISA, MC, AE, D). **Parking:** At site.

Facilities

Number of RV Sites: 100. **Number of Tent-Only Sites:** 35. **Hookups:** Electric (20, 30, 50 amps), cable TV, phone, water, 55 full hookups. **Each Site:** Fire ring, picnic table, lantern pole. **Dump Station:** Yes. **Laundry:** Yes. **Pay Phone:** Yes. **Rest Rooms and Showers:** Yes. **Fuel:** No. **Propane:** Yes. **Internal Roads:** Gravel, in good condition. **RV Service:** No. **Market:** Within 5 mi. **Restaurant:** Within 5 mi. **General Store:** Yes. **Vending:** Yes. **Playground:** Yes. **Other:** 24-hour security. **Activities:** Swimming, rec hall, coin games, fishing, basketball, bike rentals, badminton, horseshoes, hiking trails, volleyball. **Nearby Attractions:** Historic Bellefonte, Penn State University, Belleville Amish Market, Knoebels Amusement Park, Johnstown Flood National Memorial, Ashland's Pioneer Tunnel Coal Mine, Allegheny Portage Railroad, Pennsylvania Military Museum, Penn's Cave, Woodward Cave, Happy Valley Friendly Farm. **Additional Information:** Victorian Bellefonte, www.bellefonte.com.

Restrictions

Pets: On leash only. **Fires:** At site. **Alcoholic Beverages:** At site. **Vehicle Maximum Length:** None. **Other:** None.

To Get There

From I-80, take Exit 24 and go north two mi. on Hwy. 26. Entrance is on the left.

BOWMANSVILLE

Lake-In-Wood Camping Resort

576 Yellow Hill Rd., Narvon 17555. T: (717) 445-5525; www.lakeinwoodcampground.com; lakeinwoodcamp@juno.com.

RV ★★★★★ Tent ★★★★★

Beauty: ★★★★	Site Privacy: ★★★
Spaciousness: ★★★★	Quiet: ★★★★
Security: ★★★★	Cleanliness: ★★★★
Insect Control: ★★★★	Facilities: ★★★★★

Located near Bowmansville in Lancaster County, Lake-In-Wood is another campground nestled in the heart of Pennsylvania Dutch Country—and one of the best. In fact, with its cleanliness, natural splendor, and abundance of activities and amenities, Lake-In-Wood Camping Resort is one of the finest properties in the mid-Atlantic. Of Lake-In-Wood's 325 RV sites—some open, others shaded—36 handle pull-throughs and 200 accommodate double slideouts. Partial to staying near the water, we like the sites alongside the six-acre lake, where rowboats and pedal boats can be rented. For those people who do not own a tent or an RV but enjoy the camping experience, we like the novelty rental units at Lake-In-Wood. Chances are you haven't slept in a double-decker bus, a shipwreck, or a caboose. Also, though you've likely played mini-golf, perhaps you haven't tried chucker golf—a game more suited for those who cannot crush Tiger Woods-like drives. Chucker golf is played on a smaller course and is suited for beginners.

Basics

Operated By: Klaas Bakker. **Open:** Apr. 1–Nov. 1. **Site Assignment:** Reservation and walk-ins accepted. **Registration:** At park office. **Fee:** $28 (VISA, MC, D). **Parking:** At site.

Facilities

Number of RV Sites: 325. **Number of Tent-Only Sites:** 18. **Hookups:** Electric (20, 30, 50 amps), cable TV, phone, water, 285 full hookups. **Each Site:** Picnic table, fire ring, lantern pole. **Dump Station:** Yes. **Laundry:** Yes. **Pay Phone:** Yes. **Rest Rooms and Showers:** Yes. **Fuel:** No. **Propane:** No. **Internal Roads:** Gravel and paved, in good condition. **RV Service:** No. **Market:** 4 mi. in Blue Ball. **Restaurant:** 4 mi. in Blue Ball. **General Store:** Yes. **Vending:** Yes. **Playground:** Yes. **Other:** Fire engine rides, church services, themed rental units (double-decker bus, shipwreck, treehouse, etc). **Activities:** Rec hall, coin games, swimming pool, wading pool, whirlpool, boating, canoeing, rowboat and pedal boat rentals, shuffleboard, badminton, horseshoes, sports field, hiking trails, fitness trail, volleyball, basketball, mini-golf, chucker golf. **Nearby Attractions:** Pennsylvania Dutch Country, Pennsylvania Rail Museum, Landis Valley Museum, Valley Forge, Reading outlet malls, Onyx Cave, Crystal Cave, Gettysburg Battlefield, Pennsylvania Farm Museum, Longwood Gardens, Daniel Boone Homestead, Dorney Water Park. **Additional Information:** Pennsylvania Dutch CVB, (800) PADUTCH, www.padutchcountry.com; Valley Forge CVB, (888) VISITVF, www.valleyforge.org.

Restrictions

Pets: On leash only. **Fires:** None. **Alcoholic Beverages:** None. **Vehicle Maximum Length:** 45 ft. **Other:** Check-in 3–9 p.m.; arrivals before noon will be charged a full night fee; arrivals noon–3 p.m. will be charged half-day fee.

To Get There

From SR 23, go 4.5 mi. north on SR 625, 1 mi. northeast on Oaklyn Dr., and 1.5 mi. east on Yellow Hill Rd.

BOWMANSVILLE

Oak Creek Campground

P.O. Box 128, Bowmansville 17507. T: (717) 445-6161 or (800) 446-8365; F: (717) 445-4544; www.gocampingamerica.com/oakcreekcg; oakcreekcg@gocampingamerica.com.

RV ★★★★ Tent ★★★★

Beauty: ★★★★	Site Privacy: ★★★
Spaciousness: ★★★	Quiet: ★★★★
Security: ★★★★★	Cleanliness: ★★★★★
Insect Control: ★★★★	Facilities: ★★★★

In a region defined by natural beauty, with rolling green hills, towering trees, and rippling streams, Oak Creek Campground is a must-stay for campers who yearn for shady campsites and peaceful surroundings. Located outside of Bowmansville and covering 200 acres, the campground actually overlooks Oak Creek from a hillside densely packed with forest and nature trails. All RV sites are spacious and wooded. There are eight pull-through sites, and 100 accommodate double slideouts. A cluster of sites along the pond and another cluster of sites at the northwest tip of the campground along Oak Creek are ideal. Near the center of the campground, there are sites on both sides of the creek, but these sites offer little privacy. With its creek, swimming pool, and colorful hiking trails, Oak Creek is a quiet and fun park to stay at while in Dutch Country. Oakley, the Amish cricket, is Oak Creek's unofficial mascot and can be heard and seen at the campground.

Basics

Operated By: Dennis and Sue Cramer. **Open:** All year. **Site Assignment:** Reservations recommended. **Registration:** At campground office. **Fee:** $29 (VISA, MC, D). **Parking:** At site.

Facilities

Number of RV Sites: 307. **Number of Tent-Only Sites:** 20. **Hookups:** Electric (30, 50 amps), cable TV, water, 152 full hookups. **Each Site:** Fire ring, picnic table. **Dump Station:** Yes. **Laundry:** Yes. **Pay Phone:** Yes. **Rest Rooms and Showers:** Yes. **Fuel:** No. **Propane:** Yes. **Internal Roads:** Gravel and paved, in good condition. **RV Service:** No. **Market:** Within 6 mi. **Restaurant:** Within 6 mi. **General Store:** Yes. **Vending:** Yes. **Playground:** Yes. **Other:** Adult TV lounge, teen arcade. **Activities:** Rec hall, coin games, swimming, pond and stream fishing, shuffleboard, badminton, sports field, horseshoes, hiking trails, volleyball, basketball. **Nearby Attractions:** Pennsylvania Dutch Country, Rockvale Square Outlets, HersheyPark and Chocolate World, Strasburg Railroad, National Toy Train Museum, Dutch Wonderland Family Fun Park, The Amazing Maize Maze, Longwood Gardens, Gast Classic Motorcars Museum, Stoudt's Brewery. **Additional Information:** Pennsylvania Dutch CVB, (800) PADUTCH, www.padutchcountry.com.

Restrictions

Pets: On leash only. **Fires:** At site. **Alcoholic Beverages:** At site. **Vehicle Maximum Length:** 36 ft. **Other:** Check-in and check-out are both at 3 p.m.; early arrivals and late departures subject to half-day charge.

To Get There

At SR 625 and Maple Grove Rd., go 1.5 mi. east on Maple Grove. Entrance to Oak Creek is at the end.

BOWMANSVILLE

Sun Valley Campground

451 E. Maple Grove Rd. Box 708, Bowmansville 17507. T: (717) 445-6262; F: (717) 445-5854; www.sunvalleycampground.net; sunvallecampground@sunvalleycampground.net.

RV ★★★★★ Tent ★★★★

Beauty: ★★★★	Site Privacy: ★★
Spaciousness: ★★★	Quiet: ★★★
Security: ★★★★	Cleanliness: ★★★★
Insect Control: ★★★★	Facilities: ★★★★★

Located near Oak Creek Campground outside of Bowmansville, Sun Valley Campground is a family haven where hayrides, pond fishing, and sand volleyball are among the activities offered. Overall, Sun Valley has fewer sites than Lake-In-Wood Camping Resort and Oak Creek Campground, but it does not take a back seat in cleanliness, beauty, and excitement. Sun Valley has a full-time activities director. The campground is semi-wooded with shaded and open sites—all level, some grass and some gravel. There are nine pull-through sites. Like its fellow Bowmansville campgrounds, Sun Valley is centrally located between Hershey (45 mi.), Gettysburg (50 mi.), Valley Forge (40 mi.), Philadelphia (50 mi.), Reading (15 mi.), and Lancaster (20 mi.).

Basics

Operated By: Private operator. **Open:** All year. **Site Assignment:** Reservations recommended; walk-ins accepted on first-come, first-served basis. **Registration:** At campground office. **Fee:** $29 (VISA, MC, D). **Parking:** At site.

Facilities

Number of RV Sites: 265. **Number of Tent-Only Sites:** 21. **Hookups:** Electric (20, 30, 50 amps), cable TV, phone, water, 200 full hookups. **Each Site:** Fire ring, picnic table, lantern pole. **Dump Station:** Yes. **Laundry:** Yes. **Pay Phone:** Yes. **Rest Rooms and Showers:** Yes. **Fuel:** No. **Propane:** Yes. **Internal Roads:** Gravel and paved, in good condition. **RV Service:** No. **Market:** Within 2 mi. **Restaurant:** Within 2 mi. **General Store:** Yes. **Vending:** Yes. **Playground:** Yes. **Other:** Sun Valley has a full-time activities director on staff The campground has a petting zoo Cabin, cottage and pop-up rentals are available. **Activities:** Rec hall, coin games, swimming, pond fishing, basketball, badminton, sports field, hayrides, hiking trail, basketball, volleyball, horseshoes. **Nearby Attractions:** Pennsylvania Dutch Country, Dorney Park, Reading outlet malls, Gettysburg Battlefield, Valley Forge, Strasburg Railroad, golf courses, Sesame Place. **Additional Information:** Pennsylvania Dutch CVB, (800) PADUTCH, www.padutchcountry.com.

Restrictions

Pets: On leash only. **Fires:** At site. **Alcoholic Beverages:** At site. **Vehicle Maximum Length:** 35 ft. **Other:** None.

To Get There

From I-76, take Exit 22. Go south 1 mi. on Rte. 10 to SR 23, west 7.4 mi. to SR625, north 5.8 mi. to E. Maple Grove Rd., and east 2 mi. to campground entrance on the left.

BUTLER

Buttercup Woodlands Campground

854 Evans City Rd., Renfrew 16053. T: (724) 789-9340; F: (724) 789-9330; www.buttercup.org; buttcup@zbzoom.net.

RV ★★★★ Tent ★★★★

Beauty: ★★★★ Site Privacy: ★★
Spaciousness: ★★★ Quiet: ★★★
Security: ★★★★ Cleanliness: ★★★★
Insect Control: ★★★ Facilities: ★★★★

Located about 30 miles northeast of Pittsburgh and 10 miles southeast of Moraine State Park and Lake Arthur, Butler's Buttercup Woodlands Campground features spacious grassy sites. Among the amenities are a library, a new playground, a dance hall, and trolley rides. Buttercup's proximity to Moraine State Park is one of its top draws. Moraine State Park features 3,225-acre Lake Arthur, an outstanding warm water fishery that is also ideal for sailing and boating. Visitors sometimes see osprey that were reintroduced to the park. Of special interest is the Frank Preston Conservation Area and a seven-mile paved bike trail that winds around the north shore of the lake. The gently rolling hills, lush forests, and sparkling waters disguise a land that has endured the effects of continental glaciers and massive mineral extraction.

Basics

Operated By: Ed, Barb and Christy Tanski. **Open:** Apr. 15–Oct. 15. **Site Assignment:** Reservations accepted; walk-ins accepted. **Registration:** At campground headquarters. **Fee:** $24. **Parking:** At site.

Facilities

Number of RV Sites: 330. **Number of Tent-Only Sites:** None. **Hookups:** Electric (30, 50 amps), cable TV, phone, 300 full hookups. **Each Site:** Fire ring, picnic table. **Dump Station:** Yes. **Laundry:** Yes. **Pay Phone:** Yes. **Rest Rooms and Showers:** Yes. **Fuel:** No. **Propane:** Yes. **Internal Roads:** Gravel and paved, in good condition. **RV Service:** No. **Market:** Within 3 mi. **Restaurant:** Within 3 mi. **General Store:** Yes. **Vending:** Yes. **Playground:** Yes. **Other:** Cabins and RV available for rent. **Activities:** Rec room, trolley rides, coin games, swimming, lake fishing, basketball, sports field, badminton, horseshoes, volleyball, shuffleboard. **Nearby Attractions:** Pittsburgh, Moraine State Park, Lake Arthur, golf courses, Prime Outlets at Grove City, Butler County, Historic Zelienople. **Additional Information:** Greater Pittsburgh CVB, (800) 366-0093. www.visitpittsburgh.com; Butler County Tourist Promotion Agency, (888) 741-6772, www.butlercountychamber.com.

Restrictions

Pets: On leash only. **Fires:** At site. **Alcoholic Beverages:** At site. **Vehicle Maximum Length:** 65 ft. **Other:** No carpet permitted on grass.

To Get There

From I-79, take Exit 27 and follow SR 528 1.5 mi. to SR 68. Go east on SR 68 and follow for 8 miles. Campground is on the left.

CARLISLE

Western Village RV Park

200 Greenview Dr., Carlisle 17013. T: (717) 243-1179; www.westernvillagervpark.com; cowboytrain@aol.com.

RV ★★★ Tent ★★★

Beauty: ★★★ Site Privacy: ★
Spaciousness: ★★ Quiet: ★★★
Security: ★★★★ Cleanliness: ★★★
Insect Control: ★★★★ Facilities: ★★★★

Fishing is a favorite pastime in Pennsylvania, and trout fishing at the Yellow Breeches is a favorite activity of many guests who flock to the Western Village RV Park in Carlisle. Western Village is clean and comfortable, with mini-golf and a large pavilion to accommodate groups. Kids like the new, expansive game room. Of the 250 RV sites, there are 22 spacious pull-throughs and 150 that handle double slideouts. Sites on the park's eastern side of the most spacious, but, while clean, they offer little privacy. The game room at Western Village is newer and very large, and there is a swimming pool and a nature trail. A tent area is located at the northern tip of the campground.

Basics

Operated By: Larry and Maggie. **Open:** All year. **Site Assignment:** Reservations and walk-ins accepted. **Registration:** At campground office. **Fee:** $24 (VISA, MC). **Parking:** At site.

Facilities

Number of RV Sites: 250. **Number of Tent-Only Sites:** None. **Hookups:** Electric (20, 30 amps), phone, water, 140 full hookups. **Each Site:** Fire ring, picnic table. **Dump Station:** Yes. **Laundry:** Yes. **Pay Phone:** Yes. **Rest Rooms and Showers:** Yes. **Fuel:** No. **Propane:** Yes. **Internal Roads:** Gravel, in good condition. **RV Service:** No. **Market:** Within 2 mi. **Restaurant:** Within 2 mi. **General Store:** Yes. **Vending:** Yes. **Playground:** Yes. **Other:** Church service Sun. at 10 am. **Activities:** Mini-golf, hiking trails, rec hall, coin games, swimming, basketball, sports field, horseshoes, volleyball. **Nearby Attractions:** Trout fishing at the Yellow Breeches, Allenberry Dinner Theater, golf courses, hiking on Appalachian Trail and rail trails, Carlisle Theater, Harrisburg, Hershey, Lancaster County. **Additional Information:** Harrisburg-Hershey-Carlisle-Perry Co. Tourism and Convention Bureau, (800) 995-0969, www.visithhc.com.

Restrictions

Pets: On leash only. **Fires:** At site. **Alcoholic Beverages:** At site. **Vehicle Maximum Length:** None. **Other:** No clotheslines permitted.

To Get There

From I-81, take Exit 13 and go 1.5 mi. southwest on Walnut Bottom Rd. Follow signs on Greenview Dr. Entrance is at the end.

CLARION

Kalyumet Campground

8630 Miola Rd., Lucinda 16235. T: (814) 744-9622; F: (814) 744-3656; www.kalyumet.com; camp@kalyumet.com.

RV ★★★ Tent ★★★

Beauty: ★★★★ Site Privacy: ★★
Spaciousness: ★★★ Quiet: ★★★★
Security: ★★★ Cleanliness: ★★★
Insect Control: ★★★ Facilities: ★★★

Located outside of Clarion, 11.5 miles north of Interstate 80, Kalyumet Campground is an ideal base for outdoor enthusiasts longing to embark on a wilderness adventure. Kalyumet is not far from the Allegheny National Forest, and the campground is even closer to Cook Forest State Park. Bordered by the Clarion River, Cook Forest is rich with old-growth timber and is a National Natural Landmark. Adorned with a mix of open and shaded sites graced by towering pines, Kalyumet has 20 sites that accommodate pull-throughs and 20 sites that handle double slideouts. The office and activity centers (including basketball and volleyball courts) are located near the entrance of Kalyumet. A large cluster of sites is located in five rows in the center of the campground. A tent area is nestled in the woods at the northern edge.

Basics

Operated By: Mark and Becky Wineman. **Open:** May 1–Oct. 31. **Site Assignment:** Reservations recommended. **Registration:** At campground office. **Fee:** $20 (VISA, MC, D). **Parking:** At site.

Facilities

Number of RV Sites: 150. **Number of Tent-Only Sites:** 30. **Hookups:** Electric (20, 30 amps), phone, water. **Each Site:** Fire ring, picnic table. **Dump Station:** Yes. **Laundry:** Yes. **Pay Phone:** Yes. **Rest Rooms and Showers:** Yes. **Fuel:** No. **Propane:** Yes. **Internal Roads:** Gravel, in good condition. **RV Service:** No. **Market:** Within 6 mi. **Restaurant:** Within 6 mi. **General Store:** Yes. **Vending:** Yes. **Playground:** Yes. **Other:** Banquet hall, dance hall. **Activities:** Rec hall, basketball, bike rentals, planned activities on weekends, badminton, volleyball, horseshoes, sports field, hiking trails. **Nearby Attractions:** Cook Forest State Park, Clarion River, golf courses, Sawmill Center for the Arts, Sawmill Theatre, Allegheny National Forest. **Additional Information:** Allegheny National Forest Vacation Bureau, (814) 368-9370, www.allegheny-vacation.com.

Restrictions

Pets: On leash only. **Fires:** At site. **Alcoholic Beverages:** At site. **Vehicle Maximum Length:** 40 ft. **Other:** None.

To Get There

From I-80, take Exit 9 and go 1.5 mi. north on Fifth Ave., which becomes Miola Rd. Entrance to Kalyumet is on right.

COATESVILLE

Beechwood Campground

105 Beechwood Dr., Coatesville 19320. T: (610) 384-1457 or (800) CAMP248; www.beechwood-campground.com; beechwoodc@aol.com.

RV: ★★★★ Tent: ★★★★

Beauty: ★★★★ Site Privacy: ★
Spaciousness: ★★ Quiet: ★★★★
Security: ★★★★ Cleanliness: ★★★★
Insect Control: ★★★★ Facilities: ★★★★

Beechwood is dotted with peaceful, grassy, and shaded sites; 59 accommodate pull-throughs and 120 accommodate double slideouts. Two rec halls and an open pavilion are perfect for groups. In fact, when we were at Beechwood, the halls and pavilion were alive with families enjoying parties and reunions. Attractions in Beechwood's region are unique. Longwood Gardens is a horticultural display on 1,050 acres which offers 40 indoor/outdoor gardens, breathtaking conservatory, spectacular fountains, festivals. and holiday displays. Revolutionary War history is plentiful, including Valley Forge National Historical Park and Brandywine Battlefield Park. Brandywine is a 52-acre park containing historic houses used as headquarters by General Washington and quarters by General Lafayette during the largest battle of the American Revolutionary War.

Basics

Operated By: Fred Anderson. **Open:** Apr. 6–Oct. 28. **Site Assignment:** Reservations recommended, walk-ins accepted. **Registration:** At campground headquarters. **Fee:** $24 (VISA, MC). **Parking:** At site.

Facilities

Number of RV Sites: 251. **Number of Tent-Only Sites:** 15. **Hookups:** Electric (30 amps), cable TV, phone, water, 120 full hookups. **Each Site:** Fire ring, picnic table. **Dump Station:** Yes. **Laundry:** Yes. **Pay Phone:** Yes. **Rest Rooms and Showers:** Yes. **Fuel:** No. **Propane:** Yes. **Internal Roads:** Gravel and paved, in fair condition. **RV Service:** Yes. **Market:** Within 3 mi. **Restaurant:** Within 3 mi. **General Store:** Yes. **Vending:** Yes. **Playground:** Yes. **Other:** Two rec halls, open pavilion. **Activities:** Coin games, swimming, basketball, badminton, planned activities, volleyball, horseshoes, sports field. **Nearby Attractions:** Philadelphia, HersheyPark, Dorney Park, Valley Forge, Brandywine Battlefield, King of Prussia Mall, Dutch Wonderland, Rockvale outlets, Lancaster County, Longwood Gardens. **Additional Information:** Chester Co. Conference and Visitors Bureau, (800) 228-9933, www.brandywinevalley.com.

Restrictions

Pets: On leash only. **Fires:** At site. **Alcoholic Beverages:** At site. **Vehicle Maximum Length:** None. **Other:** Electric is metered.

To Get There

From Hwy. 82, take US 30 and go 1.75 mi. east to Veterans Hospital exit, 1.5 mi. north on Reeseville Rd., and 0.25 mi. east on paved road. Entrance to Beechwood is on right.

COOKSBURG

Cook Forest State Park

P.O. Box 120, Cooksburg 16217. T: (888) PAPARKS or (814) 744-8407; www.dcnr.state.pa.us/stateparks; cookforestsp@state.pa.us.

RV: ★★★★ Tent: ★★★★

Beauty: ★★★★ Site Privacy: ★★★
Spaciousness: ★★★ Quiet: ★★★
Security: ★★★ Cleanliness: ★★★★
Insect Control: ★★★★ Facilities: ★★★

Cook Forest State Park encompasses 7,182 acres in northwest Pennsylvania. Bordered by the picturesque Clarion River, the park is most known for old growth white pine and hemlock forests. Classified as a National Natural Landmark by the National Park Service, Cook Forest State Park is often referred to as the "Black Forest" of Pennsylvania. Ridge Camp, the park's campground, is open year-round. On-site hookups are not available and winter access is not guaranteed. There are two cabin areas at Cook Forest. The River Cabins are on a hillside overlooking the Clarion River. These are large cabins with four rooms and a fireplace. They will sleep either six or eight people. The Indian Cabins are smaller one-room structures which will accommodate four people. These cabins are found along Tom's Run located behind the park office. All cabins are rented with a minimum of furniture, including beds, mattresses, a gas stove, refrigerator, tables, and chairs. Occupants must provide their own bedding, cookware, and tableware.

Basics

Operated By: State of Pennsylvania. **Open:** All year. **Site Assignment:** Reservations and walk-ins accepted. **Registration:** At campground office. **Fee:** $15–$17 (VISA, MC). **Parking:** At designated spot.

Facilities

Number of RV Sites: 226. **Number of Tent-Only Sites:** None. **Hookups:** Electric (30, 50 amps). **Each Site:** Fire ring, picnic table. **Dump Station:** Yes. **Laundry:** No. **Pay Phone:** Yes. **Rest Rooms and Showers:** Yes. **Fuel:** No. **Propane:** No. **Internal Roads:** Gravel and dirt, in good condition. **RV Service:** No. **Market:** Within 3 mi. **Restaurant:** Within 3 mi. **General Store:** No. **Vending:** Yes. **Playground:** Yes. **Other:** None. **Activities:** Hiking, river and stream fishing, swimming, planned activities on weekends, sports field. **Nearby Attractions:** Cook Forest Sawmill Center for the Arts, Eldred World War II Museum, Allegheny River Islands Wilderness, Historic Brookville Walking Tour, Raccoon Creek State Park, Punxsutawney. **Additional Information:** Northwest Pennsylvania's Great Outdoors Visitors Bureau, (800) 348-9393, www.pagreatoutdoors.com.

Restrictions

Pets: No pets permitted. **Fires:** At site. **Alcoholic Beverages:** No alcohol permitted. **Vehicle Maximum Length:** 45 ft. **Other:** None.

To Get There

From Clarion River Bridge in Cooksburg, go 1 mi. northwest on Hwy. 36 north. Entrance is on the right.

COOKSBURG

Deer Meadow Campground

2761 Forest Rd., Cooksburg 16217. T: (814) 927-8125 or (866) 4DM-CAMP; F: (814) 927-2250; www.deermeadow.com; trcedbtz@penn.com.

RV: ★★★★ Tent: ★★★★

Beauty: ★★★★ Site Privacy: ★
Spaciousness: ★★★ Quiet: ★★★

Security: ★★★★ Cleanliness: ★★★★
Insect Control: ★★★★ Facilities: ★★★★

Amid the majestic white pines and hemlocks of Cook Forest State Park, Deer Meadow Campground is an oasis for outdoor enthusiasts searching for a wealth of activities and a clean and spacious campground to enjoy them in. With 500 sites, Deer Meadow is the largest campground in the Cook Forest area. The 65-acre campground borders the 6,422-acre Cook Forest. A hiking trail even wanders from Deer Meadow to other trails that lead deep into Cook Forest. Overall, there are 27 miles of hiking trails in Cook Forest. Canoeing, tubing, fishing, and swimming are available in the Clarion River at the state park. Of course, a full slate of activities are offered at Deer Meadow, including a heated pool and mini-golf. Deer Meadow has open and shaded sites, and many are wooded. There are no pull-through sites, but there are 350 double slideout sites. Most sites are laid out in rows, except for a cluster of sites on the eastern side which are situated in a circle.

Basics

Operated By: Ed, Tracy, and Andy Betz. **Open:** May 1–Oct. 15. **Site Assignment:** Reservations and walk-ins accepted. **Registration:** At campground office. **Fee:** $22. VISA, MC). **Parking:** At site.

Facilities

Number of RV Sites: 500. **Number of Tent-Only Sites:** 72. **Hookups:** Electric (20, 30 amps), cable TV, phone, water, 265 full hookups. **Each Site:** Fire ring, picnic table. **Dump Station:** Yes. **Laundry:** Yes. **Pay Phone:** Yes. **Rest Rooms and Showers:** Yes. **Fuel:** No. **Propane:** Yes. **Internal Roads:** Gravel and paved, in good condition. **RV Service:** No. **Market:** Within 7 mi. **Restaurant:** Within 7 mi. **General Store:** Yes. **Vending:** Yes. **Playground:** Yes. **Other:** Church services, hayrides. **Activities:** Rec hall, coin games, swimming, mini-golf, shuffleboard, basketball, planned activities, horseshoes, hiking trails, badminton, volleyball. **Nearby Attractions:** Cook Forest State Park, Leeper Flea Market, Sawmill Center for the Arts, Clear Creek State Forest, Deer Ranch, Kinzua Bridge State Park, antique shops. **Additional Information:** Allegheny National Forest Vacation Bureau, (814) 368-9370, www.allegheny-vacation.com.

Restrictions

Pets: On leash only. **Fires:** At site. **Alcoholic Beverages:** Under control at campsite. **Vehicle Maximum Length:** 40 ft. **Other:** Reservations required for Memorial Day and Labor Day.

To Get There

At Hwy. 36 and Clarion River Bridge, go 0.1 mi. northwest on Hwy. 36 and 3 mi. north on Forest Rd. Deer Meadow entrance is on left.

DENVER

Hickory Run Family Camping Resort

285 Greenville Rd., Denver 17517. T: (717) 336-5564 or (800) 458-0612; www.pacampgrounds.com.

RV ★★★★ Tent ★★★★

Beauty: ★★★★★ Site Privacy: ★★★
Spaciousness: ★★★★ Quiet: ★★★★
Security: ★★★★ Cleanliness: ★★★★
Insect Control: ★★★★ Facilities: ★★★★

Located in the pristine countryside of northern Lancaster County, Hickory Run is only a short drive away from many local attractions. Sites are shaded and open. Our favorite sites are along Upper Lake View Dr., where campers have privacy and are still a short distance from the fishing lake and boating lake. Paddleboats and rowboats are available to rent on Hickory Run's 3-acre bass-stocked lake. Of course, the Amish way of life is alive and well in Lancaster County. You can also tour an operating farm, travel through scenic farm country on an authentic steam train or by horse and buggy, or spend the day with a knight in the 16th century England at the Renaissance Faire. Enjoy German bands and great food at the Bavarian Beer Festival in nearby Adamstown, which is also the home of the 30,000-dealer Antique Row.

Basics

Operated By: Private operator. **Open:** Apr. 1–Nov. 1. **Site Assignment:** Reservations accepted, walk-ins accepted on first-come, first-served basis. **Registration:** At campground office. **Fee:** $25 (VISA, MC). **Parking:** At site.

Facilities

Number of RV Sites: 170. **Number of Tent-Only Sites:** 20. **Hookups:** Electric (20, 30 amps), phone, water, 85 full hookups. **Each Site:** Fire ring, picnic table. **Dump Station:** Yes. **Laundry:** Yes. **Pay Phone:** Yes. **Rest Rooms and Showers:** Yes. **Fuel:** No. **Propane:** Yes. **Internal Roads:** Gravel and paved, in good condition. **RV Service:** No. **Market:** 5 mi. in Denver. **Restaurant:** 5 mi. in Denver. **General Store:** Yes. **Vending:** Yes. **Playground:** Yes. **Other:** RV and cabin rentals. **Activities:** Rec hall, pavilion, coin games, swimming, wading pool, rowboat and pedal boat rentals, canoeing, planned activities, tennis, sports field, volleyball, horseshoes, hiking trail, hayrides, mini-golf. **Nearby Attractions:** Amish Village, Amish Farm and House, Middle Creek Wildlife Preserve, Strasburg Railroad, Pennsylvania Dutch Country, Dorney Park, Green Dragon Farmer's Market, Eagle Falls Adventure Park, Kitchen Kettle Village, Living Waters Theatre, Choo-Choo Barn/Traintown USA, Longwood Gardens, National Toy Train Museum, Railroad Museum of Pennsylvania. **Additional Information:** Pennsylvania Dutch CVB, (800) PADUTCH, www.padutchcountry.com.

Restrictions

Pets: On leash only. **Fires:** No. **Alcoholic Beverages:** At site. **Vehicle Maximum Length:** 45 ft. **Other:** Rates for standard site with electric and water increase to $27 Memorial Day–Labor Day.

To Get There

From I-76, take Exit 21 and follow Hwy. 272 1.75 mi. south, then 2 mi. west on Church/Main St., then follow signs for 2 mi. on paved road. Entrance to Hickory Run is on left.

DOVER

Gettysburg Farm Campground/ Outdoor World

6200 Big Mount Rd., Dover 17315. T: (717) 292-7191; F: (717) 292-2948; www.outdoorworld.com.

RV ★★★★ Tent ★★★★

Beauty: ★★★★ Site Privacy: ★★★
Spaciousness: ★★★ Quiet: ★★★★
Security: ★★★★ Cleanliness: ★★★★
Insect Control: ★★★★ Facilities: ★★★★★

Few places have more history in the United States than Gettysburg, and Gettysburg Farm Campground is located adjacent to the Black Horse Tavern, a historical landmark used as an inn and hospital during the Civil War. Operated by Outdoor World, Gettysburg Farm Campground is actually a living farm, where guests can enjoy horse-drawn hayrides and pony rides, visit with farm animals at the petting zoo, and watch the planting and harvesting of crops. Though located on a farm, this campground is kept clean, and the facilities are well-maintained. The country store is well-stocked, and activities ranging from mini-golf, fishing, and canoeing to events in the recreation center and video arcade offer enough variety to keep children happily occupied. Gettysburg Farm has a mix of gravel and grassy sites, some shaded and others open. Twelve sites accommodate pull-throughs, and 174 handle double slideouts.

Basics

Operated By: Outdoor World. **Open:** Apr. 14–Oct. 23. **Site Assignment:** Reservations encouraged, walk-ins accepted. **Registration:** At campground office. **Fee:** $25 (VISA, MC, AE, D). **Parking:** At site.

Facilities

Number of RV Sites: 265. **Number of Tent-Only Sites:** 20. **Hookups:** Electric (20, 30, 50 amps), water, 174 full hookups. **Each Site:** Fire ring, grill, picnic table. **Dump Station:** Yes. **Laundry:** Yes. **Pay Phone:** Yes. **Rest Rooms and Showers:** Yes. **Fuel:** No. **Propane:** Yes. **Internal Roads:** Gravel and paved, in good condition. **RV Service:** Yes. **Market:** Within 5 mi. **Restaurant:** Within 5 mi. **General Store:** Yes. **Vending:** Yes. **Playground:** Yes. **Other:** Living farm with pony rides and petting zoo. **Activities:** Swimming, wading pool, mini-golf, canoeing, basketball, volleyball, shuffleboard, horseshoes, fishing, video arcade, hayrides, rec center. **Nearby Attractions:** Gettysburg Battlefield Tours, National Civil War Wax Museum, Historic Downtown York, Harley Davidson Museum, Lincoln Train Scenic Ride, Utz Potato Chip Factory, Magic Town, Land of Little Horses. **Additional Information:** Gettysburg CVB, (717) 334-6274, www.gettysburg.com.

Restrictions

Pets: On leash only. **Fires:** At site. **Alcoholic Beverages:** At site. **Vehicle Maximum Length:** 40 ft.

To Get There

From Hwy. 194, go 4 mi. east on Hwy. 234 and 2

mi. north on Big Mount Rd. Campground entrance is on left.

EAST STROUDSBURG
Foxwood Family Campground

400 Mt. Nebo Rd., East Stroudsburg 18301.
T: (570) 421-1424 or (800) 845-4938; F: (570) 420-9830; www.foxwoodcampground.com; foxwood@gocampingamerica.com.

RV ★★★ Tent ★★★

Beauty: ★★★ Site Privacy: ★★
Spaciousness: ★★ Quiet: ★★★★
Security: ★★★ Cleanliness: ★★★★
Insect Control: ★★★ Facilities: ★★★

Fox Family Campground is located in the Pocono Mountains. Guests can fish for largemouth bass in a well-stocked pond, swim in a full size in-ground pool, or explore acres and acres of wooded trails. Kids can participate in the Fox 500 mini-car races, candy bar bingo, and family fishing tournaments. The rolling terrain offers spectacular mountain views and has open and shaded sites. There are no double slideout sites, but there are 50 sites that accommodate pull-throughs. Sites at the southern end of the campground offer the most privacy, and they are just a short walk from the rec hall, camp store, mini-golf course, and other activities. Of course, the Pocono Mountains region is teeming with adventure possibilities, including 14 waterfalls, nine state parks, 13 rafting tours, four Victorian towns, and the Pocono International Raceway.

Basics

Operated By: Randy and Peggy Kulp. **Open:** All year. **Site Assignment:** Reservations recommended, walk-ins accepted. **Registration:** At campground office. **Fee:** $22 (VISA, MC). **Parking:** At site.

Facilities

Number of RV Sites: 200. **Number of Tent-Only Sites:** 75. **Hookups:** Electric (20, 30 amps), cable TV, phone, water, 40 full hookups. **Each Site:** Fire ring, picnic table. **Dump Station:** Yes. **Laundry:** Yes. **Pay Phone:** Yes. **Rest Rooms and Showers:** Yes. **Fuel:** No. **Propane:** Yes. **Internal Roads:** Gravel and paved, in good condition. **RV Service:** Yes. **Market:** Within 3 mi. **Restaurant:** Within 3 mi. **General Store:** Yes. **Vending:** Yes. **Playground:** Yes. **Other:** Rally field can accommodate up to 50 units for family reunions, rallies and other special events. **Activities:** Rec hall, game room, pond fishing, mini-golf, basketball, planned activities, volleyball, sports field, horseshoes. **Nearby Attractions:** Pocono Mountains, candy and candle factories, Tocks Island National Reserve, Pocono International Raceway, golf courses, horseback riding. **Additional Information:** Pocono Mountains Vacation Bureau, (800) POCONOS, www.800poconos.org.

Restrictions

Pets: On leash only. **Fires:** At site. **Alcoholic Beverages:** At site. **Vehicle Maximum Length:** None. **Other:** Cutting or gathering wood in the park is prohibited.

To Get There

From I-80, take Exit 52 and go 1.5 mi. north on US 209, 0.25 mi. east on Buttermilk Falls Rd., and 1 mi. north on Mt. Nebo Rd. Entrance to campground is on left.

EAST STROUDSBURG
KOA—Delaware Water Gap

233 Hollow Rd., East Stroudsburg 18301.
T: (570) 223-8000 or (800) 562-0375; www.koa.com; dwgkoa@epix.net.

RV ★★★★ Tent ★★★★

Beauty: ★★★ Site Privacy: ★★
Spaciousness: ★★★ Quiet: ★★★
Security: ★★★★ Cleanliness: ★★★★
Insect Control: ★★★ Facilities: ★★★★

Located near the Delaware River outside of East Stroudsburg, KOA—Delaware Water Gap offers clean, and well-spaced open and partially shaded sites. There are 50 pull-through sites. The campground has standard activities, such as basketball, horseshoes, badminton, and mini-golf, but its proximity to numerous Delaware Water Gap and Pocono Mountains attractions and events is what attracts many visitors. The Delaware Water Gap preserves 40 miles of the middle Delaware River and almost 70,000 acres of land along the river's New Jersey and Pennsylvania shores. At the south end of the park, the river cuts eastward through a scenic water gap in the Appalachian Mountains. Canoeing, camping, fishing, swimming, hiking; viewing wildlife, geologic features and natural scenery—all this and more await visitors. The park includes historic Millbrook Village and several environmental education centers.

Basics

Operated By: Carmen and Carla Prato. **Open:** All year. **Site Assignment:** Reservations and walk-ins accepted. **Registration:** At campground office. **Fee:** $32. **Parking:** At designated spot.

Facilities

Number of RV Sites: 164. **Number of Tent-Only Sites:** 7. **Hookups:** Electric (20, 30, 50 amps), cable TV, phone. **Each Site:** Fire ring, picnic table. **Dump Station:** Yes. **Laundry:** Yes. **Pay Phone:** Yes. **Rest Rooms and Showers:** Yes. **Fuel:** No. **Propane:** Yes. **Internal Roads:** Gravel and paved, in good condition. **RV Service:** No. **Market:** Within 6 mi. **Restaurant:** Within 6 mi. **General Store:** Yes. **Vending:** Yes. **Playground:** Yes. **Other:** Cabins available for rent. **Activities:** Rec room, coin games, mini-golf, sports field, basketball, volleyball, hiking trails, horseshoes, badminton. **Nearby Attractions:** Delaware River, Pocono Mountains, Bushkill Falls, Shawnee Place, Pocono International Raceway, golf courses, horseback riding. **Additional Information:** Pocono Mountains Vacation Bureau, (800) POCONOS, www.800poconos.org.

Restrictions

Pets: On leash only. **Fires:** At site. **Alcoholic Beverages:** At site. **Vehicle Maximum Length:** None.

To Get There

From I-80, take Exit 52 and go 6 mi. north on US209 and 1 mi. east on Hollow Rd. Entrance is on left.

EAST STROUDSBURG
Mountain Vista Campground

RD 2 Box 2190, East Stroudsburg 18301.
T: (570) 223-0111; www.mtnvistacampground.com; info@mtnvistacampground.com.

RV ★★★★ Tent ★★★★

Beauty: ★★★★ Site Privacy: ★★★★
Spaciousness: ★★★★ Quiet: ★★★★
Security: ★★★★ Cleanliness: ★★★★
Insect Control: ★★★★ Facilities: ★★★★

Expansive wooded sites dominate the landscape at Mountain Vista Campground, which is within 15 minutes of the Delaware Water Gap National Recreation Area. The view of the mountains from the campground's sundeck is breathtaking. Throughout the year, the campground hosts special events like the Chili Fest, Italian Fest, Irish Fest, Oktoberfest, and Luau. There are 12 pull-through sites and 65 spots for double slideouts. Mountain Vista is also near the Appalachian Trail, Delaware State Forest, and the Delaware River— a popular spot for canoeing, rafting, and tubing. Across the border in New Jersey (about a half-hour drive from Mountain Vista) is Waterloo Village, a National Registered Historic Site in Allamuchy Mountain State Park.

Basics

Operated By: Vaughan family. **Open:** Apr. 1–Nov. 1. **Site Assignment:** Reservations accepted (1-night's payment to accompany reservation), walk-ins accepted. **Registration:** At campground headquarters. **Fee:** $25–$31 (VISA, MC). **Parking:** At site.

Facilities

Number of RV Sites: 185. **Number of Tent-Only Sites:** 15. **Hookups:** Electric (20, 30, 50 amps), phone, water, 100 full hookups. **Each Site:** Fire ring, grill. **Dump Station:** Yes. **Laundry:** Yes. **Pay Phone:** Yes. **Rest Rooms and Showers:** Yes. **Fuel:** No. **Propane:** No. **Internal Roads:** Gravel and paved, in good condition. **RV Service:** No. **Market:** Within 3 mi. **Restaurant:** Within 3 mi. **General Store:** Yes. **Vending:** Yes. **Playground:** Yes. **Other:** None. **Activities:** Rec hall, game room, swimming, boating, canoeing, float trips, pond fishing, basketball, shuffleboard, planned activities, tennis, badminton, sports field, horseshoes, hiking trails, volleyball. **Nearby Attractions:** Delaware Water Gap, Delaware River, Bushkill Falls, Appalachian Trail, Camelbeach and Alpine Slide, Memorytown USA, antique shops, factory outlets. **Additional Information:** Pocono Mountains Vacation Bureau, (800) POCONOS, www.800poconos.org.

Restrictions

Pets: On leash only. **Fires:** At site. **Alcoholic Beverages:** At site. **Vehicle Maximum Length:** None.

To Get There

From I-80, take Exit 52 and go 0.1 mi. north on US 209, 2 mi. northwest on Hwy. 447, 3 mi. north on Business US 209, 1 mi. west on Craig's Meadow Rd., and 500 ft. south on paved road. Entrance is on the right.

EAST STROUDSBURG

Pocono Vacation Park

RD 5 Box 5214, East Stroudsburg 18360.
T: (570) 424-2587; F: (570) 476-2932;
www.poconovacationpark.com; carlet@ptd.net.

RV ★★★★ Tent ★★★★

Beauty: ★★★★★ Site Privacy: ★★★
Spaciousness: ★★★ Quiet: ★★★★★
Security: ★★★★ Cleanliness: ★★★★
Insect Control: ★★★★ Facilities: ★★★★

Located about 50 miles south of Scranton near the Delaware Water Gap, Pocono Vacation Park has 140 level pull-through sites. Weekly performances from professional entertainers, free chip-and-putt golf, and a comfortably-sized swimming pool are among the activities. The park offers hayrides twice a week and bingo every Friday. With its proximity to the Delaware Water Gap and the Delaware River—and its perch in the Pocono Mountains—Pocono Vacation Park is central to numerous hiking, boating, and fishing spots. For a unique side trip, head to Scranton and visit the Houdini Museum. An expert on Harry Houdini hosts a two-hour tour, describing stories about the famous magician's life and career. Some of Houdini's secrets are revealed, followed by a demonstration and magic show.

Basics

Operated By: Carl Willis. **Open:** All year. **Site Assignment:** Reservations recommended (stay 6 days and get 7th day free), walk-ins accepted. **Registration:** At campground office. **Fee:** $22–$27 (VISA, MC). **Parking:** At designated spot.

Facilities

Number of RV Sites: 300. **Number of Tent-Only Sites:** 10. **Hookups:** Electric (20, 30 amps), cable TV, phone, water, 175 full hookups. **Each Site:** Fire ring, picnic table. **Dump Station:** Yes. **Laundry:** Yes. **Pay Phone:** Yes. **Rest Rooms and Showers:** Yes. **Fuel:** No. **Propane:** Yes. **Internal Roads:** Gravel, in good condition. **RV Service:** No. **Market:** Within 6 mi. **Restaurant:** Within 2 mi. **General Store:** Yes. **Vending:** Yes. **Playground:** Yes. **Other:** None. **Activities:** Rec hall, game room, swimming, wading pool, putting green, basketball, shuffleboard, planned activities on weekends, sports field, horseshoes, volleyball. **Nearby Attractions:** Delaware Water Gap, Delaware River, Bushkill Falls, Appalachian Trail, Camelbeach and Alpine Slide, Memorytown USA, antique shops, factory outlets. **Additional Information:** Pocono Mountains Vacation Bureau, (800) POCONOS, www.800poconos.org.

Restrictions

Pets: On leash only. **Fires:** At site. **Alcoholic Beverages:** At site. **Vehicle Maximum Length:** 40 ft.

To Get There

From I-80, take Exit 48 and go 2 mi. south on Business US 209 and 0.5 mi. west on Shafer's School House Rd. Entrance is on the left.

ELIZABETHTOWN

Rustic Meadows Camping and Golf Resort

1980 Turnpike Rd., Elizabethtown 17022.
T: (717) 367-7718; www.gocampingamerica.com/rusticmeadows; rusticmeadows@msn.com.

RV ★★★★ Tent ★★★★

Beauty: ★★★★ Site Privacy: ★★★
Spaciousness: ★★★ Quiet: ★★★
Security: ★★★★ Cleanliness: ★★★★
Insect Control: ★★★★ Facilities: ★★★★

Located in southeastern Pennsylvania—central to Gettysburg, Harrisburg, Lancaster County, Hershey. and Philadelphia—Rustic Meadows Camping and Golf Resort offers spacious open and shaded sites amid rolling terrain. Hayrides, bonfires, and pond fishing are among the family-oriented activities. Linksters will like the 3-par, 9-hole golf course. If the golfing experience humbles you, perhaps you can restore your pride at the mini-golf course. The Civil War sites at Gettysburg, historic Harrisburg, and even Philadelphia are a comfortable drive from Rustic Meadows. Among our favorite attractions is the Harley-Davidson Museum and Plant. The antique motorcycle museum features the history and heritage of America's top motorcycle manufacturer, and the plant tour shows the final assembly of the famous Harley-Davidson motorcycles. Of course, Chocolate World is equally interesting. Here, you can discover HersheyPark, the Hershey Museum, Hershey Gardens, and ZooAmerica North American Wildlife Park.

Basics

Operated By: Karl and Linda Schmidt. **Open:** All year. **Site Assignment:** Reservations and walk-ins accepted. **Registration:** At campground office. **Fee:** $29 (VISA, MC, D). **Parking:** At site.

Facilities

Number of RV Sites: 134. **Number of Tent-Only Sites:** 14. **Hookups:** Electric (20, 30, 50 amps), phone, water, 51 full hookups. **Each Site:** Fire ring, picnic table. **Dump Station:** Yes. **Laundry:** Yes. **Pay Phone:** Yes. **Rest Rooms and Showers:** Yes. **Fuel:** No. **Propane:** Yes. **Internal Roads:** Gravel, in fair condition. **RV Service:** No. **Market:** Within 5 mi. **Restaurant:** Within 5 mi. **General Store:** Yes. **Vending:** Yes. **Playground:** Yes. **Other:** Par 3 golf course. **Activities:** Golf, mini-golf, swimming, hayrides, pond fishing, coin games, basketball, sports field, badminton, horseshoes, hiking trails, volleyball, movies, planned activities. **Nearby Attractions:** Chocolate World, HersheyPark, Hershey Museum, Hershey Gardens, ZooAmerica North American Wildlife Park, Harrisburg, Pennsylvania Renaissance Faire, Harley-Davidson Museum and Plant Tour, Pennsylvania Dutch Country, Gettysburg. **Additional Information:** Pennsylvania Dutch CVB, (800) PADUTCH, www.padutchcountry.com.

Restrictions

Pets: On leash only. **Fires:** At site. **Alcoholic Beverages:** At site. **Vehicle Maximum Length:** None. **Other:** Early arrivals and late departures are subject to availability and additional charges.

To Get There

From junction of Hwy. 283 and Hwy. 743, go 1.5 mi. south on Hwy. 743, 0.5 mi. southwest on Hwy. 241. and 2.5 mi. northwest on Turnpike Rd. Entrance is on left.

ELVERSON

French Creek State Park

843 Park Rd., Elverson 19520-9523. T: (610) 582-9680 or (888) PAPARKS;
www.dcnr.state.pa.us/stateparks;
frenchcreeksp@state.pa.us.

RV ★★★ Tent ★★★★

Beauty: ★★★★ Site Privacy: ★★★
Spaciousness: ★★★★ Quiet: ★★★★
Security: ★★★★ Cleanliness: ★★★
Insect Control: ★★★★ Facilities: ★★★

Set amid rolling farmland of southeast Pennsylvania, French Creek State Park is home to Hopewell Lake, Scotts Run Lake, dense forests, and almost 40 miles of hiking trails. Adjacent to the park lies Hopewell Furnace National Historic Site, where a cold-blast furnace is restored to its 1830s appearance. Towering oak, poplar, hickory, maple, and beech trees cover much of the park. Wetlands and pristine streams flowing through rich creek valleys offer additional habitats for plants and animals. Of the campground's 201 sites, 50 have electric hookups. These sites are shaded by mature trees and are central to bathroom and shower facilities. Though the campground itself does not have a swimming pool, there is a pool along the shores of Hopewell Lake (open between Memorial Day and Labor Day).

Basics

Operated By: State of Pennsylvania. **Open:** All year. **Site Assignment:** Reservations and walk-ins accepted. **Registration:** At campground office. **Fee:** $15–$17 (VISA, MC). **Parking:** At site.

Facilities

Number of RV Sites: 201. **Number of Tent-Only Sites:** 18. **Hookups:** Electric (50 amps). **Each Site:** Fire ring, picnic table. **Dump Station:** Yes. **Laundry:** No. **Pay Phone:** Yes. **Rest Rooms and Showers:** Yes. **Fuel:** No. **Propane:** No. **Internal Roads:** Paved, in fair condition. **RV Service:** No. **Market:** Within 7 mi. **Restaurant:** Within 7 mi. **General Store:** No. **Vending:** No. **Playground:** No. **Other:** None. **Activities:** Boating, canoeing, boat rentals, lake fishing, planned activities on weekends, hiking trails. **Nearby Attractions:** Hopewell Furnace National Historic Site. **Additional Information:** Reading and Berks Co. Visitors Bureau, (610) 375-4085.

Restrictions

Pets: No pets permitted. **Fires:** At site. **Alcoholic Beverages:** No alcohol permitted. **Vehicle Maximum Length:** 35 ft.

To Get There

From Hwy. 23, go north on Hwy. 345. Entrance is on the right.

ENTRIKEN

Lake Raystown Resort and Lodge

100 Chipmunk Crossing Rte. 994, Entriken 16638. T: (814) 658-3500; F: (814) 658-3584; www.raystownresort.com; raystown@uplink.net.

RV: ★★★★ Tent: ★★★★

Beauty: ★★★★ Site Privacy: ★★★
Spaciousness: ★★★★ Quiet: ★★★★
Security: ★★★★★ Cleanliness: ★★★★
Insect Control: ★★★★ Facilities: ★★★★★

Located in central Pennsylvania between Harrisburg and Pittsburgh in Entriken, Lake Raystown Resort and Lodge is situated on Pennsylvania's largest inland lake, with 118 miles of scenic shoreline and thousands of acres of pristine woodlands and streams. With the vast menu of activities, many visitors never leave the lakeside campground. The Proud Mary Showboat offers cruises on Lake Raystown. Wild River Water park features Caddy's Revenge 19-hole mini-golf, two 380-foot-long twisting slides, two 70-foot high speed slides, the White Water Innertube Ride, an in-ground heated swimming pool, and the Children's Splash and Play Pool. The campground has 210 double slideout sites and nine pull-through sites. Werecommend the sites located on the water. Shaded by towering trees, these sites ooze tranquility. Primitive sites are available, as are platform tent rentals.

Basics

Operated By: Samantha Ocelus. **Open:** Apr. 1–Nov. 1. **Site Assignment:** Reservations recommended. **Registration:** At campground headquarters. **Fee:** $30 (VISA, MC, AE). **Parking:** In designated spot.

Facilities

Number of RV Sites: 272. **Number of Tent-Only Sites:** 47. **Hookups:** Electric (20, 30, 50 amps), cable TV, phone, water. **Each Site:** Picnic table, fire ring, grill. **Dump Station:** Yes. **Laundry:** Yes. **Pay Phone:** Yes. **Rest Rooms and Showers:** Yes. **Fuel:** Yes. **Propane:** No. **Internal Roads:** Gravel and paved, in good condition. **RV Service:** No. **Market:** Within 7 mi. **Restaurant:** Two on premises. **General Store:** Yes. **Vending:** Yes. **Playground:** Yes. **Other:** Water park, marina, showboat, lodge, cabins, cottages, houseboats, meeting facilities. **Activities:** Wild River Water Park, boat rentals, canoeing, rec room, game room, lake fishing, mini-golf, planned activities, badminton, basketball, volleyball, horseshoes, hiking trails. **Nearby Attractions:** Lake Raystown, Penn's Cave, Lincoln Caverns. **Additional Information:** Laurel Highlands Visitors Bureau, (800) 925-7669, www.laurelhighlands.org.

Restrictions

Pets: On leash only. **Fires:** At site. **Alcoholic Beverages:** At site. **Vehicle Max. Length:** None.

To Get There

From Hwy. 26 and Hwy. 994, go 4 mi. east on Hwy. 994. Entrance is on right.

ERIE

KOA—Erie

6645 West Rd., McKean 16426. T: (814) 476-7706; www.koakampgrounds.com; engelkoa@aol.com.

RV: ★★★★ Tent: ★★★★

Beauty: ★★★★ Site Privacy: ★
Spaciousness: ★★ Quiet: ★★★
Security: ★★★★ Cleanliness: ★★★
Insect Control: ★★★★ Facilities: ★★★

With shaded sites for RVs and a mix of wooded and open sites for tents, KOA—Erie is located outside of Erie and nine miles from Presque Isle State Park. The camp store is well-stocked and the grounds are clean and well-kept. This campground is rated in the top 10% among all KOAs. Beyond the standard offerings—heated pool and kiddie pool, pedal boat rentals, lake fishing—there are not many activities. However, the campground is within a convenient distance to Presque Isle, Lake Erie beaches, and Erie itself. Presque Isle was named a top 20 fishing spot by Field & Stream and one of the nation's top 100 swimming holes by Condé Nast Traveler. Presque Isle has seven miles of lifeguarded sandy beaches and 21 miles of recreational and hiking trails.

Basics

Operated By: KOA. **Open:** May 4–Oct. 1. **Site Assignment:** Reservations and walk-ins accepted. **Registration:** At campground office. **Fee:** $29 (VISA, MC, AE, D). **Parking:** At site.

Facilities

Number of RV Sites: 100. **Number of Tent-Only Sites:** 20. **Hookups:** Electric (15, 20, 30 amps), phone, water. **Each Site:** Fire ring, picnic table. **Dump Station:** Yes. **Laundry:** Yes. **Pay Phone:** Yes. **Rest Rooms and Showers:** Yes. **Fuel:** No. **Propane:** Yes. **Internal Roads:** Gravel and paved, in good condition. **RV Service:** No. **Market:** Within 3 mi. **Restaurant:** Within 3 mi. **General Store:** Yes. **Vending:** Yes. **Playground:** Yes. **Other:** Cabins available for rent. **Activities:** Rec hall, game room, swimming, wading pool, pedal boat rentals, fishing, planned activities, volleyball, horseshoes. **Nearby Attractions:** Presque Isle State Park, Lake Erie beaches, Waldameer Park and Water World, Mazza Winery, Penn Shore Winery, Erie Zoo, minor league baseball, golf courses, Flagship Niagara, Erie Walking Tour, Girard-Lake City, Wooden Nickel Buffalo Farm, Oil Creek and Titusville Railroad/Drakes Well Museum. **Additional Information:** Erie Area CVB, (800) 542-ERIE, www.tourerie.com.

Restrictions

Pets: On leash only. **Fires:** At site. **Alcoholic Beverages:** At site. **Vehicle Maximum Length:** None.

To Get There

From I-90, take Exit 5 and go 1 mi. south on Hwy. 832 and 0.5 mi. east on West Rd. Entrance is on the right.

FRUGALITY

Prince Gallitzin State Park

966 Marina Rd., Patton 16668-6317. T: (888) PAPARKS or (814) 674-1007; www.dcnr.state.pa.us/stateparks; princegallitzinsp@state.pa.us.

RV: ★★★★ Tent: ★★★★

Beauty: ★★★★ Site Privacy: ★★★
Spaciousness: ★★★ Quiet: ★★★★
Security: ★★★★ Cleanliness: ★★★★
Insect Control: ★★★ Facilities: ★★★★

The 6,249-acre Prince Gallitzin State Park is located in the Allegheny Plateau Region of Pennsylvania. The major attractions of the park are the 1,600-acre Lake Glendale and the spacious campground. Consisting of 437 sites, the campground features a camp store with coin-operated laundry, guarded swimming beach, boat mooring area, showers, and flush toilets. Ten modern cabins are available for rent year-round. Cabins are furnished with a living area, kitchen/dining area, shower room, and two or three bedrooms. Two-bedroom cabins provide sleeping accommodations for six (one double bed and two bunks), while three-bedroom cabins provide sleep eight (one double bed and three bunks). Johnstown offers an interesting side trip for Prince Gallitzin campers. Especially interesting are the Johnstown Flood Museum and the Johnstown Flood Memorial, a somber tribute to those people who lost their lives in the infamous flood.

Basics

Operated By: State of Pennsylvania. **Open:** Apr. 15–Dec. 15. **Site Assignment:** Reservations and walk-ins accepted. **Registration:** At campground office. **Fee:** $15–$17. VISA, MC). **Parking:** At designated spot.

Facilities

Number of RV Sites: 85. **Number of Tent-Only Sites:** 352. **Hookups:** Electric (30, 50 amps). **Each Site:** Fire ring, picnic table. **Dump Station:** Yes. **Laundry:** Yes. **Pay Phone:** Yes. **Rest Rooms and Showers:** Yes. **Fuel:** No. **Propane:** No. **Internal Roads:** Gravel, in good condition. **RV Service:** No. **Market:** Within 6 mi. **Restaurant:** Within 6 mi. **General Store:** Yes. **Vending:** Yes. **Playground:** Yes. **Other:** None. **Activities:** Canoeing, kayaking, fishing, river swimming, beach volleyball, basketball, badminton, croquet, tubing, mountain biking, soccer, football, softball. **Nearby Attractions:** Johnstown Flood Museum, Johnstown Flood Memorial, Fort Necessity Battlefield, Admiral Peary Monument, Allegheny Portage Railroad National Historic Site. **Additional Information:** Greater Johnstown/Cambria Co. CVB, (800) 237-8590, www.visitjohnstownpa.com.

Restrictions

Pets: No pets permitted. **Fires:** At site. **Alcoholic Beverages:** No alcohol permitted. **Vehicle Maximum Length:** None.

To Get There

From Hwy. 253, go 1.75 mi. south on Hwy. 53 and 3 mi. west on Marina Rd. Follow signs to campground.

GALETON

Ole Bull State Park

HCR 62 Box 9, Cross Fork 17729-9701. T: (814) 435-5000 or (888) PAPARKS; www.dcnr.pa.us/stateparks; olebullsp@state.pa.us.

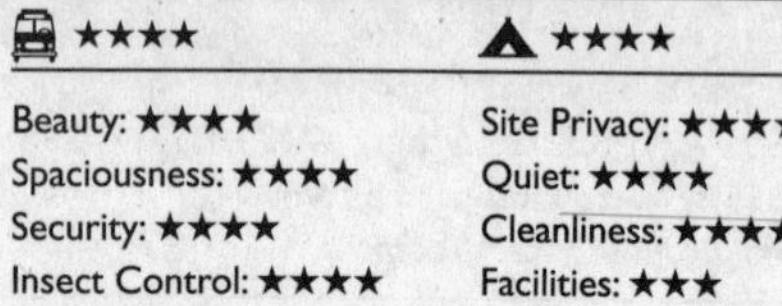

RV: ★★★★ Tent: ★★★★

Beauty: ★★★★ Site Privacy: ★★★★
Spaciousness: ★★★★ Quiet: ★★★★
Security: ★★★★ Cleanliness: ★★★★
Insect Control: ★★★★ Facilities: ★★★

Located in Galeton, Ole Bull State Park is referred to as the Black Forest of Pennsylvania. Its dense tree cover and mountainous terrain attract thousands of campers who bask in the serenity of the forested scenery along Kettle Creek. Camping is permitted year-round. Two camping areas along Kettle Creek provide sunny and shaded sites. There are 24 sites with electric hookups in Area 2. Area 1 has two sites with electric for people with disabilities. The 1.5-story Ole Bull Cabin is available for rent year-round. The cabin has a modern kitchen and bath and sleeps 10 people. The Beaver Dam Nature Trail provides an introduction to the habitats along Kettle Creek. This flat, three-quarter-mile trail starts at the concrete fordway. Go to the environmental education and interpretation center for more information. The sandy beach along Kettle Creek is open from Memorial Day weekend to Labor Day unless posted otherwise. Susquehannock State Forest surrounds Ole Bull State Park and offers hiking on a variety of trails.

Basics

Operated By: State of Pennsylvania. **Open:** All year. **Site Assignment:** Reservations and walk-ins accepted. **Registration:** At campground office. **Fee:** $15–$17.VISA, MC). **Parking:** At site.

Facilities

Number of RV Sites: 81. **Number of Tent-Only Sites:** None. **Hookups:** Electric (20, 30, 50 amps). **Each Site:** Fire ring, picnic table. **Dump Station:** Yes. **Laundry:** No. **Pay Phone:** Yes. **Rest Rooms and Showers:** No. **Fuel:** No. **Propane:** No. **Internal Roads:** Gravel, in fair condition. **RV Service:** No. **Market:** Within 2 mi. **Restaurant:** Within 2 mi. **General Store:** No. **Vending:** No. **Playground:** Yes. **Other:** None. **Activities:** River swimming, stream fishing, horseshoes, hiking trails, planned activities, sports field. **Nearby Attractions:** Susquehannock State Forest, Kettle Creek State Park, Lyman Run State Park, Pennsylvania Lumber Museum. **Additional Information:** Potter Co.Visitors Assoc., (888) POTTER2, www.pottercountypa.org.

Restrictions

Pets: No pets permitted. **Fires:** At site. **Alcoholic Beverages:** No alcohol permitted. **Vehicle Maximum Length:** 36 ft.

To Get There

From US 6, go 20 mi. south on Hwy. 144. Follow signs.

GETTYSBURG

Artillery Ridge Camping Resort

610 Taneytown Rd., Gettysburg 17325. T: (717) 334-1288; www.artilleryridge.com.

RV: ★★★★ Tent: ★★★★

Beauty: ★★★★ Site Privacy: ★★
Spaciousness: ★★★ Quiet: ★★★★
Security: ★★★★★ Cleanliness: ★★★★
Insect Control: ★★★★ Facilities: ★★★★

The closest campground to the Gettysburg Battlefield, Artillery Ridge Camping Resort is a haven for outdoor-minded Civil War enthusiasts. The campground has a mix of open and shaded grassy sites. 46 of which are pull-throughs. There is a large open area for tents, and the campground also has a few secluded tenting sites. Actively remembering Gettysburg's role in the Civil War is obviously the main purpose at Artillery Ridge. Battlefield tours (some on horseback) embark from the campground. Bringing Civil War history to life, the Gettysburg Battle Diorama Museum is truly one of the most unique and interesting attractions we have seen at any campground in Pennsylvania. The diorama features more than 750 square feet of model displays and about 20,000 hand-painted soldiers, horses, buildings, and other scenery on the battlefields and in Gettysburg itself. The diorama provides a bird's-eye view of the three days of battles with dramatic narration and impressive light and sound effects. The diorama is a learning tool for children and adults alike. If you savor Civil War history, you will especially enjoy Artillery Ridge.

Basics

Operated By: Ray Sterner. **Open:** Apr. 1–Nov. 1. **Site Assignment:** Reservations recommended, walk-ins accepted. **Registration:** At campground store. **Fee:** $23 (VISA, MC, D). **Parking:** At site.

Facilities

Number of RV Sites: 107. **Number of Tent-Only Sites:** 42. **Hookups:** Electric (20, 30 amps), phone, water. **Each Site:** Fire ring, picnic table. **Dump Station:** Yes. **Laundry:** Yes. **Pay Phone:** Yes. **Rest Rooms and Showers:** Yes. **Fuel:** No. **Propane:** No. **Internal Roads:** Gravel, in good condition. **RV Service:** No. **Market:** Within 5 mi. **Restaurant:** Within 2 mi. **General Store:** Yes. **Vending:** Yes. **Playground:** Yes. **Other:** Horse stalls available, camping with horses allowed. **Activities:** Rec room, swimming, pedal boat rentals, planned activities, horseback riding trails, horse rentals, sports field, badminton, hiking trails, horseshoes, volleyball, battlefield tours. **Nearby Attractions:** Gettysburg Civil War attractions. **Additional Information:** Gettysburg CVB, (717) 334-6274, www.gettysburg.com.

Restrictions

Pets: On leash only. **Fires:** At site. **Alcoholic Beverages:** At site. **Vehicle Maximum Length:** 40 ft.

To Get There

From US 30, go 1.5 mi. south on Business US 15 and 1.25 mi. southeast on Hwy. 134. Campground entrance is on left.

GETTYSBURG

Drummer Boy Camping Resort

1300 Hanover Rd., Gettysburg 17325. T: (800) 293-2808; F: (717) 334-9524; www.drummerboycamping.com; drummer@cun.net.

RV: ★★★★★ Tent: ★★★★

Beauty: ★★★★★ Site Privacy: ★★
Spaciousness: ★★★ Quiet: ★★★★
Security: ★★★★ Cleanliness: ★★★★
Insect Control: ★★★★ Facilities: ★★★★★

Drummer Boy Camping Resort is a full-service outdoor resort with 300 shaded and partially shaded sites located on 100 acres of beautiful woodlands one mile east of Gettysburg. Accommodations include spacious campsites for RVers and tenters, camping cabins, and housekeeping cottages. Of RV sites, 120 are full hookup (including 45 pull-throughs) and 115 sites offer water and electric; the remainder are primitive sites. There are four clean bathhouses and three dump stations. If you would like to camp along the fishing pond, three sites at the northwest side offer adequate space. Sites at the far eastern end border the hiking trails and offer the most privacy. Baltimore, Harper's Ferry, and Hershey are no more than an hour's drive away, and Washington, D.C. is about 1.5 hours away. Bus tours to Gettysburg battlefield and Washington, D.C. embark from the campground, and battlefield audio tapes are available. An activities director is on staff daily during summer and weekends during the spring and fall.

Basics

Operated By: Ron Gilbert. **Open:** Apr. 1–Oct. 31. **Site Assignment:** Reservations accepted; walk-ins on first-come, first-served basis. **Registration:** At campground office. **Fee:** $26 (VISA, MC, D). **Parking:** At designated spot.

Facilities

Number of RV Sites: 240. **Number of Tent-Only Sites:** 60. **Hookups:** Electric (20, 30, 50 amps), cable TV, phone, water, 100 full hookups. **Each Site:** Fire ring, picnic table. **Dump Station:** Yes. **Laundry:** Yes. **Pay Phone:** Yes. **Rest Rooms and Showers:** Yes. **Fuel:** No. **Propane:** No. **Internal Roads:** Gravel and paved, in good condition. **RV Service:** No. **Market:** Within 4 mi. **Restaurant:** Within 4 mi. **General Store:** Yes. **Vending:** Yes. **Playground:** Yes. **Other:** Tours of Gettysburg battlefield and Washington, D.C.. **Activities:** Rec hall, game room, swimming, whirlpool, pond fishing, mini-golf, basketball, bike rentals, planned activities, movies, badminton, sports field, horseshoes, hiking trails, volleyball. **Nearby Attractions:** Gettysburg battlefield and Civil War sites, Washington, D.C., Baltimore, Amish Country, Harper's Ferry, Hershey, Battlefield Bus Tours from camp, Washington, D.C. Bus Tours from camp, Battlefield Auto Tape available. **Additional Informa-**

tion: Gettysburg CVB, (717) 334-6274, www.gettysburg.com.

Restrictions

Pets: On leash only. **Fires:** At site. **Alcoholic Beverages:** At site. **Vehicle Maximum Length:** 45 ft.

To Get There

From US 15, go 100 yards east on Hwy. 116 and 0.1 mi. north on Rocky Grove Rd. Entrance is on the left.

GETTYSBURG

Gettysburg Campground

2030 Fairfield Rd./Rte. 116W, Gettysburg 17325. T: (717) 334-3304; www.gettysburgcampground.com.

RV ★★★★ Tent ★★★★

Beauty: ★★★★★ Site Privacy: ★★
Spaciousness: ★★ Quiet: ★★★
Security: ★★★★ Cleanliness: ★★★★
Insect Control: ★★★★ Facilities: ★★★★★

Located just three miles from the battlefield, Gettysburg Campground lies along tranquil Marsh Creek in the shadow of the South Mountains, where soldiers from both sides rested between battles. There are 240 level sites, both shaded and sunny, with 25 pull-throughs. Full hookup sites on the campground's north side along Marsh Creek are our favorites. Some of the sites in the primitive tenting area on the northeast side border the creek. If you prefer camping along the banks, waterfront sites are located at the northern and western ends. There is also a cluster of full-hookup sites surrounding the activity centers. In downtown Gettysburg, a walking tour illustrates the impact the Battle of Gettysburg had on this small rural community during those fateful days of 1863, offering a sampling of Gettysburg's battle-related sites.

Basics

Operated By: Joe, Lori, and Lorraine. **Open:** Apr. 7–Nov. 18. **Site Assignment:** Reservations recommended, walk-ins accepted. **Registration:** At campground office. **Fee:** $28 (VISA, MC). **Parking:** At site.

Facilities

Number of RV Sites: 230. **Number of Tent-Only Sites:** 21. **Hookups:** Electric (20, 30, 50 amps), phone, water, 50 full hookups. **Each Site:** Fire ring, picnic table. **Dump Station:** Yes. **Laundry:** Yes. **Pay Phone:** Yes. **Rest Rooms and Showers:** Yes. **Fuel:** No. **Propane:** Yes. **Internal Roads:** Gravel and paved, in good condition. **RV Service:** Yes. **Market:** Within 5 mi. **Restaurant:** Within 5 mi. **General Store:** Yes. **Vending:** Yes. **Playground:** Yes. **Other:** Ice cream parlor, RV and cabin rentals. **Activities:** Rec hall, game room, swimming, stream fishing, shuffleboard, planned activities, basketball, movies, sports field, badminton, volleyball, mini-golf. **Nearby Attractions:** Gettysburg battlefields, Baltimore, Hershey, Washington, D.C., Lancaster County. **Additional Information:** Gettysburg CVB, (717) 334-6274, www.gettysburg.com.

Restrictions

Pets: On leash only. **Fires:** At site. **Alcoholic Beverages:** At site. **Vehicle Maximum Length:** None.

To Get There

From Business US 15, go 3 mi. west on Hwy. 116. Entrance is on the left.

GETTYSBURG

Granite Hill Campground and Adventure Golf

3340 W. Fairfield Rd., Gettysburg 17325. T: (717) 642-8749 or (800) 642-TENT; F: (717) 642-8025; www.granitehillcampground.com; gburggrass@aol.com.

RV ★★★★★ Tent ★★★★

Beauty: ★★★★ Site Privacy: ★★★
Spaciousness: ★★★ Quiet: ★★★★
Security: ★★★★ Cleanliness: ★★★★★
Insect Control: ★★★★ Facilities: ★★★★★

Located 6 miles from historic Gettysburg and home of the Gettysburg Bluegrass Festival, Granite Hill Campground and Adventure Golf offers 300 campsites spread over 150 acres, creating an uncrowded feeling even at the busiest time of the year. Granite Hill features many recreational options—including boat rentals, pond fishing and lake fishing—but the highlight is its new 18-hole Adventure Golf Course, which rivals the best mini-golf courses we have seen. Granite Hill has wooded sites, shaded sites with manicured grass, and a large, open, grassy overflow used when the regular campsites fill up, or when club rallies and special events require more space. Granite Hill offers a convenient pick-up service for guests purchasing Gettysburg Battlefield Tour tickets at the camp store. Package tickets are also available along with information on the many museums and attractions in the area. The campground offers a free shuttle to Gettysburg.

Basics

Operated By: Private operator. **Open:** All year. **Site Assignment:** Reservations and walk-ins accepted. **Registration:** At campground headquarters. **Fee:** $28 (VISA, MC). **Parking:** At designated spot.

Facilities

Number of RV Sites: 250. **Number of Tent-Only Sites:** 50. **Hookups:** Electric (20, 30, 50 amps), water, 100 full hookups. **Each Site:** Fire ring, picnic table. **Dump Station:** Yes. **Laundry:** Yes. **Pay Phone:** Yes. **Rest Rooms and Showers:** Yes. **Fuel:** Yes. **Propane:** Yes. **Internal Roads:** Gravel and paved, in good condition. **RV Service:** No. **Market:** Within 2 mi. **Restaurant:** Within 2 mi. **General Store:** Yes. **Vending:** Yes. **Playground:** Yes. **Other:** Three dump stations, large general store. **Activities:** Rec hall, game room, swimming, wading pool, lake swimming, boat rentals, pond fishing, mini-golf, basketball, planned activities, shuffleboard, sports field, badminton, hiking trails, horseshoes, tennis, movies, volleyball. **Nearby Attractions:** Gettysburg battlefields, Civil War sites. **Additional Information:** Gettysburg CVB, (717) 334-6274, www.gettysburg.com.

Restrictions

Pets: On leash only. **Fires:** At site. **Alcoholic Beverages:** At site. **Vehicle Maximum Length:** 50 ft.

To Get There

From Business US 15, go 6 mi. west on Hwy. 116. Entrance is on the left.

GETTYSBURG

Round Top Campground

180 Knight Rd., Gettysburg 17325. T: (717) 334-9565; www.roundtopcamp.com; info@roundtopcamp.com.

RV ★★★★ Tent ★★★★

Beauty: ★★★★ Site Privacy: ★★★
Spaciousness: ★★ Quiet: ★★★
Security: ★★★★ Cleanliness: ★★★★
Insect Control: ★★★★ Facilities: ★★★★★

Located three miles from the Gettysburg Battlefield Visitors Center and offering battlefield and Washington, D.C. tours from the park, Round Top Campground is remarkably clean and has spacious, semi-wooded open and shaded sites. We most like the sites that border the pond on the east side of the campground. They offer privacy, and yet they are within a short walking distance of most of Round Top's activities, which include mini-golf, tennis, and shuffleboard. The cavernous recreation lodge overlooks the pool and can accommodate groups and special events.

Basics

Operated By: Kenny and Judy Caudill, Steve and Wendy Dutterer. **Open:** All year. **Site Assignment:** Reservations encouraged, walk-ins accepted. **Registration:** At campground office. **Fee:** $26 (VISA, MC, D). **Parking:** At site.

Facilities

Number of RV Sites: 260. **Number of Tent-Only Sites:** 16. **Hookups:** Electric (20, 30, 50 amps), phone, water, 202 full hookups. **Each Site:** Fire ring, picnic table. **Dump Station:** Yes. **Laundry:** Yes. **Pay Phone:** Yes. **Rest Rooms and Showers:** Yes. **Fuel:** No. **Propane:** Yes. **Internal Roads:** Paved, in good condition. **RV Service:** No. **Market:** Within 5 mi. **Restaurant:** Within 1 mi. **General Store:** Yes. **Vending:** Yes. **Playground:** Yes. **Other:** Park models and primitive cabins available for rent. **Activities:** Tennis, rec hall, game room, swimming, wading pool, mini-golf, basketball, shuffleboard, planned activities on weekends, sports field, badminton, horseshoes, volleyball. **Nearby Attractions:** Gettysburg battlefields and Civil War sites, 110-store outlet center 2 mi. away. **Additional Information:** Gettysburg CVB, (717) 334-6274, www.gettysburg.com.

Restrictions

Pets: On leash. **Fires:** At site. **Alcoholic Beverages:** At site. **Vehicle Max. Length:** 40 ft. **Other:** Pets not permitted in buildings or pool area.

To Get There

From US 15, go 0.1 mi. north on Hwy. 134 and 0.5 mi. west on Knight Rd. Entrance is on the left.

GREENTOWN

Promised Land State Park

RR 1 Box 96, Greentown 18426. T: (570) 676-3428 or (888) PAPARKS; www.dcnr.state.pa.us/stateparks; promisedlandsp@state.pa.us.

RV ★★★★ Tent ★★★★

Beauty: ★★★★★ Site Privacy: ★★★
Spaciousness: ★★★ Quiet: ★★★★
Security: ★★★★ Cleanliness: ★★★
Insect Control: ★★★ Facilities: ★★★★

Located amid the Pocono Mountains, Promised Land State Park is approximately 3,000 acres, 1,800 feet above sea level. The forest consists primarily of beech, oak, maple, and hemlock trees. Promised Land Lake is 422 acres and Lower Lake is 173 acres. All campgrounds are near swimming, boating, fishing, and hiking facilities. The Pines Campground is located at the northwestern end of Promised Land Lake, within walking distance of the day-use area and main beach. Pickerel Point Campground is located on a peninsula and provides patrons with the park's most primitive camping experience. Deerfield Campground is on a slight rise, near the old CCC (Civilian Conservation Corps) camp. Lower Lake Campground is found at the western edge of the Lower Lake and contains modern restrooms with showers. Nestled in hemlocks adjacent to Lower Lake, the Bear Wallow Cabin Colony contains 12 rustic rental cabins constructed by the CCC. These primitive cabins each have a fireplace, electricity, and an adjacent private bath.

Basics

Operated By: State of Pennsylvania. **Open:** All year. **Site Assignment:** Reservations and walk-ins accepted. **Registration:** At campground office. **Fee:** $15–$17, VISA, MC). **Parking:** At designated spot.

Facilities

Number of RV Sites: 102. **Number of Tent-Only Sites:** 385. **Hookups:** Electric (30, 50 amps). **Each Site:** Fire ring, picnic table. **Dump Station:** Yes. **Laundry:** No. **Pay Phone:** Yes. **Rest Rooms and Showers:** Yes. **Fuel:** No. **Propane:** No. **Internal Roads:** Gravel, in good condition. **RV Service:** No. **Market:** Within 5 mi. **Restaurant:** Within 5 mi. **General Store:** No. **Vending:** Yes. **Playground:** Yes. **Other:** None. **Activities:** Lake swimming, boating, canoeing, boat rentals, lake fishing, planned activities, hiking trails, volleyball, bicycling. **Nearby Attractions:** Delaware State Forest, Delaware Water Gap National Recreation Area, Lake Wallenpaupack. **Additional Information:** Pocono Mountains Vacation Bureau, (800) POCONOS, www.800poconos.org.

Restrictions

Pets: No pets permitted. **Fires:** At site. **Alcoholic Beverages:** No alcohol permitted. **Vehicle Maximum Length:** 35 ft.

To Get There

From I-84, take Exit 7 and go 5 mi. south on Hwy. 390. Follow signs to campground.

HANOVER

Codorus State Park

1066 Blooming Grove Rd., Hanover 17331-9545. T: (717) 637-2418; www.dcnr.state.pa.us/stateparks; codorussp@state.pa.us.

RV ★★★★ Tent ★★★★

Beauty: ★★★★ Site Privacy: ★★★
Spaciousness: ★★★ Quiet: ★★★★
Security: ★★★★ Cleanliness: ★★★★
Insect Control: ★★★ Facilities: ★★★★

Codorus State Park, located three miles southeast of Hanover, boasts the 1,275-acre Lake Marburg—a hot spot for anglers, boaters and swimmers with 26 miles of shoreline. The forests of Codorus stand in tall contrast to the surrounding farmlands. The 3,326-acre Codorus State Park is in the southwest corner of York County. The 198-site campground opens the second Friday in Apr. and closes the third Sunday in Oct. Thirteen walk-in sites are available for tents only. Hot showers, flush toilets, and a sanitary dump station are available. Many campsites have electric hookups. Eight campsites with electricity can accommodate people with disabilities. A 27-hole disc golf course is located along Marina Rd. Score cards are at the first hole, which is next to the first parking lot on the right side of Marina Rd.

Basics

Operated By: State of Pennsylvania. **Open:** All year. **Site Assignment:** Reservations and walk-ins accepted. **Registration:** At campground office. **Fee:** $15–$17 (VISA, MC). **Parking:** In designated area.

Facilities

Number of RV Sites: 185. **Number of Tent-Only Sites:** 13. **Hookups:** Electric (30, 50 amps). **Each Site:** Fire ring, picnic table. **Dump Station:** Yes. **Laundry:** No. **Pay Phone:** Yes. **Rest Rooms and Showers:** Yes. **Fuel:** No. **Propane:** No. **Internal Roads:** Paved, in good condition. **RV Service:** No. **Market:** Within 5 mi. **Restaurant:** Within 5 mi. **General Store:** No. **Vending:** Yes. **Playground:** No. **Other:** Lake Marburg. **Activities:** Pavilion, swimming, boating, boat rentals, lake fishing, hiking trails. **Nearby Attractions:** Factory tours (Frito-Lay, Crayola, Martin's Potato Chips and Harley-Davidson among others), factory outlet stores, factory-related museums. **Additional Information:** York County CVB, (888) 858-YORK, www.yorkpa.org.

Restrictions

Pets: No pets permitted. **Fires:** At site. **Alcoholic Beverages:** No alcohol permitted. **Vehicle Maximum Length:** 50 ft. **Other:** 14-day max. stay Memorial Day–Labor Day.

To Get There

From Hwy. 116, go 2 mi. east on Hwy. 216 and 0.5 mi. south on Dubb's Church Rd. Entrance is on the right.

HERSHEY

Hershey Highmeadow Campground

P.O. Box 866, Hershey 17033. T: (717) 534-8999; F: (717) 534-8998; www.hersheypa.com; hersheycamp@gocampingamerica.com.

RV ★★★★ Tent ★★★★

Beauty: ★★★★ Site Privacy: ★★
Spaciousness: ★★ Quiet: ★★
Security: ★★★★★ Cleanliness: ★★★★★
Insect Control: ★★★★ Facilities: ★★★★★

Hershey bills itself as the sweetest place on Earth, and Hershey Highmeadow Campground is the lone campground within the sweetest city's limits. The campground has 300 open and shaded sites; the best are those away from the active freight railroad that borders the campground. Sites with no hookups along Swatara Creek are tranquil, as are pull-through sites bordered by pine trees off Matlack Rd. Hershey's attractions are plentiful, and they are not limited to the thrill rides of HersheyPark and the exotic animals of ZooAmerica and North American Wildlife Park. One of the attractions is Founder's Hall, where the story of Milton Hershey is detailed. Hershey was a beloved philanthropist. Of course, he is best known for founding the renowned chocolate company. A ride aboard the Hershey Trolley takes visitors to Hershey's Chocolate World, where you can learn the secrets of chocolate making, enjoy a free sample, and buy a five-pound chocolate bar in the gift shop.

Basics

Operated By: Mark Panassow. **Open:** All year. **Site Assignment:** Reservations encouraged, walk-ins accepted on first-come, first-served basis. **Registration:** At campground office. **Fee:** $30 (VISA, MC, AE, D). **Parking:** At designated spot.

Facilities

Number of RV Sites: 223. **Number of Tent-Only Sites:** 72. **Hookups:** Electric (20, 30, 50 amps), cable TV, water, 87 full hookups. **Each Site:** Grill, picnic table. **Dump Station:** Yes. **Laundry:** Yes. **Pay Phone:** Yes. **Rest Rooms and Showers:** Yes. **Fuel:** No. **Propane:** Yes. **Internal Roads:** Gravel and paved, in good condition. **RV Service:** No. **Market:** Within 1 mi. **Restaurant:** Within 1 mi. **General Store:** Yes. **Vending:** Yes. **Playground:** Yes. **Other:** Hershey tours. **Activities:** Rec room, two swimming pools, shuffleboard, game room, planned activities on weekends, volleyball. **Nearby Attractions:** Founder's Hall, Hershey Gardens, Hershey Museum of American Life, HersheyPark, Hershey's Chocolate World Visitors Center, Trolley Works, ZooAmerica and American Wildlife Park. **Additional Information:** Harrisburg-Hershey-Carlisle-Perry Co. Tourism and Convention Bureau, (800) 995-0969, www.visithhc.com.

Restrictions

Pets: On leash only. **Fires:** At site. **Alcoholic Beverages:** At site. **Vehicle Maximum Length:** 60 ft.

To Get There

From junction of US 422, US 322, and Hwy. 39,

go 0.5 mi. northwest on Hwy. 39. Entrance is on the left.

HERSHEY

Thousands Trails—Hershey

493 South Mt Pleasant Rd., Lebanon 17042. T: (800) 884-4451; www.thousandtrails.com.

RV ★★★★ Tent ★★★★

Beauty: ★★★★ Site Privacy: ★★★
Spaciousness: ★★★ Quiet: ★★★★
Security: ★★★★★ Cleanliness: ★★★★
Insect Control: ★★★★ Facilities: ★★★★★

Situated on 200 acres of rolling farmland in the heart of Pennsylvania Dutch Country, Thousand Trails—Hershey is enclosed in a natural valley of grassy fields, sloping down to a small fishing lake. Located six miles from Hershey attractions like Hershey's Chocolate World and ZooAmerica, the campground is also near nature-oriented places such as Indian Echo Caverns, Stony Valley Wilderness Site, and Hawk Mountain. Dinosaur Rock and Middle Creek Wildlife Preserve are also worth a visit. At the campground, the adult lodge and family center brims with activity year-round. During warmer months, there are lots of outdoor activities, including canoeing, pond fishing, and enjoying the swimming pool and whirlpool. The campground features grassy open and shaded sites, including 20 pull-throughs.

Basics

Operated By: Thousands Trails. **Open:** All year. **Site Assignment:** Reservations recommended. **Registration:** At campground office. **Fee:** $20 (VISA, MC, AE, D). **Parking:** At designated spot.

Facilities

Number of RV Sites: 204. **Number of Tent-Only Sites:** 92. **Hookups:** Electric (30, 50 amps), phone, water, 200 full hookups. **Each Site:** Fire ring, picnic table. **Dump Station:** Yes. **Laundry:** Yes. **Pay Phone:** Yes. **Rest Rooms and Showers:** Yes. **Fuel:** No. **Propane:** Yes. **Internal Roads:** Gravel and paved, in good condition. **RV Service:** No. **Market:** Within 2 mi. **Restaurant:** Within 2 mi. **General Store:** Yes. **Vending:** Yes. **Playground:** Yes. **Other:** Adult lodge and family center. **Activities:** Rec hall, game room, swimming, wading pool, whirlpool, boat and canoe rentals, pond fishing, basketball, mini-golf, planned activities, shuffleboard, movies, volleyball, tennis, horseshoes. **Nearby Attractions:** Hershey attractions, Horseshoe Trail, Governor Dick and Dinosaur Rock Lookouts, Indian Echo Caverns, The Union Canal Tunnel, Susquehanna River, Stony Valley Wilderness Site in Cold Springs Township, Middle Creek Wildlife Preserve, Hawk Mountain, Gettysburg battlefields, Pennsylvania Grand Canyon. **Additional Information:** Harrisburg-Hershey-Carlisle-Perry Co. Tourism and Convention Bureau, (800) 995-0969, www.visithhc.com.

Restrictions

Pets: On leash only. **Fires:** At site. **Alcoholic Beverages:** At site. **Vehicle Maximum Length:** 40 ft.

To Get There

From Hwy. 743, go 6.5 mi. east on US 322 and 1.25 mi. south on Mt. Pleasant Rd. Entrance is at the end.

HOBBIE

Moyer's Grove Campground and Country RV

RR 2 Box 95, Wapwallopen 18660. T: (800) 722-1912; F: (570) 379-3127; www.moyercgrv.com; info@moyercgrv.com.

RV ★★★★ Tent ★★★★

Beauty: ★★★★ Site Privacy: ★★★
Spaciousness: ★★★ Quiet: ★★★
Security: ★★★★ Cleanliness: ★★★★
Insect Control: ★★★★ Facilities: ★★★★

Located in northeastern Pennsylvania about 20 miles southwest of Wilkes-Barre, Moyer's Grove Campground and Country RV is clean and boasts friendly customer service. Many of the 150 sites are perched alongside a babbling brook, which provides a perfect harmony for a good night's sleep—at least when it's warm enough to leave your RV's windows open. The campground has two ponds, one for fishing and the other for boating. Pedal boats and canoes are available for rent, as are kayaks. For beginners, the calm waters of the Moyer's Grove pond is ideal for learning kayaking techniques before venturing to the more challenging Lackawanna River. Moyer's Grove has an on-premises RV sales and service facility. Among the more interesting attractions near Moyer's Grove are the Lackawanna Coal Mine Tour and Museum, Eckley Miner's Village, Electric City Trolley Station and Museum, and the Houdini Museum.

Basics

Operated By: Todd, Janet, and Jen Lightner. **Open:** All year. **Site Assignment:** Reservation and walk-ins accepted. **Registration:** At campground headquarters. **Fee:** $23 (VISA, MC, D). **Parking:** At site.

Facilities

Number of RV Sites: 150. **Number of Tent-Only Sites:** None. **Hookups:** Electric (20, 30, 50 amps), phone, water, 70 full hookups. **Each Site:** Fire ring, picnic table. **Dump Station:** Yes. **Laundry:** Yes. **Pay Phone:** Yes. **Rest Rooms and Showers:** Yes. **Fuel:** No. **Propane:** Yes. **Internal Roads:** Gravel, in good condition. **RV Service:** Yes. **Market:** Within 5 mi. **Restaurant:** Within 5 mi. **General Store:** Yes. **Vending:** Yes. **Playground:** Yes. **Other:** Kayak rentals. **Activities:** Rec room, game room, swimming, pond and stream fishing, mini-golf, basketball, shuffleboard, planned activities, volleyball. **Nearby Attractions:** Knoebel's Grove Amusement Park, Steamtown National Historic Site, Electric City Trolley Station and Museum, Claws and Paws Wild Animal Park, Lackawanna Coal Mine Tour and Museum, Bushkill Falls, Pocono Indian Museum, Scranton, Wilkes-Barre, Eckley Miner's Village, Houdini Museum. **Additional Information:** Luzerne Co. Tourist Promotion Agency, (888) 905-2872, www.tournepa.com.

Restrictions

Pets: On leash only. **Fires:** At site. **Alcoholic Beverages:** At site. **Vehicle Maximum Length:** 40 ft. **Other:** No pets or smoking permitted in rental cabins or trailers.

To Get There

From I-80, go 3.75 mi. northeast on Hwy. 239 and follow signs for 3.5 mi. on paved roads. Entrance is on the right.

HONEY BROOK

Brandywine Meadows Family Campground

429 Icedale Rd., Honey Brook 19344. T: (610) 273-9753 or (888) 234-6977; F: (610) 273-9570; www.gocampingamerica/brandywinemeadows.

RV ★★★★ Tent ★★★★

Beauty: ★★★★★ Site Privacy: ★★
Spaciousness: ★★ Quiet: ★★★★
Security: ★★★★★ Cleanliness: ★★★★
Insect Control: ★★★★ Facilities: ★★★★

A semi-wooded park with shaded and open sites on the west bank of Brandywine Creek, Brandywine Meadows Family Campground boasts a new, spacious clubhouse where the office, store, and game room are located. Of the 166 sites, 27 accommodate pull-throughs. Attractions in Pennsylvania Dutch Country, Philadelphia, and Valley Forge are in the vicinity of Brandywine Meadows, but Brandywine Valley—which surrounds the campground—has interesting history and attractions itself. The Brandywine Battlefield Park brings to life the largest engagement of the Revolutionary War, fought on Sept. 11, 1777, between the Continental Army led by General George Washington and the British forces headed by General William Howe. Exhibiting American art in a 19th-century grist mill, the Brandywine River Museum is internationally known for its unparalleled collection of works by three generations of Wyeths and its fine collection of American illustration, still life, and landscape painting.

Basics

Operated By: Ruth Kugler and Joseph Chambers. **Open:** Apr. 1–Oct. 31. **Site Assignment:** Reservations encouraged, walk-ins accepted. **Registration:** At campground office. **Fee:** $23 (VISA, MC). **Parking:** At site.

Facilities

Number of RV Sites: 166. **Number of Tent-Only Sites:** None. **Hookups:** Electric (20, 30 amps), phone, water, 6 full hookups. **Each Site:** Fire ring. **Dump Station:** Yes. **Laundry:** Yes. **Pay Phone:** Yes. **Rest Rooms and Showers:** Yes. **Fuel:** No. **Propane:** No. **Internal Roads:** Gravel and paved, in good condition. **RV Service:** No. **Market:** Within 4 mi. **Restaurant:** Within 1 mi. **General Store:** Yes. **Vending:** Yes. **Playground:** Yes. **Other:** New main building has office, camp store, and game room. **Activities:** Rec hall, game room, swimming, wading pool, boating, canoeing, pond fishing, mini-golf, planned activities on weekends, shuffleboard, sports field, badminton, horseshoes, volleyball. **Nearby Attractions:** Hopewell Village, covered bridges, Lancaster County/Pennsylvania Dutch County, Longwood Gardens, Brandywine River Museum, Reading outlet stores, Valley Forge, Philadelphia. **Additional Information:** Pennsylvania Dutch CVB, (800) PADUTCH, www.padutchcountry.com; Lehigh Valley CVB, (800) 747-0561, www.lehighvalleypa.org.

RESTRICTIONS

Pets: On leash only. **Fires:** At site. **Alcoholic Beverages:** At site, under control. **Vehicle Maximum Length:** 40 ft.

TO GET THERE

From Hwy. 10, go 3 mi. east on US 322, 0.5 mi. south on Birdell Rd., and 0.5 mi. east on Icedale Rd. Entrance is on the left.

HOWARD

Bald Eagle State Park (Russel P. Letterman Campground)

149 Main Park Rd., Howard 16841-9607.
T: (814) 625-2775;
www.dcnr.state.pa.us/stateparks;
baldeaglesp@state.pa.us.

RV ★★★ Tent ★★★

Beauty: ★★★★ Site Privacy: ★★★★
Spaciousness: ★★★★ Quiet: ★★★★
Security: ★★★ Cleanliness: ★★★
Insect Control: ★★★ Facilities: ★★★

The Russel P. Letterman Campground is located at Bald Eagle State Park, which is nestled amid rugged Bald Eagle Mountain and the Allegheny Plateau. The 1,730-acre Bald Eagle Lake features unlimited horsepower boating. The water is teeming with smallmouth and largemouth bass, blue gill, and crappie. Hiking and butterfly trails are teeming with colorful wildflowers and wildlife. Swimming is available at the sand beach. The Russel P. Letterman Campground has 101 sites within easy walking distance of the beach, marina, and other park facilities. It features paved camping spurs, showers, and a sanitary dump station. About half of the campsites have electrical hookups and four sites can accommodate people with disabilities. A nearby primitive campground can accommodate both tents and RVs, with 35 sites for each. The wooded and shaded Skyline Drive Picnic Area has 115 picnic tables, one picnic pavilion, four public restrooms, two playfields, one volleyball court, and horseshoe pits.

BASICS

Operated By: State of Pennsylvania. **Open:** Apr. 15–Dec. 15. **Site Assignment:** Reservations and walk-ins accepted. **Registration:** At campground office. **Fee:** $12. **Parking:** At site.

FACILITIES

Number of RV Sites: 101. **Number of Tent-Only Sites:** None. **Hookups:** Electric (50 amps). **Each Site:** Fire ring, picnic table. **Dump Station:** Yes. **Laundry:** No. **Pay Phone:** Yes. **Rest Rooms and Showers:** Yes. **Fuel:** No. **Propane:** No. **Internal Roads:** Gravel, in good condition. **RV Service:** No. **Market:** Within 10 mi. **Restaurant:** Within 10 mi. **General Store:** No. **Vending:** No. **Playground:** Yes. **Other:** None. **Activities:** Lake swimming, boating, canoeing, hiking trails, rowboat and canoe rentals, horseshoes, volleyball. **Nearby Attractions:** Curtin Mansion and Ironworks, the Pennsylvania Military Museum Woodward Caves, Penn's Cave, Pine Grove Mills Mountain and Centre Hall Mountain, Pennsylvania Fish and Boat Commission, Bald Eagle factory outlets, Penn State University. **Additional Information:** Centre Co. CVB–Penn State Country, (800) 385-5466, www.visitpennstate.org.

RESTRICTIONS

Pets: No pets permitted. **Fires:** At site. **Alcoholic Beverages:** No alcohol permitted. **Vehicle Maximum Length:** 35 ft.

TO GET THERE

From I-80, take Exit 23 and go 9 mi. north on Hwy. 150. Entrance is on the right.

JIM THORPE

Jim Thorpe Camping Resort

P.O. Box 328, Jim Thorpe 18229. T: (570) 325-2644; F: (570) 325-4702;
www.jimthorpecamping.com.

RV ★★★★ Tent ★★★★

Beauty: ★★★★ Site Privacy: ★★
Spaciousness: ★★★ Quiet: ★★★★
Security: ★★★★ Cleanliness: ★★★★
Insect Control: ★★★★ Facilities: ★★★★

Situated within the town limits of historic Jim Thorpe (formerly Mauch Chunk), Jim Thorpe Camping Resort is a 28-acre wooded campground that offers level, spacious, and wooded sites. The tent area is separate from the RV area. The campground is enlivened by blooming laurels in May and June and rhododendrons in July. A mountain stream borders the campground, and many miles of mountain bike trails wind through the facility. More than 15 miles of rail trails are available for hiking. Although the Switch Back Gravity Railroad has been gone as an operating entity for more than a half century, there are lots of places to experience the physical artifacts and memories in the region the railroad served between Jim Thorpe and Summit Hill. Downtown Jim Thorpe is an ideal starting point, and the campground arranges tours. Old Mauch Chunk Landing is located in the historic Central Railroad of New Jersey Station in downtown Jim Thorpe.

BASICS

Operated By: Harold Mauer. **Open:** Apr. 1–Dec. 15. **Site Assignment:** Reservations recommended, walk-ins accepted. **Registration:** At campground office. **Fee:** $25 (VISA, MC). **Parking:** At site.

FACILITIES

Number of RV Sites: 125. **Number of Tent-Only Sites:** 25. **Hookups:** Electric (20, 30), cable TV, phone, water, sewer. **Each Site:** Fire ring, picnic table. **Dump Station:** Yes. **Laundry:** Yes. **Pay Phone:** Yes. **Rest Rooms and Showers:** Yes. **Fuel:** No. **Propane:** Yes. **Internal Roads:** Gravel, in good condition. **RV Service:** No. **Market:** Within 2 mi. **Restaurant:** Within 2 mi. **General Store:** Yes. **Vending:** Yes. **Playground:** Yes. **Other:** Trout nursery. **Activities:** Rec hall, game room, swimming, wading pool, stream fishing, shuffleboard, planned activities on weekends, volleyball, hiking trails, badminton, horseshoes. **Nearby Attractions:** Whitewater rafting, Historic Jim Thorpe, mountain bike trails and rentals, Mauch Chunk Lake, Beltzville State Park. **Additional Information:** Pocono Mountains Vacation Bureau, (800) POCONOS, www.800poconos.org.

RESTRICTIONS

Pets: On leash only. **Fires:** At site. **Alcoholic Beverages:** At site. **Vehicle Maximum Length:** 45 ft. **Other:** All campers must have and display car pass.

TO GET THERE

From Hwy. 903, go 0.25 mi. north on US 209 and 2.25 mi. west on Broadway. Entrance is on left.

KANE

Foote Rest Campground

Rte. 219 RD #1 Box 188C, Kane 16735. T: (814) 778-5336; F: (814) 778-5111;
www.users.penn.com/~cardinal;
cardinal@penn.com.

RV ★★★★ Tent ★★★★

Beauty: ★★★★★ Site Privacy: ★★
Spaciousness: ★★ Quiet: ★★★★
Security: ★★★★ Cleanliness: ★★★★
Insect Control: ★★★★ Facilities: ★★★★

Situated on 55 acres and featuring level, shaded sites—including several pull-throughs—Foote Rest Campground is a place that truly caters to families. Children are sure to like the duck pond, where tame rabbits also frolic. Fire truck rides and hayrides are offered. Sites near the pond on Circle 3 and Circle 4 are highly recommended. The general store and gift shop is new. Tent-only sites are wooded and open. Located in the Allegheny National Forest, Foote Rest is near Kinzua Bridge State Park. Kinzua Bridge itself is designated a National Engineering Landmark. An excursion train travels through the Allegheny National Forest and over the bridge. When this viaduct was built in 1881, it was the world's highest and longest railroad bridge, at 301 feet tall and 2,053 feet long. Foote Rest offers information on train excursions.

BASICS

Operated By: James and Beverly Tarbox, Bonnie Stake. **Open:** All year. **Site Assignment:** Reservations and walk-ins accepted. **Registration:** At campground office. **Fee:** $22 (VISA, MC, D). **Parking:** At designated spot.

FACILITIES

Number of RV Sites: 162. **Number of Tent-Only Sites:** 25. **Hookups:** Electric (20, 30 amps), cable TV, phone, water, 100 full hookups. **Each Site:** Fire ring, picnic table. **Dump Station:** Yes. **Laundry:** Yes. **Pay Phone:** Yes. **Rest Rooms and Showers:** Yes. **Fuel:** No. **Propane:** Yes. **Internal Roads:** Gravel and dirt, in good condition. **RV Service:** No. **Market:** Within 4 mi. **Restaurant:** Within 4 mi. **General Store:** Yes. **Vending:** Yes. **Playground:** Yes. **Other:** Allegheny National Forest Vacation Bureau and Visitors Center display on premises. **Activities:** Rec hall, game room, mini-golf, basketball, bike rentals, shuffleboard, planned activities on weekends, movies, sports field, hiking trails, horseshoes, volleyball. **Nearby Attractions:** Kinzua Bridge State Park, America's First Christmas Store, factory outlet stores, Kinzua Dam Fish Hatchery, Penn-Brad Oil Museum, Holgate Antique Toy Museum, Allegheny National Forest attractions. **Additional Information:** Allegheny National Forest Vacation Bureau, (814) 368-9370, www.allegheny-vacation.com.

RESTRICTIONS

Pets: On leash only. **Fires:** At site. **Alcoholic Beverages:** At site. **Vehicle Maximum Length:** 60 ft.

TO GET THERE

From Hwy. 321, go 7.5 mi. east on US 6 and 0.5 mi. north on US 219. Entrance is on the left.

KNOX

Wolf's Camping Resort

308 Timberwolf Run, Knox 16232. T: (814) 797-1103; F: (814) 797-1110; www.wolfsden.com; wolfsden@clarion.net.com.

RV ★★★★ Tent ★★★★

Beauty: ★★★★★ Site Privacy: ★
Spaciousness: ★★ Quiet: ★★★
Security: ★★★★★ Cleanliness: ★★★★
Insect Control: ★★★★ Facilities: ★★★★★

Located in rural Clarion County, Wolf's Camping Resort provides all the amenities and activities RV and tent campers need. Sites are grassy—some are shaded—and there are 80 pull-throughs. Wolf's Den Restaurant and Mom's Snack Shack Restaurant are on the premises, as is an ice cream parlor and a well-stocked general store. Wolf's even has a bed and breakfast in a 19th-century house that still has the original hardwood floors in the kitchen and entrance hall. The Allegheny National Forest is the main attraction near Wolf's, and an ideal way to see the natural beauty is on the Knox, Kane, and Kinzua Railroad, which covers 96 miles.

BASICS

Operated By: John Altadonna. **Open:** All year. **Site Assignment:** Reservations recommended, walk-ins accepted. **Registration:** At camp headquarters. **Fee:** $23 (VISA, MC, D). **Parking:** At site.

FACILITIES

Number of RV Sites: 639. **Number of Tent-Only Sites:** 23. **Hookups:** Electric (20, 30 amps), cable TV, phone, water, 594 full hookups. **Each Site:** Fire ring, picnic table. **Dump Station:** Yes. **Laundry:** Yes. **Pay Phone:** Yes. **Rest Rooms and Showers:** Yes. **Fuel:** No. **Propane:** Yes. **Internal Roads:** Gravel, in good condition. **RV Service:** No. **Market:** Within 4 mi. **Restaurant:** On premises. **General Store:** Yes. **Vending:** Yes. **Playground:** Yes. **Other:** Large pavilion, bed and breakfast, restaurant, ice cream parlor. **Activities:** 9-hole golf course, boat rentals, large arcade, 300-yard driving range, mini-golf, lake fishing, rowboat and pedal boat rentals, canoeing, basketball, sports field, volleyball, horseshoes, movies, planned activities, shuffleboard, two swimming pools, wading pool, whirlpool. **Nearby Attractions:** Allegheny National Forest; Knox, Kane, and Kinzua Railroad; Oil Creek; Titusville Railroad. **Additional Information:** Allegheny National Forest Vacation Bureau, (814) 368-9370, www.allegheny-vacation.com.

RESTRICTIONS

Pets: On leash only. **Fires:** At site. **Alcoholic Beverages:** At site. **Vehicle Maximum Length:** 40 ft.

TO GET THERE

From I-80, take Exit 7 and follow Hwy. 338 0.1 mi. north. Entrance is on the right.

LANCASTER

Outdoor World—Circle M Campground

2111 Millersville Rd., Lancaster 17603. T: (717) 872-5317 or (800) 222-5557; F: (717) 872-5317; www.campoutdoorworld.com; mbrservs@ptd.net.

RV ★★★★ Tent ★★★★

Beauty: ★★★★ Site Privacy: ★
Spaciousness: ★★ Quiet: ★★★
Security: ★★★★★ Cleanliness: ★★★★★
Insect Control: ★★★★ Facilities: ★★★

In the heart of Pennsylvania Dutch Country, Circle M is one of Outdoor World's largest campgrounds. Amenities include two swimming pools, an indoor water park, a covered mini-golf course, and a 9-hole pitch-and-putt golf course. There are 25 pull-through sites. Amish-related attractions are plentiful in the area surrounding Circle M. The campgrounds helps guests make arrangements for exploring the Amish farmlands in an air-conditioned bus via Amish Living Tours. Certified guides spin entertaining and informative stories about Amish life. Stops may include Amish farms, roadside stands, craft and quilt shops, and bakeries. Another must-see attraction is the Amish Farm and House, an 1805 stone farmhouse where guided house tours and self-guided farm tours are offered. The working farm includes barns, livestock, a blacksmith shop, and the Early Americana Museum.

BASICS

Operated By: Outdoor World. **Open:** All year. **Site Assignment:** Reservations encouraged. **Registration:** At campground office. **Fee:** $30 (VISA, MC, AE, D). **Parking:** At site.

FACILITIES

Number of RV Sites: 382. **Number of Tent-Only Sites:** 30. **Hookups:** Electric (30, 50 amps), cable TV, phone, water, 266 full hookups. **Each Site:** Fire ring, picnic table. **Dump Station:** Yes. **Laundry:** Yes. **Pay Phone:** Yes. **Rest Rooms and Showers:** Yes. **Fuel:** No. **Propane:** Yes. **Internal Roads:** Gravel and paved, in good condition. **RV Service:** No. **Market:** Within 3 mi. **Restaurant:** Within 3 mi. **General Store:** Yes. **Vending:** Yes. **Playground:** Yes. **Other:** Indoor water park. **Activities:** Rec hall, two swimming pools (one indoor), wading pool, whirlpool, canoeing, kayaking, river fishing, golf, mini-golf, basketball, shuffleboard, planned activities, movies, tennis, sports field, badminton, horseshoes, volleyball. **Nearby Attractions:** Hershey Chocolate World, Zoo America, Strasburg Railroad, Indian Echo Caverns, Amish Country Living Tours, Dutch Wonderland, American Music Theater, Dutch Apple Dinner Theater, Rainbow Dinner Theater, Sight and Sound Theater, Tanger Outlet Center, Rockvale Outlet Center, Roots Farmers Market. **Additional Information:** Pennsylvania Dutch CVB, (800) PADUTCH, www.padutchcountry.com.

RESTRICTIONS

Pets: On leash only. **Fires:** At site. **Alcoholic Beverages:** At site. **Vehicle Maximum Length:** 40 ft.

TO GET THERE

From US 30, go 6 mi. east on Hwy. 741. Entrance is on the left.

LAPORTE

World's End State Park

P.O. Box 62, Forksville 18616-0062. T: (570) 924-3287 or (888) PAPARKS; www.dcnr.state.pa.us/stateparks; worldsendsp@state.pa.us.

RV ★★★ Tent ★★★★

Beauty: ★★★★ Site Privacy: ★★★★
Spaciousness: ★★★★ Quiet: ★★★★★
Security: ★★★★ Cleanliness: ★★★
Insect Control: ★★★ Facilities: ★★★

Wild and rugged, World's End State Park is located in a narrow S-shaped valley of the Loyalsock Creek just south of Forksville in Sullivan County. Hiking on the Loyalsock Trail attracts many visitors to the park. The scenery is spectacular, especially the June mountain laurel and fall foliage. Canyon Vista, reached via Mineral Spring and Cold Run Roads, provides outstanding views. The campground is located along Rte. 154, one mile east of the park office. The 19 rustic cabins there are available for rent year-round. Thirty-two campsites have electric hookups. Whitewater boaters may use the Loyalsock Creek at any time of the year, although the area by the swimming beach is closed during the summer. Due to rapid fluctuations in water level, kayakers should inquire about conditions before coming to the park with their 'yaks. The stream is not suitable for open canoes.

BASICS

Operated By: State of Pennsylvania. **Open:** All year. **Site Assignment:** Reservations and walk-ins accepted. **Registration:** At campground office. **Fee:** $15–$17. VISA, MC). **Parking:** At designated spot.

FACILITIES

Number of RV Sites: 32. **Number of Tent-Only Sites:** 38. **Hookups:** Electric (30, 50 amps). **Each Site:** Fire ring, picnic table. **Dump Station:** Yes. **Laundry:** No. **Pay Phone:** Yes. **Rest Rooms and Showers:** Yes. **Fuel:** No. **Propane:** No. **Internal Roads:** Gravel, in good condition. **RV Service:** No. **Market:** Within 4 mi. **Restaurant:**

Within 4 mi. **General Store:** No. **Vending:** Yes. **Playground:** No. **Other:** None. **Activities:** River swimming, canoeing, stream fishing, planned activities, sports field, hiking trails, snowmobiling. **Nearby Attractions:** Wyoming State Forest, Endless Mountains, Pennsylvania Bow Hunters Festival. **Additional Information:** Endless Mountains Visitors Bureau, (800) 769-8999, www.endlessmountains.org.

RESTRICTIONS

Pets: No pets permitted. **Fires:** At site. **Alcoholic Beverages:** No alcohol permitted. **Vehicle Maximum Length:** 40 ft.

TO GET THERE

From Forksville, go 2 mi. south on Hwy. 154. Entrance is on the right.

LENHARTSVILLE

Robin Hill Camping Resort

149 Robin Hill Ln., Lenhartsville 19534. T: (610) 756-6117 or (800) 732-KAMP; F: (610) 756-3434; www.gocampingamerica.com/robinhill; robinhillcamp@aol.com.

RV ★★★★ Tent ★★★★

Beauty: ★★★★★	Site Privacy: ★★
Spaciousness: ★★★★	Quiet: ★★★★
Security: ★★★★	Cleanliness: ★★★★
Insect Control: ★★★★	Facilities: ★★★★

Located in the foothills of the Blue Mountains and Pennsylvania Dutch Country, Robin Hill Camping Resort offers spacious, grassy sites, including 40 pull-throughs. We recommend the sites that offer water and electric and are located lakeside and near most of Robin Hill's activities. A bulk of the full-hookup sites are located on the campground's south end, away from the lake and activity centers. Robin Hill is surrounded by amusement parks, wineries, natural attractions, and, of course, Lancaster County's Amish-related sites. A unique attractions is the Ashland Pioneer Tunnel Coal Mine and Steam Train. Pioneer Tunnel; it ceased operation in 1931, then was retimbered and reopened as a place where visitors experience a real anthracite coal mine. The other featured attraction is a narrow-gauge steam train ride aboard the Lokie Henry Clay, which was used years ago to haul coal cars. Now it pulls passenger mine cars 3,000 feet along the side of Mahanoy Mountain.

BASICS

Operated By: Gary and Carolyn Krick. **Open:** Apr. 1–Nov. 1. **Site Assignment:** Reservations recommended, walk-ins accepted. **Registration:** At campground office. **Fee:** $28 (VISA, MC, D). **Parking:** At designated spot.

FACILITIES

Number of RV Sites: 270. **Number of Tent-Only Sites:** 10. **Hookups:** Electric (20, 30, 50 amps), cable TV, phone, water, 120 full hookups. **Each Site:** Fire ring, picnic table. **Dump Station:** Yes. **Laundry:** Yes. **Pay Phone:** Yes. **Rest Rooms and Showers:** Yes. **Fuel:** Yes. **Propane:** Yes. **Internal Roads:** Gravel and paved, in good condition. **RV Service:** No. **Market:** Within 3 mi. **Restaurant:** Within 3 mi. **General Store:** Yes. **Vending:** Yes. **Playground:** Yes. **Other:** 50 × 50 sites available, winterized lodge available for group rentals. **Activities:** Rec hall, game room, boating, canoeing, pedal boat rentals, pond fishing, planned activities on weekends, basketball, volleyball, horseshoes. **Nearby Attractions:** Dorney Park and Wildwater Kingdom, Hawk Mountain Bird Sanctuary, Knoebel's Amusement Park, Ashland Pioneer Tunnel Coal Mine and Steam Train, Blue Marsh Lake, Crayola Factory, Pat Garrett Amphitheater. **Additional Information:** Lehigh Valley CVB, (800) 747-0561, www.lehighvalleypa.org.

RESTRICTIONS

Pets: On leash only. **Fires:** At site. **Alcoholic Beverages:** At site. **Vehicle Maximum Length:** 50 ft.

TO GET THERE

From I-78, take Exit 11 and go 0.5 mi. south on Hwy. 143, 1.5 mi. east on Old US 22, and follow signs for 1 mi. on paved road.

LIVERPOOL

Ferryboat Campsites

RD 2 Box 324, Liverpool 17045. T: (717) 444-3200 or (800) 759-8707; wwwferryboatcampsitescom; ferryboat@tricountyi.net.

RV ★★★★ Tent ★★★★

Beauty: ★★★★★	Site Privacy: ★★
Spaciousness: ★★★	Quiet: ★★★★
Security: ★★★★	Cleanliness: ★★★★
Insect Control: ★★★★	Facilities: ★★★★

Ferryboat Campsites promises the finest bass fishing on the Susquehanna River. Of course, the bass will determine whether that promise is true, but the campground certainly has scenic sites along the river. Located in Liverpool near the historic Millersburg Ferry, Ferryboat Campsites features wooded sites, including 20 pull-throughs. The campground does not have a pool--nor does it need one with the river so close by. Tubing, canoeing, and kayaking are favorite activities of campground guests. A ride on the Millersburg Ferry is an event in itself. Crossing the river since the early 1800s, the ferry accommodates four vehicles and 50 passengers across the mile-wide Susquehanna. Hunter's Valley Winery is nearby, as is Harrisburg, which boasts a new Civil War museum that is a must-see for history enthusiasts.

BASICS

Operated By: Private operator. **Open:** Apr. 15–Nov. 1. **Site Assignment:** Reservations and walk-ins accepted. **Registration:** At campground store. **Fee:** $25 (VISA, MC). **Parking:** At site.

FACILITIES

Number of RV Sites: 290. **Number of Tent-Only Sites:** 15. **Hookups:** Electric (20, 30 amps), cable TV, phone, water, 287 full hookups. **Each Site:** Fire ring, picnic table. **Dump Station:** Yes. **Laundry:** Yes. **Pay Phone:** Yes. **Rest Rooms and Showers:** Yes. **Fuel:** No. **Propane:** Yes. **Internal Roads:** Gravel and paved, in fair condition. **RV Service:** No. **Market:** Within 5 mi. **Restaurant:** Within 2 mi. **General Store:** Yes. **Vending:** Yes. **Playground:** Yes. **Other:** Recreation on the Susquehanna River. **Activities:** Rec hall, game room, river swimming, river fishing, boating, canoeing, kayaking, canoe and kayak rentals, mini-golf, basketball, shuffleboard, planned activities on weekends, badminton, sports field, horseshoes, hiking trails, volleyball. **Nearby Attractions:** Millersburg Ferry, Hunter Valley Winery, Tobias Animal Haven, Knoebels Grove Amusement Park, Harrisburg State Captital, Selinsgrove Speedway, Golf Courses. City Island (Home of the Harrisburg Senators), Harrisburg Civil War Museum. **Additional Information:** Harrisburg-Hershey-Carlisle-Perry Co. Tourism and Convention Bureau, (800) 995-0969, www.visithhc.com.

RESTRICTIONS

Pets: On leash only. **Fires:** At site. **Alcoholic Beverages:** At site. **Vehicle Maximum Length:** 40 ft.

TO GET THERE

From Hwy. 17, go 2 mi. south on US 11/15 and 0.25 mi. east on paved road. Entrance is on the right.

MAHANOY CITY

Locust Lake State Park

RR 1 Box 1051, Barnesville 18214-9715. T: (888) PAPARKS or (570) 467-2404; www.dcnr.state.pa.us/stateparks; tuscarorasp@state.pa.us.

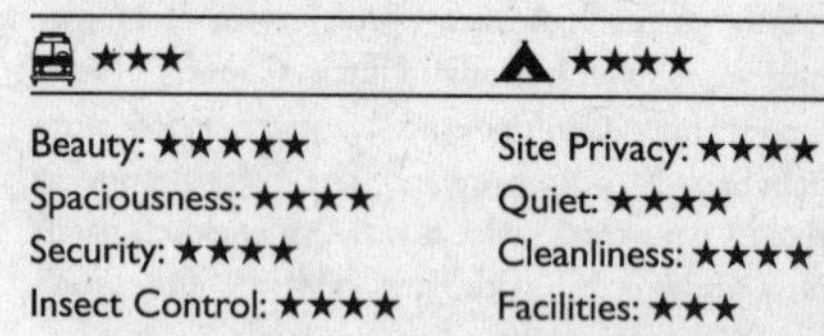

RV ★★★ Tent ★★★★

Beauty: ★★★★★	Site Privacy: ★★★★
Spaciousness: ★★★★	Quiet: ★★★★
Security: ★★★★	Cleanliness: ★★★★
Insect Control: ★★★★	Facilities: ★★★

Situated at the head of a steep, wooded valley, Locust Lake State Park is heavily forested. In fact, the only cleared area is the 52-acre lake. A bike trail and a number of hiking trails wind through the park. Known for its popular camping area, Locust Lake State Park is nestled on the side of Locust Mountain. The 282 campsites are divided into tent or trailer sides that encircle the lake. Tenting is permitted on the north side of the lake and the trailer facilities are located on the south side of the lake. Boating, hiking, and fishing are favored activities at the 1,089-acre park. Because of its location in the Appalachian Mountain section of the Ridge and Valley Province, Locust Valley is positioned along the migration route used by many species of birds of prey, including red-shouldered hawks, red-tailed hawks, merlins, and osprey. Screech owls and great-horned owls are year-round residents.

BASICS

Operated By: State of Pennsylvania. **Open:** Apr.–Oct. **Site Assignment:** Reservations accepted. **Registration:** At campground office. **Fee:** $19 (VISA, MC). **Parking:** At designated spot.

FACILITIES

Number of RV Sites: 80. **Number of Tent-Only Sites:** 202. **Hookups:** Electric (20 amps). **Each Site:** Fire ring, picnic table. **Dump Station:** Yes. **Laundry:** No. **Pay Phone:** Yes. **Rest Rooms**

and Showers: Yes. **Fuel:** No. **Propane:** No. **Internal Roads:** Paved, in good condition. **RV Service:** No. **Market:** Within 5 mi. **Restaurant:** Within 5 mi. **General Store:** Yes. **Vending:** Yes. **Playground:** Yes. **Other:** None. **Activities:** Boating, fishing, lake swimming, hiking, boat rentals. **Nearby Attractions:** Tuscarora State Park, Weiser State Forest. **Additional Information:** Schuykill County Visitors Bureau, (800) 765-7282, www.schuykill.org.

RESTRICTIONS

Pets: No pets permitted. **Fires:** At site. **Alcoholic Beverages:** No alcohol permitted. **Vehicle Maximum Length:** 35 ft.

TO GET THERE

From I-81, take Exit 37E and go 4 mi. west and south on SR 1006.

MANHEIM

Pinch Pond

3075 Pinch Rd., Manheim 17545. T: (717) 665-7640 or (800) 659-7640; www.pinchpond.com; pinchpond@gocampingamerica.com.

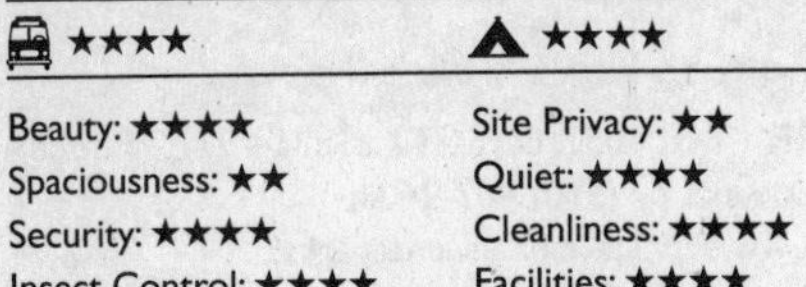

Located in the Lancaster County town of Harrisburg inside Pennsylvania Dutch Country, Pinch Pond Family Campground features shaded sites, including 30 pull-throughs. The fishing pond is stocked with trout twice a year. An enclosed pavilion permits group gatherings rain or shine. Pinch Pond's location is convenient to attractions in Harrisburg, Hershey, and Lancaster County, including the Strasburg Railroad, which takes passengers on a restored locomotive through the rolling hills of Pennsylvania Dutch Country. Also nearby is the Railroad Museum of Pennsylvania, where visitors can sit in the engineer's seat of a powerful locomotive, inspect a 62-ton engine from underneath, and relax inside an early-19th-century replica passenger depot. The museum boasts a world-class collection of more than 100 historic locomotives and rail cars displayed both indoors and outdoors.

BASICS

Operated By: Jason Sheaffer. **Open:** All year. **Site Assignment:** Reservations recommended, walk-ins accepted. **Registration:** At campground headquarters. **Fee:** $24 (VISA, MC, D). **Parking:** At site.

FACILITIES

Number of RV Sites: 211. **Number of Tent-Only Sites:** 25. **Hookups:** Electric (20, 30, 50 amps), cable TV, phone, water, 185 full hookups. **Each Site:** Fire ring, picnic table. **Dump Station:** Yes. **Laundry:** Yes. **Pay Phone:** Yes. **Rest Rooms and Showers:** Yes. **Fuel:** No. **Propane:** Yes. **Internal Roads:** Gravel and paved, in good condition. **RV Service:** No. **Market:** Within 4 mi. **Restaurant:** Within 4 mi. **General Store:** Yes. **Vending:** Yes. **Playground:** Yes. **Other:** Enclosed pavilion. **Activities:** Rec hall, game room, pond fishing, basketball, shuffleboard, planned activities on weekends, badminton, sports field, horseshoes, volleyball. **Nearby Attractions:** Hershey, Pennsylvania Dutch Country, Harrisburg, Strasburg Railroad. **Additional Information:** Pennsylvania Dutch CVB, (800) PADUTCH, www.padutchcountry.com.

RESTRICTIONS

Pets: On leash only, under control. **Fires:** At site. **Alcoholic Beverages:** At site. **Vehicle Maximum Length:** None.

TO GET THERE

From I-76, take Exit 20 and go 1 mi. south on Hwy. 72., 0.5 mi. west on Cider Press Rd., and 1 mi. north on Pinch Rd. Entrance is on the right.

MANSFIELD

Bucktail Camping Resort

1029 Mann Creek Rd., Mansfield 16933. T: (570) 662-2923; www.bucktailcamping.com; bucky@bucktailcamping.com.

RV ★★★★ Tent ★★★★

Beauty: ★★★★ Site Privacy: ★★★
Spaciousness: ★★★★ Quiet: ★★★★★
Security: ★★★★ Cleanliness: ★★★★
Insect Control: ★★★★ Facilities: ★★★★★

Bucktail Family Fun Park and Camping Resort rests in the mountains and valleys of Tioga County—otherwise known as Pennsylvania's Grand Canyon. With grassy open and shaded sites (including 12 pull-throughs), Bucktail is an attractive campground, but its amusement rides distinguish it from the typical family campground. A kiddie train winds through the grounds, and an antique carousel delights youngsters. RV and tents alike are welcome at the North Pole Rally Area at the park's northern tip. Sites that look out at the train near the batting cages and tower slide are convenient if you have children. An ideal way to marvel at canyon country is on horseback, and Tioga Trail Rides offers guided rides. Tioga Central Railroad has guided excursions through the countryside. Other family-friendly attractions near Bucktail include the Paddlewheel Riverboat Ride, Pennsylvania Lumber Museum, and Animaland Zoological Park.

BASICS

Operated By: Private operator. **Open:** Apr. 15–Oct. 31. **Site Assignment:** Reservations and walk-ins accepted. **Registration:** At campground headquarters. **Fee:** $30 (VISA, MC, AE, D). **Parking:** At site.

FACILITIES

Number of RV Sites: 190. **Number of Tent-Only Sites:** 10. **Hookups:** Electric (20, 30 amps), water, 26 full hookups. **Each Site:** Fire ring, picnic table. **Dump Station:** Yes. **Laundry:** Yes. **Pay Phone:** Yes. **Rest Rooms and Showers:** Yes. **Fuel:** No. **Propane:** No. **Internal Roads:** Gravel and dirt, in fair condition. **RV Service:** No. **Market:** Within 6 mi. **Restaurant:** Within 6 mi. **General Store:** Yes. **Vending:** Yes. **Playground:** Yes. **Other:** Kiddie train, antique carousel, other amusement rides. **Activities:** Rec hall, game room, mini-golf, basketball, planned activities on weekends, horseshoes, hiking trails, volleyball. **Nearby Attractions:** Tioga Trail Rides, Tioga Central Railroad, Pennsylvania Lumber Museum, Paddlewheel Riverboat Ride, Animaland Zoological Park. **Additional Information:** Tioga County Visitors Bureau, (888) TIOGA28, www.visittiogapa.com.

RESTRICTIONS

Pets: On leash only. **Fires:** At site. **Alcoholic Beverages:** At site. **Vehicle Maximum Length:** 40 ft.

TO GET THERE

From US 15, go 0.5 mi. east on US 6, 1.5 mi. north on Lamb's Creek Rd., and 1 mi. west on Mann Creek Rd. Entrance is on the left.

MARSHALL'S CREEK

Otter Lake Camp Resort

P.O. Box 850, Marshalls Creek 18335. T: (570) 223-0123 or (800) 345-1369; F: (570) 223-0124; www.otterlake.com.

RV ★★★★ Tent ★★★★

Beauty: ★★★★★ Site Privacy: ★★★
Spaciousness: ★★★★ Quiet: ★★★★★
Security: ★★★★ Cleanliness: ★★★★
Insect Control: ★★★★ Facilities: ★★★★★

Surrounded by the Pocono Mountains and located 10 miles from the Delaware Water Gap, Otter Lake Camp Resort has shaded sites (including 25 pull-throughs) in a wooded lakeside setting. We recommend a cluster of sites that borders the lake at the campground's northwest end. If you prefer to camp away from the activity centers but near the lake, sites on the northeast side will satisfy you. Most of the recreational facilities are located near the park's entrance at the south end of the lake. The 60-acre and private Otter Lake is on the campground property, and miles of hiking and snowmobiling trails are adjacent to the campground. Ceramics classes are held four times a week, and children are treated to free fire engine rides daily. Otter Lake and the resort are attractions themselves, but they are located near numerous Pocono Mountains and Delaware Water Gap sites. Called the "Niagara Falls of Pennsylvania," Bushkill Falls is truly one of the state's most picturesque natural wonders. Bushkill features eight waterfalls, accessible through an excellent network of hiking trails and bridges which afford fabulous views of the falls and the surrounding forest.

BASICS

Operated By: Private operator. **Open:** All year. **Site Assignment:** Reservations recommended, walk-ins accepted. **Registration:** At campground headquarters. **Fee:** $28–$35 (VISA, MC). **Parking:** At site.

FACILITIES

Number of RV Sites: 300. **Number of Tent-Only Sites:** 20. **Hookups:** Electric (20, 30 amps), cable TV, phone, water, 130 full hookups. **Each Site:** Fireplace and picnic table. **Dump Station:** Yes. **Laundry:** Yes. **Pay Phone:** Yes. **Rest Rooms and Showers:** Yes. **Fuel:** No. **Propane:** Yes. **Internal

Roads: Paved, in good condition. **RV Service:** No. **Market:** Within 7 mi. **Restaurant:** Within 7 mi. **General Store:** Yes. **Vending:** Yes. **Playground:** Yes. **Other:** Near miles of snowmobile trials. **Activities:** Rec hall, game room, 2 swimming pools (indoor and outdoor), wading pool, lake swimming, sauna, whirlpool, boating, canoeing, boat rentals, lake fishing, basketball, planned activities, shuffleboard, basketball, tennis, sports field, horseshoes, badminton, hiking trails, volleyball. **Nearby Attractions:** Bushkill Falls, Quiet Valley Living Historical Farm, golf, ice skating, skiing, horseback riding, Memorytown USA, Delaware Water Gap. **Additional Information:** Pocono Mountains Vacation Bureau, (800) POCONOS, www.800poconos.org.

Restrictions

Pets: On leash only. **Fires:** At site. **Alcoholic Beverages:** At site. **Vehicle Maximum Length:** 35 ft.

To Get There

From I-80, take Exit 52 and go 4 mi. north on US 209, 300 ft. northwest on Hwy. 402, and 7.5 mi. west on paved road. Entrance is on the left.

MEADVILLE

Brookdale Family Campground

25164 Hwy. 27, Meadville 16335. T: (814)789-3251 or (888)789-9186; F: 814-789-4494; www.brookdalecampground.com; camp@brookdalecampground.com.

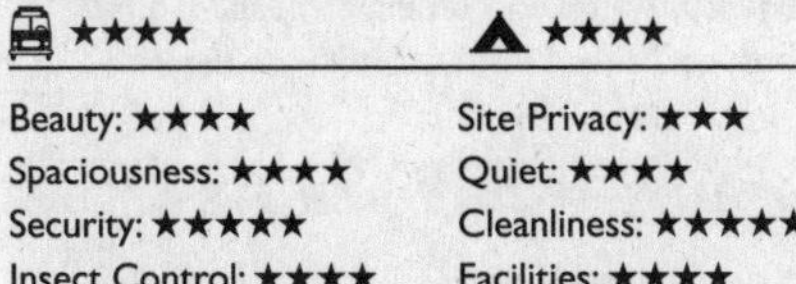

RV ★★★★ Tent ★★★★

Beauty: ★★★★ Site Privacy: ★★★
Spaciousness: ★★★★ Quiet: ★★★★
Security: ★★★★★ Cleanliness: ★★★★★
Insect Control: ★★★★ Facilities: ★★★★

Located on 62 acres seven miles east of Meadville, Brookdale Family Campground has open and shaded sites that accommodate 26 pull-throughs and 119 double slideouts. The campground store is heavily stocked with items like groceries, RV supplies, fishing supplies, and cooking supplies, including mountain pie irons and dutch ovens. Seven fishing ponds for catch and release fishing are scattered around the grounds of Brookdale, and no license is required. The campground is not far from the Crawford County Fairgrounds, which hosts one of the largest county fairs in Pennsylvania. Brookdale is also near two popular natural attractions, Pymatuning Lake and the Erie National Wildlife Refuge. Pymatuning has numerous boating, fishing, and hiking options. The Erie National Wildlife Refuge consists more than 8,700 acres of creeks, grasslands, wet meadows, and valleys teeming with birds, 47 species of mammals, 37 species of amphibians and reptiles, and several types of wildflowers.

Basics

Operated By: Private operator. **Open:** Apr. 15–Oct. 31. **Site Assignment:** Reservations and walk-ins accepted. **Registration:** At campground office. **Fee:** $24 (VISA, MC, AE, D). **Parking:** At designated spot.

Facilities

Number of RV Sites: 158. **Number of Tent-Only Sites:** 20. **Hookups:** Electric (30, 50 amps), phone, water, 35 full hookups. **Each Site:** Fire ring, picnic table. **Dump Station:** Yes. **Laundry:** Yes. **Pay Phone:** Yes. **Rest Rooms and Showers:** Yes. **Fuel:** No. **Propane:** Yes. **Internal Roads:** Gravel, in good condition. **RV Service:** No. **Market:** Within 5 mi. **Restaurant:** Within 5 mi. **General Store:** Yes. **Vending:** Yes. **Playground:** Yes. **Other:** Traffic control gate. **Activities:** Rec hall, game room, pedal boat rentals, pond fishing, basketball, planned activities on weekends, sports field, horseshoes, volleyball. **Nearby Attractions:** Erie National Wildlife Refuge, Crawford County Fairgrounds, Titusville and Oil Creek Railroad, Pymatuning Lake Spillway, rail trails in Titusville and Meadville, Thurston Classic Hot Air Balloon Event. **Additional Information:** Crawford County CVB, (800) 332-2338, www.visitcrawford.org.

Restrictions

Pets: On leash only, under control. **Fires:** At site. **Alcoholic Beverages:** At site. **Vehicle Maximum Length:** None.

To Get There

From Hwy. 77, go 5.5 mi. east on Hwy. 27. Entrance is on the left.

MIFFLINBURG

Hidden Valley Camping Resort

RR 2 Box 228, Mifflinburg 17844. T: (570) 966-1330; F: (570) 966-4985; www.gocampingamerica.com/hiddenvalleypa; hvcamp@ptd.net.

RV ★★★★ Tent ★★★★

Beauty: ★★★★ Site Privacy: ★
Spaciousness: ★★★ Quiet: ★★★
Security: ★★★★ Cleanliness: ★★★★
Insect Control: ★★★★ Facilities: ★★★★★

Located in central Pennsylvania's Buffalo Valley, Hidden Valley Camping Resort is a family-centered campground with 395 sites, including 40 pull-through sites. Wooded tent sites and primitive tent sites are also available. Full hookup sites on Stallion Ledge along the lake are especially inviting. Sites off Hidden Valley Ln. towards the entrance of the campground are most central to activities, including the petting farm and stables. Other nearby attractions include Penn's Cave, a water cavern and wildlife park explored by boat, and Hiawatha River Cruises, which board in nearby Williamsport and transport passengers on a paddle boat down the Susquehanna River.

Basics

Operated By: Private operator. **Open:** Apr. 1–Oct. 15. **Site Assignment:** Reservations and walk-ins accepted. **Registration:** At campground office. **Fee:** $23 (VISA, MC, D). **Parking:** At site.

Facilities

Number of RV Sites: 378. **Number of Tent-Only Sites:** 17. **Hookups:** Electric (20, 30 amps), cable TV, phone, water, 150 full hookups. **Each Site:** Fire ring, picnic table. **Dump Station:** Yes. **Laundry:** Yes. **Pay Phone:** Yes. **Rest Rooms and Showers:** Yes. **Fuel:** No. **Propane:** Yes. **Internal Roads:** Gravel and paved, in good condition. **RV Service:** No. **Market:** Within 5 mi. **Restaurant:** Within 5 mi. **General Store:** Yes. **Vending:** Yes. **Playground:** Yes. **Other:** Church services, gospel concerts. **Activities:** Rec room, game room, pedal boat rentals, mini-golf, lake fishing, basketball, shuffleboard, planned activities on weekends, sports field, badminton, horseshoes, hiking trails, volleyball. **Nearby Attractions:** Penn's Cave, Hiawatha River Cruises, Knoebel's Amusement Park, Clyde Peeling's Reptile Land, Pioneer Tunnel Coal Mine and Steam Train, Mifflinburg Buggy Museum, Slifer House Museum. **Additional Information:** Susquehanna Valley Visitors Bureau, (800) 525-7320, www.svvb.com.

Restrictions

Pets: On leash only, under control. **Fires:** At site. **Alcoholic Beverages:** At site. **Vehicle Maximum Length:** 40 ft.

To Get There

From US 15, go 9 mi. west on Hwy. 192. Entrance is on the left.

MILL RUN

Yogi Bear's Jellystone Park Camp and Resort—Mill Run

839 Mill Run Rd. P.O. Box 91, Mill Run 15464. T: (724) 455-2929 or (800) 439-9644; F: (724) 455-7729; www.jellystonemillrun.com; yogimillrun@gocampingamerica.com.

RV ★★★★ Tent ★★★★

Beauty: ★★★★ Site Privacy: ★★
Spaciousness: ★★ Quiet: ★★★
Security: ★★★★ Cleanliness: ★★★★
Insect Control: ★★★★ Facilities: ★★★★

Snuggled in the Laurel Highlands, Yogi Bear's Jellystone Park Camp and Resort in Mill Run has shaded sites in a wooded setting, but only one pull-through site. Sites here offer little privacy, but the campground is located in a forested environment which offers lots of welcome shade in warmer months. Like most Yogi Bear campgrounds, Yogi and Boo-Boo make occasional appearances, and the facility is located near numerous attractions. Children will love the two winding waterslides which cover 800 feet. The campground also offers train and wagon rides, and there is a mini-golf course on the grounds. A seven-mile mountain road in the Laurel Highlands connects Frank Lloyd Wright's extraordinary House on Kentuck Knob to his world renowned house on the waterfall. Kentuck Knob is an example of residential design from the final decade of Wright's career. Its pristine condition, spectacular views, and woodland setting create a memorable experience. An impressive collection of contemporary sculpture and historic artifacts enhance that experience. At Fort Necessity National Battlefield, colonial troops commanded by then-22-year-old Colonel George Washington were defeated in this French and Indian War skirmish.

BASICS

Operated By: Yogi Bear's Jellystone Park. **Open:** May 1–Oct. 31. **Site Assignment:** Reservations recommended. **Registration:** At campground office. **Fee:** $23–$31 (VISA, MC). **Parking:** At site.

FACILITIES

Number of RV Sites: 114. **Number of Tent-Only Sites:** 37. **Hookups:** Electric (20, 30 amps), water, 100 full hookups. **Each Site:** Fire ring, picnic table. **Dump Station:** Yes. **Laundry:** Yes. **Pay Phone:** Yes. **Rest Rooms and Showers:** Yes. **Fuel:** No. **Propane:** Yes. **Internal Roads:** Gravel and paved, in good condition. **RV Service:** No. **Market:** Within 2 mi. **Restaurant:** On premises. **General Store:** Yes. **Vending:** Yes. **Playground:** Yes. **Other:** Water slides. **Activities:** Rec room, game room, pond fishing, mini-golf, planned activities, badminton, horseshoes, volleyball, train and wagon rides. **Nearby Attractions:** Golf courses, Ohiopyle Falls, Fort Necessity, Fort Ligonier, Caddie Shack Family Fun Center, Living Treasures Animal Park, antique shops, bike trails. **Additional Information:** Laurel Highlands Visitors Bureau, (800) 925-7669, www.laurelhighlands.org.

RESTRICTIONS

Pets: On leash only. **Fires:** At site. **Alcoholic Beverages:** At site. **Vehicle Maximum Length:** 40 ft. **Other:** $2 fee per pet.

TO GET THERE

From Mill Run, go 0.25 mi. south on Hwy. 381. Entrance is on the right.

MILTON

Shangri-La on the Creek

RR #1 Box 245, Milton 17847-9801. T: (570) 524-4561; F: (570) 524-4522; www.shangrila-campground.com; shangri@prolog.net.

RV ★★★★ Tent ★★★★

Beauty: ★★★★★ Site Privacy: ★★★
Spaciousness: ★★★ Quiet: ★★★★
Security: ★★★★ Cleanliness: ★★★★
Insect Control: ★★★★ Facilities: ★★★★

It seems that morning, noon, and night, Shangri-La on the Creek stirs with activity. Parents and children fish on Chillisquaque Creek, and art enthusiasts learn crafts in ceramics classes. Shangri-La's 52 creekside sites and 115 additional wooded and semi-wooded sites are located at the foot of Montour Ridge along the Chillisquaque Creek. The row of water and electric sites along Chillisquaque Creek also border the recreation area for frisbee golf, basketball, and badminton. A large recreation pavilion seats 200 for special events, and the laundromat houses a tourist information center. Nearby, the Williamsport Trolley Tours take passengers past a series of lavish mansions on "Millionaire's Row" and the park where the first Little League Baseball game was played. The trolley debuted in Williamsport in 1865 and has operated ever since.

BASICS

Operated By: George and Pam Koons. **Open:** All year. **Site Assignment:** Reservations encouraged, walk-ins accepted. **Registration:** At campground office. **Fee:** $25–$29 (VISA, MC). **Parking:** At site.

FACILITIES

Number of RV Sites: 153. **Number of Tent-Only Sites:** 16. **Hookups:** Electric (20, 30, 50 amps), cable TV, phone, water, 37 full hookups. **Each Site:** Fire ring, picnic table. **Dump Station:** Yes. **Laundry:** Yes. **Pay Phone:** Yes. **Rest Rooms and Showers:** Yes. **Fuel:** No. **Propane:** Yes. **Internal Roads:** Gravel, in good condition. **RV Service:** No. **Market:** Within 7 mi. **Restaurant:** Within 7 mi. **General Store:** Yes. **Vending:** Yes. **Playground:** Yes. **Other:** Indoor and outdoor camping club areas. **Activities:** Rec hall, game room, swimming, wading pool, whirlpool, pond and stream fishing, basketball, planned activities on weekends, hiking trails, volleyball, horseshoes. **Nearby Attractions:** Williamsport, Little League Museum, Reptileland, Hiawatha Paddle Wheeler, Knoebel's Grove Amusement Park, Woodward & Penn's Caves, museums, flea and farmer's markets, restaurants, Bucknell University. **Additional Information:** Susquehanna Valley Visitors Bureau (800) 525-7320, www.svvb.com.

RESTRICTIONS

Pets: On leash only. **Fires:** At site. **Alcoholic Beverages:** At site. **Vehicle Maximum Length:** 45 ft. **Other:** No beer kegs permitted.

TO GET THERE

From I-80, take Exit 31A and go 8 mi. south on Hwy. 147, 0.25 mi. northwest on Hwy. 405, and 0.75 mi. east on paved road. Entrance is at the end.

MORGANTOWN

Warwick Woods Family Camping Resort

P.O. Box 280, St. Peters 19470. T: (610) 286-9655; www.warwickwoods.com; camp@warwickwoods.com.

RV ★★★★ Tent ★★★★

Beauty: ★★★★ Site Privacy: ★★★
Spaciousness: ★★★★ Quiet: ★★★★★
Security: ★★★★ Cleanliness: ★★★★★
Insect Control: ★★★★ Facilities: ★★★★

Located in Chester County, Warwick Woods Family Camping Resort offers 226 large, secluded sites on 100 acres. Warwick Woods has everything from primitive sites to expansive sites with full hookups. All sites are wooded, and most have foliage between them for added privacy. The renowned Horseshoe Trail meanders through the campground and can be hiked to various nearby and distant destinations. An acre in size, the campground's fishing pond is stocked with bass, trout, catfish, and bluegill. Though you likely know about the attractions in Hershey, Philadelphia, and Pennsylvania Dutch Country, you may not know about the hidden gem of small-town Kennett Square. Situated in the Brandywine Valley in southern Chester County, about three miles west of Longwood Gardens, Kennett Square is the "Mushroom Capital of the World" as well as the smallest town in America with a symphony orchestra.

BASICS

Operated By: The Daly family. **Open:** Mar. 30–Nov. 4. **Site Assignment:** Reservations and walk-ins accepted. **Registration:** At campground office. **Fee:** $24–$29 (VISA, MC). **Parking:** At designated spot.

FACILITIES

Number of RV Sites: 195. **Number of Tent-Only Sites:** 30. **Hookups:** Electric (20, 30 amps), phone, water, 18 full hookups. **Each Site:** Fire ring, picnic table. **Dump Station:** Yes. **Laundry:** Yes. **Pay Phone:** Yes. **Rest Rooms and Showers:** Yes. **Fuel:** No. **Propane:** Yes. **Internal Roads:** Gravel and paved, in good condition. **RV Service:** No. **Market:** Within 6 mi. **Restaurant:** Within 6 mi. **General Store:** Yes. **Vending:** Yes. **Playground:** Yes. **Other:** Live music and entertainment. **Activities:** Lake fishing, volleyball, basketball horseshoes, shuffleboard , two playgrounds, hiking trails, planned activities. **Nearby Attractions:** Sesame Place, Philadelphia, Pennsylvania Dutch Country, Valley Forge, Reading outlets, Hopewell Village, Hershey, Longwood Gardens. **Additional Information:** Chester Co. CVB, (800) 228-9933, www.brandywinevalley.com.

RESTRICTIONS

Pets: On leash only, under control. **Fires:** At site. **Alcoholic Beverages:** At site. **Vehicle Maximum Length:** 40 ft.

TO GET THERE

From I-76, take Exit 22 and go 1 mi. south on Hwy. 10, 7.5 mi. east on Hwy. 23, and 0.5 mi. north on Trythall Rd. Entrance is on the left.

MOUNT HOLLY SPRINGS

Mountain Creek Campground

349 Pine Grove Rd., Gardners 17324. T: (717) 486-7681; F: (717) 486-8306; www.mtncreekcg.com; mtncreekcg@aol.com.

RV ★★★★ Tent ★★★★

Beauty: ★★★★ Site Privacy: ★★★
Spaciousness: ★★★ Quiet: ★★★★
Security: ★★★★ Cleanliness: ★★★★
Insect Control: ★★★★ Facilities: ★★★★

Mountain Creek Campground is named for the stocked trout stream on the premises. When opening day of trout season comes in Apr., the campgrounds gets busy with anglers participating in fishing contests or casting just for fun. The Appalachian Trail is located just a half-mile away. Mountain Creek cuts through the middle of the campground, and sites on both sides directly bordering the creek offer spectacular views. All of the grassy sites are open or shaded. Hershey and Gettysburg are convenient to Mountain Creek, as are the lesser-known towns of Carlisle and York. York was actually the first capital of the United States, and the city has several 18th- and 19th-century buildings. Mountain Creek is an ideal base for the National Apple Harvest Festival, which is held during the first two weekends in Oct.

BASICS

Operated By: Private operator. **Open:** All year.

Site Assignment: Reservations recommended, walk-ins accepted. **Registration:** At campground headquarters. **Fee:** $25 (VISA, MC, AE, D). **Parking:** At site.

FACILITIES

Number of RV Sites: 186. **Number of Tent-Only Sites:** 14. **Hookups:** Electric (20, 30, 50 amps), phone, water. **Each Site:** Fire ring, picnic table. **Dump Station:** Yes. **Laundry:** Yes. **Pay Phone:** Yes. **Rest Rooms and Showers:** Yes. **Fuel:** No. **Propane:** Yes. **Internal Roads:** Gravel, in good condition. **RV Service:** No. **Market:** Within 5 mi. **Restaurant:** Within 5 mi. **General Store:** Yes. **Vending:** Yes. **Playground:** Yes. **Other:** Spa, stocked trout stream. **Activities:** Rec hall, game room, swimming, wading pool, pond and stream fishing, basketball, planned activities on weekends, hiking trails, horseshoes, volleyball. **Nearby Attractions:** Gettysburg battlefields, Hershey, President Eishenhower's Farm, Omar Bradley Museum, Hessian Powder Museum, York, Pennsylvania State Museum in Harrisburg, Boiling Springs, walking tour of Carlisle, Huntsdale Fish Hatchery. **Additional Information:** Harrisburg-Hershey-Carlisle-Perry Co. Tourism and Convention Bureau, (800) 995-0969, www.visithhc.com.

RESTRICTIONS

Pets: On leash only. **Fires:** At site. **Alcoholic Beverages:** No alcohol permitted. **Vehicle Maximum Length:** 45 ft.

TO GET THERE

From Hwy. 94, go 2 mi. south on Hwy. 34, 0.5 mi. west on Green Mt. Rd., and 1 mi. west on Pine Grove Rd. Entrance is on the right.

MOUNT POCONO

Mount Pocono Campground and Resort

P.O. Box 65, Mount Pocono 18344. T: (888) 55POCONO; F: (570) 839-7233; www.mountpoconocampground.com; campthemt@aol.com.

RV ★★★★ Tent ★★★★

Beauty: ★★★★ Site Privacy: ★★★
Spaciousness: ★★★★ Quiet: ★★★★
Security: ★★★ Cleanliness: ★★★★
Insect Control: ★★★★ Facilities: ★★★★

Adjacent to Devil's Hole State Game Land and perched atop Mount Pocono, Mount Pocono Campground and Resort is the region's oldest private campground, founded and still owned by the Albert family. The semi-wooded campground has open and shaded sites, including 70 pull-throughs. From the mountaintop, sunrises and moonlit nights seem more spectacular. All of the Pocono Mountains attractions are downhill from the campground. At over 2,000 feet above sea level, the air is clean and piney. Though the campground is secluded, it is not far from restaurants and grocery stores in the town of Mount Pocono, located on the other side of the mountaintop. Horseback riding is an ideal way to see a part of the Pocono Mountains not visible by car. Near Mount Pocono, Carson's Riding Stable has more than 60 miles of trails geared for everyone from beginners to seasoned riders. Free instruction is offered for first-timers.

BASICS

Operated By: John and Clara Alberts. **Open:** All year. **Site Assignment:** Reservations and walk-ins accepted. **Registration:** At campground office. **Fee:** $30–$35. **Parking:** At designated spot.

FACILITIES

Number of RV Sites: 140. **Number of Tent-Only Sites:** 15. **Hookups:** Electric (20, 30 amps), cable TV, phone, water, 70 full hookups. **Each Site:** Fire ring, picnic table. **Dump Station:** Yes. **Laundry:** Yes. **Pay Phone:** Yes. **Rest Rooms and Showers:** Yes. **Fuel:** No. **Propane:** Yes. **Internal Roads:** Gravel and paved, in good condition. **RV Service:** No. **Market:** Within 1 mi. **Restaurant:** Within 1 mi. **General Store:** Yes. **Vending:** Yes. **Playground:** Yes. **Other:** None. **Activities:** Rec hall, game room, swimming, wading pool, basketball, shuffleboard, planned activities on weekends, movies, sports field, badminton, hiking trails, horseshoes, hiking trails, volleyball. **Nearby Attractions:** Devil's Hole State Game Land, Pocono Mountains attractions. **Additional Information:** Pocono Mountains Vacation Bureau, (800) POCONOS, www.800poconos.org.

RESTRICTIONS

Pets: On leash only. **Fires:** At site. **Alcoholic Beverages:** At site. **Vehicle Maximum Length:** 40 ft.

TO GET THERE

From Hwy. 611, go 0.75 mi. north on Hwy. 196 and 0.5 mi. east on Edgewood Rd. Entrance is at the end.

NEW COLUMBIA

Nittany Mountain Campground

RR 1 Box 1383, New Columbia 17856. T: (570) 568-5541; F: (570) 568-1232; www.fun-camping.com; nittanycg@aol.com.

RV ★★★★ Tent ★★★★

Beauty: ★★★★★ Site Privacy: ★★
Spaciousness: ★★ Quiet: ★★★
Security: ★★★★ Cleanliness: ★★★★★
Insect Control: ★★★★ Facilities: ★★★★★

Located in the heart of Susquehanna Valley, Nittany Mountain Campground offers shaded and open campsites, including 20 pull-throughs. Nittany Mountain is set in wooded hills—not far from the highway, but far enough so that you hear birds singing, not automobiles. Nittany Mountain's petting zoo is a magnet that lures children to feed the goats and other farm animals. The 19-hole mini-golf course is another popular activity for children and parents alike. Every summer, the campground hosts a Sawmill Festival. Try log rolling, and then driving a golf ball on the fairway doesn't seem as hard. Nail driving (with a hammer) and crosscut sawing are among the events. For more entertainment, Knoebel's Amusement Park (free admission) in nearby Elysburg has 47 rides, including two wooden roller coasters, the Phoenix and the Twister.

BASICS

Operated By: Private operator. **Open:** All year. **Site Assignment:** Reservations recommended, walk-ins accepted. **Registration:** At campground office. **Fee:** $23–$28 (VISA, MC, D). **Parking:** At site.

FACILITIES

Number of RV Sites: 343. **Number of Tent-Only Sites:** 7. **Hookups:** Electric (20, 30, 50 amps), cable TV, phone, water, 17 full hookups. **Each Site:** Fire ring, picnic table. **Dump Station:** Yes. **Laundry:** Yes. **Pay Phone:** Yes. **Rest Rooms and Showers:** Yes. **Fuel:** No. **Propane:** Yes. **Internal Roads:** Gravel and paved, in good condition. **RV Service:** No. **Market:** Within 5 mi. **Restaurant:** Within 5 mi. **General Store:** Yes. **Vending:** Yes. **Playground:** Yes. **Other:** 19-hole mini-golf course. **Activities:** Rec hall, game room, swimming, wading pool, mini-golf, pond fishing, basketball, shuffleboard, planned activities, sports field, horseshoes, badminton, hiking trails, volleyball. **Nearby Attractions:** Knoebel's Amusement Park, Williamsport Trolleys, Pioneer Tunnel Coal Mine and Steam Train. **Additional Information:** Susquehanna Valley Visitors Bureau, (800) 525-7320, www.svvb.com.

RESTRICTIONS

Pets: On leash only. **Fires:** At site. **Alcoholic Beverages:** At site. **Vehicle Maximum Length:** 40 ft.

TO GET THERE

From I-80, take Exit 30-A and go 0.25 mi. south on US 15, 4.25 mi. west on New Columbia Rd., and 0.25 mi. north on Millers Bottom Rd. Entrance is on the right.

NEW HOLLAND

Spring Gulch Resort Campground

475 Lynch Rd., New Holland 17557. T: (717) 354-3100 or (800) 255-5744; F: (717) 355-9739; www.springgulch.com; thegulch@ptd.net.

RV ★★★★ Tent ★★★★

Beauty: ★★★★ Site Privacy: ★
Spaciousness: ★★ Quiet: ★★★★
Security: ★★★★★ Cleanliness: ★★★★
Insect Control: ★★★★ Facilities: ★★★★★

Located in the Pennsylvania Dutch Country, Spring Gulch Resort Campground has 450 open and shaded sites amid forests and farmland in Lancaster County. With two heated pools, a stocked fishing lake, a new 18-hole mini-golf course, and a dance barn, Spring Gulch boasts a wide assortment of activities. Just as guests of sister campground Mill Bridge have access to Spring Gulch amenities, Spring Gulch guests enjoy free admission to the historic Mill Bridge Village on the grounds of Mill Bridge Campground outside of Strasburg. Each May, the weekend-long Spring Gulch Folk Festival features music, campfire sing-a-longs, workshops, dancing, and crafts.

Basics

Operated By: Private operator. **Open:** Apr.–Nov. **Site Assignment:** Reservations recommended, walk-ins accepted. **Registration:** At campground office. **Fee:** $20–$40 (VISA, MC, D). **Parking:** At designated spot.

Facilities

Number of RV Sites: 350. **Number of Tent-Only Sites:** 100. **Hookups:** Electric (20, 30, 50 amps), cable TV, phone, water, 290 full hookups. **Each Site:** Fire ring, picnic table. **Dump Station:** Yes. **Laundry:** Yes. **Pay Phone:** Yes. **Rest Rooms and Showers:** Yes. **Fuel:** No. **Propane:** Yes. **Internal Roads:** Gravel and paved, in good condition. **RV Service:** No. **Market:** Within 4 mi. **Restaurant:** Within 4 mi. **General Store:** Yes. **Vending:** Yes. **Playground:** Yes. **Other:** Dance barn, stocked fishing lake. **Activities:** Rec hall, game room, two swimming pools, lake swimming, whirlpool, mini-golf, basketball, shuffleboard, planned activities on weekends, movies, tennis, sports field, badminton, horseshoes, hiking trail, volleyball. **Nearby Attractions:** Mill Bridge Village, Pennsylvania Dutch Country, Hershey. **Additional Information:** Pennsylvania Dutch CVB, (800) PADUTCH, www.padutchcountry.com.

Restrictions

Pets: On leash only. **Fires:** At site. **Alcoholic Beverages:** At site. **Vehicle Maximum Length:** 55 ft. **Other:** None.

To Get There

From Hwy. 33, go 4 mi. south on Hwy. 897 and 50 yards east on Lynch Rd. Entrance is on the left.

NEWMANSTOWN

Shady Oaks Campground

40 Round Barn Rd., Newmanstown 17073.
T: (800) 807-3177; F: (717) 949-3607;
www.shadyoakscamp.com;
shadyoaks@shadyoakscamp.com.

RV ★★★★ Tent ★★★★

Beauty: ★★★★	Site Privacy: ★★★
Spaciousness: ★★★	Quiet: ★★★★
Security: ★★★★	Cleanliness: ★★★★
Insect Control: ★★★★	Facilities: ★★★★

Nestled in the woods of Newmanstown and located in the heart of Pennsylvania Dutch Country, Shady Oaks Campground is surrounded by mountains and farmland. Shady Oaks is small compared to many campgrounds in Dutch Country, but it is clean, scenic, and quiet. Shady Oaks offers shaded and non-shaded sites, most in a wooded setting. Bath houses are clean and climate controlled, and the camp store is well-stocked and sells hand-dipped ice cream. For groups, Shady Oaks has a safari circle with water and electric hookups. The best tent sites are at the campground's north end. Shady Oaks hosts Saturday night hayrides and Sunday morning church services. Two often-overlooked attractions in the vicinity are the Pennsylvania Farm Museum and the Arrowhead Springs Trout Hatchery.

Basics

Operated By: Miller family. **Open:** Apr. 1–Nov. 1. **Site Assignment:** Reservations and walk-ins accepted. **Registration:** At campground office. **Fee:** $24 (VISA, MC, D). **Parking:** At site.

Facilities

Number of RV Sites: 87. **Number of Tent-Only Sites:** 5. **Hookups:** Electric (20, 30 amps), water, 61 full hookups. **Each Site:** Fire ring, picnic table. **Dump Station:** Yes. **Laundry:** Yes. **Pay Phone:** Yes. **Rest Rooms and Showers:** Yes. **Fuel:** No. **Propane:** Yes. **Internal Roads:** Gravel, in good condition. **RV Service:** No. **Market:** Within 4 mi. **Restaurant:** Within 4 mi. **General Store:** Yes. **Vending:** Yes. **Playground:** Yes. **Other:** None. **Activities:** Rec hall, game room, swimming, basketball, sports field, horseshoes, volleyball, planned activities on weekends. **Nearby Attractions:** Arrowhead Springs Trout Hatchery, Middle Creek Wildlife Preserve, HersheyPark, Chocolate World, Crystal Cave, Indian Echo Caverns, Ephrata Cloisters, Reading factory outlets, Blue Marsh Lake and Recreation Area, Pennsylvania Farm Museum, Summer Resort with Lake in Mt. Gretna, Harrisburg. **Additional Information:** Pennsylvania Dutch CVB, (800) PADUTCH, www.padutchcountry.com.

Restrictions

Pets: On leash only. **Fires:** At site. **Alcoholic Beverages:** At site. **Vehicle Maximum Length:** None.

To Get There

From west of Newmanstown limits, go 1 mi. southwest on paved road. Entrance is on the right.

NEWVILLE

Colonel Denning State Park

1599 Doubling Gap Rd., Newville 17241-9796.
T: (888) PAPARKS or (717) 776-5272;
www.dcnr.state.pa.us/stateparks;
coloneldenningsp@state.pa.us.

RV ★★★ Tent ★★★★

Beauty: ★★★★	Site Privacy: ★★★★
Spaciousness: ★★★★	Quiet: ★★★★
Security: ★★★★	Cleanliness: ★★★★
Insect Control: ★★★★	Facilities: ★★★

Located eight miles north of Newville, Colonel Denning State Park is nestled in a wooded area at the side of a mountain; it has a lake and well-marked hiking trails. The park has 273 acres of woodland and a 3.5-acre lake. The campground does not have showers. The mineral springs in Doubling Gap have drawn people to the area since the 1700s. Springs in the Doubling Gap area contain carbonate of soda and magnesia, glamber salt, epsom salt, carbonic acid, and bicarbonate of iron. With the advent of modern medicine, people began to learn that the bad-tasting waters were not as healing as their ancestors had thought, and the resort eventually closed in the 1920s. The main hotel still stands and is the focal point for a summer church camp.

Basics

Operated By: State of Pennsylvania. **Open:** Apr.–Dec. **Site Assignment:** Reservations and walk-ins accepted. **Registration:** At campground office. **Fee:** $15–$17. VISA, MC). **Parking:** At designated spot.

Facilities

Number of RV Sites: 18. **Number of Tent-Only Sites:** 34. **Hookups:** Electric (30, 50 amps). **Each Site:** Fire ring, picnic table. **Dump Station:** Yes. **Laundry:** No. **Pay Phone:** Yes. **Rest Rooms and Showers:** No. **Fuel:** No. **Propane:** No. **Internal Roads:** Paved, in good condition. **RV Service:** No. **Market:** Within 8 mi. **Restaurant:** Within 8 mi. **General Store:** No. **Vending:** Yes. **Playground:** Yes. **Other:** None. **Activities:** Boating, lake swimming, ice skating rink, lake fishing, hiking trails, sports field. **Nearby Attractions:** Hemlocks Natural Area, Tuscarora State Park, Doubling Gap Sulphur Springs. **Additional Information:** Pennsylvania Capital Regions Vacation Bureau, (717) 249-4801, www.pacapitalregions.com.

Restrictions

Pets: No pets permitted. **Fires:** At site. **Alcoholic Beverages:** No alcohol permitted. **Vehicle Maximum Length:** 35 ft.

To Get There

From Newville, go 8 mi. north on Hwy. 233. Follow signs to campground.

NORTHUMBERLAND

Yogi Bear's Jellystone Park Camp Resort—Yogi-on-the-River

RR 1 Box 116, Northumberland 17857. T: (570) 473-8021 or (800) 496-4320; F: (570) 473-8437; www.riverandfun.com; yogiriver@aol.com.

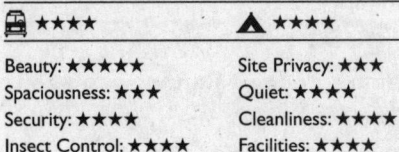

RV ★★★★ Tent ★★★★

Beauty: ★★★★★	Site Privacy: ★★★
Spaciousness: ★★★	Quiet: ★★★★
Security: ★★★★	Cleanliness: ★★★★
Insect Control: ★★★★	Facilities: ★★★★

If sites that border most of the activities are what you prefer, you'll want a location along Yogi Blvd. and Boo Boo Rd. There are 28 pull-through sites and 60 double slideouts. The sites along the lake at the south end and on the Susquehanna River at the north end are more serene and offer more privacy. At Yogi-on-the-River, you can fish in the Susquehanna River or Lake Catch-A-Fish, a stocked fishing lake where no license is required. Rowboat, canoe, and kayak rentals are also available at the lake, where you can boat around Yogi Island (which sports a statue of Yogi and his picnic basket). The campground has a full menu of special events throughout the year. One favorite is the annual Yogi Olympics, where children in various age brackets compete in events like the peanut scramble, fill the picnic basket, and string the button.

Basics

Operated By: Yogi Bear's Jellystone Park Campgrounds. **Open:** May 1–Oct. 31. **Site Assignment:** Reservations and walk-ins accepted. **Registration:** At campground office. **Fee:** $29–$35 (VISA, MC, D). **Parking:** At designated spot.

Facilities

Number of RV Sites: 150. **Number of Tent-

Only Sites: 30. **Hookups:** Electric (20, 30, 50 amps), cable TV, phone, water, 140 full hookups. **Each Site:** Fire ring, picnic table. **Dump Station:** Yes. **Laundry:** Yes. **Pay Phone:** Yes. **Rest Rooms and Showers:** Yes. **Fuel:** No. **Propane:** Yes. **Internal Roads:** Gravel and paved, in good condition. **RV Service:** No. **Market:** Within 4 mi. **Restaurant:** Within 4 mi. **General Store:** Yes. **Vending:** Yes. **Playground:** Yes. **Other:** Private fishing lake. **Activities:** Rec hall, game room, swimming, boating, canoeing, kayaking, boat rentals, lake and river fishing, mini-golf, basketball, bike rentals, planned activities, movies, sports field, badminton, horseshoes, volleyball. **Nearby Attractions:** Canoe Touring and whitewater instruction on the Susquehanna River, Clyde Peeling's Reptileand, Hiawatha Paddlewheeler Riverboat, Knoebels Amusement Park, Little League Museum & World Series, Penn's Cave, Pioneer Tunnel Coal Mine and Steam Train, T&D's Cats of the World. **Additional Information:** Susquehanna Valley Visitors Bureau, (800) 525-7320, www.svvb.com.

Restrictions

Pets: On leash only, under control. **Fires:** At site. **Alcoholic Beverages:** At site. **Vehicle Maximum Length:** 45 ft.

To Get There

From Hwy. 147, go 2.5 mi. north on US 11 and 0.25 mi. southeast on gravel road. Entrance is at the end.

OHIOPYLE

Ohiopyle State Park

P.O. Box 105, Ohiopyle 15470-0105. T: (888) PAPARKS or (724) 894-2421; F: (724) 329-8603; www.dcnr.state.pa.us/stateparks; ohiopylesp@state.pa.us.

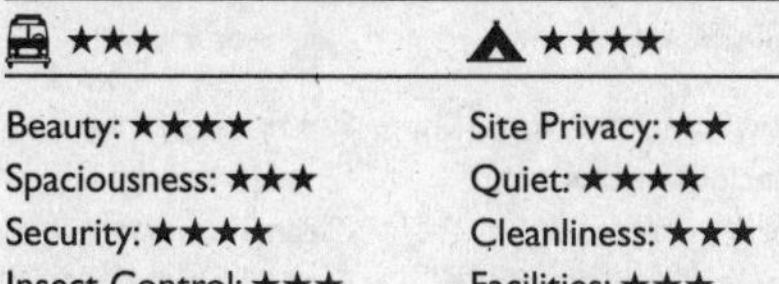

Beauty: ★★★★	Site Privacy: ★★
Spaciousness: ★★★	Quiet: ★★★★
Security: ★★★★	Cleanliness: ★★★
Insect Control: ★★★	Facilities: ★★★

More than 14 miles of the Youghiogheny River churn though the heart of Ohiopyle State Park, located in Fayette County near Ohiopyle. The famous Lower Yough, below the scenic Ohiopyle Falls, provides some of the best whitewater boating in the eastern US You can also hike or bike the 28-mile Youghiogheny River Trail. Ohiopyle State Park encompasses approximately 19,052 acres and serves as the gateway to the Laurel Mountains. Kentuck Campground is open Mar.–late Dec. There are 27 walk-in sites that have more privacy but require a short hike from your vehicle to the campsite. The campground has washhouses with hot water and flush toilets; there are also four children's play areas. A few campsites have electric hookups and more are planned for the future. There are three platform tents. These pre-pitched tents have electric hookups, dining canopy, mattresses, picnic tables, and fire ring.

Basics

Operated By: State of Pennsylvania. **Open:** Apr. 15–Dec. 15. **Site Assignment:** Reservations recommended; first-come, first-served for walk-ins. **Registration:** At campground office. **Fee:** $15–$17 (VISA, MC). **Parking:** At designated spot.

Facilities

Number of RV Sites: 226. **Number of Tent-Only Sites:** 6. **Hookups:** Electric (30, 50 amps). **Each Site:** Fire ring, picnic table. **Dump Station:** Yes. **Laundry:** No. **Pay Phone:** Yes. **Rest Rooms and Showers:** Yes. **Fuel:** No. **Propane:** No. **Internal Roads:** Gravel, in good condition. **RV Service:** No. **Market:** Within 10 mi. **Restaurant:** Within 10 mi. **General Store:** No. **Vending:** Yes. **Playground:** Yes. **Other:** None. **Activities:** Boating, swimming, hiking, bicycling, whitewater rafting, sports field, planned activities. **Nearby Attractions:** Whitewater rafting, Laurel Highlands Hiking Trail, Ferncliff Peninsula National Natural Landmark, Fort Necessity National Battlefield. **Additional Information:** Laurel Highlands Visitors Bureau, (800) 925-7669, www.laurelhighlands.org.

Restrictions

Pets: No pets permitted. **Fires:** At site. **Alcoholic Beverages:** No alcohol permitted. **Vehicle Maximum Length:** 35 ft. **Other:** 21-day max. stay.

To Get There

From I-76, take Exit 9 and go 25 mi. south on SR 381. Follow signs to park.

PARADISE

Mill Bridge Camp Resort

P.O. Box 7, Paradise 17562. T: (800) MIL-BRIG; www.millbridge.com; thegulch@ptd.net.

🚐 ★★★★ ⛺ ★★★★

Beauty: ★★★★	Site Privacy: ★★
Spaciousness: ★★	Quiet: ★★★★
Security: ★★★★	Cleanliness: ★★★★
Insect Control: ★★★★	Facilities: ★★★★

Adjacent to Mill Bridge Village (a recreated 18th-century Amish settlement), Mill Bridge Camp Resort boasts well-drained level sites, most of which are shaded and perched along Pequea Creek or amid a grove of walnut trees. Mill Bridge has 15 pull-through sites. Though Mill Bridge's amenities are not expansive (no pool), guests have free access to nearby New Holland's Spring Gulch Resort Campground, which has two heated pools, a fitness center, a dance barn, and lake swimming. Mill Bridge guests are also treated to a free Amish buggy ride and free admission to Mill Bridge Village. Of course, Mill Bridge's location is central to numerous other attractions in Pennsylvania Dutch Country, including the scenic Strasburg Railroad.

Basics

Operated By: Mill Bridge Village. **Open:** Apr. 1–Nov. 1. **Site Assignment:** Reservations and walk-ins accepted. **Registration:** At campground store. **Fee:** $24 (VISA, MC, AE, D). **Parking:** At site.

Facilities

Number of RV Sites: 100. **Number of Tent-Only Sites:** 25. **Hookups:** Electric (20, 30 amps), phone, water, 50 full hookups. **Each Site:** Fire ring, picnic table. **Dump Station:** Yes. **Laundry:** Yes. **Pay Phone:** Yes. **Rest Rooms and Showers:** Yes. **Fuel:** No. **Propane:** No. **Internal Roads:** Gravel and paved, in good condition. **RV Service:** No. **Market:** Within 2 mi. **Restaurant:** Within 2 mi. **General Store:** Yes. **Vending:** Yes. **Playground:** Yes. **Other:** Mill Bridge guests have free access to activities and amenities at Spring Gulch Resort Campground in nearby New Holland. **Activities:** Rec room, game room, boating, canoeing, stream fishing, basketball, planned activities, horseshoes. **Nearby Attractions:** Mill Bridge Village, Pennsylvania Dutch Country, Strasburg Railroad. **Additional Information:** Pennsylvania Dutch CVB, (800) PADUTCH, www.padutchcountry.com.

Restrictions

Pets: On leash only. **Fires:** At site. **Alcoholic Beverages:** At site. **Vehicle Maximum Length:** 55 ft

To Get There

From Hwy. 62, go 3.5 mi. east on US 30 and 0.5 mi. south on Ronks Rd. Entrance is on the left.

PORTERSVILLE

Bear Run Campground

184 Badger Hill Rd., Portersville 16051. T: (724) 368-3564 or (888) 737-2605; F: (724) 368-3415; www.bearruncampground.com; brcinc@earthlink.net.

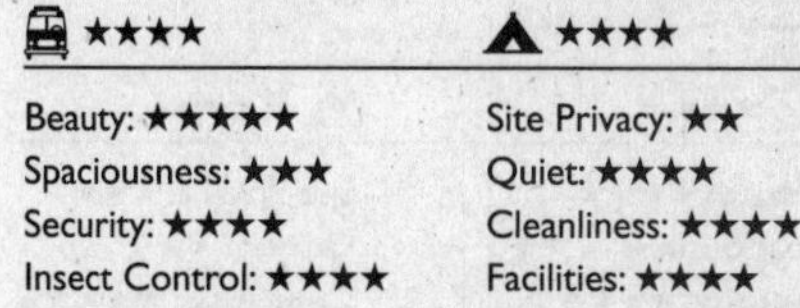

Beauty: ★★★★★	Site Privacy: ★★
Spaciousness: ★★★	Quiet: ★★★★
Security: ★★★★	Cleanliness: ★★★★
Insect Control: ★★★★	Facilities: ★★★★

Situated near Moraine State Park and Lake Arthur, Bear Run Campground consists of 60 acres of rolling hills dotted with open and shaded sites. The campground has eight pull-through sites, and 100 sites accommodate double slideouts. Moraine State Park features the 3,225-acre Lake Arthur, an outstanding warm-water fishery that is also great for sailing and boating. Visitors sometimes see osprey that were reintroduced to the park. Of special interest is the Frank Preston Conservation Area and a 7-mile paved bike trail that winds around the north shore of the lake. McConnell's Mill State Park is a five-minute drive from Bear Run. Slippery Rock Creek Gorge, a trout fisherman's paradise, is its main attraction. Bear Run is within 35 minutes of Pittsburgh and sites like Kennywood Amusement Park, Pittsburgh Zoo and Aquarium, and Carnegie museums. The Prime Outlets at Grove City are 20 minutes from Bear Run.

Basics

Operated By: Wehr family. **Open:** Apr. 15–Oct. 31. **Site Assignment:** Reservations recommended (72-hour cancellation notice required), walk-ins accepted. **Registration:** At campground office. **Fee:** $22–$33 (VISA, MC, D). **Parking:** At site.

Facilities

Number of RV Sites: 247. **Number of Tent-Only Sites:** 60. **Hookups:** Electric (20, 30 amps), phone, water, 187 full hookups. **Each Site:** Fire ring, picnic table. **Dump Station:** Yes. **Laundry:** Yes.

Pay Phone: Yes. **Rest Rooms and Showers:** Yes. **Fuel:** No. **Propane:** Yes. **Internal Roads:** Gravel and paved, in good condition. **RV Service:** No. **Market:** Within 3 mi. **Restaurant:** Within 3 mi. **General Store:** Yes. **Vending:** Yes. **Playground:** Yes. **Other:** None. **Activities:** Rec hall, game room, swimming, canoe rentals, lake fishing, planned activities on weekends, basketball, sports field, horseshoes, badminton, hiking trails, volleyball. **Nearby Attractions:** Moraine State Park, McConnelsville Mill State Park, Prime Outlets at Grove City, Living Treasures Animal Park. **Additional Information:** Butler County Tourist Promotion Agency, (888) 741-6772, www.butlercountychamber.com.

RESTRICTIONS

Pets: On leash only. **Fires:** At site. **Alcoholic Beverages:** At site. **Vehicle Maximum Length:** 35 ft. **Other:** None.

TO GET THERE

From I-79, take Exit 28 and go 50 yards east on Hwy. 488 and 0.5 mi. north on Badger Hill Rd. Entrance is on the right.

PORTLAND

Driftstone on the Delaware

2731 River Rd., Mt. Bethel 18343. T: (570) 897-6859 or (888) 355-6859; www.driftstone.com; ackdrift@epix.net.

RV ★★★★ Tent ★★★★

Beauty: ★★★★ Site Privacy: ★★★
Spaciousness: ★★★ Quiet: ★★★★
Security: ★★★★★ Cleanliness: ★★★★
Insect Control: ★★★★ Facilities: ★★★★

Set along the Delaware River, eight miles south of the Delaware Water Gap, Driftstone on the Delaware offers comfortable grassy sites, some of which are on the river. There are seven pull-through sites and 183 double slideout sites. Sites along the river are close to Driftstone Island, which can be reached with a short journey through the river. You can explore the Delaware River in a canoe, kayak, or raft during your stay at Driftstone; rentals are available to registered Driftstone campers or their paid visitors only. Driftstone also offers partial or whole day rentals from its dock. From here, you can fish and explore several miles of the Delaware. Upstream paddling is required. Campground staff members will even transport you upstream if you prefer. Driftstone offers day trips of four, eight, and fourteen miles. All trips include short sections of Class I rapids. Trip prices include rental and transportation.

BASICS

Operated By: Earl Ackerman. **Open:** May 14–Sept. 19. **Site Assignment:** Reservations recommended (deposits must be received within 1 week of date reservation made), walk-ins accepted. **Registration:** At campground office. **Fee:** $29–$32 (VISA, MC). **Parking:** At site.

FACILITIES

Number of RV Sites: 184. **Number of Tent-Only Sites:** 7. **Hookups:** Electric (20, 30 amps), phone, water. **Each Site:** Fire ring, picnic table. **Dump Station:** Yes. **Laundry:** Yes. **Pay Phone:** Yes. **Rest Rooms and Showers:** Yes. **Fuel:** No. **Propane:** Yes. **Internal Roads:** Gravel and paved, in good condition. **RV Service:** No. **Market:** Within 12 mi. **Restaurant:** Within 4 mi. **General Store:** Yes. **Vending:** Yes. **Playground:** Yes. **Other:** None. **Activities:** Rec hall, game room, swimming, wading pool, boating, canoeing, kayaking, canoe and kayak rentals, river fishing, basketball, planned activities, badminton, volleyball, horseshoes, sports field. **Nearby Attractions:** Delaware Water Gap, Shawnee Playhouse, Windrose Riding Center, Bushkill Park, Crayola Factory & Store, Crossings Factory Stores, Martin Guitar Company, National Canal Museum & Canal Boat Rides, Nazareth Speedway. **Additional Information:** Pocono Mountains Vacation Bureau, (800) POCONOS, www.800poconos.org.

RESTRICTIONS

Pets: On leash only. **Fires:** At site. **Alcoholic Beverages:** At site. **Vehicle Maximum Length:** 40 ft. **Other:** One dog per campsite.

TO GET THERE

From Hwy. 611, go 3.75 mi. south on River Rd. Entrance is on the left.

QUAKERTOWN

Quakerwoods Campground

2225 Rosedale Rd., Quakertown 18951. T: (215) 536-1984 or (800) 235-2350; F: (215) 536-5478; www.gocampingamerica/quakerwoods.

RV ★★★★ Tent ★★★★

Beauty: ★★★★ Site Privacy: ★★★
Spaciousness: ★★★ Quiet: ★★★★
Security: ★★★★ Cleanliness: ★★★★
Insect Control: ★★★★ Facilities: ★★★★

Convenient to Allentown and Philadelphia, Quakerwoods Campground in Quakertown is a quiet place nestled in a wooded setting. There are three pull-throughs and 160 double slideout sites. The bathrooms here are especially clean. When we were here, the swimming pool and fishing pond were stirring with activity. Many families use Quakerwoods as a base for visiting Philadelphia, Dorney Park, and Sesame Place. However, when mom and dad are weary from sightseeing, there is plenty for the children to do at the campground, such as basketball, volleyball, and shuffleboard. Quakerwoods offers discount tickets to Dorney Park and Sesame Place. Independence National Historic Park in Philadelphia—called the most historic square mile in America—commemorates more than 200 years of our nation's heritage. Here, you will find the Congress Hall, Independence Hall, the nation's first bank, and, of course, the Liberty Bell.

BASICS

Operated By: Tony Yu. **Open:** Apr. 1–Nov. 1. **Site Assignment:** Reservations and walk-ins accepted. **Registration:** At campground office. **Fee:** $25–$28 (VISA, MC, AE, D). **Parking:** At designated spot.

FACILITIES

Number of RV Sites: 170. **Number of Tent-Only Sites:** 15. **Hookups:** Electric (20, 30, 50 amps), cable TV, phone, water, 100 full hookups. **Each Site:** Fire ring, picnic table. **Dump Station:** Yes. **Laundry:** Yes. **Pay Phone:** Yes. **Rest Rooms and Showers:** Yes. **Fuel:** No. **Propane:** Yes. **Internal Roads:** Gravel, in good condition. **RV Service:** No. **Market:** Within 5 mi. **Restaurant:** Within 5 mi. **General Store:** Yes. **Vending:** Yes. **Playground:** Yes. **Other:** Theme weekends. **Activities:** Rec hall, game room, swimming, wading pool, pond fishing, basketball, shuffleboard, planned activities on weekends, badminton, sports field, horseshoes, hiking trails, volleyball. **Nearby Attractions:** Allentown, Philadelphia, Dorney Park, Crayola Factory, Fairmount Park, Independence National Historic Park, Neshaminy Valley Music Theatre, Sesame Place, Philadelphia Zoo. **Additional Information:** Philadelphia CVB, (800) 537-7676, www.pcvb.org.

RESTRICTIONS

Pets: On leash only. **Fires:** At site. **Alcoholic Beverages:** At site. **Vehicle Maximum Length:** 50 ft. **Other:** None.

TO GET THERE

From Hwy. 309, go 0.25 mi. southwest on Hwy. 663, 2.5 mi. north on Old Bethlehem Pk., and 0.5 mi. west on Rosedale Rd. Entrance is on the left.

ROBESONIA

Eagles Peak Family Camping Resort

397 Eagles Peak Rd., Robesonia 19551. T: (610) 589-4800 or (800) 336-0889; www.eaglespeakcampground.com; campatpeak@aol.com.

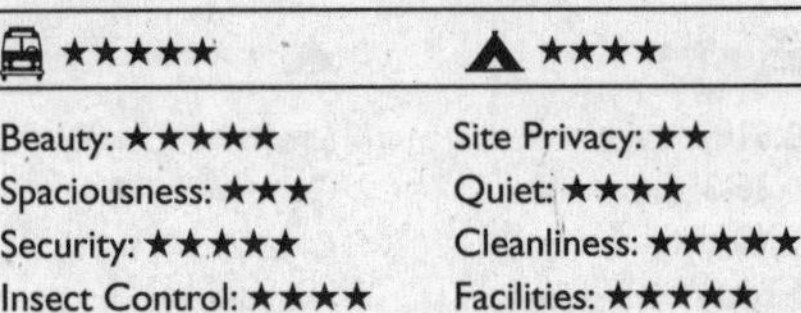

RV ★★★★★ Tent ★★★★

Beauty: ★★★★★ Site Privacy: ★★
Spaciousness: ★★★ Quiet: ★★★★
Security: ★★★★★ Cleanliness: ★★★★★
Insect Control: ★★★★ Facilities: ★★★★★

Central to Lancaster, Reading and Hershey, Eagles Peak Family Camping Resort is situated on 77 acres arranged in secluded tent areas and full hookup sites. All sites are either in meadows or wooded with a mountainside view. Sites along Mallard Ln. at the north tip of Eagles Peak (near Peak Pond) offer the most privacy. Sites in the center of the campground are closest to most of the activities. Favorite offerings include BBQ dinners and the swim-up snack bar at the swimming pool. Eagles Peak's pool has built-in benches and water volleyball, among other features. There is even a separate pool open to adults only. In nearby Amish country, you can find old-time farmer's markets and Amish-operated stores where gas lamps are used for lighting. The attractions in Hershey and Pennsylvania Dutch Country are a short drive away, as is Blue Marsh Lake, where fishing and boating are king.

BASICS

Operated By: Pete and Sue Frederick. **Open:** Apr. 10–Nov. 1. **Site Assignment:** Reservations accepted (no refund or credit given with cancellation on less than a week's notice), walk-ins accepted. **Registration:** At campground. **Fee:** $24–$34 (VISA, MC, D). **Parking:** At designated spot.

Facilities

Number of RV Sites: 320. **Number of Tent-Only Sites:** 30. **Hookups:** Electric (20, 30, 50 amps), cable TV, phone, water, 222 full hookups. **Each Site:** Fire ring, picnic table. **Dump Station:** Yes. **Laundry:** Yes. **Pay Phone:** Yes. **Rest Rooms and Showers:** Yes. **Fuel:** No. **Propane:** Yes. **Internal Roads:** Gravel and paved, in good condition. **RV Service:** No. **Market:** Within 5 mi. **Restaurant:** Within 5 mi. **General Store:** Yes. **Vending:** Yes. **Playground:** Yes. **Other:** Separate adult pool. **Activities:** Rec hall, game room, swimming, wading pool, whirlpool, boating, canoeing, pond fishing, mini-golf, basketball, shuffleboard, planned activities, movies, tennis, badminton, sports field, horseshoes, volleyball. **Nearby Attractions:** HersheyPark, Hershey Chocolate World, Dutch Wonderland, Crystal Cave, Mount Hope Estate and Winery, Lancaster County Amish attractions, Blue Marsh Lake, Daniel Boone Homestead, Reading outlets. **Additional Information:** Pennsylvania Dutch CVB, (800) PADUTCH, www.padutchcountry.com.

Restrictions

Pets: On leash only. **Fires:** At site. **Alcoholic Beverages:** At site. **Vehicle Maximum Length:** 50 ft. **Other:** None.

To Get There

From west of Robesonia, go 4 mi. west on US 422, 3 mi. south on Hwy. 419, 1.5 mi. east on Sheridan Rd., and 0.5 mi. north on Eagles Peak Rd. Entrance is on the right.

ROCKWOOD

Scottyland Camping Resort

1618 Barron Church, Rockwood 15557. T: (814) 926-3200 or (800) 242-CAMP; F: (814) 926-3491; www.scottylandrvresort.com; scotty@wpia.net.

RV ★★★★ Tent ★★★★

Beauty: ★★★★	Site Privacy: ★★★
Spaciousness: ★★★	Quiet: ★★★
Security: ★★★★	Cleanliness: ★★★★★
Insect Control: ★★★★	Facilities: ★★★★★

Scottyland Camping Resort is located in the mountainous Laurel Highlands region and situated on 311 acres. Primitive sites are located adjacent to the Laurel Hill Creek. Sites that surround the fishing lake are especially attractive, as are the sites that border the pine grove at the campground's northeast end; they offer privacy and solitude. Scottyland has an RV sales and service center with a mechanic on duty, and a snack bar with daily specials and delivery to your campsite. What is most impressive about Scottyland is the 2,000-square-foot indoor Playport designed for children 3-12. The Playport offers slides, ball pits, ropes, ladders, trolley, and tubes. Nearby is an indoor mini-golf course and skating rink. For seniors, the campground offers complimentary help with site hookup, propane, and lighting the water heater and furnace.

Basics

Operated By: Private operator. **Open:** All year. **Site Assignment:** Reservations and walk-ins accepted. **Registration:** At campground office. **Fee:** $20–$21 (VISA, MC, D). **Parking:** At designated spot.

Facilities

Number of RV Sites: 610. **Number of Tent-Only Sites:** 100. **Hookups:** Electric (20, 30 amps), cable TV, phone, water, 536 full hookups. **Each Site:** Fire ring, picnic table. **Dump Station:** Yes. **Laundry:** Yes. **Pay Phone:** Yes. **Rest Rooms and Showers:** Yes. **Fuel:** Yes. **Propane:** Yes. **Internal Roads:** Paved, in good condition. **RV Service:** Yes. **Market:** Within 10 mi. **Restaurant:** Within 10 mi. **General Store:** Yes. **Vending:** Yes. **Playground:** Yes. **Other:** Indoor mini-golf course and skating rink, Scottyland RV Sales and Service Center. **Activities:** Rec hall, game room, swimming, wading pool, lake and stream fishing, mini-golf, basketball, shuffleboard, planned activities on weekends, movies, tennis, badminton, sports field, horseshoes, hiking trails, volleyball. **Nearby Attractions:** Laurel Caverns, Seven Springs Mountain Resort, Ft. Ligonier, Idlewood Amusement Park, Ohiopyle State Park. **Additional Information:** Laurel Highlands Visitors Bureau, (800) 925-7669, www.laurelhighlands.org.

Restrictions

Pets: On leash only. **Fires:** At site. **Alcoholic Beverages:** At site. **Vehicle Maximum Length:** None. **Other:** None.

To Get There

From I-76, take Exit 10 and go 0.5 mi. south on Hwy. 601, 10 mi. south on Hwy. 281, and 1 mi. west on Hwy. 653. Entrance is on the right.

ROSE POINT

Rose Point Park Campground

RD 4 Box 410, New Castle 16101. T: (724) 924-2415 or (800) 459-1561; F: (724) 924-1309; www.rvamping.com/pa/rosepoint; rosepntprk@aol.com.

RV ★★★★ Tent ★★★★

Beauty: ★★★★	Site Privacy: ★
Spaciousness: ★★	Quiet: ★★★★
Security: ★★★★★	Cleanliness: ★★★★
Insect Control: ★★★★	Facilities: ★★★★

Located on Slippery Rock Creek near McConnell's Mill State Park and Moraine State Park near New Castle, Rose Point Park Campground has open and shaded grassy sites. There are seven pull-through sites and five double slideout sites. At McConnell's Mill State Park, you can tour the restored grist mill and covered bridges, or go hiking, rock climbing, and rappelling. Slippery Rock Gorge Trail is the longest trail in the park and extends from Hell's Hollow to Eckert Bridge. This six-mile, non-loop trail is designated as part of the North Country National Scenic Trail. Slippery Rock Creek is 49 miles long and full of slippery rocks; it's named for one exceptionally slick rock below the Armstrong Bridge.

Basics

Operated By: Yeager family. **Open:** All year. **Site Assignment:** Reservations and walk-ins accepted. **Registration:** At campground office (old white church). **Fee:** $20–$22 (VISA, MC, AE, D). **Parking:** At designated spot.

Facilities

Number of RV Sites: 142. **Number of Tent-Only Sites:** 10. **Hookups:** Electric (20, 30 amps), phone, water, 117 full hookups. **Each Site:** Fire ring, picnic table. **Dump Station:** Yes. **Laundry:** Yes. **Pay Phone:** Yes. **Rest Rooms and Showers:** Yes. **Fuel:** No. **Propane:** Yes. **Internal Roads:** Paved, in good condition. **RV Service:** No. **Market:** Within 4 mi. **Restaurant:** Within 4 mi. **General Store:** Yes. **Vending:** Yes. **Playground:** Yes. **Other:** None. **Activities:** Rec hall, game room, swimming, stream fishing, basketball, planned activities, sports field, hiking trails, horseshoes, volleyball. **Nearby Attractions:** Amish communities of New Wilmington and Volant, Grove City Outlet Shops, Harlansburg Station, Living Treasures Animal Park, McConnells Mill State Park, Moraine State Park and Lake Arthur. **Additional Information:** Pennsylvania Dutch CVB, (800) PADUTCH, www.padutchcountry.com.

Restrictions

Pets: On leash only. **Fires:** At site. **Alcoholic Beverages:** At site. **Vehicle Maximum Length:** 65 ft. **Other:** None.

To Get There

From I-79, take Exit 29 and go 3 mi. west on US 422 and 0.25 mi. north on Rose Point Rd. Entrance is on the right.

SHARTLESVILLE

Appalachian Campsites

60 Motel Dr. Box 27, Shartlesville 19554. T: (610) 488-6319 or (800) 424-5746; F: (610) 488-6238; www.appalachiancampsites.com; app2@juno.com.

RV ★★★★ Tent ★★★★

Beauty: ★★★★★	Site Privacy: ★★
Spaciousness: ★★★	Quiet: ★★★★
Security: ★★★★★	Cleanliness: ★★★★
Insect Control: ★★★★	Facilities: ★★★★★

Set in the foothills of the Blue Mountains in Dutch Country's northern Berks County, Appalachian Campsites has more than 300 wooded and open sites on 87 acres. There are 50 pull-through sites and 25 double slideout sites. Full hookup sites on the south end of the campground are near the fishing pond and a short walk away from the frog pond. Sausage and biscuits are just one of the tasty menu items at Johnny Appleseed Hall, the on-premises restaurant where breakfast is served daily (dinner on weekends). Meals are also served during annual events such as Easter dinner, autumn harvest feast, and New Year's Eve. Appalachian Campsites also has cabins, cottages, and teepees for rent.

Basics

Operated By: Jim and Sylvia Cox. **Open:** All year. **Site Assignment:** Reservations accepted (deposit must be made by credit card or check within 5 days to hold reservation), walk-ins accepted. **Registration:** At campground office. **Fee:** $23–$33 (VISA, MC, D). **Parking:** At site.

Facilities

Number of RV Sites: 300. **Number of Tent-Only Sites:** 30. **Hookups:** Electric (20, 30, 50 amps), cable TV, phone, water, 250 full hookups. **Each Site:** Fire ring, picnic table. **Dump Station:** Yes. **Laundry:** Yes. **Pay Phone:** Yes. **Rest Rooms and Showers:** Yes. **Fuel:** Yes. **Propane:** Yes. **Internal Roads:** Gravel and paved, in good condition. **RV Service:** No. **Market:** Within 7 mi. **Restaurant:** Within 1 mi. **General Store:** Yes. **Vending:** Yes. **Playground:** Yes. **Other:** New 6,500-square-ft activities center and new mini-golf course. **Activities:** Rec hall, game room, swimming, wading pool, pond fishing, mini-golf, basketball, planned activities on weekends, sports field, horseshoes, hiking trails, volleyball. **Nearby Attractions:** HersheyPark and Chocolate World, Dorney Park and Wildwater Kingdom, Shartlesville antique shops, Hawk Mountain, Crystal Cave, Pat Garrett Amphitheatre. **Additional Information:** Pennsylvania Dutch CVB, (800) PADUTCH, www.padutchcountry.com.

Restrictions

Pets: On leash only. **Fires:** At site. **Alcoholic Beverages:** At site. **Vehicle Maximum Length:** 40 ft. **Other:** None.

To Get There

From I-78, take Exit 8 and go 0.1 mi. west on N.Service Rd. Entrance is on the right.

SHARTLESVILLE

Mountain Springs Camping Resort

P.O. Box 365, Shartlesville 19554. T: (610) 488-6859; F: (610) 488-6073; www.mountain-springscampground.com; mtsprings@fast.net.

RV: ★★★★ Tent: ★★★★

Beauty: ★★★★	Site Privacy: ★★★
Spaciousness: ★★★	Quiet: ★★★★
Security: ★★★★	Cleanliness: ★★★★
Insect Control: ★★★★	Facilities: ★★★★★

Located in Pennsylvania Dutch Country near Shartlesville, Mountain Springs Camping Resort is like many of the clean and amenity-rich campgrounds central to Lancaster County and Hershey attractions. It has fishing lakes, boating, and swimming pools. What separates Mountain Springs from the other campgrounds in the region is its arena, which hosts professional and amateur rodeos, demolition derbies, horse sales, monster truck shows, and authentic Native American pow-wows. Mountain Springs also hosts bingo games and dances that aren't of the Native American variety. The campground itself has wooded and open sites on rolling hills. There are 15 pull-throughs and 50 double slideout sites. The row of water and electric sites near the cabins are convenient to the large fishing lake, while the full hookup sites on the south end of the campground of close to most of the activities (including the arena).

Basics

Operated By: Private operator. **Open:** Apr. 1–Nov. 1. **Site Assignment:** Reservations accepted (deposit due 7 days from reservation date), walk-ins accepted. **Registration:** At campground office. **Fee:** $23–$27 (VISA, MC). **Parking:** At designated spot.

Facilities

Number of RV Sites: 300. **Number of Tent-Only Sites:** 25. **Hookups:** Electric (20, 30 amps), water, 87 full hookups. **Each Site:** Fire ring, picnic table. **Dump Station:** Yes. **Laundry:** Yes. **Pay Phone:** Yes. **Rest Rooms and Showers:** Yes. **Fuel:** Yes. **Propane:** Yes. **Internal Roads:** Gravel and paved, in good condition. **RV Service:** No. **Market:** Within 3 mi. **Restaurant:** Within 3 mi. **General Store:** Yes. **Vending:** Yes. **Playground:** Yes. **Other:** Arena for rodeos, demolition derbies, and other events. **Activities:** Rec hall, game room, swimming, wading pool, boating, canoeing, pond fishing, basketball, shuffleboard, planned activities on weekends, movies, badminton, sports field, horseshoes, hiking trails, volleyball. **Nearby Attractions:** Shartlesville antique shops, Pennsylvania Dutch Country attractions, Hershey attractions. **Additional Information:** Pennsylvania Dutch CVB, (800) PADUTCH, www.padutchcountry.com.

Restrictions

Pets: On leash only. **Fires:** At site. **Alcoholic Beverages:** At site. **Vehicle Maximum Length:** None. **Other:** None.

To Get There

From I-78, take Exit 8 and go 1 mi. east on Mountain Rd. Entrance is on the left.

SOMERSET

Laurel Hill State Park

1454 Laurel Hill Park Rd., Somerset 15501. T: (814) 445-7725 or (888) PAPARKS; www.dcnr.state.pa.us/stateparks; laurelhillsp@state.pa.us.

RV: ★★★★ Tent: ★★★★

Beauty: ★★★★	Site Privacy: ★★
Spaciousness: ★★★	Quiet: ★★★★
Security: ★★★★	Cleanliness: ★★★
Insect Control: ★★★	Facilities: ★★★★

Laurel Hill State Park is home to 63-acre Laurel Hill Lake. The park consists of 3,935 acres of mountainous terrain in Somerset County. Of the 264 sites at the campground, 169 have electric hookups. There is also one walled tent available for rent. This tent sleeps six people in bunk beds and offers electricity and a refrigerator. The campground has flush toilets and hot showers. Laurel Hill has a 12-mile trail system which leads past the remains of a logging railroad. Hikers commonly see wooden crossties and rusty rail spikes along the Tramroad Trail. This railroad hauled logs from the mountains to a sawmill located at Humbert, near Confluence. A lush stand of old-growth timber may be seen along the popular Hemlock Trail. The 10-mile snowmobile trail system in the park connects with a longer trail system at Forbes State Forest, which is open for registered snowmobiles after the end of antlerless deer season in late Dec. During warmer and sunnier months, a 1,200-foot-long sandy beach is open from late-May to mid-Sept.

Basics

Operated By: State of Pennsylvania. **Open:** Apr.–Dec. **Site Assignment:** Reservations and walk-ins accepted. **Registration:** At campground office. **Fee:** $15–$17.VISA, MC). **Parking:** At designated spot.

Facilities

Number of RV Sites: 162. **Number of Tent-Only Sites:** 70. **Hookups:** Electric (20, 30, 50 amps). **Each Site:** Fire ring, picnic table. **Dump Station:** Yes. **Laundry:** No. **Pay Phone:** Yes. **Rest Rooms and Showers:** Yes. **Fuel:** No. **Propane:** No. **Internal Roads:** Paved, in good condition. **RV Service:** No. **Market:** Within 12 mi. **Restaurant:** Within 15 mi. **General Store:** No. **Vending:** Yes. **Playground:** Yes. **Other:** None. **Activities:** Lake swimming and fishing, boating, canoeing, boat rentals, stream fishing, planned activities, hiking trails. **Nearby Attractions:** Covered bridges at Barronville and Kings Bridge, Kooser State Park, Laurel Ridge State Park, Ohiopyle State Park, Frank Lloyd Wright's Falling Water house, Mt. Davis. **Additional Information:** Laurel Highlands Visitors Bureau, (800) 925-7669, www.laurelhighlands.org.

Restrictions

Pets: No pets permitted. **Fires:** At site. **Alcoholic Beverages:** No alcohol permitted. **Vehicle Maximum Length:** 30 ft. **Other:** None.

To Get There

From I-70/I-76, take Exit 10, go 10 mi. west on Hwy. 31, and follow signs 2 mi. south. Entrance is on the right.

SOMERSET

Pioneer Park Campground

273 Trent Rd., Somerset 15501. T: (814) 445-6348; F: (814) 445-6269; www.pioneerparkcampground.com; info@pioneerparkcampground.com.

RV: ★★★★ Tent: ★★★★

Beauty: ★★★★★	Site Privacy: ★★★
Spaciousness: ★★★	Quiet: ★★★★
Security: ★★★★	Cleanliness: ★★★★★
Insect Control: ★★★★	Facilities: ★★★★

Located at the foot of the Laurel Ridge Mountains, Pioneer Park Campground features well-manicured grassy open and shaded sites with spectacular mountain views. Pioneer Park's main draw is its 50 acres of spring-fed lakes. Three of the lakes are stocked with trout two times a week. The other lake is for pedal boating and children's fishing. Pioneer Park also has pedal boat races as well as some treasure hunts. Sites at the northeast end of campground are closest to the largest fishing lake. Sites at the southeast border a small lake. There are 200 full hookups and 18 level pull-through sites. Close to Seven Springs Mountain Resort and Ft. Ligonier, Pioneer Park is also near Laurel Caverns, which has three miles of underground caves open for exploration year-round.

Basics

Operated By: Frank Sujanksi. **Open:** Apr. 1–Oct. 28. **Site Assignment:** Reservations recommended, walk-ins accepted. **Registration:** At campground office. **Fee:** $20–$26 (VISA, MC). **Parking:** At designated spot.

Facilities

Number of RV Sites: 200. **Number of Tent-Only Sites:** 145. **Hookups:** Electric (20, 30, 50 amps), cable TV, phone, 200 full hookups. **Each Site:** Fire ring, picnic table. **Dump Station:** Yes. **Laundry:** Yes. **Pay Phone:** Yes. **Rest Rooms and Showers:** Yes. **Fuel:** No. **Propane:** Yes. **Internal Roads:** Gravel and paved, in good condition. **RV Service:** No. **Market:** Within 10 mi. **Restaurant:** Within 2 mi. **General Store:** Yes. **Vending:** Yes. **Playground:** Yes. **Other:** 50 acres of stocked fishing lakes. **Activities:** Lake fishing, rec hall, game room, wading pool, pedal boat rentals, mini-golf, basketball, shuffleboard, planned activities on weekends, tennis, sports field, horseshoes, hiking trails, volleyball. **Nearby Attractions:** Laurel Caverns, Seven Springs Mountain Resort, Ft. Ligonier, Idlewood Amusement Park. **Additional Information:** Laurel Highlands Visitors Bureau, (800) 925-7669, www.laurelhighlands.org.

Restrictions

Pets: On leash only. **Fires:** At site. **Alcoholic Beverages:** At site, under control. **Vehicle Maximum Length:** 40 ft. **Other:** None.

To Get There

From I-76, take Exit 10 and go 0.5 mi. south on Hwy. 601, 7 mi. west on Hwy. 31, and 0.25 mi. south on Trent Rd. Entrance is on the right.

UPPER BLACK EDDY

Colonial Woods Family Camping Resort

545 Lonely Cottage Dr., Upper Black Eddy 18972. T: (610) 847-5808 or (800) 887-2267; www.colonialwoods.com; colwoods@epix.net.

RV: ★★★★ Tent: ★★★★

Beauty: ★★★★	Site Privacy: ★★★
Spaciousness: ★★★	Quiet: ★★★
Security: ★★★★	Cleanliness: ★★★★
Insect Control: ★★★★	Facilities: ★★★★★

Rich with 18th-century history, Bucks County is called the cradle of American heritage, and Colonial Woods Family Camping Resort is in the heart of that heritage. Situated in a wooded and rolling setting, Colonial Woods offers secluded sites beneath towering timber. There are 10 pull-through sites and 175 double slideouts. Most of the water, electric, and cable sites are at the north end of the campground—close to the pond, the lakes, and most of the activities. Of course, Colonial Woods is a cozy place, so everything is a short walk away. The climate-controlled lodge is especially inviting in cold weather, when the fireplace crackles inside. Mini-golf and fishing in the pond are among the activities. Nearby, the Delaware River is ideal for tubing, boating, and swimming. Philadelphia and its wealth of attractions are less than 30 minutes away.

Basics

Operated By: Bonnie and John Haubert. **Open:** Apr. 15–Nov. 1. **Site Assignment:** Reservations accepted ($100 security deposit required, no refunds within 14 days of reservation), walk-ins accepted. **Registration:** At campground office. **Fee:** $30 (VISA, MC, AE, D). **Parking:** At site.

Facilities

Number of RV Sites: 194. **Number of Tent-Only Sites:** 30. **Hookups:** Electric (20, 30 amps), cable TV, phone, water. **Each Site:** Fire ring, picnic table. **Dump Station:** Yes. **Laundry:** Yes. **Pay Phone:** Yes. **Rest Rooms and Showers:** Yes. **Fuel:** No. **Propane:** Yes. **Internal Roads:** Gravel and paved, in good condition. **RV Service:** No. **Market:** Within 5 mi. **Restaurant:** Within 5 mi. **General Store:** Yes. **Vending:** Yes. **Playground:** Yes. **Other:** None. **Activities:** Rec hall, game room, swimming, wading pool, whirlpool, boating, canoeing, pond fishing, basketball, mini-golf, planned activities, movies, tennis, badminton, sports field, horseshoes, volleyball. **Nearby Attractions:** Philadelphia, Crayola Factory, Land of Make Believe, Lake Nockamixon State Park, Washington Crossing, Bowman's Tower, Valley Forge, Delaware River tubing, Buckingham Valley Vineyard and Winery. **Additional Information:** Bucks Co. Conference and Visitors Bureau, (800) 836-BUCKS, www.buckscountycvb.org.

Restrictions

Pets: On leash only. **Fires:** At site. **Alcoholic Beverages:** At site. **Vehicle Maximum Length:** 40 ft. **Other:** None.

To Get There

From Hwy. 412, go 2 mi. north on Hwy. 611, 1.5 mi. east on Marienstein Rd., and 0.75 mi. north on Lonely Cottage Rd. Entrance is on the right.

WATERVILLE

Little Pine State Park

4205 Little Pine Creek Rd., Waterville 17776. T: (570) 753-6000 or (888) PAPARKS; www.dcnr.state.pa.us/stateparks; littlepinesp@state.pa.us.

RV: ★★★ Tent: ★★★★

Beauty: ★★★★	Site Privacy: ★★★
Spaciousness: ★★★★	Quiet: ★★★★
Security: ★★★★	Cleanliness: ★★★
Insect Control: ★★★	Facilities: ★★★★

Set in postcard-perfect Tiadaghton State Forest in the Appalachian Mountains, the 2,158-acre Little Pine State Park is located in Lycoming County, four miles north of Rte. 44 at Waterville and eight miles south of Rte. 287 at English Center. The campground has open and shaded sites along a stream. A special attraction of the park is the trail system. Spikebuck Hollow Trail, with its picturesque vistas, outcroppings of rock, and varieties of trees and plants, is an enjoyable challenge. For parents with small children, the 0.8-mile-long Carsontown Trail is ideal. The walk is easy, a variety of wildflowers bloom, and deer are frequently seen. At 2.7 miles long, Panther Run Trail is Little Pine's most scenic hike, but it is intended for the most seasoned and conditioned hikers. Excellent views, rock formations, and a flagstone quarry can be seen along the trail.

Basics

Operated By: State of Pennsylvania. **Open:** Apr. 1–Dec. 15. **Site Assignment:** Reservations and walk-ins accepted. **Registration:** At campground office. **Fee:** $15–$17 (VISA, MC). **Parking:** At designated spot.

Facilities

Number of RV Sites: 98. **Number of Tent-Only Sites:** 6. **Hookups:** Electric (50 amps). **Each Site:** Fire ring, picnic table. **Dump Station:** Yes. **Laundry:** No. **Pay Phone:** Yes. **Rest Rooms and Showers:** Rest rooms, no showers. **Fuel:** No. **Propane:** Yes. **Internal Roads:** Paved, in good condition. **RV Service:** No. **Market:** Within 7 mi. **Restaurant:** Within 7 mi. **General Store:** Yes. **Vending:** Yes. **Playground:** Yes. **Other:** No. **Activities:** Lake swimming, boating, boat rentals, lake and stream fishing, horseshoes, hiking trails, volleyball. **Nearby Attractions:** Upper Pine Bottom State Park. **Additional Information:** Lycoming County Visitors Bureau, (800) 358-9900, www.williamsport.org.

Restrictions

Pets: No pets permitted. **Fires:** At site. **Alcoholic Beverages:** No alcohol permitted. **Vehicle Maximum Length:** 30 ft. **Other:** None.

To Get There

From Hwy. 44, go 4 mi. north on 4001. Follow signs to campground.

WAYMART

Keen Lake Camping and Cottage Resort

RR 1 Box 1976, Waymart 18472. T: (800) 443-0412 or (570) 488-5522; F: (570) 488-7077; www.keenlake.com; keenlake@socantel.net.

RV: ★★★★★ Tent: ★★★★

Beauty: ★★★★	Site Privacy: ★★★
Spaciousness: ★★★	Quiet: ★★★★★
Security: ★★★★	Cleanliness: ★★★★
Insect Control: ★★★★	Facilities: ★★★★★

Perched on a high plateau in the Pocono Mountains, Keen Lake Camping and Cottage Resort has over 300 sites on 90 acres, but the sites are by no means crowded. The open and shaded sites—which include five pull-throughs and 25 double slide-outs—are well-maintained. Campsites are nestled along a rail system's former tracks in a cluster known as Gravity Lane, named in honor of this railroad.

Keen Lake has been a part of the Keen family since 1814 when the family purchased land on what was then the Elk Forest tract. Sixth-generation members are active in the family business, and the customer service here is friendly. Other buildings of historical significance located on the resort grounds include the Island cottage located on Hermit Island, the School House cottage, and the Pre-Civil War Barn cottage. Keen Lake has a 50-foot hillslide, a scenic waterfall, train rides, and activities ranging from fishing and boating to bocce ball and arts and crafts.

Basics

Operated By: Keen family. **Open:** May 1–Oct. 1. **Site Assignment:** Reservations recommended (2-night min. reservation except major holidays), walk-ins accepted. **Registration:** At campground headquarters. **Fee:** $28–$34 (VISA, MC). **Parking:** At designated spot.

Facilities

Number of RV Sites: 300. **Number of Tent-Only Sites:** 75. **Hookups:** Electric (20, 30 amps), cable TV, phone, water, 162 full hookups. **Each Site:** Fire ring, picnic table. **Dump Station:** Yes. **Laundry:** Yes. **Pay Phone:** Yes. **Rest Rooms and Showers:** Yes. **Fuel:** No. **Propane:** No. **Internal Roads:** Gravel and paved, in good condition. **RV Service:** No. **Market:** Within 5 mi. **Restaurant:** Within 4 mi. **General Store:** Yes. **Vending:** Yes. **Playground:** Yes. **Other:** 90-acre spring-fed lake. **Activities:** Rec hall, game room, lake swimming, boating, canoeing, boat rentals, lake and stream fishing, basketball, shuffleboard, planned activities, movies, badminton, sports field, horseshoes, volleyball, hiking trails. **Nearby Attractions:** Whitewater rafting, horseback riding, Zane Grey Museum, Claws and Paws Wild Animal Park, Steamtown National Historic Site, Houdini Museum. **Additional Information:** Pocono Mountains Vacation Bureau, (800) POCONOS, www.800poconos.org.

Restrictions

Pets: On leash only. **Fires:** At site. **Alcoholic Beverages:** At site. **Vehicle Maximum Length:** None. **Other:** None.

To Get There

From Hwy. 296, go 1.5 mi. east on US 6. Entrance is on the right.

WHITE HAVEN

Hickory Run State Park

RR 1 Box 81, White Haven 18661-9712. T: (570) 443-0400 or (888) PAPARKS; www.dcnr.state.pa.us/stateparks; hickoryrunsp@state.pa.us.

RV ★★★ Tent ★★★★

Beauty: ★★★★	Site Privacy: ★★
Spaciousness: ★★★	Quiet: ★★★★
Security: ★★★★	Cleanliness: ★★★★
Insect Control: ★★★★	Facilities: ★★★

Covering 15,500 acres, Hickory Run State Park is located in Carbon County in the western foothills of the Pocono Mountains. The park has more than 40 miles of hiking trails, three state park natural areas, and miles of trout streams. The campground for RVers and tenters offers wooded and grassy open sites. Hickory Run has two group cabin areas. Camp Daddy Allen holds 124 people, and Camp Shehaqua holds 149 people. Located in a wooded setting with adjacent play fields, the camps share a swimming pool that is open from June to Labor Day. Boulder Field is actually strewn with boulders and is a national natural landmark. Some of the boulders are 26 feet long. Mud Swamp is a remote, emergent wetland dominated by spruce trees. Mud Run is a remote mountain stream lined with rhododendron and eastern hemlock. With these natural areas present, hiking is a favorite activity at Hickory Run, as are lake fishing and swimming.

Basics

Operated By: State of Pennsylvania. **Open:** Apr.–Oct. **Site Assignment:** Reservations and walk-ins accepted. **Registration:** At campground office. **Fee:** $15–$17 (VISA, MC). **Parking:** At designated spot.

Facilities

Number of RV Sites: 321. **Number of Tent-Only Sites:** 60. **Hookups:** Electric (30, 50 amps). **Each Site:** Fire ring, picnic table. **Dump Station:** Yes. **Laundry:** No. **Pay Phone:** Yes. **Rest Rooms and Showers:** Yes. **Fuel:** No. **Propane:** No. **Internal Roads:** Paved and dirt, in fair condition. **RV Service:** No. **Market:** Within 8 mi. **Restaurant:** Within 8 mi. **General Store:** Yes. **Vending:** Yes. **Playground:** Yes. **Other:** None. **Activities:** Lake swimming, lake fishing, planned activities on weekends, hiking trails. **Nearby Attractions:** Lehigh Gorge State Park, Delaware and Lehigh National Heritage Corridor. **Additional Information:** Pocono Mountains Vacation Bureau, (800) POCONOS, www.800poconos.org.

Restrictions

Pets: No pets permitted. **Fires:** At site. **Alcoholic Beverages:** No alcohol permitted. **Vehicle Maximum Length:** 35 ft. **Other:** None.

To Get There

From I-80, take Exit 41 and go 6 mi. east on Hwy. 534. Entrance is on the right.

Rhode Island

New England's smallest state, Rhode Island makes up for its tiny size by packing a lot in. For camping enthusiasts, the state offers a number of choices, and nearly all of them involve the water. With over 400 miles of coastline, it's hard to go anywhere in Rhode that's not near a beach.

Because of that, many of the campsites in the state specialize in water-based activities. There's an enormous amount of choice for boating fans and lots of places to take your canoe out for a spin. There's also plenty of campgrounds in proximity to traditional "lay out in the sand" beaches. For the most part, camping in the state works best during warm weather, but the cities and many historic attractions offer a lot when the water's cold.

Rhode Island has a national reputation for its mansions, and the city of **Newport** has long been a tourist attraction. It has numerous museums, excellent restaurants, and nearby state park land.

Those looking for a more cosmopolitan city will do well in **Providence.** While it's not New York or Boston, Providence combines small-town appeal with many of the amenities of its bigger cousins. The city also has a new park downtown that's the center of activity in the summer, with concerts and other forms of entertainment.

For campers in Rhode Island, there's an easy opportunity to combine relaxation and exploration. Because of the size of the state, everything is close to everything else, and even area attractions like the casinos in Connecticut are easily accessible.

Campground Profiles

ASHAWAY
Frontier Camper Park

180 Maxson Hill Rd., Ashaway 02804. T: (401) 377-4510.

RV: ★★★★ Tent: ★★★

Beauty: ★★ Site Privacy: ★★★
Spaciousness: ★★★ Quiet: ★★
Security: ★★★ Cleanliness: ★★★
Insect Control: ★★★ Facilities: ★★★

If you're looking for a convenient, albeit spartan place to park your trailer or pitch your tent, Frontier is literally right off the highway—and that's pretty much the best thing it has going for it. There's not much to look at here and only slightly more to do than there would be at your average motel. But the facilities are adequate if you're looking to use Frontier only as your base of operations, not a vacation in itself.

BASICS

Operated By: Janet & Bill Thompson. **Open:** May 1–Oct. 1. **Site Assignment:** Reservations, though space is usually available. **Registration:** Office. **Fee:** Varies depending on season. **Parking:** At site.

FACILITIES

Number of RV Sites: 50. **Number of Tent-Only Sites:** 60. **Hookups:** Water, electric. **Each Site:** Picnic table, fireplace. **Dump Station:** No. **Laundry:** Yes. **Pay Phone:** Yes. **Rest Rooms and Showers:** Yes. **Fuel:** No. **Propane:** Yes. **Internal Roads:** Gravel. **RV Service:** No. **Market:** Hopkinton City **General Store:** 493 Main St., Hopkinton, RI: Take a left onto Maxson Hill Rd., followed by a right onto Frontier Rd., which becomes Main St. **Restaurant:** 32 Main St., Ashaway, RI 02804: Take a left onto Maxson Hill Rd., followed by a right onto Frontier Rd., which becomes Main St. **General Store:** Yes. **Vending:** Yes. **Swimming Pool:** Yes. **Playground:** Yes. **Other:** Volleyball. **Activities:** Fishing, hiking nearby. **Nearby Attractions:** Mystic Seaport, Foxwood Casino. **Additional Information:** Beaches, I-95.

RESTRICTIONS

Pets: Allowed. **Fires:** Allowed. **Alcoholic Beverages:** Allowed. **Vehicle Maximum Length:** 35 ft. **Other:** Ask on arrival.

TO GET THERE

Take I-95 Exit 1, then go south on Rte. 3. Take a left onto Frontier Rd. and follow the camping signs.

ASHAWAY
Hollytree Campground

109 Ashaway Rd./Rte. 216, Ashaway 02804. T: (401) 596-2766.

 Tent: n/a

Beauty: ★★ Site Privacy: ★★★
Spaciousness: ★★★ Quiet: ★★★
Security: ★★★★ Cleanliness: ★★★
Insect Control: ★★★ Facilities: ★★

Leave your tent at home when visiting this fairly unspectacular but well-located campground. While not downright unattractive, the place does have a bit of a parking-lot feel. And there's really not much to do here, but there's a casino just down the road, and swimming, boating, and outdoor activities within an easy drive.

BASICS

Operated By: Private operator. **Open:** May 1–Sept. 30. **Site Assignment:** Reservation. **Registration:** At office. **Fee:** $20 & up per night. **Parking:** At site.

FACILITIES

Number of RV Sites: 140. **Number of Tent-Only Sites:** 0. **Hookups:** Water, electric, sewer. **Each Site:** Picnic tables, fireplace. **Dump Station:** Yes. **Laundry:** Yes. **Pay Phone:** Yes. **Rest Rooms and Showers:** Yes. **Fuel:** No. **Propane:** No. **Internal Roads:** None. **RV Service:** No. **Market:** Pete's Grocery, 244b Ashaway Rd., Bradford, RI 02808: Take a right on Ashaway Rd. & follow for 1.2 mi. **Restaurant:** Brick Oven, 209 Main St., Ashaway, RI 02804: Take a right on Ashaway Rd. & follow for 0.9 mi., then take a right onto Main St. **General Store:** Yes. **Vending:** Yes. **Swimming Pool:** No. **Playground:** Yes. **Other:** Rec room, video game room. **Activities:** Swimming, boating nearby. **Nearby Attractions:** Tennis courts are nearby, Foxwoods within 10 min. **Additional Information:** Call ahead.

Restrictions

Pets: Must be leashed, quiet, & cleaned up after. **Fires:** Ask on arrival. **Alcoholic Beverages:** Allowed. **Vehicle Maximum Length:** None. **Other:** Ask on arrival.

To Get There

Take Rte. 2 for 3.5 mi. to Mail Rd., take a right and go 1.5 mi., taking a right at Liberty Church Rd., going almost 1 mi. to the campground.

CHARLESTOWN

Burlingame State Park

1 Burlingame State Park Rd., Charlestown 02813. T: (401) 322-7337; www.riparks.com/burlgmcamp.htm.

RV ★★★ Tent ★★★

Beauty: ★★★★	Site Privacy: ★★★
Spaciousness: ★★★★	Quiet: ★★★★
Security: ★★★	Cleanliness: ★★★
Insect Control: ★★★	Facilities: ★★★

Burlingame State Park is monstrous, a megalopolis of campgrounds. The park itself encompasses 2,100 acres, including 755 camping sites, none with hookups. Generally speaking, the farther off the main loop throughout the park you get, the more secluded and quiet your campsite will be. Most of the sites are fairly open and certainly spacious, but there isn't much barrier between them, and the salty air and the sandy soil keep the forest from growing in too densely. There are many clusters where two or three sites will be angled in towards each other. These would be good groups of sites for large groups or families needing a couple of sites bunched together. Mention this when making your reservation if you'd like contiguous sites. Burlingame State Park is on the shores of Watchaug Pond, and it's just a few miles from Rhode Island's renowned beaches. You'll have plenty to do both within and outside of the park.

Basics

Operated By: Rhode Island Dept. of Environmental Management. **Open:** Apr. 15–Oct. 31. **Site Assignment:** First come, first served. **Registration:** At office. **Fee:** $8 state residents; $12 non residents. **Parking:** At site.

Facilities

Number of RV Sites: 755. **Number of Tent-Only Sites:** 0. **Hookups:** None. **Each Site:** Fire ring or stone hearth, picnic table. **Dump Station:** yes. **Laundry:** no. **Pay Phone:** Yes. **Rest Rooms and Showers:** Yes. **Fuel:** No. **Propane:** No. **Internal Roads:** Some paved. **RV Service:** No. **Market:** No. **Restaurant:** No. **General Store:** Yes. **Vending:** Yes. **Swimming Pool:** No. **Playground:** Yes. **Activities:** Camping, swimming, boating, fishing, hiking, picnicking, snowmobiling, scenic overlooks. **Nearby Attractions:** Several beaches. **Additional Information:** www.riparks.com/burlgmcamp.htm.

Restrictions

Pets: Not allowed. **Fires:** In fire ring. **Alcoholic Beverages:** Not allowed. **Vehicle Maximum Length:** None. **Other:** 14-day stay limit.

To Get There

Follow I-95 South to Rte. 4 South to Rte. 1 South. Follow Rte. 1 to Charlestown, and turn right at Burlingame State Park campground sign.

CHEPACHET

Bowdish Lake Camping Area

P.O. Box 25, Chepachet 02814. T: (401) 568-8890.

RV ★★★★ Tent ★★★

Beauty: ★★★	Site Privacy: ★★★★
Spaciousness: ★★★★	Quiet: ★★★★
Security: ★★★	Cleanliness: ★★★★
Insect Control: ★★★	Facilities: ★★

Located right next to the George Washington Management Area, this campground has it all for nature lovers—though the amenities are a bit sparse. Nearby, you'll find hiking trails through flat terrain, hills, and even difficult rocky terrain. Though there's no pool, there are numerous ponds to swim in—including some a bit off the beaten path—as well as plenty that offer excellent fishing. Bowdish Lake caters to RVers a bit more than tent campers, but the place is big enough for tenters to set up without being anywhere near an RV.

Basics

Operated By: Private operator. **Open:** Apr. 30–Oct. 15. **Site Assignment:** Reservations recommended. **Registration:** At office. **Fee:** Varies, depending on facilities. **Parking:** At site.

Facilities

Number of RV Sites: 350. **Number of Tent-Only Sites:** 0. **Hookups:** Water, electric, sewer. **Each Site:** Picnic table, fireplace. **Dump Station:** Yes. **Laundry:** No. **Pay Phone:** Yes. **Rest Rooms and Showers:** Yes. **Fuel:** No. **Propane:** No. **Internal Roads:** Gravel. **RV Service:** No. **Market:** Dino's Park-N-Shop, 1020 Putnam Pike, Chepachet, RI 02814: Go east on Rte. 44 for 2.9 mi. **Restaurant:** Stage Coach Tavern Restaurant, 1157 Putnam Pike, Chepachet, RI 02814: Go east on Rte. 44 for 2.2 mi. **General Store:** No. **Vending:** No. **Swimming Pool:** No. **Playground:** No. **Other:** Rec room, horseshoe pits. **Activities:** Canoe & boat rentals.

Restrictions

Pets: Allowed. **Fires:** Allowed. **Alcoholic Beverages:** Allowed. **Vehicle Maximum Length:** 60 ft. **Other:** Ask on arrival.

To Get There

Take Rte. 6 to I-395 north and follow for 10 mi. until Rte. 44 towards Woodstock/East Putnam. Follow Rte. 44 for around 9 mi.

CHEPACHET

George Washington Management Area

2185 Putnam Pike, Chepachet 02814. T: (401) 568-2013.

RV ★★★ Tent ★★★★★

Beauty: ★★★★★	Site Privacy: ★★★★
Spaciousness: ★★★★★	Quiet: ★★★★
Security: ★★★	Cleanliness: ★★★★
Insect Control: ★★★	Facilities: ★★

This state-run campground's prime offering is that it's part of an enormous (3,489 acres) wildlife management area. Beautiful but fairly spartan, it's not a resort. Though RVs are allowed, there's not much for them in the way of services. The campground is for people who want to spend time with nature, observing the enormous variety of wildlife, hiking, and swimming in the two large ponds. The entire area, known as Bowdish Reservoir, attracts big crowds of day visitors who powerboat and waterski. Still, those looking for solitude are in luck, as there's enough room for everyone here.

Basics

Operated By: State of Rhode Island. **Open:** Apr. 1–Oct. 31. **Site Assignment:** First come, first served. **Registration:** On site. **Fee:** Under $15, lower prices for RI residents. **Parking:** At site.

Facilities

Number of RV Sites: 45. **Number of Tent-Only Sites:** 0. **Hookups:** None. **Each Site:** Picnic tables, fireplace. **Dump Station:** No. **Laundry:** No. **Pay Phone:** No. **Rest Rooms and Showers:** Rest room, no showers. **Fuel:** No. **Propane:** No. **Internal Roads:** Gravel. **RV Service:** No. **Market:** Dino's Park-N-Shop, 1020 Putnam Pike, Chepachet, RI 02814: Take a left onto Rte. 44 & follow for 5.4 mi. **Restaurant:** Stateline Restaurant, 2461 Putnam Pike, Chepachet, RI 02814: Take a right onto Rte. 44 & go 1.3 mi. **General Store:** No. **Vending:** No. **Swimming Pool:** No. **Playground:** No. **Other:** Hiking trails, swimming beach, boat ramps. **Activities:** No planned activities.

Restrictions

Pets: Allowed. **Fires:** Allowed. **Alcoholic Beverages:** Allowed. **Vehicle Maximum Length:** 24 ft. **Other:** Ask on arrival.

To Get There

Take Rte. 6 to I-395 north and follow for 10 mi. until Rte. 44 towards Woodstock/East Putnam. Follow Rte. 44 for around 9 mi.

CHEPACHET

Oak Leaf Campground

43 Oakleaf Way, P.O. Box 521, Chepachet 02814. T: (401) 568-4446.

RV ★★★★ Tent ★

Beauty: ★★★	Site Privacy: ★★★
Spaciousness: ★★	Quiet: ★★★
Security: ★★★★	Cleanliness: ★★★
Insect Control: ★★★	Facilities: ★★★★

As far as trailer parks go, this is a fairly nice one. Plenty of green and lots of trees break up the parking-lot feel that many RV parks have. If you're looking for an idyllic natural setting, plenty of state-controlled land lies nearby, with places to fish, hike, and swim.

Basics

Operated By: Private operator. **Open:** Apr. 15–Oct. 31. **Site Assignment:** Reservations. **Registration:** At office. **Fee:** Starting at $18. **Parking:** At site.

Facilities

Number of RV Sites: 60. **Number of Tent-Only Sites:** 0. **Hookups:** Water, electric, sewer. **Each Site:** Picnic table, fireplace. **Dump Station:** Yes. **Laundry:** No. **Pay Phone:** Yes. **Rest Rooms and Showers:** Yes. **Fuel:** No. **Propane:** No. **Internal Roads:** Paved. **RV Service:** No. **Market:** Stop & Shop, 60 Providence Turnpike, Putnam, CT: Take a left onto Old Snake Hill Rd., then a right onto Rte. 94. Follow for 4.3 mi. & take a left onto Rte. 44 & follow for about 2 mi. **Restaurant:** McDonald's 6 Providence Turnpike, Putnam, CT: Take a left onto Old Snake Hill Rd., then a right onto Rte. 94. Follow for 4.3 mi. & take a left onto Rte. 44 & follow for about 1.6 mi. **General Store:** Yes. **Vending:** No. **Swimming Pool:** Yes. **Playground:** Yes. **Other:** Rec hall, basketball courts. **Activities:** Boating, fishing, golf nearby. **Nearby Attractions:** Historic landmarks. **Additional Information:** Call ahead.

Restrictions

Pets: Allowed. **Fires:** Allowed. **Alcoholic Beverages:** Allowed. **Vehicle Maximum Length:** 40 ft. **Other:** Ask on arrival.

To Get There

Rte. 44 to 94 South to Old Snake Hill Rd. to Oak Leaf Way (follow the signs)

COVENTRY

Colwell's Family Campground

Rte. 177, 119 Peckham Ln., Coventry 02816. T: (401) 397-4614.

RV: ★★ Tent: ★★★

Beauty: ★★★★ Site Privacy: ★★★
Spaciousness: ★★★ Quiet: ★★★
Security: ★★★ Cleanliness: ★★★★
Insect Control: ★★★ Facilities: ★★★

This basic campground is well located in the center of the state. Unfortunately, other than being situated on Johnson's Pond—a reservoir that's great for swimming—there's not much to do here. Still, if you're not looking for campground to entertain the kids, this makes a nice base of operations, with plenty to do in the surrounding area.

Basics

Operated By: The Colwell Family. **Open:** May 1–Sept. 30. **Site Assignment:** At time of registration. **Registration:** Reservation. **Fee:** $12–$15 a night. **Parking:** At site.

Facilities

Number of RV Sites: 75. **Number of Tent-Only Sites:** 0. **Hookups:** Water, electric. **Each Site:** Picnic table, fireplace. **Dump Station:** Yes. **Laundry:** No. **Pay Phone:** Yes. **Rest Rooms and Showers:** Yes. **Fuel:** No. **Propane:** No. **RV Service:** No. **Market:** Roch's Supermarket, 1475 Main St., West Warwick, RI: Take a right onto Peckham Ln., followed by a slight left onto Rte. 117. Follow for just over 6 mi. until Rte. 117 becomes Main St. **Restaurant:** Jeffrey's Restaurant, 2260 Flat River Rd. Frnt, Coventry, RI: Take a right onto Peckham Ln., followed by a slight left onto Flat River Rd. **General Store:** No. **Vending:** No. **Swimming Pool:** No. **Playground:** No. **Other:** Pond swimming. **Activities:** Boating. **Nearby Attractions:** Rodger William's Park & Zoo.

Restrictions

Pets: Allowed. **Fires:** Allowed. **Alcoholic Beverages:** Allowed. **Vehicle Maximum Length:** None. **Other:** Ask on arrival.

To Get There

I-95 North to Exit 6, left onto Rte. 3, left on Rte. 33 to Rte.117, west 4 mi. to Peckham Ln.

COVENTRY

Westwood Family Campground

2093 Harkney Hill Rd., Coventry 02816. T: (401) 397-7779.

RV: ★★★★ Tent: ★★★

Beauty: ★★★ Site Privacy: ★★★
Spaciousness: ★★★ Quiet: ★★
Security: ★★★ Cleanliness: ★★★★
Insect Control: ★★★ Facilities: ★★★★

A cross between a campground and a sports summer camp, Westwood is for the active camper. You'll find myriad games in progress at all the fields and courts, plus a golf course, batting cages, and mini-golf within easy driving distance. The campground itself is nothing special, with RVs packed in fairly tightly; even the tent areas are a bit bleak. But for families this makes an excellent choice.

Basics

Operated By: Don Thomassen. **Open:** May 1–Sept. 30. **Site Assignment:** Reservations. **Registration:** Office. **Fee:** $23 night. **Parking:** At site.

Facilities

Number of RV Sites: 60. **Number of Tent-Only Sites:** 10. **Hookups:** Water, electric, sewer. **Each Site:** Fireplace, picnic table. **Dump Station:** Yes. **Laundry:** No. **Pay Phone:** Yes. **Rest Rooms and Showers:** Yes. **Fuel:** No. **Propane:** No. **Internal Roads:** Gravel. **RV Service:** No. **Market:** P J's Country Store, 2246 Flat River Rd., Coventry, RI 02816: Take a left onto Harkney Hill Rd., followed by a right onto Rte. 102, then a right onto Flat River. Rd., which you should follow for 4.7 mi. **Restaurant:** Jeffrey's Restaurant, 2260 Flat River Rd. Frnt, Coventry, RI 02816: Take a left onto Harkney Hill Rd., a right onto Rte. 102, then a right onto Flat River Rd., which you should follow for 4.7 mi. **General Store:** No. **Vending:** No. **Swimming Pool:** No. **Playground:** No. **Other:** Sports fields of all kinds—tennis, volleyball, basketball, etc. **Activities:** Water-based activities on the nearby reservoir. **Nearby Attractions:** Quidnick Reservoir.

Restrictions

Pets: Allowed. **Fires:** Allowed. **Alcoholic Beverages:** Allowed. **Vehicle Maximum Length:** 35 ft. **Other:** Ask on arrival.

To Get There

Take I95 to Exit 5B (Rte. 102) and follow for 6.4 mi. before taking a right onto Harkeny Hill Rd.

EXETER

Peeper Pond Campground

P.O. Box 503, 159 Liberty Church Rd., Exeter 02822. T: (401) 294-5540.

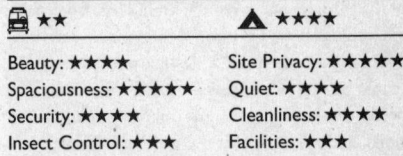

RV: ★★ Tent: ★★★★

Beauty: ★★★★ Site Privacy: ★★★★★
Spaciousness: ★★★★★ Quiet: ★★★★
Security: ★★★★ Cleanliness: ★★★★
Insect Control: ★★★ Facilities: ★★★

If you're looking for space, you'll find plenty of it at Peeper Pond. If you want activities and many facilities, however, you're out of luck, as this is a relatively bare-bones campground. In addition to having huge sites with more space than any camper would need, Peeper Pond borders beaches, a national park, and a wildlife preserve. Restaurants and the Tomaquag Indian Memorial Museum in Exeter are also relatively close.

Basics

Operated By: Private operator. **Open:** May 1–Sept. 30. **Site Assignment:** Reservations taken, but often not required. **Registration:** At office. **Fee:** $18 per night. **Parking:** At site.

Facilities

Number of RV Sites: 29. **Number of Tent-Only Sites:** 6. **Hookups:** None. **Each Site:** Picnic tables, fireplace. **Dump Station:** Yes. **Laundry:** No. **Pay Phone:** Yes. **Rest Rooms and Showers:** Yes. **Fuel:** No. **Propane:** No. **Internal Roads:** Gravel. **RV Service:** No. **Market:** L C Mart, 345 Nooseneck Hill Rd., Exeter, RI: Take a left onto Liberty Church Rd., then a left onto Sheffield Hill Rd. & a right onto Hallville Rd. Take a right onto Ten Rod Rd., which becomes Rte. 102. Follow for about 4 mi. & turn left onto Nooseneck Hill Rd. **Restaurant:** Middle of Nowhere Diner, 222 Nooseneck Hill Rd., Exeter, RI: Take a left onto Liberty Church Rd., then a left onto Sheffield Hill Rd. & a right onto Hallville Rd. Take a right onto Ten Rod Rd., which becomes Rte. 102. Follow for about 4 mi. & turn left onto Nooseneck Hill Rd. **General Store:** Limited. **Vending:** No. **Swimming Pool:** No. **Playground:** No. **Other:** Badminton, horseshoes. **Activities:** Hiking. **Nearby Attractions:** Fisherville Brook Wildlife Refuge.

Restrictions

Pets: Allowed. **Fires:** Allowed. **Alcoholic Beverages:** Allowed. **Vehicle Maximum Length:** 34 ft. **Other:** Ask on arrival.

To Get There

Located off Rte. 2 between Rtes. 102 & 138. Follow blue-and-white camping signs on Rte. 2 to Mail Rd. 1.5 mi. to Liberty Church Rd., 0.8 mi. to campground. Exit 3A off I-95 North, east on Rte. 138 North (left) on Rte. 2.

FOSTER

Ginny-B Campground

46 Johnston Rd., Foster 02825. T: (401) 397-9477; gnnyb@aol.com.

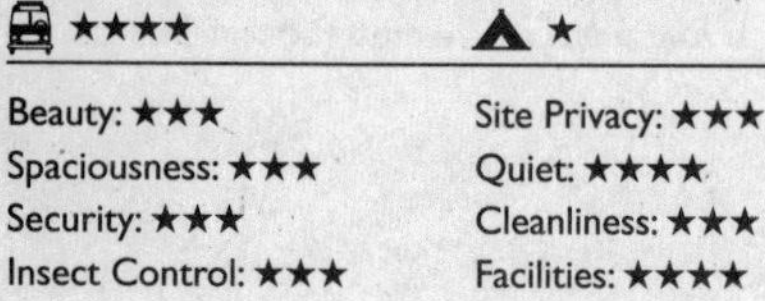

RV ★★★★ Tent ★

Beauty: ★★★ Site Privacy: ★★★
Spaciousness: ★★★ Quiet: ★★★★
Security: ★★★ Cleanliness: ★★★
Insect Control: ★★★ Facilities: ★★★★

Near the Connecticut border, Ginny-B offers a nice mix of facilities and nature. Although much of the 90 acres are covered with tall oak trees, there are still plenty of cleared areas for activities. Though it's not quite a destination in itself like many of the Connecticut areas, Ginny-B is a pretty lively campground offering many diversions, and on weekends there are usually plenty of people to share the fun. The public golf course located next to Ginny-B can get quite busy, so if you're visiting here to play golf, you might want to consider a nontraditional tee time.

BASICS

Operated By: Private operator. **Open:** May 1–Sept. 30. **Site Assignment:** Reservations recommended. **Registration:** At office. **Fee:** $16–$20. **Parking:** At site.

FACILITIES

Number of RV Sites: 200. **Number of Tent-Only Sites:** 0. **Hookups:** Water, electric (20), sewer. **Each Site:** Picnic table, fireplace. **Dump Station:** Yes. **Laundry:** Yes. **Pay Phone:** Yes. **Rest Rooms and Showers:** Yes. **Fuel:** No. **Propane:** No. **Internal Roads:** Gravel. **RV Service:** No. **Market:** P J's Country Store, 2246 Flat River Rd., Coventry, RI: Take a left onto S. Killingly Rd., followed by a slight right onto Rte. 94, then a right onto Rte. 102. Follow for 3.5 mi., then take a left onto Maple Valley Rd. & follow for 3.2 mi. Take a left onto Flat River Rd. & follow for 2 mi. **Restaurant:** Countryside Pizza & Backdraft, 110 Danielson Pike, Foster, RI: Take a left onto S. Killingly Rd., followed by a slight right onto Rte. 94 & follow for 2.2 mi. Take left onto Rte. 6 & a left onto Danielson Pike. **General Store:** Yes. **Vending:** Yes. **Swimming Pool:** Yes. **Playground:** No. **Other:** Rec rooms, pond, volleyball & basketball courts, softball diamond. **Activities:** Planned activities. **Nearby Attractions:** Next to a public golf course. **Additional Information:** Call ahead.

RESTRICTIONS

Pets: Allowed. **Fires:** Allowed. **Alcoholic Beverages:** Allowed. **Vehicle Maximum Length:** 40 ft. **Other:** Ask on arrival.

TO GET THERE

East or west on Rte. 6 (RI/CT state line): turn at the flashing light onto Cucumber Hill Rd. Follow 3.5 mi. and take a left onto Harrington Rd. Drive 0.5 mi. to Ginny-B.

FOSTER

Whippoorwill Hill Family Campground

106 Old Plainfield Pike, Foster 02825. T: (401) 397-7256; whiphicp@aol.com.

RV ★★★★ Tent ★★

Beauty: ★★★ Site Privacy: ★★★★★
Spaciousness: ★★★★ Quiet: ★★★★
Security: ★★★★ Cleanliness: ★★★★
Insect Control: ★★★ Facilities: ★★★★

Surrounded by tall pines and situated next to the huge George B. Parker Woodland, this beautiful campground caters equally to tent and RV campers. Though you'll definitely find more RVers, the large sites give everyone enough space, and some of the tent spots are very remote and private. With the preserve and its numerous trails right next door, Whippoorwill is a hiker's paradise—you could literally spend a week here and walk a new trail every day.

BASICS

Operated By: Private operator. **Open:** Apr. 15–Sept. 30. **Site Assignment:** Reservations recommended. **Registration:** At office. **Fee:** Some tent sites under $20 a night, most RV sites start at $20. **Parking:** At site.

FACILITIES

Number of RV Sites: 150. **Number of Tent-Only Sites:** 0. **Hookups:** Water, electric, sewer. **Each Site:** Fireplace, picnic table. **Dump Station:** Yes. **Laundry:** Yes. **Pay Phone:** Yes. **Rest Rooms and Showers:** Yes. **Fuel:** No. **Propane:** Yes. **Internal Roads:** Gravel. **RV Service:** No. **Market:** P J's Country Store, 2246 Flat River Rd., Coventry, RI 02816: Take a right onto Old Plainfield Pike, then a right onto Tunk Hill Rd. & a right onto Matteson Rd., which you should follow for 3 mi. Take a left onto Maple Valley Rd., followed by a left onto Flat River Rd. **Restaurant:** Jeffrey's Restaurant, 2260 Flat River Rd. Frnt, Coventry, RI 02816: Take a right onto Old Plainfield Pike, then a right onto Tunk Hill Rd. & a right onto Matteson Rd., which you should follow for 3 mi. Take a left onto Maple Valley Rd., followed by a left onto Flat River Rd. **General Store:** No. **Vending:** No. **Swimming Pool:** Yes. **Playground:** Yes. **Other:** Arcade, hiking trails, mini-golf course. **Activities:** Live bands, dances. **Nearby Attractions:** Foxwood Casino, beaches, Roger Williams Zoo. **Additional Information:** Call ahead.

RESTRICTIONS

Pets: Allowed. **Fires:** Allowed. **Alcoholic Beverages:** Allowed. **Vehicle Maximum Length:** 40 ft. **Other:** Ask on arrival.

TO GET THERE

Take Rte. 95 Exit 5 North onto Rte. 102 North—at third caution light (about 9 mi.) turn right onto Old Plainfield Pike (camp is 2 mi. in on the right).

GREENE

Hickory Ridge Family Campground

584 Victory Hwy., Greene 02827. T: (401) 391-7474; www.angelfire.com/ma2/hickoryridgecamp; hickoryridge@angelfire.com.

RV ★★★★★ Tent n/a

Beauty: ★★ Site Privacy: ★★★
Spaciousness: ★★★ Quiet: ★★★
Security: ★★★★ Cleanliness: ★★★★
Insect Control: ★★★ Facilities: ★★★★

A family campground catering to the same campers year after year, Hickory Ridge is a wonderful place if you're planning a long stay or looking for a regular spot to visit every summer. Run by the Pomfret family with a sizable staff, Hickory Ridge is like a big summer camp where everyone seems to know each other. The sites themselves are nothing special and some are even a little crowded, but this gives Hickory Ridge a sort of small-town neighborhood feel. There are no tent sites here, so this isn't the place for quiet contemplation.

BASICS

Operated By: The Pomfret family. **Open:** Apr. 1–Oct. 10. **Site Assignment:** Reservations by phone only. **Registration:** Check in at office. **Fee:** $22. **Parking:** At site.

FACILITIES

Number of RV Sites: 200. **Number of Tent-Only Sites:** 0. **Hookups:** Water, electric, sewer. **Each Site:** Picnic table, fireplace. **Dump Station:** Yes. **Laundry:** Yes. **Pay Phone:** Yes. **Rest Rooms and Showers:** Yes. **Fuel:** No. **Propane:** Yes. **Internal Roads:** Gravel. **RV Service:** No. **Market:** P J's Country Store, 2246 Flat River Rd., Coventry, RI 02816: Take a left onto Rte. 102 & follow for 1.3 mi. Turn left onto Rte. 117 & follow for 4.7 mi. **Restaurant:** Jeffrey's Restaurant, 2260 Flat River Rd. Frnt, Coventry, RI: Take a left onto Rte. 102 & follow for 1.3 mi. Turn left onto Rte. 117 & follow for 4.7 mi. **General Store:** Yes. **Vending:** No. **Swimming Pool:** Yes. **Playground:** Yes. **Other:** Softball field, volleyball, horseshoes, cool-mist tent, rec hall. **Activities:** Planned events in the rec hall on weekends. **Nearby Attractions:** Golf, benches, casinos. **Additional Information:** www.angelfire.com/ma2/HickoryRidgeCamp.

RESTRICTIONS

Pets: Allowed. **Fires:** Allowed. **Alcoholic Beverages:** Allowed. **Vehicle Maximum Length:** None. **Other:** Ask on arrival.

TO GET THERE

Take 95 to Exit 5, then go approximately 7 mi. on Rte. 102.

GREENWICH

Pine Valley RV Campground

64 Bailey Pond Rd. West, Greenwich 02817. T: (401) 397-7972.

RV ★★★ Tent ★★★

Beauty: ★★★★ Site Privacy: ★★★★
Spaciousness: ★★★ Quiet: ★★★★
Security: ★★★ Cleanliness: ★★★
Insect Control: ★★★ Facilities: ★★★★

Located between the Arcadia Management Area and Beach Pond State Park, Pine Valley has an unbelievable amount of natural scenery nearby. You could spend an entire season here and still not explore every hiking trail or see even a small selection of the wildlife. Three nearby lakes offer a variety of water-based activities. Since this is a year-round facility, Pine Valley would also make an excellent base camp for anyone who enjoys cross-country skiing.

Basics

Operated By: Private operator. **Open:** Year-round. **Site Assignment:** Reservations. **Registration:** Office. **Fee:** $10. **Parking:** At site.

Facilities

Number of RV Sites: 20. **Number of Tent-Only Sites:** 50. **Hookups:** Water, electric. **Each Site:** Picnic table, fireplace. **Dump Station:** No. **Laundry:** Yes. **Pay Phone:** No. **Rest Rooms and Showers:** Yes. **Fuel:** No. **Propane:** No. **Internal Roads:** None. **RV Service:** No. **Market:** Better Val-U Supermarket, 104 Beach Pond Rd., Voluntown, CT 06384: Take a right onto Bailey Pond Rd., followed by a right onto Hazard Rd. & a right onto Rte. 165, which becomes Beach Pond Rd. **Restaurant:** Town Pizza & Restaurant, 104 Beach Pond Rd., Voluntown, CT 06384: Take a right onto Bailey Pond Rd., followed by a right onto Hazard Rd. & a right onto Rte. 165, which becomes Beach Pond Rd. **General Store:** Yes. **Vending:** No. **Swimming Pool:** Yes. **Playground:** No. **Other:** Volleyball, tennis court, horseshoes. **Activities:** Some planned activities. **Nearby Attractions:** Beach Pond State Park. **Additional Information:** Call ahead.

Restrictions

Pets: Allowed. **Fires:** Allowed. **Alcoholic Beverages:** Allowed. **Vehicle Maximum Length:** None. **Other:** Ask on arrival.

To Get There

Take I-395 North to Rte. 14A, which becomes Rte. 14, then take a right onto Flat River Rd., followed by a right onto Hopkins Hollow Rd., then a left onto Sand Hill Rd., which becomes Plain Rd. Take a right onto Seth Brown Rd., followed by a right onto Muddy Brook Rd. and a left onto Hazard Rd., then a right onto Bailey Pond Rd.

HOPE VALLEY
Greenwood Hill Family Campground

13 A Newberry Ln. P.O. Box 141, Hope Valley 02832. T: (401) 539-7154; RathbunGHCamp@aol.com.

RV ★★★ Tent ★★★

Beauty: ★★ Site Privacy: ★★★
Spaciousness: ★★★ Quiet: ★★★
Security: ★★★ Cleanliness: ★★★
Insect Control: ★★★ Facilities: ★★

This small campground with fairly spacious sites offers group activities as well as a chance for seclusion. Though most campers at Greenwood seem to know each other and enjoy socializing, there are a handful of spartan, completely secluded sites for tents that allow complete privacy. Campers can fish and canoe nearby and enjoy easy access to most of the major attractions in the area.

Basics

Operated By: George & Ruth Rathbun. **Open:** May 15–Oct. 15. **Site Assignment:** Reservations accepted. **Registration:** Office. **Fee:** $20 & up. **Parking:** At site.

Facilities

Number of RV Sites: 40. **Number of Tent-Only Sites:** 10. **Hookups:** Water, electric. **Each Site:** Picnic table, fireplace. **Dump Station:** Yes. **Laundry:** No. **Pay Phone:** No. **Rest Rooms and Showers:** Yes. **Fuel:** No. **Propane:** No. **Internal Roads:** Gravel. **RV Service:** No. **Market:** Spring St. Market, 1 Spring St., Hope Valley, RI: Take a left onto Newberry Ln., followed by a right onto Spring St. **Restaurant:** 14 Spring St. Restaurant, 14 Spring St., Hopkinton, RI: Take a left onto Newberry Ln., followed by a right onto Spring St. **General Store:** No. **Vending:** No. **Swimming Pool:** Yes. **Playground:** Yes. **Other:** Sports fields. **Activities:** Planned weekend events & special dinners. **Nearby Attractions:** Mystic seaport, Newport, RI. **Additional Information:** Trailer rentals & camping equipment rentals.

Restrictions

Pets: Allowed. **Fires:** Allowed. **Alcoholic Beverages:** Allowed. **Vehicle Maximum Length:** None. **Other:** Ask on arrival.

To Get There

From I-95 north or south just take Exit 3B (Hope Valley/Wyoming), then RI Rte. 138 west for 3.5 mi. and follow our signs to the campground.

HOPE VALLEY
Legrand G. Reynolds Horsemen's Camping Area

260 Arcadia Rd., Hope Valley 02832. T: (401) 539-2356.

RV n/a Tent ★★★

Beauty: ★★★★ Site Privacy: ★★★★
Spaciousness: ★★★ Quiet: ★★★★★
Security: ★★★ Cleanliness: ★★★★★
Insect Control: ★★★ Facilities: none

Not for everyone, this campground was created specifically for campers with horses—you must have a horse to be allowed in. RVs are welcome (there's parking for horse trailers). Once here, you and your horse can explore miles of trails or practice for competitions in the show ring. The Arcadia Management Area, most of which is open to horses, is nearby. For those times when you need a little space from your horse, Beach Pond State Park offers swimming and other water-based recreation.

Basics

Operated By: State of Rhode Island. **Open:** Year-round. **Site Assignment:** First come, first served, max stays apply. **Registration:** By mail. **Fee:** $3 plus $10 for use of show ring. **Parking:** At site.

Facilities

Number of RV Sites: 0. **Number of Tent-Only Sites:** 20. **Hookups:** None. **Each Site:** Fireplace, picnic table. **Dump Station:** No. **Laundry:** No. **Pay Phone:** No. **Rest Rooms and Showers:** Rest room, running water. **Fuel:** No. **Propane:** No. **Internal Roads:** Gravel. **RV Service:** No. **Market:** Stop & Shop Supermarket, 3 Stillson Rd., Wyoming, RI 02898: Take a right onto Arcadia Rd., followed by a left onto Bridge St. & a left onto Rte. 3/Rte. 138, then take a left onto Stillson Rd. **Restaurant:** 3410, 1139 Main, Hope Valley, RI 02832: Take a right onto Arcadia Rd., followed by a left onto Bridge St. & a left onto Rte. 3/Rte. 138 (Main St.). **General Store:** No. **Vending:** No. **Swimming Pool:** No. **Playground:** No. **Other:** Show ring, horse trails. **Activities:** Horseback riding. **Nearby Attractions:** Beach Pond State Park. **Additional Information:** Call ahead.

Restrictions

Pets: Allowed. **Fires:** Allowed. **Alcoholic Beverages:** Allowed. **Vehicle Maximum Length:** None. **Other:** Ask on arrival.

To Get There

Take 95 to Exit 5A and follow Rte. 102 South, then take a right onto Rte. 3. Follow until Rte. 165 and take a right onto Escoheag Rd. Follow to the campground.

HOPE VALLEY
Whispering Pines Family Campground

Box 425 Saw Mill RD, Hope Valley 02832. T: (401) 539-7011; www.whisperingpinescamping.com; wpinesri@aol.com.

RV ★★★★ Tent ★★

Beauty: ★★★★ Site Privacy: ★★★
Spaciousness: ★★★ Quiet: ★★★
Security: ★★★ Cleanliness: ★★★★
Insect Control: ★★★ Facilities: ★★★★

The name Whispering Pines is appropriate since the entire campground is filled with these enormous trees. Most sites are tucked in between the pines, which can make some of them a little dark—though on a sunny day the light manages to shine through, and the trees make this a wonderful place to get out of the heat. Remote yet convenient, Whispering Pines is a fairly self-contained area with many activities, but there's not so much going on that you won't want to check out the nearby beaches or casino.

Basics

Operated By: Private operator. **Open:** June 1–Oct. 31. **Site Assignment:** Reservations. **Registration:** Office. **Fee:** $25–$29 a night depending on facilities/time of year. **Parking:** At site.

Facilities

Number of RV Sites: 180. **Number of Tent-Only Sites:** 0. **Hookups:** Water, electric, sewer.

Each Site: Picnic table, fireplace. **Dump Station:** Yes. **Laundry:** Yes. **Pay Phone:** Yes. **Rest Rooms and Showers:** Yes. **Fuel:** No. **Propane:** Yes. **Internal Roads:** Gravel. **RV Service:** No. **Market:** Spring St. Market, 1 Spring St., Hope Valley, RI: Take a left onto Highview Ave., then a left onto Main St. & follow for 0.2 mi. **Restaurant:** 3410, 1139 Main, Hope Valley, RI: Take a left onto Highview Ave., then a left onto Main St. & follow for 1.1 mi. **General Store:** Yes. **Vending:** Yes. **Swimming Pool:** Yes. **Playground:** No. **Other:** Sports field, swimming pond, rec room, tennis court, shuffleboard, beach. **Activities:** Planned recreational activities, canoe trips, swimming lessons. **Nearby Attractions:** Foxwoods Casino. **Additional Information:** www.whisperingpinescamping.com.

RESTRICTIONS

Pets: Allowed. **Fires:** Allowed. **Alcoholic Beverages:** Allowed. **Vehicle Maximum Length:** None. **Other:** Ask on arrival.

TO GET THERE

Take I-95 to Exit 3B west and follow for 3 mi.

JAMESTOWN
Fort Getty Recreation Area

P.O. Box 377, Jamestown 02835. T: (401) 423-7211.

RV: n/a | Tent: ★★★

Beauty: ★★★★ | Site Privacy: ★★★
Spaciousness: ★★★★ | Quiet: ★★★★
Security: ★★ | Cleanliness: ★★★
Insect Control: ★★★ | Facilities: ★★★

Fort Getty Recreation Area, set on windswept bluff near the southern tip of Jamestown Island in the middle of Narragansett Bay, is a beautiful oceanside campground that can be reached by car. Salty sea breezes, sunrises and sunsets to die for, and rocky beach fronts for hours of exploring all recommend it. For the historically minded, there are a couple of bunkers remaining from when Fort Getty was an ammunition depot during World War II. These are also cool little spots for older kids to play in. The land on which the campground is perched is surrounded by several other small islands dotting Narragansett Bay. In a place like this, the environment is captivating, regardless of the weather. It's brilliant on bright sunny days, cool and refreshing when the mainland is sweltering. The stars at night are crystal clear, and you'll see deeper into the universe because there isn't much light pollution out here.

BASICS

Operated By: Jamestown township. **Open:** Mid-May–Oct. 1. **Site Assignment:** First come, first served. **Registration:** At ranger station. **Fee:** $20–$30. **Parking:** At site.

FACILITIES

Number of RV Sites: 0. **Number of Tent-Only Sites:** 30. **Hookups:** Water, electric (30 amps). **Each Site:** Fire ring. **Dump Station:** Yes. **Laundry:** No. **Pay Phone:** Yes. **Rest Rooms and Showers:** Yes. **Fuel:** No. **Propane:** No. **Internal Roads:** Paved. **RV Service:** No. **Market:** No. **Restaurant:** No. **General Store:** No. **Vending:** No. **Swimming Pool:** No. **Playground:** No. **Activities:** Fishing, boating, walking trails. **Nearby Attractions:** Lighthouse at Beaver Tail. **Additional Information:** Call ahead.

RESTRICTIONS

Pets: On leash. **Fires:** In fire ring. **Alcoholic Beverages:** At site. **Vehicle Maximum Length:** 45 ft. **Other:** Ask on arrival.

TO GET THERE

From Jamestown, take N. Main St. to the south (toward Beavertail State Park). This road will cross Narragansett Rd. and turn into Southwest Ave. Follow Southwest Ave. to Beavertail Rd. The entrance for the state park and campground is on the right.

NARAGANSETT
Breakwater Village Campground

P.O. Box 563, Naragansett 02882. T: (401) 783-9527; F: (401) 783-9454.

RV: ★★★ | Tent: n/a

Beauty: ★★★ | Site Privacy: ★★★
Spaciousness: ★★★ | Quiet: ★★★
Security: ★★★★ | Cleanliness: ★★★★
Insect Control: ★★★ | Facilities: ★★

Visitors to Breakwater Village better enjoy spending time on the beach, because that's all there is to do here. For swimming, surfing, boating, and fishing, you have your choice of five town beaches. You're also close to the heart of Naragansett, which is a traditional resort community offering a variety of activities. The actual campground offers more than a place to park your RV—it's a nice (actually quite pretty) parking lot.

BASICS

Operated By: Private operator. **Open:** Apr. 15–Oct. 15. **Site Assignment:** Reservations accepted. **Registration:** At office. **Fee:** $30. **Parking:** At site.

FACILITIES

Number of RV Sites: 38. **Number of Tent-Only Sites:** 0. **Hookups:** Water, electric. **Each Site:** None. **Dump Station:** Yes. **Laundry:** No. **Pay Phone:** No. **Rest Rooms and Showers:** No. **Fuel:** No. **Propane:** No. **RV Service:** No. **Market:** Seaview Marketplace, 682 Matunuck Beach Rd., Wakefield, RI 02879: Take a left onto Point Judith Rd., followed by a left onto Woodruff Ave. & a left onto Salt Pond Rd. Merge onto Rte. 1 & follow for 5 mi. to Matunuck Beach Rd. **Restaurant:** Charlie O's Tavern-The Point, 2 Sand Hill Cove Rd., Narragansett, RI 02882: Take a right onto Point Judith Rd., followed by a right onto Sand Hill Cove Rd. **General Store:** Snack bar. **Vending:** No. **Swimming Pool:** No. **Playground:** No. **Activities:** No planned activities. **Nearby Attractions:** Lots of beaches. **Additional Information:** Call ahead.

RESTRICTIONS

Pets: On leash. **Fires:** Allowed. **Alcoholic Beverages:** Allowed. **Vehicle Max. Length:** None.

TO GET THERE

Take interstate Rte. 95 South, to Rte. 4 South, to Rte. 1 South, to Rte. 108 South, 4 mi. along 108 on right-hand side.

NARAGANSETT
Fisherman's Memorial State Park

Rte. 108, 1011 Point Judith Rd., Narragansett 02882. T: (401) 789-8374; www.riparks.com/fisherma.htm.

RV: ★★★★ | Tent: ★★★

Beauty: ★★★ | Site Privacy: ★★★
Spaciousness: ★★★★ | Quiet: ★★★
Security: ★★★ | Cleanliness: ★★★
Insect Control: ★★★ | Facilities: ★★★★

Fisherman's Memorial State Park looks like a suburban housing development with trailers and tents instead of ranches and capes. Though there are trees separating some of the sites, most are just empty patches of grass laid out along winding roads. This layout gives the campground—at least during the busy summer season—the feel of a 1950s small town. Many people stay here for more than a couple of days, and at night adults sit out on their "front porches" talking, eating, and drinking while the kids play on the street. The state of Rhode Island runs the park and keeps it well groomed despite the large crowds that can often be found.

BASICS

Operated By: Rhode Island Div. of Parks & Recreation. **Open:** Year-round. **Site Assignment:** Reservations by mail only, form available on website. **Registration:** By mail or at park office. **Fee:** $8–12 residents, $12–$16 nonresidents. **Parking:** At site.

FACILITIES

Number of RV Sites: 150. **Number of Tent-Only Sites:** 35. **Hookups:** Water, electric, sewer. **Each Site:** Picnic table, fireplace. **Dump Station:** Yes. **Laundry:** Yes. **Pay Phone:** Yes. **Rest Rooms and Showers:** Yes. **Fuel:** No. **Propane:** No. **Internal Roads:** Asphalt. **RV Service:** No. **Market:** Seaview Marketplace, 682 Matunuck Beach Rd., Wakefield, RI 02879: Take a left onto Point Judith Rd., followed by a left onto Woodruff Ave. & a left onto Salt Pond Rd. Merge onto Rte. 1 & follow for 5 mi. to Matunuck Beach Rd. **Restaurant:** Charlie O's Tavern-The Point, 2 Sand Hill Cove Rd., Narragansett, RI 02882: Take a right onto Point Judith Rd., followed by a right onto Sand Hill Cove Rd. **General Store:** No. **Vending:** No. **Swimming Pool:** No. **Playground:** Yes. **Other:** Tennis courts, basketball courts, horseshoe pit. **Activities:** Farmer's market on site, other planned activities. **Nearby Attractions:** Four beaches, city of Newport. **Additional Information:** www.riparks.com/fisherma.htm#FishermansTop.

RESTRICTIONS

Pets: Not allowed. **Fires:** Allowed. **Alcoholic Beverages:** Allowed. **Vehicle Max. Length:** None.

TO GET THERE

Take interstate Rte. 95 South, to Rte. 4 South, to Rte. 1 South, to Rte. 108 South, 4 mi. along 108 on right-hand side.

NORTH SCITUATE

Holiday Acres Campground

591 Snake Hill Rd., North Scituate 02857. T: (401) 934-0789.

RV ★★★★ Tent ★★★

Beauty: ★★★ Site Privacy: ★★★
Spaciousness: ★★★ Quiet: ★★★
Security: ★★★ Cleanliness: ★★★
Insect Control: ★★★ Facilities: ★★★★

Located on a busy freshwater lake (though motorboats aren't permitted), Holiday Acres offers a nice mix of facilities and wildlife. There are many planned activities, and the sports areas here offer a nice change from the lake, which is pretty much the center of the action for most visitors. Some sites have waterfront views, but folks looking for more privacy and a break from the action might choose a site a bit away from the lake.

Basics

Operated By: Private operator. **Open:** Year-round. **Site Assignment:** Reservations. **Registration:** At office. **Fee:** $20–$35, depending on facilities/time of year. **Parking:** At site.

Facilities

Number of RV Sites: 200. **Number of Tent-Only Sites:** 25. **Hookups:** Water, electric, sewer. **Each Site:** Picnic table, fireplace. **Dump Station:** Yes. **Laundry:** Yes. **Pay Phone:** Yes. **Rest Rooms and Showers:** Yes. **Fuel:** No. **Propane:** No. **RV Service:** No. **Market:** Dino's Park-N-Shop, 1020 Putnam Pike, Chepachet, RI 02814: Take a right onto Snake Hill Rd., then a right onto Tourtellot Hill Rd. Follow for 2.4 mi., then take a right onto Rte. 44 & follow for 0.2 mi. **Restaurant:** Harmony Restaurant, 401 Putnam Pike, Chepachet, RI 02814: Take a right onto Snake Hill Rd., followed by a left onto Sawmill Rd., then a left onto Rte. 44. **General Store:** Yes. **Vending:** Yes. **Swimming Pool:** No. **Playground:** No. **Other:** Mini-golf, horseshoes, volleyball courts. **Activities:** Canoe & paddle boat rentals.

Restrictions

Pets: On leash. **Fires:** Allowed. **Alcoholic Beverages:** Allowed. **Vehicle Max. Length:** None.

To Get There

Take Rte. 6 to a left onto Rte. 102, follow for 3.2 mi. and take a left onto Snake Hill Rd.

PASCOAG

Buck Hill Family Campground

464 Wakefield Rd., Pascoag 02859. T: (800) 387-5224; F: (828) 765-1700; www.buckhill.20m.com/contact.html; buckhill@m-y.net.

RV ★★★★ Tent ★★★

Beauty: ★★ Site Privacy: ★★
Spaciousness: ★★ Quiet: ★★
Security: ★★★ Cleanliness: ★★★
Insect Control: ★★★ Facilities: ★★★★

Located alongside the North Toe River, Buck Hill is a fairly large campground, but many of its RV sites are cramped together. This is the case mainly along the river, where camping is most desirable and you're practically bumper to bumper with other RVs. If you're looking to meet people, this proximity to your neighbor adds to the atmosphere, but you won't find much peace and quiet. For tenters and RVers looking for more privacy, there are some sites set a bit off the beaten path. An odd mix of nature and people, this campground is scenic if you get away from the crowds. The stocked river has excellent fishing.

Basics

Operated By: Private operator. **Open:** May 1–Oct. 31. **Site Assignment:** Reservations. **Registration:** Office. **Fee:** $21 w/ full hookup, discounts for extended stays. **Parking:** At site.

Facilities

Number of RV Sites: 98. **Number of Tent-Only Sites:** 0. **Hookups:** Water, electric. **Each Site:** Picnic table, fire ring. **Dump Station:** Yes. **Laundry:** Yes. **Pay Phone:** Yes. **Rest Rooms and Showers:** Yes. **Fuel:** No. **Propane:** Yes. **Internal Roads:** Gravel. **RV Service:** No. **Market:** Stop & Shop, 60 Providence Turnpike, Putnam, CT 06260: Take a left onto Wakefield Rd., followed by a left onto Buck Hill Rd. & a right onto Quaddick Town Farm Rd. Follow for around 5 mi. until it turns into Quaddick Town Farm Rd., which becomes East Putnam Rd. Follow for 1 mi. & turn left onto Rte. 44. **Restaurant:** McDonald's, 6 Providence Turnpike, Putnam, CT 06260: Take a left onto Wakefield Rd., followed by a left onto Buck Hill Rd. & a right onto Quaddick Town Farm Rd. Follow for around 5 mi. until it turns into Quaddick Town Farm Rd., which becomes East Putnam Rd. Follow for 1 mi. & turn left onto Rte. 44. **General Store:** Yes. **Vending:** No. **Swimming Pool:** No. **Playground:** Yes. **Other:** Rec room, rifle range, river. **Activities:** Swimming, fishing. **Nearby Attractions:** Mt. Mitchell. **Additional Information:** www.buckhill.20m.com/contact.html.

Restrictions

Pets: On leash. **Fires:** Allowed. **Alcoholic Beverages:** Allowed. **Vehicle Max. Length:** None.

To Get There

Take Rte. 100 to Buck Hill Rd., following for 1.75 mi., and then take a left onto Croft Rd., following for 1.5 mi. to the campground.

RICHMOND

Wawaloam Campground

510 Gardinier Rd., Richmond 02892. T: (401) 294-3039; www.wawaloam.com; wawaloam99@aol.com.

RV ★★★★ Tent n/a

Beauty: ★★★ Site Privacy: ★★★
Spaciousness: ★★★★ Quiet: ★★★★
Security: ★★★★ Cleanliness: ★★★★
Insect Control: ★★★ Facilities: ★★★★

Yet another enormous campground in Rhode Island that caters to trailers, this one might be the best of the bunch. Sites are fairly spacious, and the scenery is pleasant (with lots of trees); it's better than your average "giant parking lot," which is what many campgrounds tend to feel like. A huge swimming pool complete with water slide is as nice as anything you'd find at a resort. This makes Wawaloam a good stop for families because you can spend at least one day parked by the water without having to do anything to entertain the kids.

Basics

Operated By: Jim & Maureen Smith. **Open:** Year-round. **Site Assignment:** Reservation. **Registration:** Office. **Fee:** $32 ($2 extra for sewer hook-up). **Parking:** At site.

Facilities

Number of RV Sites: 300. **Number of Tent-Only Sites:** 0. **Hookups:** Water, electric (about half have sewer). **Each Site:** Picnic table, fireplace. **Dump Station:** Yes. **Laundry:** Yes. **Pay Phone:** Yes. **Rest Rooms and Showers:** Yes. **Fuel:** Yes. **Propane:** Yes. **Internal Roads:** Gravel. **RV Service:** No. **Market:** L C Mart 345 Nooseneck Hill Rd., Exeter, RI: Take a left onto Gardner Rd., followed by a right onto Ten Rod Rd., then a left onto Town Hall Rd., a left onto Rte. 102 & a left onto Nooseneck Hill Rd. **Restaurant:** Middle of Nowhere Diner, 222 Nooseneck Hill Rd. Exeter, RI: Take a left onto Gardner Rd., followed by a right onto Ten Rod Rd., then a left onto Town Hall Rd., a left onto Rte. 102 & a left onto Nooseneck Hill Rd. **General Store:** Yes. **Vending:** Yes. **Swimming Pool:** Yes. **Playground:** Yes. **Other:** Sports field, mini-golf, horseshoes. **Activities:** Friday night dinner, Sunday morning breakfast, fishing derbies, lots of planned activities. **Nearby Attractions:** Fairly close to Arcadia Management area, a really large state park w/ fishing, hiking, etc. **Additional Information:** www.wawaloam.com.

Restrictions

Pets: Allowed. **Fires:** Allowed. **Alcoholic Beverages:** Allowed. **Vehicle Maximum Length:** None. **Other:** Ask on arrival.

To Get There

I-95 Exit 5A to Rte. 3. Bear right on Rte. 3, take first left onto Rte. 1025, go 1.5 mi. to Town Hall Rd., bear right; Gardiner Rd. is first left after old Town Hall—follow 1.5 mi. to campground on right.

SOUTH KINGSTON

Wakamo Park Resort

697 Succotash Rd., South Kingston 02879. T: (401) 783-6688.

RV ★★★★ Tent n/a

Beauty: ★★★★ Site Privacy: ★★★★
Spaciousness: ★★★ Quiet: ★★★★
Security: ★★★★ Cleanliness: ★★★★
Insect Control: ★★★ Facilities: ★★

A beachfront resort, Wakamo Park is located near East Matunuck State Beach and the Great Swamp Management Area. The beach is one of the nicest in the state, and when it's warm it gives Wakamo a tropical island feel. For colder days and more active vacationers, the Great Swamp Management area offers hiking trails, canoeing, fishing, and more. Wakamo's small size gives it a homey feel for an RV park, making it more inviting than most.

Basics

Operated By: Private operator. **Open:** Apr. 15–Oct. 15. **Site Assignment:** Reservations accepted. **Registration:** At office. **Fee:** $40. **Parking:** At site.

Facilities

Number of RV Sites: 30. **Number of Tent-Only Sites:** 0. **Hookups:** Water, electric, sewer. **Each Site:** None. **Dump Station:** No. **Laundry:** No. **Pay Phone:** No. **Rest Rooms and Showers:** No. **Fuel:** No. **Propane:** No. **RV Service:** No. **Market:** Seaview Marketplace, 682 Matunuck Beach Rd., Wakefield, RI 02879: Take a left onto Succotash Rd., followed by a slight right onto Rte. 1 & a slight right onto Matanuck Rd. **Restaurant:** Cap'n Jack's **Restaurant:** 706 Succotash Rd., Wakefield, RI 02879: Take a right onto Succotash Rd. **General Store:** Yes. **Vending:** No. **Swimming Pool:** No. **Playground:** No. **Other:** Canoe & paddleboat rentals. **Activities:** Some planned activities. **Nearby Attractions:** Great Swamp Management Area.

Restrictions

Pets: Not allowed. **Fires:** Allowed. **Alcoholic Beverages:** Allowed. **Vehicle Max. Length:** None.

To Get There

Take I-295 south to Exit 9, Rte. 4. Take a slight right onto Tower Hill Rd., which becomes Rte. 1. Follow for 13 mi. until it becomes Succotash Rd.

WAKEFIELD

Card's Camps

1065 Worden's Pond Rd., Wakefield 02879. T: (401) 783-7158; F: (401) 783-5267; www.cardscamps.com.

RV ★★★★★ Tent n/a

Beauty: ★★★ Site Privacy: ★★★
Spaciousness: ★★★★ Quiet: ★★★
Security: ★★★ Cleanliness: ★★★
Insect Control: ★★★ Facilities: ★★★★

An enormous campground catering entirely to RVers, Card's Camp is a nicer-than-average RV park. Because it's so large and borders a nature preserve, there's enough open space here to make you feel involved in nature even though you're not sleeping outside in a tent. The campground also lies right on Worden Pond, the largest pond in the state, and pond-side campsites are available.

Basics

Operated By: Private operator. **Open:** May 1–Oct. 1. **Site Assignment:** Reservations required. **Registration:** At office. **Fee:** $38–45 for the 1st night, $22–32 for each additional. **Parking:** At site.

Facilities

Number of RV Sites: Over 250. **Number of Tent-Only Sites:** 0. **Hookups:** Water, electric, sewer. **Each Site:** Picnic table, fireplace. **Dump Station:** Yes. **Laundry:** No. **Pay Phone:** Yes. **Rest Rooms and Showers:** Yes. **Fuel:** No. **Propane:** Yes. **RV Service:** No. **Market:** 4071 Old Post Rd., Charlestown, RI: Take a right onto Wordens Pond Rd., followed by a left onto Shannock Rd., a right onto Old Coach Rd., & a left onto Narrow Ln. Then take a slight right onto Post Rd. & follow for 0.6 mi. **Restaurant:** Rojelio's Railway 3769 Old Post Rd. A, Charlestown, RI: Take a right onto Wordens Pond Rd., followed by a left onto Shannock Rd., a right onto Old Coach Rd., & a left onto Narrow Ln. Then take a slight right onto Post Rd. & follow for 0.6 mi. **General Store:** No. **Vending:** No. **Swimming Pool:** Yes. **Playground:** Yes. **Other:** Volleyball, basketball, horseshoes, freshwater pond. **Activities:** Boat rentals, fishing, hunting. **Nearby Attractions:** Great Swamp Management Area preserve. **Additional Information:** www.cardscamps.com.

Restrictions

Pets: Allowed. **Fires:** Allowed. **Alcoholic Beverages:** Allowed. **Vehicle Max. Length:** None.

To Get There

Take I-95 South to Exit 9 for Rte. 4 South. Take Rte. 4 South to Rte. 1 South. Take Rte. 1 South for approximately 12 mi. to Rte. 110 North. Take Rte. 110 North (also the U.R.I. Exit) and continue to the intersection with a flashing red light at Worden's Pond Rd. Then take a left and continue on Worden's Pond Rd. for about 2 mi. to Card's Camps on your right.

WEST GREENWICH

Oak Embers Campground

219 Escoheag Hill Rd., West Greenwich 02817. T: (401) 397-4042; F: (401) 397-4446; www.oakembers.com; info@oakembers.com.

RV ★★★ Tent ★★★

Beauty: ★★★★ Site Privacy: ★★★
Spaciousness: ★★★★ Quiet: ★★★★
Security: ★★★★ Cleanliness: ★★★★
Insect Control: ★★★ Facilities: ★★★★

Though it's set next to one of the more picturesque parts of the state, Oak Embers is not much to look at. The surrounding scenery is beautiful, but the campground itself feels much like an old summer camp, though this might be intentional on the part of the owners. Still, once you get away from the most crowded areas of the campground, you'll find plenty of trees and solitude and more than enough nature in which to lose yourself. Oak Embers combines the best of both worlds—it's near a lot of non-camping activities yet offers all the outdoor amenities as well.

Basics

Operated By: Jack & Fran Smith. **Open:** May 1–Sept. 30. **Site Assignment:** By reservation. **Registration:** Reservations required. **Fee:** $20 per night (electric), $18 (no hookups), 3 nights min. during weekends on peak season. **Parking:** At site.

Facilities

Number of RV Sites: 37. **Number of Tent-Only Sites:** 23. **Hookups:** Water, electric. **Each Site:** Picnic table, fireplace. **Dump Station:** Yes. **Laundry:** Yes. **Pay Phone:** Yes. **Rest Rooms and Showers:** Yes. **Fuel:** No. **Propane:** No. **Internal Roads:** Gravel. **RV Service:** No. **Market:** Better Val-U Supermarket, 104 Beach Pond Rd., Voluntown, CT: Take a right onto Escoheag Hill Rd., followed by a right onto Ten Rod Rd. Follow for about 4 mi. as it becomes Beach Pond Rd. **Restaurant:** Town Pizza & Restaurant, 104 Beach Pond Rd., Voluntown, CT. **General Store:** No. **Vending:** Yes. **Swimming Pool:** Yes. **Playground:** No. **Other:** Rec room, sports field. **Activities:** Hayrides, horseback riding, volleyball, theme weekends. **Nearby Attractions:** Arcadia Management Area. **Additional Information:** www.oakembers.com.

Restrictions

Pets: Allowed. **Fires:** Allowed. **Alcoholic Beverages:** Allowed. **Vehicle Maximum Length:** 40 ft.

To Get There

Take Rte. 95 South to Exit 5A onto Rte. 5, Right onto Rte. 3 to Rte. 165. Right on Rte. 165 to Escoheag Hill Rd. Right on Escoheag Hill Rd.

WESTERLY

Timber Creek RV Resort

118 Dunns Corners Rd., Westerly 02891. T: (401) 322-1877; www.timbercreekrvresort.com; timbercreek@efortress.com.

RV ★★★★ Tent n/a

Beauty: ★★★ Site Privacy: ★★★
Spaciousness: ★★★★ Quiet: ★★★
Security: ★★★ Cleanliness: ★★★
Insect Control: ★★★ Facilities: ★★★★★

With a summer camp–like setting, this RV-only park caters to families looking for a resort-type RV park. Numerous sports fields, a swimming pool, and other top-notch facilities make Timber Creek an active place to visit. Many planned activities and droves of people make this a fun place for kids. The camp is only a few years old, so most facilities are in good shape. Nature lovers might want to pick another campground since you must venture far off the grounds to hike.

Basics

Operated By: Private operator. **Open:** May 1–Oct. 31. **Site Assignment:** Reservations recommended, 7-day cancellation policy. **Registration:** Office. **Fee:** $32 . **Parking:** At site.

Facilities

Number of RV Sites: 200. **Number of Tent-Only Sites:** 0. **Hookups:** Water, electric (50 amps), sewer. **Each Site:** Picnic table, fire ring. **Dump Station:** Yes. **Laundry:** Yes. **Pay Phone:** Yes. **Rest Rooms and Showers:** Yes. **Fuel:** No. **Propane:** Yes. **Internal Roads:** Gravel. **RV Service:** No. **Market:** W. B. Cody's, 265 Post Rd., Westerly, RI 02891: Take a right onto Dunns Croner Bradford Rd. & go 1.4 mi., followed by a left onto Post Rd. **Restaurant:** On site. **General Store:** Yes. **Vending:** Yes. **Swimming Pool:** Yes. **Playground:** Yes. **Other:** Kids rec room, driving range, fishing pond, sports fields, adult lodge. **Activities:** Paddle boats, hayrides. **Nearby Attractions:** Beaches, golf.

Restrictions

Pets: Allowed. **Fires:** Allowed. **Alcoholic Beverages:** Allowed. **Vehicle Max. Length:** None.

To Get There

Take RI Exit 1, Rte. 3 south approximately 1.5 mi. Take left on Rte. 216, follow to end, bear right on Rte. 91. At traffic islands go straight through onto Dunns Corners Rd.; Resort is 0.5 mi. on right.

South Carolina

South Carolina really packs it in. Visitors encounter a small state rich in history, the arts, and outdoor beauty. Three geographical regions offer diversity not found in many larger states. The coastal low-country is known for its gorgeous live oak and marshes complete with blue heron and other birds. The rolling piedmont offers hunting and freshwater recreation. The highlands lie in the foothills of the Blue Ridge mountains and reach elevations over 3,500 feet.

South Carolina's many native peoples include the Catawba, known for their pottery which has been produced by the same techniques for almost 1,000 years.

European settlers found the South Carolina low-country perfect for rice cultivation, which began in the 1680s. Rice remained essential even as cotton production became more profitable after the invention of the cotton gin in 1793. Rice, cotton, and slave labor brought vast fortunes to Antebellum South Carolina. Many historic homes and plantations stand today and are open for touring. **Charleston's** historic district is the site of urban antebellum buildings as well as **The Dock Street Theater,** the oldest theater building in America. Notable plantations include **Middleton Place,** gathering place for southern strategists in the Revolutionary War, and **Magnolia Plantation,** home of the nation's oldest landscaped garden.

The Civil War began on April 12, 1861 when Confederates attacked Fort Sumter at Charleston Harbor. After this battle, South Carolina saw relatively little fighting, though roughly 13,000 South Carolinians died in the Civil War. In 1864, Charleston was the launch site for the H.L. Hunley, a prototypical submarine that successfully torpedoed and sank the USS Housatonic. A replica of the Hunley is on display at the **South Carolina State Museum** in Columbia.

South Carolina's economy still depends on agriculture (especially soy, tobacco, peaches, and livestock), but textiles, tourism, and numerous other industries also flourish.

Tourists and locals support performing arts in South Carolina. Fine performing arts are appreciated in the state's refurbished opera houses (in **Newberry, Abbeville,** and **Sumter**) and larger venues in **Charleston** and **Greenville**. For casual entertainment, **Myrtle Beach** stages numerous production shows.

Golfers from all over the world pilgrimage to **Hilton Head Island,** site of the Worldcom Classic—The Heritage of Golf (formerly the Heritage Classic). Of the 36 courses in the Hilton Head area, Harbor Town is instantly recognizable with its red-and-white-striped lighthouse visible from many holes. **Myrtle Beach** and the **Grand Strand** now contain over 100 courses, some excellent and others inexpensive. There are few areas in the world that offer so many golfing choices.

Not a golfer? Here are some other recreation opportunities found in South Carolina: **The Greenville County Museum of Art, Bob Jones University Museum & Gallery, Avery Research Center for African American History and Culture, Penn Center, Butterfly Pavilion, Southern Living House at Brookgreen Gardens, South Carolina Foothills Artisans Center, South Beach Adventure Amusement Park, South Carolina Aquarium, Charleston IMAX Theater, Congaree Swamp National Monument, Family Kingdom Amusement Park, Myrtle Beach Pavilion Amusement Park, Paramount's Carowinds, Myrtle Waves Waterpark, Riverbanks Zoo and Botanical Gardens, Greenville Zoo, Emerald Farm.**

The following facility accepts payment in checks or cash only:

Baker Creek State Park, McCormick

ANDERSON

Springfield Campground, Hartwell Lake

P.O. Box 278, Hartwell 30643-0278. T: (888) 893-0678; F: (706) 856-0358; www.reserveusa.com.

RV ★★★★ Tent ★★★★

Beauty: ★★★★★ Site Privacy: ★★★★
Spaciousness: ★★★★★ Quiet: ★★★★
Security: ★★★★★ Cleanliness: ★★★★
Insect Control: ★★★ Facilities: ★★★

Springfield Campground at Hartwell Lake boasts some of the most beautiful campsites we've seen. Along the shoreline, most sites have gorgeous water views. Sites 67–79 are especially stunning—huge and private with fabulous views. Sites 32–36 are less private, but have even better views. Sites 25, 26, 47, and 48 are good for families as they are roomy and close to the playground. Sites have gravel parking in pull-throughs and back-ins. There are plenty of shady trees although site privacy varies. One of three reservoirs on the Savannah River, 56,000-acre Lake Hartwell is stocked with crappie, stripers, catfish, and largemouth and hybrid bass. There are a number of other recreation areas within ten miles of the park. Security is outstanding at this rural campground. The gate is guarded by day and locked by night. Avoid Lake Hartwell on holiday weekends and during summer heat.

BASICS

Operated By: US Army Corps of Engineers. **Open:** Apr. 1–Sept. 30. **Site Assignment:** First come, first served; reservations accepted through the National Recreation Reservation Service (NRRS) at (877) 444-6777. Reservations can be made up to 240 days in advance, full payment required upon making reservation; credit card preferred (V, MC, D, AE), or pay by money order if at least 21 days in advance of arrival. $10 fee for cancellation or change of site or dates. Cancellation within 3 days of arrival charged first night, no-show charged $20 plus first night. **Registration:** Gatehouse. **Fee:** $18 peak season, $16 off-season, 10 people max., 1 wheeled camping unit or tents that fit on impact pad. **Parking:** 3 vehicles per site.

FACILITIES

Number of RV Sites: 0. **Number of Tent-Only Sites:** 0 **Number of Multipurpose Sites:** 79. **Hookups:** Water, electric (50 amps). **Each Site:** Picnic table, fire ring or grill, lantern post. **Dump Station:** Yes. **Laundry:** No. **Pay Phone:** Yes. **Rest Rooms and Showers:** Yes. **Fuel:** No. **Propane:** No. **Internal Roads:** Paved. **RV Service:** 30 mi. north in Greenville. **Market:** 7 mi. east in Anderson. **Restaurant:** 4 mi. east in Anderson. **General Store:** 1 mi. east in Anderson. **Vending:** No. **Swimming Pool:** No. **Playground:** Yes. **Other:** Boat ramp, courtesy dock, picnic area. **Activities:** Swimming beaches, fishing, swim access from most campsites. **Nearby Attractions:** Historic Pendleton, Clemson University, Anderson Flea Market, Anderson County Museum, Arts Center. **Additional Information:** Anderson Chamber of Commerce, (864) 226-3454, www.andersonsc.com.

RESTRICTIONS

Pets: Leash only. **Fires:** Campsites only. **Alcoholic Beverages:** Not allowed. **Vehicle Maximum Length:** No limit. **Other:** 14-day max. stay.

TO GET THERE

From I-85, take Exit 11 onto Hwy. 24 East. Drive 4 mi. to Hwy. 187 South. Turn right onto Hwy. 187 and drive south for 5 miles. Turn right on Providence Church Rd. Follow Providence Church Rd. to the campground.

BLACKSBURG

Kings Mountain State Park

1277 Park Rd., Blacksburg 29702. T: (803) 222-3209; F: (803) 222-6948; www.southcarolinaparks.com; kings_mountain_sp@prt.state.sc.us.

RV ★★★★ Tent ★★★★

Beauty: ★★★★ Site Privacy: ★★★
Spaciousness: ★★★ Quiet: ★★★★
Security: ★★★★★ Cleanliness: ★★★★
Insect Control: ★★★★ Facilities: ★★★★★

Bordering King's Mountain National Military Park Revolutionary War battle sight, this park is home to the "Living History Farm." This park also offers impressive outdoor activities. Situated in a gorgeous stand of white and red oak and hickory, the hilly campground includes both back-in and pull-through sites. Want a level site? Try 1, 4, 6, 8, 39, or 47 (all back-ins). If you're attached to a pull-through, you may have to deal with sloped parking. All sites are comfortably spaced with some plant growth to provide privacy between sites. Parking is on dirt or gravel. Security is excellent at rural King's Mountain; the park gates are closed at all times and campers are given a combination to open them. The campground was extremely quiet when we visited. In fact, King's Mountain only fills to capacity on holiday weekends, making it an excellent destination on other summer weekends.

BASICS

Operated By: South Carolina State Parks. **Open:** All year. **Site Assignment:** All first come, first served; reservations for handicapped accessible sites only. **Registration:** Camp store, ranger makes rounds off-season. **Fee:** $18 water & electric; $9 tent, South Carolina seniors, & disabled. **Parking:** At sites except tent sites.

FACILITIES

Number of RV Sites: 0. **Number of Tent-Only Sites:** 10 walk-in (with tent pad & fire ring). **Number of Multipurpose Sites:** 116. **Hookups:** Water, electric (20, 30 amps). **Each Site:** Picnic table. **Dump Station:** Yes. **Laundry:** Yes (in-season). **Pay Phone:** Yes. **Rest Rooms and Showers:** Yes. **Fuel:** No. **Propane:** No. **Internal Roads:** Main park roads paved, campground roads gravel. **RV Service:** 8 mi. northwest in Kings Mountain. **Market:** 8 mi. northwest in Kings Mountain. **Restaurant:** 15 mi. north in Gastonia. **General Store:** 10 mi. southeast in Clover, Ace Hardware, or Wal-Mart 16 mi. southeast in York. **Vending:** No. **Swimming Pool:** No. **Playground:** No. **Other:** Living history farm (barn, cotton gin, blacksmith/carpenter shop, gardens, livestock), park store, picnic shelters. **Activities:** Grassy swimming beach, hiking & equestrian trails, equestrian camping, fishing, fishing boat, pedal boat & canoe rentals, mini-golf. **Nearby Attractions:** Kings Mountain National Military Park, Anne Springs Close Greenway nature preserve, Historic Brattonsville, Fort Mill Confederate Park, 30 mi. from Charlotte, North Carolina. **Additional Information:** Clover Chamber of Commerce, (803) 222-3312.

RESTRICTIONS

Pets: Leash (6 ft. max.). **Fires:** Allowed. **Alcoholic Beverages:** Not Allowed. **Vehicle Maximum Length:** 40 ft.

TO GET THERE

From I-85 (NC Exit 2), drive east on State Hwy. 216. 216 turns into Park Rd. and goes through Kings Mountain National Military Park. Headquarters is on the right approx. 9 mi. from I-85.

CALHOUN FALLS

Calhoun Falls State Park

246 Maintenance Shop Rd., Calhoun Falls 29628. T: (864) 447-8267; F: (864) 447-8638; www.southcarolinaparks.com; calhoun_falls_sp@prt.state.sc.us.

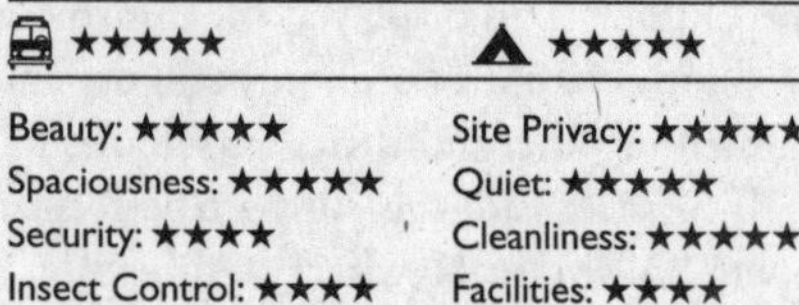

RV ★★★★★ Tent ★★★★★

Beauty: ★★★★★ Site Privacy: ★★★★★
Spaciousness: ★★★★★ Quiet: ★★★★★
Security: ★★★★ Cleanliness: ★★★★★
Insect Control: ★★★★ Facilities: ★★★★

Calhoun Falls SRA was developed jointly by the Corps of Engineers (COE) and South Carolina State Parks. The collaboration is a boon to campers, with recreation typical of state parks and large, gorgeous campsites typical of Corps campgrounds. For fishermen, Lake Russell is home to a variety of bass, bluegill, crappie, and catfish. For the children there are six playgrounds. The campground features extremely spacious sites with paved parking. Each site has a sandy picnic and tent area. Sites are afforded shade and privacy by thick, lovely woods. Campsites with hookups are found in two areas and tent-only sites in a third. Of the lakefront sites, back-ins are often more attractive than pull-throughs. Security is fair at Calhoun Falls; although the park is extremely rural and gates are locked at night, the gates are not always attended during the day. Avoid visiting on busy summer weekends.

BASICS

Operated By: South Carolina State Parks. **Open:** All year. **Site Assignment:** First come, first served; reservations accepted up to 11 months in advance, 2 night min.; full deposit required within 10 days of reservation; 48 hours notice for cancellation refund, $15 cancellation fee. **Registration:** Camp store, rangers collect after hours. **Fee:** $21 for lakefront site w/ reservation, $19 for non-lakefront site w/

reservation, $20 for lakefront sites, $18 for non–lakefront sites, $10 for tent sites, fees include 6 people. **Parking:** Site plus overflow parking.

Facilities

Number of RV Sites: 0. **Number of Tent-Only Sites:** 14. **Number of Multipurpose Sites:** 86. **Hookups:** Water, electric (20, 30 amps). **Each Site:** Picnic table, grill, fire ring, lantern holder. **Dump Station:** Yes. **Laundry:** Yes. **Pay Phone:** Yes. **Rest Rooms and Showers:** Yes. **Fuel:** No. **Propane:** No. **Internal Roads:** Paved. **RV Service:** 30 mi. north in Anderson. **Market:** 2 mi. south in Calhoun Falls. **Restaurant:** 2 mi. south in Calhoun Falls. **General Store:** Camp store. **Vending:** Beverages only. **Swimming Pool:** No. **Playground:** Yes. **Other:** Boat ramp. **Activities:** Fishing, skiing, boating, non-motorized boat rentals, swimming when lifeguard on duty, walking trail, basketball, tennis. **Nearby Attractions:** Sumter National Forest, Lake Russell Dam (Information Center in Georgia), Abbeville Historic District, walking tours. **Additional Information:** Abbeville Chamber of Commerce, (864) 459-4600.

Restrictions

Pets: Leash. **Fires:** In sites, rings only. **Alcoholic Beverages:** In sites, out of view. **Vehicle Maximum Length:** Varies. **Other:** 14-day max. stay.

To Get There

From Calhoun Falls, at the intersection of SC 81 and SC 72, take SC 81 north 1 mile. The park entrance is on the left.

CHAPIN

Dreher Island State Park

3677 State Park Rd., Prosperity 29127. T: (803) 364-4152; F: (803) 364-0756; www.southcarolinaparks.com; dreher_island_sp@prt.state.sc.us.

RV ★★★★ Tent ★★★★

Beauty: ★★★★	Site Privacy: ★★★
Spaciousness: ★★★	Quiet: ★★★★
Security: ★★★★★	Cleanliness: ★★★★
Insect Control: ★★★★	Facilities: ★★★

Recreation includes fishing and boating on Lake Murray. Fisher-folk hook catfish, bream, crappie, yellow perch and largemouth and striped bass. Day-use facilities at this 348-acre park are not extensive, but the campgrounds are lovely. Of the two camping loops, B is nicer. On loop B, we recommend the lakefront sites, which are large and secluded with pretty views. At both loops, site size and privacy vary, but none are small. Gorgeous trees include a variety of oak species, which provide plenty of shade at most sites. All parking is paved. There are a few pull-through sites and plenty of back-in sites. Located in a rural but touristy area, security is good. Gates are attended during the day and locked at night. Close to Columbia, Dreher Island stays full on summer weekends and holidays. We recommend a weekday, spring, or fall visit.

Basics

Operated By: South Carolina State Parks. **Open:** All year. **Site Assignment:** first come, first served; a few sites available for reservations for $1 extra, 2 night min., full deposit required before arrival, 24 hour cancellation notice for refund less $15 fee. **Registration:** Visitor center, late arrivals may camp in area outside gate. **Fee:** $18 for 6 people (add $1 for reservation). **Parking:** Limit 2 vehicles, overflow parking available.

Facilities

Number of RV Sites: 0. **Number of Tent-Only Sites:** 15. **Number of Multipurpose Sites:** 97. **Hookups:** Water, electric (30 amps). **Each Site:** Picnic table, fire ring. **Dump Station:** Yes. **Laundry:** No. **Pay Phone:** Yes. **Rest Rooms and Showers:** Yes. **Fuel:** Yes (automobile & boat). **Propane:** No. **Internal Roads:** Paved. **RV Service:** 30 mi. east in Columbia. **Market:** 10 mi. north in Chapin. **Restaurant:** 10 mi. north in Chapin. **General Store:** Camp store. **Vending:** No. **Swimming Pool:** No. **Playground:** Yes. **Other:** Boat ramps, tackle shop, picnic shelters, screened meeting shelter. **Activities:** Fishing, pontoon boat rentals available, walking trails. **Nearby Attractions:** Columbia historic homes, South Carolina Confederate Relic Room & Museum, Fort Jackson Museum, South Carolina State Museum. **Additional Information:** Capital City Lake Murray Country Visitor Information (803) 781-5940.

Restrictions

Pets: Leash. **Fires:** In fire rings in sites only. **Alcoholic Beverages:** Not allowed. **Vehicle Maximum Length:** 45 ft. **Other:** 14-day max. stay.

To Get There

From I-26, take Exit 91 at Chapin onto Hwy. 48 west. At Hwy. 76, turn right and look for St. Peters Church Rd. on the left. Turn left and continue until Dreher Island Rd. Turn left and look for State Park Rd. Turn left again. The park is 12 mi. from I-26.

CHARLESTON/MT. PLEASANT

Mt. Pleasant KOA

3157 Hwy. 17 North, Mt. Pleasant 29466. T: (843) 849-5177 or (800) KOA-5796; F: (843) 849-2275; www.koakampgrounds.com.

RV ★★★ Tent ★★★

Beauty: ★★★	Site Privacy: ★★
Spaciousness: ★★	Quiet: ★★★
Security: ★★★	Cleanliness: ★★★★
Insect Control: ★★★★	Facilities: ★★★

Regarding tidiness, we recommend this park over its main competitor, the KOA Charleston. This place is cleaner, though not necessarily prettier. The suburban location of this park is also nice—it's within convenient touring distance of Charleston. And plenty of restaurants and shopping are located in nearby Mount Pleasant. The campground is laid out in 11 rows of pull-throughs plus 4 back-in areas. Sites are on the small side with little privacy. A few sites have shady trees, but most are open. Parking spaces may resemble a crazy quilt—grass, gravel, and packed clay are all present. The nicest sites are B4–B7, which have nice views of the small fishing lake. This suburban campground has no gates, making security fair. Avoid touring Charleston in the humid summertime. Also avoid holiday and summer weekends.

Basics

Operated By: Gregory family. **Open:** All year. **Site Assignment:** First come, first served; reservations recommended, 2 night min. on holidays, credit card deposit required, 24 hour cancellation notice required for refund. **Registration:** Camp store, night registration available. **Fee:** $30 for sites w/ full hookups, $27 for sites w/ water & electric, $15–$19 for tent sites (cash, personal check, V, MC, D, AE). **Parking:** 2 vehicles per site, plus overflow area.

Facilities

Number of RV Sites: 60. **Number of Tent-Only Sites:** 18 (plus primitive overflow area). **Number of Multipurpose Sites:** None. **Hookups:** Water, electric (30, 50 amps), 45 sites w/ sewer, cable. **Each Site:** Picnic table, fire ring. **Dump Station:** Yes. **Laundry:** Yes. **Pay Phone:** Yes. **Rest Rooms and Showers:** Yes. **Fuel:** No. **Propane:** Yes. **Internal Roads:** Gravel. **RV Service:** 20 mi. west in Charleston. **Market:** 1 mi. west in Mt. Pleasant. **Restaurant:** 3 mi. west in Mt. Pleasant. **General Store:** Camp store. **Vending:** Beverages only. **Swimming Pool:** Yes. **Playground:** Yes. **Other:** Rec hall, kamper kitchen, boat dock. **Activities:** Bicycle & boat rentals (paddle, canoe, & kayak), walking trails, mini-golf, horseshoes, volleyball, basketball, ping pong. **Nearby Attractions:** Charleston Historic District, Charles Towne Landing, Patriot's Pointe Naval & Maritime Museum, plantation & garden tours. **Additional Information:** Charleston Area CVB, (843) 853-8000 or (800) 868-8118, www.charlestoncvb.com.

Restrictions

Pets: Leash. **Fires:** Allowed. **Alcoholic Beverages:** Allowed. **Vehicle Maximum Length:** 40 ft. **Other:** 2-week stay limit.

To Get There

From I-526, take Exit 32. Drive east on US Hwy. 17 for 5 miles. The entrance is on the right.

COLUMBIA

Sesquicentennial State Park

9564 Two Notch Rd., Columbia 29223. T: (803) 788-2706; F: (803) 788-4417; www.southcarolinaparks.com; sesquicentennial_sp@prt.state.sc.us.

RV ★★★★ Tent ★★★★

Beauty: ★★★★	Site Privacy: ★★★
Spaciousness: ★★★★	Quiet: ★★★★★
Security: ★★★★★	Cleanliness: ★★★★
Insect Control: ★★★	Facilities: ★★★★

This 1,419-acre urban green space includes a 30-acre lake stocked with bass and bream. The log house was built in 1756 in Richland County and moved to Sesquicentennial in 1961. The park's location is excellent if you like to shop and enjoy eating out. The campground consists of two loops, nicely shaded by a gorgeous stand of loblolly and longleaf pine. Campsites are large and most have back-in parking. However, we recommend the larger and more private pull-through sites. Parking is on a mixture of sand, gravel, grass, and pine straw. The campground was quiet when we visited on Labor day weekend. It's often empty in the fall, so it's a great place to stay for University of South Carolina football games or on a holiday weekend.

Basics

Operated By: South Carolina State Parks. **Open:** All year. **Site Assignment:** First come, first served; no reservations. **Registration:** Set-up first, then register at office, ranger makes rounds. **Fee:** $17 includes 6 people. **Parking:** Sites only.

Facilities

Number of Multipurpose Sites: 87. **Hookups:** Water, electric (30 amps). **Each Site:** Picnic table. **Dump Station:** Yes. **Laundry:** No. **Pay Phone:** Yes. **Rest Rooms and Showers:** Yes. **Fuel:** No. **Propane:** No. **Internal Roads:** Paved & dirt. **RV Service:** 20 mi. northeast in Elgin. **Market:** 1 mi. **Restaurant:** 0.25 mi. **General Store:** 1 mi. **Vending:** Beverages. **Swimming Pool:** No. **Playground:** Yes. **Other:** 1756 log house, picnic shelters, meeting facilities, nature center. **Activities:** Nature programs, nature trail, bicycle trail, fishing, exercise course, (non-motor) boat rentals, swimming, & paddle boat rentals when lifeguard is present. **Nearby Attractions:** Columbia historic homes, South Carolina Confederate Relic Room & Museum, Fort Jackson Museum, South Carolina State Museum. **Additional Information:** Columbia Metropolitan CVB, (803) 254-0479 or (800) 264-4884.

Restrictions

Pets: Leash. **Fires:** In sites only. **Alcoholic Beverages:** Prohibited. **Vehicle Maximum Length:** Varies, up to 40 ft. **Other:** 14-day max. stay.

To Get There

From I-77, take Exit US Hwy. 1/Two Notch Rd. northeast for 13 miles. The park entrance is on the right.

EDISTO ISLAND

Edisto Beach State Park

8377 State Cabin Rd., Edisto Island 29438. T: (843) 869-2156 or (843) 853-8000; F: (843) 869-3023; www.southcarolinaparks.com; edisto_beach_sp@prt.state.sc.us.

RV ★★★ Tent ★★★

Beauty: ★★★★★	Site Privacy: ★★
Spaciousness: ★★★	Quiet: ★★★
Security: ★★★★	Cleanliness: ★★★★
Insect Control: ★	Facilities: ★★★

This is one of the prettiest Oceanside parks we've seen. Sites in the main area are within 100 yards of the beach. Sites in the Live Oak area are within 0.25 mile of the beach. Many sites are shaded by palmetto and live oak, although there is little privacy between them. Site size varies, with most on the small side. Parking is mostly back-in, on a mishmash of packed sand and oyster shells. Sites 9 and 10 are heavenly—shady and separated from the beach only by gorgeous dunes. Sites 18–20 are also attractive—totally open with ocean views. Recreation at Edisto Beach includes hiking to 4,000-year-old Edisto Indian Mound, "Spanish Mount." Comprised of shells and pottery, it's the second oldest Indian mound in the United States. Security is good—the campground is gated and guarded. Located on a touristy little island, many restaurants are convenient to the park. Avoid this park on summer weekends and holidays.

Basics

Operated By: South Carolina State Parks. **Open:** All year. **Site Assignment:** First come, first served; no reservations accepted. **Registration:** Registration booth. **Fee:** $22 for sites w/ water & electric, $11 for tent/ walk-in sites; fees include 6 people (cash, personal checks, V, MC). **Parking:** 2 cars per site.

Facilities

Number of RV Sites: 0. **Number of Tent-Only Sites:** 5. **Number of Multipurpose Sites:** 91. **Hookups:** Water, electric (20, 30 amps). **Each Site:** Picnic table, fire ring. **Dump Station:** Yes. **Laundry:** No. **Pay Phone:** Yes. **Rest Rooms and Showers:** Yes. **Fuel:** No. **Propane:** No. **Internal Roads:** Gravel. **RV Service:** 20 mi. north toward Charleston. **Market:** 0.25 mi. **Restaurant:** 0.25 mi. **General Store:** Camp store. **Vending:** Beverages. **Swimming Pool:** No. **Playground:** Yes. **Other:** Boat ramp, picnic area. **Activities:** Indian Mound trail to Native American pottery site, fishing, swimming. **Nearby Attractions:** Edisto Island, Historic Beaufort, Charleston plantations, gardens, museums, tours, Charles Towne Landing: first English settlement in South Carolina. **Additional Information:** Charleston Area CVB, (800) 868-8118.

Restrictions

Pets: Leash, clean-up enforced. **Fires:** Fire rings only. **Alcoholic Beverages:** Not allowed. **Vehicle Maximum Length:** 40 ft. **Other:** 14-day stay limit.

To Get There

From Charlston, drive west on Hwy. 17 for 25 miles. Turn south onto Hwy. 174 and drive for 22 miles. The park entrance is at the end of the highway.

EUTAWVILLE

Rocks Pond Campground and Marina

235 Rocks Pond Rd., Eutawville 29048. T: (803) 492-7711 or (800) 982-0271; F: (803) 492-9469; www.rockspond.com.

RV ★★★★ Tent ★★

Beauty: ★★★	Site Privacy: ★★
Spaciousness: ★★★	Quiet: ★★
Security: ★★★★★	Cleanliness: ★★★★
Insect Control: ★★★★	Facilities: ★★★★

With over 250 tightly-spaced campsites, Rocks Pond has created urban crowding in rural Eutawville. And folks seem to love it, ostensibly because of extensive amenities and recreation, including live bands on the weekends and a children's fishing pond. Avoid this joint on summer weekends and holidays when the crowds are sure to be unbearable. Sites are laid out in a series of monotonous grids except for waterfront sites (numbers 109–127 and 249–268). With boat dockage, sites 128–132 are nearly impossible to obtain. Call well in advance if you'd like one of these. None of the sites are knockout beautiful—choose your site based on location. Most are treeless pull-throughs. Parking is on packed clay or grass. All are level and none have any privacy. Rest rooms are odd; each potty has it's own lavatory, but the lavatory is outside the stall door. Security is excellent—the front entrance is guarded.

Basics

Operated By: Rutledge Connor. **Open:** All year. **Site Assignment:** First come, first served; reservations accepted for 3-night min., $20 deposit; 7-day cancellation notice for refund less $5 fee. **Registration:** Office, late-comers register next morning. **Fee:** $19–$28 for RV sites based on location relative to water, $16 for tent sites, fees include 4 people, $2 per extra person up to 6 total; designated senior citizens area $10 for 2 people. **Parking:** Site plus overflow parking.

Facilities

Number of RV Sites: 226. **Number of Tent-Only Sites:** 30. **Number of Multipurpose Sites:** 226 (RV). **Hookups:** Water, electric (20, 30, 50 amps), sewer. **Each Site:** Picnic table. **Dump Station:** Yes. **Laundry:** Yes. **Pay Phone:** Yes. **Rest Rooms and Showers:** Yes. **Fuel:** Yes. **Propane:** Yes. **Internal Roads:** Paved & gravel. **RV Service:** On call service available. **Market:** 3 mi. in Eutawville. **Restaurant:** 3 mi. in Eutawville, snack bar in-season. **General Store:** Camp store. **Vending:** Beverages. **Swimming Pool:** No. **Playground:** Yes. **Other:** Marina, rec hall, gazebos, meeting rooms, fire rings on request. **Activities:** Boating (rentals available), lake swimming, mini-golf, driving range, skeet range, archery, unique soccer sports, bicycle rentals, fishing guide service (call for rates), Saturday night dances in-season. **Nearby Attractions:** Four golf courses within 25 miles, Lake Marion, Santee community, Palmetto trailhead, 1 hour from Charleston & Columbia. **Additional Information:** Santee Cooper Country Promotions (803) 854-2131.

Restrictions

Pets: Leash, clean-up enforced. **Fires:** In fire rings only (available on request). **Alcoholic Beverages:** Discouraged. **Vehicle Maximum Length:** No limit.

To Get There

From I-95, take Exit 98. Drive southeast on Hwy. 6 for 9 mi. to Eutawville. At the stop sign, go left following Hwy. 6. Look for the Rocks Pond sign and turn left on Rocks Pond Rd., then right at the dead end. The campground is 18 mi. from I-95.

FAIR PLAY

Lake Hartwell State Park

19138-A South Hwy. 11, Fair Play 29643. T: (864) 972-3352; F: (864) 972-3352; www.southcarolinaparks.com.

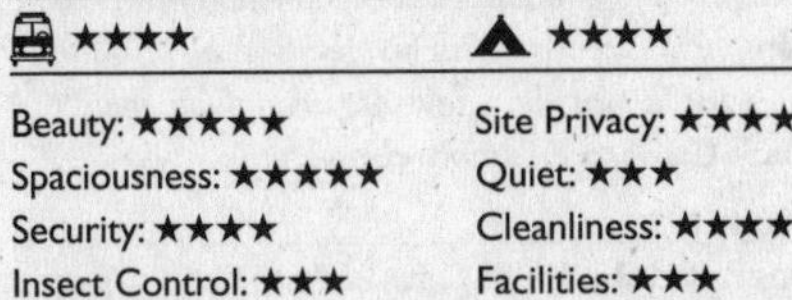

★★★★ ★★★★

Beauty: ★★★★★ Site Privacy: ★★★★
Spaciousness: ★★★★★ Quiet: ★★★
Security: ★★★★ Cleanliness: ★★★★
Insect Control: ★★★ Facilities: ★★★

This popular park is located one mile from I-85 on 56,000-acre Lake Hartwell. Activities include fishing for crappie, bream, catfish, stripers, largemouth, and hybrid bass. There are few land activities at this 680-acre park. Adrenaline lovers should consider a trip down the nearby Chattooga Wild and Scenic River. The campground is laid out in three main loops on two lake peninsulas, with many sites enjoying water views. Site size varies from ample to huge, with shady trees in most areas. Reservable sites, 69–108, are densely wooded. We recommended number 92, which is incredibly secluded (great honeymoon suite!). In the non-reservable sites, 6 and 17 are both large and private with lovely views. All parking is paved. There are both pull-through and back-in sites. Security is not great here; the park is only one mile from the interstate and has no gates. Visit on weekdays or in spring or fall for maximum peace and quiet.

BASICS

Operated By: South Carolina State Parks. **Open:** All year. **Site Assignment:** Most sites first come, first served; 40 sites available for reservation, full payment required in advance; 24-hour notice required for refund, $15 cancellation fee. **Registration:** Store, late comers register next morning. **Fee:** $17 for waterfront sites, $16 for regular sites, $8 for walk-in sites, add $1 for reserved sites, fee includes 10 people (cash, personal checks, V, MC). **Parking:** At sites except walk-in, overflow parking available.

FACILITIES

Number of RV Sites: 0. **Number of Tent-Only Sites:** 13 walk-in. **Number of Multipurpose Sites:** 108. **Hookups:** Water, electric (30 amps). **Each Site:** Picnic table, fire ring. **Dump Station:** Yes. **Laundry:** Yes. **Pay Phone:** Yes. **Rest Rooms and Showers:** Yes. **Fuel:** No. **Propane:** No. **Internal Roads:** Paved. **RV Service:** 13 mi. north toward Seneca. **Market:** 8 mi. south in Lavonia, GA. **Restaurant:** 1.5 mi. **General Store:** 17 mi. north in Seneca (Wal-Mart). **Vending:** Beverages. **Swimming Pool:** No. **Playground:** Yes. **Other:** Boat ramp, picnic shelter, park store. **Activities:** Nature trail, fishing, boating, lake swimming. **Nearby Attractions:** Anderson Historic District, Chattooga National Wild & Scenic River, Cherokee Foothills Scenic Hwy. (11), Sumter National Forest, Walhalla National Fish Hatchery, Issaqueena Falls, Clemson University. **Additional Information:** Anderson Chamber of Commerce, (864) 226-3454.

RESTRICTIONS

Pets: Leash, clean-up enforced. **Fires:** Allowed. **Alcoholic Beverages:** Not allowed. **Vehicle Maximum Length:** 45 ft. **Other:** No fire arms or fire works.

TO GET THERE

From I-85, take Exit 1 onto South Carolina Hwy. 11. Drive about 0.25 mile to the top of the hill. The park is on the left.

HUNTING ISLAND

Hunting Island State Park

2555 Sea Island Parkway, Hunting Island 29920. T: (843) 838-2011; F: (843) 838-4263; www.southcarolinaparks.com; hunting_island_sp@scprt.com.

★★★★ ★★★★

Beauty: ★★★★★ Site Privacy: ★★★
Spaciousness: ★★★ Quiet: ★★★
Security: ★★★★ Cleanliness: ★★★★
Insect Control: ★★★★ Facilities: ★★★★

The atmosphere here is deliciously mellow. The children seem more laid back than at other campgrounds. It could be the gorgeous shade provided by mature pine, palm, and palmetto or the sound of the ocean. Relax in a hammock. Get yourself off the hammock to tour the Hunting Island Lighthouse, in use from 1875 until 1933. Two of the four main loops contain sites near the beach. Site size varies, as does privacy. If you're seeking ample space and privacy, head for sites 166–173 in the back of the campground (farthest from the beach). For the nicest beachfront sites, head for 49–55, 71 and 73. All of these have pretty views of beach dunes. Most parking is back-in on packed sand and pine straw. Mosquitoes and "no-see-ums" are a nuisance, so bring insect repellent. This park is extremely popular—prepare for crowds April through October or try visiting during the week. Security is good, with gates locked at night.

BASICS

Operated By: South Carolina State Parks. **Open:** All year. **Site Assignment:** Most sites first come, first served; 40 sites available for reservation, w/ full deposit; 24-hour cancellation notice for refund less $15 fee. **Registration:** Camp store, late comers register the next morning. **Fee:** $22 for water & electric in-Season, $18 for water & electric off-season, $12 for primitive in-Season, $9 for primitive off-season, add $1 for reservation; prices for 6 people max.; seniors & disabled 50% discount. **Parking:** Limit 2 vehicles per site, overflow parking available.

FACILITIES

Number of RV Sites: 0. **Number of Tent-Only Sites:** 10. **Number of Multipurpose Sites:** 200. **Hookups:** Water, electric (30 amps). **Each Site:** Picnic table, fire ring. **Dump Station:** Yes. **Laundry:** No. **Pay Phone:** Yes. **Rest Rooms and Showers:** Yes. **Fuel:** No. **Propane:** No. **Internal Roads:** Paved, sand, & gravel. **RV Service:** 16 mi. west in Beaufort. **Market:** 12 mi. west on Lady's Island. **Restaurant:** 12 mi. west on Lady's Island. **General Store:** Park store. **Vending:** Yes. **Swimming Pool:** No. **Playground:** No. **Other:** Boat ramp, visitor's center, lighthouse, beach shop, picnic shelters. **Activities:** Lighthouse tours, hiking & bicycling trail, boardwalk, fishing pier, crabbing, boating, swimming, nature programs. **Nearby Attractions:** Historic Beaufort, boat tours, gardens, walking tours, horse-drawn carriage tours, Port Royal. **Additional Information:** Greater Beaufort Chamber of Commerce, & Visitors Center, (843) 524-3163, www.beaufortsc.org.

RESTRICTIONS

Pets: Leash. **Fires:** Fire rings only. **Alcoholic Beverages:** Not allowed. **Vehicle Maximum Length:** 40 ft. **Other:** 2-week stay limit.

TO GET THERE

From I-95, take Exit 33 and drive south on Hwy. 17, which becomes Hwy. 21. Hwy. 21 ends on Hunting Island. Once on the island, take the first left into the campground. The park is 16 mi. east of Beaufort.

McCORMICK

Baker Creek State Park

Route 3 Box 50, McCormick 29835. T: (864) 443-2457; F: (864) 443-2457; www.southcarolinaparks.com; baker_creek_sp@prt.state.sc.us.

★★★★ ★★★★

Beauty: ★★★★★ Site Privacy: ★★★★
Spaciousness: ★★★★ Quiet: ★★★
Security: ★★★★ Cleanliness: ★★★★
Insect Control: ★★★ Facilities: ★★★

Baker Creek includes 1,300 gorgeous acres of rolling forest. J. Strom Thurmond Reservoir consists of 70,000 acres stocked with crappie, catfish, bream, striper, and several bass species. Despite its rural locale, this popular park should be avoided on summer weekends and holidays. Shaded by a gorgeous stand of loblolly pine trees, campsites at Baker Creek are more spacious than average. Most offer back-in parking. Foliage provides a bit of privacy between sites. Eight sites offer pull-through parking; none are lakefront. Parking is on dirt, gravel, or pine straw. The campgrounds contain two loops forming semi-circles with lake views at many sites. In campground No. 1, the nicest sites are 32–34, 37, 38, 40, 41, and 43. In campground No. 2, the nicer sites, 86–90, are on a small peninsula. Baker Creek locks its gates at night, but the front gate is not attended during the day making security good.

BASICS

Operated By: South Carolina State Parks. **Open:** All year. **Site Assignment:** First come, first served; no reservations. **Registration:** At campsites. **Fee:** $16; South Carolina seniors & disabled 50% discount (cash or check only). **Parking:** At sites only.

FACILITIES

Number of Multipurpose Sites: 100. **Hookups:** Water, electric (20, 30 amps). **Each Site:** Picnic table, 50 sites w/ grill. **Dump Station:** Yes. **Laundry:** No. **Pay Phone:** Yes. **Rest Rooms and Showers:** Yes. **Fuel:** No. **Propane:** No. **Internal Roads:** Gravel, main roads Paved. **RV Service:** 30 mi. north in Greenwood. **Market:** 4 mi. east in

McCormick. **Restaurant:** 4 mi. east in McCormick. **General Store:** 4 mi. east in McCormick, 22 mi. to Wal-Mart. **Vending:** Beverages. **Swimming Pool:** No. **Playground:** Yes. **Other:** Boat ramps, picnic shelters, pavilion rental. **Activities:** walking & hiking trails, fishing, basketball, volleyball, horseshoes, seasonal paddle boat rentals. **Nearby Attractions:** Historic McCormick County, Revolutionary War sites, Steven's Creek Heritage Preserve. **Additional Information:** McCormick Chamber of Commerce, (864) 465-2835.

Restrictions

Pets: Leash only. **Fires:** Ground fires only. **Alcoholic Beverages:** Not allowed. **Vehicle Maximum Length:** 40 ft.

To Get There

From I-20, take Georgia Exit 200 (River Watch Pkwy.). Drive west for approx. 2 mi. and turn right onto Hwy. 28 (Furys Ferry Rd.). Drive north on Hwy. 28 to McCormick and turn left onto US Hwy. 378. Drive west on US Hwy. 378 for 4 miles, then turn right at the park sign. The park is 1 mile ahead on the left.

MODOC

Modoc Campground, J. Strom Thurmond Lake

Route 1 Box 2-D, Modoc 29838. T: (864) 333-2272; F: (864) 333-1150; www.reserveamerica.com; caewx@noaa.gov.

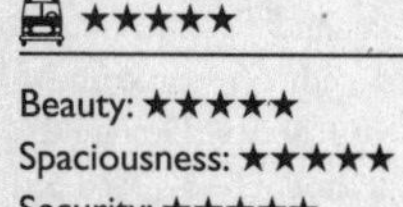

★★★★★ ▲ ★★★★★

Beauty: ★★★★★ Site Privacy: ★★★★★
Spaciousness: ★★★★★ Quiet: ★★★★★
Security: ★★★★★ Cleanliness: ★★★★
Insect Control: ★★★★ Facilities: ★★★

Modoc campground on J. Strom Thurmond Lake is one of the most beautiful campgrounds in the Southeast. Sites are incredibly spacious with a large sandy picnic and tent area. Sites are shaded and secluded by lovely loblolly and shortleaf pine and other tree species. All sites have gravel parking. Back-in sites are nice, but many of the pull-throughs are huge. The campground contains four main spurs on two peninsulas. Sites 4–10 are gorgeous, with views of a small inlet. Site 11 is one of the most beautiful we've seen anywhere—unfortunately it has no hookups. Fishermen will find smallmouth, striped, and hybrid bass. Few day-use facilities at the campground keep it blissfully quiet most of the time. Only 40 minutes from Augusta, Modoc's location is extremely rural. Security is excellent as the campground is gated and guarded. Visit Modoc anytime except holiday weekends. It rarely fills to capacity.

Basics

Operated By: US Army Corps of Engineers. **Open:** Apr. 1–Oct. 31. **Site Assignment:** First come, first served; reservations accepted through the National Recreation Reservation Service (NRRS) at (877) 444-6777. Reservations can be made up to 240 days in advance, full payment required upon making reservation; credit card preferred (V, MC, D, AE), or pay by money order if at least 21 days in advance of arrival. $10 fee for cancellation or change of site or dates. Cancellation within 3 days of arrival charged first night, no-show charged $20 plus first night. *Note:* Due to current construction, Modoc Campground may not accept reservations for the 2002 season, but will resume by 2003. **Registration:** Gatehouse, gates locked at 10 p.m. **Fee:** $18 for up to 12 people. **Parking:** At sites, 4 vehicle limit, $3 per extra vehicle, overflow parking available.

Facilities

Number of RV Sites: 0. **Number of Tent-Only Sites:** 0**Number of Multipurpose Sites:** 49. **Hookups:** Water, electric (50 amps). **Each Site:** Picnic table, grill, fire ring, utility table, lantern holder. **Dump Station:** Yes. **Laundry:** Yes. **Pay Phone:** Yes. **Rest Rooms and Showers:** Yes. **Fuel:** No. **Propane:** No. **Internal Roads:** Most Paved. **RV Service:** 20 mi. south in Augusta. **Market:** 20 mi. south in Augusta. **Restaurant:** 15 mi. north in McCormick. **General Store:** 1 mi. in Modoc. **Vending:** No. **Swimming Pool:** No. **Playground:** Yes. **Other:** Boat ramp. **Activities:** Hiking trail, beach, swimming, boating, fishing. **Nearby Attractions:** Thurmond Visitor Information Center & Dam; Golf & Gardens in Augusta, Woodrow Wilson's childhood home, Lucy Craft Laney Museum of Black History. **Additional Information:** Augusta Metropolitan CVB, (800) 726-0243.

Restrictions

Pets: Leash. **Fires:** In grills or rings in sites only. **Alcoholic Beverages:** Not allowed. **Vehicle Maximum Length:** 40 ft. **Other:** 14-day stay limit in 30-day period.

To Get There

From I-20, take Georgia Exit 200 (River Watch Pkwy.), then drive west for 2 mi. to Furys Ferry Rd. (Hwy. 28 West). Turn right and drive north for 13 mi. to Clarks Hill, SC. Continue northwest on Hwy. 221 for 4 miles. The campground entrance is on the left.

MOUNTAIN REST

Oconee State Park

624 State Park Rd., Mountain Rest 29664. T: (864) 638-5353; F: (864) 638-8776; www.southcarolinaparks.com; oconee_sp@prt.state.sc.us.

★★★★ ▲ ★★★★

Beauty: ★★★★★ Site Privacy: ★★★★
Spaciousness: ★★★★ Quiet: ★★★★★
Security: ★★★★ Cleanliness: ★★★★
Insect Control: ★★★★ Facilities: ★★★★

Oconee State Park offers large, gorgeous sites in one of the most beautifully forested campgrounds we've seen. Various oak and pine species provide shade and some privacy. A few sites have paved parking and the rest are gravel. There are pull-through and back-in campsites. Our favorite sites are 30, 31, 32, 34 and 36—totally fabulous wooded sites with pull-through, gravel parking and lovely views of the small lake. Other recommendations are 66 and 78. Unfortunately, the bathhouses were grimy during our visit. This remote, peaceful park is cherished by nature lovers. Seeking adventure? Raft the nearby Chattooga National Wild and Scenic River. In season, the gate is attended during the day and locked at night, making security good This off-the-beaten-path park is a good destination on all but the busiest summer weekends. With an elevation of 1,700 feet, the park is usually a few degrees cooler than the South Carolina Piedmont region.

Basics

Operated By: South Carolina State Parks. **Open:** All year. **Site Assignment:** 125 sites first come, first served; 30 sites available for reservation, 24 hours to 11 months in advance, deposit w/ check 10 days in advance, V or MC within 10 days; $15 cancellation fee. **Registration:** Trading post, park office off-season. **Fee:** $17 water & electric, $9 primitive tent & South Carolina seniors & disabled. **Parking:** At sites except tent sites (walk-in).

Facilities

Number of RV Sites: 0. **Number of Tent-Only Sites:** 15 walk-in sites. **Number of Multipurpose Sites:** 140. **Hookups:** Water, electric (30 amps). **Each Site:** Picnic table; walk-in sites have picnic table, grill, fire ring, lantern stand & tent pad. **Dump Station:** Yes. **Laundry:** Yes. **Pay Phone:** Yes. **Rest Rooms and Showers:** Yes. **Fuel:** No. **Propane:** No. **Internal Roads:** some Paved, some gravel. **RV Service:** 30 mi. south in Clemson. **Market:** 15 mi. south in West Union. **Restaurant:** 4 mi. west in Mountain Rest. **General Store:** 4 mi. west in Mountain Rest, Wal-Mart & K-mart 22 mi. south in Seneca. **Vending:** Beverages only. **Swimming Pool:** No. **Playground:** Yes. **Other:** Civilian Conservation Corps Museum, park store in-season, picnic shelters, multi-purpose recreation building, meeting room. **Activities:** Fishing, boating, canoe & fishing boat rentals (check w/ park about bringing your own boat), swimming & paddle boat rentals when lifeguard is present, nature trails, mini-golf, archery range. **Nearby Attractions:** Chattooga National Wildlife & Scenic River, Oconee Station state Historic Site, Cherry Hill National Forest, Devil's Fork State Park, Foothills Trail, Stumphouse Tunnel, golf courses. **Additional Information:** Greater Walhalla Area Chamber of Commerce, (864) 638-2727.

Restrictions

Pets: 6 ft. leash only. **Fires:** In designated areas only. **Alcoholic Beverages:** Not allowed. **Vehicle Maximum Length:** 35 ft.

To Get There

From I-85, take Exit 1 and drive 23 mi. north on Hwy. 11. At Hwy. 28, turn left and head west for 10 mi. At the fork at Hwy. 107, bear right and drive 2 mi. The park is on the right.

MURRELLS INLET

Huntington Beach State Park

16148 Ocean Hwy., Murrells Inlet 29576. T: (843) 237-4440; F: (843) 237-3387; www.southcarolinaparks.com; huntington_beach_sp@scprt.com.

RV ★★★★ Tent ★★★★

Beauty: ★★★★	Site Privacy: ★★★★
Spaciousness: ★★★★	Quiet: ★★★
Security: ★★★★★	Cleanliness: ★★★★
Insect Control: ★★★	Facilities: ★★★

Though Huntington Beach is more remote than Myrtle Beach State Park, it's almost as popular, with numerous activities and a pristine beach. Wildlife enthusiasts may see American alligators or loggerhead sea turtles. Bird lovers can spot many species of waterfowl, wading birds, or raptors (including bald eagles). Interpretive programs enrich the experience of low-country ecosystems. Also here is "Atalaya," the 1931 Mediterranean Moorish-style home of the Huntington family. Per Murphy's Law, the nicest campsites are the farthest from the beach. Sites 134–186 are closest to the beach and the least attractive. Walk further to the beach and choose sites 104–130. These are larger, more private and shadier than the rest of the campground and their bath house is brand new. Sites have gravel parking and most are back-in. Size varies. Gated and guarded, security at Huntington Beach is excellent. Avoid this park on summer weekends, when its popularity becomes its downfall.

Basics

Operated By: South Carolina State Parks. **Open:** All year. **Site Assignment:** First come, first served; reservations accepted for a 2-night min., w/ full deposit 2 weeks prior to reservation, $15 cancellation charge. **Registration:** Camp store, ranger on duty 24-hours. **Fee:** $28 w/ reservation for sites w/ sewer, $25 w/ reservation for sites without sewer, $27 without reservation for sites w/ sewer, $24 without reservation or sewer, $12 for all tent sites, fees include 6 people. **Parking:** Site plus overflow parking.

Facilities

Number of RV Sites: 133. **Number of Tent-Only Sites:** 6. **Number of Multipurpose Sites:** 133 (RV). **Hookups:** Water, electric (20, 30 amps), 24 sites w/ sewer. **Each Site:** Picnic table, fire ring. **Dump Station:** Yes. **Laundry:** No. **Pay Phone:** Yes. **Rest Rooms and Showers:** Yes. **Fuel:** No. **Propane:** No. **Internal Roads:** Gravel in campground, park is paved. **RV Service:** 25 mi. north in Conway. **Market:** Grocery 3 mi. north or south in Murrells Inlet, Wal-Mart 10 mi. north in Surfside. **Restaurant:** 3 mi. north or south in Murrells Inlet. **General Store:** Camp store. **Vending:** No. **Swimming Pool:** No. **Playground:** No. **Other:** Recreation room, picnic shelters. **Activities:** Beach, swimming, fishing, kayaking, canoeing, hiking trails, coastal exploration program, Atalaya Castle. **Nearby Attractions:** Water Park, Myrtle Beach, Hampton Plantation State Historic Site, Brookgreen Gardens, Pawley's Island. **Additional Information:** Myrtle Beach Area Chamber of Commerce, (843) 626-7444.

Restrictions

Pets: Leash only. **Fires:** Fire ring only. **Alcoholic Beverages:** Not allowed. **Vehicle Maximum Length:** 50 ft. **Other:** 2 weeks max. stay.

To Get There

From Georgetown, take Hwy. 17 north for 20 miles. The park entrance is on the right. From Myrtle Beach, take Hwy. 17 south for 15 miles. The park entrance is on the left.

MYRTLE BEACH

Barefoot Camping Resort

4825 Hwy. 17 South, N. Myrtle Beach 29582.
T: (843) 272-1790; F: (843) 272-4208;
www.barefootrvresort.com.

RV ★★★ Tent ★

Beauty: ★★★	Site Privacy: ★★
Spaciousness: ★★★	Quiet: ★★★★
Security: ★★	Cleanliness: ★★★
Insect Control: ★★★★	Facilities: ★★★★

Barefoot Camping Resort leases most of its sites on a seasonal/residential basis. It's in the heart of the hustle and bustle of Myrtle Beach, convenient to dining, golf, and tourist attractions. You'll experience horrendous traffic if you visit on summer weekends. The campground is laid out in numerous rows of back-in sites, with a few sites near the beach. Sites have dirt, gravel, sand, and grass parking—it's quite a mess. Most sites are shady, though sites near the beach tend to be more open. RV campers should choose sites based on desired distance from the beach. Tent campers should avoid this place altogether—tent sites are wedged into a tight strip next to noisy 48th Ave. South. Security is good at this urban resort. Gates are locked at night.

Basics

Operated By: Barefoot Resort, Inc. **Open:** All year. **Site Assignment:** First come, first served, but reservations recommended. First nights deposit holds the reservation. Cancellation fee is $5 but if cancelled within 24 hrs. of expected arrival date then the fee is $5 plus the deposit. **Registration:** At camp office. **Fee:** In-Season $36–$40 per night for 4 people (cash, checks, V, MC) $2 extra for each adult up to 8. **Parking:** 2 cars per site.

Facilities

Number of RV Sites: 215. **Number of Tent-Only Sites:** 10. **Number of Multipurpose Sites:** 205. **Hookups:** Water, electricity (30, 50 amps), sewer, cable. **Each Site:** Picnic table. **Dump Station:** Yes. **Laundry:** Yes. **Pay Phone:** Yes. **Rest Rooms and Showers:** Yes. **Fuel:** No. **Propane:** Yes. **Internal Roads:** Paved. **RV Service:** On call. **Market:** 1.5 mi. south. **Restaurant:** Cracker Barrel on site. **General Store:** Camp store. **Vending:** Yes. **Swimming Pool:** Yes. **Playground:** Yes. **Other:** Arcade, Lazy River, fitness center, spa. **Activities:** Arcade games, boating, organized activities in-season. **Nearby Attractions:** Dixie Stampede, Alabama Theater, Barefoot Landing, House of Blues. **Additional Information:** North Myrtle Beach Office Chamber of Commerce, (843) 249-3519.

Restrictions

Pets: Leash only. **Fires:** No. **Alcoholic Beverages:** Allowed. **Vehicle Maximum Length:** 40 ft.

To Get There

From I-95, exit at Florence and take US Hwy. 501 east about 60 mi. to US Hwy. 22. Take US Hwy. 22 north, which merges with US Hwy. 17. The park is 1 mi. north of the intersection of 22 and 17, at 48th Ave. South. 7 mi. north of Myrtle Beach.

MYRTLE BEACH

Lakewood Camping Resort

5901 South Kings Hwy., Myrtle Beach 29575.
T: (877) LAKEWOOD; F: (843) 447-7350;
www.lakewoodcampground.com.

RV ★★★★ Tent ★★★

Beauty: ★★★★	Site Privacy: ★★
Spaciousness: ★★★	Quiet: ★★★
Security: ★★★★★	Cleanliness: ★★★★
Insect Control: ★★★	Facilities: ★★★★★

Gigantic Lakewood is similar to its Myrtle Beach competitors in that it has scads of identical campsites. Tidy and nicely landscaped, Lakewood was awarded National Association of RV Parks and Campgrounds "National RV Park of the Year 2000–2001." Extensive amenities cater to all ages. Choose open sites in the northeastern corner of the park or shadier sites in blocks 1, 2, and 3 south. A variety of trees, including oaks, pines, dogwood, pecan, and cedar provide shade. Parking is on grass, packed sand, or dirt. Laid out in rows with mostly back-in parking, sites are small and there is little privacy. For a quaint view, try sites 2801–2867 which line the small lakes. Families should request sites near the playground. There are restaurants and tourist attractions nearby. Excellent security includes a gated entrance and 24-hour security patrols. Avoid Myrtle Beach during spring break and summer holidays. For quiet, visit in March or October.

Basics

Operated By: Lakewood Camping Resort, Inc. **Open:** All year. **Site Assignment:** First come, first served, guests may request sites; reservations accepted 48 hours to one year in advance w/ deposit, checks accepted well in advance; in-season oceanfront 7-night min., other sites 4-night min.; 48-hour notice required for refund. **Registration:** Gatehouse, express check-in also available-inquire when making reservations. **Fee:** Peak season oceanfront & prime sites $41 (off-season $22–$31), other sites $36 (off-season $22–$27); prices for 5 people (cash, personal check, V, MC, D). **Parking:** 2 vehicles per site (charge for extras in-season).

Facilities

Number of Multipurpose Sites: 1,400. **Hookups:** Water, electric (30, 50 amps), sewer, cable. **Each Site:** Picnic table. **Dump Station:** Yes. **Laundry:** Yes. **Pay Phone:** Yes. **Rest Rooms and Showers:** Yes. **Fuel:** No. **Propane:** No. **Internal Roads:** Paved. **RV Service:** 1 mi. south in Myrtle Beach. **Market:** Camp store, supermarket 0.25 mi. **Restaurant:** 0.25 mi. in Myrtle Beach. **General Store:** Camp store, Wal-Mart 2 mi. south in Myrtle Beach. **Vending:** Yes. **Swimming Pool:** Yes. **Playground:** Yes. **Other:** Hot tub, RV storage, freshwater fishing, golf-cart rentals, convention services, non-denominational ministry, snack bar. **Activities:** Mini-golf, arcade, pedal boat, kayak, & bicycle rentals, shuffleboard, basketball, horseshoes, volleyball, amphitheater, live entertainment. **Nearby Attractions:** Myrtle Beach historic tours & gardens, Grand Strand, Barefoot Landing, House of Blues, Alabama Theater, Dixie Stampede, Intracoastal Waterway. **Additional Information:** Myrtle Beach Area Chamber of Commerce, (843) 626-7444.

Restrictions

Pets: Leash (6 ft. max.). **Fires:** Allowed. **Alcoholic Beverages:** Not allowed. **Vehicle Maximum Length:** 40 ft.

To Get There

From the intersection of Hwy. 501 and Hwy. 17, drive south on 17 approx. 5 miles. The entrance is on the left.

MYRTLE BEACH

Myrtle Beach State Park

4401 South Kings Hwy., Myrtle Beach 29575. T: (843) 238-5325; F: (843) 238-9483; www.southcarolinaparks.com.

RV ★★★★ Tent ★★★★

Beauty: ★★★★ Site Privacy: ★★★★
Spaciousness: ★★★★ Quiet: ★★★
Security: ★★★★★ Cleanliness: ★★★
Insect Control: ★★★ Facilities: ★★★

Myrtle Beach State Park maintains a massive campground with large shady sites laid out in a series of semi-circles. Sweet gum, hickory, longleaf pine, and various oak species provide plenty of shade and varying amounts of privacy. Parking is on packed coquina and pine straw. A few sites offer pull-through parking. For privacy and quiet, try Circle 6 (numbers 293–336). Want to be closer to the beach? Try 166–172; these quiet sites are on a dead-end road. With plenty of recreation, Myrtle Beach State Park is popular with locals and tourists. This makes for unbearable crowds on holiday and summer weekends. We urge you to visit in the "off season," preferably autumn to avoid spring-break crowds. This urban park is convenient to restaurants, world-class golf, and other tourist attractions. Security is excellent; the front gate is attended at all times and locked at night.

Basics

Operated By: South Carolina State Parks. **Open:** All year. **Site Assignment:** First come, first served; 40 sites available for reservation 24 hours to 11 months in advance, full deposit required, $15 cancellation fee, must cancel before arrival date. **Registration:** Trading post. **Fee:** $26 w/ reservation, $25 without reservation, $20 for overflow tent sites; South Carolina seniors & disabled 50% discount (cash, personal check, V, MC). **Parking:** At sites.

Facilities

Number of RV Sites: 0. **Number of Tent-Only Sites:** 45 overflow. **Number of Multipurpose Sites:** 302. **Hookups:** Water, electric (50 amps). **Each Site:** Picnic table. **Dump Station:** Yes. **Laundry:** Yes. **Pay Phone:** Yes. **Rest Rooms and Showers:** Yes. **Fuel:** No. **Propane:** No. **Internal Roads:** Park Paved, campground packed coquina. **RV Service:** 0.25 mi. **Market:** 0.25 mi. **Restaurant:** 0.5 mi. **General Store:** 10 mi. south in Surfside (Wal-Mart). **Vending:** Yes. **Swimming Pool:** No. **Playground:** Yes. **Other:** Fishing pier, boardwalks to beach, snack bar, gift shop, picnic shelters, amphitheater, activity center. **Activities:** Nature center, nature trail, fishing. **Nearby Attractions:** Myrtle Beach historic tours & gardens, Grand Strand, Barefoot Landing, House of Blues, Alabama Theater, Dixie Stampede, Intracoastal Waterway. **Additional Information:** Myrtle Beach Area Chamber of Commerce, (843) 626-7444.

Restrictions

Pets: Leash. **Fires:** Allowed. **Alcoholic Beverages:** Not allowed. **Vehicle Maximum Length:** 50 ft.

To Get There

From the junction of Hwy. 501 and Hwy. 17, go south for 5 miles. The park is on the left.

MYRTLE BEACH

Myrtle Beach Travel Park

10108 Kings Rd., Myrtle Beach 29572. T: (800) 255-3568 or (843) 449-3714; F: (843) 497-8521; www.myrtlebeachtravelpark.com.

RV ★★★★ Tent ★★★★

Beauty: ★★★★ Site Privacy: ★★
Spaciousness: ★★★ Quiet: ★★★
Security: ★★★★★ Cleanliness: ★★★★
Insect Control: ★★★ Facilities: ★★★★★

This park and its competitors offer frighteningly similar campsites. Resolution between parks is found in activities and amenities offered. This one offers a 17-acre freshwater fishing lake. Most nightly and weekly sites lie between the lake and the ocean. Oceanside sites form 25 identical rows of pull-throughs and 3 identical rows of back-ins. Each treeless site has a covered picnic table. Sites are small and there is no privacy. Parking is on patchy grass and sand. Nicer sites enjoy views of dunes and sea grasses. The shady, nicely landscaped, back-in sites on the other side of the lake are the prettiest. Sites 700–709 and 576–588 are delightful, with pleasant views of the fishing lake.

Basics

Operated By: Myrtle Beach Travel Park. **Open:** All year. **Site Assignment:** Reservations recommended, w/ $50 deposit, 14 days in advance, 7 night min. Jun. 6–Aug. 15, off-season min. 3 nights, 7 day cancellation notice required for refund. **Registration:** Office. **Fee:** $21–42 for 4 people, $3 per extra person up to 8 total (prices vary seasonally; cash, personal check, V, MC, AE). **Parking:** 1 vehicle per site, $2/day per extra vehicle.

Facilities

Number of RV Sites: 0. **Number of Tent-Only Sites:** 10–15 (tents or pop-ups, water & electric only). **Number of Multipurpose Sites:** 650. **Hookups:** Water, electric (30, 50 amps), sewer, cable. **Each Site:** Picnic table. **Dump Station:** Yes. **Laundry:** Yes. **Pay Phone:** Yes. **Rest Rooms and Showers:** Yes. **Fuel:** No. **Propane:** Yes. **Internal Roads:** Most Paved, some coquina or gravel. **RV Service:** On site. **Market:** 2 mi. in Myrtle Beach. **Restaurant:** On site. **General Store:** On site. **Vending:** Yes. **Swimming Pool:** Yes. **Playground:** Yes. **Other:** Pavilion, recreation room, chapel, RV storage. **Activities:** Freshwater lake, beach front, arcade, paddle boat rental, activities director. **Nearby Attractions:** Myrtle Beach historic plantations, tours, Intracoastal Waterway, amusement parks, Grand Strand, Brookgreen Gardens. **Additional Information:** Myrtle Beach Area Chamber of Commerce, (843) 626-7444.

Restrictions

Pets: Leash only. **Fires:** Allowed. **Alcoholic Beverages:** At site only. **Vehicle Maximum Length:** No limit. **Other:** No fireworks.

To Get There

From the intersection of US Hwy. 501 and US Hwy. 17, drive north on US 17 approx. 5 miles to Kings Rd. Turn right and the entrance is on the left.

MYRTLE BEACH

Ocean Lakes Family Campground

6001 South Kings Hwy., Myrtle Beach 29575. T: (800) 722-1451 or (843) 238-5636; F: (843) 238-1890; www.oceanlakes.com; camping@oceanlakes.com.

RV ★★★★ Tent ★★★

Beauty: ★★★★ Site Privacy: ★★
Spaciousness: ★★★ Quiet: ★★
Security: ★★★★★ Cleanliness: ★★★★
Insect Control: ★★★ Facilities: ★★★★★

Like its competitor (Lakewood Camping Resort), Ocean Lakes has received the "National RV Park of the Year Award" from the National Association of RV Parks and Campgrounds. Campsites are pull-throughs and parking is on grass. Sites are small. Most are completely treeless, so there is no privacy between sites. Short-term sites are laid out in tidy rows on the northeast corner of the park. If you're traveling with children, we recommend a site in the HH area, which is between the pool and the beach. Otherwise choose your site according to proximity to the beach. Ocean Lakes is convenient to all Myrtle Beach attractions, restaurants and shopping. Security is excellent at this urban resort, which is gated and has 24-hour security patrols. Visits during spring break and summer holidays should be avoided completely. If you would like a little peace and quiet visit in March or October.

Basics

Operated By: Jackson Family. **Open:** All year. **Site Assignment:** Reservations recommended spring, summer, & fall (by site number), 4-night min. Jun. 15–Aug. 15, $50 deposit; 7-day cancellation notice for refund, $10 cancellation fee. **Registration:** Main gate staffed 24 hours, express check-in available—inquire when making reservations. **Fee:** Peak season rates (Memorial Day–Labor Day) ocean front $44.50 (off season $22.50–$30), 3000 section

$43.50 (off-season $21.50–$29), 4000 section $42.50 (off-season $20.50–$28); prices for 6 people, subject to 2002 increase (cash, personal check, V, MC, D). **Parking:** 2 cars per site, overflow parking available, $3 per extra car.

Facilities

Number of RV Sites: 0. **Number of Tent-Only Sites:** 2. **Number of Multipurpose Sites:** 893. **Hookups:** Water, electric (20, 30, 50 amps), sewer, cable, modem, friendly phone line (free local calls). **Each Site:** Picnic table. **Dump Station:** No. **Laundry:** Yes. **Pay Phone:** Yes. **Rest Rooms and Showers:** Yes. **Fuel:** No. **Propane:** Yes. **Internal Roads:** Paved. **RV Service:** On site. **Market:** 0.25 mi. **Restaurant:** 1 mi. **General Store:** Camp store. **Vending:** Yes. **Swimming Pool:** Yes. **Playground:** Yes. **Other:** Sailboat launch, snack bars, awning sales, golf cart, & automobile rental. **Activities:** Recreation center (full-time staff, year-round), marine life nature center, observation deck, arcade, bank fishing, freshwater lake fishing, mini-golf, golf car & bicycle rentals, basketball, volleyball, shuffleboard, horseshoes, bocci ball, weekly nondenominational church services, special event weekends, live entertainment (ask for schedules). **Nearby Attractions:** Myrtle Beach historic tours & gardens, Grand Strand, Barefoot Landing, House of Blues, Alabama Theater, Dixie Stampede, Intracoastal Waterway. **Additional Information:** Myrtle Beach Area Chamber of Commerce, (843) 626-7444.

Restrictions

Pets: Leash, clean-up enforced, no vicious breeds. **Fires:** Allowed (not encouraged). **Alcoholic Beverages:** At site only. **Vehicle Maximum Length:** 45 ft.

To Get There

From US Hwy. 501, take Hwy. 544 south until it ends at the coast at Ocean Lakes. The park is 1 mile north of Surfside Beach and 3 mi. south of downtown Myrtle Beach on South Kings Hwy. (17).

NINETY-SIX

Lake Greenwood State Recreation Area

302 State Park Rd., Ninety-Six 29666. T: (864) 543-3535; F: (864) 543-3535; www.southcarolinaparks.com; lake_greenwood_sp@prt.state.sc.us.

RV ★★★★ Tent ★★★★

Beauty: ★★★★★ Site Privacy: ★★★
Spaciousness: ★★★★ Quiet: ★★★
Security: ★★★★★ Cleanliness: ★★★★
Insect Control: ★★★★ Facilities: ★★★

The lovely campground at Lake Greenwood occupies gently rolling hills with pine straw ground cover. With shadier, prettier sites, campground No. 1 is preferable to campground No. 2. Sites are mostly back-ins with a few pull-throughs. Many have views of Lake Greenwood. Sites are spacious and all parking is paved. Though many sites are shaded by trees, privacy is poor as there is little foliage between sites. Lake Greenwood is stocked with bass, crappie, bream, perch, catfish, and stripers. Visit nearby Greenwood Museum, two-time recipient of "South Carolina Tourist Attraction of the Year" award, or the Ninety-Six National Historical site, which includes ruins of a British Fort used in the American Revolution. Security is excellent at this rural, gated, and guarded state park. This park is extremely popular and should be studiously avoided on summer holidays and weekends. Visit mid-week, in spring or fall.

Basics

Operated By: South Carolina State Parks. **Open:** All year. **Site Assignment:** Some first come, first served; some sites available for reservation w/ 2 night min., full deposit, 24-hour notice for refund, $15 cancellation fee. **Registration:** Park store, rangers make rounds, late comers register the next morning. **Fee:** $19 for waterfront sites, $18 for non-waterfront sites, fees include 6 people, South Carolina seniors & disabled pay 50%. **Parking:** 2 vehicles per site, overflow parking available.

Facilities

Number of RV Sites: 0. **Number of Tent-Only Sites:** 5 (plus primitive group camping). **Number of Multipurpose Sites:** 125. **Hookups:** Water, electric (50 amps). **Each Site:** Picnic table, fire pit. **Dump Station:** Yes. **Laundry:** No. **Pay Phone:** Yes. **Rest Rooms and Showers:** Yes. **Fuel:** No. **Propane:** No. **Internal Roads:** Paved. **RV Service:** On call. **Market:** 5 mi. west in Ninety-Six. **Restaurant:** 5 mi. west toward Greenwood. **General Store:** 1 mi. (also seasonal park store/ tackle shop). **Vending:** No. **Swimming Pool:** No. **Playground:** No. **Other:** Boat ramps, picnic shelters, recreation building, BBQ shelter. **Activities:** Nature trails, fishing wall, boating, swimming, water sports. **Nearby Attractions:** Ninety-Six historic sites, historic Abbeville, Festival of Flowers. **Additional Information:** Greenwood Chamber of Commerce, (864) 223-8431.

Restrictions

Pets: Leash. **Fires:** Allowed. **Alcoholic Beverages:** Not allowed. **Vehicle Maximum Length:** 45 ft. **Other:** 14 day max. stay in same site, swim at your own risk.

To Get There

From I-26, take Exit 74 and go west on SC Hwy. 34 for 20 miles. Turn right on SC Hwy. 702 and go north for 1 mile. The park is on the right.

PICKENS

Table Rock State Park

158 E. Ellison Ln., Pickens 20671. T: (864) 878-9813; F: (864) 878-9077; www.southcarolinaparks.com; table_rock_sp@prt.state.sc.us.

RV ★★★★ Tent ★★★★

Beauty: ★★★★ Site Privacy: ★★★
Spaciousness: ★★★ Quiet: ★★★★
Security: ★★★★ Cleanliness: ★★★★
Insect Control: ★★ Facilities: ★★★★

Nature lovers enjoy Table Rock and nearby Mountain Bridge Wilderness Area, which includes Caesar's Head State Park and Jones Gap State Park. Caesar's Head boasts dramatic granite cliffs while Jones Gap offers cool valley trails along the Middle Saluda River. A flat granite mountain serves as Table Rock's centerpiece and namesake. The campground includes two loops with mostly back-in parking. Beauty and privacy vary. The nicest section includes sites 25–40 and is heavily wooded. The park does not recommend this area for RVs. But parking spaces are level. If you have a small camper, give them a try. Sites are large, but there is little space between them. All parking is on gravel. Remote and gated, this park has excellent security. Elevations in this area range from 2,000 to 3,500 feet, so summer weather is mild. Visit in spring for solitude or in autumn for beautiful colors.

Basics

Operated By: South Carolina State Parks. **Open:** All year. **Site Assignment:** First come, first served; 25 sites available for reservation, full payment required within 10 days of reservation; 24-hour cancellation notice for 50% refund. **Registration:** Camp store or park office. **Fee:** $16 includes 6 people (cash, personal check, V, MC). **Parking:** At site, 2 vehicles max.

Facilities

Number of Multipurpose Sites: 100. **Hookups:** Electric (20, 30 amps), water. **Each Site:** Grill, picnic table, fire ring. **Dump Station:** Yes. **Laundry:** Yes. **Pay Phone:** Yes. **Rest Rooms and Showers:** Yes. **Fuel:** No. **Propane:** No. **Internal Roads:** Paved. **RV Service:** 40 mi. west in Greenville. **Market:** 10 mi. south in Pickens. **Restaurant:** On site. **General Store:** 1 mi. **Vending:** No. **Swimming Pool:** Yes. **Playground:** No. **Other:** Boat ramp, fishing pier, park store, meeting facilities, recreation center. **Activities:** Mini-golf, paddle boat, canoe & kayak rentals, nature center, year-round nature programs, hiking trails, fishing, swimming. **Nearby Attractions:** World of Energy at Lake Keowee, Issaqueena & Whitewater Falls, Foothills Trail, Sassafras Mountain. **Additional Information:** Cherokee Foothills Visitors Center/Table Rock State Park Headquarters (864) 878-9813, Pickens Chamber of Commerce (864) 878-3258.

Restrictions

Pets: Leash only. **Fires:** Allowed. **Alcoholic Beverages:** Not allowed. **Vehicle Maximum Length:** 36 ft.

To Get There

From Pickens, take Hwy. 178 north for 9 miles. Turn right and drive east on Hwy. 11 for 5 miles. The park is on the left.

PLUM BRANCH

Hamilton Branch State Park, J. Strom Thurmond Reservoir

Route 1 P.O. Box 97, Plum Branch 29845. T: (864) 333-2223; F: (864) 333-2223; www.southcarolinaparks.com; hamilton_branch_sp@scprt.com.

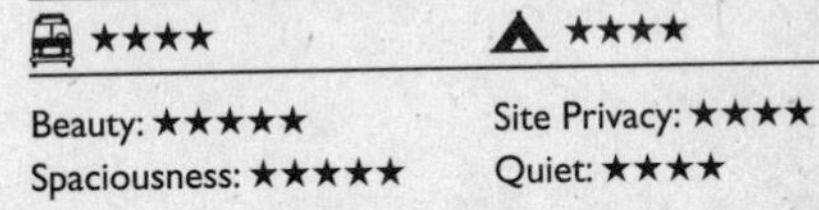

RV ★★★★ Tent ★★★★

Beauty: ★★★★★ Site Privacy: ★★★★
Spaciousness: ★★★★★ Quiet: ★★★★

Security: ★★★ Cleanliness: ★★★★
Insect Control: ★★★ Facilities: ★★★

Hamilton Branch is gorgeous. Flatter than others along the Savannah River, this campground features large sites. Loblolly pine and other species provide shade, though there is not much foliage surrounding the sites. With most sites on the waterfront, choosing the prettiest is tough. We recommend 36–54 and 71–78 for privacy and the nicest views. Most sites are laid out in pairs. Parking is on gravel or packed soil. Ten sites offer pull-through parking. Dock your boat at your campsite when lake levels permit. J. Strom Thurmond is one of the largest lakes in the southeast and is known for bream, crappie, striper, various bass, and catfish. Hamilton Branch doesn't offer many day-use activities, so explore outside the park. Remote, with gates locked at night, security is good at Hamilton Branch. This popular campground is likely to fill up on summer weekends. Plan a visit in the spring or during the week.

Basics

Operated By: South Carolina State Parks. **Open:** All year. **Site Assignment:** First come, first served; reservations accepted w/ credit card deposit, cancel anytime w/ $15 cancellation fee. **Registration:** In-season at office, off-season at sites. **Fee:** $16 ($17 w/ reservation), $8 disabled & Golden Age discount. **Parking:** At sites.

Facilities

Number of RV Sites: 0. **Number of Tent-Only Sites:** 50 (water only). **Number of Multipurpose Sites:** 130. **Hookups:** Water, electric (20, 30, 50 amps). **Each Site:** Picnic table, tent pad, fire ring (some sites), grill (some sites). **Dump Station:** Yes. **Laundry:** No. **Pay Phone:** Yes. **Rest Rooms and Showers:** Yes. **Fuel:** No. **Propane:** No. **Internal Roads:** Paved (most). **RV Service:** 30 mi. south in Augusta. **Market:** 12 mi. north in McCormick. **Restaurant:** 12 mi. north in McCormick. **General Store:** 2 mi. outside park, Wal-Mart 30 mi. south in Augusta. **Vending:** Beverages only. **Swimming Pool:** No. **Playground:** Yes. **Other:** Boat ramps, picnic shelters. **Activities:** Fishing on J. Strom Thurmond Lake, water sports. **Nearby Attractions:** Historic McCormick, Antebellum homes & museums in Edgefield, Parkseed Company & Gardens in Greenwood, 30 mi. to Augusta, Georgia. **Additional Information:** McCormick Chamber of Commerce, (864) 465-2835, Augusta Chamber of Commerce, (706) 821-1300.

Restrictions

Pets: Leash (6 ft. max.). **Fires:** Allowed. **Alcoholic Beverages:** Allowed. **Vehicle Maximum Length:** 40 ft.

To Get There

From I-20, take Georgia Exit 200 (River Watch Pkwy.), then drive west for 2 mi. to Furys Ferry Rd. (Hwy. 28 West). Turn right and drive north for 13 mi. to Clarks Hill, SC. Continue north on Hwy. 28 for 12 more mi. The park entrance is on the left.

SANTEE

Santee State Park

251 State Park Rd., Santee 29142. T: (803) 854-2408; www.southcarolinaparks.com; santee_sp@prt.state.sc.us.

RV ★★★★ Tent ★★★★

Beauty: ★★★★★ Site Privacy: ★★★
Spaciousness: ★★★ Quiet: ★★★
Security: ★★★ Cleanliness: ★★★★
Insect Control: ★★★★ Facilities: ★★★★

On Lake Marion, Santee is popular with anglers. Cypress trees and other tree stumps on the lake create a rich habitat for fish. The lake is known for its striped bass, an ocean bass which was trapped during dam construction and has since adapted to freshwater. Two delightful campgrounds offer lakefront sites. Small, quiet "Cypress View" features shady pull-through and back-in sites. "Lakeshore" features rows of mainly back-in sites. Close to the water and shaded by hickory and oak laden with Spanish moss, sites 94, 96, and 98 are especially beautiful. Site size is ample, but there is little privacy between sites. Parking is on sand, dirt, and pine straw. Despite the park's laid-back atmosphere, it's only two miles from I-95. Security is not adequate here. Gates are not attended or locked at night. This extremely popular campground stays busy. We recommend mid-week or off-season touring.

Basics

Operated By: South Carolina State Parks. **Open:** All year. **Site Assignment:** Mostly first come, first served; limited sites available for reservation for $1 extra, full deposit required within 14 days of reservation; 24-hour notice for refund, $15 cancellation fee. **Registration:** Visitor Center, after-hours registration available. **Fee:** $16 includes 6 people (cash, personal checks, V, MC). **Parking:** 2 vehicles per site, overflow parking available.

Facilities

Number of Multipurpose Sites: 163. **Hookups:** Water, electric (20, 30 amps). **Each Site:** Picnic table. **Dump Station:** Yes. **Laundry:** Yes. **Pay Phone:** Yes. **Rest Rooms and Showers:** Yes. **Fuel:** No. **Propane:** No. **Internal Roads:** Gravel. **RV Service:** On call. **Market:** 4 mi. south in Santee. **Restaurant:** 4 mi. south in Santee. **General Store:** Camp store. **Vending:** Beverages only. **Swimming Pool:** No. **Playground:** Yes. **Other:** Visitor's center, boat ramps, picnic shelters, meeting building. **Activities:** Nature & bicycle trails, fishing pier, seasonal swimming & paddle boat rentals when lifeguard on duty, tennis, nature boat tours. **Nearby Attractions:** Palmetto Trailhead, 3 golf courses, Lake Marion, Santee community, Lonestar Mercantile historic village & restaurant, one hour from Charleston & Columbia. **Additional Information:** Santee Cooper Country, (803) 854-2152, ext. 5; www.santeetourism.com.

Restrictions

Pets: Leash only. **Fires:** Allowed. **Alcoholic Beverages:** Not allowed. **Vehicle Maximum Length:** 45 ft. **Other:** 14-day max. stay.

To Get There

From I-95, take Exit 98 at Santee. Drive northwest on Hwy. 6 for about 1 mi. Turn right onto State Park Rd. The campground is 2 mi. ahead.

SPARTANBURG

Cunningham RV Park

600 Campground Rd., Spartanburg 29306. T: (864) 576-1973; F: (864) 576-1973;.

RV ★★★ Tent ★★

Beauty: ★★★ Site Privacy: ★★
Spaciousness: ★★ Quiet: ★★★★
Security: ★★ Cleanliness: ★★★★
Insect Control: ★★★★ Facilities: ★★

The campground at Cunningham RV Park is laid out in a grid, with eight rows of pull-through sites. Twelve back-in sites line the eastern perimeter of the property. About half of the sites have a shade tree. Otherwise, the sites are all the same. Choose your site based on tree preference and proximity to facilities. Parking is on grass and all sites are completely level; this park is as flat as Kansas. Sites are small and there is no privacy between sites. Cunningham's playground is fabulous, and potties are super-tidy and spacious. Two miles from the intersections of I-85 and I-26 in urban Spartanburg, Cunningham is convenient to shopping and restaurants. Security is not great here, as the park is in a developed area and has no gates. Cunningham is a convenient stop-over rather than a vacation destination. Avoid stopping here on summer holidays.

Basics

Operated By: The Cunningham Family. **Open:** All year. **Site Assignment:** First come, first served; reservations accepted up to 72 hours in advance, no deposit required. **Registration:** Camp store, self-registration after hours. **Fee:** $23 for 2 people; $2 extra for 50 amps or sewage hookup; $4 for additional adults, $2 for additional children. **Parking:** At sites, overflow parking available.

Facilities

Number of RV Sites: 0. **Number of Tent-Only Sites: Number of Tent-Only Sites:**20. **Number of Multipurpose Sites:** 69. **Hookups:** Water, electric (30, 50 amps), some sewer. **Each Site:** Picnic table, fire rings in tent sites only. **Dump Station:** Yes. **Laundry:** Yes. **Pay Phone:** Yes. **Rest Rooms and Showers:** Yes. **Fuel:** No. **Propane:** Yes. **Internal Roads:** Gravel. **RV Service:** Within 4 mi. **Market:** Grocery 3 mi. south in Spartanburg, Wal-Mart 4 mi. south in Spartanburg. **Restaurant:** 1 mi. south in Spartanburg. **General Store:** Camp store, Wal-Mart 4 mi. south in Spartanburg. **Vending:** Beverage only. **Swimming Pool:** Yes. **Playground:** Yes. **Other:** Pool table, foosball. **Activities:** Volleyball, horseshoes, nature area. **Nearby Attractions:** Foothills Trail System, historic homes & plantations, BMW plant tours, Holly Wild Animal Park, Cow Pens National Battlefield. **Additional Information:** Spartanburg CVB, (800) 374-8326.

RESTRICTIONS

Pets: Leash only. **Fires:** Fire rings at tent sites; RV campers bring your own grill. **Alcoholic Beverages:** Allowed. **Vehicle Maximum Length:** No limit.

TO GET THERE

From I-85, take Exit 70 at Spartanburg, then I-26 west 2.5 mi. to Exit 17. Head west on Hwy. 40, then left on Campground Rd. about 1 mi. to the RV park.

SUMMERTON

Santee Lakes Campground

Route 2 Box 542, Summerton 29148. T: (803) 478-2262; F: (803) 478-7197.

RV ★★★ Tent ★★★

Beauty: ★★★★ Site Privacy: ★★
Spaciousness: ★★ Quiet: ★★★
Security: ★★★★ Cleanliness: ★★★★
Insect Control: ★ Facilities: ★★★

Santee Lakes is a good alternative to Santee State Park when the latter is full. Many of the attractive sites at Santee Lakes have views of adjacent Lake Marion, and most are nicely shaded by lovely mature trees. Sites are laid out in 11 tidy rows. All but 15 sites offer pull-through parking and are deliciously shady. pull-through sites situated closest to the beach have the nicest views of the water. Site size is on the small side of average with little privacy between sites. Santee Lakes is in a touristy area, so there are plenty of nearby restaurants and shops. Security is good; the entrance is guarded during the day and the park is patrolled at night. Lake Marion is extremely popular with fisher folk, so this park stays busy. Try to visit during the week or in spring or fall.

BASICS

Operated By: The Zeiglers. **Open:** All year. **Site Assignment:** First come, first served; reservations recommended (especially holiday weekends), $25 deposit, one week cancellation notice for refund. **Registration:** Camp store, late comers self-register. **Fee:** $23 full hookup, $21 water & electric, $19 tent; fees include 2 adults, $3 per extra person (cash, personal checks, V, MC). **Parking:** 2 vehicles per site, overflow parking available.

FACILITIES

Number of Multipurpose Sites: 170. **Hookups:** Water, electric (30 amps), some sites also w/ sewer & cable. **Each Site:** Picnic tables. **Dump Station:** Yes. **Laundry:** Yes. **Pay Phone:** Yes. **Rest Rooms and Showers:** Yes. **Fuel:** No. **Propane:** No. **Internal Roads:** Dirt. **RV Service:** On call. **Market:** 4 mi. south in Santee. **Restaurant:** 0.5 mi. **General Store:** Camp store. **Vending:** Beverages only. **Swimming Pool:** Yes. **Playground:** Yes. **Other:** Boat ramp, RV storage, recreation building. **Activities:** Beach in-season, game room, swimming, mini-golf, fishing pier, hot tub. **Nearby Attractions:** Santee National Wildlife Refuge, 3 golf courses, Palmetto Trailhead, Lake Marion, Santee community, one hour from Charleston & Columbia. **Additional Information:** Santee Cooper Country Tourism Information, (803) 854-2152, ext. 5; www.santee-tourism.com.

RESTRICTIONS

Pets: Leash. **Fires:** Allowed. **Alcoholic Beverages:** Allowed. **Vehicle Maximum Length:** No limit.

TO GET THERE

From I-95, take Exit 102. Drive east on CR 400 for 0.25 miles, then turn right at the stop sign. The campground is on the left.

WINNSBORO

Lake Wateree State Recreation Area

881 State Park Rd., Winnsboro 29180. T: (803) 482-6401; F: (803) 482-6126; www.southcarolina-parks.com; lake_wateree_sp@prt.state.sc.us.

RV ★★★★ Tent ★★★★

Beauty: ★★★★★ Site Privacy: ★★★★★
Spaciousness: ★★★★ Quiet: ★★★★★
Security: ★★★★★ Cleanliness: ★★★★
Insect Control: ★★★★ Facilities: ★★★

This small state park is situated on 13,700-acre Lake Wateree, one of South Carolina's oldest and best-loved fishing lakes. Waterfowl at Lake Wateree include egrets, blue heron, mallards, and wood ducks. Here, recreation revolves around boating and fishing—there isn't even a swimming beach. But, the lake and the campground are breathtakingly gorgeous. The campground consists of one loop of paved sites. Of these, five offer pull-through parking and the remainder offer back-in parking. Site size varies from average to huge. Tree cover, consisting mainly of pine, is lovely and includes plenty of foliage to provide privacy between sites. Lakefront sites (odd numbers 11–27) and heavily wooded sites in the 50s and 60s are all gorgeous. Security is excellent at this rural state park, as gates are locked at night. For maximum peace and quiet, visit this very pretty little park on weekdays or in the spring or fall.

BASICS

Operated By: South Carolina State Parks. **Open:** All year except Christmas. **Site Assignment:** First come, first served; 36 sites available for reservations for $1 extra, 24 hours in advance, full deposit within 10 days of reservation; 24 hour cancellation notice for refund. **Registration:** Park store, late comers must have combination to open gate. **Fee:** $18 for waterfront sites (plus $1 w/ reservation), $17 for sites across from water, $16 for all other sites. **Parking:** All wheels on pavement, overflow parking available.

FACILITIES

Number of RV Sites: 72. **Number of Tent-Only Sites:** 0. **Number of Multipurpose Sites:** 72. **Hookups:** Water, electric (20, 30 amps). **Each Site:** Picnic table, fire ring. **Dump Station:** Yes. **Laundry:** No. **Pay Phone:** Yes. **Rest Rooms and Showers:** Yes. **Fuel:** No. **Propane:** No. **Internal Roads:** Paved (excellent condition). **RV Service:** 40 mi. south in Columbia. **Market:** 15 mi. west in Winnsboro. **Restaurant:** 7 mi. west in Winnsboro. **General Store:** Park store. **Vending:** Beverages. **Swimming Pool:** No. **Playground:** Yes. **Other:** Boat ramp, fueling dock, tackle shop, picnic area. **Activities:** Nature trail, fishing, boating, swimming area. **Nearby Attractions:** Ridgeway historic village, Columbia historic homes, South Carolina Confederate Relic Room & Museum, Fort Jackson Museum, South Carolina State Museum. **Additional Information:** Columbia Metropolitan CVB, (800) 264-4884 or (803) 254-0479.

RESTRICTIONS

Pets: Leash only. **Fires:** Fire rings only. **Alcoholic Beverages:** Not allowed. **Vehicle Maximum Length:** 40 ft. **Other:** 14 day max. stay.

TO GET THERE

From I-77, take Exit 41 and drive east on SC 20 for 5 mi. to Hwy. 21. Turn left (north) and drive 2 mi. until the first paved road. Turn right on River Rd. and drive 5–7 mi. The park is on the left.

South Dakota

Located in the north-central part of the United States, South Dakota is generally considered part of the Midwest. The east part of the state, with its flat or rolling soils, resembles the landscape of other states in the Midwest, while the western section lies on the Great Plains. South Dakota is filled campgrounds that take advantage of its magnificent scenery, rich natural resources, and varied wildlife.

The state's largest cities are **Sioux Falls; Rapid City,** which serves as the center of the state's resort area; and **Pierre,** where city and country collide. The Missouri River divides the state into its two major regions. The other major river is Big Sioux River. South Dakota is covered with countless other rivers and lakes providing limitless opportunities to enjoy fishing and boating.

While the bulk of South Dakota's population lies in the east, the crown jewels of the state are clearly in the southwestern part, though beautiful spots exist throughout the state. The **Badlands** and **Black Hills** typically draw the most tourists. The Black Hills are a region of deeply eroded gullies of colorful, fantastic shapes. Within are five national parks, waterfalls, abundant wildlife, acclaimed recreational trails, and trout fishing. Bison and wild horses still roam free here. The **Black Hills Caverns** and **Black Hill Maze** offer great fun for families. **Badlands National Park** is a 244,000-acre park of spires, pinnacles, buttes, and gorges. This gorgeous area was created by millions of years of erosion.

Other intriguing places include **Mt. Rushmore National Memorial,** which has the stone-carved faces of four U.S. presidents; **Jewel Cave National Monument; Wind Cave National Park,** one of the oldest caves in the world; and **Dell Rapids,** known for its beautiful scenery. One can also spend time at **Buffalo Gap** or **Grand River National Grasslands,** regions set aside to protect the state's complex ecosystem. **The Corn Palace** in **Mitchell** is a unique building that celebrates the state's rich agriculture. Finally, the state boasts of being the home of "Sue," the world famous T-rex fossil.

The state's national forests, national parks, and state parks all have facilities for camping, fishing, picnicking, and hunting. The weather is definitely a matter of extremes—cold, long winters and hot summers.

The following facilities accept payment in checks or cash only:

Mystery Mt. Resort, Rapid City

Campground Profiles

BROOKINGS

Oakwood Lakes State Park

46109 202nd St., Bruce 57220. T: (605) 627-5441; F: (605) 627-5258; www.state.sd.us/gfp/sdparks; oakwoodstp@gfp.state.sd.us.

RV ★★★★ Tent ★★★★

Beauty: ★★★★ Site Privacy: ★★★★
Spaciousness: ★★★★ Quiet: ★★★★
Security: ★★★★ Cleanliness: ★★★★
Insect Control: ★★★ Facilities: ★★

Located where Native Americans once gathered for summer camp, Oakwood Lakes State Park presents a small piece of early American history in a beautiful scenic setting. Level, asphalted camping pads under a canopy of trees make for a relaxing getaway. Within a stone's throw away are eight glacial lakes that are excellent for all water sports. In addition, there are miles of hiking trails, three Native American burial grounds, and the restored cabin of the first settler in the area, Samuel Mortimer. The campground is set in a figure-eight configuration, with most sites being back-ins. There are a limited number of pull-through sites. There is also a horse camp for those wishing to travel with their horses. Summer days average in the 80s, with nights cooling to the 50s. June is an excellent time to visit, before the bugs hatch. There is an employee in residence in addition to a camp host, offering the best of security.

BASICS

Operated By: South Dakota Game, Fish, & Parks Dept. **Open:** All year; water turned off in winter. **Site Assignment:** By reservation (800) 710-CAMP. **Registration:** At entrance booth. **Fee:** $10–$13 per camping unit (no more than 2 units per site) plus entrance fee. **Parking:** At site.

FACILITIES

Number of RV-Only Sites: 0. **Number of Tent-Only Sites:** 0. **Number of Multipurpose Sites:** 69. **Hookups:** Electric (20, 30 amps), potable water. **Each Site:** Picnic table, grated fire pits. **Dump Station:** Yes. **Laundry:** No. **Pay Phone:** Yes. **Rest Rooms and Showers:** Yes. **Fuel:** No. **Propane:** No. **Internal Roads:** Paved. **RV Service:** 17 mi. southeast in Brookings. **Market:** In Brookings. **Restaurant:** In Brookings. **General Store:** No. **Vending:** No. **Swimming Pool:** No, however there is a riverfront beach for swimming. **Playground:** Yes. **Other:** Boat ramp, picnic shelters w/ grills, amphitheater, cabins, 2 group camp areas, hiking trail, interpretive shelter, visitor center, canoe rentals. **Activities:** Water & snow skiing, boating, swimming, interpretive programs, hiking, fishing (walleye, northerns, bass), volleyball, weekly park programs, hay rides, junior naturalist program, Sunday worship services. **Nearby Attractions:** State Agricultural Heritage Museum, McCrory Gardens. **Additional Information:** South Dakota State Parks, (605) 773-3391 or Brookings Chamber of Commerce, (605) 692-6125.

RESTRICTIONS

Pets: On leash. **Fires:** In fire pits only; fires may be restricted due to weather conditions; please ask management before starting any open fires. **Alcoholic Beverages:** Yes. **Vehicle Maximum Length:** None. **Other:** 14-day stay limit.

TO GET THERE

From I-29 7 mi. north of Brookings, take Exit 140. Go west on Hwy. 30 (this will turn into CR 6) about 10 mi.; you will see a large sign for Oakwood Lake State Park. Turn north and follow signs to the campground.

CUSTER

Custer Mountain Cabins and Campground

P.O. Box 472, Custer 57730. T: (800) 239-5505 or (605) 673-5440; www.rapidnet.com/~phn.

RV ★★★ Tent ★★★★

Beauty: ★★★★★	Site Privacy: ★★★
Spaciousness: ★★★	Quiet: ★★★★★
Security: ★★★★	Cleanliness: ★★★★
Insect Control: ★★★	Facilities: ★★

Custer Mountain Cabins and Campground is an exquisite private facility. It offers deluxe modern cabins and a charming campground nestled deep in the Black Hills, two miles east of Custer. The Black Hills offer breathtaking scenic drives, wonderful wildlife, Custer State Park, and Mt. Rushmore. The campground is situated on 50 acres of pristine land encircled by stands of black hill spruces. The RV area is located in a loop near the front of the grounds, and it has both pull-through and back-in sites. Each site has a gravel camping pad, but expect to have to level it out. Large tent sites can be found among the trees, giving tent campers more seclusion and privacy. The air is crisp in the morning, and summer days are pleasant. Visitors can experience a vast array of recreational and historic activities. Inviting hosts are available to assist you with all your vacation needs.

BASICS

Operated By: Paul Nordstrom. **Open:** All year; water is turned off in winter. **Site Assignment:** By reservations; deposit required for cabins only. **Registration:** In general store. **Fee:** Tents $17, RV $23 per unit. **Parking:** At site.

FACILITIES

Number of RV-Only Sites: 21. **Number of Tent-Only Sites:** 40. **Hookups:** Electric (30, 50 amps), water, sewer, cable. **Each Site:** Picnic table, some fire pits. **Dump Station:** Yes. **Laundry:** Yes. **Pay Phone:** Yes. **Rest Rooms and Showers:** Yes. **Fuel:** 2 mi. in Custer. **Propane:** 2 mi. in Custer. **Internal Roads:** Gravel, w/ some bumps. **RV Service:** There is a mobile service based out of Rapid City. **Market:** 2 mi. in Custer. **Restaurant:** 2 mi. in Custer or in Custer State Park. **General Store:** Yes. **Vending:** General store only. **Swimming Pool:** No. **Playground:** Yes. **Other:** Very nice cabins & summer vacation homes. **Activities:** Large open recreation field, hiking, biking. **Nearby Attractions:** Custer State Park, Flinstone Village, Mt. Rushmore. **Additional Information:** Custer Chamber of Commerce, (605) 673-2244.

RESTRICTIONS

Pets: In campsites only, not in cabins. **Fires:** In designated fire pits or grills only; fires may be restricted due to weather conditions; please ask management before starting any open fires. **Alcoholic Beverages:** Yes. **Vehicle Maximum Length:** None.

TO GET THERE

The campground is 2 mi. east of Custer on Hwy. 16A.

CUSTER

Custer State Park

HC 83, Box 70, Custer 57730. T: (605) 255-4515; F: (605) 255-4460; www.state.sd.us/sdparks or www.custerresorts.com; craig.pugsley@state.sd.us or e-mail@custerresorts.com.

RV ★★★ Tent ★★★★

Beauty: ★★★★	Site Privacy: ★★★
Spaciousness: ★★★	Quiet: ★★★★
Security: ★★★★	Cleanliness: ★★★
Insect Control: ★★★	Facilities: ★★

Custer State Park is a 73,000-acre resort in the heart of the Black Hills. Created in 1913 as a game reserve, this magnificent park has become world-renowned as a showcase of the area's natural resources and wildlife. The park was named after George A. Custer, who was enthralled by the region's uncommon natural beauty. The park has eight campgrounds, including a horse camp where your equine friend is more than welcome. The majority of the campgrounds have level asphalt camping pads, potable water, laundry, evening programs, fishing, and nearby swimming. Most of the campgrounds are arranged in loops, many with sites overlooking streams, mountains, or forests. The state park works in conjunction with Custer State Park Resort Co. to offer restaurant service, group events, jeep tours, and other additional activities. There are hiking and biking trails throughout the park, as well as excellent trout fishing. The weather is typical of the area, experiencing warm summer days and cooling in the evening. The park has very tight security, and all vehicles are required to have a park license obtainable at any entrance gate.

BASICS

Operated By: South Dakota Dept. of Game, Fish & Parks. **Open:** All year. **Site Assignment:** By reservation (800) 710-2267. **Registration:** At the information station, located at the entrance to each campground. **Fee:** $12–$14 depending on which of Custers' campground you choose, plus a gate fee. **Parking:** At site.

FACILITIES

Number of Multipurpose Sites: There are 26–71 sites per campground, 354 total sites. **Hookups:** Potable water. **Each Site:** Picnic table, grated fire pits. **Dump Station:** Yes, it is located just east of the Game Lodge Resort in the maintenance complex. **Laundry:** Yes, located in Blue Bell, Game Lodge, Grace Coolidge, & Sylvan Lake. **Pay Phone:** Yes, in service area & most camping areas. **Rest Rooms and Showers:** Yes. **Fuel:** Yes, located near Blue Bell, Grace Lodge, Grace Coolidge. **Propane:** No, but in Custer. **Internal Roads:** Most roads are paved. **RV Service:** In Custer. **Market:** Sylvan Lake General Store, within the park. **Restaurant:** There are serval places to eat within the park. **General Store:** There are 3 general stores, Coolidge, Sylvan Lake, Blue Bell. **Vending:** Soft drinks. **Swimming Pool:** No, however there are 4 park beaches: Center Lake, Legion Lake, Sylvan Lake, & the Game Lodge Pond; life jackets are advised, & jumping from cliffs & rocks is strictly prohibited. **Playground:** No. **Other:** Cabins, Peter Norbeck Visitor Center, Wildlife Station Visitor Center, Black Hills Play House, 3 chapels, several restaurants, Sylvan Auditorium, mountain bike rentals, boat rentals, art gallery. **Activities:** Horseback riding, fishing (perch, crappie, bullhead, walleye, bass), boating, 4 swimming beaches, family evening programs, guided nature walks, gold panning, junior naturalist programs, interpretive trails, special events, scenic drives, Buffalo Safari Jeep Rides, Black Hills Playhouse, mountain biking. **Nearby Attractions:** Mt. Rushmore, scenic drives, Crazy Horse Memorial, natural hot springs, rodeos, shopping, museums. **Additional Information:** Custer Chamber of Commerce; (605) 673-2244; for tickets to the Black Hills Playhouse, (605) 255-4141 or www.blackhillsplayhouse.com.

RESTRICTIONS

Pets: On Leash. **Fires:** In fire pits only; fires may be restricted due to weather conditions; please ask management before starting any open fires. **Alcoholic Beverages:** Yes. **Vehicle Maximum Length:** None. **Other:** 14-day stay limit.

TO GET THERE

There are 7 entrances into this park. It is 22.3 mi. from Rapid City following Hwy. 16A south, 10.2 mi. from Hermosa following Hwy. 36 west, or you may take the scenic Needles Hwy. Most all of the campgrounds are located directly off Hwy. 16A inside the park boundaries.

GARRETSON

Palisades State Park

25495 485th Ave., Garretson 57030. T: (605) 594-3824; F: (605) 594-2369; www.state.sd.us/gfp/sdparks; palisades@gfp.state.sd.us.

Beauty: ★★★★★ Site Privacy: ★★★★
Spaciousness: ★★★★ Quiet: ★★★★
Security: ★★★★ Cleanliness: ★★★★
Insect Control: ★★ Facilities: ★★★

Palisades State Park is nestled in a unique landscape of quartzite spires cut by Split Rock Creek. It has become famous for its geological wonders and legends of the infamous Jessie James eluding a posse through Devils Gulch. Palisade State Park is located near Garretson, which has a history as unique as the land. The campground is a large loop, with both back-in and pull-through sites. The sites are spaced for optimal privacy, each with a paved parking pad and a spectacular view. The campground is well shaded with a variety of foliage. Many of the sites overlook Split Rock Creek and the magnificent quartzite spires. Palisade State Park is known for its rock climbing, and many climbers practice their scaling and rappelling. Like most of South Dakota summers, temperatures here average in the 80s, and it tends to be dry. Palisade State Park has around-the-clock security with a manager in residence.

Basics

Operated By: South Dakota Fish, Game, & Parks Dept. **Open:** All year; water may be turned off in winter. **Site Assignment:** By reservation (800) 710-CAMP. **Registration:** At the entrance gate-of the park. **Fee:** $10 no hookup, $13 w/ electric. **Parking:** At site.

Facilities

Number of Multipurpose Sites: 36. **Hookups:** Electric (20, 30 amps), potable water. **Each Site:** Picnic table, grated fire pits. **Dump Station:** Yes. **Laundry:** No. **Pay Phone:** Yes. **Rest Rooms and Showers:** Yes. **Fuel:** No. **Propane:** No. **Internal Roads:** Paved. **RV Service:** 15 mi. southwest in Sioux Falls. **Market:** Garretson or Sioux Falls. **Restaurant:** Garrettson or Sioux Falls. **General Store:** No. **Vending:** Yes. **Swimming Pool:** No. **Playground:** Yes. **Other:** Picnic area, cabins, amphitheater, 3 trails, pavilions, 1.2 billion-year-old Sioux quartzite spires, 1908 historic bridge. **Activities:** Guided hikes, summer weekend recreation programs, junior naturalist program & ECHOES program, repelling & rock climbing, fishing, s& volleyball, horseshoes. **Nearby Attractions:** Golf, Sioux Falls, Devil's Gulch, Great Plains Zoo, Jesse James River Runs (pontoon rides). **Additional Information:** Garretson Chamber of Commerce, (605) 594-6721.

Restrictions

Pets: On leash only. **Fires:** In fire pits only; fires may be restricted due to weather conditions; please ask management before starting any open fires. **Alcoholic Beverages:** Yes. **Vehicle Maximum Length:** None. **Other:** 14-day stay limit; limit of 6 people per camping site.

To Get There

From I-90 take Exit 406, go north on Hwy. 11 for 8.5 mi. then turn right and follow the signs into the park.

GETTYSBURG

West Whitlock Recreation Area

HC 3, Box 73A, Gettysburg 57442. T: (605)765-9410; F: (605) 765-2747; www.state.sd.us/gfp/sdparks/whitlock/whitlock.htm; whitlockrec@state.sd.us.

RV ★★★ Tent ★★★

Beauty: ★★★ Site Privacy: ★★★
Spaciousness: ★★★ Quiet: ★★★★
Security: ★★★★ Cleanliness: ★★★
Insect Control: ★★★ Facilities: ★★

Twenty-two miles west of Gettysburg in South Dakota's Great Lake Region, West Whitlock Recreation Area is situated on the Lake Oahe Reservoir. First explored by Lewis and Clark, this area is a small, hidden treasure and a sportsman's sanctuary. The park offers a variety of coordinated interpretive and educational programs. Lake Oahe Reservoir has over 2,000 acres of shoreline, making it ideal for boating, jet skiing, fishing, or diving. Anglers can find walleye, northern pike, chinook salmon, and bass. There is also a large variety of hunting game including pheasant, grouse, deer, and antelope. The campground is one large loop with back-in, level parking pads. Mature trees are found throughout the campground area, providing shade and adding ambiance. The weather is warm during the summer and cold in the winter. The late spring is a great time to visit before the insects come to life.

Basics

Operated By: South Dakota Game, Fish, & Parks Dept. **Open:** All year; water turned off in winter. **Site Assignment:** First come, first served. **Registration:** At entrance booth. **Fee:** $8–$11 per camping unit (no more than 2 units per site), plus entrance fee. **Parking:** At site.

Facilities

Number of Multipurpose Sites: 103. **Hookups:** Electric (20, 30 amps), potable water. **Each Site:** Picnic table, grated fire pits. **Dump Station:** Yes. **Laundry:** Next door. **Pay Phone:** Yes. **Rest Rooms and Showers:** Yes. **Fuel:** Next door. **Propane:** Next door. **Internal Roads:** Paved. **RV Service:** 22 mi. in Gettysburg. **Market:** In Gettysburg. **Restaurant:** Next door or in Gettysburg. **General Store:** No. **Vending:** Yes. **Swimming Pool:** No, but there is a swimming beach on Lake Oahe. **Playground:** Yes. **Other:** Cabins, fish-cleaning station, cross-country ski trail, boat ramp, beach, picnic area, pavilion, interpretive center, Arikara Lodge replica. **Activities:** Water & snow skiing, boating, swimming, interpretive programs, hiking, fishing (walleye, northerns, bass), biking. **Nearby Attractions:** Whitlock salmon spawning & imprinting station; annual Civil War festival. **Additional Information:** Gettysburg Chamber of Commerce, (605) 765-9309.

Restrictions

Pets: On leash. **Fires:** In fire pits only; fires may be restricted due to weather conditions; please ask management before starting any open fires. **Alcoholic Beverages:** Yes. **Vehicle Maximum Length:** None. **Other:** 14-day stay limit.

To Get There

From Gettysburg on US 212, go 18 mi. (stay on 212, do not get on 83), then take 1804N (right). Travel for 4 mi. until the pavement ends. Turn left and follow road into the park. Watch for signs.

HILL

Rafter J. Bar Ranch Campground

Box 128, Hill City 57745. T: (605)574-2527 or (888) 723-8375; F: (605) 574-3950; www.rafterj.com; info@rafter.com.

RV ★★★★ Tent ★★★★

Beauty: ★★★★★ Site Privacy: ★★★
Spaciousness: ★★★ Quiet: ★★★★
Security: ★★★★ Cleanliness: ★★★
Insect Control: ★★★ Facilities: ★★★

Located in the Black Hills, Rafter J. Bar Ranch is a huge full-service camping facility. It is divided into five camping areas, each under a canopy of large ponderosa pines. The camping areas each share beautiful commons, bike trails, hiking trails, and open meadows. The camping areas are large loops; three have their own rest rooms, showers, and laundry. Campsites, however, are not well spaced, nor are they any larger than most campground sites despite the enormous acreage of the property. The ranch offers lots of amenities, including fuel, fishing licenses, horseback riding, bike rentals, and an information center. In addition to being inclusive, it is in very close proximity to Mt. Rushmore, the Crazy Horse monument, and Custer State Park. Summer temperatures average in the mid 80s, with evenings dropping into the 60s. The ranch has staff on duty around the clock and several host families to assist with any need that may arise.

Basics

Operated By: Tom George. **Open:** May 1–Oct. 1. **Site Assignment:** By reservations held on a credit card. **Registration:** In camp office. **Fee:** Tent $23, RV $30–$32 for 2 people; extra people $3, children under age 8 free; no personal checks. **Parking:** At site.

Facilities

Number of RV-Only Sites: 160. **Number of Tent-Only Sites:** 17. **Hookups:** Electric (30, 50 amps), water, sewer, satellite TV w/ HBO, ESPN (limited number). **Each Site:** Picnic table, grated fire pits. **Dump Station:** Yes. **Laundry:** Yes. **Pay Phone:** Yes. **Rest Rooms and Showers:** Yes. **Fuel:** Yes. **Propane:** Yes. **Internal Roads:** Combination of paved & gravel. **RV Service:** Mobile repair service. **Market:** In Hill City. **Restaurant:** Snack bar on property or there are restaurants all over the Black Hills. **General Store:** Yes. **Vending:** Yes. **Swimming Pool:** Yes, & hot tub. **Playground:** Yes. **Other:** Internet data port in information room. **Activities:** Trail rides, swimming, hot tub, fishing, hiking, bike rental. **Nearby Attractions:** Mt. Rushmore, Custer State Park, Needles Dr., Iron Mountain Rd., Borglum Story Museum, Hungry Horse. **Additional Information:** Hill City Chamber of Commerce, (605) 574-2368.

RESTRICTIONS

Pets: On leash. **Fires:** Fire pits or grills only; fires may be restricted due to weather conditions; please ask management before starting any open fires. **Alcoholic Beverages:** Yes. **Vehicle Maximum Length:** None. **Other:** 14-day stay limit; 1 family unit per site; Good Sam Club.

TO GET THERE

The campground is located on Sylvan Lake–Needles Rd. (SD Hwy. 87) between the towns of Custer and Hill City.

HILL CITY

Horse Thief Campground and Resort

Needles Hwy. 87, Hill City 57745. T: (605) 574-2668 or (800) 657-5802; F: (605) 547-4376; www.horsethief.com; camp@horsethief.com.

RV ★★★★ Tent ★★★★

Beauty: ★★★★ Site Privacy: ★★★
Spaciousness: ★★★ Quiet: ★★★
Security: ★★★★ Cleanliness: ★★★
Insect Control: ★★★ Facilities: ★★★

Deep in the groves of the Black Hills is a beautiful, 50-acre camping heaven, nestled in mountains, pines, streams, and ponds. Horse Thief Campground and Resort is a secluded family getaway conveniently located near Custer State Park, Mt. Rushmore, and the Scenic Needles Hwy. The campground is a full-service facility, with both pull-through and back-in sites, a lodge, and a pool with a breathtaking view. The campground consists of an RV area where you may choose open or wooded campsites. The tent-camper's section is spectacular, with wooded campsites and a huge common area. In addition to superb camping, Horse Thief is also a horse camp—meaning there are accommodations available for equine family members. However, advance reservations must be made if traveling with your horse. The temperatures in the area average in the mid 80s for the summer and 30s in the winter. There is an entrance gate and excellent security.

BASICS

Operated By: Bob & Vicki Irvine. **Open:** May 15–Sept. 15. **Site Assignment:** By reservation held on a credit card. **Registration:** In general store. **Fee:** Tent $17, RV $20–$29 for 2 people, extra person $2.50, children under age 5 stay free. **Parking:** At site.

FACILITIES

Number of RV-Only Sites: 54. **Number of Tent-Only Sites:** 43. **Hookups:** Electric (30 amps), water, sewer, phone, TV sites. **Each Site:** Picnic table, some fire pits. **Dump Station:** Yes. **Laundry:** Yes. **Pay Phone:** Yes. **Rest Rooms and Showers:** Yes. **Fuel:** No. **Propane:** No. **Internal Roads:** Gravel w/ some bumps & parts that are not level. **RV Service:** Mobile service. **Market:** Hill City. **Restaurant:** In Hill City. **General Store:** Yes. **Vending:** No. **Swimming Pool:** Yes. **Playground:** Yes. **Other:** Huge central fire ring, fax & copy service. **Activities:** Hiking, fishing, biking. **Nearby Attractions:** Mt. Rushmore, Custer State Park, Crazy Horse, museums, hot springs, Harney Peak. **Additional Information:** South Dakota Tourism, (800) 843-1930.

RESTRICTIONS

Pets: Dogs on a short leash only; horses allowed; must show a valid health certificate for all animals; horses must have proof of current negative Coggins test. **Fires:** In approved fire pits only; fires may be restricted due to weather conditions; please ask management before starting any open fires. **Alcoholic Beverages:** Yes. **Vehicle Maximum Length:** None. **Other:** Good Sam, AAA.

TO GET THERE

From the south side of Hill City, go 3 mi. south on US 16/385; the campground entrance is on the right.

INTERIOR

Badlands National Park

P.O. Box 6, Interior 57750-0006. T: (605) 433-5361; F: (605) 433-5404; www.nps.gov/badl; badl_information@nps.gov.

RV ★★★ Tent ★★★

Beauty: ★★★ Site Privacy: ★★★
Spaciousness: ★★★ Quiet: ★★★
Security: ★★★ Cleanliness: ★★★
Insect Control: ★★ Facilities: ★

Set in the midst of what might be described as "peaks and valleys of delicately banded colors" (Thaddeus Culbertson) is the Badlands National Park campground. The wind is strong, and the terrain is a mixture of dirt and sand, yet there is an unbelievable biodiversity of both plant life and wildlife. This includes the largest remaining mixed-grass prairie in our country. The campground itself consists of two general camping loops, one group camp loop, and an amphitheater. The summers are dry and hot and the ground is brown, but in spring all is green and alive. There are no hookups in Badlands National Park; sites do have level, paved camping pads, tables on concrete pads, and wind guards. The campground is located inside the park gates, and there is a camp host during the summer months. The park offers a verity of educational and interpretive programs, including a night sky interpretive area.

BASICS

Operated By: US National Park Service. **Open:** All year. **Site Assignment:** First come, first served. **Registration:** Register at the information bulletin board; see camp host for assistance. **Fee:** $10 per site for up to 6 people; not to exceed 2 tents, or 2 vehicles per site). **Parking:** At site.

FACILITIES

Number of Multipurpose Sites: 96. **Hookups:** Potable water. **Each Site:** Picnic table, wind shelters, & patios. **Dump Station:** Yes. **Laundry:** No. **Pay Phone:** Yes. **Rest Rooms and Showers:** Yes. **Fuel:** No, 4 mi. in Interior. **Propane:** No, 30 mi. northwest in Wall. **Internal Roads:** Paved. **RV Service:** 30 mi. Northwest in Wall. **Market:** 30 mi. northwest in Wall. **Restaurant:** Cedar Pass Lodge (open mid-Apr. through mid-Oct.), or in Interior. **General Store:** Visitors center w/ ice & vending. **Vending:** No. **Swimming Pool:** No. **Playground:** No. **Other:** Amphitheater, Cedar Pass Lodge, Ben Reifel Visitor Cener. **Activities:** Ben Reifel Visitor Center w/ movies, & exhibits, horseback riding, hiking, day & evening interpretive programs, Jr. Ranger programs, guided walks. **Nearby Attractions:** Pine Ridge Indian Reservation, 80 mi. from the Black Hills & Mt. Rushmore, **Additional Information:** www.nps.gov/badl.

RESTRICTIONS

Pets: On leash; pets are not allowed in visitor centers, prairie dog towns, or Badl&s Wilderness Area. **Fires:** No open fires; fires may be restricted due to weather conditions; please ask management before starting any open fires. **Alcoholic Beverages:** Yes. **Vehicle Maximum Length:** None. **Other:** Golden Age & Golden Access Discounts; 14-day stay limit.

TO GET THERE

From I-90 Exit 131, take Hwy. 240 south about 8 mi.

INTERIOR

Badlands/White River KOA

HRC 54 Box 1, Interior 57750. T: (605) 433-5337 or (800) 562-3897; F: (605) 433-5337; www.koa.com; koa@gwtc.

RV ★★★★ Tent ★★★

Beauty: ★★★ Site Privacy: ★★★
Spaciousness: ★★★ Quiet: ★★★★
Security: ★★★★ Cleanliness: ★★★★
Insect Control: ★★★ Facilities: ★★★

Only a few miles from the Badlands National Park in the small community of Interior is the manicured landscape of the Badlands KOA. As with most KOAs, this is a full-service campground, with some of the only shade trees in the area. Due to the hard work of the owners and ongoing irrigation, the Badland KOA offers green grass and shade. There is a nice pool, mini-golf, and a courtesy phone. The campground is laid out in a series of rows and loops, with the majority of the sites being pull-through. The owners' private residence is in the middle of the property. In addition, several tent sites have electric and water hookups in what KOA refers to as a tent village. Please make note that is this campground is in a very small community, and the nearest services are 32 miles away in Wall.

BASICS

Operated By: Steve & Janet Snyder. **Open:** Apr. 22–Oct. 16. **Site Assignment:** By reservation held on a credit card. **Registration:** In general store. **Fee:** Tent $18, RV $23–$25 for 2 people, extra people $2.50, age 5 & under free. **Parking:** At site.

FACILITIES

Number of RV-Only Sites: 84. **Number of Tent-Only Sites:** 60. **Hookups:** Electric (20, 30, 50 amps), water, sewer. **Each Site:** Picnic table, some fire pits. **Dump Station:** Yes. **Laundry:** Yes.

Pay Phone: Yes. **Rest Rooms and Showers:** Yes. **Fuel:** No. **Propane:** No. **Internal Roads:** Gravel. **RV Service:** 32 mi. Northwest in Wall, SD. **Market:** 32 mi. northwest in Wall, SD. **Restaurant:** In Interior; pancake breakfast served during summer season at the campground. **General Store:** Yes. **Vending:** Soft drinks. **Swimming Pool:** Yes. **Playground:** Yes. **Other:** Internet data port in laundry, 8 cabins, game room. **Activities:** Fishing, hiking, horseshoes, basketball. **Nearby Attractions:** Badl&s National Park, Pine Ridge Indian Reservation, fossil digging. **Additional Information:** South Dakota Tourism, (800) 843-1930.

Restrictions

Pets: On leash. **Fires:** In fire pits or grills only; fires may be restricted due to weather conditions; please ask management before starting any open fires. **Alcoholic Beverages:** Yes. **Vehicle Maximum Length:** None.

To Get There

From I-90 take Exit 131, take SD 240/Badland Loop into the Badlands National Park, then take SD 377, which will become SD 44. The campground is approximately 6 mi. south of the Badlands National Park's south gate on Hwy. 44. It is approximately 10 mi. from I-90.

PIERRE

Corps of Engineers Downstream

P.O. Box 997, Pierre 57501. T: (605) 224-5862; F: (605) 224-5945; www.reserveusa.com (reservations).

RV ★★★★ Tent ★★★★★

Beauty: ★★★★ Site Privacy: ★★★★
Spaciousness: ★★★★ Quiet: ★★★★
Security: ★★★★★ Cleanliness: ★★★★
Insect Control: n/a Facilities: ★★

Corps of Engineers Downstream is a huge park located about ten miles outside of Pierre on the Oahe Dam, encompassing both the Missouri River and Lake Oahe. The Corps of Engineers Downstream Recreation Area is broken into three campgrounds with over 300 sites between them. Each site has a paved camping pad and is under a forest of mature cottonwoods and willows. There are large common areas in each campground, complete with playgrounds and comfort stations with hot showers. The campgrounds are in loops and have both pull-through and back-in sites. There is a full-service marina on the property, as well as a restaurant, convenience store, and bait shop. Each campground has a camp host, and there is a staffed entrance booth for your protection. There are four distinct seasons in Pierre, with temperatures on summer days averaging in the mid 80s. Bring insect repellent if visiting in the late summer; otherwise, the deer flies will eat you for lunch.

Basics

Operated By: US Corp of Engineers. **Open:** May–Oct. 31. **Site Assignment:** By reservations, all fees payable at that time; call National Recreation Reservation Service, (877) 444-6777 or refer to website; fees for cancellations & no-shows will apply. **Registration:** Self-registration or at the guard shack. **Fee:** $14 per site, no more than 8 people per site. **Parking:** At site.

Facilities

Number of Multipurpose Sites: 206. **Hookups:** Electric (30, 50 amps); potable water (but not on every site). **Each Site:** Picnic table, grated fire pits. **Dump Station:** Yes. **Laundry:** No. **Pay Phone:** Yes. **Rest Rooms and Showers:** Yes. **Fuel:** At the marina. **Propane:** At the marina. **Internal Roads:** Paved. **RV Service:** In Pierre. **Market:** In Pierre. **Restaurant:** At the marina, or in Pierre. **General Store:** At the marina. **Vending:** Yes. **Swimming Pool:** No, but there is a huge swimming beach on the Missouri River. **Playground:** Several. **Other:** Picnic area, Oahe Marina, archery range, rifle range, Oahe Chapel, visitors center. **Activities:** Swimming, archery, nature trails, boating, jet skiing, waterskiing, biking. **Nearby Attractions:** Fort Pierre, South Dakota Discovery Center & Aquarium, state capitol, Capitol Grounds Arboretum Trail, South Dakota Cultural Heritage Center. **Additional Information:** Pierre Chamber of Commerce, (605) 224-7361.

Restrictions

Pets: Yes. **Fires:** Fire pits only; fires may be restricted due to weather conditions; please ask management before starting any open fires. **Alcoholic Beverages:** Yes. **Vehicle Maximum Length:** None. **Other:** 50% discount w/ Golden Age or Golden Access passport.

To Get There

From Fort Pierre take Hwy. 83N to just before the river; take a left on Hwy. 14. Go about 1 mi. and take a right on 1806. The campground is about 5 mi. on the right. There are signs all the way from Fort Pierre.

PIERRE

Griffen Park

715 East Dakota Ave., Pierre 57501. T: (605) 773-7445

RV ★★★ Tent ★★★★

Beauty: ★★★ Site Privacy: ★★
Spaciousness: ★★ Quiet: ★★
Security: ★★★ Cleanliness: ★★★
Insect Control: n/a Facilities: ★★

Welcome to the state capital of Pierre, and a unique city park that offers three free nights of camping with electricity. Griffen Park is located in downtown Pierre, just a few blocks from the Capitol Building. This beautiful city park offers both a public pool and a swimming beach on the Missouri River. There are six tennis courts, 12 horseshoe pits, several picnic shelters, a softball field, a full basketball court, and a marina next door. The RV camp area is not much more than a dirt parking lot, and at the time of our visit, the showers needed some cleaning, but the park overall is very well kept and clean. The tent area is striking, as it overlooks the river. For the amenities and activities offered for free, this is a wonderful park. The weather is breezy around the riverfront, so pack a jacket.

Basics

Operated By: City of Pierre. **Open:** All year. **Site Assignment:** First come, first served. **Registration:** Read information board. **Fee:** Free (3-night limit). **Parking:** At site.

Facilities

Number of RV-Only Sites: 6. **Number of Tent-Only Sites:** 10. **Hookups:** Electric (20, 30 amps). **Each Site:** Picnic table. **Dump Station:** Yes. **Laundry:** No. **Pay Phone:** Yes. **Rest Rooms and Showers:** Yes; keep in mind that this is a public city park; there is a shower in the rest rooms located by the River Front beach & at the pool, but you will probably find that they don't meet your standards for cleanliness. **Fuel:** No. **Propane:** No. **Internal Roads:** Paved. **RV Service:** Local service. **Market:** In town. **Restaurant:** Within walking distance. **General Store:** No. **Vending:** Yes, located by the pool or across the street at the hospital. **Swimming Pool:** Yes, large city pool w/ lifeguard. **Playground:** Yes. **Other:** Large riverfront beach w/ lifeguard, on the Missouri River, covered picnic tables overlooking the river, scheduled & planned recreation, marina next door. **Activities:** Volleyball, 6 tennis courts, swimming (river or pool), horseshoes, basketball, boating, waterskiing, softball field. **Nearby Attractions:** Shopping, State Capitol, arboretum, South Dakota Cultural Center, South Dakota Discovery Center & Aquarium. **Additional Information:** Pierre Chamber of Commerce, (605) 224-7361 or www.pierrechamber.com.

Restrictions

Pets: On leash; this is a city park. **Fires:** No open fires; fires may be restricted due to weather conditions; please ask management before starting any open fires. **Alcoholic Beverages:** Yes. **Vehicle Maximum Length:** None. **Other:** 3-day stay limit.

To Get There

From the junction of US 83 & Sioux St, go east 5 blocks on Sioux St. to Washington, then go south 2 blocks.

RAPID CITY

Black Hills Jellystone RV Park

7001 South Hwy. 16, Rapid City 57702-8903. T: (605) 341-8554 or (800) 558-2954; www.jellystone.com.

RV ★★★ Tent ★★★

Beauty: ★★★ Site Privacy: ★★★
Spaciousness: ★★★ Quiet: ★★★
Security: ★★★ Cleanliness: ★★★★
Insect Control: ★★★ Facilities: ★★★

Yogi Bear and the Schneidermans welcome you their Black Hills Jellystone RV Park in Rapid City. This campground is convenient to area attractions, a nearby water park, many restaurants, Custer State Park, and Mt. Rushmore. The campground consists of level, open campsites in a rectangular configuration of several long rows, with grass and small trees separating individual sites. Sites are relatively close together, and tent sites are located very close to high-traffic areas in the campground. The majority of the sites are pull-throughs, with 12 cabins located at the front of the property. The campground offers many amenities, including children's activities, movies, a pavilion, gazebo, and a wagon train. This campground is an ideal base for travelers wishing to explore the Black Hill region. Summers days in the area have average temperatures in the mid 80s, dropping to the 60s at night. The first full week of Aug. is the Sturgis Rally, and reservations must be made about a year in advance for that time.

Basics

Operated By: Keith & S&i Schneiderman. **Open:** May 15–Oct. 1. **Site Assignment:** By reservations held w/ credit card. **Registration:** In general store. **Fee:** Tent $18, $25–$31 for 2 people. extra people $3. **Parking:** At site.

Facilities

Number of RV-Only Sites: 46. **Number of Tent-Only Sites:** 31. **Number of Multipurpose Sites:** 17. **Hookups:** Electric (30, 50 amps). **Each Site:** Picnic table, fire pits. **Dump Station:** Yes. **Laundry:** Yes. **Pay Phone:** Yes. **Rest Rooms and Showers:** Yes. **Fuel:** No. **Propane:** No. **Internal Roads:** Gravel. **RV Service:** In Rapid City. **Market:** In Rapid City. **Restaurant:** In Rapid City. **General Store:** Yes. **Vending:** Soft drinks. **Swimming Pool:** Yes. **Playground:** Yes. **Other:** 12 cabins, pavilion. **Activities:** Hot tub, swimming, pool table, game room, book exchange, children's activities. **Nearby Attractions:** Mt. Rushmore, Black Hills Maze & Amusements, Reptile Gardens. **Additional Information:** Rapid City Chamber of Commerce, (605) 343-1744.

Restrictions

Pets: On leash. **Fires:** In fire pits or grills only; fires may be restricted due to weather conditions; please ask management before starting any open fires. **Alcoholic Beverages:** Yes. **Vehicle Maximum Length:** None. **Other:** No generators.

To Get There

The campground is located 4 mi. south of Rapid City on Hwy. 16.

RAPID CITY

Mystery Mt. Resort

13752 South Hwy. 16 West, Rapid City 57702. T: (605) 342-5368 or (800)658-2267; F: (605) 348-2561; www.blackhillsresorts.com; mmresort@rapidnet.com.

RV ★★★ Tent ★★★

Beauty: ★★★★	Site Privacy: ★★
Spaciousness: ★★	Quiet: ★★★★
Security: ★★★	Cleanliness: ★★★
Insect Control: ★★★	Facilities: ★★

Mystery Mountain Resort is situated on the outskirts of Rapid City, on Hwy. 16 near the Black Hills and Mt. Rushmore. Mystery Mountain is a combination of campground, cabins, bunkhouses, and furnished reunion cottages capable of sleeping ten. The campground is integrated with other buildings, and it's configured mostly in rows. There are both pull-through and back-in sites. Many sites have concrete patios and parking pads, while other sites could use some updating and are not very level. The majority of the campground is under a canopy of pine and offers excellent shade. The campground is conveniently located near many area attractions, restaurants, state parks, and Mt. Rushmore. The weather is typical of most places in the region, with temperatures in summer averaging in the mid 80s during the day. Please also note the first full week of August is the Sturgis Rally Week; special rates will be in effect, and reservations need to be made as much as a year in advance for this time—preferably at the end of the preceding year's rally.

Basics

Operated By: Blackhills Resorts. **Open:** All year. **Site Assignment:** By reservation. **Registration:** In resort office. **Fee:** Tents $17–$22, RV $25–$32, for 2 people. **Parking:** At site.

Facilities

Number of RV-Only Sites: 75. **Number of Tent-Only Sites:** 42. **Hookups:** Electric (30, 50 amps), water, sewer. **Each Site:** Picnic table, fire pit. **Dump Station:** 2 dump stations. **Laundry:** Yes. **Pay Phone:** Yes. **Rest Rooms and Showers:** Yes. **Fuel:** No. **Propane:** No. **Internal Roads:** Gravel. **RV Service:** In Rapid City. **Market:** In Rapid City. **Restaurant:** In Rapid City. **General Store:** Yes. **Vending:** Soft drinks. **Swimming Pool:** Yes, w/ hot tub. **Playground:** Yes. **Other:** Cabins, bunkhouse, guest houses, reunion cottages, maid service. **Activities:** Basketball, horseshoes, swimming, hiking. **Nearby Attractions:** Mt. Rushmore, Childrens Science Center, Crystal Cave Park, Flintstone's Bedrock City, Cosmos of the Black Hills, Bear Country USA, Black Hills Caverns. **Additional Information:** Rapid City CVB, (800) 487-3223 or tourist@rapidcitycvb.com).

Restrictions

Pets: On leash. **Fires:** In provided fire pits or grills only; fires may be restricted due to weather conditions; please ask management before starting any open fires. **Alcoholic Beverages:** Yes. **Vehicle Maximum Length:** None.

To Get There

The campground is located 11 mi. south of Rapid City, directly off US 16W.

RAPID CITY

Rushmore Shadows Resort

P.O. Box 1696, Rapid City 57709. T: (605) 343-4544; F: (605) 348-9323; rshadows@enetis.net.

RV ★★★ Tent ★★★

Beauty: ★★★	Site Privacy: ★★
Spaciousness: ★★	Quiet: ★★★
Security: ★★★★	Cleanliness: ★★★
Insect Control: ★★★	Facilities: ★★★

Rushmore Shadow Resort is located on Hwy. 16W near Rapid City, just 16 miles from Mt. Rushmore. The resort campground is a large facility with open common areas and activities. There is a clubhouse, large heated pool, park models, and a convenience store. The campground consists of over 200 sites, laid out much like a residential subdivision with several major streets. The streets are private, and only registered guests are permitted past the registration office. Most sites are gravel with some grass between, but they are relatively close together. The common areas are generally well groomed, with a lot of room for recreation. Next door is the Old McDonald Farm, with red barns and goats that walk an overhanging bridge. The weather is not quite as extreme as the in the heart of the Black Hills, with daytime temperatures average in the mid 80s in the summer, dropping into the 60s at night.

Basics

Operated By: Private operator. **Open:** May 15–Sept. 14. **Site Assignment:** By reservation; office open 9 a.m.–5 p.m. **Registration:** At registration office. **Parking:** At site.

Facilities

Number of RV-Only Sites: 235. **Number of Tent-Only Sites:** 0. **Hookups:** Electric (20, 30 amps), water, sewer. **Each Site:** Picnic table, some grills, some fire pits. **Dump Station:** Yes. **Laundry:** Yes. **Pay Phone:** Yes. **Rest Rooms and Showers:** Yes. **Fuel:** No. **Propane:** Yes. **Internal Roads:** Combination of paved & gravel. **RV Service:** Mobile. **Market:** In Rapid City. **Restaurant:** On site or in Rapid City. **General Store:** Yes. **Vending:** Yes. **Swimming Pool:** Yes. **Playground:** Yes. **Other:** Clubhouse, Internet data port, grill, bonfire pit, barn, picnic shelter. **Activities:** Volleyball, swimming, basketball, horseshoes. **Nearby Attractions:** Badl&s National Park, Chapel in the Hills, Dinosaur Park, Museum of Geology. **Additional Information:** Rapid City CVB, (605) 343-1744, www.rapidcitycvb.com.

Restrictions

Pets: No pets allowed. **Fires:** In designated fire pits or grills only; fires may be restricted due to weather conditions; please ask management before starting any open fires. **Alcoholic Beverages:** Yes. **Vehicle Maximum Length:** None.

To Get There

The campground is located directly off Hwy. 16W in Rapid City as you are heading out of town.

SIOUX FALLS

Yogi Bear's Jellystone Park

26014 478th Ave., Brandon 57005. T: (605) 332-2233; F: (605) 332-2233; www.gocampingamerica.com/yogisiouxfalls; jellystonesiouxfalls@gocampingamerica.com.

RV ★★★ Tent ★★★

Beauty: ★★★	Site Privacy: ★★★
Spaciousness: ★★★	Quiet: ★★★
Security: ★★★★	Cleanliness: ★★★★
Insect Control: ★★★	Facilities: ★★★

Directly off I-90 only five miles east of Sioux City, Yogi Bear's Jellystone Campground is a full-service, modern facility offering a multitude of amenities and activities for the entire family. The campground is conveniently located for travelers wishing to enjoy the Sioux Falls area and neighboring state parks. The campground offers all modern hookups, including cable and phone. There are two main sections to the campground, and roads are laid out in rows. There is a tree between most sites, but at the time of our visit, they were very young and afforded little to no shade. That will obviously change with time. Most sites are pull-throughs, and there is little interference for those who wish to receive satellite TV. The campground is open year-round; however, there are limited hookups in the winter. The weather in this part of the state goes from one extreme to the other—very warm and dry in summer, and ice-cold in winter. The owners are on site during busy season, and security is good.

Basics

Operated By: Bruce Aliets. **Open:** All year; water turned off in winter. **Site Assignment:** By reservation, (800) 638-9043. **Registration:** In general store. **Fee:** Tent $16, RV $26–$28 for 2 people, extra people $2, kids age 4 & under stay free. **Parking:** At site.

Facilities

Number of RV-Only Sites: 112. **Number of Tent-Only Sites:** 33. **Hookups:** Electric (20, 30, 50 amps), water, sewer, cable, phone. **Each Site:** Picnic table, grated fire pits. **Dump Station:** Yes. **Laundry:** Yes. **Pay Phone:** Yes. **Rest Rooms and Showers:** Yes. **Fuel:** No, just down the street. **Propane:** Yes. **Internal Roads:** Gravel. **RV Service:** In Sioux Falls. **Market:** In Sioux Falls. **Restaurant:** Snack bar on site or restaurants in town. **General Store:** Yes. **Vending:** Yes. **Swimming Pool:** Yes, & hot tub. **Playground:** Yes. **Other:** 5 cabins, hot tub, indoor theatre, pavilion, arcade game room, nightly visits by Yogi, picnic area. **Activities:** Swimming, 19-hole mini-golf, volleyball, peddle bikes, planned activities in the summer, summer Sunday morning pancake breakfast. **Nearby Attractions:** Thunder Road Family Fun Park, Great Plains Zoo & Delbridge Museum, *USS South Dakota* Battleship Memorial, Falls Park. **Additional Information:** Sioux City CVB, (800) 333-2072.

Restrictions

Pets: On leash. **Fires:** In fire pits only; fires may be restricted due to weather conditions; please ask management before starting any open fires. **Alcoholic Beverages:** Yes. **Vehicle Maximum Length:** None.

To Get There

From I-90 at Exit 402, go 0.25 mi. north on City Rd. 121; the park is located on the right

WATERTOWN

Stokes-Thomas Lake City Park

90 South Lake Dr., Watertown 57201.
T: (605)882-6264

RV ★★★★★ Tent ★★★★★

Beauty: ★★★★ Site Privacy: ★★★★
Spaciousness: ★★★★ Quiet: ★★★★
Security: ★★★★ Cleanliness: ★★★★
Insect Control: n/a Facilities: ★★★

Stokes-Thomas Lake City Park is one of South Dakota's wonderful city parks. It reflects the pride South Dakota places on its towns and offers the local population, as well as travelers, a beautiful place for recreation. Stokes-Thomas is located on Lake Kampeska, about five miles out of Watertown. Watertown is a known for its rich grain fields and grasslands. The park is kept in pristine condition, with lush green grass and 42 paved camping pads, all under an awning of large, mature oak trees. New in the summer of 2002 is the introduction of full-hookup sites with all the amenities. Stokes-Thomas Lake City Park has a large boat ramp, a swimming beach, and three picnic shelters. This park is a fantastic weekend getaway. The weather is pleasant for water sports in the summer, and there is a manager in residence.

Basics

Operated By: Watertown Parks, Recreation & Forestry Dept., Kelly Stugis, Manager. **Open:** All year. **Site Assignment:** First come, first served. **Registration:** In park office. **Fee:** $13–$15 per site (limit 6 people per site). **Parking:** At site.

Facilities

Number of Multipurpose Sites: 43. **Hookups:** Electric (20, 30 amps), water, sewer. **Each Site:** Picnic table, fire pits. **Dump Station:** Yes. **Laundry:** No. **Pay Phone:** Yes. **Rest Rooms and Showers:** Yes. **Fuel:** No. **Propane:** No. **Internal Roads:** Paved. **RV Service:** In Watertown. **Market:** In Watertown. **Restaurant:** In Watertown. **General Store:** No. **Vending:** Yes. **Swimming Pool:** No, but there is a roped-off swimming beach on Lake Kampeska. **Playground:** Yes. **Other:** Boat launch, 3 picnic shelters, park manager's home/office. **Activities:** Boating, swimming, fishing, softball field, s& volleyball, horseshoes, basketball. **Nearby Attractions:** Golf, Thunder Road Family Fun Park, Bramble Park Zoo & Discovery Center. **Additional Information:** Watertown Area Chamber of Commerce, (800) 658-4505, or www.watertownsd.com.

Restrictions

Pets: On leash. **Fires:** In fire pits only; fires may be restricted due to weather conditions; please ask management before starting any open fires. **Alcoholic Beverages:** Yes. **Vehicle Maximum Length:** None. **Other:** 9-day stay limit; 5-day stay limit on holiday weekends.

To Get There

From the junction of US 81 and Hwy. 20 in Watertown, go 3 mi. northwest on Hwy. 20 to South Lake Dr.

YANKTON

Lewis & Clark Recreation Area, Resort, and Marina

43349 SD Hwy. 52, Yankton 57078. T: (605) 668-2985; F: (605) 668-3069; www.state.sd.us/gfp/sdparks; yanktonstp@gfp.state.sd.us.

RV ★★★ Tent ★★★

Beauty: ★★★ Site Privacy: ★★★
Spaciousness: ★★★ Quiet: ★★★★
Security: ★★★★ Cleanliness: ★★★
Insect Control: ★★★ Facilities: ★★

Located in one of South Dakota's most popular recreation areas, the campground at Lewis & Clark Recreation Area is a full-service modern resort facility. It's located on the Missouri River, five miles from Yankton, just north of the South Dakota/Nebraska border. Lewis & Clark Resort is broken into three areas. There's a campground consisting of 386 level, asphalted camping sites in several loop configurations, with grass common areas and plenty of trees for shade. You'll also find a concession area equipped with a marina, lodging, dining, and theater. Lastly, Gravins Point is the horse camp and day-use section of the park. The park offers many organized activities for all ages, and it rents anything from RVs to bikes. So, pack your insect repellent and sun screen, and whether you enjoy horseback riding or jet skiing down the Missouri River, Lewis & Clark Recreation Area can provide it all. During the warmer summer months, insects can be a problem. Security is excellent.

Basics

Operated By: South Dakota Game, Fish, & Parks Dept. **Open:** All year; water turned off in winter. **Site Assignment:** By reservation, (800) 710-CAMP. **Registration:** At entrance booth. **Fee:** $10–$15 per camping unit (no more than 2 units per site) plus entrance fee. **Parking:** At site.

Facilities

Number of Multipurpose Sites: 380. **Hookups:** Electric (20, 30 amps), potable water. **Each Site:** Picnic table, grated fire pits. **Dump Station:** Yes. **Laundry:** No. **Pay Phone:** Yes. **Rest Rooms and Showers:** Yes. **Fuel:** Yes, at the Marina. **Propane:** Yes, at the Marina. **Internal Roads:** Paved. **RV Service:** In Yankton. **Market:** In Yankton. **Restaurant:** Harbor Lights Restaurant on site or in Yankton. **General Store:** Yes, at the Marina. **Vending:** Yes. **Swimming Pool:** There is a pool at the Lewis & Clark Resort Hotel for guests, & there are 3 riverfront beaches available for swimming. **Playground:** Yes. **Other:** Lewis & Clark Resort Hotel, Harbor Lights Restaurant, Lewis & Clark Playhouse, marina, cabins, Horse Trail Camp, several boat ramps, convenience store, bicycle rental, boat rental, showers at the beach, picnic shelters w/ grills, amphitheater. **Activities:** Waterskiing, boating, swimming, interpretive programming, hiking, fishing (walleye, northerns, bass), 6 mi. of bike trails, 4 mi. of equestrian trails, fishing guide service, volleyball, archery, weekly park programs. **Additional Information:** South Dakota State Parks, 523 E. Capitol, Pierre, SD 57501, (605) 773-3391, or Yankton Chamber of Commerce, (605) 665-3636.

Restrictions

Pets: On leash. **Fires:** In fire pits only; fires may be restricted due to weather conditions; please ask management before starting any open fires. **Alcoholic Beverages:** Yes. **Vehicle Maximum Length:** None. **Other:** 14-day stay limit.

To Get There

The park is located 6 mi. west of Yankton, directly off SD Hwy. 52.

Tennessee

Tennessee was inhabited by Chickasaw, Cherokee, and other Native Americans when Hernando de Soto explored the shore near Memphis in 1541. From that time on, the Spanish maintained a landing site at present-day Memphis. The Spanish brought diseases that killed many Native Americans. As their populations decreased, tribes formed nations. The Cherokee Nation had a particularly strong impact on the culture and history of Tennessee.

In 1682, the French built a temporary post near Memphis under the direction of Rene-Robert Cavalier, Sieur de La Salle. After travelling to the Gulf of Mexico, La Salle claimed all of the land drained by the Mississippi for France. When Britain won the French and Indian War in 1763, it gained control of all territories between the Atlantic Ocean and the Mississippi River.

In spite of a royal proclamation banning white settlement west of the Appalachians, North Carolinians began to settle in Tennessee in the 1760s. These settlers fought against the British in the American Revolution. Though Tennessee has no official nickname, it's often referred to as The Volunteer State to commemorate the valor of native soldiers in wars dating back to the American Revolution.

In the 1770s Daniel Boone blazed the famous **Wilderness Road Trail** through Cumberland Gap to the Kentucky River. Under the leadership of William Blount, John Sevier, and Andrew Jackson, Tennessee attained statehood in 1796.

The young state experienced growth in three distinct economic and cultural regions. The western portion of the state produced cotton and was dependent upon slave labor. Due to its strong cultural and economic ties to the deep south, western Tennessee was loyal to the Confederacy during the Civil War. Central Tennessee saw diversified commercial farming, and also tended to side with the rebels in the Civil War. Hilly Eastern Tennessee was home to small subsistence farms. These independant farmers remained loyal to the Union, and tried to form their own state to avoid secession.

Tennesseans still divide their state into three main regions. Today, the flat Western region, with its fertile soil, is the most heavily farmed. As the home of **W.C. Handy** and **Elvis Presley** among others, **Memphis** has been a major hub for blues and rock 'n' roll music.

The rolling hills of Central Tennessee have an extremely diversified economy, with livestock, including the majestic **Tennessee Walking Horse,** being the most important farm product. The region is also known for automobile and parts manufacturing. In Nashville, the **Grand Ole Opry** has been around since 1925. Today, country music regularly enlivens the pop charts, and **Nashville** is still the heart and home of the industry.

Hilly-to-mountainous Eastern Tennessee is now dependent on manufacturing and tourism. The area is home to the **Cherokee National Forest** and the western half of **Great Smoky Mountains National Park,** an environmentally very important region. Botanists estimate that there are more species of plants in Great Smoky Mountains National Park than in all of Europe.

Tourist attractions in Western Tennessee include: Stax Museum of American Soul Music, **National Civil Rights Museum,** the Shipwreck of the Tennessee River, Tennessee River Folklife Museum, Casey Jones Home & Railroad Museum, Beale Street Historic District, **Graceland: Home of Elvis Presley,** Memphis Motorsports Park, Memphis Pink Palace Museum, Memphis Queen Line Riverboats, Memphis Rock 'n' Soul Museum, Mud Island River Park, The Peabody Hotel (Peabody Ducks), The Pyramid, Sun Studio, Davy Crockett Cabin-Museum, and the **Tennessee River Museum.**

Tourist attractions in Middle Tennessee include: Cumberland Science Museum, Nashville Zoo, Cordell Hull Birthplace Museum & State Park, **Cumberland River Walk in Clarksville,** Fort Donelson National Battlefield & Cemetery, The Homeplace 1850: A Living History Museum, Land Between the Lakes National Recreation Area, The Amish Community in Ethridge, James-Ben Studio and Galleries, Meriwether Lewis National Monument, Nashville Superspeedway, **Jack Daniels Distillery,** Standing Stone Monument, Rattle & Snap Plantation, Belle Meade Plantation, Country Music Hall of Fame, Frist Center for the Visual Arts, General Jackson Showboat, Governor's Executive Residence, Grand Ole Opry & Museum, **The Hermitage,** Music Valley Wax Museum & Sidewalk of the Stars, Nashville Shores, Opryland Hotel, Tennessee State Capitol, Tennessee Titans, Travellers Rest Plantation, Wildhorse Saloon, Historic Shelbyville, Tennessee Walking Horse Museum, Sam Davis Home, Saturn Welcome Center & Plant Tours, and The Arts Center of Cannon County.

Tourist attractions in Eastern Tennessee include: **Dollywood,** Knoxville Zoo, Bristol Motor Speedway, **Chattanooga Choo-**

Choo, Battles for Chattanooga Electric Map and Museum, Chickamauga-Chattanooga National Military Park, Lookout Mountain Incline Railway, **Rock City, Ruby Falls, Tennessee Aquarium,** Tennessee Valley Railroad, Cherokee Scenic Loop Tour, Museum Center at 5 Points, Ocoee Whitewater Center, Cumberland Gap National Historic Park, Christus Gardens, Great Smokies Mega Theatre, **Great Smoky Arts & Crafts Community,** Ober Gatlinburg, Ripley's Believe it or Not! Museum, President Andrew Johnson Museum and Library, Andrew Johnson National Historic Site, Rocky Mount Museum, Blount Mansion, Volunteer Landing, The Crockett Tavern Museum, American Museum of Science and Energy, Pigeon Forge/Gatlinburg headline musicians and production shows, Historic Rugby, **NASCAR Speed Park.**

The following facilities accept payment in checks or cash only:

Chilhowee Campground, Cherokee National Forest, Benton
Cosby Campground, Great Smoky Mountains National Park, Cosby
Cove Lake State Park, Caryville
Edgar Evins State Park, Silver Point
Indian Boundary Campground, Cherokee National Forest, Tellico Plains
Montgomery Bell State Park, Burns
Nathan Bedford Forrest State Park, Eva
Old Stone Fort State Archaeological Area, Manchester
Paris Landing State Resort Park, Buchanan
Pin Oak Campground, Natchez Trace State Resort Park, Wildersville
Reelfoot Lake State Park, South Campground, Tiptonville

Campground Profiles

ASHLAND CITY

Cheatham Lake Lock A Campground

1798 Cheatham Dam Rd., Ashland City 37015. T: (615) 792-3715 or (877) 444-6777 for reservations; www.reserveusa.com.

RV ★★★★ Tent ★★★★

Beauty: ★★★★★ Site Privacy: ★★★
Spaciousness: ★★★★★ Quiet: ★★★★
Security: ★★★★★ Cleanliness: ★★★★★
Insect Control: ★★★★ Facilities: ★★★

Located on Cheatham Lake, a development intended to improve navigation on the Cumberland River, Lock A campground is popular with fishermen. Catches include crappie, catfish, sauger, bream, and largemouth, striped, and white bass. Adjacent Cheatham State Wildlife Management Area provides hunting opportunities.The campground consists of two RV areas and one tent area. RV parking is paved, back-in style. RV sites are extremely large, while tent sites are a bit smaller. There are some pretty shade trees, but little foliage between sites; privacy is at a minimum while views of Cheatham Lake are optimized. For the loveliest views, head to sites 24–29. Security is excellent at this remote campground; the staff is extremely vigilant and the gates are locked at night. Central Tennessee is very hot and humid in late summer-visit in spring or fall for the nicest weather.

BASICS

Operated By: US Army Corps of Engineers. **Open:** Apr. 12–Oct. 28 (2002). **Site Assignment:** Some first come, first served; most sites available for reservation through the National Recreation Reservation Service (NRRS) at (877) 444-6777 or www.reserveusa.com. Reservations can be made up to 240 days in advance, full payment required upon making reservation; credit card preferred (V, MC, D, AE), or pay by money order if at least 21 days in advance of arrival. $10 fee for cancellation, or change of site or dates. Cancellation within 3 days of arrival charged first night, no-show charged $20 plus first night. Holidays 3-night min., weekends 2-night. **Registration:** Entrance station, gates close at 10 p.m. **Fee:** $23 waterfront, $19 non-waterfront & tent sites (cash, personal check, V, D, MC, AE). **Parking:** At site, on impact area, in parking lot.

FACILITIES

Number of RV Sites: 0. **Number of Tent-Only Sites:** 8 (w/ tent pads). **Number of Multipurpose Sites:** 36. **Hookups:** Water, electric (30 amps). **Each Site:** Picnic table, grill, fire ring, lantern pole. **Dump Station:** Yes. **Laundry:** Yes. **Pay Phone:** No. **Rest Rooms and Showers:** Yes. **Fuel:** No. **Propane:** No. **Internal Roads:** Paved. **RV Service:** 20 mi. in Nashville. **Market:** 11 mi. in Ashland City. **Restaurant:** 11 mi. in Ashland City. **General Store:** 11 mi. in Ashland City. **Vending:** No. **Swimming Pool:** No. **Playground:** Yes. **Other:** Boat launch, fish-cleaning station, amphitheater. **Activities:** Beach swimming, hiking trails, ball field, fishing, water sports, volleyball, basketball, picnic shelter, courtesy dock. **Nearby Attractions:** Nashville, Country Music Hall of Fame, The Parthenon, Belle Meade Plantation, Grand Ole Opry, Opryland Hotel, Hermitage Andrew Jackson Home. **Additional Information:** Nashville Tourism Information, (615) 259-4700.

RESTRICTIONS

Pets: Leash only, not allowed on beach. **Fires:** Allowed, in fire rings & grills only. **Alcoholic Beverages:** Allowed, at sites only. **Vehicle Maximum Length:** Varies (see www.reserveusa.com for site specifications). **Other:** 14-day stay limit.

TO GET THERE

From Nashville, take US Hwy. 12 west 15 mi. to Ashland City. Continue on 12 another 8 mi. to Cheap Hill. Turn left (southwest) on Cheatham Dam Rd. and drive 4 mi. Turn left into the campground.

BENTON

Chilhowee Campground, Cherokee National Forest

Rte. 1 Box 348-D, Benton 37307. T: (423) 338-5201; F: (423) 338-6577; www.southernregion.fs.fed.us/cherokee.

RV ★★★★ Tent ★★★★★

Beauty: ★★★★★ Site Privacy: ★★★★
Spaciousness: ★★★★★ Quiet: ★★★★★
Security: ★★★★★ Cleanliness: ★★★★
Insect Control: ★★★ Facilities: ★★★

Expansive Cherokee National Forest is divided by Great Smoky Mountains National Park and encompasses 620,000 acres of natural and recreation areas. The park includes much of the southern Appalachian Mountains that were razed by poor farming and timbering techniques in the late nineteenth century. In 1911, Congress passed the Weeks Act, establishing National Forests, and Cherokee became one of the first tracts of national forest land. Today, it supports thousands of species of flora and fauna. Breathtaking Chilhowee Campground offers both back-in and pull-through sites on a pristine mountainside. Parking is on pea gravel. Many sites also offer soft pea gravel tent pads. Sites are shaded by a variety of hardwoods and privacy is provided by foliage between sites. Though site size varies, all are spacious. For space and privacy, we recommend loops A, B, and F. Rest rooms vary; some loops have too few potties. Families should head for the extremely nice rest rooms at loops A and B. Security at Chilhowee is excellent. It's extremely remote and gated. Visit any time except summer holidays.

BASICS

Operated By: US Forest Service. **Open:** Apr.–Oct. **Site Assignment:** First come, first served; no reservations. **Registration:** Self-pay fee station. **Fee:** $15–$18 RV, $12 tent; 5 people max. (cash, personal checks). **Parking:** At site (2 cars), day-use parking lot $3 per day.

FACILITIES

Number of RV Sites: 0. **Number of Tent-Only Sites:** 58. **Number of Multipurpose Sites:** 18 (loops A & B). **Hookups:** Electric (20, 30 amps), loops A & B only. **Each Site:** Picnic table, fire ring, grill, lantern pole, tent pad. **Dump Station:** Yes. **Laundry:** No. **Pay Phone:** No. **Rest Rooms and Showers:** Yes. **Fuel:** No. **Propane:** No. **Internal Roads:** Paved. **RV Service:** 25 mi. in Cleveland. **Market:** 12 mi. in Benton. **Restaurant:** 10 mi. on Hwy. 64 West. **General Store:** 25 mi. in Cleveland. **Vending:** No. **Swimming Pool:** No. **Playground:** No. **Other:** Group picnic area. **Activities:** 7-acre private lake w/ swimming beach, boating (electric trolling motors only), fishing, hiking & mountain-biking trails. **Nearby Attractions:** Benton Falls, kayaking & rafting on the Ocoee & Hiwassee Rivers, Ocoee Whitewater center, Cherohala Skyway National Scenic Byway, Nancy Ward Grave Site, antique shopping. **Additional Information:** Polk county/Copper Basin Chamber of Commerce, (423) 338-5040; Tennessee Overhill Heritage Tourism Assoc., (423) 263-7232.

RESTRICTIONS

Pets: On leash only. **Fires:** In grills, fire rings only. **Alcoholic Beverages:** Not allowed. **Vehicle Maximum Length:** 50 ft. (sites vary).

TO GET THERE

From I-75, take Exit 20 (Cleveland) and go east on the bypass. Drive 5 mi. and take the US Hwy. 64 (Ocoee) Exit. Drive 14 mi. east on 64 to FR 77. Turn left and drive 7 mi. to the campground.

BUCHANAN

Paris Landing State Resort Park

Rte. 1, Buchanan 38222. T: (731) 641-4465 or (800) 250-8614; F: (731) 644-7390; www.tnstateparks.com.

RV: ★★★★ Tent: ★★★★

Beauty: ★★★★ Site Privacy: ★★★
Spaciousness: ★★★ Quiet: ★★★
Security: ★★★ Cleanliness: ★★★★
Insect Control: ★★★★ Facilities: ★★★★★

Paris Landing offers outstanding recreational amenities, including an 18-hole golf course which has consistently earned four stars from Golf Digest Magazine. On Kentucky Lake, the marina offers 200 rental slips plus other amenities. In the summer, the amphitheater hosts various live performances. The campground is laid out in four loops, among various tree species, including hickory, white and red oak. Most sites are nicely shaded although there is little privacy. Sites with hookups feature paved, back-in parking. Each site has a gravel patio area and sites are mid-sized. For space and privacy, we like sites 21–39 in the back of the campground. There are no gates at Paris Landing, but the park is fairly remote, making security okay. This area sees cold winters and hot summers. Try to visit in late spring or fall.

BASICS

Operated By: Tennessee State Parks. **Open:** Year round. **Site Assignment:** First come, first served; no reservations. **Registration:** At site, host or ranger makes rounds. **Fee:** $17 water & electric, $7 tent; prices for 2 people, $0.50 per additional person (under age 7, free); seniors & disabled discounts available (cash, personal checks). **Parking:** At sites.

FACILITIES

Number of RV Sites: 0. **Number of Tent-Only Sites:** 17 (primitive). **Number of Multipurpose Sites:** 43. **Hookups:** Water, electric (30 amps). **Each Site:** Picnic table, grill. **Dump Station:** Yes. **Laundry:** Yes (closed in winter). **Pay Phone:** Yes. **Rest Rooms and Showers:** Yes (closed in winter). **Fuel:** No (boat fuel available at marina). **Propane:** No. **Internal Roads:** Paved. **RV Service:** 22 mi. northwest in Murray, KY. **Market:** 18 mi. southwest in Paris. **Restaurant:** Park restaurant, also within 0.25 mi. **General Store:** 1 mi. hardware, 18 mi. southwest in Paris (Wal-Mart). **Vending:** Yes. **Swimming Pool:** Yes. **Playground:** Yes. **Other:** Marina, rental slips, boat launch, picnic grounds w/ pavilions, amphitheater. **Activities:** 18-hole golf course, driving range, practice greens, club & cart rentals, archery range, fishing, water sports, swimming beach, hiking trails, tennis, basketball. **Nearby Attractions:** Natchez Trace, Nathan Bedford Forrest, New Johnsonville, Port Royal & Dunbar Cave State Parks, Fort Donelson National Military Park, Land Between the Lakes National Recreation Area w/ over 100 mi. of mountain-biking trails. **Additional Information:** Paris/Henry County Chamber of Commerce, (731) 642-3431.

RESTRICTIONS

Pets: On leash only. **Fires:** Allowed. **Alcoholic Beverages:** Not allowed. **Vehicle Maximum Length:** 40 ft. (sites vary). **Other:** 14-day stay limit May 1–Aug. 31, no gray water.

TO GET THERE

From Memphis, take US Hwy. 79 east approximately 130 mi. The park is on the left (north) before the bridge across the Tennessee River. From I-24, take Exit 4 (40 mi. northwest of Nashville) and drive west on Hwy. 79 approximately 45 mi. The park entrance is the first right after the bridge. The campground is on the left inside the park.

BURNS

Montgomery Bell State Park

P.O. Box 39, Burns 37029. T: (615) 797-9052; F: (615) 797-3722; www.tnstateparks.com.

RV: ★★★★ Tent: ★★★★

Beauty: ★★★★★ Site Privacy: ★★★
Spaciousness: ★★★ Quiet: ★★★★
Security: ★★★★ Cleanliness: ★★★★
Insect Control: ★★★★ Facilities: ★★★★★

Montgomery Bell maintains excellent facilities, including an indoor pool (open all year) and an 18-hole golf course, which *Golf Digest* magazine has rated as one of the top 100 public courses in the US. Other interesting sites include an 1810 Presbyterian Church and reconstructed minister's home. An ancillary facility, Narrows of the Harpeth State Park, offers canoe access to the Harpeth River. The campground contains small, picturesque sites shaded by a variety of hardwoods including cedar. There is little undergrowth to provide privacy between sites. Some parking spaces are gravel, while others are paved. Most sites offer back-in parking, with the exception of two pull-throughs reserved for handicapped use. The nicest sites line Four Mile Creek, along the back of the campground. Security is fair at this rural park. A ranger is on duty at all times. Don't visit on summer weekends, when the park fills to capacity. Also avoid hot, humid July and August.

BASICS

Operated By: Tennessee State parks. **Open:** All year. **Site Assignment:** First come, first served; no reservations. **Registration:** Attendant or at site. **Fee:** $17 water & electric, $11 tent; prices for 2 people, $0.50 per additional person; senior discounts (cash, personal check). **Parking:** At site.

FACILITIES

Number of RV Sites: 0. **Number of Tent-Only Sites:** 27 (22 primitive). **Number of Multipurpose Sites:** 89. **Hookups:** Water, electric (30, 50 amps). **Each Site:** Picnic table, ground grill. **Dump Station:** Yes. **Laundry:** No. **Pay Phone:** Yes. **Rest Rooms and Showers:** Yes. **Fuel:** No. **Propane:** No. **Internal Roads:** Paved. **RV Service:** 35 mi. in Nashville. **Market:** Within 5 mi. **Restaurant:** Park Restaurant (may close winter), 6 mi. in Dickson. **General Store:** 8 mi. in Dickson or White Bluff. **Vending:** Yes. **Swimming Pool:** No. **Playground:** Yes. **Other:** Boat ramp (electric trolling motors only), conference center, picnic areas & pavilions. **Activities:** Lake swimming, fishing boat & canoe rentals (summer), 18-hole golf course, hiking trails including overnight back-country camping w/ permit, bicycling (on Park roads), tennis, basketball, croquet, shuffleboard, volleyball, ball fields, planned activities (summer). **Nearby Attractions:** Historic Franklin, Harpeth River, Country Music Hall of Fame, Grand Ole Opry, Opryland Hotel, The Parthenon, Hermitage Andrew Jackson Home, Belle Meade Plantation, Vanderbilt University. **Additional Information:** Nashville Tourism information, (615) 259-4700.

RESTRICTIONS

Pets: On leash only. **Fires:** Allowed, ground grills only. **Alcoholic Beverages:** Not allowed. **Vehicle Maximum Length:** 35–40 ft. (sites vary). **Other:** 14-day stay limit, no skateboards or rollerblades, under 13 years of age helmet required on bicycle.

TO GET THERE

From Nashville, take I-40 west 20 mi. to Exit 182. Drive 8 mi. northwest on State Hwy. 96 and turn right on State Hwy. 70. Drive 5 mi. to the park entrance on the right. From the west, take I-40 Exit 172. Drive north on State Hwy. 46 approximately 2 mi. until it intersects with Hwy. 70.

CARYVILLE
Cove Lake State Park

110 Cove Lake Ln., Caryville 37714. T: (423) 566-9701.

RV ★★★ Tent ★★★

Beauty: ★★★ Site Privacy: ★★★
Spaciousness: ★★★ Quiet: ★★★
Security: ★★★ Cleanliness: ★★★
Insect Control: ★★★ Facilities: ★★★★

Cove Lake offers nice facilities, including an Olympic-sized swimming pool and separate kiddie pool. Supporting bass, bluegill, and other species, 210-acre Cove Lake is available for bank or row-boat fishing. Hundreds of Canada Geese make Cove Lake their winter home. The campground includes some pretty lake front sites. Unfortunately, these sites have sloped parking spaces and are best for tent campers. Sites are on the small side of average, with little privacy. What's more, this campground is extremely popular. We felt claustrophobic. Sites have gravel, back-in parking. Tree cover ranges from totally shady to totally open. For RVs we recommend the large sites 23, 25, 54, 56, 57, and 59.Security is fine here, with 24-hour patrols. Cold weather aficionados should visit in the winter when hundreds of Canada Geese make Cove Lake their home. Others should visit in spring or fall to avoid the folks that flock here in the summer.

BASICS
Operated By: Tennessee State Parks. **Open:** 7 days a week, all year. **Site Assignment:** No reservations accepted, first come, first served. **Registration:** Campground office. **Fee:** $14–$17, cash or personal check only. **Parking:** 2 vehicles per site, plus an additional parking lot.

FACILITIES
Number of RV Sites: 0. **Number of Tent-Only Sites:** 4. **Number of Multipurpose Sites:** 100. **Hookups:** Electric (30 amps) & water (except in the winter). **Each Site:** Picnic table, grill. **Dump Station:** Yes. **Laundry:** No. **Pay Phone:** Yes. **Rest Rooms and Showers:** Yes. **Fuel:** No. **Propane:** No. **Internal Roads:** Paved. **RV Service:** 40 mi. south in Knoxville. **Market:** Less than 1 mi. **Restaurant:** At park. **General Store:** Less than 1 mi. **Vending:** Yes. **Swimming Pool:** Yes. **Playground:** Yes. **Other:** Softball field, basketball half-court, tennis courts, paved walking & bicycling trail, indoor pavilion w/ kitchen, picnic tables & pavilions, pool concession stand, pool bathhouse. **Activities:** Ranger programs, bank fishing, volleyball, tennis, basketball, softball, horseshoes, row boat & paddle boat rental, badminton, shuffleboard, ping pong. **Nearby Attractions:** Smoky Mountains, Pigeon Forge, Dollywood, Cumberland Gap National Park. **Additional Information:** Campbell County Chamber of Commerce, (423) 566-0329.

RESTRICTIONS
Pets: On leash only. **Fires:** At sites only. **Alcoholic Beverages:** Not allowed. **Vehicle Maximum Length:** No limit. **Other:** No guns allowed on property.

TO GET THERE
From I-75 take Exit 132, travel east on 25 West, go through the traffic light and the next left is the park's entrance.

CHATTANOOGA
Harrison Bay State Park

8411 Harrison Bay Rd., Harrison 37341. T: (423) 344-2272; F: (423) 344-6061; www.tnstateparks.com.

RV ★★★★★ Tent ★★★★★

Beauty: ★★★★★ Site Privacy: ★★★★
Spaciousness: ★★★★★ Quiet: ★★★★
Security: ★★★★ Cleanliness: ★★★★
Insect Control: ★★★★ Facilities: ★★★★★

Attractive Harrison Bay, situated on Chickamauga Lake, offers some of the finest fishing facilities in the state. The Lake supports largemouth bass, crappie, bream, striped bass, and catfish. Other recreation amenities include a swimming pool and separate children's pool. There are four camping areas. We recommend areas A and C, which offer lakefront camping. Although the waterfront sites are gorgeous, they tend to be smaller than inland sites. Luckily, all sites are spacious, but some are huge. The campgrounds are shaded by various tree species, including white oak, maple, hickory, and pine. Privacy varies from site to site. Parking is on gravel and usually back-in style. Area B contains some pull-through sites. Security is excellent at this rural park. Gates close at 10 p.m., and there is a night watchman. Visit in spring or fall for the nicest weather. Avoid the park on holiday weekends.

BASICS
Operated By: Tennessee State Parks. **Open:** All year (closed Monday & Tuesday indefinitely due to budget constraints). **Site Assignment:** First come, first served; no reservations. **Registration:** Camp store in-season, park personnel makes rounds. **Fee:** $10.50–$18 RV, $6.50 tent; prices for 2 people, $0.50 per additional person (cash, personal checks; credit cards accepted at camp store, summer only). **Parking:** At site (2 cars), in parking lot.

FACILITIES
Number of RV Sites: 0. **Number of Tent-Only Sites:** 28. **Number of Multipurpose Sites:** 135. **Hookups:** Water, electric (30 amps). **Each Site:** Picnic table, fire ring. **Dump Station:** Yes. **Laundry:** No. **Pay Phone:** Yes. **Rest Rooms and Showers:** Yes. **Fuel:** No (boat fuel at marina). **Propane:** No. **Internal Roads:** Paved. **RV Service:** 3 mi. south on Hwy. 58. **Market:** 3 mi. north on Hwy. 58. **Restaurant:** Park restaurant (seasonal), 3 mi. on Hwy. 58. **General Store:** Camp store (seasonal), 6 mi. in Chattanooga. **Vending:** Yes. **Swimming Pool:** Inquire at campground. **Playground:** Yes. **Other:** Recreation hall, marina (w/ boat fuel), boat launch, boat slips, children's pool, picnic area & shelters. **Activities:** Golf, fishing, boat rentals, hiking & bicycle trails, nature trail, ball field, badminton, tennis, volleyball, horseshoes, summer programs & entertainment. **Nearby Attractions:** Chattanooga Choo-Choo, Railroad Museum, Tennessee Aquarium, Lookout Mountain, Ruby Falls, Rock City, Incline Railway, Booker T. Washington State Park, Walnut St. Bridge, Chickamauga Battlefield. **Additional Information:** Chattanooga Area CVB, (800) 322-3344 or (423) 756-8687, www.chattanoogafun.com.

RESTRICTIONS
Pets: On leash only. **Fires:** Allowed, fire ring only. **Alcoholic Beverages:** Not allowed. **Vehicle Maximum Length:** No limit. **Other:** 4-week stay limit, firearms, & metal detectors prohibited.

TO GET THERE
From Chattanooga, take Exit 4 off I-75 onto State Rte. 153. Drive north on 153 to the sixth exit and turn north onto State Hwy. 58. Drive 12 mi. to Harrison Bay Rd. and turn left. The park entrance is 1 mi. ahead on the left.

CHATTANOOGA
Holiday Trav-L-Park of Chattanooga

1709 Mack Smith Rd., Chattanooga 37412. T: (706) 891-9766 or (800) 693-2877 for reservations; www.chattacamp.com.

RV ★★★ Tent ★★★

Beauty: ★★★ Site Privacy: ★★
Spaciousness: ★★ Quiet: ★★★★
Security: ★★★ Cleanliness: ★★★★
Insect Control: ★★★★ Facilities: ★★★

Located on a Civil War Battlefield, this park is home to a monument placed here at war's end by the 84th Indiana Volunteer Regiment to commemorate the valor of their slain comrades. The National Park Service provides a free Civil War video, which can be viewed in the campground's lobby. Best Holiday Trav-L-Park is convenient to Chattanooga attractions, restaurants, and shops. The passably attractive campground is laid out in rows of pull-through sites with gravel parking. Though sites are fairly shady, there is no privacy between sites. Sites are on the small side of average. The shadiest sites are 109, 116, 117, 122, and 134. Sites 1–15 are closest to the pool and recreation room. Security is fair at this suburban park. There are no gates, but the neighborhood is fine. Avoid autumn weekends.

BASICS
Operated By: Green Acres of America, a Limited Partnership. **Open:** All year. **Site Assignment:** First come, first served; reservations accepted w/ credit card deposit; 24-hour cancellation notice required to avoid a charge. **Registration:** Store, night self-registration, or next morning. **Fee:** $23 RV, $21 tent w/ water & electric, $17 tent no hookup; fees for 2 people, $2 charge for each additional person over age 6, cable hookup or 50 amp service (cash, personal check, V, MC). **Parking:** At site, in parking lot.

FACILITIES
Number of RV Sites: 0. **Number of Tent-Only Sites:** 18 primitive. **Number of Multipurpose Sites:** 163. **Hookups:** Water, electric (30, 50 amps), most sites have sewer, cable TV. **Each Site:** Picnic table, fire ring (primitive sites have grill & tent pad). **Dump Station:** Yes. **Laundry:** Yes. **Pay Phone:**

Yes. **Rest Rooms and Showers:** Yes. **Fuel:** No. **Propane:** Yes. **Internal Roads:** Paved & gravel. **RV Service:** Chattanooga. **Market:** 2 mi. (also camp store on-site). **Restaurant:** 0.5 mi. **General Store:** 4 mi. to Wal-Mart. **Vending:** Yes. **Swimming Pool:** Yes. **Playground:** Yes. **Other:** Arcade, pavilion. **Activities:** Civil War Battlefield & monument, covered wagon rides, basketball, badminton, horseshoes, summer activities. **Nearby Attractions:** River cruises, Chattanooga Choo-Choo, Tennessee Aquarium, Rock City, Ruby Falls, Incline Railway, Walnut St. Bridge, Chickamauga Battlefield, Booker T. Washington State Park. **Additional Information:** Chattanooga Area CVB, (800) 322-3344 or (423) 756-8687, www.chattanoogafun.com.

Restrictions

Pets: Leash only. **Fires:** Grills & fire rings only. **Alcoholic Beverages:** At site only. **Vehicle Maximum Length:** 70 ft.

To Get There

From I-75 southbound, take Tennessee Exit 1. From Northbound I-75, take Tennessee Exit 1B. Either way, turn right at the top of the ramp, then left on Mack Smith Rd. The campground is 0.5 mi. from the interstate.

COSBY

Cosby Campground, Great Smoky Mountains National Park

107 Park Headquarters Rd., Gatlinburg 37738. T: (865) 436-1200; F: (865) 436-1204; www.nps.gov/grsm.

RV ★★★★ Tent ★★★★★

Beauty: ★★★★★ Site Privacy: ★★★★
Spaciousness: ★★★★ Quiet: ★★★★
Security: ★★★★ Cleanliness: ★★★
Insect Control: ★★★★ Facilities: ★★★★

Faithful fans laud Cosby as the best kept secret in Great Smoky Mountains National Park. Cosby is rarely crowded, which makes it a fine destination for a summer weekend. The cool mountain air is always refreshing in late summer. Many of the hiking trails emanating from Cosby lead to picturesque waterfalls. The town of Cosby is rich in local lore—it was once considered the "moonshine capitol of the world." This gorgeous campground is designed primarily for tent campers, although many sites accommodate RVs. Site size ranges from large to huge. Sites are found in two sections built into a terraced mountainside. Thick woods shade the sites and provide some privacy between sites. Parking is back-in style, on gravel. Sites at the end of the loops are often more private. Security is fine at Cosby; there are no gates, but the campground is very remote.

Basics

Operated By: National Park Service. **Open:** Mid-Mar.–Oct. **Site Assignment:** First come, first served; no reservations. **Registration:** Self-register. **Fee:** $14 for 6 people max. per site, 2 tents or 1 RV & 1 tent (cash). **Parking:** At site (2 vehicles).

Facilities

Number of Multipurpose Sites: 163. **Hookups:** None. **Each Site:** Picnic table, fire ring, grill, tent pad. **Dump Station:** Yes. **Laundry:** No. **Pay Phone:** Yes. **Rest Rooms and Showers:** Rest rooms, No showers. **Fuel:** No. **Propane:** No. **Internal Roads:** Paved. **RV Service:** 20 mi. in Newport. **Market:** 20 mi. in Newport. **Restaurant:** 3 mi. in Cosby. **General Store:** 20 mi. in Newport. **Vending:** No. **Swimming Pool:** No. **Playground:** No. **Other:** Amphitheater, picnic area, horse trail, interpretive trail. **Activities:** Hiking, fishing, horseback riding, canoeing, backcountry hiking, ranger programs (seasonal). **Nearby Attractions:** Golf courses, Cades Cove, Pigeon Forge, Dollywood, Gatlinburg, whitewater rafting, Cherokee Indian Reservation. **Additional Information:** Gatlinburg Dept. of Tourism, (800) 343-1475; Park Information, (865) 436-1200.

Restrictions

Pets: 6-ft. leash only. **Fires:** Allowed, fire rings only. **Alcoholic Beverages:** Allowed. **Vehicle Maximum Length:** 25 ft.

To Get There

From US Hwy. 321 at Cosby, drive south 2 mi. and stay southeast on State Hwy. 32 another 2 mi. Stay right and continue approximately 3 mi. to the campground.

COUNCE

TVA Pickwick Dam Campground

Park Rd., Pickwick Dam. T: (256) 386-2228; F: (256) 386-2954; www.tva.gov.

RV ★★★★ Tent ★★★★

Beauty: ★★★★★ Site Privacy: ★★★
Spaciousness: ★★★★ Quiet: ★★★★
Security: ★★★ Cleanliness: ★★★★
Insect Control: ★★★★ Facilities: ★★

When we compare it to the campground at neighboring Pickwick Landing State Park, we prefer the campground at Pickwick Dam because it's enveloped in a gorgeous stand of southern pine. Although the campground is situated parallel to the Tennessee River, sites don't have water views. We recommend the quiet sites in the back of the campground, next to a lovely forest. The campground is completely flat and offers back-in parking on dilapidated gravel. Sites are larger than average. Without undergrowth, there are few privacy barriers between sites. The TVA provides little recreation, but Pickwick Landing State Park offers excellent amenities, including an 18-hole golf course and a restaurant. Pickwick Landing also provides access to mammoth Pickwick Lake and excellent fishing amenities. Fishermen catch bass, bream, catfish, crappie, and sauger. The TVA campground is popular. Avoid visiting on summer weekends. Security is marginal; there is no fence around the campground, but it's in a fairly remote area.

Basics

Operated By: Tennessee Valley Authority. **Open:** All year. **Site Assignment:** First come, first served; no reservations accepted. **Registration:** Self-registration honor system. **Fee:** $15 hookups, $11 tents; prices for 10 people max., 1 RV; Golden Age & Golden Access discounts honored. **Parking:** At sites (3 vehicles).

Facilities

Number of Multipurpose Sites: 88. **Hookups:** 66 sites w/ water, electric (50 amps). **Each Site:** Picnic table, grill, lantern pole, some fire rings. **Dump Station:** Yes. **Laundry:** No. **Pay Phone:** No. **Rest Rooms and Showers:** Yes. **Fuel:** No. **Propane:** No. **Internal Roads:** Paved. **RV Service:** 30 mi. in Burnsville, MS. **Market:** 5 mi. in Counce. **Restaurant:** 2 mi. in Pickwick Landing State Park. **General Store:** Hardware 3 mi. in Counce. **Vending:** No. **Swimming Pool:** No. **Playground:** No. **Activities:** Volleyball, horseshoes, fishing, waterfront walking & biking; water too swift for water sports at campground, 200 yards to activities at Pickwick Landing State Park above the dam. **Nearby Attractions:** Pickwick Landing State Park, Big Hill Pond State Natural Area, Shiloh National Military Park, Corinth National Cemetery & historic district, Tennessee River Museum, historic Savannah, historic Saltillo. **Additional Information:** Savannah/Hardin County CVB, (731) 925-2364.

Restrictions

Pets: 6-ft. leash max. **Fires:** Allowed. **Alcoholic Beverages:** Not allowed. **Vehicle Maximum Length:** No limit.

To Get There

From Jackson, drive approximately 40 mi. south on US Hwy. 45. Drive 21 mi. east on US Hwy. 64 to Savannah, then 10 mi. south on State Hwy. 128. Turn right at the campground (200 yards before reaching the dam).

CROSSVILLE

Bean Pot Campground

23 Bean Pot Campground Loop, Crossville 38558. T: (931) 484-7671; F: (931) 707-8399; peecehven97@multipro.com.

RV ★★★ Tent ★★★

Beauty: ★★★★ Site Privacy: ★★★
Spaciousness: ★★★ Quiet: ★★★★
Security: ★★★ Cleanliness: ★★★★
Insect Control: ★★★ Facilities: ★★★

This pleasant campground offers comfortably spaced sites and decent amenities. Bean Pot is convenient to I-40 and Crossville restaurants and shopping. The historic town of Rugby is nearby. Or trek to one of the area's popular waterfalls. Campsites are laid out in five rows of pull-throughs (full hookups), plus one row of back-in sites (water only). Sites are all the same size. Some are more level or shadier than others. All sites have gravel parking and concrete patios. The nicest sites, 5–8 and 14–18, are shady pull-throughs in the back of the park. However, families may prefer sites closer to the pool and game room in the front of the park. Security is fair. There are no gates, but the campground is not visible from the main road. Make advance reservations if you want to visit on the weekend of the world's largest yard sale (mid-Aug.), when Crossville is very congested.

Basics

Operated By: Jim & Ghislaine Gallagher. **Open:** All year. **Site Assignment:** First come, first served; reservations accepted w/ first-night deposit; cancellation by noon of arrival date for refund. **Registration:** Office, after-hours registration also. **Fee:** $19 full hookup, $18 water & electric, $15 tent; prices for 2 people, $2 per additional adult, $1 child (cash, personal check, V, MC). **Parking:** At site (2 cars), in parking lot.

Facilities

Number of RV Sites: 51. **Number of Tent-Only Sites:** 10. **Number of Multipurpose Sites:** 10. **Hookups:** Water, electric (20, 30, 50 amps). **Each Site:** Picnic table, some grills, some fire rings. **Dump Station:** Yes. **Laundry:** Yes. **Pay Phone:** Yes. **Rest Rooms and Showers:** Yes. **Fuel:** No. **Propane:** Yes. **Internal Roads:** Gravel & paved. **RV Service:** 6 mi. in Crossville. **Market:** 6 mi. in Crossville. **Restaurant:** 1.5 mi. in Crossville. **General Store:** Convenience store on-site, 6 mi. in Crossville. **Vending:** Yes. **Swimming Pool:** Yes. **Playground:** Yes. **Other:** Clubhouse, game room, RV storage. **Activities:** Nature trail, putting green, horseshoes, basketball. **Nearby Attractions:** Golf ("Golf Capital of Tennessee"), antique shopping, Historic Oak Ridge, Ozone, Fall Creek & Burgess Falls, Muddy Pond Mennonite Community, wineries. **Additional Information:** Crossville Chamber of Commerce, (931) 484-8444.

Restrictions

Pets: On leash only. **Fires:** Allowed in designated areas only. **Alcoholic Beverages:** Allowed at sites only. **Vehicle Maximum Length:** 45 ft.

To Get There

From I-40, take Exit 322. Drive north 1.5 mi. on Peavine Rd./State Hwy. 101. Turn right on Bean Pot Campground Rd. The campground is 0.25 mi. ahead on the left.

CROSSVILLE
Cumberland Mountain State Park

24 Office Dr., Crossville 38555. T: (931) 484-6138 or (800) 250-8618; F: (615) 741-1421; www.tnstateparks.com.

RV ★★★★ Tent ★★★★

Beauty: ★★★★	Site Privacy: ★★★
Spaciousness: ★★★★	Quiet: ★★★★
Security: ★★★★★	Cleanliness: ★★★★
Insect Control: ★★★★	Facilities: ★★★★★

Cumberland Mountain is home to the largest masonry structure built by the Civilian Conservation Corps, a lovely dam and bridge made of indigenous Crab Orchard stone (a type of sandstone). The park's restaurant offers picturesque lake views. On site, Bear Trace golf course was designed by Jack Nicklaus. Shore fishing on the small lake yields catfish, bass, brim, and bluegill. Unfortunately, the campground is not the most attractive area of the park. It's laid out in a series of loops with some extremely spacious sites. Other sites are average sized. Most sites are nicely shaded, although there is little foliage to provide privacy between sites. Parking is paved, back-in style. For privacy, try sites 11, 30, or 31. The park is in the small town of Crossville. Nonetheless, security is excellent; gates close at night and rangers patrol until midnight. Visit in the spring, early summer, or fall to avoid heat and humidity.

Basics

Operated By: Tennessee State Parks. **Open:** All year (closed Monday & Tuesday indefinitely). **Site Assignment:** First come, first served; no reservations accepted. **Registration:** Camp store, ranger makes rounds at night. **Fee:** $17 for 2 people, $0.50 per additional person; senior & disabled discounts available (cash, personal checks, V, MC, D, AE). **Parking:** At site (2 vehicles).

Facilities

Number of Multipurpose Sites: 142. **Hookups:** Water, electric (30 amps). **Each Site:** Picnic table, grill, some sites w/ lantern pole, fire ring & small gravel pad. **Dump Station:** Yes. **Laundry:** No. **Pay Phone:** Yes. **Rest Rooms and Showers:** Yes. **Fuel:** No. **Propane:** No. **Internal Roads:** Paved. **RV Service:** 4 mi. in Crossville. **Market:** 4 mi. in Crossville. **Restaurant:** Park restaurant (seasonal), several restaurants within 5 mi. **General Store:** Camp store, 4 mi. in Crossville. **Vending:** Yes. **Swimming Pool:** Yes. **Playground:** Yes. **Other:** Boat house, recreation lodge, picnic area. **Activities:** 18-hole golf course, ball field, tennis, volleyball, rowboat, paddleboat, & canoe rentals (no private boats), hiking & nature trails, basketball, horseshoes, summer naturalist programs. **Nearby Attractions:** Cumberland Homestead Tower Center & Museum, Crossville ("Golf Capitol of Tennessee"), Palace Theater, Chestnut Hill, Highland Manor & Stonehaus Wineries, Bledsoe & Mount Roosevelt State Forests. **Additional Information:** Crossville Chamber of Commerce, (931) 484-8444.

Restrictions

Pets: On leash & kept quiet. **Fires:** Allowed, in fire ring only. **Alcoholic Beverages:** Not allowed. **Vehicle Maximum Length:** No limit. **Other:** 14-day stay limit (except designated sites), quiet enforced.

To Get There

From I-40 (70 mi. west of Knoxville and 100 mi. east of Nashville), take Exit 317 at Crossville. Drive south 8 mi. on US Hwy. 127. The park entrance is on the right (west).

DOVER
Piney Campground, Land Between the Lakes

100 Van Morgan Dr., Golden Pond 42211. T: (270) 924-2000; F: (270) 924-2087; www.lbl.org.

RV ★★★★ Tent ★★★★

Beauty: ★★★★★	Site Privacy: ★★★
Spaciousness: ★★★★	Quiet: ★★★
Security: ★★★★★	Cleanliness: ★★★★★
Insect Control: ★★★★	Facilities: ★★★★★

Land Between the Lakes, administered by the US Department of Agriculture, offers interesting activities, including hundreds of miles of hiking, canoeing, and mountain biking trails. Other unique facilities include the planetarium and observatory (call for schedule), a nineteenth century Farm, and an elk and bison prairie. There are three multipurpose campgrounds. Piney, located at the south end of the recreation area, offers eight camping loops. Though most sites are larger than average, size varies. Lovely trees, including loblolly and shortleaf pine, shade the campgrounds. There is little foliage between sites. Most sites offer pea gravel, back-in parking. At Black Oak Loop, sites 14, 23–26, 30, and 32 are fabulous, with gorgeous views of Kentucky Lake. Tent campers should head for waterfront sites on the nearly deserted Virginia and Sweet gum loops (non-electric). Extremely remote and gated, Piney is very safe. Avoid this area on summer weekends and holidays. For solitude, plan a late spring or early fall visit.

Basics

Operated By: USDA Forest Service. **Open:** Mar. 1–Nov. 30. **Site Assignment:** First come, first served; no reservations. **Registration:** Gatehouse, campground entrance. **Fee:** $19 full hookup, $15 water & electric, $12 tent; prices for 8 people; Golden Age & Golden Access discounts available (cash, personal check, V, MC, D, AE). **Parking:** At site (2 vehicles plus camping unit, $4 per additional vehicle).

Facilities

Number of RV Sites: 44. **Number of Tent-Only Sites:** 59 primitive. **Number of Multipurpose Sites:** 281. **Hookups:** Water, electric (20, 30 amps). **Each Site:** Picnic table, fire ring, tent pad, lantern pole in primitive area. **Dump Station:** Yes. **Laundry:** Yes. **Pay Phone:** Yes. **Rest Rooms and Showers:** Yes. **Fuel:** No. **Propane:** No. **Internal Roads:** Asphalt gravel. **RV Service:** 25 mi. in Dover. **Market:** 8 mi. in Dover. **Restaurant:** 4 mi. in Dover. **General Store:** camp store, also 8 mi. in Dover. **Vending:** Yes. **Swimming Pool:** No. **Playground:** Yes. **Other:** Elk & Bison prairie, visitor canter, planetarium, The Homeplace-1850, nature center, campfire theater, boat ramps, fishing pier. **Activities:** Swimming beach, fishing, archery range, ball field, bicycle trails, mountain biking trails, equestrian trails, canoeing, hiking trails, softball, volleyball, basketball, summer recreation programs. **Nearby Attractions:** Kentucky Lake, Fort Donelson National Battlefield, Paris Landing State Resort Park, Cross Creek Wildlife Refuge. **Additional Information:** Clarksville Chamber of Commerce, (931) 647-2331; Stewart County Chamber of Commerce, (931) 232-8290; Land Between the Lakes Information, (800) LBL-7077.

Restrictions

Pets: On leash only. **Fires:** Allowed, fire rings only. **Alcoholic Beverages:** Allowed, sites only. **Vehicle Maximum Length:** No limit. **Other:** 21-day stay limit.

To Get There

From I-24, take TN Exit 4. Drive west on Hwy. 79 for 26 mi. Go through the town of Dover and drive west for 8 more mi. Turn right onto CR 100 and drive north for 4 mi. (When you enter Land between the Lakes, CR 100 turns into The Trace.)

Turn left onto Fort Henry Rd. The campground is 8 mi. ahead. From the north, take I-24 to KY Exit 31. Drive south on The Trace 35 mi. to Fort Henry Rd. Turn right and drive west for 8 mi. to Piney Campground.

EVA
Nathan Bedford Forrest State Park

1825 Pilot Knob Rd., Eva 38333. T: (731) 584-1841; F: (731) 584-1841; www.tnstateparks.com.

RV ★★★★ Tent ★★★★

Beauty: ★★★★ Site Privacy: ★★★
Spaciousness: ★★★★ Quiet: ★★★★
Security: ★★★ Cleanliness: ★★★★
Insect Control: ★★ Facilities: ★★★★

Located at the southern end of Kentucky Lake, attractive Nathan Bedford Forrest State Park offers limited recreation. Recreation within the park includes a ten-mile hiking trail. Off property, there are marinas and public boat ramps, which provide access to Kentucky Lake, known for its sauger, crappie, bream, catfish, and various bass populations. The Happy Hollow camping loop includes various sized sites under a shady cover of white and red oak, maple, cedar, sycamore, sweetgum and hackberry. However, there is little foliage between sites to provide privacy. Parking is paved, back-in style. The nicest sites, 1, 3, 5, 23, 24, and 31–35, abut the woods in the back of the campground. There are no gates at Nathan Bedford Forrest. However, the park is extremely remote, making security fair. Avoid this part of Tennessee in late summer when the weather tends to extremes of heat and humidity.

Basics

Operated By: Tennessee State Parks. **Open:** All year. **Site Assignment:** First come, first served; no reservations accepted. **Registration:** Park office or ranger makes rounds. **Fee:** $17 RV, $14 developed tent, $10 primitive; prices for 2 people, $0.50 per additional person; senior & disabled discounts available (cash, personal checks). **Parking:** At sites in designated areas only.

Facilities

Number of RV Sites: 0. **Number of Tent-Only Sites:** 13 primitive. **Number of Multipurpose Sites:** 38. **Hookups:** Water, electric (20, 30, 50 amps). **Each Site:** Picnic table, grill, concrete pad. **Dump Station:** Yes. **Laundry:** No. **Pay Phone:** Yes. **Rest Rooms and Showers:** Yes. **Fuel:** No. **Propane:** No. **Internal Roads:** Paved. **RV Service:** Local service. **Market:** 3 mi. in Eva. **Restaurant:** 8 mi. in Camden. **General Store:** 8 mi. in Camden. **Vending:** Beverages only. **Swimming Pool:** No. **Playground:** Yes. **Other:** Boat launch, folk-life museum, picnic areas, & pavilions. **Activities:** Beach swimming in designated areas, fishing, skiing, hiking trails, backpacking, softball, horseshoes, volleyball, ball field, planned programs, managed hunts. **Nearby Attractions:** Paris Landing & Natchez Trace State Parks, Fort Donelson National Historic Site, Lorretta Lynn's Dude Ranch. **Additional Information:** Camden Chamber of Commerce, (731) 584-8395.

Restrictions

Pets: On leash only. **Fires:** Allowed (subject to burn ban). **Alcoholic Beverages:** Not allowed. **Vehicle Maximum Length:** 30 ft. **Other:** No firearms.

To Get There

From Nashville, drive west on I-40 and take Exit 126. Drive north approximately 15 mi. on US Hwy. 641 straight through the by-pass. Continue 2 mi. and turn right onto Main St. Drive through town to Court Square and turn right on Local Rte. 191. This dead-ends in 9 mi. at the park.

GATLINBURG
Elkmont Campground, Great Smoky Mountains National Park

107 Park Headquarters Rd., Gatlinburg 37738. T: (865) 436-1200; F: (865) 436-1204; www.nps.gov.

RV ★★★★★ Tent ★★★★

Beauty: ★★★★★ Site Privacy: ★★★
Spaciousness: ★★★★ Quiet: ★★★
Security: ★★ Cleanliness: ★★★★
Insect Control: ★★★★ Facilities: ★★★★

Of the Great Smoky Mountains National Park campgrounds, Elkmont is the closest to the tourist attractions at Gatlinburg and Pigeon Forge and the park's Sugarland visitor's center. This campground stays busy all summer, and should be completely avoided on summer holidays. We recommend Elkmont in the spring, when crowds are minimal and wildflowers are blooming. The campground is laid out in a series of loops that are sandwiched together. Though site size is above average, the campground is often so packed with people that you may feel cramped. Shade is provided by a variety of trees, with a little foliage to provide privacy between sites. Sites offer back-in, gravel parking. For peace and quiet, we prefer sections G, H, K, L, M, and N. Security is poor at Elkmont; there are no gates. Safeguard your valuables. Also, mosquitoes can be a nuisance in late summer—bring insect repellent.

Basics

Operated By: National Park Service. **Open:** Mid-Mar.–Nov. **Site Assignment:** First come, first served; reservations accepted for May 15–Oct. 31 up to 5 months in advance, w/ full deposit; $13.25 cancellation fee w/ at least 24-hour notice, otherwise first night plus fee charged; reservations made by calling (800) 365-CAMP or at reservations.nps.gov (personal check, money order, V, D, MC). **Registration:** Self-registration. **Fee:** $14–$20 for 6 people max. per site, 2 tents or 1 tent & 1 RV; Golden Age & Golden Access discounts available (cash only during self–registration off-Season). **Parking:** At site (2 vehicles).

Facilities

Number of RV Sites: 0. **Number of Tent-Only Sites:** 5. **Number of Multipurpose Sites:** 220. **Hookups:** None. **Each Site:** Picnic table, fire ring, grill, gravel tent pad. **Dump Station:** Yes. **Laundry:** No. **Pay Phone:** Yes. **Rest Rooms and Showers:** Rest rooms, no showers. **Fuel:** No. **Propane:** No. **Internal Roads:** Paved. **RV Service:** 10 mi. in Gatlinburg. **Market:** 10 mi. in Gatlinburg. **Restaurant:** 10 mi. in Gatlinburg. **General Store:** 10 mi. in Gatlinburg. **Vending:** No. **Swimming Pool:** No. **Playground:** No. **Other:** Amphitheater, picnic areas, horse trails, interpretive trails. **Activities:** Hiking, fishing, horseback riding, canoeing, backcountry hiking, ranger programs (seasonal). **Nearby Attractions:** Golf courses, Cades Cove, Pigeon Forge, Dollywood, Gatlinburg, whitewater rafting, Cherokee Indian Reservation. **Additional Information:** Pigeon Forge Visitor information, (865) 453-5700; Park Information, (865) 436-1200.

Restrictions

Pets: 6-ft. leash only. **Fires:** Allowed, fire rings only. **Alcoholic Beverages:** Allowed. **Vehicle Maximum Length:** 32 ft.

To Get There

From Gatlinburg drive approximately 6 mi. southwest on Little River Rd. Elkmont Campground is 1 mi. south (left) off Little River Rd.

GATLINBURG
Outdoor Resorts of America

4229 Parkway East, Gatlinburg 37738. T: (865) 436-5861 or (800) 677-5861; www.gocampingamerica.com/orgatlinburg.

RV ★★★★★ Tent n/a

Beauty: ★★★★★ Site Privacy: ★★★
Spaciousness: ★★★★ Quiet: ★★★★★
Security: ★★★★★ Cleanliness: ★★★★★
Insect Control: ★★★★ Facilities: ★★★★

One of the prettiest campgrounds in Gatlinburg, Outdoor Resorts offers extremely well kept recreational facilities. Children enjoy the playground, pool, and mini-golf. Adults appreciate the carefully manicured landscaping, which includes shady weeping willow trees. The campground has two areas separated by the main road. Two creeks flow through the park, lulling campers with their soft bubbling sound. The park would be very quiet in any event—most of the spots are occupied by long-term rentals. RV sites are large, with shrubs and trees providing privacy between many. All parking is paved, back-in style. Each site has a bit of grass and a concrete patio. Ask for a creek-side site. Security is excellent; the gate is locked 24-hours a day. Gatlinburg is extremely pleasant in late summer due to its high elevation. Visit on weekdays for fall "leaf peeping"—weekend crowds are unbearable.

Basics

Operated By: Outdoor Resorts. **Open:** 7 days, all year. **Site Assignment:** Pick your site; reserve from Jan. 1; $35 deposit holds reservation (pay by check or credit card); cancel 3 days in advance for full refund. **Registration:** At camp office. **Fee:** $30 interior, $35 waterfront, fees include 4 people (cash, check, MC, V). **Parking:** At sites.

Facilities

Number of RV Sites: 376. **Number of Tent-Only Sites:** 0. **Hookups:** Water, electric, cable, sewer. **Each Site:** Picnic table, fire ring (most), concrete pad. **Dump Station:** No. **Laundry:** Yes. **Pay Phone:** Yes. **Rest Rooms and Showers:** Yes. **Fuel:** No. **Propane:** Yes. **Internal Roads:** Paved.

RV Service: Yes. **Market:** 7 mi. west in Gatlinburg. **Restaurant:** On site, in season. **General Store:** 2.5 mi. east. **Vending:** Beverages only. **Swimming Pool:** Yes. **Playground:** Yes. **Other:** Game room & lodge. **Activities:** Fishing lake, trout streams, tennis, shuffleboard, mini-golf, horseshoes, volleyball, church service in-season. **Nearby Attractions:** Gatlinburg attractions, Pigeon Forge attractions, Dollywood, Great Smoky Mountains National Park. **Additional Information:** Pigeon Forge Dept. of Tourism, (800) 251-9100.

Restrictions

Pets: On leash only. **Fires:** Fire rings only. **Alcoholic Beverages:** Not allowed. **Vehicle Maximum Length:** 40 ft.

To Get There

From I-40, take Exit 440 (Hwy. 321 South). Go south for 7 mi. and turn right before the post office. The entrance is 6.5 mi. ahead on the right.

GATLINBURG
Twin Creek RV Resort

1202 East Parkway, Gatlinburg 37738. T: (865) 436-7081 or (800) 252-8077; F: (865) 430-5742; www.twincreekrvresort.com.

RV: ★★★★ Tent: n/a

Beauty: ★★★★ Site Privacy: ★★★
Spaciousness: ★★★ Quiet: ★★★
Security: ★★★ Cleanliness: ★★★★★
Insect Control: ★★★★ Facilities: ★★★

Though it's only two miles from downtown Gatlinburg, Twin Creek feels secluded. Built in a picturesque valley, the campground is nicely landscaped and extremely tidy. The pool, whirlpool, and other facilities are in good condition. Beautiful trees shade the campground. Site size is average and there is little privacy. All parking is paved. Some sites offer parallel parking while others offer back-in. Each site has a wooden patio. The prettiest sites, 54–56, are along the creek. Gatlinburg roads become very congested on busy weekends, especially in the fall. We recommend weekday visits. If you visit on a weekend, take advantage of the trolley, which stops inside the park, and can take you all the way to outlet malls in Pigeon Forge. With no gates, security is fair.

Basics

Operated By: Twin Creek RV Resort. **Open:** Apr.–Nov. **Site Assignment:** Sites assigned; reservations recommended, deposit policy varies. **Registration:** Office, night arrival w/ reservation preferred. **Fee:** $35 peak season, prices vary; AAA, AARP, FMCA, Good Sam discounts available (cash, V, MC). **Parking:** At site (1 car, charge may apply for additional vehicles).

Facilities

Number of RV Sites: 75. **Number of Tent-Only Sites:** 0. **Number of Multipurpose Sites:** None. **Hookups:** Water, electric (30, 50 amps), sewer, cable. **Each Site:** Picnic table, fire ring, grill. **Dump Station:** No. **Laundry:** Yes. **Pay Phone:** Yes. **Rest Rooms and Showers:** Yes. **Fuel:** No. **Propane:** No. **Internal Roads:** Paved. **RV Service:** Yes. **Market:** Across the street. **Restaurant:** One block. **General Store:** Camp store, hardware 0.25 mi. **Vending:** Beverages only. **Swimming Pool:** Yes (also whirlpool & wading pool). **Playground:** Yes. **Other:** Arcade, boutique. **Activities:** Jacuzzi, children's pool, Sunday worship service. **Nearby Attractions:** Trolley to Pigeon Forge, Dollywood, Gatlinburg attractions, water park, Dixie Stampede, Elvis Museum, Kids Country, helicopter tours, white-water rafting, Cherokee Indian Reservation. **Additional Information:** Pigeon Forge Visitor information, (865) 453-5700.

Restrictions

Pets: On leash only. **Fires:** Allowed, fire rings only. **Alcoholic Beverages:** Allowed, at sites only. **Vehicle Maximum Length:** 45 ft. (sites vary). **Other:** Call ahead about pet restrictions, no motorcycles.

To Get There

From Knoxville, Take I-40 east to Exit 407 and drive approximately 20 mi. south on US Hwy. 441. Turn left on US Hwy. 321 at light No. 3 and the campground is 2 mi. on the right. From Asheville, take I-40 west to Exit 440 and turn south on Hwy. 321. The campground is approximately 25 mi. on the left.

GATLINBURG
Yogi Bear's Jellystone Park

P.O. Box 282, Gatlinburg 37738. T: (423) 487-5534 or (800) 210-2119 for reservations; gatlyogi@bellsouth.net.

RV: ★★★★ Tent: ★★★★

Beauty: ★★★★ Site Privacy: ★★★★
Spaciousness: ★★★ Quiet: ★★★
Security: ★★★★ Cleanliness: ★★★
Insect Control: ★★★★ Facilities: ★★★★★

Seasoned camping families know that Yogi Bear campgrounds offer excellent children's recreation. This park is no exception. Facilities are well maintained and activities are well planned. There are separate tent and RV camping areas. RV site size varies, but none are huge. Parking is on gravel. There are back-in and pull-through sites. Most are shady, and the nicest are along the bubbling creek. Creek-side sites 59–61 are small, but extremely pretty, while creek-side sites 41–50 are more spacious, but not as attractive. The largest site (77, a pull-through) is not creek-side. Tent sites are pretty and slightly secluded from the RV sites. There are no gates at this small-town campground, but employees are vigilant (we were questioned twice while on property). Security is good. Visit Gatlinburg in August to enjoy the cool mountain air. Avoid fall weekends, when leaf peepers cause legendary traffic jams in small mountain towns.

Basics

Operated By: Tim Gordon. **Open:** Mid-Mar.–Nov. 1, limited winter camping. **Site Assignment:** Usually assigned at check-in; reserve one year in advance; $50 deposit, refund w/ 7-day notice for cancellation (less $5 administration fee). **Registration:** At camp office. **Fee:** $25 tent (or AAA, Good Sam, Club Yogi), $31 for 2 people. **Parking:** In sites, except some walk-in tent sites.

Facilities

Number of RV Sites: 63. **Number of Tent-Only Sites:** 21. **Hookups:** Water, electric, sewer, cable. **Each Site:** Picnic table, fire ring, gravel. **Dump Station:** Yes. **Laundry:** Yes. **Pay Phone:** Yes. **Rest Rooms and Showers:** Yes. **Fuel:** No. **Propane:** No. **Internal Roads:** Gravel. **RV Service:** 30 mi. west in Sevierville. **Market:** 14 mi. east in Newport. **Restaurant:** 1 mi. west in Cosby. **General Store:** Wal-Mart, 30 mi. west in Sevierville. **Vending:** Yes. **Swimming Pool:** Yes. **Playground:** Yes. **Other:** Movie theater, pavilion. **Activities:** Children's Day Camp (in season), mini-golf, game room, swimming, fishing, hiking, basketball, horseshoes, bingo, live entertainment, wagon rides, church services (in-season). **Nearby Attractions:** Great Smoky Mountains National Park, Pigeon Forge, white-water rafting, outlet shopping, Dollywood, museums, caverns. **Additional Information:** Gatlinburg Dept. of Tourism, (800) 343-1475.

Restrictions

Pets: Not in tent area, no vicious breeds. **Fires:** Fire rings only. **Alcoholic Beverages:** In sites only. **Vehicle Maximum Length:** 40 ft. **Other:** Max. 6 people per site.

To Get There

From I-40, take Exit 435. Turn right onto Hwy. 321 and go southeast approximately 15 mi. Follow Yogi signs, right at 6 mi., left at 0.25 mi., right at 7 mi., then 2.5 mi. The entrance is on the left.

HENDERSON
Chickasaw State Park

20 Cabin Ln., Henderson 38340. T: (731) 989-5141 or (800) 458-1752; F: (731) 989-5966; www.tnstateparks.com.

RV: ★★★★ Tent: ★★★★

Beauty: ★★★★★ Site Privacy: ★★★★
Spaciousness: ★★★★ Quiet: ★★★★
Security: ★★★ Cleanliness: ★★★★
Insect Control: ★★★★ Facilities: ★★★★★

Shady tall pines and hardwoods grace the campgrounds at Chickasaw. There are separate campgrounds for RVs, tents, and equestrian use. The RV campground consists of two loops, each with its own bathhouse. Sites are on the large side of average. All parking is paved and there are pull-through and back-in sites. Foliage between some sites provides seclusion. Our favorite RV sites are the 30s and number 40, which is absolutely gorgeous. The small tent campground is nicely wooded with views of picturesque Lake Placid. With only six sites, the ratio of potties to campsites is unusually high. Lake Placid is stocked with bass and bluegill (no personally owned boats allowed). Adjoining the state park, Chickasaw State Forest contains 50 miles of roads and multi-use trails. There are no gates, but the park is off the beaten path—security is fair. Visit any time except summer holidays and hot late summer.

Basics

Operated By: Tennessee State Parks. **Open:** All year (closed Monday & Tuesday indefinitely due to budget constraints). **Site Assignment:** First come, first served; no reservations. **Registration:** At sites, ranger makes rounds. **Fee:** $17 RV & Wrangler, $11.50 tent; prices for 2 people, $0.50 per additional person; Golden Access, senior discounts (cash, personal check, V, MC, D, AE, DC, CB). **Parking:** At sites, in parking lot.

Facilities

Number of RV Sites: 0. **Number of Tent-Only Sites:** 29 (water only). **Number of Multipurpose Sites:** 53 (34 water & electric equestrian sites). **Hookups:** Water, electric (20, 30 amps). **Each Site:** Picnic table, grill. **Dump Station:** Yes. **Laundry:** No. **Pay Phone:** Yes. **Rest Rooms and Showers:** Yes. **Fuel:** No. **Propane:** No. **Internal Roads:** Paved. **RV Service:** 25 mi. in Jackson. **Market:** 3 mi. on Hwy. 100. **Restaurant:** Park restaurant, also 8 mi. in Henderson. **General Store:** 8 mi. in Henderson (hardware), 25 mi. in Jackson (Wal-Mart). **Vending:** Beverages only. **Swimming Pool:** No. **Playground:** Yes. **Other:** Stables, 18-hole golf course, boat dock (electric motors only), picnic shelters, group lodge. **Activities:** Nature trail, equestrian trails, beach, swimming (when lifeguard on duty), fishing, rowboat & paddle boat rentals, archery range, tennis, basketball, volleyball, ball field, summertime organized activities including square dancing. **Nearby Attractions:** Shiloh Military Park, Pinson Mounds State Park, Casey Jones Museum, Parker's Crossroads & Britton Lane Civil War Battlefields. **Additional Information:** Jackson Chamber of Commerce, (731) 423-2200.

Restrictions

Pets: On leash only. **Fires:** In designated areas, grills only. **Alcoholic Beverages:** Not allowed. **Vehicle Maximum Length:** Sites vary. **Other:** 2-week stay limit, no firearms.

To Get There

From US Hwy. 45 (17 mi. south of Jackson), drive west 8 mi. on State Hwy. 100. The park is on the left. From Memphis, drive 80 mi. east on US Hwy. 64, which becomes State Hwy. 100.

HILHAM

Standing Stone State Park

1674 Standing Stone Park Hwy., Hilham 38556. T: (931) 823-6347; F: (931) 823-3984; www.tnstateparks.com.

 ★★★★ ▲ ★★★★

Beauty: ★★★★ Site Privacy: ★★★★
Spaciousness: ★★★★ Quiet: ★★★★★
Security: ★★★★ Cleanliness: ★★★★
Insect Control: ★★★★ Facilities: ★★★★

Located on the Cumberland Plateau, Standing Stone offers sites with gravel, back-in parking. Though most sites are ample, size varies. However, this park is extremely remote and rarely crowded, so you're likely to have plenty of elbowroom. Most sites have some greenery to provide seclusion, and all are nicely shaded by various hardwood species. The largest sites include 1, 24, and 28. Standing Stone maintains nice facilities including an archery range and ten miles of hiking trails. They also host special events such as the Roley Hole Marble Tournament. On property, 69-acre Standing Stone Lake is stocked with bass and bluegill. Nearby, giant Dale Hollow Lake offers some of the best fishing in Tennessee and Kentucky. There are no gates at Standing Stone, making security fair. This pretty park is an excellent destination on summer weekends, though holidays should be avoided.

Basics

Operated By: Tennessee State Parks Dept. of Environment & Conservation. **Open:** All year (closed Monday & Tuesday indefinitely due to budget constraints). **Site Assignment:** First come, first served; no reservations. **Registration:** Office, or campground host will make rounds, night arrival register next morning. **Fee:** $17 RV, $14 tent; prices for 2 people, $0.50 per additional person; Golden Age & Golden Access discounts available (cash, personal check, V, MC, D, AE). **Parking:** At site (2 cars).

Facilities

Number of Multipurpose Sites: 36. **Hookups:** Water, electric (30 amps). **Each Site:** Picnic table, grill, fire ring. **Dump Station:** Yes. **Laundry:** Yes. **Pay Phone:** Yes (in park). **Rest Rooms and Showers:** Yes (closed in winter). **Fuel:** No. **Propane:** No. **Internal Roads:** Paved. **RV Service:** 21 mi. in Cookeville. **Market:** 8 mi. on Hwy. 52. **Restaurant:** 12 mi. in Livingston. **General Store:** 12 mi. in Livingston hardware or 21 mi. in Cookeville Wal-Mart. **Vending:** Beverages only. **Swimming Pool:** Yes (seasonal, wading pool also). **Playground:** Yes (3). **Other:** Picnic areas & pavilions, meeting room, rec center w/ ping pong. **Activities:** Jon boat rentals (bring your own trolling motor-electric motors only), bank fishing, hiking trails, basketball, softball field, volleyball, horseshoes, tennis, archery range, Rolley Hole Marble tournament in Sept. **Nearby Attractions:** Dale Hollow Lake, Cordell Hull Birthplace Museum & State Park, Big South Fork National River & Recreation Area, Sgt. Alvin C. York State Historic Site. **Additional Information:** Livingston/Overton County Chamber of Commerce, (931) 823-6421.

Restrictions

Pets: On leash only. **Fires:** In grills, fire rings only. **Alcoholic Beverages:** Not allowed. **Vehicle Maximum Length:** 30 ft. (sites vary). **Other:** 14-day stay limit.

To Get There

From I-40, take Exit 288 at Cookeville and drive north approximately 10 mi. on State Hwy. 111. Take the bypass to State Hwy. 52 north and drive 12 mi. to the park entrance on the left. This is Rte. 136, and the campground is 1 mi. from Hwy. 52. (This is the only access for RVs, due to a 1-lane bridge on Rte. 136 north of the park.)

HURRICANE MILLS

Loretta Lynn Dude Ranch

General Delivery, Hurricane Mills 37078. T: (931) 296-7700; F: (931) 296-3378; www.lorettalynn.com; campground@lorettalynn.com.

 ★★★★  ★★★★

Beauty: ★★★★ Site Privacy: ★★★
Spaciousness: ★★★ Quiet: ★★★
Security: ★★★ Cleanliness: ★★★★
Insect Control: ★★★ Facilities: ★★★★

Ms. Lynn's ranch and grounds are enchanting. On property, you'll find her beautifully landscaped massive neo-classical mansion complete with doric columns. The restored gristmill across the river provides idyllic photo opportunities. Inside the gristmill is a museum housing the star's memorabilia and costumes. In season, there are festivals and special events on the grounds (call for schedule). Various outdoor activities are available nearby. The massive campground features some extremely attractive sites, and some downright disappointing sites. Luckily, the less attractive sites are used only on the busiest weekends. In order to choose a pretty site, we recommend arriving a day early if you're visiting on a special event weekend. The nicer portion of the campground has a picturesque creek flowing through the middle and features average sized sites shaded by a variety of hardwoods. Parking is on gravel, and there are both back-in and pull-through sites. Loretta Lynn's Ranch is extremely remote, making gates unnecessary. Security is fine.

Basics

Operated By: Loretta Lynn Ranch, Inc. **Open:** Apr.–Oct. **Site Assignment:** First come, first served; reservations accepted w/ one-night deposit; 72-hour cancellation notice for refund. **Registration:** Main office, night arrival register next morning. **Fee:** $22 full hookup, $19 water & electric, $17 tent; prices for 2 people, $5 each additional person; seniors 10% discount (cash, personal check, V, MC, D). **Parking:** At sites (2 max.), in parking lot.

Facilities

Number of RV Sites: 200. **Number of Tent-Only Sites:** 100s of acres of primitive undesignated tent camping. **Number of Multipurpose Sites:** None. **Hookups:** Water, electric (30, 50 amps), sewer. **Each Site:** Some sites w/ picnic table, grill, fire ring. **Dump Station:** Yes. **Laundry:** Yes. **Pay Phone:** Yes. **Rest Rooms and Showers:** Yes. **Fuel:** No. **Propane:** No. **Internal Roads:** Paved & gravel. **RV Service:** 45 mi. in Dixon. **Market:** 7.5 mi. in Waverly. **Restaurant:** snack bar on-site, 7 mi. in Waverly. **General Store:** Camp store, 7 mi. in Waverly. **Vending:** Yes. **Swimming Pool:** Yes (seasonal). **Playground:** Yes. **Other:** Recreation Hall. **Activities:** Loretta Lynn Home Tour, Western town, Loretta Lynn Museum, fishing, canoeing (seasonal), mountain biking & hiking trails, campfire entertainment (seasonal), hayrides (occasional), horseshoes, softball, volleyball. **Nearby Attractions:** Humphreys County Museum & Civil War Fort, Blue Creek Nature Center, Johnsonville State Historic Park, Tennessee National Wildlife Refuge, Duck River, Nathan Bedford Forrest State Park, 65 mi. to Nashville. **Additional Information:** Waverly Chamber of Commerce, (931) 296-4865.

Restrictions

Pets: Leash only. **Fires:** Allowed in fire rings only (weather permitting). **Alcoholic Beverages:** Allowed. **Vehicle Maximum Length:** 60 ft. (sites vary). **Other:** No ATVs.

To Get There

From I-40, take Exit 143 and drive north 8 mi. on Loretta Lynn Parkway. The entrance is on the left.

JAMESTOWN

Pickett State Park

4605 Pickett Park Hwy., Jamestown 38556-4141. T: (931) 879-5821; F: (931) 879-4479; www.tnstateparks.com.

RV ★★★★ Tent ★★★★

Beauty: ★★★★	Site Privacy: ★★★
Spaciousness: ★★★★	Quiet: ★★★★★
Security: ★★★★	Cleanliness: ★★★
Insect Control: ★★★★	Facilities: ★★★★

Pickett State Park is adjacent to Daniel Boone National Forest and Big South Fork National River and Recreation Area. The park is known for its surreal rock formations, caves, and natural bridges as well as its botanical diversity. Some scientists believe that Pickett supports the second most diverse flora in the US (Great Smoky Mountains National Park has the most diverse plant life in the US). The campgrounds at Pickett are reasonably attractive, with some open sites and others shaded by white pine trees. Sites are small, but they are spaced far apart, giving campers the feeling of spaciousness. Sites have paved, back-in parking. For space and privacy, we like tent sites 20–30. RVs should head for site 1. Pickett is patrolled by rangers at night and has no gates. Nonetheless, the park's isolation makes it fairly safe. Visit Pickett State Park any time except for summer holidays—it's rarely crowded.

Basics

Operated By: Tennessee State Parks. **Open:** All year (closed Monday & Tuesday indefinitely). **Site Assignment:** First come, first served; no reservations accepted. **Registration:** Campground host makes rounds (check-in at office in winter). **Fee:** $11 for 2 people, $0.50 per additional person; senior & disabled discounts available (cash, personal checks, V, MC, D, AE). **Parking:** At sites.

Facilities

Number of Multipurpose Sites: 40. **Hookups:** Water, electric (20 amps) at most sites. **Each Site:** Picnic table, grill, fire ring. **Dump Station:** Yes. **Laundry:** Yes. **Pay Phone:** Yes. **Rest Rooms and Showers:** Yes. **Fuel:** No. **Propane:** No. **Internal Roads:** Paved. **RV Service:** 60 mi. in Cookeville. **Market:** 13 mi. in Jamestown. **Restaurant:** 13 mi. in Jamestown. **General Store:** 13 mi. in Jamestown. **Vending:** Beverages only. **Swimming Pool:** No. **Playground:** Yes. **Other:** Picnic areas & shelters, nature center, boat dock. **Activities:** Lake swimming, boating, fishing (boat rentals available), tennis, archery, hiking trail, seasonal interpretive programs, seasonal hunts. **Nearby Attractions:** Big South Fork National River & Recreation Area, Rugby, Cordell Hull Birthplace, Alvin C. York Grist Mill. **Additional Information:** Jamestown Chamber of Commerce, (931) 879-9948.

Restrictions

Pets: On leash only. **Fires:** Allowed, in fire ring only. **Alcoholic Beverages:** Not allowed. **Vehicle Maximum Length:** 25 ft. (sites vary). **Other:** 14-day stay limit.

To Get There

From I-40 Exit 317 (Crossville), drive north 35 mi. on US Hwy. 127. Turn north onto local Rte. 154 and drive another 13 mi. The park entrance is on the left.

KINGSPORT

Warrior's Path State Park

P.O. Box 5026/ Hemlock Rd., Kingsport 37663. T: (423) 239-8531; F: (423) 239-4982; www.tnstateparks.com.

RV ★★★★ Tent ★★★★

Beauty: ★★★★	Site Privacy: ★★★
Spaciousness: ★★★★	Quiet: ★★★
Security: ★★★	Cleanliness: ★★★
Insect Control: ★★	Facilities: ★★★★★

Situated on the Patrick Henry Reservoir on the Holsten River, Warrior's Path offers great recreation facilities, including an 18-hole golf course and extensive boating and fishing amenities. Fish caught in the reservoir include catfish, crappie, bass, bream, and trout. The Olympic-sized pool is next to the campground.The campground consists of one large loop and one small one. Sites are large, though size varies greatly. Although some sites are open, most are shaded by sugar maple, persimmon, tulip poplars, and various oaks. There are no natural privacy barriers. All sites have paved, back-in parking. We like sites 75–79 for pretty views of the reservoir. Others are too densely wooded to afford views of the water. Warrior's Path is popular with locals and there are no gates, which makes security fair. Insects can be a problem here when it's warm and humid. Avoid popular Warrior's Path on summer weekends.

Basics

Operated By: Tennessee State Parks. **Open:** All year (closed Monday & Tuesday indefinitely during budget constraints—call ahead). **Site Assignment:** First come, first served; no reservations. **Registration:** Camper check-in station or park office, night arrival register the next day. **Fee:** $17 water & electric, $14 overflow area; fees for 2 people, $0.50 per additional person; seniors 25% discount, disabled 50% w/ proof (cash, personal checks, traveler checks, no credit cards). **Parking:** At sites, in parking lot.

Facilities

Number of Multipurpose Sites: 135 (94 developed). **Hookups:** Water, electric (20, 30, 50 amps). **Each Site:** Picnic table, grill, fire ring. **Dump Station:** Yes. **Laundry:** No. **Pay Phone:** Yes. **Rest Rooms and Showers:** Yes. **Fuel:** No. **Propane:** No. **Internal Roads:** Paved. **RV Service:** 5 mi. in Kingsport. **Market:** 1 mi. in Kingsport. **Restaurant:** Snack bars seasonal, 1 mi. in Kingsport. **General Store:** 1.5 mi. to Wal-Mart. **Vending:** Beverages only. **Swimming Pool:** Yes (seasonal). **Playground:** Yes. **Other:** Recreation building w/ table tennis & pool tables, boat ramps, marina, riding stables, picnic area, amphitheater. **Activities:** 18-hole golf course, fishing, boating (boat rentals available, paddle boats seasonal), horseback riding (seasonal), hiking trails, mountain-bike trails, disc-golf, tennis, basketball, volleyball, horseshoes, soccer field. **Nearby Attractions:** Bays Mountain Nature Center, Allandale Mansion, Appalachian Caverns, The Netherland Inn, Steels Creek Park & Nature Center. **Additional Information:** Kingsport Chamber of Commerce, (423) 392-8820.

Restrictions

Pets: Leash only. **Fires:** Allowed, fire rings only. **Alcoholic Beverages:** Not allowed. **Vehicle Maximum Length:** 40 ft. (sites vary). **Other:** 2-week stay limit, no firearms.

To Get There

From I-81, take Exit 59 and turn north on SR 36/Fort Henry Dr. Drive 5 mi. and turn right at the fifth traffic light onto Hemlock Rd. Drive 1.5 mi. to the park entrance on the right.

LAKELAND

KOA–Memphis East

3291 Shoehorn Dr., Lakeland 38002. T: (901) 388-3053.

RV ★★★ Tent ★★

Beauty: ★★★	Site Privacy: ★★
Spaciousness: ★★	Quiet: ★★★
Security: ★★★	Cleanliness: ★★★
Insect Control: ★★★★	Facilities: ★★★

A few miles northeast of Memphis, this KOA is conveniently located for touring the river city. It's also near a large outlet mall and a public golf course. Recreational facilities are average and the park is connected to a residential mobile-home complex. Campsites are small and generally unattractive. The campground contains two rows of pull-throughs and one row of back-ins. Parking is on patchy gravel, and there are a few trees, but little privacy. For convenience, we recommend the pull-through sites closest to the pool and store, including 24F and 26F. For a little shade, we recommend sites 29–33. Security is fair at this suburban to rural park—there is no gate. Visit Memphis in spring or fall for the nicest weather. Avoid the humid summer months.

Basics

Operated By: Thomas Long. **Open:** 7 days a week, all year. **Site Assignment:** Reservations accepted w/ a credit card deposit (V, MC, or D); 24-hour cancellation required for refund; sites are first come, first served. **Registration:** At office. **Fee:** $17–$25. **Parking:** 2 vehicles per site, plus an additional parking lot.

Facilities

Number of RV Sites: 100. **Number of Tent-Only Sites:** 8. **Hookups:** Electric, water, sewer. **Each Site:** Picnic table. **Dump Station:** Yes. **Laundry:** Yes. **Pay Phone:** Yes. **Rest Rooms and Showers:** Yes. **Fuel:** No. **Propane:** Yes. **Internal Roads:** Paved. **RV Service:** 25 mi. north in Millington. **Market:** In park. **Restaurant:** 0.25 mi. north. **General Store:** In park. **Vending:** No. **Swimming Pool:** Yes. **Playground:** Yes. **Other:** Billiard table, game room. **Activities:** Fishing, pool, ping-pong, video games. **Nearby Attractions:** Graceland, Hunt-Phelan Home, Libertyland, Memphis Queen Line, The Pyramid, Sun Studio, Fire Museum of Memphis, WONDERS: The Memphis International Cultural Series, Memphis Motorsports Park, Lichterman Nature Center, Davies Manor Plantation, Memphis Music Hall of Fame, Slavehaven/Burkle Estate, W.C. Handy Home, Historic Elmwood Cemetery, The Belz Museum, Memphis Pink Palace Museum, Planetarium & IMAX Theater, Mud Island River Park, Ornamental Metal Museum, Beale St., Dixie Gallery & Gardens. **Additional Information:** Lakeland Area Chamber of Commerce, (901) 382-5027; Memphis Area Chamber of Commerce, (901) 575-3500.

Restrictions

Pets: On leash only. **Fires:** Not allowed. **Alcoholic Beverages:** At site only. **Vehicle Maximum Length:** No limit. **Other:** No swimming in lake; no generators allowed.

To Get There

Take I-40 from Memphis headed northeast. At Exit 20, 0.5 mi. south on Canada Rd., take a left on Monroe and campground is on the left.

LAWRENCEBURG

David Crockett State Park

P.O. Box 398, Lawrenceburg 38464-0398. T: (931) 762-9408; F: (931) 766-0047; www.tmstateparks.com.

RV ★★★★ Tent ★★★★

Beauty: ★★★★★	Site Privacy: ★★★★
Spaciousness: ★★★★	Quiet: ★★★★
Security: ★★★★★	Cleanliness: ★★★★
Insect Control: ★★★★	Facilities: ★★★★

Of the two campgrounds at David Crockett, Campground No. 2 is the prettiest. Flat and shady, with comfortably spaced sites, No. 2 has lovely trees. A little greenery provides barriers between some sites. All sites in No. 2 have back-in parking. The most private sites in No. 2 are 99–101. Campground No. 1 is more open and includes attractive sites along a creek (15–32). Sites 1, 2, and 3 in Campground No. 1 are the only pull-throughs. Some sites have paved parking while others have gravel. Facilities at David Crockett are very nice and include an Olympic-size swimming pool and a 40-acre fishing lake (no personally owned boats allowed, rentals available). There's a large Amish community in this area, with farm tours available. The James D. Vaughan Museum, memorializing the "Father of Southern Gospel," is also nearby. Security is excellent at remote David Crockett, with gates locked at night. Avoid the park on summer weekends. For the nicest weather, visit in spring or fall.

Basics

Operated By: Tennessee State Parks. **Open:** All year (closed Monday & Tuesday indefinitely due to budget constraints). **Site Assignment:** First come, first served; no reservations. **Registration:** Office, ranger makes rounds after hours. **Fee:** $17 RV, $14 tent; prices for 2 people, $0.50 per additional person; senior discount available (cash, personal check, V, MC, D, AE). **Parking:** At site.

Facilities

Number of RV Sites: 0. **Number of Tent-Only Sites:** 7 primitive (Campground No. 1, closed winter). **Number of Multipurpose Sites:** 107. **Hookups:** Water, electric (30 amps). **Each Site:** Picnic table, grill, fire ring. **Dump Station:** Yes. **Laundry:** No. **Pay Phone:** Yes. **Rest Rooms and Showers:** Yes. **Fuel:** No. **Propane:** No. **Internal Roads:** Paved. **RV Service:** 2 mi. east on Hwy. 64. **Market:** 2 mi. north on Hwy. 43. **Restaurant:** Park restaurant. **General Store:** 3 mi. on Hwy. 43. **Vending:** Beverages only. **Swimming Pool:** Yes. **Playground:** Yes. **Other:** Boat launch, Interpretive Center, wading pool, pool concessions, pool bathhouse. **Activities:** Fishing, paddle boat rentals (seasonal), fishing boat rentals, archery range, hiking & biking trails, tennis, softball, volleyball. **Nearby Attractions:** Historic Downtown Lawrenceburg, Amish Country farm & wagon tours, James D. Vaughan Museum ("The Birthplace of Southern Gospel Music"), Coca Cola Palace, Laurel Hill Lake, Scenic Buffalo River. **Additional Information:** South Central Tennessee Tourism Organization, (931) 762-6944.

Restrictions

Pets: On leash only. **Fires:** Allowed, grills & Campground No. 1 only. **Alcoholic Beverages:** Not allowed. **Vehicle Maximum Length:** 38 ft. **Other:** 14-day stay limit, fireworks prohibited.

To Get There

From I-65, take Exit 14 onto US Hwy. 64. Drive 30 mi. west to Lawrenceburg. The park is on the right (north) of Hwy. 64, 0.5 mi. west of Lawrenceburg.

LEBANON

Cedars of Lebanon State Park

328 Cedar Forest Rd., Lebanon 37090. T: (615) 443-2769; F: (615) 443-2793; www.tnstateparks.com.

RV ★★★★ Tent ★★★★

Beauty: ★★★★	Site Privacy: ★★★
Spaciousness: ★★★★	Quiet: ★★★★
Security: ★★★★	Cleanliness: ★★★★
Insect Control: ★★★★	Facilities: ★★★★

Named after Biblical references to dense cedar woods in ancient Lebanon, this park maintains nice facilities even though its entrance looks dumpy. There are eight miles of hiking trails, six miles of equestrian trails, and an Olympic-size pool. The park is on flat land without a major body of water; the draw here is the forest. Campgrounds 2 and 3 are the shadiest and prettiest, situated in mature tree stands consisting of about 50% cedar. Sites are large, but there is no greenery between them. There are both back-in and pull-through sites with paved parking. In campground No. 2, we liked site 18. Campground No. 3 contains the largest sites (13–15 were our favorites). There are no gates at this small town park, making security fair. A ranger is on duty at all times. Visit in spring, early summer, or fall. Avoid holiday weekends.

Basics

Operated By: Tennessee State Parks. **Open:** All year (closed Monday & Tuesday indefinitely due to budget constraints). **Site Assignment:** First come, first served; no reservations. **Registration:** Office or camp store, host will check in late comers. **Fee:** $17 RV, $14 tent; prices for 2 people, $0.50 per additional person; senior discount available (cash, personal check, V, MC, AE, D). **Parking:** At site.

Facilities

Number of RV Sites: 0. **Number of Tent-Only Sites:** 30 (tents, pop-ups, 20 amps only). **Number of Multipurpose Sites:** 87. **Hookups:** Water, electric (20, 30, 50 amps). **Each Site:** Picnic table, grill, fire ring, some lantern poles. **Dump Station:** Yes. **Laundry:** Yes. **Pay Phone:** Yes. **Rest Rooms and Showers:** Yes. **Fuel:** No. **Propane:** No. **Internal Roads:** Paved. **RV Service:** 10 mi. in Lebanon. **Market:** In Lebanon. **Restaurant:** 7 mi. in Lebanon. **General Store:** Camp store (seasonal), 8 mi. in Lebanon. **Vending:** Beverages only. **Swimming Pool:** Yes (seasonal). **Playground:** Yes. **Other:** Recreation lodge, assembly hall, nature center, picnic area & shelters, riding stables. **Activities:** Hiking trails, equestrian trails, disc-golf course, ball field, basketball, volleyball, tennis, horseshoes, organized activities in season. **Nearby Attractions:** Lebanon "Antique Capital of the South," Country Music Hall of Fame, Grand Ole Opry, Opryland Hotel, The Parthenon, Hermitage Andrew Jackson Home, Belle Meade Plantation, Vanderbilt University. **Additional Information:** Nashville Tourism information, (615) 259-4700.

Restrictions

Pets: On leash only. **Fires:** Allowed, fire ring only. **Alcoholic Beverages:** Not allowed. **Vehicle Maximum Length:** No limit. **Other:** 14-day stay limit.

To Get There

From I-40, take Exit 238 and drive south 6 mi. on US Hwy. 231. Turn left (east) on Cedar FR and drive into the park. Drive 1 mi. and turn right on WPA Rd. Drive 0.5 mi. to the campground entrance.

MANCHESTER

Old Stone Fort State Archaeological Area

732 Stone Fort Dr., Manchester 37855. T: (931) 723-5073; F: (931) 723-5075; www.tnstateparks.com.

RV ★★★★ Tent ★★★★

Beauty: ★★★★	Site Privacy: ★★★★★
Spaciousness: ★★★★★	Quiet: ★★★★
Security: ★★★	Cleanliness: ★★★★
Insect Control: ★★★★	Facilities: ★★★★

This park's namesake is a 2000-year-old Native American ceremonial site nestled into two forks of the Duck River. The Old Stone Fort consists of 50 acres of flat land enclosed by mounds, walls, and river cliffs, and was actively used for 500 years. The park maintains hiking trails for exploring the ceremonial site and area waterfalls. The campground consists of three loops near the Duck River (no water views). Campsites are commodious and very private due to nice greenery between them. Sites are heavily wooded, with various oak species and other hardwoods. All sites feature paved, back-in parking. The sites in the back of the campground (on the third circle) are the most spacious and private. Old Stone Fort is on the outskirts of Manchester. Gates are locked at night making security good. Old Stone Fort is rarely crowded, so it's a good destination for a summer weekend.

Basics

Operated By: Tennessee State Parks. **Open:** All year (closed Monday & Tuesday indefinitely). **Site Assignment:** First come, first served; no reservations accepted. **Registration:** Ranger makes rounds. **Fee:** $19 RV, $14 tent; prices for 2 people, $0.50 per additional person; senior & disabled discounts available (cash, checks). **Parking:** At sites.

Facilities

Number of RV Sites: 0. **Number of Tent-Only Sites:** Primitive area for group camping. **Number of Multipurpose Sites:** 51. **Hookups:** Water, electric (20 amps). **Each Site:** Picnic table, grill, paved pads, most have fire rings. **Dump Station:** Yes (seasonal). **Laundry:** No. **Pay Phone:** Yes. **Rest Rooms and Showers:** Yes. **Fuel:** No. **Propane:** No. **Internal Roads:** Paved. **RV Service:** 1 mi. **Market:** 3 mi. in Manchester. **Restaurant:** Within 2 mi. **General Store:** 3 mi. in Manchester. **Vending:** Beverages only. **Swimming Pool:** No. **Playground:** Yes. **Other:** Picnic areas, museum & visitor center, boat ramp. **Activities:** 9-hole golf course, pro shop (cart & club rentals), nature trails, hiking, fishing (electric trolling motors only), summer organized programs. **Nearby Attractions:** Jack Daniels Distillery, Cumberland Caverns Park, Foothills Craft Shop, Tims Ford Lake, 18-hole golf, Manchester Arts Center. **Additional Information:** Manchester Chamber of Commerce, (931) 723-1486 or (931) 728-7635.

Restrictions

Pets: On leash only. **Fires:** Allowed, fire rings only. **Alcoholic Beverages:** Not allowed. **Vehicle Maximum Length:** 30 ft. **Other:** 14-day stay limit.

To Get There

From I-24 (approximately 50 mi. south of Nashville) take Exit 110 and turn southwest on State Rte. 53. Drive 1 mi. and turn right (north) on US Hwy. 41. The park is 0.5 mi. on the left.

MANCHESTER

Manchester KOA

586 Campground Rd., Manchester 37355. T: (931) 728-9777 or (800) 562-7785; F: (931) 728-9750; www.koa.com; manchestertn@mykoa.com.

 ★★★ ▲ ★★

Beauty: ★★★ Site Privacy: ★★
Spaciousness: ★★★ Quiet: ★★★★
Security: ★★★ Cleanliness: ★★★★
Insect Control: ★★★ Facilities: ★★★

This small urban campground is a good stop-over, but if you want to enjoy outdoor recreation near Manchester, we recommend the campground at Old Stone Fort State Archeological Area. Manchester KOA includes five rows of pull-through sites with gravel parking. Sites are average sized and offer no privacy. Most sites are shady. We recommend quiet sites 38–47; these are the furthest from the road. Amenities at this KOA are not extensive, but there are plenty of restaurants, shopping, and attractions nearby, including Old Stone Fort, a 2000-year-old Native American ceremonial site nestled into two forks of the Duck River. Visit Manchester in spring, early summer, or fall for the nicest weather. Security at this KOA is fair—there are no gates, but Manchester is not a dangerous town.

Basics

Operated By: Dan & Ginny McConaughy. **Open:** All year. **Site Assignment:** Sites assigned; reservations accepted w/ credit card number to hold site, 24-hour cancellation notice required; no-show charged one night. **Registration:** Camp store, self-registration at night. **Fee:** $23–$28 RV, $19–$22 tent; prices for 2 people, $3 per additional adult & $2.50 per child; KOA Value discount available (cash, personal check, V, D, MC, AE). **Parking:** At site (1 vehicle).

Facilities

Number of RV Sites: 47. **Number of Tent-Only Sites:** 7. **Number of Multipurpose Sites:** None. **Hookups:** Water, electric (30, 50 amps), sewer, cable, instant, on phone lines. **Each Site:** Picnic table, fire ring, grills at tent sites. **Dump Station:** Yes. **Laundry:** Yes. **Pay Phone:** Yes. **Rest Rooms and Showers:** Yes. **Fuel:** No. **Propane:** Yes. **Internal Roads:** Gravel. **RV Service:** 12 mi. in Tullahoma. **Market:** Within 1 mi. **Restaurant:** Within 1 mi. **General Store:** Camp store, within 1 mi. **Vending:** Beverages only. **Swimming Pool:** Yes. **Playground:** Yes. **Other:** Camping cabins, game room w/ arcade, picnic area. **Activities:** Horseshoes, badminton, volleyball. **Nearby Attractions:** Jack Daniels Distillery, golf courses, Old Stone Fort & Tims Ford State Parks, Arnold Air Force Base, Civil War sites, Staggerwing Museum, Cumberland Caverns, antiquing in & around Manchester. **Additional Information:** Manchester Chamber of Commerce, (931) 723-1486.

Restrictions

Pets: On leash only. **Fires:** Allowed, fire ring only. **Alcoholic Beverages:** Allowed. **Vehicle Maximum Length:** No limit.

To Get There

From I-24 Exit 114, drive 100 yards southeast on US Hwy. 41. Turn north on Campground Rd. and drive 0.5 mi.

MEMPHIS

Memphis-Graceland KOA

3691 Elvis Presley Blvd., Memphis 38116. T: (901) 396-7125.

 ★★  ★

Beauty: ★★ Site Privacy: ★★
Spaciousness: ★★ Quiet: ★★
Security: ★★ Cleanliness: ★★
Insect Control: ★★★ Facilities: ★

On our visit, there was an unpleasant smell in the park. It's also a bit expensive—at $35 a night for full hookups, you could just as easily stay in the suburbs and take a taxi to Elvis's mansion. But the location can't be beat—the KOA is catty-corner to Graceland, and the staff will help you arrange shuttle service and tours of Memphis and Tunica, Mississippi. Campsites are extremely small and offer no privacy. There are no trees. Most sites are pull-thrus with untidy gravel parking. All sites are basically the same. There is no gate at this urban campground, making security poor. We urge all campers to be extremely cautious. Elvis devotees have their own religious holidays, drawing massive crowds. Avoid visits on Elvis's birthday and the anniversary of his death.

Basics

Operated By: Mary & Jim Parks. **Open:** 7 days a week, all year. **Site Assignment:** Reservations accepted w/ a $25 deposit, payable by V, MC, or D. Checks are acceptable in advance. Full refund w/ a 24-hour notice of cancellation. **Registration:** At office. **Fee:** $22–$34. **Parking:** One vehicle per site, also in the parking lot.

Facilities

Number of RV Sites: 72. **Number of Tent-Only Sites:** 50. **Hookups:** Only 13 of the RV sites w/ electric & water hookups. **Each Site:** Picnic tables. **Dump Station:** Yes. **Laundry:** Yes. **Pay Phone:** Yes. **Rest Rooms and Showers:** Yes. **Fuel:** No. **Propane:** Yes. **Internal Roads:** Paved. **RV Service:** Yes. **Market:** Yes. **Restaurant:** Across the street. **General Store:** Yes. **Vending:** Yes. **Swimming Pool:** Yes. **Playground:** Yes. **Activities:** Swimming, walking. **Nearby Attractions:** Graceland, Hunt-Phelan Home, Libertyland, Memphis Queen Line, The Pyramid, Sun Studio, Fire Museum of Memphis, WONDERS: The Memphis International Cultural Series, Memphis Motorsports Park, Lichterman Nature Center, Davies Manor Plantation, Memphis Music Hall of Fame, Slavehaven/Burkle Estate, W.C. Handy Home, Historic Elmwood Cemetery, The Belz Museum, Memphis Pink Palace Museum, Planetarium & IMAX Theater, Mud Island River Park, Ornamental Metal Museum, Beale St., Dixie Gallery & Gardens. **Additional Information:** Memphis Area Chamber of Commerce, (901) 575-3500.

Restrictions

Pets: On leash. **Fires:** Not allowed. **Alcoholic Beverages:** Allowed. **Vehicle Max. Length:** None.

To Get There

From Nashville take 40 west to 240 west to I-55 south. Take Exit 5B onto Elvis Presley Blvd. Campground is 1 mi. on the right.

MEMPHIS

T. O. Fuller State Park

1500 Mitchell Rd., Memphis 38109. T: (901) 543-5333; F: (901 785-8485; www.tnstateparks.com.

 ★★★  ★★★

Beauty: ★★★
Site Privacy: ★★★★
Spaciousness: ★★★
Quiet: ★★★★
Security: ★★
Cleanliness: ★★★★
Insect Control: ★★★
Facilities: ★★★★

Located within Memphis City Limits, T. O. Fuller was designated for African-American usage when it first opened in 1942. The park was later named for Dr. T. O. Fuller, a late-nineteenth-century minister, educator, North Carolina Senator, and committed activist. Interesting recreation and facilities include the reconstructed Chucalissa Indian Village. The campground is contained in one loop, and all sites are at least partially shaded by various hardwoods. Sites are mid-sized and some are fairly private. Sites feature gravel, back-in parking. For shade and privacy, we fancy sites 9, 11, 12, 14, 22, 23, and 24. T. O. Fuller is very popular due to its urban location in Memphis. The campground is likely to fill up for special events. Avoid visiting on "Elvis holidays" such as the King's birthday and the day he died. With no gates, security is poor, so guard your belongings.

Basics

Operated By: Tennessee State Parks. **Open:** All year (closed Monday & Tuesday indefinitely during budget constraints—call ahead). **Site Assignment:** First come, first served; no reservations accepted (except groups). **Registration:** Visitor Center, night arrival registered by ranger or host. **Fee:** $16 RV, $14 tent plus access fee $0.50 per person, $1 min. **Parking:** At sites.

Facilities

Number of Multipurpose Sites: 45. **Hookups:** Water, electric (20, 50 amps). **Each Site:** Picnic table, fire ring, grill, lantern pole. **Dump Station:** Yes. **Laundry:** Yes. **Pay Phone:** Yes. **Rest Rooms and Showers:** Yes. **Fuel:** No. **Propane:** No. **Internal Roads:** Paved. **RV Service:** 10 mi. north in Memphis. **Market:** 5 mi. north in Memphis. **Restaurant:** 5 mi. north in Memphis. **General Store:** 10 mi. north in Memphis (hardware, Wal-Mart). **Vending:** Beverages only. **Swimming Pool:** Yes (seasonal). **Playground:** Yes. **Other:** Picnic area, pavilions, Chucalissa Indian Museum, pool bathhouse & concessions, archery range. **Activities:** 18-hole golf course (club & cart rentals available, closed Dec. 24 & 25), wildlife viewing wetlands, softball, basketball, tennis, hiking trails. **Nearby Attractions:** Graceland, Beale St., Mud Island, Alex Haley House Museum, National Civil Rights Museum, Peabody Hotel. **Additional Information:** Memphis CVB, (901) 543-5333.

Restrictions

Pets: Leash only. **Fires:** Fire rings only. **Alcoholic Beverages:** Not allowed. **Vehicle Maximum Length:** No limit. **Other:** 14-day stay limit.

To Get There

From I-55 take Exit 9 and drive 4 mi. east on Mallory Ave. Turn right on Riverport and drive another 4 mi. Turn left on Plant Rd., and the campground is in 0.5 mi.

MILLINGTON

Meeman-Shelby Forest State Park

Rte. 3, Millington 38053. T: (901) 876-5215; F: (901) 876-3217; www.tnstateparks.com.

RV ★★★★ Tent ★★★★

Beauty: ★★★★
Site Privacy: ★★★★
Spaciousness: ★★★
Quiet: ★★★★
Security: ★★★★
Cleanliness: ★★★★
Insect Control: ★★★
Facilities: ★★★★

Meeman-Shelby is bordered on the west by the Chickasaw Bluffs lining the Mississippi River. The park offers lovely wooded campsites, 20 miles of hiking and bridle paths, and an Olympic-sized swimming pool. Boat ramps provide access to the Mississippi and 125-acre Poplar Tree Lake, home to bream, catfish, and largemouth bass. The park is about 15 miles from Memphis so it's a fine place to stay if you're touring the river town. The flat campground is situated in a delightful stand of shady hardwoods, including sweetgum and poplar. In most cases, foliage provides a privacy barrier between sites. Campsites are mid-sized, with paved, back-in parking. For privacy and shade, we like sites 10 and 30. Sites 33–49, which lead out of the campground, are also spacious. Rural Meeman-Shelby closes its gates at night making security good. Western Tennessee is extremely hot and humid in late summer and should be avoided. Also avoid holiday weekends.

Basics

Operated By: Tennessee State Parks Dept. of Environment & Conservation. **Open:** All year (closed Monday & Tuesday indefinitely due to budget constraints). **Site Assignment:** First come, first served; 5 sites available for reservation w/ $5 nonrefundable deposit. **Registration:** Visitor Center, night arrival register next morning. **Fee:** $16 RV, $14 tent; prices for 2 people, $0.50 per additional person up to 10 max; Golden Age & Golden Access discount, Tennessee seniors $12, out-Of-State seniors $15.50 (cash, personal check, V, MC, D, AE). **Parking:** At site (2 cars), in parking lot.

Facilities

Number of Multipurpose Sites: 49. **Hookups:** Water, electric (15, 20, 30 amps). **Each Site:** Picnic table, grill, most sites have fire ring. **Dump Station:** Yes. **Laundry:** No. **Pay Phone:** Yes. **Rest Rooms and Showers:** Yes. **Fuel:** No. **Propane:** No. **Internal Roads:** Paved. **RV Service:** 25 mi. south of Memphis. **Market:** 0.75 mi. or 9 mi. in Millington. **Restaurant:** 9 mi. in Millington. **General Store:** 9 mi. in Millington (Wal-Mart). **Vending:** Yes. **Swimming Pool:** Yes (seasonal). **Playground:** Yes. **Other:** Boat launches (electric motor only), boat dock, fishing pier, visitor center, nature center, recreation lodge, picnic shelters. **Activities:** 2 fishing lakes, fishing boat rentals (seasonal), hiking trails, bicycle trail, disc-golf, horse rentals, bridle paths, volleyball, badminton, horseshoes, softball, managed hunts. **Nearby Attractions:** Graceland, Beale St., Mud Island, Alex Haley House Museum, National Civil Rights Museum, Peabody Hotel. **Additional Information:** Memphis CVB, (901) 543-5333.

Restrictions

Pets: On leash only. **Fires:** In grills, fire rings only. **Alcoholic Beverages:** Not allowed. **Vehicle Maximum Length:** 45 ft. (sites vary). **Other:** 14-day stay limit, quiet enforced.

To Get There

From I-240, take US Hwy. 51 north 3 mi. to State Rte. 388/North Watkins. Drive north 8 mi. and turn left on Benjestown Rd. Drive 1 mi. to the 4-way stop and turn right. The park entrance is 0.75 mi. on the left. (US Hwy. 55 is accessible from the west from I-40 and I-55 as well.)

NASHVILLE

Nashville KOA Kampground

2626 Music Valley Dr., Nashville 37214. T: (615) 889-0282; F: (615) 883-9113; www.koa.com; nashvillekoa@earthlink.net.

RV ★★★★ Tent ★★

Beauty: ★★★★
Site Privacy: ★★
Spaciousness: ★★★
Quiet: ★★★★
Security: ★★
Cleanliness: ★★★★
Insect Control: ★★★★
Facilities: ★★★★

Nashville KOA campground is fairly attractive and convenient to area attractions, restaurants, and shopping. In the campground, there's a kiddie pool, a playground, and plenty of room for children to run around. Without gates, security at this suburban campground is iffy. Take care of your valuables. Nashville can become unbearably hot and humid in late summer. Visit in spring or fall for optimal weather. Sites are laid out in rows of mostly pull-throughs. All sites are the same passable size and there is no greenery to provide privacy. In other respects, sites vary. Many sites are nicely shaded by mature poplars and other hardwoods. Some sites are completely open. Most parking is paved, though some is gravel. For shade and quiet, head for 50-amp sites Z–Z27, along the back perimeter of the park. Most tent sites are very small and located near the noisy road.

Basics

Operated By: Kampgrounds of America. **Open:** All year. **Site Assignment:** First come, first served; reservations accepted w/ first-night deposit; 24-hour cancellation notice for refund. **Registration:** Store/main building, night registration also. **Fee:** $37.95 full hookup, $34.95 water & electric, $24.95 tent; prices for 2 people, $5 per additional adult, $1 child, 6 people max.; KOA discount 10% (cash, V, MC, D). **Parking:** At site (1 car), in parking lot.

Facilities

Number of RV Sites: 240. **Number of Tent-Only Sites:** 60. **Number of Multipurpose Sites:** 100 (water & electric only). **Hookups:** Water, electric (30, 50 amps), 240 sites w/ sewer. **Each Site:** Picnic table. **Dump Station:** Yes. **Laundry:** Yes. **Pay Phone:** Yes. **Rest Rooms and Showers:** Yes. **Fuel:** No. **Propane:** Yes. **Internal Roads:** Paved. **RV Service:** Next door. **Market:** 6 mi. in Nashville. **Restaurant:** At entrance. **General Store:** Convenience store w/ camp supplies on site, K-Mart 6 mi. in Nashville. **Vending:** No. **Swimming Pool:** Yes. **Playground:** Yes. **Other:** Game room, pool tables, outdoor theater,music barn. **Activities:** Basketball, horseshoes, mini-golf, bicycle rental. **Nearby Attractions:** Country Music Hall of Fame, Grand Ole Opry, Opryland Hotel, The Parthenon, Hermitage Andrew Jackson Home, Belle Meade Plantation, Vanderbilt University. **Additional Information:** Nashville Tourism information, (615) 259-4700.

RESTRICTIONS

Pets: Leash only. **Fires:** Not allowed. **Alcoholic Beverages:** Allowed. **Vehicle Maximum Length:** No limit. **Other:** Quiet hours enforced, no generators.

TO GET THERE

Interstates 40, 24, and 65 all intersect with Briley Parkway in Nashville. From Briley Pkwy., take Exit 12 and drive north (the only option) 2 mi. on Music Valley Dr. The campground is on the left.

ONEIDA

Bandy Creek Campground, Big South Fork National River and Recreation Area

4563 Leatherwood Rd., Oneida 37841. T: (931) 879-4869 or (800) 365-CAMP; F: (931) 879-9604; www.nps.gov; biso_information@nps.gov.

RV ★★★★ Tent ★★★★

Beauty: ★★★★	Site Privacy: ★★★★
Spaciousness: ★★★★★	Quiet: ★★★★
Security: ★★★★	Cleanliness: ★★★
Insect Control: ★★★★	Facilities: ★★★★

Straddling the Kentucky-Tennessee border, Big South Fork NRA is far less crowded than nearby Great Smoky Mountains National Park and offers outstanding outdoor recreation. It's known for excellent paddling, with mellow flat water and class I–IV white water. Big South Fork also has 150 miles of hiking trails. Nearby Cumberland Falls is one the most beautiful sights in the US. The campground at Bandy Creek offers attractive and extremely spacious sites. Though most sites are shady, privacy varies greatly, with some very secluded sites and others sandwiched together. There are both back-in and pull-through sites. All have gravel parking. Gorgeous Loop A is for tent campers only. The rest are multipurpose. For seclusion, we like sites 16–19 on loop D. Avoid Big South Fork on holiday weekends and fall leaf peeping weekends. Otherwise, the campground is rarely full. Security is fine at this extremely remote campground.

BASICS

Operated By: National Park Service. **Open:** All year (some areas seasonal). **Site Assignment:** First come, first served; reservations accepted Apr.–Oct. up to 5 months in advance; full deposit, $13.85 cancellation fee w/ 2-day notice or more, same day cancellation one night charged plus fee. **Registration:** Kiosk, after hours register next morning. **Fee:** $18 water & electric, $15 tent; prices for 6 people; Golden Age & Golden Access discounts available (cash, personal checks, V, MC, D). **Parking:** At site (2 cars), in parking lot.

FACILITIES

Number of RV Sites: 0. **Number of Tent-Only Sites:** 50. **Number of Multipurpose Sites:** 100. **Hookups:** Water, electric (20, 30 amps). **Each Site:** Picnic table, fire ring w/ grill, lantern pole, tent pad. **Dump Station:** Yes. **Laundry:** No. **Pay Phone:** Yes. **Rest Rooms and Showers:** Yes. **Fuel:** No. **Propane:** No. **Internal Roads:** Paved. **RV Service:** 80 mi. in Knoxville. **Market:** 12 mi. in Oneida. **Restaurant:** 12 mi. in Oneida. **General Store:** 12 mi. in Oneida. **Vending:** Yes. **Swimming Pool:** Yes (Memorial Day–Labor Day). **Playground:** Yes. **Other:** Visitor Center, stables, picnic area, covered pavilion, Big South Fork Scenic Railway, Blue Heron Outdoor Historical Museum. **Activities:** Hiking & biking trails, horseback riding, fishing, hunting, rafting, canoeing, kayaking, volleyball. **Nearby Attractions:** Highland Manor Winery, Historic Rugby restored Victorian village, Alvin York's Farm & Grist Mill, Cordell Hull Birthplace, Indian Mountain State Park, Pickett State Rustic Park, 80 mi. to Knoxville. **Additional Information:** Oneida Chamber of Commerce, (423) 569-6900; Jamestown Chamber of Commerce, (931) 879-9948.

RESTRICTIONS

Pets: On leash only. **Fires:** Allowed, fire rings only. **Alcoholic Beverages:** Allowed, at sites only. **Vehicle Maximum Length:** 45 ft. (sites vary). **Other:** 13% grade entering campground, 14-day stay limit, quiet hours enforced.

TO GET THERE

From I-75, take Exit 141 (145 from the north) and drive 20 mi. west on State Hwy. 63. At US Hwy. 27, turn right and drive 7 mi. north to Oneida. At the first traffic light, turn left onto local Rte. 297 and drive 15 mi. to the campground on the right.

PIGEON FORGE

Fort Wear RV and Campground

2630 Sequoia Rd., Pigeon Forge 37863. T: (865) 428-1951 or (800) 452-9835 for reservations; www.hometownamerica.net.

RV ★★★ Tent n/a

Beauty: ★★★★	Site Privacy: ★★★
Spaciousness: ★★★	Quiet: ★★★
Security: ★★	Cleanliness: ★★★
Insect Control: ★★★	Facilities: ★★★

Located in Pigeon Forge, Fort Wear is convenient to Dollywood, outlet malls, and restaurants. The triangular campground is nestled into a curve in Walden's Creek. Small children enjoy the kiddie pool, while older children enjoy creek fishing. The Pigeon Forge Trolley stops in front. Sites are laid out in rows of back-ins, plus one small section of pull-throughs (sites 111–116). Site size varies, but most are average-sized. All sites feature gravel parking and plenty of shade trees. For smaller RVs, we recommend 144–154, pretty sites along the creek. Large rigs will need to choose a site close to the pool and store. Security is poor-enveloped by tourist town sprawl, this campground has no gates. Avoid Pigeon Forge on fall weekends. If you can't resist leaf peeping, plan a weekday visit.

BASICS

Operated By: Hometown America. **Open:** All year. **Site Assignment:** Sites assigned; reservations recommended, w/ first night deposit, 14-day cancellation notice required for a full refund. **Registration:** Country Store (night registration by pre-arrangement preferred). **Fee:** $27 full hookup, $23.50 water & electric; Good Sam discount available (cash, personal check, V, MC, D). **Parking:** At sites, one car (plus overflow).

FACILITIES

Number of RV Sites: 160. **Number of Tent-Only Sites:** 0. **Number of Multipurpose Sites:** None. **Hookups:** Water, electric (30, 50 amps), sewer, cable TV. **Each Site:** Picnic table, fire ring. **Dump Station:** Yes. **Laundry:** Yes. **Pay Phone:** Yes. **Rest Rooms and Showers:** Yes. **Fuel:** No. **Propane:** No (soon to have propane service). **Internal Roads:** Paved. **RV Service:** Pigeon Forge. **Market:** 0.25 mi. **Restaurant:** 0.25 mi. **General Store:** 0.25 mi. hardware, 3 mi. Wal-Mart (also country store on-site). **Vending:** No. **Swimming Pool:** Yes (& wading pool). **Playground:** Yes. **Other:** Game room, trolley service to Pigeon Forge, Country Store, picnic area, RV storage. **Activities:** Fishing creek. **Nearby Attractions:** Pigeon Forge shops & theaters, Dollywood theme park, water park, Dixie Stampede, Elvis Museum, Kids Country, helicopter tours, white-water rafting, Cherokee Indian Reservation. **Additional Information:** Pigeon Forge Visitor Information, (865) 453-5700.

RESTRICTIONS

Pets: Leash only. **Fires:** Allowed, fire rings only. **Alcoholic Beverages:** Allowed, at sites only. **Vehicle Maximum Length:** 40 ft. (sites vary).

TO GET THERE

From I-40, take Exit 407 and drive south 13 mi. on US Hwy. 66. Turn right/west at third traffic light onto Wears Valley Rd. Drive 0.5 mi. and turn left/ south onto Sequoia Rd. The campground is straight ahead.

PIGEON FORGE

Riveredge RV Park

4220 Huskey St., Pigeon Forge 37863-3619. T: (800) 477-1205; www.stayriveredge.com.

RV ★★★ Tent n/a

Beauty: ★★★★	Site Privacy: ★★★
Spaciousness: ★★★	Quiet: ★★★
Security: ★★	Cleanliness: ★★★★
Insect Control: ★★★★	Facilities: ★★★

Convenient to Dollywood and outlet mall shopping, Riveredge offers attractive sites under a lovely canopy of trees, including dogwood, maple and various oak species. Though recreation facilities are not extensive, they are in good condition. The Pigeon Forge Trolley stops inside the park—let the trolley driver do the driving on busy weekends when traffic is horrendous. The campground is laid out in rows of back-in sites. The small, picturesque sites have gravel parking and a cement patio. Though the trees provide plenty of shade, there is little privacy between sites. For spaciousness, we prefer sites 41–48 for families and E40–E52 for couples. With a view of a lovely field, site E52 is our top recommendation for adults. Security is marginal—there are no gates and the park is visible from US Hwy. 441. Pigeon Forge is extremely congested on busy weekends, especially in the fall. Try to visit on weekdays.

BASICS

Operated By: Ricky & Ronald Husky. **Open:** All year. **Site Assignment:** Mostly assigned, some first come, first served; $30 credit card deposit required for reservation; 80% refund w/ 7 days notice, 3 day min. on holidays. **Registration:** Store, 8 a.m.–10 p.m. Sunday–Thursday, 8 a.m.–11 p.m. Friday & Saturday. **Fee:** $26.50 includes 2 people, $3 each additional person, children under age 3 free; no discounts. **Parking:** At sites.

FACILITIES

Number of RV Sites: 165. **Number of Tent-Only Sites:**. **Hookups:** Water, electric, sewer, cable. **Each Site:** Picnic table, concrete pad. **Dump Station:** No. **Laundry:** Yes. **Pay Phone:** Yes. **Rest Rooms and Showers:** Yes. **Fuel:** No. **Propane:** No. **Internal Roads:** Paved. **RV Service:** 10 mi. north in Sevierville. **Market:** 0.5 mi. **Restaurant:** 0.25 mi. **General Store:** Wal-Mart 5 mi. in Sevierville. **Vending:** No. **Swimming Pool:** Yes. **Playground:** Yes. **Other:** Trolley service to Pigeon Forge locations. **Activities:** Arcade, game room, fishing. **Nearby Attractions:** Dollywood, Great Smoky Mountains National Park, white water rafting, outlet shopping, museums, caverns. **Additional Information:** Pigeon Forge Dept. of Tourism, (800) 251-9100.

RESTRICTIONS

Pets: On leash only, pet walks. **Fires:** In gravel, or rings only. **Alcoholic Beverages:** Dry county. **Vehicle Maximum Length:** 40 ft. **Other:** No tents; one camping unit per site.

TO GET THERE

From I-40, take Exit 407 (Hwy. 66) and follow signs to Pigeon Forge. Turn left at the crossover between lights 9 and 10. The entrance is on the right.

PIKEVILLE

Fall Creek Falls State Park

Rte. 3 Box 300, Pikeville 37367-9803. T: (423) 881-5298 or (800) 250-8611 for reservations; F: (423) 881-5103; www.tnstateparks.com.

RV ★★★★★ Tent ★★★★★

Beauty: ★★★★★	Site Privacy: ★★★★★
Spaciousness: ★★★★★	Quiet: ★★★★★
Security: ★★★★	Cleanliness: ★★★★
Insect Control: ★★★★	Facilities: ★★★★★

This gorgeous park's namesake is the highest waterfall east of the Rocky Mountains. A moderate hike (less than two miles) leads to an area that overlooks the 256-foot waterfall. A short but difficult hike leads to the shady pool at the bottom of the waterfall. In the park are many miles of hiking, walking, road-biking, and mountain-biking trails leading to other beautiful waterfalls and gorges. The campgrounds at Fall Creek Falls are also fabulous, especially the reservation-only area, which is deliciously shaded by indigenous oak-hickory forest. Though sites are spacious and secluded, the campground often feels crowded because it's so large and popular. Most sites offer gravel, back-in parking. A few sites in areas D and E have pull-through parking. Call ahead and obtain a reservation-only site. Security is decent at this very rural park; without gates, rangers patrol nightly. Plan to visit on weekdays, in spring, or in autumn.

BASICS

Operated By: Tennessee State Parks. **Open:** All year. **Site Assignment:** 117 sites first come, first served (plus 10 walk-in sites); 109 sites available for reservation; deposit 2 nights plus $5 fee; 1 week cancellation notice for refund less $5 fee. **Registration:** Camper check-in station or headquarters, night arrivals register next day or ranger makes rounds. **Fee:** $19 full hookup, $17 water & electric, $10 walk-in; prices for 2 people $0.50 per additional person; Golden Access & Golden Age 50% discount, TN seniors 25% discount, out of state seniors $1.50 discount (cash, personal check, V, MC, D, AE). **Parking:** At sites, in parking lot.

FACILITIES

Number of RV Sites: 0. **Number of Tent-Only Sites:** 10 primitive walk-in. **Number of Multipurpose Sites:** 226. **Hookups:** Water, electric (30 amps), 55 sites w/ 50 amps & sewer. **Each Site:** Picnic table, grill, fire ring. **Dump Station:** Yes. **Laundry:** Yes. **Pay Phone:** Yes. **Rest Rooms and Showers:** Yes. **Fuel:** No. **Propane:** Yes (exchange). **Internal Roads:** Paved. **RV Service:** 60 mi. south in Chattanooga. **Market:** 17 mi. east in Pikeville. **Restaurant:** On site. **General Store:** Camp store, 17 mi. east in Pikeville. **Vending:** Yes. **Swimming Pool:** Yes (seasonal). **Playground:** Yes. **Other:** Nature center, recreation hall & arcade, picnic shelters. **Activities:** 18-hole golf course, horseback riding (seasonal), hiking trails, mountain bike trails (seasonal mountain-bike rental), lake fishing, paddle boat & canoe rentals, basketball, softball, tennis, volleyball, horseshoes, shuffleboard, ping pong, pool table, in-season organized activities. **Nearby Attractions:** Pikeville Historic District, Pumpkin Festival, Cumberland Caverns, Ocoee River rafting, 60 mi. to Chattanooga. **Additional Information:** Pikeville Chamber of Commerce, (423) 447-2791.

RESTRICTIONS

Pets: Leash only. **Fires:** Fire rings only. **Alcoholic Beverages:** Not allowed. **Vehicle Maximum Length:** 48 ft. **Other:** 2-week stay limit, except Area D.

TO GET THERE

From Chattanooga, take US Hwy. 27 north for 15 mi. Just past Soddy-Daisy, turn left onto State Hwy. 111. Drive northwest approximately 40 mi. and turn right onto State Hwy. 284. Drive east 8 mi. to the campground. From I-40, take Exit 287 and drive south 30 mi. on State Hwy. 111. Turn left on State Hwy. 284.

PULASKI

Valley KOA Kampground

2289 Hwy. 64, Pulaski 38478. T: (931) 363-4600.

RV ★★★ Tent ★★★

Beauty: ★★★	Site Privacy: ★★
Spaciousness: ★★★	Quiet: ★★★★
Security: ★★	Cleanliness: ★★★★
Insect Control: ★★★★★	Facilities: ★★★

This park is surprisingly attractive given its location 0.2 miles from I-65 in Pulaski, a small town rich in Civil War history. "Boy Hero" Sam Davis was captured here in November 1863. Today, a Civil War Museum occupies the site of his execution. There are three rows of pull-through sites plus one row of back-ins. The long, narrow sites are average sized. Parking is on untidy gravel. Landscaping needs some attention. Mature trees provide shade at most sites, but no privacy. Back-in sites 49–60 have nice field views. For full hookups, try pull-through sites 41–48 located in the back of the park; these are quiet and have pleasant views. This park is visible from I-65 and is not fenced or gated. Security is poor. The owner is serious about insect control; he used to be an exterminator. Visit in spring or fall for the nicest weather. Valley KOA Kampground is rarely full.

BASICS

Operated By: Thomas & Rochelle Talmage. **Open:** All year. **Site Assignment:** First come, first served; reservations get preferred sites, $25 deposit; 72-hour cancellation notice required for a full refund (14-day notice for holidays). **Registration:** Store, night self-registration. **Fee:** $25 full hookup, $23 water & electric, $18 tent; fees for 2 people, $2.50 per additional person (cash, personal check, V, MC, AE). **Parking:** At site (one car), in parking lot (charge may apply for extra vehicles).

FACILITIES

Number of RV Sites: 0. **Number of Tent-Only Sites:** 12. **Number of Multipurpose Sites:** 46. **Hookups:** Water, electric (20, 30 amps), some sites w/ sewer. **Each Site:** Picnic table, fire ring. **Dump Station:** Yes. **Laundry:** Yes. **Pay Phone:** Yes. **Rest Rooms and Showers:** Yes. **Fuel:** No. **Propane:** Yes. **Internal Roads:** Gravel. **RV Service:** 10 mi. in Pulaski. **Market:** 12 mi. in Pulaski. **Restaurant:** Next door. **General Store:** 12 mi. in Pulaski (also convenience store on-site w/ some camping supplies). **Vending:** Beverages only. **Swimming Pool:** Yes (plus wading pool). **Playground:** Yes. **Other:** Game room, movie rentals. **Activities:** Nature walks, horseshoes, basketball, volleyball. **Nearby Attractions:** Historic Pulaski, Civil War Museum, Fort Hill, Jack Daniels Distillery, Space Museum (Huntsville, AL). **Additional Information:** Giles County Chamber of Commerce, (931) 363-3789.

RESTRICTIONS

Pets: Leash only. **Fires:** Fire rings only. **Alcoholic Beverages:** Allowed. **Vehicle Maximum Length:** 80 ft. (sites vary).

TO GET THERE

From I-65, take Exit 14. Drive 0.25 mi. east on US Hwy. 64 directly into the campground.

ROCK ISLAND

Rock Island State Park

82 Beach Rd., Rock Island 38581. T: (931) 686-2471 or (800) 713-6065; F: (931) 686-2558; www.tnstateparks.com.

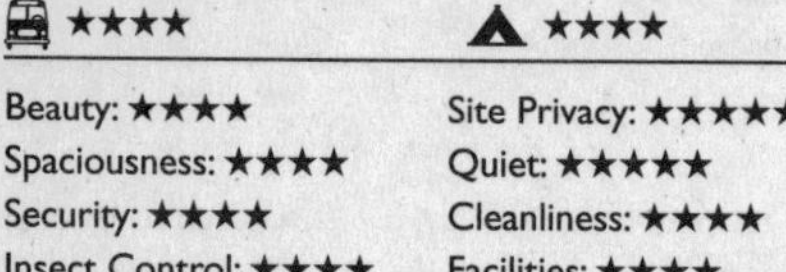

RV ★★★★ | Tent ★★★★

Beauty: ★★★★ Site Privacy: ★★★★★
Spaciousness: ★★★★ Quiet: ★★★★★
Security: ★★★★ Cleanliness: ★★★★
Insect Control: ★★★★ Facilities: ★★★★

This park's centerpiece is the Twin Falls of the Caney Fork River, a dramatic limestone gorge decked out with waterfalls. East of the park is TVA Great Falls Dam and hydroelectric plant. The Blue Hole, one of the best fishing spots in the state of Tennessee, is accessible from the park's boat launch. Nearby, Big Bone Cave offers tours by reservation. The attractive campgrounds at Rock Island include a multipurpose area and a tent-only area. Sites with hookups featured paved, back-in parking spaces. Sites and parking spaces vary greatly in size, though most are ample. The campground is nicely treed, with Virginia pine, tulip poplar, beech and ample of foliage to provide privacy between sites. The nicest sites are 21–23, 41, 43, 45, 47, 48, and 50. Though rangers close the gates nightly, they're not always locked. Rock Island is extremely remote, making security fair. Visit in spring, when heavy rains feed the waterfalls. Avoid holiday weekends.

Basics

Operated By: Tennessee State Parks. **Open:** All year (closed Monday & Tuesday indefinitely due to budget constraints). **Site Assignment:** First come, first served; reservations available w/ nonrefundable deposit of the first night plus $5. **Registration:** Park office, night arrival register next day. **Fee:** $16 for 2 people, $0.50 per additional person up to 9 max; TN seniors 25% discount, out-of-state seniors 10% (cash, personal checks, V, MC, D, AE). **Parking:** At sites, in parking lots.

Facilities

Number of Multipurpose Sites: 60. **Hookups:** Water, electric (30 amps). **Each Site:** Picnic table, grill. **Dump Station:** Yes. **Laundry:** Yes. **Pay Phone:** Yes. **Rest Rooms and Showers:** Yes. **Fuel:** No. **Propane:** No. **Internal Roads:** Paved. **RV Service:** 32 mi. in Cookeville. **Market:** 12 mi. southwest in McMinnville. **Restaurant:** Less than 2 mi. **General Store:** 12 mi. southwest in McMinnville. **Vending:** Yes. **Swimming Pool:** No. **Playground:** Yes. **Other:** Boat launch, picnic areas & pavilions. **Activities:** Beach swimming, boating, fishing, water sports, hiking trails, mountain biking, horseshoes, tennis, volleyball, basketball, multi-use fields, interpretive programs, summertime organized activities. **Nearby Attractions:** Cumberland Caverns Park, Virgin Falls Pocket Wilderness, Burgess Falls State Natural Area, Edgar Evins State Park, Fall Creek Falls State Park. **Additional Information:** McMinnville Chamber of Commerce, (931) 473-6611.

Restrictions

Pets: On leash only. **Fires:** Allowed. **Alcoholic Beverages:** Not allowed. **Vehicle Maximum Length:** No limit. **Other:** 2-week stay limit.

To Get There

From I-24, take the Cookeville Exit onto State Rte. 111 South. Drive south approximately 30 mi. and turn north on State Rte. 136. Drive 2 mi. and turn left onto State Rte. 287. Drive 2 mi. to the park entrance on the right. From I-40, take the Manchester Exit and drive northeast on State Hwy. 55/70 approximately 35 mi. to Rte. 136.

SEVIERVILLE

River Plantation RV Park

1004 Parkway, Sevierville 37862. T: (865) 429-5267 or (800) 758-5267; F: (865) 774-9174; www.riverplantationrv.com; riverrv@aol.com.

RV ★★★ | Tent ★

Beauty: ★★★ Site Privacy: ★★
Spaciousness: ★★★ Quiet: ★★★
Security: ★★★ Cleanliness: ★★★★
Insect Control: ★★★ Facilities: ★★★

River Plantation is not as attractive as many of the older campgrounds in the area. However, sites are easily maneuvered by big rigs. Some sites are shady, though many of the birch and other trees are immature. Most sites feature back-in parking, though there are a few pull-throughs. Parking is on gravel and each site has a concrete patio. Sites along the Little Pigeon River, 201–227, are the nicest, but cost extra. Featureless tent sites are not recommended. As the campground is located in nouveau urban sprawl, restaurants and outlet mall shopping are nearby. Tourist attractions, including Dollywood, charming Gatlinburg, and Great Smoky Mountains National Park are within easy driving distance. Without gates, security is fair at River Plantation. Weekend traffic can be horrendous. Avoid summer holidays and fall leaf-peeping weekends. Do yourself a favor and visit on weekdays.

Basics

Operated By: Jim & Jack Connor. **Open:** All year. **Site Assignment:** Sites assigned; reservations accepted w/ first-night deposit; 3-day cancellation notice for refund. **Registration:** Office, after-hours self-registration. **Fee:** $26 riverfront, $24 full hookup 50 amps, $22 full hookup 30 amps, $18 water & electric, $14 tent; prices for 2 people, $2.50 per additional person; Good Sam discount honored (cash, personal check, V, MC, D, AE). **Parking:** At site (2 cars).

Facilities

Number of RV Sites: 201. **Number of Tent-Only Sites:** 31. **Number of Multipurpose Sites:** None. **Hookups:** Water, electric (30, 50 amps), sewer, cable. **Each Site:** Picnic table, fire ring, concrete pad (RV sites). **Dump Station:** Yes. **Laundry:** Yes. **Pay Phone:** Yes. **Rest Rooms and Showers:** Yes. **Fuel:** No. **Propane:** Yes. **Internal Roads:** Gravel. **RV Service:** 0.25 mi. in Pigeon Forge. **Market:** 0.25 mi. in Pigeon Forge. **Restaurant:** 0.25 mi. in Pigeon Forge. **General Store:** Within 1 mi. in Pigeon Forge. **Vending:** Beverages. **Swimming Pool:** Yes (& hot tub). **Playground:** Yes. **Other:** Arcade, pavilion, hot tub, RV storage. **Activities:** Fishing in Little Pigeon River, horseshoes, basketball, badminton, volleyball. **Nearby Attractions:** Pigeon Forge shops & theaters, Dollywood theme park, water park, Dixie Stampede, Elvis Museum, Kids Country, helicopter tours, whitewater rafting, Cherokee Indian Reservation. **Additional Information:** Pigeon Forge Visitor Information, (865) 453-5700.

Restrictions

Pets: On leash only. **Fires:** Allowed, fire rings only. **Alcoholic Beverages:** Allowed. **Vehicle Maximum Length:** No limit. **Other:** 7 mph speed limit enforced.

To Get There

From I-40, take Exit 407 and drive south 12 mi. on State Rte. 66. When Rte. 66 becomes US Hwy. 441, continue another 2 mi. to the park on the left/east.

SILVER POINT

Edgar Evins State Park

1630 Edgar Evins State Park Rd., Silver Point 38582-7917. T: (800) 250-8619 or (931) 858-2446; F: (931) 858-3121; www.tnstateparks.com.

RV ★★★ | Tent ★★★

Beauty: ★★★★ Site Privacy: ★★★★
Spaciousness: ★★ Quiet: ★★★
Security: ★★★ Cleanliness: ★★★★
Insect Control: ★★★ Facilities: ★★★★

The lovely campground at Edgar Evins offers unique sites, which are built into a terraced hillside and have views of Center Hill Reservoir. Campsites consist of large wooden decks, which accommodate 36-foot campers, depending on availability. Fire rings are beside the camping deck. Although the decks confine your living space to a small area, sites are nicely spaced and buffered by foliage, so you'll have ample privacy. Most sites are plenty shady. Waterfront sites, 43–60, are worth the extra fees—views from these sites are gorgeous. Activities and facilities at Edgar Evins revolve around fishing and boating in the reservoir. Catches include largemouth bass, smallmouth bass, and walleye. The marina is open all year. Security is fair at this rural park; there are no gates, but the park is off the beaten path. This campground only fills on holiday weekends, so it's a good destination for early summer weekends.

Basics

Operated By: Tennessee State Parks. **Open:** All year (closed Monday & Tuesday indefinitely). **Site Assignment:** First come, first served; no reservations accepted. **Registration:** Campground host makes rounds. **Fee:** $19 waterfront, $17 off-water; prices for 2 people, $0.50 per additional person; senior & disabled discounts available (cash, personal checks, traveler checks). **Parking:** at site (2 vehicles).

Facilities

Number of Multipurpose Sites: 60. **Hookups:** Water, electric (30, 50 amps). **Each Site:** Picnic table, grill, fire ring. **Dump Station:** Yes. **Laundry:** No. **Pay Phone:** Yes. **Rest Rooms and Showers:** Yes. **Fuel:** No. **Propane:** No. **Internal Roads:**

Paved. **RV Service:** 60 mi. in Nashville. **Market:** 20 mi. in Cookeville. **Restaurant:** Park restaurant at marina (seasonal), 7 mi. in Silver Point. **General Store:** 20 mi. in Cookeville. **Vending:** Beverages only. **Swimming Pool:** No. **Playground:** Yes. **Other:** Marina w/ rental slips, boat ramps, visitor center, picnic areas & shelters. **Activities:** Nature trails, fishing, boating, lake swimming, horseshoes, badminton, hiking. **Nearby Attractions:** Burgess Falls State Natural Area, Rock Island State Rustic Park, Cumberland Caverns Park, Cedars of Lebanon, 60 mi. to Nashville. **Additional Information:** Cookeville/Putnam County Chamber, (931) 520-7727; Nashville Tourism Info, (615) 259-4700.

Restrictions

Pets: On leash only (no pit bulls). **Fires:** Allowed, in fire ring only (subject to burn ban). **Alcoholic Beverages:** Not allowed. **Vehicle Maximum Length:** 38 ft. (sites vary). **Other:** 14-day stay limit, quiet hours enforced, no gray water dumping, pet policy strictly enforced.

To Get There

From I-40, take Exit 268 and drive south 4.5 mi. on State Hwy. 96. At the stop sign, the park entrance is straight ahead.

SWEETWATER

Sweetwater Valley KOA

269 Murray's Chapel Rd., Sweetwater 37874.
T: (865) 213-3900; F: (865) 213-3900;
www.koa.com; sweetwaterkoa@hotmail.com.

RV ★★★ Tent ★★★

Beauty: ★★★★	Site Privacy: ★★
Spaciousness: ★★★	Quiet: ★★★★
Security: ★★★	Cleanliness: ★★★
Insect Control: ★★★	Facilities: ★★★

Located off of I-75 between Chattanooga and Knoxville, Sweetwater is a convenient stop-over. Alternately, if you want to take mountain drives along the Cherohola Skyway at the height of autumn tourist season, you could use Sweetwater as a less crowded home base. Nearby are shopping and restaurants. The campground is laid out in rows with pull-through parking. Sites are on the small side of average. Although the internal roads are gravel, most RV parking is paved. Some sites are completely shady, while others are completely open. The prettiest sites, 30–34, are located in the back corner of the park, and have gravel parking. Families should head for sites 55–65, which are near the pool and playground. Security is fair-there are no gates, but this is a quiet area. Because it stays relatively cool, eastern Tennessee is lovely in late summer. Avoid visits on holiday weekends.

Basics

Operated By: Dave & Kathy Wakeham. **Open:** All year. **Site Assignment:** Sites assigned based on RV specifics; reservations available w/ full deposit; 3-day notice for refund less $5. **Registration:** Office in store, self-registration at night. **Fee:** $26 full hookup, $23 water & electric, $19 tent; prices for 2 people, $2.50 per additional adult, $2 per additional child; KOA discount 10%. **Parking:** At site (1 car max.), in parking lot.

Facilities

Number of RV Sites: 63. **Number of Tent-Only Sites:** 9. **Number of Multipurpose Sites:** None. **Hookups:** Water, electric (30, 50 amps), some sewer. **Each Site:** Picnic table, most sites have grill &/or fire ring. **Dump Station:** Yes. **Laundry:** Yes. **Pay Phone:** Yes. **Rest Rooms and Showers:** Yes. **Fuel:** No. **Propane:** Yes. **Internal Roads:** Gravel (sites paved). **RV Service:** 2 mi. in Sweetwater. **Market:** 3.5 mi. in Sweetwater. **Restaurant:** 1 mi. at interstate. **General Store:** Convenience store w/ camp supplies on site, also 3.5 mi. in Sweetwater. **Vending:** No. **Swimming Pool:** Yes. **Playground:** Yes. **Other:** Pavilion, recreation hall w/ game room, camper kitchen. **Activities:** Volleyball, horseshoes, multipurpose recreation field, fitness room. **Nearby Attractions:** Dollywood, Pigeon Forge, The Lost Sea, Mayfield Dairy, Fort Loudon State Historic Area, 65 mi. to Chattanooga. **Additional Information:** Madisonville Chamber, (423) 442-4588.

Restrictions

Pets: 6 ft. leash only. **Fires:** Fire rings only. **Alcoholic Beverages:** Allowed at sites only. **Vehicle Maximum Length:** No limit. **Other:** Firearms not allowed.

To Get There

From I-75, take Exit 62 and drive 0.75 mi. west on Oakland/State Hwy. 322. Turn south on Murray's Chapel Rd. The campground is 0.25 mi. on the left.

TELLICO PLAINS

Indian Boundary Campground, Cherokee National Forest

250 Ranger Station Rd., Tellico Plains 37385.
T: (423) 253-2520; F: (423) 253-2804;
www.reserveusa.com.

RV ★★★★ Tent ★★★★★

Beauty: ★★★★★	Site Privacy: ★★★★★
Spaciousness: ★★★★★	Quiet: ★★★★
Security: ★★★★★	Cleanliness: ★★★★
Insect Control: ★★★★	Facilities: ★★★

Located in Cherokee National Forest, Indian Boundary is an excellent choice for those who savor solitude. The campground is gorgeous and the sites are huge—possibly the largest in the state. Most sites are shaded by thick woods, and afforded privacy by lush foliage. If you prefer a more open site, they're also available. Parking is back-in style, on pea gravel. The nicest sites, 17–20, feature views of the 70-acre lake. Recreation includes driving along the Cherohola Skyway National Scenic Hwy., which stretches from Tellico Plains, Tennessee to Robbinsville, North Carolina. Outdoor recreation abounds: world class whitewater on a number of rivers; 650 miles of trails designated for various uses, including portions of the Appalachian Trail and the John Muir National Recreation Trail; and fishing on the charming Hiwassee River. Security is excellent at remote, gated Indian Boundary campground. Avoid visiting on holiday and autumn weekends.

Basics

Operated By: US Forest Service. **Open:** Apr.–Oct. **Site Assignment:** 20 sites available first come, first served; reservations accepted through the National Recreation Reservation Service (NRRS) at (877) 444-6777 or www.reserveusa.com. Reservations can be made up to 240 days in advance, full payment required upon making reservation; credit card preferred (V, MC, D, AE), or pay by money order if at least 21 days in advance, $10 fee cancellation fee, cancellation within three days of arrival charged first night, no-show charged $20 plus first night. **Registration:** Self-service fee station. **Fee:** $15 B & C loops, $10 A & D loops; fees include 5 people, 1 sleeping unit; Golden Age & Golden Access discounts available (cash, personal checks). **Parking:** At site, 2 vehicles max.

Facilities

Number of Multipurpose Sites: 92. **Hookups:** Some sites w/ electric (20, 30 amps). **Each Site:** Picnic table, grill, lantern pole, tent pad. **Dump Station:** Yes. **Laundry:** No. **Pay Phone:** No. **Rest Rooms and Showers:** Yes. **Fuel:** No. **Propane:** No. **Internal Roads:** Paved. **RV Service:** Athens or Maryville. **Market:** 17 mi. in Tellico Plains. **Restaurant:** 17 mi. in Tellico Plains. **General Store:** Camp store, also 17 mi. in Tellico Plains or 30 mi. in Madisonville. **Vending:** Beverages only. **Swimming Pool:** No. **Playground:** No. **Other:** Boat ramp. **Activities:** Lake sports, swimming, boating (electric trolling motor only), canoe rentals, fishing, hiking, bicycling. **Nearby Attractions:** Bald River Falls, Cherohala Scenic Skyway National Scenic Byway, Fort Loudon State Historic Area, Sequoyah Birthplace Museum, The Lost Sea, Orr Mountain Winery, Coker Creek Village. **Additional Information:** Madisonville Chamber of Commerce, (423) 442-4588.

Restrictions

Pets: Leash only. **Fires:** Fire rings only. **Alcoholic Beverages:** Allowed, at sites only. **Vehicle Maximum Length:** 25 ft. (sites vary—see www.reserveusa.com for site specifications). **Other:** 14-day stay limit, must stay first night, must not leave site unattended for more than 24 hours.

To Get There

From I-75 at Sweetwater, take Exit 60 onto State Rte. 68. Drive 30 mi. southeast on 68 to Tellico Plains. Take State Rte. 165 east 17 mi. to the Indian Boundary Campground sign at Forest Rte. 345. Turn left and drive 2 mi. on 345 to the stop sign. Turn right and the campground entrance is 0.25 mi. on the right.

TIPTONVILLE

Reelfoot Lake State Park, South Campground

Rte. 1, Tiptonville 38079. T: (731) 253-7756 or (800) 250-8617; F: (731) 253-9652;
www.tnstateparks.com.

RV ★★★★ Tent ★★★★

Beauty: ★★★★★	Site Privacy: ★★★
Spaciousness: ★★★★	Quiet: ★★★
Security: ★★★	Cleanliness: ★★★★★
Insect Control: ★★	Facilities: ★★★★

Reelfoot Lake State Park is extremely remote, but it's worth the drive. This beautiful campground features cypress trees along the water and shady hardwoods in the rest of the campground. Sites are mid-sized, but feel a little cramped because the campground is often full. Most sites offer paved parking, though a few in the back have gravel parking. Five sites include pull-through parking and the rest offer back-in parking. With little undergrowth, sites are not very private. The nicest sites, 1–21, are right on the water. The most productive natural fish hatchery in the US, Reelfoot Lake supports over 50 fish species. There are no limits on crappie or bluegill. A large population of Bald Eagles winter on Reelfoot Lake. Naturalists conduct boat tours for viewing the dignified birds. This is one of the most popular parks in Tennessee, and should be avoided on summer weekends and holidays. Instead, visit in the winter or spring (when aquatic flowers bloom). Security is fine.

Basics

Operated By: Tennessee State Parks. **Open:** All year (closed Monday & Tuesday indefinitely). **Site Assignment:** First come, first served; no reservations accepted. **Registration:** Entrance station. **Fee:** $19 RV lakefront, $17 RV off lake, $16 tent lakefront, $14 tent off lake; prices for 2 people, $0.50 per additional person; senior & disabled discounts (cash, personal check). **Parking:** At site.

Facilities

Number of RV Sites: 0. **Number of Tent-Only Sites:** 20 primitive. **Number of Multipurpose Sites:** 86. **Hookups:** Water, electric (30, 50 amps). **Each Site:** Picnic table, grill, some fire rings. **Dump Station:** Yes. **Laundry:** Yes. **Pay Phone:** Yes. **Rest Rooms and Showers:** Yes. **Fuel:** No. **Propane:** No. **Internal Roads:** Paved. **RV Service:** 50 mi. in Mayfield. **Market:** 5 mi. in Tiptonville. **Restaurant:** Park restaurant, several within 5 mi. **General Store:** 5 mi. in Tiptonville, Wal-Mart 20 mi. in Union City. **Vending:** Yes. **Swimming Pool:** Yes (& wading pool). **Playground:** Yes. **Other:** Boat dock, fish-cleaning station, boat launches, picnic areas & pavilions, visitor center & auditorium. **Activities:** Fishing, boating (boat rentals available), seasonal cruise boats, swimming beach, tennis, horseshoes, ping pong, badminton, basketball, nature trails, year-round nature programs. **Nearby Attractions:** Mississippi River, Reelfoot National Wildlife Refuge & Visitor Center, Big Cypress Tree State Natural Area, golf in Union City, Dixie Gunworks Museum, Casino Aztar. **Additional Information:** Reelfoot Lake Tourism Council, (731) 253-2007, www.reelfoot-tourism.com.

Restrictions

Pets: On leash only. **Fires:** Allowed. **Alcoholic Beverages:** Not allowed. **Vehicle Maximum Length:** No limit.

To Get There

From Union City (the junction of US Hwy. 51 with US Hwy. 45), drive west 15 mi. on State Hwy. 22. The park is on the right.

TOWNSEND

Cades Cove Campground, Great Smoky Mountains National Park

107 Park Headquarters Rd., Gatlinburg 37738. T: (865) 436-1200; F: (865) 436-1204; www.nps.gov/grsm.

RV ★★★★ Tent ★★★★

Beauty: ★★★★ Site Privacy: ★★★
Spaciousness: ★★★★ Quiet: ★★★
Security: ★★ Cleanliness: ★★★★
Insect Control: ★★★ Facilities: ★★★★

Cades Cove, the flattest campground in the national park, offers the best RV maneuverability. Located in a mountain valley, this area was once heavily settled and farmed, and evidence of previous human habitation is abundant on area walks and drives. There are plenty of activities at Cades Cove, including bicycle rental and fishing in lovely mountain creeks. Cades Cove is the most popular campground in the national park. Bears are drawn here, so protect your food. With high attendance and no security precautions, you should also protect your valuables. Since the campground stays full all summer, you won't enjoy the solitude offered at Cosby. Circumvent this problem by visiting mid-week in the spring, when wildflowers bloom. The campground is laid out in rows of back-in sites with gravel parking. Pine and various oak species provide shade. Campsites are large, but not very private.

Basics

Operated By: National Park Service. **Open:** All year. **Site Assignment:** First come, first served; reservations accepted for May 15–Oct. 31 up to 5 months in advance, w/ full deposit; $13.25 cancellation fee w/ at least 24-hour notice, otherwise first night plus fee charged; reservations made by calling (800) 365-CAMP or at reservations.nps.gov (personal check, money order, V, D, MC). **Registration:** Self-registration. **Fee:** $14–$20 for 6 people max. per site, 2 tents or 1 tent & 1 RV; Golden Age & Golden Access discounts available (cash only during self–registration off-Season). **Parking:** At site (2 vehicles).

Facilities

Number of RV Sites: 0. **Number of Tent-Only Sites:** 22. **Number of Multipurpose Sites:** 139. **Hookups:** None. **Each Site:** Picnic table, fire ring, grill, pea gravel tent pad. **Dump Station:** Yes. **Laundry:** No. **Pay Phone:** Yes. **Rest Rooms and Showers:** Yes. **Fuel:** No. **Propane:** No. **Internal Roads:** Paved. **RV Service:** 23 mi. in Maryville. **Market:** 8 mi. in Townsend. **Restaurant:** 8 mi. in Townsend. **General Store:** 23 mi. in Maryville. **Vending:** Yes. **Swimming Pool:** No. **Playground:** No. **Other:** Amphitheater, picnic area, horse trail, interpretive trail. **Activities:** Hiking, fishing, horseback riding, canoeing, backcountry hiking, ranger programs (seasonal). **Nearby Attractions:** Golf courses, Cades Cove, Pigeon Forge, Dollywood, Gatlinburg, whitewater rafting, Cherokee Indian Reservation. **Additional Information:** Pigeon Forge Visitor information, (865) 453-5700; Park Information, (865) 436-1200.

Restrictions

Pets: 6-ft. leash only. **Fires:** Allowed, fire rings only. **Alcoholic Beverages:** Allowed. **Vehicle Maximum Length:** 35 ft. **Other:** Be aware of bear precautions.

To Get There

From US Hwy. 321 on the east side of Townsend, turn south on State Hwy. 73. Drive 2 mi. and turn right on Laurel Creek Rd. Continue approximately 5 mi. to the campground on the right.

TOWNSEND

Lazy Daze Campground

8429 Scenic Tennessee Hwy. 73, Townsend 37882. T: (865) 448-6061; F: (865) 448-9060; www.LazyDazecampground.com; lazydazetn@aol.com.

RV ★★★ Tent ★★★

Beauty: ★★★★ Site Privacy: ★★★
Spaciousness: ★★★ Quiet: ★★★
Security: ★★★ Cleanliness: ★★★
Insect Control: ★★★ Facilities: ★★★★

Conveniently located within one mile of the Townsend entrance to Great Smoky Mountains National Park, Lazy Daze offers small, clean sites with plenty of shade provided by sweet gum and tulip poplar. The rectangular campground offers three types of sites: those with gravel parking only, sites with gravel parking and a concrete patio, and riverside sites. Sites on the Little River are well worth the extra fees—each site has gravel parking, a concrete patio, and a charming view. All sites offer back-in parking and little privacy. Visitors can take inner tubes down the Little River, with access from the campground. Or, take a bike ride along Hwy. 73 (also known as Foothills Parkway). Townsend is an excellent home base for outdoor exploration on summer and fall weekends when the Gatlinburg area becomes unbearably crowded. Nonetheless, reservations are recommended. Holiday visits are not recommended.

Basics

Operated By: Lissa & Rodney Porter. **Open:** All year. **Site Assignment:** First come, first served; reservations accepted w/ one night deposit; 10-day notice required for cancellation refund. **Registration:** Camp store. **Fee:** $20–$29 for 2 adults & 2 children; $2 per additional adult, $1 per child; Good Sam, Family Campers, senior & group discounts available (cash, personal checks, V, MC, D). **Parking:** At site (1 vehicle), plus limited overflow.

Facilities

Number of RV Sites: 45. **Number of Tent-Only Sites:** 7. **Number of Multipurpose Sites:** 21. **Hookups:** Water, electric (20, 30 amps), sewer, cable. **Each Site:** Picnic table, fire ring, concrete pads at RV sites. **Dump Station:** Yes. **Laundry:** Yes. **Pay Phone:** Yes. **Rest Rooms and Showers:** Yes. **Fuel:** No. **Propane:** Yes. **Internal Roads:** Gravel. **RV Service:** 35 mi. in Chilhowee. **Market:**

0.5 mi. **Restaurant:** Within 1 mi. (several). **General Store:** Camp store, hardware 3.5 mi. in Townsend, Wal-Mart 30 mi. **Vending:** No. **Swimming Pool:** Yes. **Playground:** Yes. **Other:** Pavilion, game room, souvenir shop, cabins. **Activities:** River access, tubing, swimming, fishing (fishing supplies at camp store), shuffleboard, badminton, volleyball, horseshoes, basketball. **Nearby Attractions:** Golf courses, Cades Cove, Pigeon Forge, Dollywood, Gatlinburg, whitewater rafting, Cherokee Indian Reservation. **Additional Information:** Pigeon Forge Visitor information, (865) 453-5700.

RESTRICTIONS

Pets: On leash only. **Fires:** Allowed, in fire ring only. **Alcoholic Beverages:** Allowed, in site only. **Vehicle Maximum Length:** 40 ft. **Other:** No diving in the pool, family-oriented campground, quiet enforced.

TO GET THERE

Driving north on US Hwy. 321 into Townsend, continue straight at the traffic light. This becomes State Hwy. 73 and the campground is 1 mi. on left.

TOWNSEND

Little River Village

8533 State Hwy. 73, Townsend 37882. T: (865) 448-2241 or (800) 261-6370.

RV ★★★★ Tent ★★★★

Beauty: ★★★★ Site Privacy: ★★★
Spaciousness: ★★★ Quiet: ★★★
Security: ★★★ Cleanliness: ★★★★
Insect Control: ★★★★ Facilities: ★★★★

Convenient for entering Great Smoky Mountains National Park at Cades Cove, Little River Village offers nice facilities in a reasonably attractive campground. The playground is excellent for small children, while older children enjoy swimming and tubing in the Little River. The campground contains both back-in and pull-through sites, as well as an unusually large number of tent sites. Site size varies greatly, but most are long, narrow, and sandwiched together. Most are shady, but few enjoy any privacy. Parking is on gravel. Sites along the river are the prettiest. Pop-ups and small rigs should ask for sites 77–84. Tent campers should ask for 121–126. Big rigs should ask for sites 11–15. Security is fair—there are no gates, but the location is extremely rural. Visit in late summer to enjoy the cool mountain air. Visit on weekdays in the fall, when leaf peepers descend in droves.

BASICS

Operated By: Chipperfield Family. **Open:** All year. **Site Assignment:** Assigned by number, drop-ins choose; reserve up to one year in advance w/ credit card, $25 deposit; partial refund if you cancel 7 days ahead. **Registration:** At camp office. **Fee:** Off river: $20 primitive tent, $26 water & electricity, $28 full hookups. On river: $25 primitive tent, $31 water & electricity, $33 full hookups. $2 each extra person over 5. **Parking:** Yes.

FACILITIES

Number of RV Sites: 67. **Number of Tent-Only Sites:** 27 primitive. **Number of Multipurpose Sites:** 27 water & electric. **Hookups:** Water, electric, sewer, cable. **Each Site:** Picnic table, fire ring, lantern post, full hookup sites have paved patio. **Dump Station:** Yes. **Laundry:** Yes. **Pay Phone:** Yes. **Rest Rooms and Showers:** Yes. **Fuel:** Yes. **Propane:** Yes. **Internal Roads:** Paved & gravel. **RV Service:** 22 mi. west in Maryville. **Market:** On property or 3 mi. west in Townsend. **Restaurant:** Fast food on property, 2 mi. to more restaurants. **General Store:** 3.5 mi. west in Townsend. **Vending:** Yes. **Swimming Pool:** Yes. **Playground:** Yes. **Other:** Pavilion. **Activities:** Fishing, swimming, tubing (rentals), walking & bicycle trail, arcade, pool table, horseshoes, volleyball, basketball. **Nearby Attractions:** Great Smoky Mountains National Park, Pigeon Forge, Gatlinburg, Cades Cove pioneer area. **Additional Information:** Townsend Visitors Center, (865) 448-6134; Pigeon Forge Dept. of Tourism, (800) 251-9100.

RESTRICTIONS

Pets: On leash only. **Fires:** Fire rings only. **Alcoholic Beverages:** At sites only. **Vehicle Maximum Length:** 40 ft. **Other:** Max. 6 people, 2 tents.

TO GET THERE

From I-40, take Exit 386 and go south on Hwy. 129 to Maryville. After the Maryville Hospital, bear left onto 321 North and drive 18 mi. into Townsend. In Townsend, go through the stoplight. The campground is 1 mi. ahead on the left.

TOWNSEND

Tremont Hills Campground

P.O. Box 5 Hwy. 73, Townsend 37882. T: (865) 448-6363; F: (865) 448-6459; www.tremontcamp.com; tremontcamp@webtv.net.

RV ★★★★ Tent ★★★★

Beauty: ★★★★ Site Privacy: ★★★★
Spaciousness: ★★★★ Quiet: ★★★
Security: ★★★ Cleanliness: ★★★★
Insect Control: ★★★★ Facilities: ★★★

This pretty campground offers unusually large sites and is convenient to the Cades Cove entrance to Great Smoky Mountains National Park. In addition to the usual amenities, Tremont Hills offers river inner tubing. The campground consists of three areas. The tent-only and RV-only sections are adjacent to the Little River. While the riverside sites have the prettiest views, they are also the noisiest—Hwy. 73 follows the river on the park's boundary. All sites have gravel, back-in parking. Tremont Hills is nicely shaded and there is some foliage to provide privacy between sites. Like other Smoky Mountain tourist towns, Townsend becomes unbearably crowded on fall weekends. If you can't resist seeing the autumn leaves, visit on a weekday. Security is passable. There are no gates, but Townsend is a safe little town.

BASICS

Operated By: Rob & Sherry Hill. **Open:** Mar.–Nov. (cabins & self-contained rigs remain open in winter). **Site Assignment:** First come, first served; specific sites can be guaranteed w/ 6 days or more; nonrefundable deposit, varies w/ length of stay. **Registration:** Camp store, after hours register next day. **Fee:** $32 Full hookup waterfront, $28 full hookup off water, $23 water & electric, $21 tent waterfront, $18 tent off-water; prices for 2 people, $2 per additional person; FMCA discount available (cash, TN checks, V, MC, D). **Parking:** At site (one car plus camping unit), in parking lot.

FACILITIES

Number of RV Sites: 50. **Number of Tent-Only Sites:** 35. **Number of Multipurpose Sites:** 21. **Hookups:** Water, electric (30 amps), sewer, cable. **Each Site:** Picnic table, fire ring. **Dump Station:** Yes. **Laundry:** Yes. **Pay Phone:** Yes. **Rest Rooms and Showers:** Yes. **Fuel:** No. **Propane:** No. **Internal Roads:** Paved & gravel. **RV Service:** 18 mi. in Pigeon Forge. **Market:** 3 mi. in Townsend. **Restaurant:** 3 mi. in Townsend. **General Store:** Camp store, hardware 3 mi. in Townsend, Wal-Mart 18 mi. in Pigeon Forge. **Vending:** Beverages only. **Swimming Pool:** Yes. **Playground:** Yes. **Other:** Pavilion, game room. **Activities:** Fishing, river tubing, basketball, summer day-camp for children. **Nearby Attractions:** Golf courses, Cades Cove, Great Smoky Mountains National Park, Pigeon Forge, Dollywood, Gatlinburg, whitewater rafting, Cherokee Indian Reservation. **Additional Information:** Pigeon Forge Visitor Information, (865) 453-5700.

RESTRICTIONS

Pets: On leash only. **Fires:** Fire ring only. **Alcoholic Beverages:** Allowed, at sites only. **Vehicle Maximum Length:** 40 ft. (sites vary). **Other:** No parking on the grass, visitors must be registered.

TO GET THERE

From I-40, take Exit 407 and drive 13 mi. south on US Hwy. 441. At Pine Grove, turn southwest on US Hwy. 321/ Scenic Hwy. 73 and drive 16 mi. to Townsend. The campground is on the right.

UNICOI

Little Oak Campground, Cherokee National Forest

P.O. Box 400, Unicoi 37692. T: (423) 735-1500; F: (423) 735-7306; www.r8web.com/cherokee.

RV ★★★★ Tent ★★★★★

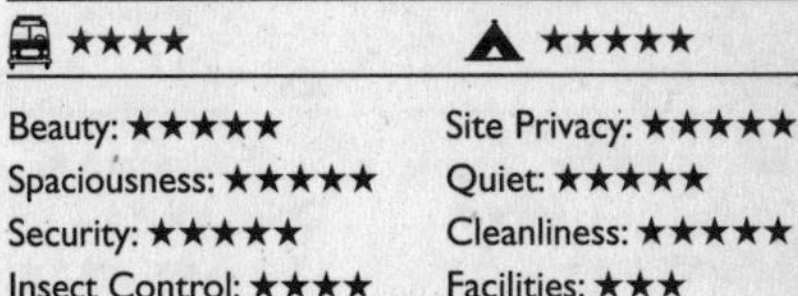

Beauty: ★★★★★ Site Privacy: ★★★★★
Spaciousness: ★★★★★ Quiet: ★★★★★
Security: ★★★★★ Cleanliness: ★★★★★
Insect Control: ★★★★ Facilities: ★★★

With few recreational amenities, the draw at this beautiful campground is the solitude. The campground is laid out on four narrow peninsulas, so almost every site has a view of South Holsten Lake. Sites are large and amply shaded by various oak species, poplar, white pine, and hemlock. Greenery provides privacy between sites. Sites have gravel, back-in parking. Although all sites here are nice, the loveliest views are found on Big Oak Loop. Huge Cherokee National Forest includes hundreds of miles of hiking, mountain biking, and equestrian trails, including the Appalachian Trail, only a few miles from the campground. A popular hike from the campground leads to the Holsten Mountain Fire tower. Security is excellent at Little Oak; the campground is extremely remote. When we visited on a May weekend, the campground was nearly deserted. This is an excellent choice for any summer weekend except for holidays.

Basics

Operated By: USDA Forest Service. **Open:** Mid-Apr.–mid-Oct. **Site Assignment:** First come, first served; no reservations. **Registration:** Self-registration at fee box. **Fee:** $12, limit 5 people per site. **Parking:** At site.

Facilities

Number of Multipurpose Sites: 72. **Hookups:** None. **Each Site:** Picnic table, fire ring, lantern pole. **Dump Station:** Yes. **Laundry:** No. **Pay Phone:** Yes. **Rest Rooms and Showers:** Yes. **Fuel:** No. **Propane:** No. **Internal Roads:** Gravel. **RV Service:** 22 mi. north in Bristol. **Market:** 22 mi. north in Bristol. **Restaurant:** 22 mi. north in Bristol. **General Store:** 22 mi. north in Bristol. **Vending:** No. **Swimming Pool:** No. **Playground:** No. **Other:** Boat ramp, amphitheater, interpretive trails. **Activities:** Hiking, boating, fishing. **Nearby Attractions:** Bristol Caverns, Bristol Motor Speedway. **Additional Information:** Bristol CVB, (423) 989-4850.

Restrictions

Pets: Leash only. **Fires:** Fire rings only. **Alcoholic Beverages:** Not allowed. **Vehicle Maximum Length:** 30 ft.

To Get There

From Bristol drive south on US Hwy. 421 for 12 mi. Turn right onto Camp Tom Howard Rd. After 0.5 mi., the road becomes gravel FR 87. Continue on 87 for 6 mi. and then turn right onto FR 87G. The campground is 1.5 mi. ahead.

WILDERSVILLE

Pin Oak Campground, Natchez Trace State Resort Park

24845 Natchez Trace Rd., Wildersville 38388. T: (731) 968-3742 or (800) 250-8616 for Pin Oak Lodge; F: (731) 967-9863; www.tnstateparks.com.

RV ★★★★ | Tent ★★★

Beauty: ★★★★	Site Privacy: ★★★
Spaciousness: ★★★★	Quiet: ★★★★
Security: ★★★	Cleanliness: ★★★★
Insect Control: ★★★★	Facilities: ★★★★★

Natchez Trace offers top-notch recreational facilities built into rolling hills and woodlands including white oak, pin oak, loblolly pine, and other species. Unique facilities include four small lakes and 250 miles of equestrian trails. The park is also the proud home of the third largest pecan tree in North America. Tidy Pin Oak Campground consists of three loops, each with views of Pin Oak Lake. Landscaping consists of meticulous grass patches and a few young hardwoods planted throughout. There is no shade or privacy. However, the campground's openness makes views of Pin Oak Lake all the more stunning. All sites are larger than average and have gravel parking. Most sites are back-in, although one loop has long narrow pull-thrus. We recommend any of the waterfront sites. Security at Pin Oak is mediocre. There are no gates, but the campground is extremely remote. Avoid western Tennessee in hot, humid late summer.

Basics

Operated By: Tennessee State Parks. **Open:** All year (closed Monday & Tuesday indefinitely). **Site Assignment:** First come, first served; no reservations accepted. **Registration:** Attendant makes rounds, self-register at night. **Fee:** $19 waterfront, $17 off water; prices for 2 people, $0.50 per additional person; senior & disabled discounts available (cash, personal checks). **Parking:** at site (2 vehicles).

Facilities

Number of Multipurpose Sites: 74. **Hookups:** Water, electric (50 amps), sewer. **Each Site:** Picnic table, grill, fire ring w/ grill, lantern pole, gravel pad. **Dump Station:** No. **Laundry:** Yes. **Pay Phone:** Yes. **Rest Rooms and Showers:** Yes. **Fuel:** Yes. **Propane:** No. **Internal Roads:** Paved. **RV Service:** 100 mi. in Nashville. **Market:** 10 mi. in Lexington. **Restaurant:** Park restaurant (seasonal), 10 mi. in Lexington. **General Store:** Park store, hardware 7 mi., Wal-Mart 10 mi. in Lexington. **Vending:** Yes. **Swimming Pool:** No. **Playground:** Yes. **Other:** Picnic shelter, boat dock, camping cabins. **Activities:** Swimming beach, fishing, hunting, hiking trails (including overnight backpacking w/ permit), roads for motorcycles & off-road vehicles, equestrian trails & horse rentals, firing range, ball field, paddle boat rentals, archery range, summer naturalist programs. **Nearby Attractions:** Nathan Bedford Forrest State Historic Area, Mousetail Landing State Rustic park, Tennessee national Wildlife Refuge, Tennessee river, Hurricane Mills Loretta Lynn Dude Ranch. **Additional Information:** Lexington Chamber of Commerce, (731) 968-2126.

Restrictions

Pets: On leash only. **Fires:** Allowed, in fire ring only. **Alcoholic Beverages:** Not allowed. **Vehicle Maximum Length:** No limit. **Other:** 14-day stay limit, quiet enforced, no parking on the grass.

To Get There

From I-40 Exit 116, drive 10 mi. south on Local Rte. 114 to Pin Oak Lodge Rd. Turn left to get to the campground.

WINCHESTER

Tims Ford State Park

570 Tims Ford. Dr., Winchester 37390-4136. T: (931) 962-1183; F: (931) 962-2704; www.tnstateparks.com.

RV ★★★★ | Tent ★★★

Beauty: ★★★	Site Privacy: ★★★★
Spaciousness: ★★★	Quiet: ★★★★
Security: ★★★	Cleanliness: ★★★
Insect Control: ★★★	Facilities: ★★★★★

Tim's Ford State Park has a passably attractive campground, w/ sites nicely shaded by red and white oak, maple, and hickory. Most sites also have a little greenery providing privacy between them. Site size varies-some are among the smallest in the Tennessee State Parks system. Others are livable. A few sites, including 34 and 35, have views of the lake. Many of the sites have very small parking pads. Sites feature paved, back-in parking. 10,700-acre Tims Ford Lake is known for excellent bass fishing, and the park provides ample fishing facilities. In addition to a large swimming pool, the park maintains a diving pool and a children's pool. The 18-hole bent grass golf course was designed by Jack Nicklaus. There are also paved multi-use trails available for exploring the rolling countryside. This park is extremely remote and has no gates. So security is fair. It's extremely popular with families and should be avoided on summer weekends.

Basics

Operated By: Tennessee State Parks. **Open:** All year. **Site Assignment:** First come, first served; no reservations accepted. **Registration:** Attendant makes rounds in-season (winter check-in at Visitor Center). **Fee:** $14–$17 RV, $14 tent; prices for 2 people, $0.50 per additional person up to 10 max.; senior & disabled discounts available (cash, personal checks, V, MC, D, AE). **Parking:** At sites, in overflow lot (not on grass).

Facilities

Number of Multipurpose Sites: 50. **Hookups:** Water, electric (20, 30 amps). **Each Site:** Picnic table, grill, fire pit, tent pad. **Dump Station:** Yes. **Laundry:** Yes. **Pay Phone:** Yes. **Rest Rooms and Showers:** Yes. **Fuel:** No. **Propane:** No. **Internal Roads:** Paved. **RV Service:** 12 mi. in Winchester. **Market:** 5 mi. **Restaurant:** Park restaurant (seasonal), 12 mi. in Winchester. **General Store:** 12 mi. in Winchester. **Vending:** Beverages only. **Swimming Pool:** Yes (Memorial Day–Mid-Aug.). **Playground:** Yes. **Other:** Picnic areas & shelters, marina w/ snack bar, bait shop & fish-cleaning station, boat dock & launch, recreation complex, visitor center. **Activities:** 18-hole golf course, bicycle trails (bicycle rentals), hiking, fishing (boat rentals), badminton, table tennis, basketball, summer interpretive programs. **Nearby Attractions:** Jack Daniels Distillery, Old Stone Fort State Archaeological Area, Falls Mill, Railroad Museum, Franklin State Forest, South Cumberland State Recreation Area, University of the South. **Additional Information:** Winchester Chamber of Commerce, (931) 967-6788.

Restrictions

Pets: On leash only. **Fires:** Allowed, fire pits & grills only. **Alcoholic Beverages:** Not allowed. **Vehicle Maximum Length:** Sites vary. **Other:** 14-day stay limit, no parking on the grass.

To Get There

From I-24 Exit 111, turn southwest on State Hwy. 55. Drive approximately 15 mi. into Tullahoma to the second traffic light (US 41A). Drive straight onto State Hwy. 130. Continue south on 130 for 0.75 mi. to Westside Dr. and turn left onto 130 and Westside Dr. Drive 3.5 mi. to the Awalt Rd. fork on the left. Drive 5.5 mi. on Awalt and turn left at Mansford Rd. Drive 1.6 mi. to the Park entrance on the right.

Texas

Texans are proud of the size of their state. Our team, a bunch of Easterners, grew more impressed as each day passed. When we hadn't reached El Paso by the 25th day of our westbound tour of Texas, we became listless and discouraged. But the discovery of Texas's natural beauty, colorful history, and rich culture is worth the drive.

Texans divide their state into seven geographic and cultural regions. Big Bend Country begins at **El Paso** and is bordered by New Mexico to the north and the Rio Grande River on the south. Big Bend Country is home to two breathtaking national parks: **Guadalupe Mountains** and **Big Bend.**

The Panhandle Plains includes **Amarillo, Lubbock, Wichita Falls,** and **Abilene.** Amarillo is the gateway to the nation's second largest canyon, **Palo Duro.** Lubbock, Wichita Falls, and Abilene experienced massive growth in the 1880s, when railroad expansion fueled the cattle industry.

The Prairies and Lakes region is bordered on the north by Oklahoma, stretches south to the Gulf Coast region, and includes the **Dallas–Fort Worth Metroplex**. Lake recreation, urban tourist attractions, and business draw millions to this area annually.

The eastern Piney Woods region borders Arkansas and Louisiana and stretches from **Texarkana** to north of **Houston.** In the heart of the rolling hills of the Piney Woods, tranquil **Angelina National Forest** surrounds massive **Sam Rayburn Reservoir.**

Texas's Gulf Coast region stretches from industrial **Beaumont** to the important agricultural area near **Brownsville.** In the 1970s the coast was transformed by OPEC's embargo on oil exported to the United States, which caused Texas oil prices to skyrocket and stimulated industrial growth.

The South Texas Plains stretch from **San Antonio** to **McAllen** and are bordered on the southwest by the Rio Grande. Greatly influenced by Mexican culture, this region has been the focus of numerous territory disputes, wars, and skirmishes. In the famous battle of the **Alamo** (1835), Texas Revolutionary forces were defeated by the Mexican army.

The Hill Country is anchored by **Austin** on its eastern border and includes the charming tourist towns of **Fredericksburg** and **Kerrville.** The **Lyndon B. Johnson National Historic Park,** near **Stonewall,** includes the president's boyhood home, grave, and family ranch. Lady Bird Johnson still occupies the ranch and greets tourists when time allows.

When planning your trip, call for the newest Texas State Travel Guide. There are so many tourist attractions in Texas that we have chosen to list only those easily accessed from major cities.

Austin attractions: **Lyndon B. Johnson Library and Museum, Lady Bird Johnson Wildflower Center, State Capitol Complex,** the **University of Texas.** Corpus Christi attractions: **Texas State Aquarium, Padre Island National Seashore,** ***USS Lexington*** **Museum on the Bay.** Dallas-Fort Worth attractions: the Dallas Cowboys, **Dallas Zoo, Fair Park, Six Flags Over Texas, Billy Bob's Texas** (world's largest honky-tonk, yahoo!), **Fort Worth Museum of Science and History, Fort Worth Zoo, Texas Motor Speedway.** El Paso attractions: **Juarez** tours, **Fort Bliss, Old Missions.** Houston attractions: **Astrodome, Downtown Houston Theater District, Museum District** (includes 14 museums, galleries, and gardens), **Six Flags AstroWorld/WaterWorld, Space Center Houston.** San Antonio attractions: **the Alamo, Military Bases Complex, Missions of San Antonio, San Antonio Zoo, Sea World of Texas, Six Flags Fiesta Texas.**

Campground Profiles

ALAMO

Alamo Palms

1341 Business Hwy. 83, Alamo, 78516. T: (956) 787-7571; F: (956) 787-7594; www.gocampingamerica.com/alamopalms, or www.alamopalms.com.

RV ★★★ Tent n/a

Beauty: ★★★
Site Privacy: ★★
Spaciousness: ★★
Quiet: ★★★★
Security: ★★★★
Cleanliness: ★★★★
Insect Control: ★★★★
Facilities: ★★★★

"Alamo Palms" is a misnomer. Incredibly, the park's brochure also boasts about its trees. Alas, the campground is almost completely treeless. But Alamo Palms does offer top-notch amenities and recreation, including 20 shuffleboard courts, eight billiard tables, and weekly ballroom dances. Alamo Palms is a community-oriented adult-only park. The campground consists of row after row of nearly identical sites. So choose your site based on location; sites in the 200s, 300s, and 400s are close to the pool and clubhouse. All RV sites are small and nondescript, with paved back-in parking. Suburban Alamo Palms is convenient to shopping and restaurants. Drive to the beach or to Mexico in about an hour. Fenced and gated at night, security is good. Don't visit south Texas in the heat of summer. Make reservations well in advance in the winter.

Basics

Operated By: Hynes Group. **Open:** All year. **Site Assignment:** Reservations for one month or more, $200 nonrefundable deposit, call (800) 780-7571. **Registration:** At office. **Fee:** $20 per night for 2 people, $1 for each additional person. **Parking:** At site.

Facilities

Number of RV Sites: 351. **Number of Tent-Only Sites:** 0. **Hookups:** Water, sewer, electric (30, 50 amps), cable TV, dataport. **Each Site:** No amenities. **Dump Station:** No. **Laundry:** Yes. **Pay Phone:** Yes. **Rest Rooms and Showers:** No showers. **Fuel:** No. **Propane:** Yes. **Internal Roads:** Paved. **RV Service:** 2 mi. **Market:** 1 mi. **Restaurant:** 1 mi. **General Store:** 0.5 mi. **Vending:** Yes. **Swimming:** Pool. **Playground:** No. **Other:** Spa, tennis courts, exercise facilities, pool room, game room, ballroom, car & RV wash area, storage facilities. **Activities:** Shuffleboard, dancing, crafts, table tennis. **Nearby Attractions:** Sabal Palm Audubon Center & Sanctuary, Gladys Porter Zoo, Brownsville Battlefields, CAF/ Confederate Air Force Rio Grande Valley Wing, Historic Brownsville Museum. **Additional Information:** Alamo Chamber of Commerce (956) 787-2117, Rio Grande Valley Chamber of Commerce, (956) 968-3141.

Restrictions

Pets: Not allowed. **Fires:** In your own grill only. **Alcoholic Beverages:** Allowed. **Vehicle Maximum Length:** 40 ft.

To Get There

Travel south on US 281 (south of San Antonio), pass the US 83 East exit, and take the next exit, Business 83 East. This will take you to Alamo. The campground is 5 mi. ahead on the right just after Cesar-Chavez Rd.

ALEDO

Cowtown RV Park

7000 I-20, Aledo, 76008. T: (817) 441-7878; F: (817) 441-6567; www.gocamopingamerica.com/cowtown; cowtown@gocampingamerica.com.

RV ★★★ | Tent n/a

Beauty: ★★★	Site Privacy: ★★★
Spaciousness: ★★★	Quiet: ★★★
Security: ★★★	Cleanliness: ★★★★
Insect Control: ★★★	Facilities: ★★★

Approximately 20 miles west of downtown Fort Worth, plain-looking Cowtown provides convenient and tidy campsites. "Cowtown" is an old nickname for Fort Worth and not descriptive of this area. A bustling suburb with plenty of restaurants and shops, Aledo is no cow-town. Arranged in two long, straight rows of pull-throughs and two smaller sections containing back-in sites, all sites are narrow and basically unattractive. Each site contains a paved parking pad, a grassy area, and a sapling. The young trees break the visual monotony, but provide no shade or privacy. For couples, we recommend sites in the 90s and 100s—furthest from the interstate, these are likely the quietest. Families should look for a site in the front, near the pool and playground. Close to I-20, with no gates and no security guard, security at Cowtown is poor. For the nicest weather, visit northeastern Texas in spring or fall.

Basics

Operated By: The Beadels. **Open:** All year. **Site Assignment:** For reservations, call (800) 781-4678; credit card number holds site, no-show charged one night. **Registration:** At office. **Fee:** $25 per night for 2 people, $1 per extra person over age 11. **Parking:** At site.

Facilities

Number of RV Sites: 104. **Number of Tent-Only Sites:** None. **Hookups:** Water, sewer, electric (30, 50 amps). **Each Site:** Some picnic tables, some grills. **Dump Station:** Yes. **Laundry:** Yes. **Pay Phone:** Yes. **Rest Rooms and Showers:** Yes. **Fuel:** No. **Propane:** Yes. **Internal Roads:** Some paved, some gravel. **RV Service:** 7 mi. east in Fort Worth. **Market:** 2 mi. in Willow Park. **Restaurant:** 2 mi. in Willow Park. **General Store:** At park. **Vending:** Yes. **Swimming:** Pool. **Playground:** Yes. **Other:** Rally room, mail service, fax service, car rental. **Activities:** volleyball, horseshoes, planned activities. **Nearby Attractions:** Trinity Meadows Race Track, Texas Opry, Six Flags Over Texas, Fort Worth Cowtown Coliseum, Fort Worth Sundance Square, Fort Worth Zoo, Fort Worth Museum of Science & History. **Additional Information:** Fort Worth CVB (800) 433-5747.

Restrictions

Pets: On leash & not allowed in playground or pool area. **Fires:** In grills only. **Alcoholic Beverages:** Not allowed inside buildings. **Vehicle Maximum Length:** 45 ft. **Other:** Speed limit 7 mph. You may rent a site for the RV price & tent-camp on it.

To Get There

From Fort Worth head west on I-30. Pass the junction of I-30 with I-20 and continue west on I-20 to exit 418 (Ranch House Rd.). Campground is one mile east on South Access Rd.

ARLINGTON

Treetops RV Village

1901 West Arbrook Rd., Arlington, 76015. T: (817) 467-7943; F: (817) 468-7607; www.flash.net/~twee tops/treetop.html; tweetops@flash.net.

RV ★★★ | Tent n/a

Beauty: ★★★★	Site Privacy: ★★★★
Spaciousness: ★★★	Quiet: ★★★
Security: ★★★	Cleanliness: ★★★★
Insect Control: ★★★	Facilities: ★★★

Convenient and attractive, Treetops is located in a thriving suburb about halfway between Dallas and Fort Worth. Spend your days off property; area shopping, dining, and tourist attractions are plentiful, while amenities at the campground are not. Sites include both back-ins and pull-throughs, and they are laid out on a winding road. Site size varies, but most are small and crowded. Even so, sites feel private thanks to 2001 shady oak trees and landscaped shrubbery between many sites. Each site contains a gravel RV parking space and a grassy area. Sites 338–361 are the furthest from busy roads and likely to be the quietest. We also recommend any of the sites along the small creek that runs through the park. There are no gates at this park, making security marginal. This park stays busy, so we recommend year-round advance reservations.

Basics

Operated By: Privately owned. **Open:** All year. **Site Assignment:** Reservations accepted, credit card number holds site, 24-hour cancellation notice required. **Registration:** At office. **Fee:** $28 per night for 2 people, $3 for each additional person over age 5. **Parking:** Gravel.

Facilities

Number of RV Sites: 165 (90 are reserved for monthly guests). **Number of Tent-Only Sites:** 0. **Hookups:** Water, sewer, electric (30, 50 amps), cable TV. **Each Site:** Picnic table, cement patio. **Dump Station:** Yes. **Laundry:** Yes. **Pay Phone:** Yes. **Rest Rooms and Showers:** Yes. **Fuel:** No. **Propane:** Yes. **Internal Roads:** Paved. **RV Service:** 15 mi. west in Fort Worth. **Market:** 0.25 mi. **Restaurant:** 0.25 mi. **General Store:** 0.25 mi. **Vending:** None. **Swimming:** Pool. **Playground:** No. **Other:** Dog walking area, dataport, mailboxes, newspaper vending, pavilion. **Activities:** Swimming. **Nearby Attractions:** Six Flags, Hurricane Harbor, Fort Worth Stockyards, Texas Motor Speedway, Texas Rangers Baseball, Lone Star Park, DFW International Airport, Dallas Mavericks, Mesquite Rodeo, Dallas Cowboys, convention centers, numerous retail shops. **Additional Information:** Fort Worth CVB (800) 433-5747, Dallas CVB (800) 232-5527.

Restrictions

Pets: Small pets only, must be on leash. **Fires:** None, bring your own grill. **Alcoholic Beverages:** Allowed. **Vehicle Maximum Length:** 45 ft. **Other:** No pop-ups or tents allowed.

To Get There

From I-20, take exit 449 (Cooper St.). Go north one block and veer left onto Melear Dr. Turn left onto Arbrook Rd. Entrance is on the right.

ATLANTA

Atlanta State Park

Rte. 1 Box 116, Atlanta 75551. T: (512) 389-8900 or (800) 792-1112; F: (512) 389-8959; www.tpwd.state.tx.us; e-mail.reservations@tpwd.state.tx.us.

RV ★★★★ | Tent ★★★★★

Beauty: ★★★★	Site Privacy: ★★★★
Spaciousness: ★★★★	Quiet: ★★★★★
Security: ★★★★	Cleanliness: ★★★★
Insect Control: ★★	Facilities: ★★★

This state park offers two of the things that all RVers love in a campsite: full hookups and pull-throughs.

(Of the nearly 60 sites in the park, about half are 110-foot pull-throughs, and nearly a third have full hookups.) While this park does not offer any sites right on the water's edge, sites 15–17 in the Kights Bluff area have decent lake views. (16 and 17 are pull-throughs.) Sites 4 and 5 are the most secluded, being 40-foot back-ins at the end of a roundabout. Sites 1 and 8 are closest to the entrance to this area and are therefore less desirable. Sites 16–23 are pull-throughs but are all quite open to the sun. The Wilkins Creek camping area offers forested pull-throughs away from the water's edge. Even-numbered sites 32–36 are particularly well-shaded. Site 65 is the only back-in in the area, and seems out of place: it looks like an outdated hookup that may not be in use. Like Knights Bluff, white Oak Ridge offers views of the lake (especially sites 51–54), but no sites on the water's edge. These sites are slightly smaller back-ins (35 feet) than in Knights Bluff, and are all pretty well-shaded. These sites, unlike the others, have a dirt floor instead of grass. Sites 52 and 53, at the end of a roundabout, are the most secluded. The rest rooms in this park are clean and have flush toilets, and each camping area has hot-water showers. This is a worthwhile destination for a family outing or a loner's getaway. There is something to suit just about anyone who doesn't mind getting out and about.

Basics

Operated By: Texas Parks & Wildlife. **Open:** All year. **Site Assignment:** First come, first served. (Credit card required to make a reservation. $3 reservation service fee; $5 cancellation fee.). **Registration:** In office. (Late arrivals use drop box at entrance.). **Fee:** RV: $13 (full), $11 (water, electric), plus $2/person entrance fee (V, MC, D accepted in the office or for reservation.). **Parking:** At site.

Facilities

Number of RV Sites: 59. **Number of Tent-Only Sites:** Combined. **Hookups:** Water, sewer, electric (20, 30 & 50 amps). **Each Site:** Picnic table, grill, fire pit, lantern post, tent pad, water. **Dump Station:** Yes. **Laundry:** No. **Pay Phone:** Yes. **Rest Rooms and Showers:** Yes. **Fuel:** No. **Propane:** No. **Internal Roads:** Paved. **RV Service:** No. **Market:** 10 mi. to Queen's City. **Restaurant:** 10 mi. to Queen's City. **General Store:** Yes. **Vending:** Yes. **Swimming:** Lake. **Playground:** Yes. **Other:** Ampitheatre, group picnic area, fish cleaning station. **Activities:** Swimming, boating, fishing, hiking, mountain biking. **Nearby Attractions:** Lake Wright Patman, Caddo Lake State Park, Starr Family State Historical Park. **Additional Information:** Park Office: (903) 796-6476.

Restrictions

Pets: On 6-ft. leash, cleaned up after. **Fires:** In grills. **Alcoholic Beverages:** None. **Vehicle Maximum Length:** None. **Other:** Each visitor must pay $2 entrance fee per day.

To Get There

From the junction of Hwy. 436 and Hwy. 59, go 1.35 mi. north on Hwy. 59 to FM 96. Turn west onto FM 96 and go 7.2 mi. Turn right onto FM 1154 and go 1.6 mi. to Park Rd. 42, which leads to the park entrance.

AUSTIN

Austin Lone Star RV Resort

7009 South IH-35, Austin, 78744. T: (512) 444-6322; F: (512) 444-8719; www.austinlonestar.com; austinlonestar@austinlonestar.com.

RV ★★★★ Tent ★★

Beauty: ★★★★	Site Privacy: ★★★★
Spaciousness: ★★★★	Quiet: ★★★
Security: ★★★	Cleanliness: ★★★★
Insect Control: ★★★★	Facilities: ★★★★

With convenient interstate access and a variety of nearby restaurants and shopping, Austin Lone Star is an excellent choice if you're touring the capital city. Sites at this pretty park are fairly spacious, with gravel parking and grassy plots at each site. Laid out in a series of tidy rows, sites include both back-ins and pull-throughs. Most sites are shaded by ash and other species. The shadiest sites include 105–138, which are bordered by trees to the south. Families should go for sites near the neat playground and other recreation at the front of the park. The rest rooms are outstanding—clean, spacious, and private. Unfortunately, the small, unattractive tent sites are not recommended. Visit Austin in spring or fall for the nicest weather. Luckily, insects are rarely a concern—Austin's famous bat community feeds on mosquitoes. With no gates, security is poor at this urban campground.

Basics

Operated By: The Rowleys. **Open:** All year. **Site Assignment:** Reservations accepted, credit card number holds site, 24-hour cancellation notice required, (800)284-0206. **Registration:** At office. **Fee:** $35 per night, RV or tent. **Parking:** At site.

Facilities

Number of RV Sites: 150 w/full hookups. **Number of Tent-Only Sites:** 4 w/electricity & water only. **Hookups:** Water, sewer, electric (30, 50 amps), phone, & cable TV. **Each Site:** Picnic tables, BBQ pits. **Dump Station:** Yes. **Laundry:** Yes. **Pay Phone:** Yes. **Rest Rooms and Showers:** Yes. **Fuel:** No. **Propane:** Yes. **Internal Roads:** Paved. **RV Service:** 0.5 mi. **Market:** 0.5 mi. **Restaurant:** In park. **General Store:** In park. **Vending:** Yes. **Swimming:** Pool. **Playground:** Yes. **Other:** Hot tub, mini-mart, gift shop, lodge. **Activities:** Tours, organized activities, pool tables, horseshoes, volleyball, basketball. **Nearby Attractions:** Texas state capitol, National Wildflower Center, Zilker Park, Pioneer Farm, Slaughter-Leftwich Winery, Mexican Free-Tailed Bat Colony, Barton Creek Greenbelt Preserve. **Additional Information:** Austin CVB (800) 926-2282.

Restrictions

Pets: On 6-ft. max. leash at all times. **Fires:** In BBQ pits only. **Alcoholic Beverages:** Allowed. **Vehicle Maximum Length:** None. **Other:** 5 mph speed limit, no bicycle riding after dark, high water pressure; suggest use of water pressure regulator, 3 day tent limit.

To Get There

If heading north on I-35, take Exit 228 and it is one block on the right side. If heading south on 35, take exit 227, make a U-turn to the left, go back under the interstate onto the service road heading north. Park is 0.5 mi. ahead on the right.

BASTROP

Bastrop State Park

P.O. Box 518, Bastrop, 78602-0518. T: (512) 321-2101; F: (512) 321-3300; www.tpwd.state.tx.us.

RV ★★★★ Tent ★★★★

Beauty: ★★★★★	Site Privacy: ★★★★
Spaciousness: ★★★★	Quiet: ★★★★
Security: ★★★	Cleanliness: ★★★★
Insect Control: ★★★	Facilities: ★★★★★

Part of a recreation complex including Lake Bastrop, Buescher State Park, and Lake Somerville State Park, the area is home to the "Lost Pines," a stand of isolated loblolly pines. Fauna includes the endangered Houston toad (mating and male trilling peak in Feb. and Mar.). The park's amenities are excellent. Though campsites at Buescher are more private and spacious than campsites here, there are fewer insects at drier Bastrop. The Piney Hill area offers RV sites with full hookups and gravel pull-throughs (we fancied sites 1, 23, 24, and 25). The Copperas Creek area includes multi-use sites with water and electric hookups and gravel back-in parking. Tent campers should "rough it" at serene Creekside campground. All sites are spacious, with lovely tree cover. There is no gate, but Bastrop's rural setting makes it reasonably safe. Visit during the week. Only 32 miles from Austin, the park stays busy weekends Mar. through Nov.

Basics

Operated By: Texas Parks & Wildlife. **Open:** All year. **Site Assignment:** Reservations (512) 389-8900; reservations must be made at least 48 hours in advance; deposit (equivalent to first night's fee) required to hold reservation; cancellations more than two days prior to reservation result in $5 fee, cancellations within two days of reservation result in loss of deposit. **Registration:** Headquarters. **Fee:** $3 per person per day for anyone aged 13 & over, $15 for sites w/water, electric, & sewer, $12 for sites w/water & electric, $9 for sites w/water only, $7 for primitive tent sites (cash, checks, D, V, MC). **Parking:** At most sites.

Facilities

Number of RV Sites: 54 sites w/full hookups. **Number of Tent-Only Sites:** 23 sites w/water at each. **Hookups:** Water, sewer, electric (30, 50 amps). **Each Site:** Picnic table, fire ring, grill. **Dump Station:** Yes. **Laundry:** No. **Pay Phone:** Yes. **Rest Rooms and Showers:** Yes. **Fuel:** No. **Propane:** No. **Internal Roads:** Paved. **RV Service:** 8 mi., west of Bastrop. **Market:** 1 mi. east in Bastrop. **Restaurant:** 1 mi. east in Bastrop. **General Store:** Wal-Mart, 1 mi. east in Bastrop. **Vending:** Beverages. **Swimming:** Pool. **Playground:** No. **Other:** 18-hole golf course (6152 yards, Bermuda greens, electric & pull carts for rent), picnic area, cabins, lodges, group barracks, group dining hall, outdoor sports area, cabins, gift shop. **Activities:** Golfing, hiking, backpacking, fishing, canoeing, swimming, road cycling, & guided tours. **Nearby Attractions:** Lake Bastrop, Buescher State Park, Lake Somerville State Park & Trailway, Austin (32 mi. west). **Additional Information:** Austin CVB (800) 926-2282, Smithville Chamber of Commerce (512) 237-2313, Bastrop Chamber of Commerce (512) 321-2419.

RESTRICTIONS

Pets: On leash only. **Fires:** In fire rings only. **Alcoholic Beverages:** prohibited. **Vehicle Maximum Length:** 50 ft.

TO GET THERE

From Bastrop, drive east on State Hwy. 21 for 1 mi. Park entrance is on the right. The park is also accessible from Buescher State Park and Hwy. 71.

BIG BEND NATIONAL PARK

Chisos Basin and Cottonwood Campgrounds

P.O. Box 129, Big Bend National Park 79834-0129. T: (915) 477-2251; F: (915) 477-1175; www.nps.gov/ bibe; bibeinformation@nps.gov.

RV ★★★★★ Tent ★★★★★

Beauty: ★★★★★ Site Privacy: ★★★
Spaciousness: ★★★★ Quiet: ★★★★★
Security: ★★★★★ Cleanliness: ★★★★★
Insect Control: ★★★★ Facilities: ★★★★

Big Bend is breathtaking. It's worth the long and sometimes desolate drive. The park's southern border is the Rio Grande River, with its dramatic cliffs. There are also vast acres of Chihuahuan desert punctuated by the Chisos Mountains (Emory Peak is the highest in the park at 7,825 feet). Flora and fauna are diverse because of extreme elevation changes and the park's location on the range borders of many Central and North American species. Each campground at Big Bend is different. Though shaded by a few cottonwood trees, the RV campground at Rio Grande Village is the least attractive of the lot. If you can forego hookups, stay elsewhere. Chisos Basin (el. 5,401 feet) offers sites with a little shade and privacy provided by high mountain junipers, small oaks, and pinions. Cottonwood campground offers little privacy, but sites are deliciously shaded by a mature stand of cottonwood trees. Gravel, back-in parking is most common. Security is not a concern. Visit in spring or fall to avoid massive crowds at the camping areas.

BASICS

Operated By: National Park Service. **Open:** All year. **Site Assignment:** First come, first served; no reservations accepted (except group camping). **Registration:** Self-registration. **Fee:** $8 for up to 9 people (cash only). **Parking:** At site (recommended no more than one car).

FACILITIES

Number of RV Sites: 94. **Number of Tent-Only Sites:** None. **Hookups:** None (water available, no generators allowed at Cottonwood). **Each Site:** Picnic table, grill. **Dump Station:** Yes (not at Cottonwood). **Laundry:** No (only at Rio Grande Village). **Pay Phone:** Yes (not at Cottonwood). **Rest Rooms and Showers:** Flush toilets at Chisos Basin, pit toilets at Cottonwood. **Fuel:** Yes (at Panther Junction & Rio Grande Village in the Park). **Propane:** Yes (at Rio Grande Village). **Internal Roads:** Paved. **RV Service:** 4 mi. outside west entrance in Study Butte/ Terlingua. **Market:** Park stores, 100 mi. in Alpine. **Restaurant:** On-site at Chisos Basin, 4 mi. outside west entrance in Terlingua. **General Store:** Hardware 100 mi. in Alpine, Wal-Mart 120 mi. in Fort Stockton. **Vending:** No. **Swimming:** No. **Playground:** No. **Other:** Visitor Center, picnic areas, amphitheaters, boat launches, gift shop. **Activities:** Nature trails, hiking, backpacking, rafting, canoeing, off-roading, scenic drive, bird-watching, historic sites, ranger programs. **Nearby Attractions:** Big Bend Ranch State Park Complex, Chihuahuan Desert Research Institute, Chinati Hot Springs, Davis Mountains Indian Lodge & Balmorhea State Parks, Alpine crafts & antiques, Museum of the Big Bend. **Additional Information:** Alpine Chamber of Commerce (800) 561-3735.

RESTRICTIONS

Pets: On leash only. **Fires:** Ground fires not allowed. **Alcoholic Beverages:** Allowed (at sites only). **Vehicle Maximum Length:** None (Chisos Basin not over 24 ft.). **Other:** 14-day stay limit, 28-days per year, quiet hours enforced (no generators at Cottonwood), no dumping of gray water.

TO GET THERE

From Alpine (junction of US 90 w/State Hwy. 118), take 118 south 80 mi. to the west entrance of the park. To get to the north entrance, take US 90 east 23 mi. and turn south on US 385. Drive approximately 45 mi. south to the north entrance. The Chisos Basin campground is 29 mi. from the west entrance and 38 mi. from the north entrance. The Cottonwood campground is 35 mi. from the west entrance and 64 mi. from the north entrance.

BLANCO

Blanco State Park

P.O. Box 493, Blanco 78606. T: (830) 833-4333 or (800) 792-1112; F: (830) 833-5388; www.tpwd. state.tx.us

RV ★★★ Tent ★★★

Beauty: ★★★ Site Privacy: ★★★
Spaciousness: ★★★ Quiet: ★★★
Security: ★ Cleanliness: ★★★
Insect Control: ★★★ Facilities: ★★★

At 104 acres, Blanco is neither large nor pretty. It feels like a city park, although original facilities were built by the Civilian Conservation Corps in the 1930s. Fishing along the Blanco River is the most popular activity. Catches include rainbow trout, perch, catfish, and bass. The campground consists of two small loops. Site size is adequate. Sites 1–10 have full hookups and are slightly smaller than sites 11–30. Most sites have paved, back-in parking (site 16 is the only pull-through). There are a few shady sites, but most are open to neighbors and the elements. Families should try for sites 27 or 31, near the playground. Otherwise, there is little difference between sites. There is no gate at Blanco, making security marginal. Visit in late spring, summer or fall, avoiding holiday weekends.

BASICS

Operated By: Texas Parks & Wildlife. **Open:** All year. **Site Assignment:** Reservations (512) 389-8900, reservations must be made at least 48 hours in advance, deposit required (equivalent to first night's fee) to hold reservation, cancellations more than two days prior to reservation result in $5 fee, cancellations within two days of reservation result in loss of deposit. **Registration:** Headquarters. **Fee:** $3 per person per day for anyone aged 13 & older, plus $12 for sites w/water & electric, $14 for sites w/water, electric, & sewer (cash, checks, D,V, MC). **Parking:** At site.

FACILITIES

Number of RV Sites: 10. Number of Tent-Only Sites. **Hookups:** Water, sewer, electric (30 & 50 amps). **Each Site:** picnic table, fire ring. **Dump Station:** Yes. **Laundry:** No. **Pay Phone:** Yes. **Rest Rooms and Showers:** Yes. **Fuel:** No. **Propane:** No. **Internal Roads:** Paved. **RV Service:** 20 mi. south in Spring Branch. **Market:** 1 mi. south. **Restaurant:** 200 yards from park. **General Store:** 40 mi. west in Fredericksburg. **Vending:** No. **Swimming:** No. **Playground:** Yes. **Other:** Gift shop, group day-use facilities, screened shelters. **Activities:** Swimming in Blanco River, picnicking, hiking, boating (electric motors only), fishing. **Nearby Attractions:** Nearby attraction include Lyndon B. Johnson State Historical Park & LBJ Ranch, Pedernales Falls & Guadalupe River state parks, Canyon Lake, Cascade Caverns, Natural Bridge Caverns, Aquarena Springs. **Additional Information:** Blanco Chamber of Commerce (830) 833-5101, www.texashillcountryinfo.com.

RESTRICTIONS

Pets: Leash Only. **Fires:** In fire rings only. **Alcoholic Beverages:** Not allowed. **Vehicle Maximum Length:** 50 ft. **Other:** Max. 8 people per campsite, Quiet time 10 p.m.–6 a.m., fourteen day stay limit, swim at your own risk, gathering of firewood prohibited.

TO GET THERE

From Austin, drive west on US 290 for 42 mi. Turn left on US 281, and go south for 10 mi. Go through Blanco, then turn right onto Park Rd. 23. The park entrance is within 200 yards. From San Antonio, drive north on US 281. Cross State Rte. 46 and continue until reaching Blanco (about 30 mi.). Cross the Blanco River and then take the first left, onto Park Rd. 23. The park entrance is within 200 yards.

BOERNE

Alamo Fiesta RV Resort

33000 IH-10 West, Boerne, 78006. T: (830) 249-4700; F: (830) 249-4654; www.alamofiestarv.com.

RV ★★★ Tent ★★★

Beauty: ★★★ Site Privacy: ★★★
Spaciousness: ★★★★ Quiet: ★★★★
Security: ★★★ Cleanliness: ★★★
Insect Control: ★★★★ Facilities: ★★★★

Alamo Fiesta is a good camping option if you would like to tour the hill country and San Antonio without switching campgrounds. Bandera, Kerrville, and Fredericksburg are within 40 miles of Boerne. Downtown San Antonio is a little closer and 6 Flags Fiesta Texas is 12 miles away. The campground consists mainly of rows of pull-throughs with back-in sites along the perimeter of the park. Sites are on the large side of average, and most have no shade. There is a bit of well-intentioned (but poorly maintained) landscaping. Each site has a grassy plot, which often bleeds haphazardly into the gravel parking spaces. Near the playground, sites 1–5 and 128–133 are good choices for families. For tranquility, obtain a back-in site in the back of the park (70–94). With no gates, this small town/suburban park has marginal security. Visit Texas Hill Country on weekdays for breezy touring.

Basics

Operated By: Cliff & Linda Dorsey. **Open:** All year. **Site Assignment:** Reservations held w/credit card number, call (800) 321-CAMP, all credit cards, checks & cash accepted; check out at 11 a.m. **Registration:** At office. **Fee:** $22 for 2 people in an RV, $2 for each extra person over age 6, $16.50 for pop-ups & vans, $15.50 for tents. **Parking:** At site.

Facilities

Number of RV Sites: 221. **Number of Tent-Only Sites:** Tent area available. **Hookups:** Water, sewer, electric (20, 30, 50 amps), cable TV, dataport. **Each Site:** Picnic table. **Dump Station:** Yes. **Laundry:** Yes. **Pay Phone:** Yes. **Rest Rooms and Showers:** Yes. **Fuel:** No. **Propane:** Yes. **Internal Roads:** Paved. **RV Service:** 1.5 mi. southeast in Boerne. **Market:** 1 mi. southeast in Boerne. **Restaurant:** 1 mi. southeast in Boerne. **General Store:** 0.5 mi. southeast in Boerne. **Vending:** Yes. **Swimming:** Pool. **Playground:** Yes. **Other:** Basketball courts, banquet rooms, soccer field, tennis court, horseshoe pit, pavilion. **Activities:** Horseshoes, washer pitching. **Nearby Attractions:** King House Museum, The Alamo, Six Flags/ Fiesta Texas, Historic Missions, Sea World, Riverwalk, Cowboy Artists of America Museum. **Additional Information:** San Antonio CVB (800) 447-3372, Boerne Chamber of Commerce (888) 842-8080.

Restrictions

Pets: On leash. **Fires:** Not allowed. **Alcoholic Beverages:** Allowed. **Vehicle Maximum Length:** 75 ft.

To Get There

From San Antonio, head west on I-10. Take Exit 542 and make an immediate right turn.

BROWNSVILLE

River Bend Resort

Rte. 8 Box 649, Brownsville, 78520. T: (956) 548-0194; F: (956) 548-0191.

RV ★★★★ Tent n/a

Beauty: ★★★★★ Site Privacy: ★★★
Spaciousness: ★★★★ Quiet: ★★★★
Security: ★★★★ Cleanliness: ★★★★★
Insect Control: ★★★★★ Facilities: ★★★★★

Seniors-only River Bend is among the most attractive parks in south Texas. The park's facilities are outstanding considering how few sites it offers. The swimming pool and clubhouse overlook a pretty bend in the Rio Grande River, and the golf course features many holes with nice river views. The campground consists of back-in sites laid out along two main roads. Sites are spacious and incredibly tidy. Landscaping at each site adds to the manicured look of the park, but provides no shade or privacy—there are no trees. All parking is paved. The nicest sites overlook the golf course. Brownsville is convenient to attractions, restaurants, and shopping galore. Gates lock at night, making security at this suburban park fair. Make reservations months in advance for winter visits. Avoid south Texas in the summer.

Basics

Operated By: John Alberg. **Open:** All year. **Site Assignment:** Reservations are required & are taken Mon–Fri. from 9 a.m.-noon; Check-in at 12 p.m.-5 p.m. firm, unless previous night registration arrangements have been made; check out at 10 a.m. **Registration:** At office. **Fee:** $21 per day for 2 people, $2.50 for each additional person, $2 A/C charge per day per unit, $4 charge per day for more than 30-amp usage. **Parking:** At site.

Facilities

Number of RV Sites: 30. **Number of Tent-Only Sites:** 0. **Hookups:** Water, sewer, electric (30, 50 amps), cable TV. **Each Site:** None. **Dump Station:** No. **Laundry:** Yes. **Pay Phone:** Yes. **Rest Rooms and Showers:** Yes. **Fuel:** No. **Propane:** No, daily service comes to the park, Mon.–Sat. **Internal Roads:** Paved. **RV Service:** 60 mi. northwest in McAllen. **Market:** 5 mi. east in Brownsville. **Restaurant:** 5 mi. east in Brownsville. **General Store:** 4 mi. east in Brownsville. **Vending:** Beverages only. **Swimming:** Pool. **Playground:** No. **Other:** 18-hole golf course, tennis courts, rec hall, dance hall. **Activities:** Horseshoes, shuffleboard, swimmimg, arts & crafts, golf. **Nearby Attractions:** Gladys Porter Zoo, CAF/Confederate Air Force Rio Grande Valley Wing, South Padre Island, Boca Chica Beach. **Additional Information:** Brownsville Chamber of Commerce (956) 542-4341.

Restrictions

Pets: On leash only. **Fires:** In grills only, bring your own. **Alcoholic Beverages:** Not allowed. **Vehicle Maximum Length:** 40 ft.

To Get There

From Hwy. US 77/83, exit at local route 802. Go west 2 mi. to US 281. Turn right on Hwy. 281 and go west 3 mi. Entrance is on the left.

BROWNWOOD

Lake Brownwood State Park

RR 5 Box 160, Lake Brownwood 76801. T: (915) 784-5223 or (800) 792-1112; F: (915) 784-6203; www.tpwd.state.tx.us

RV ★★★★ Tent ★★★★

Beauty: ★★★★ Site Privacy: ★★★
Spaciousness: ★★★★ Quiet: ★★★★
Security: ★★★★ Cleanliness: ★★★★
Insect Control: ★★ Facilities: ★★★★

Fishermen enjoy Lake Brownwood, an 8,000-acre reservoir supporting crappie, perch, catfish, and bass. There are extensive fishing and boating facilities. Landlubbers explore the shoreline, especially when adorned with spring wildflowers. There are four types of sites in three campgrounds. Those seeking peace, quiet, and full hookups should obtain a site at the Council Bluff loop. Tent campers should ask for sites 60–67—with water and electric hookups, these are the only heavily wooded sites. Boaters prefer lake level sites at Willow Point, with water and electric hookups. All sites are relatively spacious, with back-in gravel parking and at least a little shade. The park's extremely rural location makes it fairly safe even though there is no locked gate at night. The Panhandle Plains are cold in the winter and hot in the summer. Visit in spring or fall. Avoid summer weekends, when this state park more closely resembles a theme park.

Basics

Operated By: Texas Parks & Wildlife. **Open:** All year. **Site Assignment:** Reservations (512) 389-8900, reservations must be made at least 48 hours in advance, deposit required (equivalent to first night's fee) to hold reservation, cancellations more than two days prior to reservation result in $5 fee, cancellations within two days of reservation result in loss of deposit. **Registration:** Headquarters. **Fee:** $3 per person per day for anyone aged 13 & older, $8 tent-only camp sites, $11 sites w/electric, $12 sites w/electric & sewer, $2 for third vehicle at a campsite (cash, checks, D,V, MC). **Parking:** At site.

Facilities

Number of RV Sites: 8. **Number of Tent-Only Sites:** 12 sites w/water in area, 8 sites w/water, electric. **Hookups:** water, electric (30, 50 amps), sewer. **Each Site:** picnic table, grill. **Dump Station:** Yes. **Laundry:** No. **Pay Phone:** Yes. **Rest Rooms and Showers:** Yes. **Fuel:** No. **Propane:** No. **Internal Roads:** Paved. **RV Service:** Inquire at campground. **Market:** 8 mi. southwest toward Brownwood. **Restaurant:** 8 mi. southwest toward Brownwood. **General Store:** Wal-Mart 20 mi. in Brownwood. **Vending:** Beverages. **Swimming:** No. **Playground:** No. **Other:** Volleyball court, basketball court, softball field, park store, boat launches, floating boat dock w/boat slip & courtesy fuel dock, cabins, screened shelters, group camping, dining, & lodge facilities. **Activities:** picnicking, hiking, boating (motors, water skis & jet skis all allowed), fishing, swimming, bird-watching. **Nearby Attractions:** Howard Payne College, Douglas McArthur Academy of Freedom, Camp Bowie Memorial Park, Coleman City Park, Camp Colorado Museum Replica. **Additional Information:** Brownwood Chamber of Commerce (915) 646-9535.

Restrictions

Pets: Leash Only. **Fires:** In grills & fire rings only. **Alcoholic Beverages:** Prohibited. **Vehicle Maximum Length:** 65 ft. (all sites are back-in). **Other:** Max. 8 people per campsite, Quiet time 10 p.m.–6 a.m., fourteen day stay limit, gathering of firewood prohibited, special pet restrictions, number of vehicles per campsite is restricted (call for details), swim at your own risk.

To Get There

From Brownwood, go northwest on State Hwy.

279 for 16 mi. Turn right on Park Rd. 15 and follow it for 6 mi. to the park entrance.

BURNET

Inks Lake State Park

Rte. 2 Box 31, Burnet 78611. T: (512) 793-2223; F: (512) 793-2065; www.tpwd.state.tx.us.

RV ★★★★ Tent ★★★★

Beauty: ★★★★ Site Privacy: ★★★
Spaciousness: ★★★ Quiet: ★★★
Security: ★★★★ Cleanliness: ★★★★
Insect Control: ★★★★ Facilities: ★★★★

Pink granite hills, cedar and oak woodlands, and a constant level of activity: Inks Lake provide the backdrop for a variety of recreation, including a 9-hole golf course. Inks Lake supports bass, crappie, and catfish, while the land supports turkey quail and many other species. The area is famous for its spring wildflowers. Campgrounds are partially shaded, with mid-sized sites and paved back-in parking. Tent sites include paved tent pads. Tent campers looking for ample space and lake views should ask for 311, 314, 317, 333, or 346. RV campers should ask for 43, 48, 65, 67, 92, 279, or 287. Families should consider a site adjacent to one of the six playgrounds or the swimming beach. Spring and early summer are ideal times to visit, since late summer is very hot and autumn can be rainy. There is no gate at Inks Lake, but its remote location makes it fairly safe.

BASICS

Operated By: Texas Parks & Wildlife. **Open:** All year. **Site Assignment:** Reservations (512) 389-8900; reservations must be made at least 48 hours in advance; deposit (equivalent to first night's fee) required to hold reservation; cancellations more than two days prior to reservation result in $5 fee, cancellations within two days of reservation result in loss of deposit. **Registration:** Headquarters. **Fee:** $4 per person per day for anyone aged 13 & over, $15 for sites w/water & electric, $10 for sites w/water only, $8 for primitive tent sites, excess fee required for more than two vehicles per site (cash, checks, V, MC, D). **Parking:** At most sites.

FACILITIES

Number of RV Sites: 137 w/water & 50-amp hookups. **Number of Tent-Only Sites:** 50 tent only w/water at each site, 10 walk-in, tent only w/water & electric, 9 walk-in primitive. **Hookups:** Water, electric (30, 50 amps). **Each Site:** picnic table, lantern hanger, fire pit/grill combination. **Dump Station:** Yes. **Laundry:** No. **Pay Phone:** Yes. **Rest Rooms and Showers:** Yes. **Fuel:** No. **Propane:** No. **Internal Roads:** Paved. **RV Service:** 21 mi. south in Marble Falls. **Market:** 12 mi. east in Burnet. **Restaurant:** Floating restaurant on Inks Lake, 3 mi. east or west. **General Store:** In park, hardware 12 mi. in Burnet, Wal-Mart 21 Mi. in Marlboro Falls. **Vending:** Yes. **Swimming:** No. **Playground:** Yes. **Other:** 9-hole golf course, picnic area, amphitheater, fishing piers, boat ramp, mini cabins, screened shelters, park store. **Activities:** Hiking, backpacking, golf (cart & club rental available), lake swimming, fishing, waterskiing, scuba diving, guided tours at specific times, boating (canoe, paddle boat, & surfbike rentals available at park store). **Nearby Attractions:** Lyndon B. Johnson Ranch & State Historical Parks, Vanishing Texas river cruise, Lake Buchanon & Buchanon Dam, towns of Burnet, Fredericksburg, & Johnson City, numerous Hill Country lakes & state parks. **Additional Information:** Inks Lake & Lake Buchanon Chamber of Commerce (512) 793-2803, Burnet Chamber of Commerce (512) 756-4297.

RESTRICTIONS

Pets: On leash. **Fires:** In fire rings only. **Alcoholic Beverages:** Prohibited. **Vehicle Maximum Length:** 70 ft. **Other:** Follow boat launch protocol; swim at your own risk.

TO GET THERE

From Burnet, drive west on State Hwy. 29 for 9 mi. Turn left on Park Rd. 4 and drive south for 3 mi. to the park headquarters.

CADDO

Possum Kingdom State Park

P.O. Box 70, Caddo 76429. T: (940) 549-1803 or (800) 792-1112; F: (940) 549-0741; www.tpwd.state.tx.us.

RV ★★★ Tent ★★★

Beauty: ★★★ Site Privacy: ★★★
Spaciousness: ★★★ Quiet: ★★★
Security: ★★★★★ Cleanliness: ★★★
Insect Control: ★★ Facilities: ★★★★

The 20,000-acre Lake Possum Kingdom offers exceptionally clear water, attracting snorkelers and scuba divers. The lake supports crappie, perch, and various bass and catfish species. The park offers extensive fishing facilities. Five campgrounds are situated along the lakeshore. Walk-in campsites have no potties and fire-rings only. Happy with water only? Try sites 79–85 and 100, 104, 105, and 113 in the Chaparral Trail area. With full hookups and proximity to the playground and beach, the Spanish Oaks area is good for RV campers with children. Tent campers enjoy the Lakeview area, which offers water and electric hookups. Sites 22–26 have nice views. Most sites are partially shaded, with paved back-in parking. Site size varies immensely—arrive early for your choice of sites. Security is excellent due to extreme remoteness. Low year-round humidity and pleasant swimming make this park bearable (and crowded) in late summer. Visit any time except busy summer weekends.

BASICS

Operated By: Texas Parks & Wildlife. **Open:** All year. **Site Assignment:** Reservations (512) 389-8900, reservations must be made at least 48 hours in advance, deposit required (equivalent to first night's fee) to hold reservation, cancellations more than two days prior to reservation result in $5 fee, cancellations within two days of reservation result in loss of deposit. **Registration:** Headquarters. **Fee:** $3 per person per day for anyone aged 13 & older, $6 walk-in primitive tent camping, $10 water-only sites, $10 water & electric, $15 premium water & electric (cash, checks, V, MC, D). **Parking:** At most sites.

FACILITIES

Number of RV Sites: 60 sites w/water, electric. **Number of Tent-Only Sites:** 55 sites w/water close by. **Hookups:** Water, electric (30 amps). **Each Site:** Picnic table, either fire ring or grill. **Dump Station:** Yes. **Laundry:** No. **Pay Phone:** Yes. **Rest Rooms and Showers:** Yes. **Fuel:** Yes. **Propane:** No. **Internal Roads:** Paved. **RV Service:** 50 mi. east in Mineral Wells. **Market:** Marina store in park. **Restaurant:** 18 mi. North on Possum Kingdom Lake. **General Store:** Marina store in park, 32 mi. to Wal-Mart in Breckinridge or Graham. **Vending:** Beverages only. **Swimming:** No. **Playground:** Yes. **Other:** Concrete boat ramp w/courtesy dock, gas dock, covered slip rental, marina store (hours vary w/season), fishing pier, fish-cleaning facility. **Activities:** Boating (motorized & non-motorized boat rentals available), jet skiing (rentals available), fishing, waterskiing, swimming, hiking, biking. **Nearby Attractions:** Fort Griffin & Fort Richardson state historical parks. **Additional Information:** Possum Kingdom Chamber of Commerce (888) 779-8330.

RESTRICTIONS

Pets: Leash Only. **Fires:** In grills & fire rings only. **Alcoholic Beverages:** Not allowed. **Vehicle Maximum Length:** 40 ft. **Other:** Max. 8 people per campsite, Quiet time 10 p.m.–6 a.m., 14 day stay limit, swim at your own risk, follow boat launch protocol, gathering of firewood prohibited.

TO GET THERE

From I-20, take exit 414. Go west on US 180, through the towns of Weatherford and Palo Pinto. Continue to go west on 180 for 25 mi. past Palo Pinto, until you reach a blinking light. Then turn right onto Park Rd. 33. Go north on Park Rd. 33 for 17 mi. Road ends at park entrance.

CALLIHAM, THREE RIVERS

Choke Canyon State Park

P.O. Box 2, Calliham 78007. T: (361) 786-3868; F: (361) 786-3414.

RV ★★★★ Tent ★★★★

Beauty: ★★★ Site Privacy: ★★★★
Spaciousness: ★★★★ Quiet: ★★★★
Security: ★★★★★ Cleanliness: ★★★★
Insect Control: ★ Facilities: ★★★★★

Many Mexican bird species grace Choke Canyon Reservoir, which forms the northern border of their natural range. Birding is augmented with feeders and trails. Of the two park units, Calliham hosts more birds and is more densely wooded. The reservoir supports various bass, catfish, and sunfish species, as well as crappie, bluegill, carp, and gar. The park provides excellent facilities for anglers. The campgrounds aren't gorgeous, but they are tidy and functional. Sites are large, with gravel, back-in parking. Most have partial shade. For water views, head for RV sites 115–131 at Calliham. RV sites 106–108 are the most shady and private. For tents, we prefer sites 200–218, which are situated on a 75-acre lake at Calliham. Security is excellent; the park is extremely remote with locked gates at night. For the best weather, visit in spring or fall. Crowds are only a problem on holiday weekends.

BASICS

Operated By: Texas Parks & Wildlife. **Open:** All year. **Site Assignment:** Reservations (512) 389-8900, reservations must be made at least 48 hours in advance, deposit required (equivalent to first night's fee) to hold reservation, cancellations more than two days prior to reservation result in $5 fee, cancellations within two days of reservation result in loss of deposit. **Registration:** Headquarters. **Fee:** $3 per person per day for anyone aged 13 & older, $14 for sites w/water & electricity, $9 for sites w/water only (cash, checks, V, MC, D). **Parking:** At most sites.

FACILITIES

Number of RV Sites: 40 sites w/water & electricity. **Number of Tent-Only Sites:** 19 sites w/water only. **Hookups:** Water, electric (30, 50 amps). **Each Site:** Picnic table, lantern post, fire ring, shade covers at Calliham Unit. **Dump Station:** Yes. **Laundry:** No. **Pay Phone:** Yes. **Rest Rooms and Showers:** Yes. **Fuel:** 0.25 mi. outside park. **Propane:** 0.25 mi. outside park. **Internal Roads:** Paved. **RV Service:** 75 mi. southeast in Corpus Christi. **Market:** 12 mi. east in Three Rivers. **Restaurant:** 3.5 mi. east of park. **General Store:** 12 mi. east in Three Rivers. **Vending:** Beverages only. **Swimming:** Pool (Memorial Day–Labor Day). **Playground:** Yes. **Other:** Calliham Unit: screened shelters, picnic area, group picnic area, group dining hall, group rec hall, amphitheater, sports complex (including gym & stage), swimming pool bathhouse, shuffleboard, tennis, volleyball, & full basketball courts, wildlife viewing blind, bird trail w/feeders, interpretive center, boat ramps. South Shore Unit: Shaded picnic area, group picnic pavilions, concession stand, baseball diamond, volleyball court, boat ramps, canoe launch, fishing platform, fish cleaning area, overlook shelters, The North Shore Area (1700 acres includes primitive group camping, equestrian camping, boat ramps, hunting in season). **Activities:** Picnicking, boating, fishing, hiking, backpacking, birding, lake beach & pool swimming, various team sports, educational & interpretive programs. **Nearby Attractions:** Lake Corpus Christi State Park, Lipantitlan State Historical Park, San Antonio (about 80 mi.), Corpus Christi (about 70 mi.). **Additional Information:** Three Rivers Chamber of Commerce (361) 786-2528, San Antonio CVB (800) 447-3372, Corpus Christi Area Convention & Tourist Bureau (800) 678-6232.

RESTRICTIONS

Pets: On leash only. **Fires:** In fire rings only. **Alcoholic Beverages:** Prohibited. **Vehicle Maximum Length:** 50 ft.

TO GET THERE

To reach the South Shore Unit from Three Rivers, drive west on State Hwy. 72 for 3.5 mi. To reach the Callaham Unit from Three Rivers, drive west on State Hwy. 72 for 12 mi.

CANYON

Palo Duro Canyon State Park

RR 2 Box 285, Canyon, 79015. T: (806) 488-2227; F: (806) 488-2556; www.tpwd.state.tx.us.

 ★★★★  ★★★★

Beauty: ★★★★ Site Privacy: ★★★
Spaciousness: ★★★ Quiet: ★★★
Security: ★★★★★ Cleanliness: ★★★★
Insect Control: ★★★ Facilities: ★★★★

At 800 feet deep, 120 miles long, and 0.5 to 20 miles wide, Palo Duro is the second-largest canyon in the U.S. Exposed rock includes white gypsum, red claystone, and gray, yellow, and lavendar mudstone. The park's mascot is "The Lighthouse", a 300-foot rock spire. Hardwoods throughout the canyon include juniper and mesquite. The canyon rim supports short grass prairie. Campsites vary in privacy and spaciousness, with some 60 feet from neighbors and others stacked together. Low trees and brush provide no shade. Parking is paved. RV campers enjoy pull-throughs at the Hackberry area (30-amp service). Need 50-amp service? Try the Sagebrush area (sites 137 and 139 are pull-throughs). The Mesquite area has gorgeous views of red rock formations. Security is excellent— the park is in a remote area and locks its gate at night. If you're not seeing *Texas,* the musical, visit in spring or fall. Otherwise, visit during the week.

BASICS

Operated By: Texas Parks & Wildlife. **Open:** All year. **Site Assignment:** Reservations (512) 389-8900; reservations must be made at least 48 hours in advance; deposit (equivalent to first night's fee) required to hold reservation; cancellations more than two days prior to reservation result in $5 fee, cancellations within two days of reservation result in loss of deposit. **Registration:** Headquarters. **Fee:** $3 per person per day for anyone aged 13 & over, $12 for sites w/water & electric, $9 for primitive camping (checks, V, MC, D). **Parking:** At site.

FACILITIES

Number of RV Sites: 83 sites w/water & electricity. **Number of Tent-Only Sites:** 22 w/water nearby. **Hookups:** Water, electric (30, 50 amps). **Each Site:** Picnic table, grill, some have shade shelters. **Dump Station:** Yes. **Laundry:** No. **Pay Phone:** Yes. **Rest Rooms and Showers:** Yes. **Fuel:** Yes. **Propane:** No. **Internal Roads:** Paved. **RV Service:** 30 mi. north in Amarillo. **Market:** In park. **Restaurant:** In park. **General Store:** In park, or Wal-Mart 14 mi. west in Canyon. **Vending:** Yes. **Swimming:** No. **Playground:** Yes. **Other:** Equestrian area, interpretive center, gift shop, park store, picnic area, amphitheatre, historical markers, equestrian camping area, separate trails for hiking, mountain biking, & equestrian use. **Activities:** Guided tours, hiking, horseback riding, mountain biking, bird-watching, & scenic drives, TEXAS musical drama nightly during the summer (no Wed. performances). **Nearby Attractions:** Cowboy Morning at Figure 3 Ranch, Panhandle Plains Museum, Storyland Zoo for Children, Nielson Memorial Museum, Alibates Flint Quarries National Monument, Lake Meredith National Recreation Area, Amarillo. **Additional Information:** Amarillo Convention & Visitor Council (800) 692-1338, TEXAS box office (806) 655-2181.

RESTRICTIONS

Pets: On leash only. **Fires:** In grill only. **Alcoholic Beverages:** Prohibited. **Vehicle Maximum Length:** 60 ft. **Other:** Be aware of flash flood precautions & rough terrain.

TO GET THERE

From I-27, take Exit 106, State Hwy. 217. Go east on 217 for 8 mi.

CEDAR HILL

Cedar Hill State Park

1570 FM 1382, Cedar Hill, 75104. T: (972) 291-6641; F: (972) 291-0209; www.tpwd.state.tx.us.

★★★★★ ★★★★★

Beauty: ★★★★★ Site Privacy: ★★★★
Spaciousness: ★★★★ Quiet: ★★★★★
Security: ★★★★★ Cleanliness: ★★★★
Insect Control: ★★ Facilities: ★★★★★

This is one of the finest suburban parks we've seen. The 7,500-acre Lake Joe Pool supports catfish, crappie, and largemouth and white bass. The on-site Penn Farm Agricultural History Center houses a cast of farm animals, headlined by Vern the fainting goat. The park's endangered tallgrass prairie remnants include a variety of grasses and wildflowers. Four campgrounds contain 355 multi-use sites. Sites have paved, back-in parking. Most are large with shady trees and foliage between sites. For proximity to the beach and marina, RV campers prefer sites on the outside of loop G (Lakeview Camping Area). Families prefer sites on the inside of loop G, which encircles the playground. Tent campers should ask for a lake view (sites 263–265 and 267–270 are lovely). This park is perennially crowded—avoid busy summer weekends. If visiting on a holiday, book 11 months in advance. Excellent security includes vigilant peace officers and locked gates at night.

BASICS

Operated By: Texas Parks & Wildlife. **Open:** All year. **Site Assignment:** Reservations (512) 389-8900; reservations must be made at least 48 hours in advance; deposit (equivalent to first night's fee) required to hold reservation; cancellations more than two days prior to reservation result in $5 fee, cancellations within two days of reservation result in loss of deposit. **Registration:** Headquarters. **Fee:** $5 per person per day for anyone aged 13 & over, $15 for sites w/water & electric, $7 for primitive tent camping (cash, checks, V, MC, D). **Parking:** At site, except for primitive tent sites.

FACILITIES

Number of RV Sites: 325. **Number of Tent-Only Sites:** 30 walk-in primitive sites. **Hookups:** Water, electric (30 amps). **Each Site:** Fire ring/grill combination, lantern post, picnic table, tent pad. **Dump Station:** Yes. **Laundry:** No. **Pay Phone:** Yes. **Rest Rooms and Showers:** Yes. **Fuel:** Inside park at marina store. **Propane:** 1.5 mi. east in Cedar Hill. **Internal Roads:** Paved. **RV Service:** 1.5 mi. east in Cedar Hill. **Market:** 1.5 mi. east in Cedar Hill. **Restaurant:** 1.5 mi. east in Cedar Hill. **General Store:** K-Mart 1.5 mi. east in Cedar Hill. **Vending:** Yes. **Swimming:** No. **Playground:** Yes. **Other:** Penn Farm Agricultural History Center (self guided tours, farm animals, organic garden), marina store (groceries, fast food grill, boat rentals, fishing barge, gasoline), two boat ramps, picnic area, group picnic area, gift shop, extensive compost demonstration site. **Activities:** Hiking, mountain biking, picnicking, boating, waterskiing, jet skiing, fishing, lake swimming, bird-watching. **Nearby Attractions:** Dallas-Fort Worth Metroplex attractions (see Texas introduction). **Additional Information:** Joe Pool Marina Store (972) 299-9010, Dallas CVB (800) 232-5527, Fort Worth CVB (800) 433-5747.

Restrictions

Pets: On leash only. **Fires:** In fire ring only. **Alcoholic Beverages:** Prohibited. **Vehicle Maximum Length:** 50 ft.

To Get There

From I-20 take Exit 457, Hayes Rd. (FM 1382). Drive south for 4 mi. The park entrance is on the right. From Cedar Hill and US 67, exit at FM 1382 and go north for 2.5 mi. The entrance is on the left.

COMSTOCK

Seminole Canyon State Historical Park

P.O. Box 820, Comstock 78837. T: (915) 292-4464 or (800) 792-1112; F: (915) 292-4596; www.tpwd. state.tx.us.

 ★★★★★ ▲ ★★★★★

Beauty: ★★★★★ Site Privacy: ★★★★
Spaciousness: ★★★★ Quiet: ★★★★★
Security: ★★★★★ Cleanliness: ★★★★★
Insect Control: ★★★ Facilities: ★★★★

Deep canyons, big skies, and rocky terrain create a stunning landscape. Awesome vistas at Seminole Canyon belie the region's harshness (annual rainfall is 15 to 18 inches). The brochure states, "almost everything in this environment bites, stings, or scratches." Nonetheless, human habitation dates back thousands of years. Prehistoric petroglyphs endure in rock shelters (viewed by guided tour only). Diverse wildlife includes many bird species unique to Mexican borderlands. The multiuse campground contains few sites—forget about choosing your own. Sites are spacious with enough short scrubby brush between them to provide a little privacy. There is no shade here, so plan accordingly. Most every site has a stunning view. Parking is back-in and paved. Security is excellent at Seminole Canyon due to its extreme remoteness. Plan to visit in the fall, as this park experiences heavy traffic in the spring and intense heat in the summer.

Basics

Operated By: Texas Parks & Wildlife. **Open:** All year. **Site Assignment:** Reservations (512) 389-8900, reservations must be made at least 48 hours in advance, deposit required (equivalent to first night's fee) to hold reservation, cancellations more than two days prior to reservation result in $5 fee, cancellations within two days of reservation result in loss of deposit. **Registration:** Headquarters. **Fee:** $2 per person per day for anyone aged 13 & older, $11 for sites w/electricity, $8 for sites w/water only (checks, V, MC, D). **Parking:** At site.

Facilities

Number of RV Sites: 23. **Number of Tent-Only Sites:** None. **Hookups:** Water, electric (30 amps). **Each Site:** Picnic table, shade shelter, tent pad, fire ring or grill. **Dump Station:** Yes. **Laundry:** No. **Pay Phone:** Yes. **Rest Rooms and Showers:** Yes. **Fuel:** No. **Propane:** No. **Internal Roads:** Paved. **RV Service:** 42 mi. east in Del Rio. **Market:** 9 mi. east in Comstock. **Restaurant:** 9 mi. east in Comstock. **General Store:** 42 mi. east in Del Rio. **Vending:** Snacks at park headquarters 8 a.m. to 5 p.m. **Swimming:** No. **Playground:** No. **Other:** Interpretive center, picnic area, gift shop. **Activities:** Guided Tours of Seminole Canyon, Hiking, mountain biking, historical study, nature interpretation. **Nearby Attractions:** Judge Roy Bean Visitor Center in Langtry, Lake Amistad National Recreation Area (about 35 mi.), Whitehead Memorial Museum & The Old Perry Store in Del Rio (about 42 mi.). **Additional Information:** Del Rio Chamber of Commerce (830) 775-3551, Judge Roy Bean Visitor's Center (830) 291-3340.

Restrictions

Pets: Leash only. **Fires:** in designated areas only. **Alcoholic Beverages:** Not allowed. **Vehicle Maximum Length:** 45 ft. **Other:** Canyons are closed to the public except for guided tours, Max. 8 people per campsite, Quiet time 10 p.m.–6 a.m., fourteen day stay limit, gathering of firewood prohibited.

To Get There

From Del Rio drive west on US 90 for 40 mi. The park entrance is 9 mi. past the town of Comstock, just east of the Pecos River Bridge.

CONCAN

Garner State Park

HCR 70 Box 599, Concan, 78838. T: (830) 232-6132; F: (830) 232-6139; www.tpwd.state.tx.us.

★★★★ ▲ ★★★★★

Beauty: ★★★★★ Site Privacy: ★★★★
Spaciousness: ★★★★ Quiet: ★★★★
Security: ★★★★ Cleanliness: ★★★★
Insect Control: ★★★★ Facilities: ★★★★★

Garner's campgrounds are the most popular in the state. It's no wonder—the campgrounds are in a valley surrounded by beautiful rolling hills adorned with crooked Spanish and lacey oak. Garner offers unique recreation including jukebox dances and inner tubing the rapids of the Frio River. In season, the Friends of Garner State Park present the "Cowboy Sunset Serenade," celebrating American cowboys through poetry and songs. Of five camping areas, three have hookups. We prefer Live Oak area, which is quieter than Oakmont and Shady Meadows. It's also the best for families, with a playground next to the washhouse. Sites are spacious, with paved, back-in parking (pull-throughs available at other camp areas). Most are shady. We recommend even-numbered sites 334–358, which are a stone's throw from the Frio River. Security is very good at this remote park. Campgrounds are crowded spring, summer, and fall—make advance reservations.

Basics

Operated By: Texas Parks & Wildlife. **Open:** All year. **Site Assignment:** Reservations (512) 389-8900, reservations must be made at least 48 hours in advance, deposit required (equivalent to first night's fee) to hold reservation, cancellations more than two days prior to reservation result in $5 fee, cancellations within two days of reservation result in loss of deposit. **Registration:** Headquarters. **Fee:** $2 per person per day for anyone aged 13 & older, $20 for sites w/water & electricity, $10 for sites w/water only (cash, checks, V, MC, D). **Parking:** At site.

Facilities

Number of RV Sites: 146 reservable sites. **Number of Tent-Only Sites:** 205 (water only). **Hookups:** Water, electric (30 amps). **Each Site:** Picnic table, grill, fire ring, tent pad, some w/lantern hooks & shade shelters. **Dump Station:** Yes. **Laundry:** Yes. **Pay Phone:** Yes. **Rest Rooms and Showers:** Yes. **Fuel:** 9 mi. north in Leakey. **Propane:** 9 mi. north in Leakey. **Internal Roads:** Paved. **RV Service:** 100 mi. west in Del Rio. **Market:** In park. **Restaurant:** 9 mi. north in Leakey. **General Store:** 9 mi. north in Leakey. **Vending:** Beverages only. **Swimming:** No. **Playground:** Yes. **Other:** Screened shelters, overflow camping area, picnic shelter w/kitchen, dining hall, picnic sites, group camp area w/screened shelters, surfaced road area for bike riding & day hiking, unpaved hiking trails, gift shop, snack bar, mini-golf course, paddle boats & inner tubes. **Activities:** River swimming, tubing, boating, hiking, walking, bicycling, mini-golf, picnicking, fishing, & juke box dancing nightly in the summer. **Nearby Attractions:** Hill Country, Lost Maples, & Devil's Sinkhole Natural Areas, Kickapoo Cavern State Park, John Nance "Cactus Jack" Garner Museum in Uvalde, historic Mission Nuestra Senora de la C&elaria del Canon, Camp Sabinal, & Fort Inge. **Additional Information:** Frio Canyon Chamber of Commerce (830) 232-5222, Uvalde Chamber of Commerce (830) 278-3361.

Restrictions

Pets: On leash only. **Fires:** In fire rings only. **Alcoholic Beverages:** Prohibited. **Vehicle Maximum Length:** 30 ft. **Other:** Read safety warnings.

To Get There

From San Antonio take US 90 West to Sabinal. At Sabinal turn right onto US 127 and follow it for 30 mi. Turn right onto US 83 and go 8 mi. to FM 1050. Go 0.2 mi. and turn right onto Park Rd. 29.

COOPER

Cooper Lake State Park (Doctor's Creek Unit)

Rte. 3 Box 741, Cooper 75482. T: (512) 389-8900 or (800) 792-1112; F: (512) 389-8959; www.tpwd.state.tx.us; e-mail.reservations@tpwd. state.tx.us.

★★★★ ▲ ★★★★★

Beauty: ★★★★ Site Privacy: ★★★★
Spaciousness: ★★★★ Quiet: ★★★★★
Security: ★★★★ Cleanliness: ★★★★
Insect Control: ★★ Facilities: ★★★

Sites in this wilderness park are mostly grassy and forested, and they include 55-foot back-ins and

120-foot pull-throughs. Sites 1 and 42 at the entrance are well shaded, but rather close to the internal road. Site 4 is similarly close to the intersection of two internal roads, and it may not suit many campers due to the higher volume of passing traffic (which, admittedly, is still rather limited). Site 8 is reserved for the park host, and the sites on either side seem to be popular with campers either seeking the added security or the added companionship. Sites 12 and 13 are both back-ins on a concrete slab, and are very open to the sun. The best sites, depending on taste, are either 15–17 (although 17 is next to a parking area); 22 and 23, which back to the edge of the lake; or 22 (especially if 23 is unoccupied), which is well shaded, by the water, and somewhat secluded. The rest rooms are quite clean, well-lit, and spacious, with modern facilities. And as for activities in the park, there is plenty to do for anyone in the family. This park is a typical high-quality Texas state park, with water activities, sports, and hiking available. A definite destination for a family holiday.

Basics

Operated By: Texas Parks & Wildlife. **Open:** All year. **Site Assignment:** First come, first served. (Credit card required to make a reservation. $3 reservation service fee; $5 cancellation fee.). **Registration:** In office. (Late arrivals use drop box at entrance.). **Fee:** Water, electric: $12, water: $8, plus $2 entrance fee (V, MC, D accepted in the office or for reservation.). **Parking:** At site.

Facilities

Number of RV Sites: 42. **Number of Tent-Only Sites:** Combined. **Hookups:** Water, electric (30 amps). **Each Site:** Picnic table, grill, fire pit, lantern post. **Dump Station:** Yes. **Laundry:** No. **Pay Phone:** Yes. **Rest Rooms and Showers:** Yes. **Fuel:** No. **Propane:** No. **Internal Roads:** Paved. **RV Service:** No. **Market:** 3 mi. to Cooper. **Restaurant:** 3 mi. to Cooper. **General Store:** Yes. **Vending:** Yes. **Swimming:** Lake. **Playground:** Yes. **Other:** 6 shelters, 1 cottage, ampitheatre. **Activities:** Swimming, boating, fishing, hiking, mountain biking. **Nearby Attractions:** Sam Bell Maxey House State Historical Park, Bonham State Park, Lake Bob S&lin State Park. **Additional Information:** Doctor's Creek Unit Office: (903) 395-3100.

Restrictions

Pets: On 6-ft. leash, cleaned up after. **Fires:** In grills. **Alcoholic Beverages:** None. **Vehicle Maximum Length:** None. **Other:** All visitors must pay $2 entrance fee per day.

To Get There

From Business Hwy. 24 and Hwy. 154 (First and Dallas in the town square), go 1.3 mi. east on Hwy. 154 (Dallas), then turn south onto FM 1529 and go 1.6 mi. Turn right at the sign into the entrance.

CORPUS CHRISTI

Colonia del Rey RV Park

1717 Waldron Rd., Corpus Christi, 78418.
T: (361) 937-2435; F: (361) 937-2929;
www.gocamping america.com/coloniadelray;
cldelrey@intcomm.net.

RV ★★★ Tent n/a

Beauty: ★★★★	Site Privacy: ★★★
Spaciousness: ★★★	Quiet: ★★★
Security: ★★★	Cleanliness: ★★★
Insect Control: ★★	Facilities: ★★★

This suburban park is convenient to cosmopolitan Corpus Christi attractions, Corpus Christi Naval Air Station, and gorgeous beaches at Padre Island National Seashore and Mustang Island. Most of the sites at this nice-looking campground are laid out in tidy rows of pull-throughs. Sites are decent-sized and partially shaded by palm and other tree species. Parking is on grass. The most attractive sites are in section 32. Families should head for sites 16–23, large sites near the pool and playground. The quietest sites are those in section 60. With no gates and no fence around the property, security is poor at Colonia Del Rey. Although the city regularly sprays, insects can be unbearable in this area. Prepare yourself with bug spray, and avoid southern Texas in late summer.

Basics

Operated By: Jan Moya. **Open:** All year. **Site Assignment:** Advance reservations are accepted, credit card number holds site for daily or weekly camping, $50 for monthly camping; 24-hour-7-day notice for cancellation. Sites are usually assigned by the campground. Check-in after 11 a.m. Check out by noon. **Registration:** Office. **Fee:** $23.00 for 2 people. $1.50 extra per person. $2 extra for a concrete lot. **Parking:** At site.

Facilities

Number of RV Sites: 200. **Number of Tent-Only Sites:** 0. **Hookups:** Water, sewer, electric (30, 50 amps), cable TV, phone, & dataport. **Each Site:** Picnic table. **Dump Station:** Yes. **Laundry:** Yes. **Pay Phone:** Yes. **Rest Rooms and Showers:** Yes. **Fuel:** No. **Propane:** Yes. **Internal Roads:** Paved. **RV Service:** Colonia del Rey RV Sales, (361) 937-5703. **Market:** 0.5 mi. north. **Restaurant:** 0.5 mi. north. **General Store:** 0.5 mi. north Wal-Mart. **Vending:** Beverages. **Swimming:** Pool. **Playground:** Yes. **Other:** rec hall. **Activities:** Planned activities, Mexico tours, swimming. **Nearby Attractions:** USS Lexington, Texas State Aquarium, The Colombus Ships, Greyhound Racetrack, Padre Island National Seashore. **Additional Information:** Corpus Christi Area Convention & Tourist Bureau (800) 678-6232, Padre Island National Seashore (361) 949-8068.

Restrictions

Pets: Leash. **Fires:** No ground fires. **Alcoholic Beverages:** Allowed. **Vehicle Max. Length:** 50 ft.

To Get There

From I-358, exit at Waldron Rd. Go south 0.5 mi. Entrance is on the left.

DAINGERFIELD

Daingerfield State Park

Rte. 3 Box 286-B, Daingerfield 75638. T: (512) 389-8900 or (800) 792-1112; F: (512) 389-8959; www.tpwd.state.tx.us; e-mail.reservations@tpwd.state.tx.us.

RV ★★★★★ Tent ★★★★★

Beauty: ★★★★★	Site Privacy: ★★★★★
Spaciousness: ★★★★★	Quiet: ★★★★★
Security: ★★★★	Cleanliness: ★★★★
Insect Control: ★★	Facilities: ★★★

This state park has three smallish camping areas (approx 10 units each), which can all take RVs, but one of which (Big Pine) is off-limits for tents. This is just as well, since these are huge (120-foot) pull-throughs that overlook the water (1–5) or back to the water (6–10), and make the trip worthwhile for an RVer. The space is very generous, as is typical in Texas state parks, and any rig that can drive on the highway can fit into these sites. The rest room in the camping area also leaves nothing to be desired: it is big and clean, and has flush toilets and hot showers. The Dogwood camping area provides shaded electrical sites in a loop near the water. Site 17 is particularly close, while 18 and 19 have nice views of the lake. The Mountain View area is also in a loop, and offers secluded 40-foot back-ins away from the water (but with nary a mountain in view!). The best sites for someone wanting to get away from it all are 31, 33, and 34, which are on the furthest edge of a dead-end roundabout. Families, couples, and anyone with a love of the outdoors should find their way to Daingerfield State Park, which offers activities galore in a beautiful wilderness setting.

Basics

Operated By: Texas Parks & Wildlife. **Open:** All year. **Site Assignment:** First come, first served. (Credit card required to make a reservation. $3 reservation service fee; $5 cancellation fee.). **Registration:** In office. (Late arrivals use drop box at entrance.). **Fee:** RV: $14 (full), $12 (water, electric), plus $2 entrance fee (V, MC, D accepted in the office or for reservation.). **Parking:** At site.

Facilities

Number of RV Sites: 52. **Number of Tent-Only Sites:** Combined. **Hookups:** Water, sewer, electric (30 amps). **Each Site:** Picnic table, grill, fire pit, lantern post. **Dump Station:** Yes. **Laundry:** No. **Pay Phone:** Yes. **Rest Rooms and Showers:** Yes. **Fuel:** No. **Propane:** No. **Internal Roads:** Paved. **RV Service:** No. **Market:** 3 mi. to Daingerfield. **Restaurant:** 3 mi. to Daingerfield. **General Store:** Yes. **Vending:** Yes. **Swimming:** Lake. **Playground:** Yes. **Other:** Lodge, ampitheatre, boat ramp, fish cleaning station. **Activities:** Swimming, boating, fishing, hiking, mountain biking. **Nearby Attractions:** Lake Bob S&lin, Starr Mansion Historical State Park, Caddo Lake State Park, Atlanta State Park.

Restrictions

Pets: On 6-ft. leash, cleaned up after. **Fires:** In grills. **Alcoholic Beverages:** None. **Vehicle Maximum Length:** None. **Other:** All visitors must pay $2 entrance fee per day.

To Get There

From the junction of Hwy. 259 and Hwy. 49, go 2.4 mi. east on Hwy. 49. Turn right at the sign onto a paved road (the sign bearing the street name and number—Park Rd. 17—is not visible from Hwy. 49) and follow it to the entrance of the park.

DALLAS/FORT WORTH

Trader's Village RV Park and Campground

2602 Mayfield Rd., Gr& Prairie, 75052.T: (972) 647-8205; F: (972) 647-8585; www.tradersvillage.com; tvgprv@flash.net.

RV ★★★ Tent ★

Beauty: ★★★ Site Privacy: ★★
Spaciousness: ★★★ Quiet: ★★★
Security: ★★★ Cleanliness: ★★★
Insect Control: ★★★★ Facilities: ★★★

Trader's Village Flea Market covers 100 acres and accommodates 1,800 dealers. Open Sat. and Sun. all year, the flea market also offers food stands and children's rides and games. Call ahead for special event information. The campground is bland and completely flat. A few trees make the park aesthetically bearable but provide little shade. Most sites offer pull-through parking. Those on the perimeter of the campground offer back-in parking. Parking is paved, and each site has a little patch of grass. Sites in the 40s, 50s, 60s, 70s 80s, and 90s have the most mature trees. However, families should go for sites in the 200s, the closest to the pool and rec hall. We don't recommend this suburban campground unless you're buying or selling at Trader's Village. Security is fair—gates are never locked but the campground is patrolled by armed guards. Make advance reservations at Christmastime.

BASICS

Operated By: Traders Village. **Open:** All year. **Site Assignment:** Advance reservations recommended, credit card number holds site, one day cancellation notice, call from 8:30 a.m. to 8 p.m.V, MC, AE, D, personal check & cash accepted. Check-in & check-out at 1 p.m. Sites held until 6 p.m. unless previous arrangements are made. **Registration:** At office. **Fee:** $25 for RV, $16 for tent. **Parking:** At site.

FACILITIES

Number of RV Sites: 212. **Number of Tent-Only Sites:** Tent area (40 ft. × 120 ft.) w/electricity & water in area. **Hookups:** Water, sewer, electric (50 amps). **Each Site:** Picnic table, BBQ pit. **Dump Station:** Yes. **Laundry:** Yes. **Pay Phone:** Yes. **Rest Rooms and Showers:** Yes. **Fuel:** Yes, no diesel. **Propane:** Yes. **Internal Roads:** Paved. **RV Service:** 10 mi. in Dallas. **Market:** In park. **Restaurant:** 0.25 mi. **General Store:** 0.25 mi. **Vending:** Yes. **Swimming:** Pool. **Playground:** Yes. **Other:** rec hall, mini-mart, hair salon. **Activities:** Shopping on weekends, festivals. **Nearby Attractions:** Six Flags, Hurricane Harbor, Fort Worth Stockyards, Texas Motor Speedway, Texas Rangers Baseball, Lone Star Park, DFW International Airport, Dallas Mavericks, Mesquite Rodeo, Dallas Cowboys, convention centers, numerous retail shops. **Additional Information:** Fort Worth CVB (800) 433-5747, Dallas CVB (800) 232-5527.

RESTRICTIONS

Pets: 2 pets per site, on leash only, never unattended. **Fires:** Not allowed. **Alcoholic Beverages:** Allowed. **Vehicle Maximum Length:** 45 ft. **Other:** Speed limit of 10 mph strictly enforced.

TO GET THERE

From I-20, take the Great Southwest Pkwy. exit. Go north on Great Southwest Pkwy. 0.25 mi. to Mayfield Rd. Take a left on Mayfield Rd. Entrance is 300 yards on the right.

DENISON

Eisenhower State Park

50 Park Rd. 20, Denison 75020-4898.T: (512) 389-8900 or (800) 792-1112; F: (512) 389-8959; www.tpwd.state.tx.us; e-mail.reservations@tpwd.state.tx.us.

RV ★★★★ Tent ★★★★

Beauty: ★★★★ Site Privacy: ★★★
Spaciousness: ★★★★ Quiet: ★★★★★
Security: ★★★★ Cleanliness: ★★★★
Insect Control: ★★ Facilities: ★★★

This park is divided into five camping areas, along with a screened lean-to area. Armadillo Hill has 45-foot grassy back-ins. The sites are very open but are surrounded by forest. Sites 4 and 5 are very close to the playground, which some campers may not prefer. Sites 16–22 have a partial view of the water, but all sites are some distance from the water's edge. The rest rooms are clean and modern and have flush toilets, but there is no shower. Bois d'Arc Ridge has all 110-foot pull-throughs, making it the best bet for larger rigs, or anyone who doesn't want to spend time parking. These grassy sites are forested, offering good shade, but are also away from the water. The Cedar Hollow Group Trailer area consists of 110-foot pull-throughs on the blacktop, with no shade and no direct access to the water—not the prettiest camping area. Fossil Ridge, however, is much nicer, with grassy, forested sites that overlook the water (especially 152–155). The Elm Point area is similarly close to the water, with 40-foot back-ins but no shade. It would be difficult not to find a campsite to your liking in this state park, but as the office staff agree, don't come in the dead heat of Aug.!

BASICS

Operated By: Texas Parks & Wildlife. **Open:** All year. **Site Assignment:** First come, first served. (Credit card required to make a reservation. $3 reservation service fee; $5 cancellation fee.). **Registration:** In office. (Late arrivals use drop box at entrance.). **Fee:** RV: $15 (full), $13 (water, electric), water: $10, plus $2 entrance fee per person (V, MC, D accepted in the office or for reservation.). **Parking:** At site.

FACILITIES

Number of RV Sites: 214. **Number of Tent-Only Sites:** Combined. **Hookups:** Water, sewer, electric (30 amps). **Each Site:** Fire ring. **Dump Station:** Yes. **Laundry:** No. **Pay Phone:** Yes. **Rest Rooms and Showers:** Yes. **Fuel:** No. **Propane:** No. **Internal Roads:** Paved. **RV Service:** No. **Market:** 8 mi. south (Exit 69). **Restaurant:** 3 mi. across lake. **General Store:** Yes (marina). **Vending:** Yes. **Swimming:** Lake. **Playground:** Yes. **Other:** rec hall, pavillion, fish cleaning station, lighted fishing pier. **Activities:** Swimming, boating, fishing, hiking, mountain biking. **Nearby Attractions:** Eisenhower Birthplace Historical State Park, Bonham State Park, Lake Texoma, Hagerman National Wildlife Refuge. **Additional Information:** Eisenhower State Park Office: (903) 465-1956.

RESTRICTIONS

Pets: On 6-ft. leash, cleaned up after. **Fires:** In grills. **Alcoholic Beverages:** None. **Vehicle Maximum Length:** None. **Other:** All visitors must pay $2 entrance fee per day.

TO GET THERE

From Hwy. 75, take Exit 72 and turn north onto Hwy. 91. Go 1.7 mi. and turn left at the sign for the park (at the beginning of the dam). Follow the road 1.8 mi. to the park entrance.

DONNA

Victoria Palms

602 North Victoria Rd., Donna, 78537.T: (956) 464-7801; F: (956) 782-3232; www.victoriapalms.com; vicpalms@acnet.net.

RV ★★★ Tent n/a

Beauty: ★★★★ Site Privacy: ★★★
Spaciousness: ★★★★ Quiet: ★★★★
Security: ★★★★ Cleanliness: ★★★★
Insect Control: ★★★★ Facilities: ★★★★

This retirement resort in suburban Donna offers extensive and well-maintained recreational facilities. Scheduled classes and entertainment (in-season) help this large complex retain a community atmosphere. It also offers easy access to shopping and restaurants and extremely tidy sites. The spacious sites are laid out in rows, and most feature back-in parking. All parking is paved. New sites are completely open, with no shade and no privacy. We recommend the older sites, which enjoy a bit of shade and privacy. Each of the older sites contains one lovely mature palm trees and one mature grapefruit tree. Guests are encouraged to pick their own grapefruits. In all other respects, the sites are exactly alike. This gated and fenced property offers good security. Avoid the Lower Rio Grande Valley in the summer, and be sure to make advance reservations in the winter.

BASICS

Operated By: Stephen Hynes. **Open:** All year. **Site Assignment:** Reservations for 1–3 month min., w/$250 deposit, $25 cancellation fee w/notice, call (800) 551-5303. **Registration:** At office. **Fee:** $23–$30. **Parking:** At site.

FACILITIES

Number of RV Sites: 760. **Number of Tent-Only Sites:** 0. **Hookups:** Water, sewer, electric (50 amps), cable TV, dataport. **Each Site:** 1 palm tree, 1 grapefruit tree, concrete parking slots, concrete patio. **Dump Station:** No. **Laundry:** Yes. **Pay Phone:** Yes. **Rest Rooms and Showers:** Yes. **Fuel:** No. **Propane:** Yes. **Internal Roads:** Paved. **RV Service:** 5 mi. south in Donna. **Market:** 5 mi. south in Donna. **Restaurant:** On site, open in the winter only. **General Store:** 10 mi. southwest in Weslaco. **Vending:** Yes. **Swimming:** Pool. **Playground:** No. **Other:** Tennis courts, mail room, card rooms, library, ballroom, beauty & barber shop, recreation center, lounge, sewing room, billiard room, exercise facilities, computer club, poolside bar. **Activities:** Fishing, hunting, arts & crafts, dancing, shuffleboard, horseshoes, golf. **Nearby Attractions:** Sabal Palm Audubon Center & Sanctuary, Gladys Porter Zoo, Brownsville Battlefields, CAF/ Confederate Air Force Rio Grande Valley Wing, Historic Brownsville Museum. **Additional Information:** Donna Chamber of Commerce (956) 464-3272, Rio Grande Valley Chamber of Commerce (956) 968-3141.

RESTRICTIONS

Pets: On leash only. **Fires:** In your own grill only. **Alcoholic Beverages:** Allowed. **Vehicle Maximum Length:** 60 ft.

TO GET THERE

From US 83, exit at Victoria Rd. and go south 0.25 mile, entrance on the left.

EL PASO

Mission RV Park

1420 RV Dr., El Paso 79928. T: (800) 447-3795 or (915) 859-1133; F: (915) 859-5201.

RV ★★★★ Tent ★★★

Beauty: ★★★	Site Privacy: ★★★★
Spaciousness: ★★★	Quiet: ★★★★
Security: ★★★★★	Cleanliness: ★★★★★
Insect Control: ★★★★	Facilities: ★★★★★

This huge RV park is laid out like a V, with the 2 branches off-limits to pets. While most areas border nothing much to look at (there is a mobile home along the "E" strip to the south/southwest and a residential area to the northeast), there is a farily nice view of the mountains from sites E69–97, only slightly spoiled by a commercial area in the foreground. Most of the perimeter of the park is fenced off with barbed wire; in the rest of the areas, a stone or chainlink fence provides security. Pull-throughs are a good 70 feet long and 21 feet wide; back-ins are equally wide and vary up to 45 feet long. While most sites are open to the sun without any tree cover, end sites do get the benefit of trees and other vegetation and are therefore the best sites. Back-ins D49–97 also have a tree and are therefore a good choice for those willing to forego a pull-through. The recreation areas are fenced off and well maintained. Likewise, the laundry facilities are huge, modern, and clean, with plenty of space and even an ironing board. Rest rooms and showers are clean and modern. This campground is a clean, safe, and delightful campground, lacking only in shade trees to be an unbeatable destination.

BASICS

Operated By: Dan Martinez. **Open:** All year. **Site Assignment:** Assigned upon registration (Flexible). **Registration:** In office. (Late arrivals register w/security in guard box at gate.). **Fee:** Full: $24, van: $17, tent: $15. **Parking:** At site.

FACILITIES

Number of RV Sites: 188. **Number of Tent-Only Sites:** 25. **Hookups:** Water, sewer, electric (30 & 50 amps). **Each Site:** Overturned cable spool for a table. **Dump Station:** Yes. **Laundry:** Yes. **Pay Phone:** Yes. **Rest Rooms and Showers:** Yes. **Fuel:** No. **Propane:** Yes (Mon. only). **Internal Roads:** Paved, in perfect condition. **RV Service:** Yes. **Market:** 4 mi. north or south. **Restaurant:** 2 mi. west. **General Store:** Yes. **Vending:** Yes. **Swimming:** Pool (indoor). **Playground:** Yes. **Other:** Jacuzzi, wash/wax RV service, dog walk, RV storage, sell utility trailers. **Activities:** Basketball, tennis, horseshoes, Mexico tours. **Nearby Attractions:** Casinos, Mexico. **Additional Information:** El Paso Chamber of Commerce, (915) 534-0500.

RESTRICTIONS

Pets: On leash, cleaned up after, restricted from 1/2 of park. **Fires:** In grills. **Alcoholic Beverages:** At sites. **Vehicle Maximum Length:** 75 ft. **Other:** No motorcycles (Rule sheet provided inside campground map).

TO GET THERE

From I-10, take Exit 34 east onto the north loop of Americas Ave. and drive 1.8 mi. As soon as possible, get into the far left lane and take the turnaround under the overpass. Drive 1.6 mi. on Joe Battle Blvd (straight through past the Van Buren exit). Turn right onto Rojas and drive 0.2 mi. Turn right onto RV Dr., then go another 0.2 mi. and turn left at the sign into the campground entrance. Pull in as far as possible past the office on the right to allow for others to enter.

GALVESTON

Galveston Island State Park

Rte. 4 Box 156A, Galveston 77554. T: (409) 737-1222, for Information Only (800) 792-1112; F: (409) 737-5496; www.tpwd.state.tx.us.

RV ★★★ Tent ★★

Beauty: ★★★	Site Privacy: ★
Spaciousness: ★★	Quiet: ★★★
Security: ★★★	Cleanliness: ★★★
Insect Control: ★	Facilities: ★★★★

Campsites are cookie-cutter dull and extremely close to one another. The draw is the pristine beach (mere yards from campsites) and its wildlife. Over 300 species of birds have been recorded here. Observation blinds and platforms enrich the birdwatching experience. Anglers appreciate the choice of ocean or freshwater intermittently stocked with bass, catfish, perch, and rainbow trout.Each Lilliputian campsite has paved back-in parking, and absolutely no shade or privacy. There is also a group camping area. Mosquitoes and heat can be brutal here. We recommend insect repellent and a golf-style umbrella for each member of the family. Visit during the week to avoid crowds. Go during late spring, summer, or fall if you plan to sun and swim. We visited in Dec., and the weather was pleasant for beach walks. This suburban park is situated on a major roadway—valuables should be protected, though gates are locked at night.

BASICS

Operated By: Texas Parks & Wildlife. **Open:** All year. **Site Assignment:** Reservations (512) 389-8900, reservations must be made at least 48 hours in advance, deposit required (equivalent to first night's fee) to hold reservation, cancellations more than two days prior to reservation result in $5 fee, cancellations within two days of reservation result in loss of deposit. **Registration:** Headquarters. **Fee:** $3 per person per day for anyone aged 13 & over, $20 for premium sites w/50-amp hookups, $15 for premium sites w/30-amp hookups, $15 for standard sites w/50-amp hookups, $12 for standard sites w/30-amp hookups, excess fee required for more than two vehicles per site (cash, checks, D,V, MC). **Parking:** At site.

FACILITIES

Number of RV Sites: 170. **Number of Tent-Only Sites:** None. **Hookups:** water, electric (30, 50 amps). **Each Site:** Picnic table, grill, fire ring. **Dump Station:** Yes. **Laundry:** No. **Pay Phone:** Yes. **Rest Rooms and Showers:** Yes. **Fuel:** No. **Propane:** No. **Internal Roads:** Paved. **RV Service:** 25 mi. west in La Marque. **Market:** 2 mi. East in Galveston. **Restaurant:** 1 mi. East in Galveston. **General Store:** Wal-Mart 10 mi. East in Galveston. **Vending:** Beverages only. **Swimming:** No. **Playground:** No. **Other:** Bathhouse on the beach, outdoor showers, interpretive center, gift shop, screened shelters, fish cleaning shelter. **Activities:** Picnicking, fishing, bird-watching, hiking, walking, mountain biking, swimming (at your own risk). **Nearby Attractions:** Moody Gardens, numerous historical homes in Galveston, the Railroad Museum, the Str& Historical District, Tall Ship Elissa (an 1877 sailing vessel), the Seaport Museum, Ocean Star Offshore Drilling Rig & Museum, attractions in Houston & San Jacinto. **Additional Information:** Galveston Chamber of Commerce (409) 763-5326.

RESTRICTIONS

Pets: Leash. **Fires:** In grills & fire rings only. **Alcoholic Beverages:** Prohibited. **Vehicle Maximum Length:** 40 ft. **Other:** Max. 8 people per campsite, Quiet time 10 p.m.–6 a.m., 14 day stay limit, swim at your own risk, no glass on beach, beware of poisonous snakes, jellyfish, & undercurrents.

TO GET THERE

From I-45, drive south on 61st St. to Seawall Blvd. Turn right on Seawall Blvd., and then right on Seawall (FM 3005). Follow FM 3005 for 10 mi. Park entrance is on the left.

HOUSTON

Houston Leisure RV Resort

1601 South Main St., Highlands 77562. T: (281) 426-3576; F: (281) 426-5258; www.gocampingamerica.com/houstonleisure; hlrvresort@houston.rr.com.

RV ★★★ Tent ★★★

Beauty: ★★★	Site Privacy: ★★★
Spaciousness: ★★★	Quiet: ★★★
Security: ★★★	Cleanliness: ★★★★
Insect Control: ★★	Facilities: ★★★

Located in suburban Highlands, Houston Leisure is approximately 19 miles east of downtown Houston. There are restaurants and shopping within minutes of the park, and attractions such as Space Center

Houston and the Battleship *Texas* are easily accessible. The campground is attractive and consists of nine rows of long narrow pull-throughs and five rows of back-ins. Parking spaces were paved in the past, but they now more closely resemble gravel. Site size is average, and site privacy is poor. Many of the sites have a shady tree or two while a few others are completely open. Security is fair—the office is attended until 11 p.m., but there are no gates. Avoid Houston in the heat of the summer.

Basics

Operated By: LLC. **Open:** All year. **Site Assignment:** Sites assigned; credit card number holds reservation, no-show charged one night. **Registration:** Office in store, night host & self-registration. **Fee:** $25 RV, $18 tent (3 nights max.); prices for 2 people, $2 per additional person (cash, checks, V, MC, D, AE). **Parking:** At site, in parking lot.

Facilities

Number of RV Sites: 205. **Number of Tent-Only Sites:** 5. **Hookups:** Water, sewer, electric (30, 50, 100 amps). **Each Site:** Picnic table, asphalt pad. **Dump Station:** Yes. **Laundry:** Yes. **Pay Phone:** Yes. **Rest Rooms and Showers:** Yes. **Fuel:** No. **Propane:** Yes. **Internal Roads:** Paved. **RV Service:** 5 mi. in Channel View. **Market:** 1 mi. north. **Restaurant:** Within 1 mi. **General Store:** Park store, hardware 2 mi. in Highlands, Wal-Mart 10 mi. in Houston. **Vending:** No. **Swimming:** Pool. **Playground:** Yes. **Other:** Pavilion, exercise room. **Activities:** Basketball, tennis, horseshoes, shuffleboard. **Nearby Attractions:** Space Center Houston, Battleship Texas, Moody Gardens aquarium, rainforest & discovery pyramids, San Jacinto Monument & Battleground, Arm& Bayou Nature Center, Traders Village outdoor market, Lone Star Flight Museum in Galveston. **Additional Information:** Greater Houston CVB (800) 4-HOUSTON.

Restrictions

Pets: 6-ft. leash max. **Fires:** Not allowed (bring your own grill). **Alcoholic Beverages:** Allowed. **Vehicle Maximum Length:** 45 ft. (sites vary). **Other:** Quiet hours enforced.

To Get There

From Houston, take I-10 east to Exit 787/ Crosby-Lynchburg Rd. Drive north 0.5 mile on Crosby-Lynchburg Rd. and the Resort is on the right.

HUNTSVILLE

Huntsville State Park

P.O. Box 508, Huntsville 77342. T: (936) 295-5644, for information only call (800) 792-1112; F: (936) 295-9426; www.tpwd.state.tx.us.

RV ★★★★ Tent ★★★★

Beauty: ★★★★ Site Privacy: ★★★
Spaciousness: ★★★ Quiet: ★★★
Security: ★★★★ Cleanliness: ★★★
Insect Control: ★★★ Facilities: ★★★★

Because of its proximity to Houston and its rural feel, Huntsville State Park is one of the most popular state parks in Texas, with campgrounds booking to capacity months in advance. The 210-acre Lake Raven is stocked with crappie, perch, catfish, and bass. The gently sloping terrain is complemented by plenty of open space and three playgrounds. Huntsville is a great place for children to expend their seemingly limitless energy. Loblolly and shortleaf pines, trees typical of the Texas Pineywoods region, provide excellent shade cover. Campsites are spacious, with paved parking and some pull-throughs large enough to handle 56-foot RVs. The most private sites, 174 and 175, are quickly taken year-round. When planning your visit, avoid hot, humid Aug. and rainy Sep. Gates are locked at 10 p.m. making security good.

Basics

Operated By: Texas Parks & Wildlife. **Open:** All year. **Site Assignment:** Reservations (512) 389-8900, reservations must be made at least 48 hours in advance, deposit required (equivalent to first night's fee) to hold reservation, cancellations more than two days prior to reservation result in $5 fee, cancellations within two days of reservation result in loss of deposit. **Registration:** Headquarters. **Fee:** $3 per person per day for anyone aged 13 & older, plus $9 for tent-camping, $12 for RV camping (cash, checks, V, MC, D). **Parking:** At site.

Facilities

Number of RV Sites: 61. **Number of Tent-Only Sites:** 127. **Hookups:** Water, electric (20 amps). **Each Site:** Picnic table, grill, fire ring, lantern post. **Dump Station:** Yes. **Laundry:** No. **Pay Phone:** Yes. **Rest Rooms and Showers:** Yes. **Fuel:** No. **Propane:** No. **Internal Roads:** Paved. **RV Service:** 10 mi. south in New Waverly. **Market:** 5 mi. north in Huntsville. **Restaurant:** 5 mi. north in Huntsville. **General Store:** 5 mi. north in Huntsville. **Vending:** Beverages only, concession stand open May through Sep. **Swimming:** No. **Playground:** Yes. **Other:** S&y beach on lake, interpretive center, gift shop, group picnic shelter (capacity 75 people), group lodge (capacity 150 people). **Activities:** Picnicking, swimming, boating (rental of canoes, paddle boats, & flat-bottomed boats in season), fishing, hiking, biking, horseback riding. **Nearby Attractions:** General Sam Houston's Old Homestead, Sam Houston Memorial Museum, Sam Houston Visitor Center & Statue, The Walls Unit (the first Texas prison), the Prison Museum, Historic Huntsville (one of Texas' oldest towns). **Additional Information:** Horseback riding at Lake Raven Stables (936) 295-1985, Huntsville Chamber of Commerce (936) 295-8113.

Restrictions

Pets: Leash Only. **Fires:** In grills & fire rings only. **Alcoholic Beverages:** Prohibited. **Vehicle Maximum Length:** 56 ft. **Other:** Max. 8 people per campsite, Quiet time 10 p.m.–6 a.m., fourteen day stay limit, gathering of firewood prohibited.

To Get There

From Exit 109 on I-45, drive 6 mi. southwest on Park Rd. 40.

JOHNSON CITY

Pedernales Falls State Park

Rte. 1 Box 450, Johnson City 78636. T: (830) 868-7304, for information only call (800) 792-1112; F: (830) 868-4186; www.tpwd.state.tx.us.

RV ★★★★★ Tent ★★★★★

Beauty: ★★★★★ Site Privacy: ★★★★★
Spaciousness: ★★★★★ Quiet: ★★★★★
Security: ★★★ Cleanliness: ★★★★★
Insect Control: ★★★ Facilities: ★★★★

Striking limestone falls resulted from 300 million years of geological change. Hikers appreciate twenty miles of trails in this park. Ash and cypress trees are found along the river, while the drier woodlands support oak and juniper stands. Hill Country fauna includes the elusive golden-cheeked warbler. Multipurpose campsites with paved back-in parking are situated in one area. Spacious and heavily wooded, with dense foliage between each site, these are some of the most beautiful campsites in the state. The park also maintains a sponsored youth camping area. Atop the river bluffs is a hike-in primitive tent-camping area with nearby water and chemical toilets. Although there are no locked gates, security is good here because of the park's remote location (nine miles from Johnson City). Aug. and Sep. are wet and hot, and winter can be very cold here. Plan to visit in spring, early summer, or fall.

Basics

Operated By: Texas Parks & Wildlife. **Open:** All year. **Site Assignment:** Reservations (512) 389-8900, reservations must be made at least 48 hours in advance, deposit required (equivalent to first night's fee) to hold reservation, cancellations more than two days prior to reservation result in $5 fee, cancellations within two days of reservation result in loss of deposit. **Registration:** Headquarters. **Fee:** $2 per person per day for anyone aged 13 & older, $16 for sites w/water, electric, $7 for tent-camping in primitive area (cash, checks, V, MC, D). **Parking:** At most sites.

Facilities

Number of RV Sites: 66. **Number of Tent-Only Sites:** 0. **Hookups:** Water, electric (20, 30 amps). **Each Site:** Picnic tables, fire ring, flat tent pad. **Dump Station:** Yes. **Laundry:** No. **Pay Phone:** Yes. **Rest Rooms and Showers:** Yes. **Fuel:** No. **Propane:** No. **Internal Roads:** Paved. **RV Service:** 34 mi. north in Marble Falls. **Market:** 10 mi. west in Johnson City. **Restaurant:** 10 mi. west in Johnson City. **General Store:** 34 mi. north in Marble Falls. **Vending:** Beverages. **Swimming:** No. **Playground:** No. **Other:** Horse corral (day use only), covered bird viewing station, amphitheater, sponsored youth group area, gift shop. **Activities:** picnicking, hiking, river swimming, tubing, wading, mountain biking, fishing, bird-watching, horseback riding. **Nearby Attractions:** Lyndon B. Johnson National & State Historic Parks (Johnson City), Admiral Nimitz Museum & Historical Center (Fredericksburg), numerous state parks & natural areas, numerous wineries, Austin attractions. **Additional Information:** Fredericksburg CVB (830) 997-6523, Austin CVB (800) 926-2282,.

Restrictions

Pets: Leash Only. **Fires:** In grills & fire rings only. **Alcoholic Beverages:** Prohibited. **Vehicle Maximum Length:** 45 ft. **Other:** Max. 8 people per campsite, Quiet time 10 p.m.–6 a.m., fourteen day stay limit, gathering of firewood prohibited, swim at your own risk, no pets or open fires allowed in primitive camping area.

To Get There

From Austin, drive west on US 290 for 32 mi., then turn right on FM 3232. Drive north on FM 3232 for 6 mi. to the park entrance. From Johnson City drive east on FM 2766 for 9 mi. to the park entrance.

KARNACK

Caddo Lake State Park

Rte. 2 Box 15, Karnack 75661. T: (512) 389-8900 or (800) 792-1112; F: (512) 389-8959; www.tpwd.state.tx.us; e-mail.reservations@tpwd.state.tx.us.

RV ★★★★★ Tent ★★★★★

Beauty: ★★★★★ Site Privacy: ★★★★
Spaciousness: ★★★★ Quiet: ★★★★★
Security: ★★★★ Cleanliness: ★★★
Insect Control: ★★ Facilities: ★★★

Visitors to this state park who come in RVs should take note that the entrance road is quite steep in some areas, but visitors delight in the humongous pull-throughs with full hookups once they've negotiated their way in. The road is also a little more complicated because of several one-way streets, making it necessary to drive first to the day-use area (near Big Cypress Bayou), then cutting across to the left to the camping areas. The first camping area you come across is Mill Pond, which is off-limits to RVs. These are 40-foot sites that are very close to the water's edge (61–65 are right on the water), which can make them buggy. The most remote site is 60, at the end of the roundabout. The next camping area is Squirrel Haven, which merges into Armadillo Run. These two areas consist of 40-foot forested and grassy sites. Sites 37–45 are located across from a row of screened shelters. The best sites are 29 and 30, at the end of a roundabout. The last camping area, Woodpecker Hollow, is designed with the big rig in mind. These are 120-foot pull-through sites with full hookups. All sites are forested and grassy, and the best two are next to the camp host (21 and 23) at the end of the roundabout. These are probably the safest, most comfortable sites in the park. Anyone with an interest in nature or living in the wild should come to Caddo Lake State Park for a camping holiday. Boat rentals are available and make for a fun afternoon—especially if you catch sight of one of the lake's native alligators! Like other parks this far south, however, July and Aug. are unbearably hot, and Sep. and Oct. are very busy.

Basics

Operated By: Texas Parks & Wildlife. **Open:** All year. **Site Assignment:** First come, first served. (Credit card required to make a reservation. $3 reservation service fee; $5 fee.) **Registration:** In office. (Late arrivals use drop box at entrance.). **Fee:** RV: $15 (full), $12 (water, electric), water: $8, plus $2 entrance fee per person (V, MC, D accepted in the office or for reservation.). **Parking:** At site.

Facilities

Number of RV Sites: 28. **Number of Tent-Only Sites:** 20. **Hookups:** Water, sewer, electric (30 amps). **Each Site:** Picnic table, grill, fire pit. **Dump Station:** Yes. **Laundry:** No. **Pay Phone:** Yes. **Rest Rooms and Showers:** Yes. **Fuel:** No. **Propane:** No. **Internal Roads:** Paved. **RV Service:** No. **Market:** 13 mi. to Marshall. **Restaurant:** 13 mi. to Marshall. **General Store:** Yes. **Vending:** Yes. **Swimming:** Lake. **Playground:** Yes. **Other:** Canoe/boat rentals & tours, interpretive center, rec hall, cabins, ampitheatre, fishing pier. **Activities:** Swimming, boating, fishing, hiking, mountain biking, wildlife viewing. **Nearby Attractions:** Starr Family State Historical Park. **Additional Information:** Marshall Chamber of Commerce, (903) 935-7868; Caddo Lake Office, (903) 679-3351.

Restrictions

Pets: On 6-ft. leash, cleaned up after. **Fires:** In grills. **Alcoholic Beverages:** None. **Vehicle Maximum Length:** None. **Other:** All visitors must pay $2 entrance fee per day.

To Get There

From the junction of Hwy. 43/134 and FM 2198, go 0.5 mi. east on FM 2198. Turn left onto Park Rd. 2 and follow it to the park entrance.

KERRVILLE

Guadalupe River RV Resort

2605 Junction Hwy. 27, Kerrville, 78028. T: (830) 367-5676; F: (830) 367-3003; www.guadaluperiverrvresort.com; info@grrvr.com.

RV ★★★ Tent n/a

Beauty: ★★★★ Site Privacy: ★★★
Spaciousness: ★★★★ Quiet: ★★★★
Security: ★★★ Cleanliness: ★★★★
Insect Control: ★★★★ Facilities: ★★★★

This new resort offers excellent amenities, including separate adult and family swimming pools. Charming Kerrville is known as a cultural hub. With fantastic weather, Kerrville is also known as a gateway to great outdoor recreation. Lost Maples State Natural Area and Kerrville-Schreiner State Park are both nearby. Many sites at Guadalupe River are extremely attractive, while others are unappealing. Stay away from the dull, noisy sites near Hwy. 27. Instead, try to score a riverfront site (1–10 or 50–61) and enjoy the gorgeous view of the gently sloping riverbank. Riverside sites have back-in parking, but most other sites are pull-throughs. All sites are spacious, with a large patch of grass at each site. Many are shady, though few are very private. All parking is paved. Security is passable; there are no gates, but the park is very remote. Visit popular Kerrville during the week.

Basics

Operated By: Gene, Marianne, & Martin Ellis. **Open:** All year. **Site Assignment:** Credit card required to hold reservation, call (800) 582-1916. 48 hour cancellation policy. Check-out at noon. **Registration:** At office. **Fee:** $26 per night for 2 people, $2 per extra person over age 6; $.09 per kilowatt hour for electricity. Cash or personal check are the only accepted forms of payment. **Parking:** On paved area at each site.

Facilities

Number of RV Sites: 202. **Number of Tent-Only Sites:** 0. **Hookups:** Water, sewer, electric (30, 50 amps), phone, cable TV. **Each Site:** Picnic tables, BBQ pits. **Dump Station:** Yes. **Laundry:** Yes. **Pay Phone:** Yes. **Rest Rooms and Showers:** Yes. **Fuel:** Once per week, otherwise, 1 mi. away. **Propane:** Once per week, otherwise, 1 mi. away. **Internal Roads:** Paved. **RV Service:** 0.25 mi. **Market:** 0.5 mi. **Restaurant:** 1 mi. **General Store:** At park. **Vending:** Yes. **Swimming:** Pool. **Playground:** Yes. **Other:** Two group facilities, pavilion w/BBQ pit, fireplace & dance floor, health spa, jacuzzi, steam room, sauna, game room, clubhouse, adult-only area. **Activities:** fishing, walking, boating, horseshoes, tetherball, ping pong, shuffleboard, volleyball, basketball, organized activities. **Nearby Attractions:** Hill County Arts Foundation, Point Theater, Stonehenge II, Scott Schreiner Municipal Golf Course, H.E.B. Municipal Tennis Center, Texas Arts & Crafts Fair, Cowboy Artists of America Museum. **Additional Information:** Kerrville CVB (800) 221-7958.

Restrictions

Pets: On 10-ft. max. leash at all times, even in river. **Fires:** In fire pits only. **Alcoholic Beverages:** Allowed. **Vehicle Maximum Length:** 55 ft. **Other:** No tent camping allowed.

To Get There

From San Antonio, take I-10 west toward El Paso and take exit 505. Drive about 2 mi. south on FM 783. Take a right onto Hwy. 27 heading west, and the campground will be 2.5 mi. on the left.

LUMBERTON

Village Creek State Park

P.O. Box 8565, Lumberton 77657. T: (409) 755-7322; www.tpwd.state.tx.us.

RV ★★★★ Tent ★★★★

Beauty: ★★★★ Site Privacy: ★★★★
Spaciousness: ★★★★ Quiet: ★★★★★
Security: ★★★★★ Cleanliness: ★★★★
Insect Control: ★★★ Facilities: ★★★★

Village Creek is a wooded retreat surrounded by suburbia. The flat-water creek, a favorite amongst anglers and paddle-sports enthusiasts, winds southeasterly and eventually joins the Neches River. Abundant rainfall supports cypress swamps, water tupelo, and river birch. Birders spot egrets and herons. The campground includes long and narrow yet attractive sites. Site size and privacy vary—some are incredibly huge and secluded, others ho-hum. There are no creek-side RV sites due to flooding. However, tent-campers may choose walk-in sites along Village Creek. All sites are nicely wooded and shady. At the RV area, all sites are back-ins with paved parking. Sites 1 and 3 are very secluded. Security is good-the park is gated at night. Although native bats dine on mosquitoes, insects flourish after heavy rains in the warmer months. Call before you visit Village Creek to check on water levels. Make advance reservations at this extremely popular park.

Basics

Operated By: Texas Parks & Wildlife. **Open:** All

year. **Site Assignment:** Reservations (512) 389-8900; reservations must be made at least 48 hours in advance; deposit (equivalent to first night's fee) required to hold reservation; cancellations more than two days prior to reservation result in $5 fee, cancellations within two days of reservation result in loss of deposit. **Registration:** Office, after hours register next morning (gate locks at 10 p.m.). **Fee:** $10 developed, $6 primitive, plus $2 entrance fee per person 13 & older up to 8 people max. (cash, checks, V, MC, D). **Parking:** At site (2 cars), in parking lot about 75 yards from walk-in sites.

Facilities

Number of RV Sites: 25. **Number of Tent-Only Sites:** 16 walk-in primitive sites w/tent pad or clearing. **Hookups:** Water, electric (30 amps). **Each Site:** Picnic table, fire ring, lantern pole. **Dump Station:** Yes. **Laundry:** No. **Pay Phone:** Yes. **Rest Rooms and Showers:** Yes. **Fuel:** No. **Propane:** No. **Internal Roads:** Paved (gravel road to walk-in sites). **RV Service:** 2 mi. in Lumberton. **Market:** 1 mi. in Lumberton. **Restaurant:** 2 mi. in Lumberton. **General Store:** Park store, hardware & Wal-Mart 3 mi. in Lumberton. **Vending:** Beverages, ice. **Swimming:** No. **Playground:** Yes. **Other:** Picnic area, pavilion, rec hall, meeting room. **Activities:** swimming, fishing (local canoe rentals & fishing supplies), hiking, mountain biking, bird-watching, year-round nature study programs. **Nearby Attractions:** Sea Rim & Martin Dies Jr. State Parks, Big Thicket National Preserve, Cattail Marsh, Pleasure Island, Sabine Pass Battlefield, Beaumont museums, 80 mi. to Houston. **Additional Information:** Beaumont CVB (409) 880-3749 www.beaumontcvb.com.

Restrictions

Pets: 6-ft. leash max. **Fires:** Allowed, in fire rings (except under fire ban). **Alcoholic Beverages:** Not allowed. **Vehicle Maximum Length:** 55 ft. (sites vary). **Other:** No gathering firewood, dumping gray water.

To Get There

From Beaumont, drive north approximately 9 mi. on US 69/96 and take the Mitchell Rd. exit. Drive almost 0.5 mi. on the access road and turn right (east) onto Mitchell Rd. Immediately turn left (north) onto FM 3513/Village Creek Pkwy. Drive approximately 2 mi. and turn right (east) onto Alma Dr. Cross the railroad tracks, veer to the left and go 0.5 mi. to the park entrance.

MATHIS

Lake Corpus Christi State Park

Box 1167, Mathis 78368. T: (512) 547-2635; www.tpwd.state.tx.us.

RV: ★★★★ Tent: ★★★★

Beauty: ★★★★ Site Privacy: ★★★★
Spaciousness: ★★★★ Quiet: ★★★★
Security: ★★★★ Cleanliness: ★★★★
Insect Control: ★★★★ Facilities: ★★★

Anglers fish for catfish, bass, sunfish, and crappie in 21,000-acre Lake Corpus Christi. Adjacent Lake Corpus Christi State Park is instrumental in conserving the mesquite grassland ecosystem. Despite the park's gorgeous setting, there are no walking trails. There are four main camping loops: two contain full hookups and pull-through parking while the other two contain no hookups and back-in parking. For RVs, sites 1–23 are larger and more private than sites 24–48. There are no lakefront RV sites. Tent campers (or RVs foregoing hookups) should head for waterfront sites, including 57–66 and 91–99. All sites are spacious, with shade and privacy provided by mesquite trees and other brushy flora. Parking is paved and each site has a large patch of grass. Security is good at this remote park. Gates lock at night, and peace officers live on property. Convenient to Corpus Christi, the park stays busy from Feb. to Aug. Visit in autumn for tranquility.

Basics

Operated By: Texas Parks & Wildlife. **Open:** All year. **Site Assignment:** Inquire at campground. **Registration:** Inquire at campground. **Fee:** $16 for sites w/full hookups, $14 for sites w/water & electric, $8 for primitive tent sites, day use fee of $3 per person aged 13 & over. **Parking:** At site.

Facilities

Number of RV Sites: 60. **Number of Tent-Only Sites:** None. **Hookups:** Water, sewer, electric. **Each Site:** Picnic table (some covered), either BBQ pit or fire ring & grill. **Dump Station:** Yes. **Laundry:** No. **Pay Phone:** Yes. **Rest Rooms and Showers:** Yes. **Fuel:** No. **Propane:** No. **Internal Roads:** Paved. **RV Service:** 30 mi. southeast in Odem. **Market:** 3 mi. east in Mathis. **Restaurant:** 3 mi. east in Mathis. **General Store:** 3 mi. east in Mathis. **Vending:** Beverages only. **Swimming:** No. **Playground:** Yes. **Other:** Screened shelters, gift shop, picnic area, picnic pavilion, boat ramp, fishing pier, fish cleaning facility, scenic overlook. **Activities:** Lake swimming (at your own risk), fishing, boating, nature study. **Nearby Attractions:** Choke Canyon, Goose Island, & Mustang Island State parks; Fulton Mansion & Goliad State Historical parks, Padre Island National Seashore, Aransas Wildlife Refuge, Corpus Christi attractions. **Additional Information:** Corpus Christi Area Convention & Tourist Bureau (800) 678-6232.

Restrictions

Pets: Leash only. **Fires:** Fire rings, BBQ pits only. **Alcoholic Beverages:** Not allowed. **Vehicle Maximum Length:** 35 ft. **Other:** No lifeguards.

To Get There

From I-37, take exit 34 and drive southwest on TX 359 for 4 mi. Turn right onto FM 1068. The park entrance is on the left.

MEDINA

Las Avenues RV Resort

17740 State Hwy. 16 North, Medina, 78055. T: (830) 589-7766; F: (830) 589-2606; unameit@wire web.net.

RV: ★★★ Tent: n/a

Beauty: ★★★ Site Privacy: ★★★
Spaciousness: ★★★ Quiet: ★★★
Security: ★★ Cleanliness: ★★
Insect Control: ★★★★ Facilities: ★★★★

Las Avenues caters to residents, but overnighters also enjoy the nicely landscaped pool, golf course, and other amenities. Oddly, the campsites are not nearly as tidy as the recreational areas. The campground is laid out in an oblong loop with a creek flowing through the middle. Site size varies greatly, with long, tight pull-throughs and amply sized back-ins. Most sites are nicely shaded by live oak (complete with Spanish moss) and other tree species. Parking is on gravel with a grassy plot at each site. Sites 28–32 are the quietest and enjoy a lovely view of the hills. Security at Las Ave.s is fair. Gates are kept open during the day and the park is visible from Hwy. 16. Though the park has the mellow atmosphere of a retirement community, children are welcome. Visit Texas Hill Country in the spring when wildflowers are blooming.

Basics

Operated By: Private. **Open:** All year. **Site Assignment:** Reservations accepted, no deposit required, site choice is first come, first served upon check-in. V, MC, D, checks & cash are accepted forms of payment. Check-out is at noon. **Registration:** At office. **Fee:** $20 per night for two people, $2 for each additional adult. **Parking:** On site.

Facilities

Number of RV Sites: 64. **Number of Tent-Only Sites:** 0. **Hookups:** Water, sewer, electric (50 amps), phone, cable TV. **Each Site:** Picnic table. **Dump Station:** No. **Laundry:** Yes. **Pay Phone:** Yes. **Rest Rooms and Showers:** Yes. **Fuel:** No. **Propane:** Once per week, otherwise, two mi. away. **Internal Roads:** Gravel. **RV Service:** 20 mi. in Boerne. **Market:** 2 mi. **Restaurant:** 2 mi. **General Store:** 3 mi. **Vending:** Yes. **Swimming:** Pool. **Playground:** No. **Other:** 9 hole par-3 golf course, nature trails, exercise room, jacuzzi, rec hall. **Activities:** Horseshoes, shuffleboard, pool, ping-pong, fishing, card-playing, volleyball. **Nearby Attractions:** Stonehenge II, Texas Arts & Crafts Fair, Texas Cowboy Artists of America Museum, Agricultural Heritage Center Museum, Bat Railroad Tunnel, Cibolo Wilderness Trail. **Additional Information:** Kerrville CVB (800) 221-7958; Bandera Chamber of Commerce, (830) 796-3045; Boerne Chamber of Commerce, (888) 842-8080.

Restrictions

Pets: On leashes—no pit bulls, rottweilers, or German shepherds allowed. **Fires:** In grills only. **Alcoholic Beverages:** Allowed. **Vehicle Maximum Length:** 48 ft. **Other:** Speed limit 5 mph.

To Get There

From San Antonio, take I-410 (loop) Exit 13A and head northwest on State Hwy. 16. Drive approximately 50 mi. to Medina and the campground is on the right. If you are headed south on I-10, exit at Hwy. 16 south at Kerrville, then take exit Hwy. 173 heading south. From there, take FM 2828 west to Hwy. 16 north to Medina. Note that this seems round-about, but there are portions of Hwy. 16 that are unsuitable for RVs.

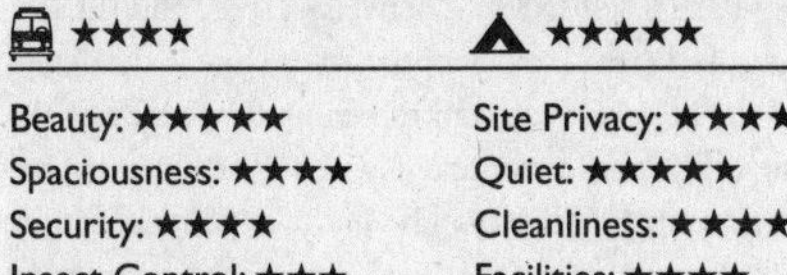

MERIDIAN

Meridian State Park

Rte. 2 Box 2465, Meridian 76665. T: (254) 435-2536; F: (254) 435-2076; www.tpwd.state.tx.us.

RV: ★★★★ Tent: ★★★★★

Beauty: ★★★★★ Site Privacy: ★★★★
Spaciousness: ★★★★ Quiet: ★★★★★
Security: ★★★★ Cleanliness: ★★★★
Insect Control: ★★★ Facilities: ★★★★

Heavily wooded with ash, juniper, oak, and other species, Meridian offers extremely attractive campgrounds. Sites are large and shady, with paved back-in and pull-through parking. Site privacy varies, with dense greenery between some and others open to neighbors. RVs should head for one of the pull-throughs with full hookups. Tent campers should head for one of the pretty lakefront sites (no hookups). Meridian's rolling woods support myriad wildlife, including golden cheeked warblers in the spring. The 72-acre lake supports bream, crappie, catfish, bass, and rainbow trout (winter only). Security is good at this extremely rural park which locks its gates at night. Visit Meridian in the spring, early summer, or fall for the nicest weather. Avoid this park on summer weekends, when the small campgrounds are likely to be crowded.

Basics

Operated By: Texas Parks & Wildlife. **Open:** All year. **Site Assignment:** Reservations (512) 389-8900; reservations must be made at least 48 hours in advance; deposit (equivalent to first night's fee) required to hold reservation; cancellations more than two days prior to reservation result in $5 fee, cancellations within two days of reservation result in loss of deposit. **Registration:** Park Headquarters, after hours self-registration (gate locks at 10 p.m.). **Fee:** $25 screened shelter, $17 pull-through (water, electric & sewer), $15 back-in (water & electric), $12 tent w/water, $10 tent without water, plus $3 entrance fee per person over 13 years (cash, personal check, V, MC, D). **Parking:** At site (2 cars).

Facilities

Number of RV Sites: 15. **Number of Tent-Only Sites:** 14 (8 w/water nearby, 6 without water or electricity). **Hookups:** Water, sewer, electric (30 amps). **Each Site:** Picnic table, fire ring. **Dump Station:** Yes. **Laundry:** No. **Pay Phone:** Yes. **Rest Rooms and Showers:** Yes. **Fuel:** No. **Propane:** No. **Internal Roads:** Paved. **RV Service:** 45 mi. in Waco. **Market:** Park store, grocery 2 mi. in Meridian. **Restaurant:** 2 mi. in Meridian. **General Store:** Hardware 2 mi. in Meridian, Wal-Mart 45 mi. in Waco. **Vending:** Beverages only. **Swimming:** No. **Playground:** No. **Other:** Screened shelters, picnic area, boat ramp, boat dock, group dining hall, gift shop. **Activities:** Lake swimming, boating (no-wake lake), pedal boat rentals summertime, fishing, bird-watching, hiking, road biking. **Nearby Attractions:** Meridian golf, Bosque County Courthouse, Norse historic Norwegian settlement, Dinosaur Valley, Lake Whitney & Cleburne State Parks, Fossil Rim, Waco historic homes, Homestead Heritage Traditional Crafts Village, Texas Sports Hall of Fame. **Additional Information:** Meridian Chamber of Commerce, (254) 435-2966; Waco CVB, (800) 321-9226.

Restrictions

Pets: 6-ft. max leash (not in shelters or buildings). **Fires:** Allowed, fire ring only. **Alcoholic Beverages:** Not allowed. **Vehicle Maximum Length:** 45 ft. (back-in sites 20 ft.). **Other:** No-wake lake.

To Get There

From Waco, take TX 6 northwest approximately 45 mi. to Meridian and turn left (southwest) on TX 22. Drive 2.5 mi. and turn right on Park Rd. 7, directly into the park.

MEXIA

Fort Parker State Park

Rte. 3 Box 95, Mexia 76667. T: (254) 562-5751; F: (254) 562-9787; www.tpwd.state.tx.us.

RV: ★★★★ Tent: ★★★★

Beauty: ★★★★★ Site Privacy: ★★★
Spaciousness: ★★★★ Quiet: ★★★★★
Security: ★★★ Cleanliness: ★★★★
Insect Control: ★★★ Facilities: ★★★★

Most campsites here offer stunning views of the sunset over 700-acre Fort Parker Lake. The lake supports crappie, bass, catfish, and trout (in season). Guided boat tours of the lake are available (call for schedule). The RV campground consists of one area alongside the lake. There are back-in and pull-through sites with paved parking. Some sites could cause mild claustrophobia, while others are amply sized. Most are nicely shaded, but none are very private. Arrive early and angle for a lakefront site, the prettiest of which is number 18—a gorgeous pull-through. The primitive tent-camping area is nicely wooded. Visit popular Fort Parker on weekdays between Mar. and June when wildfowers are blooming and crowds are at a minimum. Security is fair at this small-town park; there are no gates.

Basics

Operated By: Texas Park & Wildlife Dept. **Open:** All year. **Site Assignment:** Reservations (512) 389-8900; reservations must be made at least 48 hours in advance; deposit (equivalent to first night's fee) required to hold reservation; cancellations more than two days prior to reservation result in $5 fee, cancellations within two days of reservation result in loss of deposit. **Registration:** Park Headquarters, after hours register next morning. **Fee:** $12 developed, $8 primitive, plus entry fee $2 per adult (cash, checks, V, MC, D). **Parking:** At site, in parking lot.

Facilities

Number of RV Sites: 25. **Number of Tent-Only Sites:** 10 primitive w/picnic table. **Hookups:** Water, electric (30 amps). **Each Site:** Picnic table, fire ring grill combination, lantern pole. **Dump Station:** Yes. **Laundry:** No. **Pay Phone:** Yes. **Rest Rooms and Showers:** Yes. **Fuel:** No. **Propane:** No. **Internal Roads:** Paved. **RV Service:** 40 mi. in Waco. **Market:** 5 mi. in Groesbeck. **Restaurant:** 5 mi. in Groesbeck. **General Store:** 7 mi. in Mexia. **Vending:** Beverages only. **Swimming:** No. **Playground:** Yes. **Other:** Activity center, screened shelters, picnic area & shelter, boat ramp, fish cleaning station. **Activities:** Lake swimming, fishing, canoe & paddle boat rentals, Cynthia Ann boat tours, hiking, biking trails. **Nearby Attractions:** Confederate Reunion Grounds, Old Fort Parker Historic Site, Waco historic homes, Homestead Heritage Traditional Crafts Village, Texas Sports Hall of Fame. **Additional Information:** Waco CVB (800) 321-9226.

Restrictions

Pets: On leash only. **Fires:** Allowed, fire rings only (except under fire ban). **Alcoholic Beverages:** No. **Vehicle Maximum Length:** None (sites vary). **Other:** Texas State Park regulations apply.

To Get There

From US 84 in Mexia, turn south on TX 14. Drive 7 mi. to the park entrance on the right. The campground is one mile inside the park.

MINERAL WELLS

Lake Mineral Wells State Park and Trailway

100 Park Rd. 71, Mineral Wells 76067. T: (940) 328-1171, for information only call (800) 792-1112; F: (940) 325-8536; www.tpwd.state.tx.us.

RV: ★★★★★ Tent: ★★★★★

Beauty: ★★★★★ Site Privacy: ★★★★★
Spaciousness: ★★★★★ Quiet: ★★★★★
Security: ★★★ Cleanliness: ★★★★
Insect Control: ★★★ Facilities: ★★★★

The only major rock climbing and rappelling region in north Texas, Mineral Wells offers 85 climbs (difficulty ranges from 5.5 to 5.11d). Nearby, the State Trailway is a 20-mile "rail to trail" conversion open to pedestrians, cyclists, and equestrians. The lake supports bass, catfish, crappie, and perch. Three campgrounds are lakeside: The Post Oak tent-only area contains 11 gorgeous sites under a romantic post oak canopy. The Plateau area offers water and electric sites (ask for 59, 60, and 64–66 for the best lake views). The Live Oak area contains water-only sites (ask for 31–34 for the nicest lake views). Sites are spacious and situated on loops with back-in gravel parking. The entrance is within Mineral Wells city limits, so protect your valuables (gates lock at night). Apr. and May are the wettest months. Winters can be very cold and summers very hot. Visit in Mar., June (on weekdays), Sep., or Oct.

Basics

Operated By: Texas Parks & Wildlife. **Open:** All year. **Site Assignment:** Reservations (512) 389-8900, reservations must be made at least 48 hours in advance, deposit required (equivalent to first night's fee) to hold reservation, cancellations more than two days prior to reservation result in $5 fee, cancellations within two days of reservation result in loss of deposit. **Registration:** Headquarters. **Fee:** $3 per person per day for anyone aged 13 & older, $6 for primitive walk-in tent camping, $8 for water-only sites, $11 water & electric, $15 premium water & electric (cash, checks, D, V, MC). **Parking:** At most sites.

FACILITIES

Number of RV Sites: 108. **Number of Tent-Only Sites:** 25 hike-in (about 2.5 mi.) primitive. **Hookups:** water, electric (30 amps). **Each Site:** picnic table, fire ring, grill. **Dump Station:** Yes. **Laundry:** No. **Pay Phone:** Yes. **Rest Rooms and Showers:** Yes. **Fuel:** No. **Propane:** No. **Internal Roads:** Paved. **RV Service:** 0.5 mi. west of park. **Market:** 3 mi. west in Mineral Wells. **Restaurant:** 3 mi. west in Mineral Wells. **General Store:** Wal-Mart, 3 mi. west in Mineral Wells. **Vending:** Park concession open daily Mar. through Dec. **Swimming:** No. **Playground:** No. **Other:** Picnic sites, equestrian camp-sites, screened shelters, seasonal park store, boat ramp, fishing piers, screened shelters. **Activities:** Swimming, fishing, boating (row boat, canoe, & paddle boat rental available), rock climbing, rappelling, mountain biking, equestrian camping, horseback riding, hiking. **Nearby Attractions:** Fort Richardson State Historical Park, Lost creek Reservoir State Trailway, Possum Kingdom State Park, Cleburne State Park, Dinosaur Valley State Park, Clark Gardens, The Brazos River, Possum Kingdom Lake. **Additional Information:** Mineral Wells Area Chamber of Commerce, (800) 252-MWTX.

RESTRICTIONS

Pets: Leash Only. **Fires:** In grills & fire rings only. **Alcoholic Beverages:** Prohibited. **Vehicle Maximum Length:** 45 ft. **Other:** Max. 8 people per campsite, Quiet time 10 p.m.–6 a.m., fourteen-day stay limit, gathering of firewood prohibited, climbers & rappelers must check in at headquarters, no skiing, jet skiing, or tubing permitted.

TO GET THERE

From Mineral Wells, drive east on US 180 for 4 mi. From Weatherford, drive west on US 180 for 14 mi.

MISSION

Bentson-Rio Grande Valley State Park

P.O. Box 988, Mission 78573-0988. T: (956) 585-1107, for information only call (800) 792-1112; F: (956) 585-3448; www.tpwd.state.tx.us.

★★★★ ★★★★

Beauty: ★★★★★	Site Privacy: ★★★
Spaciousness: ★★★	Quiet: ★★★★
Security: ★★★	Cleanliness: ★★★★
Insect Control: ★	Facilities: ★★★★

Year-round warmth makes for delightful winter or early spring retreats at this campground. Situated on a resaca—a former Rio Grande River channel (now still-water)—the lush flora and varied fauna of the park are typical of the Mexican subtropics. Fish for bass and catfish in the resaca. The surrounding brushlands form natural habitats for exotic cats such as ocelot and jaguarundi. Exotic birds include paraque, groove-billed ani, black-bellied whistling duck, and scores more. The lovely campsites are large, usually shady and flat. Tent sites offer paved back-in parking and water at each site. Tent campers will find the prettiest sites lining the resaca (110–139). Searching for exotic birds and full hookups? Try sites 3–36. RV sites offer fewer trees and paved pull-through parking. In spite of its quiet feel, this suburban park is about 3 miles from afternoon traffic jams. Watch your valuables even though the gates lock at 10 p.m.

BASICS

Operated By: Texas Parks & Wildlife. **Open:** All year. **Site Assignment:** Reservations (512) 389-8900, reservations must be made at least 48 hours in advance, deposit required (equivalent to first night's fee) to hold reservation, cancellations more than two days prior to reservation result in $5 fee, cancellations within two days of reservation result in loss of deposit. **Registration:** Headquarters. **Fee:** $3 per person per day for anyone aged 13 & older, $12 per night for sites w/water, $18 per night for full hookups (cash, checks, V, MC, D). **Parking:** At site.

FACILITIES

Number of RV Sites: 78 sites w/water, electric, & sewer. **Number of Tent-Only Sites:** 65 sites w/water only. **Hookups:** Water, sewer, electric (20, 30, 50 amps). **Each Site:** Grill, picnic table, fire ring, lantern post. **Dump Station:** Yes. **Laundry:** No. **Pay Phone:** Yes. **Rest Rooms and Showers:** Yes. **Fuel:** No. **Propane:** No. **Internal Roads:** Paved. **RV Service:** 5 mi. north in Mission. **Market:** 3 mi. north in Palmview. **Restaurant:** 3 mi. north in Palmview. **General Store:** K-Mart 5 mi. north toward McAllen. **Vending:** Beverages, ice. **Swimming:** No. **Playground:** Yes. **Other:** Bicycle rental, volleyball court, shuffleboard, fish cleaning table, bird observation blinds, birding information center Dec. through Mar. **Activities:** hiking, picnicking, bird-watching, boating, bicycling, & fishing. **Nearby Attractions:** Falcon State Park, Santa Ana National Wildlife Refuge, Sabal Palm Sanctuary, Mexico attractions. **Additional Information:** Mission Chamber of Commerce, (956) 585-2727; Rio Grande Valley Chamber of Commerce, (956) 968-3141; McAllen Convention & Visitor Bureau (956) 682-2871.

RESTRICTIONS

Pets: Leash Only. **Fires:** In grills & fire rings only. **Alcoholic Beverages:** Prohibited. **Vehicle Maximum Length:** 40 ft. **Other:** Max. 8 people per campsite, Quiet time 10 p.m.–6 a.m., 14-day stay limit, gathering of firewood prohibited.

TO GET THERE

From McAllen, go west on I-83. Exit at Bentsen Palm Blvd., turn left, and drive south. After crossing Business 83, Bentsen Palm Blvd. becomes FM 2062. The park entrance is about 3 mi. from I-83.

MISSION

Chimney RV Park

4224 South Conway St., Mission, 78572. T: (956) 585-5061; F: (956) 519-8348; www.gocamping america.com/chimneypark.

 ★★★ n/a

Beauty: ★★★	Site Privacy: ★★★
Spaciousness: ★★★	Quiet: ★★★
Security: ★★★★	Cleanliness: ★★★
Insect Control: ★★★	Facilities: ★★★

Another seniors-only park in south Texas, Chimney Park is sandwiched between a levee and the Rio Grande River. However, the river view is deadened by the concrete sea wall that runs the length of the park. The park's namesake is a 1907 steam-powered water-pump chimney. The park's aged facilities are not as extensive as those at many of the competing resorts. Campsites are generally plain and small—we imagine you'll get to know your neighbors. With little shade or privacy, each site has paved back-in parking, a grassy area, and a concrete patio. Permanent park models occupy all of the riverfront sites. The nicest available sites, including 16–20, 150–154, and 261–268, have trees nearby. Fenced and guarded, security is excellent at suburban Chimney Park. Within a mile, there are restaurants and shops galore. Stay away from South Texas in the summer, and make advance reservations in the winter.

BASICS

Operated By: Private. **Open:** All year. **Site Assignment:** Reservations accepted, payable w/V, MC, D, personal check, or cash. **Registration:** At office. **Fee:** $22 per night for 2 people, $2 per night per extra person. **Parking:** On site.

FACILITIES

Number of RV Sites: 276. **Number of Tent-Only Sites:** None. **Hookups:** Water, sewer, electric, phone, dataport & cable TV. **Each Site:** Fire ring. **Dump Station:** No. **Laundry:** Yes. **Pay Phone:** Yes. **Rest Rooms and Showers:** Yes. **Fuel:** No. **Propane:** Yes. **Internal Roads:** Paved. **RV Service:** 0.5 mi. **Market:** 0.5 mi. **Restaurant:** 0.25 mi. **General Store:** 0.5 mi. **Vending:** Yes. **Swimming:** Pool. **Playground:** No. **Other:** Boat ramp, boat dock, floating dock, fishing dock, jacuzzi, game room. **Activities:** Horseshoes, shuffleboard, fishing, boating, billiards, variety shows, card games, dances, bingo, ice cream socials. **Nearby Attractions:** Azalduas Dam, Banworth Park, Mission Nature Park. **Additional Information:** Mission Chamber of Commerce, (956) 585-2727.

RESTRICTIONS

Pets: On leash. **Fires:** In grills only. **Alcoholic Beverages:** Allowed. **Vehicle Maximum Length:** 38 ft.

TO GET THERE

Traveling south from Corpus Christi or Kingville on US 77, exit onto US 83 west. Travel approxiamately 45 mi. to Mission and exit onto Conway St. The park is 0.25 mi. south on the right.

MONAHANS

Monahans Sandhills State Park

P.O. Box 1738, Monahans, 97956. T: (915) 943-2092; F: (915) 943-2806; www.tpwd.state.tx.us.

 ★★★  ★★★

Beauty: ★★★★	Site Privacy: ★★★
Spaciousness: ★★★	Quiet: ★★★

Security: ★★ Cleanliness: ★★★★
Insect Control: ★★★ Facilities: ★★★

At the end of a vast dune field which continues 200 miles northeast into New Mexico, the park contains "active dunes" that move and change seasonally because they're not anchored by vegetation. Try dusk or dawn wildlife viewing at the ponds. Look for coyote, bobcat, porcupine and others. The unique shinoak tree is mature at under four feet tall. The campgrounds are odd. Sites nestle into the dunes in pairs, with each pair sharing a shade shelter. Each site has its own picnic table. While you are nose-to-nose with your shelter-mate, dunes and ample space provide privacy between pairs of sites. Some sites offer paved pull-through parking. All others have paved back-in parking. You will be assigned a site. There are no gates, and we easily entered the park after dark. Be cautious with your valuables—the entrance is yards from the freeway exit. Visit Monahans any time but late summer.

Basics

Operated By: Texas Parks & Wildlife. **Open:** All year. **Site Assignment:** Reservations (512) 389-8900; reservations must be made at least 48 hours in advance; deposit (equivalent to first night's fee) required to hold reservation; cancellations more than two days prior to reservation result in $5 fee, cancellations within two days of reservation result in loss of deposit. **Registration:** Headquarters. **Fee:** $2 per person per day for anyone aged 13 & over, $9 for sites w/water & electric, $6 for sites w/water only (cash, checks, V, MC, D). **Parking:** At site.

Facilities

Number of RV Sites: 15. **Number of Tent-Only Sites:** 0. **Hookups:** Water, electric (20, 30, 50 amps). **Each Site:** Grill, picnic table. **Dump Station:** Yes. **Laundry:** No. **Pay Phone:** Yes. **Rest Rooms and Showers:** Yes. **Fuel:** 5 mi. west in Monahans. **Propane:** 5 mi. west in Monahans. **Internal Roads:** Paved. **RV Service:** 30 mi. east in Odessa. **Market:** 5 mi. west in Monahans. **Restaurant:** 5 mi. west in Monahans. **General Store:** 5 mi. west in Monahans. **Vending:** Yes. **Swimming:** No. **Playground:** No. **Other:** Interpretive center, equestrian day use area, group dining hall, one working oil well, picnic area, sand toboggan & disc rental. **Activities:** Hiking, picnicking, sand surfing, birdwatching at interpretive center. **Nearby Attractions:** Million Barrel Museum, Balmorhea State Park, Odessa Meteor Crater. **Additional Information:** Odessa Chamber of Commerce, (915) 332-9111; Monahans Chamber of Commerce, (915) 943-2187.

Restrictions

Pets: On leash only. **Fires:** In grill only. **Alcoholic Beverages:** Prohibited. **Vehicle Maximum Length:** 45 ft. **Other:** No "four-wheelers" or motorcycles allowed.

To Get There

From I-20, take Exit 86 to Park Rd. 41. The park entrance is visible from the interstate.

NEEDVILLE

Brazos Bend State Park

21901 FM 762, Needville, 77461. T: (979) 553-5101; F: (979) 553-5108; www.tpwd.state.tx.us.

RV ★★★★ Tent ★★★★

Beauty: ★★★★ Site Privacy: ★★★
Spaciousness: ★★★★ Quiet: ★★★
Security: ★★★★ Cleanliness: ★★★★
Insect Control: ★ Facilities: ★★★★

A nature-lover's paradise, Brazos Bend contains fascinating ecosystems, including river floodplains, upland coastal prairies, freshwater marshes, oxbow lakes, the Brazos River, and creeks. Wildlife spotted from the observation tower and viewing platforms includes feral hogs and 270 bird species. The 0.5-mile, paved Creekfeild Lake Nature Trail is handicapped accessible and includes tactile interpretive panels and audio tours. On property, George Observatory offers public star-gazing—call for schedule. Attractive campgrounds consist of two loops of back-in sites with gravel parking. Large campsites are shaded by black willow, sycamore, and cottonwood trees. There is little privacy. Many sites in both sections are situated along "Big Creek". Pretty creekside sites include101, 214, and 215. For privacy, we recommend site 105. Grassy tent pads are found at each site. Security is good at this rural park. Popular with Houston city slickers, Brazos Bend stays busy on all but the most inclement weekends. Visit on weekdays.

Basics

Operated By: Texas Parks & Wildlife. **Open:** All year. **Site Assignment:** Reservations (512) 389-8900, reservations must be made at least 48 hours in advance, deposit required (equivalent to first night's fee) to hold reservation, cancellations more than two days prior to reservation result in $5 fee, cancellations within two days of reservation result in loss of deposit. **Registration:** Headquarters. **Fee:** $3 per person per day for anyone aged 13 & older, $12 for overnight camping (cash, checks, V, MC, D). **Parking:** At site.

Facilities

Number of RV Sites: 77. **Number of Tent-Only Sites:** 0. **Hookups:** Water, electric (20, 30 amps). **Each Site:** Picnic table, fire ring, grill. **Dump Station:** Yes. **Laundry:** No. **Pay Phone:** Yes. **Rest Rooms and Showers:** Yes. **Fuel:** No. **Propane:** No. **Internal Roads:** Paved. **RV Service:** 30 mi. northeast in Sugarland. **Market:** Convenience store 1 mi. south in community of Woodrow, full market 18 mi. northwest in Needville. **Restaurant:** Deli 1 mi. south in community of Woodrow, full service 18 mi. northwest in Needville. **General Store:** Wal-Mart, 18 mi. south in West Columbia. **Vending:** Beverages only. **Swimming:** No. **Playground:** Yes. **Other:** George Observatory (call for hours), interpretive center, group dining hall, group picnic pavilions, picnic areas, screened shelters, amphitheater, gift shop, fishing piers, fish cleaning area, handicapped accessible nature trail. **Activities:** Picnicking, hiking, bicycling, mountain biking, boating, fishing, interpretive tours & educational programs, stargazing (special parties & programs). **Nearby Attractions:** San Jacinto Battleground Historical Complex including the San Jacinto Monument & Battleship "Texas", Galveston Island State Park, George Ranch, Houston. **Additional Information:** Houston CVB (800) 4-HOUSTON, Fort Bend Convention/Visitor Services (281) 491-0800.

Restrictions

Pets: On leash only. **Fires:** In fire rings only. **Alcoholic Beverages:** Prohibited. **Vehicle Maximum Length:** 45 ft. **Other:** Special alligator precautions: do not feed or molest the alligators, no swimming or wading, keep pets & children away from alligators, stay at least 30 ft. away from alligators.

To Get There

From Houston, follow TX 288 to Rosharon. At Rosharon, turn left on FM 1462 and travel west for roughly 9 mi. Park entrance on right.

PADRE ISLAND

Padre Island National Seashore, Malaquite Beach Campground

P.O. Box 181300, Corpus Christi, 78480. T: (361) 949-8068; F: (361) 949-9951; www.nps.gov/pais/pphtml/camping.html.

RV ★★★★ Tent ★★★★

Beauty: ★★★★ Site Privacy: ★★
Spaciousness: ★★★ Quiet: ★★★
Security: ★★★★ Cleanliness: ★★★★
Insect Control: ★ Facilities: ★★★★

At seventy miles long, Padre Island National Seashore is one of the largest pieces of undeveloped shoreline in the U.S. The island is rich in folklore concerning buried pirate's treasure. It's also rich in natural beauty and wildlife, including graceful waterfowl such as herons. Much of the island is accessible only by foot or four-wheel drive. Attractive Malaquite Campground is 100 feet from the beach, nestled into graceful dunes. There is no vegetation other than dune grasses. Sites have parallel paved parking and are completely open to each other. All sites are small, and there is no shade. If your RV doesn't have an awning, bring large umbrellas. Sites are all the same, so choose your site based on location. Mosquitoes thrive at Padre Island, so come prepared. Security is good—although there are no gates, the campground is extremely remote. Rarely crowded, Malaquite is an excellent destination in late spring, early summer, and autumn.

Basics

Operated By: National Park Service. **Open:** All year. **Site Assignment:** No reservations are accepted. **Registration:** Visitor Center. **Fee:** $8 per night, in addition to day use fees of $10 per car or $5 per cyclist or pedestrian. **Parking:** At site.

Facilities

Number of RV Sites: 46 plus non-designated sites on the beach. **Number of Tent-Only Sites:** Non-designated oceanfront sites. **Hookups:** None. **Each Site:** Picnic table. **Dump Station:** Yes. **Laundry:** No. **Pay Phone:** Yes. **Rest Rooms and Showers:** Yes. **Fuel:** No. **Propane:** No. **Internal**

Roads: Paved except for beach driving. **RV Service:** 18 mi. north in Corpus Christi. **Market:** In park. **Restaurant:** 10 mi. north in Corpus Christi. **General Store:** In park, 25 mi. in Corpus Christi. **Vending:** Yes. **Swimming:** No. **Playground:** No. **Other:** Visitor center, scenic drive, observation deck, bathhouses. **Activities:** Wind surfing, trash walks, picnicking, four-wheel-driving, hiking, bird-watching, beachcombing, swimming, surfing, boating, volunteering, waterskiing, fishing, guided tours, & activities. **Nearby Attractions:** Texas State Aquarium, USS Lexington, Ships of Christopher Colombus. **Additional Information:** Corpus Christi Area Convention & Tourist Bureau (800) 678-6232.

RESTRICTIONS

Pets: On leash only. **Fires:** Contained fires only. **Alcoholic Beverages:** Allowed. **Vehicle Maximum Length:** None.

TO GET THERE

From Corpus Christi, take US 358 to Rte. 22. Drive approximately 20 mi. and follow the signs to camping areas.

PORT ARANSAS

Mustang Island State Park

P.O. Box 326, Port Aransas 78373. T: (361) 749-5246; F: (361) 749-6455; www.tpwd.state.tx.us.

RV ★★★ Tent ★★★★★

Beauty: ★★★	Site Privacy: ★
Spaciousness: ★★	Quiet: ★★★
Security: ★★★	Cleanliness: ★★★★
Insect Control: ★★★	Facilities: ★★

Tent campers are in luck at Mustang Island—gorgeous beachfront tent sites include a picnic table and shade shelter at each site (call ahead regarding beach conditions). RV sites are disappointing. The RV campground is a sea of unnecessary pavement. Sites are small, extremely close together, and offer no shade or privacy. All sites are back-in, and there is no vegetation in the campground. It doesn't matter which site you choose. The beach and birding are the draws here. The park provides nice, not extensive, beach facilities and no special birding facilities. Though the park feels rural, restaurants are 10 minutes away. The mosquitoes can be oppressive here, so come prepared with insect repellant. Mustang Island is busiest in the spring and summer. For tranquility, visit in the fall. Security is good; the front gates are locked at night, and the campground is a long walk from Hwy. 361.

BASICS

Operated By: Texas Parks & Wildlife. **Open:** All year. **Site Assignment:** Reservations (512) 389-8900; reservations must be made at least 48 hours in advance; deposit (equivalent to first night's fee) required to hold reservation; cancellations more than two days prior to reservation result in $5 fee, cancellations within two days of reservation result in loss of deposit. **Registration:** Park headquarters, after hours register next morning. **Fee:** $15 developed, $7 primitve, plus $3 entrance fee per person over 13 years (cash, checks, V, MC, D). **Parking:** At site (2 cars), on beach for primitive camping.

FACILITIES

Number of RV Sites: 48. **Number of Tent-Only Sites:** 300 (beach). **Hookups:** Water, electric (50 amps). **Each Site:** Covered shelter, BBQ pit. **Dump Station:** Yes. **Laundry:** no. **Pay Phone:** Yes. **Rest Rooms and Showers:** Yes. **Fuel:** No. **Propane:** No. **Internal Roads:** Paved. **RV Service:** 15 mi. in Corpus Christi. **Market:** 10 mi. in Corpus Christi. **Restaurant:** 5 mi. in Corpus Christi. **General Store:** 10 mi. in Corpus Christi. **Vending:** Yes. **Swimming:** No. **Playground:** No. **Activities:** Fishing, swimming, surfing, beach combing, bird-watching. **Nearby Attractions:** USS Lexington, Texas State Aquarium, The Colombus Ships, Greyhound Racetrack, Padre Island National Seashore, University of Texas Marine Science Center, Port Aransas Birding Center. **Additional Information:** Port Aransas Chamber of Commerce, (361) 749-5919; Corpus Christi Area Convention & Tourist Bureau, (800) 678-6232.

RESTRICTIONS

Pets: On leash only. **Fires:** Allowed on the beach only (or grill). **Alcoholic Beverages:** No. **Vehicle Maximum Length:** 40 ft. **Other:** No lifeguards, water sports at your own risk.

TO GET THERE

From Corpus Christi, take TX 358 southeast until it becomes Park Rd. 22. Cross the causeway and drive 1 mi. to the traffic light. Turn left on TX 361 and drive 5 mi. to the park.

PORT ARANSAS

Pioneer RV Resort

120 Gulfwind Dr., Port Aransas, 78373. T: (361) 749-6248; F: (361) 749-6250; www.gocampingamerica.com/pioneerrv; info@ pioneerrvresorts.com.

RV ★★★ Tent n/a

Beauty: ★★★★	Site Privacy: ★★★
Spaciousness: ★★★	Quiet: ★★★★
Security: ★★★	Cleanliness: ★★★★
Insect Control: ★★★★	Facilities: ★★★★

Port Aransas on Mustang Island is known for its excellent birding, with boardwalks and raised observation towers at both the Port Aransas Birding Center and the Port Aransas Wetlands Park. Excellent deep-sea fishing and lovely beaches appeal to families and retirees. Pioneer's campground is attractive and tidy, with both back-in and pull-through spaces. The L-shaped campground hugs a pretty pond that attracts many birds. Sites are situated in long rows and feature paved parking. There are no trees, but each site has a grassy area. Most sites are of average size. We recommend the premium sites (the 300s), which are larger, quieter, and closer to the beach. Security is fair at Pioneer—there are no gates, but the park's serene location gives no cause for concern. Insects are not as problematic here as at nearby Mustang Island State Park. For solitude, visit Port Aransas in the fall.

BASICS

Operated By: Don Temple. **Open:** All year. **Site Assignment:** For reservations, call (888) 480-3246; credit card number holds reservation, monthly reservations require one month deposit. You may request a certain area, but not a certain site. Payment may be made by V, MC, D, personal check, or cash. **Registration:** At office. **Fee:** $21 per night for 2 people in a back-in, $23 for a pull-through, $2 for each additional adult. **Parking:** On site.

FACILITIES

Number of RV Sites: 330. **Number of Tent-Only Sites:** 0. **Hookups:** Water, sewer, electric (30, 50 amps), phone, cable TV. **Each Site:** Concrete patio, picnic table. **Dump Station:** Yes. **Laundry:** Yes. **Pay Phone:** Yes. **Rest Rooms and Showers:** Yes. **Fuel:** No. **Propane:** Yes. **Internal Roads:** Concrete. **RV Service:** 30 mi. in Corpus Christi. **Market:** 3.5 mi. north in Port Aransas. **Restaurant:** 3.5 mi. north in Port Aransas. **General Store:** 25 mi. in Aransas Pass. **Vending:** Beverages, c&y, ice, beer. **Swimming:** Pool. **Playground:** Yes. **Other:** Spa, rec hall, fish cleaning facility, trolley service. **Activities:** Birding areas, arts & crafts, deep sea fishing trips, aerobics, dancing, golf, ladies lunches, cribbage, washers, dominoes, bridge, bunko, pool, horseshoes, shuffleboard, quilting. **Nearby Attractions:** Texas State Aquarium, The USS Lexington, Corpus Christi Greyhound Racetrack, University of Texas Marine Science Center, Port Aransas Birding Center. **Additional Information:** Port Aransas Chamber of Commerce, (361) 749-5919; Corpus Christi Area Convention & Tourist Bureau (800) 678-6232.

RESTRICTIONS

Pets: On leash only; must be approved if over 50 lbs., absolutely no pit bulls, dobermans, rottweilers, chows, or wolf hybrids allowed. **Fires:** In grills only. **Alcoholic Beverages:** Allowed. **Vehicle Maximum Length:** 60 ft.

TO GET THERE

From Corpus Christi, take TX 358 which becomes Park Rd. 22. After you cross the JFK Causeway, take a left at the next traffic light (Hwy. 361) and the park will be 15 mi. on the right.

PORT ISABEL

Long Island Village

P.O. Box 695, Port Isabel 78578. T: (956) 943-6449 or (800) 292-7261; F: (956) 943-3113.

RV ★★★★ Tent n/a

Beauty: ★★★★	Site Privacy: ★★★
Spaciousness: ★★★★	Quiet: ★★★★
Security: ★★★★★	Cleanliness: ★★★★★
Insect Control: ★★★★	Facilities: ★★★★★

Ultra-tidy Long Island Village welcomes families and retirees and maintains extensive facilities, including an 18-hole golf course. Located on Long Island, south of Port Isabel, the park is convenient to South Padre Island and restaurants and shopping. Though sites are small and crowded, the campground is laid out in a series of rows dissected by picturesque canals. Waterfront sites often have private docks. The sites are extremely clean with paved, back-in parking. There are few trees. Landscaping enhances the park's beauty, though it provides no shade or privacy. Since Long Island is so large, families should look for a site near the pool. Couples should ask for a quiet site in the back. Security is excellent; the complex is gated and surrounded by water. Popular with families in the spring and summer and popular with snow birds in the winter, it's best to visit Long Island in the fall.

Basics

Operated By: Outdoor Owners Assoc. of Long Island Texas. **Open:** All year. **Site Assignment:** Lots assigned; credit card number holds lot, 48-hour cancellation notice required or fee is charged; check-in 3 p.m., check-out 11 a.m. **Registration:** Office, register w/security at night. **Fee:** $30 for 3 people, $2 per additional person, 8 people max. (cash, personal Check, V, MC, AE, D). **Parking:** At site only.

Facilities

Number of RV Sites: 200. **Number of Tent-Only Sites:** None. **Hookups:** Water, sewer, electric (50 amps), cable. **Each Site:** Concrete pad. **Dump Station:** No. **Laundry:** Yes. **Pay Phone:** Yes. **Rest Rooms and Showers:** Yes. **Fuel:** No. **Propane:** Service. **Internal Roads:** Paved. **RV Service:** 0.5 mi. in Port Isabel. **Market:** 0.5 mi. in Port Isabel. **Restaurant:** On-site (seasonal), also within one block of resort. **General Store:** Within 2 blocks. **Vending:** Yes. **Swimming:** Pool (indoor & outdoor). **Playground:** No. **Other:** Rec hall, exercise room, sauna, library, ballroom, billiard room. **Activities:** 18-hole par 3 golf course, mini-golf, tennis, shuffleboard, volleyball, basketball, horseshoes, arts & crafts. **Nearby Attractions:** Padre Island National Seashore, Port Isabel Lighthouse & Boca Chica State Parks, dolphin watching, charter fishing, Rio Grande, South Padre Island. **Additional Information:** Port Isabel Chamber of Commerce, (800) 527-6102; South Padre Island CVB, (800) SO-PADRE.

Restrictions

Pets: On leash only. **Fires:** Not allowed (bring your own grill). **Alcoholic Beverages:** Allowed. **Vehicle Maximum Length:** 60 ft. **Other:** No pop-ups, vans or tents, no fish-cleaning on picnic tables.

To Get There

From US 77/83, take TX 100 east approximately 25 mi. Just before the causeway, turn right on Garcia St. and follow it 0.5 mi. to the Resort at the end.

QUANAH

Copper Breaks State Park

RR 2 Box 480, Quanah 79252-9420. T: (940) 839-4331; www.tpwd.state.tx.us.

RV ★★★★ | Tent ★★★★

Beauty: ★★★★	Site Privacy: ★★★★
Spaciousness: ★★★★	Quiet: ★★★★
Security: ★★★★	Cleanliness: ★★★★
Insect Control: ★★★	Facilities: ★★★★

Taking its name from the copper deposits found in the area, this park boasts striking rock formations with alternating layers of gypsum, red clays, and shales. Recreation revolves around the 60-acre lake, which is stocked with rainbow trout in the winter. Lake Copper Breaks also hosts many migratory waterfowl, including great blue heron. Part of the Texas state longhorn herd lives at Copper Breaks. Comanche campground (water/electric) is not as pretty as Kiowa (no hookups). Both offer spacious, paved, back-in sites. Kiowa includes sites shaded by tall trees and secluded by foliage between many sites. Families might appreciate Kiowa's proximity to the swimming beach. Comanche's sites are cookie-cutter boring and have no shade and little privacy. Security is good at this rural park. North Texas experiences cold winters and hot summers; visit in spring, early summer, or fall.

Basics

Operated By: Texas Parks & Wildlife. **Open:** All year. **Site Assignment:** Inquire at campground. **Registration:** Headquarters. **Fee:** $11 for sites w/water & electricity, $8 for sites without water & electricity, $6 for primitive tent camping. **Parking:** At site.

Facilities

Number of RV Sites: 25. **Number of Tent-Only Sites:** 24. **Hookups:** Water, electric. **Each Site:** Fire ring, grill, picnic table. **Dump Station:** Yes. **Laundry:** No. **Pay Phone:** Yes. **Rest Rooms and Showers:** Yes. **Fuel:** No. **Propane:** No. **Internal Roads:** Yes. **RV Service:** 63 mi. northeast in Altus, OK. **Market:** 13 mi. north in Quanah. **Restaurant:** 8 mi. south in Crowell. **General Store:** 13 mi. north in Quanah. **Vending:** Yes. **Swimming:** No. **Playground:** Yes. **Other:** Visitor's center, meeting room, picnic area, picnic pavilion, swimming beach, boat ramp, boat dock, fishing pier, amphitheater, scenic overlook, group camp, equestrian camping,. **Activities:** Hiking, backpacking, equestrian trails, swimming, boating, fishing, paddle boat rental (in-season), horseshoes, basketball, volleyball. **Nearby Attractions:** Hardeman County Historical Museum, Medicine Mound (on private property), Firehall Museum in Crowell, Lake Pauline, Greenbelt Reservoir. **Additional Information:** Inquire at campground.

Restrictions

Pets: Leash only. **Fires:** Fire rings only. **Alcoholic Beverages:** Not allowed. **Vehicle Maximum Length:** 50 ft.

To Get There

From Quanah, drive south on State Hwy. 6 for 25 mi. Park Rd. 62 entrance is on the right.

QUITAQUE

Caprock Canyons State Park and Trailway

P.O. Box 204, Quitaque 79255. T: (806) 455-1492; F: (806) 455-1254; www.tpwd.state.tx.us.

RV ★★★★★ | Tent ★★★★★

Beauty: ★★★★★	Site Privacy: ★★★★
Spaciousness: ★★★★★	Quiet: ★★★★★
Security: ★★★★	Cleanliness: ★★★★★
Insect Control: ★★★	Facilities: ★★★★

This gorgeous state park is adjacent to 64-mile Caprock Canyon Trailway, a multi-use "rail to trail" conversion completed in 1993. Catering to expert hikers and mountain bikers, 25 miles of extremely rugged trails are found inside the park. Wildlife includes African aoudad sheep, a herd of pronghorn antelope, and the largest herd of buffalo in the state park system. Pretty Honea Flat campground features sites with paved back-in RV parking. Site size varies. Cottonwood trees and foliage provide shade and privacy at some sites, while others are more open. Families should go for sites 15 and 17 (near the playground and potties). Those seeking privacy should try to score site 23. The tent-only campgrounds are also very attractive. Visit Caprock on weekdays in spring, summer, or fall. Call ahead to avoid special event weekends. Security is good-there are no gates, but the park is extremely remote.

Basics

Operated By: Texas Parks & Wildlife. **Open:** All year. **Site Assignment:** Reservations (512) 389-8900; reservations must be made at least 48 hours in advance; deposit (equivalent to first night's fee) required to hold reservation; cancellations more than two days prior to reservation result in $5 fee, cancellations within two days of reservation result in loss of deposit. **Registration:** Park headquarters, after hours self-registration. **Fee:** $12 RV, $7-$10 tent, plus $2 entrance fee per additional person up to 8 max (cash, checks, V, MC, D). **Parking:** At site (2 cars, $2 per additional vehicle).

Facilities

Number of RV Sites: 35. **Number of Tent-Only Sites:** 39. **Hookups:** Water, some electric (30 amps). **Each Site:** Picnic table, fire ring, lantern pole. **Dump Station:** Yes. **Laundry:** No. **Pay Phone:** Yes. **Rest Rooms and Showers:** Yes. **Fuel:** No. **Propane:** No. **Internal Roads:** Paved. **RV Service:** Inquire at campground. **Market:** 3 mi. in Quitaque. **Restaurant:** 3 mi. in Quitaque. **General Store:** 3 mi. in Quitaque. **Vending:** Beverages only. **Swimming:** No. **Playground:** Yes. **Other:** Interpretive exhibits, gravel equestrian loop, amphitheater, backpacking trails, picnic pavilion, fishing pier boat ramp. **Activities:** hiking, horseback riding, seasonal horse rentals, mountain biking, boating, fishing, lake swimming, scenic drive, guided tours. **Nearby Attractions:** Turkey, Panhandle-Plains Historical Museum & West Texas State University in Canyon, Palo Duro Canyon & Copper Breaks State Parks, Lake Mackenzie, Ranching Heritage Center, 2 hours from Amarillo & Lubbock. **Additional Information:** Turkey City Hall (806) 423-1033, Amarillo Convention & visitors Bureau (800) 692-1338, Lubbock CVB (800) 692-4035.

Restrictions

Pets: On leash only. **Fires:** Allowed, fire rings only. **Alcoholic Beverages:** Not allowed. **Vehicle Maximum Length:** None.

To Get There

From I-27, take Exit 74 and head east on TX 86 approximately 45 mi. to Quitaque. Turn north on FM 1065 and drive 3 mi. to the park.

RUSK

Rusk Campground, Rusk/ Palestine State Park and Texas State Railroad Historical Park

P.O. Box 39, Rusk 75785. T: (903) 683-5126; F: (903) 683-2212; www.tpwd.state.tx.us.

RV ★★★★ Tent ★★★★

Beauty: ★★★★ Site Privacy: ★★★★
Spaciousness: ★★★★ Quiet: ★★★
Security: ★★★★ Cleanliness: ★★★★
Insect Control: ★★★★ Facilities: ★★★★

Rusk and Palestine recreation areas are connected by the 25-mile Texas State Railroad. The park maintains four steam engines and four antique diesel engines and offers four-hour, 50-mile round trip excursions between Rusk and Palestine (depart at either terminus). Children especially enjoy visiting the engineer and touring the steam engine cab. After the trains, explore the lake and woods. We prefer the RV campground at Rusk, which is nicer than Palestine, with tall pine trees providing shade at most sites. Pull-through sites offer full hookups and paved parking. Sites are comfortably spaced, but not huge. Sites 7–12, situated away from Hwy. 84, are the quietest. Families enjoy sites 17 and 19, which are adjacent to the playground. Site 14, the only back-in, is the most secluded. Assiduously avoid Rusk/Palestine on summer weekends. Opt for weekday and off-season visits. Security is good at this rural recreation area. Gates lock at 10 p.m.

BASICS

Operated By: Texas Parks & Wildlife Dept. **Open:** All year. **Site Assignment:** Reservations (512) 389-8900; reservations must be made at least 48 hours in advance; deposit (equivalent to first night's fee) required to hold reservation; cancellations more than two days prior to reservation result in $5 fee, cancellations within two days of reservation result in loss of deposit. **Registration:** Park Office, after hours register next morning. **Fee:** $10 plus entry fee $2 per adult (cash, checks, V, MC, D). **Parking:** At site (2 cars), in parking lot.

FACILITIES

Number of RV Sites: 34. **Number of Tent-Only Sites:** 16 water & electric. **Hookups:** Water, sewer, electric (30, 50 amps). **Each Site:** Picnic table, grill, fire ring (amenities at tent & multipurpose sites). **Dump Station:** Yes. **Laundry:** No. **Pay Phone:** Yes. **Rest Rooms and Showers:** Yes. **Fuel:** No. **Propane:** No. **Internal Roads:** Paved. **RV Service:** 30 mi. in Nacogdoches. **Market:** 4 mi. in Rusk. **Restaurant:** 5 mi. in Rusk. **General Store:** 5 mi. in Rusk. **Vending:** Beverages only. **Swimming:** No. **Playground:** Yes. **Other:** Picnic areas & pavilions, gift shop & food at train depots, group dining hall, fishing jetty, tennis courts. **Activities:** Steam engine tours (weekends Mar.-Nov.), lake swimming, fishing, pedal boat & canoe rentals, nature trails, biking, volleyball, horseshoes. **Nearby Attractions:** Mission Tejas & Caddoan Mounds State Historical Parks, Tyler & Fairfield State Parks, Museum of East Texas, NASA Scientific Balloon Base. **Additional Information:** Palestine CVB (800) 659-3484.

RESTRICTIONS

Pets: On leash only. **Fires:** Allowed, fire rings (except under fire ban). **Alcoholic Beverages:** Not allowed. **Vehicle Maximum Length:** 40 ft. (sites vary). **Other:** Checkout 2 p.m., daytime visitors must exit park by 10 p.m.

TO GET THERE

From US 84, about 1 mile west of downtown Rusk, turn south onto Park Rd. 76 and drive 0.25 mile to the park.

SABINE PASS

Sea Rim State Park

P.O. Box 1066, Sabine Pass, 77655. T: (409) 971-2559; F: (409) 971-2917; www.tpwd.state.tx.us.

RV ★★★ Tent ★★★★

Beauty: ★★★ Site Privacy: ★
Spaciousness: ★★ Quiet: ★★★
Security: ★★★ Cleanliness: ★★
Insect Control: ★ Facilities: ★★★

Spend little time in the uninspired campgrounds. Rather, enjoy the often deserted beach or explore the Sea Rim marshlands via canoe, kayak, or boardwalk. This biologically important area includes marsh grasses that inhabit a tidal zone, and it's a winter home for numerous bird species. RV sites are small and crowded. The entire campground is paved, with no trees or shrubs. Bring your own shade and live without privacy. All sites are unattractive, so pick one near the beach. Tent campers fare better—sites are more spacious and attractive, but offer little privacy. For sheer beauty, the best option for tent campers is primitive camping on the beach. Sep. is the wettest month at Sea Rim. Visit in late spring or early summer before the heat becomes unbearable. Security is good at this very rural park. We cannot overstate the terror caused by Sea Rim mosquitoes. Prepare to battle these beasts.

BASICS

Operated By: Texas Parks & Wildlife. **Open:** All year. **Site Assignment:** Reservations (512) 389-8900; reservations must be made at least 48 hours in advance; deposit (equivalent to first night's fee) required to hold reservation; cancellations more than two days prior to reservation result in $5 fee, cancellations within two days of reservation result in loss of deposit. **Registration:** Headquarters. **Fee:** $2 per person per day for anyone aged 13 & over, $11 for RV sites, $8 for tent-only sites, $6 for primitive tent camping on the beach (cash, checks, D, V, MC). **Parking:** At site.

FACILITIES

Number of RV Sites: 20. **Number of Tent-Only Sites:** 10. **Hookups:** Water, electric (30 amps). **Each Site:** Picnic table, grill, tent-only sites also have lantern hook & tent pad. **Dump Station:** Yes. **Laundry:** No. **Pay Phone:** Yes. **Rest Rooms and Showers:** Yes. **Fuel:** No. **Propane:** No. **Internal Roads:** Paved. **RV Service:** 25 mi. northeast in Port Arthur. **Market:** 10 mi. east in Sabine Pass. **Restaurant:** 10 mi. east in Sabine Pass. **General Store:** Wal-Mart 20 mi. northeast in Port Arthur. **Vending:** Yes. **Swimming:** No. **Playground:** No. **Other:** S&y swimming beach, picnic area, gift shop, visitor's center, observation deck, observation blinds for bird-watching, air boat tours (by reservation only). **Activities:** Hiking, walking, bicycling, bird-watching, beach combing, boating (canoe & kayak rentals available), beach swimming, fishing, seasonal waterfowl hunting. **Nearby Attractions:** Sabine Pass Battleground State Historical Park, festivals & historic homes in Port Arthur & surrounding towns. **Additional Information:** Port Arthur convention & Visitors Bureau (800) 235-7822.

RESTRICTIONS

Pets: On leash only. **Fires:** Ground fires allowed on beach or in fire rings. **Alcoholic Beverages:** Prohibited. **Vehicle Maximum Length:** 40 ft. **Other:** Swim at your own risk, don't approach, annoy, or feed the alligators.

TO GET THERE

From I-10, take Exit 829 at Winnie and drive 28 mi. east on TX 73. Turn south on TX 82 and drive 10 mi. to the traffic light in Sabine Pass at State Hwy. 87. Turn right and drive 10 mi. into the park.

SAN ANGELO

San Angelo State Park

3900-2 Mercedes, San Angelo 76901. T: (915) 949-4757 or (800) 792-1112; F: (915) 947-2963; www.tpwd.state.tx.us; sasp@wcc.net.

RV ★★★ Tent ★★★

Beauty: ★★★ Site Privacy: ★★★
Spaciousness: ★★★★ Quiet: ★★★★
Security: ★★★ Cleanliness: ★★★★
Insect Control: ★★★ Facilities: ★★★

Three campgrounds are situated along the North Concho River, and four are adjacent to O.C. Fisher Lake. Sites are spacious, if lackluster. RV campers looking for elbow room should ask for pull-through sites 1–11 (Red Arroyo area). Tent campers looking for lake views should head for sites 13–16 (Red Arroyo area). Many sites have partial lake views since there are few trees. Gravel parking is the norm. Ecologically diverse, this park is home to roughly 350 species of birds. The Concho River is named after indigenous freshwater mussels that produce iridescent pink or purple "Concho pearls." Also of interest are dinosaur tracks and Native American petroglyphs (access via reserved group tours). Suburban (fewer than three miles from San Angelo), but with locked gates at night, security is decent. The weather at this park can be extreme, so try to visit in spring, early summer, or fall.

BASICS

Operated By: Texas Parks & Wildlife. **Open:** All year. **Site Assignment:** Reservations (512) 389-8900, reservations must be made at least 48 hours in advance, deposit required (equivalent to first night's fee) to hold reservation, cancellations more than two days prior to reservation result in $5 fee, cancellations within two days of reservation result in loss of deposit. **Registration:** Headquarters. **Fee:** $2 per person per day for anyone aged 13 &

older, $10 for sites w/water, electric, $6 for primitive sites (cash, checks, V, MC, D). **Parking:** At site.

Facilities

Number of RV Sites: 80. **Number of Tent-Only Sites:** 100 primitive sites. **Hookups:** Water, electric. **Each Site:** Picnic table, fire ring, grill. **Dump Station:** Yes. **Laundry:** No. **Pay Phone:** Yes. **Rest Rooms and Showers:** Yes. **Fuel:** No. **Propane:** No. **Internal Roads:** Paved. **RV Service:** 3 mi. southeast in San Angelo. **Market:** Super Wal-Mart 3 mi. southeast in San Angelo. **Restaurant:** 3 mi. southeast in San Angelo. **General Store:** Super Wal-Mart, 3 mi. southeast in San Angelo. **Vending:** Beverages. **Swimming:** No. **Playground:** Yes. **Other:** High & low level boat ramps, courtesy docks, fishing platform, log shelters, group camping & picnic areas, equestrian camping, gift shop. **Activities:** Picnicking, hiking, mountain biking, horseback riding, swimming, fishing, boating, birding, group tours upon request. **Nearby Attractions:** Fort Concho, Concho Ave. shopping district, Concho River Walk, Miss Hattie's Museum. **Additional Information:** San Angelo Convention & Visitor's Bureau (800) 375-1206.

Restrictions

Pets: Must be kept on leash at all times. **Fires:** In fire rings & grills only. **Alcoholic Beverages:** Prohibited. **Vehicle Maximum Length:** 60 ft. **Other:** Max. 8 people per campsite, Quiet time 10 p.m.–6 a.m., fourteen day stay limit, gathering of firewood prohibited.

To Get There

To reach the south shore park entrance from San Angelo, take US 67 south for about 2 mi. and then turn right on FM 2288. To reach the north shore park entrance from San Angelo, go north on US 87 for about 2 mi., and then turn left on FM 2288.

SAN ANTONIO

Admiralty RV Resort

1485 North Ellison Dr., San Antonio, 78251. T: (210) 647-7878; F: (210) 521-4443; www.admiraltyresort. com; arvrllc@aol.com.

RV: ★★★ Tent: n/a

Beauty: ★★★★	Site Privacy: ★★★
Spaciousness: ★★★	Quiet: ★★★
Security: ★★★	Cleanliness: ★★★★★
Insect Control: ★★★★★	Facilities: ★★★★

This gleefully tidy park is convenient to SeaWorld, restaraunts, and shopping. Six Flags Fiesta Texas, the Alamo, and the River Walk are within 30 miles. Spending the day at the park? Facilities are well maintained. The nicely landscaped campground is laid in rows of pull-throughs, with back-ins along the perimeter of the park. Sites are small, with little privacy. Some sites enjoy shady trees, but many are open. RV parking is paved, though some internal roads are gravel. Families should head for sites 1–10, 101–110, or 201–210, the closest to the playground. Couples looking for a little solitude should go for sites in the 600s. Security is fair at this suburban campground-there are no gates, but a guard patrols the property at night. The brochures claim that San Antonio has mild weather all year, but it sometimes gets chilly in the winter; visit in spring or fall.

Basics

Operated By: Corporate. **Open:** All year. **Site Assignment:** Reservations accepted all year, (800) 999-7872; credit card number holds site, no-show charged one night; deposit & refund policies vary for weekly & monthly stays. Check out at 11 a.m. **Registration:** At office. **Fee:** $34 per night for two people, $3.50 for 3rd, 4th, & 5th person, $5 for 6th, 7th, & 8th person. **Parking:** At site.

Facilities

Number of RV Sites: 240 w/full hookups. **Number of Tent-Only Sites:** 0. **Hookups:** Water, sewer, electric (30, 50 amps), dataport, & cable TV. **Each Site:** Picnic table, concrete pads, brick patio, some grills. **Dump Station:** Yes. **Laundry:** Yes. **Pay Phone:** Yes. **Rest Rooms and Showers:** Yes. **Fuel:** No. **Propane:** No. **Internal Roads:** Paved. **RV Service:** 2 mi. west. **Market:** 2 mi. east in San Antonio. **Restaurant:** 7 mi. east in San Antonio. **General Store:** 7 mi. north in San Antonio. **Vending:** Yes. **Swimming:** Pool. **Playground:** Yes. **Other:** Game room, exercise room, adult jacuzzi, clubhouse. **Activities:** Basketball, water aerobics, volleyball, year-round schedule of activities, including bingo, crafts, dances, ice cream socials, etc. **Nearby Attractions:** The Alamo, Botanical Gardens, San Antonio Zoo & Aquarium, Sea World, Mexican-American Cultural Center, Riverwalk, McNay Art Museum, Market Square, IMAX Theater, Institute of Texan Cultures. **Additional Information:** San Antonio CVB (800) 447-3372.

Restrictions

Pets: On 6-ft. max. leash at all times. **Fires:** Only in BBQ grills. **Alcoholic Beverages:** Allowed. **Vehicle Maximum Length:** 60 ft.

To Get There

From I-410 (loop), take Exit 9A and drive northwest 2 mi. on State Hwy. 151. Turn left on Potranco Rd. and drive 2 mi. to North Ellison Rd. Turn right and the resort is one mile on the left.

SAN BENITO

Fun 'n' Sun

1400 Zillock Rd., San Benito, 78586. T: (956) 399-5125; F: (956) 399-7725; www.gocampingamerica.com/funnsun; funnsun@acnet.net.

RV: ★★★ Tent: n/a

Beauty: ★★★	Site Privacy: ★★★
Spaciousness: ★★★	Quiet: ★★★
Security: ★★★★	Cleanliness: ★★★★
Insect Control: ★	Facilities: ★★★★

Open to seniors only, Fun 'n' Sun offers activities galore and keeps its extensive facilities in good shape. South Padre Island, Brownsville, and Mexico are easy to reach, as well as a plethora of restaurants and shopping. Though Fun 'n' Sun only accepts reservations for one month or longer, there are eight overnight sites near the front gate. Sites are small and have little privacy. Some are shaded by trees. All have paved, back-in parking. Each site has a little grassy area. Ask for sites 5–8, which are away from Zillock Rd. and quieter. Security is good. The gate is attended 24-hours. Don't visit south Texas in the summer, and be prepared for major crowds in the winter.

Basics

Operated By: Lee & Jan Campbell. **Open:** All year. **Site Assignment:** Reservations for one month or more, $200 nonrefundable deposit, call (800) 399-5127; V, MC, checks, & cash accepted. **Registration:** At office, Mon–Fri., 8 a.m.–5 p.m.; at security building after hours. **Fee:** $24. **Parking:** At site.

Facilities

Number of RV Sites: 1408. **Number of Tent-Only Sites:** 0. **Hookups:** Water, sewer, electric (30, 50 amps), cable TV. **Each Site:** No amenities. **Dump Station:** No. **Laundry:** Yes. **Pay Phone:** Yes. **Rest Rooms and Showers:** Yes. **Fuel:** No. **Propane:** Yes. **Internal Roads:** Paved. **RV Service:** 15 mi. **Market:** 1 mi. **Restaurant:** 2 mi. **General Store:** 3 mi. **Vending:** Yes. **Swimming:** Pool. **Playground:** No. **Other:** Barber & beauty shops, post office, chapel, woodworking shop, music room, meeting rooms, rec hall, dance hall, sewing room, library, lapidary shop, tennis courts, hot tub, silver smithing shop. **Activities:** Dancing, pool, shuffleboard, horseshoes, bocci ball, birding. **Nearby Attractions:** South Padre Island Beaches, Gladys Porter Zoo, Mexico. **Additional Information:** San Benito Chamber of Commerce, (956) 399-5321.

Restrictions

Pets: On leash only. **Fires:** In grills only. **Alcoholic Beverages:** Allowed. **Vehicle Maximum Length:** 40 ft. **Other:** All rates are based on occupancy of 2 people per unit. One person must be at least 55 years old & the other person at least 40 years old.

To Get There

From US 77/83, take the Paso Real/Hwy. 509 exit. Stay on the frontage road 0.25 mi. past Paso Real and turn right on Zillock Rd. The campground is 0.25 mi.

SAN MARCOS

United RV Resort

1610 IH 35 North, San Marcos, 78666. T: (512) 353-5959; F: (512) 353-8271; www.gocampingamerica.com/unitedrv/index.html; united-rv@sanmarcos.net.

RV: ★★★ Tent: ★★★

Beauty: ★★★★	Site Privacy: ★★★
Spaciousness: ★★★	Quiet: ★★★
Security: ★★★	Cleanliness: ★★★
Insect Control: ★★★	Facilities: ★★★

Though clean and pretty, United lacks the recreational facilities found at many of the better parks. Just off of I-35, we recommend United as a convenient stopover or if you plan on spending most of your time outside the park. Restaurants and shopping are nearby. Most of the sites are laid out in rows of pull-throughs. However, we recommend sites in the 40s, 50s, and 60s—shady back-ins along the southern perimeter of the park. Families should consider sites 1–20, which are closer to the pool and playground. Comfortably spaced, most sites enjoy some shade and a little privacy. Parking is on gravel and each site has a long grassy area. When we visited, the suburban park was experiencing a loitering problem, raising questions about security. Visit San Marcos in the summertime if you want to take the kids to nearby Schlitterbahn Water Park.

Basics

Operated By: Ed & Josephine Morrill. **Open:** All year. **Site Assignment:** Reservations accepted (800) 344-9906, credit card number holds site, 24-hour cancellation notice required. Check-in & check-out are at noon. **Registration:** At office. **Fee:** $21.60 per night for 2 people (RV & tent sites w/electricity), $20.70 for tent sites w/water only, $3 per extra person over age 3. **Parking:** 2 places per site, gravel.

Facilities

Number of RV Sites: 100. **Number of Tent-Only Sites:** 5 w/electricity & water, 9 w/water only. **Hookups:** Water, sewer, electric (30, 50 amps), cable (91 sites w/full hookups). **Each Site:** Picnic table, some grills. **Dump Station:** Yes. **Laundry:** Yes. **Pay Phone:** Yes. **Rest Rooms and Showers:** Yes. **Fuel:** No. **Propane:** Yes. **Internal Roads:** Paved. **RV Service:** 14 mi. north in Buda. **Market:** 2 mi. north in San Marcos. **Restaurant:** 0.5 mi. north in San Marcos. **General Store:** At park. **Vending:** Yes. **Swimming:** Pool. **Playground:** Yes. **Other:** Lounge, fax, copier services, cc telephone, clubhouse, pet park, video services. **Activities:** Horseshoes, shuffleboard, Ping-Pong. **Nearby Attractions:** Aquarena Center, Camping World, Wonder World, Schlitterbahn Water Park. **Additional Information:** San Marcos CVB (888) 200-5620.

Restrictions

Pets: On leash at all times. **Fires:** In grills only. **Alcoholic Beverages:** Allowed. **Vehicle Maximum Length:** 70 ft. **Other:** Due to high water pressure, water pressure regulators are recommended.

To Get There

From San Antonio, head north on I-35 toward Austin. Take Exit 206 and stay to the right. Park will be on the right just off the service road.

SMITHVILLE

Buescher State Park

P.O. Box 75, Smithville, 78957-0075. T: (512) 237-2241; F: (512) 237-2580; www.tpwd.state.tx.us.

RV ★★★★★ Tent ★★★★★

Beauty: ★★★★★	Site Privacy: ★★★★★
Spaciousness: ★★★★★	Quiet: ★★★★★
Security: ★★★★	Cleanliness: ★★★★
Insect Control: ★	Facilities: ★★★★★

Part of a complex of state parks, Buescher connects to Bastrop State Park with a 13-mile paved, winding, hilly road that's appreciated by experienced cyclists. Unlike Bastrop, Buescher's facilities surround a small lake (approximately 25 acres) supporting catfish, bass, crappie, perch, and seasonal rainbow trout. The "Lost Pines" of Texas are prominent on the road from Bastrop. Post and live oak steal the show at Buescher. We prefer sites at Buescher over Bastrop because of their gorgeous foliage between sites. But mosquitoes are far worse here—stay at drier Bastrop if it's been raining. Three campgrounds dot the small lake. RV campers find paved, back-in sites at Cozy Circle. With shady oak trees and paved back-in parking, we prefer the multi-use sites at Oak Haven. All sites are spacious. Rural location and locked nighttime gates make security excellent. Plan to visit on weekdays to avoid the mob.

Basics

Operated By: Texas Parks & Wildlife. **Open:** All year. **Site Assignment:** Reservations (512) 389-8900; reservations must be made at least 48 hours in advance; deposit (equivalent to first night's fee) required to hold reservation; cancellations more than two days prior to reservation result in $5 fee, cancellations within two days of reservation result in loss of deposit. **Registration:** Headquarters. **Fee:** $3 per person per day for anyone aged 13 & over, $10 for sites w/water & electric, $7 for sites w/water only (cash, checks, V, MC, D). **Parking:** At most sites.

Facilities

Number of RV Sites: 40. **Number of Tent-Only Sites:** 25 sites w/water only. **Hookups:** Water, electric (30 amps). **Each Site:** Picnic table, grill, fire ring. **Dump Station:** Yes. **Laundry:** No. **Pay Phone:** Yes. **Rest Rooms and Showers:** Yes. **Fuel:** No. **Propane:** No. **Internal Roads:** Paved. **RV Service:** 45 mi. west in Austin. **Market:** 1 mi. southwest in Smithville. **Restaurant:** 1 mi. southwest in Smithville. **General Store:** 1 mi. southwest in Smithville. **Vending:** Beverages only. **Swimming:** No. **Playground:** Yes. **Other:** Picnic area, group picnic pavilion, rec hall, gift shop, screened shelters. **Activities:** Hiking, boating, fishing, lake swimming, road biking. **Nearby Attractions:** Lake Bastrop, Bastrop State Park, Lake Somerville State Park & Trailway, towns of Smithville & Bastrop, Texas state capitol Austin. **Additional Information:** Austin CVB (800) 926-2282, Smithville Chamber, (512) 237-2313; Bastrop Chamber, (512) 321-2419.

Restrictions

Pets: On leash only. **Fires:** In fire ring only. **Alcoholic Beverages:** Prohibited. **Vehicle Maximum Length:** 50 ft.

To Get There

From Smithville, go northwest on TX 71 for 2 mi. Turn right on FM 153 and go north for 0.5 mi. to Park Rd. 1.

SNYDER

Wagon Wheel Dude Ranch

5996 CR 2128, Snyder, 79549. T: (915) 573-2348; F: (915) 573-5277; www.wagonwheel.com; wagonwr @snydertex.com.

RV ★★★★ Tent ★★★★

Beauty: ★★★★	Site Privacy: ★★★
Spaciousness: ★★★★	Quiet: ★★★★
Security: ★★★	Cleanliness: ★★★★
Insect Control: ★★★★	Facilities: ★★★★★

Wagon Wheel is an excellent destination for families with energetic children. In addition to planned recreation, kids love to run around and explore the ranch. If your group is big enough (10 or more people), you can schedule a chuck wagon meal. The campground includes old and new sections, though sites at both are basically the same. Both offer pull-throughs with gravel parking and a patchy grass and dirt area. Sites are large, some a long as 90 feet. With few trees and scrubby foliage, there is little shade or privacy at the campground. Families should pick a site close to the bathrooms. Tent campers should head for the more picturesque area near the pond (no hookups). Extremely remote, security is not a problem at Wagon Wheel. The panhandle plains sometimes experience extreme weather and should be avoided during winter and late summer.

Basics

Operated By: Billy Ray & Pam Browning. **Open:** All year. **Site Assignment:** Reservations recommended, credit card deposit, one week cancellation notice required, check-in at 3 p.m., check-out at noon. **Registration:** At office. **Fee:** $19.50 for 50-amp site, $16.50 for 30-amp site, $10 for tent. **Parking:** At site.

Facilities

Number of RV Sites: 25. **Number of Tent-Only Sites:** Tenting allowed near pond or near electricity hookups. **Hookups:** Water, sewer, electric (30, 50 amps). **Each Site:** Picnic table. **Dump Station:** Yes. **Laundry:** Yes. **Pay Phone:** Yes. **Rest Rooms and Showers:** Yes. **Fuel:** No. **Propane:** No. **Internal Roads:** Gravel. **RV Service:** 8 mi. east in Snyder. **Market:** 8 mi. east in Snyder. **Restaurant:** On site. **General Store:** 8 mi. east in Snyder. **Vending:** Beverages. **Swimming:** Pool. **Playground:** Yes. **Other:** Horseback riding lessons, trail rides, paddle-boats, pleasure trails, game room, party barn. **Activities:** Washer pitching, horseshoes, softball, horseback riding, fishing, basketball, hiking, skeet shooting, quail & dove hunting. **Nearby Attractions:** Buffalo Gap Historic Village, Scurry County Museum, Abilene Zoo, Grace Museum, Dyess Air Force Base. **Additional Information:** Snyder Chamber of Commerce, (915) 573-3558; City of Snyder (915) 573-4957.

Restrictions

Pets: On leash only. **Fires:** In fire ring only. **Alcoholic Beverages:** Allowed. **Vehicle Maximum Length:** 50 ft.

To Get There

From Lubbock, take the Post Exit (US 84) off of Loop 289. Continue southeast toward Snyder. 37 mi. past the town of Post, turn left on CR 2128. Go 3 mi. to ranch; entrance on the left.

SOMERVILLE

Lake Somerville State Park and Trailway

Rte. 1 Box 499, Somerville, 77879-9713. T: (979) 535-7763; F: (979) 535-7718; www.tpwd.state.tx.us.

RV ★★★★★ Tent ★★★★★

Beauty: ★★★★★ Site Privacy: ★★★★★
Spaciousness: ★★★★★ Quiet: ★★★★★
Security: ★★★★ Cleanliness: ★★★★★
Insect Control: ★ Facilities: ★★★

Comprising over 8,700 acres, gorgeous Lake Somerville consists of three units: Nails Creek, Birch Creek, and the Somerville Wildlife Management Area (a public hunting area). Nails Creek and Birch Creek are connected by a 13-mile multi-use trail known for its spring wildflowers. Both Nails Creek and Birch Creek have lovely campgrounds with spacious sites. Exceptional privacy is provided by dense trees, including post oak, hickory, blackjack oak, and others. Each site has paved back-in parking and a large grassy area. Birch Creek is popular with college students. Families and couples prefer quieter Nails Creek. At Nails Creek, there are gorgeous lakefront sites in the Cedar Creek Loop. At Birch Creek, the prettiest views are at the Cedar Elm camping area (no hookups). Security is fair—there are no gates, but both campgrounds are extremely remote. Mosquitoes proliferate when it's rainy, so come prepared. For optimal weather, visit in spring or fall.

BASICS

Operated By: Texas Parks & Wildlife. **Open:** All year. **Site Assignment:** Reservations (512) 389-8900; reservations must be made at least 48 hours in advance; deposit (equivalent to first night's fee) required to hold reservation; cancellations more than two days prior to reservation result in $5 fee, cancellations within two days of reservation result in loss of deposit. **Registration:** Headquarters. **Fee:** $2 per person per day for everyone aged 13 & older, $12 for equestrian sites, $9 for sites w/water & electricity, $8 for sites w/water only. **Parking:** At site.

FACILITIES

Number of RV Sites: 40 sites w/water & electricity. **Number of Tent-Only Sites:** 10. **Hookups:** Water, electric (30, 50 amps). **Each Site:** Picnic table, fire ring, lantern post, tent pad. **Dump Station:** Yes. **Laundry:** No. **Pay Phone:** Yes. **Rest Rooms and Showers:** Yes. **Fuel:** No. **Propane:** No. **Internal Roads:** Paved. **RV Service:** 20 mi. west in Giddings. **Market:** 12 mi. south in Burton. **Restaurant:** 3 mi. west of park. **General Store:** 12 mi. south in Burton. **Vending:** Beverages only. **Swimming:** No. **Playground:** No. **Other:** Birch Creek Unit: equestrian camping, group picnic pavilions, group camping, group dining hall, fish cleaning shelter, boat ramps, boat dock, volleyball courts, gift shop. Nails Creek Unit: group picnic area, equestrian camping, fish cleaning shelter, boat ramp, volleyball courts, gift shop. **Activities:** Picnicking, boating, fishing, swimming, hiking, backpacking, bicycling, mountain biking, horseback riding, volleyball, group tours available. **Nearby Attractions:** Bluebell Creamery, Presidential Corridor between Austin & College Station, Bastrop & Buescher State Parks, Stephen F. Austin & Washington-on-the-Brazos State Historical Parks, Austin (about 85 mi.), College Station (about 60 mi.). **Additional Information:** Austin Convention & Visitor's Bureau (800) 926-2282, Bryan-College Station CVB, (800) 777-8292.

RESTRICTIONS

Pets: On leash only. **Fires:** In fire rings only. **Alcoholic Beverages:** Prohibited. **Vehicle Maximum Length:** 50 ft.

TO GET THERE

To access Birch Creek Unit from Somerville, drive north on State Hwy. 36 for 4 mi. to the town of Lyons. Then drive west on State Hwy. 60 for 8 mi. and turn left onto Park Rd. 57. To get to Nails Creek Unit from Giddings, head east on TX 290 for 6 mi. Turn left on FM 180 and follow it for 15 mi.

SPRING BRANCH

Guadalupe River State Park

3350 Park Rd. 31, Spring Branch 78070. T: (830) 438-2656 or (800) 792-1112; F: (830) 438-2229; www.tpwd.state.tx.us.

RV ★★★★★ Tent ★★★★★

Beauty: ★★★★★ Site Privacy: ★★★★
Spaciousness: ★★★★★ Quiet: ★★★★★
Security: ★★★★★ Cleanliness: ★★★★
Insect Control: ★ Facilities: ★★★

Three campgrounds nestle into a bend in the Guadalupe River. For tent campers only, Cedar Sage Camping area has water at each site and paved back-in parking spaces. Sites 33–37 are the roomiest, and families with children should ask for sites 24 or 26, which flank the playground. Turkey Sink camping area contains spacious sites with paved back-in parking for RVs. The Guadalupe is lined with bald cypress and limestone bluffs. A variety of hardwoods provide shade and privacy for campers. Birdwatchers look for golden-cheeked warblers who nest in the park's virgin ashe juniper woodlands. Adjacent Honey Creek State Natural Area is home to live-oak grassland, a vanishing Central Texas ecosystem (access by guided tour only). Security is excellent here, with gates that lock at 10 p.m. Only 30 miles from San Antonio, this park is an excellent, quick getaway for city folk. Plan a visit during mild spring or autumn.

BASICS

Operated By: Texas Parks & Wildlife. **Open:** All year. **Site Assignment:** Reservations (512) 389-8900, reservations must be made at least 48 hours in advance, deposit required (equivalent to first night's fee) to hold reservation, cancellations more than two days prior to reservation result in $5 fee, cancellations within two days of reservation result in loss of deposit. **Registration:** Headquarters. **Fee:** $3 per person per day for anyone aged 13 & older, $15 for sites w/water & electric, $12 for water-only or walk-in primitive camping, $4 excess vehicle charge (cash, checks, D, V, MC). **Parking:** At most sites.

FACILITIES

Number of RV Sites: 48. **Number of Tent-Only Sites:** 20 primitive walk-in sites. **Hookups:** Water, electric. **Each Site:** Picnic table, fire ring, 16-ft. × 16-ft. tent pad. **Dump Station:** Yes. **Laundry:** No. **Pay Phone:** Yes. **Rest Rooms and Showers:** Yes. **Fuel:** No. **Propane:** No. **Internal Roads:** Paved. **RV Service:** 13 mi. west in Boerne. **Market:** 7 mi. east in Bulverde. **Restaurant:** 7 mi. east in Bulverde. **General Store:** 3 mi. west in Bergheim. **Vending:** Beverages. **Swimming:** No. **Playground:** Yes. **Other:** Interpretive Center, gift shop, amphitheater. **Activities:** Canoeing, tubing, fishing, swimming, picnicking, hiking. **Nearby Attractions:** Honey Creek State Natural Area, Blanco State Park, San Antonio, Boerne, New Braunfels, & San Marcos attractions. **Additional Information:** San Antonio CVB (210) 270-8700, Boerne Convention & Visitor's Bureau (800) 842-8080, New Braunfels Convention & Visitor's Bureau (800) 572-2626, San Marcos Convention & Visitor's Bureau (888) 200-5620.

RESTRICTIONS

Pets: Leash Only. **Fires:** In fire rings only. **Alcoholic Beverages:** Prohibited. **Vehicle Maximum Length:** 58 ft. **Other:** Max. 8 people per campsite, Quiet time 10 p.m.–6 a.m., fourteen day stay limit, gathering of firewood prohibited.

TO GET THERE

From I-10 (Boerne), drive east on TX 46 for 13 mi., and then turn left on Park Rd. 31. From San Antonio, drive North on US 281, and then turn left on TX 46. Drive west on TX 46 for 8 mi., and then turn right on Park Rd. 31. The park entrance is at the north end of Park Rd. 31.

SULPHER SPRINGS

Cooper Lake State Park (South Sulpher Unit)

Rte. 3 Box 741, Sulpher Springs 75482. T: (512) 389-8900 or (800) 792-1112; F: (512) 389-8959; www.tpwd.state.tx.us; e-mail.reservations@ tpwd.state.tx.us.

RV ★★★★ Tent ★★★★★

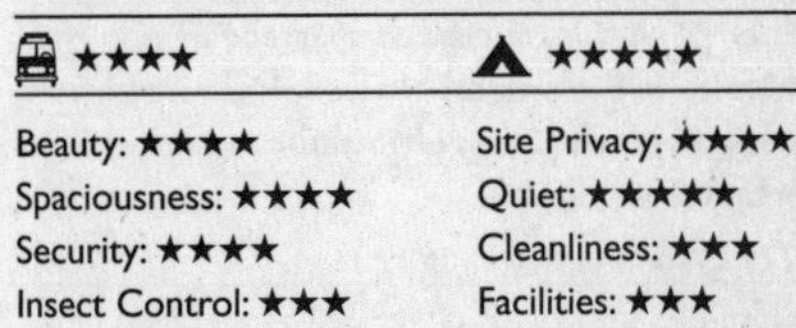

Beauty: ★★★★ Site Privacy: ★★★★
Spaciousness: ★★★★ Quiet: ★★★★★
Security: ★★★★ Cleanliness: ★★★
Insect Control: ★★★ Facilities: ★★★

This state park is divided up into four camping areas, several day-use areas, and a screened shelter and cabin area on the water's edge. RV campers will be mostly concerned with the Bright Star and Deer Haven camping areas, unless they wish to bring a horse to the Buggy Whip equestrian area. All sites are grassy and forested, although often the trees that encircle the sites do not shade them. The Bright Star area is laid out in a loop, with sites on the inside being more open to the sun. (A shaded picnic table at these sites helps reduce exposure.) Site 2 is well-shaded, but close to a dumpster. Also very well-shaded are 12–15 (which back to the lake) and 19. Of these, 14 and 15 are 110-foot pull-throughs. Nominally part of the Deer Haven area, sites 47–58 and 78–87 are located along the internal road, and are for this reason less desirable than those closer to the water and off the beaten path. Even-numbered sites 62–66, which back to the water, are the best sites in this area for their superior shade. The Oak Grove area provides walk-in tenting sites on a dirt (not grass) floor. The best sites are 92 and 94–101, which are right on the water; the least desirable is 88, right by the entrance to Oak Grove. For those campers with horses, Buggy Whip offers back-in sites as spokes around a looped road. Each site has a trailhead that leads to horse trails. More than nearly any other campground, this park offers a huge selection of activities, and everyone should enjoy their stay enough to return year after year.

Basics

Operated By: Texas Parks & Wildlife. **Open:** All year. **Site Assignment:** First come, first served. (Credit card required to make a reservation. $3 reservation service fee; $5 cancellation fee.). **Registration:** In office. (Late arrivals use drop box at entrance.). **Fee:** Water, electric: $12, water: $8, plus $3 entrance fee per person (V, MC, D accepted in the office or for reservation.). **Parking:** At site, additional parking for walk-ins.

Facilities

Number of RV Sites: 102. **Number of Tent-Only Sites:** 15. **Hookups:** Water, electric (30 amps). **Each Site:** Picnic table, grill, fire pit, lantern post. **Dump Station:** Yes. **Laundry:** No. **Pay Phone:** Yes. **Rest Rooms and Showers:** Yes. **Fuel:** No. **Propane:** No. **Internal Roads:** Paved. **RV Service:** No. **Market:** 12 mi. to Sulpher Springs. **Restaurant:** 12 mi. to Sulpher Springs. **General Store:** No. **Vending:** Yes. **Swimming:** Lake. **Playground:** Yes. **Other:** Boat ramp, fish cleaning station, pavillion, cabins, shelters, firewood. **Activities:** Swimming, boating, fishing, hiking, mountain biking. **Nearby Attractions:** Sam Bell Maxey Historical State Park, Bonham State Park, Lake Bob S&lin State Park. **Additional Information:** South Sulpher Unit Office: (903) 945-5256.

Restrictions

Pets: On 6-ft. leash, cleaned up after. **Fires:** In grills. **Alcoholic Beverages:** None. **Vehicle Maximum Length:** None. **Other:** All visitors must pay $3 entrance fee per day.

To Get There

From the junction of Hwy. 19/154 and Hwy. 71, go 4.25 mi. west on Hwy. 71. Turn north onto FM 3505 and go 1.5 mi. to the entrance.

VALLEY VIEW

Ray Roberts State Park (Johnson Branch Unit)

100 PW 4153, Valley View 76272. T: (512) 389-8900 or (800) 792-1112; F: (512) 389-8959; www.tpwd.state.tx.us; e-mail.reservations@tpwd.state.tx.us.

RV ★★★★ Tent ★★★★

Beauty: ★★★★	Site Privacy: ★★★★
Spaciousness: ★★★★	Quiet: ★★★★★
Security: ★★★★	Cleanliness: ★★★★★
Insect Control: ★★★	Facilities: ★★★

This park is divided into four camping areas. The Dogwood Canyon area is the first campground inside the entrance. It is furthest from the water, and also the most primitive, suitabale for tents but not RVs. (Sites are walk-ins.) The rest rooms have non-flush toilets. Oak Point is likewise a walk-in area suitable for tenting. Sites are open and grassy with great views of the lake. There is a small flush toilet but no showers. The Juniper Cove area is the very antithesis of Dogwood Canyon—some of its sites are right up by the water's edge (7–14), and the rest rooms are very clean and modern, with flush toilets and hot showers. These sites are 40-foot back-ins separated from the water by a row of wild bushes (except for 11–13, which are right on the water). Much less "natural" (and bordering on the ugly) are sites 1–6, 25, and 36–39, which are very open sites located on the blacktop. (Sites 5, 6, 36, 37 are pull-throughs.) While these may appeal to certain campers, they definitely miss the point of coming to such a beautiful lake. In the Walnut area, most sites are open to the sun, but sites 57 and 73 have exceptional shade. Sites 45, 49–52, and 55 have views of the water, while 41–44 and 87–89 are open blacktop sites like those described above. The rest rooms are clean and modern, like those in Juniper Cove. This campground is a delightful destination for anyone who enjoys water activities or just going "wild" for a while.

Basics

Operated By: Texas Parks & Wildlife. **Open:** All year. **Site Assignment:** First come, first served. (Credit card required to make a reservation. $3 reservation service fee; $5 cancellation fee.). **Registration:** In office. (Late arrivals use drop box at entrance.). **Fee:** Water, electric: $12, water (walk-in): $9, primitive (walk-in): $6, all add $3 entrance fee (V, MC, D accepted in the office or for reservation.). **Parking:** At site.

Facilities

Number of RV Sites: 104. **Number of Tent-Only Sites:** 83. **Hookups:** Water, electric (30 amps). **Each Site:** Picnic table, grill, fire pit, lantern post. **Dump Station:** Yes. **Laundry:** No. **Pay Phone:** Yes. **Rest Rooms and Showers:** Yes. **Fuel:** No. **Propane:** No. **Internal Roads:** Paved. **RV Service:** No. **Market:** 7 mi. to Valley View. **Restaurant:** 7 mi. to Valley View. **General Store:** Yes. **Vending:** Yes. **Playground:** Yes. **Other:** Pavillion, fish cleaning station, boat ramp. **Activities:** Swimming, boating, fishing, hiking, mountain biking. **Nearby Attractions:** Eisenhower State Park, Tioga, Frank Buck Zoo, Morton Museum. **Additional Information:** Johnson Branch Unit Office: (940) 637-2294.

Restrictions

Pets: On 6-ft. leash, cleaned up after. **Fires:** In grills. **Alcoholic Beverages:** None. **Vehicle Maximum Length:** None. **Other:** All visitors must pay $3 entrance fee per day.

To Get There

From I-35, take Exit 483 and go 6.5 mi. east on FM 3002. Turn right at the sign into the entrance.

VANDERPOOL

Lost Maples State Natural Area

HCR 1 Box 156, V&erpool 78885. T: (830) 966-3413; www.tpwd.state.tx.us.

RV ★★★★ Tent ★★★★

Beauty: ★★★★★	Site Privacy: ★★★
Spaciousness: ★★★★	Quiet: ★★★★
Security: ★★★★★	Cleanliness: ★★★★★
Insect Control: ★★	Facilities: ★★★

Famed for its isolated stand of Uvalde bigtooth maples, this natural area is popular with autumn "leaf peepers." However, the trees include other showy species such as sumac, and complement the area's striking granite outcroppings year-round. Built in a valley, the small campground offers exceptionally lovely views. The campsites are contained in one area and offer paved, back-in parking. Sites are decent-sized, with a little shade at most. Those without many trees benefit from the shaded picnic table found at each site. Few sites are very private. The most secluded are 17 and 18—we recommend these for tent campers and small RVs. Security at Lost Maples is fine. The park is so remote that gates are unnecessary. If you must visit in the fall, plan your trip for a weekday and make advance reservations. Ticks can proliferate here, so examine your hair and clothes regularly.

Basics

Operated By: Texas Parks & Wildlife. **Open:** All year. **Site Assignment:** Inquire at campground. **Registration:** Headquarters. **Fee:** $14 for sites w/water & electric, $5 per person day use fee. **Parking:** At site except primitive.

Facilities

Number of RV Sites: 30. **Number of Tent-Only Sites:** None. **Hookups:** Water, electric. **Each Site:** Shaded picnic table. **Dump Station:** Yes. **Laundry:** No. **Pay Phone:** Yes. **Rest Rooms and Showers:** Yes. **Fuel:** No. **Propane:** No. **Internal Roads:** Paved. **RV Service:** 48 mi. northeast in Kerrville. **Market:** 4 mi. south in V&erpool. **Restaurant:** 15 mi. south in Utopia. **General Store:** 15 mi. south in Utopia. **Vending:** No. **Swimming:** No. **Playground:** No. **Other:** Picnic sites, scenic drive, gift shop. **Activities:** Hiking, nature trail. **Nearby Attractions:** Garner & Kerrville-Schreiner State Parks, Hill Country State Natural Area, Frontier Times Museum, rodeos in B&era. **Additional Information:** B&era CVB (800) 364-3833.

Restrictions

Pets: Leash only. **Fires:** Fire rings only. **Alcoholic Beverages:** Not allowed. **Vehicle Maximum Length:** 50 ft. **Other:** Campfires not allowed in primitive sites.

To Get There

From Vanderpool, drive 5 mi. north on Ranch Rd. 187. The park is on the left.

WHITNEY

Lake Whitney State Park

P.O. Box 1175, Whitney, 76692. T: (254) 694-3793; F: (254) 694-6934; www.tpwd.state.tx.us.

RV ★★★ Tent ★★★

Beauty: ★★ Site Privacy: ★★★
Spaciousness: ★★★ Quiet: ★★★
Security: ★★★ Cleanliness: ★★★
Insect Control: ★★★★ Facilities: ★★★

If you don't mind the crowds, visit in the spring, when over 40 species of wildflowers bloom. The rest of the year, this is one of the least attractive state parks in Texas. The park is in a rural area, but the town of Whitney is visible from the campgrounds. Even so, the park stays busy Mar. through Oct. due to its unique offerings, including an airstrip. There are three types of campsites in a number of separate areas. No sites with full hookups have water views. We recommend the water/electric areas, which contain a number of waterfront sites. Sites are spacious and parking is paved. There are both back-in and pull-through sites. Waterfront pull-throughs 124–130 are the nicest. With very few trees in the campgrounds, snag a site with a shade shelter. Tent campers have no trouble finding a waterfront site. Security is good, with locked gates at night.

Basics

Operated By: Texas Parks & Wildlife. **Open:** All year. **Site Assignment:** Reservations (512) 389-8900, reservations must be made at least 48 hours in advance, deposit required (equivalent to first night's fee) to hold reservation, cancellations more than two days prior to reservation result in $5 fee, cancellations within two days of reservation result in loss of deposit. **Registration:** Headquarters. **Fee:** $2 per person per day for anyone aged 13 & older, $20 for sites w/full hookups & shade shelters, $13 for sites w/full hookups, $12 for sites w/water & electricity, $8 for sites w/water only (cash, checks, D,V, MC). **Parking:** At site.

Facilities

Number of RV Sites: 24 w/full hookups, 42 w/electricity & water only. **Number of Tent-Only Sites:** 71. **Hookups:** Water, sewer, electric (30 amps). **Each Site:** Fire ring, stand-up grill, some picnic tables & shade shelters. **Dump Station:** Yes. **Laundry:** No. **Pay Phone:** Yes. **Rest Rooms and Showers:** Yes. **Fuel:** No. **Propane:** No. **Internal Roads:** Paved. **RV Service:** 30 mi. north in Cleburne. **Market:** 4 mi. east in Whitney. **Restaurant:** 4 mi. east in Whitney. **General Store:** 4 mi. east in Whitney. **Vending:** Beverages, ice, & wood. **Swimming:** No. **Playground:** Yes. **Other:** Airstrip, 21 screened shelters. **Activities:** Hiking, picnicking, boating, fishing, swimming, scuba diving, waterskiing, nature study, birding, & limited mountain biking. **Nearby Attractions:** Cleburne, Meridian, Dinosaur Valley, & Mother Neff State Parks, The Confederate Museum, Texas Ranger Hall of Fame, Fossil Rim Exotic Wildlife Ranch. **Additional Information:** Lake Whitney Chamber of Commerce, (254) 694-2540.

Restrictions

Pets: Must be on leash at all times, must have proof of current shots, not allowed in swimming area. **Fires:** Allowed in fire rings only. **Alcoholic Beverages:** Not allowed. **Vehicle Maximum Length:** 100 ft.

To Get There

From I-35, take the Hillsboro exit. In Hillsboro take TX 22 west approximately 15 mi. to Whitney. At the first traffic light, turn right on TX 933 and drive 0.5 mile to FM 1244. Turn left and the park is in 3 mi.

ZAVALLA

Angelina National Forest, Boykin Springs and Sandy Creek Recreation Areas

Rte. 2 Box 242, Zavalla 75980. T: (936) 897-1068; F: (936) 897-3406; www.southernregion.fs.fed.us/texas.

RV ★★★★★ Tent ★★★★★

Beauty: ★★★★★ Site Privacy: ★★★★★
Spaciousness: ★★★★★ Quiet: ★★★★★
Security: ★★★★ Cleanliness: ★★★★
Insect Control: ★★★ Facilities: ★★★★

About 150,000 acres of national forest flank the Sam Reyburn Reservoir, with incredibly inexpensive camping areas. Boykin Springs, near man-made Boykin Lake, is the largest. Sandy Creek, a smaller camping area, contains sites with water views. The untidy campground host sites were disappointing. Sites at both campgrounds are beautiful and fairly similar, though Boykin's are often more private. The woods are lovely and provide shade at both campgrounds. Most sites are back-ins with gravel parking. Site size varies at both. At Sandy Creek, try to score site 10 (private and heavily wooded, with a lake view). At Boykin, head for sites 12, 14, and 15, bordering picturesque Boykin Creek. Security is good at Angelina National Forest owing to campground remoteness. Boykin Springs stays busy on spring and summer weekends—visit in autumn or during the week. Sandy Creek is less popular and may be visited on all but the busiest holiday weekends.

Basics

Operated By: USDA Forest Service. **Open:** All year. **Site Assignment:** First come, first served; no reservations. **Registration:** Pay station, self-registration. **Fee:** $6 for 8 people (cash, checks). **Parking:** At site (2 vehicles).

Facilities

Number of RV Sites: 48. **Number of Tent-Only Sites:** 4 (Boykin Springs). **Hookups:** None (water available). **Each Site:** Picnic table, fire ring &/or grill, tent pad. **Dump Station:** yes (at Caney Creek). **Laundry:** No. **Pay Phone:** No. **Rest Rooms and Showers:** Yes (cold only at S&y Creek). **Fuel:** No. **Propane:** No. **Internal Roads:** Paved. **RV Service:** 20 mi. in Jasper. **Market:** 20 mi. in Jasper. **Restaurant:** 20 mi. in Jasper. **General Store:** 20 mi. in Jasper. **Vending:** No. **Swimming:** No. **Playground:** No. **Other:** Sheltered picnic areas, boat launches. **Activities:** Fishing, hunting, swimming beaches (no lifeguard), horse trails, hiking, backpacking, mountain biking, canoeing, kayaking, bird-watching. **Nearby Attractions:** Jasper "Bass Fishing Capitol of the World," Museum of East Texas, Texas Forestry Museum, Millards Crossing historic Nacogdoches, antiques & flea markets, Sabine National Forest, Martin Dies Junior State Park. **Additional Information:** Lufkin/Angelina County chamber of Commerce, (936) 634-6644.

Restrictions

Pets: On leash only, must be kept quiet, not allowed on beaches. **Fires:** Allowed, fire rings, grills only. **Alcoholic Beverages:** Allowed, at sites. **Vehicle Maximum Length:** 24 ft. (sites vary). **Other:** No generators 10 p.m.–7 a.m.

To Get There

From Zavalla, drive east on State Hwy. 63. To get to Boykin Springs, drive 11 mi. and turn right (south) on Forest Service Rd. 313. Drive 2.5 mi. To get to Sandy Creek, drive 17.5 mi. and turn left (north) on Forest Service Rd. 333. Drive 3 mi.

Utah

Utah is a land of high deserts, sagebrush, mountains, mesas, canyons, weathered red-orange Navajo sandstone formations, ancient Native American rock art and ruins, internationally famous national parks, lesser-known but no less interesting state parks, Olympic ski slopes, river rafting, and enough lakes and reservoirs to make boating and fishing part of the campground experience. Southeast Utah is one of the more popular destinations, being home to **Monument Valley, Natural Bridges** and **Hovenweep National Monuments, Arches** and **Canyonlands National Parks,** the **Halls Crossing** and **Bullfrog Marina** portions of **Lake Powell,** and river rafting on the **Colorado, San Juan,** and **Green Rivers.**

River rafting, mountain biking, backpacking, and four-wheel drive and jeep explorations are popular ways of getting beyond the campground for better views of the desert washes, slickrock benches, canyons, flattop mesas, buttes, eroded spires, hoodoos, entrenched meanders, and balanced rocks beyond pavement's end. Indeed, campgrounds barely scratch the surface of **Grand-Staircase Escalante National Monument's** 1.7 million acres. But make adequate preparations and take sensible precautions, as this is a land of summer flash floods, rattlesnakes, and long distances between gas stations and fresh water.

Zion and **Bryce Canyon National Parks** in southwestern Utah are among the most popular national parks in the United States, though the red sandstone monoliths and pioneer fruit orchards of **Capitol Reef** are also spectacular. Don't overlook the sometimes spectacular scenery of lesser-known campgrounds like **Cedar Breaks National Monument,** which is like a smaller, higher-elevation version of Bryce Canyon's multi-colored sandstone amphitheaters. Similarly, little-known **Kodachrome Basin, Coral Pink Sand Dunes,** and **Goblin Valley State Parks** are among the many geologically spectacular Utah State Park camping experiences.

Utah's many lakes and reservoirs are popular with locals for boating and fishing, and summer and holiday weekends fill to capacity. But weekdays and before Memorial Day and after Labor Day it is often possible to find some solitude. Near Salt Lake City are many campground escapes, including **Antelope Island State Park** in the middle of the Great Salt Lake and **Wasatch Mountain State Park** closer to the Olympic winter sports venues. Call ahead to the parks and get reservations where available or plan to arrive early ahead of the crowds. Also, take advantage of the many excellent commercial campgrounds just outside the park boundaries.

The following facilities accept payment in checks or cash only:

- Antelope Island State Park, Syracuse
- Bullfrog Resort & Marina Campground/RV Park, Lake Powell
- Calf Creek Campground, Escalante
- Cedar Canyon Campground, Cedar City
- Dead Horse Point State Park, Moab
- Devil's Canyon, Blanding
- Devil's Garden Campground, Arches National Park
- Duck Creek Campground, Cedar City
- Escalante State Park, Escalante
- Fruita Campground, Torrey
- Goosenecks State Park, Mexican Hat
- Green River State Park, Green River
- Halls Crossing RV Park/Campground, Lake Powell
- Hovenweep Campground, Hovenweep National Monument
- Kodachrome Basin State Park, Cannonville
- Minersville State Park, Beaver
- Mitten View Campground, Monument Valley
- Natural Bridges, Natural Bridges National Monument
- North Campground, Bryce Canyon
- Oasis Campground, Yuba State Park
- Point Supreme Campground, Cedar Breaks National Monument
- Ponderosa Grove Recreation Site, Kanab
- Quail Creek State Park, St. George
- Red Canyon Campground, Bryce Canyon
- Red Cliffs Recreation Site, Leeds
- Rendezvous Beach, Bear Lake State Park
- Snow Canyon State Park, St. George
- South & Watchman Campgrounds, Zion National Park
- Squaw Flat Campground, Canyonlands National Park Needles District
- Sunset Campground, Bryce Canyon
- Virgin River Canyon Recreation Area, Littlefield
- Virgin River Canyon Recreation Area, Littlefield
- White Bridge Campground, Panguitch Lake
- Willow Flat Campground, Canyonlands National Park Island in the Sky District

The following facilities feature 50 sites or fewer:

Calf Creek Campground, Escalante
Cedar Canyon Campground, Cedar City
Goosenecks State Park, Mexican Hat
Natural Bridges, Natural Bridges National Monument
Oasis Campground, Yuba State Park
Ponderosa Grove Recreation Site, Kanab
Red Cliffs Recreation Site, Leeds
Willow Flat Campground, Canyonlands National Park Island in the Sky District

Campground Profiles

ARCHES NATIONAL PARK

Devil's Garden Campground

P.O. Box 907, Moab 84532. T: (435) 719-2299; www.nps.gov/arch.

RV ★★★★ Tent ★★★★★

Beauty: ★★★★★ Site Privacy: ★★★★★
Spaciousness: ★★★★ Quiet: ★★★★
Security: ★★★★ Cleanliness: ★★★★★
Insect Control: ★★★ Facilities: ★★

Arches National Park, where disabled Civil War veteran John Wesley Wolfe and son Fred once lived a solitary log-cabin life, grazing cattle and sheep, now gets a million visitors a year. But Devil's Garden is like paradise to self-sufficient campers eschewing the showers, shops, and amenities of Moab to show up early in the morning and snag a campsite among the sandstone fins and balanced rocks. Park parking spaces become maddeningly scarce on busy holiday weekends, but campground denizens have solar powered restrooms and their own trailheads to Broken Arch and Sand Dune Arch. Many campsites have 50-foot-long pads, though most are 12-foot-wide back-ins (some 25-foot-long sites are 20-feet wide) tucked in amongst Navajo sandstone formations and flanked with junipers, pines, and desert scrub. This is as close as it gets outside the backcountry to having a private vista of this 2,000-arch park.

BASICS

Operated By: National Park Service. **Open:** All year. **Site Assignment:** First come, first served; group site reservations. **Registration:** Self-pay fee station. **Fee:** $10 (cash or check only). **Parking:** At site.

FACILITIES

Number of RV Sites: 50. **Number of Tent-Only Sites:** 0. **Hookups:** None. **Each Site:** Table, grill. **Dump Station:** No. **Laundry:** No. **Pay Phone:** Yes. **Rest Rooms and Showers:** No showers. **Fuel:** No. **Propane:** No. **Internal Roads:** Paved, good. **RV Service:** No. **Market:** Moab, 23 mi. **Restaurant:** Moab, 23 mi. **General Store:** No. **Vending:** No. **Swimming:** No. **Playground:** No. **Other:** Amphitheater, 1 wheelchair-accessible site. **Activities:** Evening ranger programs. **Nearby Attractions:** Canyonlands, Moab. **Additional Information:** Canyonlands Natural History Assoc., (435) 259-6003, www.cnha.org; Grand County Travel Council, (800) 635-MOAB.

RESTRICTIONS

Pets: On leash under owner's control. **Fires:** Yes (in grills only, no collecting firewood). **Alcoholic Beverages:** Allowed. **Vehicle Maximum Length:** 50 ft. **Other:** 7-day max. stay, no feeding wildlife.

TO GET THERE

From Moab go 5 mi. north on US Hwy. 191, then follow park entrance road 18 mi. north.

BEAR LAKE STATE PARK

Rendezvous Beach

P.O. Box 184, Garden City 84028. T: (435) 946-3343 or (800) 322-3770 (reservations); www.nr.state.ut.us/www1/bear.htm; nrdpr.brsp@state.ut.us.

RV ★★★★★ Tent ★★★★

Beauty: ★★★★ Site Privacy: ★★★★
Spaciousness: ★★★★ Quiet: ★★★★
Security: ★★★★ Cleanliness: ★★★★
Insect Control: ★★★ Facilities: ★★★

A 28,000 year old earthquake-created freshwater lake with warm summer waters (60–70° F June–July) and 120 miles of groomed snowmobile trails in winter, Bear Lake is ringed with camping sites (mostly primitive) on both the Utah and Idaho sides. But Rendezvous Beach contains the best collection of developed campgrounds. Odd-numbered (except 29) Willow Campground tent sites are beachfront, and even-numbered sites are in deep vegetation on the opposite side of what is essentially a paved vehicle parking lot. Cottonwood Campground tent sites 5–42 are beachfront. Birch Campground has 60 50-amp sites, with 16, 18, 27, 28, 30, 38, 39, 48, 49, and 51 being the beachfront best. At Big Creek, an older (20, 30 amp) RV campground, sites 15–33 and 35–38 are beachfront. RV sites are quieter than tent sites, which get group party action on weekends and holidays, when those without reservations get shunted to more primitive and rockier East Side beaches (only South Eden has drinking water: 14 reservable sites; $7).

BASICS

Operated By: Utah State Parks & Recreation. **Open:** All year (no water or sewer after Nov., but electricity on in winter). **Site Assignment:** First come, first served; reservations recommended Mem. Day to Labor Day. **Registration:** Entrance kiosk (rangers collect fees in winter). **Fee:** $15 tent; $19 RV ($6.25 reservation fee). **Parking:** At site.

FACILITIES

Number of RV Sites: 106. **Number of Tent-Only Sites:** 75. **Hookups:** Electric (20, 30, 50 amp), water, sewer. **Each Site:** Table, fire ring. **Dump Station:** Yes. **Laundry:** No. **Pay Phone:** Yes. **Rest Rooms and Showers:** Yes. **Fuel:** No. **Propane:** No. **Internal Roads:** Paved, excellent. **RV Service:** No. **Market:** Logan, 50 mi. **Restaurant:** Garden City, 6 mi. **General Store:** No. **Vending:** Yes. **Swimming:** Lake. **Playground:** No. **Other:** Birch sites have sheltered table on cement pad, marina, boat & slip rentals. **Activities:** ATV (surrounding national forest), fishing, boating, water sports, winter sports. **Nearby Attractions:** Logan, Ogden. **Additional Information:** Rich County, (435) 793-2415.

RESTRICTIONS

Pets: On leash under owner's control. **Fires:** Yes. **Alcoholic Beverages:** Allowed. **Vehicle Maximum Length:** No limits. **Other:** Gates close 10 p.m. to 6 a.m. in summer.

TO GET THERE

From Laketown, go 2 mi. north on UT Hwy. 30.

BEAVER

Minersville State Park

P.O. Box 1531, Beaver 84713. T: (435) 438-5472; www.nr.state.ut.us.

RV ★★★★ Tent ★★★★★

Beauty: ★★★★ Site Privacy: ★★★
Spaciousness: ★★★ Quiet: ★★★★★
Security: ★★★★ Cleanliness: ★★★★
Insect Control: ★★★★ Facilities: ★★

Known for trophy rainbow and cutthroat trout that fatten up on crayfish and shrimp, Minersville is also popular for its hookups. But the lake, which holds water for downstream irrigation and freezes in cold weather, has a limit of one 20-inch trout that must be caught using only artificial lures and flies. Bicyclists from around the world brave strong winds to stop at this jewel in the sagebrush desert for the gravel campsites backed by grass strips. Tent pad users can tap into the 20-amp outlets (30-amp outlets are kept for RVs). Rock hounds hunt top-grade obsidian, chalcedony, and agates in the surrounding region. Bird-watchers flock for waterfowl like white-faced ibis, great blue herons, white pelicans, western grebes, and double-crested cormorants. Cottonwood, willow, elm, mulberry, and Russian olive trees provide shade. There are also three narrow (12 feet) wheelchair-accessible sites and a large gravel overflow area.

Basics

Operated By: Utah State Parks & Recreation. **Open:** All year (Apr.–Nov. 1 full services, depending upon weather). **Site Assignment:** First come, first served. **Registration:** Self-pay fee station. **Fee:** $14 (cash or check only). **Parking:** At site.

Facilities

Number of RV Sites: 29. **Number of Tent-Only Sites:** 0. **Hookups:** Electric (20, 30 amp), water. **Each Site:** Sheltered table, grill. **Dump Station:** Yes. **Laundry:** No. **Pay Phone:** Yes. **Rest Rooms and Showers:** Yes. **Fuel:** No. **Propane:** No. **Internal Roads:** Gravel, good. **RV Service:** No. **Market:** Beaver, 12 mi. **Restaurant:** Beaver, 12 mi. **General Store:** No. **Vending:** No. **Swimming:** In lake at own risk. **Playground:** No. **Other:** Boat ramp, horseshoes, volleyball, air compressor, 3 wheelchair-accessible sites. **Activities:** Boating, water sports, fishing, biking, bird-watching, rock hounding, golf. **Nearby Attractions:** Fishlake National Forest. **Additional Information:** Beaver County Travel Council, (435) 438-2975.

Restrictions

Pets: On leash (keep out of grass). **Fires:** Yes (in grills only, firewood available). **Alcoholic Beverages:** Allowed. **Vehicle Maximum Length:** 40 ft. **Other:** No boats inside campground, Jan. 1–May 28 no fishing (certain years).

To Get There

From Beaver go 12 mi. southwest on UT Hwy. 21.

BEAVER

United Beaver Campground

P.O. Box 1060, Beaver 84713. T: (435) 438-2808.

RV ★★★★ Tent ★★★

Beauty: ★★★★ Site Privacy: ★★★
Spaciousness: ★★★★ Quiet: ★★★★
Security: ★★★★ Cleanliness: ★★★★
Insect Control: ★★★★ Facilities: ★★★★

Situated at the gateway to Fishlake National Forest, which has a number of small high-elevation (5,900 to 9,300 feet) summer campgrounds, United Beaver is top-notch, one of the few area campgrounds open year-round with long level pull-through sites and hookups. United Beaver is also a good stopping place on the way to Great Basin National Park in Nevada, Salt Lake City, and southern destinations like the Grand Canyon and Las Vegas. Beaver is a relaxed and friendly travel stop (e.g. RV repair facilities) with two Mexican restaurants, including Kan-Kun just opposite the campground. There are grass strips between RV sites at this campground conveniently located near a highway exit at the south end of town. United Beaver is relatively quiet, with the wind blowing in the trees and chirping birds being louder than the highway. All in all, United Beaver is a friendly place where people are on a first-name basis and helpfulness prevails.

Basics

Operated By: Mary (would not give last name). **Open:** All year. **Site Assignment:** First come, first served. **Registration:** Office. **Fee:** $10.50–$13 tent, $15–$18 RV. **Parking:** At site.

Facilities

Number of RV Sites: 90. **Number of Tent-Only Sites:** Undesignated sites. **Hookups:** Electric (20, 30, 50), water, sewer. **Each Site:** Table, grill. **Dump Station:** Yes. **Laundry:** Yes. **Pay Phone:** Yes. **Rest Rooms and Showers:** Yes. **Fuel:** No. **Propane:** Yes. **Internal Roads:** Gravel, good. **RV Service:** No. **Market:** Beaver, 1 mi. **Restaurant:** Beaver, across road. **General Store:** Yes. **Vending:** Yes. **Swimming:** Pool. **Playground:** Yes. **Other:** Game room, dog run, horseshoes, Dutch oven pit in tent area. **Activities:** Golf, horseshoes, volleyball, fishing, boating, hunting, skiing, winter sports. **Nearby Attractions:** Cedar Breaks, Bryce, Paiute ATV Trail. **Additional Information:** Cedar City Ranger District, (435) 865-3200; Beaver County Travel Council, (435) 438-2975, (800) 280-2975.

Restrictions

Pets: On leash. **Fires:** Yes. **Alcoholic Beverages:** Allowed. **Vehicle Maximum Length:** 70 ft. **Other:** No parking or carpets on grass.

To Get There

From US I-15 get off at Exit 109.

BLANDING

Devil's Canyon

c/o Monticello Ranger District, 496 East Central, P.O. Box 820, Monticello 84535. T: (435) 587-2041 or (877) 446-6777 (reservations).

RV ★★ Tent ★★★★★

Beauty: ★★★★★ Site Privacy: ★★★★★
Spaciousness: ★★★ Quiet: ★★★★
Security: ★★★★ Cleanliness: ★★★★★
Insect Control: ★★★ Facilities: ★

Located in the Manti-Lasal National Forest, Devil's Canyon is a US Forest Service campground operated under permit by a private concessionaire, United Land Management (P.O. Box 970099, Orem, UT 84097). Reservations are usually not necessary, but may be a good idea during peak seasons, particularly when special events come to the area and all the campgrounds in Moab, Green River, and the surrounding environs book full. If hookups and all the amenities are a prerequisite, the numerous commercial roadside RV campgrounds between Mexican Hat and Green River are a better choice. But if the feeling of camping in the forest is paramount, then Devil's Canyon offers self-sufficient campers a good location for exploring Hovenweep, Natural Bridges, the Needles District of Canyonlands, and even Arches. Sites 9 and 10 are best for big RVs. For the most seclusion and privacy among the tall junipers and ponderosa pines choose sites 1–7.

Basics

Operated By: United Land Management. **Open:** May–Oct. **Site Assignment:** First come, first served; reservations accepted. **Registration:** Self-pay fee station. **Fee:** $10 (cash or check only). **Parking:** At site.

Facilities

Number of RV Sites: 33. **Number of Tent-Only Sites:** 0. **Hookups:** None. **Each Site:** Table, fire pit. **Dump Station:** No. **Laundry:** No. **Pay Phone:** No. **Rest Rooms and Showers:** No showers. **Fuel:** No. **Propane:** No. **Internal Roads:** Paved, rutted. **RV Service:** No. **Market:** Blanding, 10 mi. **Restaurant:** Blanding, 10 mi. **General Store:** No. **Vending:** No. **Swimming:** No. **Playground:** No. **Activities:** Hiking trails. **Nearby Attractions:** Natural Bridges, Hovenweep, Canyonlands. **Additional Information:** San Juan County Visitor Services, (435) 587-3235, (800) 574-4386.

Restrictions

Pets: On leash. **Fires:** Yes. **Alcoholic Beverages:** Allowed. **Vehicle Maximum Length:** 35 ft. **Other:** Protect food from bears, no fireworks.

To Get There

From Blanding go 9.5 mi. northeast on US Hwy. 191.

BLUFF

Cadillac Ranch RV Park

Hwy. 191, P.O. Box 157, Bluff 84512. T: (435) 672-2262 or (800) 538-6195; F: (435) 672-2417; www.bluffutah.org; ranch@sanjuan.net.

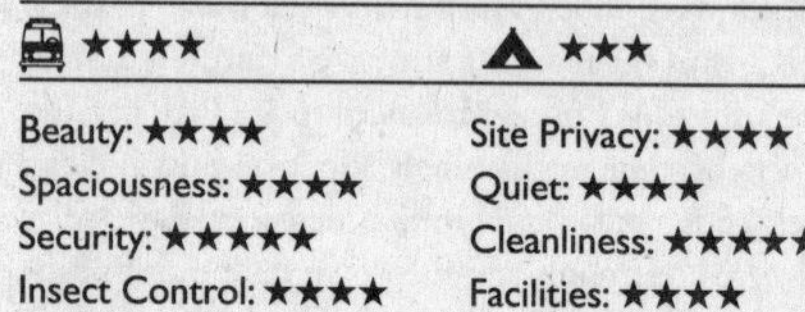

RV ★★★★ Tent ★★★

Beauty: ★★★★ Site Privacy: ★★★★
Spaciousness: ★★★★ Quiet: ★★★★
Security: ★★★★★ Cleanliness: ★★★★★
Insect Control: ★★★★ Facilities: ★★★★

A good overnight stopping place south of Moab and north of Monument Valley and Kayenta, AZ, Bluff and Cadillac Ranch also make a good base for exploring this part of southeastern Utah. Cadillac Ranch is a homey little campground with 30-foot-wide RV spaces where deer and wild turkey wander in and out on their own schedules. The atmosphere is friendly, and TV antennas pick up six channels. In the evening people sit and talk while having a drink on the office verandah overlooking the pond. The pond is available for free fishing (bass, bluegill, catfish, trout) and paddle boating, or just watching aquatic waterfowl like ducks, geese, ibis, cranes, and blue herons. The tent sites are especially attractive, being on the opposite side of the pond from the RVs, though sometimes Europeans pack their tents tightly on the lawns around the office when the official tent sites are all taken.

Basics

Operated By: Rayma Percell. **Open:** All year. **Site Assignment:** First come, first served. **Registration:** Office. **Fee:** $16 (V, MC, D). **Parking:** At site.

Facilities

Number of RV Sites: 20. **Number of Tent-Only Sites:** 10. **Hookups:** Electric (30, 50 amp), water, sewer, phone (modem). **Each Site:** Table, grill. **Dump Station:** Yes. **Laundry:** No. **Pay Phone:** Yes. **Rest Rooms and Showers:** Yes. **Fuel:** No. **Propane:** No. **Internal Roads:** Gravel, good. **RV**

Service: No. **Market:** Bluff, less than 1 mi. **Restaurant:** Bluff, less than 1 mi. **General Store:** No. **Vending:** Yes. **Swimming:** Pool. **Playground:** No. **Other:** Paddleboats. **Activities:** Horseback riding, horseshoes, volleyball, pond fishing. **Nearby Attractions:** Valley of the Gods, Monument Valley, Natural Bridges, Hovenweep, Lake Powell. **Additional Information:** San Juan County Visitor Services, (435) 587-3235, (800) 574-4386.

RESTRICTIONS

Pets: On leash under owner's control. **Fires:** Yes (firewood supplied gratis). **Alcoholic Beverages:** Allowed. **Vehicle Maximum Length:** 40 ft. **Other:** Don't let children throw or roll rocks.

TO GET THERE

On US Hwy. 191 in town.

BRYCE CANYON

Bryce Canyon Pines

P.O. Box 43, Hwy. 12, Bryce 84764. T: (800) 892-7923 or (801) 834-5441; F: (801) 834-5330.

★★★★ ★★★★

Beauty: ★★★★ Site Privacy: ★★★★
Spaciousness: ★★★★ Quiet: ★★★★
Security: ★★★★ Cleanliness: ★★★★
Insect Control: ★★★★ Facilities: ★★★★

A convenient campground for excursions into Bryce National Park (just six miles away) and Red Canyon, Bryce Canyon Pines has ample amenities and is nicely setback from the highway. The campground itself is intimate, like being in a small pine forest bisected by gravel roads. Little patches of meadow between campsites add to the rustic feel. Occasional power outages from the area's high winds are a nuisance that comes with the territory. A heated pool (at the motel, but available to campers), a restaurant, gas pumps (fill up when the power grid is working, because they are electronic) and a well-stocked store with a pool table add up to ample comforts without the crush of the crowds and tour buses at the nearby national park. In short, being outside of Bryce and away from the summer crowds is a good reason to put down here for the night.

BASICS

Operated By: Kenny & Randy Miller. **Open:** April 1–Oct. 31. **Site Assignment:** First come, first served; reservations accepted. **Registration:** In store. **Fee:** $16 tent, $22 RV (V, MC, AE, D). **Parking:** At site.

FACILITIES

Number of RV Sites: 24. **Number of Tent-Only Sites:** 15. **Hookups:** Electric (30 amp), water, sewer, phone (modem, Internet access). **Each Site:** Table. **Dump Station:** Yes. **Laundry:** Yes. **Pay Phone:** Yes. **Rest Rooms and Showers:** Yes. **Fuel:** Yes. **Propane:** No. **Internal Roads:** Gravel, good condition. **RV Service:** No. **Market:** Part of country store. **Restaurant:** At motel. **General Store:** Yes. **Vending:** Yes. **Swimming:** Heated pool in motel. **Playground:** No. **Other:** Portable grills on request. **Activities:** Horseback riding, horseshoes, game room (TV, pool table). **Nearby Attractions:** Red Canyon, Bryce. **Additional Information:** Bryce Canyon National Park, (435) 834-5322.

RESTRICTIONS

Pets: Small pets on leash. **Fires:** Yes (firewood sold). **Alcoholic Beverages:** Allowed. **Vehicle Maximum Length:** Not limited. **Other:** 11 a.m. checkout.

TO GET THERE

Go 4 mi. west on UT Hwy. 12 from the UT Hwy. 63 junction.

BRYCE CANYON

North Campground

P.O. Box 170001, Bryce Canyon 84717. T: (435) 834-5322/4801; www.nps.gov/brca.

★★★ ★★★★★

Beauty: ★★★★ Site Privacy: ★★★★
Spaciousness: ★★★★ Quiet: ★★★★
Security: ★★★★ Cleanliness: ★★★★
Insect Control: ★★★ Facilities: ★★

North Campground is in a ponderosa pine forest with pink cliffs and hoodoos at 8,000 feet elevation, where winter comes early and spring late. The primitive feel is reinforced by placement of facilities like showers a short walk outside the campground. Campsites are spread out on a tiered hillside in four loops, all of which fill up on summer weekends. Loop A is lowest, and Loop D is highest in elevation and most private. Loops A and B nearest the entrance allow only vehicles 20 feet and longer, and hum with the noise of generators from 8 a.m. to 8 p.m. Loop C bans generators. Loop D bans generators and vehicles over 20 feet, making it a haven for tent campers. The site is windy, but the cool breezes are welcomed in summer. Though the tendency is to seek shady sites, summer tent campers should opt for sunny sites so tents can dry off from thunderstorms.

BASICS

Operated By: National Park Service. **Open:** All year (Loop A only). **Site Assignment:** First come, first served. **Registration:** Self-pay entrance fee station. **Fee:** $10. **Parking:** At site.

FACILITIES

Number of RV Sites: 107. **Number of Tent-Only Sites:** 0. **Hookups:** None. **Each Site:** Table, fire pit. **Dump Station:** Yes. **Laundry:** No. **Pay Phone:** Yes. **Rest Rooms and Showers:** Yes. **Fuel:** No. **Propane:** No. **Internal Roads:** Paved, rough in spots. **RV Service:** No. **Market:** At Ruby's. **Restaurant:** At Ruby's or lodge, within 2 mi. **General Store:** No. **Vending:** No. **Swimming:** No. **Playground:** No. **Activities:** Horseback riding, ranger interpretative programs. **Nearby Attractions:** Kodachrome Basin, Red Canyon. **Additional Information:** National Park Service, www.nps.gov/brca.

RESTRICTIONS

Pets: On leash; not allowed outside campgrounds, parking lots. **Fires:** Yes. **Alcoholic Beverages:** Allowed. **Vehicle Maximum Length:** No limits, but over 40 ft. is hard to maneuver. **Other:** 15 mph speed limit enforced in campground.

TO GET THERE

Turnoff from Hwy. 63 just past Bryce Canyon National Park Visitor Center.

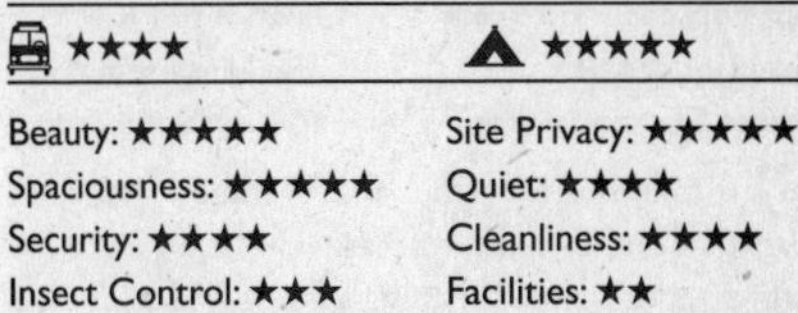

BRYCE CANYON

Red Canyon Campground

P.O. Box 80, Panguitch 84759. T: (435) 676-8815.

★★★★ ★★★★★

Beauty: ★★★★★ Site Privacy: ★★★★★
Spaciousness: ★★★★★ Quiet: ★★★★
Security: ★★★★ Cleanliness: ★★★★
Insect Control: ★★★ Facilities: ★★

This National Forest Service campground, nestled among tall pines and breathtaking red-spired sandstone hills within ten miles of Bryce, is run by a Mom and Pop concessionaire, High Country Recreation, which has been among the region's best over the past two decades. Red Canyon Campground is just a few thousand yards east of the Dixie National Forest Visitor Center, which has soda machines, a pay phone, and the short Pink Ledges Nature Walk trailhead. Campsites, some big enough for 3–4 vehicles, are on alternating sides of the road on uphill and downhill loops, with lots of sage, junipers, and pine trees offering an extra measure of privacy. Unlike Kings Creek (See appendix), which opens later in the season and gets people coming in for a week with four-wheel-drive vehicles, Red Canyon tends to be an overnight stop, though there are good trails from which a horse can be ridden into Bryce.

BASICS

Operated By: High Country Recreation. **Open:** April 15-Oct. 25 (weather permitting). **Site Assignment:** First come, first served. **Registration:** Self-pay entrance fee station. **Fee:** $10. **Parking:** At site.

FACILITIES

Number of RV Sites: 39. **Number of Tent-Only Sites:** 0. **Hookups:** None. **Each Site:** Table, grill. **Dump Station:** Yes. **Laundry:** No. **Pay Phone:** Yes. **Rest Rooms and Showers:** Yes. **Fuel:** No. **Propane:** No. **Internal Roads:** Gravel, excellent condition. **RV Service:** No. **Market:** Mile marker 10 on Hwy. 12 at Bryce Canyon Pines. **Restaurant:** Mile marker 10 on Hwy. 12 at Bryce Canyon Pines. **General Store:** No. **Vending:** Yes. **Swimming:** No. **Playground:** Yes. **Other:** asphalt bike trail. **Activities:** Horseback riding. **Nearby Attractions:** Red Canyon, Bryce, Kodachrome Basin, Escalante. **Additional Information:** Powell Ranger District, (435) 676-8815.

RESTRICTIONS

Pets: On leash under owner's control. **Fires:** Yes. **Alcoholic Beverages:** Allowed. **Vehicle Maximum Length:** 45 ft. **Other:** 14-day limit.

TO GET THERE

From junction of US Hwy. 89 & UT Hwy. 12, go 10 mi. east on Hwy. 12.

BRYCE CANYON
Ruby's RV Park & Campground

P.O. Box 22, Hwy. U-63, Bryce 84764. T: (435) 834-5301 (Apr.–Oct.) or (435) 834-5341 (Nov.–Mar.) or (800) 468-8600; F: (435) 834-5481; www.rubysinn.com; blainea@rubysinn.com.

RV ★★★★★ Tent ★★★★★

Beauty: ★★★★ Site Privacy: ★★★★
Spaciousness: ★★★★★ Quiet: ★★★★
Security: ★★★★ Cleanliness: ★★★★
Insect Control: ★★★ Facilities: ★★★★★

Just a mile north of the Park entrance, Ruby's is part of a tourist complex that includes an excellent buffet (good value; friendly staff) packed with tour buses at peak hours. The Ruby family first settled on a ranch here in 1916, seven years before Bryce became a national monument, and has been doing an excellent job in tourism ever since, now handling 1.7 million visits per year. Full hookup sites are closest to the highway, just behind the RV-park office. Electric and water sites are hidden from the tourist hordes at a lower elevation in a more rustic world of their own, with many pine trees and little depressions between sites containing bits of meadow greenery. Many of these back sites share water views with the large expanse of meadow (no designated sites) reserved for tents. Though Bryce seems hectic, with long lines of cars looking for parking in summer, Ruby's is as good as commercial camping gets.

BASICS
Operated By: The Ruby family, Shauna & Blaine. **Open:** April 1–Oct. 31. **Site Assignment:** First come, first served; reservations recommended. **Registration:** At office. **Fee:** $15 tent, $22–$25 RV (V, MC, AE, D, DC). **Parking:** At site.

FACILITIES
Number of RV Sites: 118. **Number of Tent-Only Sites:** 100. **Hookups:** Electric (20, 30, 50 amp), water, sewer. **Each Site:** Table. **Dump Station:** Yes. **Laundry:** Yes. **Pay Phone:** Yes. **Rest Rooms and Showers:** Yes. **Fuel:** Yes. **Propane:** Yes. **Internal Roads:** Gravel, good condition. **RV Service:** Yes. **Market:** Yes. **Restaurant:** Yes. **General Store:** Yes. **Vending:** Yes. **Swimming:** Pool. **Playground:** No. **Other:** ATM machine, business center, bus wash, car rentals, film processing, tram stop. **Activities:** ATV, helicopter & horseback rides, mountain biking, petting farm, gold panning, rodeo, country music dinners, cross-country skiing. **Nearby Attractions:** Bryce Canyon National Park. **Additional Information:** Bryce Canyon National Park, (435) 834-5322.

RESTRICTIONS
Pets: On leash at all times. **Fires:** Yes (charcoal). **Alcoholic Beverages:** Allowed. **Vehicle Maximum Length:** No limit. **Other:** 1 p.m. checkout.

TO GET THERE
On UT Hwy. 63, 1 mi. north of park entrance.

BRYCE CANYON
Sunset Campground

P.O. Box 170001, Bryce Canyon 84717. T: (435) 834-5322/4801; www.nps.gov/brca.

RV ★★★★ Tent ★★★★★

Beauty: ★★★★ Site Privacy: ★★★★
Spaciousness: ★★★★ Quiet: ★★★★
Security: ★★★★ Cleanliness: ★★★★
Insect Control: ★★★ Facilities: ★★

Sunset is usually the last park campground opening in the spring, after the snowfall has melted and camper demand has filled up North Campground's loops. Sunset has an isolated ponderosa pine forest feel, being furthest from Visitor Center crowds and a mile from amenities such as showers. No tents are allowed on loop A, whose widely dispersed sites are set aside for RVs and their noisy generators. The smaller and more intimate Loops B and C accommodate tents and ban generators and vehicles over 20 feet. Wheelchair accessibility, including at the group site, is another plus. Mule deer grazing under the shade of ponderosa pines are a common sight. Overall, Sunset is worthwhile because it puts some distance between campers and the park crowds, though the tradeoff is hiking, driving, or riding the new park shuttles to showers and other facilities.

BASICS
Operated By: National Park Service. **Open:** Spring–fall (exact dates depend on weather). **Site Assignment:** First come, first served; group site requires reservation. **Registration:** Self-pay entrance fee station. **Fee:** $10. **Parking:** At site.

FACILITIES
Number of RV Sites: 80. **Number of Tent-Only Sites:** 0. **Hookups:** None. **Each Site:** Table, fire ring. **Dump Station:** Yes. **Laundry:** No. **Pay Phone:** Yes. **Rest Rooms and Showers:** Yes (showers 1 mi. away). **Fuel:** No. **Propane:** No. **Internal Roads:** Paved, weathered. **RV Service:** No. **Market:** At Ruby's, 2 mi. north. **Restaurant:** At lodge, 1 mi. north. **General Store:** Yes (1 mi. away). **Vending:** No. **Swimming:** No. **Playground:** No. **Activities:** Horseback riding, ranger interpretative programs. **Nearby Attractions:** Kodachrome Basin, Red Canyon, Escalante, Cedar Breaks. **Additional Information:** National Park Service, www.nps.gov/brca.

RESTRICTIONS
Pets: On leash under owner's control; not allowed on trails. **Fires:** Yes (in grills only). **Alcoholic Beverages:** Allowed. **Vehicle Maximum Length:** No limit. **Other:** 14 day limit, no firewood gathering, don't feed squirrels or chipmunks.

TO GET THERE
From Visitor Center, go 2 mi. south on Hwy. 63.

CANNONVILLE
Cannonville/Bryce Valley KOA

P.O. Box 22, Cannonville 84718. T: (435) 679-8988 or (888) 562-4710 (reservations only); www.grandstaircasekoa.com; bvkoa@color-country.net.

RV ★★★★★ Tent ★★★★★

Beauty: ★★★★ Site Privacy: ★★★★
Spaciousness: ★★★★ Quiet: ★★★★
Security: ★★★★ Cleanliness: ★★★★
Insect Control: ★★★ Facilities: ★★★★

One of the more attractive campgrounds, public or private, this relatively new KOA (opened May 2000) integrated an old apple orchard into its front RV sites. There is a separate tent-site loop, but a dirt road leading behind the hills has even more isolated campsites that are real wilderness with good sand pads for tents. These sites are invisible from the highway and nestled among scenic red sandstone badlands, with native high-desert pinyon pine, juniper, and desert scrub. Cannonville is a town of 131 people, so campground vistas facing away from the main highway tend to be mostly banded sandstone hills and pastoral irrigated ranches, though a gas station, restaurant, and motel are only a block away. All in all, not a bad base from which to explore Bryce Canyon National Park and Kodachrome Basin State Park.

BASICS
Operated By: John Holland. **Open:** All year (pool etc. seasonal). **Site Assignment:** First come, first served; reservations accepted. **Registration:** At office. **Fee:** $17 tent, $26 RV. **Parking:** At site.

FACILITIES
Number of RV Sites: 50. **Number of Tent-Only Sites:** 25. **Hookups:** Electric (50 amp), water, sewer. **Each Site:** Table, fire ring. **Dump Station:** Yes. **Laundry:** Yes. **Pay Phone:** Yes. **Rest Rooms and Showers:** Yes. **Fuel:** No. **Propane:** Yes. **Internal Roads:** Gravel, good. **RV Service:** No. **Market:** In Cannonville. **Restaurant:** In Cannonville. **General Store:** Yes. **Vending:** Yes. **Swimming:** Heated outdoor pool. **Playground:** Yes. **Other:** Covered pavillion w/ kitchen, some grills, game room, dataports. **Activities:** Biking, horseback riding, fishing, rockhounding. **Nearby Attractions:** Bryce, Kodachrome Basin, Escalante, Boulder Mountain lakes. **Additional Information:** Escalante Interagency Office, (435) 826-5499.

RESTRICTIONS
Pets: On leash under owner's control at all times. **Fires:** Yes (firewood sold). **Alcoholic Beverages:** At site only. **Vehicle Maximum Length:** No limit. **Other:** No digging holes, disturbing ground cover, chopping vegetation, or placing doormats on grass, no firearms or fireworks, 11 a.m. checkout.

TO GET THERE
15 mi. east of Bryce at junction of UT Hwy. 12 and Red Rock Rd. in Cannonville.

CANNONVILLE
Kodachrome Basin State Park

P.O. Box 238, Cannonville 84718. T: (435) 679-8562 or (800) 322-3770 (group reservations only); F: (435) 679-8542.

RV ★★★★ Tent ★★★★★

Beauty: ★★★★★ Site Privacy: ★★★★
Spaciousness: ★★★★ Quiet: ★★★★

Security: ★★★★ Cleanliness: ★★★★
Insect Control: ★★★★ Facilities: ★★★

Named after the film, Kodachrome Basin State Park is noted for its colorful sandstone spires resembling huge chimneys. The campground is surrounded by colorful banded sandstone hills, sand pipes, and hoodoos. Big gnarly-barked junipers add privacy to the sites. There is even a wheelchair-accessible site with a raised wood tent platform with ramps. The general store, which also rents cabins, is a bit eccentric and liable to close on a whim on a busy Saturday. This is one of the few places where you are encouraged to feed an animal, namely the chukars, an introduced bird that resembles a partridge and needs help making it through the harsh winters. Dirt roads and trails lead to rock formations, coves, and colorful geyser remnants (e.g. chimneys) where the play of light changes the colors through a moody array of whites, grays, reds, and oranges. Add in the proximity to Bryce and Escalante, and this makes a fine stopping place.

BASICS

Operated By: Utah State Parks. **Open:** All year. **Site Assignment:** First come, first served; reservations for 4 group sites. **Registration:** Self-pay station. **Fee:** $13 vehicle. **Parking:** At site.

FACILITIES

Number of RV Sites: 27. **Number of Tent-Only Sites:** 0. **Hookups:** None. **Each Site:** Table, grill on cement pad. **Dump Station:** Yes. **Laundry:** No. **Pay Phone:** Yes. **Rest Rooms and Showers:** Yes. **Fuel:** No. **Propane:** No. **Internal Roads:** Pavement, excellent condition. **RV Service:** No. **Market:** 14 mi. in Tropic. **Restaurant:** 9 mi. in Cannonville. **General Store:** Yes. **Vending:** Yes. **Swimming:** No. **Playground:** No. **Other:** Wheelchair-accessible site. **Activities:** Horseback riding, mountain biking. **Nearby Attractions:** Bryce, Escalante, Cottonwood Canyon, Grosvenor Arch. **Additional Information:** Escalante Interagency Office, (435) 826-5499.

RESTRICTIONS

Pets: On leash under owner's control at all times. **Fires:** Yes. **Alcoholic Beverages:** Allowed. **Vehicle Maximum Length:** 30 ft. **Other:** 14-day max. stay, no guns, bows, slingshots, or fireworks, no firewood collecting, ATVs must remain on trailers while in park, no climbing on rocks.

TO GET THERE

From junction of UT Hwy. 12 in Cannonville, go 9 mi. southeast on Cottonwood Canyon Rd.

CANYONLANDS NATIONAL PARK, ISLAND IN THE SKY DISTRICT

Willow Flat Campground

2282 South West Resource Blvd., Moab 84532.
T: (435) 259-4712 or (435) 719-2313;
www.nps.gov/cany.

 ★★★  ★★★★

Beauty: ★★★★★ Site Privacy: ★★★★★
Spaciousness: ★★★ Quiet: ★★★★
Security: ★★★★ Cleanliness: ★★★★★
Insect Control: ★★ Facilities: ★

Set amidst flattop mesas and buttes that have eroded into spires, Willow Flat is a place of isolation and beauty for self-sufficient campers. It is best to pickup firewood and water in Moab before coming here, as the Visitors Center has only a limited number of gallon water jugs for sale. The dozen campsites are spread out along a curve for maximum privacy. Though voices tend to carry in the Canyonlands, generator noise is limited to two hours in the morning and 4–8 p.m. The longest site length is an 80-foot pull-through, but it is only 11 feet wide. There is a 50-foot-long pull-through that is 16-feet wide, and among the 33- and 35-foot-long sites are 19, 24, and 25-foot widths. Checkout time is 10 a.m., and arrival an hour or two before that is the best way to snag a space.

BASICS

Operated By: National Park Service. **Open:** All year. **Site Assignment:** First come, first served. **Registration:** Self-pay fee station. **Fee:** $5 (cash or check only). **Parking:** At site.

FACILITIES

Number of RV Sites: 12. **Number of Tent-Only Sites:** 0. **Hookups:** None. **Each Site:** Table, fire grate. **Dump Station:** No. **Laundry:** No. **Pay Phone:** Yes. **Rest Rooms and Showers:** No showers. **Fuel:** No. **Propane:** No. **Internal Roads:** Gravel, bumpy in spots. **RV Service:** No. **Market:** Moab, 46 mi. **Restaurant:** Moab, 46 mi. **General Store:** No. **Vending:** No. **Swimming:** No. **Playground:** No. **Other:** Visitor center. **Activities:** Evening campfire programs (seasonal). **Nearby Attractions:** Arches National Park, Dead Horse Point State Park, Moab. **Additional Information:** Canyonlands Natural History Assoc., (435) 259-6003, www.cnha.org.

RESTRICTIONS

Pets: On leash. **Fires:** Yes (in fire grates only, no wood gathering). **Alcoholic Beverages:** Allowed. **Vehicle Maximum Length:** 80 ft. **Other:** 14-day max. stay.

TO GET THERE

From US Hwy. 191 10 mi. north of Moab go 36 mi. southwest on UT Hwy. 313.

CANYONLANDS NATIONAL PARK, NEEDLES DISTRICT

Squaw Flat Campground

2282 South West Resource Blvd., Moab 84532.
T: (435) 259-4711 or 259-7164;
www.nps.gov/cany.

★★★★ ★★★★★

Beauty: ★★★★★ Site Privacy: ★★★★★
Spaciousness: ★★★★★ Quiet: ★★★★★
Security: ★★★★★ Cleanliness: ★★★★★
Insect Control: ★★★ Facilities: ★★

Make sure the gas tank is full and that you have enough water and firewood for the duration before turning onto UT Hwy. 211 en route to the Needles District of Canyonlands National Park. There is a small private campground catering to RVs (no hookups; $15) with gas, propane, showers, and a store with haphazard hours just outside the park boundary at Needles Outpost (call (435) 979-4007), but Squaw Flat Campground demands self-sufficiency. In return Squaw Flat offers relatively large sites, each tucked into its own little sandstone rock formation and far from its neighbor. Walk-in tent sites nestled among the orange sandstone rocks provide an even more primitive slot canyon feel. High clearance four-wheel-drive vehicles and technical driving skills are needed to visit the major geologic features; even mountain bikes quit moving in the deep sandy washes. Peak season (Mar.–May and mid-Sept.–Oct.), campsites are all snagged by 10 a.m.

BASICS

Operated By: National Park Service. **Open:** All year. **Site Assignment:** First come, first served; group site reservations. **Registration:** Self-pay fee station. **Fee:** $10 (cash or check only). **Parking:** At site; parking area near walk-in tent sites.

FACILITIES

Number of RV Sites: 20. **Number of Tent-Only Sites:** 6. **Hookups:** None. **Each Site:** Table, fire ring. **Dump Station:** No. **Laundry:** No. **Pay Phone:** Yes. **Rest Rooms and Showers:** No showers. **Fuel:** No. **Propane:** No. **Internal Roads:** Gravel, good. **RV Service:** No. **Market:** Monticello, 62 mi. **Restaurant:** Monticello, 62 mi. **General Store:** No. **Vending:** No. **Swimming:** No. **Playground:** No. **Other:** Visitor center, campfire circle. **Activities:** Four-wheel driving, mountain biking. **Nearby Attractions:** Newspaper Rock, Canyon Rims Recreation Area, Chesler Park. **Additional Information:** Canyonlands Natural History Assoc., (435) 259-6003, www.cnha.org.

RESTRICTIONS

Pets: On leash & attended at all times (not allowed on hiking trails or 4WD roads, even in a vehicle). **Fires:** Yes (only in metal fire rings, no wood gathering). **Alcoholic Beverages:** Allowed. **Vehicle Maximum Length:** 116 ft. **Other:** No ATVs, 2 vehicles & 10 people per site, 10 a.m. checkout, 14-day limit.

TO GET THERE

From US Hwy. 191 14 mi. north of Monticello go 48 mi. west on UT Hwy. 211.

CEDAR BREAKS NATIONAL MONUMENT

Point Supreme Campground

2390 West Hwy. 56, Suite 11, Cedar City 84720.
T: (435) 586-9451.

★★ ★★★★★

Beauty: ★★★★★ Site Privacy: ★★★★★
Spaciousness: ★★★★ Quiet: ★★★★
Security: ★★★★ Cleanliness: ★★★★
Insect Control: ★★★ Facilities: ★★

Just south of the renowned Brian Head ski area, where lifts carry summer mountain bikers and hikers to 100 miles of alpine meadow and aspen grove trails, 10,000-foot elevation Cedar Breaks is known for its wildflower displays and its folded, uplifted, and eroded orange and white spires, arches, columns, and canyons that have been liked to a miniature version of Bryce Canyon. A large meadow with tables and grills just off the paved road marks the entrance to Point Supreme Campground. Trees provide privacy between the campsites, though there are also good meadow views. The largest sites are 11, 12, 15, and 17. Tents must be positioned at least 20 feet from the campfire grates in order to allow campground vegetation to grow back. Besides deepening the colors of the rocks from roadside overlooks, sunrise and sunset bring deer into the campground. Snow and flash floods can close access roads.

Basics

Operated By: National Park Service. **Open:** June 15–Oct. 1. **Site Assignment:** First come, first served. **Registration:** Self-pay fee station. **Fee:** $10. **Parking:** At site.

Facilities

Number of RV Sites: 30. **Number of Tent-Only Sites:** 0. **Hookups:** None. **Each Site:** Table, grill. **Dump Station:** Yes. **Laundry:** No. **Pay Phone:** Yes. **Rest Rooms and Showers:** No showers. **Fuel:** No. **Propane:** No. **Internal Roads:** Gravel, good. **RV Service:** No. **Market:** Cedar City, 23 mi. **Restaurant:** Brian Head, 20 mi. **General Store:** No. **Vending:** No. **Swimming:** No. **Playground:** No. **Other:** Visitor center, amphitheater. **Activities:** Ranger programs, biking. **Nearby Attractions:** Panguitch Lake, Bryce, Zion. **Additional Information:** Iron County Tourism, (800) 354-4849.

Restrictions

Pets: On leash or under physical restraint at all time. **Fires:** Yes (in grills or portable barbecues only, no wood gathering). **Alcoholic Beverages:** Allowed. **Vehicle Maximum Length:** 24 ft. **Other:** No fireworks, 2 tents per site.

To Get There

From Cedar City go 18 mi. east on UT Hwy. 14 and 5 mi. north on UT Hwy. 148.

CEDAR CITY

Cedar Canyon Campground

P.O. Box 627, Cedar City 84721.T: (435) 865-3200 or (877) 444-6777 (reservations); www.fsfed.us/outernet/dixie-nf/welcome.htm.

RV ★★ Tent ★★★★

Beauty: ★★★★★	Site Privacy: ★★★★★
Spaciousness: ★★★	Quiet: ★★★★
Security: ★★★★	Cleanliness: ★★★★
Insect Control: ★★★	Facilities: ★★

Perched at 8,100-feet elevation on UT Hwy. 14, Cedar Canyon offers self-sufficient campers the best of both worlds: Cedar City's Tony Award–winning Shakespeare festival (2000 best regional theater) and the orange-and-white spires and columns of higher elevation Cedar Breaks National Monument. Cedar Canyon Campground is situated in a beautiful forest of spruce, fir, and aspen. Rocky, tree-lined Crow Creek separates the campground from the highway. Run by National Forest Service concessionaire AuDi, sites 4, 6, 7, and 17 can be reserved. For closest creek proximity select sites 2, 4, 6–8, 12, 14, or 16; site 12, one of three double sites, accommodates up to 16 people. The campground creek is not fishable, but there is a kid's fishing pond nearby at Iron County's Wood Ranch. Though water (piped in from a nearby spring) and sanitation services are shutdown after Labor Day to avoid freezing, the campground can still be used.

Basics

Operated By: AuDi, Inc. **Open:** June 15–Sept. 6. **Site Assignment:** First come, first served; group & some individual sites (4,6,7,17) can be reserved. **Registration:** Self-pay fee station. **Fee:** $8 single site, $16 double site (cash or check only). **Parking:** At site.

Facilities

Number of RV Sites: 19. **Number of Tent-Only Sites:** 0. **Hookups:** None. **Each Site:** Table, fire ring. **Dump Station:** No. **Laundry:** No. **Pay Phone:** No. **Rest Rooms and Showers:** No showers. **Fuel:** No. **Propane:** No. **Internal Roads:** Paved, excellent. **RV Service:** No. **Market:** Cedar City, 14 mi. **Restaurant:** Cedar City, 14 mi. **General Store:** No. **Vending:** No. **Swimming:** No. **Playground:** No. **Activities:** Biking, horseback riding. **Nearby Attractions:** Cedar Breaks National Monument, Virgin River Rim Trail, Brian Head, Zion. **Additional Information:** Iron County Tourism, (800) 354-4849.

Restrictions

Pets: On leash & always attended. **Fires:** Yes (in fire rings, stoves only). **Alcoholic Beverages:** Allowed. **Vehicle Maximum Length:** 24 ft. **Other:** 14-day limit, lock food away from bears.

To Get There

From Cedar City go 14 mi. east on UT Hwy. 14.

CEDAR CITY

Duck Creek Campground

P.O. Box 627, Cedar City 84721.T: (435) 865-3200 or (877) 444-6777 (reservations); www.fsfed.us/outernet/dixie-nf/welcome.htm.

RV ★★★★ Tent ★★★★

Beauty: ★★★★	Site Privacy: ★★★★
Spaciousness: ★★★★	Quiet: ★★★★
Security: ★★★★	Cleanliness: ★★★★
Insect Control: ★★	Facilities: ★★★

A large duck pond at 8,600-feet elevation and campsites heavily forested with tall aspens and spruce make Duck Creek's five loops an attractive, reservable alternative to driving gravel roads to reach the smaller 9,200-foot-elevation Te-Ah and Navajo Lake Campgrounds (See Appendix). National Forest Service concessionaire AuDi keeps Duck Creek in top shape, and added amenities like electric hookups are not too far-fetched a possibility in coming seasons. At Loop A, which is nearest the highway and has a very large picnic area, sites 4–13, 15, 17–20, and 24–37 are reservable. At smaller and more intimate Loop B, sites 38–40, 42, 43, and 46–48 can be reserved. Loops C, D and E are most primitive in feel, and only the Roundup and Wagon Train group areas can be reserved in these loops. Nearby Duck Creek Village provides many of the amenities missing at the campground.

Basics

Operated By: AuDi Inc. **Open:** June 15–Sept. 6. **Site Assignment:** First come, first served; group & some individual sites reservable. **Registration:** Self-pay entrance fee station. **Fee:** $10 single sites, $18 double sites (cash or check only). **Parking:** At site.

Facilities

Number of RV Sites: 96. **Number of Tent-Only Sites:** 0. **Hookups:** None. **Each Site:** Table, fire ring. **Dump Station:** Yes. **Laundry:** No. **Pay Phone:** Yes. **Rest Rooms and Showers:** No showers. **Fuel:** No. **Propane:** No. **Internal Roads:** Gravel, good. **RV Service:** No. **Market:** Cedar City, 30 mi. **Restaurant:** Duck Creek Village, 2 mi. **General Store:** No. **Vending:** No. **Swimming:** No. **Playground:** No. **Other:** Amphitheater, picnic area, boat ramp. **Activities:** Boating, fishing, horseback riding. **Nearby Attractions:** Cedar Breaks, Navajo Lake, Brian Head, Bryce, Zion. **Additional Information:** Iron County Tourism, (800) 354-4849.

Restrictions

Pets: On leash (pets not recommended; plague warning). **Fires:** Yes (firewood sold). **Alcoholic Beverages:** Allowed. **Vehicle Maximum Length:** 35 ft. **Other:** No fireworks.

To Get There

From Cedar City go 30 mi. east on UT Hwy. 14.

ESCALANTE

Broken Bow RV Camp

495 West Main St., P.O. Box 505, Escalante 84726.T: (888) 241-8785 or (435) 826-4959.

RV ★★★★ Tent ★★★

Beauty: ★★★	Site Privacy: ★★★
Spaciousness: ★★★	Quiet: ★★★
Security: ★★★★	Cleanliness: ★★★★
Insect Control: ★★★★	Facilities: ★★★

A small family operation on Escalante's Main Street that is easy to miss, being fronted by a handpainted wooden sign of Broken Bow Arch (the owner's favorite place) surrounded by old rusted equipment, a funky rock shop, and a tall plastic sign with the previous owner's "SSS" name adding to the obfuscation. But the Moqui Motel and Nature Sounds Drum Factory are just across the street. Though a bit hidden, the RV park is well maintained. A new pine building has pine toilet stalls, showers, and a new laundry room. A large sloping grassy strip along a fence is set aside for tents, and there is a group or extended tent area. Between the tent areas are two gravel rows of RV sites, with small grassy strips between the sites. Nothing fancy here, but the popular Cowboy Blues restaurant and the whole town are within a few block radius, making this a convenient stopping place.

Basics

Operated By: Catherine Barnes. **Open:** All year. **Site Assignment:** First come, first served. **Registration:** Office trailer. **Fee:** $11 tent, $25–$29 RV. **Parking:** At site.

Facilities

Number of RV Sites: 28. **Number of Tent-Only Sites:** 20. **Hookups:** Electric (30, 50 amp), water, sewer. **Each Site:** Table, grill. **Dump Station:** Yes. **Laundry:** Yes. **Pay Phone:** Yes. **Rest Rooms and Showers:** Yes. **Fuel:** No. **Propane:** No. **Internal Roads:** Gravel, good. **RV Service:** No. **Market:** Escalante, two blocks distant. **Restaurant:** Escalante, across the street. **General Store:** No. **Vending:** No. **Swimming:** No. **Playground:** No. **Other:** Modem access, rock shop. **Activities:** Fishing, water sports, horseback riding. **Nearby Attractions:** Grand Staircase-Escalante National Monument, Anasazi Indian Village State Park, Boulder Mountain lakes, Bryce. **Additional Information:** Escalante Interagency Office, (435) 826-5499.

Restrictions

Pets: Yes. **Fires:** Yes. **Alcoholic Beverages:** Allowed. **Vehicle Maximum Length:** 49 ft.

To Get There

At the corner of Main & 500 W St. in Escalante, where UT Hwy. 12 becomes Main St.

ESCALANTE

Calf Creek Campground

P.O. Box 225, Escalante 84726. T: (435) 826-5400; www.utso.ut.blm.gov.

RV ★ Tent ★★★★★

Beauty: ★★★★★ Site Privacy: ★★★★★
Spaciousness: ★★★★★ Quiet: ★★★★★
Security: ★★★★ Cleanliness: ★★★★
Insect Control: ★★ Facilities: ★

The natural beauty of being surrounded by Escalante sandstone cliffs and the nearness of popular trailheads makes Calf Creek Campground so popular that it fills to capacity almost every night. People turned away the night before show up early the next morning to grab the coveted spots. Fortunately, a campground host acts as traffic cop, as the small parking area fills up with day hikers and big rigs can have trouble maneuvering to turn around and exit. The campsites are coveted because they are widely dispersed on alternating sides of the road on both sides of a creek cutting through the campground. Dense vegetation scraping big vehicles on the narrow road adds extra privacy. However, many of the sites are not level, and high water or flash floods can make creek crossings and site access impossible. Long sleeves and long pants are advised, as biting deer flies breed in the creek.

Basics

Operated By: BLM. **Open:** All year. **Site Assignment:** First come, first served. **Registration:** Self-pay entrance fee station. **Fee:** $7 (exact cash or check). **Parking:** At site.

Facilities

Number of RV Sites: 10. **Number of Tent-Only Sites:** 3. **Hookups:** None. **Each Site:** Cement table, fire pit. **Dump Station:** No. **Laundry:** No. **Pay Phone:** No. **Rest Rooms and Showers:** No showers. **Fuel:** No. **Propane:** No. **Internal Roads:** Narrow in spots, w/ creek crossings. **RV Service:** No. **Market:** Escalante, 16 mi. **Restaurant:** Kiva Coffeehouse, 1 mi. **General Store:** No. **Vending:** No. **Swimming:** No. **Playground:** No. **Activities:** Fishing, water sports, horseback riding. **Nearby Attractions:** Lower Calf Creek Falls, Boynton Arch, Escalante Natural Bridge, Anasazi Indian Village State Park, Boulder Mountains, Burr Trail, Capitol Reef. **Additional Information:** Escalante Interagency Office, (435) 826-5499.

Restrictions

Pets: On leash. **Fires:** Yes. **Alcoholic Beverages:** Allowed. **Vehicle Maximum Length:** 25 ft. **Other:** 14-day limit, no firearms, fireworks, horses, or pack animals.

To Get There

16 mi. east of Escalante, on UT Hwy. 12.

ESCALANTE

Escalante State Park

710 North Reservoir Rd., Escalante 84726. T: (435) 826-4466 or (800) 322-3770.

RV ★★ Tent ★★★★★

Beauty: ★★★★★ Site Privacy: ★★★★★
Spaciousness: ★★★ Quiet: ★★★★
Security: ★★★★ Cleanliness: ★★★★
Insect Control: ★★ Facilities: ★★★

Escalante State Park stretches along the shoreline of Wide Hollow Reservoir, which supplies Escalante with its irrigation water. The Aquarius Plateau and views of red rocks add to the rugged charm of the campground, which is a short distance back from the water and slightly buffered from day users. Aside from water activities like boating and fishing for bluegill and rainbow trout, there is a popular one-mile petrified-forest trail and an array of aquatic birds ranging from loons and cormorants to spotted sandpipers and marbled godwits. The mixture of flat dirt and grassy sites, some with junipers and shade canopies and others under tall cottonwood trees, works best for tents and small vehicles. Gnats and deer flies are an occasional nuisance, but the area is still very popular with day users. All in all, a pleasant place to spend the day, or even have a picnic lunch if just passing through.

Basics

Operated By: Utah State Parks. **Open:** All year. **Site Assignment:** First come, first served; reservations (one night only; up to 16 weeks in advance of checkout date for individuals; 11 months for group site). **Registration:** Visitor Center (if open); otherwise self-pay fee station. **Fee:** $13. **Parking:** At site.

Facilities

Number of RV Sites: 22. **Number of Tent-Only Sites:** 0. **Hookups:** None. **Each Site:** Table, bench, grill on cement pad. **Dump Station:** Yes. **Laundry:** No. **Pay Phone:** Yes. **Rest Rooms and Showers:** Yes. **Fuel:** No. **Propane:** No. **Internal Roads:** Paved, excellent. **RV Service:** No. **Market:** Escalante, 2 mi. **Restaurant:** Escalante, 2 mi. **General Store:** No. **Vending:** Yes. **Swimming:** In lake. **Playground:** No. **Other:** Boat ramp, canoe rentals, shade canopies at some sites. **Activities:** Boating, waterskiing, lake fishing, aquatic bird-watching, petrified forest. **Nearby Attractions:** Grand Staircase-Escalante National Monument, Anasazi Indian Village State Park, Boulder Mountain lakes & forest, Calf Creek, Bryce. **Additional Information:** Escalante Interagency Office, (435) 826-5499.

Restrictions

Pets: On leash. **Fires:** Yes (firewood sold). **Alcoholic Beverages:** Allowed. **Vehicle Maximum Length:** 30 ft. **Other:** 14-day max. stay.

To Get There

1 mi. west of Escalante on UT Hwy. 12, then 1 mi. north on Wide Hollow Rd.

FILLMORE

Fillmore KOA

410 West 900 South, Fillmore 84631. T: (435) 743-4420 or (800) 562-1516; www.koa.com; fillmorekoa@xmission.com.

RV ★★★★ Tent ★★★★

Beauty: ★★★★★ Site Privacy: ★★★★
Spaciousness: ★★★★ Quiet: ★★★★
Security: ★★★★ Cleanliness: ★★★★★
Insect Control: ★★★ Facilities: ★★★★

Named after Millard Fillmore, a U.S. President friendly to persecuted Mormons, and briefly Utah's state capital in the 1850s, Fillmore is now the sleepy anchor for surrounding alfalfa and cattle ranches. It is easy to whiz by the I-15 Fillmore Exit without stopping at the Territorial Statehouse State Park Museum or the Fillmore KOA, a grassy poplar-shaded little gem of a campground in a windy area away from the highway. The office and general store are inside a log cabin, and the pool looks like stone (actually Gunite™ and white paint). Geology buffs should consult the host, a survivor of Mt. St. Helen's who can wax on about the geothermal ice caves, lava flows to the west, and differences in age and type between Utah and Pacific Northwest volcanoes. The town has a new golf course, and with a little luck the mini-golf course at the KOA may get finished.

Basics

Operated By: Ann & Dick Flones. **Open:** All year (limited services Dec. 15–Mar. 1; sometimes closed by snow). **Site Assignment:** First come, first served. **Registration:** Office. **Fee:** $15–$17 tent, $18–$22 RV (V, MC, AE, D). **Parking:** At site.

Facilities

Number of RV Sites: 49. **Number of Tent-Only Sites:** 7. **Hookups:** Electric (30, 50 amp), water, sewer. **Each Site:** Table. **Dump Station:** Yes. **Laundry:** Yes. **Pay Phone:** Yes. **Rest Rooms and Showers:** Yes. **Fuel:** No. **Propane:** Yes. **Internal Roads:** Gravel, good. **RV Service:** No. **Market:** Fillmore, 1 mi. **Restaurant:** Fillmore, 1 mi. **General Store:** Yes. **Vending:** Yes. **Swimming:** Pool. **Playground:** Yes (also volleyball, tetherball, game room). **Other:** Tent sites have grass pads, electric, water, sheltered tables, grills, fire rings; 5 cabins. **Activities:** Fishing, boating, hunting, golf. **Nearby Attractions:** Paiute ATV Trail, Cove Fort. **Additional Information:** Fillmore Area Chamber of Commerce, (435) 743-6121.

Restrictions

Pets: On leash. **Fires:** Yes. **Alcoholic Beverages:** Allowed. **Vehicle Maximum Length:** 90 ft.

To Get There

From US I-15 Exit163 go 0.25 mi. north on business loop and 0.5 mi. east on 900 South.

GLENDALE

Bryce/Zion KOA

P.O. Box 189, Glendale 84729. T: (435) 648-2490 or (800) 562-8635 (reservations); www.koa.com.

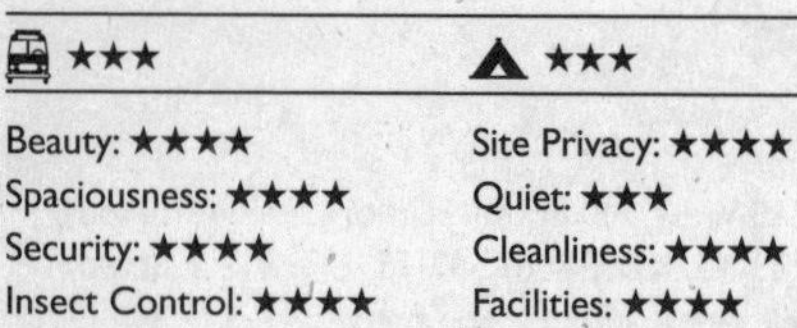

Beauty: ★★★★ Site Privacy: ★★★★
Spaciousness: ★★★★ Quiet: ★★★
Security: ★★★★ Cleanliness: ★★★★
Insect Control: ★★★★ Facilities: ★★★★

Though alongside a grade in US Hwy. 89 with tour-bus and truck engine noise, the strategic location merits careful consideration, as it is only 25 miles to Coral Pink Sand Dunes State Park, 30 miles to Zion, 35 miles to Cedar Breaks, and 45 miles to Bryce. A horse pasture and spring-fed pond border one side, and Bryce-like orange sandstone spires on the surrounding hills add a park-like ambiance. The grassy sites and gravel roads of Bryce/Zion KOA add to the impression of pastoral tranquility. Buffalo Bistro next door is known area-wide for its buffalo burgers, fruit cobblers, and rabbit-rattlesnake sausage served with spicy mustard, having been almost an east Zion institution before relocating here. The group tent sites, dog walk, car wash, and horse and hiking trails are added bonuses. Though there are some poplar trees, not every site has shade. Nevertheless, overall this is a superior stopping place.

Basics

Operated By: Ellen Lamb. **Open:** May 1–Sept. 30. **Site Assignment:** First come, first served; reservations. **Registration:** Office. **Fee:** $17 tent, $20–$22 RV (V, MC, AE, D). **Parking:** At site.

Facilities

Number of RV Sites: 62. **Number of Tent-Only Sites:** 20. **Hookups:** Electric (20, 30 amp), water, sewer. **Each Site:** Table, grill. **Dump Station:** Yes. **Laundry:** Yes. **Pay Phone:** Yes. **Rest Rooms and Showers:** Yes. **Fuel:** No. **Propane:** No. **Internal Roads:** Gravel, good condition. **RV Service:** No. **Market:** 5 mi. south in Glendale. **Restaurant:** Adjacent to Buffalo Bistro. **General Store:** Yes. **Vending:** Yes. **Swimming:** Pool. **Playground:** Yes. **Other:** Modem connection. **Activities:** Fishing, horseback riding. **Nearby Attractions:** Bryce, Zion, Cedar Breaks, Escalante. **Additional Information:** Kane County Office of Tourism, 78 S. 100 East, Kanab, UT 84741; (435) 644-5033; (800) 733-5263; kanetrav@kaneutah.com; www.kaneutah.com.

Restrictions

Pets: On leash under owner's control. **Fires:** Yes (firewood sold). **Alcoholic Beverages:** Allowed. **Vehicle Maximum Length:** 35 ft.

To Get There

5 mi. north of Glendale on US Hwy. 89.

GREEN RIVER

Green River KOA

P.O. Box 14, Green River 84525. T: (435) 564-3651 or (800) 562-3649 (reservations); www.koa.com.

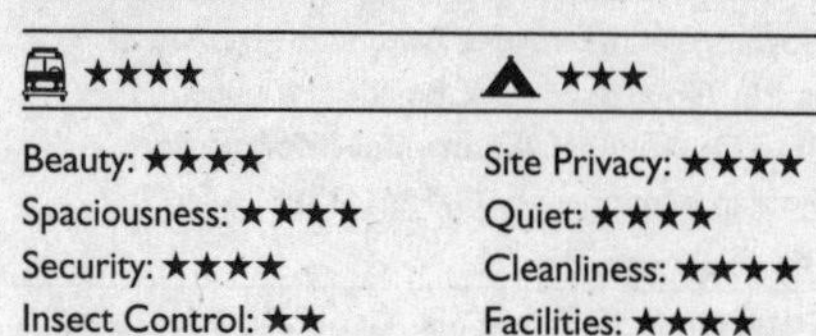

Beauty: ★★★★ Site Privacy: ★★★★
Spaciousness: ★★★★ Quiet: ★★★★
Security: ★★★★ Cleanliness: ★★★★
Insect Control: ★★ Facilities: ★★★★

Literally across the street from Green River State Park, this KOA came into existence to handle the state park's overflow, adding hookups and louder proximity to the train. Overflow camping is what Green River is about much of the time, though, being half way between Las Vegas and Denver, it attracts its fair share of the traffic plying I-70. During summer, particularly special-event weekends, Arches, Canyonlands, and Moab can fill up, leaving campers to choose between heading south towards Monticello or north towards Green River. Green River is actually closer to the Canyonlands and Arches entrances, and is a peaceful little truck-stop town compared to bustling Moab. Campers could do worse than holing up in the big grassy sites here, and might even be pleasantly surprised by the excellent River History Museum, which doubles as a Visitor Center.

Basics

Operated By: KOA franchisee. **Open:** Apr. 1–Sept. 30. **Site Assignment:** First come, first served; reservations accepted. **Registration:** At office. **Fee:** $17 tent, $19–$21 RV (V, MC, AE, D). **Parking:** At site.

Facilities

Number of RV Sites: 77. **Number of Tent-Only Sites:** 30. **Hookups:** Electric (30 amp), water, sewer, cable TV. **Each Site:** Table, grill. **Dump Station:** Yes. **Laundry:** Yes. **Pay Phone:** Yes. **Rest Rooms and Showers:** Yes. **Fuel:** No. **Propane:** No. **Internal Roads:** Gravel, good. **RV Service:** No. **Market:** Green River, 1 mi. **Restaurant:** Green River. **General Store:** Yes. **Vending:** Yes. **Swimming:** Heated pool. **Playground:** Yes. **Other:** Dog walk. **Activities:** Fishing, rockhounding, golf. **Nearby Attractions:** John Wesley Powell River History Museum, Canyonlands, Dead Horse State Park, Goblin Valley State Park, Arches, Moab. **Additional Information:** Emery County Travel Bureau, (888) 564-3600, www.emerycounty.com.

Restrictions

Pets: On leash under owner's control. **Fires:** Yes (charcoal only in grills). **Alcoholic Beverages:** Allowed. **Vehicle Maximum Length:** 105 ft. **Other:** No generator use, 11 a.m. checkout.

To Get There

From US I-70, take Green River Main St. Exit, turn south on Green River Blvd. for 0.5 mi.

GREEN RIVER

Green River State Park

P.O. Box 637, Green River 84525. T: (435) 564-3633 or (800) 322-3770 (reservations).

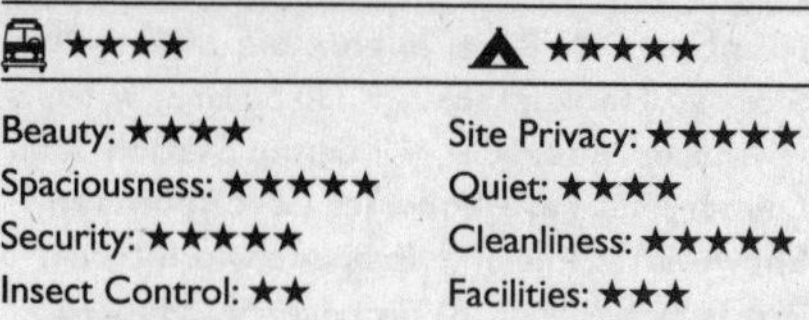

Beauty: ★★★★ Site Privacy: ★★★★★
Spaciousness: ★★★★★ Quiet: ★★★★
Security: ★★★★★ Cleanliness: ★★★★★
Insect Control: ★★ Facilities: ★★★

Muskrats, beavers, ibises, egrets, and herons share Green River State Park with golfers, campers, picnickers, boaters, rafters, and river runners. This well-run park is near the center of town, the river museum, and restaurants, but it feels away from it all, except for the pesky summer gnats (bird food) and the train that rumbles by the river. Large pull-through sites can handle the biggest rigs and are shaded by cottonwoods, willows, and Russian olive trees full of chirping birds. During summer the grass is watered at 10 a.m., and everything needs to be sealed up or put away to avoid a soaking. Tents need to be moved at least every other day anyway, to avoid killing the grass. Though hookups are lacking, this is the premier campground in Green River, and it is less than an hour from Arches.

Basics

Operated By: Utah State Parks. **Open:** All year. **Site Assignment:** First come, first served; all but 10 sites can be reserved (3–110 days in advance). **Registration:** Entrance kiosk. **Fee:** $12. **Parking:** At site.

Facilities

Number of RV Sites: 42. **Number of Tent-Only Sites:** 0. **Hookups:** None. **Each Site:** Table on cement pad, grill or fire pit. **Dump Station:** Yes. **Laundry:** No. **Pay Phone:** Yes. **Rest Rooms and Showers:** Yes. **Fuel:** No. **Propane:** No. **Internal Roads:** Paved, some ruts. **RV Service:** No. **Market:** In Green River. **Restaurant:** In Green River. **General Store:** No. **Vending:** No. **Swimming:** No. **Playground:** No. **Other:** 9-hole golf course, boat ramp & dock, vehicle storage, amphitheater, wheelchair-accessible restroom. **Activities:** River float trips, Memorial Day Friendship Cruise to Moab, Sept. Melon Days. **Nearby Attractions:** John Wesley Powell River History Museum, Canyonlands, Dead Horse State Park, Goblin Valley State Park, Arches, Moab. **Additional Information:** Emery County Travel Bureau, (888) 564-3600, www.emerycounty.com.

Restrictions

Pets: On leash under owner's control. **Fires:** Yes. **Alcoholic Beverages:** Allowed at site, but not to the point of public intoxication. **Vehicle Maximum Length:** No limit. **Other:** 14-day limit, tents must be moved every other day.

To Get There

From US I-70 Exit 162, go west on Main St., turn south on Green River Blvd.

GREEN RIVER
Shady Acres RV Park & Campground

P.O. Box 598, Green River 84525. T: (800) 537-8674 or (435) 564-8838; F: (435) 564-8838; www.shadyacresrv.com; shadya@etv.net.

RV ★★★★★ Tent ★★★★

Beauty: ★★★★ Site Privacy: ★★★★
Spaciousness: ★★★★★ Quiet: ★★★★
Security: ★★★★ Cleanliness: ★★★★
Insect Control: ★★ Facilities: ★★★★★

On the opposite side of the muddy brown Green River from United Campground and a block across the street from the truck scales and the 24-hour West Winds Restaurant (hearty trucker meals), Shady Acres shields itself from Main Street with cottonwood trees. But everything is here, including cable TV, groceries, a gas station with a submarine sandwich franchise, and RV repairs. The gravel campsites are well back from Main Street, and the cottonwood trees blowing in the wind make more noise than the steady parade of slow trucks exiting I-70. The basketball and volleyball courts among the swings and horseshoes add a touch of resort ambiance. This well-run family operation has almost zero tolerance for offensive language, and the county sheriff takes care of intoxicated troublemakers. With the Powell River History Museum down the street and the state park nearby, the range of amenities here may tip the scales for some.

BASICS
Operated By: Private family. **Open:** All year. **Site Assignment:** First come, first served; reservations recommended for long holiday weekends. **Registration:** At office. **Fee:** $10–$13 tent, $17–$22 RV (V, MC, AE, D). **Parking:** At site.

FACILITIES
Number of RV Sites: 97. **Number of Tent-Only Sites:** 14. **Hookups:** Electric (50 amp), water, sewer, cable TV. **Each Site:** Table, grill. **Dump Station:** Yes. **Laundry:** Yes. **Pay Phone:** Yes. **Rest Rooms and Showers:** Yes. **Fuel:** Yes. **Propane:** No. **Internal Roads:** Gravely pavement, good condition. **RV Service:** No. **Market:** Nearby. **Restaurant:** Across the street. **General Store:** Yes. **Vending:** Yes. **Swimming:** Pool. **Playground:** Yes. **Other:** Dog walk, wheelchair-accessible sites, Internet connection in office, car/RV wash. **Activities:** Golf. **Nearby Attractions:** Crystal Geyser, Black Dragon Pictograph, Goblin Valley, Arches, Canyonlands. **Additional Information:** Emery County Travel Bureau, (888) 564-3600, www.emerycounty.com.

RESTRICTIONS
Pets: On leash. **Fires:** Yes. **Alcoholic Beverages:** Intoxication is not tolerated. **Vehicle Maximum Length:** 100 ft. **Other:** No foul language, no changing of oil or mechanical repairs in the park.

TO GET THERE
From US I-70, exit Green River at Main St., go to 350 E. Main St.

GREEN RIVER
United Campground

P.O. Box 143, Green River 84525. T: (435) 564-8195.

RV ★★★★ Tent ★★★★

Beauty: ★★★★ Site Privacy: ★★★★
Spaciousness: ★★★★★ Quiet: ★★★
Security: ★★★★★ Cleanliness: ★★★★★
Insect Control: ★★ Facilities: ★★★★

One of the better I-70 halfway stops between Las Vegas and Denver, United is also a good overflow site for Moab, Arches, and Canyonlands (within 45 miles) on holidays like Easter. Tucked well-back from Main Street behind the Motel 6 and adjacent to an alfalfa field, the campground is a collection of large grassy sites shaded by tall trees and bisected by a gravel roadway and parking. The Tamarisk Restaurant at the Best Western next door is one of Green River's best, with seating overlooking the river bridge and colonies of swifts swooping down to catch insects (bug repellent is a good summer precaution). Across the street is the John Wesley Powell River History Museum building, which also houses a gallery and visitors center. Overall, the location is very convenient for parking and walking once settled in, and a good base for exploring the surrounding area.

BASICS
Operated By: Charles & Linda Burrage. **Open:** All year. **Site Assignment:** First come, first served; reservations recommended holiday weekends. **Registration:** At office. **Fee:** $14.50 tent, $19.50 RV. (V, MC, AE, D). **Parking:** At site.

FACILITIES
Number of RV Sites: 65. **Number of Tent-Only Sites:** 14. **Hookups:** Electric (20, 30, 50 amp), water, sewer, cable TV. **Each Site:** Table. **Dump Station:** Yes. **Laundry:** Yes. **Pay Phone:** Yes. **Rest Rooms and Showers:** Yes. **Fuel:** No. **Propane:** Yes. **Internal Roads:** Gravel, excellent. **RV Service:** No. **Market:** 2 blocks. **Restaurant:** Next door. **General Store:** Yes. **Vending:** No. **Swimming:** Pool. **Playground:** Yes. **Other:** Portable grill on request, modem hookup in office. **Activities:** Boating, river rafting. **Nearby Attractions:** Arches, Canyonlands, Capitol Reef, Goblin Valley State Park. **Additional Information:** Emery County Travel Bureau, (888) 564-3600, www.emerycounty.com.

RESTRICTIONS
Pets: On leash under owner's control. **Fires:** Yes. **Alcoholic Beverages:** Allowed. **Vehicle Maximum Length:** Over 100 ft. **Other:** 11 a.m. checkout.

TO GET THERE
Exit I-70 at Main Street in Green River, enter via driveway between Motel 6 and Best Western.

HANKSVILLE
Goblin Valley State Park

P.O. Box 637, Green River 84525. T: (435) 564-3633 or (800) 322-3770 (reservations).

RV ★★★★ Tent ★★★★★

Beauty: ★★★★★ Site Privacy: ★★★★★
Spaciousness: ★★★★★ Quiet: ★★★★★
Security: ★★★★ Cleanliness: ★★★★
Insect Control: ★★★ Facilities: ★★

The intriguing chocolate-colored goblins giving this park its name result from uneven wind and rain erosion of sandstone layers of varying hardness in this remote area once frequented by uranium miners and ancient Native Americans. The San Rafael Reef, which has steep canyons hidden inside its sawtooth swells, is also part of the Jurassic and Triassic sandstone and siltstone scenery left behind by an ancient sea in what is now the Green River Desert. The campground itself is a half loop backed by orange-and-white sandstone walls with hoodoos, spires, and a hilltop oil well pumping away next to solar panels. The restroom and hot showers are also powered by solar arrays. There is little shade from the midday sun. On hot summer days the sandstone walls surrounding the spacious campground sites radiate extra heat. But the goblins, reefs, badlands, balanced rocks, spires, and hoodoos make a colorful geologic adventure for self-sufficient campers.

BASICS
Operated By: Utah State Parks. **Open:** All year. **Site Assignment:** First come, first served; 14 sites can be reserved (up to 16 weeks in advance of checkout date for individuals; up to 11 months in advance for group site). **Registration:** Self-pay entrance fee station. **Fee:** $12. **Parking:** At site.

FACILITIES
Number of RV Sites: 21. **Number of Tent-Only Sites:** 0. **Hookups:** None. **Each Site:** Table, grill. **Dump Station:** Yes. **Laundry:** No. **Pay Phone:** No. **Rest Rooms and Showers:** Yes. **Fuel:** No. **Propane:** No. **Internal Roads:** Paved, good condition. **RV Service:** No. **Market:** Hanksville, 32 mi.; Green River, 35 mi. **Restaurant:** Hanksville, 32 mi.; Green River, 35 mi. **General Store:** No. **Vending:** No. **Swimming:** No. **Playground:** No. **Other:** Covered picnic pavilion at observation point, wheelchair-accessible rest room. **Activities:** Geologic exploration. **Nearby Attractions:** Capitol Reef, Canyonlands. **Additional Information:** Emery County Travel Bureau, (888) 564-3600, www.emerycounty.com.

RESTRICTIONS
Pets: On leash under owner's control. **Fires:** Yes. **Alcoholic Beverages:** Allowed. **Vehicle Maximum Length:** No limit. **Other:** No ground fires, 14-day limit.

TO GET THERE
Go 20 mi. north from Hanksville on UT Hwy. 24, at milepost 137 turn west onto Temple Mountain Road for 5 mi., then at intersection go 7 mi. south on graded dirt county road.

HANKSVILLE

Red Rock Restaurant and Campground

Box 55, Hanksville 84734. T: (435) 542-3235; www.hanksville.com; redrock@hanksville.com.

RV ★★★★ Tent ★★★

Beauty: ★★★ Site Privacy: ★★
Spaciousness: ★★ Quiet: ★★★★
Security: ★★★★ Cleanliness: ★★★★
Insect Control: ★★★★ Facilities: ★★★★

With gas stations, RV repair, a post office, and other amenities within blocks, this friendly restaurant with a well-maintained campground in back makes a good stopping point en route to Capitol Reef, Bullfrog Marina on Lake Powell, or Canyonlands. The restaurant has everything from steaks to beer and wine, which is handy, as there are no grills. Just behind the restaurant is a grassy area for tent camping that will suffice for a night. Three gravel rows for RVs extend further back, with a small tree between each site and a fence separating the property from an irrigated field at the rear. Though more an overnight stop, the location does lend itself to day trips to Goblin Valley State Park, Capitol Reef, and an adventurous dirt-road excursion (not to be attempted when rain threatens) heading north to Green River via the San Rafael Desert.

BASICS

Operated By: Elliot & Layne Arnoldson. **Open:** Mar. 15–Nov. 1. **Site Assignment:** First come, first served; reservations accepted. **Registration:** In restaurant. **Fee:** $10 tent, $16 RV (V, MC, D). **Parking:** At site.

FACILITIES

Number of RV Sites: 60. **Number of Tent-Only Sites:** 60. **Hookups:** Electric (30, 50 amp), water, sewer. **Each Site:** Table. **Dump Station:** Yes. **Laundry:** Yes. **Pay Phone:** Yes. **Rest Rooms and Showers:** Yes. **Fuel:** No. **Propane:** No. **Internal Roads:** Gravel, good condition. **RV Service:** No. **Market:** 1.5 blocks away. **Restaurant:** On site. **General Store:** No. **Vending:** Yes. **Swimming:** No. **Playground:** No. **Activities:** Geologic exploration. **Nearby Attractions:** Goblin Valley State Park, Capitol Reef, Canyonlands, Hite Marina, Natural Bridges. **Additional Information:** Emery County Travel Bureau, (888) 564-3600, www.emerycounty.com.

RESTRICTIONS

Pets: On leash. **Fires:** Yes. **Alcoholic Beverages:** Allowed. **Vehicle Maximum Length:** Unlimited in circle area.

TO GET THERE

Go 200 ft. west on Hwy. 24 from junction of Utah Hwys 24 & 95.

HATCH

Riverside Motel & RV Park

P.O. Box 521, Hatch 84735. T: (435) 735-4223 or (800) 824-5651; F: (435) 735-4220; brycecanyoncountry.com/accommodations/hatch; riversid@color-country.net.

RV ★★★ Tent ★★★

Beauty: ★★★★ Site Privacy: ★★★★
Spaciousness: ★★★★ Quiet: ★★★★
Security: ★★★★ Cleanliness: ★★★★
Insect Control: ★★★ Facilities: ★★★★

Strategically situated on the banks of the Sevier River just south of the Bryce Junction (where UT Hwy. 12 intersects US Hwy. 89), Riverside is a magnet for tour buses. The campground is isolated in a small valley behind an office/gift shop, motel, and restaurant and is bordered by the river on two sides. The seven designated tent sides are along the river, separated from the RVs by a large grass playing field that doubles as a tour bus group tent site. International groups, ranging from musicians to teens, like the river and distant Red Canyon mountain backdrops, as well as the group pavilion. But the campground quiets down after 10 p.m., and an occasional truck and the raging wind are about the extent of the noise most nights. The 18-foot wide pull-through sites, network TV reception, and convenient location make this a good RV stop.

BASICS

Operated By: Cordell & Julie Peters/Brent & Kathy Parkinson. **Open:** Mar. 1–Nov. 1. **Site Assignment:** First come, first served; reservations accepted. **Registration:** Office inside store. **Fee:** $13 tent, $17–$20 RV (V, MC). **Parking:** At site.

FACILITIES

Number of RV Sites: 47. **Number of Tent-Only Sites:** Undesignated sites. **Hookups:** Electric (20, 30, 50 amp), water, sewer. **Each Site:** Table, grill. **Dump Station:** Yes. **Laundry:** Yes. **Pay Phone:** Yes. **Rest Rooms and Showers:** Yes. **Fuel:** No. **Propane:** Yes. **Internal Roads:** Gravel, good. **RV Service:** No. **Market:** Panguitch, 8 mi. **Restaurant:** On site. **General Store:** Yes. **Vending:** Yes. **Swimming:** In river. **Playground:** Yes. **Other:** Horseshoe pit, basketball court, motel. **Activities:** Fishing. **Nearby Attractions:** Panguitch Lake, Red Canyon, Cedar Breaks, Bryce, Zion. **Additional Information:** Garfield County Travel Council, (800) 444-6689; Bryce Canyon National Park Headquarters, (435) 834-5322.

RESTRICTIONS

Pets: On leash under owner's control. **Fires:** Yes. **Alcoholic Beverages:** Allowed. **Vehicle Maximum Length:** Over 45 ft.

TO GET THERE

From junction w/ UT Hwy. 12, go 2 mi. south on US Hwy. 89.

HOVENWEEP NATIONAL MONUMENT

Hovenweep Campground

McElmo Rte., Cortez 81321. T: (970) 562-4282; www.nps.gov/hove.

RV ★★ Tent ★★★★

Beauty: ★★★★ Site Privacy: ★★★★
Spaciousness: ★★ Quiet: ★★★★
Security: ★★★★ Cleanliness: ★★★★★
Insect Control: ★★★ Facilities: ★★

Designed in the 1960s for tent and car camping when there was little need for pull-through sites, Hovenweep has narrow roads and tight cornering. Self-sufficiency is the watchword here, as there are sand pads for tents and some sheltered tables but neither dump stations nor showers. Only two sites are adequate for larger vehicles, but small vehicles and tent campers will do well in the small sites separated by tall junipers alive with twittering birds. High-axle or four-wheel drive vehicles are needed to reach archaeological sites like Holly, Horseshoe, and Hackberry Ruins. But regular hiking trails dotted with creamy cliff roses lead to other archaeological sites, such as Hovenweep Castle, the tall canyon-bottom Square Tower, and the double-walled Cajon sun house built near a spring at the head of a canyon. During winter, the trails get slippery from snow and ice and become dangerous near cliffs.

BASICS

Operated By: National Park Service. **Open:** All year. **Site Assignment:** First come, first served. **Registration:** Self-pay fee station. **Fee:** $10 (cash or check only). **Parking:** At site.

FACILITIES

Number of RV Sites: 31. **Number of Tent-Only Sites:** 0. **Hookups:** None. **Each Site:** Table, grill. **Dump Station:** No. **Laundry:** No. **Pay Phone:** No. **Rest Rooms and Showers:** No showers. **Fuel:** No. **Propane:** No. **Internal Roads:** Gravel, good. **RV Service:** No. **Market:** Bluff, 40 mi. **Restaurant:** Bluff, 40 mi. **General Store:** No. **Vending:** No. **Swimming:** No. **Playground:** No. **Other:** Visitor center, amphitheater, Anasazi crop garden, ranger program (summer weekends). **Activities:** Mountain biking. **Nearby Attractions:** Monument Valley, Canyonlands, Natural Bridges. **Additional Information:** Edge of the Cedars State Park, (435) 678-2238.

RESTRICTIONS

Pets: On leash (allowed on trails w/ short leashes). **Fires:** Yes (in fire grates only, no wood collection, must bring own wood or charcoal). **Alcoholic Beverages:** Allowed. **Vehicle Maximum Length:** 25 ft. **Other:** Collection of artifacts is illegal, 2 tents or 6 people per site.

TO GET THERE

From Bluff go 30 mi. east on US Hwy. 262 and then 10 mi. northeast at Aneth.

HURRICANE

Brentwood RV Resort

150 North 3700 West, Hurricane 84737. T: (435) 635-2320 or (800) 447-2239.

RV ★★★★ Tent ★★

Beauty: ★★★★ Site Privacy: ★★★★
Spaciousness: ★★★★ Quiet: ★★★★
Security: ★★★★ Cleanliness: ★★★★
Insect Control: ★★★ Facilities: ★★★★

Hurricane is located between St. George and Zion National Park and makes a good shopping place for those wanting to purchase food, hardware, and other supplies. There are many fine campground options between St. George and Zion, but Brentwood boasts a convenient roadside location, wide spaces for slide-outs, and amenities like bowling and billiards. Tent campers have a grassy area near the playground and tennis courts with mulberries and other trees still too small to provide much shade. The shadiest part of the tent area has four spaces right up against the tennis courts. Canyons RV Resort and Willowind RV Park (see Appendix) are grassier, smaller, and further back from the road. Nearby Quail Creek State Park is probably the better place for a boating weekend. If Zion National Park is the destination, then Zion River Resort in Virgin, Zion Canyon Campground in Springdale, and the two National Park Service campgrounds should be considered.

Basics

Operated By: Brentwood Resort. **Open:** All year. **Site Assignment:** First come, first served; reservations accepted. **Registration:** Office. **Fee:** $12 tent, $19 RV (V, MC, AE, D). **Parking:** At site.

Facilities

Number of RV Sites: 187. **Number of Tent-Only Sites:** Undesignated sites. **Hookups:** Electric (30, 50 amp), water, sewer, cable TV. **Each Site:** Table. **Dump Station:** Yes. **Laundry:** Yes. **Pay Phone:** Yes. **Rest Rooms and Showers:** Yes. **Fuel:** No. **Propane:** No. **Internal Roads:** Paved, good. **RV Service:** No. **Market:** Hurricane, 1 mi. **Restaurant:** Hurricane, 1 mi. **General Store:** No. **Vending:** Yes. **Swimming:** Pool. **Playground:** Yes. **Other:** Bowling, billiards, tennis, some grills. **Activities:** Golf, horseshoes, shuffleboard, boating, fishing. **Nearby Attractions:** Quail Creek SP, Zion. **Additional Information:** Washington County Travel Bureau, (435) 634-5747, (800) 869-6635.

Restrictions

Pets: On leash under owner's control. **Fires:** Yes. **Alcoholic Beverages:** Allowed. **Vehicle Maximum Length:** 60 ft. **Other:** Children under 18 must be under parental supervision.

To Get There

From US I-15 8 mi. north of St. George go east 5 mi. on UT Hwy. 9.

KANAB
Coral Pink Sand Dunes State Park

P.O. Box 95, Kanab 84741. T: (435) 648-2800 or (800) 322-3770; F: (435) 648-2801; www.parks.state.ut.us.

RV ★★★★ Tent ★★★★

Beauty: ★★★★★	Site Privacy: ★★★★★
Spaciousness: ★★★★★	Quiet: ★★★★
Security: ★★★★★	Cleanliness: ★★★★
Insect Control: ★★★	Facilities: ★★

Beautiful orange-sand dunes dotted with ponderosa pine trees and six-foot-tall dune grasses support both off-highway vehicle activity and scientific study areas with the unique Coral Pink Sand Dunes tiger beetle and Welsh milkweed. Coral Pink Sand Dunes State Park is also very popular with student groups, who come to learn about dune life from wood walkways protecting the dunes. Campsites are especially spacious, with parking loops accommodating extra long vehicles (e.g. 75–148 feet) or multiple smaller vehicles. Tall junipers growing out of the orange sand screen campsites from each other, and bicyclists pedal the paved roads. At 6,000 feet elevation, the park gets snow for winter activities. Hiking trails offer views of Zion, the Grand Canyon's North Rim, and ancient Native American pictographs. Reservations are advised at this popular park, and can be made 11 months in advance by groups or up to 16 weeks in advance of checkout date (a minimum of three days in advance of arrival) by individuals.

Basics

Operated By: Utah State Parks. **Open:** All year. **Site Assignment:** First come, first served; group reservations; specific sites can be reserved one night at a time. **Registration:** Entrance kiosk. **Fee:** $13 per vehicle (V, MC, Utah checks). **Parking:** Loops at site.

Facilities

Number of RV Sites: 22. **Number of Tent-Only Sites:** 0. **Hookups:** Water, electric (30 amp). **Each Site:** Table, grill. **Dump Station:** Yes. **Laundry:** No. **Pay Phone:** Yes. **Rest Rooms and Showers:** Yes. **Fuel:** No. **Propane:** No. **Internal Roads:** Paved, good condition. **RV Service:** No. **Market:** 22 mi. northwest in Kanab. **Restaurant:** 22 mi. northwest in Kanab. **General Store:** No. **Vending:** No. **Swimming:** No. **Playground:** No. **Other:** ADA accessible wood walkways over sand dunes, off-highway access to dunes. **Activities:** Off-highway vehicle riding, biking, snow mobiling, snow tubing. **Nearby Attractions:** Pipe Springs National Monument, Kanab, Escalante Staircase National Monument, Zion, Grand Canyon North Rim. **Additional Information:** Kane County Office of Tourism, 78 S. 100 East, Kanab, UT 84741; (435) 644-5033; (800) 733-5263; kanetrav@kaneutah.com; www.kaneutah.com.

Restrictions

Pets: On leash, never unattended. **Fires:** Yes (firewood sold). **Alcoholic Beverages:** Allowed. **Vehicle Maximum Length:** 148 ft. **Other:** 14-day limit, no wood gathering, no fireworks.

To Get There

Go 13 mi. north from Kanab on US Hwy. 89, then southwest on Hancock Rd. to Sand Dunes Rd. for 11 mi.

KANAB
Ponderosa Grove Recreation Site

318 North 1st E, Kanab 84721. T: (435) 644-2672 or (801) 539-4002; www.utso.ut.blm.gov.

RV ★★ Tent ★★★

Beauty: ★★★★	Site Privacy: ★★★★
Spaciousness: ★★★	Quiet: ★★★★
Security: ★★★	Cleanliness: ★★★★
Insect Control: ★★★★	Facilities: ★

Along with the tall grass and sand "Meadow," a big open field with pine cones where camping is free, Ponderosa Grove Recreation Site also acts as an overflow for the often full Coral Pink Sand Dunes State Park. Tall ponderosa pines and junipers give a forested feel to this 6,500-foot- elevation high-desert BLM campground. Though a primitive experience with off-road vehicle access to the rolling orange-sand dunes, Ponderosa Grove offers disabled access. Two large group sites on small loops accommodate ten vehicles each. Showers are available for a fee at Coral Pink Sand Dunes State Park. For good food, head 16 miles to Mt. Carmel Junction and the excellent honey butter scones at the Golden Hills Restaurant, or 15 miles to the many restaurants, stores, and full-hookup RV parks (see Appendix) of Kanab, where the visitor center is lined with posters of movies filmed in the area, which western film–buffs call "Little Hollywood."

Basics

Operated By: BLM. **Open:** April 1–Oct. 31. **Site Assignment:** First come, first served. **Registration:** Self-pay entrance fee station. **Fee:** $5. **Parking:** At site.

Facilities

Number of RV Sites: 9. **Number of Tent-Only Sites:** 0. **Hookups:** None. **Each Site:** Table & grills on cement pads. **Dump Station:** No. **Laundry:** No. **Pay Phone:** No. **Rest Rooms and Showers:** No shower. **Fuel:** No. **Propane:** No. **Internal Roads:** Dirt road, good condition. **RV Service:** No. **Market:** Kanab. **Restaurant:** Kanab or Mt. Carmel Junction. **General Store:** No. **Vending:** No. **Swimming:** No. **Playground:** No. **Other:** Disabled access. **Activities:** Off-highway vehicle riding. **Nearby Attractions:** Pipe Springs & Escalante Staircase National Monuments, Zion, Grand Canyon North Rim. **Additional Information:** Coral Pink Sand Dunes State Park, (435) 648-2800; Kane County Office of Tourism, 78 S. 100 East, Kanab, UT 84741; (435) 644-5033; (800) 733-5263; kanetrav@kaneutah.com; www.kaneutah.com.

Restrictions

Pets: On leash under owner's control. **Fires:** Yes. **Alcoholic Beverages:** Allowed. **Vehicle Maximum Length:** 24 ft. **Other:** 14-day max. stay.

To Get There

Go 7 mi. north from Kanab on US Hwy. 89, then 7 mi. southwest on Hancock Rd.

LAKE POWELL
Bullfrog Resort & Marina Campground/RV Park

P.O. Box 56909, Phoenix 85079. T: (435) 684-7000; F: (435) 684-2319; www.visitlakepowell.com.

RV ★★★★ Tent ★★★★

Beauty: ★★★★★	Site Privacy: ★★★★
Spaciousness: ★★★★	Quiet: ★★★★
Security: ★★★★	Cleanliness: ★★★★
Insect Control: ★★	Facilities: ★★★★★

Bullfrog Resort & Marina in Glen Canyon National Recreation Area includes the Painted Hills RV Park and Bullfrog Campground. Both are operated by Aramark Parks & Resorts, an authorized National Park Service concessionaire. The year-round RV Park has full hookups and is attractively nestled among tall conifers and low yellowish sandstone hills. The RV Park does not allow tents. Tent camping is allowed only at the seasonal Campground, which is also open to RV vehicles; sites 1–21 on Loop A have the best lake views. Tent campers must go to the village store and shell out additional money ($2) to take a shower, whereas the RV Park has showers. But it is the boating, fishing, and water sports, not campground amenities, that is the attraction here. Indeed, many locals skip the two pricey campgrounds in favor of primitive camping on the beaches (no designated sites) lining the shores of Lake Powell.

Basics

Operated By: Aramark Parks & Resorts. **Open:** All year (for RVs; tents Mar.–Oct. only). **Site Assignment:** First come, first served; reservations. **Registration:** Self-pay fee station (Campground); Lodge (RV Park). **Fee:** $16–$27 (cash only; US currency, no checks). **Parking:** At site.

Facilities

Number of RV Sites: 110. **Number of Tent-Only Sites:** 0. **Hookups:** Electric (20, 30 amp), water, sewer. **Each Site:** Table, grill. **Dump Station:** Yes. **Laundry:** Yes. **Pay Phone:** Yes. **Rest Rooms and Showers:** Yes. **Fuel:** No. **Propane:** Yes. **Internal Roads:** Paved & gravel, good. **RV Service:** No. **Market:** Blanding, 84 mi. **Restaurant:** Bullfrog Marina. **General Store:** Yes. **Vending:** Yes. **Swimming:** Lake. **Playground:** No. **Other:** Ferry, boat rental, motel. **Activities:** Boating, fishing, water sports. **Nearby Attractions:** Natural Bridges. **Additional Information:** National Park Service, (435) 684-7400; Lake Powell Ferry, (435) 684-3000; Glen Canyon Natural History Assoc., www.pagelakepowell.org.

Restrictions

Pets: On leash & under control at all times. **Fires:** Yes (in grills only, no ground fires). **Alcoholic Beverages:** Allowed. **Vehicle Maximum Length:** 35 ft. **Other:** No fireworks or loaded firearms.

To Get There

From junction of UT Hwys 95 & 276 south of Hanksville, go 46 mi. south on UT Hwy. 276.

LAKE POWELL

Halls Crossing RV Park/Campground

P.O. Box 56909, Phoenix 85079. T: (435) 684-7000; F: (435) 684-2319; www.visitlakepowell.com.

RV ★★★ Tent ★★★

Beauty: ★★★★	Site Privacy: ★★★★
Spaciousness: ★★★	Quiet: ★★★★
Security: ★★★★	Cleanliness: ★★★★
Insect Control: ★★	Facilities: ★★★★

A National Park Service concessionaire, Aramark Parks & Resorts, operates two camping areas on the Halls Crossing side of Lake Powell in the Glen Canyon National Recreation Area. Halls Crossing is most easily reached by highway from Blanding to the east, though a ferry (hours vary seasonally and are limited, ending well before nightfall) links Halls Crossing with Bullfrog Marina to the north. The gravel RV Park sites are attractively nestled in an oasis of trees providing shade and a buffer from the surrounding high-desert sagebrush and scrub. Tents are not allowed in Halls Crossing RV Park, which has full hookups. But Halls Crossing Campground, which lacks hookups, is open to both tents and self-sufficient RVs and trailers. The Campground has trees shading the tents from the hot summer sun, and good lake views looking down from an elevation across sagebrush-studded orange sands.

Basics

Operated By: Aramark Parks & Resorts. **Open:** All year (for RVs; tents Apr.–Oct. only). **Site Assignment:** First come, first served; reservations. **Registration:** Self-pay fee station. **Fee:** $18–$28 (cash only; US currency, no checks). **Parking:** At site.

Facilities

Number of RV Sites: 97. **Number of Tent-Only Sites:** 0. **Hookups:** Electric (20, 30 amp), water, sewer. **Each Site:** Table, grill. **Dump Station:** Yes. **Laundry:** Yes. **Pay Phone:** Yes. **Rest Rooms and Showers:** Yes. **Fuel:** No. **Propane:** Yes. **Internal Roads:** Paved, good. **RV Service:** No. **Market:** Blanding, 84 mi. **Restaurant:** Bullfrog Marina. **General Store:** Yes. **Vending:** Yes. **Swimming:** Lake. **Playground:** No. **Other:** Ferry, boat rental. **Activities:** Boating, fishing, water sports. **Nearby Attractions:** Natural Bridges. **Additional Information:** National Park Service, (435) 684-7400; Lake Powell Ferry, (435) 684-3000; Glen Canyon Natural History Assoc., www.pagelakepowell.org.

Restrictions

Pets: On leash (not allowed on marina or archaeological sites). **Fires:** Yes (in grills only, no ground fires). **Alcoholic Beverages:** Allowed (but not when driving a boat). **Vehicle Maximum Length:** 35 ft. **Other:** No fireworks or loaded firearms.

To Get There

From junction of UT Hwys 95 & 276 west of Blanding, go 42 mi. west on UT Hwy. 276.

LEEDS

Red Cliffs Recreation Site

225 North Bluff, St. George 84770. T: (435) 688-3246; www.utso.ut.blm.gov.

RV ★★ Tent ★★★★

Beauty: ★★★★★	Site Privacy: ★★★★★
Spaciousness: ★★	Quiet: ★★★★
Security: ★★★★	Cleanliness: ★★★★
Insect Control: ★★★	Facilities: ★

The frontage road ducks under an 11.5-foot-high tunnel under US I-15 and crosses seasonal Quail Creek on the way to Red Cliffs. But self-sufficient campers (bring your own water, as the park water is not safe for drinking) are rewarded with three trails leading through the scenic red sandstone to Anasazi ruins, an old silver-mining area and red-cliff views. The Silver Reef is particularly unusual, as the silver ore fueling an 1880s mining boom was embedded in sandstone. Though campsite 1 is large enough to accommodate any vehicle on the road, most sites are relatively small and big rigs would find maneuvering difficult, even if they squeezed through the narrow underpass tunnel. The picnic area is alongside a creek, with tall cottonwood trees providing shade and a wheelchair ramp. Winters are mild, with nighttime lows above 20° F, and snow rare. Summer temperatures can soar above 100° F.

Basics

Operated By: BLM. **Open:** All year. **Site Assignment:** First come, first served. **Registration:** Self-pay entrance fee station. **Fee:** $8 (cash or check only). **Parking:** At site.

Facilities

Number of RV Sites: 16. **Number of Tent-Only Sites:** 0. **Hookups:** None. **Each Site:** Table, grill. **Dump Station:** Yes. **Laundry:** No. **Pay Phone:** No. **Rest Rooms and Showers:** No showers. **Fuel:** No. **Propane:** No. **Internal Roads:** Paved, adequately maintained. **RV Service:** No. **Market:** St. George, 15 mi. **Restaurant:** St. George, 15 mi. **General Store:** No. **Vending:** No. **Swimming:** No. **Playground:** No. **Other:** Picnic area. **Activities:** Golf, boating, fishing. **Nearby Attractions:** Quail Creek State Park, Zion, Cedar Breaks, Brian Head. **Additional Information:** Washington County Travel Bureau, (435) 634-5747, (800) 869-6635.

Restrictions

Pets: On leash under owner's control. **Fires:** Yes (limited when high fire danger). **Alcoholic Beverages:** Allowed (at site; not allowed on trail). **Vehicle Maximum Length:** 24 ft. **Other:** Gate closed 10 p.m. to 6 a.m., no off-road vehicles or firearms.

To Get There

From St. George take US I-15 north to Exit 22 and go south on frontage road under tunnel to BLM Rd.

LEEDS

Zion West RV Park

175 South Valley Rd., P.O. Box 460721, Leeds 84746. T: (435) 879-2854.

RV ★★★★ Tent ★★★★

Beauty: ★★★★	Site Privacy: ★★★★
Spaciousness: ★★★★	Quiet: ★★★★
Security: ★★★★	Cleanliness: ★★★★
Insect Control: ★★★★	Facilities: ★★★★

Carved out of an alfalfa field belonging to the farmer next door, Zion West is still relatively new and the trees do not provide as much shade as is found at the Leeds RV Park & Motel next door. At 3,200 feet there is rarely snow, but Brian Head ski area is about an hour away, making this such a popular destination that the RV park is booked full from October to May. Indeed, many snowbirds book their October reservations when leaving in May. Tent campers have a large grassy area with tables without designated sites, as well as another area when more space is needed. Leeds RV parks make a good alternative to the roadside RV parks in nearby St. George, as they are farther back from the road. But the tradeoff for additional quietness is being further from the urban amenities of St. George.

Basics

Operated By: Jim & Gloria Parnell. **Open:** All year. **Site Assignment:** First come, first served; reservations advised Oct.-May. **Registration:** Office. **Fee:** $12 tent, $15 RV (cash or check only). **Parking:** At site.

Facilities

Number of RV Sites: 30. **Number of Tent-Only Sites:** 12. **Hookups:** Electric (30, 50 amp), water, sewer. **Each Site:** Table. **Dump Station:** Yes. **Laundry:** Yes. **Pay Phone:** Yes. **Rest Rooms and Showers:** Yes. **Fuel:** No. **Propane:** No. **Internal Roads:** Paved, good. **RV Service:** No. **Market:** St. George, 11 mi. **Restaurant:** St. George, 11 mi. **General Store:** No. **Vending:** Yes. **Swimming:** No. **Playground:** No. **Other:** Dog walk. **Activities:** Rock climbing, biking, golf, horseback riding. **Nearby Attractions:** Zion, Quail Creek, Cedar Breaks, Brian Head. **Additional Information:** Washington County Travel Bureau, (435) 634-5747, (800) 869-6635.

Restrictions

Pets: On leash (noisy pets not tolerated). **Fires:** Yes. **Alcoholic Beverages:** Allowed. **Vehicle Maximum Length:** 45 ft.

To Get There

From St. George take US I-15 11 mi. north to Exit 22, then go 0.5 mi. north on frontage road and south a block on Mulberry Lane.

LITTLEFIELD

Virgin River Canyon Recreation Area

390 North 3050 East, St. George 84770. T: (435) 688-3246.

RV ★★ Tent ★★★

Beauty: ★★★★★ Site Privacy: ★★★★
Spaciousness: ★★★★ Quiet: ★★★★
Security: ★★★★ Cleanliness: ★★★★
Insect Control: ★★★ Facilities: ★

Situated in the remote northwest corner of Arizona where US I-15 crosses from Nevada into Utah, Virgin River is popular among international rock climbers and job hunters who can't decide between Mesquite, Nevada, and St. George, Utah. Big rigs and groups can fill up the campground in spring, fall, or winter. But in summer, when temperatures top 110° F in the shade, a handful of campers typically have the three loops to themselves. Except for the clusters of four sites around the restroom with wheelchair accessibility, the sites are relatively far apart. Some truck noise can be heard from the highway, but the scenic green, orange, yellow, and white sandstone hills of the Paiute Wilderness and Beaver Dam Mountains are a visual delight. It is an easy hike to the Virgin River, cell phones work, and the area's 100 bighorn sheep occasionally make an appearance.

Basics

Operated By: BLM. **Open:** All year. **Site Assignment:** First come, first served; group reservations. **Registration:** Self-pay fee station. **Fee:** $8 (cash or check only). **Parking:** At site.

Facilities

Number of RV Sites: 71. **Number of Tent-Only Sites:** 0. **Hookups:** None. **Each Site:** Table, charcoal pit. **Dump Station:** No (gray water dump). **Laundry:** No. **Pay Phone:** No. **Rest Rooms and Showers:** No showers. **Fuel:** No. **Propane:** No. **Internal Roads:** Paved, gravelly. **RV Service:** No. **Market:** Mesquite, NV, or St. George, UT, 18 mi. **Restaurant:** Mesquite, NV, or St. George, UT, 18 mi. **General Store:** No. **Vending:** No. **Swimming:** No. **Playground:** No. **Other:** Sheltered tables, wheelchair-accessible sites. **Activities:** Rock climbing, horseback riding. **Nearby Attractions:** Nevada casinos, Utah Mormon monuments. **Additional Information:** Washington County Travel Bureau, (435) 634-5747, (800) 869-6635.

Restrictions

Pets: On leash (horses must be kept outside campground). **Fires:** Yes (in grills only, no ground fires, LPG, or big petroleum stoves). **Alcoholic Beverages:** Allowed. **Vehicle Maximum Length:** 45 ft. **Other:** Smoking only in barren areas at least 3 ft. in diameter, gate closes 9 p.m.–6 a.m.

To Get There

Go 18 mi. south from St. George, UT, or 18 mi. north from Mesquite, NV, on US I-15 to the Cedar Pockets Exit.

MANTI

Palisade State Park

2200 Palisade Rd., P.O. Box 650070, Sterling 84655. T: (835) 835-7275 or (800) 322-3770; www.nr.state.ut.us.

RV ★★★★ Tent ★★★★

Beauty: ★★★★ Site Privacy: ★★★★
Spaciousness: ★★★★ Quiet: ★★★★
Security: ★★★★ Cleanliness: ★★★★
Insect Control: ★★ Facilities: ★★★★

Started in the 1860s by rancher Daniel Funk, who built the original reservoir (Funk's Lake) and a dance pavilion at what became a popular resort in the horse-and-buggy days, Palisade State Park now boasts a golf course with a clubhouse and PGA pro a short walk from the North Campground, which has the largest pull-through sites. The South Campground, furthest from the golf course and nearest the sandy beach, has a group pavilion and tent area. Eleven double sites are spread out among the South, North, and East Campgrounds. Developers are trying to sell homes and commercial spaces on the two miles of Palisades Road leading into the park. But for now this remains a sleepy backwater campground (use peaks on summer weekends) with lakeview campsites (50–53 are best), non-motorized boating, cutthroat and rainbow trout, and ice fishing and ice skating during the winter.

Basics

Operated By: Utah State Parks & Recreation. **Open:** All year. **Site Assignment:** First come, first served; reservations for individuals (120 days in advance) & groups (1 year in advance). **Registration:** Entry kiosk (sporadically open) or self-pay fee station (the usual). **Fee:** $13 (V, MC if entry kiosk open; otherwise cash or check). **Parking:** At site.

Facilities

Number of RV Sites: 53. **Number of Tent-Only Sites:** 0. **Hookups:** None. **Each Site:** Table, grill. **Dump Station:** Yes. **Laundry:** No. **Pay Phone:** Yes. **Rest Rooms and Showers:** Yes. **Fuel:** No. **Propane:** No. **Internal Roads:** Paved, excellent. **RV Service:** No. **Market:** Manti, 7 mi. **Restaurant:** Manti, 7 mi. **General Store:** Yes. **Vending:** Yes. **Swimming:** Lake (swimmer's itch, schistosomiasis warning). **Playground:** No. **Other:** Boat ramp, canoe & paddleboat rental, golf course (18 hole, par 72) & clubhouse w/ pro, amphitheater, extensive picnic areas. **Activities:** Golf, fishing, non-motorized boating, winter sports. **Nearby Attractions:** Manti Temple, national forest. **Additional Information:** Sanpete County Heritage Council, (435) 283-4321, (800) 281-4346, www.sanpete.com.

Restrictions

Pets: On leash under owner's control (kept off beach & out of water). **Fires:** Yes (in grills or metal containers 6 inches off ground). **Alcoholic Beverages:** Allowed (but not mixed w/ boating). **Vehicle Maximum Length:** 40 ft. **Other:** No diving from rocks, no hanging or tying things to trees, personal flotation devices must be worn on boats, firearms must be unloaded & locked away.

To Get There

Go 6 mi. south of Manti on US Hwy. 89 and 2 mi. east on Palisades Rd.

MEXICAN HAT

Goosenecks State Park

c/o Edge of Cedars State Park Museum, 660 West 400 North, Blanding 84511. T: (435) 678-2238; www.nr.state.ut.us.

RV ★★ Tent ★★

Beauty: ★★★★★ Site Privacy: ★★★★
Spaciousness: ★★★ Quiet: ★★★★
Security: ★★★★ Cleanliness: ★★★★★
Insect Control: ★★★★ Facilities: ★

The view looking 1,000 feet down into the Goosenecks of the San Juan River is often photographed for geology textbooks as a classic case of an entrenched meander. Basically, tectonic plate collisions have uplifted 300-million-year-old rocks and allowed a meandering river to create a meandering river canyon. RVs must bring their own water and brace for very strong winds and summer thunderstorms when camping out at 5,000-feet elevation along the edge of the scenic overlook. Parking is pretty much anywhere in open areas with views of the wide expanse stretching south into Monument Valley. Dust devils along the road are not uncommon, and signs warn off large vehicles towing other vehicles. Indeed, unimproved roads with sharp curves and steep grades will keep big rigs from going further north on UT Hwy. 261 to explore the Valley of the Gods, whose rock formations are like a Monument Valley in miniature.

Basics

Operated By: Utah State Parks & Recreation. **Open:** All year. **Site Assignment:** First come, first served. **Registration:** Self-pay entrance fee station. **Fee:** None. **Parking:** At site.

Facilities

Number of RV Sites: 8. **Number of Tent-Only Sites:** 0. **Hookups:** None. **Each Site:** Table. **Dump Station:** Yes. **Laundry:** No. **Pay Phone:** No. **Rest Rooms and Showers:** No showers. **Fuel:** No. **Propane:** No. **Internal Roads:** Gravel, good. **RV Service:** No. **Market:** Bluff, 27 mi. **Restaurant:** Mexican Hat, 8 mi. **General Store:** No. **Vending:** No. **Swimming:** No. **Playground:** No. **Other:** Pavilion at overlook w/ sheltered table & grill. **Activities:** Picnicking, biking, off-road vehicles. **Nearby Attractions:** Edge of Cedars State Park Museum, Valley of the Gods, Monument Valley, Hovenweep, Natural Bridges. **Additional Information:** San Juan County Visitor Services, (435) 587-3235, (800) 574-4386.

Restrictions

Pets: On leash. **Fires:** Yes (in grills). **Alcoholic Beverages:** Allowed. **Vehicle Maximum Length:** No limit.

To Get There

From Mexican Hat go 3 mi. northwest on US Hwy. 163, 1 mi. north on UT Hwy. 261 and 4 mi. west on UT Hwy. 316.

MIDWAY

Wasatch Mountain State Park

P.O. Box 10, Midway 84049. T: (435) 654-1791 or (800) 322-3770 (reservations); www.nr.state.ut.us.

RV ★★★★★ Tent ★★★★★

Beauty: ★★★★★	Site Privacy: ★★★★★
Spaciousness: ★★★★★	Quiet: ★★★★
Security: ★★★★	Cleanliness: ★★★★
Insect Control: ★★★	Facilities: ★★★

Three different campgrounds with 72 holes of golf and secluded oak thickets within an hour of Salt Lake City make Wasatch Mountain so desirable that anyone without a weekend reservation is usually turned away. Park City's Olympic ski lifts and the Olympic biathlon park at Soldier Hollow are nearby, as are state parks at Jordenelle, and Deer Creek Reservoirs for water recreation. Two Wasatch Mountain campgrounds have hookups, and one loop is set aside for tents. Mahogany Campground is popular for its pull-through sites (1, 3, 5, 21, 23, 25, 27); sites 15–26 have great views across Heber Valley. Cottonwood Campground RV sites 36–47 are coveted for their tall cottonwood trees providing shade all day. Tent camping is restricted to Oak Hollow Campground's 40 sites, many enclosed in oak canopies. Children can use the playground and fish in a pond near the Visitor Center, which has a display explaining the hot springs underlying the area.

Basics

Operated By: Utah State Parks & Recreation. **Open:** Early Apr.–until snow closes (no reservations taken after Oct. 15). **Site Assignment:** First come, first served (for available sites); reservations necessary weekends (starting Friday) from Memorial Day to Labor Day. **Registration:** Entry kiosk. **Fee:** $14–$16 (V, MC; $6.25 site reservation fee). **Parking:** At site.

Facilities

Number of RV Sites: 106. **Number of Tent-Only Sites:** 0. **Hookups:** Electric (20, 30, 50 amp), water, sewer. **Each Site:** Table, grill or fire ring. **Dump Station:** Yes. **Laundry:** No. **Pay Phone:** Yes. **Rest Rooms and Showers:** Yes. **Fuel:** No. **Propane:** No. **Internal Roads:** Paved, cracks patched. **RV Service:** No. **Market:** Midway, 5 mi. **Restaurant:** Midway, 0.5 mi. **General Store:** No. **Vending:** No. **Swimming:** Homestead Resort, 2 mi. **Playground:** Yes (at Visitor Center). **Other:** 72 holes of golf, ice for sale, pavilions, amphitheater. **Activities:** Golf, horseback riding, fishing, boating. **Nearby Attractions:** Park City, Soldier Hollow, Timpanogos Cave National Monument, historic railway, reservoirs. **Additional Information:** Heber Valley Chamber of Commerce, (435) 654-3666, www.hebervalleycc.org.

Restrictions

Pets: On leash under owner's control. **Fires:** Yes (grill or fire pit only, firewood sold, no fires when extreme summer danger). **Alcoholic Beverages:** Allowed. **Vehicle Maximum Length:** 75 ft. **Other:** 10 p.m.–8 a.m. gate locked, no fireworks.

To Get There

From junction of UT Hwy. 113 and Main St. in Midway, go 6 mi. north on Pine Canyon Rd.

MOAB

Arch View Camp Park

P.O. Box 1406, Canyonlands Campground 84532. T: (435) 259-7854 or (800) 813-6622; www.moab.net/archview; archview@lasal.net.

RV ★★★★ Tent ★★★

Beauty: ★★★★	Site Privacy: ★★★★
Spaciousness: ★★★★	Quiet: ★★★
Security: ★★★★	Cleanliness: ★★★★
Insect Control: ★★★	Facilities: ★★★★

Well-positioned at the Canyonlands National Park and Dead Horse Point State Park junction (UT Hwy. 313) and just five miles north of the Arches National Park entrance, Arch View seems isolated in the countryside, surrounded by red sandstone hills. But the Moab action is only nine miles to the south. The office and general-store building was originally built as a TV movie set for "Riders of the Purple Sage," and the area is popular with film crews. There are good views of Mt. Peale and the North and South Windows in Arches National Park. Cottonwood trees between gravel RV sites and cottontail rabbits scampering into the surrounding desert scrub add to the rural ambiance, though the campground is not free from highway noise. Tent sites are shaded by tall cottonwood trees and are predominately grass, though there is some dirt. About the only amenity missing is a restaurant.

Basics

Operated By: Mitch White. **Open:** Mar.–Jan. **Site Assignment:** First come, first served; reservations recommended peak seasons & holidays. **Registration:** Office. **Fee:** $17–$20 (V, MC, AE, D, DC). **Parking:** At site.

Facilities

Number of RV Sites: 60. **Number of Tent-Only Sites:** 28. **Hookups:** Electric (20, 30, 50 amp), water, sewer, cable TV, phone (modem). **Each Site:** Table, grill. **Dump Station:** Yes. **Laundry:** Yes. **Pay Phone:** Yes. **Rest Rooms and Showers:** Yes. **Fuel:** Yes. **Propane:** Yes. **Internal Roads:** Gravel, good. **RV Service:** No. **Market:** Moab, 9 mi. **Restaurant:** Moab, 9 mi. **General Store:** Yes. **Vending:** Yes. **Swimming:** Pool. **Playground:** Yes. **Other:** Cabins. **Activities:** Horseback riding, golf, biking, fishing, boating, rafting. **Nearby Attractions:** Arches, Canyonlands, Dead Horse Point. **Additional Information:** Grand County Travel Council, (800) 635-MOAB, Canyonlands Natural History Assoc., (435) 259-6003, www.cnha.org.

Restrictions

Pets: On leash, quiet, & under owner's control at all times. **Fires:** Yes (at community fire site only, firewood sold). **Alcoholic Beverages:** Allowed. **Vehicle Maximum Length:** 50 ft. **Other:** No dirt bike, ATV riding, or firearms.

To Get There

From Moab go 9 mi. north on US Hwy. 191.

MOAB

Canyonlands Campground

555 South Main St., Moab 84532. T: (435) 259-6848 or (800) 522-6848; F: (435) 259-6848; www.moabutah.com/canyonlands/RV.html; cancamp@lasal.net.

RV ★★★★ Tent ★★★★

Beauty: ★★★	Site Privacy: ★★★
Spaciousness: ★★★	Quiet: ★★★
Security: ★★★★★	Cleanliness: ★★★★★
Insect Control: ★★★	Facilities: ★★★★★

In the center of Moab, within walking distance of bakeries with cappuccino, microbreweries, galleries, and shops, Canyonlands has tall cottonwood trees and level shaded pull-through spaces with cement pads. RV spaces in rows 5–8 can also be used for tents, and there are also two separate dirt areas for tents. The best tent sites in row G have sheltered tables. A footbridge across Pack Creek leads to 15 more secluded walk-in tent sites sharing a common sheltered eating area. Though in the center of town, Canyonlands is surprisingly quiet late at night, with less truck noise than the KOA outside of town, because speeds slow to 25 miles per hour downtown and there is no need for truckers to use noisy engine brakes. Thus, Moab's oldest campground remains very popular, and reservations are a must on holiday weekends and from June on, when Canyonlands fills up every night.

Basics

Operated By: Paul & Aggie Evans. **Open:** All year. **Site Assignment:** First come, first served; reservations recommended peak times. **Registration:** Office. **Fee:** $16–$23 (V, MC, AE, D). **Parking:** At site; separate parking for walk-in tent sites.

Facilities

Number of RV Sites: 105. **Number of Tent-Only Sites:** 28. **Hookups:** Electric (30, 50 amp), water, sewer, cable TV, phone (modem). **Each Site:** Table, grill. **Dump Station:** Yes. **Laundry:** Yes. **Pay Phone:** Yes. **Rest Rooms and Showers:** Yes.

Fuel: Yes. **Propane:** No. **Internal Roads:** Gravel, good. **RV Service:** No. **Market:** Moab, 1 block. **Restaurant:** Moab, less than 1 block. **General Store:** Yes. **Vending:** Yes. **Swimming:** Pool. **Playground:** No. **Other:** Pavilion, pet walk, horseshoes, cabins. **Activities:** Biking, boating, rafting, fishing, golf, jeep touring. **Nearby Attractions:** Arches, Canyonlands. **Additional Information:** Grand County Travel Council, (800) 635-MOAB.

Restrictions

Pets: On leash & not left unattended. **Fires:** Yes. **Alcoholic Beverages:** Allowed. **Vehicle Maximum Length:** 45 ft. **Other:** No hammocks.

To Get There

From Main (US Hwy. 191) & Center Sts. in downtown Moab, go 5 blocks south on Main St. and enter next to Amoco Station.

MOAB
Dead Horse Point State Park

P.O. Box 609, Moab 84532. T: (435) 259-2614 or (800) 322-3770 (reservations).

RV ★★★★ Tent ★★★★

Beauty: ★★★★★	Site Privacy: ★★★★
Spaciousness: ★★★★★	Quiet: ★★★★
Security: ★★★★★	Cleanliness: ★★★★★
Insect Control: ★★★	Facilities: ★★

Named after a wild mustang corral where horses died of thirst, Dead Horse Point Overlook offers a marvelous view (80–100 miles most clear days) across deep sandstone mesas and a gooseneck in the Colorado River where the silence is so complete that a lone motorized raft can be clearly heard far below. Water is scarce on this high plateau, as it has to be trucked in from Moab, so bring your own or buy it by the gallon (limited) from the Visitor Center. The campground loop has tall pinyon pines and Utah junipers separating spacious orange-sand sites, the smallest accommodating a 40-foot rig. If the crowds in Arches and Moab get too much, this is a good place to come for quiet, though noises can really travel through the campground. At the very least, this is a scenic stop en route to Canyonlands Island in the Sky District.

Basics

Operated By: Utah State Parks. **Open:** All year. **Site Assignment:** First come, first served; reservations accepted (required for group site). **Registration:** At park entrance. **Fee:** $13. **Parking:** At site.

Facilities

Number of RV Sites: 21. **Number of Tent-Only Sites:** 0. **Hookups:** None. **Each Site:** Sheltered table, charcoal grill, sand tent pad. **Dump Station:** Yes. **Laundry:** No. **Pay Phone:** Yes. **Rest Rooms and Showers:** No showers. **Fuel:** No. **Propane:** No. **Internal Roads:** Paved, good condition. **RV Service:** No. **Market:** Moab, 32 mi. **Restaurant:** Moab, 32 mi. **General Store:** No. **Vending:** Yes. **Swimming:** No. **Playground:** No. **Other:** One wheelchair-accessible site. **Activities:** Evening ranger programs in amphitheater (May–Sept.). **Nearby Attractions:** Canyonlands, Arches, Moab. **Additional Information:** Canyonlands Natural History Assoc., (435) 259-6003, www.cnha.org; Grand County Travel Council, (800) 635-MOAB.

Restrictions

Pets: On 6-ft. leash under owner's control. **Fires:** Charcoal only in grills, no ground or wood fires. **Alcoholic Beverages:** Allowed. **Vehicle Maximum Length:** 105 ft. **Other:** 8 people & 2 vehicles per site, no firearms, fireworks, or harassing wildlife.

To Get There

Go 11 mi. northwest from Moab on US Hwy. 191, then 23 mi. southwest on UT Hwy. 313.

MOAB
Moab KOA

3225 South Hwy. 191, Moab 84532. T: (435) 259-6682 or (800) 562-0372; www.moab-utah.com/koa; koa@lasal.net.

RV ★★★★ Tent ★★★

Beauty: ★★★	Site Privacy: ★★★
Spaciousness: ★★★	Quiet: ★★★
Security: ★★★★★	Cleanliness: ★★★★★
Insect Control: ★★★★	Facilities: ★★★★★

Surrounded by farms, mountains, and sagebrush-covered desert land, the Moab KOA has what appears to be an idyllic location. The gravel sites and abundance of trees reinforce the rural feel of the open countryside and surrounding mountains. There are two playgrounds, mini-golf, a pool, and more than enough amenities to make this a worthwhile base for exploring the territory both north and south of Moab. Besides, all the shops, galleries, restaurants, and microbreweries of Moab are only four miles down the road. The only drawback for those who are light sleepers is that the campground is situated alongside a steep highway grade where truckers use their noisy engine brakes late at night. But other than that, it is hard to find fault with this clean, well-maintained campground and its hard-working and helpful hosts.

Basics

Operated By: Bob & Lila Ott. **Open:** Mar.–Oct. **Site Assignment:** First come, first served; reservations accepted. **Registration:** Office. **Fee:** $20–$27 (V, MC, AE, D). **Parking:** At site.

Facilities

Number of RV Sites: 73. **Number of Tent-Only Sites:** 52. **Hookups:** Electric (30, 50 amp), water, sewer, cable TV, phone (modem). **Each Site:** Table, grill. **Dump Station:** Yes. **Laundry:** Yes. **Pay Phone:** Yes. **Rest Rooms and Showers:** Yes. **Fuel:** No. **Propane:** Yes. **Internal Roads:** Gravel, good. **RV Service:** No. **Market:** Moab, 4 mi. **Restaurant:** Moab, 4 mi. **General Store:** Yes. **Vending:** Yes. **Swimming:** Pool. **Playground:** Yes. **Other:** Game room, mini-golf, dog walk, cabins. **Activities:** Boating, rafting, horseback riding, golf, rock climbing, biking, jeep touring. **Nearby Attractions:** Arches, Canyonlands, Newspaper Rock. **Additional Information:** Grand County Travel Council, (800) 635-MOAB.

Restrictions

Pets: On leash & attended by owner at all times (not allowed in playground or store area). **Fires:** Yes (only charcoal fires in grills). **Alcoholic Beverages:** Allowed (at site only). **Vehicle Maximum Length:** 70 ft. **Other:** No wasting water or running generators, children must be supervised.

To Get There

From Moab go 4 mi. south on US Hwy. 191.

MOAB
Moab Rim Campark

1900 South Hwy. 191, Moab 84532. T: (435) 259-5002 or (888) 599-6622; F: (435) 259-5002; www.moab-utah.com/moabrimcampark.html; moabrim@moab-utah.com.

RV ★★★ Tent ★★

Beauty: ★★★★	Site Privacy: ★★★
Spaciousness: ★★★	Quiet: ★★★
Security: ★★★★	Cleanliness: ★★★★★
Insect Control: ★★★★	Facilities: ★★★

Fronted by vineyards that provide a bit of a highway noise buffer and remind of the new wine industry here, Moab Rim is attractively situated part way up a hillside across the street from the Crazy Horse Saloon. Only ten RV sites have full hookups, while nine have electric and water. Moab Rim is one of the few commercial campgrounds with more tent sites than RV sites. Fire pits are located at designated locations rather than at every site, in expectation than many travelers will partake of Moab's many restaurants and microbreweries instead of cooking for themselves after a hard day of hiking or sightseeing. In any case, the fire-pit areas are excellent locations for sitting in the evening, as they offer excellent vistas of Moab and the surrounding mountains. All in all, a good stop for those preferring a small, intimate, almost boutique type of campground.

Basics

Operated By: Jim & Sue Farrell. **Open:** Mar. 1–Nov. 30. **Site Assignment:** First come, first served; reservations recommended on weekends. **Registration:** Office. **Fee:** $15–$22 (V, MC). **Parking:** At site.

Facilities

Number of RV Sites: 22. **Number of Tent-Only Sites:** 30. **Hookups:** Electric (30, 50 amp), water, sewer. **Each Site:** Table. **Dump Station:** Yes. **Laundry:** No. **Pay Phone:** Yes. **Rest Rooms and Showers:** Yes. **Fuel:** No. **Propane:** No. **Internal Roads:** Gravel, good. **RV Service:** No. **Market:** Moab, 2 mi. **Restaurant:** Moab, 2 mi. **General Store:** Yes. **Vending:** Yes. **Swimming:** No. **Playground:** No. **Other:** Cabins, fire pits at designated locations. **Activities:** Boating, rafting, horseback riding, golf, biking. **Nearby Attractions:** Arches, Canyonlands, Newspaper Rock. **Additional Information:** Grand County Travel Council, (800) 635-MOAB.

Restrictions

Pets: On leash under owner's control. **Fires:** Yes. **Alcoholic Beverages:** Allowed. **Vehicle Maximum Length:** 35 ft. **Other:** No dishwashing in restroom sinks.

To Get There

From downtown Moab, go 2 mi. south on US Hwy. 191.

MOAB

Portal RV Park & Fishery

1261 North Hwy. 191, Moab 84532. T: (435) 259-6108 or (800) 574-2028; F: (435) 259-7931; www.portalrvpark.com; camp@portalrvpark.com.

RV: ★★★★ Tent: ★★★★

Beauty: ★★★★ Site Privacy: ★★★
Spaciousness: ★★★★ Quiet: ★★★★
Security: ★★★★ Cleanliness: ★★★★★
Insect Control: ★★★★ Facilities: ★★★★

Just south of the Colorado River Bridge and the bend in US Hwy. 191 north of Moab, Portal is positioned behind a pasture well back from the main highway, which means less noise than at the roadside Spanish Trail RV Park next door. However, Portal is only five years old and its cottonwood trees do not provide the lush shady environment found at Spanish Trail. But Portal does have fishing ponds, optional hookups to a private well with mountain spring water, trails to view birds and wildlife, horses and geese next door, and good La Sal Mountain views. Tent campers will like the grassy sheltered sites, and two group areas hold 25 tents each. Thus, Portal makes an excellent base for exploring Canyonlands and Arches National Parks and Moab. The small friendly campground is usually booked full peak season (Mar.–May) and holidays, when reservations are always recommended in Moab.

Basics

Operated By: Kent & Ann Oldham. **Open:** All year. **Site Assignment:** First come, first served; reservations recommended. **Registration:** Self-pay entrance fee station. **Fee:** $17–$25 (V, MC). **Parking:** At site.

Facilities

Number of RV Sites: 36. **Number of Tent-Only Sites:** 10. **Hookups:** Electric (30, 50 amp), water, sewer, cable TV, phone (modem). **Each Site:** Table, grill. **Dump Station:** Yes. **Laundry:** Yes. **Pay Phone:** Yes. **Rest Rooms and Showers:** Yes. **Fuel:** No. **Propane:** No. **Internal Roads:** Gravel, good. **RV Service:** No. **Market:** Moab, 2 mi. **Restaurant:** Moab, 2 mi. **General Store:** Yes. **Vending:** Yes. **Swimming:** No. **Playground:** No. **Other:** Pavilion, picnic areas, dog walk, fishing ponds, cabins. **Activities:** Horseback riding, biking, boating, rafting, golf. **Nearby Attractions:** Arches, Canyonlands. **Additional Information:** Canyonlands Natural History Assoc., (435) 259-6003, www.cnha.org; Grand County Travel Council, (800) 635-MOAB.

Restrictions

Pets: On leash under owner's control. **Fires:** Yes (only in tent site fire rings, no fires at RV sites). **Alcoholic Beverages:** Allowed (must be confined to site; no rowdiness or drunkness). **Vehicle Maximum Length:** 60 ft. **Other:** No firearms or fireworks, no dirt bike or ATV riding.

To Get There

Go 2 mi. north of Moab on US Hwy. 191.

MONUMENT VALLEY

Goulding's Monument Valley Campground

Box 360001, Monument Valley 84536. T: (435) 727-3235; F: (435) 727-3344; www.gouldings.com; gouldings@gouldings.com.

RV: ★★★★ Tent: ★★★★

Beauty: ★★★★ Site Privacy: ★★
Spaciousness: ★★★ Quiet: ★★★★
Security: ★★★★★ Cleanliness: ★★★★
Insect Control: ★★★★ Facilities: ★★★★★

Long the premier establishment in Monument Valley and headquarters for film-makers such as John Ford, whose film "Stagecoach" with John Wayne turned the area into a popular movie and TV commercial locale, Goulding's has successfully extended its quality franchise from trading post to lodge to campground. With an indoor swimming pool and nearby gas station, grocery store, restaurant, and air strip, Goulding's red-dirt campground is a compact oasis surrounded by imposing red rock sandstone formations. The only real activity here, besides touring Goulding's Trading Post Museum, watching a multi-media presentation, and visiting the tribal visitor center, is touring Monument Valley itself. While private vehicles are allowed down some of the dirt roads, half- and full-day (and longer) jeep and horseback riding tours are a popular alternative. There are obligatory stops at Navajo hogans to watch women weave, photograph Navajos (a gratuity is expected) in their finery on horseback, and view the area's geology and petroglyphs.

Basics

Operated By: Goulding's Lodge & Trading Post. **Open:** Mar. 15–Nov. 1. **Site Assignment:** First come, first served. **Registration:** Office in convenience store. **Fee:** $15 tent, $24 RV (V, MC, AE, D, DC). **Parking:** At site.

Facilities

Number of RV Sites: 66. **Number of Tent-Only Sites:** 45. **Hookups:** Electric (20, 30 amp), water, sewer, cable TV, phone (modem). **Each Site:** Table, grill. **Dump Station:** Yes. **Laundry:** Yes. **Pay Phone:** Yes. **Rest Rooms and Showers:** Yes. **Fuel:** Yes. **Propane:** Yes. **Internal Roads:** Paved, good. **RV Service:** No. **Market:** Monument Valley, 1 mi. **Restaurant:** Monument Valley, 1 mi. **General Store:** Yes. **Vending:** Yes. **Swimming:** Indoor pool. **Playground:** Yes. **Other:** Free shuttle to lodge, air strip. **Activities:** Navajo Tribal Park tours, horseback riding. **Nearby Attractions:** Navajo Tribal Park. **Additional Information:** Monument Valley Visitors Center, (435) 727-3287; Black's Hiking & Jeep Tours, (435) 739-4226, (800) 749-4226.

Restrictions

Pets: On leash at all times (not allowed in restrooms, store, laundry, or undeveloped areas). **Fires:** Yes. **Alcoholic Beverages:** Allowed. **Vehicle Maximum Length:** 36 ft. **Other:** "Do onto others as you would have them do onto you."

To Get There

From US Hwy. 163 0.5 mi. north of UT–AZ border, go 2.5 mi. west on Monument Valley Rd.

MONUMENT VALLEY

Mitten View Campground

P.O. Box 360289, Monument Valley 84536. T: (435) 727-3287 or (435) 727-3353.

RV: ★★★★ Tent: ★★★★★

Beauty: ★★★★★ Site Privacy: ★★★★
Spaciousness: ★★★★ Quiet: ★★★★
Security: ★★★★ Cleanliness: ★★★★
Insect Control: ★★★★ Facilities: ★★★

Surrounded by sandstone mesas and a panorama of red plateaus, buttes, pinnacles, and talus piles, Mitten View Campground is one of the best places to wake up to the morning light and watch the sunsets turn the sagebrush-studded land into a palette of reds, browns, and oranges. Mitten View is adjacent to the Monument Valley Visitors Center, where payment is made to drive the 17 miles of dirt road open to the public. The road is rough, and many visitor's opt for a guided tour by jeep to save the wear and tear on their vehicles and learn from the Navajo guides. Fortunately the campground has sheltered tables, as the few short junipers and desert scrub provide little shade. Indeed, tents can become virtual hothouses in hot weather. But the small tent sites ringing the perimeter have better views of the 30,000-acre Monument Valley than the larger interior pull-through sites.

Basics

Operated By: Navajo Parks & Recreation Bureau. **Open:** All year. **Site Assignment:** First come, first served; reservations advised May–Sept. **Registration:** Self-pay fee station. **Fee:** $10 (cash or check only). **Parking:** At site.

Facilities

Number of RV Sites: 52. **Number of Tent-Only Sites:** 44. **Hookups:** None. **Each Site:** Sheltered table, grill. **Dump Station:** Yes. **Laundry:** No. **Pay Phone:** No. **Rest Rooms and Showers:** Yes. **Fuel:** No. **Propane:** No. **Internal Roads:** Gravel, good. **RV Service:** No. **Market:** Goulding's, 4 mi. **Restaurant:** Goulding's, 4 mi. **General Store:** No. **Vending:** No. **Swimming:** No. **Playground:** No. **Other:** Visitor Center nearby. **Activities:** Monument Valley tours, horseback riding. **Nearby Attractions:** Goulding's Trading Post. **Additional Information:** Monument Valley Visitors Center, (435) 727-3287; Black's Hiking & Jeep Tours, (435) 739-4226, (800) 749-4226.

Restrictions

Pets: On leash. **Fires:** Yes. **Alcoholic Beverages:** Prohibited on tribal lands. **Vehicle Maximum Length:** 36 ft. **Other:** No rock climbing.

To Get There

Follow US Hwy. 163 to Monument Valley Visitors Center.

NATURAL BRIDGES NATIONAL MONUMENT

Natural Bridges

Box 1, Lake Powell 84533. T: (435) 692-1234; F: (435) 692-1111; www.nps.gov/nabr.

RV ★★ Tent ★★★★★

Beauty: ★★★★★ Site Privacy: ★★★★★
Spaciousness: ★★ Quiet: ★★★★★
Security: ★★★★ Cleanliness: ★★★★★
Insect Control: ★★★ Facilities: ★

Established as a National Monument by President Theodore Roosevelt in 1908, Natural Bridges lies at 6,000-feet elevation in a high desert where rabbitbrush and sage meet a forest of pinyon pine and Utah juniper. Formed by stream erosion, the natural bridges continue to erode and will eventually disappear. The small campground is busiest on Saturdays, but most days even mid-afternoon arrivals snag a campsite. When the campground is full, campers are shunted to a large BLM overflow area six miles away, which also accommodates vehicles longer than Natural Bridges's 26-feet limit. The flat orange-sand tent pads are good, though amenities outside the Visitor Center are few. For campgrounds with more amenities, head to Blanding or go 55 miles west to Halls Crossing or Bullfrog Marina on Lake Powell. In winter the campground stays open, but the one-way nine-mile loop drive to the natural bridge overlooks and trailheads is closed.

Basics

Operated By: National Park Service. **Open:** All year. **Site Assignment:** First come, first served. **Registration:** Self-pay fee station. **Fee:** $10 (cash or check only). **Parking:** At site.

Facilities

Number of RV Sites: 13. **Number of Tent-Only Sites:** 0. **Hookups:** None. **Each Site:** Table, grill, fire ring. **Dump Station:** Yes. **Laundry:** No. **Pay Phone:** No. **Rest Rooms and Showers:** No showers. **Fuel:** No. **Propane:** No. **Internal Roads:** Paved, good. **RV Service:** No. **Market:** Blanding, 42 mi. **Restaurant:** Fry Canyon, 20 mi. **General Store:** No. **Vending:** No. **Swimming:** No. **Playground:** No. **Other:** Visitor center, amphitheater. **Activities:** Boating, evening ranger programs. **Nearby Attractions:** Bullfrog Marina/Lake Powell, Goosenecks State Park. **Additional Information:** Canyonlands Natural History Assoc., (435) 259-6003, www.cnha.org.

Restrictions

Pets: On leash (not allowed on trails). **Fires:** Yes (in grills only, no fires allowed in dry years when high fire danger). **Alcoholic Beverages:** Allowed. **Vehicle Maximum Length:** 26 ft. **Other:** 1 vehicle & 8 people per site.

To Get There

From US Hwy. 191 4 mi. south of Blanding go 32 mi. west on UT Hwy. 95 and 6 mi. west on UT Hwy. 275.

NEPHI
Nephi KOA/Horseshoe Bar Ranch

Salt Creek Canyon, P.O. Box 309, Nephi 84648. T: (435) 623-0811.

 ★★★★ Tent ★★★★

Beauty: ★★★★★ Site Privacy: ★★★★
Spaciousness: ★★★★ Quiet: ★★★★★
Security: ★★★★ Cleanliness: ★★★★★
Insect Control: ★★★ Facilities: ★★★★

Situated on a 700-acre cattle ranch established in 1882 by the owner's grandfather, Heber B. Ockey, a Mormon pioneer who survived "Indian problems" and tough times, the over three-decade-old Nephi KOA is isolated in a canyon adjacent to a relatively quiet, scenic highway several miles from town. The friendly ambiance and canyon solitude bring repeat business from those stumbling upon the place for the first time as an overnight stop. Two creeks running through the ranch offer trout fishing possibilities, and nearby Mt. Nebo offers trails and a scenic drive. But there is no real destination draw for this off-the-beaten-track bit of wilderness, which is a good stopping place for relaxation. Nephi itself is an agricultural hub with a decent Mexican restaurant, some drive-ins, cafes, gas stations, and stores serving the surrounding farming community. Good signs from the center of town provide campground directions, but first-time around make the approach in daylight.

Basics

Operated By: Jim & Carolyn Ockey. **Open:** May–Oct. **Site Assignment:** First come, first served; reservations accepted. **Registration:** Self-pay entrance fee station. **Fee:** $17–$23 (V, MC, D). **Parking:** At site.

Facilities

Number of RV Sites: 62. **Number of Tent-Only Sites:** 20. **Hookups:** Electric (20, 30 amp), water, sewer. **Each Site:** Table. **Dump Station:** Yes. **Laundry:** Yes. **Pay Phone:** Yes. **Rest Rooms and Showers:** Yes. **Fuel:** No. **Propane:** No. **Internal Roads:** Paved, excellent. **RV Service:** No. **Market:** Nephi, 5 mi. **Restaurant:** Nephi, 5 mi. **General Store:** Yes. **Vending:** Yes. **Swimming:** Pool. **Playground:** Yes. **Other:** 7 cabins, fenced dog walk, game room, fish pond, sports field. **Activities:** Fishing, horseback riding. **Nearby Attractions:** National Forests. **Additional Information:** Nephi/Juab County Chamber, (435) 623-2411.

Restrictions

Pets: On leash under owner's control. **Fires:** Yes. **Alcoholic Beverages:** Allowed (provided not excessive). **Vehicle Maximum Length:** 55 ft. **Other:** No motor bike riding.

To Get There

From US I-15 Exit 225 at Nephi, go west 6 mi. on UT Hwy. 132.

PANGUITCH
Panguitch Big Fish KOA

P.O. Box 384, Panguitch 84759. T: (435) 676-2225 or (800) 562-1625; zionkoa@color-country.net.

RV ★★★★ Tent ★★★★

Beauty: ★★★★ Site Privacy: ★★★★
Spaciousness: ★★★★ Quiet: ★★★★
Security: ★★★★★ Cleanliness: ★★★★
Insect Control: ★★★ Facilities: ★★★★

A very well-maintained campground with plenty of shade trees and grass, Panguitch Big Fish KOA feels very rural, with distant mountains and neighboring pastures where horse and sheep graze only five blocks from town. The tent sites are grassy, and the afternoon breeze welcome in summer. Over half the clientele is European, drawn to this location because it is quiet and off the main drag, as well as near town and equidistant between important park destinations. To the west, Panguitch Lake and Cedar Breaks are less than an hour away. To the east, Bryce Canyon and Kodachrome Basin are similarly near, making this a good central location for area exploration, though not as wilderness in feel as the Red Canyon or Cannonville KOA campgrounds. Overall, this is a safe choice, reliable and well run, with ample activities (e.g. video games, pool, badminton net) for kids.

Basics

Operated By: Gregg & Jo Green. **Open:** Apr. 15–Oct. 15. **Site Assignment:** First come, first served; reservations accepted. **Registration:** At office. **Fee:** $19–$21 tent, $23–$26 RV (V, MC, AE, D). **Parking:** At site.

Facilities

Number of RV Sites: 45. **Number of Tent-Only Sites:** 14. **Hookups:** Electric (50 amp), water, sewer. **Each Site:** Table, grill. **Dump Station:** Ye[illegible] **Laundry:** Yes. **Pay Phone:** Yes. **Rest Room[illegible]** **Showers:** Yes. **Fuel:** No. **Propane:** N[illegible]ternal **Roads:** Gravel, good condition. **RV Service:** No. **Market:** In Panguitch, 5 blocks north. **Restaurant:** In Panguitch. **General Store:** Yes. **Vending:** Yes. **Swimming:** Pool. **Playground:** Yes. **Other:** Game room, Internet access, pet walk. **Activities:** Wildlife museum in town. **Nearby Attractions:** Panguitch Lake, Cedar Breaks, Red Canyon, Bryce. **Additional Information:** Garfield County Travel Council, (800) 444-6689.

Restrictions

Pets: On leash under owner's control. **Fires:** Yes (firewood sold). **Alcoholic Beverages:** Allowed. **Vehicle Maximum Length:** 65 ft. **Other:** No running of generators, noon checkout.

To Get There

From US 89 in Panguitch at intersection of Main and Center Sts., go 5 blocks south on Main St.

PANGUITCH
Red Canyon RV Park

P.O. Box 717, Panguitch 84759. T: (435) 676-2690; F: (435) 676-2765; www.redcanyon.net or www.onpages.com/thestore.

RV ★★★ Tent ★★

Beauty: ★★★ Site Privacy: ★★★
Spaciousness: ★★★★ Quiet: ★★★
Security: ★★★★ Cleanliness: ★★★★
Insect Control: ★★★ Facilities: ★★★

Red Canyon RV Park (not to be confused with the US Forest Service Red Canyon Campground) is on a relatively isolated stretch of UT Hwy. 12, just 16 miles from Bryce and 7 miles from Panguitch. The compact, well-run RV park, whose clientele is mostly seniors, has a few large pull-through sites among two short rows of RV sites. The grassy tent area is almost close enough to the highway to double as a roadside shoulder. But this is a good base camp to park the RV while biking area trails or taking a jeep or four-wheel-drive vehicle into Red Canyon. Coyote, elk, deer, cottontail, and jackrabbits visit the RV park, and red-headed woodpeckers peck away at the trees, adding a sense of wilderness to what would otherwise be a roadside stop. All in all, not a bad alternative for Red Canyon explorers and national park visitors when the campgrounds closer to Bryce fill up.

BASICS

Operated By: Arthur & Wenda Mae Tebbs. **Open:** April 1–Oct. 31 (weather permitting). **Site Assignment:** First come, first served. **Registration:** At office. **Fee:** $10 tent, $18 RV (V, MC, D). **Parking:** At site.

FACILITIES

Number of RV Sites: 40. **Number of Tent-Only Sites:** 20. **Hookups:** Water, electric (20, 30, 50 amp), sewer. **Each Site:** Table, shade canopy, grill. **Dump Station:** Yes. **Laundry:** No. **Pay Phone:** Yes. **Rest Rooms and Showers:** Yes. **Fuel:** Yes. **Propane:** No. **Internal Roads:** Gravel, excellent. **RV Service:** No. **Market:** 7 mi. northwest in Panguitch. **Restaurant:** 7 mi. northwest in Panguitch. **General Store:** Yes. **Vending:** Yes. **Swimming:** No. **Playground:** No. **Other:** Native American crafts store, rock shop, dog walk area. **Activities:** Jeep tours, bike trails. **Nearby Attractions:** Bryce, Lake Panguitch, Red Canyon. **Additional Information:** Powell Ranger District, (435) 676-8815.

RESTRICTIONS

Pets: On leash under owner's control. **Fires:** Yes. **Alcoholic Beverages:** Allowed. **Vehicle Maximum Length:** 60 ft.

TO GET THERE

Go 16 mi. west on UT Hwy. 12 from Bryce Canyon; or 1 mi. east on Hwy. 12 from the junction w/ US Hwy. 89.

PANGUITCH LAKE
Bear Paw Lakeview Resort

P.O. Box 397, 905 South Hwy. 143, Panguitch Lake 84759. T: (435) 676-2650 or (888) 553-8439; www.BearPawFishingResort.com; bearpaw@color-country.net.

RV ★★★ | Tent n/a

Beauty: ★★★★	Site Privacy: ★★★★
Spaciousness: ★★★	Quiet: ★★★★
Security: ★★★★	Cleanliness: ★★★★
Insect Control: ★★	Facilities: ★★★

Located in Dixie National Forest near an area of massive lava flows, Bear Paw Lakeview Resort is a mixture of cabins and RV sites on a hillside dotted with pine trees and sage. A rustic pine wood general store and small cafe anchor the steeply sloping hillside. A 40-foot walk crossing UT Hwy. 143 leads to Panguitch Lake's rainbow, cutthroat, brook, and brown trout (worms, tackle, and fishing licenses for sale at the general store). Ironically, the Resort's small roadside cafe serves up almost everything but lake trout, claiming Utah state law allows restaurants to serve only USDA-inspected trout from fish farms. Kids and pets do well here, but space is limited and reservations are recommended. Indeed, the 32 RV sites up the road at Rustic Lodge & RV Park, which is under the same ownership, are booked up year after year in advance by the same people, many of whom have even built their own private fenced-in decks.

BASICS

Operated By: Laura & Glenn Adams. **Open:** First week in May–Oct. 31. **Site Assignment:** First come, first served; reservations (one night; refundable one week prior to arrival). **Registration:** In store. **Fee:** $19 (V, MC, AE, D). **Parking:** At site.

FACILITIES

Number of RV Sites: 17. **Number of Tent-Only Sites:** 0. **Hookups:** Electric (20, 30 amp), water, sewer. **Each Site:** Table, fire ring. **Dump Station:** Yes. **Laundry:** Yes. **Pay Phone:** Yes. **Rest Rooms and Showers:** Yes. **Fuel:** No. **Propane:** No. **Internal Roads:** Graded gravel, on slope. **RV Service:** No. **Market:** 15 mi. in Panguitch. **Restaurant:** Resort cafe serves 3 meals. **General Store:** Yes. **Vending:** Yes. **Swimming:** In lake. **Playground:** Yes. **Other:** Boat launch, horse-riding, boat slip, boat & mountain-bike rentals. **Activities:** Trout fishing in lake & creeks. **Nearby Attractions:** Cedar Breaks, Bryce, Brian Head Ski Resort. **Additional Information:** Dixie National Forest, (435) 865-3200, www.fs.fed.us/dxnf.

RESTRICTIONS

Pets: On leash under owner's control. **Fires:** Yes. **Alcoholic Beverages:** Allowed. **Vehicle Maximum Length:** 34 ft.

TO GET THERE

17 mi. west of Panguitch or 12 mi. east of Cedar Breaks on UT Hwy. 143.

PANGUITCH LAKE
White Bridge Campground

P.O. Box 80, Panguitch Lake 84759. T: (877) 444-6777.

RV ★★★ | Tent ★★★★

Beauty: ★★★★★	Site Privacy: ★★★★
Spaciousness: ★★★★	Quiet: ★★★★★
Security: ★★★★	Cleanliness: ★★★★
Insect Control: ★★	Facilities: ★

At 7,900-feet elevation, this Dixie National Forest campground nestled among hillsides covered with gray-green desert scrub opens and closes based on local snowfall dates. Campsites are widely dispersed on alternating sides of a good gravel road. Panguitch Creek flows through White Bridge, adding a bucolic burbling backdrop. However, for the entomophobic, Utah's lake and creek ecosystems may be too much nature. Periodic hatches of mayflies and other flying insects signify a healthy ecosystem (and are not sprayed in the National Forest), and fatten the trout, lizards, birds, and other wildlife for the tough winter ahead (and were a high-protein food source gathered by ancient Native Americans). The only warm-weather alternative for those who would rather appreciate the landscape without any nuisance or DEET (insect repellent) is to stick to drier desert areas. Seasoned campers already accustomed to watching out for the region's legendary rattlers and scorpions, will find Utah's lake and creek campgrounds a pleasant base for boating, trout fishing, horseback riding, and exploring nearby national parks.

BASICS

Operated By: Aud & Di Campground Services (US Forest Service concessionaire). **Open:** May–first snow (Sept. or Oct.). **Site Assignment:** First come, first served; 11 sites can be reserved. **Registration:** Self-pay fee station at entrance. **Fee:** $10. **Parking:** At site.

FACILITIES

Number of RV Sites: 24. **Number of Tent-Only Sites:** 5. **Hookups:** None. **Each Site:** Table, grills. **Dump Station:** Yes. **Laundry:** No. **Pay Phone:** No. **Rest Rooms and Showers:** No showers. **Fuel:** No. **Propane:** No. **Internal Roads:** Gravel, good condition. **RV Service:** No. **Market:** 10 mi. northeast in Panguitch. **Restaurant:** 4 mi. west at Panguitch Lake. **General Store:** No. **Vending:** No. **Swimming:** In lake. **Playground:** No. **Activities:** Fishing. **Nearby Attractions:** Panguitch Lake, Cedar Breaks, Bryce. **Additional Information:** Dixie National Forest, (435) 865-3200, www.fs.fed.us/dxnf.

RESTRICTIONS

Pets: On leash. **Fires:** Yes. **Alcoholic Beverages:** Allowed. **Vehicle Maximum Length:** 32 ft. **Other:** No fireworks or firearms, noon checkout, 14-day limit.

TO GET THERE

Go 10 mi. southwest of Panguitch on UT Hwy. 143 or 4 mi. east from Panguitch Lake.

SALINA
Butch Cassidy Campground

1100 South State St., Salina 84654. T: (435) 529-7400 or (800) 551-6842.

RV ★★★ | Tent ★★

Beauty: ★★★★	Site Privacy: ★★★★
Spaciousness: ★★★★	Quiet: ★★★
Security: ★★★★	Cleanliness: ★★★★
Insect Control: ★★★	Facilities: ★★★★

A rural crossroads for coal, salt, and gypsum (wallboard) mining traffic, Salina is a rustic overnight stop on the long trek across Utah on I-70. Tent camping is on the grass under trees alongside the highway or in quieter back-in RV sites. The RV sites, including 26 pull-throughs, are elevated on a hillside with less highway noise. Mobile homes are on a terrace above the RVs. Trees and grass provide pleasant visuals, but the real attraction is Mom's Cafe at the corner of Main and State Streets (US Hwy. 89). Mom sits at a desk under a clock above the salad bar surveying the restaurant, and prides herself on some remarkably good road food. For breakfast try the Mad House Cafe on Main Street, where ceramics and children's art decorate the walls, and portions are large enough for a hungry trucker and a famished farmer to split (or just order blueberry pancakes at a buck apiece).

BASICS

Operated By: Lee, Danielle & Mich Crysel. **Open:** All year. **Site Assignment:** First come, first served; reservations accepted. **Registration:** Office. **Fee:** $12 tents, $15–$20 RV (V, MC). **Parking:** At site.

FACILITIES

Number of RV Sites: 38. **Number of Tent-Only Sites:** 20. **Hookups:** Electric (20, 30, 50 amp), water, sewer. **Each Site:** Table. **Dump Station:** Yes. **Laundry:** Yes. **Pay Phone:** Yes. **Rest Rooms and Showers:** Yes. **Fuel:** No. **Propane:** No. **Internal Roads:** Gravel, good. **RV Service:** No. **Market:** Salina, 1 mi. **Restaurant:** Across the street. **General Store:** Yes. **Vending:** Yes. **Swimming:** Pool. **Playground:** Yes. **Other:** Tent & back-in sites have grills. **Activities:** ATVs, fishing. **Nearby Attractions:** Fish Lake. **Additional Information:** Fish Lake National Forest, (435) 896-9233.

RESTRICTIONS

Pets: On leash at all times. **Fires:** Yes (in designated fire pits or grills). **Alcoholic Beverages:** Allowed. **Vehicle Maximum Length:** 60 ft. **Other:** No fireworks, no clothes lines.

TO GET THERE

From US I-70 Exit 54, go north 0.5 mi. on State St. (US Hwy. 89).

SPRINGDALE

Zion Canyon Campground

479 Zion Park Blvd., Springdale 84767. T: (435) 772-3237; www.zioncanyoncampground.com.

RV ★★★★ Tent ★★★★

Beauty: ★★★★ Site Privacy: ★★★★
Spaciousness: ★★★★ Quiet: ★★★★
Security: ★★★★ Cleanliness: ★★★★
Insect Control: ★★★ Facilities: ★★★★

The Zion National Park shuttle bus stops in front and the Virgin River is the back border of Zion Canyon Campground, a bustling little village run by the same family for the past three decades. A popular pizza restaurant next door to the office and store has outdoor tables bordering UT Hwy. 14 and the campground's front entrance. The showers here are very popular with campers staying at the two campgrounds inside Zion National Park. Indeed, Zion Canyon is held in such high regard that National Park overflow is sent here. While not as rustic as the National Park campgrounds, the views of Zion's sandstone mountains are still good. The campground also has plenty of trees and a pond. RV sites B20 and B21 are open-ended and can accommodate any RV currently on the road. There are also numerous grassy sites with dirt perimeters close to the river.

BASICS

Operated By: Dave & Stew Ferber. **Open:** All year. **Site Assignment:** First come, first served. **Registration:** Office. **Fee:** $16–$20 (V, MC). **Parking:** At site.

FACILITIES

Number of RV Sites: 120. **Number of Tent-Only Sites:** 100. **Hookups:** Electric (30, 50 amp), water, sewer, cable TV. **Each Site:** Table, grill. **Dump Station:** Yes. **Laundry:** Yes. **Pay Phone:** Yes. **Rest Rooms and Showers:** Yes. **Fuel:** No. **Propane:** No. **Internal Roads:** Gravel, good. **RV Service:** No. **Market:** Springdale, 1 mi. **Restaurant:** On premises. **General Store:** Yes. **Vending:** Yes. **Swimming:** Pool, river. **Playground:** Yes. **Other:** Game room, pavilion. **Activities:** Biking, horseback riding. **Nearby Attractions:** Zion National Park. **Additional Information:** Washington County Travel Bureau, (435) 634-5747, (800) 869-6635.

RESTRICTIONS

Pets: On leash (in RV area; no pets in tent area). **Fires:** Yes. **Alcoholic Beverages:** Allowed. **Vehicle Maximum Length:** No limit.

TO GET THERE

Go 0.5 mi. south of Zion National Park south entrance on UT Hwy. 9.

ST. GEORGE

Quail Creek State Park

P.O. Box 1943, St. George 84771. T: (435) 879-2378 or (800) 322-3770 (reservations); www.nr.state.ut.us.

RV ★★★★ Tent ★★★★

Beauty: ★★★★ Site Privacy: ★★★★
Spaciousness: ★★★★ Quiet: ★★★★
Security: ★★★★ Cleanliness: ★★★★
Insect Control: ★★ Facilities: ★★

Hundred-foot-deep warm blue waters and a red sandstone cliff backdrop only 15 miles northeast of St. George make 3,300-foot-elevation Quail Creek Reservoir one of Utah's most popular summer water playgrounds. The 600 acre reservoir was created in 1990 by damming Quail Creek for hydroelectric power below the lower slopes of the Pine Mountains and filling the basin behind the 202-foot-tall dam with Virgin River water. Most of the namesake quail have been hunted out of the area. But the small hillside campground and its large curving pull-through and flat tent sites command good views across waters crowded with boaters and water skiers. Sheltered picnic tables overlooking the reservoir also make this a popular day-trip party destination. Though a jaunt to Hurricane is needed for amenities, a campsite here can also be a base for exploring the Red Cliffs and Silver Reef near Leeds, as well as Zion National Park.

BASICS

Operated By: Utah State Parks & Recreation. **Open:** All year. **Site Assignment:** First come, first served; reservations advised peak times. **Registration:** Entrance kiosk. **Fee:** $10 (cash or check). **Parking:** At site.

FACILITIES

Number of RV Sites: 23. **Number of Tent-Only Sites:** 0. **Hookups:** None. **Each Site:** Sheltered table on cement pad, grill. **Dump Station:** Yes. **Laundry:** No. **Pay Phone:** No. **Rest Rooms and Showers:** No showers. **Fuel:** No. **Propane:** No. **Internal Roads:** Paved, good. **RV Service:** No. **Market:** St. George, 14 mi. **Restaurant:** St. George, 14 mi. **General Store:** No. **Vending:** No. **Swimming:** Lake. **Playground:** No. **Other:** Boat launch, fish cleaning station, 3 wheelchair-accessible sites. **Activities:** Boating, fishing. **Nearby Attractions:** Zion National Park. **Additional Information:** Washington County Travel & Convention Bureau, (435) 634-5747, (800) 869-6635.

RESTRICTIONS

Pets: On leash under owner's control. **Fires:** Yes. **Alcoholic Beverages:** Allowed. **Vehicle Maximum Length:** No limit. **Other:** 3-day limit without reservations.

TO GET THERE

From St. George go north on US I-15 to Exit 16, and then 3 mi. east on UT Hwy. 9.

ST. GEORGE

Snow Canyon State Park

1002 Snow Canyon Dr., Ivins 84738. T: (435) 628-2255 or (800) 322-3770 (reservations); parks.state.ut.us.

RV ★★★★ Tent ★★★★

Beauty: ★★★★★ Site Privacy: ★★★★
Spaciousness: ★★★★ Quiet: ★★★★★
Security: ★★★★ Cleanliness: ★★★★
Insect Control: ★★ Facilities: ★★★

Located west of Leeds among 170-million-year-old eroding red-orange sandstone mountains and white hills in the Red Cliffs Desert Reserve, Snow Canyon was chanced upon by cowboys searching for lost cattle and named after early pioneers Erastus and Lorenzo Snow. Also popular for day trips, as picnic areas as well as 25 campsites in the two loops are reservable, Snow Canyon's geologic riches include recent lava flows, deep caves, steep canyons, soft red and petrified sand dunes, and Anasazi petroglyphs. Wildlife ranges from ringtail cats to giant desert hairy scorpions (shake boots upside down in the morning before wearing). The paved sites (1–14, 3–8, and 11–14 reservable) with electric hookups at the front of the campground have sheltered tables, but their 15-foot width is too narrow for big rigs with sliders and tip-outs. A smattering of trees and desert scrub separates the other more primitive campsites.

BASICS

Operated By: Utah State Parks & Recreation. **Open:** All year. **Site Assignment:** First come, first served; some sites can be reserved (120 days in advance). **Registration:** Self-pay fee station. **Fee:** $13–$15 (cash or check only). **Parking:** At site.

FACILITIES

Number of RV Sites: 35. **Number of Tent-Only Sites:** 0. **Hookups:** Electric (30 amp), water. **Each Site:** Table, grill. **Dump Station:** Yes. **Laundry:** No. **Pay Phone:** Yes. **Rest Rooms and Showers:** Yes. **Fuel:** No. **Propane:** No. **Internal Roads:** Paved, excellent. **RV Service:** No. **Market:** St. George, 10 mi. **Restaurant:** St. George, 10 mi. **General Store:** No. **Vending:** Yes. **Swimming:** No. **Playground:** No. **Other:** Picnic area, basketball court in group area, cactus/native-plant garden. **Activities:** Biking, horseback riding. **Nearby Attractions:** Zion National Park. **Additional**

Information: Washington County Travel & Convention Bureau, (435) 634-5747, (800) 869-6635.

Restrictions

Pets: On leash (not allowed on trail). **Fires:** Yes (in grills only, no fires June 1–Sept. 15, firewood available). **Alcoholic Beverages:** Allowed. **Vehicle Maximum Length:** 60 ft. **Other:** No climbing on rocks behind campground.

To Get There

From St. George go 10 mi. north on UT Hwy. 18.

SYRACUSE

Antelope Island State Park

4528 West 1700 South, Syracuse 84075. T: (801) 773-2941 or (800) 322-3770; www.nr.state.ut.us.

RV ★★★★ Tent ★★★★

Beauty: ★★★★★ Site Privacy: ★★★★★
Spaciousness: ★★★★ Quiet: ★★★★★
Security: ★★★★★ Cleanliness: ★★★★
Insect Control: ★★★ Facilities: ★★★

An 8-mile-long two-lane causeway with swooping birds diving down and scaring drivers crosses the Great Salt Lake on the drive from the Antelope Island entrance kiosk to Bridger Bay Campground. Though the area is a popular day-use park with many migratory waterfowl and secluded turnouts and beaches for picnics, campers must bring their own water (or use the Visitor Center faucets and soft drink vending machines). Wildlife, including introduced bison and re-introduced antelope, have it better, as this largest of the 10 Great Salt Lake islands has 40 springs. The primitive campsites are widely dispersed and attractively situated among the rocky grasslands and sagebrush coming down from the hills overlooking the lake. Campsites are booked up well in advance for weekends, particularly prime vacation holidays, and visitors without reservations are frequently turned away. The sites are long and narrow, and very wide or long vehicles should call the park before coming.

Basics

Operated By: Utah State Parks & Recreation. **Open:** All year. **Site Assignment:** First come, first served; reservations (120 days in advance for individuals, 1 year for groups, an absolute necessity holidays, weekends). **Registration:** Entrance kiosk. **Fee:** $10 ($6.25 reservation fee; cash or check). **Parking:** At site.

Facilities

Number of RV Sites: 26. **Number of Tent-Only Sites:** 0. **Hookups:** None. **Each Site:** Table, fire ring w/ grill. **Dump Station:** Yes. **Laundry:** No. **Pay Phone:** No. **Rest Rooms and Showers:** Yes. **Fuel:** No. **Propane:** No. **Internal Roads:** Gravel, good. **RV Service:** No. **Market:** Syracuse, 12 mi. **Restaurant:** Buffalo Point, 2 mi. (limited hours; outdoor tables). **General Store:** No. **Vending:** No. **Swimming:** Lake. **Playground:** No. **Other:** Visitor Center, gift shop, marina, horse concessions, ranger programs. **Activities:** Biking, horseback riding, bird-watching. **Nearby Attractions:** Farmington Bay Waterfowl Management Area. **Additional Information:** Davis County Tourism, (801) 451-3286, www.co.davis.ut.us/discoverdavis; Farmington Bay Waterfowl Area, (801) 451-7386.

Restrictions

Pets: On leash (not allowed on beach). **Fires:** Yes (charcoal in fire rings or gas stoves when fire danger is low, absolutely no fires when grasslands are dry in summer). **Alcoholic Beverages:** Allowed. **Vehicle Maximum Length:** 50 ft. **Other:** Horses not allowed in campground.

To Get There

From US I-15 Exit 335 18 mi. north of Salt Lake City, go 14 mi. west on UT Hwy. 127.

TORREY

Fruita Campground

HC 70 Box 16, Torrey 84775. T: (435) 425-3791; www.nps.gov/care; interpretation@nps.gov.

RV ★★★★ Tent ★★★★

Beauty: ★★★★ Site Privacy: ★★★★
Spaciousness: ★★★ Quiet: ★★★★
Security: ★★★★ Cleanliness: ★★★★
Insect Control: ★★ Facilities: ★★

Fruita Campground is named for the surrounding historic orchards, where cherries, peaches, and other fruit can be picked in season. As the only developed campground within Capitol Reef National Park, campsites in Fruita are coveted and the campground often fills by early afternoon. Fruita is laid out alongside the Fremont River (so be prepared with bug repellent during warm months) and is noted for its many large shade trees and grassy tent sites. The three loops resemble a dense little village, with Loop C having the largest RV sites. Tent campers wanting a more primitive camping experience (no water provided) in the park may wish to head to the campgrounds at Cedar Mesa (5 no-fee tent sites; but navigating the dirt road is not advised during wet weather) or Cathedral Valley (6 no-fee sites; road conditions also a wet-weather concern). For hookups and amenities, head to Torrey.

Basics

Operated By: National Park Service. **Open:** All year. **Site Assignment:** First come, first served; reservations taken only for group site. **Registration:** Self-pay entrance fee station. **Fee:** $10 (half price for Golden Age or Golden Access; cash or check only). **Parking:** At site.

Facilities

Number of RV Sites: 70. **Number of Tent-Only Sites:** 0. **Hookups:** None. **Each Site:** Table, grill. **Dump Station:** Yes. **Laundry:** No. **Pay Phone:** Yes. **Rest Rooms and Showers:** No showers. **Fuel:** No. **Propane:** No. **Internal Roads:** Paved, good condition. **RV Service:** No. **Market:** In Torrey, 16 mi. west. **Restaurant:** In Torrey, 16 mi. west. **General Store:** No. **Vending:** No. **Swimming:** No. **Playground:** No. **Activities:** None. **Nearby Attractions:** Capitol Reef, Escalante, Goblin Valley State Park. **Additional Information:** Capitol Reef Country, (800) 858-7951, (435) 425-3365, www.capitolreef.org; Wayne County Travel Council, (800) 858-7159.

Restrictions

Pets: On leash under owner's control. **Fires:** Yes. **Alcoholic Beverages:** Allowed if over 18 years old. **Vehicle Maximum Length:** 30 ft. **Other:** Do not feed or approach wildlife, 14-day limit Apr. 1–Nov. 30, 30-day limit Dec. 1–Mar. 31.

To Get There

11 mi. east of Torrey on UT Hwy. 24, then 1 mi. south on scenic road past Visitor Center.

TORREY

Thousand Lakes RV Park

P.O. Box 750070, Torrey 84775. T: (800) 355-8995 or (435) 425-3500; www.thousandlakesrvpark.com.

RV ★★★★ Tent ★★★★

Beauty: ★★★★★ Site Privacy: ★★★★
Spaciousness: ★★★★ Quiet: ★★★★
Security: ★★★★ Cleanliness: ★★★★★
Insect Control: ★★★★ Facilities: ★★★★

Tall cottonwood trees and grass between the gravel sites lend a pleasant pastoral feel to Thousand Lakes RV Park, which boasts an exceptionally good gift shop and is within a mile of such Torrey institutions as Cafe Diablo, the Capitol Reef Inn & Cafe, and Robber's Roost Books & Beverages. Week nights from May to early October, Thousand Lakes serves up a western cookout complete with Dutch oven potatoes, cowboy beans, buttermilk scones, and entrees ranging from ribeye steak to vegetarian. With everything from horseshoes, a playground for the kids, a dog walk, and nearby espressos, guests sometimes forget that they came here for the national park and the incomparable sunrise and sunset light on the chiseled sandstone cliffs that define Capitol Reef. The combination of hookups and nearby restaurants and amenities brings a fair amount of repeat business and makes this a pleasant base camp for commuting to Capitol Reef National Park.

Basics

Operated By: John & Vally Reilly. **Open:** April 1–Oct. 31. **Site Assignment:** First come, first served; reservations accepted. **Registration:** In office. **Fee:** $12.50 tent, $15.50–$18.50 RV (V, MC, AE). **Parking:** At site.

Facilities

Number of RV Sites: 58. **Number of Tent-Only Sites:** 9. **Hookups:** Electric (30, 50 amp), water, sewer. **Each Site:** Table, grill. **Dump Station:** Yes. **Laundry:** Yes. **Pay Phone:** Yes. **Rest Rooms and Showers:** Yes. **Fuel:** No. **Propane:** No. **Internal Roads:** Gravel, good condition. **RV Service:** No. **Market:** In Torrey, 1 mi. east. **Restaurant:** Within 0.25 mi. **General Store:** Yes. **Vending:** No. **Swimming:** Heated pool. **Playground:** Yes. **Other:** Modem hookup in store, 4WD rentals, hair care. **Activities:** Western cookouts. **Nearby Attractions:** Capitol Reef, Boulder Mountain lakes, Escalante. **Additional Information:** Capitol Reef Country, (800) 858-7951, (435) 425-3365, www.capitolreef.org; Wayne County Travel Council, (800) 858-7159.

Restrictions

Pets: On leash under owner's control. **Fires:** Yes. **Alcoholic Beverages:** Allowed. **Vehicle Maximum Length:** 70 ft.

To Get There

On UT Hwy. 24, 2 mi. west of junction w/ UT Hwy. 12.

TORREY

Wonderland RV Park

Jct. of Hwys. 12 & 24, Torrey 84775. T: (435) 425-3775 or (800) 458-0216; F: (435) 425-3212; www.capitolreefwonderland.com; wonderland@color-country.net.

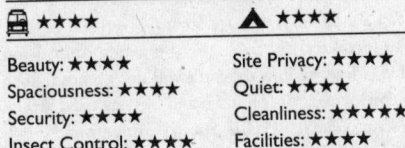

RV ★★★★ Tent ★★★★

Beauty: ★★★★
Site Privacy: ★★★★
Spaciousness: ★★★★
Quiet: ★★★★
Security: ★★★★
Cleanliness: ★★★★★
Insect Control: ★★★★
Facilities: ★★★★

Though situated at a key highway junction with a Days Inn and two gas stations with mini-marts and a Subway franchise, Wonderland RV Park looks out on a scenic vista of pasture and high desert that merges into the distant mountains. Tent sites are along a grassy strip protected by a windbreak fence. The highway gets little truck traffic, though the coyotes can howl up a storm. Almost all the amenities are here or very nearby, including use of the motel pool and restaurant, which are atop an adjacent hill. This family-run enterprise, which includes the gas station, mini-mart, and motel, also has Malfunction Junction for arranging 4WD and fishing tours with guides who have exclusive access to 25 miles of streams on the Fremont River and Boulder Creek, which is another way to see the backcountry. All in all, well situated for exploring Torrey and Capitol Reef and even the Boulder Mountains or Escalante.

Basics

Operated By: Raymond & Diane Potter. **Open:** Mar.–Nov. (or until first freeze). **Site Assignment:** First come, first served; reservations advised after June 1. **Registration:** At office or in Texaco mini-mart. **Fee:** $15 tent, $18 RV (V, MC, AE, D, DC). **Parking:** At site.

Facilities

Number of RV Sites: 33. **Number of Tent-Only Sites:** 12. **Hookups:** Electric (20, 30, 50 amp), water, sewer, cable TV. **Each Site:** Table, fire pit. **Dump Station:** Yes. **Laundry:** Yes. **Pay Phone:** Yes. **Rest Rooms and Showers:** Yes. **Fuel:** Yes. **Propane:** Yes. **Internal Roads:** Gravel, good. **RV Service:** No. **Market:** Texaco mini-mart. **Restaurant:** Several within 1 mi. **General Store:** Yes. **Vending:** Yes. **Swimming:** At Wonderland Inn (motel) pool. **Playground:** No. **Other:** 13 sites have phone (modem) hookup, RV/car wash. **Activities:** 4WD & fishing tours. **Nearby Attractions:** Capitol Reef, Boulder Mountains, Escalante. **Additional Information:** Capitol Reef Country, (800) 858-7951, (435) 425-3365, www.capitolreef.org; Wayne County Travel Council, (800) 858-7159.

Restrictions

Pets: On leash. **Fires:** Yes. **Alcoholic Beverages:** Allowed. **Vehicle Maximum Length:** 72 ft.

To Get There

At the junction of Utah Hwys 12 & 24, enter across the street from Texaco station.

VIRGIN

Zion River Resort RV Park & Campground

730 East Hwy. 9, P.O. Box 790219, Virgin 84779. T: (435) 635-8594 or (800) 838-8594; F: (435) 635-3934; www.zionriverresort.com; info@zrr.com.

RV ★★★★ Tent ★★★

Beauty: ★★★★
Site Privacy: ★★★★
Spaciousness: ★★★★
Quiet: ★★★
Security: ★★★★
Cleanliness: ★★★★★
Insect Control: ★★★
Facilities: ★★★★

With spacious pull-through sites able to handle double sliders, Zion River Resort is the place for big rigs. Even though winter night temperatures drop a few degrees below freezing, snowbirds flock here from November to March for the Zion mountain views through the surrounding trees. A well-stocked office store adds convenience, and there are enough amenities, including coin-operated video games, a pool table, and big-screen TV to keep children occupied. Tent sites 123–131 are alongside the Virgin River, while sites 118–122 are roadside. The RV sites closest to the cottonwood tree–lined Virgin River Walk are back-ins numbered 48–73 and 88–99. Budget campers will probably want to go elsewhere, as the fine facilities do not come cheap. Others will prefer camping inside Zion National Park itself, sacrificing amenities for a forested setting and closeness to park sites. Only Zion Canyon Campground in Springdale, just outside the Zion National Park entrance, offers comparable amenities.

Basics

Operated By: Robert, Todd & Ron Smith. **Open:** All year. **Site Assignment:** First come, first served; reservations accepted. **Registration:** Office. **Fee:** $20 tent, $29–$32 RV (V, MC, AE, D). **Parking:** At site.

Facilities

Number of RV Sites: 112. **Number of Tent-Only Sites:** 14. **Hookups:** Electric (30, 50 amp), water, sewer, phone (modem). **Each Site:** Table, grill. **Dump Station:** Yes. **Laundry:** No. **Pay Phone:** No. **Rest Rooms and Showers:** Yes. **Fuel:** No. **Propane:** Yes. **Internal Roads:** Paved, excellent. **RV Service:** No. **Market:** Hurricane, 9 mi. **Restaurant:** Hurricane, 9 mi. **General Store:** Yes. **Vending:** Yes. **Swimming:** Pool. **Playground:** Yes. **Other:** Cabins, teepees, whirlpool, volleyball, badminton, pet exercise area. **Activities:** Biking, horseback riding, golf, river tubing, ATV rides. **Nearby Attractions:** Zion National Park. **Additional Information:** Washington County Travel Bureau, (435) 634-5747, (800) 869-6635.

Restrictions

Pets: On leash (not allowed w/ tents). **Fires:** Yes (charcoal or wood in fire rings only). **Alcoholic Beverages:** Allowed. **Vehicle Maximum Length:** 70 ft. **Other:** No firearms, fireworks or RV storage.

To Get There

From US I-15 8 mi. north of St. George go east 18 mi. on UT Hwy. 9.

WILLARD

Willard Bay State Park

900 West 650 North Box A, Willard 84340. T: (801) 734-9494 or (801) 322-3770 or (800) 322-3770; www.nr.state.ut.us.

RV ★★★★ Tent ★★★★

Beauty: ★★★★
Site Privacy: ★★★★
Spaciousness: ★★★★
Quiet: ★★★
Security: ★★★★
Cleanliness: ★★★★
Insect Control: ★★★★
Facilities: ★★★

About a dozen miles north of Ogden and 35 miles north of Salt Lake City, Willard Bay has a more primitive tree-shaded grassy South Marina camping area favored by fishermen in the South Recreation Area (US I-15 Exit 354) and two more developed campgrounds five miles north in the North Recreation Area (US I-15 Exit 360). In the North, Cottonwood Campground has hookups, gray soil, and cottonwood trees for shade; sites 1–3, 10, 17, and 19–23 get the most highway noise. Willow Creek Campground lacks hookups but has a creek running through the campground, a pond, and sites tucked away in deep arbors of vegetation resembling coastal rainforest more than the arid grasslands and sage surrounding this Great Salt Lake floodplain. Willow Creek sites 10–35 have the best water views; sites 3–9 are nearest the pond. The bird refuge is a big attraction, and traffic picks up in January when the bald eagles start arriving.

Basics

Operated By: Utah State Parks & Recreation. **Open:** All year. **Site Assignment:** First come, first served; reservations (120 days in advance; highly recommended weekends, holidays). **Registration:** At entry kiosk. **Fee:** $10–$16 (cash or check only). **Parking:** At site.

Facilities

Number of RV Sites: 97. **Number of Tent-Only Sites:** 0. **Hookups:** Electric (30 amp), water, sewer (Cotton Campground only). **Each Site:** Table, grill or fire ring. **Dump Station:** Yes. **Laundry:** No. **Pay Phone:** No. **Rest Rooms and Showers:** Yes. **Fuel:** No. **Propane:** No. **Internal Roads:** Paved, excellent. **RV Service:** No. **Market:** Ogden, 12 mi. **Restaurant:** Willard, 1 mi. **General Store:** No. **Vending:** No. **Swimming:** Beach. **Playground:** No. **Other:** 3 boat launch ramps. **Activities:** Fishing, bird-watching. **Nearby Attractions:** Great Salt Lake. **Additional Information:** Golden Spike Empire, (801) 627-8288, www.ogdencvb.org.

Restrictions

Pets: On leash under owner's control (not allowed in public buildings). **Fires:** Yes (in fire pits & grills only). **Alcoholic Beverages:** Allowed (if over 21 years). **Vehicle Maximum Length:** 53 ft. **Other:** Off-highway vehicles & firearms prohibited.

To Get There

From US I-15 follow signs from Exit 360 into north campgrounds; take Exit 354 for more primitive south campground.

YUBA STATE PARK

Oasis Campground

P.O. Box 159, Levan 84639. T: (435) 758-2611 or (800) 322-3770 (reservations); F: (435) 758-2489; www.nr.state.ut.us.

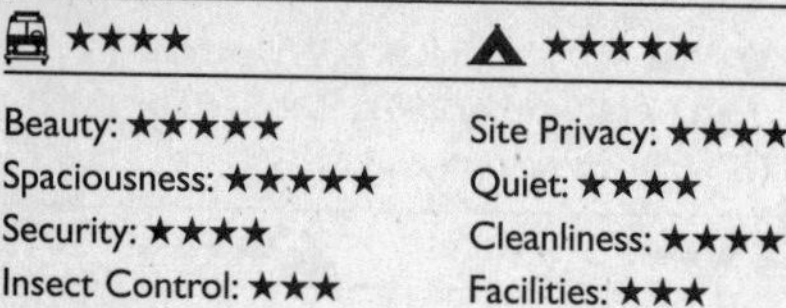

Warm (70–75° F) summer waters keep the small Oasis Campground fronting the rock-strewn sandy shores of Yuba Reservoir full most weekends and holidays during the school-vacation season. But on weekdays after the holiday crunch it is not unusual for a lone boater or two to have the whole 22-mile long, 80-foot deep lake as a private playground. Bait machines near the fish cleaning area dispense night crawlers and leeches to tempt walleye, northern pike, channel catfish, and yellow perch. Half the campground sites are over 60-feet long and the landscaping of green grass, sagebrush, cottonwood, and other trees makes this a real oasis from the seemingly distant (five miles) interstate highway for road-weary travelers. On the opposite side of the lake, Eagle View Campground's primitive boat-access-only sites 1,2,3,5,7,13, and 17 alongside a sandy day-use beach can be reserved with boat docks (sites 3 and 7 are wheelchair accessible).

Basics

Operated By: Utah State Parks & Recreation. **Open:** All year. **Site Assignment:** First come, first served; reservations recommended weekends, holidays. **Registration:** Entrance kiosk. **Fee:** $14 (cash or check; $8 for Eagle View Campground). **Parking:** At site.

Facilities

Number of RV Sites: 20. **Number of Tent-Only Sites:** 0. **Hookups:** None. **Each Site:** Table on cement pad, grill, fire ring. **Dump Station:** Yes. **Laundry:** No. **Pay Phone:** Yes. **Rest Rooms and Showers:** Yes. **Fuel:** No. **Propane:** No. **Internal Roads:** Paved, excellent. **RV Service:** No. **Market:** Nephi, 25 mi. **Restaurant:** Nephi, 25 mi. **General Store:** No. **Vending:** Yes. **Swimming:** Lake. **Playground:** No. **Other:** Boat ramp, beaches. **Activities:** Fishing, water sports. **Nearby Attractions:** Mormon Temple (Manti), Territorial Statehouse (Fillmore). **Additional Information:** Nephi/Juab County Chamber of Commerce, (435) 623-2411.

Restrictions

Pets: On leash under owner's control. **Fires:** Yes. **Alcoholic Beverages:** Allowed. **Vehicle Maximum Length:** 87 ft. **Other:** Turn in tagged walleyes for research use.

To Get There

From US I-15 Exit 202 near Mills, go 5 mi. south on reservoir perimeter road.

ZION NATIONAL PARK

Mukuntuweep RV Park & Campground

P.O. Box 193, Orderville 84758. T: (435) 648-2154; F: (435) 648-2829; www.xpressweb.com/zionpark; zionpark@xpressweb.com.

RV: ★★★ Tent: ★★★

Beauty: ★★★★ Site Privacy: ★★★★
Spaciousness: ★★★★ Quiet: ★★★★
Security: ★★★★ Cleanliness: ★★★★
Insect Control: ★★★★ Facilities: ★★★★

Mukuntuweep, the Paiute word for sacred cliffs, was the pre-Mormon name for the Zion National Park area. Mukuntuweep RV Park & Campground actually borders the park's eastern boundary, and the majestic rock-cliffs characteristic of Zion provide a scenic backdrop. Besides being the closest RV park to Zion, Mukuntuweep is somewhat of a refuge from the national park campground hustle and bustle, though it is right off the state highway. A gravel loop with pull-through sites (up to 40-feet wide) circles like a wagon train around an inner cluster of RVs near the entrance. Cottonwoods in the RV area are just getting to the size where they provide noticeable shade. Tenters have two gravel roads to choose from, and are out of sight of the RVs, with grass and junipers adding a more rugged wilderness feel. With ample amenities and diligent management living on site, Mukuntuweep makes a good base for exploring the park.

Basics

Operated By: Frank Baca. **Open:** All year. **Site Assignment:** First come, first served; reservations available. **Registration:** Office. **Fee:** $15 tent, $19 RV. **Parking:** At site.

Facilities

Number of RV Sites: 30. **Number of Tent-Only Sites:** 110. **Hookups:** Water, electric (20, 30 amp), sewer. **Each Site:** Table, grill. **Dump Station:** Yes. **Laundry:** Yes. **Pay Phone:** Yes. **Rest Rooms and Showers:** Yes. **Fuel:** Yes. **Propane:** No. **Internal Roads:** Gravel, good. **RV Service:** No (limited repairs). **Market:** Yes. **Restaurant:** Yes. **General Store:** Yes. **Vending:** Yes. **Swimming:** No. **Playground:** No. **Other:** Mountain bike rentals, horseback riding, video arcade w/ pool table, handicap accessible. **Activities:** Stream fishing, golf. **Nearby Attractions:** Zion, Bryce. **Additional Information:** Kane County Office of Tourism, 78 S. 100 East, Kanab, UT 84741; (435) 644-5033; (800) 733-5263; kanetrav@kaneutah.com; www.kaneutah.com.

Restrictions

Pets: On leash, cleaned up after, kept out of buildings. **Fires:** Yes (firewood sold). **Alcoholic Beverages:** Allowed. **Vehicle Maximum Length:** 70 ft. **Other:** 11 a.m. checkout.

To Get There

On Utah State Hwy. 9, go 0.25 mi. east from east entrance to Zion national Park; or from junction of Hwy. 9 and US Hwy. 89 at Mt. Carmel Junction, go 13 mi. west.

ZION NATIONAL PARK

South & Watchman Campgrounds

P.O. Box 1099, Springdale 84767. T: (435) 772-3256; www.nps.gov/zion.

RV: ★★★★ Tent: ★★★★★

Beauty: ★★★★★ Site Privacy: ★★★★
Spaciousness: ★★★★ Quiet: ★★★★
Security: ★★★★★ Cleanliness: ★★★★
Insect Control: ★★★★ Facilities: ★★★

Two Zion National Park campgrounds, South and Watchman, can handle RVs. But only Watchman Campground's Loop A and B have electric hookups (73 are 30 amp, two are 50 amp); Loop B has five 40-foot sites, but most are 35–36 feet. Tunnels on roads leading into the park will not accommodate vehicles over 50-feet long, and big rigs need special escort vehicles ($10). South Campground's two loops have a 24-foot length limit and tight turns difficult for large wider-bodied RVs. Watchman Loops C and D are for tent camping. Loop D's 36 sites are most coveted, being right up against scenic Mount Watchman. South Campground has three wheelchair-accessible sites (103, 114, 115) and 69 tent-only sites, including seven walk-in sites along the river. Watchman fills via reservation many days from Easter to Halloween, while South fills by 2:30 p.m. on a first-come-first-served basis.

Basics

Operated By: National Park Service. **Open:** All year (Watchman); Apr.–Oct. 15 (South). **Site Assignment:** First come, first served (South); reservations (Watchman; Easter-Halloween). **Registration:** Entry kiosk; self-pay fee station. **Fee:** $16 (cash or check only). **Parking:** At site; parking area for South Campground's 7 walk-in sites.

Facilities

Number of RV Sites: 346. **Number of Tent-Only Sites:** 7. **Hookups:** Electric (30, 50 amp). **Each Site:** Table, fire pit. **Dump Station:** Yes. **Laundry:** No. **Pay Phone:** Yes. **Rest Rooms and Showers:** No showers. **Fuel:** No. **Propane:** No. **Internal Roads:** Paved, some bumps. **RV Service:** No. **Market:** Springdale, 1 mi. **Restaurant:** Springdale, 1 mi. **General Store:** No. **Vending:** No. **Swimming:** No. **Playground:** No. **Other:** Visitor center, amphitheater, 3 wheelchair-accessible sites. **Activities:** Fishing, ranger programs. **Nearby Attractions:** Bryce. **Additional Information:** Washington County Travel Bureau, (435) 634-5747, (800) 869-6635.

Restrictions

Pets: On leash. **Fires:** Yes (in fire pit only, no wood gathering). **Alcoholic Beverages:** Allowed (at site only; zero tolerance for drinking & driving and marijuana). **Vehicle Maximum Length:** 40 ft.

To Get There

Go 0.5 mi. north of Springdale on UT Hwy. 14 to Zion National Park entrance.

Vermont

When people think of Vermont they think of the outdoors. It's hard not to picture any part of the state without seeing trees, undeveloped space, mountains, and water. That reputation is deserved, as Vermont has enormous amounts of unpopulated terrain. There are forests, mountains, lakes, and a seemingly endless amount of land—making this one of the better states for camping in the nation.

Camping in Vermont is fairly popular, and most campers in the state seek to encounter nature. Though there are some super-developed commercial campgrounds, most offer outdoors activities as the prime appeal. Even at the big RV parks with pools, rec halls, and other amenities its very rare that excellent hiking and a non-man made place to swim aren't nearby.

Vermont also has a large number of state-run campgrounds. Most of these are bare-bones facilities. For the most part, they accommodate RVs, but offer no hookups and only the barest amenities. These sites do, however, offer nature at its best. The state has maintained an enormous amount of public land—all of which remains undeveloped.

Those looking for campgrounds near a bustling metropolis will, for the most part, not find that in Vermont. Even the big "cities" in the state are relatively small, and Boston is pretty far away. Vermont does have lots of little towns with folksy charm and interesting local residents. The state is also so large that many areas don't get a lot of tourists, making them ideal spots to visit if you're looking to stay off the beaten path.

In many of the bigger towns, Vermont does have a shocking amount of antique and curiosity shops. Small cities like **Brattleboro** offer enough for a days worth of browsing, and many have regional theaters or small concert venues. In the winter months, Vermont also has some of the best skiing in the country. There are actually campgrounds affiliated with or nearby some of the mountains—though you'd have to be pretty hearty to camp in a tent during the dead of winter.

Basically, Vermont offers traditional camping with an almost endless amount of sites to choose from. Simply hiking all the trails in the state would take years, and canoeing all the rivers, climbing all the mountains, and fishing every lake would take a lifetime.

The following facilities feature 20 or fewer sites:

Knight Island State Park, St. Albans Bay

Campground Profile

ACUSTNEY

Getaway Mountain and Campground

P.O. Box 372, Ascutney 05030. T: (802) 674-2812.

RV ★★★★ Tent ★★

Beauty: ★★★ Site Privacy: ★★★
Spaciousness: ★★★ Quiet: ★★★
Security: ★★★ Cleanliness: ★★★
Insect Control: ★★★ Facilities: ★★★

A small, pleasant RV park, Getaway Mountain offers a nice alternative to large RV parking lot–type campgrounds. Most of the sites have shade trees, and though tents aren't the norm, it wouldn't be completely ridiculous to pitch one here. There's canoeing available on the nearby Connecticut River as well as easy access to hiking at Wilgus State Park.

BASICS

Operated By: Dave Fraczk. **Open:** May 1–Oct. 31. **Site Assignment:** Reservations accepted. **Registration:** At office. **Fee:** $18. **Parking:** At site.

FACILITIES

Number of RV Sites: 38. **Number of Tent-Only Sites:** 0. **Hookups:** Water, electric, sewer. **Each Site:** Fireplace. **Dump Station:** Yes. **Laundry:** No. **Pay Phone:** Yes. **Rest Rooms and Showers:** Yes. **Fuel:** No. **Propane:** No. **Internal Roads:** Entrance paved, Remainder is gravel. **RV Service:** No. **Market:** Country Village Store, Rte. 131, Ascutney, VT 05030. **Restaurant:** Mr. G's Restauraunt 202 Rte. 131 Ext 8 Ascutney, VT 05030(802) 674-2486. **General Store:** No. **Vending:** No. **Swimming Pool:** Yes. **Playground:** Yes. **Other:** Rec room, canoe rentals. **Activities:** Arcade, holiday events (hayrides, bonfires). **Nearby Attractions:** Arts & Historical Society, Fletcher Farm, Black River Academy Museum.

RESTRICTIONS

Pets: Allowed. **Fires:** Allowed. **Alcoholic Beverages:** Allowed. **Vehicle Maximum Length:** 30 ft. & plus. **Other:** Ask on arrival.

TO GET THERE

Take I-91 to Exit 8 then take Rte. 131 to Rte. 5. Go south on Rte. 5 for 2 mi.

ALBURG

Alburg RV Resort

P.O. Box 50, Blue Rock Rd., Alburg 05440. T: (802) 796-3733.

RV ★★★★ Tent ★★★

Beauty: ★★★★ Site Privacy: ★★★★
Spaciousness: ★★★★ Quiet: ★★★
Security: ★★★★ Cleanliness: ★★★★
Insect Control: ★★★ Facilities: ★★★★

The grassy sites here are located just off Lake Champlain set back in between trees. The lake is their major appeal, as there's a beach with swimming and boat access. The prime attraction, however, might be that the lake offers excellent sailing conditions. Guests with boats can hit the water right from the shore. If you have a bigger boat, there's a dock nearby. Some sites have a view of the Green Mountains—though whether you can actually see them depends on the weather. Most sites are private and there are tent-only sites, but the campground is dominated by large RVs parked for the whole season. There are a few sites available on a short term basis, you'll want to reserve early.

Basics

Operated By: Gilles R. & Francoise H. Gravel. **Open:** May 1–Oct. 1. **Site Assignment:** Reservations recommended. **Registration:** At office. **Fee:** $22–$25. **Parking:** At site.

Facilities

Number of RV Sites: 150. **Number of Tent-Only Sites:** 25. **Hookups:** Water, electric (20, 30 amps), sewer. **Each Site:** Fire ring, picnic table. **Dump Station:** Yes. **Laundry:** Yes. **Pay Phone:** Yes. **Rest Rooms and Showers:** Yes. **Fuel:** No. **Propane:** Yes. **Internal Roads:** paved/ gravel. **RV Service:** No. **Market:** Grand Union Co, 39 1st St., Swanton, VT 05488: Take a right onto Rte. 2 followed by a right onto Rte. 78. Follow for 10.6 mi. **Restaurant:** Anchorage, 164 Lake St., Rouses Point, NY 12979: Take a right onto Rte. 2 & follow it for 7.2 mi. then take a left onto Rte. 11/9-B & continue for 1.3 mi. **General Store:** Yes. **Vending:** Yes. **Swimming Pool:** Yes. **Playground:** Yes. **Other:** Lake, softball field, volleyball court, basketball court, shuffleboard, rec hall. **Activities:** Windsurfing, sailing. **Nearby Attractions:** Vermont Maple Festival (Apr.), Ethan Allen Homestead Aquarium, Moritime Museum, Lake Champlain. **Additional Information:** Call ahead.

Restrictions

Pets: Allowed.. **Fires:** Allowed. **Alcoholic Beverages:** Allowed. **Vehicle Maximum Length:** 40 ft.

To Get There

From the junction of US 2 and Hwy. 78, go 2 mi. east on Hwy. 78, then 0.5 mi. south on Blue Rock Rd.

ALBURG

Goose Point

526 US Rte. 2 South, Alburg 05440. T: (802) 796-3711.

RV: ★★★★ Tent: ★★

Beauty: ★★★★	Site Privacy: ★★★★
Spaciousness: ★★★★★	Quiet: ★★★
Security: ★★★	Cleanliness: ★★★★
Insect Control: ★★★	Facilities: ★★★★

Goose Point is big, and feels bigger. The campground, because of it size, offers something for everyone. RV sites range from grassy open spots to shaded private ones. Most of the tent sites are wooded and set off from the RVs. There's a lot of sailing done in the Missiquoi Bay of Lake Champlain, which also offers fishing—and not just your normal drop-a-line-to-catch-a-sunfish type, but the real catch-a-pike-or-trout-for-dinner variety. For tent campers who don't want to risk having their trip ruined by rain, there's also a bed-and-breakfast on the grounds where you can stay if Mother Nature doesn't cooperate.

Basics

Operated By: Gordie & Pauline Beyor. **Open:** May 1–Oct. 15. **Site Assignment:** At time of registration. **Registration:** Entrance Gate. **Fee:** $18–$20. **Parking:** At site.

Facilities

Number of RV Sites: 96. **Number of Tent-Only Sites:** 47. **Hookups:** Water, electric, sewer. **Each Site:** Picnic table, fire ring. **Dump Station:** Yes. **Laundry:** No. **Pay Phone:** Yes. **Rest Rooms and Showers:** Yes. **Fuel:** No. **Propane:** Yes. **Internal Roads:** Paved/gravel. **RV Service:** No. **Market:** Grand Union Co., 39 1st St., Swanton, VT: Take a left onto Rte. 2 then a right onto Rte. 78 & follow it for 10.8 mi. until it becomes Rte. 7. Then take a right back onto Rte. 78. **Restaurant:** Northern, Rte. 2, Alburg, VT 05440: Take a left onto Rte. 2. **General Store:** Yes. **Vending:** Yes. **Swimming Pool:** Yes. **Playground:** No. **Other:** Bait & tackle sold. **Activities:** Boating, fishing. **Nearby Attractions:** Ben & Jerry's Factory, Shelburne Museum, Appalachian Trail, Fletcher Farm. **Additional Information:** Call ahead.

Restrictions

Pets: Allowed. **Fires:** Allowed. **Alcoholic Beverages:** Allowed. **Vehicle Maximum Length:** 35 ft. **Other:** Ask on arrival.

To Get There

On Rte. 2 go 3 mi. south of the junction with Rte. 78.

BARTON

Belview Campground

P.O. Box 222, Rte. 16E, Barton 05822. T: (802) 525-3242.

RV: ★★★ Tent: ★★★★

Beauty: ★★★★★	Site Privacy: ★★★★
Spaciousness: ★★★★	Quiet: ★★★★
Security: ★★★★	Cleanliness: ★★★★
Insect Control: ★★★	Facilities: ★★★

A truly beautfiul campground, Belview has the advantage of being located a stone's throw from Crystal Lake but being set back in the woods a little bit. Though the sites are flat and fairly private, the park is offset by rolling hills on one side and farmland on the other—giving a variety of views. Though there aren't many facilities on site, there's a lot to do nearby. The lake also offers motor boating and fishing. Additionally, for those looking for smaller crowds and no power boats, there's May Pond nearby. Next to May Pond is May Pond Mountain, which offers a challenging hike.

Basics

Operated By: Bob & Joyce Morse. **Open:** May 15–Oct. 15. **Site Assignment:** Reservations accepted. **Registration:** Office Entrance. **Fee:** $14–$20. **Parking:** At site.

Facilities

Number of RV Sites: 50. **Number of Tent-Only Sites:** 0. **Hookups:** Water, electric, sewer, cable TV. **Dump Station:** Yes. **Laundry:** No. **Pay Phone:** Yes. **Rest Rooms and Showers:** Yes. **Fuel:** No. **Propane:** Nearby, but not on site. **Internal Roads:** Paved/gravel in good condition. **RV Service:** No. **Market:** Cole's Markets, 52 Main St., Orleans, VT 05860: Take a left onto Rte. 16 & follow it for 2.5 mi. to I-91 N. Follow it for 5.6 mi. to Exit 26. Take a left at the fork in the ramp & a left onto Rte. 58 East. **Restaurant:** Nickelodeon, 95 Main St., Newport, VT 05855: Take a left onto Rte. 16 & follow it for 2.5 mi. to I-91 N. Continue for 5.6 mi. to Exit 26. Take a left at the fork in the ramp & a left onto Rte. 58 East. **General Store:** No. **Vending:** No. **Swimming Pool:** No. **Playground:** Yes. **Activities:** Hiking, biking, fishing (3 lakes & ponds). **Nearby Attractions:** Concerts, Orleans County Fair (seasonal), Orleans Country Club & Barton Golf Course, Crystal Lake.

Restrictions

Pets: Allowed. **Fires:** Allowed. **Alcoholic Beverages:** Allowed. **Vehicle Maximum Length:** 40 ft. **Other:** Ask on arrival.

To Get There

Belview is located on Rte. 16E, 2 mi. from I-91 Exit 25. Go one mi. into the village, bear right on Rte. 5S for 0.5 mi., turn left over railroad tracks onto 16E. 0.5 mi. on right before going up hill.

BRANDON

Country Village Campground

40 Rte. 7, Brandon 05733. T: (802) 247-3333. cvcjb@juno.com

RV: ★★★ Tent: ★★

Beauty: ★★	Site Privacy: ★★★★
Spaciousness: ★★★	Quiet: ★★★
Security: ★★★	Cleanliness: ★★★
Insect Control: ★★★	Facilities: ★★★★

A pretty wide open campground, Country Village is supposed to be some sort of rural town. Mostly, it has RVs parked for the season in a fairly pleasant, albeit nothing special to look at setting. There's also not much at the actual campground, but there's a lot nearby. Lake Dunmore is within easy driving or long hiking distance. The campground is more of a summer camp, as most of the residents stay for the season.

Basics

Operated By: The Ceccoli Family. **Open:** May 15–Oct. 15. **Site Assignment:** Reservations recommended. **Registration:** Entrance. **Fee:** $13. **Parking:** At site.

Facilities

Number of RV Sites: 41. **Number of Tent-Only Sites:** 0. **Hookups:** Water, electric. **Each Site:** Picnic table, fire ring. **Dump Station:** Yes. **Laundry:** No. **Pay Phone:** Yes. **Rest Rooms and Showers:** Yes. **Fuel:** No. **Propane:** No. **Internal Roads:** Compressed gravel. **RV Service:** No. **Market:** Brandon Discount Foods: 2598 Franklin St. Brandon, VT 05733. **Restaurant:** Blueberry Hill Inn: Forest Rd. 32, Brandon, VT 05733, (802) 247-6735. **Gen-**

eral Store: Limited. **Vending:** No. **Swimming Pool:** Yes. **Playground:** Yes. **Other:** Mini golf, horseshoe pit. **Activities:** Mini Golf, Shuffleboard, Canoeing (nearby), dog walking, Fall Foliage. **Nearby Attractions:** Marble Exhibit, Wilson Castle, Antique Shopping, Lake Dunmole, Otter Creek.

Restrictions

Pets: Allowed. **Fires:** Allowed. **Alcoholic Beverages:** Allowed. **Vehicle Maximum Length:** 40 ft. **Other:** Ask on arrival.

To Get There

Take Rte. 7 to Rte. 73 and follow to campground

BRATTLEBORO

Fort Dummer State Park

434 Old Guilford Rd., Brattleboro 05301.
T: (802) 254-2610; www.state.vt.us.

RV ★★★ Tent ★★★

Beauty: ★★★	Site Privacy: ★★★
Spaciousness: ★★★	Quiet: ★★★
Security: ★★★	Cleanliness: ★★★★
Insect Control: ★★★	Facilities: ★★

The best part about Fort Dummer is location. The campground offers easy access to Brattelboro, which is one of Vermont's more interesting cities. The campground itself isn't very active. The facilities are sparse and there's not much there other than hiking trails. Nearby, however, there's fishing, boating, and just about everything else. The sites are well maintained, and though the campground does not stand out, it's a perfectly pleasant home base for a Brattleboro-area trip.

Basics

Operated By: State of Vermont. **Open:** late May–Sept. (Labor Day). **Site Assignment:** Reservations accepted. **Registration:** Entrance Station. **Fee:** $11. **Parking:** At site.

Facilities

Number of RV Sites: 51. **Number of Tent-Only Sites:** 10. **Hookups:** None. **Each Site:** Picnic table, fireplace. **Dump Station:** Yes. **Laundry:** No. **Pay Phone:** No. **Rest Rooms and Showers:** Yes. **Fuel:** No. **Propane:** No. **Internal Roads:** Paved, gravel. **RV Service:** No. **Market:** Price Chopper, 499 Canal St., Brattleboro, VT 05301: Take a right onto S. Main St. followed by a right onto Rte. 5 & a slight right onto Rte. 142. **Restaurant:** Ray's Diner, 105 Canal St., Brattleboro, VT 05301: Take a right onto S. Main St. followed by a left onto Rte. 5. **General Store:** No. **Vending:** No. **Swimming Pool:** No. **Playground:** Yes. **Other:** Dog walking Trail. **Activities:** Hiking Trails, Wildlife- & bird-watching, open field for games. **Nearby Attractions:** Green Mountains, Bennington Battle Monument, Townshend Dam, Basketville.

Restrictions

Pets: Allowed. **Fires:** Allowed. **Alcoholic Beverages:** Allowed. **Vehicle Maximum Length:** 30 ft. **Other:** Ask on arrival.

To Get There

Take Exit 1 on I-91 to Rte. 5 and turn right on Fairground Rd. then go right on Main St. until Old Guilford Rd.

BRATTLEBORO

Moss Hollow Campground

RD 4, Box 723, Brattleboro 05301. T: (802) 368-2418.

RV ★★★ Tent ★★★

Beauty: ★★★	Site Privacy: ★★★★
Spaciousness: ★★★★	Quiet: ★★★★
Security: ★★★	Cleanliness: ★★★★
Insect Control: ★★★	Facilities: ★★★

Located in a very rustic area, the prime attraction of this campground has to be the stream that runs through it. There's lots of fishing available as well as a swimming hole. If you're looking for more active sports, nearby Mount Snow offers hiking, mountain biking, and some trails for four-wheel ATVs. There's also an enormous network of hiking trails available as well as chair lift to the top of the mountain.

Basics

Operated By: Private operator. **Open:** May 15–Oct. 15. **Site Assignment:** Reservations recommended. **Registration:** At office. **Fee:** $15. **Parking:** At site.

Facilities

Number of RV Sites: 50. **Number of Tent-Only Sites:** 0. **Hookups:** Water, electric. **Each Site:** Picnic table, fire ring. **Dump Station:** Yes. **Laundry:** No. **Pay Phone:** Yes. **Rest Rooms and Showers:** Yes. **Fuel:** No. **Propane:** No. **Internal Roads:** Paved, dirt. **RV Service:** No. **Market:** Avenue Grocery, 82 Western Ave., Brattleboro, VT 05301: Take a right onto Abbot Rd., which becomes Greenleaf St., then take a right onto Rte. 9 & follow it for 1.5 mi. **Restaurant:** Dalem's Chalet Inc., 78 South St., Brattleboro, VT 05301: Take a right onto Abbot Rd. which becomes Greenleaf St. then take a right onto Rte. 9 & follow it for 0.3 mi. **General Store:** Yes. **Vending:** No. **Swimming Pool:** No. **Playground:** No. **Other:** Horseshoe pits. **Activities:** Fishing, swimming, biking. **Nearby Attractions:** ATV Trails. **Additional Information:** Mountain bikers must wear helmets.

Restrictions

Pets: Allowed. **Fires:** Allowed. **Alcoholic Beverages:** Allowed. **Vehicle Maximum Length:** None. **Other:** Ask on arrival.

To Get There

Take I-91 to Rte. 9 and follow for 1.5 mi. Turn left onto Green Leaf St. and follow until the end of the road. Cross the bridge and follow the dirt road to the campground.

BROWNINGTON

Will-O-Wood Campground

227 Will-O-Wood Ln., Brownington 05860.
T: (802) 525-3575;
www.will-o-woodcampground.com.

RV ★★★★ Tent ★★★

Beauty: ★★★	Site Privacy: ★★★★
Spaciousness: ★★★★	Quiet: ★★★
Security: ★★★	Cleanliness: ★★★★
Insect Control: ★★★	Facilities: ★★★★

Not quite on Lake Willoughby, Will-O-Wood offers large sites and excellent facilities. The campground is basically sits atop a grassy hill, with lots of nearby mountains for hiking as well as the lake only a half mile away. Though RVs dominate the campground, the tent sites have decent privacy and the overall spaciousness makes it a good mix for both types of campers. The campground also makes a good choice for families, as there's lots to do in and within easy access of the facility.

Basics

Operated By: Bob, Fran, Jeff, & Dave LaBerge. **Open:** May 1–Oct. 15. **Site Assignment:** Reservations accepted. **Registration:** At office. **Fee:** $18–$23. **Parking:** At site.

Facilities

Number of RV Sites: 84. **Number of Tent-Only Sites:** 33. **Hookups:** Water, electric, sewer. **Each Site:** Picnic table, fire ring, grill. **Dump Station:** Yes. **Laundry:** Yes. **Pay Phone:** Yes. **Rest Rooms and Showers:** Yes. **Fuel:** No. **Propane:** Yes. **Internal Roads:** Paved. **RV Service:** No. **Market:** Cole's Markets, 52 Main St., Orleans, VT 05860: Take a right onto Rte. 58 & go 0.1 mi. **Restaurant:** Delightful Dairy, 3556 Schoolhouse Rd. Orleans, VT 05860. **General Store:** Yes. **Vending:** Yes. **Swimming Pool:** Yes. **Playground:** Yes. **Other:** On-site trailor rental, special weekly, monthly, & seasonal rates, rec hall. **Activities:** Hiking, hunting, golf, bicycling, horseshoes. **Nearby Attractions:** Orleans Country Club, Crystal Lake, Mount Pisgah, Mount Hor, Lake Willoughby, golf courses.

Restrictions

Pets: Allowed. **Fires:** Allowed. **Alcoholic Beverages:** Allowed. **Vehicle Maximum Length:** No limit. **Other:** Ask on arrival.

To Get There

Take I-91 to Exit 26, then follow Rte. 58E for 7 mi. to Rte. 5A S and go 0.5 mi.

BURLINGTON

Burlington's North Beach Campground

60 Institute Rd., Burlington 05401. T: (802) 862-0942 or 800-571-1198; F: (802) 865-7087; www.holidayjunction.com/usa/vt/cvt0014.html.

RV ★★★ Tent ★★★

Beauty: ★★★★	Site Privacy: ★★★★
Spaciousness: ★★★★	Quiet: ★★★★
Security: ★★★	Cleanliness: ★★★★
Insect Control: ★★★	Facilities: ★★★

Burlington's North Beach Campground actually offers a nice mix of private campsites and a crowded lakefront. Though they're not secluded, the grassy sites are of a decent size and are nestled into the woods. Though it's near the busy (at least by Vermont standards) city of Burlington, North Beach feels like its in the woods. Lake Champlain, which abuts the park, has a large beach that can get quite crowded. There's also a large bike path and numerous hiking trails.

Basics

Operated By: City of Burlington. **Open:** May 1–

Oct. 15. **Site Assignment:** Reservations accepted. **Registration:** At office. **Fee:** $15–$25 (additional tents are $5 each, 2 per site max.). **Parking:** At site.

FACILITIES

Number of RV Sites: 16. **Number of Tent-Only Sites:** 137. **Hookups:** Water, electric, sewer. **Each Site:** Fireplace. **Dump Station:** Yes. **Laundry:** No. **Pay Phone:** Yes. **Rest Rooms and Showers:** Yes. **Fuel:** No. **Propane:** No. **Internal Roads:** Paved. **RV Service:** No. **Market:** Grand Union Co, 1134 North Ave., Burlington, VT 05401: Take a left onto North Ave. & follow it for 1 mi. **Restaurant:** Jimbo's Subs Wings & Things, 1130 North Ave., Burlington, VT 05401: Take a left onto North Ave. & follow it for 1 mi. **General Store:** Snack bar. **Vending:** Yes. **Swimming Pool:** No. **Playground:** Yes. **Other:** Bike path. **Activities:** Swimming, biking. **Nearby Attractions:** Historic downtown Burlington, Starr Farm Park (off-leash dog area), Paquett Arena at Leddy Park, Flynn Center. **Additional Information:** http://ci.burlington.vt.us/departments/parks/burlingtonparksandrecreation.htm.

RESTRICTIONS

Pets: Allowed. **Fires:** Allowed. **Alcoholic Beverages:** Allowed. **Vehicle Maximum Length:** 55 ft. **Other:** Ask on arrival.

TO GET THERE

From 1-89 to US 2W, take a left onto Pearl St., followed by a right onto N. Champlain St., a left onto Manhattan Dr., a left onto Pickin St., a right onto North St., and a right onto North Ave.

COLCHESTER

Lone Pine Campsites

52 Sunset View Rd., Colchester 05446. T: (802) 878-5447; www.lonepine.together.com.

RV ★★★★ Tent ★

Beauty: ★★★	Site Privacy: ★★★
Spaciousness: ★★★	Quiet: ★★★
Security: ★★★★	Cleanliness: ★★★★
Insect Control: ★★★	Facilities: ★★★★

Yet another enormous RV park, this one feels like a planned community for RVs. Sites are laid out on a grid, each with one shade tree. Campsites are grassy, and though I-89 is nearby, there's enough tree buffer to keep the camoground pretty much shielded form the noise of passing trucks. The major advantage here are the planned activities, which include a summer camp during the week for younger kids. Burlington is also pretty close by and has restaurants and shopping.

BASICS

Operated By: Bradd Rubman. **Open:** May 1–Oct. 15. **Site Assignment:** Reservations accepted. **Registration:** At office. **Fee:** $26–$35 daily or $180–$220 weekly. **Parking:** At site.

FACILITIES

Number of RV Sites: 265. **Number of Tent-Only Sites:** 0. **Hookups:** Water, electric, sewer. **Each Site:** Picnic table, fire ring, grill. **Dump Station:** Yes. **Laundry:** Yes. **Pay Phone:** Yes. **Rest Rooms and Showers:** Yes. **Fuel:** No. **Propane:** Yes. **Internal Roads:** Paved. **RV Service:** No. **Market:** Supervalu, Creek Farm Plz, Colchester, VT 05446: Take a left onto Rte. 127 & follow it for 0.2 mi. **Restaurant:** New York Pizza Oven, 288 Lakeshore Dr., Colchester, VT 05446: Take a right onto Rte. 127 & follow it for 0.9 mi. **General Store:** Yes. **Vending:** Yes. **Swimming Pool:** Yes. **Playground:** Yes. **Other:** Rec hall, game room, basketball courts, mini golf, tennis courts. **Activities:** Planned activities, fire truck rides. **Nearby Attractions:** Shelburne Museum, Vermont Teddy Bear Factory, Ben & Jerry's Factory, shopping malls, fishing charters.

RESTRICTIONS

Pets: Allowed. **Fires:** Allowed. **Alcoholic Beverages:** Allowed. **Vehicle Maximum Length:** None. **Other:** Ask on arrival.

TO GET THERE

I-89 to Exit 16, then take Rtes. 2 and 7 north for 3 mi. followed by a left onto Bay Rd. for 1 mi.

COLCHESTER

Malletts Bay Campground

88 Mallets Bay Campground Rd., Colchester 05446. T: (802) 863-6980.

RV ★★★★ Tent ★★

Beauty: ★★★	Site Privacy: ★★★
Spaciousness: ★★	Quiet: ★★★
Security: ★★★★	Cleanliness: ★★★
Insect Control: ★★★	Facilities: ★★★

On the positive side, Malletts Bay is well-located if you want to be next to a town that has a lot going on. It's also on Lake Champlain, which offers every imaginable water-based activity. The negative side is that the sites are laid out fairly close together in a grid. RVers can pick from both open and wooded spots, while tent campers are relegated to grassy fields that sometimes are a little too close to the RVs. This is not a wonderful place for tent campers—adequate at best. Still, with the lake on one side and Bayside Park on the other and the busy town nearby, there's a lot around to make this campground appealing.

BASICS

Operated By: The Handy family. **Open:** May 15–Oct. 15. **Site Assignment:** Reservations accepted. **Registration:** At office. **Fee:** $22–$29. **Parking:** At site.

FACILITIES

Number of RV Sites: 119. **Number of Tent-Only Sites:** 71. **Hookups:** Water, electric, sewer. **Each Site:** Fireplace, picnic table. **Dump Station:** Yes. **Laundry:** Yes. **Pay Phone:** Yes. **Rest Rooms and Showers:** Yes. **Fuel:** No. **Propane:** Yes. **Internal Roads:** Paved. **RV Service:** No. **Market:** Bayside Square Quick Stop, 336 Malletts Bay Ave., Colchester, VT 05446: Take a right onto Mallets Bay Ave. & follow it for 0.9 mi. **Restaurant:** Edgewater Pub, 340 Malletts Bay Ave., Colchester, VT 05446: Take a right onto Mallets Bay Ave. & follow it for 0.9 mi. **General Store:** No. **Vending:** No. **Swimming Pool:** Yes. **Playground:** Yes. **Other:** Game room, public beach. **Activities:** Tennis, boating, swimming, fishing. **Nearby Attractions:** St. Annes Shrine, Ethan Allen Homestead, Shelburne Museum, Ben & Jerry's Factory, shopping malls, tennis courts.

RESTRICTIONS

Pets: Allowed. **Fires:** Allowed. **Alcoholic Beverages:** Allowed. **Vehicle Maximum Length:** 40 ft. **Other:** Ask on arrival.

TO GET THERE

Take I-89 to Exit 16. Go north 1.5 mi. on Rte. 7. At the stop light, go left 3 mi. on Blakely Rd. Then go left on Lakeshore Dr. at the light

CONCORD

Breezy Meadows Campground

23 Wendel Rd., Concord 05824. T: (802) 695-9949 or 603-788-3624; www.gocampingamerica.com/breezymeadows; breezy@together.net.

RV ★★★★ Tent ★★★

Beauty: ★★★	Site Privacy: ★★
Spaciousness: ★★	Quiet: ★★★
Security: ★★★	Cleanliness: ★★★
Insect Control: ★★★	Facilities: ★★★★

Basically a grassy parking lot inset from the woods, Breezy Meadows is surrounded by scenery more impressive than the campground itself. RV sites tend to be a little bit close together, packed in small groups in little cutouts from the woods. Still, walk a few feet away from your vehicle and you have almost picture-perfect views of Moose River and the surrounding wilderness. Though it's a fairly small campground (additional sites are planned), Breezy Meadows has a fair amount of planned activities and the amenities of a bigger campground.

BASICS

Operated By: James & Anita Matott. **Open:** May 1–Oct. 1. **Site Assignment:** Reservations accepted. **Registration:** At office. **Fee:** $17 tent, $22-27 full hookups. **Parking:** At site.

FACILITIES

Number of RV Sites: 51. **Number of Tent-Only Sites:** 0. **Hookups:** Water, electric (20, 30, 50), sewer, cable TV. **Dump Station:** Yes. **Laundry:** Yes. **Pay Phone:** Yes. **Rest Rooms and Showers:** Yes. **Fuel:** No. **Propane:** Yes. **Internal Roads:** Gravel. **RV Service:** No. **Market:** Shop 'n' Save, 129 Portland St., St. Johnsbury, VT 05819: Take a left onto Rte. 2 & follow it for 12.5 mi. **Restaurant:** Village Pizza, 124 Portland St., St. Johnsbury, VT 05819: Take a left onto Rte. 2 & follow it for 12.5 mi. **General Store:** Yes. **Vending:** Yes. **Swimming Pool:** Yes. **Playground:** Yes. **Other:** Basketball, volleyball (sand & grass), shuffleboard. **Activities:** Canoe & paddleboat rentals. **Nearby Attractions:** Maple Groves Farms, Fairbanks Museum & Planetarium, White Mountains. **Additional Information:** Call ahead.

RESTRICTIONS

Pets: Allowed. **Fires:** Allowed. **Alcoholic Beverages:** Allowed. **Vehicle Maximum Length:** Unlimited. **Other:** Ask on arrival.

TO GET THERE

From I-91 take Exit 19 to I-93. From I-93 take Exit 1 to Rte. 2E approximately 8 mi.

CONCORD

Rustic Haven Campground

1111 Main St., Concord 05824. T: (802) 695-9933; www.campsites411.com.

RV ★★★★ Tent n/a

Beauty: ★★★ Site Privacy: ★★★
Spaciousness: ★★★★ Quiet: ★★★
Security: ★★★★ Cleanliness: ★★★★
Insect Control: ★★★ Facilities: ★★

Small, but surprisingly full-service, Rustic Haven's a pretty good choice for a family that wants some amneities but doesn't want to deal with a huge park. Sites are large, grassy, and shaded by pine trees. The campground is also well-located, with stores and restaurants out-of-sight but nearby and hiking on Kirby mountain close as well. There are also fishing spots within a few minutes away.

BASICS

Operated By: The Bacon family. **Open:** May 15–Oct. 15. **Site Assignment:** Reservations accepted. **Registration:** At office. **Fee:** $18–$24. **Parking:** At site.

FACILITIES

Number of RV Sites: 38. **Number of Tent-Only Sites:** 0. **Hookups:** Water, electric, sewer. **Each Site:** Picnic table, fireplace. **Dump Station:** Yes. **Laundry:** No. **Pay Phone:** Yes. **Rest Rooms and Showers:** Yes. **Fuel:** No. **Propane:** Yes. **Internal Roads:** Paved/good condition gravel. **RV Service:** No. **Market:** Walking distance: Goodwins' Grocery, Main St. & East St. Johnsbury, VT 05838. **Restaurant:** Walking distance: Mooselook Restaurant, 1058 Main St., Concord, VT 05824. **General Store:** Yes. **Vending:** No. **Swimming Pool:** Yes. **Playground:** Yes. **Other:** Horseshoe pits, basketball, shuffleboard, volleyball. **Activities:** Hiking, fishing. **Nearby Attractions:** White Mountains, Lake Willoughby, Fairbanks Museum & Planetarium.

RESTRICTIONS

Pets: Allowed. **Fires:** Allowed. **Alcoholic Beverages:** Allowed. **Vehicle Maximum Length:** 60 ft. **Other:** Ask on arrival.

TO GET THERE

From I-91 take Exit 20, St. Johnsbury, to Rte. 2E and follow for 7 mi.

DANVILLE

Sugar Ridge RV Village & Campground

24 Old Stagecoach Rd., Danville 05828. T: (802) 684-2550; F: (802) 684-1006; www.sugarridge rvpark.com; SugRidge@aol.com.

RV ★★★★ Tent ★★★

Beauty: ★★★★ Site Privacy: ★★★★
Spaciousness: ★★★★ Quiet: ★★★★
Security: ★★★ Cleanliness: ★★★★
Insect Control: ★★★ Facilities: ★★★★

A new campground, Sugar Ridge is located amongst a variety of trees and has some stunning natural settings along its many hiking trails. There are secluded tent sites, and even the RV locations have good privacy, as most sites are cut out from the woods. The campground, despite its natural surroundings, does not skimp on the amenities. Everything here is top-notch and has the advantage of being barely broken in. Most sites are even modem-ready. That might be more than your average camper is looking for, but it actually makes this a place you could spend the summer, working from your RV. Reservations are a must and minimum stays apply during some busy weekends.

BASICS

Operated By: Kirk Fenoss. **Open:** May 1–Oct. 31. **Site Assignment:** Reservations recommended. **Registration:** At office. **Fee:** $22.50–$29.50. **Parking:** At site.

FACILITIES

Number of RV Sites: 111. **Number of Tent-Only Sites:** 0. **Hookups:** Water, electric, sewer. **Dump Station:** Yes. **Laundry:** Yes. **Pay Phone:** Yes. **Rest Rooms and Showers:** Yes. **Fuel:** No. **Propane:** Yes. **Internal Roads:** Paved/gravel. **RV Service:** No. **Market:** White Market, 78 Portland St., St. Johnsbury, VT 05819: Take a left onto Rte. 2 then a slight right onto Rte. 28 & follow it for 2.8 mi. Turn right onto Rte. 2 & follow it for 1.5 mi. **Restaurant:** Creamery Restaurant, 46 Hill St., Danville, VT 05828: Take a right onto Rte. 2 & follow it for 2.1 mi. Then take a right onto Hill St. **General Store:** Yes. **Vending:** No. **Swimming Pool:** Yes. **Playground:** Yes. **Other:** Organized activities, crafts shop, rec hall, mini-golf course, tennis, basketball, horseshoe pits, shuffleboard, sand volleyball. **Activities:** Horse-drawn carriage rides, paddle boats. **Nearby Attractions:** Summer playhouse, Santa's Village, White mountains, Harvey's Lake, Six Gun City, Rock of Ages Granite Quarry. **Additional Information:** Information and registration available online.

RESTRICTIONS

Pets: Allowed. **Fires:** Allowed. **Alcoholic Beverages:** Allowed. **Vehicle Maximum Length:** Large RVs welcome (pease check ahead of time for accomodation). **Other:** 2 trailers & 2 pop-up tents available for rent.

TO GET THERE

From I-91, Exit 21, go 4.5 mi. west on Rte. 2; the campground is a half mi. east of Danville town.

DERBY

Fireside Campground

Box 340, Derby 05829. T: (802) 766-5109.

RV ★★★ Tent ★★★

Beauty: ★★★ Site Privacy: ★★★★
Spaciousness: ★★★ Quiet: ★★★
Security: ★★★ Cleanliness: ★★★★
Insect Control: ★★★ Facilities: ★★★

The best thing about Fireside Campground may very well be its proximity to the town of Derby, which has restaurants, tennis courts, a bowling alley, and more. The campsites aren't much to look at, but they're flat and at least somewhat private. There's not that much to do here. Being able to walk to town, is nice, but doesn't really make up for the lack of traditional campground activities. You are pretty close to the Canadian border and there's hiking and swimming nearby, but that's basically true for any location in Vermont. If however, you have friends in the area or want to attend a concert at the opera in Derby Line, where the stage is in Canada and the audience sits in the U.S.

BASICS

Operated By: Liz Willey. **Open:** May 15–Oct. 1. **Site Assignment:** First come, first served. **Registration:** At office. **Fee:** $14. **Parking:** At site.

FACILITIES

Number of RV Sites: 24. **Number of Tent-Only Sites:** 10. **Hookups:** Water, electric, sewer. **Dump Station:** Yes. **Laundry:** No. **Pay Phone:** No. **Rest Rooms and Showers:** Yes. **Fuel:** No. **Propane:** No. **Internal Roads:** Grass/gravel. **RV Service:** No. **Market:** Derby Village Store, 483 Main St., Derby, VT 05829: Take a right onto Rte. 5 & follow it for 1.6 mi. **Restaurant:** Border Restaurant, 135 Main St., Derby, VT 05829: Take a right onto Rte. 5 & follow it for 0.9 mi. **General Store:** Right off site. **Vending:** No. **Swimming Pool:** No. **Playground:** No. **Activities:** Tennis & bowling immediately nearby. **Nearby Attractions:** Derby is within walking distance.

RESTRICTIONS

Pets: Allowed. **Fires:** Allowed. **Alcoholic Beverages:** Allowed. **Vehicle Maximum Length:** 40 ft. **Other:** Ask on arrival.

TO GET THERE

Take I-91 to Exit 28 and go 0.25 mi. east on Rte. 105.

DERBY

Char-Bo Campground

P.O. Box 438, Derby 05829. T: (802) 766-8807; charbo@together.net.

RV ★★★ Tent ★★★★

Beauty: ★★★★ Site Privacy: ★★★
Spaciousness: ★★★ Quiet: ★★★
Security: ★★★ Cleanliness: ★★★★
Insect Control: ★★★ Facilities: ★★★

Located on top of a hill, Char-Bo offers excellent views of what seems like the entire state. You can see nearby Lake Salem, Lake Willoughby, and numerous mountains. Sites for RVs are nothing special—patches of grass with another RV close by. Tent sites are a lot better, private with trees offering shade. One oddball attraction that's basically walking distance away is the state's only elk farm.

BASICS

Operated By: Private operator. **Open:** May 1–Oct. 15. **Site Assignment:** Inquire at registration. **Registration:** At office. **Fee:** $21–$23. **Parking:** At site.

FACILITIES

Number of RV Sites: 33. **Number of Tent-Only Sites:** 11. **Hookups:** Water, electric, sewer. **Each Site:** Picnic table, fire ring, grill. **Dump Station:** Yes. **Laundry:** Yes. **Pay Phone:** Yes. **Rest Rooms and Showers:** Yes. **Fuel:** No. **Propane:** Yes. **Internal Roads:** Paved/gravel. **RV Service:** No. **Mar-**

ket: Derby Village Store, 483 Main St., Derby, VT 05829: Take a right onto Rte. 105 & follow it until it becomes Rte. 5. Continue for 3.9 mi. **Restaurant:** Border Restaurant, 135 Main St., Derby, VT 05829: Take a right onto Rte. 105 & follow it until it becomes Rte. 5. Follow it for 3.2 mi. **General Store:** Yes. **Vending:** Yes. **Swimming Pool:** Yes. **Playground:** Yes. **Other:** Mini golf, rec hall, boat rentals. **Activities:** Swimming, boating, canoeing. **Nearby Attractions:** Green Mountains, Fairbanks Museum & Planetarium, Craftsbury. **Additional Information:** Planned activities (weekends only).

Restrictions

Pets: Allowed. **Fires:** Allowed. **Alcoholic Beverages:** Allowed. **Vehicle Maximum Length:** 50 ft. **Other:** Boat, Canoe, & Paddleboat Rental.

To Get There

Take Exit 28 off I-91 and go three mi. east of Derby Center on Rte. 105.

ENOSBURG FALLS

Brookside Campground

680 Sand Hill Rd., Enosburg Falls 05450. T: (802) 933-4376.

RV ★★★ Tent ★★★★

Beauty: ★★★ Site Privacy: ★★★★
Spaciousness: ★★★ Quiet: ★★★★
Security: ★★★ Cleanliness: ★★★
Insect Control: ★★★ Facilities: ★★★

This entire campground was cut out from the woods along the Bogue Brook. The sites themselves are little slivers of land where the trees have been beaten back. When making a reservation here, it's best to specify what type of site you're looking for, as there's a mix of sunny and shady as well as some that are a little more private than others. Tent campers can get even more privacy, as there are some sites that are very much set away from the action.

Basics

Operated By: Private operator. **Open:** May 1–Oct. 1. **Site Assignment:** Reservations recommended. **Registration:** Entrance office. **Fee:** $10–$14. **Parking:** At site.

Facilities

Number of RV Sites: 35. **Number of Tent-Only Sites:** Unnumbered, but numerous. **Hookups:** Water, electric (20, 30), sewer. **Dump Station:** Yes. **Laundry:** Yes. **Pay Phone:** Yes. **Rest Rooms and Showers:** Yes. **Fuel:** No. **Propane:** No. **Internal Roads:** Varies. **RV Service:** No. **Market:** Uncle Floyd's, 182 Main St., Enosburg Falls, VT 05450: Take a left onto Tyler Branch Rd. & follow it for 2.9 mi. Take a right onto Rte. 108, which becomes Rte. 105. Continue 2.8 mi. **Restaurant:** Carney's Restaurant, 98 Main St., Enosburg Falls, VT 05450: Take a left onto Tyler Branch Rd. & follow it for 2.9 mi. Take a right onto Rte. 108, which becomes Rte. 105. Continue 2.5 mi. **General Store:** No. **Vending:** No. **Swimming Pool:** No. **Playground:** Yes. **Other:** Horseshoes, volleyball, **Activities:** Fishing, 2 golf courses, horseshoes. **Nearby Attractions:** Lake Champlain, historic villages, University of Vermont, Fleming Museum, cruises on the *Spirit of Ethan Allen*. **Additional Information:** Call ahead.

Restrictions

Pets: Allowed. **Fires:** Allowed. **Alcoholic Beverages:** Allowed. **Vehicle Maximum Length:** Welcomes large campers. **Other:** Ask on arrival.

To Get There

Go 0.5 mi. south across the Iron Bridge from Rte. 105, then follow signs from 108S north to Boston Post Rd. and follow signs to campground.

FAIR HAVEN

Half Moon Pond State Park

1621 Black Pond Rd., Fair Haven 05743. T: (802) 273-2848; www.vtstateparks.com.

RV ★★★★ Tent ★★★★

Beauty: ★★★★★ Site Privacy: ★★★★★
Spaciousness: ★★★★ Quiet: ★★★★
Security: ★★★★★ Cleanliness: ★★★★★
Insect Control: ★★★ Facilities: ★★★

If you're looking for a campground that will have you feeling like you've really gotten away, Half Moon State Park definitely fits the bill. And if the absolute stillness and remote location of the park are not reason enough to go, the pristine Half Moon Pond for which the park is named should convince you. Its beach area is an exceptional starting point for some relaxed paddling, fishing, and swimming. In addition, there is a fairly elaborate network of hiking trails accessible from within the park, which is surrounded by dense forest and is adjacent to the Bomoseen Wildlife Preserve. A string of ponds, marshlands, and abandoned quarry sites in the area are interconnected by hiking trails ranging in length from 0.3 mile to 4.5 miles. Both sides of the campground have some sites perched right on the shore of Half Moon Pond. These are the primo sites.

Basics

Operated By: Vermont Agency of Natural Resources. **Open:** Mid-May–Columbus Day. **Site Assignment:** Reservations or first come, first served. **Registration:** At ranger station. **Fee:** $13–$17. **Parking:** At site.

Facilities

Number of RV Sites: 60. **Number of Tent-Only Sites:** 0. **Hookups:** None. **Each Site:** Stone hearth, picnic table. **Dump Station:** Yes. **Laundry:** No. **Pay Phone:** Yes. **Rest Rooms and Showers:** Yes. **Fuel:** No. **Propane:** No. **Internal Roads:** Paved/gravel in good condition. **RV Service:** No. **Market:** No. **Restaurant:** No. **General Store:** No. **Vending:** No. **Swimming Pool:** No. **Playground:** Yes. **Other:** Boat rentals. **Activities:** Hiking, boating (no motors) limited swimming. **Nearby Attractions:** Horseback riding, Hubbardton Battlefield, Wilson Castle, Vermont Marble Exhibit, Morgan Horse Farm, Lake Champlain Ferries, Devil's Bowl Speedway, Shelburne Museum.

Restrictions

Pets: On leash. **Fires:** In fire hearth. **Alcoholic Beverages:** Ask on arrival. **Vehicle Maximum Length:** None. **Other:** Reservations 800-658-1622 (V & MC accepted).

To Get There

Between Fair Haven and Rutland on Rte. 4, take Exit 4. Go north on Rte. 30 for 6.5 mi. Turn left on Hortonia Rd. and continue for 2 mi. Turn left on Black Pond Rd. and continue for 2 mi.

FAIRFAX

Maple Grove Campground

1627 Main St., Rte. 104, Fairfax 05454. T: (802) 849-6439; www.vtwebs.com/maplegrove; heyjo@together.net.

RV ★★★★ Tent ★★★★

Beauty: ★★★★ Site Privacy: ★★★★
Spaciousness: ★★★ Quiet: ★★★★
Security: ★★★ Cleanliness: ★★★★
Insect Control: ★★★ Facilities: ★★★

Maple Grove may be small, but if offers a surprisingly nice mix of full-service RV sites and grassy, wooded sites for tent campers. There's a fair amount of privacy for all of campers because, though the sites are level, they are large and have enough trees to add privacy. The Lamoille River runs through the campground and canoers can actually take that all the way to Lake Champlain.

Basics

Operated By: Private operator. **Open:** May 1–Oct. 12. **Site Assignment:** At registration. **Registration:** Reservations accepted. **Fee:** $16–$22. **Parking:** At site.

Facilities

Number of RV Sites: 26. **Number of Tent-Only Sites:** 0. **Hookups:** Water, electric (20, 50), sewer. **Each Site:** Picnic table, fireplace. **Dump Station:** Yes. **Laundry:** Yes. **Pay Phone:** Yes. **Rest Rooms and Showers:** Yes. **Fuel:** No. **Propane:** No. **Internal Roads:** Paved/gravel in good condition. **RV Service:** No. **Market:** Lyn's Market, Main St., East Fairfield, VT 05448: Take a right onto Main St. **Restaurant:** Country Pantry, 951 Main St., Fairfax, VT 05454: Take a right onto Main St. **General Store:** Yes. **Vending:** No. **Swimming Pool:** No. **Playground:** Yes. **Other:** Horseshoes, volleyball. **Activities:** Lake Champlain, Long Trail, Green Mountains. **Nearby Attractions:** Stables, fishing, mini golf. **Additional Information:** Horsehoes, games, hiking, canoeing, fishing, rafting.

Restrictions

Pets: Allowed. **Fires:** Allowed. **Alcoholic Beverages:** Allowed. **Vehicle Maximum Length:** None. **Other:** Ask on arrival.

To Get There

From the north take Exit 19 off I-89 and go south on Rte. 104 for 8 mi. From the south, take Exit 18 off I-89 and go east on Rte. 104A for 5 mi. At a stop sign, go north on Rte. 104 for 1 mi.

FRANKLIN

Mill Pond Campground

RR No. 1 Box 2335 Mill Pond Rd., Franklin 05457. T: (802) 285-2240.

RV ★★★★ Tent n/a

Beauty: ★★★★ Site Privacy: ★★★
Spaciousness: ★★★ Quiet: ★★★

Security: ★★★ Cleanliness: ★★★
Insect Control: ★★★ Facilities: ★★★

Leave your tent at home, this campground only serves RVs. The primary clientele at Mill Pond is families looking for access to Lake Carni, which is the prime attraction here. The busy lake offers swimming, boating, and fishing and is the focal point of a stay here. You can choose from wooded or open sites (though reservations are needed if you're picky), and the campground is better looking and quieter than your average RV park.

Basics

Operated By: Phil & Doreen LeGrand. **Open:** May 1–Oct. 1. **Site Assignment:** Reservations accepted. **Registration:** At office. **Fee:** $16–$20. **Parking:** At site.

Facilities

Number of RV Sites: 58. **Number of Tent-Only Sites:** 0. **Hookups:** Water, electric. **Dump Station:** No. **Laundry:** No. **Pay Phone:** No. **Rest Rooms and Showers:** Yes. **Fuel:** No. **Propane:** No. **Internal Roads:** Compressed gravel. **RV Service:** No. **Market:** Sheldon Creek Market, 94 Bridge St., Sheldon, VT 05483. **Restaurant:** Lake Carmi. Snack Bar, 2395 Lake Rd., Franklin, VT 05457. **General Store:** Limited. **Vending:** No. **Swimming Pool:** Yes. **Playground:** Yes. **Other:** Volleyball, horseshoes, basketball, baseball, badminton, arcade, lounge. **Activities:** Planned activities, fishing, boating. **Nearby Attractions:** Shelburne Farms, University of Vermont, Fleming Museum, cruises on the *Spirit of Ethan Allen.* **Additional Information:** Call ahead.

Restrictions

Pets: Allowed. **Fires:** Allowed. **Alcoholic Beverages:** Allowed. **Vehicle Maximum Length:** 40 ft. (sometimes varies). **Other:** Ask on arrival.

To Get There

Go east on Rte. 105 out of St. Albans to the junction of Rte. 120, north of the small town of Franklin. Continue 4 mi. from Franklin east on Rte. 120.

GRAND ISLE

Champlain Adult Campground

Champlain Landing, Grand Isle 05458. T: (802) 372-5938; champlaina@aol.com.

★★★ ★★★

Beauty: ★★★★ Site Privacy: ★★★★
Spaciousness: ★★★★ Quiet: ★★★★★
Security: ★★★ Cleanliness: ★★★★
Insect Control: ★★★ Facilities: ★★★

If you're looking for a campground that isn't overun by hyperactive kids, this might be the place for you. Champlain requires guests to be over 18, and because of that gets a lot of retirees and guests looking to camp away from kids. Not surprisingly, the campground is very quiet and doesn't have much in the way of planned actiivities. There's a public golf course nearby as well as a dock for fishing, and you can take a swim in Lake Champlain if you want. The campground is set back from the lake with the private sites seperated by cedar trees.

Basics

Operated By: Emma & Jean Claude Guillon. **Open:** May 15–Oct. 15. **Site Assignment:** At time of registration. **Registration:** Entrance, reservations accepted. **Fee:** $18, no charge for WWI & WWII veterans. **Parking:** At site.

Facilities

Number of RV Sites: 79. **Number of Tent-Only Sites:** 0. **Hookups:** Water, electric, sewer. **Each Site:** Picnic table, fireplace. **Dump Station:** Yes. **Laundry:** Yes. **Pay Phone:** Yes. **Rest Rooms and Showers:** Yes. **Fuel:** No. **Propane:** No. **Internal Roads:** Paved/compressed gravel. **RV Service:** No. **Market:** Less than 2 mi. away. **Restaurant:** Less than 2 mi. away **General Store:** No. **Vending:** No. **Swimming Pool:** No. **Playground:** No. **Other:** Rec hall. **Activities:** None. **Nearby Attractions:** Hyde Log Cabin Historical Site, Shakespeare Festival, outlet center. **Additional Information:** Call ahead.

Restrictions

Pets: Allowed. **Fires:** Allowed. **Alcoholic Beverages:** Allowed. **Vehicle Maximum Length:** 34 ft. **Other:** Ask on arrival.

To Get There

From I-89 take Exit 17 and follow Rte. 2 to the Lake Champlain Islands and Rte. 314. Follow Rte. 314 for 2.5 mi. to the campground.

GRAND ISLE

Grand Isle State Park

36 East Shore Rd. South, Grand Isle 05458. T: (802) 372-4300; www.state.vt.us/anr/fpr/parks/htm/grandisle.html.

★★★ ★★★★

Beauty: ★★★ Site Privacy: ★★★
Spaciousness: ★★★★ Quiet: ★★★
Security: ★★★ Cleanliness: ★★★
Insect Control: ★★★ Facilities: ★★★★

Grand Isle is somewhat different than the other state parks in Connecticut. Though the sites still lack hookups, there's more going on at and around the campground than at any other state-run property in Vermont. Of course, there's also plenty of natural splendor, including a lake with boating, swimming, and fishing as well as tree-lined hiking trails. Even there, however, there's some development, as the trails have been organized into a fitness course. Grand Isle is also the only state park that has a rec hall—making it a good location for group events.

Basics

Operated By: State of Vermont. **Open:** May 15–Columbus Day. **Site Assignment:** Reservations recommended. **Registration:** Park office. **Fee:** $14–$20. **Parking:** At site.

Facilities

Number of RV Sites: 156. **Number of Tent-Only Sites:** 0. **Hookups:** None. **Each Site:** Table, fire ring. **Dump Station:** Yes. **Laundry:** No. **Pay Phone:** Yes. **Rest Rooms and Showers:** Yes. **Fuel:** No. **Propane:** No. **Internal Roads:** Paved. **RV Service:** No. **Market:** Cumberland Bay Market, 1544 Cumberland Head Rd., Plattsburgh, NY 12901: Take a left onto Rte. 2 followed by a right onto Pearl St. & a left onto Bell Hill Rd. Bell Hill Rd. becomes Grand Isle Ferry Rte.314 to Plattsburgh. **Restaurant:** Gus' Red Hots, 3 Cumberland Head Rd., Plattsburgh, NY 12901: Take a left onto Rte. 2 followed by a right onto Pearl St. & a left onto Bell Hill Rd. Bell Hill Rd. which becomes Grand Isle Ferry then Rte. 314 to Plattsburgh. **General Store:** No. **Vending:** Yes. **Swimming Pool:** No. **Playground:** Yes. **Other:** Rech hall, boat ramp, fitness trail. **Activities:** Activity center, fitness trail, nature walks, fishing, boat rentals. **Nearby Attractions:** Hyde Log Cabin, Shelburne Museum, State Fish Hatcherie. **Additional Information:** Call ahead.

Restrictions

Pets: Yes, w/ rabies vaccination. **Fires:** Allowed. **Alcoholic Beverages:** Allowed. **Vehicle Maximum Length:** Unlimited. **Other:** Ask on arrival.

To Get There

From Grand Isle: Go 1 mi. south on US 2

HARDWICK

Idle Hours Campground

P.O. Box 1053, Mackville Pond Rd., Hardwick 05843. T: (802) 472-6732; idlehour@together.net.

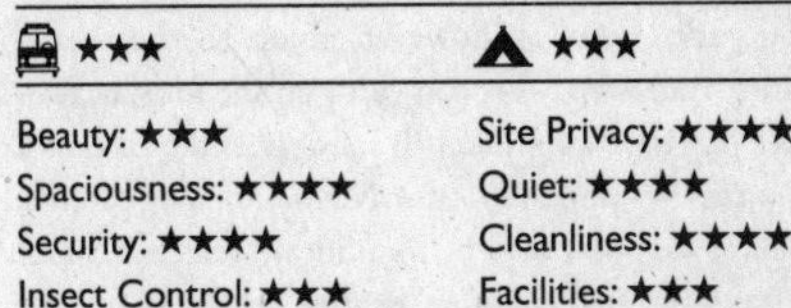

★★★ ★★★

Beauty: ★★★ Site Privacy: ★★★★
Spaciousness: ★★★★ Quiet: ★★★★
Security: ★★★★ Cleanliness: ★★★★
Insect Control: ★★★ Facilities: ★★★

This small campground caters to seasonal campers, so you almost always need a reservation. Though the activities and facilities are somewhat limited, the sites are remote and hidden by trees for near total privacy. There's also Mackville Pond, which offers a nearly empty alternative to the pool, though even the pool's never that crowded. Fisherman can cast their lines on the nearby Lamoille River. Though RVs are welcome, this is an excellent place for tenters looking for a nice mix of peace and quiet along with a reasonable amount of modern convenience.

Basics

Operated By: Barb Berthiaume. **Open:** May 27–Sept. 15. **Site Assignment:** Reservations recommended. **Registration:** Entrance. **Fee:** Starts at $15. **Parking:** At site.

Facilities

Number of RV Sites: 22. **Number of Tent-Only Sites:** 0. **Hookups:** Water, electric, sewer. **Dump Station:** Yes. **Laundry:** Yes. **Pay Phone:** Yes. **Rest Rooms and Showers:** Yes. **Fuel:** No. **Propane:** No. **Internal Roads:** Paved/gravel. **RV Service:** No. **Market:** Grand Union, Wolcott St., Hardwick, VT 05843. **Restaurant:** Egress Restaurant, 35 South Main St., Hardwick, VT 05843. **General Store:** No. **Vending:** No. **Swimming Pool:** Yes. **Playground:** Yes. **Other:** Canoeing, tubing. **Activities:** Fishing, hiking, wildlife viewing, bird-watching. **Nearby Attractions:** St. Anne Shrine, museums, galleries, Shelburne Farms & Museum. **Additional Information:** Call ahead.

Restrictions

Pets: Allowed. **Fires:** Allowed. **Alcoholic Beverages:** Allowed. **Vehicle Maximum Length:** Unlimited. **Other:** Ask on arrival.

To Get There

At junction of Rtes. 14 and 15, take Rte. 14 south for 4/10 mi., turn left onto Mackville Pond Rd. and follow for 1 mi., bearing left at pond to the campground entrance

HYDE PARK — Common Ground Camping Resort

Hwy. 100, Box 780, Hyde Park 05655. T: (802) 888-5210.

★★★★   n/a

Beauty: ★★ — Site Privacy: ★★
Spaciousness: ★★ — Quiet: ★★
Security: ★★★ — Cleanliness: ★★★
Insect Control: ★★★ — Facilities: ★★★★

Locacted next to a sort of mini amausement park, Common Ground offers a lot for kids to do. It's a small campground with decent sites, but the view is dominated by the go carts and other rides offered at the park. There is, however, access to the nearby Long Trail where—if you can pull the kids away—you can take long hikes. It's also possible to take a day trip up nearby Mount Mansfield. For parents, the main appeal may be that Stowe, which has nice restaurants and shops, is nearby, so they can have some grownup time while the kids play at the amusement park.

Basics

Operated By: Private operator. **Open:** May 1–Oct. 1. **Site Assignment:** Reservations recommended. **Registration:** At office. **Fee:** $18. **Parking:** At site.

Facilities

Number of RV Sites: 20. **Number of Tent-Only Sites:** 0. **Hookups:** Water, electric, sewer. **Dump Station:** Yes. **Laundry:** No. **Pay Phone:** Yes. **Rest Rooms and Showers:** Yes. **Fuel:** No. **Propane:** No. **Internal Roads:** Compressed gravel. **RV Service:** No. **Market:** Hyde Village **Market:** Main St. Hyde Park, VT 05655 (802) 888-5335. **Restaurant:** Charlmont Restaurant 116 Rte. 15W, Morrisville, VT 05661. **General Store:** No. **Vending:** Yes. **Swimming Pool:** Yes. **Playground:** No. **Other:** Rec hall, mini golf, volleyball. **Activities:** Go carts. **Nearby Attractions:** Ben & Jerry's Factory, museums, galleries, Maple Festival (Spring) Hyde Park Opera House, Long Trail. **Additional Information:** Call ahead.

Restrictions

Pets: Allowed. **Fires:** Allowed. **Alcoholic Beverages:** Allowed. **Vehicle Maximum Length:** Unlimited. **Other:** Ask on arrival.

To Get There

Take Rte. 15 to Rte. 100 towards Hyde Park.

ISLAND POND — Brighton State Park

102 State Park Road, Island Pond 05846.
T: (802) 723-4360 or (800) 658-6934.

★★   ★★★★

Beauty: ★★★★★ — Site Privacy: ★★★★
Spaciousness: ★★★★ — Quiet: ★★★★
Security: ★★★ — Cleanliness: ★★★★★
Insect Control: ★★★ — Facilities: ★★★

If you're looking for a wilderness campground, this might be the place for you. Though the actual campsites are on the edge of the woods, most of the surrounding area is rustic. There's no roads to speak of and most of the available activities center around the setting. There's even a naturalist who works at the park who can answer questions about the wildlife and trees. The small private beach only allows boats without a motor and the fishing hole offers some of the best catches in the state. The park headquarters also has a museum and a theater.

Basics

Operated By: State of Vermont. **Open:** Oct. 15–Columbus Day. **Site Assignment:** First come, first served. **Registration:** At office. **Fee:** $13–$17. **Parking:** At site.

Facilities

Number of RV Sites: 63. **Number of Tent-Only Sites:** 0. **Hookups:** None. **Each Site:** Picnic table, fireplace, lean-tos at some sites. **Dump Station:** Yes. **Laundry:** No. **Pay Phone:** Yes. **Rest Rooms and Showers:** Yes. **Fuel:** No. **Propane:** No. **Internal Roads:** Paved/gravel. **RV Service:** No. **Market:** John's Market, Main St. Island Pond, VT 05846. **Restaurant:** Loon's Landing, 135 Main St. Island Pond, VT 05846. **General Store:** Snack bar in park. **Vending:** In park. **Swimming Pool:** No. **Playground:** Yes. **Other:** Horsehoes. **Activities:** Hiking trails, beach, nature museum, concession stand. **Nearby Attractions:** Fishing hole, private beach. **Additional Information:** Call ahead.

Restrictions

Pets: Allowed, w/ rabies certification. **Fires:** Allowed. **Alcoholic Beverages:** Allowed. **Vehicle Maximum Length:** None. **Other:** Ask on arrival.

To Get There

Go 2 mi. east on Rte. 105 from Island Pond, then 0.75 mi. south on State Park Rd.

ISLAND POND — Lakeside Camping

1348 Rte. 105, East Brighton Rd., Island Pond 05846. T: (802) 723-6649; www.lakeside camping.com; lakecamp@together.net.

★★★★   ★★

Beauty: ★★★ — Site Privacy: ★★★
Spaciousness: ★★★★ — Quiet: ★★★
Security: ★★★★ — Cleanliness: ★★★★
Insect Control: ★★★ — Facilities: ★★★★

Surrounded by red and white pine trees, Lakeside Campground has over 1500 feet of beach. Because of that, water-based activities dominate, but there's plenty of other things to do here, including biking and hiking. Some sites are gathered in clearings, and smaller ones are interespesed with the forest. Some larger RVs can dominate the areas they're parked in, but complete solitude in the vast forest is very close.

Basics

Operated By: Private operator. **Open:** May 15–Sept. 12. **Site Assignment:** Reservations recommended. **Registration:** At office. **Fee:** $16–$22. **Parking:** At site.

Facilities

Number of RV Sites: 200. **Number of Tent-Only Sites:** 0. **Hookups:** Water, electric, sewer. **Each Site:** Picnic table, fireplace. **Dump Station:** Yes. **Laundry:** Yes. **Pay Phone:** Yes. **Rest Rooms and Showers:** Yes. **Fuel:** No. **Propane:** Yes. **Internal Roads:** Paved. **RV Service:** No. **Market:** John's Market, Main St., Island Pond, VT 05846. **Restaurant:** Cook Shack, Cross, Island Pond, VT 05846. **General Store:** No. **Vending:** Yes. **Swimming Pool:** No. **Playground:** Yes. **Other:** Game room, boat rentals. **Activities:** Boat cruises. **Nearby Attractions:** Fairbanks Museum & Planetarium, Gramby Zoo. **Additional Information:** Call ahead.

Restrictions

Pets: Allowed. **Fires:** Allowed. **Alcoholic Beverages:** Allowed. **Vehicle Maximum Length:** 40 ft. **Other:** Ask on arrival.

To Get There

Take Rte. 105 to Island Pond and go one mi.

JEFFERSONVILLE — Brewster River Campground

110 Campground Dr., Jeffersonville 05464. T: (802) 644-2126; wmckone@sover.net.

★   ★★★★

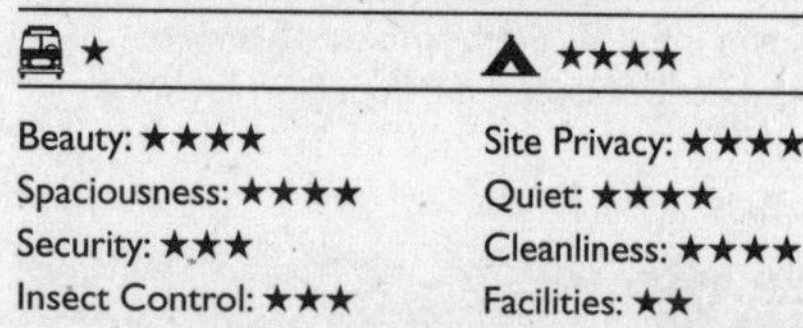

Beauty: ★★★★ — Site Privacy: ★★★★
Spaciousness: ★★★★ — Quiet: ★★★★
Security: ★★★ — Cleanliness: ★★★★
Insect Control: ★★★ — Facilities: ★★

Almost entirely domainted by tent campers, Brewster River Campground offers a spartan outdoors experience. Most of the activity here centers around the rive, suitable for swimmers as well as small boats. There are also numerous hiking opportunities nearby, and though you're out in the woods, the town is close enough you can escape the wild if you want to.

Basics

Operated By: Private operator. **Open:** May 15–Oct. 15 (winter camping by special arrangement). **Site Assignment:** Reservations accepted. **Registration:** At office. **Fee:** $20. **Parking:** At site.

Facilities

Number of RV Sites: 3. **Number of Tent-Only Sites:** 17. **Hookups:** Water, electric. **Each Site:** Picnic table, fireplace. **Dump Station:** No. **Laundry:** No. **Pay Phone:** No. **Rest Rooms and Showers:** Yes. **Fuel:** No. **Propane:** No. **Internal Roads:** Paved/gravel. **RV Service:** No. **Market:** Waterville Market, Rte. 109 Main St., Waterville, VT

05492: Take a right onto Rte. 108 which becomes Rte. 15. Then, take a left back onto Rte. 108 followed by a slight left onto Rte. 109 & follow it for 3.9 mi. **Restaurant:** Diiner's Dunn at the Windridge, Main St., Jeffersonville, VT 05464: Take a right onto Rte. 108 which becomes Rte. 15. Then, take a left back onto Rte. 108 followed by a slight left onto Rte. 109. Follow it for 3.9 mi. **General Store:** No. **Vending:** No. **Swimming Pool:** No. **Playground:** No. **Activities:** Canoeing, fishing, hiking. **Nearby Attractions:** Brewster River. **Additional Information:** Call ahead.

RESTRICTIONS

Pets: No (kennel nearby). **Fires:** Allowed. **Alcoholic Beverages:** Allowed. **Vehicle Maximum Length:** 18. **Other:** Ask on arrival.

TO GET THERE

Take Rte. 108 and go 3 mi. south of Jeffersonville. The campground is opposite Burnor Rd.

KILLINGTON

Gifford Woods State Park

34 Gifford Woods, Killington 05761. T: (802) 775-5354 (in season) or (800) 299-3071 (Jan.–May); www.vtstateparks.com.

RV: ★★★★ Tent: ★★★★★

Beauty: ★★★★★ Site Privacy: ★★★★
Spaciousness: ★★★★ Quiet: ★★★★
Security: ★★★★ Cleanliness: ★★★★
Insect Control: ★★★ Facilities: ★★★

As at other Vermont state parks, the site arrangement at Gifford Woods is a loosely spaced combination of tent sites and lean-tos named for trees. There are a lot more lean-tos in the lower loop than in the upper. Overall, the upper campground sites are a bit quieter than the lower sites. Perhaps the nicest aspect of Gifford Woods State Park is that you don't have to travel far outside the park, or even within the park for that matter, before you run across some hiking trails. The Appalachian Trail runs right through the park, and reconnects with the Long Trail approximately 1.5 miles north of the park, which makes it a perfectly situated spot from which to launch your adventures into the Green Mountains and the Killington area. Make sure to see the spectacular seven-acre stand of old growth hardwoods, located right across Rte. 100 from the campground. This pristine slice of wilderness has some massive sugar maple, beech, birch, and ash trees.

BASICS

Operated By: Vermont Agency of Natural Resources. **Open:** Mid-May–Columbus Day. **Site Assignment:** Reservations or first come, first served. **Registration:** At ranger station. **Fee:** $11–$15. **Parking:** At site.

FACILITIES

Number of RV Sites: 27. **Number of Tent-Only Sites:** 0. **Hookups:** None. **Each Site:** Fire ring or brick hearth, picnic table. **Dump Station:** Yes. **Laundry:** No. **Pay Phone:** Yes. **Rest Rooms and Showers:** Yes. **Fuel:** No. **Propane:** Yes. **Internal Roads:** Gravel. **RV Service:** No. **Market:** No. **Restaurant:** No. **General Store:** No. **Vending:** No. **Swimming Pool:** No. **Playground:** Yes. **Activities:** Hiking, fishing, wildlife viewing. **Nearby Attractions:** Killington ski gondola, Pico Alpine Slide, Vermont Marble Exhibit, Wilson's Castle, Maple Museum. **Additional Information:** Cross-country skiing is free.

RESTRICTIONS

Pets: Allowed w/ rabies vaccination. **Fires:** In fire ring. **Alcoholic Beverages:** Allowed. **Vehicle Maximum Length:** 30 ft.. **Other:** 2 day min. stay for reservations.

TO GET THERE

Gifford Woods State Park is located right off Rte. 100, just north of the access road for Killington Ski Area.

LAKE ELMORE

Elmore State Park

856 VT Rte. 12, Lake Elmore 05657. T: (802) 888-2982; www.state.vt.us/anr/fpr/parks/htm/elmore.html.

RV: ★★★ Tent: ★★★★

Beauty: ★★★★ Site Privacy: ★★★★
Spaciousness: ★★★★ Quiet: ★★★★
Security: ★★★ Cleanliness: ★★★★
Insect Control: ★★★ Facilities: ★★★★

A fairly stunning location nestled between forests and mountains, Elmore State Park gets its name from Lake Elmore. The campground sits on the lake which offers boating, swimming, and fishing. For hikers, there's Elmore mountain which offers a challenging climb to the summit as well as some easier paths for less vigorous climbs. Like most of Vermont's state parks, there are no planned activities here, but there's plenty to do as long as the weather stays nice. The sites themselves are very basic with no hookups, but some have lean-tos and they're pretty isolated from each other.

BASICS

Operated By: State of Vermont. **Open:** May 15–Columbus Day. **Site Assignment:** Reservations recommended. **Registration:** At office. **Fee:** $14–$20. **Parking:** At site.

FACILITIES

Number of RV Sites: 60. **Number of Tent-Only Sites:** 0. **Hookups:** None. **Each Site:** Picnic table, fire ring. **Dump Station:** Yes. **Laundry:** No. **Pay Phone:** Yes. **Rest Rooms and Showers:** Yes. **Fuel:** No. **Propane:** No. **Internal Roads:** Paved/gravel. **RV Service:** No. **Market:** Fisher Bridge Discount Grocery, 30 Munson Ave., Morrisville, VT 05661: Take a left onto Rte. 12 & follow it for 4.4 mi. **Restaurant:** House Of Pizza, Munson Ave., Morrisville, VT 05661: Take a left onto Rte. 12 & follow it for 4.4 mi. Then take a right onto Rte. 100 & a right onto Rte. 15. **General Store:** Snack bar. **Vending:** No. **Swimming Pool:** No. **Playground:** Yes. **Other:** Boat ramp, beach. **Activities:** Boat rentals. **Nearby Attractions:** Elmore Mountain. **Additional Information:** Call ahead.

RESTRICTIONS

Pets: Allowed w/ rabies vaccination. **Fires:** Allowed. **Alcoholic Beverages:** Allowed. **Vehicle Maximum Length:** None. **Other:** Ask on arrival.

TO GET THERE

Go 5 mi. south of Morrisville on Rte. 12.

LAKESIDE

Stillwater State Park Campground

Groton State Forest Rd., Groton 05046. T: (802) 584-3822.

RV: ★★ Tent: ★★★★

Beauty: ★★★★ Site Privacy: ★★★★
Spaciousness: ★★★★ Quiet: ★★★★
Security: ★★★ Cleanliness: ★★★★
Insect Control: ★★★ Facilities: ★★★

The main attraction here has to be Groton Lake, a very large body of water that offers boating, swimming, and fishing. The only problem is that the lake attracts an awful lot of daytrippers during the summer, making it very crowded. Still, the campsites are wooded and far enough away from the action to be private and quiet. People looking to escape the crowds at the beach can also canoe away to solitary areas or head off on hikes on the abundant trails nearby.

BASICS

Operated By: State of Vermont. **Open:** May 15–Oct. 15. **Site Assignment:** Reservations recommended. **Registration:** Entrance gate. **Fee:** $13. **Parking:** At site.

FACILITIES

Number of RV Sites: 62. **Number of Tent-Only Sites:** 14. **Hookups:** None. **Each Site:** Picnic table, fireplace. **Dump Station:** Yes. **Laundry:** No. **Pay Phone:** Yes. **Rest Rooms and Showers:** Yes. **Fuel:** No. **Propane:** No. **Internal Roads:** Paved/gravel. **RV Service:** No. **Market:** Forest Country Store, State Forest Boulder Beach Rd., Groton, VT 05046, (802) 584-4899. **Restaurant:** Upper Valley Grill, 629 Scott Hwy, Groton, VT 05046. **General Store:** Snack bar. **Vending:** No. **Swimming Pool:** No. **Playground:** Yes. **Other:** Boat ramp. **Activities:** Swimming, canoeing, hiking. **Nearby Attractions:** Trails.

RESTRICTIONS

Pets: Yes, on leash. **Fires:** Allowed. **Alcoholic Beverages:** Allowed. **Vehicle Maximum Length:** None. **Other:** Ask on arrival.

TO GET THERE

Go 12 mi. west on US Rte. 302, 6 mi. north on Rte. 232 and 0.5 mi. east on Boulder Beach Rd.

MAIDSTONE

Maidstone State Park Campground

4858 Maidstone Lake Rd., Maidstone 05905. T: (802) 676-3930.

RV: ★★ Tent: ★★★★

Beauty: ★★★ Site Privacy: ★★★★
Spaciousness: ★★★★ Quiet: ★★★★
Security: ★★★ Cleanliness: ★★★★
Insect Control: ★★★ Facilities: ★★★

Situated next to the enormous Maidstone Lake, this campground's prime attraction is water sports. There's incredible fishing, boat rentals are available, and the swimming is excellent. Most of the campsites are right off the water, which offers a nice view, but that can be a mixed blessing since during the day the public nature of the beach makes it a little noisy. The campground is surrounded by thick forest which offers hiking as well as some mountain biking opportunies.

Basics

Operated By: State of Vermont. **Open:** May 15–Labor Day. **Site Assignment:** Reservations accepted. **Registration:** Entrance gate. **Fee:** $13. **Parking:** At site.

Facilities

Number of RV Sites: 45. **Number of Tent-Only Sites:** 37. **Hookups:** None. **Each Site:** Picnic table, fireplace. **Dump Station:** Yes. **Laundry:** No. **Pay Phone:** No. **Rest Rooms and Showers:** No. **Fuel:** No. **Propane:** No. **Internal Roads:** Paved/gravel. **RV Service:** No. **Market:** Blue Mountain Variety: 892 US Rte. 3 North Stratford, NH 03590. **Restaurant:** Mountain's Restaurant: State Rte. 3, North Stratford, NH 03590. **General Store:** No. **Vending:** No. **Swimming Pool:** No. **Playground:** Yes. **Other:** Boat rentals. **Activities:** Mountain biking. **Nearby Attractions:** Trails.

Restrictions

Pets: Yes, on leash. **Fires:** Allowed. **Alcoholic Beverages:** Allowed. **Vehicle Maximum Length:** None. **Other:** Ask on arrival.

To Get There

Take Rte. 102 to State Forest Hwy.

MARSHFIELD

Covenant Hills Christian Camp

Town Rd. 49, Marshfield 05658. T: (802) 426-3340.

RV: ★ Tent: ★★★★

Beauty: ★★★★	Site Privacy: ★★★
Spaciousness: ★★★	Quiet: ★★★★
Security: ★★★★	Cleanliness: ★★★★★
Insect Control: ★★★	Facilities: ★★★★

Obviously a specialty campground, Covenant Hills Christian Camp caters to religious group retreats. Though no attempt is made to convert visitors of differing religious persuasions, this is obviously not the place to go if you're simply looking for a place to sleep. For those interested in a Christian setting, however, the campground is beautiful. The retreat center also rents motel-style rooms for those seeking a less rustic experience.

Basics

Operated By: Troy Conference of the United Methodist Church. **Open:** Year-round. **Site Assignment:** Reservations required. **Registration:** Main lodge. **Fee:** Varies. **Parking:** At main lodge.

Facilities

Number of RV Sites: Unspecified. **Number of Tent-Only Sites:** Unspecified, but numerous. **Hookups:** None. **Dump Station:** Yes. **Laundry:** Yes. **Pay Phone:** Yes. **Rest Rooms and Showers:** Yes. **Fuel:** No. **Propane:** No. **Internal Roads:** Dirt. **RV Service:** No. **Market:** Marshfield Village Store, 1425 US Rte. 2, Marshfield, VT 05658. **Restaurant:** On site. **General Store:** No. **Vending:** No. **Swimming Pool:** No. **Playground:** No. **Other:** Retreat center. **Activities:** Group activities. **Additional Information:** Call ahead.

Restrictions

Pets: Allowed. **Fires:** Allowed. **Alcoholic Beverages:** No. **Vehicle Maximum Length:** None. **Other:** Ask on arrival.

To Get There

Located 20 mi. east of Montpelier on US Rte. 2, near the village of South Cabot, about 2 mi. east of Marshfield Dam (Molly's Falls Pond on some maps). Hwy. signs mark the turn onto Houghton Rd. Follow that road 0.8 of a mi., past a sharp left curve, and the camp entrance will be on the right. Signs are posted.

MARSHFIELD

Kettle Pond State Park

4239 VT Rte. 232, Marshfield, Marshfield 05658. T: (802) 426-3042; www.state.vt.us/anr/fpr/parks/htm/groton/ketlpond.htm.html.

RV: ★★ Tent: ★★★★★

Beauty: ★★★★	Site Privacy: ★★★★★
Spaciousness: ★★★★★	Quiet: ★★★★★
Security: ★★★	Cleanliness: ★★★★
Insect Control: ★★★	Facilities: ★★

Located in an enormous state park, the campground at Kettle Pond will accomodate RVs, but the best sites are for tent campers. RVers basically get a place to park, but sites are private and the secenery is impressive. For tenters, there's a handful of remote sites that can give you total privacy. This is not a campground for people looking for a lot of activities. The facilities are sparse and the main draws are the pond, hiking trails, and wildlife.

Basics

Operated By: State of Vermont. **Open:** May 15–Columbus Day. **Site Assignment:** Reservations accepted. **Registration:** Entrance station. **Fee:** $4/person. **Parking:** At site.

Facilities

Number of RV Sites: 27. **Number of Tent-Only Sites:** 6. **Hookups:** None. **Each Site:** Lean-tos. **Dump Station:** No. **Laundry:** No. **Pay Phone:** No. **Rest Rooms and Showers:** No. **Fuel:** No. **Propane:** No. **Internal Roads:** Paved/gravel. **RV Service:** No. **Market:** Marshfield Village Store, 1425 US Rte. 2, Marshfield, VT 05658. **Restaurant:** River Run Restaurant, 3 Main St., Plainfield, VT 05667. **General Store:** No. **Vending:** No. **Swimming Pool:** No. **Playground:** Yes. **Other:** Pond. **Activities:** Boating, swimming, hiking. **Nearby Attractions:** Trails. **Additional Information:** Call ahead.

Restrictions

Pets: Allowed. **Fires:** Allowed. **Alcoholic Beverages:** Allowed. **Vehicle Maximum Length:** None. **Other:** Ask on arrival.

To Get There

From Groton, go 2 mi. west on U.S. 302, then 7.5 mi, northwest on Rte. 232.

MIDDLEBURY

Falls of Lana Campground

RR 4, Box 1260, Middlebury 05753. T: (802) 388-4362.

RV: n/a Tent: ★★★★

Beauty: ★★★★	Site Privacy: ★★★★
Spaciousness: ★★★★★	Quiet: ★★★★★
Security: ★★★	Cleanliness: ★★★★
Insect Control: ★★★	Facilities: ★

These wooded, secluded sites serve as a base camp for hikers. You can pitch your tent and then set off on day trips over a variety of hiking trails. There's also easy access to Silver Lake, which has swimming and fishing as well as a picnic area. There's absolutely nothing here in terms of facilities, so you'll only want to visit if you're looking to truly "rough it" and spend the day hiking.

Basics

Operated By: State of Vermont. **Open:** May 15–Oct. 1. **Site Assignment:** First come, first served. **Registration:** Camp entrance. **Fee:** None. **Parking:** At site.

Facilities

Number of RV Sites: 0. **Number of Tent-Only Sites:** Unspecified, but numerous. **Hookups:** None. **Dump Station:** No. **Laundry:** No. **Pay Phone:** No. **Rest Rooms and Showers:** Outhouse. **Fuel:** No. **Propane:** No. **Internal Roads:** Paved/compressed gravel. **RV Service:** No. **Market:** A&P: 260 Court St. Middlebury, VT 05753, (802) 388-9028. **Restaurant:** A&W Family Restaurant 1557 Rte. 7 S. Middlebury, VT 05753. **General Store:** No. **Vending:** No. **Swimming Pool:** No. **Playground:** No. **Activities:** None. **Nearby Attractions:** Shops in Middlebury. **Additional Information:** Call ahead.

Restrictions

Pets: Allowed. **Fires:** Allowed. **Alcoholic Beverages:** Allowed. **Vehicle Maximum Length:** 30 ft. **Other:** Ask on arrival.

To Get There

Take Rte. 7 to Rte. 125. Turn onto Rte. 32 and follow signs to the Mount Moosalamoo parking area. Go past the parking area and continue to Rte. 27 then follow signs to campgrounds.

MIDDLEBURY

Mount Moosalamoo Campground

RR 4, Box 1260, Middlebury 05753. T: (802) 388-4362.

RV: n/a Tent: ★★★★★

Beauty: ★★★★★	Site Privacy: ★★★★★
Spaciousness: ★★★★★	Quiet: ★★★★★
Security: ★★★★	Cleanliness: ★★★★★
Insect Control: ★★★	Facilities: ★

If you're looking for absolutely no frills camping, that's what you'll get at Mount Moosalamoo Campground. The "sites" are basically just areas to pitch a tent in between hikes. There's little else to do here excpet hike, but if that's what you're after, the opportunities are endless. This is not a camping area for young kids as there's very little around. Even adults coming here will want to be careful, as it's easy to get lost and, if you get hurt, there's no one to rescue you.

Basics

Operated By: State of Vermont. **Open:** May 15–Oct. 15. **Site Assignment:** First come, first served. **Registration:** Entrance gate. **Fee:** $5. **Parking:** At site.

Facilities

Number of RV Sites: 2. **Number of Tent-Only Sites:** 17. **Hookups:** None. **Dump Station:** No. **Laundry:** No. **Pay Phone:** No. **Rest Rooms and Showers:** Outhouse. **Fuel:** No. **Propane:** No. **Internal Roads:** Paved/compressed gravel. **RV Service:** No. **Market:** A&P: 260 Court St. Middlebury, VT 05753, (802) 388-9028. **Restaurant:** A&W Family Restaurant 1557 Rte. 7 S. Middlebury, VT 05753. **General Store:** No. **Vending:** No. **Swimming Pool:** No. **Playground:** No. **Activities:** Hiking. **Nearby Attractions:** Shops in Middlebury. **Additional Information:** Call ahead.

Restrictions

Pets: Allowed. **Fires:** Allowed. **Alcoholic Beverages:** Allowed. **Vehicle Maximum Length:** 30 ft. **Other:** Ask on arrival.

To Get There

Take Rte. 7 to Rte. 125. Turn onto Rte. 32 and follow the signs.

MILTON

Homestead Campground

864 Ethan Allen Hwy., Milton 05468. T: (802) 524-2356; heyjo@together.net.

RV ★★★ Tent ★★★

Beauty: ★★★ Site Privacy: ★★★
Spaciousness: ★★★ Quiet: ★★★
Security: ★★★ Cleanliness: ★★★★
Insect Control: ★★★ Facilities: ★★★★

A campground aimed at families, Homestead offers sites that are level and grassy but packed pretty close together. The main draws here are the planned activities and the fact that there's a lot for kids to do. There's also a flea market on some weekends as well as bingo and wagon rides. Though it's close to Lake Champlain and other outdoor sites, the actual campground is nothing much to look at, but with a mini golf and go-karts facility across the street, there's plenty to keep the kids busy.

Basics

Operated By: Joe & Sue Monty. **Open:** May 1–Oct. 15. **Site Assignment:** Reservations accepted. **Registration:** At office. **Fee:** Starts at $21 per night. **Parking:** At site.

Facilities

Number of RV Sites: 150. **Number of Tent-Only Sites:** 0. **Hookups:** Water, electric, sewer, cable TV. **Dump Station:** Yes. **Laundry:** Yes. **Pay Phone:** Yes. **Rest Rooms and Showers:** Yes. **Fuel:** No. **Propane:** Yes. **Internal Roads:** Paved/gravel. **RV Service:** No. **Market:** Middle Rd. Market, 69 Middle Rd., Milton, VT 05468: Take a left onto Rte. 7 & go 5.6 mi. **Restaurant:** Lucky Wok, 170 Rte. 7 S, Milton, VT 05468: Take a left onto Rte. 7 & go 5.1 mi. **General Store:** Yes. **Vending:** No. **Swimming Pool:** Yes. **Playground:** Yes. **Other:** Shuffleboard. **Activities:** Planned activities. **Nearby Attractions:** Mini golf, go-carts, & snackbar across the street. **Additional Information:** Call ahead.

Restrictions

Pets: Allowed. **Fires:** Allowed. **Alcoholic Beverages:** Allowed. **Vehicle Maximum Length:** None. **Other:** Ask on arrival.

To Get There

From Exit 18 on I-89, go 0.25 mi. south on Rte. 7.

MORRISVILLE

Mountain View Campground & Cabins

3154 Rte. 15E, Morrisville 05661. T: (802) 888-2178.

RV ★★★★ Tent ★★★★

Beauty: ★★★★ Site Privacy: ★★★
Spaciousness: ★★★ Quiet: ★★★★
Security: ★★★ Cleanliness: ★★★★
Insect Control: ★★★ Facilities: ★★★★★

One of the best campgrounds in New England for its size, Mountain View offers a rural location with all the trimmings. In addition to the mountain views that gave the campground its name, there's also the Lamoille River and Bugbee Brook. The tent sites are along the brook, which offers excellent fishing, and the wooded RV sites are closer to the river. This campground has a rare mix of natural beauty and top-notch facilities, with a heated pool, hot tub, and mini golf. If you're looking for nature, the river offers days worth of canoeing.

Basics

Operated By: The Marceau family. **Open:** June 6–Oct. 15. **Site Assignment:** Reservations accepted. **Registration:** At office. **Fee:** Starts at $22. **Parking:** At site.

Facilities

Number of RV Sites: 43. **Number of Tent-Only Sites:** 10. **Hookups:** Water, electric, sewer. **Each Site:** Picnic table, fire ring. **Dump Station:** Yes. **Laundry:** No. **Pay Phone:** Yes. **Rest Rooms and Showers:** Yes. **Fuel:** No. **Propane:** No. **Internal Roads:** Paved. **RV Service:** No. **Market:** Fisher Bridge Discount Grocery, 30 Munson Ave., Morrisville, VT 05661: Take a right onto Rte. 100 & follow it for 1 mi. until it becomes Rte. 12. **Restaurant:** On site. **General Store:** Snack bar. **Vending:** Yes. **Swimming Pool:** Yes. **Playground:** Yes. **Other:** Pavillion, mini golf, jacuzzi. **Activities:** None. **Nearby Attractions:** Alpine slide.

Restrictions

Pets: Allowed. **Fires:** Allowed. **Alcoholic Beverages:** Allowed. **Vehicle Maximum Length:** 40 ft. **Other:** Ask on arrival.

To Get There

From I-89 take Exit 10 to Rte. 100 and follow it to the junction for Rte. 15. Take a right onto Rte. 15 and continue for 3 mi.

NEWPORT

Prouty Beach Campground

Veterans Ave., Newport 05855. T: (802) 334-7951.

RV ★★★★ Tent ★★★

Beauty: ★★★★ Site Privacy: ★★★★
Spaciousness: ★★★★ Quiet: ★★★★
Security: ★★★ Cleanliness: ★★★★
Insect Control: ★★★ Facilities: ★★★★

Located along Lake Memphremagog, Prouty Beach Campground offers tremendous fishing. The lake, unfortuantely, can attract quite a crowd, so you won't be casting your line in solitude. But, it's a big body of water, so you might be able to find a quiet spot. The campground offers a lot of facilities without feeling over developed, and sites are fairly large. The big problem you'll find here is crowds at that the public beach, but this might be an ideal spot for families looking for a nice campground with lots to do that's not a barren summer camp.

Basics

Operated By: Private operator. **Open:** May 15–Oct. 15. **Site Assignment:** Reservations recommended. **Registration:** At office. **Fee:** $20. **Parking:** At site.

Facilities

Number of RV Sites: 50. **Number of Tent-Only Sites:** 0. **Hookups:** Water, electric, sewer. **Each Site:** Fire ring, grill, picnic table. **Dump Station:** Yes. **Laundry:** Yes. **Pay Phone:** Yes. **Rest Rooms and Showers:** Yes. **Fuel:** No. **Propane:** No. **Internal Roads:** Paved/gravel. **RV Service:** No. **Market:** East Main Mini Market: 477 East Main St. Newport, VT 05855 (802) 334-8460. **Restaurant:** Brown Cow: 350 East Main St. Newport, VT 05855 (802) 334-7887. **General Store:** Limited. **Vending:** No. **Swimming Pool:** No. **Playground:** Yes. **Other:** Tennis courts, sports field, volleyball courts. **Activities:** Swimming, fishing.

Restrictions

Pets: Allowed. **Fires:** Allowed. **Alcoholic Beverages:** Allowed. **Vehicle Maximum Length:** 40 ft. **Other:** Ask on arrival.

To Get There

Take I-91 to Rte. 191 and go 3 mi. then take a left onto Freeman followed by a left onto Veterans.

NORTH HERO

Kings Bay Campground

1088 Lakeview Dr., North Hero 05474. T: (802) 372-3735.

RV ★★★ Tent ★★★★

Beauty: ★★★★ Site Privacy: ★★★
Spaciousness: ★★★★ Quiet: ★★★★
Security: ★★★ Cleanliness: ★★★
Insect Control: ★★★ Facilities: ★★

Another campground dominated by seasonal campers, you'll want to make a reseration if you plan to stay here. That might be worth doing, however, as the lakeside sites are shaded and the view can spectacular. To the east you can see the Cold Hollow Mountains, which go all the way into Canada. There's plenty of hiking opportunities as well as fishing.

BASICS

Operated By: Bud Knapp. **Open:** May 15–Sept. 15. **Site Assignment:** Reservations recommended. **Registration:** At office. **Fee:** $15–$18. **Parking:** At site.

FACILITIES

Number of RV Sites: 40. **Number of Tent-Only Sites:** 0. **Hookups:** Water, electric (20), sewer. **Dump Station:** No. **Laundry:** No. **Pay Phone:** No. **Rest Rooms and Showers:** No. **Fuel:** No. **Propane:** No. **Internal Roads:** Compressed gravel. **RV Service:** No. **Market:** Grand Union Co, 39 1st St., Swanton, VT 05488: Take a left onto Lakeview Dr. followed by a right onto Bridge Rd. & a right onto Rte. 2. Continue 5.8 mi. & take a right onto Rte.78 & follow it for 10.1 mi. then follow Rte. 78 by taking a right then a left. **Restaurant:** River View Dining & Spirits, 5 Merchants Row, Swanton, VT 05488: Take a left onto Lakeview Dr. followed by a right onto Bridge Rd. & a right onto Rte. 2. Continue 5.8 mi. & take a right onto Rte. 78 & follow it for 10.1 mi. **General Store:** No. **Vending:** No. **Swimming Pool:** No. **Playground:** No. **Activities:** None. **Nearby Attractions:** Cold Hollow Mountains. **Additional Information:** Call ahead.

RESTRICTIONS

Pets: Allowed. **Fires:** Allowed. **Alcoholic Beverages:** Allowed. **Vehicle Maximum Length:** 40 ft. **Other:** Ask on arrival.

TO GET THERE

From North Hero got north on Rte. 2 for 3.3 mi., then take a right onto Lakeview Dr. and go 1 mi.

ORLEANS

White Caps Campground

5659 VT Rte. 5A, Orleans 05860. T: (802) 467-3345.

RV: ★★★★ Tent: ★★★

Beauty: ★★★★	Site Privacy: ★★★
Spaciousness: ★★★	Quiet: ★★★★
Security: ★★★	Cleanliness: ★★★★
Insect Control: ★★★	Facilities: ★★★

A small campground that's built around its access to Lake Willoughby, White Caps has the feel of a small lakeside community. Perhaps that's because though campers do interact with each other, there aren't a lot of planned activities, making for more of an individual trip in a friendly environment. The location is nearly perfect, as the lake offers, fishing, swimming, boating and anything else that can be done on water, while nearby mountains Pisgah and Hor offer hiking for all ability levels. This is an excellent place to take an active vacation, though you could also spend your time just relaxing in front of the lake staring off into the mountains.

BASICS

Operated By: John & Kathleen Binks. **Open:** May 15–Sept. 15. **Site Assignment:** Reservations accepted. **Registration:** At office. **Fee:** $17–$20. **Parking:** At site.

FACILITIES

Number of RV Sites: 35. **Number of Tent-Only Sites:** 15. **Hookups:** Water, electric, sewer. **Each Site:** Picnic tables, fireplace. **Dump Station:** Yes. **Laundry:** Yes. **Pay Phone:** Yes. **Rest Rooms and Showers:** Yes. **Fuel:** No. **Propane:** Yes. **Internal Roads:** Paved/gravel. **RV Service:** No. **Market:** Cole's Markets, 52 Main St., Orleans, VT 05860: Take a right onto Rte. 58 & follow it for 0.4 mi. **Restaurant:** 3556 Schoolhouse Rd., Orleans, VT 05860: Take a right onto Rte. 58 to Orleans. **General Store:** Yes. **Vending:** Yes. **Swimming Pool:** No. **Playground:** No. **Other:** Lake access, hiking trails. **Activities:** Water-based activities. **Nearby Attractions:** Lake Willoughby. **Additional Information:** Call ahead.

RESTRICTIONS

Pets: Allowed. **Fires:** Allowed. **Alcoholic Beverages:** Allowed. **Vehicle Maximum Length:** 40 ft. **Other:** Ask on arrival.

TO GET THERE

Take I-91 to Exit 23 and follow Rte. 5 north to West Burke, then Rte. 5A for 6 mi.

PLAINFIELD

Onion River Campground

RD 1, Box 205, Plainfield 05667. T: (802) 426-3232.

RV: ★★★ Tent: n/a

Beauty: ★★★	Site Privacy: ★★★
Spaciousness: ★★★	Quiet: ★★★
Security: ★★★	Cleanliness: ★★★
Insect Control: ★★★	Facilities: ★★★★

With sites lining the water's edge, this is a true fisherman's paradise. You can basically cast your line from your site, and the Winooski River has a nice selection of fish waiting to be caught. The River also has some excellent swimming areas and can be paddled by canoe. The campground is also next to Groton State Forest, which offers easy access to hiking and has mountain bike trails.

BASICS

Operated By: Private operator. **Open:** Apr. 10–Nov. 20. **Site Assignment:** Reservations recommended. **Registration:** At office. **Fee:** $15. **Parking:** At site.

FACILITIES

Number of RV Sites: 48. **Number of Tent-Only Sites:** 0. **Hookups:** Water, electric, sewer. **Each Site:** Picnic table, fire ring, grill. **Dump Station:** Yes. **Laundry:** Yes. **Pay Phone:** Yes. **Rest Rooms and Showers:** Yes. **Fuel:** No. **Propane:** Yes. **Internal Roads:** Paved. **RV Service:** No. **Market:** Plainfield Red Store: 230 High St., Plainfield, VT 05667 (802) 454-7886: Take a right onto Brook Rd. followed by a left onto Main St. & a left onto Rte. 2. **Restaurant:** River Run Restaurant, 3 Main St., Plainfield, VT 05667: Take a right onto Brook Rd. followed by a left onto Main St. & a right onto Rte. 2. **General Store:** Limited. **Vending:** No. **Swimming Pool:** No. **Playground:** No. **Other:** Horshoes, badminton, volleyball. **Activities:** Fishing. **Nearby Attractions:** Groton State Forest.

RESTRICTIONS

Pets: Allowed. **Fires:** Allowed. **Alcoholic Beverages:** Allowed. **Vehicle Maximum Length:** 40 ft. **Other:** Ask on arrival.

TO GET THERE

Take Rte.14 to Rte. 2E and follow for about 5 mi.

PONWAL

Pine Hollow Campground

RR 1, Box 343, Ponwal 05261. T: (802) 823-5569.

RV: ★★★★ Tent: ★★★

Beauty: ★★★	Site Privacy: ★★★
Spaciousness: ★★	Quiet: ★★★
Security: ★★★★	Cleanliness: ★★★★
Insect Control: ★★★	Facilities: ★★★★

Nature provides the prime attraction at Pine Hollow, which is built around a pond. Though the actual campground is nothing special, with fairly crowded sites and lots of RVs dotting the landscape, the surrounding area is excellent. The main attraction has to be the Long Trail, 265 miles of hiking that offers nearly endless exploration options. There's also lots of fish to be caught in the pond, which also allows swimming and non-motorized boating. Tent campers might wish for a bit more seperation from the RVs, but there's an endless amount of space once you get a little bit away from your actual campsite.

BASICS

Operated By: Ronald & Rachel Lauzon. **Open:** May 15–Oct. 15. **Site Assignment:** Reservations accepted. **Registration:** At office. **Fee:** $14–$18. **Parking:** At site.

FACILITIES

Number of RV Sites: 50. **Number of Tent-Only Sites:** 0. **Hookups:** Water, electric, sewer, cable TV. **Each Site:** Picnic table, fire ring. **Dump Station:** Yes. **Laundry:** No. **Pay Phone:** Yes. **Rest Rooms and Showers:** Yes. **Fuel:** No. **Propane:** No. **Internal Roads:** Paved/gravel. **RV Service:** No. **Market:** Winchester's Store, Rte. 7, Pownal, VT 05261. **Restaurant:** Jaeger House, Rte. 7, Pownal, VT 05261. **General Store:** No. **Vending:** No. **Swimming Pool:** No. **Playground:** Yes. **Other:** Rec hall, badminton, sports field, volleyball, pond. **Activities:** Swimming, boating. **Nearby Attractions:** Long Trail. **Additional Information:** Call ahead.

RESTRICTIONS

Pets: Yes, on leash. **Fires:** Allowed. **Alcoholic Beverages:** Allowed. **Vehicle Maximum Length:** 60 ft. **Other:** Ask on arrival.

TO GET THERE

Take Rte. 9 to Rte. 7 and go 7.5 mi. to Barbers Pond Rd. Turn right on Old Military Rd. and follow it to the campground.

POULTNEY

Lake St. Catherine State Park

RD 2 Box 1775, Poultney 05764. T: (802) 287-9158 or (800) 658-1622; www.vtstateparks.com.

RV ★★★★ Tent ★★★★

Beauty: ★★★★ Site Privacy: ★★★★
Spaciousness: ★★★★ Quiet: ★★★★
Security: ★★★ Cleanliness: ★★★
Insect Control: ★★★ Facilities: ★★★

Lake St. Catherine is a good example of the powerful combination of woods and water. The day-use area and the beachfront on the lake draw a lot of people on those hot summer days. A few sites worth noting, for various reasons, include sites 1 and 2, which are right across from one of the bathroom buildings, and site 35, which is one of the most secluded, set within a dense grove of conifers. There is an open grassy area leading in to sites 38 and 39, which makes them suitable for larger groups or for parking a boat trailer. Site 47 is a huge site, set along the side of another small grassy field area, which would make a perfect spot for a volleyball net.

Basics

Operated By: Vermont Agency of Natural Resources. **Open:** Mid-May–Columbus Day. **Site Assignment:** Reservations or first come first served. **Registration:** At ranger station. **Fee:** $13–$17. **Parking:** At site.

Facilities

Number of RV Sites: 51. **Number of Tent-Only Sites:** 0. **Hookups:** None. **Each Site:** Stone hearth, picnic table. **Dump Station:** Yes. **Laundry:** No. **Pay Phone:** Yes. **Rest Rooms and Showers:** Yes. **Fuel:** No. **Propane:** No. **Internal Roads:** Paved/gravel. **RV Service:** No. **Market:** No. **Restaurant:** Snack bar. **General Store:** No. **Vending:** No. **Swimming Pool:** No. **Playground:** Yes. **Activities:** None. **Nearby Attractions:** Equinox Mountain Dr. (Manchester) Wilson's Castle, Vermont Marble Exhibit, Hildene, Bennington Monument & Museum, Orvis.

Restrictions

Pets: On leash. **Fires:** In fire hearth. **Alcoholic Beverages:** Ask on arrival. **Vehicle Maximum Length:** Unlimited. **Other:** Ask on arrival.

To Get There

From Poultney, go 3 mi. south on Hwy. 30.

RANDOLPH

Mobile Acres Trailer Park

Hwy. 12A, Randolph 05060. T: (802) 728-5548.

RV ★★★★ Tent ★★

Beauty: ★★ Site Privacy: ★★★
Spaciousness: ★★ Quiet: ★★★
Security: ★★★ Cleanliness: ★★★
Insect Control: ★★★ Facilities: ★★★

Technically, tent camping is allowed here, but it's impossible to imagine anyone setting up a tent here. With all the RVs tightly packed, it would be a little like camping in a parking lot. Of course, for RVers looking for a friendly community to spend some time in, the park offers full hookups and sites with picnic tables and fire rings (features that do make the park more tent camper–friendly). There are plenty of organized activities, and sometimes impromptu games on the sports field.

Basics

Operated By: Private operator. **Open:** May 15–Oct. 15. **Site Assignment:** Reservations recommended. **Registration:** Entrance. **Fee:** $18. **Parking:** At site.

Facilities

Number of RV Sites: 94. **Number of Tent-Only Sites:** 0. **Hookups:** Water, electric, sewer. **Each Site:** Picnic table, fire ring. **Dump Station:** Yes. **Laundry:** Yes. **Pay Phone:** Yes. **Rest Rooms and Showers:** Yes. **Fuel:** No. **Propane:** Yes. **Internal Roads:** Paved/gravel. **RV Service:** No. **Market:** Grand Union Co., 12 North Main St., Randolph, VT 05060: Take a left onto Braintree Hill Rd. followed by a left onto Rte. 12A & a right onto Rte. 12. **Restaurant:** China Jade, 17 South Main St., Randolph, VT 05060: Take a left onto Braintree Hill Rd. followed by a left onto Rte. 12A & a right onto Rte. 12. **General Store:** No. **Vending:** Yes. **Swimming Pool:** Yes. **Playground:** Yes. **Other:** Sports field, horshoe pit. **Activities:** Lots of organized activities.

Restrictions

Pets: Allowed. **Fires:** Allowed. **Alcoholic Beverages:** Allowed. **Vehicle Maximum Length:** 35 ft. **Other:** Ask on arrival.

To Get There

From I-89, take Exit 4 to Rte. 66 and go 5 miles west, looking for the campground entrance on left.

ROCHESTER

Mountain Trails Camping Area

1375 Quarry Rd., Rochester 05767. T: (802) 767-3352; www.campusa.com/framemountaintrails.cfm.

RV ★★★ Tent ★★★

Beauty: ★★★★ Site Privacy: ★★★
Spaciousness: ★★★ Quiet: ★★★★
Security: ★★★ Cleanliness: ★★★
Insect Control: ★★★ Facilities: ★★

This is about as basic as camping gets. Though there are hookups for the RV sites, there's not much else here. There's no pool, lake, or stream, and not much to do. The tent sites are fairly wooded and secluded, but primary reason campers use it as a base camp. If you're looking to fish, the White River is nearby, and there's hunting in-season throughout the area. Hikers can also trek from the campground up Mount Cushman, which can be a challenging climb.

Basics

Operated By: Private operator. **Open:** May 1–Nov. 30. **Site Assignment:** At time of registration. **Registration:** Reservations required. **Fee:** $12–$15. **Parking:** At site.

Facilities

Number of RV Sites: 10. **Number of Tent-Only Sites:** 15. **Hookups:** Water, electric, sewer. **Each Site:** Picnic table, fireplace. **Dump Station:** Yes. **Laundry:** No. **Pay Phone:** No. **Rest Rooms and Showers:** Yes. **Fuel:** No. **Propane:** No. **Internal Roads:** Paved/gravel. **RV Service:** No. **Market:** Store of Rochester: Rte. 100, Rochester, VT 05767, (802) 767-3181. **Restaurant:** Huntington House Inn: 1806 East Park St. Rochester, VT 05767. **General Store:** No. **Vending:** No. **Swimming Pool:** No. **Playground:** Yes. **Other:** Horseshoes, badminton. **Activities:** Hiking, fishing. **Nearby Attractions:** Rochester.

Restrictions

Pets: Allowed. **Fires:** Allowed. **Alcoholic Beverages:** Allowed. **Vehicle Maximum Length:** 35 ft. **Other:** Ask on arrival.

To Get There

Take I-89 to Rte. 107 and continue west to Rte. 100. Follow Rte. 100 north for 2.75 miles.

RUTLAND

Green Mountain National Forest Campgrounds

North Main St., Rutland 05701. T: (802) 747-6700.

RV n/a Tent ★★★★★

Beauty: ★★★★★ Site Privacy: ★★★★
Spaciousness: ★★★★★ Quiet: ★★★★★
Security: ★★★ Cleanliness: ★★★★
Insect Control: ★★★ Facilities: ★★★★

Actually a collection of campsites, rather than one specific area, the Green Mountain National Forest Campgrounds cover an enormous amount of terrain. There are five specific campgrounds connected by 312 miles of hiking trails. This enormous park is an excellent place to travel light and see varying parts of the state on one trip. Areas throughout the campground offer hunting, fishing, hiking, paddling, and basically any outdoor activity you can dream up. In winter, the campground remains open and offers snowshoeing, cross country skiing, and snowmobiling in some places.

Basics

Operated By: State of Vermont. **Open:** Year-round. **Site Assignment:** Reservations accepted. **Registration:** At office. **Fee:** $4. **Parking:** Specified at Registration.

Facilities

Number of RV Sites: 0. **Number of Tent-Only Sites:** 94. **Hookups:** None. **Dump Station:** Yes. **Laundry:** No. **Pay Phone:** No. **Rest Rooms and Showers:** Yes. **Fuel:** No. **Propane:** No. **Internal Roads:** Paved/gravel. **RV Service:** No. **Market:** Bedard Cash Market, 137 Library Ave., Rutland, VT 05701. **Restaurant:** A Crust Above, 134 Woodstock Ave., Rutland, VT 05701. **General Store:** No. **Vending:** No. **Swimming Pool:** No. **Playground:** No. **Activities:** Hiking, fishing, mountain biking. **Nearby Attractions:** Mountains, trails, visitor center. **Additional Information:** Call ahead.

Restrictions

Pets: Allowed. **Fires:** Allowed. **Alcoholic Beverages:** Allowed. **Vehicle Maximum Length:** None. **Other:** Ask on arrival.

To Get There

Take Rte. 4 to Rte. 17 in Rutland

SHELBURNE

Shelburne Camping Area

4385 Shelburne Rd., Rte. 7, Shelburne 05482. T: (802) 985-2540; F: (802) 985-8132; shelbcamp@aol.com.

RV ★★★ Tent ★

Beauty: ★★★ Site Privacy: ★★★
Spaciousness: ★★★★ Quiet: ★★
Security: ★★★★ Cleanliness: ★★★★
Insect Control: ★★★ Facilities: ★★★★

Owned by the same people who own the Dutch Mill Motel and Restaurant, this campground is marked by a Dutch-style windmill at the entrance. Though that makes most people think of mini-golf, there's no course here. However, there is pretty much everything else you'd want in an RV park. Unfortunately, sites are lined up in that boring RV park grid. Still, they're grassy and bigger than average, and most have trees, so it's nice place to stay. Tent campers are technically welcome, but this is not a tent campground. The park is close to Lake Champlain, though not on it, and has access to area beaches.

Basics

Operated By: The Bissonette family. **Open:** Apr.–Nov. 1. **Site Assignment:** Reservations accepted. **Registration:** At office. **Fee:** $18–$26. **Parking:** At site.

Facilities

Number of RV Sites: 70. **Number of Tent-Only Sites:** 6. **Hookups:** Water, electric, sewer, cable TV. **Each Site:** Picnic table, fire ring. **Dump Station:** Yes. **Laundry:** Yes. **Pay Phone:** Yes. **Rest Rooms and Showers:** Yes. **Fuel:** No. **Propane:** Yes. **Internal Roads:** Paved/gravel. **RV Service:** No. **Market:** Galipeau's Grocery Store, 935 Falls Rd., Shelburne, VT 05482: Take a left onto Rte. 7 followed by a left onto Marsett Rd., which becomes Falls Rd. **Restaurant:** Buono Appetito Italian Restaurant, 3182 Shelburne Rd., Shelburne, VT 05482: Take a right onto Rte. 7 & follow it for 0.7 mi. **General Store:** Yes. **Vending:** Yes. **Swimming Pool:** Yes. **Playground:** Yes. **Other:** Rec room, basketball, volleyball, horseshoes. **Activities:** Swimming & boating. **Nearby Attractions:** Shelburne Museum. **Additional Information:** Call ahead.

Restrictions

Pets: Allowed. **Fires:** Allowed. **Alcoholic Beverages:** Allowed. **Vehicle Maximum Length:** None. **Other:** Ask on arrival.

To Get There

Take I-89 Exit 13; follow Rte. 7 south for 5 mi.

SOUTH HERO

Apple Tree Bay Campground

P.O. Box 183, 71 Rte. 2, South Hero 05486. T: (802) 372-5398; F: (802) 372-8272; www.appleislandresort.com; atbrcamp@aol.com.

RV ★★★★ Tent ★

Beauty: ★★★★ Site Privacy: ★★★
Spaciousness: ★★★ Quiet: ★★★
Security: ★★★ Cleanliness: ★★★★
Insect Control: ★★★ Facilities: ★★★★

An all-purpose resort that caters primarily to RVers, Apple Tree has tons of planned activities as well as a very busy lake. Though the lake has its share of motorboats, there's also excellent fishing, and you can hire guides to help you find the fish. It's actually possible to fish for your dinner here, though it's equally likely you'll be throwing back what you catch. Tents are allowed but not reccomended here, as the sites are really meant for RVs. You can see the Green Mountains from here as well as lots of pretty Lake Champlain scenery.

Basics

Operated By: Paul & Rick Abare. **Open:** May 1–Oct. 20. **Site Assignment:** Reservations recommended. **Registration:** Entrance. **Fee:** $20–$30. **Parking:** At site.

Facilities

Number of RV Sites: 200. **Number of Tent-Only Sites:** 0. **Hookups:** Water, electric, sewer. **Each Site:** Picnic tables, fire rings. **Dump Station:** Yes. **Laundry:** Yes. **Pay Phone:** Yes. **Rest Rooms and Showers:** Yes. **Fuel:** No. **Propane:** Yes. **Internal Roads:** Paved/gravel. **RV Service:** No. **Market:** Keeler's Bay Variety Store, 500 Rte. 2, South Hero, VT 05486: Follow Rte. 2 to number 500. **Restaurant:** Sandbar Restaurant on site. **General Store:** Yes. **Vending:** Yes. **Swimming Pool:** Yes. **Playground:** Yes. **Other:** Motel & cabins, 9 hole golf course, clubhouse, volleyball, horshoes. **Activities:** Planned activities, boat rentals, waterskiing. **Nearby Attractions:** Green Mountains.

Restrictions

Pets: Allowed. **Fires:** Allowed. **Alcoholic Beverages:** Allowed. **Vehicle Maximum Length:** 50 ft. **Other:** Ask on arrival.

To Get There

From I-89, take Exit 17 and turn right. Go 6 mi. on Rte. 2 to the end of the Sand Bar Beach Causeway.

SOUTH HERO

Camp Skyland on Lake Champlain

398 South St., South Hero 05486. T: (802) 372-4200.

RV ★★★★ Tent ★★★★

Beauty: ★★★★★ Site Privacy: ★★★★
Spaciousness: ★★★★ Quiet: ★★★★
Security: ★★★★ Cleanliness: ★★★★
Insect Control: ★★★ Facilities: ★★★

Perhaps the best looking campground in all of Vermont, Camp Skyland offers nature that has virtually undisturbed by man. Located on the Southern part of Grand Isle, the campground offers incredible views of mountains and Lake Champlain. Though RVs are allowed here, you'd be better off bringing a tent. Sites are spacious, secluded and pretty quiet. There's a boat launch as well as lake swimming and nearly endless hiking and exploration options.

Basics

Operated By: Jack, Priscilla, & Joey Arnold. **Open:** Memorial Day–Sept. 30. **Site Assignment:** Reservations. **Registration:** At office. **Fee:** Starts at $16. **Parking:** At site.

Facilities

Number of RV Sites: 22. **Number of Tent-Only Sites:** 11. **Hookups:** Water, electric, sewer. **Each Site:** Picnic tables & fire rings at tent sites. **Dump Station:** No. **Laundry:** Yes. **Pay Phone:** No. **Rest Rooms and Showers:** Yes. **Fuel:** No. **Propane:** No. **Internal Roads:** Paved/gravel. **RV Service:** No. **Market:** Brennan's Quik Stop, 50 Porters Point Ct., Colchester, VT 05446: Take a left onto Rte. 2 & follow it for 12.4 mi. Then, take a right onto Rte. 127 & follow it for 4.8 mi. **Restaurant:** Lee Zachary's Pizza House, Rte. 2 South Hero, VT 05486: Take a left onto Rte. 2 & follow it for 3 mi. **General Store:** No. **Vending:** No. **Swimming Pool:** No. **Playground:** No. **Other:** Rec hall, game room, lending library. **Activities:** Canoe & boat rentals, fishing. **Nearby Attractions:** Trails.

Restrictions

Pets: Allowed. **Fires:** Allowed. **Alcoholic Beverages:** Allowed. **Vehicle Maximum Length:** none. **Other:** Ask on arrival.

To Get There

Go 10 mi. from I-89, Exit 17, on Rte. 2, then 3.5 mi. to the campground at the end of South St.

ST. ALBANS BAY

Burton Island State Park

P.O. Box 123, St. Albans Bay 05481. T: (802) 524-6353; www.state.vt.us/anr/fpr/parks/htm/burton.html.

RV n/a Tent ★★★★

Beauty: ★★★ Site Privacy: ★★★★
Spaciousness: ★★★ Quiet: ★★★★★
Security: ★★★★ Cleanliness: ★★★★
Insect Control: ★★★ Facilities: ★★★★

Only accessible by boat (a ferry makes the trip) Burton Island offers a little something different. For tent campers it offers isolation, as the crowds never get that big due to the location. For boaters, there's electricity at the marina in the boat slips and a chance to get away from the traditional yacht club. The 253 acre park has all sorts of wildlife and a resident naturalist to explain it. There's also a beach for swimming and lots of water-based activities, since this is an island. Hikers can follow the Island's network of nature trails or get lost off the beaten path.

Basics

Operated By: State of Vermont. **Open:** May 15–

Labor Day. **Site Assignment:** Reservations accepted. **Registration:** Entrance gate. **Fee:** $14–$20. **Parking:** At site.

Facilities

Number of RV Sites: 0. **Number of Tent-Only Sites:** 42. **Hookups:** None. **Each Site:** Fireplace, picnic table. **Dump Station:** No. **Laundry:** No. **Pay Phone:** Yes. **Rest Rooms and Showers:** Yes. **Fuel:** Yes, for boats. **Propane:** No. **Internal Roads:** Paved/gravel. **RV Service:** No. **Market:** No. **Restaurant:** No. **General Store:** Yes. **Vending:** Yes. **Swimming Pool:** No. **Playground:** Yes. **Activities:** Rowboat & canoe rentals.

Restrictions

Pets: Yes, w/ rabies vaccination. **Fires:** Allowed. **Alcoholic Beverages:** Allowed. **Vehicle Maximum Length:** 60 ft. **Other:** Ask on arrival.

To Get There

Burton Island State Park is accessible only by boat. Call for ferry information.

ST. ALBANS BAY

Knight Island State Park

P.O. Box 123, St. Albans Bay 05481. T: (802) 524-6353; www.state.vt.us/anr/fpr/parks/htm/knighti.html.

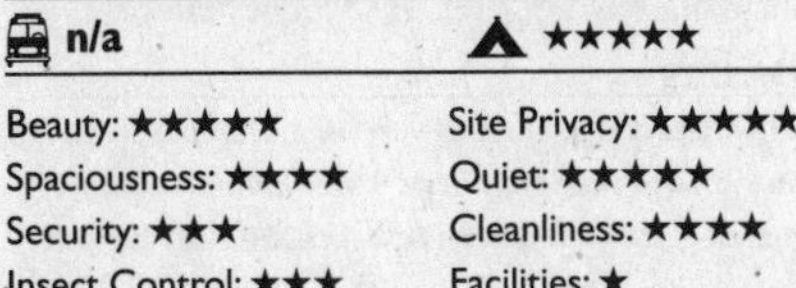

RV: n/a — Tent: ★★★★★

Beauty: ★★★★★ Site Privacy: ★★★★★
Spaciousness: ★★★★ Quiet: ★★★★★
Security: ★★★ Cleanliness: ★★★★
Insect Control: ★★★ Facilities: ★

It doesn't get much more remote than this, as you have to take a ferry to get here and once you're her you're in the middle of nowhere Of course, the basic appeal of Knight Island is solitude. There are absolutely no facilities, so you'll be completely roughing it, but the scenery might make it worth the extra effort. Each site has a private path to the shore—there's almost no need to see other people if that's what you're looking for. From the various trails that traverse the island, you get amazing views of both the Adirondacks and the Green Mountains. Don't go to Knight Island unless you're looking to get away from it all (except nature), but if that's what you want, this might be the best place in the state.

Basics

Operated By: State of Vermont. **Open:** Oct. 31–Labor Day. **Site Assignment:** Permit required. **Registration:** Island w/ caretaker. **Fee:** $12, 2 night min. **Parking:** At site.

Facilities

Number of RV Sites: 0. **Number of Tent-Only Sites:** 7. **Hookups:** None. **Each Site:** Fire ring. **Dump Station:** No. **Laundry:** No. **Pay Phone:** No. **Rest Rooms and Showers:** No. **Fuel:** No. **Propane:** No. **Internal Roads:** Paved/gravel. **RV Service:** No. **Market:** Hannaford Supermarket, Highgate Shopping Plaza, St. Albans, VT 05478. **Restaurant:** Bayside Pavillion, Lake Rd. St. Albans Bay, VT 05481. **General Store:** No. **Vending:** No. **Swimming Pool:** No. **Playground:** No. **Activities:** Fishing. **Additional Information:** Call ahead.

Restrictions

Pets: Yes, w/ rabies vaccination. **Fires:** Allowed. **Alcoholic Beverages:** Allowed. **Vehicle Maximum Length:** 60 ft. **Other:** Ask on arrival.

To Get There

Must take ferry from Burton Island

ST. JOHNSBURY

Moose River Campground

2870 Portland St., St. Johnsbury 05819. T: (802) 748-4334 (summer) or (802) 472-3139 (winter); F: (802) 748-3459 (summer) or (802) 472-6993 (winter); www.gocampingamerica.com/mooserivervt; mooservr@together.net.

RV: ★★★★ — Tent: ★★★

Beauty: ★★ Site Privacy: ★★★
Spaciousness: ★★ Quiet: ★★
Security: ★★★ Cleanliness: ★★★
Insect Control: ★★★ Facilities: ★★★

An adult campground, Moose River has a location that offers both positives and negatives. On the plus side, the campground is between the White and Green Mountains and convenient to the Connecticut River as well as the Moose River, where you can fish. The campground is actually located on a bend in the Moose River on a grassy patch. On the negative side, the sites is a little too close to Rte. 2, which can be noisy and detract from the natural atmosphere. Still, this is one of the few campgrounds that caters strictly to grownups with lots of planned activities. So those seeking such a park can usually ignore the traffic noise.

Basics

Operated By: Mary & Gary Lunderville. **Open:** May 1–Oct. 22. **Site Assignment:** Reservations accepted. **Registration:** At office. **Fee:** $15–$26. **Parking:** At site.

Facilities

Number of RV Sites: 42. **Number of Tent-Only Sites:** 8. **Hookups:** Water, electric, sewer. **Each Site:** Picnic table, fire ring. **Dump Station:** Yes. **Laundry:** No. **Pay Phone:** Yes. **Rest Rooms and Showers:** Yes. **Fuel:** No. **Propane:** Yes. **Internal Roads:** Compressed gravel. **RV Service:** No. **Market:** Shop 'n' Save, 129 Portland St., St. Johnsbury, VT 05819: Take a right onto Rte. 2. **Restaurant:** Anthony's Diner, 50 Railroad St., St. Johnsbury, VT 05819: Take a right onto Rte. 2 followed by a right onto Rte. 5. **General Store:** No. **Vending:** No. **Swimming Pool:** No. **Playground:** No. **Activities:** Lots of planned activities for grown-ups. **Nearby Attractions:** Golf course, Fairbanks Museum. **Additional Information:** Call ahead.

Restrictions

Pets: Allowed. **Fires:** Allowed. **Alcoholic Beverages:** Allowed. **Vehicle Maximum Length:** 50 ft. **Other:** No kids allowed.

To Get There

From I-93 take Exit 1, go north on Rte. 18, turn left onto Rte. 2, and follow it for 3 miles.

STOWE

Gold Brook Campground

P.O. Box 1028, Rte. 100, Stowe 05672. T: (802) 253-7683.

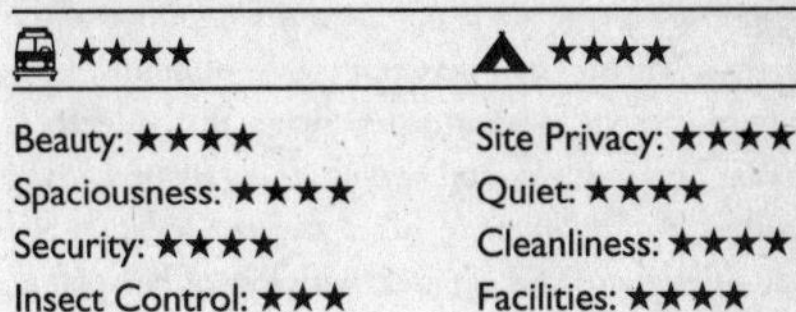

RV: ★★★★ — Tent: ★★★★

Beauty: ★★★★ Site Privacy: ★★★★
Spaciousness: ★★★★ Quiet: ★★★★
Security: ★★★★ Cleanliness: ★★★★
Insect Control: ★★★ Facilities: ★★★★

Ringed by two small rivers that offer excellent fishing, Gold Brook is the perfect campground for casual fishermen. Most sites touch the water, allowing you to cast your line while barely getting out of bed. Sites are shaded by trees, but there's a fair amount of open field space that's sometimes the scene of pick-up ballgames. Gold Brook does a heavy winter business and has a relationship with the nearby Nichols Lodge. In the winter, snowmobile rentals are available, as is hot breakfast at the lodge. There's also a lot of skiing—both downhill and cross country—easily accessible.

Basics

Operated By: John, Kay, & Mary Nichols. **Open:** Year-round. **Site Assignment:** Reservations recommended. **Registration:** At office. **Fee:** Starts at $18. **Parking:** At site.

Facilities

Number of RV Sites: 50. **Number of Tent-Only Sites:** 29. **Hookups:** Water, electric (30, 50), sewer. **Dump Station:** Yes. **Laundry:** Yes. **Pay Phone:** Yes. **Rest Rooms and Showers:** Yes. **Fuel:** No. **Propane:** Yes. **Internal Roads:** Paved/gravel. **RV Service:** No. **Market:** Gracie's Gourmutt Shop, 20 Main St., Stowe, VT 05672: Take a right onto Rte. 100, which becomes Rte. 108. Continue 1.5 mi. **Restaurant:** Swisspot Restaurant, 128 South Main St., Stowe, VT 05672: Take a right onto Rte. 100, which becomes Rte. 108. Continue 1.3 mi. **General Store:** Limited. **Vending:** Yes. **Swimming Pool:** Yes. **Playground:** Yes. **Other:** Rec hall. **Activities:** Swimming, hunting, fishing, hiking, skiing, snowmobiling. **Nearby Attractions:** Nichols Lodge.

Restrictions

Pets: Allowed. **Fires:** Allowed. **Alcoholic Beverages:** Allowed. **Vehicle Maximum Length:** 40 ft. **Other:** Ask on arrival.

To Get There

Follow Rte. 100 for 7.5 mi. north from Exit 10 off I-89.

STOWE

Smugglers' Notch State Park Campground

Box 7248 Mountain Rd., Stowe 05672. T: (802) 253-4014.

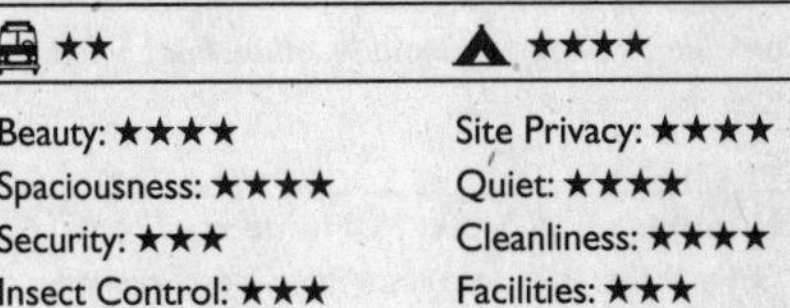

RV: ★★ — Tent: ★★★★

Beauty: ★★★★ Site Privacy: ★★★★
Spaciousness: ★★★★ Quiet: ★★★★
Security: ★★★ Cleanliness: ★★★★
Insect Control: ★★★ Facilities: ★★★

Dotted in between heavy woods, the sites here are fairly spectacular. Like all Vermont state parks, Smugglers' Notch offers very little in the way of amentities—you basically get a table, fireplace, and access to bathrooms and showers—but the natural opportunites are amazing. Even the entrance of the park, a narrow road between two mountains, visually primes visitors for experiencing this wilderness oasis. The campground makes an excellent starting point for all manner of hikes and the location is a state-designated nature area, with lots of rare plants, rock formations, and other natural phenomenons.

Basics

Operated By: State of Vermont. **Open:** May 15–Oct. 15. **Site Assignment:** Reservations recommended. **Registration:** At office. **Fee:** $12. **Parking:** At site.

Facilities

Number of RV Sites: 21. **Number of Tent-Only Sites:** 14. **Hookups:** None. **Each Site:** Picnic table, fireplace. **Dump Station:** Yes. **Laundry:** No. **Pay Phone:** No. **Rest Rooms and Showers:** Yes. **Fuel:** No. **Propane:** No. **Internal Roads:** Paved/gravel. **RV Service:** No. **Market:** Edelweiss Store, 2251 Mountain Rd., Stowe, VT 05672: Take a left onto Rte. 108. **Restaurant:** Backyard Tavern, Mountain Rd., Stowe, VT 05672: Take a left onto Rte. 108. **General Store:** Very limited. **Vending:** No. **Swimming Pool:** No. **Playground:** Yes. **Activities:** Hiking. **Nearby Attractions:** Shops in Stowe.

Restrictions

Pets: Allowed, on leash. **Fires:** Allowed. **Alcoholic Beverages:** Allowed. **Vehicle Maximum Length:** 60 ft. **Other:** Ask on arrival.

To Get There

From Stowe, follow Rte. 108 to the park entrance.

SWANTON

Champlain Valley Campground

600 Mcquam Shore Rd., Swanton 05458. T: (802) 524-5146.

RV: ★★★★ Tent: n/a

Beauty: ★★★★	Site Privacy: ★★★
Spaciousness: ★★★	Quiet: ★★★
Security: ★★★	Cleanliness: ★★★★
Insect Control: ★★★	Facilities: ★★★★

Like all of the Lake Champlain shoreline, this one has impressive views, both of the lake and of the woods around the campground. This one also offers views of Grand Isle, and it's surprisingly uncluttered for a campground that only caters to RVs. Perhaps that's because most of the campers here are staying for the season, which also makes reservations a must since there aren't that many sites available.

Basics

Operated By: Marc & Linda Bechard. **Open:** May 15–Oct. 15. **Site Assignment:** Reservations recommended. **Registration:** At office. **Fee:** Starts at $20. **Parking:** At site.

Facilities

Number of RV Sites: 79. **Number of Tent-Only Sites:** 0. **Hookups:** Water, electric, sewer. **Dump Station:** Yes. **Laundry:** Yes. **Pay Phone:** Yes. **Rest Rooms and Showers:** Yes. **Fuel:** No. **Propane:** Yes. **Internal Roads:** Paved/gravel. **RV Service:** No. **Market:** Cumberland Bay Market, 1544 Cumberland Head Rd., Plattsburgh, NY: Take a right onto Rte. 2 followed by a right onto Pearl St. & a left onto Bell Hill Rd., which becomes Grand Isle Ferry. Continue 4.8 mi. **Restaurant:** Grand Isle Ferry Dock Snackbar, 51 West Shore Rd., Grand Isle, VT 05458: Take a right onto Rte. 2 followed by a right onto Rte. 314 & follow it for 2.1 mi. **General Store:** No. **Vending:** No. **Swimming Pool:** No. **Playground:** Yes. **Other:** Rec hall. **Activities:** Fishing. **Nearby Attractions:** Lake Champlain. **Additional Information:** Call ahead.

Restrictions

Pets: Allowed. **Fires:** Allowed. **Alcoholic Beverages:** Allowed. **Vehicle Maximum Length:** 32. **Other:** Ask on arrival.

To Get There

On Rte. 36, go 5 mi. south of Swanton or 10 mi. north of St. Albans.

SWANTON

Lakewood Campground, Inc.

122 Champlain St., Swanton 05488. T: (802) 868-7270.

RV: ★★★★ Tent: ★★

Beauty: ★★★	Site Privacy: ★★★
Spaciousness: ★★★	Quiet: ★★★
Security: ★★★	Cleanliness: ★★★★
Insect Control: ★★★	Facilities: ★★★★

An enormous RV park, Lakewood is well-maintained. The whole area is manicured and surrounded by trees, with each site carefully alloted at least one tree for shade. The manufactured nature of the place lends a more urban, less wild quality, but otherwise it's a nice, large RV park. There's also the Missiquoi National Wildlife refuge nearby, so unspoiled nature is convenient if not actually within of the campground. The refuge has lots of marshes and can actually get a bit spooky at dusk, but offers tons of hiking and exploration opportunities.

Basics

Operated By: Origene & Gisele Robitaille. **Open:** May 1–Oct. 1. **Site Assignment:** Reservations accepted. **Registration:** At office. **Fee:** $15–$22. **Parking:** At site.

Facilities

Number of RV Sites: 281. **Number of Tent-Only Sites:** 0. **Hookups:** Water, electric, sewer. **Dump Station:** Yes. **Laundry:** Yes. **Pay Phone:** Yes. **Rest Rooms and Showers:** Yes. **Fuel:** No. **Propane:** Yes. **Internal Roads:** Paved. **RV Service:** No. **Market:** On site. **Restaurant:** Murphy's Country Kitchen, 9 Grand Ave., Swanton, VT 05488: Take a left onto Rte. 7 & follow it for 1.4 mi. **General Store:** Yes. **Vending:** Yes. **Swimming Pool:** Yes. **Playground:** Yes. **Other:** Rec hall, baseball field, horseshoes, tennis courts. **Activities:** Planned activities, boat rentals. **Nearby Attractions:** Golf course.

Restrictions

Pets: Allowed. **Fires:** Allowed. **Alcoholic Beverages:** Allowed. **Vehicle Maximum Length:** 35 ft. **Other:** Ask on arrival.

To Get There

Go 9 miles west of Swanton on Tabor Rd. (off Rte. 78).

WATERBURY

Little River State Park Campground

3444 Little River Rd., Waterbury 05676. T: (802) 244-7103.

RV: ★★ Tent: ★★★★

Beauty: ★★★★	Site Privacy: ★★★★
Spaciousness: ★★★★	Quiet: ★★★★
Security: ★★★	Cleanliness: ★★★★
Insect Control: ★★★	Facilities: ★★★

Located at the Waterbury Reservoir, the chief appeal here has to be the excellent waterfront area. The reservoir has its own beach and boat launch, though those areas are also open for day use, making them sometimes crowded. The sites themselves are very basic, but they're large and some are remote. If you're looking for privacy, reserve early, because the best sites go quickly. There's a lot of hiking nearby including day-long treks up Mount Mansfield.

Basics

Operated By: State of Vermont. **Open:** Varies, call ahead. **Site Assignment:** Reservations recommended. **Registration:** At office. **Fee:** $13. **Parking:** At site.

Facilities

Number of RV Sites: 100. **Number of Tent-Only Sites:** 20. **Hookups:** None. **Each Site:** Picnic table, fireplace. **Dump Station:** Yes. **Laundry:** No. **Pay Phone:** Yes. **Rest Rooms and Showers:** Yes. **Fuel:** No. **Propane:** No. **Internal Roads:** Paved/gravel. **RV Service:** No. **Market:** Champlain Farms, 1 North Main St., Waterbury, VT 05676: Take a left onto Little River Rd. followed by a left onto Rte. 2. **Restaurant:** Arvad's Spirits & Light Fare, 3 S. Main St., Waterbury, VT 05676: Take a left onto Little River Rd. followed by a left onto Rte. 2. **General Store:** Very limited. **Vending:** No. **Swimming Pool:** No. **Playground:** Yes. **Other:** Beach, boat ramp. **Activities:** Boating, swimming. **Nearby Attractions:** Ben & Jerry's Factory.

Restrictions

Pets: Yes, on leash. **Fires:** Allowed. **Alcoholic Beverages:** Allowed. **Vehicle Maximum Length:** None. **Other:** Ask on arrival.

To Get There

Take Rte. 2 to Little River Rd., turn and continue for 3.5 mi. to the campground entrance

WEST BARNET

Harvey's Lake Cabins & Campground

190 Camper's Ln., West Barnet 05821. T: (802) 633-2213; F: (802) 633-2339; harveys@together.net.

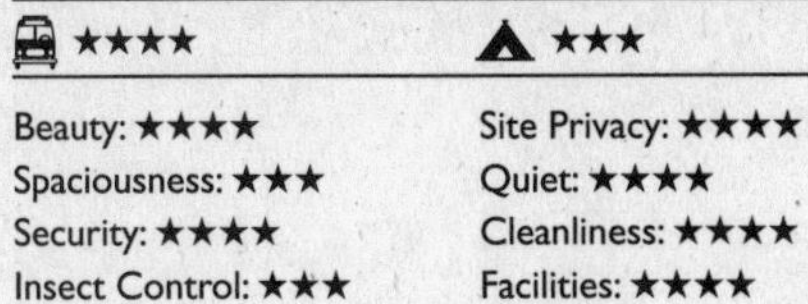

RV ★★★★ Tent ★★★

Beauty: ★★★★ Site Privacy: ★★★★
Spaciousness: ★★★ Quiet: ★★★★
Security: ★★★★ Cleanliness: ★★★★
Insect Control: ★★★ Facilities: ★★★★

Apparently, Jacques Cousteau took his first dive in Harvey's Lake, or at least that's how the locals tell it. Whether it's true or not, it's a beautiful body of water that's perfect for canoeing. You'll have to make reservations early if you want a lakefront campsite, as much of the frontage is taken up by cabins. But fortunately, the non-waterfront sites have plenty of charm. The sites are fairly small, but are surrounded by pine trees, making them private. The enormous lake has no public access, so unlike Lake Champlain it's very quiet, even during the busiest parts of summer.

Basics

Operated By: Marybeth Vereline. **Open:** May 1–Oct. 15. **Site Assignment:** Reservations recommended. **Registration:** At office. **Fee:** $18–$23. **Parking:** At site.

Facilities

Number of RV Sites: 31. **Number of Tent-Only Sites:** 12. **Hookups:** Water, electric, sewer. **Each Site:** Picnic table, fireplace, grill. **Dump Station:** Yes. **Laundry:** Yes. **Pay Phone:** Yes. **Rest Rooms and Showers:** Yes. **Fuel:** No. **Propane:** No. **Internal Roads:** Paved/gravel. **RV Service:** No. **Market:** Bayley Hazen Country Store, 24 Governer Maddocks Rd., Peacham, VT 05862. **Restaurant:** St. J Diner, Rte. 5, St. Johnsbury, VT 05819. **General Store:** No. **Vending:** Yes. **Swimming Pool:** Yes. **Playground:** Yes. **Other:** Rec hall, game room, horeshoes, pool table. **Activities:** Canoe, boat, & bike rentals. **Additional Information:** Call ahead.

Restrictions

Pets: Allowed. **Fires:** Allowed. **Alcoholic Beverages:** Allowed. **Vehicle Maximum Length:** 35 ft. **Other:** Ask on arrival.

To Get There

Take Exit 18 off I-91 and go 9 mi. from Danville on Rte. 2, then 9 mi. from Groton off Rte. 302. Go around a white church and over the bridge in West Barnet, then take the first dirt road on the right to the campground.

WEST DANVILLE

Injun Joe Court

P.O. Box 27, US Rte. 2, West Danville 05873. T: (802) 684-3430.

RV ★★ Tent n/a

Beauty: ★★★ Site Privacy: ★★★★
Spaciousness: ★★★ Quiet: ★★★
Security: ★★★ Cleanliness: ★★★
Insect Control: ★★★ Facilities: ★★

Primarily a cabin-based resort, Injun Joe Court has seven sites for fully self-contained RVs. Though the cabins themselves are nothing much to look at, the RV sites overlook Joe's Pond and there's a reonable number of hiking trails around. Still, this is likely a place to stop for a night, not the base for a long stay.

Basics

Operated By: Beth Perreault & family. **Open:** May 15–Oct. 15. **Site Assignment:** Reservations required. **Registration:** At office. **Fee:** Starts at $22. **Parking:** At site.

Facilities

Number of RV Sites: 7. **Number of Tent-Only Sites:** 0. **Hookups:** Water, electric, sewer. **Dump Station:** No. **Laundry:** No. **Pay Phone:** No. **Rest Rooms and Showers:** No. **Fuel:** No. **Propane:** No. **Internal Roads:** Paved/gravel. **RV Service:** No. **Market:** On site. **Restaurant:** On site. **General Store:** Yes. **Vending:** Yes. **Swimming Pool:** No. **Playground:** Yes. **Other:** Rowboats, paddleboats, canoes, private beach. **Activities:** No planned activities. **Nearby Attractions:** Trails. **Additional Information:** Call ahead.

Restrictions

Pets: Allowed. **Fires:** Allowed. **Alcoholic Beverages:** Allowed. **Vehicle Maximum Length:** 40 ft. **Other:** Ask on arrival.

To Get There

Ten mi. west of St. Johnsbury on US 2, the campground overlooks Joe's Pond.

WESTFIELD

Mill Brook Campground

P.O. Box 133, Westfield 05874. T: (802) 744-6673.

RV ★★★ Tent ★★★★

Beauty: ★★★★ Site Privacy: ★★★★
Spaciousness: ★★★ Quiet: ★★★★
Security: ★★★ Cleanliness: ★★★★
Insect Control: ★★★ Facilities: ★★★

A small and well laid out campground, Mill Brook is an excellent choice for both tent and RV campers. The campground offers large, open, grassy sites for RV campers along Mill Brook, which offers fishing and eventually leads to a waterfall. Tent campers get a lot more seclusion in wooded sites that are far enough away from the RVs to feel like you're at a tents-only campground. There are plenty of hiking trails for all ability levels nearby as well as bike paths.

Basics

Operated By: The Paxman family. **Open:** May 15–Sept. 15. **Site Assignment:** Reservations accepted. **Registration:** At office. **Fee:** $11.50–$15.50. **Parking:** At site.

Facilities

Number of RV Sites: 30. **Number of Tent-Only Sites:** 0. **Hookups:** Water, electric, sewer. **Each Site:** Fireplace, picnic table. **Dump Station:** Yes. **Laundry:** No. **Pay Phone:** Yes. **Rest Rooms and Showers:** Yes. **Fuel:** No. **Propane:** No. **Internal Roads:** Paved/gravel. **RV Service:** No. **Market:** Steve's Discount Center, 149 Main St., Westfield, VT 05874. **Restaurant:** Old Bobbin Mill, Rte. 100, Westfield, VT 05874. **General Store:** No. **Vending:** No. **Swimming Pool:** No. **Playground:** Yes. **Other:** Volleyball, horseshoes, badminton. **Activities:** Fishing, swimming. **Nearby Attractions:** Golf course. **Additional Information:** Call ahead.

Restrictions

Pets: Allowed. **Fires:** Allowed. **Alcoholic Beverages:** Allowed. **Vehicle Maximum Length:** 40 ft. **Other:** Ask on arrival.

To Get There

The campground entrance is on Rte. 100 in middle of the village of Westfield

WILMINGTON

Molly Stark State Park Campground

705 Hwy. 9 East, Wilmington 05363. T: (802) 464-5460.

RV ★★★ Tent ★★★★

Beauty: ★★★★ Site Privacy: ★★★★
Spaciousness: ★★★★ Quiet: ★★★★
Security: ★★★ Cleanliness: ★★★★
Insect Control: ★★★ Facilities: ★★★

A beautiful park with fairly limited camping facilities, Molly Stark offers quite a bit for those wanting to experience nature unadulterated. Because there are only a small number of sites, the campground never gets crowded and guests have to make their own fun. Much of the opportunity for that comes from the surrounding area, which offers a wide array of choices. There are open lawns for sports as well as forests for exploring. There are also trails up Mount Olga, which offer challenging, but manageable hiking. There's not much in the way of creature comforts here, but there's a lot to do for people looking for a heavy helping of the outdoors.

Basics

Operated By: State of Vermont. **Open:** May 15–Oct. 15. **Site Assignment:** Reservations accepted. **Registration:** At office. **Fee:** $11. **Parking:** At site.

Facilities

Number of RV Sites: 34. **Number of Tent-Only Sites:** 11. **Hookups:** None. **Each Site:** Fireplace, picnic table. **Dump Station:** Yes. **Laundry:** Nearby. **Pay Phone:** No. **Rest Rooms and Showers:** Yes. **Fuel:** No. **Propane:** No. **Internal Roads:** Paved/gravel. **RV Service:** No. **Market:** Shaw's, Rte. 9 Main St. Wilmington, VT 05363. **Restaurant:** Alonzo's Pasta & Grille, 10 West Main St., Wilmington, VT 05363. **General Store:** Nearby. **Vending:** No. **Swimming Pool:** No. **Playground:** Yes. **Other:** Volleyball courts, horseshoe pits. **Activities:** Hiking. **Nearby Attractions:** Mount Olga. **Additional Information:** Call ahead.

Restrictions

Pets: Allowed. **Fires:** Allowed. **Alcoholic Beverages:** Allowed. **Vehicle Maximum Length:** None. **Other:** Ask on arrival.

To Get There

Take Rte. 9 to the park entrance.

Virginia

Like Delaware and Maryland, Virginia is blessed with diverse terrain and a multitude of historical attractions. There's Shenandoah National Park and Skyline Drive in the west; Virginia Beach, Chesapeake Bay, and the three-site Colonial National Historical Park in the southeast; the culture-rich capital of Richmond; and historic areas like Arlington National Cemetery and Fredericksburg in the north. This is a state that has a little of everything for history buffs and outdoor enthusiasts alike.

The Historic Triangle in southeastern Virginia consists of three towns—Williamsburg, Jamestown, and Yorktown—linked by the 23-mile Colonial Parkway. **Williamsburg** has amusement parks **Busch Gardens** and **Water Country USA,** but it is **Colonial Williamsburg** that preserve's the city's 18th-century heritage. Colonial Williamsburg is a 173-acre reproduction of America's colonial capital—a historical theme park with about 600 restored or rebuilt structures occupied by townspeople in period dress. East of Williamsburg is the **Jamestown Settlement,** a living museum with costumed interpreters staffing buildings and ships. Your history lesson is not complete without venturing to **Yorktown,** where American and French troops under George Washington's command defeated Lord Cornwallis and his British forces in 1781.

Washington, D.C. certainly has enough attractions to keep you occupied for days, as does northern Virginia. From the nation's capital, **Arlington** is an ideal starting point. Here, you can explore **Arlington National Cemetery.** Other touring options include the **Newseum,** a 72,000-square-foot interactive facility dedicated to the history of the news; and the **Pentagon,** America's military headquarters.

In Fairfax County, George Washington's **Mt. Vernon** homestead sees more than 100,000 tourists each year. Washington's tomb is located here, as well as a small museum.

South of Fairfax County, **Fredericksburg** is a well-preserved Colonial town rich in Revolutionary War and Civil War heritage. The **Fredericksburg and Spotsylvania National Military Park** consists of sites related to four Civil War battles. Visitors centers in Chancellorsville and Fredericksburg, **Fredericksburg National Cemetery,** the **Stonewall Jackson Shrine,** and the four battlefields are points of interest. Nearby, the **Quantico Marine Corps Base** and **Marine Corps Air-Ground Museum** offer an overview of Marines history.

Richmond is easily one of America's most culturally and historically rich state capitals. The **State Capitol, Edgar Allan Poe Museum,** and **Richmond National Battlefield Park** are favorite attractions, as are the **Museum of the Confederacy** and the **White House of the Confederacy.** Presidents James Monroe and James Tyler, Confederate president Jefferson Davis, and more than 18,000 Confederate soldiers are among those buried at Richmond's **Hollywood Cemetery**. For modern excitement north of Richmond, **Paramount's Kings Dominion** has more than 100 rides, shows, and a water park.

Central and southern Virginia are primarily rural and adorned with pastoral farms and pleasant small towns. Perhaps the most famous estate in Virginia is **Monticello** in **Charlottesville.** Situated on a mountaintop, Monticello was designed and occupied by Thomas Jefferson, who started construction in 1771 and finished in 1809. Some historians believe that the **Berkeley Plantation** in **Charles City** is where the first Thanksgiving was celebrated in the New World in 1619. Attractions in **Petersburg** include the **Pamplin Park Civil War Site** and the 2,700-acre **Petersburg National Battlefield Park.** Union victories and Confederate failures in Petersburg led to Gen. Robert E. Lee's surrender to Gen. Ulysses S. Grant at the present-day **Appomattox Court House National Historic Park** in the village of **Appomattox.**

In southeast Virginia, Newport News, Norfolk, Hampton, and Virginia Beach are popular destinations in the Tidewater Peninsula. **Newport News** crown jewel is the **Mariners Museum,** which boasts a collection of more than 35,000 nautical artifacts. In **Norfolk,** guided bust tours are given at the **Norfolk Naval Base.** The **Virginia Air and Space Center** in **Hampton** is a museum and the official visitor center for the nearby **NASA Langley Research Center,** where guests can watch NASA engineers at work. With a three-mile boardwalk and 28 miles of beaches along the Atlantic Ocean and Chesapeake Bay, **Virginia Beach** is the state's finest resort area. **First Landing State Park** at Cape Henry has more than 2,700 acres of sand dunes, lagoons, and cypress trees.

Named one of the seven engineering wonders of the modern world, the **Chesapeake Bay Bridge and Tunnel** carries passengers from mainland Virginia to its eastern shore. The eastern shore sports several islands and villages, such as the Colonial-era **Accomac** and **Onancock.** Near the Maryland border, Assateague Island includes the **Chincoteague National Wildlife Refuge** and the **Assateague Island National Seashore.**

Shenandoah National Park is the highlight of western Virginia. The park is 80 miles long and features deep canyons, dense forests, majestic peaks. There are more than 200 species of birds here, as well as deer, bears, foxes, and bobcats. Campgrounds, hiking trails, and bridle trails are plentiful. The 105-mile-long **Skyline Drive** covers the entire length of Shenandoah National Park, starting at **Front Royal** to the north and connecting with the **Blue Ridge Parkway** to the south, with numerous overlooks along the way.

The following facilities accept payment in checks or cash only:

Peaks of Otter Campground, Bedford

Campground Profiles

ABINGDON

Riverside Campground

18496 N. Fork River Rd., Abingdon 24210.
T: (540) 628-5333; rverside@preferred.com.

RV ★★★★ Tent ★★★★

Beauty: ★★★★	Site Privacy: ★★
Spaciousness: ★★★	Quiet: ★★★★
Security: ★★★★★	Cleanliness: ★★★★
Insect Control: ★★★★	Facilities: ★★★★

Nestled in the Appalachian Mountains of southwest Virginia, Riverside Campground is located hear historic Abingdon along the north fork of the Holston River. Riverside has 133 level grassy and semi-wooded sites. These sites are clean and well-kept, but most offer little privacy. For families, the campground has a swimming pool, a children's pool, and a sand volleyball court. Bass fishing in the Holston River is lively, as is Abingdon itself. Nearby, the Virginia Creeper Trail is a 34.3-mile-long multiple-use trail extending from Abingdon to the Virginia–North Carolina line. Walkers, bicyclers, and horses are welcome on the trail (but not motorized vehicles). The Virginia Creeper Trail roots started as a Native American footpath. Later, pioneers like Daniel Boone used the trail, which is named for the early steam locomotives that struggled slowly up the railroad's steep grades. The Virginia Creeper engine is now showcased at the Abingdon Trailhead.

BASICS

Operated By: Private operator. **Open:** Apr. 1–Nov. 1. **Site Assignment:** Reservations and walk-ins accepted. **Registration:** At campground office. **Fee:** $17. VISA, MC). **Parking:** At designated spot.

FACILITIES

Number of RV Sites: 131. **Number of Tent-Only Sites:** 30. **Hookups:** Electric (20, 30 amps), water, phone, 96 full hookups. **Each Site:** Fire ring, picnic table. **Dump Station:** Yes. **Laundry:** Yes. **Pay Phone:** Yes. **Rest Rooms and Showers:** Yes. **Fuel:** No. **Propane:** Yes. **Internal Roads:** Gravel, in good condition. **RV Service:** No. **Market:** Within 5 mi. **Restaurant:** Within 5 mi. **General Store:** Yes. **Vending:** Yes. **Playground:** Yes. **Other:** Children's pool. **Activities:** Rec hall, game room, swimming, wading pool, river swimming, stream fishing, basketball, horseshoes, volleyball, planned activities on weekends. **Nearby Attractions:** Historic Abingdon, Virginia Creeper National Recreation Trail, White's Mill, Mt. Rogers National Recreation Area, Appalachian Trail, Barter Theater. **Additional Information:** Abingdon CVB, (800) 435-3440, www.abingdon.com.

RESTRICTIONS

Pets: On leash only. **Fires:** At site. **Alcoholic Beverages:** No alcohol permitted. **Vehicle Maximum Length:** None. **Other:** None.

TO GET THERE

From I-81, take Exit 14 and go 0.5 mi. west on Hwy. 140N, 1 mi. east on Hwy. 11, 7 mi. north on US 19, and 2 mi. east on Hwy. 611. Entrance is on the right.

APPOMATTOX

Holliday Lake State Park

Rte. 2 Box 622, Appomattox 24522. T: (804) 248-6308; www.dcr.state.va.us/parks; resvs@dcr.state.va.us.

RV ★★★★ Tent ★★★★

Beauty: ★★★★	Site Privacy: ★★★
Spaciousness: ★★★	Quiet: ★★★
Security: ★★★	Cleanliness: ★★★★
Insect Control: ★★★	Facilities: ★★★★

Twelve miles from the Appomattox Court House National Historic Park, Holliday Lake State Park boasts a 150-acre lake stocked with bass, northern pike, crappie, sunfish, and channel catfish. It also has a 30-site campground connected to the lake by the Saunders Creek Trail. The mostly open sites are level and spacious. Swimming and boating are popular activities at Holliday Lake, and boat rentals are available. The new 12-mile Carter Taylor loop trail starts across from the campground, which is near the 19,710-acre Appomattox-Buckingham State Forest. Gen. Robert E. Lee's weary and battered army passed within 1.5 miles of the present park site on its way to the Civil War's final battles. Appomattox National Court House Historic Park consists of 1,700 acres of rolling hills. The reconstructed court house serves as the park's visitor center and is located on US 24 two miles northeast of town.

BASICS

Operated By: State of Virginia. **Open:** Mar.–Dec. **Site Assignment:** Reservations accepted (no refund within 1 week of reserved date), walk-ins accepted. **Registration:** At campground office. **Fee:** $15–$18 (VISA, MC). **Parking:** At site only.

FACILITIES

Number of RV Sites: 18. **Number of Tent-Only Sites:** 12. **Hookups:** Electric. **Each Site:** Picnic table, grill, lantern pole. **Dump Station:** Yes. **Laundry:** No. **Pay Phone:** Yes. **Rest Rooms and Showers:** Yes. **Fuel:** No. **Propane:** No. **Internal Roads:** Gravel, in good condition. **RV Service:** No. **Market:** Within 12 mi. **Restaurant:** Within 10 mi. **General Store:** No. **Vending:** Yes. **Playground:** Yes. **Other:** Visitors center. **Activities:** Lake swimming, boating, hiking trails, lake fishing, boat rentals, volleyball. **Nearby Attractions:** Appomattox Courthouse National Historic Park, Booker T. Washington Monument, Monticello, Richmond, Edgar Allan Poe Museum, Museum and White House of the Confederacy. **Additional Information:** Richmond CVB, (800) 370-9004, www.richmondva.org.

RESTRICTIONS

Pets: On leash only. **Fires:** At site only. **Alcoholic Beverages:** No alcohol permitted. **Vehicle Maximum Length:** None. **Other:** 14 day max. stay in 30-day period.

TO GET THERE

From Appomattox, go 9 mi. east on Hwy. 24 and 6 mi. southeast on Hwy. 626/692. Follow signs to park entrance.

ASHLAND

Americamps Richmond North

11322 Air Park Rd., Ashland 23005. T: (800) 628-2802; www.americamps.com; americamps@aol.com.

RV ★★★★ Tent ★★★★

Beauty: ★★★★	Site Privacy: ★
Spaciousness: ★★	Quiet: ★★
Security: ★★★★	Cleanliness: ★★★★
Insect Control: ★★★★	Facilities: ★★★★

Located eight miles north of Richmond on I-95, Americamps Richmond North—a Best Holiday Trav-L-Park—bills itself as the closest full-service campground to Richmond. The campground has 146 well-maintained sites, including 98 full hookups and 32 pull-throughs. Americamps has a

400-seat pavilion for special events. With basic amenities like a swimming pool, a game room, a playground and a volleyball court (and its proximity to I-95) Though there is nothing spectacular about this campground, Americamps is ideal for overnight stays during a long journey down the interstate. Of course, it's also a central base for attractions in Richmond, like the Richmond battlefield site, the Edgar Allan Poe Museum, Paramount's Kings Dominion, and the White House of the Confederacy, where Gen. Robert E. Lee's surrender sword is among the exhibits.

Basics

Operated By: Americamps. **Open:** All year. **Site Assignment:** Reservations recommended, walk-ins accepted. **Registration:** At campground store. **Fee:** $21–$28 (VISA, MC, AE, D). **Parking:** At site.

Facilities

Number of RV Sites: 136. **Number of Tent-Only Sites:** 10. **Hookups:** Electric (20, 30, 50 amps), phone, water, 98 full hookups. **Each Site:** Fire ring, picnic table. **Dump Station:** Yes. **Laundry:** Yes. **Pay Phone:** Yes. **Rest Rooms and Showers:** Yes. **Fuel:** No. **Propane:** Yes. **Internal Roads:** Gravel and paved, in good condition. **RV Service:** No. **Market:** Within 2 mi. **Restaurant:** Within 2 mi. **General Store:** Yes. **Vending:** Yes. **Playground:** Yes. **Other:** 400-seat pavilion. **Activities:** Rec area, game room, swimming, basketball, badminton, horseshoes, volleyball. **Nearby Attractions:** Kings Dominion, Edgar Allan Poe Museum, White House of the Confederacy, Virginia State Capitol, Virginia State Fairgrounds, Virginia Museum of Fine Arts, Richmond National Battlefield Park, Richmond International Raceway. **Additional Information:** Richmond CVB, (800) 370-9004, www.richmondva.org.

Restrictions

Pets: On leash only. **Fires:** At site. **Alcoholic Beverages:** At site. **Vehicle Maximum Length:** None. **Other:** None.

To Get There

From I-95, take Exit 89 and go 0.1 mi. east on Hwy. 802 and 1 mi. south on Air Park Rd. Entrance is on the left.

BASSETT

Fairy Stone State Park

907 Fairy Stone Lake Dr., Stuart 24171-9588. T: (540) 930-2424 or (800) 933-PARK; www.dcr.state.va.us/parks; resvs@dcr.state.va.us.

RV ★★★ Tent ★★★

Beauty: ★★★	Site Privacy: ★★★
Spaciousness: ★★★	Quiet: ★★★
Security: ★★★★★	Cleanliness: ★★★★
Insect Control: ★★★	Facilities: ★★★

Fairy stones are brown staurolite, a combination of silica, iron, and aluminum. Together, these minerals crystallize in twin form, accounting for the crosslike structure. These stones are also found in the mountains of North Carolina and in Switzerland, but nowhere else in the world are they found in such abundance and shaped so nearly like crosses as in the vicinity of Fairy Stone State Park. Fairy Stone's campground has 51 sites, all which are shaded by a pine grove and scattered oaks. The best place to search for the fairy stones is within a 2.5-mile drive from the park. At Haynes Store, an old gas station on US 57, a sign leads visitors to a streambed where the crosses can be collected. Campers at Fairy Stone aren't limited to searching for rocks. The park consists of 4,868 acres, including 168-acre Fairy Stone Lake, where fishing, swimming, and boating are options.

Basics

Operated By: State of Virginia. **Open:** Mar.–Dec. 1. **Site Assignment:** Reservations and walk-ins accepted. **Registration:** At campground office. **Fee:** $15–$18, VISA, MC). **Parking:** At site.

Facilities

Number of RV Sites: 50. **Number of Tent-Only Sites:** None. **Hookups:** Electric (15 amps). **Each Site:** Fire ring, picnic table. **Dump Station:** Yes. **Laundry:** No. **Pay Phone:** Yes. **Rest Rooms and Showers:** Yes. **Fuel:** No. **Propane:** No. **Internal Roads:** Gravel, in good condition. **RV Service:** No. **Market:** Within 5 mi. **Restaurant:** Within 5 mi. **General Store:** Yes. **Vending:** Yes. **Playground:** No. **Other:** Lodge and cabins. **Activities:** Lake swimming, boating, lake fishing, canoeing, boat rentals, hiking trails. **Nearby Attractions:** Blue Ridge Parkway, Philpott Lake, Virginia Museum of Natural History, J.E.B. Stuart Birthplace, covered bridges. **Additional Information:** Roanoke Valley CVB, (800) 635-5535, www.visitroanokeva.com.

Restrictions

Pets: On leash only. **Fires:** At site. **Alcoholic Beverages:** No alcohol permitted. **Vehicle Maximum Length:** 30 ft. **Other:** 14-day stay limit in 30-day period.

To Get There

From I-81, take I-581 to US 220, turn right onto US 57 and right onto SR 346.

BEDFORD

Peaks of Otter Campground

Blue Ridge Parkway—Rte. 2 Box 163, Bedford 24523. T: (540) 586-4357.

RV ★★★ Tent ★★★★

Beauty: ★★★★	Site Privacy: ★★★
Spaciousness: ★★★	Quiet: ★★★★
Security: ★★★	Cleanliness: ★★★★
Insect Control: ★★★	Facilities: ★★★

Located near Milepost 86 of the 470-mile-long Blue Ridge Parkway, Peaks of Otter Campground is across the road from Peaks of Otter Lodge and Abbott Lake. The campground is nestled in the woods on the flanks of Sharp Top Mountain, which rises to 3,875 feet. There are 46 RV sites, but no electric or water hookups. A 1.5-mile trail leads to the top of Sharp Top; if you don't want to hike, bus rides to the top are available near the visitors center. You can also climb to the summit of 4,001-foot-high Flat Top Mountain via a 4.4-mile-long trail. At the Peaks of Otter Visitors Center at Milepost 86 of the Blue Ridge Parkway, you can see a living history demonstration on weekends at the Johnson Farm, a homestead dating back to the 1800s.

Basics

Operated By: National Park Service. **Open:** May 1–Oct. 31. **Site Assignment:** First-come, first-served. **Registration:** At campground store. **Fee:** $12 (cash only). **Parking:** At site.

Facilities

Number of RV Sites: 46. **Number of Tent-Only Sites:** 98. **Hookups:** None. **Each Site:** Grill, picnic table, and lantern pole. **Dump Station:** Yes. **Laundry:** No. **Pay Phone:** Yes. **Rest Rooms and Showers:** Rest rooms only, no showers. **Fuel:** No. **Propane:** No. **Internal Roads:** Paved, in good condition. **RV Service:** No. **Market:** Within 10 mi. **Restaurant:** Within 10 mi. **General Store:** Yes. **Vending:** Yes. **Playground:** No. **Other:** Peaks of Otter Lodge, Abbott Lake. **Activities:** Hiking trails, fishing. **Nearby Attractions:** Blue Ridge Parkway, Appalachian Trail, Booker T. Washington National Monument, Natural Bridge of Virginia. **Additional Information:** Roanoke Valley CVB, (800) 635-5535, www.visitroanokeva.com.

Restrictions

Pets: On leash only. **Fires:** At site. **Alcoholic Beverages:** At site. **Vehicle Maximum Length:** 30 ft. **Other:** Quiet hours 10 p.m.–6 a.m.

To Get There

Take the Blue Ridge Parkway to Milepost 86 and go 0.25 mi. south on Hwy. 43 to campground entrance.

BIG ISLAND

Wildwood Campground

6252 Elon Rd., Monroe 24574. T: (804) 299-5228; www.wildwoodcampground.com; wildwoodcamp@cs.com.

RV ★★★★ Tent ★★★★

Beauty: ★★★★	Site Privacy: ★★★
Spaciousness: ★★★	Quiet: ★★★★
Security: ★★★★	Cleanliness: ★★★★
Insect Control: ★★★★	Facilities: ★★★★

Surrounded by the Blue Ridge Mountains near Big Island, Wildwood Campground has 75 wooded sites for tents and RVs, including 40 pull-throughs. The area around Wildwood's stocked fishing lake is especially scenic when fall colors are their most vibrant. Wildwood has a network of hiking trails on its grounds. Natural Bridge, though, is what lures many Wildwood campers. Situated between the Blue Ridge and Appalachian Mountains, Natural Bridge is the site of Natural Bridge Cavern and the Natural Bridge of Virginia. The cavern is 34 stories below the earth's surface. Beware—the tour can be strenuous. Spanning 90 feet, the Natural Bridge of Virginia is regarded as one of the seven natural wonders of the world. If you're not weary from exploring the area's natural sites, you can visit the Natural Bridge Wax Museum, where more than 125 life-size replicas depict Native American folklore.

Basics

Operated By: Brian, Denise, and Nick Hess.

Open: All year. **Site Assignment:** Reservations accepted (7-day notice required for cancellations), walk-ins accepted. **Registration:** At campground office. **Fee:** $18–$20 (VISA, MC). **Parking:** At designated spot.

Facilities

Number of RV Sites: 67. **Number of Tent-Only Sites:** 8. **Hookups:** Electric (20, 30, 50 amps), phone, water, 27 full hookups. **Each Site:** Fire ring, picnic table. **Dump Station:** Yes. **Laundry:** Yes. **Pay Phone:** Yes. **Rest Rooms and Showers:** Yes. **Fuel:** No. **Propane:** Yes. **Internal Roads:** Gravel, in good condition. **RV Service:** No. **Market:** Within 8 mi. **Restaurant:** Within 8 mi. **General Store:** Yes. **Vending:** Yes. **Playground:** Yes. **Other:** Circus train rides. **Activities:** Rec room, game room, swimming, pond fishing, basketball, shuffleboard, badminton, horseshoes, hiking trails, volleyball. **Nearby Attractions:** Blue Ridge Parkway, Peaks of Otter, Natural Bridge of Virginia, Appalachian Trail, James River, Thomas Jefferson's Poplar Forest, Historic Appomattox, Lynchburg, Lexington Caverns. **Additional Information:** Roanoke Valley CVB, (800) 635-5535, www.visitroanokeva.com.

Restrictions

Pets: On leash only. **Fires:** At site. **Alcoholic Beverages:** At site. **Vehicle Maximum Length:** None. **Other:** None.

To Get There

From Blue Ridge Parkway, go 1 mi. east on Hwy. 130. Entrance is on the left.

BLUEFIELD

Richwood Golf Club and Campground

Rte. 2 Box 109, Bluefield 24605. T: (540) 322-4575; F: (540) 326-1814; www.richwoodgolfandcamp.com; richwood@netlinkcorp.com.

RV ★★★★ Tent ★★★★

Beauty: ★★★	Site Privacy: ★★
Spaciousness: ★★	Quiet: ★★★
Security: ★★★★	Cleanliness: ★★★★
Insect Control: ★★★★	Facilities: ★★★

Located in the Appalachian Mountains and straddling the borders of Virginia and West Virginia, Bluefield is the home of Richwood Golf Club and Campground. Founded in 1968, Richwood offers 18 sites that accommodate pull-throughs. The campground has a game room and hiking trails, but the main draw here is the adjacent 9-hole, par 35 golf course situated on 52 acres of former farmland. Even if you don't drive the ball onto the fairway, you have a beautiful view of the mountains to minimize your anger. Mayflower Seafood Restaurant is on Richwood's premises. Pipestem State Park is a short drive from Richwood. In Bluefield, the border of Virginia and West Virginia is defined by East River Mountain, which peaks at 3,400 ft.—a breathtaking site from Richwood and anywhere in Bluefield.

Basics

Operated By: Private operator. **Open:** All year. **Site Assignment:** Reservations and walk-ins accepted. **Registration:** At campground office. **Fee:** $15 (VISA, MC, D). **Parking:** At designated spot.

Facilities

Number of RV Sites: 39. **Number of Tent-Only Sites:** None. **Hookups:** Electric (15, 30, 50 amps), phone, water, sewer. **Each Site:** Picnic table. **Dump Station:** Yes. **Laundry:** Yes. **Pay Phone:** Yes. **Rest Rooms and Showers:** Yes. **Fuel:** No. **Propane:** No. **Internal Roads:** Paved, in good condition. **RV Service:** No. **Market:** Within 3 mi. **Restaurant:** On premises. **General Store:** Yes. **Vending:** Yes. **Playground:** No. **Other:** 9-hole golf course. **Activities:** Golf, putting green, hiking trails, game room. **Nearby Attractions:** Pipestem State Park, minor league baseball, Bluefield, Princeton. **Additional Information:** Mercer County Convention and Visitors Bureau, (800) 221-3206, www.mccvb.com.

Restrictions

Pets: On leash only. **Fires:** At site. **Alcoholic Beverages:** At site. **Vehicle Maximum Length:** None. **Other:** None.

To Get There

From I-77, go 2 mi. north on US 52, 7 mi. west on US 460, and 0.25 mi. north on Hockman Pike. Entrance is on the left.

BOWLING GREEN

KOA—Hidden Acres

P.O. Box 1250, Bowling Green 22427. T: (800) 562-2482 or (804) 633-7592; www.koa.com; gsbakb@bealenet.com.

RV ★★★★ Tent ★★★★

Beauty: ★★★	Site Privacy: ★★★
Spaciousness: ★★★	Quiet: ★★★★
Security: ★★★	Cleanliness: ★★★★
Insect Control: ★★★★	Facilities: ★★★★

Located near Bowling Green in northeast Virginia, KOA—Hidden Acres has 120 open and wooded sites in a setting near the roller coasters and thrill rides of Paramount's King's Dominion. Children have several options for entertainment, including the Krazy Kritter Park and Kids Water Works. Paddle boats are available for rent, and Hidden Acres has a stocked fishing pond. Fredericksburg, which was George Washington's hometown, is a short drive from Hidden Acres. The area has four Civil War battlefields at Fredericksburg and Spotsylvania Military Park, a historic district, and several antique shops. Richmond is an ideal day trip for Hidden Acres campers. In addition to King's Dominion, the city has several attractions, including the White House of the Confederacy. For campers who can't get enough thrills, Hidden Acres offers special packages in conjunction with King's Dominion.

Basics

Operated By: KOA. **Open:** All year. **Site Assignment:** Reservations and walk-ins accepted. **Registration:** At campground office. **Fee:** $25–$39, VISA, MC, AE, D). **Parking:** At site.

Facilities

Number of RV Sites: 100. **Number of Tent-Only Sites:** 26. **Hookups:** Electric (20, 30 amps), water, 37 full hookups. **Each Site:** Fire ring, picnic table. **Dump Station:** Yes. **Laundry:** Yes. **Pay Phone:** Yes. **Rest Rooms and Showers:** Yes. **Fuel:** No. **Propane:** Yes. **Internal Roads:** Gravel, in good condition. **RV Service:** No. **Market:** Within 3 mi. **Restaurant:** Within 7 mi. **General Store:** Yes. **Vending:** Yes. **Playground:** Yes. **Other:** Krazy Kritter Park. **Activities:** Rec hall, game room, swimming, boat rentals, pond fishing, mini-golf, shuffleboard, planned activities on weekends, badminton, sports field, hiking trails, volleyball, horseshoes. **Nearby Attractions:** Paramount's Kings Dominion, General Lee's Stratford Hall, Fredericksburg battlefields, Richmond, Port Royal, Monticello. **Additional Information:** Richmond CVB, (800) 370-9004, www.richmondva.org.

Restrictions

Pets: On leash only. **Fires:** At site. **Alcoholic Beverages:** At site. **Vehicle Maximum Length:** None.

To Get There

From I-95, take Exit 104 and go 11 mi. northeast on SR 207 and 2 mi. south on SR 2/US 301. Entrance is on the left.

BRACEY

Americamps—Lake Gaston

9 Lakeside Ln., Bracey 23919. T: (804) 636-2668; www.americampslakegaston.com; acamp@buggs.net.

RV ★★★★ Tent ★★★★

Beauty: ★★★★	Site Privacy: ★★★
Spaciousness: ★★★	Quiet: ★★★
Security: ★★★★★	Cleanliness: ★★★★
Insect Control: ★★★★	Facilities: ★★★★

The area around Bracey, where Americamps—Lake Gaston is located, is near acres and acres of water. To the west lies John H. Kerr Reservoir, and Lake Gaston is even closer. Lake Gaston is 35 miles long and features 350 miles of scenic shoreline wandering from Virginia into North Carolina. Fishing, boating, swimming, and hiking are among the activities here. Anglers will find Lake Gaston fishing excellent year-round for bass, northern pike, rock, crappie, walleye, and catfish. Set in the woods on the lake's north shore, Americamps—Lake Gaston is a 140-acre complex with 245 shaded sites, including 20 pull-throughs. A dip in the 200,000-gallon swimming pool is refreshing during the hot summer; there is also a children's pool. An 18-hole mini-golf course, a recreational pavilion with indoor games and pool tables, and a dance and barbecue pavilion are other popular facilities.

Basics

Operated By: Jack and Barbara Stewart. **Open:** All year. **Site Assignment:** Reservations and walk-ins accepted. **Registration:** At campground office. **Fee:** $20–$22 (VISA, MC). **Parking:** At designated spot.

Facilities

Number of RV Sites: 245. **Number of Tent-Only Sites:** None. **Hookups:** Electric (20, 30 amps), water, 60 full hookups. **Each Site:** Fireplace, picnic table. **Dump Station:** Yes. **Laundry:** Yes. **Pay Phone:** Yes. **Rest Rooms and Showers:** Yes. **Fuel:** No. **Propane:** Yes. **Internal Roads:** Gravel and paved, in good condition. **RV Service:** No. **Market:** Within 5 mi. **Restaurant:** Within 5 mi. **General Store:** Yes. **Vending:** Yes. **Playground:** Yes. **Other:** Lake Gaston. **Activities:** Rec hall, game room, swimming, wading pool, boating, canoeing, kayaking, lake fishing, mini-golf, basketball, planned activities on weekends, sports field, horseshoes, volleyball. **Nearby Attractions:** Appomattox Court House National Historic Park, Booker T. Washington National Monument, John H. Kerr Reservoir. **Additional Information:** Virginia Tourism Corp., (800) 371-8164, www.virginia.org.

Restrictions

Pets: On leash only. **Fires:** At site. **Alcoholic Beverages:** At site. **Vehicle Maximum Length:** None. **Other:** None.

To Get There

From I-85, take Exit 4 and go 5 mi. east on Hwy. 903. Entrance is on the right.

BUCHANAN

A Wonderful Life Campground

1164 Middle Creek Rd., Buchanan 24066.
T: (540) 254-2176; wonderful24@juno.com.

RV ★★★★ Tent ★★★★

Beauty: ★★★★ Site Privacy: ★★★
Spaciousness: ★★★ Quiet: ★★★★
Security: ★★★ Cleanliness: ★★★★
Insect Control: ★★★★ Facilities: ★★★★

A Wonderful Life Campground near Buchanan in western Virginia has a swimming pool and a 100-foot double-flume water slide, a mini-golf course, a stocked fishing pond, and paddle boat rentals. The sites are semi-wooded, and there are 12 pull-throughs. Nearby is the Appalachian Trail, located in the George Washington and Jefferson National Forests, where hiking and backpacking are king. Dixie Caverns is a short drive from A Wonderful Life. The tour travels up into the mountain to see the cathedral room before venturing underground to marvel at the famous wedding bell and other breathtaking formations. Of course, don't forget to visit the pottery shop before leaving.

Basics

Operated By: Herbert and Debra Worner. **Open:** All year. **Site Assignment:** Reservations and walk-ins accepted. **Registration:** At campground office. **Fee:** $25–$27 (VISA, MC). **Parking:** At site.

Facilities

Number of RV Sites: 120. **Number of Tent-Only Sites:** 18. **Hookups:** Electric (20, 30 amps), phone, water, 20 full hookups. **Each Site:** Fire ring, picnic table. **Dump Station:** Yes. **Laundry:** Yes. **Pay Phone:** Yes. **Rest Rooms and Showers:** Yes. **Fuel:** No. **Propane:** Yes. **Internal Roads:** Gravel and paved, in good condition. **RV Service:** No. **Market:** Within 10 mi. **Restaurant:** Within 10 mi. **General Store:** Yes. **Vending:** Yes. **Playground:** Yes. **Other:** 100-foot double-flume water slide. **Activities:** Swimming, rec hall, game room, pond swimming, boat rentals, pond and stream fishing, mini-golf, basketball, planned activities, movies, badminton, horseshoes, volleyball. **Nearby Attractions:** Appalachian Trail, Blue Ridge Parkway, Lee Chapel and Museum, Stonewall Jackson Home, James River, Natural Bridge of Virginia. **Additional Information:** Roanoke Valley CVB, (800) 635-5535, www.visitroanokeva.com.

Restrictions

Pets: On leash only. **Fires:** At site. **Alcoholic Beverages:** At site. **Vehicle Maximum Length:** 48 ft. **Other:** None.

To Get There

From I-81, take Exit 168 and go 5 mi. east on Hwy. 614 and 1 mi. north on CR 618. Entrance is at the end.

CENTREVILLE

Bull Run Regional Park

7700 Bull Run Dr., Centreville 22020. T: (703) 631-0550; F: (703) 273-0905; www.nvpra.org; info@nvrpa.org.

RV ★★★★ Tent ★★★★

Beauty: ★★★ Site Privacy: ★★
Spaciousness: ★★★ Quiet: ★★★
Security: ★★★★ Cleanliness: ★★★★
Insect Control: ★★★★ Facilities: ★★★★

Bull Run Regional Park is located 27 miles west of Washington, DC, but it is better known for its proximity to nearby Manassas National Battlefield Park, where two Civil War battles were fought. The heavily wooded campground, situated in the middle of the 1,500-acre park, offers spacious and level sites. Thirty miles of hiking trails and 20 miles of horseback-riding trails adorn the 4,500 acres of nearby Manassas Battlefield. Civil War enthusiasts will treasure the mile-long, self-guided walking tour of the First Manassas Battlefield. Signs and audio messages describe the scenes of this battle between Confederate and Union troops on July 21, 1861. Confederate forces prevailed, and Gen. Thomas J. Jackson earned the nickname "Stonewall." The town of Manassas is a worthwhile stop. Its visitor center is located in a refurbished train depot, where tours of Old Town Manassas begin.

Basics

Operated By: Northern Virginia Regional Park Authority. **Open:** Mar. 6–Nov. 18. **Site Assignment:** First-come, first-served. **Registration:** At campground office. **Fee:** $5 entry fee for 1st 9 people, plus $13–$16 per night (VISA, MC). **Parking:** At site.

Facilities

Number of RV Sites: 100. **Number of Tent-Only Sites:** 50. **Hookups:** Electric (15, 20, 30 amps). **Each Site:** Fire ring, picnic table. **Dump Station:** Yes. **Laundry:** Yes. **Pay Phone:** Yes. **Rest Rooms and Showers:** Yes. **Fuel:** No. **Propane:** No. **Internal Roads:** Paved, in good condition. **RV Service:** No. **Market:** Within 3 mi. **Restaurant:** Within 3 mi. **General Store:** Yes. **Vending:** Yes. **Playground:** Yes. **Other:** None. **Activities:** Swimming, wading pool, stream fishing, mini-golf, horseback riding, hiking trails, sports field, volleyball, frisbee golf, soccer. **Nearby Attractions:** Manassas National Battlefield Park, Washington, DC **Additional Information:** Prince William Co. Conference and Visitors Bureau, (703) 792-4254, www.visitpwc.com.

Restrictions

Pets: On leash only. **Fires:** At site. **Alcoholic Beverages:** No alcohol permitted. **Vehicle Maximum Length:** 45 ft. **Other:** 7-day max. stay.

To Get There

From I-66, take Centreville exit and go 3 mi. west on US 29. Entrance is on the left.

CHARLOTTESVILLE

KOA—Charlottesville

3825 Red Hill Rd., Charlottesville 22903.
T: (800) KOA-1743 or (804) 296-9881; www.koa.com; koakamp@yahoo.com.

RV ★★★★ Tent ★★★★

Beauty: ★★★ Site Privacy: ★★
Spaciousness: ★★ Quiet: ★★★★
Security: ★★★★ Cleanliness: ★★★★
Insect Control: ★★★★ Facilities: ★★★

KOA—Charlottesville is near Monticello, the home of Thomas Jefferson; Montpelier, the home of James and Dolly Madison; and Ash Lawn, the home of James Monroe. Those sites are interesting, but equally intriguing is Walton's Mountain Museum, the former home of John Walton. Yes, there actually is a Walton's Mountain. KOA—Charlottesville offers 71 wooded sites, including 18 pull-throughs. There is a swimming pool and a fishing lake. James River is a short drive away; fishing, tubing, and canoeing are among the activities there. This campground is ideal for families looking for a base as they explore the area attractions. Luray Caverns, open since 1878, offers one-hour guided tours. Should you prefer to remain in your car, the Skyline Drive meanders along the crest of the Blue Ridge Mountains, wanders through Shenandoah National Park, and continues on the Blue Ridge Parkway. If you're not tired of presidential house museums, Woodrow Wilson's one-time home is 40 miles from the campground in Staunton.

Basics

Operated By: KOA. **Open:** Mar. 1–Oct. 31. **Site Assignment:** Reservations and walk-ins accepted. **Registration:** At campground office. **Fee:** $24–$26 (VISA, MC, D). **Parking:** At designated spot.

Facilities

Number of RV Sites: 57. **Number of Tent-Only Sites:** 14. **Hookups:** Electric (20, 30 amps), water, 34 full hookups. **Each Site:** Fire ring, picnic table. **Dump Station:** Yes. **Laundry:** Yes. **Pay Phone:** Yes. **Rest Rooms and Showers:** Yes. **Fuel:** No. **Propane:** Yes. **Internal Roads:** Gravel, in good condition. **RV Service:** No. **Market:** Within 6 mi. **Restaurant:** Within 6 mi. **General**

Store: Yes. **Vending:** Yes. **Playground:** Yes. **Other:** Fishing lake. **Activities:** Rec hall, game room, swimming, pond fishing, basketball, horseshoes, volleyball, hiking trails, planned activities on weekends. **Nearby Attractions:** Monticello, Montpelier, Ash Lawn, Walton's Mountain Museum, James River, Luray Caverns. **Additional Information:** Virginia Tourism Corp., (800) 371-8164, www.virginia.org.

Restrictions

Pets: On leash only. **Fires:** At site. **Alcoholic Beverages:** At site. **Vehicle Maximum Length:** 40 ft. **Other:** None.

To Get There

From I-64, take Exit 118A and go 6 mi. south on US 29 and 4 mi. southeast on CR 708. Entrance is on the left.

CHARLOTTESVILLE

Misty Mountain Camp Resort

56 Misty Mountain Rd., Greenwood 22943. T: (888) 647-8900; www.mistycamp.com; mikemellom@cs.com.

RV ★★★★ Tent ★★★★

Beauty: ★★★★ Site Privacy: ★★★
Spaciousness: ★★★ Quiet: ★★★★
Security: ★★★★ Cleanliness: ★★★★
Insect Control: ★★★★ Facilities: ★★★★

Nestled on the mountain for which it is named, Misty Mountain Camp Resort is 50-acre park near Charlottesville. There are wooded and creekside sites, and 29 pull-throughs. A recreational building has banquet tables and chairs to accommodate groups. Hiking trails are scattered throughout the campground, and scenic vistas are plentiful. If you're hungry, Fat Sam's Pizza and Subs will deliver orders right to your campsite. Like KOA—Charlottesville, Misty Mountain is located within a half-hour drive of Washington, DC and near the presidential homes of Thomas Jefferson, James Madison, James Monroe, and Woodrow Wilson. At Walton's Mountain Museum in nearby Schuyler, the set of The Waltons television show is showcased. Though KOA and Misty Mountain offer similar recreational opportunities, Misty Mountain's facilities are cleaner, and the mountain aura is peaceful, especially at sunrise.

Basics

Operated By: Mike Mellom. **Open:** All year. **Site Assignment:** Reservations accepted (cancellation must be 7 days from reservation date for refund), walk-ins accepted. **Registration:** At campground office. **Fee:** $23–$27 (VISA, MC). **Parking:** At designated spot.

Facilities

Number of RV Sites: 79. **Number of Tent-Only Sites:** 16. **Hookups:** Electric (15, 20, 30, 50 amps), water, 41 full hookups. **Each Site:** Fire ring, picnic table. **Dump Station:** Yes. **Laundry:** Yes. **Pay Phone:** Yes. **Rest Rooms and Showers:** Yes. **Fuel:** No. **Propane:** Yes. **Internal Roads:** Gravel, in good condition. **RV Service:** No. **Market:** Within 2 mi. **Restaurant:** On premises. **General Store:** Yes. **Vending:** Yes. **Playground:** Yes. **Other:** Fat Sam's Pizza on premises. **Activities:** Rec hall, game room, wagon rides, swimming, stream fishing, planned activities, badminton, sports field, horseshoes, hiking trails, volleyball. **Nearby Attractions:** Monticello, Montpelier, Ash Lawn, Walton's Mountain Museum, James River, Luray Caverns. **Additional Information:** Virginia Tourism Corp., (800) 371-8164, www.virginia.org.

Restrictions

Pets: On leash only. **Fires:** At site. **Alcoholic Beverages:** At site. **Vehicle Maximum Length:** 65 ft. **Other:** Pets not permitted in play areas.

To Get There

From I-64, take Exit 107 and go 1 mi. west on US 250. Entrance is on the left.

CHERITON

Cherrystone Family Camping and RV Resort

P.O. Box 545, Cheriton 23316. T: (757) 331-3063; www.cherrystoneva.com; welcomecenter@cherrystoneva.com.

RV ★★★★★ Tent ★★★★★

Beauty: ★★★★ Site Privacy: ★★
Spaciousness: ★★★ Quiet: ★★★
Security: ★★★★ Cleanliness: ★★★★★
Insect Control: ★★★★ Facilities: ★★★★★

It would be hard to logically argue that Cherrystone Family Camping and RV Resort is not the overall finest campground in Virginia. Located on Chesapeake Bay, Cherrystone has 110 pull-through sites. Bayview sites located near fishing piers, an adults-only swimming pool, and a pedal boat lake. The campground's eastern side is composed of several clusters of sites that offer little privacy. You can easily and happily spend your entire vacation without leaving Cherrystone's 300-acre grounds. With Cherrystone's location on Chesapeake Bay, ocean swimming, boating, and fishing are big draws. The property is bordered on three sides by Kings Creek, Cherrystone Creek, and Chesapeake Bay. These waters are teeming with oysters, clams, crabs, and fish such as flounder, trout, croaker, and spot. The Miss Jennifer charter fishing boat departs from the Cherrystone dock Memorial Day–Labor Day. The campground has four swimming pools (including one solely for adults) and a new beach-entry family pool. An 18-hole mini-golf course, several playgrounds, volleyball and basketball courts, and a game room are also on the grounds. Cherrystone has a restaurant, snack bar, and a Farm Stand which carries fresh local vegetables, fruits, and seafood.

Basics

Operated By: Ed and Mary Davidson. **Open:** All year. **Site Assignment:** Reservations accepted (deposit required within 10 days of making reservation), walk-ins accepted. **Registration:** At campground headquarters. **Fee:** $15–$35 (VISA, MC, AE). **Parking:** At designated spot.

Facilities

Number of RV Sites: 450. **Number of Tent-Only Sites:** 200. **Hookups:** Electric (20, 30, 50 amps), phone, water, 403 full hookups. **Each Site:** Fire ring, grill. **Dump Station:** Yes. **Laundry:** Yes. **Pay Phone:** Yes. **Rest Rooms and Showers:** Yes. **Fuel:** No. **Propane:** Yes. **Internal Roads:** Gravel and paved, in good condition. **RV Service:** No. **Market:** Within 3 mi. **Restaurant:** Within 2 mi. **General Store:** Yes. **Vending:** Yes. **Playground:** Yes. **Other:** 4 pools and 4 fishing piers on Chesapeake Bay waterfront. **Activities:** Swimming at four pools and wading pool, ocean swimming, boating, canoeing, kayaking, rec hall, game room, ocean and pond fishing, mini-golf, basketball, bike rentals, shuffleboard, planned activities, movies, tennis, sports field, horseshoes, hiking trails, volleyball, fishing charter tours. **Nearby Attractions:** Chesapeake Bay, Virginia Beach, Norfolk, Williamsburg. **Additional Information:** Virginia Tourism Corp., (800) 371-8164, www.virginia.org.

Restrictions

Pets: On leash only. **Fires:** At site. **Alcoholic Beverages:** At site. **Vehicle Maximum Length:** 60 ft. **Other:** No refunds for early departures.

To Get There

From US 13 Bypass, go 1.5 mi. west on Townsfield Dr. Entrance is at the end.

CHINCOTEAGUE

Maddox Family Campground

P.O. Box 82 6742 Maddox Rd., Chincoteague 23336. T: (757) 336-3111; F: (757) 336-1980; www.chincoteague.net/i-maddox.

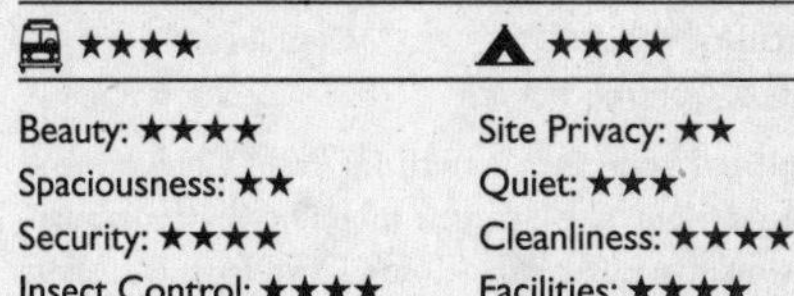

RV ★★★★ Tent ★★★★

Beauty: ★★★★ Site Privacy: ★★
Spaciousness: ★★ Quiet: ★★★
Security: ★★★★ Cleanliness: ★★★★
Insect Control: ★★★★ Facilities: ★★★★

The closest campground to Assateague Island National Seashore, Chincoteague Island's Maddox Family Campground has more than 550 open and shaded sites, including 68 pull-throughs. Wooded sites are inviting to RVers and tenters alike. The campground has a swimming pool and a playground, and the facilities are clean. Yet, many campers stay here for what the park is near, not for what it is has on the grounds. The national seashore and the national wildlife refuge are the magnets for outdoor enthusiasts. Two herds of wild horses make their home on Assateague Island, separated by a fence at the Maryland-Virginia line, and they are often seen wandering the beaches, roadways, trails, and campgrounds on the island. These small and shaggy horses have adapted to their environment over the years by eating dune and marsh grasses and drinking fresh water from ponds.

Basics

Operated By: Private operator. **Open:** Mar. 1–Nov. 30. **Site Assignment:** Reservations and walk-ins accepted. **Registration:** At campground office. **Fee:** $27–$35 (VISA, MC, D). **Parking:** At site.

Facilities

Number of RV Sites: 341. **Number of Tent-Only Sites:** 250. **Hookups:** Electric (20, 30 amps), water, 32 full hookups. **Each Site:** Fire ring, picnic table. **Dump Station:** Yes. **Laundry:** Yes. **Pay Phone:** Yes. **Rest Rooms and Showers:** Yes. **Fuel:** No. **Propane:** Yes. **Internal Roads:** Gravel, in good condition. **RV Service:** No. **Market:** Within 1 mi. **Restaurant:** Within 1 mi. **General Store:** Yes. **Vending:** Yes. **Playground:** Yes. **Other:** Duck pond, bird watching sites. **Activities:** Bird watching, crabbing, rec hall, game room, mini-golf, shuffleboard. **Nearby Attractions:** Assateague National Seashore, Chincoteague Wildlife Refuge. **Additional Information:** Eastern Shore of Virginia Tourism Commission, (757) 787-2460, www.esva.net/~esvatourism.

Restrictions

Pets: On leash only. **Fires:** At site. **Alcoholic Beverages:** At site. **Vehicle Maximum Length:** None. **Other:** None.

To Get There

From SR 175, go 0.5 mi. on Main St. to Maddox Blvd. and 1 mi. to campground.

CHINCOTEAGUE

Tom's Cove Park

P.O. Box 122, Chincoteague 23336. T: (757) 336-6498; www.tomscovepark.com; joboo@shore.intercom.net.

RV ★★★★ Tent ★★★★

Beauty: ★★★★	Site Privacy: ★
Spaciousness: ★★	Quiet: ★★★
Security: ★★★★	Cleanliness: ★★★★
Insect Control: ★★★★	Facilities: ★★★★★

Situated on the waterfront on Chincoteague Island—one of the largest migratory bird sanctuaries on the east coast—Tom's Cove Park is a short drive away from Assateague Island National Seashore and Chincoteague National Wildlife Refuge. Ocean fishing, crabbing, boating, and swimming are just a sampling of the activities offered at the 88-acre campground, home to 920 open and wooded sites. These sites are well-maintained, but they offer little privacy and can feel crowded, especially on summer weekends. The marina has a double-wide boat ramp. The campground hosts live entertainment on Saturday nights during the summer in the air-conditioned pavilion. Chincoteague Island, Virginia's only resort island, is a destination in itself. World-famous for its oyster beds and clam shoals, Chincoteague is the gateway to Assateague Island National Seashore, home to a unique breed of wild ponies. Chincoteague Island is also the home of many outstanding craftsmen and artists who produce some of the world's finest hand-carved duck decoys and reproductions of soaring wildfowl.

Basics

Operated By: Private operator. **Open:** Mar. 1–Nov. 30. **Site Assignment:** Reservations accepted (guarantees water and electric site only), walk-ins accepted. **Registration:** At campground office. **Fee:** $28–$30 (VISA, MC). **Parking:** At designated spot.

Facilities

Number of RV Sites: 865. **Number of Tent-Only Sites:** 55. **Hookups:** Electric (20, 30 amps), cable TV, phone, water, 633 full hookups. **Each Site:** Picnic table. **Dump Station:** Yes. **Laundry:** Yes. **Pay Phone:** Yes. **Rest Rooms and Showers:** Yes. **Fuel:** No. **Propane:** Yes. **Internal Roads:** Gravel and paved, in good condition. **RV Service:** No. **Market:** Within 3 mi. **Restaurant:** Within 3 mi. **General Store:** Yes. **Vending:** Yes. **Playground:** Yes. **Other:** 3 fishing and crabbing piers on Chincoteague Island. **Activities:** Ocean fishing, swimming, boating, canoeing, kayaking, bike rentals, sports field, horseshoes, rec hall, game room, crabbing. **Nearby Attractions:** Assateague National Seashore, Chincoteague Wildlife Refuge. **Additional Information:** Eastern Shore of Virginia Tourism Commission, (757) 787-2460, www.esva.net/~esvatourism.

Restrictions

Pets: On leash only. **Fires:** At site. **Alcoholic Beverages:** At site. **Vehicle Maximum Length:** None. **Other:** Use of alcohol is permitted but not preferred.

To Get There

From US 13, go 11 mi. east on SR 175, 1.25 mi. south on Main St., and 0.5 mi. east on Beebe Rd. Entrance is at the end.

CLARKSVILLE

Occoneechee State Park

1192 Occoneechee Park Rd., Clarksville 23927. T: (804) 374-2210 or (800) 933-PARK; www.dcr.state.va.us/parks; resvs@dcr.state.va.us.

RV ★★★ Tent ★★★★

Beauty: ★★★★	Site Privacy: ★★★
Spaciousness: ★★★	Quiet: ★★★★
Security: ★★★★	Cleanliness: ★★★★
Insect Control: ★★★★	Facilities: ★★★

Though it's officially named the John H. Kerr Reservoir, most people know it as Buggs Island Lake. Regardless of what it's called, the 48,000-acre body of water is the main attraction at Occoneechee State Park, located in southern Virginia near the North Carolina border. The campground has 88 sites, many shaded and some with a lake view. There are several hiking trails near the campground, including the Old Plantation Interpretive Trail (which wanders past the one-time site of a 3,105-acre plantation) and the Warriors Path Nature Trail. Swimming is not permitted from the shoreline because of hazardous drop-offs and heavy boating traffic. Buggs Island Lake and connecting Lake Gaston are famous for the number and size of fish found there. Striped and largemouth bass, bluegill, crappie, and perch are plentiful. Fishing boats with motors, canoes, paddleboats, seven-speed off-road bikes, and one- and two-person kayaks are available for rent.

Basics

Operated By: State of Virginia. **Open:** Mar.–Dec. **Site Assignment:** Upon arrival as available. **Registration:** At visitor center. **Fee:** $14–$18 (VISA, MC). **Parking:** At site.

Facilities

Number of RV Sites: 39. **Number of Tent-Only Sites:** 49. **Hookups:** Electric (15 amps). **Each Site:** Grill, picnic table, and lantern pole. **Dump Station:** Yes. **Laundry:** No. **Pay Phone:** Yes. **Rest Rooms and Showers:** Yes. **Fuel:** No. **Propane:** No. **Internal Roads:** Paved, in good condition. **RV Service:** No. **Market:** Within 1 mi. **Restaurant:** Within 1 mi. **General Store:** No. **Vending:** Yes. **Playground:** No. **Other:** Visitor center, gift shop. **Activities:** Fishing, boating, hiking trails, boat rentals. **Nearby Attractions:** Prestwood Plantation, John H. Kerr Dam. **Additional Information:** Virginia Tourism Corp., (800) 371-8164, www.virginia.org.

Restrictions

Pets: On leash only. **Fires:** At site. **Alcoholic Beverages:** No alcohol permitted. **Vehicle Maximum Length:** 30 ft. **Other:** Max. 14-day stay every 30 days.

To Get There

From Clarksville, go 1 mi. east on US 58. Follow signs to park.

CLIFTON FORGE

Douthat State Park

Rte. 1 Box 212, Millboro 24460. T: (540) 862-8100 or (800) 933-PARK; www.dcr.state.va.us/parks; resvs@dcr.state.va.us.

RV ★★★ Tent ★★★★

Beauty: ★★★★	Site Privacy: ★★★
Spaciousness: ★★★	Quiet: ★★★
Security: ★★★★	Cleanliness: ★★★★
Insect Control: ★★★★	Facilities: ★★★★

Straddling Bath and Allegheny Counties and located in a valley between Beards and Middle Mountains, Douthat State Park has received its share of recognition. Editors of the 1999 Outside Family Vacation Guide named it one of the nation's top 10 state park family vacation destinations. In addition to 50-acre Douthat Lake, more than 40 miles of hiking trails and this 77-site campground can be found in the park. Campsites are open with lake and mountain views. Douthat Lake and adjoining Wilson Creek are stocked regularly with trout, water conditions permitting. The renovated Douthat Lakeview Restaurant, one of the original CCC facilities, overlooks the lake and features a glass-enclosed porch. Adjacent to the restaurant is Douthat Camp Store. At 4.5 miles, Stony Run Trail is Douthat's longest. Mountain bikers favor the trails on Middle Mountain, which rises to more than 3,000 feet on Douthat's west end.

Basics

Operated By: State of Virginia. **Open:** Mar.–Dec. **Site Assignment:** Reservations and walk-ins accepted. **Registration:** At campground office. **Fee:** $18 (VISA, MC). **Parking:** At site.

Facilities

Number of RV Sites: 77. **Number of Tent-Only Sites:** None. **Hookups:** Electric (30 amps). **Each Site:** Picnic table, grill, lantern pole. **Dump Station:** Yes. **Laundry:** No. **Pay Phone:** Yes. **Rest Rooms and Showers:** Yes. **Fuel:** No. **Propane:** No. **Internal Roads:** Paved, in good condition. **RV Service:** No. **Market:** Within 5 mi. **Restaurant:** Within 3 mi. **General Store:** Yes. **Vending:** Yes. **Playground:** Yes. **Other:** Douthat Lake. **Activities:** Lake fishing and swimming, boating, boat rentals, horseshoes, planned activities, hiking trails. **Nearby Attractions:** The Homestead, Warm Springs Baths, Lexington, Virginia Military Institute, Lee Chapel, Stonewall Jackson House, Roanoke. **Additional Information:** Virginia Tourism Corp., (800) 371-8164, www.virginia.org.

Restrictions

Pets: On leash only. **Fires:** At site. **Alcoholic Beverages:** No alcohol permitted. **Vehicle Maximum Length:** None. **Other:** Max. 14-day stay in 30-day period.

To Get There

From US 60, go 2.5 mi. north on Hwy. 629. Follow signs to park.

COVINGTON

Morris Hill Campground

810-A Madison Ave., Covington 24426. T: (540) 962-2214.

RV ★★★ Tent ★★★★

Beauty: ★★★★	Site Privacy: ★★★
Spaciousness: ★★★	Quiet: ★★★★
Security: ★★★★	Cleanliness: ★★★★
Insect Control: ★★★★	Facilities: ★★★

Sometimes, when you hit the open road in your RV, amenities like mini-golf courses, swimming pools, rec halls—even electric hookups—can be sacrificed for solitude and serenity. This is why campers come to Morris Hill Campground near Covington in western Virginia. You'll find rest rooms and showers here, but that's about it. No phone and no swimming pool. You'll also find 2,500-acre Lake Moomaw, which is surrounded at the north by the 13,428-acre Gathright Wildlife Management Area. Formed by the construction of the Gathright Dam in 1981, Lake Moomaw is 12 miles long. Largemouth bass, crappie, bluegill, and channel catfish are among the fish that swim in the lake's waters. There is a beach at Coles Point Recreation Area. Morris Hill actually sits on a hilltop amid tall hardwoods. Though it's steep and strenuous, the 5.3-mile Oliver Mountain Trail provides stunning mountain views and a peek at Lake Moomaw.

Basics

Operated By: US Forest Service. **Open:** Apr. 30–Nov. 1. **Site Assignment:** Reservations and walk-ins accepted. **Registration:** Self-registration on site. **Fee:** $10 (VISA, MC). **Parking:** At site spur.

Facilities

Number of RV Sites: 53. **Number of Tent-Only Sites:** 2. **Hookups:** None. **Each Site:** Fire ring, picnic table. **Dump Station:** Yes. **Laundry:** No. **Pay Phone:** No. **Rest Rooms and Showers:** Yes. **Fuel:** No. **Propane:** No. **Internal Roads:** Paved, in good condition. **RV Service:** No. **Market:** Within 12 mi. **Restaurant:** Within 10 mi. **General Store:** No. **Vending:** No. **Playground:** No. **Other:** Lake Moomaw. **Activities:** Lake fishing and swimming, boating, canoeing, hiking. **Nearby Attractions:** George Washington National Forest, the Homestead, Warm Springs Baths, Lexington, Virginia Military Institute, Lee Chapel, Stonewall Jackson House, Roanoke. **Additional Information:** Virginia Tourism Corp., (800) 371-8164, www.virginia.org.

Restrictions

Pets: On leash only. **Fires:** At site. **Alcoholic Beverages:** At site. **Vehicle Maximum Length:** 22 ft. **Other:** Quiet time 10 pm.–6 a.m.

To Get There

From US 220, go 6 mi. north on Hwy. 687, 3 mi. west on Hwy. 641, and 5 mi. north on Hwy. 666. Follow signs to campground.

CULPEPER

Cedar Mountain Campground

20114 Camp Rd., Culpeper 22701. T: (540) 547-3374 or (800)-234-0968; cedarmountaincampground@juno.com.

RV ★★★★ Tent ★★★★

Beauty: ★★★★	Site Privacy: ★★
Spaciousness: ★★★	Quiet: ★★★★
Security: ★★★★	Cleanliness: ★★★★
Insect Control: ★★★★	Facilities: ★★★★

Located in a forested setting east of Shenandoah National Park and southwest of Washington, DC, Cedar Mountain Campground is near eight historic battlefields. This is a perfect base for outdoor enthusiasts who are also Civil War buffs. The 16-acre campground has room for eight pull-throughs. RVers and tenters have their choice of wooded sites that are especially cool and comfortable on sizzling summer days. Outdoor enthusiasts will like the nature walk and the fishing pond. The spacious pavilion has a fireplace and barbecue pits. Four bloody battles were fought on the soil of the Fredericksburg and Spotsylvania Military Park, about 25 miles southeast of Cedar Mountain. About 40 miles northeast of Cedar Mountain lies the Manassas National Battlefield Park, where the first and second Battles of Bull Run happened. Of course, Virginia has its share of Revolutionary War heritage too. Ferry Farm, George Washington's boyhood home, graces the banks of the Rappahannock River.

Basics

Operated By: Private operator. **Open:** All year. **Site Assignment:** Reservations and walk-ins accepted. **Registration:** At campground office. **Fee:** $15–$18 (VISA, MC). **Parking:** At designated spot.

Facilities

Number of RV Sites: 41. **Number of Tent-Only Sites:** 20. **Hookups:** Electric (30 amps), water, 39 full hookups. **Each Site:** Fire ring, picnic table. **Dump Station:** Yes. **Laundry:** No. **Pay Phone:** Yes. **Rest Rooms and Showers:** Yes. **Fuel:** No. **Propane:** Yes. **Internal Roads:** Gravel, in good condition. **RV Service:** No. **Market:** Within 5 mi. **Restaurant:** Within 5 mi. **General Store:** Yes. **Vending:** Yes. **Playground:** Yes. **Other:** Cable slides. **Activities:** Pond fishing, game room, rec hall, mini-golf, basketball, shuffleboard, badminton, sports field, horseshoes, volleyball. **Nearby Attractions:** Museum of Culpeper History, Fredericksburg and Spotsylvania battlefields, Manassas battlefields, Washington, DC, Shenandoah National Park. **Additional Information:** Virginia Tourism Corp., (800) 371-8164, www.virginia.org.

Restrictions

Pets: On leash only. **Fires:** At site. **Alcoholic Beverages:** At site. **Vehicle Maximum Length:** 40 ft.

To Get There

From Business US 29, go 3 mi. south on US 29 and 2.25 mi. east and south on CR 603/657/645/752. Follow signs. Entrance is on the right.

CUMBERLAND

Bear Creek Lake State Park

929 Oak Hill Rd., Cumberland 23040. T: (804) 492-4410; www.dcr.state.va.us/parks; resvs@dcr.state.va.us.

RV ★★★ Tent ★★★

Beauty: ★★★★	Site Privacy: ★★★
Spaciousness: ★★★	Quiet: ★★★
Security: ★★★★	Cleanliness: ★★★★
Insect Control: ★★★★	Facilities: ★★★

Situated amid the towering sweet gum, oak and tulip poplar trees of Cumberland State Forest in central Virginia, Bear Creek Lake State Park typically does not draw large crowds—all the better for campers looking for rest and relaxation. The camping area has 53 shaded sites and is actually divided in three sections. Campground A, the only campground by the lake, has 13 tent sites with no electric or water hookups, and nine sites with hookups for vehicles up to 20 ft. Campground B offers 14 sites with water and electric hookups for RVs up to 20 ft., and six sites with hookups to handle vehicles up to 35 ft. Campground C, open from Memorial Day–Labor Day, has 11 tent sites with no electric or water hookups. A campground host is available at most times in campsite A-25, adjacent to the picnic shelter. The park is surrounded by the 16,000-acre Cumberland State Forest, which is teeming with fishing and swimming areas and hiking trails.

Basics

Operated By: State of Virginia. **Open:** Mar.–Dec. **Site Assignment:** Reservations and walk-ins accepted. **Registration:** At campground office. **Fee:** $11–$15 (VISA, MC). **Parking:** At site.

Facilities

Number of RV Sites: 29. **Number of Tent-Only Sites:** 24. **Hookups:** Electric (20, 30 amps). **Each Site:** Grill, picnic table. **Dump Station:** Yes. **Laundry:** Yes, laundry sinks. **Pay Phone:** Yes. **Rest**

Rooms and Showers: Yes. **Fuel:** No. **Propane:** No. **Internal Roads:** Paved, in good condition. **RV Service:** No. **Market:** Within 7 mi. **Restaurant:** Within 7 mi. **General Store:** No. **Vending:** No. **Playground:** No. **Other:** Small market outside the park sells a limited number of groceries. **Activities:** Lake swimming and fishing, hiking trails, boating, boat rentals, canoeing. **Nearby Attractions:** Lee's Retreat Driving Tour, Farmville, Appomattox Court House National Historic Park, Richmond. **Additional Information:** Virginia Tourism Corp., (800) 371-8164, www.virginia.org.

RESTRICTIONS

Pets: On leash only. **Fires:** At site. **Alcoholic Beverages:** No alcohol permitted. **Vehicle Maximum Length:** 30 ft. **Other:** 14-day max. stay in 30-day period.

TO GET THERE

From Cumberland, go 0.5 mi. east on US 60 and 4.5 mi. west on Hwy. 622/629. Follow signs to park.

DOSWELL

Paramount's Kings Dominion Campground

10061 Kings Dominion Blvd., Doswell 23047. T: (800) 922-6710 or (804) 876-5355; www.kingsdominion.com.

RV ★★★★ Tent ★★★★

Beauty: ★★★★	Site Privacy: ★
Spaciousness: ★★	Quiet: ★★
Security: ★★★★	Cleanliness: ★★★★
Insect Control: ★★★★	Facilities: ★★★★

Located 20 miles north of Richmond, Paramount's Kings Dominion Amusement Park has its shows, more tranquil family-oriented rides and water park area, but we think that nothing compares to the assortment of thrill rides that await here. After an exhaustive day of exploring the amusement park, Paramount's Kings Dominion Campground is just a half-mile from the park's entrance. The semi-wooded campground has 37 pull-throughs and a primitive tent camping area. The facilities are well-maintained, and when campers are not frolicking in the amusement park, they can swim in the campground's pool or play mini-golf. Of course, the main reason for camping here is to have a place to rest between visits to Kings Dominion. After a long day in the park, you'll appreciate the free shuttle service back to the campground even more than when you arrived at the park that morning.

BASICS

Operated By: Paramount. **Open:** All year. **Site Assignment:** Reservations and walk-ins accepted. **Registration:** At campground headquarters. **Fee:** $20–$28 (VISA, MC, AE, D). **Parking:** At designated spot.

FACILITIES

Number of RV Sites: 190. **Number of Tent-Only Sites:** 40. **Hookups:** Electric (20, 30, 50 amps), water, 93 full hookups. **Each Site:** Picnic table. **Dump Station:** Yes. **Laundry:** Yes. **Pay Phone:** Yes. **Rest Rooms and Showers:** Yes. **Fuel:** No. **Propane:** Yes. **Internal Roads:** Gravel and paved, in good condition. **RV Service:** No. **Market:** Within 2 mi. **Restaurant:** Within 2 mi. **General Store:** Yes. **Vending:** Yes. **Playground:** Yes. **Other:** Paramount's Kings Dominion Amusement Park is 05 mi from campground entrance Shuttles available. **Activities:** Rec hall, swimming, mini-golf, horseshoes, volleyball. **Nearby Attractions:** Paramount's Kings Dominion Amusement Park, Richmond, White House of the Confederacy, Fredericksburg and Spotsylvania battlefields. **Additional Information:** Richmond CVB, (800) 370-9004, www.richmondva.org.

RESTRICTIONS

Pets: On leash only. **Fires:** At site. **Alcoholic Beverages:** At site. **Vehicle Maximum Length:** None.

TO GET THERE

From I-95, take Exit 98 and go 0.5 mi. on Hwy. 30. Entrance is on the right.

EDINBURG

Creekside Campground

108 Palmyra Rd., Edinburg 22824-0277. T: (540) 984-4299 or (540) 984-8471; www.fulltiming-america.com/creekside; cscamp@shentel.net.

RV ★★★★ Tent ★★★★

Beauty: ★★★★	Site Privacy: ★★★
Spaciousness: ★★★	Quiet: ★★★★
Security: ★★★★	Cleanliness: ★★★★
Insect Control: ★★★★	Facilities: ★★★

Creekside Campground, near Edinburgh, is an immaculately landscaped, cozy place with shaded sites situated along Stoney Creek in the Shenandoah Valley. Fishermen cast their lines at Stoney Creek and in the nearby Shenandoah River's north fork. At night, the trees at Creekside are illuminated with white lights, casting a cheerful glow on the campground. Creekside has few activities—just fishing and horseshoes—but an assortment of outdoor recreation is available at Shenandoah National Park and the George Washington National Forest. The Skyline Drive is a pleasant nearby day trip. The 105-mile highway winds from Front Royal through the Blue Ridge Mountains and the Shenandoah National Park to Waynesboro, where it stretches south on the Blue Ridge Parkway.

BASICS

Operated By: Private operator. **Open:** All year. **Site Assignment:** Reservations recommended, walk-ins accepted. **Registration:** At campground office. **Fee:** $20 (VISA, MC). **Parking:** At site.

FACILITIES

Number of RV Sites: 26. **Number of Tent-Only Sites:** 7. **Hookups:** Electric (20, 30, 50 amps), cable TV, phone, 25 full hookups. **Each Site:** Fire ring, picnic table. **Dump Station:** Yes. **Laundry:** No. **Pay Phone:** Yes. **Rest Rooms and Showers:** Yes. **Fuel:** No. **Propane:** No. **Internal Roads:** Gravel, in good condition. **RV Service:** No. **Market:** Within 1 mi. **Restaurant:** Within 1 mi. **General Store:** No. **Vending:** Yes. **Playground:** No. **Other:** Stoney Creek. **Activities:** Fishing, horseshoes. **Nearby Attractions:** Luray Caverns, George Washington National Forest, Shenandoah National Park, Edinburg, Shenandoah Vineyards. **Additional Information:** Virginia Tourism Corp., (800) 371-8164, www.virginia.org.

RESTRICTIONS

Pets: On leash only. **Fires:** At site. **Alcoholic Beverages:** At site. **Vehicle Maximum Length:** None. **Other:** None.

TO GET THERE

From I-81, take Exit 279 and go 1 mi. east on Hwy. 675, 0.75 mi. south on US 11, 0.5 mi. east on Palmyra Church Rd., and 0.25 mi. northeast on Palmyra Rd. Entrance is on the left.

EMPORIA

Yogi Bear's Jellystone Park Camp Resort

2940 Sussex Drive, Emporia 23847. T: (800) 545-4248 or (804) 634-3115; www.usastar.com/jpeva; campemporiava@mail.com.

RV ★★★★ Tent ★★★★

Beauty: ★★★★	Site Privacy: ★★★
Spaciousness: ★★★	Quiet: ★★★★
Security: ★★★★	Cleanliness: ★★★★
Insect Control: ★★★★	Facilities: ★★★★

Located a mile off Interstate 95 in Emporia, Yogi Bear's Jellystone Park Camp Resort is a clean campground with a generously sized swimming pool and a 15-acre fishing lake. There are 90 shaded and grassy sites, including 53 pull-throughs. Because of its location—the campground is about an 1.5-hour drive from Norfolk and Newport News to the west and a 45-minute drive from Lake Gaston to the west—Emporia is mostly an overnight stop for campers on the way to destinations in Florida and South Carolina. The Emporia area is home to the Virginia Pork Festival every June, and the Virginia Peanut Festival every Sept. If you choose the campground in Emporia as your base, Newport News and Norfolk are ideal day trips. Lake Gaston and John H. Kerr Reservoir to the west offer extensive boating and fishing opportunities.

BASICS

Operated By: Yogi Bear's Jellystone Park. **Open:** All year. **Site Assignment:** Reservations and walk-ins accepted. **Registration:** At campground office. **Fee:** $22–$26 (VISA, MC, D). **Parking:** At designated spot.

FACILITIES

Number of RV Sites: 80. **Number of Tent-Only Sites:** 10. **Hookups:** Electric (20, 30, 50 amps), phone, water, 44 full hookups. **Each Site:** Fire ring, picnic table. **Dump Station:** Yes. **Laundry:** Yes. **Pay Phone:** Yes. **Rest Rooms and Showers:** Yes. **Fuel:** No. **Propane:** Yes. **Internal Roads:** Gravel, in good condition. **RV Service:** No. **Market:** Within 1 mi. **Restaurant:** Within 1 mi. **General Store:** Yes. **Vending:** Yes. **Playground:** Yes. **Other:** None. **Activities:** Game room, rec hall, swimming, basketball, planned activities, movies, badminton, horseshoes, volleyball. **Nearby Attractions:** Historic Jamestown Settlement, Newport News, Norfolk, Nauticus: The National Maritime Center, Virginia Air and Space Museum. **Additional Information:** Virginia Tourism Corp., (800) 371-8164, www.virginia.org.

Restrictions

Pets: On leash only. **Fires:** At site. **Alcoholic Beverages:** At site. **Vehicle Maximum Length:** None.

To Get There

From I-95, take Exit 17 and go 1 mi. south on US 301. Entrance is on the right.

FAIRFAX

Burke Lake Park

7315 Ox Rd., Fairfax Station 22039. T: (703) 323-6600; www.co.fairfax.va.us; parkmail@co.fairfax.va.us.

RV: ★★★★ Tent: ★★★★

Beauty: ★★★★ Site Privacy: ★★
Spaciousness: ★★ Quiet: ★★★
Security: ★★★★ Cleanliness: ★★★★
Insect Control: ★★★★ Facilities: ★★★★

Relaxing in a boat somewhere on serene Burke Lake, it's hard to believe the concrete jungle and snarled traffic of Washington, DC are a short Metro Rail ride away. Fairfax County Park Authority officials promote Burke Lake Park—and its sister recreational area Lake Fairfax Park—as metropolitan DC's country side. This time, the bureaucrats are not blowing smoke. Burke Lake Park consists of 888 acres, and its centerpiece is the 218-acre Burke Lake, where boating and fishing are encouraged, but swimming is not allowed. Burke Lake Park has 163 shaded sites, including six pull-throughs. The park is ideal for families; there's a miniature train and carousel for children, and lots of hiking trails. If you want to catch the Metro Rail for a journey to Washington, DC, the closest stop from Burke Lake Park is the Springfield/Franconia station, which is about eight miles away.

Basics

Operated By: Fairfax County Park Authority. **Open:** Mar. 1–Dec. 1. **Site Assignment:** First-come, first-served; no reservations accepted. **Registration:** At campground headquarters. **Fee:** $14 (VISA, MC). **Parking:** At designated spot.

Facilities

Number of RV Sites: 103. **Number of Tent-Only Sites:** 60. **Hookups:** None. **Each Site:** Grill, picnic table. **Dump Station:** Yes. **Laundry:** Yes. **Pay Phone:** Yes. **Rest Rooms and Showers:** Yes. **Fuel:** No. **Propane:** No. **Internal Roads:** Gravel, in good condition. **RV Service:** No. **Market:** Within 2 mi. **Restaurant:** Within 1 mi. **General Store:** Yes. **Vending:** Yes. **Playground:** Yes. **Other:** Burke Lake. **Activities:** Boating, canoeing, rowboat rentals, lake fishing, golf, driving range, putting green, hiking trails, volleyball. **Nearby Attractions:** Washington, DC **Additional Information:** Washington, DC Convention and Visitors Bureau, (202) 789-7000, www.washington.org.

Restrictions

Pets: On leash only. **Fires:** At site. **Alcoholic Beverages:** At site. **Vehicle Maximum Length:** 25 ft. **Other:** No swimming permitted in lake.

To Get There

From Fairfax, go 9 mi. south on Hwy. 123 and 1.5 mi. on park road. Entrance is on the left.

FAIRFAX

Lake Fairfax Park

1400 Lake Fairfax Dr., Reston 22090. T: (703) 471-5415 or (703) 757-9242; www.co.fairfax.va.us; parkmail@co.fairfax.va.us.

RV: ★★★★ Tent: ★★★★

Beauty: ★★★★ Site Privacy: ★★
Spaciousness: ★★ Quiet: ★★★
Security: ★★★★ Cleanliness: ★★★★
Insect Control: ★★★★ Facilities: ★★★★

With a carousel, playgrounds, and one of the nicest municipal water parks you will find anywhere, Lake Fairfax Park in Reston was definitely designed with children in mind. The 20-acre Lake Fairfax provides a tranquil setting for fishing and pedal boating. The park's star attraction is the new Water Mine Family Swimmin' Hole, a western-themed activity pool with an acre of interactive play features, including Box Canyon Crossing, slides, and flumes. The water park is circled by Rattlesnake River, which has a 2.5-mile-per-hour current that gently nudges the tubes along. Kids careen off covered wagons, float on rattlesnakes, and dash through showers tipped from water-filled ore carts. Of the campground's 136 sites, 70 have electric hookups. These sites offer little privacy. With the Metro Rail, Washington, DC is a short ride away. From Lake Fairfax Park, the Metro Rail's closest stop is the Nutley St. or Dunn Loring station, about 10 miles away.

Basics

Operated By: Fairfax County Park Authority. **Open:** Mar. 1–Dec. 1. **Site Assignment:** Reservations and walk-ins accepted. **Registration:** At campground office. **Fee:** $14 (VISA, MC). **Parking:** At designated spot.

Facilities

Number of RV Sites: 136. **Number of Tent-Only Sites:** None. **Hookups:** Electric (30 amps). **Each Site:** Grill, picnic table. **Dump Station:** Yes. **Laundry:** Yes. **Pay Phone:** Yes. **Rest Rooms and Showers:** Yes. **Fuel:** No. **Propane:** No. **Internal Roads:** Gravel, in good condition. **RV Service:** No. **Market:** Within 4 mi. **Restaurant:** Within 2 mi. **General Store:** Yes. **Vending:** Yes. **Playground:** Yes. **Other:** Lake Fairfax, water park. **Activities:** Swimming, water slide, wading pool, paddle boat rentals, lake fishing, sports field, hiking trails. **Nearby Attractions:** Washington, DC **Additional Information:** Washington, DC Convention and Visitors Bureau, (202) 789-7000, www.washington.org.

Restrictions

Pets: On leash only. **Fires:** At site. **Alcoholic Beverages:** At site. **Vehicle Maximum Length:** 35 ft. **Other:** No swimming permitted in lake.

To Get There

From I-495, take Exit 10 and go 6.5 mi. northwest on Hwy. 7 and south on Hwy. 606 to Lake Fairfax Dr. Entrance is on the left.

FANCY GAP

Fox Trail Family Campground

P.O. Box 233, Fancy Gap 24328. T: (540) 728-7776; F: (540) 728-9976; www.foxtrailcg.com; rwhite@foxtrailcg.com.

RV: ★★★★ Tent: n/a

Beauty: ★★★★ Site Privacy: ★
Spaciousness: ★★ Quiet: ★★★★
Security: ★★★★ Cleanliness: ★★★★
Insect Control: ★★★★ Facilities: ★★★★

Known for stunning natural splendor, the Blue Ridge Mountains are also known as a region where bluegrass music is king. Located atop Fancy Gap Mountain near the town of Fancy Gap, Fox Trail Family Campground is near several bluegrass music events, such as the annual Old Time Fiddlers Convention in Galax. This event is regarded as the oldest and largest gathering of bluegrass music enthusiasts in the world. Many campers use Fox Trail as an overnight stopping point on their way to Myrtle Beach and Florida. Fox Trail has large, wooded sites. There's a fishing pond, hiking trails, and a nearby mountain overlook. The campground is about 10 miles from the North Carolina border, a short drive from Mayberry Days, the Autumn Leaves Festival, and Mayberry USA in Mt. Airy. Sites on the campground's north tip are the most secluded, and sites near the entrance provide a view of the pond.

Basics

Operated By: Bob and Kris White. **Open:** All year. **Site Assignment:** Reservations accepted (14-day cancellation notice required for refund), walk-ins accepted. **Registration:** At campground office. **Fee:** $22 (VISA, MC). **Parking:** At site.

Facilities

Number of RV Sites: 96. **Number of Tent-Only Sites:** None. **Hookups:** Electric (20, 30, 50 amps), water, sewer. **Each Site:** Fire ring, picnic table. **Dump Station:** Yes. **Laundry:** Yes. **Pay Phone:** Yes. **Rest Rooms and Showers:** Yes. **Fuel:** No. **Propane:** Yes. **Internal Roads:** Gravel and paved, in good condition. **RV Service:** No. **Market:** Within 2 mi. **Restaurant:** Within 3 mi. **General Store:** Yes. **Vending:** Yes. **Playground:** Yes. **Other:** Fishing pond. **Activities:** Rec hall, game room, pond fishing, horseshoes. **Nearby Attractions:** Blue Ridge Parkway, Mayberry USA, Wytheville, Historic Crab Orchard Museum and Pioneer Park. **Additional Information:** Virginia Tourism Corp., (800) 371-8164, www.virginia.org.

Restrictions

Pets: On leash only. **Fires:** At site. **Alcoholic Beverages:** At site. **Vehicle Maximum Length:** None.

To Get There

From I-77, take Exit 8 and go 1 mi. east on Rte.

148, 1 mi. south on US 52 to junction with Blue Ridge Parkway. Follow blue camping signs.

FREDERICKSBURG

KOA—Fredericksburg/ Washington, DC South

7400 Brookside Ln., Fredericksburg 22408. T: (800) 562-1889 or (540) 898-7252; www.fredericksburgkoa.com; fredbrg@koa.com.

RV ★★★★ Tent ★★★★

Beauty: ★★★★ Site Privacy: ★★★
Spaciousness: ★★★ Quiet: ★★★★
Security: ★★★★ Cleanliness: ★★★★
Insect Control: ★★★★ Facilities: ★★★★

If you prefer KOA campgrounds, KOA—Fredericksburg/Washington, DC is the closest KOA facility to the District of Columbia and all of its attractions. There are 100-plus semi-wooded sites, including 49 level and shaded pull-throughs. The birthplace of George Washington, Fredericksburg is a treasure chest of history. The town has a 40-block historic district with trolley and carriage tours. The Fredericksburg & Spotsylvania National Military Park tells the story of the Civil War battles of Fredericksburg, Chancellorsville, Wilderness, and Spotsylvania Court House. The Manassas National Battlefield Park is a short drive away. If you do choose to visit Washington, DC, the campground offers a free shuttle to the VRE Train on weekdays. This will transport you downtown, where several guided tour options await.

BASICS

Operated By: KOA. **Open:** All year. **Site Assignment:** Reservations recommended, walk-ins accepted. **Registration:** At campground office. **Fee:** $25–$34 (VISA, MC, D). **Parking:** At designated spot.

FACILITIES

Number of RV Sites: 75. **Number of Tent-Only Sites:** 25. **Hookups:** Electric (20, 30, 50 amps), water, cable TV, phone, 36 full hookups. **Each Site:** Grill, picnic table. **Dump Station:** Yes. **Laundry:** Yes. **Pay Phone:** Yes. **Rest Rooms and Showers:** Yes. **Fuel:** No. **Propane:** Yes. **Internal Roads:** Paved, in good condition. **RV Service:** No. **Market:** Within 4 mi. **Restaurant:** Within 4 mi. **General Store:** Yes. **Vending:** Yes. **Playground:** Yes. **Other:** Car rental service available. **Activities:** Game room, swimming, pedal boat rentals, pond fishing, bike rentals, sports field, horseshoes, hiking trails, volleyball. **Nearby Attractions:** Historic Fredericksburg, Washington, DC, Paramount's Kings Dominion, Mt. Vernon, golf courses, Lake Anna, Fredericksburg and Spotsylvania Military Park, Manassas National Battlefield Park. **Additional Information:** Virginia Tourism Corp., (800) 371-8164, www.virginia.org.

RESTRICTIONS

Pets: On leash only. **Fires:** At site. **Alcoholic Beverages:** At site. **Vehicle Max. Length:** None.

TO GET THERE

From I-95, take Exit 118 and go 4 mi. north on US 1 and 2.5 mi. east on Hwy. 607. Entrance is on the right.

FRONT ROYAL

KOA—Front Royal/ Washington, DC West

P.O. Box 274, Front Royal 22630. T: (800) 562-9114 or (540) 635-2741; F: (540) 635-4089; www.koa.com; frntrylkoa@aol.com.

RV ★★★★ Tent ★★★★

Beauty: ★★★★ Site Privacy: ★★
Spaciousness: ★★★ Quiet: ★★★
Security: ★★★★ Cleanliness: ★★★★
Insect Control: ★★★★ Facilities: ★★★★

Located at the north end of Skyline Drive, KOA—Front Royal/Washington, DC West is the type of campground both parents and their children can enjoy. There's a swimming pool, a whirlpool, a sauna, and a thrilling water slide. Perched on a hilltop, the campground has more than 150 open and wooded sites, including 47 pull-throughs. From Front Royal, the 105-mile-long Skyline Drive follows the crest of the Blue Ridge Mountains through Shenandoah National Park, and it continues to the Blue Ridge Parkway. Tubing, canoeing, and fishing in the Shenandoah River and hiking through Shenandoah National Park are among the activities that KOA campers partake in. Spelunkers can explore Luray Caverns and Skyline Caverns. In conjunction with its proximity to Washington, DC (about 50 miles west), KOA can arrange tours for campers.

BASICS

Operated By: KOA. **Open:** Mar. 15–Nov. 1. **Site Assignment:** Reservations and walk-ins accepted. **Registration:** At campground office. **Fee:** $27–$35 (VISA, MC, D). **Parking:** At site.

FACILITIES

Number of RV Sites: 110. **Number of Tent-Only Sites:** 40. **Hookups:** Electric (20, 30 amps), water, phone, 42 full hookups. **Each Site:** Fire rings, picnic tables. **Dump Station:** Yes. **Laundry:** Yes. **Pay Phone:** Yes. **Rest Rooms and Showers:** Yes. **Fuel:** No. **Propane:** Yes. **Internal Roads:** Gravel and paved, in good condition. **RV Service:** No. **Market:** Within 2 mi. **Restaurant:** Within 2 mi. **General Store:** Yes. **Vending:** Yes. **Playground:** Yes. **Other:** Water slide. **Activities:** Swimming, game room, rec hall, whirlpool, pond fishing, mini-golf, basketball, planned activities on weekends, horseshoes, volleyball. **Nearby Attractions:** Skyline Drive, Shenandoah River, Skyline Caverns, Luray Caverns, Shenandoah National Park, Washington, DC **Additional Information:** Shenandoah Valley Travel Assoc., (540) 740-3132, www.svta.org.

RESTRICTIONS

Pets: On leash only. **Fires:** At site. **Alcoholic Beverages:** At site. **Vehicle Max. Length:** None.

TO GET THERE

From Hwy. 55, go 2.5 mi. south on US 340 and 1 mi. southeast to entrance on the left.

GLENNS

Thousand Trails—Chesapeake Bay

12014 Trails Ln., Gloucester 23061. T: (800) 693-6901; www.thousandtrails.com.

RV ★★★★ Tent ★★★★

Beauty: ★★★★★ Site Privacy: ★★
Spaciousness: ★★★ Quiet: ★★★
Security: ★★★★ Cleanliness: ★★★★
Insect Control: ★★★★ Facilities: ★★★★★

Situated on the Piankatank River a short drive from Chesapeake Bay, Thousand Trails—Chesapeake Bay certainly doesn't have a shortage of activities and amenities. A 280-acre preserve adorned with pine, oak, and dogwood forests, the campground has two piers for fishing, boating, and water skiing; an adult lodge and a family center; indoor and outdoor swimming pools; and canoe and pedal boat rentals. RV camping is especially convenient with 355 full hookups. There are too many attractions and destinations near the campground to fit in one vacation, unless that vacation is a month long. Many campers head for Chesapeake Bay or the heritage attractions at Colonial Williamsburg and Yorktown. Busch Gardens and Water Country USA are in Williamsburg; Yorktown was the site of British General Cornwallis' surrender to Gen. George Washington. The Yorktown Victory Center is a must-see for any history enthusiast.

BASICS

Operated By: Thousand Trails. **Open:** All year. **Site Assignment:** Reservations and walk-ins accepted. **Registration:** At campground headquarters. **Fee:** $20 (VISA, MC, AE, D). **Parking:** At designated area.

FACILITIES

Number of RV Sites: 373. **Number of Tent-Only Sites:** 21. **Hookups:** Electric (30, 50 amps), phone, water, 355 full hookups. **Each Site:** Fire ring, picnic table. **Dump Station:** Yes. **Laundry:** Yes. **Pay Phone:** Yes. **Rest Rooms and Showers:** Yes. **Fuel:** No. **Propane:** Yes. **Internal Roads:** Gravel and paved, in good condition. **RV Service:** No. **Market:** Within 6 mi. **Restaurant:** On premises. **General Store:** Yes. **Vending:** Yes. **Playground:** Yes. **Other:** Adult lodge, family center, indoor spa. **Activities:** Swimming, rec hall, game room, whirlpool, boating, canoeing, kayaking, boat rentals, ocean fishing, river fishing, pond fishing, mini-golf, basketball, bike rentals, shuffleboard, planned activities on weekends, tennis, sports field, horseshoes, volleyball, hiking trails. **Nearby Attractions:** Chesapeake Bay, Colonial Williamsburg, Historic Jamestown Settlement, Fredericksburg, Williamsburg Pottery, Yorktown, Busch Gardens, Water Country USA, Paramount's Kings Dominion. **Additional Information:** Williamsburg Area CVB, (757) 253-0192, www.visitwilliamsburg.com.

RESTRICTIONS

Pets: On leash only. **Fires:** At site. **Alcoholic Beverages:** At site. **Vehicle Max. Length:** None.

TO GET THERE

From US 17, go 5.5 mi. east on Hwy. 198 and 0.5 mi. north on Dutton Rd. Entrance is on the left.

GREEN BAY

Twin Lakes State Park

Rte. 2 Box 70, Green Bay 23942. T: (804) 392-3435 or (800) 933-PARK; www.dcr.state.va.us/parks; resvs@dcr.state.va.us.

RV ★★★ Tent ★★★

Beauty: ★★★ Site Privacy: ★★
Spaciousness: ★★ Quiet: ★★★
Security: ★★★ Cleanliness: ★★★
Insect Control: ★★★ Facilities: ★★★

Green Bay is the home of Twin Lakes State Park, which operated as two parks until 1976. The land for Twin Lakes State Park was initially bought from struggling farmers by the federal government during the Great Depression. Goodwin Lake Park and Prince Edward Lake Park were created in 1939. Until the early 1960s, they were managed as two racially segregated parks. As a result, Twin Lakes State Park has two complete sets of facilities. The campground has 30 sites, all with electric and water hookups. Most of the sites are shaded. Goodwin Lake's day-use area features a 1.5-mile nature trail, a sandy beach, and a playground. A 14-mile multi-use trail winds around the adjacent 6,496-acre Prince Edward-Gallion State Forest. Nearby is Sailor's Creek Historical State Park, where Gen. Robert E. Lee's Confederate troops were soundly defeated by Union troops, leading to General Lee's surrender at Appomattox Court House three days later.

BASICS

Operated By: State of Virginia. **Open:** Mar.–Dec. **Site Assignment:** Reservations and walk-ins accepted. **Registration:** At registration point. **Fee:** $15 (VISA, MC). **Parking:** At site.

FACILITIES

Number of RV Sites: 20. **Number of Tent-Only Sites:** 10. **Hookups:** Electric (20, 30), water. **Each Site:** Fire ring, picnic table. **Dump Station:** Yes. **Laundry:** No. **Pay Phone:** Yes. **Rest Rooms and Showers:** Yes. **Fuel:** No. **Propane:** No. **Internal Roads:** Paved, in good condition. **RV Service:** No. **Market:** Within 10 mi. **Restaurant:** Within 10 mi. **General Store:** Yes. **Vending:** Yes. **Playground:** Yes. **Other:** Cedar Crest Conference Center, Mistletoe Lodge. **Activities:** Lake swimming, boating and fishing; hiking trails. **Nearby Attractions:** Sailor's Creek Battlefield State Park, Sandy River Reservoir, Briery Creek Wildlife Management Area, Prince Edward/Gallion State Forest, Lee's Retreat Driving Tour, Longwood College Visual Arts Center, Jim's Cowboy Museum. **Additional Information:** Virginia Tourism Corp., (800) 371-8164, www.virginia.org.

RESTRICTIONS

Pets: On leash only, $3 per night. **Fires:** At site. **Alcoholic Beverages:** No alcohol permitted. **Vehicle Maximum Length:** 25 ft. **Other:** Max. 14-day stay in 30-day period.

TO GET THERE

From Burkeville, take US 360 west to Hwy. 613, then go east on Hwy. 629. Entrance is on the left.

HUDDLESTON

Smith Mountain Lake State Park

1235 State Park Rd., Huddleston 24104-9547. T: (540) 297-6066; www.dcr.state.va.us/parks; resvs@dcr.state.va.us.

RV ★★★ Tent ★★★★

Beauty: ★★★ Site Privacy: ★★★
Spaciousness: ★★★ Quiet: ★★★
Security: ★★★★ Cleanliness: ★★★
Insect Control: ★★★ Facilities: ★★★

Spread out over 1,246 acres densely wooded with Virginia pine, American beech, and juniper, Smith Mountain Lake State Park is home to and named for Virginia's second largest freshwater lake. The park is located in the foothills of the Blue Ridge Mountains. There are no lake views from the 50-site campground, but the sites are situated in the woods. The park has a 500-foot sandy beach (the park's lone swimming area). There are guided night hikes, hayrides, canoe trips, and other activities. Hike to the water from the Lake View Trail and Chestnut Ridge Trail. The park's visitor center features exhibits on the history and folklore of the area and the lake's aquatic environment. A small gift shop is operated by the Friends of Smith Mountain Lake State Park. Many interpretive programs take place here or at the newly refurbished amphitheater nearby.

BASICS

Operated By: State of Virginia. **Open:** Mar.–Dec. **Site Assignment:** First-come, first-served; no reservations accepted. **Registration:** At campground office. **Fee:** $14 (VISA, MC). **Parking:** At site.

FACILITIES

Number of RV Sites: 24. **Number of Tent-Only Sites:** 26. **Hookups:** Electric (20, 30 amps). **Each Site:** Grill, picnic table. **Dump Station:** Yes. **Laundry:** No. **Pay Phone:** Yes. **Rest Rooms and Showers:** Yes. **Fuel:** No. **Propane:** No. **Internal Roads:** Paved, in good condition. **RV Service:** No. **Market:** Within 10 mi. **Restaurant:** Within 12 mi. **General Store:** No. **Vending:** Yes. **Playground:** Yes. **Other:** Cabin rentals, interpretive center. **Activities:** Lake swimming and fishing, boating, canoeing, boat rentals, hiking trails. **Nearby Attractions:** Booker T. Washington National Monument, Peaks of Otter, Blue Ridge Parkway. **Additional Information:** Roanoke Valley CVB, (800) 635-5535, www.visitroanoke.com.

RESTRICTIONS

Pets: On leash, $3 per night. **Fires:** In grills and pits. **Alcoholic Beverages:** No alcohol permitted. **Vehicle Maximum Length:** 50 ft. **Other:** Max. 14-day stay in 30-day period.

TO GET THERE

From Hwy. 43, go 14 mi. southwest on Hwy. 626. Follow signs to park.

KING & QUEEN COURTHOUSE

Rainbow Acres Camping Resort

Rte. 2 Box 16, King & Queen Courthouse 23085. T: (804) 785-9441; www.woodalls.com/a/01470_rainbowacres; rose@inna.net.

RV ★★★★ Tent ★★★★

Beauty: ★★★★ Site Privacy: ★★★
Spaciousness: ★★★ Quiet: ★★★★
Security: ★★★★ Cleanliness: ★★★★
Insect Control: ★★★★ Facilities: ★★★★

Hugging the Mattaponi River near King & Queen Courthouse, Rainbow Acres Camping Resort has 16 pull-through sites. The campground's six tent sites are located along the river. The campground is definitely a festive place, with dancing, parades, cookouts, hayrides, and bingo games. Fishing, swimming, boating and water skiing on the Mattaponi River is what draws many campers. If you want to explore the river (or other bodies of water) beyond the campground, Mattaponi Canoe & Kayak provides guided paddling excursions on both tidal and non-tidal reaches of the Mattaponi, Pamunkey, and Chickahominy Rivers, as well as the Dragon Swamp. There are also sunset paddles at the Pamunkey Indian Reservation. Rainbow Acres is about 40 miles east of Richmond and 40 miles west of Chesapeake Bay, so day trips in these areas—as well as Williamsburg, about 40 miles south—are worthwhile.

BASICS

Operated By: Rose Mary Zellner. **Open:** All year. **Site Assignment:** Reservations and walk-ins accepted. **Registration:** At campground office. **Fee:** $20 (VISA, MC, D). **Parking:** At site.

FACILITIES

Number of RV Sites: 155. **Number of Tent-Only Sites:** 6. **Hookups:** Electric (20, 30 amps), phone, 155 full hookups. **Each Site:** Fire ring, picnic table. **Dump Station:** Yes. **Laundry:** Yes. **Pay Phone:** Yes. **Rest Rooms and Showers:** Yes. **Fuel:** Yes. **Propane:** Yes. **Internal Roads:** Dirt, in good condition. **RV Service:** No. **Market:** Within 10 mi. **Restaurant:** Within 8 mi. **General Store:** Yes. **Vending:** Yes. **Playground:** Yes. **Other:** None. **Activities:** Game room, river swimming and fishing, rec hall, boating, canoeing, kayaking, basketball, planned activities on weekends, horseshoes, volleyball. **Nearby Attractions:** Mattaponi River, Richmond, Williamsburg, Chesapeake Bay. **Additional Information:** Virginia Tourism Corp., (800) 371-8164, www.virginia.org.

RESTRICTIONS

Pets: On leash only. **Fires:** At site. **Alcoholic Beverages:** At site. **Vehicle Maximum Length:** None.

TO GET THERE

From Hwy. 33, go 13 mi. northwest on Hwy. 14 and 1 mi. southwest on Fraizer Ferry Rd. Entrance is on the left.

LORTON

Pohick Bay Regional Park

6501 Pohick Bay Dr., Lorton 22709. T: (703) 339-6104; F: (703) 273-0905; www.nvrpa.org; info@nvrpa.org.

★★★★ ★★★★

Beauty: ★★★★ Site Privacy: ★★★
Spaciousness: ★★★ Quiet: ★★★
Security: ★★★★ Cleanliness: ★★★★
Insect Control: ★★★★ Facilities: ★★★★

Located 25 miles south of Washington, D.C., the Pohick Bay Regional Park is situated on a bay on the historic Mason Neck peninsula in Fairfax County. The park has a marina, boat launch, and a fleet of pedal boats, sailboats, and job boats available for rent. The campsites are nestled under pine, beech, and holly trees, providing ample shade on sweltering days. Local golf magazines have repeatedly name Pohick Bay as one of the area's most challenging courses. If you would rather explore nature without a bag of golf clubs, make a short drive to Mason Neck State Park, where more than 200 species of birds reside. Chances are you'll see great blue heron and even bald eagles. If you prefer to mix nature with visiting historic landmarks, remember that Washington, D.C. is a short drive away, and when you return to Pohick Bay, you'll appreciate nature's splendor—and serenity—even more.

BASICS

Operated By: Northern Virginia Regional Park Authority. **Open:** All year. **Site Assignment:** First-come, first-served; no reservations accepted. **Registration:** At campground office. **Fee:** $12–$15 (VISA, MC). **Parking:** At site.

FACILITIES

Number of RV Sites: 100. **Number of Tent-Only Sites:** 50. **Hookups:** Electric (30 amps). **Each Site:** Grill, picnic table. **Dump Station:** Yes. **Laundry:** Yes. **Pay Phone:** Yes. **Rest Rooms and Showers:** Yes. **Fuel:** No. **Propane:** No. **Internal Roads:** Paved, in good condition. **RV Service:** No. **Market:** Within 4 mi. **Restaurant:** On premises. **General Store:** Yes. **Vending:** Yes. **Playground:** Yes. **Other:** 18-hole golf course. **Activities:** Golf, mini-golf, frisbee golf, horseback riding, hiking trails, boating, canoeing, boat rentals, river fishing, driving range, putting green. **Nearby Attractions:** Washington, D.C. **Additional Information:** Washington, DC CVB, (202) 789-7000, ww.washington.org.

RESTRICTIONS

Pets: On leash only. **Fires:** Camp stove or fire ring. **Alcoholic Beverages:** Not permitted. **Vehicle Max. Length:** 33 ft. **Other:** 7-day max. stay.

TO GET THERE

From US 1, go 4 mi. east on Hwy. 242. Entrance is on the left.

LURAY

Big Meadows Campground

3655 US Hwy. 211 East, Luray 22835-9036. T: (540) 999-3500; F: (540) 999-3601; www.nps.gov/shen; shen_superintendent@nps.gov.

★★★★ ★★★★

Beauty: ★★★★ Site Privacy: ★★★★
Spaciousness: ★★★★ Quiet: ★★★★
Security: ★★★★ Cleanliness: ★★★★★
Insect Control: ★★★★ Facilities: ★★★★

On July 3, 1936, President Franklin D. Roosevelt helped formally open Shenandoah National Park during a ceremony at Big Meadows near Luray. Big Meadows is the park's most expansive treeless area at 640 acres. In a region dominated by mature forests, a tree-barren plateau like Big Meadows is indeed unique. Historians believe that Native Americans may have cleared the area to promote better grazing conditions. Big Meadows Campground has some grassy and open sites; others are wooded. Big Meadows Campground is the only one at the park that accepts reservations. Overall, Shenandoah National Park consists of more than 500 miles of trails, including 101 miles of the Appalachian Trail. Trails may follow a ridge crest, lead to high places with panoramic views, or wander to waterfalls in deep canyons. Many animals, including deer, black bears, and wild turkeys flourish among the rich growth of an oak-hickory forest.

BASICS

Operated By: National Park Service. **Open:** May–Oct. **Site Assignment:** Reservations recommended, walk-ins accepted. **Registration:** At campground office. **Fee:** $10 park entrance fee plus $17 (VISA, MC). **Parking:** At site.

FACILITIES

Number of RV Sites: 39. **Number of Tent-Only Sites:** 178. **Hookups:** None. **Each Site:** Grill, picnic table. **Dump Station:** Yes. **Laundry:** Yes. **Pay Phone:** Yes. **Rest Rooms and Showers:** Yes. **Fuel:** No. **Propane:** No. **Internal Roads:** Paved, in good condition. **RV Service:** No. **Market:** Within 16 mi. **Restaurant:** On premises. **General Store:** Yes. **Vending:** Yes. **Playground:** No. **Other:** Lodge and restaurant. **Activities:** Stream fishing, hiking trails. **Nearby Attractions:** Shenandoah National Park, Appalachian Trail, Skyline Drive. **Additional Information:** Shenandoah Valley Travel Assoc., (540) 740-3132, www.svta.org.

RESTRICTIONS

Pets: On leash only. **Fires:** In camp stoves and fireplaces. **Alcoholic Beverages:** At site. **Vehicle Maximum Length:** None. **Other:** Max. 6 people per site.

TO GET THERE

From US 33, go 16 mi. north on Skyline Dr. to Milepost 51. Follow signs to campground.

LURAY

Lewis Mountain Campground

3655 US Hwy. 211 East, Luray 22835-9036. T: (540) 999-3500; F: (540) 999-3601; www.nps.gov/shen; shen_superintendent@nps.gov.

★★★ ★★★★

Beauty: ★★★★ Site Privacy: ★★★
Spaciousness: ★★★ Quiet: ★★★★
Security: ★★★★ Cleanliness: ★★★★★
Insect Control: ★★★★ Facilities: ★★★★

The smallest of Shenandoah National Park's five campgrounds (and the only one with no dump station), Lewis Mountain Campground's sites are situated amid massive maple, pine, hemlock, and oak trees. No reservations are accepted at Lewis Mountain. This can pose a problem during the fall, when colors are their most vibrant and campgrounds at the park are full on weekends. The solution: arrive at Lewis Mountain on a weekday. It's difficult to miss—and important to obey—the sign at the campground that reads, "Bear Country—Protect Your Property and Food, Proper Food Storage is Required." The campground has food storage poles for tenters. If you don't have an RV or tent, Lewis Mountain has several rustic, furnished cabins with private baths. For an interesting hike, drive to Milepost 59.5 and walk along the Pocosin Mission Trail. The path leads past an old Episcopal mission from the early 1900s and an overgrown cemetery.

BASICS

Operated By: National Park Service. **Open:** May–Nov. **Site Assignment:** First-come, first-served; no reservations accepted. **Registration:** At campground office. **Fee:** $10 park entrance and $14 (VISA, MC). **Parking:** At site.

FACILITIES

Number of RV Sites: 16. **Number of Tent-Only Sites:** 16. **Hookups:** None. **Each Site:** Picnic table and fire grill. **Dump Station:** No. **Laundry:** Yes. **Pay Phone:** Yes. **Rest Rooms and Showers:** Yes. **Fuel:** No. **Propane:** No. **Internal Roads:** Paved, in good condition. **RV Service:** No. **Market:** Within 10 mi. **Restaurant:** Within 6 mi. **General Store:** Yes. **Vending:** Yes. **Playground:** No. **Other:** Cabin rentals. **Activities:** Stream fishing, hiking trails. **Nearby Attractions:** Shenandoah National Park, Appalachian Trail, Skyline Drive. **Additional Information:** Shenandoah Valley Travel Assoc., (540) 740-3132, www.svta.org.

RESTRICTIONS

Pets: On leash only. **Fires:** In camp stoves and fireplaces. **Alcoholic Beverages:** At site. **Vehicle Maximum Length:** 30 ft. **Other:** Max. 6 people per site.

TO GET THERE

From US 33, go 8 mi. northeast on Skyline Dr. to Milepost 57.5 and 1.5 mi. east on park road.

LURAY

Loft Mountain Campground

3655 US Hwy. 211 E., Luray 22835-9036. T: (540) 999-3500; F: (540) 999-3601; www.nps.gov/shen; shen_superintendent@nps.gov.

★★★ ★★★★

Beauty: ★★★★ Site Privacy: ★★★
Spaciousness: ★★★ Quiet: ★★★★
Security: ★★★★ Cleanliness: ★★★★
Insect Control: ★★★★ Facilities: ★★★

The largest campground in Shenandoah National Park, Loft Mountain Campground actually sits atop Big Flat Mountain, which affords panoramic views of the neighboring peaks and valley to east and west from 3,400 feet. Loft Mountain is the southernmost campground in the park. This mountaintop area has thick, low-growing shrubs instead of the mature hardwoods that dominate most of Shenandoah National Park's landscape. Many of the campground's 219 sites are private and spacious. Weekends—especially fall weekends—are the most difficult time to find a site. Arriving at Loft Mountain on a weekday is advisable. The 1.3-mile Deadening Nature Trail, which has two rocky observation points, and the 2.7-mile Loft Mountain Loop, which leads to a 3,290-foot lookout, are among the many hiking trails that start at or near the campground. Loft Mountain also has a visitor center with rest rooms, an information desk, and first aid items. Many ranger-led programs and hikes begin here.

Basics

Operated By: National Park Service. **Open:** May–Oct. **Site Assignment:** First-come, first-served; no reservations accepted. **Registration:** At campground office. **Fee:** $10 park entrance fee and $14 (VISA, MC). **Parking:** At site.

Facilities

Number of RV Sites: 165. **Number of Tent-Only Sites:** 54. **Hookups:** None. **Each Site:** Grill, picnic table. **Dump Station:** Yes. **Laundry:** Yes. **Pay Phone:** Yes. **Rest Rooms and Showers:** Yes. **Fuel:** No. **Propane:** No. **Internal Roads:** Paved, in good condition. **RV Service:** No. **Market:** Within 12 mi. **Restaurant:** On premises. **General Store:** Yes. **Vending:** Yes. **Playground:** No. **Other:** Restaurant. **Activities:** Stream fishing, hiking trails. **Nearby Attractions:** Shenandoah National Park, Appalachian Trail. **Additional Information:** Shenandoah Valley Travel Assoc., (540) 740-3132, www.svta.org.

Restrictions

Pets: On leash only. **Fires:** Use camp stoves and designated fireplaces. **Alcoholic Beverages:** At site. **Vehicle Maximum Length:** 30 ft. **Other:** Max. 6 people per site.

To Get There

From US 33, go 10 mi. southwest on Skyline Dr. to Milepost 79.5 and 1.5 mi. east on park road.

LURAY

Mathews Arm Campground

3655 US Hwy. 211 East, Luray 22835-9036.
T: (540) 999-3500; F: (540) 999-3601;
www.nps.gov/shen;
shen_superintendent@nps.gov.

RV ★★★ Tent ★★★★

Beauty: ★★★★ Site Privacy: ★★★
Spaciousness: ★★★ Quiet: ★★★★
Security: ★★★★ Cleanliness: ★★★★★
Insect Control: ★★★★ Facilities: ★★★

The northernmost campground in Shenandoah National Park, Mathews Arm Campground has 179 sites, most of which are level. There are no electric hookups, and no reservations are accepted. At this or any of the Shenandoah National Park campgrounds that don't accept reservations, weekends are the busiest time. The campground is shaded by hickory and oak trees, and there are many desirable sites. However, to have a wider choice of sites, consider arriving at Mathews Arm on a weekday. Several scenic hiking trails sprout near the campground. The 1.7-mile Traces Nature Trail begins near the campground registration station's parking area and connects with the Mathews Arm Trail, which in turn intersects with the Tuscarora–Overall Run Trail. A two-mile walk down this trail leads to Overall Run Falls, the tallest waterfall in Shenandoah National Park. Two miles from the campground entrance, Elkwallow Wayside has camping supplies and food service.

Basics

Operated By: National Park Service. **Open:** May–Oct. **Site Assignment:** First-come, first-served; no reservations accepted. **Registration:** At registration station. **Fee:** $10 park entrance fee and $14 (VISA, MC). **Parking:** At site.

Facilities

Number of RV Sites: 166. **Number of Tent-Only Sites:** 13. **Hookups:** None. **Each Site:** Grill, picnic table. **Dump Station:** Yes. **Laundry:** No. **Pay Phone:** Yes. **Rest Rooms and Showers:** Yes. **Fuel:** No. **Propane:** No. **Internal Roads:** Paved, in good condition. **RV Service:** No. **Market:** Within 10 mi. **Restaurant:** Within 2 mi. **General Store:** No. **Vending:** No. **Playground:** No. **Other:** Amphitheater. **Activities:** Stream fishing, hiking trails. **Nearby Attractions:** Shenandoah National Park, Appalachian Trail. **Additional Information:** Shenandoah Valley Travel Assoc., (540) 740-3132, www.svta.org.

Restrictions

Pets: On leash only. **Fires:** In camp stoves and fireplaces. **Alcoholic Beverages:** At site. **Vehicle Maximum Length:** None. **Other:** Max. 6 people per site.

To Get There

From Thornton Gap entrance to park at Milepost 31.5, go north on Skyline Dr. to campground entrance at Milepost 22.2.

LURAY

Yogi Bear's Jellystone Park Camp Resort

P.O. Box 191, Luray 22835. T: (540) 743-4002 or (800) 420-6679; F: (540) 743-2111;
www.campluray.com; yogilura@shentel.net.

RV ★★★★ Tent ★★★★

Beauty: ★★★★ Site Privacy: ★★
Spaciousness: ★★ Quiet: ★★★
Security: ★★★★ Cleanliness: ★★★★
Insect Control: ★★★★ Facilities: ★★★★★

Located at the base of the Blue Ridge Mountains five miles from the entrance to Shenandoah National Park and Skyline Drive, Yogi Bear's Jellystone Park Camp Resort in Luray has wooded and open sites that offer panoramic views of the Blue Ridge Mountains. The campground has 63 pull-through sites, a 24-hour laundromat, and a full-service camp store on the premises. Shenandoah National Park is a sanctuary for 100 varieties of trees, 200 species of birds, and 43 species of mammals. The numerous hiking trails—many accessible off Skyline Drive—lead to stunning views of mountain peaks and valleys. Luray Caverns isn't limited to its network of underground passages; the attraction also includes the Car and Carriage Museum, the Garden Maze, and the Singing Tower. The New Market Battlefield Park and Hall of Valor Museum in nearby New Market offer tours and movies about the battle and Stonewall Jackson.

Basics

Operated By: Jellystone Park. **Open:** Apr. 1–Nov. 15. **Site Assignment:** Reservations accepted (deposit forfeit for no-shows and less than 7 days cancellation notice), walk-ins accepted. **Registration:** At campground office. **Fee:** $30–$35 (VISA, MC, D). **Parking:** At site.

Facilities

Number of RV Sites: 132. **Number of Tent-Only Sites:** 68. **Hookups:** Electric (20, 30, 50 amps), water, 83 full hookups. **Each Site:** Fire ring, picnic table. **Dump Station:** Yes. **Laundry:** Yes. **Pay Phone:** Yes. **Rest Rooms and Showers:** Yes. **Fuel:** No. **Propane:** Yes. **Internal Roads:** Gravel, in good condition. **RV Service:** No. **Market:** Within 2 mi. **Restaurant:** Within 2 mi. **General Store:** Yes. **Vending:** Yes. **Playground:** Yes. **Other:** Water slide. **Activities:** Swimming, wading pool, water slide, pond fishing, boat rentals, rec hall, game room, mini-golf, planned activities, movies, sports field, horseshoes, hiking trails, volleyball. **Nearby Attractions:** Luray Caverns, Shenandoah National Park, Shenandoah River, Natural Bridge of Virginia. **Additional Information:** Shenandoah Valley Travel Assoc., (540) 740-3132, www.svta.org.

Restrictions

Pets: On leash only. **Fires:** At site. **Alcoholic Beverages:** At site. **Vehicle Maximum Length:** None. **Other:** Children must be accompanied by adult at swimming pool.

To Get There

From US 340, go 4 mi. east on US 211. Entrance is on the right.

MADISON

Shenandoah Hills Campground

RR 1 Box 7, Madison 22727. T: (540) 948-4186 or (800) 321-4186;
www.gocampingamerica.com/shenandoahhills;
shenandoah@gocampingamerica.com.

RV ★★★★ Tent ★★★★

Beauty: ★★★★★ Site Privacy: ★★★
Spaciousness: ★★★★ Quiet: ★★★★
Security: ★★★★ Cleanliness: ★★★★
Insect Control: ★★★★ Facilities: ★★★★

Located in the foothills of the Blue Ridge Mountains, Shenandoah Hills Campground has wooded and open sites, including 16 pull-throughs. There are cool and comfortable waterside sites, remote wooded tent sites, and rustic log cabin rentals. The campground is a short distance from Shenandoah National Park, Luray Caverns, and Endless Caverns. Shenandoah Hills is also near Thomas Jefferson's Monticello, a must-see for history and architectural enthusiasts. In Fredericksburg, George Washington's Mount Vernon is another presidential day trip from Shenandoah Hills. More than a dozen outbuildings are meticulously restored, including the slave quarters and greenhouse.

Basics

Operated By: Private operator. **Open:** Mar.–Dec. **Site Assignment:** Reservations recommended (3-night min. for holiday weekend), walk-ins accepted. **Registration:** At camp store. **Fee:** $21–$28 (VISA, MC). **Parking:** At site.

Facilities

Number of RV Sites: 65. **Number of Tent-Only Sites:** 16. **Hookups:** Electric (20/ 30 amps), cable TV, water, 41 full hookups. **Each Site:** Fire ring, picnic table. **Dump Station:** Yes. **Laundry:** Yes. **Pay Phone:** Yes. **Rest Rooms and Showers:** Yes. **Fuel:** No. **Propane:** Yes. **Internal Roads:** Gravel and paved, in good condition. **RV Service:** No. **Market:** Within 2 mi. **Restaurant:** Within 1 mi. **General Store:** Yes. **Vending:** Yes. **Playground:** Yes. **Other:** Hayrides. **Activities:** Game room, rec hall, swimming, basketball, planned activities on weekends, tennis, sports field, horseshoes, hiking trails, volleyball. **Nearby Attractions:** Monticello, Montpelier, Skyline Drive, Luray Caverns, Endless Caverns, Shenandoah National Park, wineries, antique shops. **Additional Information:** Shenandoah Valley Travel Assoc., (540) 740-3132, www.svta.org.

Restrictions

Pets: On leash only. **Fires:** At site. **Alcoholic Beverages:** At site. **Vehicle Maximum Length:** 45 ft.

To Get There

From Hwy. 230, go 0.1 mi. south on US 29. Entrance is on the right.

MARION

Hungry Mother State Park

2854 State Park Blvd., Marion 24354. T: (540) 781-7400 or (800) 933-PARK; www.dcr.state.va.us/parks; resvs@dcr.state.va.us.

RV ★★★★ Tent ★★★★

Beauty: ★★★★ Site Privacy: ★★★★
Spaciousness: ★★★★ Quiet: ★★★★
Security: ★★★★ Cleanliness: ★★★★
Insect Control: ★★★★ Facilities: ★★★★

According to legend, at a time when Native Americans were destroying settlements along the New River, a woman named Molly Marley and her child were captured. They later escaped and wandered through the wilderness eating only wild berries. Molly eventually collapsed, and her child later found help. The child's only words were "hungry, mother" when found. The search party found Molly dead. To honor her, the base at the mountain where she was found was named Molly's Knob, and the creek where her child followed to seek help was called Hungry Mother Creek. The creek was later dammed and renamed Hungry Mother Lake. The 108-acre lake is a popular spot for boating and fishing, and the park's 2,180 acres are ideal for hiking and horseback riding. The 43 camping sites are actually distributed over three campgrounds. The RV sites offer electric hookups, and the park has a dump station and hot showers. One of the original CCC facilities, the Restaurant at Hungry Mother overlooks the lake.

Basics

Operated By: State of Virginia. **Open:** Mar.–Dec. **Site Assignment:** First come, first served; no reservations accepted. **Registration:** At campground office. **Fee:** $14–$18 (VISA, MC). **Parking:** At site.

Facilities

Number of RV Sites: 32. **Number of Tent-Only Sites:** 11. **Hookups:** Electric (15 amps). **Each Site:** Grill, picnic table. **Dump Station:** Yes. **Laundry:** No. **Pay Phone:** Yes. **Rest Rooms and Showers:** Yes. **Fuel:** No. **Propane:** No. **Internal Roads:** Paved, in fair condition. **RV Service:** No. **Market:** Within 3 mi. **Restaurant:** On premises. **General Store:** Yes. **Vending:** Yes. **Playground:** Yes. **Other:** Hungry Mother Lake, Hemlock Haven Conference Center, Hungry Mother Lodge. **Activities:** Horseback riding, lake fishing and swimming, boating, boat rentals, planned activities, hiking trails. **Nearby Attractions:** Grayson Highlands State Park, Mt. Rogers National Recreation Area, Historic Saltville, Historic Abingdon, Wytheville, Bristol Motor Speedway. **Additional Information:** Virginia Tourism Corp. (800) 371-8164, www.virginia.org.

Restrictions

Pets: On leash only. **Fires:** In camp stove or fire ring. **Alcoholic Beverages:** No alcohol permitted. **Vehicle Maximum Length:** 30 ft. **Other:** Swimming only permitted in designated areas.

To Get There

From Marion, go 3 mi. north on Hwy. 16. Follow signs to the park.

MEADOWS OF DAN

Meadows of Dan Campground

2182 Jeb Stuart Hwy., Meadows of Dan 24120. T: (540) 952-2292; F: (540) 952-2392; www.meadowsofdancampground; kevinj@fourseasonmanagement.com.

RV ★★★★ Tent ★★★★

Beauty: ★★★★ Site Privacy: ★★★★
Spaciousness: ★★★★ Quiet: ★★★★★
Security: ★★★★★ Cleanliness: ★★★★
Insect Control: ★★★★ Facilities: ★★★★

Located in the Blue Ridge Mountains, less than a mile from the Blue Ridge Parkway, Meadows of Dan Campground is not the place to stay if you have children with visions of swimming pools, water slides, and mini-golf courses. It is ideal, though, if you are searching for solitude in a clean, scenic environment. There are two pull-through sites. The bathhouse is clean and well-kept, and there is a washer and dryer. Two cabin rentals are also available. With its proximity to the Blue Ridge Parkway, Meadows of Dan is convenient to numerous hiking trails. The Pinnacles of Dan and Lover's Leap are two nearby overlooks worth a visit. Roanoke is about 50 miles northeast, where you'll find the Virginia Museum of Transportation and its early automobiles and locomotives. For more modern transportation, a NASCAR speedway in Martinsville is nearby.

Basics

Operated By: Kevin Johnson. **Open:** All year. **Site Assignment:** Reservations and walk-ins accepted. **Registration:** At campground office. **Fee:** $16–$21 (VISA, MC, AE, D). **Parking:** At designated area.

Facilities

Number of RV Sites: 20. **Number of Tent-Only Sites:** 11. **Hookups:** Electric (30, 50 amps), water, 20 full hookups. **Each Site:** Fire ring, picnic table. **Dump Station:** Yes. **Laundry:** Yes. **Pay Phone:** Yes. **Rest Rooms and Showers:** Yes. **Fuel:** No. **Propane:** No. **Internal Roads:** Gravel and paved, in good condition. **RV Service:** No. **Market:** Within 3 mi. **Restaurant:** Within 4 mi. **General Store:** No. **Vending:** Yes. **Playground:** Yes. **Other:** Fishing pond. **Activities:** Basketball, pond fishing, badminton, horseshoes, volleyball. **Nearby Attractions:** Blue Ridge Parkway, Mayberry USA, Wytheville, Historic Crab Orchard Museum and Pioneer Park. **Additional Information:** Virginia Tourism Corp., (800) 371-8164, www.virginia.org.

Restrictions

Pets: On leash only. **Fires:** At site. **Alcoholic Beverages:** At site. **Vehicle Maximum Length:** None.

To Get There

From Blue Ridge Parkway, at Milepost 177.7 go 0.1 mi. west on US 58. Entrance is on the left.

MIDDLETOWN

Battle of Cedar Creek Campground

8950 Valley Pike, Middletown 22645. T: (540) 869-1888 or (800) 343-1562.

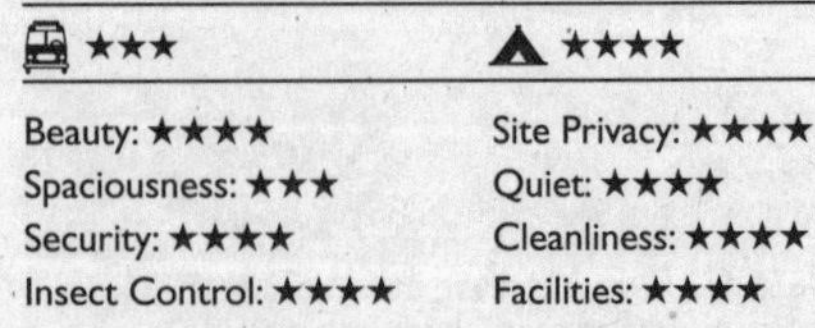

RV ★★★ Tent ★★★★

Beauty: ★★★★ Site Privacy: ★★★★
Spaciousness: ★★★ Quiet: ★★★★
Security: ★★★★ Cleanliness: ★★★★
Insect Control: ★★★★ Facilities: ★★★★

On the banks of Cedar Creek, where Union and Confederate troops clashed during the Civil War, the Battle of Cedar Creek Campground offers 59 sites, including 20 full hookups and two pull-throughs. The tent camping is especially good here, with private sites and quiet surroundings. The campground, which has a swimming pool and a mini-golf course, is not far from the entrance to the105-mile-long Skyline Drive in Front Royal, and Shenandoah National Park is a short drive away. The main attraction close to the campground is the 158-acre Cedar Creek Battlefield, which includes the Heater House and a new, 5,000-square-foot visitors center. A mile south of the campground is Belle Grove Plantation, an 18th-century grain and livestock farm. The plantation includes the main house and gardens, original outbuildings, a classic 1918 barn, an overseer's house, the slave cemetery, a heritage apple orchard, fields and meadows, and scenic mountain views.

Basics

Operated By: Private operator. **Open:** All year. **Site Assignment:** Reservations and walk-ins accepted. **Registration:** At campground office. **Fee:** $17 (VISA, MC). **Parking:** At site.

Facilities

Number of RV Sites: 46. **Number of Tent-Only Sites:** 13. **Hookups:** Electric (20, 30 amps), phone, water, 25 full hookups. **Each Site:** Fire ring, picnic table. **Dump Station:** Yes. **Laundry:** Yes. **Pay Phone:** Yes. **Rest Rooms and Showers:** Yes. **Fuel:** No. **Propane:** Yes. **Internal Roads:** Gravel, in good condition. **RV Service:** No. **Market:** Within 2 mi. **Restaurant:** Within 2 mi. **General Store:** No. **Vending:** Yes. **Playground:** Yes. **Other:** Located on Civil War battlefield. **Activities:** Swimming, rec hall, stream fishing, mini-golf, shuffleboard, horseshoes, volleyball, disc golf, tubing, canoeing. **Nearby Attractions:** Shenandoah National Park, Shenandoah River, Skyline Drive, Battle of Cedar Creek battlefield, Belle Grove Plantation, Museum of American Presidents. **Additional Information:** Shenandoah Valley Travel Assoc., (540) 740-3132, www.svta.org.

Restrictions

Pets: On leash only. **Fires:** At site. **Alcoholic Beverages:** At site. **Vehicle Maximum Length:** 42 ft.

To Get There

From I-66, go 2 mi. south on I-81 and 1 mi. north on US 11. Entrance is on the left.

MINERAL

Christopher Run Campground

7149 Zachary Taylor Hwy., Mineral 23117.
T: (540) 894-4744; F: (540) 894-4827;
www.christopherruncampground.com;
hkchilds@louisa.net or kchilds569@aol.com.

RV ★★★★ Tent ★★★★

Beauty: ★★★★ Site Privacy: ★★
Spaciousness: ★★ Quiet: ★★★★
Security: ★★★★★ Cleanliness: ★★★★
Insect Control: ★★★★ Facilities: ★★★★

With more than 200 miles of shoreline and 13,600 acres, Lake Anna is a haven for water sports, and Christopher Run Campground is in the middle of the action. The campground hosts a bluegrass festival every second weekend in June. Since Lake Anna is the campground's big draw, Christopher Run offers rowboat, canoe, and pedal boat rentals. It has a dock and a ramp for campers who own boats, and there's marine gas at the bait and tackle shop. The best spots are the cozy waterview sites looking at Lake Anna and a cluster of sites bordering a mature forest near the center of the campground. Lake Anna was formed in 1972 when the North Anna River was damned to form a cooling reservoir for the North Anna Nuclear Power Reactor The lake consists of two sections: a 3,400-acre impoundment that provides the water for the power plant's cooling, and the 9,600-acre "main lake" impoundment used to distribute the warmer water that results from the reactor cooling process. The smaller impoundment is accessible only to property owners. The larger lake is the area open to the public.

Basics

Operated By: Childs family. **Open:** Apr. 1–Oct. 31. **Site Assignment:** Reservations accepted (1-night deposit required), walk-ins accepted. **Registration:** At campground office. **Fee:** $21–$25 (VISA, MC, AE, D). **Parking:** At site.

Facilities

Number of RV Sites: 190. **Number of Tent-Only Sites:** 10. **Hookups:** Electric (20, 30 amps), water, phone, 109 full hookups. **Each Site:** Picnic table. **Dump Station:** Yes. **Laundry:** Yes. **Pay Phone:** Yes. **Rest Rooms and Showers:** Yes. **Fuel:** Yes. **Propane:** Yes. **Internal Roads:** Paved, in good condition. **RV Service:** No. **Market:** Within 5 mi. **Restaurant:** Within 3 mi. **General Store:** Yes. **Vending:** Yes. **Playground:** Yes. **Other:** Lake Anna. **Activities:** Lake swimming and fishing, boating, canoeing, kayaking, boat rentals, game room, rec hall, basketball, shuffleboard, planned activities on weekends, horseshoes, volleyball. **Nearby Attractions:** Lake Anna, Fredericksburg and Spotsylvania National Military Park, Historic Fredericksburg, North Anna Nuclear Power Station. **Additional Information:** Virginia Tourism Corp., (800) 371-8164, www.virginia.org.

Restrictions

Pets: On leash only. **Fires:** In designated areas. **Alcoholic Beverages:** At site. **Vehicle Maximum Length:** None. **Other:** Do not cross any fence lines; adjoining property is private.

To Get There

From junction of Hwy. 208 and US 522, go 5 mi. north on Hwy. 208 and 1.5 mi. north on US 522. Entrance is on the right.

NATURAL BRIDGE STATION

Campground at Natural Bridge

P.O. Box 266, Natural Bridge Station 24579.
T: (540) 291-2727; www.campnbr.com;
campnbr@rockbridge.net.

RV ★★★★ Tent ★★★★

Beauty: ★★★★ Site Privacy: ★★
Spaciousness: ★★ Quiet: ★★★★
Security: ★★★★ Cleanliness: ★★★★
Insect Control: ★★★★ Facilities: ★★★★★

In 1774, Thomas Jefferson purchased the 215-foot-high and 90-foot-long limestone arch called the Natural Bridge from King George III. Today, traffic on US 11 passes over the incredible site in the Shenandoah Valley. Located five miles from the bridge, the Campground at Natural Bridge is situated in the Blue Ridge Mountains on the James River. Some sites are along the waterfront; others are nestled deep in the woods. Several hiking trails sprout from the adjoining Jefferson National Forest. Lexington, home to Lee's Chapel and the Stonewall Jackson House, is a short drive from the campground. You can take a self-guided tour of the Natural Bridge. Other attractions include the Caverns of Natural Bridge, with passages on three levels as far as 300 feet underground; the Natural Bridge Wax Museum, where wax figures depict important people in Shenandoah Valley history; and the Natural Bridge Zoo, which is the largest zoo in Virginia.

Basics

Operated By: Private operator. **Open:** Mar. 15–Dec. 1. **Site Assignment:** Reservations recommended (1-night deposit required), walk-ins accepted. **Registration:** At campground office. **Fee:** $21–$24 (VISA, MC, D). **Parking:** At site.

Facilities

Number of RV Sites: 180. **Number of Tent-Only Sites:** 22. **Hookups:** Electric (20, 30, 50 amps), cable TV, phone, water, 77 full hookups. **Each Site:** Fire ring, picnic table. **Dump Station:** Yes. **Laundry:** Yes. **Pay Phone:** Yes. **Rest Rooms and Showers:** Yes. **Fuel:** No. **Propane:** Yes. **Internal Roads:** Gravel, in good condition. **RV Service:** No. **Market:** Within 18 mi. **Restaurant:** Within 1.5 mi. **General Store:** Yes. **Vending:** Yes. **Playground:** Yes. **Other:** Swimming lake. **Activities:** Lake swimming, river and pond fishing, boating, canoeing, kayaking, mini-golf, basketball, planned activities on weekends, horseback riding, sports field, hiking trails, horseshoes. **Nearby Attractions:** James River, Natural Bridge of Virginia, Historic Lexington, Shenandoah National Park, Roanoke, Skyline Drive, Blue Ridge Parkway, Endless Caverns, Luray Caverns. **Additional Information:** Shenandoah Valley Travel Assoc., (540) 740-3132, www.svta.org.

Restrictions

Pets: On leash only. **Fires:** At site. **Alcoholic Beverages:** At site. **Vehicle Maximum Length:** 42 ft.

To Get There

From I-81, take Exit 175 and go 2 mi. east on US 11N, 3 mi. north on Hwy. 130, and 2 mi. southeast on Hwy. 759/782. Entrance is on the left.

NEW MARKET

KOA—Harrisonburg/New Market

12480 Mountain Valley Rd., Broadway 22815.
T: (540) 896-8929 or (800) KOA-5406;
www.koa.com.

RV ★★★★ Tent ★★★★

Beauty: ★★★★ Site Privacy: ★★★
Spaciousness: ★★★ Quiet: ★★★★
Security: ★★★★ Cleanliness: ★★★★
Insect Control: ★★★★ Facilities: ★★★★

Nestled at the base of the Massanutten Mountains in the Shenandoah Valley, KOA—Harrisonburg/New Market offers spacious, wooded sites, including 17 pull-throughs. For recreation, there's a swimming pool and a fishing pond. Hiking trails lead from the campground to Jefferson National Forest. New Market is the site of New Market Battlefield State Historical Park, where on May 15, 1864, cadets from nearby Virginia Military Institute were ordered to join the Confederate attack on Union troops. The cadets, who were no older than 20, helped achieve a Confederate victory. The New Market Battlefield Military Museum is located on the actual battlefield and showcases more than 2,000 artifacts of American soldiers, from the Revolutionary War to Desert Storm. In Harrisonburg, Grand Caverns Regional Park has expansive underground chambers used by Union and Confederate troops during the Civil War. The campground is also near Endless Caverns, Luray Caverns, and Shenandoah Caverns.

Basics

Operated By: Roy and Mary Kircher. **Open:** All year. **Site Assignment:** Reservations recommended, walk-ins accepted. **Registration:** At campground office. **Fee:** $25–$28 (VISA, MC). **Parking:** At site only.

Facilities

Number of RV Sites: 52. **Number of Tent-Only Sites:** 28. **Hookups:** Electric (20, 30, 50 amps), phone, water, 26 full hookups. **Each Site:** Fire ring, picnic table. **Dump Station:** Yes. **Laundry:** Yes. **Pay Phone:** Yes. **Rest Rooms and Showers:** Yes. **Fuel:** No. **Propane:** Yes. **Internal Roads:** Paved, in fair condition. **RV Service:** No. **Market:** Within 5 mi. **Restaurant:** Within 5 mi. **General Store:** Yes. **Vending:** Yes. **Playground:** Yes. **Other:** None. **Activities:** Swimming, pond fishing, game room, rec hall, basketball, movies, badminton, horseshoes, hiking trails, volleyball. **Nearby Attractions:** Shenandoah National Park, Skyline Drive, Blue Ridge Parkway, New Market Battlefield State Historical Park, New Market Battlefield Military Museum, Endless Caverns, Shenandoah Caverns, Luray Caverns, Bedrooms of America. **Additional Information:** Shenandoah Valley Travel Assoc., (540) 740-3132, www.svta.org.

Restrictions

Pets: On leash only. **Fires:** At site only. **Alcoholic Beverages:** At site only. **Vehicle Maximum Length:** None. **Other:** No pets in cabins.

To Get There

From I-81, take Exit 257 and go 0.1 mi. north on US 11 and 3 mi. east on Hwy. 608. Entrance is at the end.

NEW POINT

New Point Campground

P.O. Box 39, New Point 23125. T: (804) 725-5120; www.newpointcampground.com; newpointcampground@newpointcampground.com.

RV ★★★★ Tent ★★★★

Beauty: ★★★★ Site Privacy: ★★
Spaciousness: ★★★ Quiet: ★★★★
Security: ★★★★ Cleanliness: ★★★★
Insect Control: ★★★★ Facilities: ★★★★

Situated at the Horn Harbor entrance to Chesapeake Bay, New Point Campground is a place where clean, salt air blows in on ocean breezes. From the campground's observation pier, the 1804 New Point comfort light graces the shoreline as a beacon for ships. Some campsites are semi-wooded, others are waterside. All sites are equipped with full hookups. Crabbing and clamming are popular activities at New Point. Of course, saltwater fishing, swimming, and boating also lure campers. New Point has an inviting white-sanded beach, as well as a spacious swimming pool. An hour east of Richmond, New Point is a short drive from attractions in Newport News, Virginia Beach, and Norfolk. Worthwhile day trips include the 25-acre Jamestown Settlement, where costumed interpreters depict life in the 17th century, and the Yorktown Victory Center, which highlights the Revolutionary War at the site of the British surrender to Gen. George Washington.

Basics

Operated By: Private operator. **Open:** Apr. 1–Oct. 31. **Site Assignment:** Reservations recommended, walk-ins accepted. **Registration:** At campground office. **Fee:** $23–$25 (VISA, MC, D). **Parking:** At site.

Facilities

Number of RV Sites: 300. **Number of Tent-Only Sites:** None. **Hookups:** Electric (30 amps), phone, 300 full hookups. **Each Site:** Fire ring, picnic table. **Dump Station:** Yes. **Laundry:** Yes. **Pay Phone:** Yes. **Rest Rooms and Showers:** Yes. **Fuel:** No. **Propane:** Yes. **Internal Roads:** Gravel and dirt, in good condition. **RV Service:** No. **Market:** Within 7 mi. **Restaurant:** Within 7 mi. **General Store:** Yes. **Vending:** Yes. **Playground:** Yes. **Other:** White-sanded beach on Chesapeake Bay. **Activities:** Crabbing, clamming, ocean fishing, game room, rec hall, wading pool, ocean swimming, mini-golf, planned activities, sports field, horseshoes, hiking trails, volleyball. **Nearby Attractions:** Chesapeake Bay, Newport News, Colonial Williamsburg, Yorktown, Historic Jamestown Settlement. **Additional Information:** Mathews County Chamber of Commerce, (804) 725-9029, www.mathewsva.org.

Restrictions

Pets: On leash only. **Fires:** At site. **Alcoholic Beverages:** At site. **Vehicle Maximum Length:** None. **Other:** N pets permitted in rental units.

To Get There

From Hwy. 198 in Mathews, go 7 mi. southeast on Hwy. 14E, 0.75 mi. east on Hwy. 602, and 500 ft. south on Hwy. 601. Entrance is on the left.

NEWPORT NEWS

Newport News Park Campground

13564 Jefferson Ave., Newport News 23603. T: (800) 203-8322; F: (757) 926-8728; www.newport-news.va.us/parks; rpoperna@ci.newport-news.va.us.

RV ★★★ Tent ★★★

Beauty: ★★★★ Site Privacy: ★★★
Spaciousness: ★★★ Quiet: ★★★
Security: ★★★★★ Cleanliness: ★★★★
Insect Control: ★★★★ Facilities: ★★★

Adjacent to the Lee Hall Reservoir, Newport News Park Campground offers 188 wooded sites in one of the largest municipal parks east of the Mississippi River. Located on the James River by the James River Bridge, the park's 200-acre slip marina offers easy access to the Hampton Roads Harbor and the Chesapeake Bay. Newport News Park has several special events throughout the year, including the Children's Festival of Friends, the Newport News Fall Festival of Folklife, and Celebration in Lights. In Newport News, visitors flock to the Mariners Museum, where the history of shipbuilding, ocean navigation, and cartography are explored; the Virginia Living Museum, which displays a 60-foot scale model of the James River; and the Virginia War Museum, which contains more than 60,000 artifacts related to US military history from the Revolutionary War to present day.

Basics

Operated By: City of Newport News. **Open:** All year. **Site Assignment:** Reservations and walk-ins accepted. **Registration:** At campground headquarters. **Fee:** $16–$18 (VISA, MC). **Parking:** At designated area.

Facilities

Number of RV Sites: 164. **Number of Tent-Only Sites:** 24. **Hookups:** Electric (20, 30 amps), water. **Each Site:** Fire ring, grill. **Dump Station:** Yes. **Laundry:** Yes. **Pay Phone:** Yes. **Rest Rooms and Showers:** Yes. **Fuel:** No. **Propane:** Yes. **Internal Roads:** Paved, in good condition. **RV Service:** No. **Market:** Within 2 mi. **Restaurant:** Within 2 mi. **General Store:** Yes. **Vending:** Yes. **Playground:** Yes. **Other:** Lee Hall Reservoir. **Activities:** Boating, canoeing, boat rentals, lake fishing, hiking trails, golf, driving range, putting green, disc golf, bike rentals, planned activities, horseback riding, sports field, horseshoes, volleyball. **Nearby Attractions:** Virginia Living Museum, Mariners Museum, Lee Hall Mansion, Norfolk, Virginia Beach, Yorktown, Historic Jamestown Settlement, Colonial Williamsburg. **Additional Information:** Virginia Tourism Corp., (800) 371-8164, www.virginia.org.

Restrictions

Pets: On leash only. **Fires:** At site. **Alcoholic Beverages:** No alcohol permitted. **Vehicle Maximum Length:** None. **Other:** 21-day max. stay.

To Get There

From I-64, take Exit 250B and go 1 mi. northwest on Hwy. 143. Entrance is on the right.

PETERSBURG

KOA—South Forty

2809 Courtland Rd., Petersburg 23805. T: (800) 562-8545 or (804) 732-8345; www.koa.com; amandcm@techcom.net.

RV ★★★ Tent ★★★

Beauty: ★★★ Site Privacy: ★★
Spaciousness: ★★ Quiet: ★★★
Security: ★★★★ Cleanliness: ★★★★
Insect Control: ★★★★ Facilities: ★★★★

Located a mile from I-95 in Petersburg, KOA—South Forty has wooded and open sites. There are 65 pull-through sites. The campground has a new clubhouse and adult lounge, a well-maintained swimming pool, a stocked fishing pond, and bike and boat rentals. Nino's Italian Restaurant is located on the premises. Nearby Petersburg National Battlefield makes for a good day trip. The visitor center has maps for self-guided tours Among the most interesting sites here are Fort Haskell, Fort Stedman, and the Crater, which is a massive hole left after Union troops tunneled beneath a Confederate artillery position and exploded four tons of powder. Petersburg has its share of architectural treasures, including the 1823 Centre Hill Mansion and the Trapezium House. Built in 1817, the Trapezium House was constructed in the form of a trapezium with no right angles and no parallel sides.

Basics

Operated By: KOA. **Open:** All year. **Site Assignment:** Reservations and walk-ins accepted. **Registration:** At campground office. **Fee:** $23–$25 (VISA, MC). **Parking:** At site.

Facilities

Number of RV Sites: 91. **Number of Tent-Only Sites:** 23. **Hookups:** Electric (20, 30, 50 amps), water, 28 full hookups. **Each Site:** Grill, picnic table. **Dump Station:** Yes. **Laundry:** Yes. **Pay Phone:** Yes. **Rest Rooms and Showers:** Yes. **Fuel:** No. **Propane:** Yes. **Internal Roads:** Gravel, in good condition. **RV Service:** No. **Market:** Within 3 mi. **Restaurant:** On premises. **General Store:** Yes. **Vending:** Yes. **Playground:** Yes. **Other:** Nino's Italian Restaurant on grounds. **Activities:** Game room, rec hall, swimming, boat rentals, lake fishing, sports field, horseshoes, hiking trails, volleyball. **Nearby Attractions:** Petersburg National Battlefield, Centre Hill Mansion, Ft. Lee, Lee's Retreat Driving Tour, National Museum of the Civil War Solider, Pamplin Park Civil War Site, Siege Museum, Trapezium House. **Additional Information:** Petersburg Visitors Center, (800) 368-3595.

Restrictions

Pets: On leash only. **Fires:** At site. **Alcoholic Beverages:** At site. **Vehicle Maximum Length:** None. **Other:** None.

To Get There

From I-95, take Exit 41 and go 0.5 mi. east on Hwy. 355. Entrance is on the right.

PETERSBURG

Picture Lake Campground

7818 Boydton Plank Rd., Petersburg 23803. T: (804) 861-0174.

RV: ★★★★ Tent: ★★★★

Beauty: ★★★★	Site Privacy: ★★
Spaciousness: ★★★	Quiet: ★★★★
Security: ★★★★	Cleanliness: ★★★★
Insect Control: ★★★★	Facilities: ★★★★

Situated on Picture Lake west of Petersburg, Picture Lake Campground has shaded sites (some located on the water), 120 of them pull-throughs. With its proximity to Petersburg, Picture Lake is near several attractions, many of which relate to the Civil War. The 2,700-acre Petersburg National Battlefield is actually the scene where 10 months of skirmishes took place on several battlefields. The visitor center is the starting point for a four-mile self-guided walking tour. If you choose to drive the countryside, an audiotape is available for a 37-mile driving tour. Pamplin Historical Park and the National Museum of the Civil War Soldier serves a dual purpose. The park preserves the battlefield of the Apr. 2, 1865 event when Union troops overwhelmed Confederate defense lines. The museum describes the daily life of a Civil War soldier. Picture Lake is also 40 miles south of Richmond and 15 miles west of water activities on the James River.

Basics

Operated By: Anne Blazek. **Open:** All year. **Site Assignment:** Reservations and walk-ins accepted. **Registration:** At campground office. **Fee:** $23–$25 (VISA, MC, AE, D). **Parking:** At site.

Facilities

Number of RV Sites: 207. **Number of Tent-Only Sites:** None. **Hookups:** Electric (20, 30, 50 amps), phone, water, 105 full hookups. **Each Site:** Fire ring, picnic table. **Dump Station:** Yes. **Laundry:** Yes. **Pay Phone:** Yes. **Rest Rooms and Showers:** Yes. **Fuel:** No. **Propane:** Yes. **Internal Roads:** Gravel and paved, in good condition. **RV Service:** No. **Market:** Within 3 mi. **Restaurant:** Within 3 mi. **General Store:** Yes. **Vending:** Yes. **Playground:** Yes. **Other:** Picture Lake. **Activities:** Swimming, boating, canoeing, kayaking, boat rentals, lake fishing, basketball, shuffleboard, badminton, sports field, horseshoes, hiking trails, volleyball. **Nearby Attractions:** Petersburg National Battlefield, Centre Hill Mansion, Ft. Lee, Lee's Retreat Driving Tour, National Museum of the Civil War Solider, Pamplin Park Civil War Site, Siege Museum, Trapezium House. **Additional Information:** Petersburg Visitors Center, (800) 368-3595.

Restrictions

Pets: On leash only. **Fires:** At site. **Alcoholic Beverages:** At site. **Vehicle Maximum Length:** None. **Other:** None.

To Get There

From I-95, go 4.5 mi. southwest on I-85 to Exit 63A. Then go 3 mi. south on US 1. Entrance is on the right.

POWHATAN

Cozy Acres Campground

2177 Ridge Rd., Powhatan 23139. T: (804) 598-2470.

RV: ★★★★ Tent: ★★★★

Beauty: ★★★★	Site Privacy: ★★★★
Spaciousness: ★★★★	Quiet: ★★★★
Security: ★★★★	Cleanliness: ★★★★
Insect Control: ★★★★	Facilities: ★★★★

Bordered on the north by the James River and on the south by the Appomattox River, Powhatan is 20 miles west of Richmond. Cozy Acres Campground is a clean and quiet park with spacious, semi-wooded sites, including 97 pull-throughs. Sites on the north end of the campground are close to two of the three ponds. With its remote location and tranquil setting, Cozy Acres is an ideal place to camp if you want to visit the attractions in Richmond but prefer to stay away from the traffic and crowds of Virginia's capitol city. The State Capitol was designed by Thomas Jefferson and is the site where Aaron Burr was tried for treason and Gen. Robert E. Lee accepted command of Virginia's forces. Another interesting spot is the Hollywood Cemetery, where notable figures like James Monroe, James Tyler, and Jefferson Davis are buried, as are 18,000 Confederate soldiers.

Basics

Operated By: Private operator. **Open:** Apr. 1–Dec. 1. **Site Assignment:** Reservations and walk-ins accepted. **Registration:** At campground office. **Fee:** $21–$25 (VISA, MC). **Parking:** At designated area.

Facilities

Number of RV Sites: 105. **Number of Tent-Only Sites:** 8. **Hookups:** Electric (20, 30, 50 amps), phone, water, 71 full hookups. **Each Site:** Fire ring, picnic table. **Dump Station:** Yes. **Laundry:** Yes. **Pay Phone:** Yes. **Rest Rooms and Showers:** Yes. **Fuel:** No. **Propane:** Yes. **Internal Roads:** Gravel and paved, in good condition. **RV Service:** No. **Market:** Within 5 mi. **Restaurant:** Within 4 mi. **General Store:** Yes. **Vending:** Yes. **Playground:** Yes. **Other:** Three fishing ponds. **Activities:** Game room, rec hall, swimming, wading pool, sports field, horseshoes, hiking trails, volleyball. **Nearby Attractions:** Richmond, Edgar Allan Poe Museum, Richmond International Speedway, Museum and White House of the Confederacy, Paramount's Kings Dominion, Virginia Museum of Fine Arts. **Additional Information:** Richmond CVB, (800) 370-9004, www.richmondva.org.

Restrictions

Pets: On leash only. **Fires:** At site. **Alcoholic Beverages:** At site. **Vehicle Maximum Length:** None. **Other:** None.

To Get There

From US 522, go 4 mi. west on US 60 and 2 mi. south on Hwy. 627. Entrance is on the right.

PROVIDENCE FORGE

Ed Allen's Campgrounds and Cottages—Chickahominy Recreational Park

13501 Campground Rd., Lanexa 23089. T: (804) 966-2582; F: (804) 966-5871; www.edallens.com; edallens@aol.com.

RV: ★★★★ Tent: ★★★★

Beauty: ★★★★	Site Privacy: ★★★★
Spaciousness: ★★★★	Quiet: ★★★★
Security: ★★★★	Cleanliness: ★★★★
Insect Control: ★★★★	Facilities: ★★★★

Located along the shores of Chickahominy Lake, which is renowned for its bass fishing, perhaps it's appropriate that Ed Allen's Campgrounds and Cottages features what it calls the world's largest bass-shaped swimming pool. Consisting of 1,100 acres, Chickahominy Lake is a stunning sight, especially with the setting sun reflecting in the glassy water. Ed Allen's is a fisherman's haven. Boat rentals are available at the lake, and there is a lakeside restaurant where prime rib, steaks, fresh seafood, and pasta grace the menu. Many of the campsites are shaded by cypress trees; there are 50 pull-throughs. Cottages and motel rooms are also available, as are lakeside tent sites. For children, Ed Allen's has a kiddie pool, a stocked fishing pond, hayrides, and a game room. Of course, most children flock to the bass-shaped swimming pool. The campground is a short drive to Colonial Williamsburg and Richmond.

Basics

Operated By: Ed Allen Jr. **Open:** Apr. 1–Nov. 1. **Site Assignment:** Reservations (online) accepted, walk-ins accepted. **Registration:** At campground headquarters. **Fee:** $16–$23 (VISA, MC). **Parking:** At designated spot.

Facilities

Number of RV Sites: 300. **Number of Tent-Only Sites:** 75. **Hookups:** Electric (20, 30 amps), phone, water, 150 full hookups. **Each Site:** Fire ring, picnic table. **Dump Station:** Yes. **Laundry:** Yes. **Pay Phone:** Yes. **Rest Rooms and Showers:** Yes. **Fuel:** Yes. **Propane:** Yes. **Internal Roads:** Gravel and paved, in good condition. **RV Service:** No. **Market:** Within 5 mi. **Restaurant:** On premises. **General Store:** Yes. **Vending:** Yes. **Playground:** Yes. **Other:** Bass-shaped swimming pool. **Activities:** Swimming, wading pool, game room, rec hall, boating, canoeing, kayaking, boat rentals, lake and pond fishing, basketball, planned activities on weekends, horseback riding, sports field, horseshoes, hiking trails, volleyball. **Nearby Attractions:** Colonial Williamsburg, Busch Gardens, Historic Jamestown Settlement, Richmond, Yorktown, James River. **Additional Information:** Virginia Tourism Corp., (800) 371-8164, www.virginia.org.

Restrictions

Pets: On leash only. **Fires:** At site. **Alcoholic Beverages:** At site. **Vehicle Maximum Length:** None. **Other:** None.

To Get There

From Hwy. 155, go 5.5 mi. east on US 60 and 0.5 mi. south on Hwy. 649. Entrance is on the right.

QUINBY

Thousand Trails—Virginia Landing

40226 Upshur Neck Rd., Quinby 23423. T: (800) 723-6226; www.thousandtrails.com.

RV ★★★★ Tent ★★★★★

Beauty: ★★★★ Site Privacy: ★★★★
Spaciousness: ★★★★ Quiet: ★★★★
Security: ★★★★★ Cleanliness: ★★★★
Insect Control: ★★★★ Facilities: ★★★★

Situated on the Virginia Peninsula along Hog Island Bay on the Atlantic Ocean, Thousand Trails—Virginia Landing is a beautiful 800-acre preserve with open and shaded sites. With its perch on the shorefront, this Thousand Trails facility offers ample boating and fishing opportunities. Located 35 miles from the Maryland line and an hour's drive from Virginia Beach, the campground has a 9-hole pitch-and-putt golf course, mini-golf course, adult lodge, and a well-stocked country store among other features. Assateague Island, which includes Chincoteague National Wildlife Refuge and Assateague Island National Seashore, is a short drive away. The 37-mile barrier island combines stretches of ocean, sand dunes, forests, and marshes teeming with wildlife, including sitka deer and the famous Chincoteague wild ponies. Thousand Trails is about an hour's drive to the NASA Visitor Center on Wallops Island.

Basics

Operated By: Thousand Trails. **Open:** Apr. 1–Oct. 31. **Site Assignment:** Reservations and walk-ins accepted. **Registration:** At campground office. **Fee:** $25 (VISA, MC, AE, D). **Parking:** At site.

Facilities

Number of RV Sites: 215. **Number of Tent-Only Sites:** None. **Hookups:** Electric (20, 30 amps), phone, water, 15 full hookups. **Each Site:** Grill, picnic table. **Dump Station:** Yes. **Laundry:** Yes. **Pay Phone:** Yes. **Rest Rooms and Showers:** Yes. **Fuel:** No. **Propane:** Yes. **Internal Roads:** Gravel and paved, in good condition. **RV Service:** No. **Market:** Within 5 mi. **Restaurant:** Within 5 mi. **General Store:** Yes. **Vending:** Yes. **Playground:** Yes. **Other:** Adult and family lodges. **Activities:** River swimming, game room, rec hall, boating, canoeing, kayaking, boat rentals, ocean and pond fishing, mini-golf, bike rentals, shuffleboard, sports field, horseshoes, hiking trails, volleyball. **Nearby Attractions:** Assateague Island National Seashore, Chincoteague National Wildlife Refuge. **Additional Information:** Eastern Shore of Virginia Tourism Commission, (757) 787-2460, www.esva.net/~esvatourism.

Restrictions

Pets: On leash only. **Fires:** At site. **Alcoholic Beverages:** At site. **Vehicle Maximum Length:** None. **Other:** None.

To Get There

From SR 182, go 6.75 mi. south on SR 605. Entrance is at the end.

REEDVILLE

KOA—Chesapeake Bay/Smith Island

382 Campground Rd., Reedville 22539. T: (804) 453-3430 or (804) 453-4051; www.eaglesnest.net/smithislandcruise or www.koa.com; chbaykoa@crosslink.net.

RV ★★★★ Tent ★★★★

Beauty: ★★★★ Site Privacy: ★★★
Spaciousness: ★★★ Quiet: ★★★★
Security: ★★★★ Cleanliness: ★★★★
Insect Control: ★★★★ Facilities: ★★★★

Located on Slough Creek near Reedville, KOA—Chesapeake Bay/Smith Island has one of the most interesting spots in Virginia. There are shaded waterfront sites, including 55 pull-throughs. Cabins are also available for rent. The campground is home to the Smith Island Cruise, which departs from the premises. Aboard the Capt. Evans, passengers see historic Smith Point, where the Potomac River meets the Chesapeake Bay, as well as the Smith Point Lighthouse two miles offshore. Known as the "Soft-Shelled Crab Capital of the World," Smith Island has three picturesque fishing villages: Ewell, Rhodes Point, and Tylerton, each on its own island in this archipelago of the Chesapeake, with interlacing creeks, canals, marsh, and meadows. Smith Island's roots date back to 1608, when Capt. John Smith sailed up Chesapeake Bay and came ashore on the island that now bears his name. The campground is also near Hughlett Point Nature Preserve on Chesapeake Bay, where hiking and bird watching are popular activities.

Basics

Operated By: KOA. **Open:** Apr. 1–Nov. 1. **Site Assignment:** Reservations and walk-ins accepted. **Registration:** At campground office. **Fee:** $24–$29 (VISA, MC). **Parking:** At designated area.

Facilities

Number of RV Sites: 86. **Number of Tent-Only Sites:** None. **Hookups:** Electric (20, 30, 50 amps), water, 25 full hookups. **Each Site:** Picnic table. **Dump Station:** Yes. **Laundry:** Yes. **Pay Phone:** Yes. **Rest Rooms and Showers:** Yes. **Fuel:** No. **Propane:** No. **Internal Roads:** Dirt and gravel, in good condition. **RV Service:** No. **Market:** Within 3 mi. **Restaurant:** Within 4 mi. **General Store:** Yes. **Vending:** Yes. **Playground:** Yes. **Other:** Smith Island Cruises. **Activities:** Swimming, boating, canoeing, boat rentals, river fishing, mini-golf, planned activities on weekends. **Nearby Attractions:** Smith Point, Smith Island, Chesapeake Bay, Colonial Williamsburg, Stratford Hall Plantation, George Washington's Birthplace and National Monument, Ingleside Winery. **Additional Information:** Virginia Tourism Corp., (800) 371-8164, www.virginia.org.

Restrictions

Pets: On leash only. **Fires:** At site. **Alcoholic Beverages:** At site. **Vehicle Maximum Length:** None. **Other:** None.

To Get There

From US 360, go 2.5 mi. east on CR 652/CR 650 and 0.5 mi. northeast on Campground Rd. Entrance is on the right.

RUSTBURG

Thousand Trails—Lynchburg

405 Mollies Creek Rd., Gladys 24554. T: (800) 615-4878 or (804) 332-6672; F: (972) 488-5124; www.thousandtrails.com.

RV ★★★★ Tent ★★★★

Beauty: ★★★★ Site Privacy: ★★
Spaciousness: ★★ Quiet: ★★★★
Security: ★★★★ Cleanliness: ★★★★
Insect Control: ★★★★ Facilities: ★★★★

Situated on Big Lake Grandview, Thousand Trails—Lynchburg is a water lover's delight. Campers can swim from the beach, fish, or rentrowboats, canoes, and kayaks. The campground also has a swimming pool, a whirlpool, an adult lodge, and a mini-golf course. The park has 191 full hookups, but there are no overflow sites. There are several interesting attractions in nearby Lynchburg, including Fort Early, the Maier Museum of Art, the Point of Honor, and the Pest House Medical Museum. Lynchburg has several 19th century residential districts. In fact, five hills of the "City of Seven Hills" are listed on the National Register of Historic Districts. Appommattox Court House National Historical Park is located about 20 miles east of Lynchburg and Thousand Trails. The 1,743-acre park includes the village of Appommattox, which is restored to look much like it did when Gen. Robert E. Lee surrendered to Gen. Ulysses S. Grant on Apr. 9, 1865, bringing an end to the Civil War.

Basics

Operated By: Thousand Trails. **Open:** May 1–Oct. 31. **Site Assignment:** Reservations accepted (online and phone), walk-ins accepted. **Registration:** At campground headquarters. **Fee:** $20 (VISA, MC, AE, D). **Parking:** At site.

Facilities

Number of RV Sites: 232. **Number of Tent-Only Sites:** 12. **Hookups:** Electric (30 amps), phone, water, 161 full hookups. **Each Site:** Grill, picnic table. **Dump Station:** Yes. **Laundry:** Yes. **Pay Phone:** Yes. **Rest Rooms and Showers:** Yes. **Fuel:** No. **Propane:** Yes. **Internal Roads:** Gravel and paved, in good condition. **RV Service:** No. **Market:** Within 7 mi. **Restaurant:** Within 7 mi. **General Store:** Yes. **Vending:** Yes. **Playground:** Yes. **Other:** Big Lake Grandview. **Activities:** Game room, rec hall, lake swimming, badminton, horseshoes, volleyball, wading pool, whirlpool, boating, canoeing, kayaking, boat rentals, lake fishing, mini-golf, basketball, shuffleboard, planned activities on weekends, tennis, sports field, hiking trails. **Nearby Attractions:** Appommattox Court House National Historic Park, Lynchburg, Blackwater Creek Natural Area, Jefferson's Polar Forest, Old Court House Museum, Pest House Medical Museum, Point of Honor. **Additional Information:** Virginia Tourism Corp., (800) 371-8164, www.virginia.org.

Restrictions

Pets: On leash only. **Fires:** At site. **Alcoholic Beverages:** At site. **Vehicle Maximum Length:** None. **Other:** None.

To Get There

From US 501, go 0.75 mi. east on Hwy. 24, 5.5 mi. south on CR 515, and 0.5 mi. southwest on CR 650. Entrance is on the right.

SALEM

Dixie Caverns Campground

5753 W. Main St., Salem 25153. T: (540) 380-2085; www.dixiecaverns.com.

RV ★★★ Tent ★★★

Beauty: ★★★★ Site Privacy: ★
Spaciousness: ★ Quiet: ★★
Security: ★★★★ Cleanliness: ★★★★
Insect Control: ★★★ Facilities: ★★★

In 1920, what is now Dixie Caverns was discovered by a dog who peered through a hole at the top of a hill. The campground has 52 sites with water and electric hookups, and there is an expansive open area for tenters. These sites are neither spacious nor private. Recreation is limited at the campground; there is no swimming pool here. The campground is centered around caverns. Tour guides take explorers through them as the caves rise up into a mountain and dip underground. There is also a shop on the grounds where antiques, rocks, pottery, and Christmas items are sold. Salem is a town rich in colonial heritage. The Salem Museum, located in the restored Williams-Brown House Store, was built in 1845 and traces Salem's history. The campground is not far from Roanoke, and the town of Salem is nestled between the Blue Ridge and Allegheny Mountains. The Blue Ridge Parkway and Skyline Drive are nearby.

Basics

Operated By: Dixie Caverns. **Open:** All year. **Site Assignment:** Reservations accepted for pull-through units, walk-ins accepted otherwise. **Registration:** At campground headquarters. **Fee:** $18 (VISA, MC, AE, D). **Parking:** At designated area.

Facilities

Number of RV Sites: 62. **Number of Tent-Only Sites:** 100. **Hookups:** Electric (20, 30, 50 amps), phone, cable TV, water. **Each Site:** Fire ring, picnic table. **Dump Station:** Yes. **Laundry:** No. **Pay Phone:** Yes. **Rest Rooms and Showers:** Yes. **Fuel:** No. **Propane:** Yes. **Internal Roads:** Gravel and paved, in good condition. **RV Service:** No. **Market:** Within 10 mi. **Restaurant:** Within 10 mi. **General Store:** No. **Vending:** Yes. **Playground:** No. **Other:** Dixie Caverns, antique mall. **Activities:** Spelunking. **Nearby Attractions:** Blue Ridge Parkway, Skyline Drive, Natural Bridge of Virginia, Roanoke, Lynchburg, Appommattox Court House National Historic Park. **Additional Information:** Virginia Tourism Corp., (800) 371-8164, www.virginia.org.

Restrictions

Pets: On leash only. **Fires:** At site. **Alcoholic Beverages:** At site. **Vehicle Maximum Length:** 70 ft. **Other:** None.

To Get There

From I-81, take Exit 132 and go 0.25 mi. south on US 460/US 11. Entrance is on the right.

SCOTTSBURG

Staunton River State Park

1170 Staunton Trail, Scottsburg 24589. T: (804) 572-4623 or (800) 933-PARK; www.dcr.state.va.us/parks; resvs@dcr.state.va.us.

RV ★★★★ Tent ★★★★

Beauty: ★★★ Site Privacy: ★★★
Spaciousness: ★★★ Quiet: ★★★
Security: ★★★★ Cleanliness: ★★★★
Insect Control: ★★★★ Facilities: ★★★

Staunton River State Park is made up of 1,597 acres along the shoreline of the John H. Kerr Reservoir (also known as Buggs Island Lake), as well as the Dan and Staunton Rivers. Set under a forest of oak and pine trees, the campsites are spread in a figure-eight, with the bathhouse and hot showers in the center. Staunton River State Park is actually located on a peninsula at the narrow end of Buggs Island Lake. Hikers, equestrians, and bikers take advantage of the 7.5-mile River Bank Multi-Use Trail, which follows the peninsula. Swimming is not allowed from the park's shoreline, so campers must cool themselves in the park's swimming pool. A short drive away is the Staunton River Battlefield Park, where Confederate soldiers stymied Union troops at a bridge that crossed the river. The 300-acre battlefield has a visitors center and a self-guided walking trail.

Basics

Operated By: State of Virginia. **Open:** Mar.–Dec. **Site Assignment:** First come, first served; no reservations accepted. **Registration:** At campground office. **Fee:** $14–$18 (VISA, MC). **Parking:** At site.

Facilities

Number of RV Sites: 34. **Number of Tent-Only Sites:** 14. **Hookups:** Electric (30 amps). **Each Site:** Fire ring, picnic table. **Dump Station:** Yes. **Laundry:** No. **Pay Phone:** Yes. **Rest Rooms and Showers:** Yes. **Fuel:** No. **Propane:** No. **Internal Roads:** Paved, in good condition. **RV Service:** No. **Market:** Within 9 mi. **Restaurant:** Within 9 mi. **General Store:** No. **Vending:** Yes. **Playground:** Yes. **Other:** John H Kerr Reservoir (Buggs Island Lake). **Activities:** Swimming, boating, canoeing, boat rentals, lake fishing, planned activities, tennis court, hiking trails. **Nearby Attractions:** John H. Kerr Reservoir, Lake Gaston. **Additional Information:** Virginia Tourism Corp., (800) 371-8164, www.virginia.org.

Restrictions

Pets: On leash only; $3 per night. **Fires:** In camp stove or fire ring. **Alcoholic Beverages:** No alcohol permitted. **Vehicle Maximum Length:** 30 ft. **Other:** 14-day stay limit in 30-day period.

To Get There

From Scottsburg, go 9 mi. southeast on Hwy. 344. Follow signs to park.

STAFFORD

Aquia Pines Camp Resort

3071 Jefferson Davis Hwy., Stafford 22554. T: (800) 726-1710 or (540) 659-3447; www.gocampingamerica.com/aquiapines; aquiapines@aol.com.

RV ★★★★ Tent ★★★★

Beauty: ★★★ Site Privacy: ★★
Spaciousness: ★★ Quiet: ★★★★
Security: ★★★★ Cleanliness: ★★★★
Insect Control: ★★★★ Facilities: ★★★★

Located southwest of Washington, D.C. and northeast of Fredericksburg, Aquia Pines Camp Resort is definitely a recommended base for exploring the nation's capitol and the surrounding historical sites. The sites are open and wooded. They are clean and well-maintained, but offer little privacy. This is a campground with very clean bathroom and shower facilities. Aquia Pines offers day-long guided tours aboard the campground's comfortable bus. Stops include the White House, Capitol Hill, and Arlington National Cemetery among other monuments. Aquia Pines also offers shuttle bus service to the Smithsonian Museum. Recreation at the campground includes a large swimming pool and a mini-golf course. Aquia Pines is 10 minutes from a free private beach on the Potomac River. The Fredericksburg and Spotsylvania National Military Park and George Washington's Mt. Vernon are a short drive from the campground, as is Washington's birthplace, Wakefield, and his childhood home, Ferry Farm.

Basics

Operated By: Private operator. **Open:** All year. **Site Assignment:** Reservations and walk-ins accepted. **Registration:** At campground headquarters. **Fee:** $26–$37 (VISA, MC). **Parking:** At designated area.

Facilities

Number of RV Sites: 102. **Number of Tent-Only Sites:** 18. **Hookups:** Electric (20, 30, 50 amps), cable TV, phone, water, 84 full hookups. **Each Site:** Picnic table. **Dump Station:** Yes. **Laundry:** Yes. **Pay Phone:** Yes. **Rest Rooms and Showers:** Yes. **Fuel:** No. **Propane:** Yes. **Internal Roads:** Gravel and paved, in good condition. **RV Service:** No. **Market:** Within 2 mi. **Restaurant:** Within 2 mi. **General Store:** Yes. **Vending:** Yes. **Playground:** Yes. **Other:** Washington, D.C. tours aboard Aquia Pines tour bus. **Activities:** Rec hall, game room, swimming, mini-golf, basketball, planned activities on weekends, horseshoes, volleyball. **Nearby Attractions:** Washington, D.C., Fredericksburg and Spotsylvania National Military Park, Manassas National Battlefield Park, Mt. Vernon. **Additional Information:** Virginia Tourism Corp., (800) 371-8164, www.virginia.org.

Restrictions

Pets: On leash only. **Fires:** At site. **Alcoholic Beverages:** At site. **Vehicle Maximum Length:** None. **Other:** None.

To Get There

From I-95, take Exit 143A, go north at light onto US 1, then 0.5 mi. north on US 1. Entrance is on the left.

STAUNTON
KOA—Shenandoah Valley

P.O. Box 98, Verona 24482. T: (540) 248-2746 or (800) 562-9949; F: (540) 248-8230; www.koa.com.

RV ★★★★ Tent ★★★★

Beauty: ★★★★	Site Privacy: ★★★
Spaciousness: ★★★	Quiet: ★★★
Security: ★★★★	Cleanliness: ★★★★
Insect Control: ★★★★	Facilities: ★★★★

Located in the Shenandoah Valley, where the Skyline Drive and Blue Ridge Parkway wind past stunning mountain vistas, KOA—Shenandoah Valley is bordered by 1.5 miles of the Middle River, where a waterfall cascades and outdoor enthusiasts enjoy tubing, boating, and fishing. The campground has its own stocked fishing lake, a new swimming pool, and four indoor whirlpools. There's also a new and spacious game room. On weekends Memorial Day–Labor Day, a country band performs on Saturday nights, and several special events are held. The mostly wooded sites include 104 pull-throughs. With its proximity to Shenandoah National Park, the campground is near numerous hiking trails and scenic overlooks. In nearby Staunton, the Museum of American Frontier Culture consists of working farms from the 17th, 18th, and 19th centuries, representing English, German, Irish, and American farmers. Presidential history enthusiasts will want to visit the Woodrow Wilson Birthplace and National Museum, also in Staunton.

Basics

Operated By: KOA. **Open:** Mar. 15–Nov. 1. **Site Assignment:** Reservations and walk-ins accepted. **Registration:** At campground office. **Fee:** $26–$29 (VISA, MC, D). **Parking:** At site.

Facilities

Number of RV Sites: 100. **Number of Tent-Only Sites:** 50. **Hookups:** Electric (20, 30, 50 amps), cable TV, phone, water, 25 full hookups. **Each Site:** Fire ring, picnic table. **Dump Station:** Yes. **Laundry:** Yes. **Pay Phone:** Yes. **Rest Rooms and Showers:** Yes. **Fuel:** No. **Propane:** Yes. **Internal Roads:** Gravel and paved, in good condition. **RV Service:** No. **Market:** Within 2 mi. **Restaurant:** Within 2 mi. **General Store:** Yes. **Vending:** Yes. **Playground:** Yes. **Other:** Middle River. **Activities:** Lake and river fishing, rec hall, game room, swimming, whirlpool, basketball, planned activities, sports field, horseshoes, hiking trails, volleyball. **Nearby Attractions:** Shenandoah National Park, Statler Brothers Museum, Blue Ridge Parkway, Skyline Drive, Frontier Culture Museum, Woodrow Wilson Birthplace and Museum. **Additional Information:** Shenandoah Valley Travel Assoc., (540) 740-3132, www.svta.org.

Restrictions

Pets: On leash only. **Fires:** At site. **Alcoholic Beverages:** At site. **Vehicle Maximum Length:** None. **Other:** None.

To Get There

From I-81, take Exit 227 and go 1 mi. west on Hwy. 612, 0.5 mi. north on US 11, and 1 mi. west on CR 781. Entrance is on the left.

STAUNTON
Walnut Hills Campground

484 Walnut Hills Rd., Staunton 24401. T: (540) 337-3920 or (800) 699-2568; www.walnuthillscampground.com; info@walnuthillscampground.com.

RV ★★★★ Tent ★★★★

Beauty: ★★★★	Site Privacy: ★★★
Spaciousness: ★★★	Quiet: ★★★★
Security: ★★★★	Cleanliness: ★★★★
Insect Control: ★★★★	Facilities: ★★★★

Located in Staunton, the "Queen City of the Shenandoah Valley," Walnut Hills Campground is a quiet and comfortable base for exploring Shenandoah National Park, Skyline Drive, and the Blue Ridge Parkway. The open and semi-wooded sites are large and level, including 20 pull-throughs. Some of the sites are situated on the waterfront, and the campground has a separate area for tenters. We most like the sites located on Kerplonken Lake; the sites on the west end are also inviting. The lake is stocked with bass, perch, blue gill, and channel catfish. Cabins and cottages are available for rent. The south tip of Shenandoah National Park is a short drive from Walnut Hills. Along Skyline Drive in Shenandoah National Park, there are an estimated 70 overlooks where you can stretch your legs and gaze at the mountains and valleys; hiking trails also sprout from numerous points in the park.

Basics

Operated By: Albrecht family. **Open:** Mar. 1–Nov. 15. **Site Assignment:** Reservations recommended (holidays require 3-night min. stay and min. deposit of $30), walk-ins accepted. **Registration:** At campground office. **Fee:** $19–$27 (VISA, MC). **Parking:** At site.

Facilities

Number of RV Sites: 108. **Number of Tent-Only Sites:** 25. **Hookups:** Electric (20, 30, 50 amps), cable TV, phone, water, 58 full hookups. **Each Site:** Fire ring, picnic table. **Dump Station:** Yes. **Laundry:** Yes. **Pay Phone:** Yes. **Rest Rooms and Showers:** Yes. **Fuel:** No. **Propane:** Yes. **Internal Roads:** Gravel and paved, in good condition. **RV Service:** No. **Market:** Within 4 mi. **Restaurant:** Within 4 mi. **General Store:** Yes. **Vending:** Yes. **Playground:** Yes. **Other:** Fishing lake. **Activities:** Swimming, game room, rec hall, lake fishing, wading pool, horseshoes, volleyball. **Nearby Attractions:** Historic Lexington, Shenandoah National Park, Statler Brothers Museum, Blue Ridge Parkway, Skyline Drive, Frontier Culture Museum, Woodrow Wilson Birthplace and Museum. **Additional Information:** Shenandoah Valley Travel Assoc., (540) 740-3132, www.svta.org.

Restrictions

Pets: On leash only. **Fires:** At site. **Alcoholic Beverages:** At site. **Vehicle Maximum Length:** 50 ft. **Other:** None.

To Get There

From I-81, take Exit 217 and go 0.5 mi. west on Hwy. 654, 1.5 mi. south on US 11, and 1 mi. east on Hwy. 655. Entrance is on the left.

TRIANGLE
Prince William Forest Park

P.O. Box 209, Triangle 22172-0209. T: (703) 221-7181; F: (703) 221-4322; www.nps.gov/prwi; prwi_info@nps.gov.

RV ★★★★ Tent ★★★★

Beauty: ★★★★	Site Privacy: ★★★
Spaciousness: ★★★	Quiet: ★★★★
Security: ★★★★	Cleanliness: ★★★
Insect Control: ★★★★	Facilities: ★★★★

Located 32 miles from Washington, D.C., 17,000-acre Prince William Forest Park certainly has an interesting menu of camping options. This national park has Oak Ridge Campground, which is operated by the National Park Service, but it also has the privately operated Prince William Travel Trailer Village. The trailer village is located on the north side of the park and provides full hookups, hot showers, a dump station, a swimming pool, laundry facilities, and a playground. Oak Ridge is situated 5.5 miles from the park visitor center; there are 80 sites, none with electric hookups, and there are no shower facilities. Sites are spacious and private, shaded by oaks and pines. If you like hiking and biking, Prince William has 37 miles of hiking trails and fire roads for mountain biking along ridges, into valleys, and alongside the two main creeks in the park. Prince William also consists of the Chopawamsic Backcountry Area, which offers 400 acres of undeveloped terrain for hiking and camping. Permits are required and can be obtained for free at the visitor center.

Basics

Operated By: National Park Service. **Open:** All year. **Site Assignment:** First come, first served; no reservations accepted. **Registration:** Self-register on site. **Fee:** $4 entry fee, $10 (VISA, MC). **Parking:** At site.

Facilities

Number of RV Sites: 100. **Number of Tent-Only Sites:** 80. **Hookups:** None. **Each Site:** Picnic table, grill, lantern pole. **Dump Station:** Yes. **Laundry:** Yes. **Pay Phone:** Yes. **Rest Rooms and Showers:** Yes. **Fuel:** No. **Propane:** Yes. **Internal Roads:** Gravel and paved, in good condition. **RV Service:** No. **Market:** Within 2 mi. **Restaurant:** Within 2 mi. **General Store:** Yes. **Vending:** Yes. **Playground:** Yes. **Other:** Separate national park campground and private RV park on park grounds. **Activities:** Lake and stream fishing, swimming pool, planned activities on weekends, hiking trails. **Nearby Attractions:** Quantico Marine Base, Washington, D.C., Fredericksburg and Spotsylvania National Military Park, Manassas National Battlefield Park, Mt. Vernon. **Additional Information:** Prince William County/Manassas CVB, (800) 432-1792, www.visitpwc.com.

Restrictions

Pets: On leash only. **Fires:** In grills. **Alcoholic Beverages:** At site. **Vehicle Maximum Length:** 30 ft. **Other:** 14-day stay limit.

To Get There

From I-95, go 0.25 mi. west on Hwy. 619 to park entrance and follow signs for 7 mi.

URBANNA

Bethpage Camp-Resort

P.O. Box 178, Urbanna 23175. T: (804) 758-4349; F: (804) 758-0209; www.bethpagecamp.com; bethpage@oonl.com.

RV: ★★★★★ Tent: n/a

Beauty: ★★★★	Site Privacy: ★★
Spaciousness: ★★★	Quiet: ★★★★
Security: ★★★★	Cleanliness: ★★★★
Insect Control: ★★★★	Facilities: ★★★★★

Set on the southern reach of the Rappahannock River near Chesapeake Bay, Bethpage Camp-Resort is not only the best all-around campground in Virginia, it is one of the top five in the mid-Atlantic region. Bethpage has 700 wooded sites on 150 acres, including 300 pull-throughs and 300 double slideouts. Many of the larger sites are located along the banks of the Rappahannock River. There are two swimming pools, a swimming lake with a soft-sanded beach, a lake pier with a band gazebo, and two recreation centers. For boaters and fisherman, the campground has a marina, fish-cleaning stations, a boat ramp, and a high-pressure boat and RV wash. Bethpage can charter fishing boat excursions too. There are numerous special events during the year. Our favorite is the Steamed Crab Feast Weekend, which features all-you-can-eat Chesapeake Bay blue crabs. Colonial Williamsburg and Jamestown are nearby. Urbanna is the site of the annual Urbanna Oyster Festival, another treat for seafood lovers.

Basics

Operated By: Private operator. **Open:** Apr. 1–Nov. 15. **Site Assignment:** Reservations accepted (3-night min. stay on holiday weekends, 2-night min. Oyster Festival Weekend, $20 deposit required), walk-ins accepted. **Registration:** At campground office. **Fee:** $25–$30 (VISA, MC). **Parking:** At designated area.

Facilities

Number of RV Sites: 700. **Number of Tent-Only Sites:** None. **Hookups:** Electric (30, 50 amps), phone, water, sewer. **Each Site:** Fire ring, picnic table. **Dump Station:** Yes. **Laundry:** Yes. **Pay Phone:** Yes. **Rest Rooms and Showers:** Yes. **Fuel:** Yes. **Propane:** Yes. **Internal Roads:** Paved, in good condition. **RV Service:** No. **Market:** On site. **Restaurant:** Within 5 mi. **General Store:** Yes. **Vending:** Yes. **Playground:** Yes. **Other:** Marina and boat ramp. **Activities:** Two swimming pools, wading pool, game room, rec hall, pond swimming, boating, boat rentals, pond and saltwater fishing, basketball, bike rentals, planned activities, tennis, shuffleboard, volleyball, sports field, horseshoes. **Nearby Attractions:** Chesapeake Bay, Colonial Williamsburg, Urbanna Oyster Festival, Busch Gardens, Historic Jamestown Settlement, Yorktown. **Additional Information:** Virginia Tourism Corp. (800) 371-8164, www.virginia.org.

Restrictions

Pets: On leash only. **Fires:** At site. **Alcoholic Beverages:** At site. **Vehicle Maximum Length:** 45 ft. **Other:** No tent sites.

To Get There

From US 17, go 4 mi. east on SR 602 and 0.5 mi. east on SR 684. Entrance is on the left.

VIRGINIA BEACH

First Landing State Park

2500 Shore Dr., Virginia Beach 23451. T: (757) 412-2300 or (800) 933-PARK; www.dcr.state.va.us/parks; resvs@dcr.state.va.us.

RV: ★★★ Tent: ★★★★

Beauty: ★★★	Site Privacy: ★★★
Spaciousness: ★★★	Quiet: ★★★
Security: ★★★	Cleanliness: ★★★
Insect Control: ★★★★	Facilities: ★★★

Virginia Beach is regarded as the world's largest resort city. Long before Virginia Beach was settled, the Virginia Company landed at a site on Chesapeake Bay on Apr. 26, 1607—more than two weeks before arriving at Jamestown. Today, that site is First Landing State Park, visited by 1.2 million people a year. Though Virginia Beach and the state park are both crowded with tourists in warmer months, First Landing's beachfront swimming area is limited to campers, which minimizes the chance you will have to step over countless sunbathers to find a patch of sand. The campground's sites are separated by small sand dunes and trees. Though there are no hookups, the campground has hot showers, a laundromat with large capacity dryers and a well-stocked camp store. There are many hiking trails; the most popular path is the 1.5-mile Bald Cypress Loop Trail, which sprouts from the visitor center and takes you along boardwalks and through cypress swamps.

Basics

Operated By: State of Virginia. **Open:** Mar.–Dec. **Site Assignment:** Reservations strongly recommended, walk-ins accepted. **Registration:** At campground office. **Fee:** $18 (VISA, MC). **Parking:** At site.

Facilities

Number of RV Sites: 233. **Number of Tent-Only Sites:** None. **Hookups:** None. **Each Site:** Grill, picnic table. **Dump Station:** No. **Laundry:** Yes. **Pay Phone:** Yes. **Rest Rooms and Showers:** Yes. **Fuel:** No. **Propane:** No. **Internal Roads:** Paved, in good condition. **RV Service:** No. **Market:** Within 5 mi. **Restaurant:** Within 5 mi. **General Store:** Yes. **Vending:** Yes. **Playground:** No. **Other:** Bay Store. **Activities:** Boating, kayaking, saltwater fishing, hiking trails, crabbing, biking, bike rentals, Chesapeake Bay swimming (at own risk). **Nearby Attractions:** Chesapeake Bay, Virginia Beach, Ocean Breeze Water Park, Old Cape Henry Lighthouse and Memorial Park, Old Coast Guard Station, Virginia Marine Science Museum, Motor World Family Thrill Park. **Additional Information:** Virginia Beach Dept. of Convention and Visitor Development, (800) 700-7702, www.vabeach.com.

Restrictions

Pets: On leash only. **Fires:** In fire rings, stoves, and grills. **Alcoholic Beverages:** No alcohol permitted. **Vehicle Maximum Length:** 34 ft. **Other:** 14-day max. stay in 30-day period.

To Get There

From I-64, take Exit 282 and go northeast on US 13 and 5 mi. east on Shore Dr. Follow signs to campground.

VIRGINIA BEACH

Holiday Trav-L-Park

1075 General Booth Blvd., Virginia Beach 23451. T: (800) 548-0223 or (757) 425-0249; F: (757) 425-5117; www.htpvabeach.com; hotrpa@pinn.net.

RV: ★★★★ Tent: ★★★★

Beauty: ★★★★	Site Privacy: ★
Spaciousness: ★	Quiet: ★★★
Security: ★★★★★	Cleanliness: ★★★★
Insect Control: ★★★★	Facilities: ★★★★★

Amid forests and meadows, Holiday Trav-L-Park in Virginia Beach is like a small town in itself, with 1,000 sites, three grocery stores, laundromats, a full-service restaurant, six playgrounds, an 18-hole mini-golf course, and more. There are 550 pull-through sites. Campers have their choice of shaded, open, and wooded sites. In the busy season, the campground is stirring with live entertainment, bingo games, and hayrides. There is a bike path that leads to the beach; campers also have access to free parking one block from the beach. The Ocean Breeze Festival Park and the Motor World Family Thrill Park are close by as well. So is the Virginia Marine Science Museum, where visitors can see sharks, sea turtles, seals, and other ocean life, in addition to enjoying a 300-seat IMAX theater.

Basics

Operated By: Holiday Trav-L-Park. **Open:** All year. **Site Assignment:** Reservations accepted (recommended Memorial Day–Labor Day), walk-ins accepted. **Registration:** At campground office. **Fee:** $18–$24 (VISA, MC, D). **Parking:** At site.

Facilities

Number of RV Sites: 700. **Number of Tent-Only Sites:** 300. **Hookups:** Electric (20, 30, 50 amps), phone, water, 280 full hookups. **Each Site:** Picnic table. **Dump Station:** Yes. **Laundry:** Yes. **Pay Phone:** Yes. **Rest Rooms and Showers:** Yes. **Fuel:** Yes. **Propane:** Yes. **Internal Roads:** Gravel and paved, in good condition. **RV Service:** No. **Market:** On site. **Restaurant:** On site. **General Store:** Yes. **Vending:** Yes. **Playground:** Yes. **Other:** Four large pools and 18-hole mini-golf course. **Activities:** Swimming, game room, rec hall, wading pool, whirlpool, mini-golf, basketball, bike rentals, shuffleboard, planned activities, movies, badminton, sports field, horseshoes, volleyball. **Nearby Attractions:** Virginia Beach, Virginia Marine Science Museum, Back Bay Wildlife Refuge, First Landing State Park, Jamestown, Yorktown, Colonial Williamsburg. **Additional Information:** Virginia Beach Dept. of Convention and Visitor Development, (800) 700-7702, www.vabeach.com.

Restrictions

Pets: On leash only. **Fires:** At site. **Alcoholic Beverages:** At site. **Vehicle Maximum Length:** None. **Other:** Max. 6 people per campsite.

To Get There

From I-264, take Exit 22 and go 3 mi. southeast on Birdneck Rd. and 0.25 mi. south on General Booth Blvd. Entrance is on the right.

VIRGINIA BEACH

KOA—Virginia Beach

1240 General Booth Blvd., Virginia Beach 23451. T: (800) 562-4150 or (757) 428-1444; www.koa.com; vbkoa@netzero.com.

RV ★★★★ Tent ★★★★

Beauty: ★★★★	Site Privacy: ★★
Spaciousness: ★★	Quiet: ★★★
Security: ★★★★	Cleanliness: ★★★★
Insect Control: ★★★★	Facilities: ★★★★

Located close to the lively resort strip on Virginia Beach, KOA—Virginia Beach has 100 acres (just like Holiday Trav-L-Park), but the campground has 600 fewer sites. Campers who want proximity to the ocean but desire a less crowded environment will likely prefer this campground. KOA does not have the wealth of amenities that Holiday boasts, but it does have two swimming pools, a laundromat, and a well-stocked store. A trolley provides free rides to the beach for campers, departing every half-hour 8 a.m.–midnight. There are 400 open and partially wooded sites, including 350 pull-throughs. Ocean Breeze Festival Park and the Virginia Marine Science Museum are nearby. Lighthouse enthusiasts will enjoy the Old Cape Henry Lighthouse, located on the grounds of the Ft. Story Military Reservation.

Basics

Operated By: KOA. **Open:** All year. **Site Assignment:** Reservations and walk-ins accepted. **Registration:** At campground office. **Fee:** $20–$40 (VISA, MC, D). **Parking:** At designated area.

Facilities

Number of RV Sites: 330. **Number of Tent-Only Sites:** 70. **Hookups:** Electric (20, 30, 50 amps), water, 125 full hookups. **Each Site:** Fire ring, picnic table. **Dump Station:** Yes. **Laundry:** Yes. **Pay Phone:** Yes. **Rest Rooms and Showers:** Yes. **Fuel:** No. **Propane:** Yes. **Internal Roads:** Gravel and paved, in good condition. **RV Service:** No. **Market:** Within 1 mi. **Restaurant:** Within 1 mi. **General Store:** Yes. **Vending:** Yes. **Playground:** Yes. **Other:** Trolley to beach. **Activities:** Swimming, mini-golf, game room, rec hall, planned activities, sports field, badminton, horseshoes, volleyball, tennis. **Nearby Attractions:** Virginia Beach, Virginia Marine Science Museum, Back Bay Wildlife Refuge, First Landing State Park, Jamestown, Yorktown, Colonial Williamsburg. **Additional Information:** Virginia Beach Dept. of Convention and Visitor Development, (800) 700-7702, www.vabeach.com.

Restrictions

Pets: On leash only. **Fires:** At site. **Alcoholic Beverages:** At site. **Vehicle Maximum Length:** None. **Other:** None.

To Get There

From Hwy. 44E, go 1 mi. south on Pacific Ave. and 3 mi. south on General Booth Blvd. Entrance is on the left.

VIRGINIA BEACH

Outdoor Resorts—Virginia Beach

3665 Sandpiper Rd., Virginia Beach 23456. T: (800) 333-7515 or (757) 721-2020; www.outdoor-resorts.com; visit@outdoor-resorts.com.

RV ★★★★ Tent n/a

Beauty: ★★★★	Site Privacy: ★★
Spaciousness: ★★	Quiet: ★★★
Security: ★★★★★	Cleanliness: ★★★★
Insect Control: ★★★★	Facilities: ★★★★

Located along the outer banks near Virginia Beach, Outdoor Resorts—Virginia Beach has 250 sites on Back Bay. The nicely landscaped grounds include two lighted tennis courts, a large swimming pool with a whirlpool and a nearby sauna, bicycle trails, and a boating ramp and dock. There are no tent sites here, and vans, pop-ups, and truck campers are not permitted. The fishing is good at this campground, with choices of casting your line into the bay, the lake, or the ocean. The campground is a short walk to Back Bay National Wildlife Refuge. The 7,000-acre preserve is bordered by the Atlantic Ocean on one side and Back Bay on the other. A network of trails and boardwalks meanders through the park. If you are longing for a unique drive, head for the Chesapeake Bay Bridge-Tunnel. Stretching 17.6 miles, the incredible engineering feat carries traffic on US 13 from Virginia Beach to Virginia's eastern shore.

Basics

Operated By: Outdoor Resorts. **Open:** All year. **Site Assignment:** Reservations recommended, walk-ins accepted. **Registration:** At campground headquarters. **Fee:** $38–$44 (VISA, MC). **Parking:** At designated spot.

Facilities

Number of RV Sites: 250. **Number of Tent-Only Sites:** None. **Hookups:** Electric (20, 30, 50 amps), water, sewer, cable TV, phone. **Each Site:** Picnic table, patio. **Dump Station:** Yes. **Laundry:** Yes. **Pay Phone:** Yes. **Rest Rooms and Showers:** Yes. **Fuel:** No. **Propane:** No. **Internal Roads:** Paved, in good condition. **RV Service:** No. **Market:** Within 6 mi. **Restaurant:** Within 5 mi. **General Store:** No. **Vending:** Yes. **Playground:** Yes. **Other:** Boating ramp and dock. **Activities:** Swimming, sauna, whirlpool, boating, ocean fishing, bike rentals, tennis. **Nearby Attractions:** Virginia Beach, Virginia Marine Science Museum, Back Bay Wildlife Refuge, First Landing State Park, Jamestown, Yorktown, Colonial Williamsburg. **Additional Information:** Virginia Beach Dept. of Convention and Visitor Development, (800) 700-7702, www.vabeach.com.

Restrictions

Pets: On leash only. **Fires:** At site. **Alcoholic Beverages:** At site. **Vehicle Maximum Length:** 18 ft. **Other:** No vans, pop-ups, or truck campers.

To Get There

From I-64, take Exit 22 and go 3.5 mi. southeast on Birdneck Rd, 7 mi. south on General Booth Blvd., 1 mi. east on Princess Anne Rd., 7 mi. east on Sandbridge Rd., and 3.5 mi. south on Sandpiper Rd. Entrance is on the right.

VOLNEY

Grayson Highlands State Park

829 Grayson Highland Ln., Mouth of Wilson 24363. T: (540) 579-7092 or (800) 933-PARK; www.dcr.state.va.us/parks; resvs@dcr.state.va.us.

RV ★★★ Tent ★★★★

Beauty: ★★★★	Site Privacy: ★★★
Spaciousness: ★★★	Quiet: ★★★
Security: ★★★★	Cleanliness: ★★★★
Insect Control: ★★★★	Facilities: ★★★

Located adjacent to the Mount Rogers National Recreation Area, Grayson Highlands State Park was originally named Mount Rogers State Park. With elevations as high as 5,089 feet, Grayson Highlands is the loftiest state park in Virginia. From the park's highest point, stunning views await of surrounding mountains—including Mt. Rogers at 5,729 feet. Though the campground itself does not offer many activities, the park does. Fishermen cast their lines into Cabin and Wilson Creeks. More than two miles of bridle paths wander through the park. The park has nine hiking trails averaging a mile in length. These trails lead to panoramic vistas, scenic waterfalls, and a 200-year-old pioneer cabin. The park also offers access to the Appalachian Trail and trails in the surrounding Jefferson National Forest. Mountain bikers love the Virginia Creeper Trail, a 33.4-mile multi-use trail extending from Whitetop to Abingdon.

Basics

Operated By: State of Virginia. **Open:** Mar.–Dec. **Site Assignment:** First come, first served; no reservations accepted. **Registration:** At campground office. **Fee:** $14–$18 (VISA, MC). **Parking:** At site.

Facilities

Number of RV Sites: 75. **Number of Tent-Only Sites:** None. **Hookups:** Electric (30 amps), water. **Each Site:** Fire ring, picnic table. **Dump Station:** Yes. **Laundry:** Yes. **Pay Phone:** Yes. **Rest Rooms and Showers:** Yes. **Fuel:** No. **Propane:** No. **Internal Roads:** Gravel, in good condition. **RV Service:** No. **Market:** Within 5 mi. **Restaurant:** Within 5 mi. **General Store:** Yes. **Vending:** Yes. **Playground:** No. **Other:** Visitor center. **Activities:** Hiking trails, biking, horseback riding, fishing, boating. **Nearby Attractions:** Blue Ridge Parkway, Barter Theatre, Bristol International Raceway, Mt. Rogers Recreation Area, Jefferson National Forest, Virginia Creeper Trail. **Additional Information:** Grayson County Visitors Bureau, (540) 773-3711, www.grayson.va.us.

Restrictions

Pets: On leash only, at campsite. **Fires:** In grills, stoves, and fire rings. **Alcoholic Beverages:** No alcohol permitted. **Vehicle Maximum Length:** 40 ft. **Other:** 14-day stay in 30-day period.

To Get There

From Hwy. 16, go 5 mi. west on US 58. Follow signs to campground.

WILLIAMSBURG
Anvil Campground

5243 Mooretown Rd., Williamsburg 23188. T: (800) 633-4442 or (757) 565-2300; F: (757) 564-9817; www.anvilcampground.com; stay@anvilcampground.com.

RV ★★★★ Tent ★★★★

Beauty: ★★★★ Site Privacy: ★★★
Spaciousness: ★★★ Quiet: ★★★★
Security: ★★★★ Cleanliness: ★★★★
Insect Control: ★★★★ Facilities: ★★★★

Brightened by azaleas and literally thousands of other perennials, Anvil Campground offers shaded and level sites adorned with mature trees. There is plenty to do at the campground, which has three playgrounds, basketball court, swimming pool, game room, and a tv room. Chances are you will want to use the campground as a base for the multitude of nearby attractions, such as Colonial Williamsburg, a 173-acre area with 600 restored or rebuilt structures that form an 18th-century colonial capitol. Instead of driving, you can ride on the Williamsburg Area Visitors Shuttle; one of the shuttle's stopping points is a short walk from Anvil. The shuttle serves the Rte. 60 Bypass and Capitol Landing Rd. from the Williamsburg Pottery Factory to Colonial Williamsburg. It also reaches Busch Gardens, Water Country USA, and several other points. The shuttle operates May 26–Labor Day, seven days a week, 9 a.m.–10 p.m.

Basics

Operated By: Private operator. **Open:** All year. **Site Assignment:** Reservations recommended (1-night deposit required), walk-ins accepted. **Registration:** At campground office. **Fee:** $24–$29 (VISA, MC, D). **Parking:** At site.

Facilities

Number of RV Sites: 63. **Number of Tent-Only Sites:** 10. **Hookups:** Electric (20, 30 amps), phone, water, 37 full hookups. **Each Site:** Fire ring, picnic table. **Dump Station:** Yes. **Laundry:** Yes. **Pay Phone:** Yes. **Rest Rooms and Showers:** Yes. **Fuel:** No. **Propane:** Yes. **Internal Roads:** Gravel, in good condition. **RV Service:** No. **Market:** Within 3 mi. **Restaurant:** Within 2 mi. **General Store:** Yes. **Vending:** Yes. **Playground:** Yes. **Other:** None. **Activities:** Rec hall, game room, , basketball, movies, badminton, horseshoes, volleyball. **Nearby Attractions:** Colonial Williamsburg, College of William and Mary, Busch Gardens, Historic Jamestown Settlement, Yorktown. **Additional Information:** Williamsburg Area CVB, (757) 253-0192, www.visitwilliamsburg.com.

Restrictions

Pets: On leash only. **Fires:** At site. **Alcoholic Beverages:** At site. **Vehicle Maximum Length:** None. **Other:** None.

To Get There

From I-64, take Exit 238 and go one block south on Hwy. 243, 1.25 mi. northwest on Rochambeau Dr., 2 mi. southwest on Hwy. 645, and 0.5 mi. south on Hwy. 603. Entrance is on the right.

WILLIAMSBURG
Jamestown Beach Campsites

P.O. Box CB, Williamsburg 23187. T: (757) 229-7609 or (800) 446-9228; www,jamestown campsites.com; jbc@wmbgva.com.

RV ★★★★ Tent ★★★★

Beauty: ★★★★ Site Privacy: ★★
Spaciousness: ★★ Quiet: ★★★★
Security: ★★★★ Cleanliness: ★★★★
Insect Control: ★★★★ Facilities: ★★★★

Situated along the James River, Jamestown Beach Campsites' location is perfect for travelers interested in visiting the area's rich historical attractions. The campground is adjacent to the Jamestown Settlement and near the Colonial Parkway that links Jamestown, Williamsburg, and Yorktown. If you like the water, Jamestown Beach Campsites has a sandy beach where you can soak in the sun and swim in the James River. There is a dock and ramp for boats, and a place to get bait and fishing supplies. Most sites are nestled in the woods and near the water. During warmer months, the campground hosts dances on the beach and live entertainment in the recreation hall. The nearby Jamestown Colonial National Historical Park is a fascinating place where the first permanent English settlement in the New World was founded on May 13, 1607. Here, you can visit a living history museum which recreates the Jamestown of the 1600s.

Basics

Operated By: T Robert Vermillion. **Open:** All year. **Site Assignment:** Reservations required. **Registration:** At campground office. **Fee:** $18–$25 (VISA, MC). **Parking:** At site.

Facilities

Number of RV Sites: 300. **Number of Tent-Only Sites:** 300. **Hookups:** Electric (20, 30, 50 amps), phone, water, 200 full hookups. **Each Site:** Fire ring, picnic table. **Dump Station:** Yes. **Laundry:** Yes. **Pay Phone:** Yes. **Rest Rooms and Showers:** Yes. **Fuel:** No. **Propane:** Yes. **Internal Roads:** Gravel and paved, in good condition. **RV Service:** No. **Market:** Within 3 mi. **Restaurant:** On site. **General Store:** Yes. **Vending:** Yes. **Playground:** Yes. **Other:** James River. **Activities:** Swimming, wading pool, boating, canoeing, kayaking, river fishing, mini-golf, game room, rec hall, shuffleboard, horseshoes, volleyball, sports field. **Nearby Attractions:** Colonial Williamsburg, College of William and Mary, Busch Gardens, Historic Jamestown Settlement, Yorktown. **Additional Information:** Williamsburg Area CVB, (757) 253-0192, www.visitwilliamsburg.com.

Restrictions

Pets: On leash only. **Fires:** At site. **Alcoholic Beverages:** At site. **Vehicle Maximum Length:** None. **Other:** None.

To Get There

From I-64, take Exit 242A and go 4 mi. west on Hwy. 199 and 4 mi. south on Hwy. 31. Entrance is on the right.

WILLIAMSBURG
KOA—Colonial Central

4000 Newman Rd., Williamsburg 23188. T: (800) 562-7609 or (757) 565-2734; www.williamsburgkoa.com; wmbgkoa.com.

RV ★★★★ Tent ★★★★

Beauty: ★★★★★ Site Privacy: ★★
Spaciousness: ★★ Quiet: ★★★
Security: ★★★★ Cleanliness: ★★★★
Insect Control: ★★★★ Facilities: ★★★★

Featuring 200 grassy and partially wooded sites, KOA—Colonial Central is connected to its sister property (KOA—Williamsburg) by a winding nature trail. Guests at one property can use facilities at the other. Colonial Central is seven miles from Colonial Williamsburg, and a short drive from an abundance of restaurants on Rte. 60. There are so many eateries on this portion of Rte. 60 that locals call it "Restaurant Row." The campground has 180 pull-through sites. Full-hookup sites with 50-amp service are located on the east end, while the remaining full hookups are situated on the west side. A free shuttle service transports campers to attractions like Colonial Williamsburg and Busch Gardens. Yorktown Battlefield, which is part of the Colonial National Historical Park which includes Williamsburg and Jamestown, is located 20 miles from the campground. KOA—Colonial Central is near several golf courses, including the much-heralded Colonial Golf Course set amid forests and tidal wetlands.

Basics

Operated By: KOA. **Open:** Mar. 1–Nov. 15. **Site Assignment:** Reservations accepted ($25 deposit required), walk-ins accepted. **Registration:** At campground office. **Fee:** $28–$38 (VISA, MC). **Parking:** At site.

Facilities

Number of RV Sites: 175. **Number of Tent-Only Sites:** 25. **Hookups:** Electric (20, 30, 50 amps), water, cable TV, phone, 61 full hookups. **Each Site:** Fire ring, picnic table. **Dump Station:** Yes. **Laundry:** Yes. **Pay Phone:** Yes. **Rest Rooms and Showers:** Yes. **Fuel:** No. **Propane:** Yes. **Internal Roads:** Gravel and paved, in good condition. **RV Service:** No. **Market:** Within 2 mi. **Restaurant:** Within 2 mi. **General Store:** Yes. **Vending:** Yes. **Playground:** Yes. **Other:** Shuttle service to Williamsburg attractions. **Activities:** Game room, rec hall, swimming , wading pool, basketball, sports field, horseshoes. **Nearby Attractions:** Colonial Williamsburg, College of William and Mary, Busch Gardens, Historic Jamestown Settlement, Yorktown. **Additional Information:** Williamsburg Area CVB, (757) 253-0192, www.visitwilliamsburg.com.

Restrictions

Pets: On leash only. **Fires:** At site. **Alcoholic Beverages:** At site. **Vehicle Maximum Length:** None. **Other:** Dogs, cats, and ferrets are only pets permitted.

To Get There

From I-64, take Exit 234 and go 1 mi. northeast on Hwy. 199, which turns into Hwy. 646. Entrance is on the right.

WILLIAMSBURG
KOA—Williamsburg

5210 Newman Rd., Williamsburg 23188. T: (757) 565-2907 or (800) 562-1733; www.williamsburgkoa.com; wmbgkoa@aol.com.

RV ★★★★ Tent ★★★★

Beauty: ★★★★ Site Privacy: ★★
Spaciousness: ★★★ Quiet: ★★★
Security: ★★★★ Cleanliness: ★★★★
Insect Control: ★★★★ Facilities: ★★★★

KOA—Williamsburg and KOA—Colonial Central are separate campgrounds connected by a nature trail. Campers have access to activities at either location. KOA—Williamsburg offers more activities than its sister property, however. At this campground, you can watch movies, fish in a creek, and enjoy cable TV at every site. There are 12 pull-through sites at KOA—Williamsburg compared to 180 at Colonial Central. Both campgrounds are elegantly landscaped, offer clean bathrooms and showers, and have nice swimming pools. Full hookup sites along the creek and near the rest rooms and showers are favorite spots at KOA—Williamsburg. The campground offers a free shuttle service to area attractions, which include Colonial Williamsburg and Busch Gardens. There are also several summer programs for children. The campground also sells tickets to area attractions.

Basics

Operated By: KOA. **Open:** Mar. 1–Oct. 31. **Site Assignment:** Reservations recommended, walk-ins accepted. **Registration:** At campground office. **Fee:** $28–$38 (VISA, MC). **Parking:** At site.

Facilities

Number of RV Sites: 140. **Number of Tent-Only Sites:** 17. **Hookups:** Electric (20, 30, 50 amps), water, cable TV, phone, 71 full hookups. **Each Site:** Picnic table. **Dump Station:** Yes. **Laundry:** Yes. **Pay Phone:** Yes. **Rest Rooms and Showers:** Yes. **Fuel:** No. **Propane:** No. **Internal Roads:** Gravel, in good condition. **RV Service:** No. **Market:** Within 3 mi. **Restaurant:** Within 3 mi. **General Store:** Yes. **Vending:** Yes. **Playground:** Yes. **Other:** Shuttle service to Williamsburg attractions. **Activities:** Game room, rec hall, swimming, basketball, planned activities, movies, horseshoes, volleyball. **Nearby Attractions:** Colonial Williamsburg, College of William and Mary, Busch Gardens, Historic Jamestown Settlement, Yorktown. **Additional Information:** Williamsburg Area CVB, (757) 253-0192, www.visitwilliamsburg.com.

Restrictions

Pets: On leash only. **Fires:** At site. **Alcoholic Beverages:** At site. **Vehicle Maximum Length:** None. **Other:** Dogs, cats, and ferrets are only pets permitted.

To Get There

From I-64, take Exit 234 and go 1.5 mi. east on Hwy. 199, which turns into Hwy. 646. Entrance is on the right.

WILLIAMSBURG
Outdoor World—Williamsburg Campground

4301 Rochambeau Dr., Williamsburg 23188. T: (800) 222-5557; www.campoutdoorworld.com; mbrservs@ptd.net.

RV ★★★★ Tent ★★★★

Beauty: ★★★★★ Site Privacy: ★★★
Spaciousness: ★★★ Quiet: ★★★★
Security: ★★★★ Cleanliness: ★★★★
Insect Control: ★★★★ Facilities: ★★★★★

Outdoor World—Williamsburg Campground sites are spacious, and there are 30 pull-throughs. What we especially like here is the menu of special events. There's a Roaring '20s Weekend, when male campers dress in gangster-like pinstripe suits and females don flapper dresses with strands of long pearls; and Disco Fever Weekend, when polyester suits and platform shoes take over and campers dance to music from the Bee Gees and the Village People. Good Old Days Weekend and Island Escape Weekend are other noteworthy special events. We were here during Star Search Weekend, but since we can't dance like Fred Astaire or Michael Jackson or sing like Frank Sinatra or Celine Dion, we chose to watch rather than participate. Of course, we could have sang a tune and entered it into the stand-up comedian category.

Basics

Operated By: Outdoor World. **Open:** All year. **Site Assignment:** Reservations recommended (3-night min. stay on holiday weekends, otherwise 2-night min. stay), walk-ins accepted. **Registration:** At campground office. **Fee:** $37 (VISA, MC, AE). **Parking:** At site.

Facilities

Number of RV Sites: 207. **Number of Tent-Only Sites:** 30. **Hookups:** Electric (20, 30, 50 amps), phone, water, 14 full hookups. **Each Site:** Fire ring, picnic table. **Dump Station:** Yes. **Laundry:** Yes. **Pay Phone:** Yes. **Rest Rooms and Showers:** Yes. **Fuel:** No. **Propane:** No. **Internal Roads:** Gravel and paved, in fair condition. **RV Service:** No. **Market:** Within 4 mi. **Restaurant:** Within 2 mi. **General Store:** Yes. **Vending:** Yes. **Playground:** Yes. **Other:** Mini-golf course. **Activities:** Swimming, wading pool, game room, rec hall, mini-golf, whirlpool, basketball, shuffleboard, planned activities, movies, sports field, horseshoes, volleyball. **Nearby Attractions:** Colonial Williamsburg, College of William and Mary, Busch Gardens, Historic Jamestown Settlement, Yorktown. **Additional Information:** Williamsburg Area CVB, (757) 253-0192, www.visitwilliamsburg.com.

Restrictions

Pets: On leash only. **Fires:** At site. **Alcoholic Beverages:** At site. **Vehicle Maximum Length:** None. **Other:** None.

To Get There

From I-64, take Exit 231A and go 0.2 mi. south on Hwy. 607 and 0.25 mi. north on Rochambeau Rd./Hwy. 30. Entrance is on the left.

WILLIAMSBURG
Williamsburg Pottery Campground

901 Lightfoot Rd., Williamsburg 23188-9017. T: (757) 565-2101 or (800) 892-0320.

RV ★★★★ Tent ★★★★

Beauty: ★★★★ Site Privacy: ★★
Spaciousness: ★★ Quiet: ★★★
Security: ★★★★ Cleanliness: ★★★★
Insect Control: ★★★★ Facilities: ★★★★

The Williamsburg Pottery Factory draws an estimated 3.5–4 million visitors a year, making it Virginia's top tourist attraction. Consisting of 32 buildings—including 25 factory outlets and a 500-seat restaurant—that occupy 200 acres, the Williamsburg Pottery Factory is a place where craftspeople create ceramics, lamps, silk and dried flower arrangements, glass-etched items, and many other arts and crafts. Located next to the pottery factory, the Williamsburg Pottery Campground has 500 shaded and open sites on 50 acres. Campsites provide little privacy, but the cleanliness of the park and the wealth of activities compensate for this. A swimming pool, fishing pond, and mini-golf course are among the recreational opportunities. The campground's rates are among the best in the Williamsburg area, making it especially attractive to families. The shopper's haven also includes 11 greenhouses, gourmet food and wine shops, and a store that sells Mexican items.

BASICS

Operated By: Holiday Trav-L-Park. **Open:** All year. **Site Assignment:** Reservations accepted (48-hour cancellation notice required), walk-ins accepted. **Registration:** At campground office. **Fee:** $16–$23 (VISA, MC, D). **Parking:** At designated area.

FACILITIES

Number of RV Sites: 450. **Number of Tent-Only Sites:** 50. **Hookups:** Electric (20, 30, 50 amps), water, phone, 213 full hookups. **Each Site:** Fire ring, picnic table. **Dump Station:** Yes. **Laundry:** Yes. **Pay Phone:** Yes. **Rest Rooms and Showers:** Yes. **Fuel:** No. **Propane:** Yes. **Internal Roads:** Gravel and paved, in good condition. **RV Service:** No. **Market:** Within 1 mi. **Restaurant:** Within 1 mi. **General Store:** Yes. **Vending:** Yes. **Playground:** Yes. **Other:** Mini-golf course. **Activities:** Mini-golf, swimming, wading pool pond fishing, basketball, badminton, sports field, horseshoes, hiking trails, volleyball. **Nearby Attractions:** Williamsburg Pottery Factory, Colonial Williamsburg, College of William and Mary, Busch Gardens, Historic Jamestown Settlement, Yorktown. **Additional Information:** Williamsburg Area CVB, (757) 253-0192, www.visitwilliamsburg.com.

RESTRICTIONS

Pets: On leash only. **Fires:** At site. **Alcoholic Beverages:** At site. **Vehicle Maximum Length:** 45 ft. **Other:** None.

TO GET THERE

From I-64, take Exit 234 and go 0.75 mi. west on Hwy. 199, 100 yds. north on West Mooretown Rd., and 250 yds. east on F-137. Entrance is on the left.

WINCHESTER

Candy Hill Campground

165 Ward Ave., Winchester 22602. T: (540) 662-8010 or (800) 462-0545; F: (540) 662-8010; www.candyhill.com; info@candyhill.com.

RV ★★★★ Tent ★★★★

Beauty: ★★★★★	Site Privacy: ★★★
Spaciousness: ★★★	Quiet: ★★★★
Security: ★★★★	Cleanliness: ★★★★
Insect Control: ★★★★	Facilities: ★★★★

Situated atop Shenandoah Valley in northern Virginia, Candy Hill Campground has 103 level sites, some open and some shaded. The facilities at Candy Hill are well-maintained and clean. Groups of 12 or more can use the Candy Hill Trolley at no cost to travel to area attractions. If you are interested in a unique lodging experience, stay in an authentic B&O Railroad caboose. Candy Hill is a short drive from the northern entrance of Skyline Drive in Front Royal. Endless Caverns and Luray Caverns are also nearby. The town of Winchester is an interesting place; it changed hands 72 times during the Civil War, including 13 times in one day. Stonewall Jackson's Headquarters is now a museum where you can peruse Confederate artifacts. Today, about 3.5 million bushels of apples are harvested in the area. The Shenandoah Apple Blossom Festival is held annually in late Apr. and early May.

BASICS

Operated By: Art and Wendy Littman. **Open:** All year. **Site Assignment:** Reservations recommended (1-night deposit required), walk-ins accepted. **Registration:** At campground office. **Fee:** $24–$31 (VISA, MC, D). **Parking:** At site.

FACILITIES

Number of RV Sites: 103. **Number of Tent-Only Sites:** None. **Hookups:** Electric (20, 30, 50 amps), phone, water, 57 full hookups. **Each Site:** Fire ring, picnic table. **Dump Station:** Yes. **Laundry:** Yes. **Pay Phone:** Yes. **Rest Rooms and Showers:** Yes. **Fuel:** No. **Propane:** Yes. **Internal Roads:** Paved, in good condition. **RV Service:** No. **Market:** Within 2 mi. **Restaurant:** Within 1 mi. **General Store:** Yes. **Vending:** Yes. **Playground:** Yes. **Other:** Cabin and caboose rentals. **Activities:** Swimming, basketball, game room, rec hall, badminton, sports field, horseshoes, volleyball. **Nearby Attractions:** Winchester Speedway, Skyline Drive, Harper's Ferry, Stonewall Jackson's Headquarters, Luray Caverns, Endless Caverns, Belle Grove Plantation. **Additional Information:** Virginia Tourism Corp., (800) 371-8164, www.virginia.org.

RESTRICTIONS

Pets: On leash only. **Fires:** At site. **Alcoholic Beverages:** At site. **Vehicle Maximum Length:** 45 ft. **Other:** None.

TO GET THERE

From I-81, take Exit 310 and go 5.5 mi. north on Hwy. 37, 300 yards west on US 50, and 0.25 mi. south on Ward Ave. Entrance is on the left.

WYTHEVILLE

KOA—Wytheville

Rt. 2 Box 122, Wytheville 24382. T: (540) 228-2601 or (800) KOA-3380; F: (540) 223-4447; www.wythevillekoa.com; wythekoa@naxs.com.

RV ★★★★ Tent ★★★★

Beauty: ★★★★	Site Privacy: ★★
Spaciousness: ★★	Quiet: ★★★
Security: ★★★★	Cleanliness: ★★★★
Insect Control: ★★★★	Facilities: ★★★★

Nestled between the Blue Ridge and Allegheny mountains in western Virginia, KOA—Wytheville is one of the cleanest KOA campgrounds you will find in Virginia and the mid-Atlantic. There are 115 RV sites, including 65 pull-throughs. While using the bathroom or taking a shower, you can listen to classical music played through the speakers. A 12,500-square-foot recreation center houses batting cages, a mini-golf course, a rock climbing wall, and the Family Fun Center with new video games, dart boards, pool tables, and skeeball. Children flock to the campground's petting zoo to see rabbits, cats, goats, lambs, and horses. Beyond the campground, scenic drives and outdoor activities beckon. Rural Retreat Lake is nearby, as is the George Washington and Jefferson National Forest. Rafting trips in "Virginia's Outback" on the New River are popular. Shot Tower Historical Park in Wytheville is perched on a bluff overlooking the New River.

BASICS

Operated By: Gene and Donna Metzger. **Open:** All year. **Site Assignment:** Reservations and walk-ins accepted. **Registration:** At campground office. **Fee:** $22–$32 (VISA, MC, AE, D). **Parking:** At site.

FACILITIES

Number of RV Sites: 110. **Number of Tent-Only Sites:** 15. **Hookups:** Electric (20, 30, 50 amps), cable TV, phone, water, 28 full hookups. **Each Site:** Fire ring, picnic table. **Dump Station:** Yes. **Laundry:** Yes. **Pay Phone:** Yes. **Rest Rooms and Showers:** Yes. **Fuel:** No. **Propane:** Yes. **Internal Roads:** Gravel and paved, in good condition. **RV Service:** No. **Market:** Within 2 mi. **Restaurant:** Within 2 mi. **General Store:** Yes. **Vending:** Yes. **Playground:** Yes. **Other:** Shuttle service to area attractions. **Activities:** Float trips, mini-golf, game room, rec hall, basketball, shuffleboard, planned activities, movies, badminton, horseshoes, hiking trails, volleyball. **Nearby Attractions:** Museum of the Middle Appalachians, Appalachian Trail, Wytheville State Fish Hatchery, New River Trail, Shot Tower Historical Park, Big Walker Lookout, Rural Retreat Lake. **Additional Information:** Wytheville-Wythe-Bland Chamber of Commerce, (540) 223-3365; www.wytheville.org/chamber.

RESTRICTIONS

Pets: On leash only. **Fires:** At site. **Alcoholic Beverages:** At site. **Vehicle Maximum Length:** 45 ft. **Other:** None.

TO GET THERE

From I-77, take Exit 77 and go 0.5 mi. south on Hwy. 758. Entrance is at the end.

Washington

Washington State, a beautiful place to tour year-round, boasts a variety of different natural and urban environments to explore. While the most popular region for tourism is the I-5 corridor, astounding natural beauty, cultural events, and man-made curiosities await across the state.

The I-5 corridor, the most widely traveled (and also promoted) section of the state, contains **Seattle, Tacoma, Olympia, Bellingham,** the Canadian border, the volcanoes, access to the **North Cascades** and **Olympic Peninsula,** and **Vancouver** (Washington). This region has mild, temperate weather all year and lots of rain.

Cities and natural attractions along the I-5 corridor abound. The northwestern region is especially beautiful, with the **San Juan Islands, Victoria** (Canada), and Bellingham. The region's geography blends mountains to the east, myriad inlets and bays to the west, and mountains rising from the islands beyond. Bellingham houses **Western Washington University** and is an interesting, small, college town. The absolute best views in the region can be had from overlooks on **Chuckanut Drive.** If you're in a small enough vehicle, continue on south through the beautiful Skagit county farmland as the road makes its way back to the interstate.

A major geographic region of the state, the Olympic Peninsula has tremendous natural beauty, vibrancy, and diversity. **Port Angeles** has the most services of any city on the northern peninsula, provides the best access to the Olympic Mountains, and, along with the surrounding area, handles the bulk of the tourist traffic. If you can only visit one area in the state, go see the peninsula; you won't be sorry.

Traveling east across Washington, the climate and environment change dramatically. The Northern Cascades have snow on the ground year-round in some places. The mountainous belt drops a couple of thousand feet into high-altitude deserts. The red earth of north-
central Washington is home to a mix of desert, valleys, canyons, farms, rivers, lakes, and the occasional ponderosa pine forest. The coulee region has scenery different from any other area, with many pullouts and vistas along **Banks Lake Road.** South-central Washington has a flat, desolate, arid terrain with lots of farms and wineries. The Yakima region of the state produces copious amounts of wine and makes a popular tourist destination. In both central and eastern Washington, lake fishing draws a lot of travelers.

Moving east from south-central Washington, the landscape changes to rolling hills around the Idaho border and the Snake River area. Moving north to **Spokane,** the landscape changes yet again to smoothly rolling farms and dry ponderosa pine forests. Although a popular escape for locals, the eastern side of the state receives very little state-sponsored tourism PR (a fact not lost on residents). Coincidentally, goods and services on the eastern side of the state don't cost quite as much as in the Puget Sound region (particularly hotels and restaurants), but the tourism infrastructure is not as developed as it is around Seattle.

The following facilities accept payment in checks or cash only:

Denny Creek Campground, North Bend

Van Mall RV Park, Vancouver

Vancouver RV Park, Vancouver

The following facilities feature 20 or fewer sites:

Corral Pass Campground, Enumclaw

Evergreen Court Campground, Ocean Park

Merrill Lake Campground, Cougar

Mounthaven Resort, Ashford

Sol Duc Resort, Port Angeles (Olympic National Park)

ANATONE

Fields Spring State Park

P.O. Box 37, Anatone 99401. T: (509) 256-3332; www.parks.wa.gov.

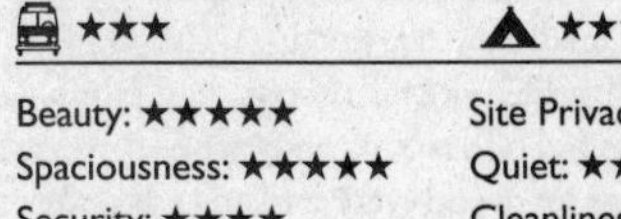

RV ★★★ Tent ★★★★

Beauty: ★★★★★	Site Privacy: ★★★
Spaciousness: ★★★★★	Quiet: ★★★★
Security: ★★★★	Cleanliness: ★★★★★
Insect Control: ★★	Facilities: ★★★

Anatone is quite small. It is the last stop for any kind of services before continuing on to Field's Spring State Park. Beyond Field's Spring to the south lies wilderness, national forest, and wild river canyons. Sitting on a basalt foundation at 4,000 feet on the eastern edge of Washington's Blue Mountains, Field's Spring State Park is a place of unusual beauty in an otherwise harsh and rugged terrain. Escaping the heat of the summer is one of the biggest draws to Field's Spring. Although the park sits on what is essentially an arid, desert-like plateau, with prickly pear cactus growing down along the Grande Ronde's banks, the difference in elevation makes all the difference in temperature. While Clarkston and Lewiston swelter in 100-degree agony in midsummer, Field's Spring rarely gets above a tolerable 85. Field's Spring is a true oasis in a region otherwise parched for camping options.

Basics

Operated By: Washington State Parks & Recreation Commission. **Open:** All year, weather permitting. **Site Assignment:** First come, first served. **Registration:** Self-registration. **Fee:** $5–$11. **Parking:** At site.

Facilities

Number of Multipurpose Sites: 20. **Hookups:** None. **Dump Station:** Yes. **Laundry:** No. **Pay Phone:** Yes. **Rest Rooms and Showers:** Yes. **Fuel:** 31 mi. in Clarkston. **Propane:** 31 mi. in Clarkston. **Internal Roads:** Paved. **RV Service:** No. **Market:** 31 mi. in Clarkston. **Restaurant:** Yes. **General Store:** 31 mi. in Clarkston. **Vending:** No. **Swimming Pool:** No. **Playground:** Yes. **Other:** 2 lodges, 2 kitchen shelters w/ electricity, 2 sheltered fire circles, teepee camp (6 can be reserved for $20 per night). **Activities:** Environmental Learning Center, hiking, biking, horseshoe pits, softball field, volleyball fields, hang gliding, paragliding. **Nearby Attractions:** Puffer Butle, Snake River. **Additional Information:** www.parks.wa.gov.

Restrictions

Pets: On leash. **Fires:** In fire pit. **Alcoholic Beverages:** Allowed. **Vehicle Maximum Length:** Call ahead for details.

To Get There

From Clarkston (roughly 110 mi. south of Spokane), follow SR 129 south through Asotin and Anatone for about 25 mi. to the park entrance.

ASHFORD

Mounthaven Resort

38210 SR 706 East, Ashford 98304. T: (360) 569-2594 or (800) 456-9380; www.mounthaven.com; info@mounthaven.com.

RV ★★★★ Tent ★

Beauty: ★★★★	Site Privacy: ★
Spaciousness: ★★★	Quiet: ★★★
Security: ★	Cleanliness: ★★★★
Insect Control: ★★	Facilities: ★★

Mounthaven Resort, half a mile west of the entrance to Mount Ranier National Park, offers a beautiful woodland setting. The quaint park lacks on-site indoor recreation, but people don't often come to the area to "stay at home". Seventeen shady RV sites are arranged in two rows. The intimate campground sits among cedars and firs, and is visited by friendly deer. Adjacent sites have dirt surfaces and come in a variety of sizes. Sites 6–13 make up the nicest sites in the park, due to size and quiet; sites 1–5 sit near the sometimes busy Hwy. 706. The campground also has an array of cabins for travelers looking for indoor accomodations. Visit during the early or late summer shoulder seasons for optimal conditions.

Basics

Operated By: Mt. Haven Resort. **Open:** All year. **Site Assignment:** On arrival or by reservation (deposit required for holidays, 15-days cancellation notice for refund). **Registration:** At office, late arrivals pay in morning. **Fee:** Full $20, extra campers (more than 4) & dogs $2; V, MC, cash. **Parking:** At site.

Facilities

Number of RV-Only Sites: 17. **Number of Tent-Only Sites:** 1. **Hookups:** Electric (20, 30 amps), water, sewer. **Each Site:** Picnic table, fire ring. **Dump Station:** Yes. **Laundry:** Yes. **Pay Phone:** Yes. **Rest Rooms and Showers:** Yes. **Fuel:** No. **Propane:** No. **Internal Roads:** Gravel, dirt. **RV Service:** No. **Market:** Convenience stores, 1–5 mi.; larger store 30 mi. west. **Restaurant:** 1–5 mi. **General Store:** No. **Vending:** Yes. **Swimming Pool:** No. **Playground:** Yes. **Other:** Cabins, firewood, horseshoes, volleyball, basketball, badminton, board games, hot tub (by reservation only, $10 per hour for 2 people). **Activities:** Mt. Rainier. **Nearby Attractions:** Mt. Rainier. **Additional Information:** Mount Ranier NPS Office, (360) 569-2212.

Restrictions

Pets: On leash only, 2 per site max. **Fires:** In fire pits only. **Alcoholic Beverages:** At site only. **Vehicle Maximum Length:** None.

To Get There

Located on SR 706, 0.5 mi. west of the southwestern park gate (Nisqually entrance).

BAKER LAKE

Panorama Point Campground

2105 WA Rte. 20, Sedro Woolley 98284. T: (360) 856-5700; www.fs.fed.us/r6/mbs or www.reserveusa.com.

RV ★★★ Tent ★★★★

Beauty: ★★★★★	Site Privacy: ★★★★
Spaciousness: ★★★★	Quiet: ★★★
Security: ★★★★	Cleanliness: ★★★★★
Insect Control: ★★★	Facilities: ★★★

Many purist northwest wilderness goers purposefully overlook camping options at places like Baker Lake simply because they don't feel that they're truly getting a pristine experience if they're within earshot of mechanized sounds. In the case of Panorama Point Campground, midway up the western shore, that sound will most likely be the gentle buzz of small outboard motors as fishermen putt-putt around in search of the best spots to hook their daily catch. They have their choice of such delights as rainbow, cutthroat, or Dolly Varden trout; kokanee salmon; and whitefish. This is, indeed, a fisherman's lake. But one can hardly complain that there's no getting away from civilization here thanks to miles and miles of Forest Service roads and trails that can lead you to soothing hot springs and deep into two designated wildernesses, a national recreation area, and a national park. Just make sure you have a good map and trail guides of the area before you find yourself at the mercy of the purists.

Basics

Operated By: Mount Baker-Snoqualmie National Forest; Conservation Resources, Inc. **Open:** May–mid-Sept. **Site Assignment:** Reservations required, call (877) 444-6777. **Registration:** Self-registration on-site. **Fee:** $7–$12. **Parking:** At site.

Facilities

Number of Multipurpose Sites: 16. **Hookups:** Water. **Dump Station:** No. **Laundry:** No. **Pay Phone:** No. **Rest Rooms and Showers:** Vault toilets. **Fuel:** 6 mi. in Concrete. **Propane:** 6 mi. in Concrete. **Internal Roads:** Paved. **RV Service:** No. **Market:** 6 mi. in Concrete. **Restaurant:** 6 mi. in Concrete. **General Store:** 6 mi. in Concrete. **Vending:** No. **Swimming Pool:** No. **Playground:** No. **Activities:** Fishing, hiking, backpacking, skiing, climbing. **Nearby Attractions:** Hot Springs, Mt. Baker, designated wildernesses, Mt. Shuksan. **Additional Information:** www.fs.fed.us/r6/mbs or www.reserveusa.com.

Restrictions

Pets: On leash only. **Fires:** In fire pits only. **Alcoholic Beverages:** Allowed. **Vehicle Maximum Length:** 21 ft. **Other:** Permit required for overnight backpacking or to park at trailhead; 2-day minimum weekend stay, 3-days on holidays.

To Get There

Drive north on Baker Lake Rd. from its junction with SR 20, about 6 mi. west of Concrete (named for the primary industry that converts local limestone into cement).

BELLINGHAM

Larrabee State Park

245 Chuckanut Dr., Bellingham 98226. T: (360) 676-2093; www.parks.wa.gov.

RV ★★★ Tent ★★★★

Beauty: ★★★★★	Site Privacy: ★★★★
Spaciousness: ★★★★	Quiet: ★★★
Security: ★★★	Cleanliness: ★★★★★
Insect Control: ★★★	Facilities: ★★★

Located on 1,885 acres along the saltwater shores of Samish Bay south of Bellingham, Larrabee is the oldest state park in Washington. Its designation in

1915 has kept protected throughout the years such a lush growth of northwest foliage that it is difficult not to feel you have ventured miles into a remote and primeval place. There are plenty of hiking trails, pebbled beaches, and rocky tide pools to explore, and sea kayaking is also an option, with numerous coves, bays, points, rocks, and islets within easy paddling range. For freshwater anglers, both Fragrance Lake and Lost Lake are stocked, but you have to take a two-mile trail to reach them. If you simply want fresh air and a look at the lay of the land, take a drive up Cleator Rd. to 1,900-foot Cyrus Gates Overlook for the best possible view of the San Juans. For views of Mount Baker and the North Cascades, take the short trail to the East Overlook.

Basics

Operated By: Washington State Parks & Recreation Commission. **Open:** All year. **Site Assignment:** First come, first served; reservations accepted mid-May–mid-Sept. **Registration:** Self-registration. **Fee:** $12–$17. **Parking:** At site.

Facilities

Number of RV-Only Sites: 26. **Number of Tent-Only Sites:** 59. **Hookups:** Electric, water, sewer. **Each Site:** Picnic table, fire pit w/ grill, shade trees. **Dump Station:** Yes. **Laundry:** No. **Pay Phone:** Yes. **Rest Rooms and Showers:** Yes. **Fuel:** 1 mi. **Propane:** 1 mi. **Internal Roads:** Paved. **RV Service:** No. **Market:** 1 mi. **Restaurant:** 1 mi. **General Store:** 1 mi. **Vending:** No. **Swimming Pool:** Yes. **Playground:** Yes. **Other:** Boat launch, security, amphitheater, working train track that runs through the park. **Activities:** Boating, hiking, fishing, diving, clamming & crabbing. **Nearby Attractions:** Frangrance Lake, Lost Lake. **Additional Information:** www.parks.wa.gov.

Restrictions

Pets: On leash only. **Fires:** In fire pits only. **Alcoholic Beverages:** In designated areas. **Vehicle Maximum Length:** None.

To Get There

Drive north on I-5 to the turnoff for Chuckanut Dr. and Fairhaven. Follow the signs to SR 11, and head south. The entrance to the park is about 7 mi. on the right.

BIRCH BAY

Birch Bay State Park

4105 Helwig, Birch Bay 98230. T: (360) 371-2800 or (888) 226-7688 for reservations; www.parks.wa.gov.

RV ★★★ Tent ★★★

Beauty: ★★★★★	Site Privacy: ★★
Spaciousness: ★★	Quiet: ★★★
Security: ★★★	Cleanliness: ★★
Insect Control: ★★	Facilities: ★★

Birch Bay State Park, incorporates an old growth forest and bay beach, both of the astounding Northwest Washington mainland variety, to provide a scenic place to stay on the U.S. side of the border. Just minutes from Blaine, the park makes a good central base for touring the surrounding area. The campground has two sections, one with a water view and the other surrounded by dense forest. The northern side of the campground (particularly sites 21, 22, 25, 63, 64, and 67) has the best view of the bay, but it also has some traffic noise during the day. The southern side has less noise and no view. Quite a few impressively large trees shade both sections, but sites lack privacy. All sites have mixed surfaces (gravel and dirt). The weather here is simple: cold and rainy. Feel special if the forecast comes out otherwise.

Basics

Operated By: Washington State Parks & Recreation. **Open:** All year (some sites seasonal). **Site Assignment:** On arrival, reservations May 15–Sept. 15 (1 night's stay deposit, 48-hours cancellation notice less $11 fee). **Registration:** At self pay station. **Fee:** Utility $19, standard $13, extra person (more than 4) $2, extra car; $6; V, MC, cash. **Parking:** At site.

Facilities

Number of RV-Only Sites: 18. **Number of Tent-Only Sites:** 0. **Number of Multipurpose Sites:** 148. **Hookups:** Electric (20, 30 amps), water. **Each Site:** Grill, picnic table. **Dump Station:** Yes. **Laundry:** No. **Pay Phone:** Yes. **Rest Rooms and Showers:** Yes. **Fuel:** No. **Propane:** No. **Internal Roads:** Paved, gravel. **RV Service:** No. **Market:** 6 mi. north in Birch Bay. **Restaurant:** 6 mi. North in Birch Bay. **General Store:** No. **Vending:** Yes. **Swimming Pool:** No. **Playground:** No. **Other:** Boat ramp, beach, basketball court. **Activities:** Shellfishing (Red Tide Hotline, (800)-562-5632). **Nearby Attractions:** Birch Bay Golf Club, water slides, scenic tours, whale-watching tours, kayaking, fishing charters, Canada, Bellingham, Mt. Baker. **Additional Information:** Bellingham/Whatcom County Visitor's Bureau, (360) 671-3990 or www.bellingham.org.

Restrictions

Pets: On leash only. **Fires:** In fire pits only. **Alcoholic Beverages:** At sites & picnic areas only. **Vehicle Maximum Length:** 55 ft. **Other:** No firewood gathering, no metal or glass on beaches; 10-day max. stay limit May–Sept., 20-day max. stay limit Oct.–Apr.

To Get There

From I-5 Exit 270, turn west onto Birch Bay Dr. and drive west 3 mi. At a stop sign, turn left on Blaine and drive south 2 mi. At a stop sign turn right on Bay Rd. and travel west 1 mi. At another stop sign, turn left on Jackson and drive 0.2 mi. south to Helwig Dr. Continue 1 mi. on Helwig to the park entrance and 0.3 mi. further to the campground.

BREMERTON

Illahee State Park

3540 Bahia Vista, Bremerton 98310. T: (360) 902-8500 or (360) 478-6460; www.parks.wa.gov.

RV ★★ Tent ★★★★

Beauty: ★★★★★	Site Privacy: ★★★★
Spaciousness: ★★★★	Quiet: ★★★★
Security: ★★★★	Cleanliness: ★★★★★
Insect Control: ★★★	Facilities: ★★

Situated on a high bluff that guards the southern entrance to Port Orchard Bay, Illahee State Park is a gem of a destination roughly an hour by ferry west of Seattle and about a half hour drive north from Tacoma. Illahee is a perfect retreat amidst towering and densely clustered maples, cedars, Douglas fir, madrona, dogwood, and rhododendron. Ferns, huckleberry, blackberry, and salmonberry provide heavy doses of understory for each of the picturesque and very private campsites. After setting up camp, with the sound of seagulls screeching overhead, take one of the park trails that leads down to the waterfront. At low tide, the clamming can be quite good. Crabbing and oystering are options, but check with park officials before eating any shellfish.

Basics

Operated By: Washington State Parks & Recreation Commission. **Open:** All year. **Site Assignment:** First come, first served. **Registration:** Self-registration. **Fee:** $5–$15. **Parking:** At site or in main lot.

Facilities

Number of RV-Only Sites: 1. **Number of Tent-Only Sites:** 24. **Hookups:** None. **Each Site:** Fire grill, picnic table, water, shade trees. **Dump Station:** Yes. **Laundry:** No. **Pay Phone:** Yes. **Rest Rooms and Showers:** Yes. **Fuel:** 1mi. **Propane:** 1 mi. **Internal Roads:** Paved. **RV Service:** No. **Market:** 1 mi. **Restaurant:** 1 mi. **General Store:** 1 mi. **Vending:** No. **Swimming Pool:** Yes. **Playground:** Yes. **Other:** Boat launch, mooring buoys, dock, covered kitchen. **Activities:** Horseshoe, ball field, boating, swimming, saltwater fishing, bird-watching. **Nearby Attractions:** Scandinavian Poulsbo, Trident Submarine Warfare Base in Bangor, golf courses, Thomas Kemper Brewing Company, antique malls in Port Orchard. **Additional Information:** www.parks.wa.gov.

Restrictions

Pets: On leash only. **Fires:** In fire pits only. **Alcoholic Beverages:** In designated areas. **Vehicle Maximum Length:** 30 ft.

To Get There

From the ferry terminal, follow SR 303 north (Warren Ave.) to SR 306 (Sylvan Way). Turn right, and follow the signs to Illahee. Total distance from the ferry terminal is about 3 mi. From Tacoma, cross the Tacoma Narrows Bridge on SR 16 and follow it for about 25 mi. to Bremerton. Take the City Center Exit (SR 304), which zigzags confusingly through town. Just keep making the obvious zigzags until you reach SR 303 (Warren Ave.). Turn left, and follow the directions above.

CASTLE ROCK

Seaquest State Park

Spirit Lake Hwy., Castle Rock 98611. T: (206) 274-8633 or (800) 452-5687 for reservations; www.parks.wa.gov

RV ★★ Tent ★★★★

Beauty: ★★★★	Site Privacy: ★★★
Spaciousness: ★★	Quiet: ★★★

Security: ★★ Cleanliness: ★★
Insect Control: ★★ Facilities: ★★

Seaquest's only drawback is it's accessibility to the interstate. Situated just off I-5, the park is 60 miles north of Portland and 100 miles south of Seattle. Still, the park is a great base camp for exploring Mount St. Helens, the famous volcano that erupted in 1980. The Mount St. Helen's Visitor Center, located across from the park entrance, offer exhibits on the cultural and historical significance of the area as well as the eruption and ensuing recovery of the area. The 475-acre park borders a one-mile section of Silver Lake. Additionally, visitors can enjoy year-round the playground and ball fields as well as the eight miles of woodland trails suitable for hiking and bicycling.

Basics

Operated By: Washington State Parks & Recreation Commission. **Open:** All year. **Site Assignment:** First come, first served; reservations (May 15–Sept. 15 (1 night's fee deposit, 48-hours cancellation policy, less $11 cancellation fee). **Registration:** At entrance or self pay station. **Fee:** Utility site $20, standard site $14, extra person (more than 4) $2, extra car $6; V, MC, check, cash. **Parking:** At site.

Facilities

Number of RV-Only Sites: 34. **Number of Tent-Only Sites:** 53. **Hookups:** Electric (20, 30 amps), water, sewer. **Each Site:** Picnic table, fire ring. **Dump Station:** Yes. **Laundry:** No. **Pay Phone:** Yes. **Rest Rooms and Showers:** Yes. **Fuel:** No. **Propane:** No. **Internal Roads:** Paved & gravel. **RV Service:** No. **Market:** 5 mi. east by I-5. **Restaurant:** 5 mi. east by I-5. **General Store:** No. **Vending:** No. **Swimming Pool:** No. **Playground:** Yes. **Other:** Horseshoe pit. **Activities:** Hiking. **Nearby Attractions:** Fishing, Mt. St. Helen's Visitor Center, Castle Rock Exhibit Hall, Mt. St. Helens Cinedome Theater, Mt. St. Helens. **Additional Information:** Castle Rock Chamber of Commerce, (360) 274-6603.

Restrictions

Pets: On 6-ft. leash only. **Fires:** Fire rings only. **Alcoholic Beverages:** At site only. **Vehicle Maximum Length:** 40 ft. **Other:** One camping unit (max. 8 people) per site, quiet hours 10p.m.–6:30 a.m.

To Get There

From I-5 Exit 49 Drive East on Hwy. 504 towards for 5.3 mi., the entrance is on left.

CENTRALIA

Midway RV Park

3200 Galvin Rd., Centralia 98531. T: (360) 736-3200; F: (360) 736-6695; www.midwayrv.com; midwayrv@cen.quik.com.

RV ★★★★ Tent n/a

Beauty: ★★★ Site Privacy: ★
Spaciousness: ★★★★ Quiet: ★★
Security: ★★★ Cleanliness: ★★★★
Insect Control: ★★ Facilities: ★★

Midway RV in Centralia has the nicest accomodations among RV parks located roughly halfway between Portland and Puget Sound. The grounds have friendly, yet not overdone, landscaping with small, manicured conifers, red Japanese Maples, and maintained grass. Sites don't have substantial privacy and lack shade, also the city location has some noise. Still, the pleasant grounds and the limited facilities have a well-maintained, newer look, and sites have lots of space. Back-ins on the back perimeter row, numbers 12-24, have the longest diagonal measurements. The rows of sites also have wide access roads. The best time to tour in the region is late summer when weather is the most amicable.

Basics

Operated By: Midway RV. **Open:** All year. **Site Assignment:** On arrival, reservations (deposit: 1 night stay; refund: 72 hours notice of cancellation). **Registration:** At office, late arrivals see sign outside office. **Fee:** $23, extra campers (more than 2) $2, Family rate $25 (2 adults & up to 3 children); V, MC, cash, personal check. **Parking:** At site.

Facilities

Number of RV-Only Sites: 60. **Number of Tent-Only Sites:** 0. **Hookups:** Electric (30, 50 amps), water, sewer, cable. **Dump Station:** No. **Laundry:** Yes. **Pay Phone:** Yes. **Rest Rooms and Showers:** Yes. **Fuel:** No. **Propane:** Yes. **Internal Roads:** Paved. **RV Service:** No. **Market:** Down the street. **Restaurant:** Down the street. **General Store:** Yes. **Vending:** Yes. **Swimming Pool:** No. **Playground:** No. **Other:** Horseshoes, movies for loan, restaurant, rec room, meeting room (reserveable). **Activities:** Monthly potluck. **Nearby Attractions:** The Vintage Antique Motorcycle Museum, skiing, wineries, casino gambling, golf, Puget Sound & big cities, Washington's Pacific coast. **Additional Information:** Centralia, Chehali,s & Greater Lewis County Chamber of Commerce, (360) 748-8885.

Restrictions

Pets: On leash only. **Fires:** No open fires. **Alcoholic Beverages:** At site only. **Vehicle Maximum Length:** None. **Other:** Do not park in grassy areas or vacant spaces.

To Get There

From I-5 Exit 82, drive west on Harrison Ave. to Galvin Rd. Turn left and continue driving for about 0.3 mi. Midway RV Park is on the left side of the road.

CLARKSTON

Granite Lake RV Resort

306 Granite Lake Dr., Clarkston 99403. T: (509) 751-1635 or reservation (800) 989-4578; F: (509) 751-1652; www.granitelakervresort.com; rvresort@clarkston.com.

RV ★★★ Tent n/a

Beauty: ★★★★ Site Privacy: ★
Spaciousness: ★★★ Quiet: ★★
Security: ★★ Cleanliness: ★★★★
Insect Control: ★★ Facilities: ★★

Granite Lake RV Resort in Clarkston (and on the Snake River) has beautiful views but very strong sunlight, no trees, and occasional air pollution from nearby industries. The park sits in downtown Clarkston and very near the Idaho-Washington border. Across the river from the campground, green, steep, rolling hills of grass drop from high altitude to the river's edge, dominating the surrounding landscape; so, the best sites, 23–38, sit on the riverbank. Consisting of a one-way loop, the whole grounds ofer little privacy, in-house recreation, shade, or much landscaping other than grass. The park has large, flat, paved sites surrounded by grass and the occasional shrub. Between the river and the park runs a bike trail, and the newer, well-maintained park has easy access to services and nearby recreation like Hell's Canyon. Summers here bring scorching, dry heat, and winters bring snow. Nights in the summer can be cool, so always have a jacket handy.

Basics

Operated By: Granite Lake Resort. **Open:** All year. **Site Assignment:** On arrival, reservation (deposit: 1 night stay; refund 72 hours notice). **Registration:** At office, after hours pay in morning. **Fee:** For 2 adults, 2 children under 14 years old, Waterfront full $27, Interior full $24, extra adult $3, 3 adults max per site, 1 pet free, second pet $1/day; V, MC, cash. **Parking:** At site.

Facilities

Number of RV-Only Sites: 75. **Number of Tent-Only Sites:** n/a. **Hookups:** Electric (20, 30, 50 amps), water, sewer, cable. **Dump Station:** No. **Laundry:** Yes. **Pay Phone:** Yes. **Rest Rooms and Showers:** Yes. **Fuel:** No. **Propane:** No. **Internal Roads:** Paved. **RV Service:** No. **Market:** A few blocks west. **Restaurant:** A few blocks west. **General Store:** No. **Vending:** Yes. **Swimming Pool:** No. **Playground:** No. **Activities:** Inquire at campground. **Nearby Attractions:** Hells Canyon, Dinner cruises, golf, casinos. **Additional Information:** Clarkston Chamber of Commerce, (800) 993-2128.

Restrictions

Pets: On leash only, no fighting breeds. **Fires:** No open fires. **Alcoholic Beverages:** At site only. **Vehicle Maximum Length:** 42 ft. **Other:** No skateboards, scooters.

To Get There

From Snake River Bridge (WA-ID border) drive 0.3 mi. on Hwy. 12 west, turn right onto 5th St. which dead-ends behind Costco; entrance on right.

CONCONULLY

Liar's Cove Resort

P.O. Box 72, Coconully 98819. T: (509) 826-1288 or (800) 830-1288; www.omakchronicle.com/liarscove; liarscr@televar.com.

RV ★★★ Tent ★★

Beauty: ★★★ Site Privacy: ★
Spaciousness: ★★ Quiet: ★★★★
Security: ★★ Cleanliness: ★★★
Insect Control: ★★★ Facilities: ★★★

Liar's Cove RV Park, 15 minutes north of Omak, offers beautiful vistas, quiet, and fishing. The campground sits on the edge of emerald-green Conconully Reservoir, surrounded by ponderosa pines, and beautiful Northern Cascade foothills covered intermittently with evergreens and grass rise sharply from the far shore. Arranged in several terraces, the park extends all the way to the lake's edge, where the best views and most spacious gravel sites (L1–L8) can be found. The whole park lacks shade or privacy between sites and the tent area consists of a small square of mostly gravel and a little grass. The least-spacious RV sites sit on the uppermost terrace (sites 1–10). The area has full-fledged winters; the best weather moves in during the summer.

BASICS

Operated By: Liar's Cove Resort. **Open:** Apr. 1–Nov. 1. **Site Assignment:** First come, first served; reservations (deposit: 1 night stay; refund: 72 hours cancellation, 2 weeks for holidays). **Registration:** At office; after hours pay in the morning. **Fee:** Rates for 2 people, Lakefront Full: $21, Middle & upper terrace full & tent: $20, extra person: $2, 7th Day free; V, MC, cash. **Parking:** At site.

FACILITIES

Number of RV-Only Sites: 30. **Number of Tent-Only Sites:** 10. **Hookups:** Electric (20, 30 amps), water, sewer. **Each Site:** Picnic table, fire ring. **Dump Station:** No. **Laundry:** No. **Pay Phone:** Yes. **Rest Rooms and Showers:** Yes. **Fuel:** No. **Propane:** No. **Internal Roads:** Gravel. **RV Service:** No. **Market:** 20 mi. south in OkaNogan. **Restaurant:** 0.5 mi. North in Conconully. **General Store:** Yes. **Vending:** Yes. **Swimming Pool:** No. **Playground:** No. **Other:** Boat launch, pontoon, paddle, row, & motor boat rentals, fish cleaning station. **Activities:** swimming, fishing, boating. **Nearby Attractions:** Snowmobiling, fishing, mining exhibitions, Colville Indian Reservation, historical points of interest. **Additional Information:** Conconully Chamber of Commerce (877)-826-9050.

RESTRICTIONS

Pets: On leash only. **Fires:** In fire pits only. **Alcoholic Beverages:** At site only. **Vehicle Maximum Length:** None. **Other:** Holidays minimum three night stay, Quiet Hours 10 p.m.–7a.m.

TO GET THERE

Off Hwy. 20/2nd Ave S. in Okanogan.

COUGAR

Merrill Lake Campground

601 Bond Rd., Castle Rock 98611. T: (360) 577-2025

RV: n/a | Tent: ★★★★

Beauty: ★★★★	Site Privacy: ★★★★
Spaciousness: ★★★★★	Quiet: ★★★★★
Security: ★★	Cleanliness: ★★★★
Insect Control: ★★★	Facilities: ★★

Campers who were enjoying the serene quiet of Merrill Lake on the fateful May morning when Mount St. Helens erupted must have been doing so with one eye nervously fixed in the direction of the mountain (which is roughly six air miles to the northeast). When the mountain blew, those lucky enough to have chosen a weekend outing on the south side probably thought that the plume of ash rising to an eventual height of 63,000 feet was the extent of the show. It wouldn't be until they returned home later that evening that television news reports showed them the full extent of the horror. Today, more than a decade later, Merrill Lake Campground sits in wooded isolation just outside the boundaries of Gifford Pinchot National Forest and Mount St. Helens National Volcanic Monument. In summer, most of the tourist throngs inundate Mount St. Helens from the north, leaving you free to explore lands around the geologic wonder in relative solitude.

BASICS

Operated By: Dept. of Natural Resources. **Open:** Memorial Day–Nov. 30. **Site Assignment:** First come, first served. **Registration:** Not necessary. **Fee:** None. **Parking:** At site.

FACILITIES

Number of RV-Only Sites: 0. **Number of Tent-Only Sites:** 7. **Hookups:** None. **Each Site:** Picnic table, fire grill, tent pad. **Dump Station:** No. **Laundry:** No. **Pay Phone:** No. **Rest Rooms and Showers:** Pit toilets. **Fuel:** No. **Propane:** No. **Internal Roads:** No. **RV Service:** No. **Market:** No. **Restaurant:** No. **General Store:** No. **Vending:** No. **Swimming Pool:** No. **Playground:** No. **Other:** Boat launch, disabled access. **Activities:** Boating, fishing, hiking, biking, caving, bird-watching. **Nearby Attractions:** Mount St. Helens, Ape Cave, Cedar Flats Northern Research Natural Area.

RESTRICTIONS

Pets: On leash. **Fires:** In fire pit. **Alcoholic Beverages:** Allowed. **Vehicle Maximum Length:** Call ahead for details. **Other:** RVs prohibited.

TO GET THERE

Take Lewis River Rd. east from Woodland off I-5 to the small settlement of Cougar. Turn north, away from Yale Lake, onto FR 81, and travel 4.5 mi. to the access road that leads to the campground.

COULEE CITY

Sun Lakes Park Resort

34228 Park Ln. Rd. Northeast, Coulee City 99115. T: (509) 632-5291; www.sunlakesparkresort.com.

RV: ★★★ | Tent: n/a

Beauty: ★★★	Site Privacy: ★
Spaciousness: ★★★	Quiet: ★★★★
Security: ★	Cleanliness: ★★★
Insect Control: ★★★	Facilities: ★★★

Sun Lakes Park Resort, a concessionaire (leased) campground located in the Sun Lakes State Park complex south of Coulee City, provides a less-rustic alternative to the state park campground next door. When compared to the park, the irrigated campground has more organization, a little more shade, longer and more spacious sites, and a cheaper base rate for full hookups. The fullhookup gravel sites lack privacy, but they have obscured views of surrounding coulee walls through the many old paper birch that shade the park. Cramped back-in sites 81–108 adjoin in the rear; the best back-ins, sites 1–16, sit on the perimeter of a grassy area. The most spacious pull-through sites, 41–80, can accommodate most large rigs. Easy access to fishing and exploration of surrounding natural wonders make this spot popular; visit just before or after summer school break to avoid both crowds and high-altitude winter weather.

BASICS

Operated By: Sunlakes Park Resort, INC. **Open:** Apr.–Sept. **Site Assignment:** Walkups, reservations starting Jan 1 for upcoming season (deposit 1 night's rate/ refund: 7 day confirmation or cancellation. **Registration:** At office, after hours pay in morning. **Fee:** For 4 people, sites 1–16 $24, sites 17–108 $22; V, AE, D, MC, cash. **Parking:** At site.

FACILITIES

Number of RV-Only Sites: 108. **Number of Tent-Only Sites:** n/a. **Hookups:** Electric (20, 30, 50 amps), water, sewer. **Each Site:** Picnic table. **Dump Station:** Yes. **Laundry:** Yes. **Pay Phone:** Yes. **Rest Rooms and Showers:** Yes. **Fuel:** No. **Propane:** Yes. **Internal Roads:** Paved, gravel. **RV Service:** No. **Market:** 5 mi. north in Coulee City. **Restaurant:** 5 mi. North in Coulee City. **General Store:** Yes. **Vending:** No. **Swimming Pool:** Yes. **Playground:** Yes. **Other:** Mini golf, boat launch & dock, 9 hole golf course, paddle & row boat rentals, fish cleaning station. **Activities:** Hiking, fishing, boating, swimming, bird-watching, picnicking, golfing. **Nearby Attractions:** Grand Coulee Dam, tons of lakes for fishing, two golf courses, hiking trails, rock climbing, various local events, Coulee Dam Casino, Coville Tribes Museum, Dry Falls Visitor's Center. **Additional Information:** Grand Coulee Dam Area Chamber of Commerce, (800) 268-5332.

RESTRICTIONS

Pets: On leash only, no dogs on grass. **Fires:** No open fires. **Alcoholic Beverages:** At site only. **Vehicle Maximum Length:** None. **Other:** Cannot guarantee specific space numbers; check in 3p.m., check out 2:45 p.m.

TO GET THERE

From the junction of Hwy. 17 and Hwy. 2 south of Coulee City, drive 3.8 mi. SW on Hwy. 17; 1.8 mi. south of Dry Falls Visitor Center, turn left onto Park Lake Rd., follow 1.1 mi., entrance on the right.

COULEE CITY

Sun Lakes State Park Campground

34875 Park Lake Rd. Northeast, Coulee City 99115. T: (509)-632-5583; www.parks.wa.gov; infocent@parks.wa.gov.

RV: ★★ | Tent: ★★

Beauty: ★★★	Site Privacy: ★
Spaciousness: ★★	Quiet: ★★★★
Security: ★★	Cleanliness: ★★★
Insect Control: ★★★	Facilities: ★★

Sun Lakes State Park south of Coulee City off of Hwy. 17 offers convenient access to many outdoor recreational activities. Many of these activities exist within the state park complex or a short walk from the campground. Most of the gravel sites have no hookups, but there are 18 gravel, full-hookup sites, and sites 49–51 have the most space and shade. Every site lacks privacy, but sites 26–33 sit in a slightly secluded area away from the rest of the grounds. An arid mix of sage-crusted hills and forbidding coulee walls make up nearby scenery, and the sun can be intense here. Sites 62–66, 163–170, and 177–180 have little to no shade. Black locust, birch, and maple create partial shade for most other sites. The flowering black locust trees bring bees in May and June, so avoid the park during this time if at risk for an allergic reaction. Management permits tents in all sites, but not on any grassy areas. Visit during late spring or early fall, when crowd volumes and temperatures and mild.

Basics

Operated By: Washington State Parks & Recreation. **Open:** All year (fully operational Apr.–Sept.). **Site Assignment:** First come, first served; reservations(during on-season only, May 15-Sept. 15; Deposit-1 night plus non refundable reservation fee; refund: 48 hours cancellation). **Registration:** At park office or self-registration station. **Fee:** For 4 people, full: $20, standard (no hookups): $14, extra person: $2, extra vehicle (over 2): $6;V, MC, check, cash. **Parking:** At site.

Facilities

Number of RV-Only Sites: 18. **Number of Tent-Only Sites:** 180. **Hookups:** Electric (20, 30 amps), water, sewer. **Each Site:** Picnic table, fire ring. **Dump Station:** Yes. **Laundry:** No. **Pay Phone:** Yes. **Rest Rooms and Showers:** Yes. **Fuel:** No. **Propane:** No. **Internal Roads:** Paved. **RV Service:** No. **Market:** 5 mi. north in Coulee City. **Restaurant:** 5 mi. North in Coulee City. **General Store:** No. **Vending:** No. **Swimming Pool:** No. **Playground:** Yes. **Other:** Horseshoes, non-improved boat launch, golf course, row boat rental. **Activities:** Hiking, extensive fishing, swimming, golf, boating, metal detecting, bird-watching. **Nearby Attractions:** Grand Coulee Dam, tons of lakes for fishing, two golf courses, hiking trails, rock climbing, various local events, Coulee Dam Casino, Coville Tribes Museum, Dry Falls Visitor's Center, Lake Lenore Caves. **Additional Information:** Grand Coulee Dam Area Chamber of Commerce, (800) 268-5332.

Restrictions

Pets: On leash only (6 ft in length). **Fires:** In fire pits only. **Alcoholic Beverages:** At site only. **Vehicle Maximum Length:** None. **Other:** Be aware of "swimmer's itch" that may occur if swimming area is contaminated by snails; max stay 10 days during summer, 20 days during winter.

To Get There

From the junction of Hwy. 17 and Hwy. 2 south of Coulee City: Drive 3.8 mi. SW on Hwy. 17; 1.8 mi. south of Dry Falls Visitor Center, turn left onto Park Lake Rd. and go 1.1 mi., entrance on the left.

COUPEVILLE

Fort Ebey State Park

395 North Fort Ebey Rd., Coupeville 98239. T: (360) 678-4636; www.parks.wa.gov.

RV: ★ Tent: ★★★★

Beauty: ★★★★★	Site Privacy: ★★★
Spaciousness: ★★★★	Quiet: ★★★
Security: ★★★★★	Cleanliness: ★★★★
Insect Control: ★★	Facilities: ★★

Situated in relatively underdeveloped waterfront beauty, Fort Ebey is increasingly popular among tent campers and others looking to escape urban life. From a tent-camping perspective, Fort Ebey is decidedly the least developed. It is evident that every attempt has been made to retain the natural beauty of the area. Old-growth Douglas fir marks this region, and an undergrowth of salal, huckleberry, Scotch broom, and rhododendron isn't dense but provides pleasant greenbelts between campsites. There are plenty of activities within the 226-acre park. Beachcombing along the driftwood-laden shoreline. Hiking the wooded trails along the bluffline. Fishing for bass in freshwater Lake Pondilla. Watching a surprising variety of wildlife, including bald eagles, deer, geese, ducks, raccoons, rabbits, pheasant, and grouse. Seeking out the varieties of cactus (yes, cactus!) that grow in this unusual "banana belt" region of western Washington. Exploring the fort's old gun emplacements. If this doesn't satisfy you, there are several other state parks in the neighborhood, too.

Basics

Operated By: Washington State Parks & Recreation Commission. **Open:** Late Feb.–Oct. 31. **Site Assignment:** First come, first served; reservations accepted mid–May–mid–Sept.; call (800) 452–5687; $6 reservation fee. **Registration:** At camp office. **Fee:** $12–$17. **Parking:** At site.

Facilities

Number of RV-Only Sites: Inquire at campground. **Number of Tent-Only Sites:** 0. **Number of Multipurpose Sites:** 50. **Hookups:** Electric (30 amps) at 4 sites. **Each Site:** Picnic table, fire grill, shade trees. **Dump Station:** No. **Laundry:** No. **Pay Phone:** Yes. **Rest Rooms and Showers:** Yes. **Fuel:** 2 mi. in Coupeville. **Propane:** 2 mi. **Internal Roads:** Paved. **RV Service:** No. **Market:** 2 mi. **Restaurant:** 2 mi. **General Store:** 2 mi. **Vending:** No. **Swimming Pool:** No. **Playground:** No. **Other:** Picnic area, boat launch. **Activities:** Fishing, boating, hiking, biking, badminton, bird-watching. **Nearby Attractions:** Lake Pondilla. **Additional Information:** www.parks.wa.gov.

Restrictions

Pets: On leash only. **Fires:** In fire pit. **Alcoholic Beverages:** Allowed. **Vehicle Maximum Length:** Call ahead for details.

To Get There

From Seattle, drive north on I-5 and WA Rtes. 526 and 525 to Mukilteo and the Washington State Ferry terminal for Whidbey Island. Once on the island, follow SR 525 north, pick up US 20 at Keystone, and continue north to Libbey Rd. and signs to the park. Total driving distance on Whidbey Island is about 35 mi. An alternative route is to take US 20 west from I-5 at Burlington (just over 60 mi. north of Seattle), and drive down the northern half of Whidbey Island through scenic Deception Pass. This route allows you to avoid ferry lines.

DAVENPORT

Two Rivers RV Park

68 B. Hwy. 25S, Davenport 99129.T: (509) 722-4029

RV: ★★★★ Tent: ★★

Beauty: ★★★	Site Privacy: ★
Spaciousness: ★★★	Quiet: ★★★★
Security: ★★	Cleanliness: ★★★★
Insect Control: ★★	Facilities: ★★★★

Two Rivers RV Resort, a half hour north of Davenport on Hwy. 25, provides a convenient location for visiting the adjacent casino and Fort Spokane. The campground sits on high bluffs overlooking the giant, gray-blue Spokane River, with an organizational scheme of several loops plus two rows of campsites surrounded by lots of grass and some small flowering shrubs. The sites lack privacy or shade, but most have views of the surrounding semi-arid rolling highlands that fall towards the river; sites with views of the river exist on G and F loops. Half the sites in section E back into a hill, diminishing their scenic views. The park has a few large pull-throughs, but it consists mostly of paved, spacious back-ins. The tent section of the campground has a cramped arrangement of picnic areas with some grassy patches for tents; sites 15–18 and 23–26 sit on the edge of bluffs overlooking the river. The park boasts two unusually large playground areas, but there's not much more in the way of on-site family recreation. Winters here are snowy and cold; visit during the late spring or summer for warm temperatures.

Basics

Operated By: Spokane Tribe of Washington. **Open:** All year. **Site Assignment:** Reservations (deposit 1 night's stay; refund). **Registration:** At office, after hours pay in morning. **Fee:** For 6 people, full pull-through: $23, full Back in: $19, tent: $14, extra person: $2, 10 people site capacity;V, MC, check, cash. **Parking:** At site, some off site.

Facilities

Number of RV-Only Sites: 100. **Number of Tent-Only Sites:** 32. **Hookups:** Electric (20, 30, 50 amps), water, sewer. **Each Site:** Picnic table, grill. **Dump Station:** Yes. **Laundry:** Yes. **Pay Phone:** Yes. **Rest Rooms and Showers:** Yes. **Fuel:** Yes. **Propane:** Yes. **Internal Roads:** Paved & gravel. **RV Service:** No. **Market:** 25 mi. south in Davenport. **Restaurant:** 25 mi. south in Davenport. **General Store:** No. **Vending:** Yes. **Swimming Pool:** No. **Playground:** Yes. **Other:** Horseshoe pit, marina w/ houseboat rentals, casino. **Activities:** Fishing, 4th of Jul. fireworks show, hiking, swimming, gambling, boating. **Nearby Attractions:** Fort Spokane, Two River's Casino, hiking, fishing. **Additional Information:** Davenport Chamber of Commerce (509) 725-6711.

Restrictions

Pets: On leash only, pick up after pets. **Fires:** In fire pits only. **Alcoholic Beverages:** At site only. **Vehicle Maximum Length:** 40 ft. **Other:** No refund once checked in; 3-day minimum stay on holidays.

To Get There

From the junction of Hwy. 2 and 25 on east side of Davenport: Drive 23.5 mi. north on Hwy. 25, then turn left on Confluence Dr. just after Fort Spokane and Spokane River Bridge, entrance to campground on left.

ELECTRIC CITY
Coulee Playland Resort

Box 457 Hwy. 155 No. 1, Electric City 99123. T: (509) 633-2671; F: (509) 633-2133; www.couleeplayland.com.

RV: ★★★	Tent: ★★
Beauty: ★★	Site Privacy: ★
Spaciousness: ★★★	Quiet: ★★
Security: ★	Cleanliness: ★★★
Insect Control: ★★★	Facilities: ★★★

Coulee Playland Resort, a couple of minutes south of Electric City, offers sites in a less crowded environment than Sunbanks resort down the road. Not as nicely furnished or landscaped as the latter, the grounds of the former consists of several rows of sites near or on the edge of Banks Lake. The general store is stocked with a wide array of fishing and boating accessories. Although the gravel RV sites lack both shade and privacy, most have the breathtaking views characteristic of the region. Water and electric sites 77–85 sit right on the water, with great views of contrasting bright-green sage and dull-colored shear coulee walls. Full-hookup sites 36–57 back into a hill, with more space than undesirable full hookups 1–18. Grassy tent sites B1–B7 sit on the deep blue lake's edge without shade or privacy. Particularly avoid water and electric back-ins 86–89, sitting as they do without a view of anything in what seems like a gravel pit. Spring, summer, and early fall make the best times to visit and avoid winter weather.

Basics

Operated By: Coulee Playland Resort. **Open:** All year, fully operational Mar.–Oct. **Site Assignment:** First come, first served; reservations (one night stay deposit, 72 hour cancellation). **Registration:** At office, after hours at drop box in front of office. **Fee:** Full $20, standard: $17.50, B**Each Site:** $18, Beach Site w/ electric: $19, Yurt: $49; V , MC, AE, D, cash. **Parking:** At site.

Facilities

Number of RV-Only Sites: 59. **Number of Tent-Only Sites:** 8. **Hookups:** Electric (20, 30 amps), water, sewer. **Each Site:** Picnic table, grill. **Dump Station:** Yes. **Laundry:** Yes. **Pay Phone:** Yes. **Rest Rooms and Showers:** Yes. **Fuel:** Yes. **Propane:** No. **Internal Roads:** Gravel & paved. **RV Service:** No. **Market:** 3 mi. north in Grand Coulee. **Restaurant:** 3 mi. north in Grand Coulee. **General Store:** Yes. **Vending:** No. **Swimming Pool:** No. **Playground:** Yes. **Other:** Boat launch & moorage, boat fuelling, store w/ fishing, boating supplies, & deli; 1 yurt, group picnic area, fishing licenses. **Activities:** Swimming, fishing, boating, picnicking. **Nearby Attractions:** Grand Coulee Dam, tons of lakes for fishing, 2 golf courses, Steamboat Rock State Park, hiking trails, rock climbing, various local events, Coulee Dam Casino, Coville Tribes Museum. **Additional Information:** Grand Coulee Dam Area Chamber of Commerce, (800) 268-5332.

Restrictions

Pets: On leash only. **Fires:** In fire pits only. **Alcoholic Beverages:** At site only. **Vehicle Maximum Length:** None. **Other:** Quiet Hours 10 p.m.–8 a.m.

To Get There

From the junction of Hwy. 174 and Hwy. 155 in Grand Coulee: Drive 1 mi. south on Hwy. 155, and take the second entrance on the right

ELECTRIC CITY
Steamboat Rock State Park Campground

P.O. Box 370, Electric City 99123-0352. T: (800) 233-0321 or reservations (800) 452-5687; www.parks.wa.gov; infocent@parks.wa.gov.

RV: ★★★	Tent: ★★★★
Beauty: ★★★★★	Site Privacy: ★
Spaciousness: ★★★	Quiet: ★★★★★
Security: ★★	Cleanliness: ★★★
Insect Control: ★★★	Facilities: ★★★

Steamboat Rock State Park Campground, 20 minutes south of Electric City, has the best local views of the surrounding coulee landscape of any campground in the area. The grounds lack shade or privacy, but this beneficially provides views of the shear, dark-toned, multicolored cliffs rising to the east and west. Site arrangement consists of cul-de-sacs of paved full-hookup sites, and standard sites on the avenues leading towards the cul-de-sacs, all cut out of a grass field. The grounds sit on the shore of huge, blue Banks Lake, and the best sites with water views include full-hookup sites 81–90, 76–79, 55–57, 41–50, and standard sites 310–312. Tents must be erected within the designated dirt areas at each site, thus protecting the irrigated grass. The best time to visit is during the summer, since winters are cold and snowy.

Basics

Operated By: Washington State Parks & Recreation. **Open:** Year-round (some seasonal sites). **Site Assignment:** First come, first served; reservations (deposit: 1 night plus non refundable reservation fee; refund: 48 hours cancellation). **Registration:** At self pay station or front gate. **Fee:** For 4 people, Utility Site (Full Hookup) $20, standard $14, extra person $2 (max. 8 people per site), Extra Vehicle $6; V, MC, check, cash. **Parking:** At site.

Facilities

Number of RV-Only Sites: 100. **Number of Tent-Only Sites:** 26. **Hookups:** Electric (20, 30 amps), water, sewer. **Each Site:** Picnic table, fire ring. **Dump Station:** Yes. **Laundry:** No. **Pay Phone:** Yes. **Rest Rooms and Showers:** Yes. **Fuel:** No. **Propane:** No. **Internal Roads:** Paved in good condition. **RV Service:** No. **Market:** 11 mi. north in Electric City. **Restaurant:** 11 mi. north in Electric City. **General Store:** Yes, in day-use area. **Vending:** No. **Swimming Pool:** No. **Playground:** No. **Other:** In State Park complex: hiking trails, boat launch & dock. **Activities:** Hiking, fishing, swimming, canoeing, water skiing, mountain biking, hiking, rock climbing. **Nearby Attractions:** Grand Coulee Dam, tons of lakes for fishing, 2 golf courses, hiking trails, rock climbing, various local events, Coulee Dam Casino, Coville Tribes Museum. **Additional Information:** Grand Coulee Dam Area Chamber of Commerce, (800) 268-5332.

Restrictions

Pets: Leash Only (6 ft. long). **Fires:** In fire pits only. **Alcoholic Beverages:** At site only. **Vehicle Maximum Length:** 45 ft. **Other:** Quiet hours 11 p.m.–6:30 a.m.; max stay 10 days during summer, 20 days during winter; check in at 2:30 p.m., check out at 1 p.m.

To Get There

From the junction of Hwy. 155 and Hwy. 174, drive 7 mi. south on Hwy. 155, after state park boat launch, entrance is 3 mi. south on Hwy. 155. Take a right turn onto unnamed road indicated by a Washington Park Service sign. Follow this road northwest for 2 mi. until reaching park gate. Past the park gate, the campground is on the right.

ELECTRIC CITY
Sunbanks Resort

57662 Hwy. 155 N, Electric City 99123. T: (888) 822-7195; F: (509) 633-3472; www.sunbanksresort.com; info@sunbanksresort.com.

RV: ★★★★	Tent: ★★★
Beauty: ★★★★	Site Privacy: ★★
Spaciousness: ★★	Quiet: ★★★★
Security: ★★★	Cleanliness: ★★★★
Insect Control: ★★★	Facilities: ★★★★★

Sunbanks Resort, on the edge of deep, blue Banks Lake just south of Electric City, comes stocked with beautiful views of surrounding scenery and nicely furnished facilities. A mix of arid and irrigated areas creates an intriguing landscape inside the grounds. Sites consist of grass or gravel in a seemingly random organization running downhill to the lake's edge. The shady, gravel, back-in, full hookups sit in cramped, adjacent rows near the office. Most RV sites on the property have water and electric hookups; of these, sites 85–95, 60–63, and 68–74 make up the least-crowded areas. Sites A and B sit on a flat hill with a crow's-nest view of shear, jagged coulee walls and the lake, but they have no hookups and access limited by vehicle size. The best tent options, sites 1–39, sit on the shores of Banks Lake in a semi-shaded, grassy area. Inter-site privacy does not exist here, and the grounds become extremely cramped when full. Just before or after the summer season make the best times to visit and avoid crowds.

Basics

Operated By: Precision Mgmt. **Open:** All year; fully operational Apr. 1–Oct. **Site Assignment:** First come, first served; reservations (deposit: 1st night's stay, non-refundable). **Registration:** At gate or lodge; after hours pay in morning. **Fee:** For 6 people, Water-electric: $30, full: $34, Waterfront tent $34, Non-waterfront tent: $30, View site: $26. **Parking:** At site.

FACILITIES

Number of RV-Only Sites: 125. **Number of Tent-Only Sites:** 82. **Hookups:** Electric (20, 30, 50 amps), water, sewer. **Each Site:** Picnic table, grated fire pits. **Dump Station:** Yes. **Laundry:** Yes. **Pay Phone:** Yes. **Rest Rooms and Showers:** Yes. **Fuel:** No. **Propane:** No. **Internal Roads:** Well-maintained gravel. **RV Service:** No. **Market:** 5 mi. north in Electric City. **Restaurant:** 5 mi. North in Electric City. **General Store:** Yes. **Vending:** Yes. **Swimming Pool:** No. **Playground:** No. **Other:** Cafe, boat launch & moorage, outdoor stage, game room (2 pool tables), paddleboat rentals, horseshoes, play field. **Activities:** Swimming, fishing, boating, water skiing & other watersports (BYOB-Bring Your Own Boat). **Nearby Attractions:** Grand Coulee Dam, tons of lakes for fishing, 2 golf courses, Steamboat Rock State Park, hiking trails, rock climbing, various local events, Coulee Dam Casino, Colville Tribes Museum. **Additional Information:** Grand Coulee Dam Area Chamber of Commerce, (800) 268-5332.

RESTRICTIONS

Pets: Leash Only. **Fires:** In fire pits only. **Alcoholic Beverages:** At site only. **Vehicle Maximum Length:** None. **Other:** Watch for no pet areas; 2 night minimum stay on all reservations; site requests not guaranteed; tents must be moved every three days.

TO GET THERE

From the junction of Hwy. 174 and Hwy. 155, go 3 mi. south on 155; entrance on right just before bridge.

ELLENSBURG

Ellensburg KOA

32 Thorp Hwy. South, Ellensburg 98926. T: (509)-925-9319; koa.com/where/wa/47129.htm.

RV: ★★ Tent: ★

Beauty: ★★★	Site Privacy: ★
Spaciousness: ★★	Quiet: ★
Security: ★★	Cleanliness: ★★★★
Insect Control: ★★	Facilities: ★★★

Ellensburg KOA, on the Yakima River, provides local access to unique recreation and sites on the river. Site arrangement consists of several parallel rows and sites on the perimeter of the grounds. The best gravel-grass perimetered full hookups, sites 4–20, sit on the banks of the green, swift river, shaded by weeping willows and pines. There also exist some quality tent spots on the river at sites T6–T13; unfortunately, these sites have a noise problem from the overpass that runs right next to site T13. Sites T1–T5 offer no shade, a definite minus in this area of intense sunlight. Patchy grass provides thin ground cover around individual sites, but in the common areas the standard seems higher. The seasonal area has hot summers and mild winters; visit during milder spring or fall months if avoiding heat is desirable.

BASICS

Operated By: Ellensburg KOA. **Open:** All year. **Site Assignment:** On arrival, reservations (deposit: 1 night's stay; refund: 24 hours cancellation). **Registration:** At office, after hours at drop by office. **Fee:** For 2 people, 1 vehicle, full $24.95, Water-electric $22.95, Tent $18, extra people/vehicle $3, Max per site 4 adults or 2 adults & 4 children (V, MC, cash). **Parking:** At site, limited off site.

FACILITIES

Number of RV-Only Sites: 90. **Number of Tent-Only Sites:** 30. **Hookups:** Electric (30, 50 amps), water, sewer. **Each Site:** Picnic table, fire pit. **Dump Station:** Yes. **Laundry:** Yes. **Pay Phone:** Yes. **Rest Rooms and Showers:** Yes. **Fuel:** No. **Propane:** No. **Internal Roads:** Gravel & paved. **RV Service:** No. **Market:** 4 mi. east in Ellensburg. **Restaurant:** 4 mi. east in Ellensburg. **General Store:** Yes. **Vending:** No. **Swimming Pool:** Yes. **Playground:** Yes. **Other:** Badminton, volleyball, horseshoes, arcade, boat ramp, kiddie pool, movie rentals. **Activities:** River fishing, swimming, boating. **Nearby Attractions:** Clymer Museum & Gallery, Gallery One, fly fishing, Ellensburg Bull Sculpture, Kittitas County Museum, Thorp Grist Mill, Chimpanzee & Human Communication Institute. **Additional Information:** Ellensburg Chamber of Commerce, (888) 925-2204.

RESTRICTIONS

Pets: On leash only. **Fires:** In fire pits only. **Alcoholic Beverages:** At site only. **Vehicle Maximum Length:** None. **Other:** No parking on grass areas.

TO GET THERE

From I-90 Exit 106, turn south (if west-bound, turn left) and drive 0.2 mi. Turn left onto Thorp Hwy.; the entrance is on the left

ENUMCLAW

Corral Pass Campground

c/o White River Ranger District, Enumclaw 98022. T: (360) 825-6585; www.fs.fed.us/r6/mbs.

RV: n/a Tent: ★★★★

Beauty: ★★★★	Site Privacy: ★★★★★
Spaciousness: ★★★★★	Quiet: ★★★★★
Security: ★★	Cleanliness: ★★★
Insect Control: ★★★	Facilities: ★★

For your own personal, unsurpassed view of the north face of Mount Rainier and for a different perspective of Crystal Mountain Ski Area, take a hard left off WA Rte. 410 about 30 miles out of Enumclaw, onto FR 7174, to Corral Pass Campground. But bring plenty of water because there is no piped water here. Hopefully, you've come to Corral Pass for the backcountry hiking options, which are plentiful. Among a number of choices, there's Norse Peak Wilderness brushing the ridgetop just east of the campground, covering more than 50,000 acres of diverse terrain dissected by 52 miles of hiking trails. There is a surprising variety of wildlife and vegetation to enjoy as well—mountain goats, elk, and deer, to name a few. The wildflowers in the meadows around Noble Knob are known to rival those at Paradise on Mount Rainier's southern slope when in full bloom (late June to early August, depending on the elevation), and berry-picking is prime in late Aug. and early Sept.

BASICS

Operated By: Mount Baker-Snoqualmie National Forest. **Open:** Jul.–late Sept. **Site Assignment:** First come, first served. **Registration:** Not necessary. **Fee:** None. **Parking:** At site.

FACILITIES

Number of RV-Only Sites: 0. **Number of Tent-Only Sites:** 20. **Hookups:** None. **Each Site:** Picnic table, fire grill. **Dump Station:** No. **Laundry:** No. **Pay Phone:** No. **Rest Rooms and Showers:** Vault toilets. **Fuel:** No. **Propane:** No. **Internal Roads:** Call ahead for details. **RV Service:** No. **Market:** No. **Restaurant:** No. **General Store:** No. **Vending:** No. **Swimming Pool:** No. **Playground:** No. **Other:** Firewood. **Activities:** Hiking, fishing, horseback riding. **Nearby Attractions:** Norse Peak Wilderness, Noble Knob, Echo Lake/Greenwater River Trail, Naches Trail. **Additional Information:** www.fs.fed.us/r6/mbs.

RESTRICTIONS

Pets: On leash only. **Fires:** In fire pit. **Alcoholic Beverages:** Allowed. **Vehicle Maximum Length:** RVs & trailers not recommended. **Other:** No piped water.

TO GET THERE

From Enumclaw (roughly 40 mi. southeast of Seattle), take SR 410 southeast for about 30 mi. Turn left onto FS 7174 and follow to its end (6 mi.). The highway marker for FS 7174 can be obscured by overhanging foliage, so keep a sharp lookout for it on the right side of the road. If you find yourself at the turnoff to Crystal Mountain Ski Area and the entrance to Mount Rainier National Park, you've gone about 1 mi. too far.

FALL CITY

Snoqualmie River Campground and RV Park

P.O.Box 16, Fall City 98024. T: (425) 222-5545

RV: ★★★ Tent: ★★

Beauty: ★★★	Site Privacy: ★
Spaciousness: ★★★	Quiet: ★★★
Security: ★	Cleanliness: ★★★
Insect Control: ★★	Facilities: ★★

Snoqualmie River Campground and RV Park, about an hour east of Seattle off I-90 in Fall City, provides a rural, mountain setting between two rivers. A flat field with sites around the perimeter comprises the campground; the center of the park has lots of wide-open grassy space. RV sites have dirt surfaces, while tent sites consist of grass. No sites have privacy, but the best sites, pull-throughs 75–92, sit near one river (no views). Sites 110–117 make up the best tent sites; avoid sites 1–21, 38–40, and tent sites 101–109, as a fence provides the only separation between this side of the park and the golf course next door. Fishing from the river sounds good, with salmon among possible catches. Of course, seasons vary. The park does receive some noise from a nearby road; the best time to visit is during the summer. Salmon usually run in late spring to early summer. Call to find out about flood schedule (this park floods every year).

Basics

Operated By: Snoqualmie River Campground. **Open:** Apr. 1–Oct. 31. **Site Assignment:** On arrival, reservation (deposit or credit card to hold). **Registration:** At office, after hours pay in morning. **Fee:** For 2 adults, Water electric $23, Tent $21, extra people $3.50, Children under 6 years of age-free, Day use fee $8 per car (max 5 people); V, MC, cash. **Parking:** At site & off site.

Facilities

Number of RV-Only Sites: 92. **Number of Tent-Only Sites:** 25. **Hookups:** Electric (30 amps), water, cable. **Each Site:** Picnic table, fire ring. **Dump Station:** Yes. **Laundry:** No. **Pay Phone:** Yes. **Rest Rooms and Showers:** Yes. **Fuel:** No. **Propane:** No. **Internal Roads:** Gravel. **RV Service:** No. **Market:** 5 mi. in Fall City. **Restaurant:** 5 mi. in Fall City. **General Store:** No. **Vending:** No. **Swimming Pool:** No. **Playground:** Yes. **Other:** Pavillion, river access nearby, large open field. **Activities:** Fishing (salmon & others, call about seasons). **Nearby Attractions:** Northwest Railway Museum, Snoqualmie Falls, fishing, rafting, river water sports, Seattle, Puget Sound, Snoqualmie Pass, Mt. Baker-Snoqualmie National Forest. **Additional Information:** Upper Snoqualmie Valley Chamber of Commerce, (425) 888-4440.

Restrictions

Pets: On leash only (no livestock please). **Fires:** In fire pits only. **Alcoholic Beverages:** At site only. **Vehicle Maximum Length:** None. **Other:** Make sure to call about flood season before arrival.

To Get There

From I-90 Exit 22, drive north on Preston-Fall City Rd. for 4.5 mi., then turn right on SE 45th PL, and drive 1 mi. until road dead-ends into campground

FEDERAL WAY

Dash Point State Park

5700 Southwest Dash Point Rd., Federal Way 98023. T: (253) 593-2206; www.parks.wa.gov.

RV ★★★ Tent ★★★★

Beauty: ★★★★ Site Privacy: ★★★
Spaciousness: ★★ Quiet: ★★★
Security: ★★ Cleanliness: ★★
Insect Control: ★★ Facilities: ★★★

For a state park near the city, Dash Point State Park provides a nicely wooded camping environment just west of Tacoma. Set in a shady forest of fir and cedar and divided into two loops, the campground also has a trail leading down to a beach on Puget Sound. The lower loop better accomodates RVs; both loops provide amiable tent accomodations. In the lower loop, one finds some water and electric sites, paved parking in every site, and a dirt area for picnicking and tenting in each site; some sites have a layout more conducive to tents, with less density in a localized area. Utility sites sit in an area with a higher site density. Based on space and privacy, lower-loop utility sites 34–49 and non-utility sites 12–28 have the most of the aforementioned traits. The upper loop houses similar sites, but with dirt parking, no utilities, and much less room for all but small RVs. Sites 119–124 sit in a high-traffic area; sites in the upper loop vary in size and have much more foliage than lower-loop sites. Visit during the summer for the best weather, but the rainy season also has a beautiful, ethereal charm.

Basics

Operated By: Washington State Parks & Recreation. **Open:** All year, upper loop open only May–Sept. **Site Assignment:** On arrival, reservations. **Registration:** At gate or self pay station. **Fee:** Water electric $20, No hookups $14, extra car $6; V, MC, cash. **Parking:** At site.

Facilities

Number of RV-Only Sites: 27. **Number of Tent-Only Sites:** 114 non-utility. **Hookups:** Electric (20, 30 amps), water. **Each Site:** Picnic table, fire ring. **Dump Station:** Yes. **Laundry:** No. **Pay Phone:** Yes. **Rest Rooms and Showers:** Yes. **Fuel:** No. **Propane:** No. **Internal Roads:** Paved. **RV Service:** No. **Market:** In Federal Way, a few mi. **Restaurant:** In Federal Way, a few mi. **General Store:** No. **Vending:** Yes. **Swimming Pool:** No. **Playground:** No. **Other:** Amphitheater, hiking trails, biking trails, beach. **Activities:** Jr. Ranger programs during summer, hiking, biking. **Nearby Attractions:** Seattle, Tacoma, Olympia, Mt's. Rainier & St. Helens, skiing, Puget Sound. **Additional Information:** Seattle Visitor Info Center, (206) 461-5840; www.seeseattle.org.

Restrictions

Pets: On leash only (6 ft. max length). **Fires:** In fire pits only. **Alcoholic Beverages:** At site only. **Vehicle Maximum Length:** 40 ft. **Other:** Remember wildlife, plants, pretty much everything in park protected by law.

To Get There

From I-5: Exit at the 320th St. Exit (Exit 143). Take 320th St. west 4 mi. When 320th St. ends at a T-intersection, make a right onto 47th St. When 47th St. ends at another T-intersection, turn left onto Hwy. 509/Dash Point Rd. Drive 2 mi. to the park. (West side of street is the campground side, and east is the day-use area.)

FERNDALE

The Cedars RV Resort

6335 Portal Way, Ferndale 98248. T: (360) 384-2622; F: (360) 380-6365.

RV ★★★ Tent ★★

Beauty: ★ Site Privacy: ★★★★
Spaciousness: ★★ Quiet: ★★
Security: ★★★ Cleanliness: ★★★
Insect Control: ★★ Facilities: ★★★

The Cedars in Ferndale makes a great place to stop in northwest Washington for travelers seeking amenities. While the campground lacks any real connection with the surrounding natural environment, grass- and gravel-surfaced sites do have cedar hedges allowing some privacy for individual campers. Utility sections A and B and sites C1–C9 have the densest and tallest hedges, but only water and electric hookups. Full-hookup sites L9–L15 have the best view of the mountains to the east, but less privacy. A different story entirely, the tenting areas consist of open grass plots interspersed throughout the grounds in random locations. Summers here come in the Indian variety (July through Sept), but even then rain and cold abound. The area plays host to year-round tourism, as travel during winter seldom gets difficult.

Basics

Operated By: Holiday Trails Resorts. **Open:** All year. **Site Assignment:** On arrival, reservations. **Registration:** At general store. **Fee:** For 2 adults, 2 children, full $26, Water, electric $24, Dry camping $18, extra adult $3, Phone (nightly)–$2, Cable (nightly)–$2; V, MC, cash. **Parking:** At site.

Facilities

Number of RV-Only Sites: 117. **Number of Tent-Only Sites:** 0. **Hookups:** Electric (30, 50 amps), water, cable, phone. **Each Site:** Picnic table. **Dump Station:** Yes. **Laundry:** Yes. **Pay Phone:** Yes. **Rest Rooms and Showers:** Yes. **Fuel:** No. **Propane:** No. **Internal Roads:** Paved & gravel. **RV Service:** No. **Market:** 6 mi. south in Ferndale. **Restaurant:** 6 mi. south in Ferndale. **General Store:** Yes. **Vending:** Yes. **Swimming Pool:** Yes. **Playground:** Yes. **Other:** Arcade, reception hall (max capacity 122 people), volleyball court. **Activities:** Horseshoes, badminton, volleyball, berry picking (in season), casino gambling (call about availability of shuttles to casinos). **Nearby Attractions:** Pioneer park, Hovander Homestead Park, Canada, The San Juan Islands, Victoria, whale-watching, fishing, Mt. Baker Ski Area & National Forest. **Additional Information:** Whatcom County Visitor's Bureau, (360) 671-3990, www.bellingham.org.

Restrictions

Pets: On leash only (no fighting breeds, no more than 2 dogs per site). **Fires:** In fire pits only. **Alcoholic Beverages:** At site, picnic areas only. **Vehicle Maximum Length:** 60 ft. **Other:** 7 day stay limit on dry camping, electric sites.

To Get There

From I-5 Exit 263, turn northeast on Portal Way, and drive 0.8 mi. The Cedars Resort will be on the left and clearly marked.

GIG HARBOR

Gig Harbor RV Resort

9515 Burnham Dr. Northwest, Gig Harbor 98332. T: (253) 858-8138 or (800) 526-8311; F: (253) 858-8399.

RV ★★★ Tent ★★

Beauty: ★★★ Site Privacy: ★★
Spaciousness: ★★★ Quiet: ★★★
Security: ★ Cleanliness: ★★★★
Insect Control: ★★ Facilities: ★★★

Gig Harbor RV Resort, located off Hwy. 16 and 45 minutes southwest of Seattle, provides lodging near a beautiful harbor area. Large terraced, gravel sites crown this park's accomodations. The park also has some adjacent sites at the top of the terraced hill. In the upper section, foliage provides a small amount of privacy; the actual terraces in the terraced section give a feeling of semi-privacy and open space. The upper section has some shade from trees; although ringed by forests of fir, the lower section has less shade and foliage among sites. Tenting within the park is limited, as the tenting area has small sites with no privacy and a little gravel, but lots of shade. Gig Harbor is a beautiful coastal area on Puget Sound. Visit during summer for the best weather.

BASICS

Operated By: PCF Mgmt. **Open:** All year. **Site Assignment:** On arrival, reservations. **Registration:** At office, after hours check welcome board out front. **Fee:** Full $37.81, Water electric $32.24, Tent $20, Cabins $30.85; V, MC, D, personal check, cash. **Parking:** At site, limited off site.

FACILITIES

Number of RV-Only Sites: 93. **Number of Tent-Only Sites:** 12. **Hookups:** Electric (20, 30, 50 amps), water, sewer. **Each Site:** Picnic table. **Dump Station:** Yes. **Laundry:** Yes. **Pay Phone:** Yes. **Rest Rooms and Showers:** Yes. **Fuel:** No. **Propane:** Yes. **Internal Roads:** Paved. **RV Service:** No. **Market:** 3 mi. west in Gig Harbor. **Restaurant:** 3 mi. west in Gig Harbor. **General Store:** Yes. **Vending:** Yes. **Swimming Pool:** Yes. **Playground:** Yes. **Other:** Basketball, volleyball, badminton, club room, horseshoes. **Activities:** Inquire at campground. **Nearby Attractions:** Scuba diving, sailing, kayaks, power boats, jet skis, wind surfing, water skiing, fishing, Seattle-Tacoma area, Puget Sound. **Additional Information:** Gig Harbor Chamber of Commerce, (253) 851-6865; Seattle Visitor Info Center, (206) 461-5840; www.seeseattle.org.

RESTRICTIONS

Pets: On leash only, no fencing or kenneling. **Fires:** No open fires, charcoal ok. **Alcoholic Beverages:** At site only. **Vehicle Maximum Length:** None.

TO GET THERE

From I-5, take Exit 132 and follow Hwy. 16 west, cross the Tacoma Narrows Bridge. Turn right at Burnham Dr.-North Rosedale Exit. Drive 1.2 mi. on Burnham; entrance is on the left.

GOLDENDALE

Brooks Memorial State Park

2465 US Hwy. 97, Goldendale 98620. T: (509) 773-4611; www.parks.wa.gov.

RV ★★★ Tent ★★★★

Beauty: ★★★★★	Site Privacy: ★★★
Spaciousness: ★★★	Quiet: ★★★★★
Security: ★★★★	Cleanliness: ★★★★★
Insect Control: ★★★	Facilities: ★★★

From its 3,000-foot location in the Simcoe Mountains, Brooks Memorial State Park is not only a good base for exploring the Klickitat Valley, but also for sights farther south to the Columbia River, west into the untamed Klickitat River region and Mount Adams, and north into the Yakima Indian Reservation and the viticultural lands of the Yakima Valley. Points of interest abound in all directions. Central to the area is Goldendale, a quiet community that is home to the Goldendale Observatory State Park Interpretive Center and has one of the largest telescopes available for public use in the country. Wildflowers bloom in the park from March until July, and there is quite a variety of park wildlife—turkeys, deer, raccoons, porcupines, beavers, bobcats, coyotes, red-tailed hawks, and owls. The Little Klickitat River follows US 97 from Brooks Memorial down into Goldendale, and it is not uncommon to observe beavers going about their business of damming the river.

BASICS

Operated By: Washington State Parks & Recreation Commission. **Open:** All year. **Site Assignment:** First come, first served. **Registration:** Self-registration at self pay station across from the rest rooms. **Fee:** $11–$16. **Parking:** At site.

FACILITIES

Number of RV-Only Sites: 23. **Number of Tent-Only Sites:** 45. **Hookups:** Electric (20 amps), water. **Dump Station:** Yes. **Laundry:** No. **Pay Phone:** Yes. **Rest Rooms and Showers:** Yes. **Fuel:** 13 mi. In Goldendale. **Propane:** 13 mi. **Internal Roads:** Paved. **RV Service:** No. **Market:** 13 mi. In Goldendale. **Restaurant:** 13 mi. **General Store:** 13 mi. **Vending:** No. **Swimming Pool:** No. **Playground:** Yes. **Other:** Kitchen shelters w/ water & electricity, group accommodations. **Activities:** Hiking, fishing, nature talks in Environmental Learning Center upon request, horseshoe pit, softball field. **Nearby Attractions:** Goldendale Observatory, Maryhill Museum, historic Columbia Hwy. **Additional Information:** www.parks.wa.gov.

RESTRICTIONS

Pets: On leash only. **Fires:** In fire pit. **Alcoholic Beverages:** At site, picnic area. **Vehicle Maximum Length:** 40 ft. **Other:** No firewood gathering.

TO GET THERE

From Yakima, follow US 97 south for 55 mi., crossing Satus Pass (elevation 3,107 ft.) to the park entrance.

GRAND COULEE

King's Court RV Park

P.O. Box 837, Grand Coulee 99133. T: (509) 633-3655 or (800) 759-2608; www.grandcouleedam.com/kingscourt; kingsco@televar.com.

RV ★ Tent ★

Beauty: ★	Site Privacy: ★
Spaciousness: ★★	Quiet: ★★
Security: ★★	Cleanliness: ★★
Insect Control: ★★	Facilities: ★★

King's Court RV Park in Grand Coulee has a location very near Grand Coulee Dam and offers shuttles to the seasonal, nightly laser shows on the dam walls. This is the main advantage of staying at this small park. None of the small gravel sites avoid the noise of nearby roads, and facilities are dated and limited. The grounds have a nice view of the low bluffs across the highway, but sites lack privacy or much shade. The best sites, full hookups 1–12, sit furthest from the road. Avoid sites 15–28, as they are right next to the nearby highway. Visit during the summer season to avoid cold, snowy weather.

BASICS

Operated By: The King's Court RV Park. **Open:** All year. **Site Assignment:** First come, first served; reservations (1 night stay deposit; 24 hour cancellation). **Registration:** At office across Hwy; After Hours see host or pay in morning. **Fee:** May 15-Sept. 15: $21, Sept. 16–May 14: $18; V, MC, AE, D, Cash. **Parking:** At site.

FACILITIES

Number of RV-Only Sites: 32. **Number of Tent-Only Sites:** n/a. **Hookups:** Electric (20, 30, 50 amps), water, sewer. **Each Site:** Picnic table. **Dump Station:** Yes. **Laundry:** Yes. **Pay Phone:** No. **Rest Rooms and Showers:** Yes. **Fuel:** No. **Propane:** Yes. **Internal Roads:** Gravel. **RV Service:** No. **Market:** 2 mi. south in Electric City. **Restaurant:** 2 mi. south in Electric City. **General Store:** No. **Vending:** Yes. **Swimming Pool:** No. **Playground:** No. **Other:** Shuttle to Grand Coulee Dam Laser Light Show. **Activities:** Laundry. **Nearby Attractions:** Grand Coulee Dam, tons of lakes for fishing, two golf courses, Steamboat Rock State Park, hiking trails, rock climbing, various local events, Coulee Dam Casino, Coville Tribes Museum. **Additional Information:** Grand Coulee Dam Area Chamber of Commerce, (800) 268-5332.

RESTRICTIONS

Pets: On leash only. **Fires:** No open fires. **Alcoholic Beverages:** At site only. **Vehicle Maximum Length:** Forty ft. **Other:** Quiet Hours 10 p.m.–7 a.m.

TO GET THERE

From the junction of Hwy. 155 and Hwy. 174: Take Hwy. 174 east for 0.7 mi.; entrance on right.

KETTLE FALLS

Hang Cove Campground

1368 South Kettle Park Rd., Kettle Falls 99141. T: (509) 738-6366; www.nps.gov/laro.

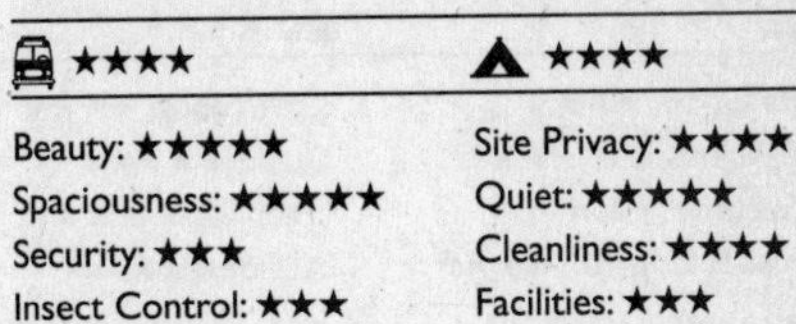

RV ★★★★ Tent ★★★★

Beauty: ★★★★★	Site Privacy: ★★★★
Spaciousness: ★★★★★	Quiet: ★★★★★
Security: ★★★	Cleanliness: ★★★★
Insect Control: ★★★	Facilities: ★★★

Set on the shore of Lake Roosevelt, against the sprawling backdrop of Colville National Forest—a 1,095,368-acre parcel in central northeastern Washington—Haag Cove is one of 32 campgrounds within the magnificent Coulee Dam National Recreation Area managed by the National Park Service. Deep canyons, sagebrush hills, and forested mountains are home to many kinds of animal and bird populations. One of the best spots for observing and shooting (with a camera) is just north of Haag Cove in Sherman Creek Habitat Management Area. The confluence of Sherman Creek and

Lake Roosevelt produces a quality fly-fishing spot. The only other campground in the vicinity is Sherman Creek. However, it is boat-in only—one of the few campgrounds in eastern Washington accessible only via watercraft. Hiking options are plentiful and relatively uncrowded in Colville National Forest. A gentler terrain, drier climate, and longer season compared to the Cascade area make for ideal conditions for treks into the backcountry here.

Basics

Operated By: National Park Service. **Open:** All year. **Site Assignment:** First come, first served. **Registration:** Not necessary. **Fee:** $10; $5 winter. **Parking:** At site.

Facilities

Number of RV-Only Sites: Inquire at campground. **Number of Tent-Only Sites:** 0. **Number of Multipurpose Sites:** 16. **Hookups:** None. **Dump Station:** Yes. **Laundry:** No. **Pay Phone:** No. **Rest Rooms and Showers:** Vault toilets. **Fuel:** 3 mi. In Kettle Falls. **Propane:** 3 mi. **Internal Roads:** Paved. **RV Service:** No. **Market:** 3 mi. In Kettle Falls. **Restaurant:** 3 mi. **General Store:** 3 mi. **Vending:** No. **Swimming Pool:** No. **Playground:** No. **Other:** Boat launch (in Kettle Falls). **Activities:** Fishing, boating, hiking, biking, badminton, bird-watching. **Nearby Attractions:** Lake Roosevelt, Colville National Forest. **Additional Information:** www.nps.gov/laro.

Restrictions

Pets: On leash only. **Fires:** In fire pit. **Alcoholic Beverages:** At site only. **Vehicle Maximum Length:** 26 ft. **Other:** Fishing license & boat launch permit required.

To Get There

From Kettle Falls (81 mi. northwest of Spokane), drive west on SR 20 across this upper portion of the Columbia River, and stay on SR 20 as it turns south along the river to the turnoff for Inchelium-Kettle Falls Rd. at about 7 mi. Take Inchelium-Kettle Falls Rd. south for 5 mi. to the campground.

LA PUSH
Mora Campground

3283 Mora Rd., Forks 98331. T: (360) 374-5460; www.northolympic.com.

RV ★★★★ Tent ★★★★

Beauty: ★★★★★ Site Privacy: ★★★★
Spaciousness: ★★★★ Quiet: ★★★★★
Security: ★★★ Cleanliness: ★★★★
Insect Control: ★★★★★ Facilities: ★★★

Mora Campground, part of the network of well-attended Olympic National Park facilities, is among the elite when it comes to its location (only a mile or so from the Pacific Ocean). For a total of 57 unspoiled and challenging miles, the saltwater frontage of the Pacific Ocean is a panoply of protruding headlands, swirling tidepools, crashing surf, and stalwart "sea-stacks." Situated at sea level, Mora is open all year and is an ideal choice for off-season travel. Actually, winter months and early spring can be some of the best times weatherwise at the Washington coast. You'll have an opportunity to watch the migratory gray whales pass on their way to southern California and Mexico. A word of warning: Coastal hiking requires a tide table at all times of the year. The "Strip of Wilderness" brochure available at the Mora Ranger Station is full of information about the pleasures and precautions of coastal hiking. Check at either the Mora station or information stations along U.S. 101 for other options in this part of Olympic National Park and the surrounding National Forest. One last word: The Native American reservations that border the Park along the coast are private property.

Basics

Operated By: Olympic National Park, National Park Service, U.S Dept of Interior. **Open:** All year. **Site Assignment:** First come, first served. **Registration:** Self-registration. **Fee:** $10. **Parking:** At site.

Facilities

Number of RV-Only Sites: 6. **Number of Tent-Only Sites:** 94. **Hookups:** None. **Dump Station:** Yes. **Laundry:** No. **Pay Phone:** No. **Rest Rooms and Showers:** Yes. **Fuel:** 12 mi. In Forks. **Propane:** 12 mi. **Internal Roads:** Paved. **RV Service:** No. **Market:** 12 mi. in Fork. **Restaurant:** 12 mi. **General Store:** 1 mi. **Vending:** No. **Swimming Pool:** No (1 mi. to coast). **Playground:** No. **Other:** Amphitheater. **Activities:** Hiking, camp fire programs, tide pool walks. **Nearby Attractions:** Olympic Wilderness Area. **Additional Information:** www.northolympic.com.

Restrictions

Pets: On leash only. **Fires:** In fire pit. **Alcoholic Beverages:** Allowed. **Vehicle Maximum Length:** 21 ft. **Other:** No vehicles allowed off of park roads, permits required for extended hikes.

To Get There

From either north or south, take US 101 around the Olympic Peninsula to the town of Forks (between 125 and 200 mi. from Seattle, depending on which route you take). About 1 mi. north of Forks, turn west onto La Push Rd., and drive for about 10 mi. to Mora Rd. Turn right onto Mora Rd., and follow the signs to the campground.

LEAVENWORTH
Icicle River RV Resort

7305 Icicle Rd., Leavenworth 98826. T: (509) 548-5420; www.icicleriverrv.com; info@icicleriverrv.com.

RV ★★★★★ Tent n/a

Beauty: ★★★★★ Site Privacy: ★
Spaciousness: ★★★ Quiet: ★★★★★
Security: ★★★ Cleanliness: ★★★★
Insect Control: ★★ Facilities: ★

Icicle River RV Resort, a few minutes from the western edge of Leavenworth, has to have the most spectacular localized scenery of any RV park in Washington State. The grounds, partially shaded by birch and pines, sit very near Wenatchee National Forest boundaries and on a small alpine river, across which beautifully gray, rocky hills rise steeply towards the sky. No truly undesirable sites exist in this park; the best full-hookup options sit on the river (sites 15–28 and 59–62). Full-hookup sites 42–56 also have spectacular views. The park has a few water and electric sites, and some sites have gravel while others have concrete surfaces. Most sites have grass perimeters and some shade. The resort provides a very quiet, mellow place to relax away from the tourist hustle of Leavenworth, feeling worlds apart from the Bavarian tourist trap; the park seldom feels crowded, even when full. Mild mountain summers make up the best time to travel here; winters bring snow and cold weather.

Basics

Operated By: Icicle River RV. **Open:** Apr. 1–Nov 30. **Site Assignment:** On arrival, reservations (deposit: $25; refund: 48 hours cancellation). **Registration:** At office, after hours ring mgmt from facility outside office. **Fee:** For 2 people, full $27, full (50 amp)–$30, Water-electric $25, extra adults $4, extra child (6-16)–$3, extra vehicle $4 (V, MC, cash). **Parking:** At site, some off site.

Facilities

Number of RV-Only Sites: 106. **Number of Tent-Only Sites:** n/a. **Hookups:** Electric (20, 30, 50 amps), water, sewer, cable, central data port. **Each Site:** Picnic table. **Dump Station:** No. **Laundry:** Yes. **Pay Phone:** Yes. **Rest Rooms and Showers:** Yes. **Fuel:** No. **Propane:** Yes. **Internal Roads:** Paved, gravel. **RV Service:** No. **Market:** East 5 min. in Leavenworth. **Restaurant:** East 5 min. in Leavenworth. **General Store:** Yes. **Vending:** No. **Swimming Pool:** No. **Playground:** No. **Other:** Small creek-side beach, hot tub, two reserveable & fully enclosed pavilions, croquet, putting green. **Activities:** Putting, river fishing, hiking, biking, river swimming. **Nearby Attractions:** Wenatchee Nat'l Forest, Leavenworth Bavarian Village, Ohme Gardens, Icicle Junction Family Fun Center. Rocky Reach Dam. **Additional Information:** Leavenworth Chamber of Commerce, (509) 548-5807.

Restrictions

Pets: On leash only. **Fires:** In fire pits only. **Alcoholic Beverages:** At site only. **Vehicle Maximum Length:** None. **Other:** No tents.

To Get There

From the center of Leavenworth, go 1 mi. west on Hwy. 2, then turn left on Icicle Rd. Icicle River RV Resorts entrance is on the Left.

LEAVENWORTH
Lake Wenatchee State Park

21588A Hwy. 207, Leavenworth 98826. T: (509) 662-0420; www.parks.wa.gov.

RV ★★★ Tent ★★★★

Beauty: ★★★★★ Site Privacy: ★★★
Spaciousness: ★★★ Quiet: ★★★
Security: ★★★★ Cleanliness: ★★★★
Insect Control: ★★ Facilities: ★★★

Although it is quite large, Lake Wenatchee State Park is a pretty nice spot with spacious, secluded campsites and oodles of choices for enjoying the outdoor recreation of one of Washington State's most scenic and untainted areas. It is a sprawling 489-acre complex divided into north and south campgrounds. The sites are available on a first come, first served basis, and if you can manage it, go for the sites in the northern section. They're closer to the river and more spacious. On this eastern slope of the Cascades, summers are hot and dry. Thunderstorms materialize out of nowhere, and lightning strikes can quickly ignite the forests in late summer and early fall. Be aware of the fire danger at all times. Also be aware that this is bear country. Food should be stored in bear-proof containers (or at least the car) when not being consumed; a tent is not much of a deterrent to a hungry bear.

Basics

Operated By: Washington State Parks & Recreation Commission. **Open:** Apr.–Sept. w/ limited facilities Oct.–Mar. **Site Assignment:** First come, first served; reservations May 15–Sept. 15; call (800) 452-5687; $6 fee. **Registration:** Self-registration. **Fee:** $12. **Parking:** At site.

Facilities

Number of RV-Only Sites: Inquire at campground. **Number of Tent-Only Sites:** 0. **Number of Multipurpose Sites:** 197. **Hookups:** None. **Dump Station:** Yes. **Laundry:** No. **Pay Phone:** Yes. **Rest Rooms and Showers:** Yes. **Fuel:** 21 mi. In Leavenworth. **Propane:** 21 mi. **Internal Roads:** Paved. **RV Service:** No. **Market:** 21 mi. In Leavenworth. **Restaurant:** Yes. **General Store:** Yes. **Vending:** No. **Swimming Pool:** No. **Playground:** Yes. **Other:** Amphitheater, boat launch, boat rentals, group camp, firewood, kitchen shelters (without electricity). **Activities:** Boating, horseback riding, campfire programs, nature walks, golf junior ranger programs, rock climbing, volleyball field. **Nearby Attractions:** Alpine Lakes Wilderness. **Additional Information:** www.parks.wa.gov.

Restrictions

Pets: On leash only. **Fires:** In fire pit. **Alcoholic Beverages:** At site or picnic area. **Vehicle Maximum Length:** None. **Other:** No firewood gathering.

To Get There

From Leavenworth (23 mi. west of Wenatchee), take US 2 west for 16 mi. to SR 207. The state park and campground are 5 mi. up SR 207.

LEAVENWORTH

Pine Village KOA Kampground

11401 River Bend Rd., Leavenworth 98826. T: (509) 548-7709 or reservations (800) 562 5709; www.koa.com.

RV ★★★★ Tent ★★★

Beauty: ★★★★	Site Privacy: ★
Spaciousness: ★★★	Quiet: ★★★
Security: ★★	Cleanliness: ★★★
Insect Control: ★★	Facilities: ★★★★

KOA Pine Village, located minutes east of the tourist mecca of Leavenworth, has to be one of the busiest campgrounds in Washington State, mostly due to its scenic location. The nearby Wenatchee National Forest houses some of the most beautiful alpine scenery around. Since it has an array of in-house recreation opportunities, the KOA stays buzzing with families, but the grounds do have some quieter areas amidst all the chaos. Sites have a seemingly arbitrary arrangement over a pine-shaded, hilly area near the Wenatchee River. Full-hookup RV sites 1–17 and 19–38 have a crowded feel, as do tent sites T4–T9 and T11–T24 located in and around a large field of grass. The least traffic-prone areas provide a less-crowded feel; gravel full-hookup sites H1–H8 and R1–R4 and and dirt tent sites R5–R21 make up the best of these. Be prepared for plenty of people regardless, as the common areas stay packed during the summer. Even so, summer provides the best season to visit this alpine area.

Basics

Operated By: Pine Village KOA. **Open:** Mar. 20–Nov. 1. **Site Assignment:** On arrival, reservations (deposit: 1 night's stay; refund: 5 days cancellation). **Registration:** At office, after hours at drop by office. **Fee:** For 2 people, full $36, Water-electric $34, Tent $29, extra adult $4.50, extra children 5-17 years old $4, extra vehicles $5, children younger than 5 stay free (V, MC, cash). **Parking:** At site, some off site.

Facilities

Number of RV-Only Sites: 135. **Number of Tent-Only Sites:** 45. **Hookups:** Electric (20, 30, 50 amps), water, sewer, cable. **Each Site:** Picnic table, grill. **Dump Station:** Yes. **Laundry:** Yes. **Pay Phone:** Yes. **Rest Rooms and Showers:** Yes. **Fuel:** No. **Propane:** No. **Internal Roads:** Paved. **RV Service:** No. **Market:** In Leavenworth 3 mi. west. **Restaurant:** In Leavenworth 3 mi. west. **General Store:** Yes. **Vending:** Yes. **Swimming Pool:** Yes. **Playground:** Yes. **Other:** Spa, game room, horseshoes, large covered pavillion, basketball, group areas, volleyball, horseshoes. **Activities:** Saturday night hay rides, train rides (small motorized cart pulling small cars), hiking, swimming, shuttle to Leavenworth, free coffee. **Nearby Attractions:** Ohme Gardens, Rocky Reach Dam, Icicle Junction Family Fun Center, Nutcracker Museum, North Central Washington Museum, Lake Wenatchee, Wenatchee National Forest. **Additional Information:** Leavenworth Chamber of Commerce, (509) 548-5807.

Restrictions

Pets: On leash only, not allowed in recreation areas. **Fires:** Fire pits, grills only. **Alcoholic Beverages:** At site only. **Vehicle Maximum Length:** None. **Other:** Don't tie clotheslines to trees or damage trees.

To Get There

From Hwy. 2 east of town heading west, turn right onto River Bend Dr., located by a Safeway. Follow signs for 0.5 mi.; entrance is on the right

LONG BEACH

Andersen's RV Park

1400 138th St., Long Beach 98631. T: (360) 642-2231 or (800) 645-6795; www.andersensrv.com; lorna@andersensrv.com.

 ★★★  ★★★

Beauty: ★★★★	Site Privacy: ★
Spaciousness: ★★	Quiet: ★★★
Security: ★★	Cleanliness: ★★★★
Insect Control: ★★	Facilities: ★★

Andersen's RV Park on the Long Beach Peninsula makes a good base for exploring the southwestern edge of the Olympic region. Natural attractions in the area draw more interest than organized recreation; the tourism infrastructure along all of the Washington Pacific Coast is, for lack of better words, second-rate and campy. Andersen's provides a small park consisting of two parallel rows of opposing back-ins, tent sites, and nearby beach access via a trail. The enormous Washington beaches form a straight line with the ocean's edge and run for miles; the surf looks like an impenetrable, high wall of fog. Everybody that has anything to say about it discourages swimming due to riptides and undertows. The gravel RV section of the campground has a slightly cramped feel and lacks shade or privacy. Tenters have it a little better; the grass sites are bigger and have more pronounced boundaries, but still no shade or privacy. Weather here aims to confuse on a daily basis, so be prepared for anything

Basics

Operated By: Andersen's RV Park. **Open:** All year. **Site Assignment:** On arrival, reservations (Encouraged; deposit: 1 night stay; refund: cancel by 12 noon on day of check-in). **Registration:** At office, after hours pay in morning. **Fee:** For 2 people, full $22, Tent $18, 6 people limit per tent site, extra people $2, Ages 6 & under free; V, MC, D, personal check, cash. **Parking:** At site.

Facilities

Number of RV-Only Sites: 58. **Number of Tent-Only Sites:** 18. **Hookups:** Electric (30 amps), water, sewer, cable. **Each Site:** Picnic table. **Dump Station:** No. **Laundry:** Yes. **Pay Phone:** Yes. **Rest Rooms and Showers:** Yes. **Fuel:** No. **Propane:** Yes. **Internal Roads:** Gravel. **RV Service:** No. **Market:** Nearby in Long Beach. **Restaurant:** Nearby in Long Beach. **General Store:** No. **Vending:** Yes. **Swimming Pool:** No. **Playground:** Yes. **Other:** Meeting room w/ pool table, fish cleaning station, beach access. **Activities:** Salt water fishing, swimming discouraged (rip tides & undertows). **Nearby Attractions:** Horseback Riding, sea kayaking, Cape Disappointment, fishing, clamming, beachcombing. **Additional Information:** Long Beach Peninsula Visitor' Info, (800) 451-2542 or (360) 642-2400.

Restrictions

Pets: On leash only. **Fires:** Not on ground in park, self contained raised fireplaces are o.k., get approval first from office. Bonfires allowed on beach, per regulation. Check w/ office. **Alcoholic Beverages:** At site only. **Vehicle Maximum Length:** None. **Other:** Do not play in driftwood, stay away from it, just leave it alone.

To Get There

Located just north of Long Beach on Hwy. 103 (northbound entrance is on the left between mile marker 4 and 5).

LONGMIRE

Cougar Rock Campground

Tahoma Woods, Star Rte., Ashford 98304-9751. T: (360) 569-2211; www.nps.gov.

RV ★★★ Tent ★★★★

Beauty: ★★★★★ Site Privacy: ★★★
Spaciousness: ★ Quiet: ★★★
Security: ★★ Cleanliness: ★★★★★
Insect Control: ★★ Facilities: ★★★

Cougar Rock Campground, operated by the National Park Service and located on the west side of Mt. Rainier National Park, offers good semi-private sites and some views of Mt. Rainier. Organized into five loops, the heavily forested campground has small sites hemmed in with foliage. This creates semi-private sites, but it decreases site roominess. Since the property is better suited for smaller RVs and tents, large RVs have trouble being comfortable here. Natural beauty abounds in this campground, with gray, jagged, rocky terra firma carpeted by green moss. Sites E1–E10 and E21–30 have obscured views of Mt. Rainier, but not much privacy. D loop houses the most private sites. All sites have dirt and gravel surfaces and receive lots of shade from firs, cedars, and pines. Summer brings the best weather for visiting the area and the largest crowds; late spring and early fall have cooler weather and beautiful displays of seasonal foliage.

BASICS

Operated By: National Park Service. **Open:** Mid May–Columbus Day. **Site Assignment:** On arrival, reservations. **Registration:** At office, at self pay station during off season. **Fee:** Reservation $15, Self pay $12; V, MC, D, cash. **Parking:** At site.

FACILITIES

Number of RV-Only Sites: 52. **Number of Tent-Only Sites:** 148 (tents & pop up campers). **Hookups:** None. **Each Site:** Picnic table, fire ring. **Dump Station:** Yes. **Laundry:** No. **Pay Phone:** Yes. **Rest Rooms and Showers:** No. **Fuel:** No. **Propane:** No. **Internal Roads:** paved. **RV Service:** No. **Market:** 15 mi. east. **Restaurant:** 15 mi. east. **General Store:** No. **Vending:** No. **Swimming Pool:** No. **Playground:** No. **Other:** Amphitheater, trails, ranger station. **Activities:** Interpretive programs (nightly during on-season). **Nearby Attractions:** Mount Rainier National Park. **Additional Information:** Mount Rainier Office, NPS (360) 569-2211.

RESTRICTIONS

Pets: On leash only (not on trails, can be walked on west side of main road). **Fires:** Pits only. **Alcoholic Beverages:** At site only. **Vehicle Maximum Length:** 35 ft. **Other:** Maximum of 6 people (or immediate family), 2 tents & 2 vehicles per site.

TO GET THERE

At 2.3 mi. north of Longmire, enter park driving on SR 706 through southwest entrance gate (Nisqually entrance) and continue, following signs to campground. Campground is 9 mi. from entrance gate.

LOPEZ

Spencer Spit State Park

Rte. 2 Box 3600, Lopez 98261. T: (360) 468-2251; www.parks.wa.gov.

RV ★★★★ Tent ★★★★

Beauty: ★★★★★ Site Privacy: ★★★★
Spaciousness: ★★★★ Quiet: ★★★★★
Security: ★★★ Cleanliness: ★★★★
Insect Control: ★★★★ Facilities: ★★★

Spencer Spit is an excellent base camp for enjoying Lopez and its sister islands by car, foot, or bicycle. The only drawback to lovely little Spencer Spit is the Washington State ferry system. Plan on becoming a veritable scholar of the ferry schedule. One of the most appealing aspects of Spencer Spit State Park is that you can camp right on the beach—in designated areas, of course. You will have to pack your gear down from the parking lot above. Lopez Island is, in our opinion, the premier bicycling island of the San Juans and can easily be covered in a day of riding if you're accustomed to 40 miles or so. A terrific excursion on Lopez is to ride out to Shark Reef Park to watch the sea lions that sprawl en masse on the offshore rocks. You can also look far across the San Juan Channel to windswept Cattle Point on San Juan Island, where the only sand dunes in the entire island group exist.

BASICS

Operated By: Washington State Parks & Recreation Commission. **Open:** Mar.–Oct. **Site Assignment:** Reservations required; call (800) 452-5687; $6. **Registration:** Self-registration. **Fee:** $6–$12. **Parking:** In campground & at some sites; parking for beach sites near trailhead.

FACILITIES

Number of Multipurpose Sites: 41. **Hookups:** Inquire at campground. **Dump Station:** Yes. **Laundry:** No. **Pay Phone:** No. **Rest Rooms and Showers:** Yes. **Fuel:** On island. **Propane:** On island. **Internal Roads:** Paved. **RV Service:** No. **Market:** On island. **Restaurant:** On island. **General Store:** On island. **Vending:** No. **Swimming Pool:** No. **Playground:** No. **Other:** 2 kitchen shelters without electricity. **Activities:** Boating, diving, fishing, clamming, crabbing, wildlife viewing, biking, water craft launch site, nightly moorage available for fee, San Juan Islands National Wildlife Refuge, Shark Reef Park, Cattle Point, Village of Lopez, Richardson & Mackay Harbor, Friday Harbor. **Nearby Attractions:** Inquire at campground. **Additional Information:** www.parks.wa.gov.

RESTRICTIONS

Pets: On leash only. **Fires:** In fire pit. **Alcoholic Beverages:** Allowed. **Vehicle Maximum Length:** 28 ft.

TO GET THERE

From the ferry terminal at the north end of Lopez Island, take Ferry Rd. south, and follow the signs to the park. The total distance from the ferry terminal is barely 5 mi.

NORTH BEND

Denny Creek Campground

42404 Southeast North Bend Way, North Bend 98045. T: (888) 206-1421

RV ★★★★ Tent ★★★

Beauty: ★★★★★ Site Privacy: ★★
Spaciousness: ★★★ Quiet: ★★★★
Security: ★★ Cleanliness: ★★
Insect Control: ★★ Facilities: ★★

Denny Creek Campground, a National Forest Campground around an hour east of Seattle and in the vicinity of Snoqualmie Pass, provides a beautiful alpine forest landscape. The limited facilities include flush toilets only, and a few electric hookups; the park's facilities almost fit a description of rustic. Of the electric sites, paved pull-throughs 30–33 have the best location. Back-in sites 16–22 sit in an area with semi-privacy for each site and near a south fork of the Snoqualmie River. All back-in sites have paved parking, with a large adjacent area used for tenting. Shaded by firs and birch, the whole park provides a peaceful, quiet retreat. Summers bring the best time to visit the area, but nights can still be cool at this altitude.

BASICS

Operated By: Recreational Resource Mgmt for National Forest Service. **Open:** Mid May–mid Oct. (weather permitting). **Site Assignment:** On arrival, reservations (877) 444-6777. **Registration:** At self pay station. **Fee:** No hookups $12, second vehicle $6, Electric $16, extra vehicle $8, Cash upon arrival. **Parking:** At site.

FACILITIES

Number of Multipurpose Sites: 33. **Hookups:** Electric (20 amps). **Each Site:** Picnic table, fire ring. **Dump Station:** No. **Laundry:** No. **Pay Phone:** No. **Rest Rooms and Showers:** Flush toilets only. **Fuel:** No. **Propane:** No. **Internal Roads:** Paved. **RV Service:** No. **Market:** Up the Interstate a few mi. **Restaurant:** Up the Interstate a few mi. **General Store:** No. **Vending:** No. **Swimming Pool:** No. **Playground:** No. **Activities:** Inquire at campground. **Nearby Attractions:** Hiking trails, Mt. Baker-Snoqualmie National Forest, skiing, fishing, golf, seattle. **Additional Information:** Washington State Tourism Office, (360) 725-5052.

RESTRICTIONS

Pets: On leash only (6 ft max length). **Fires:** In fire pits only. **Alcoholic Beverages:** At site only. **Vehicle Maximum Length:** 35 ft. (a few 40s). **Other:** Ask about collecting dead & down wood for campfires.

TO GET THERE

Take Exit 47 off I-90. Go north, then turn right at the T intersection. Travel 0.25 mi. and turn left on Denny Creek Rd. 58. Continue for 2 mi. to the campground entrance on the left.

OCEAN PARK

Evergreen Court Campground

222nd Ave. & WA Rte. 103, Ocean Park 98640.
T: (360) 665-6351

RV: n/a | Tent: ★★★

Beauty: ★★★ | Site Privacy: ★★★
Spaciousness: ★★★ | Quiet: ★★★★
Security: ★★★★★ | Cleanliness: ★★★★★
Insect Control: ★★★★ | Facilities: ★★

Long Beach Peninsula, so named by its claim to be the world's longest beach, struggles to find a workable balance between tourism promoters, real estate developers, oyster farmers, and cranberry harvesters. In the midst of this multiple-use stretch of surf and sand is Evergreen Court Campground, a five-acre haven for those willing to make the circuitous journey to this place of subtle beauty. Its proximity to Leadbetter Point State Park and the 11,000-acre Willapa National Wildlife Refuge makes Evergreen Court the perfect choice for those interested in all that these state- and federal-managed areas offer. For ocean access, Klipsan Beach Trail can be found about a half mile north of the campground, and a place to clean fish is provided for those who have a bit of luck at freshwater Loomis Lake, which is connected to the campground.

BASICS

Operated By: John & Deanna Klattenhoff. **Open:** All year. **Site Assignment:** Reservations or first come first served. **Registration:** At camp office or by mail w/ deposit. **Fee:** $12 for 2 people; $1 each add'l. **Parking:** At site or in main lot.

FACILITIES

Number of RV-Only Sites: 0. **Number of Tent-Only Sites:** 8. **Hookups:** None. **Each Site:** Picnic table, fire pit w/ grill. **Dump Station:** No. **Laundry:** No. **Pay Phone:** Yes. **Rest Rooms and Showers:** Yes. **Fuel:** No. **Propane:** No. **Internal Roads:** Gravel. **RV Service:** No. **Market:** 2 mi. in Ocean Park. **Restaurant:** 2 mi. **General Store:** 2 mi. **Vending:** No. **Swimming Pool:** No. **Playground:** Yes. **Activities:** Year-round renters participate in "community" activities. **Nearby Attractions:** Willapa National Wildlife Refuge.

RESTRICTIONS

Pets: On leash only. **Fires:** In fire pit. **Alcoholic Beverages:** Allowed. **Vehicle Maximum Length:** Call ahead for details.

TO GET THERE

From Seattle, take I-5 to Kelso/Longview (133 mi.). Go west on SR 4 for 62 mi. to Johnson's Landing. Turn south onto US 101 across the Naselle River and around the southern end of Willapa Bay to the turnoff for SR 103 and Long Beach Peninsula. Take SR 103 north. Evergreen Court Campground is 7 mi. north of Long Beach at the intersection of SR 103 and 222nd Ave. From Portland, take US 30 northwest along the Columbia River for 95 mi. to Astoria. Cross the bridge into Washington on US 101, turning left (west) onto SR 103 after 10 mi. From there, the directions are the same as from Seattle.

OLYMPIA

American Heritage Campground

9610 Kimmie St. Southwest, Olympia 98512.
T: (360) 943-8778

RV: ★★★★ | Tent: ★★★

Beauty: ★★★★ | Site Privacy: ★★★★
Spaciousness: ★★★ | Quiet: ★★
Security: ★ | Cleanliness: ★★★
Insect Control: ★★ | Facilities: ★★★★

American Heritage, the family-oriented sister campground of Olympia Campground, puts in a bid as a destination park. The older park has sites set within a well-manicured forest; the RV section has wide, paved sites, and the tenting section has a manicured yet unimproved feeling. Most sites create semi-private environments and receive lots of shade from tall conifers overhead. The best sites for both types of camping sit on the perimeters of their respective sections; sites on the medians of sections often lack any seclusion. As far as recreation goes, the "destination" section of the park kind of feels like a Florida reptile farm, but kids won't notice. The park has easy access to the interstate and a good amount of quiet; though it's only open during summer, travelers will still need a jacket for the cool western Washington nights.

BASICS

Operated By: Olymia Campgrounds. **Open:** Memorial Day–Labor Day. **Site Assignment:** On arrival, reservations. **Registration:** At office, after hours see instructions outside office. **Fee:** For 2 adults, 2 children, full $27, Water-electric $26, Tent $19, extra person $4. **Parking:** At site.

FACILITIES

Number of RV-Only Sites: 74. **Number of Tent-Only Sites:** 25. **Hookups:** Electric (20, 30 amps), water, sewer. **Each Site:** Picnic table, fire ring. **Dump Station:** Yes. **Laundry:** Yes. **Pay Phone:** Yes. **Rest Rooms and Showers:** Yes. **Fuel:** No. **Propane:** Yes. **Internal Roads:** Paved. **RV Service:** No. **Market:** 5 mi. north in Olympia. **Restaurant:** 4 mi. North in Olympia. **General Store:** Yes. **Vending:** No. **Swimming Pool:** Yes. **Playground:** Yes. **Other:** Movie room, kiddie farm, playground, bike rentals, horseshoes, volleyball, badminton, rec hall, pavillion, bike track. **Activities:** Movies nightly, hay rides, various planned activities. **Nearby Attractions:** Olympia Farmers Market, Tumwater Falls Park, Monarch Sculpture Park, Yashiro Japanese Garden, Puget Sound, Seattle. **Additional Information:** Olympia Thurston County Visitor & Convention Bureau, (360) 704-7544 or (877) 704-7500.

RESTRICTIONS

Pets: On leash only, quiet. **Fires:** In fire pits only. **Alcoholic Beverages:** At site only. **Vehicle Maximum Length:** 40 ft. **Other:** Check in at 1p.m.

TO GET THERE

Take Exit 99 off I-5, go 0.3 mi. east on 93rd Ave, then left on Kimmie St SW for 0.3 mi.; the road dead-ends into campground.

OLYMPIA

Olympia Campground

1441 83rd Ave. Southwest, Olympia 98512.
T: (360) 352-2551

RV: ★★★ | Tent: ★★★

Beauty: ★★★★ | Site Privacy: ★★★
Spaciousness: ★★★ | Quiet: ★★★
Security: ★★ | Cleanliness: ★★★
Insect Control: ★★ | Facilities: ★★★

Olympia Campground, located in the eponymous city, has flat, semiprivate sites with lots of shade. Watchtower-like Douglas firs all but block out the sky, and woody, deciduous shrubbery covers the ground in many spots and also provides some privacy among the gravel and dirt sites. Olympia Campground, like much of Olympia, has a heavily-forested but constantly upkept feel. The best sites sit in the back of the park, such as back-ins sites 50–80; the pull-through section sits near the front of the park in a more open area close to the office/convenience store/rec room/etc. This particular campground has a target audience of adults or older families; the owners have a sister park which is more family-oriented, but open summers only (see profile for American Heritage Campground). Facilities have an older, somewhat dated appearance. Weather in Olympia and all of the Puget Sound region has long, gray, wet, almost freezing winters, and short, mild summers, so a jacket (preferably of the rain-proof variety) is a good thing to keep handy.

BASICS

Operated By: Olympia Campground. **Open:** All year. **Site Assignment:** On arrival, reservations. **Registration:** At convenience store. **Fee:** For 2 people, full $25, Water-electric $24, Tent $19, extra person $4; V, MC, cash. **Parking:** At site.

FACILITIES

Number of RV-Only Sites: 96. **Number of Tent-Only Sites:** 30. **Hookups:** Electric (20, 30 amps), water, sewer. **Each Site:** Picnic table, fire ring. **Dump Station:** Yes. **Laundry:** Yes. **Pay Phone:** Yes. **Rest Rooms and Showers:** Yes. **Fuel:** Yes. **Propane:** Yes. **Internal Roads:** Paved. **RV Service:** No. **Market:** 4 mi. away. **Restaurant:** 3 mi. away. **General Store:** Yes. **Vending:** No. **Swimming Pool:** Yes. **Playground:** Yes. **Other:** Badminton, horseshoes, rec room w/ arcade & pool table, video rentals, volleyball. **Activities:** Inquire at campground. **Nearby Attractions:** State Capital, Puget Sound Region, Volcanos, skiing, casinos, Seattle. **Additional Information:** Olympia Thurston County Visitor & Convention Bureau, (360) 704-7544 or (877) 704-7500.

RESTRICTIONS

Pets: On leash only, quiet. **Fires:** In fire pits only. **Alcoholic Beverages:** At site only. **Vehicle Maximum Length:** 40 ft. **Other:** Check in at 1p.m.

TO GET THERE

Take I-5 Exit 101 (Airdustrial Way), drive 0.3 mi. east on Airdustrial, then turn right onto Center. Drive 1 mi. south on Center, then turn right onto 83rd and drive 0.2 mi. The entrance is on the left.

PACKWOOD

Ohanapecosh Campground (Mount Rainier National Park)

Tahoma Woods, Star Rte., Ashford 98304-9751. T: (360) 569-2211

RV ★★★★ Tent ★★★★

Beauty: ★★★★★ Site Privacy: ★★
Spaciousness: ★★★ Quiet: ★★★★
Security: ★★ Cleanliness: ★★★
Insect Control: ★★ Facilities: ★★★

Ohanapecosh Campground, on the east side of Mt. Rainier National Park, offers a more open feeling than Cougar Creek. Located in an old-growth forest near a rocky, cascading alpine river, the campground draws lots of campers year-round. Sites have less low-growing foliage than those at Cougar Creek, sacrificing privacy but creating a more spacious feeling below a canopy of tall evergreens. The campground has an organization of several shady loops; loop C has sites on the river, with several walk-in tent sites right on the banks. Other loops lack riverfront property but still provide a beautiful camping environment. The only loop to really avoid, B loop, has higher traffic and a location among campground facilities. Visit during the summer for the best temperatures, although a jacket still might be needed at night.

BASICS

Operated By: National Park Service. **Open:** Late May–mid Oct. (weather permitting). **Site Assignment:** On arrival, reservations highly recommended & available Jul. 1–Labor Day, call 1-(800) 365-CAMP (deposit: 1 night stay; refund: 24 hours notice of cancellation less $13.25 cancellation fee). **Registration:** At self pay station. **Fee:** Site $15 reserved, $12 self-pay; V, MC, D, cash. **Parking:** At site.

FACILITIES

Number of Multipurpose Sites: 205. **Hookups:** n/a. **Each Site:** Picnic table, fire ring. **Dump Station:** Yes. **Laundry:** No. **Pay Phone:** Yes. **Rest Rooms and Showers:** No showers, but flush toilets. **Fuel:** No. **Propane:** No. **Internal Roads:** Paved, gravel. **RV Service:** No. **Market:** 11 mi. in Packwood. **Restaurant:** 11 mi. in Packwood. **General Store:** No. **Vending:** No. **Swimming Pool:** No. **Playground:** No. **Other:** Amphitheater, hiking trails, visitor's center. **Activities:** Interpretive programs, hiking. **Nearby Attractions:** Mount Rainier, hiking, fishing, backcountry camping. **Additional Information:** Ohanapecosh Visitor Center, (360) 569-2211, ext. 2352.

RESTRICTIONS

Pets: On leash only (6 ft. max length, pets not allowed on National Park trails). **Fires:** Fire pits only, keep them small & controlled. **Alcoholic Beverages:** At site only. **Vehicle Maximum Length:** 40 ft. **Other:** Maximum of 6 people (or immediate family), two tents & two vehicles per site.

TO GET THERE

The campground is located off of Hwy. 123 in the southeast corner of the park, between mi. 4 and mi. 3. The road in the immediate area briefly changes to four lanes to accommodate park traffic; if headed southbound, campground entrance is on the right.

PASCO

Sandy Heights RV Park

P.O.Box 2487, Pasco 99301. T: (509) 542-1357 or (877) 894-1357; F: (509) 543-8335; sandyheightsrv@urx.com.

RV ★★★★ Tent ★★★

Beauty: ★★★ Site Privacy: ★
Spaciousness: ★★★ Quiet: ★★★
Security: ★★★★ Cleanliness: ★★★★★
Insect Control: ★★ Facilities: ★★★

Sandy Heights RV Park, off of I-182 in Pasco, provides a good base for exploring the tri-cities area. The grounds have a suburban park-like feel, lots of grass, the occasional red or green seedling, and newer, well-kept facilities. Recreational facilities include a basketball court with opposing goals and a large hot tub. The grass-perimetered, flat, paved, full-hookup sites come in both the pull-through and back-in variety. The park has no official "tent sites," but tents are allowed. The best back-in sites, 114–185, sit on the perimeter of the park with no neighbors to the rear; the pull-through sites lack any distinguishable differences. Security fences around the perimeter help to keep outsiders out, but also obscure views of the surrounding barren hills. Summers here stay hot, and winters stay cold; avoid visits during the hottest of summer months.

BASICS

Operated By: Sandy Heights RV. **Open:** All year. **Site Assignment:** On arrival, reservation (deposit: 1 night stay; refund: 24 hours cancellation). **Registration:** At office, after hours pay in morning. **Fee:** For 2 people, RV $22.50, Tent $18, Phone $3, Exta adult $2.50, No charge for kids (V, MC, cash). **Parking:** At site, some off site.

FACILITIES

Number of RV-Only Sites: 185. **Number of Tent-Only Sites:** 0 (Can accommodate, though). **Hookups:** Electric (20, 30, 50 amps), water, sewer, cable, phone. **Each Site:** Picnic table. **Dump Station:** Yes. **Laundry:** Yes. **Pay Phone:** Yes. **Rest Rooms and Showers:** Yes. **Fuel:** No. **Propane:** Yes. **Internal Roads:** Paved. **RV Service:** No. **Market:** 5 mi. west on I-182. **Restaurant:** 5 mi. west on I-182. **General Store:** Yes. **Vending:** No. **Swimming Pool:** Yes. **Playground:** Yes. **Other:** Hot tub, basketball court, horseshoes, volleyball, BBQ area, reserveable meeting hall. **Activities:** Occasional potluck, ice cream socials on Sundays (seasonal). **Nearby Attractions:** Wineries, golf, rodeos, boating, water skiing, fishing, Oasis Waterworks (water park), Lewis & Clark Trail historical sites. **Additional Information:** Pasco Chamber of Commerce, (509) 547-9755.

RESTRICTIONS

Pets: On leash only. **Fires:** No open fires. **Alcoholic Beverages:** At site only. **Vehicle Maximum Length:** None. **Other:** Tent max stay 3 days.

TO GET THERE

From I-182 Exit 7 (westbound, turn left) onto Broadmoor, drive 0.1 mi. south and turn at the first left onto St. Thomas Dr. Drive 1 mi. on St. Thomas, and the park is at the end of the road.

PORT ANGELES

Log Cabin Resort

3183 East Beach Rd., Port Angeles 98363. T: (360) 928-3325; F: (360) 928-2088; www.logcabinresort.net.

RV ★★★★ Tent n/a

Beauty: ★★★★★ Site Privacy: ★
Spaciousness: ★★ Quiet: ★★★★
Security: ★ Cleanliness: ★★★★
Insect Control: ★★ Facilities: ★

Log Cabin Resort, west of Port Angeles and off Hwy. 101, has a small, no-frills RV area in a beautiful fishing lodge environment. The resort also has convenient access to much of Olympic National Park. Located on big, blue Lake Crescent, the shady, rust red-painted wood lodge has non powered boat and fishing gear rentals, a restaurant (open at volume), and a laundromat. When occupancy in the RV section is low, individual sites have an outstanding view; when full, such is only a short walk away. Across the cold-blue lake, the Olympic mountains rise into the sky. And the whole joint's pretty quiet too. The area has sunny, mild weather most of the time, summers being most pleasant.

BASICS

Operated By: Log Cabin Resort for National Park Service. **Open:** Apr. 1–Oct. 31. **Site Assignment:** On arrival, reservations (deposit: one night stay; refund: full less $12 cancellation fee if 48 hours before scheduled arrival. **Registration:** At office, after hours see office door. **Fee:** Full $30.33, extra vehicle $5, Per pet $6.75, pay showers; V, MC, cash. **Parking:** At site.

FACILITIES

Number of RV-Only Sites: 38. **Number of Tent-Only Sites:** n/a. **Hookups:** Electric (30 amps), water, sewer. **Each Site:** Picnic table, fire ring. **Dump Station:** Yes. **Laundry:** Yes. **Pay Phone:** Yes. **Rest Rooms and Showers:** Yes. **Fuel:** No. **Propane:** No. **Internal Roads:** Gravel. **RV Service:** No. **Market:** East in Port Angeles. **Restaurant:** On site (May to Oct). **General Store:** Yes. **Vending:** No. **Swimming Pool:** No. **Playground:** No. **Other:** Non-powered boat rentals, fishing gear rentals, restaurant, lake access. **Activities:** Fishing, boating. **Nearby Attractions:** Olympic National Park, what else do you need?. **Additional Information:** ONP Info, (360) 452-0330; Port Angeles Chamber, (360) 452-2363.

RESTRICTIONS

Pets: On leash only (6 ft. max length), not permitted on any trails within National Park. **Fires:** In fire pits only. **Alcoholic Beverages:** At site only. **Vehicle Maximum Length:** 40 ft. (limited capacity at that length). **Other:** No tents.

TO GET THERE

From Hwy. 101 west of Port Angeles, and if driving west, turn left just after mi. marker 232 onto East Beach Rd. Drive 3.2 mi., and the entrance is on the left.

PORT ANGELES
Shadow Mountain Campground

232951 Hwy. 101, Port Angeles 98363. T: (877) 928-3043; mountain@olypen.com.

RV ★★★ Tent ★★★

Beauty: ★★★★★ Site Privacy: ★
Spaciousness: ★★ Quiet: ★★★
Security: ★ Cleanliness: ★★★★
Insect Control: ★★ Facilities: ★★

Shadow Mountain RV Park, located west of Port Angeles on Hwy. 101, makes a good accommodation when visiting Olympic National Park. The campground lacks plush or lush amenities, but it has good views of the green Olympic Mountains to the south. Sizes vary among gravel, back-in, terraced sites; terrace site 4 (the highest on the hill) and sites 1–5 have the most roominess and best view. Also, a lake across the road provides swimming (it's Hwy. 101, cross carefully—logging trucks hurt); a deli and a 9-hole mini-golf course are also on site. Campites do not have much privacy, and the tenting area, although grassy, has some hills. Just before the on-season has the best traffic conditions for seeing the park and area; after the on-season (ends Labor Day), many services discontinue.

Basics

Operated By: Shadow Mountain Campground. **Open:** All year. **Site Assignment:** Walkup, reservations (deposit: 1 night stay; refund: 24 hours cancellation. **Registration:** At store, after hours see kiosk out front. **Fee:** For 2 adults RV $18.50, Tent $13, extra adult $2, extra child $1, Pets $1 (V, MC, cash). **Parking:** At site.

Facilities

Number of RV-Only Sites: 40. **Number of Tent-Only Sites:** 10. **Hookups:** Electric (30 amps), water, sewer. **Each Site:** Picnic table, fire ring. **Dump Station:** Yes. **Laundry:** Yes. **Pay Phone:** Yes. **Rest Rooms and Showers:** Yes. **Fuel:** Yes. **Propane:** Yes. **Internal Roads:** Gravel. **RV Service:** No. **Market:** In Port Angeles. **Restaurant:** In Port Angeles. **General Store:** Yes. **Vending:** No. **Swimming Pool:** No. **Playground:** Yes. **Other:** Movie rentals, mini-golf, volleyball, badminton, basketball, horseshoes. **Activities:** swimming. **Nearby Attractions:** Port Angeles, Olympic National Park, Olympic National Forest, Dungeness Recreation Area, fishing, swimming, hiking. **Additional Information:** ONP Info, (360) 452-0330; Port Angeles Chamber of Commerce, (360) 452-2363.

Restrictions

Pets: On leash only. **Fires:** In fire pits only. **Alcoholic Beverages:** At site only. **Vehicle Maximum Length:** None.

To Get There

Located on Hwy. 101 west of Port Angeles, the Texaco/campground office is at mi. 233.

PORT ANGELES (Olympic National Park)
Altaire Campground

600 East Park Ave., Port Angeles 98362. T: (360) 452-4501; www.nps.gov.

RV ★★★ Tent ★★★★

Beauty: ★★★★★ Site Privacy: ★★
Spaciousness: ★★★ Quiet: ★★★★
Security: ★★ Cleanliness: ★★★★★
Insect Control: ★★ Facilities: ★

Altaire Campground in Olympic National Park has a beautiful setting in a less-trafficked area of the park. Surrounded by lush ferns, campsites sit among tall, vibrant, shady cedars. Sounds of the shallow, rushing Elwa River drift over the campground; the small propoerty makes up one of the river's banks. An entrance fee to the park must be paid to get to the campground, and no facilities come with the site fee, but the natural, local beauty of the surrounding landscape makes a man-made extras seem unneccessary. The site surfaces consist of dirt and fine-grit gravel. On-arrival-only registration makes it harder to obtain a specific site. Altaire also has some park-and-walk-in sites; it is a very short walk. Right after Labor Day, the National Park becomes a ghost town, and spectacular fall colors arrive shortly thereafter; just before or after the on-season provides an intimate setting to experience the Olympics.

Basics

Operated By: National Park Service. **Open:** Closed during low volume. **Site Assignment:** On arrival. **Registration:** At self pay station. **Fee:** $10. **Parking:** At site.

Facilities

Number of Multipurpose Sites: 31. **Hookups:** None. **Each Site:** Picnic table, fire ring. **Dump Station:** No. **Laundry:** No. **Pay Phone:** No. **Rest Rooms and Showers:** Non-flush only. **Fuel:** No. **Propane:** No. **Internal Roads:** Paved. **RV Service:** No. **Market:** In Port Angeles (30–45 min. driving). **Restaurant:** In Port Angeles (30 to 45 min. driving). **General Store:** No. **Vending:** No. **Swimming Pool:** No. **Playground:** No. **Activities:** Resting. **Nearby Attractions:** Olympic National Park, Olympic National Forest, lakes w/ boating, Strait of Juan De Fuca. **Additional Information:** ONP Info, (360) 452-0330; Port Angeles Chamber of Commerce, (360) 452-2363.

Restrictions

Pets: On leash only (not allowed on National Park trails). **Fires:** Fire pits only, controlled & small. **Alcoholic Beverages:** At site only. **Vehicle Maximum Length:** 25 ft. **Other:** Store all food in a bear-proof location, wash all dishes promptly & don't drop food scraps.

To Get There

From Hwy. 101 west of Port Angeles, turn Left on Olympic Hot Springs Rd., drive 2.1 mi. to entrance gate. From the park entrance, drive 2.4 mi. and the campground is on the right immediately across a bridge. Be alert, as it is not very well marked.

PORT ANGELES (Olympic National Park)
Heart of the Hills Campground

600 East Park Ave., Port Angeles 98362-6798. T: (360) 452-4501; www.nps.gov.

RV ★★★★ Tent ★★★★★

Beauty: ★★★★★ Site Privacy: ★★★
Spaciousness: ★★ Quiet: ★★★★
Security: ★★ Cleanliness: ★★★★
Insect Control: ★★ Facilities: ★

Heart o' the Hills Campground, the closest Olympic National Park campground in relation to Port Angeles (the largest city in the national park area), has the best variety in nearby recreation of any of the park campgrounds. Laid out over rolling hills, campsites sit under the canopy of an old-growth forest. Every site has a dirt area where a tent can be erected; parking areas have pavement. The surrounding forest has a vibrancy hard to find anywhere else, with lots of symbiotic plant and fungal relationships, wildlife, and atmosphere. Of the five single-loop sections, E loop has the least-open feel. All sites have at least a little privacy and lots of shade. Summers on the Olympic Peninsula bring lots of tourists, as the region has a look and feel like no other; if it's the on-season, be prepared for some crowds. Local weather is temperate ,and summers can be cool, so bring rain gear and cold-weather clothes.

Basics

Operated By: National Park Service. **Open:** All year. **Site Assignment:** On arrival. **Registration:** At self pay station. **Fee:** $10. **Parking:** At site.

Facilities

Number of Multipurpose Sites: 103. **Hookups:** None. **Each Site:** Picnic table, fire ring. **Dump Station:** No. **Laundry:** No. **Pay Phone:** At park entrance. **Rest Rooms and Showers:** No showers. **Fuel:** No. **Propane:** No. **Internal Roads:** Paved. **RV Service:** No. **Market:** In Port Angeles. **Restaurant:** In Port Angeles. **General Store:** No. **Vending:** No. **Swimming Pool:** No. **Playground:** No. **Other:** Amphitheater. **Activities:** Hiking, interpretive programs. **Nearby Attractions:** Salt water fishing, boating, Olympic National Park, Hurricane Ridge. **Additional Information:** ONP Info, (360) 452-0330; Port Angeles Chamber of Commerce, (360) 452-2363.

Restrictions

Pets: On leash only (6 ft. max length, not allowed on any park trails). **Fires:** In fire pits only. **Alcoholic Beverages:** At site only. **Vehicle Maximum Length:** 21 ft., limited availability up to 32 ft. **Other:** Store all food in a bear-proof location, wash all dishes promptly & don't drop food scraps, In campgrounds where wood is not available, dead & down wood along public roads may be collected, Max occupancy 8 people per site, Max stay limit 14 days per year.

To Get There

From Hwy. 101 southbound in Port Angeles, turn left on Race St. (at traffic light). Drive 1 mi., and after NPS Visitor's Center road forks, follow the right side of the fork. Drive 5.5 mi., through the entrance gate, and the campground is on the left.

PORT ANGELES
(Olympic National Park)
Hoh Rain Forest Campground

600 East Park Ave., Port Angeles 98362-6798. T: (360) 452-4501; www.nps.gov.

RV ★★★★★ | Tent ★★★★★

Beauty: ★★★★★ | Site Privacy: ★★★
Spaciousness: ★★ | Quiet: ★★★★★
Security: ★★ | Cleanliness: ★★★
Insect Control: ★★ | Facilities: ★

Well off Hwy. 101, on the western edge of Olympic National Park sits the Hoh Rain Forest visitor's center, and close by, the Hoh Rain Forest Campground. Although a popular spot for tourists, the area has a quiet, private feel during the off-season and the surrounding natural environment breathes beauty year-round. The campground has three loops; B and C loops have a similar layout with dense foliage, paved parking, and gravel-and-grass mixed areas for tents on many sites. A loop has more grass than the others, but it also has more open sites. The benefits of such obscured views of the mountains are best reaped in sites A1–A15. Plant life throughout the area has a unique look and wide diversity; rivers and streams abound; and many hiking trails start at the visitor's center and are usually open even if the center is not. Summer provides the mildest time to visit (it still can be rainy), but be warned: the park has lots of visitors June 17 through Labor Day.

BASICS

Operated By: National Park Service. **Open:** Year-round (some sections seasonal). **Site Assignment:** On arrival only. **Registration:** At self pay station. **Fee:** $10, Cash. **Parking:** At site, additional parking at visitor center.

FACILITIES

Number of Multipurpose Sites: 82. **Hookups:** None. **Each Site:** Picnic table, fire ring. **Dump Station:** Yes. **Laundry:** No. **Pay Phone:** No. **Rest Rooms and Showers:** Flush & Non-flush only (No shower). **Fuel:** No. **Propane:** No. **Internal Roads:** Paved. **RV Service:** No. **Market:** A long way. **Restaurant:** A long way. **General Store:** No. **Vending:** No. **Swimming Pool:** No. **Playground:** No. **Other:** Visitor center, interpretive programs. **Activities:** Interpretive programs, hiking. **Nearby Attractions:** Hoh Rain Forest, Hoh River, Olympic National Park, hiking, fishing. **Additional Information:** ONP Info, (360) 452-0330.

RESTRICTIONS

Pets: On leash only (6 ft. max length, not allowed on any park trails). **Fires:** In fire pits only. **Alcoholic Beverages:** At site only. **Vehicle Maximum Length:** 28 ft. **Other:** Store all food in a bear-proof location, wash all dishes promptly & don't drop food scraps, In campgrounds where wood is not available, dead & down wood along public roads may be collected, Max occupancy 8 people per site, Max stay limit 14 days per year.

TO GET THERE

From Hwy. 101 southbound, turn left between mile markers 179 and 178; you're looking for an unnamed (and practically unmarked) access road. Drive 12.3 mi. to the park gate; proceed through gate and drive 5.4 mi.. Campground entrance is on the right.

PORT ANGELES
(Olympic National Park)
Sol Duc Resort

600 East Park Ave., Port Angeles 98362-6798. T: (360) 452-4501; www.nps.gov.

RV ★★★ | Tent ★★

Beauty: ★★★★★ | Site Privacy: ★
Spaciousness: ★★ | Quiet: ★★★★
Security: ★ | Cleanliness: ★★★★
Insect Control: ★★ | Facilities: ★★★★

Sol Duc Resort has a small RV area and, the main attraction, an acrid-smelling pool. The pool, fed by Sol Duc Hot Spring, smells that way due to high mineral content, as does much of the water in the immediate area. People come here to relax and "take the waters"; the resort also has an in-house massage therapy operation. The resort's accommodations consist of a lodge, some cabins, and a small, cramped RV area. Sites have no privacy and sit close together in a gravel parking area near the resort. Areas directly adjacent to the RV area have a much more natural and pristine setting. Most sites receive shade from the beautiful birch grove the RV section was cut from. Picnic tables and fire rings for each site sit under the birches. The surrounding area has lots of hiking, and even catch-and-release fishing in the nearby Sol Duc river (heavily regulated, get literature from official location). Summers bring the best weather to the area, but make sure to have rain gear handy anyway.

BASICS

Operated By: Langsden Inc. under lease from NPS. **Open:** Mid Apr.–Oct. **Site Assignment:** On arrival, reservation (deposit: 1 night stay; refund: 48 hours notice of cancellation less $5 fee). **Registration:** At office (lodge), no after hours entry. **Fee:** $16, Pool use not included in fee; V, MC, cash. **Parking:** At site, some off site.

FACILITIES

Number of RV-Only Sites: 20. **Number of Tent-Only Sites:** n/a. **Hookups:** Electric (20, 30 amps), water. **Each Site:** Picnic table, fire ring. **Dump Station:** Yes. **Laundry:** No. **Pay Phone:** Yes. **Rest Rooms and Showers:** At pool. **Fuel:** No. **Propane:** No. **Internal Roads:** Gravel. **RV Service:** No. **Market:** In Port Angeles, 40 mi. east. **Restaurant:** In Port Angeles. **General Store:** Yes. **Vending:** No. **Swimming Pool:** Yes. **Playground:** No. **Other:** Hot springs pools, massage therapy, restaurant & deli. **Activities:** Taking the waters, relaxing, fishing, hiking. **Nearby Attractions:** Olympic National Park & Forest. **Additional Information:** ONP Info, (360) 452-0330; Port Angeles Chamber of Commerce, (360) 452-2363.

RESTRICTIONS

Pets: On leash only (6 ft. max length, not allowed on any park trails). **Fires:** In fire pits only. **Alcoholic Beverages:** At site only. **Vehicle Maximum Length:** 32 ft.

TO GET THERE

On Hwy. 101 just east of the National Forest Boundary and just west of Crescent Lake, turn left on Duc Hot Springs Rd. Drive 0.3 mi. to park entrance gate. Pay fee (if applicable) and continue on 12 mi.,; campground entrance is on the right.

PORT TOWNSEND
Fort Flagler State Park

10542 Flagler Rd., Nordland 98358. T: (360) 385-1259; www.parks.wa.gov; infocent@parks.wa.gov.

RV ★★★★ | Tent ★★★★★

Beauty: ★★★★★ | Site Privacy: ★★★
Spaciousness: ★★★ | Quiet: ★★★
Security: ★ | Cleanliness: ★★★
Insect Control: ★★ | Facilities: ★★

Fort Flagler, situated between Port Townsend Bay and Kilisut Harbor, has 19,100 feet of saltwater shoreline. The park has two campgrounds and both have good views. Better suited for RVs, the grassy lower campground also has better localized views than the upper. Gravel sites 97–116 have almost totally unobstructed 270° of water, horizon, and mountains (and smokestacks) rising from the Washington mainland. These sites don't have any shade; sites 52–76 have shade from short coastal pines but no view. All utility sites reside in the lower campground; the upper campground lacks utilities, is only open seasonally, and has a totally different vibe. Sitting on the edge of a lush, green, heavily forested cliff, the upper campground has limited views of the harbor below. With dirt site surfaces, narrow roads, semi-privacy, and shade, upper campground sites hold the most appeal for tent campers. Summers make the best time to visit here.

BASICS

Operated By: Washington State Parks & Recreation. **Open:** Oct. 28–Mar. 1 open for day use only. **Site Assignment:** On arrival, reservations. **Registration:** At self pay station or entrance gate. **Fee:** For 4 adults, Utility $19, standard $13, Primitive $8, extra adult $2, extra vehicle $6; V, MC, cash. **Parking:** At site, off site.

FACILITIES

Number of RV-Only Sites: 14. **Number of Tent-Only Sites:** 101. **Hookups:** Electric (20, 30 amps), water. **Each Site:** Picnic table. **Dump Station:** Yes. **Laundry:** No. **Pay Phone:** No. **Rest Rooms and Showers:** Yes. **Fuel:** No. **Propane:** No. **Internal Roads:** Paved. **RV Service:** No. **Market:** In Port Townsend. **Restaurant:** In Port Townsend. **General Store:** No. **Vending:** No. **Swimming Pool:** No. **Playground:** No. **Other:** Fort Flagler Environmental Learning Center (call for info), boat ramp, moorage. **Activities:** Boating, fishing, swimming, crabbing, clamming. **Nearby Attractions:** The ocean, boating, fishing, water-sports plus salt, Fort Worden Military Park (Historical), Olympic

National Park & Forest, ferries, golf, hiking, biking. **Additional Information:** Port Townsend Chamber of Commerce, (360) 385-2722.

RESTRICTIONS

Pets: On leash only (6 ft. max length). **Fires:** In fire pits only. **Alcoholic Beverages:** At site only. **Vehicle Maximum Length:** 40 ft. **Other:** Don't play in drift wood.

TO GET THERE

From the junction of Hwy. 20 and Hwy. 19 near Port Townsend, drive 5.4 mi. on Hwy. 19 south. Turn left onto SR 116 (Oak Bay Rd.). Go through Port Hadlock 2 mi. and take a sharp left, staying on SR 116. Follow to park entrance at end of highway. Park is about 10 mi. from Oak Bay Rd. turnoff.

PORT TOWNSEND

Fort Worden State Park

200 Battery Way, Port Townsend 98368. T: (360) 344-4400; F: (360) 385-7248; www.olympus.net/ftworden.

RV ★★★★★ Tent ★★★

Beauty: ★★★★★	Site Privacy: ★
Spaciousness: ★★★	Quiet: ★★★★
Security: ★★	Cleanliness: ★★
Insect Control: ★★	Facilities: ★★★★

Fort Worden State Park, a military history park in Port Townsend, has two campground sections. One has spectacular views—absolutely amazing views of the water and non-peninsular Washington beyond. Within the aptly titled "Beach Campground" sites, 1–17 have the most unobstructed views; sites 24–50 sit on a loop surrounded by dunes. The whole section hears the waves crashing on the flat beach, providing a peaceful aural backdrop. Waterfront areas have no shade or privacy to speak of; the upper area has some shade. Beach sites have flat, paved parking, while the upper campground sites have gravel parking, a few primitive sites, and no views. Weather here has a knack for changing, so bring cold-weather rain gear just in case.

BASICS

Operated By: Washington State Parks & Recreation. **Open:** All year. **Site Assignment:** On arrival, reservations. **Registration:** At park office or self pay station in campground. **Fee:** Apr. 1–Sept. 30 $20, Oct. 1-Mar. 30 $19, extra vehicle $6; V, MC, D, cash, check. **Parking:** At site.

FACILITIES

Number of RV-Only Sites: 85. **Number of Tent-Only Sites:** 5. **Number of Multipurpose Sites:** 35. **Hookups:** Electric (20, 30 amps), water, sewer. **Each Site:** Picnic table, fire ring. **Dump Station:** Yes. **Laundry:** No. **Pay Phone:** Yes. **Rest Rooms and Showers:** Yes. **Fuel:** No. **Propane:** No. **Internal Roads:** Paved. **RV Service:** No. **Market:** In Port Townsend, 5 mi. south. **Restaurant:** In Port Townsend, 5 mi. south. **General Store:** No. **Vending:** No. **Swimming Pool:** No. **Playground:** No. **Other:** Boat launch, beach, convention center, Military museums, hiking trails. **Activities:** Hiking, boating, fishing (check on regulations & seasons). **Nearby Attractions:** Whale-watching, fishing, boating, Olympic National Park, Olympic National Forest, shellfishing. **Additional Information:** Port Townsend Chamber of Commerce, (360) 385-2722.

RESTRICTIONS

Pets: On leash only (6 ft. max length). **Fires:** In fire pits only. **Alcoholic Beverages:** At site only. **Vehicle Maximum Length:** 40 ft. **Other:** Do not collect driftwood for fires, do not play in driftwood (very dangerous).

TO GET THERE

From I-20 east, follow hwy. into Port Towsend, turn left on Kearney St., drive 0.4 mi., then turn right on Blaine St. Drive 1 block and turn left on Walker, which changes names several times and even forks once (take the left side). When the road dead-ends, turn right and drive 1 block; campground entrance is on the left.

RANDLE

Takhlakh Campground

Cowlitz Valley Ranger District, P.O. Box 670, Randle 98377. T: (360) 497-1120; www.fs.fed.us/gpnf.

RV n/a Tent ★★★★

Beauty: ★★★★★	Site Privacy: ★★
Spaciousness: ★★★	Quiet: ★★★★★
Security: ★★★★	Cleanliness: ★★★★
Insect Control: ★★★	Facilities: ★★★

Just imagine: you're sitting at your site at Takhlakh Lake gazing out at a picture-perfect view of Mount Adams. Most of the 54 tent sites offer views of the lake and the mountain through stands of Douglas fir, Engelmann spruce, pine, and subalpine fir. There is a campground host in attendance at Takhlakh, so anything you can't find, feel free to inquire. There is no easy way to get to Takhlakh, which is part of its appeal. The confusing network of Forest Service roads can be downright irritating, too, if you don't have a good map of the area. If you've come in search of lazy fishing opportunities, Takhlakh is a treat. Only non-motorized boats are allowed on the glassy waters. With an Ansel Adams–like scene at your back, cast your line, and wait for the trout lurking in the frigid glacial depths to find you.

BASICS

Operated By: Northwest Land Management. **Open:** mid-Jun.–mid-Sept. **Site Assignment:** 70% of sites are reserveable; call (877) 444-6777; $8.25 fee. **Registration:** Not necessary. **Fee:** $11. **Parking:** At site.

FACILITIES

Number of Multipurpose Sites: 54. **Hookups:** Inquire at campground. **Dump Station:** Inquire at campground. **Laundry:** No. **Pay Phone:** No. **Rest Rooms and Showers:** No. **Fuel:** Inquire at campground. **Propane:** 3 mi. In Randle. **Internal Roads:** Paved. **RV Service:** No. **Market:** 3 mi. In Randle. **Restaurant:** 3 mi. **General Store:** Yes. **Vending:** No. **Swimming Pool:** No. **Playground:** No. **Other:** Campground host. **Activities:** Fishing, hiking, mountain biking. **Nearby Attractions:** Gifford Pinchot National Forest, Mount Adams Wilderness, Trout Lake, Lava Fields, New Takhtakh Meadow. **Additional Information:** www.fs.fed.us/gpnf.

RESTRICTIONS

Pets: On leash only. **Fires:** In fire pit. **Alcoholic Beverages:** Allowed. **Vehicle Maximum Length:** 21 ft. **Other:** Non-motorized boats only.

TO GET THERE

From Randle, take CR 3 off WA Rte. 12 at Randle. Go south for 2 mi. to FS 23. In another 29 mi., turn north onto FS 2329. The campground is a little over 1 mi. in. From Trout Lake, take FS 80 north to its intersection with FS 23. The campground is nearly the same distance from Trout Lake as from Randle, but the road twists and turns with vaguely marked intersections. The turnoff onto FS 2329 will be to the right coming from Trout Lake.

REPUBLIC

Swan Lake Campground

c/o Republic Ranger Station, P.O. Box 468, Republic 99166. T: (509) 775-3305; www.fs.fed.us/r6/colville.

RV ★★★ Tent ★★★

Beauty: ★★★	Site Privacy: ★★★
Spaciousness: ★★★	Quiet: ★★★★
Security: ★★★★	Cleanliness: ★★★★
Insect Control: ★★	Facilities: ★★★

The Swan Lake Campground has no headliner attractions. That's why people who have checked out the area come back year after year. It has a little bit of everything, but not enough of anything to attract crowds. Once a ranger station, Swan Lake retains much of the Civilian Conservation Corps' handiwork. The kitchen shelter built by the CCC in 1933 is the only structure of its kind on the Colville forest. The structure is the epicenter of all campground activit; it is a sanctuary in storms and the gathering place for everything from mountain biking groups to wedding parties. The nifty 2.2-mile trail circumnavigating the lake is particularly attractive to seniors and parents with kids. Although it's fun for mountain biking, most fat-tire enthusiasts head out to roughly 50 miles of single- and double-track trails that are blossoming on logging routes closed to motor vehicles. Popular routes go past beaver ponds, where the occasional moose can be found, and along Sheep Mountain, with views of the Kettle River Range.

BASICS

Operated By: Colville National Forest. **Open:** Apr.–Oct., but water & garbage collection only from Memorial Day–Labor Day. **Site Assignment:** First come, first served. **Registration:** Not necessary. **Fee:** $8. **Parking:** At site & at boat launch & trailhead.

FACILITIES

Number of Multipurpose Sites: 25. **Hookups:** Inquire at campground. **Dump Station:** No. **Laundry:** No. **Pay Phone:** No. **Rest Rooms and Showers:** Vault toilets. **Fuel:** No. **Propane:** No. **Internal Roads:** Paved. **RV Service:** No. **Market:** No. **Restaurant:** No. **General Store:** No. **Vend-**

ing: No. **Swimming Pool:** No. **Playground:** No. **Other:** Group site, common cooking shelter, 12 water spigots, boat launch. **Activities:** Fishing, boating, biking, hiking. **Nearby Attractions:** Long Lake (dedicated to fly-fishing only), Stonerose Interpretive Center (in Republic). **Additional Information:** www.fs.fed.us/r6/colville.

Restrictions

Pets: On leash only. **Fires:** In fire pit. **Alcoholic Beverages:** At site only. **Vehicle Maximum Length:** 24 ft., but several pull-throughs available for big rigs. **Other:** Fishing license required, gas motors prohibited.

To Get There

From Republic on SR 20, drive south on SR 21 for 8.5 mi. and turn west on Scatter Creek Rd. (No. 53). Follow this paved road about 12 mi., turning right just before Long Lake to reach the Swan Lake Campground.

ROCHESTER

Outback RV Park

19100 Huntington St. Southwest, Rochester 98579. T: (360) 273-0585; www.outbackrvpark.com; outbackrvpark@hotmail.com.

RV ★★★ Tent ★

Beauty: ★ Site Privacy: ★
Spaciousness: ★★★ Quiet: ★★
Security: ★★★ Cleanliness: ★★★★
Insect Control: ★★ Facilities: ★★

Outback RV Park, located halfway between Seattle and Portland (its claim to fame), makes a good place to stay if getting off the road sounds attractive for a night. Recreational facilities are minimal, but the park has easy access to the interstate from a rural, low-traffic area. Arranged in several parallel rows across a flat field, sites have flat, gravel surfaces and easily navigable access. The grounds have a defoliated appearance, with little shade and only patches of grass. Sites 39–55 sit closer to a major road than some; otherwise sites are indistinguishable from one another. The campground stays open all year, winters in this part of Washington have relentlessly gray, rainy, cold weather.

Basics

Operated By: Outback RV Park. **Open:** All year. **Site Assignment:** On arrival, reservations. **Registration:** At office, after hours see info outside of office. **Fee:** For 4 people, 2 adults & 2 children, full $22, Tent $14, Phone $2, extra person $2; V, MC, personal checks, cash. **Parking:** At site, limited off site.

Facilities

Number of RV-Only Sites: 58. **Number of Tent-Only Sites:** 10. **Hookups:** Electric (20, 30, 50 amps), water, cable, phone. **Dump Station:** No. **Laundry:** Yes. **Pay Phone:** Yes. **Rest Rooms and Showers:** Yes. **Fuel:** No. **Propane:** Yes. **Internal Roads:** Paved, gravel. **RV Service:** No. **Market:** 2 mi. west in Rochester. **Restaurant:** 2 mi. west in Rochester. **General Store:** Yes. **Vending:** No. **Swimming Pool:** No. **Playground:** Yes. **Other:** Club room, exercise equipment (1 Stairmaster), basketball, horseshoes, video rentals. **Activities:** Inquire at campground. **Nearby Attractions:** Olympia, Seattle, Tacoma, Puget Sound, Mt. Rainier, Washington Pacific Coast. **Additional Information:** Washington State Tourism Board, (360) 725-5052.

Restrictions

Pets: On leash only. **Fires:** Portable fire enclosures, central fire pits only, ask mgmt. **Alcoholic Beverages:** At site only. **Vehicle Maximum Length:** None.

To Get There

From I-5 Exit 88, drive 2.6 mi. west on Hwy. 12 west; the entrance is on the left.

SEATTLE

Lake Pleasant RV Park

24025 Bothell Everett Hwy. Southeast, Bothell 98021. T: (800) 742-0386 or (425) 487-1785

RV ★★★ Tent n/a

Beauty: ★★★ Site Privacy: ★★★
Spaciousness: ★★ Quiet: ★★
Security: ★★★ Cleanliness: ★★★★
Insect Control: ★★ Facilities: ★★★

Lake Pleasant RV Park, off of I-405 in the northeast suburbs of Seattle, has to be the nicest RV park in the metro area. The garden-like grounds, surrounded by oak, pine, and blackberry bramble–covered hills, sit on the edge of small, man-made Lake Pleasant. The willows on the lake's edge, the occasional red Japanese maple, and the ducks only add to the charm of this very green park with paved, grass-encircled sites. The best back-ins (sites 1–14) and the best pull-throughs (sites 15–33) have privacy created by hedges of small pines and cedars, and they sit on the lake's edge. Most other sites also have some form of privacy hedging. The least-desirable sites (back-in sites 201–228) are cramped with no privacy. The quiet grounds' location in relation to downtown Seattle is less than 20 miles, but unless the day is Sunday at six in the morning, expect lots of traffic. Chilly temperatures and rain abound in all seasons except summer, making summers the best time to visit the Puget Sound area.

Basics

Operated By: Lake Pleasant RV Park. **Open:** All Year. **Site Assignment:** First come, first served; reservations. **Registration:** At office, after hours at drop box in front of office. **Fee:** $28, Cash, check; V, MC. **Parking:** At site.

Facilities

Number of RV-Only Sites: 196. **Number of Tent-Only Sites:** n/a. **Hookups:** Electric (30 amps), water, sewer. **Each Site:** Picnic table. **Dump Station:** Yes. **Laundry:** Yes. **Pay Phone:** Yes. **Rest Rooms and Showers:** Yes. **Fuel:** No. **Propane:** Yes. **Internal Roads:** No. **RV Service:** No. **Market:** 2 mi. South in Bothell. **Restaurant:** 2 mi. south in Bothell. **General Store:** No. **Vending:** Yes. **Swimming Pool:** No. **Playground:** Yes. **Other:** Foot paths, volleyball net, horseshoe pit. **Activities:** Pancake breakfasts (monthly in summer), license-less fishing, blueberry picking, hiking. **Nearby Attractions:** Puget Sound, Seattle Center, Pike Place Market, fishing, night life, hiking, whale-watching charter. **Additional Information:** Greater Seattle Chamber of Commerce, (206) 389-7200.

Restrictions

Pets: On leash only, max length 8 ft.; no fighting breeds. **Fires:** No open fires. **Alcoholic Beverages:** At site only. **Vehicle Maximum Length:** None. **Other:** No swimming, boating in lake; no feeding of waterfowl.

To Get There

From I-405 Exit 26, drive south on Hwy. 27 for 1.2 mi.; entrance on right.

SEATTLE

Trailer Inns RV Park

15531 Southeast 37th, Bellevue 98006. T: (425) 747-9181; trailerinnsrv.uswestdex.com/page3.html.

RV ★★★★ Tent ★

Beauty: ★★ Site Privacy: ★
Spaciousness: ★★★ Quiet: ★
Security: ★★ Cleanliness: ★★★★★
Insect Control: ★★ Facilities: ★★★★★

Trailer Inns, in the east Seattle suburb of Bellevue, offers the most amenities of any park near the city. A pool table, indoor pool, and sauna are just a few of the facilities that make this park stand out. Totally paved over, the flat camping area's layout of parallel rows doesn't have any grass, but it does have some trees and landscaping. The small campground makes good use of its allotted space; campsites have a good amount of room for an urban park. Recommended sites include back-ins 2–7 and 21–42. The pull-throughs here provide less room to the sides than back-ins do. Campsites 43–66, which are back-ins with no dividers in the rear, have more of a cramped feeling than other back-ins in the park. Like all urban parks, this one has some ambient urban noise, but it's not intolerable. Also, for pop-up tent trailers or pick-up piggy backs ,there are some smaller sites near the office. Visit Seattle during summer for the best weather.

Basics

Operated By: Trailer Inns RV Park. **Open:** All year. **Site Assignment:** On arrival, reservations (deposit: $25; refund 24 hours notice for cancellation). **Registration:** At office, after hours see info at door. **Fee:** For 2 adults, 2 children & 2 pets, Supersite (largest)–$33, pull-through $31, Double $27, Single $22, Tent $18, extra people $5; V, MC, cash. **Parking:** At site.

Facilities

Number of RV-Only Sites: 109. **Number of Tent-Only Sites:** n/a. **Hookups:** Electric (30, 50 amps), water, sewer, cable. **Dump Station:** No. **Laundry:** Yes. **Pay Phone:** Yes. **Rest Rooms and Showers:** Yes. **Fuel:** No. **Propane:** Yes. **Internal Roads:** Paved. **RV Service:** No. **Market:** A few blocks west. **Restaurant:** A few blocks west. **General Store:** No. **Vending:** Yes. **Swimming Pool:** Yes. **Playground:** Yes. **Other:** Game room w/ pool table & arcade, indoor hot tub, indoor sauna, indoor BBQ, TV room w/ big screen & fireplace, outdoor gas grill. **Activities:** Inquire at campground. **Nearby Attractions:** Seattle & Puget Sound, Snoqualmie Falls, skiing. **Additional Information:** Seattle Visitor Info Center, (206) 461-5840; www.seeseattle.org.

RESTRICTIONS

Pets: On leash only, 2 pets max. **Fires:** No open fires, no charcoal. **Alcoholic Beverages:** At site only. **Vehicle Maximum Length:** None. **Other:** Properly maintained RVs only allowed on property.

TO GET THERE

From I-90 Exit 11, take the third exit ramp to 150 Ave. SE. Drive south and turn left at first light onto Frontage Rd. Drive a few blocks on Frontage; when the road separates with a median, stay on far right. The campground entrance is the third driveway after the median starts.

SEATTLE (EVERETT)

Lakeside RV Park

12321 Hwy. 99 South, Everett 98204. T: (425) 347-2970 or (425) 742-7333 or reservations only (800) 468-7275; F: (425) 347-9052.

RV: ★★★ Tent: ★★

Beauty: ★★★ Site Privacy: ★★★
Spaciousness: ★★ Quiet: ★★
Security: ★★★ Cleanliness: ★★★★
Insect Control: ★★ Facilities: ★★

Lakeside RV Park, located in the suburban burg of Everett, has easy access to services (such as groceries and shopsl) and a quick route to Seattle, some 20 minutes south. The park has laundry, bathroom facilities, and a stocked lake for fishing (runoff feeds the lake, so eat your catch at your own risk). All back-in RV sites come with paved surfaces and are divided by cedar hedges that create a little privacy. The grounds have a cramped feeling but a good location. Back-in sites 127–139 back up to a hedge of deciduous shrubbery and provide the best space and privacy. The even-numbered sites 76–104 are the best paved pull-throughs (for space). Other than the above, the RV sites have a fairly homogenous layout, and sites 1–15 sit in a high traffic area. The tenting area has fine-grit gravel pads surrounded by grass, no privacy, and cannot accommodate large tents. Seattle has tourism year-round, but summer brings the best weather and avoids the stereotypical rains of winter.

BASICS

Operated By: PFC Mgmt. **Open:** All year. **Site Assignment:** On arrival, reservations (deposit: 1 night stay; refund: 24 hours notice less $6 cancellation fee). **Registration:** At office, after hours pay in morning or drop in office door. **Fee:** Full $38.48, Tent $15.33 (V, MC, D, personal checks, cash). **Parking:** At site, additional parking available.

FACILITIES

Number of RV-Only Sites: 150. **Number of Tent-Only Sites:** 9. **Hookups:** Electric (20, 30, 50 amps), water, sewer, cable. **Dump Station:** No. **Laundry:** Yes. **Pay Phone:** Yes. **Rest Rooms and Showers:** Yes. **Fuel:** No. **Propane:** Yes. **Internal Roads:** Paved. **RV Service:** No. **Market:** South or north on Hwy. 99 (close by). **Restaurant:** South or North on Hwy. 99 (close by). **General Store:** No. **Vending:** Yes. **Swimming Pool:** No. **Playground:** Yes. **Other:** RV & boat storage, horseshoes, lake fishing, fishing dock, jogging path around lake, espresso stand (just in front of park, separate enterprise). **Activities:** Fishing (per fish charges & per site limits apply). **Nearby Attractions:** Seattle. **Additional Information:** Seattle Visitor Info Center, (206) 461-5840; www.seeseattle.org.

RESTRICTIONS

Pets: Short leash only. **Fires:** No open fires. **Alcoholic Beverages:** At site only. **Vehicle Maximum Length:** None. **Other:** Visitor parking for short term use (2 hours).

TO GET THERE

From I-5 Exit 186 (128th St. SW) drive west on 128th for 1.3 mi. Turn left on Hwy. 99 at Home Depot.

SEATTLE

Twin Cedars RV Park

17826 Hwy. 99 North, Lynnwood 98037. T: (425) 742-5540 or (800) 878-9304; F: (425) 745-2200; twincedars@pcfre.com.

RV: ★★ Tent: n/a

Beauty: ★ Site Privacy: ★
Spaciousness: ★★ Quiet: ★★
Security: ★★ Cleanliness: ★
Insect Control: ★★ Facilities: ★

Twin Cedars RV Park in Lynnwood has a very convenient location on Hwy. 99 just north of Seattle; location is only draw here. Sites consist of gravel with a small amount of surrounding grass. The best campsites, sites 10–20, are the furthest from the loud industrial facility next door; conversely, the worst, sites 58–70, sit the closest to the industrial area. The park has no landscaping, a drainage ditch running through it, and patchy grass at best. In Seattle, the best weather happens during the summer, but the city has tourist attractions open year-round.

BASICS

Operated By: PCF mgmt. **Open:** All year. **Site Assignment:** On arrival, reservations (deposit: 1 night stay; refund: 24 hours notice less $6 fee). **Registration:** At office, after hours check board at office, pay in morning. **Fee:** Full $35.08, 7th day free (V, MC, cash). **Parking:** At site, limited off site.

FACILITIES

Number of RV-Only Sites: 69. **Number of Tent-Only Sites:** n/a. **Hookups:** Electric (20, 30, 50 amps), water, sewer, cable. **Dump Station:** Yes. **Laundry:** Yes. **Pay Phone:** Yes. **Rest Rooms and Showers:** Yes. **Fuel:** No. **Propane:** Yes. **Internal Roads:** Paved. **RV Service:** No. **Market:** Across Hwy. 99. **Restaurant:** Across Hwy. 99. **General Store:** No. **Vending:** Yes. **Swimming Pool:** No. **Playground:** No. **Other:** Club house w/ TV, VCR, & small aerobic area; horseshoes, common picnic area. **Activities:** Inquire at campground. **Nearby Attractions:** Seattle. **Additional Information:** Seattle Visitor Info Center, (206) 461-5840; www.seeseattle.org.

RESTRICTIONS

Pets: On leash only. **Fires:** No open fires. **Alcoholic Beverages:** At site only. **Vehicle Maximum Length:** 40 ft.

TO GET THERE

From I-5 Exit 183, drive west 1. 6 mi. on 164th Southwest. This turns into 44th Ave West. Drive 0.5 mi., turn right on 176th St. SW, and drive 0.3 mi., then turn left on SR 99, go 0.2 mi., and the entrance is on the right behind Avis Rent-A-Car.

SEATTLE/TACOMA

Seattle-Tacoma KOA

5801 South 212th St., Kent 98032. T: (253) 872-8652; F: (253) 395-1782; www.koa.com; seattlekoa@aol.com.

RV: ★★★ Tent: ★★

Beauty: ★★ Site Privacy: ★
Spaciousness: ★★★ Quiet: ★★
Security: ★ Cleanliness: ★★★
Insect Control: ★★ Facilities: ★★

KOA Seattle-Tacoma, located between the two cities in Kent, offers easy access to the metropolitan areas. The campground consists of a flat field of sites laid out in parallel rows with two different sections. One section has more shade, but it only has dirt- and gravel-surfaced sites. The other section has paved surfaces and a more maintained appearance, but no shade. No sites have privacy. The best sites in the first section (sites 26–36) have shade from tall, bushy Japanese maples. In the less-desirable section, sites 58–109 sit furthest from the traffic noise of a nearby road. The tenting area (sites 48–57) in the back of the park have grass and dirt surfaces and lots of shade. Sites 110–133 and 1–14 sit near a road and should be avoided due to noise. Weather-wise the best time to visit the area is during the summer.

BASICS

Operated By: Seattle Tacoma KOA. **Open:** All year. **Site Assignment:** On arrival, reservations (deposit: 1 night stay; refund: 24 hours cancellation). **Registration:** At office, after hours register w/ security or pay in morning. **Fee:** For 2 people, Deluxe Full (50 amp) $42.95, Regular Full $35.95, Water-electric $32.95, No hookup $24.95, extra people over the age of 5 $2.95 (V, MC, D, cash, personal checks). **Parking:** At site, limited off site.

FACILITIES

Number of RV-Only Sites: 160. **Number of Tent-Only Sites:** 20. **Hookups:** Electric (20, 30 amps), water, sewer, cable, phone. **Each Site:** Picnic table. **Dump Station:** Yes. **Laundry:** Yes. **Pay Phone:** Yes. **Rest Rooms and Showers:** Yes. **Fuel:** No. **Propane:** Yes. **Internal Roads:** Paved. **RV Service:** No. **Market:** South in Kent. **Restaurant:** South in Kent. **General Store:** Yes. **Vending:** No. **Swimming Pool:** Yes. **Playground:** Yes. **Other:** Arcade, day room (used for movies, breakfast), tour pickups & booking, vhs rentals, bike rentals (summer). **Activities:** Nightly movies, breakfast for sale in summer. **Nearby Attractions:** Seattle. **Additional Information:** Seattle Visitor Info Center, (206) 461-5840; www.seeseattle.org.

RESTRICTIONS

Pets: On leash only. **Fires:** No open fires, charcoal ok. **Alcoholic Beverages:** At site only. **Vehicle Maximum Length:** 60 ft.

TO GET THERE

From I-5 Exit 152, take Orillia road and drive south to campground.

SEQUIM
Dungeness Recreation Area

223 East 4th St., Port Angeles 98362. T: (360) 417-2291; www.clallam.net/park/park_dungeness1.htm.

RV ★★★ Tent ★★★★

Beauty: ★★★★★ Site Privacy: ★★★★★
Spaciousness: ★★★★ Quiet: ★★★★
Security: ★★★★ Cleanliness: ★★★★
Insect Control: ★★★ Facilities: ★★

Dungeness Spit, the main attraction in the Dungeness Recreation Area/National Wildlife Re-fuge, is the longest natural sand spit in the United States. Arching nearly seven miles into the Strait of Juan de Fuca from the Olympic Peninsula, this unique landform averages only 100 yards wide for its entire length. The entire expanse of spits, tidelands, wetlands, landmarks, and adjoining surf forms Dungeness National Wildlife Refuge. The Dungeness Recreation Area campsites are well-designed around two loops, affording ultimate privacy with dense undergrowth between sites. About a third of the sites are spaced along a high bluff that overlooks the Strait of Juan de Fuca with million-dollar views. Despite the moderate year-round climate, the campground is open only from February 1 to October 1. Summer can be quite busy, so you may want to try the off-season. In addition to the ever-popular beachcombing, other activities in the park include horseback riding (separate equestrian trail and unloading area), game bird hunting in designated areas, and good old-fashioned picnicking.

BASICS

Operated By: Clallam County Parks Dept. **Open:** Feb. 1–Oct. 1. **Site Assignment:** First come, first served. **Registration:** At park information booth from daylight-dusk. **Fee:** $10. **Parking:** At site.

FACILITIES

Number of RV-Only Sites: Inquire at campground. **Number of Tent-Only Sites:** 0. **Number of Multipurpose Sites:** 67. **Hookups:** None. **Each Site:** Picnic table, fire pit, shade trees. **Dump Station:** Yes. **Laundry:** No. **Pay Phone:** Yes. **Rest Rooms and Showers:** Yes. **Fuel:** 5 mi. in Sequim. **Propane:** 5 mi. **Internal Roads:** Paved. **RV Service:** No. **Market:** 5 mi. **Restaurant:** 5 mi. **General Store:** 5 mi. **Vending:** No. **Swimming Pool:** No. **Playground:** No. **Other:** Firewood. **Activities:** Equestrian trails, hiking, hunting, shell fishing, beachcombing. **Nearby Attractions:** Dungeness Wildlife Refuge, Agriculture Tour, Cungeness Lighthouse. **Additional Information:** www.clallam.net/park/park_dungeness1.htm.

RESTRICTIONS

Pets: On leash only. **Fires:** In fire pit. **Alcoholic Beverages:** Prohibited. **Vehicle Maximum Length:** None. **Other:** No dogs on beach.

TO GET THERE

From Sequim (17 mi. east of Port Angeles), drive 5 mi. west on US 101 to Kitchen-Dick Ln. Turn north, and drive 3 mi., watching for signs to the recreation area campground entrance.

SEQUIM
Port Angeles-Sequim KOA

80 O'Brian Rd., Port Angeles 98362. T: (360) 457-5916; F: (360) 417-0759; www.koa.com; horizon@olypen.com.

RV ★★ Tent ★★

Beauty: ★★★ Site Privacy: ★
Spaciousness: ★★ Quiet: ★★
Security: ★★★ Cleanliness: ★★
Insect Control: ★★ Facilities: ★★★

KOA Port Angeles-Sequim, seven miles east of Port Angeles on Hwy. 101, has the most in-park recreational facilities near Dungeness Spit and Olympic National Park. The hotel-like recreation is not astounding, but it's an alternative to the natural or no-recreation parks that dot the rain shadow area of the northern Olympic Peninsula. The grass and gravel full hookup campsites (sites 1–18) have a view of the surrounding mountains, but they are situated without shade or privacy next to truck-heavy Hwy. 101. The quieter water and electric sites sit in grass and lightly shaded meadows with obscured or nonexistent views of the surrounding mountains. These campsites (sites 21–33) are the best, though cluttered; they sit near the next-best, which are no-hookup sites A–G. Campsites A–G have more space because they have no rear neighbors. Weather here stays mild and sunny, but most tourist attractions in the area are fully operational only in the summer.

BASICS

Operated By: KOA Port Angeles-Sequim. **Open:** Apr. 1–Oct. 31. **Site Assignment:** First come, first served: Reservations (deposit: 1 night's stay; refund: 72 hours cancellation). **Registration:** At office, after hours see directions in office window. **Fee:** For 2 people, full: $29, Water-electric: $26, No hookup: $22, Tents: $22, extra person (greater than 5 years old): $4, extra vehicle (over 1 camping unit plus 1 vehicle): $5, V, MC, cash. **Parking:** At site.

FACILITIES

Number of RV-Only Sites: 84. **Number of Tent-Only Sites:** 11. **Hookups:** Electric (20, 30 amps), water, sewer, cable. **Each Site:** Picnic table, fire ring. **Dump Station:** Yes. **Laundry:** Yes. **Pay Phone:** Yes. **Rest Rooms and Showers:** Yes. **Fuel:** No. **Propane:** Yes. **Internal Roads:** Gravel. **RV Service:** No. **Market:** 7 mi. west in Sequim. **Restaurant:** 7 mi. west in Sequim. **General Store:** Yes. **Vending:** Yes. **Swimming Pool:** Yes. **Playground:** Yes. **Other:** Game room (w/ a pool table, video games, ping pong), hot tub, video rentals, badminton, volleyball, basketball, mini-golf, banana-seat bike rentals, horseshoes, tetherball. **Activities:** Kite flying, summer hay rides, planned activities. **Nearby Attractions:** Olympic National Park, scuba diving, boating, charter fishing, hiking, Dungeness Recreation Area, seasonal local events, Deer Park, Sol Duc valley. **Additional Information:** Port Angeles Chamber of Commerce (360) 452-2363.

RESTRICTIONS

Pets: On leash only. **Fires:** In fire pits only. **Alcoholic Beverages:** At site only. **Vehicle Maximum Length:** None. **Other:** Max 6 people per site.

TO GET THERE

Located off Hwy. 101 7 mi. east of Port Angeles and 8 mi. west of Sequim very near the Washington State Patrol Sattelite office. If headed eastbound, turn right onto O'Brian Rd. and drive half a block; entrance is on right.

SEQUIM
Rainbow's End RV Park

261831 Hwy. 101, Sequim 98382. T: (360) 683-3863; rainborv@olypen.com.

RV ★★★ Tent ★★

Beauty: ★★★ Site Privacy: ★
Spaciousness: ★★ Quiet: ★★
Security: ★★★ Cleanliness: ★★★★
Insect Control: ★★ Facilities: ★★★★

Rainbow's End RV Park, a small, attractively landscaped RV park on Hwy. 101 near Sequim, lacks on-site recreation but provides a good location for access to the numerous Northern Olympic Peninsula attractions. Short coastal pines, weeping willows, and flowering hardwoods partially shade both the gravel sites and a small trout pond located in the middle of the park. The medium sized trout in the pond are for feeding only. Site layout creates a mildly cramped environment with the exception of the more spacious sites F–G. The quietest options, sites 11–21, sit furthest from the highway, and the shady tent area consists of a section of flat grass. All tent and RV sites lack privacy. The Northern Olympic Peninsula has mild weather all year, but its largest attraction—the national park,—is fully operational only in the summer.

BASICS

Operated By: Rainbow's End RV Park. **Open:** All year. **Site Assignment:** First come, first served; reservations (deposit 1 night's stay; refund: 72 hours cancellation). **Registration:** At office; after hours see host. **Fee:** For two people:, Full: $22.50, tent: $15, extra person>10 years old: $2, Under 10 years old, free. V, MC, cash, check. **Parking:** At site.

FACILITIES

Number of RV-Only Sites: 39. **Number of Tent-Only Sites:** 15. **Hookups:** Electric (20, 30, 50 amps), water, sewer, cable, phone, central data port. **Each Site:** Picnic table. **Dump Station:** Yes. **Laundry:** Yes. **Pay Phone:** Yes. **Rest Rooms and Showers:** Yes. **Fuel:** No. **Propane:** Yes. **Internal Roads:** Paved. **RV Service:** No. **Market:** 2 mi. east in Sequim. **Restaurant:** Two mi. east in Sequim. **General Store:** No. **Vending:** No. **Swimming Pool:** No. **Playground:** Yes. **Other:** Reserveable clubhouse, basketball goal, horseshoes, volleyball. **Activities:** Summer weekend BBQ's & potlucks, crafts based on tenants. **Nearby Attractions:**

Olympic National Park, Dungeness Spit, Recreation area, & National Wildlife Refuge, Olympic Game Farm, Dungeness Lighthouse, local festivals. **Additional Information:** Sequim-Dungeness Chamber of Commerce, (800) 737-8462.

Restrictions

Pets: Well behaved & On leash only. **Fires:** In fire pits in tent area only. **Alcoholic Beverages:** At site only. **Vehicle Maximum Length:** Fifty ft. **Other:** Have to have a good time or you can't leave.

To Get There

The park is located 1.5 mi. west of the western-most Sequim Exit on Hwy. 101 on the coastal side. The park has a large sign and is surrounded by privacy fencing.

SILVER CREEK

Harmony Lakeside RV Park

563 Rte. 122, Silver Creek 98585. T: (360) 983-3804; F: (360) 983-8345; www.harmonylakesidervpark.com; info@harmonylakesidervpark.com.

RV: ★★★★ Tent: ★★

Beauty: ★★★★★ Site Privacy: ★★
Spaciousness: ★★★ Quiet: ★★★★
Security: ★ Cleanliness: ★★★★
Insect Control: ★★ Facilities: ★★★

Harmony Lakeside RV Park on Mayfield Lake is between I-5 and routes to Mt. Rainier and St. Helens. The beautifully manicured grounds run up to the lake's edge; the park also has several small, river-stone-lined ponds with fountains, brightly colored koi, and small bronze statues. The sites and roads are well-maintained gravel. There are no tent sites, but tent campers can set up in a water and electric site if they don't mind the gravel. Sites 1–27 stand on two loops in a grassy field with shade and painstakingly shaped hedges. This section is often reserved well in advance, making it hard to get into. Sites 1–8 have a beautiful view of the water. The second set of loops run through a manicured fairy tale–like forest of beautiful moss interspersed with grass, tall cedars, large dead tree trunks with beautiful secondary growth, and views of the lake some 20 feet below. Sites 66–69 in this section have lots of space and sit right on the edge of the cliffs. The bonsai-like artfulness of the groundskeepers makes this already small, quiet campground even more charming. Visit late in spring or early fall for the best weather and slowest-paced days.

Basics

Operated By: Harmony Lakeside RV. **Open:** All year. **Site Assignment:** On arrival, reservations. **Registration:** At office, after hours see drop. **Fee:** Full $27, Water electric $24, Pets $2 per pet per day, V, MC, cash. **Parking:** At site.

Facilities

Number of RV-Only Sites: 80. **Number of Tent-Only Sites:** 38. **Hookups:** Electric (20, 30, 50 amps), water, sewer, cable. **Each Site:** Picnic table, fire ring. **Dump Station:** Yes. **Laundry:** No. **Pay Phone:** Yes. **Rest Rooms and Showers:** Yes. **Fuel:** No. **Propane:** No. **Internal Roads:** Gravel. **RV Service:** No. **Market:** Near Mossyrock. **Restaurant:** Near Mossyrock. **General Store:** No. **Vending:** Yes. **Swimming Pool:** No. **Playground:** No. **Other:** Reception hall, both powered & non-powered boats, volleyball, badminton, horseshoes. **Activities:** Fishing, watersports. **Nearby Attractions:** Mt. Rainier, Mt. St. Helens, fish hatcheries, Seattle, Olympia. **Additional Information:** Washington State Tourism Board, (360) 725-5052.

Restrictions

Pets: Leash Only (fee required). **Fires:** In fire pits only. **Alcoholic Beverages:** At site only. **Vehicle Maximum Length:** None. **Other:** No firewood gathering.

To Get There

On I-5, drive to Exit 68 (Hwy. 12 Morton-Yakima). Once on US 12, go east 21 mi. At the Mossyrock blinker, turn left. Drive 2.5 mi. on SR 122 and the entrance is on the left.

SKAMANIA

Beacon Rock State Park

3483L WA Rte. 14, Skamania 98648. T: (360) 902-8844; www.parks.wa.gov.

RV: ★★ Tent: ★★★★

Beauty: ★★★★ Site Privacy: ★★★★
Spaciousness: ★★★★ Quiet: ★★★★★
Security: ★★★★ Cleanliness: ★★★★★
Insect Control: ★★ Facilities: ★★

The Northwest's longest and largest river, cutting a huge sea-level pass through the Cascade Mountains, teams with the world's second-largest monolith to produce the main attractions for campers at Beacon Rock State Park. Beacon Rock, once known as Castle Rock, towers 848 feet above the mighty Columbia River in the Columbia River Gorge National Scenic Area and is second only to the Rock of Gibraltar in size. Aside from the Beacon Rock trail (which is a must), a network of other paths throughout the park's interior offers destinations to Rodney Falls and Hardy Falls. Sitting beside the falls as they cascade down Hardy Creek, a forested mountain at your back, watching birds flit and chipmunks scamper, and enjoying the fragrant wisps of campfire smoke wafting past are all ingredients for as fine a Northwest outing as anyone could hope for. The campground is tucked against a forested hillside on the north side of WA Rte. 14. Tent sites are spaced comfortably around the circular paved drive that winds up from the river. The main camp area is an older camp in a forested setting suited more for tents than RVs. There are a limited number of sites that accommodate RVs over 20 feet.

Basics

Operated By: Washington State Parks & Recreation Commission. **Open:** Apr. 1–Oct. **Site Assignment:** Reservations for group camping only; otherwise first come first served. **Registration:** Self-registration. **Fee:** $11. **Parking:** At site.

Facilities

Number of RV-Only Sites: 6. **Number of Tent-Only Sites:** 29. **Hookups:** None. **Each Site:** Picnic table, fire grill, shade trees. **Dump Station:** Yes. **Laundry:** No. **Pay Phone:** Yes. **Rest Rooms and Showers:** Yes. **Fuel:** No. **Propane:** No. **Internal Roads:** Paved. **RV Service:** No. **Market:** No. **Restaurant:** No. **General Store:** No. **Vending:** No. **Swimming Pool:** No. **Playground:** Yes. **Other:** Kitchen, showers for fee, boat launch, clock. **Activities:** Hiking, boating, mountain biking, fishing, rock climbing. **Nearby Attractions:** Rodney Falls, Hardy Falls, Table Mountain, Hamilton Mountain. **Additional Information:** www.parks.wa.gov.

Restrictions

Pets: On leash only. **Fires:** In fire pit. **Alcoholic Beverages:** Allowed. **Vehicle Maximum Length:** 50 ft.

To Get There

Go east on SR 14 from its junction with I-205 at Ellsworth. The wide expanse of the Columbia is your constant companion as you drive approximately 30 mi. on the two-lane route (Lewis and Clark Hwy.) to the park's entrance. You'll pass the base of Beacon Rock as you are watching for the signs to the turnoff for the park. Be aware that the road signs around here are a bit confusing, and traffic gets congested when motorists slow to gawk at Beacon Rock.

SKYHOMISH

Beckler River Campground

c/o Skykomish Ranger District, Box 305, Skykomish 98288. T: (360) 677-2414; www.fs.fed.us/r6/mbs or www.reserveusa.com.

RV: ★★ Tent: ★★★★

Beauty: ★★★★★ Site Privacy: ★★★
Spaciousness: ★★★ Quiet: ★★★★
Security: ★★★★★ Cleanliness: ★★★★
Insect Control: ★★ Facilities: ★★

Only 60 miles from Seattle, Beckler sits on the banks of the Beckler River three miles from the town of Skykomish. A heavy canopy of western Washington foliage drapes the area around the campground as well as the numerous steep-sided river and creek valleys that drain their tributaries into the Beckler River. Trips into the Beckler backcountry should be prefaced by a visit to the Skykomish Ranger Station. Heavy snow can often keep trails blocked longer than one would imagine. The Henry M. Jackson Wilderness (named for a former Washington State senator) lies to the north. It has 49 miles of hiking trails that were once the cross-Cascade routes used by early Native Americans and later by exploration teams. Follow the Forest Service road past Garland Hot Springs to reach the trailheads. To the south is the fabled Alpine Lakes Wilderness. Trailheads into Alpine Lakes are just west of Skykomish on Miller River Rd., which becomes FS 6412.

Basics

Operated By: Mount Baker-Snoqualmie National Forest. **Open:** Memorial Day–mid-Sept. **Site Assignment:** Reservations & fist come first served. **Registration:** At camp office. **Fee:** $12. **Parking:** At site.

Facilities

Number of RV-Only Sites: Inquire at campground. **Number of Tent-Only Sites:** 0. **Number of Multipurpose Sites:** 27. **Hookups:** None. **Each Site:** Picnic table, fire pit w/ grill, shade trees, piped water nearby. **Dump Station:** No. **Laundry:** No. **Pay Phone:** No. **Rest Rooms and Showers:** Vault toilets. **Fuel:** 1 mi. in Skykomish. **Propane:** 1 mi. **Internal Roads:** Paved. **RV Service:** No. **Market:** No. **Restaurant:** No. **General Store:** 1 mi. **Vending:** No. **Swimming Pool:** No. **Playground:** No. **Activities:** Fishing, hiking. **Nearby Attractions:** Mount Baker, Becker River. **Additional Information:** www.fs.fed.us/r6/mbs or www.reserveusa.com.

RESTRICTIONS

Pets: On leash only. **Fires:** In fire pit. **Alcoholic Beverages:** Allowed. **Vehicle Maximum Length:** 21 ft.

TO GET THERE

Drive 1 mi. east of Skykomish on US 2, turn left onto FS 65, and go 2 mi. to the campground.

SPOKANE

Yogi Bear's Camp Resort

7520 South Thomas Mallen Rd., Cheney 99004. T: (509) 747-9415 or reservations (800) 494-PARK; www.jellystonewa.com; yogi@jellystonewa.com.

RV ★★★★	Tent ★★
Beauty: ★★	Site Privacy: ★
Spaciousness: ★★	Quiet: ★★★
Security: ★★★★★	Cleanliness: ★★★
Insect Control: ★★	Facilities: ★★★★★

Yogi Bear's Camp Resort, ten miles east of Spokane, offers a wide array of in house resort-like activities. The quality of the recreational facilities here far surpasses that of competitors, with tons of planned activities during the on-season and newly furbished facilities. These facilities include a well-kept mini-golf course with lots of flowing water under the shade of ponderosa pines. Within the shady grounds, sites vary in quality, and accommodations consist of both back-in and pull-through sites. Flat, gravel pull-through rows R, G, and B make up the best sites in the campground; avoid row Y. Back-in sites exist throughout the grounds, but unfortunately many are not totally flat. The tent sites at Yogi Bear's lack a Jellystone forest feel; all have gravel floors. Additionally, the camp resort offers several varieties of permanent fixture lodging, including bungalows and cabins. The busiest time to visit is June 16 through Labor Day; visit in the late spring or early fall to avoid the crowds.

BASICS

Operated By: Private ownership of franchise rights to Jellystone Park Resorts. **Open:** All year. **Site Assignment:** First come, first served; reservations require a minimum 2 night stay (deposit 50% of total stay; refund on cancellation before 2 weeks, after 2 weeks no refund or rain check). **Registration:** At office; after hours must wait until morning-enter park. **Fee:** For 2 people Sun-Thurs, pull-through: $33, Back-in: $30, Tent site: $19, Friday or Saturday add $5-base, extra Adult: $8, extra Child: $3, extra Tent (1 per site) $11, $13 on weekends, extra Car (2 car max): $2, V, MC, cash. **Parking:** At site.

FACILITIES

Number of RV-Only Sites: 64. **Number of Tent-Only Sites:** 21. **Hookups:** Electric (20, 30, 50 amps), water, sewer, cable, phone. **Each Site:** Picnic table. **Dump Station:** Yes. **Laundry:** Yes. **Pay Phone:** Yes. **Rest Rooms and Showers:** Yes. **Fuel:** No. **Propane:** Yes. **Internal Roads:** Gravel. **RV Service:** No. **Market:** 5 mi. east on I-90. **Restaurant:** 5 mi. east on I-90. **General Store:** Yes. **Vending:** Yes. **Swimming Pool:** Yes. **Playground:** Yes. **Other:** Volleyball, pickleball, & basketball courts; 18 hole mini-golf, horseshoes, water balloon slingshot range, kiddie lagoon, hot tub, arcade w/ pool table, birthday party room, exercise room (small, equipped w/ weight, aerobic machines). **Activities:** Lots of planned activities every weekend, planned activities more frequently from Jun. 16–end of Aug. **Nearby Attractions:** Cheney Cowles Museum, Manito Park & Japanese Gardens, Riverfront Park, golf, Centennial Trail, regional special events. **Additional Information:** Spokane Chamber of Commerce (509) 624-1393.

RESTRICTIONS

Pets: On leash only. **Fires:** No open fires. **Alcoholic Beverages:** At site only. **Vehicle Maximum Length:** None. **Other:** All holiday weekends 3 night minimum stay.

TO GET THERE

From I-90 Exit 172 (eastbound turn right; westbound turn left), take next left at stop sign onto Westbow; road becomes Hallet St. Follow Hallet for 1.1 mi., and then turn right on Thomas Mallen Rd. Follow Thomas Mallen Road for 1.1 mi.; entrance is on right.

SWIFT

Lower Falls Recreation Area

42218 Northeast Yale Bridge Rd., Amboy 98601. T: (360) 247-3900; www.fs.fed.us/gpnf.

RV ★★	Tent ★★★★
Beauty: ★★★★★	Site Privacy: ★★★★
Spaciousness: ★★★★★	Quiet: ★★★★★
Security: ★★★	Cleanliness: ★★★★★
Insect Control: ★★★★	Facilities: ★★

Unfortunately, on cloudy days, there isn't much to look at on the way to the Lower Falls area except the expansive reservoirs and the clear-cut hills. However, if you are blessed with fewer clouds on your trip, views of Mount St. Helens appear at various points along the route. Once at the falls, the primary spectacle becomes a series of major waterfalls roaring off what are known geologically as "benches." Lower Falls Recreation Area has undergone some renovation recently and sports twice as many campsites as before. The original 20 sites are still the best because they are closer to the river and have more vegetation between them for ultimate privacy. Activities in the Lewis River valley include hiking, fishing, hunting, horsepacking, canoeing, and volcano watching. There are endless trails in the neighborhood. The Lewis River Trail is a popular, low-elevation meander for 13.6 miles. If you have time, check out the Mount St. Helens National Volcanic Monument Center in Swift.

BASICS

Operated By: Mount St. Helens National Volcanic Monument. **Open:** Memorial Day–Oct. **Site Assignment:** Reservations or first come first served. **Registration:** Self-registration. **Fee:** $12. **Parking:** At site.

FACILITIES

Number of RV-Only Sites: Inquire at campground. **Number of Tent-Only Sites:** 0. **Number of Multipurpose Sites:** 42. **Hookups:** None. **Each Site:** Fire pit, picnic table. **Dump Station:** No. **Laundry:** No. **Pay Phone:** No. **Rest Rooms and Showers:** Composting toilets. **Fuel:** No. **Propane:** No. **Internal Roads:** No. **RV Service:** No. **Market:** No. **Restaurant:** No. **General Store:** No. **Vending:** No. **Swimming Pool:** No. **Playground:** No. **Other:** Boardwalk to view falls. **Activities:** Hiking, fishing, wildlife viewing. **Nearby Attractions:** Indian Heaven Wilderness Area, Trout Lake, Mount St. Helens. **Additional Information:** www.fs.fed.us/gpnf.

RESTRICTIONS

Pets: On leash only. **Fires:** In fire pit. **Alcoholic Beverages:** Allowed. **Vehicle Maximum Length:** 20 ft. **Other:** Permits required for climbing Mount St. Helens.

TO GET THERE

Take the Woodland Exit off I-5, and follow SR 503 (Lewis River Rd.) to Cougar—about 45 mi. beyond Cougar, SR 503becomes FS 90. The campground is another 28 mi. past Cougar on FS 90.

VANCOUVER

Columbia Riverfront RV Resort

1881 Dike Rd., Woodland 98674. T: (360) 225-8051 or (800) 845-9842; www.columbiariverfrontrvresort.com; colriverfrontrv@aol.com.

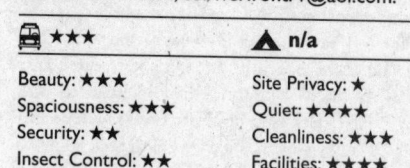

RV ★★★	Tent n/a
Beauty: ★★★	Site Privacy: ★
Spaciousness: ★★★	Quiet: ★★★★
Security: ★★	Cleanliness: ★★★
Insect Control: ★★	Facilities: ★★★★

Columbia Riverfront RV Resort, a few minutes off I-5 and a half hour north of Vancouver, sits on the south shore of the Columbia in a rural area. Across the expansive Columbia stand rolling green hills and some industrial development. The partially landscaped gravel-covered grounds consist of back-in rows with views of the river. People come to this park to watch big ships navigate up and down the industrial corridor of the river, and the best campsites for this sit near the water (sites 1–10, 50–58, and 76). Other sites in the park have limited or no views of the water, and sites 17–25 and 32–40 have a road behind them. Still, the whole area is quiet and scenic with the local pastoral lands and RV park surrounded by blunt, tree-covered hills. Weather in the area stays mild and rainy during all seasons but the summer.

BASICS

Operated By: Columbia Riverfront RV Resort.

Open: All year. **Site Assignment:** First come, first served; reservations. **Registration:** At office, after hours registration in front of office. **Fee:** Rates for 4 people, Riverfront Full: $26.27, Other Full: $24.08, extra vehicle **Fee:** $10, Pet: $1 per pet per day, extra person: $2, Cash, V, MC. **Parking:** At site.

Facilities

Number of RV-Only Sites: 76. **Number of Tent-Only Sites:** n/a. **Hookups:** Electric (20, 30, 50 amps), water, sewer, cable. **Each Site:** Picnic table. **Dump Station:** No. **Laundry:** Yes. **Pay Phone:** Yes. **Rest Rooms and Showers:** Yes. **Fuel:** No. **Propane:** Yes. **Internal Roads:** Wide, well-maintained gravel. **RV Service:** No. **Market:** 2 mi. east in Woodland. **Restaurant:** 2 mi. east in Woodland. **General Store:** No. **Vending:** No. **Swimming Pool:** Yes. **Playground:** Yes. **Other:** Riverfront beach, volleyball, horseshoe pits, clubhouse w/ kitchen (only reserveable). **Activities:** Fishing, swimming, ship watching, kite flying, hiking. **Nearby Attractions:** Golf, Mt. St. Helens, Hilda Klaegers' Lilac Gardens, The Old Grist Mill, the Columbia River, Ape Caves, Vancouver. **Additional Information:** Woodland Chamber of Commerce, (360) 225-9552.

Restrictions

Pets: On leash only. **Fires:** Beach only. **Alcoholic Beverages:** At site only. **Vehicle Maximum Length:** 40 ft. **Other:** No vehicle repairs or washing, no clotheslines, be aware of ship wakes & undertows.

To Get There

From I-5 Exit 22: northbound turn left, southbound turn right onto Dike Access Rd., and follow west for 1.7 mi. When the road forks, take the left fork and follow for another 1.1 mi.; entrance is on the right.

VANCOUVER
Van Mall RV Park

10400 Northeast 53rd St., Vancouver 98662. T: (360) 891-1091 or (888) 941-0335; F: (360) 891-2033; www.vancouverrvparks.com; vanmallrvpark@juno.com.

RV ★★ | Tent n/a

Beauty: ★	Site Privacy: ★
Spaciousness: ★	Quiet: ★★
Security: ★★★	Cleanliness: ★★★★
Insect Control: ★★	Facilities: ★★★★

Van Mall RV Park, in southeastern Vancouver off I-205, offers access to both Vancouver and Portland. The small, cramped, completely paved, urban park has an almost adjacent car dealership with a noisy loudspeaker. Even so, the car dealership closes in the evenings, and the convenient location's facilities stay in pristine condition. The quietest campsites in the park (sites 1–10) sit on the property's perimeter furthest from the dealership and nearby roads. The largest pull-through campsites (sites 37–47), form part of a row in the middle of the park. Avoid the extremely cramped sites 49–65 and 67–83. Common facilities are small but attractively decorated. The same owners operate a similar and larger facility, Vancouver RV Park (see profile), off I-5. Visit during the summer when the rains let up.

Basics

Operated By: Vancouver RV Parks. **Open:** All year. **Site Assignment:** First come, first served; reservations (no deposit). **Registration:** At office, after hours pay in morning. **Fee:** For 2 people, pull-through: $25, Back-in: $22, extra person: $2, Cash, check. **Parking:** At site.

Facilities

Number of RV-Only Sites: 83. **Number of Tent-Only Sites:** n/a. **Hookups:** Electric (20, 30, 50 amps), water, sewer, cable. **Each Site:** Concrete & pebbles. **Dump Station:** No. **Laundry:** Yes. **Pay Phone:** Yes. **Rest Rooms and Showers:** Yes. **Fuel:** No. **Propane:** No. **Internal Roads:** Paved. **RV Service:** Next door. **Market:** 1 mile east in Vancouver. **Restaurant:** 1 mi. east in Vancouver. **General Store:** No. **Vending:** Yes. **Swimming Pool:** No. **Playground:** No. **Other:** Nicely furbished reserveable rec room, horseshoes, small exercise room. **Activities:** Continental breakfast on Saturday, Sunday; Pot lucks once a month; Coffee every morning. **Nearby Attractions:** Fort Vancouver National Historic Site, Pearson Air Museum, Clark County Historic Museum, Portland, Mt. St Heles, Pomeroy Living History Farm. **Additional Information:** Southwest Washington Visitor's & Convention Bureau, (877) 600-0800.

Restrictions

Pets: On leash only. **Fires:** No fires. **Alcoholic Beverages:** At site only. **Vehicle Maximum Length:** 40 ft. **Other:** Vehicles must be (or appear) 10 years old or younger; Quiet hours 10 p.m.–7 a.m.; no firearms, fireworks, or auto repairs.

To Get There

From I-205 Exit 30, Hwy. 500E, drive 0.5 mi. on NE Fourth Plain Blvd./500 E. Turn left onto NE Gher Rd. at traffic light (YMCA on far right corner of intersection), drive less than 1 block, and turn left at Kentucky Fried Chicken. Drive 2 blocks and turn left at State Farm office, continue for 0.2 mi., and the entrance is on the left.

VANCOUVER
Vancouver RV Park

7603 Northeast 13th Ave., Vancouver 98665. T: (360) 695-1158 or (877) 756-2972; F: (360) 735-8388; www.vancouverrvparks.com; vancouverrv@juno.com.

RV ★★★ | Tent ★

Beauty: ★	Site Privacy: ★★
Spaciousness: ★★	Quiet: ★★
Security: ★★★★	Cleanliness: ★★★★
Insect Control: ★★	Facilities: ★★★★

Vancouver RV Park, located in Vancouver off of I-5, provides a quiet alternative for convenient access to Portland. RV parks in Vancouver lack the noise of northern Portland RV parks, but they do not have Portland public transit nearby. This paved park, operated by the owners of Van Mall RV Park (see profile), has better security and a little more room. A rarity in the city—the property has a few semi-private sites. Cedar hedges obscure views in back-in sites near the entrance to the park. The best of these, sites 3–19, sit further from local avenues. The largest pull-throughs, sites 62–72, also sit near the front but lack privacy. More expensive back-in deluxe sites (deluxe because they adjoin small grass islands) back into each other with a painted line on asphalt demarcating rear boundaries, creating a more cramped feeling even though these sites have more width than others. Vancouver RV Park's compact grounds waste very little space, and the new, attractive common facilities resemble their sister park's amenities with double the quantity available for double the sites.

Basics

Operated By: Vancouver RV parks. **Open:** All year. **Site Assignment:** First come, first served; Reservations. **Registration:** At office; after hours pay in morning. **Fee:** For 2 people, one camping unit & one car, Value sites (2-46): $22, Back-ins (167-178): $28, Pull-throughs (61-72 & 153-166): $28, Deluxe Sites (107-151): $32, extra person (older than 3 years old): $2, Nightly phone (limited availability): $2/night, Cash/Check only. **Parking:** At site.

Facilities

Number of Multipurpose Sites: 178. **Hookups:** Electric (20, 30, 50 amps), water, sewer, cable, phone. **Each Site:** Concrete. **Dump Station:** Yes. **Laundry:** Yes. **Pay Phone:** Yes. **Rest Rooms and Showers:** Yes. **Fuel:** No. **Propane:** No. **Internal Roads:** Paved (wide). **RV Service:** No. **Market:** North on Hwy. 99. **Restaurant:** Near entrance. **General Store:** No. **Vending:** Yes. **Swimming Pool:** No. **Playground:** No. **Other:** Reserveable Club House w/ full kitchen, big screen TV; continental breakfast on weekends, coffee served every morning. **Activities:** Planned BBQs, potlucks. **Nearby Attractions:** Officer's Row, Rocket City Neon Advertising Museum, Two Rivers Heritage Museum, Water Resource Education Center. **Additional Information:** Southwest Washington Visitor's & Convention Bureau, (877) 600-0800.

Restrictions

Pets: On leash only. **Fires:** Charcoal grills only, no open fires. **Alcoholic Beverages:** At site only. **Vehicle Maximum Length:** None. **Other:** Quiet Hours 10 p.m.–7 a.m., No firearms, fireworks, auto repairs, pets in rest rooms.

To Get There

From I-5 Exit 4, drive east on NE 78th St.; at the second light (Kentucky Fried Chicken on corner) turn right onto NE 13th Ave.; drive 1 block, and entrance is on left.

WINTHROP
Winthrop-North Cascades National Park KOA

P.O.Box 305, Winthrop 98862. T: (509) 996-2258 or reservations (800) KOA-2158; www.methownet.com/koa; campkoa@methow.com.

RV ★★★ | Tent ★★

Beauty: ★★★	Site Privacy: ★
Spaciousness: ★★	Quiet: ★★★

Security: ★★ Cleanliness: ★★★
Insect Control: ★★ Facilities: ★★★

Winthrop-North Cascades National Park KOA, located just east of the faux-Western town of Winthrop, provides convenient access to the eastern slopes of the North Cascades and nearby tourist attractions. The quiet campground consists of a grassy field surrounded by hardwoods on the banks of the narrow, glassy, rock-bottomed Methow River. None of the sites have privacy or shade. Furthest from the river sit the full-hookup options—wide pull-through sites 1–16. Most campsites on the property have water and electric or no hookups. On the river sit several no-hookup campsites (sites R8–R14) that can accept most RVs sideways, providing river views for more windows and creating some privacy. These grassy campsites, along with sites R1–R7, frequently get used as tent sites (they're the best tent options on the property). Avoid cramped water and electric sites 63–72 and the no-hookup sites 73–82. Visit during the summer; spring and fall nights can be chilly in this area, and much of the eastern side of the North Cascades stays snowed in during all but summer.

Basics

Operated By: Winthrop-North Cascades KOA under franchise from KOA. **Open:** Apr.–Nov. **Site Assignment:** First come, first served; reservations (deposit: $20 cash or credit; refund: 48 hours cancellation. **Registration:** At office; after hours at drop box in fron of office. **Fee:** For 2 people, full: $26, Water/electric: $23.50, No **Hookups:** $20, extra person ages 3-17: $2, Ages 18+: $4, Under three years old free, V, MC, AE, D, cash, check. **Parking:** At site.

Facilities

Number of RV-Only Sites: 68. **Number of Tent-Only Sites:** 35. **Hookups:** Electric (20, 30, 50 amps), water, sewer. **Each Site:** Picnic table, fire ring. **Dump Station:** Yes. **Laundry:** Yes. **Pay Phone:** Yes. **Rest Rooms and Showers:** Yes. **Fuel:** No. **Propane:** No. **Internal Roads:** Gravel. **RV Service:** No. **Market:** 0.5 mile west in Winthrop. **Restaurant:** 0.5 mi. west in Winthrop. **General Store:** Yes. **Vending:** No. **Swimming Pool:** Yes. **Playground:** Yes. **Other:** Horseshoes, volleyball, small game room, central data port, video rentals, bike rentals, shuttle service to Winthrop four times a day, local raft company drop point. **Activities:** swimming, fishing, rafting, hay rides, planned seasonal activities. **Nearby Attractions:** Shafer Museum, golf, hiking, mountain biking, North Cascades National Park, horseback riding, fish hatchery tours, Winthrop. **Additional Information:** Winthrop Chamber of Commerce, (888) 4METHOW.

Restrictions

Pets: On leash only (6 ft. max length); pick up after. **Fires:** In fire pits only. **Alcoholic Beverages:** At site only. **Vehicle Maximum Length:** None. **Other:** Quiet hours 10:30 p.m.–7 a.m., Do not tie anything–trees or shrubs.

To Get There

The campground ntrance is on Hwy. 20, 1 mi. east of downtown Winthrop (which is a remarkably small place), on the left side if traveling eastbound.

YAKIMA
Suntides RV Park

201 Pence Rd., Yakima 98908. T: (509) 966-7883

RV: ★★ Tent: n/a

Beauty: ★★ Site Privacy: ★
Spaciousness: ★★★ Quiet: ★
Security: ★★★ Cleanliness: ★★★
Insect Control: ★★ Facilities: ★★★★

Suntides RV Park, off Hwy. 12 in Yakima, provides convenient lodging for the avid golfer. The park stands adjacent to both a championship 18-hole putting course and an 18-hole full golf course. The green area looks like an oasis in the desert. Golf makes up the entireity of recreational activities at this location. The flat, paved, grass-perimetered sites lack shade, making for an intense noonday sun in the high desert. Accomodations consist of campsites in parallel rows; sites on row A sit closest to Hwy. 12 and a railroad, making them prone to noise. Sites 5D–14D are the best on the property. There are no tent-only campsites. Late spring and early fall are the best times to visit this park; summer heat here packs a punch.

Basics

Operated By: Sun Tides, Inc. **Open:** All year. **Site Assignment:** On arrival, reservations (no deposit). **Registration:** At office, after hours pay in morning. **Fee:** For 2 people, full $19.37, extra person $1 (V, MC, check, cash). **Parking:** At site.

Facilities

Number of RV-Only Sites: 68. **Number of Tent-Only Sites:** n/a. **Hookups:** Electric (30, 50 amps), water, sewer. **Dump Station:** Yes. **Laundry:** Yes. **Pay Phone:** Yes. **Rest Rooms and Showers:** Yes. **Fuel:** No. **Propane:** No. **Internal Roads:** Paved. **RV Service:** No. **Market:** 2 mi. east. **Restaurant:** Next door. **General Store:** No. **Vending:** Yes. **Swimming Pool:** No. **Playground:** No. **Other:** 18 hole golf course, 18 hole putting course, restaurant, driving range. **Activities:** Golfing. **Nearby Attractions:** Elk feeding, golf, Central WA Agricultural Museum, Yakima Electric Railway Museum, Wineries. **Additional Information:** Yakima Chamber of Commerce, (509) 248-2021.

Restrictions

Pets: On leash only. **Fires:** No open fires. **Alcoholic Beverages:** At site only. **Vehicle Maximum Length:** None. **Other:** Check w/ office before washing vehicles.

To Get There

From I-84 Exit 31 (Naches/12 West), drive 4.4 mi. on Hwy. 12 West and turn right onto Old Naches Hwy. Take an immediate right onto Pence Rd., drive 0.1 mi., and teh entrance is on the left.

YAKIMA
Trailer Inns RV Park

1610 North First St., Yakima 98901. T: (509) 451-9561 or reservations (800) 659-4784; trailerinnsrv.uswestdex.com/page3.html.

RV: ★★★★ Tent: ★★

Beauty: ★★ Site Privacy: ★
Spaciousness: ★★★ Quiet: ★★
Security: ★★★ Cleanliness: ★★★★★
Insect Control: ★★ Facilities: ★★★★★

Trailer Inns RV Park, right on the edge of downtown Yakima, offers convenient access to both the city and the interstate. The older, well-maintained facilities offer a wide array of furnishings. One of the more notable and above-average facilities, an indoor bar-b-que room, has two gas grills and a fireplace. Further, an indoor pool and two small hot tubs provide year-round swimming and relaxation. Regarding accomodations, the park's level, grassy tent sites lack shade or privacy and sit behind the office/clubhouse. The RV sites, predominately arranged into parallel rows, have some shade, and many also have adjacent grass areas. Avoid RV sites 55–71 because they lack shade and consist solely of blacktop. The best RV options are sites 103–115; they have shade, grass, and a reasonable amount of space. The high desert climate is arid and hot during the summers, and the sun's heat can be intense; visit during the spring, early summer, or early fall for optimal conditions.

Basics

Operated By: Trailer Inns. **Open:** All year. **Site Assignment:** On arrival, reservations (deposit: 1 night stay, refund: 72 hours cancellation). **Registration:** At office, after hours pay at drop or in morning. **Fee:** Call for rates (V, MC, Cash). **Parking:** At site, limited off site.

Facilities

Number of RV-Only Sites: 60. **Number of Tent-Only Sites:** 22. **Hookups:** Electric (15, 30, 50 amps), water, sewer, cable. **Each Site:** Picnic table. **Dump Station:** Yes. **Laundry:** Yes. **Pay Phone:** Yes. **Rest Rooms and Showers:** Yes. **Fuel:** No. **Propane:** Yes. **Internal Roads:** Paved. **RV Service:** No. **Market:** Nearby in Yakima. **Restaurant:** Nearby in Yakima. **General Store:** Yes. **Vending:** Yes. **Swimming Pool:** Yes, indoor. **Playground:** Yes. **Other:** Arcade, TV room, indoor BBQ room, outdoor BBQ area, indoor hot tubs (2, small), outdoor porch, shuffleboard. **Activities:** Occasional potlucks (seasonal). **Nearby Attractions:** Golfing, hunting, fishing, rafting, horseback riding, wineries, Yakima Electric Railway Museum, Yakima Valley Museum. **Additional Information:** Yakima Chamber of Commerce, (509) 248-2021.

Restrictions

Pets: On leash only, limit of 2 per space. **Fires:** No open fires, no charcoal. **Alcoholic Beverages:** At site only. **Vehicle Maximum Length:** None. **Other:** No eye-sore vehicles.

To Get There

From I-82 Exit 31, go 0.1 mi. south on First St. and the entrance is on the right.

YAKIMA

Yakama Nation Resort RV Park

280 Buster Rd., Toppenish 98948. T: (509) 865-2000 or (800) 874-3087; www.yakamanation.com; yakamarv@aol.com.

RV ★★★★ Tent ★★★

Beauty: ★★★ Site Privacy: ★
Spaciousness: ★★★ Quiet: ★★★
Security: ★★★ Cleanliness: ★★★★
Insect Control: ★★ Facilities: ★★★★★

The Yakama Nation RV Resort, located 20 miles south of Yakima off of I-84, provides easy access to Native American cultural events and obscured views of the surrounding arid hill country. The grounds consist of a flat field of grass, with paved avenues creating islands containing paved sites with grass; additional sites ring the park's perimeter. The grassy tent area has some shade from a few tall deciduous trees; the RV section has little protection from the high desert sun. The pull-through section consists of pavement with no surrounding grass. The best RV choices in the park (sites 30–54) sit furthest from nearby Hwy. 97 and on a perimeter with no rear neighbors. The park has nice and wide-ranging recreational facilities, including two very large unisex cedar saunas. The adjacent Yakama Nation Cultural Center adds to nearby recreational opportunities. Winters here stay cold and summers stay hot with cooler nights; the month of June has the largest number of Native American cultural events.

BASICS

Operated By: Private Operator. **Open:** All year. **Site Assignment:** On arrival, reservations (no deposit). **Registration:** At office, after hours pay in morning. **Fee:** Full $23 (2 people), Additional People $2, teepee $30 (5 people), additional people (up to10 people) $5, cot rentals $2, tent area $16 (4 people), Additional people per tent $5, Three years & younger free (V, MC, cash, check). **Parking:** At site.

FACILITIES

Number of RV-Only Sites: 125. **Number of Tent-Only Sites:** 10. **Hookups:** Electric (20, 30, 50 amps), water, sewer, cable. **Each Site:** Picnic table. **Dump Station:** Yes. **Laundry:** Yes. **Pay Phone:** Yes. **Rest Rooms and Showers:** Yes. **Fuel:** No. **Propane:** Yes. **Internal Roads:** Paved. **RV Service:** No. **Market:** 1 mile north on 97. **Restaurant:** Next door. **General Store:** No. **Vending:** Yes. **Swimming Pool:** Yes. **Playground:** Yes. **Other:** Hot tub, large saunas (2), exercise room, arcade, volleyball, horseshoes, basketball, running trail, putting green, 2 reserveable meeting rooms, Cultural Center adjacent to park. **Activities:** Putting, running. **Nearby Attractions:** Yakama Nation Cultural Center, Old Depot Museum, American Hop Museum, Toppenish Murals (narrated wagon rides available Apr.-Oct), golf. **Additional Information:** Yakima Chamber of Commerce, (509) 248-2021.

RESTRICTIONS

Pets: On leash only. **Fires:** In fire pits only. **Alcoholic Beverages:** Absolutely not allowed. **Vehicle Maximum Length:** None. **Other:** Teepees don't come w/ bedding, required to supply your own.

TO GET THERE

From I-82 Exit 50, drive 3.1 mi. southeast on Buena Way/East 22. Turn right at stoplight onto West 1st Ave and drive for 0.4 mi. Turn right at stoplight onto 97 North and follow 0.7 mi.; the entrance is on left through Yakima Nation Cultural Center.

West Virginia

John Denver certainly knew what he was talking about when he said that West Virginia was "Almost Heaven." Of course, there is more to West Virginia than mountain peaks and rapids. The state also boasts the therapeutic waters of White Sulphur Springs and Berkeley Springs; the subterranean wonders of Lost World Caverns, Smoke Hole Caverns, and Seneca Caverns; the Victorian historic districts and cultural heritage of Charleston, Parkersburg, and Wheeling; and the significant pre-Civil War history of Harper's Ferry.

The West Virginia nature lovers envision is best exemplified in the northern section of the state called the Highlands. Rugged and isolated, the area is defined by mountain peaks that stretch to the sky, postcard-perfect waterfalls, jutting cliffs, and unspoiled forests. The Highlands has 1.5 million acres of national parks and forests, as well as a dozen state parks. Covering 901,000 acres, **Monongahela National Forest** includes West Virginia's highest peak, the 4,862-foot **Spruce Knob.** Within the park are the **Spruce Knob/Seneca Rocks National Recreation Area** near **Petersburg** and the **Blue Bend and Lake Sherwood recreation areas** near **White Sulphur Springs,** which is also where you will find the 5,100-acre **Greenbrier State Forest** and the famous **Greenbrier resort. Marlinton** is home to the **Cass Scenic Railroad State Park.** The 43-mile **Highland National Scenic Highway,** stretching along mountaintops from **Richwood** to Cass, is an ideal way to experience the natural splendor of the Highlands.

Whitewater rafting is an integral part of West Virginia's tourism, and some of the most challenging rapids in the country are found on the New River in the **New River Gorge National River** and the Greenbrier River. Numerous outfitters operate from small towns along these rivers. **Pipestem Resort State Park** in **Pipestem, Babcock State Park** in **Clifftop,** and **Twin Falls Resort State Park** in **Beckley** are just a few of the many camping and recreational spots in the region. **Lost World Caverns** north of **Lewisburg, Organ Cave** in **Ronceverte,** and several covered bridges provide more options for travelers wanting to explore back roads.

Harper's Ferry National Historical Park is a major draw in the eastern panhandle of West Virginia. Located at the junction of the Potomac and Shenandoah rivers—where West Virginia meets Maryland and Virginia—Harper's Ferry is preserved to appear much like it did in the 19th century. In 1859, abolitionist John Brown and 16 other men seized the town's armory and rifle factory. Brown was captured by 90 Marines under the command of Robert E. Lee and J.E.B. Stuart. Ten of Brown's men were killed, and Brown was later hanged in nearby Charles Town for treason, murder, and inciting slaves to revolt. The revolt at Harper's Ferry is credited with sparking a series of events that led to the Civil War.

Charleston, the state capital, is proud of its **Capitol Building,** which is crowned by a 293-foot-high gold-leaf dome. The Kanawha River cuts through Charleston, and just minutes away from the downtown bustle is the tranquility of 9,300-acre **Kanawha State Forest.** A railroad town along the Ohio River, **Huntington** boasts the state's largest art museum. The 500-acre **Blennerhassett Island Historical State Park** in **Parkersburg,** where Aaron Burr's plan to create his own empire failed, is only accessible by sternwheeler. Other major towns in West Virginia include **Morgantown,** home of **West Virginia University** and **Cooper's Rock State Forest;** and **Wheeling,** where the famous **City of Lights** display draws thousands to **Oglebay Resort Park** during the holiday season.

The following facilities accept payment in checks or cash only:

Stonewall Jackson State Park Campground, Roanoke

The following facilities have 20 or fewer campsites:

Greenbrier River Campground, Alderson

Greenbrier River State Forest, Caldwell

ALDERSON

Greenbrier River Campground

282 Greenbrier Rd., Alderson 24343. T: (800) 775-2203; www.greenbrierriver.com; greenbrier@greenbrierriver.com.

★★★★ ★★★★

Beauty: ★★★★ Site Privacy: ★★★
Spaciousness: ★★★ Quiet: ★★★★
Security: ★★★ Cleanliness: ★★★★
Insect Control: ★★★ Facilities: ★★★★

Overlooking the Greenbrier River, the 8-acre Greenbrier River Campground offers wooded, open, and riverside grassy campsites. RV campsites average 33 × 68 feet and offer partial shading and scenic views of the river. Greenbrier's grounds are well-lighted and well-maintained. Five sites along the river are reserved for tent camping. Most campsites are equipped with electric, water, cable TV, and sewer service. River swimming is popular at Greenbrier, as are kayaking, canoeing, and tubing.

Basics

Operated By: Greenbrier River Company. **Open:** Apr. 15–Oct. 15. **Site Assignment:** Reservations and walk-ins accepted. **Registration:** At campground office. **Fee:** $22 (VISA, MC). **Parking:** At site.

Facilities

Number of RV Sites: 14. **Number of Tent-Only Sites:** 5. **Hookups:** Electric (30, 50 amps), cable TV, water, sewer. **Each Site:** Fire ring, picnic table, lantern hook. **Dump Station:** Yes. **Laundry:** Yes. **Pay Phone:** Yes. **Rest Rooms and Showers:** Yes. **Fuel:** No. **Propane:** Yes. **Internal Roads:** Gravel, in good condition. **RV Service:** No. **Market:** 4 mi. west in Alderson. **Restaurant:** 4 mi. west in Alderson. **General Store:** Yes. **Vending:** Yes. **Playground:** No. **Other:** Duckies and boats available for rent. **Activities:** Canoeing, kayaking, fishing, river swimming, beach volleyball, basketball, badminton, croquet, tubing mountain biking, soccer, football, softball. **Nearby Attractions:** Trout fishing streams, Greenbrier Valley Theater, Lewisburg, Lost World and Organ Cave, North House Museum. **Additional Information:** The Greenbrier River Company, which operates the campground, offers Class I–Class III whitewater rafting adventures on the Greenbrier River.

Restrictions

Pets: On leash only. **Fires:** At site. **Alcoholic Beverages:** At site. **Vehicle Maximum Length:** None. **Other:** None.

To Get There

From Interstate 64, take Exit 161 (Alta) and follow Rte. 12 south for 10 mi. In Alderson, turn left onto Rte. 63 east. The campground is located 4 mi. east of Alderson on Rte. 63.

BARBOURSVILLE

Beech Fork State Park

5601 Long Branch Rd., Barboursville 25504. T: (304) 528-5794 or (800) CALLWVA; www.beechforksp.com; beechfk@mail.wvnet.edu.

★★★ ★★★★

Beauty: ★★★★ Site Privacy: ★★★
Spaciousness: ★★★ Quiet: ★★★★
Security: ★★★ Cleanliness: ★★★★
Insect Control: ★★★★ Facilities: ★★★★

Located 12 miles south of Huntington and Barboursville, Beech Fork State Park has the largest camping area in West Virginia's state park system. The campground features four distinctly different areas. Approximately 80 sites front the lake. Old Orchard, a 49-site campground, is open year-round. Moxley Branch, Four Coves, and Lakeview each are equipped with newly upgraded 20- and 30-amp service. Hiking trails range from the 0.75-mile Nature Trail to the 5-mile Lost Trail; the latter is open to both hikers and mountain bikers. Beech Fork Lake is known for largemouth and hybrid striped bass, catfish, walleye, saugeye (a cross of walleye and sauger), and bluegill. A fishing license is required and is available in the Camper's Corner store located in the Administration Building. The store is open for business Mar. 15 through Oct. 31. Beech Fork also has new vacation cottages overlooking Beech Fork Lake.

Basics

Operated By: State of West Virginia. **Open:** All year. **Site Assignment:** Reservations accepted (min. 2-night stay required), walk-ins accepted. **Registration:** At campground store. **Fee:** $13–$17 (VISA, MC). **Parking:** At site.

Facilities

Number of RV Sites: 49. **Number of Tent-Only Sites:** 275. **Hookups:** Electric (20, 30, 50 amps), water, 49 full hookups. **Each Site:** Fire grate, picnic table. **Dump Station:** Yes. **Laundry:** Yes. **Pay Phone:** Yes. **Rest Rooms and Showers:** Yes. **Fuel:** No. **Propane:** No. **Internal Roads:** Paved, in fair condition. **RV Service:** No. **Market:** Within 10 mi. **Restaurant:** Within 10 mi. **General Store:** Yes. **Vending:** Yes. **Playground:** Yes. **Other:** None. **Activities:** Lake fishing and swimming, boating, rec hall, horseshoes, game room, planned activities, sports field, hiking trails, mountain biking. **Nearby Attractions:** Marshall University, Huntington Museum of Art, Pilgrim Glass and Blenko Glass factory, Ritter Park, River Front Park. **Additional Information:** Cabell Co./Huntington CVB, (800) 635-6329, www.wvvisit.org.

Restrictions

Pets: On leash only. **Fires:** At site. **Alcoholic Beverages:** No alcohol permitted. **Vehicle Maximum Length:** None. **Other:** Quiet hours 10 p.m.–7 a.m.

To Get There

From I-64, take Exit 11 and go 1.5 mi. south on WV 10. Turn right on Green Valley Rd. and follow it for 7 mi. to park entrance on right.

BOWDEN

Revelle's River Retreat

P.O. Box 96, Bowden 26254. T: (304) 636-0023; F: (304) 636-0316; www.revelles.com; revelles@hotmail.com.

★★★★ ★★★★

Beauty: ★★★★ Site Privacy: ★★
Spaciousness: ★★★ Quiet: ★★★
Security: ★★★ Cleanliness: ★★★★
Insect Control: ★★★★ Facilities: ★★★★

Located in the Potomac highlands on the banks of Shavers Fork off the Cheat River, the spacious Revelle's River Retreat is West Virginia's largest campground with more than 300 fully developed campsites. Open all year, Revelle's is an ideal place for fishing as Shaver's Fork is stocked with rainbow trout. Back-in and pull-through shaded and open campsites are available. Tent sites are available in the rear of the campground. The Bowden Train Depot, which is located on Revelle's grounds and was last operated in the early 1900s, has been restored and is open again. Passengers can board the historic Durban and Greenbrier Railroad here.

Basics

Operated By: Bruce and Nancy Ryan. **Open:** Mar. 1–Nov. 30. **Site Assignment:** Reservations accepted, otherwise first come, first served. **Registration:** At campground office. **Fee:** $17 (VISA, MC). **Parking:** At site.

Facilities

Number of RV Sites: 250. **Number of Tent-Only Sites:** 20. **Hookups:** Electric (20, 30, 50 amps), cable TV, phone. **Each Site:** Fire ring, picnic table. **Dump Station:** Yes. **Laundry:** Yes. **Pay Phone:** Yes. **Rest Rooms and Showers:** Yes. **Fuel:** No. **Propane:** Yes. **Internal Roads:** Gravel, in good condition. **RV Service:** No. **Market:** 9 mi. west in Elkins. **Restaurant:** 9 mi. west in Elkins. **General Store:** Yes. **Vending:** Yes. **Playground:** Yes. **Other:** Clubhouse; e-mail, fax, copy service. **Activities:** Hiking, fishing, canoeing, basketball, volleyball, swimming. **Nearby Attractions:** Otter Creek Wilderness Area, Smoke Hole Cavern, Bowden Cave, Blackwater Falls State Park, Rich Mountain Battlefield, Cheat Summit Fort, Durbin & Greenbrier Valley Railroad, the Old Mill, Downtown Elkins Historic District, Davis & Elkins College, Halliehurst Mansion. **Additional Information:** West Virginia Visitors Bureau, (800) CALLWVA, www.westvirginia.com.

Restrictions

Pets: On leash only. **Fires:** At site. **Alcoholic Beverages:** At site. **Vehicle Maximum Length:** 45 ft. **Other:** More than 30 sites have no hookups. Cabins and cottages also available.

To Get There

Take US 33 9 mi. east from Elkins. At the end of four-lane highway (Corridor H US 33), turn left. Drive 0.25 mi. and turn left onto Faulkner Rd.

BUCKHANNON

Audra State Park

Rte. 4 Box 564, Buckhannon 26201. T: (800) CALLWVA or (304) 457-1162; www.audrastatepark.com; audra@neumedia.net.

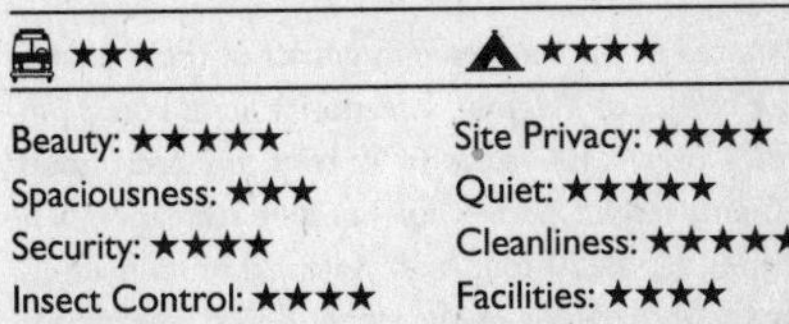

★★★ ★★★★

Beauty: ★★★★★ Site Privacy: ★★★★
Spaciousness: ★★★ Quiet: ★★★★★
Security: ★★★★ Cleanliness: ★★★★★
Insect Control: ★★★★ Facilities: ★★★★

Want solitude and modern amenities both? Head to Audra State Park, located in the northeastern part of West Virginia, six miles east off US 119 and 15 miles east of Buckhannon. The 65-site campground does not have electric hookups, but it certainly has scenery. Situated in a flat with the Middle Fork River cascading in the distance, the campground is nestled amid large boulders and thick hemlock forests. Scenic overlooks beckon along the Alum Cave Trail and the Rock Cliff Trail, the latter of which leaves the campground and climbs the bluffs behind the campsites. There is no swimming pool here, but you can swim in Middle Fork at the campground and tube downstream to a swimming beach. Remember, Audra State Park does not accept reservations. Sites are given on a first-come, first-served basis.

Basics

Operated By: State of West Virginia. **Open:** Apr.–Oct. **Site Assignment:** First come, first served. **Registration:** Ranger will greet you. **Fee:** \$13–\$17 (VISA, MC). **Parking:** At site.

Facilities

Number of RV Sites: 65. **Number of Tent-Only Sites:** None. **Hookups:** None. **Each Site:** Fire ring, picnic table. **Dump Station:** Yes. **Laundry:** Yes. **Pay Phone:** Yes. **Rest Rooms and Showers:** Yes. **Fuel:** No. **Propane:** No. **Internal Roads:** Paved, in good condition. **RV Service:** No. **Market:** Within 5 mi. **Restaurant:** Within 12 mi. **General Store:** No. **Vending:** No. **Playground:** No. **Other:** None. **Activities:** River swimming, hiking trails. **Nearby Attractions:** Carrolton Covered Bridge (Buckhannon River), Philippi Covered Bridge and Museum, Teter Creek Public Hunting and Fishing Area, Alderson-Broaddus College, West Virginia Wesleyan College, Tygart Lake State Park, Valley Falls State Park, Holly River State Park. **Additional Information:** Randolph County CVB, (800) 422-3304, www.randolphcountywv.com.

Restrictions

Pets: On leash only. **Fires:** At site. **Alcoholic Beverages:** No alcohol permitted. **Vehicle Maximum Length:** None. **Other:** 14-day stay limit.

To Get There

From I-79, take Exit 99 and follow US 33 east to Talbot Rd. Turn left and follow signs to park.

CALDWELL

Greenbrier River State Forest

HC 30 Box 154, Caldwell 24925. T: (800) CALLWVA or (304) 536-1944; www.greenbriersf.com; greenbrier@dnr.state.wv.us.

RV ★★★ Tent ★★★★

Beauty: ★★★★	Site Privacy: ★★★
Spaciousness: ★★★	Quiet: ★★★
Security: ★★★★★	Cleanliness: ★★★★★
Insect Control: ★★★★	Facilities: ★★★

Located in the southeastern corner of the state near the border of Virginia, Greenbrier State Forest provides over 5,100 acres of heavily forested, mountainous terrain perfect for outdoor recreation. The imposing, 3,280-foot-high Kate's Mountain affords magnificent views of the surrounding countryside. Greenbrier State Forest's campsites are shaded and bordered by thick forests of pine, maple, buckeye, oak, and hemlock. Twelve standard one- and two-bedroom cabins are also available. The Greenbrier River Trail is just a few miles away. Hiking and biking trails are plentiful, and the Greenbrier River is a popular canoeing spot. Worthwhile side trips include Organ Cave, used by the Confederates for saltpeter in the Civil War, and Lewisburg, where the downtown area is a National Registered Historic District. Lewisburg is home to the 1796 Old Stone Church—the oldest continuously used church west of the Alleghenies.

Basics

Operated By: State of West Virginia. **Open:** Apr. 15–Oct. 31. **Site Assignment:** Reservations accepted (min. 2-night stay), walk-ins accepted. **Registration:** At campground office. **Fee:** \$13–\$17 (VISA, MC). **Parking:** At site.

Facilities

Number of RV Sites: 16. **Number of Tent-Only Sites:** None. **Hookups:** Electric (20, 30 amps). **Each Site:** Fire grate, picnic table. **Dump Station:** Yes. **Laundry:** No. **Pay Phone:** Yes. **Rest Rooms and Showers:** Yes. **Fuel:** Yes. **Propane:** No. **Internal Roads:** Paved, in fair condition. **RV Service:** No. **Market:** Within 7 mi. **Restaurant:** Within 5 mi. **General Store:** No. **Vending:** Yes. **Playground:** Yes. **Other:** No. **Activities:** Hiking trails, badminton, horseshoes, volleyball. **Nearby Attractions:** The Greenbrier Resort, Lewisburg, Greenbrier River Trail, Moncove Lake State Park, Organ Cave, Lost World Caverns, Greenbrier River, National Fish Hatchery, Old Stone Church, West Virginia State Fair, Monongahela National Forest. **Additional Information:** Southern West Virginia CVB, (800) VISITWV, www.visitwv.org.

Restrictions

Pets: On leash only. **Fires:** At site. **Alcoholic Beverages:** No alcohol permitted. **Vehicle Maximum Length:** 30 ft. **Other:** Quite time 10 p.m.–7 a.m.

To Get There

From I-64, go 2 mi. south on Hart's Run Rd. Entrance is on the right.

CAMP CREEK

Camp Creek State Park and Forest

P.O. Box 119, Camp Creek 25820. T: (304) 425-9481 or (800) CALLWVA; www.campcreekstatepark.com; campcreek@dnr.state.wv.us.

RV ★★★★ Tent ★★★★

Beauty: ★★★	Site Privacy: ★★★
Spaciousness: ★★★	Quiet: ★★★★
Security: ★★★★	Cleanliness: ★★★★
Insect Control: ★★★★	Facilities: ★★★★

Located in the southern part of West Virginia, between Beckley and Princeton, Camp Creek State Park was formed from Camp Creek State Forest in 1987. The park is situated just two miles off I-77. Surrounded by the breathtaking mountains of southern West Virginia, Camp Creek actually has two campgrounds. Marsh Fork Campground contains 26 RV and tent sites with electrical hookups and a bathhouse with hot showers. Near Campbell Falls, the shady Blue Jay Campground consists of 12 creekside tent sites amid a forest of hemlock and ironwood. Blue Jay campers can use the showers at Marsh Fork, which is one mile away. Campbell Falls is worth the brief walk from Blue Jay. Still adjacent to the park lies Camp Creek State Forest; with about 5,300 acres of land, the state forest has several trails for hiking and mountain biking. Camp Creek is one of West Virginia's best-stocked trout streams.

Basics

Operated By: State of West Virginia. **Open:** All year. **Site Assignment:** Reservations and walk-ins accepted. **Registration:** At campground office. **Fee:** \$17 (VISA, MC). **Parking:** At site.

Facilities

Number of RV Sites: 26. **Number of Tent-Only Sites:** 12. **Hookups:** Electric (30 amps). **Each Site:** Fire ring, grill, picnic table. **Dump Station:** Yes. **Laundry:** No. **Pay Phone:** Yes. **Rest Rooms and Showers:** Yes. **Fuel:** No. **Propane:** No. **Internal Roads:** Paved, in good condition. **RV Service:** No. **Market:** Within 5 mi. **Restaurant:** Within 5 mi. **General Store:** No. **Vending:** Yes. **Playground:** Yes. **Other:** None. **Activities:** Stream fishing, shuffleboard, badminton, sports field, horseshoes, hiking trails, volleyball. **Nearby Attractions:** Beckley Exhibition Coal Mine, Bluestone State Park, Bluestone Wildlife Management Area, Bramwell Historic District, Grandview Park and Outdoor Dramas, Pipestem Resort State Park, Pinnacle Rock State Park, Twin Falls Resort State Park, New River Gorge. **Additional Information:** Southern West Virginia CVB, (800) VISITWV, www.visitwv.org.

Restrictions

Pets: On leash only. **Fires:** At site. **Alcoholic Beverages:** No alcohol permitted. **Vehicle Maximum Length:** 30 ft. **Other:** 14-day stay limit.

To Get There

From I-77, take Exit 20 and follow signs to state park.

CHARLESTON

Kanawha State Forest

Rte. 2 Box 285, Charleston 25314. T: (304) 558-3500 or (800) CALLWVA; www.kanawhastateforest.com.

RV ★★★★ Tent ★★★★

Beauty: ★★★★	Site Privacy: ★★★
Spaciousness: ★★★	Quiet: ★★★★
Security: ★★★★	Cleanliness: ★★★★★
Insect Control: ★★★★	Facilities: ★★★★

It's hard to believe that the sprawling state capitol of Charleston is only seven miles away the hills and valleys of Kanawha State Forest. With 11,000 acres of terrain, Kanawha is a haven for hikers and mountain bikers who embark along the maze of trails. Davis Creek Campground is served by two bathhouses, coin-operated laundry facilities, a swimming pool, and a well-kept playground. Hemlocks shade part of the intimate campground, which borders Davis Creek. One of the best hiking paths for families is the Spotted Salamander trail—a paved, level walkway with Braille-signed interpretive nature stations designed for both visually impaired and physically challenged guests. Store Hollow and David Creek trails sprout from the campground as well. The capitol complex and 19th-century Old Charleston Village are a short drive away from the campground.

BASICS

Operated By: State of West Virginia. **Open:** Apr. 15–Oct. 31. **Site Assignment:** Reservations and walk-ins accepted. **Registration:** At campground office. **Fee:** $13–$17 (VISA, MC). **Parking:** At site.

FACILITIES

Number of RV Sites: 25. **Number of Tent-Only Sites:** 21. **Hookups:** Electric (30 amps). **Each Site:** Fire ring, grill, picnic table. **Dump Station:** Yes. **Laundry:** No. **Pay Phone:** Yes. **Rest Rooms and Showers:** Yes. **Fuel:** No. **Propane:** No. **Internal Roads:** Paved, in good condition. **RV Service:** No. **Market:** Within 6 mi. **Restaurant:** Within 5 mi. **General Store:** Yes. **Vending:** Yes. **Playground:** Yes. **Other:** None. **Activities:** Lake fishing, hiking trails, swimming, mountain biking. **Nearby Attractions:** State Capitol, Governor's Mansion, Cultural Center with State Museum, "Mountain Stage" live radio show, Charleston East End Historical District, P.A. Denny Sternwheeler, Sunrise Museum, Charleston Sternwheel Regatta, antique malls in South Charleston and Nitro. **Additional Information:** Charleston CVB, (800) 733-5469, www.charlestonwv.com.

RESTRICTIONS

Pets: On leash only. **Fires:** At site. **Alcoholic Beverages:** No alcohol permitted. **Vehicle Maximum Length:** 30 ft. **Other:** 14-day stay limit.

TO GET THERE

From I-64, take Exit 58A and go south on US 119, east on Oakwood Rd., and follow signs for 6 mi.

CHARLESTON

Rippling Waters Church of God Campground

HC 62 Box 177, Romance 25248. T: (304) 988-2607; cogofwvga@newwave.net.

RV ★★★ Tent ★★★★

Beauty: ★★★★	Site Privacy: ★★
Spaciousness: ★★	Quiet: ★★★★
Security: ★★★	Cleanliness: ★★★
Insect Control: ★★★★	Facilities: ★★★★

Located in Romance about 10 mi. north of Charleston, Rippling Waters Church of God Campground is easily reached from I-77. Situated amid rolling, forested hills, Rippling Waters has 110 level sites, including nine pull-throughs. As indicated by its name, Rippling Waters is operated by the Church of God and is frequented by church groups. The campground has cottages, dorms, and cabins available for groups only. With two swimming pools and a lake for fishing and boating, Rippling Waters is ideal for families interested in a quiet getaway without fancy amenities. The sites—like the campground—are clean and comfortable, as is the small, charming chapel.

BASICS

Operated By: Church of God. **Open:** All year. **Site Assignment:** Reservations recommended, walk-ins accepted. **Registration:** At campground office. **Fee:** $17 (VISA, MC). **Parking:** At site.

FACILITIES

Number of RV Sites: 110. **Number of Tent-Only Sites:** None. **Hookups:** Electric (20, 30, 50 amps), phone, water, 79 full hookups. **Each Site:** Fire ring, picnic table. **Dump Station:** Yes. **Laundry:** Yes. **Pay Phone:** Yes. **Rest Rooms and Showers:** Yes. **Fuel:** No. **Propane:** Yes. **Internal Roads:** Paved and gravel, in good condition. **RV Service:** No. **Market:** Within 5 mi. **Restaurant:** Within 5 mi. **General Store:** Yes. **Vending:** Yes. **Playground:** Yes. **Other:** Small chapel. **Activities:** Lake fishing, boat rentals, badminton, sports field, horseshoes, hiking trails, volleyball, basketball. **Nearby Attractions:** State Capitol, Governor's Mansion, Cultural Center with State Museum, "Mountain Stage" live radio show, Charleston East End Historical District, P.A. Denny Sternwheeler, Sunrise Museum, Charleston Sternwheel Regatta, antique malls in South Charleston and Nitro. **Additional Information:** Charleston CVB, (800) 733-5469, www.charlestonwv.com.

RESTRICTIONS

Pets: On leash only. **Fires:** At site. **Alcoholic Beverages:** No alcohol permitted. **Vehicle Maximum Length:** None. **Other:** No smoking at campground.

TO GET THERE

From I-77, take Exit 116 and go 100 ft. east on Haines Branch Rd., 1 mi. north on Hwy. 21, and 3 mi. east on Rippling Waters/Middlefork Rd. Entrance is on the left.

CLARKSBURG

Wilderness Waterpark and Campground

Wolf Summit, Clarksburg 26301. T: (304) 622-7528; wwcg@citynet.net.

RV ★★★ Tent ★★★

Beauty: ★★★	Site Privacy: ★★★
Spaciousness: ★★★	Quiet: ★★★★
Security: ★★★	Cleanliness: ★★★
Insect Control: ★★★	Facilities: ★★★★

They call West Virginia "Mountaineer Country," and that slogan is especially fitting in the north central part of the state. This is where you will find Clarksburg and the Wilderness Waterpark and Campground. All 51 sites have full hookups and accommodate pull-throughs. The lake, created from strip mining years ago, is popular for its fishing, paddle boating, canoeing, and water slide. There are interesting historical attractions nearby. Nearby Fort New Salem is a collection of relocated log structures representing a West Virginia frontier settlement. Watters Smith Memorial State Park is a 532-acre historical park. Jackson's Mill is the boyhood home of Gen. Thomas J. "Stonewall" Jackson, complete with working grist mill and walking tours. Jackson's Mill is also the site of the Jubilee, an arts and crafts festival held on Labor Day weekend.

BASICS

Operated By: Private operator. **Open:** All year. **Site Assignment:** Reservations and walk-ins accepted. **Registration:** At campground headquarters. **Fee:** $16 (VISA, MC). **Parking:** At site.

FACILITIES

Number of RV Sites: 51. **Number of Tent-Only Sites:** None. **Hookups:** Electric (15, 30 amps), phone, water, sewer. **Each Site:** Fire ring, picnic table. **Dump Station:** Yes. **Laundry:** No. **Pay Phone:** Yes. **Rest Rooms and Showers:** Yes. **Fuel:** No. **Propane:** No. **Internal Roads:** Gravel, in good condition. **RV Service:** No. **Market:** Within 12 mi. **Restaurant:** Within 10 mi. **General Store:** Yes. **Vending:** Yes. **Playground:** Yes. **Other:** Water slide. **Activities:** Rec hall, game room, lake swimming, boating, lake fishing, basketball, planned activities on weekends, horseback riding, sports field, horseshoes, hiking trails, volleyball. **Nearby Attractions:** Historic Jackson's Mill, Stonewall Jackson Lake State Park, Clarksburg, Fort New Salem, Blennerhasset Island. **Additional Information:** Marion County CVB, (800) 834-7365, www.marioncvb.com.

RESTRICTIONS

Pets: On leash only. **Fires:** At site. **Alcoholic Beverages:** At site. **Vehicle Maximum Length:** None. **Other:** None.

TO GET THERE

From I-79, go 10 mi. west on US 50, 1 mi. south on Sycamore Rd., and follow signs for 1.5 mi. west on blacktop and then gravel road. Entrance is at the end.

CLIFFTOP

Babcock State Park

HC 35 Box 150, Clifftop 25831. T: (304) 438-3004 or (800) CALLWVA; www.babcocksp.com; babcock@mail.wvnet.edu.

RV ★★★ Tent ★★★

Beauty: ★★★★	Site Privacy: ★★★
Spaciousness: ★★	Quiet: ★★★
Security: ★★★★	Cleanliness: ★★★★
Insect Control: ★★★★	Facilities: ★★★★

One of West Virginia's first state parks, the 4,127-acre Babcock State Park borders New River Gorge National River. The park is graced with a fast-flowing trout stream in a boulder-strewn canyon, where mountainous vistas can be viewed from scenic overlooks. The 52-site campground, set amid hemlock, white pine, oak, and hickory, has open and shaded sites. The park itself has more than 20 miles of hiking and mountain biking trails. Also on the park grounds is the Glade Creek Grist Mill, which was completed in 1976 at Babcock. This fully operational replica was built by combining parts from three vintage mills. A living monument to the hundreds of mills which thrived in West Virginia at the turn of the century, the Glade Creek Grist Mill provides freshly ground cornmeal and buckwheat flour. Of course, many campers at Babcock prefer whitewater to grist mills. New River Gorge and numerous river outfitters are a short drive from Babcock.

Basics

Operated By: State of West Virginia. **Open:** Apr. 15–Oct. 31. **Site Assignment:** Reservations and walk-ins accepted. **Registration:** At campground office. **Fee:** $13–$17 (VISA, MC). **Parking:** At site.

Facilities

Number of RV Sites: 28. **Number of Tent-Only Sites:** 24. **Hookups:** Electric (20 amps). **Each Site:** Fire grate, picnic table. **Dump Station:** Yes. **Laundry:** Yes. **Pay Phone:** Yes. **Rest Rooms and Showers:** Yes. **Fuel:** No. **Propane:** No. **Internal Roads:** Paved, in good condition. **RV Service:** No. **Market:** Within 10 mi. **Restaurant:** Within 12 mi. **General Store:** Yes. **Vending:** Yes. **Playground:** Yes. **Other:** None. **Activities:** Boating, boat rentals, lake and stream fishing, shuffleboard, tennis, hiking trails, volleyball. **Nearby Attractions:** New River Gorge National River, Beckley, Exhibition Coal Mine and Coal Museum. **Additional Information:** Southern West Virginia CVB, (800) VISITWV, www.visitwv.org.

Restrictions

Pets: On leash only. **Fires:** At site. **Alcoholic Beverages:** No alcohol permitted. **Vehicle Maximum Length:** None. **Other:** 14-day stay limit.

To Get There

At the US Rte. 60 exit, travel east 10 mi. to Rte. 41 South. Babcock's campground is 2 mi. south of Rte. 60 at Clifftop, while the main park entrance is 2 mi. south of Clifftop.

DAVIS

Blackwater Falls State Park

P.O. Box 490, Davis 26260. T: (304) 259-5216 or (800) CALLWVA; www.blackwaterfalls.com; blackwater@blackwaterfalls.com.

RV ★★★ Tent ★★★

Beauty: ★★★	Site Privacy: ★★★
Spaciousness: ★★★	Quiet: ★★★★
Security: ★★★★	Cleanliness: ★★★★
Insect Control: ★★★★	Facilities: ★★★★

Located in the mountainous Potomac Highlands outside of Davis, Blackwater Falls State Park is named for the falls of the Blackwater River, whose amber-colored waters plunge five stories, then twist and tumble through an eight-mile gorge. The "black" water is a result of tannic acid from fallen hemlock and red spruce needles. The 70-site campground has 39 pull-through sites. A short walk along the Elakala Trail from the lodge will take hikers over the upper section of Elakala Falls. Pendleton Falls can be viewed at a roadside pull-off about 0.5 mile from the lodge. Like Elakala, these falls are the cascades of Pendleton Run coming from the park's swimming and boating lake. Accommodating non-RVers and tenters, Blackwater Lodge sits on the canyon's south rim, providing a sweeping view of the densely forested gorge. Each one of the 54 air-conditioned guest rooms has a private bath, phone, and color television. The lodge also features a game room, a sitting room with a cozy fireplace, and an indoor pool.

Basics

Operated By: State of West Virginia. **Open:** May 1–Oct. 31. **Site Assignment:** Reservations and walk-ins accepted. **Registration:** At campground office. **Fee:** $13–$17 (VISA, MC). **Parking:** At site.

Facilities

Number of RV Sites: 45. **Number of Tent-Only Sites:** 25. **Hookups:** Electric (20 amps). **Each Site:** Fire ring, picnic table. **Dump Station:** Yes. **Laundry:** Yes. **Pay Phone:** Yes. **Rest Rooms and Showers:** Yes. **Fuel:** No. **Propane:** No. **Internal Roads:** Paved, in good condition. **RV Service:** No. **Market:** Within 5 mi. **Restaurant:** Within 7 mi. **General Store:** Yes. **Vending:** Yes. **Playground:** Yes. **Other:** State park has lodge with indoor pool. **Activities:** Rec hall, lake swimming, boating, boat rentals, river fishing, planned activities, tennis, badminton, sports field, horseshoes, hiking trails, volleyball. **Nearby Attractions:** Harper's Old Country Store, Monongahela National Forest, Seneca Caverns. **Additional Information:** Potomac Highlands Travel Council, (304) 257-9315.

Restrictions

Pets: On leash only. **Fires:** At site. **Alcoholic Beverages:** No alcohol permitted. **Vehicle Maximum Length:** 25 ft. **Other:** 14-day stay limit.

To Get There

From Hwy. 32, go 2 mi. southwest on CR 29. Entrance is on the right.

DUNLOW

Cabwaylingo State Forest

Rte. 1 Box 85, Dunlow 25511. T: (304) 385-4255 or (800) CALLWVA; www.cabwaylingo.com.

RV ★★★ Tent ★★★★

Beauty: ★★★★	Site Privacy: ★★★
Spaciousness: ★★★	Quiet: ★★★★
Security: ★★★★	Cleanliness: ★★★★
Insect Control: ★★★★	Facilities: ★★★★

Located in Wayne County in southwestern West Virginia, Cabwaylingo State Forest is midway between Huntington and Williamson. Consisting of 8,123 densely wooded acres, the state forest offers two campgrounds to choose from. Spruce Creek is a newer 11-site campground with water and electric hookups and shower facilities. Tick Ridge is more rustic camping area surrounded by a pine and oak forest. There are about 25 miles of trails to explore at Cabwaylingo, including the Indian Trail that starts at the campground. Located near the McClintic Group Camp, the swimming area features a newly remodeled pool, bathhouse and a wading pool for children. Lifeguards are on duty during pool hours. Cabwaylingo State Forest is steeped in the history of the Civilian Conservation Corps; the CCC built log cabins with stone fireplaces, the superintendents's residence, picnic areas, hiking trails. and a fire tower.

Basics

Operated By: State of West Virginia. **Open:** Apr. 15–Oct. 31. **Site Assignment:** First-come, first-served; no reservations. **Registration:** Ranger will stop at campsite and register you. **Fee:** $13–$17 (VISA, MC). **Parking:** At site.

Facilities

Number of RV Sites: 12. **Number of Tent-Only Sites:** 22. **Hookups:** Electric (20 amps). **Each Site:** Fire grate, picnic table. **Dump Station:** Yes. **Laundry:** No. **Pay Phone:** No. **Rest Rooms and Showers:** Yes. **Fuel:** No. **Propane:** No. **Internal Roads:** Paved, in good condition. **RV Service:** No. **Market:** Within 12 mi. **Restaurant:** Within 12 mi. **General Store:** No. **Vending:** Yes. **Playground:** Yes. **Other:** None. **Activities:** Fishing, hiking trails, swimming, basketball, volleyball. **Nearby Attractions:** Huntington, Heritage Farm Museum and Village, Mountain State Mystery Train. **Additional Information:** Cabell Co./Huntington CVB, (800) 635-6329, www.wvvisit.org.

Restrictions

Pets: On leash only. **Fires:** At site. **Alcoholic Beverages:** No alcohol permitted. **Vehicle Maximum Length:** None. **Other:** 14-day stay limit.

To Get There

Follow US Rte. 152 for about 42 mi. south of Huntington and turn off at Missouri Branch.

ELKINS

Alpine Shores Campground

HC 73 Box 3, Bowden 26254. T: (304) 636-4311; www.neumedia.net~zeb/shores/main.htm; zeb@neumedia.net.

RV ★★★ Tent ★★★

Beauty: ★★★★	Site Privacy: ★★★★
Spaciousness: ★★★★	Quiet: ★★★★
Security: ★★★★	Cleanliness: ★★★
Insect Control: ★★★★	Facilities: ★★★★

Just east of Elkins, Alpine Shores Campground lies on 260 acres of beautiful mountain woodland along a mile of shoreline of the Cheat River's Shaver's Fork. The campground has 166 level, grassy, and open sites. Fishing and swimming are popular activities in Shaver's Fork. Nearby Monongahela National Forest offers a wealth of opportunities for outdoor enthusiasts, including skiing, golfing, canoeing, and whitewater rafting. Alpine Shores is a short drive from the antique shops of Elkins. Another worthwhile side trip is Spruce Knob; at 4,861 ft. above sea level, this is West Virginia's highest peak. From this rugged alpine height, you can view grassy meadows and pastures or look down on forested ridges as far as the eye can see. A stone-and-steel observation tower sits atop Spruce Knob, providing visitors with a panoramic view. The 0.5-mile Whispering Spruce Trail circles Spruce Knob, providing breathtaking views of West Virginia's mountains and valleys.

Basics

Operated By: Private operator. **Open:** Apr. 15–Nov. 15. **Site Assignment:** Reservations and walk-ins accepted. **Registration:** At campground headquarters. **Fee:** $18–$20 (VISA, MC). **Parking:** At site.

Facilities

Number of RV Sites: 141. **Number of Tent-Only Sites:** 25. **Hookups:** Electric (15, 20, 30 amps), water, 25 full hookups. **Each Site:** Fire ring, picnic table. **Dump Station:** Yes. **Laundry:** Yes.

Pay Phone: Yes. **Rest Rooms and Showers:** Yes. **Fuel:** No. **Propane:** No. **Internal Roads:** Gravel, in good condition. **RV Service:** No. **Market:** Within 7 mi. **Restaurant:** On premises. **General Store:** Yes. **Vending:** Yes. **Playground:** Yes. **Other:** Alpine Lodge. **Activities:** River swimming and fishing, basketball, horseshoes, volleyball. **Nearby Attractions:** Blackwater Falls, Seneca Caverns, Spruce Knob, Davis and Elkins historic sites, Augusta Heritage Center. **Additional Information:** Randolph County CVB, (800) 422-3304, www.randolphcountywv.com.

Restrictions

Pets: On leash only. **Fires:** At site. **Alcoholic Beverages:** At site. **Vehicle Maximum Length:** 40 ft. **Other:** None.

To Get There

From Elkins, travel east on US 33 for 7 mi. to find Alpine Shores on the right.

ELKINS

Cheat River Campground

P.O. Box 91, Bowden 26254. T: (304) 636-3624; www.neumedia.net/~lynnb; lynnb@neumedia.net.

RV ★★★★ Tent ★★★★

Beauty: ★★★★ Site Privacy: ★★★
Spaciousness: ★★★ Quiet: ★★★★
Security: ★★★ Cleanliness: ★★★
Insect Control: ★★★★ Facilities: ★★★★

Nestled in the heart of West Virginia and surrounded by the Blue Ridge Mountains, Cheat River Campground has 27 open and shaded sites, including four pull-throughs. The trout fishing is good at the campground's two lakes. Of course, many campers cast their reels on the banks of the Cheat River, where tour operators can take you whitewater rafting and canoeing. A unique way to see the region's natural splendor is on the Cass Scenic Railroad. The historic town of Cass remains relatively unchanged since the turn of the 19th century; from the country store and museum to the train station, visitors find lots to do. The passenger cars of the Cass Railroad are old logging flat-cars refurbished into passenger coaches.

Basics

Operated By: Private operator. **Open:** All year. **Site Assignment:** Reservations and walk-ins accepted. **Registration:** At campground office. **Fee:** $15–$18 (VISA, MC). **Parking:** At site.

Facilities

Number of RV Sites: 27. **Number of Tent-Only Sites:** 12. **Hookups:** Electric (20, 30 amps), cable TV, water, 18 full hookups. **Each Site:** Fire ring, picnic table. **Dump Station:** Yes. **Laundry:** No. **Pay Phone:** Yes. **Rest Rooms and Showers:** Yes. **Fuel:** No. **Propane:** No. **Internal Roads:** Gravel, in fair condition. **RV Service:** No. **Market:** Within 8 mi. **Restaurant:** Within 6 mi. **General Store:** No. **Vending:** Yes. **Playground:** Yes. **Other:** No. **Activities:** River swimming and fishing, canoeing, badminton, sports field, horseshoes, hiking trails, volleyball. **Nearby Attractions:** Cheat River, Blackwater Falls, Seneca Caverns, Spruce Knob, Davis and Elkins historic sites, Augusta Heritage Center, Cass Scenic Railroad. **Additional Information:** Randolph County CVB, (800) 422-3304, www.randolphcountywv.com.

Restrictions

Pets: On leash only. **Fires:** At site. **Alcoholic Beverages:** At site. **Vehicle Maximum Length:** None. **Other:** None.

To Get There

From US 219, go 7.5 mi. east on US 33, 0.25 mi. north on off ramp to Fawlkner Rd., and follow signs to campground. Entrance is on the right.

GAP MILLS

Moncove Lake State Park

Rte. 4 Box 73-A, Gap Mills 24941. T: (304) 772-3450; www.moncovelakestatepark.com; moncovesp@dnr.state.wv.us.

RV ★★★ Tent ★★★★

Beauty: ★★★★ Site Privacy: ★★★
Spaciousness: ★★★ Quiet: ★★★
Security: ★★★★ Cleanliness: ★★★★★
Insect Control: ★★★★ Facilities: ★★★

Located in Monroe County's Sweet Spring Valley near Gap Mills, Moncove Lake State is home to an abundance of wildlife—foxes, white-tail deer, squirrels, and beavers are among the many animals you are likely to see. The park is located near a major flyway for hawks migrating in the fall and spring. In Sept., on Peter's Mountain, hundreds of hawks can be seen daily heading south for the winter. All campsites are level; some sites are open, others are shaded by hickory and oak. The 144-acre Moncove Lake provides fishing for largemouth bass, bluegill, trout, and catfish. Rowboats and paddle boats are available for rent. Hikers flock to the Devil's Creek Trail, which departs from the campground and links with other trails such as Diamond Hollow and Roxalia Springs. Underground hiking is the draw at Organ Cave and Lost World Caverns, a short drive from Moncove Lake.

Basics

Operated By: State of West Virginia. **Open:** Apr. 15–Dec. 31. **Site Assignment:** First-come, first-served; no reservations. **Registration:** At campground office. **Fee:** $13–$17 (VISA, MC). **Parking:** At site.

Facilities

Number of RV Sites: 50. **Number of Tent-Only Sites:** None. **Hookups:** Electric (20, 30 amps). **Each Site:** Fire ring, picnic table. **Dump Station:** Yes. **Laundry:** Yes. **Pay Phone:** Yes. **Rest Rooms and Showers:** Yes. **Fuel:** No. **Propane:** No. **Internal Roads:** Gravel, in fair condition. **RV Service:** No. **Market:** Within 6 mi. **Restaurant:** Within 6 mi. **General Store:** Yes. **Vending:** Yes. **Playground:** Yes. **Other:** None. **Activities:** Lake fishing, boating, boat rentals, badminton, sports field, horseshoes, hiking trails, volleyball. **Nearby Attractions:** Greenbrier River, Greenbrier River Rail Trail, Organ Cave, Lost World Caverns, Historic Lewisburg, Harding Rock Hawk Tower on Peter's Mountain. **Additional Information:** Southern West Virginia CVB, (800) VISITWV, www.visitwv.org.

Restrictions

Pets: On leash only. **Fires:** At site. **Alcoholic Beverages:** No alcohol permitted. **Vehicle Maximum Length:** None. **Other:** 14-day stay limit.

To Get There

From Gap Mills, go 6 mi. north on Hwy. 8. Follow signs to the park.

GLENVILLE

Cedar Creek State Park

Rte. 1 Box 9, Glenville 26351. T: (304) 462-7158 or (800) CALLWVA; www.cedarcreeksp.com.

RV ★★★★ Tent ★★★★

Beauty: ★★★★ Site Privacy: ★★★
Spaciousness: ★★★ Quiet: ★★★★
Security: ★★★★ Cleanliness: ★★★★★
Insect Control: ★★★★ Facilities: ★★★★

The 2,483-acre Cedar Creek State Park is located 25 mi. west of I-79 near Glenville. The 48-site campground is clean, and there are three bathhouses, alleviating long waits at prime shower times. Some of the open and shaded sites are creekside. One of the unique aspects of the campground is the check-in station—a restored log cabin which was formerly a Gilmer County historical landmark. Further adding to the charming ambience of the park, a reconstructed one-room schoolhouse has been erected as a testimonial to the early years of education. Hikers will enjoy the Stone Trough and Park View trails. The three lakes at Cedar Creek are seasonally stocked for fishing. Trout are stocked in late winter and early spring, and muskie in summer. Bass and catfish may be caught year-round.

Basics

Operated By: State of West Virginia. **Open:** Apr. 15–Oct. 15. **Site Assignment:** Reservations and walk-ins accepted. **Registration:** At campground office. **Fee:** $13–$17 (VISA, MC). **Parking:** At site.

Facilities

Number of RV Sites: 48. **Number of Tent-Only Sites:** None. **Hookups:** Electric (20, 30 amps). **Each Site:** Fire grate, picnic table. **Dump Station:** Yes. **Laundry:** Yes. **Pay Phone:** Yes. **Rest Rooms and Showers:** Yes. **Fuel:** No. **Propane:** No. **Internal Roads:** Paved, in good condition. **RV Service:** No. **Market:** Within 10 mi. **Restaurant:** Within 8 mi. **General Store:** Yes. **Vending:** Yes. **Playground:** Yes. **Other:** Activity building. **Activities:** Boating, boat rentals, stream and pond fishing, mini-golf, planned activities, tennis, sports field, horseshoes, hiking trails, volleyball. **Nearby Attractions:** Blennerhassett Historical State Park, Bulltown Historic District. **Additional Information:** Parkersburg/Wood Co. CVB, (800) 752-4982, www.parkersburgcvb.com.

Restrictions

Pets: On leash only. **Fires:** At site. **Alcoholic Beverages:** No alcohol permitted. **Vehicle Maximum Length:** None. **Other:** 14-day stay limit.

To Get There

From Interstate 79, take the Burnsville/Glenville exit and follow Rte. 5 west to Glenville. The park is located south of Glenville and 4 mi. east of US 33/119.

GRAFTON

Tygart Lake State Park

Rte. 1 Box 260, Grafton 26354. T: (304) 265-6144 or (800) CALLWVA; www.tygartlake.com; tygartlake@wvonline.net.

RV ★★★★ Tent ★★★★

Beauty: ★★★★ Site Privacy: ★★★
Spaciousness: ★★★ Quiet: ★★★★
Security: ★★★★ Cleanliness: ★★★★
Insect Control: ★★★★ Facilities: ★★★★

Nestled in the foothills of the Allegheny Mountains in north central West Virginia near Grafton, Tygart Lake State Park is home to the 1,740-acre Tygart Lake. The centrally located bathhouse has hot showers. Though there is no general store, bagged ice and firewood are sold at the check-in station. Perched on a promontory overlooking the lake, Tygart Lake Lodge has 20 wood-paneled guest rooms. The lodge's 100-seat restaurant offers panoramic views of the waterfront. The restaurant can cater banquets and receptions for special groups such as business meetings, family reunions, and weddings. Dinner theaters are also scheduled throughout the year. The park has five hiking trails. Swimming is offered in the roped off-beach area, monitored by a staff of lifeguards. Fishing and pontoon boats can be rented from the marina. You can also hit the links at Tygart Lake Country Club.

BASICS

Operated By: State of West Virginia. **Open:** Apr. 15–Nov. 15. **Site Assignment:** First-come, first served; no reservations accepted. **Registration:** At campground office. **Fee:** $13–$17 (VISA, MC). **Parking:** At site.

FACILITIES

Number of RV Sites: 20. **Number of Tent-Only Sites:** 20. **Hookups:** Electric (20 amps). **Each Site:** Fire ring, picnic table. **Dump Station:** Yes. **Laundry:** Yes. **Pay Phone:** Yes. **Rest Rooms and Showers:** Yes. **Fuel:** No. **Propane:** No. **Internal Roads:** Paved, in good condition. **RV Service:** No. **Market:** Within 5 mi. **Restaurant:** At park lodge. **General Store:** No. **Vending:** Yes. **Playground:** Yes. **Other:** Lodge. **Activities:** Rec hall, equipped pavilion, lake swimming, boating, lake fishing, shuffleboard, planned activities, sports field, hiking trails, volleyball. **Nearby Attractions:** Tygart Lake Dam Visitors Center, International Mother's Day Shrine, Grafton National Cemetery, Pleasant Creek Wildlife Management Area, Valley Falls State Park, Pricketts Fort Memorial State Park, Phillipi Covered Bridge, Anna Jarvis House, Durbin and Greenbrier Railroads, Weston Glass Factory. **Additional Information:** Marion County CVB, (800) 834-7365, www.marioncvb.com.

RESTRICTIONS

Pets: On leash only. **Fires:** At site. **Alcoholic Beverages:** No alcohol permitted. **Vehicle Maximum Length:** 30 ft. **Other:** 14-day stay limit.

TO GET THERE

Take US 119 or Rte. 50 to Grafton. From Grafton, take Rte. 50 to South Grafton and follow signs to the park.

HACKER VALLEY

Holly River State Park

P.O. Box 70, Hacker Valley 26222. T: (304) 493-6353 or (800) CALLWVA; www.hollyriver.com; hollyriver@mountain.net.

RV ★★★ Tent ★★★★

Beauty: ★★★ Site Privacy: ★★★
Spaciousness: ★★★ Quiet: ★★★★
Security: ★★★★ Cleanliness: ★★★★
Insect Control: ★★★ Facilities: ★★★★

Located near the center of the state in Webster County, Holly River State Park is far from the hustle and bustle of city life, making it a perfect vacation getaway. Weighing in at 8,101 acres, Holly River is the second-largest park in the West Virginia park system. Nestled in a narrow valley, the park is surrounded by heavily forested mountains, some reaching heights of over 2,800 feet. Most of the campsites are stretched alongside Laurel Fork before that body of water merges with Left Fork Holly River. The campground offers a homey, wood-paneled restaurant with wood-burning fireplace for those who want a delicious break from the picnics, campsite cookouts, and cabin-cooked meals. Tecumseh and Tenskwatawa Trails, named for two legendary Native American chiefs of the area, are popular routes to view waterfalls. Another great hike is the trail to Potato Knob, featuring a view at 2,480 feet. At the bottom, you can't miss the Shupe's Chute waterfall.

BASICS

Operated By: State of West Virginia. **Open:** Apr. 15–Oct. 31. **Site Assignment:** Reservations and walk-ins accepted. **Registration:** At campground office. **Fee:** $13–$17 (VISA, MC). **Parking:** At site.

FACILITIES

Number of RV Sites: 88. **Number of Tent-Only Sites:** None. **Hookups:** Electric (20 amps). **Each Site:** Fire grate, picnic table. **Dump Station:** Yes. **Laundry:** Yes. **Pay Phone:** Yes. **Rest Rooms and Showers:** Yes. **Fuel:** No. **Propane:** No. **Internal Roads:** Paved, in good condition. **RV Service:** No. **Market:** Within 12 mi. **Restaurant:** Within 7 mi. **General Store:** Yes. **Vending:** Yes. **Playground:** Yes. **Other:** None. **Activities:** Lake fishing, hiking trails, swimming, horseshoes, planned activities, sports field, tennis, basketball, croquet. **Nearby Attractions:** Sutton Lake, Burnsville Lake, West Virginia Wildlife Center, Elk River Public Hunting and Fishing Area, Kumbrabow State Forest, Helvetia. **Additional Information:** Randolph County CVB, (800) 422-3304, www.randolphcountywv.com.

RESTRICTIONS

Pets: On leash only. **Fires:** At site. **Alcoholic Beverages:** No alcohol permitted. **Vehicle Maximum Length:** None. **Other:** 14-day stay limit.

TO GET THERE

From SR 15, go 12 mi. north on SR 20. Follow signs to the park.

HARPER'S FERRY

KOA—Harper's Ferry/ Washington, D.C. Northwest

Rte. 5 Box 1300, Harper's Ferry 25425. T: (304) 535-6895 or (800) KOA-9497; F: (304) 535-6870; www.koa.com; harpersferrykoa@gocampingamerica.com.

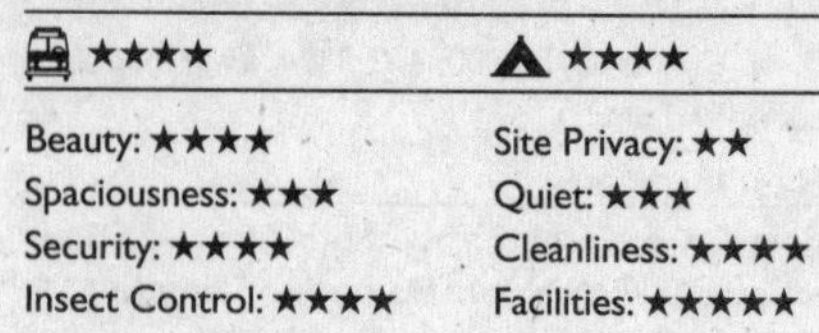

RV ★★★★ Tent ★★★★

Beauty: ★★★★ Site Privacy: ★★
Spaciousness: ★★★ Quiet: ★★★
Security: ★★★★ Cleanliness: ★★★★
Insect Control: ★★★★ Facilities: ★★★★★

Located at the confluence of the Potomac and Shenandoah Rivers, KOA—Harper's Ferry/Washington, D.C. Northwest is packed with Civil War history. With the ferry across the Potomac, the Hall Rifle Works, the Chesapeake and Ohio Canal (which connected Harper's Ferry to Washington, D.C.), and the Baltimore & Ohio Railroad, the town had definite strategic value. Usually occupied by Federal troops, Harper's Ferry also became a refugee camp for thousands of runaway slaves making their way north. The campground, one of the top three in West Virginia, is the same place where Civil War troops camped, and it's an ideal base for families exploring the Harper's Ferry area and Washington, D.C. The campground has 104 pull-through sites. A movie theater, spacious swimming pool, and well-stocked camp store are among the amenities. The campground will help arrange local and Washington, D.C. tours.

BASICS

Operated By: KOA. **Open:** All year. **Site Assignment:** Reservations recommended. **Registration:** At campground office. **Fee:** $25–$39 (VISA, MC, D). **Parking:** At site.

FACILITIES

Number of RV Sites: 209. **Number of Tent-Only Sites:** 97. **Hookups:** Electric (20, 30, 50 amps), phone, water, 142 full hookups. **Each Site:** Fire ring, picnic table. **Dump Station:** Yes. **Laundry:** Yes. **Pay Phone:** Yes. **Rest Rooms and Showers:** Yes. **Fuel:** No. **Propane:** Yes. **Internal Roads:** Gravel and paved, in good condition. **RV Service:** No. **Market:** Within 3 mi. **Restaurant:** Within 3 mi. **General Store:** Yes. **Vending:** Yes. **Playground:** Yes. **Other:** Located on Civil War battlefield. **Activities:** Rec hall, game room, swimming, wading pool, kayaking, float trips, planned activities, movies, sports field, horseshoes, hiking trail, volleyball, local tours. **Nearby Attractions:** Harper's Ferry National Historic Park, Harper's Ferry Overlook, Appalachian Trail, Antietam Battlefield, Washington, D.C., George Washington's Headquarters, National Museum of Civil War Medicine, Berkeley Castle. **Additional Information:** Jefferson Co. CVB, (800) 848-TOUR, www.jeffersoncountycvb.com.

RESTRICTIONS

Pets: On leash only. **Fires:** At site. **Alcoholic Beverages:** At site. **Vehicle Maximum Length:** 50 ft. **Other:** None.

To Get There

From the junction of US 340 and Harper's Ferry exit, go south 100 ft. to Campground Rd. Follow signs to entrance.

HINTON

Bluestone State Park

HC 78 Box 3, Hinton 25951. T: (304) 466-2805 or (800) CALLWVA; www.bluestonesp.com; bstone@stargate.net.

RV ★★★ Tent ★★★

Beauty: ★★★ Site Privacy: ★★★
Spaciousness: ★★★ Quiet: ★★★★
Security: ★★★★ Cleanliness: ★★★★
Insect Control: ★★★★ Facilities: ★★★

Adjacent to 2,000-acre Bluestone Lake, Bluestone State Park consists of 2,100 acres of rugged and mountainous terrain. Located five miles south of Hinton, the park has Meador Campground and Old Mill Campground, both with grassy sites along the Bluestone Lake. Set on the eastern shore of Bluestone Lake is a primitive 50-site campground accessible by boat only. The campgrounds are located in the flood storage basin of Bluestone Lake and are open early May–late Oct., depending on the water level. Several points of historical and recreational interest are located in the Bluestone area. Outdoor musical dramas such as "Hatfields and McCoys" are performed at Grandview Park, near Beckley. Just north of the park are Bluestone Dam, historic Hinton, and the New River Gorge National River.

Basics

Operated By: State of West Virginia. **Open:** Apr. 31–Oct. 31. **Site Assignment:** Reservations and walk-ins accepted. **Registration:** At campground office. **Fee:** $13–$17 (VISA, MC). **Parking:** At site.

Facilities

Number of RV Sites: 79. **Number of Tent-Only Sites:** 8. **Hookups:** Electric (20 amps). **Each Site:** Fire ring, picnic table, lantern pole. **Dump Station:** Yes. **Laundry:** Yes. **Pay Phone:** Yes. **Rest Rooms and Showers:** Yes. **Fuel:** No. **Propane:** No. **Internal Roads:** Paved, in good condition. **RV Service:** No. **Market:** Within 5 mi. **Restaurant:** Within 5 mi. **General Store:** Yes. **Vending:** Yes. **Playground:** Yes. **Other:** Cabin rentals. **Activities:** Rec hall, boating, canoeing, boat rentals, lake and stream fishing, planned activities, badminton, horseshoes, hiking trails, volleyball. **Nearby Attractions:** Bluestone Gorge, Hinton historic district, Pipestem Resort State Park, New River Gorge National River, Railroad Museum. **Additional Information:** Summers County CVB, (304) 466-5420, www.summerscvb.com.

Restrictions

Pets: On leash only. **Fires:** At site. **Alcoholic Beverages:** No alcohol permitted. **Vehicle Maximum Length:** 18 ft. **Other:** 14-day stay limit.

To Get There

From Hinton, go 4 mi. south on Hwy. 20. Follow signs to park entrance.

LOGAN

Chief Logan State Park

Chief Logan State Park, Logan 25601. T: (304) 792-7125 or (800) CALLWVA; www.wvparks.com/chieflogan.

RV ★★★ Tent ★★★★

Beauty: ★★★ Site Privacy: ★★★
Spaciousness: ★★★ Quiet: ★★★★
Security: ★★★★ Cleanliness: ★★★★
Insect Control: ★★★★ Facilities: ★★★

Located in West Virginia's southern coalfields near Logan, Chief Logan State Park is situated in wooded hills around Buffalo Creek. The campground has 25 sites, seven of which accommodate pull-throughs. The 3,300-acre park has 18 acres of trails for hiking and mountain biking. There's even a fitness trail dotted with exercise stations along the way. The Coal Mine Trail traces an old mine-tram road, complete with coal silo and mine openings. Chief Logan State Park has several attractions where the area's natural and Mingo Indian history are detailed. "The Aracoma Story," a play about the era when the Mingo tribe first encountered British settlers, is performed at the outdoor theater. An old steam locomotive, typical of those that once pulled coal cars from the surrounding mountains to market, is enshrined as a memorial to a bygone era. Also, a small wildlife exhibit featuring live animals native to the state—such as birds, bears, and snakes—is a much-visited attraction.

Basics

Operated By: State of West Virginia. **Open:** Mar. 1–Nov. 30. **Site Assignment:** Reservations and walk-ins accepted. **Registration:** Ranger will stop by your campsite and register you. **Fee:** $13–$17 (VISA, MC). **Parking:** At site.

Facilities

Number of RV Sites: 14. **Number of Tent-Only Sites:** 11. **Hookups:** Electric (20, 30 amps). **Each Site:** Fire grate, picnic table. **Dump Station:** Yes. **Laundry:** No. **Pay Phone:** Yes. **Rest Rooms and Showers:** Yes. **Fuel:** No. **Propane:** No. **Internal Roads:** Paved, in good condition. **RV Service:** No. **Market:** Within 4 mi. **Restaurant:** On state park grounds. **General Store:** No. **Vending:** Yes. **Playground:** Yes. **Other:** Outdoor theater. **Activities:** Mini-golf, hiking trails, tennis court. **Nearby Attractions:** Hatfield and McCoy Interpretive Driving Tour, Lost World Caverns, Organ Cave, New River Gorge National River. **Additional Information:** Southern West Virginia CVB, (800) VISITWV, www.visitwv.org.

Restrictions

Pets: On leash only. **Fires:** At site. **Alcoholic Beverages:** No alcohol permitted. **Vehicle Maximum Length:** 28 ft. **Other:** 14-day stay limit.

To Get There

From Logan, go 3 mi. north on Hwy. 10. Entrance is on the left.

LOST RIVER

Lost River Campground

HC 83 Box 2, Lost River 26810. T: (304) 897-5415; www.teetsfarms.com/campgrounds; teetsfarms@hardynet.com.

RV ★★★★ Tent ★★★★

Beauty: ★★★★ Site Privacy: ★★★
Spaciousness: ★★★ Quiet: ★★★★
Security: ★★★ Cleanliness: ★★★★
Insect Control: ★★★★ Facilities: ★★★★

Located in the eastern panhandle of West Virginia, Lost River Campground is about 10 miles north of the Virginia state line. The campground is a short drive from Lost River State Park, which has several miles of hiking trails, a swimming pool, and naturalist activities. Lost River Campground's main draw is its 63-acre stocked lake, a perfect spot for fishing and boating. The campground has 37 sites, all nice and level, and 11 pull-throughs. As is the case for most campgrounds in West Virginia, eye-catching natural wonders surround Lost River. Seneca Rocks, Spruce Knob, Smoke Hole, and Wolf Gap Recreation Area are nearby. Of course, Lost River State Park has its own share of natural splendor. One trail leads to Cranny Crow Overlook, where there are stunning views of the park from 3,200 feet up. Hikes, stream searches, films, slide shows, cookouts, campfires and family fun athletic competitions are among the park's organized events.

Basics

Operated By: Teets Farms. **Open:** All year. **Site Assignment:** Reservations and walk-ins accepted. **Registration:** At campground office. **Fee:** $16–$18 (VISA, MC). **Parking:** At site.

Facilities

Number of RV Sites: 37. **Number of Tent-Only Sites:** None. **Hookups:** Electric (20, 30, 50 amps). **Each Site:** Grill, picnic table. **Dump Station:** Yes. **Laundry:** No. **Pay Phone:** Yes. **Rest Rooms and Showers:** Yes. **Fuel:** No. **Propane:** No. **Internal Roads:** Gravel, in good condition. **RV Service:** No. **Market:** Within 8 mi. **Restaurant:** Within 6 mi. **General Store:** Yes. **Vending:** Yes. **Playground:** Yes. **Other:** 63-acre stocked lake. **Activities:** Lake and river fishing, boating, canoeing, kayaking, sports field, horseshoes, hiking trails. **Nearby Attractions:** Lost River State Park, Lost River Museum, the Potomac Eagle Train, Smoke Hole Caverns, Seneca Rocks. **Additional Information:** Potomac Highlands Travel Council, (304) 257-9315, www.potomachighlands.org.

Restrictions

Pets: On leash only. **Fires:** At site. **Alcoholic Beverages:** At site. **Vehicle Maximum Length:** None. **Other:** None.

To Get There

From SR 55, go 7 mi. south on SR 259 and 0.5 mi. west on Dove Hollow Rd. Entrance is on the left.

MILTON

Fox Fire Resort

Rte. 2 Box 655, Milton 25541. T: (304) 743-5622; F: (304) 743-5622; www.foxfirewv.com; foxfirewv@aol.com.

RV ★★★★ Tent n/a

Beauty: ★★★★ Site Privacy: ★★★
Spaciousness: ★★★ Quiet: ★★★★
Security: ★★★★★ Cleanliness: ★★★★
Insect Control: ★★★★ Facilities: ★★★★★

A 240-foot water slide. A whirlpool, sauna, and two swimming pools. Mini-golf. Hot-air balloon rides. Around-the-clock security. Clean, comfortable, open, grassy sites—all with full hookups. Consisting of 72 acres located in Milton between Huntington and Charleston, Fox Fire Resort is hands-down the finest private campground in West Virginia. Sites are spacious, and the campground accommodates 34 pull-throughs. Boating and fishing is available on Fox Fire's five spring-fed lakes, and there are several wooded trails for hikers and bikers to explore. After a long tennis match, soaking in the whirlpool is the perfect form of relaxation. For adventure, I.V. Cunningham will take you for a hot-air balloon ride. Hot-air balloon flights last about one hour or more, and it's a great way to see West Virginia's mountains.

BASICS

Operated By: Marie Cunningham. **Open:** All year. **Site Assignment:** Reservations and walk-ins accepted. **Registration:** At campground office. **Fee:** $24–$31 (VISA, MC, D). **Parking:** At designated spot.

FACILITIES

Number of RV Sites: 110. **Number of Tent-Only Sites:** None. **Hookups:** Electric (20, 30, 50 amps), phone, water, sewer. **Each Site:** Picnic table. **Dump Station:** Yes. **Laundry:** Yes. **Pay Phone:** Yes. **Rest Rooms and Showers:** Yes. **Fuel:** No. **Propane:** Yes. **Internal Roads:** Paved, in good condition. **RV Service:** No. **Market:** Within 6 mi. **Restaurant:** Within 6 mi. **General Store:** Yes. **Vending:** Yes. **Playground:** Yes. **Other:** 240-ft water slide. **Activities:** Rec hall, game room, 2 swimming pools, lake swimming, sauna, whirlpool, water slide, boat rentals, mini-golf, basketball, tennis, badminton, sports field, horseshoes, hiking trails, volleyball. **Nearby Attractions:** West Virginia Capitol Complex, West Virginia Cultural Center, Old Charleston Village, Kanawha State Forest. **Additional Information:** Charleston CVB, (800) 733-5469, www.charlestonwv.com.

RESTRICTIONS

Pets: On leash only. **Fires:** At site. **Alcoholic Beverages:** At site. **Vehicle Maximum Length:** None. **Other:** No tent camping.

TO GET THERE

From I-64, take Exit 28, go 3 mi. west on US 60, and 0.25 mi. northeast on Fox Fire Rd. Entrance is at the end.

MORGANTOWN

Chestnut Ridge Regional Park

Rte. 1 Box 267, Bruceton Mills 26525. T: (304) 594-1773 or (888) 594-3111; F: (304) 594-1711; www.chestnutridgepark.com; mail@chestnutridgepark.com.

RV ★★★★ Tent ★★★★

Beauty: ★★★ Site Privacy: ★★★
Spaciousness: ★★★ Quiet: ★★★★
Security: ★★★★ Cleanliness: ★★★★
Insect Control: ★★★★ Facilities: ★★★★

Rolling woodlands, mountain streams, and shaded trails define the landscape of 150-acre Chestnut Ridge Regional Park, located outside of Morgantown. Like nearby Sand Springs Camping Area, Chestnut Ridge is operated by Monongalia County; it features 18 graveled RV sites and 50 tent sites set on a mountainside forest. Paddle boating and fishing are options at Lake Harris and Feather Lake on the park's grounds. Sites at Area E near the Sand Springs Trail offer the most privacy. Chestnut Ridge hosts several special events, including a fishing rodeo, a 5K run, and a toboggan festival. Though Chestnut Ridge does not have a swimming pool, nearby Sand Springs has a pool and a mini-golf course, available to Chestunt Ridge campters for a fee. Hiking trails meander around Chestnut Ridge, but the best hiking nearby is at Cooper's Rock State Forest, where a lookout atop a massive rock formation looks down at the Cheat River Gorge. During college football season, the campground is swarmed when the West Virginia University Mountaineers are playing at home.

BASICS

Operated By: Monongalia County. **Open:** All year. **Site Assignment:** Reservations and walk-ins accepted. **Registration:** At park office. **Fee:** $13–$16 (VISA, MC). **Parking:** At designated spot.

FACILITIES

Number of RV Sites: 18. **Number of Tent-Only Sites:** 50. **Hookups:** Electric (30 amps). **Each Site:** Fire ring, picnic table. **Dump Station:** Yes. **Laundry:** Yes. **Pay Phone:** Yes. **Rest Rooms and Showers:** Yes. **Fuel:** No. **Propane:** No. **Internal Roads:** Gravel, in good condition. **RV Service:** No. **Market:** Within 7 mi. **Restaurant:** Within 5 mi. **General Store:** Yes. **Vending:** Yes. **Playground:** Yes. **Other:** Lodge and cabins, nature center. **Activities:** Pond swimming and boating, boat rentals, pond fishing, basketball, badminton, sports field, horseshoes, volleyball, hiking trails. **Nearby Attractions:** Morgantown, West Virginia University, Cooper's Rock State Forest, Circle H Outfitter's, Lakeview Scanticon Resort, Cheat Lake and Cheat River. **Additional Information:** Morgantown CVB, (800) 458-7373, www.mgtn.com.

RESTRICTIONS

Pets: On leash only. **Fires:** At site. **Alcoholic Beverages:** No alcohol permitted. **Vehicle Maximum Length:** 50 ft. **Other:** None.

TO GET THERE

From I-68, take Exit 15 and go 0.25 mi. east on Old Hwy. 73, 1.5 mi. on Sand Springs Rd., and left at the fork 1 mi. away. Entrance is on the left.

MULLENS

Twin Falls Resort State Park

Rte. 97 Box 1023, Mullens 25882. T: (304) 294-4000 or (800) CALLWVA; www.twinfallsresort.com; twinfalls@citynet.net.

RV ★★★★ Tent ★★★★

Beauty: ★★★★ Site Privacy: ★★★★
Spaciousness: ★★★ Quiet: ★★★★★
Security: ★★★★★ Cleanliness: ★★★★
Insect Control: ★★★★ Facilities: ★★★★★

Located southwest of Beckley, Twin Falls Resort State Park is named for the falls that majestically grace this rugged mountain wilderness. The campground features wooded and open campsites, including three pull-throughs. The contact center houses a laundromat, a small store with convenience items, and the camper registration area. Twin Falls has a swimming pool and a tennis court, but its prime recreation draw is the 18-hole, par 71 championship golf course. Nine hiking trails vary from remote wooded paths to scenic walks en route to the Twin Falls. The Pioneer Farm is a restored homeplace on Bowers Ridge; this living history farm provides a glimpse of the 1830s way of life in the Twin Falls area. Twin Falls Lodge is located on a high wooded ridge with a picturesque view of the golf course. The lodge also houses a restaurant that serves breakfast, lunch, and dinner.

BASICS

Operated By: State of West Virginia. **Open:** May 1–Oct. 15. **Site Assignment:** Reservations and walk-ins accepted. **Registration:** At campground office. **Fee:** $13–$17 (VISA, MC). **Parking:** At designated spot.

FACILITIES

Number of RV Sites: 25. **Number of Tent-Only Sites:** 25. **Hookups:** Electric (30 amps). **Each Site:** Fire ring, picnic table. **Dump Station:** Yes. **Laundry:** Yes. **Pay Phone:** Yes. **Rest Rooms and Showers:** Yes. **Fuel:** No. **Propane:** No. **Internal Roads:** Paved, in good condition. **RV Service:** No. **Market:** Within 5 mi. **Restaurant:** On park grounds. **General Store:** Yes. **Vending:** Yes. **Playground:** Yes. **Other:** Lodge and restaurant. **Activities:** Swimming, tennis, badminton, planned activities, hiking trails, volleyball. **Nearby Attractions:** Beckley, New River Gorge National River, Exhibition Coal Mine and Coal Museum. **Additional Information:** Southern West Virginia CVB, (800) VISITWV, www.visitwv.org.

RESTRICTIONS

Pets: On leash only. **Fires:** At site. **Alcoholic Beverages:** No alcohol permitted. **Vehicle Maximum Length:** 30 ft. **Other:** 14-day stay limit.

TO GET THERE

From Hwy. 54, go 5.5 mi. west on Hwy. 97. Follow signs to park.

NEW MANCHESTER

Tomlinson Run State Park

P.O. Box 97, New Manchester 26056. T: (304) 564-3651; www.wvparks.com/tomlinsonrun; harvej@wvnvm.wvnet.edu.

 ★★★★  ★★★★

Beauty: ★★★★ Site Privacy: ★★★
Spaciousness: ★★★ Quiet: ★★★★
Security: ★★★★ Cleanliness: ★★★★
Insect Control: ★★★★ Facilities: ★★★★

Located at the tip of West Virginia's northern panhandle, Tomlinson Run State Park is five miles in either direction of the Ohio and Pennsylvania borders. The spacious sites are situated at the Chief Big Foot and Chief Logan camping areas. Eleven sites accommodate pull-throughs, and there are six rent-a-camp sites with cabin-style tents sans electricity. Four ponds at Tomlinson Run are stocked with bass and bluegill. Swimming is even a unique adventure at Tomlinson Run; the Z-shaped pool can accommodate 1,600 people and has a 182-foot figure-eight water slide. Hiking trails offer spectacular views of the valleys and ridges that surround Tomlinson Run Lake. The Poe Trail, Big Foot Trail, and Laurel Trail are just a few pathways where hikers can immerse themselves in this park's natural splendor.

Basics

Operated By: State of West Virginia. **Open:** Apr. 1–Oct. 31. **Site Assignment:** Reservations and walk-ins accepted. **Registration:** At campground office. **Fee:** $13–$17 (VISA, MC). **Parking:** At site.

Facilities

Number of RV Sites: 48. **Number of Tent-Only Sites:** 6. **Hookups:** Electric (30 amps). **Each Site:** Fire grate, picnic table, lantern pole. **Dump Station:** Yes. **Laundry:** Yes. **Pay Phone:** Yes. **Rest Rooms and Showers:** Yes. **Fuel:** No. **Propane:** No. **Internal Roads:** Paved, in good condition. **RV Service:** No. **Market:** Within 8 mi. **Restaurant:** Within 8 mi. **General Store:** Yes. **Vending:** Yes. **Playground:** Yes. **Other:** Tomlinson Run Lake. **Activities:** Lake swimming, boating, boat rentals, pond and stream fishing, mini-golf, tennis courts, hiking trails, volleyball. **Nearby Attractions:** Wheeling, Oglebay Park Resort, Point Overlook Museum, Wheeling Suspension Bridge, Independence Hall. **Additional Information:** Wheeling CVB, (800) 828-3097, www.wheelingcvb.com.

Restrictions

Pets: On leash only. **Fires:** At site. **Alcoholic Beverages:** At site. **Vehicle Maximum Length:** None. **Other:** 14-day stay limit.

To Get There

From SR 2, go 3 mi. north on SR 8. Entrance is on the left.

PIPESTEM

KOA—Pipestem

HC 78 Box 37B, Pipestem 25979. T: (800) 562-5418 or (304) 466-5114; www.koa.com.

 ★★★  ★★★★

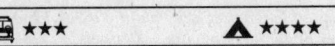

Beauty: ★★★★ Site Privacy: ★★★★
Spaciousness: ★★★ Quiet: ★★★
Security: ★★★★ Cleanliness: ★★★★
Insect Control: ★★★★ Facilities: ★★★

Located in southeast West Virginia 14 miles north of Princeton, KOA—Pipestem is smaller than most KOA campgrounds, and it has few amenities. Yet its proximity to whitewater rafting at the New River Gorge National River and outdoor activities at Pipestem Resort State Park, Bluestone Lake, and the Greenbrier River Trail make it an inviting place to stay nonetheless. KOA—Pipestem has open and shaded sites, including 21 pull-throughs. The campground has a full-service store. Nearby, Pipestem Resort State Park has two golf courses, a restaurant, an outdoor amphitheater, a nature center, and several hiking trails. New River Gorge also offers several miles of hiking trails with incredible cliff views. East of Lewisburg, where the historic district includes the 1796 Old Stone Church, the Greenbrier River Trail offers another 76 miles of trails for hiking and biking.

Basics

Operated By: KOA. **Open:** Mar. 1–Nov. 30. **Site Assignment:** Reservations and walk-ins accepted. **Registration:** At campground office. **Fee:** $20–$25 (VISA, MC). **Parking:** At designated spot.

Facilities

Number of RV Sites: 24. **Number of Tent-Only Sites:** 6. **Hookups:** Electric (20, 30 amps). **Each Site:** Fire ring, picnic table. **Dump Station:** Yes. **Laundry:** Yes. **Pay Phone:** Yes. **Rest Rooms and Showers:** Yes. **Fuel:** No. **Propane:** Yes. **Internal Roads:** Gravel, in good condition. **RV Service:** No. **Market:** Within 3 mi. **Restaurant:** Within 3 mi. **General Store:** Yes. **Vending:** Yes. **Playground:** Yes. **Other:** None. **Activities:** Hiking trails, golf. **Nearby Attractions:** Bluestone Lake, Historic Lewisburg, Greenbrier River Trail, Exhibition Coal Mine and Coal Museum, Pipestem Resort State Park. **Additional Information:** Southern West Virginia CVB, (800) VISITWV, www.visitwv.org.

Restrictions

Pets: On leash only. **Fires:** At site. **Alcoholic Beverages:** At site. **Vehicle Maximum Length:** None. **Other:** None.

To Get There

From I-77, take Exit 14 and go 3.5 mi. north on CR 7 and 13.5 northeast on SR 20. Follow signs to park entrance.

PIPESTEM

Pipestem Resort State Park

P.O. Box 150, Pipestem 25979. T: (304) 466-1800 or (800) CALLWVA; www.pipestemresort.com; pipestem@cwv.net.

 ★★★★ ▲ ★★★★

Beauty: ★★★★ Site Privacy: ★★★
Spaciousness: ★★★ Quiet: ★★★★
Security: ★★★★ Cleanliness: ★★★★
Insect Control: ★★★★ Facilities: ★★★★★

Pipestem Resort State Park is the crown jewel of West Virginia's state parks. There are several amenities, including two lodges and a full menu of recreational activities (five tennis courts, two golf courses, and mini-golf to name a few). Pipestem's scenic highlight is the aerial tramway that carries passengers on a six-minute ride over Bluestone Gorge and Bluestone River, 3,600 ft. below. The campground has 23 pull-through sites. Pipestem State Park also has two lodges. McKeever Lodge has 112 modern guest rooms and suites, some rooms with gorge views. This lodge has an indoor heated pool, game room, saunas, exercise room, a full-service restaurant, and snack bar. Mountain Creek Lodge is solely accessible by the aerial tramway; this lodge also has a restaurant. Pipestem features two golf courses—one an 18-hole, par 72 championship course with views of Bluestone Canyon, and the other a 9-hole course.

Basics

Operated By: State of West Virginia. **Open:** Memorial Day–Labor Day. **Site Assignment:** Reservations and walk-ins accepted. **Registration:** At campground office. **Fee:** $13–$19 (VISA, MC, AE, D). **Parking:** At designated spot.

Facilities

Number of RV Sites: 51. **Number of Tent-Only Sites:** 31. **Hookups:** Electric (30, 50 amps), 50 full hookups. **Each Site:** Fire ring, picnic table. **Dump Station:** Yes. **Laundry:** Yes. **Pay Phone:** Yes. **Rest Rooms and Showers:** Yes. **Fuel:** No. **Propane:** No. **Internal Roads:** Paved, in good condition. **RV Service:** No. **Market:** Within 5 mi. **Restaurant:** On park grounds. **General Store:** Yes. **Vending:** Yes. **Playground:** Yes. **Other:** 2 swimming pools, indoor and outdoor. **Activities:** Swimming, canoeing, boat rentals, lake and river fishing, shuffleboard, mini-golf, tennis courts, planned activities, badminton, horseshoes, hiking trails, volleyball, horseback riding. **Nearby Attractions:** Bluestone Lake, Historic Lewisburg, Greenbrier River Trail, Exhibition Coal Mine and Coal Museum. **Additional Information:** Southern West Virginia CVB, (800) VISITWV, www.visitwv.org.

Restrictions

Pets: On leash only. **Fires:** At site. **Alcoholic Beverages:** No alcohol permitted. **Vehicle Maximum Length:** None. **Other:** 14-day stay limit.

To Get There

From I-77, go 3.5 mi. north on CR 7 and 13.5 mi. northeast on SR 20. Follow signs to park and campgroun vd.

RICHWOOD

Summit Lake Campground

Box 110, Richwood 26261. T: (304) 846-2695; F: (304) 636-1875; www.fs.fed.us/r9/mon; tvance@fs.fed.us.

★★★ ▲ ★★★★

Beauty: ★★★ Site Privacy: ★★★
Spaciousness: ★★★ Quiet: ★★★★
Security: ★★★ Cleanliness: ★★★★
Insect Control: ★★★ Facilities: ★★★

Located about 10 miles east of Richwood in the Monongahela National Forest, Summit Lake Campground is adjacent to 43-acre Summit Lake. Many campsites are level and perched on a mountainside. Summit Lake is stocked with trout by the West Virginia Division of Natural Resources. The lake has an accessible fishing pier and boat launch. Brook trout, rainbow trout, brown trout, largemouth bass, and crappie are among the fish swimming in the lake. Hiking and mountain biking are available on Summit Lake Trail and Pocahontas Trail. Nearby are Bishop Knob Campground and Cranberry Campground. Also close is the Cranberry Backcountry, teeming with hiking and fishing spots. Overall, the Monongahela National Forest consists of 900,000 acres, including 850 miles of hiking trails.

Basics

Operated By: US Forest Service. **Open:** Mar. 15–Dec. 8. **Site Assignment:** First-come, first-served; no reservations accepted. **Registration:** At park office. **Fee:** $6 (VISA, MC). **Parking:** At designated spot.

Facilities

Number of RV Sites: 33. **Number of Tent-Only Sites:** None. **Hookups:** None. **Each Site:** Picnic table, fire ring, lantern pole. **Dump Station:** No. **Laundry:** No. **Pay Phone:** Yes. **Rest Rooms and Showers:** No. **Fuel:** No. **Propane:** No. **Internal Roads:** Paved, in good condition. **RV Service:** No. **Market:** Within 5 mi. **Restaurant:** Within 5 mi. **General Store:** No. **Vending:** No. **Playground:** No. **Other:** Summit Lake. **Activities:** Lake fishing, boating, volleyball, sports field. **Nearby Attractions:** Monongahela National Forest. **Additional Information:** Summersville CVB, (304) 872-3722, www.richwoodwv.com.

Restrictions

Pets: On leash only. **Fires:** At site. **Alcoholic Beverages:** At site. **Vehicle Maximum Length:** 22 ft. **Other:** 14-day stay limit.

To Get There

From Hwy. 39, go 2 mi. north on Hwy. 77. Follow signs to park.

ROANOKE

Stonewall Jackson State Park Campground

Rte. 1 Box 0, Roanoke 26447. T: (304) 269-0523; www.stonewalljacksonsp.com; stonewall@dnr.state.wv.us.

RV ★★★ Tent ★★★

Beauty: ★★★★	Site Privacy: ★★★
Spaciousness: ★★★	Quiet: ★★★★
Security: ★★★★	Cleanliness: ★★★★
Insect Control: ★★★	Facilities: ★★★★

Located in the heart of West Virginia about 13 miles south of Weston and named for the esteemed Civil War general, Stonewall Jackson Lake State Park Campground has 34 sites, all fully equipped. Open Apr.–Dec., the campground is near the 2,650-acre Stonewall Jackson Lake, where houseboats, pontoons, and motor boats can be rented. The lake also features a fishing pier and a fully equipped marina. Hiking and biking trails are available, as is a pavilion for picnicking and a playground for the children.

Basics

Operated By: State of West Virginia. **Open:** Apr. 1–Dec. 15. **Site Assignment:** Reservations recommended; first-come, first-served for walk-ins. **Registration:** At campground headquarters. **Fee:** $20. **Parking:** At site only.

Facilities

Number of RV Sites: 35. **Number of Tent-Only Sites:** None. **Hookups:** Electric (30 amps), water, sewer. **Each Site:** Grill, picnic table. **Dump Station:** Yes. **Laundry:** Yes. **Pay Phone:** Yes. **Rest Rooms and Showers:** Yes. **Fuel:** No. **Propane:** No. **Internal Roads:** Gravel, in fair condition. **RV Service:** No. **Market:** 2.5 mi. north in Roanoke. **Restaurant:** 2.5 mi. north in Roanoke. **General Store:** Yes. **Vending:** Yes. **Playground:** Yes. **Other:** Cottages and houseboats also available A 200-room lodge, 18-hole championship golf course, 10 cabins, and 100 additional campsites are planned in the next few years. **Activities:** Boating, swimming, hiking, bicycling. **Nearby Attractions:** Stonewall Jackson Lake, Jackson's Mill Historic Area, Lambert's Vintage Winery, Masterpiece Crystal, Glass Works Factory Outlet, Weston. **Additional Information:** Lewis County Convention and Visitors Bureau, www.stonewallcountry.com, (304) 269-7328.

Restrictions

Pets: On leash only. **Fires:** At site only. **Alcoholic Beverages:** At site only. **Vehicle Maximum Length:** 40 ft. **Other:** 14 day max. stay.

To Get There

From Interstate 79, take Exit 91 (Roanoke) and follow US 19 south for 2.5 mi. to the park entrance.

RONCEVERTE

Organ Cave Campground

417 Masters Rd., Ronceverte 24970. T: (304) 647-5551; www.organcave.com; information@organcave.com.

RV ★★★★ Tent ★★★★

Beauty: ★★★★	Site Privacy: ★★★★
Spaciousness: ★★★★	Quiet: ★★★★
Security: ★★★	Cleanliness: ★★★★
Insect Control: ★★★★	Facilities: ★★★

Organ Cave Campground, located in southeastern West Virginia's Greenbrier Valley near Ronceverte, features 37 sites—including four pull-throughs—adjoining Organ Cave, a National Natural Historic Landmark. The campground itself has no rest rooms, but its beautiful mountain setting provides lots of serenity and scenery. Tours are given in Organ Cave, one of the longest caves in the United States with more than 40 miles of mapped passageways. Pioneers have known of Organ Cave since 1704, and the cave also played a role during the Civil War. Religious services for 1,100 of Gen. Robert E. Lee's men were given in the shelter of the huge entrance room of the cave. The cave was a significant source of saltpeter, one of the ingredients necessary for making gunpowder. Organ Cave's grounds also feature a rodeo arena, where several rodeos are held throughout the year.

Basics

Operated By: Organ Cave. **Open:** All year. **Site Assignment:** Reservations and walk-ins accepted. **Registration:** At campground office. **Fee:** $15 (VISA, MC, AE, D). **Parking:** At designated spot.

Facilities

Number of RV Sites: 37. **Number of Tent-Only Sites:** None. **Hookups:** Electric (20, 30, 50 amps), water. **Each Site:** Picnic table. **Dump Station:** Yes. **Laundry:** No. **Pay Phone:** Yes. **Rest Rooms and Showers:** No. **Fuel:** No. **Propane:** No. **Internal Roads:** Paved, in good condition. **RV Service:** No. **Market:** Within 6 mi. **Restaurant:** Within 6 mi. **General Store:** Yes. **Vending:** Yes. **Playground:** Yes. **Other:** Rodeo arena, Organ Cave. **Activities:** Basketball, horseshoes, volleyball, sports field, hiking trails. **Nearby Attractions:** Organ Cave, Exhibition Coal Mine and Coal Museum, Beckley, Hinton, Lewisburg. **Additional Information:** Southern West Virginia CVB, (800) VISITWV, www.visitwv.org.

Restrictions

Pets: On leash only. **Fires:** At site. **Alcoholic Beverages:** At site. **Vehicle Maximum Length:** None. **Other:** None.

To Get There

From I-64, take Exit 169 and go 6 mi. south on Hwy. 219, 3.5 mi. east on Hwy. 219/Hwy. 63E, and 0.5 mi. east on Hwy. 63E. Entrance is on the right.

SAND SPRINGS CAMPING AREA

Morgantown

Rte. 1 Box 267, Bruceton Mills 26525. T: (304) 594-2415 or (877) 817-9395; F: (304) 594-1269; www.chestnutridgepark.com; chestnut@westvirginia.com.

RV ★★★★ Tent ★★★★

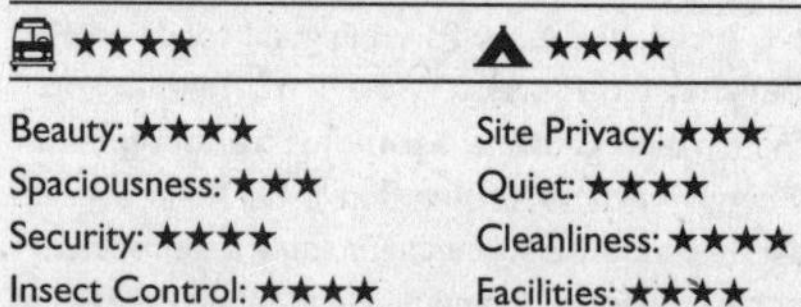

Beauty: ★★★★	Site Privacy: ★★★
Spaciousness: ★★★	Quiet: ★★★★
Security: ★★★★	Cleanliness: ★★★★
Insect Control: ★★★★	Facilities: ★★★★

Located outside of Morgantown, Sand Springs Camping Area is larger than Chestnut Ridge Regional Park, the nearby campground also operated by Monongalia County. Sand Springs has 36 RV sites, including 10 pull-throughs. Most of the RV sites are located in the center of the park. Sand Springs also offers 40 tent sites, the best being those at the northeast tip of the campground. Pond fishing and paddle boating are options at nearby Chestnut Ridge; hiking and other outdoor pursuits are available at Cooper's Rock State Forest. The Morgantown area is also home to the Allegheny Trail, which stretches 270 miles through West Virginia. Like Chestnut Ridge, Sand Springs is best visited during the spring and fall, when the colors of the mountains are especially vibrant.

Basics

Operated By: Monongalia County. **Open:** Apr. 1–Dec. 1. **Site Assignment:** Reservations and walk-ins accepted. **Registration:** At camp office. **Fee:** $20–$22 (VISA, MC). **Parking:** At designated spot.

Facilities

Number of RV Sites: 36. **Number of Tent-Only Sites:** 40. **Hookups:** Electric (20, 30, 50 amps), phone, water, 26 full hookups. **Each Site:** Fire ring, picnic table. **Dump Station:** Yes. **Laundry:** Yes. **Pay Phone:** Yes. **Rest Rooms and Showers:** Yes. **Fuel:** No. **Propane:** No. **Internal Roads:** Gravel, in good condition. **RV Service:** No. **Market:** Within 7 mi. **Restaurant:** Within 7 mi. **General Store:** Yes. **Vending:** Yes. **Playground:** Yes. **Other:** Mini-golf course. **Activities:** Rec room, game room, swimming, mini-golf, hiking trails. **Nearby Attractions:** Morgantown, West Virginia University, Cooper's Rock State Forest, Circle H Outfitters, Lakeview Scanticon Resort, Cheat Lake and Cheat River. **Additional Information:** Morgantown CVB, (800) 458-7373, www.mgtn.com.

Restrictions

Pets: On leash only. **Fires:** At site. **Alcoholic Beverages:** No alcohol permitted. **Vehicle Maximum Length:** 35 ft. **Other:** None.

To Get There

From I-68, take Exit 15 and go 0.5 mi. northeast on Old Rte. 73 and 2.25 mi. north on Sand Springs Rd. Entrance is on the right.

SENECA ROCKS

Yokum's Vacationland

HC 59 Box 3, Seneca Rocks 26884. T: (304) 567-2351 or (800) 772-8342; F: (304) 567-2642; www.yokum.com; shirley@yokum.com.

RV ★★★★ Tent ★★★★

Beauty: ★★★ Site Privacy: ★★
Spaciousness: ★★★ Quiet: ★★★★
Security: ★★★★ Cleanliness: ★★★
Insect Control: ★★★ Facilities: ★★★★

Located in the center of Pendleton County amid the Spruce Knob—Seneca Rocks National Recreation Area and Monongahela National Forest, Yokum's Vacationland is situated on a 1,000-acre cattle farm. Some sites are open, others are shaded. The campground is located along the north fork of the Potomac River. Princess Snowbird Campground, set on Seneca Creek and facing a majestic view of the Seneca Rocks, has primitive sites with teepees in the Indian Village. Fishing and swimming are popular in the river. The campground also has a new heated indoor pool. Adventure seekers have several options in the area, including whitewater rafting. Rock climbers can rent equipment and climb the 960-foot-high Seneca Rocks with qualified instructors. Seneca Caverns offers guided tours through its trails.

Basics

Operated By: Yokum family. **Open:** All year. **Site Assignment:** Reservations and walk-ins accepted. **Registration:** At campg office. **Fee:** $16–$18 (VISA, MC, AE, D). **Parking:** At designated spot.

Facilities

Number of RV Sites: 150. **Number of Tent-Only Sites:** 50. **Hookups:** Electric (15, 20, 30 amps), water, 18 full hookups. **Each Site:** Fire ring, picnic table. **Dump Station:** Yes. **Laundry:** Yes. **Pay Phone:** Yes. **Rest Rooms and Showers:** Yes. **Fuel:** No. **Propane:** No. **Internal Roads:** Paved, in good condition. **RV Service:** No. **Market:** Within 5 mi. **Restaurant:** On premises. **General Store:** Yes. **Vending:** Yes. **Playground:** Yes. **Other:** None. **Activities:** Rec room, swimming, river swimming, canoeing, river fishing, hiking trails, sports field, volleyball. **Nearby Attractions:** Seneca Caverns, Blackwater Falls, Cass Scenic Railroad, Seneca Rocks, Spruce Knob. **Additional Information:** Tucker Co. CVB, (800) 782-2775, www.canaanvalley.org.

Restrictions

Pets: On leash only. **Fires:** At site. **Alcoholic Beverages:** No alcohol permitted. **Vehicle Maximum Length:** None. **Other:** None.

To Get There

From US 33, go 0.5 mi. north on Hwy. 28. Entrance is on the right.

SUMMERSVILLE

Mountain Lake Campground

Airport Rd., Summersville 26651. T: (304) 872-4220.

RV ★★★★ Tent ★★★★

Beauty: ★★★★ Site Privacy: ★★★
Spaciousness: ★★★ Quiet: ★★★★
Security: ★★★★ Cleanliness: ★★★★
Insect Control: ★★★★ Facilities: ★★★★

Located in Summersville in south-central West Virginia, Mountain Lake Campground is situated near Summersville Lake, the largest lake in the state. The campground has shaded and open sites, including 15 pull-throughs. Campers at Mountain Lake can swim and fish in Summersville Lake, called "the little Bahamas of the East" by Skin Diver Magazine because of its excellent visibility—scuba diving is popular since the visibility in the lake is 20–45 feet (sometimes as much as 80 feet). The lake was built by the Corps of Engineers, and the dam is on Gauley River near Summersville. The dam is the second largest of its type in the eastern U.S. In fact, the dam is about as tall as a 40-story building and is 2,280 feet long. The hiking is remarkable, too, especially at the Battle Run Recreation Area.

Basics

Operated By: Private operator. **Open:** All year. **Site Assignment:** Reservations and walk-ins accepted. **Registration:** At camp headquarters. **Fee:** $13–$15 (V, MC). **Parking:** At designated spot.

Facilities

Number of RV Sites: 150. **Number of Tent-Only Sites:** 50. **Hookups:** Electric (20, 30 amps), phone, water. **Each Site:** Fire ring, picnic table. **Dump Station:** Yes. **Laundry:** Yes. **Pay Phone:** Yes. **Rest Rooms and Showers:** Yes. **Fuel:** No. **Propane:** No. **Internal Roads:** Gravel, in good condition. **RV Service:** No. **Market:** Within 4 mi. **Restaurant:** Within 4 mi. **General Store:** Yes. **Vending:** Yes. **Playground:** Yes. **Other:** None. **Activities:** Rec hall, game room, lake swimming and fishing, boating, canoeing, kayaking, mini-golf, basketball, badminton, sports field, horseshoes, hiking, volleyball. **Nearby Attractions:** New River Gorge National River, Gauley River National Recreation Area, Carniex Ferry Battlefield SP, Hawk's Nest State Park. **Additional Information:** Southern West Virginia CVB, (800) VISITWV, www.visitwv.org.

Restrictions

Pets: On leash only. **Fires:** At site. **Alcoholic Beverages:** At site. **Vehicle Max. Length:** None.

To Get There

From Summersville, go 1 mi. south on US 19 and 2 mi. west on Airport Rd. Entrance is on the right.

WESTON

Whisper Mountain Campground and RV Park

Rte. 1 Box 65, Roanoke 26423. T: (304) 452-8847 or (800) CALLWVA; www.fishingspots.net/whisper_mountain; webmaster@fishingspots.net.

RV ★★★★ Tent ★★★★

Beauty: ★★★★ Site Privacy: ★★★
Spaciousness: ★★★ Quiet: ★★★★
Security: ★★★★ Cleanliness: ★★★★
Insect Control: ★★★★ Facilities: ★★★★

Located near Stonewall Jackson Lake and State Park, and Weston, Whisper Mountain Campground and RV Park has 69 level and grassy sites with 10 pull-throughs, all situated amid mountain scenery. Hiking and biking trails (as well as boat rentals) can be found at 2,650-acre Stonewall Jackson Lake. The lake also features a fishing pier and a fully equipped marina. A short drive from Whisper Mountain, Jackson's Mill Historic Area, where Confederate Gen. Thomas "Stonewall" Jackson's boyhood home is located, also houses an assortment of 19th-century buildings.

Basics

Operated By: Chyreck family. **Open:** All year. **Site Assignment:** Reservations and walk-ins accepted. **Registration:** At campground office. **Fee:** $16–$18 (VISA, MC). **Parking:** At designated spot.

Facilities

Number of RV Sites: 49. **Number of Tent-Only Sites:** 20. **Hookups:** Electric (20, 30, 50 amps), water, 5 full hookups. **Each Site:** Fire ring, picnic table. **Dump Station:** Yes. **Laundry:** Yes. **Pay Phone:** Yes. **Rest Rooms and Showers:** Yes. **Fuel:** No. **Propane:** No. **Internal Roads:** Paved, in good condition. **RV Service:** No. **Market:** Within 6 mi. **Restaurant:** Within 6 mi. **General Store:** Yes. **Vending:** Yes. **Playground:** Yes. **Other:** None. **Activities:** Swimming, paddle boat rentals, pond fishing, sports field, horseshoes, hiking trails, volleyball. **Nearby Attractions:** Stonewall Jackson Lake and State Park, Jackson's Mill Historic Area, Weston Christmas Town, Glass Works Factory Outlet. **Additional Information:** Lewis County CVB, (304) 269-7328, www.stonewallcountry.com.

Restrictions

Pets: On leash only. **Fires:** At site. **Alcoholic Beverages:** At site. **Vehicle Max. Length:** None.

To Get There

From I-79, take Exit 91 and go 200 yds. north on US 19, 5 mi. west on Goose Pen Rd., and 100 ft. south on 3 Lick Rd. Entrance is on the left.

Wisconsin

Along with its famed cheese and cherries, Wisconsin offers a vacationer's paradise. From its rugged Door County peninsula to the state's biggest city of Milwaukee and on to the scenic Dells, America's Dairyland provides a variety of attractions.

The St. Croix River shares gorgeous gorges, rock formations, and waterfalls, while the national lakeshore has more lighthouses than any other national park. With 15,000 inland lakes and 25,000 miles of waterways—along with borders on Lakes Michigan and Superior, the St. Croix, Menomonie, and Brule Rivers, and the mighty Mississippi—Wisconsin is a water wonderland. Scuba divers explore shipwrecks waiting at "death's door," the watery passage between **Door County** and **Washington Island.** Navigable its entire length, the winding **Kickapoo** is called "the crookedest river in the world." For heights, head to **Devil's Lake State Park** near **Baraboo** for the 500-foot bluffs or to **Granddad Bluff** which towers 600 feet above **La Crosse.** Stretches of Class V rapids make the **Montreal River** a popular spot for expert kayakers. For exploration, the rugged sea caves dotting the bases of sandstone cliffs are a great choice.

To turn back the clock, visit the living history village in **New Glarus,** often called "Little Switzerland." The great architecture of Frank Lloyd Wright is preserved in **Madison** and **Spring Green,** as is circus memorabilia in **Baraboo.** Climb aboard the "Lumberjack Special" steam-powered train, puffing from the Laona historic depot to **Camp Five Museum Complex,** to learn about logging.

As Wisconsin's oldest state park, **Interstate State Park** in **St. Croix Falls** is home to an unusual rock outcropping known as the Old Man of the Dalles. Climb aboard a boat in the **Wisconsin Dells** for a cruise past rock formations, canyons, islands, and sandstone cliffs. In **Green Bay,** the Packers (founded in 1919) lay claim to being the oldest professional football team in the National Football League.

Anglers will enjoy seeing the **National Fresh Water Fishing Hall of Fame** in **Hayward.** Housed in a building designed to resemble a muskellunge, the facility is complete with an observation deck in the mouth of the giant fish. **Horicon** offers boat tours of a wetland inhabited by more than 260 species of birds.

True to its name, the lovely village of **Land O' Lakes** is surrounded by about 135 lakes. Stroll the tree-shaded streets of **Madison** where the impressive **1917 State Capitol** offers free tours showcasing state history and artwork.

The following facilities accept payment in checks or cash only:

Aqualand Camp Resort, Sister Bay
Benson's Century Camping Resort, Campbellsport
Big Lake Campground, Algoma
Chetek River Campground, Chetek
Coon's Deep Lake Campground, Oxford
Edgewater Acres Campground, Menomonie
Elmer's RV Park and Campgrounds, Eau Claire
Hickory Hills Campground, Edgerton
Hy-Land Court, Ellison Bay
Lake Chippewa Campground, Hayward
Lake Hilbert Campground, Goodman
Lakeview Campground, Milton
Maple View Campground, Norman
Mississippi Sports and Recreation, De Soto
Monument Point Camping, Sturgeon Bay
The Out-Post Campground, Tomahawk
Red Barn Campground, Shell Lake
Rivers Edge Campground, Stevens Point
Scenic View Campground, Spooner
Timber Trail Campground, Algoma
Timber Trail Campground, West Bend
Tomorrow Wood Campground, Hancock
Turtle Creek Campsite, Beloit
Veterans Memorial Campground, West Salem
Wildwood Campground, Iron River
Wolf River Trips and Campgrounds, New London

The following facilities feature 20 or fewer sites:

- Coon's Deep Lake Campground, Oxford
- Creekview Campground, Edgerton
- Elmer's RV Park and Campgrounds, Eau Claire
- Granger's Campground, Oakdale
- Ham Lake Campground, Laona
- Holiday Lodge Golf Resort, Wyeville
- Hy-Land Court, Ellison Bay
- Lost Falls Resort and Campground, Black River Falls
- Mississippi Sports and Recreation, De Soto
- Raft 'N Rest Campground and Rafting, White Lake
- Scenic View Campground, Spooner
- Wildwood Campground, Iron River
- Wolf River-Nicolet Forest Campground and Outdoor Center, White Lake

Campground Profiles

ALGOMA

Big Lake Campground

2427 Lake St., Algoma 54201. T: (920) 487-2726; mlthomas@itol.com.

RV ★★★ Tent ★★★

Beauty: ★★ Site Privacy: ★★
Spaciousness: ★★★ Quiet: ★★★
Security: ★★★ Cleanliness: ★★★★
Insect Control: None Facilities: ★★★

Located in Algoma, Big Lake Campground is surrounded by vacation land. It is only minutes from Northeast Wisconsin's many attractions—Lake Michigan and Door County, in particular. Campground sites are level, with a typical site width of 30 feet. Some sites are open, but most are shaded and back up into the woods. Laid out in a series of loops, the campground has one pull-through site. Boats also are allowed in the campground. Arrangements can be made ahead of time for charter fishing and for tee times at the local 18-hole golf course. For snowmobiling and ice-fishing enthusiasts, the campground is open from Jan. through Mar., with reservations. Tent sites are in a separate wooded area with more green space and privacy. Security measures include owners who live on site year-round and regular patrols by city police.

Basics

Operated by: Mike & Linda Thomas. **Open:** Apr. 15–Oct. 15; Jan.–Mar. w/ reservations. **Site Assignment:** Reservations w/ no deposit. **Registration:** At campground office. **Fee:** $20 (cash & check). **Parking:** At site.

Facilities

Number of RV Sites: 72. **Number of Tent-Only Sites:** 12. **Hookups:** Electric (20, 30, 50 amps), water, sewer. **Each Site:** Picnic table, fire ring. **Dump Station:** Yes. **Laundry:** Yes. **Pay Phone:** No. **Rest Rooms and Showers:** Yes. **Fuel:** No. **Propane:** No. **Internal Roads:** Gravel/dirt, in good condition. **RV Service:** No. **Market:** 0.25 mi. north in Algoma. **Restaurant:** 0.25 mi. north in Algoma. **General Store:** No. **Vending:** No. **Swimming Pool:** No. **Playground:** Yes. **Other:** Recreation field, volleyball, horseshoes, lighted fish-cleaning station, fish freezing, game room, badminton, adults room. **Activities:** None. **Nearby Attractions:** Lake Michigan, boat launch, fishing piers, beaches, golf, Door County, antiques, museums, charter fishing, cheese factories, harbor, winery, snowmobiling, ice fishing, zoo, jail museum. **Additional Information:** Algoma Area Chamber of Commerce, (920) 487-2041.

Restrictions

Pets: Leash only. **Fires:** Fire ring only. **Alcoholic Beverages:** Permitted. **Vehicle Maximum Length:** None.

To Get There

From the junction of Hwy. 54 and Hwy. 42, drive 1 mi. south on Hwy. 41. Roads are wide and well maintained w/ broad shoulders.

ALGOMA

Timber Trail Campground

N 8326 CR M, Algoma 54201. T: (920) 487-3707; timbertrail@itol.com.

RV ★★★ Tent ★★

Beauty: ★★ Site Privacy: ★★
Spaciousness: ★★★★ Quiet: ★★★
Security: ★★★★ Cleanliness: ★★★★
Insect Control: None Facilities: ★★★

Located near Algoma, Timber Trail Campground offers grassy, shaded sites close to Door County. The campground has 35 seasonal campers, four pull-through sites, and a typical site width of 40 feet. Tent sites are in a separate area with privacy from RVs and more green space. The best RV sites are 48, 49, and 50 because they are larger and more secluded in the woods. Security and safety measures include a five-mph speed limit and owners who live on site and provide regular patrols of the campground. Although part of the campground's major draw is its proximity to Door County, there are also several activities at the property. Another plus is clean bathrooms. Prices are very reasonable for being located in such a popular vacation area.

Basics

Operated by: Mike & Alisa Herrick. **Open:** Apr. 15–Oct. 15. **Site Assignment:** Reservations w/ 1-night deposit; refund w/ 2-week notice. **Registration:** At campground office. **Fee:** $20 (cash, check). **Parking:** At site.

Facilities

Number of RV Sites: 62. **Number of Tent-Only Sites:** 8. **Hookups:** Electric (20, 30, 50 amps), water. **Each Site:** Picnic table, fire ring. **Dump Station:** Yes. **Laundry:** Yes. **Pay Phone:** Yes. **Rest Rooms and Showers:** Yes. **Fuel:** No. **Propane:** Yes. **Internal Roads:** Gravel, in good condition. **RV Service:** No. **Market:** 1 mi. southeast in Algoma. **Restaurant:** 1 mi. southeast in Algoma. **General Store:** Yes. **Vending:** No. **Swimming Pool:** Yes. **Playground:** Yes. **Other:** Rec room, fishing lake/river, badminton, sports field, horseshoes, hiking trails, volleyball, riverboat launch. **Activities:** Swimming, fishing, boating (rental canoe available), hiking, scheduled weekend activities. **Nearby Attractions:** Lake Michigan, boat launch, fishing piers, beaches, golf, Door County, antiques, museums, charter fishing, cheese factories, harbor, winery, snowmobiling, ice fishing, zoo, jail museum. **Additional Information:** Algoma Area Chamber of Commerce (920) 487-2041.

Restrictions

Pets: Leash only. **Fires:** Fire ring only. **Alcoholic Beverages:** Permitted. **Vehicle Maximum Length:** None.

To Get There

From the junction of Hwy. 54 and Hwy. 42, drive 0.5 mi. north on Hwy. 42, then 1 mi. west on CR S, then 0.75 mi. north on CR M. The roads are wide and well maintained w/ broad shoulders.

BAGLEY

River of Lakes Campground and Resort

132A Packer Dr., Bagley 53801. T: (608) 996-2275

RV ★★ Tent ★★★

Beauty: ★★★ Site Privacy: ★★
Spaciousness: ★★ Quiet: ★★★
Security: ★★★ Cleanliness: ★★★
Insect Control: None Facilities: ★★★

Family owned and operated for over 40 years, River of Lakes Resort and Campground is located in the heart of the upper Mississippi bluff country in an area of lakes and backwater sloughs. That means plenty of water activities, including good fishing for bass, pike, catfish, and other panfish. However, it also means the Mississippi River sometimes leaves its banks and floods this campground one mile south of Bagley. Be sure the area is not in the midst of a flood or soon will be before you make camping plans. The entrance to the campground is over a railroad track and through an area of about 100 summer cottages and mobile homes. The campground has 75 seasonal lots in addition to the ones available for visitors. Many regulars return and bring their boats. Sites 57–59 are the most popular because they are on the riverfront.

Basics

Operated by: Rob & Gary Irish. **Open:** Apr. 15–Oct. 15. **Site Assignment:** First come, first served. **Registration:** At campground office. **Fee:** $17 (cash, check, credit cards). **Parking:** At site.

Facilities

Number of RV Sites: 120. **Number of Tent-Only Sites:** 0. **Hookups:** Electric (20, 30 amps,) water, sewer. **Each Site:** Picnic table, fire ring. **Dump Station:** Yes. **Laundry:** No. **Pay Phone:** Yes. **Rest Rooms and Showers:** Yes. **Fuel:** Yes. **Propane:** Yes. **Internal Roads:** Blacktop, in good condition. **RV Service:** No. **Market:** 17 mi. north to Prairie du Chien. **Restaurant:** 1 mi. north to Bagley. **General Store:** Yes. **Vending:** No. **Swimming Pool:** No. **Playground:** Yes. **Other:** Rec hall, pavilion, river, pond, shuffleboard, horseshoes, badminton, sports field, fish-cleaning facility, boat ramp, basketball, sandy beach & swim area. **Activities:** Swimming, fishing, boating (rental rowboats, canoes, paddleboats, motor boats available). **Nearby Attractions:** Casino, Villa Louis historical site, Kickapoo Indian Caverns, Native American Museum, car ferry, Museum of Agricultural History & Village Life. **Additional Information:** Prairie du Chien Chamber of Commerce, (800) 732-1673.

Restrictions

Pets: Leash only. **Fires:** Fire pits only. **Alcoholic Beverages:** Permitted. **Vehicle Maximum Length:** None.

To Get There

From the junction of CR X and CR A, drive 1 mi. south on CR A, then 0.75 mi. west on Willow Ln. Roads are wide and well maintained w/ broad shoulders.

BAGLEY

Syalusing State Park

13081 State Park Ln., Bagley 53801. T: (608) 996-2261

RV ★★ Tent ★★★★

Beauty: ★★★★ Site Privacy: ★★★★
Spaciousness: ★★★★ Quiet: ★★★★
Security: ★★★★ Cleanliness: ★★★
Insect Control: None Facilities: ★★

The 2,674-acre Wyalusing State Park got its name from the Munsee-Delaware Native American word meaning "home of the warrior." As with most state park campgrounds, Wyalusing is short on amenities and long on beauty and recreational opportunities. Although the park doesn't offer swimming, the Wyalusing Recreation Area two miles south of the park entrance is a county operated beach, boat ladning, and picnic area on the Mississippi River. No fees are required. Located five miles north of Bagley, the wilderness campground is covered by mature maple, cedar, oak, black walnut, and white pine trees. The best sites are atop a 500-foot bluff overlooking the Wisconsin River. Although the sites have no hookups, they are popular with both tents and RVs. Activity at Wyalusing slows during the winter but doesn't stop. Winter camping, ice fishing, cross-country skiing, sledding, snowshoeing, hiking, and wildlife observation draw campers to the park as the temperature plunges. Sevral campsites, including some with electricity, are kept plowed open all winter. Water is available near the group tent area. Winter camping here is only for the very hardy, but those numbers seem to increase each year.

Basics

Operated by: State of Wisconsin. **Open:** All year. **Site Assignment:** Reservations w/ entire stay deposit; refund (minus $9.50) w/ 4-day notice. **Registration:** At campground office. **Fee:** $13 (cash, check, credit cards), plus $5 daily park fee of $18 annual fee if Wisconsin resident; $7 daily fee or $25 annual fee if not Wisconsin resident. **Parking:** At site.

Facilities

Number of RV Sites: 34. **Number of Tent-Only Sites:** 76. **Hookups:** Electric (30 amps). **Each Site:** Picnic table, fire ring. **Dump Station:** Yes. **Laundry:** No. **Pay Phone:** Yes. **Rest Rooms and Showers:** Yes. **Fuel:** No. **Propane:** No. **Internal Roads:** Paved, in good condition. **RV Service:** No. **Market:** 12 m. west in Prairie du Chien. **Restaurant:** 5 mi. south in Bagley. **General Store:** Yes. **Vending:** Yes. **Swimming Pool:** No. **Playground:** Yes. **Other:** Backwaters of the Mississippi & Wisconsin rivers, tennis, canoe trail, boat ramp, hiking trail, shelter, nature center, bike trail. **Activities:** Fishing, boating, hiking, biking, nature education programs. **Nearby Attractions:** Casino, Villa Louis historical site, Kickapoo Indian Caverns, Native American Museum. **Additional Information:** Prairie du Chien Chamber of Commerce, (800) 732-1673.

Restrictions

Pets: Leash only. **Fires:** Fire ring only. **Alcoholic Beverages:** Permitted. **Vehicle Maximum Length:** None. **Other:** 14-day stay limit.

To Get There

From Bagley, drive 7 mi. north on CR X, then 1 mi. on CR C. Roads are in average condition w/ often narrow shoulders.

BAGLEY

Yogi Bear's Jellystone Park Camp-Resort

11354 CR X, Bagley 53801. T: (608) 996-2201; www.jellystonebagley.com; yogibagley@mailtds.net.

RV ★★★★ Tent ★★★

Beauty: ★★★ Site Privacy: ★★★
Spaciousness: ★★★ Quiet: ★★★
Security: ★★★★ Cleanliness: ★★★★
Insect Control: No Facilities: ★★★★

Campers know what to expect when they go to a Yogi Bear's Jellystone Park-Resort: clean facilities, a quiet, secure campground, and plenty of activities for children. The Bagley campground offers all that, plus a valley site with hills on both sides and the Mississippi River across the road. A railroad track also runs right by the campground. Laid out in a series of loops, the campground has sites that are flat, grassy, and mostly open. Many of the trees were wiped out by a 1998 tornado. Site sizes vary, with some as large as 40 feet wide and 100 feet deep. The campground has seven pull-throughs and 62 seasonal campers. Non-campers are allowed to use the recreational facilities for $3 per day per person, Sunday through Thursday, holidays excluded. Located one mile north of Bagley, the campground enforces quiet time from 10:30 p.m. to 8 a.m., and no mini-bikes, dirt bikes, three- or four-wheelers, or ATVs are allowed in the park at any time. Motorcycles are permitted only to and from the campsite. A five-mph speed limit includes bicycles, too. Security measures include a campground gate that is closed after 10 p.m. as well as "rangers" who patrol the park regularly.

Basics

Operated by: Mike & Kim Esler. **Open:** May 1–Oct. 15. **Site Assignment:** Reservations w/ 1-night deposit; refunds w/ 14-day notice. **Registration:** At campground office. **Fee:** $32 (cash,check, credit cards). **Parking:** At site.

Facilities

Number of RV Sites: 206. **Number of Tent-Only Sites:** 11. **Hookups:** Electric (30 amps), water, sewer. **Each Site:** Picnic table, fire ring. **Dump Station:** Yes. **Laundry:** Yes. **Pay Phone:** Yes. **Rest Rooms and Showers:** Yes. **Fuel:** No. **Propane:** Yes. **Internal Roads:** Paved/gravel, in good condition. **RV Service:** No. **Market:** 15 mi. north in Prairie du Chien. **Restaurant:** 1 mi. south in Bagley. **General Store:** Yes. **Vending:** Yes. **Swimming Pool:** Yes. **Playground:** Yes. **Other:** Pavilion, mini-golf, Yogi cartoons at outdoor theatreamphitheatre, ranger station w/ fireplace & lounge, game room, snack bar, shuffleboard, horseshoes, ping-pong, basketball, volleyball, walking trails, rental cabins. **Activities:** Swimming, activity director, scheduled activities. **Nearby Attractions:** House on the Rock, Villa Louis, Mississippi River boat rides, antiques, state parks, golf, caves, minies, locks & dams, fishing, water sports. **Additional Information:** Prairie du Chien Chamber of Commerce, (800) 732-1673.

Restrictions

Pets: Leash only. **Fires:** Fire ring only. **Alcoholic Beverages:** At sites only. **Vehicle Maximum Length:** None.

To Get There

From the junction of CR A and CR X in Bagley, drive 1 mi. north on on CR X. Roads are wide and well maintained w/ good shoulders.

BAILEYS HARBOR

Baileys Bluff Campground and RV Park

2701 CR EE, Baileys Harbor 54202. T: (920) 839-2109

RV ★★★ Tent ★★★

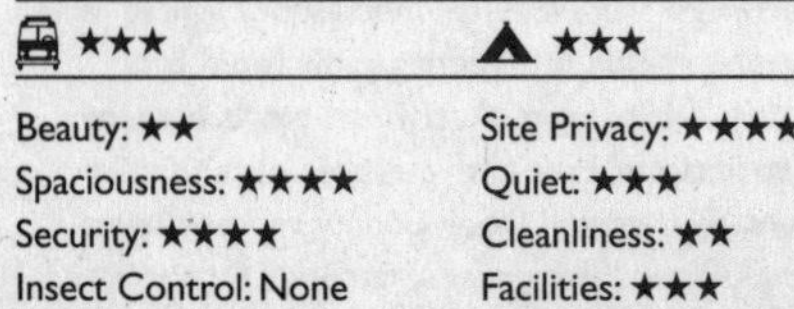

Beauty: ★★ Site Privacy: ★★★★
Spaciousness: ★★★★ Quiet: ★★★
Security: ★★★★ Cleanliness: ★★
Insect Control: None Facilities: ★★★

Baileys Bluff Campground and RV Park really is up on a bluff, about one mile west of Baileys Harbor. Drive slowly up the entrance and look back at the view. In the right spots, you have a 20-mile vista. The campground itself is very wooded and not suitable for satellite TV. The wilderness sites have a typical site width of 30 feet; there are 16 seasonal sites and two pull-throughs. Laid out in a series of loops, most sites have plenty of natural screening with trees, bushes, and other greenery. As one of Wisconsin's finest fishing areas, Baileys Bluff provides a fish-cleaning station and free freezer space for catches. A five-mph speed limit is enforced, and campers should be extra cautious driving up and down the bluff entrance. For security measures, the campground has one entrance/exit,, and owners who live on site and provide regular campground patrols.

Basics

Operated by: Bob & Cheryl Hook. **Open:** Apr. 15–Oct. 20. **Site Assignment:** Reservations w/ 1-night deposit; refund w/ 2-week notice. **Registration:** At campground office. **Fee:** $24 (cash, check, credit cards). **Parking:** At site.

Facilities

Number of RV Sites: 52. **Number of Tent-Only Sites:** 33. **Hookups:** Electric (30 amps), water. **Each Site:** Picnic table, fire ring. **Dump Station:** Yes. **Laundry:** Yes. **Pay Phone:** Yes. **Rest Rooms and Showers:** Yes. **Fuel:** No. **Propane:** No. **Internal Roads:** Gravel, in good condition. **RV Service:** No. **Market:** 1 mi. east in Baileys Harbor. **Restaurant:** 1 mi. east in Baileys Harbor. **General Store:** Yes, limited. **Vending:** Yes. **Swimming Pool:** No. **Playground:** Yes. **Other:** Fish cleaning & freezing, badminton, horseshoes, hiking trails, volleyball, game room, recreation field, rental trailers. **Activities:** Hiking. **Nearby Attractions:** Golf, Door County, nature sanctuary, Lake Michigan, fishing, swimming, beaches, bike routes, Moonlight & North bays, sport fishing, antiques, arts & crafts, cherry orchards, cheese. **Additional Information:** Baileys Harbor Visitor Information Center, (920) 839-2366.

Restrictions

Pets: Leash only. **Fires:** Fire ring only. **Alcoholic Beverages:** Permitted. **Vehicle Maximum Length:** 36 ft. **Other:** No arrivals after 10 p.m. without advance approval.

To Get There

From the junction of Hwy. 57 and CR F/EE, drive 0.75 mi. west on CR F/EE, then 0.25 mi. west on CR EE. Roads are wide and well maintained w/ broad shoulders.

BAILEYS HARBOR

Baileys Grove Travel Park and Campground

2552 CR F & EE, Baileys Harbor 54202. T: (866) 839-2559; F: (920) 839-1339; campnowwi@yahoo.com.

RV: ★★★ Tent: ★★★

Beauty: ★★	Site Privacy: ★★
Spaciousness: ★★★	Quiet: ★★★
Security: ★★★★	Cleanliness: ★★★★
Insect Control: None	Facilities: ★★★

Baileys Grove Travel Park and Campground offers convenience and easy access to northern Door County and Lake Michigan. Less than a mile from Baileys Grove, the campground is right off the country road, next to a small private airport. Campsites are level and grassy with a shade tree on every site for a wooded (not wilderness) setting. A tree buffer around the campground helps provide quiet and privacy. Baileys Grove has 16 seasonal campers and 25 pull-throughs, with a typical site width of 40 feet. As a popular destination for fishing, the campground offers a fish-cleaning station and freezing facilities. A five-mph speed limit is enforced, as are quiet hours from 10 p.m. to 7 a.m. Security measures include one entrance/exit road and an owner who lives on site and provides regular patrols.

Basics

Operated by: Elwyn & Leann Kropuenske. **Open:** May 1–Oct. 15. **Site Assignment:** Reservations w/ 1-night deposit; refund w/ 7-day notice. **Registration:** At campground office. **Fee:** $24 (cash, check, credit cards). **Parking:** At site.

Facilities

Number of RV Sites: 59. **Number of Tent-Only Sites:** 12. **Hookups:** Electric (30 amps), water, sewer. **Each Site:** Picnic table, fire ring. **Dump Station:** Yes. **Laundry:** Yes. **Pay Phone:** Yes. **Rest Rooms and Showers:** Yes. **Fuel:** No. **Propane:** No. **Internal Roads:** Gravel, in good condition. **RV Service:** No. **Market:** 1 mi. north in Baileys Harbor. **Restaurant:** 1 mi. north in Baileys Harbor. **General Store:** Yes, limited. **Vending:** Yes. **Swimming Pool:** Yes. **Playground:** Yes. **Other:** Fish-cleaning station & freezing, game room, adults room, horseshoes, badminton, volleyball. **Activities:** Swimming. **Nearby Attractions:** Golf, Door County, nature sanctuary, Lake Michigan, fishing, beaches, bike routes, Moonlight & North bays, sport fishing, antiques, arts & crafts, cherry orchards, cheese. **Additional Information:** Baileys Harbor Visitor Information Center, (920) 839-2366.

Restrictions

Pets: Leash only. **Fires:** Fire rings only, must be extinguished by 11 p.m. **Alcoholic Beverages:** Permitted. **Vehicle Maximum Length:** None.

To Get There

From the junction of Hwy. 57 and CR F/EE, drive 0.7 mi. west on CR F/EE. Roads are wide and well maintained w/ broad shoulders.

BANCROFT

Vista Royalle Campground

8025 Isherwod Rd., Bancroft 54921. T: (715) 335-6860

RV: ★★★★ Tent: ★★★★

Beauty: ★★★★	Site Privacy: ★★★★
Spaciousness: ★★★★	Quiet: ★★★★
Security: ★★★★★	Cleanliness: ★★★★★
Insect Control: Yes	Facilities: ★★★★★

As avid campers, Jim and Judy Kollock decided 26 years ago to open a campground with the amenities they looked for when camping. To be sure they got off on the right foot, the Kollocks worked with a landscape architect to create the initial layout. It shows. Tall pine trees, spacious (40 × 60 feet) sites and a man-made lake with a sandy bottom and big sandy beach set Vista Royalle Campground apart from others. The lake is aerated and treated to keep it clean. Favorite RV campsites for families are sites 1–10 along the beach. A lodge with a fireplace, video games, movies, and a television welcome children (wholesome, non-"raunchy" movies and games only). Security is also tops, as the campground has one video-monitored access road and owners who live on site and patrol.

Basics

Operated by: Jim & Judy Kollock. **Open:** Apr. 20–Oct. 20. **Site Assignment:** Reservations w/ 1-night deposit. Refund w/ 3-day notice or 7-day notice on holidays. **Registration:** At campground office. **Fee:** $26 (cash, check, credit cards). **Parking:** At site.

Facilities

Number of RV Sites: 200. **Number of Tent-Only Sites:** 0. **Hookups:** Electric (20, 30, 50 amps), water, sewer. **Each Site:** Picnic table, fire ring. **Dump Station:** Yes. **Laundry:** Yes. **Pay Phone:** Yes. **Rest Rooms and Showers:** Yes. **Fuel:** No. **Propane:** Yes. **Internal Roads:** Gravel, in good condition. **RV Service:** No. **Market:** 1 mi. south to Bancroft. **Restaurant:** 1 mi. south to Bancroft. **General Store:** Yes. **Vending:** Yes. **Swimming Pool:** No. **Playground:** Yes. **Other:** Swimming pond w/ sandy beach, mini-golf, snack shack, fishing pond, rec hall, shuffleboard, horseshoes, shelter house, video games, basketball. **Activities:** Swimming, fishing, planned activities. **Nearby Attractions:** Chain of lakes, several golf courses, water park, tours of vegetable farming & paper mills. **Additional Information:** Stevens Point Area CVB, (715) 344-2556.

Restrictions

Pets: Leash only. **Fires:** Fire ring only. **Alcoholic Beverages:** Permitted. **Vehicle Maximum Length:** 50 ft.

To Get There

From Exit 143 at the junction of US 51 and CR W, drive east 0.75 mi. to Isherwood Rd., drive north 1 mi. Roads are wide and well maintained w/ broad shoulders.

BELOIT

Turtle Creek Campsite

3513 East CR S, Beloit 53511. T: (608) 362-7768

RV: ★★★ Tent: ★★★

Beauty: ★★★	Site Privacy: ★★★
Spaciousness: ★★★	Quiet: ★★★
Security: ★★★★	Cleanliness: ★★★★
Insect Control: None	Facilities: ★★★

Located 500 feet off I-90 in Beloit, Turtle Creek Campsite is a good stopping-off point, as well as a destination for campers seeking activities along the creek. With such a convenient highway location, however, the sounds of traffic do float over the campground. The facility has 75 pull-through sites and a typical site width of 30 feet. Spots are level, grassy, and semi-wooded. An open field is popular with big rigs and campers with satellite TV. Laid out in a series of loops, the campground offers sites right along Turtle Creek and in a beautiful oak grove. Paddlers can access the creek here for a leisurely canoe trip (no motors allowed). Safety and security measures include quiet time enforced at 10:30 p.m., one entrance/exit road, and owners who live on site and provide regular patrols. Visitors must register and pay $2 per adult and child but are not allowed to use the swimming facilities and must leave at dark.

BASICS

Operated by: The George Denu family. **Open:** May 15–Oct. 1. **Site Assignment:** Reservations w/ 1-night deposit; no refunds. **Registration:** At campground office. **Fee:** $18 (cash). **Parking:** At site.

FACILITIES

Number of RV Sites: 48. **Number of Tent-Only Sites:** 52. **Hookups:** Electric (20, 30 amps), water. **Each Site:** Picnic table, fire ring. **Dump Station:** Yes. **Laundry:** No. **Pay Phone:** Yes. **Rest Rooms and Showers:** Yes. **Fuel:** No. **Propane:** No. **Internal Roads:** Gravel, in good condition. **RV Service:** No. **Market:** 3 mi. west in Beloit. **Restaurant:** 3 mi. west in Beloit. **General Store:** No. **Vending:** No. **Swimming Pool:** Yes. **Playground:** Yes. **Other:** Turtle Creek, air-conditioned rec hall, pavilion, coin games, fishing river, basketball, sports field, horseshoes, hiking trails, volleyball. **Activities:** Swimming, hiking, fishing, boating (no motors). **Nearby Attractions:** Golf, the Angel Museum, Beloit College, historic districts, Logan Museum of Anthropology, Pohlman Field, self-guided walking tours, antiques, arts & crafts. **Additional Information:** Beloit Convention & Visitor Bureau, (800) 423-5648.

RESTRICTIONS

Pets: Leash only; 1 pet to a site. **Fires:** Fire ring only. **Alcoholic Beverages:** Permitted. **Vehicle Maximum Length:** None. **Other:** 3-day stay limit for tents.

TO GET THERE

From the junction of I-43 and I-90, take Exit 183 (Shopiere Rd.), drive 2 mi. north on I-90, then 500 feet east on CR S. Roads are wide and well maintained w/ broad shoulders.

BLACK RIVER FALLS

Lost Falls Resort and Campground

N2974 Sunnyvale Rd., Black River Falls 54615.
T: (800) 329-3911

RV ★★ Tent ★★★

Beauty: ★★★	Site Privacy: ★★★
Spaciousness: ★★★	Quiet: ★★★★
Security: ★★★★	Cleanliness: ★★★
Insect Control: None	Facilities: ★★★

Lost Falls Resort and Campground, ten miles west of Black River Falls, is a destination in itself. It may be too far from the interstate for some campers, and the gravel road leading down to the campground is quite narrow (as are the interior roads). The Black River is the center of activities for Lost Falls Resort and Campground, and outdoor activities abound. RV sites are generally grassy, shaded, and spacious (50 × 50), but the campground offers only one pull-through site. The best spots for tent campers are in the woods and along the river. However, RVs are not allowed by the river. Be sure and bring all the food and supplies you need, as the campstore sells mostly candy, ice cream, and snacks.

BASICS

Operated by: Ed & Rose Schaper. **Open:** May 1–Oct. 1. **Site Assignment:** Reservations w/ 1-night deposit; full refund if vacancy is filled. No refund on holiday weekends. **Registration:** At campground office. **Fee:** $22 (cash, check, credit cards). **Parking:** At site.

FACILITIES

Number of RV Sites: 20. **Number of Tent-Only Sites:** 10. **Hookups:** Electric (20, 30 amps), water, sewer. **Each Site:** Picnic table, fire ring. **Dump Station:** No. **Laundry:** No. **Pay Phone:** No. **Rest Rooms and Showers:** Yes. **Fuel:** No. **Propane:** No. **Internal Roads:** Gravel, in fair condition. **RV Service:** No. **Market:** 10 mi. east in Black River Falls. **Restaurant:** 6 mi. west in Melrose. **General Store:** Yes. **Vending:** Yes. **Swimming Pool:** No. **Playground:** Yes. **Other:** River, hiking trails, badminton, horseshoes, basketball, canoe landing. **Activities:** Fishing, swimming, boating (rental canoes, kayaks & tubes available), hiking, storytelling every Saturday night by Rose Schaper. **Nearby Attractions:** State forest, bike/ATV trails, water park. **Additional Information:** Black River Falls Area Chamber of Commerce, (800) 404-4008.

RESTRICTIONS

Pets: Leash only. **Fires:** Fire ring only. **Alcoholic Beverages:** Permitted. **Vehicle Maximum Length:** None.

TO GET THERE

From the junction of I-94 and Hwy. 54, take Exit 116, drive 10.5 mi. west and south on Hwy. 54, then 0.25 mi. south on Sunnyvale Rd. Roads are wide and well maintained w/ good shoulders.

BLACK RIVER FALLS

Parkland Village Campground

N6150 Julianna Rd., Black River Falls 54615. T: (715) 284-9700

RV ★★ Tent ★★★

Beauty: ★★★	Site Privacy: ★★★★
Spaciousness: ★★★★	Quiet: ★★★
Security: ★★★	Cleanliness: ★★★★
Insect Control: None	Facilities: ★★★

Located halfway between the Madison/Milwaukee metro area and Minneapolis/St. Paul, Parkland Village Campground must be a welcome sight for snowbirds heading south for the winter or back home in the summer. The campground is a short distance from the interstate, yet its tree buffer makes it quiet enough to get some rest. The entrance is through a mobile home park. Twenty large (65 × 60 feet) pull-through sites offer easy in-and-out for overnight campers. Although a dump station is located nearby, it would be handy to have one in the campground. An important note is that Parkland Village is open all year. Water is shut off in the campground, but campers still have access to showers, rest rooms and other campground facilities. Most winter campers are late-traveling snowbirds or outdoor enthusiasts wanting to hunt, snowmobile, and cross-country ski. Parkland Village doesn't offer scheduled activities, preferring to let campers devise their own entertainment.

BASICS

Operated by: Dan & Barb Potkonak. **Open:** All year. **Site Assignment:** Reservation w/ 1-night deposit; no refund. **Registration:** At campground office. **Fee:** $23 (cash, check, credit cards). **Parking:** At site.

FACILITIES

Number of RV Sites: 80. **Number of Tent-Only Sites:** 0. **Hookups:** Electric (20, 30, 50 amps), water, sewer. **Each Site:** Picnic table, fire ring. **Dump Station:** No. **Laundry:** Yes. **Pay Phone:** Yes. **Rest Rooms and Showers:** Yes. **Fuel:** No. **Propane:** No. **Internal Roads:** Gravel, in good condition. **RV Service:** No. **Market:** 0.5 mi. north in Black River Falls. **Restaurant:** Next door. **General Store:** No. **Vending:** Yes. **Swimming Pool:** Yes. **Playground:** Yes. **Other:** TV & game room, pond, patio, ATV & snowmobile trails. **Activities:** Swimming, hiking, fishing, snowmobiling & ATV riding. **Nearby Attractions:** Cross-country ski trails, scuba diving, casino, golf, roller skating, Tufts Museum, water sports, shopping, cranberry marshes. **Additional Information:** Warrens Area Business Assoc., (608) 378-4200.

RESTRICTIONS

Pets: Leash only. **Fires:** Fire pits only. **Alcoholic Beverages:** Permitted. **Vehicle Maximum Length:** None.

TO GET THERE

From the junction of I-94 and Hwy. 54, take Exit 116 and drive 300 yards east on Hwy. 54, then 0.25 mi. south on Oasis Rd. Roads are wide and well maintained w/ broad shoulders.

BOULDER JUNCTION

Camp Holiday

P.O. Box 67, Boulder Junction 54512. T: (715) 385-2264; F: (715) 385-2966; www.campholiday.com; campholiday@centurytel.net.

RV ★★★★ Tent ★★★

Beauty: ★★★	Site Privacy: ★★★
Spaciousness: ★★★	Quiet: ★★★
Security: ★★★★	Cleanliness: ★★★
Insect Control: None	Facilities: ★★★★

Set in the heart of the Northern Highland-American Legion State Forest, Camp Holiday has nearly 200 lakes within a ten-mile radius. The campground, four miles southwest of Boulder Junction, offers a choice of shaded or open sites alongside Rudolph Lake. Camp Holiday has 100 seasonal campers, 21 pull-through sites, and a typical site width of 40 feet. The lake offers excellent fishing for largemouth bass and panfish and the area is known as the musky capital of the world. Laid out in a series of loops, the facility's most popular sites are by the lake. Sightings of eagles, nesting loons, and beaver are common in the area. Security and safety measures include a ten-mph speed limit (rather high with all the activities going on), a ban on motors on the lake, quiet time from 10:30 p.m. to 7:30 a.m., and owners who live on site and offer regular patrols of the campground. Since it is open until Nov. 1, Camp Holiday is a good place to enjoy the fall foliage.

BASICS

Operated by: Al & Lila Vehrs. **Open:** May 1–Nov. 1. **Site Assignment:** Reservations held w/ 1-night deposit on credit card; no fee w/ 7-day notice of cancellation. **Registration:** At campground office. **Fee:** $25 (cash, check, credit cards). **Parking:** At site.

FACILITIES

Number of RV Sites: 159. **Number of Tent-Only Sites:** 2. **Hookups:** Electric (30, 50 amps), water, sewer, phone. **Each Site:** Picnic table, fire ring. **Dump Station:** Yes. **Laundry:** Yes. **Pay Phone:** Yes. **Rest Rooms and Showers:** Yes. **Fuel:** No. **Propane:** Yes. **Internal Roads:** Paved/gravel, in good condition. **RV Service:** No. **Market:** 4 mi. northeast in Boulder Junction. **Restaurant:** 4 mi. northeast in Boulder Junction. **General Store:** Yes, limited. **Vending:** No. **Swimming Pool:** No. **Playground:** Yes. **Other:** Rudolph Lake, swimming beach, horseshoes, volleyball, basketball, shuffleboard, rec hall, game room, trails, boat launch, fishing lake. **Activities:** Swimming, fishing, boating (rental rowboats, canoes, kayaks available), scheduled weekend activities, hiking. **Nearby Attractions:** Lakes, forest, antiques, hiking, boating, cross-county skiing, bicycling, arts & crafts, scenic drive. **Additional Information:** Boulder Junction Chamber of Commerce, (800) 466-8579.

RESTRICTIONS

Pets: Leash only. **Fires:** Fire ring only. **Alcoholic Beverages:** Permitted. **Vehicle Maximum Length:** 45 ft.

TO GET THERE

From the junction of US 51 and CR H, drive 3 mi. northeast on CR H, then 500 feet east on Rudolph Lake Ln. Roads are generally wide and well maintained w/ narrow shoulders in some areas.

BRISTOL

Happy Acres Kampground

22230 45th St., Bristol 53104. T: (262) 857-7373; www.happyacres.com; info@happyacres.com.

RV ★★★ Tent ★★★

Beauty: ★★★	Site Privacy: ★★★
Spaciousness: ★★★	Quiet: ★★★★
Security: ★★★★	Cleanliness: ★★★
Insect Control: Yes	Facilities: ★★★

Established by veteran campers in 1970, Happy Acres Kampground is a popular place with families. Reservations are recommended for all weekends between Memorial Day and Labor Day. Reservations are mandatory and must be finalized at least two weeks prior to a holiday weekend. Located halfway between Chicago and Milwaukee about nine miles off I-94, Happy Acres offers convenient access for travelers. Laid out in a series of loops, the campground has 46 seasonal campers and 13 pull-through sites. A rolling grassy campground, Happy Acres has open and wooded sites. The best sites are 61, 62, and 64 because they are by the lake and offer more green space. A separate tenting area allows privacy from RVs and more trees and greenery. The campground has 25 acres of walking trails. The speed limit is ten mph, and rules note that the facility "is not a drivers education training site." Mini-bikes, dirt bikes, mopeds, go-carts, and golf carts are not allowed. Quiet time from 10 p.m. to 9 a.m. is strictly enforced. The owners live on site and provide 24-hour security protection for the campground.

BASICS

Operated by: Bill & Irene Davis. **Open:** May 1–Sept. 30. **Site Assignment:** Reservations w/ 1-night deposit; refund (minus $5) w/ 7-day notice. **Registration:** At campground office. **Fee:** $30 (cash, check, credit cards). **Parking:** At site.

FACILITIES

Number of RV Sites: 150. **Number of Tent-Only Sites:** 18. **Hookups:** Electric (20, 30 amps), water. **Each Site:** Picnic table, fire ring. **Dump Station:** Yes. **Laundry:** Yes. **Pay Phone:** Yes. **Rest Rooms and Showers:** Yes. **Fuel:** No. **Propane:** Yes. **Internal Roads:** Gravel, in good condition. **RV Service:** No. **Market:** 3 mi. south in Padlock Lake. **Restaurant:** 1 mi. east. **General Store:** Yes. **Vending:** Yes. **Swimming Pool:** Yes. **Playground:** Yes. **Other:** Mini zoo, pond, hiking trails, pavilion, swimming beach, mini golf, horseshoes, volleyball, basketball, lounge, game room, boat dock, rental cabins, rental trailers. **Activities:** Swimming, fishing, hiking, boating (rental rowboats, paddleboats available), scheduled weekend activities. **Nearby Attractions:** Six Flags Great America, Milwaukee Zoo, Dairyland Dog Track, Lake Geneva, Lake Michigan, outlet malls, antiques, arts & crafts, golf, scenic drive. **Additional Information:** Kenosha Area Chamber of Commerce, (800) 654-7309.

RESTRICTIONS

Pets: Leash only, "leave nervous watch dogs home". **Fires:** Fire ring only. **Alcoholic Beverages:** Permitted. **Vehicle Maximum Length:** None.

TO GET THERE

From the junction of Hwy. 50 and US 45, drive 2 mi. north on US 45, then 1.5 mi. west on CR NN. Roads are wide and well maintained w/ sometimes narrow shoulders.

BRUSSELS

Quietwoods South Camping Resort

9245 Lovers Ln., Brussels 54204. T: (888) 378-2005

RV ★★★ Tent ★★★

Beauty: ★★★	Site Privacy: ★★★
Spaciousness: ★★★	Quiet: ★★★
Security: ★★★★	Cleanliness: ★★★★
Insect Control: Yes	Facilities: ★★★

Quietwoods South Camping Resort, located four miles north of Brussels, is the first campground as you enter Door County. Many of its campers are returnees, along with 65 seasonals. The campground offers secluded, wooded sites in a rural area. The typical site width is 36 feet, with eight pull-throughs. Tents are in a separate area with more green space and privacy. Security measures include one-way roads and an owner who lives on site and provides regular patrols of the campground.

BASICS

Operated by: Michael & Christine Marant. **Open:** May 1–Oct. 15. **Site Assignment:** Reservations w/ $20 deposit; refund w/ 1-week notice. **Registration:** At campground office. **Fee:** $23 (cash, check, credit cards). **Parking:** At site.

FACILITIES

Number of RV Sites: 150. **Number of Tent-Only Sites:** 10. **Hookups:** Electric (30 amps), water. **Each Site:** Picnic table, fire ring. **Dump Station:** Yes. **Laundry:** Yes. **Pay Phone:** Yes. **Rest Rooms and Showers:** Yes. **Fuel:** No. **Propane:** No. **Internal Roads:** Paved/gravel, in good condition. **RV Service:** No. **Market:** 4 mi. south in Brussels. **Restaurant:** 4 mi. south in Brussels. **General Store:** Yes. **Vending:** Yes. **Swimming Pool:** Yes. **Playground:** Yes. **Other:** Game room, pavilion, mini-golf, volleyball, game room, adult lounge, horseshoes, baseball, fishing pond, rental trailers & pop-ups, small bar. **Activities:** Swimming, fishing, scheduled weekend activities. **Nearby Attractions:** Door County, cherry & apple orchards, fishing, golf, hiking, boating, Lake Michigan, Green Bay, historic sites, antiques, arts & crafts shops, summer stock theatre, parks, bike trails. **Additional Information:** Door County Chamber of Commerce, (800) 527-3529.

RESTRICTIONS

Pets: Leash only. **Fires:** Fire ring only. **Alcoholic Beverages:** Permitted. **Vehicle Maximum Length:** None.

TO GET THERE

From the junction of Hwy. 57 and CR C, drive 2.5 mi. north on CR C, then 1.5 mi. east on CR K, then 0.5 mi. north on Lovers Ln. The roads are wide and well maintained w/ broad shoulders.

CALEDONIA

Yogi Bear's Jellystone Park Camp-Resort

8425 WI 38, Caledonia 53108. T: (262) 835-2565; www.jellystone-caledonia.com; yogipark@aol.com.

RV ★★★★ Tent ★★★

Beauty: ★★★	Site Privacy: ★★★
Spaciousness: ★★★	Quiet: ★★★
Security: ★★★★	Cleanliness: ★★★
Insect Control: None	Facilities: ★★★★

Located one mile south of Oak Creek, Yogi Bear's Jellystone Camp-Resort is a popular destination in itself as well as a camping spot for Milwaukee visitors. Most sites are level and shaded with gravel spots for RVs. The campground has no seasonal campers and offers 22 pull-throughs. Tent campers have a separate area with more green space and privacy. The best sites for RVs are on Jellystone Ave. because they are bigger and located near the pool and other facilities. A five-mph speed limit is enforced, as is quiet time from 11 p.m. to 8 a.m. Ill-mannered conduct is not tolerated, nor is the use of foul language. Security measures include one entrance/exit to the campground, security guards, and a park manager who lives on site.

Basics

Operated by: Jim & Ellen Votaw. **Open:** Apr. 15–Oct. 15. **Site Assignment:** Reservations w/ $50 deposit, $75 for holidays; refund (minus $5 fee) w/ 7-day notice. **Registration:** At campground office. **Fee:** $38 (cash, check, credit cards). **Parking:** At site.

Facilities

Number of RV Sites: 222. **Number of Tent-Only Sites:** 25. **Hookups:** Electric (30, 50 amps), water, sewer. **Each Site:** Picnic table, fire ring. **Dump Station:** Yes. **Laundry:** Yes. **Pay Phone:** Yes. **Rest Rooms and Showers:** Yes. **Fuel:** No. **Propane:** Yes. **Internal Roads:** Paved/gravel, in good condition. **RV Service:** No. **Market:** 1 mi. north in Oak Creek. **Restaurant:** 1 mi. north in Oak Creek. **General Store:** Yes. **Vending:** Yes. **Swimming Pool:** Yes. **Playground:** Yes. **Other:** Adult lounge, cafe, mini golf, volleyball, basketball, game room, fishing pond, rental cabins, kiddie pool, recreation field, cartoon theatre. **Activities:** Swimming, kiddie fishing, scheduled activities. **Nearby Attractions:** Zoo, brewery tours, golf, antiques, arts & crafts, museum, historic homes, nature center, baseball. **Additional Information:** Greater Milwaukee CVB, (800) 554-1448.

Restrictions

Pets: Leash only. **Fires:** Fire ring only. **Alcoholic Beverages:** At sites only. **Vehicle Maximum Length:** 40 ft.

To Get There

From I-94, take Exit 326 and drive 2 mi. east on Seven Mile Rd., then 0.25 mi. north on Hwy. 38. Roads are wide and well maintained w/ broad shoulders.

CAMPBELLSPORT

Benson's Century Camping Resort

N3845 Hwy. 67, Campbellsport 53010. T: (920) 533-8597

RV ★★ Tent ★★★

Beauty: ★★★ Site Privacy: ★★★
Spaciousness: ★★★ Quiet: ★★★★
Security: ★★★★ Cleanliness: ★★★★
Insect Control: None Facilities: ★★

Long Lake forms the centerpiece of Benson's Century Camping Resort, located nine miles east of Campbellsport. Arranged in a series of loops, the campground offers mostly shaded, grassy sites, with three pull-throughs and 100 seasonal campers. The typical site width is 35 feet. Safety measures include a five-mph speed limit, no mini-bikes allowed, and no parking on roadway. Throwing stones in the campground or lake is also prohibited. Tent sites are in a separate area away from RVs with more trees and green space. Security includes one entrance/exit past the office, owners who live on site providing regular campground patrols, and police officers who keep an eye on the campground.

Basics

Operated by: Nancy Benson. **Open:** May 15–Oct. 15. **Site Assignment:** Reservations w/ 1-night deposit; no refund. **Registration:** At campground office. **Fee:** $20 (cash, check). **Parking:** At site.

Facilities

Number of RV Sites: 168. **Number of Tent-Only Sites:** 82. **Hookups:** Electric (50 amps), water. **Each Site:** Picnic table, fire ring. **Dump Station:** Yes. **Laundry:** No. **Pay Phone:** Yes. **Rest Rooms and Showers:** Yes. **Fuel:** No. **Propane:** Yes. **Internal Roads:** Paved, in good condition. **RV Service:** No. **Market:** 9 mi. west in Campbellsport. **Restaurant:** Next door. **General Store:** Yes, limited. **Vending:** Yes. **Swimming Pool:** No. **Playground:** Yes. **Other:** Long Lake, boat launch, pier, beach, rec room, snack bar, horseshoes, volleyball, game room, sports field. **Activities:** Swimming, fishing, boating (rental fishing boats, canoes, paddleboats available). **Nearby Attractions:** Riding stables, golf, hiking trails, trout ponds, Kettle Moraine, historic homes, museums, antiques, arts & crafts. **Additional Information:** Fond du Lac Area CVB, (800) 937-9123.

Restrictions

Pets: Leash only. **Fires:** Fire ring only. **Alcoholic Beverages:** Permitted. **Vehicle Maximum Length:** 38 ft.

To Get There

From the junction of US 45 and Hwy. 67, drive 6 mi. northeast on Hwy. 67

CHETEK

Chetek River Campground

590 24th St., Chetek 54728. T: (715) 924-2440; www.chetekriver.com; camp@chetekriver.com.

RV ★★★★ Tent ★★★

Beauty: ★★★ Site Privacy: ★★★★
Spaciousness: ★★★★ Quiet: ★★★★
Security: ★★★★ Cleanliness: ★★★★
Insect Control: None Facilities: ★★★

Chetek River Campground does so many little things right, and that all adds up to a very pleasant campground. Some of the extras: guests may visit campers free of charge (there is a $2 charge to swim), and free "doggie bags" for cleaning up after pets are available at the office. The campground is chock full of activities for children, including a local high school basketball coach who offers clinics and games every Saturday. Located less than a mile west of Chetek, the campground is situated on the Chetek River, where you can take a tubing trip or rent a canoe. The rural campground has 50 seasonals and is booked up almost every weekend, so reservations are strongly recommended. Laid out in a series of loops, the campground has a typical site width of 36 feet, with back-in, grassy, open sites. A popular spot for family reunions, the campground has a giant grill that can hold 50 pieces of chicken. Quiet hours from 10 p.m. to 8 a.m. are enforced, as is a five-mph speed limit. Owners live on site and provide 24-hour security. With all those children enjoying river activities and other outdoors play, it sure would be nice to have laundry facilities at such a top-notch family campground.

Basics

Operated by: Jan Gebhardt & Christine Gay. **Open:** May 1–Sept. 30. **Site Assignment:** Reservations w/ 1-night deposit; refund w/ 7-day notice. **Registration:** At campground office. **Fee:** $22 (cash, check). **Parking:** At site.

Facilities

Number of RV Sites: 100. **Number of Tent-Only Sites:** 0. **Hookups:** Electric (20, 30 amps), water. **Each Site:** Picnic table, fire ring. **Dump Station:** Yes. **Laundry:** No. **Pay Phone:** Yes. **Rest Rooms and Showers:** yes. **Fuel:** No. **Propane:** No. **Internal Roads:** Paved/gravel, in good condition. **RV Service:** No. **Market:** 1 mi. east in Chetek. **Restaurant:** 1 mi. east in Chetek. **General Store:** No. **Vending:** Yes. **Swimming Pool:** Yes. **Playground:** Yes. **Other:** Red Cedar River, basketball, volleyball, shuffleboard, horseshoes, mini-golf, pool table, ping pong, air hockey, video games, TV room, badminton, recreation field, scheduled weekend activities. **Activities:** Swimming, fishing, tubing trips, boating (rental canoes available), biking, (rental pedal karts available). **Nearby Attractions:** Museums, golf, fishing lakes, antiques. **Additional Information:** Chippewa Valley CVB, (888) 523-3866.

Restrictions

Pets: Leash only. **Fires:** Fire ring only. **Alcoholic Beverages:** Permitted. **Vehicle Maximum Length:** 40 ft. **Other:** Bury fish guts in a designated area. Shovels are provided.

To Get There

From the junction of US 53 and Hwy. 1, take Exit 126, drive 0.25 mi. south on Hwy. 1 to River Rd., then 0.75 mi. south on River Rd. Roads are wide and well maintained w/ good shoulders.

CHIPPEWA FALLS

O'Neil Creek Campground & RV Park

14956 105th Ave., Chippewa Falls 54729. T: (715) 723-6581; www.discover-net.net/~oneilcreek; oneilcreek@discover-net.net.

RV ★★★★ Tent ★★★★

Beauty: ★★★★ Site Privacy: ★★★
Spaciousness: ★★★ Quiet: ★★★★
Security: ★★★★ Cleanliness: ★★★★
Insect Control: None Facilities: ★★★★

Located four miles north of Chippewa Falls, O'Neil Creek Campground & RV Park has level, shaded, wooded sites, some along a gently flowing creek. The campground has 200 seasonal campers, 16 pull-through sites, and a typical site width of 28 feet. Be aware that all full hookups are occupied by seasonals. Campers have direct access to Lake Wissota and the Chippewa River system. Motor downstream from the campground on O'Neil Creek to Lake Wissota (15 miles long and three miles wide) and the Chippewa River system. Tent sites are in a separate area with privacy from RVs and more green space. Showers and rest rooms are tiled and very clean. A nice benefit is no visitor fee. However, all visitors must leave the campground by 11 p.m., or they will be charged as an overnight guest.

BASICS

Operated by: Mike & Judy Rabska. **Open:** Apr. 15–Oct. 15. **Site Assignment:** Reservations w/ 1-night deposit; refund (minus $5) w/ 7-day notice. **Registration:** At campground office. **Fee:** $30 (cash, check, credit cards). **Parking:** At site.

FACILITIES

Number of RV Sites: 390. **Number of Tent-Only Sites:** 35. **Hookups:** Electric (20, 30, 50 amps), water, sewer, phone. **Each Site:** Picnic table, fire ring. **Dump Station:** Yes. **Laundry:** Yes. **Pay Phone:** Yes. **Rest Rooms and Showers:** Yes. **Fuel:** No. **Propane:** Yes. **Internal Roads:** Paved/gravel, in good condition. **RV Service:** No. **Market:** 4 mi. south in Chippewa Falls. **Restaurant:** 4 mi. south in Chippewa Falls. **General Store:** Yes. **Vending:** Yes. **Swimming Pool:** No. **Playground:** Yes. **Other:** O'Neil Creek, nature trails, boat ramp, rec room, horseshoes, volleyball, mini golf, boat dock, rental cabins, pavilion, coin games, basketball, sports field. **Activities:** Swimming, hiking, boating (rental paddleboats, rowboats & canoes available), fishing, float trips, scheduled activities. **Nearby Attractions:** Golf, Lake Wissota, Chippewa Rose Society Garden, Irvine Park, zoo, swimming pool, tennis, Glen Loch Dam aned Overlook, museum, Leinenkugel Brewery, antiques, arts & crafts. **Additional Information:** Chippewa Falls Area Chamber of Commerce, (888) 723-0024.

RESTRICTIONS

Pets: Leash only. **Fires:** Fire ring only. **Alcoholic Beverages:** Permitted. **Vehicle Maximum Length:** None.

TO GET THERE

From the junction of Hwy. 124 and US 53, drive 5 mi. north on US 53, then 2 mi. east on County Trunk S, then 2 mi. north on Hwy. 124, then 0.75 mi. east on 105th Ave. Roads are generally wide and well maintained w/ broad shoulders, though there is one bad curve down to campground.

COLOMA

Coloma Camperland

N 1130 5th Rd., Coloma 54930. T: (715) 228-3611; www.colomacamperland.com; colomarv@uniontel.net.

RV ★★★ Tent ★★★

Beauty: ★★★	Site Privacy: ★★★
Spaciousness: ★★★	Quiet: ★★★★
Security: ★★★★	Cleanliness: ★★★★
Insect Control: None	Facilities: ★★★

It's not a pleasant subject to mention, but if an RV had to break down, this would be the place to do it. Coloma Camperland offers camper sales, RV parts, supplies and services—along with being a nice place to stay. Located off Hwy. 39 and 21 in Coloma, Camperland has six large (40 × 50 feet), grassy pull-through sites, the most requested ones in the campground. Laid out in a series of loops, the campground offers both wooded and open sites. A family campground and a comfortable spot for overnight travelers, Camperland has good security with only one way into the facility, owners who live on site, and patrols by night personnel. For safety, bike riding is not allowed in the campground after dark.

BASICS

Operated by: Chris & Carole Johnson. **Open:** Apr. 1–Dec. 1. **Site Assignment:** Reservations w/ $20 deposit, refund w/ 2-week notice. **Registration:** At campground office. **Fee:** $20. **Parking:** At site.

FACILITIES

Number of RV Sites: 85. **Number of Tent-Only Sites:** 10. **Hookups:** Electric (30 amps), water, sewer. **Each Site:** Picnic table, fire ring. **Dump Station:** Yes. **Laundry:** Yes. **Pay Phone:** Yes. **Rest Rooms and Showers:** Yes. **Fuel:** No. **Propane:** Yes. **Internal Roads:** Gravel, in fair condition. **RV Service:** Yes. **Market:** 0.5 mi. north in Coloma. **Restaurant:** 0.5 mi. north in Coloma. **General Store:** Yes. **Vending:** Yes. **Swimming Pool:** Yes. **Playground:** Yes. **Other:** Game room, shelter, volleyball, shuffleboard, horseshoes, sports field. **Activities:** Swimming, planned weekend activities. **Nearby Attractions:** Fishing, hunting, snowmobile trail, golf, biking, horseback riding, scenic drive, 35 minutes to casino, Wisconsin Dells. **Additional Information:** Wisconsin Dells Visitor & Convention Bureau, (800) 223-3557.

RESTRICTIONS

Pets: Leash only. **Fires:** Fire pits only. **Alcoholic Beverages:** At sites only. **Vehicle Maximum Length:** None.

TO GET THERE

From the junction of Hwy. 51 and 21, drive 0.25 mi. east on Hwy. 21, then 1 mi. south on CR CH. Roads are wide and well maintained w/ good shoulders.

CRIVITZ

High Falls Family Camping

W11594 Archer Ln., Crivitz 54114. T: (715) 757-3399; www.exploringthenorth.com/highfalls/campground.html; hffc@cybrzn.com.

RV ★ Tent ★★

Beauty: ★★★	Site Privacy: ★★
Spaciousness: ★★	Quiet: ★★
Security: ★★★	Cleanliness: ★★
Insect Control: None	Facilities: ★★

Located 13 miles west of Crivitz, High Falls Family Campground is starting an expansion project to provide new bathrooms and showers, a laundry and new store. The result should be a more user-friendly campground. The campground offers wooded and open sites in a rural setting. Laid out in a series of loops, the grassy campground has one pull-through site and 39 seasonal campers. A primitive tent camping area also includes walk-in sites for a more secluded spot. Security measures include a five-mph speed limit and one-way roads. Quiet hours are 10 p.m. to 8 a.m. Paths leading to the lake are on property owned by Wisconsin Public Service Corporation, and visitors must respect the land and avoid littering. Boats must be moored at public landings and not along the shoreline. Security includes owners who live on site and provide regular campground patrols.

BASICS

Operated by: Ed & Cheryl Wruk & Leonard & Cindy Wahl. **Open:** May 1–Oct. 15. **Site Assignment:** Reservations w/ 50 percent deposit, 100 percent on holidays; refund (less $4 fee) w/ 10-day notice. **Registration:** At campground office. **Fee:** $15 (cash, check, credit cards). **Parking:** At site.

FACILITIES

Number of RV Sites: 88. **Number of Tent-Only Sites:** 8. **Hookups:** Electric (20, 30, 50 amps), water. **Each Site:** Picnic table, fire ring. **Dump Station:** Yes. **Laundry:** No. **Pay Phone:** Yes. **Rest Rooms and Showers:** No. **Fuel:** No. **Propane:** No. **Internal Roads:** Gravel, in fair condition. **RV Service:** No. **Market:** 13 mi. east in Crivitz. **Restaurant:** 1 mi. northwest. **General Store:** Yes, limited. **Vending:** Yes. **Swimming Pool:** No. **Playground:** Yes. **Other:** Nature trails, volleyball, horseshoes, basketball, lake. **Activities:** Swimming, hiking, fishing, boating (rental hydrobikes & canoes available), scheduled weekend activities. **Nearby Attractions:** Golf, tennis, water ski shows, river & lake fishing, white water rafting, horseback riding, flea markets, antiques, museums, waterfalls. **Additional Information:** Marinette County Area Chamber of Commerce, (800) 236-6681.

RESTRICTIONS

Pets: Leash only. **Fires:** Fire ring only. **Alcoholic Beverages:** Permitted. **Vehicle Maximum Length:** 36 ft.

TO GET THERE

From the junction of US 141 and CR W, drive 0.5 mi. west on CR W, then 8 mi. northwest on CR A, then 3.5 mi. west on CR X, then 0.25 mi. south on Boat Landing Rd. 3, then 0.25 mi. west on Archer Ln. Roads are wide and well maintained w/ broad shoulders.

CRIVITZ

Peshtigo River Campground

W7948 Airport Rd., Crivitz 54114. T: (715) 854-2986; F: (715) 854-3120; peshti@cybrzn.com.

RV ★★★ Tent ★★★★

Beauty: ★★★	Site Privacy: ★★★
Spaciousness: ★★★★	Quiet: ★★★
Security: ★★★★	Cleanliness: ★★★★
Insect Control: Yes	Facilities: ★★★

The Peshtigo River Campground calls it "stress reduction therapy"—floating down the historic Pestigo River in a big innertube, stopping along the way for a sandbar picnic, if you want. After the two- to six-hour trip, all pressure (except that in the tubes) should be gone, they say. The campground offers free shuttles to the put-in. Camping sites are level and shaded, with most backing up into the woods. To ensure future shade, small trees have been planted, and campers are welcome to "adopt" a tree and water it during their stay. The typical site width is 50 feet, with eight pull-throughs and 40 seasonal campers. A separate area for tent campers provides more green space and privacy. Some open sites for RVs are located near the front of the campground, which is one mile south of Crivitz. Quiet time between 11 p.m. and 7 a.m. is enforced Safety measures include one-way roads and a ten-mph speed limit, rather high for such a child-friendly campground. Security is provided by one entrance and exit, regular patrols, and an owner (a retired police officer) who lives on site.

Basics

Operated by: Rick Greene. **Open:** May 1–Dec. 1. **Site Assignment:** Reservations w/ $20 deposit; refund (minus 20 percent service charge) w/ 2-week notice. **Registration:** At campground office. **Fee:** $20 (cash, check, credit cards). **Parking:** At site.

Facilities

Number of RV Sites: 100. **Number of Tent-Only Sites:** 10. **Hookups:** Electric (20, 30 amps), water. **Each Site:** Picnic table, fire ring. **Dump Station:** Yes. **Laundry:** Yes. **Pay Phone:** Yes. **Rest Rooms and Showers:** Yes. **Fuel:** No. **Propane:** No. **Internal Roads:** Gravel, in good condition. **RV Service:** Yes. **Market:** 1 mi. north in Crivitz. **Restaurant:** 1 mi. north in Crivitz. **General Store:** Yes. **Vending:** Yes. **Swimming Pool:** No. **Playground:** Yes. **Other:** Peshtigo River, swimming area, horseshoes, volleyball, nature trails, fish freezer, rental cabins, rec room, pavilion, sports field. **Activities:** Swimming, river tubing (rental tubes available), boating (rental canoes available), fishing, hiking, scheduled activities. **Nearby Attractions:** Golf, tennis, water ski shows, river & lake fishing, white water rafting, riding stables, flea markets, antiques, museums, waterfalls. **Additional Information:** Marinette County Area Chamber of Commerce, (800) 236-6681.

Restrictions

Pets: Leash only. **Fires:** Fire ring only. **Alcoholic Beverages:** Permitted. **Vehicle Maximum Length:** None.

To Get There

From the junction of US 141 and CR W, drive 2 mi. south on US 141, then 500 feet west on Airport Rd. Roads are wide and well maintained w/ broad shoulders.

DE SOTO

Mississippi Sports and Recreation

E870 Hwy. 35, De Sota 54624. T: (608) 648-3630; tghelf@aol.com.

RV ★★ Tent ★★★

Beauty: ★★ Site Privacy: ★★
Spaciousness: ★★★ Quiet: ★★★
Security: ★★★★ Cleanliness: ★★★
Insect Control: None Facilities: ★★★

Mississippi Sports and Recreation is a work in progress. Started in 1999 by an energetic young man, the campground has three important things going for it—convenience, price, and access to the Mississippi River. An easy pull-in off Hwy. 35, the campground is near the Mississippi River and offers campsites with electric hookups for a low $10. With river activities as its primary draw, the campground offers a very well-stocked tackle shop along with a marina and boat rentals. The idea is for a camper to be able to put a boat in the river, moor it in a boat slip, and leave it for a weekend or full week of water activities. Not just a summer resort, this campground two miles north of De Soto attracts RV campers in the winter for ice fishing and snowmobiling. Laid out in a series of loops, the campground offers back-in and pull-through sites, but the sites are rather small and not well screened by greenery yet.

Basics

Operated by: Thomas L. Ghelf. **Open:** All year. **Site Assignment:** Reservations w/ no deposit. **Registration:** At campground office. **Fee:** $10 (cash, check). **Parking:** At site.

Facilities

Number of RV Sites: 25. **Number of Tent-Only Sites:** 20. **Hookups:** Electric (30 amps), water. **Each Site:** Picnic table, fire ring. **Dump Station:** No. **Laundry:** Yes. **Pay Phone:** Yes. **Rest Rooms and Showers:** Yes. **Fuel:** No. **Propane:** No. **Internal Roads:** Gravel, in good condition. **RV Service:** No. **Market:** 7 mi. south in Lansing. **Restaurant:** 2 mi. south in DeSoto. **General Store:** Yes. **Vending:** No. **Swimming Pool:** No. **Playground:** Yes. **Other:** Bait & tackle store, full-service marina repair, walking trails, fish-cleaning facility, pond, boat dock, marina. **Activities:** Fishing, boating (rental motor boats available), hiking, fishing tournaments, live music twice a month. **Nearby Attractions:** State parks, museums, historic homes, golf, scenic drives. **Additional Information:** Prairie du Chien Chamber of Commerce, (800) 732-1673.

Restrictions

Pets: Yes. **Fires:** Fire pits only. **Alcoholic Beverages:** Permitted. **Vehicle Maximum Length:** None.

To Get There

Take Hwy. 35 and drive 2 mi. north of De Soto. Roads are wide and well maintained w/ good shoulders.

EAGLE RIVER

Pine Aire Resort & Campground

4443 Chain O' Lakes Rd., Eagle River 54521. T: (800) 597-6777; F: (715) 479-2658; www.pine-aire.com; vacation@pine-aire.com.

RV ★★★★ Tent ★★★★

Beauty: ★★★★ Site Privacy: ★★★
Spaciousness: ★★★ Quiet: ★★★★
Security: ★★★★ Cleanliness: ★★★★
Insect Control: ★★★ Facilities: ★★★★

Located in the beautiful Northwoods lakes region two miles north of Eagle River, Pine Aire Resort and Campground seems an unlikely place to find a gourmet restaurant. But the Logging Camp Kitchen & Still features surprising dining choices, such as veal Chardonnay with wild mushrooms and barley risotto, plus special cranberry applesauce and chutney made in the kitchen. Craft workshops at the Calico Cottage also let you know this is not an ordinary campground. Laid out in a series of loops, the campground has a choice of open or shaded sites. It has 19 seasonal campers, 13 pull-through sites, and a typical site width of 20 feet. Some lakeside campsites are available. The campground is a popular spot because of the wealth of recreational activities available and because of its quiet, natural surroundings. Regular night security keeps a close eye on the campground.

Basics

Operated by: Ron & Cindy Meinholz. **Open:** All year. **Site Assignment:** Reservations w/ $25 deposit; refund w/ 2-week notice. **Registration:** At campground office. **Fee:** $42 (cash, check, credit cards). **Parking:** At site.

Facilities

Number of RV Sites: 121. **Number of Tent-Only Sites:** 15. **Hookups:** Electric (15, 20, 30 amps), water, sewer. **Each Site:** Picnic table, fire ring. **Dump Station:** Yes. **Laundry:** Yes. **Pay Phone:** Yes. **Rest Rooms and Showers:** Yes. **Fuel:** No. **Propane:** Yes. **Internal Roads:** Paved/gravel, in good condition. **RV Service:** No. **Market:** 2 mi. south in Eagle River. **Restaurant:** On site. **General Store:** Yes, limited. **Vending:** Yes. **Swimming Pool:** No. **Playground:** Yes. **Other:** Swimming lake, rec room, restaurant, volleyball, basketball, lounge, game room, tennis, marina, snack bar, bar, pavilion, trails, boat launch, rental cottages,. **Activities:** Swimming, fishing, hiking, boating (rental motor boats, canoes, paddleboats, rowboats, pontoons, ski boats, wave runners, acqua cycles available), scheduled activities. **Nearby Attractions:** Casinos, golf, historic boathouses, Nicolet National Forest, Ottawa National Forest, scenic drives, antiques, arts & crafts, ski trails, Trees For Tomorrow Environmental Education Center. **Additional Information:** Eagle River Area Chamber of Commerce, (800) 359-6315.

Restrictions

Pets: Leash only. **Fires:** Fire ring only. **Alcoholic Beverages:** Permitted. **Vehicle Maximum Length:** None.

To Get There

From the junction of Hwy. 70 and Northbound US 45, drive 3 mi. north on US 45, then 0.1 mi. east on Chain-O-Lakes road. Roads are mostly wide and well maintained w/ narrow shoulders in spots.

EAU CLAIRE

Elmer's RV Park and Campgrounds

8027 Hwy. 12, Fall Creek 54742. T: (715) 832-6277

Beauty: ★★ Site Privacy: ★★
Spaciousness: ★★ Quiet: ★★★
Security: ★★★ Cleanliness: ★★★
Insect Control: None Facilities: ★★

Elmer Backstrom went broke growing beans on this property, so 35 years ago he turned it into a campground. He knows most every birch, pine, and poplar tree on the site because he planted them himself. The major pluses for the campground are the convenience it offers, easy access from US 53, and eight pull-through sites, in addition to a very reasonable price. The major minuses are small sites (some 22 × 50 feet) = located too close together and no general store or swimming pool. Sites are generally grassy and shady. Most campers who stay at Elmer's are either overnight travelers or people who are visiting the area for family and friends. Elmer lives on the site and keeps a close eye on the comings and goings.

Basics

Operated by: Elmer Backstrom. **Open:** Apr. 15–Oct. 15. **Site Assignment:** First come, first served. **Registration:** At campground office. **Fee:** $14 (cash, check). **Parking:** At site.

Facilities

Number of RV Sites: 30. **Number of Tent-Only Sites:** 5. **Hookups:** Electric (30 amps), water, sewer. **Each Site:** Picnic table, fire ring. **Dump Station:** No. **Laundry:** Yes. **Pay Phone:** Yes. **Rest Rooms and Showers:** Yes. **Fuel:** No. **Propane:** No. **Internal Roads:** Gravel, in good condition. **RV Service:** No. **Market:** 4 mi. west in Eau Claire. **Restaurant:** 4 mi. west in Eau Claire. **General Store:** No. **Vending:** Yes. **Swimming Pool:** No. **Playground:** Yes. **Activities:** None. **Nearby Attractions:** Park, Chippewa Valley Museum, Paul Bunyan Logging Camp & Interpretive Center. **Additional Information:** Chippewa Valley CVB, (888) 523-3866.

Restrictions

Pets: Leash only. **Fires:** Fire ring only. **Alcoholic Beverages:** Permitted. **Vehicle Maximum Length:** None.

To Get There

From the junction of US 53 and Hwy. 12, drive east 4.5 mi. on Hwy. 12. Roads are wide and well maintained w/ broad shoulders

EDGERTON
Creekview Campground

748 Albion Rd., Edgerton 53534. T: (608) 884-3288

RV ★★ Tent ★★

Beauty: ★★ Site Privacy: ★★
Spaciousness: ★★ Quiet: ★★★★
Security: ★★★★ Cleanliness: ★★★
Insect Control: None Facilities: ★★

Creekview Campground is so low-key it doesn't even have a brochure. It did at one time, but most folks who stay at Creekview have either stayed there before or were told about the place by someone who did. With its easy access to a major interstate, it wouldn't be a bad place to spend the night while going or coming from someplace else. Located in a quiet country setting beside a creek, the campground caters to senior citizens. Eight of its sites are taken by seasonals who like the peaceful area. The level sites are grassy, shady, and there are a couple of pull-throughs. There are no planned activities, but there is a golf course within walking distance. Tent campers don't have a separate place set aside for them but are welcome to any of the sites. The favorite campsites are the eight by the creek. Security is good, since the owners live in a house in front of the campground; there is only one access road, and the grounds are patrolled. It also helps that the campground doesn't seem to attract campers who want to make noise.

Basics

Operated by: Howard & Jeanne Richardson. **Open:** Apr. 15–Oct. 31. **Site Assignment:** Reservations w/ no deposit. **Registration:** At campground office. **Fee:** $15. **Parking:** At site.

Facilities

Number of RV Sites: 25. **Number of Tent-Only Sites:** 0. **Hookups:** Electric (20, 30, 50 amps), water. **Each Site:** Picnic table, fire ring. **Dump Station:** Yes. **Laundry:** No. **Pay Phone:** No. **Rest Rooms and Showers:** Yes. **Fuel:** No. **Propane:** No. **Internal Roads:** Gravel, in fair condition. **RV Service:** No. **Market:** 4 mi. south in Edgerton. **Restaurant:** 2 mi. northeast in Stoughton. **General Store:** No. **Vending:** No. **Swimming Pool:** No. **Playground:** No. **Other:** Rec room, pavilion, sports field, horseshoes, hiking trail. **Activities:** None. **Nearby Attractions:** Golf, swimming, boating, horseback riding, historic Milton House, Lake Koshkonong. **Additional Information:** Milton Area Chamber of Commerce, (608) 868-6222.

Restrictions

Pets: Leash only. **Fires:** Fire ring only. **Alcoholic Beverages:** Permitted. **Vehicle Maximum Length:** None.

To Get There

From the junction of I-90 and Hwy. 51-73, take Exit 160 N, then drive 300 feet west and 1.5 mi. north on Albion Rd. Roads are in good condition w/ good shoulders.

EDGERTON
Hickory Hills Campground

856 Hillside Rd., Edgerton 53534. T: (608) 884-6327

RV ★★★★ Tent ★★★★

Beauty: ★★★★ Site Privacy: ★★★★★
Spaciousness: ★★★★★ Quiet: ★★★★★
Security: ★★★★★ Cleanliness: ★★★★★
Insect Control: None Facilities: ★★★★

Hickory Hills Campground, located four miles north of Edgerton, certainly has personality. It's not all neatly laid out with same-size, same-look sites. Most sites are spacious, ranging from 40 × 60 to 30 × 45 feet. About evenly split between grassy and gravel sites, the wilderness setting offers mostly shady spots sheltered by mature hickory and oak trees. The campground store is not a jumble of odds and ends but an attractive arrangement of light groceries, ice cream, snacks, pop, camping supplies, toiletries, and bait, along with souvenirs and gift items. About half the camping sites are occupied by seasonals. All campers probably wish that Hickory Hills offered laundry facilities.

Basics

Operated by: Richard & Cynthia Poff. **Open:** May 1–Oct. 15. **Site Assignment:** Reservations for 2 nights or more w/ 1-night deposit; no refund but a camping credit if notified 48 hours in advance. **Registration:** At campground office. **Fee:** $28 (cash, check). **Parking:** At site.

Facilities

Number of RV Sites: 300. **Number of Tent-Only Sites:** 0. **Hookups:** Electric (20, 30, 50 amps), water, sewer. **Each Site:** Picnic table. **Dump Station:** Yes. **Laundry:** No. **Pay Phone:** Yes. **Rest Rooms and Showers:** Yes. **Fuel:** No. **Propane:** Yes. **Internal Roads:** Gravel/paved, in good condition. **RV Service:** No. **Market:** 4 mi. south in Edgerton. **Restaurant:** 4 mi. south in Edgerton. **General Store:** Yes. **Vending:** Yes. **Swimming Pool:** Yes. **Playground:** Yes. **Other:** Mini-golf, shuffleboard, gameroom, snack bar, spring fed lake, juke box, lodge, horseshoes. **Activities:** Swimming, biking (rental bikes available) fishing, boating (rental boats available), planned weekend activities. **Nearby Attractions:** Horseback riding, golf, Lake Koshkonong, historic Milton House. **Additional Information:** Milton Area Chamber of Commerce, (608) 868-6222.

Restrictions

Pets: Leash only. **Fires:** Fire ring only. **Alcoholic Beverages:** Permitted. **Vehicle Maximum Length:** None.

To Get There

From the junction of I-90 and Hwy. 73, take Exit 160, drive 0.5 mi. north on Hwy. 73, then 0.75 mi. east on Hwy. 106, then 0.75 mi. north on Hillside Rd. Roads are wide and well maintained w/ broad shoulders.

EGG HARBOR
Camp-Tel Family Campground

8164 Hwy. 42, Egg Harbor 54209. T: (920) 868-3278; FamilyCampground.homestead.com/Camptel.html; camptel@dcemail.com.

RV ★★ Tent ★★★

Beauty: ★★★ Site Privacy: ★★
Spaciousness: ★★ Quiet: ★★★
Security: ★★★★ Cleanliness: ★★★★
Insect Control: None Facilities: ★★★

Located in the heart of the Door County Peninsula, Camp-Tel Family Campground is one mile north of Egg Harbor, right off Hwy. 42. Sites are mostly shaded and gravel with two pull-throughs and 39 seasonal campers. The typical site width is 25 feet. Laid out in a series of loops, Camp-Tel offers a separate area for tent campers with more green space and privacy. For safety, a five-mph speed limit is enforced, and mini-bikes and skateboards are not permitted. Quiet time is from 10:30 p.m. to 7 a.m., and all children and teenagers are required to be at their sites during those hours. Be aware that running electric heaters and air conditioners is not allowed. Security includes one entrance/exit, owners who live on site, and a campground patrol. The owners also offer a reward for information leading to the arrest, conviction, and restitution in connection with damage to Camp-Tel property.

BASICS

Operated by: Rich & Marian Irmens. **Open:** May 15–Oct. 15. **Site Assignment:** Reservations w/ 1-night deposit; refund (minus $5 service fee) w/ 7-day notice. **Registration:** At campground office. **Fee:** $19 (cash, check, credit cards). **Parking:** At site.

FACILITIES

Number of RV Sites: 104. **Number of Tent-Only Sites:** 17. **Hookups:** Electric (20 amps), water. **Each Site:** Picnic table, fire ring. **Dump Station:** Yes. **Laundry:** Yes. **Pay Phone:** Yes. **Rest Rooms and Showers:** Yes. **Fuel:** No. **Propane:** No. **Internal Roads:** Paved/gravel, in good condition. **RV Service:** No. **Market:** 1 mi. south in Egg Harbor. **Restaurant:** 1 mi. south in Egg Harbor. **General Store:** Yes. **Vending:** Yes. **Swimming Pool:** Yes. **Playground:** Yes. **Other:** Rec room, TV room, volleyball, badminton, basketball, horseshoes, rental A frames, recreation field. **Activities:** Swimming. **Nearby Attractions:** Door County, cherry & apple orchards, fishing, golf, bird-watching, hiking, boating, Lake Michigan, Green Bay, historic sites, antiques, arts & crafts shops, stock theatre, parks, bike trails. **Additional Information:** Door County Chamber of Commerce, (800) 527-3529.

RESTRICTIONS

Pets: Leash only. **Fires:** Fire ring only. **Alcoholic Beverages:** Permitted. **Vehicle Maximum Length:** None. **Other:** No air conditioners or heaters.

TO GET THERE

From the junction of CR E and Hwy. 42, drive 1.5 mi. north on Hwy. 42. Roads are wide and well maintained w/ broad shoulders.

EGG HARBOR
Door County Camping Retreat

4906 Court Rd., Egg Harbor 54209. T: (866) 830-5145; www.doorcountrycamp.com; office@doorcountycamp.com.

RV ★★★★ Tent ★★★

Beauty: ★★★★	Site Privacy: ★★★★
Spaciousness: ★★★★	Quiet: ★★★★
Security: ★★★★	Cleanliness: ★★★★
Insect Control: None	Facilities: ★★★★

Door County Camping Retreat, located three miles south of Egg Harbor, offers wooded campsites and a grassy, open meadow. Average site width is 30 feet, with 12 pull-throughs and 30 seasonal campers. Sites generally have a nice buffer of trees and bushes for privacy. Tent sites are separate from RV area with more green space. Speed limit is five mph, and quiet hours are 10 p.m. to 8 a.m. All radios, TVs, and stereos must be off by 10 p.m., and children must be on sites by 10:30 p.m. Only one warning for noise will be given, and then violators will be evicted without refund. Profanity also is not tolerated, and violators will be evicted without refund. Security measures include one entrance/exit, one-way roads, and regular patrols of the campground.

BASICS

Operated by: John Moravec. **Open:** May 1–Oct. 20. **Site Assignment:** Reservations w/ $25 deposit; no refund but will put it on account for next stay. **Registration:** At campground office. **Fee:** $25 (cash, check, credit cards). **Parking:** At site.

FACILITIES

Number of RV Sites: 160. **Number of Tent-Only Sites:** 50. **Hookups:** Electric (30, 50 amps), water, sewer. **Each Site:** Picnic table, fire ring. **Dump Station:** Yes. **Laundry:** Yes. **Pay Phone:** Yes. **Rest Rooms and Showers:** Yes. **Fuel:** No. **Propane:** Yes. **Internal Roads:** Gravel, in good condition. **RV Service:** No. **Market:** 3 mi. north in Egg Harbor. **Restaurant:** 3 mi. north in Egg Harbor. **General Store:** Yes. **Vending:** Yes. **Swimming Pool:** Yes. **Playground:** Yes. **Other:** Nature trails, pavilion, game room, arcade games, pool table, pop-up rentals, camping cabins, volleyball, basketball, horseshoes, badminton, sports field. **Activities:** Swimming, hiking, biking (rental bikes available), scheduled weekend activities. **Nearby Attractions:** Door County, cherry & apple orchards, fishing, golf, hiking, boating, Lake Michigan, historic sites, antiques, arts & crafts, parks, bike trails, museums. **Additional Information:** Door County Chamber of Commerce, (800) 527-3529.

RESTRICTIONS

Pets: Leash only. **Fires:** Fire ring only. **Alcoholic Beverages:** Permitted. **Vehicle Maximum Length:** 40 ft. **Other:** No bug lights allowed.

TO GET THERE

From the junction of CR E and Hwy. 42, drive 3.75 mi. south on Hwy. 42, then 0.25 mi. east on Sunny Point Rd., then 0.5 mi. north on Court Rd. Roads are wide and well maintained w/ broad shoulders.

EGG HARBOR
Frontier Wilderness Campground

4375 Hillside Rd., Egg Harbor 54209. T: (920) 868-3349

RV ★★★★★ Tent ★★★★

Beauty: ★★★★	Site Privacy: ★★★★
Spaciousness: ★★★★	Quiet: ★★★★
Security: ★★★★	Cleanliness: ★★★★★
Insect Control: Yes	Facilities: ★★★★★

Nope, it was no hallucination. The voice of Clint Black was actually singing in the women's outhouse at Frontier Wilderness Campground. The campground, located 2.5 miles south of Egg Harbor, has the distinction of providing music in its outhouses. Ask the owners how they do it. That is just one indication that this is no run-of-the-mill camping spot. Other special touches are a big indoor pool, complete with sauna and exercise site; a dumpster station inside a fancy little wooden enclosure; toilet rooms with real slate floors and blue fixtures; and private washrooms with mirrors. Instead of shower stalls with concrete floors and peek-a-boo curtains, Frontier Wilderness offers individual private shower rooms. An adult center has TV, carpet, reading chairs, sofas, tables, and other quality furnishings, instead of just a couple of rickety old chairs and worn-out furniture often found in some facilities. The campground has a typical site width of 36 feet, seven pull-throughs, and 180 seasonal campers. Laid out in a series of loops, the campground offers gravel sites for RVs and sand-bed sites for tents—either a drive-up site or a short walk-in site. A five-mph speed limit is enforced, as are quiet hours from 10 p.m. to 8 a.m. Security measures include surveillance cameras, one entrance/exit, owners who live on site, and regular patrols. Although Frontier Wilderness Campground lacks some amenities, such as sewer and 50-amp electric hookups, it more than makes up for those deficits with an abundance of other features, including top-notch cleanliness, beautiful landscaping with real flowers, and hanging baskets even at the outhouses.

BASICS

Operated by: Ray & Carla Kempen. **Open:** May 1–Oct. 31. **Site Assignment:** Reservations w/ 1-night deposit; refund w/ 7-day notice. **Registration:** At campground office. **Fee:** $23 (cash, check, credit cards). **Parking:** At site.

FACILITIES

Number of RV Sites: 250. **Number of Tent-Only Sites:** 0. **Hookups:** Electric (20, 30 amps), water. **Each Site:** Picnic table, fire ring. **Dump Station:** Yes. **Laundry:** Yes. **Pay Phone:** Yes. **Rest Rooms and Showers:** Yes. **Fuel:** No. **Propane:** No. **Internal Roads:** Paved/gravel, in good condition. **RV Service:** No. **Market:** 2.5 mi. north in Egg Harbor. **Restaurant:** 2.5 mi. north in Egg Harbor. **General Store:** Yes. **Vending:** Yes. **Swimming Pool:** Yes. **Playground:** Yes. **Other:** Cedar-lined sauna, exercise dome, mini golf, game room, pavilion, activity center, adult lounge, badminton, sports field, volleyball, recreation field. **Activities:** Swimming, live music on holiday weekends. **Nearby Attractions:** Door County, Lake Michigan, cherry & apple orchards, golf, fishing, hiking, boating, historic sites, antiques, arts & crafts, bike trails, Green Bay, parks. **Additional Information:** Door County Chamber of Commerce, (800) 527-3529.

RESTRICTIONS

Pets: Leash only. **Fires:** Fire ring only. **Alcoholic Beverages:** Permitted. **Vehicle Maximum Length:** None. **Other:** No smoking in any public buildings.

TO GET THERE

From the junction of CR E and Hwy. 42, drive 2.5 mi. south on Hwy. 42, then 1.5 mi. east on Hillside Rd. Roads are wide and well maintained w/ broad shoulders.

ELLISON BAY
Hy-Land Court

11563 Hwy. 42, Ellison Bay 54210. T: (920) 854-4850

RV ★★ Tent ★

Beauty: ★★	Site Privacy: ★★
Spaciousness: ★★	Quiet: ★★★
Security: ★★★	Cleanliness: ★★★★
Insect Control: None	Facilities: ★★

Located two miles south of Ellison Bay, Hy-Land Court is part of a mobile home park. Many of the campers are repeat business, so it is best to make reservations well in advance. The wooded campground features shaded, level sites with grass and gravel pads for RVs. The typical site width is 20 feet, and the campground has six pull-throughs and two seasonal campers. Speed limit is five mph. Quiet hours are in constant effect and "absolute silence" is required after 10 p.m., according to campground rules. Pets are not encouraged, but "if you must have a pet," it must be leashed at all times and not walked anywhere in the park. The campground has two entrance/exit roads. Security measures include an owner who lives on site and regular patrols of the campground.

BASICS

Operated by: Dale Hilander. **Open:** May 1–Nov. 1. **Site Assignment:** Reservations w/ 1-night deposit; refund w/ 7-day notice. **Registration:** At campground office. **Fee:** $23 (cash, check). **Parking:** At site.

FACILITIES

Number of RV Sites: 28. **Number of Tent-Only Sites:** 0. **Hookups:** Electric (20, 30, 50 amps), water, sewer. **Each Site:** Picnic table, fire ring. **Dump Station:** Yes. **Laundry:** No. **Pay Phone:** No. **Rest Rooms and Showers:** Yes. **Fuel:** No. **Propane:** No. **Internal Roads:** Paved/gravel, in good condition. **RV Service:** No. **Market:** 2 mi. north in Ellison Bay. **Restaurant:** 2 mi. north in Ellison Bay. **General Store:** No. **Vending:** No. **Swimming Pool:** No. **Playground:** No. **Activities:** None. **Nearby Attractions:** Door County, cherry & apple orchards, fishing, golf, hiking, boating, Lake Michigan, historic sites, antiques, arts & crafts, parks, bike trails. **Additional Information:** Door County Chamber of Commerce, (800) 527-3529.

RESTRICTIONS

Pets: Leash only but pets are not encouraged. **Fires:** Fire ring only. **Alcoholic Beverages:** At sites only. **Vehicle Maximum Length:** None.

TO GET THERE

From the junction of Hwy. 57 and Hwy. 42 (Sister Bay), drive 3.5 mi. north on Hwy. 42. Roads are wide and well maintained w/ broad shoulders.

ELLISON BAY

Wagon Trail Campground

1190 Hwy. ZZ, Ellison Bay 54210. T: (920) 854-4818; www.wagontrailcampground.com; wtc@dcwis.com.

RV ★★★★ Tent ★★★★

Beauty: ★★★★	Site Privacy: ★★★★
Spaciousness: ★★★★	Quiet: ★★★★
Security: ★★★★	Cleanliness: ★★★★★
Insect Control: None	Facilities: ★★★★

Think of the things you want in a campground, and Wagon Trail probably has most of them. Secluded and wooded with an average site width of 30 feet, Wagon Trail is the northernmost campground on the Door County peninsula. Most sites are sandy, with some grassy ones for tents. Laid out in a series of loops, Wagon Trail has four pull-throughs and 26 seasonals in a separate area. Located three-and-a-half miles northwest of Ellison Bay, Wagon Trail is one of the few campgrounds with direct access to the water (trails lead right to the lake). With a name like Wagon Trail, it's no surprise the campground features a western motif, including tree branches for curtain rods, branch-trim bed frames, and mirrors in the rest rooms. Other nice touches include a heated bathroom and rec room. Fresh-brewed coffee is served mornings in the well-stocked camp store, and the bathroom features free hot showers with plenty of electric outlets. The best RV sites are on Lady Slipper Ln., which is more secluded. The best tent sites are the three hideaways that have their own driveway for more privacy. Quiet time is from 10 p.m. to 8 a.m., with no radios allowed during those hours. Owners and the manager walk the grounds at night to be sure it is quiet and safe. Campfires must be out by midnight. Dogs are not allowed to sleep outside the camping unit at night.

BASICS

Operated by: Dick Bartlett & Cheri Ault. **Open:** May 5–Oct. 15. **Site Assignment:** Reservations w/ 1-night deposit; refund (minus $8) w/ 7-day notice. **Registration:** At campground office. **Fee:** $36 (cash, check, credit cards). **Parking:** At site.

FACILITIES

Number of RV Sites: 88. **Number of Tent-Only Sites:** 28. **Hookups:** Electric (30, 50 amps), water, sewer. **Each Site:** Picnic table, fire ring. **Dump Station:** Yes. **Laundry:** Yes. **Pay Phone:** Yes. **Rest Rooms and Showers:** Yes. **Fuel:** No. **Propane:** Yes. **Internal Roads:** Paved/gravel, in good condition. **RV Service:** No. **Market:** 3.5 mi. northwest in Ellison Bay. **Restaurant:** Walking distance. **General Store:** Yes. **Vending:** Yes. **Swimming Pool:** No. **Playground:** Yes. **Other:** Lake, swimming beach, rec room, hiking trails, volleyball, recreation field, rental cabins, badminton, horseshoes, adults room. **Activities:** Swimming, fishing, hiking. **Nearby Attractions:** Door County, Lake Michigan, cherry & apple orchards, fishing, boating, golf, historic sites, antiques, arts & crafts, parks, bike trails, nature conservancy. **Additional Information:** Door County Chamber of Commerce, (800) 527-3529.

RESTRICTIONS

Pets: Leash only. **Fires:** Fire ring only. **Alcoholic Beverages:** Permitted. **Vehicle Maximum Length:** 45 ft.

TO GET THERE

From the junction of Hwy. 42 and CR ZZ in Sister Bay, drive 6 mi. northeast on CR ZZ. Roads are wide and well maintained w/ broad shoulders.

FISH CREEK

Path O' Pines Campground

3709 CR F, Fish Creek 54212. T: (800) 868-7802; doorcountycampgrounds.com; crimp@dcwis.com.

RV ★★★ Tent ★★★

Beauty: ★★★	Site Privacy: ★★★
Spaciousness: ★★★	Quiet: ★★★
Security: ★★★	Cleanliness: ★★★
Insect Control: None	Facilities: ★★★

Located in the heart of Wisconsin vacationland, Path O' Pines Campground offers level, mostly shaded spots near a good access road. About a mile east of Fish Creek, the campground has 20 seasonal campers, 40 pull-through sites, and a typical site width of 30 feet. Laid out in a series of loops, the campground has gravel sites for RVs to park on. Security and safety measures include a five-mph speed limit and owners who live on site. The office staff is very good about sharing information oncerning activities in Door County. Although the campground doesn't offer swimming, it is located near three beaches within a one- to three-mile area. Quiet hours beginning at 10 p.m. are enforced. Violators receive one warning, then are asked to leave if the disturbance continues.

BASICS

Operated by: Tim & Janet Johnson. **Open:** May 15–Oct. 10. **Site Assignment:** Reservations w/ $25 deposit (2-night min.); refund (minus $5) w/ 5-day notice. **Registration:** At campground office. **Fee:** $30 (cash, check, credit cards). **Parking:** At site.

FACILITIES

Number of RV Sites: 85. **Number of Tent-Only Sites:** 10. **Hookups:** Electric (30 amps), water. **Each Site:** Picnic table, fire ring. **Dump Station:** Yes. **Laundry:** Yes. **Pay Phone:** Yes. **Rest Rooms and Showers:** Yes. **Fuel:** No. **Propane:** Yes. **Internal Roads:** Paved/gravel, in good condition. **RV Service:** No. **Market:** 1 mi. west in Fish Creek. **Restaurant:** 1 mi. west in Fish Creek. **General Store:** Yes. **Vending:** Yes. **Swimming Pool:** No. **Playground:** Yes. **Other:** Fish Creek, rec room, TV & game room, adults room, recreation field. **Activities:** None. **Nearby Attractions:** Door County, cherry & apple orchards, fishing, swimming, hiking, golf, boating, Lake Michigan, historic sites, antiques, arts & crafts, parks, bike trails. **Additional Information:** Fish Creek Information Center (800) 577-1880.

RESTRICTIONS

Pets: Leash only. **Fires:** Fire ring only. **Alcoholic Beverages:** Permitted. **Vehicle Maximum Length:** None.

TO GET THERE

From the junction of Hwy. 42 and CR F, drive 0.5 mi. east on CR F. Road is wide and well maintained w/ broad shoulders.

FOND DU LAC

Westward Ho Camp Resort

N5456 Division Rd., Glenbeulah 53023. T: (920) 526-3407

RV ★★★★ Tent ★★★★

Beauty: ★★★★	Site Privacy: ★★★★
Spaciousness: ★★★★	Quiet: ★★★★
Security: ★★★★	Cleanliness: ★★★★
Insect Control: None	Facilities: ★★★★

The first all-western theme park in Wisconsin and nestled in the North Kettle Moraine, Westward Ho Camp Resort is only minutes away from the historic Wade House—the old stagecoach stop for the early settlers going west or east. The rolling grassy campground offers a choice of wooded, semi-wooded, or open sites, and enough activities to wear out any child or parent. The typical site width is 40 feet, and there are no pull-throughs. Laid out in a series of loops, the campground has a five-mph speed limit and permits no skateboards. Rollerblades and bikes are not allowed after dark. Quiet time is 10:30 to 8 a.m., with no radios after 10:30 p.m. The Trading Post offers a pool table and color TV, plus a well-stocked general store and souvenir shop. Security includes one entrance/exit with a gate that is locked from 11 p.m. to 8 a.m., owners who live on site, and a sheriff's patrol of the campgrounds.

Basics

Operated by: James & Linda Schott. **Open:** May 15–Sept. 30. **Site Assignment:** Reservations w/ full deposit; refunds (minus $15) w/ 14-day notice. **Registration:** At campground office. **Fee:** $38 (cash, check, credit cards). **Parking:** At site.

Facilities

Number of RV Sites: 234. **Number of Tent-Only Sites:** 66. **Hookups:** Electric (30, 50 amps), water, sewer. **Each Site:** Picnic table, fire ring. **Dump Station:** Yes. **Laundry:** Yes. **Pay Phone:** Yes. **Rest Rooms and Showers:** Yes. **Fuel:** No. **Propane:** No. **Internal Roads:** Paved, in good condition. **RV Service:** No. **Market:** 12 mi. east in Plymouth. **Restaurant:** 5 mi. north in St. Cloud. **General Store:** Yes. **Vending:** Yes. **Swimming Pool:** Yes. **Playground:** Yes. **Other:** Frontier Theater, live petting farm, chuck wagon, music hall, game room, children's fishing ond, 10-station exercise trail, mini golf, movie, tetherball, baseball, basketball, volleyball, shuffleboard, horseshoes, hiking trail, wading pool, coin games. **Activities:** Swimming, fishing, hiking, movies, scheduled activities. **Nearby Attractions:** Wildlife refuge, trout & coho fishing, museums, horseback riding, Lake Michigan, sailing, summer stock theatre, antiques, arts & crafts, historic site. **Additional Information:** Fond du Lac Area CVB, (800) 937-9123.

Restrictions

Pets: Leash only. **Fires:** Fire rings only; fires not permitted past midnight (township ordinance). **Alcoholic Beverages:** Permitted. **Vehicle Maximum Length:** 40 ft.

To Get There

From the junction of US 41 and Hwy. 23, drive 16 mi. east on Hwy. 23, then 3 mi. south on CR G, then 0.5 mi. east on CR T. Roads are wide and well maintained w/ broad shoulders.

FORT ATKINSON

Jellystone Park at Fort Atkinson

N551 Wishing Well Dr., Fort Atkinson 53538.
T: (920) 568-4100; www.bearsatfort.com.

★★★★ ★★★★

Beauty: ★★★★	Site Privacy: ★★★★
Spaciousness: ★★★★	Quiet: ★★★★
Security: ★★★★	Cleanliness: ★★★★
Insect Control: None	Facilities: ★★★★

Check out the facilities and the activities, and you'll see why so many seasonal campers (380) chose to stay at Jellystone Park of Fort Atkinson. With a full-time activities director, the campground has enough going on to keep anyone busy. The grassy hilltop campground is pleasant enough just to sit around and do nothing. The campground has back-in sites and a typical site width of 35 feet. Laid out in a series of loops, the campground has level sites with a choice of shaded or open. Security and safety measures include a ban on motorcycles and scooters, proof of license and insurance for golf cart drivers, and a nightly quiet time. All guests/visitors must wear wristbands, and all vehicles must display a vehicle pass. Rangers patrol the campground.

Basics

Operated by: Steve Cline. **Open:** May 15–Sept. 15. **Site Assignment:** Reservations w/ 1-night deposit; refund (minus $5) w/ 10-day notice. **Registration:** At campground office. **Fee:** $26 (cash, check, credit cards). **Parking:** At site.

Facilities

Number of RV Sites: 569. **Number of Tent-Only Sites:** 20. **Hookups:** Electric (30, 50 amps), water. **Each Site:** Picnic table, fire ring. **Dump Station:** Yes. **Laundry:** Yes. **Pay Phone:** Yes. **Rest Rooms and Showers:** Yes. **Fuel:** No. **Propane:** Yes. **Internal Roads:** Paved/gravel, in good condition. **RV Service:** No. **Market:** 4 mi. north in Fort Atkinson. **Restaurant:** 4 mi. north in Fort Atkinson. **General Store:** Yes. **Vending:** Yes. **Swimming Pool:** Yes. **Playground:** Yes. **Other:** Pond, snack bar, baseball, full-time activities director, mini golf, tennis, horsehsoes, volleyball, basketball, shuffleboard, lounge, game room, pavilion, trails, kids/ fishing pond, rangers kitchen, wading pool, coin games. **Activities:** Swimming, hiking, fishing, movies, scheduled activities. **Nearby Attractions:** Aquatic park, boat launch, horseback riding, Lake Koshkonong, Fireside Dinner Theatre, golf, bicycle trails, roller skating, bowling, hang gliding, archery range, Hoard Historical Museum, National Dairy Shrine & Jones Dairy Farm, Dwight Foster House, Milton House Museum, Hexagon Stagecoach Inn, Replica of Old Fort Koshkonong. **Additional Information:** Fort Atkinson Area Chamber of Commerce, (888) 733-3678.

Restrictions

Pets: Leash only. **Fires:** Fire ring only. **Alcoholic Beverages:** At sites only. **Vehicle Maximum Length:** None.

To Get There

From the junction of US 12 and Hwy. 26, drive 5.25 mi. southwest on Hwy. 26, then 0.75 mi. west on Koshkonong Lake Rd., then 0.25 mi. south on Wishing Well Dr. Roads are wide and well maintained w/ broad shoulders.

FREMONT

Yogi Bear's Jellystone Park Camp-Resort

P.O. Box 497, Fremont 54940. T: (800) 258-3315; F: (920) 446-3450; www.fremontjellystone.com.

Beauty: ★★★★	Site Privacy: ★★★★
Spaciousness: ★★★★	Quiet: ★★★★
Security: ★★★★	Cleanliness: ★★★★
Insect Control: ★★★★	Facilities: ★★★★

Campers can usually count on a wealth of activities at Yogi Bear campgrounds. The Yogi Bear Jellystone Park Camp-Resort at Fremont has a huge bonus by being located on the shores of Partridge Lake. The 990-acre lake is part of the Wolf River Flowage. From the Yogi Bear boat ramp, there is more than 125 miles of navigable waterways. Not surprisingly, the most popular sites are the ones on the lake with private docks. Laid out in a series of loops, the campground has 50 seasonal campers, 28 pull-through sites, and a typical site width of 50 feet. Sites are level, with a choice of open or shaded. To accompany its water wonderland, the campground has a bait and tackle shop and an array of rental boats with enough good fishing to keep big and little kids happy. Quiet hours from 11 p.m. to 7 a.m. are enforced. Security is tops, with rangers who keep a close eye on the campground.

Basics

Operated by: John & Alyssa Harlan. **Open:** Apr. 15–Oct. 15. **Site Assignment:** Reservations w/ 50 percent deposit of total reservation; refund (minus $7) w/ 7-day notice. If less than 7-day notice given, full refund less 1 night will be returned. Reservations w/ 2-night min. on weekends; 3-night min. on holidays. **Registration:** At campground office. **Fee:** $45 (cash, check, credit cards). **Parking:** At site.

Facilities

Number of RV Sites: 251. **Number of Tent-Only Sites:** 31. **Hookups:** Electric (20, 30, 50 amps), water, sewer. **Each Site:** Picnic table, fire ring. **Dump Station:** Yes. **Laundry:** Yes. **Pay Phone:** Yes. **Rest Rooms and Showers:** Yes. **Fuel:** No. **Propane:** Yes. **Internal Roads:** Paved/gravel, in good condition. **RV Service:** No. **Market:** 2 mi. east in Fremont. **Restaurant:** 2 mi. east in Fremont. **General Store:** Yes. **Vending:** Yes. **Swimming Pool:** Yes. **Playground:** Yes. **Other:** Partridge Lake, arcade, mini golf, horseshoes, volleyball, basketball, shuffleboard, rec hall, game room, pavilion, nature trails, boat launch, gift shop, rental cabins, rental cottages, bait & tackle shop, boat ramp, badminton, sports field. **Activities:** Swimming, fishing (fishing guides available), hiking, boating (rental pontoons, rowboats, canoes, kayaks, jon boats available), scheduled activities. **Nearby Attractions:** Golf, horseback riding, waterslide, go-karts, cheese factories, bowling, canoeing, tubing, outlet mall, biking trails, Amish arts & crafts, antiques, harbor boat rides, Green Bay Packer Hall of Fame, zoo. **Additional Information:** Fremont Chamber of Commerce, (920) 446-3838.

Restrictions

Pets: Leash only; $2 per night. **Fires:** Fire ring only. **Alcoholic Beverages:** Permitted. **Vehicle Maximum Length:** None.

To Get There

From the junction of CR H & US 10, drive 1.5 mi. west on US 10. Roads are wide and well maintained w/ broad shoulders.

GALESVILLE

Rivers Edge Campground & Resort

W16751 Pow Wow Ln., Galesville 54630. T: (608) 582-2995

★★ ★★

Beauty: ★★ Site Privacy: ★★★
Spaciousness: ★★★ Quiet: ★★★
Security: ★★★★ Cleanliness: ★★
Insect Control: None Facilities: ★★

Located three miles south of Galesville, Rivers Edge Campground & Resort is a wooded campground with mostly grassy, shaded sites. Seasonals occupy 34 sites. The typical site width is 24 feet, with tall pine trees providing buffers between sites in many areas. Arranged in a series of loops, the campground offers nine pull-throughs and the Rivers Edge Bar, which is open all year to serve fast food and drinks. Most of the campers at Rivers Edge are local people and families who have been going there for years. Security measures include owners who live on site, regular patrols, and a gate that is locked from 11 p.m. to 8 a.m.

Basics

Operated by: Tom & Yvette Sulser. **Open:** May 15–Sept. 15. **Site Assignment:** Reservations accepted w/ no deposit. **Registration:** At campground office. **Fee:** $19 (cash, check, credit cards). **Parking:** At site.

Facilities

Number of RV Sites: 54. **Number of Tent-Only Sites:** 40. **Hookups:** Electric (20, 30 amps), water. **Each Site:** Picnic table, fire ring. **Dump Station:** Yes. **Laundry:** No. **Pay Phone:** Yes. **Rest Rooms and Showers:** Yes. **Fuel:** No. **Propane:** No. **Internal Roads:** Paved, in good condition. **RV Service:** No. **Market:** 3 mi. north in Galesville. **Restaurant:** 3 mi. north in Galesville. **General Store:** No. **Vending:** Yes. **Swimming Pool:** Yes. **Playground:** Yes. **Other:** Black River, beach, game room, rec hall, adults room, horseshoes, sports field, hiking trails, mini-golf, badminton, volleyball, basketball. **Activities:** Fishing, swimming, boating (rental canoes available). **Nearby Attractions:** Museums, antiques, zoo, paddlewheel boat. **Additional Information:** La Crosse Area CVB, (800) 658-9424.

Restrictions

Pets: Leash only. **Fires:** Fire ring only. **Alcoholic Beverages:** Permitted. **Vehicle Maximum Length:** None.

To Get There

From the junction of Hwys 54, 35, and 53, drive 3 mi. southeast on Hwy. 53. Roads are wide and well maintained w/ broad shoulders.

GOODMAN

Lake Hilbert Campground

N20470 Town Pike Rd., Fence 54541. T: (715) 336-3013

Beauty: ★★ Site Privacy: ★★
Spaciousness: ★★ Quiet: ★★★
Security: ★★ Cleanliness: ★★★
Insect Control: None Facilities: ★★

Located four miles north of Armstrong Creek, Lake Hilbert Campground offers mostly shady, grassy sites. Laid out in a series of loops, the campground has ten pull-throughs and 22 seasonal campers. The best thing the campground has going for it is Lake Hilbert, which has a large park, boat landing, recreational area, fishing, and waterskiing. Quiet hours are from 10 p.m. to 6 a.m., and no loud music is allowed at any time. A ten-mph speed limit seems a bit high for a campground with children. Picnic tables may not be moved from other sites, unless you want to pay a $5 fee for the extra table. For security measures, the owner lives on site, and the campground has one entrance/exit road. Campground regulations also require that no personal belongings be left outside when the campsite is not in use.

Basics

Operated by: Mike Kocken. **Open:** Apr. 1–Nov. 31. **Site Assignment:** Reservations w/ 1-night deposit; refund w/ 14-day notice. **Registration:** At campground office. **Fee:** $16 (cash, check). **Parking:** At site.

Facilities

Number of RV Sites: 50. **Number of Tent-Only Sites:** 20. **Hookups:** Electric (30, 50 amps), water. **Each Site:** Picnic table, fire ring. **Dump Station:** Yes. **Laundry:** No. **Pay Phone:** Yes. **Rest Rooms and Showers:** Yes. **Fuel:** No. **Propane:** No. **Internal Roads:** Paved/gravel, in good condition. **RV Service:** No. **Market:** 4 mi. south in Armstrong. **Restaurant:** Next door. **General Store:** No. **Vending:** Yes. **Swimming Pool:** No. **Playground:** Yes. **Other:** Lake Hilbert, swimming beach, game room, rental cabins. **Activities:** Swimming, fishing, boating. **Nearby Attractions:** Train rides, logging museum, gambling casinos, nature center, bird refuge, Chequamegon-Nicolet National Forest. **Additional Information:** Laona Chamber of Commerce, (715) 674-3007.

Restrictions

Pets: Leash only. **Fires:** Fire ring only. **Alcoholic Beverages:** Permitted. **Vehicle Maximum Length:** None.

To Get There

Take Hwy. 141 to Pembine, drive 20 mi. west on Hwy. 8 to Goodman, and drive 3 mi. north on CR H. Roads are wide and well maintained w/ broad shoulders.

HANCOCK

Tomorrow Wood Campground

N 3845 7th Dr., Hancock 54943. T: (715) 249-5954

★★ ★★

Beauty: ★★ Site Privacy: ★★★
Spaciousness: ★★★ Quiet: ★★★
Security: ★★★ Cleanliness: ★★★★
Insect Control: None Facilities: ★★

A rustic rural campground on Fish Lake four miles southwest of Hancock, Tomorrow Wood Campground is popular as a fishing destination. The lake has bass, crappie, and lots of other pan fish. All the sewer sites are taken by seasonals. Laid out in a series of loops, the campground offers tall pine, oak, and other hardwood trees. All sites are wooded, with a typical width of 40 feet and no pull-throughs. Quiet hours from 11 p.m. to 8 a.m. are enforced, as is a five-mph speed limit. Owners live on the site and provide regular patrols, as well as seasonals who keep an eye on the campground. The best RV sites are 312 and 410 because they are bigger and offer more space. The best tent sites are P423 and 427 because they are more secluded and located away from RVs.

Basics

Operated by: Edward & Bonnie Zdroik. **Open:** May 1–Oct. 1. **Site Assignment:** Reservations w/ 1-night deposit; refund w/ 7-day notice. **Registration:** At campground office. **Fee:** $19 (cash, check). **Parking:** At site.

Facilities

Number of RV Sites: 115. **Number of Tent-Only Sites:** 30. **Hookups:** Electric (30, 50 amps), water, sewer. **Each Site:** Picnic table, fire ring. **Dump Station:** Yes. **Laundry:** Yes. **Pay Phone:** Yes. **Rest Rooms and Showers:** Yes. **Fuel:** No. **Propane:** Yes. **Internal Roads:** Gravel, in good condition. **RV Service:** No. **Market:** 4 mi. northeast in Hancock. **Restaurant:** 4 mi. northeast in Hancock. **General Store:** Yes. **Vending:** No. **Swimming Pool:** No. **Playground:** Yes. **Other:** Fish Lake, basketball, horseshoes, volleyball, pavilion, sandy beach, pavilion, sports field. **Activities:** Swimming, fishing, boating (rental rowboats available), scheduled weekend activities. **Nearby Attractions:** Rainbow Falls Water Park, golf, Mead Wildlife Refuge, Grotto Shrine, manufacturers mall. **Additional Information:** Stevens Point Area CVB, (800) 236-4626.

Restrictions

Pets: Leash only. **Fires:** Fire ring only. **Alcoholic Beverages:** Permitted. **Vehicle Maximum Length:** None.

To Get There

At the junction of Hwy. 51 and CR V, drive 1.25 mi. east on CR V, then 2 mi. southeast on CR GG, then 0.5 mi. south on 7th Dr. Roads are wide and well maintained w/ adequate shoulders.

HAYWARD

Lake Chippewa Campground

8380 North CTH CC, Hayward 54843. T: (715) 462-3672; www.lakechip.com; lakechip@pctcnet.net.

★★★★ ★★★★

Beauty: ★★★★ Site Privacy: ★★★★
Spaciousness: ★★★★ Quiet: ★★★★
Security: ★★★★ Cleanliness: ★★★★
Insect Control: None Facilities: ★★★★

Lake Chippewa Campground is located on an island in the heart of Lake Chippewa. Connected by a bridge and a causeway to the mainland, the campground offers great water activities. The 17,000-acre Chippewa Flowage is Wisconsin's largest wilderness lake, with most of its lakeshore undeveloped, wild, and scenic. The campground offers level, shaded, wooded sites, with 16 seasonal campers, 20 pull-through sites, and a typical site width of 30 feet. Campers can beach their boat or canoe right outside their RV door. Unobstructed views of water and seasonal foliage are also available. Reservations are recommended, especially for weekends and holidays. Since the campground stays open until Nov. 1, campers can enjoy the great fall foliage. Muskie is king here, but other popular fish are walleye, crappie, bluegill, and perch. The best sites, of course, are by the lake.

Basics

Operated by: Don & Judy Robinson. **Open:** May 1–Nov. 1. **Site Assignment:** Reservations w/ 1-night deposit; refund (minus $5) w/ 7-day notice. **Registration:** At campground office. **Fee:** $25 (cash, check). **Parking:** At site.

Facilities

Number of RV Sites: 170. **Number of Tent-Only Sites:** 10. **Hookups:** Electric (20, 30, 50 amps), water, sewer. **Each Site:** Picnic table, fire ring. **Dump Station:** Yes. **Laundry:** Yes. **Pay Phone:** Yes. **Rest Rooms and Showers:** Yes. **Fuel:** No. **Propane:** No. **Internal Roads:** Paved/gravel, in good condition. **RV Service:** No. **Market:** 7 mi. south. **Restaurant:** 2 mi. **General Store:** Yes, limited. **Vending:** Yes. **Swimming Pool:** No. **Playground:** Yes. **Other:** Chippewa Flowage, snack shop, sandy beach, baseball, mini golf, horseshoes, volleyball, basketball, rec hall, game room, trails, fish-cleaning station, rental RVs, rental cabins, boat landing, boat dock. **Activities:** Swimming, fishing, boating (rental motorboats, canoes, paddleboats available), scheduled activities. **Nearby Attractions:** National Freshwater Fishing Hall of Fame, lumberjack shows, zoo, golf, horseback riding, national forest, fishing, casinos, antiques, arts & crafts, Sawyer County Historical Society & Museum. **Additional Information:** Hayward Area Chamber of Commerce, (715) 634-8662.

Restrictions

Pets: Leash only. **Fires:** Fire ring only. **Alcoholic Beverages:** Permitted. **Vehicle Maximum Length:** None.

To Get There

From the junction of US 63 and Hwy. 27, drive 0.5 mi. south on Hwy. 27, then 13 mi. east on CR B, then 5 mi. south on CR CC. Roads are mostly wide and well maintained w/ narrow shoulders in spots.

HIXTON

Hixton-Alma Center KOA

N9657 State Rd. 95, Alma Center 54611. T: (800) 562-2680

RV ★★★★ Tent ★★★★

Beauty: ★★★★	Site Privacy: ★★★★
Spaciousness: ★★★★	Quiet: ★★★★
Security: ★★★★	Cleanliness: ★★★★★
Insect Control: Yes	Facilities: ★★★★

This is not a "party" campground. The Hixton-Alma Center KOA, 12 miles east of Black River Falls, is where families and campers come to enjoy a peaceful country setting with plenty of birds and flowers. The campground owner has an iron fist when it comes to rowdiness, but she also has a green thumb and spends a good number of hours tending her tulips and lilacs. She feeds birds year-round and uses a garlic spray to control mosquitos without harming wildlife. A small spring-fed pond provides catch-and-release fishing for youngsters. An immaculate bathroom not only has shiny waxed floors, but also features bouquets of fresh flowers. Each large (40 × 50 feet) campsite has a tree, grass, and a gravel pad for RVs; most are pull-throughs. Secluded wilderness sites are available for tent campers.

Basics

Operated by: Jim & Donna Rankin. **Open:** Apr. 1–Nov. 30. **Site Assignment:** Reservations w/ 1-night deposit; refund w/ 24-hour notice. **Registration:** At campground office. **Fee:** $24 (cash, check, credit cards). **Parking:** At site.

Facilities

Number of RV Sites: 50. **Number of Tent-Only Sites:** 16. **Hookups:** Electric (30, 50 amps), water, sewer. **Each Site:** Picnic table, fire ring. **Dump Station:** Yes. **Laundry:** Yes. **Pay Phone:** Yes. **Rest Rooms and Showers:** Yes. **Fuel:** No. **Propane:** No. **Internal Roads:** Gravel, in good condition. **RV Service:** No. **Market:** 12 mi. west in Black River Falls. **Restaurant:** 12 mi. west in Black River Falls. **General Store:** Yes. **Vending:** No. **Swimming Pool:** Yes. **Playground:** Yes. **Other:** Hiking trails, small fishing pond for children, volleyball, horseshoes, pavilion w/ juke box, videos, pool table. **Activities:** Hiking, swimming, fishing, birdwatching, biking (rental bikes available). **Nearby Attractions:** Golf, diving, canoeing, orchard, casino, Thunderbird Museum, antique & craft shops. **Additional Information:** Black River Falls Area Chamber of Commerce, (800) 404-4008.

Restrictions

Pets: Leash only. **Fires:** Fire ring only. **Alcoholic Beverages:** At sites only. **Vehicle Maximum Length:** None.

To Get There

From the junction of I-94 and Hwy. 95, take Exit 105, drive 3.5 mi. east on Hwy. 95. The roads are wide and well maintained w/ broad shoulders.

IRON RIVER

Wildwood Campground

9505 Wildwood Rd., Iron River 54847. T: (715) 372-4072; wildcamp@win.bright.net.

RV ★★ Tent ★★

Beauty: ★★★	Site Privacy: ★★★
Spaciousness: ★★★	Quiet: ★★★
Security: ★★★	Cleanliness: ★★★
Insect Control: ★★★	Facilities: ★★

Located two miles outside Iron River, Wildwood Campground has a beautiful spot on 18-acre Peterson Lake. There is no highway noise, and no jet skis or power boats are permitted on the lake. That means the campground is peaceful and quiet—except when ATVs roar off. Local ATV trails are accessible directly from the campgrounds. The closer to the lake, the better for most campers. Sites are level with plenty of shade, and typical site width of 30 feet.

Basics

Operated by: Carl & Sandra Westlund. **Open:** May 1–Oct. 15. **Site Assignment:** Reservations w/ 1-night deposit; refund (minus $5) w/ 7-day notice. **Registration:** At campground office. **Fee:** $14 (cash). **Parking:** At site.

Facilities

Number of RV Sites: 23. **Number of Tent-Only Sites:** 2. **Hookups:** Electric (20, 30 amps), water, sewer. **Each Site:** Picnic table, fire ring. **Dump Station:** Yes. **Laundry:** No. **Pay Phone:** Yes. **Rest Rooms and Showers:** Yes. **Fuel:** No. **Propane:** No. **Internal Roads:** Gravel, in good condition. **RV Service:** No. **Market:** 2 mi. west in Iron River. **Restaurant:** 2 mi. west in Iron River. **General Store:** Yes, limited. **Vending:** Yes. **Swimming Pool:** No. **Playground:** Yes. **Other:** Peterson Lake, swim beach, pavilion, ATV trails, hiking trails, rental camper bus. **Activities:** Swimming, fishing, boating (rental paddleboats, rowboats, canoes available). **Nearby Attractions:** Apostle Islands, Brule River, waterfalls, ferry boats, musuems, Big Top Chautauqua, fish hatcheries, scenic drives, antiques. **Additional Information:** Iron River Area Chamber of Commerce, (715) 372-8558.

Restrictions

Pets: Leash. **Fires:** Fire ring only. **Alcoholic Beverages:** Permitted. **Vehicle Max. Length:** None.

To Get There

From the junction of Hwy. 2 and Wayside Rd., drive 2.75 mi. south on Wayside Rd., then 0.5 mi. east on Wildwood Dr. Roads are mostly wide and well maintained w/ narrow shoulders in spots.

KEWAUNEE

Cedar Valley Campground

5098 Cedar Valley Rd., Kewaunee 54216. T: (920) 388-4983

RV ★★★ Tent ★★★

Beauty: ★★	Site Privacy: ★★★
Spaciousness: ★★★	Quiet: ★★★
Security: ★★★★	Cleanliness: ★★★
Insect Control: None	Facilities: ★★★

A rural campground along the Kewaunee River, Cedar Valley Campground offers level, grassy, mostly shaded sites. Located six miles west of Kewaunee, the campground has 64 seasonal campers, 30 pull-through sites, and a typical site width of 30 feet. The river serves as the campground's focal point and provides fishing and swimming; there's also a swimming pool. The most popular campsites for both tents and RVs are along the river, where spots are more secluded and offer more green space. The campground is in the heart of Wisconsin vacationland, but it also offers a fair amount of activities on site. Safety and security measures include a five-mph speed limit, speed bumps, a manager who lives on site, a traffic-control gate, and regular patrols of the campground.

BASICS

Operated by: John Pagel. **Open:** Apr. 25–Oct. 15. **Site Assignment:** Reservations w/ 1-night deposit; refund w/ 7-day notice. **Registration:** At campground office. **Fee:** $20 (cash, check, credit cards). **Parking:** At site.

FACILITIES

Number of RV Sites: 115. **Number of Tent-Only Sites:** 25. **Hookups:** Electric (30 amps), water. **Each Site:** Picnic table, fire ring. **Dump Station:** Yes. **Laundry:** Yes. **Pay Phone:** Yes. **Rest Rooms and Showers:** Yes. **Fuel:** No. **Propane:** Yes. **Internal Roads:** Gravel/sand, in good condition. **RV Service:** No. **Market:** 6 mi. east in Kewaunee. **Restaurant:** 6 mi. east in Kewaunee. **General Store:** Yes, limited. **Vending:** No. **Swimming Pool:** Yes. **Playground:** Yes. **Other:** Kewaunee River, mini golf, badminton, sports field, horseshoes, hiking trails, volleyball, basketball. **Activities:** Swimming, fishing, hiking, scheduled weekend activities. **Nearby Attractions:** Lake Michigan, boating, charter fishing, harbor, boat launch, cheese factories, antiques, arts & crafts, Door County, zoo, jail museum, golf, nautical museum, nature walk. **Additional Information:** Kewaunee Chamber of Commerce, (800) 666-8214.

RESTRICTIONS

Pets: Leash only. **Fires:** Fire ring only. **Alcoholic Beverages:** Permitted. **Vehicle Maximum Length:** None.

TO GET THERE

From the junction of Hwy. 42 and Hwy. 29, drive 0.75 mi. west on Hwy. 29, then 5 mi. northwest on CR C, then 0.75 mi. north on Cedar Valley Rd. (CR B). Roads are wide and well maintained w/ mostly broad shoulders.

KEWAUNEE

Kewaunee Village RV Park

333 Terraqua Dr., Kewaunee 54216. T: (800) 274-9684; F: (920) 388-4853; www.kewauneevillage.com; info@kewauneevillage.com.

RV ★★★★ Tent ★★★

Beauty: ★★★	Site Privacy: ★★
Spaciousness: ★★	Quiet: ★★★
Security: ★★★★	Cleanliness: ★★★★
Insect Control: None	Facilities: ★★★★

Location is everything, and Kewaunee Village RV Park certainly has a prime spot. Situated just over one mile north of downtown Kewaunee, the campground is right off the main road of Hwy. 42. It also is next to Lake Michigan on a beautiful harbor with a boat launch, charter fishing, and marina facilities. There is even a fish-cleaning house at the harbor and fish-freezing services for campers at the campground. Camp sites are level and mostly open, with a typical site width of 40 feet. Kewaunee Village RV Park has 64 pull-through sites, 24 seasonal campers, and city water and sewer. The campground has some shade trees, but it is not a wooded facility. RVs must be parked only on gravel pad areas, not on the grass. A ten-mph speed limit is enforced (a lower one might be better with so many children on site), as is quiet time from 11 p.m. to 7 a.m. Young adults and children must be on their sites by 10 p.m. Security measures include one entrance/exit, a regular patrol, and owners who live on site.

BASICS

Operated by: Dean, Nanette & Katie Kulm; Warren & Kathy Clark. **Open:** May 15–Oct. 15. **Site Assignment:** Reservations w/ 1-night deposit; refund w/ 3-day notice. **Registration:** At campground office. **Fee:** $27 (cash, check, credit card). **Parking:** At site.

FACILITIES

Number of RV Sites: 74. **Number of Tent-Only Sites:** 15. **Hookups:** Electric (20, 30, 50 amps), water, sewer. **Each Site:** Picnic table, fire ring. **Dump Station:** Yes. **Laundry:** Yes. **Pay Phone:** Yes. **Rest Rooms and Showers:** Yes. **Fuel:** No. **Propane:** Yes. **Internal Roads:** Paved/gravel, in good condition. **RV Service:** No. **Market:** 1.5 mi. south in Kewaunee. **Restaurant:** 1.5 mi. south in Kewaunee. **General Store:** Yes. **Vending:** No. **Swimming Pool:** Yes. **Playground:** Yes. **Other:** Pavilion, game & video room, mini golf, recreation field, horseshoes, fish freezing, shuffleboard. **Activities:** Swimming, sheduled weekend activities. **Nearby Attractions:** Lake Michigan, boating, charter fishing, harbor, boat launch, cheese factories, antiques, arts & crafts shops, Door County, zoo, jail museum, golf, art galleries, nautical museum, nature walk. **Additional Information:** Kewaunee Chamber of Commerce, (800) 666-8214.

RESTRICTIONS

Pets: Leash only, max. of 2 pets per site. **Fires:** Fire rings only. All fires must be extinguished by 11 p.m. Must be put out w/ water & no glowing embers remain. **Alcoholic Beverages:** Permitted. **Vehicle Maximum Length:** None. **Other:** Generators may not be used in the campground.

TO GET THERE

From the junction of Hwy. 29 and Hwy. 42, drive 0.75 mi. north on Hwy. 42. Roads are wide and well maintained w/ broad shoulders.

LAKEWOOD

Heaven's Up North Family Campground

18344 Lake John Rd., Lakewood 54138. T: (715) 276-6556; www.heavensupnorth.com; heavnsupno@ez.net.com.

RV ★★★★ Tent ★★★★

Beauty: ★★★★	Site Privacy: ★★★★
Spaciousness: ★★★★	Quiet: ★★★★
Security: ★★★★	Cleanliness: ★★★★★
Insect Control: No	Facilities: ★★★★

Located three miles west of Lakewood, Heaven's Up North Family Campground is a wooded, rolling facility with some steep hills leading to some of the campsites. But that hilly terrain also adds to the beauty. Quiet is maintained at the wilderness campground by having plenty of trees and other green space as buffers between sites and by enforcing 10 p.m. to 7 a.m. quiet times. No loud or amplified music is allowed at any time. Group-camping sites are not available in order to cut down on noise. The typical site width is 50 feet, and the campground has four pull-through sites and 76 seasonal campers. Laid out in a series of loops, the campground has a five-mph speed limit and one-way roads. Security measures include one entrance/exit, owners who live on site, and regular campground patrols. Open year-round, the campground is kept plowed in the winter for campers who want to hunt or go snowmobiling or ice fishing.

BASICS

Operated by: Marlene Sauriol. **Open:** All year. **Site Assignment:** Reservations w/ 2-night deposit; no refunds. **Registration:** At campground office. **Fee:** $23 (cash, check, credit cards). **Parking:** At site.

FACILITIES

Number of RV Sites: 110. **Number of Tent-Only Sites:** 5. **Hookups:** Electric (20, 30 amps), water. **Each Site:** Picnic table, fire ring. **Dump Station:** Yes. **Laundry:** Yes. **Pay Phone:** Yes. **Rest Rooms and Showers:** Yes. **Fuel:** No. **Propane:** No. **Internal Roads:** Gravel, in good condition. **RV Service:** No. **Market:** 3 mi. east in Lakewood. **Restaurant:** 3 mi. east in Lakewood. **General Store:** Yes, limited. **Vending:** Yes. **Swimming Pool:** Yes. **Playground:** Yes. **Other:** Game room, coin games, mini golf, horseshoes, recreation field, volleyball. **Activities:** Swimming. **Nearby Attractions:** Casino, bingo, gingerbread houses, fish hatchery, logging camp, golf, fishing & boating lakes, winery, art studio. **Additional Information:** Lakewood Area Chamber of Commerce, (715) 276-6500.

RESTRICTIONS

Pets: Leash only. **Fires:** Fire ring only. **Alcoholic Beverages:** Permitted. **Vehicle Maximum Length:** 36 ft.

TO GET THERE

From the junction of Hwy. 32 and CR F in Lakewood, drive 2 mi. northeast on CR F, then 3 mi. north on Lake John Rd. Roads are wide and well maintained w/ broad shoulders.

LAKEWOOD

Maple Heights Campground

P.O. Box 130, Lakewood 54138. T: (715) 276-6441

RV ★★★ Tent ★★★

Beauty: ★★★	Site Privacy: ★★★
Spaciousness: ★★★	Quiet: ★★★★
Security: ★★★★	Cleanliness: ★★★★
Insect Control: None	Facilities: ★★★

Maple Heights Campground, located 1.5 miles north of Lakewood, has two notable landmarks—a canopy of huge maple, beech, and hemlock trees, and a giant statue of Paul Bunyan's Babe the Blue Ox, a favorite photo op. The campground borders the Nicolet National Forest and offers a wealth of nearby water activities. Over 60 lakes are within ten miles. The McCas-lin Brook trout stream meanders around the campground, and it is located between two popular rafting rivers, the Wolf and Peshtigo. The campground's 50-foot heated pool is also hard to ignore. Laid out in a series of loops, Maple

Heights offers a typical site width of 30 feet, 85 pull-throughs, and 50 seasonal campers. Sites in the secluded, wooded campground are level and mostly shady. Seasonal campers are mostly clumped in sections. The best RV site is LB because it is larger, has water and electricity, and is close to the pool and other facilities. The best tent site is B13 because it is large and backs up into the national forest. Speed limit is five mph, and quiet time between 11 p.m. and 7:30 a.m. means music must be turned off and voices kept low. Security includes one entrance/exit road, owners who live on site, and regular patrols of the campground.

Basics

Operated by: Mike & Carolyn Kubitz. **Open:** Apr. 1–Dec. 1. **Site Assignment:** Reservations w/ $20 deposit; refund w/ 7-day notice. **Registration:** At campground office. **Fee:** $20 (cash, check, credit cards). **Parking:** At site.

Facilities

Number of RV Sites: 93. **Number of Tent-Only Sites:** 7. **Hookups:** Electric (20, 30, 50 amps), water. **Each Site:** Picnic table, fire ring. **Dump Station:** Yes. **Laundry:** Yes. **Pay Phone:** Yes. **Rest Rooms and Showers:** Yes. **Fuel:** No. **Propane:** No. **Internal Roads:** Gravel, in good condition. **RV Service:** No. **Market:** 1.5 mi. south in Lakewood. **Restaurant:** 1.5 mi. south in Lakewood. **General Store:** Yes. **Vending:** Yes. **Swimming Pool:** Yes. **Playground:** Yes. **Other:** McCaslin Brook trout stream, rec room, snack bar, mini golf, volleyball, horseshoes, ping pong, pavilion, hiking trail, sports field. **Activities:** Swimming, fishing, hiking. **Nearby Attractions:** Casino, bingo, gingerbread houses, fish hatchery, logging camp, golf, fishing & boating lakes, winery, art studio. **Additional Information:** Lakewood Area Chamber of Commerce, (715) 276-6500.

Restrictions

Pets: Leash only. **Fires:** Fire ring only. **Alcoholic Beverages:** Permitted. **Vehicle Maximum Length:** None.

To Get There

From the junction of CR F and Hwy. 32, drive 2 mi. north on Hwy. 32. Roads are wide and well maintained w/ broad shoulders.

LAONA

Ham Lake Campground

RR 1 Box 434, Wabeno 54566. T: (715) 674-2201; F: (715) 674-5028; hamlake@newnorth.net.

RV ★★★ Tent ★★★

Beauty: ★★ Site Privacy: ★★★
Spaciousness: ★★★ Quiet: ★★★
Security: ★★★★ Cleanliness: ★★★
Insect Control: None Facilities: ★★★

With easy access off Hwy. 32, Ham Lake Campground is a rural facility four miles south of Laona. Located on Ham Lake, the campground offers level, grassy sites with a choice of shade or open. The campground has 22 seasonal campers, 11 pull-through sites, and a typical site width of 30 feet. The mini golf set up could definitely use some work. The road going to sites R, T, K, and S has a steep, narrow hill that requires slow, careful maneuvering. The best RV site is B5 because it is a pull-through near the lake. The campground is a popular place to stay because it is conveniently near a wealth of recreational opportunities, as well as offering many on site. Security includes owners who live on site and keep a close watch on the campground.

Basics

Operated by: Terry & Judy Collins. **Open:** May 1–Oct. 15. **Site Assignment:** Reservations w/ $25 deposit; refund w/ 7-day notice. **Registration:** At campground office. **Fee:** $20 (cash, check, credit cards). **Parking:** At site.

Facilities

Number of RV Sites: 44. **Number of Tent-Only Sites:** 1. **Hookups:** Electric (30 amps), water, sewer. **Each Site:** Picnic table, fire ring. **Dump Station:** Yes. **Laundry:** Yes. **Pay Phone:** Yes. **Rest Rooms and Showers:** Yes. **Fuel:** No. **Propane:** Yes. **Internal Roads:** Paved/gravel, in good condition. **RV Service:** No. **Market:** 4 mi. north in Laona. **Restaurant:** 4 mi. north in Laona. **General Store:** Yes, limited. **Vending:** No. **Swimming Pool:** No. **Playground:** Yes. **Other:** Ham Lake, swimming beach, rec room, pavilion, mini golf, badminton, sports field, horseshoes, hiking trail, rental cabin & cottages, volleyball, fishing lake, boat dock. **Activities:** Swimming, fishing, hiking, boating (rental rowboats, canoes & paddleboats available). **Nearby Attractions:** Chequamegon-Nicolet National Forest, steam-powered train, lumberjack museum, bird refuge, casino, golf, snowmobile & cross-country ski trails, fishing, hunting, canoeing, antiques, arts & crafts, scenic drive, trout fishing. **Additional Information:** Laona Chamber of Commerce, (715) 674-3007.

Restrictions

Pets: Leash only. **Fires:** Fire ring only. **Alcoholic Beverages:** Permitted. **Vehicle Maximum Length:** None.

To Get There

From the junction of US 8 and Hwy. 32, drive 4 mi. south on Hwy. 32. Road is wide and well maintained w/ broad shoulders.

MENOMONIE

Edgewater Acres Campground

E5468 670th Ave., Menomonie 54751. T: (715) 235-3291; www.mycampground.com; info@mycampground.com.

RV ★★★ Tent ★★★★

Beauty: ★★★★ Site Privacy: ★★★
Spaciousness: ★★★ Quiet: ★★★
Security: ★★★ Cleanliness: ★★★
Insect Control: ★★★ Facilities: ★★★

Located an hour from the Twin Cities and a half hour from Eau Claire, Edgewater Acres Campground is a handy stopping point. Many campers also choose Edgewater Acres because of its water activities. Secluded sites are available on the Red Cedar River. The campground is seven miles from the start of the Red Cedar Bike Trail. Laid out in a series of loops, the campground has 38 seasonal campers and a typical site width of 30 feet. A separate tent area offers more greenery and privacy. A separate group area also allows group campers to have adjoining sites. The campground offers great fishing and a nice shoreline for children to fish from. Sites are level with a choice of shade or sun. The best sites are located on the shoreline.

Basics

Operated by: Tina King. **Open:** May 1–Oct. 1. **Site Assignment:** Reservations w/ 1-night deposit; refund w/ 7-day notice. **Registration:** At campground office. **Fee:** $22 (cash). **Parking:** At site.

Facilities

Number of RV Sites: 55. **Number of Tent-Only Sites:** 17. **Hookups:** Electric (15, 20 amps), water. **Each Site:** Picnic table, fire ring. **Dump Station:** Yes. **Laundry:** No. **Pay Phone:** Yes. **Rest Rooms and Showers:** Yes. **Fuel:** No. **Propane:** No. **Internal Roads:** Gravel, in good condition. **RV Service:** No. **Market:** 3 mi. north in Menonomie. **Restaurant:** 3 mi. north in Menonomie. **General Store:** Yes, limited. **Vending:** Yes. **Swimming Pool:** Yes. **Playground:** Yes. **Other:** Fish-cleaning house, boat launch, horseshoes, volleyball, basketball, rec hall, game room, fishing lake, fishing river, sports field. **Activities:** Fishing, swimming, boating (rental canoes, paddleboats, rowboats available). **Nearby Attractions:** Golf, antiques, Empire in Pine Lumber Museum, Wakanda Water Park, go-cart races, stock car races, Crystal Cave, Wilson Place Museum, Caddie Woodlawn Historic Park, Mabel Tainter Theater, state park. **Additional Information:** Menomonie Area Local Tourism, (800) 283-1862.

Restrictions

Pets: Leash only. **Fires:** Fire ring only. **Alcoholic Beverages:** Permitted. **Vehicle Maximum Length:** None.

To Get There

From the junction of I-94 and Hwy. 25, take Exit 41, drive 2 mi. north on Hwy. 25, then 1.5 mi. east on CR BB, then 0.75 mi. south on Cedar Falls Rd. (530th St.), then 0.5 mi. east on gravel road. Roads are mostly wide and well maintained w/ good shoulders.

MILTON

Hidden Valley RV Resort and Campground

872 East Hwy. 59, Milton 53563. T: (800) 469-5515; www.hiddenvalleyrvresort.com.

RV ★★★★ Tent ★★★

Beauty: ★★★★ Site Privacy: ★★★★★
Spaciousness: ★★★★★ Quiet: ★★★★★
Security: ★★★★★ Cleanliness: ★★★★★
Insect Control: None Facilities: ★★★★★

Hidden Valley RV Resort and Campground, two miles east of Edgerton, makes a wonderful first impression with its stone waterfall at the entrance. And the rural campground lives up that impression. Grounds are manicured almost like a golf course; sites are spacious (40 feet wide), mostly grassy with gravel pads, and adjoin a grassy park area. The campground opened in 1993, and most of the trees are still rather small to provide much shade. Exceptionally clean, modern facilities along with a large, three-level clubhouse add luxury touches. Tent campers are permitted to use RV sites, but the campground may be a bit too organized for many tent enthusiasts. The campground has a manager who lives on site, regular patrols, and one-way roads throughout the facility for security.

Basics

Operated by: Jim & Marcia Kersten. **Open:** Apr. 15–Oct. 15. **Site Assignment:** Reservations accepted w/ 1-night deposit; refund (minus $10 fee) w/ 7-day notice. **Registration:** At campground office. **Fee:** $29 (cash, check, credit cards). **Parking:** At site.

Facilities

Number of RV Sites: 175. **Number of Tent-Only Sites:** 0. **Hookups:** Electric (20, 30, 50 amps), water, sewer. **Each Site:** Picnic table, fire ring. **Dump Station:** Yes. **Laundry:** Yes. **Pay Phone:** Yes. **Rest Rooms and Showers:** Yes. **Fuel:** No. **Propane:** Yes. **Internal Roads:** Gravel, in good condition. **RV Service:** No. **Market:** 2 mi. west in Edgerton. **Restaurant:** 0.1 mi. any direction. **General Store:** Yes. **Vending:** No. **Swimming Pool:** Yes. **Playground:** Yes. **Other:** Hot tub, video game room, lounge areas, meeting room, deck, TV room, 4-acre recreations area including softball, volleyball, horseshoes. **Activities:** Swimming, biking (rental bikes available), planned weekly activities. **Nearby Attractions:** Waterskiing, boating, fishing, swimming on Lake Koshkonong, golf, Milton House Museum. **Additional Information:** Milton Area Chamber of Commerce, (608) 868-6222.

Restrictions

Pets: Leash only. **Fires:** Fire ring only. **Alcoholic Beverages:** Permitted. **Vehicle Maximum Length:** None.

To Get There

From the junction of I-90 and Hwy. 59, take Exit 163 and drive 0.75 mi. east on Hwy. 59. Roads are wide and well maintained w/ broad shoulders.

MILTON

Lakeland Camping Resort

1948 West Hwy. 59, Milton 53563. T: (608) 868-4700

RV ★★★ Tent n/a

Beauty: ★★★ Site Privacy: ★★★
Spaciousness: ★★★ Quiet: ★★★★
Security: ★★★★ Cleanliness: ★★★★
Insect Control: None Facilities: ★★★★

The statistics are impressive: about 575 total campground sites on beautiful Lake Kosh-konong (the state's second largest lake), a well-stocked campground store, and wealth of recreational activities. But Lakeland Camping Resort is filled mostly with seasonal campers. Only 30 overnight sites are available, so reservations are strongly recommended. The sites are mostly shaded, with nine pull-throughs (30 × 60 feet) and eight with sewer. Laid out in a series of loops, the campground offers a pleasant wilderness/rural setting with over a mile of lakeshore. Tents are not permitted. The complex, 2.5 miles north of Edgerton, includes Lakeland Custom Coach RV Sales and Service Center.

Basics

Operated by: Lakeland Leisure Corp. **Open:** May 1–Nov. 1. **Site Assignment:** Reservations w/ 1-night deposit, 3-night deposit for holidays; refund w/ week notice. **Registration:** At campground office. **Fee:** $33.15 (cash, check, credit cards). **Parking:** At site.

Facilities

Number of RV Sites: 500. **Number of Tent-Only Sites:** 0. **Hookups:** Electric (20, 30, 50 amps), water, sewer. **Each Site:** Picnic table, fire ring. **Dump Station:** Yes. **Laundry:** Yes. **Pay Phone:** Yes. **Rest Rooms and Showers:** Yes. **Fuel:** No. **Propane:** Yes. **Internal Roads:** Paved, in good condition. **RV Service:** Yes. **Market:** 2.5 mi. west in Edgerton. **Restaurant:** 2.5 mi. west in Edgerton. **General Store:** Yes. **Vending:** Yes. **Swimming Pool:** Yes. **Playground:** Yes. **Other:** Lake, sandy beach, tennis courts, recreation center, boat launch, game room, nature trails, cross-country & snowmobile trails, bait shop. **Activities:** Swimming, fishing, boating (rental boats available), hiking, planned. **Nearby Attractions:** Golf, Milton House Museum, hunting preserve, horseback riding, antique shops, county fairs & festivals, 35 mi. to Madison. **Additional Information:** Greater Madison CVB, (800) 373-6376.

Restrictions

Pets: Leash. **Fires:** Fire pits only. **Alcoholic Beverages:** Permitted. **Vehicle Maximum Length:** None. **Other:** No tents. Limit of 2 trout per day, per person in pond. Pets must be on 7-ft. leash.

To Get There

From the junction of I-90 and East State Rd 59, drive 2 mi. east on 59. Roads are wide and well-maintained w/ broad shoulders

MILTON

Lakeview Campground

1901 East WI 59, Milton 53563. T: (608) 868-7899

RV ★★ Tent ★★

Beauty: ★★★ Site Privacy: ★★
Spaciousness: ★★ Quiet: ★★★
Security: ★★★ Cleanliness: ★★★
Insect Control: None Facilities: ★★

Located on the shore of Lake Koshkonong, Lakeview Campground offers mooring facilities a short walk from campsite. Docks are provided for easy entry and exit from the boats. RV sites are level, mostly grassy, and shaded, with two pull-throughs. Both primitive and improved sites are available for tent campers. Tent sites on the shore are most popular with tent campers. Lakeview's 800 feet of shoreline boasts two beaches. The main beach, located directly in front of the lodge, is best for swimming and picnics on provided picnic benches. The smaller secluded beach to the northwest of the camp is a rustic retreat used mostly for tanning or quiet times. Check out the "window wall" of the lodge offering a panoramic view that stretches up to ten miles

Basics

Operated by: Dorothy Zaccari. **Open:** Apr. 1–Oct. 31. **Site Assignment:** Reservations w/ 1-night fee; refunds w/ 7-day notice. **Registration:** At campground office. **Fee:** $26 (cash). **Parking:** At site.

Facilities

Number of RV Sites: 75. **Number of Tent-Only Sites:** 30. **Hookups:** Electric (30, 50 amps). **Each Site:** Picnic table, fire ring. **Dump Station:** Yes. **Laundry:** No. **Pay Phone:** No. **Rest Rooms and Showers:** Yes. **Fuel:** Yes. **Propane:** No. **Internal Roads:** Gravel, in good condition. **RV Service:** No. **Market:** 4 mi. west in Milton. **Restaurant:** 4 mi. west in Milton. **General Store:** No. **Vending:** No. **Swimming Pool:** No. **Playground:** Yes. **Other:** Lake Koshkonong, rec room, boat dock, gameroom, lodge, snack bar. **Activities:** Swimming, fishing, boating, lodge. **Nearby Attractions:** Waterskiing, golf, Milton House Museum, horseback riding, skeet shooting. **Additional Information:** Milton Area Chamber of Commerce, (800) 868-6222.

Restrictions

Pets: Leash only. **Fires:** Fire ring only. **Alcoholic Beverages:** Permitted. **Vehicle Maximum Length:** None.

To Get There

From the junction of I-90 and Hwy. 59, take Exit 163, then drive 1.5 mi. east on Hwy. 59. Roads are wide and well maintained w/ broad shoulders.

MINOCQUA

Patricia Lake Campground

8505 Camp Pinemere Rd., Minocqua 54548. T: (715) 356-3198; F: (715) 358-3149; patlake@newnorth.net.

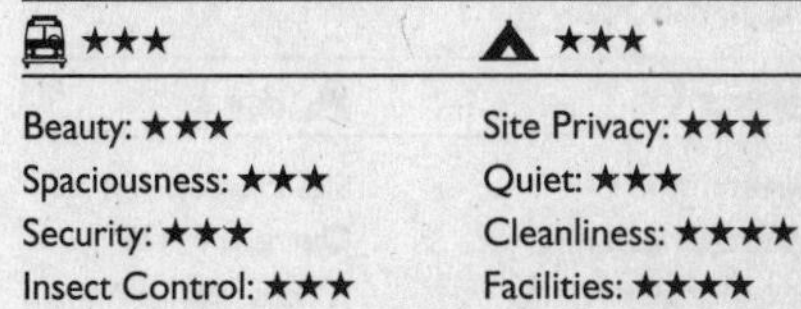

RV ★★★ Tent ★★★

Beauty: ★★★ Site Privacy: ★★★
Spaciousness: ★★★ Quiet: ★★★
Security: ★★★ Cleanliness: ★★★★
Insect Control: ★★★ Facilities: ★★★★

Situated on the Oneida/Vilas County border near Chequamegon National Forest in Minocqua, Patricia Lake Campground features wooded sites on Patricia Lake. A small, deep, spring-fed lake with no wake, Patricia Lake has good fishing for bass, northern pike and crappies. Nearby is the famous Minocqua Chain of Lakes for excellent fishing. Sites are level and mostly wooded. A separate tenting area offers tenters more green space and privacy. The campground has four pull-through sites, 69 seasonal campers, and a typical site width of 30 feet. The campground is conveniently located one mile from an 18-hole golf course and petting zoo and three miles from downtown shops. Most popular sites are closest to the lake. Campground owners provide security and make sure the campground is kept quiet and family oriented.

Basics

Operated by: David & Joy Taber. **Open:** May 1–Oct. 15. **Site Assignment:** Reservations w/ 1-night deposit; refund w/ 2-week notice. **Registra-**

tion: At campground office. **Fee:** $23 (cash, check, credit cards). **Parking:** At site.

Facilities

Number of RV Sites: 97. **Number of Tent-Only Sites:** 3. **Hookups:** Electric (20, 30 amps), water, sewer. **Each Site:** Picnic table, fire ring. **Dump Station:** Yes. **Laundry:** Yes. **Pay Phone:** Yes. **Rest Rooms and Showers:** Yes. **Fuel:** Yes. **Propane:** Yes. **Internal Roads:** Gravel, in fair condition. **RV Service:** No. **Market:** 3 mi. south. **Restaurant:** 3 mi. south. **General Store:** Yes. **Vending:** Yes. **Swimming Pool:** No. **Playground:** Yes. **Other:** Patricia Lake, swimming beach, horseshoes, volleyball, basketball, game room, pavilion, boat launch, recreation field, hiking trails. **Activities:** Swimming, fishing, hiking, boating (rental canoes, paddleboats, rowboats available). **Nearby Attractions:** Golf, Peck's Wildwood Wildlife Park & Nature Center, casino, antiques, arts & crafts, cross-country skiing, snowmobiling, professional repertory theater, Circle M Corral amusement park. **Additional Information:** Minocqua-Arbor Vitae-Woodrull Area Chamber of Commerce, (800) 446-6784.

Restrictions

Pets: Leash only; small pets only. **Fires:** Fire ring only. **Alcoholic Beverages:** Permitted. **Vehicle Maximum Length:** None.

To Get There

From south junction US 51 and Hwy. 70, drive 2.5 mi. west on Hwy. 70, then 0.5 mi. south on Camp Pinemere Rd. Roads are mostly wide and well maintained w/ borad shoulders.

MONTELLO

Buffalo Lake Camping Resort

555 Lake Ave., Montello 53949. T: (888) 297-2915; F: (608) 297-9072; buffalolakecamping.com; lake@maqs.net.

RV ★★★★ Tent ★★★

Beauty: ★★★★	Site Privacy: ★★★★
Spaciousness: ★★★★	Quiet: ★★★★
Security: ★★★★★	Cleanliness: ★★★★
Insect Control: No	Facilities: ★★★★

Buffalo Lake Camping Resort has the benefits of being located within the town of Montello, without the drawbacks of city noise and traffic. With a barrier of trees and large grassy areas, the campground is secluded and quiet. The campground is situated on 2,200-acre Buffalo Lake, the largest in Marquette County (called a "Sportsman's Paradise"), and the lake is well known for its northern pike, bass, crappie, bluegill, and perch. A well-stocked campground store carries groceries, beer, ice, firewood, camping supplies, snacks, clothing, souvenirs, fishing licenses, live bait, tackle, and boat rentals. A new laundry, rest rooms, and showers are kept clean, and rules about cleanliness and quiet are enforced. Recycling is mandatory, with recycling areas located throughout the campground. Quiet hours are 11 p.m. to 7 p.m. and children under 18 years old must remain in their campsite with adult supervision after 10 p.m. Owners live next door, the back gate to the campground is locked at night, and city police patrol the campground for security.

Basics

Operated by: Linda & Gary Doudna. **Open:** Apr. 12–Oct. 14. **Site Assignment:** Reservations w/ 2-night deposit; refund (minus $5 fee) w/ 14-day notice. **Registration:** At campground office. **Fee:** $28 (cash, check, credit cards). **Parking:** At site.

Facilities

Number of RV Sites: 111. **Number of Tent-Only Sites:** 0. **Hookups:** Electric (20, 30, 50 amps), water, sewer. **Each Site:** Picnic table, fire ring. **Dump Station:** Yes. **Laundry:** Yes. **Pay Phone:** Yes. **Rest Rooms and Showers:** Yes. **Fuel:** No. **Propane:** Yes. **Internal Roads:** Gravel, in good condition. **RV Service:** No. **Market:** 1 mi. south in Montello. **Restaurant:** Across the road. **General Store:** Yes. **Vending:** Yes. **Swimming Pool:** Yes. **Playground:** Yes. **Other:** Arcade, bait & tackle, horseshoes, covered pavilion, basketball, volleyball, lake boat dock, 4 piers, boat ramp, fish-cleaning house. **Activities:** Swimming, fishing, boating (rental canoes, kayaks & rowboats available), planned activities. **Nearby Attractions:** Rivers & trout streams, scenic country roads, 30 mi. to Wisconsin Dells. **Additional Information:** Wisconsin Dells Visitor & Convention Bureau, (800) 223-3557.

Restrictions

Pets: Leash only. **Fires:** Fire pits only. **Alcoholic Beverages:** Permitted. **Vehicle Maximum Length:** None.

To Get There

From Madison, take 1-90/94 to Exit 108B to WI 23 East, drive 8 mi. to CR C (Lake Ave.), 0.75 mi. to entrance. Roads are wide and well maintained w/ broad shoulders.

MONTELLO

Kilby Lake Campground

N4492 Fern Ave., Montello 53949. T: (877) 497-2344; www.kilbylake.com; klcg@yahoo.com.

RV ★★★★ Tent ★★★★

Beauty: ★★★★	Site Privacy: ★★★★
Spaciousness: ★★★★	Quiet: ★★★★
Security: ★★★★★	Cleanliness: ★★★★★
Insect Control: None	Facilities: ★★★★★

Since opening their campground in 1993, Jim and Sharon Caulfield have tried to add a little something every year for campers. The results are obvious. Located two miles west of Montello, Kilby Lake Campground has the wilderness beauty of a state park with extras usually not found at such facilities. Rustic sites are generally spacious (some 30 × 60 feet) and separated by mature oak trees. The 50-acre Kilby Lake is restricted to no wake to ensure cleanliness and great fishing. Known as a family campground, Kilby Lake Campground also sets aside and enforces "adult times." Friday and Saturday from 8 p.m. to 10 p.m., the heated swimming pool is reserved for adults only. Children may not be in the pool area during that time. Children under 16 also are not allowed in the whirlpool at any time. The 2001 addition was a bird sanctuary located just off the hiking trail behind the petting zoo. The campground offers scheduled birding tours and owl calling evenings. With all it has going for it, Kilby Lake Campground suffers from the results of popularity—66 of the full-hookup sites are occupied by seasonals, leaving only seven for visiting campers. Reservations are definitely recommended.

Basics

Operated by: Jim & Sharon Caulfield. **Open:** Apr. 15–Dec. 1. **Site Assignment:** Reservations w/ 50 percent deposit, special event & holiday weekend 100 percent deposit; refunds (minus $5 fee) w/ 7-day notice or 14 days prior to holiday & special events. **Registration:** At campground office. **Fee:** $28 (cash, check, credit cards). **Parking:** At site.

Facilities

Number of RV Sites: 122. **Number of Tent-Only Sites:** 0. **Hookups:** Electric (20, 30, 50 amps), water, sewer. **Each Site:** Picnic table, fire ring. **Dump Station:** Yes. **Laundry:** Yes. **Pay Phone:** Yes. **Rest Rooms and Showers:** Yes. **Fuel:** No. **Propane:** Yes. **Internal Roads:** Gravel, in good condition. **RV Service:** No. **Market:** 2 mi. east in Montello. **Restaurant:** 2 mi. east in Montello. **General Store:** Yes. **Vending:** Yes. **Swimming Pool:** Yes. **Playground:** Yes. **Other:** Farm animal petting zoo, whirlpool, lake, bird sanctuary, mini-golf, game room, shelter, horsehoes, hiking trail, beach house, beach, piers. **Activities:** Swimming, fishing, boating (rental rowboats, canoes & paddleboats available), bird-watching, hiking, scheduled activities. **Nearby Attractions:** Rivers & trout streams, scenic country roads, 30 mi. to Wisconsin Dells. **Additional Information:** Wisconsin Dells CVB, (800) 223-3557.

Restrictions

Pets: Leash only. **Fires:** Fire ring only. **Alcoholic Beverages:** Permitted. **Vehicle Maximum Length:** 40 ft. **Other:** 3-night min. on Memorial Day, Raspberry Fest & Labor Day, 4-night min. on 4th of July.

To Get There

From the junction of Hwy. 23 and Hwy. 50/49, drive 6 mi. east on Hwy. 23 to Fern Ave. Drive north on Fern 0.4 mi. Roads are wide and well maintained w/ broad shoulders.

MONTELLO

Wilderness Campground

N 1499 State Hwy. 22, Montello 53949. T: (608) 297-2002; www.wildernesscampground.com; wildrnes@palacenet.net.

RV ★★★★ Tent ★★★★

Beauty: ★★★★	Site Privacy: ★★★★
Spaciousness: ★★★★	Quiet: ★★★★
Security: ★★★★	Cleanliness: ★★★★
Insect Control: None	Facilities: ★★★★

Under the same ownership for more than three decades, Wilderness Campground offers easy access and a quiet facility away from highway noise. Located seven miles south of Montello, in the heart of Wisconsin's vacation land, the campground is on the shores of beautiful Bonnie and Hidden Lakes. The three private lakes provide plenty of water recreation, along with a large heated swimming pool. Laid out in a series of loops, the campground has 100 seasonal campers, 75 pull-through sites, and a typical site width of 45 feet. Sites are grassy, level, and mostly shaded in a rambling oak woodland. A separate tent area provides privacy from RVs and more green space. The best sites for tents and RVs are along the lakes. Tons of turtles and frogs keep down the mosquito population without insecticides. Security and safety measures include a 10 p.m. curfew for youngsters, a ban on bicycles on the roads after 8 p.m., quiet time starting 11 p.m., and owners who live on site and provide regular campground patrols.

Basics

Operated by: Bea Weiss. **Open:** Apr. 15–Oct. 15. **Site Assignment:** Reservations w/ 50 percent deposit; refund (minus $5) w/ 14-day notice. **Registration:** At campground office. **Fee:** $30 (cash, check, credit cards). **Parking:** At site.

Facilities

Number of RV Sites: 290. **Number of Tent-Only Sites:** 10. **Hookups:** Electric (15, 20, 30, 50 amps), water, sewer, phone. **Each Site:** Picnic table, fire ring. **Dump Station:** Yes. **Laundry:** Yes. **Pay Phone:** Yes. **Rest Rooms and Showers:** Yes. **Fuel:** No. **Propane:** Yes. **Internal Roads:** Paved/gravel, in good condition. **RV Service:** No. **Market:** 6 mi. north in Montello. **Restaurant:** 6 mi. north in Montello. **General Store:** Yes. **Vending:** Yes. **Swimming Pool:** Yes. **Playground:** Yes. **Other:** Three private lakes, dance hall, petting zoo, hiking trails, rental cabins, rental RVs, mini golf, rec hall, mini farm, pavilion, coin games, snack bar, boat ramp, badminton, sports field, volleyball, sandy beach. **Activities:** Hiking, swimming, fishing, boating (no motors allowed, rental rowboats, canoes & paddleboats available), scheduled activities. **Nearby Attractions:** Wisconsin Dells, golf, horseback riding, wildlife refuge, granite quarries, historic homes, museums, fish hatchery, Circus World museum, Devil's Lake, casino, stock car racing, antiques, arts & crafts. **Additional Information:** Wisconsin Dells Visitor & Convention Bureau, (800) 223-3557.

Restrictions

Pets: Leash only. **Fires:** Fire ring only. **Alcoholic Beverages:** Permitted. **Vehicle Maximum Length:** None.

To Get There

From the junction of Hwy. 23 and Hwy. 22 southbound, drive 7 mi. south on Hwy. 22. Roads are wide and well maintained w/ mostly broad shoulders.

NEW LONDON

Wolf River Trips and Campgrounds

E8041 County Hwy. X, New London 54961. T: (920) 982-2458; F: (920) 982-6122; rivertrips@yahoo.com.

RV ★★★ Tent ★★★

Beauty: ★★★	Site Privacy: ★★★
Spaciousness: ★★★	Quiet: ★★★
Security: ★★★★	Cleanliness: ★★★★
Insect Control: None	Facilities: ★★★

Located five miles southwest of New London, Little Wolf Trips and Campground offers wooded sites along Little Wolf River and rustic sites on Big Wolf River. Tubing trips start at the campground, where a shuttle bus takes tubers to the put-in point on the Wolf River. From there, the river takes tubers through rocks, rapids and quiet drifting areas back to the campground. The typical site width is 24 feet, and the campground has ten pull-throughs and 20 seasonal campers. The most desirable sites for both RVs and tents are along the river. All sites are either grassy or sand. An on-site lounge serves fast food and drinks. Security measures include one entrance/exit road, owners who live on site, regular patrols, and a 24-hour staffed security phone.

Basics

Operated by: Mark & Gary Flease & Janet Koplien. **Open:** May 1–Oct. 1. **Site Assignment:** Reservations w/ 1-night deposit; refund w/ 10-day notice. **Registration:** At campground office. **Fee:** $20 (cash, check). **Parking:** At site.

Facilities

Number of RV Sites: 105. **Number of Tent-Only Sites:** 30. **Hookups:** Electric (15, 30, 50 amps), water, sewer. **Each Site:** Picnic table, fire ring. **Dump Station:** Yes. **Laundry:** Yes. **Pay Phone:** Yes. **Rest Rooms and Showers:** Yes. **Fuel:** No. **Propane:** No. **Internal Roads:** Paved/gravel, in good condition. **RV Service:** No. **Market:** 5 mi. northeast in New London. **Restaurant:** 5 mi. northeast in New London. **General Store:** Yes, limited. **Vending:** Yes. **Swimming Pool:** No. **Playground:** Yes. **Other:** Wolf River, tennis, ball diamond, volleyball, rec hall, lounge, horseshoes, shuffleboard, pavilion, hiking trails. **Activities:** Swimming, fishing, canoeing (rental canoes available), tubing, boat ramp, boat dock,. **Nearby Attractions:** Chapel in the Woods, covered bridges, snowmobile trails, Red Mill, sternwheeler cruises, golf, museums, historic sites, antiques, Wisconsin Veterans Museum. **Additional Information:** Waupaca Area Chamber of Commerce, (888) 417-4040.

Restrictions

Pets: Leash only. **Fires:** Fire ring only. **Alcoholic Beverages:** Permitted. **Vehicle Maximum Length:** None.

To Get There

From the junction of US 45 and Hwy. 54, drive 4 mi. west on Hwy. 54, then 1 mi. south on Larry Rd., then 2 blocks west on CR X. The roads are wide and well maintained w/ broad shoulders.

NORMAN

Maple View Campground

N1460 Hwy. B, Kewaunee 54216. T: (920) 776-1588

RV ★★★ Tent ★★★

Beauty: ★★★	Site Privacy: ★★★★
Spaciousness: ★★★★	Quiet: ★★★★
Security: ★★★	Cleanliness: ★★★
Insect Control: None	Facilities: ★★★

Perched on a high ridge, Maple View Campground is wooded with maple trees, of course. It may be the only campground that makes its own maple syrup from its own maple trees. The syrup is for sale in the camp store. Located eight miles south of Kewaunee, Maple View has level sites; mostl are shaded, but some open ones are available for those who worry about satellite TV reception. Laid out in a series of loops, the campground offers four pull-throughs, 35 seasonals, and a typical site width of 36 feet. Most sites have a green buffer of trees and bushes for privacy and quietness. The best RV site is 22, known as the "honeymoon suite," offering a bigger spot and closeness to facilities. But you don't have to be a newlywed to stay there. The best tent sites are in a separate area down by the lake where they offer privacy away from RVs. Facilities are smoke-free. You don't need a license to fish in the private lake, which is stocked with perch, bluegill, and largemouth bass. Quiet time is 11 p.m. to 8 a.m., the speed limit is five mph, and the owners live on site to ensure safety and quietness.

Basics

Operated by: Joyce LaCrosse. **Open:** May 1–Oct. 15. **Site Assignment:** Reservations w/ 1-night deposit; refund w/ 7-day notice. **Registration:** At campground office. **Fee:** $18 (cash & check). **Parking:** At site.

Facilities

Number of RV Sites: 65. **Number of Tent-Only Sites:** 10. **Hookups:** Electric (20, 30, 50 amps), water. **Each Site:** Picnic table, fire ring. **Dump Station:** Yes. **Laundry:** Yes. **Pay Phone:** Yes. **Rest Rooms and Showers:** Yes. **Fuel:** No. **Propane:** No. **Internal Roads:** Gravel, in good condition. **RV Service:** No. **Market:** 8 mi. north in Kewaunee. **Restaurant:** 8 mi. north in Kewaunee. **General Store:** Yes, limited. **Vending:** Yes. **Swimming Pool:** No. **Playground:** Yes. **Other:** Lake, swimming beach, pavilion, ball diamond, horseshoes, volleyball, basketball, rental cabins, hiking trails, badminton. **Activities:** Swimming, fishing, hiking, boating (no motors), scheduled weekend activities. **Nearby Attractions:** Lake Michigan, boating, charter fishing, harbor, boat launch, cheese factories, antiques, arts & crafts, Door County, zoo, jail museum, golf, nautical museum,nature walk. **Additional Information:** Kewaunee Chamber of Commerce, (800) 666-8214.

Restrictions

Pets: Leash only. **Fires:** Fire ring only. **Alcoholic Beverages:** Permitted. **Vehicle Maximum Length:** None.

To Get There

From the junction of Hwy. 42 and CR G, drive 3 mi. west on CR G, then 500 feet south on Norman Rd. Roads are wide and well maintained w/ broad shoulders.

OAKDALE

Granger's Campground

Rte. 3, Tomah 54660. T: (608) 372-4511

RV ★★ Tent ★★

Beauty: ★★	Site Privacy: ★★
Spaciousness: ★★	Quiet: ★★★

Security: ★★★ Cleanliness: ★★
Insect Control: None Facilities: ★★★

Level grassy sites in a rural location with handy interstate access make this a good spot for travelers looking for an overnight stay. Granger's Campground also offers RV repair service and is located next to Granger's outdoor power equipment business. But don't count on Dwayne Granger being able to quickly work in a last-minute repair—the shop has a waiting list. Thirty-five large (50 × 80 feet) pull-through sites arranged in a series of loops provide easy in-and-out for RVs. Located six miles east of Tomah, the campground features few recreational outlets or activities and doesn't offer much privacy for tent campers. Security is good, with lights on the premises and an owner who lives on site and patrols the facilities. Noise can be a bit bothersome, depending on the interstate traffic and vehicles driving down the county road by the campground.

Basics

Operated by: Grangers LLC. **Open:** Apr. 1–Dec. 1. **Site Assignment:** Reservation w/ one-night deposit, refund w/ 7-day notice. **Registration:** At campground office. **Fee:** $13.66 (cash, check, credit cards). **Parking:** At site.

Facilities

Number of RV Sites: 45. **Number of Tent-Only Sites:** 3. **Hookups:** Electric (30 amps), water, sewer. **Each Site:** Picnic table, fire ring. **Dump Station:** Yes. **Laundry:** Yes. **Pay Phone:** Yes. **Rest Rooms and Showers:** Yes. **Fuel:** No. **Propane:** Yes. **Internal Roads:** Gravel, in good condition. **RV Service:** Yes. **Market:** 6 mi. west in Tomah. **Restaurant:** 6 mi. west in Tomah. **General Store:** Yes. **Vending:** No. **Swimming Pool:** No. **Playground:** Yes. **Other:** Pavilion, horseshoes, basketball, volleyball, badminton. **Activities:** Pancake breakfast on holidays, hayrides on holidays & weekends. **Nearby Attractions:** Bike trail, cranberry museum, golf, roller rink, cranberry festival, 45 min. drive to Wisconsin Dells. **Additional Information:** Warrens Area Business Assoc., (608) 378-4878.

Restrictions

Pets: Leash only. **Fires:** Fire ring only. **Alcoholic Beverages:** At sites only. **Vehicle Maximum Length:** 55 ft.

To Get There

From the junction of I-90/94 and CR PP, take Exit 48, drive 0.4 mi. north on CR PP. The roads are wide and well maintained w/ good shoulders.

OAKDALE

Oakdale KOA

P.O. Box 150, Oakdale 54649. T: (800) KOA-1737

RV ★★★★ Tent ★★

Beauty: ★★★ Site Privacy: ★★★
Spaciousness: ★★★ Quiet: ★★
Security: ★★★★ Cleanliness: ★★★★
Insect Control: None Facilities: ★★★★

It's inevitable: Access this convenient (just one block) to the interstate also means a noisy campground with the rumbling of trucks and cars passing by. This is probably more of a distraction for tent campers than RVs. But convenience is what Oakdale KOA has in abundance. Located in the heart of cranberry country, six miles southeast of Tomah, the campground is a popular site during the annual Cranberry Festival in Sept., as well as for bike riders on the nearby state bike trails. The pluses are mature pine and oak trees (with beautiful fall foliage) and mostly pull-through, level sites with new water and electric hookups. Shade is abundant, but some trees have been newly cut for those RVs with satellite dishes. New tent sites with concrete curbing outlining tent placement areas offer dependability for campers.

Basics

Operated by: William Rood. **Open:** May 11–Oct. 15. **Site Assignment:** Reservations w/ 1-night deposit; refunds w/ 24-hour notice. **Registration:** At campground office. **Fee:** $24 (cash, check, credit cards). **Parking:** At site.

Facilities

Number of RV Sites: 47. **Number of Tent-Only Sites:** 6. **Hookups:** Electric (20, 30, 50 amps), water, sewer, cable TV, phone. **Each Site:** Picnic table, fire ring. **Dump Station:** Yes. **Laundry:** Yes. **Pay Phone:** Yes. **Rest Rooms and Showers:** Yes. **Fuel:** No. **Propane:** Yes. **Internal Roads:** Gravel, in good condition. **RV Service:** No. **Market:** 6 mi. northwest in Tomah. **Restaurant:** 6 mi. northwest in Tomah. **General Store:** Yes. **Vending:** No. **Swimming Pool:** Yes. **Playground:** Yes. **Other:** Game room, heated & air-conditioned pavilion, horseshoes, volleyball. **Activities:** Swimming, biking. **Nearby Attractions:** State bike trails, cranberry festival & tours, Tomah tractor pull, golf, roller skating. **Additional Information:** Warrens Area Business Assoc. (608) 378-4878.

Restrictions

Pets: Leash only. **Fires:** Fire pits only. **Alcoholic Beverages:** At sites only. **Vehicle Maximum Length:** None.

To Get There

From the junction of I-90/94 and CR PP, take Exit 48, drive 1 block n on CR PP, then 2 blocks east on Woody Dr., 1 block south on Jay Street. Roads are well maintained w/ broad shoulders.

ONTARIO

Brush Creek Campground

S190 Opal Rd., Ontario 54651. T: (608) 337-4344

RV ★★ Tent ★★★★

Beauty: ★★★ Site Privacy: ★★★★
Spaciousness: ★★★★ Quiet: ★★★★
Security: ★★★★ Cleanliness: ★★★
Insect Control: None Facilities: ★★★

A self-described "Mom and Pop" operation, Brush Creek Campground caters to tent campers. Campers can choose between terraced sites on a hill or more level sites by a creek. Located in the Kickapoo Valley, 24 miles east of Sparta, the wilderness campground has spring-fed creeks, wooded hills, and rolling meadows, with plenty of room to breathe and enjoy the peace and quiet. Special tent sites are reserved in the woods and along the creek. Campers are not permitted to carry in firewood because the owner says they often bring in too much wood and leave it dumped on site, or bring in wood that won't burn. Plentiful stacks of firewood can be bought at the campground for a couple of dollars. Security is good, as the campground is located on a dead-end country road, and the owners live on site and patrol the area.

Basics

Operated by: Bud & Sis Kalb. **Open:** May 1–Oct. 31. **Site Assignment:** Reservations w/ $20, refund w/ 7-day notice. **Registration:** At campground office. **Fee:** $16. **Parking:** At site.

Facilities

Number of RV Sites: 35. **Number of Tent-Only Sites:** 70. **Hookups:** Electric (20, 30, 50 amps), water, sewer. **Each Site:** Many picnic table, fire ring. **Dump Station:** Yes. **Laundry:** Yes. **Pay Phone:** Yes. **Rest Rooms and Showers:** Yes. **Fuel:** No. **Propane:** No. **Internal Roads:** Gravel, in rough condition. **RV Service:** No. **Market:** 24 mi. west in Sparta. **Restaurant:** 2 mi. east in Ontario. **General Store:** Yes. **Vending:** Yes. **Swimming Pool:** No. **Playground:** Yes. **Other:** Pond, creeks, rec room, snack bar, hiking trails, horseshoes, volleyball, cable swing on lake. **Activities:** Swimming, fishing, hiking, kayak rentals, biking, scheduled weekend activities. **Nearby Attractions:** Golf, horseback riding, boating (rental kayaks available), Amish community, scenic drives. **Additional Information:** La Crosse Area CVB, (800) 658-9424.

Restrictions

Pets: Leash only. **Fires:** Fire pits only. **Alcoholic Beverages:** Permitted. **Vehicle Maximum Length:** 33 ft. **Other:** 2-night min. on all reservations, 3-night min. on holidays. No firewood can be brought in, must be bought on premises.

To Get There

From the junction of Hwy. 131 and 33, drive 3 mi. west on Hwy. 33, then 0.5 mi. south on Opal Rd. Hwy. 33 is good road but watch out for Amish buggies sharing the roadway

OSHKOSH

Kalbus' Country Harbor

5309 Lake Rd., Oshkosh 54902. T: (920) 426-0062; F: (920) 426-4162.

RV ★★★ Tent ★★★

Beauty: ★★★ Site Privacy: ★★
Spaciousness: ★★★ Quiet: ★★★★
Security: ★★★ Cleanliness: ★★★★
Insect Control: None Facilities: ★★★

Seeing the lines of empty boat trailers sitting at the entrance to Kalbus' County Harbor lets you know one of the main attractions of this campground. Located seven miles south of Oshkosh, Country Harbor is the only campground on the west side of Lake Winnebago. Owned by the Kalbus family since the 1940s, the campground offers lake views from every site. Easy-access boat launching and docking is located in the center of the campground on a man-made channel. The beach area has a sandy shore and sand bottom, making it popular with snorkelers. The typical site width is 35 feet, and the campground has eight pull-through sites and 22 seasonal campers. All sites seem about equally good. Security measures include an owner who lives on site and provides regular patrols of the campground.

Basics

Operated by: Jerry Kalbus. **Open:** May 1–Oct. 31. **Site Assignment:** Reservations w/ 1-night deposit plus $5; refund (minus $5) w/ 7-day notice. **Registration:** At campground office. **Fee:** $25 (cash, check, credit cards). **Parking:** At site.

Facilities

Number of RV Sites: 49. **Number of Tent-Only Sites:** 8. **Hookups:** Electric (20, 30, 50 amps), water, sewer. **Each Site:** Picnic table, fire ring. **Dump Station:** Yes. **Laundry:** Yes. **Pay Phone:** Yes. **Rest Rooms and Showers:** Yes. **Fuel:** Yes. **Propane:** Yes. **Internal Roads:** Gravel, in good condition. **RV Service:** No. **Market:** 6 mi. north in Oshkosh. **Restaurant:** 6 mi. north in Oshkosh. **General Store:** No. **Vending:** Yes. **Swimming Pool:** No. **Playground:** No. **Other:** Lake Winnebago, beach, boat launch, dock, fish-cleaning facilities. **Activities:** Swimming, fishing, boating (rental boats available). **Nearby Attractions:** Golf, The Morgan House, Grand Opera House, art center, arboretum, park, antiques, zoo, Military Veterans Museum, arts & crafts, EAA Air Adventure Museum. **Additional Information:** Oshkosh CVB, (877) 303-9200.

Restrictions

Pets: Leash only. **Fires:** Fire ring only. **Alcoholic Beverages:** Permitted. **Vehicle Maximum Length:** 40 ft.

To Get There

From the junction of US 41/Hwy. 26/CR N, drive 3 mi. east on CR N (becomes Fisk Rd.), then 1.5 mi. south on US 45, then 0.5 mi. east on Nekimi Ave., then 0.25 mi. north on Lake Rd. Roads are wide and well maintained w/ broad shoulders.

OSSEO

Osseo Camping Resort

50483 Oak Grove Rd., Osseo 54758. T: (715) 597-2102

RV ★★★ Tent ★★★

Beauty: ★★★★ Site Privacy: ★★★
Spaciousness: ★★★ Quiet: ★★★★
Security: ★★★★ Cleanliness: ★★★
Insect Control: Yes Facilities: ★★★

Osseo Camping Resort already has the basis for a good campground, and the new owners are embarking on major projects to make it even better. In 2001, they started adding new camping sections, a new office, new pool, and other improvements. Then they plan to start on the existing campground area. With a typical site size of 40 × 60 feet, the campground features mostly shaded, level, grassy sites. With one entrance, owners who live on site, and a night patrol, the campground boasts a good safety record. Remote wooded sites also are available for tent campers. The campground is conveniently located near I-90, one mile east of Osseo. It is 90 miles from the Wisconsin Dells, 156 miles from Madison, 88 miles from the Minnesota state line, and 125 miles from the Mall of America.

Basics

Operated by: Tom & Joy Levake. **Open:** Apr. 15–Oct. 31. **Site Assignment:** Reservations w/ 1-night deposit; refunds w/ 1-week notice. **Registration:** At campground office. **Fee:** $22 (cash, check, credit cards). **Parking:** At site.

Facilities

Number of RV Sites: 104. **Number of Tent-Only Sites:** 20. **Hookups:** Electric (20, 30 amps), water, sewer. **Each Site:** Picnic table, fire ring. **Dump Station:** Yes. **Laundry:** Yes. **Pay Phone:** Yes. **Rest Rooms and Showers:** Yes. **Fuel:** No. **Propane:** Yes. **Internal Roads:** Gravel, in good condition. **RV Service:** No. **Market:** 1 mi. west in Osseo. **Restaurant:** 1 mi. west in Osseo. **General Store:** Yes. **Vending:** No. **Swimming Pool:** Yes. **Playground:** Yes. **Other:** Video & TV game room, basketball, volleyball, horseshoes, outdoor stage, community fire ring, mini-golf, nature trails. **Activities:** Swimming, hiking, Saturday hayrides & dances, theme weekends. **Nearby Attractions:** Lakes, Northland Fishing Museum, golf, buffalo farm, hunting, Amish shops & farm tours, casino, antique & craft shops. **Additional Information:** Chippewa Valley CVB, (999) 523-3866.

Restrictions

Pets: Leash only. **Fires:** Fire ring only. **Alcoholic Beverages:** Permitted. **Vehicle Maximum Length:** None. **Other:** Other.

To Get There

From the junction of I-94 and US 10, take Exit 88, drive 0.25 mi. east on US 10, then 0.25 mi. south on Oak Grove Rd. Roads are wide and well maintained w/ broad shoulders.

OXFORD

Coon's Deep Lake Campground

348 Fish Ln., Oxford 53952. T: (608) 586-5644

RV ★★★ Tent ★★★

Beauty: ★★★ Site Privacy: ★★★
Spaciousness: ★★★ Quiet: ★★★★
Security: ★★★★ Cleanliness: ★★★★
Insect Control: None Facilities: ★★★

First off, Coon's Deep Lake Campground has 30 seasonal campers, which leaves only ten sites for other RVs. The place is popular because of its lake for fishing and swimming. Arranged in three layers of terraces, the campground overlooks the lake which is down the hillside. Sites are grassy, shaded, and level. The campground is surrounded by farm fields and woods, which gives it a quiet setting. Quiet hours are between 10 p.m. and 7 a.m. The best tent sites are in the woods away from RVs. The best available RV sites are 17-22 because they are larger and offer a nice view. There are no pull-through sites. A family-owned campground three miles west of Oxford, Coon's Deep Lake Campground is about 15 minutes from the Wisconsin Dells. But given the scarcity of overnight sites, it is recommended that you call ahead for reservations.

Basics

Operated by: George & Delores Benish. **Open:** May 1–Sept. 10. **Site Assignment:** Reservation w/ 2-night deposit; refund w/ 7-day notice. **Registration:** At campground office. **Fee:** $18 (cash, check). **Parking:** At site.

Facilities

Number of RV Sites: 40. **Number of Tent-Only Sites:** 10. **Hookups:** Electric (30, 50 amps), water. **Each Site:** Picnic table, fire ring. **Dump Station:** Yes. **Laundry:** Yes. **Pay Phone:** No. **Rest Rooms and Showers:** Yes. **Fuel:** No. **Propane:** No. **Internal Roads:** Gravel, in good condition. **RV Service:** No. **Market:** 3 mi. east in Oxford. **Restaurant:** 3 mi. east in Oxford. **General Store:** No. **Vending:** Yes. **Swimming Pool:** No. **Playground:** Yes. **Other:** Deep Lake, swimming beach, rec room, sports field, horseshoes. **Activities:** Swimming, fishing, boating (rental rowboats, canoe, paddleboats available). **Nearby Attractions:** Wisconsin Dells, scenic drives, golf. **Additional Information:** Wisconsin Dells Visitor & Convention Bureau, (800) 223-3557.

Restrictions

Pets: Leash only. **Fires:** Fire ring only. **Alcoholic Beverages:** Permitted. **Vehicle Maximum Length:** None.

To Get There

From the junction of CR A and Hwy. 82, drive 4 mi. west on Hwy. 82, then 1,000 feet north on paved access road. Roads are wide and well maintained w/ adequate shoulders.

PITTSVILLE

Dexter Park

400 Market St., Wisconsin Rapids 54495. T: (715) 421-8422; co.wood.wi.us.

RV ★★★ Tent ★★★★

Beauty: ★★★★ Site Privacy: ★★★★
Spaciousness: ★★★★ Quiet: ★★★★
Security: ★★★★ Cleanliness: ★★★
Insect Control: None Facilities: ★★★

Dexter Park is long on scenic beauty and short on man-made amenities. But that is exactly what some campers are seeking. Others should be forewarned that there is no handy laundry for those wet and dirty clothes, no well-stocked campstore for forgotten or used-up items, and no heated swimming pool for when it is too cold to set foot in the lake. Water and sewer hookups for RVs are non-existent, the electricity is 30 amps, and the rest room/shower facilities are adequate and passably clean. The beauty, however, is top-rate. The park is located on 1,235 acres around the 298-acre Lake Dexter, five miles south of Pittsville, and it offers over over 1,000 acres of wild or undeveloped land with abundant wildlife and game fish. Internal roads are paved and in excellent condition, and blacktop camp pads are provided on all campsites, most of which are wooded and secluded.

Basics

Operated by: Wood County. **Open:** May 1–Nov. 30. **Site Assignment:** Reservations w/ 1-night fee plus $5. Reservations cannot be made at campgrounds, must be made by telephone (715) 421-8422 or in person at county office Monday through

Friday 9 a.m. to 3 p.m. Refund (minus the $5 fee) w/ 7-day notice. **Registration:** At park rangers station. **Fee:** $13 (cash, Wisconsin check) credit cards accepted only for reservation. **Parking:** At site.

FACILITIES

Number of RV Sites: 69. **Number of Tent-Only Sites:** 28. **Hookups:** Electric (30 amp). **Each Site:** Some picnic table, fire ring. **Dump Station:** Yes. **Laundry:** No. **Pay Phone:** Yes. **Rest Rooms and Showers:** Yes. **Fuel:** No. **Propane:** No. **Internal Roads:** Paved, in excellent condition. **RV Service:** No. **Market:** 5 mi. north in Pittsville. **Restaurant:** 1 mi. north in Lakeside. **General Store:** No. **Vending:** Yes. **Swimming Pool:** No. **Playground:** Yes. **Other:** Dexter Lake, beach, enclosed shelter, tennis courts, hiking trail, volleyball court, fish-cleaning house, basketball court, boat launch. **Activities:** Swimming, fishing, hiking, boating. **Nearby Attractions:** Hunting, berry picking, all-terrain vehicle areas, speedway, snowmobiling, golf, zoo. **Additional Information:** Wisconsin Rapids Area CVB, (800) 554-4484.

RESTRICTIONS

Pets: Leash only. **Fires:** Fire pits only. **Alcoholic Beverages:** Permitted. **Vehicle Maximum Length:** None. **Other:** 2-night min. for weekends, 3-night for holidays.

TO GET THERE

From the junction of Hwy. 80 and 54, drive 0.5 mi. west on 54. Roads are wide and well-maintained w/ broad shoulders.

RICE LAKE

Rice Lake-Haugen KOA

1876 29 3/4 Ave., Rice Lake 54868. T: (715) 234-2360; www.koa.com; ricelakekoa@aol.com.

RV ★★★★ Tent ★★★★

Beauty: ★★★★	Site Privacy: ★★★★
Spaciousness: ★★★★	Quiet: ★★★★
Security: ★★★★	Cleanliness: ★★★★
Insect Control: ★★★★	Facilities: ★★★★

Rice Lake-Haugen KOA, located ten miles north of Rice Lake, offers relief from highway noise. Situated on Upper Devil's Lake, the campground has a nice beach and a dock where campers can fish. There is no charge to fish—a welcome break from campgrounds that charge that extra fee. The most popular camping spots are as close to the lake as possible. The campground has ten seasonal campers, eight pull-through sites, and a typical site width of 30 feet. The semi-wooded campground offers level, open, or shaded sites. Security is good—owners keep an eye on the facility and ensure that it is a quiet, family spot.

BASICS

Operated by: Dave & Mary Jo Nelson. **Open:** Apr. 15–Oct. 15. **Site Assignment:** Reservations w/ 1-night deposit; refund w/ 7-day notice. **Registration:** At campground office. **Fee:** $28 (cash, check, credit cards). **Parking:** At site.

FACILITIES

Number of RV Sites: 99. **Number of Tent-Only Sites:** 11. **Hookups:** Electric (20, 30, 50 amps), water, sewer. **Each Site:** Picnic table, fire ring. **Dump Station:** Yes. **Laundry:** Yes. **Pay Phone:** Yes. **Rest Rooms and Showers:** Yes. **Fuel:** No. **Propane:** Yes. **Internal Roads:** Gravel, in good condition. **RV Service:** No. **Market:** 10 mi. south in Rice Lake. **Restaurant:** 10 mi. south in Rice Lake. **General Store:** Yes, limited. **Vending:** Yes. **Swimming Pool:** Yes. **Playground:** Yes. **Other:** Upper Devil's Lake, beach, horseshoes, volleyball, basketball, game room, hiking trails, biking trails, boat launch, rental cabins, rental cottages, snack bar, sports field. **Activities:** Swimming, fishing, hiking, boating (rental rowboats, canoes, paddleboats available), scheduled activities. **Nearby Attractions:** Golf, stock car racing, nature preserve, horseback riding, Museum of Woodcarving, Barron County Historical Society Pioneer Village Museum, amusement center, casinos, antiques, cheese factories. **Additional Information:** Rice Lake Area Chamber of Commerce, (800) 523-6318.

RESTRICTIONS

Pets: Leash only. **Fires:** Fire ring only. **Alcoholic Beverages:** Permitted. **Vehicle Maximum Length:** None.

TO GET THERE

From the junction of US 53 and Hwy. 48, drive 10 mi. north on Hwy. 53, then 1 mi. east on the campground driveway. Roads are mostly wide and well maintained w/ broad shoulders.

SHAWANO

Kellogg's Kampsites

N1840 Airport Rd., Shawano 54166. T: (715) 526-2824

RV ★★ Tent ★★

Beauty: ★★★	Site Privacy: ★★
Spaciousness: ★★	Quiet: ★★★
Security: ★★★★	Cleanliness: ★★
Insect Control: None	Facilities: ★★

Located one mile south of Shawano, Kellogg's Kampsites offers level sites on Shawano Lake. Over 65% of the sites are located on the water, either on the 500-plus feet of lakefront or the 0.1-mile channel. Campers can park their boats a few feet behind the camper. For those who camp in the center grove area, there's full acess to the lake only 100 feet away. Kellogg's also provides a boat launch to campers and free boat docking. At more than 6,000 acres, Shawano Lake is a great fishing spot and is big enough to handle boaters without feeling crowded. All sites come with a moveable metal "burning pad" for campfires. The typical site width is 24 feet, with no pull-throughs and 45 seasonal campers. Laid out in a series of loops, the campground has a five-mph speed limit. Security includes one entrance/exit road, owners who live on site, and regular patrols by city police.

BASICS

Operated by: Klayton Kellogg. **Open:** Apr. 15–Oct. 15. **Site Assignment:** Reservations w/ 1-night deposit; refunds w/ 7-day notice. **Registration:** At campground office. **Fee:** $22 (cash, check, credit cards). **Parking:** At site.

FACILITIES

Number of RV Sites: 75. **Number of Tent-Only Sites:** 6. **Hookups:** Electric (30 amps), water, sewer. **Each Site:** Picnic table, fire ring. **Dump Station:** Yes. **Laundry:** No. **Pay Phone:** No. **Rest Rooms and Showers:** Yes. **Fuel:** No. **Propane:** No. **Internal Roads:** Gravel, in fair condition. **RV Service:** No. **Market:** 1 mi. north in Shawano. **Restaurant:** 1 mi. north in Shawano. **General Store:** Yes. **Vending:** No. **Swimming Pool:** No. **Playground:** Yes. **Other:** Shawano Lake, beach, game room, fishing pier, horseshoes, rec hall, boat ramp, boat dock, sports field, volleyball, video games, fish-cleaning facilities. **Activities:** Swimming, boating (rental paddleboats available), some scheduled weekend activities. **Nearby Attractions:** Casino, go-karts, white water rafting, Wolf River, flea market, stock car races, farmers market, golf, hunting, fishing, museums, ATV trails. **Additional Information:** Shawano County Tourism Council, (800) 235-8528.

RESTRICTIONS

Pets: Leash only. **Fires:** Fire ring only. **Alcoholic Beverages:** At sites only. **Vehicle Maximum Length:** 35 ft. **Other:** Air conditioners are not allowed.

TO GET THERE

From the junction of Hwy. Bus 29 and CR H and CR HHH (Aiport Rd.), drive 1 mi. north on CR HHH. Roads are wide and well maintained w/ broad shoulders.

SHELL LAKE

Red Barn Campground

W6820 CR B, Shell Lake 54871. T: (715) 468-2575; www.redbarncampground.com.

RV ★★★ Tent ★★★

Beauty: ★★★	Site Privacy: ★★★
Spaciousness: ★★★★	Quiet: ★★★★
Security: ★★★★	Cleanliness: ★★★
Insect Control: ★★★	Facilities: ★★★

Many youngsters don't have a grandma and grandpa to visit on the farm. The Red Barn Campground gives them a taste of that farm life. Located two miles east of Shell Lake, the Red Barn has rabbits, goats, chickens, horses, and other animals to pet. A rooster's crow greets the break of dawn, and children can gather their own egg for breakfast. Campers also can pick strawberries in season (late June through early July) in the U-Pick Patch. The campground has 15 seasonal campers, ten pull-through sites, and a typical site width of 30 feet. A grassy, semi-wooded facility, the Red Barn offers a choice of open or shaded sites. A separate tent area allows for more green space and privacy. Lake access is available, as are nature trails through the woods and fields.

BASICS

Operated by: Lee & Dotty Swan. **Open:** May 15–Sept. 15. **Site Assignment:** Reservations w/ 1-night deposit; refund w/ 7-day notice. **Registration:** At campground office. **Fee:** $23 (cash, check). **Parking:** At site.

FACILITIES

Number of RV Sites: 45. **Number of Tent-Only Sites:** 25. **Hookups:** Electric (15, 20, 30, 50 amps), water. **Each Site:** Picnic table, fire ring. **Dump Station: Yes. **Laundry:** No. **Pay Phone:** Yes. **Rest Rooms and Showers:** Yes. **Fuel:** No. **Propane:** No. **Internal Roads:** Gravel, in good condition. **RV Service:** No. **Market:** 2 mi. west in Shell Lake. **Restaurant:** 2 mi. west in Shell Lake. **General Store:** No. **Vending:** No. **Swimming Pool:** No. **Playground:** Yes. **Other:** Petting zoo, mini golf, horseshoes, volleyball, basketball, sports field, hiking trails. **Activities:** Hiking, schedule activities. **Nearby Attractions:** Shell Lake beach, golf, walking tour, historic sites, Railroad Memories Museum, float trip, Wisconsin Great Northern Railroad, Museum of Woodcarving, Indianhead Art Center, fish hatchery. **Additional Information:** Washburn County Tourism Information Center, (800) 367-3306.

Restrictions

Pets: Leash only. **Fires:** Fire ring only. **Alcoholic Beverages:** Permitted. **Vehicle Maximum Length:** None.

To Get There

From center of town, drive 0.5 mi. north on US 63, then 2 mi. east on CR B. Roads are wide and well maintained w/ mostly broad shoulders.

SISTER BAY

Aqualand Camp Resort

Box 538, Sister Bay 54234. T: (920) 854-4573

RV ★★★ Tent ★★

Beauty: ★★★★	Site Privacy: ★★★
Spaciousness: ★★★	Quiet: ★★★★
Security: ★★★★	Cleanliness: ★★★★
Insect Control: None	Facilities: ★★★

In the heart of scenic Door County, Aqualand Camp Resort is a semi-wooded campground with level, gravel sites. The campground is occupied by almost all seasonals. Only ten sites are left for overnighters, so reservations are recommended. The typical site width is 40 feet, and the campground has seven pull-throughs. Seasonal campers take good care of their sites, including landscaping and other knick-knacks, which adds to the beauty of the campground. The speed limit is five mph, and quiet times are enforced between 10 p.m. to 8 a.m., requiring "absolute quiet," according to campground rules. Just in time to provide supper, rainbow trout fishing is allowed, (with no license required) between the hours of 2–4 p.m. The campground furnishes the poles and bait and even cleans the fish. You only pay for what you catch at $4 a fish—but you must keep all the fish you catch. Security includes one entrance/exit road, owners who live on site, and regular patrols of the campground.

Basics

Operated by: Mike & Karen McAndrews. **Open:** May 25–Oct. 15. **Site Assignment:** Reservations w/ 2-night deposit; refund w/ 1-week notice. **Registration:** At campground office. **Fee:** $26 (cash, check). **Parking:** At site.

Facilities

Number of RV Sites: 150. **Number of Tent-Only Sites:** 0. **Hookups:** Electric (30, 50 amps), water. **Each Site:** Picnic table, fire ring. **Dump Station:** Yes. **Laundry:** No. **Pay Phone:** Yes. **Rest Rooms and Showers:** Yes. **Fuel:** No. **Propane:** No. **Internal Roads:** Gravel, in good condition. **RV Service:** No. **Market:** 2 mi. north in Sister Bay. **Restaurant:** 2 mi. north in Sister Bay. **General Store:** No. **Vending:** No. **Swimming Pool:** Yes. **Playground:** Yes. **Other:** Fish-cleaning station, fish freezer, trout ponds, shuffleboard, sports field, volleyball. **Activities:** Swimming, fishing. **Nearby Attractions:** Door County, cherry & apple orchards, fishing, golf, hiking, boating, Lake Michigan, historic sites, antiques, arts & crafts, parks, bike trails. **Additional Information:** Door County Chamber of Commerce, (800) 527-3529.

Restrictions

Pets: Leash only. **Fires:** Fire rings only; fires must be extinguished by midnight. **Alcoholic Beverages:** Permitted. **Vehicle Maximum Length:** None.

To Get There

From the junction of Hwy. 42 and Hwy. 57, drive 2.25 mi. south on Hwy. 57, then 0.25 mi. east on CR Q. Roads are wide and well maintained w/ broad shoulders.

SPARTA

Leon Valley Campground

9050 Jancing Ave., Sparta 54656. T: (608) 269-6400; www.campleonvalley.com.

RV ★★★ Tent ★★★★

Beauty: ★★★★	Site Privacy: ★★★★
Spaciousness: ★★★	Quiet: ★★★★
Security: ★★★★	Cleanliness: ★★★★★
Insect Control: None	Facilities: ★★★

Leon Valley is out in the middle of nowhere, a valley surrounded by trees and hills. It's a great location for a peaceful, scenic campground. An attractive entranceway has an old wagon wheel, shrubs, and bushes. Thirty of the 105 RV sites are taken by seasonals. Sites are grassy with gravel pads for RVs, mostly shady, and level. Laid out in a series of loops, the campground offers a wilderness setting with 12 pull-through sites and an average site of 27 × 50 feet. The best RV sites are in the A 40 section near the playground and bathrooms. Tent sites are spread out in the campground, including some secluded areas. The best tent sites are B 1–37 because they are more wooded and away from people. Security measures are good since the owners live on site, have a regular patrol, and lock up the entrance gate at midnight.

Basics

Operated by: Bernard & JoAnn Waege. **Open:** Apr. 1–Nov. 30. **Site Assignment:** Reservations w/ 1-night deposit; refund w/ 7-day notice, 14-day notice for holidays. **Registration:** At campground office. **Fee:** $22 (cash, check, credit cards). **Parking:** At site.

Facilities

Number of RV Sites: 105. **Number of Tent-Only Sites:** 20. **Hookups:** Electric (30, 50 amps), water. **Each Site:** Picnic table, fire ring. **Dump Station:** Yes. **Laundry:** No. **Pay Phone:** Yes. **Rest Rooms and Showers:** Yes. **Fuel:** No. **Propane:** No. **Internal Roads:** Gravel, in good condition. **RV Service:** No. **Market:** 4 mi. north in Sparta. **Restaurant:** 4 mi. north in Sparta. **General Store:** Yes. **Vending:** Yes. **Swimming Pool:** Yes. **Playground:** Yes. **Other:** Basketball, volleyball, pavilion, horseshoes, snack bar, game room, hiking trail, sports field. **Activities:** Swimming, hiking. **Nearby Attractions:** Fort McCoy, 32-mi. bike trail, fishing, boating, hunting, horseback riding, canoeing, specialty shops, museums, craft mall, tennis, trap shooting, two self-guided historical walking tours. **Additional Information:** Sparta Tourism Bureau, (800) 354-BIKE.

Restrictions

Pets: Leash only. **Fires:** Fire ring only. **Alcoholic Beverages:** Permitted. **Vehicle Maximum Length:** None.

To Get There

From the junction of I-90 and Hwy. 27, drive 4 mi. south on Hwy. 27, then 1.25 mi. east on Jancing Ave. Roads are wide and well maintained w/ broad shoulders (except for the paved access road, which has little shoulder room). The road also takes a couple of whopping big turns on the way in.

SPOONER

Scenic View Campground

24560 Scenic View Ln., Spooner 54801. T: (715) 468-2510; www.scenicviewcampground.com; cline@spacestar.net.

RV ★★★ Tent ★★★★

Beauty: ★★★★	Site Privacy: ★★★
Spaciousness: ★★★	Quiet: ★★★
Security: ★★★	Cleanliness: ★★★
Insect Control: ★★★	Facilities: ★★★

Activities revolve around Poquette Lake at Scenic View Campground, located nine miles west of Spooner. Laid out in a series of loops, the campground has 20 seasonal campers and two pull-through sites. The best sites for tent campers are Areas 5 and 6, which offer more privacy and green space. Sites 5 and 6 offer no water or electric hookups, but water is handy nearby. The best RV sites are in Area 1, which features shaded, level spots overlooking the beautiful 100-acre lake. The sites are also near the beach and the main building which houses the bar and bathrooms. RVers that are camping with friends and might want several sites together would probably prefer Area 2 which is west of the main building and has sites with greater depth. Fed with clean, sparkling water, Poquette Lake is ideal for swimming and water sports. It has a sandy beach, swimming raft, and roped-off area for small children. The lake is brimming with bass, walleye, northern pike, and panfish. Check out the 11-pound pike caught in the lake and now hanging on a wall in the bar. Security measures include one way in and out past the owners' home.

Basics

Operated by: Tom & Carol Haseltine. **Open:** May 1–Oct. 10. **Site Assignment:** Reservations w/ 1-night deposit; refund (minus $5) w/ 2-week notice.

Registration: At campground office. **Fee:** $22 (cash). **Parking:** At site.

Facilities

Number of RV Sites: 40. **Number of Tent-Only Sites:** 5. **Hookups:** Electric (30 amps), water. **Each Site:** Picnic table, fire ring. **Dump Station:** Yes. **Laundry:** No. **Pay Phone:** Yes. **Rest Rooms and Showers:** Yes. **Fuel:** No. **Propane:** Yes. **Internal Roads:** Gravel, in good condition. **RV Service:** No. **Market:** 9 mi. east in Spooner. **Restaurant:** 9 mi. east in Spooner. **General Store:** Yes, limited. **Vending:** Yes. **Swimming Pool:** No. **Playground:** Yes. **Other:** Swimming beach, pavilion, lounge, boat ramp, boat dock, horseshoes, volleyball, basketball, rec hall, game room rental campers, fishing lake, badminton, hiking trails. **Activities:** Swimming, fishing, hiking, boating (rental rowboats, paddleboats, motorboats available). **Nearby Attractions:** Golf, casinos, supper clubs, walking tour, historic sites, Wisconsin Great Northern Railroad, Railroad Memories Museum, fish hatchery, Indianhead Art Center, snowmobile trails, horseback riding. **Additional Information:** Burnett County Tourism Office, (800) 788-3164.

Restrictions

Pets: Leash only. **Fires:** Fire ring only. **Alcoholic Beverages:** Permitted. **Vehicle Maximum Length:** None.

To Get There

From the junction of US 63 and Hwy. 70, drive 9.25 mi. west on Hwy. 70, then 0.5 mi. south on Scenic View Ln. Hwy. 70 is mostly wide and well maintained w/ broad shoulders. Scenic View Ln. has narrow shoulders in spots.

ST. GERMAIN

Lynn Ann's Campground

P.O. Box 8, St. Germain 54558. T: (715) 542-3456; F: (715) 542-2317; www.Lynnannscampground.com; heather@lynnannscampground.com.

RV ★★★ Tent ★★★

Beauty: ★★★ Site Privacy: ★★★
Spaciousness: ★★★ Quiet: ★★★
Security: ★★★ Cleanliness: ★★★★
Insect Control: ★★★ Facilities: ★★★★

Located on Big St. Germain Lake in St. Germain, Lynn Ann's Campground offers open and wooded sites. The facility has ten seasonal campers, one pull-through site, and a typical site width of 36 feet. Laid out in a series of loops, camp sites are level and grassy. The campground offers a variety of water activities and rents boats and other water equipment. The lake is a popular fishing spot for muskies, walleye, bass, northerns, and panfish. No glass, bottles, or cans are permitted near the beach or water. To ensure a neat appearance, the campground requires that campsites be cleaned daily. Ceramic-tiled showers are a nice touch, but the showers are coin-operated. Owners keep a close watch on the campground for security measures.

Basics

Operated by: Mike & Heather Davidson. **Open:** May 5–Oct. 10. **Site Assignment:** Reservations w/ 1-night deposit; refund w/ 10-day notice. **Registration:** At campground office. **Fee:** $25 (cash, check, credit cards). **Parking:** At site.

Facilities

Number of RV Sites: 90. **Number of Tent-Only Sites:** 0. **Hookups:** Electric (30 amps), water, sewer, Internet, cable TV. **Each Site:** Picnic table, fire ring. **Dump Station:** Yes. **Laundry:** Yes. **Pay Phone:** Yes. **Rest Rooms and Showers:** Yes. **Fuel:** Yes. **Propane:** Yes. **Internal Roads:** Gravel, in good condition. **RV Service:** No. **Market:** 3 mi. south. **Restaurant:** 3 mi. south. **General Store:** Yes. **Vending:** Yes. **Swimming Pool:** No. **Playground:** Yes. **Other:** Sandy beach, game room, hiking trails, horseshoes, volleyball, basketball, shuffleboard, boat launch, boat harbor, marina, rental trailers. **Activities:** Swimming, fishing, hiking, boating (rental pontoons, kayaks, wave runners, tubes, motor boats, sailboats, waterskis, canoes available). **Nearby Attractions:** Golf, casino, tennis, historic sites, national forest, museums, snowmobile trails, antiques, arts & crafts. **Additional Information:** St. Germain Chamber of Commerce, (800) 727-7203.

Restrictions

Pets: Leash only. **Fires:** Fire ring only. **Alcoholic Beverages:** Permitted. **Vehicle Maximum Length:** None. **Other:** No oversized tents, trailers must provide drain containers.

To Get There

From the junction of Hwy. 70 and Hwy. 155, drive 2 mi. west on Hwy. 70, then 0.5 mi. north on Normandy Court, then 0.25 mi. east on South Shore Dr. Roads are mostly wide and well maintained w/ broad shoulders.

STEVENS POINT

Rivers Edge Campground

3368 Campsite Dr., Stevens Point 54481. T: (715) 344-8058

RV ★★★ Tent ★★★

Beauty: ★★★★ Site Privacy: ★★★
Spaciousness: ★★★ Quiet: ★★★
Security: ★★★★ Cleanliness: ★★★★
Insect Control: None Facilities: ★★

With 12 miles of frontage on the beautiful Wisconsin River, Rivers Edge Campground has a head start on appealing to campers. The river is known for its good fishing and boating. The campground, located seven miles north of Stevens Point, offers waterfront or wooded campsites featuring a tree buffer to muffle highway noise. Easy access off I-51 and well-maintained connecting roads also give the campground an edge. Rivers Edge could really use a laundry and general store for the convenience of its campers and seasonal residents. Security gets high marks because the campground has one entrance, the manager lives on site, access to the fenced swimming pool is only through the office, and the grounds are patrolled. In addition, there are two rules that are strictly enforced: a speed limit of five mph (or violators will be asked to leave), and a 10 p.m. quiet time on weekdays (11 p.m. on Fridays and Saturdays).

Basics

Operated by: Jerry Fahrner. **Open:** May 1–Oct. 7. **Site Assignment:** Reservations w/ $20 deposit; refund w/ 48-hour notice. Full deposit in advance for holiday weekends. **Registration:** At campground office. **Fee:** $21 (cash, check). **Parking:** At site.

Facilities

Number of RV Sites: 108. **Number of Tent-Only Sites:** 6. **Hookups:** Electric (20, 30, 50 amps), water. **Each Site:** Picnic table, fire ring. **Dump Station:** Yes. **Laundry:** No. **Pay Phone:** Yes. **Rest Rooms and Showers:** Yes. **Fuel:** No. **Propane:** Yes. **Internal Roads:** Gravel, in good condition. **RV Service:** No. **Market:** 7 mi. south in Stevens Point. **Restaurant:** Next door. **General Store:** No. **Vending:** Yes. **Swimming Pool:** Yes. **Playground:** Yes. **Other:** Boat launch, boat docks, rec hall w/ game room, sandy beach, volleyball courts, horseshoes. **Activities:** Swimming, fishing, boating, waterskiing, planned weekend activities. **Nearby Attractions:** 4 public golf courses within 25-mi. radius, Cedar Creek Manufacturer's Direct Mall, Rainbow Falls Water Park, Rib Mountain, Grotto Shrine, Mead Wildlife Refuge. **Additional Information:** Stevens Point Area CVB, (800) 236-4626.

Restrictions

Pets: Leash only. **Fires:** Fire pits only. **Alcoholic Beverages:** Permitted. **Vehicle Max. Length:** 30 ft. **Other:** 3-day min. on holiday weekends.

To Get There

From Exit 165 on US 51 northbound, drive 0.4 mi. east on CR X, 20.5 mi. north on Sunset Drive, 0.5 mi. west on Maple Dr., 0.25 mi. north on Campsite Dr. Roads are wide and well maintained w/ good shoulders.

STURGEON BAY

Monument Point Camping

5718 West Monument Point Rd., Sturgeon Bay 54235. T: (920) 743-9411

RV ★★★ Tent ★★★★

Beauty: ★★★ Site Privacy: ★★★★
Spaciousness: ★★★★ Quiet: ★★★★
Security: ★★★★ Cleanliness: ★★★★
Insect Control: None Facilities: ★★★

Located five miles south of Egg Harbor, Monument Point Camping offers secluded, wooded spots in the Door County area. Sites are level and surrounded by green space for little private nooks. Tall trees, shrubs, and other greenery help buffer noise and add to privacy. Laid out in a series of loops, the campground features gravel RV pads and dirt tent pads. The typical site width is 50 feet, with five pull-throughs and 24 seasonal campers. The biggest drawbacks include no water hookups, pool, or laundry, but the tradeoff might be worth it for the serenity of the camping site. The speed limit is five mph, with quiet hours from 10:30 p.m. to 8 a.m. Recycling is a state law in Wisconsin. Security measures include one entrance/exit, one-way roads, owners who live on site, and regular patrols of the campground.

Basics

Operated by: Doug & Debbie Krauel. **Open:** May 1–Oct. 20. **Site Assignment:** Reservations w/ $10 deposit; refunds (minus $5) w/ 7-day notice. **Registration:** At campground office. **Fee:** $22 (cash, check). **Parking:** At site.

Facilities

Number of RV Sites: 76. **Number of Tent-Only Sites:** 9. **Hookups:** Electric (30 amps). **Each Site:** Picnic table, fire ring. **Dump Station:** Yes. **Laundry:** No. **Pay Phone:** No. **Rest Rooms and Showers:** Yes. **Fuel:** No. **Propane:** No. **Internal Roads:** Gravel, in good condition. **RV Service:** No. **Market:** 5 mi. north in Egg Harbor. **Restaurant:** 5 mi. north in Egg Harbor. **General Store:** Yes, limited. **Vending:** Yes. **Swimming Pool:** No. **Playground:** Yes. **Other:** Game room, volleyball, horseshoes, recreation field, badminton, hiking trails. **Activities:** Hiking. **Nearby Attractions:** Door County, cherry & apple orchards, fishing, golf, hiking, boating, swimming, Lake Michigan, historic sites, antiques, arts & crafts, parks, Green Bay. **Additional Information:** Door County Chamber of Commerce (800) 527-3529.

Restrictions

Pets: Leash only. **Fires:** Fire ring only. **Alcoholic Beverages:** Permitted. **Vehicle Maximum Length:** 40 ft.

To Get There

From north junction of Hwy. 42 and Hwy. 57 near Sturgeon Bay, drive 8 mi. north on Hwy. 42, then 1.25 mi. northwest on Monument Point Rd. Roads are wide and well maintained w/ broad shoulders.

STURGEON BAY
Potawatomi State Park Daisy Field Campground

3740 CR PD, Sturgeon Bay 54235. T: (920) 746-2890

RV ★★★★ Tent ★★★★

Beauty: ★★★★	Site Privacy: ★★★
Spaciousness: ★★★	Quiet: ★★★★
Security: ★★★★	Cleanliness: ★★★★
Insect Control: None	Facilities: ★★★

Natural beauty is the basic asset of Potawatomi State Park. Located only a few miles from Sturgeon Bay on the Wisconsin Door County peninsula, the park consists of 1,200 acres of flat to gently rolling upland terrain bordered by steep slopes and rugged limestone cliffs along Sturgeon Bay. Laid out in a series of loops, campsites are level and mostly shaded, with two pull-through sites. The park also offers two camping options for people with accessibility limitations. Two accessible campsites are located in the south campground adjacent to the toilet/shower building. In addition, the Cabin by the Bay is a fully accessible indoor facility which can be reserved by people who are unable to use the more traditional campsites. The biggest drawback of the park and campground is lack of swimming facilities. Since there is not a sandy beach, swimming is not recommended. However, park staff will direct campers to the nearest public beach. The rest room facilities are cleaner than most state facilities, and the campground has excellent security, including one entrance/exit road past the ranger station, along with regular campground patrols by rangers.

Basics

Operated by: State of Wisconsin. **Open:** All year. **Site Assignment:** Reservations w/ entire stay deposit (2-night min.); refund (minus $9.50) w/ 2-day notice. **Registration:** At campground office. **Fee:** $13 (cash, check, credit cards), plus $5 daily park fee or $18 annual fee if Wisconsin resident; $7 daily fee or $25 annual fee if not Wisconsin resident. **Parking:** At site.

Facilities

Number of RV Sites: 25. **Number of Tent-Only Sites:** 98. **Hookups:** Electric (20, 30 amps). **Each Site:** Picnic table, fire ring. **Dump Station:** Yes. **Laundry:** No. **Pay Phone:** Yes. **Rest Rooms and Showers:** Yes. **Fuel:** No. **Propane:** No. **Internal Roads:** Paved, in good condition. **RV Service:** No. **Market:** 3 mi. northeast in Sturgeon Bay. **Restaurant:** 3 mi. northeast in Sturgeon Bay. **General Store:** Yes, limited. **Vending:** No. **Swimming Pool:** No. **Playground:** Yes. **Other:** Sturgeon Bay, fishing lake, hiking trails, boat launch, observation tower, nature center, bike trails, pavilion, boat dock. **Activities:** Fishing, hiking, biking, boating, scheduled activities. **Nearby Attractions:** Lake Michigan, hiking trails, biking trails, fishing, Door County, golf, antiques, arts & crafts, historic sites, swimming. **Additional Information:** Door County Chamber of Commerce, (800) 527-3526.

Restrictions

Pets: Leash only, some areas are pet free. **Fires:** Fire ring only. **Alcoholic Beverages:** Permitted. **Vehicle Maximum Length:** None. **Other:** 21-day stay limit.

To Get There

From Sturgeon Bay, drive 1.5 mi. west on CR C, then 2 mi. north on park road. Roads are wide and well maintained w/ mostly broad shoulders.

STURGEON BAY
Quietwoods North Camping Resort

3668 Grondin Rd., Sturgeon Bay 54235. T: (800) 986-2267; www.quietwoodsnorth.com.

RV ★★★ Tent ★★★

Beauty: ★★★	Site Privacy: ★★
Spaciousness: ★★★	Quiet: ★★★★
Security: ★★★★	Cleanliness: ★★★★
Insect Control: None	Facilities: ★★★

Located in the heart of Door County overlooking Sturgeon Bay waters, Quietwoods North Camping Resort offers a satisfaction guarantee. Within one hour of check-in, if campers are not satisfied with their site, campground services, or facilities, the problems will be corrected to the campers satisfaction or a refund will be given. Located two miles west of Sturgeon Bay, Quietwoods North offers a choice of full-sun or wooded sites and grassy or gravel spots. The typical site width is 30 feet, with five pull-throughs and 105 seasonal campers. Although Quietwoods North and Quietwoods South used to have the same owners, the two campgrounds are no longer affiliated. The best tent site is 420 because of its lush green setting and view of the bluff. The best RV site is S24 because it is bigger, offers full hookups, and borders on Potawatomi State Park. Quiet hours are 11 p.m. to 8 a.m., and the speed limit is ten mph—but motorists are encouraged to drive slower in the campground, according to the campground brochure. Security is provided by one entrance/exit that is locked at night and owners who live on site and perform regular patrols.

Basics

Operated by: The McClelland family. **Open:** May 1–Oct. 15. **Site Assignment:** Reservations w/ $25 deposit; refund (minus $5) w/ 7-day notice. **Registration:** At campground office. **Fee:** $30 (cash, check, credit cards). **Parking:** At site.

Facilities

Number of RV Sites: 275. **Number of Tent-Only Sites:** 31. **Hookups:** Electric (20, 30, 50 amps), water, sewer. **Each Site:** Picnic table, fire ring. **Dump Station:** Yes. **Laundry:** Yes. **Pay Phone:** Yes. **Rest Rooms and Showers:** Yes. **Fuel:** No. **Propane:** No. **Internal Roads:** Paved/gravel, in good condition. **RV Service:** No. **Market:** 2 mi. east in Sturgeon Bay. **Restaurant:** 2 mi. east in Sturgeon Bay. **General Store:** Yes. **Vending:** Yes. **Swimming Pool:** Yes. **Playground:** Yes. **Other:** Game room, wading pool, snack bar, pavilion, mini golf, horseshoes, volleyball, basketball, tetherball, coin games, rental cabins, trailers & park models. **Activities:** Swimming, biking (rental bikes available), scheduled weekend activities. **Nearby Attractions:** Potawatomi State Park, hiking trails, biking trails, fishing, boat launch, Door County, golf, Sturgeon Bay, Lake Michigan, antiques, arts & crafts, historic sites. **Additional Information:** Door County Chamber of Commerce, (800) 527-3529.

Restrictions

Pets: Leash only; large breeds, such as pitbulls, dobermans & rottweilers, require prior management approval. **Fires:** Fire rings only; fires must be extinguished by 1 a.m. **Alcoholic Beverages:** Permitted. **Vehicle Maximum Length:** 45 ft.

To Get There

From the junction of Hwy. 42/57 and CR PD, drive 1.25 mi. north on CR PD, then 1 mi. east on CR C, then 0.75 mi. north on Grondin Rd. Roads are wide and well maintained w/ broad shoulders.

STURGEON BAY
Yogi Bear's Jellystone Park Camp-Resort

3677 May Rd., Sturgeon Bay 54235. T: (920) 743-9001; www.campdoorcounty.com/yogibear.

RV ★★★ Tent ★★

Beauty: ★★★	Site Privacy: ★★
Spaciousness: ★★	Quiet: ★★★
Security: ★★★★	Cleanliness: ★★★
Insect Control: None	Facilities: ★★★

Yogi Bear's Jellystone Park Camp-Resort has enough activities to wear out any parent or child. It also is located in Door County, eight miles south of Sturgeon Bay, which means even more choices for recreation. The campground is semi-wooded, with some nicely shaded sites and some sitting right out in an open field. Laid out in a series of loops, the campground has two pull-through sites and 100 seasonal campers. The typical site width is 40 feet. The best RV site is 91 because it is in the woods and offers more space and privacy. Tent campers can use any site, but it is hard to pick unless you look to see what is beside it at the moment. Quiet hours are from 10:30 p.m. to 7 a.m.; campfires are to be extinguished by 1 a.m., and all activities ceased by the 1 a.m. curfew. Mopeds, mini-bikes, ATVs, skateboards, and golf carts are prohibited at all times. Security measures include one entrance/exit road, and owners who live on site provide regular campground patrols.

Basics

Operated by: Dick & Sylvia Himes. **Open:** May 15–Oct. 15. **Site Assignment:** Reservations w/ $25 deposit; refund w/ 8-day notice. **Registration:** At campground office. **Fee:** $28 (cash, check, credit cards). **Parking:** At site.

Facilities

Number of RV Sites: 289. **Number of Tent-Only Sites:** 0. **Hookups:** Electric (30, 50 amps), water, sewer. **Each Site:** Picnic talbe, fire ring. **Dump Station:** Yes. **Laundry:** Yes. **Pay Phone:** Yes. **Rest Rooms and Showers:** Yes. **Fuel:** No. **Propane:** No. **Internal Roads:** Paved/gravel, in good condition. **RV Service:** No. **Market:** 8 mi. north in Sturgeon Bay. **Restaurant:** 8 mi. north in Sturgeon Bay. **General Store:** Yes. **Vending:** Yes. **Swimming Pool:** Yes. **Playground:** Yes. **Other:** Goodie Shoppe, Yogi's theater, mini-golf, horseshoes, funnelball, tetherball, ping pong, football, hiking trails, softball, shuffleboard, volleyball, game room, kiddie pool, pavilion. **Activities:** Swimming, hiking, scheduled activities. **Nearby Attractions:** Door County, Lake Michian, historic sites, cherry & apple orchards, boating, fishing, golf, hiking, historic sites, antiques, arts & crafts shops, parks, summer stock theater, bike trails, Green Bay. **Additional Information:** Door County Chamber, (800) 527-3529.

Restrictions

Pets: Leash only. **Fires:** Fire ring only. **Alcoholic Beverages:** Permitted. **Vehicle Maximum Length:** None.

To Get There

From the junction of Hwy. 42/57 and CR C, drive 1 mi. north and 3 mi. west on CR C, then 1 mi. north on CR M, then 2 mi. west on Sand Bay Rd., then 500 feet south on May Rd. The roads are wide and well maintained w/ broad shoulders.

TOMAHAWK

The Out-Post Campground

9507 Hwy. N, Tomahawk 54497. T: (715) 453-3468

RV: ★★★ Tent: ★★★

Beauty: ★★★ Site Privacy: ★★★
Spaciousness: ★★★ Quiet: ★★★
Security: ★★★ Cleanliness: ★★★
Insect Control: ★★★ Facilities: ★★★

Located on Deer Lake and Lake Nokomis three miles west of Tomahawk, the Out-Post Campground features a wide array of water activities. Sites are level and mostly shaded. The campground has 30 seasonal campers, 31 pull-through sites, and a typical site width of 30 feet. A separate area for tents offers more green space and privacy. The wooded campground offers plenty of hot water in its free showers. A rental housekeeping cottage is available year-round for winter enthusiasts. A concrete launching pad offers easy access to the water. Folks say fishing is good in the area, and swimmers like the sandy beach. The most popular sites are closest to the water. Security measures include a traffic-control gate.

Basics

Operated by: Lou & Kitty Miller. **Open:** Apr. 15–Oct. 15. **Site Assignment:** Reservations w/ 1-night deposit; refund w/ 2- week notice. **Registration:** At campground office. **Fee:** $33 (cash & check). **Parking:** At site.

Facilities

Number of RV Sites: 230. **Number of Tent-Only Sites:** 40. **Hookups:** Electric (20, 30, 50 amps), water, sewer. **Each Site:** Picnic table, fire ring. **Dump Station:** Yes. **Laundry:** Yes. **Pay Phone:** Yes. **Rest Rooms and Showers:** Yes. **Fuel:** No. **Propane:** Yes. **Internal Roads:** Gravel, in fair condition. **RV Service:** No. **Market:** 3 mi. east in Tomahawk. **Restaurant:** 3 mi. east in Tomahawk. **General Store:** Yes, limited. **Vending:** Yes. **Swimming Pool:** No. **Playground:** Yes. **Other:** Snack bar, swimming beach, Lake Nokomis, Deer Lake, restaurant, marina, horseshoes, volleyball, basketball, shuffleboard, rec hall, lounge, game room, boat launch, hiking trail, bar. **Activities:** Swimming, fishing, boating (rental paddleboats, canoes, motorboats, rowboats available). **Nearby Attractions:** Golf, local park, Hiawatha Bike Trail, snowmobiling, antiques, arts & crafts, water ski shows, cross-country skiing, ice fishing. **Additional Information:** Tomahawk Regional Chamber of Commerce, (800) 569-2160.

Restrictions

Pets: Leash only. **Fires:** Fire ring only. **Alcoholic Beverages:** Permitted. **Vehicle Maximum Length:** None.

To Get There

From the junction of US 51 and US 8 West, drive 3 mi. west on US 8, then 0.25 mi. north on CR L, then 1 mi. east on CR N. Roads are mostly wide and well maintained w/ adequate shoulders.

TURTLE LAKE

Turtle Lake RV Park

P.O. Box 526, Turtle Lake 54889. T: (715) 986-4140; speedys@chibardun.net.

RV: ★★★ Tent: ★

Beauty: ★★ Site Privacy: ★★
Spaciousness: ★★★ Quiet: ★★★
Security: ★★★★ Cleanliness: ★★★★
Insect Control: Yes Facilities: ★★★

Turtle Lake RV Park is a campground with an amusement center attached—Speedy's Family Fun Center. Many of the amusements require additional money. Laid out in a series of loops, the campground is mostly a flat, open field with gravel RV pads on grassy lots and a few trees. The typical site width is 30 feet, and the campground has 30 pull-throughs. Tents are allowed on any site, but there are few natural amenities to make it pleasant for tent campers. Located two blocks west of Turtle Lake, the campground offers excellent access from main roads. The St. Croix Casino is nearby, which may account for the campground rule that children under the age of 14 are not to be left unattended. Children under 14 also must be accompanied by an adult in the pool area. Quiet hours are enforced from 10 p.m. to 8 a.m. A ten-mph speed limit might be better reduced to half that since children probably spend much time going back and forth from the campground to the family fun center.

Basics

Operated by: Richard & Linda Phillips. **Open:** Apr. 15–Oct. 15. **Site Assignment:** Reservations w/ 1-night deposit; no refunds. **Registration:** At campground office. **Fee:** $18 (cash, credit cards). **Parking:** At site.

Facilities

Number of RV Sites: 102. **Number of Tent-Only Sites:** 0. **Hookups:** Electric (30, 50 amps), water, sewer. **Each Site:** Picnic table, fire ring. **Dump Station:** Yes. **Laundry:** No. **Pay Phone:** Yes. **Rest Rooms and Showers:** Yes. **Fuel:** No. **Propane:** No. **Internal Roads:** Gravel, in good condition. **RV Service:** No. **Market:** 2 blocks east in Turtle Lake. **Restaurant:** Next door. **General Store:** Yes. **Vending:** No. **Swimming Pool:** Yes. **Playground:** No. **Other:** Recreation field, pavilion, coin games, mini-golf, driving range, basketball, go-karts, bumper boats, bumper cars, ATV mud track, water games. **Activities:** Swimming. **Nearby Attractions:** Lakes, boating, fishing, winter sports, art galleries, ATV & snowmobile trails, Polk County Museum, antiques, Pioneer Village Museum, St. Croix Casino & Hotel. **Additional Information:** Turtle Lake Village Hall, (715) 986-2241.

Restrictions

Pets: Leash only. **Fires:** Fire ring only. **Alcoholic Beverages:** At sites only. **Vehicle Maximum Length:** None. **Other:** Must shower w/ soap & water before entering pool.

To Get There

At the junction of US 63 and US 8, drive 500 feet east on US 8. Roads are wide and well maintained w/ broad shoulders.

WARRENS

Yogi Bear's Jellystone Park Camp-Resort

CR EW Box 67, Warrens 54666. T: (888) FUN-YOGI; www.jellystonewarrens.com.

RV: ★★★★★ Tent: ★★★★

Beauty: ★★★★ Site Privacy: ★★★★
Spaciousness: ★★★★ Quiet: ★★★★

Security: ★★★★★ Cleanliness: ★★★★★
Insect Control: None Facilities: ★★★★★

Ask a child to design the perfect campground, and this might be the result. Yogi Bear's Jellystone Park Camp Resort is a children's wonderland. With a full-time summer activity director, the campground offers a huge smorgasbord of activities, handy snack bars, heated swimming pools, and a lake with a big sandy beach. Fifty pull-through sites (35 × 65 feet) and back ins (40 × 50 feet) offer easy access and a fair amount of privacy. Arranged in a series of loops, the nicely landscaped campground features mostly shady, grassy sites. One entrance to the campground and a security patrol help keep the campground safe and quiet. For such a popular family facility with a large number of children, the campground is surprisingly peaceful, mainly because most of the play areas are located in a clump away from the campsites.

Basics

Operated by: Ed Van Der Molen. **Open:** All year. **Site Assignment:** Reservations w/ 1-night fee; refunds (minus $10 charge) w/ 14-day notice. Reservations require a 2-night min., 3-nights on holidays. **Registration:** At campground office. **Fee:** $33 (cash, check, credit cards). **Parking:** At site.

Facilities

Number of RV Sites: 490. **Number of Tent-Only Sites:** 100. **Hookups:** Electric (30, 50 amps), water, sewer. **Each Site:** Picnic table, fire ring. **Dump Station:** Yes. **Laundry:** Yes. **Pay Phone:** Yes. **Rest Rooms and Showers:** Yes. **Fuel:** No. **Propane:** Yes. **Internal Roads:** 98 percent paved, rest gravel, in good condition. **RV Service:** No. **Market:** 8 mi. south in Tomah. **Restaurant:** In campground. **General Store:** Yes. **Vending:** Yes. **Swimming Pool:** Yes. **Playground:** Yes. **Other:** 400-ft. waterslide, adventure golf, mini-golf, game room, Yogi's playroom, sand volleyball court, shuffleboard, horseshoes, pavilions, basketball, tennis, baseball, bandstand. **Activities:** Swimming, paddleboat rental, a full-time activity director w/ over 100 activities offered weekly. **Nearby Attractions:** Cranberry festival, cranberry bog tours, Amish country, antique shops, art galleries, golf, casino. **Additional Information:** Tomah CVB, (800) 04-TOMAH.

Restrictions

Pets: Leash only. **Fires:** Fire pits only. **Alcoholic Beverages:** Permitted. **Vehicle Maximum Length:** 45 ft.

To Get There

From the junction of I-94 and CR E, take Exit 135 and drive 0.5 mi. east on CR EW.

WEST BEND

Lake Lenwood Beach and Campground

7053 Lenwood Dr., West Bend 53090. T: (262) 334-1335; www.lakelenwood.com.

 ★★★★  ★★★★

Beauty: ★★★★ Site Privacy: ★★★★
Spaciousness: ★★★★ Quiet: ★★★★
Security: ★★★★ Cleanliness: ★★★★
Insect Control: None Facilities: ★★★★

Want to know if a campground is well maintained? Check out the bathrooms. At Lake Lenwood Beach and Campground, the rest rooms are clean and nicely decorated. and so is the rest of the campground. Located 1.5 miles southwest of West Bend, the campground offers shaded and open sites around a beautiful lake. Almost every site has a tree or a shrub, the typical site width is 45 feet, there are gravel pads for RVs, and the campground has ten pull-throughs and 55 seasonal campers. An unusual 25-foot-high enclosed tower with a spiral slide is a thriller for children. The best RV sites are on the lakefront; the best tent sites are on the lakeshore in a isolated area. Quiet time is enforced between 9:30 p.m. and 8 a.m., with no radios allowed. Children must be at their campsite after dark. Owners are serious about no barking dogs allowed. Security includes one entrance/exit road, owners who live on site, and regular patrols of the campground.

Basics

Operated by: Mike & Mary Dricken. **Open:** Apr. 20–Oct. 12. **Site Assignment:** Reservations w/ 2-day min. & 2-day deposit; refunds (minus 15 percent charge) w/ 2-week notice. **Registration:** At campground office. **Fee:** $28 (cash, check, credit cards). **Parking:** At site.

Facilities

Number of RV Sites: 125. **Number of Tent-Only Sites:** 30. **Hookups:** Electric (30, 50 amps), water, sewer, cable TV, phone. **Each Site:** Picnic table, fire ring. **Dump Station:** Yes. **Laundry:** Yes. **Pay Phone:** Yes. **Rest Rooms and Showers:** Yes. **Fuel:** No. **Propane:** No. **Internal Roads:** Gravel, in good condition. **RV Service:** No. **Market:** 1.5 mi. northwest in West Bend. **Restaurant:** 1 block. **General Store:** Yes, limited. **Vending:** Yes. **Swimming Pool:** No. **Playground:** Yes. **Other:** Lake Lenwood, beach, pier, basketball, horseshoes, hiking trails, volleyball, pavilion, sports field. **Activities:** Swimming, fishing, hiking, boating (rental fishing boats, canoes, kayaks, paddleboats, hydro-bikes & innertubes available). **Nearby Attractions:** Parks, Old Courthouse Square Museum, art museum, golf, indoor go karts, historic homes, antiques, arts & crafts, bike trail, hiking trail, outlet shops, nature areas. **Additional Information:** West Bend Chamber of Commerce, (888) 338-8666.

Restrictions

Pets: Leash only, non-barking only. **Fires:** Fire ring only. **Alcoholic Beverages:** Permitted. **Vehicle Maximum Length:** None.

To Get There

From the junction of US 45 and CR D, drive 1 mi. east on CR D, then 1 mi. north on Hwy. 144, then 1 block east on Wallace Lake Rd. Roads are wide and well maintained w/ broad shoulders.

WEST BEND

Lazy Days Campground

1475 Lakeview Rd., West Bend 53090. T: (262) 675-6511; F: (262) 675-9133; www.wisvacations.com/lazydays; lazydays@ticon.net.

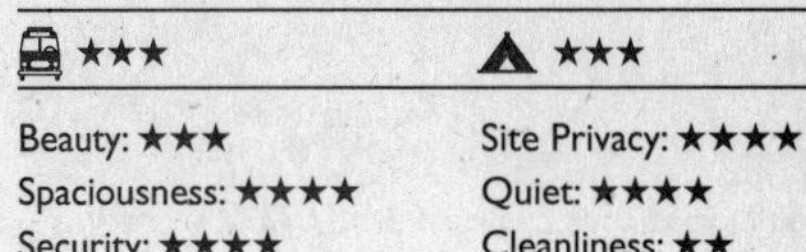 ★★★ ★★★

Beauty: ★★★ Site Privacy: ★★★★
Spaciousness: ★★★★ Quiet: ★★★★
Security: ★★★★ Cleanliness: ★★
Insect Control: None Facilities: ★★★

Located on a beautiful lake five miles south of West Bend, Lazy Days Campground offers grassy open or wooded sites in a wilderness setting. The gently rolling terrain has a typical site width of 50 feet, 40 pull-throughs, and 194 seasonal campers. Laid out in a series of loops, the campground has a separate section for tents with more green space and privacy. A few tent sites are spread out in other sections. Almost four decades in the same family, Lazy Days tries to ensure a tranquil campground by enforcing quiet time between 10 p.m. to 8 a.m., when no radios, TV, voices, or sounds should carry beyond the site. A nine-mph speed limit seems a bit high for a family-friendly campground, but the rutted roads may discourage anyone from driving over a crawl. Security measures include a guard shack, video surveillance cameras, and regular campground patrols, including drive-throughs by the local sheriff's department. Plus, the owner is a big fella who doesn't put up with any nonsense.

Basics

Operated by: Eric Waters. **Open:** Apr. 1–Oct. 31. **Site Assignment:** Reservations w/ no deposit; holiday reservations require 3-night deposit; refund w/ 7-day notice. **Registration:** At campground office. **Fee:** $27 (cash, check, credit cards). **Parking:** At site.

Facilities

Number of RV Sites: 300. **Number of Tent-Only Sites:** 42. **Hookups:** Electric (30 amps), water, sewer. **Each Site:** Picnic table, fire ring. **Dump Station:** Yes. **Laundry:** Yes. **Pay Phone:** Yes. **Rest Rooms and Showers:** Yes. **Fuel:** Yes. **Propane:** Yes. **Internal Roads:** Gravel, in poor condition. **RV Service:** Yes. **Market:** 5 mi. north in West Bend. **Restaurant:** 2.5 mi. north towards West Bend. **General Store:** Yes. **Vending:** Yes. **Swimming Pool:** No. **Playground:** Yes. **Other:** Green Lake, sandy beach, game room, pavilion, dock, mini golf, volleyball, sports field, hiking trails. **Activities:** Swimming, fishing, hiking, boating (rental rowboats & paddleboats available), biking (rental bikes available), scheduled weekend activities. **Nearby Attractions:** Parks, Old Courthouse Square Museum, art museum, golf, indoor go karts, historic homes, antiques, arts & crafts, bike trail, hiking trail, outlet shops, nature areas. **Additional Information:** West Bend Area Chmber of Commerce, (888) 338-8666.

Restrictions

Pets: Leash only. **Fires:** Fire ring only. **Alcoholic Beverages:** Permitted. **Vehicle Maximum Length:** None. **Other:** No electric heaters in the campground.

To Get There

From the junction of US 45 and eastbound Hwy. 144, drive 2.75 mi. northeast on Hwy. 144, then 2 mi. east on CR A, then 0.5 mi. south on Lakeview Rd. Roads are wide and well maintained w/ mostly good shoulders.

WEST BEND

Timber Trail Campground

7590 Good Luck Ln., West Bend 53090. T: (262) 338-8561

RV ★★★ Tent ★★★

Beauty: ★★★ Site Privacy: ★★★★
Spaciousness: ★★★★ Quiet: ★★★★
Security: ★★★★ Cleanliness: ★★★★
Insect Control: None Facilities: ★★★

Timber Trail Campground is like camping under a canopy of maple and beechwood trees, except that 100 seasonal campers are there too. Located adjacent to Kettle Moraine Ice Age Trail four miles northwest of West Bend, Timber Trail offers mostly wooded gravel sites. If you're looking for an open spot for that satellite dish, this is not the place for you. But it is a very secluded, woodsy campground. Laid out in a series of loops, the rural campground has two pull-throughs and a typical site width of 45 feet. The best RV site is 216 because it offers full hookups and is close to facilities. The best tent site is 42 because it is very wooded and private, with a sandy spot for the tent. Tent-only sites are available in two separate areas. Security measures include owners who live on site and provide regular patrols of the campground.

BASICS

Operated by: Brent & Judy Lange. **Open:** May 15–Oct. 15. **Site Assignment:** Reservations w/ 1-night deposit; refund w/ 7-day notice. **Registration:** At campground office. **Fee:** $22 (cash, check). **Parking:** At site.

FACILITIES

Number of RV Sites: 130. **Number of Tent-Only Sites:** 5. **Hookups:** Electric (30 amps), water, sewer. **Each Site:** Picnic table, fire ring. **Dump Station:** Yes. **Laundry:** Yes. **Pay Phone:** Yes. **Rest Rooms and Showers:** Yes. **Fuel:** No. **Propane:** Yes. **Internal Roads:** Paved/gravel, in good condition. **RV Service:** No. **Market:** 5 mi. southeast in West Bend. **Restaurant:** 5 mi. southeast in West Bend. **General Store:** Yes, limited. **Vending:** Yes. **Swimming Pool:** Yes. **Playground:** Yes. **Other:** Whirlpool, recreation building, snack bar, ball field, tennis court, basketball, volleyball, hiking trails, horseshoes, fishing pond. **Activities:** Swimming, hiking, fishing, boating (no motors), scheduled weekend activities. **Nearby Attractions:** Parks, Old Courthouse Square Museum, art museum, golf, indoor go-karts, historic homes, antiques, arts & crafts, bike trail, hiking trail, outlet shops, nature areas, Kettle Moraine Ice Age Trail. **Additional Information:** West Bend Chamber of Commerce, (888) 338-8666.

RESTRICTIONS

Pets: Leash only. **Fires:** Fire ring only. **Alcoholic Beverages:** Permitted. **Vehicle Maximum Length:** None.

TO GET THERE

From the junction of US 45 and CR D, drive 1.5 mi. west on CR D, then 0.75 mi. north on Good Luck Ln. Roads are wide and well maintained w/ broad shoulders, but they are winding in spots.

WEST SALEM

Neshonoc Lakeside Campground

N5334 Neshonoc Rd., West Salem 54669. T: (888) 783-0035; neshcamp@aol.com.

RV ★★★★★ Tent ★★★★

Beauty: ★★★★★ Site Privacy: ★★★★★
Spaciousness: ★★★★★ Quiet: ★★★★★
Security: ★★★★★ Cleanliness: ★★★★★
Insect Control: None Facilities: ★★★★★

Neshonoc Lakeside Camp has natural beauty galore, along with some great touches added by the owners over their 30 years. Located on Lake Neshonoc one mile east of West Salem, the campground offers beautiful views of the water and bluffs on the other shore. Not surprisingly, the most popular sites are 168–205 up on the hillside, where campers can see spectacular sunsets over the 600-acre lake. Also, not surprisingly, the most desirable lakeside spots have been snapped up by seasonal campers. Tent campers might yearn for a more wilderness section that affords some privacy away from RV campers. Exceptionally manicured grounds, mighty clean bathrooms, and color-coordinated reddish-brown paint on campground facilities adds to the visual appeal. Lighted wooden stairs with railings on both sides provide safe passage from the hillside to the heated pool and well-stocked camp store, which features cappuccino every day and sweet rolls from a local bakery on every weekend.

BASICS

Operated by: Bob & Paula Martell. **Open:** Apr. 15–Oct. 15. **Site Assignment:** Reservations w/ 1-night deposit, refund w/ 72-hour notice. **Registration:** At campground office. **Fee:** $26 (cash, check, credit cards). **Parking:** At site.

FACILITIES

Number of RV Sites: 240. **Number of Tent-Only Sites:** 0. **Hookups:** Electric (20, 30, 50 amps), water, sewer. **Each Site:** Picnic table, fire ring. **Dump Station:** Yes. **Laundry:** Yes. **Pay Phone:** Yes. **Rest Rooms and Showers:** Yes. **Fuel:** No. **Propane:** Yes. **Internal Roads:** Paved, in good condition. **RV Service:** No. **Market:** 1 mi. west in West Salem. **Restaurant:** 2.5 mi. west in West Salem. **General Store:** Yes. **Vending:** Yes. **Swimming Pool:** Yes. **Playground:** Yes. **Other:** Sandy beach, boat dock, video game room, sand volleyball court, horseshoes, basketball, croquet, softball. **Activities:** Swimming, boating (rental rowboats, paddleboats, kayaks & canoes available), haywagon rides, scheduled activities. **Nearby Attractions:** Bike trails, shopping center, golf, speedway, zoo, boat tours, historic homes, La Crosse's Riverfest & Oktoberfest. **Additional Information:** Onalaska Center for Commerce & Tourism, (800) 873-1901.

RESTRICTIONS

Pets: Leash only. **Fires:** Fire pits only. **Alcoholic Beverages:** Permitted. **Vehicle Maximum Length:** None.

TO GET THERE

From the junction of I-90 and CR 3, take Exit 12, drive 1.5 mi. north on CR C through village, then 1.5 mi. east on Hwy. 16, then 1,000 feet south on paved road. Roads are wide and well maintained w/ broad shoulders

WEST SALEM

Veterans Memorial Campground

N4668 CR VP, West Salem 54669. T: (608) 786-4011

RV ★★★ Tent ★★★★

Beauty: ★★★★ Site Privacy: ★★★★
Spaciousness: ★★★ Quiet: ★★★★
Security: ★★★★ Cleanliness: ★★★★
Insect Control: Yes Facilities: ★★★

At Veterans Memorial Campground, visitors can camp so close to the La Crosse River that they can almost fish from their RV or tent. The La Crosse County park, located in West Salem, lacks many of the amenities campers often want—a laundry, swimming pool, general store, games, and activities—but it has that beautiful river. Wonderful views and unfettered access to the river more than compensate for the shortage of amenities. Located less than three miles from I-90, the campground offers easy access for travelers, including 50 pull-through sites. The most popular sites, of course, are on the river, and tenters have private areas of their own. Security is tops, as a manager lives on site and city police patrol every night. As a friendly touch, the campground provides free firewood—and a little wagon to haul it to the campsite.

BASICS

Operated by: La Crosse County. **Open:** Apr. 15–Oct. 15. **Site Assignment:** First come, first served. **Registration:** At campground office. **Fee:** $16 (cash, check). **Parking:** At site.

FACILITIES

Number of RV Sites: 90. **Number of Tent-Only Sites:** 10. **Hookups:** Electric (20, 30, 50 amps). **Each Site:** Picnic table, fire ring. **Dump Station:** Yes. **Laundry:** No. **Pay Phone:** Yes. **Rest Rooms and Showers:** Yes. **Fuel:** No. **Propane:** No. **Internal Roads:** Paved, in good condition. **RV Service:** No. **Market:** 1.5 mi. east in West Salem. **Restaurant:** 1.5 mi. east in West Salem. **General Store:** Yes. **Vending:** Yes. **Swimming Pool:** No. **Playground:** Yes. **Other:** Shelter house, 4-acre fishing pond, shuffleboard, volleyball, canoe landing, state bike trail. **Activities:** Fishing, biking, scheduled twice-monthly activities. **Nearby Attractions:** Biking, hunting, birdwatching, golf, Onalaska Historical Society Museum, historic homes, aquatic center w/ 200-ft. water slide, antique shops. **Additional Information:** Onalaska Center for Commerce & Tourism, (800) 873-1901.

RESTRICTIONS

Pets: Leash only. **Fires:** Fire ring only. **Alcoholic Beverages:** At sites only. **Vehicle Maximum Length:** None.

TO GET THERE

From the junction of I-90 and CR C, drive 1.5 mi. north and west on CR C, then 2 mi. west on Hwy. 16, Roads are wide and well maintained w/ broad shoulders

WHITE LAKE

Raft 'N Rest Campground and Rafting

N4327 Hwy. 55, White Lake 54491. T: (715) 882-5613

RV ★★ Tent ★★★

Beauty: ★★★ Site Privacy: ★★★
Spaciousness: ★★★ Quiet: ★★
Security: ★★★★ Cleanliness: ★★★
Insect Control: None Facilities: ★★

Proximity to river rafting is what Raft 'N Rest Campground and Rafting has going for it. Located two miles east of White Lake, the campground is on rolling terrain with mostly open, grassy sites in a big field for RVs. Wooded tent sites offer more green space and privacy. A limited playground includes swings and a sandbox. Laundry facilities are limited to two dryers. Laid out in a series of loops, the campground has a typical site width of 30 feet, no pull-throughs, and two seasonal campers. Special activities and parties are sometimes scheduled, such as a pig roast and rafting party with a disc jockey. Beer kegs are available upon request. During the week, the campground is fairly quiet, but it can get rowdy on weekends with camping/rafting groups. Security measures include one entrance/exit, a manager living on site, and regular patrols (including local police) on the weekends.

BASICS

Operated by: Robb & Sharon Rose. **Open:** May 1–Sept. 30. **Site Assignment:** Reservations w/ 1-night deposit; refunds w/ 7-day notice. **Registration:** At campground office. **Fee:** $20 (cash, check, credit cards). **Parking:** At site.

FACILITIES

Number of RV Sites: 12. **Number of Tent-Only Sites:** 33. **Hookups:** Electric (20, 30 amps), water. **Each Site:** Picnic table, fire ring. **Dump Station:** Yes. **Laundry:** 2 dryers only. **Pay Phone:** No. **Rest Rooms and Showers:** Yes. **Fuel:** No. **Propane:** No. **Internal Roads:** Gravel, in poor condition. **RV Service:** No. **Market:** 2 mi. west in White Lake. **Restaurant:** 2 mi. west in White Lake. **General Store:** Yes, limited. **Vending:** No. **Swimming Pool:** No. **Playground:** Yes, limited. **Other:** Volleyball, pavilion, sports field. **Activities:** Scheduled activities sometimes. **Nearby Attractions:** Wolf River, rafting, hiking & biking trails, Nicolet National Forest, golf, casinos, fish hatchery, horseback riding, fishing, swimming, hunting. **Additional Information:** Troutland Assoc., (715) 882-8901.

RESTRICTIONS

Pets: Leash only. **Fires:** Fire ring only. **Alcoholic Beverages:** Permitted. **Vehicle Maximum Length:** None.

TO GET THERE

From the junction of Hwy. 64 and Hwy. 55, drive 0.4 mi. south on Hwy. 55. Roads are wide and well maintained w/ broad shoulders.

WHITE LAKE

River Forest Rafting Campground

N2755 Sunny Waters Ln., White Lake 54491. T: (715) 882-3351; www.wolfriverrafting.com; riverfor@aol.com.

RV ★ Tent ★★★

Beauty: ★★★ Site Privacy: ★★★★
Spaciousness: ★★★★ Quiet: ★★★★
Security: ★★★ Cleanliness: ★★
Insect Control: None Facilities: ★

River Forest Rafting Campground has so much going for it. It is located by Wolf River, six miles southeast of White Lake, in the midst of a natural wonderland. A narrow dirt and gravel road leads uphill to the wilderness campsites, like camping in a state forest. When we visited one bathroom and one shower were out of order. Sites are mostly shady and level with no seasonals. Quiet time is from 10 p.m. to 7 a.m., and the speed limit is five mph. Be aware that no pets are permitted. Security includes one entrance road past the office and a campground gate that may be locked at 11 p.m. Cars arriving after that hour will be parked near the registration building and campers should carry a flashlight with them to assist on the walk back to camp.

BASICS

Operated by: John Stecher. **Open:** May 1–Sept. 15. **Site Assignment:** Reservations w/ $5 per person deposit; refund (minus $5) w/ 10-day notice. **Registration:** At campground office. **Fee:** $6.25 per person. **Parking:** At site.

FACILITIES

Number of RV Sites: 9. **Number of Tent-Only Sites:** 31. **Hookups:** Electric (20 amps). **Each Site:** Picnic table, fire ring. **Dump Station:** Yes. **Laundry:** No. **Pay Phone:** No. **Rest Rooms and Showers:** Yes. **Fuel:** No. **Propane:** Yes. **Internal Roads:** Gravel, in fair condition. **RV Service:** No. **Market:** 6 mi. northwest in White Lake. **Restaurant:** 0.25 mi. south. **General Store:** Yes, limited. **Vending:** Yes. **Swimming Pool:** No. **Playground:** No. **Other:** Hiking trails, river. **Activities:** River swimming, fishing, boating (rental canoes & kayaks available), rafting (rental rubber rafts available). **Nearby Attractions:** Nicolet Forest, ATV trail, lakes, hunting, mountain biking, trout streams, horseback riding, golf, casinos, fish hatchery. **Additional Information:** Troutland Assoc., (715) 882-8901.

RESTRICTIONS

Pets: Not allowed. **Fires:** Fire ring only. **Alcoholic Beverages:** Permitted. **Vehicle Maximum Length:** 38 ft.

TO GET THERE

From the junction of CR WW and Hwy. 55, drive 300 feet north on Hwy. 55. Roads are wide and well maintained w/ broad shoulders.

WHITE LAKE

Wolf River-Nicolet Forest Campground and Outdoor Center

N3116 Hwy. 55, White Lake 54491. T: (715) 882-4002

RV ★★ Tent ★★★★

Beauty: ★★★ Site Privacy: ★★★★
Spaciousness: ★★★★ Quiet: ★★★★
Security: ★★★★ Cleanliness: ★★★
Insect Control: None Facilities: ★★

First off, Wolf River-Nicolet Forest Campground and Outdoor Center is not affiliated with Nicolet National Forest Campgrounds. It is a private campground located 8.5 miles southeast of White Lake and nestled in the Nicolet National Forest. It offers secluded, wooded, primitive campsites near a river. Sites with electric hookups are mostly grassy and shaded, with three pull-throughs and six seasonal campers. For rafters, the Wolf River is 1.5 miles away. A rustic trail takes about 15 minutes to walk from the campground to the river. The campground also offers a "pet-sitting" service for rafters and other campers. For a donation, the pet is walked and tied up outside the office while campers are gone rafting or enjoying other area activities. During the winter season, the campground is plowed, so campers can stay while enjoying local snowmobiling and cross-country skiing. Security measures include one entrance/exit, an owner who lives on site, and regular patrols, including local police who drive through the campground frequently.

BASICS

Operated by: Janet Williams. **Open:** All year. **Site Assignment:** Reservations w/ 1-night deposit; refund w/ 14-day notice. **Registration:** At campground office. **Fee:** $16 (cash, check, credit cards). **Parking:** At site.

FACILITIES

Number of RV Sites: 12. **Number of Tent-Only Sites:** 30. **Hookups:** Electric (30 amps). **Each Site:** Picnic table, fire ring. **Dump Station:** No. **Laundry:** Yes. **Pay Phone:** Yes. **Rest Rooms and Showers:** Yes. **Fuel:** No. **Propane:** Yes. **Internal Roads:** Gravel, in fair condition. **RV Service:** No. **Market:** 8 mi. northwest in White Lake. **Restaurant:** 1.5 mi. south. **General Store:** Yes, limited. **Vending:** Yes. **Swimming Pool:** No. **Playground:** Yes. **Other:** Volleyball, arcade room, mini golf, rental cabins, rental rooms, rental camper, horseshoes, nature trails, basketball, pool table. **Activities:** Hiking, scheduled weekend activities. **Nearby Attractions:** Wolf River, hiking & biking trails, Nicolet National Forest, golf, casinos, fish hatchery, horseback riding, fishing, rafting, swimming, hunting, snowmobiling. **Additional Information:** Troutland Assoc., (715) 882-8901.

RESTRICTIONS

Pets: Leash only. **Fires:** Fire ring only. **Alcoholic Beverages:** Permitted. **Vehicle Maximum Length:** None.

To Get There

From the junction of Hwy. 64 and Hwy. 55, drive 5 mi. south on Hwy. 55. Roads are wide and well maintained w/ broad shoulders.

WILTON

Tunnel Trail Campground

Rte. 1, Box 185, Wilton 54670. T: (608) 435-6829; www.tunneltrail.com; questions@tunneltrail.com.

RV ★★★★ | Tent ★★★★

Beauty: ★★★★ | Site Privacy: ★★★
Spaciousness: ★★★ | Quiet: ★★★★
Security: ★★★★ | Cleanliness: ★★★
Insect Control: None | Facilities: ★★★★

A rural campground adjacent to the Elroy-Sparta State Bicycle Trail, Tunnel Trail Campground offers terraced, shaded sites in a valley. Located four miles east of Wilton, the campground has nine pull-throughs and a typical site width of 30 feet. Sites are level and grassy in a quiet, park-like setting. Besides the convenient access from the highway, the campground has a major plus in its proximity to the popular bike trail, formerly the old Chicago-Northwestern railroad bed. The trail is 32 level miles in length and passes through three tunnels and the beautiful hills of the Coulee Region. For campers who don't feel like hauling bikes, the campground rents well-maintained mountain bikes, hybrids, bike trailers, third-wheels, tandems, and recunbent bikes. The campground is also blessed by being relatively free of mosquitos without having to use insecticides. Quiet hours are from 10:30 p.m. to 7 a.m., with all radios required to be off after 10:30 p.m.

Basics

Operated by: Scott & Julie Grenon. **Open:** May 1–Oct. 15. **Site Assignment:** Reservations w/ $40 deposit, 2-night min. on weekend, 3-night min. on holidays; refund (minus $5) w/ 2-week notice. **Registration:** At campground office. **Fee:** $25 (cash, check, credit cards). **Parking:** At site.

Facilities

Number of RV Sites: 63. **Number of Tent-Only Sites:** 12. **Hookups:** Electric (20, 30 amps), water. **Each Site:** Picnic table, fire ring. **Dump Station:** Yes. **Laundry:** Yes. **Pay Phone:** Yes. **Rest Rooms and Showers:** Yes. **Fuel:** No. **Propane:** No. **Internal Roads:** Paved/gravel, in good condition. **RV Service:** No. **Market:** 4 mi. west in Wilton. **Restaurant:** 4 mi. west in Wilton. **General Store:** Yes, limited. **Vending:** Yes. **Swimming Pool:** Yes. **Playground:** Yes. **Other:** Mini golf, horseshoes, volleyball, basketball, game room, trails, rental cabins, pavilion, badminton, sports field, adults room. **Activities:** Swimming, hiking, biking (rental bikes available). **Nearby Attractions:** Kickapoo River, horseback riding, canoeing, fishing, Amish community, scenic drive, antiques, arts & crafts. **Additional Information:** La Crosse Area CVB, (800) 658-9424.

Restrictions

Pets: Leash only. **Fires:** Fire ring only. **Alcoholic Beverages:** Permitted. **Vehicle Maximum Length:** None.

To Get There

From the east junction of Hwy. 131 and Hwy. 71, drive 1 mi. east on Hwy. 71. Roads are wide and well maintained w/ broad shoulders.

WYEVILLE

Holiday Lodge Golf Resort

10555 Freedom Rd., Tomah 54660. T: (608) 374-4390

RV ★★★ | Tent n/a

Beauty: ★★★ | Site Privacy: ★★★
Spaciousness: ★★★ | Quiet: ★★★★
Security: ★★★ | Cleanliness: ★★★
Insect Control: None | Facilities: ★★★

The name says it all. Holiday Lodge Golf Resort caters to golfers or campers looking for a quiet overnight stay. No other activities are offered. Located six miles east of Tomah, the campground is across the street from an 18-hole golf course, a well-stocked pro shop, and a lounge serving sandwiches and drinks. The 71-par course offers gas carts, rental clubs, and watered fairways. Thirty-six holes per day, which includes green fees and a cart, cost $36 per person with a discount for campground guests. The campground's flat, shaded sites are generally spacious (36 feet wide) with 14 full hookups and 14 pull-throughs. The most popular sites are 12–22 because they are larger pull-throughs. The campground offers good security, with one entrance, a manager who lives on site, and a night patrol. For someone who wants to golf and sleep, Holiday Lodge Golf Resort is a popular destination.

Basics

Operated by: Holiday Lodge Inc. **Open:** Apr. 15–Oct. 15. **Site Assignment:** Reservations accepted w/ no deposit. **Registration:** At campground office. **Fee:** $17 (cash, check, credit cards). **Parking:** At site.

Facilities

Number of RV Sites: 30. **Number of Tent-Only Sites:** 0. **Hookups:** Electric (30 amps), water, sewer. **Each Site:** Picnic table, fire ring. **Dump Station:** Yes. **Laundry:** Yes. **Pay Phone:** Yes. **Rest Rooms and Showers:** Yes. **Fuel:** No. **Propane:** No. **Internal Roads:** Gravel, in good condition. **RV Service:** No. **Market:** 6 mi. west in Tomah. **Restaurant:** 6 mi. west in Tomah. **General Store:** No. **Vending:** Yes. **Swimming Pool:** No. **Playground:** No. **Other:** Golf course, pro shop. **Activities:** Golfing. **Nearby Attractions:** Telecommunications Historical Museum, tractor pull, bicycle trails, cranberry fest,. **Additional Information:** Warrens Area Business Assoc. (608) 378-4878.

Restrictions

Pets: Leash only. **Fires:** Fire pits only. **Alcoholic Beverages:** Permitted. **Vehicle Maximum Length:** None. **Other:** No tents allowed.

To Get There

From the junction of I-94 and Hwy. 21, drive 6 mi. east on Hwy. 21, then 0.75 mi. south on Excelsior Ave. Roads are wide and well maintained w/ broad shoulders.

Wyoming

Wyoming's clean, geometric borders belie the geographical variety found in its interior. With an amalgam of winding rivers, scenic gorges, vast plains, craggy mountain peaks, pristine lakes, and lonely buttes, Wyoming is a prime destination for campers and outdoor enthusiasts. Wyoming is probably most popular for containing the nation's first national park, **Yellowstone National Park,** whose **Old Faithful Geyser** is as popular as any theme park ride. However, if touring the state, it is important to give yourself plenty of time to visit the other points of interest available. In **Shoshone National Forest** on the eastern border of Yellowstone, you'll find the Absakora and Wind River Mountain Ranges as well as the Shoshone River's north and south forks. Camping here provides easy access to hiking, rafting, fishing, and exploration. Just south of Yellowstone on I-89 is the **Grand Teton National Park,** where the majestic Tetons stand 7,000 feet tall and shadow the famous ski area of **Jackson Hole.** Here, off I-191, are the headwaters of the Snake River, making this an ideal spot for campers interested in hiking, river rafting, and fishing. The **National Elk Preserve,** located in **Jackson,** might give you the opportunity to view a herd of elk or to hear their strange bugle call.

Farther south, the **Fossil Butte National Monument** is an interesting sight for curious observers and budding archeologists. **Flaming Gorge National Recreation Area** near the Green River is a veritable outdoors playground. Both the Flaming Gorge Lake, 90 miles long with 375 miles of shoreline, and the Green River provide limitless water recreation. Campers here enjoy watching the sun and shadows dance among the rock formations, transforming the area into a festival of lights and color. In the southeast corner of Wyoming is **Cheyenne,** the state's capital. The capitol building was modeled after its national equivalent in Washington, D.C.

Through central Wyoming, you can travel the **Oregon Trail** and view the land as Oregon-bound pioneers would have. There are a number of historical sites and opportunities for recreation. **Sinks Canyon State Park,** six miles south of Lander off Hwy. 131, is where the Popo Agie River flows from the Wind River Mountains into a limestone cavern in the Sink Canyon. The are offers numerous opportunities for camping, hiking, and fishing. **Casper,** Wyoming's second-largest city, is a nice stop too. In eastern Wyoming, you'll find **Thunder Basin National Grassland,** where a number of private campgrounds are located. And north from there, **Devil's Tower** and **Buffalo Bill Country** provide opportunity for picnics, scenic drives, fishing, and views of waterfalls. No matter the direction or destination, Wyoming is rich with opportunity to experience the beauty of a scenic outdoors.

Campground Profiles

BUFFALO

Buffalo KOA Kampground

P.O. Box 189, Buffalo 82834. T: (307) 684-5423 or (800) 562-5403; www.koa.com.

RV ★★★★ Tent ★★★★

Beauty: ★★★ Site Privacy: ★★★★
Spaciousness: ★★★★ Quiet: ★★★★
Security: ★★★★ Cleanliness: ★★★★
Insect Control: ★★★★ Facilities: ★★★★

Just east of town, set in an attractive and inviting atmosphere, is the Buffalo KOA Kampground. This KOA campground has truly earned its gold rating. In a state where grass is a luxury, this KOA is beautifully landscaped and impeccably kept. There are Russian olives and quaking aspen trees giving shade and adding warmth. Campsites are set in a series of rows, with a separate tenting area. All sites have a level parking pad, covered picnic table, and grill. There are both pull-through and back-in sites, most being pull-throughs. In addition, the campground has the only deluxe campsite in the KOA system with a private fence, yard, patio, and hot tub (special rates apply). The campground offers a daily pancake breakfast June–Aug., and propane service 8 a.m. to dusk. The weather is always windy, and summers are smoldering. The camp staff are friendly and happy to assist.

BASICS

Operated By: Don and Sue Gill. **Open:** Apr.–Oct. **Site Assignment:** By reservation. **Registration:** In the camp store. **Fee:** Tent $17–$20, RVs $21–$28, per 2 people, extra people over age 6 $3. each. **Parking:** Yes, there is a $5 extra vehicle fee.

FACILITIES

Number of RV-Only Sites: 63. **Number of Tent-Only Sites:** 28. **Hookups:** Electric (20, 30, 50 amps), water, sewer. **Each Site:** Picnic tables, and a some fire pits. **Dump Station:** Yes. **Laundry:** Yes. **Pay Phone:** Yes. **Rest Rooms and Showers:** Yes. **Fuel:** No. **Propane:** Yes. **Internal Roads:** Gravel, in good condition. **RV Service:** Local service. **Market:** In town. **Restaurant:** In town. **General Store:** Yes. **Vending:** Yes. **Swimming Pool:** Yes w/ a hot tub. **Playground:** Yes. **Other:** 5 cabins, a fishing stream, covered picnic areas, camp kitchen, teepees, and a wonderful deluxe site w/ hot tub, Internet data port. **Activities:** Fishing, hiking, game room, playground, horseshoes, mini-golf. **Nearby Attractions:** The White Buffalo, Jim Gatchell Museum, the rodeo. **Additional Information:** Buffalo Chamber of Commerce, (307) 684-5544.

RESTRICTIONS

Pets: On leash. **Fires:** In fire rings only. **Alcoholic Beverages:** Yes. **Vehicle Maximum Length:** None.

To Get There

On Hwy. 16 between I-90 Exit 58 and I-25 Exit 299.

BUFFALO

Lake DeSmet, Lake Stop Resort

P.O.Box 578, Buffalo 82834. T: (307) 684-9051; lakeshop@vcn.com.

RV ★★★ Tent ★★★

Beauty: ★★★★ Site Privacy: ★★★★
Spaciousness: ★★★★ Quiet: ★★★★
Security: ★★★★ Cleanliness: ★★★
Insect Control: ★★★ Facilities: ★★★

Lake DeSmet, "the Lake Stop," is positioned at the base of the Big Horn Mountains on the splendid Lake DeSmet. This small lakeside campground is only a small part of the Lake Stop experience, which offers an 18-site circular campground with full hookups, pool, and clean facilities. The campsites are on a bed of red shale, and each have a table and light post. Although the campsites are not on the lake, there is lake access and boat launch. There is also a full-service bait/tack shop, cafe, motel, boat repair shop, professional fishing outfitters, and boat rentals. The Lake Stop has a small decorative pond up by the campground, and the motel beautifully landscaped with a nice grotto. The owners also have their own private residence across from the campground and are there to assist in any way. Lake DeSmet is six miles north of Buffalo, which is a nice community that offers a variety of activities, rodeos, and Native American history.

Basics

Operated By: Ted and Bambi Schumacher. **Open:** Year-round. **Site Assignment:** By reservation. **Registration:** In the lake shop. **Fee:** Tent $10, RV $19 per unit. **Parking:** At site.

Facilities

Number of RV-Only Sites: 18. **Number of Tent-Only Sites:** Open tent area. **Hookups:** Electric (20, 30, 50 amps), water, sewer. **Each Site:** Picnic tables, grills, and light posts. **Dump Station:** Yes. **Laundry:** Yes. **Pay Phone:** Yes. **Rest Rooms and Showers:** Yes. **Fuel:** Yes. **Propane:** Yes. **Internal Roads:** Red Shale. **RV Service:** Buffalo. **Market:** In town. **Restaurant:** On site. **General Store:** Yes. **Vending:** Yes. **Swimming Pool:** Yes. **Playground:** Yes. **Other:** Full service grocery store, tack shop, boat repair shop, boat ramp, motel, and a small pond w/ a grotto. **Activities:** Fishing (Rainbow, brown, and eagle lake trout), guided fishing tours, boating, jet skiing, basketball, volleyball, lake access. **Nearby Attractions:** 6 mi. from Buffalo, stream fishing, golf, scenic drives, rodeo. **Additional Information:** Buffalo Chamber of Commerce, (307) 684-5544.

Restrictions

Pets: On leash. **Fires:** Grills only. **Alcoholic Beverages:** Yes. **Vehicle Maximum Length:** 40 ft., limited room for extra long RV. **Other:** Fishing Packages.

To Get There

Off I-90 (Exit 51) then follow signs 7 mi. north.

CHEYENNE

A B Camping

1503 West College Dr., Cheyenne 82007. T: (307) 634-7035

RV ★★★ Tent ★★★

Beauty: ★★ Site Privacy: ★★★
Spaciousness: ★★★ Quiet: ★★★★
Security: ★★★★ Cleanliness: ★★★★
Insect Control: ★★★ Facilities: ★★★

The A.B. Campground is a quite, clean facility with a full array of camping amenities. The campground is configured in rows, with large gravel parking spurs at every site, lush green grass, and a perimeter of large pines that offer a nice buffer from the sun and wind. The campground has a large recreation area and playground with a covered pavilion and barbeque. The campground takes part in the annual Frontier Days Celebration (last ten days in July). The nearby city of Cheyenne is the capital of Wyoming, and it's also the largest city in the state, boasting a variety of activties and events. There are several state and federal parks in the area, as well as museums and galleries. Several tours of the area include downtown and the Wyoming state capitol building and grounds. Cheyenne has a very dry climate with relentless winds. The winters can be very harsh and the summers very warm.

Basics

Operated By: Larry and Kay Colboch. **Open:** Mar.–Oct. 31. **Site Assignment:** By reservation. **Registration:** In the camp store. **Fee:** Tent $13.50, RVs $14.50–$22.50, per 2 people, extra people over age of 5 $2 each. **Parking:** At site.

Facilities

Number of RV-Only Sites: 132. **Number of Tent-Only Sites:** Open tent area. **Hookups:** Electric (20, 30, 50 amps), water, sewer. **Each Site:** Picnic tables, and grills. **Dump Station:** Yes. **Laundry:** Yes. **Pay Phone:** Yes. **Rest Rooms and Showers:** Yes. **Fuel:** In town. **Propane:** Yes. **Internal Roads:** Gravel, in good condition. **RV Service:** Next door. **Market:** In town. **Restaurant:** In town. **General Store:** Yes. **Vending:** Yes. **Swimming Pool:** No. **Playground:** Yes. **Other:** 4 cabins, store, Internet dataport, pavilion w/ grills, movie rentals. **Activities:** Playground, horseshoes. **Nearby Attractions:** Golf, State Capitol, trolley tours. **Additional Information:** Cheyenne Chamber of Commerce, (307) 638-3388.

Restrictions

Pets: On leash. **Fires:** In fire rings only. **Alcoholic Beverages:** Yes. **Vehicle Maximum Length:** None. **Other:** Good Sam, AAA, AARP, special rates apply for Frontier Days and reservations need to be made up to a year in advance. (the last 10 days in July).

To Get There

From I-25 Exit 7, go east on SR 212 (W. College Dr.) about 1.7 mi. to the campground.

CHEYENNE

Cheyenne KOA

8800 Archer Frontage Rd., Cheyenne 82007. T: (307) 638-8840 or (800) 562-1507; F: (307) 432-9746; www.cheyennekoa.com; manager@cheyennekoa.com.

RV ★★★★ Tent ★★★

Beauty: ★★★ Site Privacy: ★★★★
Spaciousness: ★★★★ Quiet: ★★★
Security: ★★★★ Cleanliness: ★★★★★
Insect Control: ★★★★ Facilities: ★★★★★

Conveniently located of I-80, the Cheyenne KOA presents a comfortable and well-maintained campground with full amenities to meet the entire family's needs. The Cheyenne KOA has reasonably sized gravel camping sites with some lawn and trees, configured into rows with both back-in and pull-through sites. The campground has several cabins, a snack bar, pool, and mini-golf. The nearby city of Cheyenne is the capital of Wyoming, and it's also the largest city in the state, boasting a variety of activties and events. There are several state and federal parks in the area, as well as museums and galleries. Several tours of the area include downtown and the Wyoming state capitol building and grounds. Cheyenne has a very dry climate with relentless winds. The winters can be very harsh and the summers very warm. The staff at the Cheyenne KOA are friendly and helpful, and the campground is secure.

Basics

Operated By: Mike and Donna Lawrance and Don Lonergan. **Open:** Year-round. **Site Assignment:** By reservation. **Registration:** In the camp store. **Fee:** Tent $21, RVs $17–$28, per 2 people, extra people over age of 5 $3 each. **Parking:** At site.

Facilities

Number of RV-Only Sites: 42. **Number of Tent-Only Sites:** 11. **Hookups:** Electric (20, 30, 50 amps), water, sewer. **Each Site:** Picnic tables, and grills in the tent and cabin area. **Dump Station:** Yes. **Laundry:** Yes. **Pay Phone:** Yes. **Rest Rooms and Showers:** Yes. **Fuel:** 3 mi. east in town. **Propane:** Yes. **Internal Roads:** Gravel, in good condition. **RV Service:** Local service. **Market:** In town. **Restaurant:** In town. **General Store:** Yes. **Vending:** Yes. **Swimming Pool:** Yes. **Playground:** Yes. **Other:** 6 cabins, store, Internet dataport, pavilion w/ kitchen. **Activities:** Game room, playground, horseshoes, mini-golf, basketball. **Nearby Attractions:** Golf, State Capitol, trolley tours. **Additional Information:** Cheyenne Chamber of Commerce, (307) 638-3388.

Restrictions

Pets: On leash. **Fires:** In fire rings only. **Alcoholic Beverages:** Yes. **Vehicle Maximum Length:** None.

To Get There

Right off I-80 Exit 367 on the north side.

CODY
Cody KOA

5561 Greybull Hwy., Cody 82414. T: (307) 587-2369 or (800) 562-8507; F: (307) 587-2369; www.koa.com; codykoa@aol.com.

★★★ ★★★

Beauty: ★★★ Site Privacy: ★★★
Spaciousness: ★★★ Quiet: ★★★
Security: ★★★ Cleanliness: ★★★
Insect Control: ★★★ Facilities: ★★★

The Cody KOA is just east of Cody, conveniently located off Hwy 20. This full-service campground comes fully equipped to meet your needs. The campground offers close to 200 sites, 20 cabins, and a cottage. The comfortable sites come in both back-in and pull-through flavors, with quite a bit of grass and shade for the region. Each campsite has a gravel parking area. There is a large pool with a hot tub to escape Wyoming's blistering summer heat, as well as a game room and trail rides for your enjoyment. The community of Cody is warm and friendly, and there are a number of shops and restaurants to enjoy. Cody also conducts a nightly summer rodeo and serves as the east entrance to Yellowstone National Park.

BASICS

Operated By: Jean Mickelson- manager. **Open:** May–Oct. 1. **Site Assignment:** By reservation. **Registration:** In camp store. **Fee:** Tents $23–$29 RV $28–$36 per 2 people extra child $3, Adult $3. **Parking:** At site.

FACILITIES

Number of RV-Only Sites: 120. **Number of Tent-Only Sites:** 84. **Hookups:** Electric (20, 30 amps), water, sewer. **Each Site:** Picnic tables, and fire pits in tent sites. **Dump Station:** Yes. **Laundry:** Yes. **Pay Phone:** Yes. **Rest Rooms and Showers:** Yes. **Fuel:** No. **Propane:** Yes. **Internal Roads:** Gravel, in good condition. **RV Service:** In Cody. **Market:** In Cody. **Restaurant:** In Cody. **General Store:** Yes. **Vending:** Yes. **Swimming Pool:** Yes, w/ hot tub. **Playground:** Yes. **Other:** 20 cabins, 1 cottage, covered pavilion w/ 2 gas grills, game room w/ TV and cable, hot tub, dish sink, data port. **Activities:** Swimming, playground, games, trail rides, volleyball, horseshoes. **Nearby Attractions:** The east entrance to Yellowstone National Park, nightly summer rodeo, float trips, Buffalo Bills Historical Center. **Additional Information:** Cody Chamber of Commerce, (307) 587-2777.

RESTRICTIONS

Pets: On leash only. **Fires:** In fire pits only. **Alcoholic Beverages:** Yes. **Vehicle Maximum Length:** 45 ft.

TO GET THERE

On US 20 just east of Cody.

CODY
Ponderosa Campground

1815 Yellowstone Ave., Cody 82414. T: (307) 587-9203; F: (307) 436-5779.

★★★ ★★★

Beauty: ★★★ Site Privacy: ★★
Spaciousness: ★★ Quiet: ★★★
Security: ★★★★ Cleanliness: ★★★
Insect Control: ★★★ Facilities: ★★★

Smack dab in the middle of Cody is the Ponderosa Campground. This large and busy place is in the center of all the activities Cody has to offer. There is shopping and fine dining just around the corner. In the summers, Cody host a nightly rodeo and other special events and festivals designed to entertain tourists. Cody is the main gate to Yellowstone National Park in the east, and the Ponderosa is the premiere full-service campground in the area. The Ponderosa's sites are relatively close together, and due to high traffic and hot dry weather, there is little grass. In addition, much for the same reason there are few trees, and little shade. The campground is well maintained, and the facilities are clean. It is recommended that reservations are made as far in advance as possible, since they do operate at full capacity most of the time. The campground is staffed around the clock, and they are very helpful and considerate.

BASICS

Operated By: The Richardsons. **Open:** Apr.–Oct. 15. **Site Assignment:** By reservation. **Registration:** In the camp store. **Fee:** Tent $17, RV $27 per 2 people extra people over 8 $2. **Parking:** At site.

FACILITIES

Number of RV-Only Sites: 140. **Number of Tent-Only Sites:** Open tent area. **Hookups:** Electric (20, 30, 50 amps), water, sewer. **Each Site:** Picnic table. **Dump Station:** Yes. **Laundry:** Yes. **Pay Phone:** Yes. **Rest Rooms and Showers:** Yes. **Fuel:** No, down the street. **Propane:** No. **Internal Roads:** Gravel, in good condition. **RV Service:** In town. **Market:** In town. **Restaurant:** In town. **General Store:** Yes. **Vending:** Yes. **Swimming Pool:** No. **Playground:** Yes. **Other:** Arcade, trading post, store, 7 cabins, 6 teepees. **Activities:** Games, playground. **Nearby Attractions:** Yellowstone National Park, nightly summer rodeos, Horse Rides and Chuckwagon Dinner, Buffalo Bill Historical Center. **Additional Information:** Cody Chamber of Commerce, (307) 587-2297.

RESTRICTIONS

Pets: On leash. **Fires:** No fires in the city limit. **Alcoholic Beverages:** Yes. **Vehicle Maximum Length:** None. **Other:** Good Sam and AAA.

TO GET THERE

Located on US 14 in Cody near 16th St. and Sheridan Ave.

DOUGLAS
Douglas Jackalope KOA Campground

P.O. Box 1190, Douglas 82007. T: (307) 358-2164 or (800) 562-2469; F: (307) 358-2164; www.koa.com.

 ★★★  ★★★

Beauty: ★★★ Site Privacy: ★★★
Spaciousness: ★★★ Quiet: ★★★
Security: ★★★ Cleanliness: ★★★
Insect Control: ★★★ Facilities: ★★★

If you are looking for a quiet place to stay or just passing through, the Douglas KOA is a delightful, well-maintained, and comfortable place to lodge. The Douglas KOA offers a more rustic, woodsy setting, with all the amenities you would expect from a full-service campground. The campsites are moderate in size and have gravel parking spurs; there are both pull-through and back-in sites. The community of Douglas is listed as number 72 in Norman Crampton's *The 100 Best Small Towns in America,* and it's home to Fort Fetterman and the Wyoming Pioneer Memorial Museum. This area of Wyoming is rich in Native American history, and the Oregon, Emigrant, Mormon, and Bozeman trails, which cross through the area, are full of untold stories. The Douglas KOA has a safe and secure atmosphere and a kind and caring staff.

BASICS

Operated By: Bob and Delores Kessner. **Open:** Apr. 1–Nov. 1. **Site Assignment:** By reservation. **Registration:** In the camp store. **Fee:** Tent $17, RVs $22–$26, per 2 people, extra people $3 each. **Parking:** At site.

FACILITIES

Number of RV-Only Sites: 68. **Number of Tent-Only Sites:** 16. **Hookups:** Electric (20, 30, 50 amps), water, sewer, cable. **Each Site:** Picnic tables, and grills in the tent and cabin area. **Dump Station:** Yes. **Laundry:** Yes. **Pay Phone:** Yes. **Rest Rooms and Showers:** Yes. **Fuel:** No. **Propane:** Yes. **Internal Roads:** Gravel, in good condition. **RV Service:** Casper. **Market:** In town. **Restaurant:** In town. **General Store:** Yes. **Vending:** Yes. **Swimming Pool:** Yes. **Playground:** Yes. **Other:** 1 cabin, store, Internet dataport, pavilion. **Activities:** Game room, playground, horseshoes, mini-golf, basketball. **Nearby Attractions:** Pioneer Museum, natural bridge, national speedway, Ft Fetterman. **Additional Information:** Douglas Chamber of Commerce, (307) 358-2950.

RESTRICTIONS

Pets: On leash. **Fires:** No open wood fires. **Alcoholic Beverages:** Yes. **Vehicle Maximum Length:** None.

TO GET THERE

From I-25 take Exit 140, go right on Hwy. 91, and drive for about 1.5 mi.

GLENROCK
Deer Creek Village RV Park

P.O. Box 1003, Glenrock 82637. T: (307) 436-8121; F: (307) 436-5779.

★★★ ★★

Beauty: ★★★ Site Privacy: ★★★
Spaciousness: ★★★ Quiet: ★★★
Security: ★★★ Cleanliness: ★★★
Insect Control: ★★★ Facilities: ★★

Deer Creek Village RV Park is nestled behind a large community park in Glenrock. Deer Creek has the advantage of activities offered by the Glenrock Community Park while maintaining a separate private area for its visitors. The Deer Creek RV Park has extra-large sites, with lush green grass and large, hearty shade trees. In addition, it offers full hookups and cable TV at an exceptionally reasonable price. The facilities are adequately maintained, and the owner resides on the property. The Glenrock Community Park has a large playground, baseball diamond, and tennis courts, all in walking distance from any campsite. There is plenty of room for children to ride bikes without the fear of major road traffic. There are a few full-time residents in the RV park as well as a few mobile homes. The weather has a tendency to be cool in the evening, and Wyoming is always windy.

Basics

Operated By: Cindy Yuker. **Open:** Mar. 15–Nov. 15. **Site Assignment:** By reservation. **Registration:** In the camp store. **Fee:** $12 no hookups, $16 w/ hookups, $1 extra for cable and $3-the heat. **Parking:** At site.

Facilities

Number of RV-Only Sites: 80. **Number of Tent-Only Sites:** 10. **Hookups:** Electric (20, 30, 50 amps), water, sewer, cable. **Each Site:** None. **Dump Station:** No. **Laundry:** Yes. **Pay Phone:** No. **Rest Rooms and Showers:** Yes. **Fuel:** No. **Propane:** Yes. **Internal Roads:** Gravel, in good condition. **RV Service:** In Casper. **Market:** In town. **Restaurant:** In town. **General Store:** Yes. **Vending:** Yes. **Swimming Pool:** No. **Playground:** Yes. **Other:** Gift shop. **Activities:** Next door to a nice city park w/ basketball, baseball, tennis, walking trails. **Nearby Attractions:** A Mane Attraction in Casper, Wagon Wheel Roller Skating in Mills. **Additional Information:** Glenrock Chamber of Commerce, (307) 436-5652.

Restrictions

Pets: On leash. **Fires:** In approved sites only. **Alcoholic Beverages:** Yes. **Vehicle Maximum Length:** None.

To Get There

From I-25, take US 20/26/87 into Glenrock. Campground is behind Glenrock Community Park.

GREYBULL

Greybull KOA Campground

P.O. Box 387, Greybull 82426. T: (307) 765-2555 or (800) 562-7508; F: (307) 765-2555; www.koa.com.

RV ★★★ | Tent ★★★

Beauty: ★★★	Site Privacy: ★★★
Spaciousness: ★★★	Quiet: ★★★
Security: ★★★	Cleanliness: ★★★
Insect Control: ★★★	Facilities: ★★★

Situated just outside of the Big Horn National Forest and the Cloud Peak Wilderness, Greybull KOA, is an excellent base camp for the outdoor sports enthusiast. This area of Northeast Wyo-ming is renowned for its blue-ribbon trout fishing, its miles of hiking trails, and rocks that would challenge even the most experienced rock climbers. It offers excellent mountain biking for the serious biker, and there's also great snow in the winter for those who like to ski. Greybull KOA is a full-service RV park with full amenities, a pool, a snack bar, and cable TV. They offer a comfortable, affordable, well-maintained campground. The staff is friendly, helpful, and always willing to make your visit more pleasurable. The campground offers both pull-through and back-in sites, as well as gravel parking spurs. There is some grass; however, grass is not very common due to dry weather (so don't forget to pack the lotion).

Basics

Operated By: Bob and Marilyn Patterson. **Open:** Apr. 15–Oct. 30. **Site Assignment:** By reservation. **Registration:** In the camp store. **Fee:** Tent $20, RVs $25–$28, per 2 people, extra people over the age of 3 $3 each (no personal checks). **Parking:** At site.

Facilities

Number of RV-Only Sites: 33. **Number of Tent-Only Sites:** 24. **Hookups:** Electric (20, 30 amps), water, sewer, cable, phone, Internet. **Each Site:** Picnic tables, and grills. **Dump Station:** Yes. **Laundry:** Yes. **Pay Phone:** Yes. **Rest Rooms and Showers:** Yes. **Fuel:** No. **Propane:** Yes. **Internal Roads:** Gravel, in good condition. **RV Service:** In town. **Market:** In town. **Restaurant:** In town. **General Store:** Yes. **Vending:** No. **Swimming Pool:** Yes. **Playground:** Yes. **Other:** 3 cabins, store, café, Internet dataport. **Activities:** Game room, playground, horseshoes, volleyball, basketball. **Nearby Attractions:** Dinosaur Beds, Shell Falls, horseback riding. **Additional Information:** Greybull Chamber of Commerce (307) 765-2100.

Restrictions

Pets: On leash. **Fires:** In approved sites only. **Alcoholic Beverages:** Yes. **Vehicle Maximum Length:** None.

To Get There

Go four blocks north of Hwy. 14 off of 2nd St. or four blocks east of Hwy. 16/20 off 3rd Ave. in Greybull.

JACKSON HOLE

Snake River Park KOA (Jackson/Hoback Junction KOA)

9705 South Hwy. 89, Jackson Hole 83001. T: (307) 733-7078; F: (307) 733-0412; www.srkoa.com; srpinformation@aol.com.

RV ★★★★ | Tent ★★★★

Beauty: ★★★★	Site Privacy: ★★★★
Spaciousness: ★★★★	Quiet: ★★★★
Security: ★★★★	Cleanliness: ★★★★
Insect Control: ★★★★	Facilities: ★★★★

Snake River Park KOA is positioned between the Snake River and Horse Creek only a few short miles south of Jackson Hole. The Snake River runs directly behind the facility and adds to the rustic atmosphere. The Snake River Park KOA is a full-service camping facility that offers grass sites and large shade trees along the water's edge. All sites have a gravel parking area, and both pull-through and back-in sites are available. This particular KOA is also a fully licensed float trip outfitter by the Bridger-Teton National Forest and specializes in packaged float trips both for individuals and for groups. They have Coast Guard–approved equipment and provide both food and transportation. The campground itself has a large convenience store, gift shop, game room, and snacks. This is a very lively KOA that caters to patrons utilizing their float service.

Basics

Operated By: Snake River Park, Inc. **Open:** Apr.–mid Oct. **Site Assignment:** By reservations, $30–$50 per site or cabin deposit required. Checks will be taken on deposits only until Apr. 1th. **Registration:** In camp store. **Fee:** Tents $30.95, RVs $39.95–$47.95 per 2 people, extra people over age 5 are $6 each w/ a max. of 6 people per site. **Parking:** Yes, but there is a $10 extra vehicle fee, campers are allowed 1 tow.

Facilities

Number of RV-Only Sites: 47. **Number of Tent-Only Sites:** 28. **Hookups:** Electric (30, 50 amps), water, sewer. **Each Site:** Picnic table, fire pits. **Dump Station:** Yes. **Laundry:** Yes. **Pay Phone:** Yes. **Rest Rooms and Showers:** Yes. **Fuel:** 1 mi. south in town. **Propane:** 1 mi. south in town. **Internal Roads:** Gravel, in good condition. **RV Service:** Mobile service from Jackson. **Market:** In Jackson. **Restaurant:** There is a café on site and another restaurant across the street, or in Jackson. **General Store:** Yes. **Vending:** General Store only. **Swimming Pool:** No. **Playground:** Yes. **Other:** River Access, whitewater rafting outfitters, 17 cabins, float packages. **Activities:** Rafting, fishing, tubing. **Nearby Attractions:** Jackson Hole, skiing, the Grand Tetons, Yellowstone National Park. **Additional Information:** Jackson Hole Chamber of Commerce, (307) 733-3316.

Restrictions

Pets: On Leash only. **Fires:** In approved sites only. **Alcoholic Beverages:** Yes. **Vehicle Maximum Length:** None. **Other:** 10 day max. stay, KOA discount.

To Get There

From Jackson, go south on US 26/89 for about 5 mi.; campground is on you right.

JACKSON HOLE

Virginian Lodge and RV Resort

P.O. Box 1052, Jackson 83001. T: (307) 733-7189 or (800) 321-6982 in the summer or (800) 262-4999 in the winter; F: (307) 733-4063; virginian@wyoming.com.

RV ★★★ | Tent ★★

Beauty: ★★★	Site Privacy: ★★★
Spaciousness: ★★	Quiet: ★★★
Security: ★★★	Cleanliness: ★★★
Insect Control: ★★★	Facilities: ★★★

The Virginian Lodge and RV Resort is suitably located in downtown Jackson Hole. The property is convenientl to a vast number of novelty shops and excellent restaurants. The campground is open to RVs only and offers a full array of camping amenities. The campsites are gravel with some grass and shade. The facility offers both pull-through and back-in sites and has room to accommodate large RVs. There is a nice-sized swimming pool, hot tub, and full-service lodge. Jackson Hole is but a short drive from the Grand Teton National Park and serves as the south entrance to Yellowstone National Park. The area is a great base camp for those patrons wishing to experience the parks or take a float trip down the Snake River. The resort staff is very friendly and will be more than happy to assist with any needs. The weather can be a bit windy and dry, so it is always best to be prepared.

Basics

Operated By: Wayne and Lynn Simons. **Open:** May 1–Oct. 15. **Site Assignment:** By reservation. **Registration:** In camp registration office, located at the front gate. **Fee:** $37–$45 per unit (no personal checks). **Parking:** At site.

Facilities

Number of RV-Only Sites: 103. **Number of Tent-Only Sites:** 0. **Hookups:** Electric (20, 30, 50 amps), water, sewer, cable. **Each Site:** Picnic tables, and grills. **Dump Station:** Yes. **Laundry:** Yes. **Pay Phone:** Yes. **Rest Rooms and Showers:** Yes. **Fuel:** Less than a mi. in any direction. **Propane:** Same as above. **Internal Roads:** Gravel, in good condition. **RV Service:** 65 mi. west in Idaho Falls, ID. **Market:** In Jackson. **Restaurant:** On site or there is a large selection in town. **General Store:** No. **Vending:** Yes. **Swimming Pool:** Yes w/ Jacuzzi at the lodge. **Playground:** Yes. **Other:** Hotel, meeting rooms, central data port in office. **Activities:** There are no activities on site other than the pool and playground on site. **Nearby Attractions:** Yellowstone National Park, the Grand Tetons, Jackson Hole, Jackson National Fish Hatchery, National Museum of Wildlife Art, Snow King Mountain Ski Area, Jackson Hole Ski Area. **Additional Information:** Jackson Hole Chamber of Commerce (307) 733-3316.

Restrictions

Pets: On leash only. **Fires:** No open fires, charcoal grills only. **Alcoholic Beverages:** Yes. **Vehicle Maximum Length:** 45 ft. **Other:** AAA, Good Sam.

To Get There

Once in Jackson Hole, US 26/89 will be W. Broadway. The campground is behind the lodge on Virginian Ln., heading northeast towards the Tetons.

LARAMIE

Laramie KOA

P.O. Box 1134, Laramie 82073. T: (307) 742-6553 or (800) 562-4153; www.koa.com; koalaramie.vcn.com.

RV ★★ Tent ★★

Beauty: ★★	Site Privacy: ★★
Spaciousness: ★★	Quiet: ★★★
Security: ★★★	Cleanliness: ★★★
Insect Control: ★★★	Facilities: ★★★

Directly off the highway, the Laramie KOA offers clean and affordable lodging. The Laramie KOA offers over 100 pull-through RV sites with cable and phone hookups. There is a playground, recreation hall, laundry, and locked rest rooms. The campground backs right up to I-80 and is behind a mobile home area. The campground is gravel for the most part—the exception being the cabin area, which has a small lawn and a flower garden. Sites are level and configured in long rows, resembling a large parking lot. The staff is very friendly, and they work hard to maintain a nice campground in a desert region. The Laramie area has many attractions and festivals, such as the fair in Aug., and the Wyoming Children's Museum & Nature Center. There is also the Laramie Wyoming Territorial Prison and Old West Park with a horse barn dinner theatre.

Basics

Operated By: Greg Milliken. **Open:** Apr.–Nov 1. **Site Assignment:** By reservation. **Registration:** In the camp store. **Fee:** Tent $15, RVs $23, per 2 people, extra people over age 8 $2 each. **Parking:** At site.

Facilities

Number of RV-Only Sites: 116. **Number of Tent-Only Sites:** Open tent area. **Hookups:** Electric (20, 30, 50 amps), water, sewer. **Each Site:** Picnic tables, and fire pits in the tent and cabin area. **Dump Station:** Yes. **Laundry:** Yes. **Pay Phone:** Yes. **Rest Rooms and Showers:** Yes. **Fuel:** No. **Propane:** Yes. **Internal Roads:** Gravel, in good condition. **RV Service:** Local service. **Market:** In town. **Restaurant:** In town. **General Store:** Yes. **Vending:** Yes. **Swimming Pool:** No. **Playground:** Yes. **Other:** 8 cabins, store, Internet data port, rec hall, garage, flower garden. **Activities:** Game room, playground, horseshoes. **Nearby Attractions:** Laramie Wyoming Territorial Prison and Old West Park, Medicine Bow-Routt National Forests and Thunder Basin National Grassland. **Additional Information:** Laramie Chamber of Commerce (307) 745-7339.

Restrictions

Pets: On leash. **Fires:** In fire rings only. **Alcoholic Beverages:** Yes. **Vehicle Maximum Length:** None.

To Get There

From I-80 take Exit 310, go east on Curtis St, then turn right on McCue St at the Pilot. The KOA can be seen from I-80.

LYMAN

Lyman KOA

HC 66 Box 55, Lyman 82937. T: (307) 786-2762 or (800) 562-2762; www.koa.com; larkmary@buea.net.

RV ★★★★ Tent ★★★

Beauty: ★★★	Site Privacy: ★★★
Spaciousness: ★★★	Quiet: ★★★★
Security: ★★★★	Cleanliness: ★★★
Insect Control: ★★★	Facilities: ★★★

Located between Evanston and Rock Springs is delightful medium-sized campground, set in a rural atmosphere. The Lyman KOA is charming and inviting. The campground has a beautiful green lawn, with just enough shade from a few large trees, and a large outdoor swimming pool. The owners are friendly and genuinely pleased to assist their customers. Each campsite has a gravel parking area, and both pull-through and back-in sites are available. There is a large covered pavilion great for family outings, along with a small basketball court and other games. The town of Lyman is small, and this is a great place to read a book and enjoy a nice spring breeze. The historic Ft. Bridger is only a short drive away, and the Mountain Man Rendezvous is celebrated Labor Day weekend.

Basics

Operated By: Clark Anderson. **Open:** May 15–Oct. 1. **Site Assignment:** By reservation. **Registration:** In the camp store. **Fee:** Tent $17, RVs $21, per 2 people, extra people over age 4 $1.50 each. **Parking:** At site.

Facilities

Number of RV-Only Sites: 36. **Number of Tent-Only Sites:** 17. **Hookups:** Electric (20, 30, 50 amps), water, sewer. **Each Site:** Picnic tables, and a some fire pits. **Dump Station:** Yes. **Laundry:** Yes. **Pay Phone:** Yes. **Rest Rooms and Showers:** Yes. **Fuel:** No, 7 mi. in Mt. View. **Propane:** No, 7 mi. in Mt. View. **Internal Roads:** Gravel, in good condition. **RV Service:** Local service. **Market:** Mt. View. **Restaurant:** In town. **General Store:** Yes. **Vending:** Yes. **Swimming Pool:** Yes. **Playground:** Yes. **Other:** 2 cabins, pavilion w/ kitchen, horseshoes, Internet dataport. **Activities:** Game room, playground, horseshoes, basketball, volleyball. **Nearby Attractions:** Flaming Gorge, Rock City. **Additional Information:** Bridger Valley Chamber of Commerce, (307) 787-6738.

Restrictions

Pets: On leash. **Fires:** In fire rings only. **Alcoholic Beverages:** Yes. **Vehicle Maximum Length:** None.

To Get There

Campground is 1 mi. south of I-80 at Exit 44.

MOOSE

Grand Tetons

P.O. Drawer 170, Moose 83012. T: (307) 739-3300; F: (307) 739-3438; www.grand.teton.national-park.com; grte_info@nps.gov.

RV ★★★ Tent ★★★★

Beauty: ★★★★★	Site Privacy: ★★★
Spaciousness: ★★	Quiet: ★★★
Security: ★★★★	Cleanliness: ★★★
Insect Control: n/a	Facilities: ★★★

Regal and proud, the Grand Tetons stand tall over the Snake River and peer down from the heavens. This natural marvel represents most intact temperate ecosystem in North America. Renowned for its world-famous wildlife viewing and unparalleled beauty, the Grand Teton National Park portrays an image of strength and majesty unscathed by man. The park has a total of six large campgrounds with over 1,000 camsites among them. The sites range from primitive to modern, with Colter Bay Trailer Village offering full hookups. The Grand Teton Lodge Company is the in-park concessionaire and oversees the majority of guest services, including camping reservations in three of the six campgrounds. The campgrounds are configured in loops, with paved parking pads, potable water, and rest room facilities. Showers are available in the Colter Bay Service Area at the laundry. The Grand Tetons, like any national park, is home and refuge to many forms of wildlife—including bear, moose, and elk—and therefore it is very important for your safety to please follow all the regulations put forth by the National Park Service.

Basics

Operated By: National Park Service. **Open:** The park is open year round, most camping areas are open mid May–end of Sept. **Site Assignment:** Camping is first come, first served w/ the exception of Colter Bay Trailer Village (307) 739-3399 Visitor Information (There is a Colter Bay Campground and a Colter Bay Trailer Village, all in the Colter Bay Village Area). **Registration:** Each campground has a registration office. **Fee:** $10–$30. based on which campground is chosen and the amenities they provide. **Parking:** At site.

Facilities

Number of RV-Only Sites: 112. **Number of Tent-Only Sites:** 0. **Number of Multipurpose Sites:** 905. **Hookups:** Electric (20, 30, 50 amps), water, sewer in Colter Bay Trailer Village Park only. There are no hookups at the other 5 campgrounds inside the park. **Each Site:** Picnic tables, fire pits (except Colter Bay trailer Village). **Dump Station:** Yes, at Gros Ventre, Signal Mountain, and Colter Bay. **Laundry:** Yes, in the service area at Colter Bay. **Pay Phone:** Pay phones are located throughout the park, but Not necessarily at each campground, primarily in the service areas. **Rest Rooms and Showers:** There are rest rooms located in every campground, and showers in the service areas near Colter Bay for a fee. **Fuel:** Yes, there 3 service areas through out the park Colter Bay, Jenny Lake, and Moose Junction. **Propane:** Yes, in several service areas through out the park. **Internal Roads:** The majority are paved but in need of repair. **RV Service:** Minor repair service available at Colter Bay. **Market:** There are several in the park, or in Jackson Hole, WY. **Restaurant:** There are several restaurants in the park, Jenny Lake Lodge, Signal Mountain Lodge, Jackson Lake Lodge and Flagg Ranch. **General Store:** There are 3 general stores at Colter Bay, Jenny Lake, Jackson Lake. **Vending:** Yes in the major service areas of the park. **Swimming Pool:** No. **Playground:** No. **Other:** The Grand Teton National Park is a its own community w/ lodging, food, transportation, laundry, stores, restaurants, and medical clinic. Each guest will be given a newsletter upon arrival w/ a complete listing of the parks amenities and services. **Activities:** Horseback riding, motor coach tours, photo safaris, hiking, backpacking, Ranger led programs, evening programs, photo hikes, lectures, boating tennis, golf, biking tours. **Nearby Attractions:** Yellowstone National Park, Jackson Hole, Jackson National Fish Hatchery, National Museum of Wildlife Art, Snow King Mountain Ski Area, Jackson Hole Ski Area. **Additional Information:** Grand Teton Lodge Company, (307) 543-2811; Jackson Hole Chamber of Commerce, (307) 733-3316; National Park Service US Dept. of the Interior, or there are over 50 Internet links to Yellowstone National Park through www.yahoo.com or www.google.com.

Restrictions

Pets: Although pets are allowed in The Grand Teton Nation; Park on a leash only, however we strongly discouraged bringing them. Pets are not allowed out of the camping ares areas or off the main roads. Pets are not allowed in the backcountry or in any public viewing area. **Fires:** In fire pits only (fires may be prohibited due to weather conditions, please ask before starting any open fire). **Alcoholic Beverages:** Yes. **Vehicle Maximum Length:** Depends on the campground of your choice but never longer than 45ft. **Other:** National Park passes honored for entrance fees, golden age and golden access cards are *not* honored at all the campgrounds, including Colter Bay Trailer Village.

To Get There

There are three main gates into the Grand Tetons.; the most popular is through Jackson on Hwy. 191.

MORAN
The Flagg Ranch Resort

P.O.Box 187, Moran 83013.T: (800) 443-2311 or (307) 543-2861; F: (307) 543-2356; www.flaggranch.com; info@flaggranch.com.

RV ★★★ Tent ★★★

Beauty: ★★★★★	Site Privacy: ★★★
Spaciousness: ★★★	Quiet: ★★★★
Security: ★★★	Cleanliness: ★★★
Insect Control: ★★★	Facilities: ★★★

The Flagg Ranch Resort Campground is in one of the most ideal locations in Wyoming. It is situated between the Grand Tetons National Park and the south entrance to Yellowstone National Park along Hwy 89. This campground is privately owned in conjunction with a full-service lodge and service station. The campground sits in a forest of large evergreens and offers a real sense of tranquility. A great base for visiting both national parks, this campground offers all the amenities expected of a full-service RV camp. Each campsite has a gravel parking pad, hookups, and fire ring, as well as a natural forest floor and towering pines. Due to the location of this camping facility and the fact that there is only one trailer campground with hookups in either park, reservations must be made far in advance. Also, there is no access to this campground except through one of the national parks; therefore, expect to pay a park entrance fee.

Basics

Operated By: Bob Walker. **Open:** Year-round. **Site Assignment:** By reservation. **Registration:** In camp store. **Fee:** Tents $20 RV $35 per 2 people, extra child $2, Adult $2. **Parking:** At site.

Facilities

Number of RV-Only Sites: 97. **Number of Tent-Only Sites:** 74. **Hookups:** Electric (20, 30 amps), water, sewer. **Each Site:** Picnic tables, and fire pits in tent sites. **Dump Station:** No. **Laundry:** Yes. **Pay Phone:** Yes. **Rest Rooms and Showers:** Yes. **Fuel:** Yes. **Propane:** Yes. **Internal Roads:** Gravel, in good condition. **RV Service:** At Colter Bay Village. **Market:** At Colter Bay Village. **Restaurant:** On site at the lodge. **General Store:** Yes. **Vending:** Yes. **Swimming Pool:** No. **Playground:** Yes. **Other:** Main lodge w/ dining area, fireplace, gift shop, store, service station, meeting rooms, cabins, hotel, Internet data ports. **Activities:** Fishing, hiking, float tours, biking, horseback riding, coach tours. **Nearby Attractions:** Yellowstone National Park, the Grand Tetons, Jackson Hole, Jackson National Fish Hatchery, National Museum of Wildlife Art, Snow King Mountain Ski Area, Jackson Hole Ski Area, fishing, float trips, covered wagon cookouts. **Additional Information:** Jackson Hole Chamber of Commerce, (307) 733-3316.

Restrictions

Pets: On leash only. **Fires:** In fire pits only. **Alcoholic Beverages:** Yes. **Vehicle Maximum Length:** 45 ft. **Other:** Expect to pay a national park entrance fee, unless you have a park pass.

To Get There

The campground is located directly between the south gate of Yellowstone National Park and north gate of the Grand Tetons National Park on Hwy. 89 (you will have to enter through one of the two parks, so expect to pay a park entrance fee).

MORAN
Grand Teton Park RV Resort

P.O.Box 83013, Moran 83013.T: (800) (563) 6469 or (307) 733-1980; F: (307) 543-0927; www.yellowstonerv.com; gtprv@blissnet.com.

RV ★★★ Tent ★★★

Beauty: ★★★★★	Site Privacy: ★★★
Spaciousness: ★★★	Quiet: ★★★★
Security: ★★★	Cleanliness: ★★★
Insect Control: ★★★	Facilities: ★★★

The Grand Teton Park RV Resort is just one mile east of the Grand Tetons National Park and 32 miles from the south gate of Yellowstone. Few other full-service RV campgrounds are more convenient to the national parks (though there is at least one—see profile for Flagg Ranch Resort). The Grand Teton Park RV Resort offers a spectacular panoramic view of the majestic Grand Tetons, in addition to comfortable and affordable lodging year-round. The campground offers over 200 campsites, large, open tenting areas, and five teepees. They have both pull-through and back-in sites, as well as level parking spaces. The campground has full amenities, including a deli, pizza, and fuel. The property also offers a variety of services such as snowmobile and van rentals. This campground is also in close proximity to the scenic Snake River and many rafting outfitters. The weather in summer is comfortable, and the winter is harsh—but regardless of season, this campground is always inviting, and the people are great.

Basics

Operated By: Private Operator. **Open:** Year-round. **Site Assignment:** By reservation. **Regis-

tration: In camp store. **Fee:** Tents $29 RV $32–$40 per 2 people extra child $4, Adult $5. **Parking:** At site.

Facilities

Number of RV-Only Sites: 140. **Number of Tent-Only Sites:** 60. **Hookups:** Electric (20, 30, 50 amps), water, sewer. **Each Site:** Picnic tables, and fire pits in tent sites. **Dump Station:** Yes. **Laundry:** Yes. **Pay Phone:** Yes. **Rest Rooms and Showers:** Yes. **Fuel:** Yes. **Propane:** Yes. **Internal Roads:** Gravel, in good condition. **RV Service:** Mobile service. **Market:** 36 mi. southwest in Jackson. **Restaurant:** 2 mi. in any direction, but The Buffalo Valley Ranch Café is a wonderful find w/ good prices and excellent service. **General Store:** Yes. **Vending:** No. **Swimming Pool:** Yes w/ hot tub. **Playground:** Yes. **Other:** 18 cabins, game room, 5 tepees, Pizza and deli, central data port in office. **Activities:** There are no activities on site other than the pool and playground on site. **Nearby Attractions:** Yellowstone National Park, the Grand Tetons, Jackson Hole, Jackson National Fish Hatchery, National Museum of Wildlife Art, Snow King Mountain Ski Area, Jackson Hole Ski Area, fishing, float trips, covered wagon cookouts. **Additional Information:** Jackson Hole Chamber of Commerce, (307) 733-3316.

Restrictions

Pets: On leash only. **Fires:** In fire pits only. **Alcoholic Beverages:** Yes. **Vehicle Maximum Length:** 45 ft. **Other:** AAA, Good Sam, KOA discounts.

To Get There

The campground is 6 mi. east of the Moran junction on Hwy. 26 & 287.

RAWLINS
Rawlins KOA

205 East Hwy. 71, Rawlins 82301. T: (307) 328-2021 or (800) 562-7559; www.koa.com; gattfarr@vcn.com.

RV ★★★ Tent ★★

Beauty: ★★★	Site Privacy: ★★★
Spaciousness: ★★★	Quiet: ★★★
Security: ★★★★	Cleanliness: ★★★
Insect Control: ★★★	Facilities: ★★★★

The Rawlins KOA is located directly off I-80 and offers convenient lodging in a clean and well-maintained atmosphere. The Rawlins KOA is nicely landscaped in a desert area where it is hard for anything to grow. The campsites have recently been upgraded and lengthened to accommodate newer and longer RVs. Each site has a level, gravel parking area, as well as free cable TV. The tents sites have tent pads and wind shields. The weather is very dry, and there is a considerable amount of sand in this region. In addition, the campground has a nice swimming pool and a camp kitchen. There is fishing in the Seminoe Reservoir or the North Platte River nearby, and hunting for antelope and deer. The community of Rawlins is full of interesting places to see, such as the Frontier Prison or Fort Steele.

Basics

Operated By: Fran and Jean Farrell. **Open:** Apr.–Oct. 31. **Site Assignment:** By reservation. **Registration:** In the camp store. **Fee:** Tent $18, RVs $21–$23, per 2 people, extra people over age 5 $3 each. **Parking:** At site.

Facilities

Number of RV-Only Sites: 56. **Number of Tent-Only Sites:** 6. **Hookups:** Electric (20, 30, 50 amps), water, sewer. **Each Site:** Picnic tables, and fire pits in the tent and cabin area. **Dump Station:** Yes. **Laundry:** Yes. **Pay Phone:** Yes. **Rest Rooms and Showers:** Yes. **Fuel:** No. **Propane:** Yes. **Internal Roads:** Gravel, in good condition. **RV Service:** Larime. **Market:** In town. **Restaurant:** In town. **General Store:** Yes. **Vending:** Yes. **Swimming Pool:** Yes. **Playground:** Yes. **Other:** 5 cabin, store, Internet dataport. **Activities:** Game room, playground, horseshoes, basketball. **Nearby Attractions:** Carbon County Museum, Frontier Prison, Snowy Ridge Scenic Byway. **Additional Information:** Rawlins Chamber of Commerce, (307) 324-4111 or (800) 935-4821.

Restrictions

Pets: On leash. **Fires:** In fire rings only. **Alcoholic Beverages:** Yes. **Vehicle Maximum Length:** None.

To Get There

The campground is near Exit 214 off I-80 in central Rawlins.

RAWLINS
Western Hills Campground and Trailer Court

P.O. Box 760, Rawlins 82301. T: (307) 324-2592 or (888) 568-3040; members.tripod.com/~wyo_camping/index.htm#local; whc@trib.com.

RV ★★★ Tent ★★

Beauty: ★★	Site Privacy: ★★
Spaciousness: ★★★	Quiet: ★★★★
Security: ★★★	Cleanliness: ★★★
Insect Control: ★★★	Facilities: ★★★

Located directly off I-80 in Rawlins, Western Hills Campground is ideal for the night. The campground is clean and well maintained, with activities the entire family can enjoy. The campsites are mostly gravel with no trees, but this is very common for this particular part of Wyoming. The air is very hot in the summer, with little precipitation and large gusts of wind. The campground has a mini-golf course and wildlife viewing area. There is fishing in the Seminoe Reservoir or the North Platte River nearby, and hunting for antelope and deer. The community of Rawlins is full of interesting places to see, such as the Frontier Prison or Fort Steele. It is also home to several small museums. The Carbon County Fair and Rodeo are held the first week in Aug., an event well worth planning to attend.

Basics

Operated By: John and Doreen McDade. **Open:** Year-round w/ limited service Nov.–Mar. 1. **Site Assignment:** By reservation. **Registration:** In camp office. **Fee:** Tent $14, RV $18–$22 per 2 people, children under 5 stay free (cash, credit, check). **Parking:** At site.

Facilities

Number of RV-Only Sites: 139. **Number of Tent-Only Sites:** Open tent area. **Hookups:** Electric (30, 50 amps), water, sewer, cable, phone. **Each Site:** Picnic table. **Dump Station:** No. **Laundry:** Yes. **Pay Phone:** Yes. **Rest Rooms and Showers:** Yes. **Fuel:** No. **Propane:** No. **Internal Roads:** Gravel, in good condition. **RV Service:** 150 mi. east in Cheyenne. **Market:** 6 mi. east in town. **Restaurant:** There are over 30 restaurants in the Rawlins area. **General Store:** Yes w/ a photo shop. **Vending:** Yes. **Swimming Pool:** No. **Playground:** Yes. **Other:** Game room, dog walk, pavilion, wildlife viewing area. **Activities:** Games, horseshoes, mini-golf. **Nearby Attractions:** The Historic Fort Steele, The Carbon County Museum. **Additional Information:** Rawlins Chamber of Commerce, (800) 935-4821.

Restrictions

Pets: Yes on leash only. **Fires:** No open fires. **Alcoholic Beverages:** Yes. **Vehicle Maximum Length:** None. **Other:** Good Sam.

To Get There

From I-80 Exit 211, go west on W. Spruce St. (SR 789), then bear left onto S. Wagon Rd.

RIVERTON
Owl Creek

11124 US Hwy. 26/789, Riverton 82501. T: (307) 856-2869; campowlcreek@tcinc.net.

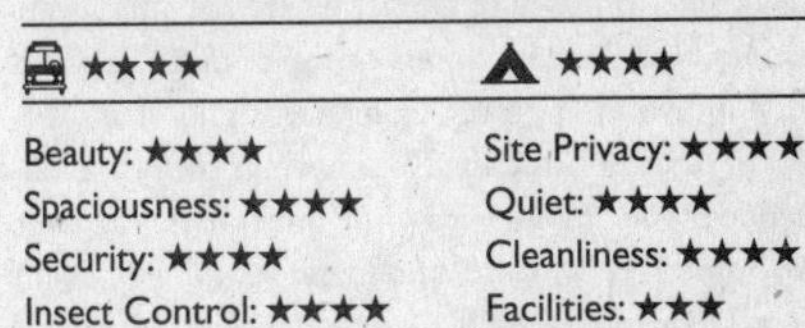

RV ★★★★ Tent ★★★★

Beauty: ★★★★	Site Privacy: ★★★★
Spaciousness: ★★★★	Quiet: ★★★★
Security: ★★★★	Cleanliness: ★★★★
Insect Control: ★★★★	Facilities: ★★★

Owl Creek Campground in Riverton is a lovely, established campground. Owl Creek was one of the original KOA campgrounds, and although it is no longer a member of the franchise, the original KOA structure and open breezeway still stand. The campground is one of the only campgrounds in Wyoming with thick, lush, green grass and mature, large, deciduous shade trees. The campground is beautifully maintained, but it has nostalgia for the past. This reminiscence is apparent in the owners' display of antiques and the older facilities. The owners' live in a large colonial home on the property, and the house the focal point of the park. Owl Creek caters to more mature visitors that appreciate the calm atmosphere and picturesque setting. Simply due to the age of this campground, sites needed to accommodate large RVs are very limited.

Basics

Operated By: Frank and Pat Petek. **Open:** May 15–Sept. 15. **Site Assignment:** By reservation. **Registration:** In the camp office. **Fee:** $18.50 per 2 people. **Parking:** At site.

Facilities

Number of RV-Only Sites: 21. **Number of**

Tent-Only Sites: 20. **Number of Multipurpose Sites:** 11. **Hookups:** Electric (20, 30, 50 amps), water, sewer, a few phone. **Each Site:** Picnic tables, and grills. **Dump Station:** Yes. **Laundry:** Yes. **Pay Phone:** Yes. **Rest Rooms and Showers:** Yes. **Fuel:** No, but in town. **Propane:** No. **Internal Roads:** Paved. **RV Service:** Local service. **Market:** In town. **Restaurant:** In town. **General Store:** Yes. **Vending:** Yes. **Swimming Pool:** No. **Playground:** Yes. **Other:** Orchard, utility sink. **Activities:** Playground, tetherball. **Nearby Attractions:** Fishing, hunting, boating, biking, hiking, and scenic byways. **Additional Information:** Riverton Chamber of Commerce, (307) 856-4801.

RESTRICTIONS

Pets: On leash. **Fires:** In approved sites. **Alcoholic Beverages:** Yes. **Vehicle Maximum Length:** 40 ft., limited room for extra long RV.

TO GET THERE

The campground is 5 mi. northeast of Riverton on Hwy. 26.

ROCK SPRINGS
Rock Springs KOA

P.O. Box 2910, Rock Springs 82902. T: (307) 362-3063 or (800) 562-8699; F: (307) 362-5799; www.koa.com.

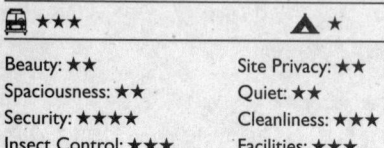

RV ★★★ Tent ★

Beauty: ★★	Site Privacy: ★★
Spaciousness: ★★	Quiet: ★★
Security: ★★★★	Cleanliness: ★★★
Insect Control: ★★★	Facilities: ★★★

Welcome to the high desert, where the sun always shines, and there is seldom a drop of rain. The air is dry and wind is strong. Conveniently located off I-80 in Rock Springs, the Rock Springs KOA is a full-service RV park with full amenities, a large swimming pool, store, and game room. This KOA is a large facility, well maintained and clean. The sites are gravel, and there is no grass anywhere in the park, including the tent sites or in front of the cabins. In addition, there are no trees, but we've been told there is great satellite television reception. The park does overlook some smaller mountains to the rear, but there is Conoco oil plant in the front. Sites are lined up in rows, with no real dividers. Rock City is a fairly large metropolis for Wyoming, offering movies, shopping, museums, and many special events and festivals.

BASICS

Operated By: Dale and Bonnie Whitley. **Open:** Apr. 1–Oct. 15. **Site Assignment:** By reservation. **Registration:** In the camp store. **Fee:** Tent $18, RVs $21–$28, per 2 people, extra people over age of 6 $3 each. **Parking:** At site.

FACILITIES

Number of RV-Only Sites: 86. **Number of Tent-Only Sites:** 10. **Number of Multipurpose Sites:** 11. **Hookups:** Electric (20, 30, 50 amps), water, sewer, cable. **Each Site:** Picnic tables, and grills in the tent and cabin area. **Dump Station:** Yes. **Laundry:** Yes. **Pay Phone:** Yes. **Rest Rooms and Showers:** Yes. **Fuel:** No, but in town. **Propane:** Yes. **Internal Roads:** Gravel, in good condition. **RV Service:** Local service. **Market:** In town. **Restaurant:** In town. **General Store:** Yes. **Vending:** Yes. **Swimming Pool:** Yes. **Playground:** Yes. **Other:** 6 cabins, store, Internet dataport, pavilion w/ kitchen, tent wind shelters, chuck wagon, hot tub. **Activities:** Game room, playground, horseshoes, basketball, nature trails. **Nearby Attractions:** Fort Bridger, shopping, stock car races, the rodeo, golf, museums, Flaming Gorge, and scenic byways. **Additional Information:** Rock Springs Chamber of Commerce (800) 46-DUNES.

RESTRICTIONS

Pets: On leash. **Fires:** No open fires. **Alcoholic Beverages:** Yes. **Vehicle Maximum Length:** None.

TO GET THERE

From I-80 Exit 99, follow signs for 1 mi. northeast.

THERMOPOLIS
Country Campin' RV Park

710 East Sunnyside Ln., Thermopolis 82443. T: (800) 609-2244; F: (307) 864-2416; w3.trib.com/~camp; camp@trib.com.

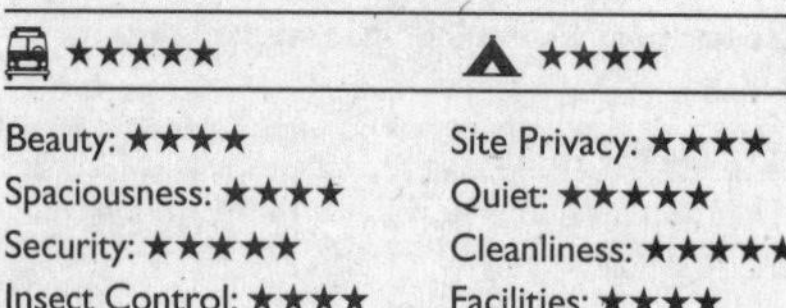

RV ★★★★★ Tent ★★★★

Beauty: ★★★★	Site Privacy: ★★★★
Spaciousness: ★★★★	Quiet: ★★★★★
Security: ★★★★★	Cleanliness: ★★★★★
Insect Control: ★★★★	Facilities: ★★★★

Located on the owners' private ranch, Country Campin' RV is a charming, small, private campground five miles north of Thermopolis. The campground offers full amenities with waterfront access. Campsites are mostly pull-throughs, large, level, and with gravel parking spurs. There is a small store and gift shop, laundry, and clean rest rooms and showers. The owners have a few farm animals for children to pet and two friendly dogs that watch over the campground. The campground is nicely landscaped, and the sprinklers are on frequently. There is a small boat dock for non-motorized boats, and there's great fishing along the Big Horn River. The campground has a large open common area, and it's decorated with large, colorful dinosaur statues. Thermopolis is home of the world's largest mineral hot springs, which are open 365 days a year, and Wyoming's Dinosaur Center.

BASICS

Operated By: Darvin and Spring Longwell. **Open:** May–Nov. 1. **Site Assignment:** Reservation. **Registration:** In the camp store. **Fee:** Tent $15, RV $20 per 2 people, extra people $1.50. **Parking:** At site.

FACILITIES

Number of RV-Only Sites: 42. **Number of Tent-Only Sites:** 12. **Hookups:** Electric (20, 30, 50 amps), water, sewer. **Each Site:** Picnic table. **Dump Station:** Yes. **Laundry:** Yes. **Pay Phone:** Yes. **Rest Rooms and Showers:** Yes. **Fuel:** No, but local. **Propane:** No. **Internal Roads:** Gravel, in good condition. **RV Service:** In town. **Market:** In town. **Restaurant:** In town. **General Store:** Yes. **Vending:** Yes. **Swimming Pool:** No, and please do Not swim in the river. **Playground:** Yes. **Other:** Boat launch, petting zoo, gift shop, teepees. **Activities:** playground, hiking, Blue Ribbon Trout Fishing, boating. **Nearby Attractions:** World's largest mineral hot spring, Wyoming's Dinosaur Center. **Additional Information:** Thermopolis Chamber of Commerce, (307) 864-3192.

RESTRICTIONS

Pets: On leash. **Fires:** In approved areas and out by 10 p.m.. **Alcoholic Beverages:** Yes. **Vehicle Maximum Length:** None. **Other:** Good Sam and AAA.

TO GET THERE

5.4 mi. north of Thermopolis off US 20 on E. Sunnyside Ln. This campground is on a private farm.

THERMOPOLIS
Eagle RV Park

204 Hwy. 20 South, Thermopolis 82443. T: (307) 864-2325 or (888) 865-5707; F: (307) 864-5262; www.eaglervpark.com; eaglervpark@wyoming.com.

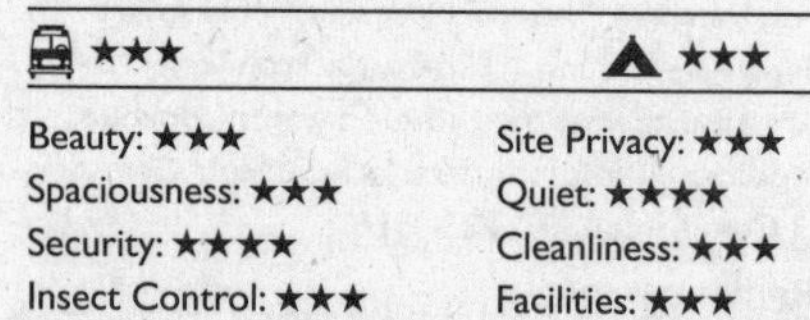

RV ★★★ Tent ★★★

Beauty: ★★★	Site Privacy: ★★★
Spaciousness: ★★★	Quiet: ★★★★
Security: ★★★★	Cleanliness: ★★★
Insect Control: ★★★	Facilities: ★★★

Eagle RV Park is located in the city of Thermopolis on Hwy. 20. Thermopolis is home of the worlds largest mineral pool and hot springs. Eagle RV Park is only a few miles from Hot Springs State Park, where visitors from all over the world come to see and enjoy the pools. The Eagle RV Park is convenient to the Big Horn River and offers float trip packages to its patrons. The campground is an older facility, but the owners are working diligently to update their facilities. Just in the past year, the internal roads have been asphalted, and a pool is being built for the new season. Rest rooms and showers are clean, and the grounds are well kept. Campites are being updated, but there was still a lot of work to be done when we visited. The owners are very gracious hosts, and they are always there to assist. The weather is dry here, and skin protection is always needed, especially in the mineral pools.

BASICS

Operated By: The Schneider Family. **Open:** Year-round. **Site Assignment:** By reservation. **Registration:** In the camp office. **Fee:** Tent $13, RV $19 per 2 people, extra person $1.50. **Parking:** At site.

FACILITIES

Number of RV-Only Sites: 50. **Number of Tent-Only Sites:** 15. **Hookups:** Electric (20, 30, 50 amps), water, sewer, cable, phone. **Each Site:** Picnic tables, and grills. **Dump Station:** Yes. **Laundry:** Yes. **Pay Phone:** Yes. **Rest Rooms and Showers:** Yes. **Fuel:** No, but in town. **Propane:** Yes. **Internal Roads:** Paved asphalt. **RV Service:** Local service. **Market:** In town. **Restaurant:** In town. **General Store:** Yes. **Vending:** Yes. **Swimming Pool:** New pool!!! we hope. They were digging when we visited. **Playground:** Yes. **Other:** Tube rentals, float trips, 4 cabins. **Activities:** Playground, rafting. **Nearby Attractions:** Thermopolis hot springs, Wyoming Dinosaur Center, several small museums, blur ribbon trout fishing, golf, Hot Springs

State Park. **Additional Information:** Thermopolis Chamber of Commerce, (307) 864-3192.

Restrictions

Pets: On leash. **Fires:** In approved sites. **Alcoholic Beverages:** Yes. **Vehicle Maximum Length:** 40 ft., limited room for extra long RV.

To Get There

The campground is ocated on Hwy. 20 on the south side of Thermopolis.

YELLOWSTONE

Fishing Bridge

P.O. Box 165, Yellowstone 82190. T: (307) 344-7311 or 303-338-6000; F: (307) 344-7456 or (303) 338-2045; www.travelyellowstone.com/fishing_bridge_campground; information@amfac.com or camp@travelyellowstone.com.

RV ★★★ Tent n/a

Beauty: ★★★ Site Privacy: ★
Spaciousness: ★ Quiet: ★★★
Security: ★★★★ Cleanliness: ★★★
Insect Control: ★★★ Facilities: ★★★

Fishing Bridge RV Park is one of 12 campgrounds inside Yellowstone National Park. However, Fishing Bridge is the only one to offer full hookups for hard-shelled RVs only. The campground itself is a simple, no-frills, concrete parking lot with 344 sites and barley enough room for slide-outs. There are no trees except on the outer perimeter, and trailers are parked back to back. On the upside of things, Fishing Bridge is in a very central location within Yellowstone and is in close proximity to fuel, groceries, showers, laundry, and an amphitheater with evening interpretive programs. It is also very close to the visitor's center and museum, as well as the Lake Hotel, which has a large dinning room and cafeteria. Amfac Parks and Resorts are the primary in-park concessionaire and provide the majority of guest services, which includes overseeing this campground.

Basics

Operated By: Amfac Parks & Resorts. **Open:** Mid May–mid Sept. **Site Assignment:** By reservations, reservations need to be made up to a year in advance. **Registration:** There is a registration desk. **Fee:** $30.24. **Parking:** Yes, but there is a vehicle fee for all vehicles.

Facilities

Number of RV-Only Sites: 334. **Number of Tent-Only Sites:** n/a. **Hookups:** Electric (20, 30, 50 amps), water, sewer. **Each Site:** A place to park. **Dump Station:** Yes. **Laundry:** Yes. **Pay Phone:** Yes. **Rest Rooms and Showers:** Yes, showers cost $3 and are open to the public. **Fuel:** Yes. **Propane:** Yes. **Internal Roads:** Paved. **RV Service:** Limited on site service. **Market:** In Yellowstone, about 2 blocks away at Hamiltons. **Restaurant:** There are several restaurants in Yellowstone a 3 close by. **General Store:** No. **Vending:** Yes. **Swimming Pool:** No. **Playground:** No. **Other:** Please see the profile on Yellowstone National Park. **Activities:** Please see the profile on Yellowstone National Park. **Nearby Attractions:** Jackson Hole, skiing, the Grand Tetons. **Additional Information:** Jackson Hole Chamber, (307) 733-3316 or Yellowstone Visitor Info, (307) 344-7381, (TDD) (307) 344-2386.

Restrictions

Pets: On leash only, pets are not allowed off the main roads anywhere in Yellowstone. **Fires:** No open fires. **Alcoholic Beverages:** Yes. **Vehicle Maximum Length:** 40 ft. **Other:** Only hard-sided units only, Golden age and golden access discounts are *not* honored by Amfac.

To Get There

There are 5 entrances into Yellowstone; visit www.travelyellowstone.com for directions, or call to request a park map.

YELLOWSTONE

Yellowstone National Park

P.O. Box 168, Yellowstone National Park 82190-0168. T: (307) 344-7381 or (TDD) (307) 344-2386; F: (307) 344-2005; www.nps.gov/yell/index.htm; yell_visitor_services@nps.gov or www.travelyellowstone.com.

RV ★★★ Tent ★★★★

Beauty: ★★★★★ Site Privacy: ★★★
Spaciousness: ★★ Quiet: ★★★
Security: ★★★★ Cleanliness: ★★★
Insect Control: n/a Facilities: ★★★

Yellowstone National Park encompasses the entire northwestern corner of Wyoming, with over 2.2 million acres of federal land serving as the world's first and oldest national park. The park has five major entrances and a total of 12 campgrounds with over a 2,000 campsites among them. The campsites range from very primitive to full hookups. Most are RV-friendly, with level parking pads, grated fire pits, potable water, and rest rooms in a wooded location. Most all of the campgrounds are configured as large multiple loops. Amfac Parks and Resorts are the primary in-park concessionaire and provide the majority of guest services, overseeing the five major campgrounds. Campsites managed by Amfac maybe reserved up to a year in advance. Yellowstone Park is open year-round; however, there is very limited camping after Sept. Yellowstone National Park is wonderful natural attraction, but first and foremost it is a home and refuge to the wildlife that inhabit its land. Therefore, we are all guests of these majestic animals and must respect the regulations put forth by the National Park Service for our protection as well as that of the wildlife. If you're considering a trip to Yellowstone National Park, please plan far in advance and contact visitor services.

Basics

Operated By: National Park Service. **Open:** The park is open year round, most camping areas are open mid May–end of Sept. Mommoth is open all year. Fishing Lodge May 18–Sept. 23. **Site Assignment:** Bridge Bay, Canyon, Grant Village, Madison, and Fishing Bridge RV Park. Fishing Bridge RV Park are by reservation and concessioned by Amfac Parks and Resorts. For reservations call (800) 329-9205 or (307) 344-7311. **Registration:** At registration office. **Fee:** $10–$30. **Parking:** At site.

Facilities

Number of RV-Only Sites: 340 (Fishing Bridge Only). **Number of Tent-Only Sites:** 454. **Number of Multipurpose Sites:** 1406 both RV and tent w/no hookups. **Hookups:** Electric (20, 30, 50 amps), water, sewer at Fishing Bridge RV Park only. There are no hookups at the other 11 campgrounds inside the park. **Each Site:** Picnic tables, fire pits (except Fishing Bridge). **Dump Station:** Yes, at Bridge Bay, Canyon, Fishing Bridge, Grant Village, and Madison. **Laundry:** Yes, in the service area near Canyon, Fishing Bridge, and Grant Village. **Pay Phone:** Pay phones are located throughout the park, but Not necessarily at each campground. **Rest Rooms and Showers:** There are rest rooms located in every campground, and showers in the service areas near Canyon, Fishing Bridge, and Grants Village. **Fuel:** Yes, there a 8 service areas through out the park. **Propane:** Yes, in several service areas through out the park. **Internal Roads:** The majority are paved. **RV Service:** There are several repair stations in the park. **Market:** There are several in the park, or West Yellowstone, MT. **Restaurant:** There are 17 restaurants in the park, 5 by Old Faithful, 2 in Grants Village, 3 in Canyon Village, 3 in Lake Village, 2 in Tower Roosevelt. **General Store:** There are 13 general stores throughout the park. **Vending:** Yes in the major service areas of the park. **Swimming Pool:** No. **Playground:** No. **Other:** Yellowstone National Park is a its own community w/ lodging, food, transportation, laundry, stores, restaurants, and hospital. Each guest will be given a newsletter upon arrival w/ a complete listing of the parks amenities and services. **Activities:** Horseback riding, Stagecoach rides, Bridge Bay Guided Fishing Trips, motor coach tours, old West Cookouts, photo safaris, hiking, backpacking, Ranger led programs, evening programs, Yellowstone for kids, photo hikes, lectures,. **Nearby Attractions:** West Yellowstone, MT, visitors center, Imax, 15 museums, rodeos, the Grand Tetons, Jackson Hole, WY, Cody, WY, shopping. **Additional Information:** West Yellowstone Chamber, (406) 646-7701, or there are over 45 Internet links to Yellowstone National Park through yahoo or google.com.

Restrictions

Pets: Although pets are allowed in Yellowstone National Park on a leash only, we strongly discouraged bringing them. Pets are not allowed out of the camping ares areas or off the main roads. Pets are not allowed in the backcountry or in any public viewing area. **Fires:** In fire pits only in approved areas, there are no open fires in Fishing Bridge (fires may be prohibited due to weather conditions, please ask before starting any open fire). **Alcoholic Beverages:** Yes. **Vehicle Maximum Length:** Depends on the campground of your choice, call and ask over the reservation line 800-329-9205 or 307-344-7311. **Other:** National Park passes are honored for entrance fees, golden age and golden access cards are *not* honored at all the campgrounds concessioned by Amfac, including Fishing Bridge.

To Get There

There are 5 entrances into Yellowstone; visit www.travelyellowstone.com for directions, or call to request a park map.

British Columbia

The region of Southwest British Columbia, as covered in this book, extends from the southeast end of the Fraser Valley in Hope, through the start of the Coast Mountains just north of Vancouver and ending in Pemberton. Within this small section of the large province of British Columbia, travelers can find a diverse array of activities and sights from cosmopolitan to wilderness.

Squamish and **Whistler** provide the major eco-tourism and outdoor sport centers for southwest British Columbia. Squamish prides itself on being cheaper than Whistler, and yet it's only a short drive away. Squamish has the same outdoor opportunities as Whistler, with one exception—skiing. Whistler is the province's premier western ski resort town. Organized recreation north of Whistler exists, but on a smaller scale.

Finally, a note on customs. Some products commercially available in the United States will cause trouble at the border. Melatonin is one, alligator meat is another. Anything that seems like drugs or paraphernalia without prescription will cause trouble. *Do not* take weapons into Canada. If arrested by customs for anything, you will be summarily fined, detained until you pay the fine, and your vehicle will be impounded (to be extricated only by payment of another, usually larger fine). If the offense is deemed large enough, the RCMP will be called and criminal charges may also be brought.

Additional Information

If travelling between Whistler and Pemberton, make sure to have plenty of gas in the tank. Though the distance is short, filling stations come in short supply anywhere north of Whistler. In some of northern British Colubmia and the Yukon, it is a good idea to fill up at every gas station along the way.

When going from Vancouver to Alaska or the Yukon, travellers have an alternative to the British Columbia leg of the Alaska Highway. Take the Cassiar Highway (Highway 37) running south from Highway 1 near Upper Liard, Yukon to Highway 16 and continuing on to Prince George, However be advised, this road is extremely rugged (both in environment and construction), very long, and scarcely populated or traversed along the northernmost 550 miles. Services exist, but just barely.

Camping in northern British Columbia and the Yukon involves little more than stopping at a pull out (*do not* camp in a slow vehicle turn out). Empty septic tanks at designated dump stations only, pack *all* trash to a commercial waste disposal pickup (gas station, etc.), be aware of bears and other animals (consider any wild animal potentially dangerous upon approach or confrontation), help people out with car trouble in wilderness areas (other wise they may be stuck for hours), and carry plenty of water. But if time doesn't permit the lengthy trip through the north country, enjoy the stay in southwest British Columbia.

The following facilities accept payment in checks or cash only:

Alice Lake Provincial Park, Squamish
Brandywine Falls Provincial Park, Whistler/Squamish
Gold Creek Campground (Golden Ears Provincial Park), Maple Ridge
Nairn Falls Provincial Park, Pemberton
Porteau Cove Provincial Park, Britannia Beach

Campground Profiles

ABBOTSFORD

Abbotsford Campground and RV

36114 Lower Sumas Mountain Rd., Abbotsford V3G 2J3. T: (604) 855-3330; F: (604) 855-7251.

RV ★★★★ | Tent ★★★★

Beauty: ★★★★ | Site Privacy: ★★★
Spaciousness: ★★★ | Quiet: ★★★
Security: ★★★ | Cleanliness: ★★★★
Insect Control: ★★ | Facilities: ★★★

Abbotsford Campground, 10 minutes north of the Sumas border crossing and just off Hwy. 1, has attractive landscaping and private tent sites. The hilly grounds have an enormous pool, two smaller hot tubs, a little shade from cedar trees, beautifully maintained grass, and a subtle scheme of potted flowers and shrubs. RV sites come in several flavors: flat grass, gravel, or paved, each with full hookups, and all positioned over gently rolling hills. Most RV sites lack privacy; sites 53–59 lack the flatness most other sites provide. The best paved, grass sites with full hookups, 60–69, sit on the south edge of the park. Extremely thick, tall cedar hedges mark the bounderies for most grass tent sites, creating walls of privacy. On the south edge of the park, there is a hill providing a small viewpoint with a spectacular view of Snowy Mount Baker rising from the horizon (no individual sites have any particularly striking views). Tent sites A1–A10 have the best privacy with cedar hedges on two sides and a hill on the third. Summer provides the best weather for visiting the area, however some grass RV sites may be closed during rainy periods.

Basics

Operated By: Abbotsford Camp and RV Park. **Open:** All year. **Site Assignment:** Walk up, reservations (deposit: 1 night stay; refund: 72 hours cancellation). **Registration:** At office, after hours pay in morning. **Fee:** For 2 people, full $27, water-electric $25, tent $21, MC, V, cash, personal checks (Canadian). **Parking:** At site, limited off site.

Facilities

Number of RV-Only Sites: 71. **Number of Tent-Only Sites:** 17. **Hookups:** Electric (15, 30 amps), water, sewer, cable. **Each Site:** Picnic table. **Dump Station:** Inquire at campground. **Laundry:** Inquire at campground. **Pay Phone:** Inquire at campground. **Rest Rooms and Showers:** Inquire at campground. **Fuel:** Inquire at campground. **Propane:** Inquire at campground. **Internal Roads:** Call ahead for details. **RV Service:** No. **Market:** 4 mi. west. **Restaurant:** 1 mi. south. **General Store:** No. **Vending:** Yes. **Swimming Pool:** Yes. **Playground:** Yes. **Other:** 2 hot tubs, reservable cabin (meeting hall), view point. **Activities:** Swimming. **Nearby Attractions:** Vancouver (45 minutes east), BC Farm Machinery and Agricultural Museum, Aldergrove Telephone Museum, Cheam Lake Wetlands Regional Park, Minter Gardens, golf. **Additional Information:** Fraser Valley Guide, (604) 820-0206; www.fraservalleyguide.com (very good site).

Restrictions

Pets: Leash only. **Fires:** No open fires. **Alcoholic Beverages:** At site. **Vehicle Maximum Length:** None. **Other:** Gates closed 11 p.m. to 7 a.m.

To Get There

From Hwy. 1 Exit 95 (Whatcom Road), go north 3 mi. and take first right onto Lower Sumas Mountain, drive 0.1 mi. and entrance is on the right.

BRITANNIA BEACH

Porteau Cove Provincial Park

Box 220, Brackendale V0I 1H0. T: (604) 898-3678; F: (604) 898-4171; wlapwww.gov.bc.ca/bcparks/explore/parkpgs/porteau.htm; gsdinfo@victoria1.gov.bc.ca.

RV ★★★ Tent ★★★

Beauty: ★★★★★	Site Privacy: ★★
Spaciousness: ★★★	Quiet: ★
Security: ★★	Cleanliness: ★★★
Insect Control: ★★	Facilities: ★★

Porteau Cove Provincial Park, located between Squamish and Vancouver, offers a large number of waterfront sites with beautiful views of silty Howe Sound and cloud-ringed, steep, evergreen-forested mountains rising sharply from the sea to the sky. The down side to the campground sits just to the east—the BC Rail tracks runs right next to the campground. The best sites within the grounds definitely have to be those by the water; sites 10, 11, 13, 14, and 17 sit furthest from the tracks (but are still very close). Sites 24–30 sit closest to the railroad. The campground has 16 walk in tent sites, but they lack fire pits and picnic tables, sit too close together, have little privacy, are very near the train tracks, and the sites themselves are small. With the exception of the noise, the campgrounds provide a beautiful, mild summer experience of BC's unique scenery.

Basics

Operated By: Peak To Valley Recreations for BC Parks. **Open:** All year, fully operational (with flush bathrooms, showers) Mar. 1–Oct. 31. **Site Assignment:** Walk in, reservations (Reservation service and campsite fees must be paid in full by V or MC at time of booking, campers are charged a non-refundable reservation service fee of $6.42 per night to a max of $19.26; refund: cancellation 7 days prior to arrival less $6.42 cancellation fee). **Registration:** At gate or collected at sites by attendant or at self pay station. **Fee:** Prices for 4 adults, 4 children, Sites–$18.50, Extra vehicle–$9.25, Adults ages 16 and over if traveling by themselves, Cash. **Parking:** At site.

Facilities

Number of RV-Only Sites: 0. **Number of Tent-Only Sites:** 16. **Number of Multipurpose Sites:** 44. **Hookups:** None. **Each Site:** Picnic table, grated fire pits. **Dump Station:** Inquire at campground. **Laundry:** Inquire at campground. **Pay Phone:** Inquire at campground. **Rest Rooms and Showers:** Inquire at campground. **Fuel:** Inquire at campground. **Propane:** Inquire at campground. **Internal Roads:** Call ahead for details. **RV Service:** No. **Market:** 10 mi. north. **Restaurant:** 6 mi. north. **General Store:** No. **Vending:** No. **Swimming Pool:** No. **Playground:** No. **Other:** Boat ramp, amphitheater, beach. **Activities:** Hiking, boating, salt water swimming, fishing (off boats only), scuba diving. **Nearby Attractions:** Scuba diving, BC Museum of Mining, ecotourism, Vancouver, Squamish, Whistler. **Additional Information:** Squamish Chamber of Commerce, (604) 892-9244.

Restrictions

Pets: Leash only. **Fires:** Fire pits only. **Alcoholic Beverages:** At site. **Vehicle Maximum Length:** 40 ft. **Other:** Don't gather dead or downed wood.

To Get There

The park entrance, driving north bound on Hwy. 99, is on the left 38 km (23.6 mi.) north of Vancouver and 8.5 (5.2 mi.) km south of Britannia Beach. 20 km (12.4 mi.) south of Squamish.

BURNABY (VANCOUVER)

Burnaby Cariboo RV Park

8765 Cariboo Place, Burnaby V3N 4T2. T: (604) 420-1722 or reservations (800) 667-9901; F: (604) 420-4782; www.bcrvpark.com; camping@bcrvpark.com.

RV ★★★ Tent ★★

Beauty: ★★★	Site Privacy: ★★★
Spaciousness: ★★★	Quiet: ★
Security: ★★★	Cleanliness: ★★★★
Insect Control: ★★	Facilities: ★★★

Burnaby Cariboo RV Park, or BC RV, located within close proximity to downtown Vancouver, offers an array of well-furnished facilities in a convenient location. However, active railroad runs near the facility, so noise here can be a problem. Paved, grass-bordered RV sites offer a large amount of privacy with thick cedar hedges on at least two sides, making the park look like a maze. The best RV sites ring the perimeter of the park with privacy on three sides and more area per site than those positioned on islands within the grounds; sites contained on islands vary greatly in size. Tenters have a small grassy area with open sites, and fine-grit gravel pads of varying sizes. Sites within the tenting area have little elbow room, but the section has a covered area with two large kitchen sinks for meal preparation. Vancouver has year-round tourist activities, but summer offers more amiable temperatures and less rain than the rest of the year.

Basics

Operated By: BCRV inc. **Open:** All year. **Site Assignment:** Walk up, reservations (deposit: 1 night stay; refund: 24 hours notice). **Registration:** At store, after hours see info on store front. **Fee:** For 2 people, Full–$34.75, Tent–$23, Cable–$2, Phone–$3, Ages 6 and younger–free, Ages 7-14–$2.50, Ages 15 and up–$3.50, RVs over 31 feet add $2.25/day, MC, V, D, Cash. **Parking:** At site and off site.

Facilities

Number of RV-Only Sites: 217. **Number of Tent-Only Sites:** 24. **Hookups:** Electric (30 amps), water, sewer, cable. **Each Site:** Picnic table. **Dump Station:** Inquire at campground. **Laundry:** Inquire at campground. **Pay Phone:** Inquire at campground. **Rest Rooms and Showers:** Inquire at campground. **Fuel:** Inquire at campground. **Propane:** Inquire at campground. **Internal Roads:** Call ahead for details. **RV Service:** No. **Market:** 4 mi. in Burnaby. **Restaurant:** 4 mi. in Burnaby. **General Store:** Yes. **Vending:** Yes. **Swimming Pool:** Yes, indoor. **Playground:** Yes. **Other:** Indoor pool, meeting room (large and nice), fitness room, Jacuzzi, sun bathing deck, tour bookings, rental car reservations, golf bookings, RV wash, horseshoes, outdoor cooking area. **Activities:** Aquafit classes once a week. **Nearby Attractions:** Golf, Simon Fraser University, Vancouver. **Additional Information:** Vancouver Tourist Info Center (604) 683-2000; www.tourism-vancouver.org.

Restrictions

Pets: Leash only, prefer small dogs. **Fires:** No open fires. **Alcoholic Beverages:** At site. **Vehicle Maximum Length:** 40 ft. **Other:** No boats in tow. No dogs in tenting area.

To Get There

From Hwy. 1, take Exit 37 and go north on Garlar and turn right at first light. Drive and turn left at first light onto Cariboo Rd. Drive 0.3 mi., turn right at light onto Cariboo Place and drive 0.1 mi., road dead ends into park.

CULTUS LAKE

Sunnyside Family Campground

3405 Columbia Valley Hwy., Cultus Lake V2R 5A3. T: (604) 858-5253; F: (604) 858-5263; www.cultuslake.bc.ca; cultuslake@dowco.com.

RV ★★★★ Tent ★★★

Beauty: ★★★★★ Site Privacy: ★
Spaciousness: ★★★ Quiet: ★★★
Security: ★★★★ Cleanliness: ★★★
Insect Control: ★★ Facilities: ★★★

Sunnyside Campground, a few minutes south of Hwy. 1 in the Fraser Valley, sits in the very popular vacation area of Cultus Lake. During summer, there exists no chance of entrance without a reservation; the campground teems with people and remains a cluttered sea of trailers and tents. The campground receives shade from a thick canopy of evergreens; individual sites consist of mostly dirt, with some gravel surfaces in the RV areas. In the overnighter area, RV sites sit arranged in parallel rows and tent sites line several avenues winding their way down to the lakefront. The best RV sites, numbered 1–18, back up to the northern perimeter of the park. Tent sites 121–127 sit very near the lake, isolated from the rest of the grounds; all tent sites have close neighbors and no privacy. The lengthy beach and some tent sites have beautiful vistas of the mountains that rise sharply beyond Cultus Lake's southern banks. In addition to the lake, the campground has an arcade, a large general store and a rec room frequently hosting family oriented planned activities. The best time for good weather and swimming is during the summer, and the best time to avoid crowds is a weekday during the off season.

BASICS

Operated By: Cultus Lakes Parks Board. **Open:** Apr. 1–Oct. 1. **Site Assignment:** Walk up, reservations (highly recommended; deposit: 1 night or ten percent of reservation; refund: 7 days cancellation). **Registration:** At gate, no after hours entrance without prior notification of office. **Fee:** For 2 people, Full–$30, Tenting regular–$22, Tenting, view–$25, Tenting waterfront–$28, Children under 16 free, Extra vehicle-1/2 of site charge, Extra RV or tent-Full site charge, Extra adults–$3, Pets–$2, MC, V, cash. **Parking:** At site.

FACILITIES

Number of RV-Only Sites: 104. **Number of Tent-Only Sites:** 132. **Hookups:** Electric (30 amps), water, sewer. **Each Site:** Picnic table, fire ring. **Dump Station:** Inquire at campground. **Laundry:** Inquire at campground. **Pay Phone:** Inquire at campground. **Rest Rooms and Showers:** Inquire at campground. **Fuel:** Inquire at campground. **Propane:** Inquire at campground. **Internal Roads:** Call ahead for details. **RV Service:** No. **Market:** 3 mi. north. **Restaurant:** 1.5 mi. North. **General Store:** Yes. **Vending:** Yes. **Swimming Pool:** No. **Playground:** Yes. **Other:** Boat launch, horseshoes, basketball, rec room, group BBQ, arcade, beach, moorage. **Activities:** Swimming, planned activities, daily kids programs. **Nearby Attractions:** Golf, water sports, hiking, Cultus Lake Provincial Park, Bridal Veil Falls, sport fishing, mountain biking, bird watching, mountain climbing, ATV's. **Additional Information:** Chilliwack Visitor Info Center (800) 567-9535; www.tourismchilliwack.com.

RESTRICTIONS

Pets: Leash only, not allowed on beach. **Fires:** Fire pits only. **Alcoholic Beverages:** At site. **Vehicle Maximum Length:** 45 ft. **Other:** No fishing from shore. No semi's pulling fifth wheels.

TO GET THERE

From Hwy. 1, take Exit 119B (Cultus Lake/Sardis), drive 3.8 mi. south on Vedder Rd. Turn left at light onto Cultus Lake Rd. Drive 2.8 mi. south on Cultus Lake, entrance on right with big wooden sign.

HARRISON HOT SPRINGS

Sasquatch Springs RV Resort

P.O.Box 400, Harrison Hot Springs V0M 1K0. T: (604) 796-9228; F: (604) 796-2040.

RV ★★★ Tent ★★

Beauty: ★★★★ Site Privacy: ★
Spaciousness: ★★ Quiet: ★★★
Security: ★★ Cleanliness: ★★★★
Insect Control: ★★ Facilities: ★★★

Sasquatch Springs RV Resort, in scenic Harrison Hot Springs, provides nearby access to Harrison Lake and the hot springs pool a few blocks away. The green park sits in one of the many valleys of the beautiful Northern Cascades and the property backs up to a steep, forested hill; in front of the park flows the narrow, silty, meandering Meama River. Campers can rent canoes to explore the river. There also exist several other recreational opportunities. Sites receive a small amount of shade from cedars and Japanese maples; they contain a mixture of gravel and grass with manicured, grassy perimeters, but lack privacy. The best full-hookup sites, numbered 53–68, line the banks of the river. Grass tent sites T11–T16 also line the river, but these sites sit in a higher traffic area; grassy, electric sites 92–97 provide amicable tent accommodations, backing up to the steep mountain behind the park. Avoid full hookup sites 18–21 because of their close proximity to each other. Weather during the summers tends to be cool and often overcast, so don't forget rain gear.

BASICS

Operated By: Sasquatch Springs RV Park. **Open:** Mar. 15–Oct. 30. **Site Assignment:** Walk up, reservation (deposit: 100 percent of reservation; refund: 10 days cancellation for 90% of deposit) Two day minimum on reservations in July and August. **Registration:** At office, no entry after 10 p.m. **Fee:** For 2 people, Full mountain side–$24, Full riverbank–$26, No hookup and tent–$19, Extra persons age 6-12–$2.50, Extra persons age 13 and older–$3, Under 6 years old-free, Cable–$2.50, MC, V, cash. **Parking:** At site, limited off site.

FACILITIES

Number of RV-Only Sites: 78. **Number of Tent-Only Sites:** 22. **Hookups:** Electric (15, 20, 30 amps), water, sewer, cable. **Each Site:** Picnic table, fire ring. **Dump Station:** Inquire at campground. **Laundry:** Inquire at campground. **Pay Phone:** Inquire at campground. **Rest Rooms and Showers:** Inquire at campground. **Fuel:** Inquire at campground. **Propane:** Inquire at campground. **Internal Roads:** Call ahead for details. **RV Service:** No. **Market:** 1 block north. **Restaurant:** Across the street. **General Store:** Yes. **Vending:** Yes. **Swimming Pool:** No. **Playground:** No. **Other:** Small arcade, pool, ping pong, TV/rec room, canoe rentals, horseshoes, badmitton, lawn games. **Activities:** Occasional planned activities, boating (no power). **Nearby Attractions:** Harrison Lake, Agassiz-Harrison Museum, Agassiz Agriculture Research Center, Dino Town, Hells Gate Airtram, Hemlock Valley Ski Resort, Sandsculpture Competition (September). **Additional Information:** Harrison, Agassiz Chamber of Commerce (604) 796-3425; www.harrison.ca; Fraser Valley Guide (604) 820-0206; www.fraservalleyguide.com (very good site).

RESTRICTIONS

Pets: Leash only. **Fires:** Only use wood purchased from office; in fire pits only. **Alcoholic Beverages:** At site. **Vehicle Maximum Length:** None. **Other:** Check in 12 p.m. Gate closed 10 p.m. (11 p.m. weekends).

TO GET THERE

From Hwy. 1 Exit 135, drive 10.7 mi. north on Hwy. 9. Hwy. 9 changes roads several times, the entrance is on the left just before downtown Harrison

HOPE

Hope Valley Campground

62280 Flood-Hope Rd., RR No. 2, Hope V0X 1L0. T: (604) 869-9857 or (866) 869-6660; F: (604) 869-7458.

RV ★★★ Tent ★★★

Beauty: ★★★★ Site Privacy: ★★★
Spaciousness: ★★★ Quiet: ★★★
Security: ★★ Cleanliness: ★★★
Insect Control: ★★ Facilities: ★★★

Hope Valley Campground, just off Hwy.1 in Hope, provides family-oriented accommodations on the edge of the wilderness. The melee of sites within the grounds have lots of thick shade and ground foliage, creating some privacy but sacrificing views; the older facilities have a well-maintained look. Consisting of pull-throughs near the front of the park, the small full hookup area has less of the rustic, woodland feel one finds throughout the rest of the park. Most RV sites have only water-electric hookups. The best water-electric sites consist of numbers 48–63 because of their privacy and intrasite spaciousness. Grass tent-only sites, T1–T22, along with water-electric sites 117–130, make up some of the most open sites on the property. All non T-prefixed sites consist of a mix of gravel and grass. Visit during the summer, but be aware that summers consist of cool and often rainy weather.

BASICS

Operated By: Hope Valley Campground. **Open:** Mar. 1–Oct. 31. **Site Assignment:** Walk up, reservation (deposit: 1 night stay; refund: 24 hours cancellation, 48 on holidays). **Registration:** At office. **Fee:**

For 2 people, Full–$25.50, Water-electric–$22.50, Extra children 4-17–$2, Extra adults–$3, Children under 3 free, MC,V, Cash. **Parking:** At site.

Facilities

Number of RV-Only Sites: 100. **Number of Tent-Only Sites:** 40. **Hookups:** Electric (15, 30 amps), water, sewer, cable. **Each Site:** Picnic table, fire ring. **Dump Station:** Inquire at campground. **Laundry:** Inquire at campground. **Pay Phone:** Inquire at campground. **Rest Rooms and Showers:** Inquire at campground. **Fuel:** Inquire at campground. **Propane:** Inquire at campground. **Internal Roads:** Call ahead for details. **RV Service:** No. **Market:** In Hope. **Restaurant:** In Hope. **General Store:** Yes. **Vending:** No. **Swimming Pool:** Yes. **Playground:** Yes. **Other:** Rec room with an arcade, 2 pool tables, volleyball, bike rentals. **Activities:** Swimming. **Nearby Attractions:** Chainsaw carvings, Cheam Lake Wetlands Regional Park, Coquihalla Canyon Provincial Park, Hell's Gate Air-Tram, golf, tons of ecotourism. **Additional Information:** Hope Visitor Info Center, (604) 869-2021; www.fraservalleyguide.com.

Restrictions

Pets: Leash only. **Fires:** Fire pits only. **Alcoholic Beverages:** Sites only. **Vehicle Maximum Length:** 45 ft. **Other:** Don't wash RVs.

To Get There

From Hwy. 1 west take Exit 165 and turn left off exit ramp. Road dead ends after 0.1 mi. Turn right onto Flood Hope Rd., drive 0.2 mi. and entrance is on the right. From Hwy. 1 East, take Exit 168 and turn right onto Flood Hope Rd., drive 1 mi. to entrance on left.

HOPE

Wild Rose Campground

62030 Flood Hope Rd., Hope V0X 1L2. T: (604) 869-9842; F: (604) 869-3171; wildrose@uniserve.com.

RV ★★★★ Tent ★★★

Beauty: ★★★★ Site Privacy: ★★
Spaciousness: ★★★ Quiet: ★★★
Security: ★★ Cleanliness: ★★★★
Insect Control: ★★ Facilities: ★★

Wild Rose Campground, off of Hwy.1 in Hope, offers a more adult-oriented setting in the beautiful, wild landscape of Hope. Lacking the in-house recreation most families seek, Wild Rose consists primarily of two rows of well manicured, grassy sites. Much of the grounds receives shade from numerous beautiful fir trees, and most sites have good views of the rugged mountains surrounding the Fraser Valley. The tent section, numbers 61–68, lacks an abundance of shade, but individual sites have some privacy created by cedars and the best, unobstructed mountain views. The largest RV sites, 22–26 and 41–45, have a mixture of shade and views. The pull-through section is extremely shady. The least attractive sites, 51-60, receive such a label due to their smaller size. Even during the summer the weather tends to be cool and rainy, so make sure and keep rain gear handy.

Basics

Operated By: Wild Rose Campground. **Open:** Apr. 1–Sept 30. **Site Assignment:** Walk up, reservations (deposit: 1 night stay; refund 48 hours cancellation). **Registration:** At office. **Fee:** For 2 people, Full–$24, No hookup–$20, Extra person–$2, MC,V, cash. **Parking:** At site.

Facilities

Number of RV-Only Sites: 60. **Number of Tent-Only Sites:** 8. **Hookups:** Electric (15, 30 amps), water, sewer, cable. **Each Site:** Picnic table. **Dump Station:** Inquire at campground. **Laundry:** Inquire at campground. **Pay Phone:** Inquire at campground. **Rest Rooms and Showers:** Inquire at campground. **Fuel:** Inquire at campground. **Propane:** Inquire at campground. **Internal Roads:** Call ahead for details. **RV Service:** No. **Market:** 3 mi. east in Hope. **Restaurant:** 0.1 mi. west. **General Store:** Yes. **Vending:** No. **Swimming Pool:** No. **Playground:** Yes. **Other:** Rec room, volleyball, horseshoes. **Activities:** Inquire at campground. **Nearby Attractions:** Dinotown, Hell's Gate Air-Tram, Hiking, Japanese Friendship Gardens, Trans-Canada Water Slide, (Rambo: First Blood was filmed in Hope). **Additional Information:** Hope Visitor Info Center, (604) 869-2021; www.fraservalleyguide.com.

Restrictions

Pets: Short leash only, quiet dogs only. **Fires:** Fire pits only. **Alcoholic Beverages:** At site. **Vehicle Maximum Length:** None. **Other:** No outdoor music.

To Get There

From Hwy. 1 west, take Exit 165 and turn left off exit ramp. Road dead ends after 0.1 mi.. Turn right onto Flood Hope road, drive 0.5 mi. and entrance is on the right From Hwy. 1 East, take Exit 168 and turn right onto Flood Hope Rd., drive 1.3 mi. and entrance on left.

MAPLE RIDGE

Gold Creek Campground (Golden Ears Provincial Park)

1610 Mt. Seymour Rd., North Vancouver V7G 2R9. T: (604) 924-2200; F: (604) 924-2244; wlapwww.gov.bc.ca/bcparks/explore/parkpgs/golden.htm; lmdinfo@victoria1.gov.bc.ca.

RV ★★★ Tent ★★★★

Beauty: ★★★★★ Site Privacy: ★★
Spaciousness: ★★★ Quiet: ★★★★
Security: ★★ Cleanliness: ★★★
Insect Control: ★★ Facilities: ★★

Golden Ears Provincial Park, located northeast of Vancouver, offers a very quiet, wilderness environment near the city. The park has three separate campgrounds, all close to one another; Gold Creek Campground has the only showers and flushers in the park. Sites have an arrangement on parallel, one-way avenues with numbers relative to the avenue's initials. All sites have the setting of a beautiful, heavily shaded cedar forest with a green floor resulting from moss and lichen growth on feeder logs, a very delicate environment to maintain effectively. The flat, gravel sites look like those of most provincial parks. This park is a highly popular and stays crowded during the summer, but two days after labor day the park turns into a ghost-town. The only sites to avoid sit on Trilium Drive, the main access loop to the rest of the grounds, and on Plantain Lane, another high traffic area. Sites do not adjoin, but they lack visual privacy due to the land formation in the campground. Summers here have cool temperatures, magnified by the shadiness of the area so make sure to pack accordingly.

Basics

Operated By: BC Parks. **Open:** All year, fully operational Apr. 6–Oct. 8. **Site Assignment:** Walk up, reservations available Apr. 6-Sept. 15 (Reservation service and campsite fees must be paid in full by V or MC at time of booking; campers are charged a non-refundable reservation service fee $6.42 per night to a max of $19.26; refund: cancellation 7 days prior to arrival less $6.42 cancellation fee). **Registration:** At gate or self pay stations. **Fee:** For four adults, Site–$18.50, extra vehicle–$9.25, rates for 4 adults and 4 children (under 16 years old, cash only upon arrival. **Parking:** At site.

Facilities

Number of RV-Only Sites: 0. **Number of Tent-Only Sites:** 0. **Number of Multipurpose Sites:** 138. **Hookups:** None. **Each Site:** Picnic table, fire ring. **Dump Station:** Inquire at campground. **Laundry:** Inquire at campground. **Pay Phone:** Inquire at campground. **Rest Rooms and Showers:** Inquire at campground. **Fuel:** Inquire at campground. **Propane:** Inquire at campground. **Internal Roads:** Call ahead for details. **RV Service:** No. **Market:** 20 mi. south in Maple Ridge. **Restaurant:** 20 mi. south in Maple Ridge. **General Store:** No. **Vending:** No. **Swimming Pool:** No. **Playground:** No. **Other:** Free firewood, hiking trails, interpretive trails, beach, Amphitheater. **Activities:** Interpretive programs in summer, hiking, swimming, biking. **Nearby Attractions:** Mountain Biking, canoeing, fishing, golfing, the Haney House (Homestead museum), hiking, horseback riding, skydiving, UBC Research Forest. **Additional Information:** Pitt Meadows Visitor Information Centre, (604) 460-8300.

Restrictions

Pets: Leash only. **Fires:** Fire pits only. **Alcoholic Beverages:** At site. **Vehicle Maximum Length:** 40 ft. **Other:** Don't gather dead or downed foliage.

To Get There

From Maple Ridge (located on Hwy. 7 north of Fraser River), drive east on Golden Ears Pkwy to entrance.

NORTH VANCOUVER

Capilano RV Park

295 North Tomahawk Ave., North Vancouver V7P 1C5. T: (604) 987-4722; F: (604) 987-2015; www.capilanorvpark.com; capilanorvpark.com.

RV ★★★ Tent ★★

Beauty: ★★ Site Privacy: ★
Spaciousness: ★★★ Quiet: ★★

Security: ★★★ Cleanliness: ★★★★
Insect Control: ★★ Facilities: ★★★★

Capilano RV Park, located in Metro Northwest Vancouver, offers convenient access to shopping and the city. The park has an indoor hot tub, a shopping mall within walking distance, and wide, easily navigable roads. Paved, grass perimetered back-in sites with full hookups sit back to back; cedar hedges provide some rear privacy, but no privacy on the sides or shade above. Sites 1-105 provide the best accommodations. A slight view of mountains to the north (largely eclipsed by tall condos) provides a backdrop for the urban campground, although individual sites have a view of little more than their neighbors. The tenting section lies on park's perimeter, with grass sites and gravel parking; sites 128-140 have partial shade. Because of its urban location, the park receives some noise from the surrounding city. Visit Vancouver during the summer, but even then weather can be crisp or rainy.

Basics

Operated By: Capilano RV Park. **Open:** All year. **Site Assignment:** Walk in, reservations (No deposit, will hold reservation after 6 p.m. on arrival date with credit card only; cancel as soon as possible). **Registration:** At office. **Fee:** For two people, Full–$38, Water-electric–$33, Extra vehicle–$10, Pet–$2/day, No hookup and tent–$28, Extra persons–$3.50, Five years old or younger–Free, V, MC, cash, Canadian travelers checks. **Parking:** At site, off site parking at additional charge.

Facilities

Number of RV-Only Sites: 208. **Number of Tent-Only Sites:** 29. **Hookups:** Electric (15, 30, 50 amps), water, sewer, cable. **Each Site:** Picnic table. **Dump Station:** Inquire at campground. **Laundry:** Inquire at campground. **Pay Phone:** Inquire at campground. **Rest Rooms and Showers:** Inquire at campground. **Fuel:** Inquire at campground. **Propane:** Inquire at campground. **Internal Roads:** Call ahead for details. **RV Service:** No. **Market:** Next door. **Restaurant:** Next door. **General Store:** No. **Vending:** Yes. **Swimming Pool:** Yes. **Playground:** Yes. **Other:** Small arcade, Jacuzzi, TV room. **Activities:** Swimming. **Nearby Attractions:** Lions Gate Bridge, False Creek, Point Grey, Stanley Park, Vancouver Harbor, Vancouver International Wine Festival, Capilano Salmon Hatchery, Chinatown, skiing. **Additional Information:** Vancouver Tourist Info Center, (604) 683-2000; www.tourism-vancouver.org.

Restrictions

Pets: Leash only. **Fires:** No open fires. **Alcoholic Beverages:** At site. **Vehicle Maximum Length:** 48 ft. **Other:** Quiet hours 9 p.m.–8 a.m.

To Get There

From Hwy. 99, take Exit 14 (just west of Lion's Gate Bridge) to Capilano Rd. Go south on Capilano 0.6 mi. and go through Marine intersection and take left fork. Drive 0.4 mi. to a stop and turn right on Welch Street. Drive 0.4 mi. to a stop and turn right following RV park signs. Drive 0.2 mi. and turn right following RV park signs, entrance is just across a right angle turn.

PEMBERTON

Nairn Falls Provincial Park

Box 220, Brackendale V0N 1H0. T: (604) 898-3678 or reservations (800) 689-9025; F: (604) 898-4171; www.env.gov.bc.ca/bcparks/explore/parkpgs/nairn.htm; gsdinfo@victoria1.gov.bc.ca.

RV ★★★★ Tent ★★★★

Beauty: ★★★★★ Site Privacy: ★★★
Spaciousness: ★★★ Quiet: ★★★★
Security: ★★★ Cleanliness: ★★★
Insect Control: ★★ Facilities: ★★

Nairn Falls Provincial Park, just south of Pemberton, offers a quiet, wilderness setting just out of reach of the heavy tourist traffic found to the south in Whistler. Best described as primitive, the campground does not have flush toilets but does have potable water. Non-adjacent sites sit in an arrangement of parallel rows, creating a semi-private environment. Further, some sites have amazing views of nearby Green River and the mountains. These sites, 48–51, lack the privacy that can be found in the rest of the park and sit on a ridge, subject to a cold breeze at times. Sites with the most privacy sit on the exterior perimeters of the park and have no neighbors to the rear. All sites have gravel surfaces, a fair amount of room, and lots of shade from the overhead forest. The scenery here is incredible. The summers provide the best time to visit; even so, the mountain weather seldom gets very warm, so be prepared for cool temperatures.

Basics

Operated By: BC Parks. **Open:** May 1–Sept. 30. **Site Assignment:** Walk up, reservations (Reservation service and campsite fees must be paid in full by V or MC at time of booking, campers are charged a non-refundable reservation service fee $6.42 per night to a max of $19.26; refund: cancellation 7 days prior to arrival less $6.42 cancellation fee). **Registration:** Fees collected at sites by attendants, after hours pay in morning—host or drop box located by info station. **Fee:** For 4 adults, 4 children (under 16 years old), Site–$12, Extra vehicle–$6, cash only upon arrival. **Parking:** At site, limited off site.

Facilities

Number of RV-Only Sites: 0. **Number of Tent-Only Sites:** 0. **Number of Multipurpose Sites:** 88. **Hookups:** None. **Each Site:** Picnic table, fire ring. **Dump Station:** Inquire at campground. **Laundry:** Inquire at campground. **Pay Phone:** Inquire at campground. **Rest Rooms and Showers:** Inquire at campground. **Fuel:** Inquire at campground. **Propane:** Inquire at campground. **Internal Roads:** Call ahead for details. **RV Service:** No. **Market:** North in Pemberton; limited. **Restaurant:** North in Pemberton, limited. **General Store:** No. **Vending:** No. **Swimming Pool:** No. **Playground:** No. **Other:** Hiking trails. **Activities:** Fishing, hiking, wildlife viewing, birdwatching. **Nearby Attractions:** Horseback riding, river rafting, mountain biking, ecotourism. **Additional Information:** Pemberton and District Chamber of Commerce, (604) 894-6175.

Restrictions

Pets: Leash only. **Fires:** Fire pits only. **Alcoholic Beverages:** At site. **Vehicle Maximum Length:** 38 ft. **Other:** Be aware of areas designated no pets. Do not gather dead or down foliage, habitat sensitive. Use suitable grey water containers. Be aware of bear procedures.

To Get There

Driving north on Hwy. 99, entrance is on right just south of Pemberton and about 30 minutes north of Whistler

ROSEDALE (CHILLIWACK)

Chilliwack RV Park and Campground

50850 Hack Brown Rd., Rosedale V0X 1X0. T: (604) 794-7800; F: (604) 794-7800.

RV ★★★ Tent ★

Beauty: ★★★ Site Privacy: ★★
Spaciousness: ★★★ Quiet: ★★★
Security: ★★ Cleanliness: ★★★
Insect Control: ★★ Facilities: ★★

Chilliwack RV Park and Campground, just off the Trans-Canadian Highway in Chilliwack, provides a base for day trips to the surrounding areas. The park receives some noise from nearby Hwy. 1 and can be a little dusty, but also has beautiful panoramic views of the surrounding mountains. Limited recreational facilities make this property less family oriented than other parks in the area. Numbers 36–50, the best gravel full hookup sites, climb up a shady, gentle hill in the back of the park but have only obscured views of the surrounding scenery and no privacy. With less shade, sites 12–18 have some privacy provided by shrubbery and less obscured views of the distant scenery. The grass tent sites lack good shade or any privacy. The mild summers can be rainy here, so make sure to have rain gear handy.

Basics

Operated By: Chilliwack RV Park. **Open:** All year. **Site Assignment:** Walk up, reservation (deposit: 1 night stay; refund: 7 days notice of cancellation. **Registration:** At office, after hours pay in morning. **Fee:** For 2 people, Full–$22, Water-electric–$20, Tent–$18, Extra person–$2, Cable $2 extra, Pets–$1 per pet per day, Max 4 adults per site, MC, V, cash. **Parking:** At site.

Facilities

Number of RV-Only Sites: 58. **Number of Tent-Only Sites:** 15. **Hookups:** Electric (15, 30 amps), water, sewer, cable. **Each Site:** Picnic table, fire ring. **Dump Station:** Inquire at campground. **Laundry:** Inquire at campground. **Pay Phone:** Inquire at campground. **Rest Rooms and Showers:** Inquire at campground. **Fuel:** Inquire at campground. **Propane:** Inquire at campground. **Internal Roads:** Call ahead for details. **RV Service:** No. **Market:** 4 mi. north in Rosedale. **Restaurant:** 4 mi. North in Rosedale. **General Store:** Yes. **Vending:** No. **Swimming Pool:** No. **Playground:** Yes. **Other:** Horseshoe pits, meeting room, gazebo. **Activities:** Blackberry picking (in season). **Nearby Attractions:** Bridal Veil Falls Provincial Park, Minter Gardens, Trans Canada Water Slide, Harrison Watersports, Chilliwack River Rafting. **Additional Information: Tourism Chilliwack Info Center (800) 567-9535; www.fraservalleyguide.com.

Restrictions

Pets: Leash only, max 2 per site. **Fires:** Fire pits only. **Alcoholic Beverages:** At site. **Vehicle Maximum Length:** None. **Other:** Inquire at campground.

To Get There

From Hwy. 1 Exit 129 (west bound turn left), cross Annis road, go down Hwy. 1 east entrance ramp and take right fork onto Hack-Brown Rd., drive 0.3 mi. and entrance is on right

SQUAMISH

Alice Lake Provincial Park

Box 220, Brackendale V0N 1H0. T: (604) 898-3678 or reservations (800) 689-9025; F: (604) 898-4171; www.env.gov.bc.ca/bcparks/explore/parkpgs/alicelk.htm; gsdinfo@victoria1.gov.bc.ca.

RV ★★★ Tent ★★★★

Beauty: ★★★★ Site Privacy: ★★
Spaciousness: ★★★ Quiet: ★★★★
Security: ★★★ Cleanliness: ★★★
Insect Control: ★★ Facilities: ★★

Alice Lake Provincial Park, just minutes north of Squamish, offers the widest array of facilities of any provincial park in the area. Translated, this means flush toilets and showers. The campground has an organization of loops off a main road and non-adjacent, shady, semi-private gravel sites in a beautifully forested area. Sites 56–96 make up a loop with less site density than the other main section, sites 1–55. Within the former, sites 79–86 have the most privacy of any in the grounds. There also exist some sites near Alice Lake, numbered 61–68, but these get quite chilly with the wind they receive from the lake. In the latter section, sites 9–55 have a very high site density and not much privacy. The park has walk-in tent sites, and although these sit in an area slightly segregated from the main sections, they have no privacy within their area. Busy during the summer, the campground buzzes with families, especially on weekends. Otherwise, the campground stays free of ambient environmental noise. Summers are the best time to visit, but even then the weather has a crisp feel.

Basics

Operated By: Ben Hubbard for BC Parks. **Open:** Maintained with showers, flushers Mar. 1–Oct. 31; accessible all year. **Site Assignment:** Walk in, reservations highly recommended 90 days prior to arrival (Reservation service and campsite fees must be paid in full by V or MC at time of booking, campers are charged a non-refundable reservation service fee $6.42 per night to a max of $19.26; refund: cancellation 7 days prior to arrival less $6.42 cancellation fee). **Registration:** At gate, after hours pay in morning if entrance possible, sites available. **Fee:** For four adults, Site–$18.50, Extra vehicle–$9.25, rates for 4 adults and 4 children (under 16 years old), cash only upon arrival, reserved sites already paid in full upon arrival. **Parking:** At site.

Facilities

Number of RV-Only Sites: 0. **Number of Tent-Only Sites:** 11. **Number of Multipurpose Sites:** 96. **Hookups:** None. **Each Site:** Picnic table, fire ring. **Dump Station:** Inquire at campground. **Laundry:** Inquire at campground. **Pay Phone:** Inquire at campground. **Rest Rooms and Showers:** Inquire at campground. **Fuel:** Inquire at campground. **Propane:** Inquire at campground. **Internal Roads:** Call ahead for details. **RV Service:** No. **Market:** 10 min. south in Squamish. **Restaurant:** 10 min. south in Squamish. **General Store:** No. **Vending:** No. **Swimming Pool:** No. **Playground:** Yes. **Other:** Hiking trails, amphitheater, firewood (free), kayak rentals, changing rooms at beach. **Activities:** Hiking, interpretive programs (Thursday-Sunday in summers), fishing, swimming, mountain biking, kayaking, canoeing. **Nearby Attractions:** Hiking, mountain biking, fishing, rock climbing, adventure tours, ecotourism, Garibaldi Provincial Park. **Additional Information:** Squamish Chamber of Commerce, (604) 892-9244; www.squamishchamber.bc.ca/main.htm.

Restrictions

Pets: Leash only. **Fires:** Fire pits only. **Alcoholic Beverages:** At site. **Vehicle Maximum Length:** 40 ft. **Other:** Gates closed 11p.m. to 7 a.m., page security for entry. Be aware of areas designated no pets. Do not gather dead or down foliage, habitat sensitive. Use suitable grey water containers. Be aware of bear procedures.

To Get There

From Hwy. 99N, turn right on Alice Lake Rd. approx. 7 mi. north of Squamish. Drive 0.7 mi. and take left fork, drive 0.3 mi. further and entrance is on the right at gate house

SQUAMISH

Dryden Creek Resort and Campground

P.O.Box 1012, Garibaldi Highlands V0N 1T0. T: (604) 898-9726; F: (604) 898-9780; www.drydencreek.com; dryden@uniserve.com.

RV ★★★★ Tent ★★★

Beauty: ★★★★ Site Privacy: ★★
Spaciousness: ★★★ Quiet: ★★★
Security: ★★ Cleanliness: ★★★★
Insect Control: ★★ Facilities: ★★

Dryden Creek Resort and Campground, located just north of Squamish on Hwy. 99, offers close access to a plethora of outdoor recreation. The small campground has a quaint, enchanted forest feel, and offers a variety of sites. On top of backing up to a beautiful gray, rocky ridge forested with evergreens, the park also has a Salmon spawning creek running through it. RV sites in the west section of the park offer a more forested feel, but sit in a higher traffic area. The best gravel RV sites, E1–E8, sit in the east section of the park, half of which back up to the cliffs at the rear of the park. These sites have an open feel, no privacy, and grass perimeters. Within the tenting section there exist two types of sites, ones positioned in a grassy area with little shade or privacy, and ones that sit in a wooded area with more privacy but also gravel and dirt surfaces. The latter, sites N10–N14, have the most shade from tall cedars characteristic of the area. Surrounding areas provides year-round outdoor recreation, summers have mild and sometimes rainy weather, winters bring snow and world-class skiing.

Basics

Operated By: Dryden Creek Resorts. **Open:** All year. **Site Assignment:** Walk up, reservations (deposit: full cost of stay; refund: 48 hours less $6 cancellation fee). **Registration:** At office, after hours arrival call ahead before close. **Fee:** For 2 people, full $24, tent $18.50, weekly rates 10% off, extra people older than 18 or traveling without parents $2.20, extra people 18 and younger $1.12, V, MC, cash. **Parking:** At site.

Facilities

Number of RV-Only Sites: 29. **Number of Tent-Only Sites:** 20. **Hookups:** Electric (30 amps), water, sewer, cable. **Each Site:** Picnic table, fire ring. **Dump Station:** Inquire at campground. **Laundry:** Inquire at campground. **Pay Phone:** Inquire at campground. **Rest Rooms and Showers:** Inquire at campground. **Fuel:** Inquire at campground. **Propane:** Inquire at campground. **Internal Roads:** Call ahead for details. **RV Service:** No. **Market:** South in Squamish. **Restaurant:** South in Squamish. **General Store:** Yes. **Vending:** No. **Swimming Pool:** No. **Playground:** No. **Other:** Motel, group camping, one canoe for rental, German and Spanish speaking staff. **Activities:** Occasional church on Sundays, stream fishing. **Nearby Attractions:** Mountain Biking, wind surfing, rock climbing, salmon spawning trails, ecotourism. **Additional Information:** Squamish Chamber of Commerce, (604) 892-9244; www.squamishchamber.bc.ca.

Restrictions

Pets: Leash only. **Fires:** Fire pits only. **Alcoholic Beverages:** At site. **Vehicle Maximum Length:** 40 ft. **Other:** Check in 3 p.m. Stream regulated for fishing, check with office before fishing.

To Get There

On Hwy. 99, drive 1.7 mi. north of Burger King on north edge of Squamish/Brackendale. Turn right onto Depot Rd., take an almost immediate left and drive up entry drive into campground.

VANCOUVER (RICHMOND)

Richmond RV Park

6200 River Rd., Richmond V7C 5G1. T: (604) 270-7878 or voice mail (800) 755-4905; F: (604) 244-9713; www.richmondrvpark.com; richmondrv@aol.com.

RV ★★★ Tent ★★

Beauty: ★★ Site Privacy: ★
Spaciousness: ★★★ Quiet: ★★
Security: ★★★ Cleanliness: ★★★
Insect Control: ★★ Facilities: ★

Richmond RV Park, located in what can be considered downtown Vancouver, offers easy access to the city. The park has a good, relatively secure location. Constant, heavy traffic in surrounding areas and urban noise such as airliners overhead make the grounds unsuitable for travelers looking for exceptional quiet and slow moving relaxation; management assures the train tracks in the back of the park have been dead for some time. The pull-through sites 205–275 have a very cramped feeling. The grounds contain a multitude of back-ins with homogenous attributes; a flat field makes up the gravel and grass sites. The bare-bones park has a design lending itself to little more than a jumping off point for the city. Grass tent sites 276–292 (even numbered only) sit around the perimeter of the park; the best offer a reasonable amount of space. The bathrooms here have lots of stalls, no waiting in line for a shower. Vancouver has tourism year-round, but summer offers the most activities.

BASICS

Operated By: Richmond RV Park. **Open:** Apr. 1–Oct. 31. **Site Assignment:** Walk in, reservations (deposit: 1 nights stay; refund: 24 hours notice). **Registration:** At office, after hours see instructions on office door. **Fee:** For 2 people, Back-in (RVs 22 feet and over)–$25, Back-in (RVs 21 feet and under)–$23, Pull-through–$27, No hookup and tent–$17, Additional persons 7 years and older–$3, Under 7 years old–free, V, MC, U.S and Canadian cash, travelers checks. **Parking:** At site, off site available.

FACILITIES

Number of RV-Only Sites: 200. **Number of Tent-Only Sites:** 75. **Hookups:** Electric (15, 30 amps), water. **Each Site:** Picnic table. **Dump Station:** Inquire at campground. **Laundry:** Inquire at campground. **Pay Phone:** Inquire at campground. **Rest Rooms and Showers:** Inquire at campground. **Fuel:** Inquire at campground. **Propane:** Inquire at campground. **Internal Roads:** Call ahead for details. **RV Service:** No. **Market:** 3 mi. east. **Restaurant:** 3 mi. east. **General Store:** Yes. **Vending:** No. **Swimming Pool:** No. **Playground:** No. **Other:** Tour booking, gameroom, shuttle to Alaska Ferry Cruise dock and RV storage ($), mobile dump station, grill loans. **Activities:** Inquire at campground. **Nearby Attractions:** IMAX Theatre, Watermania, Steverson Fishing Village, Stanley Park, Lion's Gate Bridge, Queen Elizabeth Park, Gastown, Downtown Vancouver. **Additional Information:** Vancouver Tourist Info Center (604) 683-2000; www.tourism-vancouver.org.

RESTRICTIONS

Pets: Leash only. **Fires:** No open fires. **Alcoholic Beverages:** At site. **Vehicle Maximum Length:** None. **Other:** 30 day max stay limit.

TO GET THERE

From Hwy. 99, take Exit 36 (Westminster Hwy., always high traffic) and drive 3.4 mi. west on Westminster Hwy. Turn right on No 2 Rd, drive less than 1 block and take off ramp to the right to River Road. Turn right onto River Road and drive 0.3 mi., entrance on the right.

VANCOUVER (SURREY)

Dogwood Campground and RV Park

15151 112th Ave., Surrey V3R 6G8. T: (604) 583-5585; F: (604) 583-4725.

RV ★★ Tent ★★

Beauty: ★★	Site Privacy: ★
Spaciousness: ★★★	Quiet: ★★★
Security: ★★★	Cleanliness: ★
Insect Control: ★★	Facilities: ★★

Dogwood Campground in Surry, located about 20 minutes east of municipal Vancouver, offers a convenient location just outside the city. The park has areas for both overnight and seasonal accommodations, in addition to grassy tent sites that make up the perimeter of the park. The homogenous overnight section of the park consists of four rows of back-in sites, either grass or paved and surrounded by grass, open and adjacent on two sides. Overnighters can be put in a seasonal site if one is requested and available. Essential facilities have a clean, reasonably well kept interior appearance, but the grounds and building exteriors look quite run down and in need of cosmetic maintenance. Regarding tent sites, they lack privacy and many lack shade; the shadiest sites, 178–193, sit under oak and elm. Avoid tent sites 333–351 as they sit near the highway with some noise issues. Vancouver has a beautiful mild summer and rainy, cool to cold weather every other season.

BASICS

Operated By: Dogwood Campground. **Open:** All year. **Site Assignment:** Walk in, reservations (deposit: 1 night stay; refund: 24 hour notice). **Registration:** At office, after hours see instructions posted outside office. **Fee:** Full–$30, For 2 people (regarding tents only), Tent–$19.50, Extra persons 12 years or older tenting–$3. **Parking:** At site.

FACILITIES

Number of RV-Only Sites: 209. **Number of Tent-Only Sites:** 150. **Hookups:** Electric (30 amps), water, sewer, cable. **Each Site:** Picnic table. **Dump Station:** Inquire at campground. **Laundry:** Inquire at campground. **Pay Phone:** Inquire at campground. **Rest Rooms and Showers:** Inquire at campground. **Fuel:** Inquire at campground. **Propane:** Inquire at campground. **Internal Roads:** Call ahead for details. **RV Service:** No. **Market:** 2 mi. east in Surrey. **Restaurant:** 2 mi. east in Surrey. **General Store:** Yes. **Vending:** Yes. **Swimming Pool:** Yes. **Playground:** Yes. **Other:** Jacuzzi, rec. hall, arcade, volleyball, badmitton, horseshoes, tour bookings, Gray Line tours pick-up. **Activities:** Swimming, lawn games. **Nearby Attractions:** Stanley Park and Aquarium, Vancouver Aquarium, Grouse Mountain Chairlift, Capilano Suspension Bridge, Downtown Vancouver. **Additional Information:** City of Surrey, (604) 591-4811; www.city.surrey.bc.ca; Vancouver Tourist Info Center (604) 683-2000; www.tourism-vancouver.org.

RESTRICTIONS

Pets: Leash only. **Fires:** No open fires. **Alcoholic Beverages:** At site. **Vehicle Maximum Length:** 45 ft.

TO GET THERE

From the Hwy. 1 Exit, go north on 160th Street for 0.7 mi. and turn left on 108th Ave at the light with ScotiaBank. Follow 108th Ave for 1 mi., where it turns into 154th St. Drive 0.2 mi. on 154th St and turn left on 112th Ave which dead ends into the campground.

VANCOUVER (SURREY)

Hazelmere RV Park and Campground

18843 8th Ave., Surrey V4P 1M7. T: (604) 538-1167; F: (604) 538-1080; www.globalserve.net/~hazelmere; hazelmere@globalserve.net.

RV ★★★ Tent ★★

Beauty: ★★★	Site Privacy: ★
Spaciousness: ★★★	Quiet: ★★★
Security: ★★★	Cleanliness: ★★★★
Insect Control: ★★★	Facilities: ★★★★

Hazelmere RV Park, located in a rural area of Surrey and just south of Vancouver, offers large open spaces and a unique summer attraction. The campground has two large open grassy areas, accounting for much of the acreage; one field gets use as a group camping area and the other frequently hosts hot air balloon launches during the summer months. The park includes a large seasonal area (monthly rentals) and a smaller overnight section. Sites in the overnight section have gravel surfaces surrounded by grass, with a little shade and no privacy. The tent section consists of sites on the edge of the group camping area. The better RV sites, numbers 112–115 and 127–129, offer the best of the partial shade available. Sitting in the back of the park, the overnight section offers quiet, and backs up to a small river. Tent sites 152–155 sit on a slope and are not very flat. Summer is the best time to come to the Vancouver area.

BASICS

Operated By: Hazelmere RV Park. **Open:** All year. **Site Assignment:** Walk in, reservations (deposit: 1 night's stay; refund: cancel 4 days before arrival). **Registration:** At office, after hours at drop box or see caretaker. **Fee:** For 2 people: Full–$27.82, Electric-water RV–$24.61, Electric-water Tent–$23.54, Tent–$21.40, Extra people 7 years and up–$2, under 7 free, max 4 people per site, MC, V, cash. **Parking:** At site, limited off site.

FACILITIES

Number of RV-Only Sites: 160. **Number of Tent-Only Sites:** 8-plus. **Hookups:** Electric (15, 30 amps), water, sewer, cable. **Each Site:** Picnic table, fire ring. **Dump Station:** Inquire at campground. **Laundry:** Inquire at campground. **Pay Phone:** Inquire at campground. **Rest Rooms and Showers:** Inquire at campground. **Fuel:** Inquire at campground. **Propane:** Inquire at campground. **Internal Roads:** Call ahead for details. **RV Service:** No. **Market:** 10 min. north in Surrey. **Restaurant:** 10 min. North in Surrey. **General Store:** Yes. **Vending:** No. **Swimming Pool:** Yes. **Playground:** Yes. **Other:** Volleyball, basketball, soccer, horseshoes, rec room w/ pool table and 3 arcade games, picnic shelter, hot tub, exercise room, hot air balloon rides (summer), trails to fish hatchery. **Activities:** Ballooning, hiking. **Nearby Attractions:** Golf, Peace Arch Park, Bear Creek Park, Green Timbers Urban Forest, Redwood Park, Vancouver, Semiahmoo Fish Hatchery. **Additional Information:** City of Surrey, (604) 591-4811, www.city.surrey.bc.ca; Vancouver Tourist Info Center (604) 683-2000; www.tourism-vancouver.org.

RESTRICTIONS

Pets: Leash only (except for dog exercise area). **Fires:** Fire pits only. **Alcoholic Beverages:** At site, picnic areas. **Vehicle Maximum Length:** None. **Other:** Check in 12 p.m.

TO GET THERE

From Hwy. 15 just north of Blaine border crossing, turn right (east) on 8th Ave and drive 1.5 mi., entrance on the left. From Hwy. 99 just north of the border, take Exit 2 (8th Ave) and drive 2.5 mi. east, entrance on the left.

VANCOUVER (SURREY)

Peace Arch RV Park

14601 40th Ave., Surrey V4P 2J9. T: (604) 594-7009; F: (604) 597-4220; www.peacearchrvpark.com; info@peacearchrvpark.com.

RV ★★★★ Tent ★★

Beauty: ★★★ Site Privacy: ★★★★
Spaciousness: ★★★ Quiet: ★★★
Security: ★★★ Cleanliness: ★★★★
Insect Control: ★★ Facilities: ★★★★

Peace Arch RV Park, located about 10 minutes north of the Blaine, WA border crossing, houses beautiful, flowering shrubs and many private pull-throughs. Colored by densely packed flowers, the common areas stay in bloom throughout the summer. Facilities have a well-kept, clean appearance. The sites are arranged in many rows of gravel pull-throughs and back-ins parallel to each other. Back-in sites lack much shade or privacy, but all pull-through sites, rows B–D, have huge fir tree buffers on either side, creating a private, almost forest feeling and shade; they also have some grass within each site. The firs have an overgrown look, but do not encroach upon the spaciousness of the sites. Tent sites in the park sit in a small field without much shade or privacy; this field does, however, have many seedling hardwoods. Also, the tenting section has a small covered area with a sink for dishes. Summers bring flowers and the best time to visit the Vancouver area, but nights can be especially chilly even in August.

BASICS

Operated By: Peace Arch RV Park. **Open:** All year. **Site Assignment:** Walk in, reservation (deposit: 1 night stay; refund: 24 hour cancellation policy). **Registration:** At office, after hours at drop box. **Fee:** For 2 people, Full–$24.50, Tents–$18.50, Extra people over 7 years old–$2, Under 7 years old-free, V, MC, US and Canadian cash and travelers checks. **Parking:** At site, off site.

FACILITIES

Number of RV-Only Sites: 202. **Number of Tent-Only Sites:** 50. **Hookups:** Electric (30 amps), water, sewer, phone (pull-throughs only), cable. **Each Site:** Picnic table. **Dump Station:** Inquire at campground. **Laundry:** Inquire at campground. **Pay Phone:** Inquire at campground. **Rest Rooms and Showers:** Inquire at campground. **Fuel:** Inquire at campground. **Propane:** Inquire at campground. **Internal Roads:** Call ahead for details. **RV Service:** No. **Market:** 5 min. north in Cloverdale. **Restaurant:** 5 min. North in Cloverdale. **General Store:** No. **Vending:** Yes. **Swimming Pool:** Yes. **Playground:** Yes. **Other:** Mini golf, horseshoes, basketball, rec room w/ pool table and 2 arcade games, RV storage. **Activities:** Winter social clubs, occasional BBQs in summer. **Nearby Attractions:** Stanley Park and Zoo, Vancouver Aquarium, Transportation Museum, Capilano Suspension Bridge, Gastown, White Rock Beach. **Additional Information:** City of Surrey, (604) 591-4811, www.city.surrey.bc.ca; Vancouver Tourist Info Center (604) 683-2000; www.tourism-vancouver.org.

RESTRICTIONS

Pets: Leash only. **Fires:** No Fires. **Alcoholic Beverages:** At site. **Vehicle Maximum Length:** None. **Other:** No parking on grass, do not tie any lines to trees.

TO GET THERE

From Hwy. 99, take Exit 10, turn onto 99A northbound. After less than one block, turn right onto 40th Ave, drive 0.5 mi., entrance on the left

VANCOUVER (SURREY)

Tynehead RV Camp

16275 102nd Ave., Surrey V4N 2K7. T: (604) 589-1161; F: (604) 589-1161; www.tynehead.bc.ca.

RV ★★★ Tent ★★

Beauty: ★★★ Site Privacy: ★★
Spaciousness: ★★★ Quiet: ★★
Security: ★★★ Cleanliness: ★★★★
Insect Control: ★★ Facilities: ★★★

Tynehead RV Camp, located southeast of Vancouver in the suburb of Surrey, offers a quiet environment and easy access to Downtown Vancouver. Attractively landscaped and arranged in parallel rows, the park offers gravel pull-through and back-in full hookup sites with a small amount of privacy generated by cedar hedges. Still, there exists little shade for RV sites, and sites are not particularly flat. The best RV sites, back-ins 9–19, have the most shade and sit on a perimeter; the absence of rear neighbors creates more privacy. The back of the property has a little traffic noise. The tenting section consists of a grass field with sites interspersed throughout, none have particularly striking qualities. The best time to visit Vancouver has to be summer, when the weather is largely clear and mild.

BASICS

Operated By: Tynehead RV Camp. **Open:** All year. **Site Assignment:** Walk in, reservations (deposit: 10% of stay or 1 night; refund: call about varying policy). **Registration:** At office, after hours ring buzzer outside. **Fee:** For 2 people, Full–$30, Partial–$27, Tent–$20, Extra person–$3, Large dogs–$2, Children 5 and under free, Group rate if more than 10 people in a tent site, MC, V, cash. **Parking:** At site, limited off site parking.

FACILITIES

Number of RV-Only Sites: 120. **Number of Tent-Only Sites:** 53. **Hookups:** Electric (30 amps), water, sewer, cable. **Each Site:** Picnic table. **Dump Station:** Inquire at campground. **Laundry:** Inquire at campground. **Pay Phone:** Inquire at campground. **Rest Rooms and Showers:** Inquire at campground. **Fuel:** Inquire at campground. **Propane:** Inquire at campground. **Internal Roads:** Call ahead for details. **RV Service:** No. **Market:** Nearby in Surrey. **Restaurant:** Nearby in Surrey. **General Store:** Yes. **Vending:** No. **Swimming Pool:** Yes. **Playground:** Yes. **Other:** Spa (indoor), mini-golf. **Activities:** Inquire at campground. **Nearby Attractions:** Greater Vancouver Zoological Centre, Science World, Queen Elizabeth and Bloedel Conservatory, Lynn Canyon Suspension Bridge, Chinatown, Vancouver. **Additional Information:** City of Surrey, (604) 591-4811; www.city.surrey.bc.ca; Vancouver Tourist Info Center (604) 683-2000; www.tourism-vancouver.org.

RESTRICTIONS

Pets: Leash only. **Fires:** In pits only. **Alcoholic Beverages:** At site. **Vehicle Maximum Length:** 40 ft. **Other:** Do not park vehicles on grass.

TO GET THERE

From Hwy. 1 Exit 501, turn south on 160th street and drive 0.15 mi.. Turn left on 103rd Ave. and drive 0.3 mi., then turn left on 102nd Ave and drive 0.2 mi., entrance on the left.

VANCOUVER (WHITE ROCK)

Seacrest Motel and RV Park

864 160th St. (Stayte Rd.), White Rock V4A 4W4. T: (604) 531-4720; F: (604) 531-4735; www.seacrestmotel.bc.ca; seacrest@uniserve.com.

RV ★★★ Tent n/a

Beauty: ★★ Site Privacy: ★
Spaciousness: ★★★ Quiet: ★★★
Security: ★★★ Cleanliness: ★★★★
Insect Control: ★★★ Facilities: ★★

Seacrest Motel and RV Park, just across the border in White Rock, has quiet, no frills lodging in a beach-side community about a half hour south of Vancouver. A walk to the beach takes only a few minutes. Sites exist in two rows in two sections on paved blacktop with no grass or privacy. The surrounding motel has attractive landscaping and a small laundry facility (one set of machines). The whole grounds have a very quaint, quiet feel to them, neither pretentious nor dated, perfect for people who want to see Vancouver but not stay within it's municipality. All sites have a pretty similar setting, with the exception of sites 101 and 107, which sit near a road. Visit during the summer for optimal meteorological conditions.

BASICS

Operated By: Seacrest Motel. **Open:** All year. **Site Assignment:** Walk in, reservations (deposit: 1 night stay; refund: 48 hours notice). **Registration:**

At office, after hours pay in morning. **Fee:** Full–$24. **Parking:** At site.

Facilities

Number of RV-Only Sites: 32. **Number of Tent-Only Sites:** 0. **Hookups:** Electric (30 amps), water, sewer, cable. **Each Site:** Picnic table. **Dump Station:** Inquire at campground. **Laundry:** Inquire at campground. **Pay Phone:** Inquire at campground. **Rest Rooms and Showers:** Inquire at campground. **Fuel:** Inquire at campground. **Propane:** Inquire at campground. **Internal Roads:** Call ahead for details. **RV Service:** No. **Market:** a few mi. west in White Rock. **Restaurant:** A couple of blocks in either direction. **General Store:** No. **Vending:** No. **Swimming Pool:** No. **Playground:** No. **Other:** Inquire at campground. **Activities:** Inquire at campground. **Nearby Attractions:** White Rock Beach, pier and promenade, shopping and restaurants near waterfront, Peace Arch Park, Golf, fishing, crabbing, Vancouver. **Additional Information:** City of White Rock, (604) 541-2142, www.city.whiterock.bc.ca; Vancouver Tourist Info Center (604) 683-2000; www.tourism-vancouver.org.

Restrictions

Pets: Leash only, no loud dogs. **Fires:** No fires. **Alcoholic Beverages:** At site. **Vehicle Maximum Length:** 40 ft. **Other:** Check in at 1 p.m.

To Get There

From Hwy. 99 Exit 2, drive 0.7 mi. west on 8th Ave. Turn right on Stayte Rd and drive less than 1 block; entrance is on the right

WHISTLER

Riverside RV Resort and Campground

8018 Mons Rd., Whistler V0N 1B0. T: (604) 905-5533 or (877) 905-5533; F: (604) 905-5539; www.whistlercamping.com; info@whistlercamping.com.

RV ★★★★ Tent ★★★★

Beauty: ★★★★	Site Privacy: ★★★
Spaciousness: ★★	Quiet: ★★★
Security: ★★★	Cleanliness: ★★★★★
Insect Control: ★★	Facilities: ★★★★★

Riverside RV Resort and Campground, located in the expensive resort town of Whistler, provides convenient access to world class, year-round outdoor recreation, restaurants and clubs. This new campground has top-of-the-line, well equipped facilities and a variety of in-house recreation—notably a high-quality, all-grass, 18-hole putting course. Landscaping within the grounds is garden-like, well maintained, and classy. The RV section has obscured views of the surrounding mountains. In the RV section, consisting of several parallel rows of flat, paved back-in sites, the best sites, D1–D9 and E1–E8, sit toward the back of the grounds with some shade trees overhead and a little privacy. The tenting area, heavily shaded by pine and birch, consists of walk-in, semi-private dirt and gravel sites; the only sites to avoid, T1, T25, and T26, lack the privacy found in other sites. Any time makes a good time to visit Whistler; the town draws crowds for both summer and winter recreation.

Basics

Operated By: Riverside RV Resort. **Open:** All year. **Site Assignment:** Walk up, reservation (deposit: 1 night stay to hold; refund:cancel before 2 weeks for refund of *total* cost of stay, less than 2 weeks 50% of total stay, after 48 hours prior to arrival cancellation billed for total cost of stay). **Registration:** At office, after hours info in front of office. **Fee:** For 2 people, Full–$40, Overflow RV–$25, Extra RV adults–$5, Tent–$25, Extra tent adults–$7.50 (16 years and older, flexible for families). **Parking:** At site; tent sites walk-in with seperate parking lot.

Facilities

Number of RV-Only Sites: 60. **Number of Tent-Only Sites:** 31. **Hookups:** Electric (15, 30, 50 amps), water, sewer, cable ($2/day). **Each Site:** Picnic table, fire ring. **Dump Station:** Inquire at campground. **Laundry:** Inquire at campground. **Pay Phone:** Inquire at campground. **Rest Rooms and Showers:** Inquire at campground. **Fuel:** Inquire at campground. **Propane:** Inquire at campground. **Internal Roads:** Call ahead for details. **RV Service:** No. **Market:** Across street. **Restaurant:** On grounds. **General Store:** Yes. **Vending:** Yes. **Swimming Pool:** No. **Playground:** Yes. **Other:** PGA regulation 18-hole grass putting green, arcade with pool table, Internet terminal, cafe, rentals (roller blades, foot scooters, mountain bikes, movies, TVs, VCRs). **Activities:** Putting, volleyball, horseshoes, free shuttles to and from Whistler Village twice in morning and twice in afternoon. **Nearby Attractions:** Mountain biking, golf, hiking, fishing, tons of winter recreation (in winter), ecotourism; restaurants, shopping, and nightlife at Whistler resort complex. **Additional Information:** Tourism Whistler, (800)-WHISTLER; www.tourism.whistler.com; Squamish Chamber of Commerce, (604) 892-9244; www.squamishchamber.bc.ca.

Restrictions

Pets: Leash only; not allowed in beach (stream), playground area. **Fires:** At site, in pits. **Alcoholic Beverages:** At site. **Vehicle Maximum Length:** None. **Other:** Be aware of bear regulations. No refunds for early departures.

To Get There

On Hwy. 99 heading north, drive 1.1 mi. north of Whistler Village (main entrance to the north edge of town) and turn right onto Spruce Grove Park/Blackcomb Way. Take an almost immediate left onto the access road and follow for 0.3 mi. to entrance

WHISTLER/SQUAMISH

Brandywine Falls Provincial Park

Box 220, Brackendale V0N 1H0. T: (604) 898-3678; F: (604) 898-4171; www.elp.gov.bc.ca/bcparks/explore/parkpgs/brandywi.htm; gsdinfo@victoria1.gov.bc.ca.

RV ★★ Tent ★★

Beauty: ★★★	Site Privacy: ★★
Spaciousness: ★★★	Quiet: ★★★
Security: ★	Cleanliness: ★★
Insect Control: ★★	Facilities: ★

Brandywine Falls Provincial Park, located about 15 minutes south of Whistler, offers an overflow area within a very busy tourist corridor. Blink and you'll miss this small campground of 15 sites. The campground consists of a loop with sites on the perimeter and a central island. Individual sites lack elbow room and privacy, but do have some shade from firs and cedars. Sites 1–6 sit near busy Hwy. 99, but sites 7–15 are more removed from the major provincial artery. There are no facilities of any kind save vault toilets. The provincial park itself seems more like a rest area than a park, but it does have a couple of trails to hike. Year-round outdoor recreation abounds in the surrounding areas.

Basics

Operated By: Markim Ventures for BC Parks. **Open:** May 15–Oct. 15, off season gate closed, can walk in; no services and no fees. **Site Assignment:** Walk up. **Registration:** Attendant will collect fees at site, or pay in morning-attendant (host) or at self-pay box by info station. **Fee:** For 4 adults, 4 children, Site–$12, Extra vehicle–$6, cash only upon arrival. **Parking:** At site.

Facilities

Number of RV-Only Sites: 0. **Number of Tent-Only Sites:** 0. **Number of Multipurpose Sites:** 15. **Hookups:** None. **Each Site:** Picnic table, fire ring. **Dump Station:** Inquire at campground. **Laundry:** Inquire at campground. **Pay Phone:** Inquire at campground. **Rest Rooms and Showers:** Inquire at campground. **Fuel:** Inquire at campground. **Propane:** Inquire at campground. **Internal Roads:** Call ahead for details. **RV Service:** No. **Market:** 15 min. north in Whistler. **Restaurant:** 15 min. North in Whistler. **General Store:** No. **Vending:** No. **Swimming Pool:** No. **Playground:** No. **Other:** Hiking trails to Brandywine Falls and surrounding areas. **Activities:** Hiking. **Nearby Attractions:** Whistler and Squamish areas with lots of ecotourism, outdoor sport activities. **Additional Information:** Tourism Whistler, (800)-WHISTLER; www.tourism.whistler.com; Squamish Chamber of Commerce, (604) 892-9244; www.squamishchamber.bc.ca.

Restrictions

Pets: Leash only. **Fires:** Fire pits only. **Alcoholic Beverages:** At site. **Vehicle Maximum Length:** 38 ft. **Other:** Pitch tents only in designated pads. Max stay 14 days.

To Get There

Located about 15 minutes south of Whistler. If travelling north on Hwy. 99, entrance is on the right.

Supplemental Directory of Campgrounds

ALABAMA

Alberta

Chilatchee Creek Park, off CR 29, 36720. T: (334) 573-2562. www.sam.usace.army.mil/op/rec/al_lakes/camp.htm. RV/tent: 53. $8–$14. Hookups: water, electric (30 amps).

Aliceville

Cochrane Campground, 707 Tenntom Park Rd., 35442. T: (205) 373-8806. RV/tent: 59. $8–$12. Hookups: water, electric (50 amps).

Alpine

Logan Landing RV Resort & Campground, 1036 Bear Bryant Rd., 35014. T: (256) 268-0045. RV/tent: 140. $15–$18. Hookups: sewer, electric (30, 50 amps), water, phone.

Andalusia

Conecuh National Forest (Open Pond Campground), Rte. 5 Box 157, 36420. T: (334) 222-2555. RV/tent: 66. $5–$12. Hookups: water, electric.

Ariton

Camp Bama RV Resort & Campgrounds, Hwy. 231, 36311. T: (800) 435-8259. RV/tent: 16. $10. Hookups: water, electric (20, 30 amps), sewer.

Athens

Lucy's Branch Resort & Marina, 5381 Bay Village Dr., 35611. T: (256) 729-6443. RV/tent: 204. $20. Hookups: water, electric (20, 30, 50 amps), sewer.

Atmore

Claude D. Kelley State Park, 580 H. Kyle, 36502. T: (251) 862-2511. www.alapark.com. RV/tent: 25. $11. Hookups: water, electric, sewer.

Auburn

Chewacla State Park, 124 Shell Toomer Pkwy., 36830. T: (334) 887-5621. www.alapark.com. RV/tent: 36. $15. Hookups: water, electric (20, 30 amps), sewer.

Leisure Time Campgrounds, 2670 South College St., 36830. T: (334) 821-2267. RV/tent: 60. $18–$20. Hookups: water, electric (20, 30, 50 amps), sewer, phone.

Birmingham

M & J RV Park, 556 Bessemer Super Hwy., 35228. T: (205) 788-2605. RV/tent: 72. $12–$20. Hookups: water, electric (50 amps), sewer, phone.

Boaz

Barclay RV Parking, 104 South Main St., 35957. T: (256) 593-8769. RV/tent: 22. $12–$15. Hookups: water, electric (30, 50 amps), sewer.

Castleberry

Country Sunshine RV Park, Rte. 2 Box 290, 36432. T: (251) 966-5540. RV/tent: 11. $15. Hookups: water, electric (30, 50 amps), sewer.

Centre

John's Campground & Grocery, 6480 CR 22, 35960. T: (256) 475-3234. RV/tent: 58. $25. Hookups: water, electric (30, 50 amps), sewer, cable.

Centreville

Talladega National Forest (Payne Lake West Side), Oakmulgee Ranger District, US 82/AL 5 North, 35042. T: (205) 926-9765. RV/tent: 77. $4. Hookups: none.

Citronelle

Citronelle Lakeview RV Park, 17850 Municipal Park Dr., 36522. T: (251) 866-9647. RV/tent: 32. $15. Hookups: water, electric (30, 50 amps), sewer.

Clio

Blue Springs State Park, 2595 Hwy. 10, 36017. T: (334) 397-4875. www.alapark.com. RV/tent: 50. $11. Hookups: water, electric (30 amps), sewer.

Coaling

Candy Mountain RV Park, 11742 Hagler Coaling Rd., 35449. T: (205) 553-5428. RV/tent: 40. $17. Hookups: water, electric (30, 50 amps), sewer.

Cottondale

Sunset II Travel Park, 5001 JVC Rd., 35453. T: (205) 553-9233. RV/tent: 36. $20. Hookups: water, electric (20, 30, 50 amps), sewer.

Creola

I-65 RV Campground, 730 Jackson Rd., 36525. T: (800) 287-3208. www.i65campground.com. RV/tent: 76. $17–$19. Hookups: electric (20, 30, 50 amps), sewer, phone.

KOA–Mobile North/River Delta, 2350 Dead Lake Marina Rd., 36525. T: (800) KOA-0362. www.koa.com. RV/tent: 42. $18–$20. Hookups: water, electric (20, 30, 50 amps), sewer.

Cullman

Cullman Campground, 215 CR 1185, 35056. T: (256) 734-9794. RV/tent: 75. $13–$15. Hookups: water, electric (20, 30, 50 amps), sewer, phone.

Good Hope Campground, 330 Super Saver Rd., 35055. T: (256) 739-1319. RV/tent: 50. $13–$16. Hookups: water, electric (15, 30 amps), sewer, phone.

Hames Marina & RV Park, 850 CR 248, 35057. T: (256) 287-9785. RV/tent: 48. $10–$15. Hookups: water, electric (30, 50 amps), sewer.

Dauphin Island

Dauphin Island Campground, 109 Bienville Blvd., 36528. T: (251) 861-2742. RV/tent: 150. $15–$22. Hookups: water, electric (30, 50 amps), sewer.

Decatur

Point Mallard Campground, 1800 Point Mallard Dr., 35601. T: (256) 351-7772. RV/tent: 210. $12–$15. Hookups: water, electric (20, 30, 50 amps), sewer.

Demopolis

Forkland Park, Off US 43, 12 miles north of Demopolis, 36732. T: (334) 289-5530. www.sam.usace.army.mil/op/rec. RV/tent: 42. $12–$14. Hookups: water, electric (20, 30 amps).

Foscue Creek Park, 1800 Lockin Dam Rd., 36732. T: (334) 289-5535. www.sam.usace.army.mil/ op/rec. RV/tent: 45. $12. Hookups: water, electric (20, 30 amps).

Dothan

Clean Park RV Park, 4100 South Oates St., 36301. T: (334) 792-2000. RV/tent: 150. $15. Hookups: water, electric (30, 50 amps), sewer, cable.

ALABAMA (continued)

Elberta

Lazy Acres RV Park & Campground, 12160 Wortel Rd., 36530. T: (877) 986-5266. www.lazyacres campground.com. RV/tent: 54. $12. Hookups: water, electric (20, 30, 50 amps), sewer, phone.

Elkmont

Mill Creek RV Park, 28861 Veto Rd., 35620. T: (256) 732-3686. www.millcreekrv.com. RV/tent: 125. $10–$18. Hookups: sewer, electric (30, 50 amps), water, phone.

Equality

Lakeway Pub & Grill and RV Park, P.O. Box 176, 36026. T: (334) 541-2010. RV/tent: 13. $15. Hookups: water, electric (30, 50 amps), sewer.

Eufaula

Lake Eufaula Campground, 151 West Chewalla Creek Dr., 36027. T: (334) 687-4425. RV/tent: 100. $14–$17. Hookups: water, electric (30 amps), sewer.

Fairhope

Driftwood RV Park, 9318 Hwy. 98, 36532. T: (251) 928-8233. RV/tent: 24. $14. Hookups: water, electric (30, 50 amps), sewer.

East Park Plaza, 7625 Parker Rd., 36532. T: (251) 928-7619. RV/tent: 15. $14. Hookups: water, electric (30, 50 amps), sewer.

Safe Harbor RV Resort & Marina, 11401 US Hwy. 98, 36532. T: (800) 928-4544. www.safeharbour resort.com. RV/tent: 105. $20. Hookups: water, electric (30, 50 amps), sewer.

Florala

Florala State Park, P.O. Box 322, 36442-0322. T: (334) 858-6425. RV/tent: 23. $14. Hookups: water, electric (30 amps).

Florence

McFarland Park, South Seminary St., 35630. T: (256) 760-6416. RV/tent: 50. $8–$12. Hookups: water, electric (20, 30 amps).

Veterans Memorial Park, Wilson Dam Rd., 35630. T: (256) 760-6416. RV/tent: 22. $8–$12. Hookups: water, electric (20, 30 amps).

Foley

Helen's RV Park, 10340 South Juniper St., 36535. T: (251) 943-1227. RV/tent: 18. $12. Hookups: sewer, electric (30, 50 amps), water, phone.

Palm Lake RV Court, 15810 Hwy. 59, 36535. T: (251) 970-3773. F: (251) 970-1704. RV/tent: 62. $18. Hookups: water, electric (20, 30, 50 amps), sewer, phone.

Franklin

Isaac Creek Park, Rte. 1 Box 51B, 36444. T: (251) 282-4254. www.sam.usace.army.mil/op/rec/al_lakes/camp.htm. RV/tent: 50. $12–$14. Hookups: water, electric (30, 50 amps).

Gadsden

River Country Campground, 1 River Rd., 35901. T: (256) 543-7111. www.rivercountrycampground.com. RV/tent: 112. $16–$22. Hookups: sewer, electric (30, 50 amps), water, phone.

Gallion

Chickasaw State Park, 26955 US Hwy. 43, 36742. T: (334) 295-8230. www.alapark.com. RV/tent: 8. $10. Hookups: water, electric (30 amps).

Gardendale

Gardendale Kampground, 2128 Moncrief Rd., 35071. T: (205) 631-7364. RV/tent: 30. $19. Hookups: water, electric (20, 30 amps), sewer.

Gulf Shores

Luxury RV Resort, 590 Gulf Shores Pkwy., 36542. T: (800) 982-3510. RV/tent: 89. $22–$25. Hookups: sewer, electric (30, 50 amps), water, phone.

Southport Campgrounds, 108 West 28th Ave., 36542. T: (251) 968-6220. RV/tent: 116. $13–$17. Hookups: water, electric (20, 30 amps), sewer, phone.

Sun Runners RV Park, 19436 CR 8, 36542. T: (251) 955-5257. RV/tent: 60. $14. Hookups: water, electric (20, 30 amps), sewer.

Guntersville

Seibold Campground, 54 Seibold Creek Rd., 35976. T: (256) 582-0040. RV/tent: 102. $17–$20. Hookups: water, electric (20, 30, 50 amps).

Hamilton

US 78 Campgrounds, 3194 CR 55, 35570. T: (205) 921-2718. RV/tent: 14. $10. Hookups: water, electric (20, 30, 50 amps), sewer.

Hanceville

Country RV Park, 15959 Hwy. 91, 35077. T: (256) 352-4678. RV/tent: 40. $15–$20. Hookups: sewer, electric (30, 50 amps), water, phone, cable.

Heflin

Talladega National Forest (Coleman Lake), Shoal Creek Ranger District, 2309 Hwy. 46, 36264. T: (256) 463-2272. RV/tent: 39. $12. Hookups: water, electric (30, 50 amps).

Talladega National Forest (Pine Glen), Shoal Creek Ranger District, 2309 Hwy. 46, 36264. T: (256) 463-2272. RV/tent: 31. $3. Hookups: none.

Helena

Cherokee Beach Kamper Village, 2800 Hwy. 93, 35080. T: (205) 428-8339. RV/tent: 80. $14. Hookups: water, electric (30 amps), sewer.

Hope Hull

KOA–Montgomery, 250 Fischer Rd., 36043. T: (800) KOA-5032. F: (334) 286-1133. www.koa.com. RV/tent: 125. $19–$35. Hookups: water, electric (20, 30, 50 amps), sewer, phone.

Huntsville

Ditto Landing Marina Campground, 293 Ditto Landing Rd., 35815. T: (256) 883-9420. www.nservice.com/ditto_landing. RV/tent: 26. $14. Hookups: water, electric (30 amps).

Ider

Thunder Canyon Campground, 583 Thunder Canyon Rd., 35981. T: (256) 632-2103. RV/tent: 50. $12–$14. Hookups: water, electric (20, 30, 50 amps), sewer.

Jemison

Peach Queen Campground, 12986 CR 42, 35085. T: (205) 688-2573. RV/tent: 92. $20–$24. Hookups: water, electric (20, 30, 50 amps), sewer, phone.

Langston

South Sauty Creek Resort, 6845 South Sauty Rd., 35755. T: (256) 582-3367. RV/tent: 85. $18. Hookups: water, electric (20, 30, 50 amps).

Leeds

Holiday Trav-L-Park, 900 Old Ashville Rd., 35094. T: (205) 640-5300. RV/tent: 137. $17–$20. Hookups: water, electric (20, 30 amps), sewer.

Leroy

Double R Campground, HC 63 Box 247, 36548. T: (251) 246-9175. RV/tent: 40. $15. Hookups: water, electric (20, 30, 50 amps), sewer.

Magnolia Springs

Southwind RV Park, 12821 CR 9N, 36555. T: (251) 988-1216. RV/tent: 120. $18. Hookups: water, electric (20, 30, 50 amps), sewer.

McCalla

KOA–McCalla/Tannehill, 22191 Hwy. 216, 35111. T: (800) KOA-9505. www.koa.com. RV/tent: 62. $17–$24. Hookups: sewer, electric (30, 50 amps), water, phone.

Millbrook

K & K RV Park, 1810 I-65 Service Rd. East, 36054. T: (334) 285-5251. RV/tent: 46. $19. Hookups: water, electric (20, 30, 50 amps), sewer, phone.

Mobile

Brown's RV Park, 1619 Jasper Rd., 36618. T: (251) 342-3383. www.brownsrvpark.com. RV/tent: 34. $17. Hookups: sewer, electric (30, 50 amps), water, phone, cable.

Pala Verde RV Park, 3525 Demetropolis Rd., 36693. T: (251) 660-7148. RV/tent: 19. $15. Hookups: water, electric (30, 50 amps), sewer.

ALABAMA (continued)

Montgomery

Gunter Hill Park, 561 Booth Rd., 36108. T: (334) 269-1053. www.sam.usace.army.mil/op/rec/al_lakes/camp.htm. RV/tent: 146. $8–$14. Hookups: water, electric (30, 50 amps).

Moundville

Moundville Archaeological Park, 13075 Moundville Arch Park, 35474. T: (205) 371-2572. www.ua.edu/mndville.htm. RV/tent: 34. $10. Hookups: water, electric (20, 30 amps), sewer.

Muscle Shoals

Mallard Creek, P.O. Box 1010 SB1H, 35662. T: (256) 386-2221. RV/tent: 56. $15. Hookups: water, electric (30 amps).

Ohatchee

Coosa Willow Point Campground & Marina, 138 Willow Point Dr., Hwy. 77 North, 36271. T: (800) 566-9906. RV/tent: 74. $15. Hookups: water, electric (20, 30, 50 amps).

Opelika

Lakeside RV Park, 5664 US Hwy. 280 East, 36801. T: (334) 745-5414. RV/tent: 20. $20. Hookups: water, electric (30, 50 amps), sewer.

Opp

Frank Jackson State Park, Rte. 3 Box 73-C, 36467. T: (334) 493-6988. www.dcnr.state.al.us/parks/frank_jackson_1a.html. RV/tent: 26. $15. Hookups: water, electric (30 amps).

Orange Beach

Beech Camping, 4224 Orange Beach Blvd., #50, 36561. T: (251) 981-4136. RV/tent: 90. $20. Hookups: water, electric (20, 30, 50 amps), sewer.

Ozark

Ozark Trav-L-Park, 4000 US 231 North, 36360. T: (800) 359-3218. www.trav-l-park.com. RV/tent: 45. $21. Hookups: sewer, electric (30, 50 amps), water, phone, cable.

Pelham

KOA–Birmingham South, 222 Hwy. 33, 35124. T: (205) 664-8832. F: (205) 620-1103. www.koa.com. RV/tent: 113. $25–$45. Hookups: water, electric (20, 30, 50 amps), sewer, phone.

Pittsview

Bluff Creek Park, 144 Bluff Creek Rd., 36871. T: (334) 855-2746. RV/tent: 88. $14. Hookups: water, electric (20, 30 amps).

Robertsdale

Hilltop RV Park, 23420 CR 64, 36567. T: (251) 960-1129. RV/tent: 72. $16. Hookups: water, electric (20, 30, 50 amps), sewer, phone.

Russellville

Bear Creek Development Authority, 111 CR 88, 35653. T: (256) 332-4392. F: (256) 332-4372. www.bearcreeklakes.com. RV/tent: 160. $7.50–$12. Hookups: water, electric (30 amps), sewer.

Scottsboro

Crawford RV Park, 4320 South Broad St., 35759-7421. T: (256) 574-5366. www.crawfordrv.com. RV/tent: 12. $18. Hookups: water, electric (30, 50 amps), sewer, cable.

Goose Pond Colony, 417 Ed Hembree Dr., 35769. T: (256) 259-1808. F: (256) 259-3127. www.goosepond.org. RV/tent: 117. $15–$17. Hookups: water, electric (20, 30 amps), sewer, phone.

Selma

Lake Lanier Travel Park, 655 Lake Lanier Rd., 36701. T: (334) 875-1618. RV/tent: 55. $12–$18. Hookups: water, electric (20, 30, 50 amps), sewer.

Paul M. Grist State Park, 1546 Grist Rd., 36701. T: (334) 872-5846. www.dcnr.state.al.us/parks/paul_m_grist_1a.html. RV/tent: 6. $8–$16. Hookups: water, electric (30 amps), sewer.

Shorter

Wind Drift Campground, At Jct. of I-85 & US 80, 36075. T: (334) 724-9428. RV/tent: 33. $17. Hookups: water, electric (20, 30, 50 amps), sewer, phone.

Siles

Service Park Campground, US Hwy. 84, 36919. T: (251) 754-9658. RV/tent: 32. $12. Hookups: water, electric (20, 30 amps).

Theodore

I-10 Kampground, 6430 Theodore Dawes Rd., 36582. T: (800) 272-1263. RV/tent: 193. $21. Hookups: sewer, electric (30, 50 amps), water, phone.

Town Creek

Doublehead Resort, 145 CR 314, 35672. T: (800) 685-9267. www.doublehead.com. RV/tent: 30. $15. Hookups: water, electric (30, 50 amps).

Troy

Deer Run RV Park, 3736 Hwy. 231 North, 36081. T: (800) 552-3036. F: (334) 670-6759. www.deer

ALASKA

Anchor Point

Kyllonen's RV Park, 74160 Anchor Point Beach Rd., 99556. T: (907) 235-7762 or (907) 235-7451. F: (907) 235-6435. www.kyllonenrvpark.com. susank@xyz.net. RV/tent: 23. $24. Hookups: electric (30 amps), water, sewer.

Anchorage

Centennial Campground, 8300 Glenn Hwy., 99519. T: (907) 343-4474. RV/tent: 129. $13–$15. Hookups: none.

Electronic Solutions Midtown RV Park, 545 East Northern Lights, Suite C, 99503. T: (907) 277-2407. RV/tent: 42. $22. Hookups: electric (20 amps), water, sewer.

Golden Nugget Camper Park, 4100 Debarr, 99508. T: (907) 333-2012 or (800) 449-2012. F: (907) 333-1016. www.alaskan.com/camperpark. Gnugget@alaska.net. RV/tent: 215. $17–$27. Hookups: electric (20, 30, 50 amps), water, sewer.

Hillside on Gambell Motel & RV Park, 2150 Gambell St., 99503. T: (907) 258-6006 or (800) 478-6005. F: (907) 279-8972. www.hillside-alaska.com. info@hillside-alaska.com. RV/tent: 67. $20–$24. Hookups: electric (20, 30, 50 amps), water, sewer.

Auke Bay

Auke Bay RV Park, 11930 Glacier Hwy., 99821. T: (907) 789-9467. RV/tent: 40. $22. Hookups: electric (20, 30 amps), water, sewer.

Cantwell

Cantwell RV Park, Mile 209.9 Parks Hwy., 99729. T: (907) 768-2210 (summer) or (800) 940-2210. F: (907) 262-5149. www.alaskaone.com/cantwellrv. jodinepp@corecom.net. RV/tent: 82. $10–$21. Hookups: water, electric (20, 30 amps).

Cooper Landing

Cooper Creek Campground, Sterling Hwy. Mile 51, 99572. T: (800) 280-CAMP. www.reserveusa.com. RV/tent: 29. $15. Hookups: none.

Russian River Campground, Mile 53 Sterling Hwy., 99572. T: (800) 280-CAMP. www.reserveusa.com. RV/tent: 110. $13–$20. Hookups: none.

Sunrise Inn RV Park, P.O. Box 832, 99572. T: (907) 595-1222. RV/tent: 27. $18–$22. Hookups: electric (20, 30, 50 amps), water, sewer.

Copper Center

Kenny Lake Mercantile/RV Park, Mile 7.5 Edgerton Hwy., 99573. T: (907) 822-3313. www.alaskaoutdoors.com/KennyLake.knnylake@alaska.net. RV/tent: 19. $15–$18. Hookups: electric (20 amps).

ALASKA (continued)

Delta Junction

Smith's Green Acres, 2428 Richardson Hwy. Mile 268, 99737. T: (907) 895-4369 or (800) 895-4369. F: (907) 895-4110. www.greenacresrvpark.com. garvpark@wildak.net. RV/tent: 97. $13–$22. Hookups: electric (30 amps), water, sewer.

Fairbanks

Chena Hotsprings Resort, P.O. Box 58740, 99711. T: (907) 452-7867 or (800) 478-4681. F: (907) 456-3122. www.chenahotsprings.com. chenahs@polar-net.com. RV/tent: 80. $20. Hookups: none.

Chena Marina RV Park, 1145 Shypoke Dr., 99709. T: (907) 479-4653. F: (907) 479-0575. www.chenarvpark.com. chenarv@mosquitonet.com. RV/tent: 67. $15–$32. Hookups: electric (30 amps), water, sewer, cable, phone.

Tanana Valley Campground, 1800 College Rd., 99709. T: (907) 456-7956 (summer) or (907) 452-3750 (winter). F: (907) 456-7971. www.tananavalleyfair.org/campground. tvcg@tananavalleyfair.org. RV/tent: 50. $8–$15. Hookups: electric (30 amps).

Girdwood

GIRDWOOD, Crow Creek Mine, 99587. T: (907) 278-8060. F: (907) 278-8061. www.crowcreek goldmine.com. cynthia2@ptialaska.net. RV/tent: 15. $5. Hookups: none.

Glennallen

Tazlina River RV Park, Mile 110.2 Richardson Hwy., 99588. T: (907) 822-3546. radigan@alaska.net. RV/tent: 12. $7–$15. Hookups: electric (20 amps), water.

Haines

Haines Hitch-Up RV Park, 851 Main St., 99827. T: (907) 766-2882. F: (907) 766-2515. www.hitchuprv.com. hitchuprv@aol.com. RV/tent: 92. $22-plus. Hookups: electric (30, 50 amps), water, sewer, cable, phone.

Port Chilkoot Camper Park, P.O. Box 1589, 99827. T: (907) 766-2755 or (800) 542-6363. F: (907) 766-2445. www.haines.ak.us/halsingland. halsinglan@aol.com. RV/tent: 25. $14–$19. Hookups: electric (20, 30, 50 amps), water, sewer.

Salmon Run Campground & Cabins, Mile 6.5 Lutak Rd., 99827. T: (907) 766-3240. salmonrun@whitebear.com. RV/tent: 30. $14. Hookups: none.

Healy

Carlo Creek Lodge and Campground, Mile 223.9 Parks Hwy., 99743. T: (907) 683-2576 (summer) or (907) 683-2573 (winter). F: (907) 683-2573. www.alaskaone.com/carlocreek. carlocreek@hotmail.com. RV/tent: 25. $17-plus. Hookups: electric (20 amps).

McKinley RV and Campground, Mile 248.3 Parks Hwy., 99743. T: (907) 683-2379 or (800) 478-2562. F: (907) 683-2281. RV/tent: 100. $18–$27. Hookups: electric (20, 30 amps), water, sewer.

Homer

Driftwood Inn RV Park, 135 West Bunnell Ave., 99603. T: (907) 235-8019 or (800) 478-8019. www.thedriftwoodinn.com. driftinn@xyz.net. RV/tent: 27. $26–$29. Hookups: electric (20, 30, 50 amps), water, sewer, cable.

Hope

Henry's One Stop, Mile 15.5 Hope Hwy., 99605. T: (907) 782-3222. RV/tent: 12. $17. Hookups: electric (20 amps), water, sewer.

Hyder

Camp Run-A-Muck, 1001 Premier Ave., 99923. T: (250) 636-9006 or (888) 393-1199. F: (250) 636-9003. www.sealaskainn.com. sealaskainn@yahoo.com. RV/tent: 65. $8–$17. Hookups: electric (30 amps), water, sewer.

Juneau

Spruce Meadow RV Park, 10200 Mendenhall Loop Rd., 99801. T: (907) 789-1990. F: (907) 790-7231. www.juneaurv.com. juneaurv@aol.com. RV/tent: 69. $24-plus. Hookups: electric (30 amps), water, sewer, cable.

Kasilof

Crooked Creek RV Park, 111 Sterling Hwy., 99610. T: (907) 262-1299. RV/tent: 45. $15–$20. Hookups: electric (20, 30, 50 amps), water, sewer.

Ketchikan

Clover Pass Resort, P.O. Box 7322, 99901. T: (907) 247-2234 or (800) 410-2234. F: (907) 247-0793. www.cloverpassresort.com. info@cloverpassresort.com. RV/tent: 32. $26. Hookups: electric (30 amps), water, sewer, cable.

Moose Pass

Moose Pass RV Park, Mile 29 Seward Hwy., 99631. T: (907) 288-5624. www.moosepassrvpark.com. moosepassrvpark@yahoo.com. RV/tent: 31. $12–$17. Hookups: electric (30 amps).

Ptarmigan Creek, Mile 23 Seward Hwy., 99631. T: (800) 280-CAMP. www.reserveusa.com. RV/tent: 16. $10. Hookups: none.

Trail River Campground, Mile 24 Seward Hwy., 99631. T: (800) 280-CAMP. www.reserveusa.com. RV/tent: 65. $10. Hookups: none.

Ninilchik

Alaskan Angler RV Resort, P.O. Box 39388, 99639. T: (907) 567-3393 or (800) 347-4114. F: (907) 347-4114. www.afishunt.com. info@afishunt.com. RV/tent: 70. $10–$27. Hookups: electric (20, 30, 50 amps), water, sewer, cable, phone.

North Pole

Riverview RV Park, 1316 Badger Rd., 99707. T: (907) 488-6281 or (888) 488-6392. F: (907) 488-0555. www.alaskaone.com/riverview. dfickes@mosquitonet.com. RV/tent: 180. $16–$24.95. Hookups: electric (20, 30, 50 amps), water, sewer, cable.

Road's End RV Park, 1463 Westcott Ln., 99705. T: (907) 488-0295. www.roadsendrvpark.com. kentgaverett@hotmail.com. RV/tent: 73. $10–$20. Hookups: electric (20, 30, 50 amps), water, sewer.

Santaland RV Park, 125 St. Nicholas Dr., 99705. T: (907) 488-9123 or (888) 488-9123. F: (907) 488-7947. www.santalandrv.com. info@santalandrv.com. RV/tent: 94. $15–$25. Hookups: electric (20, 30, 50 amps), water, sewer, cable.

Palmer

Grandview Lodge & RV Park, Mile 109.75 Glenn Hwy., 99645. T: (907) 746-4480. www.grandviewrv.com. RV/tent: 19. $18–$21. Hookups: electric (30, 50 amps), water, sewer.

The Homestead RV Park, P.O. Box 354, 99645. T: (907) 745-6005. RV/tent: 64. $21. Hookups: electric (30 amps), water.

Petersburg

Twin Creek RV Park, Mile 7 Mitkof Hwy., 99833. T: (907) 772-3244. RV/tent: 22. $16–$21. Hookups: electric (30 amps), water, sewer, cable.

Prince Wales Island

Log Cabin Resort, P.O. Box 54, 99925. T: (907) 755-2205 or (800) 544-2205. F: (907) 755-2218. www.logcabinresortandrv.com. lcresak@aptalaska.net. RV/tent: 14. $7-plus. Hookups: electric (30 amps), water, sewer.

Seward

Miller's Landing Campground, P.O. Box 81, 99664. T: (907) 224-5739. F: (907) 224-5739. www.millerslandingak.com. miland@ptialaska.net. RV/tent: 53. $20-plus. Hookups: electric (25 amps).

Sitka

Sitka Sportsman's Association RV Park, P.O. Box 3030, 99835. T: (907) 747-6033. www.ptialaska.net/~ssport. ssport@ptialaska.net. RV/tent: 16. $14–$18. Hookups: electric (30 amps), water.

Skagway

Garden City RV Park, P.O. Box 228, 99840. T: (907) 983-2378. F: (907) 983-3378. www.gardencityrv.com. gcrv@aptalaska.net. RV/tent: 96. $24. Hookups: electric (30 amps), water, sewer, cable.

Skagway Mountainview RV Park, 12th and Broadway, 99840. T: (907) 983-3333 or (888) 778-7700. F: (907) 983-2224. www.alaskarv.com. alaskarv@aol.com. RV/tent: 147. $14–$23. Hookups: electric (20, 30, 50 amps), water, sewer.

ALASKA (continued)

Soldotna

Diamond M Ranch, B&B, Cabins and RV Park, Mile 16.5 Kalifornsky Beach Rd., 99669. T: (907) 283-9424. F: (907) 283-9330. www.diamondmranch.com. martin@diamondmranch.com. RV/tent: 33. $20. Hookups: electric (30, 50 amps), water, sewer, phone.

Kasilof RV Park, P.O. Box 1333, 99669. T: (907) 262-0418 or (800) 264-0418. www.kasilofrvpark.com. kasilofrv@ak.net. RV/tent: 39. $18-plus. Hookups: electric (30 amps), water, sewer.

River Terrace RV Park, 44761 Sterling Hwy. (Kenai River Bridge), 99669. T: (907) 262-5593. F: (907) 262-8873. RV/tent: 70. $20–$35. Hookups: electric (20, 30, 50 amps), water, sewer.

Talkeetna

Talkeetna River Adventures Campground, P.O. Box 473, 99676. T: (907) 733-2604. RV/tent: 40. $12. Hookups: none.

Tok

Bull Shooter RV Park, 1313 Alaska Hwy., 99780. T: (907) 883-5625. F: (907) 883-5620. www.tokalaska.com. bullshooter@tokalaska.com. RV/tent: 25. $18–$20. Hookups: electric (30 amps), water, sewer.

Sourdough Campground, Mile 122.8 Tok Cutoff Rd., 99780. T: (907) 883-5543 or (800) 789-5543. www.tokalaska.com. sourdough@tokalaska.com. RV/tent: 75. $16–$24. Hookups: electric (20, 30 amps), water, sewer.

Tok RV Village, Mile 1313.4 Alaska Hwy., 99780. T: (907) 883-5877. F: (907) 883-5878. RV/tent: 150. $22–$25. Hookups: electric (30, 50 amps), water, sewer.

Tundra RV Park, Mile 1315 Alaska Hwy., 99780. T: (907) 883-7875 (summer) or (907) 883-5885 (winter). F: (907) 883-7876. www.tokalaska.com. tundrarv@aptalaska.net. RV/tent: 78. $14–$20. Hookups: electric (20, 30, 50 amps), water, sewer.

Two Rivers

Pleasant Valley RV Park, 7435 Chena Hot Springs Rd., 99716. T: (907) 488-8198. F: (907) 488-8198. RV/tent: 16. $20. Hookups: electric (30 amps), water.

Valdez

Bear Paw Camper Park, 101 North Harbor Dr., 99686. T: (907) 835-2530. F: (907) 835-5266. www.alaska.net/~bpawcamp. bpawcamp@alaska.net. RV/tent: 140. $17–$25. Hookups: electric (30 amps), water, sewer, cable.

Eagle's Rest RV Park, 630 East Pioneer Dr., 99686. T: (800) 553-7275 or (907) 835-2373. F: (907) 835-5267. www.eaglesrestrv.com. rvpark@alaska.net. RV/tent: 390. $17–$26. Hookups: electric (20, 30, 50 amps), water, sewer, cable, phone.

Wasilla

Bestview RV Park, 7701 Parks Hwy., 99687. T: (907) 745-7400 or (800) 478-6600. F: (907) 745-3512. RV/tent: 61. $18–$21. Hookups: electric (30 amps), water, sewer.

Iceworm RV Park & Country Store, Mile 50.2 Parks Hwy., 99687. T: (907) 892-8200. F: (907) 892-8200. RV/tent: 24. $18. Hookups: electric (30, 50 amps), water, sewer, phone.

Willow

Pioneer Lodge, Inc., Mile 71.4 Parks Hwy., 99688. T: (907) 495-1000. RV/tent: 47. $20. Hookups: electric (30 amps), water, sewer.

Susitna Landing, Mile 82.5 Parks Hwy., 99688. T: (907) 495-7700. F: (907) 495-5000. www.ronsriverboat.com. info@ronsriverboat.com. RV/tent: 30. $10–$16. Hookups: electric (30 amps).

Wrangell

Wrangell RV Park, P.O. Box 531, 99929. T: (907) 874-2444. F: (907) 874-3186. parksrec@aptak.net. RV/tent: 26. $6–$10. Hookups: electric (30 amps).

ARIZONA

Aguila

Fairhaven RV Park, 52227 West Hwy. US 60 P.O. (P.O. Box 38), 85320. T: (520) 685-2412. RV/tent: 55. $15–$16. Hookups: electric (30 amp), water, sewer.

Ajo

Ajo Heights RV Park, 2000 North Hwy. 85, 85321. T: (520) 387-6796. rose@ajorvparks.com. RV/tent: 40. $20. Hookups: electric (30, 50 amp), water, sewer, cable TV, phone.

Belly Acres RV Park, 2050 North Hwy. 85, 85321. T: (520) 387-6062. del-sur@tabletoptelephone.com. RV/tent: 55. $16. Hookups: electric (30 amp), water, sewer, cable TV.

La Siesta Motel & RV Resort, 2561 North Ajo-Gila Bend Hwy., 85321. T: (520) 387-6569. RV/tent: 29. $18–$20. Hookups: electric (30 amp), water, sewer, cable TV.

Shadow Ridge RV Resort, 431 North 2nd Ave., 85321. T: (520) 387-6569. F: (520) 387-5055. RV/tent: 125. $20. Hookups: electric (30, 50 amp), water, sewer, cable TV.

Apache Junction

Apache Skies Mobile Home Park, 102 South Ironwood, 85219. T: (480) 982-6916 or (800) 625-7264. F: (480) 982-5735. RV/tent: 38. $25. Hookups: water, electric (20, 30, 50 amp), sewer, phone (modem).

Arizonian Travel Trailer Resort, 15976 East Hwy. 60, 85219. T: (520) 463-2585. RV/tent: 75. $24. Hookups: water, electric (30, 50 amp), sewer.

Budget RV Park, Old West Hwy., 85219. T: (480) 982-5856. RV/tent: 175. $20. Hookups: water, electric (30, 50 amp), sewer.

Countryside Travel Trailer Resort, Idaho Rd., 85219. T: (480) 982-1537. RV/tent: 560. $29. Hookups: electric (30, 50 amp), water, sewer, phone.

Dana's Trailer Ranch, Apache Trail, 85219. T: (480) 986-1471. RV/tent: 60. $20. Hookups: water, electric (20, 30 amp), sewer, phone.

Gold Canyon RV Resort, 7151 East Hwy. 60, 85219. T: (480) 982-5800 or (877) 465-3266. RV/tent: 754. $32. Hookups: electric (30, 50 amp), water, sewer.

Golden Sun RV Resort, 999 West Broadway, 85220. T: (480) 983-3760. RV/tent: 330. $25. Hookups: electric (30, 50 amp), water, sewer, phone.

La Hacienda RV Resort, 1797 West 28th Ave., 85220. T: (480) 982-2808. www.hacienda-RV.com. information@hacienda-RV.com. RV/tent: 280. $30. Hookups: electric (30, 50 amp), water, sewer, cable TV, phone (modem).

Rock Shadows RV Resort, 600 South Idaho Rd., 85219. T: (480) 982-0450. rockrv1@aol.com. RV/tent: 683. $29. Hookups: electric (30, 50 amp), water, sewer, phone.

Sunrise RV Resort, 1403 West Broadway, 85220. T: (480) 983-2500 or (877) 633-3133. RV/tent: 483. $27. Hookups: electric (30, 50 amp), water, sewer.

Superstition Lookout RV Resort, 1371 East Fourth Ave., 85219. T: (480) 982-2008. RV/tent: 192. $31. Hookups: electric (30, 50 amp), water, sewer, phone.

Superstition Sunrise RV Resort, 702 South Meridian Dr., 85220. T: (480) 986-8404 or (800) 624-7027. supersun01@aol.com. RV/tent: 1119. $35. Hookups: electric (30, 50 amp), water, sewer, cable TV, phone (modem).

VIP RV Resort, 401 South Ironwood Dr., 85220. T: (480) 983-0847. RV/tent: 128. $19. Hookups: water, electric (20, 30, 50 amp), sewer, phone (modem).

Weaver's Needle Travel Trailer Resort, 250 South Tomahawk Rd., 85219. T: (480) 982-3683. RV/tent: 400. $29. Hookups: water, electric (20, 30, 50 amp), sewer, phone (modem).

Arizona City

Quail Run RV Resort, 14010 South Amado Blvd., 85223. T: (520) 466-6000 or (800) 301-8114. RV/tent: 324. $22–$25. Hookups: electric (20, 30, 50 amp), water, sewer, phone (modem).

ARIZONA (continued)

Benson

Benson I-10 RV Park, 840 North Ocotillo, 85602. T: (520) 586-4262. RV/tent: 88. $12.50–$20.50. Hookups: electric (30, 50 amp), water, sewer.

Benson KOA, 180 Four Feathers Ln., 85602. T: (520) 586-9815. F: (520) 586-3977. www.koakampgrounds.com/where/az/3133.html. djsunkular@theriver.com. RV/tent: 107. $19–$23.50. Hookups: electric (20, 30, 50 amp), water, sewer, cable TV, phone (modem).

Butterfield RV Resort, 251 South Ocotillo Ave., 85602. T: (520) 507-6161. RV/tent: 173. $29. Hookups: electric (30, 50 amp), water, sewer, cable TV, phone (modem).

Pato Blanco Lakes RV Park, 635 East Pearl St., 85602. T: (520) 586-8966 or (800) 229-9368. www.patoblanco.com. patoblancolakes@theriver.com. RV/tent: 103. $18. Hookups: electric (20, 30, 50 amp), water, sewer, cable TV, phone (modem).

Quarter Horse RV Park, 800 West 4th St., 85602. T: (520) 586-3371 or (800) 527-5025. qhrvpark@theriver.com. RV/tent: 50. $16. Hookups: electric (20, 30, 50 amp), water, sewer, cable TV, phone (modem)

Red Barn Campground, Campground Rd., 85602. T: (520) 586-2035. RV/tent: 49. $13. Hookups: electric (30 amp), water, sewer.

San Pedro Territory 55+ Mobile Home & RV Resort, 1110 South Hwy. 80 Box 1, 85602. T: (520) 586-9546 or (877) 235-9100. RV/tent: 169. $17. Hookups: electric (20, 30, 50 amp), water, sewer.

Bisbee

San Jose Lodge & RV Park, 1002 Naco Hwy., 85603. T: (520) 432-5761. F: (520) 432-4302. www.sanjoselodge.com. info@sanjoselodge.com. RV/tent: 50. $14. Hookups: electric, water, sewer, cable TV.

Brenda

Desert Gold RV Park, 46628 East Hwy. 60, 85348. T: (520) 927-7800 or (800) 927-2101. www.g7inc.org. RV/tent: 425. $20. Hookups: water, electric (30, 50 amp), sewer, modem, cable TV.

Buckeye

Destiny Phoenix RV Resort, 416 North Citrus Rd., 85326. T: (888) 667-2454. www.destinyrv.com. RV/tent: 284. $30–$37. Hookups: water, electric (20, 30, 50 amp), sewer, phone (modem).

Leaf Verde RV Park, 1500 South Apache Rd., 85326. T: (623) 386-3132. leafrv@aol.com. RV/tent: 400. $20. Hookups: electric (30, 50 amp), water, sewer, cable TV, phone (modem).

Bullhead City

Blackstone RV Park, 3299 Boundary Cone Rd., 86426. T: (520) 768-3303. www.bullheadcityaz.com/blackstonervpark. blackstonervpark@yahoo.com. RV/tent: 136. $15. Hookups: water, electric (20, 30, 50 amp), sewer, phone (modem).

Ridgeview RV Resort, 775 Bullhead Parkway, 86429. T: (520) 754-2595 or (800) 392-8560. ridgerv@ctaz.com. RV/tent: 302. $18. Hookups: water, electric (30, 50 amp), sewer, phone (modem), cable TV.

River City RV Park, 2225 Merrill Ave., 86442. T: (520) 754-2121. RV/tent: 134. $16. Hookups: water, electric (30, 50 amp), sewer.

Silver Creek RV Park, 1515 Gold Rush Rd., 86442. T: (520) 763-2444. RV/tent: 140. $15. Hookups: none.

Snowbird RV Resort, 1600 Joy Ln., 86426. T: (520) 768-7141. F: (520) 768-7145. RV/tent: 135. $16. Hookups: water, electric (30, 50 amp), sewer, phone (modem).

Casa Grande

Campground Buena Tierra, 1995 South Cox Rd., 85222. T: (520) 836-3500 or (888) 520-8360. RV/tent: 266. $14–$19. Hookups: water, electric (20, 30, 50 amp), sewer.

Fiesta Grande, 1511 East Florence Blvd., 85222. T: (520) 426-7000 or (888) 934-3782. RV/tent: 767. $26. Hookups: electric (30, 50 amp), water, sewer, phone (modem).

Foothills West RV Resort, 19501 West Hopi Dr., 85222. T: (520) 836-2531. F: (520) 836-0471. www.foothillswest.com. veli@c2i2.com. RV/tent: 180. $22. Hookups: electric (30, 50 amp), water, sewer, phone (modem).

Leisure Valley RV Resort, 9985 North Pinal Ave., 85222. T: (520) 836-9449 or (800) 993-9449. RV/tent: 125. $20. Hookups: water, electric (20, 30, 50 amp), sewer.

Palm Creek Golf and RV Resort, 1110 North Henness Rd., 85222. T: (800) 421-7004. www.palmcreekgolf.com. RV/tent: 1089. $28. Hookups: electric (30, 50 amp), water, sewer, cable TV, phone (modem).

Sundance 1 RV Resort, 1920 North Thornton Rd., 85222. T: (520) 426-9662 or (888) 332-5335. sundance@c2i2.com. RV/tent: 711. $20. Hookups: electric (30, 50 amp), water, sewer.

Val Vista Winter Village RV Resort, 16680 West Val Vista Rd., 85222. T: (520) 836-7800 or (877) 836-7801. F: (520) 836-2638. RV/tent: 345. $25. Hookups: water, electric (20, 30, 50 amp), sewer, phone (modem).

Chloride

Chloride Western RV Park, 5123 Tennessee Ave., P.O. Box 498, 86431. T: (520) 565-4492. RV/tent: 93. $7–$13. Hookups: water, electric (30, 50 amp), sewer.

Shep's RV Park, 9827 2nd St., 86431. T: (877) 565-4251. jmcn1122@aol.com. RV/tent: 7. $10–$15. Hookups: water, electric, sewer.

Dateland

The Oasis at Aztec Hills, P.O. Box 324, 85333. T: (520) 454-2229. RV/tent: 37. $19. Hookups: electric (30, 50 amp), water, sewer, phone (modem).

Dewey

Orchard RV Ranch, 11250 East Hwy. 69, 86327. T: (520) 772-8266 or (800) 352-6305. F: (480) 924-2044. RV/tent: 315. $24–$26. Hookups: water, electric (20, 30, 50 amp), sewer, phone (modem), cable TV.

Ehrenberg

Ehrenberg/Colorado River KOA, 50238 Ehrenberg-Parker Hwy., 85334. T: (520) 923-7213 or (800) 562-8651. RV/tent: 169. $20–$33. Hookups: electric (20, 30, 50 amp), water, sewer.

Flagstaff

Flagstaff KOA, 5803 North Hwy. 89, 86004. T: (520) 526-9926 or (800) KOA-FLAG. F: (520) 527-8356. jsatkoaflag@aol.com. RV/tent: 150. $20–$26. Hookups: water, electric (20, 30 amp), sewer, phone (modem).

J&H RV Park, 7901 North Hwy. 89, 86004. T: (520) 526-1829 or (800) 243-5264 or (623) 879-3215 (winter). F: (623) 879-3215 (winter). j&h@flagstaffrvparks.com. RV/tent: 64. $24–$30. Hookups: water, electric (20, 30, 50 amp), sewer, phone (modem).

Woody Mountain Campground & RV Park, 2727 West Rte. 66, 86001. T: (520) 774-7727 or (800) 732-7986. F: (520) 773-9882. woodymtnrvpark@webtv.net. RV/tent: 146. $17–$23. Hookups: water, electric (20, 30 amp), sewer, phone (modem).

Florence

Desert Gardens RV Park, P.O. Box 1186, 85232. T: (520) 868-3800 or (800) 868-1018. RV/tent: 84. $10–$18. Hookups: water, electric (20, 30, 50 amp), sewer, phone (modem).

Globe

Gila County RV Park & Batting Range, 300 South Pine St., 85501. T: (800) 436-8083. RV/tent: 24. $13–$16. Hookups: water, electric (30, 50 amp), sewer, modem, cable TV.

Gold Canyon

Canyon Vistas RV Resort, 6601 East Hwy. 60, 85219. T: (480) 288-8844. F: (480) 648-5590. www.cal-am.com. reservations@cal-am.com. RV/tent: 637. $20–$30. Hookups: electric (30, 50 amp), water, sewer, cable TV, phone (modem).

Golden Valley

Adobe RV Park, 4950 Apache Way, 86413. T: (520) 565-3010. RV/tent: 75. $16. Hookups: electric (20, 30, 50 amp), water, sewer.

Grand Canyon

Desert View, P.O. Box 129, 86023. T: (520) 638-7888. RV/tent: 50. $10. Hookups: none.

Grand Canyon Camper Village, Box 490, 86023. T: (520) 638-2887. RV/tent: 300. $15–$25. Hookups: water, electric (20, 30 amp), sewer, phone (modem).

Ten-X, FR7302C, 86023. T: (520) 638-2443. RV/tent: 70. $10. Hookups: none.

ARIZONA (continued)

Happy Jack

Happy Jack Lodge & RV Resort, P.O. Box 19569, 86024. T: (520) 477-2805 or (800) 430-0385. RV/tent: 73. $21. Hookups: water, electric (20, 30, 50 amp), sewer.

Hereford

Lakeview Campground, 5990 South Hwy. 92, 85615. T: (520) 378-0311. www.fs.fed.us/r3/coronado. RV/tent: 65. $10. Hookups: none.

Huachuca City

Mountain View RV Park, Post 309, Hwy. 90, 85616. T: (520) 456-2860 or (800) 772-4103. RV/tent: 100. $17. Hookups: electric (30, 50 amp), water, sewer, cable TV, phone (modem).

Tombstone Territories RV Park, 2111 East Hwy. 82, 85616. T: (520) 457-2584 or (877) 316-6714. F: (520) 457-2584. TTRVPARK@yahoo.com. RV/tent: 102. $23. Hookups: electric (20, 30, 50 amp), water, sewer, phone (modem).

Kingman

A Quality Star RV Park, 3131 McDonald Ave., 86401. T: (520) 753-2277. F: (520) 753-4142. RV/tent: 49. $14–$18. Hookups: water, electric (20, 30 amp), sewer, phone (modem), cable TV.

Blake RV Ranch, I-40 & Blake Ranch Rd., 86401. T: (520) 565-3010 or (800) 270-1332. RV/tent: 58. $17. Hookups: electric (20, 30, 50 amp), water, sewer.

Hualapai Mountain Park, P.O. Box 7000, 86402. T: (520) 757-3859. RV/tent: 75. $9–$16. Hookups: electric (30 amp), water, sewer.

Zuni Village RV, 2840 Airway Ave., 86401. T: (520) 692-6202. RV/tent: 84. $17. Hookups: electric (20, 30, 50 amp), water, sewer.

Lake Havasu City

Beachcomber RV Resort, 601 Beachcomber Blvd., 86403. T: (520) 855-2322. F: (520) 855-3707. RV/tent: 50. $28–$33. Hookups: water, electric (30 amp), sewer, phone (modem), cable TV.

Cattail Cove State Park, P.O. Box 1990, 86405. T: (520) 855-1223. F: (520) 855-1730. RV/tent: 101. $8–$16. Hookups: Electric (30 amp), water.

Crazy Horse Campgrounds, 1534 Beachcomber Blvd., 86403. T: (520) 855-4033. www.crazy horsecampgrounds.com. RV/tent: 777. $24–$38. Hookups: electric (20, 30, 50 amp), water, sewer, cable TV, phone.

London Bridge RV Park, 3405 London Bridge Rd., 86405. T: (520) 764-3700. RV/tent: 56. $25. Hookups: water, electric (20, 30 amp), sewer.

Marana

A Bar A RV Park, 9015 West Tangerine Rd., 85653. T: (520) 682-4333. F: (520) 682-4332. abaraaz@netscape.com. RV/tent: 85. $19. Hookups: electric (20, 30, 50 amp), water, sewer, phone (modem).

Valley of the Sun RV Mobile Home Park, 13377 North Sandario Rd., 85653. T: (520) 682-3434. RV/tent: 65. $20. Hookups: electric (30, 50 amp), water, sewer, phone (modem).

McNeal

Double Adobe Campground, 5057 West Double Adobe Rd., 85617. T: (520) 364-4000 or (800) 694-4242. www.theriver.com/doubleadobe. doubleadobe@theriver.com. RV/tent: 70. $10–$14. Hookups: electric (30 amp), water, sewer, cable TV.

Mesa

The Resort, 1101 South Ellsworth Rd., 85208. T: (480) 986-8404. RV/tent: 792. $30. Hookups: electric (30, 50 amp), water, sewer, cable TV, phone (modem).

Apache Wells RV Resort, 2656 North 56th St., 85215. T: (480) 832-4324. RV/tent: 320. $34. Hookups: electric (30, 50 amp), water, sewer, phone (modem).

Canyon Lake Marina, P.O. Box 5800, 26 North MacDonald, 85211. T: (602) 467-2511 or (602) 379-6446. RV/tent: 115. $10. Hookups: none.

Fiesta RV Resort, 3811 East University Dr., 85205. T: (480) 832-6490 or (877) 506-0071. RV/tent: 336. $28. Hookups: water, electric (20, 50 amp), sewer, phone (modem).

Good Life RV Resort, 3403 East Main St., 85213. T: (480) 832-4990 or (800) 999-4990. RV/tent: 1184. $32. Hookups: electric (30, 50 amp), water, sewer, phone (modem).

Greenfield Village RV Resort, 111 South Greenfield Rd., 85206. T: (480) 832-4990 or (800) 999-4990. RV/tent: 1184. $35. Hookups: electric (30, 50 amp), water, sewer.

Las Palmas Grand, 2550 South Ellsworth Rd., 85212. T: (480) 380-3000 or (800) 982-2250. RV/tent: 63. $30. Hookups: electric (20, 30, 50 amp), water.

Mesa Regal RV Resort, 4700 East Main, 85205. T: (480) 830-2821 or (800) 845-4752. RV/tent: 2005. $35. Hookups: electric (30, 50 amp), water, sewer, phone (modem).

Orangewood Shadows RV Resort, 3165 East University, 85213. T: (480) 832-9080 or (800) 826-0909. RV/tent: 474. $31. Hookups: electric (30, 50 amp), water, sewer.

Palm Gardens Mobile Home/RV Community, 2929 East Main St., 85213. T: (480) 832-0290. RV/tent: 115. $35. Hookups: electric (30, 50 amp), water, sewer, phone (modem).

Paradise Palms Resort, 1608 East Main St., 85203. T: (480) 964-3552. RV/tent: 25. $16. Hookups: electric (30 amp), water, sewer, phone (modem).

Park Place RV Resort, 306 South Recker Rd., 85206. T: (480) 830-1080. RV/tent: 288. $16. Hookups: electric (30, 50 amp), water, sewer.

Silveridge RV Resort, 8265 East Southern, 85208. T: (480) 373-7000. F: (480) 373-7647. www.silveridge.com. RV/tent: 687. $30. Hookups: electric (30, 50 amp), water, sewer, cable TV, phone (modem).

Sun Life RV Resort, 5055 East University, 85205. T: (480) 981-9500. RV/tent: 761. $25. Hookups: electric (30, 50 amp), water, sewer, phone (modem).

Tortilla, P.O. Box 5800, 26 North MacDonald, 85211. T: (602) 467-2511 or (602) 379-6446. RV/tent: 77. $8. Hookups: water.

Towerpoint RV Resort, 4860 East Main, 85205. T: (480) 832-4996. www.towerpointresort.com. RV/tent: 1115. $30. Hookups: water, electric (20, 30, 50 amp), sewer, phone (modem).

Trailer Village, 3020 East Main St., 85213. T: (480) 832-1770 or (877) 924-6709. RV/tent: 1800. $16–$32. Hookups: water, electric (20, 30, 50 amp), sewer, phone (modem).

Trailing Ranch, 8730 East Apache Trail, 85208. T: (480) 984-0592:(800) 625-7266. F: (480) 984-2592. RV/tent: 55. $25. Hookups: electric (30, 50 amp), water, sewer, phone (modem).

Val Vista Village RV Resort, 233 North Val Vista Dr., 85213. T: (480) 832-2547. RV/tent: 1016. $30. Hookups: electric (30, 50 amp), water, sewer, phone (modem).

Valle de Oro RV Resort, 1452 South Ellsworth, 85208. T: (480) 984-1146:(800) 626-6686. www.valledeloro.com. RV/tent: 1802. $35. Hookups: electric (30, 50 amp), water, sewer, phone (modem).

Venture Out, 5001 East Main St., 85205. T: (480) 832-0200. RV/tent: 1749. $20–$30. Hookups: electric (30, 50 amp), water, sewer.

View Point RV & Golf Resort, 8700 East University, 85207. T: (480) 373-8700. RV/tent: 1784. $35. Hookups: electric (30, 50 amp), water, sewer, cable TV, phone (modem).

Mormon Lake

Mormon Lake Lodge RV Park and Campground, P.O. Box 38102, Main St., 86038. T: (520) 354-2227. www.foreverresorts.com. scott.gold@inetmail.att.net. RV/tent: 86. $8–$24. Hookups: water, electric (20, 30, 50 amp), sewer, phone (modem).

Naco

Turquoise Valley Golf Course & RV Park, P.O. Box 727, 85620. T: (520) 432-3091. www.turquoisevalley.com. golfer@turquoisevalley.com. RV/tent: 100. $15. Hookups: electric (30, 50 amp), water, sewer, cable TV, phone (modem).

Overgaard

Elk Pines RV Resort, P.O. Box 422, 2256 East Hwy. 260, 85933. T: (520) 535-3833. elkpines@pinenet.com. RV/tent: 68. $21. Hookups: water, electric (20, 30, 50 amp), sewer, phone (modem).

Page

Page-Lake Powell Campground, 849 South Coppermine Rd., 86040. T: (928) 645-3374. F: (928) 645-2588. campground.page-lakepowell.com. RV/tent: 133. $17–$26. Hookups: water, electric (20, 30, 50 amp), sewer, modem, cable TV.

Parker

Fox's Pierpoint Landing, 6350 Riverside Dr., 85344. T: (520) 667-3444. F: (520) 667-4100. RV/tent: 70. $20–$25. Hookups: electric (20, 30, 50 amp), water, sewer.

ARIZONA (continued)

Parker (continued)

Tony's Road Runner RV Park, 7000 Riverside Dr., 85344. T: (520) 667-4252. F: (520) 667-3293. www.roadrunnerfloating.com. RV/tent: 35. $27–$30. Hookups: electric (20, 30 amp), water, sewer, phone (modem), cable TV.

Peoria

Pleasant Harbor RV Resort, 8708 West Harbor Blvd., 85382. T: (800) 475-3272 or (602) 269-0077. F: (602) 269-0838. www.pleasantharbor.com. mwd@pleasantharbor.com. RV/tent: 200. $25–$32. Hookups: water, electric (20, 30, 50 amp), sewer, phone (modem).

Quality Inn RV Park, Grand Ave., 85382. T: (800) 572-9295. RV/tent: 72. $26. Hookups: water, electric (20, 30 amp), sewer.

Sundial Mobil & RV Park, 75th Ave., 85382. T: (623) 979-1921. RV/tent: 102. $16. Hookups: water, electric (30, 50 amp), sewer.

Phoenix

Desert Shadows Travel Trailer Resort, 19203 North 29th Ave., 85027. T: (623) 869-8178 or (800) 595-7290. RV/tent: 638. $25. Hookups: water, electric (30, 50 amp), sewer.

Desert's Edge RV Park, 22623 North Black Canyon Hwy., 85027. T: (623) 587-0940. F: (623) 587-0029. RV/tent: 250. $22. Hookups: water, electric (30, 50 amp), sewer, phone (modem).

Prescott

Point of Rocks Campground, 3025 North Hwy. 89, 86301. T: (520) 445-9018. www.northlink.com/~rhorsely. RV/tent: 96. $18. Hookups: water, electric (20, 30 amp), sewer.

Willow Lake RV & Camping Park, 1617 Heritage Park Rd., 86301. T: (520) 445-6311 or (800) 940-2845. RV/tent: 200. $20. Hookups: water, electric (20, 30, 50 amp), sewer, phone (modem), cable TV.

Quartzsite

88 Shades RV Park, 575 West Main St., 85346. T: (520) 927-6336 or (800) 457-4392. RV/tent: 250. $18–$22. Hookups: electric (30 amp), water, sewer.

B-10 Campground, P.O. Box 4613, 85359. T: (520) 927-4393. RV/tent: 174. $16–$23. Hookups: electric (30, 50 amp), water, sewer.

Desert Gardens, P.O. Box 619, 85346. T: (520) 927-6361. RV/tent: 270. $18. Hookups: electric (20, 30, 50 amp), water, sewer, phone (modem).

Holiday Palms RV Park, P.O. Box 4800, 85346. T: (520) 927-5666. RV/tent: 254. $18–$22. Hookups: electric (20, 30 amp), water, sewer.

Queen Valley

Encore RV Park, 50 West Oro Viejo Dr., 85219. T: (877) 337-2757. F: (520) 463-2331. www.rvonthego.com. RV/tent: 210. $18–$24. Hookups: water, electric (30, 50 amp), sewer, phone (modem).

Roosevelt

Apache Lake Resort, Hwy. 88, HCO 2 Box 4800, 85545. T: (602) 467-2511 or (520) 467-3200. RV/tent: 12. $2. Hookups: yes (unspecified).

Safford

Roper Lake State Park, Rte 2 Box 712, 85546. T: (520) 428-6760. RV/tent: 71. $4–$15. Hookups: none.

Sahuarita

Rancho Resort RV Park, 1300 West Sahuarita Rd., 85629. T: (888) 363-8616 or (520) 399-3900. www.ranchoresort.com. info@ranchoresort.com. RV/tent: 100. $19–$30. Hookups: water, electric, sewer, cable TV, phone.

Salome

Desert Palms Golf & RV Resort, 39258 Harquahala Rd., 85348. T: (520) 859-2000. F: (520) 859-2001. desertpalmssp@netscape.net. RV/tent: 750. $18. Hookups: electric (30, 50 amp), water, sewer.

Tomahawk RV Park, I-10 & Exit 45 at Vicksburg Rd., P.O. Box A4, 85348. T: (520) 859-3843 or (800) 925-2407. RV/tent: 95. $19. Hookups: electric (20, 30, 50 amp), water, sewer.

Sedona

Rancho Sedona RV Park, 135 Bear Wallow Ln., 86336. T: (520) 282-7255 or (888) 641-4261. www.ranchosedona.com. ranchosedona@kachina.net. RV/tent: 84. $27. Hookups: water, electric (30, 50 amp), sewer, modem, cable TV.

Show Low

K-Bar RV Park, 300 North 15th Ave., 85901. T: (520) 537-2886. RV/tent: 92. $20. Hookups: electric (20, 30, 50 amp), water, sewer, cable TV, phone (modem).

Waltner's RV Park, 4800 South 28th St., 85901. T: (520) 537-4611. RV/tent: 145. $25. Hookups: electric (30 amp), water, sewer, cable TV, phone (modem).

Sierra Vista

Pueblo del Sol RV Resort, 3400 Resort Dr., 85650. T: (520) 378-0282 or (888) 551-1432. www.pdsrvresort.com. pdsrv@C2I2.com. RV/tent: 135. $19–$27. Hookups: water, electric (30, 50 amp), sewer, cable TV, phone (modem).

St. David

Holy Trinity Monastery/Monte Cassino RV Park, P.O. Box 298, Hwy. 80-303, 85630. T: (520) 720-4016. F: (520) 720-4202. RV/tent: 23. $13. Hookups: water, electric (20, 30 amp), sewer.

Sun City

Paradise RV Resort, 10950 West Union Hills Dr., 85373. T: (623) 977-0344 or (800) 847-2280. RV/tent: 950. $35. Hookups: electric (30, 50 amp), water, sewer, cable TV, phone (modem).

Surprise

Donorma RV Park, 15637 Norma Ln., 85374. T: (623) 583-8195. F: (623) 583-0649. RV/tent: 66. $23. Hookups: water, electric (20, 30, 50 amp), sewer, phone (modem).

Sunflower Resort, 16501 North El Mirage Rd., 85374. T: (623) 583-0100 or (800) 627-8637. F: (623) 583-2007. Sunflowr@doitnow.com. RV/tent: 1156. $24–$32. Hookups: electric (30, 50 amp), water, sewer, cable TV, phone (modem).

Tempe

Apache Palms RV Park, 1836 East Apache Blvd., 85281. T: (480) 966-7399. apacheplms@aol.com. RV/tent: 75. $19–$29. Hookups: electric (20, 30, 50 amp), water, sewer, cable TV, phone (modem).

Tombstone

Stampede RV Park, 201 West Allen, P.O. Box 1247, 85638. T: (520) 457-3738. stampederv@desert-gold.com. RV/tent: 22. $22. Hookups: water, electric (20, 30, 50 amp), sewer, phone (modem).

Tombstone Hills RV Park & Campground, P.O. Box 99, 85638. T: (520) 457-3829. RV/tent: 86. $20. Hookups: water, electric (50 amp), sewer.

Tonopah

Saddle Mountain RV Park, 3607 North 411th St., P.O. Box 146, 85354. T: (623) 386-3892. www.saddlemountain.com. RV/tent: 139. $10–$20. Hookups: electric (30, 50 amp), water, sewer, phone (modem).

Stage Stop RV Park, 2614 South Wintersberg Rd., 85354. T: (623) 386-1601. F: (623) 386-1612. RV/tent: 146. $23. Hookups: water, electric (20, 30, 50 amp), sewer, phone (modem).

Tucson

Beaudry RV Resort, 5151 South Country Club Rd., 85706. T: (520)806-8156 or (877) 806-8156. www. beaudryrvresort.com. RV/tent: 400. $30. Hookups: water, electric (50 amp), sewer, cable TV, phone (modem).

Cactus Country RV Resort, 10195 South Houghton Rd., 85747. T: (520) 574-3000 or (800) 777-8799. F: (520) 574-9004. www.arizonguide.com/cactusco. RV/tent: 263. $26. Hookups: water, electric (20, 30, 50 amp), sewer, cable TV, phone (modem).

Far Horizons Trailer Village, 555 North Pantano Rd., 85710. T: (520) 296-1234. F: (520) 733-9003. farhorizonstv@worldnet.att.net. RV/tent: 514. $26. Hookups: water, electric (30, 50 amp), sewer, phone (modem).

Justin's RV Park & WaterWorld, 3551 South San Joaquin Rd., 85735. T: (520) 883-8340 or (888) 883-8340. RV/tent: 220. $10–$18. Hookups: water, electric (30, 50 amp), sewer, phone (modem).

Miracle RV Park, 333 West Glenn St., 85705. T: (520) 624-0142 or (888) 624-0142. RV/tent: 86. $16. Hookups: water, electric (20, 30 amp), sewer, phone (modem).

ARIZONA (continued)

Mission RV Resort, 31 West Los Reales Rd., 85735. T: (800) 444-8439. missnview@aol.com. RV/tent: 152. $28. Hookups: water, electric (30, 50 amp), sewer.

Prince of Tucson, 3501 North Freeway, 85705. T: (520) 887-3501 or (800) 955-3501. princeoftucson@worldnet.att.net. RV/tent: 212. $22. Hookups: water, electric (20, 30, 50 amp), sewer.

Rincon Country East RV Resort, 8989 East Escalante, 85730. T: (520) 886-8431. eastinfo@rinconcountry.com. RV/tent: 460. $28. Hookups: water, electric (30, 50 amp), sewer.

Rincon Country West RV Resort, 4555 South Mission Rd., 85746. T: (520) 294-5608 or (800) 782-7275. westinfo@rinconcountry.com. RV/tent: 1100. $26–$29. Hookups: water, electric (30, 50 amp), sewer, cable TV, phone (modem).

Rose Canyon, Mile Post 17 Catalina Hwy., 85750. T: (520) 749-8700. www.azstarnet.com.public/nonprofit/coronado/d5home1.htm. RV/tent: 74. $7. Hookups: none.

South Forty RV Ranch, 3600 West Orange Grove Rd., 85741. T: (520) 297-2503. south40rv@theriver.com. RV/tent: 229. $22–$26. Hookups: water, electric (20, 30 amp), sewer, phone (modem).

Spencer Canyon, Mile Post 22 Catalina Hwy., 85750. T: (520) 749-8700. www.azstarnet.com.public/nonprofit/coronado/d5home1.htm RV/tent: 77. $7. Hookups: none.

Western Way RV Resort, 3100 South Kinney Rd., 85713. T: (520) 578-1715 or (800) 292-8616. accenth@azstarnet.com. RV/tent: 300. $15–$25. Hookups: water, electric (20, 30 amp), sewer.

Whispering Palms RV Trailer Park, 3445 North Romero Rd., 85705. T: (520) 888-2500 or (800) 266-8577. RV/tent: 103. $15–$19. Hookups: water, electric (30 amp), sewer.

Wellton

M&M RV Village, 28541 West AZ Ave., 85356. T: (520) 785-4273. F: (520) 785-9651. tsmangine@aol.com. RV/tent: 90. $15. Hookups: water, electric (30 amp), sewer, phone (modem).

West Sedona

Lo Lo Mai Springs Outdoor Resort, P.O. Box 3169, 86340. T: (520) 634-4700. www.lolomai.com. lolomai@sedona.net. RV/tent: 90. $23–$32. Hookups: electric (30 amp), water, sewer.

Why

Coyote Howls Campground, P.O Box 1134, US Hwy. 86, 85321. T: (520) 387-5209. coyosurf@tabletoptelephone.com. RV/tent: 550. $8. Hookups: none.

Hickiwan Trails RV Park, South US Hwy. 86, 85321. T: (520) 362-3267. RV/tent: 95. $15. Hookups: water, electric (20, 30 amp), sewer.

Las Palmas RV Park, Hwy. 85, 85321. T: (520) 387-3300. RV/tent: 47. $15. Hookups: water, electric (20, 30 amp), sewer.

Roberts Ranch Resort, 1600 South US Hwy. 86, 85321. T: (800) 699-7983. RV/tent: 85. $6–$18. Hookups: water, electric (20, 30, 50 amp), sewer.

Wickenburg

Desert Cypress Trailer Ranch, 610 Jack Burden Rd., space No. 1, 85390. T: (520) 684-2153. RV/tent: 32. $20. Hookups: water, electric (20, 30, 50 amp), sewer, cable TV.

Willcox

Fort Willcox RV Park, RR2 Box 512, 85643. T: (520) 384-4986. F: (520) 384-4986. RV/tent: 35. $10–$15. Hookups: water, electric (20, 30, 50 amp), sewer.

Grande Vista RV Park, 711 Prescott Ave. North, 85643. T: (520) 384-4002. F: (520) 384-0458. connet1@vtc.net. RV/tent: 37. $16. Hookups: water, electric (30, 50 amp), sewer, cable TV, phone (modem).

Lifestyle RV Resort, 622 North Haskell Ave., 85643. T: (520) 384-3303. F: (520) 384-0740. RV/tent: 60. $13–$21. Hookups: water, electric (30, 50 amp), sewer.

Magic Circle RV Park, 700 North Virginia Ave., 85643. T: (520) 384-3212 or (800) 333-4720. Magic1@vtc.net. RV/tent: 56. $20. Hookups: water, electric (20, 30, 50 amp), sewer, cable TV, phone (modem).

Williams

Canyon Gateway RV Park, 1060 North Grand Canyon Blvd., 86046. T: (888) 635-0329. F: (520) 635-2733. RV/tent: 101. $18. Hookups: water, electric (30, 50 amp), sewer.

Circle Pines KOA, 1000 Circle Pines Rd., 86046. T: (520) 635-2626 or (800) 562-9379. F: (520) 635-2627. CABA66@aol.com. RV/tent: 149. $18–$27. Hookups: water, electric (20, 30 amp), sewer, phone (modem).

Flinstone's Bedrock City, HCR-34 Box A, 86046. T: (520) 635-2600. F: (520) 635-2600. RV/tent: 60. $16. Hookups: electric (30 amp).

Railside RV Ranch, 877 Rodeo Rd., 86046. T: (520) 635-4077 or (888) 635-4077. www.thegrandcanyon.com/railside. railside@thegrandcanyon.com. RV/tent: 100. $15–$20. Hookups: water, electric (20, 30, 50 amp), sewer, modem, cable TV.

Yuma

Araby Acres Travel Trailer Park, 6649 East Hwy. 80, 85365. T: (520) 344-8666. arabyacres@aol.com. RV/tent: 338. $28. Hookups: electric (30, 50 amp), water, sewer, phone (modem).

Arizona Sands RV Park, 5510 East 32nd St., 85365. T: (520) 726-0286. azsandsrvparks@aol.com. RV/tent: 200. $20–$25. Hookups: electric (30, 50 amp), water, sewer.

Blue Sky RV Park, 10247 South Frontage Rd., 85365. T: (877) 367-5220. RV/tent: 287. $25–$40. Hookups: electric (30, 50 amp), water, sewer.

Bonita Mesa RV Resort, 9400 East North Frontage Rd., 85365. T: (520) 342-2999. RV/tent: 472. $24. Hookups: water, electric (30, 50 amp), sewer, phone (modem), cable TV.

Caravan Oasis RV Park, 10500 North East Frontage Rd., 85365. T: (520) 342-1480. RV/tent: 742. $21. Hookups: water, electric (30, 50 amp), sewer, phone (modem), cable TV.

Cocopah RV & Golf Resort, 6800 Strand Ave., 85364. T: (520) 343-9300 or (800) 537-7901. RV/tent: 806. $27. Hookups: water, electric (30, 50 amp), sewer, phone (modem), cable TV.

Desert Paradise RV Resort, 10537 South Ave. 9E, 85367. T: (520) 342-9313. dprvresort@aol.com. RV/tent: 260. $25. Hookups: water, electric (30, 50 amp), sewer, phone (modem), cable TV.

El Prado Estates RV Park, 6200 East Hwy. 95, 85365. T: (520) 726-4006. F: (602) 978-0613. RV/tent: 120. $14. Hookups: electric (30 amp), water, sewer.

Fortuna de Oro RV Resort, 13650 North Frontage Rd., 85367. T: (520) 342-5051. RV/tent: 763. $20. Hookups: water, electric (20, 30, 50 amp), sewer.

Friendly Acres Trailer Park, 2779 West Eighth St., 85364. T: (520) 783-8414. RV/tent: 280. $16. Hookups: water, electric (30 amp), sewer, phone (modem), cable TV.

Hidden Shores RV Village, Star Rte. 4 Box 40, 85365. T: (520) 783-1448. F: (520) 329-4654. RV/tent: 354. $12–$21. Hookups: water, electric (20, 30, 50 amp), sewer, phone (modem).

Las Quintas Oasis RV Park, 1442 North Frontage Rd., 85365. T: (520) 305-9005 or (877) 975-9005. RV/tent: 460. $21. Hookups: water, electric (30, 50 amp), sewer, phone (modem), cable TV.

Shangri-La RV Resort, 10498 North Frontage Rd., 85365. T: (520) 340-9123. RV/tent: 302. $21–$25. Hookups: water, electric (30, 50 amp), sewer.

Sun Vista RV Resort, 7201 East Hwy. 80, 85365. T: (520) 726-8920 or (800) 423-8382. RV/tent: 1230. $29. Hookups: water, electric (30, 50 amp), sewer, phone (modem), cable TV.

Villa Alameda RV Resort, 11451 South Ave. 5E, 85365. T: (520) 344-8081. RV/tent: 302. $23. Hookups: water, electric (30, 50 amp), sewer, phone (modem), cable TV.

West Wind RV & Golf Resort, 9797 East Frontage Rd., 85365. T: (520) 342-2992. RV/tent: 1083. $27. Hookups: water, electric (20, 30, 50 amp), sewer, phone (modem), cable TV.

Wind Have RV Park, 6580 East Hwy. 80, 85365. T: (520) 726-0284. F: (520) 726-6622. RV/tent: 135. $27. Hookups: water, electric (20, 30, 50 amp), sewer.

Yuma Mesa RV Park, 5990 East Hwy. 80, 85365. T: (520) 344-3369. RV/tent: 183. $23. Hookups: water, electric (30 amp), sewer.

ARKANSAS

Alma

Alma RV Park, 405 Heather Ln., 72921. T: (501) 632-0909. RV/tent: 50. $5–$22. Hookups: electric (30, 50 amps), water, sewer.

Ft. Smith/Alma KOA, 3539 North Hwy. 71, 72921. T: (800) 562-2703 or (501) 632-2704. www.koa.com/where/AR/04110. RV/tent: 78. $20–$24. Hookups: electric (30, 50 amps), water, sewer.

Indian Creek Campground, 13324 Indian Creek Rd., 72732. T: (501) 656-3145. www.ReserveUSA.com/nrrs/ar/ind2. RV/tent: 20. $13–$15. Hookups: electric (30 amps).

Arkadelphia

Alpine Ridge Campground, 729 Channel Rd., 71923. T: (870) 246-5501. www.ReserveUSA.com/nrrs/ar/alpr. RV/tent: 49. $10–$14. Hookups: electric (20, 30 amps).

Arlie Moore Campground, 729 Channel Rd., 71923. T: (870) 246-5501. www.ReserveUSA.com/nrrs/ar/arli. RV/tent: 71. $10–$14. Hookups: electric (20, 30 amps).

Caddo Drive Campground, 729 Channel Rd., 71923. T: (870) 246-5501. www.ReserveUSA.com/nrrs/ar/cadv. RV/tent: 72. $10. Hookups: electric (20, 30 amps).

Edgewood Campground, 729 Channel Rd., 71923. T: (870) 246-5501. www.ReserveUSA.com/nrrs/ar/edge. RV/tent: 51. $10–$14. Hookups: electric (20, 30 amps).

Iron Mountain Campground, 729 Channel Rd., 71923. T: (870) 246-5501. www.ReserveUSA.com/nrrs/ar/irom. RV/tent: 69. $10–$14. Hookups: electric (20, 30 amps).

Shouse Ford Campground, 729 Channel Rd., 71923. T: (870) 246-5501. www.ReserveUSA.com/nrrs/ar/shou. RV/tent: 100. $10–$14. Hookups: electric (20, 30, 50 amps).

Ashdown

Beards Bluff Campground, 1528 Hwy. 32 East, 71822. T: (870) 388-9556. www.ReserveUSA.com/nrrs/ar/beab. RV/tent: 30. $9–$14. Hookups: electric (20, 30 amps).

Cottonshed, 1528 Hwy. 32 East, 71822. T: (870) 287-7118. www.ReserveUSA.com/nrrs/ar/cotn. RV/tent: 46. $13–$15. Hookups: electric (20, 30 amps), water.

Millwood State Park, 1564 Hwy. 32 East, 71822. T: (870) 898-2800. www.ArkansasStateParks.com. RV/tent: 117. $9–$17. Hookups: electric (30 amps), water.

Benton

JB's RV Park & Campground, 8601 J.B. Baxely Rd., 72015. T: (501) 778-6050. RV/tent: 44. $14–$16. Hookups: electric (30, 50 amps), water, sewer.

Bismarck

DeGray State Park, 2027 State Park Entrance Rd., 71929. T: (501) 865-2801. www.ArkansasStateParks.com. RV/tent: 113. $14–$16. Hookups: electric (30 amps), water.

Bluff City

White Oak Lake State Park, Rte. 2 Box 28, 71722. T: (870) 685-2748 or (870) 685-2132. www.ArkansasStateParks.com. RV/tent: 45. $6–$14. Hookups: electric (30 amps), water.

Blytheville

Knights of the Road RV Park, 3801 South Division, 72315. T: (501) 763-7161. RV/tent: 12. $18. Hookups: electric (20, 30, 50 amps), water, sewer.

Brinkley

Super 8 RV Park, P.O. Box 828, 72021. T: (501) 734-4680. RV/tent: 34. $13–$17. Hookups: electric (30 amps), water, sewer.

Cotter

White River Campground & Cottages, P.O. Box 99, 72626. T: (870) 453-2299. F: (870) 453-3232. RV/tent: 86. $17. Hookups: electric (30, 50 amps), water, sewer.

Dardanelle

Mount Nebo State Park, No. 1 State Park Dr., 72834. T: (501) 229-3655. www.ArkansasStateParks.com. RV/tent: 35. $6–$12. Hookups: electric (30 amps), water.

DeQueen

Bellah Mine Campground, 706 DeQueen Lake Rd., 71832. T: (870) 584-4161. www.ReserveUSA.com/nrrs/ar/bell. RV/tent: 20. $10–$14. Hookups: electric (20, 30 amps), water.

Cossatot Reefs Campground, 706 DeQueen Lake Rd., 71832. T: (870) 584-4161. www.ReserveUSA.com/nrrs/ar/coss. RV/tent: 26. $9–$15. Hookups: electric (20, 30 amps), water.

Big Coon Creek Campground, 706 DeQueen Lake Rd., 71832. T: (870) 584-4161. www.ReserveUSA.com/nrrs/ar/bigc. RV/tent: 31. $13–$15. Hookups: electric (20, 30 amps), water.

Dierks

Blue Ridge Campground, 952 Lake Rd. P.O. Box 8, 71833. T: (870) 286-2346. www.ReserveUSA.com/nrrs/ar/blur. RV/tent: 17. $9–$13. Hookups: electric (20, 30 amps), water.

Eureka Springs

Green Tree Lodge & RV Park, Rte. 6 Box 130, 72632. T: (501) 253-8807. RV/tent: 24. $17–$19. Hookups: electric (20, 30, 50 amps), water, sewer.

Hidden Cove, 700 C.R. 1089, 72632. T: (501) 253-2939. F: (501) 253-0591. www.eurekaweb.com/hiddencove. RV/tent: 80. Hookups: electric (20, 30, 50 amps), water, sewer.

Kettle Campground, Hwy. 62 East, Rte. 4 Box 615, 72632. T: (800) 899-CAMP or (501) 253-9100. www.eureka-net.com/kettle. RV/tent: 80. $12–$19. Hookups: electric (20, 30, 50 amps), water, sewer.

Starkey Campground, 3994 Mundell Rd., 72631. T: (501) 253-5866. www.ReserveUSA.com/nrrs/ar/star. RV/tent: 23. $11. Hookups: electric (20, 30 amps).

Wanderlust RV Park, Rte. 1 Box 946, 72632. T: (800) 253-7385. RV/tent: 90. $19. Hookups: electric (20, 30, 50 amps), water, sewer.

Fairfield Bay

Golden Pond RV Park, Box 1520, 72088. T: (501) 723-8212. F: (501) 723-8414. www.goldenpond.com. RV/tent: 35. $19. Hookups: electric (30, 50 amps), water, sewer.

Flippin

Cedar Hollow RV Park, 76 MC 8119, 72634. T: (877) 747-3633 or (870) 453-8643. www.billyhill.com/cedarhollowrv. RV/tent: 26. $17. Hookups: electric (20, 30, 50 amps), water, sewer.

Garfield

Lost Bridge South Campground, 12001 Buckhorn Cir., 72732. T: (501) 359-3312. www.ReserveUSA.com/nrrs/ar/loss. RV/tent: 36. $13. Hookups: electric (20, 30 amps).

Gilbert

Buffalo Camping and Canoeing, P.O. Box 45, 72636. T: (870) 439-2888 or (870) 439-2386. www.gilbertstore.com/lodging.htm. RV/tent: 86. $5–$15. Hookups: electric (30 amps), water.

Greenbrier

Woolly Hollow State Park, 82 Woolly Hollow Rd., 72058. T: (501) 679-2098. www.ArkansasStateParks.com. RV/tent: 32. $9–$14. Hookups: electric (30 amps), water.

Hampton

Silver Eagle RV Campground, P.O. Box 1165, 71744. T: (870) 798-3798. www.silvereaglerv.com. RV/tent: 35. $18. Hookups: electric (20, 30, 50 amps), water, sewer.

Harrisburg

Lake Poinsett State Park, 5752 State Park Ln., 72432. T: (870) 578-2064. www.ArkansasStateParks.com. RV/tent: 30. $12–$16. Hookups: electric (30 amps), water.

Harrison

Harrison Village Campground, Rte. 4 Box 15, 72601. T: (501) 743-3388. RV/tent: 79. $18. Hookups: electric (20, 30, 50 amps), water, sewer.

ARKANSAS (continued)

Shady Oaks Campground and RV Park, 960 Hwy. 206 East, 72601. T: (870) 743-2343. www.camptheoaks.com. RV/tent: 50. $12–$22. Hookups: electric (20, 30, 50 amps), water, sewer.

Heber Springs

Devils Fork Campground, 700 Heber Springs Rd. North, 72543. T: (501) 362-2416. www.ReserveUSA.com/nrrs/ar/devf. RV/tent: 56. $12–$17. Hookups: electric (20, 30 amps).

Hill Creek Campground, 700 Heber Springs Rd. North, 72543. T: (501) 362-2416. www.ReserveUSA.com/nrrs/ar/hill. RV/tent: 41. $12–$15. Hookups: electric (30, 50 amps), water, sewer.

John F Kennedy Campground, 700 Heber Springs Rd. North, 72543. T: (501) 362-2416. www.ReserveUSA.com/nrrs/ar/john. RV/tent: 74. $15–$18. Hookups: electric (20, 30 amps), water.

Hot Springs

Camp Lake Hamilton, 6191 Central Ave., 71901. T: (501) 525-8204. RV/tent: 80. $12. Hookups: electric (30, 50 amps), water, sewer.

Hot Springs KOA, 838 McClendon Rd., 71901. T: (800) 562-5903 or (501) 624-5912. www.koa.com/where/AR/04106. RV/tent: 86. $24–$26. Hookups: electric (20, 30, 50 amps), water, sewer.

Lake Catherine State Park, 1200 Catherine Park Rd., 71913. T: (501) 844-4176. www.ArkansasStateParks.com. RV/tent: 70. $14–$16. Hookups: electric (30 amps), water.

Lakeside Trailer Park & Cottages, Inc., 451 Lakeland Dr., 71901. T: (501) 525-8878. RV/tent: 20. $13. Hookups: electric (30 amps), water, sewer.

Mill Pond Mobile Home & RV Village, 1 Peakness Dr., 71901. T: (501) 525-3959. RV/tent: 21. $10. Hookups: electric (30, 50 amps), water, sewer.

Pit Stop RV Park & Restaurant, 3040 Albert Pike, 71901. T: (501) 767-6830. RV/tent: 15. $18. Hookups: electric (30, 50 amps), water.

River View Paradise RV Park & Condos, 200 River Oaks Dr., 71901. T: (501) 767-9821. RV/tent: 65. $20. Hookups: electric (30 amps), water, sewer.

Timbercrest RV & Mobile Home Park, 3921 Central Ave., 71901. T: (501) 525-8361. RV/tent: 53. $15. Hookups: electric (50 amps), water, sewer.

Wagon Wheel RV Park, 205 Treasure Isle Rd. No. 99, 71913. T: (501) 767-6852. RV/tent: 62. $15–$18. Hookups: electric (30 amps), water, sewer.

Huntsville

Withrow Springs State Park, Rte. 3 Box 29, 72750. T: (501) 559-2593. www.ArkansasStateParks.com. RV/tent: 26. $6–$14. Hookups: electric (30 amps), water.

Jonesboro

Lake Frierson State Park, 7904 Hwy. 141, 72401. T: (870) 932-2615. www.ArkansasStateParks.com. RV/tent: 12. $12. Hookups: electric (30 amps), water.

Perkins RV Park, 1821 Parker Rd., 72404. T: (870) 935-4152. RV/tent: 44. $8–$19. Hookups: electric (30, 50 amps), water, sewer.

Kirby

Daisy State Park, 103 East Park, 71950. T: (870) 398-4487. www.ArkansasStateParks.com. RV/tent: 117. $6–$16. Hookups: electric (30 amps), water.

Lake Village

Lake Chicot State Park, 2542 Hwy. 257, 71653. T: (870) 265-5480. www.ArkansasStateParks.com. RV/tent: 127. $6–$17. Hookups: electric (30 amps), water, sewer.

Lakeview

Bull Shoals State Park, 129 Bull Shoals Park, 72756. T: (870) 431-5521. www.ArkansasStateParks.com. RV/tent: 105. $6–$16. Hookups: electric (30 amps), water, sewer.

Riverside Mobile/RV Park, 449 River Rd., 72642. T: (870) 431-5419. F: (870) 431-5419. www.riversidervpark.com. RV/tent: 21. $10–$15. Hookups: electric (20, 30, 50 amps), water, sewer.

Lamar

Dad's Dream RV Park, Rte. 2 Box 19, 72846. T: (501) 865-2322. RV/tent: 40. $12. Hookups: electric (30, 50 amps), water, sewer.

Lowell

Green Country RV Park, 110 Pleasant Grove Rd., 72745. T: (501) 659-8850. RV/tent: 71. $16–$18. Hookups: electric (30, 50 amps), water, sewer.

Hickory Creek Park, 12618 Hickory Creek Rd., 72745. T: (501) 750-2943. www.ReserveUSA.com/nrrs/ar/hic2. RV/tent: 61. $13–$15. Hookups: electric (20, 30amps).

Magnolia

Coachman's Inn & RV Park, 420 East Main St., 71753. T: (870) 234-6122. RV/tent: 10. $15. Hookups: electric (30, 50 amps), water, sewer.

Mena

Queen Wilhelmina State Park, 3877 Hwy. 88 West, 71953. T: (501) 394-2863. www.ArkansasStateParks.com. RV/tent: 41. $6–$14. Hookups: electric (30 amps), water.

Morrilton

Cherokee Campground, 1 Quincy Rd., 72110. T: (501) 329-2986. www.ReserveUSA.com/nrrs/ar/che3. RV/tent: 33. $16. Hookups: electric (20, 30 amps), water.

Lewisburg Bay RV Park, 1020 South Bridge St., 72110. T: (501) 354-5601. RV/tent: 20. $11. Hookups: electric (30 amps), water, sewer.

Mount Ida

Marilyn's RV Park, 3551 Hwy. 270 West, 71957. T: (870) 867-0168. F: (870) 867-0168. RV/tent: 12. $15. Hookups: electric (15 amps), water.

Mountain Home

Bidwell Point Campground, P.O. Box 2070, 72654. T: (870) 467-5375. www.ReserveUSA.com/nrrs/ar/bidw. RV/tent: 48. $14. Hookups: electric (20, 30 amps).

Buck Creek Campground, P.O. Box 2070, 72654. T: (870) 785-4313. www.ReserveUSA.com/nrrs/ar/buck. RV/tent: 42. $9–$16. Hookups: electric (20, 30 amps).

Cranfield Park Campground, P.O. Box 2070, 72654. T: (870) 492-4191. www.ReserveUSA.com/nrrs/ar/cran. RV/tent: 69. $13–$16. Hookups: electric (20, 30 amps).

Gamaliel Campground, P.O. Box 2070, 72654. T: (870) 425-2700. www.ReserveUSA.com/nrrs/ar/gama. RV/tent: 64. $13–$16. Hookups: electric (20, 30 amps).

Jordan Park Campground, P.O. Box 2070, 72654. T: (870) 499-7223. www.ReserveUSA.com/nrrs/ar/jord. RV/tent: 33. $11–$14. Hookups: electric (20, 30 amps).

Panther Bay Campground, P.O. Box 2070, 72654. T: (870) 425-2700. www.ReserveUSA.com/nrrs/ar/pant. RV/tent: 22. $11. Hookups: electric (20, 30 amps).

Robinson Point Campground, P.O. Box 2070, 72654. T: (870) 492-6853. www.ReserveUSA.com/nrrs/ar/robp. RV/tent: 102. $13–$16. Hookups: electric (20, 30 amps).

White Buffalo Resort and Campground, 418 White Buffalo Tr., 72653. T: (870) 425-8555. RV/tent: 52. $18–$23. Hookups: electric (20, 30, 50 amps), water, sewer.

Mountain Pine

Lake Ouachita State Park, 5451 Mountain Pine Rd., 71956. T: (501) 767-9366. www.ArkansasStateParks.com. RV/tent: 118. $6–$17. Hookups: electric (30 amps), water, sewer.

Mountain View

Blue Sky RV Park, HC 72 Box 136, 72113. T: (870) 269-8132. www.blueskyrvpark.com. RV/tent: 87. $17. Hookups: electric (20, 30 amps), water, sewer.

Ozark RV Park, HC 71 Box 540, 72560. T: (501) 269-2542. RV/tent: 56. $14. Hookups: electric (20, 30 amps), water, sewer.

ARKANSAS (continued)

Mountainburg

Lake Fort State Park, P.O. Box 4, 72946. T: (501) 369-2469. www.ArkansasStateParks.com. RV/tent: 12. $14. Hookups: electric (30 amps), water.

Murfreesboro

Cowhide Cove Campground, Rte. 1, 71958. T: (870) 285-2151. www.ReserveUSA.com/nrrs/ar/cown. RV/tent: 50. $8–$14. Hookups: electric (20, 30 amps).

Crater of Diamonds State Park, 209 State Park Rd., 71958. T: (870) 285-3113. www.ArkansasStateParks.com. RV/tent: 60. $14.00. Hookups: electric (30 amps), water.

Self Creek Campground, Rte. 1, 71958. T: (870) 285-2151. www.ReserveUSA.com/nrrs/ar/self. RV/tent: 72. $12–$14. Hookups: electric (20, 30 amps).

Omaha

Ozark Vue RV Park, Rte. 1 Box 126D, 72662. T: (501) 426-5166. RV/tent: 31. $14. Hookups: electric (20, 30, 50 amps), water, sewer.

Cricket Creek Campground, 20110 Boat Dock Rd., 72662. T: (870) 426-3331. www.ReserveUSA.com/nrrs/ar/cric. RV/tent: 35. $11–$14. Hookups: electric (20, 30 amps).

Ozark

Aux Arc Campground, 6042 Lock and Dam Rd., 72949. T: (501) 667-2129. www.ReserveUSA.com/nrrs/ar/auxa. RV/tent: 63. $14–$19. Hookups: electric (20, 30, 50 amps), water, sewer.

Perryville

Coffee Creek Landing & Resort, P.O. Box 31, 72126. T: (501) 889-2745. F: (501) 889-5485. www.coffeecreekresort.com. RV/tent: 63. $15. Hookups: electric (20, 30, 50 amps), water, sewer.

Plainview

Quarry Cove Campground, Nimrod Lake Quarry Cove Park, 3 Hwy. 7 South, 72857. T: (501) 272-4233. www.ReserveUSA.com/nrrs/ar/quar. RV/tent: 31. $14. Hookups: electric (20, 30 amps), water.

Sunlight Bay Campground, Sunlight Bay 3 Hwy. 7 South, 72857. T: (501) 272-4234. www.ReserveUSA.com/nrrs/ar/sunl. RV/tent: 28. $14. Hookups: electric (20, 30 amps), water.

Powhatan

Lake Charles State Park, 3705 Hwy. 25, 72458. T: (870) 878-6595. www.ArkansasStateParks.com. RV/tent: 61. $14–$16. Hookups: electric (30 amps), water.

Rogers

Lost Bridge North Campground, 2260 North 2nd, 72756. T: (501) 359-3312. www.ReserveUSA.com/nrrs/ar/lost. RV/tent: 48. $13–$15. Hookups: electric (20, 30 amps).

Royal

Brady Mountain Campground, 1201 Blakely Dam Rd., 71968. T: (501) 767-2108. www.ReserveUSA.com/nrrs/ar/bran. RV/tent: 74. $12–$14. Hookups: electric (20, 30 amps).

Denby Point Campground, 1201 Blakely Dam Rd., 71968. T: (501)767-2108. www.ReserveUSA.com/nrrs/ar/denb. RV/tent: 67. $8–$14. Hookups: electric (20, 30 amps).

Russellville

Lake Dardanelle State Park, 2428 Marina Rd., 72802. T: (501) 967-5516. www.ArkansasStateParks.com. RV/tent: 83. $14–$17. Hookups: electric (30 amps), water, sewer.

Piney Bay Campground, 1598 Lock And Dam Rd., 72802. T: (501) 885-3029. www.ReserveUSA.com/nrrs/ar/pinb. RV/tent: 91. $13–$16. Hookups: electric (20, 30 amps), water.

Siloam Springs

Greentree RV Park, 1800 West Hwy. 412, 72761. T: (501) 524-8898. RV/tent: 37. $17–$19. Hookups: electric (30, 50 amps), water, sewer.

South Plainview

Carter Cove Campground, 3 Hwy. 7, 72857. T: (501) 272-4983. www.ReserveUSA.com/nrrs/ar/cart. RV/tent: 34. $14. Hookups: electric (20, 30 amps), water.

County Line, 3 Hwy. 7, 72857. T: (501) 272-4945. www.ReserveUSA.com/nrrs/ar/coul. RV/tent: 20. $14. Hookups: electric (20, 30 amps), water.

Springdale

Springdale Whisler RV Park, 1101 South Old Missouri Rd., 72764. T: (501) 751-9081. F: (501) 756-9388. RV/tent: 64. $15. Hookups: electric (30, 50 amps), water, sewer.

Star City

Cane Creek State Park, P.O. Box 96, 71667. T: (870) 628-4714. www.ArkansasStateParks.com. RV/tent: 30. $14–$16. Hookups: electric (30 amps), water.

Van Buren

Park Ridge RV Campground, 1616 Rena Rd., 72956. T: (501) 410-GORV (4678). F: (501) 474-2282. RV/tent: 28. $16–$24. Hookups: electric (30, 50 amps), water, sewer.

West Fork

Devil's Den State Park, 11333 West Hwy. 74, 72774. T: (501) 761-3325. www.ArkansasStateParks.com. RV/tent: 148. $6–$16. Hookups: electric (30 amps), water.

West Memphis

Tom Sawyer's Mississippi River RV Park, 1286 South 8th, 72301. T: (870) 735-9770. RV/tent: 90. $20–$22. Hookups: electric (30, 50 amps), water, sewer.

CALIFORNIA

Acton

The Californian RV Resort, 1535 West Sierra Hwy., 93510. T: (888) RVRV-FUN or (661) 269-0919. www.calrv.com. RV/tent: 73. $33. Hookups: water, electric (20, 30, 50 amp), sewer, cable TV, phone.

Adin

Lower Rush Creek, County Rd. 198A, 96006. T: (530) 299-3215. F: (530) 299-8409. www.r5.fs.fed.us/modoc. RV/tent: 15. $6. Hookups: none.

Allensworth

Colonel Allensworth State Historic Park, Palmer Ave., 93219. T: (800) 444-7275 or (661) 634-3795. F: (661) 849-3433. www.reserveamerica.com. RV/tent: 15. $8. Hookups: none.

Anaheim

Anaheim Harbor RV Park, 1009 South Harbor Blvd., 92805. T: (714) 535-6495. F: (714) 535-4239. www.anaheimharborrvpark.com. RV/tent: 198. $24–$38 . Hookups: water, electric (30, 50 amp), sewer, cable TV, phone.

Anaheim Resort RV Park, 200 West Midway Dr., 92805. T: (714) 774-3860. F: (714) 774-5970. www.anaheimresortrvpark.com. RV/tent: 150. $36. Hookups: water, electric (20, 30, 50 amp), sewer, cable TV, phone.

Angels Camp

Angels Camp RV & Camping Resort, 3069 South Hwy. 49, 95222. T: (888) 398-0404 or (209) 736-0404. F: (209) 736-2849. www.gocampingamerica.com/angelscamp/. RV/tent: 44. $25. Hookups: water, electric (20, 30, 50 amp), sewer.

CALIFORNIA (continued)

Angelus Oaks

Barton Flats, Hwy. 38, 92305. T: (877) 444-6777 or (909) 794-1123. F: (909) 794-1125. www.reserveusa.com. RV/tent: 47. $20. Hookups: none.

Heart Bar Family Camp, FR 1N02, 92305. T: (877) 444-6777 or (909) 794-1123. F: (909) 794-1125. www.reserveusa.com. RV/tent: 94. $15. Hookups: none.

San Gorgonio, Hwy. 38, 92305. T: (877) 444-6777 or (909) 794-1123. F: (909) 794-1125. www.reserveusa.com. RV/tent: 55. $20. Hookups: none.

South Fork, Hwy. 38, 92305. T: (877) 444-6777 or (909) 794-1123. F: (909) 794-1125. www.reserveusa.com. RV/tent: 24. $15. Hookups: none.

Anza

Kamp-Anza RV Resort, 41560 Terwilliger Rd., 92539. T: (909) 763-4819. www.koan.com/. RV/tent: 115. $12–$18. Hookups: water, electric (30 amp), sewer, TV, phone.

Arcadia

Santa Anita Village & RV Park, 4241 East Live Oak Ave., 91006. T: (626) 447-3878. RV/tent: 100. $25. Hookups: water, electric (30 amp), sewer, phone.

Arcata

Mad River Rapids RV Park, 3501 Janes Rd., 95521. T: (800) 822-7776 or (707) 822-7275. F: (707) 822-7286. www.madriverrv.com. RV/tent: 92. $29. Hookups: water, electric (30, 50 amp), sewer, cable TV, phone.

Auburn

Auburn KOA, 3550 KOA Way, 95602. T: (800) 562-6671 or (530) 885-0990. www.koa.com. RV/tent: 80. $25–$35. Hookups: water, electric (20, 30, 50 amp), sewer.

Bakersfield

Bakersfield Palms RV Park, 250 Fairfax Rd., 93307. T: (888) 725-6778 or (661) 366-6700. F: (661) 366-6704. www.palmsrv.com. RV/tent: 116. $20–$22. Hookups: water, electric (30, 50 amp), sewer, cable TV, phone.

Bakersfield Trav-L-Park, 8633 East Brundage Ln., 93307. T: (800) 962-4546 (CA only) or (661) 366-3550. www.bakersfieldtravelpark.com/. RV/tent: 126. $19. Hookups: water, electric (20, 30, 50 amp), sewer, cable TV, phone.

Orange Grove RV Park, 1452 South Edison Rd., 93307. T: (800) 553-7126 or (661) 366-4662. F: (661) 366-8915. www.orangegrovervpark.com/. RV/tent: 146. $22. Hookups: water, electric (50 amp), sewer, cable TV, phone.

Southland RV Park, 9901 Southland Court, 93307. T: (877) 834-4868. www.gocampingamerica.com/southlandrvpk/. RV/tent: 91. $22. Hookups: water, electric (30, 50 amp), sewer, TV, phone.

Banning

Stagecoach RV Park, 1455 South San Gorgonio Ave., 92220. T: (909) 849-7513. F: (909) 849-7998. RV/tent: 97. $14–$19.50. Hookups: water, electric (20, 30, 50 amp), sewer, cable TV, phone.

Bard

Senator Wash Recreation Area, Senator Wash Rd., 92222. T: (520) 317-3200. F: (520) 317-3250. www.ca.blm.gov/caso/information.html. RV/tent: undesignated. $5. Hookups: none.

Squaw Lake, Senator Wash Rd., 92222. T: (520) 317-3200. F: (520) 317-3250. www.ca.blm.gov/caso/information.html. RV/tent: 80. $5. Hookups: none.

Barstow

Shady Lane RV Camp, 36445 Soap Mine Rd, 92311. T: (760) 256-5332. RV/tent: 33. $19–$20. Hookups: water, electric (20, 30 amp), sewer, phone.

Bass Lake

Chilkoot, Beasore Rd., 93604. T: (559) 877-2218. F: (559) 877-3108. www.r5.fs.fed.us/sierra. RV/tent: 14. $12. Hookups: none.

Forks, County Rd. 222, 93604. T: (559) 877-2218. F: (559) 877-3108. www.r5.fs.fed.us/sierra. RV/tent: 31. $16. Hookups: none.

Spring Cove, County Rd. 222, 93604. T: (559) 877-2218. F: (559) 877-3108. www.r5.fs.fed.us/sierra. RV/tent: 65. $16. Hookups: none.

Wishon Point, County Rd. 222, 93604. T: (559) 877-2218. F: (559) 877-3108. www.r5.fs.fed.us/sierra. RV/tent: 47. $16. Hookups: none.

Beckwourth

Grizzly, Lake Davis Rd., 96129. T: (530) 836-2575. F: (530) 836-0493. www.r5.fs.fed.us/plumas. RV/tent: 55. $13. Hookups: none.

Lightning Tree, Lake Davis Rd., 96129. T: (530) 836-2575. F: (530) 836-0493. www.r5.fs.fed.us/plumas. RV/tent: 38. $6. Hookups: none.

Bethel Island

Lundborg Landing, 6777 Riverview Rd, 94511. T: (925) 684-9351. F: (925) 684-9366. www.lundborglanding.com. RV/tent: 96. $16–$20. Hookups: water, electric (30 amp), sewer.

Big Bear Lake

Holloway's Marina & RV Park, 398 Edgemoor Rd., 92325. T: (800) 448-5335 or (909) 866-5706. www.bigbearboating.com/. RV/tent: 99. $25–$40. Hookups: water, electric (20, 30, 50 amp), sewer, cable TV.

Big Pine

Sage Flat, Glacier Lodge Rd., 93513. T: (760) 873-2500. F: (760) 873-2563. www.r5.fs.fed.us/inyo. RV/tent: 28. $11. Hookups: none.

Upper Sage Flat, Glacier Lodge Rd., 93513. T: (760) 873-2500. F: (760) 873-2563. www.r5.fs.fed.us/inyo. RV/tent: 21. $11. Hookups: none.

Big Sur

Big Sur Campgrounds & Cabins, Hwy. 1, 93920. T: (831) 667-2322. www.bigsurcalifornia.org/camping.html. RV/tent: 81. $26–$29. Hookups: water, electric (20, 30 amp).

Bishop

Big Trees, Hwy. 168, 93514. T: (760) 873-2500. F: (760) 873-2563. www.r5.fs.fed.us/inyo. RV/tent: 9. $12. Hookups: none.

Bishop Park, Hwy. 168, 93514. T: (760) 873-2500. F: (760) 873-2563. www.r5.fs.fed.us/inyo. RV/tent: 20. $12. Hookups: none.

Brown's Millpond Campground, Sawmill Rd., 93514. T: (760) 872-6911. F: (760) 872-1373. www.thesierraweb.com/recreation/browns/millpond.html. RV/tent: 74. $14–$19. Hookups: water, electric (30 amp).

Brown's Owens River Campground, Benton Crossing Rd., 93514. T: (760) 920-0975 or (760) 872-6911. F: (760) 872-1373. www.thesierraweb.com/recreation/browns/owens.html. RV/tent: 75. $14–$19. Hookups: water, electric (30 amp).

Brown's Town, Schober n., 93514. T: (760) 873-8522. F: (760) 872-1373. www.thesierraweb.com/recreation/browns/browns.html. RV/tent: 155. $14. Hookups: water, electric (30 amp).

Creekside RV Park, South Lake Rd., 93514. T: (760) 873-4483. www.thesierraweb.com/lodging/creekside/. RV/tent: 49. $20–$28. Hookups: water, electric (15, 30 amp), sewer.

Forks, Hwy. 168, 93514. T: (760) 873-2500. F: (760) 873-2563. www.r5.fs.fed.us/inyo. RV/tent: 8. $12. Hookups: none.

Four Jeffrey, South Lake Rd., 93514. T: (760) 873-2500. F: (760) 873-2563. www.r5.fs.fed.us/inyo. RV/tent: 106. $12. Hookups: none.

Highlands RV Park, 2275 North Sierra Hwy., 93514. T: (760) 873-7616. RV/tent: 103. $24. Hookups: water, electric (15, 30, 50 amp), sewer, cable TV.

Intake, Hwy. 168, 93514. T: (760) 873-2500. F: (760) 873-2563. www.r5.fs.fed.us/inyo. RV/tent: 15. $12. Hookups: none.

North Lake, FR 8S02, 93514. T: (760) 873-2500. F: (760) 873-2563. www.r5.fs.fed.us/inyo. RV/tent: 11. $12. Hookups: none.

Sabrina, Hwy. 168, 93514. T: (760) 873-2500. F: (760) 873-2563. www.r5.fs.fed.us/inyo. RV/tent: 18. $12. Hookups: none.

Blythe

Coon Hollow, Wiley's Well Rd., 92225. T: (760) 251-4800. F: (760) 251-4899. www.ca.blm.gov/caso/information.html. RV/tent: 27. $20. Hookups: none.

Destiny's McIntyre RV Resort, 8750 East 26th Ave., 92225. T: (760) 922-8205. www.destinyrv.com/River2.htm. RV/tent: 161. $29–$37. Hookups: water, electric (30 amp), sewer.

CALIFORNIA (continued)

Blythe (continued)

Destiny's Riviera RV Resort & Marina, 14100 Riviera Dr., 92225. T: (760) 922-5350. www.destinyrv.com/River2.htm. RV/tent: 268. $32–$39. Hookups: water, electric (30, 50 amp), sewer, cable TV, phone.

Wiley's Well, Wiley's Well Rd., 92225. T: (760) 251-4800. F: (760) 251-4899. www.ca.blm.gov/caso/information.html. RV/tent: 13. $20. Hookups: none.

Boca

Boca, County Rd. 73, 96161. T: (877) 444-6777 or (530) 587-3558. F: (530) 587-6914. www.r5.fs.fed.us/tahoe; www.reserveusa.com. RV/tent: 22. $10. Hookups: none.

Boca Rest Campground, County Rd. 270, 96161. T: (877) 444-6777 or (530) 587-3558. F: (530) 587-6914. www.r5.fs.fed.us/tahoe; www.reserveusa.com. RV/tent: 31. $8. Hookups: none.

Boyington Mill, County Rd. 270, 96161. T: (877) 444-6777 or (530) 587-3558. F: (530) 587-6914. www.r5.fs.fed.us/tahoe; www.reserveusa.com. RV/tent: 10. $10. Hookups: none.

Cold Creek, Hwy. 89, 96161. T: (877) 444-6777 or (530) 587-3558. F: (530) 587-6914. www.r5.fs.fed.us/tahoe; www.reserveusa.com. RV/tent: 13. $10. Hookups: none.

Lower Little Truckee, Hwy. 89, 96161. T: (877) 444-6777 or (530) 587-3558. F: (530) 587-6914. www.r5.fs.fed.us/tahoe; www.reserveusa.com. RV/tent: 15. $10. Hookups: none.

Upper Little Truckee, Hwy. 89, 96161. T: (877) 444-6777 or (530) 587-3558. F: (530) 587-6914. www.r5.fs.fed.us/tahoe; www.reserveusa.com. RV/tent: 26. $10. Hookups: none.

Bodega Bay

Bodega Bay RV Park, 2001 Hwy. 1, 94923. T: (800) 201-6864 or (707) 875-3701. F: (707) 875-9811. www.bodegabayrvpark.com. RV/tent: 72. $25–$31. Hookups: water, electric (30, 50 amp), sewer, TV.

Doran Regional Park, Hwy. 1, 94923. T: (707) 875-3540. www.sonomacounty.org. RV/tent: 134. $16. Hookups: none.

Sonoma Coast State Beach, Wrights Beach, Hwy. 1, 94923. T: (707) 875-3483 or (800) 444-7275. www.cal-parks.ca.gov; www.reserveamerica.com. RV/tent: 30. $12. Hookups: none.

Westside Regional Park, Bay Flat Rd., 94923. T: (707) 875-3540. www.sonomacounty.org. RV/tent: 47. $16. Hookups: none.

Borrego Springs

Anza-Borrego Desert State Park, Arroyo Salado Primitive Camp, County Rd. S22, 92004. T: (760) 767-5311. F: (760) 767-3427. www.cal-parks.ca.gov. RV/tent: Dispersed. $5. Hookups: none.

Anza-Borrego Desert State Park, Tamarisk Grove, Hwy. 78 and Yaqui Pass Rd., 92004. T: (760) 767-5311. F: (760) 767-3427. www.cal-parks.ca.gov. RV/tent: 27. $10. Hookups: none.

Anza-Borrego Desert State Park, Yaqui Pass Primitive Camp, Yaqui Pass Rd., 92004. T: (760) 767-5311. F: (760) 767-3427. www.cal- parks.ca.gov. RV/tent: dispersed. $5. Hookups: none.

Anza-Borrego Desert State Park, Yaqui Well Primitive Camp, Yaqui Pass Rd., 92004. T: (760) 767-5311. F: (760) 767-3427. www.cal-parks.ca.gov. RV/tent: dispersed. $5. Hookups: none.

Palm Canyon Resort RV Park, 221 Palm Canyon Dr., 92004. T: (800) 242-0044 or (760) 767-5341. F: (760) 767-4073. www.pcresort.com/. RV/tent: 132. $29. Hookups: water, electric (30 amp), sewer, cable TV, phone (long-term only).

Bradley

Lake Nacimiento Resort, 10625 Nacimiento Lake Dr., 93426. T: (800) 323-3839 or (805) 238-3256. www.nacimientoresort.com/. RV/tent: 340. $18–$30. Hookups: water, electric (30 amp), sewer.

Bridgeport

Crags, Twin Lakes Rd., 93517. T: (760) 932-7070. F: (760) 932-1299. www.r5.fs.fed.us/htnf/honecamp.htm. RV/tent: 26. $9. Hookups: none.

Lower Twin Lake, Twin Lakes Rd., 93517. T: (760) 932-7070. F: (760) 932-1299. www.r5.fs.fed.us/htnf/honecamp.htm. RV/tent: 14. $9. Hookups: none.

Paha, Twin Lakes Rd., 93517. T: (760) 932-7070. F: (760) 932-1299. www.r5.fs.fed.us/htnf/honecamp.htm. RV/tent: 22. $9. Hookups: none.

Robinson Creek, Twin Lakes Rd., 93517. T: (760) 932-7070. F: (760) 932-1299. www.r5.fs.fed.us/htnf/honecamp.htm. RV/tent: 54. $9. Hookups: none.

Bucks Lake

Grizzly Creek, Oroville-Quincy Rd./FR 33, 95971. T: (530) 283-0555. F: (530) 283-1821. www.r5.fs.fed.us/plumas. RV/tent: 8. $14. Hookups: none.

Haskins Valley, Bucks Lake Rd., 95971. T: (530) 283-0555. F: (530) 283-1821. www.r5.fs.fed.us/plumas. RV/tent: 65. $15. Hookups: none.

Lower Bucks, Bucks Lake Dam Rd./FR 33, 95971. T: (530) 283-0555. F: (530) 283-1821. www.r5.fs.fed.us/plumas. RV/tent: 6. $10. Hookups: none.

Mill Creek, Bucks Lake Dam Rd./FR 33, 95971. T: (530) 283-0555. F: (530) 283-1821. www.r5.fs.fed.us/plumas. RV/tent: 8. $14. Hookups: none.

Sundew, Bucks Lake Dam Rd./FR 33, 95971. T: (530) 283-0555. F: (530) 283-1821. www.r5.fs.fed.us/plumas. RV/tent: 19. $13. Hookups: none.

Whitehorse, Bucks Lake Rd., 95971. T: (530) 283-0555. F: (530) 283-1821. www.r5.fs.fed.us/plumas. RV/tent: 20. $14. Hookups: none.

Buellton

Flying Flags RV Park & Campground, 180 Avenue of the Flags, 93427. T: (805) 688-3716. F: (805) 688-9245. www.flyingflags.com. RV/tent: 300. $18–$26. Hookups: water, electric (20, 30, 50 amp), sewer, TV, phone.

Camp Nelson

Belknap, Nelson Dr., 93208. T: (559)539-2607. www.r5.fs.fed.us/sequoia. RV/tent: 15. $12. Hookups: none.Nelson

Coy Flat, Coy Flat Rd., 93208. T: (559)539-2607. www.r5.fs.fed.us/sequoia. RV/tent: 20. $10. Hookups: none.

Lower Peppermint, Lloyd Meadow Rd., 93208. T: (559)539-2607. www.r5.fs.fed.us/sequoia. RV/tent: 17. $12. Hookups: none.

Camptonville

Cal-Ida, Cal-Ida Rd., 95922. T: (530) 288-3231. F: (530) 288-0727. www.r5.fs.fed.us/tahoe. RV/tent: 20. $12. Hookups: none.

Carlton, Hwy. 49, 95922. T: (530) 288-3231. F: (530) 288-0727. www.r5.fs.fed.us/tahoe. RV/tent: 21. $12. Hookups: none.

Dark Day, Dark Day Rd., 95922. T: (530) 692-3200 or (530) 288-3231. F: (530) 288-0727. www.r5.fs.fed.us/tahoe. RV/tent: 16. $14. Hookups: none.

Fiddle Creek, Hwy. 49, 95922. T: (530) 288-3231. F: (530) 288-0727. www.r5.fs.fed.us/tahoe. RV/tent: 15. $12. Hookups: none.

Indian Valley, Hwy. 49, 95922. T: (530) 288-3231. F: (530) 288-0727. www.r5.fs.fed.us/tahoe. RV/tent: 17. $12. Hookups: none.

Ramshorn, Hwy. 49, 95922. T: (530) 288-3231. F: (530) 288-0727. www.r5.fs.fed.us/tahoe. RV/tent: 16. $12. Hookups: none.

Rocky Nest, Hwy. 49, 95922. T: (530) 288-3231. F: (530) 288-0727. www.r5.fs.fed.us/tahoe. RV/tent: 10. $12. Hookups: none.

Carmel

Carmel by the River RV Park, 27680 Schulte Rd., 93923. T: (831) 624-9329. F: (831) 624-8416. RV/tent: 35. $40–$45. Hookups: water, electric (20, 30 amp), sewer, cable TV, phone.

Carrville

Eagle Creek, Hwy. 3, 96091. T: (530) 623-2121. F: (530) 623-6010. www.r5.fs.fed.us/shasta-trinity. RV/tent: 17. $8. Hookups: none.

Trinity River, Hwy. 3, 96091. T: (530) 623-2121. F: (530) 623-6010. www.r5.fs.fed.us/shasta-trinity. RV/tent: 7. $8. Hookups: none.

Castaic

Castaic Lake RV Park, 31540 Ridge Rte. Rd., 91384. T: (661) 257-3340 or (877) 450-3340. F: (661) 257-1077. www.gocampingamerica.com/castaiclake/. RV/tent: 103. $18–$25. Hookups: water, electric (30 amp), sewer, cable TV, phone.

CALIFORNIA (continued)

Cathedral City

Palm Springs Oasis RV Resort, 36100 Date Palm Dr., 92234. T: (800) 680-0144 or (760) 328-4813. F: (760) 328-8455. RV/tent: 140. $25–$32. Hookups: water, electric (20, 30, 50 amp), sewer, cable TV, phone.

Chester

Benner Creek, Juniper Lake Rd., 96020. T: (530) 258-2141. F: (530) 258-5194. www.r5.fs.fed.us/lassen. RV/tent: 9. $9. Hookups: none.

Domingo Springs, County Rd. 311, 96020. T: (530) 258-2141. F: (530) 258-5194. www.r5.fs.fed.us/lassen. RV/tent: 18. $11. Hookups: none.

High Bridge, County Rd. 312, 96020. T: (530) 258-2141. F: (530) 258-5194. www.r5.fs.fed.us/lassen. RV/tent: 12. $11. Hookups: none.

North Shore Campground, Hwy. 36, 96020. T: (530) 258-3376. www.gocamping america.com/northshorecpgrd/. RV/tent: 128. $17–$20. Hookups: water, electric (20, 30 amp), phone.

Warner Creek, County Rd. 311, 96020. T: (530) 258-2141. F: (530) 258-5194. www.r5.fs.fed. us/lassen. RV/tent: 13. $9. Hookups: none.

Chico

Almond Tree RV Park, 3124 Esplanade, 95973. T: (530) 899-1271. F: (530) 892-0523. http://now2000.com/rvpark/. RV/tent: 42. $24. Hookups: water, electric (30, 50 amp), sewer, TV, phone.

Chula Vista

Chula Vista RV Resort & Marina, 460 Sandpiper Way, 91910. T: (619) 422-0111. F: (619) 422-8872. www.gocampingamerica.com/chulavista/. RV/tent: 237. $28.50–$47.50. Hookups: water, electric (30, 50 amp), sewer, TV, phone.

KOA San Diego Metropolitan, 111 North Second St., 91910. T: (800) KOA-9877 or (619) 427-3601. F: (619) 427-3622. www.sandiegokoa.com. RV/tent: 270. $26–$45. Hookups: water, electric (30, 50 amp), sewer, cable TV.

Sweetwater Regional Park-Summit Site (San Diego County Park), Summit Meadow Rd., 91910. T: (877) 565-3600 or (858) 694-3049. www.co.sandiego.ca.us/cnty/cntydepts/landuse/parks/camping/sweetwater/. RV/tent: 60. $16. Hookups: water, electric (30 amp).

Cloverdale

KOA Cloverdale Camping Resort, 26460 River Rd., 95425. T: (800) 562-4042 or (707) 894-3337. www.koa.com. RV/tent: 151. $28–$42. Hookups: water, electric (30, 50 amp).

Coleville

Bootleg, US 395, 96107. T: (760) 932-7070. F: (760) 932-1299. www.r5.fs.fed.us/htnf/soncamp.htm. RV/tent: 63. $10. Hookups: none.

Chris Flat, US 395, 96107. T: (760) 932-7070. F: (760) 932-1299. www.r5.fs.fed.us/htnf/son camp.htm. RV/tent: 15. $10. Hookups: none.

Obsidian, US 395, 96107. T: (760) 932-7070. F: (760) 932-1299. www.r5.fs.fed.us/htnf/son camp.htm. RV/tent: 14. $5. Hookups: none.

Coloma

Coloma Resort & RV Park, 6921 Mt. Murphy Rd., 95613. T: (530) 621-2267 or (800) 238-2298. F: (530) 621-4960. www.colomaresort.com. RV/tent: 165. $26–$30. Hookups: water, electric (30 amp), sewer.

Columbia

49er RV Ranch, 23223 Italian Bar Rd., 95310. T: (209) 532-4978. F: (209) 532-4978. www.49rv.com. RV/tent: 45. $27.50. Hookups: water, electric (30 amp), sewer, cable TV.

Marble Quarry RV Park, 11551 Yankee Hill Rd., 95310. T: (209) 532-9539. F: (209) 532-8631. www.marblequarry.com. RV/tent: 87. $17–$30. Hookups: water, electric (30, 50 amp), sewer, satellite TV.

Colusa

Colusa-Sacramento River State Recreation Area, 10th St., 95932. T: (800) 444-7275 or (530) 458-4927. F: (530) 538-2200. www.reserveamerica.com. RV/tent: 14. $10. Hookups: none.

Crescent City

Bayside RV Park, Citizen Dock Rd., 95531. T: (800) 446-9482. RV/tent: 110. $ 15–$20. Hookups: water, electric (30 amp), sewer, phone.

Hiouchi Hamlet RV Resort, 2000 Hwy. 199, 95531. T: (707) 458-3321. F: (707) 458-4223. RV/tent: 120. $15–$25. Hookups: water, electric (20, 30, 50 amp), sewer, cable TV, phone.

KOA-Crescent City Redwoods, 4241 Hwy. 101 North, 95531. T: (800) 562-5754 or (707) 464-5744. www.koa.com. RV/tent: 94. $20–$27. Hookups: water, electric (15, 20, 30 amp), sewer, cable TV.

Sunset Harbor RV Park, 205 King St., 95531. T: (707) 464-3423. F: (707) 464-2084. RV/tent: 69. $20. Hookups: water, electric (30, 50 amp), sewer, cable TV, phone.

Village Camper Inn, 1543 Parkway Dr., 95531. T: (707) 464-3544. RV/tent: 158. $14.50–$18.50. Hookups: water, electric (20, 30, 50 amp), sewer, cable TV, phone.

Dardanelle

Baker, Hwy. 108, 95314. T: (209) 965-3434. F: (209) 965-3372. www.r5.fs.fed.us/stanislaus. RV/tent: 44. $10. Hookups: none.

Brightman Flat, Hwy. 108, 95314. T: (209) 965-3434. F: (209) 965-3372. www.r5.fs.fed.us/stanislaus. RV/tent: 33. $10. Hookups: none.

Cascade Peak, Hwy. 108, 95314. T: (209) 965-3434. F: (209) 965-3372. www.r5.fs.fed.us /stanislaus. RV/tent: 14. $5. Hookups: none.

Dardanelle, Hwy. 108, 95314. T: (209) 965-3434. F: (209) 965-3372. www.r5.fs.fed.us/stanislaus. RV/tent: 28. $14. Hookups: none.

Deadman, Kennedy Meadow Rd., 95314. T: (209) 965-3434. F: (209) 965-3372. www.r5.fs.fed.us/stanislaus. RV/tent: 17. $11. Hookups: none.

Eureka Valley, Hwy. 108, 95314. T: (209) 965-3434. F: (209) 965-3372. www.r5.fs.fed.us/stanislaus. RV/tent: 28. $12. Hookups: none.

Fence Creek, FR 6N06, 95314. T: (209) 965-3434. F: (209) 965-3372. www.r5.fs.fed.us/stanislaus. RV/tent: 34. $5. Hookups: none.

Pigeon Flat, Hwy. 108, 95314. T: (209) 965-3434. F: (209) 965-3372. www.r5.fs.fed.us/stanislaus. RV/tent: 7. $8. Hookups: none.

Sand Flat, Clark Fork Rd., 95314. T: (209) 965-3434. F: (209) 965-3372. www.r5.fs.fed.us/stanislaus. RV/tent: 68. $7. Hookups: none.

Death Valley

Stovepipe Wells, Hwy. 190, 92328. T: (800) 365-2267 or (760) 786-2331. F: (760) 786-3283. www.nps.gov/deva; reservations.nps.gov. RV/tent: 199. $10. Hookups: none.

Sunset, Hwy. 190, 92328. T: (800) 365-2267 or (760) 786-2331. F: (760) 786-3283. www.nps.gov/deva; reservations.nps.gov. RV/tent: 1000. $10. Hookups: none.

Texas Spring, Hwy. 190, 92328. T: (800) 365-2267 or (760) 786-2331. F: (760) 786-3283. www.nps.gov/deva; reservations.nps.gov. RV/tent: 92. $10. Hookups: none.

Delhi

McConnell State Recreation Area, Pepper St., 95315. T: (800) 444-7275 or (209) 394-7755. www.reserveamerica.com. RV/tent: 19. $12. Hookups: none.

Dunnigan

Campers Inn RV & Golf Resort, 2501 CR 88, 95937. T: (800) 79-GOLF-3 or (530) 724-3350. F: (530) 724-3110. www.campersinnrv.com. RV/tent: 85. $15–$21. Hookups: water, electric (30, 50 amp), sewer.

Dunsmuir

Railroad Park Resort, 100 Railroad Park Rd., 96025. T: (530) 235-9983. F: (530) 235-4470. www.rrpark.com. RV/tent: 60. $16–$24. Hookups: water, electric (20, 30 amp), sewer, cable TV.

El Cajon

Circle RV Ranch, 1835 East Main St., 92021. T: (800) 422-1835 or (619) 440-0040. F: (619) 440-8050. www.gocampingamerica.com/circlervranch/. RV/tent: 179. $27. Hookups: water, electric (30, 50 amp), sewer, TV, phone.

Oak Creek RV Resort, 15379 Oak Creek Rd., 92021. T: (619) 390-7132. F: (619) 390-7171. www.oakcreekrv.com. RV/tent: 120. $25–$29. Hookups: water, electric (30, 50 amp), sewer, cable TV, phone.

El Centro

Desert Trails RV Park & Country Club, 225 Wake Ave., 92243. T: (760) 352-7275. RV/tent: 388. $26. Hookups: water, electric (30, 50 amp), sewer, TV, phone.

CALIFORNIA (continued)

Encinitas

San Elijo State Beach, US 101, 92023. T: (800) 444-7275 or (760) 753-5091. www.reserveamerica.com. RV/tent: 150. $12–$18. Hookups: water, electric (30 amp).

Escondido

Escondido RV Resort, 1740 Seven Oaks Rd., 92026. T: (760) 740-5000. F: (760) 740-5982. www.escondidorv.com. RV/tent: 67. $29.50–$34.50. Hookups: water, electric (20, 30, 50 amp), sewer, cable TV, phone (long term).

Essex

Providence Mountains State Recreation Area, Essex Rd., 92332. T: (760) 928-2586. F: (661) 940-7327. RV/tent: 6. $12. Hookups: none.

Etna

Mountain Village RV Park, 30 Commercial Way, 96027. T: (877) 386-2787. F: (530) 467-6402. www.etnarvp.com. RV/tent: 44. $22. Hookups: water, electric (20, 30, 50 amp), sewer, cable TV, phone.

Eureka

KOA-Eureka, 4050 Hwy. 101 North, 95503. T: (800) 562-3136 or (707) 822-4243. F: (707) 822-0126. www.koa.com. RV/tent: 156. $20–$26. Hookups: water, electric (20, 30, 50 amp), sewer, cable TV, phone.

Redwood Acres Fairground, 3750 Harris St., 95503. T: (707) 445-3037. F: (707) 445-1583. www.redwoodacres.com. RV/tent: 52. $15. Hookups: water, electric (30, 50 amp), sewer.

Felton

Cotillion Gardens Recreational Vehicle Park, 300 Old Big Trees Rd., 95018. T: (831) 335-7669. RV/tent: 80. $29–$31. Hookups: water, electric (20, 30 amp), sewer, cable TV, phone.

Fort Bragg

Pomo RV Park & Campground, 17999 Tregoning Ln., 95437. T: (707) 964-3373. www.infortbragg.com/pomo/. RV/tent: 125. $ 20–$27. Hookups: water, electric (20, 30, 50 amp), sewer, cable TV, phone.

Woodside RV Park & Campgrounds, 17900 North Hwy. 1, 95437. T: (707) 964-3684. F: (707) 964-5221. www.gocampingamerica.com/woodsiderv/. RV/tent: 104. $19–$22. Hookups: water, electric (15, 30 amp), sewer, TV, phone.

Fouts Springs

Letts Lake, FR 17N02, 95979. T: (530) 963-3128. F: (530) 963-3173. www.r5.fs.fed.us/mendocino. RV/tent: 40. $8. Hookups: none.

Mill Valley, FR 17N02, 95979. T: (530) 963-3128. F: (530) 963-3173. www.r5.fs.fed.us/mendocino. RV/tent: 15. $5. Hookups: none.

Frazier Park

McGill, Mount Piños Hwy., 93222. T: (661) 245-3731. F: (661) 245-1526. RV/tent: 73. $8. Hookups: none.

Mount Piños, Mount Piños Hwy., 93222. T: (661) 245-3731. F: (661) 245-1526. RV/tent: 19. $8. Hookups: none.

Fresno

West Olive Mobile/RV Park, 3147 West Olive Ave., 93722. T: (559) 275-0154. RV/tent: 55. $15. Hookups: water, electric (20, 30, 50 amp), sewer, phone.

Garbervile

Benbow Valley RV Resort & Golf Course, 7000 Benbow Dr., 95542. T: (866) BENBOWRV or (707) 923-2777. F: (707)923-2821. www.benbowrv.com. RV/tent: 112. $28.90–$43.50. Hookups: water, electric (20, 30, 50 amp), sewer, cable TV, phone.

Gasquet

Smith River National Recreation Area, Big Flat, FR 15N59, 95543. T: (707) 457-3131. F: (707) 457-3794. www.r5.fs.fed.us/sixrivers. RV/tent: 28. $8. Hookups: none.

Smith River National Recreation Area, Grassy Flat, US 199, 95543. T: (877) 444-6777 or (707) 457-3131. F: (707) 457-3794. www.r5.fs.fed.us/sixrivers; www.reserveusa.com. RV/tent: 19. $10. Hookups: none.

Smith River National Recreation Area, Patrick Creek, US 199, 95543. T: (877) 444-6777 or (707) 457-3131. F: (707) 457-3794. www.r5.fs.fed.us/sixrivers; www.reserveusa.com. RV/tent: 13. $13. Hookups: none.

Gorman

Los Alamos, Smokey Bear Rd., 93243. T: (661) 245-3731. F: (661) 245-1526. RV/tent: 93. $10. Hookups: none.

Groveland

Dimond "O", Evergreen Rd., 95321. T: (209) 962-7825. F: (209) 962-6406. www.r5.fs.fed.us/stanislaus. RV/tent: 38. $13. Hookups: none.

Lost Claim, Hwy. 120, 95321. T: (209) 962-7825. F: (209) 962-6406. www.r5.fs.fed.us/stanislaus. RV/tent: 10. $9. Hookups: none.

Sweetwater, Hwy. 120, 95321. T: (209) 962-7825. F: (209) 962-6406. www.r5.fs.fed.us/stanislaus. RV/tent: 13. $11. Hookups: none.

Thousand Trails-Yosemite Lakes, Hwy. 120, 95321. T: (800) 533-1001. www.1000trails.com. RV/tent: 445. $25. Hookups: water, electric (20, 30, 50 amp), sewer, phone.

Yosemite Pines RV Resort, 20450 Old Hwy. 120, 95321. T: (800) 368-5386 or (209) 962-5042. F: (209) 962-5269. www.yosemitepines.com. RV/tent: 214. $17–$32. Hookups: water, electric (20, 30, 50 amp), sewer, cable TV, phone.

Grover Beach

Le Sage Riviera RV Park, 319 Hwy. 1, 93433. T: (805) 489-5506. RV/tent: 82. $25–$30. Hookups: water, electric (20, 30 amp), sewer, phone.

Gustine

San Luis Reservoir State Recreation Area, Basalt Campground, Hwy. 152, 95322-9737. T: (800) 444-7275 or (209) 826-1196. F: (209) 826-0284. www.cal-parks.ca.gov; www.reserveamerica.com. RV/tent: 79. $12. Hookups: none.

San Luis Reservoir State Recreation Area, Medeiros Campground, Hwy. 33, 95322-9737. T: (209) 826-1196. F: (209) 826-0284. www.cal-parks.ca.gov. RV/tent: 350. $7. Hookups: none.

Half Moon Bay

Half Moon Bay State Beach, Kelly Ave., 94019. T: (650) 726-8820. F: (415) 330-6300. RV/tent: 55. $12. Hookups: none.

Hamburg

O'Neil Creek, Hwy. 96, 96086. T: (877) 444-6777 or (530) 493-2243. F: (530) 493-1796. www.r5.fs.fed.us/klamath. RV/tent: 18. $4. Hookups: none.

Happy Camp

Curly Jack, Curly Jack Rd., 96039. T: (530) 493-2243. F: (530) 493-1796. www.r5.fs.fed.us/klamath. RV/tent: 17. $10. Hookups: none.

West Branch, Indian Creek Rd., 96039. T: (530) 493-2243. F: (530) 493-1796. www.r5.fs.fed.us/klamath. RV/tent: 15. $4. Hookups: none.

Hat Creek

Rancheria RV Park, 15565 Black Angus Ln., 96040. T: (800) 346-3430 or (530) 335-7418. www.rancheriarv.com. RV/tent: 75. $20–$22. Hookups: water, electric (30, 50 amp), sewer, satellite TV.

Hemet

Casa del Sol RV Resort, 2750 West Acacia, 92545. T: (909) 925-2515. www.casadelsolrvpark.com. RV/tent: 358. $15–$23. Hookups: water, electric (30, 50 amp), sewer, cable TV, phone.

Golden Village Palms RV Resort, 3600 West Florida Ave., 92545. T: (800) 323-9610 or (909) 925-2518. F: (909) 929-5672. www.goldenvillagepalms.com/. RV/tent: 1,019. $33. Hookups: water, electric (20, 30, 50 amp), sewer, cable TV, phone.

Mountain Valley RV Park, 235 South Lyon Ave., 92543. T: (800) 926-5593 or (909)-925-5812. F: (909) 658-6272. www.mountainvalleyrvp.com/. RV/tent: 170. $30. Hookups: water, electric (20, 30, 50 amp), sewer, cable TV, phone.

Hesperia

Hesperia Lake Park & Campground, Arrowhead Lake Rd., 92345. T: (800) 521-6332 or (760) 244-5951. www.hesperiaparks.com/pages/PG12.HTM. RV/tent: 86. $12–$15. Hookups: water, electric (30 amp).

Hollister

Casa De Fruta RV Orchard Resort, 10031 Pacheco Pass Hwy., 95023. T: (800) 548-3813 or (408) 842-9316. F: (408) 842-3793. www.casadefruta.com/orchardresort.asp. RV/tent: 301. $29–$31. Hookups: water, electric (20, 30 amp), sewer, satellite TV.

CALIFORNIA (continued)

Huntington Beach

Huntington By The Sea RV Park, 21871 Newland St., 92646. T: (714) 536-8316 or (800) 439-3486. F: (714) 846-8874. www.gocampingamerica.com/huntingtonbythesea/. RV/tent: 140. $24–$38. Hookups: water, electric (30 amp), sewer, cable TV, phone.

Idyllwild

Boulder Basin, FR 4S01, 92549. T: (909) 659-2117. F: (909) 659-2107. www.r5.fs.fed.us/sanbernardino. RV/tent: 34. $10. Hookups: none.

Dark Canyon, FR 4S02, 92549. T: (909) 659-2117. F: (909) 659-2107. www.r5.fs.fed.us/sanbernardino. RV/tent: 21. $12. Hookups: none.

Fern Basin, FR 4S02, 92549. T: (909) 659-2117. F: (909) 659-2107. www.r5.fs.fed.us/san bernardino. RV/tent: 22. $10. Hookups: none.

Marion Mountain, FR 4S02, 92549. T: (909) 659-2117. F: (909) 659-2107. www.r5.fs.fed.us/san bernardino. RV/tent: 24. $10. Hookups: none.

Mount San Jacinto State Park, Idyllwild Campground, Hwy. 243, 92549. T: (909) 659-2607; reservations (800) 444-7275. F: (909) 659-4769. www.sanjac.statepark.org/. RV/tent: 33. $12. Hookups: none.

Piñon Flat, Hwy. 74, 92549. T: (909) 659-2117. F: (909) 659-2107. www.r5.fs.fed.us/san bernardino. RV/tent: 18. $8. Hookups: none.

Indio

Fiesta RV Park, 46-421 Madison St., 92201. T: (760) 342-2345. F: (760) 342 - 2712. www.fiestarvpark.com. RV/tent: 200. $25–$35. Hookups: water, electric (30, 50 amp), sewer, cable TV, phone.

Jamestown

Lake Tulloch RV Campground and Marina, 14448 Tulloch Rd., 95327. T: (800) 894-2267 or (209) 881-0107. F: (209) 881-0107. www.laketullochcampground.com. RV/tent: 130. $17.50–$27.50. Hookups: water, electric (50 amp), sewer.

Julian

Pinezanita Trailer Ranch, 4446 Hwy. 79, 92036. T: (760) 765-0429. F: (760) 765-2426. www.pinezanita.com. RV/tent: 230. $18–$24. Hookups: water, electric (20, 30 amp), sewer.

June Lake

Gull Lake, Hwy. 158, 93529. T: (760) 647-2408. F: (760) 647-3046. www.r5.fs.fed.us/inyo. RV/tent: 11. $12. Hookups: none.

June Lake, Hwy. 158, 93529. T: (760) 647-2408. F: (760) 647-3046. www.r5.fs.fed.us/inyo. RV/tent: 28. $12. Hookups: none.

Oh! Ridge, Oh! Ridge Rd., 93529. T: (760) 647-2408. F: (760) 647-3046. www.r5.fs.fed.us/inyo. RV/tent: 148. $12. Hookups: none.

Reversed Creek, Hwy. 158, 93529. T: (760) 647-2408. F: (760) 647-3046. www.r5.fs.fed.us/inyo. RV/tent: 17. $12. Hookups: none.

Silver Lake, Hwy. 158, 93529. T: (760) 647-2408. F: (760) 647-3046. www.r5.fs.fed.us/inyo. RV/tent: 63. $12. Hookups: none.

Kelseyville

Edgewater Resort & RV Park, 6420 Soda Bay Rd., 95451. T: (800) 396-6224 or (707) 279-0208. F: (707) 279-0138. www.edgewaterresort.net. RV/tent: 61. $25–$35. Hookups: water, electric (20, 30 amp), sewer, cable TV, phone.

Kernville

Camp 3, Sierra Way Rd., 93238. T: (760) 376-3781. F: (760) 376-3795. www.r5.fs.fed.us/sequoia. RV/tent: 52. $12–$14. Hookups: none.

Headquarters, Sierra Way Rd., 93238. T: (760) 376-3781. F: (760) 376-3795. www.r5.fs.fed.us/sequoia. RV/tent: 44. $12–$14. Hookups: none.

Hospital Flat, Sierra Way Rd., 93238. T: (760) 376-3781. F: (760) 376-3795. www.r5.fs.fed.us/sequoia. RV/tent: 40. $12–$14. Hookups: none.

Rivernook Campground, 14001 Sierra Way, 93238. T: (760) 376-2705. RV/tent: 269. $17–$23. Hookups: water, electric (20, 30, 50 amp), sewer, cable TV.

King City

Ciudad Del Rey, 50557 Wild Horse Rd., 93930. T: (831) 385-4827. RV/tent: 38. $25. Hookups: water, electric (20, 30, 50 amp), sewer, phone.

Kings Canyon National Park

Crystal Springs, Hwy. 180, Grant Grove Village, 93633. T: (559) 565-3341. www.nps.gov/seki. RV/tent: 67. $14. Hookups: none.

Moraine, Hwy. 180, Cedar Grove Village, 93633. T: (559) 565-3341. www.nps.gov/seki. RV/tent: 120. $14. Hookups: none.

Sentinel, Hwy. 180, Cedar Grove Village, 93633. T: (559) 565-3341. www.nps.gov/seki. RV/tent: 83. $14. Hookups: none.

Sheep Creek, Hwy. 180, Cedar Grove Village, 93633. T: (559) 565-3341. www.nps.gov/seki. RV/tent: 111. $14. Hookups: none.

Sunset, Hwy. 180, Grant Grove Village, 93633. T: (559) 565-3341. www.nps.gov/seki. RV/tent: 214. $14. Hookups: none.

Kingsburg

Riverland, 38743 West Frontage Rd., 93631. T: (559) 897-5166. www.riverlandresorts.com. RV/tent: 196. $19.95–$29.95. Hookups: water, electric (15, 30, 50 amp), sewer.

Kit Carson

Caples Lake, Hwy. 88, 95644. T: (209) 295-4251. F: (209) 295-5994. RV/tent: 35. $12. Hookups: none.

East Silver Lake, Hwy. 88, 95644. T: (877) 444-6777 or (209) 295-4251. F: (209) 295-5994. www.reserveusa.com. RV/tent: 62. $12. Hookups: none.

Kirkwood Lake, Hwy. 88, 95644. T: (209) 295-4251. F: (209) 295-5994. RV/tent: 12. $11. Hookups: none.

Woods Lake, Woods Lake Turnoff, 95644. T: (209) 295-4251. F: (209) 295-5994. RV/tent: 25. $11. Hookups: none.

Klamath

Camp Marigold Garden Cottages & RV Park, 16101 Hwy. 101 S, 95548. T: (800) 621-8513 or (707) 482-3585. www.clia.com/Camp-Marigold-Klamath/. RV/tent: 45. $15. Hookups: water, electric (30 amp), sewer, cable TV.

Chinook RV Resort, 17465 Hwy. 101, 95548. T: (707) 482-3511. www.rvdestinations.com/chinook/. RV/tent: 80. $18. Hookups: water, electric (30 amp), sewer, cable TV, phone.

Klamath's Camper Corral, Hwy. 101 at 169 Interchange, 95548. T: (707) 482-5741 or (800) 701-PARK. www.rvdestinations.com/campercorral/. RV/tent: 120. $14–$22.25. Hookups: water, electric (30 amp), sewer, cable TV.

Mystic Forest RV Park, 15875 US 101, 95548. T: (707) 482-4901. F: (707) 482-0704. www.rvdestinations.com/mysticforest/. RV/tent: 44. $16. Hookups: water, electric (20, 30 amp), sewer, cable TV, phone.

La Grange

Turlock Lake State Recreation Area, Lake Rd., 95329. T: (800) 444-7275 or (209) 874-2008. F: (818) 874-2611. www.reserveamerica.com. RV/tent: 66. $12. Hookups: none.

La Porte

Black Rock, County Rd. 514/Little Grass Valley Rd., 95981. T: (530) 534-6500. F: (530) 532-1210. www.r5.fs.fed.us/plumas. RV/tent: 30. $12. Hookups: none.

Little Beaver, County Rd. 514/Little Grass Valley Rd., 95981. T: (530) 534-6500. F: (530) 532-1210. www.r5.fs.fed.us/plumas. RV/tent: 120. $13–$15. Hookups: none.

Peninsula Tent, County Rd. 514/Little Grass Valley Rd., 95981. T: (530) 534-6500. F: (530) 532-1210. www.r5.fs.fed.us/plumas. RV/tent: 25. $12. Hookups: none.

Red Feather Camp, County Rd. 514/Little Grass Valley Rd., 95981. T: (530) 534-6500. F: (530) 532-1210. www.r5.fs.fed.us/plumas. RV/tent: 60. $13–$15. Hookups: none.

Running Deer, FR 22N57, 95981. T: (877) 444-6777 or (530) 534-6500. F: (530) 532-1210. www.r5.fs.fed.us/plumas; www.reserveusa.com. RV/tent: 40. $13–$15. Hookups: none.

Wyandotte, County Rd. 514/Little Grass Valley Rd., 95981. T: (530) 534-6500. F: (530) 532-1210. www.r5.fs.fed.us/plumas. RV/tent: 28. $13–$22. Hookups: none.

Lake Elsinore

Lake Elsinore West Marina, 32700 Riverside Dr., 92530. T: (800) 328-6844 or (909) 678-1300. F: (909) 678-6377. www.gocampingamerica.com/elsinorewest/. RV/tent: 197. $27.50–$32.50. Hookups: water, electric (30, 50 amp), sewer, cable TV, phone.

CALIFORNIA (continued)

Lake Isabella

Lake Isabella RV Resort, 11936 Hwy. 178, 93240. T: (800) 787-9920. F: (760) 379-2046. www.lakeisabellarv.com. RV/tent: 91. $24. Hookups: water, electric (30, 50 amp), sewer, cable TV, phone.

Lakehead

Lakeshore Villa RV Park, 20672 Lakeshore Dr., 96051. T: (800) 238-8688. F: (530) 238-8688. www.gocampingamerica.com/lakeshorevilla/. RV/tent: 92. $17.50–$19.50. Hookups: water, electric (30, 50 amp), sewer, cable TV, phone.

Shasta Lake RV Resort & Campground, 20433 Lakeshore Dr., 96051. T: (800) 374-2782 or (530) 238-8500. F: (530) 238-2083. www.shastacounty.com/shastalake/. RV/tent: 70. $16–$24. Hookups: water, electric (30 amp), sewer.

Lakeside

Rancho Los Coches RV Park, 13468 Hwy. 8 Business, 92040. T: (800) 630-0448 or (619) 443-2025. F: (619) 443-8440. www.rancholoscochesrv.com/. RV/tent: 147. $23–$35. Hookups: water, electric (30, 50 amp), sewer, cable TV, phone.

Lancaster

Saddleback Butte State Park, Ave. J, 93535. T: (661) 942-0662. F: (661) 940-7327. RV/tent: 50. $10. Hookups: none.

Lee Vining

Big Bend, Hwy. 120, 93541. T: (760) 932-5451. F: (760) 932-5458. RV/tent: 17. $11. Hookups: none.

Boulder, Hwy. 120, 93541. T: (760) 932-5451. F: (760) 932-5458. RV/tent: 32. $7. Hookups: none.

Cattle Guard, Hwy. 120, 93541. T: (760) 932-5451. F: (760) 932-5458. RV/tent: 17. $7. Hookups: none.

Junction, Saddlebag Lake Rd., 93541. T: (760) 873-2400 or (760) 647-3044. F: (760) 647-3046. www.r5.fs.fed.us/inyo. RV/tent: 13. $6. Hookups: none.

Lower Lee Vining, Hwy. 120, 93541. T: (760) 932-5451. F: (760) 932-5458. RV/tent: 74. $7. Hookups: none.

Mono Vista RV Park, US 395, 93541. T: (760) 647-6401. www.thesierraweb.com/recreation/monovista/. RV/tent: 63. $13–$23. Hookups: water, electric (20, 30, 50 amp), sewer, cable TV.

Morraine, Hwy. 120, 93541. T: (760) 932-5451. F: (760) 932-5458. RV/tent: 20. $7. Hookups: none.

Saddlebag Lake, Saddlebag Lake Rd., 93541. T: (760) 873-2400 or (760) 647-3044. F: (760) 647-3046. ww.r5.fs.fed.us/inyo. RV/tent: 20. $11. Hookups: none.

Tioga Lake, Hwy. 120, 93541. T: (760) 873-2400 or (760) 647-3044. F: (760) 647-3046. www.r5.fs.fed.us/inyo. RV/tent: 25. $11. Hookups: none.

Leggett

Redwoods River Resort & Campground, 75000 Hwy. 101, 95585. T: (707) 925-6249. F: (707) 925-6413. www.rvdestinations.com/redwoodsriver/. RV/tent: 60. $17–$26. Hookups: water, electric (20, 30, 50 amp), sewer.

Lewiston

Ackerman, Trinity Dam Blvd., 96052. T: (530) 623-2121. F: (530) 623-6010. www.r5.fs.fed.us/shastatrinity. RV/tent: 66. $10. Hookups: none.

Mary Smith, Trinity Dam Blvd., 96052. T: (530) 623-2121. F: (530) 623-6010. www.r5.fs.fed.us/shastatrinity. RV/tent: 18. $9. Hookups: none.

Tunnel Rock, Trinity Dam Blvd., 96052. T: (530) 623-2121. F: (530) 623-6010. www.r5.fs.fed.us/shastatrinity. RV/tent: 6. $5. Hookups: none.

Lodi

Tower Park Resort, 14900 West Hwy. 12, 95242. T: (209) 369-1041. F: (209) 943-5656. RV/tent: 442. $22–$26. Hookups: water, electric (20, 30 amp), sewer.

Loma Linda

Mission RV Park, Redlands Blvd., 92354. T: (909) 796-7570. www.woodalls.com. RV/tent: 79. $20. Hookups: water, electric (20, 30, 50 amp), sewer, phone.

Lone Pine

Boulder Creek RV Resort, 2550 South Hwy. 395, 93545. T: (800) 648-8965 or (760) 876-4243. www.395.com/bouldercreek/. RV/tent: 65. $24. Hookups: water, electric (30, 50 amp), sewer, cable TV, phone.

Lone Pine, Whitney Portal Rd., 93545. T: (760) 876-6200. F: (760) 876-6202. www.r5.fs.fed.us/inyo. RV/tent: 43. $10. Hookups: none.

Loomis

KOA Loomis, 3945 Taylor Rd., 95650. T: (916) 652-6737. F: (916) 652-5026. www.koa.com. RV/tent: 78. $26–$28. Hookups: water, electric (20, 30 amp), sewer.

Lucia

Limekiln State Park, Hwy. 1, 93921. T: (877) 444-6777 or (831) 667-2403. www.reserveusa.com. RV/tent: 43. $12. Hookups: none.

Nacimiento, Nacimiento Fergusson Rd., 93921. T: (831) 385-5434. F: (831) 385-0628. www.r5.fs.fed.us/lospadres/. RV/tent: 17. $5. Hookups: none.

Plaskett Creek, Hwy. 1, 93921. T: (831) 385-5434. F: (831) 385-0628. www.r5.fs.fed.us/lospadres/. RV/tent: 43. $16. Hookups: none.

Mammoth Lakes

Agnew Meadows, Minaret Summit Rd., 93546. T: (760) 924-5500. F: (760) 924-5537. www.r5.fs.fed.us/inyo. RV/tent: 21. $12. Hookups: none.

Coldwater, Lake Mary Rd., 93546. T: (760) 924-5500. F: (760) 924-5537. www.r5.fs.fed.us/inyo. RV/tent: 78. $13. Hookups: none.

Lake George, Lake Mary Rd., 93546. T: (760) 924-5500. F: (760) 924-5537. www.r5.fs.fed.us/inyo. RV/tent: 16. $13. Hookups: none.

Lake Mary, Lake Mary Rd., 93546. T: (760) 924-5500. F: (760) 924-5537. www.r5.fs.fed.us/inyo. RV/tent: 48. $13. Hookups: none.

Mammoth Mountain RV Park, Hwy. 203, 93546. T: (760) 934-3822. F: (760) 934-1896. www.mammothweb.com/lodging/mammothrv/mammothrv.html. RV/tent: 183. $18–$28. Hookups: water, electric (30, 50 amp), sewer, cable TV.

Minaret Falls, Minaret Summit Rd., 93546. T: (760) 924-5500. F: (760) 924-5537. www.r5.fs.fed.us/inyo. RV/tent: 28. $12. Hookups: none.

New Shady Rest, Sawmill Cutoff, 93546. T: (760) 924-5500. F: (760) 924-5537. www.r5.fs.fed.us/inyo. RV/tent: 95. $12. Hookups: none.

Old Shady Rest, Sawmill Cutoff, 93546. T: (760) 924-5500. F: (760) 924-5537. www.r5.fs.fed.us/inyo. RV/tent: 51. $12. Hookups: none.

Pine City, Lake Mary Rd., 93546. T: (760) 924-5500. F: (760) 924-5537. www.r5.fs.fed.us/inyo. RV/tent: 10. $13. Hookups: none.

Pine Glen, Sawmill Cutoff, 93546. T: (760) 924-5500. F: (760) 924-5537. www.r5.fs.fed.us/inyo. RV/tent: 11. $12. Hookups: none.

Pumice Flat, Minaret Summit Rd., 93546. T: (760) 924-5500. F: (760) 924-5537. www.r5.fs.fed.us/inyo. RV/tent: 17. $12. Hookups: none.

Red's Meadow, Minaret Summit Rd., 93546. T: (760) 924-5500. F: (760) 924-5537. www.r5.fs.fed.us/inyo. RV/tent: 56. $12. Hookups: none.

Upper Soda Springs, Minaret Summit Rd., 93546. T: (760) 924-5500. F: (760) 924-5537. www.r5.fs.fed.us/inyo. RV/tent: 29. $12. Hookups: none.

Manchester

KOA Manchester Beach, 44300 Kinney Rd., 95459. T: (800) KOA-4188 or (707) 882-2375. F: (707) 882-3104. www.koa.com. RV/tent: 125. $27–$41. Hookups: water, electric (20, 30 amp), sewer, cable TV, phone.

Manchester State Park, Kinney Ln., 95468. T: (707) 937-5804. F: (707) 937-2953. RV/tent: 46. $12. Hookups: none.

Manteca

Oakwood Lake RV Campround, 874 East Woodward Ave., 95337. T: (800) 626-5253 or (209) 249-2500 ext. 308. www.oakwoodlake.com. RV/tent: 357. $19–$31. Hookups: water, electric (20, 30 amp), sewer, phone.

CALIFORNIA (continued)

Marina

Marina Dunes RV Park, 3330 Dunes Dr., 93933. T: (831) 384-6914. F: (831) 384-0285. RV/tent: 75. $29.50–$39. Hookups: water, electric (20, 30 amp), sewer, cable TV, phone.

Mariposa

Mariposa Fairgrounds, 5007 Fairgrounds Rd., 95338. T: (209) 966-2432. F: (209) 966-6273. www.mariposafair.com/camping.htm. RV/tent: 350. $18. Hookups: water, electric (20, 30, 50 amp).

Markleeville

Markleeville, Hwy. 89, 96120. T: (775) 882-2766. F: (775) 884-8199. RV/tent: 10. $9. Hookups: none.

McCloud

Ah-Di-Na, Lake McCloud Rd., 96057. T: (530) 964-2184. F: (530) 964-2938. www.r5.fs.fed.us/shastatrinity. RV/tent: 16. $8. Hookups: none.

Cattle Camp, Hwy. 89, 96057. T: (530) 964-2184. F: (530) 964-2938. www.r5.fs.fed.us/shastatrinity. RV/tent: 29. $10. Hookups: none.

Meeks Bay

Kaspian, Hwy. 89, West Shore Lake Tahoe, 96142. T: (877) 444-6777 or (530) 573-2674. F: (530) 573-2693. www.r5.fs.fed.us/ltbmu; www.reserveusa.com. RV/tent: 10. $12. Hookups: none.

Mendocino

Caspar Beach RV Park, 14441 Point Cabrillo Dr., 95460. T: (707) 964-3306. F: (707) 964-0526. www.casparbeachrvpark.com. RV/tent: 118. $22–$29.50. Hookups: water, electric (30 amp), sewer, cable TV, phone.

Mineral

Crags, Lassen Volcanic National Park, Lassen Park Rd., 96063. T: (530) 595-4444. F: (530) 595-3262. www.nps.gov/lavo. RV/tent: 45. $8. Hookups: none.

Juniper Lake, Juniper Lake Rd., 96063. T: (530) 595-4444. F: (530) 595-3262. www.nps.gov/lavo. RV/tent: 18. $10. Hookups: none.

North Summit Lake, Lassen Park Rd., 96063. T: (530) 595-4444. F: (530) 595-3262. www.nps.gov/lavo. RV/tent: 46. $14. Hookups: none.

South Summit Lake, Lassen Park Rd., 96063. T: (530) 595-4444. F: (530) 595-3262. www.nps.gov/lavo. RV/tent: 48. $12. Hookups: none.

Southwest, Lassen Park Rd., 96063. T: (530) 595-4444. F: (530) 595-3262. www.nps.gov/lavo. RV/tent: 21. $12. Hookups: none.

Volcano Country RV Park & Campground, Hwy. 36 East, 96063. T: (530) 595-3347. F: (530) 595-4452. RV/tent: 30. $16–$21. Hookups: water, electric (20, 30 amp), sewer.

Warner Valley, Warner Valley Rd., 96063. T: (530) 595-4444. F: (530) 595-3262. www.nps.gov/lavo. RV/tent: 18. $12. Hookups: none.

Mojave National Preserve

Mid Hills, Black Canyon Rd., 92311. T: (760) 255-8801. www.nps.gov/moja. RV/tent: 26. $10. Hookups: none.

Monterey

Cypress Tree Inn of Monterey, 2227 North Fremont St., 93940. T: (800) 446-8303 (CA only) or (831) 372-7586. F: (831 372-2940. www.cyprestreeinn.com/rv.html. RV/tent: 25. $20–$40. Hookups: water, electric (20, 30 amp).

Morro Bay

Bay Pines Travel Trailer Park, 1502 Quintana Rd., 93442. T: (805) 772-3223. F: (805) 772-0288. www.baypinesrv.com/. RV/tent: 112. $23. Hookups: water, electric (30 amp), sewer, satellite TV, phone.

Morro Bay State Park, State Park Rd., 93443. T: (805) 772-7434; reservations (800) 444-7275. F: (805) 772-5760. www.reserveamerica.com. RV/tent: 125. $7. Hookups: water, electric (30 amp).

Morro Dunes RV Park, 1700 Embarcadero, 93442. T: (805) 772-2722. F: (805) 772-5319. www.rvdestinations.com/morrodunes/. RV/tent: 226. $17.60–$26.40. Hookups: water, electric (15, 30 amp), sewer, cable TV, phone.

Mount Laguna

Agua Dulce, Sunrise Hwy./Laguna Mountain Rd., 91948. T: (877) 444-6777 or (619) 445-6235. F: (619) 445-1753. www.r5.fs.fed.us/cleveland. RV/tent: 5. $13. Hookups: none.

Burnt Rancheria, Sunrise Hwy./Laguna Mountain Rd., 91948. T: (877) 444-6777 or (619) 445-6235. F: (619) 445-1753. www.r5.fs.fed.us/cleveland; www.reserveusa.com. RV/tent: 109. $14. Hookups: none.

Cibbets Flat, Kitchen Creek Rd., 91948. T: (619) 445-6235. F: (619) 445-1753. www.r5.fs.fed.us/cleveland. RV/tent: 23. $10. Hookups: none.

Laguna, Sunrise Hwy./Laguna Mountain Rd., 91948. T: (877) 444-6777 or (619) 445-6235. F: (619) 445-1753. www.r5.fs.fed.us/cleveland; www.reserveusa.com. RV/tent: 103. $14. Hookups: none.

Napa

Spanish Flat Resort, 4290 Knoxville Rd., 94558. T: (707) 966-7700. F: (707) 966-7704. www.spanishflatresort.com. RV/tent: 120. $21–$26. Hookups: water, electric (50 amp).

Needles

KOA Needles, 5400 National Old Trails Hwy., 92363. T: (800) 562-3407 or (760) 326-4207. F: (460) 326-6329. www.koa.com. RV/tent: 101. $18–$26. Hookups: water, electric (30 amp), sewer, phone.

Rainbo Beach Resort, Rte. 4 Box 139 River Rd., 92363. T: (760) 326-3101. F: (760) 326-5085. www. coloradoriverinfo.com/needles/rainbobeach/. RV/tent: 64. $22. Hookups: water, electric (20, 30, 50 amp), sewer, phone.

Niland

Fountain of Youth Spa, 10249 Coachella Canal Rd., 92257. T: (888) 800-0772. F: (760) 354-1558. www.foyspa.com. RV/tent: 1000. $16–$30. Hookups: water, electric (50 amp), sewer, cable TV.

North Shore

Salton Sea State Recreation Area, Corvina Beach, Hwy. 111, 92254. T: (760) 393-3052. F: (760) 393-2466. www.saltonsea.statepark.org/. RV/tent: 500. $10. Hookups: none.

Recreation Area, Mecca Beach, Hwy. 111, 92254. T: (760) 393-3052. F: (760) 393-2466. www.saltonsea.statepark.org/. RV/tent: 110. $10. Hookups: water, electric (30 amp).

Salton Sea State Recreation Area, Salt Creek Primitive Area, Hwy. 111, 92254. T: (760) 393-3052. F: (760) 393-2466. www.saltonsea.statepark.org/. RV/tent: 150. $10. Hookups: none.

Northridge

Walnut RV Park, 19130 Nordhoff St., 91324. T: (800)-868-2749. F: (818) 775- 0384. www.walnutrvpark.com. RV/tent: 114. $35. Hookups: water, electric (50 amp), sewer, cable TV, phone (long term).

Novato

Novato RV Park, 1530 Armstrong Ave., 94945. T: (800) 733-6787 or (415) 897-1271. F: (415) 897-5500. http://209.24.94.35/novatorvpark/. RV/tent: 86. $3050–$36.50. Hookups: water, electric (20, 30, 50 amp), sewer, TV, phone.

O'Brien

Antlers, Antlers Rd., 96070. T: (877) 444-6777 or (530) 275-1587. www.r5.fs.fed.us/shastatrinity; www.reserveusa.com. RV/tent: 59. $15. Hookups: none.

Gregory Creek, Gregory Creek Rd., 96070. T: (877) 444-6777 or (530) 275-1587. www.r5.fs.fed.us/shastatrinity; www.reserveusa.com. RV/tent: 18. $12. Hookups: none.

Lakeshore East, Lakeshore Dr., 96070. T: (877) 444-6777 or (530) 275-1587. www.r5.fs.fed.us/shastatrinity; www.reserveusa.com. RV/tent: 25. $15. Hookups: none.

Moore Creek, Gilman Rd., 96070. T: (877) 444-6777 or (530) 275-1587. www.r5.fs.fed.us/shastatrinity; www.reserveusa.com. RV/tent: 12. $12. Hookups: none.

Old Station

Big Pine Camp, Hwy. 89, 96071. T: (530) 336-5521. F: (530) 335-4518. www.r5.fs.fed.us/lassen. RV/tent: 19. $10. Hookups: none.

Bridge Camp, Hwy. 89, 96071. T: (530) 336-5521. F: (530) 335-4518. www.r5.fs.fed.us/lassen. RV/tent: 25. $11. Hookups: none.

Cave Camp, Hwy. 89, 96071. T: (530) 336-5521. F: (530) 335-4518. www.r5.fs.fed.us/lassen. RV/tent: 46. $13. Hookups: none.

CALIFORNIA (continued)

Old Station (continued)

Crater Lake, FR 32N08, 96071. T: (530) 257-4188. F: (530) 252-5803. www.r5.fs.fed.us/lassen. RV/tent: 32. $11. Hookups: none.

Hat Creek, Hwy. 89, 96071. T: (877) 444-6777 or (530) 336-5521. F: (530) 335-4518. www.r5.fs.fed.us/lassen; www.reserveusa.com. RV/tent: 73. $13. Hookups: none.

Honn, Hwy. 89, 96071. T: (530) 336-5521. F: (530) 335-4518. www.r5.fs.fed.us/lassen. RV/tent: 6. $8. Hookups: none.

Orick

Prairie Creek Redwoods State Park, Gold Bluff Beach, Newton B. Drury Scenic Parkway, 95555. T: (707) 464-6101 ext. 5301 or 5064. www.cal-parks.ca.gov. RV/tent: 25. $12. Hookups: none.

Orland

Old Orchard RV Park, 4490 County Rd. HH, 95963. T: (530) 865-5335. F: (530) 865-5335. RV/tent: 72. $12–$22. Hookups: water, electric (30, 50amp), sewer.

Orland Buttes, Newville Rd./Rd. 200, 95963-8901. T: (877) 444-6777 or (530) 865-4781. F: (530) 865-5283. www.spk.usace.army.mil/cespkco/lakes/black-butte.html; www.reserveusa.com. RV/tent: 39. $14. Hookups: none.

Orleans

Aikens Creek West, Hwy. 96, 95556. T: (530) 626-3291. F: (530) 627-3401. www.r5.fs.fed.us/sixrivers. RV/tent: 0. $7. Hookups: none.

Dillon Creek, Hwy. 96, 95556. T: (530) 626-3291. F: (530) 627-3401. www.r5.fs.fed.us/sixrivers. RV/tent: 21. $9. Hookups: none.

E-Ne-Luck, Hwy. 96, 95556. T: (530) 626-3291. F: (530) 627-3401. www.r5.fs.fed.us/sixrivers. RV/tent: 11. $9. Hookups: none.

Fish Lake, Fish Lake Rd., 95556. T: (530) 626-3291. F: (530) 627-3401. www.r5.fs.fed.us/sixrivers. RV/tent: 24. $9. Hookups: none.

Oxnard

Evergreen RV Park, 2135 Oxnard Blvd., 93030. T: (805) 485-1936. www.caohwy.com/e/evergtrp.htm. RV/tent: 81. $30. Hookups: water, electric (30 amp), sewer.

Palmdale

Saddleback Butte State Park, Ave. J, 93551. T: (661) 942-0662. F: (661) 940-7327. RV/tent: 50. $10. Hookups: none.

Paso Robles

Wine Country RV Resort, Airport Rd., 93446. T: (805) 238-4560. RV/tent: 82. $28–$30. Hookups: water, electric (30, 50 amp), sewer.

Petaluma

KOA San Francisco North-Petaluma, 20 Rainsville Rd., 94952. T: (800) 992-2267 or (707) 763-1492. www.sanfranciscokoa.com. RV/tent: 312. $31–$38. Hookups: water, electric (20, 30, 50 amp), sewer, cable TV, phone.

Pine Valley

Boulder Oaks, Old Hwy. 80, 91962. T: (877) 444-6777 or (619) 445-6235. F: (619) 445-1753. www.r5.fs.fed.us/cleveland; www.reserveusa.com. RV/tent: 18. $10–$12. Hookups: none.

Pismo Beach

Pismo State Beach, Oceano Campground, Pier Ave., 93445. T: (800) 444-7275 or (805) 489-2684. www.cal-parks.ca.gov; www.reserveamerica.com. RV/tent: 82. $12–$18. Hookups: water, electric (30 amp).

Pollock Pines

Jones Fork, Ice House Rd., 95726. T: (530) 644-2349. F: (530) 647-5405. www.r5.fs.fed.us/eldorado. RV/tent: 10. $5. Hookups: none.

Northwind, Ice House Rd., 95726. T: (530) 644-2349. F: (530) 647-5405. www.r5.fs.fed.us/eldorado. RV/tent: 9. $5. Hookups: none.

Silver Creek, Ice House Rd., 95726. T: (530) 644-2349. F: (530) 647-5405. www.r5.fs.fed.us/eldorado. RV/tent: 12. $6. Hookups: water, electric (20, 30, 50), phone, cable TV.

Strawberry Point, Ice House Rd., 95726. T: (530) 644-2349. F: (530) 647-5405. www.r5.fs.fed.us/eldorado. RV/tent: 10. $5. Hookups: none.

Wench Creek, Ice House Rd., 95726. T: (530) 644-2349. F: (530) 647-5405. www.r5.fs.fed.us/eldorado. RV/tent: 100. $13–$20. Hookups: none.

Wolf Creek, Union Valley Rd., 95726. T: (877) 444-6777 or (530) 644-2349. F: (530) 647-5405. www.r5.fs.fed.us/eldorado; www.reserveusa.com. RV/tent: 42. $13–$20. Hookups: none.

Yellowjacket, Union Valley Rd., 95726. T: (877) 444-6777 or (530) 644-2349. F: (530) 647-5405. www.r5.fs.fed.us/eldorado; www.reserveusa.com. RV/tent: 40. $13–$20. Hookups: none.

Pomona

KOA Pomona-Fairplex, 2200 North White Ave., 91768. T: (909) 593-8915 or (888) 562-4230. www.koa.com. RV/tent: 185. $25–$40. Hookups: water, electric (30, 50 amp), sewer, phone.

Port Hueneme

Point Mugu State Park, Big Sycamore Canyon Campground, Hwy. 1, 93043. T: (800) 444-7275 or (818) 880-0350. F: (818) 880-6165. www.reserveamerica.com. RV/tent: 55. $12. Hookups: none.

Point Mugu State Park, Thornhill Broome Campground, Hwy. 1, 93043. T: (800) 444-7275 or (818) 880-0350. F: (818) 880-6165. www.reserveamerica.com. RV/tent: 88. $7–$12. Hookups: none.

Porterville

Deer Creek RV Park, 10679 Main St., 93257. T: (559) 781-3337. RV/tent: 78. $18. Hookups: water, electric (20, 30, 50 amp), sewer, phone.

Portola

Sierra Springs Trailer Resort, 70099 Hwy. 70, 96122. T: (530) 836-2747. F: (530) 836-2559. www.psln.com/sstr/. RV/tent: 40. $20. Hookups: water, electric (20, 30 amp), sewer, cable TV, phone.

Pratville

Cool Springs, Butt Valley Rd., 95923. T: (916) 386-5164. www.r5.fs.fed.us/lassen. RV/tent: 30. $15. Hookups: none.

Last Chance Creek, Lake Almanor Causeway, 95923. T: (916) 386-5164. www.r5.fs.fed.us/lassen. RV/tent: 12. $13. Hookups: none.

Ponderosa Flat, Butt Valley Rd., 95923. T: (916) 386-5164. www.r5.fs.fed.us/lassen. RV/tent: 63. $15. Hookups: none.

Yellow Creek, County Rd. 307, 95923. T: (916) 386-5164. www.r5.fs.fed.us/lassen. RV/tent: 10. $13. Hookups: none.

Redding

JGW RV Park, 6612 Riverland Dr., 96002. T: (800) 469-5910 or (530) 365-7965. F: (530) 244-0420. RV/tent: 65. $25. Hookups: water, electric (20, 30, 50 amp), sewer, cable TV, phone.

Mountain Gate RV Park, 14161 Holiday Rd., 96003. T: (800) 404-6040 or (530) 275 4600. F: (530) 275-1905. www.mt-gatervpark.com/. RV/tent: 122. $23.50 . Hookups: water, electric (30, 50 amp), sewer, satellite TV, phone.

Redding RV Park, 11075 Campers Ct., 96003. T: (800) 428-2089 or (530) 241-0707. F: (530) 243-2781. www.gocampingamerica.com/redding/. RV/tent: 110. $22–$23. Hookups: water, electric (30, 50 amp), sewer, satellite TV, phone.

Redwood City

Trailer Villa, 3401 East Bayshore Rd., 94063. T: (800) 366-7880. F: (650) 366-7948. www.gocampingamerica.com/trailervillarv/. RV/tent: 90. $26. Hookups: water, electric (20, 30 amp), sewer, phone.

Sacramento

Oak Haven RV Park, 2145 Auburn Blvd., 95821. T: (916) 922-0814. F: (916) 924-0814. www.gocampingamerica.com/oakhavenrv/. RV/tent: 90. $19–$21. Hookups: water, electric (30, 50 amp), sewer, TV, phone.

Stillman Adult RV Park, 3880 Stillman Park Cir., 95824. T: (916) 392-2820 or (800) 570-6562. www.gocampingamerica.com/stillman/. RV/tent: 65. $29. Hookups: water, electric (20, 30, 50 amp), sewer, TV, phone.

CALIFORNIA (continued)

Salinas

Laguna Seca Recreation Area, Hwy. 68, 93901. T: (831) 755-4895. www.carmelfun.com/parks.html. RV/tent: 177. $18–$22. Hookups: water, electric (20, 30 amp).

San Bernardino

KOA San Bernardino, 1707 Cable Canyon Rd., 92407. T: (800) KOA-4155 or (909) 887-4098. F: (909) 887-8499. www.koa.com. RV/tent: 153. $19–$32. Hookups: water, electric (20, 30, 50 amp), sewer, phone.

San Diego

Campland on the Bay, 2211 Pacific Beach Dr., 92109. T: (800) 4-BAY-FUN. F: (858) 581-4264. www.campland.com. RV/tent: 750. $36–$155. Hookups: water, electric (50 amp), sewer, cable TV, phone.

De Anza Harbor Resort, De Anza Dr., 92109. T: (858) 273-3211. RV/tent: 262. $20–$72. Hookups: water, electric (20, 30 amp), sewer, phone.

La Pacifica RV Park, 1010 West San Ysidro Blvd., 92109. T: (619) 428-4413. F: (619) 428-4413. www.gocampingamerica.com/lapacificarvpk/. RV/tent: 177. $20. Hookups: water, electric (30, 50 amp), sewer, phone, satellite TV.

San Fernando

Buckhorn, Hwy. 2, 91342. T: (818) 899-1900. F: (818) 896-6727. www.r5.fs.fed.us/angeles. RV/tent: 38. $12. Hookups: none.

Chilao, Hwy. 2, 91342. T: (818) 899-1900. F: (818) 896-6727. www.r5.fs.fed.us/angeles. RV/tent: 110. $12. Hookups: none.

Horse Flats, Santa Clara Divide Rd., 91342. T: (818) 899-1900. F: (818) 896-6727. www.r5.fs.fed.us/angeles. RV/tent: 25. $10. Hookups: none.

Messenger Flats, Santa Clara Divide Rd., 91342. T: (818) 899-1900. F: (818) 896-6727. www.r5.fs.fed.us/angeles. RV/tent: 10. $5. Hookups: none.

San Juan Bautista

Betabel RV Resort, 9664 Betabel Rd., 95045. T: (800) 278-7275. F: (831) 623-2028. www.betabel.com. RV/tent: 155. $30–$32. Hookups: water, electric (30, 50 amp), sewer, satellite TV, phone.

Fremont Peak State Park, San Juan Canyon Rd., 95045. T: (831) 623-4255. F: (831) 623-4612. RV/tent: 25. $7. Hookups: none.

Mission Farm RV Park, 400 San Juan-Hollister Rd., 95045. T: (831) 623-4456. www.mission-farm.com. RV/tent: 165. $25–$28. Hookups: water, electric (20, 30 amp), sewer, cable TV, phone.

San Luis Obispo

Avila Valley Hot Springs Spa & RV Resort, 250 Avila Beach Dr., 93405. T: (805) 595-2359 or (800) 332-2359 or (800) 543-2359. F: (805) 595-7914. www.rvdestinations.com/avila/. RV/tent: 100. $30–$40. Hookups: water, electric (20, 30 amp), sewer, cable TV.

San Rafael

China Camp State Park, North San Pedro Rd., 94903. T: (800) 444-7275 or (415) 456-0766. F: (415) 456-1743. www.reserveamerica.com. RV/tent: 30. $1 per person. Hookups: none.

San Simeon

San Simeon State Park, Washburn Campground, San Simeon Creek Rd., 93452. T: (800) 444-7275; (805) 927-2035 or (805) 927-2020. www.cal-parks.ca.gov; www.reserveamerica.com. RV/tent: 70. $7. Hookups: none.

Santa Barbara

Santa Barbara Sunrise RV Park, 516 South Salinas, 93103. T: (800) 345-5018 or (805) 966-9954. F: (805) 966-7950. www.gocampingamerica.com/santabarbara/. RV/tent: 33. $35. Hookups: water, electric (20, 30 amp), sewer, cable TV, phone.

Scott Bar

Indian Scotty, Scott River Rd., 96085. T: (530) 468-5351. F: (530) 468-1290. www.r5.fs.fed.us/klamath. RV/tent: 28. $6. Hookups: none.

Scotts Valley

Carbonero Creek RV Park, 917 Disc Dr., 95066. T: (408) 438-1288 / (800) 546-1288. F: (408) 438-2877. www.gocampingamerica.com/carbonero/. RV/tent: 104. $22–$29. Hookups: water, electric (20, 30 amp), sewer, cable TV, phone.

Sequoia National Park

Atwell Mill, Mineral King Rd., 93262. T: (559) 565-3341. www.nps.gov/seki. RV/tent: 21. $8. Hookups: none.

Buckeye Flat, Hwy. 198, 93262. T: (559) 565-3341. www.nps.gov/seki. RV/tent: 28. $14. Hookups: none.

Cold Springs, Mineral King Rd., 93262. T: (559) 565-3341. www.nps.gov/seki. RV/tent: 40. $8. Hookups: none.

Dorst, Generals Hwy., 93262. T: (559) 565-3341. www.nps.gov/seki. RV/tent: 218. $16. Hookups: none.

Lodgepole, Generals Hwy., 93262. T: (559) 565-3341. www.nps.gov/seki. RV/tent: 214. $16. Hookups: none.

South Fork, South Fork Rd., 93262. T: (559) 565-3341. www.nps.gov/seki. RV/tent: 13. $8. Hookups: none.

Shelter Cove

Horse Mountain, Kings Peak Rd., 95589. T: (707) 986-7731or (707) 825-2300. F: (707) 825-2301. www.ca.blm.gov/arcata/campground.html. RV/tent: 9. $5. Hookups: none.

Nadelos, Chemise Mountain Rd., 95589. T: (707) 986-7731 or (707) 825-2300. F: (707) 825-2301. www.ca.blm.gov/arcata/campground.html. RV/tent: 8. $8. Hookups: none.

Wailaki, Chemise Mountain Rd., 95589. T: (707) 986-7731 or (707) 825-2300. F: (707) 825-2301. www.ca.blm.gov/arcata/campground.html. RV/tent: 13. $8. Hookups: none.

Sierra City

Loganville, Hwy. 49, 96125. T: (530) 288-3231 or (530) 993-1410. F: (530) 288-0727. www.r5.fs.fed.us/tahoe. RV/tent: 20. $12. Hookups: none.

Stockton

Tiki Lagun Resort & Marina, 12988 West McDonald Rd., 95206. T: (877) 444-TIKI or (209) 941-8975. F: (209) 941-4575. www.tiki-marina.com. RV/tent: 103. $25. Hookups: water, electric (30 amp), sewer, cable TV.

Susanville

Christie, County Rd. 231, 96130. T: (877) 444-6777 or (530) 257-4188. F: (530) 252-5803. www.r5.fs.fed.us/lassen; www.reserveusa.com. RV/tent: 69. $14. Hookups: none.

Mariners Resort, 509-725 Stones Rd., 96130. T: (800) 700-5253. F: (530) 825-3397. www.marinersresort.com. RV/tent: 67. $25–$30. Hookups: water, electric (30, 50 amp), sewer, satellite TV, phone.

Mountain View RV Park, 3075 Johnstonville Rd., 96130. T: (877) 686-7878. F: (530) 251-0796. RV/tent: 77. $24. Hookups: water, electric (30, 50 amp), sewer, cable TV, phone.

Tahoe City

Tahoe State Recreation Area, Hwy. 28, 96145. T: (530) 583-3074. www.reserveamerica.com. RV/tent: 38. $12. Hookups: none.

William Kent, Hwy. 89, West Shore Lake Tahoe, 96145. T: (877) 444-6777; (530) 573-2674 or (530) 583-3642. F: (530) 573-2693. www.r5.fs.fed.us/ltbmu; www.reserveusa.com. RV/tent: 95. $14. Hookups: none.

Tahoma

Emerald Bay State Park, Hwy. 89, West Shore Lake Tahoe, 96142. T: (800) 444-7275; (530) 525-7277 or (530) 525-7232. www.cal-parks.ca.gov; www.reserveamerica.com. RV/tent: 120. $12. Hookups: none.

Temecula

Indian Oaks Trailer Ranch Campground, 38120 East Benton Rd., 92593. T: (909) 302-5399. F: (909) 302-5399. www.gocampingamerica.com/indianoaks/. RV/tent: 62. $18–$25. Hookups: water, electric (20, 30 amp), sewer, phone.

Pechanga RV Resort, 45000 Pala Rd., 92592. T: (909) 587-0484 or (877) 997-8386. F: (909) 587-8204. www.pechangarvresort.com/. RV/tent: 170. $32. Hookups: water, electric (20, 30, 50 amp), sewer, cable TV, phone.

Three Rivers

Three Rivers Motel & RV Park, 43365 Sierra Dr., 93271. T: (559) 561-4413. RV/tent: 26. $14–$20. Hookups: water, electric (15, 30 amp), sewer, TV, phone.

CALIFORNIA (continued)

Toms Place

Big Meadow, Rock Creek Rd., 93514. T: (760) 873-2500. F: (760) 873-2563. www.r5.fs.fed.us/inyo. RV/tent: 11. $12. Hookups: none.

French Camp, Rock Creek Rd., 93514. T: (760) 873-2500. F: (760) 873-2563. www.r5.fs.fed.us/inyo. RV/tent: 86. $12. Hookups: none.

Holiday, Rock Creek Rd., 93514. T: (760) 873-2500. F: (760) 873-2563. www.r5.fs.fed.us/inyo. RV/tent: 35. $12. Hookups: none.

Iris Meadows, Rock Creek Rd., 93514. T: (760) 873-2500. F: (760) 873-2563. www.r5.fs.fed.us/inyo. RV/tent: 14. $12. Hookups: none.

Palisade, Rock Creek Rd., 93514. T: (760) 873-2500. F: (760) 873-2563. www.r5.fs.fed.us/inyo. RV/tent: 5. $12. Hookups: none.

Pine Grove, Rock Creek Rd., 93514. T: (760) 873-2500. F: (760) 873-2563. www.r5.fs.fed.us/inyo. RV/tent: 11. $12. Hookups: none.

Rock Creek Lake, Rock Creek Rd., 93514. T: (760) 873-2500. F: (760) 873-2563. www.r5.fs.fed.us/inyo. RV/tent: 28. $12. Hookups: none.

Tuff, US 395, 93514. T: (760) 873-2500. F: (760) 873-2563. www.r5.fs.fed.us/inyo. RV/tent: 34. $12. Hookups: none.

Upper Pine Grove, Rock Creek Rd., 93514. T: (760) 873-2500. F: (760) 873-2563. www.r5.fs.fed.us/inyo. RV/tent: 8. $12. Hookups: none.

Trinidad

Azalea Glen RV Park & Campground, 3883 Patricks Point Dr., 95570. T: (707) 677-3068. www.azaleaglen.com. RV/tent: 42. $15–$24. Hookups: water, electric (30, 50 amp), sewer, cable TV, phone.

Truckee

Goose Meadows, Hwy. 89, 96161. T: (877) 444-6777; (530) 587-3558 or (530) 544-0426. F: (530) 587-6914. www.r5.fs.fed.us/tahoe; www.reserveamerica.com. RV/tent: 24. $10. Hookups: none.

Granite Flat, Hwy. 89, 96161. T: (877) 444-6777; (530) 587-3558 or (530) 544-0426. F: (530) 587-6914. www.r5.fs.fed.us/tahoe www.reserveamerica.com. RV/tent: 75. $12. Hookups: none.

Silver Creek, Hwy. 89, 96161. T: (877) 444-6777; (530) 587-3558 or (530) 544-0426. F: (530) 587-6914. www.r5.fs.fed.us/tahoe; www.reserveamerica.com. RV/tent: 21. $10. Hookups: none.

Tulare

Sun & Fun RV Park, 1000 East Rankin Ave., 93274. T: (559) 686-5779. www.tldirectory.com/campgrounds/sunandfun/. RV/tent: 64. $23. Hookups: water, electric (30, 50 amp), sewer, cable TV, phone.

Tulelake

A.H. Hogue, FR 49/Medicine Lake Rd., 96134. T: (530) 667-2246. F: (530) 667-8609. www.r5.fs.fed.us/modoc. RV/tent: 24. $7. Hookups: none.

Headquarters, FR 49/Medicine Lake Rd., 96134. T: (530) 667-2246. F: (530) 667-8609. www.r5.fs.fed.us/modoc. RV/tent: 9. $7. Hookups: none.

Hemlock, FR 49/Medicine Lake Rd., 96134. T: (530) 667-2246. F: (530) 667-8609. www.r5.fs.fed.us/modoc. RV/tent: 19. $7. Hookups: none.

Medicine, FR 49/Medicine Lake Rd., 96134. T: (530) 667-2246. F: (530) 667-8609. www.r5.fs.fed.us/modoc. RV/tent: 22. $7. Hookups: none.

Tuttletown

Tuttletown Recreation Area; Big Oak Campground, Glory Hole Rd., 95222. T: (209) 536-9094. F: (209) 536-9652. www.recreation.gov. RV/tent: 55. $14. Hookups: none.

Tuttletown Recreation Area; Glory Hole Campground, Glory Hole Rd., 95222. T: (209) 536-9094. F: (209) 536-9652. www.recreation.gov. RV/tent: 20. $14. Hookups: none.

Tuttletown Recreation Area; Ironhorse Campground, Glory Hole Rd., 95222. T: (209) 536-9094. F: (209) 536-9652. www.recreation.gov. RV/tent: 89. $14. Hookups: none.

Twentynine Palms

29 Palms RV and Golf Resort, 4949 Desert Knoll Ave., 92277. T: (800) 874-4548 or (760) 367-3320. www.29palmsrvgolfresort.com/. RV/tent: 197. $27. Hookups: water, electric (30, 50 amp), sewer, phone.

Black Rock Canyon, Joshua Tree National Park, Black Rock Canyon Rd., 92277-3597. T: (760) 367-5525. F: (760) 367-5583. www.nps.gov/jotr. RV/tent: 100. $10. Hookups: none.

Indian Cove, Indian Cove Rd., Joshua Tree National Park, 92277-3597. T: (760) 367-5525. F: (760) 367-5583. www.nps.gov/jotr. RV/tent: 101. $10. Hookups: none.

Ukiah

Bu-Shay, Inlet Rd., 95482-9404. T: (877) 444-6777 or (707) 462-7581. F: (707) 462-3372. www.spn.usace.army.mil/mendocino.html; www.reserveusa.com. RV/tent: 164. $16. Hookups: none.

Che-Ka-Ka, Lake Mendocino Dr., 95482-9404. T: (877) 444-6777 ot (07) 462-7581. F: (707) 462-3372. www.spn.usace.army.mil/mendocino.html; www.reserveusa.com. RV/tent: 22. $8. Hookups: none.

Valencia

Valencia Travel Village, 27946 Henry Mayo Dr., 91384. T: (661) 257-3333. RV/tent: 460. $22–$42. Hookups: water, electric (20, 30, 50 amp), sewer, cable TV, phone.

Vallejo

Tradewinds RV Park of Vallejo, 239 Lincoln Rd. West, 94590. T: (707) 643-4000. www.gocampingamerica.com/tradewinds/. RV/tent: 78. $25. Hookups: water, electric (30, 50 amp), sewer, phone.

Ventura

Emma Wood State Beach, State Beach Rd., 93005. T: (805) 648-4807. RV/tent: 94. $12. Hookups: none.

Ventura Beach RV Resort, 800 W Main St., 93001. T: (805) 643-9137. F: (805) 643-7479. www.caohwy.com/v/venbearv.htm. RV/tent: 168. $22–$32. Hookups: water, electric (50 amp), sewer.

Visalia

KOA Visalia-Fresno South, 7480 Ave 308, 93291. T: (800) 562-0540 or (559) 651-0544. F: (559) 651-1080. www.koa.com. RV/tent: 137. $20–$28. Hookups: water, electric (20, 30 amp), sewer, cable TV.

Watsonville

KOA SantaCruz-Monterey Bay, 1186 San Andreas Rd., 95076. T: (800) 562-7701 or (831)722-0551. F: (831)722-0989. www.koa.com. RV/tent: 230. $32–$50. Hookups: water, electric (30, 50 amp), sewer.

Weaverville

Alpine View, Gun Covington Dr., 96093. T: (877) 444-6777 or (530) 623-2121. F: (530) 623-6010. www.r5.fs.fed.us/shastatrinity; www.reserveusa.com. RV/tent: 66. $12–$18. Hookups: none.

Hayward Flat, FR 35N26Y, 96093. T: (877) 444-6777 or (530) 623-2121. F: (530) 623-6010. www.r5.fs.fed.us/shastatrinity; www.reserveusa.com. RV/tent: 97. $12–$18. Hookups: none.

Preacher Meadow, Hwy. 3, 96093. T: (877) 444-6777 or (530) 623-2121. F: (530) 623-6010. www.r5.fs.fed.us/shastatrinity; www.reserveusa.com. RV/tent: 45. $8. Hookups: none.

Sidney Gulch RV Park, Hwy. 299 West & Tinnen St., 96093. T: (530) 623-6621. RV/tent: 40. $19. Hookups: water, electric (20, 30 amp), sewer, cable TV, phone.

Stoney Point, Hwy. 3, 96093. T: (530) 623-2121. F: (530) 623-6010. www.r5.fs.fed.us/shasta-trinity. RV/tent: 22. $10. Hookups: none.

Weott

Humboldt Redwoods State Park, Albee Creek Campground, Avenue of the Giants, 95571. T: (800) 444-7275; (707) 946-2409 or (707) 946-2015. F: (707) 946-2326. www.cal-parks.ca.gov; www.reserveamerica.com. RV/tent: 72. $12. Hookups: none.

Humboldt Redwoods State Park, Hidden Springs Campground, Avenue of the Giants, 95571. T: (800) 444-7275; (707) 946-2409 or (707) 946-2015. F: (707) 946-2326. www.cal-parks.ca.gov; www.reserveamerica.com. RV/tent: 154. $12. Hookups: none.

CALIFORNIA (continued)

West Sacramento

KOA Sacramento-Metropolitan, 3951 Lake Rd., 95691. T: (800) KOA-2747 or (916) 371-6771. F: (916) 371-0622. www.koa.com. RV/tent: 122. $25–$33. Hookups: water, electric (20, 30 amp), sewer, cable TV, phone.

Sherwood Harbor Marina & RV Park, 35050 South River Rd., 95691. T: (916) 371-3471. F: (916) 372-0997. www.sherwoodharbor.com/rvpark.html. RV/tent: 40. $22. Hookups: water, electric (20 amp).

Westport

Westport-Union Landing State Beach, Hwy. 1, 95488. T: (707) 937-5804. F: (707) 937-2953. RV/tent: 130. $12. Hookups: none.

Winterhaven

Picacho State Recreation Area, Picacho Rd., 92283. T: (760) 393-3059. RV/tent: 58. $12. Hookups: none.

Wofford Heights

Boulder Gulch, Hwy. 155, 93285. T: (760) 379-5646. F: (760) 379-8597. www.r5.fs.fed.us/sequoia. RV/tent: 78. $14. Hookups: none.

Camp 9, Sierra Way, 93285. T: (877) 444-6777 or (760) 379-5646. F: (760) 379-8597. www.r5.fs.fed.us/sequoia. RV/tent: 109. $8. Hookups: none.

Hungry Gulch, Hwy. 155, 93285. T: (760) 379-5646. F: (760) 379-8597. www.r5.fs.fed.us/sequoia. RV/tent: 78. $14. Hookups: none.

Pioneer Point, Hwy. 155, 93285. T: (760) 379-5646. F: (760) 379-8597. www.r5.fs.fed.us/sequoia. RV/tent: 78. $14. Hookups: none.

Woodfords

Crystal Springs, Hwy. 88, 96120. T: (775) 882-2766. F: (775) 884-8199. www.r5.fed.fs.us/htnf. RV/tent: 20. $9. Hookups: none.

Kit Carson, Hwy. 88, 96120. T: (775) 882-2766. F: (775) 884-8199. www.r5.fed.fs.us/htnf. RV/tent: 12. $9. Hookups: none.

Wrightwood

Lake, Big Pines Hwy., 92397. T: (661) 944-2187. F: (661) 944-4698. www.r5.fs.fed.us/angeles. RV/tent: 18. $10. Hookups: none.

Table Mountain, Table Mountain Rd., 92397. T: (661) 944-2187. F: (661) 944-4698. www.r5.fs.fed.us/angeles. RV/tent: 115. $12. Hookups: none.

Yermo

KOA Barstow-Calico, 35250 Outer Hwy. 15, 92398. T: (800) 562-0059 or (760) 254-2311. F: (760) 254-2247. www.koa.com. RV/tent: 78. $18–$26. Hookups: water, electric (20, 30, 50 amp), sewer, phone.

Yosemite National Park

Bridalveil Creek, Mineral King Rd., 95389. T: (800) 436-7275 or (209) 372-0265. F: (209) 372-0371. www.nps.gov/yose; www.reservations.nps.gov. RV/tent: 74. $14. Hookups: none.

Crane Flat, Hwy. 120, 95389. T: (800) 436-7275 or (209) 372-0265. F: (209) 372-0371. www.nps.gov/yose; www.reservations.nps.gov. RV/tent: 166. $18. Hookups: none.

Hodgdon Meadow, Hwy. 120, 95389. T: (800) 436-7275 or (209) 372-0265. F: (209) 372-0371. www.nps.gov/yose; www.reservations.nps.gov. RV/tent: 105. $18. Hookups: none.

Lower Pines, Southside Dr., Yosemite Valley, 95389. T: (800) 436-7275 or (209) 372-0265. F: (209) 372-0371. www.nps.gov/yose; www.reservations.nps.gov. RV/tent: 60. $18. Hookups: none.

Porcupine Flat, Tioga Rd./Hwy. 120, 95389. T: (800) 436-7275 or (209) 372-0265. F: (209) 372-0371. www.nps.gov/yose; www.reservations.nps.gov. RV/tent: 52. $6. Hookups: none.

Upper Pines, Southside Dr., Yosemite Valley, 95389. T: (800) 436-7275 or (209) 372-0265. F: (209) 372-0371. www.nps.gov/yose; www.reservations.nps.gov. RV/tent: 238. $18. Hookups: none.

White Wolf, White Wolf Rd., 95389. T: (800) 436-7275 or (209) 372-0265. F: (209) 372-0371. www.nps.gov/yose; www.reservations.nps.gov. RV/tent: 87. $10. Hookups: none.

Yosemite Creek, Yosemite Creek Campground Rd., 95389. T: (800) 436-7275 or (209) 372-0265. F: (209) 372-0371. www.nps.gov/yose; www.reservations.nps.gov. RV/tent: 75. $6–$8. Hook ups: none.

COLORADO

Amargosa Valley

Fort Amargosa, P.O. Box 245, 89020. T: (775) 372-1178. F: (775) 372-1166. RV/tent: 98. $14. Hookups: electric (20, 30, 50 amp), water, sewer.

Alamosa

Alamosa Economy Campground, 12532 Hwy. 160 East, 81101. T: (719) 589-5574. RV/tent: 30. $10–$15. Hookups: electric (20, 30, 50 amps), water.

Almont

Three Rivers Resort & Outfitting, Rafting, Fishing, Kayaking, P.O. Box 339, 81210. T: (888) 761-3474 or (970) 641-1303. RV/tent: 62. $20. Hookups: electric (20, 30 amps), water, sewer.

Antonito

Camp Twin Rivers Cabins & RV Park, 34044 Hwy. 17, 81120. T: (888) 689-6787 or (719) 376-5710. F: (719) 376-5954. RV/tent: 46. $13–$18. Hookups: electric (20, 30, 50 amps), water, sewer.

Narrow Gauge RR Inn & RV Park, 5200 CO 285, P.O. Box 636, 81120. T: (800) 323-9469 or (719) 376-5441. F: (719) 376-5443. RV/tent: 10. $12. Hookups: electric (20, 30 amps), water, sewer.

Ponderosa Campground & Cabins, 18234 West Hwy. 17, 81120. T: (719) 376-5857. RV/tent: 34. $16–$22. Hookups: electric (20, 30 amps), water.

Arboles

Arboles Campground, Navajo State Park, 1526 CR 982, Box 1697, 81121. T: (970) 883-2208. http://parks.state.co.us/navajo. RV/tent: 52. $18. Hookups: electric (30 amps).

Mancos State Park, 1526 CR 982, Box 1697, 81121. T: (970) 883-2208. http://parks.state.co.us/mancos. RV/tent: 25. $18. Hookups: none.

Piñon Park Campground, RV Resort & Lodging, P.O. Box 1729, 81121. T: (888) 926-1749 or (970) 883-3636. RV/tent: 55. $12–$20. Hookups: electric (20, 30, 50 amps), water, sewer.

Aurora

Cherry Creek State Park (Cherry Creek Campground), 4201 South Parker Rd., 80014. T: (303) 699-3860. http://parks.state.co.us/cherry_creek. RV/tent: 102. $18. Hookups: electric (30 amps).

Denver Meadows RV Park, 2075 Potomac St., 80011. T: (800) 364-9487 or (303) 364-9483. F: (303) 366-7289. RV/tent: 278. $25. Hookups: electric (20, 30, 50 amps), water, sewer.

Bayfield

Riverside RV Park, 41743 Hwy. 160, P.O. Box 919, 81122. T: (888) 884-2475 or (970) 884-2475. F: (970) 884-6163. RV/tent: 97. $12–$19. Hookups: electric (20, 30 amps), water, sewer.

COLORADO

Bayfield (continued)

Vallecito Resort, 13030 CR 501, 81122. T: (970) 884-9458 (Apr–Sept) or (480) 671-9848 (Oct–Apr). RV/tent: 213. $15–$33. Hookups: electric (20, 30, 50 amps), water, sewer.

Bellevue

Archer's Poudre River Resort, 33021 Poudre Canyon Hwy., 80512. T: (888) 822-0588 or (970) 881-2139. RV/tent: 9. $17–$25. Hookups: electric (20, 30, 50 amps), water, sewer.

Home Moraine Trailer Park, 37797 Poudre Canyon Hwy., 80512. T: (970) 881-2356. RV/tent: 32. $15. Hookups: electric (20, 30, 50 amps), water, sewer.

Mountain Park, Hwy. 14, 80512. T: (970) 881-2157. www.ReserveUSA.com/nrrs/co/mout. RV/tent: 55. $18. Hookups: electric (20, 30 amps).

Rustic Resort, Restaurant, Lounge, & Store, 31443 Poudre Canyon Hwy., 80512. T: (970) 881-2179. RV/tent: 18. $14–$16. Hookups: electric (20, 30 amps), water, sewer.

Sportsman's Lodge & Store, 44174 Poudre Canyon Hwy., 80512. T: (800) 270-2272 or (970) 881-2272. RV/tent: 14. $25. Hookups: electric (20, 30 amps), water, sewer.

Blanca

Blanca RV Park, 521 Main St., 81123. T: (719) 379-3201. RV/tent: 36. $15. Hookups: electric (20, 30, 50 amps), water, sewer.

Brighton

Barr Lake Campground, 17180 East 136th Ave., 80601. T: (800) 654-7988 or (303) 659-6180. RV/tent: 108. $19–$28. Hookups: electric (20, 30, 50 amps), water, sewer.

Buena Vista

Buena Vista KOA, 27700 CR 303, 81211. T: (800) 562-2672 or (719) 395-8318. F: (719) 395-2192. www.koa.com. RV/tent: 87. $18–$27. Hookups: electric (50 amps), water, sewer.

Crazy Horse Camping Resort, 33975 Hwy. 24 North, 81211. T: (800) 888-7320. www.crazyhorseresort.com. RV/tent: 85. $19–$28. Hookups: electric (20, 30 amps), water, sewer.

Mt. Princeton RV Park, 30380 CR 383, 81211. T: (719) 395-6206. RV/tent: 86. $20. Hookups: electric (30, 50 amps), water, sewer.

Snowy Peaks RV & Mobile Park, 30430 North Hwy. 24, 81211. T: (719) 395-8481. www.snowypeaksrvpark.com. RV/tent: 65. $18–$20. Hookups: electric (20, 30, 50 amps), water, sewer.

Canon City

Buffalo Bill's Royal Gorge Campground, 30 CR 3-A, 81212. T: (800) 787-0880 or (719) 269-3211. F: (719) 269-3211. www.camproyalgorge.com. RV/tent: 46. $20–$22. Hookups: electric (20, 30, 50 amps), water, sewer.

Conejos River Campground, 26714 Hwy. 17, 81120. T: (719) 376-5943. RV/tent: 56. $18. Hookups: electric (30, 50 amps), water, sewer.

Fort Gorge Campground & RV Park, 45044 Hwy. 50, 81212. T: (719) 275-5111. F: (719) 276-3069. RV/tent: 90. $15–$22. Hookups: electric (20, 30, 50 amps), water, sewer.

Indian Springs Ranch, P.O. Box 405, 81215. T: (719) 372-3907. www.coloradodirectory.com/indianspringsranch. RV/tent: 80. $15–$20. Hookups: electric (20, 30, 50 amps), water, sewer.

Royal Gorge/Canon City KOA, P.O. Box 528, 81215. T: (800) 562-5689. F: (719) 275-6116. www.koa.com. RV/tent: 153. $20–$27. Hookups: electric (20, 30, 50 amps), water, sewer.

Royal View Camp Resort, 43590 Hwy. 50 West, 81212. T: (866) 290-2461 or (719) 275-1900. F: (719) 275-0498. www.royalviewcampground.com. RV/tent: 53. $15–$35. Hookups: electric (20, 30, 50 amps), water, sewer.

Yogi Bear's Jellystone Park, 43595 Hwy. 50, 81212. T: (719) 275-2128. RV/tent: 81. $22–$31. Hookups: electric (20, 30 amps), water, sewer.

Cascade

Lone Duck Campground & Fishing Pond, P.O. Box 25, 80809. T: (800) 776-5925 or (719) 684-9907. RV/tent: 99. $19–$25. Hookups: electric (20, 30, 50 amps), water, sewer.

Cedaredge

Alexander Lake Lodge, P.O. Box 900, 81413. T: (970) 856-2539. F: (970) 856-2540. RV/tent: 17. $20. Hookups: electric (20, 30, 50 amps), water, sewer.

Mesa View RV Park, 195 Southwest 15th Cir., 81413. T: (970) 856-7689. F: (970) 856-7693. RV/tent: 10. $15. Hookups: electric (20, 30 amps), water, sewer.

Shady Creek, 205 North Grand Mesa Dr. (Hwy. 65), 81413. T: (970) 856-7522. F: (970) 856-7563. RV/tent: 16. $20. Hookups: electric (30, 50 amps), water, sewer.

Central City

Central City/Blackhawk KOA, 661 Hwy. 46, 80403. T: (800) 562-1620 or (303) 582-9979. F: (303) 582-3475. www.koa.com. RV/tent: 37. $16–$24. Hookups: electric (15, 20, 50 amps), water, sewer.

Cimarron

Black Canyon RV Park & Campground, P.O. Box 128, 81220. T: (970) 249-1147. RV/tent: 31. $15–$22. Hookups: electric (20, 30, 50 amps), water, sewer.

Clark

Pearl Lake State Park Lower Loop, P.O. Box 750, 80428. T: (970) 879-3922. http://parks.state.co.us/pearl. RV/tent: 15. $14. Hookups: none.

Pearl Lake State Park Upper Loop, P.O. Box 750, 80428. T: (970) 879-3922. http://parks.state.co.us/pearl. RV/tent: 21. $14. Hookups: none.

Coaldale

Hidden Valley Campground & Trail Rides, P.O. Box 220, 81222. T: (719) 942-4171. RV/tent: 63. $14–$19. Hookups: electric (20, 30, 50 amps), water, sewer.

Collbran

Wallace Guides & Outfitters, P.O. Box 380, 81624. T: (970) 487-3235. F: (970) 487-0118. RV/tent: 4. $10. Hookups: electric (20, 30 amps), water.

Colorado Springs

Conifer Ridge Campground, Mueller State Park, P.O. Box 39, 80814. T: (719) 687-2366. http://parks.state.co.us/mueller. RV/tent: 28. $18. Hookups: electric (30 amps).

Cross Creek Campground, Eleven Mile State Park, 4229 CR 92, 80827. T: (719) 748-3401. http://parks.state.co.us/eleven_mile. RV/tent: 13. $14. Hookups: none.

Fountain Creek RV Park, 3023 1/2 West Colorado Ave., 80904. T: (719) 633-2192. RV/tent: 114. $24–$28. Hookups: electric (20, 30, 50 amps), water, sewer.

Goldfield Campground, 411 South 26th, 80904. T: (719) 471-0495. RV/tent: 50. $20–$23. Hookups: electric (20, 30, 50 amps), water, sewer.

Grouse Mountain Campground, Mueller State Park, P.O. Box 39, 80814. T: (719) 687-2366. http://parks.state.co.us/mueller. RV/tent: 32. $18. Hookups: electric (30 amps).

Howbert Point Campground, Eleven Mile State Park, 4229 CR 92, 80827. T: (719) 748-3401. http://parks.state.co.us/eleven_mile. RV/tent: 10. $14. Hookups: none.

Lazy Boy Campground, Eleven Mile State Park, 4229 CR 92, 80827. T: (719) 748-3401. http://parks.state.co.us/eleven_mile. RV/tent: 14. $14. Hookups: none.

Mountaindale Campground & Cabins, 2000 Barrett Rd., 80926. T: (719) 576-0619. F: (719) 576-0619. RV/tent: 93. $15–$22. Hookups: electric (20, 30, 50 amps), water, sewer.

North Shore Campground, Eleven Mile State Park, 4229 CR 92, 80827. T: (719) 748-3401. http://parks.state.co.us/eleven_mile. RV/tent: 89. $14. Hookups: none.

Northwoods Village RV Park, 3100 Wood Ave., 80907. T: (719) 633-7564. RV/tent: 143. $20. Hookups: electric (50 amps), water, sewer.

COLORADO (continued)

Peak View Campground, Mueller State Park, P.O. Box 39, 80814. T: (719) 687-2366. http://parks.state.co.us/mueller. RV/tent: 5. $18. Hookups: electric (30 amps).

Peak View Inn & RV Park, 4950 North Nevada Ave., 80918. T: (800) 551-CAMP or (719) 598-1434. RV/tent: 120. $20–$25. Hookups: electric (20, 30 amps), water, sewer.

Revenuers Ridge Campground, Mueller State Park, P.O. Box 39, 80814. T: (719) 687-2366. http://parks.state.co.us/mueller. RV/tent: 34. $18. Hookups: electric (30 amps).

Rocking Chair Campground, Eleven Mile State Park, 4229 CR 92, 80827. T: (719) 748-3401. http://parks.state.co.us/eleven_mile. RV/tent: 13. $14. Hookups: none.

Rocky Ridge Campground, Eleven Mile State Park, 4229 CR 92, 80827. T: (719) 748-3401. http://parks.state.co.us/eleven_mile. RV/tent: 140. $14. Hookups: electric (30 amps).

Witcher Cove Campground, Eleven Mile State Park, 4229 CR 92, 80827. T: (719) 748-3401. http://parks.state.co.us/eleven_mile. RV/tent: 26. $14. Hookups: none.

Wrangler RV Ranch & Motel, 6225 East Platte Ave. (Hwy. 24), 80915. T: (719) 591-1402. RV/tent: 110. $26–$28. Hookups: electric (20, 30, 50 amps), water, sewer.

Cortez

La Mesa Campground, 2430 East Main St., 81321. T: (970) 565-3610. RV/tent: 45. $19. Hookups: electric (20, 30 amps), water, sewer.

Lazy G Campground, P.O. Box 1048, 81321. T: (800) 628-2183 or (970) 565-8577. F: (970) 565-0123. RV/tent: 79. $14–$20. Hookups: electric (20, 30, 50 amps), water, sewer.

Sundance RV Park, 815 East Main, 81321. T: (800) 880-9413 or (970) 565-0997. RV/tent: 68. $24. Hookups: electric (20, 30, 50 amps), water, sewer.

Creede

Antlers Rio Grande Resort, 26222 Hwy. 149, 81130. T: (719) 658-2423. F: (719) 658-0804. RV/tent: 24. $23. Hookups: electric (30, 50 amps), water, sewer.

Broken Arrow Ranch, HC 70, 32728 Hwy. 149, 81130. T: (719) 658-2484. RV/tent: 10. $15. Hookups: electric (20, 30, 50 amps), water, sewer.

Cripple Creek

Cripple Creek Gold Campground & Horse Company, P.O. Box 601, 80813. T: (719) 689-2342 or (719) 689-0131. RV/tent: 25. $12–$14. Hookups: electric (20, 30 amps).

Cripple Creek Hospitality House & Travel Park, P.O. Box 957, 80813. T: (800) 500-2513 or (719) 689-2513. RV/tent: 88. $16–$19. Hookups: electric (20, 30, 50 amps), water, sewer.

Cripple Creek KOA, P.O. Box 699, 80813. T: (800) 562-9125 or (719) 689-3376. www.koa.com. RV/tent: 82. $20–$25. Hookups: electric (20, 30, 50 amps), water, sewer.

Prospectors RV Park, P.O. Box 1237, 80813. T: (719) 689-2006. RV/tent: 27. $5–$20. Hookups: electric (20, 30 amps), water, sewer.

Del Norte

Woods & River Campground, P.O. Box 64, 81132. T: (877) 354-6922 or (719) 657-4530 or (719) 657-4530. RV/tent: 46. $12–$19. Hookups: electric (20, 30 amps), water, sewer.

Delta

Four Seasons River Inn & RV Park, 676 Hwy. 50 North, 81416. T: (888) 340-4689 or (970) 874-9659. RV/tent: 30. $18–$21. Hookups: electric (30, 50 amps), water, sewer.

Over-The-Hill RV Ranch, 1675 Hwy. 92, 81416. T: (970) 874-0200. RV/tent: 51. $18–$21. Hookups: electric (20, 30, 50 amps), water, sewer.

Riverwood Inn and RV Park, 677 Hwy. 50 North, 81416. T: (888) 213-2124 or (970) 874-5787. F: (970) 874-4872. www.riverwoodn.com/rvpark.htm. RV/tent: 39. $11–$22. Hookups: electric (30, 50 amps), water, sewer.

Divide

Alpine Lakes Resort, 4145 Omer Rd., P.O. Box 669, 80814. T: (719) 687-7337. RV/tent: 85. $18–$24. Hookups: electric (20, 30, 50 amps), water.

Dolores

Dolores River RV Park & Cabins, 18680 Hwy. 145, 81323. T: (800) 200-2399 or (970) 882-7761. F: (970) 882-4829. RV/tent: 91. $14–$25. Hookups: electric (20, 30, 50 amps), water, sewer.

Groundhog Lake Fishing Camp & Outfitters, P.O. Box 27, 81323. T: (970) 882-4379. RV/tent: 10. $7–$13. Hookups: electric (20, 30 amps).

Outpost Motel, Cabins, & RV Park, 1800 Central Ave., 81323. T: (800) 382-4892 or (970) 882-7271. RV/tent: 16. $25. Hookups: electric (20, 30 amps), water, sewer.

Priest Gulch Campground & RV Park, 27646 Hwy. 145, 81323. T: (970) 562-3810. www.priestgulch.com. RV/tent: 93. $18–$23. Hookups: electric (20, 30, 50 amps), water, sewer.

Stoner Creek Cafe, Store, Cabins, & RV Park, 25113 Hwy. 145, 81323. T: (970) 882-2204. F: (970) 882-2204. RV/tent: 35. $13–$20. Hookups: electric (20, 30, 50 amps), water, sewer.

Durango

Alpen Rose RV Park, 27847 Hwy. 550 North, 81301. T: (877) 259-5791 or (970) 247-5540. RV/tent: 100. $29. Hookups: electric (30, 50 amps), water, sewer.

Bueno Tiempo Ranch, 27846 Hwy. 550, 81301. T: (877) 247-9796 or (970) 247-9796. RV/tent: 118. $12–$25. Hookups: electric (20, 30 amps), water.

Cottonwood Camper Park, 21636 US 160, P.O. Box 1456, 81302. T: (970) 247-1977. RV/tent: 75. $17–$22. Hookups: electric (20, 30, 50 amps), water, sewer.

Durango North KOA, 13391 CR 250, 81301. T: (800) 562-2792 or (970) 247-4499. F: (970) 259-9545. www.koa.com. RV/tent: 131. $19–$29. Hookups: electric (20, 30 amps), water, sewer.

Five Branches Camper Park & Cabins, 4677 CR 501-A, 81122. T: (800) 582-9580 or (970) 884-2582. F: (970) 884-9765. RV/tent: 108. $13–$17. Hookups: electric (20, 30 amps), water, sewer.

Golden Terrace South, 17801 West Colfax, 80401. T: (303) 279-6279. RV/tent: 167. $25. Hookups: electric (30, 50 amps), water, sewer.

Hermosa Meadows Camper Park & Camper Cabins, 31420 Hwy. 550, 81301. T: (800) 748-2853 or (970) 247-3055. RV/tent: 150. $21–$30. Hookups: electric (20, 30, 50 amps), water, sewer.

Lightner Creek Campground, 1567 CR 207, 81301. T: (970) 247-5406. RV/tent: 97. $22–$27. Hookups: electric (20, 30 amps), water, sewer.

United Campground of Durango, 1322 Animas View Dr., 81301. T: (970) 247-3853. RV/tent: 193. $19–$31. Hookups: electric (20, 30, 50 amps), water, sewer.

Empire

Conestoga Wagon Stop RV Campground & Cabin Lodging, 7364 US 40, P.O. Box 334, 80438. T: (888) 428-9604 or (303) 569-3066. F: (303) 569-0251. RV/tent: 20. $13–$19. Hookups: electric (20, 30, 50 amps), water, sewer.

Mountain Meadow Campground, P.O. Box 2, 80438. T: (877) 931-2500 or (303) 569-2424. F: (303) 569-2424. RV/tent: 45. $16–$26. Hookups: electric (20, 30 amps), water, sewer.

Englewood

Flying Saucer RV Park, 2500 West Hampden, 80110. T: (303) 789-1707. RV/tent: 150. $24. Hookups: electric (20, 30, 50 amps), water, sewer.

COLORADO (continued)

Estes Park

Blue Arrow, 1665 Hwy. 66, 80517. T: (800) 582-5342 or (970) 586-5342. www.estes-park.com. RV/tent: 175. $20–$31. Hookups: electric (30, 50 amps), water, sewer.

Estes Park Campground, P.O. Box 3517, 80517. T: (888) 815-2029 or (970) 586-4188. www.estes-park.com/epcampground. RV/tent: 68. $21–$24. Hookups: electric (20, 30 amps), water.

Manor RV Park & Motel, 815 Riverside Dr., 80517. T: (800) 344-3256 or (970) 586-3251. RV/tent: 110. $28–$31. Hookups: electric (20, 30 amps), water, sewer.

Mary's Lake Campground & RV Park, P.O. Box 2514, 80517. T: (800) 445-6279 or (970) 586-4411. RV/tent: 150. $20–$26. Hookups: electric (20, 30, 50 amps), water, sewer.

National Park Resort Campground & Cabins, 3501 Fall River Rd., 80517. T: (970) 586-4563. RV/tent: 96. $25–$27. Hookups: electric (20, 30 amps), water, sewer.

Paradise RV Park & Motel, 815 East Riverside Dr., 80517. T: (800) 344-3256 or (970) 586-3251. www.campestespark.com. RV/tent: 110. $27. Hookups: electric (30 amps), water, sewer.

Spruce Lake RV Park, 1050 Mary's Lake Rd., 80517. T: (970) 586-2889. www.estes-park.com/sprucelake. RV/tent: 110. $22–$32. Hookups: electric (30 amps), water, sewer.

Yogi Bear's Jellystone Park of Estes, 5495 US 36, 80517. T: (800) 722-2928. www.jellystone-ofestes.com. RV/tent: 99. $25–$35. Hookups: electric (20, 30, 50 amps), water, sewer.

Falcon

Falcon Meadow Campground, 11150 Hwy. 24, 80831. T: (719) 495-2694. www.campcolorado.com. RV/tent: 30. $12–$17. Hookups: electric (20, 30 amps), water, sewer.

Fort Collins

Blue Spruce Mobile Home & RV Park, 2730 North Shields, 80524. T: (970) 221-3723. RV/tent: 14. $15. Hookups: electric (20, 30, 50 amps), water, sewer.

Heron Lake RV Park, P.O. Box 1100, 80522. T: (877) 254-4063. RV/tent: 190. $26–$28. Hookups: electric (20, 30, 50 amps), water, sewer.

Fort Garland

Ute Creek Campground, P.O. Box 188, 81133. T: (719) 379-3238. F: (719) 379-3238. RV/tent: 32. $10–$15. Hookups: electric (20, 30 amps), water, sewer.

Ft. Collins KOA, Box 600, 6670 North Hwy. 287, 80535. T: (800) 562-2648. F: (970) 493-9758. www.koa.com. RV/tent: 59. $19–$25. Hookups: electric (20, 30, 50 amps), water, sewer.

Glenwood Springs

Rock Gardens Campground, Rafting, & Jeep Tours, 1308 CR 129, 81601. T: (800) 958-6737 or (970) 945-6737. F: (970) 945-2413. RV/tent: 77. $21–$25. Hookups: electric (20, 30, 50 amps), water, sewer.

Golden

Dakota Ridge RV Park, 17700 West Colfax Ave., 80401. T: (800) 398-1625 or (303) 279-1625. RV/tent: 141. $32. Hookups: electric (20, 30, 50 amps), water, sewer.

Reverends Ridge Campground, Golden Gate Canyon, 3873 Hwy. 46, 80403. T: (303) 582-3707. http://parks.state.co.us/golden_gate. RV/tent: 62. $18. Hookups: electric (30 amps).

Granby

Arapaho Bay, c/o USFS P.O. Box 10, 80446. T: (970) 887-4100. www.ReserveUSA.com/nrrs/co/arap. RV/tent: 84. $12. Hookups: none.

Grand Junction

Aspen Grove Campground, Vega State Park Box 186, 81624. T: (970) 487-3407. http://parks.state.co.us/vega. RV/tent: 29. $14. Hookups: none.

Big J RV Park, 2819 Hwy. 50, 81503. T: (877) 240-2527. F: (970) 263-0566. RV/tent: 90. $21. Hookups: electric (20, 30, 50 amps), water, sewer.

Bookcliff Campground, Highline Lake State Park, 1800 11.8 Rd., 81524. T: (970) 858-7208. http://parks.state.co.us/highline. RV/tent: 28. $14. Hookups: none.

Early Settlers Campground, Vega State Park Box 186, 81624. T: (970) 487-3407. http://parks.state.co.us/vega. RV/tent: 34. $18. Hookups: electric (30 amps).

Island Acres Campground, Colorado River State Park, P.O. Box 700, 81520. T: (970) 434-3388. http://parks.state.co.us/Colorado_River. RV/tent: 74. $18. Hookups: electric (30 amps).

Junction West RV Park, 793-22 Rd., 81505. T: (970) 245-8531. RV/tent: 66. $21. Hookups: electric (20, 30, 50 amps), water, sewer.

Mobile City RV Home Park, 2322 Hwys. 6 and 50, 81505. T: (970) 242-9291. RV/tent: 90. $22. Hookups: electric (30 amps), water, sewer.

Oak Point Campground, Vega State Park Box 186, 81624. T: (970) 487-3407. http://parks.state.co.us/vega. RV/tent: 38. $14. Hookups: none.

Grand Lake

Winding River Resort Village & Snowmobiling, P.O. Box 629, 80447. T: (800) 282-5121 or (970) 627-3215 or (303) 623-1121. F: (970) 627-5003. RV/tent: 186. $20–$25. Hookups: electric (20, 30 amps), water, sewer.

Green Mountain Falls

Rocky Top Motel and Campground, P.O. Box 215, 80819. T: (719) 684-9044. RV/tent: 78. $11–$18. Hookups: electric (20, 30 amps), water, sewer.

Gunnison

Gunnison Lakeside Resort, 28357 Hwy. 50 West, 81230. T: (877) 641-0488 or (970) 641-0477. RV/tent: 43. $12–$25. Hookups: electric (20, 30, 50 amps), water, sewer.

Mesa Campground, 36128 West Hwy. 50, 81230. T: (970) 641-3186. www.coloradodirectory.com/mesacamp. RV/tent: 150. $17–$26. Hookups: electric (30, 50 amps), water, sewer.

Rockey River Resort, 4359 CR 10, 81230. T: (970) 641-0174. RV/tent: 26. $20. Hookups: electric (20, 30 amps), water, sewer.

Shady Island Resort, Cabins, & RV Park, 2776 Hwy. 135 North, 81230. T: (970) 641-0416. RV/tent: 40. $20. Hookups: electric (20, 30 amps), water, sewer.

Tall Texan Campground, 194 CR 11, 81230. T: (970) 641 2927. F: (970) 641 2927. RV/tent: 118. Hookups: electric (20, 30, 50 amps), water, sewer.

Hayden

Juniper Springs Campground, Yampa River State Park, P.O. Box 759, 81639. T: (970) 276-2061. http://parks.state.co.us/Yampa. RV/tent: 6. $14. Hookups: none.

Maybell Bridge Campground, Yampa River State Park, P.O. Box 759, 81639. T: (970) 276-2061. http://parks.state.co.us/Yampa. RV/tent: 5. $14. Hookups: none.

The Elks Campground, Yampa River State Park, P.O. Box 759, 81639. T: (970) 276-2061.http://parks.state.co.us/Yampa. RV/tent: 15. $14. Hookups: none.

Yampa River State Park Headquarters, P.O. Box 759, 81639. T: (970) 276-2061. http://parks.state.co.us/Yampa. RV/tent: 35. $18. Hookups: electric (30 amps).

Hooper

UFO Watchtower & Campground, P.O. Box 583, 81136. T: (719) 378-2271. www.ufowatchtower.com. RV/tent: 24. $10. Hookups: electric (20, 30 amps), water, sewer.

Hotchkiss

Clear Fork Campground, CrawfoRd. State Park, P.O. Box 147, 81415. T: (970) 921-5721. http://parks.state.co.us/crawford. RV/tent: 16. Hookups: none.

Iron Creek Campground, CrawfoRd. State Park, P.O. Box 147, 81415. T: (970) 921-5721. http://parks.state.co.us/crawford. RV/tent: 16. $18. Hookups: electric (30 amps).

COLORADO (continued)

Howard

Pleasant Valley RV Park of Howard, 0018 CR 47, 81233. T: (719) 942-3484. RV/tent: 61. $12–$21. Hookups: electric (20, 30, 50 amps), water, sewer.

Idaho Springs

Cottonwood RV Park, 1485 Hwy. 103, 80452. T: (303) 567-2617. RV/tent: 20. $18–$25. Hookups: electric (20, 30, 50 amps), water, sewer.

Indian Springs Resort & Campground, P.O. Box 1990, 80452. T: (303) 989-6666. RV/tent: 32. $18. Hookups: electric (20, 30 amps), water.

Kremmling

Red Mountain RV Park, P.O. Box 1267, 80459. T: (970) 724-9593. RV/tent: 65. $12–$19. Hookups: electric (20, 30, 50 amps), water, sewer.

La Jara

Aspen Glade, Conejos Peak Rd., 15571 CR T-5, 81140. www.ReserveUSA.com/nrrs/co/asgl. RV/tent: 34. $14. Hookups: none.

La Veta

Elk Valley RV Park & Fly Shop, 5535 Hwy. 12, 81055. T: (866) 733-5533. RV/tent: 12. $22. Hookups: electric (20, 30, 50 amps), water, sewer.

Rustic Shack Cabins & RV Park, 404 South Oak, P.O. Box 397, 81055. T: (877) 460-6221 or (719) 742-6221. RV/tent: 14. $15–$20. Hookups: electric (20, 30 amps), water, sewer.

Lake City

Castle Lakes Campground Resort & Cabins, CR 30, P.O. Box 909, 81235. T: (800) 862-6166 or (970) 944-2622. RV/tent: 51. $17–$22. Hookups: electric (20, 30, 50 amps), water, sewer.

Highlander RV Campground, Jeep Rentals, & Gifts, P.O. Box 880, 81235. T: (888) 580-4636 or (970) 944-2878. RV/tent: 28. $20–$25. Hookups: electric (20, 30, 50 amps), water, sewer.

Woodlake Park Campground & Cabins, P.O. Box 400, 81235. T: (800) 201-2694 or (970) 944-2283 (June–Sept) or (817) 536-4079 (Oct–May). RV/tent: 25. $19. Hookups: electric (20, 30 amps), water, sewer.

Lake George

Lake George Cabins & RV Park, 8966 CR 90, 80827. T: (719) 748-3822. F: (719) 748-3822. RV/tent: 13. $15–$20. Hookups: electric (20, 30 amps), water, sewer.

Lamar

Lamar Country Acre's, 29151 US 28, 81052. T: (719) 336-1031. RV/tent: 8. $16–$18. Hookups: electric (20, 30, 50 amps), water, sewer.

Leadville

Baby Doe, Tourquoise Lake, 80461. www.ReserveUSA.com/nrrs/co/baby. RV/tent: 50. $15. Hookups: none.

Sugar Loafin' RV Park and Campground, 303 Hwy. 300, 80461. F: (719) 486-0919. www. sugarloafin@leadville.com. RV/tent: 98. $22–$26. Hookups: electric (20, 30, 50 amps), water, sewer.

Littleton

Chatfield State Park, 11500 North Roxborough Park Rd., 80125. T: (303) 791-7275. www.parks.state.co.us/Chatfield/camping.asp #Individual. RV/tent: 153. $18. Hookups: electric (30 amps).

Longmont

Westwood Inn Motel & Campground, 1550 North Main, 80501. T: (303) 776-2185. RV/tent: 20. $20. Hookups: electric (20, 30, 50 amps), water, sewer.

Loveland

Boyd Lake State Park, 3720 North CR 11-C, 80538. T: (970) 669-1739. www.parks.state.co.us/Boyd/camping.asp. RV/tent: 148. $18. Hookups: electric (30 amps).

Fireside RV Park & Cabins, 6850 West Hwy. 34, 80537. T: (970) 667-2903. RV/tent: 36. $18–$22. Hookups: electric (20, 30, 50 amps), water, sewer.

Loveland RV Village, 4421 East Hwy. 34, 80537. T: (970) 667-1204. RV/tent: 190. $20–$24. Hookups: electric (30, 50 amps), water, sewer.

Riverview RV Park & Campground, 7806 West Hwy. 34, 80537. T: (800) 447-9910 or (970) 667-9910. F: (970) 613-2023. RV/tent: 160. $20–$27. Hookups: electric (20, 30, 50 amps), water, sewer.

Lyons

Stone Mountain Lodge & Cabins, 18055 North St. Vrain Dr., 80540. T: (800) 282-5612 or (303) 823-6091. www.stonemountain lodge.com. RV/tent: 16. $15–$20. Hookups: electric (20, 30 amps).

Mancos

A & A Mesa Verde RV Park, 34979 Hwy. 160, 81328. T: (800) 972-6620. F: (970) 565-7141. RV/tent: 70. $20–$25. Hookups: electric (30, 50 amps), water, sewer.

Echo Basin Guest Ranch Resort & RV Park, 43747 Rd. M, 81328. T: (800) 426-1890 or (970) 533-7000. RV/tent: 100. $17–$25. Hookups: electric (20, 30, 50 amps), water, sewer.

Morefield Campground in Mesa Verde, P.O. Box 277, 81328. T: (800) 449-2288. F: (970) 533-7831. www.visitmesaverde.com. RV/tent: 440. $16–$23. Hookups: electric (20, 30 amps), water, sewer.

Marble

Meri Daes RV Park, 220 West Park, 81623. T: June–Sept (970) 963-1831 or Oct–May (303) 756-0566. RV/tent: 15. $18. Hookups: electric (20, 30 amps), water.

Meeker

Buford Hunting & Fishing Lodge, Store, Chuckwagon, & Horse Boarding, 20474 CR 8, 81641. T: (970) 878-4745. RV/tent: 8. $20. Hookups: electric (20, 30 amps), water.

North Fork Campground and Group Site, CR 8, 81641. T: (970) 878-4039. www.Reserve USA.com/nrrs/co/nor2. RV/tent: 40. $12. Hookups: none.

Ute Lodge, Horses, Fishing, and Pack Trips, 393 CR 75, 81641. T: (888) 414-2022 or (970) 878-4669. RV/tent: 12. $15–$25. Hookups: electric (20, 30, 50 amps), water, sewer.

Mesa

Sundance RV Camp & Cabins, 11674 Hwy. 65, 81643. T: (970) 268-5651. RV/tent: 37. $15–$25. Hookups: electric (20, 30, 50 amps), water, sewer.

Montrose

Cedar Creek RV Park & Mini Golf, 126 Rose Ln., 81401. T: (877) 426-3884 or (970) 249-3884. F: (970) 856-6386. RV/tent: 55. $19–$22. Hookups: electric (20, 30, 50 amps), water, sewer.

Hangin Tree RV Park, Campground, Convenience Store, & Gas, 17250 Hwy. 550 South, 81401. T: (888) 657-4131. F: (970) 249-1865. RV/tent: 31. $16–$22. Hookups: electric (20, 30, 50 amps), water, sewer.

King's River Bend RV Park, 65100 Old Chipeta Tr., 81401. T: (970) 249-8235. RV/tent: 70. $15–$19. Hookups: electric (20, 30, 50 amps), water, sewer.

Monument

Lake of the Rockies Retreat, Camping, & Cabin Resort, 99 Mitchell Ave., 80132. T: (800) 429-4228 or (719) 481-4227. F: (719) 481-0039. RV/tent: 235. $18–$30. Hookups: electric (20, 30, 50 amps), water, sewer.

Mosca

Great Sand Dunes Oasis, 5400 Hwy. 150 North, 81146. T: (719) 378-2222. F: (719) 378-2901. RV/tent: 90. $12–$19. Hookups: electric (20, 30, 50 amps), water, sewer.

Nathrop

Brown's Family Campground, Box 39, 11430 CR 197, 81236. T: (800) 643-9727 or (719) 395-8301. F: (719) 395-8337. RV/tent: 75. $16–$25. Hookups: electric (20, 30 amps), water, sewer.

COLORADO (continued)

New Castle

New Castle/Glenwood Springs KOA, 0581 CR 241, 81647. T: (800) 562-3240 or (970) 984-2240. F: (970) 984-0349. www.koa.com. RV/tent: 57. $16–$24. Hookups: electric (20, 30, 50 amps), water, sewer.

Ohio City

Rowe's RV Park, Gun Shop, & 1886 Gen'l Store, P.O. Box 61, 81237. T: (970) 641-4272. RV/tent: 8. $13. Hookups: electric (20, 30, 50 amps), water, sewer.

Orchard

Dunes Campground, Jackson Lake State Park, 26363 CR 3, 80649. T: (970) 645-2551. http://parks.state.co.us/jackson. RV/tent: 18. $14. Hookups: none.

Foxhills Campground, Jackson Lake State Park, 26363 CR 3, 80649. T: (970) 645-2551. http://parks.state.co.us/jackson. RV/tent: 89. $14. Hookups: none.

Lakeside Campground, Jackson Lake State Park, 26363 CR 3, 80649. T: (970) 645-2551. http://parks.state.co.us/jackson. RV/tent: 58. $14. Hookups: none.

Northview Campground, Jackson Lake State Park, 26363 CR 3, 80649. T: (970) 645-2551. http://parks.state.co.us/jackson. RV/tent: 10. $18. Hookups: electric (30 amps).

Pelican Campground, Jackson Lake State Park, 26363 CR 3, 80649. T: (970) 645-2551. http://parks.state.co.us/jackson. RV/tent: 33. $14. Hookups: none.

Sandpiper Campground, Jackson Lake State Park, 26363 CR 3, 80649. T: (970) 645-2551. http://parks.state.co.us/jackson. RV/tent: 28. $18. Hookups: electric (30 amps).

Ouray

Ouray KOA, P.O. Box J, 81427. T: (800) 562-8026 or (970) 325-4736. F: (970) 325-0461. www.koa.com. RV/tent: 123. $19–$26. Hookups: electric (20, 30 amps), water, sewer.

Pagosa Springs

160 West Adult RV Park, P.O. Box 28, 81147. T: (970) 264-5873. F: (970) 264-7225. RV/tent: 28. $22. Hookups: electric (20, 30, 50 amps), water, sewer.

Acres Green RV Park, 10 Leisure Ct., 81147. T: (888) 724-6727 or (970) 264-9264. F: (970) 264-9265. RV/tent: 20. $18. Hookups: electric (30, 50 amps), water, sewer.

Blanco River RV Park, 97 Leisure Ct., 81147. T: (800) 280-9429 or (970) 264-5547. RV/tent: 64. $14–$20. Hookups: electric (20, 30, 50 amps), water, sewer.

Elk Meadows Campground, P.O. Box 238, 81147. T: (970) 264-5482. RV/tent: 35. $15–$18. Hookups: electric (20, 30, 50 amps), water, sewer.

Happy Camper RV Park & Cabin, 9260 West Hwy. 160, 81147. T: (970) 731-5822. F: (970) 731-5620. RV/tent: 90. $12–$18. Hookups: electric (20, 30 amps), water, sewer.

Hide-A-Way RV Park & Campground, P.O. Box 1931, 81147. T: (970) 731-5112. RV/tent: 40. $10–$15. Hookups: electric (20, 30, 50 amps), water, sewer.

Pagosa Riverside Campground & Camper Cabins, P.O. Box 268, 81147. T: (888) 785-3234 or (970) 264-5874. F: (970) 264-5874. RV/tent: 87. $16–$26. Hookups: electric (20, 30 amps), water, sewer.

Sportsman's Supply, Campground, & Cabins, 2095 Taylor Ln., 81147. T: (970) 731-2300. RV/tent: 40. $16–$25. Hookups: electric (20, 30 amps), water, sewer.

The Spa @ Pagosa Springs, Destination Spa & RV Resort, 317 Hot Springs Blvd., P.O. Box 37, 81147. T: (800) 832-5523 or (970) 264-5910. RV/tent: 8. $23. Hookups: electric (20, 30, 50 amps), water, sewer.

Paonia

Redwood Arms Motel & RV Park, 1478 Hwy. 133, P.O. Box 1390, 81428. T: (970) 527-4148. F: (970) 527-4181. RV/tent: 20. $20. Hookups: electric (20, 30, 50 amps), water, sewer.

Parlin

7-11 Ranch, 5291 CR 76, 81239. T: (970) 641-0666. RV/tent: 11. $10. Hookups: electric (20, 30 amps), water, sewer.

Penrose

Floyd's RV Park, 1438 Hwy. 50, 81240. T: (719) 372-3385. F: (719) 372-3385. RV/tent: 47. $12–$20. Hookups: electric (20, 30 amps), water, sewer.

Piru

Green Ridge, P.O. Box 249, 93040. T: (970) 887-4100. www.ReserveUSA.com/nrrs/co/grer. RV/tent: 78. $5. Hookups: none.

Pueblo

Arkansas Point Campground, Lake Pueblo State Park, 640 Pueblo Reservoir Rd., 81005. T: (719) 561-9320. http://parks.state.co.us/pueblo. RV/tent: 95. $18. Hookups: electric (30 amps).

Fort's RV Park, 3015 Lake Ave., 81004. T: (719) 564-2327. RV/tent: 55. $21–$25. Hookups: electric (20, 30, 50 amps), water, sewer.

Fowler RV Park, P.O. Box 306, 81039. T: (719) 263-4287. RV/tent: 41. $10–$20. Hookups: electric (20, 30 amps), water, sewer.

Haggard's RV Campground, 7910 West Hwy. 50, 81007. T: (719) 547-2101. RV/tent: 180. $20–$23. Hookups: electric (20, 30 amps), water, sewer.

Juniper Breaks Campground, Lake Pueblo State Park, 640 Pueblo Reservoir Rd., 81005. T: (719) 561-9320. http://parks.state.co.us/pueblo. RV/tent: 84. $14. Hookups: none.

Kettle Creek Campground, Lake Pueblo State Park, 640 Pueblo Reservoir Rd., 81005. T: (719) 561-9320. http://parks.state.co.us/pueblo. RV/tent: 27. $14. Hookups: none.

Prairie Ridge Campground, Lake Pueblo State Park, 640 Pueblo Reservoir Rd., 81005. T: (719) 561-9320. http://parks.state.co.us/pueblo. RV/tent: 82. $18. Hookups: electric (30 amps).

Pueblo South/Colorado City KOA, 9040 I-25 South, 81004. T: (800) 562-8646 or (719) 676-3376. www.koa.com. RV/tent: 109. $18–$32. Hookups: electric (30, 50 amps), water, sewer.

Pueblo West Campground, Cabins, & Arena, 480 East McCulloch Blvd., 81007. T: (877) 547-7070 or (719) 547-9887. RV/tent: 63. $17–$20. Hookups: electric (20, 30, 50 amps), water, sewer.

Yucca Flats Campground, Lake Pueblo State Park, 640 Pueblo Reservoir Rd., 81005. T: (719) 561-9320. http://parks.state.co.us/pueblo. RV/tent: 86. $18. Hookups: electric (30 amps).

Red Feather Lakes

Alpine Lodge, P.O. Box 180, 80545. T: (970) 881-2933. RV/tent: 10. $5–$15. Hookups: electric (20, 30 amps), water, sewer.

Rifle

Elk Run Campground, Sylvan Lake State Park, 0050 CR 219, 81650. T: (970) 625-1607. http://parks.state.co.us/sylvan. RV/tent: 33. $14. Hookups: none.

Fishermans Paradise Campground, Sylvan Lake State Park, 0050 CR 219, 81650. T: (970) 625-1607. http://parks.state.co.us/sylvan. RV/tent: 11. $14. Hookups: none.

Rye

Lodge at San Isabel, RV Park & General Store, 59 CR 371, 81069. T: (719) 489-2280 (lodge) or (719) 489-2601 (store). RV/tent: 15. $15. Hookups: electric (20, 30 amps), water, sewer.

Salida

Five Points Campground, Arkansas Headwaters Recreation Area, 307 West Sackett, 81201. T: (719) 539-7289. www.parks.state.co.us/arkansas/camping.asp. RV/tent: 16. $14. Hookups: none.

Heart of the Rockies Campground, 16105 Hwy. 50, 81201. T: (800) 496-2245 or (719) 539-4051. RV/tent: 65. $14–$20. Hookups: electric (20, 30 amps), water, sewer.

Helca Junction Campground, Arkansas Headwaters Recreation Area, 307 West Sackett, 81201. T: (719) 539-7289. www.parks.state.co.us/arkansas/camping.asp. RV/tent: 11. $14. Hookups: none.

COLORADO (continued)

Monarch Spur RV Park and Campground, 18989 West Hwy. 50, 81201. T: (888) 814-3001. www.monarchspurrvpark.com. RV/tent: 49. $17–$25. Hookups: electric (50 amps), water, sewer.

Railroad Bridge Campground, Arkansas Headwaters Recreation Area, 307 West Sackett, 81201. T: (719) 539-7289. www.parks.state.co.us/arkansas/camping.asp. RV/tent: 7. $14. Hookups: none.

Rincon Campground, Arkansas Headwaters Recreation Area, 307 West Sackett, 81201. T: (719) 539-7289. www.parks.state.co.us/arkansas/camping.asp. RV/tent: 4. $14. Hookups: none.

Ruby Mountain Campground, Arkansas Headwaters Recreation Area, 307 West Sackett, 81201. T: (719) 539-7289. www.parks.state.co.us/arkansas/camping.asp. RV/tent: 12. $14. Hookups: none.

Silt

Viking RV Park & Campground, 32958 River Frontage Rd., 81652. T: (970) 876-2443. F: (970) 963-2139. RV/tent: 77. $15–$25. Hookups: electric (20, 30, 50 amps), water, sewer.

Silverton

Molas Lake Camping, Camper Cabins, Stables, Snowmobile Tours, P.O. Box 776, 81433. T: (800) 846-2177 or (970) 387-5848. RV/tent: 78. $14. Hookups: electric (20, 30 amps), water, sewer.

Red Mountain Motel, Cabins, RV Park, Jeep & Snowmobile Rental, P.O. Box 346, 81433. T: (888) 970-5512 or (970) 387-5512. RV/tent: 20. $15–$22. Hookups: electric (20, 30, 50 amps), water, sewer.

Silverton Lakes Campground, P.O. Box 126, 81433. T: (888) 551-CAMP or (970) 387-5721. RV/tent: 75. $14–$17. Hookups: electric (20, 30, 50 amps), water, sewer.

Somerset

Crystal Meadows Resort, 30682 CR 12, 81434. T: (970) 929-5656. F: (970) 929-5957. RV/tent: 45. $27–$30. Hookups: electric (20, 30, 50 amps), water, sewer.

South Fork

AspenRidge Cabins & RV Park, 0710 West Hwy. 149, 81154. T: (719) 873-5921. F: (719) 813-1148. RV/tent: 40. $17. Hookups: electric (20, 30, 50 amps), water, sewer.

Blue Creek Lodge, Cabins, RV Park, & Campground, 11682 Hwy. 149, 81154. T: (800) 326-6408 or (719) 658-2479. F: (719) 658-2915. RV/tent: 33. $20. Hookups: electric (20, 30, 50 amps), water, sewer.

Budget Host—Ute Bluff Lodge, Cabins, Motel, & RV Park, 27680 West Hwy. 160, 81154. T: (800) 473-0595. RV/tent: 42. $17–$19. Hookups: electric (20, 30, 50 amps), water, sewer.

Chinook Lodge, Cabins, Smokehouse, RV Park, & Trail Rides, Box 1214, 81154. T: (888) 890-9110 or (719) 873-9993. F: (719) 873-1706. RV/tent: 26. $12–$18. Hookups: electric (20, 30, 50 amps), water, sewer.

Cottonwood Cove Lodge, Cabins, Restaurant, Jeeps, & Rafts, 13046 Hwy. 149, 81154. T: (719) 658-2242. F: (719) 658-0802. RV/tent: 25. $20. Hookups: electric (20, 30 amps), water, sewer.

Goodnight's Lonesome Dove Cabins & RVs, P.O. Box 157, 81154. T: (800) 551-3683 or (719) 873-1072. F: (719) 873-1170. RV/tent: 42. $15–$18. Hookups: electric (20, 30 amps), water, sewer.

Moon Valley Ranch Resort Campground & Guided Fishing & Hunting, P.O. Box 265, 81154. T: (719) 873-5216. RV/tent: 61. $15. Hookups: electric (20, 30 amps), water, sewer.

Rainbow Lodge, Cabins, & RV Park, P.O. Box 224, 81154. T: (888) 873-5174 or (719) 873-5571. F: (719) 873-5125. RV/tent: 24. $20. Hookups: electric (20, 30 amps), water, sewer.

Riverbend Resort Cabins & RV Park, P.O. Box 1270, 81154. T: (800) 621-6512 or (719) 873-5344. F: (719) 873-5770. RV/tent: 57. $18–$22. Hookups: electric (20, 30 amps), water, sewer.

Steamboat Springs

Hahns Peak Lake, FR 486. T: (970) 870-2161. www.ReserveUSA.com/nrrs/co/hahn. RV/tent: 26. $10. Hookups: none.

Harding Spur Campground, Stagecoach State Park, 25500 R CR 14 (P.O. Box 98), 80467. T: (970) 736-2436. http://parks.state.co.us/stagecoach. RV/tent: 18. $14. Hookups: none.

Junction City Campground, Stagecoach State Park, 25500 R CR 14 (P.O. Box 98), 80467. T: (970) 736-2436. http://parks.state.co.us/stagecoach. RV/tent: 27. $18. Hookups: electric (30 amps).

Pinnacle Campground, Stagecoach State Park, 25500 R CR 14 (P.O. Box 98), 80467. T: (970) 736-2436. http://parks.state.co.us/stagecoach. RV/tent: 38. $18. Hookups: electric (30 amps).

Sterling

Chimney Grove Campground, North Sterling State Park, 24005 CR 330, 80751. T: (970) 522-3657. http://parks.state.co.us/north_sterling. RV/tent: 44. $14. Hookups: none.

Elks Campground, North Sterling State Park, 24005 CR 330, 80751. T: (970) 522-3657. http://parks.state.co.us/north_sterling. RV/tent: 50. $18. Hookups: electric (30 amps).

Inlet Grove Campground, North Sterling State Park, 24005 CR 330, 80751. T: (970) 522-3657. http://parks.state.co.us/north_sterling. RV/tent: 47. $18. Hookups: electric (30 amps).

Strasburg

Denver East/Strasburg KOA, P.O. Box 597, 80136. T: (800) 562-6538 or (303) 622-9274. F: (303) 622-9274. www.koa.com. RV/tent: 75. $18–$27. Hookups: electric (20, 30, 50 amps), water, sewer.

Stratton

Marshall Ash Village RV Park, 818 Colorado Ave., 80836. T: (800) 577-5795 or (719) 348-5141. RV/tent: 33. $19–$25. Hookups: electric (30, 50 amps), water, sewer.

Texas Creek

Whispering Pines Resort, 24871 Hwy. 50 West, 81223. T: (888) 275-3827 or (719) 275-3827. RV/tent: 118. $9–$18. Hookups: electric (20, 30 amps), water, sewer.

Trinidad

Budget Host—Derrick RV Park & Motel, 10301 Santa Fe Trail Dr., 81082. T: (719) 846-3307. F: (719) 846-3309. RV/tent: 20. $17–$25. Hookups: electric (20, 30, 50 amps), water, sewer.

Carpios Ridge Campground, Trinidad Lake State Park, 32610 Hwy. 12, 81082. T: (719) 846-6951. http://parks.state.co.us/trinidad. RV/tent: 62. $18. Hookups: electric (30 amps).

Walden

Bockman Campground, State Forest State Park, 2746 CR 41, 80480. T: (970) 723-8366. http://parks.state.co.us/state_forest. RV/tent: 52. $14. Hookups: none.

CONNECTICUT

Baltic

Salt Rock Family Camping, Rte. 97, 06330. T: (860) 822-8728. RV/tent: 125. $20–$25. Hookups: water, electric, sewer.

Bantam

Looking Glass Hill Campgrounds, 14 Cozy Hill, 06750. T: (860) 567-2050. RV/tent: 50. $15. Hookups: water, electric.

Bozrah

Odetah, 38 Bozrah St. Ext., 06334. T: (860) 889-4144. RV/tent: 250. $20–$25. Hookups: water, electric, sewer.

Chaplin

Nickerson Park Camp Grounds, 1036 Phoenixville Rd., 06235. T: (860) 455-0007. RV/tent: 112. $15–$20. Hookups: water, electric, sewer, cable.

Clinton

River Road Camp Sites, 13 River Rd., 06413. T: (860) 669-2956. RV/tent: 50. $20. Hookups: water, electric.

Riverdale Farm Camp Sites, 111 River Rd., 06413. T: (860) 669-5388. RV/tent: 250. $23. Hookups: water, electric, sewer.

Cornwall Bridge

Housatonic Meadows State Park, Rte. 7, 06754. T: (860) 676-6772. RV/tent: 95. $10. Hookups: none.

Deep River

Dale River Camp Sites, River Rd., 06417. T: (860) 669-5388. RV/tent: 96. $25–$32. Hookups: water, electric (30, 50 amps), sewer, cable TV.

East Hampton

Markham Meadows Campgrounds, 7 Markham Rd., 06424. T: (860) 267-9738. RV/tent: 100. $22. Hookups: water, electric.

Nelson's Family Campground, 71 Mott Hill Rd., 06424. T: (860) 267-5300. F: (860) 267-5312. www.nelsonscampground.com. RV/tent: 90. $27. Hookups: water, electric (30, 50 amps), sewer, cable TV.

East Killingly

Stateline Campresort, Rte. 101, 06243. T: (860) 774-3016. F: (860) 774-6470. anewman@localnet.com. RV/tent: 226. $25. Hookups: water, electric, sewer, phone.

Eastford

Silvermine Horse Camp, Star Rte. Pilfershire Rd., 06242. T: (860) 974-1562. RV/tent: 30. No fee. Hookups: none.

Goshen

Mohawk Campground, 708 Sharon Turnpike, 06756. T: (860) 491-2231. RV/tent: 80. $15. Hookups: water, electric.

Valley in the Pines Campground, Lucas Rd., 06756. T: (860) 491-2032. RV/tent: 30. $25. Hookups: water, electric, sewer.

Haddam

Devil's Hopyard State Park, 366 Hopyard Rd., 06423. T: (860) 873-8566. RV/tent: 21. $9. Hookups: none.

Higganum

Little City Campground, 733 Little City Rd., 06438. T: (860) 345-8469. RV/tent: 55. $30–$33. Hookups: water, electric (15, 30 amps), sewer.

Jewett City

Ross Hill Park, 170 Ross Hill Rd., 06351. T: (860) 376-9606. RV/tent: 250. $20. Hookups: water, electric, sewer.

Hopeville Pond State Park, 193 Roode Rd., 06351. T: (860) 376-0313. RV/tent: 82. $13. Hookups: water, electric, sewer.

Kent

Macedonia Brook State Park, 159 Macedonia Brook Rd., 06757. T: (860) 927-4100. RV/tent: 80. $9. Hookups: none.

Kent

Treetops Campground, Spectacle Lake, 06757. T: (860) 927-3555. RV/tent: 262. $20. Hookups: water, electric, sewer.

Lebanon

Waters Edge Family Campground, 271 Leonard Bridge Rd., 06249. T: (860) 642-7470. RV/tent: 170. $23–$26. Hookups: water, electric.

Litchfield

White Memorial Campground, P.O. Box 368, 06759. T: (860) 567-0069. RV/tent: 65. $8–$15. Hookups: none.

Madison

Hammonasset Beach State Park/William F. Miller Campground, Box 271, 06443. T: (203) 245-1817. RV/tent: 558. $12. Hookups: water, electric, sewer.

New Preston

Lake Waramaug State Park, 30 Lake Waramaug Rd., 06777. T: (860) 868-0220. RV/tent: 78. $10. Hookups: water, electric, sewer.

Niantic

Rocky Neck State Park, Box 676, 06357. T: (860) 739-5471. RV/tent: 160. $12. Hookups: water, electric, sewer.

North Grosvenor

West Thompson Lake Campground, RFD 1, 06255. T: (203) 923-2982. RV/tent: 30. $20. Hookups: water, electric.

Oakdale

Laurel-Lock Campgrounds, 15 Cottage Rd., 06370. T: (860) 859-1424. RV/tent: 130. $22. Hookups: water, electric, sewer, cable.

Pequot Ledge Campgrounds, 157 Doyle Rd., 06370. T: (860) 859-0682. RV/tent: 92. $25. Hookups: water, electric, sewer.

Oneco

River Bend Campground, P.O. Box 23, 06373. T: (860) 564-3440. RV/tent: 160. $25. Hookups: water, electric, sewer.

Pleasant Valley

American Legion State Forest/Austin F. Hawes Memorial Campground, P.O. Box 161, 06063. T: (860) 379-0922. RV/tent: 30. $10. Hookups: water, electric, sewer.

Pomfret Center

Mashamoquet Brook State Park/Mashamoquet Brook Campground, 147 Wolf Den Drive, 06259. T: (860) 928-6121. RV/tent: 20. $9. Hookups: water, sewer.

Preston

Strawberry Park Resort Campground, 42 Pierce Rd., 06365. T: (860) 886-1944. RV/tent: 440. $20–$40. Hookups: water, electric, sewer.

Salem

Salem Farms Campground Inc., 39 Alexander Rd., 06420. T: (860) 859-2320. RV/tent: 186. $21. Hookups: water, electric, sewer.

Witch Meadow Lake Campsites, 139 Witch Meadow Rd., 06420. T: (860) 859-1542. RV/tent: 280. $23. Hookups: water, electric, sewer.

Southbury

Kettletown State Park, 175 Quaker Farms Rd., 06488. T: (203) 264-5678. RV/tent: 72. $10. Hookups: water, sewer.

Stafford Springs

Mineral Springs Family Campground, 135 Leonard Rd., 06076. T: (860) 684-2993. RV/tent: 150. $17. Hookups: water, electric.

Sterling

Sterling Park Campground, 177 Gibson Hill Rd., 06377. T: (860) 564-8777. RV/tent: 100. $25. Hookups: water, electric, sewer, cable.

Thomaston

Black Rock State Park, Rte. 6, 06787. T: (860) 283-8088. RV/tent: 96. $10. Hookups: none.

Torrington

Burr Pond State Park/Taylor Brook Campground, 385 Burr Mountain Rd., 06790. T: (860) 379-0172. RV/tent: 40. $10. Hookups: water, electric, sewer.

Voluntown

Frog Hollow Horse Camp, RFD 1, 06384. T: (860) 376-4075. RV/tent: 18. $9. Hookups: water, electric, sewer.

Nature's Camp Site, Rte. 49, 06384. T: (860) 376-4203. RV/tent: 185. $24. Hookups: water, electric, sewer.

Pachaug State Forest/Green Falls Campground, P.O. Box 5, 06384. T: (860) 376-4075. RV/tent: 18. $13. Hookups: water, electric, sewer.

Pachaug State Forest/Mt. Misery Campground, P.O. Box 5, 06384. T: (860) 376-4075. RV/tent: 22. $11. Hookups: water, electric, sewer.

CONNECTICUT (continued)

Wethersfield

Roaring Brook, 308 Silas Deane Hwy., 06109. T: (860) 563-2199. RV/tent: 400. $12. Hookups: water, electric, sewer.

Willington

Moosemeadow Camping Resort, 28 Kechkes Rd., 06279. T: (860) 429-7451. RV/tent: 100. $25–$33. Hookups: water, electric (20, 30 amps), sewer, cable TV.

Rainbow Acres Family Campground, 166 Village Hill Rd., 06279. T: (860) 684-5704. RV/tent: 135. $20. Hookups: water, electric.

Woodstock

Manna Campground, 1728 Hwy. 198, 06281. T: (860) 928-9174. RV/tent: 26. $20. Hookups: water, electric, sewer.

Solair Family Nudist Campground, 65 Ide Perrin Rd., 06281. T: (860) 928-9174. RV/tent: 150. $20. Hookups: water, electric.

DELAWARE

Fenwick Island

Lost Lands RV Park, Bearhole Rd., 19975. T: (302) 436-9450 or (302) 242-8912. F: (302) 678-8037. www.lostlandsrvpark.com. RV/tent: 66. $33. Hookups: water, electric, sewer.

Georgetown

Homestead Camping, Harbeson, 19951. T: (302) 684-4278. RV/tent: 158. $20. Hookups: water, electric (20, 30 amps), sewer.

Harrington

G & R Campground, Gun and Rod Club Rd., 19954. T: (302) 398-8108. RV/tent: 109. $20–$25. Hookups: water, electric (30, 50 amps), sewer.

Long Neck

Leisure Point Resort, Box A-1 Leisure Point, 19966. T: (302) 945-2000. F: (302) 945-4011. www.leisurepoint.com. RV/tent: 319. $33. Hookups: water, electric, sewer.

Milford

Pine Haven Campground, Pine Haven Trailer Park, 19963. T: (302) 422-7117. RV/tent: 140. $22. Hookups: water, electric (20, 30 amps).

Millsboro

Shawn's Hideaway Trailer, RR 24, 19966. T: (302) 945-3133. RV/tent: 4. $25. Hookups: water, electric (20, 30 amps).

Milton

Eagles Nest Family Campground, Rtes. 1 & 16, 19968. T: (302) 684-4031. RV/tent: 67. $19. Hookups: water, electric (20, 30 amps).

Ocean View

Bayshore RV Campground, RR 1 Box 252, 19970. T: (302) 539-7200. RV/tent: 324. $25. Hookups: water, electric (30 amps), sewer.

Pine Tree Campsites, RR 1 Box 331, 19970. T: (302) 539-7006. RV/tent: 115. $25. Hookups: water, electric (20, 30 amps), sewer.

FLORIDA

Alligator Point

KOA–Alligator Point Kampground Resort, 1320 Alligator Dr., 32346. T: (850) 349-2525. F: (850) 349-2067. www.alligatorpointkoa.com. RV/tent: 148. $18–$25. Hookups: water, electric (30, 50 amps), sewer.

Arcadia

Lettuce Lake Travel Resort, 8644 SW Reese St., 34269. T: (863-494-6057. F: (863) 494-4254. RV/tent: 50. $24. Hookups: water, electric (30, 50 amps), sewer, phone.

Riverside RV Resort and Campground, 9770 SW CR 769 (Kings Hwy.), 34269. T: (863) 993-2111 or (800) 795-9733. F: (863) 993-2021. www.river sidervresort.com. RV/tent: 250. $27–$35. Hookups: water, electric (30, 50 amps), sewer, phone.

Astor

St. Johns River Campground, 1520 SR 40, 32102. T: (904) 749-3995. F: (352) 759-3419. www.stjohnsrivercampground.com. RV/tent: 85. $20. Hookups: water, electric (20, 30, 50 amps), sewer.

Big Pine Key

Bahia Honda State Park, 36850 Overseas Hwy., 33043. T: (305) 872-2353 or (800) 326-3521. www.reserveamerica.com or www.myflorida.com. RV/tent: 80. $29. Hookups: water, electric.

Big Pine Key Fishing Lodge, Box 430513, 33043. T: (305) 872-2351. RV/tent: 156. $37. Hookups: water, electric (30 amps), solar, cable.

Bokeelia

Tropic Isle RV Park, 15175 Stringfellow Rd. (CR 767), 33922. T: (941) 283-4456. F: (941) 283-7262. RV/tent: 145. $30–$35. Hookups: water, electric (30 amps), sewer.

Bradenton

Encore RV Resort–Sarasota North, 800 Kay Rd. Northeast, 34202. T: (941) 745-2600 or (800) 678-2131. F: (941) 748-8964. www.rvonthego.com. RV/tent: 415. $23–$40. Hookups: water, electric (30, 50 amps), sewer, cable TV, phone.

Pleasant Lake RV Resort, 6653 53rd. Ave. East, 34203. T: (941) 756-5076. F: (941) 727-8520. RV/tent: 343. $34. Hookups: water, electric (30, 50 amps), sewer, cable TV, phone.

Cape Canaveral

Mango Manor, 190 Oak Manor Dr., 32920. T: (321) 799-0741. F: (321) 783-8671. RV/tent: 51. $22. Hookups: water, electric (20, 30, 50 amps), sewer, cable TV, phone.

Cape San Blas

Cape San Blas Camping Resort, 1342 Cape San Blas Rd., 32457. T/F: (850) 229-6800. www.capesanblas.com/capecamp. RV/tent: 44. $14–$16. Hookups: water, electric (20, 30 amps), sewer.

Carrabelle

Ho-Hum RV Park, 2132 Hwy. 98E, 32322. T: (850) 697-3926. www.hohorvpark.com. RV/tent: 50. $19–$21. Hookups: water, electric, sewer.

Chattahoochee

KOA–Chattachoochee, 2309 Flat Creek Rd., 32324. T: (850) 442-6657. F: (850) 442-6653. RV/tent: 46. $21–$24. Hookups: water, electric (30, 50 amps), sewer.

Clearwater

Travel World RV Park, 12400 US 19 North, 33764. T: (727) 536-1765. F: (727) 532-9385. RV/tent: 200. $20. Hookups: water, electric (50 amps), sewer, cable TV, phone.

FLORIDA (continued)

Clewiston

Clewiston/Lake Okeechobee Holiday Trav-L Park, Rte. 2 Box 242, 33440. T: (863) 983-7078. F: (863) 983-9108. RV/tent: 124. $15–$26. Hookups: water, electric (30 amps), sewer, phone.

Crooked Hook RV Resort, 51700 US Hwy. 27, 33440. T: (941) 983-7112. F: (941) 983-3022. RV/tent: 180. $25. Hookups: water, electric (30 amps), sewer.

Cocoa Beach

Oceanus Mobile Village Campground, 152 Crescent Beach Dr. (23rd), 32931. T: (321) 783-3871. F: (321) 799-0818. RV/tent: 38. $28. Hookups: water, electric, sewer.

Dade City

Traveler's Rest Resort, 29129 Johnston Rd., 33525. T: (352) 588-2013. F: (352) 588-3462. www.travelersrestresort.com. RV/tent: 537. $23. Hookups: water, electric (30, 50 amps), sewer, cable TV.

Davenport

Fort Summit Camping Resort, 4200 US 27 North, 33837. T: (863) 424-1880. F: (863) 424-3336. www.koa.com. RV/tent: 300. $29–$33. Hookups: water, electric (50 amps), cable TV, phone.

Daytona Beach

Daytona Beach Campground, 4601 Clyde Morris Blvd., 32129. T: (386) 761-2663. F: (386) 761-2663. RV/tent: 285. $24. Hookups: water, electric (30, 50 amps), sewer, cable TV.

International RV Park and Campground, 3175 West International Speedway, 32124. T: (386) 239-0249. F: (386) 253-7073. RV/tent: 137. $20–$50. Hookups: water, electric (30, 50 amps), sewer.

Nova Family Campground, 1190 Herbert, 32129. T: (386) 767-0095. F: (386) 767-1666. www.gocampingamerica.com/novafamily-campground. RV/tent: 200. $22. Hookups: water, electric, cable TV.

DeBary

High Banks Marina & Campresort, 488 West High Banks Rd., 32713. T: (386) 668-4491. F: (386) 668-5072. RV/tent: 227. $22–$25. Hookups: water, electric (30, 50 amps), sewer.

Delray Beach

Del-Raton Travel Trailer Park, 2998 South Federal Hwy., 33483. T: (561) 278-4633. RV/tent: 60. $33. Hookups: water, electric (20, 30, 50 amps), sewer, phone.

Destin

Camping on the Gulf Holiday Travel Park, 10005 West Emerald Coast Pkwy., 32541. T: (850) 837-6334. F: (850) 654-5048. www.campgulf.com. RV/tent: 192. $29–$62. Hookups: water, electric (20, 30, 50 amps), sewer.

Dover

Citrus Hills RV Park, 5311 ST 60 East, 33527. T: (813) 737-4770. F: (813) 681-8310. RV/tent: 183. $20. Hookups: water, electric (30, 50 amps), sewer.

Dunedin

Dunedin Beach Campground, 2920 Alternate 19 North, 34698. T: (727) 784-3719. F: (727) 787-9821. RV/tent: 233. $29. Hookups: water, electric (50 amps), sewer, cable TV, phone.

Flagler Beach

Bulow Resort, 345 Old Kings Rd. South, 32136. T: (386) 439-9200. F: (386) 439-6757. www.bulow.com. RV/tent: 350. $22. Hookups: water, electric, cable TV.

Picnickers Campground/Shelltown, 2455 North Oceanshore Blvd., 32136. T: (386) 439-5337. F: (386) 439-0853. RV/tent: 56. $20–$23. Hookups: water, electric, sewer.

Fort Lauderdale

Yacht Haven Park & Marina, 2323 State Rd. 84, 33312-4889. T: (954) 583-2322. RV/tent: 250. $24–$35. Hookups: water, electric (20, 30, 50 amps), sewer.

Fort Myers

Shady Acres RV Travel Park, 19370 South Tamiami Trail, 33908. T: (941) 267-8448. F: (941) 267-7016. www.shadyacresfl.com. RV/tent: 316. $28. Hookups: water, electric (20, 30, 50 amps), sewer, cable TV, phone.

The Groves RV Resort, 16175 John Morris Rd., 33908. T: (941) 466-4300. F: (941) 466-6310. RV/tent: 150. $15–$32. Hookups: water, electric (50 amps), sewer, cab le TV, phone.

Fort Myers Beach

Red Coconut RV Resort on the Beach, 3001 Estero Blvd., 33931. T: (941) 463-7200. F: (941) 463-2609. www.redcoconut.com. RV/tent: 250. $25–$52. Hookups: water, electric (50 amps), sewer, cable TV, phone.

Fort Pierce

Road Runner Travel Resort, 5500 St. Lucie Blvd., 34946. T: (561) 464-0969. F: (561) 464-0987. www.roadrunnertravelresort.com. RV/tent: 450. $25. Hookups: water, electric (50 amps), sewer, cable TV, phone.

Fort Walton Beach

Playground RV Park, 777 North Beal Pkwy., 32547. T: (850) 862-3513. F: (850) 864-2468. RV/tent: 56. $22. Hookups: water, electric (50 amps), sewer, cable TV.

Fountain

Pine Lake RV Park, 21036 US Hwy. 231, 32428. T: (850) 722-1401. F: (850) 722-1403. RV/tent: 75. $16. Hookups: water, electric (30 amps), sewer, cable TV.

Freeport

Lazy Days RV Park, 18655 US Hwy. 331 South, 32439. T: (850) 835-4606. F: (850) 835-4605. www.lazydaysrv.net. RV/tent: 27. $20. Hookups: water, electric, sewer, cable TV, phone.

Georgetown

Riverwood RV Village, 1389 CR 309, 32139. T: (386) 467-7144. F: (386) 467-7143. RV/tent: 25. $18. Hookups: water, electric (30, 50 amps), sewer.

Gulf Islands National Seashore

Fort Pickens Area Campground, 1400 Fort Pickens Rd., 32561. T: (850) 934-2622. F: (850) 934-2653. www.nps.gov/guis/pphtml/camping.html. RV/tent: 200. $20. Hookups: water, electric.

Haines City

Paradise Island RV Park, 2900 South Hwy. 27, 33844. T: (863) 439-1350. RV/tent: 62. $20. Hookups: water, electric (50 amps), sewer, cable TV, phone.

High Springs

Ginnie Springs Resort, 7300 Northeast Ginnie Springs Rd., 32643. T: (386) 454-2202. F: (386) 454-3201. www.ginniesprings.com. RV/tent: 252. $16. Hookups: water, electric (20, 30, 50 amps).

O'Leno State Park, Rte. 2 Box 1010, 32643. T: (386) 454-1853 or (800) 326-3521. F: (386) 454-2565. www.reserveamerica.com or www.myflorida.com. RV/tent: 59. $10. Hookups: water, electric.

Holiday

Holiday Travel Park, 1622 Aires Dr., 34690. T: (727) 934-6782. F: (727) 939-0278. www.campgulf.com. RV/tent: 703. $28.19–$62. Hookups: water, electric (50 amps), sewer, cable TV, phone.

Holt

River's Edge RV Campground, 4001 Log Lake Rd., 32564. T: (850) 537-2267. RV/tent: 114. $15. Hookups: water, electric, sewer, phone.

Homosassa

Camp 'N' Water Outdoor Resort, 11465 West Priest Ln., 34448. T: (352) 628-2000. F: (352) 628-0066. RV/tent: 95. $21. Hookups: water, electric (50 amps), sewer, cable TV, phone.

Chassahowitzka River Campground, 8600 Miss Maggie Dr., 32623. T: (352) 382-2200. F: (352) 382-2200. www.cclib.org/cccs/parks/facilities/campground/campground.html. RV/tent: 85. $18. Hookups: water, electric, sewer.

Indian Rocks Beach

Indian Rocks Beach RV Resort, 601 Gulf Blvd., 33785. T: (727) 596-7743. F: (727) 593-2896. RV/tent: 55. $30–$50. Hookups: water, electric (30, 50 amps), sewer, cable TV, phone.

FLORIDA (continued)

Jacksonville

Flamingo Lake RV Resort Park, 3640 Newcomb Rd., 32218. T: (904) 766-0672 or (800) 326-3521. F: (904) 766-8909. www.flamingolake.com. RV/tent: 157. $26. Hookups: water, electric (20, 30, 50 amps), sewer, cable TV, phone.

Huguenot Memorial Park, 10980 Heckscher Dr., 32226. T: (904) 251-3335. F: (904) 251-3019. RV/tent: 71. $6–$8. Hookups: none.

Little Talbot Island State Park, 12157 Heckscher Dr., 32226. T: (904) 251-2320. www.myflorida.com. RV/tent: 40. $10–$14. Hookups: water, electric.

Jennings

Jennings Outdoor Resort, Rte. 1 Box 221, 32053. T: (386) 938-3321. F: (386) 938-3322. RV/tent: 112. $19. Hookups: water, electric (20, 30, 50 amps), sewer, cable TV, phone.

Juno Beach

Juno Beach RV Park, 900 Juno Ocean Walk, 33408. T: (561) 622-7500. RV/tent: 246. $26–$39. Hookups: water, electric (30, 50 amps), sewer.

Jupiter

West Jupiter Camping Resort, 17801 130th Ave. North, 33478. T: (888) 746-6073. F: (561) 743-3738. www.westjupitercampingresort.com. RV/tent: 103. $25–$32. Hookups: water, electric (20, 30, 50 amps), sewer, cable TV, phone.

Key West

Boyd's Key West Campground, 6401 Maloney Ave., 33040. T: (305) 294-1465. F: (305) 293-9301. RV/tent: 124. $56–$70. Hookups: water, electric (30, 50 amps), sewer, cable TV, phone.

Jabours Trailer Court, 223 Elizabeth St., 33040. T: (305) 294-5723. F: (305) 296-7965. www.kwcamp.com. RV/tent: 90. $40–$74. Hookups: water, electric (30 amps), sewer.

Kissimmee

Cypress Cove Nudist Resort, 4425 South Pleasant Hill Rd., 34746. T: (407) 933-5870. F: (407) 933-3559. www.gocampingamerica.com. RV/tent: 100. $54. Hookups: water, electric, sewer.

Mill Creek RV Resort, 2775 Michigan Ave., 34744. T: (407) 847-6288. F: (407) 847-6683. RV/tent: 183. $22. Hookups: water, electric (30 amps), sewer, phone.

Raccoon Lake Camp Resorts, 8555 West Irlo Bronson Hwy., 34747. T: (407) 239-4148. F: (407) 239-0223. RV/tent: 587. $25–$32. Hookups: water, electric (20, 30, 50 amps), sewer.

Southport Campground and Marina, 2001 East Southport Rd., 34746. T: (407) 933-5822. F: (407) 847-4010. www.southportpark.com. RV/tent: 61. $17. Hookups: water, electric (30, 50 amps), sewer.

Tropical Palms Resort, 2650 Holiday Trail, 34746. T: (407) 396-4595. F: (407) 396-8938. RV/tent: 500. $39. Hookups: water, electric (50 amps), sewer, cable TV, phone.

LaBelle

Whisper Creek RV Resort, 1980 Hickory Dr., 33935. T: (863) 675-6888. F: (863) 675-2323. www.whisper creek.com. RV/tent: 396. $21. Hookups: water, electric (30, 50 amps), sewer, cable TV, phone.

Lake City

Waynes RV Resort, Inc., Rte. 21 Box 501, 32024. T: (386) 752-5721. F: (386) 752-5721. RV/tent: 102. $14–$17. Hookups: water, electric, sewer.

Lake Placid

Camp Florida Resort/Lake Placid, 1525 US Hwy. 27 South, 33852. T: (863) 699-1991. F: (863) 699-1995. www.campfla.com. RV/tent: 396. $28. Hookups: water, electric (30, 50 amps) sewer, phone.

Lake Worth

Camping Resort of the Palm Beaches, 5332 Lake Worth Rd., 33463. T: (561) 965-1653. F: (561) 965-9095. RV/tent: 150. $35. Hookups: water, electric (30 amps), sewer, cable TV, phone.

Lakeland

Sanlan Ranch Campground, 3929 US 98 South, 33813. T: (863) 665-1726. F: (863) 665-0604. www.sanlan.com. RV/tent: 315. $22–$32. Hookups: water, electric (50 amps), sewer, phone.

Lakeport

Aruba RV Resort, 1825 Old Lakeport Rd., 33471. T: (863) 946-1324. F: (863) 946-1270. www.okeedirect.com/arubarv. RV/tent: 156. $20. Hookups: water, electric (30, 50 amps), sewer, cable TV, phone.

Lamont

A Camper's World Campground, Rte. 1 Box 164B, 32336. T: (850) 997-3300. RV/tent: 38. $19. Hookups: water, electric (20, 30, 50 amps), sewer, phone.

Largo

Indian Rocks Travel Park, 12121 Vonn Rd., 33774. T: (727) 595-2228. RV/tent: 30. $19–$22. Hookups: water, electric (30 amps), sewer, cable TV, phone.

Yankee Traveler RV Park, 8500 Ulmerton Rd. (Hwy. 688), 33771. T/F: (727) 531-7998. RV/tent: 210. $20–$22. Hookups: water, electric (30, 50 amps), sewer.

Leesburg

Holiday Travel Resort, 28229 CR 33, 34748. T: (352) 787-5151. F: (352) 787-1052. www.holidaytravel resort.com. RV/tent: 935. $26. Hookups: water, electric (30 amps), sewer, cable TV, phone.

Long Key

KOA–Fiesta Key Kampground, Mile Marker 70, 33001. T: (305) 664-4922 or (800) 562-7730. F: (305) 664-8741. www.koa.com/where/fl/09250.html. RV/tent: 341. $63–$88. Hookups: water, electric, sewer, cable TV, phone.

Marathon

Jolly Roger Travel Park, 59275 Overseas Hwy., 33050-9756. T: (305) 289-0404. F: (305) 743-6913. RV/tent: 131. $31–$48. Hookups: water, electric (20, 30, 50 amps), sewer.

Mexico Beach

Islander RV Park, 2600 US 98, 32410. T: (850) 648-4006. RV/tent: 40. $20. Hookups: water, electric (30 amps), sewer, phone, cable TV.

Miami

Larry and Penny Thompson Park and Campground, 12451 SW 184th St., 33177. T: (305) 232-1049. F: (305) 235-8667. www.co.miami-dade.fl.us/parks/mparks2.htm. RV/tent: 264. $19. Hookups: water, electric (20, 30, 50 amps), sewer.

Milton

Adventures Unlimited, Rte. 6 Box 283, 32570. T: (850) 623-6197. F: (850) 626-3124. www.adventuresunlimited.com. RV/tent: 30. $20. Hookups: water, electric (30 amps).

Mims

KOA–Cape Kennedy, 4513 West Main St., 32754. T: (352) 269-7361. F: (321) 269-1123. www.koa.com. RV/tent: 100. $19–$23. Hookups: water, electric (50 amps), sewer, cable TV, phone.

Naples

Club Naples RV Resort, 3180 Beck Blvd., 34114. T: (941) 455-7275. F: (941) 455-7271. www.club napleserv.com. RV/tent: 309. $24–$38. Hookups: water, electric, cable TV, phone.

Greystone Park, 13300 East Tamiami Trail, 34104. T: (941) 774-4044. RV/tent: 40. $28. Hookups: water, electric, sewer.

Kountree Kampinn RV Resort, 8230 Collier Blvd., 34114. T: (941) 775-4340. F: (941) 775-2269. RV/tent: 161. $27–$35. Hookups: water, electric (30 amps), sewer.

KOA–Naples/Marco Island, 1700 Barefoot Wiliams Rd., 34113. T: (941) 774-5455. F: (941) 774-0788. RV/tent: 186. $29–$47. Hookups: water, electric (20, 30 amps), sewer.

Port of the Islands RV Resort, 12425 Union Rd., 34114. T: (941) 642-5343. F: (941) 642-5343. www.portoftheislands.com/rvresort/. RV/tent: 99. $30. Hookups: water, electric (30 amps), sewer, phone.

Navarre

Navarre Beach Campground, 9201 Navarre Parkway, 32566. T: (850) 939-2188. F: (850) 939-4712. www.navarrebeachcampground.com. RV/tent: 160. $33. Hookups: water, electric (20, 30, 50 amps), sewer, cable TV.

FLORIDA (continued)

Nokomis

Encore SuperPark–Sarasota, 1070 Laurel Rd., 34275. T: (800) 548-8678. F: (941) 485-5678. www.rvonthego.com. RV/tent: 558. $25–$46. Hookups: water, electric (30, 50 amps), cable TV, phone.

Stay-N-Play RV Resort, 899 Knights Trail, 34275. T: (941) 485-1800. F: (941) 488-1813. www.stay–play.com. RV/tent: 398. $30–$52. Hookups: water, electric (50 amps), cable TV, phone.

O'Brien

Ichetucknee Family Campground, RR 1 Box 1576, 32071. T: (386) 497-2150. F: (386) 497-2150. www.ichetuckneeriver.com. RV/tent: 50. $18–$21.50. Hookups: water, electric (30, 50 amps), sewer.

Ocala

KOA–Silver Springs, 3200 SW 38th Ave., 34474. T: (352) 237-2138. F: (352) 237-9894. RV/tent: 205. $33–$37. Hookups: water, electric (20, 30 amps), sewer.

Okeechobee

Bob's Big Bass RV Park, 12766 Southeast Hwy. 441, 34974. T: (863) 763-2638. RV/tent: 43. $15. Hookups: water, electric (20, 30, 50 amps), sewer.

Buckhead Ridge Marina, 670 Hwy. 78B, 34974. T: (863) 763-2826. F: (863) 467-5555. RV/tent: 112. $15–$25. Hookups: water, electric (20, 30 amps), sewer.

KOA–Okeechobee Kampground and Golf Course, 4276 Hwy. 441 South, 34974. T: (863) 763-0231. F: (863) 763-0531. www.koa.com. RV/tent: 465. $29–$65. Hookups: water, electric (30, 50 amps) sewer, cable TV, phone.

Ormond Beach

Encore Superpark Daytona Beach North, 1701 North US 1, 32174. T: (386) 672-3045. F: (386) 672-3026. www.encorerv.com/superparks/florida/daytonabeachnorth/. RV/tent: 336. $30. Hookups: water, electric, sewer, cable TV, phone.

Ormond-by-the-Sea

Ocean Village Camper Resort, 2162 Ocean Shore Blvd., 32176. T: (386) 441-1808. RV/tent: 80. $25. Hookups: water, electric (30 amps), sewer, cable TV.

Osprey

Oscar Scherer State Recreation Area, 1843 North Tamiami Trail, 34229. T: (941) 483-5956 or (800) 326-3521. F: (941) 480-3007. www.reserveameri ca.com or www.myflorida.com. RV/tent: 104. $25. Hookups: water, electric, sewer.

Palm Harbor

Caladesi RV Park, 205 Dempsey Rd., 34683. T: (727) 784-3622. F: (727) 784-3622. RV/tent: 46. $27. Hookups: water, electric (20, 30 amps), sewer.

Palmetto

Frog Creek Campground, 8515 Bayshore Rd., 34221. T: (941) 722-6154. F: (941) 723-5820. www.frogcreekrv.com. RV/tent: 190. $22. Hookups: water, electric (30 amps), sewer, phone.

Panacea

Holiday Campground, 14 Coastal Hwy., 32346. T: (850) 984-5757. F: (850) 984-5757. RV/tent: 80. $24. Hookups: water, electric (30, 50 amps), sewer.

Panama City Beach

Ocean Park RV Resort, 23026 Panama City Beach Pkwy., 32413. T: (850) 235-0306. RV/tent: 160. $30. Hookups: water, electric (30 amps), sewer, cable TV.

Pensacola

Playa del Rio Park and Yacht Club, Perdido Key, 32507. T: (850) 492-0904. F: (850) 492-4471. www.playadelrio.com. RV/tent: 30. $19–$35. Hookups: water, electric (20, 30 50 amps), sewer, cable TV, phone.

Perdido Key

All Star Campground / Perdido Key, 13621 Perdido Key Dr., 32507. T: (850) 492-0041. www.allstar-rv.com. RV/tent: 182. $24–$70. Hookups: water, electric (20, 30, 50 amps), sewer, cable TV, phone.

Perry

Southern Oaks RV Campground and Resort, 3641 Hwy. 19 South, 32347. T: (850) 584-3221. F: (850) 584-3224. RV/tent: 100. $23. Hookups: water, electric (15, 30, 50 amps), sewer, cable TV, phone.

Port Richey

Suncoast RV Resort, 9029 US 19, 34668. T: (727) 842-9324. RV/tent: 142. $22. Hookups: water, electric (20, 30, 50 amps), sewer, cable TV, phone.

Port St. Joe

Presnell's Bayside Marina and RV Resort, 2115 Hwy. C30, 32456. T: (850) 229-2710. RV/tent: 27. $12. Hookups: water, electric (50 amps).

Punta Gorda

Waters Edge RV of Punta Gorda, 6800 Golf Course Blvd., 33982. T: (941) 637-4677. F: (941) 637-9543. RV/tent: 131. $20–$29. Hookups: water, electric (20, 30, 50 amps), sewer.

Waters Edge RV Resort, Punta Gorda, 33982. T: (941) 637-4677. F: (941) 637-9543. www.watersedgervresort.com. RV/tent: 176. $25. Hookups: water, electric (30, 50 amps), sewer, phone.

Riverview

Alafia River RV Resort, 9812 Gibsonton Dr., 33569-5399. T: (813) 677-1997. F: (813) 677-1997. RV/tent: 203. $21. Hookups: water, electric (20, 30 amps), sewer.

Hidden River Travel Resort, 12500 McMullen Loop, 33569. T: (813) 677-1515. RV/tent: 340. $21. Hookups: water, electric (20, 30, 50 amps), sewer.

Rockledge

Space Coast RV Resort, 820 Barnes Blvd., 32955. T: (321) 636-2873. F: (321) 636-0275. www.usa star.com/spacecoast/. RV/tent: 240. $35. Hookups: water, electric (50 amps), sewer.

Ruskin

Hide-A-Way RV Resort, 2206 Chaney Dr., 33570. T: (813) 645-6037. F: (813) 645-6037. RV/tent: 292. $22. Hookups: water, electric (30, 50 amps), sewer, cable TV, phone.

River Oaks RV Resort, 201 Stephens Rd., 33570. T: (813) 645-2439. RV/tent: 97. $13–$20. Hookups: water, electric (20, 30, 50 amps), sewer.

Salt Springs

Elite Resorts at Salt Springs, 25250 East Hwy. 316, 32134. T: (352) 685-1900. F: (352) 685-0557. www.eliteresorts.com. RV/tent: 470. $20. Hookups: water, electric (20, 30 amps), sewer.

Sanford

Twelve Oaks RV Resort, 6300 State Rte. 46 West, 32771-9290. T: (407) 323-0880. RV/tent: 281. $22. Hookups: water, electric (30, 50 amps), sewer.

Sarastoa/Siesta Key

Gulf Beach Campground, 8862 Midnight Pass Rd., 34242. T: (941) 349-3839. RV/tent: 48. $19–$57. Hookups: water, electric (20, 30, 50 amps), sewer, cable TV, phone.

Sopchoppy

Ochlockonee River State Park, P.O. Box 5, 32358. T: (850) 962-2771 or (800) 326-3521. F: (850) 962-2403. www.reserveamerica.com or www.myflorida.com. RV/tent: 30. $20. Hookups: water, electric, sewer.

South Bay

South Bay RV Park, 100 Levee Rd., 33493. T: (561) 992-9045. F: (561) 992-9277. RV/tent: 96. $16.50–$17.60. Hookups: water, electric (30 amps), cable TV.

St. Augustine

North Beach Camp Resort, 4125 Coastal Hwy. (A1A), 32084. T: (904) 824-1806. F: (904) 826-0897. RV/tent: 121. $35. Hookups: water, electric (30, 50 amps), sewer, cable TV, phone.

St. Augustine Beach

Bryn Mawr Ocean Resort, 4850 A1A South, 32800. T: (904) 471-3353. F: (904) 471-8730. www.brynmawroceanresort.com. RV/tent: 130. $34–$42. Hookups: water, electric (20, 30, 50 amps), sewer, cable TV, phone.

FLORIDA (continued)

Cooksey's Camping Resort, 2795 A1A South, 32080. T: (904) 471-3171. RV/tent: 244. $30. Hookups: water, electric (15, 30, 50 amps), sewer, phone.

Ocean Grove Camp Resort, 4225 Hwy. A1A South, 32084. T: (904) 471-3414. F: (904) 461-8403. www.oceangroveresort.com. RV/tent: 198. $35. Hookups: water, electric (20, 30, 50 amps), sewer, cable TV, phone.

KOA–St. Augustine Beach Kampground Resort, 525 West Pope Rd., 32080. T: (904) 471-3113. F: (904) 471-1715. www.koa.com. RV/tent: 71. $36. Hookups: water, electric (30, 50 amps), sewer, cable TV.

St. Petersburg

Robert's Mobile Home and RV Resort, 3390 Gandy Blvd., 33702. T: (727) 577-6820. F: (727) 577-2621. RV/tent: 430. $20. Hookups: water, electric (30, 50 amps), sewer, cable TV, phone.

KOA–St. Petersburg/Madeira Beach Kampground, 5400 95th St. North, 33708. T: (727) 392-2233. F: (727) 398-6081. www.koa.com. RV/tent: 390. $37–$65. Hookups: water, electric (20, 30, 50 amps), phone.

Thonotassa

Happy Traveler RV Park, 9401 Fowler Ave., 33592. T: (813) 986-3094. F: (813) 986-9077. RV/tent: 224. $21. Hookups: water, electric (20, 30, 50 amps), sewer, phone.

Titusville

The Great Outdoors RV and Golf Resort, 135 Plantation Dr., 32780. T: (800) 621-2267 or 321-269-5004. F: (321) 269-5004. www.tgoresort.com. RV/tent: 200. $35. Hookups: water, electric (30, 50 amps), sewer, cable TV.

Venice

Venice Campground and RV Park, 4085 East Venice Ave., 34292. T: (941) 488-0850. F: (941) 485-1666. www.campvenice.com/index.shtml. RV/tent: 133. $28–$36. Hookups: water, electric (30 amps), sewer.

Wabasso

Vero Beach Kamp RV Resort, 8850 North US Hwy. 1, 32970. T: (561) 589-5665. F: (561) 388-5722. RV/tent: 120. $20. Hookups: water, electric (30, 50 amps), cable TV.

West Palm Beach

Pine Lake Camp Resort, 7000 Okeechobee Blvd., 33411. T: (561) 686-0714. RV/tent: 194. $20. Hookups: water, electric (20, 30 amps), sewer, phone.

White Springs

Kelly's RV Park, Rte. 1 Box 370, Rte. 41 South, 32096. T: (386) 397-2616. F: (386) 397-1261. RV/tent: 76. $16. Hookups: water, electric (30, 50 amps), sewer, phone.

Yulee

Hance's First in Florida RV Park, 3111 Hance Pkwy. (US 17), 32097. T: (904) 225-2080. F: (904) 225-2080. RV/tent: 73. $27. Hookups: water, electric (30, 50 amps), sewer, cable TV, phone.

Zephyrhills

Jim's RV Park, 35120 Hwy. 54 West, 33541-1400. T: (813) 782-5610. RV/tent: 156. $17. Hookups: water, electric (20, 30 amps), sewer.

GEORGIA

Acworth

Holiday Marina Harbor & Campground, 5989 Groover's landing, 30102. T: (770) 974-2575. RV/tent: 47. $16–$19. Hookups: water, electric (20, 30 amps), sewer, phone.

Lakemont Campground, 5134 North Shores Rd., 30101. T/F: (770) 966-0302. lakemontjc@aol.com. RV/tent: 100. $16–$21. Hookups: water, electric (20, 30, 50 amps), sewer, phone (modem).

Adel

Reed Bingham State Park, P.O. Box 394, B-1, Rte. 2, 31620. T: (912) 896-3551. reedpark@surfsouth.com. RV/tent: 46. $18–$21. Hookups: water, electric (20, 30 amps), sewer, cable TV, phone.

1021Albany

Albany RV Resort, 1218 Liberty Expressway Southeast, 31705. T: (800) 424-6301. atrv@surfsouth.com. RV/tent: 31. $17–$19. Hookups: water, electric (20, 30, 50 amps), sewer, cable TV, phone (modem).

Creekside Plantation RV Campground, 2700 Liberty Expressway Southeast, 31705. T: (912) 883-7996. RV/tent: 60. $16. Hookups: water, electric (30, 50 amps), sewer, cable TV, phone (modem).

Devencrest Travel Park, 1833 Liberty Expressway Southeast, 31705. T: (912) 432-2641. RV/tent: 100. $16–$18. Hookups: water, electric (15, 20, 30, 50 amps), sewer, laundry.

Americus

Brickyard Plantation RV & Tent Campground, 1619 US Hwy. 280 East, 31709. T: (912) 874-1234. www.brickyardgolfclub.com. RV/tent: 12. $16. Hookups: water, electric (20, 30 amps), sewer.

Andersonville

City Campground, Rte. 1 Box 800, 31711. T: (912) 924-2558. RV/tent: 40. $14–$16. Hookups: water, electric (15, 20 amps), sewer.

Arabi

Southen Gates RV Park & Campground, 138 Campsite Rd., 31712. T: (912) 273-6464. RV/tent: 55. $19–$21. Hookups: water, electric (20, 30, 50 amps), sewer, phone (modem).

Ashburn

Knights Inn & RV Park, 1971 North St., 31714. T: (229) 567-3334. RV/tent: 77. $10–$12. Hookups: water, electric (20, 30 amps), sewer.

Augusta

Flynn's Inn Camping Village, 3746 Peach Orchard Rd., 30906. T: (706) 798-6912. RV/tent: 61. $12–$14. Hookups: water, electric (30, 50 amps), sewer, phone (modem).

Austell

Arrowhead Campground, 7400 Six Flags Dr. SW, 30001. T: (800) 631-8956. F: (770) 745-8752. acg@arrowheadcampground.com. RV/tent: 200. $28. Hookups: water, electric (20, 30, 50 amps), sewer, phone (modem).

Barnesville

High Falls Campground, 1046 High Falls Park Rd., 30204. T: (770) 358-2205. RV/tent: 122. $21–$24. Hookups: water, electric (20, 30, 50 amps), sewer, phone, laundry.

Blairsville

Goose Creek Campgrounds, 7061 Goose Creek, 30512. T: (706) 745-5111. RV/tent: 24. $16–$18. Hookups: water, electric (20 amps), sewer.

Lake Nottely RV Park, 350 Haley Cir., 30512. T: (706) 745-8899. F: (706) 745-8806. www.lakenot telyrv.com. RV/tent: 80. $16. Hookups: water, electric (20, 30, 50 amps), sewer, phone (modem).

Mountain Oak Cabins & Campgrouds, 2388 Mulky Gap Rd., 30512. T: (888) 781-6867. www.moun tainoak.com. mofcc@alltel.net. RV/tent: 35. $15–$21. Hookups: water, electric (20, 30, 50 amps), sewer, phone (modem).

Trackrock Campgrounds & Cabins, 4887 Trackrock Campground Rd., 30512. T: (706) 745-2420. www.trackrock.com. trackroc@alltel.net. RV/tent: 90. $16–$18. Hookups: water, electric (20, 30 amps), sewer, phone (modem), laundry.

GEORGIA (continued)

Blakely

Kolomoki Mounds State Park, Temple Mound Rd., 31723. T: (229) 724-2150. kolomoki@alltel.net. RV/tent: 43. $15. Hookups: water, electric (30 amps), sewer, phone.

Blue Ridge

Cooper Creek Campground, US Forest Service, 650 Appalachian Hwy., 30513. T: (706) 632-3031. RV/tent: 27. $8–$12. Hookups: water, picnic table, restrooms, showers, tent pads.

Deep Hole Campground, US Forest Service, 650 Appalachian Hwy., 30513. T: (706) 632-3031. RV/tent: 12. $8–$12. Hookups: water, picnic table, restrooms, showers, tent pads.

Frank Gross Campground, US Forest Service, 650 Appalachian Hwy., 30513. T: (706) 632-3031. RV/tent: 9. $8–$12. Hookups: water, picnic table, restrooms, showers, tent pads.

Morganton Point, US Forest Service, 650 Appalachian Hwy., 30513. T: (706) 632-3031. RV/tent: 43. $8–$12. Hookups: water, picnic table, restrooms, showers, tent pads.

Mulky Campground, US Forest Service, 650 Appalachian Hwy., 30513. T: (706) 632-3031. RV/tent: 21. $8–$12. Hookups: water, picnic table, restrooms, showers, tent pads.

Whispering Pines Campground, 290 Whipering Pines Rd., 30513. T: (706) 374-6494. RV/tent: 30. $16. Hookups: water, electric (15, 20 amps), sewer, phone.

Brunswick

Golden Isles Vacation Park, 7445 Blythe Hwy., 31523. T: (912) 261-1025. RV/tent: 110. $19–$21. Hookups: water, electric (20, 30, 50 amps), sewer, cable TV.

Ocean Breeze Campround, Dover Bluff Rd., 31523. T: (912) 264-6692. RV/tent: 37. $17. Hookups: water, electric (20, 30 amps), sewer, phone.

Buena Vista

Country Vista Campground, Rte. 1 Box 14, 31803. T: (229) 649-2267. RV/tent: 44. $17–$19. Hookups: water, electric (20, 30, 50 amps), sewer, phone (modem), cable TV.

Buford

Bolding Mill Campground, P.O. Box 567, 30515-0567. T: (404) 532-3650. RV/tent: 97. $14–$22. Hookups: water, electric (20 amps), sewer, laundry.

Byron

Interstate Camping, 305 Chapman Rd., 31008. T: (229) 956-5511. www.interstatervcenter. irvcenter@aol.com. RV/tent: 104. $20–$22. Hookups: water, electric (30, 50 amps), sewer, phone (modem).

Calhoun

KOA–Calhoun, 2523 Redbud Rd. Northeast, 30701. T: (800) 562-7512. RV/tent: 87. $21–$24. Hookups: water, electric (15, 20, 30 amps), sewer, laundry.

Carrollton

John Tanner State Park, 354 Tanners Beach Rd., 30117. T: (770) 830-2222. RV/tent: 32. $16–$20. Hookups: water, electric (30, 50 amps), sewer, cable TV.

Cartersville

Clark Creek South, P.O. Box 487, 30120-0487. T: (770) 382-4700. RV/tent: 40. $14–$20. Hookups: water, electric (30 amps), sewer.

KOA–Cartersville, 800 Cassville-White Rd., 30121. T: (404) 382-7333. RV/tent: 117. $20–$22. Hookups: water, electric (20, 30, 50 amps), sewer, laundry.

McKinney Campground, P.O. Box 487, 30120. T: (770) 382-4700. RV/tent: 150. $18–$20. Hookups: water, electric (30, 50 amps), sewer.

Payne Campground, P.O. Box 487, 30120. T: (770) 382-4700. RV/tent: 60. $20. Hookups: water, electric (30 amps), sewer.

Cave Spring

Cedar Creek Park, 6770 Cave Springs Rd., 30124. T: (706) 777-3030. cdrcrkpark@aol.com. RV/tent: 60. $15. Hookups: water, electric (30, 50 amps), sewer.

Cecil

Cecil Bay RV Park, Old Coffee Rd., 31627. T: (229) 794-1484. RV/tent: 100. $14–$16. Hookups: water, electric (20, 30, 50 amps), sewer.

Chatsworth

Fort Mountain State Park, 181 Ft. Mountain Park Rd., 30705. T: (706) 695-2621. fortmtpk@aol.com. RV/tent: 79. $14. Hookups: water, electric (30 amps), sewer, cable TV.

Lake Conasauga Campground, Chattahoochee National Forest, 1755 Cleveland Hwy., 30501. T: (706) 695-6736. www.fs.fed.u/conf/consauga_host.htm. madavis@fs.fed.us. RV/tent: 35. $12–$16. Hookups: water sources, bathhouse, firewood, grill, sewer, table, tent pad.

Chauncey

Jaybird Springs Resort, 1221 Jaybird Springs Rd., 31011. T: (229) 868-2728. RV/tent: 22. $14–$16. Hookups: water, electric (15, 30 amps), sewer, phone.

Clarkesville

Moccasin Creek State Park, Rte. 1 Box 1634, 30523. T: (706) 947-3194. www.georgia.com/parks/moccasin.html. mocccrkpk@stc.net. RV/tent: 54. $12–$16. Hookups: water, electric (30 amps), sewer, firewood, grill.

Clayton

Black Rock Mountain State Park, 3085 Black Rock Mountain Pkwy., 30562. T: (706) 746-2141. brmp@stc.net. RV/tent: 59. $12–$14. Hookups: water, electric (30 amps), sewer, cable TV, laundry, phone.

Cleveland

Crystal Springs Campground, 4542 Hwy. 129 North, 30528. T: (706) 865-6955. RV/tent: 62. $12–$16. Hookups: water, sewer, laundry, pet friendly.

Gold 'n' Gem Grubbin, 75 Gold Nugget Ln., 30528. T: (800) 942-4436. www.goldngem.com. RV/tent: 50. $10–$22. Hookups: water, electric (20, 30, 50 amps), sewer, bathhouse.

Jenny's Creek Family Campground, 4542 Hwy. 129 North, 30528. T: (706) 865-6955. www.jennys creek.com. RV/tent: 70. $14–$18. Hookups: water, electric (15, 20, 30 amps), sewer, laundry.

Leisure Acres Campground, 3840 Westmoreland Rd., 30528. T: (706) 865-4114. F: (706) 865-9544. leisure@aol.com. RV/tent: 92. $18–$20. Hookups: water, electric (30, 50 amps), sewer, phone (modem).

Mountain Creek Grove, 258 Grove Ln., 30528. T: (706) 865-6930. F: (706) 865-5521. www.cyber nude.com/resorts/mtncreek. mtncreek@stc.net. RV/tent: 17. $18–$24. Hookups: water, electric (20, 30, 50 amps), sewer.

Mountain Creek Grove Campgrounds, 338 Mountain Creek Cir., 30528. T: (706) 865-6930. www.mountaincreekgrove.com. mtncreek@alltel.net. RV/tent: 110. $7–$15. Hookups: water, electric (30 amps), sewer, shower, bathhouse.

Serendipity Nudist Resort, 95 Cedar Hollow Rd., 30528. T: (706) 219-3993. office@serendipity-park.com. RV/tent: 42. $18–$21. Hookups: water, electric (50 amps), sewer, phone (modem).

Turner Campsite, 142 Turner Campsite Rd., 30528. T: (706) 865-4757. RV/tent: 126. $16–$20. Hookups: water, electric 30 amps), sewer, laundry.

Colquitt

Emerald Lake RV Park & Music Showcase, 698 Enterprise Rd., 31737. T: (229) 758-2929. RV/tent: 20. $16. Hookups: water, electric (30, 50 amps), sewer, laundry.

Lake Pines RV Park & Campground, 6404 Garrett Rd., 31820. T: (706) 561-9675. www.lakepines.net. RV/tent: 68. $18–$20. Hookups: water, electric (20, 30, 50 amps), sewer, phone (modem).

Comer

Watson Mill Bridge State Park, 650 Watson Mill Rd., 30629. T: (706) 783-5349. www.negia.net/~watson/. watson@negia.net. RV/tent: 24. $15. Hookups: water, electric (30 amps), sewer, laundry.

Commerce

KOA–Commerce/Athens Campground, CR 466, 30529. T: (706) 335-5535. RV/tent: 71. $18–$24. Hookups: water, electric (20, 30, 50 amps), sewer, phone (modem).

GEORGIA (continued)

Cordele

KOA–Cordele, 373 Rockhouse Rd., 31015. T: (800) 562-0275. RV/tent: 73. $22–$24. Hookups: water, electric (20, 30 amps), sewer.

Cornelia

Lake Russell Campground, 1756 Cleveland Hwy., 30501. T: (706) 754-6221. RV/tent: 42. $10–$12. Hookups: water, sewer, table, grill.

Covington

Riverside Estates RV & Camping, 1891-2 Access Rd., 30014. T: (770) 787-3707. RV/tent: 172. $18–$20. Hookups: water, electric (20, 30, 50 amps), sewer, phone (modem), cable TV.

Crawfordsville

Alexander H. Stephens State Historic Park, Hwy. 22 & US 278, 30631. T: (706) 456-2602. ahssp@ g-net.net. RV/tent: 25. $12–$16. Hookups: water, electric (20, 30 amps), sewer, laundry.

Cumming

Sawnee Campground, P.O. Box 567, 30515-0567. T: (770) 887-0592. RV/tent: 56. $16–$22. Hookups: water, electric (20 amps), sewer, laundry.

Shady Grove Campground, P.O. Box 567, 30515-0567. T: (770) 887-2067. RV/tent: 115. $14–$22. Hookups: water, electric (20 amps), sewer, laundry.

Twin Lakes RV Park, 3300 Shore Dr., 30040. T: (770) 887-4400. RV/tent: 90. $16–$18. Hookups: water, electric (30, 50 amps), sewer.

Darien

Tall Pines Campground, Hwy. 251, 31305. T: (912) 437-3966. RV/tent: 45. $16–$18. Hookups: water, electric (30, 50 amps), sewer, laundry.

Dawsonville

Amicalola Falls State Park & Lodge, 418 Amicalola Falls Lodge Rd., 30534. T: (706) 265-4703. www.ngeorgia.com/parks/amicalola.html. RV/tent: 20. $12–$16. Hookups: water, electric (20, 30 amps), sewer, laundry.

Dillard

River Vista Mountain Village, 960 Hwy. 246, 30537. T: (888) 850-7275. www.rvmountainvillage.com. relax@rvmountainvillage.com. RV/tent: 127. $25. Hookups: water, electric (30, 50 amps), sewer, cable TV, laundry.

Donalsonville

Seminole Sportsman Lodge, Marina & Campground, 7966 Marina Rd., 31745. T: (229) 861-3862. F: (229) 861-3501. www.seminolesportsmanlodge.com. brandimist2000@yahoo.com. RV/tent: 24. $16. Hookups: water, electric (20, 30 amps), gas, sewer, modem.

Seminole State Park, Rte. 2 & Hwy. 39, 31745. T: (229) 861-3137. RV/tent: 50. $12–$16. Hookups: water, electric (30 amps), sewer, firewood, grill, laundry.

Eatonton

Lawrence Shoals Park, Junction US 129 & Hwy. 16, 31024. T: (706) 485-5494. RV/tent: 49. $14–$16. Hookups: water, electric (20, 30 amps), sewer, firewood, grill, laundry.

Oconee Springs Park at Lake Sinclair, US 129 & Hwy. 16, 31024. T: (706) 485-8423. www.lakesin clair.org. RV/tent: 52. $12–$25. Hookups: water, electric (20, 30 amps), sewer, firewood, grill, laundry (No Pets).

Old Federal Rd. Park, Junction Hwy. 369 & Hwy. 53, 31024. T: (770) 967-6757. RV/tent: 84. $16. Hookups: water, electric (30, 50 amps), sewer, laundry.

Ellijay

Camp Cherry Log, Little Rock Creek Rd., 30540. T: (706) 635-5006. RV/tent: 43. $18–$22. Hookups: water, electric (30, 50 amps), sewer.

Plum Nelly Campground, 15828 South Hwy. 515, 30540. T: (404) 317-2458. RV/tent: 32. $16–$18. Hookups: water, electric (30, 50 amps), sewer.

Fitzgerald

Colony City Campground, Perry House Rd., 31750. T: (229) 423-5050. RV/tent: 36. $12–$16. Hookups: water, electric (30 amps), sewer, firewood, grill, laundry (No Showers).

Florence

Florence Marina State Park, Junction 39 C & Hwy. 39, 31821. T: (229) 838-6870. flmarina@sowega.net. RV/tent: 44. $16. Hookups: water, electric (30, 50 amps), sewer.

Folkston

Okefenokee Pastimes, Rte. 2 Box 3090, 31537. T: (229) 496-4472. www.okefenokee.com. overnight@okefenokee.com. RV/tent: 22. $18–$22. Hookups: water, electric (30 amps), sewer, firewood, grill, laundry.

Forsyth

L & D RV Park & Campgrounds, Rte. 3 Box 62A, 31029. T: (921) 994-5401. RV/tent: 29. $16–$18. Hookups: water, electric (20, 30, 50 amps), sewer, laundry.

Fort Benning

Uche Creek Campground/Fort Benning Manor, Miller Hall Bldg. 241, 31905. T: (706) 545-4053. F: (706) 545-3057. RV/tent: 85. $18–$22. Hookups: water, electric (30, 50 amps), sewer, cable TV, phone (modem).

Gainesville

Duckett Mill Campground, Hwy. 400 & Duckett Mill Rd., 30506. T: (770) 532-9802. RV/tent: 54. $12–$14. Hookups: table, tent pad, grill, sewer.

Lake Blue Ridge Campground, 1755 Cleveland Hwy., 30501. T: (770) 257-3000. www.fs.fed.us. spayne@fs.fed.us. RV/tent: 58. $10–$12. Hookups: water, rest rooms, showers, tent pads.

Hephzibah

Fox Hollow Campgrounds, 4032 Peach Orchard Rd., 30815. T: (706) 592-4563. RV/tent: 21. $14. Hookups: water, electric (30 amps), phone (modem).

Hiawassee

Enota Campground & Resort, 1000 Hwy. 180, 30546. T: (706) 896-9966. RV/tent: 92. $22–$28. Hookups: water, electric (30, 50 amps), laundry, sewer, phone.

Georgia Mountain Campground, P.O. Box 444, 30546. T: (706) 896-4191. RV/tent: 96. $14–$18. Hookups: water, electric (20, 30 amps), sewer, cable TV, phone (modem).

La Grange

Three Creeks Campground, 305 Old Roanoke Rd., 30241. T: (706) 884-0899. alltel.net. RV/tent: 34. $19–$21. Hookups: water, electric (30, 50 amps), sewer, phone, laundry.

Metter

Beaver Run RV Park & Campground, Rte. 3 Box 168, 30439. T: (912) 685-2594. www.turnstonecabins.com/beaverrun.html. bvrunpk@pineland.net. RV/tent: 71. $20. Hookups: water, electric (30, 50 amps), sewer, phone (modem).

Perry

Boland's Perry Overnight Park, 800 Perimeter Rd., 31069. T: (770) 987-3371. RV/tent: 65. $18. Hookups: water, electric (20, 30 amps), laundry, sewer, cable TV, phone (modem).

Crossroads Travel Park, 1513 Sam Nunn Blvd., 31069. T: (912) 987-3141. RV/tent: 56. $20–$22. Hookups: water, electric (20, 30 amps), sewer, phone (modem).

Rincon

Green Peace RV Park, 155 Caroni Dr., 31326. T: (912) 826-5540. pkavali@aol.com. RV/tent: 50. $11–$14. Hookups: water, electric (30 amps), sewer, phone (modem).

Whispering Pines RV Park, 1755 Hodgeville Rd., 31326. T: (912) 728-7562. F: (912) 728-5519. RV/tent: 53. $23–$25. Hookups: water, electric (20, 30, 50 amps), sewer, phone (modem).

Rome

Coosa River Campground, 181 Lock & Dam Rd., 30161. T: (706) 234-5001. RV/tent: 31. $16–$18. Hookups: water, electric (30, 50 amps), sewer, phone (modem), laundry.

Sautee

Cherokee Campground of White County, 45 Bethel Rd., 30571. T: (706) 878-2267. F: (706) 878-1880. www.mindlessdrivel.org. RV/tent: 48. $18–$20. Hookups: water, electric (20, 30 amps), sewer, cable TV, phone (modem).

Creekwood Cabins & Campground, 5730 Hwy. 356, 30571. T: (706) 878-2164. db.cornerpost.com. creekwoodcamp@yahoo.com. RV/tent: 168. $12–$25. Hookups: water, electric (30, 50 amps), sewer, cable TV, bathhouse.

GEORGIA (continued)

Sautee (continued)

Sleepy Hollow Campground, 307 Sleepy Hollow Rd., 30571. T: (706) 878-2618. RV/tent: 73. $17–$20. Hookups: water, electric (20, 30 amps), sewer, hot showers, playground.

St. George

Hidden River Ranch, 885 Reynolds Bridge Road St., 31646. T: (912) 843-2603. web.infoave.net/~hiddenriver/index.html. hiddenriver@planettel.net. RV/tent: 30. $10–$17. Hookups: water, electric (30, 50 amps), sewer, phone (modem), laundry.

Statesboro

Parkwood Motel & RV Park, 12188 Hwy. 301 South, 30458. T: (912) 681-3105. parkwood@frontiernet.net. RV/tent: 37. $15–$19. Hookups: water, electric (30, 50 amps), sewer, cable TV, phone.

Tifton

Amy's South Georgia RV Park, 4632 Union Rd., 31794. T: (912) 386-8441. amysrvpark@planttel.com. RV/tent: 86. $18–$20. Hookups: water, electric (20, 30, 50 amps), sewer, phone.

Townsend

Lake Harmony RV Park, Rte. 3 Box 3128, 31331. T: (912) 832-4338. www.lakeharmonypark.com. RV/tent: 50. $18–$21. Hookups: water, electric (30 amps), sewer, cable TV, phone (modem).

McIntosh Lake Campgrounds, Rte. 3 Box 3112, 31331. T: (229) 832-6215. RV/tent: 39. $12. Hookups: water, electric (15, 30 amps), sewer, cable TV, phone (modem).

Tybee Island

River's End Campground & RV Park, 915 Polk St., 31328-0988. T: (912) 786-5518. F: (706) 786-4126. riversendga@gocamping america.com. RV/tent: 127. $25–$35. Hookups: water, electric (20, 30, 50 amps), sewer, phone (modem).

Unadilla

South Prong Creek Campground, 627 Hwy. 230, 31091. T: (912) 783-2551. www.southprong.com. tom@southprong.com. RV/tent: 150. $11–$16. Hookups: water, electric (30, 50 amps), sewer, laundry.

Yatesville

Heart of Georgia RV Park, 6722 Hwy. 74, 31097. T: (706) 472-3437. RV/tent: 33. $17–$19. Hookups: water, electric (30, 50 amps), sewer, laundry

IDAHO

American Falls

Indian Springs RV Campground, 3249 Indian Springs Rd., 83211. T: (208) 226-2174. indian@gemstate.net. RV/tent: 125. $16–$18. Hookups: electric (15, 20, 30 amps), water, sewer.

Massacre Rocks State Park, 3592 North Park Ln., 83211. T: (208) 548-2672. mas@id.state.id.us. RV/tent: 48. $12–$16. Hookups: electric (30, 50 amps), water, sewer.

Willow Bay Recreation Area, 550 North Oregon Trail, 83211. T: (208) 226-2688. F: (208) 226-2548. RV/tent: 26. $11–$18. Hookups: electric (30 amps), water, sewer.

Arco

Landing Zone RV Park, 2424 No. 3000 West, 83213. T: (877) 563-0663. www.geocities.com/landingzone_2000. lzrvpark@ida.net. RV/tent: 37. $13–$16. Hookups: electric (30 amps), water, sewer, modem.

Mountain View RV Park, P.O. Box 284, 83213. T: (800) 845-1460 or (208) 527-3707. mtview@atcnet.net. RV/tent: 40. $15–$17. Hookups: electric (20, 30 amps), water, sewer, modem.

Ashton

Jessen's RV Park, Box 11, 83420. T: (800) 747-3356 or (208) 652-3356. RV/tent: 55. $15–$17. Hookups: electric (30 amps), water, sewer, modem.

Boise

Americana RV Park, 3600 Americana Ter., 83706. T: (208) 344-5733. www.americanarvpark.com. ak83706@cyberHwy.net. RV/tent: 107. $18. Hookups: electric (30, 50 amps), water, sewer, modem.

Fiesta RV Park, 11101 Fairview Ave., 83713. T: (888) 784-3246 or (208) 375-8207. F: (208) 322-2499. fiestarv@earthlink.net. RV/tent: 109. $23–$29. Hookups: electric (20, 30 amps), water, sewer, modem.

Hi Valley RV Park, 10555 Horshoe Bend Rd., 83703. T: (888) 457-5959 or (208) 939-8080. www.idahoheartland.net. RV/tent: 194. $23. Hookups: electric (30, 50 amps), water, sewer, cable, phone.

On The River RV Park, 6000 North Glenwood, 83714. T: (800) 375-7432. otrrvpark@internetoutlet.net. RV/tent: 223. $15–$22. Hookups: electric (30, 50 amps), water, sewer, cable, modem.

Bonners Ferry

Blue Lake Camp & RV Park, HCR 61 Box 277, 83847. T: (208) 267-2029. RV/tent: 55. $17–$20. Hookups: electric (20, 30 amps), water, sewer.

Deep Creek Resort, Rte. 4 Box 628, 83805. T: (800) 689-2729 or (208) 267-2729. RV/tent: 52. $9–$13. Hookups: electric, water, sewer.

Idyl Acres RV Park, HCR 61 Box 170, 83805. T: (208) 267-3629. RV/tent: 10. $15. Hookups: electric (20, 30 amps), water, sewer.

Caldwell

Caldwell Campground, 218 Town Cir., 83606. T: (888) 675-0279 or (208) 454-0279. RV/tent: 125. $17–$20. Hookups: electric (30, 50 amps), water, sewer, cable, modem.

Country Corners Campground, 17671 Oasis Rd., 83607. T: (208) 453-8791. www.rvers choice.com/id/countrycornersrv.park. RV/tent: 69. $18. Hookups: electric (30, 50 amps), water, sewer, cable, modem.

Challis

Challis Hot Springs Campground, HC Box 1779, 83226. T: (208) 879-4442. RV/tent: 36. $20. Hookups: electric (30 amps), water, modem.

Challis Valley RV Park, Box 928, 83226. T: (208) 879-2393. RV/tent: 48. $20. Hookups: electric (30, 50 amps), water, sewer, cable.

Clark Fork

River Delta Resort, 60190 Hwy. 200, 83811. T: (208) 266-1335. RV/tent: 57. $18. Hookups: electric (30, 50 amps), water, sewer.

River Lake RV Park, 145 North River Lake Rd., 83811. T: (208) 266-1115. RV/tent: 25. $16. Hookups: electric (30 amps), water, sewer.

Clayton

Torrey's Burnt Creek Inn, HC 67 Box 725, 83227. T: (208) 836-2313. RV/tent: 27. $15. Hookups: electric (30, 50 amps), water, sewer.

Cocolalla

Sandy Beach Resort, 4405 Loop Rd., 83813. T: (208) 263-4328. F: (208) 263-3253. RV/tent: 90. $16–$20. Hookups: electric, water, sewer.

Coeur d'Alene

Bambi RV Park, 3113 North Government Way, 83815. T: (877) 381-5534 or (208) 664-6527. RV/tent: 21. $16. Hookups: electric, water, sewer.

IDAHO (continued)

Blackwell Island RV Park, 800 South Marina Dr., 83814. T: (888) 571-2900 or (208) 665-1300. F: (208) 667-5853. www.idahorvpark.com. rvpark@ior.com. RV/tent: 122. $21–$30. Hookups: electric (20, 30, 50 amps), water, sewer, cable, modem.

River Walk RV Park, 1214 Mill Ave., 83814. T: (888) 567-8700 or (208) 765-6538. riverparkrvpark@yahoo.com. RV/tent: 42. $22–$26. Hookups: electric (30, 50 amps), water, sewer, cable, modem.

Robin Hood Campground & RV Park, 703 Lincoln Way, 83814. T: (208) 664-2306. RV/tent: 80. $19–$20. Hookups: electric (20, 30, 50 amps).

Shady Acres RV Park, 3630 North Government Way, 83814. T: (877) 212-0523 or (206) 664-3087. www.angelfire.com/id2/shadyacresrv. shadyacresrv@yahoo.com. RV/tent: 30. $17. Hookups: electric, water, sewer.

Squaw Bay Camping Resort, P.O. Box 174, 83816. T: (208) 664-6782. F: (208) 664-6728. RV/tent: 50. $15–$28. Hookups: electric, water, sewer, cable, modem.

Wolf Lodge Campground, 12425 East Interstate 90, 83814. T: (208) 664-2812. RV/tent: 100. $13–$23. Hookups: electric, water, sewer, cable, modem.

Declo

Travel Stop 216 RV Park, Exit 216 Interstate 84, 83323. T: (208) 654-2133. F: (208) 887-3525. www.travelstop216.com. manager@travelstop216.com. RV/tent: 165. $25. Hookups: electric (30, 50 amps), water, sewer, cable.

Donnelly

Chalet RV Resort, P.O. Box 100, 83615. T: (888) 457-5959 or (208) 325-8223. RV/tent: 76. $19. Hookups: electric (30 amps), water, sewer.

Mountain View RV Park, P.O. Box 488, 83615. T: (208) 325-8373. RV/tent: 40. $15-plus. Hookups: electric, water, sewer.

Southwestern Idaho Senior Citizens Recreation Association, P.O. Box 625, 83615. T: (208) 325-9518. RV/tent: 175. $3–$5. Hookups: electric, water, sewer.

Downey

Downata Hot Springs, 25900 Downata Rd., 83234. T: (208) 897-5736. F: (208) 897-5072. www.downatahotsprings.com. downata@poky.srv.net. RV/tent: 90. $16. Hookups: electric (20, 30 amps), water, modem.

Eden

Anderson Best Holiday Trav-L-Park, 1188 East 990 South, 83325. T: (888) 480-9400 or (208) 825-9800. F: (208) 825-9715. andercamo@cyberHwy.net. RV/tent: 155. $19–$24. Hookups: electric (30, 50 amps), water, sewer, modem.

Fruitland

Neet Retreat RV Park, 2701 Alder Space, 83619. T: (800) 433-7806 or (208) 452-4324. RV/tent: 80. $20. Hookups: electric (30, 50 amps), water, sewer, cable, modem.

Glenns Ferry

Trails West RV Park, 510 North Bannock Ave., 83623. T: (208) 366-2002. RV/tent: 52. $10–$15. Hookups: electric, water, sewer, cable.

Grangeville

Mountain View RV Park, 127 Cunningham St. No. 4, 83530. T: (208) 983-2328. RV/tent: 75. $15. Hookups: electric (15, 30, 50 amps), water, sewer.

Hagerman

Hagerman RV Village, P.O. Box 297, 83332. T: (208) 837-4906 or (208) 837-4412. F: (208) 837-4551. RV/tent: 54. $17. Hookups: electric (30, 50 amps), water, sewer, modem.

Harvard

Pines RV Park & Campground, 4510 Hwy. 6, 83834. T: (208) 875-0831. RV/tent: 17. $12. Hookups: electric (15, 30 amps).

Hayden Lake

Coeur D'Alene North/Hayden Lake KOA, 4850 East Garwood Rd., 83825. T: (800) KOA-0250 or (208) 772-4557. RV/tent: 66. $16–$20. Hookups: electric (30 amps), water, sewer, modem.

Heise

Heise Hot Springs, 5116 Heise Rd. East, 83443. T: (208) 538-7312. www.srv.net/~heise/heise.html. heise@srv.net. RV/tent: 50. $15–$20. Hookups: electric, water, sewer.

Homedale

Snake River RV Resort, Rte. 1 Box 1062, 83628. T: (208) 337-3744. rvresort@cyberHwy.net. RV/tent: 52. $20. Hookups: electric (30, 50 amps), water, sewer, modem.

Hope

Beyond Hope Resort, 248 Beyond Hope, 83836. T: (877) 270-HOPE or (208) 264-5251. www.beyondhoperesort.com. bhresort@aol.com. RV/tent: 91. $24–$26. Hookups: electric (30, 50 amps), water, sewer, cable, modem.

Idaho Country Resort, 141 Idaho Country Rd., 83836. T: (800) (307) 3050 or (208) 264-5505. www.keokee.com/edahoresorts. RV/tent: 90. $15–$31. Hookups: electric (30 amps), water, sewer, cable.

Sam Owen Campground, Idaho Panhandle National Forest, 83836. T: 877-444-6777 or (208) 264-0209. www.reserveusa.com. claudia@americanll.com. RV/tent: 80. $12. Hookups: none.

Idaho Falls

Idaho Falls KOA, 1440 Lindsey Blvd., 83402. T: (800) 562-7644 or (208) 523-3362. RV/tent: 183. $24–$30. Hookups: electric (30 amps), water, sewer, modem.

Sunnyside Acres Park, 905 West Sunnyside Rd., 83401. T: (208) 523-8403. RV/tent: 25. $20. Hookups: electric (30, 50 amps), water, sewer.

Island Park

Aspen Lodge, HC 66 Box 269, 83429. T: (208) 558-7406. RV/tent: 8. $39. Hookups: electric, water, sewer.

Big Springs (Caribou National Forest), Big Springs Loop Rd., 83429. T: (208) 558-7301. RV/tent: 29. $7–$16. Hookups: none.

Red Rock RV & Camping Park, HC 66 Box 256, 83429. T: (800) 473-3762 or (208) 558-7442. www.8004redrock.com/.reservations@8004redrock.com. RV/tent: 52. $14–$16. Hookups: electric (20, 30 amps), water, sewer, modem.

Snowy River Campground, 3502 North Hwy. 20, 83429. T: (208) 558-7112 or (888) 797-3434. marleen@ida.net. RV/tent: 57. $15–$16. Hookups: electric (20, 30 amps), water, sewer, modem.

Valley View General Store & RV Park, HC 66 Box 26, 83429. T: (208) 558-7443. RV/tent: 53. $10–$20. Hookups: electric, water, sewer.

Jerome

Twin Falls/Jerone KOA, 5431 US 93, 83338. T: (800) 562-4169 or (208) 324-4169. RV/tent: 91. $24–$25. Hookups: electric (30, 50 amps), water, sewer, satelite, modem.

Kamiah

Lewis-Clark Resort, Rte. 1 Box 17X, 83536. T: (208) 935-2556. www.tenting-hostels.com/tvc. lcresort@camasnet.com. RV/tent: 190. $18. Hookups: electric (30 amps), water, sewer, modem.

Ketchum

The Meadows RV Park, P.O. Box 1440, 83353. T: (208) 726-5445. RV/tent: 45. $18. Hookups: electric (30 amps), water, sewer, cable.

Sun Valley RV Resort, P.O. Box 548, 83340. T: (208) 726-3429. RV/tent: 80. $19–$27. Hookups: electric, water, sewer, cable, modem.

Kooskia

Harpster Riverside RV Park, HC 66 Box 337, 83539. T: (800) 983-1918. RV/tent: 29. $18. Hookups: electric (30, 50 amps), water, sewer, satelite, modem.

River Junction RV Park, P.O. Box 413, 83539. T: (208) 926-7865. RV/tent: 29. $6–$14. Hookups: electric, water, sewer.

Lava Hot Springs

Cottonwood Family Campground, Box 307, 83246. T: (208) 776-5295. RV/tent: 116. $24–$27. Hookups: electric (20, 30 amps), water, sewer.

Lucille

Prospector's Gold RV & Campground, P.O. Box 313, 83542. T: (208) 628-3773. RV/tent: 24. $15. Hookups: electric (30, 50 amps), water, modem.

IDAHO (continued)

McCall

Lakeview Village RV Park, 8 Pearl St., 83638. T: (208) 634-5280. RV/tent: 84. $12–$16. Hookups: electric (30 amps), water, sewer.

McCall Campground, 190 Krahn Ln., 83638. T: (208) 634-5165. RV/tent: 36. $14–$16. Hookups: electric, water, sewer.

Melba

Given's Hot Springs, HC 79 Box 103, 83641. T: (800) 874-6046 or (208) 495-2000. F: (208) 286-0925. RV/tent: 18. $8–$13. Hookups: electric, water, sewer.

Meridian

The Playground RV Park, 1780 East Overland Rd., 83642. T: (800) 668-PLAY or (208) 887-1022. playgroundrv@juno.com. RV/tent: 72. $20. Hookups: electric (30 amps), water, sewer, satellite, modem.

Montpelier

Emigration (Caribou National Forest), 322 North 4th, 83254. T: (877) 444-6777 or (208) 847-0375. RV/tent: 23. $8–$16. Hookups: none.

Montpelier Canyon (Caribou National Forest), 322 North 4th, 83254. T: (877) 444-6777 or (208) 847-0375. RV/tent: 14. $4. Hookups: none.

Scout Mountain (Caribou National Forest/Pocatello), 322 North 4th, 83254. T: (877) 444-6777 or (208) 236-7500. RV/tent: 32. $6–$18. Hookups: none.

Summit View (Caribou National Forest/Intermountain), 322 North 4th, 83254. T: (877) 444-6777 or (208) 847-0375. RV/tent: 19. $8. Hookups: none.

Willow Flat (Caribou National Forest/Preston), 322 North 4th, 83254. T: (877) 444-6777 or (208) 847-0375. RV/tent: 47. $4–$20. Hookups: none.

Moyle Springs

Herman Lake Campground, HCR 62 Box 246, 83845. T: (208) 267-1205. RV/tent: 10. $10–$25. Hookups: electric, water, sewer.

Twin Rivers Canyon Resort, HCR 62 Box 25, 83845. T: (208) 267-5932. RV/tent: 65. $13–$19. Hookups: electric, water, sewer.

Nampa

Garrity RV Park, 3515 Garrity Blvd., 83687. T: (877) 442-9090 or (208) 442-9000. F: (208) 442-1617. RV/tent: 98. $18–$20. Hookups: electric (30, 50 amps), water, sewer, cable, phone.

Mason Creek RV Park, 807 Franklin Blvd., 83687. T: (208) 465-7199. RV/tent: 88. $14–$19. Hookups: electric (30, 50 amps), water, sewer, cable, modem.

New Meadows

Meadows RV Park, P.O. Box 60, 83654. T: (208) 347-2325 or (800) 603-2325. RV/tent: 37. $17. Hookups: electric (30 amps), water, sewer, modem.

Zim's Hot Springs, P.O. Box 314, 83654. T: (208) 347-2686. RV/tent: 62. $10–$16. Hookups: electric (30 amps), water.

Nordman

Kaniksu Resort, HCO 1 Box 152, 83848. T: (208) 443-2121. F: (208) 443-3864. kaniksu@nidlink.com. RV/tent: 111. $18–$24. Hookups: electric (30, 50 amps), water, sewer.

North Fork

Wagonhammer Springs Campground, P.O. Box 173, 83466. T: (208) 865-2477. RV/tent: 28. $15–$17. Hookups: electric (20, 30 amps), water, sewer.

Obsidian

Sessions Lodge, HC 64 Box 9696, 83340. T: (208) 774-3366. RV/tent: 13. $12. Hookups: electric (30 amps), water, sewer.

Orofino

Freeman Creek Campground (Dworshak SP), P.O. Box 2028, 83544. T: (208) 476-5994. RV/tent: 108. $12–$16. Hookups: electric (20, 30 amps), water.

Osburn

Blue Anchor Trailer & RV Park, P.O. Box 645, 83849. T: (208) 752-3443. RV/tent: 38. $14–$20. Hookups: electric (30, 50 amps), water, sewer, cable.

Paris

Bear Lake State Park, P.O. Box 297, 83261. T: (208) 847-1045. F: (208) 847-1056. BEA@idpr.state.id/us. RV/tent: 100. 8–$16. Hookups: none.

Pinehurst

KOA Kellogg/Silver Valley Kampground, P.O. Box 949, 83850. T: (800) 562-0799. F: (208) 682-9464. kelloggkoa@aol.com. RV/tent: 57. $20–$29. Hookups: electric (20, 30, 50 amps), water, sewer, cable, modem.

Pocatello

Cowboy RV Park, 845 Barton Rd., 83204. T: (208) 232-4587. F: (208) 232-6731. RV/tent: 41. $22. Hookups: electric (30, 50 amps), water, sewer, cable, modem.

Post Falls

Suntree RV Park, 401 Idahine, 83854. T: (208) 773-9982. suntree@micron.net. RV/tent: 81. $23. Hookups: electric (30 amps), water, sewer, modem.

Priest Lake

Priest Lake RV Resort & Marina, HCR 5 Box 172, 83856. T: (208) 443-2405. F: (208) 443-2299. RV/tent: 16. $10–$13. Hookups: electric, water, sewer.

Priest River

Luby Bay (Idaho Panhandle National Forest), 5538 West Lakeshore Rd., 83856. T: (800) 280-2267 or (208) 443-1801. www.reserveusa.com. RV/tent: 50. $12. Hookups: none.

Rexburg

Rainbow Lake & Campground, 2245 South 2000 West, 83440. T: (208) 356-3681. RV/tent: 85. $15–$17. Hookups: electric (30 amps), water, sewer, modem.

Sheffield RV Park, 5362 South Hwy. 191, 83440. T: (208) 356-4182. sheffieldbb@msn.com. RV/tent: 27. $18. Hookups: electric (30, 50 amps), water, sewer, modem.

Ririe

7N Ranch, 5156 East Heise Rd., 83443. T: (208) 538-5097. RV/tent: 50. $12–$17. Hookups: electric (20, 30, 50 amps), water.

Mountain River Ranch RV Park, 98 North 5050 East, 83443. T: (208) 538-7337. RV/tent: 39. $17. Hookups: electric (30 amps), water.

Rogerson

Desert Hot Springs, General Delivery, 83302. T: (208) 857-2233. RV/tent: 12. $10–$15. Hookups: electric, water, sewer.

Sagle

Alpine Trailer Park, P.O. Box 585, 83860. T: (208) 265-0179. RV/tent: 15. $15. Hookups: electric, water, sewer.

Salmon

Century II Campground, 603 Hwy. 93 North, 83467. T: (208) 756-3063. RV/tent: 76. $17. Hookups: electric (30, 50 amps), water, sewer.

Heald's Haven, HC 61 Box 15, 83467. T: (208) 756-3929. RV/tent: 34. $12–$15. Hookups: electric (20, 30 amps), water.

Salmon Meadows

Salmon Meadows Campground, Rte. 1 Box 25AB, 83467. T: (888) 723-2640 or (208) 756-2640. F: (208) 756-3771. smeadows@ida.net. RV/tent: 71. $20. Hookups: electric (30, 50 amps), water, sewer, modem.

Sandpoint

Travel America Plaza, P.O. Box 199, 83860. T: (208) 263-6522. RV/tent: 79. $14–$15. Hookups: electric (20, 30, 50 amps), water, sewer, modem.

Spirit Lake

Silver Beach Resort, 8350 West Spirit Lake Rd., 83869. T: (208) 623-4842. www.silverbeach-resort.com. info@silver-beach-resort.com. RV/tent: 40. $17–$20. Hookups: electric, water, sewer.

St. Anthony

Riverside Campground (Targhee National Forest), P.O. Box 208, 83445. T: (208) 652-7442. RV/tent: 63. $8–$10. Hookups: none.

St. Charles

Bear Lake North RV Park & Campgrounds, P.O. Box 60, 83201. T: (208) 945-2941. brite_83272@yahoo.com. RV/tent: 66. $18. Hookups: electric (20, 30 amps), water.

IDAHO (continued)

Cedars & Shade Campground, P.O. Box 219, 83272. T: (208) 945-2608. RV/tent: 100. $8–$12. Hookups: none.

Twin Falls

Nat-Soo-Pah Hot Springs, 3738 East 2400 North, 83301. T: (208) 655-4337. RV/tent: 75. $12. Hookups: electric (30 amps), water.

Oregon Trail Campground & Family Fun Center, 2733 Kimberly Rd., 83301. T: (800) 733-0853 or (208) 733-0853. RV/tent: 50. $15. Hookups: electric, water, sewer.

Victor

Teton Valley Campground, 128 Hwy. 31 or P.O. Box 49, 83455. T: (877) 787-3036 or (208) 787-2647. F: (208) 787-3036. www.tentinghostels.com/tve. tvcampground@pdt.net. RV/tent: 70. $20–$31. Hookups: electric (20, 30, 50 amps), water, sewer, modem.

Wallace

Down by the Depot RV Park, 108 Nine Mile Rd., 83873. T: (208) 753-7121. RV/tent: 43. $20–$22. Hookups: electric (30 amps), water, sewer, cable.

Weiser

Gateway RV Park, 229 East 7th St., 83672. T: (208) 549-2539. RV/tent: 24. $14–$18. Hookups: electric (20, 30 amps), water, sewer, cable.

Monroe Creek Campground & RV Park, 822 US Hwy. 95, 83672. T: (208) 549-2026. mccrvpark@rurainetwork.net. RV/tent: 66. $18. Hookups: electric (30 amps), water, modem.

Wendell

Intermountain RV Park, 1894 North Frontage Rd., 83355. T: (208) 536-2301. mike@idahorv.com. RV/tent: 55. $12. Hookups: electric (20, 30 amps), water, modem.

Wilder

Rivers Edge RV Park, 28522 Lower Pleasant Rd., 83676. T: (208) 482-6560. www.riversedgervpark.com. riverrv@riversedgervpark.com. RV/tent: 24. $13. Hookups: electric (30, 50 amps), water, sewer.

ILLINOIS

Algonquin

Buffalo Park, 4 Alan Dr., 60102. T: (847) 658-9640. RV/tent: 170. $15. Hookups: water, electric (30 amps).

Amboy

Mendota Hills Resort, 642 US 52, 61310. T: (815) 849-5930. F: (815) 849-9037. RV/tent: 198. $30. Hookups: water, electric (30, 50 amps) sewer, phone.

Arcola

Arcola Camper Stop, 472 Davis St., 61910. T: (217) 268-4616. RV/tent: 30. $14. Hookups: water, electric (20, 30 amps), sewer, cable TV.

Campalot, 55 Industrial Dr., 61910. T: (217) 268-3563. RV/tent: 10. $15. Hookups: water, electric (20, 30, 50 amps), sewer.

Atlanta

Hickory Lane Camping, RR 2, 61723. T: (217) 648-2778. RV/tent: 178. $15. Hookups: water, electric (20, 30, 50 amps), sewer.

Barstow

Lundeen's Landing (East Moline), P.O. Box 182, 61236. T: (309) 496-9956. RV/tent: 68. $15. Hookups: water, electric (30 amps).

Belvidere

Holiday Acres, 7050 Epworth Rd., 61038. T: (815) 547-7846. RV/tent: 520. $25. Hookups: water, electric (20, 30 amps).

Outdoor World-Pine Country Campground, 5710 Shattuck Rd., 61008. T: (800) 222-5557. F: (815) 544-8019. www.campoutdoor.com. RV/tent: 107. $15. Hookups: water, electric (30 amps), sewer.

Benton

Gun Creek Recreation Area, 12220 Rend City Rd., 62812. T: (618) 724-2493. RV/tent: 100. $18. Hookups: electric (20, 30, 50 amps).

North Sandusky Creek Recreation Area, State Rd. 154, 62812. T: (618) 625-6115. RV/tent: 141. $18. Hookups: water, electric (30 amps), sewer.

South Marcum Recreation Area, 11623 Trail Head Ln., 62812. T: (618) 435-3549. RV/tent: 143. $14. Hookups: electric (50 amps).

South Sandusky Creek Recreation Area, Red Oak Ln., 62812. T: (618) 625-3011. RV/tent: 121. $18. Hookups: water, electric (50 amps), sewer.

Biggsville

Hend-CoHills, Rte. 34, 61418. T: (309) 627-2779. RV/tent: 34. $15. Hookups: water, electric (20, 30 amps), sewer.

Bourbonnais

Kankakee River State Park, 5314 West Rte. 102, 60914. T: (815) 933-1383. F: (815) 933-9809. RV/tent: 250. $15. Hookups: Electric (30 amps).

Bushnell

Timberview Lakes Campground, 23200 North 2000 Rd., 61422. T: (309) 772-3609. F: (309) 772- 3609. timberviewlakes@aol.com, www.timberviewlakes.com. RV/tent: 108. $18. Hookups: water, electric (20, 30, 50 amps), sewer, phone.

Byron

Lake Louise, 8840 Rte. 2, 61010. T: (815) 234-8483. F: (815) 234-2503. www.lakelouise.com. RV/tent: 317. $28. Hookups: water, electric (20, 30, 50 amps), sewer.

Cahokia

Cahokia RV Parque, 4060 Mississippi Ave., 62206. T: (618) 332-7700. cahokiarv@aol.com. RV/tent: 116. $25. Hookups: water, electric (30, 50 amps), sewer.

Cambridge

Gibson's RV Park and Campground, 10768 East 1600 St., 61238. T: (309) 937-2314. gibsonscmp@msn.com, www.hometown.aol.com/gibsoncmp. RV/tent: 190. $17. Hookups: water, electric (20, 30 amps).

Carbondale

Crab Orchard Lake Campground, 10067 Campground Dr., 62901. T: (618) 997-3344. RV/tent: 250. $12. Hookups: water, electric (20, 30 amps).

Little Grassy Campground and Boatdock, 788 Hidden Bay, 62958. T: (618) 457-6655. RV/tent: 152. $10. Hookups: water, electric (30 amps), sewer.

Carlyle

Cole's Creek Recreation Area (Boulder), 16225 Coles Creek Rd., 62231. T: (618) 226-3211. RV/tent: 148. $15. Hookups: water, electric (30, 50 amps), sewer.

Dam West Recreation Area, 801 Lake Rd., 62231. T: (618) 594-4410. RV/tent: 113. $20. Hookups: electric (30 amps).

Eldon Hazlet State Park, 20100 Hazlet Park Rd., 62231. T: (618) 594-3015. RV/tent: 363. $20. Hookups: electric (30, 50 amps).

McNair Campground, 801 Lake Rd., 62231. T: (618) 594-2484. RV/tent: 25. $20. Hookups: water, electric (30 amps).

Carmi

Burrell Park Campground, Sixth & Stewart Sts, 62821. T: (618) 382-2693. RV/tent: 25. $18. Hookups: water, electric (30 amps), sewer.

Champaign

D & W Camping and Fishing Lake, 411 West Hensley Rd., 61821. T: (217) 356-3732. RV/tent: 60. $15. Hookups: water, electric (20, 30, 50 amps), sewer.

Clayton

Siloam State Park, RR 1 Box 204, 62324. T: (217) 894-6205. RV/tent: 230. $11. Hookups: electric (30 amps).

ILLINOIS (continued)

Clinton

Weldon Springs State Park, RR 2 Box 87, 61727. T: (217) 935-2644. RV/tent: 98. $11. Hookups: electric (30 amps).

Crete

Emerald Trails Campground, 3132 East Goodnow Rd., 60417. T: (800) 870-8357. RV/tent: 94. $25. Hookups: water, electric (30 amps), sewer.

Danville

Kickapoo State Park, 10906 Kickapoo Park Rd., 61858. T: (217) 442-4915. RV/tent: 201. $11. Hookups: electric (30 amps).

De Witt

Clinton Lake-Mascoutin State Recreation Complex, R. R. 1 Box 4, 61735. T: (217) 935-8722. RV/tent: 308. $11. Hookups: Electric (20, 30, 50 amps).

Durand

Sugar Shores Camping Resort, 9938 West Winslow Rd., 61024. T: (815) 629-2568. RV/tent: 90. $17. Hookups: water, electric (20, 30, 50 amps), phone.

East St. Louis

Casino Queen RV Park, 200 South Front St., 62201. T: (618) 874-5000. www.casinoqueen.com. RV/tent: 90. $15. Hookups: water, electric (50 amps), cable TV, Internet.

Edwardsville

Red Barn Rendezvous, 3955 Blackburn Rd., 62025. T: (618) 692-9015. RV/tent: 45. $18. Hookups: water, electric (20, 30, 50 amps), sewer.

Effingham

Lake Sara Campground and Beach, 70 Wildwood Dr., 62401. T: (217) 868-2964. RV/tent: 315. $20. Hookups: water, electric (20, 30 amps), sewer.

Fithian

Five Bridges Campground, State Hwy. 49 North, 61844. T: (217) 583-3200. RV/tent: 37. $20. Hookups: water, electric (30 amps).

Gages Lake

Gages Lake Camping, 18887 West Gages Lake Rd., 60030. T: (847) 223-5541. F: (847) 223-5564. RV/tent: 100. $29. Hookups: water, electric (30 amps).

Garden Prairie

Paradise Park, 11122 Station St., 61038. T: (815) 597-1671. www.paradiservpark.com. RV/tent: 170. $25. Hookups: water, electric (15, 20, 30, 50 amps).

Genesco

Geneseo Campground, 22978 Illinois Hwy. 82, 61254. T: (309) 944-6465. w6465@geneseo.net; www.fultiming-america.com/genesco. RV/tent: 63. $16. Hookups:water, electric (20, 30, 50 amps), sewer, phone, Internet.

Spirit in the Oaks, 27340 East 1350 St., 61254. T: (309) 944-3889. RV/tent: 90. $22. Hookups: water, electric (20, 30, 50 amps), sewer.

Glenarm

Holiday RV Center & Trav-L-Park, 9683 Palm Rd., 62629. T: (219) 483-9998. RV/tent: 110. $18. Hookups: water, electric (50 amps), sewer.

Golconda

Dixon Springs State Park (Dixon), RR 2, 62938. T: (618) 949-3394. RV/tent: 50. $10. Hookups: electric (30 amps).

Goreville

Ferne Clyffe State Park, P.O. Box 10, 62939. T: (618) 995-2411. RV/tent: 65. $11. Hookups: electric (30 amps).

Hilltop Campgrounds, 255 Baker Ln., 62939. T: (618) 995-2189. RV/tent: 52. $16. Hookups: water, electric (30, 50 amps), sewer.

Grafton

Pere Marquette State Park, P.O. Box 158, 62037. T: (618) 786-3323. RV/tent: 117. $11. Hookups: electric (30 amps).

Havana

Evening Star Camping Resort, 16474 Walker Rd., 61567. T: (309) 562-7590. estar@casscomm.com. RV/tent: 403. $15. Hookups: water, electric (20, 30, 50 amps), sewer.

Havana Park District Riverfront Park Campground, South Schrader Ave., 62644. T: (309) 543-6240. RV/tent: 12. $12. Hookups: water, electric (30 amps).

Ina

Sherwood Camping Resort, 411 Main St., 62846. T: (618) 437-5530. RV/tent: 81. $15. Hookups: water, electric (30 amps), sewer.

Joliet

Martin Campground, 725 Cherry Hill Rd., 60433. T: (815) 726-3173. RV/tent: 110. $25. Hookups: water, electric (20, 30 amps) sewer.

Le Roy

Moraine View State Park, R. R. 2, 61752. T: (309) 724-8032. F: (309) 724-8039. RV/tent: 199. $15. Hookups: electric (30 amps).

Leland

Hi-Tide Recreation, 4611 East 22nd Rd., 60531. T: (815) 495-9032. RV/tent: 33. $23. Hookups: water, electric (20, 30, 50 amps), sewer, phone.

Lincoln

Camp-A-While, 1779 1250 Ave., 62656. T: (888) 593-5102. camp-a-while@yahoo.com. RV/tent: 27. $16. Hookups: water, electric (20, 30, 50 amps), sewer.

Litchfield

Kamper Kompanion Campground, 18388 East Frontage Rd., 62056. T: (217) 324-4747. RV/tent: 24. $15. Hookups: water, electric (20, 30 amp), sewer.

Mackinaw

Kentuckiana Campground (Hopedale), 27585 Kentuckiana Rd., 61755. T: (309) 449-3274. RV/tent: 330. $17. Hookups: water, electric (20, 30, 50 amps), sewer.

Makanda

Giant City State Park, 235 Grant City Rd., 62958. T: (618) 457-4836. RV/tent: 99. $7. Hookups: electric (20, 30, 50 amps).

Marengo

Best Holiday Lehman's Lakeside RV Resort, 19609 Harmony Rd., 60152. T: (877) 242-8533. RV/tent: 290. $30. Hookups: water, electric (20, 30, 50 amps), sewer, cable TV, phone.

Marion

Motel Marion Campground, 2100 West Main St., 62959. T: (618) 993-2101. RV/tent: 25. $15. Hookups: water, electric (30, 50 amps), sewer.

Marseilles

Illini State Park, 2660 East 2350th Rd., 61341. T: (815) 795-2448. RV/tent: 102. $15. Hookups: electric (30 amps).

Whispering Pines Campground, 2776 East 2625 Rd., 61341. T: (815) 795-5720. RV/tent: 400. $20. Hookups: water, electric (15, 20, 30, 50 amps), sewer.

Marshall

Mill Creek Park Campground, 20482 North Park Rd. Entrance, 62441. T: (217) 889-3601. F: (217) 889-3601. RV/tent: 139. $15. Hookups: electric (20, 30 amps).

Mendon

Whispering Oaks Campground, 2124 East 1300th Place, 62351. T: (217) 936-2500. RV/tent: 197. $15. Hookups: water, electric (30 amps).

Millbrook

Yogi Bear Jellystone Camp-Resort Chicago-Millbrook, 8574 Millbrook Rd., 60536. T: (800) 438-9644. www.jellystonechicago.com. RV/tent: 356. $37. Hookups: water, electric (20, 30, 50 amps), sewer.

ILLINOIS (continued)

Miller City
Horseshoe Lake State Conservation Area (Cairo), P.O. Box 85, 62962. T: (618) 776-5689. RV/tent: 178. $11. Hookups: electric (30 amps).

Mt. Vernon
Quality Times, 9746 East IL Hwy. 15, 62864. T: (618) 244-0399. F: (618) 244-7422. RV/tent: 43. $17. Hookups: water, electric (20, 30 amps), sewer, phone.

Murphysboro
Lake Murphysboro State Park, 52 Cinda Hill Dr., 62966. T: (618) 684-2867. RV/tent: 74. $11. Hookups: electric (50 amps).

Nauvoo
Nauvoo Campground, 2205 Mulholland St., 62354. T: (217) 453-2263. F: (217) 453-2253. Ajbate@aol.com. RV/tent: 28. $15. Hookups: water, electric (20, 30, 50 amps), sewer.

New Windsor
Shady Lakes Camping & Recreation, 3355 75th Ave., 61465. T: (309) 667-2709. F: (309) 667-2809. shadylak@winco.net; www.web.winco.net/~shadylak. RV/tent: 253. $16. Hookups: water, electric (20, 30, 50 amps).

Oakland
Hebron Hills Camping, 14349 North City Rd. 2350 E, 61943. T: (217) 346-3385. www.HebronHills.com. RV/tent: 55. $16. Hookups: water, electric (20, 30, 50 amps), sewer, phone.

Onarga
Lake Arrowhead, Frontage Rd. North, 60955. T: (815) 268-4849. RV/tent: 61. $15. Hookups: water, electric (30 amps).

Oquawka
Delabar State Park, R. R. 2, 91469. T: (309) 867-3671. RV/tent: 124. $8. Hookups: electric (30 amps).

Oregon
Hansen's Hide Away Ranch & Family Campground, 2936 Harmony Rd., 61061. T: (815) 732-6489. RV/tent: 102. $16. Hookups: water, electric (20, 30 amps), sewer.

Pearl City
Emerald Acres Campground, 33351 South Mill Grove Rd., 61062. T: (815) 443-2550. RV/tent: 60. $22. Hookups: water, electric (30 amps).

Peoria
Mt. Hawley RV Park, 8327 North Knoxville Ave., 61615. T: (309) 692-2223. RV/tent: 90. $20. Hookups: water, electric (30, 50 amps), sewer.

Plainview
Beaver Dam State Park, 14548 Beaver Dam Ln., 62676. T: (217) 854-8020. RV/tent: 84. $11. Hookups: electric (30 amps).

Rochester
KOA Springfield (Springfield), 4320 KOA Rd., 62563. T: (800) 562-7212. RV/tent: 96. $20. Hookups: water, electric (20, 30 amps), sewer, phone.

Rock
Cave-In-Rock State Park, New State Park Rd., 62919. T: (618) 289-4325. F: (618) 289-4315. RV/tent: 48. $10. Hookups: electric (30 amps).

Rock Falls
Leisure Lake Campground, 2304 French St., 61071. T: (815) 626-0005. RV/tent: 68. $16. Hookups: water, electric (20, 30 amps), sewer, phone.

Rock Island
Camelot Campground & Recreation, 2311 78 Ave. West, 61201. T: (309) 787-0665. F: (309) 787-1320. RV/tent: 158. $17. Hookups: water, electric (30, 50 amps), sewer, phone.

Rockford
Blackhawk Valley Campground, 6540 Valley Trail Rd., 61109. T: (815) 874-9767. RV/tent: 170. $20. Hookups: water, electric (30 amps), sewer.

Salem
Stephen A. Forbes State Park, 4577 Rte. 84N, 61074. T: (618) 547-33381. RV/tent: 146. $11. Hookups: electric (30 amps).

Shelbyville
Bo Wood Recreation Area, R. R. 4, 62565. T: (217) 774-2014. RV/tent: 82. $14. Hookups: electric (30 amps).

Sheridan
Mallard Bend Campground & RV Park, 2838 North 4351st St., 60551. T: (815) 496-2496. F: (630) 964-6487. www.mallardbend.com. RV/tent: 168. $25. Hookups: water, electric (20, 30, 50 amps), sewer.

Sheridan
Rolling Oaks Campground, 2743 North4251 1st Rd., 60551. T: (815) 496-2334. RV/tent: 670. $17. Hookups: water, electric (20, 30 amps), sewer.

Spring Grove
Chain O'Lakes State Park, Oak Point (Fox Lake), 8916 Wilmot Rd., 60081. T: (847) 587-5512. RV/tent: 206. $11. Hookups: electric (30 amps).

St. Elmo
Bell's Timberline Lake Campground, P. O. Box 15, 62458. T: (618) 829-3383. RV/tent: 100. $14. Hookups: water, electric (30 amps), sewer.

Sumner
Red Hills Lake State Park (Lawrencville), R. R. 2, 62466. T: (618) 936-2469. RV/tent: 247. $11. Hookups: electric (20, 30 amps).

Tinley Park
Windy City Campground & Beach, 18701 South 80th Ave., 60477. T: (708) 720-0030. F: (708) 720-0431. RV/tent: 100. $25. Hookups: water, electric (20, 30, 50s), sewer, phone.

Union
KOA-Chicago Northwest (Marengo), 8404 South Union Rd., 60180. T: (800) KOA-2827. RV/tent: 138. $25. Hookups: water, electric (15, 20, 30, 50 amps), phone.

Wilmington
Fossil Rock Campground, 24615 West Strip Mine Rd., 60481. T: (815) 476-6784. F: (815) 476-6704. RV/tent: 275. $25. Hookups: water, electric (20, 30, 50 amps), sewer, phone.

Windsor
Wolf Creek State Park (Findlay), R. R. 1 Box 99, 61957. T: (217) 459-2831. RV/tent: 406. $11. Hookups: electric (30 amps).

Yorkville
Hide-A-Way Lakes, 8045 Van Emmon Rd., 60560. T: (630) 553-6323. RV/tent: 800. $20. Hookups: water, electric (20, 30, 50 amps), sewer, phone.

INDIANA

Albion

Chain O'Lakes State Park, 2355 East 75S, 46701. T: (219) 636-2654. RV/tent: 413. $11.00. Hookups: electric (30 amps).

Anderson

Mounds State Park, 4306 Mounds Rd., 46017. T: (765) 642-6627. RV/tent: 75. $11. Hookups: electric (30 amps).

Andrews

Lost Bridge West S.R.A. Salamonie Lake, 9214 West Lost Bridge W, 46702. T: (219) 468-2125. RV/tent: 276. $11. Hookups: electric (30 amps).

Angola

Camp Sack-In, 8740 E 40S, 46703. T: (219) 665-5166. RV/tent: 170. $20. Hookups: water, electric (30 amps).

Circle B Park, 340 Ln. 100, 46703. T: (219) 665-5353. RV/tent: 250. $24. Hookups: water, sewer, electric (50 amps).

Cook's Happy Acres RV Park, 1940 South 300W, 46703. T: (888) 318-8797. RV/tent: 100. $24. Hookups: water, sewer, electric (50 amps).

Pokagon State Park, 450 Ln. 100 Lake James, 46703. T: (219) 833-2012. RV/tent: 273. $11. Hookups: electric (30 amps).

Attica

Summers Campground, 5509 North 200E, 47918. T: (765) 762-2832. RV/tent: 100. $18. Hookups: water, electric (30 amps).

Birdseye

Newton-Stewart S.R.A. Patoka Lake, RR 1, 47513. T: (812) 685-2464. RV/tent: 563. $8. Hookups: electric (30 amps).

Bloomington

Paynetown State Recreation Area, 4850 South SR 446, 47401. T: (812) 837-9546. RV/tent: 320. $8. Hookups: electric (30 amps).

Bluffton

Quabache State Park, 4930 East SR 210, 46714. T: (219) 824-0926. RV/tent: 124. $11. Hookups: electric (30 amps).

Boonville

Scales Lake Park, 800 West Tennyson Rd., 47601. T: (812) 897-6200. RV/tent: 141. $13. Hookups: electric (30 amps), sewer.

Borden

Deam Lake State Recreation Area, RR 2, 47106. T: (812) 246-5421. RV/tent: 286. $11. Hookups: electric (30 amps).

Bremen

Rupert's Resort Campground, 3408 West Shore Dr., 46506. T: (219) 546-2657. RV/tent: 120. $20. Hookups: water, electric (30 amps).

Brookville

Mounds State Recreation Area, Brookville Lake, P.O. Box 100, 47012. T: (765) 647-2657. RV/tent: 379. $10. Hookups: water, electric (30 amps), sewer.

Cedar Lake

Cedar Lake Bible Conference, 13701 Lauerman, 46303. T: (219) 374-5941. RV/tent: 40. $22. Hookups: water, sewer, electric (30 amps).

Charlestown

Charlestown State Park, P.O. Box 38, 47111. T: (812) 256-5600. RV/tent: 219. $13. Hookups: water, sewer, electric (30 amps).

Chesteron

Indiana Dune State Park, 1600 North 25E, 46304. T: (219) 926-1952. RV/tent: 286. $11. Hookups: electric (30 amps).

Sand Creek Campground, 1000 North 350E, 46304. T: (219) 926-7482. RV/tent: 146. $20. Hookups: water, sewer, electric (50 amps).

Cicero

White River Campground, 11299 East 234th St., 46034. T: (317) 984-2705. RV/tent: 116. $22. Hookups: water, sewer, electric (30 amps).

Clarksville

Louisville Metro KOA Kampground, 900 Marriott Dr., 47129. T: (812) 282-4474. RV/tent: 92. $21. Hookups: water, electric (50 amps), sewer.

Cloverdale

Blackhawk Campground, 2046 West CR 1050S, 46120. T: (765) 795-4795. RV/tent: 158. $20. Hookups: water, electric (30 amps), sewer.

Colfax

Broadview Lake, 4850 South Broadview Rd., 46035. T: (317) 324-2622. RV/tent: 170. $20. Hookups: water, sewer, electric (30 amps).

Dillsboro

Brownings Camp, 3622 East CR 200S, 47018. T: (812) 689-6464. RV/tent: 281. $15. Hookups: water, sewer, electric (50 amps).

Edinburgh

Driftwood Camp-RV Park, 12180 US 31N, 46124. T: (812) 526-6422. RV/tent: 62. $13. Hookups: water, electric (30 amps), sewer.

Elkhart

Elkhart Campground, 25608 CR 4E, 46514. T: (219) 264-2914. RV/tent: 450. $20. Hookups: water, sewer, electric (50 amps).

Fort Wayne

Gordon's Camping, 1010 Ansely Dr., 46804. T: (219) 351-3383. RV/tent: 321. $30. Hookups: water, electric (50 amps).

Frankton

Miami Camp, 8851 West 400N, 46044. T: (765) 734-1365. RV/tent: 100. $18. Hookups: water, electric (30 amps), sewer.

Garrett

Indian Springs Campground, P.O. Box 216, 46738. T: (219) 357-5194. RV/tent: 365. $25. Hookups: water, electric (50 amps), sewer.

Geneva

Amishville USA, 844 East 900S, 46740. T: (219) 589-3536. RV/tent: 284. $15. Hookups: water, electric (30 amps).

Granger

South Bend East KOA, 50707 Princess Way, 46530. T: (219) 277-1335. RV/tent: 80. $25. Hookups: water, electric (30 amps).

Greenfield

Heartland Resort, 1613 West 300N, 46140. T: (317) 326-3181. RV/tent: 309. $25. Hookups: water, sewer, electric (50 amps).

Mohawk Campground & RV Park, CR 375N, 46140. T: (317) 326-3393. RV/tent: 104. $18. Hookups: water, sewer, electric (30 amps).

Hartford City

Wildwood Acres Campground, 520 West 300N, 47348. T: (765) 348-2100. RV/tent: 169. $15. Hookups: water, sewer, electric (50 amps).

Indianapolis

Indiana State Fairgrounds Campground, 1202 East 38th St., 46205. T: (317) 927-7510. RV/tent: 170. $15. Hookups: water, electric (20 amps).

Jasonville

Shakamak State Park, 6265 West SR 48, 47438. T: (812) 665-2158. RV/tent: 196. $11. Hookups: electric (30 amps).

Knox

Bass Lake State Park, 5838 South SR 10, 46534. T: (219) 772-3382. RV/tent: 60. $11. Hookups: electric (30 amps).

Kokomo

Springhill Campground, 623 South 750 W, 46901. T: (765) 883-7433. RV/tent: 122. $16. Hookups: water, sewer, electric (30 amps).

Kouts

Donna-Jo Camping Area, 1255 South CR 350E, 46347. T: (219) 766-2186. RV/tent: 75. $20. Hookups: water, electric (50 amps).

Liberty

Whitewater Memorial State Park, 1418 South SR 101, 47353. T: (765) 458-5565. RV/tent: 279. $11. Hookups: electric (30 amps).

Lincoln City

Lincoln State Park, P.O. Box 216, 47552. T: (812) 937-4710. RV/tent: 270. $11. Hookups: electric (30 amps), water.

Logansport

France Park, 4505 US 24W, 46947. T: (219) 753-2928. RV/tent: 300. $12. Hookups: water, electric (30 amps).

INDIANA (continued)

Tall Sycamore Campground, 355 South CR 600E, 46947. T: (219) 753-4898. RV/tent: 125. $16. Hookups: electric (50 amps), water.

Loogootee

West Boggs Park, P.O. Box 245, 47553. T: (812) 295-3421. RV/tent: 220. $18. Hookups: electric (30 amps), water, sewer.

Lynnville

Lynville Park, P.O. Box 309, 47619. T: (812) 922-5144. RV/tent: 47. $12. Hookups: water, electric (30 amps), sewer.

Marshall

Turkey Run State Park, P.O. Box 37, 47859. T: (765) 597-2635. RV/tent: 253. $11. Hookups: electric (30 amps).

Michigan City

Michigan City Campground, 1601 US 421N, 46360. T: (219) 872-7600. RV/tent: 150. $20. Hookups: water, electric (30 amps), sewer.

Middlebury

Elkhart Co./Middlebury Exit KOA, 52867 SR 13, 46540. T: (219) 825-5932. RV/tent: 120. $30. Hookups: water, electric (50 amps), sewer.

Mitchell

Spring Mill State Park, P.O. Box 376, 47446. T: (812) 849-4129. RV/tent: 224. $13. Hookups: electric (30 amps).

Modoc

Kamp Modoc, 8773 South 800W, 47358. T: (765) 853-5290. RV/tent: 260. $20. Hookups: water, electric (30 amps).

Montgomery

Glendale State Fish & Wildlife Area, P.O. Box 300, 47558. T: (812) 644-7711. RV/tent: 121. $10. Hookups: electric (30 amps).

Monticello

Arrowhead Campground, CR 400 East, 47960. T: (219) 583-5198. RV/tent: 194. $25. Hookups: water, electric (30 amps), sewer.

Holiday Resort, Lakeside Dr., 47960. T: (219) 583-7396. RV/tent: 36. $20. Hookups: water, electric (30 amps).

Indiana Beach Camp Resort, 5224 East Indiana Beach Rd., 47960. T: (219) 583-8306. RV/tent: 301. $30. Hookups: water, sewer, electric (50 amps).

Nashville

Brown County State Park, P.O. Box 608, 47448. T: (812) 988-6406. RV/tent: 412. $12. Hookups: electric (30 amps).

Westward Ho Campground, 4557 East SR 46, 47448. T: (812) 988-0008. RV/tent: 122. $25. Hookups: water, electric (50 amps), sewer.

New Carlisle

Mini Mountain Camp Resort, 32351 State Rd. 2, 46552. T: (219) 654-3307. RV/tent: 199. $22. Hookups: water, sewer, electric (50 amps).

New Castle

Summit Lake State Park, 5993 North Messick Rd., 47362. T: (765) 766-5873. RV/tent: 125. $11. Hookups: electric (30 amps).

Walnut Ridge Resort Campground, 408 North CR 300W, 47362. T: (765) 533-6611. RV/tent: 150. $20. Hookups: water, electric (30 amps).

New Harmony

Harmonie State Park, 3451 Harmonie State Park Rd., 47631. T: (812) 682-4821. RV/tent: 200. $12. Hookups: electric (30 amps).

North Liberty

Potato Creek State Park, 25601 SR 4, 46554. T: (219) 656-8186. RV/tent: 287. $11. Hookups: electric (30 amps).

Orland

Manapogo Park, 5495 West 760 North, 46776. T: (219) 833-3902. RV/tent: 300. $30. Hookups: water, sewer, electric (30 amps).

Pendletown

Glowood Campground, 9384 West 700S, 46064. T: (317) 485-5239. RV/tent: 100. $23. Hookups: water, electric (30 amps).

Peru

Mississinewa Lake-Miami Recreation Area, Box 194, 46970. T: (765) 473-6528. RV/tent: 620. $15. Hookups: water, sewer, electric (50 amps).

Pierceton

Yogi Bear's Jellystone Park Camp-Resort, 1916 North 850E, 46562. T: (219) 594-2124. RV/tent: 150. $35. Hookups: water, electric (30 amps), sewer.

Portland

Hickory Grove Lakes Campground, 7424 South 300E, 47371. T: (219) 335-2639. RV/tent: 152. $20. Hookups: water, sewer, electric (30 amps).

Richmond

Deer Ridge Camping Resort, 3696 Smyma Rd., 47374. T: (765) 939-0888. RV/tent: 64. $24. Hookups: water, electric (30 amps), sewer.

Grandpa's Farm, 4244 SR 227 North, 47374. T: (765) 962-7907. RV/tent: 55. $20. Hookups: water, sewer, electric (30 amps).

Indiana-Ohio KOA Kampground, 3101 Cart Rd., 47374. T: (765) 962-1219. RV/tent: 75. $25. Hookups: water, electric (30 amps), sewer.

Rockville

Covered Bridge Campground, 211H South Erie St., 47872. T: (765) 569-3911. RV/tent: 100. $22. Hookups: water, sewer, electric (30 amps).

Raccoon State Recreation Area, 160 South Raccoon Parkway, 47872. T: (765) 344-1412. RV/tent: 350. $12. Hookups: electric (30 amps).

Scottsburg

Hardy Lake State Recreation Area, Box 174, 47170. T: (812) 794-3800. RV/tent: 167. $10. Hookups: electric (30 amps).

Yogi Bear's Jellystone Park at Raintree Lake, 4577 West SR 56, 47170. T: (812) 752-4062. RV/tent: 91. $35. Hookups: water, electric (30 amps), sewer.

Shelbyville

Fairland Recreation Park, 3779 North Frontage Rd., 46176. T: (317) 392-0525. RV/tent: 44. $22. Hookups: water, electric (30 amps).

Shipshewana

Riverside Campground, 5910 North CR 450W, 46565. T: (219) 562-3742. RV/tent: 30. $18. Hookups: water, electric (30 amps).

Shipshewana Campground & Amish Log Cabin Lodging, P.O. Box 172, 46565. T: (219) 768-7770. RV/tent: 45. $28. Hookups: water, sewer, electric (30 amps).

Shipshewana Campground South, 1105 South VanBuren St., 46565. T: (219) 768-4669. RV/tent: 68. $25. Hookups: water, electric (30 amps).

Spencer

McCormick's Creek State Park, RR 5 Box 282, 47460. T: (812) 829-2235. RV/tent: 289. $11. Hookups: electric (30 amps).

St. Paul

Hidden Paradise Campground, 802 East Jefferson St., 47272. T: (765) 525-6582. RV/tent: 168. $20. Hookups: water, sewer, electric (50 amps).

Terre Haute

Terre Haute KOA, 5995 East Sony Dr., 47802. T: (812) 232-2457. RV/tent: 77. $35. Hookups: water, sewer, electric (30 amps).

Thorntown

Old Mill Run Park, 8544 West 690N, 46071. T: (800) 874-7343. RV/tent: 385. $25. Hookups: water, sewer, electric (30 amps).

Unionville

Riddle Point Park on Lake Lemon, 7599 North Tunnel Rd., 47468. T: (812) 332-5220. RV/tent: 100. $16. Hookups: water, electric (30 amps).

Vallonia

Starve Hollow State Recreation Area, 4345 South County Rd. 275W, 47281. T: (812) 358-3464. RV/tent: 185. $12. Hookups: electric (30 amps).

Valparaiso

Candy Stripe Campsite, 446 West Division Dr., 46383. T: (219) 462-0784. RV/tent: 100. $22. Hookups: water, sewer, electric (50 amps).

Warsaw

Hoffman Lake Camp, 7638 West 300N, 46582. T: (800) 289-8256. RV/tent: 193. $22. Hookups: water, sewer, electric (30 amps).

INDIANA (continued)

Warsaw (continued)

Pic-A-Spot Campground, 6402 East McKenna Rd., 46580. T: (219) 594-2635. RV/tent: 172. $20. Hookups: water, electric (30 amps).

Pike Lake Campground, 117 East Canal St., 46580. T: (219) 269-1439. RV/tent: 110. $14. Hookups: water, electric (30 amps).

Winamac

Tippecanoe River State Park, 4200 North US 35, 46996. T: (219) 946-3213. RV/tent: 122. $11. Hookups: electric (30 amps).

Williams Broken Arrow Campground, RR 1 Box 391, 46996. T: (219) 946-4566. RV/tent: 990. $22. Hookups: water, sewer, electric (50 amps).

IOWA

Allerton

Bobwhite State Park, RR1 P.O. Box 124 A, 50008. T: (641) 873-4670. RV/tent: 32. $9–$14. Hookups: electric.

Amana

Amana Colonies RV Park, P.O. Box 400, 52203. T: (319) 622-7616. RV/tent: 144. $10–$18. Hookups: full.

Anita

Lake Anita State Park, RR1, 50020. T: (712) 762-3564. RV/tent: 144. $6–$14. Hookups: full.

Arnolds Park

City Park, P.O. Box 437, 51331. T: (712) 762-3564. RV/tent: 52. $9–$14. Hookups: electric.

Auburn

Grants Park (Sac County Park), 3531 365th St., 51433. T: (712) 662-4530. RV/tent: 30. $9–$14. Hookups: electric, water.

Augusta

Lower Skunk River Access (Des Moines County Park), 512 North Main St., Burlington, 52601. T: (319) 753-8260. RV/tent: 47. $9–$14. Hookups: electric.

Avoca

Parkway Campground, 857 South Chestnut St., 51521. T: (712) 343-6652. RV/tent: 50. $15–$21. Hookups: full.

Bedford

Lake of Three Fires State Park, 2303 State Hwy. 49, 50833. T: (712) 523-2700. RV/tent: 140. $9–$14. Hookups: full.

Bellevue

Bellevue State Park, 21466 429th Ave., 52031. T: (563) 872-4019. RV/tent: 48. $9–$14. Hookups: electric, water.

Pleasant Creek, 11995 US Hwy. 52, 52031. T: (563) 872-5782. RV/tent: 60. $13–$17. Hookups: none.

Spruce Creek (Jackson County Park), Jackson County Courthouse, 52060. T: (563) 872-3621. RV/tent: 86. $9–$14. Hookups: electric (30 amps).

Blairstown

Hannen Park (Benton County Park), RR1 Box 37 B1, Vinton, 52349. T: (563) 454-6382. RV/tent: 55. $9–$14. Hookups: electric.

Bloomfield

Lakeside Village Campground, Rte. 3 Box 39, 52537. T: (647) 664-3364. RV/tent: 180. $10–$15. Hookups: full.

Boone

Ledges State Park, 1519 250th St., Madrid, 50126. T: (515) 432-1852. RV/tent: 94. $9–$14. Hookups: electric.

Brighton

Lake Darling State Park, 110 Lake Darling Rd., 52540. T: (319) 694-2323. RV/tent: 118. $9–$14. Hookups: electric.

Clermont

Skip-A-Way RV Park and Campground, Box 324, 52135. T: (800) 728-1167. RV/tent: 156. $13–$17. Hookups: electric (20, 30, 50 amps), water.

Colo

Twin Anchors RV Park, 68132 US Hwy. 30, 50023. T: (641) 372-2243. RV/tent: 210. $13–$20. Hookups: electric (30, 50 amps), water.

Council Bluffs

Bluffs Run RV Park, 2701 23rd Ave., 51501. T: (800) 238-2946. RV/tent: 123. $17–$20. Hookups: electric (20, 30, 50 amps), water.

Tomes Country Club Acres, 706 South Omaha Bridge Rd., 51501. T: (712) 366-0363. RV/tent: 25. $19. Hookups: electric (15, 20, 30 amps).

Crescent

Honey Creek Campground, 28120 145th St., 51526. T: (712) 545-9400. RV/tent: 66. $16–$18. Hookups: electric (20, 30, 50 amps), water.

Decorah

Chimney Rock Canoe Rental and Campground, 3312 Chimney Rock Rd., 52136. T: (319) 735-5786. RV/tent: 28. $10–$15. Hookups: electric (20 amps).

Des Moines

Timberline Best Holiday Trav-L-Park Campground, 3165 Ashworth Rd., 50263. T: (515) 987-1714. RV/tent: 100. $16–$22. Hookups: full.

Dubuque

Dubuque Yacht Basin and RV Park, 1630 East 16th, 52001. T: (319) 556-7708. RV/tent: 56. $21–$24. Hookups: full.

Forest City

Three Fingers Campground, 14300 355th St., 50436. T: (641) 581-5856. RV/tent: 75. $12. Hookups: electric, water.

Fort Madison

Hilltop Campground, 2182 US Hwy. 61, 52627. T: (319) 372-4227. RV/tent: 17. $10–$14. Hookups: electric (20, 30, 50 amps).

Garnavillo

J-Wood Campground, 31848 Clayton Rd., 52046. T: (319) 964-2236. RV/tent: 97. $15. Hookups: electric, water.

Paradise Valley, 19745 Keystone Rd. Unit 4, 52049. T: (319) 873-9632. RV/tent: 210. $11–$14. Hookups: electric (30 amps), water.

Harlan

Nielson RV Park, 1244 F32, 51537. T: (712) 627-4640. RV/tent: 17. $10–$15. Hookups: electric (20, 30 amps).

Kalona

Windmill Ridge Campground, P.O. Box 772, 52247. T: (319) 656-4488. RV/tent: 70. $8–$10. Hookups: electric (15, 30, 50 amps).

Kellogg

Lake Pla-Mor, 12725 Killdeer Ave., 50135. T: (641) 526-3169. RV/tent: 84. $7–$11. Hookups: electric (20, 30 amps), water.

Keokuk

Hickory Haven Campground, 2413 353rd St., 52632. T: (800) 890-8469. RV/tent: 45. $13. Hookups: electric (20, 30, 50 amps), water.

Lansing

Red Barn Resort, 2609 Main St., 52151. T: (319) 538-4956. RV/tent: 117. $12–$20. Hookups: electric (20, 30, 50 amps), water.

Little Sioux

Woodland Campground, 1449 Benton Ln., 51545. T: (712) 649-2594. RV/tent: 27. $15. Hookups: electric (30 amps), water.

Marshalltown

Shady Oaks Camping, 2370 Shady Oaks Rd., 50138. T: (641) 752-2946. RV/tent: 22. $16. Hookups: electric (20, 30, 50 amps).

IOWA (continued)

McCregor

Spook Cave and Campground, 13899 Spook Cave Rd., 52157. T: (319) 873-2114. RV/tent: 73. $10–$15. Hookups: electric (15, 20, 30, 50 amps), water.

Monticello

Walnut Acres, P.O. Box 624, 52310. T: (319) 465-4665. RV/tent: 255. $13–$20. Hookups: electric (20, 30 amps), water.

Mount Pleasant

J & J Camping, 105 North J & J Ln., 52641. T: (319) 986-6398. RV/tent: 100. $17. Hookups: electric, water.

Nashua

River Ranch Camping, 2575 Cheyenne Ave., 50658. T: (641) 435-2108. RV/tent: 111. $9–$14. Hookups: electric, water.

Newton

Rolling Acres RV Park and Campground, 1601 East 36th St. South, 50208. T: (641) 792-2428. RV/tent: 82. $17–$19. Hookups: electric (20, 30 , 50 amps), water.

North Liberty

Colony County Campground, 1275 Forevergreen Rd., Iowa City, 52240. T: (319) 626-2221. RV/tent: 45. $15–$22. Hookups: electric (20, 30 amps), water.

Jolly Roger Campground and Harper's Marina, 1858 Scales Bend Rd., 52317. T: (319) 626-2171. RV/tent: 190. $12–$20. Hookups: electric (15, 20, 30, 50 amps), water.

Onawa

Interchange RV Park, Box 324, 51040. T: (712) 423-1387. RV/tent: 28. $13–$16. Hookups: electric (20, 30, 50 amps), water.

Oxford

Sleepy Hollow RV Park and Campground, 3340 Black Hawk Ave., 52322. T: (319) 828-4400. RV/tent: 143. $14–$20. Hookups: electric (30, 50 amps), water.

KANSAS

Arkansas City

Lou Ann's Campground, 9423 292nd Rd., 67005. T: (620) 442-4458. RV/tent: 20. $15. Hookups: electric (30 amps), water, sewer.

Assaria

Shepherd's Gate RV & Recreational Park, 1288 East Lapsley Rd., 67416. T: (785) 667-5795 or (785) 822-8463. F: (785) 667-5796. RV/tent: 35. $10–$15. Hookups: electric (30 amps), water, sewer.

Bird City

Right Motel & RV Park, Hwy. 36, 67731. T: (785) 734-2344. RV/tent: 19. $15–$20. Hookups: electric (30, 50 amps), water, sewer.

Bonner Springs

Cottonwood Camping RV Park & Campground, 115 South 130th St., 66012. T: (913) 422-8038. www.cottonwoodcamping.com. RV/tent: 100. $18–$22. Hookups: electric (20, 30, 50 amps), water, sewer.

Burlington

Damsite Campground, 1565 Embankment Rd. Southwest, 66839. T: (316) 364-8613. www.ReserveUSA.com/nrrs/ks/dams/index.html. RV/tent: 26. $10–$15. Hookups: electric (30 amps), water.

Riverside East Campground, 1565 Embankment Rd. Southwest, 66839. T: (316) 364-8613. www.ReserveUSA.com/nrrs/ks/riea. RV/tent: 53. $10–$15. Hookups: electric (30 amps), water.

Riverside West Campground, 1565 Embankment Rd. Southwest, 66839. T: (316) 364-8613. RV/tent: 43. $10–$15. Hookups: electric (30 amps).

Cherryvale

Big Hill Lake (Overlook Campground), P.O. Box 426, 67335-0426. T: (316) 336-2741. www.ReserveUSA.com/nrrs/ks/chpa. RV/tent: 30. $12. Hookups: electric (20 amps).

Coffeyville

Walter Johnson Park Campground, P.O. Box 307, 508 Park, 67337. T: (800) 626-3357. www.coffeyville.com. RV/tent: 72. $4. Hookups: electric (20, 30, 50 amps), water.

Columbus

T&S RV Park, 1308 East Hwy. 160, 66725. T: (620) 674-3304. F: (620) 674-3342. RV/tent: 23. $15. Hookups: electric (30, 40, 50 amps), water, sewer.

Council Grove

Canning Creek, 945 Lake Rd., 66846. T: (620) 767-5195. www.ReserveUSA.com/nrrs/ks/cank. RV/tent: 42. $10–$16. Hookups: electric (20, 30 amps), water.

Richey Cove, 945 Lake Rd., 66846. T: (620) 767-5195. www.ReserveUSA.com/nrrs/ks/ricv. RV/tent: 49. $10–$15. Hookups: electric (20, 30 amps), water.

Santa Fe Trail Campground, 945 Lake Rd., 66846. T: (620) 767-5195. www.ReserveUSA.com/nrrs/ks/sant. RV/tent: 39. $9–$16. Hookups: electric (20, 30, 50 amps), water, sewer.

Dodge City

Gunsmoke Trav-L Park, 11070 108 Rd., 67801. T: (800) 789-8247 or (316) 227-8247. RV/tent: 110. $18–$20. Hookups: electric (50 amps), water, sewer.

El Dorado

Bluestem Point Campground, Rte. 3, 67042. T: (316) 321-7180. RV/tent: 286. $15–$16. Hookups: electric (20, 30 amps), water, sewer.

Walnut River Campground, Rte. 3, 67042. T: (316) 321-7180. RV/tent: 177. $15–$16. Hookups: electric (20, 30 amps), water, sewer.

Ellis

Cedar Bluff State Park, Rte. 2 Box 76A, 67637. T: (785) 726-3212. RV/tent: 121. $10–$16. Hookups: electric (20, 30, 50 amps), water, sewer.

Ellis Lakeside Campground, Rte. 2 Box 76A, 67637. T: (785) 726-3212. RV/tent: 28. $7–$10. Hookups: electric (20 amps).

Fall River

Damsite, P.O. Box 37, 67047. T: (620) 658-4445. www.ReserveUSA.com/nrrs/ks/damr. RV/tent: 33. $10–$18. Hookups: electric (20, 30, 50 amps), water, sewer.

Whitehall Bay, P.O. Box 37, 67047. T: (620) 658-4445. www.ReserveUSA.com/nrrs/ks/whha. RV/tent: 29. $10–$18. Hookups: electric (20, 30, 50 amps), water, sewer.

Fredonia

Cottonwood Court, P.O. Box 5, 1002 North 8th St., 66736. T: (620) 378-3468. RV/tent: 13. $10. Hookups: electric (20, 30, 50 amps), water, sewer.

Garden City

Garden City KOA, 4100 East Hwy. 50, 67846. T: (800) KOA-3361 or (316) 276-8741. www.koa.com. RV/tent: 96. $15–$22. Hookups: electric (50 amps), water, sewer.

Goodland

Mid-America Camp Inn, 2802 Commerce Rd., 67735. T: (785) 899-5431. RV/tent: 109. $13–$19. Hookups: electric (20, 30, 50 amps), water, sewer.

KANSAS (continued)

Halstead

Spring Lake Campground, Rte. 2, 67056. T: (316) 835-3272. RV/tent: 131. $15. Hookups: electric (30, 50 amps), water, sewer.

Hays

El Charro RV Park, 2020 East 8th St., 67601. T: (785) 625-3423. RV/tent: 5. $16. Hookups: electric (30, 50 amps), water, sewer.

Sunflower Creek Campground & RV Park, 501 Vine St., 67601. T: (785) 623-4769. RV/tent: 24. $15–$20. Hookups: electric (30, 50 amps), water, sewer.

Hesston

Cottonwood Grove Campground, 1001 East Lincoln Blvd., 67062. T: (620) 327-4173. RV/tent: 32. $5–$15. Hookups: electric (30 amps), water, sewer.

Horton

Horse Thief Campground, 200 Horse Thief Rd., 67464. T: (785) 546-2565. F: (785) 546-2343. RV/tent: 40. $7–$15. Hookups: electric (30 amps).

Junction City

Curtis Creek Park, 4020 West Hwy. K-57, 66441. T: (785) 238-4636. www.ReserveUSA.com/nrrs/ks/curc. RV/tent: 78. $10–$16. Hookups: electric (20, 30 amps), water.

Dam Site, 2105 North Pawnee Rd., 66839. T: (316) 364-8613. RV/tent: 32. $10–$15. Hookups: electric (20, 30 amps), water.

Rolling Hills Park West, 4020 West Hwy. K-57, 66441. T: (785) 238-5714. www.ReserveUSA.com/nrrs/ks/rolh. RV/tent: 62. $10–$16. Hookups: electric (30 amps).

Thunderbird Marina, West Rolling Hills Rd., 66441. T: (785) 238-5864. RV/tent: 80. $14. Hookups: electric (15, 20, 30, 50 amps), water.

La Crosse

Double D RV Park, P.O. Box 699, 67548. T: (785) 222-2457. RV/tent: 14. $13–$17. Hookups: electric (20, 30 amps), water, sewer.

Lawrence

Cedar Ridge, 872 North 1402 Rd., 66049. T: (785) 843-7665. www.ReserveUSA.com/nrrs/ks/cdri. RV/tent: 100. $16. Hookups: electric (20, 30 amps), water.

Hickory Campground, 872 North 1402 Rd., 66049. T: (785) 843-7665. www.ReserveUSA.com/nrrs/ks/hick. RV/tent: 196. $10–$14. Hookups: electric (30 amps).

Walnut, 872 North 1402 Rd., 66049. T: (785) 843-7665. www.ReserveUSA.com/nrrs/ks/waln. RV/tent: 100. $8–$14. Hookups: electric (30 amps).

Leavenworth

Leavenworth RV Park, 24836 Tonganoxie Rd., 66048. T: (913) 351-0505. RV/tent: 5. $22. Hookups: electric (30 amps), water.

Lebo

Sundance Campground, 31051 Melvern Lake Pkwy., 66510-9179. T: (785) 549-3318. RV/tent: 30. $10. Hookups: none.

Lindsborg

Coronado Motel/RV Park, 305 Harrison, 67456. T: (800) 747-2793 or (785) 227-3943. RV/tent: 18. $17. Hookups: electric (20, 30, 50 amps), water, sewer.

Louisburg

Middle Creek RV Park, 33565 South Metcalf, 66053. T: (866) 888-6779 or (913) 376-3304. F: (913) 376-3304. www.rutlateroutpost.com. RV/tent: 24. $20–$22. Hookups: electric (30, 50 amps), water, sewer.

Lucas

Lucas RV Park & Laundry, 119 North Wolf, 67648. T: (785) 525-6396. RV/tent: 5. $17. Hookups: electric (20, 50 amps), water, sewer.

Lyndon

Crossroads RV Park & Campground Inc., P.O. Box 721, 66451. T: (785) 221-5482. RV/tent: 65. $15–$23. Hookups: electric (20, 30, 50 amps), water, sewer.

Marion

Cottonwood Point, 2105 North Pawnee, 66861. T: (620) 382-2101. www.ReserveUSA.com/nrrs/ks/cotp. RV/tent: 94. $14–$16. Hookups: electric (20, 30, 50 amps).

Hillsboro Cove, 2105 North Pawnee, 66861. T: (620) 382-2101. www.ReserveUSA.com/nrrs/ks/hilc. RV/tent: 52. $14. Hookups: electric (20, 30 amps).

Marquette

Riverside, 105 Riverside Dr., 67464. T: (785) 546-2294. www.ReserveUSA.com/nrrs/ks/rive. RV/tent: 40. $10–$14. Hookups: electric (20, 30 amps).

Venango Park, 105 Riverside Dr., 67464. T: (785) 546-2294. RV/tent: 236. $10–$16. Hookups: electric (20, 30 amps).

Mayetta

Prairie Schooner RV Park & Campground, 15680 Pacific St., 66509. T: (785) 966-2952. RV/tent: 39. $18. Hookups: electric (20, 30, 50 amps), water, sewer.

McPherson

Mustang Mobile Park, 1909 Millers Ln., 67460. T: (316) 241-0237. RV/tent: 28. $12. Hookups: electric (20, 50 amps), water, sewer.

Melvern

Arrow Rock Campground, 31051 Melvern Lake Pkwy., 66510-9179. T: (785) 549-3318. RV/tent: 45. $10–$14. Hookups: electric (30 amps).

Coeur d'Alene Campground, 31051 Melvern Lake Pkwy., 66510-9179. T: (785) 549-3318. www.ReserveUSA.com/nrrs/ks/coeu. RV/tent: 60. $10–$14. Hookups: electric (30 amps).

Eisenhower Campground, 31051 Melvern Lake Pkwy., 66510-9179. T: (785) 528-4102. RV/tent: 190. $9–$16. Hookups: electric (30, 50 amps), water, sewer.

Outlet Campground, 31051 Melvern Lake Pkwy., 66510-9179. T: (785) 549-3318. www.ReserveUSA.com/nrrs/ks/oult. RV/tent: 150. $15–$18. Hookups: electric (20, 30 amps), water, sewer.

Turkey Point Campground, 31051 Melvern Lake Pkwy., 66510-9179. T: (785) 549-3318. www.ReserveUSA.com/nrrs/ks/turp. RV/tent: 50. $10–$16. Hookups: electric (20, 30, 50 amps), water.

Merriam

Walnut Grove RV Park, 10218 Johnson Dr., 66203. T: (913) 262-3023. F: (913) 432-5269. www.walnutgroverv.com. RV/tent: 55. $20–$22. Hookups: electric (30, 50 amps), water, sewer.

Milford

Flagstop Resort & RV Park, P.O. Box 329, 66514. T: (800) 293-1465. www.members.xoom.com/flagstop. RV/tent: 190. $16. Hookups: electric (50 amps), water, sewer.

Langley Point, 4020 West Hwy. K57, 66441. T: (785) 238-5714. RV/tent: 57. $7–$16. Hookups: electric (20, 30, 50 amps), water, sewer.

Timber Creek Park, 4020 West Hwy. K57, 66441. T: (785) 238-5714. RV/tent: $7–$16. Hookups: electric (20, 30, 50 amps), water, sewer.

Morrill

Mulberry Creek Family Retreat, 551 270th St., 66515. T: (888) 459-1595 or (785) 459-2279. RV/tent: 70. $15. Hookups: electric (30, 50 amps), water, sewer.

Mound Valley

Big Hill Lake, P.O. Box 426, 67335. T: (316) 336-2741. www.ReserveUSA.com/nrrs/ks/mova. RV/tent: 72. $12–$17. Hookups: electric (20, 30, 50 amps), water, sewer.

Nickerson

Hendrick's Capybara Lake, 7910 North Roy L. Smith Rd., 67561. T: (888) 489-8039. www.hedricks.com/lake. RV/tent: 16. $15. Hookups: electric (20, 30, 50 amps), water, sewer.

KANSAS (continued)

Oakley

Kansas Kountry Inn, 3538 Hwy. 40, 67748. T: (800) 211-6917 or (785) 672-3131. F: (785) 672-3134. RV/tent: 16. $10. Hookups: electric (20, 30, 50 amps), water, sewer.

Paola

Hillsdale State Park, 26001 West 255th St., 66071. T: (913) 783-4507. www.kdwparks.state.ks.us. RV/tent: 80. $10–$17. Hookups: electric (20, 30, 50 amps), water.

Paxico

Mill Creek Campground, Rte. 1 Box 54, 66526. T: (785) 636-5321. RV/tent: 46. $18. Hookups: electric (20, 30, 50 amps), water, sewer.

Perry

Locust Campground, 10419 Perry Park Dr., 66073. T: (785) 597-5144. www.ReserveUSA.com/nrrs/ks/slou. RV/tent: 14. $15. Hookups: electric (20, 30 amps), water.

Longview, 10419 Perry Park Dr., 66073. T: (785) 597-5144. www.ReserveUSA.com/nrrs/ks/lonv. RV/tent: 52. $10–$14. Hookups: electric (20, 30 amps).

Old Town, 10419 Perry Park Dr., 66073. T: (785) 597-5144. www.ReserveUSA.com/nrrs/ks/oldt. RV/tent: 77. $10–$14. Hookups: electric (20, 30 amps).

Rock Creek Peninsula Campground, 10419 Perry Park Dr., 66073. T: (785) 597-5144. www.ReserveUSA.com/nrrs/ks/rocr. RV/tent: 77. $10–$14. Hookups: electric (20, 30 amps), water.

Slough Creek Campground, 10419 Perry Park Dr., 66073. T: (785) 597-5144. www.ReserveUSA.com/nrrs/ks/slou. RV/tent: 273. $10–$15. Hookups: electric (20, 30 amps), water.

Perry

Southpoint Campground, 10419 Perry Park Dr., 66073. T: (785) 597-5144. www.ReserveUSA.com/nrrs/ks/slou. RV/tent: 24. $15. Hookups: electric (20, 30 amps), water.

Worthington Campground, 10419 Perry Park Dr., 66073. T: (785) 597-5144. www.ReserveUSA.com/nrrs/ks/slou. RV/tent: 62. $15. Hookups: electric (20, 30 amps).

Quinter

Sunflower Campground, 1130 Castle Rock Rd., 67752-9400. T: (913) 754-3451. RV/tent: 40. $13–$17. Hookups: electric (30 amps), water, sewer.

Rexford

Shepherd's Staff RV Park, 315 Main St., 67753. T: (888) 687-2565 or (785) 687-2565. RV/tent: 12. $18. Hookups: electric (20, 30, 50 amps), water, sewer.

Richmond

V&P RV Park, 532 East South St., 66080. T: (785) 835-6369. RV/tent: 25. $15. Hookups: electric (30, 50 amps), water, sewer.

Russel

Dumler Estates RV Park, P.O. Box 180, 67665. T: (785) 483-2603. RV/tent: 35. $15. Hookups: electric (20, 30, 50 amps), water, sewer.

Salina

Salina KOA, 1109 West Diamond Dr., 67401. T: (800) 562-3126 or (785) 827-3182. www.koa.com. RV/tent: 82. $16–$21. Hookups: electric (20, 30, 50 amps), water, sewer.

Sundowner West Park, P.O. Box 2388, 67402. T: (785) 823-8335. RV/tent: 91. $20. Hookups: electric (30, 50 amps), water, sewer.

Scott City

Pine Tree RV Park, 402 North Main St., 67871. T: (620) 872-3076. RV/tent: 25. $17. Hookups: electric (20, 30, 50 amps), water, sewer.

Smith Center

Sunset Park Campground, West Hwy. 36, 705 White Rock, 66967. T: (785) 282-6037. RV/tent: 16. $14. Hookups: electric (20, 30 amps), water, sewer.

South Haven

Oasis RV Park, Hwy. 166 East of I-35, 67140. T: (620) 892-5115. RV/tent: 25. $14. Hookups: electric (20, 30, 50 amps), water, sewer.

St. Francis

Homesteader Motel & RV Park, 414 West Hwy. 36, 67756. T: (800) 750-2169 or (785) 332-2168. RV/tent: 9. $15. Hookups: electric (30, 50 amps), water, sewer.

St. John

Pine Haven Retreat, Rte. 2 Box 140A, 67576. T: (88) 549-CAMP or (620) 549-3444. F: (620) 549-3571. RV/tent: 50. $10–$16. Hookups: electric (20, 30, 50 amps), water, sewer.

Sylvan Grove

Lucas Park, 4860 Outlet Blvd., 67481. T: (785) 658-2551. www.ReserveUSA.com/nrrs/ks/luca. RV/tent: 116. $10–$16. Hookups: electric (20, 30 amps), water.

Minooka Park, 4860 Outlet Blvd., 67481. T: (785) 658-2551. www.ReserveUSA.com/nrrs/ks/mino. RV/tent: 235. $10–$16. Hookups: electric (20, 30 amps), water.

Topeka

Capital City RV Park, 1949 Southwest 49th St., 66609. T: (785) 862-KAMP. RV/tent: 51. $14–$19. Hookups: electric (20, 30, 50 amps), water, sewer.

Lake Shawnee Camping Area, 3435 Southeast Edge Rd., 66609. T: (913) 267-1859. RV/tent: 154. $10. Hookups: electric (30 amps), water.

Toronto

Holiday Hill Campground, 144 Hwy. 105, 66777. T: (316) 637-2213. RV/tent: 30. $7–$10. Hookups: electric (30 amps).

Toronto Point Campground, 144 Hwy. 105, 66777. T: (316) 637-2213. RV/tent: 200. $7–$10. Hookups: electric (20, 30 amps), water.

Vassar

Carbolyn Park, 5260 Pomona Dam Rd., 66543. T: (785) 453-2201. www.ReserveUSA.com/nrrs/ks/carb. RV/tent: 32. $10–$16. Hookups: electric (20, 30 amps), water.

Michigan Valley, 5260 Pomona Dam Rd., 66543. T: (785) 453-2201. www.ReserveUSA.com/nrrs/ks/mich. RV/tent: 158. $10–$16. Hookups: electric (20, 30 amps), water.

Pomona Lake Outlet Campground, 5260 Pomona Dam Rd., 66543. T: (785) 453-2201. www.ReserveUSA.com/nrrs/ks/out2. RV/tent: 36. $14. Hookups: electric (20, 30 amps), water.

Wolf Creek, 5260 Pomona Dam Rd., 66543. T: (785) 453-2201. www.ReserveUSA.com/nrrs/ks/wocr. RV/tent: 87. $10–$14. Hookups: electric (20, 30 amps).

Washington

Rose Garden RV Camp, 127 East Ninth St., 66968. T: (785) 325-2411. RV/tent: 9. $15. Hookups: electric (20, 30, 50 amps), water, sewer.

Wellington

Wheatlands of Wellington RV Park, Rte. 1 Box 227, 67152. T: (877) 914-6114 or (316) 326-6114. RV/tent: 72. $24. Hookups: electric (30, 50 amps), water, sewer.

Wichita

All Seasons RV Park, 15520 Maple Ave., 67052. T: (316) 722-1154. RV/tent: 76. $19–$22. Hookups: electric (20, 30, 50 amps), water, sewer.

Blasi Campgrounds, 11209 West Hwy. 54, 67209. T: (316) 722-2681. RV/tent: 110. $19–$23. Hookups: electric (20, 30, 50 amps), water, sewer.

K & R Tratel RV Park, 3200 Southeast Blvd., 67216. T: (316) 684-1531. RV/tent: 66. $16. Hookups: electric (30, 50 amps), water, sewer.

Waco Wego Campground, 9747 South Broadway, 67120. T: (316) 522-1400. RV/tent: 9. $16. Hookups: electric (20, 30, 50 amps), water, sewer.

Wilson

Hell Creek Campground, Rte. 1 Box 181, 67841. T: (785) 658-2465. RV/tent: 400. $7–$10. Hookups: electric (20, 30 amps), water.

KANSAS (continued)

Wilson (continued)

Otoe Campground, Rte. 1 Box 181, 67841. T: (785) 658-2465. RV/tent: 235. $7–$10. Hookups: electric (20, 30 amps), water.

KENTUCKY

Aurora

Aurora Oaks Campground, 55 KOA Ln., 42048. T: (888) 886-8704. RV/tent: 60. $15–$18. Hookups: water, electric.

Lakeside Campground & Marina, 12363 US Hwy. 68 East, 42025. T: (270) 354-8157. RV/tent: 140. $19–$21. Hookups: water, electric.

Bardstown

Holt's Campground, 2351 Templin Ave., 40004. T: (502) 348-6717. RV/tent: 60. $16. Hookups: water, electric.

White Acres Campground, 3022 Boston Rd., 62 West, 40004. T: (502) 348-9677. RV/tent: 82. $10–$14. Hookups: water, electric.

Benton

Big Bear Resort, 30 Big Bear Resort Rd., 42025. T: (800) 922-BEAR. RV/tent: 75. $17.29. Hookups: water, electric.

Berea

Oh Kentucky Campground, 1142 Hwy. 21 West, 40403. T: (606) 986-1150. RV/tent: 152. $10–$12. Hookups: water, electric.

Walnut Meadow Campground, 1201 Paint Lick Rd., 40403. T: (606) 986-6180. RV/tent: 123. $8–$12. Hookups: water, electric.

Bowling Green

Beech Bend Family Campground, 798 Beech Bend Rd., 42101. T: (270) 781-7634. RV/tent: 439. $20. Hookups: water, electric.

Buckhorn

Buckhorn Dam Recreation Area (Corps of Engineers–Buckhorn Lake), 104 Tailwater Camp Rd., 41721. T: (606) 398-7251. RV/tent: 31. $16. Hookups: water, electric.

Burkesville

Sulphur Creek Resort, 3498 Sulphur Creek Rd., 42717. T: (270) 433-7200. RV/tent: 22. $20. Hookups: water, electric.

Burnside

Lake Cumberland RV Park, P.O. Box 394 499 Gibson Ln., 42518. T: (606) 561-8222. RV/tent: 40. $15–$20. Hookups: water, electric.

Cadiz

Hurricane Creek Recreational Area (Corps of Engineers–Lake Barkle), Box 218, 42045. T: (270) 362-4236. RV/tent: 45. $10–$20. Hookups: water, electric.

Prizer Point Marina & Resort, 1777 Prizer Point Rd., 42211. T: (270) 522-3762. RV/tent: 102. $18. Hookups: water, electric.

Rockcastle RV Resort & Campground, 1049 Goose Hollow Rd., 42211. T: (270) 522-5530. RV/tent: 57. $8–$15. Hookups: water, electric.

Calvert City

Cypress Lakes RV Park, 54 Scillion Dr., 42029. T: (270) 395-4267. RV/tent: 130. $14–$16. Hookups: water, electric.

KOA–KY Lake Dam/Paducah, 4793 US Hwy. 62, 42029. T: (270) 395-5841. RV/tent: 85. $18.50–$24.50. Hookups: water, electric.

Campbellsville

Green River Lake State Park, Green River Lake State Park, 42718. T: (270) 465-8255. RV/tent: 156. $18. Hookups: water, electric.

Smith Ridge (Corps of Engineers–Green River Lake), 2882 Smith Ridge Rd., 42718. T: (270) 789-2743. RV/tent: 80. $16–$19. Hookups: water, electric.

Canton

Devil's Elbow Campground (Corps of Engineers–Trigg), 100 Devil's Elbow Rd., 42211. T: (270) 924-5878. RV/tent: 22. $10–$13. Hookups: water, electric.

Corbin

Grove Campground, Daniel Boone National Forest, 1700 Bypass Rd., 40391. T: (800) 280-CAMP. RV/tent: 56. $15–$25. Hookups: water, electric.

Danville

Pioneer Playhouse Trailer Park, 840 Stanford Rd./US Hwy. 150, 40422. T: (606) 236-2747. RV/tent: 70. $13. Hookups: water, electric.

Dry Ridge

75 Camper Village, 940 Curry Ln., 41035. T: (606) 824-5836. RV/tent: 70. $15–$20. Hookups: water, electric.

Dunmor

Dogwood Lake & Campground, Box 150, 42339. T: (270) 657-8380. RV/tent: 95. $10–$14. Hookups: water, electric.

Eddyville

Holiday Hills Resort, 5631 KY 93 South, 42038. T: (800) 337-8550. RV/tent: 150. $18–$20. Hookups: water, electric.

Lake Barkley RV Resort, 4481 State Rte. 93 South, 42038. T: (800) 910-PARK. RV/tent: 114. $14–$17. Hookups: water, electric.

Elizabethtown

Glendale Campground, 4566 Sportsman Lake Rd., 42701. T: (270) 369-7755. RV/tent: 100. $16–$20. Hookups: water, electric.

KOA–Elizabethtown, 209 Tunnel Hill Rd., 42701. T: (270) 737-7600. RV/tent: 68. $16–$24.50. Hookups: water, electric.

Falls of Rough

Cave Creek (Corps of Engineers–Rough River Lake), 14500 Falls of Rough R, 40119-6313. T: (270) 257-2061. RV/tent: 86. $8–$12. Hookups: water, electric.

Frankfort

Elkhorn Campground, 165 Scruggs Ln., 40601. T: (502) 695-9154. RV/tent: 125. $17–$21. Hookups: water, electric.

Franklin

KOA–Franklin, P.O. Box 346, 42135. T: (800) 562-5631. RV/tent: 104. $16.50–$22. Hookups: water, electric.

Golden Pond

Energy Lake (LBL) National Recreation Area, 100 Van Morgan Dr., 42211. T: (270) 924-2270. RV/tent: 48. $12–$15. Hookups: water, electric.

Fenton (LBL) National Recreation Area, 100 Van Morgan Dr., 42211. T: (270) 924-2000. RV/tent: 29. $8–$11. Hookups: water, electric.

Rushing Creek (LBL) National Recreation Area, 100 Van Morgan Dr., 42211. T: (270) 924-2000. RV/tent: 40. $9. Hookups: water, electric.

Wrangler (LBL) National Recreation Area, 100 Van Morgan Dr., 42211. T: (270) 924-2000. RV/tent: 163. $11–$18. Hookups: water, electric.

Grand Rivers

Birmingham Ferry (LBL) National Recreation Area, 100 Van Morgan Dr., 42211. T: (270) 924-2000. RV/tent: 46. $8. Hookups: water, electric.

Cravens Bay (LBL) National Recreation Area, 100 Van Morgan Dr., 42211. T: (270) 924-2000. RV/tent: 31. $8. Hookups: water, electric.

Hillman Ferry (LBL) National Recreation Area, 100 Van Morgan Dr., 42211. T: (270) 362-8230. RV/tent: 379. $12–$19. Hookups: water, electric.

KENTUCKY (continued)

Harrodsburg

Chimney Rock Campground, 160 Chimney Rock Rd., 40330. T: (606) 748-5252. RV/tent: 70. $15. Hookups: water, electric.

Cummins Ferry Campground & Marina, 2528 Cummins Ferry Rd., 40372. T: (859) 748-6243. RV/tent: 120. $15–$20. Hookups: water, electric.

Hartford

Ohio County Park, 1802 Country Club Ln., 42347. T: (270) 298-4466. RV/tent: 50. $10–$14. Hookups: water, electric.

Hodgenville

Cruise Inn Campground & Motel, 2784 Lincoln Farm Rd., 42748. T: (270) 358-9998. RV/tent: 20. $14. Hookups: water, electric.

Horse Cave

KOA–Horse Cave, Box 87, 42749. T: (270) 786-2819. RV/tent: 100. $16–$20. Hookups: water, electric.

Hyden

Trace Branch (Corps of Engineers–Buckhorn Lake), 1325 Buckham Dam Rd., 41721. T: (606) 398-7251. RV/tent: 30. free. Hookups: none.

Jamestown

Kendall Recreation Area (Corps of Engineers–Lake Cumberland), 855 Boat Dock Rd., 42501-0450. T: (270) 343-4660. RV/tent: 77. $14–$24. Hookups: water, electric.

Kuttawa

Boyds Landing Campground (Corps of Engineers), P.O. Box 218, 42045-0218. T: (270) 388-2721. RV/tent: 14. $12–$15. Hookups: water, electric.

Leitchfield

Dog Creek (Corps of Engineers–Nolin River Lake), 2150 Nolin Dam Rd., 42207. T: (270) 524-5454. RV/tent: 70. $11–$17. Hookups: water, electric.

Wax Site (Corps of Engineers–Nolin River Lake), 14008 Peonia Rd., 42726. T: (270) 242-7205. RV/tent: 110. $13–$20. Hookups: water, electric.

London

Daniel Boone National Forest (Holly Bay Rec. Area), London Ranger District, 40744. T: (800) 280-CAMP. RV/tent: 94. $5–$10. Hookups: water, electric.

Westgate RV Camping, 254 West Daniel Boone Pkwy, 40741. T: (606) 878-7330. RV/tent: 14. $19.95. Hookups: full.

White Oak Boat-In Campground, Daniel Boone National Forest, Stearns Ranger District Office, P.O. Box 429, Whitley, 42653. T: (606) 864-4163. RV/tent: 51. $6–$9. Hookups: none.

Louisa

The Falls Campground, P.O. Box 643, SR 3, 41230. T: (606) 686-3398. RV/tent: 111. $10.50–$21. Hookups: water, electric.

McDaniels

Axtel Campground (Corps of Engineers–Rough River Lake), Hwy. 79, 40152. T: (270) 257-2584. RV/tent: 158. $15–$22. Hookups: water, electric.

Laurel Branch Campground (Corps of Engineers–Rough River Lake), Hwy. 110, 40152. T: (270) 257-8839. RV/tent: 77. $11–$24. Hookups: water, electric.

Monticello

Conley Bottom Resort, Rte. 5 Box 5360, 42633. T: (606) 348-6351. RV/tent: 170. $15–$25. Hookups: water, electric.

Morehead

Buckskin Run Campground, 1750 801 South, 40351. T: (606) 784-7476. RV/tent: 30. $12–$16. Hookups: water, electric.

Mortons Gap

Pennyrile Campground, P.O. Box 612, 42440. T: (270) 258-5201. RV/tent: 15. $15. Hookups: water, electric.

Mount Olivet

Blue Licks Battlefield State Park, P.O. Box 66, 41064-0066. T: (606) 289-5507. RV/tent: 51. $8.50–$16. Hookups: water, electric.

Mount Vernon

Nicely's Campground, Rte. 2 Box 38, 40456. T: (606) 256-5637. RV/tent: 99. $13.95–$16.95. Hookups: water, electric.

Muldraugh

Military Park (Camp Carlson Army Travel Camp), 9186 US Hwy. 60, 40155. T: (502) 624-4836. RV/tent: 25. $9.50. Hookups: water, electric.

Murray

Wildcat Creek Rec Area, 28 Wildcat Beach Rd., 42071. T: (270) 436-5628. RV/tent: 50. $19. Hookups: water, electric.

Owensboro

Diamond Lake Resort Campground, P.O. Box 211, 42377. T: (270) 229-4961. RV/tent: 440. $19.50. Hookups: water, electric.

Windy Hollow Campground & Recreation Area, 5141 Windy Hollow Rd., 42301. T: (270) 785-4150. RV/tent: 300. $18. Hookups: water, electric.

Paducah

Fern Lake Campground, 5535 Cairo Rd., 42001. T: (270) 444-7939. RV/tent: 70. $20. Hookups: water, electric.

Park City

Cedar Hill Campground, P.O. Box 305, 42160. T: (270) 749-3114. RV/tent: 117. $14.25–$19. Hookups: water, electric.

Pineville

Pine Mountain State Resort Park, 1050 State Park Rd., 40977-0610. T: (606) 337-3066. RV/tent: 32. $10. Hookups: none.

Renfro Valley

Renfro Valley RV Park, US Hwy. 25, 40473. T: (800) 765-7464. RV/tent: 199. $21.20–$23.32. Hookups: water, electric.

Salt Lick

The Outpost RV Park, 340 Cave Run Lake Rd., 40371. T: (606) 683-2311. RV/tent: 89. $15. Hookups: water, electric.

Zilpo Recreation Area, Daniel Boone National Forest, P.O. Box 218, 40371. T: (606) 784-7788. RV/tent: 172. $12–$20. Hookups: water, electric.

Sanders

Eagle Valley Camping Resort, 1100 Eagle Valley Rd., 41083. T: (502) 347-9361. RV/tent: 225. $15. Hookups: water, electric.

Scottsville

Bailey's Point Campground (Corps of Engineers–Barren River Lake), 3147 Baileys Point Rd., 42164. T: (270) 622-6959. RV/tent: 215. $16–$19. Hookups: water, electric.

Shelbyville

Guist Creek Marina & Campground, 11990 Boat Dock Rd., 40065. T: (502) 633-1934. RV/tent: 50. $15–$16.50. Hookups: water, electric.

Slade

Koomer Ridge Campground, Daniel Boone National Forest, 705 West College Ave., 40380. T: (606) 663-2852. RV/tent: 54. $10–$15. Hookups: none.

Somerset

Cumberland Point Public Use Area (Corps of Engineers–Lake Cumberland), Rte. 8 Box 173T, 42501. T: (606) 871-7886. RV/tent: 30. $17–$23. Hookups: water, electric.

Fishing Creek Public Use Area (Corps of Engineers–Lake Cumberland), 1611 Hwy. 1248, 42501-0450. T: (606) 679-5174. RV/tent: 44. $17–$24. Hookups: water, electric.

Waitsboro Rec Area (Corps of Engineers–Lake Cumberland), 500 Waitsboro Rd., 42501. T: (606) 561-5513. RV/tent: 26. $14–$24. Hookups: water, electric.

Stearns

Big South Forks Nat'l. River & Rec. Area (Blue Heron), Park Headquarters, 4564 Leatherwood Rd., 37841. T: (423) 569-9778. RV/tent: 45. $15–$18. Hookups: water, electric.

KENTUCKY (continued)

Walton

Oak Creek Campground, P.O. Box 161, 41094. T: (859) 485-9131. RV/tent: 105. $17.50–$21. Hookups: water, electric.

Williamsburg

Williamsburg Travel Trailer Park, 50 Balltown Rd., 40769. T: (800) 426-3267. RV/tent: 56. $12. Hookups: water, electric.

LOUISIANA

Abbeville

Abbeville RV Park, 1004 Jacqulyn St., 70510. T: (337) 898-4042. www.abbevillervpark.com. abbrv@abbevillervpark.com. RV/tent: 55. $14–$17. Hookups: water, electric (30, 50 amps), sewer.

Betty's RV Park, 2118 South State St., 70510. T: (337) 893-7057. www.bettysrvpark.com. bettybernard@cox-internet.com. RV/tent: 68. $12–$14. Hookups: water, electric (30, 50 amps), sewer, cable TV.

Herbert's Cajun Haven RV Park, South State & Trahan St., 70510. T: (337) 893-3504. RV/tent: 110. $8–$12. Hookups: water, electric (30, 50 amps), sewer, laundry.

Abita Springs

Family Time Resorts, 24150 Hwy. 435, 70420. T: (504) 892-3565. RV/tent: 68. $12–$14. Hookups: water, electric (30, 50 amps)sewer, phone (modem), laundry.

Alexandria

Fish'n Heav'n RV Park, Robinson Bridge Rd., 71303. T: (318) 448-9269. RV/tent: 31. $18. Hookups: water, electric (30, 50 amps), sewer, laundry, row boat rentals.

KOA–Kincaid Lake Campground, South Kisatchie Ln., 71303. T: (318) 445-5227. RV/tent: 57. $18–$24. Hookups: water, electric (20, 30, 50 amps), sewer, laundry.

Angie

Great Southern RC & Bluegrass Park, Hwy. 21 & Main St., 70426. T: (504) 986-8411. RV/tent: 100. $12–$14. Hookups: water, electric (30, 50 amps), sewer, phone (modem).

Arcadia

Bonnie & Clyde Trade Days & Campground, South Hwy. 9, 71001. T: (318) 263-2437. RV/tent: 97. $15–$20. Hookups: water, electric (30, 50 amps), sewer, phone (modem).

Avoyselles

Grand Avoyelles RV Resort, Southeast & Hwy. 1, 70648. T: (800) 578-7275. RV/tent: 186. $14–$18. Hookups: water, electric (20, 30, 50 amps), sewer, cable TV, phone (modem), playground.

Baker

Azalea Mobile Home and RV Park, 3300 Baker Blvd., 70714. T: (504) 775-1123. RV/tent: 52. $12–$18. Hookups: water, electric (20, 30 amps), sewer, laundry.

Baton Rouge

Farr Park Campground, 6400 River Rd., 70820. T: (225) 769-7805. www.brec.org. RV/tent: 150. $12–$16. Hookups: water, electric (30 amps), sewer, phone (modem), laundry, playground.

Greenwood Park, 13350 Louisiana Hwy. 19, 70821. T: (225) 775-9166. www.brec.org. RV/tent: 75. $10–$12. Hookups: water, electric (30, 50 amps), sewer, phone (modem), laundry.

Knight's RV and Mobile Home Park, 14740 Florida Blvd., 70819. T: (504) 275-0679. RV/tent: 78. $11–$15. Hookups: water, electric (20, 30, 50 amps), sewer.

Beauregard

Longville Lake Park, Hwy. 110, 70652. T: (337) 725-3395. RV/tent: 175. $16. Hookups: water, electric (30, 50 amps).

Benton

Cypress–Black Bayou Recreation, 135 Cypress Park Dr., 71006. T: (318) 965-0007. www.cypressblackbayou.com. RV/tent: 73. $8–$13. Hookups: water, electric (20, 30, 50 amps), sewer.

Bogalusa

Clear Water Creek Resort Inc., 60407 Spring Valley Rd., 70427. T: (504) 732-5555. RV/tent: 55. $10–$16. Hookups: water, electric (20, 30 amps), sewer, bathhouse, showers.

Bossier

Maplewood RV Park, 452 Maplewood Dr., 71111. T: (800) 569-2264. RV/tent: 42. $17. Hookups: water, electric (30, 50 amps), sewer, phone.

Bourg

Grand Bois Campsite, 470 Hwy. 24, 70343. T: (504) 594-7410. RV/tent: 41. $9–$12. Hookups: water, electric.

Boyce

KOA–Alexandria West, 64 Kisatchie Ln., 71409. T: (800) 401-6450. RV/tent: 52. $15–$27. Hookups: water, electric, sewer.

Broussard

Maxie's Campground, P.O. Box, 70518. T: (337) 837-6200. www.maxiescampground.com. maxiescamp@aol.com. RV/tent: 70. $18. Hookups: water, electric (20, 30, 50 amps)sewer, phone (modem), laundry.

De Ridder

Sadler RV Park and Mobile Home, 7196 Main St., 70634. T: (318) 463-5561. RV/tent: 72. $12–$18. Hookups: water, electric (30, 50 amps), sewer, laundry.

Evangeline

Crooked Creek Campground, Hwy. 3187/Parish Police Jury, 70537. T: (337) 599-2661. RV/tent: 100. $12–$16. Hookups: water, electric (30 amps), sewer, laundry.

Florien

Hodges Wilderness Campground, P.O. Box 340, 71429. T: (318) 586-3523. www.hodges park.com. Hodges@cp.tel.net. RV/tent: 19. $16–$18. Hookups: water, electric (30, 50 amps), sewer, boat rentals.

Greenwood

Kelly's RV Park, 8560 Greenwood Rd., 71033. T: (318) 938-6360. RV/tent: 45. $18. Hookups: water, electric, sewer.

Hammond

Punkin Park Campground, 43037 North Billville Rd., 70404. T: (888) 585 5519. RV/tent: 52. $20. Hookups: water, electric, sewer.

Haughton

Pine Hill Mobile Home and RV, 2 Pine Hill Cir., 71037. T: (318) 949-3916. RV/tent: 28. $10–$14. Hookups: water, electric (20, 30 amps), sewer, bathhouse, showers.

Kinder

Grand Casino Coushatta Luxury RV Resort, 1240 711 Pow Wow Pkwy., 70648. T: (888) 867-8727. RV/tent: 156. $15–$19. Hookups: water, electric, sewer.

Quiet Oaks RV Park, 18159 TV Tower Rd., 70648. T: (318) 756-2230. www.quietoaks.com. RV/tent: 40. $12–$16. Hookups: water, electric (30, 50 amps), sewer, boat rentals.

Leesville

Shady Lake RV Park, 168 Sapphire Ln., 71446. T: (337) 239-4674. RV/tent: 25. $16. Hookups: water, electric (30, 50 amps), sewer, phone (modem).

Many

Cypress Bend Park (Toledo Bend Lake), 3462 Cypress Bend Dr., 71449. T: (318) 256-4118. F: (318) 256-4179. www.toledo-bend.com. srala@toledo-bend.com. RV/tent: 63. $14–$18. Hookups: water, electric (20, 30 amps), sewer, playground.

Marthaville

Country Livin' RV Park, 1115 Hwy. 174, 71450. T: (318) 796-2543. F: (318) 796-2543. RV/tent: 18. $15. Hookups: water, electric (30, 50 amps), sewer, laundry.

LOUISIANA (continued)

Monroe

Monroe Shilo RV and Travel, 7300 Frontage Rd., 71202. T: (318) 343-6098. RV/tent: 92. $18. Hookups: water, electric (30 amps), sewer.

Morgan City

Morgan City RV Park, 5428 Hwy. 6, 70380. T: (504) 385-4813. RV/tent: 99. $15–$16. Hookups: water, electric (30, 50 amps), sewer.

Natchitoches

Nakatosh RV Park, 5428 Hwy. 6, 71457. T: (318) 352-0911. RV/tent: 41. $12–$15. Hookups: water, electric, sewer.

New Orleans

Parc D'Orleans Campground, 7676 Chef Menteur Hwy., 70126. T: (504) 244-7434. RV/tent: 71. $16. Hookups: water, electric (20, 30 amps), sewer.

River Boat Travel Park, 6232 Chef Menteur Hwy., 70126. T: (504) 246-2628. RV/tent: 111. $10–$16. Hookups: water, electric (20 amps), sewer, laundry.

Port Allen

Cajun Country Campground, 4667 Rebelle Ln., 71001. T: (800) 264-8554. RV/tent: 77. $20–$22. Hookups: water, electric (30, 50 amps), sewer, phone (modem), laundry.

Ruston

Lincoln Parish Park, 198 Parish Park Rd., 71270. T: (318) 251-5156. RV/tent: 33. $12. Hookups: water, electric, sewer.

Shreveport

Campers RV Center, 7700 West 70th St., 71129. T: (318) 687-4567. RV/tent: 58. $17. Hookups: water, electric, sewer.

Tallulah

Roudaway RV Park, Hwy. 602, 71282. T: (318) 574-9026. RV/tent: 48. $10–$12. Hookups: water, electric (20 amps), sewer, laundry.

West Monroe

Cheniere Lake Park–Area 1, 337 Well Rd., 71292. T: (318) 387-2383. RV/tent: 10. $12–$10. Hookups: water, electric.

Pavilion RV Park, 309 Well Rd., 71292. T: (318) 322-4216. RV/tent: 60. $20. Hookups: water, electric (30, 50 amps), sewer.

MAINE

Acton

Apple Valley Campground, P.O. Box 92, 04001. T: (207) 636-2285. RV/tent: 145. $21. Hookups: water, electric (30 amps), sewer, cable TV.

Addison

Pleasant River RV Park, West Side Rd., 04606. T: (207) 483-4083. www.camp.com/pleasant river. RV/tent: 6. $20. Hookups: water, electric (20, 30, 50 amps), sewer, phone.

Alfred

Bunganut Lake Campground, P.O. Box 141, 04002. T: (207) 247-3875. www.camp.com/bunganutlake. RV/tent: 110. $24. Hookups: water, electric (20, 30 amps).

Scott's Cove Camping Area, Box 761, 04002. T: (207) 324-6594. www.scottscove camping.com. RV/tent: 50. $24. Hookups: water, electric (20, 30 amps), sewer.

Walnut Grove Campground, 599 Gore Rd., 04002. T: (207) 324-1207. www.gocamping america.com/walnutgroveme. RV/tent: 93. $18. Hookups: water, electric (20, 30 amps).

Baileyville

Sunset Acres Campground, 162 Airline Rd., 04694. T: (207) 454-1440. www.camp.com/sunsetacres. RV/tent: 15. $12. Hookups: water, electric (30, 50 amps), sewer.

Bangor

Shady Acres RV & Campground, RR 2 Box 7890, 04419. T: (207) 848-5515. RV/tent: 50. $18–$20. Hookups: water, electric (30 amps), sewer.

Wheeler Stream Camping Area, RR 2 Box 2800, 04401. T: (207) 848-3713. RV/tent: 25. $16. Hookups: water, electric (20, 30 amps).

Berwick

Beaver Dam Campground, 551 Rte. 9, 03901. T: (207) 698-2267. www.beaverdamcamp ground.com. RV/tent: 40. $22. Hookups: water, electric (20, 30, 50 amps), sewer.

Bethel

Bethel Outdoor Adventures & Campground, 121 Mayville Rd., 04217. T: (207) 824-4224. www.betheloutdooradventure.com. RV/tent: 34. $14. Hookups: water, electric (50 amps), sewer.

Biddeford

Homestead by the River, Rte. 5, 04072. T: (207) 282-6445. F: (207) 283-1287. www.homesteadbytheriver.com. RV/tent: 110. $20. Hookups: water, electric (30, 50 amps), sewer.

Shamrock RV Park, 391 West St., 04005. T: (207) 284-4282. www.lamere.net/shamrock. RV/tent: 60. $20. Hookups: water, electric (20, 30 amps), sewer.

Boothbay

Camper's Cove Campground, P.O. Box 136, 04537. T: (207) 633-5013 or (207) 633-0050. RV/tent: 56. $18. Hookups: water, electric (30 amps), sewer.

Bridgton

Vicki-Lin Camping Area, RR 2, P.O. Box 449, 04009. T: (207) 647-2630. RV/tent: 87. $25. Hookups: water, electric (30 amps), sewer.

Brownfield

Shannon's Saco River Sanctuary, Rte. 160 North, 04010. T: (207) 452-2274. www.angel fire.com/me3/shannonsanctuary. RV/tent: 55. $24. Hookups: water, electric (30 amps).

Bucksport

Masthead Campground, RR 2 Box 1590, 04416. T: (207) 469-3482. RV/tent: 38. $14. Hookups: water, electric (15, 20 amps).

Calais

Hilltop Campground, RR 1 Box 298, 04671. T: (207) 454-3985. www.hilltopcamping.com. RV/tent: 81. $15. Hookups: water, electric (20, 30, 50 amps), sewer.

Danforth

Greenland Cove Campground, East Grand Lake, 04424. T: (207) 448-2863. F: (207) 532-4456. www.rec.com/gcc. RV/tent: 85. $21. Hookups: water, electric (20, 30 amps).

Deer Isle

Sunshine Campground, RR 2 Box 521E, 04627. T: (207) 348-2663. RV/tent: 22. $16. Hookups: water, electric (15, 20 amps).

Denmark

Granger Pond Camping Area, P.O. Box 47, 04022. T: (207) 452-2342. RV/tent: 45. $12. Hookups: water, electric (15 amps), sewer.

Pleasant Mountain Camping Area, RR 1, 04022. T: (207) 452-2170. RV/tent: 40. $20. Hookups: water, electric (30 amps), sewer.

Dixfield

Mountain View Campground, 208 Weld St., 04224. T: (207) 562-8285. www.explore.com/~jenndon/mountainview. RV/tent: 45. $19. Hookups: water, electric (50 amps), sewer.

East Hebron

Hebron Pines Campground, RR 1, 04238. T: (207) 966-2179. RV/tent: 24. $21. Hookups: water, electric (30 amps).

East Machias

River's Edge Campground, HCR 74, Box 265, 04630. T: (207) 255-5987. RV/tent: 38. $13. Hookups: water, electric (20, 30, 50 amps), sewer.

Eastbrook

Eastbrook Campground, RR 1 Box 465M, 04634. T: (207) 565-3509 or (888) 565-2319. www.eastbrookcamp.com. RV/tent: 5. $10–$24. Hookups: water, electric (20, 30, 50 amps), sewer.

MAINE (continued)

Eastport

Seaview Campground, 16 Norwood Rd., 04631. T: (207) 853-4471. www.Eastport.com. RV/tent: 74. $18. Hookups: water, electric (20, 30 amps), sewer, cable TV.

Ellsworth

Hospitality Woods RV Park, 2 Our Way, 04605. T: (207) 667-2668 or (800) 773-2668. www.cT:net/~dandan. RV/tent: 47. $25. Hookups: water, electric (20, 30, 50 amps), sewer, cable TV, phone.

Farmingdale

Foggy Bottom RV Campground, 195 AQ Ave., 04344. T: (207) 582-0075. F: (207) 582-8584. RV/tent: 9. $20. Hookups: water, electric (50 amps), sewer.

Troll Valley Campground, RR 4, 04938. T: (207) 778-3656. RV/tent: 25. $17. Hookups: water, electric (50 amps).

Freeport

Big Skye Acres Campground, 1430 Hallowell, 04222. T: (207) 688-4288. F: Fax (207) 688-3323. www.bigskyeacres.com. RV/tent: 212. $23. Hookups: water, electric (30 amps), sewer.

Blueberry Pond Campground, 218 Poland Range Rd., 04069. T: (207) 688-4421 or (877) 290-1381. F: Fax (207) 688-4063. www.blueberrycampground.com. RV/tent: 97. $19. Hookups: water, electric (20, 30 amps), sewer.

Recompence Shore Campsites, 134 Burnett Rd., 04032. T: (207) 865-9307. www.freeportcamping.com. RV/tent: 104. $14. Hookups: water, electric (15 amps).

Fryeburg

Canal Bridge Campground, Rte. 5, 04037. T: (207) 935-2286. RV/tent: 50. $20. Hookups: water, electric (20 amps).

Georgetown

Sagahadoc Bay Campground, Sagahadoc Bay Rd., 04548. T: (207) 371-2014. www.sagbaycamping.com. RV/tent: 36. $24. Hookups: water, electric (50 amps), sewer.

Gray

Twin Brooks Camping Area, P.O. Box 194, 04039. T: (207) 428-3832. RV/tent: 52. $20. Hookups: water, electric (20 amps), sewer.

Greenville

Allagash Gateway Campsite, P.O. Box 675, 04441. T: (207) 723-9215. www.allagashgateway.com. RV/tent: 30. $12. Hookups: none.

Frost Pond Campground, P.O. Box 620, HCR 76, 04441. T: (207) 695-2821. www.frostpondcamps.com. RV/tent: 10. $15. Hookups: none.

Moosehead Family Campground, P.O. Box 307, 04441. T: (207) 695-2210. F: (207) 695-2007. www.mooseheadcampground.com. RV/tent: 35. $15. Hookups: water, electric (50 amps).

Greenwood

Littlefield Beaches Campground, 13 Littlefield Ln., 04255. T: (207) 875-3290. www.littlefieldbeaches.com. RV/tent: 170. $21. Hookups: water, electric (30 amps), sewer.

Hanover

Stony Brook Recreation, 42 Powell Pl., 04237. T: (207) 824-2836 or (888) 439-5625 ext 0604. F: (207) 824-6898. www.stonybrookrec.com. RV/tent: 140. $18. Hookups: water, electric (30 amps), sewer, cable TV.

Harrison

Bear Mountain Village Cabins and Sites, RR 2, P.O. Box 745, 04040. T: (207) 583-2541. RV/tent: 71. $10–$12. Hookups: water, electric (30 amps).

Vacationland Campground, 233 Vacationland Rd., 04040. T: (207) 583-4953. www.vacationlandcampground.com. RV/tent: 90. $18. Hookups: water, electric (30 amps), sewer, phone, modem.

Hermon

Pumpkin Patch RV Resort, 149 Billings Rd., 04401. T: (207) 848-2231. F: (207) 848-7731. www.pumpkinpatchrv.com. RV/tent: 35. $22. Hookups: water, electric (30, 50 amps), sewer, cable TV.

Holden

Red Barn RV Park, 602 Main Rd., 04429. T: (207) 843-6011. F: (207) 843-6011. RV/tent: 125. $15. Hookups: water, electric (20, 30, 50 amps), sewer, cable TV, phone.

Jackman

Jackman Landing, P.O. Box 567, Main St., 04945. T: (207) 668-3301. RV/tent: 24. $15. Hookups: water, electric (30 amps).

John's Four Season Accomodations, 37 John St., 04945. T: (207) 668-7683 or (888) 668-0098. F: (207) 668-7683. RV/tent: 14. $15. Hookups: water, electric (30 amps), sewer, cable TV.

Loon Echo Family Campground, Rte. 201, P.O. Box 711, 04945. T: (207) 668-4829. RV/tent: 15. $16. Hookups: none.

Moose Alley Campground, Rte. 201, P.O. Box 298, 04945. T: (207) 668-2781. RV/tent: 21. $15. Hookups: water, electric (30 amps), cable TV.

Jefferson

Town Line Campsites, 483 East Pond Rd., 04348. T: (207) 832-7055. RV/tent: 55. $13. Hookups: water, electric (15 amps).

Kennebunk

Hemlock Grove Campground, 1299 Portland Rd., 04046. T: (207) 985-0398. RV/tent: 54. $18. Hookups: water, electric (30, 50 amps), sewer.

Red Apple Campground, 111 Sinnott Rd., 04046. T: (207) 967-4927. F: (207) 967-8905. www.redapplecampground.com. RV/tent: 37. $16. Hookups: water, electric (20, 30 amps), sewer, cable TV, phone.

Salty Acres, 272 Mills Rd., Rte. 9, 04046. T: (207) 967-2483. F: (207) 967-2500. RV/tent: 140. $18. Hookups: water, electric (20, 30 amps), sewer.

Kezar Falls

Windsong Campground, P.O. Box 547, 04047. T: (207) 625-4389. RV/tent: 35. $13. Hookups: water, electric (20, 30 amps).

Kingfield

Deer Farm Campground, Tufts Pond Rd., 04947. T: (207) 265-4599. www.deerfarmcamps.com. RV/tent: 47. $16. Hookups: water, electric (30 amps).

Lebanon

Heavenlee Acres Campground, 75 Cemetery Rd., 04027. T: (207) 457-1260. F: (207) 457-3088. www.gocampingamerica.com/heavenlee. RV/tent: 140. $17. Hookups: water, electric (30, 50 amps), sewer.

King & Queens Court Resort, 21 Flat Rock Bridge Rd., 04027. T: (207) 339-9465. F: (207) 339-9583. www.kingandqueenscamping.com. RV/tent: 70. $30. Hookups: water, electric (20 amps), sewer.

Potter's Place Adult Camping Area, 89 Baker's Grant Rd., 04027. T: (207) 457-1341. RV/tent: 100. $16. Hookups: water, electric (20, 30 amps).

Lee

Sleeping Bear Camping, P.O. Box 37, 04455. T: (207) 738-3148. RV/tent: 9. $12. Hookups: water, electric (30 amps).

Lewiston

Lewiston/Auburn North Allen Pond Campground, 102 North Mountain Rd., 04236. T: (207) 946-7439. RV/tent: 65. $18. Hookups: water, electric (30 amps).

Lincoln

Lakeside Camping and Cabins, P.O. Box 38, 04457. T: (207) 732-4241. RV/tent: 40. $15. Hookups: water, electric (15 amps), sewer.

Litchfield

Birches Family Campground, Norris Point Rd., 04350. T: (207) 268-4330. www.thebirches.com. RV/tent: 115. $8. Hookups: water, electric (30 amps), modem.

Livermore

Rol-Lin Hills, RR 2, P.O. Box 3300, 04254. T: (207) 897-6394. RV/tent: 30. $13. Hookups: water, electric (30 amps), sewer.

Lubec

South Bay Campground, RR 1 Box 6565, 04652. T: (207) 733-1037. F: (207) 733-1038. www.ne.com/southbay. RV/tent: 42. $15. Hookups: water, electric (20, 30 amps), sewer.

Sunset Point Trailer Park, P.O. Box 180, 04652. T: (207) 733-2272. RV/tent: 45. $19. Hookups: water, electric (20, 50 amps).

Madison

Abnaki Family Camping Center, Abnaki Rd., 04950. T: (207) 474-2070. RV/tent: 95. $13–$20. Hookups: water, electric (20 amps).

MAINE (continued)

Medway

Pine Grove Campground and Cottages, P.O. Box 604, 04460. T: (207) 746-5172. RV/tent: 43. $16. Hookups: water, electric (30 amps), sewer, modem.

Millinocket

Abol Bridge Campground, Bowater Great Northern Paper Co. Rd., 04462. T: No phone. RV/tent: 36. $15. Hookups: none.

Hidden Springs Campground, 224 Central St., 04462. T: (207) 723-6337 or (888) 685-4488. www.hiddenspring.com. RV/tent: 103. $15. Hookups: water, electric (50 amps).

Jo-Mary Lake Campground, P.O. Box 329, 04462. T: (207) 723-8117. RV/tent: 60. $15. Hookups: none.

Pray's Big Eddy Campground, P.O. Box 548, 04462. T: (207) 723-9581. www.eastmill.com/pages/pray. RV/tent: 80. $8 per person. Hookups: water, electric (15 amps).

Moody

Outdoor World-Moody Beach Campground, US 1, 04054. T: (207) 646-4586. F: (207) 646-0637. www.campoutdoorworld.com. RV/tent: 150. $20. Hookups: water, electric (30, 50 amps), sewer.

Mount Vernon

Five Seasons Family Resort, RR 2, 04352. T: (207) 685-9141. www.5seasonsfamily resort.com. RV/tent: 54. $24. Hookups: water, electric (30 amps).

Naples

Brandy Pond Park, P.O. Box 1617, 04055. T: (207) 693-3129. RV/tent: 75. $10–$12. Hookups: water, electric (20 amps), sewer.

Colonial Mast Campground, Kansas Rd., 04055. T: (207) 693-6652. RV/tent: 79. $26. Hookups: water, electric (30 amps), sewer.

Loon's Haven Family Campground, Rte. 114, 04055. T: (207) 693-6881. RV/tent: 37. $23. Hookups: water, electric (20 amps).

New Harbor

Pemaquid Point Campground, 9 Pemaquid Point Campground Rd., 04554. T: (207) 677-CAMP. RV/tent: 51. $26. Hookups: water, electric (50 amps).

Newport

Christies Campground, Rte. 2 Box 565, 04953. T: (207) 368-4645. F: (207) 368-4251. www.camp.com/christies. RV/tent: 80. $14. Hookups: water, electric (20, 30 amps), sewer.

Tent Village Travel Trailer Park, RR 2 Box 580, 04953. T: (207) 368-5047 or (800) 319-9333. www.camp.com/village. RV/tent: 52. $15. Hookups: water, electric (20, 30 amps), sewer.

Nobleboro

Duck Puddle Campground, P.O. Box 176, 04555. T: (207) 563-5608. www.duckpuddlecamp ground.com. RV/tent: 120. $22. Hookups: water, electric (30 amps), sewer.

North Bridgton

Lakeside Pines Campground, P.O. Box 182, 04057. T: (207) 647-3935. www.lakeside-pinescamping.com. RV/tent: 185. $31. Hookups: water, electric (30 amps), sewer.

Old Orchard Beach

Acorn Village, 42 Walnut St., 04064. T: (207) 934-4154. www.camp.com/acornvillage. RV/tent: 75. $23. Hookups: water, electric (20 amps) sewer.

Ne're Beach Family Campground, 38 Saco Ave. (Rte. 5), 04064. T: (207) 934-7614. RV/tent: 58. $27. Hookups: water, electric (20, 30 amps), sewer.

Virginia Tent & Trailer Park, Box 242, 04064. T: (207) 934-4791. www.virginiaparkcamp-ground.com. RV/tent: 130. $24. Hookups: water, electric (20, 30, 50 amps), sewer.

Wagon Wheel Campground & Cabins, 3 Old Orchard Rd., 04064. T: (207) 934-2160. F: (207) 934-4578. www.gocampingamerica.com/wagonwheel. RV/tent: 54. $32. Hookups: water, electric (20, 30 amps), sewer.

Oxford

Mirror Pond Campground, 210 Tiger Hill Rd., 04270. T: (207) 539-4888. RV/tent: 40. $15. Hookups: water, electric (30 amps).

Parsonfield

Locklin Camping Area, Tripp Town Rd., 04047. T: (207) 625-8622. RV/tent: 50. $18. Hookups: water, electric (50 amps).

Patten

Shin Pond Village Campground & Cottages, Shin Pond Rd., 04765. T: (207) 528-2900. www.shinpond.com. RV/tent: 30. $6–$20. Hookups: water, electric (30 amps).

Perry

Knowlton's Campground, RR 1 Box 171, 04667. T: (207) 726-4756. RV/tent: 80. $14. Hookups: water, electric (20, 30 amps), sewer.

Phippsburg

Ocean View Park/Popham Beach, Rte. 209, 04562. T: (207) 389-2564 (summer) or (207) 443-1000 (winter). RV/tent: 48. $21. Hookups: water, electric (20 amps), sewer.

Poland

Range Pond Campground, 94 Plains Rd., 04274. T: (207) 998-2624. www.rangepondcamp.com. RV/tent: 90. $18. Hookups: water, electric (30 amps), sewer.

Richmond

Nesowadnehunk Lake Wilderness Campground, Langdon Rd., 04357. T: (207) 458-1551. RV/tent: 46. $8 per person, $16 mini- mum. Hookups: water, electric (15 amps).

Rockwood

Old Mill Campground, Cabins & Marina, Rte. 15, 04478. T: (207) 534-7333. F: (207) 534-9792. RV/tent: 50. $16. Hookups: water, electric (20 amps), sewer.

Seboomook Wilderness Campground, P.O. Box 560, HC 85, 04478. T: (207) 534-8824. www.seboomookwilderness.com. RV/tent: 39. $20. Hookups: water, electric (15 amps), sewer.

Roxbury

Silver Lake Campground, P.O. Box 32, 04275. T: (207) 545-0416. RV/tent: 25. $14. Hookups: water, electric (30 amps).

Rumford

Madison Resort Inn & Campground, Rte. 2, 04276. T: (207) 364-7973 or (800) 258-MADI-SON. F: (207) 369-0341. www.madison inn.com. RV/tent: 61. $20. Hookups: water, electric (50 amps).

Sanford

Apache Campground, 165 Bernier Rd., 04073. T: (207) 324-5652. www.camp.com/ apachecampground. RV/tent: 150. $17. Hookups: water, electric (20, 30 amps) sewer.

Jellystone Park Camp Resort, 1175 Main St., 04073. T: (207) 324-7782. www.jelly-stoneme.com. RV/tent: 102. $17. Hookups: water, electric (30, 50 amps), sewer.

Sand Pond Campground, P.O. Box 741., 04073. T: (207) 324-1752. F: (207) 324-17. www.sandpond.com. RV/tent: 48. $21. Hookups: water, electric (30, 50 amps), sewer.

Scarborough

Wild Duck Campground, 39 Dunstan Landing Rd., 04074. T: (207) 883-4432. RV/tent: 70. $23. Hookups: water, electric (30 amps), sewer.

Sebago

Nason's Beach & Campground, 771 Sebago Rd., 04029. T: (207) 787-2345. RV/tent: 50. $22. Hookups: water, electric (30 amps).

Skowhegan

Eaton Mountain Ski Area and Campground, HCR 71, P.O. Box 128, 04976. T: (207) 474-2666. www.eatonmountain.com. RV/tent: 32. $15. Hookups: water, electric (30 amps), sewer.

Two Rivers Campground, HCR 71, P.O. Box 14, 04976. T: (207) 474-6482. www.twors.com. RV/tent: 65. $18. Hookups: water, electric (30 amps), cable TV, phone.

Yonder Hill Campground, 17 Parlin St., 04976. T: (207) 474-7353. RV/tent: 70. $18. Hookups: water, electric (30 amps), sewer.

Solon

The Evergreens Campground, Rte. 201 A, 04979. T: (207) 643-2324. www.Kynd.com/ ~evrgrncp. RV/tent: 40. $20. Hookups: water, electric (30 amps).

South Thomaston

Lobster Buoy Campsites, HC 33, P.O. Box 625, 04858. T: (207) 594-7546. RV/tent: 40. $16. Hookups: water, electric (30 amps).

MAINE (continued)

Stetson

Stetson Shores, P.O. Box 86M, 04488. T: (207) 296-2041. www.camp.com/stetson. RV/tent: 47. $19. Hookups: water, electric (20, 30 amps), sewer.

Steuben

Mainayr Campground, 321 Village Rd., 04680. T: (207) 546-2690. F: (207) 546-3780. www.mainayr.com. RV/tent: 100. $17. Hookups: water, electric (20, 30 amps), sewer.

Stonington

Greenlaw's RV Tent & Rental, P.O. Box 72, 04681. T: (207) 367-5049. RV/tent: 27. $18. Hookups: water, electric (15, 20, 30 amps), sewer.

The Forks

Indian Pond Campground, HCR 63, P.O. Box 52, 04985. T: (800) 371-7774. F: (207) 237-3269. RV/tent: 27. $14. Hookups: none.

Northern Outdoors Adventure Resort, Rte. 201, 04985. T: (800) 765-7238. F: (207) 663-2244. www.northernoutdoors.com. RV/tent: 10. $11 per person. Hookups: none.

Tremont

Quietside Campground & Cabins, P.O. Box 10, 04653. T: (207) 244-5992. RV/tent: 35. $18–$22. Hookups: water, electric (20, 30 amps).

Vassalboro

Green Valley Campground, Cross Hill Rd., 04989. T: (207) 923-3000. RV/tent: 80. $22. Hookups: water, electric (30 amps), sewer.

Warren

Sandy Shores RV Resort, 459 Sandy Shores Rd., 04864. T: (207) 273-2073. F: (207) 845-2019. www.midcoast.com/sandyshores. RV/tent: 29. $25. Hookups: water, electric (50 amps), sewer, cable TV.

Waterville

Countryside Campground, West River Rd., 04903. T: (207) 873-4603. RV/tent: 25. $12. Hookups: water, electric (30 amps), sewer, phone, cable TV.

Weld

Dummer's Beach Campground, P.O. Box 82, 04285. T: (207) 585-2200. RV/tent: 200. $17. Hookups: water, electric (30 amps).

Wells

Beach Acres Campground, 563M Post Rd., 04090. T: (207) 646-5612. F: Fax (207) 646-2288. www.beachacres.com. RV/tent: 71. $20. Hookups: water, electric (20, 30, 50 amps), sewer.

Gregoire's Campground, 697 Sanford, 04090. T: (207) 646-3711. RV/tent: 100. $15. Hookups: water, electric (20, 30 amps), sewer.

Pinederosa Camping Area, 128 North Village Rd., 04090. T: (207) 646-2492. www.pinederosa.com. RV/tent: 122. $20. Hookups: water, electric (20, 30 amps), sewer.

Riverside Campground, 2295 Post Rd., 04090. T: (207) 646-3145. www.riversidecampgroundwells.com. RV/tent: 125. $21. Hookups: water, electric (20, 30, 50 amps), sewer, cable TV, phone.

Stadig Mobile Park & Campground, 146 Bypass Rd., 04090. T: (207) 646-2298. www.stadig.com. RV/tent: 150. $18. Hookups: water, electric (20, 30 amps), sewer.

West Bethel

Pleasant River Campground, P.O. Box 92, 04286. T: (207) 836-2000. RV/tent: 75. $18. Hookups: water, electric (50 amps), sewer.

West Poland

Hemlocks Camping Area, P.O. Box 58, 04291. T: (207) 998-2384 or (888) 578-9251. www.hemlockscampground.com. RV/tent: 75. $17. Hookups: water, electric (30 amps), sewer.

Mac's Campground, P.O. Box 87, 04291. T: (207) 998-4238. RV/tent: 33. $18. Hookups: water, electric (20 amps), sewer.

Wilsons Mills

Aziscoos Valley Camping Area, HCR 10, P.O. Box 302, 03579. T: (207) 486-3271. RV/tent: 31. $9. Hookups: water, electric (30 amps).

Windham

Highland Lake Park, 19 Roosevelt Trail, 04062. T: (207) 892-8911. RV/tent: 40. $16. Hookups: water, electric (20 amps), sewer, cable TV.

Winslow

Giordano's Camping and Recreation, RR 2, 04901. T: (207) 873-2408. www.campanddance.com. RV/tent: 45. $16. Hookups: water, electric (15 amps).

Winthrop

Augusta West Kampground, P.O. Box 232, 04364. T: (207) 377-9993. RV/tent: 81. $19. Hookups: water, electric (30 amps), sewer, phone, modem.

York Beach

York Beach Camper Park, 11 Cappy's Ln., 03910. T: (207) 363-1343. RV/tent: 39. $25. Hookups: water, electric (30, 50 amps), sewer.

York Harbor

Camp Eaton, Rte. 1A, 03911. T: (207) 363-3424. www.campeaton.com. RV/tent: 307. $32. Hookups: water, electric (30, 50 amps), sewer, cable TV.

MARYLAND

Big Pool

Indian Springs Campground, 10809 Big Pool Rd., 21711. T: (301) 842-3336 or (800) 760-9051. RV/tent: 90. Hookups: water, electric, sewer.

Callaway

Take-It-Easy Campground, P.O. Box 357, 20620. T: (301) 994-0494. RV/tent: 250. Hookups: water, electric, sewer.

Delmar

Woodlawn Campground, 1209 Walnut St., 21875. T: (410) 896-2979. RV/tent: 35. $15. Hookups: water, electric (30 amps).

Elkton

Woodlands Camping Resort, 265 Starkey Ln., 21921. T: (410) 398-4414 or (800)-972-2674. RV/tent: 155. $21. Hookups: water, electric (30, 50 amps), sewer.

Frostburg

Mason Dixon Campground, 4121 Greenville, 21532. T: (888) MAPLECAMP. RV/tent: 70. $15–$20. Hookups: water, electric (20, 30 amps), sewer.

Goldsboro

Lake Bonnie Campsites, P.O. Box 142, 21636. T: (410) 482-8479. RV/tent: 110. $16. Hookups: water, electric (20, 30 amps).

Grantsville

New Germany State Park, 349 Headquarters Ln., 21536. T: (301) 895-5453. www.dnr.state.md.us. RV/tent: 37. $15. Hookups: none.

Hancock

Happy Hills Campground, 12617 Seavolt Rd., 21750. T: (301) 678-7760. RV/tent: 205. $21–$24. Hookups: water, electric (20, 30 amps), sewer.

Indian Springs

Indian Springs Campground, 10809 Big Pool Rd., 21711. T: (301) 842-3336. RV/tent: 95. $15. Hookups: water, electric (20, 30 amps), sewer.

Leonardtown

LaGrande Estate Camping Resort, Rte. 5, 20650. T: (301) 475-8550. RV/tent: 109. $19–$20. Hookups: water, electric (30 amps), sewer.

Newburg

Aqua-Land Campground, US 301 South, 20664. T: (301) 259-2575. RV/tent: 136. $20–$23. Hookups: water, electric (20, 30, 50 amps), sewer.

MARYLAND (continued)

North East

Elk Nest State Park, 4395 Turkey Point Rd., 21901. T: (410) 287-5333. RV/tent: 279. $18–$25. Hookups: water, electric (20), sewer.

Perryville

Riverview Campground, 1200 Frenchtown Rd., 21903. T: (410) 642-6200. RV/tent: 64. $22. Hookups: water, electric (30, 50 amps), sewer.

Pocomoke

Lake Somerset Campground, US 13 South, 21851. T: (410) 957-9897. RV/tent: 127. $23. Hookups: water, electric (30 amps).

Queen Anne

Tuckahoe State Park, 13070 Crouse Mill Rd., 21657. T: (410) 820-1668. RV/tent: 35. $13–$18. Hookups: none.

Snow Hill

Pocomoke River State Park, 3461 Worecester Hwy., 21863. T: (410) 632-2566. RV/tent: 200. $13–23. Hookups: electric (20, 30 amps).

Thurmont

Catoctin Mountain National Park, 6602 Foxville Rd., 21788. T: (301) 663-9388. RV/tent: 51. $12. Hookups: none.

Crow's Nest Campground, Box 145, Rte. 77W, 21788. T: (301) 271-7632 or (800) 866-1959. RV/tent: 110. $20–$22. Hookups: water, electric (15, 20, 30 amps), sewer.

MASSACHUSETTS

Amesbury

Powow Cove Campground, 2 Powow Cove Ln., 01913. T: (978) 399-4022. RV/tent: 73. $25. Hookups: water, electric (30 amps).

Ashburnham

Howe's Camping, 133 Sherbert Rd., 01430. T: (978) 827-4558 or (800) 766-4807. RV/tent: 30. $18. Hookups: water, electric (20 amps).

Ashby

The Pines, 39 Davis Rd., 01431. T: (978) 386-7702. F: (978) 386-2354. RV/tent: 59. $23. Hookups: water, electric (50 amps).

Assonet

Forge Pond Campground, 62 Forge Rd., 02702. T: (508) 644-2969. RV/tent: 65. $20. Hookups: water, electric (15 amps).

Barre

Coldbrook Campground, 864 Old Coldbrook Rd., 01005. T: (978) 355-2090. www.coldbrookcountry.com. RV/tent: 195. $23. Hookups: water, electric (30 amps).

Becket

Bonny Rigg Campground, P.O. Box 14, 01011. T: (413) 623-5366. www.bonnyrigg.com. RV/tent: 200. $21. Hookups: water, electric (30 amps).

Bedford

Military Park (Hanscom AFB FAM-CAMP), P.O. Box 479, 02047. T: (617) 377-4670. RV/tent: 73. $6–$12. Hookups: water, electric (20, 30, 50 amps).

Bernardston

Purple Meadow Campground, P.O. Box 192, 01337. T: (413) 648-9289. RV/tent: 40. $10–$13. Hookups: water, electric (15, 20, 30 amps).

Travelers Woods of New England, P.O. Box 88, 152 River St., 01337. T: (413) 648-9105. RV/tent: 94. $18. Hookups: water, electric (30 amps), sewer.

Bolton

Crystal Springs Campground, P.O. Box 279, 01740. T: (978) 779-2711. RV/tent: 200. $17. Hookups: water, electric (30 amps), sewer.

Brimfield

Village Green Family Campground, 228 Sturbridge Rd. Rte. 20, 01010. T: (413) 245-3504. F: (413) 245-0115. www.villagegreencampground.com. RV/tent: 131. $20. Hookups: water, electric (30 amps).

Charlemont

Mohawk Park, P.O. Box 668, 01339. T: (413) 339-4470. RV/tent: 81. $20. Hookups: water, electric (20 amps), sewer.

Dennisport

Grindell's Ocean View Park, 61 Old Wharf Rd., 02639. T: (508) 398-2671. RV/tent: 160. $30. Hookups: water, electric (20 amps), sewer, cable TV.

East Douglas

Lake Manchaug Camping, 76 Oak St., 01516. T: (508) 476-2471. RV/tent: 190. $30. Hookups: water, electric (50 amps), sewer.

East Otis

Laurel Ridge Camping Area, 40 Old Blandford Rd., 01029. T: (413) 269-4804 or (800) 538-CAMP. RV/tent: 181. $22. Hookups: water, electric (30 amps).

East Wareham

Maple Park Family Campground, RFD. 2, 02538. T: (508) 295-4945 or (508) 291-CAMP. RV/tent: 400. $22. Hookups: water, electric (20 amps), sewer.

Granville

Granville State Forest, 323 West Hartland Rd., 01034. T: (413) 357-6611. RV/tent: 36. $12. Hookups: none.

Hancock

Berkshire Vista Nude Resort, P.O. Box 1177, 01237. T: (413) 738-5154. F: (413) 232-7860. www.berkshirevista.com. RV/tent: 180. $57. Hookups: water, electric (50 amps), sewer.

Hinsdale

Fernwood Forest, P.O. Box 896, 01235. T: (413) 655-2292. www.topcities.com/Busines/fernwood/index.htm. RV/tent: 36. $15. Hookups: water, electric (30 amps).

Mashpee

Johns Pond Campground/Otis Trailer Village, P.O. Box 586, 02541. T: (508) 477-0444. F: (508) 457-4233. www.johnspondcampground.com. RV/tent: 90. $20. Hookups: water, electric (30 amps), sewer.

Monson

Partridge Hollow, P.O. Box 41, Munn Rd., 01057. T: (413) 267-5122. RV/tent: 240. $23. Hookups: water, electric (50 amps).

North Egremont

Prospect Lake Park, 50 Prospect Lake Rd., 02152. T: (413) 528-4158 or (877) 860-4757. F: (413) 528-3666. RV/tent: 140. $24. Hookups: water, electric (30 amps), sewer.

North Rutland

Pout & Trout Family Campground, 94 River Rd., 01543. T: (508) 886-6677. F: (508) 886-6931. RV/tent: 156. $20. Hookups: water, electric (30 amps).

North Truro

North of Highland, 52 Head of the Meadow Rd., 02652. T: (508) 487-1191. RV/tent: 237. $20. Hookups: none.

Northfield

Barton Cove Campground and Canoe Shuttle Service, 90 Millers Falls Rd., 01360. T: (413) 863-9300. RV/tent: 31. $15. Hookups: none.

Otis

Camp Overflow, P.O. Box 645, 01253. T: (413) 269-4036. RV/tent: 175. $13–$18. Hookups: water, electric (20 amps), dump station.

Mountain View Campground, P.O. Box 162, 01253. T: (413) 269-8928. www.otismass.com; www.berkshire.com. RV/tent: 54. $25. Hookups: water, electric (50 amps), sewer.

MASSACHUSETTS (continued)

Phillipston

Lamb City Campground, 85 Royalston Rd., 01331. T: (978) 249-2049 or (800) 292-5262. www.lambcity.com. RV/tent: 212. $22. Hookups: water, electric (30 amps), sewer, cable TV.

Pittsfield

Bonnie Brae Cabins & Campsites, 108 Broadway St., 01201. T: (413) 442-3754. www.hometown.aol.com/honey44/myhomepage/business.html. RV/tent: 42. $26. Hookups: water, electric (30 amps), sewer.

Plymouth

Indianhead Resort, 1929 State Rd., 02360. T: (508) 888-3688. F: (508) 888-5907. RV/tent: 200. $20. Hookups: water, electric (50 amps).

Shady Pond Campground, 834 Bourne Rd., 02360. T: (503) 759-9336. www.shadypond.com. RV/tent: 200. $22–$28. Hookups: water, electric (50 amps), sewer.

Rochester

Knight and Look Campground, 241 Marion Rd., 02770. T: (508) 763-2454. RV/tent: 120. $23–$26. Hookups: water, electric (20 amps), sewer.

Sandwich

Dunroamin' Trailer Park, 5 John Ewer Rd., 02563. T: (508) 477-0541 or (508) 477-0859. F: (508) 477-9659. RV/tent: 64. $30. Hookups: water, electric (30 amps), sewer.

South Dennis

Airline Mobile Home Park, 310 Chartham Rd., 02660. T: (508) 385-3616. RV/tent: 50. $17–$27. Hookups: water, electric (15, 30 amps).

South Wellfleet

Paine's Campground, P.O. Box 201, 02663. T: (508) 349-3007. F: (508) 349-0246. www.campingcapecod.com. RV/tent: 50. $18. Hookups: water, electric (30 amps).

Southwick

Southwick Acres, College Hwy., 01077. T: (413) 569-6339. F: (413) 569-2987. www.southwickacres.com. RV/tent: 40. $33. Hookups: water, electric (30 amps).

Townsend

Pearl Hill State Park, New Fitchburg Rd., 01469. T: (978) 597-8802. RV/tent: 51. $12. Hookups: none.

Vineyard Haven

Martha's Vineyard Family Campground, Inc., Edgartown Rd., 02568. T: (508) 693-3772. F: (508) 693-5767. www.campmvfc.com. RV/tent: 40. $32. Hookups: water, electric (30 amps), sewer, cable TV, modem.

Warwick

Wagon Wheel Camping Area, 909 Wendell Rd., 01378. T: (978) 544-3425. RV/tent: 102. $18. Hookups: water, electric (30 amps), sewer.

Washington

Summit Hill Campground, Summit Hill Rd., 01223. T: (413) 623-5761. RV/tent: 106. $20. Hookups: water, electric (15 amps).

West Brookfield

Highview Campground, 58 John Gilbert Rd., 01585. T: (508) 867-7800. RV/tent: 212. $27. Hookups: water, electric (30 amps).

The Old Sawmill Campground, Long Hill Rd., 01585. T: (508) 867-2427. RV/tent: 120. $19. Hookups: water, electric (20, 30 amps).

West Sutton

Sutton Falls Camping Area, 90 Manchaug Rd., 01590. T: (508) 865-3898. www.suttonfalls.com. RV/tent: 119. $19. Hookups: water, electric (15 amps).

Westhampton

Windy Acres Campground, 139 South St., 01027. T: (413) 527-9862. RV/tent: 127. $22. Hookups: water, electric (30 amps).

Whately/Deerfield

White Birch Campground, 214 North St., 01093. T: (413) 665-4941. RV/tent: 60. $22. Hookups: water, electric (30 amps).

Windsor

Windsor State Forest, River Rd., 01270. T: (413) 684-0948 (summer) or (413) 442-8928 (Oct.–Apr.). RV/tent: 24. $12. Hookups: water.

Worthington

Berkshire Park Camping Area, 350 Harvey Rd., 01237. T: (413) 238-5918. F: (413) 238-0132. www.erols.com/bpca. RV/tent: 134. $18. Hookups: water, electric (30 amps).

MICHIGAN

Acme

Traverse Bay RV Park, P.O. Box 515, 49610. T: (231) 938-5800. RV/tent: 133. $25. Hookups: water, sewer, electric (50 amps).

Alanson

Crooked River RV Park, 5397 Cheboygan St., 49706. T: (231) 548-5534. RV/tent: 15. $15. Hookups: electric (30 amps).

Alger

Greenwood Campground, 636 West Greenwood Rd., 48610. T: (989) 345-2778. RV/tent: 45. $22. Hookups: water, sewer, electric (50 amps).

Algonac

Algonac State Park, 8732 River Rd., 48039. T: (810) 765-5605. RV/tent: 300. $15. Hookups: electric (30 amps).

Aloha

Aloha State Park, 4347 Third St., 49721. T: (231) 625-2522. RV/tent: 287. $14. Hookups: electric (30 amps).

Alpena

Thunder Bay RV Park & Campground, 4250 US 23 South, 49707. T: (989) 354-2528. RV/tent: 45. $18. Hookups: water, electric (30 amps).

Alto

Tyler Creek Golf Club & Campground, 13495 92nd St., 49302. T: (616) 868-6751. RV/tent: 206. $25. Hookups: water, electric (30 amps).

Atlanta

Clear Lake State Park, 20500 M-33, 49709. T: (517) 785-4388. RV/tent: 200. $12. Hookups: electric (30 amps).

Au Gres

Pt Au Gres Marina & Fish Camp, 2325 Green Dr., 48703. T: (989) 876-7314. RV/tent: 44. $20. Hookups: water, electric (30 amps).

Augusta

Fort Custer Recreation Area, 5163 West Fort Custer Dr., 49012. T: (616) 731-4200. RV/tent: 217. $12. Hookups: electric (30 amps).

Shady Bend Campground, 15320 Augusta Dr., 49012. T: (616) 731-4503. RV/tent: 62. $18. Hookups: water, electric (30 amps).

Baraga

Baraga State Park, 1300 US 41S, 49908. T: (906) 353-6558. RV/tent: 119. $11. Hookups: electric (30 amps).

Bark River

Bayside Resort & Campground, 376 Hwy. M-35, 49807. T: (906) 786-7831. RV/tent: 30. $20. Hookups: water, sewer, electric (30 amps).

Bay City

Bay City State Park, 3582 State Park Dr., 48706. T: (517) 684-3020. RV/tent: 193. $12. Hookups: electric (30 amps).

Bay View

Petoskey KOA, 1800 NorthUS 31, 49770. T: (231) 347-0005. RV/tent: 206. $25. Hookups: water, sewer, electric (50 amps), phone, cable TV.

MICHIGAN (continued)

Beaverton

Lost Haven Campground, 5300 Townhall Rd., 48612. T: (989) 435-7623. RV/tent: 100. $20. Hookups: water, electric (30 amps).

Bellaire

Chain-O-Lakes Campground, 7231 S M-88, 49615. T: (231) 533-8432. RV/tent: 78. $24. Hookups: water, sewer, electric (50 amps).

Belmont

Grand Rogue Campground/Canoe & Tube Livery, 6400 West River Dr., 49306. T: (616) 361-1053. RV/tent: 82. $25. Hookups: water, electric (30 amps).

Benzonia

Timberline Campground, 2788 Benzie Hwy, 49616. T: (231) 882-9548. RV/tent: 190. $18. Hookups: water, electric.

Beulah

Turtle Lake Campground, 854 Miller Rd., 49617. T: (231) 275-7353. RV/tent: 59. $15. Hookups: electric (30 amps).

Birch Run

Pine Ridge RV Campground, 11700 Gera Rd., 48415. T: (517) 624-9029. RV/tent: 157. $30. Hookups: water, sewer, electric (50 amps), phone.

Bitely

Pettibone Lake, Pettibone Lake Rd., 51408. T: (231) 689-2021. RV/tent: 16. $10. Hookups: electric (30 amps).

Pickerel Lake Lakeside Campground & Cottages, 12666 North Woodbridge, 49309. T: (231) 745-7268. RV/tent: 42. $14. Hookups: electric (30 amps).

Boyne City

Young State Park, 2280 Boyne City Rd., 49712. T: (231) 582-7523. RV/tent: 240. $15. Hookups: electric (30 amps).

Breckenridge

River Ridge Campground, 1989 West Pine River Rd., 48615. T: (989) 842-5184. RV/tent: 82. $24. Hookups: water, sewer, electric (50 amps).

Brighton

Brighton State Recreation Area, 6360 Chilson Rd., 48116. T: (313) 229-6566. RV/tent: 213. $12. Hookups: electric (30 amps).

Brimley

Brimley State Park, 9200 West 6 Mile Rd., 49715. T: (906) 248-3422. RV/tent: 269. $12. Hookups: electric (30 amps).

Buchanan

Three Braves Campground, 400 Able Rd., 49107. T: (616) 695-9895. RV/tent: 156. $19. Hookups: water, electric.

Buckley

Traverse City South KOA, 9700 M-37, 49620. T: (800) 249-3203. RV/tent: 110. $38. Hookups: water, sewer, electric (50 amps).

Byron Center

Dome World Campground, 400 84th St. Southwest, 49315. T: (616) 878-1518. RV/tent: 50. $20. Hookups: water, sewer, electric (30 amps), phone, cable TV.

Woodchip Campground, 7501 Burlingame Southwest, 49315. T: (616) 878-9050. RV/tent: 108. $19. Hookups: water, electric (30 amps).

Cadillac

Birchwood Resort and Campground, 6545 East M-115, 49601. T: (231) 775-9101. RV/tent: 28. $25. Hookups: water, sewer, electric (50 amps).

Mitchell State Park, 6093 E-M115, 49601. T: (231) 775-7911. RV/tent: 215. $15. Hookups: electric (30 amps).

Calumet

McLain State Park, RT 1 Box 82, M-203, 49930. T: (906) 482-0278. RV/tent: 103. $14. Hookups: electric (30 amps).

Carp Lake

Wilderness State Park, 898 Wilderness Park Dr., 49718. T: (231) 436-5381. RV/tent: 250. $15. Hookups: electric (30 amps).

Caseville

Sleeper State Park, 6573 State Park Rd., 48725. T: (517) 856-4411. RV/tent: 223. $15. Hookups: electric (30 amps).

Cedar River

J.W. Wells State Park, North 7670 Hwy. M-35, 49813. T: (906) 863-9747. RV/tent: 178. $12. Hookups: electric (30 amps).

Cedar Springs

Duke Creek Campground, 15190 White Creek Ave., 49319. T: (616) 696-2115. RV/tent: 114. $22. Hookups: water, sewer, electric (30 amps).

Cedarville

Cedarville RV Park & Campground, Box 328, 49719. T: (800) 906-3351. RV/tent: 57. $20. Hookups: water, sewer, electric (50 amps).

Lazy Days Campground, 266 Mary, 49719. T: (888) 813-2564. RV/tent: 22. $16. Hookups: water, electric (30 amps).

Champion

Van Riper State Park, P.O. Box 88, 49814. T: (906) 339-4461. RV/tent: 189. $12. Hookups: electric (30 amps).

Cheboygan

Cheboygan State Park, 4490 Beach Rd., 49721. T: (231) 627-2811. RV/tent: 78. $11. Hookups: electric (30 amps).

Chelsea

Waterloo State Recreation Area Portage Campground, 16345 McClure Rd., 48118. T: (734) 475-8307. RV/tent: 194. $14. Hookups: electric (30 amps).

Waterloo State Recreation Area Sugarloaf Campground, 16345 McClure Rd., 48118. T: (734) 475-8307. RV/tent: 180. $12. Hookups: electric (30 amps).

Clare

Herrick Recreation Area, 6320 East Herrick Rd., 48617. T: (517) 772-0911. RV/tent: 73. $11. Hookups: electric (30 amps).

Clarkston

Holly State Recreation Area, 8100 Grange Hall Rd., 48442. T: (248) 634-8811. RV/tent: 159. $12. Hookups: water, electric (30 amps).

Clinton

W. J. Hayes State Park, 1220 Wampler's Lake Rd., 49265. T: (517) 467-7401. RV/tent: 185. $15. Hookups: electric (30 amps).

Clyde

Fort Trodd Family Campground Resort, Inc., 6350 Lapeer Rd., 48049. T: (810) 987-4889. RV/tent: 120. $22. Hookups: water, sewer, electric (50 amps).

Cooks

Fish Dam Campground, Box 24, 49817. T: (906) 644-7660. RV/tent: 19. $14. Hookups: electric (30 amps).

Coopersville

Conestoga Grand River Campground, 9720 Oriole Dr., 49404. T: (616) 837-6323. RV/tent: 81. $25. Hookups: water, sewer, electric (50 amps).

Copper Harbor

Fort Wilkins State Park, P.O. Box 71, 49918. T: (906) 289-4215. RV/tent: 165. $14. Hookups: electric (30 amps).

Lake Fanny Hooe Resort & Campground, P.O. Box 31, 49918. T: (800) 426-4451. RV/tent: 64. $25. Hookups: water, sewer, electric (50 amps), cable TV.

Crystal Falls

Bewabic State Park, 1933 US 2 W, 49920. T: (906) 875-3324. RV/tent: 144. $11. Hookups: electric (30 amps).

Pentoga Park, 1630 CR 424, 49920. T: (906) 265-3979. RV/tent: 100. $12. Hookups: water, electric (30 amps).

Dafter

Clear Lake Campground, 13301 South Mackinaw Trail, 49724. T: (906) 635-0201. RV/tent: 60. $20. Hookups: water, electric (30 amps).

Davison

Timber Wolf Campground, 7004 North Irish Rd., 48463. T: (734) 736-7100. RV/tent: 196. $17. Hookups: water, sewer, electric (30 amps).

MICHIGAN (continued)

Davison (continued)

Wolverine Campground, G-7698 North Baxter Rd., 48506. T: (810) 736-7100. RV/tent: 195. $16. Hookups: electric (30 amps).

Dundee

Wilderness Retreat Campground, 1350 Meanwell Rd., 48131. T: (734) 529-5122. RV/tent: 44. $20. Hookups: water, electric (30 amps).

East Tawas

East Tawas City Park, 407 West Bay, 48730. T: (517) 362-5562. RV/tent: 170. $20. Hookups: water, sewer, electric (30 amps), cable TV.

Tawas Point State Park, 686 Tawas Beach Rd., 48730. T: (517) 362-5041. RV/tent: 205. $15. Hookups: electric (30 amps).

Elk Rapids

Vacation Village Campground, 509 Lake St., 49629. T: (231) 264-8636. RV/tent: 31. $21. Hookups: water, sewer, electric (30 amps).

Emmett

Beech Grove Family Campground & RV Park, 3864 Breen Rd., 48022. T: (810) 395-7042. RV/tent: 100. $20. Hookups: water, electric (30 amps).

Escanaba

Park Place of the North, E4575 Hwy. M-35, 49829. T: (906) 786-8453. RV/tent: 25. $15. Hookups: water, electric (30 amps).

Evart

Muskegon River Camp & Canoe, 6281 River Rd., 49631. T: (231) 734-3808. RV/tent: 116. $20. Hookups: water, sewer, electric (30 amps).

Farwell

Evergreen Acres Campground & RV Park, 78 West Ludington Dr., 48622. T: (517) 588-9702. RV/tent: 25. $22. Hookups: water, sewer, electric (30 amps).

Fenton

Seven Lakes, 2220 Tinsman, 48430. T: (810) 634-7271. RV/tent: 71. $12. Hookups: electric (50 amps).

Forester

Forester Park, 2820 North Lakeshore Dr., 48419. T: (810) 622-8715. RV/tent: 120. $16. Hookups: electric (30 amps).

Fountain

Timber Surf Campground, 6575 Dewey Rd., 48410. T: (231) 462-3468. RV/tent: 75. $19. Hookups: water, sewer, electric (30 amps).

Frankfort

Betsie River Campsite, 1923 River Rd., 49635. T: (231) 352-9535. RV/tent: 100. $18. Hookups: water, electric (20 amps).

Garden

Fayette State Park, 13700 13.25 Ln., 49835. T: (906) 644-2603. RV/tent: 61. $9. Hookups: electric (30 amps).

Gaylord

Gaylord Alpine RV Park & Campground, 1315 M-32 W, 49735. T: (517) 731-1772. RV/tent: 130. $14. Hookups: water, sewer, electric (30 amps).

Otsego Lake State Park, RT. 3 Box 414, 49735. T: (517) 732-5485. RV/tent: 156. $14. Hookups: electric (30 amps).

Germfask

Big Cedar Campground & Canoe Livery, P.O. Box 7, 49836. T: (906) 586-6684. RV/tent: 52. $20. Hookups: water, electric (30 amps).

Northland Outfitters Camping Resort, Hwy. M-77, 49836. T: (800) 808-3FUN. RV/tent: 15. $20. Hookups: water, electric (30 amps).

Gladwin

River Valley RV Park, 2165 South Bailey Lake Ave., 48624. T: (517) 386-7844. RV/tent: 68. $23. Hookups: water, sewer, electric (30 amps).

Glennie

Alcona Park-Modern Area, 2550 South Au Sable Rd., 48737. T: (517) 735-3881. RV/tent: 104. $13. Hookups: electric (30 amps).

Alcona Park-Full Service Area, 2550 South Au Sable Rd., 48737. T: (517) 735-3881. RV/tent: 48. $18. Hookups: water, sewer, electric (50 amps).

Gordonville

River Ridge Campground, 1989 West Pine River Rd., 48615. T: (517) 842-5184. RV/tent: 73. $19. Hookups: water, sewer, electric (50 amps).

Gould City

Michihistrigan Campground, HCR Box 20, 49838. T: (906) 477-6983. RV/tent: 34. $18. Hookups: water, sewer, electric (30 amps).

Gowen

Camp Concordia, 13400 Pinewood Northeast, 49326. T: (616) 754-3785. RV/tent: 38. $15. Hookups: electric (50 amps).

Grand Haven

Grand Haven State Park, 1001 Harbor Ave., 49417. T: (231) 798-3711. RV/tent: 174. $14. Hookups: electric (30 amps).

Yogi Bear's Jellystone Park Camp–Grand Haven, 10990 US 31 North, 49417. T: (616) 842-9395. RV/tent: 165. $37. Hookups: water, sewer, electric (50 amps), phone.

Grant

Chinook Camping, 5471 West 112th St., 49327. T: (231) 834-7505. RV/tent: 56. $18. Hookups: water, electric (30 amps).

Salmon Run Campground & Vic's Canoes, 8845 Felch Ave., 49327. T: (231) 834-5494. RV/tent: 80. $21. Hookups: water, electric (30 amps).

Grass Lake

Applecreek Resort & RV Park, 11185 Orban Rd., 49240. T: (517) 522-3467. RV/tent: 95. $22. Hookups: water, electric (30 amps).

Hideaway RV Park, 3500 Updyke Rd., 49240. T: (517) 522-5858. RV/tent: 55. $25. Hookups: water, sewer, electric (50 amps).

Grayling

Hartwick Pines State Park, 4216 Ranger Rd., 49738. T: (517) 348-7068. RV/tent: 100. $14. Hookups: electric (30 amps).

Greenville

Three Seasons RV Park, 6956 Fuller Rd., 48838. T: (616) 754-5717. RV/tent: 25. $18. Hookups: water, electric (30 amps).

Gwinn

Horseshoe Lake Campground, 840 North Horseshoe Lake Rd., 49841. T: (906) 346-9937. RV/tent: 125. $20. Hookups: water, sewer, electric (30 amps).

Hanover

Twin Pines Campground & Canoe Livery, 9800 Wheeler Rd., 49241. T: (517) 524-6298. RV/tent: 81. $15. Hookups: water, electric (30 amps).

Harbor Beach

North Park Campground, 836 North Huron Ave., 48441. T: (517) 479-9554. RV/tent: 184. $16. Hookups: water, sewer, electric (50 amps), cable TV.

Harrisville

Harrisville State Park, P.O. Box 326, 48740. T: (517) 724-5126. RV/tent: 200. $14. Hookups: electric (30 amps).

Hastings

Camp Michawana, 5800 Head Lake Rd., 49058. T: (616) 623-5168. RV/tent: 54. $22. Hookups: water, sewer, electric (30 amps).

Hesperia

Leisure Haven Campground, 3056 E M-20, 49421. T: (231) 861-7262. RV/tent: 47. $14. Hookups: electric (30 amps).

Hillman

Heine's Landing, 24650 Landing Rd., 49746. T: (517) 742-4029. RV/tent: 62. $14. Hookups: electric (30 amps).

Sorensen's Grass Lake Resort, 18680 Sorensen Rd., 49746. T: (989) 742-3412. RV/tent: 20. $20. Hookups: water, electric (30 amps).

Holland

Drew's Country Camping, 12850 Ransom Rd., 49424. T: (616) 399-1886. RV/tent: 75. $20. Hookups: water, electric (30 amps).

MICHIGAN (continued)

Holland State Park, Lake Michigan Campground, 2215 Ottawa Beach Rd., 49424. T: (616) 399-9390. RV/tent: 310. $15. Hookups: electric (30 amps).

Holly

Groveland Oaks County Park, 14555 Dixie Hwy., 48442. T: (248) 634-9811. RV/tent: 269. $23. Hookups: water, electric (50 amps).

Hopkins

Miller Lake Campground, 2130 Miller Lake Rd., 49328. T: (616) 672-7139. RV/tent: 42. $22. Hookups: water, sewer, electric (50 amps).

Indian River

Burt Lake State Park, 6635 State Park Dr., 49749. T: (231) 238-9392. RV/tent: 333. $12. Hookups: electric (30 amps).

Interlochen

Interlochen State Park, SR 137, 49647. T: (231) 276-9511. RV/tent: 490. $14. Hookups: electric (30 amps).

Ionia

Ionia Recreation, 2880 David Hwy., 48846. T: (616) 527-3750. RV/tent: 100. $12. Hookups: electric (30 amps).

Iron Mountain

Lake Antoine Park, N3393 Lake Antoine Rd., 49801. T: (906) 774-8875. RV/tent: 90. $8. Hookups: water, electric (30 amps).

Summer Breeze, LLC, W8576 Twin Falls Rd., 49801. T: (906) 774-7701. RV/tent: 65. $20. Hookups: water, sewer, electric (30 amps).

Irons

Leisure Time Campground, 9214 West 5 Mile Rd., 49644. T: (800) 266-8214. RV/tent: 100. $24. Hookups: water, sewer, electric (50 amps).

Ironwood

Curry Park, Cloverland Dr., 49938. T: (906) 932-5050. RV/tent: 56. $9. Hookups: water, sewer, electric (30 amps).

Jackson

Greenwood Acres, 2401 Hilton Rd., 49201. T: (517) 522-8600. RV/tent: 1160. $25. Hookups: water, sewer, electric (50 amps).

Pleasant Lake County Park & Campground, Styles Rd., 49201. T: (517) 769-2401. RV/tent: 69. $18. Hookups: water, electric (30 amps).

Swains Lake County Park & Campground, South Concord Rd., 49201. T: (517) 524-7666. RV/tent: 60. $18. Hookups: water, electric (30 amps).

Jones

Camelot Campground LLC, 14630 M-60, 49061. T: (616) 476-2473. RV/tent: 101. $22. Hookups: water, sewer, electric (50 amps).

Kinross

Kinross RV Park East, Riley Rd., 49783. T: (906) 495-5504. RV/tent: 174. $12. Hookups: water, sewer, electric (30 amps).

Laingsburg

Sleepy Hollow State Park, 7835 East Price Rd., 48848. T: (517) 651-6217. RV/tent: 181. $12. Hookups: electric (30 amps).

Lake City

Maple Grove Campground, East Union St., 49651. T: (231) 839-4429. RV/tent: 23. $20. Hookups: water, electric (30 amps).

Lansing

Lansing Cottonwood Campground, 5339 South Aurelius Rd., 48911. T: (517) 393-3200. RV/tent: 110. $21. Hookups: water, sewer, electric (30 amps).

Lapeer

Hilltop Campground, 1260 Piper Dr., 48446. T: (810) 664-2782. RV/tent: 60. $20. Hookups: water, electric (20 amps).

Leonard

Addison Days, 1480 West Romeo Rd., 48367. T: (248) 693-2432. RV/tent: 133. $22. Hookups: water, electric (30 amps).

Family Park Campground, 120 Yule Rd., 48367. T: (248) 628-4204. RV/tent: 30. $22. Hookups: water, electric (20 amps).

Lewiston

Lewiston Shady Acres Campground & Cottages, 4329 North Red Oak Rd., 49756. T: (800) 357-2494. RV/tent: 40. $25. Hookups: water, sewer, electric (50 amps), cable TV.

Lexington

Lexington RV Resort, 7181 Lexington Blvd., 48450. T: (810) 359-2054. RV/tent: 30. $15. Hookups: water, sewer, electric (50 amps).

Linwood

Hoyle's Marina & Campground, 135 South Linwood Beach Rd., 48634. T: (989) 697-3153. RV/tent: 78. $24. Hookups: water, sewer, electric (50 amps).

Ludington

Kibby Creek Travel Park, 4900 Deren Rd., 49431. T: (231) 843-3995. RV/tent: 113. $22. Hookups: water, sewer, electric (30 amps).

Lakeview Campsite, 6181 Peterson Rd., 49431. T: (231) 843-3702. RV/tent: 60. $22. Hookups: water, sewer, electric (30 amps).

Ludington State Park, P.O. Box 709, 49431. T: (231) 843-8671. RV/tent: 341. $15. Hookups: electric (30 amps).

Mason County Campground, 5906 West Chauvez Rd., 49431. T: (231) 845-7609. RV/tent: 50. $15. Hookups: electric (30 amps).

Tamarac Village Mobile Homes & RV Park, 2875 North Lakeshore Dr., 49431. T: (231) 843-4990. RV/tent: 20. $15. Hookups: water, sewer, electric (30 amps).

Mackinaw City

Mackinaw City KOA, 566 Trailsend Rd., 49701. T: (231) 436-5643. RV/tent: 110. $29. Hookups: water, sewer, electric (50 amps).

Mancelona

Rapid River Campground/Cabins, 7182 US 131, 49659. T: (231) 258-2042. RV/tent: 63. $19. Hookups: electric (30 amps).

Manistee

Orchard Beach State Park, 2064 Lakeshore Dr., 49660. T: (231) 723-7422. RV/tent: 168. $12. Hookups: electric (30 amps).

Manistique

Indian Lake Travel Resort, HC-01 Box 3286, 49854. T: (906) 341-2807. RV/tent: 50. $15. Hookups: water, sewer, electric (30 amps).

Kewadin Inn Campground, Rte. 1 Box 1938, 49854. T: (906) 341-6911. RV/tent: 40. $18. Hookups: water, sewer, electric (30 amps).

Matson's Big Manistee River Campground, 2680 Bialik Rd., 49660. T: (888) 556-2424. RV/tent: 55. $22. Hookups: water, sewer, electric (50 amps).

Woodstar Beach Campground, Little Harbor Rd., 49854. T: (906) 341-6514. RV/tent: 41. $14. Hookups: electric (30 amps).

Marenisco

Lake Gogebic State Park, HC 1 Box 139, 49947. T: (906) 842-3341. RV/tent: 127. $11. Hookups: electric (30 amps).

Marquette

Gitche Gumee RV Park & Campground, 2048 SR 28E, 49855. T: (906) 249-9102. RV/tent: 55. $28. Hookups: water, sewer, electric (50 amps).

Marquette Tourist Park & Campground, CR 550, 49855. T: (906) 228-0465. RV/tent: 110. $13. Hookups: water, sewer, electric (30 amps).

Martin

Schnable Lake Family Campground, 1476 115th Ave., 49070. T: (616) 672-7367. RV/tent: 62. $17. Hookups: water, sewer, electric (50 amps).

Mears

Hide-A-Way Campground/Waterslide, 9671 West Silver Lake Rd., 49436. T: (231) 873-4428. RV/tent: 86. $20. Hookups: water, electric (30 amps).

Silver Hills Camp/Resort, 7594 West Hazel Rd., 49436. T: (800) 637-3976. RV/tent: 105. $25. Hookups: water, electric (50 amps).

Silver Lake II Campground, 1786 North 34th Ave., 49436. T: (800) 359-1909. RV/tent: 270. $20. Hookups: water, electric (30 amps).

Silver Lake State Park, Rte. 1 Box 67, 49420. T: (231) 873-3083. RV/tent: 156. $15. Hookups: electric (30 amps).

Yogi Bear's Jellystone Park Silver Lake, 8329 West Hazel Rd., 49436. T: (231) 873-4502. RV/tent: 180. $34. Hookups: water, sewer, electric (30 amps).

MICHIGAN (continued)

Mecosta

Blue Gill Lake Campground, 15854 Pretty Lake Dr., 49332. T: (231) 972-7410. RV/tent: 60. $15. Hookups: water, electric (20 amps).

School Section Lake Park, SR 20, 49332. T: (231) 972-7450. RV/tent: 90. $14. Hookups: water, electric (30 amps).

Mesick

Mesick RV Park, 285 Manistee River Dr., 49668. T: (231) 885-1199. RV/tent: 190. $15. Hookups: water, electric (30 amps).

Metamora

Metamora-Hadley Recreation Area, 3871 Hurd Rd., 48455. T: (810) 797-4439. RV/tent: 220. $12. Hookups: electric (30 amps).

Middleville

Gun Lake Parkside Park, 2430 Briggs Rd., 49333. T: (616) 795-3140. RV/tent: 25. $15. Hookups: water, sewer, electric (30 amps).

Yankee Springs State Recreational Area, 2104 Gun Lake Rd., 49058. T: (616) 795-9081. RV/tent: 345. $10. Hookups: electric (30 amps).

Milford

Proud Lake State Recreation Area, 3500 Wixom Rd., 48382. T: (248) 685-2433. RV/tent: 130. $15. Hookups: electric (30 amps).

Mio

Mio Pines Acres, 1215 West 8th St., 48647. T: (800) 289-2845. RV/tent: 90. $20. Hookups: water, electric (30 amps).

Monroe

Harbortown RV Resort, 14931 LaPlaisance Rd., 48161. T: (734) 384-4700. RV/tent: 250. $30. Hookups: water, sewer, electric (50 amps).

Sterling State Park, 2800 State Park Rd., 48161. T: (734) 289-2715. RV/tent: 288. $14. Hookups: electric (30 amps).

Montague

White River Campground, 735 Fruitvale Rd., 49437. T: (231) 894-4708. RV/tent: 182. $25. Hookups: water, electric (30 amps).

Morley

Mecosta Pines RV Park, 550 South Talcott, 49336. T: (231) 856-4556. RV/tent: 30. $20. Hookups: water, electric (50 amps).

Mount Pleasant

Coldwater Lake Family Park, 1703 North Littlefield, 48893. T: (517) 772-0911. RV/tent: 95. $20. Hookups: water, electric (30 amps).

Munising

Buckhorn/Otter Lake Campground, HC 50, 49862. T: (906) 387-3559. RV/tent: 72. $15. Hookups: electric (30 amps).

Wandering Wheels Campground, P.O. Box 419, 49862. T: (906) 387-3315. RV/tent: 100. $22. Hookups: water, sewer, electric (30 amps).

Munith

The Oaks Resort, 7800 Cutler Rd., 49259. T: (517) 596-2747. RV/tent: 65. $18. Hookups: water, electric (30 amps).

Muskegon

Hoffmaster State Park, 6585 Lake Harbor Rd., 49441. T: (231) 798-3711. RV/tent: 293. $15. Hookups: electric (30 amps).

Muskegon KOA, 3500 North Strand, 49445. T: (231) 766-3900. RV/tent: 82. $24. Hookups: water, sewer, electric (30 amps).

Nashville

Camp Thornapple Inc., 5625 Thornapple Lake Rd., 49073. T: (517) 852-9645. RV/tent: 143. $20. Hookups: water, sewer, electric (50 amps).

New Era

Stony Haven Campground, 8079 West Stony Lake Rd., 49446. T: (800) 962-1117. RV/tent: 45. $20. Hookups: water, electric (30 amps).

New Hudson

Green Valley Park, P.O. Box 298, 48165. T: (248) 437-4136. RV/tent: 32. $22. Hookups: water, sewer, electric (30 amps).

Haas Lake Park, 25800 Haas Rd., 48165. T: (248) 437-0900. RV/tent: 110. $30. Hookups: water, sewer, electric (50 amps).

Newaygo

Ed H. Henning Park, 500 East Croton Rd., 49337. T: (231) 652-1202. RV/tent: 60. $11. Hookups: electric (30 amps).

Little Switzerland Resort and Campground, 254 Pickeral Lake Dr., 49337. T: (231) 652-7939. RV/tent: 80. $20. Hookups: water, electric (30 amps).

Muskallonge Lake State Park, P.O. Box 245, 49868. T: (906) 658-3338. RV/tent: 175. $11. Hookups: electric (30 amps).

Mystery Creek Campground, 9419 Wisner, 49337. T: (231) 652-6915. RV/tent: 65. $20. Hookups: water, electric (30 amps).

Northcountry Campground & Cabins, RR 1 Box 94, 49868. T: (906) 293-8562. RV/tent: 50. $18. Hookups: water, sewer, electric (30 amps).

Newberry

Newberry KOA, Box 783 M-28, 49868. T: (800) 562-5853. RV/tent: 130. $22. Hookups: water, electric (50 amps).

Niles

Spaulding Lake Campground, 2305 Bell Rd., 49120. T: (616) 684-1393. RV/tent: 120. $20. Hookups: water, sewer, electric (50 amps).

North Branch

Sutter's Recreation Area, 1601 Tozer Rd., 48461. T: (810) 688-3761. RV/tent: 40. $19. Hookups: water, sewer, electric (30 amps).

North Muskegon

Muskegon State Park, 3560 Memorial Dr., 49445. T: (231) 744-3483. RV/tent: 284. $14. Hookups: electric (30 amps).

Omer

Big Bend Campground, 513 Conrad Rd., 48658. T: (517) 653-2267. RV/tent: 70. $19. Hookups: water, electric (20 amps).

Riverbend Campground & Canoe Rental, P.O. Box 6, 48749. T: (517) 653-2576. RV/tent: 80. $20. Hookups: water, sewer, electric (30 amps).

Russell's Canoe & Campground, 146 Carrington, 48749. T: (517) 653-2644. RV/tent: 30. $16. Hookups: electric (30 amps).

Onaway

Onaway State Park, Rte. 1 Box 112, 49765. T: (517) 733-8279. RV/tent: 98. $11. Hookups: electric (30 amps).

Onsted

Lake Hudson Recreation Area, 1220 Wampler, 49265. T: (517) 445-2265. RV/tent: 50. $9. Hookups: electric (30 amps).

Ossineke

Paul Bunyan Campgrounds, 6969 North Huron, 48762. T: (517) 471-2921. RV/tent: 80. $17. Hookups: water, sewer, electric (30 amps).

Otter Lake

Genesee Otterlake Campground, 12260 Farrand Rd., 48464. T: (810) 793-2725. RV/tent: 129. $18. Hookups: water, electric (30 amps).

Paradise

Tahquamenon Falls State Park, Lower Falls, P.O. Box 57, 49768. T: (906) 492-3415. RV/tent: 171. $14. Hookups: electric (30 amps).

Tahquamenon Falls State Park, River Mouth Unit, P.O. Box 57, 49768. T: (906) 492-3415. RV/tent: 130. $14. Hookups: electric (30 amps).

Paris

Paris Park Campground, US 131, 49512. T: (231) 796-3420. RV/tent: 68. $13. Hookups: water, sewer, electric (30 amps).

Pentwater

Hill & Hollow Campground, 8915 North Business 31, 49449. T: (231) 869-5811. RV/tent: 150. $28. Hookups: water, sewer, electric (30 amps).

Mears State Park, P.O. Box 370, 49449. T: (231) 869-2051. RV/tent: 179. $15. Hookups: electric (30 amps).

Perry

Hickory Lake Camping, 11433 South Beardslee Rd., 48872. T: (517) 625-3113. RV/tent: 62. $17. Hookups: water, sewer, electric (30 amsp).

MICHIGAN (continued)

Petoskey

Petoskey State Park, Rte. 4 Box 121 A, 49770. T: (231) 347-2311. RV/tent: 170. $15. Hookups: electric (30 amps).

Pinckney

Pinckney Recreation Area, 8555 Silver Hill, 48169. T: (734) 426-4913. RV/tent: 225. $14. Hookups: electric (30 amps).

Port Austin

Port Crescent State Park, 1775 Port Austin Rd., 48467. T: (517) 738-8663. RV/tent: 135. $15. Hookups: electric (30 amps).

Port Huron

Lakeport State Park, 7605 Lakeshore Rd., 48060. T: (810) 327-6224. RV/tent: 284. $14. Hookups: electric (30 amps).

Rapid River

Camper's Paradise Resort, 8733 EE 25 Rd., 49878. T: (906) 474-6106. RV/tent: 19. $18. Hookups: water, electric (30 amps).

Vagabond Resort & Campground, 8935 CR 513T, 49878. T: (906) 474-6122. RV/tent: 50. $25. Hookups: water, sewer, electric (50 amps).

Whispering Valley Campground & RV Park, 8410 US 2, 49878. T: (906) 474-7044. RV/tent: 26. $22. Hookups: water, sewer, electric (50 amps).

Riverdale

Half Moon Lake Campground & RV Park, 11394 Lumberjack Rd., 48877. T: (989) 833-7852. RV/tent: 42. $24. Hookups: water, electric (30 amps).

Riverside

Benton Harbor KOA, 3527 Coloma Rd., 49084. T: (616) 849-3333. RV/tent: 113. $32. Hookups: water, sewer, electric (30 amps).

Rogers City

Hoeft State Park, US 23 North, 49779. T: (517) 734-2543. RV/tent: 144. $11. Hookups: electric (30 amps).

Roscommon

Great Circle Campground, 5370 Marl Lake Rd., 48653. T: (800) 272-5428. RV/tent: 45. $20. Hookups: water, sewer, electric (30 amps).

Higgins Hills RV Park, 3800 West Federal Hwy, 48653. T: (800) 478-8151. RV/tent: 98. $22. Hookups: water, sewer, electric (30 amps).

Higgins Lake Family Campground & Mobile Resort, 2380 West Burdell Rd., 48653. T: (517) 821-6891. RV/tent: 35. $17. Hookups: water, electric (20 amps).

North Higgins Lake State Park, RR 1 Box 436, 48653. T: (517) 821-6125. RV/tent: 195. $14. Hookups: electric (30 amps).

Paddle Brave Campground & Canoe Livery, 10610 Steckert Bridge Rd., 48653. T: (517) 275-5273. RV/tent: 45. $16. Hookups: electric (30 amps).

South Higgins Lake State Park, RR 2 Box 360, 48653. T: (517) 821-6374. RV/tent: 395. $14. Hookups: electric (30 amps).

Rose City

Rifle River State Recreation Area, P.O. Box 98, 48635. T: (517) 473-2258. RV/tent: 181. $12. Hookups: electric (30 amps).

Rothbury

Back Forty Ranch at the Double JJ Resort, 5900 Water Rd., 49452. T: (800) DOUBLE JJ. RV/tent: 50. $25. Hookups: water, sewer, electric (50 amps).

Saugatuck

Saugatuck RV Resort, P.O. Box 683, 49453. T: (616) 857-3315. RV/tent: 195. $35. Hookups: water, sewer, electric (50 amps).

Sault Ste. Marie

Chippewa Campground, P.O. Box 786, 49783. T: (906) 632-8581. RV/tent: 100. $22. Hookups: water, sewer, electric (50 amps).

Sawyer

New Life Campground, 12033 Red Arrow Hwy., 49125. T: (616) 426-4971. RV/tent: 110. $21. Hookups: water, sewer, electric (30 amps).

Warren Dunes State Park, 12032 Red Arrow Hwy., 49125. T: (616) 426-4013. RV/tent: 280. $15. Hookups: electric (30 amps).

Scottville

Crystal Lake Campground, 1884 West Hansen Rd., 49454. T: (231) 757-4510. RV/tent: 130. $26. Hookups: water, sewer, electric (30 amps).

Scottville Riverside Park, 105 North Main St., 49454. T: (231) 757-4729. RV/tent: 52. $12. Hookups: water, electric (30 amps).

Sears

Merrill Lake Park, SR 66, 49679. T: (517) 382-7158. RV/tent: 74. $13. Hookups: water, electric (30 amps).

Shepherd

Salt River Acres Inc., 926 Greendale Rd., 48883. T: (989) 631-7659. RV/tent: 88. $15. Hookups: water, electric (30 amps).

Silver City

Porcupine Mountains Wilderness State Park, 412 South Boundry Rd., 49953. T: (906) 885-5275. RV/tent: 188. $14. Hookups: electric (30 amps).

South Boardman

Ranch Rudolf Campground, 6841 Brownbridge Rd., 49686. T: (231) 947-9529. RV/tent: 25. $30. Hookups: water, electric (30 amps).

South Haven

Van Buren State Park, Rte. 3 Box 122B, 49090. T: (616) 637-2788. RV/tent: 220. $12. Hookups: electric (30 amps).

St. Ignace

Lakeshore Park, 416 Pte LaBarbe Rd., 49781. T: (800) 643-9522. RV/tent: 100. $22. Hookups: water, sewer, electric (50 amps).

Straits State Park, 720 Church St., 49781. T: (906) 643-8620. RV/tent: 275. $14. Hookups: electric (30 amps).

Tiki Travel Park, 200 South Airport Rd., 49781. T: (906) 643-7808. RV/tent: 100. $17. Hookups: water, sewer, electric (30 amps.

Stanwood

Brower County Park, 8 Mile and Old State Rd., 49346. T: (231) 823-2561. RV/tent: 230. $15. Hookups: water, electric (50 amps).

Sterling

Rifle River AAA Canoe Rental, 2148 South School Rd., 48659. T: (989) 654-2333. RV/tent: 65. $20. Hookups: water, electric (30 amps).

River View Campground and Canoe Livery, 5755 Townline Rd., 48659. T: (988) 654-2447. RV/tent: 250. $22. Hookups: water, sewer, electric (30 amps).

Sturgis

Green Valley Campgrounds, 25499 West Fawn River Rd., 49091. T: (616) 651-8760. RV/tent: 220. $19. Hookups: water, electric (20 amps).

Tawas City

Brown's Landing RV Park, 1129 Dyer Rd., 48763. T: (989) 362-3737. RV/tent: 74. $24. Hookups: water, sewer, electric (50 amps).

Tawas RV Park, 1453 Townline Rd., 48673. T: (989) 362-3848. RV/tent: 39. $25. Hookups: water, sewer, electric (30 amps).

Tecumseh

Indian Creek Camp & Conference Center, 9415 Tangent Hwy, 49286. T: (517) 423-5659. RV/tent: 47. $25. Hookups: water, sewer, electric (30 amps).

Thompson

Indian Lake State Park, South Campground, Rte. 2 Box 2500, 49854. T: (906) 341-2355. RV/tent: 302. $15. Hookups: electric (30 amps).

Tipton

Ja Do Campground, 5603 US 12, 49287. T: (517) 431-2111. RV/tent: 100. $25. Hookups: water, electric (20 amps).

Traverse City

Traverse City State Park, 1132 US 31 North, 49686. T: (231) 922-5270. RV/tent: 342. $15. Hookups: electric (30 amps).

Tustin

Cadillac KOA, 13163 M-115, 49688. T: (231) 825-2012. RV/tent: 35. $27. Hookups: water, electric (30 amps).

MICHIGAN (continued)

Union

Hollywood Shores Resort, 70901 Wayne St., 49130. T: (616) 641-7307. RV/tent: 28. $18. Hookups: water, electric (20 amps).

Union City

Rustic Potawatomie Recreation Area, 1126 Bell Rd., 49094. T: (517) 278-4289. RV/tent: 70. $18. Hookups: water, sewer, electric (50 amps).

Vassar

Ber-Wa-Ga-Na Campground, 3526 Sanilac Rd., 48768. T: (517) 673-7125. RV/tent: 74. $22. Hookups: water, sewer, electric (30 amps).

Vicksburg

Oak Shores Resort Campground, 13496 28th St., 49097. T: (616) 649-4689. RV/tent: 90. $23. Hookups: water, sewer, electric (50 amps).

Wakefield

Sunday Lake Trailer Park, M28, 49968. T: (906) 229-5131. RV/tent: 84. $12. Hookups: water, electric (30 amps).

Walkerville

Pine Haven Campground, 7792 North 186th Ave., 49459. T: (231) 898-2722. RV/tent: 25. $20. Hookups: water, sewer, electric (30 amps).

Waterford

Pontiac Lake State Recreation Area, 7800 Gale Rd., 48054. T: (248) 666-1020. RV/tent: 176. $11. Hookups: electric (30 amps).

Wellston

Sportsman's Port Canoes & Campground, 10487 West M-55 Hwy, 49689. T: (888) 226-6301. RV/tent: 51. $15. Hookups: electric (30 amps).

Twin Oaks Campground, 233 Moss Rd., 49689. T: (231) 848-4124. RV/tent: 60. $15. Hookups: electric (30 amps).

West Branch

Lake George Campground, 3070 Elm Dr., 48661. T: (517) 345-2700. RV/tent: 97. $24. Hookups:

MINNESOTA

Adrian

Adrian Campground and Recreation Park, P.O. Box 187, 56110. T: (507) 483-2820. RV/tent: 120. $15. Hookups: electric (30 amps), sewer.

Aitkin

Big "K" Campground, RR 2 Box 965, 56431. T: (218) 927-6001. RV/tent: 55. $19. Hookups: water, electric (30 amps), sewer.

Edgewater Resort & RV Park, RR 3 Box 890, 56431. T: (800) 639-4337. RV/tent: 47. $25. Hookups: water, electric (50 amps), sewer.

Farm Island Lake Resort & Campground, Rte. 2 Box 225, 56431. T: (218) 927-3841. RV/tent: 40. $18. Hookups: water, electric (30 amps), sewer.

Albert Lea

Myre Big Island, Rte. 3 Box 33, 56007. T: (507) 379-3403. RV/tent: 99. $13. Hookups: electric (30 amps).

Alexandria

Hillcrest RV Park, 715 Birch Ave., 56038. T: (320) 763-6330. RV/tent: 55. $20. Hookups: water, electric (30 amps), sewer.

Andover

Bay Shore, 7124 Pymatuning Lake Rd., 44003. T: (440) 293-7202. RV/tent: 250. $35. Hookups: water, electric (30 amps), sewer.

Pymatuning State Park, P.O. Box 1000, 44003. T: (440) 293-6030. RV/tent: 373. $14. Hookups: electric (20 amps).

Wildwood Acres, RD 1 Marvin Rd., 44003. T: (440) 293-6838. RV/tent: 102. $18. Hookups: water, electric (30 amps).

Ashtabula

Hide-A-Way Lakes Campground, 2034 South Ridge W, 44004. T: (440) 992-4431. RV/tent: 100. $24. Hookups: water, electric (30 amps).

Aurora

Silverhorn Camping Resort, 250 Treat Rd., 44202. T: (330) 562-4423. RV/tent: 300. $32. Hookups: water, electric (30 amps).

Woodside Lake Park, 2256 Frost Rd., 44241. T: (330) 626-4251. RV/tent: 125. $24. Hookups: water, electric (30 amps).

Bainbridge

Paint Creek State Park, 14265 US Rt 50, 45612. T: (937) 365-1401. RV/tent: 199. $14. Hookups: electric (20 amps).

Pike Lake State Park, 1847 Pike Ln. Rd., 45612. T: (740) 493-2212. RV/tent: 213. $12. Hookups: electric (20 amps).

Baltimore

Rippling Stream Campground, 3640 Reyn-Bait Rd., 43105. T: (740) 862-6065. RV/tent: 132. $14. Hookups: water, electric (20 amps).

Bellefontaine

Eagles Club of Ohio-Alken Lakes, 5118 US 68 North, 43311. T: (937) 593-1565. RV/tent: 263. $15. Hookups: water, electric (30 amps).

Bellville

Yogi Bear's Jellystone Park Camp-Resort, SR 546 at Black Rd., 44813. T: (419) 886-2267. RV/tent: 90. $30. Hookups: water, electric (50 amps), sewer.

Belmont

Barkcamp State Park, 65330 Barkcamp Park Rd., 43718. T: (740) 484-4064. RV/tent: 150. $12. Hookups: electric (50 amps).

Blue Rock

Muskingum River Campgrounds, 11206 South River Rd., 43720. T: (740) 674-6918. RV/tent: 24. $10. Hookups: water, sewer, electric (30 amps).

Bowerston

Clow's Marina & Campground, 4131 Deer Rd. Southwest, 44695. T: (740) 269-5371. RV/tent: 88. $13. Hookups: electric (20 amps).

Buckeye Lake

Buckeye Lake KOA, 4460 Walnut Rd., 43008. T: (740) 928-0706. RV/tent: 205. $35. Hookups: water, sewer, electric (50 amps).

Camden

Cross's Campground Inc., 7777 SR 127, 45311. T: (937) 452-1535. RV/tent: 55. $14. Hookups: water, electric (30 amps).

Canfield

Dreamiee Acres, 9727 Columbiana-Canfield Rd., 44406. T: (330) 533-9366. RV/tent: 24. $15. Hookups: water, electric (20 amps).

Carrollton

Camper's Paradise Campground, 4105 Fresno Rd. Northwest, 44615. T: (330) 753-3220. RV/tent: 55. $14. Hookups: water, electric (30 amps).

Cozy Ridge Campground, 4145 Fresno Rd. Northwest, 44615. T: (330) 735-2553. RV/tent: 70. $15. Hookups: water, sewer, electric (30 amps).

Petersburg Boat Landing, 2126 Azalea Rd. Southwest, 44615. T: (330) 627-4270. RV/tent: 78. $12. Hookups: electric (30 amps).

Twin Valley Campground, 2330 Apollo Rd. Southeast, 44615. T: (330) 739-2811. RV/tent: 130. $22. Hookups: water, sewer electric (50 amps).

Chillicothe

Scioto Trail State Park, 144 Lake Rd., 45601. T: (740) 663-2125. RV/tent: 75. $13. Hookups: electric (30 amps).

MINNESOTA (continued)

Circleville

A.W. Marion State Park, 7317 Warner-Huffer Rd., 43113. T: (740) 474-3386. RV/tent: 59. $13. Hookups: electric (20 amps).

Clyde

Traveland Family Campground, 3681 CR 213, 43410. T: (419) 626-1133. RV/tent: 300. $31. Hookups: water, sewer, electric (50 amps).

College Corner

Hueston Woods State Park, Rte. 1, 45003. T: (513) 523-6347. RV/tent: 491. $15. Hookups: electric (30 amps).

Conneaut

Evergreen Lake Park, 703 Center Rd., 44030. T: (440) 599-8802. RV/tent: 100. $20. Hookups: water, electric (50 amps).

Deersville

Tappan Lake Park Campground, US 250, 44693. T: (740) 922-3649. RV/tent: 550. $21. Hookups: electric (30 amps).

Delaware

Delaware State Park, 5202 US 23N, 43015. T: (740) 369-2761. RV/tent: 214. $15. Hookups: electric (20 amps).

East Rochester

Bob Boord's Park, 25067 Buffalo Rd., 44625. T: (330) 894-2360. RV/tent: 250. $21. Hookups: water, sewer, electric (30 amps).

Paradise Lake Park, 6940 Rochester Rd., 44625. T: (330) 525-7726. RV/tent: 200. $20. Hookups: water, electric (30 amps).

East Sparta

Bear Creek Ranch KOA, 3232 Downing St. Southwest, 44626. T: (330) 484-3901. RV/tent: 103. $31. Hookups: water, electric (50 amps), sewer.

Fayette

Harrison Lake State Park, 26246 Harrison Lake Rd., 43521. T: (419) 237-2593. RV/tent: 193. $14. Hookups: electric (20 amps).

Fort Loramie

Hickory Hill Lakes, 7103 SR 66, 45845. T: (937) 295-3820. RV/tent: 121. $20. Hookups: water, electric (30 amps).

Frankfort

Lake Hill Campground, 2466 Mussieman Station Rd., 45628. T: (740) 998-5648. RV/tent: 100. $16. Hookups: water, electric (50 amps), sewer.

Freeport

Clendening Lake Marina Campground, 79100 Bose Rd., 43973. T: (740) 658-3691. RV/tent: 100. $15. Hookups: electric (30 amps).

Piedmont Lake Marina & Campground, SR 8, 43973. T: (740) 658-3735. RV/tent: 67. $18. Hookups: electric (30 amps).

Twin Hills Park, 77720 Cummins Rd., 43973. T: (740) 658-3275. RV/tent: 100. $13. Hookups: water, electric (30 amps).

Fresno

Forest Hill Lake & Campground, 52176 CR 425, 43824. T: (740) 545-9642. RV/tent: 76. $18. Hookups: water, electric (20 amps).

Geneva

Audubon Lakes Campground, 3935 North Broadway, 44041. T: (440) 466-1293. RV/tent: 125. $20. Hookups: water, electric (30 amps).

Geneva State Park, P.O. Box 429, 44041. T: (440) 466-8400. RV/tent: 91. $18. Hookups: electric (20 amps).

Kenisee's Grand River Camp & Canoe, 4680 RT. 307E, 44041. T: (440) 466-2320. RV/tent: 120. $22. Hookups: water, electric (50 amps).

R & R Camping, 4455 Rte. 307, 44041. T: (440) 466-2550. RV/tent: 120. $22. Hookups: water, sewer, electric (30 amps).

Geneva-On-The-Lake

Indian Creek Camping & Resort, 4710 Lake Rd. East, 44041. T: (440) 466-8191. RV/tent: 573. $32. Hookups: water, sewer, electric (50 amps).

Granville

Lazy R. Campground, 2340 Dry Creek Rd. Northeast, 43023. T: (740) 366-4385. RV/tent: 195. $19. Hookups: water, sewer, electric (50 amps).

Green

Pine Valley Lake Park, 4936 South Arlington Rd., 44720. T: (330) 896-1381. RV/tent: 90. $23. Hookups: water, electric (30 amps), sewer.

Greenville

Wildcat Woods Campground, 1355 Wildcat Rd., 45331. T: (937) 548-7921. RV/tent: 78. $18. Hookups: water, electric (30 amps), sewer.

Homerville

Wild Wood Lake Campground, 11450 Crawford Rd., 44235. T: (330) 625-2817. RV/tent: 60. $19. Hookups: water, electric (50 amps).

Howard

Kokosing Valley Camp & Canoe, 25860 Coshocton Rd., 43028. T: (740) 599-7056. RV/tent: 170. $18. Hookups: water, electric (20 amps).

Hubbard

Homestead Campground, 1436 Brookfield Rd., 44425. T: (330) 448-2938. RV/tent: 30. $18. Hookups: water, sewer, electric (30 amps).

Jefferson

Buccaneer Campsites, P.O. Box 352, 44047. T: (440) 576-2881. RV/tent: 170. $20. Hookups: water, sewer, electric (30 amps).

Kings Mill

Paramount's Kings Island Campground, 6300 Kings Island Dr., 45034. T: (513) 754-5901. RV/tent: 349. $41. Hookups: water, sewer, electric (30 amps).

Lakeside

East Harbor State Park, 1169 North Buck Rd., 43440. T: (419) 734-4424. RV/tent: 570. $17. Hookups: electric (330 amps).

Lakeview

Indian Lake State Park, 12744 SR 235 North, 43331. T: (937) 843-2717. RV/tent: 443. $14. Hookups: electric (30 amps).

Lancaster

Lakeview RV Park and Campground, 2715 Sugar Grove Rd., 43130. T: (740) 653-4519. RV/tent: 100. $25. Hookups: water, sewer, electric (50 amps).

Lancaster Campground, 2151 West Fair Ave., 43130. T: (740) 653-2119. RV/tent: 24. $15. Hookups: water, electric (30 amps).

Latham

Cave Lake Park, 1132 Bell Hollow Rd., 45133. T: (937) 588-3252. RV/tent: 300. $19. Hookups: water, electric (30 amps).

Long's Retreat Family Resort, 50 Bell Hollow Rd., 45133. T: (937) 588-3725. RV/tent: 450. $14. Hookups: water, sewer, electric (20 amps).

Laurelville

Tar Hollow State Park, 16396 Tar Hollow Rd., 43135. T: (614) 887-4818. RV/tent: 113. $15. Hookups: electric (50 amps).

Lebanon

Cedarbrook Campground, 760 Franklin Rd., 45036. T: (513) 932-7717. RV/tent: 150. $21. Hookups: water, sewer, electric (50 amps).

Lisbon

Lock 30 Woodlands RV Campground Resort, 45529 Middle Beaver Rd., 44432. T: (970) 424-9197. RV/tent: 65. $30. Hookups: water, electric (50 amps), sewer.

Logan

Hocking Hills State Park, Old Man's Cave, 20160 SR 664, 43138. T: (614) 385-6165. RV/tent: 170. $17. Hookups: electric (30 amps).

Scenic View Campground, 29150 Pattor Rd., 43138. T: (740) 385-4295. RV/tent: 70. $37. Hookups: water, sewer, electric (30 amps).

Lore City

Salt Fork State Park, 14755 Cadiz Rd., 43725. T: (740) 439-3521. RV/tent: 212. $16. Hookups: electric (50 amps).

Loudonville

Camp Toodik Family Campground & Canoe Livery, 7700 TR 462, 44842. T: (419) 994-3835. RV/tent: 153. $17. Hookups: water, electric (50 amps), sewer.

MINNESOTA (continued)

Loudonville (continued)

Lake Wapusun, 10787 Molter Rd., 44676. T: (330) 496-2355. RV/tent: 150. $17. Hookups: water, electric (30 amps).

Long Lake Park & Campground, 8974 Long Lake Dr., 44638. T: (419) 827-2278. RV/tent: 75. $22. Hookups: water, electric (30 amps).

Mohican Campground & Cabins, 3058 SR 3, 44842. T: (419) 994-2267. RV/tent: 146. $27. Hookups: water, sewer, electric (30 amps).

Mohican State Park, 3116 SR 3, 44842. T: (419) 994-5125. RV/tent: 167. $20. Hookups: electric (50 amps).

River Run Family Campground, 3064 Wally Rd., 44842. T: (419) 994-5257. RV/tent: 98. $24. Hookups: water, electric (50 amps).

Mansfield

Charles Mill Lake Park Camp Area, 1271 SR 430, 44903. T: (419) 368-6885. RV/tent: 527. $19. Hookups: electric (30 amps).

Marietta

Camp Civitan, 922 Front St., 45750. T: (740) 373-7937. RV/tent: 42. $15. Hookups: water, electric (30 amps).

Marion

Hickory Grove Lake Family Campground, 805 Hoch Rd., 43302. T: (740) 382-8584. RV/tent: 88. $19. Hookups: water, electric (50 amps), sewer.

McArthur

Lake Hope State Park, 22331 SR 278, 45651. T: (740) 596-4938. RV/tent: 126. $13. Hookups: electric (30 amps).

Medina

Pier-lon Park, 5960 Vandemark Rd., 44256. T: (330) 667-2311. RV/tent: 150. $20. Hookups: water, sewer, electric (50 amps).

Milan

Milan Trav-L-Park, 11404 SR 250N, 44846. T: (419) 433-4277. RV/tent: 142. $30. Hookups: water, sewer, electric (50 amps).

Mineral City

Atwood Lake Park, 4956 Shop Rd., 44656. T: (330) 343-6780. RV/tent: 569. $23. Hookups: electric (30 amps).

Minster

Lake Loramie State Park, 11221 SR 362, 45865. T: (937) 295-2011. RV/tent: 166. $14. Hookups: water, electric (30 amps).

Montville

Tri-County Kamp Inn, 17147 Gar Hwy, 44064. T: (440) 968-3400. RV/tent: 155. $24. Hookups: water, electric (30 amps).

Mount Gilead

Dogwood Valley, 4185 Twp Rd 99, 43338. T: (419) 946-5230. RV/tent: 95. $22. Hookups: water, sewer, electric (30 amps).

Mount Gilead State Park, 4119 SR 95, 43338. T: (419) 946-1961. RV/tent: 60. $12. Hookups: electric (50 amps).

Mount Sterling

Deer Creek State Park, 20635 Waterloo Rd., 43143. T: (740) 869-3124. RV/tent: 232. $16. Hookups: electric (30 amps).

Mount Vernon

Rustic Knolls Campsites, 8664 Keys Rd., 43050. T: (740) 397-9318. RV/tent: 150. $14. Hookups: water, electric (30 amps), sewer.

Nashport

Dillon State Park, 5265 Dillon Hills Dr., 43830. T: (740) 453-4377. RV/tent: 195. $15. Hookups: electric (20 amps).

Wild Bill's Resort, 6819 Newark Rd., 43830. T: (740) 452-0113. RV/tent: 150. $18. Hookups: water, electric (30 amps), sewer.

Navarre

Baylor Beach Park, 8725 Manchester Southwest, 44662. T: (330) 767-3031. RV/tent: 50. $20. Hookups: water, electric (30 amps).

Nelsonville

Happy Hills Family Campground, 22245 SR 278, 45764. T: (740) 385-6720. RV/tent: 63. $20. Hookups: water, electric (30 amps).

Nevada

Foxfire Family Fun Park, 3699 Crawford-Wyandot Rd., 44849. T: (740) 482-2190. RV/tent: 120. $30. Hookups: water, electric (30 amps), sewer.

New London

Indian Trail Campground, 1400 US 250S, 44851. T: (419) 929-1135. RV/tent: 176. $25. Hookups: water, sewer, electric (30 amps).

New Paris

Arrowhead Campground, 1361 Thomas Rd., 45347. T: (937) 996-6203. RV/tent: 33. $21. Hookups: water, sewer, electric (30 amps).

New Washington

Auburn Lake Park, 555 Michael Ave., 44854. T: (419) 492-2110. RV/tent: 28. $18. Hookups: water, electric (30 amps).

Newbury

Punderson State Park, 11755 Kinsman Rd., 44065. T: (440) 564-2279. RV/tent: 201. $15. Hookups: electric (20 amps).

Newton Falls

Ridge Ranch Campground, 5219 SR 303 Northwest, 44444. T: (330) 898-8080. RV/tent: 176. $20. Hookups: water, electric (30 amps), sewer.

Oak Harbor

Paradise Acres, 4225 North Rider Rd., 43449. T: (419) 898-6411. RV/tent: 74. $15. Hookups: water, sewer, electric (30 amps).

Oberlin

Schaun Acres Campground, 51468 SR 303, 44074. T: (440) 775-7122. RV/tent: 53. $21. Hookups: water, electric (30 amps), sewer.

Oregon

Maumee Bay State Park, 1400 State Park Rd., 43618. T: (419) 836-7305. RV/tent: 256. $16. Hookups: electric (20 amps).

Oregonia

Olive Branch Campground, 6985 Wilmington Rd., 45054. T: (513) 932-2267. RV/tent: 138. $22. Hookups: water, sewer, electric (50 amps).

Orwell

Pine Lakes Campground, 3001 Hague Rd., 44076. T: (440) 437-6218. RV/tent: 70. $16. Hookups: water, electric (30 amps).

Oxford

Camp America, Box 47, 45056. T: (800) 818-2267. RV/tent: 24. $15. Hookups: water, electric (30 amps).

Parkman

Kool Lakes Family Camping & Recreation Resort, P.O. Box 673, 44080. T: (440) 548-8436. RV/tent: 97. $19. Hookups: water, electric (50 amps), sewer.

Paulding

Woodbridge Campground, 8656 Rd. 137, 45879. T: (419) 399-2267. RV/tent: 65. $19. Hookups: water, electric (30 amps).

Peebles

Mineral Springs Lake Resort, 162 Bluegill Rd., 45660. T: (937) 587-3132. RV/tent: 53. $26. Hookups: water, sewer, electric (30 amps).

Perrysburg

Stony Ridge KOA Campgrounds, 24787 Luckey Rd., 43551. T: (419) 837-6848. RV/tent: 58. $26. Hookups: water, sewer, electric (30 amps).

Perrysville

Pleasant Hill Lake, 3431 SR 95, 44864. T: (419) 938-7884. RV/tent: 382. $20. Hookups: electric (30 amps).

Pioneer

Funny Farm Campground, 19452 CR 12, 43554. T: (419) 737-2467. RV/tent: 200. $22. Hookups: water, sewer, electric (30 amps).

Lazy River Campground, 12-808 SR #20, 43554. T: (419) 485-4411. RV/tent: 350. $23. Hookups: water, sewer, electric (30 amps).

Port Clinton

Cedarlane Campground, 2926 Northeast Catawba Rd., 43452. T: (419) 797-9907. RV/tent: 175. $26. Hookups: water, electric (50 amps).

MINNESOTA (continued)

Tall Timbers Campground, 340 Christy Chapel Rd., 43452. T: (419) 732-3938. RV/tent: 150. $22. Hookups: water, electric (30 amps).

Portsmouth

Shawnee Village RV Park & Campground, 13610 US 52, 45663. T: (740) 858-5542. RV/tent: 100. $22. Hookups: water, electric (30 amps).

Randolph

Friendship Acres Campground, 2210 SR 44, 44201. T: (330) 325-9527. RV/tent: 150. $22. Hookups: water, electric (30 amps).

Ravenna

Country Acres Campground, 9850 Minyoung Rd., 44266. T: (330) 358-2774. RV/tent: 100. $22. Hookups: water, electric (50 amps), sewer.

Republic

Clinton Lake Camping, 4990 East Twp Rd 122, 44867. T: (419) 585-3331. RV/tent: 50. $17. Hookups: water, electric (30 amps).

Rogers

Camp Frederick, P.O. Box 258, 44455. T: (330) 227-3633. RV/tent: 11. $20. Hookups: water, electric (30 amps).

Rushsylvania

Back Forty Ltd, 959 CR 111E, 43347. T: (937) 468-7492. RV/tent: 52. $18. Hookups: water, electric (30 amps).

Salem

Chaparral Family Campground, 10136 Middletown Rd., 44460. T: (330) 337-9381. RV/tent: 230. $23. Hookups: water, sewer, electric (30 amps).

Timashamie Family Campground, 28251 Georgetown Rd., 44460. T: (330) 525-7054. RV/tent: 55. $21. Hookups: water, electric (50 amps), sewer.

Sandusky

Bayshore Estates Campground, 2311 Cleveland Rd., 44870. T: (419) 625-7906. RV/tent: 380. $35. Hookups: water, sewer, electric (50 amps).

Crystal Campground, 710 Crystal Rock Rd., 44870. T: (419) 684-7177. RV/tent: 124. $28. Hookups: water, sewer, electric (30 amps).

Senecaville

Seneca Lake Marina Point, SR 313, 43780. T: (740) 685-6013. RV/tent: 320. $14. Hookups: electric (30 amps).

Shelby

Wagon Wheel Campground, 6787 Baker, 44875. T: (419) 347-1392. RV/tent: 50. $20. Hookups: water, sewer, electric (50 amps).

South Bloomingville

Top O' The Caves Family Campground/Resort, 26780 Chapel Ridge Rd., 43152. T: (740) 385-6566. RV/tent: 200. $22. Hookups: water, electric (30 amps), sewer.

Southington

Valley Lake Park, 3959 SR 305, 44470. T: (330) 898-1819. RV/tent: 22. $15. Hookups: water, sewer, electric (30 amps).

Spencer

Sunset Lake Campground, 5566 Root Rd., 44275. T: (330) 667-2686. RV/tent: 80. $19. Hookups: electric (30 amps) water.

Springfield

Buck Creek State Park, 1901 Buck Creek Ln., 45502. T: (937) 322-5284. RV/tent: 100. $16. Hookups: electric (30 amps).

St. Mary's

Grand Lake-St. Mary's State Park, P.O. Box 308, 45885. T: (419) 394-3611. RV/tent: 206. $14. Hookups: electric (50 amps).

Streetsboro

Mar-Lynn Lake Park, 187 SR 303, 44241. T: (330) 650-2522. RV/tent: 120. $32. Hookups: electric (50 amps), sewer, water.

Thompson

Heritage Hills Campground, 6445 Ledge Rd., 44086. T: (440) 298-1311. RV/tent: 150. $23. Hookups: water, electric (50 amps), sewer.

Tiffin

Walnut Grove Campground, 7325 South Twp Rd 131, 44883. T: (419) 448-1014. RV/tent: 30. $18. Hookups: water, sewer, electric (30 amps).

Toronto

Austin Lake Park & Campground, 1002 Twp Rd 285A, 43964. T: (740) 544-5253. RV/tent: 55. $20. Hookups: water, electric (50 amps).

Urbana

Meadow Lake Resort, 4739 Woodville Pike, 43078. T: (937) 652-3400. RV/tent: 300. $23. Hookups: water, sewer, electric (50 amps).

Van Wert

Pleasant Grove Campground, 10856A Liberty-Union Rd., 45891. T: (419) 238-1124. RV/tent: 53. $19. Hookups: water, sewer, electric (30 amps).

Versailles

Cottonwood Lakes, 8549 Althoff Rd., 45380. T: (419) 582-2610. RV/tent: 40. $14. Hookups: water, electric (30 amps).

Wellington

Rustic Lakes Campground, 44901 New London Eastern Rd., 44880. T: (440) 647-3804. RV/tent: 100. $23. Hookups: water, electric (30 amps).

Williamstown

Sulphur Lake Camp, P.O. Box 19, 45897. T: (419) 365-5374. RV/tent: 100. $20. Hookups: water, sewer, electric (50 amps).

Wilmington

Beechwood Acres, P.O. Box 227, 45177. T: (937) 289-2202. RV/tent: 95. $16. Hookups: water, electric (50 amps).

Winesburg

Amish Country Campsite, 1930 US 62, 44690. T: (330) 359-5226. RV/tent: 60. $15. Hookups: water, electric (30 amps).

Zanesville

Campers Grove, Hopewell National Rd. RT. 40, 43701. T: (740) 453-3973. RV/tent: 45. $12. Hookups: water.

Wolfies Family Kamping, 101 Buckeye Dr., 43701. T: (740) 454-0925. RV/tent: 39. $16. Hookups: electric (30 amps), sewer, water.

MISSISSIPPI

Bay St. Louis

Bay Marina & RV Park & Lodging, 100 Bay Marina Dr., 39520. T: (228) 466-4970. RV/tent: 33. $20. Hookups: electric (20, 30, 50 amps).

KOA–Bay St. Louis/Gulfport, 814 Hwy. 90, 39520. T: (800) 562-2790. RV/tent: 78. $24. Hookups: electric (20, 30, 50 amps).

McLeod Water Park (Pearl River Basin Dev. Dist.), Texas Flat Rd., 39520. T: (228) 467-1894. RV/tent: 58. $6–$11. Hookups: water, electric.

Biloxi

Biloxi RV Park & Biloxi Travel Inn, 2010 Beach Blvd., 39531. T: (228) 388-5531. RV/tent: 36. $22. Hookups: electric (20, 30, 50 amps).

Cajun RV Park, 1860 Beach Blvd., 39531. T: (228) 388-5590. RV/tent: 126. $24.50–$26.64. Hookups: electric (20, 30, 50 amps).

Fox's RV Park & Complex, 190 Beauvoir Rd., 39531. T: (800) 736-7275. RV/tent: 144. $20. Hookups: electric (30, 50 amps).

MISSISSIPPI (continued)

Biloxi (continued)

Southern Comfort Camping Resort, 1766 Beach Blvd., 39531. T: (877) 302-1700. RV/tent: 123. $18–$24. Hookups: water, electric (20, 30, 50 amps).

Clinton

Springridge RV Park, 499 Springridge Rd., 39056. T: (601) 924-0947. RV/tent: 42. $18. Hookups: electric (20, 30, 50 amps).

Coldwater

Dub Patton Campground (Corps of Engineers–Arkabutla Lake), 3905 Arkabutla Dam Rd., 38668. T: (662) 562-6261. RV/tent: 66. $12–$18. Hookups: water, electric.

Hernando Point (Corps of Engineers–Arkabutla Lake), 3905 Arkabutla Dam Rd., 38668. T: (662) 562-6261. RV/tent: 83. $12–$18. Hookups: water, electric.

Columbia

Whispering Pines RV Park, 7836 Hwy. 49 South, 39402-9169. T: (601) 943-6290. RV/tent: 10. $20. Hookups: water, electric (20, 50 amps).

Columbus

Brown's RV Trailer Park, 2002 Bluecutt Rd., 39705. T: (662) 328-1976. RV/tent: 24. $14. Hookups: electric (20, 30 amps).

Decatur

Turkey Creek Water Park (Pat Harrison Waterway District), 142 Parkway Dr., 39327. T: (601) 635-3314. RV/tent: 22. $8. Hookups: electric (20 amps).

Durant

Holmes County State Park, Old Holmes Park Rd., 39063. T: (662) 653-3351. RV/tent: 28. $10–$13. Hookups: electric (50 amps).

Edwards

Askew's Landing Campground, 3412 Askew Ferry Rd., 39066. T: (601) 852-2331. RV/tent: 89. $14–$16. Hookups: electric (20, 30, 50 amps).

Enid

Chickasaw Hill Campground, 931 CR 36, 38606. T: (662) 563-4571. RV/tent: 51. $12. Hookups: water, electric (30 amps).

Persimmon Hill–South Abutment, 931 CR 36, 38606. T: (662) 563-4571. RV/tent: 72. $12. Hookups: water, electric (30 amps).

Water Valley Landing Campground, 931 CR 36, 38606. T: (662) 563-4571. RV/tent: 29. $12. Hookups: water, electric (30 amps).

Enterprise

Dunn's Falls Water Park (Pat Harrison Waterway District), 6890 Dunn's Falls Rd., 39330. T: (601) 655-9511. RV/tent: 15. $8. Hookups: none.

Escatawpa

Riverbend RV Resort, 10707 Hwy. 613, 39552. T: (228) 475-2429. RV/tent: 77. $16. Hookups: electric (20, 30, 50 amps).

Flora

Mississippi Petrified Forest Campground, 124 Forest Park Rd., 39071. T: (601) 879-8189. RV/tent: 37. $12–$15. Hookups: water, electric (20 amps).

Forest

Bienville National Forest, 246 Mimosa Dr., 39153. T: (601) 469-3811. RV/tent: 35. $7–$13. Hookups: water, electric (20, 30 amps).

Greenville

Delta Village Park, 3836 Hwy. 82 West, 38701. T: (662) 378-3655. RV/tent: 16. $11. Hookups: electric (20, 30, 50 amps).

Grenada

Hugh White State Park, 3170 Hugh White State Park Rd., 38901. T: (662) 226-4934. RV/tent: 200. $13. Hookups: water, electric 30, 50 amps).

Oxbow RV Park, 601 Hwy. 7 North, 38901-8656. T: (662) 226-0751. RV/tent: 49. $17.75. Hookups: electric (20, 30, 50 amps).

Gulfport

Campground of the South, 10406 Three Rivers Rd., 39503. T: (228) 539-2922. RV/tent: 90. $20. Hookups: electric (20, 30, 50 amps).

Country Side RV Park & Tradin' Post, 20278 Hwy. 49, 39574. T: (228) 539-0807. RV/tent: 32. $16. Hookups: electric (20, 30, 50 amps).

San Beach RV Park, 1020 Beach Dr., 39507. T: (228) 896-7551. RV/tent: 102. $22.47. Hookups: electric (20, 30, 50 amps).

Hattiesburg

Military Park, 1001 Lee Ave., 39407-5500. T: (601) 558-2540. RV/tent: 25. $10. Hookups: full.

Quilla's RV Park, 558 South Gate Rd., 39401-9410. T: (601) 544-6837. RV/tent: 28. $15. Hookups: water, electric (20, 30, 50 amps).

Shady Cove RV Park, 7836 Hwy. 49 North, 39405. T: (877) 251-8169. RV/tent: 53. $16. Hookups: water, electric (20, 30, 50 amps).

Hernando

Memphis South Campground & RV Park, 1250 Mt Pleasant Rd. Northeast, 38632. T: (662) 622-0056. RV/tent: 47. $18. Hookups: water, electric (20, 30 amps).

Hollandale

Leroy Percy State Park, Hwy. 12 West, 38748. T: (662) 827-5436. RV/tent: 16. $9–$13. Hookups: water, electric (20, 30 amps).

Holly Springs

Wall Doxey State Park, 3946 Hwy. 7 South, 38635. T: (662) 252-4231. RV/tent: 64. $9–$13. Hookups: water, electric (20, 30 amps).

Houston

Tombigbee National Forest, Hwy. 15 South, 39735. T: (662) 285-3264. RV/tent: 28. $13. Hookups: water, electric (30, 50 amps).

Iuka

JP Coleman State Park, 607 CR 321, 38852. T: (662) 423-6515. RV/tent: 57. $14. Hookups: water, electric.

Jackson

Goshen Springs Campground (Pearl River Valley Water Supply District), 1684 Hwy. 43 North, 39042. T: (601) 829-2751. RV/tent: 68. $16. Hookups: water, electric (30 amps).

Swinging Bridge RV Park, 5750 I-55, 39211. T: (601) 502-1101. RV/tent: 35. $22. Hookups: water, electric.

Laurel

KOA–Laurel, 2920 Hwy. 11 North, 39440. T: (800) 562-0378. RV/tent: 88. $24–$27. Hookups: full.

Long Beach

Plantation Pines Campground and RV Park, 19391 28 St., 39560. T: (228) 863-6550. RV/tent: 70. $20. Hookups: full.

Louisville

Legion State Park, Old Hwy. 25 North, 39339. T: (662) 773-8323. RV/tent: 10. $6. Hookups: water, electric.

Ludlow

Coal Bluff Park (Pearl River Valley Water Supply District), 1319 Coal Bluff Rd., 39200. T: (601) 654-7726. RV/tent: 68. $10–$13. Hookups: water, electric (20, 30 amps).

Lumberton

Little Black Creek Water Park (Pat Harrison Waterway District), 2159 Little Black Creek Rd., 39475. T: (601) 794-2957. RV/tent: 125. $14–$17.50. Hookups: water, electric (30 amps).

Mendenhall

D'Lo Water Park, P.O. Box 278, 39062. T: (601) 847-4310. RV/tent: 12. $10. Hookups: water, electric.

Meridian

Campground RV and Trailer Park, Hwy. 45 North, 39301. T: (601) 485-4549. RV/tent: 58. $15–$17. Hookups: full.

Nanabe Creek Campground, 1933 Russell–Mt. Gilead Rd., 39301. T: (601) 485-4711. RV/tent: 95. $14–$18. Hookups: water, electric (20, 30, 50 amps).

Mount Olive

Dry Creek Water Park (Pat Harrison Waterway District), Hwy. 35, 39119. T: (601) 797-4619. RV/tent: 28. $8–$14. Hookups: water, electric (20 amps).

Natchez

Natchez State Park, 40 Wickcliff Rd., 39120. T: (601) 442-2658. RV/tent: 21. $10–$13. Hookups: water, electric (20, 30 amps).

Traceway Campground, 1113 Hwy. 61 North, 39120. T: (601) 445-8278. RV/tent: 40. $14–$17.12. Hookups: water, electric (15, 20, 30, 50 amps).

MISSISSIPPI (continued)

Ocean Springs

RV-Tel, 2302 Beinville Blvd., 39565-9340. T: (228) 875-2772. RV/tent: 20. $22.50. Hookups: electric (20, 30, 50 amps).

Philadelphia

Frog Level RV Park, 1532 Hwy. 16 West, 39350. T: (601) 650-9621. RV/tent: 52. $18. Hookups: full.

Port Gibson

Grand Gulf Military Park Campground (State), 12006 Grand Gulf Rd., 39150. T: (601) 437-5911. RV/tent: 42. $5–$15. Hookups: electric (20, 30, 50 amps).

Quitman

Clarkco State Park, Hwy. 45 North, 39355. T: (601) 776-6651. RV/tent: 43. $13. Hookups: water, electric (20, 30 amps).

Rosedale

Great River Road State Park, Hwy. 1 South, 38769. T: (662) 759-6762. RV/tent: 61. $13. Hookups: water, electric (30 amps).

Tishomingo

Tishomingo State Park, 105 CR 90, 38873. T: (662) 438-6914. RV/tent: 62. $9–$13. Hookups: water, electric (20, 30, 50 amps).

Tunica

Hollywood Casino RV Resort, P.O. Box 28, 38676. T: (800) 871-0711. RV/tent: 123. $16.20. Hookups: full.

Sam's Town RV Park, 1477 Casino Strip Resorts Blvd., 38664. T: (800) 456-0711. RV/tent: 100. $8. Hookups: full.

Tupelo

Natchez Trace RV Park, P.O. Box 2564, 38803. T: (601) 769-8609. RV/tent: 72. $15.45. Hookups: water, electric (20, 30, 50 amps).

RV Campground at Barnes Crossing, 125 Rd. 1698, 38801. T: (662) 844-6063 or (662) 767-8609. RV/tent: 40. $15. Hookups: full.

Trace State Park, Rte. 1 P.O. Box 254, 39200. T: (662) 489-2958. RV/tent: 25. $10–$13. Hookups: water, electric (20, 30 amps).

Vaiden

Vaiden Campground, P.O. Box 227, 39176. T: (662) 464-9336. RV/tent: 90. $14–$17. Hookups: water, electric (20, 30, 50 amps).

Vicksburg

Vicksburg Battlefield Kampground, 4407 I-20 Frontage Rd., 39183. T: (601) 636-2025. RV/tent: 81. $15–$17. Hookups: water, electric (20, 30 amps).

Wesson

Lake Lincoln State Park, 2573 Sunset Rd. Northeast, 39191. T: (601) 643-9044 or (601) 735-4365. RV/ tent: 61. $13. Hookups: water, electric (30 amps).

Wiggins

Flint Creek Water Park (Pat Harrison Waterway District), 1216 Parkway Dr., 39577. T: (601) 928-3051. RV/tent: 170. $18. Hookups: water, electric (30 amps).

MISSOURI

Anderson

Indian Creek RV Park & Campground, Hwy. 71, 64831. T: (417) 845-6400. RV/tent: 120. $12. Hookups: electric (20, 30, 50 amps), water, sewer.

Arrow Rock

Arrow Rock State Historic Site State Park, P.O. Box 1, 65320. T: (660) 837-3330. RV/tent: 45. $12–$15. Hookups: electric (20, 30 amps), water.

Blue Eye

Old Hwy. 86, HCR 2 Box 136, 65615. T: (417) 779-5376. www.ReserveUSA.com/nrrs/mo/ol86. RV/tent: 71. $12–$16. Hookups: electric (20, 30 amps).

Bonne Terre

St. Francois State Park, 8920 US 67 North, 63628. T: (573) 358-2173. RV/tent: 110. $12–$15. Hookups: electric (20, 30 amps), water.

Branson

Acorn Acres, 159 Acorn Acres Ln., 65737. T: (417) 338-2500. RV/tent: 77. $17–$23. Hookups: electric (30, 50 amps), water, sewer.

America's Best Campground, 499 Buena Vista Rd., 65616. T: (417) 339-2296 or (800) 671-4399. F: (417) 336-6581. www.abc-branson.com. RV/tent: 166. $18–$30. Hookups: electric (30, 50 amps), water, sewer.

Andrew's Landing Resort & RV Park, 5329 Hwy. 165, 65616. T: (800) 678-9780 or (417) 334-5071. www.andrewslanding.com. RV/tent: 25. $16. Hookups: electric (20, 30, 50 amps), water, sewer.

Bar M Resort & Campground, HCR 4 Box 2990; Hwy. DD-24, 65737. T: (417) 338-2593. www.Barmresort.com. RV/tent: 12. $17–$20. Hookups: electric (30 amps), water, sewer.

Branson City Campground, 300 Boxcar Willie Dr., 65616. T: (417) 334-2915. RV/tent: 350. $18. Hookups: electric (30, 50 amps), water, sewer.

Branson KOA, 1025 Headwaters Rd., 65616. T: (800) 562-4177 or (417) 334-7450. F: (417) 334-7457. www.koa.com. RV/tent: 169. $19–$28. Hookups: electric (30, 50 amps), water, sewer.

Branson Shenanigans RV Park, 3675 Keeter St., 65616. T: (800) 338-7275 or (417) 334-1920. www.bransonrvpark.com. RV/tent: 30. $20–$25. Hookups: electric (30, 50 amps), water, sewer.

Branson Stagecoach RV Park, 5751 Hwy. 165, 65616. T: (800) 446-7110 or (417) 335-8185. RV/tent: 47. $22–$25. Hookups: electric (30, 50 amps), water, sewer.

Branson View Campground, 2362 Hwy. 265, 65616. T: (800) 992-9055 or (417) 338-8716. F: (417) 338-2016. www.bransonview.com. RV/tent: 42. $19–$25. Hookups: electric (30, 50 amps), water, sewer.

Compton Ridge Campground, 5040 Hwy. 265, 65616. T: (800) 233-8648 or (417) 338-2911. www.comptonridge.com. RV/tent: 227. $19–$27. Hookups: electric (20, 30, 50 amps), water, sewer.

Cooper Creek Resort & Campground, 471 Cooper Creek Rd., 65616. T: (800) 261-8398 or (417) 334 5250. RV/tent: 91. $20–$27. Hookups: electric (20, 30, 50 amps), water, sewer.

Gerth Campground & Camper Park, 139 Irish Ln., 65616. T: (417) 334-5849. RV/tent: 200. $18. Hookups: electric (30, 50 amps), water, sewer.

Indian Point, 3125 Indian Point Rd., 65616. T: (417) 338-2121. www.ReserveUSA.com/nrrs/ mo/indp. RV/tent: 78. $16. Hookups: electric (20, 30 amps).

Lakeview Campground, 2820 Indian Point Rd., 65616. T: (800) 396-2232. www.lakeview campground.com. RV/tent: 45. $13–$18. Hookups: electric (30, 50 amps), water, sewer.

Musicland Kampground, 116 North Gretna Rd., 65616. T: (888) 248-9080. www.musicland-kampground.com. RV/tent: 112. $26–$32. Hookups: electric (50 amps), water, sewer.

MISSOURI (continued)

Branson (continued)

Ozark Country Campground, 679 Quebec Dr., 65616. T: (800) 968-1300 or (417) 334-4681. www.natins.com/campground/country. RV/tent: 67. $13–$25. Hookups: electric (20, 30, 50 amps), water, sewer.

Stormy Point Camp & Resort, 1318 Stormy Point Rd., 65616. T: (417) 338-2255. www.stormypoint.com. RV/tent: 60. $17–$25. Hookups: electric (20, 30, 50 amps), water, sewer.

Tall Pines Campground, 5558 Hwy. 265, 65616. T: (800) 425-2300. RV/tent: 83. $15–$24. Hookups: electric (30, 50 amps), water, sewer.

Trail's End Resort & RV Park, 71 Dogwood Park Tr., 65616. T: (800) 888-1891 or (417) 338-2633. RV/tent: 12. $12–$16. Hookups: electric (30, 50 amps), water, sewer.

Table Rock State Park, 5272 Hwy. 165, 65616. T: (417) 334-4704. RV/tent: 143. $12–$15. Hookups: electric (20, 30, 50 amps), water, sewer.

Camdenton

Bull Run Bluff RV Park & Campground, 54–82 Lake Rd., HCR 80 Box 775. T: (573) 346-7815. www.funlake.com/accommodations/bullrunbluff. RV/tent: 72. $17–$22. Hookups: electric (30, 50 amps), water, sewer.

Cameron

Wallace State Park, 10621 Northeast Hwy. 121, 64429. T: (816) 632-3745. RV/tent: 87. $12–$15. Hookups: electric (20, 30 amps), water.

Cape Fair

Cape Fair, 1092 Shadrack Rd., 65624. T: (417) 538-9999. www.ReserveUSA.com/nrrs/mo/cape. RV/tent: 82. $12–$17. Hookups: electric (20, 30 amps), water.

Carthage

Big Red Barn RV Park, 5089 CL 138, 64836. T: (888) 244-2276 or (417) 358-2432. www.bigbarnrvpark.com. RV/tent: 63. $14–$17. Hookups: electric (30, 50 amps), water, sewer.

Cassville

Big M, HCR 81 Box 9251, 65625. T: (417) 271-3190. www.ReserveUSA.com/nrrs/mo/bigm. RV/tent: 92. $11–$17. Hookups: electric (20, 30 amps).

Roaring River State Park, Rte. 4 Box 4100, 65625. T: (417) 847-2539. RV/tent: 185. $12–$15. Hookups: electric (20, 30 amps), water.

Columbia

Finger Lakes State Park, 1505 East Peabody Rd., 65202. T: (573) 443-5315. RV/tent: 36. $12–$15. Hookups: electric (20, 30 amps), water.

Craig

Big Lake State Park, 204 Lake Shore Dr., 64437. T: (660) 442-3770. RV/tent: 75. $12–$15. Hookups: electric (20, 30 amps).

Cuba

Blue Moon RV & Horse Park, 355 Hwy. F, 65453. T: (877) 440-CAMP or (573) 885-3752. F: (573) 885-3752. www.fidnet.com/~blmoonrv. RV/tent: 55. $10–$19. Hookups: electric (30, 50 amps), water, sewer.

Dadeville

Stockton State Park, Rte. 1 Box 1715, 65635. T: (417) 276-4259. RV/tent: 75. $12–$15. Hookups: electric (20, 30 amps), water.

Danville

Graham Cave State Park, 217 Hwy. TT, 63361. T: (573) 564-3476. RV/tent: 52. $12–$15. Hookups: electric (20, 30 amps), water.

DeSoto

Washington State Park, Rte. 2 Box 450, 63020. T: (636) 586-2995. RV/tent: 51. $12–$15. Hookups: electric (20, 30 amps), water.

Eagle Rock

Eagle Rock, HC 1 Box 1037, 65641. T: (417) 271-3215. www.ReserveUSA.com/nrrs/mo/eagr. RV/tent: 63. $12–$18. Hookups: electric (20, 30 amps), water, sewer.

Paradise Cove Camping Resort, HCR 1 Box 1067, 65641. T: (417) 271-4888. RV/tent: 21. $10–$15. Hookups: electric (20, 30 amps), water, sewer.

Forsyth

Forsyth KOA, 11020 MO 76, 65653. T: (800) 562-7560 or (417) 546-5364. www.koa.com. RV/tent: 67. $22–$25. Hookups: electric (20, 30, 50 amps), water, sewer.

Genevieve

Hawn State Park, 12096 Park Dr., 63670. T: (573) 883-3603. RV/tent: 50. $12–$15. Hookups: electric (20, 30 amps), water.

Golden

Viney Creek, Rte. 1 Box 1023, 65658. T: (417) 271-3860. www.ReserveUSA.com/nrrs/mo/vinc. RV/tent: 46. $11–$16. Hookups: electric (20, 30 amps), water.

Hermitage

Damsite, Rte. 2 Box 2160, 65668. T: (417) 745-2244. www.ReserveUSA.com/nrrs/mo/da10. RV/tent: 130. $10–$18. Hookups: electric (20, 30 amps), water.

Lightfoot Landing, Rte. 2 Box 2160, 65668. T: (417) 282-6890. www.ReserveUSA.com/nrrs/mo/ligl. RV/tent: 35. $10–$12. Hookups: electric (20, 30 amps).

Nemo Landing, Rte. 2 Box 2160, 65668. T: (417) 993-5529. www.ReserveUSA.com/nrrs/mo/nemo. RV/tent: 121. $10–$18. Hookups: electric (20, 30 amps), water, sewer.

Outlet Park, Rte. 2 Box 2160, 65668. T: (417) 745-2290. www.ReserveUSA.com/nrrs/mo/oua2. RV/tent: 28. $8–$10. Hookups: electric (20, 30 amps).

Wheatland Park, Rte. 2 Box 2160, 65668. T: (417) 282-5267. www.ReserveUSA.com/nrrs/mo/whea. RV/tent: 86. $10–$18. Hookups: electric (20, 30 amps), water.

Jamesport

Countryside RV Park, 106 East Second, 64648. T: (660) 684 6392. RV/tent: 16. $13. Hookups: electric (20, 30 amps), water, sewer.

Jonesburg

Jonesburg/Warrenton KOA, P.O. Box H, 63351. T: (800) 562-5634 or (636) 488-5630. www.koa.com/where/MO/25105. RV/tent: 52. $17–$24. Hookups: electric (20, 30, 50 amps), water, sewer.

Joplin

Joplin KOA, 4359 Hwy. 43, 64804. T: (800) 562-5675 or (417) 623-2246. www.koa.com. RV/tent: 74. $18–$26. Hookups: electric (20, 30, 50 amps), water, sewer.

Kaiser

Lake of the Ozarks State Park, P.O. Box 170, 65047. T: (573) 348-2694. RV/tent: 182. $12–$15. Hookups: electric (20, 30 amps), water.

Kimberling City

Kimberling City KOA, HCR 5 Box 465, 65686. T: (800) 562-5685 or (417) 739-4627. www.koa.com/where/MO/25107. RV/tent: 94. $18–$25. Hookups: electric (30, 50 amps), water, sewer.

Knob Noster

Knob Noster State Park, 801 Southeast Hwy. 10, 65336. T: (660) 563-2463. RV/tent: 77. $12–$15. Hookups: electric (20, 30 amps), water.

Laclede

Pershing State Park, 29277 Hwy. 130, 64651. T: (660) 963-2299. RV/tent: 39. $12–$15. Hookups: electric (20, 30 amps), water.

LaGrange

Wakonda State Park, Rte. 1 Box 242, 63448. T: (573) 655-2280. RV/tent: 79. $12–$15. Hookups: electric (20, 30 amps), water.

Lake Ozark

Cross Creek RV Park, P.O. Box 936, 65049. T: (888) 250-3885. RV/tent: 76. $10–$15. Hookups: electric (30, 50 amps), water, sewer.

MISSOURI (continued)

Majestic Oaks Park, P.O. Box 525, 65049. T: (573) 365-1890. F: (573) 365-9609. www.majesticoakspark.com. RV/tent: 85. $16–$22. Hookups: electric (30, 50 amps), water, sewer.

Lampe

Baxter Campground, HCR 1 171-A, 65681. T: (417) 779-5370. www.ReserveUSA.com/nrrs/mo/baxt. RV/tent: 54. $11–$15. Hookups: electric (20, 30 amps).

Mill Creek, HCR Box 1059, 65681. T: (417) 779-5378. www.ReserveUSA.com/nrrs/mo/mil2. RV/tent: 68. $12–$16. Hookups: electric (20, 30 amps).

Lawson

Watkins Woolen Mill State Park, 26600 Park Rd. North, 64602. T: (816) 296-3357. RV/tent: 98. $12–$15. Hookups: electric (20, 30 amps), water.

Leasburg

Ozark Outdoors, 200 Ozark Outdoor Ln., 65535. T: (800) 888-0023 or (573) 245-6839. www.ozarkoutdoors.net. RV/tent: 260. $7–$16. Hookups: electric (20, 30, 50 amps), water, sewer.

Onondaga Cave State Park, 7556 Hwy. H, 65535. T: (573) 245-6576. RV/tent: 71. $12–$15. Hookups: electric (20, 30 amps), water.

Lebanon

Bennett Spring State Park, 26250 Hwy. 64A, 65536. T: (417) 532-4338. RV/tent: 140. $12–$15. Hookups: electric (20, 30 amps), water, sewer.

Mansfield

Mansfield House B&B/RV Park, 2991 Hwy. A, 65704. T: (417) 924-2222. F: (417) 924-8619. RV/tent: 52. $18–$20. Hookups: electric (20, 30, 50 amps), water, sewer.

Miami

Van Meter State Park, 65344. T: (660) 886-7537. RV/tent: 21. $12–$15. Hookups: electric (20, 30 amps), water.

Monroe City

Frank Russell, 20642 Hwy. J, 63456. T: (573) 735-4097. www.ReserveUSA.com/nrrs/mo/frar. RV/tent: 60. $12. Hookups: electric (20, 30 amps).

Indian Creek, 20642 Hwy. J, 63456. T: (573) 735-4097. www.ReserveUSA.com/nrrs/mo/ind4. RV/tent: 190. $14. Hookups: electric (20, 30 amps).

Ray Behrens, 20642 Hwy. J, 63456. T: (573) 735-4097. www.ReserveUSA.com/nrrs/mo/rabe. RV/tent: 168. $14. Hookups: electric (20, 30 amps).

Mountain Home

Beaver Creek, P.O. Box 2070, 72654. T: (870) 546-3708. www.ReserveUSA.com/nrrs/mo/bec3. RV/tent: 37. $13–$16. Hookups: electric (20, 30 amps).

Pontiac Park, P.O. Box 2070, 72654. T: (870) 425-2700. www.ReserveUSA.com/nrrs/mo/pont. RV/tent: 38. $9–$16. Hookups: electric (20, 30 amps).

River Run, P.O. Box 2070, 72654. T: (870) 546-3646. www.ReserveUSA.com/nrrs/mo/rivn. RV/tent: 32. $8–$16. Hookups: electric (20, 30 amps).

Mountain View

Weaver's RV Park, 5400 CR 3200 No. 19, 65548. T: (417) 469-3351. RV/tent: 15. $12. Hookups: electric (20, 30 amps), water, sewer.

Newburg

Arlington RV Campground, 13003 Arlington Outer Rd., 65550. T: (573) 762-2714. www.arlingtonrvcampground.com. RV/tent: 60. $4–$14. Hookups: electric (30 amps), water, sewer.

Park Hills

St. Joe State Park, 2800 Pimville Rd., 63601. T: (573) 431-1069. RV/tent: 80. $12–$15. Hookups: electric (20, 30 amps), water.

Patterson

Sam A. Baker State Park, RFD 1 Box 114, 63956. T: (573) 856-4411. RV/tent: 192. $12–$15. Hookups: electric (20, 30 amps).

Piedmont

Bluff View (Clearwater Lake), Rte. 3 Box 3559-D, 63957. T: (573) 223-7777. www.ReserveUSA.com/nrrs/mo/blu2. RV/tent: 69. $10–$15. Hookups: electric (20, 30, 50 amps), water.

Highway K, Rte. 3 Box 3559-D, 63957. T: (573) 223-7777. www.ReserveUSA.com/nrrs/mo/higw. RV/tent: 61. $10–$13. Hookups: electric (20, 30 amps).

River Road L. Bank, Rte. 3 Box 3559-D, 63957. T: (573) 223-7777. www.ReserveUSA.com/nrrs/mo/rilb. RV/tent: 120. $10–$14. Hookups: electric (20, 30 amps).

Webb Creek, Rte. 3 Box 3559-D, 63957. T: (573) 223-7777. www.ReserveUSA.com/nrrs/mo/webb. RV/tent: 39. $10–$13. Hookups: electric (20, 30 amps), water.

Pittsburg

Pomme de Terre State Park, HC 77 Box 890, 65724. T: (417) 852-4291. RV/tent: 257. $12–$15. Hookups: electric (20, 30 amps), water.

Poplar Bluff

Camelot RV Campground, 1217 Rte. 6, 63901. T: (573) 785-1016. RV/tent: 70. $15–$19. Hookups: electric (30, 50 amps), water, sewer.

Reeds Spring

Aunts Creek, Rte. 5 Box 585, 65737. T: (417) 739-2792. www.ReserveUSA.com/nrrs/mo/aunt. RV/tent: 56. $12–$16. Hookups: electric (20, 30 amps).

Ridgedale

Long Creek, 1036 Long Creek Rd., 65639. T: (417) 334-8427. www.ReserveUSA.com/nrrs/mo/lonc. RV/tent: 47. $12–$17. Hookups: electric (20, 30, 50 amps), water.

Robertsville

Robertsville State Park, P.O. Box 186, 63072. T: (636) 257-3788. RV/tent: 27. $12–$15. Hookups: electric (20, 30 amps), water.

Rock Port

Rock Port KOA, 1409 Hwy. 136 West, 64482. T: (800) 562-5415 or (660) 744-5485. www.koa.com/where/MO/25148. RV/tent: 56. $16–$24. Hookups: electric (20, 30, 50 amps), water, sewer.

Rushville

Lewis and Clark State Park, 801 Lake Crest Blvd., 64484. T: (816) 579-5564. RV/tent: 70. $12–$15. Hookups: electric (20, 30 amps), water.

Salem

Jason Place Campground, HCR 81 Box 90, 65560. T: (800) 333-5628 or (573) 858-3224. F: (573) 858-3341. RV/tent: 175. $11–$24. Hookups: electric (20, 30 amps), water.

Montauk State Park, Rte. 5 Box 279, 65560-9025. T: (573) 548-2201. RV/tent: 154. $12–$15. Hookups: electric (20, 30 amps), water.

Sarcoxie

WAC RV Park, 2041 Cimarron Rd., 64862. T: (417) 548-2258. RV/tent: 144. $14. Hookups: electric (20, 30, 50 amps), water, sewer.

Sedalia

Chaplin's RVs, 22415 Main St., 65301. T: (660) 826-8549. RV/tent: 15. $12. Hookups: electric (30, 50 amps), water, sewer.

Shell Knob

Campbell Point, 792 Campbell Point Rd., 65747. T: (417) 858-3903. www.ReserveUSA.com/nrrs/mo/camb. RV/tent: 765. $12–$18. Hookups: electric (20, 30 amps).

MISSOURI (continued)

Shell Knob (continued)

Viola, Rte. 5 Box 5210, 65747. T: (417) 858-3904. www.ReserveUSA.com/nrrs/mo/viol. RV/tent: 57. $11–$16. Hookups: electric (20, 30 amps), water.

Sikeston

Town & Country Camping & RV Park, Hwy. 62 East, P.O. Box 1223, 63801. T: (800) 771-1339 or (573) 472-1339. F: (573) 472-2240. RV/tent: 60. $15. Hookups: electric (30, 50 amps), water, sewer.

Springfield

Springfield KOA, 5775 West Farm Rd., 65802. T: (800) 562-1228 or (417) 831-3645. F: (417) 863-0295. www.koa.com. RV/tent: 99. $18–$26. Hookups: electric (20, 30, 50 amps), water, sewer.

St. Louis

KOA St. Louis West at Six Flags, Box 128, 63025. T: (800) 562-6249 or (636) 257-3018. F: (636) 257-6575. www.koa.com. RV/tent: 159. $19–$24. Hookups: electric (20, 30, 50 amps), water, sewer.

KOA St. Louis South, 8000 Metropolitan Blvd., 63012. T: (800) 562-3049 or (636) 479-4449. www.koa.com. RV/tent: 113. $15–$23. Hookups: electric (20, 30, 50 amps), water, sewer.

St. Charles

Sundermeier RV Park & Conference Center, 111 Transit St., 63301. T: (800) 929-0832 or (314) 940-0111. RV/tent: 106. $34–$37. Hookups: electric (30, 50 amps), water, sewer.

Stanton

Stanton/Meramec KOA, Box 177, 63079. T: (800) 562-4498 or (573) 927-5215. F: (573) 927-5215. www.koa.com. RV/tent: 51. $16–$21. Hookups: electric (20, 30, 50 amps), water, sewer.

Stockton

Cedar Ridge, 16435 East Stockton Lake Dr., 65785. T: (417) 995-2045. www.ReserveUSA.com/nrrs/mo/cemo. RV/tent: 54. $10–$16. Hookups: electric (20, 30 amps), water.

Crabtree Cove, 16435 East Stockton Lake Dr., 65785. T: (417) 276-6799. www.ReserveUSA.com/nrrs/mo/crat. RV/tent: 58. $10–$16. Hookups: electric (20, 30 amps), water.

Hawker Point, 16435 East Stockton Lake Dr., 65785. T: (417) 276-7266. www.ReserveUSA.com/nrrs/mo/hawk. RV/tent: 62. $10–$16. Hookups: electric (20, 30 amps).

Ruark Bluff East, 16435 East Stockton Lake Dr., 65785. T: (417) 637-5303. www.ReserveUSA.com/nrrs/mo/ruar. RV/tent: 91. $10–$16. Hookups: electric (20, 30 amps).

Ruark Bluff West, 16435 East Stockton Lake Dr., 65785. T: (417) 637-5279. www.ReserveUSA.com/nrrs/mo/ruaw. RV/tent: 66. $10–$16. Hookups: electric (20, 30 amps).

Stoutsville

Mark Twain State Park, 20057 State Park Office Rd., 65283. T: (573) 565-3440. RV/tent: 101. $12–$15. Hookups: electric (20, 30 amps), water.

Sullivan

Meramec State Park, 2800 South Hwy. 185, 63080. T: (573) 468-6072. RV/tent: 190. $12–$15. Hookups: electric (20, 30, 50 amps), water, sewer.

Trenton

Crowder State Park, 76 Hwy. 128, 64683. T: (660) 359-6473. RV/tent: 42. $7–$12. Hookups: electric (30 amps).

Troy

Cuivre River State Park, 678 SR 147, 63379. T: (636) 528-7247. RV/tent: 80. $12–$15. Hookups: electric (20, 30, 50 amps), water, sewer.

Wappapello

Peoples Creek Campground, HC 2 Box 2349, 63966. T: (573) 222-8234. www.ReserveUSA.com/nrrs/mo/pecr/pecr2. RV/tent: 37. $14. Hookups: electric (20, 30 amps).

Peoples Creek Upper Campground, HC 2 Box 2349, 63966. T: (573) 222-8234. www.Reserve USA.com/nrrs/mo/pecr/pecr1. RV/tent: 20. $14. Hookups: electric (20, 30 amps).

Redman Creek East, HC 2 Box 2349, 63966. T: (573) 222-8233. www.ReserveUSA.com/nrrs/mo/red2/red21. RV/tent: 68. $14. Hookups: electric (20, 30 amps).

Redman Creek West, HC 2 Box 2349, 63966. T: (573) 222-8233. www.ReserveUSA.com/nrrs/mo/red2/red22. RV/tent: 38. $14. Hookups: electric (20, 30 amps).

Warsaw

Berry Bend, Rte. 2 Box 29A, 65355. T: (660) 438-7317. www.ReserveUSA.com/nrrs/mo/berr. RV/tent: 113. $10–$16. Hookups: electric (20, 30 amps).

Bucksaw, Rte. 2 Box 29A, 65355. T: (660) 438-7317. www.ReserveUSA.com/nrrs/mo/bucs. RV/tent: 136. $10–$16. Hookups: electric (20, 30 amps).

Long Shoal, Rte. 2 Box 29A, 65355. T: (660) 438-7317. www.ReserveUSA.com/nrrs/mo/losh. RV/tent: 123. $10–$16. Hookups: electric (20, 30, 50 amps), water.

Osage Bluff, Rte. 2 Box 29A, 65355. T: (660) 438-7317. www.ReserveUSA.com/nrrs/mo/osag. RV/tent: 68. $10–$16. Hookups: electric (20, 30 amps).

Talley Bend, Rte. 2 Box 29A, 65355. T: (417) 438-7317. www.ReserveUSA.com/nrrs/mo/tale. RV/tent: 76. $10–$16. Hookups: electric (20, 30 amps).

Thibaut Point, Rte. 2 Box 29A, 65355. T: (660) 438-7317. www.ReserveUSA.com/nrrs/mo/thib. RV/tent: 51. $10–$16. Hookups: electric (20, 30 amps).

Harry S Truman State Park, HCR 66 Box 14, 65355. T: (660) 438-7711. RV/tent: 201. $12–$15. Hookups: electric (20, 30 amps), water.

Weston

Weston Bend State Park, P.O. Box 115, 16600 Hwy. 45 North, 64098. T: (816) 640-5443. RV/tent: 36. $12–$15. Hookups: electric (20, 30 amps), water.

Wildwood

Dr. Edmund A Babler Memorial State Park, 800 Guy Park Dr., 63005. T: (636) 458-3813. RV/tent: 77. $12–$15. Hookups: electric (20, 30 amps).

MONTANA

Arlee

Jocko Hollow, Old Hwy. 93, 59821. T: (406) 726-3336. F: (406) 726-3334. RV/tent: 16. $15. Hookups: electric (20 amps).

Augusta

Lewis & Clark National Forest (Benchmark Campground), P.O. Box 869, 59403. T: (406) 466-5341. RV/tent: 25. $6. Hookups: none.

Basin

Merry Widow Health Mine Campground & Motel, Box 129, 59631. T: (406) 225-3220. RV/tent: 55. $6–$10. Hookups: electric (30 amps).

Big Sky

Gallatin/Red Cliff, US Hwy. 191, 59718. T: (406) 522-2520. RV/tent: 68. $9–$13. Hookups: electric, water.

Greek Creek/Deerlodge National Forest, US Rte. 191 North, 59718. T: (877) 444-6777. RV/tent: 14. $9. Hookups: none.

Big Timber

Spring Creek Campground and Trout Ranch, P.O. Box 1435, 59011. T: (406) 932-4387. RV/tent: 25. $15–$26. Hookups: full.

MONTANA (continued)

Bigfork

Outback Montana, 27202 East Lakeshore, 59911. T: (888) 900-6973 or (406) 837-6973. outback@cyberport.net. RV/tent: 50. $11–$16. Hookups: electric (20, 30, 50 amps), water, sewer.

Timbers RV Park & Campground, 8550 Hwy. 35 South, 59911. T: (800) 821-4546. RV/tent: 35. $18. Hookups: electric (20, 30, 50 amps), water, modem.

Billings

Big Sky Campground, 5516 Laurel Rd., 59101. T: (406) 259-4110. RV/tent: 54. $18–$23. Hookups: electric (30, 50 amps), water, sewer.

Bozeman

Bear Canyon Campground, 4000 Bozeman Trail Rd., 59715. T: (800) 438-1575 or (406) 587-1575. F: (406) 556-8133. www.bearcanyon campground.com/. bearcc@gomontana.com. RV/tent: 130. $15–$22. Hookups: electric (30, 50 amps), water.

Sunrise Campground, 31842 Frontage Rd., 59715. T: (877) 437-2095. RV/tent: 70. $15–$19. Hookups: electric (20, 30, 50 amps), water, sewer, phone.

Broadus

Wayside Park, Box 568, 59317. T: (406) 436-2510. RV/tent: 21. $8–$12. Hookups: electric (20, 30, 50 amps), water.

White Buffalo Campground, P.O. Box 387, 59317. T: (406) 436-2595. RV/tent: 17. $12. Hookups: electric, water, sewer.

Browning

Chewing Black Bones Resort & Campground, P.O. Box 2809, 59417. T: (406) 732-9263. F: (406) 338-7206. RV/tent: 127. $12–$16. Hookups: electric, water, sewer, cable, phone.

Sleeping Wolf Campground, Box 607, 59417. T: (406) 338-7933. RV/tent: 21. $13–$18. Hookups: electric (20, 30, 50 amps), water.

Butte

2 Bar Lazy H RV Park, 122015 West Browns Gulch Rd., 59701. T: (406) 782-5464. RV/tent: 24. $18–$20. Hookups: electric (30, 50 amps), phone.

Choteau

Choteau KOA, 85 MT Hwy. 221, 59422. T: (800) 562-4156. F: (406) 466-5635. RV/tent: 55. $16–$22. Hookups: full.

Clancy

Alhambra RV Park, Hwy. 282 South No. 515, 59634. T: (406) 933-8020-. RV/tent: 38. $10–$16. Hookups: electric (20, 30 amps), water.

Clinton

Beaver Hill State Park, 3201 Spurgin Rd., 59804. T: (406) 542-5500. RV/tent: 28. $12. Hookups: none.

Elkhorn RV Ranch, 408 Rock Creek Rd., 59825. T: (406) 825-3220. www.montana.com/elkhorn. c/n3224@montana.com. RV/tent: 90. $20–$25. Hookups: electric (20, 30 amps), water, sewer, modem.

Columbia Falls

Glacer Mountain Shadows Resort, 7285 Hwy. 2 East, 59912. T: (406) 892-7686. RV/tent: 28. $16–$20. Hookups: electric (20, 30 amps), water, sewer, cable.

Glacier Peaks Campground, P.O. Box 492, 59912. T: (800) 268-4849. RV/tent: 76. $8–$19. Hookups: electric (30, 50 amps), water, cable, phone.

Dillon

Red Mountain Campgrounds, 1005 Selway Dr., 59725. T: (406) 683-2337. www.blm/for/state. RV/tent: 14. $5. Hookups: electric, water.

Sky-line RV Park Campground, 3525 North US Hwy. 91, 59725. T: (406) 683-4692. RV/tent: 34. $15. Hookups: electric (30 amps), water, sewer, cable.

Drummond

Good Time Camping & RV Park, 239 Frontage Rd. West, 59832. T: (406) 288-3608. RV/tent: 16. $15. Hookups: electric (20, 30, 50 amps), water, phone.

East Glacier Park

Firebrand Campground, P.O. Box 146, 59434. T: (406) 226-5573. RV/tent: 30. $10–$15. Hookups: electric (20, 30 amps).

Glacier/Two Medicine, P.O. Box 128, 59936. T: (406) 888-7800. RV/tent: 99. $14. Hookups: none.

Three Forks Campground, P.O. Box 124, 59434. T: (406) 226-4479. RV/tent: 42. $13–$16. Hookups: electric (20, 39 amps), water, sewer, modem.

Y Lazy R Camper Trailer Park, P.O. Box 146, 59434. T: (406) 226-5573. RV/tent: 41. $10–$15. Hookups: electric (20, 30 amps), water.

Gardiner

Rocky Mountain Campground, 14 Jardine Rd., 59030. T: (406) 848-7251. bertgini@earth link.net. RV/tent: 87. $20–$26. Hookups: electric (30 amps), water, sewer, modem.

Georgetown

Georgetown Lake Lodge, 2015 Dentons Point Rd., 59711. T: (406) 563-6030. RV/tent: 63. $20–$25. Hookups: electric (30, 50 amps) water, sewer, modem.

Glasgow

Trails West Campground, Rte. 1-4404, 59230. T: (406) 228-2778. hrc@nemontel.net. RV/tent: 66. $13–$19. Hookups: electric (30, 50 amps), water, sewer, modem.

Glendive

Green Valley Campground, P.O. Box 1396, 59330. T: (406) 377-1944. RV/tent: 87. $13–$16. Hookups: electric (20, 30, 50 amps), water.

Great Falls

Dick's RV Park, 1403 11th St. South, 59404. T: (406) 452-0333. F: (406) 727-7340. RV/tent: 148. $22. Hookups: electric (30, 50 amps), water, sewer, modem.

Hamilton

Angler's Roost Campground, 815 US Hwy. 93 South, 59840. T: (406) 363-1268. RV/tent: 70. $19–$21. Hookups: full.

Bitterroot Family Campground, 1744 Hwy. 93 South, 59840. T: (800) 453-2430. RV/tent: 52. $10–$16. Hookups: electric (15, 20, 30 amps), water.

Lick Creek Campground, 2251 US Hwy. 93 South, 59840. T: (406) 821-3840. RV/tent: 54. $13–$15. Hookups: electric (20 amps), water, sewer.

Hardin

Grandview Campground, 1002 North Mitchell Ave., 59034. T: (406) 622-9890. www.grand viewcamp.com. grandviewcamp@mcn.net. RV/tent: 50. $13–$20. Hookups: electric (30, 50 amps), water, sewer, cable, modem.

Harlowton

Chief Joseph Park, Box 292, 59036. T: (406) 632-5523. RV/tent: 23. $3–$8. Hookups: electric (20, 30 amps).

Havre

Havre Family Campground, HC Box 200, 59501. T: (406) 265-9722. havrefamilycampground@ hotmail.com. RV/tent: 108. $14–$18. Hookups: electric (30 amps), water, sewer.

Helena

Hauser Lake SRA/Black Sandy, 930 Custer Ave., 59620. T: (406) 444-4720. www.fwp.state. mt.us/. RV/tent: 33. $12. Hookups: electric, water.

Hungry Horse

Flathead/Lid Creek, Ranger District, Box 190340, 59919. T: (406) 387-5243. RV/tent: 22. $7. Hookups: electric, water.

Joliet

Cooney Reservoir State Park, P.O. Box 253, 59041. T: (406) 247-2940. www.fwp.state. mt.us/. RV/tent: 75. $7. Hookups: none.

Kalispell

Glacier Pines RV Park, 1850 Hwy. 35 East, 59901. T: (800) 533-4029 or (406) 752-2760. RV/tent: 160. $20–$22. Hookups: electric (20, 30 amps), modem.

Greenwood Village Campgrounds, 1100 East Oregon St., 59901. T: (406) 257-7719. RV/tent: 38. $11–$18. Hookups: electric (20, 30, 50 amps), phone.

Rocky Mountain HI Campground, 825 Helena Flats Rd., 59901. T: (800) 968-5637 or (406) 755-9573. F: (406) 755-8816. kalispell.bigsky. net/rmhc/. rmhc@bigsky.net. RV/tent: 102. $15–$20. Hookups: electric (20, 30 amps), water, TV, phone.

MONTANA (continued)

Kalispell (continued)

Spruce Park Campground, 1985 Hwy. 35, 59901. T: (888) 752-6321 or (406) 752-6321. F: (406) 756-0480. sprucepk@digisys.net. RV/tent: 160. $13–$18. Hookups: electric (15, 30, 50 amps), water, sewer, cable, phone.

Laurel

Clark's Riverfront Campground & Resort, 3001 Thiel Rd., 59044. T: (406) 628-2984. prk@imt.net. RV/tent: 33. $15. Hookups: electric.

Pelican's RV Campground, 3444 South Frontage Rd., 59044. T: (406) 628-4324. RV/tent: 54. $16. Hookups: electric (30, 50 amps), water, sewer.

Lewiston

Mountain Acres Campground, 103 Rocklyn Ave., 59457. T: (406) 538-7591. RV/tent: 36. $20. Hookups: electric (20, 30 amps), water, sewer.

Libby

Two Bit Outfit RV Park, 716 Hwy. 2 West, 59923. T: (406) 293-8323. www.twobitcamping.com. TwoBit@libby.org. RV/tent: 40. $12–$20. Hookups: electric.

Libby Mountain

Sportsman's RV Park, 11741 Hwy. 37, 59923. T: (406) 293-2267. RV/tent: 22. $16–$20. Hookups: full.

Livingston

Livingston Campground, 11 Rogers Ln., 59047. T: (406) 222-1122. livingstoncampground@hotmail.com. RV/tent: 42. $18–$26. Hookups: electric (20, 50 amps), water, sewer, cable.

Osen's Campground, 20 Merrill Ln., 59047. T: (406) 222-0591. RV/tent: 55. $18–$24. Hookups: electric (20, 30, 50 amps), water, sewer, cable+M60.

Rock Canyon Campground, 5070 US Hwy. 89 South, 59047. T: (406) 222-1096. RV/tent: 39. $17–$20. Hookups: electric (30 amps), water, sewer.

Lolo

Lolo Hot Springs RV Park & Campground, 38500 Hwy. 12 West, 59847. T: (406) 273-2294. www.lolohotsprings.net/. RV/tent: 116. $13–$19. Hookups: electric (20, 30 amps), water.

Square & Round Dance Center & RV Park, 9955 Hwy. 12 West, 59847. T: (406) 273-0141. missoula.bigsky.net/sqrdance. sqrdance@bigsky.net. RV/tent: 71. $12–$19. Hookups: electric (20, 30 amps), water, sewer, cable, modem.

Marion

Moose Crossing, 8405 Hwy. 2 West, 59925. T: (406) 854-2070. RV/tent: 22. $22. Hookups: electric, water, phone.

Miles City

Big Sky Camp & RV Park, RR 1 Hwy. 12, 59301. T: (406) 232-1511. RV/tent: 74. $11–$12. Hookups: electric (30 amps), water.

Missoula

Jim & Mary's RV Park, 9800 US Hwy. 93 North, 59802. T: (406) 549-4416. jimandmary@montana.com. RV/tent: 45. $19–$21. Hookups: electric (30, 50 amps), water, sewer, modem.

Outpost Campground, 11600 US Hwy. 93 North, 59802. T: (406) 549-2016. RV/tent: 65. $15–$16. Hookups: electric (20, 30 amps), water, sewer.

Yogi Bear's Jellystone Park, 10955 Hwy. 93 North, 59802. T: (406) 543- 9400 or (800) 318-9644. F: (406) 543-9400. www.campjellystonemt.com. RV/tent: 110. $21–$26. Hookups: electric (20, 30, 50 amps), water, sewer, phone.

Noxon

Cabinet Gorge RV Park & Campground, 30 Blue Jay Ln., 59853. T: (406) 847-2294. gardensock@blackfoot.netq. RV/tent: 26. $16. Hookups: electric (30, 50 amps), water, sewer, modem.

Philipsburg

Deerlodge/Piney Campground, Phillipsburg Ranger District H, 59851. T: (406) 859-3211. RV/tent: 47. $10. Hookups: none.

Polson

Flathead River Resort, P.O. Box 940, 59860. T: (406) 883-6400. RV/tent: 36. $24. Hookups: electric (20, 30, 50 amps), phone.

Paradise Pines Resort, 6913 East Shore Rte., 59860. T: (406) 887-2537. RV/tent: 87. $12–$18. Hookups: electric (20, 30 amps), water ,modem.

Red Lodge

Perry's RV Park & Campground, HC 49 Box 3586, 59068. T: (406) 446-2722. RV/tent: 40. $18. Hookups: electric (20 amps), water.

Rexford

Mariners Haven Campground, 101 Mariners Dr., 59930. T: (406) 296-3252. RV/tent: 65. $13–$20. Hookups: electric (20, 30 amps), water, sewer.

Ronan

Mission Meadows, 298 Mission Meadows Dr., 59364. T: (406) 676-5182. RV/tent: 42. $13–$18. Hookups: electric (20, 30 amps), water.

Pipestone Campground, 41 Bluebird Ln., 59759. T: (406) 287-5224. RV/tent: 75. $18–$22. Hookups: electric (20, 30, 50 amps), phone.

Shelby

Lake Shel-oole Campground, City of Shelby Box 743, 59474. T: (406) 434-5222. F: (406) 434-2143. RV/tent: 56. $12. Hookups: electric (30 amps), water.

Silver Star

Jefferson River Camp, 5162 State Hwy. 41, 59751. T: (406) 684-5225. RV/tent: 14. $15. Hookups: electric (20, 30 amps), water, phone.

St. Ignatius

St. Ignatius Campground & Hostel, 33076 Hwy. 93, 59865. T: (406) 745-3959. F: (406) 745-0024. campground@stignatius.net. RV/tent: 14. $16–$25. Hookups: electric (30 amps), water, sewer.

Sula

Lost Trail Hot Springs Resort, 8321 Hwy. 93 South, 59871. T: (800) 825-3574. RV/tent: 20. $20. Hookups: electric (20, 30 amps), phone.

Moosehead Campground, 6457 Hwy. 93 South, 59827. T: (406) 821-3327. RV/tent: 91. $20. Hookups: electric (20 amps), water, sewer.

Terry

Terry's RV Oasis, 510 Jane St., 59349. T: (406) 637-5520. RV/tent: 18. $12–$18. Hookups: electric (30, 50 amps), water, sewer, cable.

Thompson Falls

The Riverfront, P.O. Box 22, 59873. T: (406) 827-3460. RV/tent: 11. $19. Hookups: electric (20, 30, 50 amps), phone.

Three Forks

Fort Three Forks RV Park & Motel, 10776 Hwy. 287, 59752. T: (800) 477-5690 or (406) 285-3233. www.fortthreeforks.com. info@fortthreeforks.com. RV/tent: 12. $18. Hookups: electric (30, 50 amps) water, sewer.

Townsend

Roadrunner RV Park, 704 Nort Front Rd., 59644. T: (406) 266-9900. RV/tent: 25. $14. Hookups: electric (30, 50 amps), water, sewer.

Silos RV Park & Fishing Camp, 81 Silos Rd., 59644. T: (406) 266-3100. RV/tent: 41. $9–$14. Hookups: electric (30 amps), water, sewer.

Troy

Kootenai River Campground, 2898 Hwy. 2 North, 59935. T: (406) 295-4090. RV/tent: 48. $15–$18. Hookups: electric (20, 30 amps), water.

Valier

Lake Francis City Park Campground, P.O. Box 512, 59486. T: (406) 279-3361. RV/tent: 32. $8. Hookups: electric.

Virginia City

Virginia City Campground & RV Park, P.O. 188, 59755. T: (888) 833-5493. vccamp@3rivers.net. RV/tent: 17. $16–$32. Hookups: electric (30 amps), water, sewer.

West Glacier

San-Suz-Ed Trailer Park & Campground, P.O. Box 387, 59936. T: (800) 305-4616. www.san-suz-edrvpark.com. RV/tent: 68. $20–$22. Hookups: electric (30, 50 amps), water, phone.

Sundance RV Park & Campground, P.O. Box 130037, 59913. T: (406) 387-5016. RV/tent: 64. $16. Hookups: electric (20, 30 amps), water.

MONTANA (continued)

West Yellowstone

Gallatin/Beaver Creek, P.O. Box 520, 59758. T: (406) 646-7369. RV/tent: 65. $10. Hookups: none.

Hideaway RV Park, 310 Electric, 59758. T: (406) 646-9049. www.wyellowstone.com/hideaway. joe@hideawayrv.com. RV/tent: 17. $15–$25. Hookups: electric (20, 50 amps), water, sewer, cable.

Rustic Wagon RV, Campground & Cabins, 634 Hwy. 20 & Gibbon Ave., 59758. T: (406) 646-7387. www.wyellowstone.com/rusticwagon. rusticwagon@wyellowstone.com. RV/tent: 52. $20–$32. Hookups: electric (20, 30, 50 amps), water.

Wagon Wheel RV Campground & Cabins, 408 Gibbon Ave., 59758. T: (406) 646-7872. www.wyellowstone.com. wagonwheel@wyellowstone.com. RV/tent: 51. $28–$32. Hookups: electric (20, 30 amps), water, sewer, cable, modem.

Yellowstone Holiday RV Campground & Marina, P.O. Box 759, 59758. T: (877) 646-4242 or (406) 646-4242. F: (406) 646-4242. yhr@wyellowstone.com. RV/tent: 60. $15–$28. Hookups: electric (20, 30, 50 amps), water, sewer, modem.

White Sulpher Springs

Conestoga Campground, Box 508, 59645. T: (406) 547-3890 or (800) 548-2289. RV/tent: 77. $10–$17. Hookups: electric (20, 30, 50 amps), water.

Wolf Point

Rainbow Campground, P.O. Box C26456, 59201. T: (406) 525-3740. RV/tent: 9. $12–$18. Hookups: electric, water.

Rancho Campground, Hwy. 2, 59201. T: (406) 653-1382. RV/tent: 19. $16. Hookups: electric (30 amps), water, sewer.

NEBRASKA

Alliance

J&C RV Park, 2491 South US Hwy. 385, 69301. T: (308) 762-3860. RV/tent: 13. $20. Hookups: none.

Anselmo

Victoria Springs State Recreation Area, HC 69 P.O. Box 117, 68813. T: (308) 749-2235. RV/tent: 75. $8–$11. Hookups: electric.

Bellevue

Haworth Park, 210 West Misson Ave., 68005. T: (402) 293-3098. RV/tent: 129. $10. Hookups: electric, water.

Big Springs

McGreer Camper Park, Rte. 2 Box 96, 69122. T: (308) 889-3605. RV/tent: 40. $12–$16. Hookups: electric, water.

Bridgeport

Golden Acres Motel and RV Park, Rte. 1 Box 196, 69336. T: (308) 262-0410. RV/tent: 18. $14–$16. Hookups: electric, water.

Broken Bow

Wagon Wheel Motel and Campground, 1545 South "E" St., 68822. T: (308) 872-2433. RV/tent: 10. $11. Hookups: electric.

Brule

Riverside Park, 1000 South State St., 69127. T: (308) 287-2474. RV/tent: 38. $13–$17. Hookups: electric.

Burwell

Calamus Reservoir State Recreation Area, HC 79 P.O. Box 20-C, 68823. T: (308) 346-5666. RV/tent: 177. $4–$13. Hookups: electric.

Chadron

J&L RV Park, J&L No. 13, 69337. T: (308) 432-4349. RV/tent: 58. $12. Hookups: none.

Chappell

Creekside RV Park and Campground, P.O. Box 238, 69129. T: (308) 874-camp. RV/tent: 55. $18. Hookups: none.

Elm Creek

Sunny Meadows Campground, 234 East Front St., 68836. T: (308) 856-4792. RV/tent: 30. $12. Hookups: none.

Gibbon

Windmill State Recreation Area, 2625 Lowell Rd., 68840. T: (308) 468-5700. RV/tent: 89. $9–$13. Hookups: electric.

Grand Island

Grand Island KOA, 904 South B Rd., Doniphan, 68832. T: (402) 886-2249. RV/tent: 71. $17–$22. Hookups: none.

Gretna

West Omaha KOA, 14601 Hwy. 6, 68028. T: (402) 332-3010. RV/tent: 86. $18–$28. Hookups: electric, water.

Halsey

NA National Forest, P.O. Box 38, 69142. T: (308) 533-2257. RV/tent: 33. $8–$11. Hookups: none.

Harrison

Corral Campground, P.O. Box 115, 69346. T: (308) 668-2441. RV/tent: 12. $12. Hookups: none.

Hastings

Hastings Campground, 302 East 26th, 68901. T: (402) 462-5621. RV/tent: 63. $16–$21. Hookups: full.

Hemingford

Box Butte Reservoir State Recreation Area, P.O. Box 392, Crawford, 69339. T: (308) 665-2903. RV/tent: 50. $9–$17. Hookups: electric.

Kearrey

Claude and Vi's Campground, P.O. Box 834, 68848. T: (308) 234-1532. RV/tent: 110. $15–$20. Hookups: electric, water.

Kimball

KOA-Kimball, Rte. 1 Box 128 D, 69145. T: (308) 235-4404. RV/tent: 45. $17–$24. Hookups: electric, water.

Maxwell

Fort McPherson Campground, 12568 Valley View Rd., 69151. T: (308) 582-4320. RV/tent: 79. $14–$20. Hookups: electric.

Minden

Pioneer Village Motel and Campground, Harold Wrap Memorial Dr., 68959. T: (800) 445-4447. RV/tent: 165. $12–$23. Hookups: electric, water.

Nebraska City

Victorian Acres RV Park and Campground, 6591 Hwy. 2, 68410. T: (402) 873-6860. RV/tent: 70. $10–$15. Hookups: electric, water.

North Plate

A-1 Sunset RV Park, 3120 Rodeo Rd., 69101. T: (308) 532-9180. RV/tent: 24. $16. Hookups: none.

Holiday Park, 601 Hullingan Dr., 69101. T: (800) 424-4531. RV/tent: 98. $16–$22. Hookups: none.

The Rockin' DH Campground, 3800 Hadley Dr., 69101. T: (877) 994-2267. RV/tent: 57. $20. Hookups: electric, water.

Ogallala

Area's Finest Meyer Camper Court, 120 Rd. East 80, 69153. T: (308) 284-2415. RV/tent: 112. $12–$21. Hookups: none.

Corral Campground and RV Park, 221 Rd. East 85, 69153. T: (308) 284-4327. RV/tent: 68. $15–$17. Hookups: none.

NEBRASKA (continued)

Ogallala (continued)

Van's Lakeview Fishing Camp, No. 1 Lakeview, Brule, 69127. T: (308) 284-4965. RV/tent: 122. $17–$20. Hookups: electric, water.

Paxton

Ole's Lodge and RV Park, 851 Paxton-Elsie Rd., 69155. T: (308) 239-4510. RV/tent: 12. $10–$15. Hookups: full.

Schuyler

Schuyler Campground, 1103 B St., 68661. T: (402) 352-2057. RV/tent: 30. $5. Hookups: electric.

Shubert

Indian Cave State Park, RR 2 Box 30, 68437. T: (402) 883-2575. RV/tent: 274. $8–$13. Hookups: electric.

Sidney

Bear Family RV Park, 919 Greenwood, 69162. T: (308) 254-6000. RV/tent: 44. $17. Hookups: none.

Cabela's RV Park, 1 Anglers Ln., 69162. T: (308) 254-7177. RV/tent: 37. $25. Hookups: full.

South Sioux

Scenic Park, 1615 1st Ave., 68776. T: (402) 494-7531. RV/tent: 53. $10–$17. Hookups: full.

Sutherland

Oregon Trail Trading Post and Campground, Rte. 1 Box 606, 69165. T: (308) 386-4653. RV/tent: 30. $8. Hookups: electric.

Valentine

River of Life Camp, HC 37 Box 3, 96201. T: (402) 376-2958. RV/tent: 37. $15–$25. Hookups: electric, water.

Valentine Motel and RV Park, P.O. Box A, 69201. T: (800) 376-2450. RV/tent: 36. $20. Hookups: none.

Wacky West Travel Park, 224 North Wood St., 69201. T: (402) 376-1771. RV/tent: 22. $17. Hookups: electric, water.

York

Double Nickel Campground and County Store, 907 Rd. South, 68460. T: (402) 728-5558. RV/tent: 110. $15–$23. Hookups: electric, water.

NEVADA

Amargosa Valley

Fort Amargosa, P.O. Box 245, 89020. T: (775) 372-1178. F: (775) 372-1166. RV/tent: 98. $14. Hookups: electric (20, 30, 50 amp), water, sewer.

Austin

Austin RV Park, US Hwy. 50, 89310. T: (775) 964-1011. F: (775) 964-2601. tdw@austin.igate.com. RV/tent: 21. $10–$16. Hookups: electric (20, 30 amp), water, sewer.

Big Creek Campground, P.O. Box 130, 89310. T: (702) 964-2671. RV/tent: 6. $3. Hookups: none.

Bob Scott Campground, P.O. Box 130, 89310. T: (702) 964-2671. RV/tent: 10. $4. Hookups: none.

Baker

Baker Creek Campground, Superintendent, Great Basin National Park, 89311. T: (775) 234-7331. www.nps.gov/grba. RV/tent: 30. $10. Hookups: none.

Wheeler Creek Campground, Superintendent, Great Basin National Park, 89311. T: (775) 234-7331. www.nps.gov/grba. RV/tent: 37. $10. Hookups: none.

Whispering Elms RV Park, P.O. Box 105, 89311. T: (775) 234-7343. RV/tent: 20. $10–$16. Hookups: electric (20, 30 amp), water, sewer.

Battle Mountain

Broadway Flying J Service Center, 650 West Front, 89820. T: (775) 635-5424. F: (775) 635-0371. RV/tent: 96. $15. Hookups: electric (20, 30, 50 amp), water, sewer.

Beatty

Burro Inn, US Hwy. 95, P.O. Box 7, 89003. T: (775) 553-2225 or (800) 843-2078. F: (775) 553-2892. www. burroinn.com. RV/tent: 43. $15. Hookups: electric (20, 30, 50 amp), water, sewer.

Kay's Korral RV Park, US Hwy. 95, 89003. T: (775) 553-2732. kskorral@parhump.com. RV/tent: 25. $12. Hookups: electric, water, sewer.

Rio Rancho RV Park, US Hwy. 95 North, P.O. Box 905, 89003. T: (775) 553-2238 or (800) 448-4423. RV/tent: 35. $16. Hookups: electric (30, 50 amp), water, sewer.

Space Station RV Park & Market, US Hwy. 95, P.O. Box 568, 89003. T: (775) 553-9039. RV/tent: 24. $15. Hookups: electric (30 amp), water, sewer.

Boulder City

Boulder Oaks RV Resort, 1010 Industrial Rd., 89005. T: (702) 294-4425 or (800) 478-5687(outside NV). www.aardvarkrv/boulder oaks. boulderoaksrv@yahoo.com. RV/tent: 275. $28. Hookups: electric (30, 50 amp), water, sewer, cable TV, phone (modem).

Canyon Trail RV Park, 1200 Industrial Rd., 89005. T: (702) 293-1200. F: (702) 293-1954. RV/tent: 156. $18. Hookups: electric (30, 50 amp), water, sewer.

Lakeshore Trailer Village, 268 Lakeshore Rd., 89005. T: (702) 293-2540. RV/tent: 80. $18. Hookups: electric (30 amp), water, sewer, cable TV.

Cal Nev Ari

Cal Nev Ari, US Hwy. 95, P.O. Box 430, 89039. T: (702) 297-1115. F: (702) 297-1167. RV/tent: 58. $13. Hookups: electric (20, 30, 50 amp), water, sewer, cable TV.

Caliente

Agua Caliente Trailer Park, US Hwy. 93 North, 89008. T: (775) 726-3399. F: (775) 726-3205. RV/tent: 5. $10–$15. Hookups: electric (20 amp), water, sewer.

Carson City

Camp-N-Town, 2438 North Carson St., 89706. T: (775) 883-1132 or (800) 872-1132. F: (775) 883-1123. RV/tent: 130. $20–$25. Hookups: electric (30, 50 amp), water, sewer, cable TV, phone (modem).

Comstock Country RV Resort, 5400 South Carson St., 89701. T: (775) 882-2445 or (800) NEVADA-1. F: (775) 882-1197. www.comstocknv.com. RV/tent: 166. $18–$24. Hookups: electric (20, 30, 50 amp), water, sewer, cable TV.

Crystal Springs Campground, 1536 South Carson St., 89701. T: (775) 882-2766. RV/tent: 22. $8. Hookups: none.

Indian Creek Campground, 5665 Morgan Hill Rd., 89701. T: (775) 885-6000. RV/tent: 29. $8–$10. Hookups: none.

Kit Carson Campground, 1536 South Carson St., 89701. T: (775) 882-2766. RV/tent: 12. $6. Hookups: none.

Mount Rose Campground, 1536 South Carson St., 89701. T: (775) 882-2766. RV/tent: 24. $8. Hookups: none.

Oasis RV Park, 4550 South Carson St., 89701. T: (775) 882-1375. RV/tent: 20. $10–$17. Hookups: electric (20, 30 amp), water, sewer, cable TV.

Pinon Plaza Casino Resort & RV Park, 2171 US Hwy. 50 East, 89701. T: (775) 885-9000 x-1037 or (877) 519-5567. F: (775) 888-8003. www.pinonplaza.com. RV/tent: 70. $18–$21. Hookups: electric (30, 50 amp), water, sewer, cable TV, phone (modem).

Cottonwood Cove

Cottonwood Cove Marina & Resort, P.O. Box 1000, 89046. T: (702) 297-1464. www.foreverresorts.com. RV/tent: 73. $17–$20. Hookups: electric (30, 50 amp), water, sewer.

NEVADA (continued)

Dayton

Dayton State Park, P.O. Box 412, 89403. T: (775) 687-4379. RV/tent: 10. $9. Hookups: none.

Denio

Royal Peacock RV Park, Virgin Valley Rd., 89404. T: (775) 941-0374 or (775) 272-3201. RV/tent: 20. $9–$16. Hookups: electric (20, 30 amp), water, sewer.

Elko

Best Western Gold Country RV Park, Inn & Casino, 2050 Idaho St., 89801. T: (775) 738-8421 or (800) 621-1332. F: (775) 738-1798. www.bestwesternnevada.com. RV/tent: 26. $20. Hookups: electric (20, 30, 50 amp), water, sewer.

Double Dice RV Park, 3730 East Idaho St., 89801. T: (775) 738-5642 or (888) 738-3423. F: (775) 753-0055. www.gocamping america.com/doubledice. RV/tent: 150. $20–$23. Hookups: electric (30, 50 amp), water, sewer, cable TV, phone (modem).

Dunn's Wildhorse Resort, HC 31 Box 213 (62 mi. north of Elko), 89801. T: (775) 758-6472. F: (775) 758-5400. RV/tent: 34. $9–$18. Hookups: electric (20, 30 amp), water, sewer.

Hidden Valley Guest & RV Resort, P.O. Box 1454, 89803. T: (775) 738-2347. RV/tent: 27. $10–$20. Hookups: electric (30 amp), water, sewer.

North Wildhorse Campground, 3900 East Idaho St., 89801. T: (775) 753-0200. RV/tent: 18. $6. Hookups: none.

Ryndon RV Park, 303-11 Ryndon, P.O. Box 1656, 89801. T: (775) 738-3448. F: (775) 738-4825. RV/tent: 54. $17–$20. Hookups: electric (30, 50 amp), water, sewer, phone (modem).

South Fork State Recreation Area, HC 30 353-8, 89801. T: (775) 744-4346. RV/tent: 25. $9. Hookups: none.

Wildhorse State Recreation Area, HC 31 Box 265 (67 mi. north of Elko), 89801. T: (775) 758-6493. RV/tent: 33. $9. Hookups: none.

Wilson Reservoir Campground, 3900 East Idaho St., 89801. T: (775) 753-0200. RV/tent: 15. $5. Hookups: none.

Ely

El Dorado Service, HC 31 Box 31020, 89301. T: (775) 237-7253. RV/tent: 14. $10–$16. Hookups: electric (30 amp), water, sewer.

Harry's Wilderness RV, No. 58 McGill Hwy., 89301. T: (775) 289-8727. RV/tent: 10. $10–$16. Hookups: electric (30 amp), water, sewer.

KOA of Ely, US Hwy. 93S, 89301. T: (775) 289-3413 or (800) 526-3413. www.elykoa.com. elykoa@netxxpress.net. RV/tent: 107. $16–$22. Hookups: electric (20, 30, 50 amp), water, sewer, cable TV, phone (modem).

Lanes Ranch Motel, HC 34 (Preston) Box 34145, 89301. T: (775) 238-5246. F: (775) 238-5248. RV/tent: 7. $8–$15. Hookups: electric (30 amp), water, sewer.

Major's Station RV Park, US Hwy. 93 & US Hwy. 50 Junction, 89301. T: (775) 591-0430. RV/tent: 7. $10. Hookups: electric (30 amp), water, sewer, phone.

Prospector Casino RV Park (Holiday Inn), US Hwy. 93, 89301. T: (775) 289-8900. F: (775) 289-4607. RV/tent: 22. $10. Hookups: electric (20, 30, 50 amp), water, sewer.

Stage Stop, HCR 33 Box 33900, 89301. T: (775) 591-0397. F: (775) 591-0401. RV/tent: 4. $10–$15. Hookups: electric (30 amp), water, sewer.

Timber Creek, 350 8th St., P.O. Box 539, 89301. T: (702) 289-3031. RV/tent: 15. $4. Hookups: none.

Valley View RV Park, No. 65 McGill Hwy., 89301. T: (775) 289-3303. RV/tent: 46. $15. Hookups: electric (20, 30, 50 amp), water, sewer, cable TV, phone (modem).

West End RV Park, No. 50 Aultman St., 89301. T: (775) 289-8900. RV/tent: 11. $10. Hookups: electric (30 amp), water, sewer.

Eureka

Eureka RV Park, P.O. Box 734, 89316. T: (775) 237-7203. RV/tent: 25. $10–$20. Hookups: electric (30 amp), water, sewer, cable TV.

Pita RV, P.O. Box 27, 89316. T: (775) 237-5281. F: (775) 237-7001. RV/tent: 11. $10–$16. Hookups: electric (30 amp), water, sewer, cable TV.

Silver Sky RV Park, P.O. Box 573, 89316. T: (775) 237-7146. RV/tent: 15. $8–$15. Hookups: electric (30 amp), water, sewer.

T/C Trailer Park, P.O. Box 176, 89316. T: (775) 237-5331. RV/tent: 14. $10–$17. Hookups: electric (30 amp), water, sewer, cable TV.

Fallon

Bonanza RV Park, 855 West Williams, 89407. T: (775) 423-6031. F: (775) 423-6282. RV/tent: 20. $12. Hookups: electric (30 amp), water, sewer.

Fallon RV Park, 5787 Reno Hwy., 89406. T: (775) 867-2332. F: (775) 867-4392. RV/tent: 64. $18–$20. Hookups: electric (30, 50 amp), water, sewer.

The Hub Totel RV Park, 4800 Reno Hwy. (US Hwy. 50), 89406. T: (775) 867-3636. RV/tent: 44. $19. Hookups: electric (20, 30 amp), water, sewer, cable TV, phone (modem).

Fernley

Desert Rose RV Park, 3285 Hwy. 50 East, 89408. T: (877) 767-3478. www.desert roserv.com. RV/tent: 112. $20–$22. Hookups: electric (30, 50 amp), water, sewer, cable TV, phone (modem).

Fernley RV Park, 550 West Main St., 89408. T: (775) 575-5222. RV/tent: 40. $21. Hookups: electric (30, 50 amp), water, sewer, cable TV, phone (modem).

Gardnerville

Topaz Lodge & Casino RV Park, 1995 US Hwy. 395 South, P.O. Box 187, 89410. T: (775) 266-3338 or (800) 962-0732. F: (775) 266-3046. www.enterit.com. RV/tent: 59. $10–$17. Hookups: electric, water, sewer, cable TV.

Goldfield

Goldfield RV Park, P.O. Box 315, 89013. T: (775) 485-3280. F: (775) 485-3279. home.earth-link.net/~siebert. RV/tent: 10. $10. Hookups: electric (30, 50 amp), water, sewer.

Hawthorne

Desert Lake Campground, US Hwy. 95 Walker Lake, P.O. Box 647, 89415. T: (775) 945-3373. RV/tent: 25. $8–$15. Hookups: electric (30 amp), water, sewer.

Frontier RV Park, Fifth & L St., 89415. T: (775) 945-2733. RV/tent: 27. $10–$15. Hookups: electric (30, 50 amp), water, sewer.

Scotty's RV Park, 1101 5th St., 89415. T: (775) 945-2079. RV/tent: 16. $15. Hookups: electric (20, 30, 50 amp), water, sewer, cable TV.

Henderson

Desert Sands RV Park, 1940 North Boulder Hwy., 89015. T: (702) 565-1945. F: (702) 565-3534. RV/tent: 300. $15–$21. Hookups: electric (20, 30, 50 amp), water, sewer.

Jackpot

Cactus Pete's Saquaro RV Park, 1385 Hwy. 93, 89825. T: (775) 755-2321 or (800) 821-1103. www.ameristarcasinos.com/cactus_petes.asp. RV/tent: 91. $10–$14. Hookups: electric (20, 30 amp), water, sewer, cable TV, phone (modem).

Spanish Gardens RV Park, P.O. Box 390, 89825. T: (775) 755-2396 or (800) 422-8233. F: (775) 755-2630. RV/tent: 38. $14. Hookups: electric (30, 50 amp), water, sewer, cable TV.

Las Vegas

Arizona Charlie's East Hotel, Casino & RV Park, 4575 Boulder Hwy., 89121. T: (702) 951-5911 or (800) 970-7280. F: (702) 951-9211. RV/tent: 239. $18. Hookups: electric (20, 30, 50 amp), water, sewer, phone (modem).

Boulder Lakes RV Resort, 6201 Boulder Hwy., 89122. T: (702) 435-1157. F: (702) 435-1125. RV/tent: 417. $20–$25. Hookups: electric (20, 30, 50 amp), water, sewer, cable TV, phone (modem).

Castaways RV Park, 2960 Fremont St., 89104. T: (702) 383-9333 or (800) 826-2800. F: (702) 385-9163. www.showboat-lv.com. RV/tent: 84. $18–$20. Hookups: electric (20, 30, 50 amp), water, sewer, cable TV, phone (modem).

Circusland RV Park, 500 Circus Circus Dr., 89109. T: (702) 794-3757 or (800) 444-CIRCUS. F: (702) 792-2280. RV/tent: 365. $13–$24. Hookups: electric (30, 50 amp), water, sewer, phone (modem).

Destiny's Oasis Las Vegas RV Resort, 2711 Windmill Rd., 89123. T: (702) 260-2020 or (800) 566-4747. F: (702) 263-5160. www.destinyrv.com. RV/tent: 701. $20–$56. Hookups: electric (30, 50 amp), water, sewer, cable TV, phone (modem).

NEVADA (continued)

Las Vegas (continued)

Hitchin' Post RV Park, 3640 Las Vegas Blvd. North, 89115. T: (702) 644-1043 or (888) 433-8402. F: (702) 644-8359. RV/tent: 196. $18. Hookups: electric (20, 30, 50 amp), water, sewer, cable TV, phone (modem).

Holiday Travel Park, 3890 South Nellis Blvd., 89121. T: (702) 451-8005. F: (702) 451-5806. RV/tent: 403. $18. Hookups: electric (30, 50 amp), water, sewer, phone (modem).

KOA Las Vegas, 4315 Boulder Hwy., 89121. T: (702) 451-5527 or (800) 562-7782. F: (702) 434-8729. RV/tent: 300. $25–$33. Hookups: electric (20, 30, 50 amp), water, sewer, phone (modem).

Nevada Palace VIP Travel Trailer Park, 5325 Boulder Hwy., 89122. T: (702) 451-0232 or (800) 634-6283. F: (702) 458-3361. www.nvpalace.com. RV/tent: 168. $14. Hookups: electric (30 amp), water, sewer.

Riviera RV Park, 2200 Palm, 89104. T: (702) 457-8700. F: (702) 457-1488. RV/tent: 135. $20. Hookups: electric (20, 30, 50 amp), water, sewer, phone (modem).

Road Runner RV Park, 4711 Boulder Hwy., 89121. T: (702) 456-4711. RV/tent: 200. $15–$20. Hookups: electric (30, 50 amp), water, sewer.

Sam's Town Boulder RV Park, 5225 Boulder Hwy., 89122. T: (702) 454-7777 or (800) 634-6371. F: (702) 456-5665. RV/tent: 291. $18. Hookups: electric (20, 30, 50 amp), water, sewer, cable TV.

Sam's Town Nellis RV Park, 4040 South Nellis Blvd., 89121. T: (702) 456-7777 or (800) 634-6371. F: (702) 456-5665. RV/tent: 207. $18. Hookups: electric (20, 30, 50 amp), water, sewer, cable TV.

Sunrise RV Park, 4445 Boulder Hwy., 89121. T: (702) 458-7275 or (800) 970-7280. F: (702) 898-7275. RV/tent: 239. $18. Hookups: electric (30, 50 amp), water, sewer, phone (modem).

Western RV Park, 1023 East Fremont, 89104. T: (702) 384-1033. RV/tent: 69. $10. Hookups: electric (20, 30, 50 amp), water, sewer.

Laughlin

Avi RV Park, P.O. Box 77011, 89028. T: (702) 535-5555. F: (702) 535-5400. RV/tent: 240. $17–$27. Hookups: electric (50 amp), water, sewer, cable TV, phone (modem).

Lovelock

Rye Patch Reservoir State Recreation Area, 2505 Rye Patch Reservoir Rd., 89419. T: (775) 538-7321. RV/tent: 44. $4–$10. Hookups: none.

Mesquite

Casablanca RV Park, 950 West Mesquite Blvd., P.O. Box 2737, 89024. T: (702) 346-7529 or (800) 459-7529. F: (702) 346-6862. www.casablancaresort.com. RV/tent: 45. $12. Hookups: electric (20, 30, 50 amp), water, sewer, cable TV.

Desert Skies RV Resort, 99 Peppermill Palms Dr., P.O. Box 3780, 89024. T: (520) 347-6000 or (800) 818-2773. F: (520) 347-6002. RV/tent: 189. $20–$24. Hookups: electric (20, 30, 50 amp), water, sewer, cable TV.

Si Redd's Oasis Resort RV Park, P.O. Box 360, 89024. T: (702) 346-5232 or (800) 21-OASIS. F: (702) 346-2746. www.oasisresort.com. RV/tent: 91. $14. Hookups: electric (20, 30, 50 amp), water, sewer, cable TV.

Virgin River RV Park, I-15 Exit 122, 89024. T: (702) 346-7777 or (800) 346-7721. F: (702) 346-7780. www.virginriver.com. RV/tent: 55. $10. Hookups: electric (20, 30 amp), water, sewer, cable TV.

Mina

Sunrise Valley RV Park LLC, US Hwy. 95, P.O. Box 345, 89422. T: (775) 573-2214. F: (775) 573-2602. www.sunrisevalley.com. RV/tent: 27. $18. Hookups: electric (30, 50 amp), water, sewer, cable TV.

Minden

Carson Valley Inn Hotel Casino RV Resort, 1627 US Hwy. 395 North, 89423. T: (775) 782-9711 or (800) 321-6983. www.cvinn.com. RV/tent: 60. $16. Hookups: electric (20, 30, 50 amp), water, sewer, cable TV, phone (modem).

Silver City RV Resort, 3165 Hwy. 395, 89423. T: (800) 997-6393. www.silvercityrvresort.com. RV/tent: 206. $20–$25. Hookups: electric (30, 50 amp), water, sewer, cable TV, phone (modem).

Overton

Robbin's Nest Mobile Village, P.O. Box 130, 479 South Moapa Dr., 89040. T: (702) 397-2364. www.robbinsnestmv.com. rnmv@robbinsnestmv.com. RV/tent: 50. $14. Hookups: electric (30, 50 amp), water, sewer, phone (modem).

Pahrump

Pahrump Station RV Park, P.O. Box 38, 89041. T: (775) 727-5100. F: (775) 751-1325. RV/tent: 48. $18. Hookups: electric (20, 30, 50 amp), water, sewer, cable TV, phone (modem).

Saddle West Hotel, Casino, RV Resort, 1220 South Hwy. 160, 89048. T: (775) 727-1111 or (800) 433-3987. www.saddlewest.com. RV/tent: 80. $18. Hookups: electric (20, 30, 50 amp), water, sewer, cable TV.

Seven Palms RV Park, 101 South Linda St., 89048. T: (775) 727-6091. RV/tent: 59. $15. Hookups: electric (20, 30, 50 amp), water, sewer.

Terrible's Lakeside Casino & RV Resort, 5870 South Homestead Rd., 89048. T: (775) 751-7770 or (888) 558-LAKE. F: (775) 751-7746. www.terribleherbst.com. RV/tent: 160. $19. Hookups: electric (50 amp), water, sewer, cable TV, phone (modem).

Panaca

Beaver Dam State Park, P.O. Box 176, 89042. T: (775) 728-4467. www.state.nv.us/stparks/. RV/tent: 42. $8. Hookups: none.

Primm

Primadonna RV Village, P.O. Box 93718, 89193. T: (702) 382-1212 or (800) 386-7867. F: (702) 679-5195. www.primadonna.com. RV/tent: 197. $12–$15. Hookups: electric (30, 50 amp), water, sewer, cable TV.

Reno

Bordertown Casino RV Resort, 19575 US Hwy. 395 N, 89506. T: (775) 677-0169 or (800) 218-9339. RV/tent: 50. $15–$25. Hookups: electric (20, 30, 50 amp), water, sewer, cable TV, phone (modem).

Chism Trailer Park, 1300 West 2nd St., 89503. T: (775) 322-2281 or (800) 638-2281. F: (775) 322-6376. www.chismtrailerpark.com. RV/tent: 152. $19. Hookups: electric (20, 30, 50 amp), water, sewer, cable TV.

Keystone RV Park, 1455 West Fourth St., 89503. T: (775) 324-5000 or (800) 686-8559. RV/tent: 102. $21–$23. Hookups: electric (20, 30, 50 amp), water, sewer, cable TV, phone (modem).

KOA at the Reno Hilton, 2500 East 2nd St., 89595. T: (775) 789-2000 or (888) 562-5698. F: (775) 789-2418. RV/tent: 230. $15–$28. Hookups: electric (30, 50 amp), water, sewer, phone (modem).

Reno RV Park, 735 Mill St., 89502. T: (775) 323-3381 or (800) 445-3381. F: (775) 323-7266. RV/tent: 46. $23. Hookups: electric (30 amp), water, sewer, cable TV, phone (modem).

Shamrock RV Park, 260 Parr Blvd., 89512. T: (775) 329-5222 or (800) 322-8248. F: (775) 329-9065. RV/tent: 121. $19–$22. Hookups: electric (20, 30, 50 amp), water, sewer, cable TV, phone (modem).

Silver Sage RV Park, 2760 South Virginia St., 89502. T: (775) 829-1919. www.cris.com/~rvparks/. RV/tent: 43. $18–$22. Hookups: electric (30, 50 amp), water, sewer, cable TV, phone (modem).

Ruth

Copperpit RV Park, 5 Main St., 89319. T: (775) 289-6032. RV/tent: 17. $8–$14. Hookups: electric (20, 30 amp), water, sewer, cable TV.

Searchlight

Cree's, US Hwy. 164, 89046. T: (702) 297-1532. F: (702) 297-1532. RV/tent: 10. $10–$13. Hookups: electric (20, 30 amp), water, sewer, cable TV.

Smith

Walker River Resort, P.O. Box 90, 89430. T: (775) 465-2573 or (800) 465-2573. RV/tent: 130. $16–$18. Hookups: electric (30, 50 amp), water, sewer, phone (modem).

South Lake Tahoe

Nevada Beach Campground, P.O. Box 14000, 94301. T: (775) 588-5562 or (877) 444-6777. RV/tent: 54. $18–$20. Hookups: none.

NEVADA (continued)

Sparks

Rivers Edge RV Park, 1405 South Rock Blvd., 89431. T: (775) 358-8533 or (800) 621-4792. F: (775) 358-3168. RV/tent: 164. $21. Hookups: electric (30, 50 amp), water, sewer, phone (modem).

Victorian RV Park, 205 Nichols Blvd., 89431. T: (775) 356-6400 or (800) 955-6405. F: (775) 358-1542. RV/tent: 92. $20. Hookups: electric (20, 30, 50 amp), water, sewer.

Tonopah

Twister Inn RV Park, Ketten Rd. & US Hwy. 6, 89049. T: (775) 482-9444. RV/tent: 13. $10–$16. Hookups: electric (30 amp), water, sewer, cable TV.

Verdi

Boomtown RV Park, P.O. Box 399, 89439. T: (775) 345-8650 or (887) 626-6686. F: (775) 345-8666. www.boomtowncasinos.com. RV/tent: 203. $28. Hookups: electric (30, 50 amp), water, sewer, cable TV, phone (modem).

Gold Ranch Casino RV Park, I-80 Exit 2, 89439. T: (775) 345-6789. RV/tent: 155. $20–$30. Hookups: electric (20, 30, 50 amp), water, sewer, cable TV, phone (modem).

Virginia City

Virginia City RV Park, 355 North F St., P.O. Box 1070, 89440. T: (775) 847-0999 or (800) 889-1240. www.vcrvpark.com. RV/tent: 56. $12–$20. Hookups: electric (30, 50 amp), water, sewer, phone (modem).

Wells

Angel Creek Campground, P.O. Box 246, 89825. T: (775) 752-3357. RV/tent: 19. $7. Hookups: none.

Angel Lake Campground, P.O. Box 246, 89825. T: (775) 752-3357. RV/tent: 37. $7. Hookups: none.

Beverly Hills RV Ranch, I-80 Exit 348, 89825. T: (775) 752-3800. RV/tent: 55. $18. Hookups: electric (20, 30 amp), water, sewer, phone (modem).

Crossroads RV Park, P.O. Box 161, 89835. T: (775) 752-3012. RV/tent: 24. $16. Hookups: electric (30 amp), water, sewer.

Thomas Canyon Campground, P.O. Box 246, 89825. T: (702) 752-3357. RV/tent: 42. $6. Hookups: none.

Wendover

Stateline RV Park, P.O. Box 789, 89883. T: (775) 664-2221 or (800) 848-7300. RV/tent: 56. $17–$20. Hookups: electric (30, 50 amp), water, sewer.

Wendover KOA, 651 North Camper Dr., 89883. T: (775) 664-3221 or (800) 562-8552. F: (775) 664-3712. RV/tent: 122. $17–$28. Hookups: electric (20, 30, 50 amp), water, sewer.

Winnemucca

Model T Hotel/Casino/RV Park, 1130 West Winnemucca Blvd., 89445. T: (775) 623-2588. www.ModelT.com. RV/tent: 58. $22. Hookups: electric (30, 50 amp), water, sewer, cable TV, phone (modem).

Westerner Trailer Lodge, 800 East Fourth St., 89445. T: (775) 623-2907. RV/tent: 20. $14. Hookups: electric (30 amp), water, sewer.

Winnemucca RV Park, 5255 East Winnemucca Blvd., 89445. T: (775) 623-4458 or (877) 787-2750. wmcarvpark@the-onramp.net. RV/tent: 121. $16–$23. Hookups: electric (30, 50 amp), water, sewer, cable TV, phone (modem).

NEW HAMPSHIRE

Alton Bay

Viewland Campground, P.O. Box 26, Bay Hill Rd., 03810. T: (603) 875-7100. RV/tent: 56. $20. Hookups: water, electric, sewer.

Ashland

Squam Lakes Camp Resort, RFD 1 Box 42, 03217. T: (603) 968-7227. F: (603) 968-3464. RV/tent: 119. $14. Hookups: water, electric (20, 30, 50 amps), sewer, cable TV.

Bath

Twin River Campground & Cottages, P.O. Box 212, 03740. T: (603) 747-3640 or (800) 811-1040. F: (603) 747-2160. www.ucampnh.com/twinriver. RV/tent: 116. $18. Hookups: water, electric (20, 30, 50 amps), sewer, modem.

Bethlehem

Apple Hill Campground, P.O. Box 388, 03574. T: (603) 869-2238. www.musar.com/applehill. RV/tent: 66. $18. Hookups: water, electric (20, 30 amps), sewer.

Snowy Mountain Campground & Motel, 1225 Main St., 03574. T: (603) 444-7789. RV/tent: 40. $16. Hookups: water, electric (15 amps).

Bristol

Davidson's Countryside Campground, 100 Schofield Rd., 03222. T: (603) 744-2403. F: (603) 744-0071. www.worldpath.net/~davcamp. RV/tent: 273. $24. Hookups: water, electric (20, 30 amps), sewer.

Brookline

Field & Stream Park, 5 Dupaw Gould Rd., 03033. T: (603) 673-4677. F: (603) 673-6217. www.fieldnstream.hypermart.net. RV/tent: 40. $24. Hookups: water, electric (20, 30 amps), sewer, cable TV, modem.

Campton

Branch Brook Four Season Campground, P.O. Box 390, 03223. T: (603) 726-7001. F: (603) 726-4093. www.campnh.com. RV/tent: 50. $23. Hookups: water, electric (20, 30, 50 amps), sewer.

Canaan

Crescent Campsites, P.O. Box 238, 03741. T: (603) 523-9910 or (800) 494-5118. www.endor.com/~crescent. RV/tent: 80. $22. Hookups: water, electric (20, 30 amps), sewer.

Center Ossipee

Deer Cap Campground, P.O. Box 332, 03814. T: (603) 539-6030. www.ucampnh.com. RV/tent: 75. $15. Hookups: water, electric (30 amps), sewer.

Terrace Pines Campground, P.O. Box 98 Z, 03814. T: (603) 539-6210. F: (603) 539-6325. www.terracepines.com. RV/tent: 65. $27. Hookups: water, electric (20, 30 amps), sewer, cable TV.

Chester

Silver Sands Campground, 603 Raymond Rd., 03036. T: (603) 887-3638. F: (603) 887-3638. RV/tent: 206. $18. Hookups: water, electric (30 amps), sewer.

Colebrook

Maplewoods Scenic Campground and Bed & Breakfast, Box 114, 03576. T: (603) 237-4237. F: (603) 237-4237. www.maplewoodsci-cg.com. RV/tent: 450. $15. Hookups: water, electric (30 amps), sewer.

Conway Lake

Cove Camping Area, P.O. Box 778A, 03818. T: (603) 447-6734. F: (603) 447-5169. www.covecamping.com. RV/tent: 155. $20. Hookups: water, electric (20, 30 amps).

Derry

Hidden Valley Campground, 81 Damren Rd., 03038. T: (603) 887-3767. F: (603) 887-8115. www.ucampnh.com/hiddenvalley. RV/tent: 72. $25. Hookups: water, electric (20, 30 amps) sewer.

Dover

Old Stage Campground, 46 Old Stage Rd., 03820. T: (603) 742-4050. www.ucampnh.com/oldstage. RV/tent: 157. $24. Hookups: water, electric (20, 30 amps), sewer.

Durham/Lee

Forest Glen Campground, P.O. Box 676, 03824. T: (603) 659-3416. RV/tent: 130. $25. Hookups: water, electric (30 amps), sewer, cable TV.

NEW HAMPSHIRE (continued)

East Lempster

Tamarack Trails Campground, P.O. Box 24, 03605. T: (603) 863-6443. RV/tent: 28. $15. Hookups: water, electric (30 amps), sewer.

East Wakefield

Beachwood Shores Campground, HC Box 228, 03830. T: (603) 539-4272 or (800) 371-4282. www.ucampnh.com/beachwoodshores. RV/tent: 90. $28. Hookups: water, electric (20, 30 amps), sewer.

Lake Forest Resort, North Shore Rd., 03839. T: (603) 522-3306. www.ucampnh.com/lake-forest. RV/tent: 130. $21. Hookups: water, electric (30, 50 amps), sewer.

Epsom

Blake's Brook Campground, 76 Mountain Rd., 03234. T: (603) 736-4793 or (888) 425-2537. F: (603) 736-4083. www.blakesbrook.com. RV/tent: 68. $21. Hookups: water, electric (20, 30 amps), sewer.

Errol

Log Haven Campground, P.O. Box 239, 03579. T: (603) 482-3294. www.loghaven.com. RV/tent: 55. $15. Hookups: water, electric (20, 30 amps), sewer.

Exeter

Green Gate Camping Area, P.O. Box 185, 03833. T: (603) 772-2100. www.greengatecamp.com. RV/tent: 127. $24. Hookups: water, electric (20, 30 amps), sewer.

Fitzwilliam

Laurel Lake Campground, P.O. Box 114, 03447. T: (603) 585-3304. RV/tent: 65. $22. Hookups: water, electric (20, 30 amps), sewer.

Franconia

Fransted Campground, P.O. Box 155, 03580. T: (603) 823-5675. F: (603) 823-5676. www.franstedcampground.com. RV/tent: 95. $18. Hookups: water, electric (20, 30 amps), sewer.

Franklin

Thousand Acres Campground, 1079 South Main St., 03235. T: (603) 934-4440. www.thousand acrescamp.com. RV/tent: 150. $20. Hookups: water, electric (20, 30 amps), sewer.

Glen

Green Meadow Camping Area, P.O. Box 246, 03838. T: (603) 383-6801. www.ucampnh.com/greenmeadow. RV/tent: 92. $20. Hookups: water, electric (15 amps), sewer, cable TV.

Hampstead

Sanborn Shore Acres Campground, Main St., 03841. T: (603) 329-5247. F: (603) 329-9497. RV/tent: 140. $25. Hookups: water, electric (amps), sewer.

Sunset Park Campground, 104 Emerson Rd., 03841. T: (603) 329-6941. RV/tent: 151. $18. Hookups: water, electric (30 amps), sewer.

Hampton

Shel-Al Camping Area, Rte. 1, 03862. T: (603) 964-5730. www.ucampnh.com. RV/tent: 208. $23. Hookups: water, electric (20, 30 amps), sewer.

Holderness

Bethel Woods Campground, Rte. 3, 03245. T: (603) 279-6266. F: (603) 279-6266. www.bethelwoods.com. RV/tent: 380. $22. Hookups: water, electric (20, 30 amps), sewer.

Jaffrey

Emerald Acres, 39 Ridgecrest Rd., 03452. T: (603) 532-8838. RV/tent: 52. $14. Hookups: water, electric (20, 30 amps), sewer.

Jefferson

Israel River Campground, RR 1 Box 179A, 03583. T: (603) 586-7977. F: (603) 586-7187. RV/tent: 119. $18. Hookups: water, electric (30 amps), sewer.

Jefferson Campground, Box 112A, 03583. T: (603) 586-4510. F: (603) 586-7044. www.jeffersoncampground.com. RV/tent: 192. $16. Hookups: water, electric (20, 30 amps), sewer.

Kingston

Country Shore Camping Area, P.O. Box 550, 03865. T: (603) 642-5072. F: (603) 642-6745. www.ucampnh.com/countryshore. RV/tent: 100. $27. Hookups: water, electric (20, 30, 50 amps), sewer.

Laconia

Hack-Ma-Tack Campground, 713 Endicott St. North, 03246. T: (603) 366-5977. RV/tent: 80. $24. Hookups: water, electric (30 amps), sewer.

Paugus Bay Campground, 96 Hilliard Rd., 03246. T: (603) 366-4757. www.geocities.com/weirs_pbc. RV/tent: 173. $30. Hookups: water, electric (20, 30 amps), sewer.

Lancaster

Beaver Trails Campground, RR 2 Box 315, 03584. T: (603) 788-3815. F: (603) 788-2808. www.greatnorthwoods.org/beavertrails. RV/tent: 350. $20. Hookups: water, electric (20, 30, 50 amps), sewer, modem.

Lee

Wadleigh Falls Campground, 16 Campground Rd., 03824. T: (603) 659-1751. F: (603) 659-4045. www.wadleighfalls.com. RV/tent: 50. $23. Hookups: water, electric (20, 30, 50 amps), sewer.

Lincoln

Country Bumpkins Campground & Cabins, Rte. 3, 03251. T: (603) 745-8837. www.country-bumpkins.com. RV/tent: 45. $19. Hookups: water, electric (20, 30 amps), sewer.

Lochmere

Silver Lake Park Campground, 389 Jamestown Rd., 03252. T: (603) 524-6289. www.ucampnh.com/silverlake. RV/tent: 77. $21. Hookups: water, electric (20, 30 amps), sewer.

Milan

Nay Pond Campground, 7 Nay Pond Rd., 03588. T: (603) 449-2122. RV/tent: 33. $15. Hookups: water, electric (30 amps), sewer.

Moultonboro

Pine Woods Campground, P.O. Box 776, 03254. T: (603) 253-6251. www.pinewoods.com. RV/tent: 97. $23. Hookups: water, electric (20, 30, 50 amps), sewer.

Newport

Northstar Campground, 43 Coonbrook Rd., 03773. T: (603) 863-4001. www.northstar.com. RV/tent: 69. $22. Hookups: water, electric (20, 30 amps), sewer.

Orford

Jacobs Brook Campground, High Bridge Rd., 03777. T: (603) 353-9210. www.outdoors.at/jacobsbrook. RV/tent: 65. $20. Hookups: water, electric (20, 30 amps), sewer.

Pittsburg

Mountain View Cabins & Campground, RR 1 Box 30, 03592. T: (603) 538-6305. F: (603) 538-1157. RV/tent: 53. $14. Hookups: water, electric (20 amps), sewer.

Plymouth

Plymouth Sands Campground, 3 Quincy Rd., 03264. T: (603) 536-2605. RV/tent: 84. $16. Hookups: water, electric (20 amps), sewer.

Rochester

Crown Point Campground, 44 First Crown Point Rd., 03867. T: (603) 332-0405. RV/tent: 135. $24. Hookups: water, electric (20, 30 amps), sewer.

Grand View Camping Area, 51 Four Rod Rd., 03867. T: (603) 332-1263. F: (603) 332- 7947. www.grandviewcamping.com. RV/tent: 70. $28. Hookups: water, electric (20, 30 amps), sewer.

Rumney

Baker River Campground, 56 Campground Rd., 03266. T: (603) 786-9707. www.ucampnh.com/bakerriver. RV/tent: 60. $18. Hookups: water, electric (20, 30 amps), sewer.

Sandown

Angle Pond Grove Camping Area, P.O. Box 173, 03826. T: (603) 887-4434. F: (603) 887-4434. www.anglepondgrove.com. RV/tent: 15. $20. Hookups: water, electric (30, 50 amps), sewer.

Shelburne

White Birches Camping Park, 218 SR 2, 03581. T: (603) 466-2022. F: (603) 466-3441. www.gocampingamerica/whitebirches. RV/tent: 91. $15. Hookups: water, electric (30 amps), sewer.

NEW HAMPSHIRE (continued)

Tamworth

Foothills Campground, 506 Maple Rd., 03886. T: (603) 323-8322. F: (603) 323-8194. www.thefoothills.com. RV/tent: 40. $18. Hookups: water, electric (20, 30 amps), sewer.

Tamworth Camping Area, P.O. Box 99, 03886. T: (603) 323-8031. F: (603) 323-7500. www.tamworthcampingarea.com. RV/tent: 38. $21. Hookups: water, electric (20, 30 amps), sewer.

Thornton

Pemi River Campground, RFD 1 Box 926, 03223. T: (603) 726-7015. RV/tent: 71. $22. Hookups: water, electric (15, 30, 50 amps).

Twin Mountain

Ammonoosuc Campground, P.O. Box 178 North, 03595. T: (603) 846-5527. www.ucampnh.com/ammonoosuc. RV/tent: 112. $20. Hookups: water, electric (20, 30 amps), sewer.

Warren

Scenic View Campground, 193AA South Main St., 03279. T: (603) 764-9380. www.usastar.com/scenicview. RV/tent: 98. $23. Hookups: water, electric (20, 30 amps), cable TV, phone, modem.

Washington

Happy Days Campground, 928 Valley Rd., 03280. T: (603) 495-0150. F: (603) 495-0261. www.ucampnh.com/happydays. RV/tent: 185. $20. Hookups: water, electric (20, 30 amps), sewer.

Weare

Autumn Hills Campground, 285 South Stark Hwy., 03281. T: (603) 529-2425. F: (603) 529-5877. www.autumnhillscampground.com. RV/tent: 159. $21. Hookups: water, electric (20, 30 amps), sewer.

Webster

Cold Brook Campground, 539 Battle St., 03303. T: (603) 746-3390. www.coldbrookcampground.com. RV/tent: 50. $15. Hookups: water, electric (15, 20 amps), sewer.

Weirs Beach

Weirs Beach Tent and Trailer Park, 198 Endicott St., 03246. T: (603) 366-4747. www.wbttp.com. RV/tent: 184. $22. Hookups: water, electric (30 amps), sewer.

West Ossipee

Bearcamp River Campground, P.O. Box 104, 03890. T: (603) 539-4898. F: (603) 539-6025. www.bearcamp.com. RV/tent: 112. $23. Hookups: water, electric (20, 30 amps), sewer.

Whitefield

Burns Lake Campground, RR 2 Box 620A, 03598. T: (603) 837-9037. RV/tent: 70. $14. Hookups: water, electric (20, 30 amps).

Winchester

Forest Lake Campground, 331 Keene Rd., 03470. T: (603) 239-4267. RV/tent: 150. $20. Hookups: water, electric (20, 30 amps), sewer.

Wolfeboro

Robie's RV Park, 139 Governor Wentworth Hwy., 03894. T: (603) 569-2732. F: (603) 569-4354. RV/tent: 50. $24. Hookups: water, electric (30, 50 amps), sewer.

Willey Brook Campground, 883 Center St., 03894. T: (603) 569-9493. www.WilleyBrookCampground.com. RV/tent: 33. $16. Hookups: water, electric (30 amps), sewer.

NEW JERSEY

Andover

Columbia Valley Campground, 3 Ghost Pony Rd., 07821. T: (201) 691-0596. RV/tent: 123. $20. Hookups: water, electric, sewer.

Barnegat

Brookville Campground, 224 Jones Rd., 09005. T: (609) 698-3134. RV/tent: 100. $15–20. Hookups: water, electric (20, 30 amps), sewer.

Beach Haven

Long Beach Island Trailer Park, 19 Harding Ave., 08008. T: (609) 492-9151. RV/tent: 140. $37. Hookups: water, electric (30 amps), sewer.

Cape May

Cape May Mobile Homes, 755 Rte. 9, 08204. T: (609) 884-3203. F: (609) 884-7017. www.cm mobileestates.com. RV/tent: 86. $25. Hookups: water, electric (20, 30 amps), sewer.

Lake Laurie Campground, 669 Rte. 9, 08204. T: (609) 884-3567. RV/tent: 700. $23.50–$31. Hookups: water, electric, sewer.

Cape May Court House

Ponderosa Campground, 18 West Beaver Dam Rd., 08210. T: (609) 465-7794. www.ponderosacamp ground.com. RV/tent: 100. $21–25. Hookups: water, electric, sewer.

Shellbay Campground, Shellbay Ave., 08210. T: (609) 465-4770. RV/tent: 300. $27. Hookups: water electric (20, 30, 50 amps), sewer.

Clermont

Avalon Campground, 1917 North Rte. 9, 08210. T: (609) 624-0075. RV/tent: 360. $29–$36. Hookups: water, electric (20, 30, 50 amps), sewer.

Clinton

Round Valley State Recreational Area, 1220 Lebanon-Stanton Rd., 08833-3115. T: (908) 236-6355. RV/tent: 106. $8. Hookups: none.

Spruce Run State Recreation Area, 1 Van Syckels Rd., 08809. T: (908) 638-8572. RV/tent: 70. $10. Hookups: none.

Colesville

High Point State Park, Rte. 23, 07461. T: (973) 875-4800. RV/tent: 50. $10. Hookups: none.

Columbia

Worthington State Forest, HC 62, P.O. Box 2, 07832. T: (908) 841-9575. RV/tent: 69. $8–$10. Hookups: none.

Delaware

Delaware River Family Campground, 100 Rte. 46, P.O. Box 142, 07833. T: (908) 475-4517. RV/tent: 171. $24. Hookups: water, electric.

Egg Harbor

Union Hill Campground, 163 Leektown Rd., 08215. T: (609) 296-8599. F: (609) 296-8939. RV/tent: 25. $15. Hookups: water, electric, sewer.

Farmingdale

Alaire State Park, P.O. Box 220, 07727. T: (732) 938 2371. RV/tent: 55. $10. Hookups: none.

Freehold

Pine Cone Campground, 340 Georgia Rd., 07728. T: (732) 462-2230. RV/tent: 125. $26–$28. Hookups: water, electric (20, 30 amps), sewer.

Turkey Swamp/Monmouth County Park, 66 Nomoco Rd., 07728. T: (732) 462-7286. RV/tent: 64. $21–$23. Hookups: water, electric (30 amps).

Great Meadow

Jenny Jump State Forest, 330 State Park Rd., 07844. T: (908) 459-4366. RV/tent: 23. $10. Hookups: none.

Hackettstown

Stephens State Park, 800 Willow Grove St., 07840. T: (908) 852-3790. RV/tent: 40. $10. Hookups: none.

NEW JERSEY (continued)

Highbridge
Voorhees State Park, 251 Circle-513, 08826. T: (908) 638-6969. RV/tent: 50. $10. Hookups: none.

Jackson
Maple Lake Campground, 980 East Veterans Hwy., 08527. T: (732) 367-0177. RV/tent: 150. $29–$31. Hookups: water, electric (20, 30 amps), sewer.

Monroeville
Old Cedar Campground, 274 Richwood Rd., 08343. T: (856) 538-4881 or (856) 358-2406. RV/tent: 200. $21–$22. Hookups: water, electric 15,20,30 amps, sewer.

Montague
Cedar Ridge Campground, 205 River Rd., 07827. T: (973) 293-3512. RV/tent: 220. $21–$23. Hookups: water, electric (20, 30 amps), sewer.

Netcong
Fla-Net-Park Campground, 23 Flanders Netcong Rd., 07836. T: (973) 347-4467. RV/tent: 100. $25. Hookups: water, electric (20, 30 amps), sewer.

New Gretna
Chips Folly Family Campgrounds, P.O. Box 56, 08224. T: (609) 296-4434. F: (609) 296-2067. RV/tent: 300. $22–$23. Hookups: water, electric (20, 30, 50 amps), sewer.

Pilgrims Lake Campground, P.O. Box 17, 08224. T: (609) 296-4725. RV/tent: 116. $18–$22. Hookups: water, electric (30 amps), sewer.

Newton
Swartswood State Park, P.O. Box 123, 07860. T: (973) 383-5230. RV/tent: 70. $10–$20. Hookups: none.

Ocean View
Tamerlane Campground, P.O. Box 510, 2241 US-9, 08230. T: (609) 604-0767. RV/tent: 280. $23–27. Hookups: water, electric (20, 30 amps), sewer.

Parkerstown
Baker's Acres Campground, 230 Willets Ave., 08087. T: (609) 296-2664 or (800) 648-2227. F: (609) 296-1990. RV/tent: 250. $22–$27. Hookups: water, electric, sewer.

Pemberton
Lebanon State Forest, Rte. 72, 08064. T: (609) 726-1191. RV/tent: 82. $10. Hookups: none.

Pilesgrove
Four Seasons Campground, 158 Woodstown-Daretown Rd., 08098. T: (856) 769-3635 or (888) FSC-CAMP. RV/tent: 480. $18–$22. Hookups: water, electric, sewer.

Pomona
Evergreen Woods Lakefront Resort, P.O. Box 197, 08240. T: (609) 624-0767. RV/tent: 175. $24–$26. Hookups: water, electric (20, 30 amps), sewer.

Pomona Campground, P.O. Box 675, 08240. T: (609) 965-2123. RV/tent: 125. $22. Hookups: water, electric (30 amps), sewer.

Port Republic
Atlantic City Blueberry Hill Campground, P.O. Box 219, 08241. T: (609) 652-1644. RV/tent: 171. $31. Hookups: water, electric (20, 30, 50 amps), sewer.

Sewell
Lake Kandle Campground, 250 Chapel Heights Rd., 08080. T: (800) 905-2653 or (856) 589-2158. RV/tent: 150. $27–$28. Hookups: water, electric, sewer.

Stockton
Delaware & Raritan Canal State Park, Canal Rd., 08873. T: (732) 873-3050. RV/tent: 75. $10. Hookups: none.

Toms River
Albocondo Campground, 1480 Whitesville Rd., 08755. T: (732) 349-4079. RV/tent: 186. $27–$30. Hookups: water, electric (20, 30 amps), sewer.

NEW MEXICO

Alamogordo
Cimmarron Campground, Carson National Forest Community Affairs Office, 208 Cruz Alta Rd., 87571. T: (505) 758-6200. www.fs.fed.us/r3/carson/html_main/list_camping2.html. RV/tent: 36. $10. Hookups: none.

Evergreen Park, 2200 North Florida Ave. No. 50, 88310. T: (505) 437-3721. RV/tent: 45. $16. Hookups: electric (20, 30, 50 amps), water, sewer.

Oliver Lee Memorial State Park, 409 Dog Canyon, 88310. T: (505) 437-8284. www.emnrd.state.nm.us/nmparks/pages/parks/oliver/oliver.htm. RV/tent: 44. $8–$18. Hookups: electric (20, 30 amps).

White Sands Community, 607 South White Sands Blvd., 88310. T: (505) 437-8388. RV/tent: 290. $17–$20. Hookups: electric (30 amps), water, sewer.

Albuquerque
Albuquerque North/Bernalillo KOA, P.O. Box 758, 87004. T: (800) 562-3616 or (505) 867-5227. www.koa.com. RV/tent: 89. $21–$31. Hookups: electric (20, 30, 50 amps), water, sewer.

American RV Park of Albuquerque, 13500 Coronado Fwy. Southwest, 87121. T: (800) 282-8885 or (501) 831-3545. F: (501) 836-6095. www.americanrvpark.com. RV/tent: 202. $26–$30. Hookups: electric (20, 30, 50 amps), water, sewer.

Balloon View RV Park, 500 Tyler Rd. Northeast, 87121. T: (800) 932-9523 or (505) 345-3716. F: (505) 345-3718. RV/tent: 87. $23–$26. Hookups: electric (30, 50 amps), water, sewer.

Best Western American Motor Inn & RV Park, 12999 Central Ave. Northeast, 87123. T: (505) 298-7426. F: (505) 298-0212. RV/tent: 13. $24–$28. Hookups: electric (30, 50 amps), water, sewer, cable.

Enchanted Trails Camping Resort, 14305 Central NW, 87121. T: (800) 326-6317 or (505) 831-6314. F: (505) 831-1000. www.enchantedtrails.com. RV/tent: 135. $20–$22. Hookups: electric (30 amps), water, sewer.

Palisades RV Park, 9201 Central NW, 87121. T: (888) 922-9595 or (505) 831-5000. RV/tent: 112. $22–$24. Hookups: electric (30, 50 amps), water, sewer.

Alto
Elk Run Cabins & RV Park, P.O. Box 406, 88312. T: (800) 687-0620 or (505) 336-4240. www.ruidoso.net/elkrun. RV/tent: 20. $20–$25. Hookups: electric (30, 50 amps), water, sewer.

Angel Fire
Monte Verde RV Park, P.O. Box 520, 87710. T: (505) 377-3404. www.aardvarkrv.com/monteverderv. RV/tent: 28. $18. Hookups: electric (30 amps), water, sewer.

Anthony
El Paso West RV Park, 1415 Anthony Dr., 88021. T: (505) 882-7172. RV/tent: 100. $20. Hookups: electric (30, 50 amps), water, sewer.

Arrey
Arrey RV Park, MM 19, Hwy. 87, 87930. T: (866) 267-1049 or (505) 267-1049. www.zianet.com/mmoyle. RV/tent: 10. $8.50. Hookups: electric (20, 30, 50 amps), water, sewer.

NEW MEXICO (continued)

Aztec

Ruins Road RV Park, 312 Ruins Rd., 87410. T: (505) 334-3160. F: (505) 334-3160. RV/tent: 45. $15. Hookups: electric (30, 50 amps), water, sewer.

Bloomfield

Bloomfield KOA, 1900 East Blanco Blvd., 87413. T: (800) 562-8513 or (505) 632-8339. www.koa.com/where/NM/31156. RV/tent: 84. $16–$23. Hookups: electric (20, 30, 50 amps), water, sewer.

Caballo

Caballo Lake State Park, P.O. Box 32, 87931. T: (505) 743-3942. www.emnrd.state.nm.us/nmparks/pages/parks/caballo/caballo.htm. RV/tent: 200. $8–$18. Hookups: electric (20, 30 amps).

Percha Dam State Park, P.O. Box 32, 87931. T: (505) 743-3942. www.emnrd.state.nm.us/nmparks/pages/parks/percha/percha.htm. RV/tent: 29. $8–$18. Hookups: electric (20, 30 amps).

Canjilon

Canjilon Lakes Campground, Carson National Forest Community Affairs Office, 208 Cruz Alta Rd., 87571. T: (505) 758-6200. www.fs.fed.us/r3/carson/html_main/list_camping2.html. RV/tent: 40. $10. Hookups: none.

Echo Ampitheater Campground, Carson National Forest Community Affairs Office, 208 Cruz Alta Rd., 87571. T: (505) 758-6200. www.fs.fed.us/r3/carson/html_main/list_camping2.html. RV/tent: 10. $10. Hookups: none.

Capitan

Mountain High RV Park, HC 71 Box 1220, 88316. T: (505) 336-4236. RV/tent: 39. $20. Hookups: electric (30 amps), water, sewer.

Carlsbad

Brantley Lake State Park, P.O. Box 2288, 88221. T: (505) 457-2384. www.emnrd.state.nm.us/nmparks/pages/parks/brantley/Brantley.htm. RV/tent: 11. $8–$18. Hookups: electric (20, 30 amps).

Cavern Estates Mobile Home & RV Park, 3022 National Parks Hwy., 88220. T: (505) 887-3274. RV/tent: 50. $15–$17. Hookups: electric (30, 50 amps), water, sewer.

Edeal's Pecos River RV Park & Minimart, 320 East Greene St., 88220. T: (505) 885-5201. RV/tent: 16. $19. Hookups: electric (20, 30, 50 amps), water, sewer.

Windmill RV Park, 3624 National Parks Hwy., 88220. T: (888) 349-7275 or (505) 887-1387. RV/tent: 61. $18–$22. Hookups: electric (30, 50 amps), water, sewer.

Carrizozo

Valley of Fires Recreation Area, P.O. Box 63, 88301. T: (505) 648-2241. F: (505) 648-2241. RV/tent: 25. $10. Hookups: electric (30 amps).

Cedar Crest

Turquoise Trail Campground & RV Park, P.O. Box 582, 22 Calvary Rd., 87008. T: (505) 281-2005. RV/tent: 87. $19. Hookups: electric (20, 30, 50 amps), water, sewer.

Chama

El Vado Lake State Park, P.O. Box 367, 87575. T: (505) 588-7247. www.emnrd.state.nm.us/nmparks/pages/parks/elvado/elvado.htm. RV/tent: 64. $8–$18. Hookups: electric (20, 30 amps).

Little Creel Resort, P.O. Box 781, 87520. T: (505) 756-2382. RV/tent: 67. $15–$35. Hookups: electric (20, 30, 50 amps), water, sewer.

Rio Chama RV Park, 182 North Hwy. 17, 87520. T: (505) 756-2303. RV/tent: 90. $16–$20. Hookups: electric (30, 50 amps), water, sewer.

Twin Rivers RV Park & Campground, P.O. Box 26, 87520. T: (505) 756-2218. RV/tent: 85. $15. Hookups: electric (15, 20, 30, 50 amps), water, sewer.

Church Rock

Red Rock State Park, Box 10, 57311. T: (505) 722-3839. RV/tent: 135. $14. Hookups: electric (30, 50 amps), water.

Cimarron

Cimarron Inn & RV Park, 204 Hwy. 64, 87714. T: (505) 376-2268. F: (505) 376-4504. RV/tent: 12. $17. Hookups: electric (20, 30 amps), water, sewer.

Cloudcroft

Apache Campground, Lincoln Forest, 1101 New York Ave., 88310-6992. T: (505) 682-2551. F: (505) 434-7218. RV/tent: 26. $10. Hookups: none.

Deerhead Campground, Lincoln Forest, 1101 New York Ave., 88310-6992. T: (505) 682-2551. F: (505) 434-7218. RV/tent: 35. $10. Hookups: none.

Pines Campground, Lincoln Forest, 1101 New York Ave., 88310-6992. T: (505) 682-2551. F: (505) 434-7218. RV/tent: 48. $10. Hookups: none.

Silver Campground, Lincoln Forest, 1101 New York Ave., 88310-6992. T: (505) 682-2551. F: (505) 434-7218. RV/tent: 32. $10. Hookups: none.

Sleepy Grass Campground, Lincoln Forest, 1101 New York Ave., 88310-6992. T: (505) 682-2551. F: (505) 434-7218. RV/tent: 45. $10. Hookups: none.

Clovis

West Park Inn RV Park, 1500 West 7th St., 88101. T: (505) 763-7218. RV/tent: 18. $18. Hookups: electric (20, 30 amps), water, sewer, cable.

Conchas Dam

Conchas Lake State Park, P.O. Box 976, 88416. T: (505) 868-2270. www.emnrd.state.nm.us/nmparks/pages/parks/conchas/conchas.htm. RV/tent: 215. $8–$18. Hookups: electric (20, 30 amps).

Deming

81 Palms RV Resort, 2800 West Pine St., 88030. T: (505) 546-7434. RV/tent: 106. $16–$18. Hookups: electric (20, 30, 50 amps), water, sewer.

A Deming Roadrunner RV Park, 2849 East Motel Dr., 88030. T: (800) 226-9937. F: (505) 546-6960. www.zianet.com/roadrunnerrv. RV/tent: 109. $10–$16. Hookups: electric (20, 30, 50 amps), water, sewer.

A Little Vineyard RV Park & Resort, 2901 Motel Dr. East, 88030. T: (800) 413-0312. www.zianet.com/cjbailey. RV/tent: 153. $12. Hookups: electric (20, 30, 50 amps), water, sewer.

Dream Catcher Escapees RV Park, 4400 East Motel Dr., 88030. T: (505) 544-4004. www.escapees.com. RV/tent: 132. $10. Hookups: electric (20, 30, 50 amps), water, sewer.

Hitchin' Post RV Park, 611 West Pine St., 88030. T: (505) 546-9145. RV/tent: 40. $11–$14. Hookups: electric (30 amps), water, sewer.

Rockhound State Park, P.O. Box 1064, 88030. T: (505) 546-6182. www.emnrd.state.nm.us/nmparks/pages/parks/rockh/rockh.htm. RV/tent: 36. $8–$18. Hookups: electric (20, 30 amps).

Starlight Village Resort, P.O. Drawer 1139, 88031. T: (505) 546-0867. F: (505) 546-6029. RV/tent: 64. $17. Hookups: electric (30, 50 amps), water, sewer.

Vista Floridas RV Park, 545 O'Kelley Rd. Southeast, 88030. T: (505) 544-8366. RV/tent: 21. $15. Hookups: electric (20, 30, 50 amps), water, sewer.

Eagle Nest

Eagle Gem RV Park, HCR 71 Box 3, 87718. T: (505) 377-2214 or (505) 377-0522. RV/tent: 60. $17. Hookups: electric (20, 30, 50 amps), water, sewer.

Golden Eagle RV Park, Box 458, 87718. T: (800) 388-6188 or (505) 377-6188. RV/tent: 53. $20. Hookups: electric (30, 50 amps), water, sewer.

Lost Eagle RV Park, 155 East Therma Dr., 87718. T: (800) 581-2374 or (505) 377-2374. RV/tent: 41. $15–$17. Hookups: electric (30, 50 amps), water, sewer.

NEW MEXICO (continued)

Elephant Butte

Cozy Cove, Box 427, 87935. T: (505) 740-0745. RV/tent: 29. $13. Hookups: electric (20, 30, 50 amps), water, sewer.

Elephant Butte Lake State Park, P.O. Box 13, 87935. T: (505) 744-5421. www.emnrd.state.nm.us/nmparks/pages/parks/butte/butte.htm. RV/tent: 223. $8–$18. Hookups: electric (20, 30 amps).

Enchanted Views RV Park, P.O. Box 250, 87935. T: (505) 744-5876. RV/tent: 37. $14–$16. Hookups: electric (30, 50 amps), water, sewer.

Espanola

Ohkay RV Park, North Riverside Dr., 87532. T: (505) 753-5067. RV/tent: 84. $21. Hookups: electric (30, 50 amps), water, sewer.

Farmington

Dad & Ann's RV Park, 202 East Pinon, 87401. T: (888) 326-3237. F: (505) 326-1870. RV/tent: 10. $15. Hookups: electric (30 amps), water, sewer.

Downs Hair Salon & RV Park, 5701 Hwy. 64, 87401. T: (505) 325-7094. RV/tent: 42. $17. Hookups: electric (30, 50 amps), water, sewer.

Mom & Pop RV Park, 901 Illinois Ave., 87401. T: (800) 748-2807. RV/tent: 33. $14. Hookups: electric (30 amps), water, sewer.

Paramount RV Park, North Rd. 6220, 87401. T: (505) 598-9824. F: (505) 598-6515. RV/tent: 16. $15. Hookups: electric (20, 30, 50 amps), water, sewer.

Faywood

City of Rocks State Park, P.O. Box 50, 88034. T: (505) 536-2800. www.emnrd.state.nm.us/nmparks/pages/parks/cityrock/cityrock.htm. RV/tent: 57. $8–$18. Hookups: electric (20, 30 amps).

Fort Sumner

Sumner Lake State Park, HC 64 Box 125, 88119. T: (505) 355-2541. www.emnrd.state.nm.us/nmparks/pages/parks/sumner/sumner.htm. RV/tent: 106. $8–$18. Hookups: electric (20, 30 amps).

Gila Hot Springs

Gila Hot Springs RV Park & Vacation Center, HC 68 Box 80, 88061. T: (505) 536-9551. RV/tent: 16. $17. Hookups: electric (30, 50 amps), water, sewer.

Grants

Bar S RV Park, I-40, Exit 79, 87020. T: (505) 876-6002. RV/tent: 51. $12. Hookups: electric (20, 30, 50 amps), water, sewer.

Blue Spruce RV Park, I-40, Exit 81, 87020. T: (505) 287-2560. RV/tent: 23. $11. Hookups: electric (20, 30, 50 amps), water, sewer.

Cibola Sands RV Park, P.O. Box 179, 87020. T: (505) 287-4376. www.cibolarv.com. RV/tent: 46. $16–$20. Hookups: electric (20, 30, 50 amps), water, sewer.

Valencia Village Mobile & RV Park, 1400 East Roosevelt Ave., 87020. T: (505) 287-2744. RV/tent: 60. $15. Hookups: electric (30, 50 amps), water, sewer.

Guadalupita

Coyote Creek State Park, P.O. Box 477, 87722. T: (505) 387-2328. www.emnrd.state.nm.us/nmparks/pages/parks/coyote/coyote.htm. RV/tent: 50. $8–$18. Hookups: electric (20, 30 amps).

Morphy Lake State Park, P.O. Box 477, 87722. T: (505) 387-2328. RV/tent: 60. $8–$18. Hookups: none.

Hobbs

Burnell's RV Park, 100 South Marlind Blvd., 88240. T: (505) 393-3226. F: (505) 393-3226. RV/tent: 27. $16. Hookups: electric (30, 50 amps), water, sewer.

Conner RV Sales & Park, 100 South Marland Blvd., 88240-6349. T: (505) 393-3226. RV/tent: 5. $16. Hookups: electric (30, 50 amps), water, sewer.

Jims RV Park, 615 North Marland Blvd., 88240-5404. T: (505) 397-2551. RV/tent: 21. $13. Hooksups: electric (20, 30, 50 amps), water, sewer.

Jemez Springs

Fenton Lake State Park, 455 Fenton Lake Rd., 87025. T: (505) 829-3630. www.emnrd.state.nm.us/nmparks/pages/parks/fenton/fenton.htm. RV/tent: 40. $8–$18. Hookups: electric (20, 30 amps).

Lakewood

7 Rivers Cove RV Resort at Brantley Lake, P.O. Box 103, 88254. T: (877) 457-2002 or (505) 457-2000. RV/tent: 30. $20–$22. Hookups: electric (30, 50 amps), water, sewer.

Las Cruces

Coachlight Motel & RV Park, 301 South Motel Blvd., 88005. T: (505) 526-3301. RV/tent: 47. $20. Hookups: electric (30, 50 amps), water, sewer.

Dalmonts RV Trailer Corral, 2224 South Valley, 88005. T: (505) 523-2992. RV/tent: 26. $16. Hookups: electric (15, 20, 30 amps), water, sewer.

RV Doc's Park & Service Center, 1475 Ave. de Mesilla, 88005. T: (888) 2RV-DOCS or (505) 526-8401. RV/tent: 66. $20–$23. Hookups: electric (30, 50 amps), water, sewer.

Siesta RV Park, 1551 Ave. de Mesilla, 88005. T: (800) 414-6816 or (505) 523-6816. F: (505) 523-0599. RV/tent: 54. $21–$23. Hookups: electric (30 amps), water, sewer.

Sunny Acres Mobile Village, 595 North Valley Dr., 88005. T: (877) 800-1716 or (505) 534-1716. F: (505) 524-3099. RV/tent: 24. $20. Hookups: electric (30, 50 amps), water, sewer.

Las Vegas

Las Vegas KOA, HC 31 Box 16, 87701. T: (800) 562-3423 or (505) 454-0180. www.koa.com. RV/tent: 60. $19–$27. Hookups: electric (20, 30 amps), water, sewer.

Storrie Lake State Park, HC33 Box 109 No. 2, 87701. T: (505) 425-7278. www.emnrd.state.nm.us/nmparks/pages/parks/storrie/storrie.htm. RV/tent: 112. $8–$18. Hookups: electric (20, 30 amps).

Vegas RV Park, 504 Harris Rd., 87701. T: (505) 425-5640. RV/tent: 33. $18. Hookups: electric (30 amps), water, sewer.

Westward Ho RV Park, 857 AirpoRte. Rd., 87701. T: (505) 425-6978. www.members.tripod.com/~dukesrv. RV/tent: 20. $20. Hookups: electric (30, 50 amps), water, sewer.

Los Alamos

Bandelier National Monument, HCR 1 Box 1, Suite 50, 87544. T: (505) 672-3861. F: (505) 672-9607. RV/tent: 93. $20. Hookups: none.

Los Ojos

Heron Lake State Park, P.O. Box 159, 87511. T: (505) 588-7470. www.emnrd.state.nm.us/nmparks/pages/parks/heron/heron.htm. RV/tent: 400. $8–$18. Hookups: electric (20, 30 amps).

Mesilla

Hacienda RV Resort, P.O. Box 1479, 88046. T: (888) 686-9090 or (505) 528-5800. www.haciendarv.com. RV/tent: 113. $25–$27. Hookups: electric (30, 50 amps), water, sewer.

Moriarty

Zia RV Park & Campground, HC 81 Box 165, 87035. T: (505) 832-9796. RV/tent: 58. $15–$17. Hookups: electric (30, 50 amps), water, sewer.

Navajo Dam

Navajo Lake State Park, 1448 NM 511 No. 1, 87419. T: (505) 632-2278. www.emnrd.state.nm.us/nmparks/pages/parks/navajo/navajo.htm. RV/tent: 451. $8–$18. Hookups: electric (20, 30 amps).

Nogal

Alto Hombre Gordito, P.O. Box 1445, 88341. T: (877) 466-2734 or (505) 336 7877. www.hombregordito.com. RV/tent: 20. $35. Hookups: electric (20, 30, 50 amps), water, sewer.

NEW MEXICO (continued)

North Pecos

Santa Barbara Campground, Carson National Forest Community Affairs Office, 208 Cruz Alta Rd., 87571. T: (505) 758-6200. www.fs.fed.us/r3/carson/html_main/list_camping2.html. RV/tent: 22. $10. Hookups: none.

Pena Blanca

Cochiti Area, 82 Dam Crest Rd., 87041. T: (505) 465-0307. www.ReserveUSA.com/nrrs/nm/coca. RV/tent: 60. $5–$11. Hookups: electric (20, 30 amps).

Tetilla Peak, 82 Dam Crest Rd., 87041. T: (505) 465-0307. www.ReserveUSA.com/nrrs/nm/tpea. RV/tent: 52. $7–$11. Hookups: electric (20, 30 amps).

Portales

Oasis State Park, 1882 Oasis Rd., 88130. T: (505) 356-5331. www.emnrd.state.nm.us/nmparks/pages/parks/oasis/oasis.htm. RV/tent: 23. $8–$18. Hookups: electric (20, 30 amps).

Wagon Wheel RV Park, Northeast Hwy. 70, 88130. T: (505) 356-3700. RV/tent: 21. $16. Hookups: electric (20, 30, 50 amps), water, sewer.

Radium Springs

Leasburg Dam State Park, P.O. Box 6, 88054. T: (505) 524-4068. www.emnrd.state.nm.us/nmparks/pages/parks/leasburg/leasburg.htm. RV/tent: 54. $8–$18. Hookups: electric (20, 30 amps).

Ranchos de Taos

Taos RV Park, P.O. Box 729 TL, 87557. T: (800) 323-6009 or (505) 758-1667. F: (505) 758-1989. RV/tent: 24. $21–$23. Hookups: electric (20, 30 amps), water, sewer.

Raton

Kickback RV Park, 1025 Frontage Rd., 87740. T: (505) 445-1200. RV/tent: 45. $20–$22. Hookups: electric (30, 50 amps), water, sewer.

Raton KOA, 1330 South 2nd St., 87740. T: (800) 562-9033 or (505) 445-3488. www.koa.com. RV/tent: 54. $15–$25. Hookups: electric (20, 30, 50 amps), water, sewer.

Sugarite Canyon State Park, HCR 63 Box 386, 87740. T: (505) 445-5607. www.emnrd.state.nm.us/nmparks/pages/parks/sugarite/sugarite.htm. RV/tent: 40. $8–$18. Hookups: electric (20, 30 amps).

Red River

River Ranch, Box 69, 87558. T: (505) 754-2293. www.redrivernm.com/riverranch. RV/tent: 31. $23–$27. Hookups: electric (30, 50 amps), water, sewer.

Red River Canyon

Columbine Campground, Carson National Forest Community Affairs Office, 208 Cruz Alta Rd., 87571. T: (505) 758-6200. www.fs.fed.us/r3/carson/html_main/list_camping2.html. RV/tent: 27. $10. Hookups: none.

Elephant Rock Campground, Carson National Forest Community Affairs Office, 208 Cruz Alta Rd., 87571. T: (505) 758-6200. www.fs.fed.us/r3/carson/html_main/list_camping2.html. RV/tent: 22. $10. Hookups: none.

Fawn Lakes Campground, Carson National Forest Community Affairs Office, 208 Cruz Alta Rd., 87571. T: (505) 758-6200. www.fs.fed.us/r3/carson/html_main/list_camping2.html. RV/tent: 21. $10. Hookups: none.

Junebug Campground, Carson National Forest Community Affairs Office, 208 Cruz Alta Rd., 87571. T: (505) 758-6200. www.fs.fed.us/r3/carson/html_main/list_camping2.html. RV/tent: 22. $10. Hookups: none.

Rio Grande Gorge

BLM Orilla Verde, Carson National Forest Community Affairs Office, 208 Cruz Alta Rd., 87571. T: (505) 758-6200. www.fs.fed.us/r3/carson/html_main/list_camping2.html. RV/tent: 23. $10. Hookups: none.

BLM Wild Rivers Campground, Carson National Forest Community Affairs Office, 208 Cruz Alta Rd., 87571. T: (505) 758-6200. www.fs.fed.us/r3/carson/html_main/list_camping2.html. RV/tent: 35. $10. Hookups: none.

Rio Pueblo

Comales Campground, Carson National Forest Community Affairs Office, 208 Cruz Alta Rd., 87571. T: (505) 758-6200. www.fs.fed.us/r3/carson/html_main/list_camping2.html. RV/tent: 13. $10. Hookups: none.

Duran Canyon Campground, Carson National Forest Community Affairs Office, 208 Cruz Alta Rd., 87571. T: (505) 758-6200. www.fs.fed.us/r3/carson/html_main/list_camping2.html. RV/tent: 12. $10. Hookups: none.

La Junta Campground, Carson National Forest Community Affairs Office, 208 Cruz Alta Rd., 87571. T: (505) 758-6200. www.fs.fed.us/r3/carson/html_main/list_camping2.html. RV/tent: 8. $10. Hookups: none.

Rio Rancho

Stagecoach Stop RV Resort, 3650 Hwy. 528, 87124. T: (888) 272-PARK. F: (505) 867-1890. RV/tent: 85. $21–$25. Hookups: electric (30, 50 amps), water, sewer.

Rociada

Pendaries RV Park, P.O. Box 697, 87742. T: (800) 820-8304 or (505) 454-8304. F: (505) 425-6989. www.pendariesrvpark.com. RV/tent: 30. $25. Hookups: electric (20, 30, 50 amps), water, sewer.

Rodeo

Mountain Valley Lodge, 88056. T: (505) 557-2267. www.rodeonewmexico.com/rvparks. RV/tent: 13. $6–$12. Hookups: electric (30, 50 amps), water, sewer.

Roswell

Bottomless Lakes State Park, HC 12 Box 1200, 88201. T: (505) 624-6058. www.emnrd.state.nm.us/nmparks. RV/tent: 76. $8–$18. Hookups: electric (20, 30 amps).

Town & Country RV Park, 331 West Brasher Rd., 88203. T: (800) 499-4364 or (505) 624-1833. www.roswell-usa.com/tandcrv. RV/tent: 131. $18–$20. Hookups: electric (30, 50 amps), water, sewer.

Ruidoso

Blue Spruce RV Park, 302 Mechem, 88345. T: (505) 257-7993. RV/tent: 23. $17. Hookups: electric (30 amps), water, sewer.

Bonito Hollow RV Park, P.O. Box 349, 88312. T: (505) 336-4325. RV/tent: 71. $18–$23. Hookups: electric (20, 30, 50 amps), water, sewer.

Pine Ridge RV Campground, 124 Glade Dr., 88345. T: (505) 378-4164. RV/tent: 73. $16–$21. Hookups: electric (20, 30, 50 amps), water, sewer.

Twin Spruce RV Park, 621 Hwy. 70 West, 88245. T: (505) 257-4310. RV/tent: 102. $25–$26. Hookups: electric (20, 30, 50 amps), water, sewer.

Ruidoso Downs

Circle B RV Park, Box 1800, 88346. T: (505) 378-4990. RV/tent: 202. $18. Hookups: electric (20, 30, 50 amps), water, sewer.

Seeping Springs Trout Lakes & Campground, P.O. Box 997, 88346. T: (505) 378-4216. RV/tent: 65. $20. Hookups: electric (30 amps), water, sewer.

Santa Fe

Hyde Memorial State Park, 740 Hyde Park Rd., 87501. T: (505) 983-7175. www.emnrd.state.nm.us/nmparks/pages/parks/hyde/hyde.htm. RV/tent: 50. $8–$18. Hookups: electric (20, 30 amps).

Los Campos de Santa Fe RV Park, 3574 Cerrillos Rd., 87505. T: (800) 852-8160 or (505) 473-1949. F: (505) 471-9220. RV/tent: 95. $25. Hookups: electric (30, 50 amps), water, sewer.

Rancheros de Santa Fe Campground, 736 Old Las Vegas Hwy., 87505. T: (800) 426-9259 or (505) 466-3482. www.rancheros.com. RV/tent: 121. $26. Hookups: electric (15, 20, 30, 50 amps), water, sewer.

Santa Fe KOA, 934 Old Las Vegas Hwy., 87505. T: (800) 562-1514 or (505) 466-1419. www.koa.com/where/NM/31159. RV/tent: 51. $20–$30. Hookups: electric (30, 50 amps), water, sewer.

NEW MEXICO (continued)

Santa Fe (continued)

Trailer Ranch RV Park, 3471 Cerrillos Rd., 87505. T: (505) 471-9970. www.trailler ranch.com. RV/tent: 42. $25–$28. Hookups: electric (30, 50 amps), water, sewer.

Santa Rosa

Santa Rosa KOA, Box 423, 88435. T: (800) 562-0836 or (505) 472-3126. F: (505) 472-3883. www.koa.com/where/NM/31143. RV/tent: 100. $18–$25. Hookups: electric (20, 30, 50 amps), water, sewer.

Santa Rosa Lake State Park, P.O. Box 384, 88433. T: (505) 472-3110. www.emnrd.state.nm.us/nmparks/pages/parks/santa/Santa.htm. RV/tent: 90. $8–$18. Hookups: electric (20, 30 amps).

Seneca

Clayton Lake State Park, Rte. Box 20, 88437. T: (505) 374-8808. www.emnrd.state.nm.us/nmparks/pages/parks/clayton/clayton.htm. RV/tent: 33. $8–$18. Hookups: electric (20, 30 amps).

Silver City

Cedar Ridge RV Park & Campground, 2789 South Hwy. 90, 88061. T: (505) 388-4013. RV/tent: 15. $12. Hookups: electric (20, 30 amps), water, sewer.

Silver City KOA, 11824 Hwy. 180 East, 88061. T: (800) 562-7623 or (505) 388-3351. F: (505) 388-0461. www.koa.com. RV/tent: 77. $18–$27. Hookups: electric (20, 30, 50 amps), water, sewer.

Socorro

Casey's Socorro RV Park, P.O. Box 641, 87801. T: (800) 687-2696 or (505) 835-2234. F: (505) 835-2234. RV/tent: 103. $13. Hookups: electric (30 amps), water, sewer, cable.

Western Motel & RV Park, 404 1st St., 87825. T: (505) 854-2417. F: (505) 854-3217. RV/tent: 12. $15. Hookups: electric (20, 30, 50 amps), water, sewer.

Taos

Enchanted Moon RV Park, 7 Valle Escondido Rd., 87571. T: (505) 758-3338. RV/tent: 69. $20. Hookups: electric (20, 30, 50 amps), water, sewer.

Taos Valley RV Park & Campground, Box 7204 NDCBU, 120 Este Es Rd., 87571. T: (800) 999-7571 or (505) 758-4469. www.camp taos.com/rv. RV/tent: 92. $22–$27. Hookups: electric (20, 30, 50 amps), water, sewer.

Taos Canyon

Capulin Campground, Carson National Forest Community Affairs Office, 208 Cruz Alta Rd., 87571. T: (505) 758-6200. www.fs.fed.us/r3/carson/html_main/list_camping2.html. RV/tent: 11. $10. Hookups: none.

La Sombra Campground, Carson National Forest Community Affairs Office, 208 Cruz Alta Rd., 87571. T: (505) 758-6200. www.fs.fed.us/r3/carson/html_main/list_camping2.html. RV/tent: 13. $10. Hookups: none.

Las Petacas Campground, Carson National Forest Community Affairs Office, 208 Cruz Alta Rd., 87571. T: (505) 758-6200. www.fs.fed.us/r3/carson/html_main/list_camping2.html. RV/tent: 9. $10. Hookups: none.

Tijeras

Hidden Valley Resort, 844B East Hwy. 66, 87059. T: (800) 326-2024 or (505) 281-3363. RV/tent: 99. $18–$23. Hookups: electric (30, 50 amps), water, sewer.

Mountain View Campground & RV Park, 768 Hwy. 66 East, 87059. T: (888) 284-2343 or (505) 281-2343. RV/tent: 24. $15–$18. Hookups: electric (30 amps), water, sewer.

Truth or Consequences

Cielo Vista RV Park, 501 South Broadway, 97901. T: (888) 414-8478 or (505) 894-3738. RV/tent: 72. $21. Hookups: electric (30, 50 amps), water, sewer.

RJ RV Park, 2103 South Broadway, 87901. T: (505) 894-9777. RV/tent: 47. $21. Hookups: electric (30, 50 amps), water, sewer.

Tucumcari

Tucumcari KOA, 6299 Quay Rd., 88401. T: (800) 562-1871 or (505) 461-1841. www.koa.com. RV/tent: 111. $15–$25. Hookups: electric (20, 30, 50 amps), water, sewer.

Tularosa

Mountain Meadow RV Park, 240 Mountain Meadow, 88352. T: (505) 585-4979. RV/tent: 32. $13. Hookups: electric (30 amps), water, sewer.

Vado

Vado RV Park, 16201 Las Aleuras, 88072. T: (505) 233-2573. RV/tent: 71. $16. Hookups: electric (30 amps), water, sewer.

Valle Vidal

Cimmarron Campground, Carson National Forest Community Affairs Office, 208 Cruz Alta Rd., 87571. T: (505) 758-6200. www.fs.fed.us/r3/carson/html_main/list_camping2.html. RV/tent: 36. $10. Hookups: none.

McCrystal Campground, Carson National Forest Community Affairs Office, 208 Cruz Alta Rd., 87571. T: (505) 758-6200. www.fs.fed.us/r3/carson/html_main/list_camping2.html. RV/tent: 60. $10. Hookups: none.

Villanueva

Villanueva State Park, P.O. Box 40, 87583. T: (505) 421-2957. www.emnrd.state.nm.us/nmparks/pages/parks/villanue/villanue.htm. RV/tent: 60. $8–$18. Hookups: electric (20, 30 amps).

Williamsburg

Shady Corner RV Park, Broadway & Rio Grande, 87942. T: (505) 894-7698. RV/tent: 6. $12. Hookups: electric (30, 50 amps), water, sewer.

NEW YORK

Acra

Whip-O-Will Campsite, P.O. Box 327, 12473-0327. T: (518) 622-3277 or (800) WOW-CAMP. RV/tent: 304. $20–$24. Hookups: water, electric (20, 30, 50 amps), sewer.

Addison

Sunflower Acres Family Campground, 8355 Tinkertown Rd., 14801. T: (607) 523-7756. RV/tent: 71. $16–$20. Hookups: water, electric (20, 30, 50 amps), sewer.

Afton

Kellystone Park Campsite, 51 Hawkins Rd., 13813-1602. T: (607) 639-1090. RV/tent: 95. $17–$21. Hookups: water, electric (15, 20, 30 amps) sewer.

Akron

Sleepy Hollow Lake Campground, 13801 Siehl Rd., 14001. T: (716) 542-4336. RV/tent: 200. $17–$21. Hookups: water, electric (20, 30, 50 amps).

Altamont

Thompson's Lake State Park, 68 Thompson's Lake, 12059. T: (518) 872-1674. RV/tent: 140. $13. Hookups: none.

Angelica

Evergreen Trails Campground, RD 1, Box 236, 14709. T: (716) 466-7993. RV/tent: 75. $18. Hookups: water, electric (20, 30 amps).

Angola

Evangola State Park, Shaw Rd., 14081. T: (716) 549-1802. RV/tent: 80. $13–$17. Hookups: electric (20 amps).

NEW YORK (continued)

Ausable

Holiday Travel Park, 428 Rte. 373, 12944. T: (518) 834-9216. RV/tent: 48. $15–$17. Hookups: water, electric (20, 30 amps), sewer.

Bainbridge

Oquaga Creek State Park, RD 2 Box 255, 13733. T: (607) 467-4160. RV/tent: 95. $13. Hookups: none.

Riverside RV Camping, 1303 Cr 39, 13733. T: (607) 967-2102. RV/tent: 14. $19. Hookups: water, electric (20, 30 amps), sewer.

Baldwinsville

Sunset Park Campground, 455 Sprague Rd., 13112-9746. T: (315) 635-6450. RV/tent: 233. $17–$19. Hookups: water, electric (20 amps).

Bath

Babcock Hollow Campground, 5932 Babcock Hollow Rd., 14910. T: (607) 776-7185. RV/tent: 93. $19.50. Hookups: water, electric (20, 30 amps), sewer.

Campers Haven, 6832 Cr-15 Knight Settlement Rd., 14910. T: (607) 776-0328. RV/tent: 136. $17.50–$19.50. Hookups: water, electric (15,20), sewer.

Bemus Point

Wildwood Acres, 506 Brown Rd., 14712. T: (716) 386-7037. RV/tent: 88. $20. Hookups: water, electric (20, 30, 50 amps), sewer.

Bloomingburg

Rainbow Valley Campground, 61 High St., 12721. T: (845) 733-4767. RV/tent: 85. $27. Hookups: water, electric (15, 20, 30 amps), sewer.

Bolton Landing

Scenic View Campground, P.O. Box 172, Rte. 9 North, 12814. T: (518) 644-2115. RV/tent: 100. $22–$32. Hookups: water, electric (20, 30 amps).

Boonville

Pixley Falls State Park, 11430 State Hwy. 46, 13309. T: (315) 942-4713. RV/tent: 22. $13–$17. Hookups: none.

Bristol Center

Bristol Woodlands Campground, 3300 Eastlake Rd., No. 4C, 14424. T: (716) 229-2290. RV/tent: 86. $15–$22. Hookups: water, electric (30 amps), sewer.

Brockton

Lake Erie State Park, RD 1, 14716. T: (716) 792-9214. RV/tent: 97. $13–$17. Hookups: electric.

Cambridge

Battenkill Sports Quarters/Campground, 937 State Rte. 313, 12816. T: (800) 676-8768. RV/tent: 60. $20. Hookups: water, electric (15 amps).

Canandaigua

Creek Side Campground, 2528 Wheeler Station Rd., 14469-9326. T: (716) 657-7746. RV/tent: 40. $12–$15. Hookups: water, electric (20, 30 amps), sewer.

Candor

Buckridge Nudist Park, 215 Turtle Hill Rd., 13743. T: (888) 231-3268. RV/tent: 40. $32–$39. Hookups: water, electric (20 amps).

Cape Vincent

Burnham Point State Park, 34075 State Rte. 12e, 13618. T: (315) 654-2522. RV/tent: 49. $13–$17. Hookups: electric.

Caroga Lake

Caroga Lake Campgrounds, Co Hwy. 343, 12032. T: (518) 835-4241. RV/tent: 161. $9. Hookups: none.

Cazenovia

Chittenango Falls State Park, 2300 Rathbun Rd., 13035. T: (315) 655-9620. RV/tent: 22. $13. Hookups: none.

Central Bridge

Hide-A-Way Campsites, P.O. Box 58, 12035. T: (518) 868-0075. RV/tent: 50. $18. Hookups: water, electric (20, 30, 50 amps).

Locust Park Campground, Box 225, 12035. T: (518) 668-9927. RV/tent: 32. $15–$19. Hookups: water, electric (20, 30 amps), sewer.

Chateaugay

High Falls Park Campground, Box 918, 12920. T: (518) 497-3156. RV/tent: 217. $16–$18. Hookups: water, electric (20, 30, 50 amps), sewer.

Chestertown

Rancho Pines, Schroon River Rd., 12817. T: (518) 494-3545. www.ranchopines.com. RV/tent: 55. $18–$23. Hookups: water, electric (20, 30 amps), sewer, cable.

Riverside Pines Campsites, 3 Carl Turner Rd., 12817. T: (518) 654-2280. RV/tent: 70. $21. Hookups: water, electric (20, 30 amps), sewer.

Clayton

Cedar Point State Park, 36661 Cedar Point Dr, 13624. T: (315) 654-2522. RV/tent: 176. $19–$22. Hookups: water, electric, sewer.

Riverside Acres Campground & Motel, 38447 State Hwy. 12e, 13624. T: (315) 686-4001. RV/tent: 72. $18. Hookups: water, electric (20, 30 amps), sewer.

Cohocton

Tumble Hill Campground, 10551 Atlanta Back Rd., 14826. T: (716) 384-5248. RV/tent: 40. $22. Hookups: water, electric (15, 20, 30 amps), sewer.

Cold Spring

Clarence Fahnestock Memorial State Park, Rte. 301, 10512. T: (845) 225-7207. RV/tent: 81. $10–$13. Hookups: none.

Cooperstown

Cooperstown Famous Family Tent & Trailer Campground, 230 Petkewec Rd., 13326. T: (607) 293-7766. RV/tent: 100. $22–$24. Hookups: water, electric (30, 50 amps), sewer.

Cooperstown Ringwood Farms Campground, RD 2, Box 721, 13326. T: (800) 231-9114. RV/tent: 86. $25. Hookups: water, electric (20, 30 amps), sewer.

Corinth

River Road Campground, 5254 Rte. 9 North, 12822. T: (518) 654-6630. RV/tent: 80. $25–$28. Hookups: water, electric (20, 30 amps), sewer.

Rustic Barn Campsites, 4757 Rte. 9 North South, 12822. T: (518) 654-6588. RV/tent: 55. $21. Hookups: water, electric (20, 30 amps).

Cortland

Yellow Lantern Kampground, 1770 State Hwy. 13 North, 13045. T: (607) 756-2959. RV/tent: 250. $18–$20. Hookups: water, electric (20, 30 amps), sewer.

Cuba

Uncle Bo's RV Park, 5239 Maple Ln., 14727. T: (716) 968-1677. RV/tent: 34. $20. Hookups: water, electric (30, 50 amps).

Cuddebackville

Oakland Valley Campground, 399 Oakland Valley Rd., 12729. T: (845) 754-8732 or (800) 832-2254. F: (845) 754-7821. RV/tent: 110. $25–$35. Hookups: water, electric (15, 30 amps).

Cutchogue

Cliff & Ed's Trailer Park, P.O. Box 751, 11935. T: (631) 298-4091. RV/tent: 23. $25. Hookups: water, electric (30, 50 amps), sewer.

Dansville

Skybrook Campground, 0861 Mccurdy Rd., 14437. T: (716) 335-6880. RV/tent: 470. $20–$25. Hookups: water, electric (15, 20, 30 amps), sewer.

Stony Brook State Park, 10820 Rte. 36 South, 14437. T: (716) 335-8111. RV/tent: 125. $13–$15. Hookups: water, electric (15, 20 amps), sewer.

Darien Center

Darien Lake State Park, 10289 Harlow Rd., 14040. T: (716) 547-9242. RV/tent: 158. $13–$15. Hookups: water, electric (20, 30, 50 amps).

Delevan

Arrowhead Camping Area, Rte. 16, 14042. T: (716) 492-3715. RV/tent: 250. $15–$20. Hookups: water, electric (20, 30 amps).

NEW YORK (continued)

Downsville

Catskill Mountain Kampground, P.O. Box 356, 13755. T: (607) 363-2599. RV/tent: 100. $16–$21. Hookups: water, electric (15, 20, 30 amps), sewer.

Delaware Valley Campsite, HC 89, Box 36, 13755. T: (607) 363-2306. RV/tent: 88. $24. Hookups: water, electric (15, 20 amps), sewer.

Duane

Meacham Lake Campground, P.O. Box 53A, 12970. T: (518) 483-5116. RV/tent: 224. $10–$12. Hookups: none.

East Islap

Heckscher State Park, Heckscher Pkwy Prkng Field No. 1, 11730. T: (631) 581-2100. RV/tent: 69. $10–$13. Hookups: none.

East Springfield

Glimmerglass State Park, 1527 County Hwy. 31, 13333. T: (607) 547-8662. RV/tent: 36. $13. Hookups: none.

Elizaville

Brook–Wood Family Campground, County Rd. 8, 12523. T: (518) 537-6896 or (888) 588-8622. RV/tent: 138. $20–$24. Hookups: water, electric (15, 30, 50 amps), sewer.

Findley Lake

Paradise Bay Park, P.O. Box 446, Shadyside Rd., 14736. T: (716) 769-7582. RV/tent: 100. $20–$22. Hookups: water, electric (15, 20, 30, 50 amps).

Forestport

Kayuta Lake Campground, 10892 Campground Rd., 13338. T: (315) 831-5077. RV/tent: 164. $18–$25. Hookups: water, electric (20, 30, 50 amps), sewer.

Fort Ann

Fort Ann Campground, Clay Hill Rd., 12827. T: (518) 639-8840. RV/tent: 50. $19–$22. Hookups: water, electric (15, 20, 30 amps), sewer.

Franklinville

Memory Lake Campground, 3900 Jarecki Rd., Rte. 98, 14737. T: (716) 676-2776. RV/tent: 150. $20. Hookups: water, electric (30, 50 amps), sewer.

Gabriels

Buck Pond, Onchiota, 12939. T: (518) 891-3449. RV/tent: 116. $10–$12. Hookups: none.

Gainesville

Woodstream Campsites, 5440 School Rd., 14066. T: (877)-CAMPNOW. RV/tent: 200. $17–$22. Hookups: water, electric (15, 20, 30, 50 amps).

Galway

McConchies Heritage Acres, 2501 Northline Rd., 12074. T: (518) 882-6605. RV/tent: 190. $14–$20. Hookups: water, electric (15, 20, 30 amps).

Pop's Lake Campground, 518 Centerline Rd., 12074. T: (518) 883-8678. RV/tent: 80. $16–$18. Hookups: water, electric (15, 20 amps), sewer.

Gilboa

Nickerson Park Campground, Stryker Rd., 12076. T: (607) 588-7327. RV/tent: 200. $15–421. Hookups: water, electric (15, 20, 30 amps), sewer.

Glens Falls

Moreau Lake State Park, 605 Old Saratoga Rd., 12831. T: (518) 793-0511. RV/tent: 148. $13. Hookups: none.

Godeffroy

American Family Campground, 110 Guymard Turnpike, 12739. T: (845) 754-8388. RV/tent: 135. $28–$39. Hookups: water, electric (20, 30 amps), sewer.

Haines Falls

North/South Lake Campground, P.O. Box 347, 12436. T: (518) 589-5058. RV/tent: 219. $10–$16. Hookups: none.

Hamlin

Hamlin Beach Sate Park, 1 Camp Rd., 14464. T: (716) 964-2462. RV/tent: 264. $10–$13. Hookups: electric.

Hammond

McLear Cottage Colony & Campground, 2477 County Rte. 6, 13646. T: (315) 375-6508. RV/tent: 40. $20–$26. Hookups: water, electric (15, 20, 30 amps), sewer.

Harpursville

Belden Hill Campground, 1843 Rte. 7, 13787. T: (607) 693-1645. RV/tent: 142. $20–$28. Hookups: water, electric (20, 30 amps), sewer.

Henderson Harbor

Association Island RV Resort & Marina, Snowshoe Rd., 13651. T: (315) 938-5887. RV/tent: 307. Call for rate. Hookups: water, electric (20, 30, 50 amps), sewer.

Himrod

Back-Achers Campsite, 3112 Rte. 14, 14842. T: (607) 243-7926. RV/tent: 40. $17. Hookups: water, electric (30 amps).

Hubbardsville

Canaan Campground, Green Rd., 13355. T: (315) 691-2005. RV/tent: 48. $20. Hookups: water, electric (30 amps), sewer.

Hudson

Lake Taghkanic State Park, 1528 State Rte. 82, 12502-5103. T: (518) 851-3631. RV/tent: 51. $10–$12. Hookups: none.

Indian Lake

Lewey Public Campground, Rte. 30, 12864. T: (518) 648-5266. RV/tent: 209. $10–$12. Hookups: none.

Inlet

Limekiln Lake, Rte. 28, 13360. T: (315) 357-4401. RV/tent: 271. $12. Hookups: none.

Ithaca

Buttermilk Falls State Park, RD 10, 14850. T: (607) 273-5761. RV/tent: 46. $13. Hookups: none.

Robert H. Treman State Park, RD 10, 14850. T: (607) 273-3440. RV/tent: 72. $13–$15. Hookups: electric.

Taughannock Falls State Park, P.O. Box 1055, 14886-1055. T: (607) 387-6739. RV/tent: 79. $10–$13. Hookups: electric.

Jamestown

Hidden Valley Camping Area, 299 Kiantone Rd., 14701. T: (716) 569-5433. RV/tent: 215. $18–$23. Hookups: water, electric (20, 30 amps).

Johnstown

Royal Mountain Campsite, 4948 Hwy. 29, 12095. T: (518) 762-1946. RV/tent: 65. $17. Hookups: water, electric (15, 20 amps).

Keeseville

Poke-O-Moonshine, Box 163B, 12944. T: (518) 834-9045. RV/tent: 25. $10–$13. Hookups: none.

Kendaia

Sampson State Park, 6096 Rte. 96a, 14541. T: (315) 585-6392. RV/tent: 309. $13–$16. Hookups: none.

Kennedy

Forest Haven Campground, 2329 Page Rd., 14747. T: (716) 267-5902. RV/tent: 102. $12–$17. Hookups: water, electric (20, 30 amps), sewer.

Keuka

Keuka Lake State Park, 3370 Pepper Rd., 14478. T: (315) 536-3666. RV/tent: 150. $13–$16. Hookups: water, electric.

Lake George

King Phillips Family Campsite, P.O. Box 592, 12845. T: (518) 668-5763. RV/tent: 170. $27. Hookups: water, electric (20, 30 amps), sewer.

Lake George Battleground Campground, Box 220, 12845. T: (518) 668-3348. RV/tent: 60. $10–$16. Hookups: none.

Rainbow View Family Campground, Rte. 9, 12845. T: (518) 623-9444. RV/tent: 130. $28–$31. Hookups: water, electric (30 amps), sewer.

Whippoorwill Campground, RR 3 Box 3347, 12845. T: (518) 668-5565. RV/tent: 45. $20–$25. Hookups: water, electric (20, 30 amps) sewer.

Lake Luzerne

Lake Luzerne State Park, Hudson St. Ext., 12885. T: (518) 696-2031. RV/tent: 174. $12–15. Hookups: none.

NEW YORK (continued)

Mt. Kenyon Family Campground, Warrensburg, 12845. T: (518) 696-2905. RV/tent: 110. $20–$23. Hookups: water, electric (15, 20 amps), sewer.

Lake Placid

Whispering Pines Campground, Cascade Rd., Rte. 73, 12946. T: (518) 523-9322. RV/tent: 80. $20–$25. Hookups: water, electric (15, 20 amps), sewer.

Lake Pleasant

Little Sand Point, Lake Pleasant, 12108. T: (518) 548-7585. RV/tent: 78. $10. Hookups: none.

Moffitt Beach Campground, Rte. 8 Page St., 12164. T: (518) 548-7102. RV/tent: 260. $10–$12. Hookups: none.

Lakeville

Conesus Lake Campground, 5609 East Lake Rd., 14435. T: (716) 346-5472. RV/tent: 115. $20–$25. Hookups: water, electric (15, 20 amps).

Lewis

Magic Pines Family Campground, P.O. Box 411, 12950. T: (518) 873-2288. RV/tent: 37. $20–$34. Hookups: water, electric (20, 30 amps), sewer.

Livingston Manor

Beaverkill Campground, Rr3 Box 243, 12776. T: (914) 439-4281. RV/tent: 115. $12. Hookups: none.

Lockport

Niagara County Camping Resort, 7369 Wheeler Rd., 14094. T: (716) 434-3991. RV/tent: 154. $15–$21. Hookups: water, electric (30, 50 amps), sewer.

Long Lake

Lake Eaton Campground, Rte. 30, 12847. T: (518) 624-2641. RV/tent: 135. $10–$12. Hookups: none.

Lake Harris Campground, Long Lake, 12847. T: (518) 582-2403. RV/tent: 89. $10–$12. Hookups: none.

Lowville

Whetstone Gulf State Park, RD 2, Box 69, 13367. T: (315) 376-6630. RV/tent: 56. $13. Hookups: none.

Marathon

Country Hills Campground, 1165 Muckey Rd., 13803. T: (607) 849-3300. RV/tent: 119. $15–$22. Hookups: water, electric (20, 30, 50 amps). sewer.

Massena

Robert Moses State Park, Box 548, 13662. T: (315) 769-8663. RV/tent: 168. $13–$17. Hookups: electric.

Mexico

KOA-Mexico Campground, 291 Tubbs Rd., 13114. T: (315) 963-3509. RV/tent: 75. $18–$28. Hookups: water, electric (20, 30, 50), sewer.

Middleburgh

Max V. Shaul State Park, Box 23, 12071. T: (518) 827-4711. RV/tent: 30. $13. Hookups: none.

Millerton

Copake Falls Area (Taconic State Park), Millerton, 12546. T: (518) 329-3993. RV/tent: 112. $13–$14. Hookups: none.

Montauk

Hither Hill State Park, RR 2 Box 206a, 11954. T: (613) 668-3781. RV/tent: 165. $16. Hookups: none.

Montezuma

Hejamada Campground & RV Park, P.O. Box 429, 748 McDonald Rd., 13117. T: (315) 776-5887. RV/tent: 185. $21–$28. Hookups: water, electric (20, 30, 50 amps), sewer.

Montgomery

Winding Hills Park, 211 Rte. 416, 12549. T: (914) 457-4918. RV/tent: 51. $10–15. Hookups: water, electric (15 amps).

Moravia

Fillmore Glen State Park, RD 3, Box 26, 13118. T: (315) 497-0130. RV/tent: 60. $13. Hookups: none.

Morristown

Jacques Cartier State Park, River Rd., Box 178, 13664. T: (315) 375-6371. RV/tent: 92. $13–17. Hookups: electric.

Morrisville

Cedar Valley Campsites, RD 1 Box 176, 13408. T: (315) 684-3033. RV/tent: 55. $12–$18. Hookups: water, electric (30 amps), sewer.

Nassau

Dingmans Family Campground, RD 2 Box 459, 12123. T: (518) 766-2310. RV/tent: 60. $20. Hookups: water, electric (20, 30 amps).

Niagara Falls

Cinderella Campsite & Motel, 2797 Grand Island Blvd., 14072. T: (716) 773-4095. RV/tent: 90. $33–$35. Hookups: water, electric (15, 30, 50), sewer.

Niagara Falls Campground & Motel, 2405 Niagara Falls Blvd., 14304. T: (716) 731-3434. RV/tent: 65. $22–$28. Hookups: water, electric (15, 20, 30 amps), sewer.

North Java

Rolling Pines Campground & Resort, 5204 Youngers Rd., 14113. T: (716) 457-9644. RV/tent: 200. $23–$26. Hookups: water, electric (20, 15, 20, 30 amps), sewer.

Odessa

Cool-Lea Camps, Rte. 228, 14869. T: (607) 594-3500. F: (607) 594-4673. RV/tent: 57. $20–$22. Hookups: water, electric.

Ogdensburg

Eel Weir State Park, Eel Weir Rd., 13669. T: (315) 393-1138. RV/tent: 35. $13–15. Hookups: none.

KOA—Thousand Islands, 4707 Hwy. 37, 13669. T: (315) 393-3951. RV/tent: 105. $19–$27. Hookups: water, electric (15, 20, 30 amps) sewer.

Old Forge

Singing Waters Campground, Box 411, 13420. T: (315) 369-6618. RV/tent: 132. $22–$30. Hookups: water, electric (15, 20 amps), sewer.

Oneonta

Gilbert Lake State Park, 18 Ccc Rd., 13796. T: (607) 432-2114. RV/tent: 221. $13–15. Hookups: electric.

Susquehanna Trail Campsites, 4292 St. Hwy. 7, 13820. T: (607) 432-1122. RV/tent: 40. $20–$23. Hookups: water, electric (15, 30 amps), sewer.

Oswego

Sunset RV Park, 45 County Rd. 89, 13126. T: (315) 343-2166. RV/tent: 38. $19. Hookups: water, electric (15, 30 amps) sewer.

Ovid

Ridgewood Campground, 6590 South Cayuga Lake Rd., 14521. T: (607) 869-9787. RV/tent: 84. $20–$22. Hookups: water, electric (20, 30 amps), sewer.

Oxford

Bowman Lake State Park, 745 Bliven Sherman, 13830. T: (607) 334-2718. RV/tent: 198. $10–13. Hookups: none.

Palenville

Pine Hollow Campground, Hcr 1 Box 54, 12463. T: (518) 678-2245. RV/tent: 31. $19–$22. Hookups: water, electric (20, 30 amps).

Penn Yan

Wigwam Keuka Lake Campground, 3324 Esperanza Rd., 14478. T: (315) 536-6352. RV/tent: 60. $17–$21. Hookups: water, electric (30 amps).

Peru

Ausable Pines Campground, 3281 Lakeshore, 12972. T: (518) 561-1188. RV/tent: 130. $17–$19. Hookups: water, electric (30 amps), sewer.

Ausable Point Campground, RD 2, Box 152, 12972. T: (518) 561-7080. RV/tent: 123. $10–$19. Hookups: electric.

Iroquois RV & Campground, 270 Bear Swamp Rd., 12972. T: (518) 643-9057. RV/tent: 160. $22. Hookups: water, electric (20, 30 amps), sewer.

Petersburgh

Broken Wheel Campground, 61 Broken Wheel Rd., 12138. T: (518) 658-2925. RV/tent: 75. $15–$18. Hookups: water, electric (15, 20 amps).

Vista Valley Campground, 82 Armsby Rd., 12138. T: (518) 658-3559 or (877) 646-0653. RV/tent: 156. $20–$24. Hookups: water, electric (50 amps).

NEW YORK (continued)

Phelps

Junius Ponds Cabins & Campground, 1475 West Townline Rd., 14532. T: (315) 781-5120 or (315) 539-9008. RV/tent: 110. $21–$22. Hookups: water, electric (30, 50 amps), sewer.

Pike

Rolling Acres Golf & Campground, 7795 Dewitt Rd., 14130. T: (716) 567-5240. RV/tent: 100. $19. Hookups: water, electric (20, 30 amps).

Plattsburgh

Cumberland Bay State Park, 152 Cumberland Head Rd., 12901. T: (518) 563-5240. RV/tent: 208. $13–$15. Hookups: none.

Plattsburgh RV Park, 3 Crestview Dr, 12901. T: (518) 563-3915. RV/tent: 200. $15–$20. Hookups: water, electric (20, 30 amps), sewer.

Shady Oaks RV Park, 70 Moffit Rd., 12901. T: (518) 562-0561 or (888) 329-0899. F: (518) 562-3207. RV/tent: 103. $20. Hookups: water, electric (20, 30 amps).

Port Kent

Port Kent Campsite, 93 Rte. 373, P.O. Box 166, 12975. T: (518) 834-9011. RV/tent: 127. $18–$20. Hookups: water, electric (20, 30 amps), sewer.

Potter

Flint Creek Campgrounds, 1455 Phelps Rd., 14507. T: (716) 554-3567. RV/tent: 133. $17–$19. Hookups: water, electric (20, 30 amps) sewer.

Pottersville

Ideal Campground, Box 113, 12860. T: (518) 494-2096. RV/tent: 68. $19. Hookups: water, electric (20, 30 amps), sewer.

Wakonda Family Campground, 3901 East Schroon River Rd., 12860. T: (518) 494-2610. www.wakondacampground.com. RV/tent: 134. $27–$31. Hookups: water, electric (20, 30 amps), sewer.

Prattsburgh

Wagon Wheel Campground, 10378 Presler Rd., 14873. T: (607) 522-3270. RV/tent: 95. $17–$21. Hookups: water, electric (30, 50 amps).

Pulaski

Bear's Sleepy Hollow RV Park, 7065 SR-3, 13142. T: (315) 298-5560. RV/tent: 65. $15–$22. Hookups: water, electric (20, 30 amps), sewer.

Rainbow Shores Campsite, 348 Rainbow Shores Rd., 13142. T: (315) 298-4407. RV/tent: 144. $20. Hookups: water, electric (15, 20, 30), sewer.

Randolph

JJ's Pope Haven, Rte. 241 Pope Rd., 14772. T: (716) 358-4900. F: (716) 358-2313. RV/tent: 130. $19–$21. Hookups: water, electric (30, 50 amps).

Raquette Lake

Brown Tract Pond Campground, Raquette Lake, 13436. T: (315) 354-4412. RV/tent: 90. $10–$13. Hookups: none.

Golden Beach, Raquette Lake, 13436. T: (315) 354-4230. RV/tent: 205. $10–$14. Hookups: none.

Rhinebeck

Interlake RV Park, 428 Lake Dr., 12572. T: (845) 266-5387. www.interlakervpark.com. RV/tent: 159. $28–$31. Hookups: water, electric (20, 30 amps), sewer.

Ripley

Lakeside Campground, 10768 Rte. 5, 14775. T: (716) 736-3362 or (800) 669-5404. F: (716) 736-3362. RV/tent: 75. $15–$21. Hookups: electric (30, 50 amps), sewer.

Rome

Delta Lake State Park, 8797 State Rte. 46, 13440. T: (315) 337-4670. RV/tent: 101. $13–$15. Hookups: none.

Sackets Harbor

Allen's Boat Livery & Campground, 16750 Allen Dr, 13685. T: (315) 646-2486. RV/tent: 155. $10–$14. Hookups: water, electric (15, 20, 30 amps), sewer.

Wescott Beach State Park, Sackets Harbor, 13685. T: (315) 938-5083. RV/tent: 166. $10–$13. Hookups: electric.

Salamanca

Allegany State Park (Quaker Area), 2373 Rte. 1, 14779. T: (716) 354-2182. RV/tent: 64. $10–$13. Hookups: electric (20 amps).

Allegany State Park (Redhouse Cabins), 2373 Asp Rte. 1, 14779. T: (716) 354-9121. RV/tent: 133. $10–$13. Hookups: electric.

Saranac

Baker's Acres Campground, P.O. Box 115, 12981. T: (518) 293-6471. RV/tent: 50. $15. Hookups: water, electric (15 amps), sewer.

Saranac Lake

Meadowbrook Campground, Saranac Lake, 12983. T: (518) 891-4351. RV/tent: 62. $10. Hookups: none.

Schroon Lake

Sharp Bridge Campground, Rte. 9, 12855. T: (518) 532-7538. RV/tent: 40. $9. Hookups: none.

Schuyler Falls

Macomb Reservation State Park, 201 Campsite Rd., 12985. T: (518) 643-9952. RV/tent: 175. $13–$14. Hookups: none.

Schuylerville

Schuyler Yacht & Campground, 1 Ferry St., 12871. T: (518) 695-3193. RV/tent: 31. $20. Hookups: water, electric (15, 20 amps), sewer.

Scotia

Arrowhead Marina & RV Park, 2 Van Buren Ln., 12302. T: (518) 382-8966. RV/tent: 68. $16–$18. Hookups: water, electric (20, 30 amps), sewer.

Seneca Falls

Cayuga Lake Campground, 2546 State Rte. 89, 13148. T: (315) 568-0919. RV/tent: 74. $18–$20. Hookups: water, electric (15, 20 amps), sewer.

Cayuga Lake State Park, 2678 Lower Lake Rd., 13148. T: (315) 568-5163. RV/tent: 286. $15. Hookups: electric.

Oak Orchard Marina & Campground, P.O. Box 148, Rte. 89 at Mays Point, 13148. T: (315) 365-3000. RV/tent: 75. $19–$25. Hookups: water, electric (15, 20, 30 amps), sewer.

Smithtown

Blydenburgh, Suffolk Cnty Pks Box 144, 11796. T: (631) 853-4966. RV/tent: 50. $13–$23. Hookups: none.

Sodus Point

South Shore RV Park, 7867 Lake Rd., 14555. T: (315) 483-8649. RV/tent: 68. $20–$24. Hookups: water, electric (20, 30 amps), sewer.

South Colton

Higley Flow State Park, South Colton, 13687. T: (315) 262-2880. RV/tent: 135. $13–$19. Hookups: electric.

Springwater

Holiday Hill Campground, 7818 Marvin Hill Rd., 14560. T: (716) 669-2600. RV/tent: 100. $25–$28. Hookups: water, electric (20, 30 amps).

Stone Ridge

So-Hi Campground, P.O. Box 379, 12484. T: (845) 687-7377. RV/tent: 130. $20–$22. Hookups: water, electric (20, 30 amps), sewer.

Stony Point

Harriman State Park, Stony Point, 10980. T: (845) 786-2701. RV/tent: 200. $16. Hookups: none.

Swan Lake

Swan Lake Campground, P.O. Box 336W, 12783. T: (800) 733-0604 or (845) 292-4681. RV/tent: 100. $24–$26. Hookups: water, electric (30 amps), sewer, cable TV.

Sylvan Beach

Ta-Ga-Soke Campgrounds, 7820 Higginsville Rd., 13308. T: (800) 831-1744. RV/tent: 150. $21–$24. Hookups: water, electric (15, 20, 50 amps).

The Landing Campground, Kellogg Rd., 13157. T: (315) 245-9951. RV/tent: 94. $17–$25. Hookups: water, electric (15, 20, 30 amps), sewer, phone, cable TV.

NEW YORK (continued)

Syracuse

Foland Trailer Park, 407 North Midler Ave., 13206. T: (315) 463-1892. RV/tent: 10. $16.50. Hookups: water, electric (15, 20, 30 amps), sewer.

Three Mile Bay

Long Point State Park, 7495 State Park Rd., 13693. T: (315) 649-5258. RV/tent: 93. $13–$15. Hookups: none.

Ticonderoga

Paradox Lake Campground, Rte. 74, 12872. T: (518) 532-7451. RV/tent: 58. $9–$13. Hookups: none.

Putnam Pond Campsite, R.D. Chilson, 12818. T: (518) 585-7280. RV/tent: 72. $10–$12. Hookups: none.

Rogers Rock Campground, Rte. 9 North, 12836. T: (518) 585-6746. RV/tent: 321. $9–$13. Hookups: none.

Tupper Lake

Fish Creek Ponds Campgrounds, Star Rte. Box 75, 12983. T: (518) 891-4560. RV/tent: 355. $10–$16. Hookups: none.

Rollins Pond Campground, Star Rte. Box 75, 12983. T: (518) 891-3239. RV/tent: 288. $10–$14. Hookups: none.

Unadilla

KOA—Unadilla/I-88 Campground, RD 1 Box 186, 13775. T: (800) KOA-9032. RV/tent: 72. $24–$28. Hookups: water, electric (20, 30, 50 amps).

Utica

Elmtree Campsites, 131 Elmwood Rd., 13340. T: (315) 724-6678. RV/tent: 36. $18–$25. Hookups: water, electric (20, 30, 50 amps), sewer.

Verona

KOA—Rome/Verona Campground, 6591 Blackman's Corner Rd., 13478. T: (315) 336-7318. RV/tent: 93. $27. Hookups: water, electric (15, 20, 30, 50 amps), sewer.

Wadding River

Wildwood State Park, Box 518, 11792. T: (631) 929-4314. RV/tent: 320. $13–$18. Hookups: water, electric (15 amps), sewer.

Waddington

Coles Creek State Park, Rte. 37, P.O. Box 442, 13694. T: (315) 388-5636. RV/tent: 235. $13–$17. Hookups: electric.

Walton

Bear Spring Mountain, HC 63 Box 30, 13755. T: (607) 865-6989. RV/tent: 41. $10–$12. Hookups: none.

Warrensburg

Daggett Lake Campsites, 660 Glen Athol Rd., 12885. T: (518) 623-2198. www.daggettlake.com. RV/tent: 60. $18–$25. Hookups: water, electric (20 amps), sewer.

Glen Hudson Campsite, 564 River Rd., P.O. Box 35, 12885. T: (518) 623-9871. RV/tent: 100. $18–$22. Hookups: water, electric (15, 20, 30, 50 amps), sewer.

Warrensburg Travel Park, P.O. Box 277, 12885. T: (518) 623-9833. www.warrensburgtravelpark.com. RV/tent: 140. $25. Hookups: water, electric (15, 20 amps), sewer, cable TV.

Warsaw

Dream Lake Campground, 4391 Old Buffalo Rd., 14569. T: (716) 786-5172. RV/tent: 85. $21. Hookups: water, electric (15, 20, 30 amps), sewer.

Waterloo

Welcome Traveler Campground, 672 Packwood Rd., 13165. T: (315) 789-2102. RV/tent: 32. $15–$17. Hookups: water, electric (20, 30 amps).

Watertown

Kelly RV Park, 556 Eastern Blvd., 13601. T: (315) 782-5317. RV/tent: 17. $17. Hookups: water, electric (30 amps), sewer.

Weedsport

Riverforest Park Campground, 2526 River Forest Rd., 13166. T: (315) 834-9458. RV/tent: 250. $19–$22. Hookups: water, electric (20, 30 amps).

Wellsville

Breezy Point Campsite, 2749 Wolf Spring Rd., 14895. T: (716) 593-3085. RV/tent: 200. $18. Hookups: water, electric (20, 30 amps), sewer.

Westfield

Brookside Beach Campground, P.O. Box 130, 14787. T: (716) 326-3096. RV/tent: 70. $17–$22. Hookups: water, electric (30, 50 amps).

Westport

Barber Homestead Campground, P.O. Box 214, 12993. T: (518) 962-8989. RV/tent: 40. $22. Hookups: water, electric (20, 30, 50 amps).

Windham

White Birches Campsites, Nauvoo Rd., Box 35, 12496. T: (518) 734-3266. RV/tent: 130. $20. Hookups: water, electric (15, 20 amps).

Windsor

Pine Crest Campground, 280 NY 79, 13865. T: (607) 655-1515. RV/tent: 70. $19–$20. Hookups: water, electric (15 amps), sewer.

White Birches Campground, Box 35, Princess Nauvoo Rd., 13865. T: (607) 655-1515. RV/tent: 68. $20. Hookups: water, electric (20, 30 amps), sewer.

Wolcott

Cherry Grove Campground, Ridge Rd. East, 14590. T: (315) 594-8320. RV/tent: 90. $20–$22. Hookups: water, electric (20, 30 amps), sewer.

Lake Bluff Campground, 7150 Garner Rd., 14590. T: (888) 588-4517. RV/tent: 115. $20–$25. Hookups: water, electric (20, 30 amps), sewer.

Woodridge

Lazy "G" Campground, P.O. Box 563, 12789. T: (845) 434-3390. RV/tent: 70. $25. Hookups: water, electric (20, 30), sewer.

Woodville

Southwick State Park, 8119 Southwick Pl., 13650. T: (315) 938-5083. RV/tent: 112. $13–$15. Hookups: electric.

Youngstown

Niagara Frontier State Park, 1 Maintenance Ave., 14174. T: (716) 745-7273. RV/tent: 266. $13. Hookups: electric (15 amps).

NORTH CAROLINA

Advance

Thousand Trails–Forest Lake, 192 Thousand Trails Dr., 27006. T: (800) 722-6411. RV/tent: 265. $20. Hookups: water, electric (20, 30, 50 amps).

Almond

Turkey Creek Campground, P.O. Box 93, 28702-0093. T: (828) 488-8966. RV/tent: 60. $15–$17. Hookups: water, electric (20 amps).

Apex

Jordan Lake State Recreation Area (Parkers Creek), 280 State Park Rd., 27502. T: (919) 362-0586. ils.unc.edu/parkproject/ncparks.html. RV/tent: 250. $12–$17. Hookups: water, electric (20, 30 amps).

Jordan Lake State Recreation Area (Vista Point), 280 State Park Rd., 27502. T: (919) 362-0586. ils.unc.edu/parkproject/ncparks.html. RV/tent: 55. $12–$17. Hookups: water, electric (20, 30 amps).

Ararat

Homeplace Recreational Park, 136 Homeplace Park Rd., 27007. T: (336) 374-5173. www.homeplacerecreationpark.com. RV/tent: 152. $18–$20. Hookups: water, electric (30, 50 amps).

NORTH CAROLINA (continued)

Asheboro

Deep River Campground & RV Park, 814 McDowell Country Trail, 27203. T: (336) 629-4069. www.kiz.com/deepriver. RV/tent: 62. $16–$18. Hookups: water, electric (20, 30, 50 amps).

Holly Bluff Family Campground, 4846 NC Hwy. 49 South, 27203. T: (336) 857-2761. RV/tent: 85. $18. Hookups: water, electric 15, 20, 30, 50 amps).

Zooland Family Campground, 3671 Pisgah–Covered Bridge Rd., 27203. T: (336) 381-3422. RV/tent: 100. $14.50–$17. Hookups: water, electric (20, 30 amps).

Asheville

Asheville–Bear Creek RV Park, 81 South Bear Creek Rd., 28806. T: (828) 253-0798. RV/tent: 106. $26–$27. Hookups: water, electric (15, 20, 30, 50 amps).

Campfire Lodgings, 7 Appalachian Village Rd., 28804. T: (800) 933-8012. www.campfirelodgings.com. RV/tent: 21. $23–$35. Hookups: water, electric (20, 30, 50 amps).

Taps RV Park, P.O. Box 865, 28711. T: (828) 299-8277. RV/tent: 52. $23.50. Hookups: water, electric (15, 20, 30, 50 amps).

The French Broad River Campground, 1030 Old Marshall Hwy., 28804. T: (828) 658-0772. RV/tent: 53. $20–$21. Hookups: water, electric.

Avon

Sands of Time Campground, 125 North End Rd., 27915. T: (252) 995-5596. www.sandsoftimecampground.com. RV/tent: 36. $16–$24. Hookups: water, electric (20, 30, 50 amps), sewer.

Balsam

Moonshine Creek Campground, P.O. Box 10, 28707. T: (828) 586-6666. RV/tent: 92. $24. Hookups: water, electric (15, 20, 30 amps).

Boone

Appalachian Campground, 150 Hires Dr., 28607. T: (828) 264-4505. RV/tent: 75. $22. Hookups: water, electric (20, 30 amps).

Flintlock Family Campground, 171 Flintlock Campground Dr., 28607. T: (828) 963-5325. RV/tent: 100. $22. Hookups: water, electric (15, 20, 30, 50 amps).

KOA–Boone, 123 Harmony Mtn Ln., 28607. T: (828) 264-7250. RV/tent: 118. $24–$29. Hookups: water, electric (15, 20, 30, 50 amps).

Waterwheel RV Park, 1655 Hwy. 194 North, 28607. T: (828) 264-5165. RV/tent: 24. $17. Hookups: water, electric (15, 30 amps).

Boonville

Holly Ridge Family Campground, 5140 River Rd., 27011. T: (336) 367-7756. RV/tent: 62. $17.50–$21. Hookups: water, electric (20, 30, 50 amps).

Bryson City

Deep Creek Tube Center & Campground, P.O. Box 105, 28713. T: (828) 488-6055. RV/tent: 37. $18–$21.50. Hookups: water, electric (20, 30 amps).

Smoky Mountain Meadows Family Campground, 755 East Alarka Rd., 28713. T: (828) 488-3672. RV/tent: 53. $14–$15. Hookups: water, electric (15, 30 amps), sewer.

Burnsville

Black Mountain Campground, Pisgah National Forest, Appalachian Ranger District, Toecane Ranger Station, P.O. Box 128, 28714. T: (828) 682-6146. www.cs.unca.edu/nfsnc. RV/tent: 46. $13. Hookups: none.

Carolina Hemlock Park, Pisgah National Forest, Appalachian Ranger District, Toecane Ranger Station, P.O. Box 128, 28714. T: (828) 682-6146. www.cs.unca.edu/nfsnc. RV/tent: 32. $13. Hookups: none.

Candler

KOA–Asheville West, 309 Wiggins Rd., 28715. T: (828) 665-7015. RV/tent: 78. $22–$25. Hookups: water, electric (20, 30, 50 amps).

Cedar Island

Driftwood Campground, Hwy. 12 North, 28520. T: (252) 225-4861. RV/tent: 65. $14–$16. Hookups: water, electric (15, 20, 30 amps).

Cedar Mountain

Black Forest Family Camping Resort, P.O. Box 709, 28718. T: (828) 884-2267. RV/tent: 90. $22. Hookups: water, electric (20, 30, 50 amps).

Charlotte

Elmore Mobile Home Park, 4826 North Tryon St., 28213. T: (704) 597-1323. RV/tent: 25. $20. Hookups: water, electric (15, 20, 30, 50 amps).

Fleetwood RV Racing Camping Resort, 6550 Speedway Blvd., 28027. T: (704) 455-4445. www.gospeedway.com. RV/tent: 254. $15–$25. Hookups: water, electric.

Cherokee

Adventure Trail Campground, P.O. Box 1673, 28719. T: (828) 497-3651. RV/tent: 90. $22. Hookups: water, electric (15, 20, 30 amps).

Bradley's Campground, P.O. Box 88, 28719. T: (828) 497-6051. RV/tent: 42. $14–$15. Hookups: water, electric (15, 20, 30 amps).

Cherokee Campground, P.O. Box 516, 28719. T: (828) 497-9838. RV/tent: 70. $22. Hook--ups: water, electric (15, 20, 30 amps).

Flaming Arrow Campground, P.O. Box 533, 28719. T: (877) 497-6161. RV/tent: 85. $22.50–$27. Hookups: water, electric (20, 30, 50 amps).

Fort Wilderness Campground and RV Resort, P.O. Box 1657, 28719. T: (828) 497-9331. RV/tent: 120. $23. Hookups: water, electric (15, 30, 50 amps).

Great Smoky Mountain RV Camping Resort, 17 Old Soco Rd., 28789. T: (828) 497-2470. RV/tent: 251. $19. Hookups: water, electric (20, 30 amps).

Indian Creek Campground, 1367 Bunches Creek Rd., 28719. T: (828) 497-4361. RV/tent: 69. $16–$17. Hookups: water, electric (15 amps).

River Valley Campground, P.O. Box 471, 28719. T: (828) 497-3540. RV/tent: 200. $18.50–$21. Hookups: water, electric (20, 30, 50 amps).

Riverside Campground, P.O. Box 58, 28719. T: (828) 497-9311. RV/tent: 30. $18. Hookups: water, electric (15, 30 amps).

Chimney Rock

Creekside Mountain Camping, P.O. Box 251, 28710. T: (800) 248-8118. www.creeksidecamping.com. RV/tent: 90. $21–$23. Hookups: water, electric (15, 20, 30 amps).

Lake Lure RV Park & Campground, 176 Boys Camp Rd., 28746. T: (828) 625-9160. RV/tent: 70. $26–$35. Hookups: water, electric (15, 30 amps).

Coinjock

Hampton Lodge Camping Resort, 1631 Waterlily Rd., 27923. T: (252) 453-2732. RV/tent: 268. $18–$20. Hookups: water, electric (20, 30 amps).

Columbus

Silver Creek Campground, 410 Silver Creek Rd., 28756. T: (800) 510-1603. RV/tent: 62. $19–$21. Hookups: water, electric (20, 30 amps).

Denver

Wildlife Woods Campground, 4582 Beaver Blvd., 28673. T: (704) 483-5611. RV/tent: 305. $22–$27. Hookups: water, electric (15, 20, 30, 50 amps).

Elizabethtown

Jones Lake State Park, 113 Jones Lake Dr., 28337. T: (910) 588-4550. ils.unc.edu/parkproject/ncparks.html. RV/tent: 20. $12. Hookups: none.

Enfield

KOA–Enfield/Rocky Mtn., 101 Bell Acres, 27823. T: (252) 445-5925. RV/tent: 78. $17–$24. Hookups: water, electric (15, 20, 30 amps).

Fayetteville

Fayetteville Spring Valley Park, 4504 US Hwy. 301 South, 28348. T: (910) 425-1505. RV/tent: 36. $18.95–$23.75. Hookups: water, electric (20, 30 amps).

Fletcher

Rutledge Lake Travel Park, 170 Rutledge Rd., 28732. T: (828) 654-7873. www.campingnorthcarolina.com. RV/tent: 75. $20–$30. Hookups: water, electric (20, 30, 50 amps).

Fontana Village

Cable Cove Campground, Nantahala National Forest, Cheoah Ranger District, Rte. 1 Box 16-A, 28721. T: (828) 479-6431. www.cs.unca.edu/nfsnc. RV/tent: 26. $8. Hookups: none.

NORTH CAROLINA (continued)

Fort Mill

KOA–Charlotte/Fort Mill, 940 Gold Hill Rd., 29715. T: (803) 548-1148. RV/tent: 209. $22–$26. Hookups: water, electric (20, 30, 50 amps).

Foscoe

Grandfather Mountain Campground, P.O. Box 2060, 28607. T: (800) 788-2582. RV/tent: 149. $18.50–$22. Hookups: water, electric (20, 30, 50 amps).

Franklin

Carolina Village RV Resort, 20 Carolina Village Cir., 28734. T: (828) 369-5858 or (888) 818-5228. RV/tent: 16. $25. Hookups: water, electric (20, 30, 50 amps).

Cartoogechaye Creek Campground, 91 No Name Rd., 28734. T: (828) 524-8553. RV/tent: 103. $14–$16. Hookups: water, electric (30 amps).

Franklin RV Park, 145 Addington Bridge Rd., 28734. T: (828) 369-5841. RV/tent: 25. $14. Hookups: water, electric (20, 30 amps).

Mi Mountain Campground, 151 Mi Mountain Rd., 28734. T: (828) 524-6155. RV/tent: 48. $19.50. Hookups: water, electric (15, 30 amps).

Old Corundum Mill Campground, 80-33 Nickajack Rd., 28734. T: (828) 524-4663. www.travel.to/oldcorundum. RV/tent: 86. $18. Hookups: water, electric (20, 30 amps).

Rainbow Springs Campground, 7984 West Old Murphy Rd., 28734. T: (828) 524-6376. RV/tent: 51. $17. Hookups: water, electric (15, 30 amps).

Standing Indian Campground, Nantahala National Forest, Wayah Ranger District, 90 Sloan Rd., 28734. T: (828) 524-6441. www.cs.unca.edu/nfsnc. RV/tent: 84. $12. Hookups: none.

Frisco

Frisco Woods Campground, Cape Hatteras National Seashore, Hwy. 12, P.O. Box 159, 27936. T: (252) 995-5208. www.nps.gov/caha. RV/tent: 225. $22–$37. Hookups: water, electric (15, 20, 30 amps), sewer.

Hatteras Sands Camping Resort, P.O. Box 295, 27943. T: (252) 986-2422. hatsandscg@aol.com. RV/tent: 124. $31.20–$42.95. Hookups: water, electric (15, 20, 30, 50 amps).

Gatesville

Merchants Millpond State Park, 71 US Hwy. 158 East, 27938. T: (252) 357-1191. ils.unc.edu/parkproject/ncparks.html. RV/tent: 20. $12. Hookups: none.

Gatlinburg

Balsam Mountain (Cherokee, NC), Great Smoky Mountains National Park, 107 Park Headquarters Rd., 37738. T: (423) 436-1200. www.nps.gov/grsm. RV/tent: 46. $14. Hookups: none.

Deep Creek Camp (Bryson City, NC), Great Smoky Mountains National Park, 107 Park Headquarters Rd., 37738. T: (423) 436-1200. www.nps.gov/grsm. RV/tent: 92. $14. Hookups: none.

Glendale Springs

Raccoon Holler, P.O. Box 16, 28629. T: (336) 982-2706. RV/tent: 189. $16–$18. Hookups: water, electric (20, 30 amps).

Goldsboro

Cliffs of the Neuse State Park, 345-A Park Entrance Rd., 28578. T: (919) 778-6234. ils.unc.edu/parkproject/ncparks.html. RV/tent: 35. $12. Hookups: none.

Eastern Carolina Athletic Park, P.O. Box 160, 27863. T: (919) 580-1100. RV/tent: 22. $20. Hookups: water, electric (20, 30, 50 amps).

Grandy

Yogi Bear Jellystone/Currituck Resort Shores, 6671 Caratoke Hwy., 27939. T: (252) 453-226. RV/tent: 138. $26.50. Hookups: water, electric (20, 30, 50 amps).

Greensboro

Fields RV Campground, 2317 Campground Rd., 27406. T: (336) 292-1381. RV/tent: 29. $13. Hookups: water, electric (20, 30 amps).

Greensboro Campground, 1896 Trox St., 27406. T: (336) 274-4143. RV/tent: 117. $16–$21.50. Hookups: water, electric (20, 30, 50 amps).

Hayesville

Ho Hum Campground, 47 Ho Hum Loop, 28904. T: (828) 389-6740. RV/tent: 88. $20. Hookups: water, electric (15, 20, 30 amps).

Tusquittee Campground & Cabins, 9594 Tusquittee Rd., 28904. T: (828) 389-8520. RV/tent: 18. $15. Hookups: water, electric (15, 20, 30 amps).

Henderson

Bullocksville, Kerr State Recreation Area, 269 Glasshouse Rd., 27536. T: (252) 438-7791. ils.unc.edu/parkproject/ncparks.html. RV/tent: 69. $17. Hookups: water, electric (30 amps).

Henderson Point, Kerr State Recreation Area, 6254 Satterwhite Point Rd., 27536. T: (252) 438-7791. ils.unc.edu/parkproject/ncparks.html. RV/tent: 79. $17. Hookups: water, electric (30 amps).

Nutbush Bridge, Kerr State Recreation Area, 6254 Satterwhite Point Rd., 27536. T: (252) 438-7791. ils.unc.edu/parkproject/ncparks.html. RV/tent: 103. $17. Hookups: water, electric (30 amps).

Satterwhite Point, Kerr State Recreation Area, 269 Glasshouse Rd., 27536. T: (252) 438-7791. ils.unc.edu/parkproject/ncparks.html. RV/tent: 118. $17. Hookups: water, electric (30 amps).

Apple Valley Travel Park, 1 Apple Orchard Rd., 28792. T: (828) 685-8000. RV/tent: 93. $20. Hookups: water, electric (30 amps).

Lazy Boy Travel Park, 110 Old Sunset Hill Rd., 28792. T: (828) 697-7165. RV/tent: 83. $15. Hookups: water, electric (20, 30 amps).

Park Place RV Park, Rte. 2 Box 152B, 28731. T: (828) 693-3831. RV/tent: 48. $16. Hookups: water, electric (20, 30, 50 amps).

Phil & Ann's RV, 818 Tracy Grove Rd., 28731-9618. T: (800) 753-8373. RV/tent: 31. $11.99. Hookups: water, electric (15, 30 amps).

Red Gates RV Park, Rte. 19 Box 89, 28792. T: (828) 685-8787. RV/tent: 18. $14–$15. Hookups: water, electric (20, 30 amps).

Town Mountain Travel Park, 2030 Old Spartanburg Rd., 28792. T: (828) 697-6692. RV/tent: 26. $17. Hookups: water, electric (20, 30, 50 amps).

Highlands

Highlands RV Park, 651 Chestnut St., 28741. T: (828) 526-5985. RV/tent: 6. $40. Hookups: water, electric (20, 30, 50 amps).

Hot Springs

Hot Springs RV Park & Campground, P.O. Box 428, 28743. T: (828) 622-7676. RV/tent: 110. $20. Hookups: water, electric (15, 20, 30 amps).

Rocky Bluff Campground, Pisgah National Forest, Appalachian Ranger District, French Broad Ranger Station, P.O. Box 128, 28743. T: (828) 622-3202. www.cs.unca.edu/nfsnc. RV/tent: 30. $8. Hookups: none.

Jacksonville

Cabin Creek Campground & Mobile Home Park, 3200 Wilmington Hwy., 28540. T: (910) 346-4808. RV/tent: 81. $24. Hookups: water, electric (15, 30, 50 amps).

Kitty Hawk

Adventure Bound Campground, 1004 West Kitty Hawk Rd., 27949. T: (252) 255-1130. RV/tent: 20. $12. Hookups: none.

Colington Park Campground, 1608 Colington Rd., 27948. T: (252) 441-6128. RV/tent: 90. $18. Hookups: water, electric (15, 20, 30 amps).

Lake Toxaway

Outdoor Resorts–Blue Ridge, 1 Resorts Blvd., 28747. T: (828) 966-9350. RV/tent: 82. $48. Hookups: water, electric (20, 30, 50 amps).

Laurel Springs

Doughton Park Camp, Blue Ridge National Parkway, Blue Ridge Pkwy., Milepost 239.2, 28644. T: (336) 372-8568. www.nps.gov/blri. RV/tent: 135. $12. Hookups: none.

Linville Falls

Linville Falls Camp, Blue Ridge National Parkway, Blue Ridge Pkwy., Milepost 316.5, 28647. T: (828) 298-0398. www.nps.gov/blri. RV/tent: 70. $12. Hookups: none.

Linville Falls Trailer Lodge & Campground, P.O. Box 205, 28647. T: (828) 765-2681. RV/tent: 46. $20. Hookups: water, electric (15, 20, 30 amps).

NORTH CAROLINA (continued)

Little Switzerland

Crabtree Meadows Camp, Blue Ridge National Parkway, Blue Ridge Pkwy., Milepost 339.5, 28749. T: (828) 298-0398. www.nps.gov/blri. RV/tent: 93. $12. Hookups: none.

Littleton

Outdoor World–Lake Gaston Campground, Rte. 6 Box 236, 27850. T: (252) 586-4121. RV/tent: 191. $25. Hookups: water, electric (30, 50 amps).

Lumberton

Sleepy Bear's Family Campground, 465 Kenric Rd., 28360. T: (910) 739-4372. RV/tent: 80. $19. Hookups: water, electric (20, 30, 50 amps).

Maggie Valley

Meadowbrook Resort, 102 Meadowbrook Loop, 28751. T: (828) 926-1821. RV/tent: 28. $16. Hookups: water, electric (15, 20, 30 amps).

Stone Bridge RV Park, 1786 Soco Rd. US Hwy. 19, 28751. T: (828) 926-1904. RV/tent: 308. $20–$25. Hookups: water, electric (20, 30 amps).

Manteo

Cypress Cove Campground, 818 US 64, 27954. T: (252) 473-5231. www.outerbankscamping.com. RV/tent: 58. $17–$24. Hookups: water, electric (15, 20, 30 amps).

Marion

Buck Creek Campground, 1020 Tom's Creek Rd., 28752. T: (828) 724-4888. RV/tent: 64. $20. Hookups: water, electric (15, 20, 30, 50 amps).

Hidden Valley Campground and Waterpark, Rte. 1 Box 377, 28752. T: (828) 652-7208. RV/tent: 75. $21. Hookups: water, electric (20, 30 amps).

Mocksville

Lake Myers RV Resort, 150 Fred Lanier Rd., 27028. T: (336) 492-7736. RV/tent: 425. $26. Hookups: water, electric (20, 30 amps).

Morehead City

Waters Edge RV Park, 1463 Hwy. 24, 28570. T: (252) 247-0494. RV/tent: 86. $20–$25. Hookups: water, electric (20, 30, 50 amps).

Whispering Pines Family Campground, 25 Whispering Pines, 28570. T: (252) 726-4902. www.ncpines.com. RV/tent: 135. $22–$26. Hookups: water, electric (15, 20, 30, 50 amps).

Murphy

Creekside RV Park, 68 Old Peachtree Rd., 28905. T: (828) 837-4123. RV/tent: 23. $22. Hookups: water, electric (15, 20, 30, 50 amps).

Hanging Dog Campground, Nantahala National Forest, Tusquitee Ranger District, 123 Woodland Dr., 28906. T: (828) 837-5152. www.cs.unca.edu/nfsnc. RV/tent: 67. $8. Hookups: none.

Jackrabbit Mountain Camp, Nantahala National Forest, Tusquitee Ranger District, 123 Woodland Dr., 28906. T: (828) 837-5152. www.cs.unca.edu/nfsnc. RV/tent: 101. $12. Hookups: none.

Peace Valley Campground, P.O. Box 606, 28906. T: (828) 837-6223. RV/tent: 87. $18–$20. Hookups: water, electric (15, 30 amps).

Nebo

Lake James State Park, Rte. 2 Lake James Rd., Hwy. 126, 28761. T: (828) 652-5047. ils.unc.edu/parkproject/ncparks.html. RV/tent: 20. $12. Hookups: none.

New Bern

Neuse River Campground, 1565 B St., 28560. T: (252) 638-2556. RV/tent: 93. $17–$19. Hookups: water, electric (20, 30 amps), sewer.

Norlina

County Line Park, Kerr State Recreation Area, 6254 Satterwhite Point Rd., 27536. T: (252) 438-7791. ils.unc.edu/parkproject/ncparks.html. RV/tent: 82. $17. Hookups: water, electric (30 amps).

Kimball Point Park, Kerr State Recreation Area, 6254 Satterwhite Point Rd., 27536. T: (252) 438-7791. ils.unc.edu/parkproject/ncparks.html. RV/tent: 91. $17. Hookups: water, electric (30 amps).

Oak Island

Long Beach Campground, 5011 East Oak Island Dr., 28465. T: (910) 278-5737. RV/tent: 184. $18–$25. Hookups: water, electric (15, 20, 30 amps).

Ocracoke

Beachcomber Campground, P.O. Box 203, 27960. T: (252) 928-4031. RV/tent: 29. $20. Hookups: water, electric (30 amps).

Old Fort

Catawba Falls Campground, Rte. 3 Box 230, 28762. T: (828) 668-4831. RV/tent: 41. $12.50–$15.50. Hookups: water, electric (20, 30 amps).

Pinehurst

Village of Pinehurst RV Park, P.O. Box 5170, 28374. T: (910) 295-5452. RV/tent: 80. $21. Hookups: water, electric (20, 30, 50 amps).

Piney Creek

RiverCamp USA, P.O. Box 9, 28663-0009. T: (336) 359-2267. www.rivercamp.net. RV/tent: 74. $20. Hookups: water, electric (20, 30 amps).

Pink Hill

Maxwell's Mill Campground, 142 Maxwell's Mill Campground Rd., 28572. T: (252) 568-2022. RV/tent: 56. $20. Hookups: water, electric (20, 30, 50 amps).

Pinnacle

Pilot Mountain State Park, 1792 Pilot Knob Park Rd., 27043. T: (336) 325-2355. ils.unc.edu/parkproject/ncparks.html. RV/tent: 49. $12. Hookups: none.

Raleigh

William B. Umstead State Park, 8801 Glenwood Ave., 27612. T: (919) 571-4170. ils.unc.edu/parkproject/ncparks.html. RV/tent: 28. $12. Hookups: none.

Roaring Gap

Stone Mountain State Park, 3042 Frank Pkwy., 28668. T: (336) 957-8185. ils.unc.edu/parkproject/ncparks.html. RV/tent: 37. $12. Hookups: none.

Robbinsville

Cheoah Point Recreation Area, Nantahala National Forest, Cheoah Ranger District, Rte. 1 Box 16A, 28721. T: (828) 479-6431. www.cs.unca.edu/nfsnc. RV/tent: 26. $8. Hookups: none.

Hidden Waters RV Park & Campground, Rte. 3 Box 81, 28771. T: (828) 479-3509. RV/tent: 12. $15. Hookups: water, electric (30 amps).

Tsali Recreational Area, Nantahala National Forest, Cheoah Ranger District, Rte. 1 Box 16A, 28721. T: (828) 479-6431. www.cs.unca.edu/nfsnc. RV/tent: 42. $15. Hookups: none.

Rodanthe

Camp Hatteras, P.O. Box 10, 27968. T: (252) 987-2777. RV/tent: 336. $25.95–$45. Hookups: water, electric (30, 50 amps).

Ocean Waves Campground, P.O. Box 3576, 27982. T: (252) 987-2556. RV/tent: 68. $20–$22. Hookups: water, electric (20, 30, 50 amps).

Rodanthe Shoreline Campground, P.O. Box 272, 27968. T: (252) 987-1431. RV/tent: 10. $14.50–$18.25. Hookups: water, electric (30 amps).

Salisbury

Dan Nicholas Park (Rowan County Park), 6800 Bringle Ferry Rd., 28146. T: (704) 636-0154. RV/tent: 80. $15. Hookups: water, electric (20, 30 amps).

Salter Path

Arrowhead Campground, 1550 Salter Path Rd., 28512. T: (252) 247-3838. RV/tent: 171. $19. Hookups: water, electric (20, 30 amps).

Salter Path Family Campground, P.O. Box 2323, 28512-2323. T: (252) 247-3525. www.salterpathcamping.com. RV/tent: 205. $26–$38. Hookups: water, electric (20, 30 amps).

Sealevel

Cedar Creek Campground & Marina, 111 Canal Dr., 28577. T: (252) 225-9571. RV/tent: 70. $18. Hookups: water, electric (20, 30 amps).

NORTH CAROLINA (continued)

Selma

KOA–Selma/Smithfield, 428 Campground Rd., 27576. T: (919) 965-5923 or (800) 562-5897. RV/tent: 93. $18.50–$24.50. Hookups: water, electric (20, 30, 50 amps).

Shallotte

S & W RV Park, 532 Holden Beach Rd., 28470-1713. T: (910) 754-8576. RV/tent: 22. $16. Hookups: water, electric (30 amps).

Sea Mist Camping Resort, P.O. Box 1481, 28459. T: (910) 754-8916. RV/tent: 250. $18–$27. Hookups: water, electric (15, 30 amps).

Smithfield

Holiday Trav-L-Park Smithfield, 497 US Hwy. 701, 27524. T: (919) 934-3181. RV/tent: 104. $19.25–$20.75. Hookups: water, electric (20, 30 amps).

Spruce Pine

Bear Den Campground, R.F.D. 3 Box 284, 28777. T: (828) 765-2888. RV/tent: 144. $25–$31. Hookups: water, electric (15, 20, 30, 50 amps).

Buck Hill Campground, P.O. Box 238, 28664. T: (800) 387-5224. RV/tent: 59. $21. Hookups: water, electric (15, 20, 30 amps).

Secluded Valley Campground, 8551 19E South, 28657. T: (828) 765-4810. RV/tent: 58. $14. Hookups: water, electric (20, 30 amps).

Statesville

KOA–Statesville, 162 KOA Ln., 28677. T: (704) 873-556 or (800) KOA-5705. RV/tent: 88. $23–$27. Hookups: water, electric (20, 30, 50 amps).

Midway Campground & RV Resort, 114 Midway Dr., 28625. T: (704) 546-7615. RV/tent: 83. $27–$37. Hookups: water, electric (20, 30, 50 amps).

Stoneville

Dan River Campground, 724 Webster Rd., 27048. T: (336) 427-8530. RV/tent: 40. $15. Hookups: water, electric (20, 30, 50 amps).

Sunset Beach

Wishing Well Campground, 520 Seaside Rd. SW, 28468. T: (910) 579-7982. RV/tent: 39. $15. Hookups: water, electric (20, 30 amps).

Swannanoa

Mama Gertie's Hideaway Campground, 620 Patton Cove Rd., 28778. T: (828) 686-4258. RV/tent: 28. $18.50–$22.50. Hookups: water, electric (15, 20, 30, 50 amps).

Miles Motors RV Center & Campground, 15 Patton Cove Rd., 28778. T: (828) 686-3414. RV/tent: 61. $20. Hookups: water, electric (20, 30, 50 amps).

Swansboro

Waterway RV Park, P.O. Box 4847, 28594. T: (252) 393-8715. RV/tent: 334. $25. Hookups: water, electric (15, 20, 30, 50 amps).

Topton

Brookside Campground & Rafting, P.O. Box 93, 28781. T: (828) 321-5209. RV/tent: 46. $14. Hookups: water, electric (15, 20 amps).

Union Grove

Fiddlers Grove Campground, P.O. Box 11, 28689. T: (704) 539-4417. RV/tent: 40. $17–$20. Hookups: water, electric (15, 20, 30, 50 amps).

Van Hoy Farms Family Campground, P.O. Box 38, 28689. T: (704) 539-5493. RV/tent: 147. $21. Hookups: water, electric (15, 30, 50 amps).

Vilas

Vanderpool Campground, 1173 Charlie Thompson Rd., 28692. T: (828) 297-3486. RV/tent: 44. $18. Hookups: water, electric (30 amps).

Wade

KOA–Fayetteville, P.O. Box 67, 28395. T: (910) 484-5500 or (800) KOA-5350. RV/tent: 90. $24–$26. Hookups: water, electric (20, 30, 50 amps).

Washington

Twin Lakes Camping Resort & Yacht Basin, 1618 Memory Ln., 27817. T: (252) 946-5700. www.twinlakesnc.com. RV/tent: 379. $20–$28. Hookups: water, electric (20, 30, 50 amps).

Whichard's Beach Campground, P.O. Box 746, 27889. T: (252) 946-0011. www.whichards beach.com. RV/tent: 118. $20–$23. Hookups: water, electric (20, 30, 50 amps).

Waxhaw

Cane Creek Park (Union County Park), 5213 Harkey Rd., 28173. T: (704) 843-3919. RV/tent: 120. $14–$24. Hookups: water, electric (20, 30 amps), sewer.

Waynesville

Winngray Family Campground, 26 Winngray Ln., 28785. T: (828) 926-3170. RV/tent: 150. $20. Hookups: water, electric (15, 20, 30, 50 amps).

White Lake

Camp Clearwater Family Campground, 2038 White Lake Dr., 28337. T: (336) 862-3365. www.campclearwater.com. RV/tent: 910. $25–$35. Hookups: water, electric (20, 30, 50 amps), sewer.

Whittier

Holly Cove Campground & RV Resort, 341 Holly Cove Rd., 28789. T: (828) 631-0692. RV/tent: 49. $20. Hookups: water, electric (15, 30 amps).

Timberlake Campground, 3270 Conleys Creek Rd., 28789. T: (828) 497-7320. RV/tent: 54. $16.50–$20.50. Hookups: water, electric (15, 20, 30 amps).

Wilkesboro

Warrior Creek Park (Corps of Engineers–West Kerr Scott Reservoir), 499 Reservoir Rd., 28697. T: (336) 921-2177. www.reserveusa.com. RV/tent: 88. $12–$16. Hookups: water, electric (30 amps).

Wilmington

Camelot RV Park, 7415 Market St., 28411. T: (910) 686-7705. RV/tent: 107. $24–$28. Hookups: water, electric (15, 20, 30 amps).

NORTH DAKOTA

Arvilla

Turtle River State Park, 3084 Park Ave., 58214. T: (701) 594-4445. F: (701) 594-2556. trsp@state.nd.us. RV/tent: 125. $5–$12. Hookups: electric (20, 30, 50 amps), water.

Beulah

Dakota Waters Resort, P.O. Box 576, 58523. T: (800) 473-5803. RV/tent: 45. $8–$12. Hookups: electric (30 amps).

Bismarck

Bismark KOA, 3720 Centennial Rd., 58501. T: (701) 575-4261. bismkoa@aol.com. RV/tent: 128. $18–$25. Hookups: electric (30, 50 amps), water, sewer, modem.

General Sibley RV Park, 5001 South Washington St., 58504. T: (701) 222-1844. RV/tent: 19. $15. Hookups: electric (20, 30 amps), water, sewer.

Hill Crest Acres Campground, 5700 East Main Ave., 58501. T: (701) 255-4334. RV/tent: 57. $14. Hookups: electric (30, 50 amps), water, sewer.

Bowman

Twin Butte Campground & Antiques, Box 983, 58623. T: (701) 523-5569. RV/tent: 26. $12. Hookups: electric (20, 30 amps).

NORTH DAKOTA (continued)

Cavalier

Icelandic State Park, 13571 Hwy. 5, 58220. T: (800) 807-4723 or (701) 265-4561. isp@state.nd.us. RV/tent: 167. $7–$12. Hookups: electric (20, 30, 50 amps), water.

Church's Ferry

Wild Goose RV Park, HCR 1 Box 10, 58325. T: (701) 466-2324. RV/tent: 15. $10–$12. Hookups: electric (20, 30 amps).

Devils Lake

Graham's Island State Recreation Area, 152 South Duncan Dr., 58301. T: (800) 807-4723 or (701) 766-4015. www.state.nd.us/nd parks/Parks/DLSP.htm. dlsp@state.nd.us. RV/tent: 55. $3. Hookups: electric (30 amps), water.

Dickinson

Camp on the Heart, P.O. Box 1074, 58602. T: (701) 225-9600. camp@camponthe heart.com. RV/tent: 18. $18–$26. Hookups: electric (20, 30, 50 amps), water, sewer, cable, modem.

Dunseith

International Peace Garden Campground, Rte. 1 Box 116, 58367. T: (701) 263-4390. RV/tent: 4. $9–$14. Hookups: electric (20 amps), water.

Eckelson

Praire Haven Family Campground, 10121 36th St. East, 58481. T: (701) 646-2267. prairhvn@ictc.com. RV/tent: 51. $20. Hookups: electric (20, 30, 50 amps), water, sewer, modem.

Grafton

Leistikow Park Campground, P.O. Box 122, 58237. T: (701) 352-1842. RV/tent: 38. $9–$12. Hookups: electric (30, 50 amps), water, sewer.

Grand Forks

Grand Forks Campground & RV Park, Rte. 1 Box 227, 58201. T: (701) 772-6108. RV/tent: 149. $19. Hookups: electric (20, 30, 50 amps), water, sewer, modem.

Hillsboro

Hillsboro Campground & RV Park, 203 6th St. Southwest, 58045. T: (888) 430-5205 or (701) 436-5205. www.gocampingamerica.com/hills-borocampground. hillsborocampground@gocampingamerica.com. RV/tent: 35. $15. Hookups: electric (20, 30 amps), water, sewer, modem.

Jamestown

Frontier Fort Campground, P.O. Box 143, 58401. T: (701) 252-7492. RV/tent: 71. $16. Hookups: electric (30, 50 amps), water, sewer.

Jamestown Dam/Lakeside Marina, 3225 East Lakeside Rd., 58401. T: (701) 252-9200. RV/tent: 48. $9–$14. Hookups: electric (20, 30 amps), water.

Jamestown KOA, 3605 80th Ave. North, 58401. T: (701) 752-6262. ahc@pocketmail.com. RV/tent: 68. $18–$27. Hookups: electric (30, 50 amps), water, sewer, modem.

Lamoure

Lamoure County Memorial Park, P.O. Box 128, 58458. T: (701) 683-5856. RV/tent: 9. $8. Hookups: electric (15, 20 amps).

Linton

Sunrise Mobile Home Park & RV Camp, 146 Sunrise Ln., 58552. T: (701) 254-4439. RV/tent: 13. $8. Hookups: electric (30 amps).

Mandan

Colonial Campground, 4631 Memorial Hwy., 58554. T: (701) 663-9824 or (800) 377-9824. RV/tent: 42. $15. Hookups: electric (30, 50 amps).

Fort Abraham Lincoln State Park, 4480 Fort Lincoln Rd., 58554. T: (800) 807-4723 or (701) 663-9571. falsp@state.nd.us. RV/tent: 95. $11–$16. Hookups: electric (30 amps).

Medora

Medora Campground, P.O. Box 198, 58645. T: (800) 633-6721 or (701) 623-4444. RV/tent: 185. $22. Hookups: electric (20, 30, 50 amps), water, sewer, modem.

Red Trail Campground, Box 367 G, 58645. T: (800) 621-4317 or (701) 623-4317. F: (701) 623-4833. RV/tent: 98. $14–$26. Hookups: electric (20, 30, 50 amps), water, sewer, cable, modem.

Theodore Roosevelt/Cottonwood Campground, Watford City, 58854. T: (701) 842-2333 or (701) 623-4466. www.usparks.com/US_National_Parks/theodore/theodore_north_unit.shtml. RV/tent: 5. $10. Hookups: none.

Menoken

A Prairie Breeze RV Park, 2810 158th St. Northeast, 58558. T: (701) 224-8215. rafarm@btigate.com. RV/tent: 41. $12. Hookups: electric (30, 50 amps), water, sewer.

Minot

Casa Motel & Campground, 1900 Hwy. 2 & 52 West, 58701. T: (701) 852-2352. RV/tent: 15. $18. Hookups: electric (30 amps), water, sewer.

Minot KOA, 5261 Hwy. 52 South, 58701. T: (701) 839-7400. RV/tent: 74. $16–$20. Hookups: electric (30 amps), water, sewer, modem.

Pat's Motel & Campground, 2025 27th St. Southeast, 58701. T: (701) 838-5800. RV/tent: 45. $10–$16. Hookups: electric (30 amps), water, sewer.

Roughrider Campground, 500 54th St. West, 58703. T: (701) 852-8442. F: (701) 852-9482. www.minot.com/~roughrid. roughrid@minot.com. RV/tent: 94. $15–$21. Hookups: electric (30 amps), water, sewer, modem.

Ray

Red Mike's RV Park, Hwy. 1840, 58849. T: (701) 568-2600. www.redmike.com/. redmike@nccray.com. RV/tent: 13. $19. Hookups: electric (30, 50 amps), water, sewer.

Ross

Dakota West RV Park & General Store, P.O. Box 36, 58776. T: (701) 755-3407. RV/tent: 21. $10–$15. Hookups: electric (20, 30, 50 amps).

Steele

OK Motel & Campground, 301 3rd Ave. Northeast, 58482. T: (701) 475-2440. RV/tent: 17. $11. Hookups: electric (30, 50 amps).

Warwick

East Bay Campground, 3892 East Bay Rd., 58381. T: (701) 398-5184 or (701) 740-8368. www.eastbaycampground.com. woodfarm@stellarnet.com. RV/tent: 16. $14. Hookups: electric (20, 30 amps), water, sewer.

Williston

Buffalo Trails Campground, 6700 2nd Ave. West, 58801. T: (701) 572-3206. RV/tent: 149. $13–$19. Hookups: electric (20, 30, 50 amps), water, sewer, modem.

Prairie Acres RV Park, 13853 US Hwy. 2, 58801. T: (701) 572-4860. RV/tent: 37. $12. Hookups: electric (30, 50 amps), water, sewer.

OHIO

Andover

Bunker Hills Campground, 550 Bunker Lake Blvd., 55304. T: (612) 757-3920. RV/tent: 50. $20. Hookups: water, electric (30 amps).

Annandale

Schroeder County Park, 9201 Ireland Ave. Northwest, 55302. T: (320) 274-8870. RV/tent: 50. $15. Hookups: electric (30 amps).

Apple Valley

Lebanon Hills Regional Park, 12100 Johnny Cake Ridge Rd., 55124. T: (612) 454-9211. RV/tent: 92. $20. Hookups: electric (30 amps).

Argyle

Old Mill State Park, Rte. 1 Box 43, 56713. T: (218) 437-8174. RV/tent: 26. $10. Hookups: electric (30 amps), water.

Ashby

Sundown RV Park & Campground, Rte. 1 Box 145, 56309. T: (218) 747-2931. RV/tent: 30. $18. Hookups: water, electric (30 amps), sewer.

Babbitt

Timber Wolf Lodge, 9130 Escape Rd., 55706. T: (218) 827-3512. RV/tent: 15. $28. Hookups: water, electric (30 amps).

Backus

Barrett Lake Resort & Campground, 3781 State 87 Northwest, 56435. T: (320) 528-2598. RV/tent: 34. $16. Hookups: water, electric (50 amps), sewer.

Eagle Wing Campground, 1588 36th Ave. Southwest, 56435. T: (218) 587-2090. RV/tent: 45. $20. Hookups: water, electric (30 amps).

Lindsey Lake Campground, 3781 State 87 Northwest, 56435. T: (218) 947-4728. RV/tent: 40. $15. Hookups: water, electric (30 amps).

Barnum

Bent Trout Lake Campground, 2928 Bent Trout Lake Rd., 55707. T: (218) 389-6322. RV/tent: 30. $17. Hookups: water, electric (30 amps).

Battle Lake

Battle Lake Sunset Beach Resort & Campground, RR 3 Box 181, 56515. T: (888) 583-2750. RV/tent: 20. $20. Hookups: water, electric (30 amps), sewer.

Baudette

Zippel Bay Resort, HC2 Box 51, 56686. T: (800) 222-2537. RV/tent: 57. $20. Hookups: water, electric (30 amps).

Bemidji

Hamilton's Fox Lake Campground, 2555 Island View Dr. Northeast, 56601. T: (218) 586-2231. RV/tent: 35. $20. Hookups: water, electric (30 amps).

Lake Bemidji State Park, 3401 State Park Rd. Northeast, 56601. T: (218) 755-3843. RV/tent: 98. $15. Hookups: electric (30 amps.).

Bena

New Leech Lake Campground, HC 1 Box 75, 56626. T: (800) 272-3785. RV/tent: 73. $23. Hookups: water, electric (30 amps), sewer.

Big Lake

Shady River Campground, 21535 CO 5, 55309. T: (612) 263-3705. RV/tent: 75. $18. Hookups: water, electric (50 amps).

Bigfork

Scenic State Park, HCR 2 Box 17, 56628. T: (218) 743-3362. RV/tent: 117. $9. Hookups: electric (30 amps).

Blackduck

Lost Acres Resort & Campground, HC 3 Box 162D Kitchi Lake, 56630. T: (800) 835-6414. F: (218) 835-6414. RV/tent: 8. $20. Hookups: water, electric (30 amps).

Blooming Prairie

Brookside Campground, 52482 320th St., 55917. T: (507) 583-2979. RV/tent: 60. $20. Hookups: water, electric (30 amps).

Brainerd

Crow Wing State Park, 7100 State Park Rd. Southwest, 56401. T: (218) 829-8022. RV/tent: 61. $13. Hookups: electric (30 amps).

Hidden Paradise Resort & Campground, 1388 Ojibwa Rd. North, 56401. T: (218) 963-3180. RV/tent: 10. $27. Hookups: water, electric (50 amps), sewer.

Lum Park Campground, 1619 Northeast Washington St., 56401. T: (218) 828-2320. F: (218) 828-2791. RV/tent: 25. $15. Hookups: water, electric (30 amps), sewer, cable TV.

Breezy Point

Highview Campground & RV Park, HC 83 Box 1084, 56472. T: (877) 543-4526. F: (218) 543-4526. RV/tent: 132. $22. Hookups: water, electric (30 amps), sewer.

Burtrum

Big Swan Lake Resort, RR 1 Box 256, 56318. T: (320) 732-6065. RV/tent: 21. $20. Hookups: water, electric (30 amps), sewer.

Caledonia

Beaver Creek Valley State Park, Rte. 2 Box 57, 55921. T: (507) 724-2107. RV/tent: 42. $13. Hookups: electric (30 amps).

Dunromin' Park, RR 1 Box 146, 55921. T: (800) 822-2514. F: (507) 724-5560. RV/tent: 90. $22. Hookups: water, electric (30 amps).

Canby

Stonehill Regional Park, Box 2, 56220. T: (507) 223-7586. RV/tent: 40. $14. Hookups: water, electric (30 amps).

Cannon Falls

Cannon Falls Campground, 30365 Oak Ln., 30365. T: (507) 263-3145. RV/tent: 100. $21. Hookups: water, electric (50 amps).

Lake Byllesby Regional Park Campground, 7650 Echo Point Rd., 55009. T: (507) 263-4447. RV/tent: 57. $17. Hookups: electric (30 amps).

Carlos

Lake Carlos State Park, 2601 CO 38 Northeast, 56319. T: (320) 852-7200. RV/tent: 126. $15. Hookups: electric (30 amps).

Cass Lake

Cass Lake Lodge Resort & RV Park, 16293 60th Ave. Northwest, 56633. T: (218) 335-6658. RV/tent: 49. $20. Hookups: water, electric (30 amps), sewer.

Marclay Point Campground, Rte. 2 Box 80, 56633. T: (218) 335-6589. RV/tent: 75. $18. Hookups: water, electric (30 amps).

Center City

Wild River State Park, 39755 Park Trace, 55012. T: (651) 583-2125. RV/tent: 96. $15. Hookups: electric (30 amps).

Clearwater

St. Cloud-Clearwater KOA, 2454 CO 143, 55320. T: (320) 558-2876. RV/tent: 93. $27. Hookups: water, electric (50 amps), sewer.

Cokato

Collinwood Regional Park, 17251 70th St. Southwest, 55320. T: (320) 286-2801. RV/tent: 50. $15. Hookups: electric (30 amps).

Crane Lake

Beddow's Campground, 7516 Bayside Dr., 55725. T: (218) 993-2389. RV/tent: 22. $20. Hookups: water, electric (30 amps), sewer.

Cromwell

Island Lake Campground, 1391 Middle Rd., 55726. T: (218) 644-3543. RV/tent: 15. $20. Hookups: water, electric (50 amps).

Currie

Lake Shetek State Park, 163 State Park Rd., 56123. T: (507) 763-3256. RV/tent: 108. $15. Hookups: electric (30 amps).

Schreler's on Shetek, 35 Resort Rd., 56123. T: (507) 763-3817. RV/tent: 110. $17. Hookups: water, electric (50 amps), sewer.

Cushing

Fish Trap Campground, RR 1 Box 17, 56443. T: (218) 575-2603. RV/tent: 90. $26. Hookups: water, electric (50 amps), sewer.

Fish Trap Lake Campground, 30894 Fish Trap Lake Dr., 56443. T: (218) 575-2603. RV/tent: 47. $25. Hookups: water, electric (30 amps), sewer.

OHIO (continued)

Dassel

Lake Dale Campground, 24473 CSAH 4, 55325. T: (320) 275-3387. RV/tent: 45. $15. Hookups: electric (30 amps).

Deer River

Jessie View Resort & Campground, 45756 CO 35, 56636. T: (218) 832-3678. RV/tent: 37. $20. Hookups: water, electric (30 amps), sewer.

Lake Winnibigoshish Recreation Area, 34385 US Hwy. 2, 56636. T: (218) 326-6565. F: (218) 326-6565. RV/tent: 44. $12. Hookups: electric (30 amps).

Deerwood

Camp Holiday Resort & Campground, 17467 Round Lake Rd., 56444. T: (218) 678-2495. RV/tent: 40. $21. Hookups: water, electric (30 amps), sewer.

Sisselbagamah RV Resort on Bay Lake, 685 Katrine Dr. Northeast, 56444. T: (218) 678-3393. RV/tent: 35. $20. Hookups: water, electric (30 amps), sewer.

Detroit Lakes

American Legion Campground, 810 West Lake Dr., 56501. T: (218) 847-3759. RV/tent: 97. $19. Hookups: water, electric (30 amps), sewer, cable TV.

Duluth

Duluth Tent & Trailer Camp, 8411 Congdon Blvd., 55804. T: (218) 525-1350. RV/tent: 64. $19. Hookups: water, electric (30 amps), sewer.

Indian Point Campground, 902 South 69th Ave., 55807. T: (218) 624-5637. RV/tent: 70. $20. Hookups: water, electric (30 amps), sewer.

Elbow Lake

Tipsinah Mounds Campground & Park, Rte. 2 Box 52A, 56531. T: (218) 685-5114. RV/tent: 68. $20. Hookups: water, electric (30 amps), sewer.

Elk River

Wapiti Park Campground, 18746 Troy St., 55330. T: (612) 441-1396. RV/tent: 142. $20. Hookups: water, electric (30 amps), sewer.

Ely

Canoe Country Campground & Cabins, Box 30, 55731. T: (800) 725-2306. RV/tent: 15. $20. Hookups: water, electric (30 amps), sewer.

Erskine

Lake Cameron RV Park & Campground, RR 3 Box 24, 56535. T: (218) 687-4555. RV/tent: 36. $18. Hookups: water, electric (50 amps), sewer, cable TV.

Esko

Knife Island Campgrounds, 234 Hwy. 61 Box 361, 55733. T: (218) 879-6063. RV/tent: 20. $16. Hookups: water, electric (30 amps).

Fairfax

Valley View Campground, 60861 State Hwy. 4, 55332. T: (507) 426-7420. RV/tent: 42. $22. Hookups: water, electric (30 amps).

Fairmont

Dawson's Lakeside Campground, 248 Cottonwood Rd., 56031. T: (507) 235-5753. RV/tent: 140. $20. Hookups: water, electric (50 amps), sewer.

Flying Goose Campground, 2521 115th St., 56031. T: (507) 235-3458. RV/tent: 95. $20. Hookups: water, electric (50 amps), sewer.

Faribault

Camp Faribo, 21851 Bagley Ave., 55021. T: (507) 332-8453. RV/tent: 62. $19. Hookups: water, electric (50 amps), sewer.

Camp Maiden Rock, 22661 Dodge Court, 55021. T: (800) 657-4776. RV/tent: 100. $21. Hookups: water, electric (30 amps), sewer.

Roberds Lake Resort & Campground, 18192 Roberds Lake Blvd., 55021. T: (800) 879-5091. RV/tent: 40. $24. Hookups: water, electric (50 amps), sewer.

Fergus Falls

Elks Point, P.O. Box 502 Rte. 1, 56537. T: (218) 736-4292. RV/tent: 40. $20. Hookups: water, electric (30 amps).

Fifty Lakes

Fifty Lakes Campground, P.O. Box 158, 56448. T: (218) 763-2616. RV/tent: 82. $22. Hookups: water, electric (50 amps), sewer.

Forest Lake

Timm's Marina & Campground, 9080 North Jewel Ln., 55025. T: (612) 464-3890. RV/tent: 30. $20. Hookups: water, electric (30 amps), sewer.

Frazee

Birchmere Family Resort & Campground, 18346 Birchmere Rd., 56544. T: (800) 642-9554. RV/tent: 30. $20. Hookups: water, electric (30 amps), sewer.

Garden City

Shady Oaks Campground, P.O. Box 284, 56034. T: (507) 546-3986. RV/tent: 55. $20. Hookups: water, electric (30 amps), sewer.

Garfield

Oak Park Campground, 9561 CO 8 Northwest, 56332. T: (320) 834-2345. RV/tent: 55. $17. Hookups: water, electric (30 amps), sewer.

Garrison

Wilderness of Minnesota, Box 387, 56450. T: (320) 692-4347. RV/tent: 132. $15. Hookups: water, electric (50 amps), sewer.

Glenwood

Chalet Campground, Hwy. 104, 56334. T: (651) 634-5433. RV/tent: 36. $16. Hookups: water, electric (30 amps), sewer.

Grand Marais

Grand Marais RV Park & Campground, P.O. Box 820, 55604. T: (218) 387-1712. F: (218) 387-1310. RV/tent: 200. $30. Hookups: water, electric (50 amps), sewer.

Gunflint Pines Resort & Campground, 217 South Gunflint Lake Rd., 55604. T: (218) 388-4454. RV/tent: 20. $25. Hookups: water, electric (15 amps).

Grand Rapids

Birch Cove Resort & Campground, 32382 Southwood Rd., 55744. T: (218) 326-8754. RV/tent: 14. $19. Hookups: water, electric (20 amps), sewer.

Pokegama Recreation Area, 34385 US Hwy. 2, 55744. T: (218) 326-6128. F: (218) 326-6565. RV/tent: 40. $16. Hookups: electric (30 amps).

Sal's Campground, P.O. Box 363, 55744. T: (218) 492-4297. RV/tent: 44. $20. Hookups: water, electric (30 amps), sewer.

Hackensack

Quietwoods Campground, 4755 Alder Ln. Northwest, 56452. T: (218) 675-6240. RV/tent: 20. $15. Hookups: water, electric (20 amps).

Ham Lake

Ham Lake Campground, 2400 Constance Blvd., 55304. T: (612) 434-5337. RV/tent: 130. $19. Hookups: water, electric (50 amps).

Hastings

St. Croix Bluffs Regional Park Campground, 10191 St. Croix Trail, 55033. T: (651) 430-8240. F: (651) 430-8239. RV/tent: 73. $18. Hookups: water, electric (50 amps).

Hawick

Old Wagon Campground, 21611 132nd St. Northeast, 56246. T: (320) 354-2165. RV/tent: 25. $19. Hookups: water, electric (30 amps).

International Falls

Arnold's Campground & RV Park, Hwy. 53 and 21st St., 56649. T: (218) 285-9100. RV/tent: 24. $15. Hookups: water, electric (30 amps), sewer.

Isanti

Country Camping RV Tent & RV Park on the Rum River, 750 273rd Ave., 55040. T: (612) 444-9626. RV/tent: 58. $16. Hookups: water, electric (30 amps).

Isle

Father Hennepin State Park, P.O. Box 397, 56342. T: (320) 676-8763. RV/tent: 103. $15. Hookups: electric (30 amps).

Jackson

Jackson KOA Campground, 2035 Hwy. 71, 56143. T: (507) 847-3825. RV/tent: 60. $22. Hookups: water, electric (30 amps), sewer.

Loon Lake Campground, 405 4th St., 56143. T: (507) 847-2240. RV/tent: 80. $20. Hookups: water, electric (30 amps).

OHIO (continued)

Jasper

Split Rock Creek State Park, 336 50th Ave., 56144. T: (507) 348-7908. RV/tent: 28. $13. Hookups: electric (30 amps).

Jordan

Minneapolis S.W. KOA, 3315 West 166th St., 55352. T: (612) 492-6440. RV/tent: 111. $26. Hookups: water, electric (50 amps).

Kabetogama Lake

Cedar Cove Campsites & Resort, 9940 Gappa Rd., 56669. T: (218) 875-3851. RV/tent: 30. $25. Hookups: water, electric (30 amps), sewer.

Kandiyohi

Kandiyohi County Park No. 3, 6920 CO 4, 56251. T: (612) 974-8520. RV/tent: 65. $16. Hookups: electric (30 amps).

Kelliher

Rogers' On Red Lake Campground & RV Park, HC 78 Box 20, 56650. T: (800) 678-1871. RV/tent: 51. $16. Hookups: water, electric (30 amps), sewer.

Kerrick

Hoffman's Oak Lake Campground, HC1 Box 80, 55756. T: (218) 496-5678. RV/tent: 14. $18. Hookups: water, electric (30 amps), sewer.

Knife River

Depot Campground, P.O. Box 115, 56149. T: (218) 834-5044. RV/tent: 32. $18. Hookups: water, electric (30 amps).

Lake Benton

Hole-in-the-Mountain County Park, Hwy. 14 W, 56149. T: (507) 368-9350. RV/tent: 70. $11. Hookups: water, electric (30 amps).

Lake Bronson

Lake Bronson State Park, Box 9, 56734. T: (218) 754-2200. RV/tent: 194. $13. Hookups: electric (30 amps).

Lakefield

Kilen Woods State Park, Rte. 1 Box 122, 56150. T: (507) 662-6258. RV/tent: 33. $13. Hookups: electric (30 amps).

Lanesboro

Sylvan Park, P.O. Box 333, 55949. T: (507) 467-3722. RV/tent: 42. $13. Hookups: electric (30 amps).

Le Roy

Lake Louise State Park, 12385 766th Ave., 55951. T: (507) 324-5249. RV/tent: 22. $13. Hookups: electric (30 amps).

Le Sueur

Peaceful Valley Campsite, 213 Peaceful Valley Rd., 56058. T: (507) 665-2297. F: (612) 388-5605. RV/tent: 38. $18. Hookups: water, electric (50 amps), sewer.

Lindstrom

Hillscrest RV Park, 32741 North Lakes Trail, 55045. T: (651) 257-5352. RV/tent: 70. $20. Hookups: water, electric (30 amps), sewer.

Lino Lakes

Rice Creek Campground, 7401 Main St., 55038. T: (612) 757-3928. RV/tent: 78. $20. Hookups: water, electric (30 amps).

Mahnomen

Shooting Star Casino Hotel & RV Park, 777 Casino Dr., 56557. T: (800) 453-STAR. RV/tent: 47. $13. Hookups: water, electric (30 amps), sewer.

Mankato

Minneopa State Park, RR 9 Box 143, 56001. T: (507) 389-5464. RV/tent: 62. $13. Hookups: electric (30 amps).

Maple Plain

Baker Park Reserve, 2931 CO 19, 55359. T: (612) 479-2258. RV/tent: 213. $17. Hookups: electric (30 amps).

Marine on St. Croix

William O'Brien State Park, 16821 O'Brien Trail North, 55047. T: (651) 433-0500. RV/tent: 125. $15. Hookups: electric (30 amps).

Mazeppa

Ponderosa Campground, RR 1 Box 209, 55956. T: (800) 895-0328. RV/tent: 80. $17. Hookups: water, electric (50 amps).

McGregor

Sandy Lake Recreation Area, HCR 4 Box 362, 55760. T: (218) 426-3482. F: (218) 426-4815. RV/tent: 110. $18. Hookups: electric (30 amps).

Savanna Portage State Park, HCR 3 Box 591, 55760. T: (218) 426-3271. RV/tent: 72. $13. Hookups: electric (30 amps).

Merrifield

Shing Wako Resort & Campground, HC 87 Box 9580, 51465. T: (218) 765-3226. RV/tent: 33. $21. Hookups: water, electric (30 amps), sewer.

Sunset Bay Resort & Campground, HC 86 Box 1000, 56465. T: (800) 715-2267. RV/tent: 75. $25. Hookups: water, electric (30 amps), sewer.

Montevideo

Lac Qui Parle State Park, Rte. 5 Box 74A, 56265. T: (612) 752-4736. RV/tent: 66. $13. Hookups: electric (30 amps).

Moorhead

Buffalo River State Park, P.O. Box 352, 56547. T: (218) 498-2124. RV/tent: 44. $13. Hookups: electric (30 amps).

Fargo-Moorhead KOA, Rte. 4 Box 168, 56560. T: (218) 233-0671. RV/tent: 95. $30. Hookups: water, electric (50 amps), sewer, cable TV.

Mora

Camperville, 2351 310th Ave., 55051. T: (320) 679-2326. RV/tent: 49. $20. Hookups: water, electric (50 amps).

Captain Dan's Crow's Nest Resort, 2743 Hwy. 65, 55051. T: (320) 679-1977. RV/tent: 51. $22. Hookups: water, electric (30 amps), sewer.

Morton

Jackpot Junction Casino Hotel Campground, 39375 CO 24, 56270. T: (507) 644-3000. F: (507) 644-2648. RV/tent: 42. $12. Hookups: water, electric (30 amps), sewer.

Nerstrand

Nerstrand Big Woods State Park, 9700 170th St. East, 55053. T: (507) 334-8848. RV/tent: 68. $13. Hookups: water, electric (30 amps).

Nevis

Whispering Pines Resort & Campgrounds, Rte. 1 Box 83, 56467. T: (218) 652-4362. RV/tent: 10. $23. Hookups: water, electric (30 amps), sewer.

New London

Hide-Away Campground, 199th Ave. Northeast, 56273. T: (320) 354-2148. RV/tent: 11. $18. Hookups: water, electric (30 amps).

Sibley State Park, 800 Sibley Park Rd., 56273. T: (320) 354-2055. RV/tent: 138. $15. Hookups: electric (30 amps).

New Ulm

Flandrau State Park, 1300 Summit Ave., 56073. T: (507) 233-9800. RV/tent: 90. $13. Hookups: electric (30 amps).

Ogema

Woodland Trails Resort & Campground, Rte. 1 Box 71 E, 56569. T: (218) 983-3230. RV/tent: 35. $15. Hookups: water, electric (30 amps), sewer.

Orr

Cabin O'Pines Resort & Campground, 4378 Pelican Rd., 55771. T: (800) 757-3122. RV/tent: 30. $20. Hookups: water, electric (30 amps).

Pine Acres Resort & Campground, 4498 Pine Acres Rd., 55771. T: (218) 757-3144. RV/tent: 80. $20. Hookups: water, electric (30 amps), sewer.

Ortonville

Big Stone Lake State Park, RR 1 Box 153, 56278. T: (612) 839-3663. RV/tent: 40. $13. Hookups: electric (30 amps).

Osage

R&D Resort & Campground, 54097 Grant St., 56570. T: (218) 573-3182. RV/tent: 26. $10. Hookups: water, electric (30 amps).

Osakis

Black's Cresent Beach, P.O. Box 416, 56360. T: (320) 859-2127. RV/tent: 10. $22. Hookups: water, electric (30 amps), sewer.

OHIO (continued)

Osakis (continued)

Midway Beach Resort & Campground, 1821 Lake St., 56360. T: (320) 859-4410. RV/tent: 9. $20. Hookups: water, electric (30 amps), sewer.

Owatonna

Owatonna Campground, 2554 Southwest 28th St., 55060. T: (507) 451-8050. RV/tent: 142. $20. Hookups: water, electric (50 amps), sewer.

Park Rapids

Breeze Camping & RV Resort on Eagle Lake, HCO 5 Box 321, 56470. T: (218) 732-5888. RV/tent: 69. $22. Hookups: water, electric (20 amps), sewer.

Pelican Rapids

Pelican Hills Park, RR 4 Box 218B, 56572. T: (800) 430-2267. RV/tent: 83. $20. Hookups: water, electric (30 amps), sewer.

Pengilly

Swan Lake Campground & Resort, 29995 East Shore Dr., 55775. T: (218) 885-3385. RV/tent: 24. $15. Hookups: water, electric (30 amps).

Perham

Golden Eagle Vacationland, Golden Eagle Rd., 56573. T: (218) 346-4386. RV/tent: 131. $18. Hookups: water, electric (30 amps), sewer.

Preston

Forestville Mystery Cave State Park, Rte. 2 Box 128, 55965. T: (507) 352-5111. RV/tent: 73. $15. Hookups: electric (30 amps).

Prior Lake

Dakotah Meadows Campground, 2341 Park Place, 55372. T: (800) 653-CAMP. F: (612) 496-6857. RV/tent: 48. $22. Hookups: water, electric (50 amps), sewer.

Red Wing

Haycreek Valley Campground, 31673 Hwy. 58 Blvd., 55066. T: (651) 388-3998. RV/tent: 122. $22. Hookups: water, electric (50 amps).

Richmond

Cozy Corners, 19897 Hwy. 22, 56368. T: (320) 597-3587. RV/tent: 17. $24. Hookups: water, electric (30 amps).

Your Haven Campground, 18337 SR 22, 56368. T: (320) 597-2450. RV/tent: 18. $20. Hookups: water, electric (30 amps), sewer.

Rochester

Brookside RV Park, 516 17th Ave., 55901. T: (507) 288-1413. F: (507) 288-3166. RV/tent: 25. $25. Hookups: water, electric (50 amps), sewer, cable TV, telephone.

Roger

Minneapolis Northwest/Maple Grove KOA, 10410 Brockton Ln., 55374. T: (612) 420-2255. RV/tent: 160. $29. Hookups: water, electric (50 amps), sewer, phone.

Roseau

Roseau City Park, 900 11th St. Southeast, 56751. T: (218) 463-1791. RV/tent: 20. $16. Hookups: water, electric (30 amps).

Rutledge

Pine River Campground, 7201 Hwy. 61, 55795. T: (320) 233-7678. RV/tent: 70. $18. Hookups: water, electric (30 amps).

Sandstone

Banning State Park, P.O. Box 643, 55072. T: (612) 245-2668. RV/tent: 39. $13. Hookups: electric (30 amps).

Savage

Town and Country Campground, 12630 Boone Ave., 55378. T: (612) 445-1756. RV/tent: 46. $25. Hookups: water, electric (30 amps), sewer.

Sebeka

Sebeka Municipal Park, P.O. Box 305, 56477. T: (218) 837-5773. RV/tent: 10. $16. Hookups: electric (30 amps).

Silver Bay

Northern Exposure Campground, 5346 Hwy. 61, 55614. T: (218) 226-3324. RV/tent: 55. $20. Hookups: water, electric (30 amps), sewer.

South Haven

Timberwoods Resort & Campground, 10255 Nevens Ave. Northwest, 55382. T: (320) 274-5140. RV/tent: 40. $20. Hookups: water, electric (30 amps), sewer.

South Isle

South Isle Family Campground, 39002 SR 47, 56342. T: (320) 676-8538. RV/tent: 47. $18. Hookups: water, electric (30 amps).

Starbuck

Glacial Lakes State Park, 25022 CO 41, 56381. T: (320) 239-2860. RV/tent: 46. $13. Hookups: electric (30 amps).

Tenstrike

Gull Lake Campground, Rte. 1 Box 28, 56683. T: (218) 586-2842. RV/tent: 92. $20. Hookups: water, electric (30 amps), sewer.

Moen's Birch Haven Campground & Resort, Rte. 1 Box 138, 56683. T: (218) 586-2863. RV/tent: 42. $16. Hookups: water, electric (30 amps).

Thief River Falls

Thief River Falls Tourist Park, Oakland Park Rd., 56701. T: (218) 681-2519. RV/tent: 64. $13. Hookups: water, electric (30 amps), sewer.

Two Harbors

Burlington Bay Campsite, 522 1st Ave., 55616. T: (218) 834-2021. RV/tent: 111. $16. Hookups: water, electric (30 amps), sewer.

Penmarallter Campsite, 725 Scenic Dr., 55616. T: (218) 834-4603. RV/tent: 19. $18. Hookups: water, electric (30 amps).

Walker

Waters Edge RV Park, 10634 SR 371, 56484. T: (218) 547-3552. RV/tent: 10. $16. Hookups: water, electric (30 amps), sewer.

Warroad

Warroad Campground, P.O. Box 50, 56763. T: (218) 386-1004. RV/tent: 153. $18. Hookups: water, electric (30 amps), sewer.

Waterville

Sakatah Lake State Park, RR 2 Box 19, 56096. T: (507) 362-4438. RV/tent: 68. $13. Hookups: electric (30 amps).

Waubun

Elk Horn Resort & Campground, Rte. 2 Box 323, 56589. T: (218) 935-5437. RV/tent: 24. $20. Hookups: water, electric (30 amps), sewer.

Woodbury

St. Paul East KOA, 568 Cottage Grove Dr., 55129. T: (651) 436-6436. RV/tent: 76. $30. Hookups: water, electric (50 amps), sewer, telephone.

Zimmerman

Camp in the Woods, 14791 289th Ave., 55398. T: (612) 427-5050. RV/tent: 78. $25. Hookups: water, electric (30 amps), sewer.

Zumbrota

Shades of Sherwood Camping Park, 14334 Sherwood Trace, 55992. T: (507) 732-5100. RV/tent: 140. $20. Hookups: water, electric (30 amps).

OKLAHOMA

Afton

Grand Country Mobile & RV Park, Rte. 3 Box 163, 74331. T: (918) 257-5164. RV/tent: 16. $12. Hookups: electric (20, 30, 50 amps), water, sewer.

Canton

Big Bend, P.O. Box 69, 73724. T: (580) 886-3576. www.reserveusa.com/nrrs/ok/biok. RV/tent: 115. $11–$16. Hookups: electric (20, 30 amps), water.

Canadian, P.O. Box 69, 73724. T: (580) 886-2989. www.reserveusa.com/nrrs/ok/caok. RV/tent: 77. $11–$15. Hookups: electric (20, 30 amps).

Sandy Cove, P.O. Box 69, 73724. T: (580) 274-3576. www.reserveusa.com/nrrs/ok/saco. RV/tent: 37. $14. Hookups: electric (20, 30 amps).

Checotah

Terra Starr Park, Rte. 2 Box 2130, 74426. T: (918) 689-2164 or (918) 689-7094. RV/tent: 300. $13. Hookups: electric (20, 30 amps), water, sewer.

Checotah/Henryetta

Checotah/Henryetta KOA, Box 750, 74426. T: (800) 562-7510 or (918) 473-6511. www.koa.com. RV/tent: 83. $18–$20. Hookups: electric (20, 30, 50 amps), water, sewer.

Claremore

Claremore Expo Center, 400 Veterans Pkwy., 74017. T: (918) 342-5357. RV/tent: 44. $15. Hookups: electric (20, 30, 50 amps), water, sewer.

Clayton

Potato Hills Central, HC 60 Box 175, 74536. T: (918) 569-4131. www.reserveusa.com/nrrs/ok/pota. RV/tent: 94. $15. Hookups: electric (20, 30 amps), water.

Copan

Post Oak Park, Rte. 1 Box 260, 74022. T: (918) 532-4334. www.reserveusa.com/nrrs/ok/post. RV/tent: 20. $14–$18. Hookups: electric (20, 30 amps), water.

Washington Cove, Rte. 1 Box 260, 74022. T: (918) 532-4129. www.reserveusa.com/nrrs/ok/wash. RV/tent: 101. $14–$16. Hookups: electric (20, 30, 50 amps), water.

Davis

Turner Falls Park, I-35 Exit 47 or 51. T: (580) 369-2917 or (580) 369-2988. www.turnerfallspark.com. RV/tent: 344. $8–$10. Hookups: electric (30 amps), water.

El Reno

Cherokee KOA, Box 6, 73036. T: (800) 562-5736 or (405) 884-2595. www.koa.com. RV/tent: 79. $15–$21. Hookups: electric (20, 30, 50 amps), water, sewer.

Hensley's RV Park, Country Club Rd., 73036. T: (405) 262-6490. RV/tent: 26. $21. Hookups: electric (30, 50 amps), water, sewer.

Elk City

Elk City/Clinton KOA, P.O. Box 137, 73626. T: (800) 562-4149 or (580) 592-4409. F: (580) 592-4530. www.koa.com. RV/tent: 90. $17–$28. Hookups: electric (20, 30, 50 amps), water, sewer.

Elk Creek RV Park, 20th & South Main, 73644. T: (888) 4RV-OKLA or (580) 225-3160. RV/tent: 74. $17–$19. Hookups: electric (30, 50 amps), water, sewer.

Fort Gibson

Blue Bill Point, Rte. 1 Box 3900, 74434. T: (918) 682-4314. www.reserveusa.com/nrrs/ok/blpo. RV/tent: 43. $11–$16. Hookups: electric (20, 30 amps), water.

Dam Site (Fort Gibson Lake), Rte. 1 Box 3900, 74434. T: (918) 682-4314. www.reserveusa.com/nrrs/ok/dami. RV/tent: 47. $15. Hookups: electric (20, 30 amps).

Flat Rock Creek, Rte. 1 Box 3900, 74434. T: (918) 682-4314. www.reserveusa.com/nrrs/ok/flat. RV/tent: 36. $15–$16. Hookups: electric (20, 30 amps), water.

Rocky Point, Rte. 1 Box 3900, 74434. T: (918) 682-4314. www.reserveusa.com/nrrs/ok/rocy. RV/tent: 63. $16. Hookups: electric (20, 30 amps), water.

Taylor Ferry, Rte. 1 Box 3900, 74434. T: (918) 682-4314. www.reserveusa.com/nrrs/ok/tafe. RV/tent: 102. $11–$16. Hookups: electric (20, 30, 50 amps), water.

Wildwood, Rte. 1 Box 3900, 74434. T: (918) 682-4314. www.reserveusa.com/nrrs/ok/wilw. RV/tent: 30. $16. Hookups: electric (20, 30, 50 amps), water.

Fort Supply

Supply Park, P.O. Box 248, 73841. T: (580) 766-2001. www.reserveusa.com/nrrs/ok/supp. RV/tent: 110. $10–$15. Hookups: electric (20, 30 amps), water.

Gore

Afton Landing, Rte. 2 Box 21, 74435. T: (918) 489-5541. www.reserveusa.com/nrrs/ok/afto. RV/tent: 20. $10–$15. Hookups: electric (20, 30 amps), water.

Applegate Cove, Rte. 2 Box 21, 74435. T: (918) 489-5541. www.reserveusa.com/nrrs/ok/appg. RV/tent: 27. $15. Hookups: electric (20, 30 amps), water.

Bluff Landing, Rte. 2 Box 21, 74435. T: (918) 489-5541. www.reserveusa.com/nrrs/ok/blla. RV/tent: 21. $15. Hookups: electric (20, 30 amps).

Brewers Bend, Rte. 2 Box 21, 74435. T: (918) 489-5541. www.reserveusa.com/nrrs/ok/brew. RV/tent: 42. $10–$15. Hookups: electric (20, 30 amps).

Chicken Creek, Rte. 1 Box 259, 74435. T: (918) 487-5252. www.reserveusa.com/nrrs/ok/chok. RV/tent: 102. $13–$18. Hookups: electric (20, 30, 50 amps), water.

Cookson Bend, Rte. 1 Box 259, 74435. T: (918) 487-5252. www.reserveusa.com/nrrs/ok/cobe. RV/tent: 121. $10–$18. Hookups: electric (20, 30, 50 amps).

Cowlington Point, Rte. 2 Box 21, 74435. T: (918) 489-5541. www.reserveusa.com/nrrs/ok/cowl. RV/tent: 38. $8–$13. Hookups: electric (20, 30 amps), water.

Elk Creek Landing, Rte. 1 Box 259, 74435. T: (918) 487-5252. www.reserveusa.com/nrrs/ok/elcl. RV/tent: 42. $10–$15. Hookups: electric (20, 30 amps).

Pettit Bay, Rte. 1 Box 259, 74435. T: (918) 487-5252. www.reserveusa.com/nrrs/ok/pett. RV/tent: 55. $10–$18. Hookups: electric (20, 30, 50 amps), water, sewer.

Short Mountain Cove, Rte. 2 Box 21, 74435. T: (918) 489-5541. www.reserveusa.com/nrrs/ok/shmc. RV/tent: 32. $8–$12. Hookups: electric (20, 30 amps).

Snake Creek, Rte. 1 Box 259, 74435. T: (918) 487-5252. www.reserveusa.com/nrrs/ok/sank. RV/tent: 82. $10–$18. Hookups: electric (20, 30, 50 amps), water, sewer.

Spaniard Creek, Rte. 2 Box 21, 74435. T: (918) 489-5541. www.reserveusa.com/nrrs/ok/span. RV/tent: 35. $15. Hookups: electric (20, 30 amps), water.

Strayhorn Landing, Rte. 1 Box 259, 74435. T: (918) 487-5252. www.reserveusa.com/nrrs/ok/strl. RV/tent: 38. $15–$18. Hookups: electric (20, 30 amps), water, sewer.

Grove

Lee's Grand Lake Resort, 24800 South 630 Rd., 74344. T: (918) 786-4289. RV/tent: 25. $18–$20. Hookups: electric (30, 50 amps), water, sewer.

Kansas

Spencer Ridge Resort, Rte. 1 Box 222, 74347. T: (800) 964-6670 or (918) 597-2269. RV/tent: 32. $14. Hookups: electric (20, 30, 50 amps), water, sewer.

Kellyville

Heyburn Park, Rte. 2 Box 140, 74039. T: (918) 247-6601. www.reserveusa.com/nrrs/ok/heyb. RV/tent: 47. $14–$16. Hookups: electric (20, 30 amps), water.

Sheppard Point, 27349 Heyburn Lake Rd., 74039. T: (918) 247-4551. www.reserveusa.com/nrrs/ok/shep. RV/tent: 37. $16. Hookups: electric (20, 30 amps), water.

OKLAHOMA (continued)

Kingston

Buncombe Creek, 351 Corps Rd., 75020. T: (903) 465-4990. www.reserveusa.com/nrrs/ok/bunc. RV/tent: 51. $10–$15. Hookups: electric (20, 30 amps), water.

Burns Run East, 351 Corps Rd., 75020. T: (903) 465-4990. www.reserveusa.com/nrrs/ok/burr. RV/tent: 54. $11–$20. Hookups: electric (20, 30 amps), water.

Burns Run West, 351 Corps Rd., 75020. T: (903) 465-4990. www.reserveusa.com/nrrs/ok/burw. RV/tent: 127. $11–$20. Hookups: electric (20, 30 amps), water.

Caney Creek, 351 Corps Rd., 75020. T: (903) 465-4990. www.reserveusa.com/nrrs/ok/caek. RV/tent: 52. $10–$18. Hookups: electric (20, 30 amps), water.

Johnson Creek, 351 Corps Rd., 75020. T: (903) 465-4990. www.reserveusa.com/nrrs/ok/jocr. RV/tent: 40. $18. Hookups: electric (20, 30 amps), water.

Lakeside, 351 Corps Rd., 75020. T: (903) 465-4990. www.reserveusa.com/nrrs/ok/lasd. RV/tent: 127. $11–$20. Hookups: electric (20, 30 amps), water.

Platter Flats, 351 Corps Rd., 75020. T: (903) 465-4990. www.reserveusa.com/nrrs/ok/plat. RV/tent: 57. $10–$15. Hookups: electric (20, 30, 50 amps), water.

McAlester

Super 8 Motel & RV Park, US 69 Business South, 2400 South Main, 74502. T: (918) 426-5400. RV/tent: 40. $12. Hookups: electric (20, 30 amps), water, sewer.

Miami

Miami Mobile Home & RV Park, 2001 East Steve Owens, 74354. T: (800) 515-2287 or (918) 542-2287. RV/tent: 48. $14. Hookups: electric (30, 50 amps), water, sewer.

Muskogee

Meadowbrook RV Park, 1305 South 32nd St., 74401. T: (918) 681-4574. RV/tent: 39. $15. Hookups: electric (30, 50 amps), water, sewer.

Oklahoma City

A-OK RV Park, 721 South Rockwell, 73128. T: (405) 787-7356. RV/tent: 34. $14. Hookups: electric (30, 50 amps), water, sewer.

Briscoe's RV Park, 6002 I-35 South, 73149. T: (800) 622-6073. RV/tent: 60. $18. Hookups: electric (20, 30, 50 amps), water, sewer.

Council Road RV Park, 8108 Southwest 8th St., 73128. T: (405) 789-2103. RV/tent: 102. $16. Hookups: electric (20, 30, 50 amps), water, sewer.

Eastland Hills RV Park, 3100 South Douglas Blvd., 73150. T: (405) 736-1013. RV/tent: 53. $12–$15. Hookups: electric (20, 30, 50 amps), water, sewer.

Okie RV Park & Camp Ground, 9824 Southeast 29th St., 73129. T: (405) 732-3093. RV/tent: 35. $8. Hookups: electric (30, 50 amps), water, sewer.

Oklahoma City East KOA, 6200 South Choctaw Rd., 73020. T: (800) 562-5076 or (405) 391-5000. F: (405) 391-5004. www.koa.com. RV/tent: 85. $15–$29. Hookups: electric (20, 30, 50 amps), water, sewer.

Roadrunner RV Park, 4800 South I-35, 73129. T: (405) 677-2373. RV/tent: 80. $19–$21. Hookups: electric (30, 50 amps), water, sewer.

Rockwell RV Park, 720 South Rockwell, 73128. T: (888) 684-3251 or (405) 787-5992. www.campusa.com/ok/rockwell. RV/tent: 126. $20–$24. Hookups: electric (30, 50 amps), water, sewer.

Oologah

Blue Creek, P.O. Box 700, 74053. T: (918) 341-4244. www.reserveusa.com/nrrs/ok/blcr. RV/tent: 61. $12–$16. Hookups: electric (20, 30 amps).

Hawthorn Bluff, P.O. Box 700, 74053. T: (918) 443-2319. www.reserveusa.com/nrrs/ok/hawt. RV/tent: 93. $14–$18. Hookups: electric (20, 30 amps).

Spencer Creek, P.O. Box 700, 74053. T: (918) 341-3690. www.reserveusa.com/nrrs/ok/spen. RV/tent: 84. $12–$16. Hookups: electric (20, 30 amps).

Ouachita

Cedar Lake (Oklahoma), Choctaw Ranger District, HC 63 Box 5184, 74939. T: (918) 653-2991. www.reserveusa.com/nrrs/ok/ced3. RV/tent: 24. $10–$20. Hookups: electric (20, 30, 50 amps), water, sewer.

Ponca City

Bear Creek Cove, 9400 Lake Rd., 74604. T: (580) 762-5611. www.reserveusa.com/nrrs/ok/brcc. RV/tent: 22. $15. Hookups: electric (20, 30 amps), water.

Coon Creek, 9400 Lake Rd., 74604. T: (580) 762-5611. www.reserveusa.com/nrrs/ok/cooe. RV/tent: 304. $16–$18. Hookups: electric (20, 30 amps), water.

Osage Cove, 9400 Lake Rd., 74604. T: (580) 762-5611. www.reserveusa.com/nrrs/ok/osac. RV/tent: 94. $16. Hookups: electric (20, 30 amps).

Sarge Creek, 9400 Lake Rd., 74604. T: (580) 762-5611. www.reserveusa.com/nrrs/ok/sarg. RV/tent: 301. $16. Hookups: electric (20, 30 amps), water.

Washunga Bay, 9400 Lake Rd., 74604. T: (580) 762-5611. www.reserveusa.com/nrrs/ok/waba. RV/tent: 62. $11–$15. Hookups: electric (20, 30, 50 amps), water.

Sallisaw

Sallisaw KOA, P.O. Box 88, 74955. T: (800) 562-2797 or (918) 775-2792. www.koa.com. RV/tent: 82. $15–$21. Hookups: electric (20, 30, 50 amps), water, sewer.

Sand Springs

New Mannford Ramp, 23115 West Wekiwa Rd., 74063. T: (918) 865-2621. www.reserveusa.com/nrrs/ok/newm. RV/tent: 39. $10–$17. Hookups: electric (20, 30 amps), water.

Salt Creek North, 23115 West Wekiwa Rd., 74063. T: (918) 865-2621. www.reserveusa.com/nrrs/ok/salc. RV/tent: 126. $11–$16. Hookups: electric (20, 30 amps), water.

Washington Irving S Campground, 23115 West Wekiwa Rd., 74063. T: (918) 865-2621. www.reserveusa.com/nrrs/ok/wasi. RV/tent: 41. $11–$16. Hookups: electric (20, 30 amps).

Sawyer

Kiamichi Park, P.O. Box 99, 74756. T: (580) 326-3345. www.reserveusa.com/nrrs/ok/kiam. RV/tent: 91. $9–$15. Hookups: electric (20, 30 amps), water.

Virgil Point, P.O. Box 99, 74756. T: (580) 326-3345. www.reserveusa.com/nrrs/ok/virp. RV/tent: 51. $15. Hookups: electric (20, 30 amps).

Skiatook

Birch Cove, HC 67 Box 135, 74070. T: (918) 396-3170. www.reserveusa.com/nrrs/ok/birc. RV/tent: 84. $16. Hookups: electric (20, 30 amps).

Tall Chief Cove, HC 67 Box 135, 74070. T: (918) 288-6820. www.reserveusa.com/nrrs/ok/tall. RV/tent: 57. $18. Hookups: electric (20, 30 amps), water.

Twin Points, HC 67 Box 135, 74070. T: (918) 396-3170. www.reserveusa.com/nrrs/ok/twpo. RV/tent: 54. $14. Hookups: electric (20, 30 amps).

Stigler

Belle Starr, Rte. 4 Box 5500, 74462. T: (918) 799-5843. www.reserveusa.com/nrrs/ok/bels. RV/tent: 68. $16–$18. Hookups: electric (20, 30, 50 amps), water.

Brooken Cove, Rte. 4 Box 5500, 74462. T: (918) 799-5843. wwwreserveusa.com/nrrs/ok/brco. RV/tent: 71. $16. Hookups: electric (20, 30 amps), water.

Dam Site South (Eufaula Lake), Rte. 4 Box 5500, 74462. T: (918) 799-5843. www.reserveusa.com/nrrs/ok/dam9. RV/tent: 57. $11–$16. Hookups: electric (20, 30 amps), water.

Gentry Creek, Rte. 4 Box 5500, 74462. T: (918) 799-5843. www.reserveusa.com/nrrs/ok/gent. RV/tent: 40. $10–$14. Hookups: electric (20, 30 amps), water.

OKLAHOMA (continued)

Highway 9 Landing, Rte. 4 Box 5500, 74462. T: (918) 799-5843. www.reserveusa.com/nrrs/ok/hinl. RV/tent: 73. $10–$16. Hookups: electric (20, 30 amps), water.

Porum Landing, Rte. 4 Box 5500, 74462. T: (918) 799-5843. www.reserveusa.com/nrrs/ok/poru. RV/tent: 53. $10–$16. Hookups: electric (20, 30 amps), water.

Tahlequah

Arrowhead Camp, 7704 Hwy. 10, 74464. T: (800) 749-1140 or (918) 456-1140. RV/tent: 281. $12–$17. Hookups: electric (15, 20, 30 amps), water, sewer.

Diamondhead Resort, 10281 Hwy. 10, 74464. T: (800) 722-2411 or (918) 456-4545. RV/tent: 118. $12–$15. Hookups: electric (30 amps).

Eagle Bluff Resort, 9800 Hwy. 10, 74464. T: (800) 366-3031. RV/tent: 155. $13–$17. Hookups: electric (30, 50 amps), water, sewer.

Hanging Rock Camp, 7453 Hwy. 10, 74464. T: (800) 375-3088 or (918) 456-3088. F: (918) 456-3670. RV/tent: 506. $3–$15. Hookups: electric (30 amps), water, sewer.

Peyton's Place, 10298 Hwy. 10, 74464. T: (800) 359-0866 or (918) 456-3847. F: (918) 456-4950. RV/tent: 85. $3–$15. Hookups: electric (20, 30, 40 amps), water, sewer.

Riverside Camp, 5116 Hwy. 10, 74464. T: (800) 749-CAMP. RV/tent: 48. $10–$15. Hookups: electric (30 amps).

Sparrowhawk Camp, 21985 North Ben George Rd., 74464. T: (800) 722-9635 or (918) 456-8371. www.sparrowhawkcamp.com. RV/tent: 100. $10–$16. Hookups: electric (30 amps).

Tahlequah Floats, One Plaza South, Ste. 243, 74464. T: (800) 375-6949 or (918) 456-6949. RV/tent: 158. $3/person. Hookups: electric (30 amps).

War Eagle Resort, 13020 Hwy. 10, 74464. T: (800) 722-3834 or (918) 456-6272. www.shopoklahoma.com/wareagle.htm. RV/tent: 532. $10–$16. Hookups: electric (30 amps), water.

Tulsa

Estes Park, 1710 South 79th East Ave., 74112. T: (918) 627-3150. RV/tent: 21. $18. Hookups: electric (30, 50 amps), water, sewer.

Mingo RV Park, 801 North Mingo Rd., 74116. T: (800) 932-8824 or (918) 832-8824. RV/tent: 100. $22. Hookups: electric (30, 50 amps), water, sewer.

Valliant

Little River Park, Rte. 1 Box 400, 74764. T: (580) 876-3720. www.reserveusa.com/nrrs/ok/lirp. RV/tent: 89. $10–$15. Hookups: electric (20, 30 amps), water.

Lost Rapids, Rte. 1 Box 400, 74764. T: (580) 876-3720. www.reserveusa.com/nrrs/ok/losr. RV/tent: 30. $8–$13. Hookups: electric (20, 30 amps), water.

Pine Creek Cove, Rte. 1 Box 400, 74764. T: (580) 933-4215. www.reserveusa.com/nrrs/ok/picr. RV/tent: 40. $10–$15. Hookups: electric (20, 30 amps), water.

Turkey Creek, Rte. 1 Box 400, 74764. T: (580) 876-3720. www.reserveusa.com/nrrs/ok/turk. RV/tent: 34. $8–$12. Hookups: electric (20, 30 amps).

Watonga

Roman Nose, Rte. 1, 73772. T: (800) 892-8690 or (580) 623-4215. RV/tent: 175. $7–$21. Hookups: electric (20, 30, 50 amps), water, sewer.

Waurika

Chisholm Trail Ridge, P.O. Box 29, 73573. T: (580) 439-8040. www.reserveusa.com/nrrs/ok/chis. RV/tent: 95. $14–$16. Hookups: electric (20, 30 amps), water.

Kiowa Park I, P.O. Box 29, 73573. T: (580) 963-9031. www.reserveusa.com/nrrs/ok/kiow. RV/tent: 180. $14–$16. Hookups: electric (20, 30 amps), water.

Woodward

Cottonwood RV Park, Rte. 1 Box 195, 73801. T: (580) 256-1068. RV/tent: 22. $12. Hookups: electric (30, 50 amps), water, sewer.

OREGON

Agness

Agness RV Park, 04125 Agness Rd., 97406. T: (541) 247-2813. camping@agnessrv.com. RV/tent: 90. $17. Hookups: electric (30 amps), water.

Albany

Blue Ox RV Park, 4000 Blue Ox Dr. Southeast, 97321. T: (800) 336-2881. RV/tent: 149. $24. Hookups: full.

Ashland

Ashland Regency Inn and RV Park, 50 Lowe Rd., 97520. T: (800) 482-4701. RV/tent: 12. $17–$18. Hookups: electric (20, 30 amps), water.

Howard Prarie Lake Resort, P.O. Box 4709, Medford, 97501. T: (541) 482-1979. RV/tent: 268. $12–$19. Hookups: electric (20 amps), water, dump station.

Hyatt Lake Resort, 7979 Hyatt Prarie Rd., 97520. T: (541) 482-3331. RV/tent: 80. $20–$23. Hookups: electric (20, 30, 50 amps), water, dump station.

Astoria

Fort Stevens State Park, US 30, 97121. T: (503) 861-1671. park.info@state.or.us. RV/tent: 518. $18–$29. Hookups: full.

Baker City

Mountain View Holiday Trav-L-Park, 2845 Hughes Ln, 97814. T: (541) 523-4824. www.ohwy.com/or/m/mtviewrv.htm. RV/tent: 91. $21. Hookups: electric (20, 30, 50 amps).

Oregon Trails West RV Park, 42534 North Cedar Rd., 97814. T: (888) 523-3236. RV/tent: 61. $17. Hookups: full.

Wallowa-Whitman National Forest-Union Creek Campground, P.O. Box 907, 97814. T: (541) 894-2260. RV/tent: 58. $14–$19. Hookups: electric (20, 30 amps).

Bandon

Bandon-Port Orford-KOA, 46612 Hwy. 101, Langlois, 97450. T: (800) 562-3298. RV/tent: 72. $24–$26. Hookups: electric (20, 30 amps), water.

Bullards Beach State Park, Hwy. 101 North, 97411. T: (541) 347-2209. park.info@state.or.us. RV/tent: 185. $19. Hookups: full.

Beaver

Camper Cove, P.O. Box 42, 97108. T: (503) 398-5334. RV/tent: 18. $15–$18. Hookups: electric (20, 30, 50 amps), water.

Belknap Springs

Belknap Lodge and Hot Springs, Box No. 1, McKenzie Bridge, 97413. T: (541) 822-3512. RV/tent: 52. $12–$18. Hookups: electric (30), water.

Bend

Crane Prarie Campground (Deschutes National Forest), FR 4270, 97701. T: (541) 382-9443. RV/tent: 146. $13–$19. Hookups: none.

Crane Prarie Resort, Crane Prarie Lake Rd., 97701. T: (541) 383-3939. RV/tent: 39. $22. Hookups: full.

Crown Villa RV Park, 60801 Brosterhaus Rd., 97702. T: (541) 388-1131. RV/tent: 131. $17–$31. Hookups: full.

OREGON (continued)

Bend (continued)

Curtis Lake Campground (Deschutes National Forest), FR 4635, 97701. T: (541) 382-9443. RV/tent: 55. $13–$19. Hookups: none.

Gull Point Campground (Deschutes National Forest), FR 4262, 97701. T: (541) 382-9443. RV/tent: 81. $13–$19. Hookups: none.

Lava Lake Campground (Deschutes National Forest), FR 514, 97701. T: (541) 382-9443. RV/tent: 45. $13–$19. Hookups: none.

Quinn River Campground (Deschutes National Forest), Hwy. 46, 97701. T: (541) 382-9443. RV/tent: 41. $13–$19. Hookups: none.

Rock Creek Campground (Deschutes National Forest), Hwy. 46, 97701. T: (541) 382-9443. RV/tent: 32. $13–$19. Hookups: none.

Scandia RV and Mobile Park, 61415 South Hwy. 97, 97702. T: (541) 382-6206. RV/tent: 75. $20. Hookups: full.

South Twin Lake Recreation Complex (Deschutes National Forest), FR 4260, 97701. T: (541) 382-9443. RV/tent: 45. $13–$19. Hookups: none.

Boardman

Driftwood RV Park, 800 West Kunze, 97818. T: (800) 684-5583. RV/tent: 123. $22–$28. Hookups: electric (20, 30, 50 amps).

Bonanza

Gerber Reservoir Campground, 2795 Anderson Ave., Klamath Falls, 97603. T: (541) 883-6916. RV/tent: 50. $13–$20. Hookups: none.

Brookings

Port of Brookings Harbor Beachfront RV Park, P.O. Box 848, 97415. T: (541) 469-5867. RV/tent: 147. $14–$27. Hookups: electric (30 amps), water.

At Rivers Edge RV Resort, 98203 South Bank Chetco, 97415. T: (888) 295-1441. RV/tent: 121. $20–$25. Hookups: electric (20, 30, 50 amps).

Portside RV Park, 16219 Lower Harbor Rd., 97415. T: (887) 787-2752. portsiderv@wave.net. RV/tent: 104. $16–$28. Hookups: full.

Whaleshead Beach Resort, 19921 Whaleshead Rd., 97415. T: (800) 943-4325. RV/tent: 110. $20–$25. Hookups: electric (30, 50 amps).

Canby

Riverside RV Park, 24310 Hwy. 99 East, 97013. T: (800) 425-2250. bj06990080@aol.com. RV/tent: 118. $22. Hookups: full.

Canyonville

Seven Feathers Casino Resort, 146 Chief Miwaleta Ln., 97417. T: (541) 839-1111. www.sevenfeathers.com. info@sevenfeathers.com. RV/tent: 32. $14–$16. Hookups: electric (20, 30 amps).

Stanton Park (Douglas County Park), P.O. Box 800, 97495. T: (541) 839-4483. RV/tent: 40. $11–$14. Hookups: none.

Cascade Summit

Shelter Cove Resort, West Odell Lake Rd., Hwy. 58, 97425. T: (800) 647-2729. RV/tent: 69. $12–$19. Hookups: electric (20, 30 amps).

Cave Junction

Country Hills, 7901 Caves Hwy., 97523. T: (541) 592-3406. RV/tent: 28. $17–$18. Hookups: electric (15, 20, 30 amps), water.

Grayback US Forest and Campground, 11575 Caves Hwy., 97523. T: (541) 592-3311. RV/tent: 34. $15. Hookups: none.

Shady Acres RV Park, 27550 Redwood Hwy., 97523. T: (541) 592-3702. RV/tent: 30. $15. Hookups: electric (20, 30 amps).

Charleston

Sunset Bay State Park, 10965 Cape Arago Hwy., 97420. T: (541) 888-4902. RV/tent: 131. $15–$27. Hookups: electric, water.

Chiloquin

Agency Lake Resort, 37000 Modoc Point Rd., 97642. T: (541) 783-2489. RV/tent: 25. $16. Hookups: electric (20, 30 amps), water.

Melita's Highway 97 RV Park, 39500 Hwy. 97, 97624. T: (541) 783-2401. RV/tent: 27. $16. Hookups: electric (30 amps), water.

Walt's Cozy Camp, P.O. Box 243, 97624. T: (541) 783-2537. RV/tent: 34. $14. Hookups: electric (20 amps), water.

Water Wheel Campground, 200 Williamson River Dr., 97624. T: (541) 783-2738. RV/tent: 40. $15–$21. Hookups: electric (30, 50 amps), water.

Coos Bay

Alder Acres, 1800 28th Ct., 97420. T: (541) 269-0999. RV/tent: 33. $19. Hookups: electric (30, 50 amps).

Oregon Dunes KOA, 4135 Coast US Hwy.101, North Bend, 97459. T: (541) 756-4851. www.oregondunesKOA.com. RV/tent: 66. $26–$31. Hookups: electric (30, 50 amps), water.

Cottage Grove

Village Green RV Park, 725 Row River Rd., 97424. T: (541) 942-2491. RV/tent: 42. $24. Hookups: electric (20, 30, 50 amps).

Crater Lake

Mazama Campground, 1211 Ave. C., White City, 97503. T: (541) 594-2511. RV/tent: 196. $14. Hookups: none.

Crescent

Big Pines RV Park, 135151 Hwy. 97 North, 97733. T: (800) 351-2785. Bgpnsrvprk@aol.com. RV/tent: 21. $20. Hookups: full.

Williamette Pass Inn and RV, P.O. Box 35, 97425. T: (541) 443-2211. RV/tent: 19. $20. Hookups: electric (20, 30, 50 amps), water.

Dale

Meadowbrook Lodge Inc., P.O. Box 37, 97880. T: (541) 421-3104. RV/tent: 31. $18–$23. Hookups: electric (20 amps).

Depoe Bay

Fogarty Creek RV Park, 3340 North Hwy. 101, 97341. T: (888) 675-7034. RV/tent: 53. $17–$25. Hookups: electric (20, 30 amps).

Sea and Sand RV Park, US Hwy. 101, 97388. T: (541) 764-2313. RV/tent: 109. $21–$24. Hookups: full.

Detroit

Detroit Lake State Park, 711 North Santiam Hwy., 97342. T: (503) 854-3346. RV/tent: 238. $14–$22. Hookups: full.

Detroit RV Park, 100 Breinbenbush Rd., 97342. T: (503) 855-3002. RV/tent: 17. $17–$22. Hookups: full.

Dexter

Dexter Shores Mobile and RV Park, 39140 Dexter Rd., 97431. T: (541) 937-3711. RV/tent: 56. $24. Hookups: full.

Diamond Lake

Diamond Lake RV Park, 3500 Diamond Lake Loop, 97731. T: (541) 793-3318. F: (541) 793-3088. www.diamondlakervpark.com. RV/tent: 115. $22. Hookups: full.

Dodson

Ainsworth State Park, P.O. Box 100, 97019. T: (503) 695-2301. RV/tent: 50. $14–$19. Hookups: full.

Dufur

Dufur RV Park, P.O. Box 192, 97021. T: (541) 467-2449. RV/tent: 26. $14. Hookups: electric (20, 30 amps).

Elkton

Elkton RV Park, 450 River Dr., 97436. T: (541) 584-2832. RV/tent: 50. $20. Hookups: electric (20, 30, 50 amps).

Sawyers Rapids RV Resort, 24828 State Hwy. 38, 97436. T: (541) 584-2226. RV/tent: 32. $18. Hookups: full.

Enterprise

Outpost RV, 66258 Lewiston Hwy., 97828. T: (541) 426-4027. RV/tent: 60. $19. Hookups: full.

Estacada

Promontory Park, 40600 East Hwy. 224, 97023. T: (503) 630-7229. RV/tent: 48. $15. Hookups: none.

Silver Fox RV Park, 40505 Southeast Hwy. 224, 97023. T: (503) 630-7000. RV/tent: 70. $21. Hookups: electric (20, 30, 50 amps).

Eugene

Coburg Hills RV Park, 33022 Van Duyn Rd., 97408. T: (541) 686-3152. RV/tent: 141. $22. Hookups: full.

OREGON (continued)

Deerwood RV Park, 35059 Seavey Loop Rd., 97405. T: (877) 988-1139. RV/tent: 50. $23–$26. Hookups: full.

KOA Sherwood Forest, 298 East Oregon Ave., Creswell, 97426. T: (541) 895-4110. RV/tent: 143. $17–$23. Hookups: electric, cable.

Shamrock Village, 4531 Franklin Blvd., 97403. T: (541) 747-7473. RV/tent: 115. $22. Hookups: electric (20, 30, 50 amps), water.

Fairview

Portland Fairview RV Park, 21401 Northeast Sandy Blvd., 97401. T: (503) 661-1047. www.portlandviewrv.com. info@portlandviewrv.com. RV/tent: 407. $25. Hookups: electric (20, 30, 50 amps), cable.

Rolling Hills Mobile Terrace and RV Park, 20145 Northeast Sandy Blvd., 97024. T: (503) 666-7282. RV/tent: 101. $22. Hookups: full.

Florence

Carl G. Washburne State Park, Hwy. 101 South, 97439. T: (541) 997-3641. RV/tent: 65. $14–$19. Hookups: full.

Darlings Resort and RV Park, 4879 Darlings Loop, 97439. T: (541) 997-2841. RV/tent: 41. $18. Hookups: electric (20, 30 amps).

Happy Place RV Park, 4044 Hwy. 101, 97439. T: (541) 997-1434. F: (541) 997-4044. happyplacerv@aol.com. RV/tent: 52. $25–$27. Hookups: full.

Lakeshore RV Park, 83763 US Hwy. 107, 97439. T: (541) 997-2741. RV/tent: 20. $18. Hookups: electric (30 amps).

Thousand Trails—South Jetty, 05010 South Jetty Rd., 97439. T: (541) 997-8333. RV/tent: 192. $20. Hookups: electric (20, 30 amps), water.

Woahink Lake RV Resort, 83570 Hwy. 101 South, 97439. T: (541) 997-6454. RV/tent: 76. $23. Hookups: electric (30, 50 amps).

Fort Klamath

Crater Lake Resort at Fort Creek Campground, 50711 State Hwy. 62, 97626. T: (541) 381-2349. RV/tent: 43. $16–$20. Hookups: electric (20, 30, 50 amps), water.

Fort Klamath Lodge and RV Park, P.O. Box 428, 97626. T: (541) 381-2234. RV/tent: 13. $15. Hookups: electric (20 amps).

Glendale

Meadow Wood RV and Campground, P.O. Box 885, 97442. T: (541) 832-3114. RV/tent: 64. $17–$19. Hookups: electric (20, 30, 50 amps), water.

Glide

Susan Creek (BLM), 777 Northwest Garden Valley Blvd., Roseburg, 97470. T: (541) 440-4930. RV/tent: 31. $11–$14. Hookups: none.

Gold Beach

Four Seasons RV Resort, 96526 North Bank Rogue, 97444. T: (800) 248-4503. www.fourseasonsrv.com. fourseasons@harbourside.com. RV/tent: 51. $22–$31. Hookups: full.

Honey Bear Campground, P.O. Box 97, 97464. T: (800) 822-4444. RV/tent: 120. $20–$22. Hookups: electric (20,30 amps), water.

Indian Creek, 94680 Jerry's Flat Rd., 97444. T: (541) 247-7704. RV/tent: 125. $22–$24. Hookups: electric (20, 30 amps), water.

Irelands Oceanview RV Park, 29272 Ellensburg Ave., 97444. T: (541) 247-0148. RV/tent: 33. $15–$22. Hookups: full.

Kimball Creek Bend RV Resort, North Bank Rogue River Rd., 97444. T: (541) 247-7580. RV/tent: 69. $23. Hookups: full.

Lucky Lodge RV Park, 32040 Watson Ln., 97444. T: (541) 247-7618. RV/tent: 36. $17–$22. Hookups: full.

Turtle Rock RV Resort, Hunter Creek Loop Rd., 97444. T: (800) 353-9754. www.turtlerockresorts.com. turtlerv@harbourside.com. RV/tent: 50. $18–$23. Hookups: full.

Gold Hill

KOA-Medford/Gold Hill, P.O. Box 320, 97525. T: (800) KOA-7608. RV/tent: 69. $19–$23. Hookups: electric (15, 20, 30 amps).

Lazy Acres RV Park and Motel, 1550 Second Ave., 97525. T: (541) 855-7000. RV/tent: 75. $16–$18. Hookups: electric (30, 50 amps), phone, modem, dump station.

Grants Pass

Moon Mountain RV Resort, 3290 Pearce Park Rd., 97526. T: (541) 479-1145. RV/tent: 50. $20. Hookups: electric (20, 30, 50 amps), water, dump station.

Rogue Valley Overnighters, 1806 Northwest Sixth, 97526. T: (541) 479-2208. RV/tent: 110. $20. Hookups: electric (20, 30, 50 amps), cable.

Twin Pines RV Park, 2630 Merlin Rd., 97526. T: (541) 956-0710. RV/tent: 22. $18. Hookups: electric (30, 50 amps).

Hermiston

Hat Rock Campground, Hat Rock Rd., 97838. T: (541) 567-0917. RV/tent: 65. $14–$15. Hookups: full.

Huntington

Farewell Bend State Park, Hwy. 30 East, 97907. T: (541) 869-2365. park.info@state.or.us. RV/tent: 136. $14–$23. Hookups: electric, water.

Idleyld Park

Elk Have RV Resort, 22020 North Umpqua Hwy., 97477. T: (541) 496-3096. RV/tent: 42. $20. Hookups: electric (20, 30, 50 amps), water.

Klamath Falls

Klamath Falls KOA, 3435 Shasta Way, 97603. T: (800) KOA-9036. RV/tent: 84. $18–$23. Hookups: electric (20, 30, 50 amps), water, dump station, cable.

Lake of the Woods Resort, 950 Harriman Rte., 97601. T: (541) 949-8300. RV/tent: 39. $20. Hookups: electric (30, 50 amps).

Oregon 8 RV Park, 5225 Hwy. 97 North, 97601. T: (541) 883-3431. RV/tent: 30. $22. Hookups: electric (20, 30 amps), water.

La Grande

Hot Lake RV Resort, 65182 Hot Lake Ln., 97805. T: (800) 994-5253. RV/tent: 120. $23. Hookups: full.

La Pine

Cascade Meadows RV Resort, 53750 Hwy. 97, 97739. T: (541) 536-2244. F: (541) 536-2747. oregonrv@bendnet. RV/tent: 100. $17–$24. Hookups: full.

Lakeside

Eel Creek RV Park and Campground, 67760 Spin Reel Rd., 97449. T: (541) 759-4462. RV/tent: 41. $15. Hookups: full.

Osprey Point RV Resort, 1505 North Lake Rd., 97449. T: (541) 759-2801. RV/tent: 164. $18–$30. Hookups: full.

Lakeview

Goose Lake Park, US 395, 97630. T: (541) 937-3111. RV/tent: 47. $16–$22. Hookups: electric, water.

Hunter's RV Park, US 395, 97630. T: (541) 947-4968. RV/tent: 133. $15–$17. Hookups: full.

Lincoln City

Devils Lake State Park, 1450 Northeast 6th Dr., 97366. T: (541) 994-2002. RV/tent: 87. $22–$25. Hookups: full.

KOA-Lincoln City, 5298 Northeast Parklane, 97368. T: (541) 944-2961. www.koa.com. RV/tent: 76. $19. Hookups: full.

McMinnville

Mulkey RV Park, 1325 Southwest Hwy. 18, 97128. T: (887) 472-2475. RV/tent: 86. $15–$20. Hookups: full.

Olde Stone Village RV Park, 4155 Three Mile Ln., 97128. T: (503) 472-4315. RV/tent: 71. $20. Hookups: full.

Medford

Fish Lake Resort, P.O. Box 40, 97501. T: (541) 949-8500. RV/tent: 51. $15–$23. Hookups: electric (20, 30 amps).

Holiday RV Park, Box 1020, 97535. T: (800) 452-7970. RV/tent: 110. $25. Hookups: electric (20, 50 amps).

Lakewood RV Park, 2564 Merry Ln., White City, 97503. T: (541) 830-1957. RV/tent: 45. $22. Hookups: electric (20, 30, 50 amps).

Medford Oaks RV Park, 7049 State Hwy. 140, Eagle Point, 97524. T: (541) 826-5103. RV/tent: 70. $12–$23. Hookups: electric (20, 30, 50 amps), water, phone, modem.

Pear Tree Motel and RV Park, 3730 Fern Valley, 97504. T: (541) 535-4445. RV/tent: 31. $23. Hookups: electric (20, 30 50 amps).

Myrtle Creek

Rivers West RV Park, 333 Ruckles Dr., 97457. T: (888) 863-7602. RV/tent: 120. $20–$23. Hookups: electric (30, 50 amps), water.

OREGON (continued)

Newport

Harbor Village RV Park, 923 Southeast Bay Blvd., 97365. T: (541) 265-5088. RV/tent: 140. $17. Hookups: full.

Pacific City

Cape Kiwanda RV Park, 33315 Cape Kiwanda Dr., 97135. T: (503) 965-6230. F: (503) 965-6235. pacificcity.net/capekiwandarvpark. capekiwanda@oregoncoast.com. RV/tent: 180. $21.50–$23. Hookups: full.

Pendleton

Mountain View RV Park, 1375 Southeast 3rd St., 97801. T: (541) 216-1041. F: (541) 966-8820. rvpark@oregontrail.com. RV/tent: 100. $20–$25. Hookups: full.

Prineville

Crook County RV Park, 1040 South Main, 97754. T: (800) 609-2599. RV/tent: 32. $19. Hookups: full.

Prospect

Rogue River National Forest (Farewell Bend Campground), 333 West Eighth St., 97501. T: (541) 560-3400. RV/tent: 61. $12–$17. Hookups: none.

Rogue River

Circle W RV Park, 8110 Rogue River Hwy., Grants Pass, 97527. T: (541) 582-1686. RV/tent: 25. $17–$22. Hookups: electric (20, 30, 50 amps), water, dump station.

Cypress Grove RV Park, 1679 Rogue River Hwy., Gold Hill, 97525. T: (800) 758-0719. RV/tent: 45. $20–$22. Hookups: electric (30, 50 amps), cable.

Roseburg

Mt. Nebo RV Park, 2071 Norheast Stephena, 97470. T: (541) 673-4108. RV/tent: 35. $17. Hookups: electric (30 amps).

Rising River RV Park, 5579 Grange Rd., 97470. T: (800) 854-4279. www.risingriverrv.com. risingrv@rosenet.net. RV/tent: 69. $20. Hookups: full.

Twin Rivers Vacation Park, 433 River Forks Park Rd., 97470. T: (541) 673-3811. F: (541) 672-0261. twinrv@internetcds.com. RV/tent: 80. $15–$28. Hookups: full.

Western Star RV Park, 101 LADD, 97470. T: (541) 679-6159. RV/tent: 15. $16. Hookups: electric (20, 30, 50 amps).

Salem

Eola Bend RV Resort, 4700 Salem, Dallas Hwy. 22, 97304. T: (877) 364-9990. RV/tent: 180. $25. Hookups: full.

Salem Campground and RV, 3700 Hagers Grove Rd. Southeast, 97301. T: (800) 826-9605. F: (888) 827-9605. www.salemrv.com. salemrv@salemrv.com. RV/tent: 187. $14–$20. Hookups: full.

Shady Cove

Fly Casters RV Park, 21655 Crater Lake Hwy. 62, 97539. T: (800) 806-4705. RV/tent: 50. $18–$28. Hookups: electric (30, 50 amps), cable.

Rogue River RV Park and Resort, 21800 Crater Lake Hwy. 62, 97539. T: (541) 878-2404. RV/tent: 70. $18–$25. Hookups: electric (30, 50 amps).

Shady Trails RV Park and Campground, 1 Meadow Ln., 97539. T: (800) 606-2206. RV/tent: 50. $18–$22. Hookups: electric (20, 30 amps), water, dump station.

Sunny Valley

Grants Pass/Sunny Valley KOA, 140 Old Stage Rd., 97497. T: (800) 562-7557. RV/tent: 70. $17–$22. Hookups: electric (20, 40 amps), water, dump station.

Trail

Bear Mountain RV Park, 27301 Hwy. 62, 97541. T: (800) 586-2327. RV/tent: 43. $12–$16. Hookups: electric (20, 30, 50 amps), water.

Tualatin

Roamer's Rest RV Park, 17585 Southwest Pacific Hwy., 97062. T: (877) 4RV-PARK. RV/tent: 93. $23. Hookups: full.

Waldport

Waldport/Newport KOA, Hwy. 101–P.O. Box 397, 97394. T: (800) 562-3443. www.oregoncoastkoa.com. orcostkoa@casco.net. RV/tent: 84. $19–$30. Hookups: full.

Wilderville

Grants Pass/Redwood Hwy. KOA, 13370 Redwood Hwy., 97543. T: (541) 476-6508. RV/tent: 40. $17–$22. Hookups: electric (30, 50 amps), water, dump station.

Wilsonville

Pheasant Ridge RV Park, 8275 Southwest Elligen Rd., 97070. T: (800) 532-7829. RV/tent: 130. $26. Hookups: full.

Winston

On the River RV Park, P.O. Box 1614, 97470. T: (541) 679-6634. RV/tent: 36. $17–$21. Hookups: electric (20, 30 amps), water, dump station.

River Bend RV Park, 31 Southeast Thompson, 97496. T: (541) 679-4000. RV/tent: 63. $20. Hookups: electric (20, 30, 50 amps), dump station.

Umpqua Safari RV Park, P.O. Box 886, 97496. T: (541) 679-6328. RV/tent: 30. $17–$19. Hookups: electric (20, 30, 50 amps).

Wildlife Safari RV Area, P.O. Box 1600, 97496. T: (800) 350-4848. RV/tent: 24. $8–$10. Hookups: electric (20, 30 amps).

Wolf Creek

Creekside RV Resort, 999 Old Hwy. 99, 97497. T: (541) 866-2655. RV/tent: 42. $17.50. Hookups: electric (20, 30, 50 amps).

Woodburn

Woodburn I-5 RV Park, 115 North Arney Rd., 97071. T: (888) 988-0002. www.woodburnrv.com. RV/tent: 148. $21–$22. Hookups: full.

Yachats

Sea Perch Campground/RV Park, 95480 US 101 South, 97498. T: (541) 547-3505. RV/tent: 38. $28. Hookups: full.

Yamhill

Flying M Ranch, 23029 Northwest Flying M Rd., 97148. T: (503) 662-3222. RV/tent: 100. $12. Hookups: none.

PENNSYLVANIA

Airville

Otter Creek Campground, 1101 Furnace Rd., 17302. T: (717) 862-3628. RV/tent: 85. $20. Hookups: water, electric (20, 30 amps).

Allentown

KOA Allentown—Lehigh Valley Kampground, Rte. 100, 18066. T: (610) 298-2160. RV/tent: 103. $25–$31. Hookups: water, electric (20, 30, 50 amps), sewer, phone.

Altoona

Sanderbeck's Campground, Spencer Creek Dr., 16635. T: (814) 695-0501. RV/tent: 20. $20–$22. Hookups: water, electric (20, 30 amps), sewer, phone.

Wright's Orchard Station Campground, US 220, 16635. T: (814) 695-2628. www.gocampingamerica.com/wrightsorchard. wrightcamp@aol.com. RV/tent: 42. $20–$22. Hookups: water, electric (20, 30, 50 amps) sewer.

Bangor

Camp Charles Campground, 1020 Blue Mountain Rd., 18013. T: (610) 588-0553. RV/tent: 155. $22. Hookups: water, electric.

Bath

Evergreen Lake Camping, 2375 Benders Dr., 18014. T: (610) 837-6401. RV/tent: 375. $20–$27. Hookups: water, electric (20, 30), sewer, phone.

PENNSYLVANIA (continued)

Beavertown

Gray Squirrel Campsites, RR 1 Box 1699, 17813. T: (570) 837-0333. RV/tent: 240. $16–$20. Hookups: water, electric, sewer

Bedford

Choice Camping Court, 209 Choice Campground Rd., 15550. T: (814) 623-9272. RV/tent: 197. $14. Hookups: water, electric (20, 30 amps) sewer, phone.

Bellefonte

Fort Bellefonte Campground, 2023 Jacksonville Rd., 16823. T: (814) 355-9820. RV/tent: 100. $20–$25. Hookups: water, electric, sewer, phone.

Bentleyville

Campground 70, 824 Bentleyville Rd., 15022. T: (800) 327-6053. RV/tent: 47. $14. Hookups: water, electric, sewer.

Benton

Whispering Pines Camping Estates, 1969 Henderson Ave., 15301. T: (570) 925-6810. RV/tent: 56. $18–$21. Hookups: water, electric, sewer, phone.

Blakeslee

Fern Ridge Campground, P.O. Box 707, 18610. T: (570) 646-2267. RV/tent: 225. $18–$21. Hookups: water, electric.

WT Family Camping, Rte. 115, 18610. T: (570) 646-9255. RV/tent: 110. $23–$27. Hookups: water, electric, sewer.

Bloomsburg

Deihl's Camping Resort, RD 4, 17815. T: (717) 683-5212. RV/tent: 101. $20. Hookups: water, electric (30 amps), sewer, phone.

Indian Head Recreational Campground, 340 Reading St., 17815. T: (570) 784-6150. RV/tent: 229. $20–$25. Hookups: water, electric, sewer.

Shady Rest Campground, 119 Eyers Grove Rd., 17846. T: (570) 458-6327. RV/tent: 100. $12–$13. Hookups: water, electric.

Turner High View Camping Area, RR 4, 17815. T: (570) 784-6940. RV/tent: 92. $18. Hookups: water, electric.

Boyertown

Schlegel's Grove & Campsites, 102 Township Line Rd., 19505. T: (610) 367-8576. RV/tent: 175. $17–$22. Hookups: water, electric, sewer.

Bradford

KOA Kinzua East, Kinuza Hts. Rte. 59, 16701. T: (814) 368-3662. RV/tent: 120. $28–$30. Hookups: water, electric, sewer, phone.

Breezewood

Way Bridge Campground, P.O. Box 102, 15522. T: (814) 735-2768. RV/tent: 50. $16. Hookups: none.

Brodheadsville

Chestnut Lake Campground, Frantz Rd., 18322. T: (570) 992-6179. RV/tent: 200. $20–$25. Hookups: water, electric, sewer.

Silver Valley Campsites, 4214 Silver Valley Dr., 18353. T: (570) 992-4824. RV/tent: 125. $18–$25. Hookups: water, electric, sewer, phone.

Bushkill

Outdoor World—Timothy Lake South Campground, RD 6 Box 6627, 18301. T: (570) 699-1617. RV/tent: 216. $25. Hookups: water, electric, sewer.

Carlisle

Bienvenu Canadian, 200 Greenview Dr., 17013. T: (717) 243-1179. RV/tent: 256. $23–$24. Hookups: water, electric (20, 30 mps) sewer, phone.

Carlisle Campground, 1075 Harrisburg Pike, 17013. T: (717) 249-4563. RV/tent: 115. $21–$23. Hookups: water, electric, sewer, phone.

Catawissa

J&D Campground, RD 2 Box 358, 17820. T: (717) 356-7700. RV/tent: 225. $25. Hookups: water, electric, phone.

Chambersburg

Twin Bridge Meadow Family Campground, 1345 Twin Bridge Rd., 17201. T: (717) 369-2216. RV/tent: 132. $15. Hookups: water, electric, sewer.

Clarks Mills

Camp Wilhelm, 1401 Creek Rd., 16114. T: (724) 253-2886. RV/tent: 147. $16–$20. Hookups: water, electric, sewer.

Claysville

Four Seasons Camping Resort, 3 Camp Resort Rd., Unit 3, 15377. T: (877) 660-4407. RV/tent: 200. $19–$23. Hookups: water, electric, sewer.

Coatesville

Birchview Farm Campground, RD 9 Box 266, 19320. T: (610) 384-0500. RV/tent: 185. $19–$24. Hookups: water, electric, sewer, phone.

Hidden Acres Camping Grounds, RD 2, 19320. T: (610) 857-3990. RV/tent: 255. $19–$24. Hookups: water, electric, sewer.

Cocalico

Cocalico Creek Campground, 560 Cocalico Rd., 17517. T: (717) 336-2014. RV/tent: 130. $22. Hookups: water, electric, sewer.

Columbia

Prospect Valley Farm Campground, 1334 Prospect Rd., 17512. T: (717) 684-8893. RV/tent: 148. $17–$21. Hookups: water, electric (20, 30 amps), sewer, phone.

Connellsville

River's Edge Family Campground, 1101 River's Edge Rd., 15425. T: (412) 628-4880. RV/tent: 157. $15–$22. Hookups: water, electric, (30 amps) sewer.

White's Haven Campground & Cabins, HC 1Box 81D, 15828. T: (814) 752-2205. RV/tent: 120. $18. Hookups: water, electric, sewer.

Corry

Hare Creek Campground, 375 Sciota St., 16407. T: (814) 664-9684. harecreek@tbscc.com. RV/tent: 160. $18–$22. Hookups: water, electric, sewer, phone, cable TV.

Covington

Tanglewood Camping, Tanglewood Rd., 16917. T: (570) 549-8299. RV/tent: 100. $18–$20. Hookups: water, electric.

Cranberry Township

Pittsburgh North Campground, 6610 Mars Rd., 16066. T: (724) 776-1150. RV/tent: 126. $18–$26. Hookups: water, electric (30 amps), sewer.

Darlington

Crawfords Camping Park, 273 Hodgson Rd., 16115. T: (724) 846-5964. RV/tent: 125. $18. Hookups: water, electric, sewer.

Denver

Lancaster/Reading KOA, 3 Denver Rd., 17517. T: (800) 562-1621. RV/tent: 144. $21–$28. Hookups: water, electric (30 amps), sewer.

Dingmans Ferry

Dingmans Campground, Rte. 209, 18328. T: (570) 828-2266. RV/tent: 45. $17. Hookups: water, electric, sewer.

Donegal

Donegal Campground, Rte. 31, HC 63 Box 104, 15628. T: (412) 593-7717. RV/tent: 45. $17. Hookups: water,electric (20, 50 Amps) sewer.

Laurel Highlands Campground, Rte. 31 East, 15628. T: (724) 593-6325. RV/tent: 300. $24. Hookups: water, electric, sewer.

Downingtown

Shady Acres Camp Ground, Rte. 282, 19335. T: (610) 269-1800. RV/tent: 50. $28. Hookups: water, electric, sewer.

Drums

Hazelton/Wilkes-Barre Campground, 718 North Old Turnpike Rd., 18222. T: (570) 788-3382. RV/tent: 87. $22–$28. Hookups: water, electric, sewer, phone.

Hazleton KOA, RR 1 Box 1405, 18222. T: (800) 562-9751. RV/tent: 148. $21–$29. Hookups: water, electric (20, 30 amps), sewer.

Du Bois

Clearview Campground, RD 2 Box 355, 15801. T: (814) 371-9947. RV/tent: 70. $12–$14. Hookups: water, electric, sewer.

PENNSYLVANIA (continued)

East Berlin

Conewago Isle Campground, Bigmount Rd., 17315. T: (717) 292-1461. RV/tent: 95. $18. Hookups: water, electric, sewer.

Outdoor World—Gettysburg Farm Campground, 6200 Big Mount Rd., 17315. T: (717) 292-7191. RV/tent: 275. $25. Hookups: water, electric, sewer.

East Lancaster

Old Mill Stream Camping Manor, 2249 Rte. 30, 17602. T: (717) 299-2314. www.oldmillstreamcamping.com. infooc@oldmillstreamcamping.com. RV/tent: 65. $23–$32. Hookups: water, electric (30, 50 amps), sewer, cable TV.

East Springfield

Pine Lane Campground, 1709 West Lake Rd., 16411. T: (814) 774-4808. www.virthost.alts.net/pine/ane. RV/tent: 45. $15–$23. Hookups: water, electric (20 amps).

Ebensburg

Woodland Park, 220 Campground Rd., 15931. T: (814) 472-9857. www.paonline.com/jwv. woodlandparkinc@paonline.com. RV/tent: 36. $12–$16. Hookups: water, electric (20, 30 amps), sewer, phone.

Elizabethtown

Ridge Run Family Campground, 867 Schwanger Rd., 17022. T: (717) 367-3454. RV/tent: 138. $19–$22. Hookups: water, electric, sewer, phone.

Elysburg

Knoebels Grove Campground, Hwy. 487, 17824. T: (570) 672-9555. RV/tent: 500. $24. Hookups: electric.

Emlenton

Gas Light Campground, RD 2 Box 10, 16373. T: (724) 867-6981. RV/tent: 158. $20–$23. Hookups: water, electric (30 amps), sewer.

Entriken

Hemlock Hideaway Camp, Box 189 B1, 16657. T: (814) 658-3663. RV/tent: 63. $15–$30. Hookups: water, electric.

Ephrata

Starlite Camping Resort, 1500 Furnace Hill Rd., 17578. T: (800) 521-3599. RV/tent: 220. $27. Hookups: water, electric, sewer.

Erie

Hill's Family Campground, 6300 Sterrittania Rd., 16415. T: (814) 833-3272. RV/tent: 136. $21–$22. Hookups: water, electric, sewer.

Etters

Park Away Park Family Campground, 1300 Old Trail Rd., 17319. T: (717) 938-1686. parkaway park@ webtv.net. RV/tent: 203. $13–$22. Hookups: water, electric (20, 30 amps), sewer.

Everett

Triangle Acres Family Campground, Bridge St., 15537. T: (814) 784-3363. RV/tent: 25. $13.50–$15. Hookups: water, electric.

Farmington

Benner's Meadow Run Camping & Cabins, 315 Nelson Rd., 15437. T: (724) 329-4097. F: (724) 329-8101. RV/tent: 200. $19–$29. Hookups: water, electric, sewer:.

Florence

Bennett Acres Campground, RD 1, Rte. 18 North, 15021. T: (412) 947-5120. RV/tent: 515. $15–$18. Hookups: water, electric (30 amps).

Forksville

Almost Heaven Campground, P.O. Box 63, 18616. T: (717) 924-3458. RV/tent: 200. $15–$18. Hookups: water, electric (20, 30 amps).

Fort Littleton

Ye Olde Mill Campground, 599 Gristmill Rd., 17215. T: (717) 987-3244. RV/tent: 30. $15. Hookups: water, electric.

Gaines

Kearse's Campground, Rte. 6, 16921. T: (814) 435-2550. RV/tent: 150. $14.

Kenshire Kampsite, RR 1, 16921. T: (814) 435-6764. RV/tent: 117. $14–$16. Hookups: water, electric.

Pine Creek Vista Campgrounds, Elk Run Rd., 16921. T: (814) 435-6398. RV/tent: 88. $10–$14. Hookups: water, electric.

Gettysburg

Gettysburg Battlefield Resort, 1960 Emmitsburg Rd., 17325. T: (717) 337-3363. RV/tent: 300. $18–$37. Hookups: water, electric, sewer.

Gettysburg KOA, 20 Knox Rd., 17325. T: (800) 562-1869. gettykoa@cvzz.net. RV/tent: 93. $24–$34. Hookups: water, electric (30 amps), sewer, cable TV.

Glen Iron

Penn's Creek Campground, RD 1 Box 363, 17845. T: (570) 922-1371. RV/tent: 87. $18–$20. Hookups: water, electric, sewer.

Gordonville

Country Aces Family Campground, 20 Leven Rd., 17529. T: (717) 687-8014. country-acrescamp@ aol.com. RV/tent: 60. $18–$23. Hookups: water, electric (30 amps), sewer.

Greencastle

Keystone RV Campground, 15799 Young Rd., 17225. T: (800) 232-3279. RV/tent: 25. $15. Hookups: water, electric.

Greentown

Ironwood Point Recreation Area (PP&L), RR 3 Box 344, 18426. T: (570) 857-0880. RV/tent: 60. $16. Hookups: electric.

Ledgedale Recreation Area, RR 3 Box 379 C, 18426. T: (570) 689-2181. RV/tent: 70. $16. Hookups: electric.

Harmony

Indian Brave Campground, Mercer St., 16037. T: (724) 452-9204. RV/tent: 250. $22. Hookups: water, electric, sewer.

Harrisburg

Harrisburg East Campground, 1134 Highspire Rd., 17111. T: (717) 939-4331. RV/tent: 74. $22. Hookups: water, electric, sewer.

Harrisville

Kozy Rest Kampground, 449 Campground Rd., 16038. T: (724) 735-2417. RV/tent: 203. $18–$20. Hookups: water, electric, sewer.

Hatfield

Village Scene Park, 2151 Koffel Rd., 19440. T: (215) 362-6030. RV/tent: 10. $18. Hookups: water, electric, sewer.

Hawley

Wilsonville Recreation Area, HC 6 Box 6114, 18428. T: (570) 226-4382. RV/tent: 168. $16. Hookups: electric.

Hegins

Camp-A-While, RD 3 Box 334, 17938. T: (570) 682-8696. RV/tent: 106. $21. Hookups: water, electric, sewer.

Hershey

KOA Hershey/Conewago, Hwy. 743, 17033. T: (717) 367-1179. RV/tent: 151. $22–$29. Hookups: water, electric, sewer.

Hesston

Pleasant Hills Resort, P.O. Box 86, 16647. T: (814) 658-3986. RV/tent: 110. $18–$21. Hookups: water, electric, sewer.

Holtwood

Muddy Run Recreation Park, 172 Bethesda Church Rd. West, 17532. T: (717) 284-4325. RV/tent: 163. $20. Hookups: water, electric, sewer.

Tucquan Park Family Campground, 917 River Rd., 17532. T: (717) 284-2156. RV/tent: 198. $19–$23. Hookups: water, electric, sewer, phone.

Honesdale

Countryside Family Campground, RR 1, 18431. T: (570) 253-0424. RV/tent: 70. $20. Hookups: water, electric.

Ponderosa Pines Campground, Alden Lake Rd., 18431. T: (570) 253-2080. RV/tent: 88. $21. Hookups: water, electric.

Honey Brook

The Berry Patch Campground, Ross Rd., 19344. T: (610) 273-3720. RV/tent: 125. $20–$26. Hookups: water, electric, sewer.

Two Log Campground, 960 Beaver Dam Rd., 19344. T: (610) 273-3068. RV/tent: 75. $15. Hookups: water, electric.

PENNSYLVANIA (continued)

Hop Bottom

Shore Forest Campground, P.O. Box 366, 18824. T: (717) 289-4666. RV/tent: 160. $23. Hookups: water, electric, sewer, phone.

Indiana

L&M Campgrounds, 2743 Campground Rd., 15765. T: (724) 479-3264. RV/tent: 239. $12–$15. Hookups: water, electric (20, 30 amps), sewer.

Intercourse

Beacon Camping, P.O. Box 494, West Newport Rd./Rte. 772, 17534. T: (717) 768-8775. www.800padutch.com/beacon.html. beacon 8@aol.com. RV/tent: 44. $24–$27. Hookups: water, electric (30, 50 amps), sewer.

Irwin

Dusty Rhodes Mobile Home Village, 14940 US Hwy. 30, 15647. T: (412) 824-7078. RV/tent: 18. $20. Hookups: water, electric, sewer.

Rustic Acres Campground, P.O. Box 253, 15642. T: (814) 226-9850. RV/tent: 132. $10–$15. Hookups: water, electric (30 amps), sewer.

Jamestown

Shangri-La by the Lake Campground, 1824 Williamsfield Rd., 16134. T: (724) 932-5044. RV/tent: 280. $16. Hookups: water, electric, sewer.

Jonestown KOA, 500 Old Rte. 22 East, 17038. T: (717) 865-2526. RV/tent: 129. $21–$26. Hookups: water, electric, sewer, phone.

Kinzers

Roamers Retreat Campground, 5005 Lincoln Hwy., 17535. T: (717) 442-4287. www.rvcamping. com/pa/roamers.html. roamersr@epix.net. RV/tent: 170. $12–$26. Hookups: water, electric (30, 50 amps), sewer.

Kutztown

Pine Hill Campground, 268 Old Rte. 22, 19530. T: (610) 285-6776. RV/tent: 125. $27. Hookups: water, electric, sewer, phone.

Sacony Park Campsites, RD 3 Box 306, 19530. T: (610) 683-3939. drbrown_1@msn.com. RV/tent: 113. $15–$22. Hookups: water, electric (20, 30 amps).

Lake City

Camp Eriez, 9356 West Lake Rd./Rte. 5, 16423. T: (814) 774-8381. RV/tent: 190. $20. Hookups: water, electric.

Laporte

Pioneer Campground, Rte. 220, P.O. Box 185, 18626. T: (717) 946-9971. RV/tent: 95. $19–$23. Hookups: water, electric, sewer, phone.

Lenhartsville

Blue Rocks Family Campground, 341 Sousley Rd., 19534. T: (610) 756-6366. RV/tent: 200. $25–$27. Hookups: water, electric, sewer.

Loganton

Holiday Pines Campground, RR 1, 17747. T: (570) 725-CAMP. RV/tent: 74. $19–$21. Hookups: water, electric, sewer, phone.

Manheim

Tall Oaks Campground, 2649 Camp Rd., 17545. T: (717) 665-7120. RV/tent: 40. $12–$14. Hookups: water, electric, sewer.

Matamoras

Tri-State RV Park, 400 Shay Ln., 18336. T: (800) 562-2663. RV/tent: 130. $23–$25. Hookups: water, electric, sewer, phone.

Mercer

Junction 19-80 Campground, 1266 Old Mercer Rd., 16137. T: (412) 748-4174. RV/tent: 161. $15–$23. Hookups: water, electric, sewer, phone.

Mercer/Grove City KOA, 1337 Butler Pike, 16137. T: (724) 748-3160. RV/tent: 173. $33–$28. Hookups: water, electric, sewer.

Rocky Springs Campground, 84 Rocky Spring Rd./Rte. 318, 16137. T: (412) 662-4415. users.nowonline.net/rockysprings/rocky.htm. rockysprings@nowonline.net. RV/tent: 115. $15–$20. Hookups: water, electric (30 amps), sewer.

Meshoppen

Slumber Valley Campground, RR 2, 18630. T: (570) 833-5208. RV/tent: 70. $18–$22. Hookups: water, electric, phone.

Milford

River Beach Campsites, Rte. 209 Box 382, 18337. T: (717) 296-7421. RV/tent: 165. $23. Hookups: water, electric, phone.

Montgomery

Riverside Campground, 125 South Main St., 17752. T: (717) 547-6289. www.riverside-campground. com. reservations@riverside-campground.com. RV/tent: 172. $14–$23. Hookups: water, electric (30 amps), sewer, cable TV.

New Castle

Willow Lake Campground, RD 1 Box 551, 17856. T: (717) 538-2790. RV/tent: 100. $13–$21. Hookups: water, electric (20, 30 amps), sewer.

New Holland

Country Haven Campsite, 354 Springville Rd., 17557. T: (717) 354-7926. RV/tent: 55. $20–$28. Hookups: water, electric, sewer, phone.

New Stanton

Fox Den Acres RV Resort, RD 1, 15672. T: (412) 925-7054. RV/tent: 350. $20. Hookups: water, electric, sewer, phone.

North East

Creekside Campgrounds, 10834 Rte. 89, 16428. T: (814) 725-5523. RV/tent: 100. $15–$19. Hookups: water, electric.

Ottsville

Beaver Valley Family Campground, 80 Clay Ridge Rd., 18942. T: (610) 847-5643. RV/tent: 85. $22.50. Hookups: water, electric.

Palmerton

Don Laine Family Campground, 790 57 Dr., 18071. T: (610) 318-3381 or (800) 635-0152. www.donlaine.com. dlaine@ptd.net. RV/tent: 92. $21–$22. Hookups: water, electric (30 amps), sewer.

Pequea

Pequea Creek Campground, 86 Fox Hollow Rd., 17565. T: (717) 284-4587. RV/tent: 99. $18–$20. Hookups: water, electric.

Portland

Shady Acres Campground, 1078 Turkey Ridge Rd., P.O. Box 417, 18351. T: (570) 897-6230. RV/tent: 110. $21–$23. Hookups: water, electric, phone.

Quakertown

Melody Lakes Country Estates, 1045 North West End Blvd./US 309, 18951. T: (215) 536-6640. RV/tent: 16. $15. Hookups: water, electric (30 amps), sewer.

Tohickon Family Campground, 8308 Covered Bridge Rd., 18951. T: (215) 536-7951. RV/tent: 200. $25–$30. Hookups: water, electric, sewer, phone.

Quarryville

Yogi Bear's Jellystone Park Camp Resort, Blackburn Rd., 17566. T: (717) 786-3458. RV/tent: 145. $26–$30. Hookups: water, electric, sewer, phone.

Ruffsdale

Madison/Pittsburgh SE KOA, RR 2 Box 560, 15679. T: (800) 562-4034. RV/tent: 106. $23–$31. Hookups: water, electric, sewer, phone.

Russell

Red Oak Campground, RD 1 Box 1724, 16345. T: (814) 757-8507. redoak@gocampingamerica. com. RV/tent: 109. $16–$22. Hookups: water, electric (20, 30 amps), sewer.

Sandy Lake

Goddard Park Vacationland Campground, 867 Georgetown Rd., 16145. T: (724) 253-4645. RV/tent: 534. $18–$23. Hookups: water, electric, sewer.

Schellsburg

Shawnee Sleepy Hollow Campground, RD 1 Box 121, 15559. T: (814) 733-4380. www.dcnr.state.pa. us/stateparks/parks/index.htm. shawneesp@ state.pa.us. RV/tent: 314. $13–$18. Hookups: electric (30 amps).

Scotrun

Four Seasons Campground, Babbling Brook Rd., 18355. T: (570) 629-2504. RV/tent: 125. $24–$26. Hookups: water, electric, sewer.

PENNSYLVANIA (continued)

Shelocta

Wheel-In Campground, RD 2 Box 147, 15774. T: (412) 354-3693. RV/tent: 100. $17–$19. Hookups: water, electric, sewer, phone.

Sigel

Camper's Paradise Campground & Cabins, RD 1 Rte. 949, 15860. T: (814) 752-2393. users.penn.com/~campers. RV/tent: 136. $15–$23. Hookups: water, electric (30 amps), sewer.

Strasburg

White Oak Campground, P.O. Box 90, 17579. T: (717) 687-6207. RV/tent: 180. $18–$22. Hookups: water, electric, sewer, phone.

Stroudsburg

Arrowhead Campground, Beaver Valley Rd., 18360. T: (570) 992-7949. RV/tent: 47. $19. Hookups: water, electric, sewer, phone.

Sunbury

Fantasy Island Campground, 401 Park Dr., 17801. T: (717) 286-1307. fantasy4@sunlink.net. RV/tent: 35. $17–$19. Hookups: water, electric (20, 30 amps).

Tamaqua

Rosemount Camping Resort, Valley Rd., 18252. T: (570) 668-2580. RV/tent: 200. $23–$24. Hookups: water, electric, sewer, phone.

Tioga

TNT Scenic View Campground, Scenic View Dr., 16946. T: (570) 835-5863. RV/tent: 220. $18–$20. Hookups: water, electric, sewer, phone.

Titusville

Oil Creek Camp Resort, RD 3, 16354. T: (814) 827-1023. RV/tent: 100. $16–$20. Hookups: water, electric, sewer.

Tobyhanna

Hemlock Campground & Cottages, 362 Hemlock Dr., 18466. T: (570) 894-4388. RV/tent: 81. $18–$24. Hookups: water, electric, sewer.

Towanda

Riverside Acres Campground, RR 2 Box 211, 18848. T: (570) 265-3235. www.riversideacres.com. camp@riversideacrescom. RV/tent: 41. $14–$21. Hookups: water, electric (30 amps), sewer.

Tunkhannock

Tunkhannock KOA, Box 768, 18657. T: (570) 836-4122. RV/tent: 181. $19–$26. Hookups: water, electric, sewer, phone.

Unionville

Philadelphia/West Chester KOA, P.O. Box 920D, 19375. T: (800) 562-1726. koa@aol.com. RV/tent: 126. $22–$31. Hookups: water, electric (20, 30 amps), sewer.

Upper Black Eddy

Ringing Rocks Family Campground, 75 Woodland Dr., 18972. T: (610) 982-5552. RV/tent: 128. $22–$25. Hookups: water, electric.

Washington

Washington KOA, 7 Koa Rd., 15301. T: (800) 562-0254. koa@wpcd.com. RV/tent: 167. $18–$27. Hookups: water, electric (20, 30 amps), sewer.

Wellsboro

Canyon Country Campground, RD 6 Box 186, 16901. T: (717) 724-3818. cccinpa@epix.net. RV/tent: 99. $16–$22. Hookups: water, electric (20, 30 amps), sewer.

West Sunbury

Yogi Bear's Jellystone Park Camp & Resort, 236 Peaceful Valley Rd., 16061. T: (412) 894-2421. RV/tent: 85. $18–$25. Hookups: water, electric (30 amps), sewer.

White Haven

Lehigh Gorge Campground, Rte. 940, 18661. T: (570) 443-9191. RV/tent: 150. $22–$27. Hookups: water, electric, sewer, phone.

Woodland

Woodland Campground, RR 1 Box 474, 16881. T: (814) 757-5388. RV/tent: 90. $18. Hookups: water, electric, phone.

York

Indian Rock Campground, 436 Indian Rock Dam Rd., 17403. T: (717) 741-1764. RV/tent: 50. $22. Hookups: water, electric, sewer, phone.

York Springs

Hershey's Fur Center, 8164 Carlisle Pike, 17372. T: (717) 528-4412. RV/tent: 25. $21–$25. Hookups: water, electric, sewer.

RHODE ISLAND

Charlestown

Charlestown Breachway, Burlingame State Park, 02908. T: (401) 364-7000. RV/tent: 75. $8–$12. Hookups: water, electric.

Ninigret Conservation Area, East Beach Rd., 02813. T: (401) 322-0450 or (401) 322-8910. RV/tent: 20. $12. Hookups: water, electric.

Chepachet

Camp Ponagansett, Bungy Rd., 02814. T: (401) 647-7377. RV/tent: 40. $15. Hookups: water, electric.

Foster

Dyer Woods Nudist Campground, 114 Johnson Rd., 02825. T: (401) 397-3007. RV/tent: 16. $10. Hookups: water, electric.

Middletown

Meadowlark Park, 132 Prospect Ave., 02842. T: (401) 846-9455. RV/tent: 40. $20. Hookups: water, electric, sewer.

Paradise Motel and Campground, 459 Aquidneck Ave., 02842. T: (401) 847-1500. RV/tent: 16. $25. Hookups: water, electric, sewer.

Middletown Campground, Second Beach, 02842. T: (401) 846-6273. RV/tent: 44. Seasonal rates on request. Hookups: water, electric.

Narragansett

Long Cove Campsite and Marina, 325 Point Judith Rd., 02882. T: (401) 783-4902. RV/tent: 150. $19. Hookups: water, electric, sewer.

Pascoag

Echo Lake Campground, 180 Moroney Rd., 02859. T: (401) 568-7109. RV/tent: 150. $20. Hookups: water, electric, sewer.

Portsmouth

Melville Campground Recreation, 181 Bradford Ave., 02871. T: (401) 682-2424. RV/tent: 133. $15–$23. Hookups: water, electric, sewer.

Melville Ponds Campground, Rte. 114, 02835. T: (401) 849-8212. RV/tent: 128. $21–$25. Hookups: water, electric.

Wakefield

Worden's Pond Family Campground, 416 Wordens Pond Rd. No. A, 02879. T: (401) 789-9113. RV/tent: 200. $20. Hookups: water, electric, sewer.

SOUTH CAROLINA

Aiken

Aiken State Natural Area, 1145 State Park Rd., 29856. T: (803) 649-2857. RV/tent: 25. $12. Hookups: water, electric (20, 30 amps).

Crossroads RV Park & Mobile Home Community, 569 Crossreads Park Dr., 29803. T: (803) 642-5702. RV/tent: 22. $18. Hookups: water, electric (20, 30, 50 amps).

Pine Acres Campground, 213 Duke Dr., 29801. T: (803) 648-5715. RV/tent: 30. $18. Hookups: water, electric (20, 30, 50 amps).

Anderson

KOA–Anderson/Lake Hartwell, 200 Wham Rd., 29625. T: (864) 287-3161. www.koa.com. alhkon@carol.net. RV/tent: 70. $21–$29. Hookups: water, electric (30, 50 amps).

Hartwell Four Seasons Campground, 400 Ponderosa Point Rd., 29689. T: (864) 287-3223. RV/tent: 108. $17–$21. Hookups: water, electric (20, 30 amps).

Sadlers Creek State Recreation Park, 940 Sadlers Creek Park Rd., 29626. T: (864) 226-8950. RV/tent: 37. $13.40–$17.15. Hookups: water, electric (30 amps).

Beaufort

Tuck in the Wood Campground, 22 Tuc in de Wood Ln., 29920. T: (843) 838-2267. RV/tent: 75. $21–$23. Hookups: water, electric (30, 50 amps).

Bishopville

Lee State Natural Area, 487 Loop Rd., 29101. T: (803) 428-5307. RV/tent: 25. $11. Hookups: water, electric (30 amps).

Blackville

Barnwell State Park, 223 State Park Rd., 29817. T: (803) 284-2212. RV/tent: 25. $13. Hookups: water, electric (30 amps).

Bluffton

Stoney Crest Plantation Campground, 419 May River Rd., 29910. T: (843) 757-3249. RV/tent: 30. $17. Hookups: water, electric (20, 30 amps).

Camden

Columbia/Camden RV Park, Box 1210, 29301. T: (803) 438-8774 (call collect). RVColaCamden@earthlink.net. RV/tent: 34. $19. Hookups: water, electric (30, 50 amps).

Canadys

Colleton State Park, 147 Wayside Ln., 29433. T: (843) 538-8206. RV/tent: 25. $13. Hookups: water, electric (20 amps).

Shuman's RV Trailer Park, Hwy. 15 North, 29433. T: (843) 538-8731. RV/tent: 15. $10. Hookups: water, electric (20, 30, 50 amps).

Charleston

Campground at James Island County Park, 871 Riverland Dr., 29412. T: (843) 795-7275. www.ccprc.com. RV/tent: 125. $22–$26. Hookups: water, electric (30, 50 amps).

Fain's RV Park, 6309 Fain Blvd., 29406-4986. T: (843) 744-1005. RV/tent: 34. $22. Hookups: water, electric (30, 50 amps).

Lake Aire RV Park and Campground, 4375 Hwy. 162, 29449. T: (843) 571-1271. www.lakeairerv.com. lakeairerv@juno.com. RV/tent: 117. $12–$24.50. Hookups: water, electric (20, 30, 50 amps).

Oak Plantation Campground, 3540 Savannah Hwy., 29455. T: (843) 766-5936. RV/tent: 304. $13.50–$20. Hookups: water, electric (30, 50 amps).

Cheraw

Cheraw State Recreation Area, 100 State Park Rd., 29520. T: (800) 868-9630. RV/tent: 17. $13. Hookups: water, electric (20, 30 amps).

Chester

Chester State Park, 759 State Park Dr., 29706. T: (803) 385-2680. RV/tent: 25. $11. Hookups: water, electric (30 amps).

Clemson

Twin Lakes Campground, US Hwy. 76, 5 miles west of Pendleton, 29670. T: (888) 893-0678 or (706) 856-0300. RV/tent: 102. $12–18. Hookups: water, electric (20, 30 amps).

Columbia

Barnyard RV Park, 4414 Augusta Rd., 29073-7345. T: (803) 957-1238. RV/tent: 97. $17–$18. Hookups: water, electric (20, 30, 50 amps).

Wood Smoke Family Campground, 11302 Broad River Rd., 29063. T: (803) 781-9921. RV/tent: 37. $11–$18. Hookups: water, electric (15, 20, 30 amps).

Conway

Big Cypress Lake RV Park & Fishing Retreat, Cates Bay Hwy., 29527. T: (843) 397-1800. RV/tent: 23. $20–$35. Hookups: water, electric (20, 30, 50 amps).

Dillon

Bass Lake RV Campground, 1149 Bass Lake Pl., 29536. T: (843) 774-2690. RV/tent: 68. $16. Hookups: water, electric (20, 30 amps).

Little Pee Dee State Park, 1298 State Park Rd., 29436. T: (843) 774-8872. RV/tent: 50. $7–$12. Hookups: water, electric (30 amps).

Ehrhardt

Rivers Bridge State Historic Site, Rte. 1, Boox 190, 29801. T: (803) 267-3675. RV/tent: 25. $12. Hookups: water, electric (20, 30 amps).

Fair Play

Lakeshore Campground, 231 Lakeshore Dr., 29543-2747. T: (864) 972-3330. RV/tent: 50. $22. Hookups: water, electric (20, 30 amps).

Thousand Trails–Carolina Landing, 120 Carolina Landing Dr., 29643-2703. T: (864) 972-3717. RV/tent: 250. $24. Hookups: water, electric (30 amps).

Florence

KOA–Florence, 1115 East Campground Rd., 29506. T: (843) 665-7007. RV/tent: 135. $17–$25. Hookups: water, electric (20, 30, 50 amps).

Swamp Fox Camping, 1600 Gateway Rd., 29501-8123. T: (877) 251-2251 or (843) 665-7007. RV/tent: 61. $15–$16.69. Hookups: water, electric (20, 30, 50 amps).

Fort Mill

KOA–Charlotte/Fort Mill, 940 Gold Hill Rd., 29708. T: (803) 548-1148. RV/tent: 209. $22–$26. Hookups: water, electric (20, 30, 50 amps).

SPM Defender Lakeside Lodges & Campground, 9600 Regent Parkway, 29715. T: (803) 547-3500. RV/tent: 127. $18. Hookups: water, electric (30 amps).

Gaffney

Pine Cone Campground, 160 Sarrett School Rd., 29341. T: (864) 489-2022. pineconerv@aol.com. RV/tent: 91. $20–$23. Hookups: water, electric (20, 30, 50 amps).

Green Pond

Wood Brothers Campground, 8446 Ace Basin Parkway, 29446. T: (843) 844-2208. RV/tent: 42. $15. Hookups: water, electric (20, 30 amps).

Greenville

Flowermill RV Park, 31 Stallings Rd., 29687. T: (864) 877-5079. RV/tent: 30. $14. Hookups: water, electric (20, 30 amps).

Paris Mountain State Park, 2401 State Park Rd., 29609. T: (864) 244-5565. RV/tent: 50. $12. Hookups: water, electric (20, 30 amps).

Rainbow RV Park, 3553 Rutherford Rd., 29687. T: (864) 244-1271. RV/tent: 50. $20. Hookups: water, electric (30, 50 amps).

Scuffletown USA, 603 Scuffle Town Rd., 29681. T: (864) 967-2276. RV/tent: 55. $21. Hookups: water, electric (30, 50 amps).

Springwood RV Park, 800 Donaldson Rd., 29605. T: (864) 277-9789. RV/tent: 55. $18. Hookups: water, electric (30, 50 amps).

Hilton Head Island

Outdoor Resorts/Hilton Head Island Motor Coach Resort, 19 Arrow Rd., 29928-3245. T: (800) 722-2365 or (843) 785-7699. RV/tent: 401. $28–$34. Hookups: water, electric (20, 30, 50 amps).

Outdoor RV Resort & Yacht Club, 43 Jenkins Rd., 29925. T: (843) 681-3256 or (800) 845-9560. www.outdoor-rv.com. outdoorresort@aol.com. RV/tent: 200. $32–$38. Hookups: water, electric (30, 50 amps).

Lancaster

Andrew Jackson State Park, 196 Andrew Jackson Park Rd., 29720. T: (803) 285-3344. RV/tent: 25. $13. Hookups: water, electric (30 amps).

SOUTH CAROLINA (continued)

Leesville
Cedar Pond Campground, 4721 Fairview Rd., 29070. T: (803) 657-5993. RV/tent: 32. $16. Hookups: water, electric (30, 50 amps).

Lexington
Edmund RV Park & Campground, 5920 Edmund Hwy., 29073. T: (800) 955-7957. RV/tent: 260. $10–$13. Hookups: water, electric (20, 30, 50 amps).

Liberty Hill
Wateree Lake Campground, P.O. Box 242, 29074. T: (803) 273-3013. RV/tent: 38. $17. Hookups: water, electric (30 amps).

Manning
Campers Paradise, Rte. 6 Box 870, 29102. T: (803) 473-3550. RV/tent: 60. $14–$15. Hookups: water, electric (30 amps).

McCormick
Hickory Knob State Resort Park, Rte. 1 Box 199B, 29835. T: (800) 491-1764. RV/tent: 75. $18. Hookups: water, electric (20, 30 amps).

Myrtle Beach
Apache Family Campground, 900 Kings Rd., 29572. T: (800) 553-1749. RV/tent: 268. $19–$36. Hookups: water, electric (20, 30 amps).

Orangeburg
Sweetwater Lake Campground, Rte. 5, 29135. T: (803) 874-3547 or (800) 553-1749. RV/tent: 50. $15. Hookups: water, electric (15, 20, 50 amps).

Pelion
River Bottom Farms RV Park & Campground, 357 Cedar Creek Rd., 29160. T: (803) 568-4182. riverbottomfarmsr.v.park@myexcel.com. RV/tent: 60. $22. Hookups: water, electric (30 amps).

Pickens
Keowee–Toxaway State Natural Area, 108 Residence Dr., 29685. T: (864) 868-2605. RV/tent: 24. $7–$12. Hookups: water, electric (30 amps).

Point South
KOA–Point South, P.O. Box 1760, 29945. T: (843) 726-5733 or (800) KOA-2948. pointsouthkoa@gocampingamerica.com. RV/tent: 54. $18.90–45. Hookups: water, electric (50 amps).

The Oaks at Point South RV Resort, Rte. 1, 29945. T: (843) 726-5728. RV/tent: 83. $20.95. Hookups: water, electric (30, 50 amps).

Ridgeway
Ridgeway Campground, P.O. Box 472, 29130. T: (803) 337-8585. RV/tent: 24. $14. Hookups: water, electric (20, 30 amps).

Roebuck
Pine Ridge Campground, 199 Pine Ridge Campground Rd., 29367. T: (864) 576-0302. RV/tent: 45. $16–$22.50. Hookups: water, electric (30, 50 amps).

Santee
Lake Marion Resort & Marina, 510 Rag Time Trail, 29142. T: (803) 854-2136. RV/tent: 65. $16. Hookups: water, electric (20, 30 amps).

Seneca
Crooked Creek RV Park, 777 Arve Ln., 29696. T: (864) 882-5040. RV/tent: 110. $32. Hookups: water, electric (20, 30, 50 amps).

South Of The Border
Camp Pedro, P.O. Box 8, 29547. T: (843) 774-2411 or (800) 845-6011. RV/tent: 100. $17.50. Hookups: water, electric (20, 30, 50 amps).

Spartanburg
Pine Cone Campground, Rte. 4, 29302. T: (864) 585-1283. RV/tent: 12. $12. Hookups: water, electric (30 amps).

Summerton
Taw Caw Campground & Marina, Rte. 4 Box 1740, Summerton, 29148. T: (803) 478-2171. tawcaw@ftc-I.net. RV/tent: 63. $18. Hookups: water, electric (20, 30 amps).

Summerville
Givhans Ferry State Park, 746 Givhans Ferry Rd., 29472. T: (843) 873-0692. RV/tent: 25. $13. Hookups: water, electric (30 amps).

Sumter
Military Park, 314 Lance Ave., 29152. T: (803) 432-7976. RV/tent: 13. $11. Hookups: water electric (20, 30 amps).

Timmonsville
Lake Honey Dew Campground, 2028 Cale Yarborough Hwy., 29161-8223. T: (843) 346-0700. RV/tent: 16. $15. Hookups: water, electric (20, 30, 50 amps).

Townville
Coneross Campground, P.O. Box 278, 30643-0278. T: (888) 893-0678 or (706) 856-0300. RV/tent: 106. $10–18. Hookups: water, electric (20, 30 amps).

Travelers Rest
Holly Hill RV Park, 219 Stamey Valley Rd., 29690. T: (864) 834-0776. RV/tent: 18. $18.50. Hookups: water, electric (20, 30, 50 amps).

Walhalla
Devils Fork State Park, 161 Holcombe Cir., 29676. T: (864) 944-2639. RV/tent: 59. $18. Hookups: water, electric (30 amps).

Walterboro
Green Acres Family Campground, 396 Campground Rd., 29488. T: (800) 474-3450 or (843) 538-3450. RV/tent: 135. $14–$15. Hookups: water, electric (15, 30, 50 amps).

Wedgefield
Poinsett State Park, 6660 Poionsett Park Rd., 29168. T: (803) 494-8177. RV/tent: 50. $8–$$11. Hookups: water, electric (20, 30 amps).

Whitmire
Brickhouse Campground, US Forest Service, 20 Work Center Rd., 29178. T: (864) 427-9858. RV/tent: 23. $5. Hookups: none.

SOUTH DAKOTA

Aberdeen
Wylie Park, 616 Southeast 10th Ave., 57401. T: (888) 326-9693. www.aberdeen.sd.us/parks/wylie.html. RV/tent: 92. $16. Hookups: electric (30, 50 amps), water, sewer.

Akaska
D & S Campground, Rte. Box 55H, 57420. T: (605) 229-1739. dscamp@hdc.net. RV/tent: 16. $15. Hookups: electric (30, 50 amps).

Belle Fourche
Riverside Campground & RV Park, 418 9th Ave., 57717. T: (605) 892-6446. www.ohwy.com/sd/r/rivecamp.htm. RV/tent: 75. $10–$15. Hookups: electric (15, 20, 30, 50 amps).

Beresford
Windmill Campground, 505 Southwest 13th St., 57004. T: (605) 763-2029. RV/tent: 53. $10–$18. Hookups: electric (20, 30, 50 amps), water.

Black Hawk
Fort WeLikIt Family Campground, P.O. Box 381, 57718. T: (888) 946-2267. www.blackhillssrv.com. gocamp@blackhillssrv.com. RV/tent: 100. $18–$27. Hookups: electric (20, 30, 50 amps), water, cable, sewer.

Chamberlain
Happy Campers Campground, 110 West Clemmer Ave., 57325. T: (888) 734-6655. RV/tent: 80. $10–$18. Hookups: electric (20, 30, 50 amps), water.

SOUTH DAKOTA (continued)

Custer

Beaver Lake Campground, 12005 West US Hwy. 16, 57730. T: (800) 346-4383. www.beaverlakecampground.net. beaverlake@gwtc.net. RV/tent: 83. $16–$24. Hookups: electric (15,20,30 amps).

Big Pine Campground, Rte. 1 Box 52, 57730. T: (800) 235-3981. RV/tent: 90. $16–$20. Hookups: electric (20, 30 amps).

Custer-Crazy Horse Campground, Rte. 2 Box 3030, 57730. T: (866) 526-7377. RV/tent: 106. $17–$23. Hookups: electric (20, 30, 50 amps), water, sewer.

Deadwood

Fish'n Fry Campground, HC 73 Box 801, 57732. T: (605) 578-2150. www.deadwood.net/fishnfry/. fishnfry@deadwood.net. RV/tent: 65. $12–$14. Hookups: electric, water, sewer.

Hermosa

Heartland Campground and RV Park, 24743 Hwy. 79, 57744. T: (605) 255-5460. Rving@rapidnet.com. RV/tent: 150. $15–$25. Hookups: electric (20, 30, 50 amps), water, sewer, cable, phone.

Hot Springs

Angostura Reservoir, P.O. Box 131-A, 57747. T: (605) 745-6996. RV/tent: 159. $11–$13. Hookups: electric.

Larive Lake Resort and Campground, P.O. Box 33, 57747. T: (605) 745-3993. RV/tent: 40. $13–$21. Hookups: electric (20, 30 amps).

Interior

Badlands/White River KOA, HC 54 Box 1, 57750. T: (800) KOA-3897. RV/tent: 138. $18–$25. Hookups: electric (20, 30, 50 amps), water, phone.

Keystone

Spokane Creek Resort, P.O. Box 927, 57750. T: (800) 261-9331. www.spokanecreekresort.com. RV/tent: 15. $14–$24. Hookups: electric (15 amps).

Kimball

Parkway Campground, P.O. Box 136, 57355. T: (605) 778-6312. RV/tent: 26. $10–$15. Hookups: electric (20, 30, 50 amps).

Mitchell

R & R Campground, Box 867, 57301. T: (605) 996-8895. RV/tent: 53. $16–$22. Hookups: electric (20, 30, 50 amps), cable, water, sewer.

Mobridge

Kountry Kampging and Kabins, P.O. Box 907, 57601. T: (800) 648-2267. RV/tent: 33. $14–$16. Hookups: electric, water.

Murdo

Camp McKin-Z, P.O. Box 262, 57559. T: (605) 669-2573. RV/tent: 95. $15–$16. Hookups: electric (30, 50 amps), phone.

Oacoma

Familyland Campground, P.O. Box 97, 57365. T: (800) 675-6959. RV/tent: 100. $9–$13. Hookups: electric (30 amps), cable.

Oasis Campground, P.O. Box 97, 57365. T: (800) 675-6959. F: (605) 734-6927. RV/tent: 97. $12–$25. Hookups: electric (20,30, 50 amps), water, cable.

Pierre

Lighthouse Pointe, 19602 Lake Place, 57501. T: (888) 420-9340. www.lighthousepoint.com. lodge@lighthousepoint.com. RV/tent: 45. $12–$25. Hookups: electric (50 amps).

Rapid City

Lake Park Campground, 2850 Chapel Ln., 57702. T: (800) 644-2267. F: (605) 394-8871. campnelson@ rapidnet.com. RV/tent: 48. $19–$29. Hookups: electric (20, 30, 50 amps), water, sewer.

Salem

Camp America Campground, 25495 US Hwy. 57058, 57058. T: (605) 425-9085. cmpsalem@rapidnet.com. RV/tent: 62. $11–$18. Hookups: electric (30, 50 amps), water, phone, cable, modem.

Sisseton

Camp Dakotah, Rte. 1 Box 184, 57262. T: (877) 698-3507. RV/tent: 25. $10–$14. Hookups: electric (30, 50 amps), water, sewer.

Sturgis

Hog Heaven Resort, P.O. Box 477, 57785. T: (800) 551-1283. RV/tent: 100. $15–$35. Hookups: electric (30 & 50 amps), water, sewer.

Wall

Sleepy Hollow Campground, P.O. Box 101, 57790. T: (605) 279-2531. RV/tent: 93. $15–$20. Hookups: electric (20, 30 amps), water, cable, phone.

TENNESSEE

Allons

Deep Valley Park & Trout Farm, 755 Hunters Cove Rd., 38541. T: (931) 823-6053. RV/tent: 29. $10–$12. Hookups: water, electric (20, 30 amps), sewer.

Lillydale Campground, 5199 Lillydale Rd., 38541. T: (931) 823-4155. www.reserveusa.com. RV/tent: 114. $13–$22. Hookups: water, electric (20, 30 amps).

Williow Grove, 9997 Willow Grove Rd., 38541. T: (931) 823-4285. www.reserveusa.com. RV/tent: 83. $10–$22. Hookups: water, electric (30, 50 amps).

Athens

Athens I-75 Campground, 2509 Decatur Pike, Hwy. 30, 37303. T: (423) 745-9199. RV/tent: 63. $16–$20. Hookups: water, electric (20, 30 amps), sewer.

Over-Niter RV Park, 316 Mt Verd Rd., Hwy. 305, 37303. T: (423) 507-0069. RV/tent: 16. $14–$16. Hookups: water, electric (20, 30, 50 amps), sewer.

Baileyton

Baileyton Camp Inn, 7485 Horton Hwy., 37745. T: (423) 234-4992. RV/tent: 44. $16–$19. Hookups: water, electric (20, 30, 50 amps), sewer, modem.

Blountville

KOA–Bristol/Kingsport, 425 Rocky Branch Rd., 37617. T: (423) 323-7790. F: (423) 323-7790. www.koa.com. RV/tent: 73. $19–$28. Hookups: water, electric (20, 30, 50 amps), sewer, modem.

Rocky Top Campground, 496 Pearl Ln., 37617. T: (800) 452-6456. F: (423) 323-9965. RV/tent: 35. $15–$20. Hookups: water, electric (20, 30, 50 amps), sewer.

Buchanan

Paris Landing State Park, 16055 Hwy. 79 North, 38222. T: (731) 644-7359. www.tnstateparks.com. RV/tent: 44. $14–$17. Hookups: water, electric (30 amps).

Bumpus Mills

Bumpus Mills Recreational Area, 764 Forest Trace, 37028. T: (931) 232-8831. www.reserveusa.com. RV/tent: 33. $10–$18. Hookups: water, electric (30 amps).

Carthage

Defeated Creek Park (Corps of Engineers), State Rte. 85, 37030. T: (615) 774-3141. www.reserveusa.com. RV/tent: 155. $13–$23. Hookups: water, electric (20, 30 amps), sewer.

Indian Creek Park, US 53, north of Chestnut Mound, 37030. T: (615) 897-2233. www.reserveusa.com. RV/tent: 53. $9–$20. Hookups: water, electric (30 amps).

Castalian Springs

Shady Cove Resort & Marina, 1115 Shady Cove Rd., 37031. T: (615) 452-8010. F: (615) 452-4524. RV/tent: 95. $12–$20. Hookups: water, electric (20, 30, 50 amps), sewer, modem.

TENNESSEE (continued)

Celina

Dale Hollow Dam Campground, 5050 Dale Hollow Dam Rd., 38551. T: (931) 243-3554. www.reserveusa.com. RV/tent: 79. $15–$22. Hookups: water, electric.

Chattanooga

Lookout Valley RV Park, 3714 Cummings Hwy., 37419. T: (423) 821-3100. F: (423) 821-5774. RV/tent: 126. $22. Hookups: water, electric (30, 50 amps), sewer, modem.

Raccoon Mountain Campground & RV Park, 319 West Hills Dr., 37419. T: (423) 821-9403. www.raccoonmountain.com. RV/tent: 124. $14–$23. Hookups: water, electric (20, 30, 50 amps), sewer.

Shipp's RV Center & Campground, 3728 Ringgold Rd., 37412. T: (800) 222-4551. www.shippsrv.com. RV/tent: 120. $20–$23. Hookups: water, electric (20, 30, 50 amps), sewer.

Clarksville

Clarksville RV Park & Campground, 1270 Tylertown Rd., 37040. T: (931) 648-8638. RV/tent: 59. $19–$21. Hookups: water, electric (20, 30, 50 amps), sewer, modem.

Clinton

Fox Inn Campground, 2423 Andersonville Hwy., 37716. T: (865) 494-9386. F: (865) 494-6794. www.foxinncampground.com. RV/tent: 93. $15–$24. Hookups: water, electric (20, 30, 50 amps), sewer, modem.

Cornersville

Texas T Campground, 2499 Lynnville Hwy., 37047. T: (931) 293-2500. RV/tent: 40. $14–$16. Hookups: water, electric (30, 50 amps), sewer.

Cosby

Fox Den Campground, 311 South Hwy. 32, 37722. T: (888) 369-3661. RV/tent: 74. $12–$20. Hookups: water, electric (15, 30, 50 amps), sewer.

Crossville

Ballyhoo Family Campground, 256 Werthwyle, 38555. T: (888) 336-3703. RV/tent: 74. $15–$20. Hookups: water, electric (20, 30, 50 amps), sewer.

Roam & Roost RV Campground, 255 Fairview Dr., 38558. T: (877) 707-1414. RV/tent: 24. $13–$18. Hookups: water, electric (30, 50 amps), sewer, modem.

Delano

Hiawassee State Scenic River & Ocoee River (Gee Creek Campground), Spring Creek Rd., 37325. T: (423) 263-0050. F: (423) 263-0103. www.tnstateparks.com. RV/tent: 43. $11. Hookups: none.

Dickson

Dickson RV Park, 2340 Hwy. 46 South, 37055. T: (615) 446-9925. RV/tent: 60. $17–$25. Hookups: water, electric (20, 30 amps), sewer, modem.

Tanbark Campground, 125 South Spradlin Rd., 37055. T: (615) 441-1613. RV/tent: 30. $10–$15. Hookups: water, electric (20, 30, 50 amps), sewer.

Gainesboro

Salt Lick Creek Campground, Smith Bend Rd., 38562. T: (931) 678-4718. www.reserveusa.com. RV/tent: 150. $13–$23. Hookups: water, electric (30 amps), sewer.

Gallatin

Cages Bend Campground, 1125 Benders Ferry Rd., 37066. T: (615) 824-4989. www.reserveusa.com. RV/tent: 43. $19–$23. Hookups: water, electric, sewer.

Gatlinburg

Arrow Creek Campground, 4721 East Pkwy., 37738. T: (865) 430-7433. RV/tent: 63. $16–$20. Hookups: water, electric (20, 30 amps), sewer.

Crazy Horse Campground & RV Resort, 4609 East Pkwy., 37738. T: (800) 528-9003. www.crazyhorsecampground.com. RV/tent: 229. $15–$38. Hookups: water, electric (20, 30, 50 amps), sewer.

Great Smoky Mountains National Park (Cataloochee Camp, Cove Creek, NC), 107 Park Headquarters Rd., 37738. T: (423) 436-1200. www.nps.gov/grsm. RV/tent: 27. $12. Hookups: none.

Greenbrier Island Campground, 2353 East Pkwy., 37738. T: (865) 436-4243. RV/tent: 116. $15–$16. Hookups: water, electric (20, 30 amps), sewer.

Le Conte Vista Campground Resort, 1739 East Pkwy., 37738. T: (865) 436-5437. RV/tent: 75. $19–$23. Hookups: water, electric (15, 30 amps), sewer.

Greenback

Lotterdale Cove, P.O. Box 61, 37742. T: (865) 856-3832. RV/tent: 90. $15. Hookups: electric (20, 30, 50 amps).

Heiskell

Jellystone Camping Resort, 9514 Diggs Gap Rd., 37754. T: (865) 938-6600. RV/tent: 100. $15–$22. Hookups: water, electric (30, 50 amps), sewer.

Henning

Fort Pillow State Park, 3122 Park Rd., 38041. T: (731) 738-5581. F: (731) 738-9117. www.tnstateparks.com. RV/tent: 38. $7. Hookups: none.

Hermitage

Seven Points Campground, Stewarts Ferry Pike, 37076. T: (615) 889-5198. www.reserveusa.com. RV/tent: 60. $17–$25. Hookups: water, electric (30, 50 amps).

Hixson

Chester Frost County Park, 2318 Gold Point Cir. North, 37343. T: (423) 842-0177. RV/tent: 188. $12. Hookups: water, electric (20 amps).

Hohenwald

Thousand Trails–Natchez Trace, 1363 Napier Rd., 38462. T: (931) 796-3212. www.thousandtrails.com. RV/tent: 494. $20. Hookups: water, electric (30 amps), sewer.

Hurricane Mills

KOA–Buffalo, 473 Barren Hollow Rd., 37078. T: (931) 296-1306. www.koa.com. RV/tent: 62. $17–$27. Hookups: water, electric (20, 30, 50 amps), sewer, modem.

Jackson

Jackson Mobile Village & RV Park, 2223 Hollywood Dr., 38305. T: (731) 668-1147. RV/tent: 14. $14. Hookups: water, electric (15, 30 amps), sewer.

Whispering Pines RV Park, 129 McKenzie Rd., 38301. T: (731) 422-3682. RV/tent: 30. $15. Hookups: water, electric (30, 50 amps), sewer.

Jamestown

Maple Hill RV Park, 1386 North York Hwy., US 127, 38556. T: (931) 879-3025. RV/tent: 22. $18–$23. Hookups: water, electric (20, 30, 50 amps), sewer.

Kingston

Four Seasons Campground, 120 Farmer Rd., 37763. T: (800) 990-CAMP. RV/tent: 50. $16–$18. Hookups: water, electric (20, 30 amps), sewer.

Knoxville

Southlake RV Park, 3730 Maryville Pike, 37920. T: (865) 573-1837. RV/tent: 125. $19–$23. Hookups: water, electric (30, 50 amps), sewer, modem.

Kodak

KOA–Knoxville East, 241 KOA Dr., 37764. T: (865) 933-6393. www.koa.com. RV/tent: 153. $19–$27. Hookups: water, electric (20, 30, 50 amps), sewer.

Smoky Mountain Campground, 194 Foretravel Dr., 37764. T: (800) 864-2267. RV/tent: 280. $16. Hookups: water, electric (30, 50 amps), sewer.

Lancaster

Long Branch Campground, 478 Lancaster Rd., 38569. T: (615) 548-8002. www.reserveusa.com. RV/tent: 57. $16–$20. Hookups: water, electric (20, 30 amps).

Lebanon

Countryside Resort, 2100 Safari Camp Rd., 37090. T: (615) 449-5527. www.gocampingamerica.com/countrysidetn. RV/tent: 120. $17–$21. Hookups: water, electric (20, 30, 50 amps), sewer.

Lenoir City

The Crosseyed Cricket, 751 Country Ln., 37771. T: (865) 986-5435. RV/tent: 50. $16–$18. Hookups: water, electric (30, 50 amps), sewer.

TENNESSEE (continued)

Limestone

Davy Crockett Birthplace State Park, 1245 Davy Crockett Park Rd., 37681. T: (423) 257-2167. www.tnstateparks.com. RV/tent: 73. $14–$17. Hookups: water, electric (30 amps), sewer.

Linden

Mousetail Landing State Park, Rte. 3 Box 280B, 37096. T: (731) 847-0841. F: (731) 847-0771. www.tnstateparks.com. RV/tent: 45. $13. Hookups: water, electric (30, 50 amps), sewer.

Manchester

KOA–Manchester, 586 Kampground Rd., 37355. T: (931) 728-9777. F: (931) 728-9750. www.koa.com. RV/tent: 43. $19–$27. Hookups: water, electric (20, 30, 50 amps), sewer, modem.

Whispering Oaks Campground, 812 16th Model Rd., 37355. T: (931) 728-0225. RV/tent: 49. $14–$17. Hookups: water, electric (20, 30 amps), sewer, modem.

Memphis

Camp Memphis/Agricenter International, 7777 Walnut Grove Rd., 38120. T: (901) 757-7790. www.agricenter.org. RV/tent: 600. $18. Hookups: water, electric (30 amps).

Middleton

Thousand Trails–Cherokee Landing, Cherokee Landing Rd., 38052. T: (731) 376-0935. www.thousandtrails.com. RV/tent: 296. $20. Hookups: water, electric (30 amps), sewer.

Monroe

Obey River Campground, 100 Park Rd., 38573. T: (931) 864-6388. www.reserveusa.com. RV/tent: 132. $10–$22. Hookups: water, electric (20, 30 amps).

Mt. Juliet

Cedar Creek Campground, 9264 Saundersville Rd., 37122. T: (615) 754-4947. RV/tent: 60. $19–$23. Hookups: water, electric (30 amps).

Nashville

Anderson Road Campground, Anderson Rd., 37217. T: (615) 361-1980. www.reserve usa.com. RV/tent: 37. $11–$13. Hookups: none.

Holiday Nashville Travel Park, 2572 Music Valley Dr., 37214. T: (800) 547-4480. www.city search.com/nas/holidaypark. RV/tent: 238. $20–$34. Hookups: water, electric (20, 30, 50 amps), sewer.

Nashville Shores, 4001 Bell Rd., 37076. T: (615) 889-7050. www.nashvilleshores.com. RV/tent: 100. $20–$35. Hookups: water, electric (20, 30, 50 amps), sewer.

Two Rivers Campground, 2616 Music Valley Dr., 37214. T: (615) 883-8559. RV/tent: 105. $20–$28. Hookups: water, electric (20, 30, 50 amps), sewer.

Newport

KOA–Newport I-40/Smoky Mtns, 240 KOA Ln., 37821. T: (423) 623-9004. www.koa.com. RV/tent: 99. $19–$24. Hookups: water, electric (20, 30, 50 amps), sewer, modem.

Triple Creek Campground, 141 Lower Bogard Rd., 37821. T: (423) 623-2020. RV/tent: 79. $10–$15. Hookups: water, electric (20, 30, 50 amps), sewer.

Old Hickory

Shutes Branch Campground, 501 Weather Station Rd., 37075. T: (615) 754-4847. www.reserveusa.com. RV/tent: 35. $11–$17. Hookups: water, electric (30, 50 amps), sewer.

Pickwick Dam

Pickwick Landing State Park, Park Rd., 38365. T: (731) 689-3129. www.tnstateparks.com. RV/tent: 48. $14–$17. Hookups: water, electric (20, 30, 50 amps).

Pigeon Forge

Alpine Hideaway Campground, 251 Spring Valley Rd., 37863. T: (865) 428-3285. RV/tent: 80. $19. Hookups: water, electric (20, 30, 50 amps), sewer.

Clabough's Campground & Market, 405 Wears Valley Rd., 37863. T: (800) 965-8524. RV/tent: 170. $19–$25. Hookups: water, electric (30, 50 amps), sewer.

Creekside Campground, 2475 Henderson Springs Rd., 37863. T: (800) 498-4801. RV/tent: 75. $20–$24. Hookups: water, electric (30, 50 amps), sewer, modem.

Eagle's Nest Campground, 1111 Wears Valley Rd., 37863. T: (865) 428-5841. RV/tent: 200. $17–$22.50. Hookups: water, electric (20, 30 amps), sewer.

Foothills Campground & Cabins, 4235 Huskey St., 37863. T: (888) 428-3818. RV/tent: 39. $20. Hookups: water, electric (20, 30 amps), sewer.

King's Holly Haven RV Park, 647 Wears Valley Rd., 37863. T: (865) 453-5352. RV/tent: 170. $16–$23.40. Hookups: water, electric (20, 30, 50 amps), sewer.

Riverbend Campground, 2479 Riverbend Loop 1, 37863. T: (865) 453-1224. www.smokymtn-mall.com/mall/river.html. RV/tent: 120. $16. Hookups: water, electric (30, 50 amps), sewer.

Z Buda's Smokies Campground, 4020 Pkwy., 37863. T: (865) 453-4129. RV/tent: 308. $18. Hookups: water, electric (15, 20, 30 amps), sewer.

Pocahontas

Big Hill Pond State Park, 984 John Howell Rd., 38061. T: (731) 645-7967. www.tnstateparks.com. RV/tent: 30. $10. Hookups: none.

Roan Mountain

Roan Mountain State Resort Park, 1015 Hwy. 143, 37687. T: (423) 772-4178. www.tnstateparks.com. RV/tent: 107. $14–$17. Hookups: water, electric (30 amps).

Sevierville

Ripplin' Waters Campground, 1930 Winfield Dunn Pkwy., 37876. T: (888) RIPPLIN. RV/tent: 156. $18–$19. Hookups: water, electric (20, 30, 50 amps), sewer.

Riverside RV Park & Resort, 4280 Boyds Creek Hwy., 37876. T: (800) 341-7534. www.riversidecamp.com. RV/tent: 180. $16–$20. Hookups: water, electric (30, 50 amps), sewer, modem.

Silver Point

Floating Mill Park Campground, 430 Floating Mill Ln., 38582. T: (931) 858-4845. www.reserveusa.com. RV/tent: 118. $14–$20. Hookups: water, electric (20, 30 amps).

Smithville

Holmes Creek, 2620 Casey Cove Rd., 37166. T: (615) 597-7191. www.reserveusa.com. RV/tent: 97. $14–$20. Hookups: water, electric (20 amps).

Smyrna

Nashville I-24 Campground, 1130 Rocky Fork Rd., 37167. T: (615) 459-5818. RV/tent: 150. $13–$18. Hookups: water, electric (20, 30, 50 amps), sewer, modem.

Springville

Buchanan Resort, 785 Buchanan Resort Rd., 38256. T: (731) 642-2828. www.buchananresort.com. RV/tent: 38. $20. Hookups: water, electric (20, 30, 50 amps), sewer.

Ten Mile

Fooshee Pass (TVA), Rte. 1 Box 504, 37880. T: (423) 334-4842. RV/tent: 55. $11–$15. Hookups: electric (30 amps).

Hornsby Hollow (TVA-Watts Bar Lake), Rte. 1 Box 61, 37880. T: (423) 334-1709. RV/tent: 99. $11–$15. Hookups: water, electric (30, 50 amps).

Townsend

Big Meadow Family Campground, 8215 Cedar Creek Rd., 37882. T: (888) 497-0625. F: (865) 448-3346. www.bigmeadowcampground.com. RV/tent: 86. $24–$35. Hookups: water, electric (30, 50 amps), sewer, modem.

Lazy Daze Campground, 8429 Hwy. 73, 37882. T: (865) 448-6061. F: (865) 448-9060. www.gocampingamerica.com/lazydaze. RV/tent: 74. $18–$25. Hookups: water, electric (20, 30 amps), sewer.

Mountaineer Campground, 8451 Hwy. 73, 37882. T: (865) 448-6421. F: (865) 448-2386. www.gocampingamerica.com/mountaineer. RV/tent: 49. $19–$26. Hookups: water, electric (30 amps), sewer.

Tuckaleechee Campground, 7301 Punkin Ln., 37882. T: (865) 448-9608. RV/tent: 134. $12–$20. Hookups: water, electric (20, 30 amps), sewer.

TENNESSEE (continued)

Vonore

Notchy Creek Campground, 1235 Corntassle, 37885. T: (423) 884-6280. RV/tent: 51. $15. Hookups: electric (30, 50 amps).

Toqua Beach Campground, Hwy. 360, 37885. T: (423) 884-2344. RV/tent: 25. $15. Hookups: water, electric (30, 50 amps).

Wildersville

Natchez Trace State Park, 24845 Natchez Trace Rd., 38388. T: (731) 968-8176. www.tnstateparks.com. RV/tent: 210. $14–$19. Hookups: water, electric (20, 30, 50 amps), sewer.

Winchester

Tims Ford State Park, 570 Tims Ford Dr., 37398. T: (931) 962-1181. www.tnstateparks.com. RV/tent: 50. $14–$17. Hookups: water, electric (20, 30 amps).

Yuma

Parker's Crossroads Campground, 22580 Hwy. 22 North, 38390. T: (731) 968-9939. home.aeneas.net/~wksmith/pcamp.htm. RV/tent: 75. $14–$19. Hookups: water, electric (20, 30, 50 amps), sewer

TEXAS

Abilene

Abilene RV Park, 6195 East Int. Hwy. 20, 79601. T: (915) 672-0657. RV/tent: 60. $18. Hookups: electric (20, 30, 50 amps), phone (modem).

Abilene State Park, 150 Park Rd. 32, Tuscola, 79562. T: (915) 572-3204. RV/tent: 107. $6–12. Hookups: electric, water.

KOA-Abilene, 4851 West Stamford St., 79603. T: (915) 672-3681. RV/tent: 81. $24. Hookups: electric (20, 30, 50 amps), water, cable TV, central phone (modem), phone (modem).

Alamo

Alamo Rec-Veh Park, 1320 West Frontage Rd., 78516. T: (956) 787-8221. RV/tent: 440. $17. Hookups: electric (20, 30 amps), phone (modem).

Casa Del Valle, 1048 North Alamo Rd., 78516. T: (956) 783-5008. RV/tent: 175. $20. Hookups: electric (30, 50 amps).

Morningside Mobile & RV Park, 105 North Cesar Chavez, San Juan, 78589. T: (956) 787-5784. RV/tent: 504. $18. Hookups: electric (30, 50 amps).

Alpine

Lost Alskan RV Resort, 2401 North Hwy. 118, 79830. T: (800) 837-3604. RV/tent: 93. $18. Hookups: electric (30, 50 amps), cable TV, central phone (modem), phone (modem).

KOA-Amarillo, 1100 Folsom Rd., 79108. T: (800) 335-1792. RV/tent: 142. $19–24. Hookups: electric (20, 30, 50 amps), water.

Overnite RV Park, 900 South Lakeside Dr., 79118. T: (806) 373-1431. elens@juno.com. RV/tent: 77. $23. Hookups: electric (20, 30, 50 amps), water, cable TV, central phone (modem), modem.

Amarillo

The Village East RV Park, 1414 Sunrise Dr., 79104. T: (806) 373-4962. RV/tent: 90. $22. Hookups: electric (20, 30, 50 amps), cable TV, central phone (modem).

Westview RV Park, P.O. Box 2891, 79105. T: (806) 352-8567. RV/tent: 54. $13. Hookups: electric (30, 50 amps).

Aransas Pass

Icw RV Park, 427 East Ransom Rd., 78336. T: (361) 758-1044. RV/tent: 134. $16–21. Hookups: electric (20, 30, 50 amps).

Portobelo Village RV & Mobile Home Park, 2009 West Wheeler (Hwy. 35 West), 78336. T: (361) 758-3378. RV/tent: 125. $16–18. Hookups: electric (100 amps).

Argyle

Paradise RV Park, 1217 FM 407W, 76226. T: (940) 648-3573. RV/tent: 91. $15. Hookups: electric (20, 30, 50 amps).

Arroyo City

Seaway RV Village, 35375 FM 2925 Rio Hondo, 78583-3474. T: (956) 748-2276. cjtenna@attglobal.net. RV/tent: 75. $18. Hookups: electric (20, 30, 50 amps), central phone (modem), phone (modem).

Austin

McKinney Falls State Park, 5808 McKinney Falls Pkwy, 78744. T: (512) 243-1643. RV/tent: 84. $12. Hookups: electric, water.

Oak Forest RV Park, 8207 Canoga Ave., 78724. T: (512) 926-8984. RV/tent: 88. $20. Hookups: electric (30, 50 amps), cable TV, phone (modem).

Pecan Grove RV Park, 1518 BaRte.on Springs Rd., 78704. T: (512) 472-1067. RV/tent: 93. $20. Hookups: electric (30 amps), cable TV, central phone (modem), phone (modem).

Bacliff

Bayside RV Park, 5437 East FM 646, 77518. T: (281) 339-2131. RV/tent: 87. $25–30. Hookups: electric (30, 50 amps), central phone (modem).

Bandera

Pomarosa RV Park, P.O. Box 1118, 78003. T: (830) 796-4339. RV/tent: 50. $18. Hookups: electric (30,50 amps), phone (modem).

Skyline Ranch RV Park, Drawer 1990, 78003. T: (830) 796-4958. skyline@indian-creek.net. RV/tent: 85. $15. Hookups: electric (20, 30, 50 amps), cable TV, central phone (modem), phone (modem).

Yogi Bear's Jellystone Camp-Resort-Bandera, P.O. Box 1687, 78003. T: (830) 796-3751. RV/tent: 210. $17–19. Hookups: electric (20, 30, amps), water.

Baytown

Willow Creek RV Park, 2305 Hwy. 146 North, 77520. T: (281) 422-5423. RV/tent: 62. $15. Hookups: electric (30, 50 amps).

Beaumont

East Lucas RV Park, 2590 East Lucas Dr., 77703-1126. T: (409) 899-9209. d.sorensen@worldnet.att.net. RV/tent: 65. $20. Hookups: electric (20, 30, 50 amps), cable TV, central phone (modem), phone (modem).

Belton

KOA-Belton/Temple/Killeen, P.O. Box 118, 76513. T: (254) 939-1961. RV/tent: 99. $21–22. Hookups: electric (20, 30, 50 amps), water, cable TV, central phone (modem), phone (modem).

Benbrook

Holiday Park, 76126-0619. T: (817) 292-2400. RV/tent: 105. $10–20. Hookups: electric, water.

Big Spring

Texas RV Park Of Big Spring, 4100 South US Highway 87, 79720. T: (915) 267-7900. rbworthy@msn.com. RV/tent: 106. $21. Hookups: electric (20, 30, 50 amps), cable TV, central phone (modem), phone (modem).

Brackettville

Fort Clark Springs, P.O. Box 345, 78832. T: (800) 937-1590. fcsa@ms1.hilconet.com. RV/tent: 84. $17. Hookups: electric (20, 30, 50 amps), cable TV, phone (modem).

Breckenridge

Bridgeview RV Park, 5300 Hwy. 180 W, 76424. T: (254) 559-8582. RV/tent: 43. $15–16. Hookups: electric (30, 50 amps), water.

TEXAS (continued)

Brenham

Artesian Park RV Campground, 8601 Hwy. 290 W, 77833. T: (979) 836-0680. RV/tent: 59. $12–14. Hookups: electric (20, 30, 50 amps), water, central phone (modem), phone (modem).

Brookeland

Mill Creek Park, Route 3 P.O. Box 486, Jasper, 75951-9598. T: (409) 384-5716. RV/tent: 110. $11–15. Hookups: electric.

Brookshire

KOA-Houston West Campground, 35303 Cooper Rd., 77423. T: (281) 375-5678. RV/tent: 84. $20–23. Hookups: electric (20, 30, 50 amps), water, central phone (modem), phone (modem).

Brownsville

4 Seasons Mobile Home Park & RV Resort, 6900 Coffee Port Rd., 78521. T: (956) 831-4918. coffeeport@aol.com. RV/tent: 125. $20. Hookups: electric (30 amps), cable TV, phone (modem).

Breeze Lake Campground, 1710 North Vermillion, 78521. T: (877) 296-3329. breeze lake@worldnet.att.net. RV/tent: 189. $18–20. Hookups: electric (20, 30, 50 amps), cable TV, central phone (modem), phone (modem).

Crooked Tree Campland, 605 FM 802, 78520. T: (956) 546-9617. RV/tent: 200. $24–28. Hookups: electric (20, 30, 50 amps), central phone (modem), phone (modem).

Paul's RV Park, 1129 North Minnesota Ave., 78521. T: (956) 831-4852. paulrvpark@aol.com. RV/tent: 135. $15–27. Hookups: electric (20, 30, 50 amps), cable TV, central phone (modem), phone (modem).

Rio RV Park, 8801 East Boca Chica, 78521. T: (956) 831-4653. riorvpark@aol.com. RV/tent: 112. $15–27. Hookups: electric (20, 30, 50 amps), cable TV, central phone (modem), phone (modem).

Bryan

Primrose Lane RV & MH Park, 2929 Stevens Dr., 77803. T: (888)782-2671. RV/tent: 117. $20. Hookups: electric (20, 30, 50 amps).

Buchanan Dam

Shady Oaks RV Park, P.O. Box 725, 78609. T: (512) 793-2718. RV/tent: 64. $17. Hookups: electric (20, 30, 50 amps), cable TV, phone (modem).

Bulverde

Texas 281 RV Park, P.O. BOX 420, 78163. T: (830) 980-2282. RV/tent: 159. $20. Hookups: electric (30, 50 amps), water.

Burleson

Mockingbird Hill Mobile Home & RV Park, 1990 South Burleson Blvd No. 20, 76028. T: (877) 736-7699. RV/tent: 59. $18. Hookups: electric (20, 30, 50 amps), phone (modem).

Caddo Mills

Dallas Northeast Campground, 4268 FM 36 South, 75135-6782. T: (800) 309-0714. RV/tent: 85. $19. Hookups: electric (20, 30, 50 amps), central phone (modem), phone (modem).

Canton

Canton Campground, 30488 State Hwy. 64 Wills Point, 75169. T: (903) 865-1511. cmpcnton@gte.net. RV/tent: 74. $15–18. Hookups: electric (20, 30, 50 amps), water, central phone (modem).

Canyon Lake

Maricopa Ranch Resort, P.O. Box 1659, 78130. T: (830) 964-3731. RV/tent: 142. $15–25. Hookups: electric (30, 50 amps).

Cleburne

Cleburne State Park, 5800 Park Rd. 21, 76031. T: (817) 645-4215. RV/tent: 58. $11–17. Hookups: electric, water.

Clint

Cotton Valley RV Park, P.O. Box 1189, 79836. T: (915) 851-2137. RV/tent: 75. $18. Hookups: electric (20, 30, 50 amps), water.

College Station

University RV Park, 19191 Hwy. 6 South, 77845. T: (409) 690-6056. RV/tent: 42. $18. Hookups: electric (20, 30 amps), water.

Colorado City

Lake Colorado City State Park, 4582 FM 2836, 79512. T: (915) 728-3931. RV/tent: 132. $8–11. Hookups: electric, water.

Columbus

Columbus RV Park & Campground, 2800 Hwy. 71S, 78934. T: (800) 657-6108. RV/tent: 50. $20. Hookups: electric (30, 50 amps).

Comanche

Copperas Creek Park, Route 1, P.O. Box 71 A, 76442-9210. T: (817) 893-7545. RV/tent: 60. $14–32. Hookups: electric (30 amps), water.

Comfort

RV Park USA, 108 Blue Ridge, 78013. T: (830) 995-2900. RV/tent: 52. $16.50. Hookups: electric (20, 30, 50 amps).

Conroe

Convenience RV Park & Repair Center At The Fish Ponds, 17091 State Hwy. 75 North Willis, 77378. T: (936) 344-2027. RV/tent: 52. $18. Hookups: electric (20, 30, 50 amps), phone (modem).

Park on The Lake, 12351 FM 830 Willis, 77378. T: (409) 890-2375, rvpark@flex.net. RV/tent: 85. $15. Hookups: electric (30, 50 amps), central phone (modem), phone (modem).

Corpus Christi

Greyhound RV Park, 5402 LeopaRd. St, 78408. T: (361) 289-2076. RV/tent: 90. $18. Hookups: electric (20, 30, 50 amps), central phone (modem), phone (modem).

Hatch RV Park, 3101 Up River Rd., 78408. T: (800) 332-4509. bettyemcl@msn.com. RV/tent: 130. $25–27. Hookups: electric (20, 30, 50 amps), central phone (modem), phone (modem), cable TV.

Marina Village Park, 78418. T: (361) 937-2560. RV/tent: 135. $17. Hookups: electric (20, 30, 50 amps), central phone (modem).

Puerto Del Sol RV Park, 5100 Timon Blvd, 78402. T: (361) 882-5373. ptdelsol@int comm.net. RV/tent: 59. $19–21. Hookups: electric (20, 30, 50 amps), water, entral phone (modem), phone (modem).

Corsicana

American RV Park, 4345 West Highway 31, 75110. T: (888) 872-0233. american.rv.@air mail.net. RV/tent: 95. $22.50. Hookups: electric (20, 30, 50 amps), central phone (modem), phone (modem).

Dallas

Dallas Hi Ho RV Park, 200 West Bear Creek Rd. Glenn Heights, 75154-8112. T: (877) 619-3900. RV/tent: 127. $20. Hookups: electric (20, 30, 50 amps), water, central phone (modem), phone (modem).

Sandy Lake RV Park, 1915 Sandy Lake Rd. Carrollton, 75006. T: (972) 242-6808. sandylrv@ nationwide.net. RV/tent: 260. $20–22. Hookups: electric (20, 30, 50 amps), central phone (modem), phone (modem).

Dawson

Wolf Creek Park, 1175 FM 667, 76679-9707. T: (817) 578-1431. RV/tent: 74. $10–15. Hookups: electric (20, 30 amps), water.

Del Rio

American Campground, HCR 3 Box 44, 78840. T: (830) 775-6484. amercamp@delrio.com. RV/tent: 123. $17.95. Hookups: electric (20, 30, 50 amps), water, cable TV, central phone (modem), phone (modem).

Holiday Trav-L-Park, HCR 3 Box 40, 78840. T: (830) 775-7275. RV/tent: 176. $18. Hookups: electric (30, 50 amps), water.

Denton

Dallas Destiny RV Park, 7100 I-35 E, 76205. T: (888) 238-1532. dstnydall@aol.com. RV/tent: 193. $31–34. Hookups: electric (20, 30, 50 amps).

TEXAS (continued)

Diana

Brushy Creek Park, 2669 FM 726, Jefferson, 75657. T: (903) 777-3491. RV/tent: 111. $10–20. Hookups: electric, water.

Dickinson

Green Caye RV Park, 2415 Caroline St, 77539. T: (281) 337-0289. RV/tent: 74. $18. Hookups: electric (30, 50 amps), central phone (modem).

Donna

Bit-O-Heaven RV & Mobile Home Park, Rte. 4 Box 4750, 78537. T: (956) 464-5191. RV/tent: 700. $18. Hookups: electric (20, 30, 50 amps).

Palm Shadows RV Park, Rte. 4 Box 4452, 78537. T: (956) 464-3324. RV/tent: 469. $25. Hookups: electric (30, 50 amps), phone (modems).

Dumas

Yerby's Mobile Home & RV Park, Box 774, 79029. T: (806) 935-4940. RV/tent: 52. $12–14. Hookups: electric (30, 50 amps), phone (modems).

Edinburg

Orange Groove RV Park, 4901 East State Highway 107, 78539. T: (956) 383-7931. RV/tent: 524. $22. Hookups: electric (20, 30 amps).

Edna

Lake Texana State Park, P.O. Box 760, 77957-0760. T: (361) 782-5718. RV/tent: 141. $9–12. Hookups: electric, water.

El Paso

El Paso Roadrunner RV Park, 1212 Lafayette Dr., 79907. T: (915) 598-4469. elpasorv@aol.com. RV/tent: 136. $20. Hookups: electric (20, 30 amps), water, central phone (modem), phone (modem).

Ennis

Waxahachie Creek Park, 4000 Observation Dr., 75119-9563. T: (214) 875-5711. RV/tent: 58. $12–16. Hookups: electric (20, 30 amps), water.

Eustace

Purtis Creek State Park, 14225 FM 316, 75124. T: (903) 425-2332. RV/tent: 71. $6–12. Hookups: electric, water.

Fentress

Leisure Camp And RV Park, P.O. Box 277, 78622. T: (512) 488-2563. leisure@thrifty.net. RV/tent: 108. $17–19. Hookups: electric (20, 30, 50 amps), water, central phone (modem), phone (modem).

Fort Davis

Davis Mountains State Park, P.O. Box 1458, 79734. T: (915) 426-3337. RV/tent: 88. $15. Hookups: electric, water.

Fort Stockton

Comanche Land RV Park, 700 North Gillis, 79735. T: (915) 336-6403. RV/tent: 58. $10. Hookups: electric (30 amps).

KOA-Fort Stockton, P.O. Box 627, 79735. T: (915) 395-2494. jokar@netwest.com. RV/tent: 79. $15.50–19.50. Hookups: electric (20, 30, 50 amps), water, central phone (modem), phone (modem).

Fort Worth

Sunset RV Park, 4921 White Settlement Rd., No. 46, 76114. T: (800) 738-0567. sunsetrvpark@earthlink.net. RV/tent: 69. $16. Hookups: electric (20, 30, 50 amps), cable TV, central phone (modem), phone (modem).

Fredericksburg

Fredericksburg-KOA, 5681 East US Highway 290, 78624. T: (830) 997-4796. RV/tent: 109. $25–29. Hookups: electric (20, 30, 50 amps), water, cable TV, central phone (modem), phone (modem).

Oakwood RV Resort, 78 FM 2093, 78624-7154. T: (830) 997-9817. oakwood@ktc.com. RV/tent: 134. $19.50–23. Hookups: electric (20, 30, 50 amps), cable TV, central phone (modem), phone (modem).

Fulton

Goose Island State Park, HC 4 Box 105 Rockport, 78382. T: (361) 729-2858. RV/tent: 127. $8–15. Hookups: electric, water.

Galveston

Bayou Shores RV Resort, 6310 HeaRd.s Ln., 77551. T: (888) 744-2837. RV/tent: 84. $18–22. Hookups: electric (20, 30, 50 amps), cable TV, central phone (modem), phone (modem).

Glen Rose

Oakdale Park, P.O. Box 548, 76043. T: (254) 897-2321. RV/tent: 300. $16. Hookups: electric (20, 30 amps), water.

Tres Rios RV River Resort, 2322 CR 312, 76043. T: (254) 897-4253. RV/tent: 537. $18–20. Hookups: electric (30, 50 amps), water, central phone (modem).

Goliad

Coleto Creek Reservoir and Park, P.O. Box 68 Fannin, 77960. T: (361) 575-6366. RV/tent: 58. $14–22. Hookups: electric, water (15, 30, 50 amps).

Grapeland

Salmon Lake Park, P.O. Box 483, 75844. T: (936) 687-2594. RV/tent: 525. $16. Hookups: electric (20, 30 amps), water.

Grapevine

Silver Lake Park, 1501 North Dooley, 76051. T: (817) 329-8993. RV/tent: 59. $15. Hookups: electric (30 amps), water.

Harlingen

Encore RV Park Harlington, 1900 Grace Ave., 78550. T: (956) 428-4137. nhctxss@msn.com. RV/tent: 1066. $20. Hookups: electric (30, 50, 100 amps), central phone (modem), phone (modem).

Paradise Park Harlingen, 1201 North Expressway 77, 78552. T: (956) 425-6881. nhctxpp@msn.com. RV/tent: 309. $22. Hookups: electric (30,50 amps), central phone (modem), phone (modem).

Sunburst RV Park, 4525 Graham Rd., 78552. T: (956) 423-1170. nhctxlw@swbell.net. RV/tent: 300. $20. Hookups: electric (30, 50 amps), central phone (modem), phone (modem).

Tropic Winds Mobile Home & RV Park, 1501 North Loop 499, 78552. T: (956) 423-4020. tropicwsrv@aol.com. RV/tent: 477. $22. Hookups: electric (20, 30, 50 amps), cable TV, central phone (modem), phone (modem).

Hempstead

Yogi Bear's Jellystone Park, Rte. 3 Box 83A, 77445. T: (409) 826-4111. RV/tent: 151. $17. Hookups: electric (20, 30, 50 amps), water.

Houston

All Star RV Resort, 10515 Southwest Fwy., 77074. T: (713) 981-6814. allstar@allstar-rv.com. RV/tent: 120. $34–39. Hookups: electric (20, 30, 50 amps), cable TV, central phone (modem), phone (modem).

KOA-Houston Central, 1620 Peachleaf, 77039. T: (281) 442-3700. RV/tent: 75. $18–24. Hookups: electric (20, 30, 50 amps), water, central phone (modem), phone (modem).

South Main RV Park, 10100 South Main, 77025. T: (713) 667-0120. smrvpark@flash.net. RV/tent: 108. $27.95. Hookups: electric (20, 30, 50 amps), water, central phone (modem).

Traders Village, 7979 Eldridge Rd., 77041. T: (281) 890-8846. tvhops@flash.net. RV/tent: 307. $17.95–20. Hookups: electric (20, 30, 50 amps), water, central phone (modem).

Jasper

Martin Dies Jr. State Park, Rte. 4 Box 274, 75951. T: (409) 384-5231. RV/tent: 85. $12. Hookups: electric, water.

Jefferson

Buckhorn Creek, Farm 726, 75657. T: (903) 665-8261. RV/tent: 100. $12–20. Hookups: electric, water.

Johnson Creek Camping Area, 2669 FM, 75657-9780. T: (903) 755-2435. RV/tent: 85. $12–20. Hookups: electric, water.

Johnson City

Roadrunner RV Park, P.O. Box 161, 78636. T: (830) 868-7449. rvpark1@yahoo.com. RV/tent: 52. $16–18. Hookups: electric (20, 30, 50 amps), central phone (modem).

TEXAS (continued)

Junction

KOA-Junction, 2145 North Main St., 76849. T: (800) 562-7506. RV/tent: 61. $19.95–21.45. Hookups: electric (20, 30, 50 amps), water.

South Llano River State Park, HC 15 Box 224, 76849. T: (915) 446-3994. RV/tent: 70. $6–12. Hookups: electric, water.

Kerrville

Buckhorn Lake Resort, 4071 Goat Creek Rd., 78028. T: (800) 568-6458. buckhorn@ktc.com. RV/tent: 225. $27. Hookups: electric (20, 30, 50 amps), cable TV, central phone (modem), phone (modem).

By the River RV Campground, P.O. Box 2126, 78029. T: (830) 367-5566. RV/tent: 75. $20. Hookups: electric (30 amps), cable TV, central phone (modem).

Take-It-Easy Resort, 703 Junction Hwy., 78028. T: (800) 828-6984. tie@ktc.com. RV/tent: 81. $20. Hookups: electric (20, 30, 50 amps), cable TV, central phone (modem), phone (modem).

Kingsville

Oasis RV & Mobile Home Park, P.O. Box 1689, 78363. T: (361) 592-0764. nomad1@intcomm.net. RV/tent: 147. $15. Hookups: electric (20, 30, 50 amps), phone (modem).

La Feria

Kenwood RV & Mobile Home Plaza Llc, 1221 North Main No. 100, 78559. T: (956) 797-1851. RV/tent: 293. $20. Hookups: electric (20, 30, 50 amps), cable TV, phone (modem).

La Feria RV Park, 450 East Frontage Rd., 78559. T: (956) 797-1043. RV/tent: 153. $20. Hookups: electric (20, 30, 50 amps).

Vip Park, 600 East Frontage Rd., 78559. T: (956) 797-1401. RV/tent: 155. $20. Hookups: electric (20, 30, 50 amps).

La Marque

Little Thicket Travel Park, 408 Volney, 77568. T: (409) 935-5375. RV/tent: 59. $16.50. Hookups: electric (20, 30, 50 amps).

Lajitas

Lajitas On The Rio Grande RV Park, HC 70 Box 435, 79852. T: (915) 424-3471. RV/tent: 78. $18. Hookups: electric (20, 30, 50 amps), cable TV, phone (modem).

Laredo

Lake Casa Blanca International State Park, P.O. Box 1844, 78044. T: (956) 725-3826. RV/tent: 300. $12. Hookups: electric (30 amps), water.

Lavon

Lavonia, 3375 Skyview Dr., 75098-7575. T: (972) 442-3141. RV/tent: 53. $8–16. Hookups: electric, water.

League City

Space Center RV Resort, 301 Gulf Freeway, 77573. T: (888) 846-3478. scrvp@flash.net. RV/tent: 125. $20–32. Hookups: electric (20, 30, 50, 100 amps), cable TV, phone and modem.

Los Fresnos

Palmdale RV Resort, P.O. Box 308, 78566. T: (956) 399-8694. info@PalmdaleRVResort.com. RV/tent: 200. $21. Hookups: electric (30, 50 amps), central phone (modem), phone (modem).

Lubbock

KOA-Lubbock, 5502 County Rd. 6300, 79416. T: (806) 762-8653. RV/tent: 87. $18.95–25.95. Hookups: electric (20, 30, 50 amps), water.

Loop 289 RV Park, 3436 West Loop 289, 79407. T: (806) 792-4348. RV/tent: 85. $19. Hookups: electric (20, 30, 50 amps).

Luling

Riverbend RV Park, P.O. Box 1062, 78648. T: (830) 875-9548. RV/tent: 80. $12–18. Hookups: electric (30, 50 amps), water.

Manvel

Almost Heaven Resort, 4202 Del Bello Rd., 77578. T: (800) 895-CAMP. almostheaven@orbitworld.net. RV/tent: 138. $21.50. Hookups: electric (20, 30, 50 amps), water, central phone (modem).

Marathon

Stillwell Ranch Campground, HC 65 Box 430, Alpine, 79830. T: (915) 376-2244. RV/tent: 66. $13–14. Hookups: electric (30 amps), water.

Marshall

Country Pines RV Park, 5935 US Hwy. 59 North, 75670. T: (800) 848-7087. RV/tent: 100. $13–17. Hookups: electric (20, 30, 50 amps), water, central phone (modem).

Mathis

KOA-Lake Corpus Christi, P.O. Box 1167, 78368. T: (361) 547-5201. RV/tent: 108. $22. Hookups: electric (20, 30, 50 amps), water.

Wilderness Lakes RV Resort, P.O. Box 519, 78368. T: (361) 547-9995. RV/tent: 123. $18. Hookups: electric (20, 30, 50 amps).

McAllen

Citrus Valley RV Park, 2901 State Hwy. 107, 78504. T: (956) 383-8189. RV/tent: 233. $22. Hookups: electric (20, 30 amps).

McAllen Mobile Park, 4900 North McColl Rd., 78504. T: (956) 682-3304. mmpdavid@aol.com. RV/tent: 318. $19. Hookups: electric (20, 30, 50 amps), phone (modem).

McKinney

Lighthouse RV Resort, Box 350, 1020 US Hwy. 75 North, 75454. T: (800) 844-2196. rvresorttx@aol.com. RV/tent: 114. $24.50–26.50. Hookups: electric (20, 30, 50 amps), water, phone (modem).

Mercedes

Encore RV Park-Mercedes, 8000 Paradise South, 78570. T: (956) 565-2044. nhctxps@msn.com. RV/tent: 490. $10–21. Hookups: electric (30, 50 amps), phone (modem).

Llano Grande Lake Park, 489 Yolanda, 78570. T: (956) 565-2638. RV/tent: 870. $20. Hookups: electric (30, 50 amps).

Midland

Midessa Oil Patch RV Park, 4220 South CR 1290, Odessa, 79765. T: (915) 5632368. RV/tent: 135. $24. Hookups: electric (20, 30, 50 amps), central phone (modem), phone (modem).

Mission

Bentsen Grove Trailer Park, 810 North Bentsen Palm Dr., 78572. T: (956) 585-7011. bentsengrv@aol.com. RV/tent: 850. $20. Hookups: electric (30, 50 amps), cable TV, central phone (modem), phone (modem).

Circle T RV Park, 1820 Clay Tolle St., 78572. T: (956) 585-5381. RV/tent: 268. $15. Hookups: electric (20, 30, 50 amps), phone (modem).

Eldorado Acres RV Park, 2404 North Goodwin Rd. (FM 492), 78572. T: (956) 581-6718. RV/tent: 122. $16. Hookups: electric (30 amps).

Seven Oaks Resort & Country Club, 1300 Circle Dr., 78572. T: (956) 581-0068. RV/tent: 232. $20. Hookups: electric (30 amps).

Montgomery

Havens Landing RV Resort, 19785 Hwy. 105 W, 77316. T: (936) 582-6307. lea.bivins@gte.net. RV/tent: 170. $25. Hookups: electric (20, 30, 50 amps).

Mount Pleasant

Lake Bob Sandlin State Recreation Area, Rte. 5 Box 224, 75686. T: (903) 572-5531. RV/tent: 75. $12–14. Hookups: electric, water.

New Braunfels

Hill Country RV Resort, 131 South Ruekle Rd., 78130. T: (830) 625-1919. RV/tent: 300. $18. Hookups: electric (20, 30, 50 amps).

New Caney

Lone Star Lakes RV Park, 20842 US Highway 59, 77357. T: (800) 290-9301. RV/tent: 78. $17. Hookups: electric (20, 30, 50 amps), water, cable TV, phone (modem).

TEXAS (continued)

Orange

Oak Leaf Park Campground, 6900 Oak Leaf Dr., 77632. T: (409) 886-4082. RV/tent: 115. $19. Hookups: electric (20, 30, 50 amps), water, phone (modem).

Ozona

Circle Bar RV Park, P.O. Box 1498, 76943. T: (915) 392-2611. RV/tent: 128. $20. Hookups: electric (20, 30, 50 amps).

Palacios

Serendipity RV Park & Marina, 1001 Main St, 77465. T: (800) 556-0534. RV/tent: 162. $16.50–18.50. Hookups: electric (30, 50 amps).

Paris

Sanders Cove Park, P.O. Box 129, Powderly. T: (903) 732-3020. RV/tent: 89. $10–15. Hookups: electric, water.

Pecos

Trapark RV Park, 3100 Moore St, 79772. T: (915) 447-2137. RV/tent: 61. $15. Hookups: electric (20, 30, 50 amps), water, cable TV, central phone (modem).

Perrin

Mitchell RV Park, P.O. Box 68, 76486. T: (940) 798-4615. dheinz@wf.net. RV/tent: 245. $16. Hookups: electric (20, 30 amps), water, central phone (modem), phone (modem).

Pineland

San Augustine Park, Route 3, P.O. Box 486, Jasper, 75951-9598. T: (409) 384-5716. RV/tent: 100. $12–17. Hookups: electric, water.

Port Aransas

Island RV Resort, Box 1377, 78373. T: (361) 749-5600. RV/tent: 199. $20. Hookups: electric (20, 30, 50 amps), cable TV, phone (modem).

Surfside RV Resort, P.O. Box 179, 78373. T: (888) 565-5929. RV/tent: 45. $20–22. Hookups: electric (50 amps), cable TV, phone (modem).

Port Isabel

Port Isabel Park Center, P.O. Box 295, 78578. T: (956) 943-7340. Pipkcenter@aol.com. RV/tent: 225. $13–14. Hookups: electric (30, 50 amps), cable TV, central phone (modem), phone (modem).

Portland

Sea Breeze RV Park, 1026 Seabreeze Ln., 78374. T: (361) 643-0744. seabreezrv@aol.com. RV/tent: 142. $20. Hookups: electric (30, 50 amps), water, cable TV, central phone (modem), phone (modem).

Proctor

Sowell Creek Park, Route 1, P.O. Box 71 A, Comancle, 76442-9210. T: (817) 879-2322. RV/tent: 60. $14–50. Hookups: electric (30 amps), water.

Rio Hondo

River Ranch RV Resort, 20054 Reynolds, 78583-3106. T: (956) 748-2286. RV/tent: 125. $20. Hookups: electric (30, 50 amps).

Rockport

Lagoons RV Resort, 600 Enterprise Blvd., 78382. T: (361) 729-7834. lagoonsrv@the-i.net. RV/tent: 298. $21.50–23. Hookups: electric (30, 50 amps), cable TV, central phone (modem), phone (modem).

Woody Acres Mobile Home & RV Resort, Box 236 Fulton, 78358. T: (800) 526-9264. woodyacres@interconnect.net. RV/tent: 225. $17.50–24. Hookups: electric (20, 30, 50 amps), cable TV, central phone (modem), phone (modem).

San Angelo

Spring Creek Marina & RV Park, 45 Fishermans Rd., 76904. T: (800) 500-7801. sprcreek@wcc.net. RV/tent: 83. $18.50–22. Hookups: electric (20, 30, 50 amps), water, cable TV, central phone (modem), phone (modem).

San Antonio

Blazing Star Luxury RV Resort, 1120 West Loop 1604 North, 78251. T: (877) 387-5777. bfurci@express-news.net. RV/tent: 260. $27–35. Hookups: electric (30, 50 amps), cable TV, central phone (modem), phone (modem).

Traveler's World RV Resort, 2617 Roosevelt Ave., 78214. T: (210) 532-8310. tvrwrld@aol.com. RV/tent: 170. $24.50–27. Hookups: electric (30, 50 amps), central phone (modem), phone (modem).

Sanger

Ray Roberts Lake State Park, 100 PW 4137 Pilot Point, 76258-8944. T: (940) 686-2148. RV/tent: 151. $10–14. Hookups: electric (20, 30 amps), water.

Schertz

Stone Creek RV Park, 18905 IH-35 North, 78154. T: (830) 609-7759. stonecrk@onr.com. RV/tent: 256. $19.50–21.50. Hookups: electric (30, 50 amps), central phone (modem), phone (modem).

Seguin

River Shade RV Park, 3995 State Hwy. 123 Bypass, 78155. T: (800) 364-7275. rivershade@prodigy.net. RV/tent: 78. $20–22. Hookups: electric (30, 50 amps), cable TV, central phone (modem), phone (modem).

South Padre Island

Destination South Padre Island, One Padre Blvd., 78597. T: (800) 867-2373. RV/tent: 190. $28–38. Hookups: electric (20, 30, 50 amps).

Spring

Spring Oaks RV & Mobile Home Community, 22014 Spring Oaks Dr., 77389. T: (281) 350-2606. RV/tent: 67. $18. Hookups: electric (30, 50 amps), central phone (modem), phone (modem).

Sugar Land

USA RV Park, 20825 Southwest Fwy., 77479. T: (281) 343-0626. RV/tent: 114. $14.50. Hookups: electric (30, 50 amps).

Surfside Beach

San Luis Pass County Park, 14001 CR 257 Freeport, 77541. T: (800) 372-7578. RV/tent: 89. $17–20. Hookups: electric (20, 30, 50 amps).

Terlingua

Big Bend Motor Inn & RV Campground, Box 336, 79852. T: (915) 371-2218. RV/tent: 166. $16. Hookups: electric (20, 30, 50 amps), water, cable TV, central phone (modem), phone (modem).

Texarkana

Clear Springs Recreational Area, P.O. Box 1817, 75504-1817. T: (903) 838-8636. RV/tent: 101. $12. Hookups: electric (20, 30 amps), water.

The Colony

Hidden Cove Park, Rte. 2 Box 353H, Frisco, 75034. T: (972) 294-1155. RV/tent: 50. $16–28. Hookups: electric (20, 30 amps), water.

Tyler

Tyler State Park, 789 Park Rd. 16, 75706-9141. T: (903) 597-5338. RV/tent: 149. $8–12. Hookups: electric (20, 30 amps), water.

Whispering Pines Campground & Resort, 5583 FM 16 East, 75706. T: (800) 559-3817. wpines@gower.net. RV/tent: 140. $17–20. Hookups: electric (20, 30, 50 amps), water, central phone (modem), phone (modem).

Uvalde

Park Chalk Bluff, HCR 33 Box 566, 78801. T: (830) 278-5515. fgwallac@peppersnet.com. RV/tent: 87. $10–18. Hookups: electric (30, 50 amps), water.

Van Horn

KOA-Van Horn, P.O. Box 265, 79855. T: (915) 283-2728. RV/tent: 70. $18.50. Hookups: electric (20, 30, 50 amps), water.

Vernon

Rocking A RV Park, 3725 Harrison, 76384. T: (940) 552-2821. rockinga@chipshot.net. RV/tent: 83. $18–20. Hookups: electric (20, 30, 50 amps), water, central phone (modem), phone (modem).

TEXAS (continued)

Victoria

Dad's RV Park, 203 Hopkins, 77901. T: (361) 573-1231. dadrv@txer.lnet. RV/tent: 50. $14–17. Hookups: electric (20, 30, 50 amps), water, cable TV, central phone (modem), phone (modem).

Waco

Speegleville I Park, P.O. Box 8221, 76714. T: (817) 756-5359. RV/tent: 99. $13–16. Hookups: electric (30 amps), water.

Waco North-KOA, P.O. Box 157 West, 76691. T: (254) 826-3869. RV/tent: 76. $20–21. Hookups: electric (20, 30, 50 amps), water, central phone (modem), phone (modem).

Wallisville

Turtle Bayou RV Park, P.O. Box 185, 77597. T: (409) 389-2468. RV/tent: 63. $24. Hookups: electric (30, 50 amps), water.

Weslaco

Magic Valley Park, 2300 East State Hwy. 83, 78596. T: (956) 968-8242. RV/tent: 387. $17. Hookups: electric (20, 30 amps), phone (modem).

Snow to Sun RV & Mobile Home Community, 1701 North International Blvd., 78596. T: (956) 968-0322. RV/tent: 316. $25. Hookups: electric (50 amps), phone (modem), central phone (modem).

Whitney

Lake Whitney RV Resort, P.O. Box 1309, 76692-1309. T: (800) 999-9259. RV/tent: 75. $18. Hookups: electric (20, 30, 50 amps).

Wichita Falls

Wichita Falls RV Park, 2944 Seymour Hwy., 76301. T: (800) 252-1532. RV/tent: 135. $20–22.50. Hookups: electric (20, 30, 50 amps), cable TV.

Wylie

East Fork Park, P.0. Box 742585, 75374. T: (972) 442-3141. RV/tent: 63. $8–16. Hookups: electric, water.

Zapata

4 Seasons RV Park, P.O. Box 1007, 78076. T: (956) 765-4241. RV/tent: 175. $15. Hookups: electric (20, 30, 50 amps), water, cable TV, phone (modem)

UTAH

American Fork

American Campground, 418 East 620 South, 84003. T: (801) 756-5502. RV/tent: 52. $18–$20. Hookups: electric (20, 30 amp), water, sewer, phone (modem).

Antimony

Antimony Mercantile Campground, 700 North Hwy. 22, 84712. T: (435) 624-3253. RV/tent: 24. $10–$15. Hookups: electric (30 amp), water, sewer.

Otter Creek RV & Marina, P.O. Box 43, 84712. T: (435) 624-3268. RV/tent: 32. $15. Hookups: electric (15, 30 amp), water, sewer.

Otter Creek State Park, Hwy. 22, 84712. T: (800) 441-3292. RV/tent: 30. $10–$12. Hookups: none.

Beaver

Anderson Meadow, 575 South Main, P.O. Box E, 84713. T: (435) 438-2436. RV/tent: 10. $6. Hookups: none.

Beaver Canyon Campground, 1419 East Canyon Rd., P.O. Box 1528, 84713. T: (435) 438-5654. RV/tent: 105. $10–$12. Hookups: electric (20, 30 amp), water, sewer.

Kents Lake, 575 South Main, P.O. Box E, 84713. T: (435) 438-2436. RV/tent: 38. $8. Hookups: none.

KOA Beaver, Manderfield Rd., 84713. T: (435) 438-2924. RV/tent: 75. $16–$20. Hookups: electric (20, 30 amp), water, sewer.

Blanding

Kampark, 861 South Main St., 84511. T: (435) 678-2770. RV/tent: 69. $11–$15. Hookups: electric (20, 30, 50 amp), water, sewer, phone (modem).

Bluff

Cottonwood RV Park, P.O. Box 6, 84512. T: (435) 672-2287. RV/tent: 41. $14–$16. Hookups: Electric (20, 30, 50 amp), water, sewer, phone (modem).

Boulder

Boulder Exchange, 425 North Hwy. 12 Box 1418, 84716. T: (435) 335-7304. RV/tent: 6. $10–$20. Hookups: electric (20 amp), water, sewer.

Brigham City

Brigham City/Perry South KOA, Box 579, 84302. T: (435) 723-5503 or (800) 562-0903. RV/tent: 102. $19–$23. Hookups: electric (20, 30 amp), water, sewer.

Crystal Hot Springs, 8215 North Hwy. 38, 84314. T: (435) 279-8104. RV/tent: 120. $9–$19. Hookups: electric (20, 30 amp), water, sewer.

Golden Spike RV Park, 1100 South 905 West, 84302. T: (435) 723-8858. RV/tent: 60. $13–$24. Hookups: electric (20, 30, 50 amp), water, sewer, cable TV, phone (modem).

Caineville

Sleepy Hollow Campground, HC 70 Box 40, 84775. T: (435) 456-9130. RV/tent: 39. $12. Hookups: electric (30 amp).

Cedar City

Best Western Town & Country RV Park, 200 North Main St., 84720. T: (435) 586-9900. F: (435) 586-1664. RV/tent: 10. $26 (includes breakfast). Hookups: electric (20, 30, 50 amp), water, sewer, cable TV, phone (modem).

KOA Cedar City, 1121 North Main, 84720. T: (435) 586-9872. RV/tent: 129. $18–$22. Hookups: electric (20, 30 amp), water, sewer, phone.

Navajo Lake, P.O. Box 627, 84721. T: (435) 865-3200. www.fsfed.us/outernet/dixie-nf/welcome.htm. RV/tent: 28. $7. Hookups: none.

Te-Ah, P.O. Box 627, 84721. T: (435) 865-3200. www.fsfed.us/outernet/dixie-nf/welcome.htm. RV/tent: 42. $7. Hookups: none.

Delta

Antelope Valley RV Park, 776 West Main, P.O. Box 843, 84624. T: (435) 864-1813. RV/tent: 96. $20. Hookups: water, electric (20, 30, 50 amp), sewer.

Duchesne

Aspen Grove Campground, 85 West Main, P.O. Box 981, 84021. T: (435) 738-2482. RV/tent: 33. $6–$9. Hookups: none.

Hades Campground, 85 West Main, P.O. Box 981, 84021. T: (435) 738-2482. RV/tent: 17. $6. Hookups: none.

Iron Mine Campground, 85 West Main, P.O. Box 981, 84021. T: (435) 738-2482. RV/tent: 27. $6. Hookups: none.

Moon Lake Campground, 85 West Main, P.O. Box 981, 84021. T: (435) 738-2482. RV/tent: 51. $8. Hookups: none.

South Fork Campground, 85 West Main, P.O. Box 981, 84021. T: (435) 738-2482. RV/tent: 5. $8. Hookups: none.

Starvation State Park, P.O. Box 584, 84021. T: (435) 738-2326. RV/tent: 54. $12. Hookups: none.

UTAH (continued)

Duchesne (continued)

Yellowpine Campground, 85 West Main, P.O. Box 981, 84021. T: (435) 738-2482. RV/tent: 29. $8. Hookups: none.

Escalante

Blue Spruce Campground, P.O. Box 246, 84726. T: (435) 826-5400 or (877) 444-6777. RV/tent: 6. $7. Hookups: none.

Moqui Motel & RV Park, 480 West Main St. Box 434, 84726. T: (435) 826-4210. RV/tent: 7. $20–$29. Hookups: electric (20, 30 amp), water, sewer.

Pine Lake Campground, P.O. Box 246, 84726. T: (435) 826-5600 or (877) 444-6777. RV/tent: 33. $9. Hookups: none.

Posey Lake Campground, P.O. Box 246, 84726. T: (435) 826-5400 or (877) 444-6777. RV/tent: 23. $8. Hookups: none.

Farmington

Lagoon RV Park & Campground, 375 North Lagoon Dr., 84025. T: (801) 451-8100 or (800) 748-5246. RV/tent: 208. $18–$26. Hookups: electric (20, 30, 50 amp), water, sewer.

Fillmore

Wagons West RV Park and Campground, 545 North Main, 84631. T: (435) 743-6188. RV/tent: 50. $20. Hookups: electric (20, 30, 50 amp), water, sewer, cable TV, phone (modem).

Garden City

Bear Lake KOA, 485 North Bear Lake Blvd., 84028. T: (435) 946-3454 or (800) 562-3442. F: (435) 946-3454. RV/tent: 160. $17–$26. Hookups: electric (30, 50 amp), water, sewer.

Sweetwater RV Park & Marina, Ideal Beach, South Shore, 84028. T: (435) 946-8735. RV/tent: 19. $25. Hookups: electric (30 amp), water, sewer.

Hanksville

Starr Spring Campground, 100 West 400 S, 84734. T: (435) 542-3461. www.utso.ut.blm.gov. RV/tent: 12. $4. Hookups: none.

Hatch

Bryce-Zion Midway Resort, US Hwy. 89, 84735. T: (888) 299-3531 or (435) 735-4199. F: (435) 735-4198. www.netutah.com/bzrhatch. bzmrhatch@juno.com. RV/tent: 20. $19. Hookups: electric (30 amp), water, sewer.

Heber City

Currant Creek Campground, 2460 South Hwy. 40, 84032. T: (435) 654-0470. RV/tent: 99. $10. Hookups: none.

Heber Valley RV Park Resort, 7000 North Hwy. 40, 84032. T: (435) 654-4049. F: (435) 654-5496. RV/tent: 120. $20. Hookups: electric (20, 30, 50 amp), water, sewer.

High Country Inn & RV Park, 1000 South Main, 84032. T: (435) 654-0201 or (800) 345-9198. RV/tent: 38. $20–$25. Hookups: electric (20, 30, 50 amp), water, sewer.

Jordenelle State Park–Hailstone Campground, SR 319, No. 515 Box 4, 84032. T: (435) 649-9540. RV/tent: 186. $15–$17. Hookups: electric (20, 30, 50 amp), water, sewer.

Lodgepole Campground, 2460 South Hwy. 40, 84032. T: (435) 654-0470. RV/tent: 50. $7–$10. Hookups: none.

Mill Hollow, 2460 South Hwy. 40, 84032. T: (435) 654-0470. RV/tent: 26. $7. Hookups: none.

Soldier Creek, 2460 South Hwy. 40, 84032. T: (435) 654-0470. RV/tent: 165. $10. Hookups: none.

Strawberry Bay, 2460 South Hwy. 40, 84032. T: (435) 654-0470. RV/tent: 357. $10. Hookups: none.

Huntington

Huntington State Park, P.O. Box 1343, 84528. T: (435) 687-2491. RV/tent: 22. $13. Hookups: none.

Millsite State Park, P.O. Box 1343, 84528. T: (435) 687-2491. RV/tent: 20. $13. Hookups: none.

Hurricane

The Canyons RV Resort, Box 331-2, 84737. T: (435) 635-0200. RV/tent: 20. $15–$20. Hookups: Electric (30, 50 amp), water, sewer.

Hyrum

Hyrum State Park, 405 West 300 South, 84319. T: (435) 245-6866. RV/tent: 32. $12. Hookups: none.

Jensen

Bedrock Campground & RV Park, 9650 East 6000 South, 84035. T: (435) 781-6000 or (800) 852-7336. RV/tent: 131. $12–$16. Hookups: electric (20, 30, 50 amp), water, sewer.

Kamas

Beaver View Campground, 50 East Center, P.O. Box 68, 84036. T: (801) 783-4338. RV/tent: 8. $10. Hookups: none.

Butterfly Lake Campground, 50 East Center, P.O. Box 68, 84036. T: (801) 783-4338. RV/tent: 20. $7. Hookups: none.

Christmas Meadows Campground, 50 East Center, P.O. Box 68, 84036. T: (801) 783-4338. RV/tent: 21. $10. Hookups: none.

Cobble Rest Campground, 50 East Center, P.O. Box 68, 84036. T: (801) 783-4338. RV/tent: 18. $10. Hookups: none.

Hayden Fork Campground, 50 East Center, P.O. Box 68, 84036. T: (801) 783-4338. RV/tent: 9. $10. Hookups: none.

Ledgefork Campground, 50 East Center, P.O. Box 68, 84036. T: (801) 783-4338. RV/tent: 73. $11. Hookups: none.

Lost Lake Campground, 50 East Center, P.O. Box 68, 84036. T: (801) 783-4338. RV/tent: 34. $10. Hookups: none.

Mirror Lake Campground, 50 East Center, P.O. Box 68, 84036. T: (801) 783-4338. RV/tent: 85. $11. Hookups: none.

Moose Horn Lake Campground, 50 East Center, P.O. Box 68, 84036. T: (801) 783-4338. RV/tent: 33. $9. Hookups: none.

Shady Dell Campground, 50 East Center, P.O. Box 68, 84036. T: (801) 783-4338. RV/tent: 20. $11. Hookups: none.

Shingle Creek Campground, 50 East Center, P.O. Box 68, 84036. T: (801) 783-4338. RV/tent: 21. $10. Hookups: none.

Smith and Moorehouse Campground, 50 East Center, P.O. Box 68, 84036. T: (801) 783-4338. RV/tent: 34. $13. Hookups: none.

Soapstone Campground, 50 East Center, P.O. Box 68, 84036. T: (801) 783-4338. RV/tent: 33. $11. Hookups: none.

Stillwater Campground, 50 East Center, P.O. Box 68, 84036. T: (801) 783-4338. RV/tent: 21. $10. Hookups: none.

Sulphur Campground, 50 East Center, P.O. Box 68, 84036. T: (801) 783-4338. RV/tent: 21. $10. Hookups: none.

Trial Lake Soapstone Campground, 50 East Center, P.O. Box 68, 84036. T: (801) 783-4338. RV/tent: 60. $11. Hookups: none.

Kanab

Hitchin' Post RV Park, 196 East 300 South, 84741. T: (435) 644-2142. RV/tent: 50. $12–$16. Hookups: water, electric (20, 30, 50 amp), sewer.

Kanab RV Corral, 483 South 100 East, 84741. T: (435) 644-5330 or (888) 818-5330. F: (435) 644-5464. rvcoral@xpressweb.com. RV/tent: 40. $17–$20. Hookups: water, electric (20, 30, 50 amp), sewer, phone (modem).

Kanarraville

Red Ledge RV Park & Campground, 15 North Main, 84742. T: (435) 586-9150. RV/tent: 22. $12–$19. Hookups: water, electric (30, 50 amp), sewer.

Leeds

Leeds RV Park & Motel, 97 South Valley Rd., 84746. T: (435) 673-2970. leedsrv@infowest.com. RV/tent: 59. $15. Hookups: water, electric (20, 30, 50 amp), sewer, phone (modem).

Loa

Bowery Campground, 138 South Main St., 84747. T: (801) 836-2811. RV/tent: 43. $9. Hookups: none.

Doctor Creek Campground, 138 South Main St., 84747. T: (801) 836-2811. RV/tent: 30. $9. Hookups: none.

Mackinaw Campground, 138 South Main St., 84747. T: (801) 836-2811. RV/tent: 68. $9. Hookups: none.

Piute Campground, 138 South Main St., 84747. T: (801) 836-2811. RV/tent: 48. $4. Hookups: none.

Logan

Box Elder Campground, 1500 East Hwy. 89, 84327. T: (435) 755-3620. RV/tent: 26. $6. Hookups: none.

UTAH (continued)

Bridger Campground, 1500 East Hwy. 89, 84327. T: (435) 755-3620. RV/tent: 10. $9–$12. Hookups: none.

Guinavah-Malibu Campground, 1500 East Hwy. 89, 84327. T: (435) 755-3620. RV/tent: 40. $8. Hookups: none.

Lewis M. Turner Campground, 1500 East Hwy. 89, 84327. T: (435) 755-3620. RV/tent: 10. $8. Hookups: none.

Lodge Campground, 1500 East Hwy. 89, 84327. T: (435) 755-3620. RV/tent: 10. $7. Hookups: none.

LW's Phillips 66, 1936 North Main (US Hwy. 91), 84327. T: (435) 753-1025. RV/tent: 13. $15. Hookups: water, electric (20, 50 amp), sewer.

Pioneer Campground, 1500 East Hwy. 89, 84327. T: (435) 755-3620. RV/tent: 15. $6. Hookups: none.

Red Banks Campground, 1500 East Hwy. 89, 84327. T: (435) 755-3620. RV/tent: 12. $7. Hookup: none.

Riverside RV Park & Campground, 447 West 1700 South, 84327. T: (435) 245-4469. RV/tent: 14. $17–$19. Hookups: water, electric (20, 30 amp), sewer.

Spring Hollow Campground, 1500 East Hwy. 89, 84327. T: (435) 755-3620. RV/tent: 12. $8. Hookups: none.

Sunrise Campground, 1500 East Hwy. 89, 84327. T: (435) 755-3620 or (877) 444-6777. RV/tent: 27. $9–$12. Hookups: none.

Tony Grove Lake, 1500 East Hwy. 89, 84327. T: (435) 755-3620. RV/tent: 36. $10. Hookups: none.

Traveland RV Park, 2020 South Hwy. 89-91, 84321. T: (435) 787-2060. F: (435) 787-4590. RV/tent: 52. $15–$22. Hookups: electric (20, 30, 50 amp), water, sewer.

Western Park Campground, 350 West 800 South, 84321. T: (435) 752-6424. RV/tent: 13. $17. Hookups: water, electric (20, 30 amp), sewer.

Manila

Antelope Flat Campground, P.O. Box 279, 84046. T: (801) 784-3448. RV/tent: 126. $9. Hookups: none.

Canyon Rim Campground, P.O. Box 279, 84046. T: (801) 784-3448. RV/tent: 19. $9. Hookups: none.

Deep Creek, P.O. Box 279, 84046. T: (801) 784-3448. RV/tent: 17. $9. Hookups: none.

Dripping Springs Campground, P.O. Box 279, 84046. T: (801) 784-3448. RV/tent: 25. $10. Hookups: none.

Firefighters Memorial Campground, P.O. Box 279, 84046. T: (801) 784-3448. RV/tent: 94. $11. Hookups: none.

Flaming Gorge KOA, P.O. Box 157, 84046. T: (435) 784-3184 or (800) 562-3254. RV/tent: 50. $17–$27. Hookups: electric (20, 30, 50 amp), water, sewer.

Greens Lake Campground, P.O. Box 279, 84046. T: (801) 784-3448. RV/tent: 20. $9. Hookups: none.

Lucerne Valley Campground, P.O. Box 279, 84046. T: (801) 784-3448. RV/tent: 147. $11. Hookups: none.

Mustang Ridge Campground, P.O. Box 279, 84046. T: (801) 784-3448. RV/tent: 73. $11. Hookups: none.

Skull Creek Campground, P.O. Box 279, 84046. T: (801) 784-3448. RV/tent: 17. $9. Hookups: none.

Spirit Lake Campground, P.O. Box 279, 84046. T: (801) 784-3448. RV/tent: 24. $6. Hookups: none.

Manti

Manti Campground & RV Park, 490 North 250 East, P.O. Box 126, 84642. T: (435) 835-2267. RV/tent: 71. $10–$19. Hookups: water, electric (20, 30 amp), sewer.

Mantua

Mountain Haven RV Park & Country Store, 130 North Main, 84324. T: (435) 723-1292. RV/tent: 57. $17. Hookups: electric (15 amp), water, sewer.

Midway

Deer Creek State Park, P.O. Box 257, 84049. T: (435) 654-0171. RV/tent: 35. $12. Hookups: none.

Moab

Devil's Canyon Campground, 2290 South West Resource Blvd., 84532. T: (435) 259-7155. RV/tent: 33. $6. Hookups: none.

Moab Valley RV & Campark, 1773 North Hwy. 191, 84532. T: (435) 259-4469. RV/tent: 128. $16–$24. Hookups: electric (20, 30, 50 amp), water, sewer.

O.K. RV Park & Canyonlands Stables, 3310 Spanish Valley Dr., 84532. T: (435) 259-1400. RV/tent: 45. $17–$20. Hookups: electric (20, 30, 50 amp), water, sewer.

Park Creek Campground & RV Park, Murphy Ln., 84532. T: (435) 259-2982. RV/tent: 48. $17–$20. Hookups: electric (20, 30 amp), water, sewer.

Price Canyon, 82 East Dogwood Rd., 84501. T: (435) 637-4584. RV/tent: 18. $6. Hookups: none.

Riverside Oasis RV Park, P.O. Box 412, 84532. T: (435) 259-3424. F: (435) 259-2305. www.moab:ut.com/riversideoasis. Rsoasis@lasal.net. RV/tent: 60. $20. Hookups: electric (20, 30, 50 amp), water, sewer, cable TV, phone (modem).

Slickrock Campground, 1301 1/2 North Hwy. 191, 84532. T: (435) 259-7660 or (800) 448-8873. www.slickrockcampground. RV/tent: 173. $16–$18. Hookups: electric (20, 30 amp), water, sewer, cable TV, phone (modem).

Spanish Trail RV Park & Campground, 2980 South Hwy. 191, 84532. T: (800) 787-2751. F: (435) 259-2710. RV/tent: 73. $24. Hookups: electric (20, 30, 50 amp), water, sewer, cable TV, phone (modem).

Morgan

East Canyon State Park, 5535 South Hwy. 66, 84050. T: (801) 829-6866. RV/tent: 59. $12. Hookups: none.

Mount Carmel

East Zion RV Park, Junction of US Hwy. 69 & State Hwy. 9, 84755. T: (435) 648-2326. RV/tent: 20. $15. Hookups: water, electric (30 amp), sewer.

Ogden

Anderson Cove, 507 25th St., suite 103, P.O. Box 1433, 84401. T: (801) 625-5112. RV/tent: 74. $8. Hookups: none.

Century RV Park & Campground, 1399 West 2100 South, 84401. T: (801) 731-3800. cp1399@aol.com. RV/tent: 168. $17–$23. Hookups: electric (20, 30, 50 amp), water, sewer, cable TV, phone (modem).

Maple Grove, 2501 Wall Ave., 84401. T: (435) 743-5721. RV/tent: 11. $5. Hookups: none.

Meadows Campground, 507 25th St., suite 103, 84401. T: (801) 625-5110. RV/tent: 26. $11. Hookups: none.

Monte Cristo Campground, 507 25th St., suite 103, 84401. T: (801) 625-5110. RV/tent: 47. $9. Hookups: none.

Oak Creek, 2501 Wall Ave., 84401. T: (435) 743-5721. RV/tent: 23. $5. Hookups: none.

Perception Park Campground, 507 25th St., suite 103, 84401. T: (801) 625-5110. RV/tent: 60. $11. Hookups: none.

Panguitch

Hitch-N-Post Campground, 420 North Main St., 84759. T: (435) 676-2436. RV/tent: 48. $15–$18. Hookups: electric (20, 30, 50 amp), water, sewer.

Kings Creek Campground, P.O. Box 80, 84759. T: (435) 676-8815. RV/tent: 38. $9. Hookups: none.

Panguitch Lake General Store, Gift Shop & RV Park, 53 West Hwy. 143, P.O. Box 688, 84759. T: (435) 676-2464. www.panguitchlake.net. RV/tent: 14. $22. Hookups: electric (20, 30 amp), water, sewer.

Panguitch Lake Resort, P.O. Box 567, 84759. T: (435) 676-2657. F: (435) 676-2000. www.panguitchlake.net. babe@colorcountry.net. RV/tent: 62. $23. Hookups: electric (20, 30 amp), water, sewer.

Paradise RV Park & Campground, 2153 North Hwy. 89, 84759. T: (435) 676-8348. F: (435) 676-8092. www.brycecanyonparadiserv.com. RV/tent: 67. $18. Hookups: electric (20, 30, 50 amp), water, sewer.

Park City

Hidden Haven Campground, 2200 Rasmussen Rd., 84098. T: (435) 649-8935 or (800) 553-8269. redlandsrvpark.com. RV/tent: 88. $15–$21. Hookups: electric (20, 30, 50 amp), water, sewer, cable TV, phone (modem).

UTAH (continued)

Parowan

Sportsmen's Country RV Park & Restaurant, 492 North Main, P.O. Box 888, 84761. T: (435) 477-3714. RV/tent: 56. $10–$15. Hookups: electric (20, 30 amp), water, sewer, cable TV, phone (modem).

Peoa

Rockport State Park, 9040 North Hwy. 302, 84061. T: (435) 336-2241. RV/tent: 102. $8–$15. Hookups: electric (20, 30 amp), water, sewer.

Price

Budget Host Inn & RV Park, 145 North Carbonville Rd., 84501. T: (435) 637-2424. RV/tent: 40. $18–$20. Hookups: electric (20, 30, 50 amp), water, sewer.

Flat Canyon Campground, 599 West Price River Dr., 84501. T: (801) 637-2817. RV/tent: 12. $10. Hookups: none.

Price

Old Folks Flat Campground, 599 West Price River Dr., 84501. T: (801) 637-2817. RV/tent: 8. $10. Hookups: none.

Scofield State Park, P.O. Box 166, 84501. T: (435) 448-9449(summer) or (435) 637-2732(winter). RV/tent: 70. $11–$13. Hookups: none.

Provo

Granite Flat Campground, 88 West 100 North, 84601. T: (801) 342-5100. RV/tent: 32. $12. Hookups: none.

Hope Campground, 88 West 100 North, 84601. T: (801) 342-5100. RV/tent: 24. $6. Hookups: none.

Lakeside RV Campground, 4000 West Center, 84601. T: (801) 373-5267 or (800) 906-5267. www.lakesidervcampground.com. RV/tent: 145. $16–$21. Hookups: electric (20, 30 amp), water, sewer, phone (modem).

Little Mill Campground, 88 West 100 North, 84601. T: (801) 342-5100. RV/tent: 79. $6–$12. Hookups: none.

Mt. Timpanogos Campground, 88 West 100 North, 84601. T: (801) 342-5100. RV/tent: 27. $6–$12. Hookups: none.

Payson Lakes Campground, 88 West 100 North, 84601. T: (801) 342-5100. RV/tent: 88. $8. Hookups: none.

Provo KOA, 320 N. 2050 West, 84601. T: (801) 375-2994 or (800) 562-1894. F: (801) 375-1373. RV/tent: 95. $19–$27. Hookups: electric (20, 30 amp), water, sewer.

Timpooneke Campground, 88 West 100 North, 84601. T: (801) 342-5100. RV/tent: 32. $6–$12. Hookups: none.

Utah Lake State Park, 4400 West Center St., 84601. T: (801) 375-0731. RV/tent: 54. $11–$13. Hookups: none.

Richfield

JR Munchies Convenience Store, US Hwy. 89, 84701. T: (435) 896-9340. RV/tent: 21. $16. Hookups: electric (30, 50 amp), water, sewer.

KOA Richfield, 600 West 600 South, 84701. T: (435) 896-6674. RV/tent: 141. $18–$26. Hookups: electric (20, 30, 50 amp), water, sewer.

Roosevelt

Swift Creek Campground, 244 West Hwy. 40, 84066. T: (801) 722-5018. RV/tent: 13. $6. Hookups: none.

Yellowstone Campground, 244 West Hwy. 40, 84066. T: (801) 722-5018. RV/tent: 14. $6. Hookups: none.

Salina

Salina Creek RV Camp, State St., 84654. T: (435) 529-3711 or (888) 529-3711. RV/tent: 27. $16. Hookups: electric (20, 30, 50 amp), water, sewer.

Albion Basin Campground, 6944 South 300 East, 84121. T: (801) 943-1794. RV/tent: 24. $10. Hookups: none.

Big Bend Recreation Site, 324 South State St., 84145. T: (435) 259-6111. RV/tent: 22. $5. Hookups: none.

Bountiful Peak Campground, 6944 South 300 East, 84121. T: (801) 943-1794. RV/tent: 26. $10. Hookups: none.

Bridge Hollow Campground, 324 South State St., 84145. T: (435) 781-4400. RV/tent: 12. $5. Hookups: none.

Camp VIP Salt Lake City, 1400 West North Temple St., 84116. T: (801) 328-0224 or (800) 226-7752. F: (801) 355-1055. RV/tent: 413. $25–$29. Hookups: electric (20, 30, 50 amp), water, sewer, cable TV, phone (modem).

Deer Creek Campground, 324 South State St., 84145. T: (801) 539-4002. www.utso.ut.blm.gov. RV/tent: 7. $5. Hookups: none.

Oasis Campground (Little Sahara Recreation Area), 324 South State St., 84145. T: (435) 896-1551. www.utso.ut.blm.gov. RV/tent: 114. $6. Hookups: none.

Redman Campground, 6944 South 300 East, 84121. T: (801) 943-1794. RV/tent: 37. $12. Hookups: none.

Spruces Campground, 6944 South 300 East, 84121. T: (801) 943-1794. RV/tent: 86. $14. Hookups: none.

Sunset Campground, 6944 South 300 East, 84121. T: (801) 943-1794. RV/tent: 32. $10. Hookups: none.

Tanner's Flat Campground, 6944 South 300 East, 84121. T: (801) 943-1794. RV/tent: 36. $12. Hookups: none.

White Sands Campground (Little Sahara Recreation Area), 324 South State St., 84145. T: (435) 896-1551. www.utso.ut.blm.gov. RV/tent: 99. $6. Hookups: none.

Sandy

Ardell Brown's Quail Run RV Park, 9230 South State St., 84070. T: (801) 255-9300. rvpark@abrv.com. RV/tent: 69. $25. Hookups: electric (20, 30, 50 amp), water, sewer, cable TV, phone (modem).

Santa Clara

Gunlock State Park, P.O. Box 637, 84525. T: (435) 564-3633. RV/tent: 30. $8. Hookups: none.

Sevier

Fremont Indian State Park & Museum, 11550 West Clear Creek Canyon Rd., 84766. T: (435) 527-4631. RV/tent: 31. $10. Hookups: none.

Snowville

Lottie-Dell Campground, 490 West Main St Box 601, 84336. T: (435) 872-8273. RV/tent: 76. $18–$20. Hookups: electric (15, 20, 30 amp), water, sewer, phone (modem).

Springville

East Bay RV Park, 1750 West 1600 North, 84663. T: (801) 491-0700. F: (801) 491-0800. www.estbayrvpark.com. RV/tent: 230. $16–$22. Hookups: electric (20, 30, 50 amp), water, sewer, cable TV, phone (modem).

St. George

Baker Dam, 225 North Bluff, 84770. T: (435) 673-4654. RV/tent: 20. $6. Hookups: none.

McArthur's Temple View RV Resort, 975 South Main, 84770. T: (435) 673-6400 or (888) 255-2552. RV/tent: 266. $19–$27. Hookups: electric (20, 30, 50 amp), water, sewer, cable TV, phone (modem).

Redlands RV Park, 650 West Telegraph, 84770. T: (435) 673-9700 or (800) 553-8269. Redlandsrvpark.com. RV/tent: 200. $16–$22. Hookups: electric (20, 30, 50 amp), water, sewer, cable TV, phone (modem).

Settler's RV Park, 1333 East 100 South, 84790. T: (435) 628-1624 or (800) 628-2255. RV/tent: 175. $21. Hookups: electric (20, 30, 50 amp), water, sewer.

St. George RV Park & Campground, 2100 East Middleton Dr., 84770. T: (435) 673-2970. RV/tent: 135. $15–$25. Hookups: electric (20, 30 amp), water, sewer, cable TV, phone (modem).

Teasdale

Oak Creek Campground, 138 East Main, P.O. Box 99, 84773. T: (435) 425-3702. RV/tent: 9. $10. Hookups: none.

Pleasant Creek Campground, 138 East Main, P.O. Box 99, 84773. T: (435) 425-3702. RV/tent: 19. $10. Hookups: none.

Single Tree Campground, 138 East Main, P.O. Box 99, 84773. T: (435) 425-3702 or (877) 444-6777. RV/tent: 33. $11. Hookups: none.

Ticaboo

Ticaboo Resort, Restaurant & Campground, Hwy. 276 Box 2110-T, 84533. T: (877) 842-2267. RV/tent: 22. $20–$30. Hookups: electric (30 amp), water, sewer.

UTAH (continued)

Torrey

Sand Creek RV Park, Campground & Hostel, 540 Hwy. 24, P.O. Box 750276, 84775. T: (435) 425-3577 or (877) 425-3578. RV/tent: 24. $9, $15–$18. Hookups: electric (30, 50 amp), water, sewer.

Vernal

Dinosaurland KOA, 930 North Vernal Ave., 84078. T: (435) 789-2148. RV/tent: 110. $17–$22. Hookups: electric (20, 30, 50 amp), water, sewer, cable TV.

East Park, 353 N. Vernal Ave., 84078. T: (801) 789-1181. RV/tent: 21. $8. Hookups: none.

Fossil Valley RV Park, 999 West Hwy. 40, 84078. T: (435) 789-6450. RV/tent: 34. $17–$20. Hookups: electric (30, 50 amp), water, sewer.

Lodgepole Springs Campground, 353 North Vernal Ave., 84078. T: (801) 789-1181. RV/tent: 35. $8. Hookups: none.

Oaks Park, 353 N. Vernal Ave., 84078. T: (801) 789-1181. RV/tent: 11. $8. Hookups: none.

Red Fleet State Park, 8750 North Hwy. 191, 84078. T: (435) 789-4432. F: (435) 789-4475. RV/tent: 39. $10. Hookups: none.

Steinaker State Park, 4355 North Hwy. 191, 84078. T: (435) 789-4432. F: (435) 789-4475. RV/tent: 31. $10. Hookups: none.

Wellington

Mountain View RV Park, 50 South 700 East, 84542. T: (435) 637-7980. RV/tent: 24. $17. Hookups: water, electric (20, 30 amp), sewer

VERMONT

Addison

Ten Acres Campground, RR 1 Box 356, 05491. T: (802) 759-2662. RV/tent: 87. $16. Hookups: water, electric, sewer.

Andover

Horseshoe Acres Campgrounds, 1978 Weston Andover Rd., 05143. T: (802) 875-2960. RV/tent: 120. $16–$23. Hookups: water, electric, sewer.

Arlington

Camping on the Battenkill, Rte. 7A, 05250. T: (802) 375-6663 or (800) 830-6663. RV/tent: 96. $20. Hookups: water, electric, sewer.

Howell's Camping Area, No Name Rd., 05250. T: (802) 375-6469. RV/tent: 77. $17. Hookups: water, electric, sewer.

Ascutney

Running Bear Camping Area, 6248 Rte. 5, 05030. T: (802) 674-6417. RV/tent: 90. $16–$20. Hookups: water, electric, sewer.

Wilgus State Park Campground, P.O. Box 196, 05030. T: (802) 674-5422. RV/tent: 29. $12. Hookups: none.

Barnard

Silver Lake Family Campground, Stage Rd., 05031. T: (802) 234-9974. RV/tent: 67. $17. Hookups: water, electric, sewer.

Silver Lake State Park Campground, Town Rd., 05031. T: (802) 234-9451. RV/tent: 47. $13. Hookups: none.

Barton

Sugar Mill Farm, Box 26, 05822. T: (800) 688-7978. RV/tent: 18. $17. Hookups: water, electric.

Bennington

Greenwood Lodge and Campsites, Rte. 9, 05201. T: (802) 442-2547. F: (802) 442-2547. RV/tent: 20. $14. Hookups: water, electric, sewer.

Bomoseen

Lake Bomoseen Campground, Rte. 30, 05732. T: (802) 273-2061. RV/tent: 99. $20. Hookups: water, electric, sewer, phone.

Brandon

Branbury State Park, RD 2 Box 242, 05743. T: (802) 247-5925. RV/tent: 39. $3. Hookups: none.

Smoke Rise Farm Campground, Rte. 7 North, 05733. T: (802) 247-6472. RV/tent: 50. $10. Hookups: water, electric, sewer.

Brattleboro

Hidden Acres Campground, 792 US Rte. 5, 05301. T: (802) 254-2098. RV/tent: 40. $19–25. Hookups: water, electric, sewer.

Bristol

Elephant Mountain Camping Area, RD 3 Box 850, 05443. T: (802) 453-3123. RV/tent: 50. $15. Hookups: water, electric, sewer.

Maple Hill Campground, 690 Quaker St., 05443. T: (802) 453-3687. RV/tent: 13. $16. Hookups: electric.

Brookfield

Allis State Park Campground, RD 2 Box 192, 05036. T: (802) 276-3175. RV/tent: 27. $11. Hookups: none.

Burlington

North Beach Campground, Lakeview Terrace, 05401. T: (800) 571-1198. RV/tent: 137. $18–$25. Hookups: water, electric (30, 50 amps), sewer.

Cavendish

Caton Place Campground, RR 1 Box 107, 05142. T: (802) 226-7767. RV/tent: 85. $14–$15. Hookups: water, electric (15, 20, 30 amps), sewer.

Charlotte

Mt. Philo State Park, 5425 Mt. Philo Rd., 05445. T: (802) 425-2390. www.state.vt.us/anr/fpr/parks/htm/philo.html. RV/tent: 7. $12–18. Hookups: none.

Old Lantern Campground, P.O. Box 221, 5445. T: (802) 425-2120. RV/tent: 95. $15–$20. Hookups: water, electric, sewer.

Chester

Hidden Valley Campgrounds, 1924 Mattson Rd., 05143. T: (802) 886-2497. RV/tent: 32. $15. Hookups: water, electric.

Danby

Otter Creek Campground, Rte. 7, 05739. T: (802) 293-5041. RV/tent: 50. $14 (higher in winter). Hookups: water, electric.

Dorset

Dorset RV Park, 1567 Rte. 30, 05251-9802. T: (802) 867-5754. RV/tent: 40. $10–$19. Hookups: water, electric, sewer.

East Burkes

Burke Mountain Campgrounds, Mountain Rd., 05832. T: (802) 626-1204. RV/tent: 25. $10. Hookups: water, electric, sewer.

East Dummerston

KOA Campground, 1238 US 5, 05346. T: (802) 254-5908. RV/tent: 42. $24–$32. Hookups: water, electric (20, 30, 50 amps), sewer.

East Montpelier

Green Valley Campground, RR 2, P.O. Box 21, 05651. T: (802) 223-6217. F: (802) 223-1702. RV/tent: 36. $15–$25. Hookups: water, electric, sewer, phone.

East Thetford

Rest n' Nest Campground, Latham Rd., 05043. T: (802) 785-2997. RV/tent: 90. $20. Hookups: water, electric, sewer.

Enosburg Falls

Lake Carmi, 460 Marsh Farm Rd., 05450. T: (802) 933-8383. RV/tent: 140. $13–$17. Hookups: none.

Fair Haven

Bomoseen State Park, RR 1 Box 2620, 05743. T: (802) 265-4242. RV/tent: 66. $13. Hookups: none.

VERMONT (continued)

Gaysville

White River Valley Camping, Box 106T, 05746. T: (802) 234-9115. RV/tent: 40. $17–$22. Hookups: water, electric, sewer.

Graniteville

Lazy Lions Campground, 281 Middle Rd., 05654-9801. T: (802) 479-2823. F: (802) 479-2870. www.campusa.com/frame northbeach.cfm. RV/tent: 180. $20 RV, $15 tent. Hookups: water, electric, sewer, phone.

Groton

Ricker Pond State Park, 526 State Forest Rd., 05046. T: (802) 584-3821. RV/tent: 55. $17. Hookups: none.

Hartford

Quechee Gorge State Park Campground, 190 Dewey Mills Rd., 05001. T: (802) 295-2990 or (800) 299-3071. RV/tent: 54. $12–$18. Hookups: none.

Isle La Motte

Lakehurst Campground, 204 Lakehurst Rd., 05463. T: (802) 928-3266. www.campusa.com/framenorthbeach.cfm. RV/tent: 160. $15–$20. Hookups: water, electric, sewer.

Summer Place Campground & Cabins, P.O. Box 30, 05463. T: (802) 928-3300. RV/tent: 70. $14. Hookups: water, electric.

Jamaica

Jamaica State Park Campground, P.O. Box 45, 05343. T: (802) 874-4600. RV/tent: 61. $13. Hookups: none.

Killington

Gifford Woods State Park, Hwy. 100, 05751. T: (802) 775-5354. RV/tent: 48. $15. Hookups: none.

Killington Campground at Alpenhof Lodge, Box 2880, Killington Rd., 05751. T: (802) 422-9787. RV/tent: 10. $20. Hookups: water, electric.

Ludlow

Hideaway Squirrel Hill Camp, 176 Bixby Rd., 05149. T: (802) 228-8800. RV/tent: 24. $10–$15. Hookups: water, electric.

Manchester Center

Greendale Campground, 2539 Depot St., 05255. T: (802) 362-2307. RV/tent: 11. $5. Hookups: water.

Marshfield

Groton Forest Road Campground, RD 1 Box 402, Hwy. 232, 05658. T: (802) 426-4122. RV/tent: 35. $14. Hookups: water, electric.

Larry & Sons Campground, Rte. 2, 05658. T: (802) 426-3514. RV/tent: 23. $10. Hookups: water, electric.

Middlebury

Rivers Bend Campground, 1000 Dog Team Rd., 05653. T: (802) 388-9092. RV/tent: 65. $20–$24. Hookups: water, electric (20, 30 amps).

Newfane

Kenolie Village Campground, 16 Kenolie Campground Rd., 05345. T: (802) 365-7671. RV/tent: 150. $13. Hookups: water, electric (20, 30 amps).

North Clarendon

Iroquios Land Family, 2334 East Clarendon Rd., 05759. T: (802) 773-2832. RV/tent: 35. $20. Hookups: water, electric, sewer.

North Dorset

Emerald Lake State Park Campground, RD 485, 05251. T: (802) 362-1655. RV/tent: 105. $13. Hookups: none.

North Hero

Carry Bay Campground & Cottages, 5289 Rte. 2, 05474. T: (802) 372-8233. RV/tent: 30. $20 RV, $12 tent. Hookups: water, electric, sewer.

North Hero State Park, 3803 Lakeview Drive, 05474-9698. T: (802) 372-8727. RV/tent: 99. $12–$17. Hookups: none.

Perkinsville

Crown Point Camping Area, 131 Bishops Camp Rd., 05151. T: (802) 263-5555. RV/tent: 36. $15. Hookups: water, electric, sewer.

Winhall Brook Camping Area, RR 1 Box 164B, 05151. T: (802) 874-4881. RV/tent: 109. $10. Hookups: none.

Peru

Green Mountain/Red Mill Brook, 231 North Main St., 05701-2417. T: (802) 362-2307. RV/tent: 20. $5. Hookups: none.

Hapgood Pond Recreation Area, P.O. Box 248, 05152. T: (802) 824-6456. RV/tent: 28. $10. Hookups: water.

Plymouth

Coolidge State Park, Rte. A, 05056. T: (802) 672-3612. RV/tent: 60. $11–$15. Hookups: none.

Sugarhouse Campground, Rte. 100, 05056. T: (802) 672-5043. RV/tent: 45. $15 (higher rates jn winter). Hookups: water, electric.

Randolph Center

Lake Champagne Campground, Furnace Pt., 05061. T: (802) 728-5293. F: (802) 479-2870. RV/tent: 68. $18–$28. Hookups: water, electric, sewer.

Rochester

Chittendon Brook Recreation Area, Rte. 100, 05767. T: (802) 767-4261. RV/tent: 17. $9. Hookups: none.

Salisbury

Branbury State Park, 3570 Lake Dunmore Rd., 05769. T: (802) 247-5925. RV/tent: 45. $13–$17. Hookups: none.

Lake Dunmore Kampersville, RR 1, 05769-9801. T: (802) 352-4501 or (877) 250-2568. RV/tent: 120. $17. Hookups: water, electric, sewer.

Waterhouse Campground & Marina, 937 West Shore Rd., 05769. T: (802) 352-4433. RV/tent: 60. $17–$25. Hookups: water, electric, sewer.

Shaftsbury

Lake Shaftsbury State Park, RR 1 Box 266, 05262. T: (802) 375-9978. RV/tent: 15. $16. Hookups: none.

South Hero

Apple Island, Rte. 2, 05486-4008. T: (802) 372-5398. F: (802) 372-8272. RV/tent: 200. $25–$30. Hookups: water, electric, sewer.

South Londonderry

Ball Mountain Lake Project Campground, 98 Reservoir Rd., Springfield, Vermon, 05156-2210. T: (802) 824-4570. RV/tent: 111. $12–$18. Hookups: water, electric (20, 30 amps), sewer.

Springfield

Tree Farm Campground, 53 Skitchewaug Trail, 05156. T: (802) 885-2889. RV/tent: 118. $17. Hookups: water, electric, sewer.

Thetford

Thetford Hill State Park Campground, P.O. Box 132, 05074. T: (802) 785-2266. RV/tent: 16. $11. Hookups: none.

Townshend

Bald Mountain Campground, 1760 State Forest Rd., 05353. T: (802) 365-7510. RV/tent: 200. $18. Hookups: water, electric, sewer.

Camperama, Depot Rd., 05353. T: (802) 365-4315 or (800) 632-2677. RV/tent: 205. $20–$23. Hookups: water, electric, sewer.

Townshend State Park Campground, RD 1 Box 2650, 05353. T: (802) 365-7500. RV/tent: 35. $11. Hookups: none.

Underhill

South Hill Riverside Campground, RD 2 Box 287, 05489. T: (802) 899-2232. RV/tent: 50. $20. Hookups: water, electric, sewer.

Vergennes

Button Bay State Park, RD 3 Box 4075, 05491. T: (802) 475-2377. RV/tent: 72. $13–$17. Hookups: none.

D.A.R. State Park, RD 2 Box 3493, 05491. T: (802) 759-2354. RV/tent: 70. $12–$16. Hookups: none.

Whispering Pines Campground, 1072 Panton Rd., 05491. T: (802) 475-2264. RV/tent: 40. $12. Hookups: water, electric.

Waterbury

Duxbury Campground, 2542 VT 100, 05676. T: (802) 244-7546. RV/tent: 16. $10. Hookups: water, electric.

Waterbury Center

The Long Trail, 4711 Waterbury-Stowe Rd., 05677. T: (802) 244-7037. RV/tent: 70. $4. Hookups: none.

Wells River

Pleasant Valley Camp Grounds, 964 Wallace Hill Rd., 05081. T: (802) 584-3884 or (802) 866-5991. RV/tent: 37. $12–$19. Hookups: water, electric, sewer.

VERMONT (continued)

Westfield

Barrewood Campground, 3201 VT 100, 05874-9801. T: (802) 744-6340. RV/tent: 46. $12–$18. Hookups: water, electric, sewer.

White Junction

Maple Leaf Motel & Campground, Rte. 5 South, 05001. T: (802) 295-2817. RV/tent: 14. $19. Hookups: water, electric, sewer.

White River Junction

Pine Valley RV Resort, 400 Woodstock Rd., 05001. T: (802) 296-6711. RV/tent: 90. $12–$26. Hookups: water, electric, sewer.

Williamstown

Limehurst Lake, 4104 Rte. 14, 05679. T: (802) 433-6662 or (800) 242-9876. RV/tent: 76. $18–$23. Hookups: water, electric, sewer.

Windsor

Ascutney State Park, Box 186, HCR 71, 05089. T: (802) 674-2060. RV/tent: 39. $11. Hookups: none.

Woodford

Greenwood Lodge and Campsites, Box 246, 05201. T: (802) 442-2547. grnwd@compuserve.com. RV/tent: 20. $16–$22. Hookups: water, electric (30, 50 amps).

Woodford State Park Campground, HCR 65, Box 928, 05201. T: (802) 447-7169. RV/tent: 103. $13. Hookups: none.

VIRGINIA

Appomattox

Paradise Lake Family Campground, P.O. Box 478, 24522. T: (804) 993-3332. RV/tent: 117. $22. Hookups: water, electric (20, 30, 50 amps), sewer.

Bassett

Goose Point/Philpott Lake, 4780 Goose Point Rd., 24055. T: (540) 629-2703. www.reserveusa.com. RV/tent: 61. $12–$18. Hookups: water, electric (30 amps).

Bentonville

Low Water Bridge Campground, 192 Panhandle Rd., 22610. T: (540) 635-7277. F: (540) 635-9606. www.lowwaterbridge.com. RV/tent: 60. $21. Hookups: none.

Bowling Green

Campground 721, 22085 Sparta Rd., 22514. T: (804) 633-9516. RV/tent: 53. $9–$16. Hookups: water, electric, sewer.

Boydton

Ivy Hill Campground, 1930 Mays Chapel Rd., 23917. T: (434) 738-6144. RV/tent: 25. $8. Hookups: none.

Longwood Recreation Area, 1930 Mays Chapel Rd., 23917. T: (434) 738-6144. RV/tent: 55. $12–$14. Hookups: water, electric (30 amps).

North Bend Park, 1930 Mays Chapel Rd., 23917. T: (434) 738-6144. RV/tent: 249. $12–$14. Hookups: water, electric (20, 30 amps).

Bristol

Lee Hwy. Campground, 2671 Lee Hwy., 24203. T: (540) 669-3616 or (540) 669-1800. RV/tent: 19. $20. Hookups: water, electric (20, 30 amps), sewer.

Broadway

Harrisonburg/New Market KOA, 12480 Mountain Valley Rd., 22815. T: (540) 896-8929 or (540) KOA-5406. www.koa.com. RV/tent: 48. $19–$28. Hookups: water, electric (30, 50 amps), sewer.

Buena Vista

Glen Maury Park, 2039 Sycamore Ave., 24416. T: (540) 261-7321. RV/tent: 52. $12–$17. Hookups: water, electric (20, 30 amps), sewer.

Chesapeake

Chesapeake Campground, 693 South George Washington Pkwy., 23323. T: (757) 485-0149. RV/tent: 133. $20–$30. Hookups: water, electric (20, 30 amps), sewer.

Chincoteague

Pine Grove Campround & Waterfowl Park, 5283 Deep Hole Rd., 23336. T: (757) 336-5200. www.pinegrovecampground.com. RV/tent: 150. $20–$28. Hookups: water, electric (15, 20, 30 amps), sewer.

Christiansburg

Interstate Overnight Park, 2705 Roakoke St., 24073. T: (540) 382-1554. RV/tent: 32. $16. Hookups: water, electric (20, 30, 50 amps), sewer.

Colonial Beach

Monroe Bay Campground, 551 Lafayette St., 22443. T: (804) 224-7418 or (804) 224-7544. RV/tent: 310 RV. $17. Hookups: water, electric (30 amps), sewer.

Outdoor World—Harbor View Campground, 15 Harbor View Cir., 22443. T: (800) 222-5557 or (804) 224-8164. www.campoutdoorworld.com. RV/tent: 144. $20. Hookups: water, electric (30, 50 amps), sewer.

Cross Junction

Log Cabin Campground, 2058 Morgan Frederick Grade, 22625. T: (540) 888-3461. RV/tent: 60. $10–$14. Hookups: water, electric (15, 20 amps).

Damascus

Ironhorse Family Campground, 30460 Blossom Rd., 24236. T: (276) 475-6008. RV/tent: 18. $18. Hookups: water, electric (30 amps), sewer.

Dublin

Claytor Lake State Park, 2400 State Park Rd., 24084. T: (540) 674-5492. www.dcr.state.va.us/ parks/claytor.htm. RV/tent: 110. $14–$18. Hookups: water, electric (20, 30 amps).

Duffield

Natural Tunnel State Park, Rte. 3 Box 250, 24244. T: (276) 940-2674. www.dcr.state.va.us/parks/ naturalt.htm. RV/tent: 22. $11–$15. Hookups: water, electric (20, 30 amps).

Dumfries

Prince William Travel Trailer Village & RV Park, 160 Dumfries Rd., 22026. T: (703) 221-2474 or (888) 737-5730. RV/tent: 75. $19–$22. Hookups, water, electric (20, 30 amps), sewer.

Ferrum

Horseshoe Point/Philpott Lake, 3950 Horseshoe Point Rd., 24102. T: (540) 629-2703. www.reserveusa.com. RV/tent: 49. $12–$18. Hookups: water, electric (30 amps).

Gainesville

Hillwood Camping Park, 14222 Lee Hwy., 20155-1799. T: (703) 754-6105. F: (801) 457-1034. RV/tent: 140. $23. Hookups: electric, water, sewer.

Hayes

Gloucester Point Campground, 3149 Campground Rd., 23072. T: (800) 332-4316. F: (804) 642-4316. RV/tent: 230 RV. $18–$20. Hookups: water, electric (30, 50 amps), sewer.

Haymarket

Greenville Farm Family Campground, 14004 Shelter Ln., 20189. T: (703) 754-7944. RV/tent: 165 RV. $20–$24, tent. Hookups: water, electric (20, 30, 50 amps), sewer.

VIRGINIA (continued)

Henry

Salthouse Branch Park/Philpott Lake, 620 Salthouse Branch Rd., 24102. T: (540) 629-2703. www.reserveusa.com. RV/tent: 93. $12–$18. Hookups: water, electric (30 amps).

Hillsville

Carrollwood Campground, P.O. Box 175, 24343. T: (540) 728-9312. RV/tent: 100. $19–$21. Hookups: water, electric (20, 30, 50 amps), sewer.

Hot Springs

Bolar Mountain Campground/George Washington National Forest, Warm Springs Ranger District, Hwy. 220 South, Rte. 2 Box 30, 24445. T: (540) 839-2521. RV/tent: 91. $16–$20. Hookups: electric (30 amps).

Hidden Valley Campgrounds/George Washington National Forest, Warm Springs Ranger District, Hwy. 220 South, Rte. 2 Box 30, 24445. T: (540) 839-2521. RV/tent: 30. $6. Hookups: none.

Lexington

Lake A. Willis Robertson Recreation Area/Rockbridge County Park, Rte. 2 Box 251, 24450. T: (540) 463-4164. RV/tent: 53. $15–$20. Hookups: water, electric (20, 30 amps), sewer.

Louisa

Small Country Campground, 4400 Byrd Mill Rd., 23093. T: (540) 967-2431. F: (540) 967-1667. www.smallcountry.com. RV/tent: 157. $24–$28. Hookups: water, electric (20, 30 amps), sewer.

Luray

The Country Waye RV Resort, 3402 Kimball Rd., 22835. T: (888) 765-7222. F: (540) 743-2734. www.countrywaye.com. RV/tent: 97. $27. Hookups: water, electric (30, 50 amps), sewer.

Marion

Beartree Campground/Mount Rogers National Recreation Area, 3714 Hwy. 16, 24354. T: (540) 783-5196. RV/tent: 84. $7–$14. Hookups: none.

Grindstone Campground/Mount Rogers National Recreation Area, Rte. 1 Box 303, 24354. T: (540) 783-5196. RV/tent: 98. $14–$28. Hookups: none.

Martinsville

David & Julia's RV Park, P.O. Box 3091, Beckham Church Rd., 24115. T: (540) 632-8718. www.kimbanet.com/~rvpark. RV/tent: 10. $18–$20. Hookups: water, electric (20, 30, 50 amps), sewer.

Max Meadows

Fort Chiswell RV Campground, 312 Ft. Chiswell Rd., 24360. T: (540) 637-6868. RV/tent: 92. $22. Hookups: water, electric (20 amps), sewer.

Moneta

Campers Paradise, 1336 Campers Paradise Tr., 24121. T: (540) 297-6109. www.campers paradise. com. RV/tent: 35. $17–$22. Hookups: water, electric (15, 20, 30, 50 amps), sewer.

Montebello

Montebello Camping Resort, Crabtree Falls Hwy., Rte. 56, 22964. T: (540) 377-2650. www.montebellova.com. RV/tent: 60. $16–$23. Hookups: water, electric (30 amps), sewer.

Montross

Westmoreland State Park, 1650 State Park Rd., 22520. T: (804) 493-8821. www.dcr.state.va.us/parks/westmore.htm. RV/tent: 133. $14–$18. Hookups: water, electric (20, 30 amps), sewer.

Natural Bridge

Cave Mountain Lake/Jefferson National Forest, Glenwood Ranger District, Box 10, 24579. T: (540) 291-2189. RV/tent: 42. $10. Hookups: none.

KOA—Natural Bridge Campground, Oak Bank Dr., Rte. F-232, 24578. T: (540) 291-2770. www.koa.com. RV/tent: 97. $19–$25. Hookups: water, electric (20, 30 amps), sewer.

Shernando Campgrounds/George Washington National Forest, Pedlar Ranger District, P.O. Box 10, 24579. T: (540) 291-2189. RV/tent: 65. $15–$30. Hookups: electric (30 amps).

New Market

Rancho Campground, 15554 Valley Pike, US 115, 22844. T: (540) 740-8313. RV/tent: 65. $19–$21. Hookups: water, electric (20, 30, 50 amps), sewer.

Petersburg

Spring Gardens Mobile Home Park, 2178 Country Dr., 23803. T: (804) 732-8908. RV/tent: 44. $18. Hookups: water, electric (20, 30, 50 amps), sewer.

Saluda

Dublfun Campground, Hcr 67 Box 2206, 23079. T: (804) 758-5432. RV/tent: 150. $15–$22. Hookups: water, electric (20, 30 amps), sewer.

Sanford

Tall Pines Harbor Waterfront Campground, Box 375, 23426. T: (757) 824-0777. RV/tent: 90. $15–$21. Hookups: water, electric (30 amps), sewer.

Skippers

Cattail RV Park and Campground, 3901 Moore's Ferry Rd., 23879. T: (804) 634-9935 or (877) 888-0324. F: (804) 634-9935. RV/tent: 60 RV. $17–$18. Hookups: Water, electric, sewer.

Stanardsville

Heavenly Acres Campground, 2010 Madison Rd., 22973. T: (804) 985-6601. www.heavenly acres.net. RV/tent: 35. $22–$23. Hookups: water, electric (20, 30 amps), sewer.

Sugar Grove

Raccoon Branch/Mount Rogers National Recreation Area, 3714 Hwy. 16, 24354. T: (540) 783-5196. RV/tent: 20. $6–$12. Hookups: none.

Vesuvius

Tye River Gap Campground, P.O. Box 334, 24483. T: (540) 377-6168. RV/tent: 50 RV. $20. Hookups: water, electric, sewer.

Vinton

Roanoke Mountain Campground, 2551 Mountain View Rd., 24179. T: (540) 982-9242. RV/tent: 104. $12. Hookups: none.

Virginia Beach

Shore Campground, 3257 Colechester Rd., 23456. T: (757) 426-7911. RV/tent: 140 RV. $18–$25. Hookups: water, electric (20, 30 amps).

Warsaw

Naylors Beach Campground, 4011 Naylors Beach Rd., 22572. T: (804) 333-3951. RV/tent: 100. $20. Hookups: water, electric (15, 20, 30 amps).

Waynesboro

Waynesboro North 340 Campground, Rte. 340 North, 22980. T: (540) 943-9573. RV/tent: 175. $19. Hookups: water, electric (15, 20, 50 amps), sewer.

Williamsburg

American Heritage RV Park, 146 Maxton Ln., 23188. T: (888) 530-CAMP. F: (757) 566-1338. RV/tent: 95. $17–$23. Hookups: water, electric, sewer.

Four Winds Trading Post & Campground, 8758 Pocahontas Tr. Rte. 60, 23185. T: (757) 220-0386 or (888) 999-6236. RV/tent: 50 RV. $23–$25. Hookups: water, electric (20, 30, 50 amps), sewer.

Williamsburg Campsites, 6967 Richmond Rd., 23188. T: (757) 564-3101. RV/tent: 285. $19–$20. Hookups: water, electric (20, 30 amps), sewer.

Willis

Daddy Rabbit's Campground, 2015 Union School Rd. Southwest, 24380. T: (540) 789-4150. RV/tent: 57. $15–$20. Hookups: water, electric (20, 30 amps), sewer.

Wise

Cane Patch Campground/Jefferson National Forest, Clinch Ranger District, 9416 Darden Dr., 24293. T: (540) 328-2931. RV/tent: 35. $8. Hookups: none.

VIRGINIA (continued)

Cave Springs Campground/Jefferson National Forest, Clinch Ranger District, 9416 Darden Dr., 24293. T: (540) 328-2931. RV/tent: 41. $8. Hookups: none.

Woolwine

Deer Run Campgrounds, P.O. Box 6, 24185. T: (540) 930-1235. RV/tent: 72. $16–$17. Hookups: water, electric (20, 30, 50 amps), sewer

WASHINGTON

Amanda Park

Graves Creek Campground, 1835 Black Lake Blvd. SW, Olympia, 98512-5623. T: (360) 452-0330. RV/tent: 30. $10. Hookups: none.

American River

Bumping Lake Campground, 215 Melody Ln., 98801. T: (509) 653-2205. RV/tent: 45. $4–$8. Hookups: none.

Anacortes

Fidalgo Bay Resort, 7337 Miller Rd., 98221. T: (888) 777-5355. RV/tent: 67. $22–$25. Hookups: electric, water.

Artic

Artic RV Park and Campground, 893 US Hwy. 101, Cosmopolis, 98537. T: (360) 533-4470. RV/tent: 20. $14–$16. Hookups: full.

Ashford

Mouthaven Resort, 38210 State Hwy. 706 East, 98304. T: (800) 456-9380. RV/tent: 19. $20. Hookups: full.

Bay Center

KOA-Bay Center, P.O. Box 315, 98527. T: (800) 562-7810. RV/tent: 28. $21–$24. Hookups: electric, water.

Belfair

Snooze Junction RV Park, P.O. Box 880, 98528. T: (360) 275-2381. RV/tent: 36. $20. Hookups: full.

Birch Bay

Thousand Trails-Birch Bay, 8418 Harborview Rd., Blaine, 98230. T: (360) 371-7432. RV/tent: 180. $22. Hookups: full.

Burlington

KOA-Burlington, 6397 North Green Rd., 98233. T: (800) 562-9154. RV/tent: 40. $20. Hookups: electric, water.

Chehalis

Chehalis-KOA, 118 Hwy. 12, 98532. T: (800) KOA-9120. RV/tent: 19. $21–$24. Hookups: electric, water.

Cheney

Williams Lake Resort, 18607 Williams Lake Rd., 99004-9762. T: (509) 235-2391. RV/tent: 46. $15–$19. Hookups: electric, water.

Chinook

River's End Campground and RV Park, P.O. Box 280, 98614. T: (360) 777-8317. RV/tent: 72. $14–$18. Hookups: electric, water.

Clarkston

Granite Lake RV Resort, 306 Granite Lake Dr, 99403. T: (509) 751-1635. RV/tent: 75. $18–$26. Hookups: electric.

Conconully

Conconully Lake Resort, P.O. Box 131, 98819. T: (800) 850-0813. RV/tent: 11. $19. Hookups: electric.

Shady Pines Resort, P.O. Box 44, 98819. T: (800) 552-2287. RV/tent: 23. $19. Hookups: electric, water.

Concrete

Baker Lake Resort, 46110 East Main St., 98237. T: (360) 853-8341. RV/tent: 90. $15–$20. Hookups: electric, water.

Copalis Beach

Rod's Beach Resort, P.O. Box 507, 98535. T: (360) 289-2222. RV/tent: 90. $18. Hookups: electric.

Cougar

Lone Fit Resort, 16806 Lewis River Rd., 98616. T: (360) 238-5210. RV/tent: 31. $16. Hookups: electric.

Coulee

Laurent's Sun Village Resort, 33575 Park Lake Rd. Northeast, 99115. T: (888) 632-5664. RV/tent: 100. $18. Hookups: full.

Cusick

Blueslide Resort, 400041 Hwy. 20, 99119. T: (509) 445-1327. RV/tent: 56. $15–$16. Hookups: full.

Easton

RV Town, P.O. Box 1203, 98925. T: (509) 656-2360. RV/tent: 72. $18. Hookups: electric, water.

Eastsound

Moran State Park, SR Box 22, 98245. T: (360) 376-2326. RV/tent: 151. $13–$19. Hookups: none.

Ellensburg

KOA-Ellensburg, 32 Thorp Hwy. South, 98926. T: (800) 562-7616. RV/tent: 152. $23–$25. Hookups: full.

Elma

Elma RV Park, P.O. Box 1135, 98541. T: (360) 482-4053. RV/tent: 102. $18. Hookups: electric.

Everett

Lakeside RV Park, 12321 Hwy. 99 South, 98204. T: (800) HOT-PARK. RV/tent: 164. $33. Hookups: electric.

Forks

Bogachiel State Park, Hwy. 101, 98331. T: (360) 374-6356. RV/tent: 42. $13–$19. Hookups: none.

Glacier

Yogi Bear Jellystone Park at Mt. Baker, 10443 Mt. Baker Hwy., 98244-0021. T: (360) 599-1908. RV/tent: 30. $21–$24. Hookups: full.

Goldendale

Maryhill State Park, 50 US Hwy. 97, 98620. T: (509) 773-5007. RV/tent: 70. $13–$19. Hookups: electric.

Graham

Benbow Campground, 32919 Benbow Dr. East, 98338. T: (360) 879-5426. RV/tent: 54. $18–$20. Hookups: full.

Granite Falls

Gold Basin Camground, 33515 Mt. Loop Hwy., 98252. T: (877) 444-6777. RV/tent: 94. $14–$24. Hookups: none.

Grayland

Ocean Gate Resort, P.O. Box 57, 98547. T: (800) 473-1956. RV/tent: 55. $19. Hookups: electric.

Ilwaco

Fort Canby State Park, P.O. Box 488, 98624. T: (360) 642-3078. RV/tent: 250. 23–$29. Hookups: full.

KOA-Ilwaco, P.O. Box 549, 98624. T: (360) 642-3292. RV/tent: 164. $3–$29. Hookups: full.

Inchelium

Rainbow Beach Resort, 18 North Twin Lakes Rd., 99138. T: (509) 722-5901. RV/tent: 19. $16. Hookups: full.

Ione

Colville National Forest, 755 South Main St., 99114. T: (509) 684-4557. RV/tent: 30. $14–$19. Hookups: none.

Issaquah

Blue Sky RV and Resorts, 9002 302nd Ave. Southeast, 98027. T: (425) 222-7910. RV/tent: 51. $28. Hookups: full.

WASHINGTON (continued)

Kelso

Brookhollow RV Park, 2506 Allen St., 98626. T: (800) 867-0453. RV/tent: 132. $22. Hookups: electric.

Cedars RV Park, 115 Beauvais Rd., 98626. T: (360) 274-5136. RV/tent: 26. $15. Hookups: none.

Kent

KOA-Seattle/Tacoma, 5801 South 212th, 98032. T: (253) 872-8652. RV/tent: 160. $28–$40. Hookups: full.

La Conner

Blake's RV Park and Marina, 13739 Rawlins Rd., 98273. T: (360) 445-6533. RV/tent: 76. $15–$25. Hookups: full.

Thousand Trails La Conner, 16362 Shee Oosh Rd., 98257. T: (360) 446-3558. RV/tent: 298. $20. Hookups: electric (20, 30 amps), water.

La Push

Lonesome Creek RV Park, P.O. Box 250, 98350. T: (360) 374-4338. RV/tent: 55. $20–$29. Hookups: full.

Leavenworth

Blu-Shastin RV Park, 3300 Hwy. 97, 98826. T: (888) 548-4184. RV/tent: 82. $22. Hookups: full.

Thousand Trails, 20752-4 Chiwawa Loop Rd., 98826. T: (509) 7633217. RV/tent: 308. $20. Hookups: full.

Long Beach

Anderson's on the Ocean, 1400 138th St., 98631. T: (800) 645-6795. RV/tent: 75. $20. Hookups: full.

Driftwood RV Park, P.O. Box 296, 98631. T: (888) 567-1902. RV/tent: 55. $20. Hookups: full.

Loomis

Rainbow Resort, 761 Loomis Hwy., Tonasket, 98855. T: (509) 223-3700. RV/tent: 54. $16. Hookups: full.

Loon Lake

Deer Lake Resort, 3908 North Deer Lake Rd., 99148. T: (509) 233-2081. RV/tent: 65. $18. Hookups: full.

Shore Acres Resort, P.O. Box 900, 99148. T: (800) 900-2474. RV/tent: 30. $20. Hookups: electric.

Lynden

Lynden KOA, 8717 Line Rd., 98264. T: (800) 563-4779. RV/tent: 160. $28. Hookups: full.

Lynn Wood

Twin Cedars RV Park, 17826 Hwy. 99, 98037. T: (800) 878-9304. twincedar@pcfre.com. RV/tent: 69. $27–$30. Hookups: full.

Mazama

Okanogan National Forest, 1240 South 2nd Ave., 98840. T: (509) 996-4000. RV/tent: 46. $3–$8. Hookups: none.

Medical Lake

Rainbow Cove Resort, 12514 South Clear Lake Rd., 99022. T: (509) 299-3717. RV/tent: 17. $15–$18. Hookups: electric, water.

Montesano

Friends Landing, 300 Katon Rd., 98563. T: (360) 249-5117. RV/tent: 29. $20. Hookups: electric, water.

Lake Sylvia State Park, P.O. Box 701, 98563. T: (360) 249-3621. RV/tent: 35. $13–$19. Hookups: none.

Moses Lake

Mar Don Resort, 8198 State Hwy. 262 Southeast, Othello, 99344. T: (800) 416-2736. RV/tent: 273. $20. Hookups: full.

Mossyrock

Harmony Lakeside RV Park, 563 St. Rte. 122, Silver Creek, 98585. T: (360) 983-3804. RV/tent: 80. $19–$22. Hookups: electric, water.

Mount Vernon

Thousand Trails-Mount Vernon, 5409 North Darrk Ln., Bow, 98232. T: (360) 724-331. RV/tent: 240. $20. Hookups: electric, water.

Naches

Squaw Rock Resort, 45070 State Rte. 410, 98937. T: (509) 658-2926. RV/tent: 64. $20. Hookups: electric, water.

Neaah Bay

Snow Creek Campground, P.O. Box 248, 98357. T: (800) 883-1464. RV/tent: 81. $19–$23. Hookups: electric, water.

Newhalem

North Cascades NP-Ross Lake NRA, 810 St. Rte. 20, 98284. T: (360) 856-5700. RV/tent: 164. $10–$12. Hookups: none.

Newport

Thousand Trails-Little Diamond, 1002 McGowen Rd., 99156. T: (509) 447-4813. RV/tent: 312. $20. Hookups: electric, water.

North Bend

Denny Creek Campground, 33515 Mountain Loop Hwy., 98252. T: (877) 444-6777. RV/tent: 34. $12–$14. Hookups: none.

Tinkham Campground, 33515 Mountain Loop Hwy., Granite Falls, 98252. T: (877) 444-6777. RV/tent: 48. $12. Hookups: none.

Northport

Homeland RV Park and Camping, 4706 Northport Waneta Rd., 99157. T: (509) 732-4367. RV/tent: 28. $16. Hookups: none.

Oak Harbor

Military Park, 3515 Princeton St. Bldg. 2641, 98278-1900. T: (360) 257-2434. RV/tent: 26. $5–$10. Hookups: electric, water.

Ocean Park

Ocean Park Resort, P.O. Box 339, 98640. T: (800) 835-4634. info@opresort.com. RV/tent: 83. $18–$21. Hookups: full.

Ocean Shores

Yesterday's RV Park, 3377 Bethel Rd. Southeast 223, Port Orchard, 98366. T: (360) 289-9227. RV/tent: 48. $17–$20. Hookups: full.

Olympia

American Heritage Campground, 9610 Kimmie St. Southwest, 98512. T: (360) 943-8778. RV/tent: 99. $25–$26. Hookups: electric, water.

Olympia Campground, 1441 83rd Ave. Southwest, 98512. T: (360) 352-2551. RV/tent: 99. $20–$24. Hookups: electric, water.

Omak

Eastside Park, P.O. Box 1456, 98841. T: (509) 826-0804. RV/tent: 68. $7–$12. Hookups: full.

Orcas Island

West Beach Resort, 190 Waterfront Way, 98245. T: (360) 376-2240. RV/tent: 45. $30–$35. Hookups: electric, water.

Oroville

Orchard RV Park, 25A Thorndike Loop Rd., 98844. T: (509) 476-2669. RV/tent: 41. $13–$16. Hookups: full.

Sun Cove Resort and Guest Ranch, 93 East Wannacut Ln., 98844. T: (509) 476-2223. suncove@nvinet.com. RV/tent: 38. $18. Hookups: full.

Pacific Beach

Pacific Beach State Park, 148 St. Rte. 115, Hoquiam, 98550. T: (360) 276-4297. RV/tent: 64. $13–$19. Hookups: electric.

Pasco

Arrowhead RV Park, 3120 Commercial Ave., 99301. T: (509) 545-8206. RV/tent: 64. $30. Hookups: none.

Sandy Heights RV Park, 8801 St. Thomas Dr., 99301. T: (877) 894-1357. sandyheightsrv@urx.com. RV/tent: 185. $20–$25. Hookups: full.

Pateros

Alta Lake State Park, 191A Alta Lake Rd., 98846. T: (509) 923-2473. RV/tent: 189. $3–$9. Hookups: none.

Port Angeles

Crescent Beach and RV Park, 2860 Crescent Beach Rd., 98363-8703. T: (360) 928-3344. RV/tent: 64. $30. Hookups: none.

Lyre River Park, 596 West Lyre River Rd., 98363. T: (360) 938-3436. RV/tent: 86. $17–$25. Hookups: full.

Peabody Creek RV Park, 127 South Lincoln, 98362. T: (800) 392-2361. patm@tenf. RV/tent: 44. $21. Hookups: full.

WASHINGTON (continued)

Port Orchard
Manchester State Park, P.O. Box 338, 98353. T: (360) 871-4065. RV/tent: 53. $13–$19. Hookups: none.

Poulsbo
Eagle Tree RV Park, 16280 St. Hwy. 305, 98370. T: (360) 598-5988. RV/tent: 93. $25. Hookups: electric.

Quinault
Lake Quinault's Rain Forest Resort Village, 516 South Shore Rd., Lake Quinault, 98575. T: (360) 288-2535. RV/tent: 30. $16. Hookups: electric, water.

Quincy
Crescent Bar Resort Campground, 8894 Crescent Bar Rd. Northwest, Suite 1, 98848. T: (800) 824-7090. RV/tent: 60. $30. Hookups: none.

Raymond
Timberland RV Park, 850 Crescent St., 98577. T: (800) 563-3325. RV/tent: 29. $15. Hookups: full.

Republic
Black Beach Resort, 80 Black Beach Rd., 99166. T: (509) 775-3989. bbresort@televar.com. RV/tent: 87. $16–$18. Hookups: full.

Pine Point Resort, 38 Pine Point Resort Rd., 99166. T: (877) 775-3643. RV/tent: 52. $17. Hookups: full.

Tiffany's Resort, 58 Tiffany Rd., 99166. T: (509) 775-3152. RV/tent: 17. $17. Hookups: full.

Riverside
Glenwood RV Park, P.O. Box 278, 98849. T: (509) 826-5228. RV/tent: 20. $15. Hookups: full.

Roosevelt
Crow Butte State Park, 1 Crow Butte State Park Rd., Paterson, 99345. T: (509) 875-2644. RV/tent: 50. $13–$19. Hookups: full.

Salkum
Barrier Dam Campground, 273 Fuller Rd., 98582. T: (360) 985-2495. RV/tent: 27. $20. Hookups: electric, water.

San Juan Island
Lakedale Resort, Friday Harbor, 98250. T: (800) 617-2267. RV/tent: 129. $23–$28. Hookups: none.

Seabeck
Scenic Beach State Park, P.O. Box 701, 98380. T: (360) 830-5079. RV/tent: 52. $13–$19. Hookups: none.

Seaview
Thousand Trails-Long Beach Preserve, 2215 Willows Rd., 98644. T: (360) 642-3091. RV/tent: 120. $20. Hookups: full.

Sekiu
Shipwreck Point Campground, 6850 Hwy. 112, 98381. T: (360) 963-2688. RV/tent: 48. $18. Hookups: none.

Selah
Stagecoach RV Park, P.O. Box 806, 98937. T: (509) 697-9650. RV/tent: 24. $15. Hookups: full.

Sequim
Dungeness Recreation Area, 554 Voice of America Rd., 98383. T: (360) 683-5847. RV/tent: 67. $13–$19. Hookups: none.

Shelton
Lake Nahatzel Resort, West 12900 Shelton Matlock Rd., 98584. T: (360) 426-8323. RV/tent: 17. $20–$22. Hookups: none.

Potlatch State Park, P.O. Box 1051, 98548-1051. T: (360) 877-5361. RV/tent: 35. $13–$19. Hookups: none.

Silver Lake
Seaquest State Park, 3030 Spirit Lake Hwy., 98611. T: (360) 274-8633. RV/tent: 92. $13–$19. Hookups: none.

Skamania
Beacon Rock Resort, 62 Moorage Rd., 98648. T: (509) 427-8473. RV/tent: 57. $15. Hookups: none.

South Prairie
Prairie Creek RV Park, P.O. Box 17, 98358. T: (888) 270-8465. RV/tent: 125. $18. Hookups: electric.

Spokane
KOA-Spokane, 3025 North Barker Rd., Otis Orchards, 99027. T: (509) 924-4722. RV/tent: 196. $23–$28. Hookups: electric, water.

Sprague
Four Sesasons Campround, 2384 North Bob Lee Rd., 99032. T: (509) 257-2332. RV/tent: 38. $17–$19. Hookups: none.

Stanwood
Cedar Grove Shores RV Park, 16529 West Lake Goodwin Rd., 98292. T: (360) 652-7083. RV/tent: 60. $19–$26. Hookups: electric, water.

Starbuck
Lyons Ferry Marina, P.O. Box 189, 99359. T: (509) 399-2001. RV/tent: 60. $14. Hookups: electric.

Sultan
Lake Bronson Club Family Nudist Park, P.O. Box 1135, 98294. T: (360) 793-0286. RV/tent: 26. $40–$50. Hookups: electric, water.

Sumas
Sumas RV Park and Campground, 9600 Easterbrook, 98295. T: (360) 988-8875. RV/tent: 60. $12–$18. Hookups: none.

Tenino
Offut Lake RV Resort, 4005 120th Ave. Southeast, 98589. T: (360) 264-2438. RV/tent: 66. $20. Hookups: none.

Tonasket
Spectacle Lake Resort, 10 McCammon Rd., 98855. T: (509) 223-3433. RV/tent: 40. $15. Hookups: none.

Toppenish
Yakama Nation RV Resort, 280 Buster Rd., 98948. T: (800) 874-3087. RV/tent: 125. $18–$25. Hookups: electric.

Trout Lake
Elk Meadows RV Park and Campground, 78 Trout Lake Creek Rd., 98650. T: (509) 395-2400. RV/tent: 63. $15–$17. Hookups: electric, water.

Twisp
Riverbend RV Park, 19961 Hwy. 20, 98856. T: (800) 686-4498. RV/tent: 104. $14–$19. Hookups: none.

Valley
Silver Beach Resort, 3323 Waitts Lake Rd., 99181. T: (509) 937-2811. RV/tent: 40. $19. Hookups: electric.

Winona Beach Resort, 33022 Winona Beach Rd., 99181. T: (509) 937-2231. RV/tent: 54. $19. Hookups: none.

Vantage
Vantage Riverstone Campground, P.O. Box 135, 98950. T: (509) 856-2800. RV/tent: 75. $21–$23. Hookups: electric.

Wanapum State Park, P.O. Box 1203, 98950. T: (509) 856-2700. RV/tent: 50. $13–$19. Hookups: none.

Walla Walla
RV Resort Four Seasons, 1440 Dallas Military Rd., 99362. T: (509) 529-6072. RV/tent: 89. $23. Hookups: electric.

Wenatchee
Daroga State Park, 1 South Daroga Park Rd., Orondo, 98843. T: (509) 664-6380. RV/tent: 28. $13–$19. Hookups: electric, water.

Lincoln Rock State Park, 1253 US Hwy. 2, 98802. T: (509) 884-8702. RV/tent: 93. $13–$19. Hookups: electric, water.

Westpoint
Jolly Rogers Fishing Camp, P.O. Box 342, 98595. T: (360) 268-0265. RV/tent: 22. $16–$18. Hookups: electric.

Westport
Coho RV Park, P.O. Box 1087, 98595. T: (800) 572-0177. RV/tent: 76. $18–$20. Hookups: electric.

Twin Harbors State Park, 420 St. Rte. 105, 98595. T: (360) 268-9717. RV/tent: 302. $13–$19. Hookups: electric, water.

WASHINGTON (continued)

White Salmon

Bridge RV Park and Campground, 65271 Hwy. 14, 98672. T: (509) 483-1111. RV/tent: 50. $21–$25. Hookups: electric.

Wilbur

Bell RV Park, 712 Southeast Railroad, 99185. T: (509) 647-5888. RV/tent: 30. $18. Hookups: electric.

Winthrop

Big Twin Lake Campground, Rt 2 Box 705, 98862. T: (509) 996-2650. RV/tent: 89. $18. Hookups: electric, water.

Jeffrey's Silberline Resort, 677 Bear Creek Rd., 98862. T: (509) 996-2448. RV/tent: 122. $18–$20. Hookups: none.

KOA-Methow River, P.O. Box 305, 98862. T: (800) 562-2158. RV/tent: 90. $20–$26. Hookups: electric, water.

Woodland

Columbia Riverfront RV Park, 1881 Dike Rd., 98674. T: (800) 845-9842. RV/tent: 76. $22–$24. Hookups: electric.

Paradise Point State Park, 33914 New Paradise Park Rd., Ridgefield, 98642. T: (360) 263-2350. RV/tent: 70. $13–$19. Hookups: electric, water.

Yakima

Circle H RV Ranch, 1107 South 18th St., 98901. T: (509) 457-3683. RV/tent: 76. $18. Hookups: electric.

Yakima-KOA, 1500 Keys, 98901. T: (800) 562-5773. RV/tent: 148. $22–$28. Hookups: electric, water.

WEST VIRGINIA

Beckley

Beckley Exhibition Coal Mine & Campground, New River Park, 25802. T: (304) 256-1747. RV/tent: 17. $15. Hookups: water, electric (20, 30 amps), sewer.

Lake Stephens Campground, RR 3 Box 350, 25801. T: (304) 934-5322. RV/tent: 113. $15. Hookups: water, electric (30 amps), sewer.

Belington

Twin Lakes Campground, Audra Rd., 26250. T: (304) 823-2021. RV/tent: 185. $14–$16. Hookups: water, electric (20, 30 amps), sewer.

Bruceton Mills

Glade Farms Campground, P.O. Box 455, 26525. T: (304) 379-9375. RV/tent: 85. $12. Hookups: water, electric (20, 30 amps), sewer.

Buckhannon

Stonecoal Campground, Rte. 7, 26201. T: (304) 472-7226. RV/tent: 33. $10–$12. Hookups: none.

Circleville

Milstead's Grocery & Camping, P.O. Box 125, 26804. T: (304) 567-3171. RV/tent: 38. $10–$15. Hookups: water, electric (20 amps), sewer.

Spruce Knob Lake Campground/Monongahela National Forest, HC 59 Box 240, 26804. T: (304) 257-4488. www.fs.fed.us/r9/mnf. RV/tent: 46. $7–$14. Hookups: none.

Davis

Canaan Valley Resort Park, Rte. 1 Box 330, 26260. T: (304) 866-4121. www.canaanresort.com. RV/tent: 34. $14–$19. Hookups: water, electric (20, 30, 50 amps), sewer.

Dawson

Summer Wind, Rte. 1 Box 120 1, 25976. T: (304) 392-2005. RV/tent: 20. $19. Hookups: water, electric (30, 50 amps).

Dunmore

Seneca State Forest, Rte. 1 Box 140, 24934. T: (304) 799-6213. www.senecastateforest.com. RV/tent: 10. $11. Hookups: none.

Durbin

East Fork River Campgrounds, Box 177, 26264. T: (304) 456-3101. RV/tent: 36. $12–$20. Hookups: water, electric (20, 30, 50 amps).

Fairmont

Prickett's Creek Campground, RR 3, 26554. T: (304) 363-1910. RV/tent: 16. $16–$18. Hookups: water, electric (20, 30, 50 amps).

Falling Waters

Falling Waters Campsite, 7685 Williamsport Pike, 25419. T: (304) 274-2791. RV/tent: 47. $19–$22. Hookups: water, electric (20, 30, 50 amps), sewer.

Fayetteville

Mountain Laurel Campground, Rte. 2 Box 68, 25840. T: (304) 574-0188. RV/tent: 23. $15. Hookups: water, electric (20 amps).

New River Gorge Campgrounds, P.O. Box 300, Miller Ridge Rd., 25840. T: (304) 658-5919. RV/ tent: 100. $8–$15. Hookups: electric (15, 30 amp).

Rifrafters Campground, Rte. 2 Box 140a, 25840. T: (304) 574-1065. F: (304) 574-1007. RV/tent: 6 RV. $7–$15. Hookups: water, electric (30 amps).

Glen Jean

Whitewater Campground, Box 637, 25951. T: (800) 292-0880. RV/tent: 50. $6–$15. Hookups: water, electric (20, 30 amps).

Harrisville

North Bend State Park, Rte. 1 Box 221, 26337. T: (304) 643-2391. www.northbendsp.com. RV/tent: 75. $13–17. Hookups: electric.

Hazelton

Pine Hill Campground & Cabins, RD 3 Box 233aa, 26525. T: (304) 379-4612. RV/tent: 180. $14–$16. Hookups: water, electric (20, 30, 50 amps).

Hinton

Bass Lake Park, Hwy. 20 North, 25951. T: (304) 466-4475. RV/tent: 200. $20. Hookups: water, electric (15, 20, 30 amps), sewer.

Huntersville

Watoga State Park, HC 82 Box 252, 24954. T: (304) 799-4087. www.wotaga.com. RV/tent: 88. $14–18. Hookups: electric (20 amps).

Huttonsville

Kumbrabow State Forest, P.O. Box 65, 26273. T: (304) 335-2219. RV/tent: 13. $8–$10. Hookups: none.

Inwood

Lazy A Campground, 2741 Back Creek Valley Rd., 25427. T: (304) 229-8185. RV/tent: 58. $16. Hookups: water, electric (20, 30 amps).

Marlinton

Tea Creek Campground/Monongahela National Forest, Marlinton Ranger District, P.O. Box 10, 24954. T: (304) 799-4334. www.fs.fed.us/r9/mnf. RV/tent: 29. $6. Hookups: none.

Morgantown

Coopers Rock State Forest, Rte. 1 Box 270, 26525. T: (304) 594-1561. www.coopersrock-state forest.com. RV/tent: 25. $13–$17. Hookups: electric (20 amps).

Panther

Panther State Forest, Box 287, 24872. T: (304) 938-2252. www.pantherstateforest.com. RV/tent: 6. $8–$10. Hookups: electric (30 amps).

Parkersburg

Trailer Center Campground, P.O. Box 3312, 26101. T: (304) 448-8203. RV/tent: 33. $18. Hookups: water, electric (20, 30 amps).

WEST VIRGINIA (continued)

Paw Paw

Avalon Campground, P.O. Box 369, 25434. T: (304) 947-5600. F: (304) 947-5579. www.avalon-nude.com. RV/tent: 40. $10–$52. Hookups: water, electric (30, 50 amps), sewer.

Pax

Plum Orchard Lake State Wildlife Management Area, Rte. 1 Box 186, 25917. T: (304) 469-9905. RV/tent: 43. $8–$10. Hookups: none.

Point Pleasant

Krodel Park, 400 Viand St., 25550. T: (304) 675-1068. RV/tent: 55. $14–$16. Hookups: water, electric (20, 30, 50 amps), sewer.

Oldtown Campground, Rte. 1 Box 662, Country Club Rd., 25550. T: (304) 675-7153. RV/tent: 80. $10. Hookups: water, electric (20, 30 amps), sewer.

Princeton

Green Acres RV Park & Campground, 5127 Eads Mill Rd., 24740. T: (304) 384-7994. RV/tent: 56. $10–$18. Hookups: water, electric (20, 30 amps), sewer.

Ripley

Ruby Lake Campground, Rte. 2 Box 51, 27275. T: (304) 273-3427. RV/tent: 29. $10–$14. Hookups: water, electric (30 amps), sewer.

Romney

Middle Ridge Campground, HC 65 Box 4960, 26757. T: (304) 822-8020. RV/tent: 21. $15. Hookups: water, electric (30, 50 amps), sewer.

Wapocoma Campgrounds, River Rd., 26757. T: (304) 822-5528. RV/tent: 200. $11–$13. Hookups: water, electric (30, 50 amps).

Seneca Rocks

Seneca Shadows Campground/Monongahela National Forest, US Rte. 33, 26884. T: (304) 257-4488. www.fs.fed.us/r9/mnf. RV/tent: 81. $8–$15. Hookups: electric (20 amps).

Summersville

Battle Run Recreation Area, Rte. 2 Box 470, 26651. T: (304) 872-3579. www.reserveusa.com. RV/tent: 117. $14–$18. Hookups: electric (30 amps).

Summersville Music Park Campground, State Rte. 41 North, 26651. T: (304) 872-3145. RV/tent: 300. $15. Hookups: water, electric (20, 30 amps).

Weston

Briar Point Campground/Stonewall Jackson Lake State Park, 100 State Park Tr., 26447. T: (304) 269-0523. www.stonewalljacksonsp.com. RV/tent: 34. $21. Hookups: water, electric (20, 30 amps), sewer.

Broken Wheel Campground & Country Store, Rte. 3 Box 299, 26452. T: (304) 269-6097. RV/tent: 46. $17. Hookups: water, electric (30 amps).

Wheeling

Dallas Pike Campground, RD 1 Box 231, Mccutcheon Rd., 26059. T: (800) 233-0940. RV/tent: 148. $21–$24. Hookups: water, electric (20, 30, 50 amps), sewer.

White Sulphur Springs

Greenbrier Mountainaire Campground, HC 30 Box 155, 24925. T: (304) 536-1512. RV/tent: 33. $10–$18. Hookups: water, electric (20, 30 amps).

Twilight Overnight Campground, US Rte. 60 East, 24986. T: (304) 536-1731. RV/tent: 15. $14–$22. Hookups: water, electric (20, 30, 50 amps)

WISCONSIN

Algoma

Ahnapee River Trails Camp Resort Inc., 6053 West Wilson Rd., 54201. T: (920) 487-5777. RV/tent: 65. $18. Hookups: water, electric (30 amps).

Alma Center

KOA Hixton/Alma Center, North 9657 State Hwy. 95, 54611. T: (715) 964-2508. RV/tent: 66. $24. Hookups: water, electric (30 amps), sewer.

Amherst Junction

Lake Emily Park, 3961 Park Dr., 54407. T: (715) 346-1433. RV/tent: 49. $13. Hookups: electric (30 amps).

Arbor Vitae

Arbor Vitae Campground, 10545 Big Arbor Vitae Dr., 54568. T: (715) 356-5146. RV/tent: 90. $20. Hookups: water, electric (30 amps), sewer.

Fox Fire Campground, 11180 Fox Fire Rd., 54568. T: (715) 356-6470. RV/tent: 50. $23. Hookups: water, electric (30 amps), sewer.

Ashland

Evergreen Acres Campground, Rte. 3 Box 353, 54806. T: (715) 682-4658. RV/tent: 20. $16. Hookups: water, electric (20 amps).

Kreher RV Park, 601 Main St. W, 54806. T: (715) 682-7071. RV/tent: 35. $15. Hookups: electric (20 amps).

Prentice Park, 601 Main St. W, 54806. T: (715) 682-7071. RV/tent: 25. $15. Hookups: electric (20 amps).

Athelstane

Kosir's Rapid Rafts, W 14073 Cty Hwy. C, 54104. T: (715) 757-3431. RV/tent: 32. $11. Hookups: water, electric (20 amps).

McCaslin Mountain Campground, W 15720 County F, 54104. T: (715) 757-3734. RV/tent: 114. $15. Hookups: water, sewer, electric (20 amps).

Augusta

Coon Fork Lake Campground, CR CF, 54722. T: (715) 839-4738. RV/tent: 88. $13. Hookups: electric (30 amps).

Sandy Hill Campground, E2100 ND Rd., 54722. T: (715) 286-2495. RV/tent: 28. $15. Hookups: water, electric (30 amps).

Babcock

Country Aire Campground, P.O. Box 88, 54413. T: (715) 884-2300. RV/tent: 39. $17. Hookups: water, electric (30 amps).

Balsam Lake

Apple River Campground North, 956 165th Ave., 54810. T: (715) 268-8980. RV/tent: 28. $12. Hookups: water, electric (30 amps).

Baraboo

Baraboo Hills Campground, E 10545 Terrytowne Rd., 53913. T: (608) 356-8505. RV/tent: 180. $25. Hookups: water, sewer, electric (50 amps).

Devil's Lake State Park, 5975 Park Rd., 53913. T: (608) 356-8301. RV/tent: 407. $15. Hookups: electric (30 amps).

Fox Hill RV Park, 11371 North Reedsburg Rd., 53913. T: (608) 356-5890. RV/tent: 50. $27. Hookups: water, electric (30 amps).

Mirror Lake State Park, 10320 East Fern Dell Rd., 53913. T: (608) 254-2333. RV/tent: 148. $15. Hookups: electric (30 amps).

Nordic Pines, E11740 County DL, 53913. T: (608) 356-5810. RV/tent: 140. $20. Hookups: electric (20 amps).

Red Oak Campground, South 2350 US Hwy. 12, 53913. T: (608) 356-7304. RV/tent: 121. $18. Hookups: water, sewer, electric (50 amps).

Rocky Arbor State Park, 10320 Fern Dell Rd., 53913. T: (608) 254-8001. RV/tent: 48. $21. Hookups: electric (30 amps).

WISCONSIN (continued)

Barron

Barron Motel & RV Campground, 1521 East Division Ave., 54812. T: (715) 637-3154. RV/tent: 17. $14. Hookups: water, sewer, electric (30 amps).

Bayfield

Apostle Islands Area Campground, HC 64 Box 8, 54814. T: (715) 779-5524. RV/tent: 59. $22. Hookups: water, sewer, electric (50 amps).

Buffalo Bay Campground & Marina, P.O. Box 529, 54814. T: (715) 779-3743. RV/tent: 50. $15. Hookups: water, electric (30 amps).

Belmont

Lake Joy Campground, 24192 Lake Joy Ln., 53510. T: (608) 762-5150. RV/tent: 78. $18. Hookups: water, electric (30 amps).

Big Flats

Pineland Camping Park, 916 Hwy. 13, 54613. T: (608) 564-7818. RV/tent: 175. $20. Hookups: waters, sewer, electric (50 amps).

Birchwood

Doolittle Park, P.O. Box 6, 54817. T: (715) 354-3300. RV/tent: 34. $14. Hookups: electric (30 amps).

Spider Lake Resort & Campground, N2603 CTH T, 54817. T: (715) 354-3723. RV/tent: 45. $16. Hookups: water, electric (20 amps).

Black River Falls

Black River State Forest, Castle Mound Rec. Area, 910 Hwy. 54 East, 54615. T: (715) 284-4103. RV/tent: 38. $15. Hookups: electric (30 amps).

Jamboree Campground, Hwy. 12, 54615. T: (715) 284-7138. RV/tent: 200. $25. Hookups: water, sewer, electric (30 amps).

Blair

Riverside Memorial Park, P.O. Box 147, 54616. T: (608) 989-2517. RV/tent: 24. $11. Hookups: electric (30 amps).

Blue Mounds

Blue Mounds State Park, 4350 Mounds Park Rd., 53517. T: (608) 437-5711. RV/tent: 123. $14. Hookups: electric (30 amps).

Blue River

Eagle Cave Natural Park, 16320 Cavern Ln., 53518. T: (608) 537-2988. RV/tent: 50. $15. Hookups: water, electric (15 amps).

Briggsville

Lake Mason Campground, 4035 First Ln., 53920. T: (608) 981-2444. RV/tent: 50. $16. Hookups: water, sewer, electric (30 amps).

Wagon Wheel Campground, 4016 1st Dr., 53920. T: (608) 981-2161. RV/tent: 150. $16. Hookups: water, sewer, electric (30 amps).

Brodhead

Crazy Horse Campground, N3201 Crazy Horse Ln., 53520. T: (608) 897-2207. RV/tent: 196. $18. Hookups: water, sewer, electric (30 amps).

Sweet Minni Ha Ha Campground, N4697 County E, 53520. T: (608) 862-3769. RV/tent: 117. $20. Hookups: water, electric (30 amps).

Bruce

Bruce Park, P.O. Box 238, 54819. T: (715) 868-2185. RV/tent: 8. $10. Hookups: electric (20 amps).

Brule

Brule River Motel & Campground, P.O. Box 126, 54820. T: (715) 372-4815. RV/tent: 65. $15. Hookups: water, electric (30 amps), sewer.

Burlington

Meadowlark Acres Campground, N 5146 North Rd., 53105. T: (262) 763-7200. RV/tent: 84. $22. Hookups: water, electric (30 amps).

Butternut

Butternut Lake Campground, Rte. 1 Box 129 A, 54514. T: (715) 769-3448. RV/tent: 24. $19. Hookups: water, sewer, electric (20 amps).

Camp Douglas

Mill Bluff State Park, 15819 Funnel Rd., 54651. T: (608) 427-6692. RV/tent: 21. $10. Hookups: electric (20 amps).

Cascade

Hilly Haven Campground, N 2827 Dusty Ln., 53011. T: (920) 528-8966. RV/tent: 70. $20. Hookups: water, sewer, electric (50 amps).

Hoeft's Resort & Campground, W9070 Crooked Lake Dr., 53011. T: (262) 626-2221. RV/tent: 96. $17. Hookups: water, electric (50 amps).

Cassville

K-7 Korral, 10895 Jack Oak Rd., 53806. T: (608) 725-2267. RV/tent: 35. $20. Hookups: water, electric (30 amps).

Nelson Dewey State Park, County Trunk VV, 53806. T: (608) 725-5374. RV/tent: 43. $15. Hookups: electric (30 amps).

Chetek

Northern Exposure Resort & Campground, P.O. Box 222, 54728. T: (715) 859-2887. RV/tent: 20. $18. Hookups: water, electric (30 amps).

Six Lakes Resort & Campground, 25358 8th Ave., 54728. T: (800) 203-4624. RV/tent: 180. $20. Hookups: water, sewer, electric (30 amps).

Chippewa Falls

Lake Wissota State Park, 18127 CR O, 54729. T: (715) 382-4574. RV/tent: 81. $15. Hookups: electric (30 amps).

Pine Harbor Campground, 7181 185th St., 54729. T: (715) 723-9865. RV/tent: 26. $14. Hookups: water, electric (30 amps).

Conover

Buckatabon Lodge & Lighthouse Inn, 5630 Rush Rd., 54519. T: (715) 479-4660. RV/tent: 51. $19. Hookups: water, sewer, electric (20 amps).

Cornell

Brunet Island State Park, 23125 255th St., 54732. T: (715) 239-6888. RV/tent: 69. $12. Hookups: electric (30 amps).

Cumberland

Camp Brigadoon, 2554 4th St., 54829. T: (800) 715-BRIG. RV/tent: 131. $18. Hookups: water, electric (30 amps).

De Pere

Brown County Fairgrounds, Ft. Howard Ave., 54115. T: (920) 336-3283. RV/tent: 40. $15. Hookups: water, electric (30 amps), sewer.

Happy Hollow Camping Resort, 3831 CR U, 54115. T: (920) 532-4386. RV/tent: 125. $23. Hookups: water, sewer, electric (30 amps).

De Soto

Blackhawk Park, RFD 1, 54624. T: (608) 648-3314. RV/tent: 175. $16. Hookups: electric (30 amps).

Deerbrook

Veterans Memorial Park, P.O. Box 460, 54409. T: (715) 623-6214. RV/tent: 41. $10. Hookups: electric (30 amps).

Delavan

Snug Harbor Inn Campground on Turtle Lake, W7772-2C Wisc Pkwy, 53115. T: (608) 883-6999. RV/tent: 43. $35. Hookups: water, electric (50 amps).

Dells

American World RV Park & Resort, 400 Wisconsin Dells Parkway, 53965. T: (608) 253-4451. RV/tent: 52. $54. Hookups: water, sewer, electric (50 amps).

Arrowhead Resort Campground, P.O. Box 295, 53965. T: (608) 254-7344. RV/tent: 285. $28. Hookups: water, sewer, electric (30 amps).

Blue Lake Campground, 3531 Hwy. G, 53965. T: (608) 586-4376. RV/tent: 45. $20. Hookups: water, sewer, electric (30 amps).

Bonanza Campground, P.O. Box 453, 53965. T: (608) 254-8124. RV/tent: 150. $22. Hookups: water, sewer, electric (50 amps).

Dell-Boo Campground, P.O. Box 407, 53965. T: (608) 356-5898. RV/tent: 138. $31. Hookups: water, sewer, electric (30 amps).

Erickson's Tepee Park Campground, 10096 Trout Rd., 53965. T: (608) 253-3122. RV/tent: 113. $25. Hookups: water, sewer, electric (30 amps).

Holiday Shores Campground & Resort, 3901 River Rd., 53965. T: (608) 254-2717. RV/tent: 140. $26. Hookups: water, electric (30 amps).

K & L Campground, 3503 County Rd. G, 53965. T: (608) 586-4720. RV/tent: 96. $25. Hookups: water, sewer, electric (30 amps).

Lake of the Dells Camping Resort, 3879 Hwy. 13, 53965. T: (608) 254-6485. RV/tent: 200. $30. Hookups: water, sewer, electric (50 amps).

River Bay Resort Campground, Marina and RV Park, P.O. Box 456, 53965. T: (608) 254-7193. RV/tent: 158. $31. Hookups: water, sewer, electric (50 amps).

WISCONSIN (continued)

Sherwood Forest Campground, 352 Hwys 12 & 16, 53965. T: (608) 254-7080. RV/tent: 189. $31. Hookups: water, sewer, electric (50 amps).

Stand Rock Campground, 570 Hwy. N, 53965. T: (608) 253-2169. RV/tent: 140. $25. Hookups: water, sewer, electric (30 amps).

Wisconsin Dells KOA, 235 Stand Rock Rd., 53965. T: (608) 254-4177. RV/tent: 147. $40. Hookups: water, sewer, electric (50 amps).

Denmark

Shady Acres Campsites, 5422 Shady Acre Ln., 54208. T: (920) 863-8143. RV/tent: 25. $17. Hookups: water, sewer, electric (30 amps).

Dodgeville

Governor Dodge State Park, 4175 SSR 23N, 53533. T: (608) 935-2315. RV/tent: 268. $15. Hookups: electric (30 amps).

Eagle

Kettle Moraine State Forest-Southern Unit Headquarters, 39091 West Hwy. 59, 53119. T: (262) 594-6200. RV/tent: 260. $15. Hookups: electric (30 amps).

Eagle River

Chain-O-Lakes Resort & Campground, 3165 Campground Rd., 54521. T: (715) 479-6708. RV/tent: 100. $20. Hookups: water, electric (30 amps).

Elkhart Lake

Plymouth Rock Camping Resort, 7271 North Lando St., 53073. T: (920) 892-4252. RV/tent: 270. $30. Hookups: water, sewer, electric (50 amps).

Elton

Glacier Wilderness Campground, P.O. Box 5, 54430. T: (715) 882-4781. RV/tent: 11. $20. Hookups: water, electric (30 amps).

Exeland

Windfall Lake Family Camping, 632 North SR 40, 54835. T: (715) 943-2625. RV/tent: 25. $13. Hookups: electric (15 amps).

Fish Creek

Peninsula State Park Campgrounds, P.O. Box 218, 54212. T: (920) 868-3258. RV/tent: 469. $14. Hookups: electric (30 amps).

Florence

Keyes Lake Campground, HCl Box 162, 54121. T: (715) 528-4907. RV/tent: 35. $15. Hookups: water, electric (30 amps).

Fort Atkinson

Pilgrim's Campground LLC, W 7271 Hwy. C, 53538. T: (920) 563-8122. RV/tent: 103. $27. Hookups: water, sewer, electric (50 amps).

Fremont

Blue Top Resort & Campground, 1460 Wolf River Dr., 54940. T: (920) 446-3343. RV/tent: 50. $21. Hookups: water, electric (30 amps).

Galesville

Pow-Wow Campground, W 16751 Pow-Wow Ln., 54630. T: (608) 582-2995. RV/tent: 128. $18. Hookups: water, electric (30 amps).

Glidden

Northern Lure Resort & Campground, P.O. Box 5, 54527. T: (715) 264-3677. RV/tent: 19. $20. Hookups: water, sewer, electric (30 amps).

Gordon

Adventureland, 7440 E CR Y, 54838. T: (715) 376-4528. RV/tent: 50. $18. Hookups: water, electric (30 amps).

Grantsburg

Cedar Point Resort & Campground, 12480 Cedar Point Ln., 54840. T: (715) 488-2224. RV/tent: 30. $18. Hookups: water, sewer, electric (30 amps).

James N. McNally Campground, 316 South Brad St., 54840. T: (715) 463-2405. RV/tent: 38. $15. Hookups: water, sewer, electric (50 amps).

Green Lake

Green Lake Campground, W2360 Hwy. 23, 54941. T: (920) 294-3543. RV/tent: 200. $30. Hookups: water, sewer, electric (30 amps).

Greenbush

Westward Ho Camp Resort, 5456 North Division Rd., 53023. T: (920) 526-3407. RV/tent: 175. $35. Hookups: water, sewer, electric (50 amps).

Hayward

The Hayward KOA, 11544 North Hwy. 63, 54843. T: (715) 634-2331. RV/tent: 142. $35. Hookups: water, sewer, electric (50 amps).

Nelson Lake Lodge, 12980 North Lodge Rd., 54843. T: (715) 634-3750. RV/tent: 52. $27. Hookups: water, sewer, electric (30 amps).

Revelle's Landing Resort & Campground, 15249 W. Bills Rd., 54843. T: (715) 634-4216. RV/tent: 48. $16. Hookups: water, sewer, electric (30 amps).

Sisko's Pine Point Resort, 8677 North County Rd. CC, 54843. T: (715) 462-3700. RV/tent: 33. $19. Hookups: water, sewer, electric (30 amps).

Sunrise Bay Campground & RV Park, 16269 W. Jolly Fisherman Rd., 54843. T: (715) 634-2213. RV/tent: 51. $18. Hookups: water, sewer, electric (30 amps).

Trail's End Resort & Campground, 8080 North CR K, 54843. T: (715) 634-2423. RV/tent: 65. $30. Hookups: water, sewer, electric (30 amps).

Hazelhurst

Cedar Falls Campground, 6051 Cedar Falls Rd., 54531. T: (715) 356-4953. RV/tent: 42. $18. Hookups: electric (20 amps).

Hilbert

Calumet County Park, 6150 City EE, 54129. T: (920) 439-1008. RV/tent: 71. $16. Hookups: electric (30 amps).

Hiles

Hiles Pine Lake Campground, 8896 West Pine Lake Rd., 54511. T: (715) 649-3319. RV/tent: 80. $18. Hookups: water, electric (30 amps).

Hixton

Triple R Resort, N11818 Hixton-Levis Rd., 54635. T: (715) 964-8777. RV/tent: 25. $21. Hookups: water, electric (50 amps).

Holmen

Sandman's Campground, 8905 Hwy. 53 & 93, 54636. T: (608) 526-4956. RV/tent: 50. $14. Hookups: water, electric (30 amps).

Horicon

The Playful Goose Campground, 2001 South Main St., 53032. T: (920) 485-4744. RV/tent: 192. $26. Hookups: water, sewwer, electric (30 amps).

Hudson

Willow River State Park, 1034 CR A, 54016. T: (715) 386-5931. RV/tent: 55. $15. Hookups: electric (30 amps).

Iola

Iola Pines Campground Inc., 100 Fairway Dr., 54945. T: (715) 445-3489. RV/tent: 50. $16. Hookups: water, sewer, electric (30 amps).

Iron River

Wildwood Campground, RR 2 Box 18, 54847. T: (715) 372-4072. RV/tent: 25. $14. Hookups: water, sewer, electric (30 amps).

Jefferson

Bark River Campground, 2340 W. Hansen Rd., 53549. T: (262) 593-2421. RV/tent: 250. $20. Hookups: water, sewer, electric (30 amps).

Kansasville

Bong State Recreation Area, 26313 Burlington Rd., 53139. T: (262) 878-5600. RV/tent: 192. $15. Hookups: electric (30 amps).

Kewaskum

Kettle Moraine State Forest, Mauthe Lake Recreation Area, CR Hwy. G, 53010. T: (262) 626-4305. RV/tent: 147. $14. Hookups: electric (30 amps).

Kettle Moraine State Forest-North, 1765 CR Hwy. G, 53010. T: (262) 626-2116. RV/tent: 341. $14. Hookups: electric (30 amps).

Kewaunee

Mapleview Campsites, N1460 Hwy. B, 54216. T: (920) 776-1588. RV/tent: 75. $21. Hookups: water, electric (30 amps).

Kieler

Rustic Barn Campground, 3854 Dry Hollow Rd., 53812. T: (608) 568-7797. RV/tent: 58. $18. Hookups: water, electric (30 amps).

Kingston

Grand Valley Campground, 5855 CR B, 53926. T: (920) 394-3643. RV/tent: 200. $21. Hookups: water, electric (30 amps).

WISCONSIN (continued)

La Crosse

Bluebird Springs Recreation Area, N 2833 Smith Valley Rd., 54601. T: (608) 781-CAMP. RV/tent: 148. $20. Hookups: water, sewer, electric (50 amps).

Goose Island Camp, Hwy. 35, 54601. T: (608) 788-7018. RV/tent: 400. $15. Hookups: electric (30 amps).

Pettibone Resort & Campground, 333 Park Plaza Dr., 54601. T: (608) 782-5858. RV/tent: 170. $28. Hookups: water, electric (50 amps).

Lac Du Flambeau

Lac Du Flambeau Tribal Campground, P.O. Box 67, 54538. T: (715) 588-9611. RV/tent: 72. $18. Hookups: water, sewer, electric (30 amps).

Ladysmith

Flambeau River Lodge, N7870 Flambeau Rd., 54848. T: (715) 532-5392. RV/tent: 25. $15. Hookups: water, sewer, electric (30 amps).

Thornapple River Campground, N6599 Hwy. 27, 54848. T: (715) 532-7034. RV/tent: 25. $17. Hookups: water, electric (30 amps).

Westcove Campground, 1011 Edgewood Ave., Hwy. 8, 54848. T: (715) 532-7812. RV/tent: 15. $14. Hookups: waters, sewer, electric (30 amps).

Lake Delton

Yogi Bear's Jellystone Park Camp-Resort, 51915 Ishnala Rd., 53940. T: (608) 254-2568. RV/tent: 229. $58. Hookups: water, sewer, electric (50 amps).

Lake Geneva

Coachman's Terrace Park, W 3540 SR 50W, 53147. T: (262) 248-3636. RV/tent: 63. $25. Hookups: water, sewer, electric (30 amps).

Lancaster

Klondyke Secluded Acres, 6656 Pine Knob Rd., 53813. T: (608) 723-2844. RV/tent: 37. $18. Hookups: water, electric (30 amps).

Land O'Lakes

Borderline RV Park, P.O. Box 552, 54540. T: (715) 547-6169. RV/tent: 25. $19. Hookups: water, sewer, electric (30 amps).

Lodi

Crystal Lake Campground, P.O. Box 188, 53555. T: (608) 592-5607. RV/tent: 65. $32. Hookups: water, electric (30 amps).

Smokey Hollow Campground, Inc., 9935 McGowan, 53555. T: (608) 635-4806. RV/tent: 100. $19. Hookups: water, electric (30 amps).

Lyndon Station

Bass Lake Campground, 1497 Southern Rd., 53944. T: (608) 666-2311. RV/tent: 50. $30. Hookups: water, electric (30 amps).

Yukon Trails Camping, 2330 Hwy. HH, 53944. T: (608) 666-3261. RV/tent: 65. $30. Hookups: water, sewer, electric (30 amps).

Lynxville

River Hills Estates Campground, Box 171, 54626. T: (608) 874-4197. RV/tent: 40. $15. Hookups: water, sewer, electric (30 amps).

Manawa

Bear Lake Campground, N4715 Hwy. 22-110, 54949. T: (920) 596-3308. RV/tent: 150. $24. Hookups: water, electric (30 amps).

Maribel

Devil's River Campers Park, 16612 CTH R, 54227. T: (920) 863-2812. RV/tent: 80. $25. Hookups: water, electric (30 amps).

Marion

Kastle Kampground, N11301 Kinney Lake Rd., 54950. T: (715) 754-5900. RV/tent: 365. $23. Hookups: water, sewer, electric (50 amps).

Markesan

Shady Oaks Campground, N 2770 Park Rd., 53946. T: (920) 398-3138. RV/tent: 151. $20. Hookups: water, sewer, electric (30 amps).

Marquette

Sportsman's Resort LLC, 222 Lyon St., 53947. T: (920) 394-3421. RV/tent: 30. $25. Hookups: water, sewer, electric (50 amps).

Mauston

Bavarian Campsites, W 4796 Hwy. G, 53948. T: (608) 847-7039. RV/tent: 70. $20. Hookups: electric (20 amps).

Mellen

Copper Falls State Park, RR 1 Box 17AA, 54546. T: (715) 274-5123. RV/tent: 56. $18. Hookups: electric (30 amps).

Menomonie

Menomonie KOA, 2501 Broadway St. North, 54751. T: (715) 235-6360. RV/tent: 94. $30. Hookups: water, sewer, electric (30 amps).

Twin Springs Resort Campground, 530th St., 54751. T: (715) 235-9321. RV/tent: 75. $24. Hookups: water, sewer, electric (50 amps).

Mercer

Lake of the Falls, County Trunk FF, 54547. T: (715) 561-2695. RV/tent: 30. $9. Hookups: electric (30 amps).

Merrill

Council Grounds State Park, N1895 Council Grounds Dr., 54452. T: (715) 356-8773. RV/tent: 55. $15. Hookups: electric (30 amps).

Merrimac

Merry Mac's Camp'N, E 12540 Halweg Rd., 53561. T: (608) 493-2367. RV/tent: 110. $22. Hookups: water, electric (30 amps).

Milton

Blackhawk Campground, 3407 Blackhawk Dr., 53563. T: (608) 868-2586. RV/tent: 50. $27. Hookups: water, electric (30 amps).

Montello

Lake Arrowhead Campground, 781 Fox Court, 53949. T: (920) 295-3000. RV/tent: 115. $27. Hookups: water, sewer, electric (30 amps).

Lakeside Campground, N3510 East Tomahawk Trail, 53949. T: (920) 295-3389. RV/tent: 95. $30. Hookups: water, sewer, electric (50 amps).

Wilderness County Park, N 1499 State Hwy. 22, 53949. T: (608) 297-2002. RV/tent: 159. $15. Hookups: electric (30 amps).

Mosinee

Lake DuBay Shores Campground, 1713 DuBay Dr., 54455. T: (715) 457-2484. RV/tent: 150. $26. Hookups: water, sewer, electric (30 amps).

Mountain

Chute Pond Park, 12436 Chute Dam Rd., 54149. T: (715) 276-6261. RV/tent: 100. $18. Hookups: water, electric (30 amps).

Mukwonago

Country View Campground, 26400 Craig Ave., 53149. T: (262) 662-3654. RV/tent: 150. $26. Hookups: water, sewer, electric (30 amps).

Muscoda

Riverside Park, P.O. Box 293, 53573. T: (608) 739-3786. RV/tent: 36. $10. Hookups: electric (30 amps).

Necedah

Buckhorn Campground Resort Inc., 8410 CR G, 54646. T: (608) 565-2090. RV/tent: 24. $20. Hookups: water, electric (50 amps).

Ken's Marina, Campground & Pontoon Rental, W4240 Marina Ln., 54646. T: (608) 565-2426. RV/tent: 35. $15. Hookups: water, electric (30 amps).

St. Joseph Resort, P.O. Box 467, 54646. T: (608) 565-7258. RV/tent: 40. $18. Hookups: water, electric (30 amps).

Neillsville

Greenwood Park, Hwy. 73, 54456. T: (715) 743-5140. RV/tent: 24. $12. Hookups: electric (30 amps).

Mead Lake Park, CR G, 54456. T: (715) 743-5140. RV/tent: 75. $12. Hookups: electric (30 amps).

Rock Dam Park, Rock Dam Lake, 54456. T: (715) 743-5140. RV/tent: 140. $17. Hookups: water, sewer, electric (30 amps).

Russell Memorial Park, County Trunk J, 54456. T: (715) 743-5140. RV/tent: 200. $20. Hookups: water, sewer, electric (30 amps).

Sherwood Park, County Trunk Z, 54456. T: (715) 743-5140. RV/tent: 38. $12. Hookups: electric (30 amps).

Snyder Park, US 10, 54456. T: (715) 743-5140. RV/tent: 37. $12. Hookups: electric (30 amps).

WISCONSIN (continued)

Nekoosa

Deer Trail Park Campground, 13846 CR Z, 54457. T: (715) 886-3871. RV/tent: 160. $19. Hookups: water, electric (50 amps).

New Lisbon

Fischer's Campground, 7989 Hwy. 80, 53950. T: (608) 562-5355. RV/tent: 50. $20. Hookups: water, electric (30 amps).

Oakdale

Oakdale KOA, P.O. Box 150, 54649. T: (608) 372-5622. RV/tent: 84. $22. Hookups: water, sewer, electric (50 amps).

Oconto

Holtwood Campsite, Holtwood Way, 54153. T: (920) 834-7732. RV/tent: 150. $18. Hookups: water, electric (30 amps).

North Bay Shore Park, County Trunk Y, 54153. T: (920) 834-6825. RV/tent: 33. $17. Hookups: water, electric (30 amps).

Osceola

Schillberg's Brookside Campground, 409 10th Ave., 54020. T: (715) 755-2260. RV/tent: 120. $17. Hookups: electric (30 amps).

Oshkosh

Circle R Campground, 1185 Old Knapp Rd., 54902. T: (920) 235-8909. RV/tent: 100. $19. Hookups: water, sewer, electric (30 amps).

Hickory Oaks Fly In and Campground, 555 Glendale Ave., 54901. T: (920) 235-8076. RV/tent: 50. $18. Hookups: water, electric (30 amps).

Palmyra

Circle K Campground, W 1316 Island Rd., 53156. T: (262) 495-2896. RV/tent: 80. $20. Hookups: water, sewer, electric (30 amps).

Pardeeville

Duck Creek Campground, 6560 County Hwy. G, 53954. T: (608) 429-2425. RV/tent: 50. $20. Hookups: water, electric (30 amps).

Indian Trails Campground, 6445 Haynes Rd., 53954. T: (608) 429-3244. RV/tent: 168. $21. Hookups: water, electric (30 amps).

Pelican Lake

Weaver's Resort & Campground, 1001 Weaver Rd., 54463. T: (715) 487-5217. RV/tent: 9. $25. Hookups: water, sewer, electric (30 amps).

Pembine

Tranquil Vista Campground, P.O. Box 98, 54156. T: (715) 324-6430. RV/tent: 25. $12. Hookups: water, electric (30 amps).

Phillips

Solberg Lake County Park, 104 South Eyder Ave., 54555. T: (715) 339-6371. RV/tent: 45. $15. Hookups: electric (30 amps).

Plover

Ridgewood Campground, 4800 River Ridge Rd., 54467. T: (715) 344-8750. RV/tent: 70. $22. Hookups: water, electric (30 amps).

Portage

Kamp Dakota, W 10670 Tritz Rd., 53901. T: (608) 742-5599. RV/tent: 125. $18. Hookups: water, sewer, electric (30 amps).

Pride of America Camping Resort, 7584 W. Bush Rd., 53901. T: (608) 742-6395. RV/tent: 120. $27. Hookups: water, sewer, electric (50 amps).

Sky High Camping Resort, 5740 Sky High Dr., 53901. T: (608) 742-2572. RV/tent: 100. $30. Hookups: water, sewer, electric (50 amps).

Prairie Du Chien

Wyalusing State Park, 13081 State Park Ln., 53801. T: (608) 996-2261. RV/tent: 82. $15. Hookups: electric (30 amps).

Rapids

Dexter Park, Hwys 80 & 54, 54494. T: (715) 421-8422. RV/tent: 96. $13. Hookups: electric (30 amps).

North Wood County Park, CR A, 54494. T: (715) 421-8422. RV/tent: 91. $13. Hookups: electric (320 amps).

South Wood Park-Lake Wazeecha, CR W, 54494. T: (715) 421-8422. RV/tent: 71. $13. Hookups: electric (20 amps).

Redgranite

Flanagan's Pearl Lake Campsite, W 4585 South Pearl Lake Rd., 54970. T: (920) 566-2758. RV/tent: 100. $17. Hookups: water, electric (50 amps).

Reedsburg

Lighthouse Rock Campground, 2330 CR V, 53959. T: (608) 524-4203. RV/tent: 98. $21. Hookups: water, sewer, electric (30 amps).

Reedsville

Rainbow's End Campground, 18227 US Hwy. 10, 54230. T: (920) 754-4142. RV/tent: 40. $18. Hookups: water, electric (30 amps).

Rhinelander

Lake George Campsites, 4008 Bassett Rd., 54501. T: (715) 362-6152. RV/tent: 37. $16. Hookups: water, electric (30 amps).

West Bay Camping Resort, 4330 South Shore Dr., 54501. T: (715) 362-3481. RV/tent: 79. $18. Hookups: water, sewer, electric (50 amps).

Richland Center

Alana Springs Lodge & Campground, 22628 Covered Bridge Rd., 53581. T: (608) 647-2600. RV/tent: 23. $20. Hookups: water, electric (20 amps).

Rio

Little Bluff Campground, N4003 Traut Rd., 53960. T: (920) 992-5157. RV/tent: 135. $19. Hookups: water, sewer, electric (30 amps).

Silver Springs Campsites, N5048 Ludwig Rd., 53960. T: (920) 992-3537. RV/tent: 300. $26. Hookups: water, sewer, electric (30 amps).

Willow Mill Campsite, 5830 CR SS, 53960. T: (920) 992-5355. RV/tent: 60. $26. Hookups: water, electric (30 amps).

Saxon

Frontier Bar & Campground, HC 1 Box 477, 54559. T: (715) 893-2461. RV/tent: 25. $16. Hookups: water, sewer, electric (30 amps).

Shawano

Brady's Pine Grove Campground, N5999 Campground Rd., 54166. T: (715) 787-4555. RV/tent: 200. $24. Hookups: water, electric (30 amps).

Shawano County Park Campground, CR H, 54166. T: (715) 524-4986. RV/tent: 90. $10. Hookups: electric (30 amps).

Sheboygan

Kohler/Andre State Park, 1520 Old Park Rd., 53081. T: (920) 451-4080. RV/tent: 95. $15. Hookups: electric (30 amps).

Sherwood

High Cliff State Park, 7650 State Park Rd., 54169. T: (920) 989-1106. RV/tent: 83. $15. Hookups: electric (30 amps).

Solon Springs

Swanson's Motel & Campground, P.O. Box 296, 54873. T: (715) 378-2215. RV/tent: 21. $16. Hookups: water, sewer, electric (30 amps).

Somerset

River's Edge Camp Resort, P.O. Box 67, 54025. T: (715) 247-3305. RV/tent: 277. $20. Hookups: water, electric (30 amps).

Spooner

Country House Lodging & RV Park, 717 South Hwy. 63, 54801. T: (715) 635-8721. RV/tent: 21. $18. Hookups: water, electric (30 amps).

Highland Park Campground, 8050 Carlton Rd., 54801. T: (715) 635-2462. RV/tent: 45. $30. Hookups: water, sewer, electric (30 amps).

Totogatic Park, CR 1, 54801. T: (715) 466-2822. RV/tent: 71. $13. Hookups: electric (30 amps).

Spring Green

Highland Ridge Campground, P.O. Box 190, 54767. T: (715) 778-5562. RV/tent: 45. $14. Hookups: electric (30 amps).

Valley RV Park, E5016 Hwy. 14 & 23, 53588. T: (608) 588-2717. RV/tent: 18. $19. Hookups: water, sewer, electric (30 amps).

Spruce

Holt Park, 9601 Holt Park Rd., 54174. T: (920) 842-4433. RV/tent: 50. $7. Hookups: water, electric (30 amps).

Stevens Point

Collins Park, CR 1, 54481. T: (715) 346-1433. RV/tent: 25. $11. Hookups: electric (30 amps).

Dubay Park, CR E, 54481. T: (715) 346-1433. RV/tent: 31. $11. Hookups: electric (30 amps).

Jordan Park, SR 66, 54481. T: (715) 346-1433. RV/tent: 25. $13. Hookups: electric (30 amps).

WISCONSIN (continued)

Stoughton

Kamp Kegonsa, 2671 Circle Dr., 53589. T: (608) 873-5800. RV/tent: 100. $23. Hookups: water, electric (30 amps).

Lake Kegonsa State Park, 2405 Door Creek Rd., 53589. T: (608) 873-9695. RV/tent: 80. $14. Hookups: electric (30 amps).

Viking Village Campground & Resort Inc., 1648 County Trunk N, 53589. T: (608) 873-6601. RV/tent: 77. $29. Hookups: water, sewer, electric (50 amps).

Sturgeon Bay

Door County Yogi Bear's Jellystone Park, 3677 May Rd., 54235. T: (920) 743-9001. RV/tent: 175. $25. Hookups: water, sewer, electric (50 amps).

Monument Point Camping, 5718 West Monument Point Rd., 54235. T: (920) 743-9411. RV/tent: 84. $20. Hookups: electric (30 amps).

Sturtevant

Cliffside Park, 14200 Washington Ave., 53177. T: (262) 886-8440. RV/tent: 92. $13. Hookups: water, electric (30 amps).

Travelers' Inn Motel and Campground, 14017 Durand Ave., 53177. T: (262) 878-1415. RV/tent: 25. $17. Hookups: water, electric (30 amps).

Superior

Pattison State Park, 6294 South SR 35, 54880. T: (715) 399-3111. RV/tent: 50. $15. Hookups: electric (20 amps).

Tilleda

Tilleda Falls Campground, P.O. Box 76, 54978. T: (715) 787-4143. RV/tent: 40. $21. Hookups: water, electric (30 amps).

Tomah

Holiday Lodge Golf Resort & RV Park, 10558 Freedom Rd., 54660. T: (608) 372-9314. RV/tent: 28. $17. Hookups: water, sewer, electric (30 amps).

Tomahawk

Birkensee Resort & Camping, 9350 CR H, 54487. T: (715) 453-5103. RV/tent: 45. $20. Hookups: water, sewer, electric (30 amps).

Terrace View Campsites, W5220 Terrace View Rd., 54487. T: (715) 453-8352. RV/tent: 42. $18. Hookups: water, electric (30 amps).

Trego

Bay Park Resort & Campground, 8347 Bay Park Rd., 54888. T: (715) 635-2840. RV/tent: 52. $25. Hookups: water, sewer, electric (30 amps).

Eagle Lodge Resort & Campground, 8234 Bald Eagle Dr., 54888. T: (715) 466-2728. RV/tent: 17. $25. Hookups: water, sewer, electric (30 amps).

Trego Town Park & Campground, 5665 Trego Park Rd., 54888. T: (715) 635-9931. RV/tent: 49. $15. Hookups: water, electric (30 amps).

Trempealeau

Perrot State Park, P.O. Box 407, 54661. T: (608) 534-6409. RV/tent: 97. $15. Hookups: electric (30 amps).

Tripoli

Buck Snort Resort & Campground, 5129 Boyle Rd., 54564. T: (715) 564-2262. RV/tent: 33. $18. Hookups: water, sewer, electric (30 amps).

Two Rivers

Point Beach State Forest, 9400 CTHO, 54241. T: (920) 794-7480. RV/tent: 127. $15. Hookups: water, sewer, electric (30 amps).

Viola

Banker Park, P.O. Box 38, 54664. T: (608) 627-1831. RV/tent: 45. $5. Hookups: electric (30 amps).

Wabeno

Ham Lake Campground, 3490 Hwy. 32, 54566. T: (715) 674-2201. RV/tent: 31. $23. Hookups: water, sewer, electric (30 amps).

Washington Island

Washington Island Campground, RR 1 Box 144, 54246. T: (920) 847-2622. RV/tent: 80. $33. Hookups: water, electric (30 amps).

Waupaca

Deerhaven Campground, N 3185 Butts Dr., 54981. T: (715) 256-1412. RV/tent: 40. $18. Hookups: water, sewer, electric (30 amps).

Royal Oaks Golf Resort Inc., N4440 Oakland Dr., 54981. T: (715) 258-5103. RV/tent: 25. $17. Hookups: water, sewer, electric (30 amps).

Rustic Woods, E 2585 Southwood Dr., 54981. T: (715) 258-2442. RV/tent: 164. $23. Hookups: water, sewer, electric (30 amps).

Wapaca Camping Park, 2411 Holmes Rd., 54981. T: (715) 258-8010. RV/tent: 133. $24. Hookups: water, sewer, electric (30 amps).

Wausau

Dells of the Eau Claire Park, CR Y, 54401. T: (715) 449-2293. RV/tent: 26. $8. Hookups: electric (30 amps).

Marathon Park, SR 29 W, 54401. T: (715) 261-1570. RV/tent: 45. $11. Hookups: electric (30 amps).

Rib Mountain State Park, 4200 Park Rd., 54401. T: (715) 842-2522. RV/tent: 40. $11. Hookups: electric (20 amps).

Wautoma

Land of the Woods Campground, 9070 14th Ave., 54982. T: (920) 787-3601. RV/tent: 150. $23. Hookups: water, electric (20 amps).

Webster

Wagner's Port Sand, 4904 Hwy. 70, 54893. T: (715) 349-2395. RV/tent: 60. $20. Hookups: water, sewer, electric (30 amps).

White Lake

River Forest Rafts & Campground, N2765 Sunny Waters Ln., 54491. T: (715) 882-3351. RV/tent: 45. $6. Hookups: electric (15 amps).

Whitewater

Scenic Ridge Campground, W7991 R & W Townline Rd., 53190. T: (608) 883-2920. RV/tent: 187. $9. Hookups: water, electric (30 amps).

Wild Rose

Evergreen Campsites, W5449 Archer Ln., 54984. T: (920) 622-3498. RV/tent: 400. $20. Hookups: water, electric (30 amps).

Wonewoc

Chapparal Campground & Resort, S320 Hwy. 33, 53968. T: (888) 283-0755. RV/tent: 72. $24. Hookups: water, sewer, electric (50 amps).

Woodruff

Hiawatha Trailer Resort, P.O. Box 590, 54568. T: (715) 356-6111. RV/tent: 60. $30. Hookups: water, sewer, electric (50 amps).

Indian Shores Resort & RV Sales, P.O. Box 12, 54568. T: (715) 356-5552. RV/tent: 150. $26. Hookups: water, sewer, electric (30 amps)

WYOMING

Arlington

Arlington Outpost, Hwy. 13, 82083. T: (307) 378-2350. RV/tent: 76. $15–$17. Hookups: full.

Beulah

Camp Fish, Main St., 82712. T: (888) BEU-LAHW. RV/tent: 16. $15–$20. Hookups: electric (20, 30 amps), water.

Buffalo

Big Horn Mountains Campground, 8935 US 16 West, 82834. T: (307) 684-2307. RV/tent: 83. $15–$18. Hookups: full.

Buffalo KOA Campground, 87 Hwy. 16 East, 82443. T: (800) 562-5403. www.buffalokoa.com. RV/tent: 91. $20–$26. Hookups: full.

WYOMING (continued)

Deer Park, US 16, 82834. T: (800) 222-9960. information@deerparkrv.com. RV/tent: 97. $16–$25. Hookups: full.

Indian Campground, US 16, 82834. T: (307) 684-9601. steveng@trib.com. RV/tent: 122. $16–$25. Hookups: full.

Mountain View Motel, Cabins, and Campground, US 16, 82834. T: (307) 684-2881. RV/tent: 18. $15–$18. Hookups: full.

Caspar

Caspar KOA, 2800 East Yellowstone, 82609. T: (800) KOA-3259. www.koa.com. RV/tent: 110. $16–$20. Hookups: full.

Fort Caspar Campground, 4205 Fort Caspar Rd., 82604. T: (888) 243-7709. RV/tent: 165. $13–$19. Hookups: full.

Cheyenne

A B Camping, College Dr., 82207. T: (307) 634-7035. RV/tent: 194. $15–$21. Hookups: full.

Greenway Trailor Park, College Dr., 82207. T: (307) 634-6696. RV/tent: 42. $14. Hookups: full.

Jolley Rogers RV Campground, US 30, 82207. T: (307) 634-8457. RV/tent: 69. $15. Hookups: full.

KOA-Cheyenne, Campstool Rd., 82207. T: (307) 638-8840. manager@cheyennekoa.com. RV/tent: 53. $26–$28. Hookups: electric (20, 30, 50 amps), water.

Restway Travel Park, Whitney Rd., 82207. T: (800) 443-2751. RV/tent: 121. $15–$19. Hookups: full.

T-Joe's RV Park, P.O. Box 2267, 82003. T: (307) 635-8750. RV/tent: 54. $18–$20. Hookups: electric (20, 30, 50 amps), water.

WYC Campground, Box 5201, 82003. T: (307) 547-2244. RV/tent: 100. $15–$23. Hookups: electric (20, 30, 50 amps).

Chugwater

Diamond Guest Ranch, Box 236, 82210. T: (800) YEA-HAAA. RV/tent: 121. $18. Hookups: electric (20, 30, 50 amps), water.

Cody

7 K's RV Park, 232 West Yellowstone Ave., 82414. T: (307) 587-5890. RV/tent: 54. $20. Hookups: electric (20, 30 amps).

Absaroka Bay RV Park, P.O. Box 953, 82414. T: (800) 557-7440. www.cody-wy.com. campground@wyoming.com. RV/tent: 99. $19. Hookups: electric (30, 50).

Camp Cody Campground, 415 Yellowstone Ave., 82414. T: (888) 231-CAMP. RV/tent: 63. $15. Hookups: electric (20, 30, 50 amps), water.

Elk Valley Inn, RV Park, and Cabins, 3256 Yellowstone Hwy., 82414. T: (307) 587-4149. RV/tent: 70. $14–$23. Hookups: electric (20, 30, 50 amps), water.

Gateway Motel and Campground, P.O. Box 2348, 82414. T: (307) 587-2561. RV/tent: 87. $16–$20. Hookups: electric (20, 30 amps).

KOA-Cody, 5561 Greybull Hwy., 82414. T: (800) KOA-8507. RV/tent: 228. $22–$33. Hookups: electric (20, 30, 50 amps), water.

Parkway Village and RV Campground, 132 Yellowstone Ave., 82414. T: (307) 527-5927. RV/tent: 25. $10–$14. Hookups: electric (20, 30, 50 amps), water.

Ponderosa Campground, P.O. Box 1477, 82414. T: (307) 587-9203. RV/tent: 165. $17–$25. Hookups: electric (20, 30, 50 amps).

Dayton

Foothills Motel and Campground, Box 174, 82836. T: (307) 655-2347. www.fiberpip.net/~foothill/Home.htm. RV/tent: 45. $12–$17. Hookups: electric (20, 30, 50 amps), water.

Devils Tower

Fort Devils Tower Campground, 601 Hwy. 24, 82714. T: (307) 467-5655. RV/tent: 32. $15. Hookups: electric (20, 50 amps).

KOA—Devils Tower, P.O. Box 100, 82714. T: (800) 562-5785. RV/tent: 145. $20–$26. Hookups: electric (20, 30, 50 amps), water.

Douglas

Douglas Jackalope KOA Kampground, P.O. Box 1150, 82633. T: (800) 562-2469. RV/tent: 101. $21–$22. Hookups: electric (20, 30, 50 amps), water.

Dubois

Circle Up Camper Court, P.O. Box 1520, 82513. T: (307) 455-2238. RV/tent: 117. $17–$23. Hookups: electric (20, 30, 50 amps), water.

Pinnicale Buttes Lodge and Campground, 3577 US Hwy. 26, 82513. T: (800) 934-3569. RV/tent: 21. $12–$19. Hookups: electric (15. 20, 30, 50), water.

Evanston

Phillips RV Park, 225 Bear River Dr., 82930. T: (307) 789-3805. RV/tent: 58. $19. Hookups: electric (20, 30, 50).

Fort Bridger

Fort Bridger RV Camp, P.O. Box 244, 82933. T: (800) 578-6535. RV/tent: 23. $18. Hookups: electric (20, 30, 50 amps).

Fort Laramie

Chuckwagon RV Park, P.O. Box 142, 82212. T: (307) 837-2828. RV/tent: 12. $12. Hookups: electric (20, 30, 50 amps), water.

Pony Soldier RV Park, RR1 Box 33 US Hwy. 26, Lingle, 82223. T: (307) 837-3078. RV/tent: 65. $15–$16. Hookups: electric (20, 30, 50 amps), water.

Gillette

Green Tree's Crazy Woman Campground, 1001 West 2nd St., 82716. T: (307) 682-3665. RV/-tent: 124. $16–$28. Hookups: electric (20, 30, 50 amps), water.

Glenrock

Deer Creek Village RV Park, P.O. Box 1003, 82637. T: (307) 436-8121. RV/tent: 95. $16. Hookups: electric (20, 30, 50 amps).

Green River

Buckbord Marina, HCR 65 Box 100, 82935. T: (307) 865-6927. RV/tent: 40. $22. Hookups: electric (30, 50 amps).

Tex's Travel Camp, Star Rte. 2 Box 101, 82935. T: (307) 875-2630. RV/tent: 89. $16–$25. Hookups: electric (20, 30, 50 amps), water.

Greybull

Green Oasis Campground, 540 12th Ave. North, 82426. T: (888) 765-2856. RV/tent: 32. $13–$21. Hookups: electric (20, 30, 50 amps), water.

KOA-Greybull, Box 387, 82426. T: (800) 562-7508. RV/tent: 57. $22–$23. Hookups: electric (30 amps), water.

Jackson

KOA-Snake River Park, 9705 South US Hwy. 89, 83001. T: (800) 562-1878. RV/tent: 96. $36–$39. Hookups: electric (20, 30, 50 amps), water.

Lone Eagle Resort, 13055 South US Hwy. 191, 83001. T: (800) 321-3800. RV/tent: 154. $41. Hookups: electric (20, 30 amps).

Lander

Hart Ranch Hideout RV Park and Campground, 7192 Hwy. 789/287, 82520. T: (800) 914-9226. RV/tent: 85. $23–$24. Hookups: electric (20, 30, 50 amps), water.

Maverick Mobile Home and RV Park, 1104 North 2nd St., 82520. T: (307) 332-3142. RV/tent: 45. $15. Hookups: electric (15, 20, 30 amps), water.

Rocky Acres Campground, P.O. Box 1565, 82520. T: (307) 332-6953. RV/tent: 30. $13. Hookups: electric (15,20, 30 amps).

Sleeping Bear RV Park and Campground, 715 East Main, 82520. T: (888) SLP-BEAR. RV/tent: 54. $26. Hookups: electric (20, 30 ,50 amps), water.

Laramie

KOA-Laramie, P.O. Box 1134, 82073. T: (800) KOA-4153. RV/tent: 146. $18–$22. Hookups: electric (20, 30, 50 amps).

Lusk

Prairie View Campground, Box 1168, 82225. T: (307) 334-3174. RV/tent: 29. $18. Hookups: electric (15, 20, 30 amps), water.

Lyman

KOA-Lyman, HC 66 Box 55, 82937. T: (307) 786-2188. RV/tent: 51. $16–$20. Hookups: electric (20, 30, 50 amps), water.

Madison Junction

Madison Junction Campground, P.O. Box 165, Yellowstone National Park, 82190. T: (307) 344-7311. RV/tent: 280. $15. Hookups: none.

Moran Junction

Colter Bay RV Park, P.O. Box 250, 83013. T: (800) 628-9988. RV/tent: 112. $32–$34. Hookups: electric (20, 30, 50 amps).

WYOMING (continued)

Moran Junction (continued)

Grand Teton Park RV Resort, P.O. Box 92, 83013. T: (800) 563-6469. RV/tent: 204. $27–$38. Hookups: electric (20, 30, 50 amps), water.

Newcastle

Crystal Park Campground, 2 Fountain Plaza, 82701. T: (307) 746-3339. RV/tent: 100. $13–$16. Hookups: electric (20, 30 amps), water.

Rimrock RV, 2206 West Main, 82701. T: (307) 746-2007. RV/tent: 58. $15–$18. Hookups: electric (20, 30 amps), water.

Pine Bluffs

Pine Bluffs RV Park, P.O. Box 806, 82082. T: (800) 294-4968. RV/tent: 108. $20. Hookups: electric (20, 30, 50 amps).

Pinedale

Pinedale RV, P.O. Box 248, 82941. T: (307) 367-4555. RV/tent: 64. $18–$20. Hookups: electric (20, 30, 50 amps), water.

Ranchester

Lazy R Campground, P.O. Box 286, 82839. T: (888) 655-9284. RV/tent: 22. $15. Hookups: electric (30, 50 amps).

Rawlins

American Presidents Camp, 2346 West Spruce St., 82301. T: (307) 324-3218. RV/tent: 67. $8–$15. Hookups: electric (20, 30, 50 amps), water.

KOA-Rawlins, 205 East Hwy. 71, 82301. T: (800) 562-7559. RV/tent: 57. $15–$22. Hookups: electric (20, 30, 50 amps), water.

RV World Campground, P.O. Box 1282, 82301. T: (307) 328-1091. RV/tent: 60. $14–$20. Hookups: electric (20, 30, 50 amps), water.

Western Hills Campground, P.O. Box 760, 82301. T: (888) 568-3040. RV/tent: 179. $12–$17. Hookups: electric (20, 30, 50 amps).

Riverside

Lazy Acres Campground, P.O. Box 641, 82325. T: (307) 327-5968. RV/tent: 34. $13–$18. Hookups: electric (15, 20, 30, 50 amps).

Riverton

Owl Creek Kampground, 11124 US Hwy. 26, 82501. T: (307) 856-9769. RV/tent: 40. $17. Hookups: electric (20, 30 amps), water.

Rudy's Camper Court, 622 East Lincoln, 82501. T: (307) 856-9764. RV/tent: 24. $11–$18. Hookups: electric (20, 30 amps).

Wind River RV Park, 1618 East Park, 82501. T: (800) 528-3913. RV/tent: 60. $22–$25. Hookups: electric (20, 30, 50 amps).

Rock Springs

Rock Springs KOA, 86 Foothill Blvd., 82901. T: (800) 562-8699. RV/tent: 115. $18–$28. Hookups: full.

Thermopolis

Country Campin' RV and Tent Park, 710 East Sunnyside Ln., 82443. T: (800) 609-2244. RV/tent: 62. $18. Hookups: electric (20, 30, 50 amps), water.

Eagle RV Park, 204 Hwy. 20 South, 82443. T: (307) 864-5262. RV/tent: 45. $15–$18. Hookups: electric (20, 30 amps), water.

Fountain of Youth RV Park, 250 US Hwy. 20 North, 82443. T: (307) 864-3265. F: (307) 864-3388. w3.trib.com/~foyrvpark. foyrv-park@trib.com. RV/tent: 66. $19.50. Hookups: full.

The Wyoming Waltz RV Park, 720 Shoshoni Hwy. 20 South, 82443. T: (307) 864-2778. RV/tent: 13. $14. Hookups: full

BRITISH COLUMBIA

Balfour

Birch Grove Campground, RR 3 Site 33 Comp 18, Nelson, V1L 5P6. T: (250) 229-4275. RV/tent: 50. $19–$25. Hookups: full.

Barkerville

Becker's Lodge, P.O. Box 129, Wells, V0K 2R0. T: (800) 808-4761. becker@beckers.bc.ca. RV/tent: 17. $18–$20. Hookups: none.

Barriere

Dee Jay Camp and Trailer Park, 626 Yellowhead Hwy., V0E 1E0. T: (250) 672-5685. RV/tent: 75. $15–$18. Hookups: electric, water.

Bell II

Bell II Lodge, P.O. Box 1118, Vernon, V1T 6N4. T: (600) 700-3298. www.bell2lodge.com. info@bell2lodge.com. RV/tent: 10. $18. Hookups: full.

Blue River

Eleanor Lake Campsite, 1 Herb Bilton Way, V0E 1J0. T: (250) 673-8316. RV/tent: 60. $12–$19. Hookups: none.

Boston Bar

Blue Lake Resort, 63452 Blue Lake, V0K 1C0. T: (877) 867-9246. RV/tent: 75. $15–$20. Hookups: electric (15 amps), water.

Canyon Alpine RV Park & Campground, Hwy. 1, V0K 1C0. T: (800) 644-PARK. RV/tent: 31. $22. Hookups: full.

Boswell

Mountain Shores Resort and Marina, 13485 Hwy. 3A, V0B 1A0. T: (250) 223-8258. RV/tent: 87. $18–$24. Hookups: full.

Burnaby

Burnaby Cariboo RV Park, Cariboo Place, V5K 1A1. T: (604) 420-1722. camping@bcrvpark.com. RV/tent: 241. $22–$35. Hookups: full.

Burns Lake

Beaver Point Resort, P.O. Box 587, V0J 1E0. T: (250) 698-7665. RV/tent: 39. $13–$16. Hookups: electric, water.

Burns Lake KOA, P.O. Box 491, V0J 1E0. T: (800) 562-0905. RV/tent: 36. $16–$22. Hookups: full.

Cache Creek

Brookside Campsite, P.O. Box 737, V0K 1H0. T: (250) 457-6633. RV/tent: 95. $12–$19. Hookups: none.

Campbell River

Shelter Bay Resort, 3860 South Island Hwy., V9H 1M2. T: (250) 923-5338. RV/tent: 50. $22. Hookups: full.

Canim Lake

Canim Lake Resort, P.O. Box 248, V0K 1J0. T: (250) 397-2355. RV/tent: 25. $15–$24. Hookups: full.

Reynolds Resort, North Canim Lake Rd., V0K 1M0. T: (250) 397-2244. RV/tent: 29. $13–$20. Hookups: full.

Castlegar

Pine Grove Resort, 1142 Pine Grove, Scotch Creek, V0E 3L0. T: (250) 955-2306. RV/tent: 15. $26. Hookups: full.

Chilanko Forks

Poplar Grove Resort, P.O. Box 70, V0L 1H0. T: (250) 481-1186. RV/tent: 18. $12–$15. Hookups: electric, water.

Chilliwack

Cottonwood Meadows RV Country Club, 44280 Luckakuck Way, V2R 4A7. T: (604) 824-7275. www.cottonwoodrvpark.com. camping@cottonwoodrvpark.com. RV/tent: 107. $19–$24. Hookups: full.

Christina Lake

Skands Court, 64 Johnson Rd., V0H 1V2. T: (250) 447-9295. RV/tent: 84. $19–$21. Hookups: electric, water.

BRITISH COLUMBIA (continued)

Clearwater

Birch Island Campground, 88 Walker Rd., V0E 1N0. T: (250) 674-3991. RV/tent: 42. $15–$20. Hookups: full.

Clinton

Cache Creek, Cariboo Hwy., V0K 1H0. T: (250) 752-6707. RV/tent: 22. $14–$18. Hookups: full.

Courtenay

Hideaway Resort, 9413 Bracken Rd., Black Creek, V9I 1E3. T: (250) 337-5360. RV/tent: 67. $18–$20. Hookups: none.

Fairmont Hot Springs

Hoodoos Mountain Resort, P.O. Box 67, V0B 1L0. T: (250) 345-6631. www.realtystar.com/hoodoos. RV/tent: 75. $13–$20. Hookups: electric, water.

Spruce Grove Resort, P.O. Box 993, V0B 1L0. T: (250) 345-6561. www.sprucegrove resort.com. RV/tent: 160. $19–$27. Hookups: electric, water.

Fanny Bay

Pepper Land Outdoor Resort, 8256 South Island Hwy., V0R 1W0. T: (250) 336-1521. RV/tent: 24. $15–$19. Hookups: full.

Fort Fraser

Pipers Glen RV Resort, West Hwy. 16, V0J 1N0. T: (250) 690-7565. RV/tent: 32. $12–$15. Hookups: electric (15, 30 amps), water.

Fort Langley

Fort Camping, 9451 Glover Rd., V1M 352. T: (604) 888-3678. RV/tent: 300. $18–$21. Hookups: full.

Fort Nelson

Westend Campground, Mile 300.5 Alaska Hwy., V0C 1R0. T: (250) 774-2340. RV/tent: 139. $13–$20. Hookups: full.

Fort St. James

Pitka Bay Resort, Pitka Bay Rd., V0J 1P0. T: (250) 996-8585. RV/tent: 17. $12–$16. Hookups: full.

Stuart River Campground, Roberts Rd., V0J 1P0. T: (250) 996-8690. RV/tent: 34. $13–$15. Hookups: full.

Fort St. John

Sourdough Pete's RV Park, Box 6911, V1J 4J3. T: (800) 227-8388. RV/tent: 88. $12–$20. Hookups: full.

Fort Steele

Fort Steele Campground and RV Park, 335 Kelly Rd., V0B 1N0. T: (250) 426-5117. RV/tent: 63. $15–$21. Hookups: full.

Fraser Lake

Birch Bay Resort, Birch Bay Rd., V0J 1S0. T: (250) 699-8484. RV/tent: 31. $14–$17. Hookups: electric (15, 30 amps), water.

Francois Lake Resort, Francois Lake Rd., V0J 1S0. T: (250) 699-6551. RV/tent: 30. $14–$17. Hookups: full.

Nithi on the Lake, Francois Lake Rd., V0J 1S0. T: (250) 699-6675. RV/tent: 30. $13–$17. Hookups: full.

Golden

Whispering Spruce Campground and RV Park, 1430 Golden View Rd., V0A 1H1. T: (250) 344-6680. RV/tent: 135. $16–$21. Hookups: full.

Grand Forks

Riviera RV Park, 6331 Hwy. 3, V0H 1H0. T: (250) 442-2158. RV/tent: 36. $15–$20. Hookups: full.

Harrison Hot Springs

Bigfoot Campground, 670 Hot Springs, V0M 1K0. T: (604) 796-9767. RV/tent: 200. $16–$22. Hookups: full.

Hixon

Canyon Creek Campgound, 39035 Hwy. 97 South, V0K 1S0. T: (250) 998-4384. www.canyoncreekcampground.com. rvpark@canyoncreekcampground.com. RV/tent: 55. $10–$18. Hookups: electric (30 amps), water.

Hope

Coquihalla Campsite, 800 Kawkawa Lake Rd., V0X 1L0. T: (604) 869-7119. RV/tent: 122. $16–$20. Hookups: electric (15, 30 amps), water,

Kawkawa Lake Resort, P.O. Box 788, V0X 1L0. T: (604) 869-9930. RV/tent: 120. $15–$25. Hookups: none.

Hornby Island

Bradsdadsland, 1980 Shingle Spit Rd., V0R 1Z0. T: (250) 335-0757. RV/tent: 50. $24–$27. Hookups: electric (15 amps), water.

Kaslo

Mirror Lake Campground, 5777 Arcola, V0G 1M0. T: (250) 353-7102. RV/tent: 114. $15–$17. Hookups: electric (15 amps), water.

Madeira Park

Sunshine Coast Resort, 12695 Hwy. 101, P.O. Box 213, V0N 2H0. T: (604) 883-9177. RV/tent: 30. $21–$28. Hookups: full.

Monte Lake

Heritage Campsite and RV Park, P.O. Box 42, V0E 2N0. T: (877) 881-5150. RV/tent: 36. $14–$17. Hookups: full.

Nakusp

Coachman Campsite, 1701 Hwy. 23, V0G 1R0. T: (250) 265-4212. RV/tent: 44. $24. Hookups: full.

Osoyoos

Wild Rapids Campground, RR 1 Lakeshore Dr., V0H 1R0. T: (250) 495-7696. RV/tent: 155. $19–$26. Hookups: electric, water.

Parksville

Park Sands Beach Resort, P.O. Box 179, 105 East Island Hwy., V9P 2G4. T: (250) 248-3171. www.parksands.com. RV/tent: 99. $20–$40. Hookups: full.

Port Alberni

Arrowvak Riverside Campground, 5955 Hector Rd., RR 3, V9Y 7L7. T: (250) 723-7948. RV/tent: 37. $15–$18. Hookups: none.

Prince George

Sintich Trailer Park, P.O. Box 1022, V2L 4V1. T: (250) 963-9862. www.sintichpark.bc.ca. info@sintichpark.bc.ca. RV/tent: 51. $15–$22. Hookups: full.

Quesnel

Cariboo Place Campsite, 6905 Hwy. 97 South, V2J 6M2. T: (250) 747-8555. RV/tent: 70. $14–$17. Hookups: electric, water.

Revelstoke

Williamson's Lake Campground, P.O. Box 1791, V0E 2S0. T: (250) 837-5512. RV/tent: 41. $15–$18. Hookups: none.

Salmon Arm

Salmon Arm KOA, 381 Hwy. 97 B, V1E 4M4. T: (250) 832-6489. RV/tent: 78. $26–$31. Hookups: electric, water.

Sicamous

Cedars Campground, P.O. Box 749, V0E 2V0. T: (250) 836-2265. cedars@sicamous.com. RV/tent: 105. $14. Hookups: electric, water.

Surrey

Dogwood Campground and RV Park, 15151-112 Ave., V3R 6G8. T: (604) 583-5585. RV/tent: 300. $19.50–$30. Hookups: full.

Peace Arch RV Park, 14601 40th Ave., V4P 2J9. T: (604) 594-7009. RV/tent: 255. $19–$25. Hookups: full.

Victoria

Weir's Beach RV Resort, 5191 William Head Rd., V9C 4H5. T: (250) 478-3323. office@weirsbeachrvresort.bc.ca. RV/tent: 61. $25–$35. Hookups: full.

Westbay Marine Village RV Park, 453 Head St., V9A 5S1. T: (250) 385-1831. www.westbay.bc.ca. info@westbay.bc.ca. RV/tent: 61. $20–$35. Hookups: full.

Index

Arizona

Arizona (continued)

Arkansas

California

***California** (continued)*

California (continued)

Colorado

***Colorado** (continued)*

Connecticutt

Delaware

Florida

Florida (continued)

Georgia

Idaho

Indiana

Kentucky

***Kentucky** (continued)*

Louisiana

Maine

Maryland

Maryland (continued)

Massachusetts

Michigan

Michigan (continued)

Minnesota

Mississippi

Mississippi (continued)

Missouri

Montana

New Hampshire

New Hampshire (continued)

New Jersey

New Mexico

New York

New York (continued)

North Carolina

North Carolina (continued)

North Dakota

Ohio

***Oregon** (continued)*

Pennsylvania

Rhode Island

South Carolina

South Carolina (continued)

South Dakota

Tennessee

Texas

Texas (continued)

Utah

Utah (continued)

Vermont

Virginia

Washington

West Virginia

Wisconsin

***Wisconsin** (continued)*

Wyoming

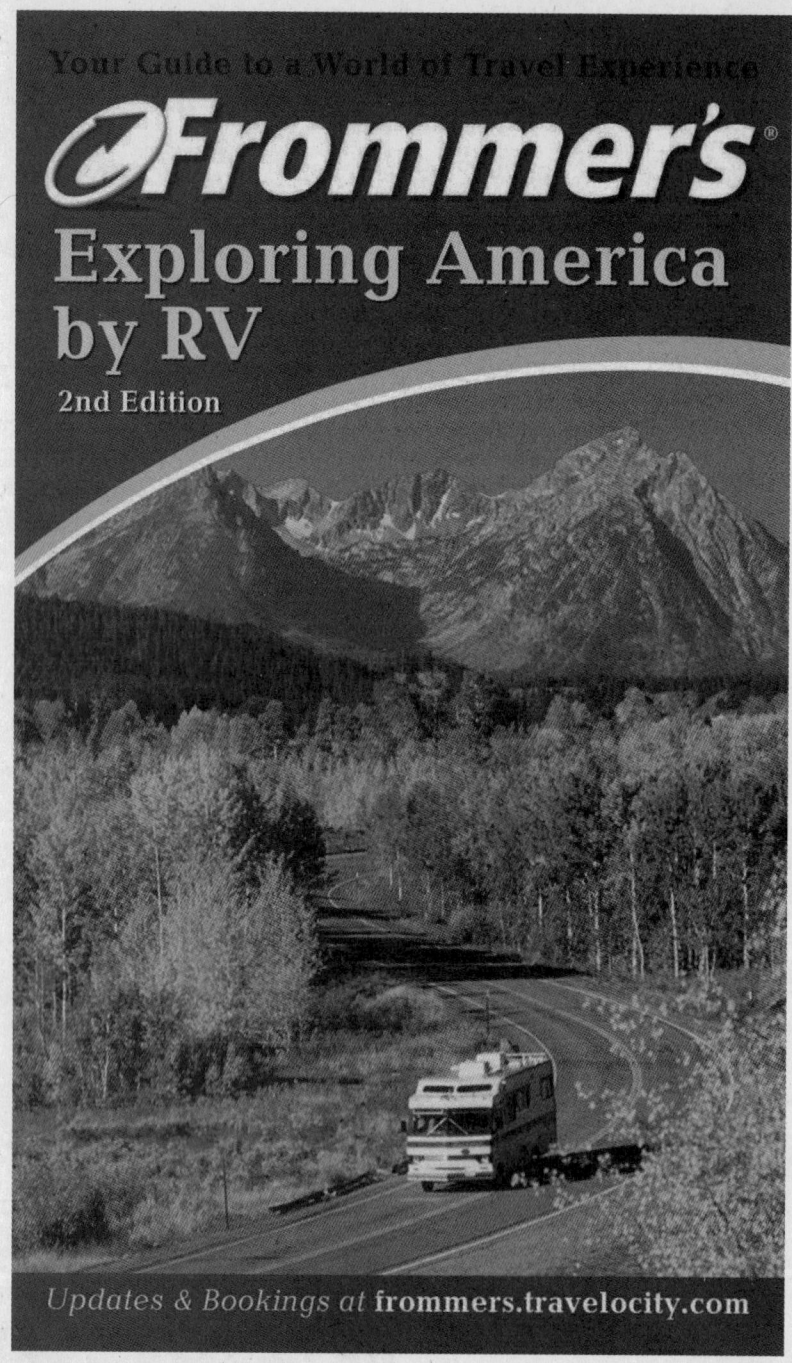